WHO'S WHO 1987

WHO WAS WHO

Seven volumes containing the biographies
removed from WHO'S WHO each year on
account of death, with final details and date of
death added. Also a Cumulated Index to the seven
volumes giving name, years of birth and death, and
the volume in which each entry is to be found.

VOL. I.   1897-1915
VOL. II.   1916-1928
VOL. III.   1929-1940
VOL. IV.   1941-1950
VOL. V.   1951-1960
VOL. VI.   1961-1970
VOL. VII.   1971-1980
A CUMULATED INDEX 1897-1980

WHO'S WHO 1987

AN ANNUAL
BIOGRAPHICAL DICTIONARY

ONE HUNDRED AND THIRTY-NINTH
YEAR OF ISSUE

A & C BLACK
LONDON

PUBLISHED BY A&C BLACK (PUBLISHERS) LIMITED
35 BEDFORD ROW LONDON WC1

COPYRIGHT © 1987 A&C BLACK (PUBLISHERS) LTD

"WHO'S WHO" IS A REGISTERED TRADE MARK
IN THE UNITED KINGDOM

ISBN 0–7136–2870–7

The United States
ST. MARTIN'S PRESS, NEW YORK

Australia
EDWARD ARNOLD (AUSTRALIA) LTD, CAULFIELD EAST, VICTORIA

New Zealand
BOOK REPS (NEW ZEALAND) LTD, AUCKLAND

Canada
COLLIER MACMILLAN (CANADA) INC.,
CAMBRIDGE, ONTARIO

Southern Africa
BOOK PROMOTIONS (PTY) LTD, CLAREMONT, CAPE TOWN

Middle East
EURAB LTD, CHORLEYWOOD, ENGLAND

India
ALLIED PUBLISHERS PRIVATE LTD, NEW DELHI

Hong Kong
UNITED PUBLISHERS SERVICES (HONG KONG) LTD,

Singapore, Malaysia
FEDERAL PUBLICATIONS (S) PTE LTD, SINGAPORE

Japan
WESTERN PUBLICATIONS DISTRIBUTION AGENCY, TOKYO

TYPESET BY CLOWES COMPUTER COMPOSITION,
PRINTED AND BOUND IN GREAT BRITAIN BY
WILLIAM CLOWES LIMITED, BECCLES AND LONDON

CONTENTS

EDITORS' NOTE

A proof of each entry is posted to its subject every year for personal revision, but this cannot be sent unless an address is recorded. It should be noted that the numbers given of the children of a marriage are, unless otherwise indicated, those of the sons and daughters now living; also, that it is the practice to print the names of London clubs unaccompanied by the word London. Forenames printed within brackets are those which the subject of the entry does not commonly use. While every care is taken to ensure accuracy, neither the publishers nor the printers can admit liability for any loss incurred through misprint or other circumstances.

It cannot be stated too emphatically that inclusion in *Who's Who* has never at any time been a matter for payment or of obligation to purchase the volume.

PREFACE

The first edition of *Who's Who* was published in 1849. It consisted of an Almanack, followed by 39 lists of ranks and appointments and the names of those holding them. As might be expected there were lists of Peers, Members of the House of Commons, Archbishops, Bishops and Judges. Additionally, however, there were the names of the Governor and Board of Directors of the Bank of England, of British Ministers abroad, of the Directors of the East India Company and of the officers (including the actuaries) of the life and fire assurance companies in London.

In 1897 substantial changes were made to the nature and content of the book. The range of lists had been expanded over the years to more than 250, to include, amongst others, the Police Commissioners, the officers of the principal railways, the members of the London School Board and the Crown Agents – together with the editors of significant newspapers and magazines whose names, the editor noted, were "given here, not for contributors, but that the public may know who lead public opinion". The major change, however, was the addition of a section of biographies in which details were given of the lives of some five and a half thousand leading figures of the day.

The book had, by this early date, set the pattern it has followed to this day, aiming to list those who, through their careers, affect the political, economic, scientific and artistic life of the country; the first invitations to prepare biographies for the 1897 edition were sent to such people. The origin explains the nature of *Who's Who:* it places its emphasis on careers whilst giving opportunity for the inclusion of family and other individual details, such as the recreations which have become a distinctive feature of the book.

Once established, the essential character of *Who's Who* has been consistently maintained. It seeks to be a detailed, comprehensive and accurate reference book of those people whose lives are of particular interest, whether because they decide our destinies, spend our money, influence our taste or because they are especially prominent in their fields – the arts, education, medicine, sport, the trade unions . . .

An invitation to appear in *Who's Who* has, on occasion, been thought of as conferring distinction; that is the last thing it can do. It recognises distinction and influence. The attitude of the present editorial board remains that of the editor of the 1897 edition, who stated in his preface that the book seeks to recognise people "whether their prominence is inherited, or depending upon office, or the result of ability which singles them out from their fellows in occupations open to every educated man or woman".

It cannot be stated too emphatically that inclusion in *Who's Who* has never at any time been a matter for payment or of obligation to purchase the volume.

INDEX TO ADVERTISERS

ABBREVIATIONS USED IN THIS BOOK

Some of the designatory letters in this list are used merely for economy of space and do not necessarily imply any professional or other qualification.

A

AA — Anti-Aircraft; Automobile Association; Architectural Association; Augustinians of the Assumption
AAA — Amateur Athletic Association; American Accounting Association
AAAL — American Academy of Arts and Letters (*now see* AAIL)
AA&QMG — Assistant Adjutant and Quartermaster-General
AAAS — American Association for the Advancement of Science
AACCA — Associate, Association of Certified and Corporate Accountants (*now see* ACCA)
AACE — Association for Adult and Continuing Education
AAF — Auxiliary Air Force (*now see* RAuxAF)
AAG — Assistant Adjutant-General
AAI — Associate, Chartered Auctioneers' and Estate Agents' Institute (*now* (after amalgamation) *see* ARICS)
AAIL — American Academy and Institute of Arts and Letters
AAM — Association of Assistant Mistresses in Secondary Schools
AAMC — Australian Army Medical Corps (*now see* RAAMC)
A&AEE — Aeroplane and Armament Experimental Establishment
AASA — Associate, Australian Society of Accountants
AASC — Australian Army Service Corps
AAUQ — Associate in Accountancy, University of Queensland
AB — Bachelor of Arts (US); able-bodied seaman
ABA — Amateur Boxing Association; Antiquarian Booksellers' Association; American Bar Association
ABC — Australian Broadcasting Commission
ABCA — Army Bureau of Current Affairs
ABCC — Association of British Chambers of Commerce
ABCFM — American Board of Commissioners for Foreign Missions
ABIA — Associate, Bankers' Institute of Australasia
ABINZ — Associate, Bankers' Institute of New Zealand
ABNM — American Board of Nuclear Medicine
ABP — Associated British Ports
Abp — Archbishop
ABPsS — Associate, British Psychological Society
ABRC — Advisory Board for the Research Councils
ABS — Associate, Building Societies' Institute (*now see* ACBSI)
ABSI — Associate, Boot and Shoe Institution
ABSM — Associate, Birmingham and Midland Institute School of Music
ABTAPL — Association of British Theological and Philosophical Libraries
AC — Companion of the Order of Australia; *Ante Christum* (before Christ)
ACA — Associate, Institute of Chartered Accountants
Acad. — Academy
ACARD — Advisory Council for Applied Research and Development
ACAS — Advisory, Conciliation and Arbitration Service; Assistant Chief of the Air Staff
ACBSI — Associate, Chartered Building Societies Institute
ACC — Association of County Councils; Anglican Consultative Council
ACCA — Associate, Association of Certified Accountants
ACCM — Advisory Council for the Church's Ministry
ACCS — Associate, Corporation of Secretaries (formerly of Certified Secretaries)
ACDP — Australian Committee of Directors and Principals
ACDS — Assistant Chief of Defence Staff
ACE — Association of Consulting Engineers; Member, Association of Conference Executives
ACF — Army Cadet Force
ACFA — Army Cadet Force Association
ACFAS — Association Canadienne-Française pour l'avancement des sciences
ACG — Assistant Chaplain-General
ACGI — Associate, City and Guilds of London Institute
ACGS — Assistant Chief of the General Staff
ACIArb — Associate, Chartered Institute of Arbitrators
ACII — Associate, Chartered Insurance Institute
ACIS — Associate, Institute of Chartered Secretaries and Administrators (*formerly* Chartered Institute of Secretaries)
ACIT — Associate, Chartered Institute of Transport
ACLS — American Council of Learned Societies
ACM — Association of Computing Machinery
ACMA — Associate, Institute of Cost and Management Accountants
ACNS — Assistant Chief of Naval Staff
ACommA — Associate, Society of Commercial Accountants (*now see* ASCA)
ACORD — Advisory Committee on Research and Development
ACOS — Assistant Chief of Staff
ACP — Association of Clinical Pathologists; Associate, College of Preceptors; African/Caribbean/Pacific
ACPO — Association of Chief Police Officers
ACS — American Chemical Society; Additional Curates Society

ACSEA — Allied Command South East Asia
ACSM — Associate, Camborne School of Mines
ACT — Australian Capital Territory; Australian College of Theology; Associate, College of Technology; Association of Corporate Treasurers
ACTT — Association of Cinematograph, Television and Allied Technicians
ACTU — Australian Council of Trade Unions
ACU — Association of Commonwealth Universities
ACWA — Associate, Institute of Cost and Works Accountants (*now see* ACMA)
AD — Dame of the Order of Australia; *Anno Domini*; Air Defence
aD — ausser Dienst
ADAS — Agricultural Development and Advisory Service
ADB — Asian Development Bank
ADB/F — African Development Bank/Fund
ADC — Aide-de-camp
ADCM — Archbishop of Canterbury's Diploma in Church Music
AD Corps — Army Dental Corps (*now* RADC)
ADC(P) — Personal Aide-de-camp to HM The Queen
Ad eund — *Ad eundem gradum*; and *see under* aeg
ADFManc — Art and Design Fellow, Manchester
ADFW — Assistant Director of Fortifications and Works
ADGB — Air Defence of Great Britain
ADGMS — Assistant Director-General of Medical Services
ADH — Assistant Director of Hygiene
Adjt — Adjutant
ADJAG — Assistant Deputy Judge Advocate General
ADK — Order of Ahli Darjah Kinabalu
Adm. — Admiral
ADMS — Assistant Director of Medical Services
ADOS — Assistant Director of Ordnance Services
ADP — Automatic Data Processing
ADS&T — Assistant Director of Supplies and Transport
Adv. — Advisory; Advocate
ADVS — Assistant Director of Veterinary Services
ADWE&M — Assistant Director of Works, Electrical and Mechanical
AE — Air Efficiency Award
AEA — Atomic Energy Authority; Air Efficiency Award (*now see* AE)
AEAF — Allied Expeditionary Air Force
AEC — Agriculture Executive Council; Army Educational Corps (*now see* RAEC)
AECMA — Association Européenne des Constructeurs de Matériel Aérospatial
AEF — Amalgamated Union of Engineering and Foundry Workers (*now see* AEU); American Expeditionary Forces
aeg — *ad eundem gradum* (to the same degree—of the admission of a graduate of one university to the same degree at another without examination)
AEGIS — Aid for the Elderly in Government Institutions
AEI — Associated Electrical Industries
AEM — Air Efficiency Medal
AER — Army Emergency Reserve
AERE — Atomic Energy Research Establishment (Harwell)
Æt., Ætat. — *Ætatis* (aged)
AEU — Amalgamated Engineering Union
AFA — Amateur Football Alliance
AFAIAA — Associate Fellow, American Institute of Aeronautics and Astronautics
AFC — Air Force Cross; Association Football Club
AFCAI — Associate Fellow, Canadian Aeronautical Institute
AFCEA — Armed Forces Communications and Electronics Association
AFCENT — Allied Forces in Central Europe
AFD — Doctor of Fine Arts (US)
AFHQ — Allied Force Headquarters
AFI — American Film Institute
AFIA — Associate, Federal Institute of Accountants (Australia)
AFIAP — Artiste, Fédération Internationale de l'Art Photographique
AFIAS — Associate Fellow, Institute of Aeronautical Sciences (US) (*now see* AFAIAA)
AFICD — Associate Fellow, Institute of Civil Defence
AFIMA — Associate Fellow, Institute of Mathematics and its Applications
AFM — Air Force Medal
AFOM — Associate, Faculty of Occupational Medicine
AFRAeS — Associate Fellow, Royal Aeronautical Society (*now see* MRAeS)
AFRC — Agricultural and Food Research Council
AFV — Armoured Fighting Vehicles
AG — Attorney-General
AGAC — American Guild of Authors and Composers
AGARD — Advisory Group for Aerospace Research and Development
AGH — Australian General Hospital
AGI — Artistes Graphiques Internationaux; Associate, Institute of Certificated Grocers

AGR	Advanced Gas-cooled Reactor
AGRA	Army Group Royal Artillery; Association of Genealogists and Record Agents
AGSM	Associate, Guildhall School of Music and Drama; Australian Graduate School of Management
AHA	Area Health Authority; American Hospitals Association; Associate, Institute of Health Service Administrators (*now see* AHSM)
AHA(T)	Area Health Authority (Teaching)
AHQ	Army Headquarters
AHSM	Associate, Institute of Health Services Management
AH-WC	Associate, Heriot-Watt College, Edinburgh
ai	*ad interim*
AIA	Associate, Institute of Actuaries; American Institute of Architects; Association of International Artists
AIAA	American Institute of Aeronautics and Astronautics
AIAgrE	Associate, Institution of Agricultural Engineers
AIAL	Associate Member, International Institute of Arts and Letters
AIArb	Associate, Institute of Arbitrators (*now see* ACIArb)
AIAS	Associate Surveyor Member, Incorporated Association of Architects and Surveyors
AIB	Associate, Institute of Bankers
AIBD	Associate, Institute of British Decorators
AIBP	Associate, Institute of British Photographers
AIBScot	Associate, Institute of Bankers in Scotland
AIC	Agricultural Improvement Council; Associate of the Institute of Chemistry (later ARIC, MRIC; *now see* MRSC)
AICA	Associate Member, Commonwealth Institute of Accountants; Association Internationale des Critiques d'Art
AICC	All-India Congress Committee
AICE	Associate, Institution of Civil Engineers
AICPA	American Institute of Certified Public Accountants
AICS	Associate, Institute of Chartered Shipbrokers
AICTA	Associate, Imperial College of Tropical Agriculture
AIE	Associate, Institute of Education
AIEE	Associate, Institution of Electrical Engineers
AIF	Australian Imperial Forces
AIG	Adjutant-Inspector-General
AIIA	Associate, Insurance Institute of America
AIInfSc	Associate, Institute of Information Scientists
AIL	Associate, Institute of Linguists
AILA	Associate, Institute of Landscape Architects (*now see* ALI)
AILocoE	Associate, Institution of Locomotive Engineers
AIM	Associate, Institution of Metallurgists (*now see* MIM)
AIMarE	Associate, Institute of Marine Engineers
AIME	American Institute of Mechanical Engineers
AIMSW	Associate, Institute of Medical Social Workers
AInstM	Associate Member, Institute of Marketing
AInstP	Associate, Institute of Physics
AInstPI	Associate, Institute of Patentees and Inventors
AIProdE	Associate, Institution of Production Engineers
AIQS	Associate Member, Institute of Quantity Surveyors
AIRTE	Associate, Institute of Road Transport Engineers
AIRTO	Association of Industrial Research and Technology Organizations
AIS	Associate, Institute of Statisticians (*now see* MIS)
AISA	Associate, Incorporated Secretaries' Association
AIStructE	Associate, Institution of Structural Engineers
AJAG	Assistant Judge Advocate General
AJEX	Association of Jewish Ex-Service Men and Women
AK	Knight of the Order of Australia
AKC	Associate, King's College London
ALA	Associate, Library Association
Ala	Alabama (US)
ALAA	Associate, Library Association of Australia
ALAM	Associate, London Academy of Music and Dramatic Art
ALCD	Associate, London College of Divinity
ALCM	Associate, London College of Music
ALCS	Authors Lending and Copyright Society
ALFSEA	Allied Land Forces South-East Asia
ALI	Argyll Light Infantry; Associate, Landscape Institute
ALICE	Autistic and Language Impaired Children's Education
ALLC	Association for Literary and Linguistic Computing
ALP	Australian Labor Party
ALPSP	Association of Learned and Professional Society Publishers
ALS	Associate, Linnean Society
Alta	Alberta
AM	Albert Medal; Member of the Order of Australia; Master of Arts (US); Alpes Maritimes
AMA	Association of Metropolitan Authorities; Assistant Masters Association; Associate of the Museums Association; Australian Medical Association
Amb.	Ambulance; Ambassador
AMBIM	Associate Member, British Institute of Management (*now see* MBIM)
AMBritIRE	Associate Member, British Institution of Radio Engineers (*now see* AMIERE)
AMC	Association of Municipal Corporations
AMCT	Associate, Manchester College of Technology
AME	Association of Municipal Engineers
AMEME	Association of Mining Electrical and Mechanical Engineers
AMet	Associate of Metallurgy
AMF	Australian Military Forces
AMGOT	Allied Military Government of Occupied Territory
AMIAE	Associate Member, Institution of Automobile Engineers
AMIAgrE	Associate Member, Institution of Agricultural Engineers
AMIBF	Associate Member, Institute of British Foundrymen
AMICE	Associate Member, Institution of Civil Engineers (*now see* MICE)
AMIChemE	Associate Member, Institution of Chemical Engineers
AMIE(Aust)	Associate Member, Institution of Engineers, Australia
AMIED	Associate Member, Institution of Engineering Designers
AMIEE	Associate Member, Institution of Electrical Engineers (*now see* MIEE)
AMIE(Ind)	Associate Member, Institution of Engineers, India
AMIERE	Associate Member, Institution of Electronic and Radio Engineers
AMIH	Associate Member, Institute of Housing
AMIMechE	Associate Member, Institution of Mechanical Engineers (*now see* MIMechE)
AMIMinE	Associate Member, Institution of Mining Engineers
AMIMM	Associate Member, Institution of Mining and Metallurgy
AMInstBE	Associate Member, Institution of British Engineers
AMInstCE	Associate Member, Institution of Civil Engineers (*now see* MICE)
AmInstEE	American Institute of Electrical Engineers
AMInstR	Associate Member, Institute of Refrigeration
AMInstT	Associate Member, Institute of Transport (*now see* ACIT)
AMInstTA	Associate Member, Institute of Traffic Adminstration
AMINucE	Associate Member, Institution of Nuclear Engineers
AMIStructE	Associate Member, Institution of Structural Engineers
AMN	Ahli Mangku Negara (Malaysia)
AMP	Advanced Management Program
AMRINA	Associate Member, Royal Institution of Naval Architects
AMS	Assistant Military Secretary; Army Medical Services
AMTE	Admiralty Marine Technology Establishment
ANA	Associate National Academician (America)
ANAF	Arab Non-Arab Friendship
Anat.	Anatomy; Anatomical
ANC	African National Congress
ANECInst	Associate, NE Coast Institution of Engineers and Shipbuilders
ANGAU	Australian New Guinea Administrative Unit
Anon.	Anonymously
ANU	Australian National University
ANZAAS	Australian and New Zealand Association for the Advancement of Science
Anzac	Australian and New Zealand Army Corps
AO	Officer of the Order of Australia; Air Officer
AOA	Air Officer in charge of Administration
AOC	Air Officer Commanding
AOC-in-C	Air Officer Commanding-in-Chief
AOD	Army Ordnance Department
AOER	Army Officers Emergency Reserve
APA	American Psychiatric Association
APCK	Association for Promoting Christian Knowledge, Church of Ireland
APD	Army Pay Department
APEX	Association of Professional, Executive, Clerical and Computer Staff
APHA	American Public Health Association
APM	Assistant Provost Marshal
APMI	Associate, Pensions Management Institute
APS	Aborigines Protection Society
APsSI	Associate, Psychological Society of Ireland
APSW	Association of Psychiatric Social Workers
APT&C	Administrative, Professional, Technical and Clerical
APTC	Army Physical Training Corps
AQ	Administration and Quartering
AQMG	Assistant Quartermaster-General
AR	Associated Rediffusion (Television)
ARA	Associate, Royal Academy
ARACI	Associate, Royal Australian Chemical Institute
ARAD	Associate, Royal Academy of Dancing
ARAeS	Associate, Royal Aeronautical Society
ARAM	Associate, Royal Academy of Music
ARAS	Associate, Royal Astronomical Society
ARBA	Associate, Royal Society of British Artists
ARBC	Associate, Royal British Colonial Society of Artists
ARBS	Associate, Royal Society of British Sculptors
ARC	Architects' Registration Council; Agricultural Research Council (*now see* AFRC); Aeronautical Research Council
ARCA	Associate, Royal College of Art; Associate, Royal Canadian Academy
ARCamA	Associate, Royal Cambrian Academy of Art
ARCE	Academical Rank of Civil Engineer
ARCIC	Anglican-Roman Catholic International Commission
ARCM	Associate, Royal College of Music
ARCO	Associate, Royal College of Organists
ARCO(CHM)	Associate, Royal College of Organists with Diploma in Choir Training
ARCPsych	Associate Member, Royal College of Psychiatrists
ARCS	Associate, Royal College of Science
ARCST	Associate, Royal College of Science and Technology (Glasgow)
ARCUK	Architects' Registration Council of the United Kingdom
ARCVS	Associate, Royal College of Veterinary Surgeons
ARE	Associate, Royal Society of Painter-Etchers and Engravers; Arab Republic of Egypt
ARELS	Association of Recognised English Language Schools
ARIAS	Associate, Royal Incorporation of Architects in Scotland
ARIBA	Associate, Royal Institute of British Architects (*now see* RIBA)
ARIC	Associate, Royal Institute of Chemistry (later MRIC; *now see* MRSC)

ARICS	Professional Associate, Royal Institution of Chartered Surveyors
ARINA	Associate, Royal Institution of Naval Architects
Ark	Arkansas (US)
ARLT	Association for the Reform of Latin Teaching
ARMS	Associate, Royal Society of Miniature Painters
ARP	Air Raid Precautions
ARPS	Associate, Royal Photographic Society
ARR	Association of Radiation Research
ARRC	Associate, Royal Red Cross
ARSA	Associate, Royal Scottish Academy
ARSCM	Associate, Royal School of Church Music
ARSM	Associate, Royal School of Mines
ARTC	Associate, Royal Technical College (Glasgow) (now see ARCST)
ARVIA	Associate, Royal Victoria Institute of Architects
ARWA	Associate, Royal West of England Academy
ARWS	Associate, Royal Society of Painters in Water-Colours
AS	Anglo-Saxon
ASA	Associate Member, Society of Actuaries; Associate of Society of Actuaries (US); Australian Society of Accountants; Army Sailing Asssociation
ASAA	Associate, Society of Incorporated Accountants and Auditors
ASAM	Associate, Society of Art Masters
AS&TS of SA	Associated Scientific and Technical Societies of South Africa
ASBAH	Association for Spina Bifida and Hydrocephalus
ASC	Administrative Staff College, Henley
ASCA	Associate, Society of Company and Commercial Accountants
ASCAB	Armed Services Consultant Approval Board
ASCAP	American Society of Composers, Authors and Publishers
ASCE	American Society of Civil Engineers
AScW	Association of Scientific Workers (now see ASTMS)
ASD	Armament Supply Department
ASE	Amalgamated Society of Engineers (now see AUEW)
ASEAN	Association of South East Asian Nations
ASH	Action on Smoking and Health
ASIAD	Associate, Society of Industrial Artists and Designers
ASIA(Ed)	Associate, Society of Industrial Artists (Education)
ASLE	American Society of Lubrication Engineers
ASLEF	Associated Society of Locomotive Engineers and Firemen
ASLIB or Aslib	Association for Information Management (formerly Association of Special Libraries and Information Bureaux)
ASM	Association of Senior Members
ASME	American Society of Mechanical Engineers; Association for the Study of Medical Education
ASO	Air Staff Officer
ASSC	Accounting Standards Steering Committee
ASSET	Association of Supervisory Staffs, Executives and Technicians (now see ASTMS)
AssocISI	Associate, Iron and Steel Institute
AssocMCT	Associateship of Manchester College of Technology
AssocMIAeE	Associate Member, Institution of Aeronautical Engineers
AssocRINA	Associate, Royal Institution of Naval Architects
AssocSc	Associate in Science
Asst	Assistant
ASTC	Administrative Service Training Course
ASTMS	Association of Scientific, Technical and Managerial Staffs
ASVU	Army Security Vetting Unit
ASWE	Admiralty Surface Weapons Establishment
ATA	Air Transport Auxiliary
ATAE	Association of Tutors in Adult Education
ATAF	Allied Tactical Air Force
ATC	Air Training Corps; Art Teacher's Certificate
ATCDE	Association of Teachers in Colleges and Departments of Education (now see NATFHE)
ATCL	Associate, Trinity College of Music, London
ATD	Art Teacher's Diploma
ATI	Associate, Textile Institute
ATII	Associate Member, Institute of Taxation
ato	Ammunition Technical Officer
ATS	Auxiliary Territorial Service (now see WRAC)
ATTI	Association of Teachers in Technical Institutions (now see NATFHE)
ATV	Associated TeleVision
AUA	American Urological Association
AUCAS	Association of University Clinical Academic Staff
AUEW	Amalgamated Union of Engineering Workers (now see AEU)
AUEW(TASS)	Amalgamated Union of Engineering Workers (Technical, Administrative and Supervisory Section), now TASS – The Manufacturing Union
AUS	Army of the United States
AUT	Association of University Teachers
AVCC	Australian Vice-Chancellors' Committee
AVCM	Associate, Victoria College of Music
AVD	Army Veterinary Department
AVLA	Audio Visual Language Association
AVR	Army Volunteer Reserve
AWA	Anglian Water Authority
AWRE	Atomic Weapons Research Establishment
aws	Graduate of Air Warfare Course

B

b	born; brother
BA	Bachelor of Arts
BAA	British Airports Authority
BAAB	British Amateur Athletic Board
BAAL	British Association for Applied Linguistics
BAAS	British Association for the Advancement of Science
BAB	British Airways Board
BAC	British Aircraft Corporation
BACM	British Association of Colliery Management
BAe	British Aerospace
B&FBS	British and Foreign Bible Society
BAFO	British Air Forces of Occupation
BAFPA	British Association of Fitness Promotion Agencies
BAFTA	British Academy of Film and Television Arts
BAG	Business Art Galleries
BAI	*Baccalarius in Arte Ingeniaria* (Bachelor of Engineering)
BAIE	British Association of Industrial Editors
BALPA	British Air Line Pilots' Association
BAO	Bachelor of Art of Obstetrics
BAOMS	British Association of Oral and Maxillo-Facial Surgeons
BAOR	British Army of the Rhine (formerly *on* the Rhine)
BAOS	British Association of Oral Surgeons (now see BAOMS)
BAppSc(MT)	Bachelor of Applied Science (Medical Technology)
BARC	British Automobile Racing Club
Bart	Baronet
BAS	Bachelor in Agricultural Science
BASc	Bachelor of Applied Science
BASW	British Association of Social Workers
Batt.	Battery
BBA	British Bankers' Association; Bachelor of Business Administration
BB&CIRly	Bombay, Baroda and Central India Railway
BBB of C	British Boxing Board of Control
BBC	British Broadcasting Corporation
BBM	Bintang Bakti Masharakat (Public Service Star) (Singapore)
BBS	Bachelor of Business Studies
BC	Before Christ; British Columbia
BCC	British Council of Churches
BCE	Bachelor of Civil Engineering
BCh or BChir	Bachelor of Surgery
BCL	Bachelor of Civil Law
BCMF	British Ceramic Manufacturers' Federation
BCMS	Bible Churchmen's Missionary Society
BCOF	British Commonwealth Occupation Force
BCom or BComm	Bachelor of Commerce
BComSc	Bachelor of Commercial Science
BCS	Bengal Civil Service; British Computer Society
BCSA	British Constructional Steelwork Association
BCURA	British Coal Utilization Research Association
BCYC	British Corinthian Yacht Club
BD	Bachelor of Divinity
Bd	Board
BDA	British Dental Association
Bde	Brigade
BDS	Bachelor of Dental Surgery
BDSc	Bachelor of Dental Science
BE	Bachelor of Engineering; British Element
BEA	British East Africa; British European Airways; British Epilepsy Association
BEAMA	Federation of British Electrotechnical and Allied Manufacturers' Associations (formerly British Electrical and Allied Manufacturers' Association)
BE&A	Bachelor of Engineering and Architecture (Malta)
BEAS	British Educational Administration Society
BEC	Business Education Council (now see BTEC)
BEc	Bachelor of Economics
BEd	Bachelor of Education
Beds	Bedfordshire
BEE	Bachelor of Electrical Engineering
BEF	British Expeditionary Force; British Equestrian Federation
BEM	British Empire Medal
BEMAS	British Education Management and Administration Society
BEME	Brigade Electrical and Mechanical Engineer
BEO	Base Engineer Officer
Berks	Berkshire
BFI	British Film Institute
BFMIRA	British Food Manufacturing Industries Research Association
BFPO	British Forces Post Office
BFSS	British Field Sports Society
BGS	Brigadier General Staff
Bhd	Berhad
BHRA	British Hydromechanics Research Association
BHRCA	British Hotels, Restaurants and Caterers' Association
BHS	British Horse Society
BICC	British Insulated Callender's Cables
BICERA	British Internal Combustion Engine Research Association
BICSc	British Institute of Cleaning Science
BIF	British Industries Fair
BIFU	Banking Insurance and Finance Union
BIM	British Institute of Management
BIR	British Institute of Radiology
BIS	Bank for International Settlements

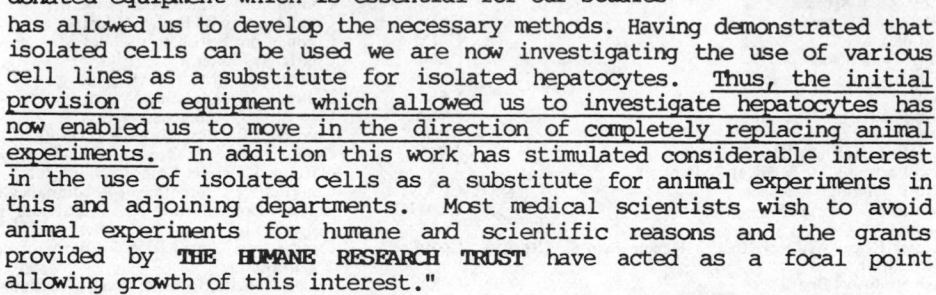
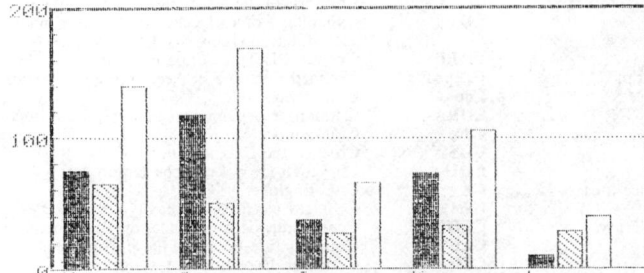

BISF	British Iron and Steel Federation	CA	Central America; County Alderman; Chartered Accountant (Scotland and Canada)
BISFA	British Industrial and Scientific Film Association		
BISPA	British Independent Steel Producers Association	CAA	Civil Aviation Authority
BISRA	British Iron and Steel Research Association	CAABU	Council for the Advancement of Arab and British Understanding
BJ	Bachelor of Journalism		
BJSM	British Joint Services Mission	CAAV	Central Association of Agricultural Valuers; *also* Member of the Association
BKSTS	British Kinematograph, Sound and Television Society		
BL	Bachelor of Law	CAB	Citizens' Advice Bureau
BLA	British Liberation Army	CACTM	Central Advisory Council of Training for the Ministry (*now see* ACCM)
BLE	Brotherhood of Locomotive Engineers; Bachelor of Land Economy		
		CAER	Conservative Action for Electoral Reform
BLESMA	British Limbless Ex-Servicemen's Association	CALE	Canadian Army Liaison Executive
BLitt	Bachelor of Letters	Cambs	Cambridgeshire
BM	British Museum; Bachelor of Medicine; Brigade Major; British Monomark	CAMC	Canadian Army Medical Corps
		CAMRA	Campaign for Real Ale
BMA	British Medical Association	CAMS	Certificate of Advanced Musical Study
BMEO	British Middle East Office	CAMW	Central Association for Mental Welfare
BMet	Bachelor of Metallurgy	Cantab	*Cantabrigiensis* (of Cambridge)
BMEWS	Ballistic Missile Early Warning System	Cantuar	*Cantuariensis* (of Canterbury)
BMH	British Military Hospital	CARD	Campaign against Racial Discrimination
BMJ	British Medical Journal	CARE	Cottage and Rural Enterprises
BMM	British Military Mission	CARICOM	Caribbean Community
BMRA	Brigade Major Royal Artillery	CARIFTA	Caribbean Free Trade Area (*now see* CARICOM)
Bn	Battalion	CAS	Chief of the Air Staff
BNAF	British North Africa Force	CASI	Canadian Aeronautics and Space Institute
BNC	Brasenose College	Cav.	Cavalry
BNEC	British National Export Council	CAWU	Clerical and Administrative Workers' Union (*now see* APEX)
BNFL	British Nuclear Fuels Ltd		
BNOC	British National Oil Corporation; British National Opera Company	CB	Companion of the Order of the Bath; County Borough
		CBC	County Borough Council
BOAC	British Overseas Airways Corporation	CBCO	Central Board for Conscientious Objectors
BomCS	Bombay Civil Service	CBE	Commander of the Order of the British Empire
BomSC	Bombay Staff Corps	CBI	Confederation of British Industry
BoT	Board of Trade	CBIM	Companion, British Institute of Management
Bot.	Botany; Botanical	CBiol	Chartered Biologist
BOTB	British Overseas Trade Board	CBNS	Commander British Navy Staff
Bp	Bishop	CBS	Columbia Broadcasting System
BPA	British Paediatric Association	CBSA	Clay Bird Shooting Association
BPharm	Bachelor of Pharmacy	CBSI	Chartered Building Societies Institute
BPIF	British Printing Industries Federation	CC	Companion of the Order of Canada; City Council; County Council; Cricket Club; Cycling Club; County Court
BPMF	British Postgraduate Medical Federation		
BPsS	British Psychological Society	CCAB	Consultative Committee of Accountancy Bodies
BR	British Rail	CCAHC	Central Council for Agricultural and Horticultural Co-operation
Br.	Branch		
BRA	Brigadier Royal Artillery; British Rheumatism & Arthritis Association	CCBE	Commission Consultative des Barreaux de la Communauté Européenne
BRB	British Railways Board	CCC	Corpus Christi College; Central Criminal Court; County Cricket Club
BRCS	British Red Cross Society		
BRE	Building Research Establishment	CCE	Chartered Civil Engineer
Brig.	Brigadier	CCF	Combined Cadet Force
BritIRE	British Institution of Radio Engineers (*now see* IERE)	CCFM	Combined Cadet Forces Medal
BRNC	Britannia Royal Naval College	CCG	Control Commission Germany
BRS	British Road Services	CCH	Cacique's Crown of Honour, Order of Service of Guyana
BS	Bachelor of Surgery; Bachelor of Science	CChem	Chartered Chemist
BSA	Bachelor of Scientific Agriculture; Birmingham Small Arms; Building Societies' Association	CCHMS	Central Committee for Hospital Medical Services
		CCIA	Commission of Churches on International Affairs
BSAA	British South American Airways	CCJ	Council of Christians and Jews
BSAP	British South Africa Police	CCPR	Central Council of Physical Recreation
BSC	British Steel Corporation; Bengal Staff Corps	CCRA	Commander Corps of Royal Artillery
BSc	Bachelor of Science	CCRE	Commander Corps of Royal Engineers
BScA	Bachelor of Science in Agriculture	CCRSigs	Commander Corps of Royal Signals
BSc(Dent)	Bachelor of Science in Dentistry	CCS	Casualty Clearing Station; Ceylon Civil Service
BSE	Bachelor of Science in Engineering (US)	CCSU	Council of Civil Service Unions
BSF	British Salonica Force	CCTA	Commission de Coopération Technique pour l'Afrique
BSFA	British Science Fiction Association	CD	Canadian Forces Decoration; Commander of the Order of Distinction (Jamaica); Civil Defence
BSI	British Standards Institution		
BSJA	British Show Jumping Association	CDEE	Chemical Defence Experimental Establishment
BSME	Bachelor of Science in Mechanical Engineering	CDipAF	Certified Diploma in Accounting and Finance
BSNS	Bachelor of Naval Science	Cdo	Commando
BSocSc	Bachelor of Social Science	CDRA	Committee of Directors of Research Associations
BSRA	British Ship Research Association	Cdre	Commodore
BSS	Bachelor of Science (Social Science)	CDS	Chief of the Defence Staff
BST	Bachelor of Sacred Theology	CDU	Christlich-Demokratische Union
BT	Bachelor of Teaching; British Telecommunications	CE	Civil Engineer
Bt	Baronet; Brevet	CEA	Central Electricity Authority
BTA	British Tourist Authority (*formerly* British Travel Association)	CEDEP	Centre Européen d'Education Permanente
		CEE	Communauté Economique Européenne
BTC	British Transport Commission	CEF	Canadian Expeditionary Force
BTCV	British Trust for Conservation Volunteers	CEFIC	Conseil Européen des Fédérations de l'Industrie Chimique
BTDB	British Transport Docks Board (*now see* ABP)	CEGB	Central Electricity Generating Board
BTEC	Business and Technician Education Council	CEI	Council of Engineering Institutions
BTh	Bachelor of Theology	CEIR	Corporation for Economic and Industrial Research
Btss	Baronetess	CEM	Council of European Municipalities (*now see* CEMR)
BUAS	British Universities Association of Slavists	CEMA	Council for the Encouragement of Music and the Arts
BUPA	British United Provident Association	CEMR	Council of European Municipalities and Regions
BVA	British Veterinary Association	CEMS	Church of England Men's Society
BVM	Blessed Virgin Mary	CEN	Comité Européen de Normalisation
BVMS	Bachelor of Veterinary Medicine and Surgery	CEng	Chartered Engineer
Bucks	Buckinghamshire	Cento	Central Treaty Organisation
BWI	British West Indies	CEPT	Conférence Européenne des Postes et des Télécommunications
BWM	British War Medal		
		CERL	Central Electricity Research Laboratories

C

		CERN	Organisation (*formerly* Centre) Européenne pour la Recherche Nucléaire
		CERT	Charities Effectiveness Review Trust
(C)	Conservative; 100	Cert Ed	Certificate of Education
c	Child; cousin; *circa* (about)	CET	Council for Educational Technology
		CETS	Church of England Temperance Society

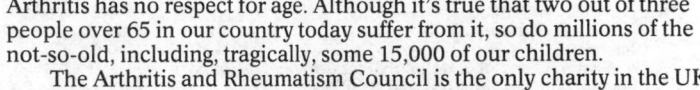

CF	Chaplain to the Forces
CFA	Canadian Field Artillery
CFE	Central Fighter Establishment
CFM	Cadet Forces Medal
CFR	Commander of the Order of the Federal Republic of Nigeria
CFS	Central Flying School
CGA	Community of the Glorious Ascension; Country Gentlemen's Association
CGH	Order of the Golden Heart of Kenya (1st class)
CGIA	Insignia Award of City and Guilds of London Institute
CGLI	City and Guilds of London Institute
CGM	Conspicuous Gallantry Medal
CGRM	Commandant-General Royal Marines
CGS	Chief of the General Staff
CH	Companion of Honour
Chanc.	Chancellor; Chancery
Chap.	Chaplain
ChapStJ	Chaplain of Order of St John of Jerusalem (now see ChStJ)
CHAR	Campaign for the Homeless and Rootless
CHB	Companion of Honour of Barbados
ChB	Bachelor of Surgery
CHC	Community Health Council
Ch.Ch.	Christ Church
Ch.Coll.	Christ's College
CHE	Campaign for Homosexual Equality
CHM	Chevalier of Honour and Merit (Haiti)
(CHM)	See under ARCO(CHM), FRCO(CHM)
ChM	Master of Surgery
Chm.	Chairman
CHSC	Central Health Services Council
ChStJ	Chaplain of the Most Venerable Order of the Hospital of St John of Jerusalem
CI	Imperial Order of the Crown of India; Channel Islands
CIA	Chemical Industries Association; Central Intelligence Agency
CIAD	Central Institute of Art and Design
CIAgrE	Companion, Institution of Agricultural Engineers
CIAL	Corresponding Member of the International Institute of Arts and Letters
CIArb	Chartered Institute of Arbitrators
CIBS	Chartered Institution of Building Services (now see CIBSE)
CIBSE	Chartered Institution of Building Services Engineers
CIC	Chemical Institute of Canada
CICHE	Committee for International Co-operation in Higher Education
CID	Criminal Investigation Department
CIDEC	Conseil International pour le Développement du Cuivre
CIE	Companion of the Order of the Indian Empire; Confédération Internationale des Etudiants
CIFRS	Comité International de la Rayonne et des Fibres Synthétiques
CIGasE	Companion, Institution of Gas Engineers
CIGRE	Conférence Internationale des Grands Réseaux Electriques
CIGS	Chief of the Imperial General Staff (now see CGS)
CIIA	Canadian Institute of International Affairs
CIM	China Inland Mission
CIMarE	Companion, Institute of Marine Engineers
CIMEMME	Companion, Institution of Mining Electrical and Mining Mechanical Engineers
CIMGTechE	Companion, Institution of Mechanical and General Technician Engineers
C-in-C	Commander-in-Chief
CINCHAN	Allied Commander-in-Chief Channel
CIOB	Chartered Institute of Building
CIPFA	Chartered Institute of Public Finance and Accountancy
CIPL	Comité International Permanent des Linguistes
CIPM	Companion, Institute of Personnel Management
CIR	Commission on Industrial Relations
CIRIA	Construction Industry Research and Information Association
CIS	Institute of Chartered Secretaries and Administrators (formerly Chartered Institute of Secretaries); Command Control Communications and Information Systems
CISAC	Confédération Internationale des Sociétés d'Auteurs et Compositeurs
CIT	Chartered Institute of Transport; California Institute of Technology
CIU	Club and Institute Union
CIV	City Imperial Volunteers
CJ	Chief Justice
CJM	Congregation of Jesus and Mary (Eudist Fathers)
CL	Commander of Order of Leopold
cl	cum laude
Cl.	Class
CLA	Country Landowners' Association
CLit	Companion of Literature (Royal Society of Literature Award)
CLJ	Commander, Order of St Lazarus of Jerusalem
CLP	Constituency Labour Party
CLRAE	Conference of Local and Regional Authorities of Europe
CM	Member of the Order of Canada; Congregation of the Mission (Vincentians); Master in Surgery; Certificated Master; Canadian Militia
CMA	Canadian Medical Association; Cost and Management Accountant (NZ)
CMAC	Catholic Marriage Advisory Council
CMB	Central Midwives' Board
CMF	Commonwealth Military Forces; Central Mediterranean Force
CMG	Companion of the Order of St Michael and St George
CMLJ	Commander of Merit, Order of St Lazarus of Jerusalem
CMM	Commander, Order of Military Merit (Canada)
CMO	Chief Medical Officer
CMP	Corps of Military Police (now see CRMP)
CMS	Church Missionary Society; Certificate in Management Studies
CMT	Chaconia Medal of Trinidad
CNAA	Council for National Academic Awards
CND	Campaign for Nuclear Disarmament
CNI	Companion, Nautical Institute
CNR	Canadian National Railways
CNRS	Centre National du Recherche Scientifique
CO	Commanding Officer; Commonwealth Office (after Aug. 1966) (now see FCO); Colonial Office (before Aug. 1966); Conscientious Objector
Co.	County; Company
C of E	Church of England
C of S	Chief of Staff
Coal.L or Co.L	Coalition Liberal
COHSE	Confederation of Health Service Employees
COI	Central Office of Information
CoID	Council of Industrial Design (now Design Council)
Col	Colonel
Coll.	College; Collegiate
Colo	Colorado (US)
Col.-Sergt	Colour-Sergeant
Com	Communist
Comd	Command
Comdg	Commanding
Comdr	Commander
Comdt	Commandant
COMEC	Council of the Military Education Committees of the Universities of the UK
COMET	Committee for Middle East Trade
Commn	Commission
Commnd	Commissioned
CompAMEME	Companion, Association of Mining Electrical and Mechanical Engineers
CompICE	Companion, Institution of Civil Engineers
CompIEE	Companion, Institution of Electrical Engineers
CompIERE	Companion, Institution of Electronic and Radio Engineers
CompIMechE	Companion, Institution of Mechanical Engineers
CompIWES	Companion, Institution of Water Engineers and Scientists
CompTI	Companion of the Textile Institute
Comr	Commissioner
Comy-Gen.	Commissary-General
CON	Commander, Order of the Niger
Conn	Connecticut (US)
Const.	Constitutional
Co-op.	Co-operative
COPA	Comité des Organisations Professionels Agricoles de la CEE
COPEC	Conference of Politics, Economics and Christianity
Corp.	Corporation; Corporal
Corresp. Mem.	Corresponding Member
COS	Chief of Staff; Charity Organization Society
COSA	Colliery Officials and Staffs Association
CoSIRA	Council for Small Industries in Rural Areas
COSLA	Convention of Scottish Local Authorities
COSPAR	Committee on Space Research
COSSAC	Chief of Staff to Supreme Allied Commander
COTC	Canadian Officers' Training Corps
Coal.U or Co.U	Coalition Unionist
CP	Central Provinces; Cape Province
CPA	Commonwealth Parliamentary Association; Chartered Patent Agent; Certified Public Accountant (Canada) (now see CA)
CPAS	Church Pastoral Aid Society
CPC	Conservative Political Centre
CPhys	Chartered Physicist
CPL	Chief Personnel and Logistics
CPM	Colonial Police Medal
CPR	Canadian Pacific Railway
CPRE	Council for the Protection of Rural England
CPSA	Civil and Public Services Association
CPSU	Communist Party of the Soviet Union
CPU	Commonwealth Press Union
CQSW	Certificate of Qualification in Social Work
CR	Community of the Resurrection
cr	created or creation
CRA	Commander, Royal Artillery
CRAeS	Companion, Royal Aeronautical Society
CRASC	Commander, Royal Army Service Corps
CRC	Cancer Research Campaign; Community Relations Council
CRCP(C)	Certificant, Royal College of Physicians of Canada
CRE	Commander, Royal Engineers; Commission for Racial Equality; Commercial Relations and Exports
Cres.	Crescent
CRMP	Corps of Royal Military Police
CRNCM	Companion, Royal Northern College of Music
CRO	Commonwealth Relations Office (before Aug. 1966; now see FCO)
CS	Civil Service; Clerk to the Signet
CSA	Confederate States of America

CSB	Bachelor of Christian Science
CSC	Conspicuous Service Cross; Congregation of the Holy Cross
CSCA	Civil Service Clerical Association (now see CPSA)
CSCE	Conference on Security and Cooperation in Europe
CSD	Civil Service Department; Cooperative Secretaries Diploma
CSEU	Confederation of Shipbuilding and Engineering Unions
CSG	Companion of the Order of the Star of Ghana; Company of the Servants of God
CSI	Companion of the Order of the Star of India
CSIR	Commonwealth Council for Scientific and Industrial Research (now see CSIRO)
CSIRO	Commonwealth Scientific and Industrial Research Organization (Australia)
CSO	Chief Scientific Officer; Chief Signal Officer; Chief Staff Officer
CSP	Chartered Society of Physiotherapists; Civil Service of Pakistan
CSS	Companion of the Star of Sarawak; Council for Science and Society
CSSB	Civil Service Selection Board
CSSp	Holy Ghost Father
CSSR	Congregation of the Most Holy Redeemer (Redemptorist Order)
CSTI	Council of Science and Technology Institutes
CStJ	Commander of the Most Venerable Order of the Hospital of St John of Jerusalem
CSU	Christlich-Soziale Union in Bayern
CSV	Community Service Volunteers
CTA	Chaplain Territorial Army
CTB	College of Teachers of the Blind
CTC	Cyclists' Touring Club; Commando Training Centre
CText	Chartered Textile Technologist
CTR(Harwell)	Controlled Thermonuclear Research
CU	Cambridge University
CUAC	Cambridge University Athletic Club
CUAFC	Cambridge University Association Football Club
CUBC	Cambridge University Boat Club
CUCC	Cambridge University Cricket Club
CUF	Common University Fund
CUHC	Cambridge University Hockey Club
CUMS	Cambridge University Musical Society
CUP	Cambridge University Press
CURUFC	Cambridge University Rugby Union Football Club
CV	Cross of Valour (Canada)
CVCP	Committee of Vice-Chancellors and Principals of the Universities of the United Kingdom
CVO	Commander of the Royal Victorian Order
CVS	Council of Voluntary Service
CWA	Crime Writers Association
CWGC	Commonwealth War Graves Commission
CWS	Co-operative Wholesale Society

D

D	Duke
d	Died; daughter
DA	Diploma in Anaesthesia; Diploma in Art
DAA&QMG	Deputy Assistant Adjutant and Quartermaster-General
DAAG	Deputy Assistant Adjutant-General
DA&QMG	Deputy Adjutant and Quartermaster-General
DAC	Development Assistance Committee
DACG	Deputy Assistant Chaplain-General
DAD	Deputy Assistant Director
DAdmin	Doctor of Administration
DADMS	Deputy Assistant Director of Medical Services
DADOS	Deputy Assistant Director of Ordnance Services
DADQ	Deputy Assistant Director of Quartering
DADST	Deputy Assistant Director of Supplies and Transport
DAG	Deputy Adjutant-General
DAgr	Doctor of Agriculture
DAMS	Deputy Assistant Military Secretary
DandAD	Designers and Art Directors Association
DAppSc	Doctor of Applied Science
DAQMG	Deputy Assistant Quartermaster-General
DASc	Doctor in Agricultural Sciences
DATA	Draughtsmen's and Allied Technicians' Association (now see AUEW(TASS))
DATEC	Art and Design Committee, Technician Education Council
DBA	Doctor of Business Administration
DBE	Dame Commander Order of the British Empire
DC	District Council; District of Columbia (US)
DCAe	Diploma of College of Aeronautics
DCAS	Deputy Chief of the Air Staff
DCB	Dame Commander of the Order of the Bath
DCG	Deputy Chaplain-General
DCGRM	Department of the Commandant General Royal Marines
DCGS	Deputy Chief of the General Staff
DCh	Doctor of Surgery
DCH	Diploma in Child Health
DCIGS	Deputy Chief of the Imperial General Staff (now see DCGS)
DCL	Doctor of Civil Law
DCLI	Duke of Cornwall's Light Infantry
DCM	Distinguished Conduct Medal
DCMG	Dame Commander of the Order of St Michael and St George
DCMHE	Diploma of Contents and Methods in Health Education
DCnL	Doctor of Canon Law
DCP	Diploma in Clinical Pathology; Diploma in Conservation of Paintings
DCS	Deputy Chief of Staff; Doctor of Commercial Sciences
DCSO	Deputy Chief Scientific Officer
DCT	Doctor of Christian Theology
DCVO	Dame Commander of Royal Victorian Order
DD	Doctor of Divinity
DDGAMS	Deputy Director General, Army Medical Services
DDL	Deputy Director of Labour
DDME	Deputy Director of Mechanical Engineering
DDMI	Deputy Director of Military Intelligence
DDMS	Deputy Director of Medical Services
DDMT	Deputy Director of Military Training
DDNI	Deputy Director of Naval Intelligence
DDO	Diploma in Dental Orthopaedics
DDPH	Diploma in Dental Public Health
DDPR	Deputy Director of Public Relations
DDPS	Deputy Director of Personal Services
DDR	Deutsche Demokratische Republik
DDRA	Deputy Director Royal Artillery
DDS	Doctor of Dental Surgery; Director of Dental Services
DDSc	Doctor of Dental Science
DDSD	Deputy Director Staff Duties
DDSM	Defense Distinguished Service Medal
DDST	Deputy Director of Supplies and Transport
DDWE&M	Deputy Director of Works, Electrical and Mechanical
DE	Doctor of Engineering
DEA	Department of Economic Affairs
decd	deceased
DEconSc	Doctor of Economic Science
DEd	Doctor of Education
Del	Delaware (US)
Deleg.	Delegate
DEMS	Defensively Equipped Merchant Ships
(DemU)	Democratic Unionist
DEng	Doctor of Engineering
DenM	Docteur en Médicine
DEOVR	Duke of Edinburgh's Own Volunteer Rifles
DEP	Department of Employment and Productivity; European Progressive Democrats
Dep.	Deputy
DES	Department of Education and Science
DèsL	Docteur ès lettres
DèsS	Docteur ès sciences
DesRCA	Designer of the Royal College of Art
DFA	Doctor of Fine Arts
DFC	Distinguished Flying Cross
DFH	Diploma of Faraday House
DFLS	Day Fighter Leaders' School
DFM	Distinguished Flying Medal
DG	Director General; Dragoon Guards
DGAA	Distressed Gentlefolks Aid Association
DGAMS	Director-General Army Medical Services
DGLP(A)	Director General Logistic Policy (Army)
DGMS	Director-General of Medical Services
DGMT	Director-General of Military Training
DGMW	Director-General of Military Works
DGNPS	Director-General of Naval Personal Services
DGP	Director-General of Personnel
DGPS	Director-General of Personal Services
DGS	Diploma in Graduate Studies
DGStJ	Dame of Grace, Order of St John of Jerusalem (now see DStJ)
DGU	Doctor of Griffith University
DH	Doctor of Humanities
DHA	District Health Authority
Dhc	Doctor honoris causa
DHEW	Department of Health Education and Welfare (US)
DHL	Doctor of Humane Letters; Doctor of Hebrew Literature
DHM	Dean Hole Medal
DHMSA	Diploma in the History of Medicine (Society of Apothecaries)
DHQ	District Headquarters
DHSS	Department of Health and Social Security
DIAS	Dublin Institute of Advanced Sciences
DIC	Diploma of the Imperial College
DICTA	Diploma of Imperial College of Tropical Agriculture
DIG	Deputy Inspector-General
DIH	Diploma in Industrial Health
DIMP	Darjah Indera Mahkota Pahang
Dio.	Diocese
DipAD	Diploma in Art and Design
DipAe	Diploma in Aeronautics
DipASE	Diploma in Advanced Study of Education, College of Preceptors
DipAvMed	Diploma of Aviation Medicine, Royal College of Physicians
DipBA	Diploma in Business Administration
DipBS	Diploma in Fine Art, Byam Shaw School
DipCAM	Diploma in Communications, Advertising and Marketing of CAM Foundation
DipCC	Diploma of the Central College
DipCD	Diploma in Civic Design
DipCE	Diploma in Civil Engineering
DipEcon	Diploma in Economics
DipEd	Diploma in Education
DipEl	Diploma in Electronics
DipESL	Diploma in English as a Second Language
DipEth	Diploma in Ethnology

WE, THE LIMBLESS, LOOK TO YOU FOR HELP

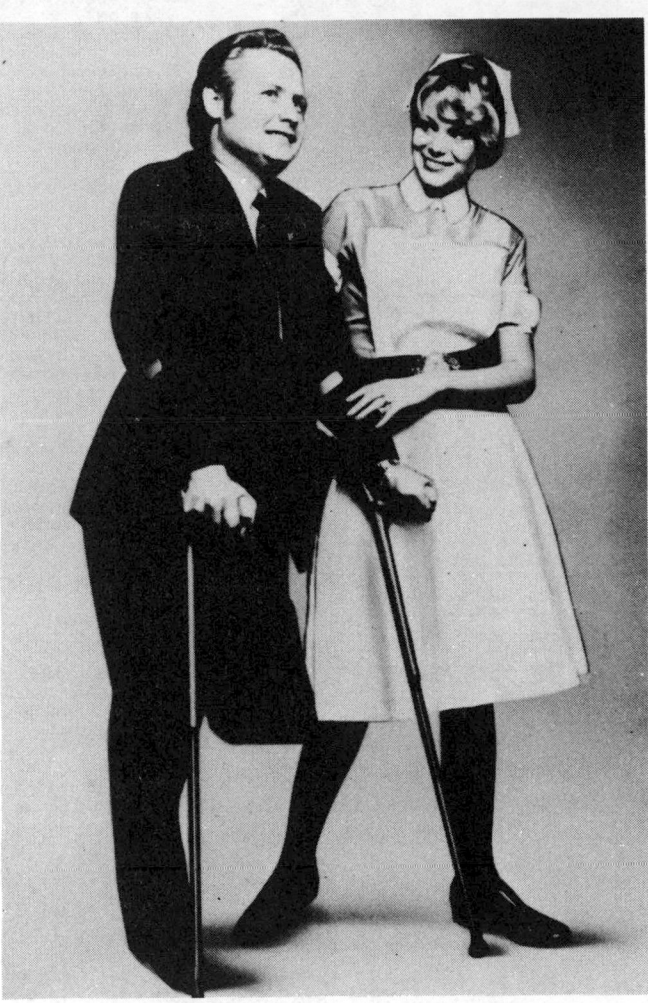

We come from both world wars. We come from Korea, Kenya, Malaya, Aden, Cyprus, Ulster and from the Falklands.

Now, disabled, we must look to you for help. Please help by helping our Association.

BLESMA looks after the limbless from all the Services. It helps to overcome the shock of losing arms, or legs or an eye. And, for the severely handicapped, it provides Residential Homes where they can live in peace and dignity.

Help the disabled by helping BLESMA. We promise you that not one penny of your donation will be wasted.

Donations and information:
The Chairman, BLESMA,
Midland Bank Ltd.,
60 West Smithfield, London EC1A 9DX

Give to those who gave – please.

50 years in the service of Disabled Ex-Service Men

BLESMA 1932-1982 GOLDEN JUBILEE

BLESMA
BRITISH LIMBLESS
EX-SERVICE MEN'S ASSOCIATION

DipFE	Diploma in Further Education
DipGSM	Diploma in Music, Guildhall School of Music and Drama
DipLA	Diploma in Landscape Architecture
DipLib	Diploma of Librarianship
DipM	Diploma in Marketing
DipN	Diploma in Nursing
DipNEC	Diploma of Northampton Engineering College (*now* City University)
DipPA	Diploma of Practitioners in Advertising (*now see* DipCAM)
DipREM	Diploma in Rural Estate Management
DipTA	Diploma in Tropical Agriculture
DipT&CP	Diploma in Town and Country Planning
DipTh	Diploma in Theology
DipTP	Diploma in Town Planning
DipTPT	Diploma in Theory and Practice of Teaching
DistTP	Distinction in Town Planning
Div.	Division; Divorced
DJAG	Deputy Judge Advocate General
DJStJ	Dame of Justice, Order of St John of Jerusalem (*now see* DStJ)
DJur	*Doctor Juris*
DK	Most Esteemed Family Order (Brunei)
DL	Deputy Lieutenant
DLC	Diploma Loughborough College
DLES	Doctor of Letters in Economic Studies
DLI	Durham Light Infantry
DLit or DLitt	Doctor of Literature; Doctor of Letters
DLJ	Dame of Grace, Order of St Lazarus of Jerusalem
DLO	Diploma in Laryngology and Otology
DM	Doctor of Medicine
DMA	Diploma in Municipal Administration
DMD	Doctor of Medical Dentistry (Australia)
DME	Director of Mechanical Engineering
DMet	Doctor of Metallurgy
DMI	Director of Military Intelligence
DMin	Doctor of Ministry
DMJ	Diploma in Medical Jurisprudence
DMJ(Path)	Diploma in Medical Jurisprudence (Pathology)
DMO	Director of Military Operations
DMR	Diploma in Medical Radiology
DMRD	Diploma in Medical Radiological Diagnosis
DMRE	Diploma in Medical Radiology and Electrology
DMRT	Diploma in Medical Radio-Therapy
DMS	Director of Medical Services; Decoration for Meritorious Service (South Africa); Diploma in Management Studies
DMSSB	Direct Mail Services Standards Board
DMT	Director of Military Training
DMus	Doctor of Music
DNB	Dictionary of National Biography
DNE	Director of Naval Equipment
DNI	Director of Naval Intelligence
DO	Diploma in Ophthalmology
DOAE	Defence Operational Analysis Establishment
DObstRCOG	Diploma Royal College of Obstetricians and Gynaecologists
DOC	District Officer Commanding
DocEng	Doctor of Engineering
DoE	Department of the Environment
DoI	Department of Industry
DOL	Doctor of Oriental Learning
Dom.	*Dominus*
DOMS	Diploma in Ophthalmic Medicine and Surgery
DOR	Director of Operational Requirements
DOS	Director of Ordnance Services
Dow.	Dowager
DPA	Diploma in Public Administration; Discharged Prisoners' Aid
DPD	Diploma in Public Dentistry
DPEc	Doctor of Political Economy
DPed	Doctor of Pedagogy
DPH	Diploma in Public Health
DPh or DPhil	Doctor of Philosophy
DPLG	Diplômé par le Gouvernement
DPM	Diploma in Psychological Medicine
DPR	Director of Public Relations
DPS	Director of Postal Services; Director of Personal Services; Doctor of Public Service
DQMG	Deputy Quartermaster-General
Dr	Doctor
DRAC	Director Royal Armoured Corps
DRC	Diploma of Royal College of Science and Technology, Glasgow
DRD	Diploma in Restorative Dentistry
Dr ing	Doctor of Engineering
Dr jur	Doctor of Laws
Dr ŒcPol	*Doctor Œconomiæ Politicæ*
Dr rer. nat.	Doctor of Natural Science
DRSAMD	Diploma of the Royal Scottish Academy of Music and Drama
DS	Directing Staff
DSA	Diploma in Social Administration
DSAO	Diplomatic Service Adinistration Office
DSC	Distinguished Service Cross
DSc	Doctor of Science
DScA	Docteur en sciences agricoles
DSCHE	Diploma of the Scottish Council for Health Education
DScMil	Doctor of Military Science

DSD	Director Staff Duties
DSIR	Department of Scientific and Industrial Research (later SRC; *now see* SERC)
DSL	Doctor of Sacred Letters
DSLJ	Dato Seri Laila Jasa Brunei
DSM	Distinguished Service Medal
DSNB	Dato Setia Negara Brunei
DSO	Companion of the Distinguished Service Order
DSocSc	Doctor of Social Science
DSP	Director of Selection of Personnel; Docteur en sciences politiques (Montreal)
dsp	*decessit sine prole* (died without issue)
DSS	Doctor of Sacred Scripture
Dss	Deaconess
DSSc	Doctor of Social Science (USA)
DST	Director of Supplies and Transport
DStJ	Dame of Grace, Most Venerable Order of the Hospital of St John of Jerusalem; Dame of Justice, Most Venerable Order of the Hospital of St John of Jerusalem
DTA	Diploma in Tropical Agriculture
DTD	Dekoratie voor Trouwe Dienst (Decoration for Devoted Service)
DTech	Doctor of Technology
DTH	Diploma in Tropical Hygiene
DTheol	Doctor of Theology
DThPT	Diploma in Theory and Practice of Teaching
DTI	Department of Trade and Industry
DTM&H	Diploma in Tropical Medicine and Hygiene
DU	Doctor of the University
Dunelm	*Dunelmensis* (of Durham)
DUniv	Doctor of the University
DUP	Docteur de l'Université de Paris
(DUP)	Democratic Unionist Party
DVA	Diploma of Veterinary Anaesthesia
DVH	Diploma in Veterinary Hygiene
DVLC	Driver and Vehicle Licensing Centre
DVM	Doctor of Veterinary Medicine
DVMS	Doctor of Veterinary Medicine and Surgery
DVR	Diploma in Veterinary Radiology
DVSc	Doctor of Veterinary Science
DVSM	Diploma in Veterinary State Medicine

E

E	East; Earl; England
e	eldest
EAA	Edinburgh Architectural Association
EAHY	European Architectural Heritage Year
EAP	East Africa Protectorate
EAW	Electrical Association for Women
EBC	English Benedictine Congregation
Ebor	*Eboracensis* (of York)
EBU	European Broadcasting Union
EC	Etoile du Courage (Canada); European Commission; Emergency Commission
ECA	Economic Co–operation Administration; Economic Commission for Africa
ECAFE	Economic Commission for Asia and the Far East (*now see* ESCAP)
ECE	Economic Commission for Europe
ECGD	Export Credits Guarantee Department
ECLA	Economic Commission for Latin America
ECOVAST	European Council for the Village and Small Town
ECSC	European Coal and Steel Community
ECU	English Church Union
ED	Efficiency Decoration; Doctor of Engineering (US); European Democrat
ed	edited
EdB	Bachelor of Education
EDC	Economic Development Committee
EdD	Doctor of Education
EDF	European Development Fund
EDG	European Democratic Group
Edin.	Edinburgh
Edn	Edition
EDP	Executive Development Programme
Educ	Educated
Educn	Education
EEC	European Economic Community; Commission of the European Communities
EEF	Engineering Employers' Federation; Egyptian Expeditionary Force
EETPU	Electrical Electronic Telecommunication & Plumbing Union
EETS	Early English Text Society
EFCE	European Federation of Chemical Engineering
EFTA	European Free Trade Association
eh	ehrenhalber (honorary)
EI	East Indian; East Indies
EIB	European Investment Bank
EICS	East India Company's Service
E-in-C	Engineer-in-Chief
EIS	Educational Institute of Scotland
EISCAT	European Incoherent Scatter Association
EIU	Economist Intelligence Unit
ELBS	English Language Book Society
ELSE	European Life Science Editors

ROSEMARY FOR REMEMBRANCE

Sue Ryder Foundation

Founder: Lady Ryder, of Warsaw, CMG, OBE

In aid of the sick and disabled of all ages.

The Sue Ryder Foundation was established by Lady Ryder during the post-war years after she had been doing social relief work on the Continent. Its purpose was, and is, the relief of suffering on a wide scale by means of personal service, helping the sick and disabled everywhere, irrespective of race, religion or age, and thus serving as a **Living Memorial** to all those who suffered or died in the two World Wars and to those who undergo persecution or die in defence of human values today.

Domiciliary care is also undertaken.

New homes are planned in Birmingham, The North-East, Kent, Lancashire, Leicestershire, London and Scotland.

At present there are Homes in Britain in **Berks, Bedfordshire, Cambridgeshire, Cumbria, Gloucestershire, Hampshire, Hertfordshire, Lancashire, Norfolk, Suffolk, Yorkshire and Wembley,** but many more are needed. They care for **physically handicapped, cancer patients** both terminal and convalescent, the **mentally ill, handicapped children,** and the **elderly.**

In addition to its work in Britain, the Foundation also works in many countries overseas where the needs are even greater.

These and all our patients desperately need your help—with a legacy, deed of covenant or donation in finance or kind.

Please write for any further information to

The Sue Ryder Foundation
Cavendish, Suffolk CO10 8AY

ELT	English Language Teaching
EM	Edward Medal; Earl Marshal
EMBO	European Molecular Biology Organisation
EMS	Emergency Medical Service
Enc.Brit.	Encyclopaedia Britannica
Eng.	England
Engr	Engineer
ENO	English National Opera
ENSA	Entertainments National Service Association
ENT	Ear Nose and Throat
EOPH	Examined Officer of Public Health
EORTC	European Organisation for Research on Treatment of Cancer
EPP	European People's Party
er	elder
ER	Eastern Region (BR)
ERA	Electrical Research Association
ERC	Electronics Research Council
ERD	Emergency Reserve Decoration (Army)
ESA	European Space Agency
ESCAP	Economic and Social Commission for Asia and the Pacific
ESRC	Economic and Social Research Council
ESRO	European Space Research Organization (*now see* ESA)
E-SU	English-Speaking Union
ETH	Eidgenössische Technische Hochschule
ETUC	European Trade Union Confederation
EUDISED	European Documentation and Information Service for Education
Euratom	European Atomic Energy Community
EUROM	European Federation for Optics and Precision Mechanics
EUW	European Union of Women
eV	eingetragener Verein
Ext	Extinct

F

FA	Football Association
FAA	Fellow, Australian Academy of Science; Fleet Air Arm
FAAAS	Fellow, American Association for the Advancement of Science
FAAVCT	Fellow, American Academy of Veterinary and Comparative Toxicology
FACC	Fellow, American College of Cardiology
FACCA	Fellow, Association of Certified and Corporate Accountants (*now see* FCCA)
FACCP	Fellow, American College of Chest Physicians
FACD	Fellow, American College of Dentistry
FACDS	Fellow, Australian College of Dental Surgeons (*now see* FRACDS)
FACE	Fellow, Australian College of Education
FACI	Fellow, Australian Chemical Institute (*now see* FRACI)
FACMA	Fellow, Australian College of Medical Administrators (*now see* FRACMA)
FACOG	Fellow, American College of Obstetricians and Gynæcologists
FACOM	Fellow, Australian College of Occupational Medicine
FACP	Fellow, American College of Physicians
FACR	Fellow, American College of Radiology
FACRM	Fellow, Australian College of Rehabilitation Medicine
FACS	Fellow, American College of Surgeons
FACVT	Fellow, American College of Veterinary Toxicology (*now see* FAAVCT)
FAGO	Fellowship in Australia in Obstetrics and Gynaecology
FAGS	Fellow, American Geographical Society
FAHA	Fellow, Australian Academy of the Humanities
FAI	Fellow, Chartered Auctioneers' and Estate Agents' Institute (*now* (after amalgamation) *see* FRICS); Fédération Aéronautique Internationale
FAIA	Fellow, American Institute of Architects
FAIAA	Fellow, American Institute of Aeronautics and Astronautics
FAIAS	Fellow, Australian Institute of Agricultural Science
FAIE	Fellow, Australian Institute of Energy
FAIEx	Fellow, Australian Institute of Export
FAIFST	Fellow, Australian Institute of Food Science and Technology
FAIM	Fellow, Australian Institute of Management
FAIP	Fellow, Australian Institute of Physics
FAMA	Fellow, Australian Medical Association
FAMI	Fellow, Australian Marketing Institute
FAmNucSoc	Fellow, American Nuclear Society
FAMS	Fellow, Ancient Monuments Society
F and GP	Finance and General Purposes
FANY	First Aid Nursing Yeomanry
FANZCP	Fellow, Australian and New Zealand College of Psychiatrists (*now see* FRANZCP)
FAO	Food and Agriculture Organization of the United Nations
FAPA	Fellow, American Psychiatric Association
FAPHA	Fellow, American Public Health Association
FAPI	Fellow, Australian Planning Institute (*now see* FRAPI)
FAPS	Fellow, American Phytopathological Society
FArborA	Fellow, Arboricultural Association
FARE	Federation of Alcoholic Rehabilitation Establishments
FARELF	Far East Land Forces
FAS	Fellow, Antiquarian Society; Fellow, Nigerian Academy of Science
FASA	Fellow, Australian Society of Accountants
FASc	Fellow, Indian Academy of Sciences

FASCE	Fellow, American Society of Civil Engineers
FASSA	Fellow, Academy of the Social Sciences in Australia
FAustCOG	Fellow, Australian College of Obstetricians and Gynæcologists (*now see* FRACOG)
FBA	Fellow, British Academy; Federation of British Artists
FBCO	Fellow, British College of Ophthalmic Opticians (Optometrists)
FBCS	Fellow, British Computer Society
FBEC(S)	Fellow, Business Education Council (Scotland)
FBHI	Fellow, British Horological Institute
FBHS	Fellow, British Horse Society
FBI	Federation of British Industries (*now see* CBI)
FBIA	Fellow, Bankers' Institute of Australasia
FBIBA	Fellow, British Insurance Brokers' Association
FBID	Fellow, British Institute of Interior Design
FBIM	Fellow, British Institute of Management
FBINZ	Fellow, Bankers' Institute of New Zealand
FBIPP	Fellow, British Institute of Professional Photography
FBIRA	Fellow, British Institute of Regulatory Affairs
FBIS	Fellow, British Interplanetary Society
FBKS	Fellow, British Kinematograph Society (*now see* FBKSTS)
FBKSTS	Fellow, British Kinematograph, Sound and Television Society
FBOA	Fellow, British Optical Association
FBOU	Fellow, British Ornithologists' Union
FBritIRE	Fellow, British Institution of Radio Engineers (*now see* FIERE)
FBPsS	Fellow, British Psychological Society
FBS	Fellow, Building Societies Institute (*now see* FCBSI)
FBSI	Fellow, Boot and Shoe Institution (*now see* FCFI)
FBSM	Fellow, Birmingham School of Music
FC	Football Club
FCA	Fellow, Institute of Chartered Accountants; Fellow, Institute of Chartered Accountants in Australia; Fellow, New Zealand Society of Accountants
FCAI	Fellow, New Zealand Institute of Cost Accountants; Fellow, Canadian Aeronautical Institute (*now see* FCASI)
FCAM	Fellow, CAM Foundation
FCASI	Fellow, Canadian Aeronautics and Space Institute
FCBSI	Fellow, Chartered Building Societies Institute
FCCA	Fellow, Association of Certified Accountants
FCCEA	Fellow, Commonwealth Council for Educational Administration
FCCS	Fellow, Corporation of Secretaries (*formerly* of Certified Secretaries)
FCCT	Fellow, Canadian College of Teachers
FCEC	Federation of Civil Engineering Contractors
FCFI	Fellow, Clothing and Footwear Institute
FCGI	Fellow, City and Guilds of London Institute
FCGP	Fellow, College of General Practitioners (*now see* FRCGP)
FCH	Fellow, Coopers Hill College
FChS	Fellow, Society of Chiropodists
FCI	Fellow, Institute of Commerce
FCIA	Fellow, Corporation of Insurance Agents
FCIArb	Fellow, Chartered Institute of Arbitrators
FCIB	Fellow, Corporation of Insurance Brokers
FCIBS	Fellow, Chartered Institution of Building Services (*now see* FCIBSE)
FCIBSE	Fellow, Chartered Institution of Building Services Engineers
FCIC	Fellow, Chemical Institute of Canada (*formerly* Canadian Institute of Chemistry)
FCII	Fellow, Chartered Insurance Institute
FCILA	Fellow, Chartered Institute of Loss Adjusters
FCIOB	Fellow, Chartered Institute of Building
FCIPA	Fellow, Chartered Institute of Patent Agents (*now see* CPA)
FCIS	Fellow, Institute of Chartered Secretaries and Administrators (*formerly* Chartered Institute of Secretaries)
FCIT	Fellow, Chartered Institute of Transport
FCM	Faculty of Community Medicine
FCMA	Fellow, Institute of Cost and Management Accountants
FCNA	Fellow, College of Nursing, Australia
FCO	Foreign and Commonwealth Office (departments merged Oct. 1968)
FCOG(SA)	Fellow, South African College of Obstetrics and Gynæcology
FCollP	Fellow, College of Preceptors
FCommA	Fellow, Society of Commercial Accountants (*now see* FSCA)
FCP	Fellow, College of Preceptors
FCPath	Fellow, College of Pathologists (*now see* FRCPath)
FCPS	Fellow, College of Physicians and Surgeons
FCP(SoAf)	Fellow, College of Physicians, South Africa
FCPSO(SoAf)	Fellow, College of Physicians and Surgeons and Obstetricians, South Africa
FCRA	Fellow, College of Radiologists of Australia (*now see* FRACR)
FCS	Federation of Conservative Students
FCS or FChemSoc	Fellow, Chemical Society (now absorbed into Royal Society of Chemistry)
FCSP	Fellow, Chartered Society of Physiotherapy
FCSSA, or FCS(SoAf)	Fellow, College of Surgeons, South Africa
FCST	Fellow, College of Speech Therapists
FCT	Federal Capital Territory (*now see* ACT); Fellow, Association of Corporate Treasurers
FCTB	Fellow, College of Teachers of the Blind
FCU	Fighter Control Unit
FCWA	Fellow, Institute of Cost and Works Accountants (*now see* FCMA)

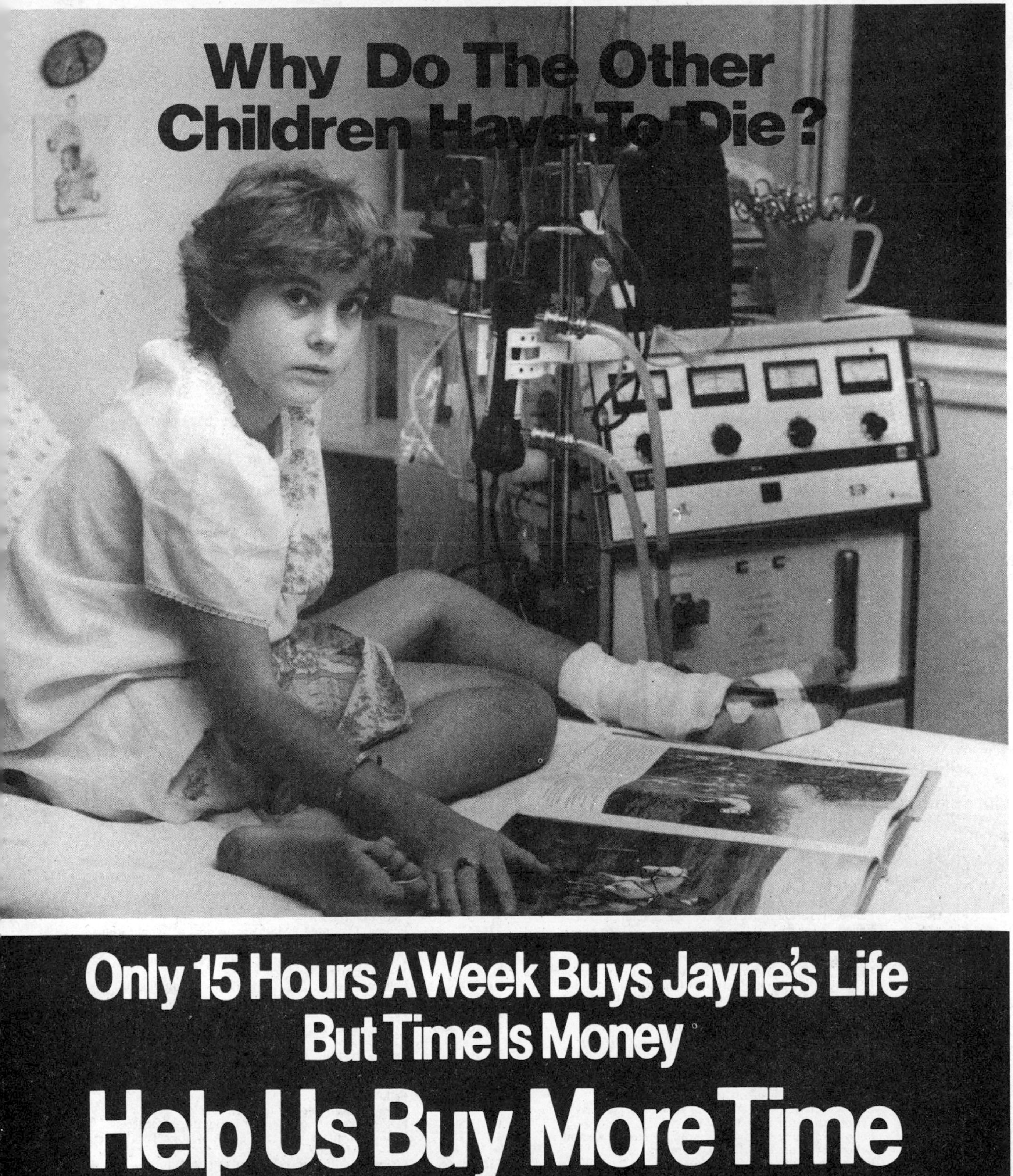
Why Do The Other
Children Have To Die?
Only 15 Hours A Week Buys Jayne's Life
But Time Is Money
Help Us Buy More Time
Send your donation to
The British Kidney Patient Association
Bordon, Hants. Tele: 04203 2022
B.K.P.A.

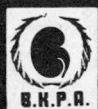

FDI	Fédération Dentaire Internationale
FDS	Fellow in Dental Surgery
FDSRCPSGlas	Fellow in Dental Surgery, Royal College of Physicians and Surgeons of Glasgow
FDSRCS or FDS RCS	Fellow in Dental Surgery, Royal College of Surgeons of England
FDSRCSE	Fellow in Dental Surgery, Royal College of Surgeons of Edinburgh
FEAF	Far East Air Force
FEBS	Federation of European Biochemical Societies
FEF	Far East Fleet
FEI	Fédération Equestre Internationale
FEIS	Fellow, Educational Institute of Scotland
FEng	Fellow, Fellowship of Engineering
FES	Fellow, Entomological Society; Fellow, Ethnological Society
FF	Fianna Fáil; Field Force
FFA	Fellow, Faculty of Actuaries (in Scotland)
FFARACS	Fellow, Faculty of Anaesthetists, Royal Australian College of Surgeons
FFARCS	Fellow, Faculty of Anaesthetists, Royal College of Surgeons of England
FFARCSI	Fellow, Faculty of Anaesthetists, Royal College of Surgeons in Ireland
FFAS	Fellow, Faculty of Architects and Surveyors, London
FFB	Fellow, Faculty of Building
FFCM	Fellow, Faculty of Community Medicine
FFDRCSI	Fellow, Faculty of Dentistry, Royal College of Surgeons in Ireland
FFF	Free French Forces
FFHC	Freedom from Hunger Campaign
FFHom	Fellow, Faculty of Homœopathy
FFI	French Forces of the Interior; Finance for Industry
FFOM	Fellow, Faculty of Occupational Medicine
FFPath, RCPI	Fellow, Faculty of Pathologists of the Royal College of Physicians of Ireland
FFPS	Fauna and Flora Preservation Society
FFR	Fellow, Faculty of Radiologists (now see FRCR)
FG	Fine Gael
FGA	Fellow, Gemmological Association
FGDS	Fédération de la Gauche Démocratique et Socialiste
FGGE	Fellow, Guild of Glass Engineers
FGI	Fellow, Institute of Certificated Grocers
FGS	Fellow, Geological Society
FGSM	Fellow, Guildhall School of Music and Drama
FGSM(MT)	Fellow, Guildhall School of Music and Drama (Music Therapy)
FHA	Fellow, Institute of Health Service Administrators (formerly Hospital Administrators, now see FHSM)
FHAS	Fellow, Highland and Agricultural Society of Scotland
FHCIMA	Fellow, Hotel Catering and Institutional Management Association
FHFS	Fellow, Human Factors Society
FHKIE	Fellow, Hong Kong Institution of Engineers
FHMAAAS	Foreign Honorary Member, American Academy of Arts and Sciences
FHS	Fellow, Heraldry Society
FHSM	Fellow, Institute of Health Service Management
FH-WC	Fellow, Heriot-Watt College (now University), Edinburgh
FIA	Fellow, Institute of Actuaries
FIAA	Fellow, Institute of Actuaries of Australia
FIAAS	Fellow, Institute of Australian Agricultural Science
FIAA&S	Fellow, Incorporated Association of Architects and Surveyors
FIAgrE	Fellow, Institution of Agricultural Engineers
FIAI	Fellow, Institute of Industrial and Commercial Accountants
FIAL	Fellow, International Institute of Arts and Letters
FIAM	Fellow, Institute of Administrative Management; Fellow, International Academy of Management
FIAP	Fellow, Institution of Analysts and Programmers
FIArb	Fellow, Institute of Arbitrators (now see FCIArb)
FIArbA	Fellow, Institute of Arbitrators of Australia
FIAS	Fellow, Institute of Aeronautical Sciences (US) (now see FAIAA)
FIASc	Fellow, Indian Academy of Sciences
FIAWS	Fellow, International Academy of Wood Sciences
FIB	Fellow, Institute of Bankers
FIBA	Fellow, Institute of Business Administration, Australia
FIBD	Fellow, Institute of British Decorators
FIBP	Fellow, Institute of British Photographers
FIBiol	Fellow, Institute of Biology
FIBScot	Fellow, Institute of Bankers in Scotland
FIC	Fellow, Institute of Chemistry (now see FRIC, FRSC); Fellow, Imperial College, London
FICA	Fellow, Commonwealth Institute of Accountants; Fellow, Institute of Chartered Accountants in England and Wales (now see FCA)
FICAI	Fellow, Institute of Chartered Accountants in Ireland
FICD	Fellow, Institute of Civil Defence; Fellow, Indian College of Dentists
FICE	Fellow, Institution of Civil Engineers
FICeram	Fellow, Institute of Ceramics
FICFor	Fellow, Institute of Chartered Foresters
FIChemE	Fellow, Institution of Chemical Engineers
FICI	Fellow, Institute of Chemistry of Ireland; Fellow, International Colonial Institute
FICMA	Fellow, Institute of Cost and Management Accountants
FICorrST	Fellow, Institution of Corrosion Science and Technology

FICS	Fellow, Institute of Chartered Shipbrokers; Fellow, International College of Surgeons
FICT	Fellow, Institute of Concrete Technologists
FICW	Fellow, Institute of Clerks of Works of Great Britain
FIDA	Fellow, Institute of Directors, Australia
FIDCA	Fellow, Industrial Design Council of Australia
FIDE	Fédération Internationale des Echecs
FIE(Aust)	Fellow, Institution of Engineers, Australia
FIEC	Fellow, Institute of Employment Consultants
FIED	Fellow, Institution of Engineering Designers
FIEE	Fellow, Institution of Electrical Engineers
FIEEE	Fellow, Institute of Electrical and Electronics Engineers (NY)
FIElecIE	Fellow, Institution of Electronic Incorporated Engineers
FIEI	Fellow, Institution of Engineering Inspection (now see FIQA); Fellow, Institution of Engineers of Ireland
FIEJ	Fédération Internationale des Editeurs de Journaux et Publications
FIERE	Fellow, Institution of Electronic and Radio Engineers
FIES	Fellow, Illuminating Engineering Society (later FIllumES, now see FCIBSE)
FIET	Fédération Internationale des Employés, Techniciens et Cadres
FIEx	Fellow, Institute of Export
FIExpE	Fellow, Institute of Explosives Engineers
FIFA	Fédération Internationale de Football Association
FIFF	Fellow, Institute of Freight Forwarders
FIFireE	Fellow, Institution of Fire Engineers
FIFM	Fellow, Institute of Fisheries Management
FIFor	Fellow, Institute of Foresters (now see FICFor)
FIFST	Fellow, Institute of Food Science and Technology
FIGasE	Fellow, Institution of Gas Engineers
FIGCM	Fellow, Incorporated Guild of Church Musicians
FIGD	Fellow, Institute of Grocery Distribution
FIGO	International Federation of Gynaecology and Obstetrics
FIH	Fellow, Institute of Housing; Fellow, Institute of the Horse
FIHE	Fellow, Institute of Health Education
FIHM	Fellow, Institute of Housing Managers (now see FIH)
FIHort	Fellow, Institute of Horticulture
FIHospE	Fellow, Institute of Hospital Engineering
FIHT	Fellow, Institution of Highways and Transportation
FIHVE	Fellow, Institution of Heating & Ventilating Engineers (now see FCIBS and MCIBS)
FIIA	Fellow, Institute of Industrial Administration (now see CBIM and FBIM); Fellow, Institute of Internal Auditors
FIIC	Fellow, International Institute for Conservation of Historic and Artistic Works
FIIM	Fellow, Institution of Industrial Managers
FIInfSc	Fellow, Institute of Information Scientists
FIInst	Fellow, Imperial Institute
FIIP	Fellow, Institute of Incorporated Photographers (now see FBIPP)
FIIPE	Fellow, Indian Institution of Production Engineers
FIL	Fellow, Institute of Linguists
FILA	Fellow, Institute of Landscape Architects (now see FLI)
Fil.Hed.	Filosofie Hedersdoktor
FILLM	Fédération Internationale des Langues et Littératures Modernes
FIllumES	Fellow, Illuminating Engineering Society (now see FCIBSE)
FIM	Fellow, Institute of Metals (formerly Institution of Metallurgists)
FIMA	Fellow, Institute of Mathematics and its Applications
FIMarE	Fellow, Institute of Marine Engineers
FIMBRA	Financial Intermediaries, Managers and Brokers Regulatory Association
FIMC	Fellow, Institute of Management Consultants
FIMechE	Fellow, Institution of Mechanical Engineers
FIMFT	Fellow, Institute of Maxillo-facial Technology
FIMGTechE	Fellow, Institution of Mechanical and General Technician Engineers
FIMH	Fellow, Institute of Materials Handling; Fellow, Institute of Military History
FIMI	Fellow, Institute of the Motor Industry
FIMinE	Fellow, Institution of Mining Engineers
FIMIT	Fellow, Institute of Musical Instrument Technology
FIMLS	Fellow, Institute of Medical Laboratory Sciences
FIMLT	Fellow, Institute of Medical Laboratory Technology (now see FIMLS)
FIMM	Fellow, Institution of Mining and Metallurgy
FIMS	Fellow, Institute of Mathematical Statistics
FIMT	Fellow, Institute of the Motor Trade (now see FIMI)
FIMTA	Fellow, Institute of Municipal Treasurers and Accountants (now see IPFA)
FIMunE	Fellow, Institution of Municipal Engineers (now amalgamated with Institution of Civil Engineers)
FIN	Fellow, Institute of Navigation (now see FRIN)
FInstAM	Fellow, Institute of Administrative Management
FInstB	Fellow, Institution of Buyers
FInstBiol	Fellow, Institute of Biology (now see FIBiol)
FInstD	Fellow, Institute of Directors
FInstE	Fellow, Institute of Energy
FInstF	Fellow, Institute of Fuel (now see FInstE)
FInstFF	Fellow, Institute of Freight Forwarders Ltd
FInstHE	Fellow, Institution of Highways Engineers (now see FIHT)
FInstLEx	Fellow, Institute of Legal Executives
FInstM	Fellow, Institute of Meat; Fellow, Institute of Marketing
FInstMC	Fellow, Institute of Measurement and Control

The Malcolm Sargent Cancer Fund for Children

Over 850 new cases are accepted by the Fund each year.
Grants are made for warm clothing, heating bills, beds and bedding, nourishing foods, convalescent holidays, etc.

A Social Worker wrote:

"As I am leaving this department I would like to thank you and your staff and the Trustees of the Fund for all the help which you have given to the families with whom I have been working. I must say that the Fund really is the most wonderful charity with which I have ever worked. It enables one to give reassurance to families that day to day expenses need not be yet a further problem to them when they are trying to use their energies to cope with the awfulness of the illness which is affecting their child. The families themselves are helped by knowing that there are other people who care and who want to help them with their difficulties."

PLEASE help the Fund to continue its practical work and send a donation and/or a request for further information to:

The Malcolm Sargent Cancer Fund for Children
14 Abingdon Road, London W8 6AF
Telephone: 01-937 4548

FInstMSM   Fellow, Institute of Marketing and Sales Management (*now see* FInstM)
FInstMet   Fellow, Institute of Metals (later part of Metals Society, *now see* FIM)
FInstP   Fellow, Institute of Physics
FInstPet   Fellow, Institute of Petroleum
FInstPI   Fellow, Institute of Patentees and Inventors
FInstPS   Fellow, Institute of Purchasing and Supply
FInstSM   Fellow, Institute of Sales Management (*now see* FInstSMM)
FInstSMM   Fellow, Institute of Sales and Marketing Management
FInstW   Fellow, Institute of Welding (*now see* FWeldI)
FINucE   Fellow, Institution of Nuclear Engineers
FIOA   Fellow, Institute of Acoustics
FIOB   Fellow, Institute of Building (*now see* FCIOB)
FIOM   Fellow, Institute of Office Management (*now see* FIAM)
FIOP   Fellow, Institute of Printing
FIP   Fellow, Australian Institute of Petroleum
FIPA   Fellow, Institute of Practitioners in Advertising
FIPDM   Fellow, Institute of Physical Distribution Management
FIPENZ   Fellow, Institution of Professional Engineers, New Zealand
FIPG   Fellow, Institute of Professional Goldsmiths
FIPHE   Fellow, Institution of Public Health Engineers
FIPlantE   Fellow, Institution of Plant Engineers (*now see* FIIM)
FIPM   Fellow, Institute of Personnel Management
FIPR   Fellow, Institute of Public Relations
FIProdE   Fellow, Institution of Production Engineers
FIQ   Fellow, Institute of Quarrying
FIQA   Fellow, Institute of Quality Assurance
FIQS   Fellow, Institute of Quantity Surveyors
FIRA(Ind)   Fellow, Institute of Railway Auditors and Accountants (India)
FIRE(Aust)   Fellow, Institution of Radio Engineers (Australia) (*now see* FIREE(Aust)
FIREE(Aust)   Fellow, Institution of Radio and Electronics Engineers (Australia)
FIRI   Fellow, Institution of the Rubber Industry (*now see* FPRI)
FIRTE   Fellow, Institute of Road Transport Engineers
FIS   Fellow, Institute of Statisticians
FISA   Fellow, Incorporated Secretaries' Association
FISE   Fellow, Institution of Sales Engineers; Fellow, Institution of Sanitary Engineers
FISP   Fédération Internationale des Sociétés de Philosophie
FIST   Fellow, Institute of Science Technology
FISTC   Fellow, Institute of Scientific and Technical Communicators
FIStructE   Fellow, Institution of Structural Engineers
FISW   Fellow, Institute of Social Work
FITD   Fellow, Institute of Training and Development
FITE   Fellow, Institution of Electrical and Electronics Technician Engineers
FIW   Fellow, Welding Institute (*now see* FWeldI)
FIWE   Fellow, Institution of Water Engineers (*now see* FIWES)
FIWES   Fellow, Institution of Water Engineers and Scientists
FIWM   Fellow, Institution of Works Managers (*now see* FIIM)
FIWPC   Fellow, Institute of Water Pollution Control
FIWSc   Fellow, Institute of Wood Science
FIWSP   Fellow, Institute of Work Study Practitioners (*now see* FMS)
FJI   Fellow, Institute of Journalists
FJIE   Fellow, Junior Institution of Engineers (*now see* CIMG-TechE)
FKC   Fellow, King's College London
FKCHMS   Fellow, King's College Hospital Medical School
FLA   Fellow, Library Association
Fla   Florida (US)
FLAI   Fellow, Library Association of Ireland
FLAS   Fellow, Chartered Land Agents' Society (*now* (after amalgamation) *see* FRICS)
FLCM   Fellow, London College of Music
FLHS   Fellow, London Historical Society
FLI   Fellow, Landscape Institute
FLIA   Fellow, Life Insurance Association
FLS   Fellow, Linnean Society
Flt   Flight
FM   Field-Marshal
FMA   Fellow, Museums Association
FMANZ   Fellow, Medical Association of New Zealand
FMF   Fiji Military Forces
FMS   Federated Malay States; Fellow, Medical Society; Fellow, Institute of Management Services
FMSA   Fellow, Mineralogical Society of America
FNA   Fellow, Indian National Science Academy
FNCO   Fleet Naval Constructor Officer
FNECInst   Fellow, North East Coast Institution of Engineers and Shipbuilders
FNI   Fellow, Nautical Institute; Fellow, National Institute of Sciences in India (*now see* FNA)
FNIA   Fellow, Nigerian Institute of Architects
FNZIA   Fellow, New Zealand Institute of Architects
FNZIAS   Fellow, New Zealand Institute of Agricultural Science
FNZIC   Fellow, New Zealand Institute of Chemistry
FNZIE   Fellow, New Zealand Institution of Engineers
FNZIM   Fellow, New Zealand Institute of Management
FO   Foreign Office (*now see* FCO); Field Officer; Flying Officer
FOIC   Flag Officer in charge
FOR   Fellowship of Operational Research
For.   Foreign
FPA   Family Planning Association
FPC   Family Practitioner Committee
FPEA   Fellow, Physical Education Association

FPhS   Fellow, Philosophical Society of England
FPI   Fellow, Plastics Institute (*now see* FPRI)
FPMI   Fellow, Pensions Management Institute
FPRI   Fellow, Plastics and Rubber Institute
FPS   Fellow, Pharmaceutical Society; Fauna Preservation Society (*now see* FFPS)
FPhysS   Fellow, Physical Society
f r   fuori ruole
FRACDS   Fellow, Royal Australian College of Dental Surgeons
FRACGP   Fellow, Royal Australian College of General Practitioners
FRACI   Fellow, Royal Australian Chemical Institute
FRACMA   Fellow, Royal Australian College of Medical Administrators
FRACO   Fellow, Royal Australian College of Ophthalmologists
FRACOG   Fellow, Royal Australian College of Obstetricians and Gynaecologists
FRACP   Fellow, Royal Australasian College of Physicians
FRACR   Fellow, Royal Australasian College of Radiologists
FRACS   Fellow, Royal Australasian College of Surgeons
FRAD   Fellow, Royal Academy of Dancing
FRAeS   Fellow, Royal Aeronautical Society
FRAgS   Fellow, Royal Agricultural Societies (*ie* of England, Scotland and Wales)
FRAHS   Fellow, Royal Australian Historical Society
FRAI   Fellow, Royal Anthropological Institute
FRAIA   Fellow, Royal Australian Institute of Architects
FRAIB   Fellow, Royal Australian Institute of Building
FRAIC   Fellow, Royal Architectural Institute of Canada
FRAM   Fellow, Royal Academy of Music
FRAME   Fund for the Replacement of Animals in Medical Experiments
FRANZCP   Fellow, Royal Australian and New Zealand College of Psychiatrists
FRAPI   Fellow, Royal Australian Planning Institute
FRAS   Fellow, Royal Astronomical Society; Fellow, Royal Asiatic Society
FRASB   Fellow, Royal Asiatic Society of Bengal
FRASE   Fellow, Royal Agricultural Society of England
FRBS   Fellow, Royal Society of British Sculptors; Fellow, Royal Botanic Society
FRCCO   Fellow, Royal Canadian College of Organists
FRCGP   Fellow, Royal College of General Practitioners
FRCM   Fellow, Royal College of Music
FRCN   Fellow, Royal College of Nursing
FRCO   Fellow, Royal College of Organists
FRCO(CHM)   Fellow, Royal College of Organists with Diploma in Choir Training
FRCOG   Fellow, Royal College of Obstetricians and Gynaecologists
FRCP   Fellow, Royal College of Physicians, London
FRCPA   Fellow, Royal College of Pathologists of Australasia
FRCP&S (Canada)   Fellow, Royal College of Physicians and Surgeons of Canada
FRCPath   Fellow, Royal College of Pathologists
FRCP(C)   Fellow, Royal College of Physicians of Canada
FRCPE or FRCPEd   Fellow, Royal College of Physicians, Edinburgh
FRCPGlas   Fellow, Royal College of Physicians and Surgeons of Glasgow
FRCPI   Fellow, Royal College of Physicians of Ireland
FRCPS(Hon.)   Hon. Fellow, Royal College of Physicians and Surgeons of Glasgow
FRCPsych   Fellow, Royal College of Psychiatrists
FRCR   Fellow, Royal College of Radiologists
FRCS   Fellow, Royal College of Surgeons of England
FRCSCan   Fellow, Royal College of Surgeons of Canada
FRCSE or FRCSEd   Fellow, Royal College of Surgeons of Edinburgh
FRCSGlas   Fellow, Royal College of Physicians and Surgeons of Glasgow
FRCSI   Fellow, Royal College of Surgeons in Ireland
FRCSoc   Fellow, Royal Commonwealth Society
FRCUS   Fellow, Royal College of University Surgeons (Denmark)
FRCVS   Fellow, Royal College of Veterinary Surgeons
FREconS   Fellow, Royal Economic Society
FREI   Fellow, Real Estate Institute (Australia)
FRES   Fellow, Royal Entomological Society of London
FRFPSG   Fellow, Royal Faculty of Physicians and Surgeons, Glasgow (*now see* FRCPGlas)
FRG   Federal Republic of Germany
FRGS   Fellow, Royal Geographical Society
FRGSA   Fellow, Royal Geographical Society of Australasia
FRHistS   Fellow, Royal Historical Society
FRHS   Fellow, Royal Horticultural Society
FRHSV   Fellow, Royal Historical Society of Victoria
FRIAS   Fellow, Royal Incorporation of Architects of Scotland
FRIBA   Fellow, Royal Institute of British Architects (*and see* RIBA)
FRIC   Fellow, Royal Institute of Chemistry (*now see* FRSC)
FRICS   Fellow, Royal Institution of Chartered Surveyors
FRIH   Fellow, Royal Institute of Horticulture (NZ)
FRIN   Fellow, Royal Institute of Navigation
FRINA   Fellow, Royal Institution of Naval Architects
FRIPA   Fellow, Royal Institute of Public Administration (the Institute no longer has Fellows)
FRIPHH   Fellow, Royal Institute of Public Health and Hygiene
FRMCM   Fellow, Royal Manchester College of Music
FRMedSoc   Fellow, Royal Medical Society
FRMetS   Fellow, Royal Meteorological Society
FRMIA   Fellow, Retail Management Institute of Australia
FRMS   Fellow, Royal Microscopical Society

FRNCM	Fellow, Royal Northern College of Music
FRNS	Fellow, Royal Numismatic Society
FRPS	Fellow, Royal Photographic Society
FRPSL	Fellow, Royal Philatelic Society, London
FRS	Fellow, Royal Society
FRSA	Fellow, Royal Society of Arts
FRSAI	Fellow, Royal Society of Antiquaries of Ireland
FRSAMD	Fellow, Royal Scottish Academy of Music and Drama
FRSanI	Fellow, Royal Sanitary Institute (*now see* FRSH)
FRSC	Fellow, Royal Society of Canada; Fellow, Royal Society of Chemistry
FRS(Can)	Fellow, Royal Society of Canada (used when a person is also a Fellow of the Royal Society of Chemistry)
FRSCM	Fellow, Royal School of Church Music
FRSC (UK)	Fellow, Royal Society of Chemistry (used when a person is also a Fellow of the Royal Society of Canada)
FRSE	Fellow, Royal Society of Edinburgh
FRSGS	Fellow, Royal Scottish Geographical Society
FRSH	Fellow, Royal Society for the Promotion of Health
FRSL	Fellow, Royal Society of Literature
FRSM or FRSocMed	Fellow, Royal Society of Medicine
FRSNZ	Fellow, Royal Society of New Zealand
FRSSAf	Fellow, Royal Society of South Africa
FRST	Fellow, Royal Society of Teachers
FRSTM&H	Fellow, Royal Society of Tropical Medicine and Hygiene
FRTPI	Fellow, Royal Town Planning Institute
FRTS	Fellow, Royal Television Society
FRVA	Fellow, Rating and Valuation Association
FRVC	Fellow, Royal Veterinary College
FRVIA	Fellow, Royal Victorian Institute of Architects
FRZSScot	Fellow, Royal Zoological Society of Scotland
FS	Field Security
fs	Graduate, Royal Air Force Staff College
FSA	Fellow, Society of Antiquaries
FSAA	Fellow, Society of Incorporated Accountants and Auditors
FSAE	Fellow, Society of Automotive Engineers; Fellow, Society of Art Education
FSAIEE	Fellow, South African Institute of Electrical Engineers
FSAM	Fellow, Society of Art Masters
FSArc	Fellow, Society of Architects (merged with the RIBA 1952)
FSAScot	Fellow, Society of Antiquaries of Scotland
FSASM	Fellow, South Australian School of Mines
FSBI	Fellow, Savings Banks Institute
fsc	Foreign Staff College
FSCA	Fellow, Society of Company and Commercial Accountants
FSDC	Fellow, Society of Dyers and Colourists
FSE	Fellow, Society of Engineers
FSG	Fellow, Society of Genealogists
FSGT	Fellow, Society of Glass Technology
FSI	Fellow, Chartered Surveyors' Institution (*now see* FRICS)
FSIAD	Fellow, Society of Industrial Artists and Designers
FSLAET	Fellow, Society of Licensed Aircraft Engineers and Technologists
FSMA	Fellow, Incorporated Sales Managers' Association (later FInstMSM, *now see* FInstM)
FSMC	Freeman of the Spectacle-Makers' Company
FSS	Fellow, Royal Statistical Society
FSTD	Fellow, Society of Typographic Designers
FSVA	Fellow, Incorporated Society of Valuers and Auctioneers
FTC	Flying Training Command
FTCD	Fellow, Trinity College, Dublin
FTCL	Fellow, Trinity College of Music, London
FTI	Fellow, Textile Institute
FTII	Fellow, Institute of Taxation
FTP	Fellow, Thames Polytechnic
FTS	Fellow, Australian Academy of Technological Sciences; Flying Training School
FUCUA	Federation of University Conservative and Unionist Associations (*now see* FCS)
FUMIST	Fellow, University of Manchester Institute of Science and Technology
FWA	Fellow, World Academy of Arts and Sciences
FWACP	Fellow, West African College of Physicians
FWeldI	Fellow, Welding Institute
FWSOM	Fellow, Institute of Practitioners in Work Study, Organisation and Method (*now see* FMS)
FZS	Fellow, Zoological Society
FZSScot	Fellow, Zoological Society of Scotland (*now see* FRZSScot)

G

GA	Geologists' Association; Gaelic Athletic (Club)
Ga	Georgia (US)
GAP	Gap Activity Projects
GAPAN	Guild of Air Pilots and Air Navigators
GATT	General Agreement on Tariffs and Trade
GB	Great Britain
GBA	Governing Bodies Association
GBE	Knight or Dame Grand Cross of the Order of the British Empire
GBGSA	Association of Governing Bodies of Girls' Public Schools
GBSM	Graduate of Birmingham and Midland Institute School of Music
GC	George Cross
GCB	Knight or Dame Grand Cross of the Order of the Bath

GCFR	Grand Commander of the Order of the Federal Republic of Nigeria
GCH	Knight Grand Cross of the Hanoverian Order
GCHQ	Government Communications Headquarters
GCIE	Knight Grand Commander of the Order of the Indian Empire
GCLJ	Grand Cross, St Lazarus of Jerusalem
GCLM	Grand Commander, Order of the Legion of Merit of Rhodesia
GCM	Gold Crown of Merit (Barbados)
GCMG	Knight or Dame Grand Cross of the Order of St Michael and St George
GCON	Grand Cross, Order of the Niger
GCSE	General Certificate of Secondary Education
GCSG	Knight Grand Cross of the Order of St Gregory the Great
GCSI	Knight Grand Commander of the Order of the Star of India
GCSJ	Knight Grand Cross of Justice, Order of St John of Jerusalem (Knights Hospitaller)
GCStJ	Bailiff or Dame Grand Cross of the Most Venerable Order of the Hospital of St John of Jerusalem
GCVO	Knight or Dame Grand Cross of the Royal Victorian Order
g d	grand-daughter
GDC	General Dental Council
Gdns	Gardens
GDR	German Democratic Republic
Gen.	General
Ges.	Gesellschaft
GFS	Girls' Friendly Society
g g d	great-grand-daughter
g g s	great-grandson
GGSM	Graduate in Music, Guildhall School of Music and Drama
GHQ	General Headquarters
Gib.	Gibraltar
GIMechE	Graduate Institution of Mechanical Engineers
GL	Grand Lodge
GLAA	Greater London Arts Association
GLC	Greater London Council
Glos	Gloucestershire
GM	George Medal; Grand Medal (Ghana)
GMBATU	General, Municipal, Boilermakers and Allied Trades Union
GmbH	Gesellschaft mit beschränkter Hoftung
GMC	General Medical Council; Guild of Memorial Craftsmen
GMIE	Grand Master, Order of the Indian Empire
GMSI	Grand Master, Order of the Star of India
GMWU	General and Municipal Workers' Union (*now see* GMBATU)
GNC	General Nursing Council
GOC	General Officer Commanding
GOC-in-C	General Officer Commanding-in-Chief
GOE	General Ordination Examination
Gov.	Governor
Govt	Government
GP	General Practitioner; Grand Prix
GPDST	Girls' Public Day School Trust
GPO	General Post Office
GQG	Grand Quartier Général
Gr.	Greek
GRSM	Graduate of the Royal Schools of Music
GS	General Staff; Grammar School
g s	grandson
GSA	Girls' Schools Association
GSM	General Service Medal; Guildhall School of Music and Drama (also Member of the School)
GSMD	Guildhall School of Music and Drama
GSO	General Staff Officer
GTCL	Graduate, Trinity College of Music
GTS	General Theological Seminary (New York)
GUI	Golfing Union of Ireland
GWR	Great Western Railway

H

HA	Historical Association; Health Authority
HAA	Heavy Anti-Aircraft
HAC	Honourable Artillery Company
Hants	Hampshire
HARCVS	Honorary Associate, Royal College of Veterinary Surgeons
Harv.	Harvard
HBM	His (or Her) Britannic Majesty (Majesty's); Humming Bird Gold Medal (Trinidad)
hc	*honoris causa*
HCEG	Honourable Company of Edinburgh Golfers
HCF	Honorary Chaplain to the Forces
HCIMA	Hotel, Catering and Institutional Management Association
HDA	Hawkesbury Diploma in Agriculture (Australia)
HDD	Higher Dental Diploma
HDipEd	Higher Diploma in Education
HE	His (or Her) Excellency; His Eminence
HEC	Ecole des Hautes Etudes Commerciales
HEH	His (or Her) Exalted Highness
HEIC	Honourable East India Company
HEICS	Honourable East India Company's Service
Heir-pres.	Heir-presumptive
Herts	Hertfordshire
HFARA	Honorary Foreign Associate of the Royal Academy
HFRA	Honorary Foreign Member of the Royal Academy

MEMBER OF THE BRITISH ANTIQUE DEALERS' ASSOCIATION

INIMICUM · NISI · IGNORANTIAM · ARS · NON · HABET

BENVENUTO CELLINI

Follow The Sign . . .

Confident that our 500 members throughout the country are all elected for their knowledge and integrity.

Confident that all members are experts in their field, that you will obtain the soundest advice and help, that you can both buy and sell with the utmost confidence.

Re-election to membership is reviewed annually.

A list of members is sent free on receipt of a s.a.e.
The British Antique Dealers' Association Ltd., 20 Rutland Gate, London SW7 1BD
Telephone: 01-589 4128

HG	Home Guard
HGTAC	Home Grown Timber Advisory Committee
HH	His (or Her) Highness; His Holiness; Member, Hesketh Hubbard Art Society
HHA	Historic Houses Association
HHD	Doctor of Humanities (US)
HIH	His (or Her) Imperial Highness
HIM	His (or Her) Imperial Majesty
HJ	Hilal-e-Jurat (Pakistan)
HKIA	Hong Kong Institute of Architects
HKIPM	Hong Kong Institute of Personnel Management
HLD	Doctor of Humane Letters
HLI	Highland Light Infantry
HM	His (or Her) Majesty, or Majesty's
HMA	Head Masters' Association
HMAS	His (or Her) Majesty's Australian Ship
HMC	Headmasters' Conference; Hospital Management Committee
HMCIC	His (or Her) Majesty's Chief Inspector of Constabulary
HMCS	His (or Her) Majesty's Canadian Ship
HMHS	His (or Her) Majesty's Hospital Ship
HMI	His (or Her) Majesty's Inspector
HMIED	Honorary Member, Institute of Engineering Designers
HMOCS	His (or Her) Majesty's Overseas Civil Service
HMS	His (or Her) Majesty's Ship
HMSO	His (or Her) Majesty's Stationery Office
HNC	Higher National Certificate
HND	Higher National Diploma
H of C	House of Commons
H of L	House of Lords
Hon.	Honourable; Honorary
HPk	Hilal-e-Pakistan
HQ	Headquarters
HQA	Hilal-i-Quaid-i-Azam (Pakistan)
(HR)	Home Rule
HRCA	Honorary Royal Cambrian Academician
HRH	His (or Her) Royal Highness
HRHA	Honorary Member, Royal Hibernian Academy
HRI	Honorary Member, Royal Institute of Painters in Water Colours
HROI	Honorary Member, Royal Institute of Oil Painters
HRSA	Honorary Member, Royal Scottish Academy
HRSW	Honorary Member, Royal Scottish Water Colour Society
HSC	Health and Safety Commission
HSE	Health and Safety Executive
HSH	His (or Her) Serene Highness
Hum.	Humanity, Humanities (Classics)
Hunts	Huntingdonshire
HVCert	Health Visitor's Certificate
Hy	Heavy

I

I	Island; Ireland
Ia	Iowa (US)
IA	Indian Army
IAC	Indian Armoured Corps; Institute of Amateur Cinematographers
IACP	International Association of Chiefs of Police
IADR	International Association for Dental Research
IAEA	International Atomic Energy Agency
IAF	Indian Air Force; Indian Auxiliary Force
IAHM	Incorporated Association of Headmasters
IAM	Institute of Advanced Motorists
IAMC	Indian Army Medical Corps
IAMTACT	Institute of Advanced Machine Tool and Control Technology
IAO	Incorporated Association of Organists
IAOC	Indian Army Ordnance Corps
IAPS	Incorporated Association of Preparatory Schools
IARO	Indian Army Reserve of Officers
IAS	Indian Administrative Service
IASS	International Association for Scandinavian Studies
IATA	International Air Transport Association
IATUL	International Association of Technical University Libraries
IAU	International Astronomical Union
IAWPRC	International Association on Water Pollution Research and Control
ib. or ibid.	ibidem (in the same place)
IBA	Independent Broadcasting Authority; International Bar Association
IBG	Institute of British Geographers
IBRD	International Bank for Reconstruction and Development (World Bank)
IBRO	International Bank Research Organisation; International Brain Research Organisation
i/c	in charge; in command
ICA	Institute of Contemporary Arts; Institute of Chartered Accountants in England and Wales
ICAA	Invalid Children's Aid Association
ICAI	Institute of Chartered Accountants in Ireland
ICAO	International Civil Aviation Organization
ICBP	International Council for Bird Preservation
ICBS	Irish Christian Brothers' School
ICC	International Chamber of Commerce

ICCROM	International Centre for Conservation at Rome
ICD	Iuris Canonici Doctor; Independence Commemorative Decoration (Rhodesia)
ICE	Institution of Civil Engineers
ICED	International Council for Educational Development
ICEF	International Federation of Chemical, Energy and General Workers' Unions
Icel.	Icelandic
ICES	International Council for the Exploration of the Sea
ICF	International Federation of Chemical and General Workers' Unions (now see ICEF)
ICFC	Industrial and Commercial Finance Corporation (later part of Investors in Industry)
ICFTU	International Confederation of Free Trade Unions
ICHCA	International Cargo Handling Co-ordination Association
IChemE	Institution of Chemical Engineers
ICI	Imperial Chemical Industries
ICL	International Computers Ltd
ICM	International Confederation of Midwives
ICMA	Institute of Cost and Management Accountants
ICME	International Commission for Mathematical Education
ICOM	International Council of Museums
ICOMOS	International Council of Monuments and Sites
ICorrST	Institution of Corrosion Science and Technology
ICPO	International Criminal Police Organization (Interpol)
ICRC	International Committee of the Red Cross
ICS	Indian Civil Service
ICSA	Institute of Chartered Secretaries and Administrators
ICSID	International Council of Societies of Industrial Design
ICSS	International Committee for the Sociology of Sport
ICSU	International Council of Scientific Unions
ICT	International Computers and Tabulators Ltd (now see ICL)
Id	Idaho (US)
ID	Independence Decoration (Rhodesia)
IDA	International Development Association
IDB	Internal Drainage Board
IDC	Imperial Defence College (now see RCDS); Inter-Diocesan Certificate
idc	Completed a Course at, or served for a year on the Staff of, the Imperial Defence College (now see rcds)
IDS	Institute of Development Studies
IEC	International Electrotechnical Commission
IEE	Institution of Electrical Engineers
IEEE	Institute of Electrical and Electronics Engineers (NY)
IEEIE	Institution of Electrical and Electronics Incorporated Engineers
IEETE	Institution of Electrical and Electronics Technician Engineers (now see IEEIE)
IEI	Institution of Engineers of Ireland
IEME	Inspectorate of Electrical and Mechanical Engineering
IERE	Institution of Electronic and Radio Engineers
IES	Indian Educational Service; Institution of Engineers and Shipbuilders in Scotland
IExpE	Institute of Explosives Engineers
IFAC	International Federation of Automatic Control
IFAD	International Fund for Agricultural Development
IFAW	International Fund for Animal Welfare
IFC	International Finance Corporation
IFIAS	International Federation of Institutes of Advanced Study
IFIP	International Federation for Information Processing
IFL	International Friendship League
IFLA	International Federation of Library Associations
IFORS	International Federation of Operational Research Societies
IFPI	International Federation of the Phonographic Industry
IFS	Irish Free State; Indian Forest Service
IG	Instructor in Gunnery
IGasE	Institution of Gas Engineers
IGPP	Institute of Geophysics and Planetary Physics
IGS	Independent Grammar School
IGU	International Geographical Union; International Gas Union
IHA	Institute of Health Service Administrators
IHospE	Institute of Hospital Engineering
IHVE	Institution of Heating and Ventilating Engineers (now see CIBS)
IIM	Institution of Industrial Managers
IIMT	International Institute for the Management of Technology
IInfSc	Institute of Information Scientists
IIS	International Institute of Sociology
IISS	International Institute of Strategic Studies
ILA	International Law Association
ILEA	Inner London Education Authority
ILEC	Inner London Education Committee
Ill	Illinois (US)
ILO	International Labour Office; International Labour Organisation
ILP	Independent Labour Party
ILR	Independent Local Radio; International Labour Review
IM	Individual Merit
IMA	International Music Association; Institute of Mathematics and its Applications
IMCO	Inter-Governmental Maritime Consultative Organization (now see IMO)
IMEA	Incorporated Municipal Electrical Association
IMechE	Institution of Mechanical Engineers
IMEDE	Institut pour l'Etude des Méthodes de Direction de l'Entreprise
IMF	International Monetary Fund
IMGTechE	Institution of Mechanical and General Technician Engineers

EVENINGS ARE FOR ELEGANCE

There are many ways to enjoy an evening's entertainment but a memorable meal will always make the perfect ending, whether with friends or someone very special.

Come early for, say, a glass of wine and a starter to get you in the mood or try The Champagne Bar – the perfect place to meet and greet.

Or come later, for dinner or supper. At The Restaurant you'll find we're as flexible as you are. It helps if you can book.

Sheraton Park Tower Ⓢ

THE RESTAURANT

101 KNIGHTSBRIDGE, LONDON SW1X 7RN TELEPHONE (01) 235 8050.
The hospitality people of **ITT**

IMinE	Institution of Mining Engineers
IMM	Institution of Mining and Metallurgy
IMMLEP	Immunology of Leprosy
IMMTS	Indian Mercantile Marine Training Ship
IMO	International Maritime Organization
Imp.	Imperial
IMRO	Investment Management Regulatory Organisation
IMS	Indian Medical Service; Institute of Management Services; International Military Staff
IMTA	Institute of Municipal Treasurers and Accountants (now see CIPFA)
IMU	International Mathematical Union
IMunE	Institution of Municipal Engineers (now amalgamated with Institution of Civil Engineers)
IN	Indian Navy
Inc.	Incorporated
INCA	International Newspaper Colour Association
Incog.	Incognito
Ind.	Independent; Indiana (US)
Inf.	Infantry
INSA	Indian National Science Academy
INSEA	International Society for Education through Art
INSEAD or Insead	Institut Européen d'Administration des Affaires
Insp.	Inspector
Inst.	Institute
Instn	Institution
InstSMM	Institute of Sales and Marketing Management
InstT	Institute of Transport
IOB	Institute of Building (now see CIOB)
IOCD	International Organisation for Chemical Science in Development
IODE	Imperial Order of the Daughters of the Empire
I of M	Isle of Man
IOGT	International Order of Good Templars
IOM	Isle of Man; Indian Order of Merit
IOOF	Independent Order of Odd-fellows
IOP	Institute of Painters in Oil Colours
IoW	Isle of Wight
IPA	International Publishers' Association
IPCS	Institution of Professional Civil Servants
IPFA	Member or Associate, Chartered Institute of Public Finance and Accountancy
IPHE	Institution of Public Health Engineers
IPI	International Press Institute
IPlantE	Institution of Plant Engineers (now see IIM)
IPM	Institute of Personnel Management
IPPA	Independent Programme Producers' Association
IPPF	International Planned Parenthood Federation
IPPS	Institute of Physics and The Physical Society
IProdE	Institution of Production Engineers
IPS	Indian Police Service; Indian Political Service; Institute of Purchasing and Supply
IPU	Inter-Parliamentary Union
IRA	Irish Republican Army
IRAD	Institute for Research on Animal Diseases
IRC	Industrial Reorganization Corporation
IRCert	Industrial Relations Certificate
IREE(Aust)	Institution of Radio and Electronics Engineers (Australia)
IRI	Institution of the Rubber Industry (now see PRI)
IRO	International Refugee Organization
IRPA	International Radiation Protection Association
IRTE	Institute of Road Transport Engineers
Is	Island(s)
IS	International Society of Sculptors, Painters and Gravers
ISBA	Incorporated Society of British Advertisers
ISC	Imperial Service College, Haileybury; Indian Staff Corps
ISCM	International Society for Contemporary Music
ISCO	Independent Schools Careers Organisation
ISE	Indian Service of Engineers
ISI	International Statistical Institute
ISIS	Independent Schools Information Service
ISJC	Independent Schools Joint Council
ISM	Incorporated Society of Musicians
ISME	International Society for Musical Education
ISMRC	Inter-Services Metallurgical Research Council
ISO	Imperial Service Order; International Organization for Standardization
ISSTIP	International Society for Study of Tension in Performance
ISTC	Iron and Steel Trades Confederation; Institute of Scientific and Technical Communicators
ISTD	Imperial Society of Teachers of Dancing
IStructE	Institution of Structural Engineers
IT	Information Technology; Indian Territory (US)
ITA	Independent Television Authority (now see IBA)
Ital. or It.	Italian
ITB	Industry Training Board
ITC	International Trade Centre
ITCA	Independent Television Companies Association Ltd
ITDG	Intermediate Technology Development Group
ITEME	Institution of Technician Engineers in Mechanical Engineering
ITF	International Transport Workers' Federation
ITN	Independent Television News
ITO	International Trade Organization
ITU	International Telecommunication Union
ITV	Independent Television

IUA	International Union of Architects
IUB	International Union of Biochemistry
IUC	Inter-University Council for Higher Education Overseas (now see IUPC)
IUCN	International Union for the Conservation of Nature and Natural Resources
IUCW	International Union for Child Welfare
IUGS	International Union of Geological Sciences
IUHPS	International Union of the History and Philosophy of Science
IULA	International Union of Local Authorities
IUP	Association of Independent Unionist Peers
IUPAC	International Union of Pure and Applied Chemistry
IUPAP	International Union of Pure and Applied Physics
IUPC	Inter-University and Polytechnic Council for Higher Education Overseas
IUPS	International Union of Physiological Sciences
IUTAM	International Union of Theoretical and Applied Mechanics
IVS	International Voluntary Service
IWES	Institution of Water Engineers and Scientists
IWGC	Imperial War Graves Commission (now see CWGC)
IWM	Institution of Works Managers (now see IIM)
IWPC	Institute of Water Pollution Control
IWSOM	Institute of Practitioners in Work Study Organisation and Methods (now see IMS)
IWSP	Institute of Work Study Practitioners (now see IMS)
IY	Imperial Yeomanry
IZ	I Zingari

J

JA	Judge Advocate
JACT	Joint Association of Classical Teachers
JAG	Judge Advocate General
Jas	James
JCB	*Juris Canonici* (or *Civilis*) *Baccalaureus* (Bachelor of Canon (or Civil) Law)
JCS	Journal of the Chemical Society
JCD	*Juris Canonici* (or *Civilis*) *Doctor* (Doctor of Canon (or Civil) Law)
JCI	Junior Chamber International
JCL	*Juris Canonici* (or *Civilis*) *Licentiatus* (Licentiate in Canon (or Civil) Law)
JCO	Joint Consultative Organisation (of AFRC, MAFF, and Department of Agriculture and Fisheries for Scotland)
JD	Doctor of Jurisprudence
JDipMA	Joint Diploma in Management Accounting Services
JG	Junior Grade
JInstE	Junior Institution of Engineers (now see IMGTechE)
jls	journals
JMN	Johan Mangku Negara (Malaysia)
Joh. or Jno.	John
JP	Justice of the Peace
Jr	Junior
jsc	Qualified at a Junior Staff Course, or the equivalent, 1942–46
JSD	Doctor of Juristic Science
JSDC	Joint Service Defence College
jsdc	Completed a course at Joint Service Defence College
JSLS	Joint Services Liaison Staff
JSM	Johan Setia Mahkota (Malaysia)
JSPS	Japan Society for the Promotion of Science
JSSC	Joint Services Staff College
jssc	Completed a course at Joint Services Staff College
jt, jtly	joint, jointly
JWS or jws	Joint Warfare Staff
JUD	*Juris Utriusque Doctor*, Doctor of Both Laws (Canon and Civil)
Jun.	Junior
Jun.Opt.	Junior Optime

K

KA	Knight of St Andrew in the Order of Barbados
Kans	Kansas (US)
KAR	King's African Rifles
KBE	Knight Commander Order of the British Empire
KC	King's Counsel
KCB	Knight Commander of the Order of the Bath
KCC	Commander of Order of Crown, Belgium and Congo Free State
KCH	King's College Hospital; Knight Commander of the Hanoverian Order
KCHS	Knight Commander, Order of the Holy Sepulchre
KCIE	Knight Commander, Order of the Indian Empire
KCL	King's College London
KCLJ	Knight Commander, Order of St Lazarus of Jerusalem
KCMG	Knight Commander, Order of St Michael and St George
KCSA	Knight Commander, Military Order of the Collar of St Agatha of Paterna
KCSG	Knight Commander, Order of St Gregory the Great
KCSI	Knight Commander, Order of the Star of India
KCSS	Knight Commander, Order of St Silvester
KCVO	Knight Commander, Royal Victorian Order

Cheshire Homes are all about caring... in so many ways

Founder, Group Captain Leonard Cheshire, VC, OM, DSO, DFC

The residents in Leonard Cheshire Homes are very severely handicapped men, women and children suffering from a wide range of conditions. Sometimes unable to speak, or to move much more than a hand or foot.

A Cheshire Home offers them much more than just physical care. It gives them the dignity and freedom that is their right as individuals, the opportunity of friendship, a sense of purpose and a chance to participate.

There are 75 Cheshire Homes in the United Kingdom and a further 147 in 45 countries throughout the world. All of them have been made possible by the efforts of dedicated volunteers and by generous charitable donations.

We also reach out to elderly and disabled people living in their own homes, and to families with a handicapped member who may be struggling alone in isolation and despair. 19 Family Support Services in England provide vital part-time help at crucial times of the day – a lifeline indeed. But many, many more services are needed to plug the yawning gaps in state provision. Only 2.37% of our income is spent on administering this large charity. This means that almost all the money we receive goes in *direct* help to those in need. PLEASE HELP US TO GO ON CARING AND EXPANDING.

Donations, legacies and covenants will be most gratefully received, either for the Home or Family Support Service of your choice, or to the Cheshire Foundation for use wherever the need is greatest.

Send to Hon. Treasurer, Room NLJ,
The Leonard Cheshire Foundation,
26-29 Maunsel Street, London SW1P 2QN.

Society for the Assistance of Ladies in Reduced Circumstances

(Founded by the late Miss Smallwood)

Patron: Her Majesty the Queen

This Society is entirely supported by Voluntary Contributions

Since it was founded in 1886, this Society has helped thousands of elderly and infirm ladies. Assistance is given to those living in their own homes or in Rest Homes or Nursing Homes. Single Grants are also given for special purposes. Many ladies have no one else to turn to when in distress and there is always a need for our Work. Perhaps you know of someone who is having difficulty in managing and you can share in our work by making a Donation, Covenanted Subscription or a Bequest.

All investments are held in the name of the Official Custodian for Charities.

Please make cheques payable to:

S.A.L.R.C.

LANCASTER HOUSE (AW), 25 HORNYOLD ROAD, MALVERN, WORCESTERSHIRE WR14 1QQ.
Charity Registration No. 205798

KCVSA	King's Commendation for Valuable Services in the Air
KDG	King's Dragoon Guards
KEH	King Edward's Horse
KEO	King Edward's Own
KG	Knight of the Order of the Garter
KGStJ	Knight of Grace, Order of St John of Jerusalem (*now see* KStJ)
KH	Knight of the Hanoverian Order
KHC	Hon. Chaplain to the King
KHDS	Hon. Dental Surgeon to the King
KHNS	Hon. Nursing Sister to the King
KHP	Hon. Physician to the King
KHS	Hon. Surgeon to the King; Knight of the Order of the Holy Sepulchre
K-i-H	Kaisar-i-Hind
KJStJ	Knight of Justice, Order of St John of Jerusalem (*now see* KStJ)
KLJ	Knight, St Lazarus of Jerusalem
KM	Knight of Malta
KORR	King's Own Royal Regiment
KOSB	King's Own Scottish Borderers
KOYLI	King's Own Yorkshire Light Infantry
KP	Knight of the Order of St Patrick
KPM	King's Police Medal
KRRC	King's Royal Rifle Corps
KS	King's Scholar
KSC	Knight of St Columba
KSG	Knight of the Order of St Gregory the Great
KSJ	Knight of the Order of St John of Jerusalem (Knights Hospitaller)
KSLI	King's Shropshire Light Infantry
KSS	Knight of the Order of St Silvester
KStJ	Knight of the Most Venerable Order of the Hospital of St John of Jerusalem
KStJ(A)	Associate Knight of Justice of the Most Venerable Order of the Hospital of St John of Jerusalem
KT	Knight of the Order of the Thistle
Kt	Knight
Ky	Kentucky (US)

L

(L)	Liberal
LA	Los Angeles; Library Association; Literate in Arts; Liverpool Academy
La	Louisiana (US)
(Lab)	Labour
LAC	London Athletic Club
LACSAB	Local Authorities Conditions of Service Advisory Board
LAMDA	London Academy of Music and Dramatic Art
LAMSAC	Local Authorities' Management Services and Computer Committee
LAMTPI	Legal Associate Member, Town Planning Institute (*now see* LMRTPI)
L-Corp. or Lance-Corp.	Lance-Corporal
Lancs	Lancashire
LARSP	Language Assessment, Remediation and Screening Procedure
Lautro	Life Assurance and Unit Trust Regulatory Organization
LBC	London Broadcasting Company
LC	Cross of Leo
LCAD	London Certificate in Art and Design (University of London)
LCC	London County Council (later GLC)
LCh	Licentiate in Surgery
LCJ	Lord Chief Justice
LCL	Licentiate of Canon Law
LCP	Licentiate, College of Preceptors
LCSP	London and Counties Society of Physiologists
LCST	Licentiate, College of Speech Therapists
LD	Liberal and Democratic
LDiv	Licentiate in Divinity
LDS	Licentiate in Dental Surgery
LDV	Local Defence Volunteers
LEA	Local Education Authority
LEPRA	British Leprosy Relief Association
LèsL	Licencié ès lettres
LGSM	Licentiate, Guildhall School of Music and Drama
LGTB	Local Government Training Board
LH	Light Horse
LHD	*Literarum Humaniorum Doctor* (Doctor of Literature)
LI	Light Infantry; Long Island
LIBER	Ligue des Bibliothèques Européennes de Recherche
LicMed	Licentiate in Medicine
Lieut	Lieutenant
LIFFE	London International Financial Futures Exchange
Lincs	Lincolnshire
LIOB	Licentiate, Institute of Building
Lit.	Literature; Literary
LitD	Doctor of Literature; Doctor of Letters
Lit.Hum.	*Literae Humaniores* (Classics)
LittD	Doctor of Literature; Doctor of Letters
LJ	Lord Justice
LLA	Lady Literate in Arts
LLB	Bachelor of Laws

LLCM	Licentiate, London College of Music
LLD	Doctor of Laws
LLL	Licentiate in Laws
LLM	Master of Laws
LM	Licentiate in Midwifery
LMBC	Lady Margaret Boat Club
LMC	Local Medical Committee
LMCC	Licentiate, Medical Council of Canada
LMed	Licentiate in Medicine
LMR	London Midland Region (BR)
LMS	London, Midland and Scottish Railway; London Missionary Society
LMSSA	Licentiate in Medicine and Surgery, Society of Apothecaries
LMRTPI	Legal Member, Royal Town Planning Institute
(LNat)	Liberal National
LNER	London and North Eastern Railway
LOB	Location of Offices Bureau
L of C	Library of Congress; Lines of Communication
LPTB	London Passenger Transport Board (later LTE, *now see* LRT)
LRAD	Licentiate, Royal Academy of Dancing
LRAM	Licentiate, Royal Academy of Music
LRCP	Licentiate, Royal College of Physicians, London
LRCPE	Licentiate, Royal College of Physicians, Edinburgh
LRCPI	Licentiate, Royal College of Physicians of Ireland
LRCPSGlas	Licentiate, Royal College of Physicians and Surgeons of Glasgow
LRCS	Licentiate, Royal College of Surgeons of England
LRCSE	Licentiate, Royal College of Surgeons, Edinburgh
LRCSI	Licentiate, Royal College of Surgeons in Ireland
LRFPS(G)	Licentiate, Royal Faculty of Physicians and Surgeons, Glasgow (*now see* LRCPSGlas)
LRIBA	Licentiate, Royal Institute of British Architects (*now see* RIBA)
LRPS	Licentiate, Royal Photographic Society
LRT	London Regional Transport
LSA	Licentiate, Society of Apothecaries; Licence in Agricultural Sciences
LSE	London School of Economics and Political Science
LSHTM	London School of Hygiene and Tropical Medicine
LSO	London Symphony Orchestra
Lt	Lieutenant; Light
LT	London Transport (*now see* LRT); Licentiate in Teaching
LTA	Lawn Tennis Association
LTB	London Transport Board (later LTE, *now see* LRT)
LTCL	Licentiate of Trinity College of Music, London
Lt-Col	Lieutenant-Colonel
LTE	London Transport Executive (*now see* LRT)
Lt-Gen.	Lieutenant-General
LTh	Licentiate in Theology
(LU)	Liberal Unionist
LUOTC	London University Officers' Training Corps
LVO	Lieutenant, Royal Victorian Order (*formerly* MVO (Fourth Class))
LWT	London Weekend Television
LXX	Septuagint

M

M	Marquess; Member; Monsieur
m	married
MA	Master of Arts; Military Assistant
MAA	Manufacturers' Agents Association of Great Britain
MAAF	Mediterranean Allied Air Forces
MAAT	Member, Association of Accounting Technicians
MACE	Member, Australian College of Education; Member, Association of Conference Executives
MACI	Member, American Concrete Institute
MACM	Member, Association of Computing Machines
MACS	Member, American Chemical Society
MADO	Member, Association of Dispensing Opticians
MAEE	Marine Aircraft Experimental Establishment
MAF	Ministry of Agriculture and Fisheries
MAFF	Ministry of Agriculture, Fisheries and Food
MAI	*Magister in Arte Ingeniaria* (Master of Engineering)
MAIAA	Member, American Institute of Aeronautics and Astronautics
MAICE	Member, American Institute of Consulting Engineers
MAIChE	Member, American Institute of Chemical Engineers
Maj.-Gen.	Major-General
Man	Manitoba (Canada)
MAO	Master of Obstetric Art
MAOT	Member, Association of Occupational Therapists
MAOU	Member, American Ornithologists' Union
MAP	Ministry of Aircraft Production
MAPsS	Member, Australian Psychological Society
MArch	Master of Architecture
Marq.	Marquess
MASAE	Member, American Society of Agricultural Engineers
MASC	Member, Australian Society of Calligraphers
MASCE	Member, American Society of Civil Engineers
MASME	Member, American Society of Mechanical Engineers
Mass	Massachusetts (US)
Math.	Mathematics; Mathematical
MATSA	Managerial Administrative Technical Staff Association
MAusIMM	Member, Australasian Institute of Mining and Metallurgy

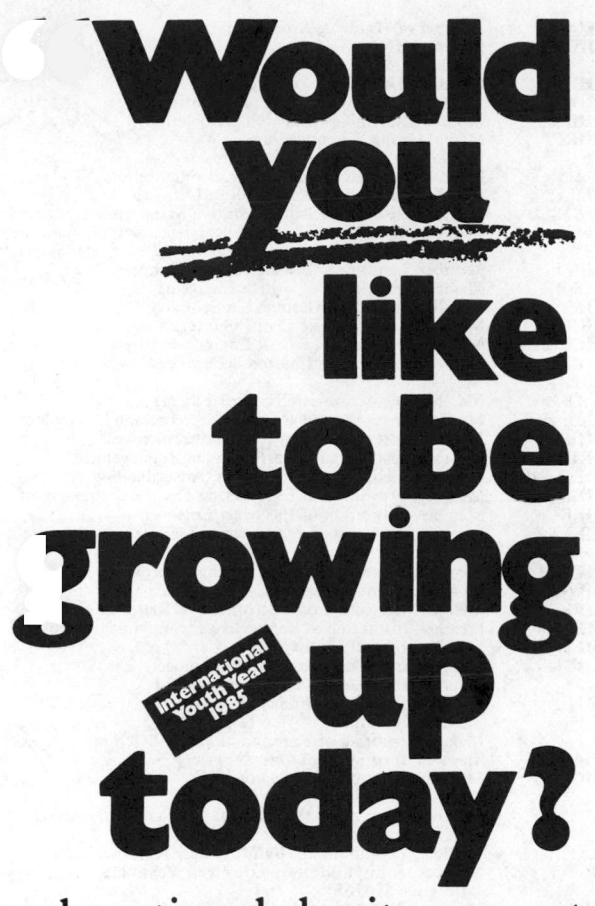

"Would you like to be growing up today?

International Youth Year 1985

Growing up is more depressing and difficult today than ever before. Housing conditions are often appalling, recreational facilities are often lacking; many young people are homeless while others live in unhappy homes. For most, secondary education sends them out ill-prepared for adult life and work. Worst of all is the extent of unemployment facing school-leavers.

In these circumstances, it is hardly surprising that some young people end up in trouble with the law.

The Rainer Foundation is the only national charity concentrating exclusively on these important problems of adolescence. Our pioneering projects help many hundreds of young people every year to find their feet. In our early days as the 'London Police Court Mission' one of our first tasks was the establishment of the Probation Service.

But we are seriously short of funds and must ask for your support — by covenant, legacy or donation. Your help will give someone a chance in life. "

The Rt. Hon. Lord Hunt of Llanfair Waterdine.
Patron — HRH Prince Philip, Duke of Edinburgh.
President — The Lord Henniker K.C.M.G., C.V.O., M.C.

The Rainer Foundation
(Reg. Charity 213133),
Attn. Christopher Naylor,
227-239 Tooley Street,
London SE1 2JX,
01-403 4434

the **Rainer** foundation

MB	Medal of Bravery (Canada); Bachelor of Medicine
MBA	Master of Business Administration
MBASW	Member, British Association of Social Workers
MBCS	Member, British Computer Society
MBE	Member, Order of the British Empire
MBFR	Mutual and Balanced Force Reductions (negotiations)
MBHI	Member, British Horological Institute
MBIM	Member, British Institute of Management (*now see* FBIM)
MBKS	Member, British Kinematograph Society (*now see* MBKSTS)
MBKSTS	Member, British Kinematograph, Sound and Television Society
MBOU	Member, British Ornithologists' Union
MBritIRE	Member, British Institution of Radio Engineers (*now see* MIERE)
MBS	Member, Building Societies Institute (*now see* MCBSI)
MC	Military Cross; Missionaries of Charity
MCAM	Member, CAM Foundation
MCB	Master in Clinical Biochemistry
MCBSI	Member, Chartered Building Societies Institute
MCC	Marylebone Cricket Club; Metropolitan County Council
MCD	Master of Civic Design
MCE	Master of Civil Engineering
MCFP	Member, College of Family Physicians (Canada)
MCh or MChir	Master in Surgery
MChE	Master of Chemical Engineering
MChemA	Master in Chemical Analysis
MChOrth	Master of Orthopaedic Surgery
MCIBS	Member, Chartered Institution of Building Services (*now see* MCIBSE)
MCIBSE	Member, Chartered Institution of Building Services Engineers
MCIOB	Member, Chartered Institute of Building
M.CIRP	Member, International Institution for Production Engineering Research
MCIS	Member, Institute of Chartered Secretaries and Administrators
MCIT	Member, Chartered Institute of Transport
MCL	Master in Civil Law
MCMES	Member, Civil and Mechanical Engineers' Society
MCom	Master of Commerce
MConsE	Member, Association of Consulting Engineers
MCP	Member of Colonial Parliament; Master of City Planning (US)
MCPA	Member, College of Pathologists of Australia (*now see* MRCPA)
MCPath	Member, College of Pathologists (*now see* MRCPath)
MCPS	Member, College of Physicians and Surgeons
MCS	Madras Civil Service; Malayan Civil Service
MCSEE	Member, Canadian Society of Electrical Engineers
MCSP	Member, Chartered Society of Physiotherapy
MCST	Member, College of Speech Therapists
MCT	Member, Association of Corporate Treasurers
MD	Doctor of Medicine; Military District
Md	Maryland (US)
MDC	Metropolitan District Council
MDes	Master of Design
MDS	Master of Dental Surgery
Me	Maine (US)
ME	Mining Engineer; Middle East; Master of Engineering
MEAF	Middle East Air Force
MEC	Member of Executive Council; Middle East Command
MEc	Master of Economics
MECAS	Middle East Centre for Arab Studies
Mech.	Mechanics; Mechanical
MECI	Member, Institute of Employment Consultants
Med.	Medical
MEd	Master of Education
MEF	Middle East Force
MEIC	Member, Engineering Institute of Canada
MELF	Middle East Land Forces
Mencap	Royal Society for Mentally Handicapped Children and Adults
MEng	Master of Engineering
MEO	Marine Engineering Officer
MEP	Member of the European Parliament
MetR	Metropolitan Railway
MetSoc	Metals Society (formed by amalgamation of Institute of Metals and Iron and Steel Institute; now merged with Institution of Metallurgists to form Institute of Metals)
MEXE	Military Engineering Experimental Establishment
MFA	Master of Fine Arts
MFC	Mastership in Food Control
MFCM	Member, Faculty of Community Medicine
MFGB	Miners' Federation of Great Britain (*now see* NUM)
MFH	Master of Foxhounds
MFHom	Member, Faculty of Homeopathy
MFOM	Member, Faculty of Occupational Medicine
MGA	Major-General in charge of Administration
MGC	Machine Gun Corps
MGDS RCS	Member in General Dental Surgery, Royal College of Surgeons
MGGS	Major-General, General Staff
MGI	Member, Institute of Certificated Grocers
MGO	Master General of the Ordnance; Master of Gynaecology and Obstetrics
Mgr	Monsignor
MHA	Member of House of Assembly
MHCIMA	Member, Hotel Catering and Institutional Management Association
MHK	Member of the House of Keys
MHR	Member of the House of Representatives
MHRA	Modern Humanities Research Association
MHRF	Mental Health Research Fund
MI	Military Intelligence
MIAeE	Member, Institute of Aeronautical Engineers
MIAgrE	Member, Institution of Agricultural Engineers
MIAM	Member, Institute of Administrative Management
MIAS	Member, Institute of Aeronautical Science (US) (*now see* MAIAA)
MIBF	Member, Institute of British Foundrymen
MIBritE	Member, Institution of British Engineers
MIBS	Member, Institute of Bankers in Scotland
MICE	Member, Institution of Civil Engineers
MICEI	Member, Institution of Civil Engineers of Ireland
MICFor	Member, Institute of Chartered Foresters
Mich	Michigan (US)
MIChemE	Member, Institution of Chemical Engineers
MICorrST	Member, Institution of Corrosion Science and Technology
MICS	Member, Institute of Chartered Shipbrokers
MIDPM	Member, Institute of Data Processing Management
MIE(Aust)	Member, Institution of Engineers, Australia
MIED	Member, Institution of Engineering Designers
MIEE	Member, Institution of Electrical Engineers
MIEEE	Member, Institute of Electrical and Electronics Engineers (NY)
MIEI	Member, Institution of Engineering Inspection
MIE(Ind)	Member, Institution of Engineers, India
MIERE	Member, Institution of Electronic and Radio Engineers
MIES	Member, Institution of Engineers and Shipbuilders, Scotland
MIEx	Member, Institute of Export
MIExpE	Member, Institute of Explosives Engineers
MIFA	Member, Institute of Field Archaeologists
MIFF	Member, Institute of Freight Forwarders
MIFireE	Member, Institution of Fire Engineers
MIFor	Member, Institute of Foresters (*now see* MICFor)
MIGasE	Member, Institution of Gas Engineers
MIGeol	Member, Institution of Geologists
MIH	Member, Institute of Housing
MIHM	Member, Institute of Housing Managers (*now see* MIH)
MIHort	Member, Institute of Horticulture
MIHT	Member, Institution of Highways and Transportation
MIHVE	Member, Institution of Heating and Ventilating Engineers (*now see* MCIBS)
MIIA	Member, Institute of Industrial Administration (*now see* FBIM)
MIIM	Member, Institution of Industrial Managers
MIInfSc	Member, Institute of Information Sciences
MIL	Member, Institute of Linguists
Mil.	Military
MILGA	Member, Institute of Local Government Administrators
MILocoE	Member, Institution of Locomotive Engineers
MIM	Member, Institute of Metals (*formerly* Institution of Metallurgists)
MIMarE	Member, Institute of Marine Engineers
MIMC	Member, Institute of Management Consultants
MIMechE	Member, Institution of Mechanical Engineers
MIMGTechE	Member, Institution of Mechanical and General Technician Engineers
MIMI	Member, Institute of the Motor Industry
MIMinE	Member, Institution of Mining Engineers
MIMM	Member, Institution of Mining and Metallurgy
MIMunE	Member, Institution of Municipal Engineers (now amalgamated with Institution of Civil Engineers)
Min.	Ministry
MIN	Member, Institute of Navigation (*now see* MRIN)
Minn	Minnesota (US)
MInstAM	Member, Institute of Administrative Management
MInstBE	Member, Institution of British Engineers
MInstCE	Member, Institution of Civil Engineers (*now see* FICE)
MInstD	Member, Institute of Directors
MInstE	Member, Institute of Energy
MInstEnvSci	Member, Institute of Environmental Sciences
MInstF	Member, Institute of Fuel (*now see* MInstE)
MInstHE	Member, Institution of Highway Engineers (*now see* MIHT)
MInstM	Member, Institute of Marketing
MInstMC	Member, Institute of Measurement and Control
MInstME	Member, Institution of Mining Engineers
MInstMet	Member, Institute of Metals (later part of Metals Society, *now see* MIM)
MInstP	Member, Institute of Physics
MInstPet	Member, Institute of Petroleum
MInstPI	Member, Institute of Patentees and Inventors
MInstPkg	Member, Institute of Packaging
MInstPS	Member, Institute of Purchasing and Supply
MInstR	Member, Institute of Refrigeration
MInstRA	Member, Institute of Registered Architects
MInstT	Member, Institute of Transport
MInstTM	Member, Institute of Travel Managers in Industry and Commerce
MInstW	Member, Institute of Welding (*now see* MWeldI)
MInstWM	Member, Institute of Wastes Management
MINucE	Member, Institution of Nuclear Engineers
MIOB	Member, Institute of Building (*now see* MCIOB)
MIOM	Member, Institute of Office Management (*now see* MIAM)

MIPA	Member, Institute of Practitioners in Advertising
MIPlantE	Member, Institution of Plant Engineers (*now see* MIIM)
MIPM	Member, Institute of Personnel Management
MIPR	Member, Institute of Public Relations
MIProdE	Member, Institution of Production Engineers
MIQ	Member, Institute of Quarrying
MIRE	Member, Institution of Radio Engineers (*now see* MIERE)
MIREE(Aust)	Member, Institution of Radio and Electronics Engineers (Australia)
MIRT	Member, Institute of Reprographic Technicians
MIRTE	Member, Institute of Road Transport Engineers
MIS	Member, Institute of Statisticians
MISI	Member, Iron and Steel Institute (now part of Metals Society)
MIS(India)	Member, Institution of Surveyors of India
Miss	Mississippi (US)
MIStructE	Member, Institution of Structural Engineers
MIT	Massachusetts Institute of Technology
MITA	Member, Industrial Transport Association
MITD	Member, Institute of Training and Development
MITE	Member, Institution of Electrical and Electronics Technician Engineers
MITT	Member, Institute of Travel and Tourism
MIWE	Member, Institution of Water Engineers (*now see* MIWES)
MIWES	Member, Institution of Water Engineers and Scientists
MIWM	Member, Institution of Works Managers (*now see* MIIM)
MIWPC	Member, Institute of Water Pollution Control
MIWSP	Member, Institute of Work Study Practitioners (*now see* MMS)
MJI	Member, Institute of Journalists
MJIE	Member, Junior Institution of Engineers (*now see* MIG-TechE)
MJS	Member, Japan Society
MJur	*Magister Juris*
ML	Licentiate in Medicine; Master of Laws
MLA	Member of Legislative Assembly; Modern Language Association; Master in Landscape Architecture
MLC	Member of Legislative Council
MLitt	Master of Letters
Mlle	Mademoiselle (Miss)
MLM	Member, Order of the Legion of Merit (Rhodesia)
MLO	Military Liaison Officer
MLR	Modern Language Review
MM	Military Medal
MMA	Metropolitan Museum of Art
MMB	Milk Marketing Board
MME	Master of Mining Engineering
Mme	Madame
MMechE	Master of Mechanical Engineering
MMet	Master of Metallurgy
MMGI	Member, Mining, Geological and Metallurgical Institute of India
MMM	Member, Order of Military Merit (Canada)
MMS	Member, Institute of Management Services
MMSA	Master of Midwifery, Society of Apothecaries
MN	Merchant Navy
MNAS	Member, National Academy of Sciences (US)
MNECInst	Member, North East Coast Institution of Engineers and Shipbuilders
MNI	Member, Nautical Institute
MNSE	Member, Nigerian Society of Engineers
MO	Medical Officer; Military Operations
Mo	Missouri (US)
MoD	Ministry of Defence
Mods	Moderations (Oxford)
MOF	Ministry of Food
MOH	Medical Officer(s) of Health
MOI	Ministry of Information
Mon	Monmouthshire
Mont	Montana (US); Montgomeryshire
MOP	Ministry of Power
MoS	Ministry of Supply
Most Rev.	Most Reverend
MoT	Ministry of Transport
MP	Member of Parliament
MPA	Master of Public Administration; Member, Parliamentary Assembly, Northern Ireland
MPBW	Ministry of Public Building and Works
MPH	Master of Public Health
MPIA	Master of Public and International Affairs
MPO	Management and Personnel Office
MPP	Member, Provincial Parliament
MPRISA	Member, Public Relations Institute of South Africa
MPS	Member, Pharmaceutical Society
MR	Master of the Rolls; Municipal Reform
MRAC	Member, Royal Agricultural College
MRACP	Member, Royal Australasian College of Physicians
MRACS	Member, Royal Australasian College of Surgeons
MRAeS	Member, Royal Aeronautical Society
MRAIC	Member, Royal Architectural Institute of Canada
MRAS	Member, Royal Asiatic Society
MRC	Medical Research Council
MRCA	Multi-Role Combat Aircraft
MRCGP	Member, Royal College of General Practitioners
MRCOG	Member, Royal College of Obstetricians and Gynaecologists
MRCP	Member, Royal College of Physicians, London
MRCPA	Member, Royal College of Pathologists of Australia
MRCPE	Member, Royal College of Physicians, Edinburgh
MRCPGlas	Member, Royal College of Physicians and Surgeons of Glasgow
MRCPI	Member, Royal College of Physicians of Ireland
MRCPsych	Member, Royal College of Psychiatrists
MRCS	Member, Royal College of Surgeons of England
MRCSE	Member, Royal College of Surgeons of Edinburgh
MRCSI	Member, Royal College of Surgeons in Ireland
MRCVS	Member, Royal College of Veterinary Surgeons
MRE	Master of Religious Education
MRES or MREmpS	Member, Royal Empire Society
MRI	Member, Royal Institution
MRIA	Member, Royal Irish Academy
MRIAI	Member, Royal Institute of the Architects of Ireland
MRIC	Member, Royal Institute of Chemistry (*now see* MRSC)
MRIN	Member, Royal Institute of Navigation
MRINA	Member, Royal Institution of Naval Architects
MRSanI	Member, Royal Sanitary Institute (*now see* MRSH)
MRSC	Member, Royal Society of Chemistry
MRSH	Member, Royal Society for the Promotion of Health
MRSL	Member, Order of the Republic of Sierra Leone
MRSM or MRSocMed	Member, Royal Society of Medicine
MRST	Member, Royal Society of Teachers
MRTPI	Member, Royal Town Planning Institute
MRUSI	Member, Royal United Service Institution
MRVA	Member, Rating and Valuation Association
MS	Master of Surgery; Master of Science (US)
MS, MSS	Manuscript, Manuscripts
MSA	Master of Science, Agriculture (US); Mineralogical Society of America
MSAE	Member, Society of Automotive Engineers (US)
MSAICE	Member, South African Institution of Civil Engineers
MSAInstMM	Member, South African Institute of Mining and Metallurgy
MS&R	Merchant Shipbuilding and Repairs
MSAutE	Member, Society of Automobile Engineers
MSC	Manpower Services Commission; Missionaries of the Sacred Heart; Madras Staff Corps
MSc	Master of Science
MScD	Master of Dental Science
MSE	Master of Science in Engineering (US)
MSH	Master of Stag Hounds
MSIAD	Member, Society of Industrial Artists and Designers
MSINZ	Member, Surveyors' Institute of New Zealand
MSIT	Member, Society of Instrument Technology (*now see* MInstMC)
MSM	Meritorious Service Medal; Madras Sappers and Miners
MSocIS	Member, Société des Ingénieurs et Scientifiques de France
MSocSc	Master of Social Sciences
MSR	Member, Society of Radiographers
MSTD	Member, Society of Typographic Designers
Mt	Mount, Mountain
MT	Mechanical Transport
MTA	Music Trades Association
MTAI	Member, Institute of Travel Agents
MTB	Motor Torpedo Boat
MTCA	Ministry of Transport and Civil Aviation
MTD	Midwife Teachers' Diploma
MTEFL	Master in the Teaching of English as a Foreign or Second Language
MTh	Master of Theology
MTIRA	Machine Tool Industry Research Association
MTPI	Member, Town Planning Institute (*now see* MRTPI)
MTS	Master of Theological Studies
MUniv	Master of the University
MusB	Bachelor of Music
MusD	Doctor of Music
MusM	Master of Music
MV	Merchant Vessel, Motor Vessel (naval)
MVO	Member, Royal Victorian Order
MVSc	Master of Veterinary Science
MWA	Mystery Writers of America
MWeldI	Member, Welding Institute
MWSOM	Member, Institute of Practitioners in Work Study Organisation and Methods (*now see* MMS)

N

(N)	Nationalist; Navigating Duties
N	North
n	Nephew
NA	National Academician (America)
NAACP	National Association for the Advancement of Colored People
NAAFI	Navy, Army and Air Force Institutes
NAAS	National Agricultural Advisory Service
NABC	National Association of Boys' Clubs
NAC	National Agriculture Centre
NACCB	National Accreditation Council for Certification Bodies
NACRO	National Association for the Care and Resettlement of Offenders
NADFAS	National Association of Decorative and Fine Arts Societies
NAEW	Nato Airborn Early Warning
NAHA	National Association of Health Authorities
NALGO or Nalgo	National and Local Government Officers' Association

A Fine Gold and Ruby bracelet
Van Cleef & Arpel, c. 1940

A Rare Diamond and Emerald bracelet
by Lacloche Freres, c. 1920

NAMAS	National Measurement and Accreditation Service
NAMCW	National Association for Maternal and Child Welfare
NAMH	MIND (National Association for Mental Health)
NAMMA	NATO MRCA Management Agency
NAPT	National Association for the Prevention of Tuberculosis
NASA	National Aeronautics and Space Administration (US)
NAS/UWT	National Association of Schoolmasters/Union of Women Teachers
NATCS	National Air Traffic Control Services (*now see* NATS)
NATFHE	National Association of Teachers in Further and Higher Education (combining ATCDE and ATTI)
NATLAS	National Testing Laboratory Accreditation Scheme
NATO	North Atlantic Treaty Organisation
NATS	National Air Traffic Services
Nat. Sci.	Natural Sciences
NATSOPA	National Society of Operative Printers, Graphical and Media Personnel (*formerly* of Operative Printers and Assistants)
NAYC	National Association of Youth Clubs
NB	New Brunswick
NBA	North British Academy
NBC	National Book Council (*now see* NBL); National Broadcasting Company (US)
NBL	National Book League
NBPI	National Board for Prices and Incomes
NC	National Certificate; North Carolina (US)
NCA	National Certificate of Agriculture
NCB	National Coal Board
NCC	National Computing Centre
NCCI	National Committee for Commonwealth Immigrants
NCCL	National Council for Civil Liberties
NCDAD	National Council for Diplomas in Art and Design
NCLC	National Council of Labour Colleges
NCSE	National Council for Special Education
NCTA	National Community Television Association (US)
NCU	National Cyclists' Union
NCVO	National Council for Voluntary Organisations
NDA	National Diploma in Agriculture
NDak	North Dakota (US)
ndc	National Defence College
NDD	National Diploma in Dairying; National Diploma in Design
NDH	National Diploma in Horticulture
NDIC	National Defence Industries Council
NDTA	National Defense Transportation Association (US)
NE	North-east
NEAC	New English Art Club
NEAF	Near East Air Force
NEB	National Enterprise Board
Neb	Nebraska (US)
NEBSS	National Examinations Board for Supervisory Studies
NEC	National Executive Committee
NECCTA	National Educational Closed Circuit Television Association
NECInst	North East Coast Institution of Engineers and Shipbuilders
NEDC	National Economic Development Council; North East Development Council
NEDO	National Economic Development Office
NEH	National Endowment for the Humanities
NEL	National Engineering Laboratory
NERC	Natural Environment Research Council
Nev	Nevada (US)
New M	New Mexico (US)
NFC	National Freight Consortium (*formerly* Corporation, then Company)
NFER	National Foundation for Educational Research
NFMS	National Federation of Music Societies
NFS	National Fire Service
NFT	National Film Theatre
NFU	National Farmers' Union
NFWI	National Federation of Women's Institutes
NGO	Non-Governmental Organisation(s)
NH	New Hampshire (US)
NHBC	National House-Building Council
NHS	National Health Service
NI	Northern Ireland; Native Infantry
NIAB	National Institute of Agricultural Botany
NIACRO	Northern Ireland Association for the Care and Resettlement of Offenders
NIAE	National Institute of Agricultural Engineering
NICEC	National Institute for Careers Education and Counselling
NICG	Nationalised Industries Chairmen's Group
NICS	Northern Ireland Civil Service
NID	Naval Intelligence Division; National Institute for the Deaf; Northern Ireland District
NIESR	National Institute of Economic and Social Research
NIH	National Institutes of Health (US)
NII	Nuclear Installations Inspectorate
NILP	Northern Ireland Labour Party
NISTRO	Northern Ireland Science and Technology Regional Organisation
NJ	New Jersey (US)
NL	National Liberal
NLF	National Liberal Federation
NLYL	National League of Young Liberals
NNMA	Nigerian National Merit Award
NNOM	Nigerian National Order of Merit
Northants	Northamptonshire
NOTB	National Ophthalmic Treatment Board
Notts	Nottinghamshire
NP	Notary Public

NPFA	National Playing Fields Association
NPk	Nishan-e-Pakistan
NPL	National Physical Laboratory
NRA	National Rifle Association; National Recovery Administration (US)
NRCC	National Research Council of Canada
NRD	National Registered Designer
NRDC	National Research Development Corporation
NRPB	National Radiological Protection Board
NRR	Northern Rhodesia Regiment
NS	Nova Scotia; New Style in the Calendar (in Great Britain since 1752); National Society; National Service
ns	Graduate of Royal Naval Staff College, Greenwich
NSA	National Skating Association
NSAIV	Distinguished Order of Shaheed Ali (Maldives)
NSF	National Science Foundation (US)
NSMHC	National Society for Mentally Handicapped Children (*now see* Mencap, RSMHCA)
NSPCC	National Society for Prevention of Cruelty to Children
NSRA	National Small-bore Rifle Association
N/SSF	Novice, Society of St Francis
NSTC	Nova Scotia Technical College
NSW	New South Wales
NT	New Testament; Northern Territory (Australia); National Theatre; National Trust
NTDA	National Trade Development Association
NUAAW	National Union of Agricultural and Allied Workers
NUBE	National Union of Bank Employees (*now see* BIFU)
NUFLAT	National Union of Footwear Leather and Allied Trades
NUGMW	National Union of General and Municipal Workers (*now see* GMBATU)
NUHKW	National Union of Hosiery and Knitwear Workers
NUI	National University of Ireland
NUJ	National Union of Journalists
NUJMB	Northern Universities Joint Matriculation Board
NUM	National Union of Mineworkers
NUPE	National Union of Public Employees
NUR	National Union of Railwaymen
NUT	National Union of Teachers
NUTG	National Union of Townswomen's Guilds
NUTN	National Union of Trained Nurses
NUU	New University of Ulster
NW	North-west
NWFP	North-West Frontier Province
NWP	North-Western Province
NWT	North-Western Territories
NY	New York
NYC	New York City
NYO	National Youth Orchestra
NZ	New Zealand
NZEF	New Zealand Expeditionary Force
NZIA	New Zealand Institute of Architects

O

O	Ohio (US)
o	only
OA	Officier d'Académie
O & E	Operations and Engineers (US)
O & M	organisation and method
O & O	Oriental and Occidental Steamship Co.
OAS	Organisation of American States; On Active Service
OAU	Organisation for African Unity
ob	*obiit* (died)
OBE	Officer, Order of the British Empire
OBI	Order of British India
OC	Officer of the Order of Canada (equivalent to former award SM)
o c	only child
OC or	
o/c	Officer Commanding
OCA	Old Comrades Association
OCDS or	
ocds Can	Overseas College of Defence Studies (Canada)
OCF	Officiating Chaplain to the Forces
OCSS	Oxford and Cambridge Shakespeare Society
OCTU	Officer Cadet Training Unit
OCU	Operational Conversion Unit
OD	Officer of the Order of Distinction (Jamaica)
ODA	Overseas Development Administration
ODI	Overseas Development Institute
ODM	Ministry of Overseas Development
OE	Order of Excellence (Guyana)
OEA	Overseas Education Association
OECD	Organization for Economic Co-operation and Development
OEEC	Organization for European Economic Co-operation (*now see* OECD)
OFEMA	Office Française d'Exportation de Matériel Aéronautique
OFM	Order of Friars Minor (Franciscans)
OFMCap	Order of Friars Minor Capuchin (Franciscans)
OFMConv	Order of Friars Minor Conventual (Franciscans)
OFR	Order of the Federal Republic of Nigeria
OFS	Orange Free State
OFT	Office of Fair Trading
Oftel	Office of Telecommunications
OHMS	On His (or Her) Majesty's Service

Your gift to the BDA will give deaf people a stronger voice

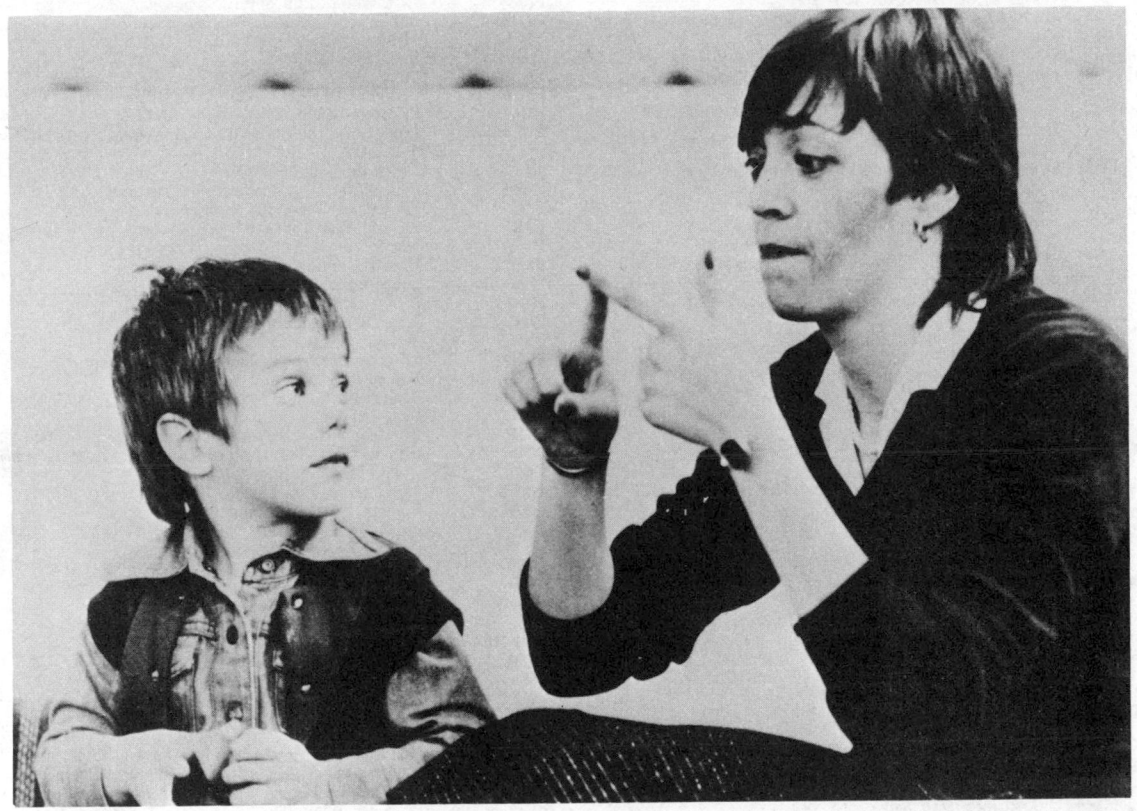

Photo by Yorkshire Post Newspapers Ltd (1985)

There are many charities helping deaf people. But we are the only charity with thousands of deaf members organised in over 170 local branches.

Because we are part of the deaf community, and because we have nearly 100 years of experience (formerly as The British Deaf & Dumb Association), we are able to provide the services deaf people most want and need:

Our education programme offers school-leaver courses, vocational and leadership training, and summer schools. We work with Special Schools for the Deaf. And we help hearing children in ordinary schools to understand what deafness means and feels like.

We support deaf people and their families with counselling and small grants, and low-cost holidays for those in need.

We promote British Sign Language (BSL) because it is the best way for deaf people to acquire language. We train BSL teachers, produce videos with BSL interpretation, and have nearly completed a unique BSL Dictionary.

We take up cases of deaf people who have been unjustly treated.

Whether you are hearing or deaf, you can share in this work. With a legacy for tomorrow. Or a donation for the here-and-now. Both will help the BDA to speak for deaf people with a stronger voice, to advance their interests, and to help them become more self-reliant.

The British Deaf Association

38, Victoria Place, Carlisle CA1 1HU

Patron: HRH The Princess of Wales   Registered charity number: 220820

O i/c	Officer in charge	pfc	Graduate of RAF Flying College
OJ	Order of Jamaica	PFE	Program for Executives
OL	Officer of the Order of Leopold	PGA	Professional Golfers' Association
OLM	Officer of Legion of Merit (Rhodesia)	PGCE	Post Graduate Certificate of Education
OM	Order of Merit	PH	Presidential Order of Honour (Botswana)
OMI	Oblate of Mary Immaculate	PHAB	Physically Handicapped & Able-bodied
OMM	Officer, Order of Military Merit (Canada)	PhB	Bachelor of Philosophy
ON	Order of the Nation (Jamaica)	PhC	Pharmaceutical Chemist
OND	Ordinary National Diploma	PhD	Doctor of Philosophy
Ont	Ontario	Phil.	Philology, Philological; Philosophy, Philosophical
OON	Officer of the Order of the Niger	PhL	Licentiate of Philosophy
OP	*Ordinis Praedicatorum*: of the Order of Preachers (Dominican); Observation Post	PHLS	Public Health Laboratory Service
		PhM	Master of Philosophy (USA)
OPCON	Operational Control	PhmB	Bachelor of Pharmacy
OPCS	Office of Population Censuses and Surveys	Phys.	Physical
OQ	Officer of the National Order of Quebec	PIARC	Permanent International Association of Road Congresses
OR	Order of Rorima (Guyana); Operational Research	PIB	Prices and Incomes Board (*see* NBPI)
ORC	Orange River Colony	PICAO	Provisional International Civil Aviation Organization (*now* ICAO)
Ore	Oregon (US)		
ORGALIME	Organisme de Liaison des Industries Métalliques Européennes	pinx.	*Pinxit* (he painted it)
		PIRA	Paper Industries Research Association
ORS	Operational Research Society	PJG	Pingat Jasa Gemilang (Singapore)
ORSL	Order of the Republic of Sierra Leone	PJK	Pingkat Jasa Kebaktian (Malaysia)
ORT	Organization for Rehabilitation by Training	Pl.	Place; Plural
ORTF	Office de la Radiodiffusion et Télévision Française	PLA	Port of London Authority
o s	only son	PLC, plc	public limited company
OSA	Order of St Augustine (Augustinian); Ontario Society of Artists	Plen.	Plenipotentiary
		PLP	Parliamentary Labour Party
OSB	Order of St Benedict (Benedictine)	PMC	Personnel Management Centre
osc	Graduate of Overseas Staff College	PMD	Programme of Management Development
OSFC	Franciscan (Capuchin) Order	PMG	Postmaster-General
O/Sig	Ordinary Signalman	PMN	Panglima Mangku Negara (Malaysia)
OSNC	Orient Steam Navigation Co.	PMO	Principal Medical Officer
o s p	*obiit sine prole* (died without issue)	PMRAFNS	Princess Mary's Royal Air Force Nursing Service
OSRD	Office of Scientific Research and Development	PMS	Presidential Order of Meritorious Service (Botswana); President, Miniature Society
OSS	Office of Strategic Services		
OStJ	Officer of the Most Venerable Order of the Hospital of St John of Jerusalem	PNBS	Panglima Negara Bintang Sarawak
		PNEU	Parents' National Educational Union
OSUK	Ophthalmological Society of the United Kingdom	PNG	Papua New Guinea
OT	Old Testament	PNP	People's National Party
OTC	Officers' Training Corps	PO	Post Office
OTL	Officer of the Order of Toussaint L'Ouverture (Haiti)	POB	Presidential Order of Botswana
OTU	Operational Training Unit	POMEF	Political Office Middle East Force
OTWSA	Ou-Testamentiese Werkgemeenskap in Suider-Afrika	Pop.	Population
OU	Oxford University; Open University	POUNC	Post Office Users' National Council
OUAC	Oxford University Athletic Club	POW	Prisoner of War; Prince of Wales's
OUAFC	Oxford University Association Football Club	PP	Parish Priest; Past President
OUBC	Oxford University Boat Club	Pp	Pages
OUCC	Oxford University Cricket Club	PPCLI	Princess Patricia's Canadian Light Infantry
OUDS	Oxford University Dramatic Society	PPE	Philosophy, Politics and Economics
OUP	Oxford University Press; Official Unionist Party	PPInstHE	Past President, Institution of Highway Engineers
OURC	Oxford University Rifle Club	PPIStructE	Past President, Institution of Structural Engineers
OURFC	Oxford University Rugby Football Club	PPITB	Printing and Publishing Industry Training Board
Oxon	Oxfordshire; *Oxoniensis* (of Oxford)	PPP	Private Patients Plan
		PPRA	Past President, Royal Academy
		PPRBA	Past President, Royal Society of British Artists
		PPRBS	Past President, Royal Society of British Sculptors
		PPRE	Past President, Royal Society of Painter-Etchers and Engravers

P

		PPROI	Past President, Royal Institute of Oil Painters
PA	Pakistan Army; Personal Assistant	PPRTPI	Past President, Royal Town Planning Institute
Pa	Pennsylvania (US)	PPS	Parliamentary Private Secretary
PAA	President, Australian Academy of Science	PPSIAD	Past President, Society of Industrial Artists and Designers
pac	passed the final examination of the Advanced Class, The Military College of Science	PQ	Province of Quebec
		PR	Public Relations
PACE	Protestant and Catholic Encounter	PRA	President, Royal Academy
PAg	Professional Agronomist	PRBS	President, Royal Society of British Sculptors
P&O	Peninsular and Oriental Steamship Co.	PRCS	President, Royal College of Surgeons
P&OSNCo.	Peninsular and Oriental Steam Navigation Co.	PRE	President, Royal Society of Painter-Etchers and Engravers
PAO	Prince Albert's Own	Preb.	Prebendary
PASI	Professional Associate, Chartered Surveyors' Institution (*now see* ARICS)	PrEng.	Professional Engineer
		Pres.	President
PBS	Public Broadcasting Service	PRHA	President, Royal Hibernian Academy
PC	Privy Counsellor; Police Constable; Perpetual Curate; Peace Commissioner (Ireland); Progressive Conservative (Canada)	PRI	President, Royal Institute of Painters in Water Colours; Plastics and Rubber Institute
		PRIA	President, Royal Irish Academy
pc	*per centum* (in the hundred)	PRIAS	President, Royal Incorporation of Architects in Scotland
PCC	Parochial Church Council	Prin.	Principal
PCE	Postgraduate Certificate of Education	PRISA	Public Relations Institute of South Africa
PCMO	Principal Colonial Medical Officer	PRO	Public Relations Officer; Public Records Office
PdD	Doctor of Pedagogy (US)	Proc.	Proctor; Proceedings
PDG	Président Directeur Général	Prof.	Professor; Professional
PDR	People's Democratic Republic	PROI	President, Royal Institute of Oil Painters
PDRA	post doctoral research assistant	PRORM	Pay and Records Office, Royal Marines
PDSA	People's Dispensary for Sick Animals	Pro tem.	*Pro tempore* (for the time being)
PDTC	Professional Dancer's Training Course Diploma	Prov.	Provost; Provincial
PE	Procurement Executive	Prox.	*Proximo* (next)
PEI	Prince Edward Island	Prox.acc.	*Proxime accessit* (next in order of merit to the winner)
PEN	Poets, Playwrights, Editors, Essayists, Novelists (Club)	PRS	President, Royal Society; Performing Right Society Ltd
PEng	Registered Professional Engineer (Canada); Member, Society of Professional Engineers	PRSA	President, Royal Scottish Academy
		PRSE	President, Royal Society of Edinburgh
Penn	Pennsylvania	PRSH	President, Royal Society for the Promotion of Health
PEP	Political and Economic Planning (*now see* PSI)	PRSW	President, Royal Scottish Water Colour Society
PER	Professional and Executive Recruitment	PRUAA	President, Royal Ulster Academy of Arts
PEST	Pressure for Economic and Social Toryism	PRWA	President, Royal West of England Academy
PETRAS	Polytechnic Educational Technology Resources Advisory Service	PRWS	President, Royal Society of Painters in Water Colours
		PS	Pastel Society; Paddle Steamer
PF	Procurator-Fiscal	ps	passed School of Instruction (of Officers)
PFA	Professional Footballers' Association		

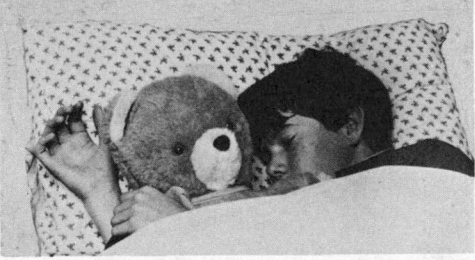

PSA	Property Services Agency
psa	Graduate of RAF Staff College
psc	Graduate of Staff College (†indicates Graduate of Senior Wing Staff College)
PSD	Petty Sessional Division
PSGB	Pharmaceutical Society of Great Britain
PSI	Policy Studies Institute
PSIAD	President, Society of Industrial Artists and Designers
PSM	Panglima Setia Mahkota (Malaysia)
psm	Certificate of Royal Military School of Music
PSMA	President, Society of Marine Artists
PSNC	Pacific Steam Navigation Co.
PSO	Principal Scientific Officer; Personal Staff Officer
PSSC	Personal Social Services Council
PTA	Passenger Transport Authority; Parent-Teacher Association
PTE	Passenger Transport Executive
Pte	Private
ptsc	passed Technical Staff College
Pty	Proprietary
PUP	People's United Party
PVSM	Param Vishishc Seva Medal (India)
PWD	Public Works Department
PWE	Political Welfare Executive
PWO	Prince of Wales's Own
PWR	Pressurized Water Reactor

Q

Q	Queen
QAIMNS	Queen Alexandra's Imperial Military Nursing Service
QALAS	Qualified Associate Chartered Land Agents' Society (now (after amalgamation) see ARICS)
QARANC	Queen Alexandra's Royal Army Nursing Corps
QARNNS	Queen Alexandra's Royal Naval Nursing Service
QBD	Queen's Bench Division
QC	Queen's Counsel
QCVSA	Queen's Commendation for Valuable Service in the Air
QFSM	Queen's Fire Service Medal for Distinguished Service
QGM	Queen's Gallantry Medal
QHC	Queen's Honorary Chaplain
QHDS	Queen's Honorary Dental Surgeon
QHNS	Queen's Honorary Nursing Sister
QHP	Queen's Honorary Physician
QHS	Queen's Honorary Surgeon
Qld	Queensland
Qly	Quarterly
QMAAC	Queen Mary's Army Auxiliary Corps
QMC	Queen Mary College, London
QMG	Quartermaster-General
QO	Qualified Officer
QOOH	Queen's Own Oxfordshire Hussars
Q(ops)	Quartering (operations)
QPM	Queen's Police Medal
Qr	Quarter
QRIH	Queen's Royal Irish Hussars
QRV	Qualified Valuer, Real Estate Institute of New South Wales
QS	Quarter Sessions
qs	RAF graduates of the Military or Naval Staff College
QSM	Queen's Service Medal (NZ)
QSO	Queen's Service Order (NZ)
QUB	Queen's University, Belfast
qv	*quod vide* (which see)

R

(R)	Reserve
RA	Royal Academician; Royal Artillery
RAA	Regional Arts Association
RAAF	Royal Australian Air Force
RAAMC	Royal Australian Army Medical Corps
RABI	Royal Agricultural Benevolent Institution
RAC	Royal Automobile Club; Royal Agricultural College; Royal Armoured Corps
RACGP	Royal Australian College of General Practitioners
RAChD	Royal Army Chaplains' Department
RACI	Royal Australian Chemical Institute
RACOG	Royal Australian College of Obstetricians and Gynae-cologists
RACP	Royal Australasian College of Physicians
RACS	Royal Australasian College of Surgeons; Royal Arsenal Co-operative Society
RADA	Royal Academy of Dramatic Art
RADAR	Royal Association for Disability and Rehabilitation
RADC	Royal Army Dental Corps
RAE	Royal Australian Engineers; Royal Aircraft Establishment
RAEC	Royal Army Educational Corps
RAeS	Royal Aeronautical Society
RAF	Royal Air Force
RAFA	Royal Air Force Association
RAFO	Reserve of Air Force Officers (now see RAFRO)
RAFRO	Royal Air Force Reserve of Officers
RAFVR	Royal Air Force Volunteer Reserve
RAI	Royal Anthropological Institute; Radio Audizioni Italiane
RAIA	Royal Australian Institute of Architects
RAIC	Royal Architectural Institute of Canada

RAM	(Member of) Royal Academy of Music
RAMC	Royal Army Medical Corps
RAN	Royal Australian Navy
R&D	Research and Development
RANR	Royal Australian Naval Reserve
RANVR	Royal Australian Naval Volunteer Reserve
RAOC	Royal Army Ordnance Corps
RAPC	Royal Army Pay Corps
RARDE	Royal Armament Research and Development Establishment
RARO	Regular Army Reserve of Officers
RAS	Royal Astronomical Society; Royal Asiatic Society
RASC	Royal Army Service Corps (now see RCT)
RASE	Royal Agricultural Society of England
RAuxAF	Royal Auxiliary Air Force
RAVC	Royal Army Veterinary Corps
RB	Rifle Brigade
RBA	Member, Royal Society of British Artists
RBC	Royal British Colonial Society of Artists
RBK&C	Royal Borough of Kensington and Chelsea
RBS	Royal Society of British Sculptors
RBSA	Royal Birmingham Society of Artists
RBY	Royal Bucks Yeomanry
RC	Roman Catholic
RCA	Member, Royal Canadian Academy of Arts; Royal College of Art; Royal Cambrian Academy (now see RCamA)
RCAC	Royal Canadian Armoured Corps
RCAF	Royal Canadian Air Force
RCamA	Member, Royal Cambrian Academy
RCAS	Royal Central Asian Society (now see RSAA)
RCDS	Royal College of Defence Studies
rcds	Completed a Course at, or served for a year on the Staff of, the Royal College of Defence Studies
RCGP	Royal College of General Practitioners
RCHA	Royal Canadian Horse Artillery
RCHM	Royal Commission on Historical Monuments
RCM	Royal College of Music
RCN	Royal Canadian Navy; Royal College of Nursing
RCNC	Royal Corps of Naval Constructors
RCNR	Royal Canadian Naval Reserve
RCNVR	Royal Canadian Naval Volunteer Reserve
RCO	Royal College of Organists
RCOG	Royal College of Obstetricians and Gynaecologists
RCP	Royal College of Physicians, London
RCPath	Royal College of Pathologists
RCPE or RCPEd	Royal College of Physicians, Edinburgh
RCPI	Royal College of Physicians of Ireland
RCPSG	Royal College of Physicians and Surgeons of Glasgow
RCR	Royal College of Radiologists
RCS	Royal College of Surgeons of England; Royal Corps of Signals; Royal College of Science
RCSE or RCSEd	Royal College of Surgeons of Edinburgh
RCSI	Royal College of Surgeons in Ireland
RCT	Royal Corps of Transport
RCVS	Royal College of Veterinary Surgeons
RD	Rural Dean; Royal Naval and Royal Marine Forces Reserve Decoration
Rd	Road
RDA	Royal Defence Academy
RDC	Rural District Council
RDF	Royal Dublin Fusiliers
RDI	Royal Designer for Industry (Royal Society of Arts)
RDS	Royal Dublin Society
RE	Royal Engineers; Fellow, Royal Society of Painter-Etchers and Engravers; Religious Education
Rear-Adm.	Rear-Admiral
REconS	Royal Economic Society
Reg. Prof.	Regius Professor
Regt	Regiment
REME	Royal Electrical and Mechanical Engineers
REPC	Regional Economic Planning Council
RERO	Royal Engineers Reserve of Officers
RES	Royal Empire Society (now Royal Commonwealth Society)
Res.	Resigned; Reserve; Resident; Research
RETI	Association of Traditional Industrial Regions
Rev.	Reverend; Review
RFA	Royal Field Artillery
RFC	Royal Flying Corps (now RAF); Rugby Football Club
RFN	Registered Fever Nurse
RFPS(G)	Royal Faculty of Physicians and Surgeons, Glasgow (now see RCPGlas)
RFR	Rassemblement des Français pour la République
RFU	Rugby Football Union
RGA	Royal Garrison Artillery
RGI	Royal Glasgow Institute of the Fine Arts
RGJ	Royal Green Jackets
RGN	Registered General Nurse
RGS	Royal Geographical Society
RGSA	Royal Geographical Society of Australasia
RHA	Royal Hibernian Academy; Royal Horse Artillery; Regional Health Authority
RHAS	Royal Highland and Agricultural Society of Scotland
RHB	Regional Hospital Board
RHBNC	Royal Holloway and Bedford New College, London
RHC	Royal Holloway College, London (now see RHBNC)
RHF	Royal Highland Fusiliers
RHG	Royal Horse Guards

NATIONAL ASSOCIATION OF VOLUNTARY HOSTELS
and
HELP THE HOMELESS

The National Association of Voluntary Hostels operates the only national placement agency for the single homeless. It was founded in 1962 and it has, over the years, concentrated on solving placement problems that have defied the resources and knowledge of statutory agencies and other organisations in the voluntary sector. It is the agency of last resort and through its unrivalled data base and relationships with other agencies it has helped over 135,000 men and women find security and hope for a better life.

NAVH also advises and supports other voluntary agencies in achieving their aims and objectives for their clients. It is a Membership organisation and currently has 282 voluntary agencies in Corporate Membership, 67 statutory agencies in Associate Membership and 99 individuals in Personal Membership. Through this extensive network NAVH are able to remain aware of the wide range of needs in our society and, more importantly, help in many ways to meet those needs.

NAVH is funded by Government Departments, the "Richmond Scheme", a number of London Boroughs and voluntary donations. As with most voluntary agencies our funding does not meet our costs.

To help overcome that problem a sister charity, Help the Homeless, was formed in 1978. A national appeal, chaired by Sir Robert Mark, GBE, raised a capital sum that has since helped NAVH and many of its member organisations.

The resources for helping the single homeless and organisations providing accommodation for that large group in our society are under ever greater pressures. No one, however great their disabilities, is refused help and NAVH does find appropriate solutions to almost all the problems presented to them.

NAVH is a Company Limited by Guarantee No. 1239130 and a Registered Charity No. 271136.

Help the Homeless is a Company Limited by Guarantee No. 1238563 and a Registered Charity No. 271988.

Registered Office: 3 Long Acre, London, WC2E 9LA.

Telephone No: 01-240 0665

RHistS	Royal Historical Society
RHR	Royal Highland Regiment
RHS	Royal Horticultural Society; Royal Humane Society
RI	Member, Royal Institute of Painters in Water Colours; Rhode Island
RIA	Royal Irish Academy
RIAI	Royal Institute of the Architects of Ireland
RIAM	Royal Irish Academy of Music
RIAS	Royal Incorporation of Architects in Scotland
RIASC	Royal Indian Army Service Corps
RIBA	Royal Institute of British Architects; *also* Member of the Institute
RIBI	Rotary International in Great Britain and Ireland
RIC	Royal Irish Constabulary; Royal Institute of Chemistry (*now see* RSC)
RICS	Royal Institution of Chartered Surveyors
RIE	Royal Indian Engineering (College)
RIF	Royal Inniskilling Fusiliers
RIIA	Royal Institute of International Affairs
RIM	Royal Indian Marines
RIN	Royal Indian Navy
RINA	Royal Institution of Naval Architects
RINVR	Royal Indian Naval Volunteer Reserve
RIPA	Royal Institute of Public Administration
RIPH&H	Royal Institute of Public Health and Hygiene
RIrF	Royal Irish Fusiliers
RLSS	Royal Life Saving Society
RM	Royal Marines; Resident Magistrate
RMA	Royal Marine Artillery; Royal Military Academy Sandhurst (*now* incorporating Royal Military Academy, Woolwich)
RMB	Rural Mail Base
RMC	Royal Military College Sandhurst (*now see* RMA)
RMCS	Royal Military College of Science
RMedSoc	Royal Medical Society, Edinburgh
RMetS	Royal Meterological Society
RMFVR	Royal Marine Forces Volunteer Reserve
RMIT	Royal Melbourne Institute of Technology
RMLI	Royal Marine Light Infantry
RMN	Registered Mental Nurse
RMO	Resident Medical Officer(s)
RMP	Royal Military Police
RMPA	Royal Medico-Psychological Association
RMS	Royal Microscopical Society; Royal Mail Steamer; Royal Society of Miniature Painters
RN	Royal Navy; Royal Naval
RNAS	Royal Naval Air Service
RNAY	Royal Naval Aircraft Yard
RNC	Royal Naval College
RNCM	(Member of) Royal Northern College of Music
RNEC	Royal Naval Engineering College
RNIB	Royal National Institute for the Blind
RNID	Royal National Institute for the Deaf
RNLI	Royal National Life-boat Institution
RNLO	Royal Naval Liaison Officer
RNR	Royal Naval Reserve
RNS	Royal Numismatic Society
RNSA	Royal Naval Sailing Association
RNSC	Royal Naval Staff College
RNT	Registered Nurse Tutor
RNUR	Régie Nationale des Usines Renault
RNVR	Royal Naval Volunteer Reserve
RNVSR	Royal Naval Volunteer Supplementary Reserve
RNXS	Royal Naval Auxiliary Service
RNZAC	Royal New Zealand Armoured Corps
RNZAF	Royal New Zealand Air Force
RNZIR	Royal New Zealand Infantry Regiment
RNZN	Royal New Zealand Navy
RNZNVR	Royal New Zealand Naval Volunteer Reserve
ROC	Royal Observer Corps
ROF	Royal Ordnance Factories
R of O	Reserve of Officers
ROI	Member, Royal Institute of Oil Painters
RoSPA	Royal Society for the Prevention of Accidents
(Rot.)	Rotunda Hospital, Dublin (after degree)
RP	Member, Royal Society of Portrait Painters
RPC	Royal Pioneer Corps
RPMS	Royal Postgraduate Medical School
RPO	Royal Philharmonic Orchestra
RPR	Rassemblement pour la République
RPS	Royal Photographic Society
RRC	Royal Red Cross
RRE	Royal Radar Establishment (*now see* RSRE)
RRF	Royal Regiment of Fusiliers
RRS	Royal Research Ship
RSA	Royal Scottish Academician; Royal Society of Arts; Republic of South Africa
RSAA	Royal Society for Asian Affairs
RSAF	Royal Small Arms Factory
RSAI	Royal Society of Antiquaries of Ireland
RSAMD	Royal Scottish Academy of Music and Drama
RSanI	Royal Sanitary Institute (*now see* RSH)
RSC	Royal Society of Canada; Royal Society of Chemistry; Royal Shakespeare Company
RSCM	Royal School of Church Music
RSCN	Registered Sick Children's Nurse
RSE	Royal Society of Edinburgh
RSF	Royal Scots Fusiliers
RSFSR	Russian Socialist Federated Soviet Republic

RSGS	Royal Scottish Geographical Society
RSH	Royal Society for the Promotion of Health
RSL	Royal Society of Literature; Returned Services League of Australia
RSM	Royal School of Mines
RSM or	
RSocMed	Royal Society of Medicine
RSMA	Royal Society of Marine Artists
RSME	Royal School of Military Engineering
RSMHCA	Royal Society for Mentally Handicapped Children and Adults (*see* Mencap)
RSNC	Royal Society for Nature Conservation
RSO	Rural Sub-Office; Railway Sub-Office; Resident Surgical Officer
RSPB	Royal Society for Protection of Birds
RSPCA	Royal Society for Prevention of Cruelty to Animals
RSRE	Royal Signals and Radar Establishment
RSSAILA	Returned Sailors, Soldiers and Airmen's Imperial League of Australia (*now see* RSL)
RSSPCC	Royal Scottish Society for Prevention of Cruelty to Children
RSTM&H	Royal Society of Tropical Medicine and Hygiene
RSW	Member, Royal Scottish Society of Painters in Water Colours
RTE	Radio Telefis Eireann
Rt Hon.	Right Honourable
RTL	Radio-Télévision Luxembourg
RTO	Railway Transport Officer
RTPI	Royal Town Planning Institute
RTR	Royal Tank Regiment
Rt Rev.	Right Reverend
RTS	Religious Tract Society; Royal Toxophilite Society; Royal Television Society
RTYC	Royal Thames Yacht Club
RU	Rugby Union
RUC	Royal Ulster Constabulary
RUI	Royal University of Ireland
RUKBA	Royal United Kingdom Beneficent Association
RUR	Royal Ulster Regiment
RUSI	Royal United Services Institute for Defence Studies (*formerly* Royal United Service Institution)
RVC	Royal Veterinary College
RWA (RWEA)	Member, Royal West of England Academy
RWAFF	Royal West African Frontier Force
RWF	Royal Welch Fusiliers
RWS	Member, Royal Society of Painters in Water Colours
RYA	Royal Yachting Association
RYS	Royal Yacht Squadron
RZSScot	Royal Zoological Society of Scotland

S

(S)	(in Navy) Paymaster; Scotland
S	Succeeded; South; Saint
s	Son
SA	South Australia; South Africa; Société Anonyme
SAAF	South African Air Force
SABC	South African Broadcasting Corporation
sac	Qualified at small arms technical long course
SACEUR	Supreme Allied Commander Europe
SACLANT	Supreme Allied Commander Atlantic
SACSEA	Supreme Allied Command, SE Asia
SA de CV	sociedad anónima de capital variable
SADF	Sudanese Auxiliary Defence Force
SADG	Société des Architectes Diplômés par le Gouvernement
SAE	Society of Automobile Engineers (US)
SAMC	South African Medical Corps
Sarum	Salisbury
SAS	Special Air Service
Sask	Saskatchewan
SASO	Senior Air Staff Officer
SAT	Senior Member, Association of Accounting Technicians
SATRO	Science and Technology Regional Organisation
SB	Bachelor of Science (US)
SBAC	Society of British Aerospace Companies (*formerly* Society of British Aircraft Constructors)
SBStJ	Serving Brother, Most Venerable Order of the Hospital of St John of Jerusalem
SC	Star of Courage (Canada); Senior Counsel (Eire, Guyana, South Africa); South Carolina (US)
sc	Student at the Staff College
SCAO	Senior Civil Affairs Officer
SCAPA	Society for Checking the Abuses of Public Advertising
SCAR	Scientific Committee for Antarctic Research
ScD	Doctor of Science
SCDC	Schools Curriculum Development Committee
SCF	Senior Chaplain to the Forces; Save the Children Fund
Sch.	School
SCI	Society of Chemical Industry
SCL	Student in Civil Law
SCM	State Certified Midwife; Student Christian Movement
SCONUL	Standing Conference of National and University Libraries
Scot.	Scotland
ScotBIC	Scottish Business in the Community
SD	Staff Duties
SDA	Social Democratic Alliance
SDak	South Dakota (US)

SDB	Salesian of Don Bosco
SDF	Sudan Defence Force; Social Democratic Federation
SDI	Strategic Defence Initiative
SDLP	Social Democratic and Labour Party
SDP	Social Democratic Party
SE	South-east
SEAC	South-East Asia Command
SEALF	South-East Asia Land Forces
SEATO	South-East Asia Treaty Organization
Sec.	Secretary
SEE.	Society of Environmental Engineers
SEN	State Enrolled Nurse
SEPM	Society of Economic Palaeontologists and Mineralogists
SERC	Science and Engineering Research Council
SESO	Senior Equipment Staff Officer
SFInstE	Senior Fellow, Institute of Energy
SFInstF	Senior Fellow, Institute of Fuel (now see SFInstE)
SFTA	Society of Film and Television Arts (now see BAFTA)
SFTCD	Senior Fellow, Trinity College Dublin
SG	Solicitor-General
SGA	Member, Society of Graphic Art
SGBI	Schoolmistresses' and Governesses' Benevolent Institution
Sgt	Sergeant
SHA	Secondary Heads Association; Special Health Authority
SHAC	London Housing Aid Centre
SHAEF	Supreme Headquarters, Allied Expeditionary Force
SHAPE	Supreme Headquarters, Allied Powers, Europe
SHHD	Scottish Home and Health Department
SIAD	Society of Industrial Artists and Designers
SIAM	Society of Industrial and Applied Mathematics (US)
SIB	Shipbuilding Industry Board
SICOT	Société Internationale de Chirurgie Orthopédique et de Traumatologie
SID	Society for International Development
SIMA	Scientific Instrument Manufacturers' Association of Great Britain
SIME	Security Intelligence Middle East
SIMG	Societas Internationalis Medicinae Generalis
SinDrs	Doctor of Chinese
SITA	Société Internationale de Télécommunications Aéro-nautiques
SITPRO	Simplification of International Trade Procedures
SJ	Society of Jesus (Jesuits)
SJAB	St John Ambulance Brigade
SJD	Doctor of Juristic Science
SL	Serjeant-at-Law
SLA	Special Libraries Association
SLAC	Stanford Linear Accelerator Centre
SLAET	Society of Licensed Aircraft Engineers and Technologists
SLAS	Society for Latin-American Studies
SLP	Scottish Labour Party
SM	Medal of Service (Canada) (now see OC); Master of Science; Officer qualified for Submarine Duties
SMA	Society of Marine Artists (now see RSMA)
SMB	Setia Mahkota Brunei
SME	School of Military Engineering (now see RSME)
SMIEEE	Senior Member, Institute of Electrical and Electronics Engineers (New York)
SMIRE	Senior Member, Institute of Radio Engineers (New York)
SMMT	Society of Motor Manufacturers and Traders Ltd
SMN	Seri Maharaja Mangku Negara (Malaysia)
SMO	Senior Medical Officer; Sovereign Military Order
SMPTE	Society of Motion Picture and Television Engineers (US)
SMRTB	Ship and Marine Requirements Technology Board
SNAME	Society of Naval Architects and Marine Engineers (US)
SNCF	Société Nationale des Chemins de Fer Français
SNP	Scottish National Party
SNTS	Society for New Testament Studies
SO	Staff Officer
SOAS	School of Oriental and African Studies
Soc.	Society
SocCE(France)	Société des Ingénieurs Civils de France
SODEPAX	Committee on Society, Development and Peace
SOE	Special Operations Executive
SOGAT	Society of Graphical and Allied Trades
SOLACE or Solace	Society of Local Authority Chief Executives
SOTS	Society for Old Testament Study
sowc	Senior Officers' War Course
sp	sine prole (without issue)
SP	Self-Propelled (Anti-Tank Regiment)
SpA	Società per Azioni
SPAB	Society for the Protection of Ancient Buildings
SPCK	Society for Promoting Christian Knowledge
SPCM	Darjah Seri Paduka Cura Si Manja Kini (Malaysia)
SPD	Salisbury Plain District
SPDK	Seri Panglima Darjal Kinabalu
SPG	Society for the Propagation of the Gospel (now see USPG)
SPk	Sitara-e-Pakistan
SPMB	Seri Paduka Makhota Brunei
SPMO	Senior Principal Medical Officer
SPNC	Society for the Promotion of Nature Conservation (now see RSNC)
SPNM	Society for the Promotion of New Music
SPR	Society for Psychical Research
SPRC	Society for Prevention and Relief of Cancer
sprl	société de personnes à responsabilité limitée
SPSO	Senior Principal Scientific Officer

SPTL	Society of Public Teachers of Law
Sq.	Square
sq	staff qualified
SQA	Sitara-i-Quaid-i-Azam (Pakistan)
Sqdn or Sqn	Squadron
SR	Special Reserve; Southern Railway; Southern Region (BR)
SRC	Science Research Council (now see SERC); Students' Representative Council
SRHE	Society for Research into Higher Education
SRN	State Registered Nurse
SRNA	Shipbuilders and Repairers National Association
SRO	Supplementary Reserve of Officers
SRP	State Registered Physiotherapist
SRY	Sherwood Rangers Yeomanry
SS	Saints; Straits Settlements; Steamship
SSA	Society of Scottish Artists
SSAFA or SS&AFA	Soldiers', Sailors', and Airmen's Families Association
SSC	Solicitor before Supreme Court (Scotland); Sculptors Society of Canada; Societas Sanctae Crucis (Society of the Holy Cross)
SSEB	South of Scotland Electricity Board
SSEES	School of Slavonic and East European Studies
SSF	Society of St Francis
SSJE	Society of St John the Evangelist
SSM	Society of the Sacred Mission; Seri Setia Mahkota (Malaysia)
SSO	Senior Supply Officer
SSRC	Social Science Research Council (now see ESRC)
SSStJ	Serving Sister, Most Venerable Order of the Hospital of St John of Jerusalem
St	Street; Saint
STB	Sacrae Theologiae Baccalaureus (Bachelor of Sacred Theology)
STC	Senior Training Corps
STD	Sacrae Theologiae Doctor (Doctor of Sacred Theology)
STh	Scholar in Theology
Stip.	Stipend; Stipendiary
STL	Sacrae Theologiae Lector (Reader or a Professor of Sacred Theology)
STM	Sacrae Theologiae Magister (Master of Sacred Theology)
STP	Sacrae Theologiae Professor (Professor of Divinity, old form of DD)
STRIVE	Society for Preservation of Rural Industries and Village Enterprises
STSO	Senior Technical Staff Officer
STV	Scottish Television
SUNY	State University of New York
Supp. Res.	Supplementary Reserve (of Officers)
Supt	Superintendent
Surg.	Surgeon
Surv.	Surviving
SW	South-west
SWET	Society of West End Theatre
SWIA	Society of Wildlife Artists
SWPA	South West Pacific Area
SWRB	Sadler's Wells Royal Ballet
Syd.	Sydney

T

T	Telephone; Territorial
TA	Telegraphic Address; Territorial Army
TAA	Territorial Army Association
TA&VRA	Territorial Auxiliary and Volunteer Reserve Association
TAF	Tactical Air Force
T&AFA	Territorial and Auxiliary Forces Association
T&AVR	Territorial and Army Volunteer Reserve
TANS	Territorial Army Nursing Service
TANU	Tanganyika African National Union
TARO	Territorial Army Reserve of Officers
TAS	Torpedo and Anti Submarine Course
TC	Order of the Trinity Cross (Trinidad and Tobago)
TCCB	Test and County Cricket Board
TCD	Trinity College, Dublin (University of Dublin, Trinity College)
TCF	Temporary Chaplain to the Forces
TCPA	Town and Country Planning Association
TD	Territorial Efficiency Decoration; Efficiency Decoration (T&AVR) (since April 1967); Teachta Dala (Member of the Dáil, Eire)
TDD	Tubercular Diseases Diploma
TEAC	Technical Educational Advisory Council
TEC	Technician Education Council (now see BTEC)
Tech(CEI)	Technician
TEM	Territorial Efficiency Medal
TEMA	Telecommunication Engineering and Manufacturing Association
Temp.	Temperature; Temporary
TEng(CEI)	Technician Engineer
Tenn	Tennessee (US)
TeolD	Doctor of Theology
TES	Times Educational Supplement
TET	Teacher of Electrotherapy
Tex	Texas (US)

TF	Territorial Force
TFR	Territorial Force Reserve
TGEW	Timber Growers England and Wales Ltd
TGO	Timber Growers' Organisation (*now see* TGEW)
TGWU	Transport and General Workers' Union
THED	Transvaal Higher Education Diploma
THELEP	Therapy of Leprosy
THES	Times Higher Education Supplement
ThL	Theological Licentiate
ThSchol	Scholar in Theology
TIMS	The Institute of Management Sciences
TLS	Times Literary Supplement
TMMG	Teacher of Massage and Medical Gymnastics
TNC	Theatres National Committee
TOSD	Tertiary Order of St Dominic
TP	Transvaal Province
TPI	Town Planning Institute (*now see* RTPI)
Trans.	Translation; Translated
Transf.	Transferred
TRC	Thames Rowing Club
TRE	Telecommunications Research Establishment (*now see* RRE)
TRH	Their Royal Highnesses
Trin.	Trinity
TRRL	Transport and Road Research Laboratory
TSB	Trustee Savings Bank
tsc	passed a Territorial Army Course in Staff Duties
TSD	Tertiary of St Dominic
TSSA	Transport Salaried Staffs' Association
TUC	Trades Union Congress
TULV	Trade Unions for a Labour Victory
TV	Television
TVEI	Technical and Vocational Education Initiative
TWA	Thames Water Authority
TYC	Thames Yacht Club (*now see* RTYC)

U

(U)	Unionist
u	Uncle
UAE	United Arab Emirates
UAR	United Arab Republic
UAU	Universities Athletic Union
UBI	Understanding British Industry
UC	University College
UCCA	Universities Central Council on Admissions
UCET	Universities Council for Education of Teachers
UCH	University College Hospital (London)
UCL	University College London
UCLA	University of California at Los Angeles
UCNS	Universities' Council for Non-academic Staff
UCNW	University College of North Wales
UCRN	University College of Rhodesia and Nyasaland
UCS	University College School
UCW	University College of Wales; Union of Communication Workers
UDC	Urban District Council
UDF	Union Defence Force
UDR	Ulster Defence Regiment; Union des Démocrates pour la Vème République (*now see* RFR)
UDSR	Union Démocratique et Socialiste de la Résistance
UEA	University of East Anglia
UED	University Education Diploma
UEFA	Union of European Football Associations
UF	United Free Church
UFAW	Universities Federation of Animal Welfare
UGC	University Grants Committee
UIAA	Union Internationale des Associations d'Alpinisme
UICC	Union Internationale contre le Cancer
UIE	Union Internationale des Etudiants
UJD	*Utriusque Juris Doctor* (Doctor of both Laws, Doctor of Canon and Civil Law)
UK	United Kingdom
UKAC	United Kingdom Automation Council
UKAEA	United Kingdom Atomic Energy Authority
UKCC	United Kingdom Central Council for Nurses, Midwives and Health Visitors
UKISC	United Kingdom Industrial Space Committee
UKLF	United Kingdom Land Forces
UKMF(L)	United Kingdom Military Forces (Land)
UKMIS	United Kingdom Mission
UKSLS	United Kingdom Services Liaison Staff
ULCI	Union of Lancashire and Cheshire Institutes
UMDS	United Medical and Dental Schools
UMIST	University of Manchester Institute of Science and Technology
UN	United Nations
UNA	United Nations Association
UNCAST	United Nations Conference on the Applications of Science and Technology
UNCIO	United Nations Conference on International Organisation
UNCITRAL	United Nations Commission on International Trade Law
UNCSTD	United Nations Conference on Science and Technology for Development
UNCTAD or Unctad	United Nations Commission for Trade and Development
UNDP	United Nations Development Programme

UNDRO	United Nations Disaster Relief Organisation
UNECA	United Nations Economic Commission for Asia
UNEP	United Nations Environment Programme
UNESCO or Unesco	United Nations Educational, Scientific and Cultural Organisation
UNFAO	United Nations Food and Agriculture Organisation
UNFICYP	United Nations Force in Cyprus
UNHCR	United Nations High Commissioner for Refugees
UNICE	Union des Industries de la Communauté Européenne
UNICEF or Unicef	United Nations Children's Fund (*formerly* United Nations International Children's Emergency Fund)
UNIDO	United Nations Industrial Development Organisation
UNIDROIT	Institut International pour l'Unification du Droit Privé
UNIPEDE	Union Internationale des Producteurs et Distributeurs d'Energie Electrique
UNISIST	Universal System for Information in Science and Technology
UNITAR	United Nations Institute of Training and Research
Univ.	University
UNRRA	United Nations Relief and Rehabilitation Administration
UNRWA	United Nations Relief and Works Agency
UNSCOB	United Nations Special Commission on the Balkans
UP	United Provinces; Uttar Pradesh; United Presbyterian
UPGC	University and Polytechnic Grants Committee
UPNI	Unionist Party of Northern Ireland
(UPUP)	Ulster Popular Unionist Party
URC	United Reformed Church
URSI	Union Radio-Scientifique Internationale
US	United States
USA	United States of America
USAAF	United States Army Air Force
USAF	United States Air Force
USAID	United States Agency for International Development
USAR	United States Army Reserve
USC	University of Southern California
USDAW	Union of Shop Distributive and Allied Workers
USMA	United States Military Academy
USN	United States Navy
USNR	United States Naval Reserve
USPG	United Society for the Propagation of the Gospel
USPHS	United States Public Health Service
USS	United States Ship
USSR	Union of Soviet Socialist Republics
USVI	United States Virgin Islands
UTC	University Training Corps
(UU)	Ulster Unionist
(UUUC)	United Ulster Unionist Coalition
(UUUP)	United Ulster Unionist Party
UWIST	University of Wales Institute of Science and Technology
UWT	Union of Women Teachers

V

V	Five (Roman numerals); Version; Vicar; Viscount; Vice
v	*versus* (against)
v or vid.	*vide* (see)
Va	Virginia (US)
VAD	Voluntary Aid Detachment
V&A	Victoria and Albert
VAT	Value Added Tax
VC	Victoria Cross
VCAS	Vice-Chief of the Air Staff
VCDS	Vice-Chief of the Defence Staff
VCGS	Vice-Chief of the General Staff
VCNS	Vice-Chief of Naval Staff
VD	Royal Naval Volunteer Reserve Officers' Decoration (*now* VRD); Volunteer Officers' Decoration; Victorian Decoration
VDC	Volunteer Defence Corps
Ven.	Venerable
Vet.	Veterinary
VG	Vicar-General
VHS	Hon. Surgeon to Viceroy of India
VIC	Victoria Institute of Colleges
Vice-Adm.	Vice-Admiral
Visc.	Viscount
VM	Victory Medal
VMH	Victoria Medal of Honour (Royal Horticultural Society)
Vol.	Volume; Volunteers
VP	Vice-President
VPP	Volunteer Political Party
VPRP	Vice-President, Royal Society of Portrait Painters
VQMG	Vice-Quartermaster-General
VR	*Victoria Regina* (Queen Victoria)
VRD	Royal Naval Volunteer Reserve Officers' Decoration
VSO	Voluntary Service Overseas
Vt	Vermont (US)
(VUP)	Vanguard Unionist Party

W

W	West
WA	Western Australia
WAAF	Women's Auxiliary Air Force (*now see* WRAF)

Wash	Washington State (US)
WCC	World Council of Churches
W/Cdr	Wing Commander
WEA	Workers' Educational Association; Royal West of England Academy
WES/PNEU	Worldwide Education Service of Parents' National Educational Union
WEU	Western European Union
WFSW	World Federation of Scientific Workers
WFTU	World Federation of Trade Unions
WhF	Whitworth Fellow
WHO	World Health Organization
WhSch	Whitworth Scholar
WI	West Indies; Women's Institute
Wilts	Wiltshire
WIPO	World Intellectual Property Organization
Wis	Wisconsin (US)
Wits	Witwatersrand
WJEC	Welsh Joint Education Committee
WLA	Women's Land Army
WLF	Women's Liberal Federation
Wm	William
WMO	World Meteorological Organization
WNO	Welsh National Opera
WO	War Office
Worcs	Worcestershire
WOSB	War Office Selection Board
WR	West Riding; Western Region (BR)
WRAC	Women's Royal Army Corps
WRAF	Women's Royal Air Force
WRNS	Women's Royal Naval Service
WRVS	Women's Royal Voluntary Service
WS	Writer to the Signet
WSPU	Women's Social and Political Union
WUS	World University Service

WVa	West Virginia (US)
WVS	Women's Voluntary Services (*now see* WRVS)
WWF	World Wildlife Fund
Wyo	Wyoming (US)

X

X	Ten (Roman numerals)
XO	Executive Officer

Y

y	youngest
YC	Young Conservative
YCNAC	Young Conservatives National Advisory Committee
Yeo.	Yeomanry
YES	Youth Enterprise Scheme
YHA	Youth Hostels Association
YMCA	Young Men's Christian Association
Yorks	Yorkshire
YPTES	Young People's Trust for Endangered Species
yr	younger
yrs	years
YTS	Youth Training Scheme
YVFF	Young Volunteer Force Foundation
YWCA	Young Women's Christian Association

Z

ZANU	Zimbabwe African National Union
ZAPU	Zimbabwe African People's Union

OBITUARY

Deaths notified from the beginning of December 1985 to late October 1986.

Abbott, Arthur William, CMG, CBE, 8 Oct. 1986.
Abel Smith, Vice-Adm. Sir (Edward Michael) Conolly, GCVO, CB, 3 Dec. 1985.
Abercrombie, Nigel James, 17 Feb. 1986.
Abraham, Robert John Elliot   [*Deceased.*
Acutt, Sir Keith Courtney, KBE, 21 July 1986.
Adam, Hon. Sir Alexander Duncan Grant, 20 Sept. 1986.
Agra, Archbishop of, (RC); Most Rev. Dominic Romuald Athaide, OFMCap   [*Deceased.*
Ainley, Eric Stephen, 26 March 1986.
Aird, Ronald, MC, TD, 16 Aug. 1986.
Aitken, Ian Hugh, CBE, 12 June 1986.
Aldenham, 5th Baron; Antony Durant Gibbs, 25 Jan. 1986.
Alexander, Duncan Hubert David, CBE, TD, 18 Dec. 1985.
Allen, Brig. Ronald Lewis, CBE, 19 June 1986.
Allen, W(alter) Godfrey, 12 June 1986.
Anderson, Prof. David Steel, 11 Feb. 1986.
Anderson, Hugh Fraser, 1 July 1986.
Andrews, Rt Hon. Sir John Lawson Ormrod, KBE, PC (NI), 12 Jan. 1986.
Annamunthodo, Sir Harry, 6 Sept. 1986.
Archer, Maj.-Gen. Gilbert Thomas Lancelot, CB, 5 June 1986.
Armstrong, Brig. Charles Douglas, CBE, DSO, MC, 11 Dec. 1985.
Armstrong, Christopher Wyborne, OBE, 8 July 1986.
Arnold, Prof. Denis Midgley, CBE, FBA, 28 April 1986.
Askew, Herbert Royston, QC, 18 Aug. 1986.
Astbury, Sir George, 20 Dec. 1985.
Aves, Dame Geraldine Maitland, DBE, 23 June 1986.
Ayers, Herbert Wilfred, CB, CBE, 27 June 1986.

Baddeley, Hermione, 19 Aug. 1986.
Baker, Prof. Arthur Semprière Lancey, 20 May 1986.
Baker, Rt Rev. John Gilbert Hindley, 29 April 1986.
Balfour-Lynn, Dr Stanley, 23 Feb. 1986.
Barlow, Sir John Denman, 2nd Bt, 5 Jan. 1986.
Barnett, Richard David, CBE, FBA, 29 July 1986.
Barrett, Anthony Arthur, 25 May 1986.
Barrett, Edwin Cyril Geddes, CMG, 8 Feb. 1986.
Barrington, Prof. Ernest James William, FRS, 15 Dec. 1985.
Bartlett, Peter Geoffrey, 25 June 1986.
Barton, Sidney James, 20 Jan. 1986.
Bate, Henry, OBE, 19 May 1986.
Bateson, Air Vice-Marshal Robert Norman, CB, DSO, DFC, 6 March 1986.
Batho, Edith Clara, 21 Jan. 1986.
Beale, Evelyn Martin Lansdowne, FRS, 23 Dec. 1985.
Bearsted, 3rd Viscount; Marcus Richard Samuel, TD, 15 Oct. 1986.
Beattie, Prof. William, CBE, 28 March 1986.
Beauvoir, Simone de, 14 April 1986.
Beddard, Dr Frederick Denys, CB, 29 Dec. 1985.
Beeck, Sir Marcus Truby, 3 May 1986.
Bell, His Honour P(hilip) Ingress, TD, QC, 12 Sept. 1986.
Bemrose, Sir Max, (John Maxwell), 13 July 1986.
Beney, Frederick William, CBE, QC, 5 April 1986.
Bennett, Daniel   [*Deceased.*
Bennett, Air Vice-Marshal Donald Clifford Tyndall, CB, CBE, DSO, 15 Sept. 1986.
Bennett, Joan, 20 July 1986.
Bergin, John Alexander, CB, 24 May 1986.
Bergner, Elisabeth, 12 May 1986.
Bibby, Major Sir (Arthur) Harold, 1st Bt, DSO, 7 March 1986.
Billam, John Bertram Hardy, CB, DFC, 7 July 1986.
Binns, John, 6 Aug. 1986.
Bird, Lt-Gen. Sir Clarence August, KCIE, CB, DSO, 30 July 1986.
Bird, Veronica, 30 Aug. 1986.
Birgi, Muharrem Nuri, 30 Sept. 1986.
Black, (Ian) Hervey Stuart, TD, 14 Feb. 1986.
Blackwell, John Kenneth, CBE, 14 April 1986.
Blackwood, Dame Margaret, DBE, 1 June 1986.
Blough, Roger M.   [*Deceased.*
Blyde, Sir Henry Ernest, KBE   [*Deceased.*
Blyth, Charles Henry, OBE, 24 Sept. 1986.
Boase, Arthur Joseph, CMG, OBE, 31 Jan. 1986.
Boland, Frederick Henry, 4 Dec. 1985.
Bolte, Dame Edith Lilian, (Lady Bolte), DBE, 14 Aug. 1986.

Boothby, Baron (Life Peer); Robert John Graham Boothby, KBE, 16 July 1986.
Boothby, Sir Hugo Robert Brooke, 15th Bt, 30 May 1986.
Borges, Jorge Luis, 14 June 1986.
Borwick, Lt-Col Michael George, 20 April 1986.
Bosanquet, Charles Ion Carr, 9 April 1986.
Bosch, Baron Jean van den, Hon. GCVO, 15 Dec. 1985.
Bosworth, George Simms, CBE, 15 May 1986.
Bowles, Chester, 25 May 1986.
Bradford, Ernle, 8 May 1986.
Braye, 7th Baron; Thomas Adrian Verney-Cave, 19 Dec. 1985.
Brennan, Lt-Gen. Michael, 24 Oct. 1986.
Brewis, John Fenwick, CMG, CVO, 11 Jan. 1986.
Bricker, John William, 22 March 1986.
Brinton, Dr Denis Hubert, 13 March 1986.
Brown, Air Cdre Sir Vernon, CB, OBE, 26 Aug. 1986.
Browne, Rev. Prof. Laurence Edward, 29 May 1986.
Browne, Stanley George, CMG, OBE, 29 Jan. 1986.
Bruhn, Erik Belton Evers, 1 April 1986.
Bryden, Sir William James, CBE, QC (Scot.), 27 May 1986.
Buckley, Hon. Dame Ruth Burton, DBE, 11 July 1986.
Bull, Sir George, 3rd Bt, 9 Sept. 1986.
Bullock, Prof. Kenneth   [*Deceased.*
Burrow, Prof. Thomas, FBA, 8 June 1986.
Bury, Hon. Leslie Harry Ernest, CMG, 7 Sept. 1986.
Bush, Ronald Paul, CMG, OBE, 18 Aug. 1986.
Butler, Rt Rev. (Basil) Christopher, OSB, 20 Sept. 1986.
Byam Shaw, Glencairn Alexander, CBE, 29 April 1986.

Cage, Edward Edwin Henry   [*Deceased.*
Campbell, Ian George Hallyburton, TD, QC, 16 Oct. 1986.
Campbell, Dame Kate Isabel, DBE, 12 July 1986.
Canfield, Cass, 27 March 1986.
Canning, Victor, 21 Feb. 1986.
Cannon, Air Vice-Marshal Leslie William, CB, CBE, 27 Jan. 1986.
Carey, Denis, 28 Sept. 1986.
Carne, Colonel James Power, VC, DSO, 19 April 1986.
Carpenter, Trevor Charles, 27 Feb. 1986.
Carr, Herbert Reginald Culling, 23 April 1986.
Carter, Air Cdre North, CB, DFC   [*Deceased.*
Carter, William Stovold, CMG, CVO, 13 Dec. 1985.
Cartwright, Rt Hon. John Robert, CC (Can.), MC, PC (Can.)   [*Deceased.*
Cawston, (Edwin) Richard, CVO, 7 June 1986.
Cecil, Lord (Edward Christian) David (Gascoyne), CH, CLit, 1 Jan. 1986.
Chadwick, Sir Albert Edward, CMG   [*Deceased.*
Chadwyck-Healey, Sir Charles Arthur, 4th Bt, OBE, TD, 14 Aug. 1986.
Chalmers, William John, CB, CVO, CBE, 8 Jan. 1986.
Chapling, Norman Charles, CBE, 29 April 1986.
Charlemont, 13th Viscount; Charles Wilberforce Caulfeild   [*Deceased.*
Chauncy, Major Frederick Charles Leslie, CBE, 4 June 1986.
Checkland, Prof. Sydney George, FBA, 22 March 1986.
Chegwidden, Sir Thomas Sidney, CB, CVO, 4 Jan. 1986.
Chester, Sir (Daniel) Norman, CBE, 20 Sept. 1986.
Christie, Prof. Ronald Victor, 27 Sept. 1986.
Clark, David Allen Richard, 15 Feb. 1986.
Clark, Sir (Gordon Colvin) Lindesay, AC, KBE, CMG, MC, 3 Jan. 1986.
Clayden, Rt Hon. Sir (Henry) John, PC, 11 July 1986.
Clayton, Prof. Sir Stanley George, 12 Sept. 1986.
Clegg, Sir Alec, (Alexander Bradshaw Clegg), 20 Jan. 1986.
Clegg, Sir Cuthbert Barwick, TD, 9 Jan. 1986.
Clifford, Sir (Geoffrey) Miles, KBE, CMG, ED, 21 Feb. 1986.
Cocker, Prof. Ralph, CBE, 29 July 1986.
Cocking, Prof. John Martin, 28 Jan. 1986.
Codrington, Prof. Kenneth de Burgh, 1 Jan. 1986.
Cohen, Prof. John, 19 Dec. 1985.
Collar, Prof. (Arthur) Roderick, CBE, FRS, 12 Feb. 1986.
Collier, Air Vice-Marshal Sir (Alfred) Conrad, KCB, CBE, 16 Sept. 1986.
Collingwood, Lt-Gen. Sir (Richard) George, KBE, CB, DSO, 21 April 1986.
Collingwood, Brig. Sydney, CMG, CBE, MC, 12 Jan. 1986.

Coltart, James Milne, 6 Sept. 1986.
Colton, Gladys M., 24 April 1986.
Compston, Dr Nigel Dean, CBE, 17 Oct. 1986.
Cooper, Sqdn Ldr Albert Edward, MBE, 12 May 1986.
Cooper, Lady Diana, (Diana, Viscountess Norwich), 16 June 1986.
Cooper, Martin Du Pré, CBE, 15 March 1986.
Cornish, Prof. Ronald James, 8 May 1986.
Coulson, Prof. Noel James, 30 Aug. 1986.
Cousins, Rt Hon. Frank, PC, 11 June 1986.
Coutts, Gen. Frederick, CBE, 6 Feb. 1986.
Cowern, Raymond Teague, RA, 8 June 1986.
Cox, Air Vice-Marshal Joseph, CB, OBE, DFC, 22 April 1986.
Cox, Thomas Richard Fisher, CMG, 12 May 1986.
Craig, Clifford, CMG, 5 Sept. 1986.
Cramer, Dame Mary Theresa, DBE   [*Deceased.*
Crawshaw of Aintree, Baron (Life Peer); Lt-Col Richard Crawshaw, OBE, TD, 16 July 1986.
Creasey, Gen. Sir Timothy May, KCB, OBE, 5 Oct. 1986.
Creswell, Sir Michael Justin, KCMG, 25 April 1986.
Cronin, John Desmond, 3 Jan. 1986.
Crooks, Very Rev. Samuel Bennett, OBE, TD, 21 Aug. 1986.
Croom, Sir John Halliday, TD, 12 April 1986.
Crutchley, Adm. Sir Victor Alexander Charles, VC, KCB, DSC, 24 Jan. 1986.
Curtis, Brig. Francis Cockburn, CBE, 24 Sept. 1986.
Curtis-Raleigh, Nigel Hugh; His Honour Judge Curtis-Raleigh, 1 Sept. 1986.

D'Aeth, Air Vice-Marshal Narbrough Hughes, CB, CBE, 21 Jan. 1986.
Dahlgaard, Tyge, 20 Dec. 1985.
Daniels, David Kingsley, CBE, 27 July 1986.
Daniels, Jeffery, 3 Feb. 1986.
Dann, Howard Ernest, CBE, 18 April 1986.
Daventry, 2nd Viscount; Robert Oliver Fitz Roy, 19 Jan. 1986.
Davidson, Hon. Sir Charles William, KBE   [*Deceased.*
Davies, Elwyn, 18 Sept. 1986.
Davis, Brig. Cyril Elliott, CBE, 29 June 1986.
Davison, His Honour William Norris, 16 Sept. 1986.
Davitt, Cahir, 1 March 1986.
Dean, Col Donald John, VC, OBE, TD, 9 Dec. 1985.
de Courcy-Ireland, Lt-Col Gerald Blakeney, LVO, MC, 28 March 1986.
Defferre, Gaston, 7 May 1986.
de Gale, Sir Leo Victor, GCMG, CBE, 22 March 1986.
de Gex, Maj.-Gen. George Francis, CB, OBE, 16 Aug. 1986.
de la Mare, Richard Herbert Ingpen, 22 March 1986.
Denholm, Col Sir William Lang, TD, 9 Aug. 1986.
d'Entrèves, Prof. Alexander Passerin, 15 Dec. 1985.
Derry, Warren, 9 July 1986.
Derwent, 4th Baron; Patrick Robin Gilbert Vanden-Bempde-Johnstone, CBE, 2 Jan. 1986.
de Wolff, Brig. Charles Esmond, CB, CBE, 12 Oct. 1986.
Dick, Alick Sydney, 8 March 1986.
Dickens, Prof. Frank, FRS, 25 June 1986.
Dickinson, Prof. Robert Eric   [*Deceased.*
Dickinson, Ronald Arthur, CMG, 31 July 1986.
Dingwall, Eric John, 7 Aug. 1986.
Dixon, Prof. Malcolm, FRS, 7 Dec. 1985.
Doisy, Prof. Edward A., 23 Oct. 1986.
Donald, David William Alexander, OBE, TD, 25 April 1986.
Doughty, Dame Adelaide, DBE, 12 Aug. 1986.
Douglas, Very Rev. Hugh Osborne, KCVO, CBE, 4 Jan. 1986.
Douglas, Sir Sholto Courtenay Mackenzie, 5th Bt, MC, 9 June 1986 (*ext*).
Downes, Dr Ronald Geoffrey, CB, 2 May 1986.
Dowse, Maj.-Gen. Sir Maurice Brian, KCVO, CB, CBE, 24 Sept. 1986.
D'Oyly, Sir John Rochfort, 13th Bt, 29 April 1986.
Drewe, Geoffrey Grabham, CIE, CBE, 28 Jan. 1986.
Dudding, Sir John Scarbrough, 26 June 1986.
Dundonald, 14th Earl of; Ian Douglas Leonard Cochrane, 4 Oct. 1986.
Dunham, Cyril John, 30 Jan. 1986.
Durlacher, Adm. Sir Laurence George, KCB, OBE, DSC, 16 Jan. 1986.
Dyson, Edith Mary Beatrice, OBE, RRC, 14 Sept. 1986.

Easterbrook, Prof. William Thomas James   [*Deceased.*
Elder, Hugh, 7 Feb. 1986.
Emminger, Otmar, 2 Aug. 1986.
Everett, Rear-Adm. Douglas Henry, CB, CBE, DSO, 26 Aug. 1986.

Fairn, (Richard) Duncan, 12 April 1986.
Falshaw, Sir Donald   [*Deceased.*
Farquhar, Lt-Col Sir Peter Walter, 6th Bt, DSO, OBE, 2 June 1986.
Fearnley, John Thorn, 22 May 1986.
Fell, Dame Honor Bridget, DBE, FRS, 22 April 1986.

Fellowes, Sir William Albemarle, KCVO, 6 April 1986.
ffrench, 7th Baron; Peter Martin Joseph Charles John Mary ffrench, 30 Jan. 1986.
Field, Stanley Alfred, CBE, 7 Jan. 1986.
Filson, Alexander Warnock, 29 March 1986.
Finley, Sir Moses, FBA, 23 June 1986.
Fitzherbert, Cuthbert, 23 July 1986.
Fletcher, Richard Cawthorne, OBE, 18 July 1986.
Flory, Prof. Paul John   [*Deceased.*
Foggin, (Wilhelm) Myers, CBE, 17 July 1986.
Forbes, Dr Gilbert, 30 Aug. 1986.
Forbes, Hon. Sir Hugh Harry Valentine; Hon. Mr Justice Forbes, 13 Dec. 1985.
Ford, Sir Edward, OBE, 27 Aug. 1986.
Ford, Air Vice-Marshal Howard, CB, CBE, AFC, 28 March 1986.
Fournier, Pierre, 8 Jan. 1986.
Fraenkel, Heinrich, 25 May 1986.
Francis, Hugh Elvet, QC, 7 June 1986.
Freeman, Sir (Nathaniel) Bernard, CBE   [*Deceased.*
Freeth, H. Andrew, RA, 26 March 1986.
Fulton, Baron (Life Peer); John Scott Fulton, 14 March 1986.
Furnivall, Maj.-Gen. Lewis Trevor, CB, DSO, 12 July 1986.

Gadd, Maj.-Gen. Alfred Lockwood, (David), CBE, 15 March 1986.
Gailey, Thomas William Hamilton, CBE, 18 Sept. 1986.
Galsworthy, Sir Arthur Norman, KCMG, 7 Oct. 1986.
Gandell, Captain Wilfrid Pearse, CBE, RN, 9 June 1986.
Gander, L(eonard) Marsland, March 1986.
Gardiner, Lt-Col Christopher John, DSO, OBE, TD, 19 May 1986.
Gardner, Dame Helen Louise, DBE, FBA, 4 June 1986.
Gardner, Hugh, CB, CBE, 5 Aug. 1986.
Garrett, Alexander Adnett, MBE, 5 June 1986.
Garside, Air Vice-Marshal Kenneth Vernon, CB, DFC, 2 Aug. 1986.
Gash, Robert Walker, 19 April 1986.
Gemmell, Prof. Alan Robertson, OBE, 5 July 1986.
Gibb, George Dutton, CB, 25 Feb. 1986.
Gilchrist, John   [*Deceased.*
Gilmour, John Scott Lennox, 3 June 1986.
Glazebrook, Reginald Field, 2 March 1986.
Glubb, Lt-Gen. Sir John Bagot, KCB, CMG, DSO, OBE, MC, 17 March 1986.
Glynn, Prudence Loveday, (The Lady Windlesham), 24 Sept. 1986.
Goode, Sir William Allmond Codrington, GCMG, 15 Sept. 1986.
Goodson, Lt-Col Sir Alfred Lassam, 2nd Bt, 17 Feb. 1986.
Goodwin, Sir Reginald Eustace, CBE, 29 Sept. 1986.
Gordon, Sir John Charles, 9th Bt   [*Deceased.*
Gosnay, Maxwell; His Honour Judge Gosnay, 17 May 1986.
Gould, Sir Ronald, 11 April 1986.
Goulden, Gontran Iceton, OBE, TD, 19 April 1986.
Graham, Lt-Gen. Howard Douglas, OC, CVO, CBE, DSO, ED, CD, QC (Can.), 28 Sept. 1986.
Graham-Dixon, Leslie Charles, QC, 15 Feb. 1986.
Grant, Alexander Ludovic, TD, 6 March 1986.
Grant, Frank, CB, OBE, 2 Jan. 1986.
Grant, Captain, John Moreau, CBE, RCN, 2 Feb. 1986.
Graves, Robert Ranke, 7 Dec. 1985.
Gregory, Philip Herries, FRS, 9 Feb. 1986.
Gwynne-Evans, Sir Ian William, 3rd Bt, 27 Dec. 1985.

Haddington, 12th Earl of; George Baillie-Hamilton, KT, MC, TD, 17 April 1986.
Haight, Prof. Gordon Sherman, 28 Dec. 1985.
Hakewill Smith, Maj.-Gen. Sir Edmund, KCVO, CB, CBE, MC, 15 April 1986.
Hamilton, Maj.-Gen. Godfrey John, CB, CBE, DSO, 21 Dec. 1985.
Hamilton, Iain (Bertram), 15 July 1986.
Hamilton Stubber, Lt-Col John Henry, 3 Oct. 1986.
Hamper, Rev. Richard John, 25 Feb. 1986.
Harding, Sir Harold John Boyer, 27 March 1986.
Hardy, Sir James Douglas, CBE, 28 Feb. 1986.
Hare, Prof. Ronald, 13 March 1986.
Harland, Rt Rev. Maurice Henry, 29 Sept. 1986.
Harmer, Cyril Henry Carrington, 17 Sept. 1986.
Harper, George Clifford, 3 Aug. 1986.
Harriman, (William) Averell, 26 July 1986.
Harris, Sir Charles Joseph William, KBE, 14 Jan. 1986.
Harrison, Rev. Cecil Marriott, 15 Aug. 1986.
Hartnett, Sir Laurence John, CBE, 4 April 1986.
Harvey, Prof. Leslie Arthur, 19 March 1986.
Harvey, Richard Jon Stanley, QC, 21 Feb. 1986.
Hawes, Maj.-Gen. Leonard Arthur, CBE, DSO, MC, 7 Aug. 1986.
Hay, Sir (Alan) Philip, KCVO, TD, 7 April 1986.
Headlam-Morley, Prof. Agnes, 21 Feb. 1986.

Hein, Sir (Charles Henri) Raymond, QC   [*Deceased.*
Helpmann, Sir Robert Murray, CBE, 28 Sept. 1986.
Henderson, Rt Rev. Edward Barry, DSC, 13 June 1986.
Henderson, Sir Neville Vicars, CBE, 15 Aug. 1986.
Henderson, Rupert Albert Geary, 9 Sept. 1986.
Hentschel, Christopher Carl, 21 July 1986.
Herklots, Geoffrey Alton Craig, CBE, 14 Jan. 1986.
Hewer, Christopher Langton, 28 Jan. 1986.
Heywood, Geoffrey Henry, CBE, 20 June 1986.
Hickey, Nancy Maureen, OBE, 22 Sept. 1986.
Hicks, Donald, OBE, 30 Jan. 1986.
Higgs, Godfrey Walter, CBE, 4 May 1986.
Higgs, Sir John Walter Yeoman, KCVO, 6 June 1986.
Hilliard, Christopher Richard; His Honour Judge Hilliard, 4 Dec. 1985.
Hillier, Arthur, OBE, 7 June 1986.
Hills, Prof. Edwin Sherbon, CBE, FRS, 1 May 1986.
Hilton, Sir Derek Percy, MBE, 10 April 1986.
Hintz, Orton Sutherland, CMG   [*Deceased.*
Hobson, Alec, CBE, MVO, 11 Sept. 1986.
Hodson, Prof. Cecil John, 1 Dec. 1985.
Hogan, Hon. Sir Michael Joseph Patrick, CMG, 27 Sept. 1986.
Holder, Sir John Eric Duncan, 3rd Bt, 10 May 1986.
Hollis, Rt Rev. (Arthur) Michael, 11 Feb. 1986.
Hollis, Hugh, 6 Oct. 1986.
Horsbrugh-Porter, Sir Andrew Marshall, 3rd Bt, DSO, 5 Feb. 1986.
Horsfall, Geoffrey Jonas, CBE   [*Deceased.*
Hothfield, 4th Baron; Thomas Sackville Tufton, 16 May 1986.
Howard, Sir John, 2 Jan. 1986.
Howland, Robert Leslie, 7 March 1986.
Hucker, Ernest George, CBE, 24 Feb. 1986.
Hughes, Rear-Adm. Henry Hugh, CB, 17 May 1986.
Hughes Hallett, Vice-Adm. Sir (Cecil) Charles, KCB, CBE, 2 Dec. 1985.
Hughes-Parry, Dr Robert, 1 May 1986.
Hunnings, Prof. Gordon, 16 April 1986.
Hunt, Prof. (Jack) Naylor, 14 April 1986.
Hurley, Ven. Alfred Vincent, CBE, TD, 24 Feb. 1986.
Hutchinson, William James, TD   [*Deceased.*
Hutchison, James Seller, 1 April 1986.
Hutton, Maurice, 21 Feb. 1986.

Incledon-Webber, Lt-Col Godfrey Sturdy, TD, 28 April 1986.
Ingoldby, Eric, CIE, 13 May 1986.
Inness, Air Cdre William Innes Cosmo, CB, OBE, 13 April 1986.
Irving, David Blair, 9 June 1986.
Isherwood, Christopher, 4 Jan. 1986.
Ivins, Prof. John Derek, CBE, 22 April 1986.

Jackson, Prof. Richard Meredith, FBA, 8 May 1986.
Jameson, (Margaret) Storm, 30 Sept. 1986.
Jardine of Applegirth, Col Sir William Edward, 11th Bt, OBE, TD, 19 April 1986.
Jarvis, Mrs Doris Annie, CBE   [*Deceased.*
Jeffery, Lilian Hamilton, FBA, 29 Sept. 1986.
Jeffreys, 2nd Baron; Mark George Christopher Jeffreys, 13 Feb. 1986.
Jessup, Philip C(aryl), 31 Jan. 1986.
John, DeWitt   [*Deceased.*
Johnston, Sir Charles Hepburn, GCMG, 23 April 1986.
Johnston, Rt Rev. William, 23 May 1986.
Jolly, Dr Hugh Reginald, 4 March 1986.
Jones, Tom, CBE   [*Deceased.*
Joslin, Ivy Collin, 17 July 1986.
Jowett, Ronald Edward, CBE, 29 Aug 1986.

Kaldor, Baron (Life Peer); Nicholas Kaldor, FBA, 30 Sept. 1986.
Kantorovich, Prof. Leonid Vitaljevich, 7 April 1986.
Karasek, Dr Franz, 11 March 1986.
Kawamata, Katsuji, 29 March 1986.
Kearns, Prof. Howard George Henry, OBE, 15 July 1986.
Kelsey, Emanuel, 11 Dec. 1985.
Kennedy, John Norman   [*Deceased.*
Kent, Sir Percy Edward, (Sir Peter Kent), FRS, 9 July 1986.
Kershaw, His Honour Philip Charles Stones, 1 July 1986.
Kessel, Prof. Lipmann, MBE, MC, 5 June 1986.
Key, Maj.-Gen. Berthold Wells, CB, DSO, MC, 26 Sept. 1986.
Kier, Olaf, CBE, 3 May 1986.
Kilner, Cyril   [*Deceased.*
Knight, Henry Lougher, 22 March 1986.
Knutsford, 5th Viscount; Julian Thurstan Holland-Hibbert, CBE, 8 March 1986.
Krishnamurti, Jiddu, 17 Feb. 1986.

Lambart, Sir Oliver Francis, 2nd Bt, 16 March 1986 (*ext*).

Lambert, Jack Walter, CBE, DSC, 3 Aug. 1986.
Lancaster, Sir Osbert, CBE, 27 July 1986.
Langton, Thomas Bennett, MC, 14 Feb. 1986.
Larkin, Philip Arthur, CH, CBE, CLit, 2 Dec. 1985.
Lascelles, Daniel Richard, CBE   [*Deceased.*
Lash, Rt Rev. William Quinlan, 5 Oct. 1986.
Lattin, Francis Joseph, CMG, 19 April 1986.
Lavrin, Prof. Janko (John), 13 Aug. 1986.
Lawson, Lt-Col Harold Andrew Balvaird, 28 Dec. 1985.
Layton, Dr (Lt-Col) Basil Douglas Bailey, CD, 9 Feb. 1986.
Lee, Sir (George) Wilton, TD, 15 Jan. 1986.
Leechman, Hon. Lord; James Graham Leechman, 15 May 1986.
Lees, David, CBE, 18 Jan. 1986.
Le Fèvre, Prof. Raymond James Wood, FRS, 26 Aug. 1986.
Le Marchant, Sir Spencer, 7 Sept. 1986.
Leonard, Sir Reginald Byron, CMG, OBE, 12 March 1986.
Lerner, Alan Jay, 14 June 1986.
Lewis, Henry Gethin, 20 March 1986.
Lillie, Very Rev. Henry Alexander, 8 Jan. 1986.
Lipmann, Prof. Fritz (Albert), 24 July 1986.
Lister, Laurier, OBE, 30 Sept. 1986.
Little, Prof. Alan Neville, 18 Oct. 1986.
Llewellyn, Col Sir (Robert) Godfrey, 1st Bt, CB, CBE, MC, TD, 3 Oct. 1986.
Lloyd, (Charles) Christopher, 31 March 1986.
Lloyd-Jones, Sir (Harry) Vincent, 23 Sept. 1986.
Lloyd-Roberts, George Charles, 12 Jan. 1986.
Loewen, Gen. Sir Charles Falkland, GCB, KBE, DSO, 17 Aug. 1986.
Loewy, Raymond, 14 July 1986.
Lovett, Robert Abercrombie, 7 May 1986.
Lowe, Sir Francis Reginald Gordon, 3rd Bt, 28 May 1986.
Lowthian, George Henry, CBE, 11 June 1986.
Luft, Rev. Canon Hyam Mark, 19 April 1986.
Lyon, (Percy) Hugh (Beverley), MC, 18 Jan. 1986.

McAllister, Sir Reginald Basil, CMG, CVO   [*Deceased.*
Macaulay, Sir Hamilton, CBE, 19 Sept. 1986.
McEleney, Most Rev. John, SJ, 5 Oct. 1986.
McFarland, Sir Basil Alexander Talbot, 2nd Bt, CBE, ERD, 5 March 1986.
McGillivray, Hon. William Alexander   [*Deceased.*
McIntyre, Surgeon Rear-Adm. William Percival Edwin, CB, 2 March 1986.
Mackay, Ian Keith, CMG   [*Deceased.*
Mackay, Sir James Mackerron, KBE, CB, 24 Dec. 1985.
Mackenzie, Dr Alastair Stewart, (Sandy), 31 Jan. 1986.
MacKenzie, Norman Archibald MacRae, CC (Can.), CMG, MM, CD, QC, 26 Jan. 1986.
Mackenzie, Captain Sir Roderick Edward François McQuhae, 11th Bt, CBE, DSC, RN, 7 Jan. 1986.
Mackley, Garnet Hercules, CMG, 24 April 1986.
McLaren, Prof. Hugh Cameron, 8 June 1986.
Maclean, Ian Albert Druce, 31 Jan. 1986.
Maclean, Col John Francis, 9 March 1986.
MacLysaght, Edward Anthony, 3 March 1986.
MacMillan of MacMillan, Gen. Sir Gordon Holmes Alexander, KCB, KCVO, CBE, DSO, MC, 21 Jan. 1986.
Madoc, Maj.-Gen. Reginald William, CB, DSO, OBE, 24 May 1986.
Mahon, Simon, 19 Oct. 1986.
Mair, Prof. Lucy Philip, 1 April 1986.
Malamud, Bernard, 18 March 1986.
Man, Morgan Charles Garnet, CMG, 24 Aug. 1986.
Margetson, Major Sir Philip Reginald, KCVO, MC, QPM, 5 Dec. 1985.
Marjolin, Robert Ernest, 15 April 1986.
Marlow, Roger Douglas Frederick, DSC, 12 Feb. 1986.
Marnham, John Ewart, CMG, MC, TD, 28 Dec. 1985.
Marshall, Sir Hugo Frank, KBE, CMG, 10 June 1986.
Marshall-Cornwall, Gen. Sir James Handyside, KCB, CBE, DSO, MC, 25 Dec. 1985.
Marten, Rt Hon. Sir Neil, PC, 22 Dec. 1985.
Maston, Charles James, CB, CBE, 6 July 1986.
Matthews, Sir Bryan Harold Cabot, CBE, FRS, 23 July 1986.
Maude, His Honour John Cyril, QC, 16 Aug. 1986.
Maxwell, William Wayland, 15 Oct. 1986.
Maybray-King, Baron (Life Peer); Horace Maybray Maybray-King, PC, 3 Sept. 1986.
Mayers, Norman, CMG, 11 Aug. 1986.
Medlycott, Sir (James) Christopher, 8th Bt, 11 April 1986.
Mellor, Sir John Serocold Paget, 2nd Bt, 15 July 1986.
Merton, Air Chief Marshal Sir Walter Hugh, GBE, KCB, 23 March 1986.
Milland, Raymond Alton, (Ray Milland), 10 March 1986.

Miller, Rear-Adm. Andrew John, 1 July 1986.
Miller, Desmond Campbell, TD, QC, 15 Jan. 1986.
Millis, Sir Leonard William Francis, CBE, 30 July 1986.
Milne, James, 14 April 1986.
Milner, George Andrew; His Honour Judge Milner, 14 Feb. 1986.
Minio-Paluello, Lorenzo, FBA, 6 May 1986.
Mitford-Slade, Col Cecil Townley, 13 Aug. 1986.
Monroe, Elizabeth, (Mrs Humphrey Neame), CMG, 10 March 1986.
Montague, Leslie Clarence, 3 Oct. 1986.
Montague-Smith, Patrick Wykeham, 26 Jan. 1986.
Moon, Lieut Rupert Vance, VC, 28 Feb. 1986.
Moore, Brig. Guy Newton, CBE, DFC, ED   [*Deceased.*
Moore, Henry, OM, CH, FBA, 31 Aug. 1986.
Morant, Dame Mary Maud, (Sister Mary Regis), DBE   [*Deceased.*
Morgan, Sir Clifford Naunton, 24 Feb. 1986.
Morgan, William Stanley, CMG, 16 June 1986.
Mowlem, Rainsford, 6 Feb. 1986.
Muir, Air Commodore Adam, CB, 20 March 1986.
Muir, Sir David John, CMG, 23 March 1986.
Munro, Robert Wilson, CMG, 25 Dec. 1985.
Munrow, William Davis, CBE, 15 Sept. 1986.
Muntz, Thomas Godric Aylett, CMG, OBE, 19 June 1986.
Murphy, Lionel Keith, 21 Oct. 1986.
Musgrave, Sir (Frank) Cyril, KCB, 20 July 1986.
Myrdal, Alva, 1 Feb. 1986.

Napier, Sir Joseph William Lennox, 4th Bt, OBE, 13 Oct. 1986.
Neagle, Dame Anna, (Dame Marjorie Wilcox), DBE, 3 June 1986.
Newburgh, 11th Earl of; Don Giulio Cesare Taddeo Cosimo Maria
   Rospigliosi, 18 April 1986.
Newton, John Mordaunt, CB, 7 March 1986.
Nicholson, Sir John Charles, 3rd Bt, TD, 16 March 1986 (*ext*).
Nixon, Rear-Adm. Harry Desmond, CB, LVO, 6 Oct. 1986.
North, Roger, 15 Dec. 1985.

O'Donnell, Peadar, 13 May 1986.
O'Hara, Rear-Adm. Derek, CB, 1 Feb. 1986.
O'Keeffe, Georgia, 6 March 1986.
Onians, Prof. Richard Broxton, 21 May 1986.
Osmond-Clarke, Sir Henry, KCVO, CBE, 24 Oct. 1986.
Otter, Rt Rev. Anthony, 9 March 1986.
Owen, Peter Granville, CMG, QPM, CPM, 25 May 1986.
Oxfuird, 12th Viscount of; (John) Donald (Alexander Arthur) Makgill,
   24 Jan. 1986.

Pagan, Brig. Sir John Ernest, CMG, MBE, ED, 26 June 1986.
Palme, (Sven) Olof (Joachim), 28 Feb. 1986.
Parke, Prof. Herbert William, 20 Jan. 1986.
Parshall, Horace Field, TD, 18 Feb. 1986.
Paton, His Honour Harold William, DSC, 16 March 1986.
Paton, Sir Leonard Cecil, CBE, MC, 18 Jan. 1986.
Pawson, Albert Guy, CMG, 25 Feb. 1986.
Pears, Sir Peter, CBE, 3 April 1986.
Pendred, Air Marshal Sir Lawrence Fleming, KBE, CB, DFC, 19 Sept.
   1986.
Pennington-Ramsden, Major Sir (Geoffrey) William, 7th Bt, 13 Jan.
   1986.
Perkins, (George) Dudley (Gwynne), 15 April 1986.
Peterson, Sir Arthur William, KCB, LVO, 8 May 1986.
Phemister, James, 18 May 1986.
Phillips, Sir John Grant, KBE, Oct. 1986.
Phillips, Prof. Owen Hood, QC, 25 May 1986.
Phipps, John Constantine, 30 July 1986.
Pickford, Prof. Ralph William, 7 June 1986.
Pike, Rt Rev. Victor Joseph, CB, CBE, 25 Feb. 1986.
Pitman, Sir Hubert, OBE, 19 March 1986.
Pitt, Terence John, 3 Oct. 1986.
Plant, Baron (Life Peer); Cyril Thomas Howe Plant, CBE, 9 Aug. 1986.
Pocock, Most Rev. Philip F.   [*Deceased.*
Pond, Sir Desmond Arthur, 29 June 1986.
Pottinger, John Inglis Drever, (Don Pottinger), LVO, 14 June 1986.
Preminger, Otto (Ludwig), 23 April 1986.
Preston, Aston Zachariah, 24 June 1986.
Price, Captain Henry Ryan, MC, 16 Aug. 1986.
Prior-Palmer, Brig. Sir Otho Leslie, DSO, 29 Jan. 1986.
Proctor, Sir (George) Philip, KBE, 22 June 1986.
Pugh, Rt Rev. William Edward Augustus, 4 Jan. 1986.

Quick-Smith, George William, CBE, 15 July 1986.

Raikes, Sir (Henry) Victor (Alpin MacKinnon), KBE, 18 April 1986.
Rainbird, George Meadus, 20 Aug. 1986.
Ram, Jagjivan, 6 July 1986.

Ramgoolam, Dr Rt Hon. Sir Seewoosagur, GCMG, PC, 15 Dec. 1985.
Ramsay, Cdre Sir James Maxwell, KCMG, KCVO, CBE, DSC, 1 May
   1986.
Ramsay, Sir Neis Alexander, 12th Bt, 7 March 1986.
Ramsey, Robert John, CBE, 7 May 1986.
Randrup, Michael   [*Deceased.*
Rankin, Dame Annabelle Jane Mary, DBE, 30 Aug. 1986.
Ransom, Charles Frederick George, CMG, OBE, 20 July 1986.
Ratter, John, CBE, ERD, 25 Dec. 1985.
Rawlinson, Sir Anthony Keith, KCB, 22 Feb. 1986.
Redgrave, William Archibald, 20 June 1986.
Redman, Lt-Gen. Sir Harold, KCB, CBE, 24 Aug. 1986.
Reed, Michael, CB, 4 Dec. 1985.
Rees, His Honour Richard Geraint, 27 March 1986.
Reid, George Smith, 20 Dec. 1985.
Reid, Prof. Louis Arnaud, 26 Jan. 1986.
Renton, Lady; Claire Cicely Renton, 24 April 1986.
Revington, Air Commodore Arthur Pethick, CB, CBE, 21 April 1986.
Reynolds, Doris Livesey, (Mrs Arthur Holmes)   [*Deceased.*
Richardson, Sir (H.) Frank   [*Deceased.*
Richardson, Sir William Robert, 16 Jan. 1986.
Richmond, Vice-Adm. Sir Maxwell, KBE, CB, DSO, 15 May 1986.
Rickards, Oscar Stanley Norman, CBE, 9 Jan. 1986.
Riley, Harry Lister, 25 March 1986.
Roberts, Captain Gilbert Howland, CBE, RD, RN, 22 Jan. 1986.
Roberts, Gen. Sir Ouvry Lindfield, GCB, KBE, DSO, 16 March 1986.
Robertson, Catherine Christian, 4 Dec. 1985.
Rochford, James Donald Henry, 21 April 1986.
Rogers, Prof. Neville William, 22 Dec. 1985.
Room, Prof. Thomas Gerald, FRS, 2 April 1986.
Rose, (Edward) Michael, CMG, 25 March 1986.
Rous, Sir Stanley Ford, CBE, 18 July 1986.
Rowett, Geoffrey Charles, 19 June 1986.
Rowlandson, Sir (Stanley) Graham, MBE, 29 Jan. 1986.
Rowley, John Hewitt, CBE, 6 July 1986.
Roy, Maurice Paul Mary   [*Deceased.*
Rubbra, Edmund, CBE, 16 Feb. 1986.
Rugg, Sir (Edward) Percy, 7 Sept. 1986.
Russell of Killowen, Baron (Life Peer); Charles Ritchie Russell, PC,
   23 June 1986.
Ryder, Captain Robert Edward Dudley, VC, RN, 29 June 1986.
Ryley, Air Vice-Marshal Douglas William Robert, CB, CBE, 29 Dec.
   1985.

Sacher, Michael Moses, 29 July 1986.
St Johnston, Sir (Thomas) Eric, CBE, QPM, 17 March 1986.
Salt, Mrs Emmaline Juanita, CBE, Feb. 1986.
Samuels, Sir Alexander, CBE, 18 June 1986.
Sandford, Sir Folliott Herbert, KBE, CMG, 5 July 1986.
Sansom, Lt-Gen. Ernest William, CB, DSO, CD   [*Deceased.*
Saw, Prof. Ruth Lydia, 23 March 1986.
Sawyerr, Rev. Prof. Canon Harry Alphonso Ebun, CBE, 22 Aug. 1986.
Scarfe, Prof. Francis Harold, CBE, 13 March 1986.
Scorgie, Mervyn Nelson, OBE, 30 March 1986.
Scott, Sir David John Montagu Douglas, KCMG, OBE, 22 Aug. 1986.
Scott, J(ames) M(aurice), OBE, 12 March 1986.
Seifert, Jaroslav, 10 Jan. 1986.
Seuffert, Stanislaus, QC, 22 Sept. 1986.
Seymour, Derek Robert Gurth, 5 Feb. 1986.
Shackleton, Prof. Robert, CBE, FBA, 9 Sept. 1986.
Shankland, Sir Thomas Murray, CMG, 13 Oct. 1986.
Shaw, Sinclair, QC (Scot.)   [*Deceased.*
Shea, Patrick, CB, OBE, 31 May 1986.
Sheppard, Leslie Alfred, 3 Dec. 1985.
Shinwell, Baron (Life Peer); Emanuel Shinwell, CH, PC, 8 May 1986.
Simpson, Gen. Sir Frank Ernest Wallace, GBE, KCB, DSO, 28 July
   1986.
Simpson, Maj.-Gen. Hamilton Wilkie, CB, DSO, 8 June 1986.
Sinker, Rt Rev. George, 19 Jan. 1986.
Sixsmith, Maj.-Gen. Eric Keir Gilborne, CB, CBE, 6 April 1986.
Skinner, Hon. Sir Henry Albert; Hon. Mr Justice Skinner, 15 March
   1986.
Smith, David MacLeish, FRS, 3 Aug. 1986.
Smith, His Honour Edgar Dennis, 1 June 1986.
Smith, Sir Henry Thompson, KBE, CB, 4 Oct. 1986.
Smithers, Donald William, CB, 10 Sept. 1986.
Snell, Ven. Basil Clark, 12 June 1986.
Soddy, Dr Kenneth, 10 April 1986.
Somerville, Mrs (Katherine) Lilian, CMG, OBE, 15 Dec. 1985.
Sorel Cameron, Brig. John, CBE, DSO, 30 May 1986.
Sparkman, John J(ackson)   [*Deceased.*
Spence, John Deane, MP, 4 March 1986.
Spencer, Noël, 18 Feb. 1986.

Spinelli, Altiero, 23 May 1986.
Spragg, Cyril Douglas, CBE, 21 April 1986.
Spurling, Hon. Sir (Arthur) Dudley, CBE, 20 May 1986.
Stafford, 14th Baron; Basil Francis Nicholas Fitzherbert, 8 Jan. 1986.
Stamm, Air Vice-Marshal William Percivale, CBE, 10 March 1986.
Stamp, Prof. Edward, 10 Jan. 1986.
Stanbridge, Air Vice-Marshal Reginald Horace, CB, OBE, 3 Jan. 1986.
Starling, Brigadier John Sieveking, CBE, 4 March 1986.
Steel, Sir (Joseph) Lincoln (Spedding), 27 Dec. 1985.
Steele, Sir Kenneth Charles, DFC, 4 June 1986.
Stevens, Martin, MP, 10 Jan. 1986.
Stevenson, Robert, 30 April 1986.
Stewart, Sir Iain Maxwell, 18 Dec. 1985.
Stewart, Potter, 7 Dec. 1985.
Stiles, Walter Stanley, OBE, FRS, 15 Dec. 1985.
Stirling, Sir Charles Norman, KCMG, KCVO, 5 April 1986.
Stone, Baron (Life Peer); Joseph Ellis Stone, 17 July 1986.
Storrar, Air Vice-Marshal Ronald Charles, CB, OBE, 1 Dec. 1985.
Stranks, Prof. Donald Richard, AO, 9 Aug. 1986.
Streatfeild, (Mary) Noel, OBE, 11 Sept. 1986.
Streit, Clarence Kirshman, 6 July 1986.
Stuchbery, Arthur Leslie, CBE, 12 May 1986.
Sturge, Arthur Collwyn, MC, 21 Feb. 1986.
Style, Sir William Montague, 12th Bt   [*Deceased.*
Summerson, Thomas Hawksley, OBE, 3 March 1986.
Sutherland, Carol Humphrey Vivian, CBE, FBA, 14 May 1986.
Sutherland, Sir Iain Johnstone Macbeth, KCMG, 1 July 1986.
Svenningsen, Nils Thomas   [*Deceased.*
Swann, Robert Swinney, MBE, 3 Oct. 1986.
Sycamore, Thomas Andrew Harding, CBE, 17 Feb. 1986.
Syme, Sir Colin York, AK, 19 Jan. 1986.
Symonds, Joseph Bede, OBE   [*Deceased.*
Symons, Noel Victor Housman, CIE, MC, 24 Jan. 1986.
Szent-Györgyi, Albert, 22 Oct. 1986.

Taplin, Walter, 19 Jan. 1986.
Taylor, Rupert Sutton, OBE, TD, 4 April 1986.
Tenzing Norgay, GM, 9 May 1986.
Thorpe, Prof. William Homan, FRS, 7 April 1986.
Tobias, Prof. Stephen Albert, 24 April 1986.
Tonks, Rt Rev. Basil   [*Deceased.*
Toothill, Sir John Norman, CBE, 5 July 1986.
Totman, Grenfell William, CMG, OBE, 14 Jan. 1986.
Toynbee, Prof. Jocelyn Mary Catherine, FBA, 31 Dec. 1985.
Trapnell, His Honour Alan Stewart, 18 Oct. 1986.
Trent, Group Captain Leonard Henry, VC, DFC, 20 May 1986.
Trusted, Sir Harry Herbert, QC, 8 Dec. 1985.
Tucker, Hon. Sir Henry James, KBE, 9 Jan. 1986.
Tudor Price, Hon. Sir David William; Hon. Mr Justice Tudor Price, 13 Feb. 1986.
Turner, James Grant Smith, CMG, 25 Dec. 1985.
Turner, Theodore Francis, QC, 19 May 1986.

Urwin, Rt Hon. Thomas William, PC, 14 Dec. 1985.

Vaughan Wilkes, Rev. John Comyn, 24 Jan. 1986.
Vibert, McInroy Este, 29 March 1986.
Vivian, Arthur Henry Seymour, 22 Dec. 1985.

Wackett, Air Vice-Marshal Ellis Charles, CB, CBE   [*Deceased.*

Wade, Col Sir George Albert, MC, 27 Jan. 1986.
Wakefield, Roger Cuthbert, CMG, OBE, 1 July 1986.
Walsh, Leslie, 4 Jan. 1986.
Walsh, Prof. William Henry, FBA, 7 April 1986.
Walwyn, Rear-Adm. James Humphrey, CB, OBE, 24 Feb. 1986.
Ward, Frederick John, 5 Sept. 1986.
Wardlaw, Prof. Claude Wilson, 16 Dec. 1985.
Warner, Rex, 24 June 1986.
Warrack, Guy Douglas Hamilton, 12 Feb. 1986.
Wates, Sir Ronald Wallace, 25 Jan. 1986.
Watson, (John) Steven, 12 June 1986.
Webster, Rev. Canon Douglas, 27 Feb. 1986.
Webster, Sir Richard James, DSO, 17 Jan. 1986.
Weck, Richard, CBE, FRS, 9 Jan. 1986.
Welsh, Dame (Ruth) Mary (Eldridge), DBE, TD, 25 June 1986.
Westall, Gen. Sir John Chaddesley, KCB, CBE, 30 Sept. 1986.
Wheldon, Sir Huw Pyrs, OBE, MC, 14 March 1986.
Wheler, Captain Sir Trevor Wood, 13th Bt, 14 Jan. 1986.
Whittle, Dr Claude Howard, 1 March 1986.
Whyte, Gabriel Thomas   [*Deceased.*
Wilcockson, Rear-Adm. Kenneth Dilworth East, CBE, 22 Sept. 1986.
Wilcox, Sir Malcolm George, CBE, 23 May 1986.
Wilkinson, Sir Harold, CMG, 9 May 1986.
Wilkinson, Prof. James Hardy, FRS, 5 Oct. 1986.
Wilks, Dick Lloyd, 18 Dec. 1985.
Williams, Stuart Graeme, OBE, 15 May 1986.
Williams, Sir (William) Thomas, QC; His Honour Judge Sir Thomas Williams, 28 Feb. 1986.
Willis, Harold Infield, QC, 12 Feb. 1986.
Willoughby de Broke, 20th Baron; John Henry Peyto Verney, MC, AFC, AE, 25 May 1986.
Wilson, Rear-Adm. Guy Austen Moore, CB, 11 Jan. 1986.
Wilson, Percy, CB, 1 July 1986.
Wilson-Haffenden, Maj.-Gen. Donald James, CBE, 27 May 1986.
Windsor-Aubrey, Henry Miles, 3 Jan. 1986.
Winneke, Hon. Sir Henry Arthur, AC, KCMG, KCVO, OBE, QC (Aust.), 28 Dec. 1985.
Wittrick, Prof. William Henry, FRS, 2 July 1986.
Wollen, Sir (Ernest) Russell (Storey), KBE, 28 May 1986.
Wolverton, 5th Baron; Nigel Reginald Victor Glyn, 18 Aug. 1986.
Wood, Sir Ian Jeffreys, MBE, 1 Sept. 1986.
Wood, Sir Kenneth Millns, 27 May 1986.
Woodifield, Rear-Admiral Anthony, CB, CBE, LVO, 7 May 1986.
Woods, Reginald Salisbury, (Rex Woods), 21 Sept. 1986.
Woollcombe, Dame Jocelyn May, DBE, 30 Jan. 1986.
Woolley, Baron (Life Peer); Harold Woolley, CBE, 31 July 1986.
Woolley, Rev. (Alfred) Russell, 27 Jan. 1986.
Woolley, Richard, 30 Jan. 1986.
Wrangham, Sir Geoffrey Walter, 22 Aug. 1986.
Wright, Thomas Erskine, 27 Jan. 1986.

Yates, William   [*Deceased.*
Yonge, Sir (Charles) Maurice, CBE, FRS, 17 March 1986.
Young, Dr Carmichael Aretas, 11 Aug. 1986.
Young, Eric Edgar, 12 July 1986.
Young, Mary Lavinia Bessie, OBE, 10 June 1986.
Young, Stuart, 29 Aug. 1986.

Zimmern, Archibald, CBE, 20 Dec. 1985.

THE ROYAL FAMILY

THE SOVEREIGN

	Born
Her Majesty Queen Elizabeth II, (Elizabeth Alexandra Mary)	21 April 1926

    Succeeded her father, King George VI, 6 February 1952

    Married 20 Nov. 1947, HRH The Duke of Edinburgh, *now* HRH The Prince Philip, Duke of Edinburgh, KG, KT, OM, GBE, PC (*b* 10 June 1921; *s* of HRH Prince Andrew of Greece (*d* 1944) and of HRH Princess Andrew of Greece (*d* 1969), *g g-d* of Queen Victoria; *cr* 1947, Baron Greenwich, Earl of Merioneth and Duke of Edinburgh)

    Residences: Buckingham Palace, SW1; Windsor Castle, Berkshire; Sandringham House, Norfolk; Balmoral Castle, Aberdeenshire.

SONS AND DAUGHTER OF HER MAJESTY

HRH The Prince of Wales, (Prince Charles Philip Arthur George), KG, KT, GCB, PC; . .	14 Nov. 1948

cr 1958, Prince of Wales and Earl of Chester; Duke of Cornwall; Duke of Rothesay, Earl of Carrick and Baron of Renfrew; Lord of the Isles and Great Steward of Scotland

    Married 29 July 1981, Lady Diana Frances Spencer, *now* HRH The Princess of Wales (*b* 1 July 1961; *y d* of 8th Earl Spencer, *qv*), and has issue –

HRH PRINCE WILLIAM OF WALES, (PRINCE WILLIAM ARTHUR PHILIP LOUIS) .	21 June 1982
HRH PRINCE HENRY OF WALES, (PRINCE HENRY CHARLES ALBERT DAVID) . . .	15 Sept. 1984

    Office: Buckingham Palace, SW1; *residence:* Highgrove, Doughton, Tetbury, Gloucestershire GL8 8TG.

HRH The Duke of York, (Prince Andrew Albert Christian Edward), CVO;	19 Feb. 1960

cr 1986, Baron Killyleagh, Earl of Inverness and Duke of York

    Married 23 July 1986, Sarah Margaret, 2nd *d* of Major Ronald Ivor Ferguson, Life Guards (retired)

    Residence: Buckingham Palace, SW1.

HRH The Prince Edward (Antony Richard Louis)	10 March 1964
HRH The Princess Anne (Elizabeth Alice Louise), Mrs Mark Phillips, GCVO	15 Aug. 1950

    Married 14 Nov. 1973, Mark Anthony Peter Phillips, *qv*, and has issue

PETER MARK ANDREW PHILLIPS	15 Nov. 1977
ZARA ANNE ELIZABETH PHILLIPS	15 May 1981

    Office: Buckingham Palace, SW1; *residence:* Gatcombe Park, Minchinhampton, Stroud, Gloucestershire GL6 9AT.

SISTER OF HER MAJESTY

HRH The Princess Margaret (Rose), Countess of Snowdon, CI, GCVO	21 Aug. 1930

    Married 6 May 1960, Antony Charles Robert Armstrong-Jones, *now* 1st Earl of Snowdon, *qv* (marriage dissolved, 1978), and has issue –

DAVID ALBERT CHARLES ARMSTRONG-JONES, (VISCOUNT LINLEY, *qv*)	3 Nov. 1961
SARAH FRANCES ELIZABETH ARMSTRONG-JONES, (LADY SARAH ARMSTRONG-JONES) .	1 May 1964

    Residence: Kensington Palace, W8 4PU.

MOTHER OF HER MAJESTY

Her Majesty Queen Elizabeth The Queen Mother, (Elizabeth Angela Marguerite), . . .	4 Aug. 1900

    Lady of the Order of the Garter, Lady of the Order of the Thistle, CI, GCVO, GBE

    Married 26 April 1923 (as Lady Elizabeth Bowes-Lyon, *d* of 14th Earl of Strathmore and Kinghorne), HRH The Duke of York (Prince Albert), who succeeded as King George VI, 11 Dec. 1936 and *d* 6 Feb. 1952

    Residences: Clarence House, St James's, SW1; Royal Lodge, Windsor Great Park, Berkshire; Castle of Mey, Caithness-shire.

WIDOWS OF UNCLES OF HER MAJESTY

HRH Princess Alice (Christabel), Duchess of Gloucester, GCB, CI, GCVO, GBE, . . . 25 Dec. 1901
3rd *d* of 7th Duke of Buccleuch

   Married 6 Nov. 1935, HRH The Duke of Gloucester (Prince Henry William Frederick Albert, *b* 31 March 1900, *d* 10 June 1974), and has issue –

   HRH PRINCE WILLIAM OF GLOUCESTER, (PRINCE WILLIAM HENRY ANDREW FREDERICK), *b* 18 Dec. 1941; *d* 28 Aug. 1972

   HRH THE DUKE OF GLOUCESTER, (PRINCE RICHARD ALEXANDER WALTER GEORGE) (*see below*)

   Residences: Kensington Palace, W8 4PU; Barnwell Manor, Peterborough PE8 5PJ.

COUSINS OF HER MAJESTY

Child of HRH The Duke of Gloucester and of HRH Princess Alice Duchess of Gloucester (*see above*)

HRH The Duke of Gloucester, (Prince Richard Alexander Walter George), GCVO . . . 26 Aug. 1944

   Married 8 July 1972, Birgitte Eva van Deurs, *d* of Asger Preben Wissing Henriksen, and has issue –

   ALEXANDER PATRICK GREGERS RICHARD, (EARL OF ULSTER, *qv*) . . . . . 24 Oct. 1974
   DAVINA ELIZABETH ALICE BENEDIKTE, (LADY DAVINA WINDSOR) . . . 19 Nov. 1977
   ROSE VICTORIA BIRGITTE LOUISE, (LADY ROSE WINDSOR) . . . 1 March 1980

   Residences: Kensington Palace, W8 4PU; Barnwell Manor, Peterborough PE8 5PJ.

Children of HRH The Duke of Kent (Prince George Edward Alexander Edmund, *b* 20 Dec. 1902, *d* 25 Aug. 1942) and HRH Princess Marina, Duchess of Kent (*b* 13 Dec. 1906, *d* 27 Aug. 1968), *y d* of late Prince Nicholas of Greece

HRH The Duke of Kent, (Prince Edward George Nicholas Paul Patrick), KG, GCMG, GCVO . 9 Oct. 1935

   Married 8 June 1961, Katharine Lucy Mary Worsley, GCVO (*b* 22 Feb. 1933, *o d* of Sir William Worsley, 4th Bt) and has issue –

   GEORGE PHILIP NICHOLAS, (EARL OF ST ANDREWS, *qv*) . . . . . . 26 June 1962
   NICHOLAS CHARLES EDWARD JONATHAN, (LORD NICHOLAS WINDSOR) . . . 25 July 1970
   HELEN MARINA LUCY, (LADY HELEN WINDSOR) . . . . . . 28 April 1964

   Residences: York House, St James's Palace, SW1; Anmer Hall, King's Lynn, Norfolk PE31 6RW.

HRH Prince Michael of Kent, (Prince Michael George Charles Franklin) . . . . 4 July 1942

   Married 30 June 1978, Baroness Marie-Christine Agnes Hedwig Ida von Reibnitz, *d* of Baron Günther Hubertus von Reibnitz, and has issue –

   FREDERICK MICHAEL GEORGE DAVID LOUIS, (LORD FREDERICK WINDSOR) . . . 6 April 1979
   GABRIELLA MARINA ALEXANDRA OPHELIA, (LADY GABRIELLA WINDSOR) . . . 23 April 1981

   Residences: Kensington Palace, W8 4PU; Nether Lypiatt Manor, Stroud, Gloucestershire GL6 7LS.

HRH Princess Alexandra (Helen Elizabeth Olga Christabel), the Hon. Mrs Angus Ogilvy, GCVO 25 Dec. 1936

   Married 24 April 1963, Hon. Angus James Bruce Ogilvy, *qv*, and has issue –

   JAMES ROBERT BRUCE OGILVY . . . . 29 Feb. 1964
   MARINA VICTORIA ALEXANDRA OGILVY . . . . 31 July 1966

   Office: 22 Friary Court, St James's Palace, SW1; *residence:* Thatched House Lodge, Richmond, Surrey.

A

AARON, Richard Ithamar, MA, DPhil; FBA 1955; Professor of Philosophy, University College of Wales, Aberystwyth, 1932–69; *b* 6 Nov. 1901; *s* of William and Margaret Aaron, Ynystawe, Swansea; *m* Rhiannon, *d* of Dr M. J. Morgan, Aberystwyth; two *s* three *d. Educ:* Ystalyfera Grammar School; Cardiff University College; Oriel College, Oxford. Fellow, Univ. of Wales, 1923; Lectr at Swansea, 1926; Chm., Central Adv. Coun. for Educn (Wales), 1946–52; Mem., Coun. for Wales, 1956–63 (Chm., 1960–63); Chm. Library Advisory Council (Wales), 1965–72; Mem. Gen. Advisory Council, BBC, 1962–73, and TV Research Council, 1963–69; Mem. Council, National Library of Wales, 1953–73; Vice-Chm., Coleg Harlech Residential Coll.; Chm., Pembroke and Cardigan Agricultural Wages Cttee, 1962–73. Vis. Prof. in Philosophy, Yale Univ., US, 1952–53 (Fell. of Pierson Coll.). Pres., Mind Assoc., 1955–56; Pres., Aristotelian Society, London, 1957–58. Hon. DLitt Wales, 1973. *Publications:* The Nature of Knowing, 1930; Hanes Athroniaeth, 1932; An Early Draft of Locke's Essay (with Jocelyn Gibb), 1936; John Locke, 1937, 3rd rev. edn 1971; The Limitations of Locke's Rationalism, in Seventeenth Century Studies, 1938; Our Knowledge of Universals, Annual Philosophical Lecture to British Academy, 1945; The Theory of Universals, 1952, 2nd rev. edn 1967; The True and the Valid, Friends of Dr Williams's Library Lecture, 1954; Knowing and the Function of Reason, 1971; Editor, Efrydiau Athronyddol, 1938–68; contributor to Mind, Proc. Arist. Soc., Philosophy, Mod. Lang. Rev., Llenor, etc. *Address:* Garth Celyn, Aberystwyth, Dyfed. *T:* 3535.

AARONSON, Graham Raphael; QC 1982; Advisor on tax reform to Treasury, Israel, since 1986; *b* 31 Dec. 1944; *s* of late John Aaronson and of Dora Aaronson (*née* Franks); *m* 1967, Linda Esther Smith; two *s* one *d. Educ:* City of London Sch.; Trinity Hall, Cambridge (Thomas Waraker Law Schol.; MA). Called to the Bar, Middle Temple, 1966; practised Revenue law, 1968–73 and 1978–. Founder, Standford Grange residential rehabilitation centre for ex-offenders, 1974; Man. Dir, Worldwide Plastics Development, 1974–77. *Publication:* contrib. Chitty on Contracts, 23rd edn 1968. *Recreations:* photography, sitting in the sun and staring at the sea and sometimes swimming under it. *Address:* Queen Elizabeth Building, Temple, EC4Y 9BS. *T:* 01–353 0551.

AARVOLD, His Honour Sir Carl (Douglas), Kt 1968; OBE 1945; TD 1950; DL; Recorder of London, 1964–75; *b* 7 June 1907; *s* of late O. P. Aarvold and late J. M. Aarvold, West Hartlepool, County Durham; *m* 1934, Noeline Etrenne Hill, Denton Park, Yorks; three *s. Educ:* Durham Sch.; Emmanuel College, Cambridge (Hon. Fellow, 1976). Called to the Bar, Inner Temple, 1932; North Eastern Circuit. Master of the Bench, Inner Temple, 1959. Recorder of Pontefract, 1951–54; a Judge of the Mayor's and City of London Court, 1954–59; Common Serjeant, City of London, 1959–64; Chm., City of London QS, 1969–71. Chm., Inner London Probation Cttee, 1965–75; Pres., Central Council of Probation Cttees, 1968–75; Chm., Home Sec.'s Adv. Bd on Restricted Patients, 1978–81. Chairman: RAC, 1978–81; Statutory Cttee, Pharmaceutical Soc., 1981–86. DL Surrey, 1973. Hon. LLD Dalhousie, 1962; Hon. DCL Durham, 1965. Pres., Lawn Tennis Assoc., 1962–81. *Recreations:* golf, tennis, gardening. *Address:* The Coach House, Crabtree Lane, Westhumble, Dorking, Surrey. *T:* Dorking 882771.

ABBADO, Claudio; Principal Conductor, Vienna Philharmonic Orchestra, since 1971; *b* 26 June 1933; *m;* two *s* one *d. Educ:* Conservatorio G. Verdi, Milan; Musical Academy, Vienna. Guest Conductor of principal orchestras in Europe and America: conductor at principal festivals and opera houses, 1961–. Music Dir, La Scala, Milan, 1968–86; Musical Dir, European Community Youth Orch., 1977–; Music Dir, LSO, 1983– (Principal Conductor, 1979–83); Musical Dir, Vienna State Opera, 1986–. Principal Guest Conductor, Chicago Symphony Orch., 1982–85. Sergei Koussewitzky Prize, Tanglewood, 1958; Dimitri Mitropoulos Prize, 1963; Mozart-Medaille, Mozart-Gemeinde, Vienna, 1973; winner of major international prizes for recordings (Diapason, Deutscher Schalplatten-Preis, Grand Prix du Disque, Grammy, USA, etc), 1965–. *Address:* Piazzetta Bossi 1, 20121 Milan, Italy.

ABBOT, Dermot Charles Hyatt, CB 1959; Assistant Under-Secretary of State, Department of Health and Social Security, 1968–69 (Under-Secretary, Ministry of Pensions and National Insurance, 1955–66, Ministry of Social Security, 1966–68); retired 1969; *b* 8 Sept. 1908; *e s* of late Reginald Arthur Brame Abbot and late Sarah Ethel Abbot; *m* 1947, Elsie Myrtle Arnott (Dame Elsie Abbot) (*d* 1983). *Educ:* High School, Newcastle-under-Lyme; High School, Southend-on-Sea; University College, London. Post Office, 1929–40 and 1945–49; transferred to Ministry of Pensions and National Insurance, 1949. *Recreations:* gardening, fishing, travel. *Address:* 4 Constable Close, NW11. *T:* 01–455 9413. *Club:* Royal Automobile.

ABBOTT, Sir Albert (Francis), Kt 1981; CBE 1974; Mayor, City of Mackay, Queensland, since 1970; *b* Marvel Loch, WA, 10 Dec. 1913; *s* of late Albert Victor and Diana Abbott; *m* 1941, Gwendoline Joyce Maclean; two *s* four *d. Educ:* Mount Martin and Mackay State Schs, Qld. Served RAAF, 1941–45. Sugar cane farmer, 1950–; has given twenty years service to sugar industry organisations. Member: Picture, Theatre and Films Commn, 1975–; Qld Local Govt Grants Commn, 1977–. Returned Services League of Australia: Mem., 1946–; Pres., Mackay Sub-Br., 1960–65; Dist Pres., Mackay, 1965–74; Pres., Qld State, 1974–. President: N Qld Local Govt Assoc., 1975–84; Qld Local Govt Assoc., 1983–. Mem., Mackay Rotary Club. Governor, Utah Foundn, 1975 . *Recreations:* golf, tennis, racing. *Address:* 2 Tudor Court, Mackay, Qld 4740, Australia. *Clubs:* United Services (Brisbane); RSL Ex-Services, Bowls, Golf, Trotting, Turf, Amateur Race, Diggers Race, Legacy (all in Mackay).

ABBOTT, Anthony Cecil, MC 1945; RDI 1972; RIBA; Senior Designer, BBC Television, since 1962 (Designer, 1954–62); *b* 21 Aug. 1923; *s* of Col Albert Leigh Abbott, MC, and Alice Elizabeth Abbott. *Educ:* Dulwich Coll.; Architectural Assoc. (AADip Hons). Served Army, 1939–45 (Captain). AA, 1946–51; Architects' Dept, LCC; private practice, designing new Kuwait, 1952–54. *Work includes: opera:* Billy Budd, 1966; Rigoletto, La Bohème, Faust, 1968; Otello, 1969; *drama:* Horror of Darkness, 1964; Brothers Karamazov, Poet Game, 1965; The Idiot, Somerset Maugham, 1984, Out of the Unknown, Ross, 1966; Richard II, Beyond the Sunrise, 1968; Rembrandt, Vortex, 1969; St Joan, The Tempest, Somerset Maugham, 1970; Traitor, The General's Day, Sextet, 1971; Oh Fat White Woman, The Grievance, The Merchant of Venice, Lady Windermere's Fan, 1972; Caucasian Chalk Circle, Loyalties, Secrets, An Imaginative Woman (film), Twelfth Night, 1973; The Applecart, Forget-Me-Not-Lane, Savages, 1974; A Story to Frighten the Children (film), Look Back in Anger, 1975; 84 Charing Cross Road, A Picture of Dorian Gray, Abide with Me (film), Rogue Male (film), 1976; Heartbreak House, She Fell Amongst Thieves (film), 1977; Beaux Stratagem, Richard II, Julius Caesar, 1978; Crime and Punishment, 1979; Dr Jekyll and Mr Hyde, The Crucible, The Fatal Spring, 1980; Timon of Athens, Little Eyolf, Baal, 1981; Accounts, 1982; Shibear–Going Home; A Fellow by the Name of (film); Mr Pye (film), 1985; *theatre work includes:* Hotel in Amsterdam, Time Present, This Story is Yours, Look Back in Anger, 1968; Fidelio (opera), The Marquise, So What About Love, 1969; The Entertainer, 1974; The Exorcism, 1975; Julius Caesar (opera) 1984. Awards: Guild of TV Directors and Producers: Designer of the Year, for The Idiot, 1984, Billy Budd, 1966; Pye Colour Award: Best Colour Prodn, for Otello, 1969; Soc. of Film and TV Arts: Designer of the Year, for Vortex, Rembrandt, 1970. *Recreations:* gardening, travel. *Address:* 4 The Hamlet, Champion Hill, SE5 8AW. *T:* 01–733 4216.

ABBOTT, Hon. Douglas Charles, PC (Can.) 1945; QC 1939; BCL (McGill); Hon. LLD, Hon. DCL; Justice of the Supreme Court, Canada, 1954–73; *b* Lennoxville, PQ, 29 May 1899; *s* of Lewis Duff Abbott and Mary Jane Pearce; *m* 1st, 1925, Mary Winifred Chisholm (*d* 1980); two *s* one *d;* 2nd, 1981, Elizabeth Peters. *Educ:* Bishop's College; McGill University; Dijon University, France. Elected to House of Commons, 1940; re-elected, 1945, 1949 and 1953. Minister of National Defence for Naval Services, April 1945; Minister of National Defence (Army), Aug. 1945; Min. of Finance, Canada, 1946–54. Practised law in Montreal with firm of Robertson, Abbott, Brierley and O'Connor. Chancellor, Bishop's Univ., 1958–68. *Recreations:* fishing, curling, golf. *Address:* 45 Lakeway Drive, Ottawa K1L 5A9, Canada. *TA:* Ottawa Canada. *T:* 746–6271. *Clubs:* University, Royal Montreal Curling (Montreal); Rideau (Ottawa).

ABBOTT, James Alan, PhD; Manager and Director of Research, Koninklijk/Shell Laboratorium, Amsterdam, Shell Research BV, since 1981; *b* 2 Dec. 1928; *s* of George Oswald and Eva Abbott; *m* 1954, Rita Marjorie Galloway; one *s* one *d. Educ:* Ilkeston Grammar School; University of Nottingham (BSc, PhD). Post-doctoral research, Univ. of Durham, 1952–53; served Royal Air Force, 1953–56 (Flt Lt RAF Technical Coll., Henlow). Shell companies, UK and Holland, 1956–; Dir, Shell Research Ltd, Sittingbourne Research Centre, 1980–81. *Publications:* papers in Trans Faraday Soc., Proc. Royal Society. *Recreations:* farming, golf. *Address:* Shell Research BV, Koninklijk/Shell-Laboratorium, Postbus 3003, 1003 AA Amsterdam-Noord, Netherlands.

ABBOTT, Morris Percy; Chairman, Bryanston Insurance Co. Ltd, since 1985; Director, The Bell Group International Ltd (formerly Associated Communications Corporation Ltd), since 1983; Hogg Robinson & Gardner Mountain Ltd, since 1971; National Westminster Bank (City and West region), since 1980; *b* 3 May 1922; *s* of Harry Abbott and Agnes Maud Breeze; *m* 1944, Marjorie Leven; one *s* one *d. Educ:* Rothesay Academy. MIBS. Bank of Scotland, 1939–49. Served War as Pilot, 1941–46; Flight Lieut, RAF; seconded to US Navy at Pensacola Naval Air Station, Florida. Senior Executive with National Bank of India (now Grindlays Bank) in India and East Africa, 1949–59. Managing Director: Credit Insurance Assoc. Ltd, 1969; Hogg Robinson & Gardner Mountain Ltd, 1971; Hogg Robinson Group Ltd: Group Man. Dir, 1973; Chief Exec., 1974–83; Chm., 1977–83. *Recreations:* music, golf, tennis, sailing. *Address:* Castlemans, Sedlescombe, Battle, Sussex. *T:* Sedlescombe 501. *Clubs:* City of London, Caledonian; Royal and Ancient Golf, Prestwick Golf, Rye Golf, Royal Calcutta Golf.

ABBOTT, Roderick Evelyn; Director, Directorate-General of External Relations, EEC Commission, Brussels, since 1982; *b* 16 April 1938; *e s* of Stuart Evelyn Abbott, OBE; *m* 1963, Elizabeth Isobel McLean; three *d. Educ:* Rugby Sch.; Merton Coll., Oxford. Board of Trade, 1962–68 (Private Sec. to Pres. of BoT, 1965–66; seconded to DEA, 1966–68); UK Mission to UN, Geneva, 1968–71; Foreign Office, London, 1971–73; EEC, 1973–75; EEC Delegation, Geneva, 1975–79; EEC, 1980–. *Recreation:* travel. *Address:* c/o EEC Commission, Berlaymont (DG I), 1049 Brussels, Belgium. *Club:* Royal Commonwealth Society.

ABBOTT, Ronald William, CBE 1979; FIA, ASA, FPMI; Consultant Partner, Bacon & Woodrow, Consulting Actuaries, since 1982 (Senior Partner, 1972–81); Chairman, Occupational Pensions Board, since 1982 (Deputy Chairman, 1973–82); *b* 18 Jan. 1917; *s* of late Edgar Abbott and Susan Mary Ann Abbott; *m* 1st, 1948, Hilda Mary Hampson (*d* 1972), *d* of late William George Clarke and Emily Jane Clarke; two *d;* 2nd, 1973, Barbara Constance, *d* of late Gilbert Hugh Clough and Harriet Clough. *Educ:* St Olave's and St Saviour's Grammar Sch. FIA 1946; FPMI 1976. Actuarial Assistant: Atlas Assce Co., 1934–38; Friends Provident & Century Life Office, 1938–46; Sen. Actuary, Bacon & Woodrow, 1946, Partner 1948. Mem., Deptl Cttee on Property Bonds and Equity Linked Life Assce, 1971–73. Mem. Council: Inst. of Actuaries, 1966–74 (Hon. Treasurer, 1971–73); Indust. Soc., 1964–84; Pensions Management Inst., 1977–81 (Vice-Pres.,

1978–80). *Publications:* contrib. to Jl of Inst. of Actuaries. *Recreation:* music. *Address:* 21 The Byway, Sutton, Surrey. *T:* 01–642 3910. *Club:* Royal Automobile.

ABDELA, His Honour Jack Samuel Ronald, TD 1948; QC 1966; a Circuit Judge, Central Criminal Court (formerly Deputy Chairman, Inner London Quarter Sessions), 1970–86; *b* 9 Oct. 1913; *s* of Joseph and Dorothy Abdela, Manchester; *m* 1942, Enid Hope Russell, *y d* of Edgar Dodd Russell, London; one *s* (and one *s* decd). *Educ:* Manchester Gram. Sch.; Milton Sch., Bulawayo; Fitzwilliam House, Cambridge (MA). Called to the Bar, Gray's Inn, 1935. 2nd Lieut, Lancashire Fusiliers (TA), 1938; Lieut-Col. Comdt 55 Div. Battle School, 1943; 7th Bn Royal Welch Fusiliers, NW Europe, 1944–46; Major, Inns of Court Regt. (TA), 1946–52. Liveryman, The Worshipful Company of Painter-Stainers. *Recreations:* swimming, tennis, gardening. *Address:* 4 South Square, Gray's Inn, WC1R 5PH. *T:* 01–405 3627; Tall Trees, Shipton-under-Wychwood, Oxfordshire; Central Criminal Court, EC4. *Club:* Savage.

ABDUL JAMIL RAIS, Tan Sri Dato', PMN; Chairman, Penang Port Commission, since 1971; High Commissioner for Malaysia in the UK, 1967–71; *b* 14 Jan. 1912; *s* of Abdul Rais and Saodah; *m* 1936, Norhimah Abdul Jamil; four *s* six *d* (and one *s* decd). *Educ:* Clifford Sch.; Jesus Coll., Oxford. Joined Govt service, 1932; State Sec., Perlis, 1951–52; State Financial Officer, Selangor, 1954–55; State Sec., Selangor, 1955–56; Chief Minister, Selangor, 1957–59; Sec. to Treasury, 1961–64; Chief Sec. to Malaysian Govt and Sec. to Cabinet, 1964–67. *Recreations:* golf, tennis. *Address:* Jamnor, 32 Jalan Kia Beng, Kuala Lumpur, Malaysia.

ABDUL RAHMAN PUTRA, Tunku (Prince), CH 1961; Order of the National Crown, Malaysia; Kedah Order of Merit; Secretary General, Islamic Conference of Foreign Ministers, 1969–73; Prime Minister of Malaysia, 1963–70; Chairman, Star Publications, Penang; *b* 8 Feb. 1903; *m* 3rd, 1939, Puan Sharifah Rodziah binti Syed Alwi Barakbah; one *s* one *d* (both by 1st wife); one *s* three *d* (all adopted). *Educ:* Alor Star; Bangkok; St Catharine's Coll., Cambridge (Research Fellow, 1980); Inner Temple, London (Hon. Master, 1971). Joined Kedah State Civil Service, 1931, District Officer. During the occupation, when the Japanese returned Kedah to Siam, he served as Supt of Educn and Dir of Passive Defence until the reoccupation, Sept. 1945; opposed British Govt fusion of States and Colonies to form the Malayan Union and took a leading part in formation of United Malays National Organisation (UMNO); when the Malayan Union gave way to the Federation of Malaya in 1949, he became Chairman of UMNO in Kedah; after being called to Bar (Inner Temple), he returned to Kedah and was seconded to Federal Legal Dept as a Dep. Public Prosecutor, 1949; President of UMNO, 1951; resigned from CS and a year later was apptd an unofficial Mem. Federal Executive and Legislative Councils; leader of the Alliance Party (UMNO, Malayan Chinese Association, Malayan Indian Congress), 1954; Mem., Federal Legislative Council, 1955–73; became Chief Minister and Minister of Home Affairs; in reshuffle of 1956 also took portfolio of Minister for Internal Defence and Security; was also Chm. Emergency Ops Council which decides on policy in fighting Malayan Communist Party; headed Alliance deleg. to London to negotiate Independence for the Federation, Dec. 1955; after Independence on 31 Aug. 1957, became Prime Minister and Minister of External Affairs and continued to be Chm. Emergency Ops Council; resigned as Prime Minister in Feb. 1959 to prepare for general elections in Aug.; became Prime Minister for second time, Aug. 1959, and in Sept. initiated Min. of Rural Development; became also Minister of Ext. Affairs, Nov. 1960, and Minister of Information and Broadcasting, June 1961; Prime Minister, Federation of Malaya, until it became Malaysia, 1963; became Prime Minister for third time, April 1964, following Gen. Elections in States of Malaya, also Minister of External Affairs and Minister of Culture, Youth and Sports. Attended Prime Ministers' Conferences in London, May 1960 and March 1961; Head of mission to London to discuss and agree in principle proposed formation of Federation of Malaysia, Nov. 1961; Head of second mission to London on formation of Malaysia, July 1962; attended Prime Ministers' Confs, London, 1965, 1966. Apptd Chancellor, Univ. Malaya, 1962. Pres., Football Assoc. of Malaya; Pres., Asian Football Confedn; Vice-Pres. (for life), Royal Commonwealth Society. Dr of Law, Univ. of Malaya; Hon. LLD: Araneta Univ., 1958; Cambridge Univ., 1960; Univ. of Sydney, 1960; Univ. of Saigon, 1961; Aligarh Muslim Univ., 1962; Univ. Sains, Malaysia, 1975; Hon. DLitt, Seoul National Univ., 1965; Hon. DCL Oxford, 1970. Holds various foreign Orders. *Publications:* Mahsuri (imaginary play of Malaya; performed on stage in North Malaya throughout 1941; filmed in Malaya, 1958); Raja Bersiong (filmed 1966). *Relevant publication:* Prince and Premier (Biography) by Harry Miller, 1959. *Recreations:* golf, football, tennis, walking, swimming, racing, motor-boating, photography (both cine and still); collector of ancient weapons, particularly the Malay kris. *Address:* 1 Jalan Tunku, Kuala Lumpur, Malaysia; 16 Ayer Rajah Road, Penang, Malaysia.

ABDULAH, Frank Owen; Permanent Secretary, Ministry of External Affairs, Trinidad, since 1985; *b* 8 Nov. 1928; *m* (separated); four *d*. *Educ:* Queen's Royal Coll., Trinidad; Oxford (MA, DipEd Oxon). Held several govt posts, 1953–62, before entering Diplomatic Service at Trinidad and Tobago's Independence, 1962; Dep. Perm. Rep. (Minister Counsellor), 1970–73, Perm. Rep. (Ambassador), 1975–83, Trinidad and Tobago Perm. Mission to UN, NY; Perm. Sec. (Acting), Ministry of External Affairs, Port of Spain, 1973–75; High Comr for Trinidad and Tobago in London with concurrent accreditations as Ambassador to Denmark, Finland, France, FRG, Norway and Sweden, 1983–85. *Recreations:* music, sports. *Address:* Ministry of External Affairs, Queen's Park West, Port of Spain, Trinidad.

ABDULLAH bin Ali, Datuk; Director, Guthrie Ropel Berhad, since 1979; *b* Johore State, 31 Aug. 1922; *m* Datin Badariah binti Haji Abdul Aziz; two *s* two *d*. *Educ:* Raffles Coll., Singapore; ANU, Canberra. Entered Johore Civil Service, 1949, later Malayan Civil Service; with Independence of Malaysia joined Malaysian Foreign Service; served in India, Australia, Indonesia, Thailand, and as Head of Mission in Ethiopia, Morocco; Chief of Protocol and Dep. Sec.-Gen. (Admin and Gen Affairs), Min. of Foreign Affairs, Kuala Lumpur, 1969–71; High Comr to Singapore, 1971–74; Ambassador to Fed. Rep. of Germany, 1975; High Comr in London and Ambassador to Ireland, 1975–79. Has attended many foreign confs, incl. UNO in NY. Holds Orders: Panglima Setia DiRaja (Order of the Sovereign of Malaysia); Dato Paduka Mahkota Johore (Order of Crown of Johore, Malaysia); Kesatria Mangku Negara (Order of Upholder of Realm, Malaysia); Order of Sacred Heart (Japan). *Address:* 1 Jalan Setiajaya, Damansara Heights, Kuala Lumpur, Malaysia.

ABDY, Sir Valentine (Robert Duff), 6th Bt *cr* 1850; *b* 11 Sept. 1937; *s* of Sir Robert Henry Edward Abdy, 5th Bt, and Lady Diana Bridgeman (*d* 1967), *e d* of 5th Earl of Bradford; *S* father, 1976; *m* 1971, Mathilde Coche de la Ferté; one *s*. *Educ:* Eton. *Heir:* *s* Robert Etienne Eric Abdy, *b* 22 Feb. 1978. *Address:* Newton Ferrers, Callington, Cornwall; 3 Brock Road, St Peter Port, Guernsey, Channel Islands; 13 villa Molitor, Paris 16, France. *Clubs:* Travellers', Jockey (Paris).

ABEL-SMITH, Prof. Brian; Professor of Social Administration, University of London, at the London School of Economics, since 1965; *b* 6 Nov. 1926; *s* of late Brig.-Gen. Lionel Abel-Smith. *Educ:* Haileybury Coll.; Clare Coll., Cambridge. MA, PhD, 1955. Served Army: Private 1945; commissioned Oxford and Bucks Light Inf., 1946; Mil. Asst to Dep. Comr, Allied Commn for Austria (Capt.), 1947–48. Res. Fellow, Nat. Inst. of Economic and Social Res., collecting economic evidence for Guillebaud Cttee (cost of NHS), 1953–55. LSE: Asst Lectr in Social Science, 1955; Lectr, 1957; Reader in Social Administration, University of London, 1961. Assoc. Prof., Yale Law Sch., Yale Univ., 1961. Consultant and Expert Adv. to WHO on costs of med. care, 1957–; Consultant: to Social Affairs Div. of UN, 1959, 1961; to ILO, 1967 and 1981–83; Special Adviser: to Sec. of State for Social Services, 1968–70, 1974–78; to Sec. of State for the Environment, 1978–79; Adviser to Comr for Social Affairs, EEC, 1977–80. Member: SW Metrop. Reg. Hosp. Bd, 1956–63; Cent. Health Services Coun. Sub-Cttee on Prescribing Statistics, 1960–64; Sainsbury Cttee (Relationship of Pharmaceut. Industry with NHS), 1965–67; Long-term Study Group (to advise on long-term develt of NHS), 1965–68; Hunter Cttee (Functions of Medical Administrators,) 1970–72; Fisher Cttee (Abuse of Social Security Benefits), 1971–73. Chm., Chelsea and Kensington HMC, 1961–62; Governor: St Thomas' Hosp., 1957–68; Maudsley Hosp. and Inst. of Psychiatry, 1963–67. Hon. MD Limburg, 1981. *Publications:* (with R. M. Titmuss) The Cost of the National Health Service in England and Wales, 1956; A History of the Nursing Profession, 1960; (with R. M. Titmuss) Social Policy and Population Growth in Mauritius, 1961; Paying for Health Services (for WHO), 1963; The Hospitals, 1800–1948, 1964; (with R. M. Titmuss *et al.*) The Health Services of Tanganyika, 1964; (with K. Gales) British Doctors at Home and Abroad, 1964; (with P. Townsend) The Poor and the Poorest, 1965; (with R. Stevens) Lawyers and the Courts, 1967; An International Study of Health Expenditure (for WHO), 1967; (with R. Stevens) In Search of Justice, 1968; (with M. Zander and R. Brooke) Legal Problems and the Citizen, 1973; People Without Choice, 1974; Value for Money in Health Services, 1976; Poverty Development and Health Policy, 1978; National Health Service: the first thirty years, 1978; (with P. Grandjeat) Pharmaceutical Consumption, 1978; (with A. Maynard) The Organisation, Financing and Cost of Health Care in the European Community, 1979; Sharing Health Care Costs, 1980; (with E. Mach) Planning the Finances of the Health Sector, 1984; Cost Containment in Health Care, 1984; pamphlets for Fabian Soc., 1953–; articles. *Recreations:* skiing, swimming. *Address:* London School of Economics, Houghton Street, WC2. *T:* 01–405 7686.

ABEL SMITH, Henriette Alice, (Lady Abel Smith), DCVO 1977 (CVO 1964); JP; a Lady-in-Waiting to the Queen (formerly as HRH Princess Elizabeth), 1949–85; *b* 6 June 1914; *d* of late Comdr Francis Charles Cadogan, RN, and late Ruth Evelyn (*née* Howard, *widow* of Captain Gardner Sebastian Bazley); *m* 1st, 1939, Sir Anthony Frederick Mark Palmer, 4th Bt (killed in action, 1941); one *s* one *d*; 2nd, 1953, Sir Alexander Abel Smith, KCVO, TD (*d* 1980); one *s* one *d*. JP Tunbridge Wells 1955, Gloucestershire 1971. *Address:* The Garden House, Quenington, Cirencester, Glos. *T:* Coln St Aldwyns 231.

See also Sir T. S. Bazley, Bt, Sir C. M. Palmer, Bt.

ABEL SMITH, Col Sir Henry, KCMG 1961; KCVO 1950; DSO 1945; DL; late Royal Horse Guards; Governor of Queensland, 1958–66; Administrator, Australian Commonwealth, during part of 1965; *b* 8 March 1900; *er s* of late Francis Abel Smith and Madeline St Maur, *d* of late Rev. Henry Seymour; *m* 1931, Lady May Cambridge, *o* surv. *c* of Earl of Athlone, KG, PC, GCB, GCMG, GCVO, DSO, FRS (*d* 1957), and Princess Alice, Countess of Athlone, VA, GCVO, GBE (*d* 1981); one *s* two *d*. *Educ:* RMC, Sandhurst. Entered RHG, 1919; Capt. 1930; Major, 1934; Temp. Lieut-Col 1941; Lieut-Col 1944; Acting Colonel, Corps of Household Cavalry, 1946; retired, 1950. ADC to Earl of Athlone, Governor-General of S Africa, 1928–31. DL Berks 1953. KStJ 1958; Hon. LLD Univ. of Queensland, 1962. Hon. Air Cdre, RAAF, 1966. *Recreations:* hunting, shooting, fishing, polo. *Address:* Barton Lodge, Winkfield, Windsor, Berks SL4 4RL. *T:* Winkfield Row 882632. *Club:* Turf.

ABELES, Sir (Emil Herbert) Peter, Kt 1972; Managing Director and Chief Executive, TNT (formerly Thomas Nationwide Transport Ltd), Australia, and associated companies, since 1967; Joint Managing Director, since 1980 and Joint Chairman, since 1981, Ansett Transport Industries Ltd; *b* 25 April 1924; *s* of late Alexander Abel and of Mrs Anna Deakin; *m* 1969, Katalin Ottilia (*née* Fischer); two *d*. *Educ:* Budapest. Scrap metal industry, Hungary; emigrated to Australia, Sept. 1949; formed Alltrans Pty Ltd, 1950. Director: TNT Ltd Group; Ansett Transport Industries Ltd Group; Bliss Welded Products; Reserve Bank of Australia. Dir, Opera Foundn of Australia. *Recreations:* swimming, bridge. *Address:* TNT Ltd, Tower One, 10th Floor, TNT Plaza, Lawson Square, Redfern, NSW 2016, Australia. *Clubs:* Carlton; American National, Royal Automobile of Australia, Royal Motor Yacht, Tattersalls, Australian Jockey (Sydney).

ABELL, Sir Anthony (Foster), KCMG 1952 (CMG 1950); Gentleman Usher of the Blue Rod, in the Order of St Michael and St George, 1972–79; *b* 11 Dec. 1906; 2nd *s* of late G. F. Abell, JP, Foxcote Manor, Andoversford, Glos; unmarried. *Educ:* Repton; Magdalen Coll., Oxford. Joined Colonial Admin. Service, Nigeria, 1929. Resident, Oyo Province, Nigeria, 1949; Governor and C-in-C, Sarawak, 1950–59; High Commissioner, Brunei, 1950–58. Family Order of Brunei (First Class), 1954. *Address:* Gavel House, Wherwell, Andover, Hants. *Clubs:* MCC, Royal Over-Seas League, United Oxford & Cambridge University.

See also Sir George Abell.

ABELL, Charles, OBE 1948; CEng, Hon. FRAeS; Consultant, British Airways Overseas Division, 1974–77; *b* 1 Dec. 1910; *s* of late Major George Henry Abell and Muriel Abell (*née* Griesbach); *m* 1st, 1939, Beryl Anne Boyce (*d* 1973); one *s*; 2nd, 1976, M. A. Newbery. *Educ:* Sherborne Sch. Imperial Airways, 1934–39; BOAC 1939–74: Manager No 3 Line, 1946–51; Dep. Operations Dir (Engineering), 1951–55; Chief Engineer, 1955–68; Engineering Dir, 1968–74; Board Mem., 1972–74; Chm., British Airways Engine Overhaul Ltd, 1972–74. Hon FRAeS (Pres., 1976–77; Vice-Pres., 1972–74); Hon. FSLAET (Pres. 1973–74). British Silver Medal for Aeronautics, RAeS, 1957. *Recreation:* sailing. *Address:* Five Oaks, Woodlands Road West, Virginia Water, Surrey. *T:* Wentworth 2560. *Clubs:* Cruising Association; Royal Lymington Yacht.

ABELL, David; *see* Abell, J. D.

ABELL, Sir George (Edmond Brackenbury), KCIE 1947 (CIE 1946); OBE 1943; Hon. LLD (Aberdeen), 1947; First Civil Service Commissioner, 1964–67; *b* 22 June 1904; *s* of late G. F. Abell, JP, Foxcote Manor, Andoversford, Glos; *m* 1928, Susan Norman-Butler; two *s* one *d*. *Educ:* Marlborough; Corpus Christi Coll., Oxford (Hon. Fellow, 1971). Joined Indian Civil Service, 1928; Private Sec. to the Viceroy, 1945–47. Advisor, 1948–52, Director, 1952–64, Bank of England; Dir, Portals Hldgs, 1968–76. Rhodes Trustee, 1949–74 (Chm., 1969–74). Pres. Council, Reading Univ., 1969–74; Mem. Council, 1955–77, Chm., 1974–77, Marlborough Coll. *Address:* Whittonditch House, Ramsbury, Wilts. *T:* Marlborough 20449. *Club:* Oriental.

See also Sir Anthony Abell, J. N. Abell.

ABELL, (John) David; Chairman and Chief Executive, Suter plc (formerly Suter Electrical), since 1981; *b* 15 Dec. 1942; *s* of Leonard Abell and Irene (*née* Anderson); *m* 1967, Anne Janette Priestley (marr. diss. 1977); three *s*; *m* 1981, Sandra Dawn Abell (*née* Atkinson); one *s* one *d*. *Educ:* Univ. of Leeds (BAEcon); London School of Economics

(Dip. Business Admin). Assistant to Cash and Investment Manager, Ford Motor Co., 1962–65; Asst, Treasurer's Office, AEI, 1965–67; British Leyland: Central Staffs, 1968–69; Manager, Investments and Banking, 1969–70; Chm. and Chief Exec., Prestcold Div., 1970–72; Corporate Treasurer, 1972; First Nat. Finance Corp., Nov. 1972–Aug. 1973; re-joined British Leyland as Man. Dir, Leyland Australia, 1974–75; Group Man. Dir, Leyland Special Products, 1975; Man. Dir, BL Commercial Vehicles, Chm. and Chief Exec., Leyland Vehicles Ltd, 1978–81. *Recreations:* horse breeding (and racing), riding, tennis, music. *Address:* c/o Suter plc, The Priory, Market Place, Grantham, Lincs NG31 6LJ.

ABELL, John Norman; Vice-Chairman, Wood Gundy Inc., since 1986; *b* 18 Sept. 1931; *s* of Sir George Edmond Brackenbury Abell, *qv*; m 1957, Mora Delia (*née* Clifton-Brown); two *s* one *d*. *Educ:* Marlborough Coll.; Worcester Coll., Oxford (MA). Wood Gundy Ltd: joined in Vancouver, Canada, 1955; Internat. Man. Dir, Toronto, 1962; Director and Vice-Pres., 1966; Pres., Wood Gundy Inc., New York, 1966; Vice-Chm., Wood Gundy Ltd, Toronto, 1977; Dir, Echo Bay Mines Ltd, Edmonton, Canada, 1980; Dep. Chm. and Chief Exec., Orion Royal Bank Ltd, 1982, Chm. and Chief Exec. Officer, 1983–85; Director: Massey-Ferguson Ltd, Toronto, 1983; Minerals & Resources Corp. Ltd, 1985; Mem., Securities and Investments Bd, 1985–86. Chm., Arthritis Soc. of Canada, 1981–82. Dir, London House for Overseas Graduates, 1984; Mem. Council, Reading Univ., 1984. *Address:* 63 Warwick Square, SW1. *T:* (office) 01–628 4030. *Clubs:* Toronto, York (Toronto); India House (New York).

ABER, Prof. Geoffrey Michael, FRCP; Professor of Renal Medicine and Head of Department of Postgraduate Medicine, University of Keele, since 1982; *b* 19 Feb. 1928; *s* of David and Hilda Aber; *m* 1964, Eleanor Maureen; one *s* one *d*. *Educ:* Leeds Grammar School; University of Leeds (MB, ChB, MD with distinction); PhD Birmingham. Leeds Gen. Infirmary, 1952–54; RAMC, 1954–56; Queen Elizabeth Hosp., Birmingham (Univ. of Birmingham), 1956–57, 1958–65; Brompton Hosp., London, 1957–58; Research Fellow: Univ. of Birmingham (Depts of Expt Path. and Medicine), 1958–59 and 1960–64; McGill Univ., 1959–60; Wellcome Sen. Res. Fellow in Clinical Sci., 1964–65; Prof. and Adviser in Clinical Res., Univ. of Keele, 1979–82. *Publications:* contribs to: Recent Advances in Renal Medicine, 1983; Postgraduate Nephrology, 1985; Textbook of Genitourinary Surgery, 1985; scientific papers in learned jls. *Recreations:* music, sport, motor cars. *Address:* University of Keele, Department of Postgraduate Medicine, North Staffordshire Medical Institute, Hartshill Road, Hartshill, Stoke-on-Trent, Staffs. *T:* (Univ.) Stoke-on-Trent 49144; (home) Stoke-on-Trent 613692.

ABERCONWAY, 3rd Baron, *cr* 1911, of Bodnant; **Charles Melville McLaren,** Bt 1902; JP; President, John Brown & Co. Ltd (Director, 1939–85; Chairman, 1953–78); Director since 1935 and President since 1984, English China Clays Ltd (Chairman, 1953–84); Commissioner-General, International Garden Festival of Liverpool 1984; Director, National Garden Festival (Stoke on Trent) 1986 Ltd; President, Royal Horticultural Society, 1961–84, now President Emeritus; *b* 16 April 1913; *e s* of 2nd Baron Aberconway, CBE, LLD and Christabel (*d* 1974), *y d* of Sir Melville Macnaghten, CB; *S* father, 1953; *m* 1st, 1941, Deirdre Knewstub (marr. diss. 1949); one *s* two *d*; 2nd, 1949, Ann Lindsay Bullard, *o d* of Mrs A. L. Aymer, New York City; one *s*. *Educ:* Eton; New Coll., Oxford. Barrister, Middle Temple, 1937. Served War of 1939–45, 2nd Lieut RA. Deputy Chairman: Sun Alliance & London Insurance, 1976–85 (Dir, London Assurance, 1953); Westland Aircraft, 1979–84 (Dir, 1947–85); Dir, National Westminster Bank (formerly National Provincial Bank), 1953–83. JP Denbighshire 1946; High Sheriff of Denbighshire 1950. *Recreations:* gardening, travel, motoring. *Heir:* *s* Hon. Henry Charles McLaren [*b* 26 May 1948; *m* 1981, Sally, *yr d* of Captain C. N. Lentaigne; one *s* two *d*]. *Address:* 25 Egerton Terrace, SW3; Bodnant, Tal-y-cafn, Colwyn Bay, Clwyd.

ABERCORN, 5th Duke of, *cr* 1868; **James Hamilton;** Lord of Paisley, 1587; Lord of Abercorn, 1603; Earl of Abercorn and Lord of Hamilton, Mountcastle and Kilpatrick, 1606; Baron of Strabane, 1617; Viscount of Strabane, 1701; Viscount Hamilton, 1786; Marquess of Abercorn, 1790; Marquess of Hamilton, 1868; Bt 1660; company director; *b* 4 July 1934; *er s* of 4th Duke of Abercorn, and of Lady Mary Kathleen Crichton (Dowager Duchess of Abercorn, GCVO); *S* father, 1979; *m* 1966, Anastasia Alexandra, *e d* of late Lt-Col Harold Phillips, Checkendon Court, Reading; two *s* one *d*. *Educ:* Eton Coll.; Royal Agricultural Coll., Cirencester, Glos. Joined HM Army, Oct. 1952; Lieut, Grenadier Guards. MP (UU) Fermanagh and South Tyrone, 1964–70. Dir, NI Industrial Devlt Bd, 1982–. Member: Council of Europe, 1968–70; European Economic and Social Cttee, 1973–78. Pres. Royal UK Beneficent Assoc., 1979–. High Sheriff of Co. Tyrone, 1970. *Recreations:* shooting, water ski-ing. *Heir:* *s* Marquess of Hamilton, *qv*. *Address:* Barons Court, Omagh, Northern Ireland BT78 4EZ. *T:* Newtownstewart 61470; 10 Little Chester Street, SW1. *T:* 01-235 5518. *Clubs:* Royal Automobile, Brooks's.

ABERCROMBIE, Prof. David; Professor of Phonetics, Edinburgh University, 1964–80, now Emeritus Professor; *b* 19 Dec. 1909; *e s* of Lascelles Abercrombie, FBA, and Catherine Abercrombie; *m* 1944, Mary, *d* of Eugene and Mary Marble, Carmel, Calif; no *c*. *Educ:* Leeds Grammar Sch.; Leeds Univ.; University Coll., London; Sorbonne. Asst Lectr in English, LSE, 1934–38; Dir of Studies, Inst. of English Studies, Athens, 1938–40; Lectr in English: Cairo Univ., 1940–45; LSE, 1945–47; Lectr in Phonetics, Leeds Univ., 1947–48; Edinburgh Univ.: Lectr in Phonetics, 1948–51; Sen. Lectr 1951–57; Reader, 1957–63. Lectr in Linguistics and Phonetics, Glasgow Univ., 1980–81. *Publications:* Isaac Pitman: a Pioneer in the Scientific Study of Language, 1937; Problems and Principles in Language Study, 1956; English Phonetic Texts, 1964; Studies in Phonetics and Linguistics, 1965; Elements of General Phonetics, 1967. *Address:* 13 Grosvenor Crescent, Edinburgh EH12 5EL. *T:* 031-337 4864.

ABERCROMBIE, Robert James, CMG 1964; General Manager, Bank of New South Wales, 1962–64, retired; *b* 9 July 1898; *s* of P. M. Abercrombie, Whitburn, Scotland; *m* 1924, Dorothy, *d* of H. F. Oldham; two *d*. *Educ:* Sydney Grammar School; Scotch Coll., Melbourne. Chairman, Consultative Council of Export Payments Insurance Corporation, 1958–64; Chairman, Australian Bankers' Assoc., 1964. *Recreation:* golf. *Address:* 1 Hillside Avenue, Vaucluse, NSW 2030, Australia. *Clubs:* Union (Sydney); Australian, Athenæum (Melbourne).

ABERCROMBY, Sir Ian George, 10th Bt *cr* 1636, of Birkenbog; *b* 30 June 1925; *s* of Robert Ogilvie Abercromby (*g s* of 5th Bt); *S* kinsman, 1972; *m* 1st, 1950, Joyce Beryl, *d* of Leonard Griffiths; 2nd, Fanny Mary, *d* of late Dr Graham Udale-Smith; one *d*; 3rd, 1976, Diana Marjorie, *d* of H. G. Cockell, and *widow* of Captain Ian Charles Palliser Galloway. *Educ:* Lancing Coll.; Bloxham Sch. *Heir:* none. *Address:* c/o National Westminster Bank, Sloane Square, SW1; El Amador, Marbella, Spain. *Clubs:* Ski Club of Great Britain; Kandahar; Kildare Street (Dublin).

ABERDARE, 4th Baron, *cr* 1873, of Duffryn; **Morys George Lyndhurst Bruce,** KBE 1984; PC 1974; DL; Chairman of Committees, House of Lords, since 1976; Prior for Wales, Order of St John; *b* 16 June 1919; *s* of 3rd Baron Aberdare, GBE, and Margaret Bethune (*née* Black); *S* father 1957; *m* 1946, Maud Helen Sarah, *o d* of Sir John Dashwood, 10th Bt, CVO; four *s*. *Educ:* Winchester; New College, Oxford (MA). Welsh Guards, 1939–46. Minister of State, DHSS, 1970–74; Minister Without Portfolio, 1974. Chm., Albany Life Assurance Co. Ltd, 1975–. Chairman: The Football Trust, 1979–; Ye Olde Cheshire Cheese; President: Welsh Nat. Council of YMCAs; Kidney Res. Unit for Wales Foundn; Tennis and Rackets Assoc.; British Assoc. of Physical Trng. Hon. LLD Wales, 1985. DL Dyfed, 1985. Bailiff Grand Cross, OStJ, 1974. *Publications:* The Story of Tennis, 1959; Willis Faber Book of Tennis and Rackets, 1980. *Recreations:* real tennis and rackets. *Heir:* *s* Hon. Alastair John Lyndhurst Bruce [*b* 2 May 1947; *m* 1971, Elizabeth Mary Culbert, *d* of John Foulkes; one *s* one *d*]. *Address:* 32 Elthiron Road, SW6 4BW. *T:* 01–736 0825. *Clubs:* Lansdowne, MCC, Queen's.

ABERDEEN, Bishop of, (RC), since 1977; **Rt. Rev. Mario Joseph Conti;** *b* Elgin, Moray, 20 March 1934; *s* of Louis Joseph Conti and Josephine Quintilia Panicali. *Educ:* St Marie's Convent School and Springfield, Elgin; Blairs Coll., Aberdeen; Pontifical Gregorian Univ. (Scots College), Rome. PhL 1955, STL 1959. Ordained, Rome, 1958; Curate, St Mary's Cathedral, Aberdeen, 1959–62; Parish Priest, St Joachim's, Wick and St Anne's, Thurso (joint charge), 1962–77. Chairman: Scottish Catholic Heritage Commn, 1980–; Commn for the Pastoral Care of Migrant Workers and Tourists (incl. Apostleship of the Sea, Scotland), 1978–85; Pres.-Treasurer, Scottish Catholic Internat. Aid Fund, 1978–85; Pres., National Liturgy Commn, 1981–85; Scottish Mem., Episcopal Bd, Internat. Commn for English in the Liturgy, 1978–; Mem., Bishops' Jt Cttee for Bio-ethical Issues, 1982–; Pres., Nat. Christian Doctrine and Unity Commn, 1985–; Consultor-Mem., Secretariat for Promotion of Christian Unity (Rome), 1984–. Commendatore, Order of Merit of the Italian Republic, 1982. *Recreations:* music, art, book browsing, TV, travel, swimming. *Address:* 156 King's Gate, Aberdeen AB2 6BR. *T:* Aberdeen 319154.

ABERDEEN, (St Andrew's Cathedral), Provost of; *see* Howard, Very Rev. Donald.

ABERDEEN AND ORKNEY, Bishop of, since 1978; **Rt. Rev. Frederick Charles Darwent;** *b* Liverpool, 20 April 1927; *y s* of Samuel Darwent and Edith Emily Darwent (*née* Malcolm); *m* 1st, 1949, Edna Lilian (*d* 1981), *o c* of David Waugh and Lily Elizabeth Waugh (*née* McIndoe); twin *d*; 2nd, 1983, Roma Evelyn, *er d* of John Michie and Evelyn Michie (*née* Stephen). *Educ:* Warbreck Sch., Liverpool; Ormskirk Grammar Sch., Lancs; Wells Theological Coll., Somerset. Followed a Banking career, 1943–61 (War service in Far East with Royal Inniskilling Fusiliers, 1945–48). Deacon 1963; priest 1964, Diocese of Liverpool; Curate of Pemberton, Wigan, 1963–65 (in charge of St Francis, Kitt Green, 1964–65); Rector of: Strichen, 1965–71; New Pitsligo, 1965–78; Fraserburgh, 1971–78; Canon of St Andrew's Cathedral, Aberdeen, 1971; Dean of Aberdeen and Orkney, 1973–78. Hon. LTh, St Mark's Inst. of Theology, 1974. *Recreations:* amateur stage (acting and production), music (especially jazz), calligraphy. *Address:* Bishop's House, 107 Osborne Place, Aberdeen AB2 4DD. *T:* Aberdeen 646497. *Clubs:* Rotary International; Club of Deir (Aberdeens).

ABERDEEN AND TEMAIR, 6th Marquess of, *cr* 1916; **Alastair Ninian John Gordon;** Bt (NS) 1642; Earl of Aberdeen, Viscount Formartine, Lord Haddo, Methlic, Tarves and Kellie, 1682 (Scot.); Viscount Gordon 1814, Earl of Haddo 1916 (UK); painter; *b* 20 July 1920; *s* of 3rd Marquess of Aberdeen and Temair, DSO, and Cécile Elizabeth (*d* 1948), *d* of George Drummond, Swaylands, Penshurst, Kent; *S* brother, 1984; *m* 1950, Anne, *d* of late Lt-Col Gerald Barry, MC; one *s* two *d*. *Educ:* Harrow. Served War of 1939–45, Captain Scots Guards. Mem., Internat. Assoc. of Art Critics. *Recreations:* wine, women and song. *Heir:* *s* Earl of Haddo, *qv*. *Address:* Quick's Green, near Pangbourne, Berks.

ABERDEEN AND TEMAIR, June Marchioness of; (Beatrice Mary) June Gordon, MBE 1971; DL; Musical Director and Conductor, Haddo House Choral Society, since 1945; *d* of Arthur Paul Boissier, MA, and Dorothy Christina Leslie Smith; *m* 1939, David George Ian Alexander Gordon (later 4th Marquess of Aberdeen and Temair, CBE, TD) (*d* 1974); two adopted *s* two adopted *d*. *Educ:* Southlands School, Harrow; Royal Coll. of Music. GRSM, ARCM. Teacher of Music, Bromley High School for Girls, 1936–39. Director of Haddo House Choral and Operatic Soc. and Arts Centre, 1945–. Chairman: Scottish Children's League, 1969–; NE Scotland Music School, 1975–; Adv. Council, Scottish Opera, 1979–; Chm. (local), Adv. Cttee, Aberdeen Internat. Festival of Music and the Performing Arts, 1980–. Governor: Gordonstoun Sch., 1971–86; Royal Scottish Acad. of Music and Drama, 1979–82. FRCM 1967; FRSE 1983; FRSAMD 1985. DStJ 1977. DL Aberdeenshire, 1971. Hon. LLD Aberdeen, 1968. *Publications:* contribs to Aberdeen Univ. Jl, RCM magazine. *Address:* Haddo House, Aberdeen AB4 0ER. *T:* Tarves 216. *Club:* Naval & Military.

ABERDEEN, David du Rieu, FRIBA, MRTPI; Architect (Private Practice); *b* 13 Aug. 1913; *s* of David Aberdeen and Lilian du Rieu; *m* 1940, Phyllis Irene Westbrook (*née* Buller), *widow*; two step *c*. *Educ:* privately; Sch. of Architecture, London Univ. (BA Hons, Arch.). RIBA Donaldson Medallist, 1934; RIBA Alfred Bossom Research Fell., 1946–47. Works include: Brabazon Hangars, Filton, for Bristol Aeroplane Co.; TUC Headquarters, London, won in open architectural competition, 1948 (RIBA London Architecture Bronze Medal, 1958); 13–storey point block flats, New Southgate; housing for Basildon and Harlow New Towns. Architect for: new headquarters in City for Swiss Bank Corp.; redevelopment of Paddington Gen. Hosp.; New Gen. Market Hall, Shrewsbury; Swiss Centre, cultural and trade Headquarters, Leicester Square; First National City Bank of NY, London Office. Lectr, Atelier of Advanced Design, Sch. of Architecture, London Univ., 1947–53. *Publications:* contrib. to architectural press. *Address:* 20 Green Moor Link, N21.

ABERDOUR, Lord; John Stewart Sholto Douglas; *b* 17 Jan. 1952; *s* and *heir* of 22nd Earl of Morton, *qv*; *m* 1985, Amanda, *yr d* of David Mitchell, Kirkcudbright; one *s*. *Educ:* Dunrobin Castle School. Studied Agriculture, Aberdeen Univ. *Heir:* *s* Master of Aberdour, *qv*. *Address:* Haggs Farm, Kirknewton, Midlothian.

ABERDOUR, Master of; Hon. John David Sholto Douglas; *b* 28 May 1986; *s* and *heir* of Lord Aberdour, *qv*.

ABERGAVENNY, 5th Marquess of, *cr* 1876; **John Henry Guy Nevill,** KG 1974; OBE 1945; JP; Baron Abergavenny, 1450; Earl of Abergavenny and Viscount Nevill, 1784; Earl of Lewes, 1876; Lt-Col late Life Guards; Lord-Lieutenant of East Sussex, since 1974 (Vice-Lieutenant of Sussex, 1970–74); Chancellor, Order of the Garter, since 1977; *b* 8 Nov. 1914; *er s* of 4th Marquess and Isabel Nellie (*d* 1953), *d* of James Walker Larnach; *S* father, 1954; *m* 1938, Patricia (*see* Marchioness of Abergavenny); three *d* (and one *s* one *d* decd). *Educ:* Eton; Trinity Coll., Cambridge. Joined Life Guards, 1936; served War of 1939–45 (despatches, OBE); Lt-Col, retired 1946; Hon. Col, Kent & Co. of London Yeomanry, 1948–62. Director: Massey-Ferguson Holdings Ltd, 1955–85; Lloyds Bank Ltd, 1962–85; Lloyds Bank UK Management, 1962–85; Lloyds Bank SE Regional Bd (Chm.), 1962–85; Whitbread Investment Co. Trustee, Ascot Authority, 1953–; HM Representative at Ascot, 1972–82; President: Royal Assoc. of British Dairy Farmers, 1955 and 1963; Assoc. of Agriculture, 1961–63; Royal Agric. Soc. of England, 1967 (Dep. Pres. 1968, 1972); Hunters' Improvement Soc., 1959; British Horse Soc., 1970–71; Vice-Chm., Turf Bd, 1967–68; Mem. Nat. Hunt Cttee, 1942 (Senior Steward, 1953 and 1963); Mem.

Jockey Club, 1952. Member: E Sussex CC, 1947–54 (Alderman 1954–62); E Sussex Agric. Cttee, 1948–54. JP Sussex, 1948; DL Sussex, 1955. KStJ 1976 (Pres. Council, Order of St John, Sussex, 1975). *Heir: nephew* Guy Rupert Gerard Nevill [*b* 29 March 1945; *s* of Lord Rupert Nevill, CVO (*d* 1982); *m* 1982, Lady Beatrix Lambton, *d* of Viscount Lambton, *qv*]. *Address:* (seat) Eridge Park, Tunbridge Wells, East Sussex. *T:* Tunbridge Wells 27378; Flat 2, 46 Pont Street, SW1. *T:* 01–581 3967. *Club:* White's.

See also Earl of Cottenham.

ABERGAVENNY, Marchioness of; Mary Patricia Nevill, DCVO 1981 (CVO 1970); Lady of the Bedchamber to the Queen since 1966 (an Extra Lady of the Bedchamber, 1960–66); *b* 20 Oct. 1915; *d* of late Lt-Col John Fenwick Harrison, Royal Horse Guards, and Hon. Margery Olive Edith, *d* of 3rd Baron Burnham, DSO; *m* 1938, Marquess of Abergavenny, *qv*; three *d* (and one *s* one *d* decd). *Address:* Eridge Park, Tunbridge Wells, East Sussex; Flat 2, 46 Pont Street, SW1.

ABERNETHY, William Leslie, CBE 1972; FCA, IPFA; Managing Trustee, Municipal Mutual Insurance Ltd, since 1973, and Director of associated companies; Comptroller of Financial Services, Greater London Council, 1972–73 (Treasurer, 1964–72) and Chief Financial Officer, Inner London Education Authority, 1967–73; *b* 10 June 1910; *s* of Robert and Margaret Abernethy; *m* 1937, Irene Holden; one *s*. *Educ:* Darwen Grammar Sch., Lancs. Hindle & Jepson, Chartered Accts, Darwen, 1925–31; Borough Treasurer's Dept, Darwen, 1931–37; Derbyshire CC, Treasurer's Dept, 1937–48 (Dep. Co. Treas., 1944–48); 1st Treas., Newcastle upon Tyne Regional Hosp. Bd, 1948–50. LCC: Asst Comptroller, 1950–56; Dep. Comptroller, 1956–64; Comptroller, Sept. 1964–Mar. 1965. Hon. Life Mem., Roy. Inst. of Public Admin (Chm. Exec. Coun., 1959–60). Mem. Council, IMTA, 1966–73. *Publications:* Housing Finance and Accounts (with A. R. Holmes), 1953; Internal Audit in Local Authorities and Hospitals, 1957; Internal Audit in the Public Boards, 1957; contribs professional jls. *Address:* 6 Ballakeyll, Colby, Isle of Man. *T:* 832792.

ABINGDON, Earl of; *see* Lindsey and Abingdon, Earl of.

ABINGER, 8th Baron, *cr* 1835; **James Richard Scarlett,** DL; Lt-Col, late Royal Artillery; farmer and company director; *b* 28 Sept. 1914; *e s* of 7th Baron and Marjorie (*d* 1965), 2nd *d* of John McPhillamy, Blair Athol, Bathurst, NSW; *S* father, 1943; *m* 1957, Isla Carolyn, *o d* of late Vice-Adm. J. W. Rivett-Carnac, CB, CBE, DSC; two *s*. *Educ:* Eton; Magdalene College, Cambridge (MA 1952). India, France, Airborne Corps, and attached RAF; RNXS, 1968. DL Essex, 1968. KStJ. *Heir: s* Hon. James Harry Scarlett, *b* 28 May 1959. *Address:* Clees Hall, Bures, Suffolk. *T:* Bures 227227; 1a Portman Mansions, Chiltern Street, W1. *T:* 01–487 3585. *Clubs:* Carlton, Royal Automobile.

See also Hon. J. L. C. Scarlett.

ABNEY-HASTINGS, family name of **Countess of Loudoun.**

ABOU-SEÉDA, Hassan A. H.; Order of Merit, First Class (Egypt), 1979; Star of Honour (Egypt) and King Abdel Aziz Alsaud Order, First Class (for performance during 1973 October War), 1973; Order of Liberation (Egypt), 1957; fourteen military medals; Ambassador; Ministry of Defence, Arab Republic of Egypt; *b* 13 Oct. 1930; *s* of Aly Hassan Abou-Seéda and Fatimah Salamah; *m* 1973, Sohair A. A. el-Etriby; one *s*. *Educ:* Military College, Cairo (BA mil. sciences, MA mil. sciences). Fellow: Higher War Studies College; Nasser Academy. Military service with promotion all through command structure of Egyptian Armed Forces, 1949–79: Division Commander, 1971; Commander of an army, 1976; Chief of Military Operations and Dep. Chief of Staff of Armed Forces, 1978. Ambassador in Foreign Ministry, 1979; Ambassador to the UK, 1980–84. *Publications:* several research papers on the 1973 October War and on military strategy (Egypt). *Recreations:* reading (strategy, economics and history), chess, painting, tennis. *Address:* 14 Sarayah el-Azbakeyah, off Mohamed Farid, Down Town Cairo, Egypt. *T:* Cairo 911 644. *Clubs:* Royal Automobile; Gezirah, Armed Forces Officers', Tahrir (Cairo).

ABOYADE, Prof. Ojetunji, CON 1977; PhD; Professor of Economics, University of Ibadan, 1966–75 and 1978–81; *b* 9 Sept. 1931; *s* of Mr and Mrs Aboyade, Awe, Oyo, Nigeria; *m* 1961, Olabimpe (*née* Odubanjo); two *s* two *d*. *Educ:* The University, Hull (Groves Prize, Best Perf. Econs Dept, 1957; BSc Hons Econs 1st Cl.); Pembroke Coll., Cambridge (PhD 1960). Govt Scholar, 1953–60. Res. Asst, Nigerian National Income Accounts, Fed. Office of Statistics, Lagos, 1958–59; University of Ibadan, Nigeria: Lectr, Grade II and I, 1960–64; Sen. Lectr, 1964–66; Head, Dept of Econs, 1966–71; Dean of Social Sciences, 1972–74; Vice-Chancellor and Professor, Univ. of Ife, 1975–78. Head, National Econ. Planning, Fed. Govt of Nigeria (Econ. Develt), 1969–70. Vis. Asst Prof. and Res. Fellow, Dept of Econs, Univ. of Mich, Ann Arbor, 1963–64; Vis. Consultant (Econ.), World Bank, USA, 1971–72. Editor, Nigerian Jl of Economic and Social Studies, 1961–71. Pres., Nigerian Econ. Soc., 1973–74; Member: Bd of Trustees, Internat. Food Policy Research Inst., USA; Internat. Assoc. for Res. and Income, 1964–; Council, Assoc. of Commonwealth Univs; Chm., Tech. Cttee on Revenue Allocation, 1977. *Publications:* Foundations of an African Economy: a study of investment and growth in Nigeria, 1967 (USA); Issues in the Development of an African Economy, 1976 (Nigeria); chapters in and essay contribs to books, and articles in professional jls, 1961–75. *Recreations:* hobbies include farming. *Address:* c/o University of Ibadan, Ibadan, Nigeria.

ABOYNE, Earl of; Granville Charles Gomer Gordon; *b* 4 Feb. 1944; *s* and *heir* of 12th Marquess of Huntly, *qv; m* 1972, Jane Elizabeth Angela, *d* of late Col Alistair Gibb and Lady McCorquodale of Newton; two *s* two *d*. *Educ:* Gordonstoun. *Heir: s* Lord Strathavon and Glenlivet, *b* 26 July 1973. *Address:* Aboyne Castle, Aberdeenshire. *T:* Aboyne 2118.

See also Baron Cranworth.

ABRAHAM, Sir Edward (Penley), Kt 1980; CBE 1973; FRS 1958; MA, DPhil (Oxon); Fellow of Lincoln College, Oxford, 1948–80, Honorary Fellow, since 1980; Professor of Chemical Pathology, Oxford, 1964–80; *b* 10 June 1913; *s* of Albert Penley Abraham and Mary Abraham (*née* Hearn); *m* 1939, Asbjörg Harung, Bergen, Norway; one *s*. *Educ:* King Edward VI School, Southampton; The Queen's College, Oxford (1st cl. Hons Sch. of Natural Science), Hon. Fellow 1973. Rockefeller Foundation Travelling Fellow at Universities of Stockholm (1939) and California (1948). Ciba lecturer at Rutgers University, NJ, 1957; Guest lecturer, Univ. of Sydney, 1960; Reader in Chemical Pathology, Oxford, 1960–64; Rennebohm Lectr, Univ. of Wisconsin, 1966–67; Squibb Lectr, Rutgers Univ., 1972; Perlman Lectr, Univ. of Wisconsin, 1985. Hon. Fellow: Linacre Coll., Oxford, 1976; Lady Margaret Hall, Oxford, 1978; Wolfson Coll., Oxford, 1982; St Peter's Coll., Oxford, 1983. For. Hon. Mem., Amer. Acad. of Arts and Scis, 1983. Hon. DSc: Exeter, 1980; Oxon, 1984. Royal Medal, Royal Soc., 1973; Mullard Prize and Medal, Royal Soc., 1980; Scheele Medal, Swedish Academy of Pharmaceut. Sciences, 1975; Chemical Soc. Award in Medicinal Chemistry, 1975; Internat. Soc. Chemotherapy Award, 1983. *Publications:* Biochemistry of Some Peptide and Steroid Antibiotics, 1957; Biosynthesis and Enzymic Hydrolysis of Penicillins and Cephalosporins, 1974; contribs to: Antibiotics, 1949; The Chemistry of Penicillin, 1949; General Pathology, 1957, 4th edn 1970; Cephalosporins and Penicillins, Chemistry and Biology, 1972; scientific papers on the biochemistry of natural products, incl. penicillins and cephalosporins. *Recreations:* walking, ski-ing. *Address:* Badger's Wood, Bedwells Heath, Boars Hill, Oxford. *T:* Oxford 735395. *Club:* Athenæum.

ABRAHAM, Gerald Ernest Heal, CBE 1974; MA; FBA 1972; FTCL; President, Royal Musical Association, 1970–74; *b* 9 March 1904; *s* of Ernest and Dorothy Mary Abraham; *m* 1936, Isobel Patsie Robinson; one *d*. Asst Editor, Radio Times, 1935–39; Dep. Editor, The Listener, 1939–42; Director of Gramophone Dept, BBC, 1942–47; James and Constance Alsop Prof. of Music, Liverpool Univ., 1947–62; BBC Asst Controller of Music, 1962–67; Music Critic, The Daily Telegraph, 1967–68; Ernest Bloch Prof. of Music, Univ. of Calif (Berkeley), 1968–69. Chairman, Music Section of the Critics' Circle, 1944–46. Editor, Monthly Musical Record, 1945–60; Editor, Music of the Masters (series of books); General Editor: The History of Music in Sound (gramophone records and handbooks); New Oxford History of Music; Chm., Early English Church Music Cttee, 1970–80; Mem. Editorial Cttee, Musica Britannica. President, International Society for Music Education, 1958–61; Dep. Chm. Haydn Institute (Cologne), 1961–68; Mem. Directorium, Internat. Musicological Soc., 1967–77; Corr. Mem., Amer. Musicological Soc., 1980; Governor, Dolmetsch Foundn, 1970–73. Hon. RAM 1970. Hon. DMus: Dunelm, 1961; Liverpool, 1978; Southampton, 1979; Hon. Dr of Fine Arts, California (Berkeley), 1969. *Publications:* This Modern Stuff, 1933; Nietzsche, 1933; Studies in Russian Music, 1935; Tolstoy, 1935; Masters of Russian Music (with M. D. Calvocoressi), 1936; Dostoevsky, 1936; A Hundred Years of Music, 1938; On Russian Music, 1939; Chopin's Musical Style, 1939; Beethoven's Second-Period Quartets, 1942; Eight Soviet Composers, 1943; Tchaikovsky, 1944; Rimsky-Korsakov, 1945; Design in Music, 1949; Slavonic and Romantic Music, 1968; The Tradition of Western Music, 1974; The Concise Oxford History of Music, 1979; Essays on Russian and East European Music, 1984; (ed) New Oxford History of Music: (with Dom Anselm Hughes) Vol. III (Ars Nova and the Renaissance), 1960; Vol. IV (The Age of Humanism), 1968; Vol. VIII (The Age of Beethoven), 1982; Vol. VI (Concert Music: 1630–1750), 1985. *Recreations:* walking, languages, military history. *Address:* The Old School House, Ebernoe, near Petworth, West Sussex. *T:* North Chapel 325.

ABRAHAM, Maj.-Gen. (Sutton) Martin (O'Heguerty), CB 1973; MC 1942 and Bar, 1943; Secretary, Bedford College, University of London, 1976–82, retired; *b* 26 Jan. 1919; *s* of Capt. E. G. F. Abraham, CB, late Indian Civil Service, and Ruth Eostre Abraham; *m* 1950, Iona Margaret, *d* of Sir John Stirling, KT, MBE; two *s* one *d*. *Educ:* Durnford; Eton; Trinity Coll., Cambridge (BA Modern Languages). Commissioned in RA, 1939; transf. to 12th Royal Lancers, 1941; Egypt, 1941; Armoured Car Troop Leader, desert campaigns; Armoured Car Sqdn 2nd-in-Comd, Italian campaign, Sangro Valley, Rimini, Po Valley; accepted surrender of Trieste (Sqdn Ldr); Mil. Asst to C-in-C Austria, and accompanied him to BAOR, 1946; psc 1948; Mem. Chiefs of Staff Secretariat, 1949–52; Sqdn Ldr 12th Lancers, Malaya, 1953–54; Mem. Staff Coll. Directing Staff, 1955–57; 2nd-in-Comd 12th Lancers, 1957–58; CO 12th Lancers, 1958–62 (Cyprus, 1959–60); Asst Mil. Sec., Southern Comd, 1960–62; GSO1, Staff Coll. (Minley Div.), 1960–62; Comdr RAC (Brig.), 1st Brit. Corps, Germany, 1964–66; idc 1967; Dir, Combat Develt (Army), MoD, 1968–71; Chief of Jt Services Liaison Orgn, BAOR, 1971–73; Mil. Adviser to Arms Control and Disarmament Res. Unit and Western Organisations Dept, FCO, 1973–76, retd. Col, 9/12 Royal Lancers, 1977–81. Governor, Bedford Coll., 1982–85. *Recreations:* painting, reading, sundry practical country pursuits and chores, shooting. *Address:* c/o C. Hoare & Co., 37 Fleet Street, EC4. *T:* 01–353 4522. *Club:* Cavalry and Guards.

ABRAHAMS, Allan Rose, CMG 1962; *b* 29 Nov. 1908; *s* of late Mr and Mrs Frank Abrahams; *m* 1948, Norma Adeline Neita; one *s* two *d*. *Educ:* Jamaica College, Jamaica. Joined Civil Service, 1927; Permanent Secretary, Ministry of Communications and Works, Jamaica, 1955–64, retired. *Recreation:* gardening. *Address:* 20 Widcombe Road, Kingston 6, Jamaica. *T:* 78214. *Club:* Kingston (Kingston, Jamaica).

ABRAHAMS, Anthony Claud Walter; Governor since 1966, and Chairman since 1978 of the Harpur Trust (the Bedford Charity); *b* 16 June 1923; *s* of late Rt Hon. Sir Sidney Abrahams, QC, and of Ruth Bowman; *m* 1st, 1950, Laila Myking; two *s* one *d*; 2nd, 1982, Elizabeth, *d* of late Comdr A. E. Bryant, RN. *Educ:* Bedford Sch.; Emmanuel Coll., Cambridge (MA). Barrister-at-law. Served War: Wavell Cadet, Bangalore, 1942–43; commnd 3/12 Royal Bn, Frontier Force Regt, 1943–45; India, N Africa, Italy, Greece (despatches). Called to the Bar, Middle Temple, 1951; practised Midland Circuit, 1951–64; Centre for British Teachers: Founder, 1964; Dir, 1973–82; Life Pres., 1982; Chm., Colchester and Bedford English Study Centres, 1982–84 (Man. Dir, 1968–82). Liveryman, Worshipful Co. of Glaziers. *Recreations:* Rugby, cricket, golf, Rugby fives, English language learning. *Address:* Goldsmith Building, Temple, EC4Y 7BL. *T:* 01–353 7913. *Clubs:* Garrick, MCC, Jesters.

ABRAHAMS, Gerald Milton, CBE 1967; Chairman and Managing Director, Aquascutum Group, plc, since 1947; *b* 20 June 1917; *s* of late Isidor Abrahams; *m* 1st, 1946, Doris, *d* of Mark Cole, Brookline, Mass, USA; two *d*; 2nd, 1972, Marianne Wilson, *d* of David Kay, London. *Educ:* Westminster Sch. Served War of 1939–45, Major HAC, RHA, in Greece, W Desert and Ceylon. Member: Council, FBI, 1962–65, CBI, 1965–; British Menswear Guild (Chm., 1959–61, 1964–66); Clothing Export Council (Chm., 1966–70; Vice-Pres., 1970–); Clothing Manufacturers Fedn of GB, 1960–82 (Chm., 1965–66); EDC for Clothing Industry, 1966–69; British Clothing Industry Assoc., 1982–; BNEC Cttee for Exports to Canada, 1965–70; North American Adv. Gp, BOTB, 1978– (Vice Chm., 1983–). FRSA 1972; CBIM 1973. *Recreations:* golf, tennis. *Address:* 100 Regent Street, W1A 2AQ. *T:* 01–734 6090. *Club:* Buck's.

ABRAMS, Mark Alexander, PhD; Director of Research Unit, Age Concern, since 1976; *b* 27 April 1906; *s* of Abram Abrams and Anne (*née* Jackson); *m* 1st, 1931, Una Strugnell (marr. diss. 1951); one *s* one *d*; 2nd, 1951, Jean Bird; one *d*. *Educ:* Latymer Sch., Edmonton; London Sch. of Economics, Univ. of London. Fellow, Brookings Institute, Washington, DC, 1931–33; Research Department, London Press Exchange, 1933–39; BBC Overseas Dept, 1939–41; Psychological Warfare Board and SHAEF, 1941–46; Man. Dir, then Chm., Research Services Ltd, 1946–70; Dir, Survey Res. Unit, SSRC, 1970–76. Member: Metrication Bd, 1969–79; Council, PSI, 1978–; Exec. Council, Austrian Soc. for Social Sci. Res.; Business Educn Council, 1974–77. *Publications:* Condition of the British People, 1911–1946, 1947; Social Surveys and Social Action, 1951; Beyond Three Score and Ten, 1980; People in Their Sixties, 1983. *Recreation:* listening to music. *Address:* 12 Pelham Square, Brighton, East Sussex BN1 4ET. *T:* Brighton 684537. *Clubs:* Reform, Civil Service.

ABRAMS, Dr Michael Ellis, FRCP, FFCM; Deputy Chief Medical Officer, Department of Health and Social Security, since 1985; *b* 17 Sept. 1932; *s* of late Sam Philip and Ruhamah Emmie Abrams; *m* 1962, Rosalind J. Beckman; four *c*. *Educ:* King Edward's Sch., Birmingham; Univ. of Birmingham (BSc 1st Cl. Anat. and Physiol. 1953; MB ChB Distinction in Medicine 1956). FRCP 1972; MFCM (Founder Mem.) 1972, FFCM 1983.

Ho. Officer posts in United Birmingham Hosps, 1957–58; Univ. Research Fellow, Dept of Exp. Pathology, Univ. of Birmingham, and Medical Registrar, Queen Elizabeth Hosp., Birmingham, 1959; Medical Registrar and MRC Clinical Res. Fellow, Queen Elizabeth Hosp., Birmingham, 1959–62; MRC Clin. Res. Fellow, Dept of Medicine, Guy's Hosp., London, 1962–63; Rockefeller Travelling Fellow, Cardiovascular Res. Inst., Univ. of California Med. Centre, San Francisco, 1963–64; Lectr/Sen. Lectr and Hon. Cons. Phys., Guy's Hosp., 1964–75; Chief Med. Adviser, Guy's Hosp./Essex Gen. Practice Computing Unit, 1968–73; Dir, Inter-Deptl Laboratory, Guy's Hosp., 1971–75; DHSS: SMO, 1975–78; PMO, 1978 79; SPMO, 1979–85. Hon. Cons. Phys. Emeritus, Guy's Hosp. and Hon. Lectr in Medicine, Guy's Hosp. Med. Sch.; Examr in Human Communication, London Univ., 1972–84. President, Section of Measurement in Medicine, RSM, 1981–83; Chm., Computer Cttee, RCP, 1981–. *Publications:* (ed) Medical Computing Progress and Problems, 1970; (ed) Spectrum 71, 1971; (ed) The Computer in the Doctor's Office, 1980; articles on biomedical computing, pulmonary surfactant and glucose tolerance in diabetes. *Recreations:* reading, gardening, beachcombing. *Address:* 97 Wood Vale, N10 3DL. *T:* 01–883 2392.

ABRAMSON, Sidney, CMG 1979; retired from Department of Trade (Under Secretary, 1972–81); *b* 14 Sept. 1921; *s* of Jacob and Rebecca Abramson; *m* 1st, 1946, Lerine Freedman (marr. diss. 1958); two *s*; 2nd, 1960, Violet Ellen Eatly. *Educ:* Emanuel Sch., London; Queen's Coll., Oxford. Joined Civil Service, 1948; served Board of Trade, later Dept of Trade, 1950–81, including delegns to OEEC and EFTA, and GATT Secretariat. *Recreations:* music, gardening, writing. *Address:* 75a Holden Road, N12. *T:* 01–445 1264.

ABSE, Dr Dannie, FRSL; Specialist in charge of chest clinic, Central Medical Establishment, London, since 1954; writer; *b* 22 Sept. 1923; *s* of Rudolph Abse and Kate (*née* Shepherd); *m* 1951, Joan (née Mercer); one *s* two *d. Educ:* St Illtyd's Coll., Cardiff; University Coll., Cardiff; King's Coll., London; Westminster Hosp., London. MRCS, LRCP. First book of poems accepted for publication, 1946. Qualified at Westminster Hosp., 1950; RAF, 1951–54, Sqdn Ldr; Sen. Fellow of the Humanities, Princeton Univ., 1973–74. Pres., Poetry Soc., 1978–. FRSL 1983. *Publications: poetry:* After Every Green Thing, 1948; Walking Under Water, 1952; Tenants of the House, 1957; Poems, Golders Green, 1962; A Small Desperation, 1968; Funland and other Poems, 1973; Collected Poems, 1977; Way Out in the Centre, 1981; Ask the Bloody Horse, 1986; *prose:* Ash on a Young Man's Sleeve, 1954; Public Journals, 1986; *novels:* Some Corner of an English Field, 1957; O. Jones, O. Jones, 1970; *autobiography:* A Poet in the Family, 1974; A Strong Dose of Myself, 1983; *plays:* House of Cowards, (first prod.) Questors Theatre, Ealing, 1960; The Dogs of Pavlov, (first prod.) Questors, 1969; Pythagoras, (first prod.) Birmingham Rep. Th., 1976; Gone in January, (first prod.) Young Vic, 1978. *Recreations:* chess, bowls, watching Cardiff City FC. *Address:* 85 Hodford Road, NW11; Green Hollows, Craig-yr-Eos Road, Ogmore-by-Sea, Glamorgan, South Wales.
See also Leo Abse.

ABSE, Leo; MP (Lab) Torfaen, since 1983 (Pontypool, Nov. 1958–1983); *b* 22 April 1917; *s* of Rudolph and Kate Abse; *m* 1955, Marjorie Davies; one *s* one *d. Educ:* Howard Gardens High Sch.; LSE. Served RAF, 1940–45 (arrest for political activities in ME, 1944, precipitated parly debate). Solicitor; sen. partner in Cardiff law firm. Chm., Cardiff City Lab Party, 1952–53; Mem., Cardiff CC, 1955–58. Contested (Lab) Cardiff N, 1955. Chm., Welsh Parly Party, 1976–. Mem., Home Office Adv. Cttees on the Penal System, 1968, on adoption, 1972; first Chm., Select Cttee on Welsh Affairs, 1980; Mem., Select Cttee on Abortion, 1975–76; Sec., British-Taiwan Parly Gp, 1983. Sponsor or co-sponsor of Private Mem.'s Acts relating to divorce, homosexuality, family planning, legitimacy, widows' damages, industrial injuries, congenital disabilities and relief from forfeiture; sponsored Children's Bill, 1973, later taken over by govt to become Children's Act, 1975; initiated first Commons debates on genetic engineering, Windscale, *in vitro* pregnancies. Led Labour anti-devolution campaign in Wales, 1979. Mem. Council, Inst. for Study and Treatment of Delinquency, 1964–; Trustee, Winnicott Clinic of Psychotherapy, 1980–; Pres., National Council for the Divorced and Separated; Vice-Pres., British Assoc. for Counselling, 1985; Chm., Parly Friends of WNO. Governor, Nat. Museum of Wales, 1981–; Member of Court: Univ. of Wales; UWIST. Regents' Lectr, Univ. of Calif, 1984. Received best dressed man award of Clothing Fedn, 1962. *Publications:* Private Member: a psychoanalytically orientated study of contemporary politics, 1973; (contrib.) In Vitro Fertilisation: past, present and future, 1986. *Recreations:* Italian wines, psycho-biography. *Address:* 54 Strand-on-the-Green, W4 3PD. *T:* 01–994 1166; 91 Via Poggio di Mezzo, Nugola Vecchia, Livorno, Italy. *T:* Livorno 586 977022.
See also D. Abse.

ABUBAKAR, Prof. Iya; Wali of Mubi; Minister of Defence, Nigeria, 1979–82; *b* 14 Dec. 1934; *s* of Buba Abubakar, Wali of Mubi, and Fatima Abubakar; *m* 1963, Ummu; one *s* three *d. Educ:* Univ. of Ibadan (BSc London (External)); Cambridge Univ. (PhD). FRAS, FIMA. Ahmadu Bello Univ., Zaria, Nigeria: Prof. of Maths, 1967–75, 1978–; Dean, Faculty of Science, 1968–69, 1973–75; Vice-Chancellor, 1975–78. Visiting Professor: Univ. of Michigan, 1965–66; City Univ. of New York, 1971–72. Chm., Natural Sciences Reg. Council of Nigeria, 1972–75. Mem., Nigerian Univs Commn, 1968–73. Dir, Central Bank of Nigeria, 1972–75. Hon. DSc Univ. of Ife, 1977. *Publications:* Entebbe Modern Mathematics, 1970; several research papers on mathematics in internat. jls. *Recreations:* chess, golf, horse riding. *Address:* c/o PO Box 221, Yola, Nigeria.

ABU BAKAR, Datuk Jamaluddin, PNBS 1977; JMN 1967; AMN 1965; High Commissioner for Malaysia in United Kingdom and Ambassador to Ireland, since 1986; *b* Seremban, 19 May 1929; *m* Datin Rahmah Jamaluddin; one *s* two *d. Educ:* Univ. of Malaya (BA Hons History); LSE (Internat. Relns). Min. of For. Affairs, Malaya, 1957; Second Sec., Bangkok, 1958; Consul, Songkhla, 1961; First Sec., Cairo, 1963; Prin. Asst Sec., Min. of For. Affairs, 1966; Counsellor, Washington, 1969; Dep. Sec.-Gen. (Gen. Affairs), Min. of For. Affairs, Apr. 1971; Sec.-Gen. Min. of Culture, Youth and Sports, Nov. 1971; Sec.-Gen., Min. of Nat. Unity, 1973; Ambassador to Kuwait, 1974; High Comr to India, Feb. 1978; seconded to Bintulu Develt Authy, Sarawak, Oct. 1978; Ambassador to Tokyo, 1981. *Recreation:* sports, including golf and tennis. *Address:* 1 Templewood Gardens, NW3 7XB. *T:* 01–435 7074,

ACHEBE, Prof. Chinua, FRSL 1983, author; Professor of English, University of Nigeria, Nsukka, 1973–81; Professor Emeritus, since 1984; *b* 16 Nov. 1930; *s* of Isaiah and Janet Achebe; *m* 1961, Christiana Okoli; two *s* two *d. Educ:* Univ. of Ibadan. Nigerian Broadcasting Corp.: Talks Producer, 1954; Controller, 1959; Dir, 1961–66. Rockefeller Fellowship, 1960; Unesco Fellowship, 1963; Prof. of English, Univ. of Massachusetts, 1972–75; Prof. of English, Univ. of Connecticut, Storrs, 1975–76. Chairman: Soc. of Nigerian Authors, 1966; Assoc. of Nigerian Authors, 1982–. Member: Council, Univ. of Lagos, 1966; Exec. Cttee, Commonwealth Arts Orgn, London, 1981–; Internat. Social Prospects Acad., Geneva, 1983–. Neil Gunn Internat. Fellowship, Scottish Arts Council, 1975; Hon. Fellow: Modern Language Assoc. of America, 1975; Amer. Acad. and Inst. of Arts and Letters, 1982. Editor, Okike, 1971–. Patron, Writers and Scholars Educnl Trust, London, and Writers and Scholars Internat., 1972–; Governor, Newsconcern

Internat. Foundn, London, 1983–. Hon. DLitt: Dartmouth Coll., 1972; Southampton, 1975; Ife, 1978; Nigeria, 1981; Kent, 1982; Guelph and Mount Allison, 1984; Franklin Pierce Coll., 1985; DUniv Stirling, 1975; Hon. LLD Prince Edward Island, 1976; Hon. DHL Massachusetts, 1977. Jock Campbell New Statesman Award, 1965; Commonwealth Poetry Prize, 1972; Commonwealth Foundn Sen. Vis. Practitioner Award, 1983. Nigerian Nat. Merit Award, 1979; Order of the Fed. Repub. (Nigeria), 1979. *Publications:* Things Fall Apart, 1958; No Longer at Ease, 1960; Arrow of God, 1964; A Man of the People, 1966; Beware Soul-brother (poems), 1971; (jtly) The Insider, 1972; Girls at War, 1972; Morning Yet on Creation Day (essays), 1975; The Trouble with Nigeria (essays), 1983; *for children:* Chike and the River, 1966; (jt) How the Leopard Got its Claws, 1971; The Flute, 1978; The Drum, 1978. *Recreation:* music. *Address:* PO Box 53, Nsukka, Nigeria.

ACHESON, family name of **Earl of Gosford.**

ACHESON, Sir (Ernest) Donald, KBE 1986; Chief Medical Officer, Department of Health and Social Security, Department of Education and Science and Home Office, since 1984; *b* 17 Sept. 1926; *s* of Malcolm King Acheson, MC, MD, and Dorothy Josephine Rennoldson; *m* Barbara Mary Castle; one *s* five *d. Educ:* Merchiston Castle Sch., Edinburgh; Brasenose Coll., Oxford (Theodore Williams Schol. in pathology, 1946; MA, DM); Middlesex Hospital (Sen. Broderip Schol. in Med., Surg. and Pathol., 1950). FRCP; FFCM; FFOM. Sqdn Leader, RAF Med. Br., 1953–55. Medical Practitioner, 1951; various clinical posts at Middlesex Hosp.; Radcliffe Trav. Fellow of University Coll., Oxford, 1957–59; Medical Tutor, Nuffield Dept of Medicine, Radcliffe Infirmary, Oxford, 1960; Dir, Oxford Record Linkage Study and Unit of Clin. Epidemiology, 1962; May Reader in Medicine, 1965; Fellow, Brasenose Coll., Oxford, 1968; Prof. of Clinical Epidemiology, Univ. of Southampton, and Hon. Consultant Physician, Royal South Hants Hosp., 1968–83; Foundation Dean, Faculty of Med., Southampton Univ., 1968–78; Dir, MRC Unit in Environmental Epidemiology, 1979–83. Member: Wessex Regional Hosp. Bd, 1968–74; Hampshire AHA (Teaching) 1974–78, Chm., SW Hants and Southampton DHA, 1981–83; Member: Adv. Cttee on Asbestos, Health and Safety Exec., 1978; Royal Commn on Environmental Pollution, 1979–83; UGC, 1982–83; GMC, 1984–; MRC, 1984–; Chairman: Slow Virus Group, DHSS, 1979–80; Primary Health Care Inner London Gp, DHSS, 1980–81. R. Samuel McLaughlin Vis. Prof., McMaster Univ., 1977; King's Fund Travelling Fellow, NZ Postgrad. Med. Fedn, 1979; Lectures: inaugural Adolf Streicher Meml, Stoke-on-Trent, 1978; Walter Hubert, British Assoc. for Cancer Res., 1981; Christie Gordon, Univ. of Birmingham, 1982, etc. Examiner in Community Medicine: Univ. of Aberdeen, 1971–74; Univ. of Leicester, 1981–82; Examiner in Medicine, Univ. of Newcastle upon Tyne, 1975. Mem., Assoc. of Physicians of GB and Ire, 1965– (Pres. 1979). Hon. DM Southampton, 1984; Hon. DSc Newcastle, 1984. *Publications:* Medical Record Linkage, 1967; Multiple Sclerosis, a reappraisal, 1966; Medicine, an outline for the intending student, 1970; scientific papers on epidemiology of cancer and chronic disease, medical education and organisation of medical care. *Recreations:* family, gardening, music. *Address:* Alexander Fleming House, Elephant and Castle, SE1 6BY. *Club:* Athenæum.
See also R. M. Acheson.

ACHESON, Prof. Roy Malcolm, ScD, DM; FRCP, FFCM, FFOM; Professor of Community Medicine, University of Cambridge, since 1976; Fellow, Churchill College, Cambridge, since 1976; *b* 18 Aug. 1921; *s* of Malcolm King Acheson, MC, MD and Dorothy Rennoldson; *m* 1950, Fiona Marigo O'Brien; two *s* one *d. Educ:* Merchiston Castle Sch., Edinburgh; TCD (MA, ScD); Brasenose Coll., Oxford (MA, DM); Radcliffe Infirmary, Oxford. FRCP 1973; FFCM 1972; FFOM (by distinction) 1984. Clin. and res. posts, Radcliffe Infirmary and Univ. of Oxford; Rockefeller Trav. Fellow, Western Reserve and Harvard Univs, 1955–56; Radcliffe Trav. Fellow, University Coll., Oxford, 1955–57; Lectr in Social Med., Univ. of Dublin, 1955–59; FTCD, 1957–59; Sen. Lectr, then Reader in Social and Preventive Med., Guy's Hosp. Med. Sch. and London Sch. of Hygiene and Trop. Med., 1959–62; Yale University: Associate Prof. of Epidemiology, 1962; Prof. of Epidemiology, 1964–72; Fellow, Jonathan Edwards Coll., 1966–75; London Sch. of Hygiene and Tropical Medicine: Commonwealth Fund Sen. Trav. Fellow in Med., 1968–69; Dir, Centre for Extension Trng in Community Med., 1972–76. Hon. Cons. in Community Med., NE Thames RHA (formerly NE Metrop. RHB), 1972–76, E Anglian RHA, 1976–; Prof. of Health Service Studies, Univ. of London, 1974–76. Samuel R. McLaughlin Vis. Prof. in Med., McMaster Univ., Hamilton, Ont, 1976. Member: Exec. Cttee and Council, Internat. Epidemiol Soc., 1964–75; Expert Cttee, Methods in Chronic Disease Epidemiol., WHO, 1966; Mem., GMC, 1979– (Mem. Exec. Cttee, 1979–; Mem. Educn Cttee, 1979–); Mem., GDC, 1985– (Mem. Educn Cttee, 1985–); Cons., Argentina, Colombia, Guatemala, India, Venezuela, WHO, 1965–. Faculty of Community Medicine: Mem. Bd, 1974–84; Sec. to Examrs, 1974–77; and Mem., numerous other cttees. Hon. MA Yale, 1964. *Publications:* (ed) Comparability in International Epidemiology, 1965; Seminars in Community Medicine: (ed with L. Aird) I: Sociology, 1976; (ed with L. Aird and D. J. Hall) II: Health Information, Planning and Monitoring, 1971; (ed with S. Hagard) Health, Society and Medicine: an introduction to community medicine, 1985; (jtly) Costs and Benefits of the Heart Transplantation Programmes at Harefield and Papworth Hospitals, 1985. *Recreations:* golf (when time permits); country matters; meditating in the bath. *Address:* Department of Community Medicine, New Addenbrooke's Hospital, Hills Road, Cambridge CB2 2QQ. *T:* Cambridge 45171. *Club:* United Oxford & Cambridge University.
See also Sir E. D. Acheson.

ACHONRY, Bishop of, (RC), since 1977; **Most Rev. Thomas Flynn,** DD; *b* 8 July 1931; *s* of Robert and Margaret Flynn. *Educ:* St Nathy's, Ballaghaderreen; Maynooth College. BD, LPh, MA. Diocesan Religious Inspector of Schools, 1957–64; teaching in St Nathy's College, Ballaghaderreen, 1964–73; President and Headmaster of St Nathy's Coll., 1973–77. DD 1977. *Recreations:* gardening, fishing, golf. *Address:* St Nathy's, Ballaghaderreen, Co. Roscommon, Eire. *T:* Ballaghaderreen 21.

ACKERMANN, Georg K.; *see* Kahn-Ackermann.

ACKERS, James George; Chairman, Ackers Jarrett Leasing Ltd, since 1982, Chairman, West Midlands Regional Health Authority, since 1982; *b* 20 Oct. 1935; *s* of James Ackers and Vera Harriet Ackers (*née* Edwards). *Educ:* Oundle Sch., Northants; LSE. Bsc(Econ). Man. Dir, 1963–, Chm., 1974–, Ackers Jarrett Ltd; Vice Pres., Michael Doud Gill & Associates, Washington, DC, 1968–71. Pres., Walsall Chamber of Industry and Commerce, 1978; Chairman: West Midlands Chambers of Industry and Commerce, 1980–82; Assoc. of British Chambers of Commerce, 1984– (Dep. Chm., 1982–84); Chm., Economic and Industrial Cttee, 1981–84); Member: Cttee of Inquiry into Civil Service Pay, 1981–; Monopolies and Mergers Commn, 1981–. Chm., Fedn of Univ. Conservative Assocs, 1958; Vice-Chm., Bow Group, 1962–63. Pres., Jerome K. Jerome Soc., 1985–. *Address:* 5 Wrekin Court, Walsall Road, Sutton Coldfield, West Midlands B74 4QN; 21A Greycoat Gardens, Greycoat Street, SW1. *Club:* Carlton.

ACKLAND, Joss, (Sidney Edmond Jocelyn); actor; *b* 29 Feb. 1928; *s* of Major Norman Ackland, Journalist, Daily Telegraph and Morning Post, and Ruth Izod; *m* 1951 Rosemary

Jean Kirkcaldy, actress; one *s* five *d* (and one *s* decd). *Educ:* Cork Grammar Sch.; Dame Alice Owens Sch.; Central Sch. of Speech Training and Dramatic Art. *Plays:* The Hasty Heart, Aldwych, 1945; The Rising Sun, Arts, 1946; Dir, Winterset, 20th Century, 1946; Shakespeare Fest., Stratford-on-Avon, 1947; various try-out plays at Irving, Q, and Watergate Theatres, and toured, with Easy Money, in Germany, 1948; acted for Anthony Hawtrey, Embassy, Buxton and Croydon; then Arts Council tour, first Pitlochry Fest.; tours, and Repertory at Windsor, Chesterfield and Coventry. Went, with family, to Malawi, Central Africa, to work as a tea planter, 1954. S Africa: acting, directing, script writing and disc-jockeying, 1955–57; returned to England and joined Oxford Playhouse Co., 1957. Old Vic Co.: (incl. tours of America, Canada, USSR, Yugoslavia and Poland) Falstaff, Toby Belch, Caliban, Pistol, etc, 1958–61; Associate Dir, Mermaid Theatre: casting, choosing plays, Dir, Plough and the Stars, and playing numerous leading rôles, 1961–63. In 1963 his house burnt down so concentrated on television and did not return to theatre until 1965. Leading rôles on London stage: The Professor, in The Professor, 1966; Jorrocks, in Jorrocks, 1967; Hotel in Amsterdam, 1968–69; Come As You Are, 1969–70; Brassbound, in Captain Brassbound's Conversion, 1971; The Collaborators, 1973; Mitch, in A Streetcar Named Desire, 1974; Frederick, in A Little Night Music, 1975–76; The Madras House, 1977; Juan Perón, in Evita, 1978; Falstaff, in Henry IV Pts 1 and 2, RSC, opening of Barbican Theatre, 1982; Captain Hook and Mr Darling, in Peter Pan, Barbican, 1982; Romain Gary, in Jean Seberg, NT, 1983; Stewart, in Pack of Lies, 1984; Captain Hook in Peter Pan, 1985; tours: Petruchio, in The Taming of the Shrew, 1977; Sir, in The Dresser; Gaev in The Cherry Orchard, Chichester, 1981. *Films:* Seven Days to Noon, 1949; Crescendo, 1969; The House that Dripped Blood, Villain, 1970; The Happiness Cage, England Made Me, 1971; Penny Gold, The Little Prince, The Black Windmill, S-P-Y-S, The Three Musketeers, 1973; Great Expectations, One of our Dinosaurs is Missing, 1974; Operation Daybreak, Royal Flash, 1975; The Silver Bears, 1976; The End of Civilisation as we know it, The Greek Tycoon, Someone is killing the Great Chefs of Europe, 1977; Saint Jack, The Apple, Rough Cut, 1978; Lady Jane, 1984; A Zed and Two Noughts, 1985. Numerous appearances on TV, incl. Barrett in The Barretts of Wimpole Street, C. S. Lewis in Shadowland, and series: Kipling; The Crezz; Tinker, Tailor, Soldier, Spy; Shroud for a Nightingale; The Adventures of Sherlock Holmes. *Recreations:* his children, writing, painting. *Club:* Garrick.

ACKLAND, Rodney; Playwright; *b* 18 May 1908; *m* 1952, Mab (*d* 1972), *d* of Frederick Lonsdale. First play, Improper People, Arts, 1929; Marionella, Players, 1930; Dance With No Music, Arts and Embassy, 1931; Strange Orchestra, Embassy and St Martin's, 1932; Ballerina, adapted from Lady Eleanor Smith's novel, Gaiety, 1933; Birthday, Cambridge, 1934; The Old Ladies, adapted from Sir Hugh Walpole's novel, New and St Martin's, 1935; After October, Criterion and Aldwych, 1936; Plot Twenty-One, Embassy, 1936; The White Guard, adapted from the Russian play by Michael Bulgakov, Phœnix, 1938; Remembrance of Things Past, Globe, 1938; Sixth Floor, adapted from the French play by Alfred Gehri, St James's, 1939; The Dark River, Whitehall, 1943; Crime and Punishment, adapted from Dostoevsky, New, 1946; (with Robert G. Newton) Cupid and Mars, Arts, 1947; Diary of a Scoundrel, based on a comedy by Ostrovsky, Arts, 1949; Before the Party, adapted from Somerset Maugham's short story, St Martin's, 1949, revived, Queen's and Apollo, 1980; The Pink Room, Lyric, Hammersmith, 1952; A Dead Secret, Piccadilly, 1957; adapted Farewell, Farewell, Eugene, Garrick, 1959; Smithereens, Theatre Royal, Windsor. *Publications:* Improper People; Dance With No Music; Strange Orchestra; The Old Ladies; Birthday; After October; The Dark River; Crime and Punishment; Cupid and Mars; Diary of a Scoundrel; Before the Party; Farewell, Farewell, Eugene; The Celluloid Mistress (autobiography); The Other Palace. *Address:* c/o Eric Glass Ltd, 28 Berkeley Square, W1X 6HD.

ACKNER, family name of Baron Ackner

ACKNER, Baron *cr* 1986 (Life Peer), of Sutton in the county of West Sussex; **Desmond James Conrad Ackner;** Kt 1971; PC 1980; a Lord of Appeal in Ordinary, since 1986; *b* 18 Sept. 1920; *s* of Dr Conrad and Rhoda Ackner; *m* 1946, Joan, *d* of late John Evans, JP, and widow of K. B. Spence; one *s* two *d. Educ:* Highgate Sch.; Clare Coll., Cambridge (MA; Hon. Fellow, 1983). Served in RA, 1941–42; Admty Naval Law Br., 1942–45. Called to Bar, Middle Temple, 1945; QC 1961; Recorder of Swindon, 1962–71; Judge of Courts of Appeal of Jersey and Guernsey, 1967–71; a Judge of the High Court of Justice, Queen's Bench Div., 1971–80; Judge of the Commercial Court, 1973–80; Presiding Judge, Western Circuit, 1976–79; a Lord Justice of Appeal, 1980–86. Mem. Gen. Council of Bar, 1957–61, 1963–70 (Hon. Treas., 1964–66); Vice-Chm., 1966–68; Chm., 1968–70); Bencher Middle Temple, 1965, Dep. Treasurer, 1983, Treasurer, 1984; Mem. Senate of the Four Inns of Court, 1966–70 (Vice-Pres., 1968–70); Pres., Senate of the Inns of Court and the Bar, 1980–82. Chm., Law Adv. Cttee, British Council, 1980–. Hon. Mem., Canadian Bar Assoc., 1973–. *Recreations:* swimming, sailing, gardening, theatre. *Address:* 7 Rivermill, 151 Grosvenor Road, SW1. *T:* 01–821 8068; Browns House, Sutton, near Pulborough, West Sussex. *T:* Sutton (Sussex) 206. *Club:* Birdham Yacht.

ACKRILL, Prof. John Lloyd, FBA 1981; Professor of the History of Philosophy, Oxford University, since 1966; Fellow of Brasenose College, Oxford, since 1966; *b* 30 Dec. 1921; *s* of late Frederick William Ackrill and Jessie Anne Ackrill; *m* 1953, Margaret Walker Kerr; one *s* three *d. Educ:* Reading School; St John's Coll., Oxford (Scholar) (1940–41 and 1945–48). War service (Royal Berks Regt and GS, Capt.), 1941–45. Assistant Lecturer in Logic, Glasgow Univ., 1948–49; Univ. Lectr in Ancient Philosophy, Oxford, 1951–52; Tutorial Fellow, Brasenose Coll., 1953–66. Mem., Inst. for Adv. Study, Princeton, 1950–51, 1961–62; Fellow Coun. of Humanities, and Vis. Prof., Princeton Univ., 1955, 1964. *Publications:* Aristotle's *Categories* and *De Interpretatione* (trans. with notes), 1963; Aristotle's Ethics, 1973; Aristotle the Philosopher, 1981; articles in philos. and class. jls. *Address:* 22 Charlbury Road, Oxford. *T:* 56098.

ACKROYD, Dame (Dorothy) Elizabeth, DBE 1970; MA, BLitt (Oxon); Chairman, Patients Association, since 1978; *d* of late Major Charles Harris Ackroyd, MC. *Educ:* privately; St Hugh's Coll., Oxford. Civil servant, 1940–70 (Under-Sec., 1952); Commonwealth Fund Fellow, 1949–50; Dir of Steel and Power Div., Economic Commn for Europe, 1950–51; UK Delegn to High Authority of ECSC, 1952–55; Dir, Consumer Council, 1963–71. Chairman: Bloodstock and Racehorse Industries Confedn Ltd, 1977–78; Cinematograph Films Council, 1981–85 (Mem., 1970–85); SE Electricity Consultative Council, 1972–84; Indep. Mem., Council for the Securities Industry, 1978–83; Vice-Pres., Consumers' Assoc., 1970–; Member: PO Users' Nat. Council, 1970–84; Seeboard, 1972–84; Bedford Coll. Council, 1970–85; Royal Holloway and Bedford New Coll. Council, 1985–; Horserace Totalisator Bd, 1975–84; Waltham Forest Community Health Council, 1974–; Council, RSA, 1975–81; Exec. Cttee, Nat. Council for Voluntary Organisations, 1980–; Governor, Birkbeck Coll., 1973–; Vice-Chm., London Voluntary Service Council, 1977–; Pres., Patients Assoc., 1971–78; Hon. Treasurer, Pedestrians' Assoc. for Road Safety, 1971–. *Address:* 73 St James's Street, SW1A 1PH. *T:* 01–493 6686. *Club:* Jockey.

ACKROYD, Sir John (Robert Whyte), 2nd Bt *cr* 1956; Chairman and Managing Director, Ackroyd Underwriting Agencies Ltd, since 1978; Director, Martingale Productions Ltd, since 1984; *b* 2 March 1932; *s* of Sir Cuthbert Lowell Ackroyd, 1st Bt, and Joyce Wallace (*d* 1979), *d* of Robert Whyte; S father, 1973; *m* 1956, Jennifer Eileen MacLeod, *d* of H. G. S. Bishop; two *s* two *d. Educ:* Bradfield Coll.; Worcester Coll., Oxford (BA 1955, MA 1958). Commissioned RA, 1951; Sword of Honour, Mons Officer Cadet Sch., 1951; served in Jordan, 1951–52. Oxford Univ., 1952; Steward, OUDS, 1954. Lloyd's, 1955–68, re-elected 1981; joined Engineer Planning & Resources Ltd, 1968–75. Hon. Secretary, The Pilgrims of Gt Britain, 1966; Mem. Gen. Council, Victoria League for Commonwealth Friendship, 1973. Mem. Council, Royal Coll. of Music, 1981–; Patron, London and Internat. Sch. of Acting, 1983–. Church Warden: St Mary-le-Bow, Cheapside, 1973–; The Church of All Hallows, 1973–. FZS 1970. Freeman of the City of London; Liveryman Carpenters' Co. *Publication:* (ed) Jordan, 1978 (to commemorate Silver Jubilee of HM King Hussein of Jordan). *Recreations:* music, theatre. *Heir: er s* Timothy Robert Whyte Ackroyd, *b* 7 Oct. 1958. *Address:* 43 Lansdowne Crescent, Holland Park, W11 2NN. *T:* 01–727 5465. *Club:* (Life Mem.) Union Society (Oxford).

ACKROYD, Peter; writer; Chief Book Reviewer, The Times, since 1986; *b* 5 Oct. 1949; *s* of Graham Ackroyd and Audrey Whiteside. *Educ:* St Benedict's Sch., Ealing; Clare Coll., Cambridge (MA); Yale Univ. (Mellon Fellow). Literary Editor, 1973–77, Jt Managing Editor, 1978–82, The Spectator. FRSL 1984. *Publications: poetry:* London Lickpenny, 1973; Country Life, 1978; The Diversions of Purley, 1987; *novels:* The Great Fire of London, 1982; The Last Testament of Oscar Wilde, 1983 (Somerset Maugham Prize, 1984); Hawksmoor, 1985 (Whitbread Award; Guardian Fiction Prize); *non-fiction:* Notes for a New Culture, 1976; Dressing Up, 1979; Ezra Pound and his World, 1980; T. S. Eliot, 1984 (Whitbread Award; Heinemann Award). *Address:* c/o Anthony Sheil Associates Ltd, 43 Doughty Street, WC1N 2LF. *T:* 01–405 9351.

ACKROYD, Rev. Prof. Peter Runham, MA, PhD Cantab, BD, MTh, DD London; Samuel Davidson Professor of Old Testament Studies, University of London, 1961–82, now Emeritus Professor; *b* 15 Sept. 1917; *s* of Jabez Robert Ackroyd and Winifred (*née* Brown); *m* 1940, Evelyn Alice Nutt, BSc (Manch.), *d* of William Young Nutt; two *s* three *d. Educ:* Harrow County School for Boys; Downing and Trinity Colleges, Cambridge. Open Exhibition in Modern Languages, Downing Coll., Cambridge, 1935; Mod. and Med. Langs Tripos, Pt I, 1936, Pt II, 1938; BDHons London, 1940; Stanton Student, Trin. Coll., Cambridge, 1941–43; Dr Williams's Trust Exhibnr, 1941; MTh London, 1942; PhD Cambridge, 1945; DD London, 1970. Minister of: Roydon Congregational Church, Essex, 1943–47; Balham Congregational Church, London, 1947–48; Lectr in Old Testament and Biblical Hebrew, Leeds Univ., 1948–52; Cambridge University: Univ. Lectr in Divinity, 1952–61; Select Preacher, 1955; Mem. Council of Senate, 1957–61; Hulsean Lectr, 1960–62; Select Preacher, Oxford, 1962, 1981 (McBride Sermon); Dean of Faculty of Theology, King's Coll., London, 1968–69; FKC 1969; Mem. Senate, London Univ., 1971–79; Dean, Univ. Faculty of Theology, 1976–80. Vis. Professor: Lutheran Sch. of Theology, Chicago, 1967 and 1976; Univ. of Toronto, 1972; Univ. of Notre Dame, Indiana, 1982; Emory Univ., Atlanta, 1984. Lectures: Selwyn, NZ, 1970; Ethel M. Wood, Univ. of London, 1982; (first) Walter S. Williams, Denver, 1982; Tübingen, 1983; series of lectures, Japan, 1983. External Examiner, Belfast, Bristol, Durham, Cambridge, Edinburgh, Leeds, Nottingham, Exeter, West Indies. Ordained Deacon, 1957; Priest, 1958; Hon. Curate, Holy Trinity, Cambridge, 1957–61. Proctor in Convocation, Cambridge Univ., 1960–64. Pres., Soc. for Old Testament Study, 1972; Hon. Mem., Soc. of Biblical Literature, 1982–; Chairman: Council, British Sch. of Archaeology in Jerusalem, 1979–83; Palestine Exploration Fund, 1986– (Hon. Sec., 1962–70). Hon. DD St Andrews, 1970. *Publications:* Freedom in Action, 1951; The People of the Old Testament, 1959, new edn 1981; Continuity, 1962; The Old Testament Tradition, 1963; Exile and Restoration, 1968; Israel under Babylon and Persia, 1970; 1 & 2 Chronicles, Ezra, Nehemiah, Ruth, Jonah, Maccabees, 1970; 1 Samuel (Cambridge Bible Commentary), 1971; I & II Chronicles, Ezra, Nehemiah (Torch Bible Commentary), 1973; 2 Samuel, 1977; Doors of Perception, 1978, new edn 1983; articles and reviews in various learned jls, dictionaries, etc; *translations:* E. Würthein's The Text of the Old Testament, 1957; L. Köhler's Hebrew Man, 1957, repr. 1973; O. Eissfeldt's The Old Testament: An Introduction, 1965; *editor:* Bible Key Words, 1961–64; Society for Old Testament Study Book List, 1967–73; Palestine Exploration Quarterly, 1971–86; *joint editor:* SCM Press OT Library, 1960–; Cambridge Bible Commentary, 1961–79; SCM Studies in Biblical Theol., 1962–77; Words and Meanings: Essays presented to D. W. Thomas, 1968; Cambridge History of the Bible: vol. I, 1970; Oxford Bible Series, 1979–; Cambridge Commentaries: Jewish and Christian Writings of the period 200 BC to AD 200, 1979–. *Recreations:* reading, music. *Address:* Lavender Cottage, Middleton, Saxmundham, Suffolk IP17 3NQ. *T:* Westleton 458.

ACLAND, Sir Antony (Arthur), GCMG 1986 (KCMG 1982; CMG 1976); KCVO 1976; HM Diplomatic Service; Ambassador to Washington, since 1986; *b* 12 March 1930; *s* of Brig. P. B. E. Acland, *qv; m* 1956, Clare Anne Verdon (*d* 1984); two *s* one *d. Educ:* Eton; Christ Church, Oxford (MA 1956). Joined Diplomatic Service, 1953; ME Centre for Arab Studies, 1954; Dubai, 1955; Kuwait, 1956; FO, 1958–62; Asst Private Sec. to Sec. of State, 1959–62; UK Mission to UN, 1962–66; Head of Chancery, UK Mission, Geneva, 1966–68; FCO, 1968, Hd of Arabian Dept, 1970–72; Principal Private Sec. to Foreign and Commonwealth Sec., 1972–75; Ambassador to Luxembourg, 1975–77, to Spain, 1977–79; Deputy Under-Sec. of State, FCO, 1980–82, Perm. Under-Sec. of State, FCO, and Head of Diplomatic Service, 1982–86. *Address:* c/o Foreign and Commonwealth Office, SW1. *Club:* Brooks's.
    See also Maj.-Gen. Sir J. H. B. Acland.

ACLAND, Major Sir (Christopher) Guy (Dyke), 6th Bt *cr* 1890; Major, RHA; *b* 24 March 1946; *s* of Major Sir Antony Guy Acland, 5th Bt, and of Margaret Joan, *e d* of late Major Nelson Rooke; S father, 1983; *m* 1971, Christine Mary Carden, *y d* of Dr John Waring, Totland Bay, Isle of Wight; two *s. Educ:* Allhallows School; RMA Sandhurst. Commissioned RA, 1966; served BAOR (26 Field Regt), 1967–70; UK and Hong Kong, (3 RHA), 1970–73; BAOR and UK (22 AD Regt), 1974–77; Staff Coll., Camberley, 1978 (psc); served on Staff of HQ Eastern District, 1979–80; commanded Q (Sanna's Post) Bty in BAOR (5 Regt), 1981–83; SO2, Army Staff Duties Directorate, MoD, 1983–85. *Recreations:* sailing, cricket, gardening. *Heir: s* Alexander John Dyke Acland, *b* 29 May 1973. *Club:* Royal Artillery Yacht.

ACLAND, Maj.-Gen. Sir John (Hugh Bevil), KCB 1980; CBE 1978; DL; farmer; Director of Liaison Research, Allied Vintners (formerly Allied Breweries), since 1982; *b* 26 Nov. 1928; *s* of Brig. Peter Acland, *qv; m* 1953, Myrtle Christian Euing, *d* of Brig. and Mrs Alastair Crawford, Auchentroig, Stirlingshire; one *s* one *d. Educ:* Eton. Enlisted Scots Guards, 1946; commnd, 1948; served with 1st or 2nd Bn in Malaya, Cyprus, Egypt, Germany, Kenya, Zanzibar and NI, 1949–70; Equerry to the Duke of Gloucester, 1957; Staff Coll., 1959; Bde Major, 4th Guards Armoured Bde, 1964–66; CO 2nd Bn Scots Guards, 1968–71; Col GS ASD, MoD, 1971–74; BGS, MoD, 1975; Comd Land Forces and Dep. Comd British Forces Cyprus, 1976–78; GOC South West Dist, 1978–81; Comd Monitoring Force, Southern Rhodesia, and Military Advr to the Governor, 1979–80.

Hon. Colonel: Exeter Univ. OTC, 1980–; Royal Devon Yeomanry, 1983–. Pres., Royal British Legion, Devon, 1982–; Mem., Dartmoor National Park Authority, 1986. Governor, Allhallows Sch., 1982–. DL Devon, 1984. *Publications:* articles in British Army Review and other jls. *Recreations:* fishing, arboriculture, destroying vermin. *Address:* Feniton Court, Honiton, Devon.

See also Sir Antony Acland.

ACLAND, Brigadier Peter Bevil Edward, OBE 1945; MC 1941; TD; Vice-Lord-Lieutenant of Devon, 1962–78; *b* 9 July 1902; *s* of late Col A. D. Acland, CBE; *m* 1927, Bridget Susan Barnett (served ME, 1940–43; despatches), *d* of late Canon H. Barnett; two *s*. *Educ:* Eton; Christ Church, Oxford. Sudan Political Service, 1924–40. Served War of 1939–45: Abyssinia, Western Desert, Ægean (wounded, despatches). Comd Royal Devon Yeomanry, 1947–51, Hon. Col, 1953; Chairman, Devon AEC, 1948–58; Member, National Parks Commission, 1953–60; Chairman, Devon T&AFA, 1960. DL Devon, 1948; High Sheriff for Devon, 1961; JP 1962. 4th Class Order of the Nile; Greek War Cross. *Address:* Little Court, Feniton, Honiton, Devon.

See also Sir A. A. Acland, Maj.-Gen. Sir J. H. B. Acland.

ACLAND, Sir Richard Thomas Dyke, 15th Bt, *cr* 1644; *b* 26 Nov. 1906; *e s* of Rt Hon. Sir Francis Acland, 14th Bt, MP; *S* father, 1939; *m* 1936, Anne Stella Alford; three *s*. *Educ:* Rugby; Balliol Coll., Oxford. MP (L) Barnstaple Div. Devon, 1935–45; contested: Torquay Div., 1929; Barnstaple, 1931; Putney, 1945; MP (Lab) Gravesend Division of Kent, 1947–55. Sen. Lectr, St Luke's College of Educn, Exeter, 1959–74. Second Church Estates Commissioner, 1950–51. *Publications:* Unser Kampf, 1940; The Forward March, 1941; What It Will Be Like, 1942; How It Can Be Done, 1943; Public Speaking, 1946; Nothing Left to Believe?, 1949; Why So Angry?, 1958; Waging Peace, 1958; We Teach Them Wrong: religion and the young, 1963; (with others) Sexual Morality: three views, 1965; Curriculum or Life, 1966; Moves to the Integrated Curriculum, 1967; The Next Step, 1974. *Heir: s* John Dyke Acland [*b* 13 May 1939; *m* 1961, Virginia, *d* of Roland Forge; two *s* one *d*]. *Address:* College, Broadclyst, Exeter. *T:* Exeter 61452.

A'COURT; *see* Holmes a'Court.

ACTON, 3rd Baron, *cr* 1869, of Aldenham, Salop; **John Emerich Henry Lyon-Dalberg-Acton;** Bt 1643; CMG 1963; MBE 1945; TD 1949; Hereditary Duke of Dalberg; Patrician of Naples; Major RA, TA; Director, Canadian Overseas Packaging Industries, since 1983; Trustee, Cold Comfort Farm Society, since 1967; *b* 15 Dec. 1907; *e s* of 2nd Baron Acton, KCVO, and Dorothy (*d* 1923), *d* of late T. H. Lyon, Appleton Hall, Cheshire; *S* father, 1924; *m* 1931, Daphne Strutt, *o d* of 4th Baron Rayleigh, FRS, and late Mary Hilda, 2nd *d* of 4th Earl of Leitrim; five *s* five *d*. *Educ:* Downside; RMC Sandhurst; Trinity Coll., Cambridge. Served War of 1939–45, Italy; Major, Shropshire Yeo. (MBE). Partner, Barham & Brooks, Mem. Birmingham Stock Exchange, 1936–47; emigrated S Rhodesia, 1947; Dir, Amal. Packaging Industries Ltd, 1950–67; Chm. and Man. Dir, API (Rhodesia) Ltd, Central Africa Paper Sacks Ltd, 1951–67; Director: Canadian Overseas Packaging Industries Ltd, 1962–65; Monterrey Packaging (Zambia) Ltd, 1964–67; Rhodesian Bd Standard Bank Ltd, 1958–67; Discount Co. of Rhodesia Ltd, 1960–67; East African Packaging, Jamaica Packaging Ltd, Caribbean Packaging Ltd, to 1965; Old Mutual Fire and General Insurance (Rhodesia) Ltd, to 1967; Chairman: Colcom Ltd, 1959–67; Rhodesian Insurances Ltd, Wright Dean (Rhodesia) Ltd, to 1967. Pres., Rhodesian Royal Agricl Show Soc., 1960–64; qualified Judge of Jersey cattle and pigs; Chairman: Gwebi Agricl Coll., 1958–62; Chibero Agricl Coll., 1960–65 (resigned on illegal declaration of independence); Mem. African Farm Develt Cttee, 1964–67; Chm., BRCS Rhodesia Council Br., 1962–68 (Life Mem. BRCS, 1966); Founding Chm., National (non-racial) Club, Salisbury, 1962; served SR Legal Aid and Welfare Cttee (detainees), 1965–67. Patron, Rhodesian Coll. of Music, to 1967. Chm., Mashonaland Owners and Trainers Assoc., 1956–57; Steward, Mashonaland Turf Club, 1957–67. Emigrated to Swaziland, 1967. Chairman: NEOPAC (Swaziland) Ltd, 1968–70; Swaziland Bd, Standard Bank Ltd, 1968–70; Dir, Swaziland Building Soc., 1968–70. Dir, Swaziland Br., BRCS, 1967–70; Founding Chm., Tattersalls Swaziland, 1969. Retired to Majorca, 1971. *Recreations:* music, bridge, roulette. *Heir: s* Hon. Richard Gerald Lyon-Dalberg-Acton [*b* 30 July 1941; *m* 1st, 1965, Hilary Juliet Sarah Cookson (*d* 1973); one *s*; 2nd, 1974, Judith (writer), *d* of Hon. Sir Garfield Todd, *qv*. *Educ:* St George's Coll., Salisbury, Rhodesia; Trinity Coll., Oxford (BA Hist. 1963). Called to Bar, Inner Temple, 1976. Dir, Coutts & Co., 1970–74]. *Address:* Ca-Na Rosalinda, Pollensa, Mallorca. *T:* 531071. *Clubs:* Royal Commonwealth Society; British American (Palma).

ACTON, Sir Harold (Mario Mitchell), Kt 1974; CBE 1965; author; *b* 5 July 1904; *s* of Arthur Mario Acton and Hortense Mitchell, La Pietra, Florence. *Educ:* Eton Coll.; Christ Church, Oxford (BA). FRSL. Lectr in English Literature, National University of Peking and Peking Normal College, 1933–35. Lived for seven years in Peking, devoting much time to Chinese Classical Theatre. Served in RAF during War of 1939–45, chiefly in Far East. Hon. DLitt New York Univ., 1973. Grand Officer, Republic of Italy; Kt of the Constantinian Order. *Publications:* Aquarium, 1923; An Indian Ass, 1925; Five Saints and an Appendix, 1927; Humdrum, 1928; Cornelian, 1928; This Chaos, 1930; The Last Medici, 1932, new edn 1958; (in collab.) Modern Chinese Poetry, 1936; (in collab.) Famous Chinese Plays, 1937; Peonies and Ponies, 1941; Glue and Lacquer, 1941 (Four Cautionary Tales, 1947, reprint of former); Memoirs of an Aesthete, 1948; Prince Isidore, 1950; The Bourbons of Naples, 1956; The Last Bourbons of Naples, 1961; Florence (an essay), 1961; Old Lamps for New, 1965; More Memoirs of an Aesthete, 1970; Tit for Tat, 1972; Tuscan Villas, 1973, repr. as The Villas of Tuscany, 1984; Nancy Mitford: a memoir, 1975; (in collab.) The Peach Blossom Fan, 1976; The Pazzi Conspiracy, 1979; The Soul's Gymnasium (short stories), 1982; Three Extraordinary Ambassadors, 1984. *Recreations:* jettatura, hunting the Philistines. *Address:* La Pietra, Florence, Italy. *T:* 474448. *Club:* Savile.

ACTON, William Antony; *b* 8 April 1904; *o s* of late William Walter Acton, Wolverton Hall, Pershore, Worcs; *m* 1932, Joan, *o c* of late Hon. Francis Geoffrey Pearson; one *d*. *Educ:* Eton; Trinity College, Cambridge. HM Treasury, 1939–45. Managing Director, Lazard Bros & Co. Ltd, 1945–53; Director: The National Bank Ltd, 1945–70 (Chm. 1964–70); Bank of London and South America Ltd, 1953–70; Standard Bank Ltd, 1953–70; Ottoman Bank, 1953–58; Bank of London and Montreal Ltd., 1959–64; Bank of West Africa Ltd, 1954–70; Bank of Ireland, 1966–70; National Commercial Bank of Scotland, 1967–70; National and Commercial Banking Group Ltd, 1969–70; The Whitehall Trust, 1945–70. High Sheriff, County of London, 1955. *Recreation:* travelling. *Address:* Poste Restante, Corfu, Greece. *T:* Corfu 91–236. *Club:* White's.

ADAIR, Maj.-Gen. Sir Allan (Henry Shafto), 6th Bt, *cr* 1838; GCVO 1974 (KCVO 1967; CVO 1957); CB 1945; DSO 1940; MC; DL; JP; Lieutenant of HM Bodyguard of the Yeomen of the Guard, 1951–67; *b* 3 Nov. 1897; *o s* of Sir R. Shafto Adair, 5th Bt and Mary (*d* 1950), *d* of Henry Anstey Bosanquet; *S* father, 1949; *m* Enid (*d* 1984), *d* of late Hon. Mrs Dudley Ward; three *d* (one *s* killed in action, 1943). *Educ:* Harrow. Grenadier Guards, 1916–41; commanded 3rd Battalion, 1940; Comdr 30 Guards Brigade, 1941; Comdr 6 Guards Brigade, 1942; Comdr Guards Armoured Division 1942–45; retired pay, 1947. Colonel of the Grenadier Guards, 1961–74. DL for Co. Antrim; JP for Suffolk. Governor of Harrow School, 1947–52. Dep. Grand Master, United Grand Lodge of Freemasons, 1969–76. *Address:* 55 Green Street, W1. *T:* 01–629 3860; Denton Lodge, Harleston, Norfolk. *Clubs:* Turf, Cavalry and Guards.

See also Brig. Sir J. L. Darell, Bt.

ADAM, Sir Christopher Eric Forbes, 3rd Bt *cr* 1917; *b* 12 Feb. 1920; *s* of Eric Graham Forbes Adam, CMG (*d* 1925) (2nd *s* of 1st Bt) and of Agatha Perrin, *d* of Reginald Walter Macan; *S* uncle, 1982; *m* 1957, Patricia Ann Wreford, *y d* of late John Neville Wreford Brown; one adopted *d*. *Heir: cousin* Rev. (Stephen) Timothy Beilby Forbes Adam [*b* 19 Nov. 1923; *m* 1954, Penelope, *d* of George Campbell Munday, MC; four *d*]. *Address:* 46 Rawlings Street, SW3.

ADAM, (David Stuart) Gordon; Director, Barclays Bank UK, since 1977; Chairman, International Trust Group Ltd, since 1983; *b* 21 Dec. 1927; *o s* of late James Adam, RCNC and Florence (*née* Kilpatrick); *m* 1965, Rosanne, *er d* of late William Watson of Ardlamont; two *s* one *d*. *Educ:* Upper Canada College; Queen's Univ., Belfast (LLB); Trinity Hall, Cambridge (MA, LLB). Called to the Bar, Gray's Inn, 1951 (scholar and exhibnr). War Office, 1952–53; joined Barclays Bank, 1954; Southern and Central Africa, 1956–57; Local Dir, 1959, Gen. Man., 1968–, Dep. Chm., 1977–82, Barclays Bank Trust Co.; Chm., Barclays Internat. Devlt Fund, 1985–; Dir, various cos in Barclays' Group. Mem. Council, CBI, 1972–77. Chairman: Council, Wycombe Abbey Sch., 1981–; Girls Education Co., 1981– (Dir, 1977–). *Recreations:* mainly Alpine, and getting there. *Address:* Mulberry Hill, Wendover, Bucks. *T:* Wendover 623200. *Clubs:* Boodle's, Kandahar.

ADAM, Gordon; *see* Adam, D. S. G.

ADAM, Gordon Johnston, PhD; Member (Lab) Northumbria, European Parliament, since 1979; *b* 28 March 1934; *s* of John Craig Adam and Deborah Armstrong Johnston; *m* 1973, Sarah Jane Seely; one *s*. *Educ:* Leeds Univ. (BSc Hons, PhD). CEng, MIMinE. Mining Engr, NCB, 1959–79. Mem., Whitley Bay Bor. Council, 1971–74; Mem. 1973–80, and Dep. Leader 1975–80, North Tyneside Metrop. Bor. Council (Chm., 1973–74; Mayor, 1974–75). Chm., Whitley Bay Playhouse Theatre Trust, 1975–80; Vice-Chm., Energy, Res. and Technol. Cttee, Eur. Parlt, 1984–; Member: Northern Econ. Planning Council, 1974–79; Northern Arts Gen. Council, 1975–; Northern Sinfonia Management Cttee, 1978–80. Parly Labour Candidate: Tynemouth, 1966; Berwick-upon-Tweed, Nov. 1973 (by-election), and Feb. 1974. *Recreation:* gardening. *Address:* 2 Queens Road, Whitley Bay, Tyne and Wear. *T:* Tyneside 2528616; (office) 10 Coach Road, Wallsend, Tyne and Wear NE28 6JA. *T:* Tyneside 2635838.

ADAM, Madge Gertrude, MA, DPhil; FRAS; University Lecturer (Astronomy), Department of Astrophysics, University Observatory, Oxford, 1947–79; Research Fellow of St Hugh's College, 1957–79, now Emeritus Fellow; *b* 6 March 1912; 2nd *d* of late John Gill Simpson and late Gertrude Adam; unmarried. *Educ:* Municipal High School, Doncaster; St Hugh's College, Oxford (Scholar). Research Scholar, Lady Margaret Hall, 1935–37; Junior British Scholarship, 1936–37; Assistant Tutor of St Hugh's College and Research Assistant at Oxford University Observatory, 1937; lately Fellow and Tutor, St Hugh's College. *Publications:* papers in Monthly Notices of Royal Astronomical Society from 1937. *Address:* 17 Dovehouse Close, Upper Wolvercote, Oxford OX2 8BG.

ADAM, Robert Wilson, (Robin); Chairman: MEPC plc, since 1984 (Director since 1982); London & Scottish Marine Oil PLC, since 1985 (Director since 1984); *b* 21 May 1923; *s* of R. R. W. Adam; *m* 1957, Marion Nancy Scott. *Educ:* Fettes, Edinburgh. Royal Scots, 1942; commnd RIASC 1942; served in India and Burma (Major). Chartered Accountant 1950. Joined British Petroleum Co. Ltd, 1950; Pres., BP North America Inc. New York, 1969–72; Director: BP Canada, 1969–84 (Chm., 1981); BP Trading Ltd, 1973–75; The Standard Oil Co. (Sohio), 1972–76 and 1978–83; a Man. Dir, 1975–83, and Dep. Chm. 1981–83, British Petroleum Co. plc; Director: BP Southern Africa (Pty) Ltd, 1984–; General Accident, 1980–; Motherwell Bridge Holdings Ltd, 1984–; Royal Bank of Canada, 1984–. Lay Mem., Stock Exchange Council, 1983–85. Mem., British N America Cttee, 1980–; Trustee, Foundn for Canadian Studies, 1975–80. *Address:* 25 Onslow Square, SW7. *Clubs:* Brooks's, MCC.

ADAM SMITH, Janet (Buchanan), (Mrs John Carleton), OBE 1982; author and journalist; *b* 9 Dec. 1905; *d* of late Very Rev. Sir George Adam Smith, Principal of Aberdeen Univ. and late Lady Adam Smith; *m* 1st, 1935, Michael Roberts (*d* 1948); three *s* one *d*; 2nd, 1965, John Carleton (*d* 1974). *Educ:* Cheltenham Ladies' College (scholar); Somerville College, Oxford (exhibitioner). BBC, 1928–35; Asst Editor, The Listener, 1930–35; Asst Literary Editor, New Statesman and Nation, 1949–52, Literary Editor, 1952–60. Virginia Gildersleeve Vis. Prof., Barnard Coll., New York, 1961 and 1964. Trustee, National Library of Scotland, 1950–85; Pres., Royal Literary Fund, 1976–84. Hon. LLD Aberdeen, 1962. *Publications:* Poems of Tomorrow (ed), 1935; R. L. Stevenson, 1937; Mountain Holidays, 1946; Life Among the Scots, 1946; Henry James and Robert Louis Stevenson (ed) 1948; Collected Poems of R. L. Stevenson (ed), 1950; Faber Book of Children's Verse (ed), 1953; Collected Poems of Michael Roberts (ed), 1958; John Buchan: a Biography, 1965; John Buchan and his World, 1979. *Recreation:* mountain walking. *Address:* 57 Lansdowne Road, W11 2LG. *T:* 01–727 9324. *Club:* Alpine (Vice-Pres., 1978–80).

See also E. A. Roberts.

ADAMI, Edward F.; *see* Fenech-Adami, E.

ADAMS, Rt. Rev. (Albert) James; Acting Vicar, Ridgeway Team Ministry, Diocese of Salisbury, since 1984; *b* 9 Nov. 1915; *s* of James and Evelyn Adams, Rayleigh, Essex; *m* 1943, Malvena Jones; three *s*. *Educ:* Brentwood Sch.; King's Coll., London; Community of St Andrew, Whittlesford, Cambridge. Ordained Deacon, 1942; Priest, 1943; Curate of Walkley, Sheffield, 1942–44; Succentor, 1944, Precentor, 1945–47, Sheffield Cathedral. Rector of Bermondsey, 1947–55; Rural Dean of Bermondsey, 1954–55; Rector of: Stoke Damerel, Devonport, 1955–63; Wanstead, 1963–71. Sub-Dean, Wanstead and Woodford, 1968–69; Asst Rural Dean, Redbridge, 1970–71; Archdeacon of West Ham, 1970–75; Bishop Suffragan of Barking, 1975–83. *Address:* The Vicarage, Ogbourne St George, Marlborough, Wilts SN8 1SU. *T:* Ogbourne St George 248.

ADAMS, Alec Cecil Stanley, CMG 1960; CBE 1952; HM Diplomatic Service, retired; *b* 25 July 1909; *e s* of late Stanley A. Adams. *Educ:* King's School, Canterbury; Corpus Christi Coll., Cambridge. One of HM Vice-Consuls in Siam, 1933; served in Portuguese East Africa (acting Consul at Beira, June 1936–Feb. 1937); local rank 2nd Secretary, Bangkok Legation, 1937; Acting Consul, Sourabaya, 1938; Bangkok Legation, 1939–40; Foreign Office, Ministry of Information, 1940; Consul, in Foreign Office, 1945; Bangkok, 1946, Acting Consul-General and Chargé d'Affaires, 1948; Consul, Cincinnati, 1949; HM Chargé d'Affaires in Korea, 1950; HM Consul-General at Houston, Texas, 1953–55; Counsellor and Consul-General at HM Embassy, Bangkok, 1956–62; Deputy Commissioner-General for South East Asia, 1962–63; Political Advisor to C-in-C (Far East) at Singapore, 1963–67; retired 1967. *Address:* Flat 513, 97 Southampton Row, WC1B 4HH. *Club:* Travellers'.

ADAMS, Air Vice-Marshal Alexander Annan, CB 1957; DFC 1944; *b* 14 Nov. 1908; *s* of Capt. Norman Anderson Adams, Durham; *m* 1933, Eileen Mary O'Neill; one *s* (one *d* decd). *Educ:* Beechmont, Sevenoaks; Bellerive, Switzerland; Austria. Commnd RAF, 1930; 54 Fighter Sqdn, 1931–32; 604 Aux. Sqdn, Hendon, 1933–35; CFS, 1935; Asst Air Attaché, Berlin, Brussels, The Hague, Berne, 1938–40; Ops, Air Min., 1940; British Embassy, Washington, 1941–42; in comd 49 (Lancaster) Sqdn, 1943–44; RAF Staff Coll., 1945; Head of RAF Intelligence, Germany, 1946–48; in comd RAF Binbrook, 1948–50; NATO Standing Gp, Washington, DC, 1951–53; idc, 1954; Air Attaché, Bonn, 1955; Min. of Defence, 1956; Chief of Staff, Far East Air Force, 1957–59. Hawker Siddeley Aviation, 1961–66. Dir, Mental Health Trust and Res. Fund, later Mental Health Foundn, 1970–77. Comdr Order of Orange Nassau, 1950. *Recreations:* golf, painting. *Address:* The Lodge, Fairford, Glos GL7 4BT. *Club:* Royal Air Force.

ADAMS, Allen S.; MP (Lab) Paisley North, since 1983 (Paisley, 1979–83); computer analyst; *b* 16 Feb. 1946; *m* 1968, Irene; one *s* two *d*. *Educ:* Camphill High Sch., Paisley; Reid-Kerr Technical Coll., Paisley. Labour Scottish Whip. *Recreations:* boating, gardening. *Address:* House of Commons, SW1A 0AA; Oaklands, Hunterhill Road, Paisley.

ADAMS, Prof. Anthony Peter, FFARCS; Professor of Anaesthetics in the University of London, at the United Medical and Dental Schools of Guy's and St Thomas's Hospitals (formerly at Guy's Hospital Medical School), since 1979; Chairman: Division of Anaesthetics, United Medical and Dental Schools, since 1984; Association of Professors of Anaesthesia, since 1984; *b* 17 Oct. 1936; *s* of late H. W. J. Adams and of W. L. Adams; *m* 1973, Veronica Rosemary John; three *s* one *d*. *Educ:* Epsom College; London Univ. MB BS, PhD; DA; MRCS, LRCP, FFARCS. Wellcome Res. Fellow, RPMS, 1964–66; Consultant Anaesthetist and Clinical Lectr, Nuffield Dept of Anaesthetics, Univ. of Oxford, 1968–79. Member: Standing Cttee, Bd of Studies in Surgery, London Univ., 1979–; Academic Bd of Medicine, London Univ., 1980–83; Jt Cttee for Higher Trng of Anaesthetists, 1985–; Specialist Adv. Cttee on Accident and Emergency Medicine, Jt Cttee for Higher Trng in Medicine, 1986–; Exec. Cttee, Fedn of Assocs of Clin. Profs, 1979–; Exec. Cttee, Anaesthetic Res. Soc., 1983–; Council, Assoc. of Anaesthetists of GB and Ireland, 1984–; Senator, Eur. Acad. of Anaesthesiology, 1985–. Regional Educnl Adviser (SE Thames RHA) to Faculty of Anaesthetists of RCS, 1980–; Examiner: FFARCS, 1974–86; DVA, 1986–. Asst Editor, Anaesthesia, 1976–82; Associate Editor, Survey of Anesthesiology, 1984–; Mem. Editl Bd, British Jl of Anaesthesia, 1984–. *Publications:* Principles and Practice of Blood Gas Analysis, 1979, 2nd edn 1982; Intensive Care, 1984; (ed jtly) Recent Advances in Anaesthesia and Analgesia, 1984; Emergency Anaesthesia, 1986; contribs to medical jls. *Recreations:* badger watching, English castles, history, tennis, croquet, cinema, theatre. *Address:* Department of Anaesthetics, Guy's Hospital, London Bridge, SE1 9RT. *T:* 01–407 7600. *Clubs:* Royal Society of Medicine; Halifax House (Oxford).

ADAMS, Bernard Charles; architect; consultant to architects Messrs Steel, Coleman and Davis; *b* 29 Oct. 1915; *s* of late Charles Willoughby Adams and Emily Alice (*née* Ambrose); *m* 1942, Marjorie Barrett Weller (*d* 1986); one *d* (and two *d* decd). *Educ:* King James I Sch., Newport, IoW. ARIBA 1948, FRIBA 1968. TA, 1938–39; served 1939–41, 57 (Wessex) HAA Regt, RA; commissioned 1941; served 1941–46, 107 HAA Regt RA, France (Normandy), Belgium, Holland, Germany; Captain RA (despatches). Sen. Architect, Derbs CC, 1951–54; Asst County Architect, Kent CC, 1954–59; Dep. County Architect, Herts CC, 1959–60; County Architect, Somerset CC, 1960–80. Mem. Council, RIBA, 1963–69 and 1970–76 (Vice-Pres., 1970–72; Chm., S-W Regional Council, 1972–74); Chm., Structure of the Profession Study, RIBA, 1976–79; Mem., Nat. Consultative Council for Building and Civil Engrg Industries, 1974–80; Pres., County Architects' Soc., 1973–74 (Vice-Pres., 1971–73); Hon. Mem., Soc. of Ch. Architects of Local Authorities (founded 1974), 1983 (Sen. Vice-Pres., 1974–75; Pres. 1975–76); Architect Adviser to ACC, 1971–80; Mem., Bd of Architectural Studies, Bristol Univ., 1964–74; Founder Chm., Architects' Cttee, Consortium for Method Building, 1961–68. Founder Mem., Taunton Theatre Trust, 1972. RIBA Architecture Award, 1970, and Commendation, 1974; Heritage Year Award (EAHY), 1975; Civic Trust Awards, 1962, 1968, 1971, and Commendation, 1965. FRSA 1972. *Publications:* contrib. Jl of RIBA and other jls. *Recreations:* arts, music, theatre, travel, languages. *Address:* Meadowside, Wild Oak Lane, Trull, Taunton, Somerset TA3 7JT. *T:* Taunton 72485.

ADAMS, Prof. Colin Wallace Maitland, MD, DSc; FRCP, FRCPath; Sir William Dunn Professor of Pathology, Guy's Campus, since 1965, and Chairman, Division of Histopathology, United Medical and Dental Schools of Guy's and St Thomas's Hospitals, since 1984, University of London; *b* 17 Feb. 1928; *s* of Sidney Ewart Adams and Gladys Alethea Fletcher Adams; *m* 1953, Anne Brownhill; one *s*. *Educ:* Oundle School; Christ's College, Cambridge. Sir Lionel Whitby Medal, Cambridge Univ., 1959–60; MD Cantab, 1960; DSc London, 1967. FRCP 1977; FRCPath 1975. Visiting Scientist, National Institutes of Health, Bethesda, USA, 1960–61. *Publications:* Neurohistochemistry, 1965; Vascular Histochemistry, 1967; Research on Multiple Sclerosis, 1972; (jtly) Multiple Sclerosis, Pathology, Diagnosis and Treatment, 1982; papers on arterial diseases, neuropathology and microscopical chemistry in medical and biological journals. *Address:* The Priory, Braxted Road, Tiptree, Essex. *T:* Tiptree 818446; 15 Hasker Street, SW3. *T:* 01-589 1775.

ADAMS, Air Commodore Cyril Douglas, CB 1948; OBE 1942; retired; *b* 18 Sept. 1897; British; *m* 1927, D. M. Le Brocq (*d* 1957), Highfield, Jersey; one *s* one *d*; *m* 1968, Mrs K. E. Webster, NZ. *Educ:* Parkstone Grammar School. Served European War in Army, 1915–18, Egypt, Palestine; Commissioned RFC, 1918; Flying Instructor, 1918–25; Staff Duties, Iraq Command, 1925–27; Staff and Flying Duties, Halton Comd, 1928–35; CO 15 Sqdn, 1936–38; HQ Bomber Comd, 1938; CO 38 Sqdn, 1938–39; Sen. Officer i/c Administration, No 3 Group, 1939–40; Station Comdr, Kemble, Oakington, Abingdon, 1940–44; Base Comdr, Marston Moor and North Luffenham, 1944–45; India Command, AOA, AHQ, 1945–46; Base Comdr, Bombay, 1946; AOC No 2 Indian Group, 1946–47 (despatches 6 times, OBE (immediate award for gallantry)); Air Officer Commanding No 85 Group, BAFO, 1948–49; retired, 1949. *Recreations:* represented: RAF (Rugby, cricket, athletics); Hampshire (Rugby); Dorset and minor counties (cricket); keen golfer. *Address:* 6 Solent Pines, Whitby Road, Milford-on-Sea, Lymington, Hants. *T:* Milford-on-Sea 43754.

ADAMS, Ernest Victor, CB 1978; Deputy Secretary and Commissioner, Inland Revenue, 1975–81; *b* 17 Jan. 1920; *s* of Ernest and Amelia Adams; *m* 1943, Joan Bastin, Halesworth, Suffolk; one *s* one *d*. *Educ:* Manchester Grammar Sch.; Keble Coll., Oxford (MA). HM Forces, RA, 1940–45. Inland Revenue Dept, 1947; Sen. Inspector of Taxes, 1956; Principal Inspector of Taxes, 1961; Sen. Principal Inspector of Taxes, 1966; Dep. Chief Inspector of Taxes, 1969. *Address:* 34 Sloane Court West, Chelsea, SW3. *T:* 01–730 6482.

ADAMS, Frank Alexander, CB 1964; Member, Public Health Laboratory Service Board, 1968–79; *b* 9 July 1907; *m* 1928, Esther Metcalfe; two *d*. *Educ:* Selhurst Grammar Sch.; London School of Economics, Univ. of London. HM Inspector of Taxes, 1928; Assistant Secretary, Board of Inland Revenue, 1945; Counsellor (Economic and Financial), UK Delegation to OEEC, Paris, 1957–59; Director, Civil Service Pay Research Unit, 1960–63; Under-Sec. (Finance) and Accountant-General, Min. of Health, 1963–67. *Address:* 6 Magpie Way, Winslow, Buckingham. *T:* Winslow 3848. *Clubs:* Climbers'; Swiss Alpine (Geneva).

ADAMS, Frederick Baldwin, Jr; Director, Pierpont Morgan Library, 1948–69, now Emeritus; *b* 28 March 1910; *s* of Frederick B. Adams and Ellen Walters Delano; *m* 1st, 1933, Ruth Potter; 2nd, 1941, Betty Abbott; four *d*; 3rd, 1969, Marie-Louise de Croy. *Educ:* St Paul's Sch.; Yale Univ. (BA). Empl. Air Reduction Co. Inc., 1933–48. President: New-York Historical Soc., 1963–71; Bd Governors, Yale University Press, 1959–71; Hon. Pres., Assoc. Internationale de Bibliophilie; Trustee, Yale Univ., 1964–71; Fellow: Amer. Acad. Arts and Sciences; Amer. Philosophical Soc.; Amer. Antiquarian Soc.; Mass. Historical Soc.; Mem., Phi Beta Kappa. Hon. degrees: LittD: Hofstra Coll., 1959; Williams Coll., 1966; DFA, Union Coll., 1959; MA, Yale Univ., 1965; LHD, New York Univ., 1966. Chevalier, Légion d'Honneur, 1950; Comdr, Order of the Crown of Belgium, 1979. *Publications:* Radical Literature in America, 1939; One Hundred Influential American Books (with Streeter and Wilson), 1947; To Russia with Frost, 1963; contrib. to books and jls in bibliography, printing, collecting. *Address:* 208 rue de Rivoli, 75001 Paris, France. *Clubs:* Athenæum, Roxburghe; Century, Grolier (NY).

ADAMS, Gerald Edward, PhD, DSc; Director, Medical Research Council Radiobiology Unit, Chilton, Oxon, since 1982; *b* 8 March 1930; *m* 1955, Margaret Ray; three *s*. *Educ:* Royal Technical Coll., Salford (BSc London, 1955); Univ. of Manchester (PhD 1958, DSc 1970). Post-doctoral Fellow, Argonne National Lab., USA, 1958–60; Vis. Scientist, Centre d'Etude Nucléaire, Saclay, France, 1961–62; Lectr, 1962–66, Sen. Lectr, 1966–70, Cancer Campaign Res. Unit in Radiobiol., Mount Vernon Hosp. (later CRC Gray Lab.); Dir of Molecular Radiobiol., 1970–72, Dep. Dir of Lab., 1972–76, CRC Gray Lab.; Prof. of Physics as Applied to Medicine, Inst. of Cancer Res. (Univ. of London), Sutton, 1976–82. Lectures: 2nd Milford Schulz Annual, Harvard Med. Sch., 1979; Maurice Lenz Annual, Columbia Univ., NY, 1981. Hon. Doctorate, Univ. of Bologna, 1982. Hon. FACR 1981. Radiation Res. Award, Radiation Res. Soc., USA, 1969; David Anderson-Berry Prize, RSE, 1969; Silvanus Thompson Medal, British Inst. of Radiol., 1979. Specialist Editor, Encyc. of Pharmacology and Therapeutics, 1975–; Mem. Editorial Board: Internat. Jl of Radiation Oncology, Biology and Physics, 1978–; British Jl of Cancer, 1981–; Internat. Jl of Radiation Biology, 1983–. *Recreations:* music, golf, walking. *Address:* MRC Radiobiology Unit, Chilton, Didcot, Oxon OX11 0RD. *T:* Abingdon 834393.

ADAMS, Hervey Cadwallader, RBA 1932; FRSA 1951; landscape painter; lecturer on art; *b* Kensington, 1903; *o s* of late Cadwallader Edmund Adams and Dorothy Jane, *y d* of Rev. J. W. Knight; *m* 1928, Iris Gabrielle, (*d* 1984), *y d* of late F. V. Bruce, St Fagans, Glamorgan; two *s*. *Educ:* Charterhouse. Studied languages and singing in France and Spain, 1922–26; studied painting under Bernard Adams, 1929. Art Master, Tonbridge Sch., 1940–63. *Publications:* The Student's Approach to Landscape Painting, 1938; Art and Everyman, 1945; Eighteenth Century Painting, 1949; Nineteenth Century Painting, 1949; The Adventure of Looking, 1949. *Address:* Pummel, Houndscroft, near Stroud, Glos.

ADAMS, Rt. Rev. James; *see* Adams, Rt Rev. A. J.

ADAMS, Jennifer; Superintendent, Central Royal Parks, Department of the Environment, since 1983; *b* 1 Feb. 1948; *d* of Arthur Roy Thomas Crisp and Joyce Muriel Crisp (*née* Davey); *m* 1968, Terence William Adams. *Educ:* City of London School for Girls. Final Diploma, Inst. of Leisure and Amenity (FILAM DipPRA); MIHort. Various positions in Parks Dept, London Borough of Wandsworth, 1971–83. *Recreations:* walking, gardening, nature conservation. *Club:* Soroptimists' International.

ADAMS, John Crawford, MD, MS, FRCS; Honorary Consulting Orthopædic Surgeon, St Mary's Hospital, London; Hon. Civil Consultant in Orthopædic Surgery, Royal Air Force; Member, Council, Journal of Bone and Joint Surgery (formerly Production Editor); *m* 1940, Joan Bowen Elphinstone (*d* 1981); *m* 1985, Valerie le Maistre. MB, BS 1937; MRCS 1937; LRCP 1937; FRCS 1941; MD (London) 1943; MS (London) 1965. Formerly: Chief Asst, Orthopædic and Accident Dept, London Hosp.; Orthopædic Specialist, RAFVR; Resident Surgical Officer, Wingfield-Morris Orthopædic Hosp., Oxford. FRSM; Fellow, British Orthopædic Assoc. (Hon. Sec., 1959–62; Vice-Pres., 1974–75). OBE 1977. *Publications:* Outline of Orthopædics, 1956, 10th edn 1986; Outline of Fractures, 1957, 8th edn 1983; Ischio-femoral Arthrodesis, 1966; Arthritis and Back Pain, 1972; Standard Orthopaedic Operations, 1976, 3rd edn 1985; Recurrent Dislocation of Shoulder (chapter in Techniques in British Surgery, ed Maingot), 1950; Associate Editor and Contributor Operative Surgery (ed Rob and Smith); contributions to the Journal of Bone and Joint Surgery, etc. *Address:* White Lion Farm, Halland, near Lewes, Sussex BN8 6JQ.

ADAMS, John Douglas Richard; Registrar of Civil Appeals, since 1982; *b* 19 March 1940; *o s* of late Gordon Arthur Richard Adams and Marjorie Ethel Adams (*née* Ongley); *m* 1966, Anne Easton Todd, *o d* of late Robert Easton Todd and Mary Ann Margaret Todd (*née* Isaac); two *d*. *Educ:* Watford Grammar School; Durham Univ. (LLB 1963). Called to Bar, Lincoln's Inn, 1967. Lecturer: Newcastle Univ., 1963–71; University College London, 1971–78; also practised at Revenue Bar until 1978; Special Comr of Income Tax, 1978–82. Hon. Lecturer, St Edmund Hall, Oxford, 1978–. *Publications:* (with J. Whalley) The International Taxation of Multinational Enterprises, 1977; (contrib.) Atkin's Court Forms, 1984.; (ed jtly) Supreme Court Practice, 1985. *Recreations:* music, walking, dining. *Address:* Royal Courts of Justice, Strand, WC2A 2LL.

ADAMS, Prof. John Frank, MA, ScD; FRS 1964; Lowndean Professor of Astronomy and Geometry, Cambridge University, since 1970; Fellow of Trinity College, Cambridge; *b* 5 Nov. 1930; *m* 1953, Grace Rhoda, BA, BD, AAPSW, MBASW; one *s* three *d*. *Educ:* Bedford School; Trinity College, Cambridge; The Institute for Advanced Study, Princeton. Junior Lecturer, Oxford, 1955–56; Research Fellow, Trinity College, Cambridge, 1955–58; Commonwealth Fund Fellow, 1957–58; Assistant Lecturer, Cambridge, and Director of Studies in Mathematics, Trinity Hall, Cambridge, 1958–61; Reader, Manchester, 1962–64; Fielden Prof. of Pure Mathematics, Manchester Univ., 1964–71. For. Associate, Nat. Acad. of Scis, USA, 1985. Hon. ScD Heidelberg, 1986. Sylvester Medal, Royal Society, 1982. *Publications:* Stable Homotopy Theory, 1964; Lectures on Lie Groups, 1969; Algebraic Topology, 1972; Stable Homotopy and Generalised Homology, 1974; Infinite Loop Spaces, 1978; papers in mathematical jls. *Recreations:* walking, climbing, enamel. *Address:* 7 Westmeare, Hemingford Grey, Huntingdon PE18 9BZ.

ADAMS, Rear-Adm. John Harold, CB 1967; LVO 1957; Director, DUO (UK) Ltd, since 1983; *b* Newcastle-on-Tyne, 19 Dec. 1918; *m* 1st, 1943, Mary Parker (marr. diss. 1961); one *s* decd; 2nd, 1961, Ione Eadie, MVO, JP; two *s* two *d*. *Educ:* Glenalmond. Joined Navy, 1936; Home Fleet, 1937–39; Western Approaches, Channel and N Africa, 1939–42 (despatches); Staff Capt. (D), Liverpool, 1943–45; Staff Course, Greenwich,

1945; jssc 1949; Comdr, HM Yacht Britannia, 1954–57; Asst Dir, Underwater Weapons Matériel Dept, 1957–58; Capt. (SM) 3rd Submarine Sqdn, HMS Adamant, 1958–60; Captain Supt, Underwater Detection Estab., Portland, subseq. Admty Underwater Weapons Estab., 1960–62; idc 1963; comd HMS Albion, 1964–66; Asst Chief of Naval Staff (Policy), 1966–68; retd 1968. Lieut 1941; Lieut-Comdr 1949; Comdr 1951; Capt. 1957; Rear-Adm. 1966. Dir, Paper and Paper Products Industry Training Bd, 1968–71; Dir, Employers' Federation of Papermakers and Boardmakers, 1972–73; Dir Gen., British Paper and Board Industry Fedn, 1974–83. FIPM 1975. Chm. Governors, Cheam Sch, 1975–. *Recreations:* shooting, fishing, photography. *Address:* The Oxdrove House, Burghclere, Newbury, Berks. *T:* Burghclere 385. *Club:* Army and Navy.

ADAMS, John Kenneth; Editor of Country Life, 1958–73; Editorial Director, Country Life Ltd, 1959–73; *b* 3 June 1915; *o c* of late Thomas John Adams and late Mabel Adams (*née* Jarvis), Oxford; *m* 1944, Margaret, *o c* of late Edward Claude Fortescue, Banbury, Oxon. *Educ:* City of Oxford Sch.; Balliol Coll., Oxford. Asst Master, Stonyhurst Coll., 1939–40; served with RAFVR, 1940–41 (invalided); Asst Master, Wellington Coll., 1941–44; attached to Manchester Guardian as Leader-writer, 1942–44; Leader-writer, The Scotsman, 1944–46; joined editorial staff of Country Life, 1946; Asst Editor, 1952; Deputy Editor, 1956; Editor, 1958; Editorial Director, 1959. *Recreations:* gardening, ornithology, travel. *Address:* 95 Alleyn Park, West Dulwich, SE21 8AA. *T:* 01–693 1736. *Club:* Athenæum.

ADAMS, John Nicholas William B.; *see* Bridges-Adams.

ADAMS, John Roderick Seton; a Recorder of the Crown Court, since 1980; *b* 29 Feb. 1936; *s* of George Adams and Winifred (*née* Wilson); *m* 1965, Pamela Bridget, *e d* of Rev. D. E. Rice, MC; three *s*. *Educ:* Whitgift Sch., Croydon; Trinity Coll., Cambridge. BA (Hons) Classics and Law, 1959, MA 1963. Commnd, Seaforth Highlanders, 1955–56; Parachute Regt, TA, 1959–66. Legal Adviser in industry, 1960–66; Sec., Media Computer Services Ltd, 1966. Called to the Bar, Inner Temple, 1962; began practice at the Bar, 1967; Dep. Circuit Judge, 1978–80. *Recreations:* music, fishing, growing old roses. *Address:* 78 South Croxted Road, Dulwich, SE21. *T:* 01–670 4130; 6 Pump Court, Temple, EC4. *T:* 01–353 2510.

ADAMS, Major Kenneth Galt, CVO 1979; Comino Fellow of the Royal Society of Arts, since 1979; *b* 6 Jan. 1920; *s* of late William Adams, OBE, and Christina Elisabeth (*née* Hall); unmarried. *Educ:* Doncaster Grammar Sch.; Staff Coll., Camberley (psc 1953). MA (Lambeth); CBIM, FMS, FRSA, FCIT. Served RASC, 1940–59: War Service, ME and N Africa; DADST WO, 1946–48; DAA&QMG, Aldershot, 1952; DAQMG HQ Northern Comd, 1954–56; Sen. Instr, RASC Officers Sch., 1956–59. Sec., S London Indust. Mission, 1959–61; Proprietors of Hay's Wharf Ltd, 1960–70, Exec. Dir, 1966–70; Dir of Studies, 1969–76, Fellow, 1976–82, St George's House, Windsor Castle; Consultant, Mirror Gp Newspapers, 1976–83. Chm., Indust. Christian Fellowship, 1977–; Vice Chairman: Archbishops' Council on Evangelism, 1965–77; Southwark Cathedral Council, 1967–70; Member: Indust. Cttee, Bd for Social Responsibility of C of E, 1973–81; Bldg EDC, NEDC, 1977–81; Prof. Standards Cttee, BIM, 1976–81; Dept of Employment's Services Resettlement Cttee for SE England, 1967–77; Trustee, Industrial Trng Foundn, 1980–. Gilbreth Meml Lecture, IMS, 1980. *Publications:* papers on business ethics and attitudes to industry in Britain. *Recreations:* reading, gardening. *Address:* 7 Datchet Road, Windsor, Berks SL4 1QB. *T:* Windsor 69708. *Club:* Army and Navy.

ADAMS, Surg. Rear-Adm. Maurice Henry, CB 1965; MB, BCh, DOMS; *b* 16 July 1908; *s* of Henry Adams and Dorothea (*née* Whitehouse); *m* 1938, Kathleen Mary (*née* Hardy); one *s* two *d*. *Educ:* Campbell Coll.; Queen's University, Belfast. MB, BCh, 1930. RN Medical Service 1933; HMS Cornwall, 1934; HMS Barham, 1936; Central Air Medical Board, 1940; HMS Activity, 1942; RN Hospital, Haslar, 1944; Med. Dept, Admiralty, 1946; RN Hospital: Malta, 1950; Chatham, 1952; MO i/c Trincomalee, 1957; Med. Dept, Admiralty, 1958; Medical Officer-in-Charge, Royal Naval Hosp., Malta, 1963; QHS, 1963–66; retd 1966. *Recreations:* sailing, golf. *Address:* Canberra, Rock, Cornwall.

ADAMS, Air Vice-Marshal Michael Keith, CB 1986; AFC 1970; FRAeS; Senior Directing Staff (Air), Royal College of Defence Studies, since 1987; *b* 23 Jan. 1934; *s* of late William Frederick Adams and Jean Mary Adams; *m* 1966, Susan (*née* Trudgian); two *s* one *d*. *Educ:* Bedford Sch.; City of London Sch. FRAeS 1978. Joined RAF, 1952; qualified Pilot, 1954; Flying Instr, 1960; Test Pilot, 1963; Staff Coll., Toronto, 1969; CO Empire Test Pilots' Sch., 1975; Dir of Operational Requirements, 1978–81; RCDS, 1982; Asst Chief of Air Staff, 1984; ACDS (Air), MoD, 1985–86. *Recreations:* walking, climbing, skiing.

ADAMS, Norman (Edward Albert), RA 1972 (ARA 1967); ARCA 1951; artist (painter and ceramic sculptor); Professor of Fine Art and Director of King Edward VII College (formerly School), University of Newcastle, since 1981; *b* 9 Feb. 1927; *s* of Albert Henry Adams and Winifred Elizabeth Rose Adams; *m* 1947, Anna Theresa; two *s*. *Educ:* Royal Coll. of Art. Head of Sch. of Painting, Manchester Coll. of Art and Design, 1962–70; Lectr, Leeds Univ., 1975–. Exhibitions in most European capitals, also in America (New York, Pittsburgh); Retrospective exhibns, Royal College of Art, 1969, Whitechapel Gall. Paintings in collections of: most British Provincial Art Galleries; Tate Gall., London; Nat. Galls, New Zealand; work purchased by: Arts Coun. of Gt Brit.; Contemp. Art Soc.; Chantrey Bequest; various Educn Authorities. Murals at: Broad Lane Comprehensive Sch., Coventry; St Anselm's Church, S London; Our Lady of Lourdes, Milton Keynes. Decor for ballets, Covent Garden and Sadler's Wells. *Publications:* Alibis and Convictions, 1978; A Decade of Painting, 1971–81, 1981. *Address:* Butts, Horton-in-Ribblesdale, Settle, North Yorks. *T:* Horton-in-Ribblesdale 284; 6 Belle Grove Terrace, Spital Tongues, Newcastle upon Tyne.

ADAMS, Sir Philip (George Doyne), KCMG 1969 (CMG 1959); HM Diplomatic Service, retired; *b* 17 Dec. 1915; *s* of late George Basil Doyne Adams, MD, and Arline Maud Adams (*née* Dodgson); *m* 1954, Hon. (Mary) Elizabeth Lawrence, *e d* of Baron Trevethin and Oaksey (3rd and 1st Baron respectively); two *s* two *d*. *Educ:* Lancing Coll.; Christ Church, Oxford. Entered Consular Service, 1939; served at: Beirut, 1939; Cairo, 1941; Jedda, 1945; FO, 1947; First Sec., 1948; Vienna, 1951; Counsellor, Khartoum, 1954; Beirut, 1956; FO, 1959; Chicago, 1963; Ambassador to Jordan, 1966–70; Asst Under-Sec., FCO, 1970; Dep. Sec., Cabinet Office, 1971–72; Ambassador to Egypt, 1973–75. Dir, Ditchley Foundn, 1977–82. Member: Board, British Council, 1977–82; Marshall Aid Commem. Commn, 1979–. *Address:* 78 Sussex Square, W2; The Malt House, Ditchley, Enstone, Oxford. *Club:* Brooks's.

ADAMS, Richard Borlase, CBE 1983; Managing Director, Peninsular & Oriental Steam Navigation Co., 1979–84 (Director, 1970, Deputy Managing Director, 1974); *b* 9 Sept. 1921; *s* of James Elwin Cokayne Adams and Susan Mercer Porter; *m* 1951, Susan Elizabeth Lambert; two *s* one *d*. *Educ:* Winchester Coll.; Trinity Coll., Oxford, 1940. War service, Rifle Bde, 1940–46 (Major). Mackinnon Mackenzie Gp of Cos, Calcutta, New Delhi and Hongkong, 1947–63; Chm., Islay Kerr & Co. Ltd, Singapore, 1963–66; British India Steam Navigation Co. Ltd: Dir, 1966; Man. Dir, 1969; Chm., 1970. Dir, Clerical, Medical & General Life Assurance Soc., 1975. *Recreations:* gardening, tennis, golf. *Address:* Beacon House, Bethersden, Ashford, Kent TN26 3AE. *T:* Bethersden 247. *Club:* Oriental.

ADAMS, Richard George; author; *b* 9 May 1920; *s* of Evelyn George Beadon Adams, FRCS, and Lilian Rosa Adams (*née* Button); *m* 1949, Barbara Elizabeth Acland; two *d*. *Educ:* Bradfield Coll., Berks; Worcester Coll., Oxford (MA, Mod. Hist.). Entered Home Civil Service, 1948; retd as Asst Sec., DoE, 1974. Writer-in-residence: Univ. of Florida, 1975; Hollins Univ., Virginia, 1976. Pres., RSPCA, 1980–82. Carnegie Medal, 1972; Guardian Award for Children's Literature, 1972. FRSL 1975. *Publications:* Watership Down, 1972 (numerous subseq. edns in various languages; filmed 1978); Shardik, 1974; Nature through the Seasons, 1975; The Tyger Voyage, 1976; The Ship's Cat, 1977; The Plague Dogs, 1977 (filmed 1982); Nature Day and Night, 1978; The Girl in a Swing, 1980; The Iron Wolf, 1980; (with Ronald Lockley) Voyage through the Antarctic, 1982; Maia, 1984; The Bureaucats, 1985; A Nature Diary, 1985; (ed and contrib.) Occasional Poets (anthology), 1986. *Recreations:* folk-song, chess, country pursuits, fly-fishing, travel. *Address:* 26 Church Street, Whitchurch, Hants. *Clubs:* MCC, Savile.

ADAMS, Richard John Moreton G.; *see* Goold-Adams.

ADAMS, Sherman; Chairman and Chief Executive Officer, Loon Mountain Corporation, since 1980 (President, 1966–80); *b* 8 Jan. 1899; *s* of Clyde H. Adams and Winnie Marion (*née* Sherman); *m* 1923, Rachel Leona White; one *s* three *d*. *Educ:* Dartmouth College (Montgomery Fellow, 1980). Graduated, 1920; Manager, timberland and lumber operations, The Parker-Young Co., Lincoln, NH, 1928–45. Mem., New Hampshire House of Representatives, 1941–44; Chm. Cttee on Labor, 1941–42; Speaker of House, 1943–44; mem. 79th Congress, 2nd New Hampshire Dist; Gov. of New Hampshire, 1949–53; Chief of White House Staff, Asst to President of US, 1953–58, resigned. Chairman: Conf. of New England Govs, 1951–52; Mt Washington Commn, 1969–. Director (life), Northeastern Lumber Mfrs Assoc., New England Council. Served with US Marine Corps, 1918. First Robert Frost Award, Plymouth State Coll., 1970. Holds several hon. degrees. *Publications:* First Hand Report, 1961 (Gt Brit. 1962); articles in Life, American Forests, Appalachia, 1958–70. *Recreations:* golf, fishing, ski-ing. *Address:* Pollard Road, Lincoln, New Hampshire 03251, USA.

ADAMS, William James, CMG 1976; HM Diplomatic Service; Ambassador to Tunisia, since 1984; *b* 30 April 1932; *s* of late William Adams and late Norah (*née* Walker); *m* 1961, Donatella, *d* of late Andrea Pais-Tarsilia; two *s* one *d*. *Educ:* Shrewsbury Sch.; Queen's Coll., Oxford. HM Forces, 1950–51. Foreign Office, 1954; MECAS, 1955; 3rd Sec., Bahrain, 1956; Asst Political Agent, Trucial States, 1957; FO, 1958; 2nd Sec., 1959; Manila, 1960; 1st Sec. and Private Sec. to Minister of State, FO, 1963; 1st Sec. (Information), Paris, 1965–69; FCO, 1969; Counsellor, 1971; Head of European Integration Dept (2), FCO, 1971–72; seconded to Economic Commn for Africa, Addis Ababa, 1972–73; Counsellor (Developing Countries), UK Permanent Representation to EEC, 1973–77; Head of Chancery and Counsellor (Economic), Rome, 1977–80; Asst Under-Sec. of State, FCO, 1980–84. Order of the Star of Honour (Hon.), Ethiopia, 1965; Order of the Two Niles (Hon.), Sudan, 1965. *Address:* c/o Foreign and Commonwealth Office, SW1A 2AL. *Club:* Reform.

ADAMS-SCHNEIDER, Rt. Hon. Sir Lancelot (Raymond), KCMG 1984; PC 1980; Ambassador of New Zealand to the United States, 1982–84; *b* Wellington, NZ, 11 Nov. 1919; *s* of A. A. Adams; *m* 1945, Shirley Lois, *d* of L. A. Brunton; two *s* one *d*. *Educ:* Mt Albert Grammar School. Served War of 1939–45, NZ Medical Corps. Formerly Gen. Manager of department store, Taumarunui; Mem. Borough Council and Pres., Chamber of Commerce, Taumarunui; Exec. Member, NZ Retailers' Fedn. Vice-Chm. of Nat. Party in Waitomo electorate; Mem. S Auckland Div. Exec.; MP for Hamilton, 1959–69, for Waikato, 1969–81; Minister of Broadcasting, and Assistant to Minister of Customs, 1969; Minister of Customs, Asst Minister of Industries and Commerce, 1969–72; Minister of Health, Social Security and Social Welfare, Feb.-Nov. 1972; Opposition Spokesman on Health and Social Welfare, 1972–75, and on Industry, Commerce and Customs, 1974–75; Minister of Trade and Industry, 1975–81. *Address:* 41 Kanpur Road, Broadmeadows, Wellington 4, New Zealand.

ADAMSON, Sir Campbell; *see* Adamson, Sir W. O. C.

ADAMSON, Estelle Inez Ommanney, OBE 1962; Director of Nursing, St Thomas' Hospital, London, 1965–70, retired; *b* 21 May 1910; *d* of late R. O. Adamson, MA, MD, and late Evelyn Mary Ommanney. *Educ:* Benenden School, Cranbrook, Kent. Nurse training, St Thomas' Hosp., 1932–35; Sister, etc, St Thomas' Hosp., 1936–43; Asst Matron, King Edward VII Sanatorium, Midhurst, Sussex, 1943–45; Secretary, Nursing Recruitment Service, Nuffield Provincial Hospitals Trust, Scotland, 1946–51; Matron, Western General Hosp., Edinburgh, 1951–65. *Address:* 19 Millers Close, Goring-on-Thames, Oxon.

ADAMSON, Norman Joseph, CB 1981; QC (Scot.) 1979; Legal Secretary to the Lord Advocate and First Parliamentary Draftsman for Scotland, since 1979; *b* 29 Sept. 1930; *o s* of Joseph Adamson, wine and spirit merchant, and Lily Thorrat, Glasgow; *m* 1961, Patricia Mary, *er d* of Walter Scott Murray Guthrie and Christine Gillies Greenfield, Edinburgh; four *d*. *Educ:* Hillhead High Sch., Glasgow; Glasgow Univ. MA (Hons Philosophy and Economics) 1952; LLB 1955; Faculty of Advocates, Scotland, 1957; called to English Bar, Gray's Inn, 1959. Army Legal Aid (Civil) (UK), 1956–57; practice at Scottish Bar, 1957–65; Standing Jun. Counsel, Bible Board, 1962; Standing Jun. Counsel, MoD (Army), 1963–65; Hon. Sheriff Substitute, 1963–65; Parly Draftsman and Legal Sec., Lord Advocate's Dept, London, 1965–. Elder of the Church of Scotland. *Recreations:* music, theatre. *Address:* Whiteways, White Lane, Guildford, Surrey GU4 8PS. *T:* Guildford 65301. *Clubs:* Royal Over-Seas League (London and Edinburgh), College (Glasgow).

ADAMSON, Rt. Rev. Mgr. Canon Thomas; Canon, Liverpool Metropolitan Cathedral, since 1950; Parish Priest of St Clare's, Liverpool, since 1945; *b* 30 Sept. 1901; *s* of George and Teresa Adamson, Alston Lane, near Preston. *Educ:* St Edward's College, Liverpool; Upholland College; Oscott College, Birmingham; Gregorian University, Rome. Ordained Priest, 1926; Beda College, Rome, 1926–28; Private Secretary to Archbishop of Liverpool, 1928–45; Privy Chamberlain to Pope Pius XI, 1932; Domestic Prelate to the Pope, 1955; Vicar General to Archbishops of Liverpool, 1955–65; Protonotary Apostolic to the Pope, 1966.

ADAMSON, Sir (William Owen) Campbell, Kt 1976; Chairman: Abbey National Building Society, since 1978; Renold Ltd, since 1982 (Director, since 1976; Deputy Chairman, 1981–82); Director: Lazard Bros & Co. Ltd, since 1977; Tarmac plc, since 1980; *b* 26 June 1922; *o s* of late John Adamson, CA; *m* 1st, 1945, Gilvray (*née* Allan) (marr. diss. 1984); two *s* two *d*; 2nd, 1984, Mrs J. (Mimi) Lloyd-Chandler. *Educ:* Rugby Sch.; Corpus Christi Coll., Cambridge. Royal Inst. of Internat. Affairs, 1944–45; Baldwins Ltd as Management Trainee, 1945; successive managerial appts with Richard Thomas & Baldwins Ltd and Steel Co. of Wales Ltd, 1947–69; Gen. Man. i/c of construction and future operation of Spencer Steelworks, Llanwern; Dir, Richard Thomas & Baldwins Ltd, 1959–69, seconded as Dep. Under-Sec. of State, and Co-ordinator of Industrial Advisers, DEA, 1967–69; Dir-Gen., CBI, 1969–76. Dir, Imperial Group, 1976–86. Member: BBC Adv. Cttee, 1964–67 and 1967–75; SSRC (on formation), 1965–69; NEDC, 1969–76; Council, Industrial Soc.; Design Council, 1971–73; Council, Iron and Steel Inst., 1960–72; Iron and Steel Industry Delegn to Russia, 1956, and to India, 1968; Vice-Chm., National Savings Cttee for England and Wales, 1975–77. Vis. Fellow: Lancaster Univ., 1970; Nuffield Coll., Oxford, 1971–79. Governor: Rugby Sch., 1979–; Bedford Coll., London Univ., 1983–85. *Publications:* various technical articles. *Recreations:* brass rubbing, tennis, music, arguing. *Address:* 13 Henning Street, SW11 3DR.

ADAMSON-MACEDO, Prof. Colin, DSc; engineering and higher education consultant; Overseas Advisor to the University of Salford, since 1983; *b* 23 Nov. 1922; British; *m* 1983, Dr Elvidina Nabuco Macedo; one *s* (and one *s* one *d* of former marriage). *Educ:* Pocklington Sch., Yorks. BSc 1947, MSc(Eng.) 1952, London; DSc Manchester, 1961. REME (Capt.), 1942–46. Asst Lectr, then with A. Reyrolle & Co. (power systems analysis), 1946–52; Sen. Lectr, then Reader, in Electrical Power Systems Engrg, UMIST, 1952–61; Chm., Dept of Electrical Engineering and Electronics, Univ. of Manchester Institute of Science and Technology, 1961–70; Rector, The Polytechnic of Central London, 1970–83. Mem., Conference Internationale des Grands Réseaux Electriques; Chm. of Consultants, Educational Overseas Services, 1975–; Chm. of Panel 1 (and Mem. Council), British Calibration Service, 1969–83. Mem., Exec. Cttee, Inter-Univ. Council for Service Overseas, 1972–82. Mem., Bd of Trustees, Ecole Supérieure Interafricaine d'Electricité, Abidjan, 1979–; UN Team leader for Yarmouk Univ. of Technology, Jordan, 1978–. Vis. Professor: Univ. of Roorkee, India, 1954–55; Univs of Washington and Wisconsin, 1959; Middle East Techn. Univ., Ankara, 1967–68; Univ. of Technology, Baghdad, 1975–; Fed. Univ. of Rio de Janeiro, 1983–; Mahidol Univ., Thailand, 1984–. *Publications:* (jtly) High Voltage Direct Current Power Transmission, 1960; High Voltage DC Power Convertors and Systems, 1963; University Perspectives, 1970; UNESCO reports: Higher Technical Education (Egypt), 1972; Alternative University Structures (UK), 1973, 3rd edn 1977; Technical Higher Education (Iraq), 1974; Post-secondary Education for Persons Gainfully-employed, 1976 and 1977; contribs to Proc. IEE and other learned jls. *Recreations:* yachting, oriental science and technology. *Address:* Ridge Top Farm, Hayfield, Derbyshire SK12 5JT. *Clubs:* Athenæum, Royal Automobile; Royal Mersey Yacht.

ADCOCK, Sir Robert (Henry), Kt 1950; CBE 1941; retired as Clerk of County Council, Lancashire (1944–60), also as Clerk of the Peace for Lancashire and Clerk of the Lancashire Lieutenancy; *b* 27 Sept. 1899; *s* of late Henry Adcock, Polesworth, Warwicks; *m* Mary, *d* of late R. K. Wadsworth, Handforth Hall, Cheshire; one *s* two *d*. *Educ:* Atherstone, Warwicks. Asst Solicitor, Manchester, 1923; Asst Solicitor and Asst Clerk of the Peace, Notts CC, 1926; Senior Asst Solicitor, Manchester, 1929; Deputy Town Clerk, Manchester, 1931; Town Clerk, Manchester, 1938. DL Lancs, 1950–74. *Recreation:* golf. *Address:* Summer Place, Rock End, Torquay, Devon. *T:* 22775.

See also R. W. Adcock.

ADCOCK, Robert Wadsworth; DL; Chief Executive and Clerk, Essex County Council, since 1976; *b* 29 Dec. 1932; *s* of Sir Robert Adcock, *qv*; *m* 1957, Valerie Colston Robins; one *s* one *d*. *Educ:* Rugby Sch. Solicitor. Asst Solicitor, Lancs CC, 1955–56; Asst Solicitor, Manchester City Council, 1956–59; Sen. Solicitor, Berks CC, 1959–63; Asst Clerk, later Dep. Clerk, Northumberland CC, 1963–70; Dep. Chief Exec., Essex CC, 1970–76. DL Essex, 1978–85. *Recreations:* gardening, ornithology. *Address:* The Christmas Cottage, Great Sampford, Saffron Walden, Essex. *T:* Great Sampford 363. *Club:* Law Society.

ADDERLEY, family name of **Baron Norton.**

ADDINGTON, family name of **Viscount Sidmouth.**

ADDINGTON, 6th Baron *cr* 1887; **Dominic Bryce Hubbard;** *b* 24 Aug. 1963; *s* of 5th Baron Addington and of Alexandra Patricia, *yr d* of late Norman Ford Millar; *S* father, 1982. *Heir:* *b* Hon. Michael Walter Leslie Hubbard, *b* 6 July 1965. *Address:* 9/11 Chalk Hill Road, Norwich NR1 1SL.

ADDISON, family name of **Viscount Addison.**

ADDISON, 3rd Viscount *cr* 1945 of Stallingborough; **Michael Addison;** Baron Addison 1937; *b* 12 April 1914; 2nd *s* of 1st Viscount Addison, KG, PC, MD, FRCS, and Isobel McKinnon (*d* 1934), *d* of late Archibald Gray; *S* brother, 1976; *m* 1936, Kathleen Amy, *d* of Rt Rev. and Rt Hon. J. W. C. Wand, PC, KCVO, and late Amy Agnes Wiggins; one *s* two *d*. *Educ:* Hele's School, Exeter; Balliol Coll., Oxford. BA (PPE) 1935, MA 1965. Min. of Labour, 1935; War Damage Commission, 1940. Served RAFVR, 1941–45, FO Intell. Branch. War Damage Commn and Central Land Bd, 1945–51; Min. of Supply/Aviation, 1951–63; HM Treasury, 1963–65; Sen. Lectr, Polytechnic of Central London (School of Management Studies), 1965–76; retired, 1976. Member: Royal Inst. of Public Administration; Assoc. of Teachers of Management. *Recreation:* gardening. *Heir:* *s* Hon. William Matthew Wand Addison [*b* 13 June 1945; *m* 1970, Joanna Mary, *e d* of late J. I. C. Dickinson; one *s* two *d*]. *Address:* Old Stables, Maplehurst, Horsham, West Sussex. *T:* Lower Beeding 298. *Club:* Oxford Union Society.

ADDISON, Prof. Cyril Clifford, PhD, DSc (Dunelm); FRS 1970; FInstP; FRSC; Professor of Inorganic Chemistry, University of Nottingham, 1960–78, Dean of Faculty of Pure Science, 1968–71, Leverhulme Emeritus Fellow, 1978; *b* 28 Nov. 1913; *s* of late Edward Thomas Addison and Olive Clifford; *m* 1939, Marjorie Whineray Thompson; one *s* one *d*. *Educ:* Workington and Millom Grammar Schools, Cumberland; University of Durham (Hatfield College). Scientific Officer, British Launderers' Research Assoc., 1936–38; Lectr, Harris Inst., Preston, 1938–39; Ministry of Supply, Chemical Inspection Dept, 1939–45; Chemical Defence Research Establ., 1945; Univ. of Nottingham: Lectr, 1946; Reader in Inorganic Chemistry, 1952. Lectures: Corday-Morgan, E Africa, 1969; Liversidge, 1976; Dist. Vis. Prof., Auburn Univ., Alabama, 1979–80. Member: Chemical Soc. Council, 1954–57 (Pres. 1976–77); Inst. of Chemistry Council, 1948–51 and 1962–65 (Vice-Pres., 1965–67). Hon. DSc: Dunelm, 1977; Warwick, 1979. *Publications:* The Chemistry of the Liquid Alkali Metals, 1984. Numerous papers in Jl Chemical Soc., Trans. Faraday Soc., etc. *Recreations:* mountain walking, gardening. *Address:* Department of Chemistry, The University, Nottingham. *T:* Nottingham 506101.

ADDISON, Air Vice-Marshal Edward Barker, CB 1945; CBE 1942 (OBE 1938); MA; CEng, FIEE; RAF, retired; *b* 4 Oct. 1898; *m* 1926, Marie-Blanche Marguerite Rosain; one *s* one *d*. *Educ:* Sidney Sussex Coll., Cambridge. Served European War, 1915–18, RFC and RAF; Cambridge Univ., 1918–21; BA (Cantab), 1921; MA (Cantab), 1926; Ingénieur Diplomé de l'Ecole Supérieure d'Electricité, Paris, 1927; re-commissioned RAF, 1921; retd from RAF, 1955; Dir and Div. Manager, Redifon Ltd, 1956–63, retd; Director, Intercontinental Technical Services Ltd, 1964–75, retd; Consultant to Vocational Guidance Assoc., 1966–72. AMIEE 1933; MIEE 1941; FIEE 1966. Commander of US Legion of Merit, 1947. *Address:* 7 Hall Place Drive, Weybridge, Surrey. *T:* Weybridge 47450.

ADDISON, Kenneth George, OBE 1978; Director, since 1971 and Deputy Chief General Manager, 1976–84, Sun Alliance & London Insurance Group; *b* 1 Jan. 1923; *s* of Herbert George Addison and Ruby (*née* Leathers); *m* 1945, Maureen Newman; one *s* one *d*. *Educ:* Felixstowe Grammar Sch. LLB London. Served RAF, 1942–46. Joined Alliance Assurance Co. Ltd, 1939; various subsequent appts; Asst Sec., Law Fire Insurance Office, 1960–64; Gen. Manager, Sun Alliance & London Insurance Group, 1971. Chairman: Fire Insurers' Res. & Testing Orgn, 1977–84; Management Cttee, Associated Insurers (British Electricity), 1977–84; Internat. Oil Insurers, 1979–82; Dir, Insurance Technical Bureau, 1977–84; Chm., Hearing Aid Council, 1971–78. FCIS; FCII (Pres., 1980); FCIArb (Pres., 1968–69). *Publications:* papers on insurance and allied subjects. *Recreations:* swimming, carpentry, gardening. *Address:* Ockley, 13 Hillcroft Avenue, Purley, Surrey. *T:* 01–660 2793.

ADDISON, Dr Philip Harold, MRCS, LRCP; Hon. Consulting Secretary, The Medical Defence Union, since 1974 (Secretary, 1959–74); *b* 28 June 1909; 2nd *s* of late Dr Joseph Bartlett Addison and Mauricia Renée Addison; *m* 1934, Mary Norah Ryan; one *s* one *d*. *Educ:* Clifton Coll., Bristol; St Mary's Hosp. Medical Sch. MRCS, LRCP 1933; Gold Medallist, Military Medicine and Bronze Medallist Pathology, Army Medical Sch., Millbank, SW1, 1935. Permanent Commission, IMS, 1935; served Burma Campaign, 1943–45 (despatches). Chm., Ethical Cttee of Family Planning Assoc., 1956–60; Vice-Pres., Medico-Legal Soc., 1965–74. *Publications:* Professional Negligence, in Compendium of Emergencies, 1971; The Medico-Legal Aspects of General Anaesthesia, in, Clinical Practice of General Anaesthesia, 1971; contrib. Brit. Med. Jl, Irish Med. Jl, Proc. R.Soc.Med, Medico-Legal Jl, Lancet. *Recreations:* fishing, golf, bridge. *Address:* Red-Wyn-Byn, Monkmead Lane, West Chiltington, Pulborough, West Sussex. *T:* West Chiltington 3047. *Clubs:* East India, Devonshire, Sports and Public Schools; Shark Angling Club of Gt Britain; West Sussex Golf; BMA Bridge (Founder Mem.).

ADDISON, Sir William (Wilkinson), Kt 1974; JP; DL; Chairman of Council, The Magistrates' Association, 1970–76; *b* Mitton, WR Yorks, 4 April 1905; *s* of Joseph Addison, Bashall Eaves; *m* 1929, Phoebe, *d* of Robert Dean, Rimington, WR Yorks. Verderer of Epping Forest, 1957–84. Chm., Epping Petty Sessions, 1955–, combined Epping and Ongar Petty Sessions, 1968–76; Magistrates' Assoc.: Mem. Coun., 1959–76; Dep. Chm. of Coun., 1966–70; Chm., Treatment of Offenders Cttee, 1961–68; Chm. Exec. Cttee, 1968–75. Member: Hill Hall Prison Board of Visitors, 1955–70; Chelmsford Prison, 1958–77; Bullwood Hall Borstal, 1962–76; Home Sec.'s Adv. Coun. on Probation and After-Care, 1964–67; Lord Chancellor's Adv. Coun. on Trng of Magistrates, 1964–73; Magistrates' Courts Rule Cttee, 1968–74; Council, Commonwealth Magistrates Assoc., 1970–75; Assessor to Deptl Cttee on Liquor Licensing, 1971. Member: Court, Univ. of Essex, 1965–; Adv. Council, Univ. of Cambridge Inst. of Criminology, 1972–78; Vice-Pres., 1980, Pres., 1985–, Assoc. of Genealogists and Records Agents; Mem. Council, Essex Archaeol Soc., 1949–71 (Pres., 1964–67); Vice-Pres., Council for the Protection of Rural England (Essex), 1984–; Pres. or Chm. of several bodies connected with local history and the preservation of antiquities in Essex, inc. Victoria County History and Friends of Essex Churches. JP 1949, DL 1973, Essex. FSA 1965; FRHistS 1965. *Publications:* Epping Forest, 1945; The English Country Parson, 1947; Essex Heyday, 1949; Suffolk, 1950; Worthy Dr Fuller, 1951; English Spas, 1951; Audley End, 1953; English Fairs and Markets, 1953; Thames Estuary, 1953; In the Steps of Charles Dickens, 1955; Wanstead Park, 1973; Essex Worthies, 1973; Portrait of Epping Forest, 1977; Understanding English Place-Names, 1978; Understanding English Surnames, 1978; The Old Roads of England, 1980; Local Styles of the English Parish Church, 1982. *Recreation:* exploring the English countryside for evidence of local history. *Address:* Ravensmere, Epping, Essex. *T:* Epping 73439.

ADDLESHAW, His Honour John Lawrence; a Circuit Judge (formerly County Court Judge), 1960–75; *b* 30 Oct. 1902; *s* of Harold Pope Addleshaw, Solicitor and Mary Gertrude (*née* Shore), Manchester; unmarried. *Educ:* Shrewsbury School; University College, Oxford (BA). Called to the Bar, Inner Temple, 1925. Auxiliary Air Force, 1939–45. *Recreations:* golf, walking. *Address:* 3 College House, Southdowns Road, Bowdon, Altrincham, Cheshire WA14 3DZ. *T:* 061–928 2139. *Club:* St James's (Manchester).

ADEANE, Hon. (George) Edward, CVO 1985; an Extra Equerry to HRH the Prince of Wales, since 1985; Director: Hambros Bank Ltd, since 1986; Guardian Royal Exchange Assurance plc; English and Scottish Investors plc; *b* 4 Oct. 1939; *s* of Baron Adeane, GCB, GCVO, PC and of Lady Adeane. *Educ:* Eton; Magdalene College, Cambridge (MA). Called to Bar, Middle Temple, July 1962. Page of Honour to HM the Queen, 1954–55; Private Sec. and Treas. to HRH the Prince of Wales, 1979–85; Treas. to TRH the Prince and Princess of Wales, 1981–85; Private Sec. to HRH the Princess of Wales, 1984–85. *Address:* B4 Albany, Piccadilly, W1. *T:* 01–734 9410.

ADEBO, Simeon Olaosebikan, Chief; The Okanlomo of Egbaland, CFR 1979; CMG 1959; Chancellor, University of Lagos, Nigeria, since 1984; *b* 5 Oct. 1913; *s* of late Chief Adebo, the Okanlomo of Itoko, Abeokuta; *m* 1941, Regina Abimbola, *d* of Chief D. A. Majekodunmi, Abeokuta; three *s* one *d*. *Educ:* St Peter's Sch., Ake, Abeokuta; Abeokuta Grammar Sch.; King's Coll., Lagos, Nigeria. BA Hons (London) 1939; LLB Hons (London) 1946. Called to Bar, Gray's Inn, 1949. Accountant in trg, Nigerian Rly, 1933; Admin. Officer Cadet, Nigerian Govt, 1942; Asst Fin. Sec. to Govt of Nigeria, 1954; Western Nigeria: Admin. Officer, Class I, 1955; Perm. Sec., Min. of Finance, 1957; Perm. Sec. to Treasury and Head of Civil Service, 1958; Head of Civil Service and Chief Secretary to Government, 1961; Permanent Representative of Nigeria at UN and Comr-Gen. for Economic Affairs, 1962–67; UN Under-Secretary-General and Exec. Dir of UNITAR, 1968–72. Chancellor, Univ. of Ife, 1982–84. Mem., Constituent Assembly on draft constitution of Nigeria, 1977. Chairman: Nat. Universities Commn of Nigeria, 1975–77; Nat. Inst. for Policy and Strategic Studies, 1979–82. Mem., Soc. for Internat. Devélt. Hon. LLD: Western Michigan, 1963; Nigeria, Nsukka, 1965; Fordham, 1966; Lincoln, 1966; Beaver Coll., 1966; Ife, 1968; Ibadan, 1969; Columbia, 1971; Ahmadu Bello (Nigeria), 1973; Open Univ., 1975; Lagos, Nigeria, 1978; Hon. DCL, Union Coll., 1965. *Publication:* (with Sir Sydney Phillipson) Report on the Nigerianisation of the Nigerian Civil Service, 1953. *Recreations:* swimming, tennis, cricket. *Address:* Abimbola Lodge, Ibara, PO Box 139, Abeokuta, Nigeria. *Clubs:* Royal Commonwealth Society; Nigeria Society (Lagos); Abeokuta Sports.

ADELAIDE, Archbishop of, and Metropolitan of South Australia, since 1975; **Most Rev. Keith Rayner;** *b* 22 Nov. 1929; *s* of Sidney and Gladys Rayner, Brisbane; *m* 1963, Audrey Fletcher; one *s* two *d*. *Educ:* C of E Grammar Sch., Brisbane; Univ. of Queensland. BA 1951; PhD 1964. Deacon, 1953; Priest, 1953. Chaplain, St Francis' Theol Coll., Brisbane, 1954; Mem., Brotherhood of St John, Dalby, 1955–58; Vice-Warden, St John's Coll., Brisbane, 1958; Rotary Foundn Fellow, Harvard Univ., 1958–59; Vicar, St Barnabas', Sunnybank, 1959–63; Rector, St Peter's, Wynnum, 1963–69; Bishop of Wangaratta, 1969–75. Pres., Christian Conference of Asia, 1977–81; Chm., International Anglican Theological and Doctrinal Commission, 1980–. *Recreation:* tennis. *Address:* Bishop's Court, North Adelaide, SA 5006, Australia.

ADELAIDE, Archbishop of, (RC), since 1985; **Most Rev. Leonard Anthony Faulkner;** *b* Booleroo Centre, South Australia, 5 Dec. 1926. *Educ:* Sacred Heart Coll., Glenelg; Corpus Christi Coll., Werribee; Pontifical Urban University, Rome. Ordained Propaganda Fide Coll., Rome, 1 Jan. 1950. Asst Priest, Woodville, SA, 1950–57; Administrator, St Francis Xavier Cathedral, Adelaide, 1957–67; Diocesan Chaplain, Young Christian Workers, 1955–67; Mem., Nat. Fitness Council of SA, 1958–67; Bishop of Townsville, 1967–83; Coadjutor Archbishop of Adelaide, 1983–85. Chm., Aust. Episcopal Conference Cttee for Laity, 1982– (Sec., 1968–82); Sec., Aust. Episcopal Conference Cttee for Aborigines, 1975–. *Address:* Archbishop's House, 91 West Terrace, Adelaide, SA 5000, Australia.

ADELSTEIN, Abraham Manie, MD; FRCP; FFCM; Visiting Professor, London School of Hygiene and Tropical Medicine, 1981–84, retired 1985; *b* 28 March 1916; *s* of Nathan Adelstein and Rosa Cohen; *m* 1942, Cynthia Gladys Miller; one *s* one *d. Educ:* Univ. of Witwatersrand. MB, ChB, MD. SAMC, 1941–45; Health Officer (res. and medical statistics), SA Railways, 1947–61; Sen. Lectr, Univ. of Manchester, 1961–67; OPCS, 1967–81 (SPMO and Chief Medical Statistician, 1975–81). Donald Reid Medal, LSHTM, 1979; Bisset Hawkins Medal, RCP, 1982. *Publications:* Thesis on Accident Proneness, 1950; papers in scientific jls on the distribution and aetiology of various diseases (diseases of heart, nervous system, respiratory system, cancer, accidents) and of methods of collecting, analysing and publishing national statistics. *Address:* 21 Dunstan Road, NW11 8AG. *T:* 01–455 9983.

ADEMOLA, Rt. Hon. Sir Adetokunbo (Adegboyega), GCON 1972; CFR 1963; PC 1963; KBE 1963; Kt 1957; Chancellor, University of Nigeria, since 1975; *b* 1 Feb. 1906; *e s* of late Sir Ladapo Ademola, Alake of Abeokuta, KBE, CMG; *m* 1939, Kofoworola, *yr d* of late Eric Olawolu Moore, CBE; three *s* two *d. Educ:* King's Coll., Lagos, Nigeria; Selwyn Coll., Cambridge. Attached to Attorney-General's Chambers, Lagos, Nigeria, 1934–35; Assistant Secretary, Secretariat, Southern Provinces, Nigeria, 1935–36; private law practice, Nigeria, 1936–39; Magistrate, Nigeria, 1939; served on commn for Revision of Courts Legislation, Nigeria, 1948; served on commn to enquire into Enugu (Nigeria) disturbances, 1949; Puisne Judge, Nigeria, 1949; Chief Justice, Western Region, Nigeria, 1955–58; Chief Justice of Nigeria, 1958–72. Deputy Chm., United Bank for Africa, 1972–74. Hon. Bencher, Middle Temple, 1959–. Chairman: Commonwealth Foundn, 1978–; Adv. Cttee on Conventions and Regulations of the ILO (Mem., 1962–); Member: Internat. Commn of Jurists, 1961– (now Hon. Mem.); Internat. Olympic Cttee, 1963–. Hon. LLD Ahmadu Bello, Nigeria, 1962; Hon. DSc Benin, 1972. *Recreations:* golf, horse racing. *Address:* The Close, Adetokunbo Ademola Street, Victoria Island, Lagos, Nigeria. *T:* Lagos 52219. *Clubs:* Island, Metropolitan, Yoruba Tennis (Lagos); Ibadan Recreation, Ibadan (Ibadan).

ADEY, (Arthur) Victor; Director: Ampex Corporation (USA), 1973–85; Motability and Motability Finance Ltd, 1978–85; *b* 2 May 1912; *s* of Arthur Frederick and Pollie Adey; *m* 1936, Kathleen Mary Lewis; one *s* one *d. Educ:* Wolverhampton Secondary Sch. Articled clerk, Crombie, Lacon & Stevens, 1928; Office Manager and Accountant, Attwoods Factors Ltd, 1933; Branch Man., Mercantile Union Guarantee Corp., 1937; Man. Dir, Mercantile Credit Co. of Ireland Ltd, 1949; Mercantile Credit Co. Ltd: Dir, Bd of Management, 1955; Director, 1957–; Man. Dir, 1964; Dep. Chm. and Man. Dir, 1973; Chm. and Man. Dir, 1975–77; Chm., 1977–80; Dir, Barclays Bank UK Management Ltd, 1975–79. *Recreations:* shooting, fishing. *Address:* Rosemount, Burtons Lane, Chalfont St Giles, Bucks HP8 4BN. *T:* Little Chalfont 2160.

ADIE, Jack Jesson, CMG 1962; BA (Oxon); *b* 1 May 1913; *s* of late P. J. Adie; *m* 1940, Patricia McLoughlin; one *s* two *d. Educ:* Shrewsbury Sch.; Magdalen Coll., Oxford. Entered Colonial Administrative Service, 1938; served in Zanzibar, 1938–48 (on military service, 1940–42 in Kenya Regt, KAR and Occupied Territory Administration), posts included: Private Sec. to The Sultan, Private Sec. to British Resident and Sen. Asst Sec.; seconded to Colonial Office, 1949–51, as Principal; Asst Sec., Kenya, 1951; Sec. for Educn and Labour, Kenya, 1952; Sec. for Educn, Labour and Lands, Kenya, 1954; acted as Minister for Educn, Labour and Lands, Kenya, Sept. 1955–Feb. 1956; Chief Sec., Barbados, 1957; Perm. Sec. for Forest Development, Game and Fisheries, Kenya, April-Dec. 1958; for Agriculture, Animal Husbandry and Water Resources, and Chm. African Land Development Bd, Dec. 1958–July 1959; for Housing, and Chm. Central Housing Bd, Nov. 1959–April 1960; for Housing, Common Services, Probation and Approved Schools, April 1960–April 1961; for Labour and Housing, 1961–62; acted as Minister for Labour and Housing, Jan.-April 1962; Perm. Sec. for Labour, 1962–63; retd from HMOCS, Jan 1964; Temp. Principal, Min. of Overseas Develt, 1964–69. Brilliant Star of Zanzibar, 4th class, 1947. *Address:* 3 Braemar, Kersfield Road, Putney, SW15.

ADIE, Rt. Rev. Michael Edgar; *see* Guildford, Bishop of.

ADISESHIAH, Dr Malcolm Sathianathan; Member of Parliament, Rajya Sabha, 1978–84; Vice-Chancellor, University of Madras, 1975–78; Director, Institute of Development Studies, Madras, 1971–78, now Chairman and Fellow; *b* 18 April 1910; *s* of Varanasi Adiseshiah and Nesammah Adiseshiah; *m* 1951, Sanchu Pothan. *Educ:* Univ. of Madras (MA); LSE, London Univ. (PhD). Lectr in Econs, St Paul's Coll., Calcutta, 1931–36; Prof. of Econs, Madras Christian Coll., 1940–46; Associate Gen. Sec., World Univ. Service, Geneva, 1946–48; Unesco, Paris: Dep. Dir, Dept of Exchange of Persons, 1948–50; Dir, Dept of Tech. Assistance, 1950–54; Asst Dir-Gen., 1954–63; Dep. Dir-Gen., 1963–70. Chairman: Tamil Nadu State Council for Science and Technology, 1984–; Governing Bd, Internat. Inst. for Educnl Planning, 1981–. *Publications:* Demand for Money, 1938; Agricultural Development, 1941; Rural Credit, 1943; Planning Industrial Development, 1944; Non-political UN, 1964; Economics of Indian and Industrial Natural Resources, 1966; Education and National Development, 1967; Adult Education, 1968; Let My Country Awake, 1970; It is Time to Begin, 1972; Techniques of Perspective Planning, 1973; Plan Implementation Problems and Prospects for the Fifth Plan, 1974; Science in the Battle against Poverty, 1974; Literacy Discussion, 1976; Towards a Functional Learning Society, 1976; Backdrop to Learning Society: educational perspectives for Tamil Nadu, 1977; Adult Education faces Inequality, 1980; Mid Term Appraisal of the VI Plan, 1982; Mid Year Review of the Economy, 1976–83; Some Thoughts on the VII Five Year Plan 1985–86 to 1989–90, 1985; Shaping National Events—the economy, 1985; VII Plan Perspectives, 1985; Mid-Year Review of the Economy, 1985, 1986; Comments on the Black Economy, 1986; Madras Development Seminar Series, 1971–. *Address:* 21 Cenotaph Road, Madras-600018, India. *T:* Madras 440144.

ADLER, George Fritz Werner, OBE 1982; FEng, FIMechE; FICE; Director of Research, British Hydromechanics Research Association, 1971–86; *b* 12 Jan. 1926; *s* of Fritz Jacob Sigismund Adler and Hildegard Julie Adler (*née* Lippmann); *m* 1949, June Moonaheim Margaret Nash; three *d. Educ:* Penarth County School; Cardiff Technical Coll.; University Coll., Cardiff; Imperial Coll., London. BSc (Eng), DIC. Design Engineer, 1948, Chief, Mechanical Develt, 1953, English Electric, Rugby; Chief Mechanical Engineer, 1958, Gen. Manager Mech. Products, Marconi, 1962; Manager, Mech. Products Div., English Electric, 1966. Dir, Fluid Engineering Products Ltd, 1982–84. Vice-Pres., 1979, Pres., 1983, IMechE; Chm., CDRA (Fedn of Technology Centres), 1981–83; Mem., Engineering Council, 1986–. FBIM; FInstD. *Publications:* chapter, Water Turbines (jtly), in Kempe's Engineers' Year Book, 1956; articles in technical jls. *Recreations:* gardening, swimming, music. *Address:* The Dower House, Shenley Church End, Bucks MK5 6AB. *T:* Milton Keynes 501469. *Club:* Carlton.

ADLER, Larry, (Lawrence Cecil Adler); mouth organist; *b* 10 Feb. 1914; *s* of Louis Adler and Sadie Hack; *m* 1st, 1938, Eileen Walser (marr. diss. 1961); one *s* two *d;* 2nd, 1969, Sally Cline (marr. diss. 1977); one *d. Educ:* Baltimore City Coll. Won Maryland Harmonica Championship, 1927; first stage appearance, 1928 (NY); first British appearance, 1934 (in C. B. Cochran's Streamline revue); first appearance as soloist with Symphony Orchestra, Sydney, Australia, 1939; jt recital tours with dancer Paul Draper, US, 1941–49; soloist with NY Philharmonic and other major US Orchestras, also orchestras in England, Japan and Europe; war tours for Allied Troops, 1943, 1944, 1945; Germany, 1947, 1949; Korea (Brit. Commonwealth Div.), 1951; Israel (Six Day War), 1967; (Yom Kippur War), 1973; articles and book reviews in Sunday Times, New Statesman, Spectator, New Society; restaurant critic: Harpers & Queen, London Portrait; Chamber Life; columnist: What's On in London, Jazz Express, Jewish Gazette; numerous TV One Man Shows; soloist, Edinburgh Festival, playing first performance of unpublished Gershwin quartet (MS gift to Adler from I. Gershwin, 1963; works composed for Adler by: Dr Ralph Vaughan Williams, Malcolm Arnold, Darius Milhaud, Arthur Benjamin, Gordon Jacob and others. Diploma: Peabody Conservatory of Music, Baltimore; City Coll., Baltimore, 1986. *Compositions:* film scores: Genevieve; King and Country; High Wind in Jamaica; The Great Chase, etc; TV scores: Midnight Men (BBC serial); various TV plays and documentaries; music for TV commercials, children's records, stage plays, etc; concert music: Theme and Variations; Camera III; One Man Show, From Hand to Mouth, Edinburgh Festival, 1965 (other festivals, 1965–). *Publications:* How I Play, 1937; Larry Adler's Own Arrangements, 1960; Jokes and How to Tell Them, 1963; It Ain't Necessarily So (autobiog.), 1985. *Recreations:* tennis, journalism, cycling, conversation; obsession: writing letters to Private Eye. *Address:* c/o MBA Literary Agents Ltd, 118 Tottenham Court Road, W1. *T:* 01–387 2076.

ADLEY, Robert James; MP (C) Christchurch, since 1983 (Bristol North East, 1970–74; Christchurch and Lymington, 1974–83); Director and Marketing Consultant, Commonwealth Holiday Inns of Canada Ltd; *b* 2 March 1935; *s* of Harry and Marie Adley; *m* 1961, Jane Elizabeth Pople; two *s. Educ:* Falconbury; Uppingham. Lived and worked in: Malaya, Singapore, Thailand; established Pearl & Dean (Thailand) Ltd, 1956; Sales Director, May Fair Hotel, 1960–64; Director: Alexander James & Dexter Ltd, 1984–; William Jacks plc, 1984–. Chairman: Parly Tourism Cttee; British-Jordanian Parly Gp; British-Chinese Parly Gp; Pres., Western Area Young Conservatives, 1972. Member: Nat. Council, British Hotels, Restaurants and Caterers Assoc.; Railway Correspondence and Travel Soc.; Cttee, National Railway Museum; Founder and First Chm., Brunel Soc.; Trustee, Brunel Engineering Centre Trust; Patron, SS Great Britain Project. *Publications:* Hotels, the Case for Aid, 1966; One Man, No Vote, 1976; A Policy for Tourism, 1977; British Steam in Cameracolour 1962–68, 1979; Take It or Leave It, 1980; In Search of Steam, 1981; The Call of Steam, 1982; To China for Steam, 1983; All Change Hong Kong, 1984; In Praise of Steam, 1985. *Recreations:* railway photography, railway enthusiast. *Address:* House of Commons, SW1A 0AA. *T:* 01–219 4438. *Club:* Carlton.

ADMANI, Dr Haji (Abdul) Karim, JP; Consultant Physician, Sheffield Area Health Authority (Teaching), since 1970; Hon. Clinical Lecturer in Medicine, Sheffield University Medical School, since 1972; *b* 19 Sept. 1937; *s* of late Haji Abdul Razzak Admani (Electrical Engr in India), and of Hajiani Rahima Admani; *m* 1968, Seema (*née* Robson; Nursing Dir); one *s* one *d. Educ:* Gujarat Univ., India (BSc 1st Cl. Hons 1956); Karachi Univ., Pakistan (MB, BS 1962). DTM&H 1963; MRCPE (Neurology), 1967; FRCPE 1979; Associate MRCP. Sec. Med. Div., Northern Dist, Sheffield, 1972–75; Mem. Dist Med. Cttee, N Dist, 1975–; Area Rep. and Mem. Exec. Cttee, BMA, Sheffield, 1975–; Member: Sheffield AHA, 1977–82; GMC, 1979–. President: British Red Cross Soc. for Co. of S Yorks, 1982– (County MO, 1974–82); Muslim Council of Sheffield, Rotherham and dist, 1977– (Chm., 1970–76); Sheffield and N Reg., Pakistan Med. Soc. in UK, 1972–; Anglo-Asian Soc., Sheffield, 1973–; Union of Pakistani Orgns in UK and Europe, 1979– (Sen. Vice Pres., 1978–79). Chairman: Islamic Centre Man. Cttee, Sheffield, 1973–; Overseas Doctors' Assoc. in UK, 1981– (Vice-Chm., 1975–81; Chm. Post-grad. Med. Sub-Cttee, 1975; Chm. S Yorks Div., 1976–; Chm., Inf., Advice and Welfare Centre, 1977–82); BBC Radio Sheffield Adv. Council, 1982–. Vice-Chairman: National Org. of Afro-Asian-Caribbean People in UK, 1977; Sheffield Cttee for Racial Equality, 1981–. Member: Exec. Cttee, Standing Conf. of Pakistani Orgs in UK, 1976– (Chm. Standing Conf., 1974–76); Asian Action Cttee (National), 1976; Exec. Cttee, Sheffield Community Relations Council, 1974–76; Adv. Council, IBA for Radio Hallam, Sheffield, 1975–81; National Cttee for Campaign against Rickets and Osteomalacia, 1980– (Chm., Sheffield Cttee, 1981–); Central Cttee for Hosp. Med. Services in UK, 1979–. Pres., Sheffield Stroke Club, 1977. Member: British Geriatric Soc.; Medico-Chirurgical Soc. Sheffield; Abbeydale Rotary Club, Sheffield; BMA; Collegiate Cttee of Edinburgh; Magistrates' Assoc. JP City of Sheffield, 1974. *Recreations:* tennis, cricket, chess, football, golf, table tennis. *Address:* 1 Derriman Glen, Silverdale Road, Sheffield S11 9LQ. *T:* Sheffield 360465.

ADRIAN, family name of **Baron Adrian.**

ADRIAN, 2nd Baron, *cr* 1955, of Cambridge; **Richard Hume Adrian,** MD; FRS 1977; Professor of Cell Physiology, University of Cambridge, since 1978; Master of Pembroke College, since 1981; Vice-Chancellor, University of Cambridge, 1985–Oct. 1987; *b* 16 Oct. 1927; *o s* of 1st Baron Adrian, OM, FRS, FRCP, and Hester Agnes, DBE 1965 (*d* 1966), *o d* of late Hume C. and Dame Ellen Pinsent, DBE, Birmingham; *S* father, 1977; *m* 1967, Lucy Caroe, MA, PhD. *Educ:* Swarthmore High Sch., USA; Westminster Sch.; Trinity Coll., Cambridge (MA). MB, BChir Cantab. UCH, 1951; National Service, RAMC, 1952–54; Univ. of Cambridge: G. H. Lewes Student, Physiol Lab., 1954; Univ. Demonstr, 1956; Fellow, Corpus Christi Coll., 1956; Univ. Lectr, 1961; Reader in Exptl Biophysics, 1968; Fellow of Churchill Coll., 1961–81, Hon. Fellow 1985. Trustee: British Museum, 1979–; British Museum (Nat. Hist.), 1984–; Mem. Council, Royal Soc., 1984. Docteur *hc* Poitiers, 1975. *Publications:* articles in Jl of Physiol. *Recreations:* sailing, skiing. *Address:* The Master's Lodge, Pembroke College, Cambridge CB2 1RF. *T:* Cambridge 352241; Umgeni, Cley, Holt, Norfolk.

ADRIEN, Sir J. F. M. L.; *see* Latour-Adrien.

ADSHEAD, Mary; engaged on painting a series of house portraits; *m* 1929, Stephen Bone (*d* 1958). Trained at Slade School under Prof. Henry Tonks. Mural paintings in public and private buildings; illustrations, designs for GPO stamps. Chief works: murals in: Restaurant at Luton Hoo; St Peter's Church, Vauxhall Estate, Luton; Civic Centre, Plymouth; Town Hall, Totnes; Commonwealth Inst.; Messrs Costain & Sons; The Post House, Leicester; Beatson Mural, Beatson Walk Underpass, Rotherhithe, 1982 (mosaic mural depicting the return of the Fighting Temeraire to Rotherhithe; mediums used were mosaics, high fired tiles, cast iron; mould for canon and aluminium strip framework for ships; also various screeds; work carried out for Southwark Council in conjunction with Land Use Consultants).

ADYE, John Anthony; Under Secretary, Government Communications Headquarters, since 1983; *b* 24 Oct. 1939; *s* of Arthur Francis Capel Adye and Hilda Marjorie Adye (*née* Elkes); *m* 1961, Anne Barbara, *d* of Dr John Aeschlimann, Montclair, NJ; two *s* one *d*. *Educ:* Leighton Park Sch.; Lincoln Coll., Oxford (MA). Joined GCHQ, 1962; Principal, 1968; British Embassy, Washington, 1973–75; Nat. Defence Coll., Latimer, 1975–76; Asst Sec., 1977–83. *Recreations:* book-collecting and restoration, drawing, history, early travellers to Greece. *Address:* Government Communications Headquarters, Priors Road, Cheltenham, Glos. *Club:* Naval and Military.

AGA KHAN (IV), His Highness Prince Karim, granted title His Highness by the Queen, 1957, granted title His Royal Highness by the Shah of Iran, 1959; *b* 13 Dec. 1936; *s* of late Prince Aly Salomon Khan and of Princess Joan Aly Khan (*née* Joan Barbara Yarde-Buller, *e d* of 3rd Baron Churston, MVO, OBE); became Aga Khan, spiritual leader and Imam of Ismaili Muslims all over the world on the death of his grandfather, Sir Sultan Mohamed Shah, Aga Khan III, GCSI, GCIE, GCVO, 11 July 1957; *m* 1969, Sarah Frances Croker Poole, *o d* of Lt-Col A. E. Croker Poole; two *s* one *d*. *Educ:* Le Rosey, Switzerland; Harvard University (BA Hons). Leading owner and breeder of race horses in France, UK and Ireland; won 1981 Derby (Shergar) and 1982 Prix de L'Arc de Triomphe (Akiyda). President: Aga Khan Foundn, Geneva, 1967 (also branches in Bangladesh, Canada, India, Kenya, Pakistan, Portugal, UK and US); Aga Khan Award for Architecture, 1976–; Inst. of Ismaili Studies, 1977–; Aga Khan Fund for Economic Develt, Geneva, 1984. Commandeur, Ordre du Mérite Mauritanien, 1960; Grand Croix: Order of Prince Henry the Navigator, Portugal, 1960; l'Ordre National de la Côte d'Ivoire, 1965; l'Ordre National de la Haute-Volta, 1965; l'Ordre Malgache, 1966; l'Ordre du Croissant Vert des Comores, 1966; Grand Officier, l'Ordre National du Lion, Sénégal, 1982; Grand Cordon, Order of the Taj, Iran, 1967; Cavaliere di Gran Croce della Republica Italiana, 1977; Nishan-i-Imtiaz, Pakistan, 1970; Nishan-e-Pakistan, Pakistan, 1983. Hon. Fellow, Coll. of Physicians and Surgeons of Pakistan, 1985; Doctor of Laws (*hc*): Peshawar Univ., Pakistan, 1967; Sind Univ., Pakistan, 1970; McGill Univ., Canada, 1983. Architecture Award, Thomas Jefferson Meml Foundn, 1984; Inst. Honor, AIA, 1984. Prix de Jockey Club: Charlottesville, 1960; Top Ville, 1979; Darshaan, 1984; Mouktar, 1985. *Recreations:* tennis, ski-ing, yachting. *Address:* Aiglemont, 60270 Gouvieux, France. *Clubs:* Royal Yacht Squadron; Yacht Club Costa Smeralda (Founder Pres.) (Sardinia); Pevero Golf (Founder Pres.) (Sardinia).

AGA KHAN, Prince Sadruddin; Consultant to the Secretary-General of the UN, since 1978; Founding Member and President, Groupe de Bellerive; Founding Member and Chairman, Independent Commission on Internal Humanitarian Issues, 1983; *b* 17 Jan. 1933; *s* of His late Highness Sir Sultan Mohamed Shah, Aga Khan III, GCSI, GCIE, GCVO and of Andrée Joséphine Caron; *m* 1957, Nina Sheila Dyer (marr. diss., 1962); *m* 1972, Catherine Aleya Sursock. *Educ:* Harvard Univ. (BA); Harvard Grad. Sch. Arts and Sciences; Centre of Middle Eastern Studies. Unesco Consultant for Afro-Asian Projects, 1958; Head of Mission and Adviser to UN High Comr for Refugees, 1959–60; Unesco Special Consultant to Dir-Gen., 1961; Exec. Sec., Internat. Action Cttee for Preservation of Nubian Monuments, 1961; UN Dep. High Comr for Refugees, 1962–65; UN High Comr for Refugees, 1965–77. Vice Pres., WWF. Hon. Citizen Geneva, 1978. UN Human Rights Award, 1978; Hammarsköld Medal, German UN Assoc., 1979; Olympia Prize, Alexander S. Onassis Foundn, 1982. Grand Cross: Order of St Silvestro (Papal), 1963; Order of Homayoun (Iran), 1967; Order of the Royal Star of Great Comoro (Comoro Is), 1970; Order of the Two Niles (First Class) Sudan, 1973; Commander's Cross with Star, Order of Merit of Polish People's Republic, 1977; Commandeur de la Légion d'Honneur (France), 1979. *Publications:* Lectures on refugee problems delivered to RSA and Acad. Internat. Law, The Hague; Violations of Human Rights and Mass Exodus, study for UN Commn on Human Rights, 1981. *Recreations:* Islamic art, sailing, ski-ing, hiking, kite-flying. *Address:* Château de Bellerive, 1245 Collonge-Bellerive, Canton of Geneva, Switzerland. *Clubs:* Travellers' (Paris); Knickerbocker (New York).

AGAR, family name of **Earl of Normanton.**

AGER, Rear-Adm. Kenneth Gordon, CB 1977; retired Royal Navy 1977; *b* 22 May 1920; *s* of Harold Stoddart Ager and Nellie Maud (*née* Tate); *m* 1944, Muriel Lydia Lanham; one *s* one *d*. *Educ:* Dulwich Central Sch. and Royal Navy. Called up for War Service, RN, 1940; Sub Lt (Special Br.) RNVR, 1943; Lieut (Electrical) RN, 1944; Weapons and Elect. Engr; Comdr (WE) 1958; Captain (E) 1966; Fleet Weapons and Elect. Engr Officer, 1969–71; Sen. Officers' War Course, 1971–72; CSO (Eng) to Flag Off. Scotland and NI, and Captain Fleet Maintenance, Rosyth, 1972–75; Rear-Adm. (E) 1975; Flag Off., Admiralty Interview Bd, 1975–77. *Recreations:* golf, bowls, reading. *Address:* South View, Washington Road, Storrington, West Sussex RH20 4DE. *Club:* Royal Naval and Royal Albert Yacht (Portsmouth).

AGLIONBY, Francis John; His Honour Judge Aglionby; a Circuit Judge, since 1980; *b* 17 May 1932; *s* of Francis Basil and Marjorie Wycliffe Aglionby; *m* 1967, Susan Victoria Mary Vaughan; one *s* one *d*. *Educ:* Charterhouse; Corpus Christi Coll., Oxford (MA). Barrister, Inner Temple, 1956, Bencher, 1976; a Recorder of the Crown Court, 1975–80. Chancellor of Diocese of Birmingham, 1971–; also of Portsmouth, 1978–. Held Home Office enquiry into Horserace Totalisator Bd's bets transmissions procedures, 1979. *Recreations:* variable. *Address:* 36 Bark Place, W2 4AT. *T:* 01–229 7303. *Club:* Brooks's.

AGNELLI, Dr Giovanni; industrialist; car manufacturer, Italy; Chairman: Fiat, since 1966; Istituto Finanziario Industriale, since 1959; IFI International, Luxembourg; Agnelli Foundation, since 1968; Chairman, Editrice La Stampa; *b* Turin, Italy, 12 March 1921; *s* of Edoardo Agnelli, and *g s* of Giovanni Agnelli, founder of Fabbrica Italiana Automobili Torino (FIAT); *m* 1953, Princess Marella Caracciolo di Castagneto; one *s* one *d*. *Educ:* Turin. DrJur, Univ. of Turin, 1943. Member Board: SKF, Göteborg, 1965–; Eurafrance, Paris, 1972–; Mediobanca, 1962–; Credito Italiano, 1967–; Assonime; Unione Industriale di Torino; Member: Internat. Adv. Cttee, Chase Manhattan Bank, NY; Eur. Adv. Council, United Technologies Corp., 1983–; Internat. Indust. Conf., San Francisco; Exec. Cttee, Trilateral Commn, Paris; Groupe des Présidents des Grandes Entreprises Européennes, Bruxelles. Governor, Atlantic Inst. for Internat. Affairs, Paris. *Address:* 10 Corso Marconi, Turin, Italy. *T:* 65651.

AGNEW, Sir Anthony Stuart; *see* Agnew, Sir J. A. S.

AGNEW OF LOCHNAW, Sir Crispin Hamlyn, 11th Bt *cr* 1629; Chief of the Name and Arms of Agnew; Advocate; Unicorn Pursuivant of Arms, since 1981; *b* 13 May 1944; *s* of (Sir) Fulque Melville Gerald Noel Agnew of Lochnaw, 10th Bt and of Swanzie, *d* of late Major Esmé Nourse Erskine, CMG, MC; *S* father, 1975; *m* 1980, Susan (journalist, broadcaster; formerly Advertising Exec.), *yr d* of J. W. Strang Steel, Logie, Kirriemuir, Angus; one *d*. *Educ:* Uppingham; RMA, Sandhurst. Major RARO (retd

1981), late RHF. Slains Pursuivant of Arms to Lord High Constable of Scotland, 1978–81. Leader: Army Expedn to E Greenland, 1968; Jt Services Expedn to Chilean Patagonia, 1972–73; Army Expedn to Api, NW Nepal, 1980; Member: RN Expedn to E Greenland, 1966; Jt Services to Elephant Island (Antarctica), 1970–71; Army Nuptse Expedn, 1975; Jt British and Royal Nepalese Army Everest Expedn, 1976 (reached the South Col). *Publications:* articles in newspapers and magazines, and in legal and heraldic jls. *Recreations:* mountaineering, sailing (Yacht Pippa's Song), heraldry. *Heir: cousin* Andrew David Quentin Agnew, PhD [*b* 31 Dec. 1929; *m* 1957, Shirley, *d* of late James Arnold Smithson; three *s*]. *Address:* 6 Palmerston Road, Edinburgh EH9 1TN. *Clubs:* Army and Navy, Alpine, Alpine Ski.

AGNEW, Sir Garrick; *see* Agnew, Sir R. D. G.

AGNEW, Sir Geoffrey (William Gerald), Kt 1973; Chairman, Thos Agnew & Sons, Ltd (Fine Art Dealers), 1965–82; *b* 11 July 1908; *er s* of late Charles Gerald Agnew and Olive Mary (*née* Danks); *m* 1934, Hon. Doreen Maud Jessel, *y d* of 1st Baron Jessel, CB, CMG; two *s* one *d*. *Educ:* Eton (Oppidan Scholar, 1923; Hon. Fellow, 1976); Trinity College, Cambridge (BA 1930; MA 1971); Munich. Joined Thos Agnew & Sons (Fine Art Dealers), 1931, a Managing Director, 1937–. Assistant master (History), Eton College, 1939–45. Chairman, Evelyn (Agnew) Nursing Home, Cambridge, 1955–81, Pres., 1981–. A Permanent Steward, 1955– and a Vice-Pres., 1968–, Artists' General Benevolent Institution; President, Fine Art Provident Institution, 1963–66; Chairman: St George's Arts Trust, King's Lynn, 1966–73; Society of London Art Dealers, 1970–74; Friends of the Courtauld Institute, 1970–; Vice-Pres., Guildhall of St George, King's Lynn, 1975–. *Publications:* Agnew's 1817–1967, 1967; various broadcasts on art published in the Listener. *Recreations:* works of art, travel, gardening. *Address:* Flat 3, 6 Onslow Square, SW7. *T:* 01–589 8536; Egmere Farm House, Walsingham, Norfolk. *T:* Walsingham 247. *Clubs:* Brooks's, Garrick.

AGNEW, Sir Godfrey; *see* Agnew, Sir W. G.

AGNEW, Sir (John) Anthony Stuart, 4th Bt, *cr* 1895; *b* 25 July 1914; *s* of Sir John Stuart Agnew, 3rd Bt, TD, DL, and Kathleen (*d* 1971), *d* of late I. W. H. White, Leeds; *S* father, 1957. *Educ:* privately in Switzerland. *Heir: b* Major George Keith Agnew, TD [*b* 25 Nov. 1918; *m* 1948, Anne Merete Louise, *yr d* of Baron Johann Schaffalitzky de Muckadell, Fyn, Denmark; two *s*]. *Address:* c/o Blackthorpe Farm, Rougham, Bury St Edmunds, Suffolk.

AGNEW, Commander Sir Peter (Garnett), 1st Bt *cr* 1957; *b* 9 July 1900; *s* of late C. L. Agnew; *m* 1st, 1928, Enid Frances (*d* 1982), *d* of late Henry Boan, Perth, Western Australia, and *widow* of Lt Col O. Marescaux; one *s*; 2nd, 1984, Mrs Julie Marie Watson. *Educ:* Repton. Entered Royal Navy, 1918; ADC to Governor of Jamaica, 1927–28; retired, 1931; returned to service at sea, Aug. 1939 (despatches). MP (C) Camborne Div. of Cornwall, 1931–50; PPS to Rt Hon. Walter Runciman, President of Board of Trade, 1935–37, and to Rt Hon. Sir Philip Sassoon, First Commissioner of Works, 1937–39; an Assistant Government Whip, May-July, 1945; a Conservative Whip, Aug. 1945–Feb. 1950; contested (C) Falmouth and Camborne Div., Feb. 1950; MP (C) South Worcs, 1955–66. Member of House of Laity, Church Assembly, 1935–65; a Church Comr for England, 1948–68; Trustee, Historic Churches Preservation Trust, 1968–. Chm., Iran Society, 1966–73; Internat. Pres., European Centre of Documentation and Information, 1974–76. Order of Homayoun (Iran), 1973; Kt Grand Cross, Order of Civil Merit (Spain), 1977. *Recreation:* travelling. *Heir: s* Quentin Charles Agnew-Somerville [*b* 8 March 1929; *m* 1963, Hon. April, *y d* of 15th Baron Strange; one *s* two *d*. *Educ:* RNC Dartmouth]. *Address:* 2 Smith Square, SW1P 3HS. *T:* 01–222 7179. *Clubs:* Carlton, Buck's.

AGNEW, Peter Graeme, MBE 1946; BA; retired; Deputy Chairman, Bradbury Agnew & Co. Ltd (Proprietors of Punch), 1969–84; *b* 7 April 1914; *s* of late Alan Graeme Agnew; *m* 1937, Mary Diana (*née* Hervey); two *s* two *d*. *Educ:* Kingsmead, Seaford; Stowe School; Trinity College, Cambridge. Student Printer, 1935–37. Joined Bradbury Agnew & Co. Ltd, 1937. RAFVR 1937. Served War of 1939–45; Demobilised, 1945, as Wing Commander. *Recreations:* sailing, gardening. *Address:* The Old House, Manaccan, Helston, Cornwall TR12 6HR. *T:* Manaccan 468.

See also Col N. T. Davies.

AGNEW, Sir (Robert David) Garrick, Kt 1983; CBE 1978; Director, Australian Bank Ltd (Founding Chairman, 1981–85); *b* 21 Sept. 1930; *s* of late R. Agnew; *m* 1959, Fay (*d* 1981), *d* of Colin Ferguson; two *s* one *d* (and one *d* decd). *Educ:* Perth Modern Sch.; Univ. of WA; Ohio State Univ. (BS); Harvard Business Sch. Chm., Agnew Clough; Dir, Qantas Airways; former Dir, Australian Industry Develt Corp. *Recreation:* swimming (rep. Australia, Olympic Games, 1948, 1952 and Commonwealth Games, 1950). *Address:* 16 Victoria Avenue, Claremont, WA 6010, Australia. *Club:* Weld (Perth).

AGNEW, Rudolph Ion Joseph; Chairman, since 1983, Group Chief Executive, since 1978, and Member, Committee of Managing Directors, since 1986, Consolidated Gold Fields PLC; *b* 12 March 1934; *s* of Rudolph John Agnew and Pamela Geraldine (*née* Campbell); *m* 1980, Whitney Warren. *Educ:* Downside School. Commissioned officer, 8th King's Royal Irish Hussars, 1953–57. Joined Consolidated Gold Fields, 1957; Dep. Chm., 1978–82. FBIM; Fellow of the Game Conservancy. Trustee, WWF, 1983–. *Recreation:* shooting. *Address:* (office) 31 Charles II Street, St James's Square, SW17 4AG. *Club:* Cavalry and Guards.

AGNEW, Spiro Theodore, (Ted); *b* Baltimore, Md, 9 Nov. 1918; *s* of Theodore S. Agnew and Margaret Akers; *m* 1942, Elinor Isabel Judefind; one *s* three *d*. *Educ:* Forest Park High Sch., Baltimore; Johns Hopkins Univ.; Law Sch., Univ. Baltimore (LLB). Served War of 1939–45 with 8th and 10th Armd Divs, 1941–46, company combat comdr in France and Germany (Bronze Star). Apptd to Zoning Bd of Appeals of Baltimore County, 1957 (Chm., 1958–61); County Executive, Baltimore County, 1962–66; Governor of Maryland, 1967–68; Vice-President of the United States, 1969–73. Republican. With Pathlite Inc., Crofton, Md, 1974–. *Publication:* The Canfield Decision, 1976. *Recreations:* golf, tennis.

AGNEW, Stanley Clarke, CB 1985; FEng 1985; FICE; Chief Engineer, Scottish Development Department, since 1976; *b* 18 May 1926; *s* of Christopher Gerald Agnew and Margaret Eleanor Agnew (*née* Clarke); *m* 1950, Isbell Evelyn Parker (*née* Davidson); two *d*. *Educ:* Royal Belfast Academical Instn; Queen's Univ., Belfast (BSc Civil Eng., 1947). FIWE, FIPHE; Hon. FIWPC. Site Engr, Farrans Ltd, 1947–50; Asst Engr, Fife CC, 1950–52; Site Agent, R. J. McLeod (Contractors) Ltd, 1952–53; Sen. Asst Engr, Dumfries CC, 1953–57; Resident Engr, Blyth & Blyth, 1957–59; Engr to Dungannon and Clogher RDCs, 1959–62; Eng. Inspector, Scottish Develt Dept, 1962–68, Dep. Chief Engr, 1968–75. *Recreations:* golf, photography, motoring, gardening. *Address:* Duncraig, 52 Blinkbonny Road, Edinburgh EH4 3HX. *T:* 031–332 4072. *Clubs:* Royal Commonwealth Society; Murrayfield Golf (Edinburgh).

AGNEW, Sir (William) Godfrey, KCVO 1965 (CVO 1953); CB 1975; Chairman, Lady Clare Ltd, since 1970; Vice-Chairman, Sun Life Assurance Society plc, 1983–84 (Director, 1974–84); Director, Sun Life Properties Ltd, 1980–84; *b* 11 Oct. 1913; *o s* of late Lennox Edelsten Agnew and Elsie Blyth (*née* Nott), Tunbridge Wells; *m* 1st, 1939, Ruth Mary (*d* 1962), *e d* of late Charles J. H. O'H. Moore, CVO, MC, and late Lady Dorothie Moore; three *s* three *d;* 2nd, 1965, Lady (Nancy Veronica) Tyrwhitt, *widow* of Adm. Sir St John Reginald Joseph Tyrwhitt, 2nd Bt, KCB, DSO, DSC; two step *s* one step *d. Educ:* Tonbridge. Solicitor, 1935; entered Public Trustee Office, 1936. Served RA and Surrey and Sussex Yeomanry, 1939–46; Major, 1945. Senior Clerk, Privy Council Office, 1946–51; Clerk of the Privy Council, 1953–74 (Deputy Clerk, 1951–53); Dep. Sec., Cabinet Office, 1972–74. Director: Seaway Shipping Agencies Ltd, 1971–80; Seaway Holdings Ltd, 1971–80; Artagen Properties Ltd, 1976–80. Chairman, Sembal Trust, 1967–73. Mem., Bd of Hon. Tutors, Council of Legal Educn, Univ. of WI, 1973–; Consultant: CEI, 1974–79; University Coll., Cardiff, 1982–84; Univ. of Wales Inst. of Science and Technol., 1982–84. Hon. FIMechE, 1968; Hon. FIMunE, 1974; Hon. FCIBSE (formerly Hon. FCIBS), 1975; Hon. FICE, 1984. *Address:* Pinehurst, Friary Road, South Ascot, Berks SL5 9HD. *T:* Ascot 20036. *Clubs:* Army and Navy; Swinley Forest Golf; Rye Golf.

See also Sir J. M. H. Pollen, Bt, Sir Reginald Tyrwhitt, Bt.

AGUIRRE, Marcelino O.; *see* Oreja Aguirre.

AGUTTER, Jennifer Ann; actress; *b* 20 Dec. 1952; *d* of Derek and Catherine Agutter. *Educ:* Elmhurst Ballet School, Camberley. *Films:* East of Sudan, 1964; Ballerina, 1964; Gates of Paradise, 1967; Star, 1968; Walkabout, I Start Counting, The Railway Children, 1969 (Royal Variety Club Most Promising Artist, 1971); Logan's Run, 1975; The Eagle Has Landed, Equus (BAFTA Best Supporting Actress, 1977), 1976; Dominique, Clayton and Catherine, 1977; The Riddle of the Sands, Sweet William, 1978; The Survivor, 1980; An American Werewolf in London, 1981; Secret Places, 1983; *stage:* School for Scandal, 1972; Rooted, Arms and the Man, The Ride Across Lake Constance, 1973; National Theatre: The Tempest, Spring Awakening, 1974; Hedda, Betrayal, 1980; Breaking the Silence, 1985; Royal Shakespeare Co.: Arden of Faversham, Lear, King Lear, The Body, 1982–83; *television includes:* Long After Summer, 1967; The Wild Duck, The Cherry Orchard, The Snow Goose (Emmy Best Supporting Actress), 1971; A War of Children, 1972; The Man In The Iron Mask, 1976; School Play, 1979; Amy, 1980; Love's Labours Lost, This Office Life, 1984; Silas Marner, 1985. *Publication:* Snap, 1983.

AH-CHUEN, Sir Moi Lin Jean (Etienne), Kt 1980; Minister of Local Government, Mauritius, 1969–76; Chairman: Chue Wing & Co. Ltd, since 1977; Oceania Travel Agents Ltd, since 1977; The Mauritius Union Assurance Co. Ltd, since 1977; *b* 22 Feb. 1911. *Educ:* De La Salle School; Mauritius. Mem., Mauritius Legislative Assembly, 1948–76. Founder (Chm. and Man. Dir), ABC Store (Chue Wing & Co. Ltd), 1931–68; Dir, Chinese Daily News, 1942–. Alternately Pres. and Vice-Pres., Chinese Chamber of Commerce, 1942–64. Chairman: Union Shipping Ltd; ABC Motors Co. Chm., Chinese Nat. Coll. Pres., Chinese Cultural Centre, 1968–; mem. or past-mem., various other social and charitable organisations. *Recreations:* bridge, travelling, sports. *Address:* 5 Reverend Lebrun Street, Rose Hill, Mauritius. *T:* 4–3804. *Clubs:* Mauritius Turf, Chinese Traders (Mauritius).

AHERN, Most Rev. John; *see* Cloyne, Bishop of, (RC).

AHMAD, Khurshid; Chairman, Institute of Policy Studies, Islamabad, Pakistan, since 1979; Chairman, Board of Trustees, Islamic Foundation, Leicester; Member, Senate of Pakistan; *b* 23 March 1934; three *s* three *d. Educ:* Karachi Univ. (LLB; MA Economics; MA Islamic Studies); Leicester Univ. Dir-Gen., Islamic Foundn, 1973–78; Federal Minister for Planning and Develt and Dep. Chm., Planning Commn, Govt of Pakistan, 1978–79. *Publications:* Essays on Pakistan Economy (Karachi), 1958; An Analysis of Munir Report (Lahore), 1958; (ed) Studies in the Family Law of Islam (Karachi), 1960; (ed) The Quran: an Introduction (Karachi), 1966; The Prophet of Islam (Karachi), 1967; Principles of Islamic Education (Lahore), 1970; Fanaticism, Intolerance and Islam (Lahore), 1970; Islam and the West (Lahore), 1972; The Religion of Islam (Lahore), 1973; (ed) Islam: its meaning and message (London, Islamic Council of Europe), 1976; Development Strategy for the Sixth Plan (Islamabad), 1983; *for Islamic Foundation, Leicester:* Islam: Basic Principles and Characteristics, 1974; Family Life in Islam, 1974; Islamic Perspectives: Studies in honour of Maulana Mawdudi, 1979; The Quran: Basic Teachings, 1979; Studies in Islamic Economics, 1980; contrib. The Third World's Dilemma of Development, Non-Aligned Third World Annual, (USA) 1970. *Recreations:* travelling, reading. *Address:* 223 London Road, Leicester LE2 1ZE. *T:* Leicester 700725; Institute of Policy Studies, House No 3, Street No 56, Shalimar 6/4, Islamabad, Pakistan. *T:* Islamabad 051-824930.

'AHO, Siaosi Taimani; High Commissioner for Tonga in London, since 1986; concurrently Ambassador for Tonga to EEC, Belgium, FRG, France, USSR, Denmark, Italy, Luxemburg, USA; *b* 18 Jan. 1939; *s* of Tenita Kilisimari 'Aho and Otolose 'Aho; *m* 1984, Sitola 'Aho; one *s. Educ:* Auckland Grammar Sch.; Auckland Teachers' Coll., Auckland Univ. (BA). Asst Teacher, Tonga High Sch., 1965; Asst Sec., Min. of Health, 1972; 1st Sec., Tonga High Commn, London, 1976; Asst Sec., Min. of For. Affairs, 1980; Sec. to Cabinet, 1982; Sec. for For. Affairs, 1983. *Recreations:* watching sports, playing snooker, fishing, gardening. *Address:* Greenbanks, Lyndale, NW2. *T:* 01–794 9291.

AHRENDS, Peter; Partner, Ahrends Burton & Koralek, Architects, since 1961; Professor of Architecture, Bartlett School of Architecture and Planning, University College London, since 1986; *b* 30 April 1933; *s* of Steffen Bruno Ahrends and Margarete Marie Sophie Ahrends; *m* 1954, Elizabeth Robertson; two *d. Educ:* Architectural Assoc. Sch. of Architecture (Dipl., Hons). ARIBA 1959. Architecture carried out by Ahrends Burton & Koralek in fields of educn, libraries, housing, planning, industrial bldgs, etc, 1961–; exhibitions of drawings and works of Ahrends Burton & Koralek: RIBA Heinz Gall., 1980; RIAI, 1981; Museum of Finnish Arch., 1982; Alvar Aalto Museum, Finland, 1982. Part-time teaching posts and workshops in schs of arch. in Britain and abroad, 1960–; ext. examr, schs of arch., 1965–; Hon. Vis. Prof., Kingston Polytechnic Sch. of Arch., 1982–83. *Publications:* papers and articles in RIBA Jl and other prof. jls. *Recreation:* architecture. *Address:* 7 Chalcot Road, NW1 8LH. *T:* 01–586 3311. *Club:* Architectural Association.

AIKEN, Joan Delano, (Mrs Julius Goldstein); writer of historical, mystery and children's novels, plays and poetry; *b* 4 Sept. 1924; *d* of Conrad Potter Aiken and Jessie McDonald; *m* 1st, 1945, Ronald George Brown (*d* 1955); one *s* one *d;* 2nd, 1976, Julius Goldstein. *Educ:* Wychwood Sch., Oxford. Inf. Officer, subseq. Librarian, UN London Inf. Centre, 1943–49; Features Editor, Argosy magazine, 1955–60; Copy-writer, J. Walter Thompson London office, 1960–61; time thereafter devoted to writing. Mem., Soc. of Authors. Guardian Award for Children's Literature, 1969; Lewis Carroll Award, 1970. *Publications:* (most also published in USA and as paperbacks): The Silence of Herondale, 1964; The Fortune Hunters, 1965; Trouble with Product X, 1966 (Beware of the Bouquet, USA 1966); Hate Begins at Home, 1967 (Dark Interval, USA 1967); The Ribs of Death, 1967 (The Crystal Crow, USA 1968); The Windscreen Weepers (stories), 1969; The Embroidered Sunset, 1970; The Butterfly Picnic, 1970 (A Cluster of Separate Sparks, USA 1972); Died on a Rainy Sunday, 1972; Voices in an Empty House, 1975; Castle Barebane, 1976; Last Movement, 1977; The Five-Minute Marriage, 1977; The Smile of the Stranger, 1978; A Touch of Chill (horror stories), 1979; The Lightning Tree, 1980 (The Weeping Ash, USA); The Girl from Paris, 1982; The Way to Write for Children, 1982; A Whisper in the Night, 1982; Foul Matter, 1983; Mansfield Revisited, 1984; *for children:* (many also published in USA): All You've Ever Wanted (stories), 1953; More Than You Bargained For (stories), 1955; The Kingdom and the Cave, 1960; The Wolves of Willoughby Chase, 1962; Black Hearts in Battersea, 1964; Night Birds on Nantucket, 1966; The Whispering Mountain, 1968; A Necklace of Raindrops (stories), 1968; A Small Pinch of Weather (stories), 1969; Night Fall, 1969; Armitage, Armitage, Fly Away Home (stories), USA 1970; Smoke From Cromwell's Time, USA 1970; The Cuckoo Tree, 1971; The Kingdom Under the Sea (folktales), 1971; The Green Flash (fantasy and horror stories), USA 1971; A Harp of Fishbones (stories), 1972; Winterthing (play), USA 1972; The Mooncusser's Daughter (play), USA 1973; Winterthing & The Mooncusser's Daughter, 1973; Midnight is a Place, 1974; Arabel's Raven, USA 1974; Tales of Arabel's Raven, 1974; Not What You Expected (stories), USA 1974; Tale of a One-Way Street (stories), 1976; The Skin Spinners (poems), USA 1976; A Bundle of Nerves (horror stories), 1976; The Angel Inn (trans. from French), 1976; The Faithless Lollybird (stories), 1977; Mice and Mendelson, 1978; Go Saddle the Sea, 1978; Street (play), USA 1978; Arabel and Mortimer, 1979; The Shadow Guests, 1980; The Stolen Lake, 1981; Mortimer's Cross, 1983; Bridle the Wind, 1983; Up the Chimney Down and Other Stories, 1984; Fog Hounds, Wind Cat, Sea Mice, 1984; The Kitchen Warriors, 1984; The Last Slice of Rainbow, 1985; Mortimer Says Nothing, 1985; Dido and Pa, 1986; Past Eight O'Clock, 1986. *Recreations:* listening to music, looking at art, travel, reading, gardening, walking, talking to friends. *Address:* The Hermitage, East Street, Petworth, West Sussex GU28 0AB. *T:* Petworth 42279. *Clubs:* Society of Authors, Writers' Guild, Crime Writers' Association, PEN; Mystery Writers of America.

AIKEN, Air Chief Marshal Sir John (Alexander Carlisle), KCB 1973 (CB 1967); Director General of Intelligence, Ministry of Defence, 1978–81; *b* 22 Dec. 1921; *s* of Thomas Leonard and Margaret Aiken; *m* 1948, Pamela Jane (*née* Bartlett); one *s* one *d. Educ:* Birkenhead School. Joined RAF, 1941; Fighter Sqdns, Europe and Far East, 1942–45; Fighter Comd, 1946–47; CFS, 1948; Staff of RAF Coll., Cranwell, 1948–50; OC Univ. of Birmingham Air Sqdn, 1950–52; Staff Coll., 1953; HQ Fighter Comd, 1954–55; OC 29 Fighter Sqdn, 1956–57; jssc 1958; Headquarters AF North, 1958–60; Air Min., 1960–63; Station Comdr, RAF Finningley, 1963–64; Air Cdre Intelligence, Min. of Defence, 1965–67; idc 1968; Dep. Comdr, RAF, Germany, 1969–71; Dir-Gen. Training, RAF, 1971–72; Head of Economy Project Team (RAF), 1972–73; AOC-in-C, NEAF, Comdr British Forces Near East, and Administrator, Sovereign Base Areas, Cyprus, 1973–76; Air Member for Personnel, 1976–78. Pres., RAFA, 1984–85 (Chm., Central Council, 1981–84). Mem. Council, Chatham House, 1984–. *Recreations:* ski-ing, music. *Club:* Royal Air Force.

AIKENS, Richard John Pearson; QC 1986; *b* 28 Aug. 1948; *s* of late Basil Aikens and of Jean Eleanor Aikens; *m* 1979, Penelope Anne Hartley Rockley (*née* Baker); two *s* two step *d. Educ:* Norwich Sch.; St John's Coll., Cambridge (MA). Called to Bar, Middle Temple, 1973; Harmsworth scholarship, 1974; in practice, 1974–; a Junior Counsel to the Crown, Common Law, 1981–86. Mem., Supreme Court Rules Cttee, 1984–. *Recreations:* music, gardening, wine. *Address:* 1 Brick Court, Temple, EC4. *T:* 01–583 0777. *Club:* Leander.

AIKIN, Olga Lindholm, (Mrs J. M. Driver); Visiting Lecturer, London Business School, since 1985; Director, General Law Division, Lion International (Keiser Enterprises Inc.), since 1985; Council Member, Advisory Conciliation and Arbitration Service, since 1982; *b* 10 Sept. 1934; *d* of Sidney Richard Daly and Lilian May Daly (*née* Lindholm); *m* 1st, 1959, Ronald Sidney Aikin (marr. diss. 1979); one *d;* 2nd, 1982, John Michael Driver; one step *d. Educ:* London School of Economics (LLB); King's Coll., London. Called to Bar, Gray's Inn, 1956. Assistant Lecturer, King's Coll., London, 1956–59; Lecturer, London School of Economics, 1959–70; London Business School: Sloan Fellowship Programme, 1970–71; Vis. Lectr, 1971–79; Lectr in Law, 1979–85. *Publications:* Employment, Welfare and Safety at Work, 1971 (with Judith Reid); articles in Personnel Management. *Recreation:* collecting cookery books and pressed glass. *Address:* 22 St Luke's Road, W11 1DP. *T:* 01–727 9791.

See also Hon. Francis Daly.

AIKMAN, Colin Campbell, PhD; consultant; *b* 24 Feb. 1919; *s* of Colin Campbell Aikman and Bertha Egmont Aikman (*née* Harwood); *m* 1952, Betty Alicia, *d* of R. Y. James; three *d* (one *s* decd). *Educ:* Palmerston North Boys' High Sch.; Victoria University Coll., Wellington, NZ (LLM); London Sch. of Economics (PhD). Law Clerk in Legal Offices, 1935–41; Barrister and Solicitor of Supreme Court of New Zealand, 1940–41; Personal Asst to Air Secretary, Air Dept (NZ), 1942–43; Prime Minister's Dept and Dept of External Affairs (Legal Adviser, 1949–55), 1943–55; Mem. NZ Delgn to San Francisco Conf., 1945; Prof. of Jurisprudence and Constitutional Law, Victoria Univ. of Wellington (Dean of Law Faculty, 1957–59, 1962–67), 1955–68; Mem. Council, NZ Inst. of Internat. Affairs (Nat. Pres., 1960–63, Dir. 1979–84), 1955–; Advr to NZ Govt on Constitutional Develt of Cook Is, Western Samoa and Niue, 1956–68, 1975; Vice-Chancellor, The Univ. of the South Pacific, Suva, Fiji, 1968–74; NZ High Comr to India, accredited also to Bangladesh and Nepal, 1975–78. Member: Council of Volunteer Service Abroad (Inc.) (Chm. 1962–65), 1962–68; NZ Nat. Commn for UNESCO, 1957–65; Univ. of Waikato Academic Cttee, Council and Professorial Bd, 1963–66; (Chm.) Nat. Adv. Council on Teacher Trng, 1963–68; Law Revision Commn and Public and Administrative Law Reform Cttee, 1966–68; Adv. Cttee on External Aid and Develt, 1980–. Trustee, Norman Kirk Meml Trust, 1979–. Queen's Silver Jubilee Medal. *Publications:* (co-author): A Report to Members of the Legislative Assembly of the Cook Islands on Constitutional Development, 1963; New Zealand, The Development of its Laws and Constitution (ed Robson), 1967 (2nd edn); New Zealand's Record in the Pacific Islands in the Twentieth Century (ed Angus Ross), 1969; contribs to NZ Internat. Review. *Recreations:* golf, cricket, carpentry. *Address:* 28 Korokoro Road, Petone, New Zealand. *Clubs:* Wellington; Wellington Golf (Heretaunga).

AILESBURY, 8th Marquess of, *cr* 1821; **Michael Sydney Cedric Brudenell-Bruce;** Bt 1611; Baron Brudenell 1628; Earl of Cardigan 1661; Baron Bruce 1746; Earl of Ailesbury 1776; Earl Bruce 1821; Viscount Savernake 1821; 30th Hereditary Warden of Savernake Forest; Lt RHG, 1946; Member London Stock Exchange since 1954; *b* 31 March 1926; *e s* of 7th Marquess of Ailesbury and Joan (*d* 1937), *d* of Stephen Salter, Ryde, Isle of Wight; *S* father, 1974; *m* 1st, 1952, Edwina Sylvia de Winton (from whom he obtained a divorce, 1961), *yr d* of Lt-Col Sir (Ernest) Edward de Winton Wills, 4th Bt; one *s* two *d;* 2nd, 1963, Juliet Adrienne (marr. diss. 1974), *d* of late Hilary Lethbridge Kingsford and of Mrs Latham Hobrow, Marlborough; two *d;* 3rd, 1974, Mrs Caroline Elizabeth Romilly, *d* of late Commander O. F. M. Wethered, RN, DL, JP. *Educ:* Eton. *Heir:* *s* Earl of Cardigan, *qv. Address:* Stable Block, Tottenham House, near Marlborough, Wilts. *Club:* Sloane.

AILSA, 7th Marquess of, *cr* 1831; **Archibald David Kennedy,** OBE 1968; Baron Kennedy, 1452; Earl of Cassillis, 1509; Baron Ailsa (UK), 1806; *b* 3 Dec. 1925; *s* of 6th Marquess of Ailsa and Gertrude Millicent (*d* 1957), *d* of Gervas Weir Cooper, Wordwell Hall, Bury St Edmunds; *S* father 1957; *m* 1954, Mary, 7th *c* of John Burn, Amble; two *s* one *d*. *Educ:* Nautical Coll., Pangbourne. Scots Guards, 1943–47; Royal Northumberland Fusiliers, 1950–52. National Trust for Scotland, 1953–56. Territorial Army, 1958–68; Hon. Col, Ayrshire Battalion ACF, 1980–. Patron, Isle of Man Railway Soc., 1978–; Chm., Scottish Assoc. of Boys Clubs, 1978–82. *Recreations:* walking, motoring, modelling, sailing. *Heir:* *s* Earl of Cassillis, *qv*. *Address:* Blanefield, Kirkoswald, Ayrshire KA19 8HH. *Clubs:* Carlton; New (Edinburgh); Royal Yacht Squadron.
See also Rev. N. W. Drummond.

AILWYN, 4th Baron *cr* 1921; **Carol Arthur Fellowes,** TD 1946; *b* 23 Nov. 1896; 4th *s* of 1st Baron Ailwyn, PC, KCVO, KBE, 2nd *s* of 1st Baron de Ramsey, and Hon. Agatha Eleanor Augusta Jolliffe, *d* of 2nd Baron Hylton; *S* brother, 1976; *m* 1936, Caroline (Cudemore) (*d* 1985), *d* of late Maynard Cowan, Victoria, BC; one adopted step *d*. *Educ:* Royal Naval Colls, Osborne and Dartmouth. Lieut, 3rd and 2nd Norfolk Regt., 1916–19; served in Mesopotamia, 1917–19. Subsequently fruit farmer; Agent to Earl of Strafford, 1930–52. Formed 334 (Barnet) AA Company, RE (T), 1937; served War as Major RA (T) comdg 334 Co. and on staff of Anti-Aircraft Command, 1939–44. Asst Sec., RASE, 1952–59; Sec., Norfolk Club, Norwich, 1964–69; Trustee, Lord Wandsworth Coll., 1955–72; Governor, Felixstowe Coll., 1960–74 (Chm., 1966–72). Late JP Herts and Middlesex. *Heir:* none. *Address:* The Depperhaugh, Hoxne, Eye, Suffolk IP21 5BX. *Club:* (Hon. Member) Norfolk (Norwich).

AINLEY, Sir (Alfred) John, Kt 1957; MC 1940; Chief Justice, Kenya, 1963–68; retired; Chairman of Industrial Tribunals, 1972–76; *b* 10 May 1906; *o s* of late Rev. A. Ainley, Cockermouth, Cumb; *m* 1935, Mona Sybil Wood (*d* 1981); one *s* two *d*. *Educ:* St Bees Sch.; Corpus Christi, Oxford. Called to Bar, 1928; Magistrate, Gold Coast, 1935; Crown Counsel (Gold Coast), 1936; Puisne Judge, Uganda, 1946–55; Chief Justice of Eastern Region, Nigeria, 1955–59; Combined Judiciary of Sarawak, N Borneo and Brunei, 1959–62. Served War of 1939–45, West African Forces, E Africa and Burma. *Address:* Horrock Wood, Watermillock, Penrith, Cumbria.

AINLEY, David Geoffrey, CEng, FIMechE, FRAeS; Deputy Director (Projects and Research), Military Vehicles and Engineering Establishment, Chertsey, 1978–84; *b* 5 July 1924; *s* of Cyril Edward and Constance Ainley; *m* 1st, 1948, Dorothy Emily (*née* Roberts); one *s* one *d*; 2nd, 1959, Diana Margery Hill (*née* Sayles); one *d*. *Educ:* Brentwood Sch., Essex; Queen Mary Coll., London Univ. (BSc, 1st Cl. Hons). Engine Dept, RAE, Farnborough, 1943–44; Power Jets (R&D) Ltd, 1944–46; National Gas Turbine Estabt, Pyestock, 1946–66; idc 1967; Dir of Engine Develt, MoD (Procurement Exec.), 1968–78. George Stephenson Research Prize, IMechE, 1953. *Publications:* contrib. books and learned jls on gas turbine technology. *Recreations:* painting, sketching, golf. *Address:* 20 Hampton Close, Church Crookham, Aldershot, Hants GU13 0LB. *T:* Fleet 622577.

AINLEY, Sir John; *see* Ainley, Sir A. J.

AINSCOW, Robert Morrison; Deputy Secretary, Overseas Development Administration, Foreign and Commonwealth Office, since 1986; *b* 3 June 1936; *s* of Robert M. Ainscow and Hilda Ainscow (*née* Cleminson); *m* 1965, Faye Bider; one *s* one *d*. *Educ:* Salford Grammar School; Liverpool Univ. (BA Econ Hons). Statistician: Govt of Rhodesia and Nyasaland, 1957–61; UN Secretariat, New York, 1961–65 and 1966–68; Dept of Economic Affairs, London, 1965–66. Ministry of Overseas Development: Economic Adviser, 1968–70; Senior Economic Adviser, 1971–76; Head, South Asia Dept, 1976–79; Under Secretary, FCO (ODA), 1979–86. Chm., OECD (DAC) Working Party on Financial Aspects of Develt Assistance, 1982–86. *Address:* Overseas Development Administration, Eland House, Stag Place, SW1E 5DH.

AINSWORTH, Sir David; *see* Ainsworth, Sir T. D.

AINSWORTH, Sir (Thomas) David, 4th Bt *cr* 1916; *b* 22 Aug. 1926; *s* of Sir Thomas Ainsworth, 2nd Bt, and Marie Eleanor (May) (*d* 1969), *d* of Compton Charles Domvile; *S* half-brother, 1981; *m* 1957, Sarah Mary, *d* of late Lt-Col H. C. Walford; two *s* two *d*. *Educ:* Eton. Formerly Lt 11th Hussars. *Recreations:* shooting, fishing. *Heir:* *s* Anthony Thomas Hugh Ainsworth, *b* 30 March 1962. *Address:* Ballyneale House, Ballingarry, Co. Limerick; 80 Elm Park Gardens, SW10. *Club:* Cavalry and Guards.

AIRD, Captain Sir Alastair (Sturgis), KCVO 1984 (CVO 1977; LVO 1969); Comptroller to Queen Elizabeth the Queen Mother since 1974; *b* 14 Jan. 1931; *s* of Col Malcolm Aird; *m* 1963, Fiona Violet, LVO 1980, *d* of Lt-Col Ririd Myddelton, *qv*; two *d*. *Educ:* Eton; RMA Sandhurst. Commnd 9th Queen's Royal Lancers, 1951; served in BAOR; Adjt 9th Lancers, 1956–59; retd from Army, 1964. Equerry to Queen Elizabeth the Queen Mother, 1960; Asst Private Sec. to the Queen Mother, 1964. *Recreations:* shooting, fishing, golf. *Address:* 31B St James's Palace, SW1A 1BA. *T:* 01–839 6700.

AIRD, Sir (George) John, 4th Bt *cr* 1901; Chairman and Managing Director, Sir John Aird & Co Ltd, since 1969; *b* 30 Jan. 1940; *e s* of Sir John Renton Aird, 3rd Bt, MVO, MC, and of Lady Priscilla Aird, *yr d* of 2nd Earl of Ancaster; *S* father, 1973; *m* 1968, Margaret, *yr d* of Sir John Muir, Bt, *qv*; one *s* two *d*. *Educ:* Eton; Oxford Univ.; Harvard Business Sch. MICE. Trainee, Sir Alexander Gibb & Partners, 1961–65; Manager, John Laing & Son Ltd, 1967–69. *Recreations:* farming, skiing. *Heir:* *s* James John Aird, *b* 12 June 1978. *Address:* Grange Farm, Evenlode, Moreton-in-Marsh, Glos GL56 0NT. *T:* Moreton-in-Marsh 50607. *Club:* White's.

AIREDALE, 4th Baron, *cr* 1907; **Oliver James Vandeleur Kitson;** Bt, *cr* 1886; Deputy Chairman of Committees, House of Lords, since 1961; Deputy Speaker, House of Lords, since 1962; *b* 22 April 1915; *o s* of 3rd Baron Airedale, DSO, MC, and Sheila Grace (*d* 1935), *d* of late Frank E. Vandeleur, London; *S* father, 1958; unmarried. *Educ:* Eton; Trinity College, Cambridge. Major, The Green Howards. Called to the Bar, Inner Temple, 1941. *Heir:* none. *Address:* (seat) Ufford Hall, Stamford, Lincs.

AIREY OF ABINGDON, Baroness *cr* 1979 (Life Peer), of Abingdon in the County of Oxford; **Diana Josceline Barbara Neave Airey;** *b* 7 July 1919; *d* of late Thomas A. W. Giffard, MBE, JP, and late Angela Erskine Giffard (*née* Trollope); *m* 1942, Airey Middleton Sheffield Neave, DSO, OBE, MC (assassinated, March 1979), MP Abingdon; two *s* one *d*. *Educ:* privately and abroad. Quartermaster, RAF Hospital, 1939; later with Foreign Office (PWE) and Polish Ministry of Information, London. Then, in politics with her husband. Member: N Atlantic Assembly, 1983–84; Select Cttee on Eur. Communities (Sub-Cttee F), 1986–. Trustee: Nat. Heritage Meml Fund, 1980–; Imperial War Mus., 1984–; Dorney Wood Trust, 1980–; Stansted Park Foundn, 1983–. Governor: St Mary's Sch., Wantage, 1959–; Abingdon Sch., 1981–. Freedom, City of London, 1980. *Recreations:* reading, theatre, opera. *Address:* House of Lords, SW1.

AIREY, Sir Lawrence, KCB 1978 (CB 1976); Chairman of the Board of Inland Revenue, 1980–86; *b* 10 March 1926; *s* of late Lawrence Clark Airey and Isabella Marshall Pearson; *m* 1953, Patricia Anne, *d* of late Edward George Williams and Mary Selway; two *s* one *d*. *Educ:* Newcastle Royal Grammar Sch.; Peterhouse, Cambridge. Entered Civil Service, 1949; General Register Office, 1949–56; Cabinet Office, 1956–58; HM Treasury, 1958–79: Under-Sec., 1969–73; Dep. Sec., 1973–77; Second Perm. Sec., 1977–79. Research Fellow, Nuffield Coll., Oxford, 1961–62. Mem., Bd of British Nat. Oil Corp., 1976–77. *Recreations:* collecting books; music. *Address:* Lions House, Berwick-on-Tweed, Northumberland.

AIRLIE, 13th Earl of, *cr* 1639 (*de facto* 10th Earl, 13th but for the Attainder); **David George Coke Patrick Ogilvy,** KT 1985; GCVO 1984; PC 1984; DL; Baron Ogilvy of Airlie, 1491; Captain late Scots Guards; Lord Chamberlain of HM Household, since 1984; Chancellor, Royal Victorian Order, since 1984; *b* 17 May 1926; *e s* of 12th (*de facto* 9th) Earl of Airlie, KT, GCVO, MC, and Lady Alexandra Marie Bridget Coke (*d* 1984), *d* of 3rd Earl of Leicester, GCVO; *S* father, 1968; *m* 1952, Virginia Fortune Ryan (*see* Countess of Airlie); three *s* three *d*. *Educ:* Eton. Lieutenant Scots Guards, 1944; serving 2nd Battalion Germany, 1945; Captain, ADC to High Comr and C-in-C Austria, 1947–48; Malaya, 1948–49; resigned commission, 1950. Ensign, 1975–85, Lieutenant, 1985–, Queen's Body Guard for Scotland, Royal Company of Archers. Chm., Schroders plc, 1977–84; Dep. Chm., Gen. Accident Fire & Life Assurance Corp. Ltd., 1975–; Chm., Ashdown Investment Trust Ltd, 1968–82; Director: J. Henry Schroder Wagg & Co. Ltd, 1961–84 (Chm., 1973–77); Scottish & Newcastle Breweries plc, 1969–83; The Royal Bank of Scotland Gp, 1983–. Treasurer, Scouts Assoc. DL Angus, 1964. Governor, Nuffield Nursing Homes Trust, 1985–. *Heir:* *s* Lord Ogilvy, *qv*. *Address:* Cortachy Castle, Kirriemuir, Angus, Scotland. *T:* Cortachy 231; 5 Swan Walk, Chelsea SW3 4JJ.
See also Hon. Angus Ogilvy, Sir Hereward Wake.

AIRLIE, Countess of; Virginia Fortune Ogilvy, CVO 1983; Lady of the Bedchamber to the Queen since 1973; *b* 9 Feb. 1933; *d* of John Barry Ryan, Newport, RI, USA; *m* 1952, Lord Ogilvy (now Earl of Airlie, *qv*); three *s* three *d*. *Educ:* Brearley School, New York City. Founder Governor, Cobham School, Kent, 1958. Member: Royal Fine Art Commission, 1975–; Industrial Design Panel, British Rail, 1974–; Scottish Board, British Council, 1974–. Trustee, Tate Gallery, 1983– (Chm. Friends of Tate Gallery, 1978–83). *Address:* Cortachy Castle, Kirriemuir, Angus, Scotland; 5 Swan Walk, SW3.

AISHER, Sir Owen (Arthur), Kt 1981; Founder Member, Marley Ltd, 1934, Chairman, 1945–82, now Life President, Marley plc; *b* 28 May 1900; *s* of late Owen Aisher, Branksome Park, Poole; *m* 1921, Ann Allingham; two *s* two *d*. Mem. Court of Paviors; Pres., RYA, 1970–75; has had many successes in off-shore racing, inc. Fastnet Race, 1951; was elected Yachtsman of the Year, 1958. *Recreations:* sailing, fishing, shooting. *Address:* Faygate, South Godstone, Surrey. *Clubs:* Reform, City Livery; Royal Thames Yacht; RORC (Adm. 1969–75); Ranelagh Sailing; Little Ship (Pres.); Royal Southern Yacht (Hamble); Royal Yacht Squadron, Royal London Yacht, Island Sailing (Adm.) (Cowes); Bembridge Sailing; Royal Motor Yacht (Poole); New York YC, Seawanhaka Corinthian Yacht (USA); Royal St George Yacht (Eire); Royal Cape Yacht (South Africa).

AITCHISON, Sir Charles (Walter de Lancey), 4th Bt, *cr* 1938; *b* 27 May 1951; *er s* of Sir Stephen Charles de Lancey Aitchison, 3rd Bt, and (Elizabeth) Anne (Milburn), *er d* of late Lt-Col Edward Reed, Ghyllheugh, Longhorsley, Northumberland; *S* father 1958; *m* Susan, *yr d* of late Edward Ellis; one *s* one *d*. Lieut, 15/19th The King's Royal Hussars, 1974; RARO 1974–78. *Recreations:* motor sport, shooting. *Heir:* *s* Rory Edward Aitchison, *b* 7 March 1986. *Address:* Howden Dene, Corbridge, Northumberland. *Club:* Northern Counties.
See also R. A. Cookson.

AITCHISON, Craigie (Ronald John), ARA 1978; painter; *b* 13 Jan. 1926; *yr s* of late Rt Hon. Lord Aitchison, PC, KC, LLD. *Educ:* Scotland; Slade Sch. of Fine Art. British Council Italian Govt Scholarship for painting, 1955; Edwin Austin Abbey Premier Scholarship, 1965; Lorne Scholarship, 1974–75. One-man Exhibitions: Beaux Arts Gall., 1959, 1960, 1964; Marlborough Fine Art (London) Ltd, 1968; Compass Gall., Glasgow, 1970; Basil Jacobs Gall., 1971; Rutland Gall., 1975; Knoedler Gall., 1977; Kettle's Yard Gall., Cambridge, 1979; Serpentine Gall. (major retrospective, 1953–81), 1981–82; Artis, Monte Carlo, Monaco, 1986. Exhibited: Galouste Gulbenkian Internat. Exhibn, 1964; Il Tempo del imagine, 2nd Internat. Biennale, Bologna, 1967; Modern British Painters, Tokyo, Japan, 1969; 23rd Salon Actualité de l'Esprit, Paris, 1975. Pictures in public collections: Tate Gall., Arts Council, Contemp. Art Soc., Scottish National Gall. of Modern Art, and Nat. Gall. of Melbourne, Australia. 1st Johnson Wax Prize, Royal Acad., 1982. *Address:* 32 St Mary's Gardens, SE11. *T:* 01–582 3708; Montecastelli San Gusme, Siena, Italy.

AITCHISON, June Rosemary, (Mrs T. J. Aitchison); *see* Whitfield, J. R.

AITHRIE, Viscount; Andrew Victor Arthur Charles Hope; *b* 22 May 1969; *s* and *heir* of Earl of Hopetoun, *qv*. A Page of Honour to the Queen Mother, 1985–.

AITKEN, family name of **Baron Beaverbrook.**

AITKEN, Ian Levack; Political Editor, The Guardian, since 1975; *b* 19 Sept. 1927; *s* of George Aitken and Agnes Levack Aitken; *m* 1956, Dr Catherine Hay Mackie, *y d* of late Maitland Mackie, OBE; two *d*. *Educ:* King Alfred Sch., Hampstead; Regent Street Polytechnic; Lincoln Coll., Oxford (BA PPE); LSE. Served Fleet Air Arm, 1945–48. HM Inspector of Factories, 1951; Res. Officer, CSEU, 1952; Industrial Reporter, Tribune, 1953–54; Industrial Reporter, subseq. Foreign Correspondent and Political Correspondent, Daily Express, 1954–64; political staff, The Guardian, 1964–. Gerald Barry Award for journalism, 1984. *Recreation:* music. *Address:* 52A North Hill, N6. *T:* 01–340 5914. *Clubs:* Garrick, Wig and Pen.
See also Baron John-Mackie, Baron Mackie of Benshie, Sir M. Mackie.

AITKEN, Prof. John Thomas; Professor of Anatomy, University of London at University College, 1965–80, now Emeritus; *b* 6 May 1913; *s* of David and Helen Aitken; *m* 1941, Doreen Violet Whitaker; two *s* two *d*. *Educ:* High School, Glasgow; Grammar School, Hull; Glasgow University. MB, ChB 1936, MD 1950. University College, London, 1940–80. *Publications:* Manual of Human Anatomy (in collab.); Essential Anatomy (in collab.); papers on regeneration of nerves and muscles, in various jls. *Recreation:* gardening. *Address:* Woodpeckers Cottage, Sway Road, Brockenhurst, Hants SO4 7RX. *T:* Lymington 22493.

AITKEN, Jonathan William Patrick; MP (C) Thanet South, since 1983 (Thanet East, Feb. 1974–1983); *b* 30 Aug. 1942; *s* of late Sir William Aitken, KBE and of Hon. Lady Aitken, MBE, JP; *m* 1979, Lolicia Olivera, *d* of Mr and Mrs O. Azucki, Zürich; one *s* two *d*. *Educ:* Eton Coll.; Christ Church, Oxford. MA Hons Law. Private Sec. to Selwyn Lloyd, 1964–66; Foreign Corresp., London Evening Standard, 1966–71; Man. Dir, Slater Walker (Middle East) Ltd, 1973–75; Co-founder and Chm., Aitken Hume Internat., 1980–; Chm., Aitken Hume PLC, 1981–; Dir, TV-am Ltd, 1981–. Mem., Select Cttee on Employment, 1979–82. Pres., London Road Runners Club, 1984–. *Publications:* A Short Walk on the Campus, 1966; The Young Meteors, 1967; Land of Fortune: A Study of

Australia, 1969; Officially Secret, 1970; articles in Spectator, Sunday Telegraph, Sydney Morning Herald, Washington Post, etc. *Recreations:* squash, ski-ing, marathon running. *Address:* 8 Lord North Street, SW1. *Clubs:* Pratt's, Turf, Beefsteak.

AITKEN, Prof. Martin Jim, FRS 1983; FSA; Professor of Archaeometry, since 1985, and Deputy Director, Research Laboratory for Archaeology, since 1957, Oxford University; Fellow of Linacre College, Oxford, since 1965; *b* 11 March 1922; *s* of Percy Aitken and Ethel Brittain; *m* Joan Killick; one *s* four *d*. *Educ:* Stamford Sch., Lincs; Wadham Coll. and Clarendon Lab., Oxford Univ. (MA, DPhil). Served War, RAF Radar Officer, 1942–46 (Burma Star, 1945). Mem., Former Physical Soc., 1951–; MRI, 1972–. Editor, Archaeometry, 1958–. *Publications:* Physics and Archaeology, 1961, 2nd edn 1974; Thermoluminescence Dating, 1985. *Recreations:* sailing, dinghy-racing. *Address:* White Cottage, Islip, Oxford OX5 2SY.

AITKEN, Sir Robert (Stevenson), Kt 1960; MD (New Zealand), DPhil (Oxford); FRCP, FRACP; DL; retired; *b* NZ; *s* of late Rev. James Aitken; *m* 1929, Margaret G. Kane; one *s* two *d*. *Educ:* Gisborne High School, Gisborne, NZ; University of Otago, Dunedin, NZ; Oxford. Medical Qualification in New Zealand, 1922; Rhodes Scholar, Balliol College, Oxford, 1924–26; attached to Medical Unit, The London Hospital, 1926–34; Reader in Medicine, British Post-Graduate Medical School, Univ. of London, 1935–38; Regius Prof. of Medicine, Univ. of Aberdeen, 1939–48; Vice-Chancellor, Univ. of Otago, Dunedin, NZ, 1948–53; Vice-Chancellor, Univ. of Birmingham, 1953–68. Vice-Chm. Association of Univs of the British Commonwealth, 1955–58; Dep. Chm., UGC, 1968–73; Chairman: Committee of Vice-Chancellors and Principals, 1958–61; Birmingham Repertory Theatre, 1962–74. DL Co. Warwick, 1967, West Midlands, 1974. Hon. FRCPE; Hon. FDSRCS; Hon. DCL Oxford; Hon. LLD: Dalhousie, Melbourne, Panjab, McGill, Pennsylvania, Aberdeen, Newfoundland, Leicester, Birmingham, Otago; Hon. DSc: Sydney, Liverpool. *Publications:* papers in medical and scientific journals. *Address:* 6 Hintlesham Avenue, Birmingham B15 2PH.

AJAYI, Prof. Jacob Festus Ade; Professor of History, University of Ibadan, since 1963; *b* 26 May 1929; *s* of Chief E. Ade Ajayi and late Mrs C. Bolajoko Ajayi; *m* 1956, Christie Aduke Martins; one *s* four *d*. *Educ:* University College, Ibadan; University College, Leicester; Univ. of London; BA, PhD (London). Research Fellow, Inst. of Historical Research, London, 1957–58; Lectr, Univ. of Ibadan, 1958–62, Sen. Lectr, 1962–63; Dean, Faculty of Arts, 1964–66; Asst to Vice-Chancellor, 1966–68. Fellow, Centre for Advanced Study in the Behavioural Sciences, Stanford, Calif, 1970–71; Vice-Chancellor, Univ. of Lagos, 1972–78. Member: UN University Council, 1974–80 (Chm., 1976–77); Nat. Archives Cttee, Nigeria, 1961–72; Nat. Antiquities Commn, Nigeria, 1970–74; Exec. Council, Internat. African Inst. London, 1971– (Chm., 1975–); Exec. Bd, Assoc. of African Univs, 1974–80; Admin. Bd., Internat. Assoc. of Univs, 1980–; Pres., Historical Soc. of Nigeria, 1972–81; Pres., Internat. Congress of African Studies, 1978–85. Hon. LLD Leicester, 1975; Hon. DLitt Birmingham, 1984. Fellow, Hist. Soc. of Nigeria, 1980; Overseas FRHistS, 1982. Traditional titles, Bobapitan of Ikole-Ekiti and Onikoyi of Ife, 1983. *Publications:* Milestones in Nigerian History, 1962; (ed, with Ian Espie) A Thousand Years of West African History, 1964; (with R. S. Smith) Yoruba Warfare in the Nineteenth Century, 1964; Christian Missions in Nigeria: the making of a new elite, 1965; (ed, with Michael Crowder) A History of West Africa, vol. I, 1972; vol. II, 1974; (ed jtly) The University of Ibadan, 1948–73, 1973; (ed with Bashir Ikara) Evolution of Political Culture in Nigeria, 1985; (ed with M. Crowder) A Historical Atlas of Africa, 1985; contribs to Jl Historical Soc. of Nigeria, Jl of African History, etc. *Recreations:* dancing, tennis. *Address:* History Department, University of Ibadan, Nigeria.

AKEHURST, Lt. Gen. Sir John (Bryan), KCB 1984; CBE 1976; Commander, UK Field Army and Inspector General, Territorial Army, since 1984; *b* 12 Feb. 1930; *s* of late Geoffrey and Doris Akehurst; *m* 1955, Shirley Ann, *er d* of late Major W. G. Webb, MBE, and of Ethel Webb; one *s* one *d* decd. *Educ:* Cranbrook Sch.; RMA, Sandhurst. Commnd Northamptonshire Regt, 1949; Malay Regt (despatches), 1952–55; Adjt, 5th Northamptonshire Regt (TA), 1959–60; Staff Coll., Camberley, 1961; Brigade Major, 12 Infantry Bde Gp, 1962–64; Instructor, Staff Coll., Camberley, 1966–68; commanded 2nd Royal Anglian Regt, 1968–70; Directing Staff, IDC/RCDS, 1970–72; Comdt, Jun. Div., Staff Coll., 1972–74; Comdr, Dhofar Bde, Sultan of Oman's Armed Forces, 1974–76; Dep. Mil. Sec. (A), MoD (Army), 1976–79; GOC 4th Armoured Div., BAOR, 1979–81; Comdt, The Staff Coll., Camberley, 1982–83. Sen. Mil. Visitor to Saudi Arabia, 1985–. Dep. Col, Royal Anglian Regt, 1981–. Mem. Council, RUSI, 1985–. Chm., 1982–84, Pres., 1984–, Army Golf Assoc.; Vice Patron, Army Officers' Golf Soc., 1986– (Pres., 1983). Governor, Harrow Sch., 1982–. Order of Oman, 3rd Class (mil.), 1976. *Publication:* We Won a War, 1982. *Recreations:* golf, trout fishing, travel, avoiding MoD. *Address:* Dresden Cottage, 46 Vicarage Street, Warminster, Wilts BA12 8JF. *Clubs:* Army and Navy; Tidworth Golf.

AKERLOF, Prof. George Arthur, PhD; Cassel Professor of Economics, London School of Economics and Political Science, 1978–81; *b* 17 June 1940; *s* of Gosta C. Akerlof and Rosalie C. Akerlof; *m* 1978, Janet Yellen. *Educ:* Yale Univ. (BA 1962); MIT (PhD 1966). Fellowships: Woodrow Wilson, 1962–63; National Science Co-op., 1963–66; Fulbright, 1967–68; Guggenheim, 1973–74. Univ. of Calif, Berkeley: Asst Prof. of Econs, 1966–70; Associate Prof., 1970–77; Prof., 1977–78. Vis. Prof., Indian Statistical Inst., New Delhi, 1967–68. Sen. Economist, Council of Econ. Advisors, USA, 1973–74; Vis. Economist, Bd of Governors of Fed. Reserve System, USA, 1977–78. *Publications:* contrib. American Econ. Rev., Econ. Jl, Qly Jl Econs, Jl Polit. Econ., Rev. of Econ. Studies, Internat. Econ. Rev., Jl Econ. Theory, Indian Econ. Rev., and Rev. of Econs and Stats. *Club:* Piggy (Center Harbor, NH, USA).

AKERS, John Fellows; Chairman, International Business Machines Corp., since 1986; *b* 1934; *m* 1960, Susan Davis; one *s* two *d*. *Educ:* Yale Univ. (BS). International Business Machines Corp., 1960–: Vice Pres., Data Processing Div., 1973–74, Pres. 1974–76; IBM Vice Pres., Asst Gp Exec., Data Processing Product Gp, 1976–78; IBM Vice Pres., Gp Exec., Data Processing Marketing Gp, 1978–81, Inf. Systems and Communications Gp, 1981–82, IBM Sen. Vice Pres., 1982–83; Dir, IBM, 1983–; Pres., 1983–; Chief Exec. Officer, 1985–. Director: Council for Financial Aid to Educn, 1984–; New York Times Co., 1985–; Trustee: MMA; CIT; Inst. for Advanced Study; Adv. Bd, Yale Sch. of Org. and Management; Governor, United Way of America. *Address:* (office) IBM Corp., Old Orchard Road, Armonk, NY 10504, USA.

AKERS-DOUGLAS, family name of **Viscount Chilston.**

AKERS-JONES, Sir David, KBE 1985; CMG 1978; Chief Secretary, Hong Kong, since 1985; *b* 14 April 1927; *s* of Walter George and Dorothy Jones; *m* 1951, Jane Spickernell; one *d* (one *s* decd). *Educ:* Worthing High Sch.; Brasenose Coll., Oxford (MA). British India Steam Navigation Co., 1945–49. Malayan Civil Service (studied Hokkien and Malay), 1954–57; Hong Kong Civil Service, 1957–; Government Secretary: for City and New Territories, 1973–83; for Dist Admin, 1983–85. Vice-Pres. Hong Kong Football Assoc., 1967–. *Recreations:* painting, gardening, walking, music. *Address:* Government Secretariat, Hong Kong. *Clubs:* Athenæum, Oriental, Royal Over-Seas League; Hong Kong (Hong Kong).

AKHTAR, Prof. Muhammad, FRS 1980; Professor of Biochemistry, since 1973, and Chairman of the School of Biochemical and Physiological Sciences, since 1983, University of Southampton; *b* 23 Feb. 1933; *m* 1963, Monika E. Schurmann; two *s*. *Educ:* Punjab Univ., Pakistan (MSc 1st class 1954); Imperial College, London (PhD, DIC 1959). Research Scientist, Inst. for Medicine and Chemistry, Cambridge, Mass, USA, 1959–63; University of Southampton: Lecturer in Biochemistry, 1963–66; Senior Lectr, 1966–68; Reader, 1968–73. Member: Chemical Soc. of GB; American Chemical Soc.; Biochemical Soc. of GB; Council, Royal Soc., 1984–; Founding Fellow, Third World Acad. of Sciences. Sitara-I-Imtiaz (Pakistan), 1981. *Publications:* numerous works on: enzyme mechanisms; synthesis and biosynthesis of steroids and porphyrins; biochemistry of vision; synthesis of anti-microbial compounds. *Address:* Department of Biochemistry, University of Southampton, Southampton SO9 3TU. *T:* Southampton 559122, ext. 8338.

AKINKUGBE, Prof. Oladipo Olujimi, CON 1979; Officier de l'Ordre National de la République de Côte d'Ivoire, 1981; MD, DPhil; FRCP, FWACP, FAS; Professor of Medicine, University of Ibadan, Nigeria, since 1968; *b* 17 July 1933; *s* of late Chief David Akinbobola and of Chief (Mrs) Grace Akinkugbe; *m* 1965, Dr Folasade Modupeore Dina; two *s*. *Educ:* Univs of Ibadan, London (MD), Liverpool (DTM&H) and Oxford (DPhil). FRCP 1968; FWACP 1975; FAS 1980. House Phys., London Hosp., 1958; House Surg., King's Coll. Hosp., London, 1959; Commonwealth Res. Fellow, Balliol Coll. and Regius Dept of Medicine, Oxford, 1962–64; Head of Dept of Medicine, 1972, Dean of Medicine, 1970–74, and Chm., Cttee of Deans, 1972–74, Univ. of Ibadan; Vice-Chancellor: Univ. of Ilorin, 1977–78 (Principal, 1975–77); Ahmadu Bello Univ., Zaria, 1978–79. Rockefeller Vis. Fellow, US Renal Centres, 1966; Vis. Fellow in Medicine, Univs of Manchester, Cambridge and London, 1969; Vis. Prof. of Medicine, Harvard Univ., 1974–75; Vis. Fellow, Balliol Coll., Oxford, 1981–82. Adviser on Postgrad. Med. Educn to Fed. Govt of Nigeria, 1972–75; Member: Univ. Grants Commn, Uganda Govt; OAU Scientific Panels on Health Manpower Develt; Council, Internat. Soc. of Hypertension, 1982–; internat. socs of hypertension, cardiology, and nephrology; Med. Res. Soc. of GB; Scientific Adv. Panel, CIBA Foundn; WHO Expert Adv. Panels on Cardiovascular Diseases, 1973–78, on Health Manpower 1979–; Sec. to WHO 1984 Technical Discussions. Pro-Chancellor, and Chm. of Council, Univ. of Port-Harcourt, Nigeria, 1986–. Hon. DSc Ilorin, 1982. *Publications:* High Blood Pressure in the African, 1972; (ed) Priorities in National Health Planning, 1974; (ed) Cardiovascular Disease in Africa, 1976; papers on hypertension and renal disease in African, Eur. and Amer. med. jls, and papers on med. and higher educn. *Recreations:* music, gardening. *Address:* Department of Medicine, University of Ibadan, Ibadan, Nigeria. *T:* 400550. *Clubs:* Rotary International; Dining (Ibadan).

ALANBROOKE, 3rd Viscount *cr* 1946; **Alan Victor Harold Brooke;** Baron Alanbrooke, 1945; *b* 24 Nov. 1932; *s* of 1st Viscount Alanbrooke, KG, GCB, OM, GCVO, DSO, and Benita Blanche (*d* 1968), *d* of Sir Harold Pelly, 4th Bt; *S* half-brother, 1972. *Educ:* Harrow; Bristol Univ. (BEd Hons 1976). Qualified teacher, 1975. Served Army, 1952–72; Captain RA, retired. *Heir:* none.

ALBEE, Edward; American dramatist; *b* 12 March 1928. *Publications: plays:* The Zoo Story, 1959; The Death of Bessie Smith, 1960; The Sandbox, 1961; The American Dream, 1961; Who's Afraid of Virginia Woolf?, 1962; (adapted from Carson McCullers' novella) The Ballad of the Sad Café, 1963; Tiny Alice, 1964; (adapted from the novel by James Purdy) Malcolm, 1965; A Delicate Balance, 1966 (Pulitzer Prize, 1967); (adapted from the play by Giles Cooper) Everything in the Garden, 1967; Box and Quotations from Chairman Mao Tse-Tung, 1968; All Over, 1972; Seascape, 1975 (Pulitzer Prize, 1975); Listening, 1975; Counting the Ways, 1976; The Lady from Dubuque, 1978; Lolita (adapted from V. Nabakov), 1979; The Man Who Had Three Arms, 1980; Finding the Sun, 1981; Walking, 1982. *Address:* 14 Harrison Street, New York, NY 10013, USA.

ALBEMARLE, 10th Earl of, *cr* 1696; **Rufus Arnold Alexis Keppel;** Baron Ashford, 1696; Viscount Bury, 1696; *b* 16 July 1965; *s* of Derek William Charles Keppel, Viscount Bury (*d* 1968), and Marina, *yr d* of late Count Serge Orloff-Davidoff; *S* grandfather, 1979. *Heir: uncle* Hon. Walter Arnold Crispian Keppel, DSC [*b* 6 Dec. 1914; *m* 1941, Aline Lucy, *d* of late Brig.-Gen. John Harington, CB, CMG, DSO; two *s* one *d*]. *Address:* Piazza di Bellosguardo 10, 50124 Florence, Italy.

ALBEMARLE, Countess of, (Diana Cicely), DBE 1956; Chairman: Development Commission, 1948–74; The Drama Board, 1964–78; *b* 6 Aug. 1909; *o c* of John Archibald Grove; *m* 1931, 9th Earl of Albemarle, MC (*d* 1979); one *d*. *Educ:* Sherborne Sch. for Girls. Norfolk County Organiser, WVS, 1939–44. Chairman: Exec. Cttee, Nat. Fedn of Women's Institutes, 1946–51; Departmental Cttee on Youth Service, 1958–60; Nat. Youth Employment Council, 1962–68. Vice-Chm., British Council, 1959–74. Member: Arts Council, 1951; Royal Commn on Civil Service, 1954; Harkness Fellowship Cttee of Award, 1963–69; UGC, 1956–70; Standing Commn on Museums and Galleries, 1958–71; English Local Govt Boundary Commn, 1971–77; Youth Develt Council, 1960–68; Council, Univ. of E Anglia, 1964–72. Life Trustee, Carnegie UK Trust (Chm., 1977–82); Trustee of: The Observer until 1977; Glyndebourne Arts Trust, 1968–80. RD Councillor, Wayland, Norfolk, 1935–46. Hon. DLitt Reading, 1959; Hon. DCL Oxon, 1960; Hon. LLD London, 1960. *Recreations:* gardening, reading. *Address:* Seymours, Melton, Woodbridge, Suffolk. *T:* Woodbridge 2151.

See also Sir Hew Hamilton-Dalrymple.

ALBERT, Sir Alexis (François), Kt 1972; CMG 1967; VRD 1942; Chairman and Governing Director, Albert Investments (formerly J. Albert & Son Pty Ltd), Sydney, since 1962; Chairman, The Australian Broadcasting Company Pty Ltd, Sydney; *b* 15 Oct. 1904; *s* of late M. F. and M. E. Albert, Sydney; *m* 1934, Elsa K. R. (decd), *d* of late Capt. A. E. Lundgren, Sydney; three *s*. *Educ:* Knox College, Sydney; St Paul's College, University of Sydney. BEc 1930. Director: Amalgamated Television Services Pty Ltd, 1955–; Australasian Performing Right Association Ltd, 1946–76. Underwriting Member of Lloyd's, 1944–74; President, Royal Blind Soc. of NSW, 1962–78; Fellow of Council, St Paul's Coll., Univ. of Sydney, 1965–; Council, Nat. Heart Foundn of Aust., NSW Div. 1959–. RANR, 1918–49; Lt-Comdr, retd. Hon. ADC to Governors of NSW, 1937–57. KStJ 1985 (CStJ 1980; OStJ 1976). *Recreations:* swimming, yachting. *Address:* 25 Coolong Road, Vaucluse, NSW 2030, Australia; (office) 175 Macquarie Street, Sydney, NSW 2000. *T:* 232 2144. *Clubs:* Naval and Military; Australian, Union (Sydney); Royal Sydney Golf, Royal Sydney Yacht Squadron (Commodore 1971–75); New York Yacht.

ALBERT, Carl (Bert); Speaker, US House of Representatives, 1970–76; Member, Third Oklahoma District, 1947–76 (Democratic Whip, 1955–62; Majority Leader, 1962–71); *b* 10 May 1908, McAlester, Oklahoma; *s* of Ernest Homer and Leona Ann (Scott) Albert; *m* 1942, Mary Sue Greene Harmon; one *s* one *d*. *Educ:* Univ. of Oklahoma (AB 1931); Oxford Univ. (Rhodes Scholar, BA 1933, BCL 1934). Served US Army, 1941–46. Admitted Oklahoma Bar, 1935; Legal Clerk, Fed. Housing Admin, 1935–37; attorney and accountant, Sayre Oil Co., 1937–38; legal dept, Ohio Oil Co., 1939–40. Practised law: Oklahoma City, 1938; Mattoon, Ill, 1938–39; McAlester, Oklahoma, 1946–47. Bronze Star, 1945. *Recreation:* reading. *Address:* Route two, McAlester, Oklahoma 74501, USA.

ALBERTYN, Rt. Rev. Charles Henry; a Bishop Suffragan, Diocese of Cape Town, since 1983; *b* 24 Dec. 1928; *s* of Adam and Annie Albertyn; *m* 1965, Berenice Lategan; one *s* two *d*. *Educ:* Hewat Training College (Teacher's Diploma 1948); Diocesan Clergy School, Cape Town (LTh 1956). Teaching, 1948–52. Deacon 1955, priest 1956; Assistant, St Nicholas, Matroosfontein, 1955–60; Priest-in-charge, St Helena Bay, 1960–64; Assistant, St George's, Silvertown, 1965–70; Rector: Church of Holy Spirit, Heideveld, 1970–75; St Mary's, Kraaifontein, 1975–78; Church of Resurrection, Bonteheuwel, 1978–83; Canon of St George Cathedral, Cape Town, 1972–83; Archdeacon of Bellville, 1981–83. *Recreation:* watching soccer. *Address:* Bishopsholme, 18 Rue Ursula, Glenhaven, Bellville, Cape, S Africa. *T:* (021) 940184.

ALBERY, Sir Donald (Arthur Rolleston), Kt 1977; Former Chairman and Managing Director, The Wyndham Theatres Ltd, Donmar Productions Ltd and associated companies and Piccadilly Theatre Ltd; Director, Anglia Television Ltd, 1958–78; Chairman, Theatres' National Committee, 1974–78; *b* London, 19 June 1914; *s* of late Sir Bronson Albery and Una Gwen, *d* of T. W. Rolleston; *g s* of James Albery, dramatist and Mary Moore (Lady Wyndham), actress; *m* 1935, Rubina McGilchrist (decd); one *s*; *m* 1946, Heather Boys (marr. diss. 1974); two *s* one *d*; *m* 1978, Nobuko Uenishi. *Educ:* Alpine Coll., Switzerland. Gen. Man., Sadler's Wells Ballet, 1941–45; formerly Dir-Gen., London's Festival Ballet; Jt Patron with Dame Ninette de Valois of the Royal Ballet Benevolent Fund. Has presented or jtly presented plays: The Living Room, 1953; Birthday Honours, 1953; I Am a Camera, The Living Room (NY, with Gilbert Miller), 1954; The Remarkable Mr Pennypacker, Lucky Strike, Waiting for Godot, 1955; The Waltz of the Toreadors, Gigi, Grab Me a Gondola, 1956; Zuleika, Tea and Sympathy, Dinner With the Family, Paddle Your Own Canoe, 1957; The Potting Shed, George Dillon, Irma La Douce (NY, 1960), 1958; The Rose Tattoo, A Taste of Honey (NY, 1960), The Hostage (NY, 1960), The Complaisant Lover, One to Another, The Ring of Truth, The World of Suzie Wong, Make Me an Offer, 1959; Fings Ain't Wot They Used T' Be, A Passage to India, Call It Love, The Art of Living, Oliver! (NY, 1963; tour, 1965), The Tinker, 1960; The Miracle Worker, Breakfast for One, Sparrers Can't Sing, Beyond the Fringe (NY, 1962), Celebration, Bonne Soupe, 1961; Not to Worry, Blitz!, Semi-Detached, Fiorello!, 1962; Licence to Murder, The Perils of Scobie Prilt (tour), A Severed Head (NY, 1964), The Time of the Barracudas (US), 1963; The Fourth of June, The Poker Session, Who's Afraid of Virginia Woolf?, A Little Winter Love (tour), Entertaining Mr Sloane (NY, 1965), Instant Marriage, Carving a Statue, The Diplomatic Baggage, Portrait of a Queen, Jorrocks, The Prime of Miss Jean Brodie, 1966; Mrs Wilson's Diary, Spring and Port Wine, The Restoration of Arnold Middleton, 1967; The Italian Girl, Man of La Mancha, 1968; Conduct Unbecoming (NY, 1970; Australia, 1971), 1969; It's a Two Foot Six Inches Above the Ground World, Mandrake, Poor Horace, 1970; Popkiss, 1972; Very Good Eddie, The Thoughts of Chairman Alf, 1976. *Address:* 31 Avenue Princesse Grace, Monte Carlo, Monaco. *T:* 507082. *Club:* Garrick.

ALBERY, Prof. Wyndham John, FRS 1985; FRSC; Professor of Physical Chemistry, Imperial College of Science and Technology, since 1978; *b* 5 April 1936; *s* of late Michael James Albery, QC, and of Mary Lawton Albery. *Educ:* Winchester Coll.; Balliol Coll., Oxford (MA, DPhil). Weir Jun. Research Fellow, 1963, Fellow, 1964, University Coll., Oxford; Lectr, Phys. Chem., Univ. of Oxford, 1964. Vis. Fellow, Univ. of Minnesota, 1965; Vis. Prof., Harvard Univ., 1976. Tilden Lectr, RSC, 1979; Staff Orator, Imperial Coll., 1980; Sherman Fairchild Schol. Calif. Inst. of Tech., 1985. Chairman: SERC Chemistry Cttee, 1982; Electrochem. Gp, RSC, 1985. Mem. Council, Royal Instn, 1985. Writer for television series That Was The Week That Was, 1963–64; also (with John Gould) two musicals, Who Was That Lady?, and On The Boil. Curator, Oxford Playhouse, 1974–78; Governor, Old Vic, 1979. *Publications:* Ring-Disc Electrodes, 1971; Electrode Kinetics, 1975; papers in jls: Faraday I, Nature, and Jls of Electrochemical Soc., Electroanalytical Chemistry, etc. *Recreations:* theatre, skiing. *Address:* Flat 8, 53 Queens Gardens, W2. *T:* 01–402 0230. *Club:* Garrick.

ALBRECHT, Ralph Gerhart; American lawyer, barrister and international legal consultant; *b* Jersey City, NJ, 11 Aug. 1896; *s* of J. Robert Albrecht and Gertrude A. F. Richter; *m* 1936, Aillinn, *d* of late William Elderkin Leffingwell, Watkins Glen, NY; one *s*. *Educ:* Pennsylvania Univ. (AB); Harvard Univ. (JD). Admitted to Bar of NY, 1924, US Supreme Court, 1927; senior partner, Peaslee, Albrecht & McMahon, 1931–61, counsel to firm, 1961; gen. practice, specializing in foreign causes and internat. law. Special Dep. Attorney-Gen. of New York, 1926; Special Asst to US Attorney-Gen., 1945; Mem. US War Crimes Commn and leading trial counsel in Prosecution of Major Nazi War Criminals, before Internat. Mil. Tribunal, Nuremberg, 1945–46, prosecuted Hermann Goering; counsel to German steel, coal and chem. industries in decartelization procs before Allied High Commn for Germany, 1950–53. Mem. Republican County Cttee, NY Co., 1933–35; Harvard Univ. Overseers' Visiting Cttee to Faculty of Germanic Langs and Lits, 1949–63. Apprentice Seaman, USN Res. Force, 1918; served with Sqdn A (101st Cavalry, NY Nat. Guard), 1924–30; Comdr USNR, on active duty, 1941–45; Naval Observer, American Embassy, London, 1942 (letter of commendation from Chief of Naval Ops); Asst Dir OSS (War Crimes), 1945. Member: NY City Bar Assoc.; Amer. Bar Assoc.; Amer. Soc. of Internat. Law (Donor of Manley O. Hudson Gold Medal Award; Chm., Medal Cttee, 1958–78); Internat. Bar Assoc.; International Law Assoc.; World Peace Through Law Center (Cttee on Conciliation and Mediation of Disputes). Fellow: Nat. Audubon Society; Massachusetts Audubon Soc.; Amer. Geog. Soc., etc. Delegate, First Internat. Congress Comparative Law, The Hague, 1932. Republican; Mason. *Publications:* (with Prof. Walter B. Pitkin) Studies for Vocational Guidance of Recent School and College Graduates; contrib. Peter Markham's (pseud.) America Next, 1940. *Address:* 520 East 86th Street, New York, NY 10028, USA. *Clubs:* University, Harvard, Pilgrims of the US, Squadron A (all in NY).

ALBROW, Desmond; Assistant Editor, Sunday Telegraph, since 1976; *b* 22 Jan. 1925; *er s* of Frederick and Agnes Albrow; *m* 1950, Aileen Mary Jennings; one *s* three *d*. *Educ:* St Bede's Grammar Sch., Bradford; Keble Coll., Oxford (MA). On the Editorial Staff of the Yorkshire Observer, 1950–51, Manchester Guardian, 1951–56, Daily Telegraph, 1956–60; Sunday Telegraph, 1960–66: Chief Sub-Editor, News Editor, and Night Editor; Editor, Catholic Herald, 1966–71; Features Editor, Sunday Telegraph, 1971–76. *Recreations:* drinking in moderation and talking to excess; watching other people cultivate their gardens. *Address:* Totyngton Cottage, Victoria Road, Teddington, Mddx. *T:* 01–977 4220. *Clubs:* Garrick, Presscala.

ALBU, Austen Harry, BSc (Eng.); FCGI, CEng; *b* London, 21 Sept. 1903; *s* of Ferdinand and Beatrice Rachel Albu; *m* 1st, 1929, Rose (*d* 1956), *d* of Simon Marks, Newcastle; two *s*; 2nd, 1958, Dr Marie Jahoda, *qv*. *Educ:* Tonbridge School; City and Guilds College (Imperial College of Science and Technology). Works Manager, Aladdin Industries, Greenford, 1930–46. Dep. Pres., Govtl Sub-Commn, CCG, 1946–47. Dep. Dir, British Institute of Management, Feb.-Nov. 1948. MP (Lab) Edmonton, 1948–Feb. 1974; Minister of State, Dept of Economic Affairs, 1965–67. Fellow, Imp. Coll. of Science and Technology. DUniv Surrey, 1966. *Address:* 17 The Crescent, Keymer, Sussex BN6 8RB.

ALBU, Sir George, 3rd Bt, *cr* (UK) 1912, of Grosvenor Place, City of Westminster, and Johannesburg, Province of Transvaal, South Africa; farmer; *b* 5 June 1944; *o s* of Major Sir George Werner Albu, 2nd Bt, and Kathleen Betty (*d* 1956), *d* of Edward Charles Dicey, Parktown, Johannesburg; *S* father, 1963; *m* 1969, Joan Valerie Millar, London; two *d*. *Recreations:* horse racing, tennis, golf. *Heir:* none. *Address:* Glen Hamish Farm, PO Box 62, Richmond, Natal, 3780, South Africa. *T:* Richmond (Natal) 287. *Clubs:* Victoria (Pietermaritzburg, Natal); Richmond Country (Richmond, Natal).

ALBU, Marie, (Mrs A. H. Albu); *see* Jahoda, Prof. Marie.

ALCOCK, Prof. Leslie; Professor of Archaeology, University of Glasgow, since 1973; *b* 24 April 1925; *o s* of Philip John Alcock and Mary Ethel (*née* Bagley); *m* 1950, Elizabeth A. Blair; one *s* one *d*. *Educ:* Manchester Grammar Sch.; Brasenose Coll., Oxford. BA 1949, MA 1950. Supt of Exploration, Dept of Archaeology, Govt of Pakistan, 1950; Curator, Abbey House Museum, Leeds, 1952; Asst Lectr, etc, UC Cardiff, 1953. Prof. of Archaeology, UC Cardiff, 1973. Member: Bd of Trustees, Nat. Mus. of Antiquities, Scotland, 1973–85; Ancient Monuments Bd, Scotland, 1974–; Royal Commn on Ancient and Historical Monuments of Scotland, 1977–; Royal Commn on Ancient and Historical Monuments in Wales, 1986–. President: Cambrian Archaeological Assoc., 1982; Glasgow Archaeological Soc., 1984–85; Soc. of Antiquaries, Scotland, 1984–. FSA 1957; FRHistS 1969; FRSE 1976. *Publications:* Dinas Powys, 1963; Arthur's Britain, 1971; Cadbury/Camelot, 1972; articles and reviews in British and Amer. jls. *Recreations:* mountain and coastal scenery, baroque and jazz music. *Address:* 29 Hamilton Drive, Hillhead, Glasgow G12 8DN.

ALCOCK, Air Vice-Marshal Robert James Michael; Director General of Communications, Information Systems and Organisation (RAF), since 1985; *b* 11 July 1936; *s* of late William George and Doris Alcock; *m* 1965, Pauline Mary Oades; two *d*. *Educ:* Victoria College, Jersey; Royal Aircraft Establishment. CEng, FIMechE. Commissioned, Engineer Branch, RAF, 1959; RAF Tech. Coll., Henlow, 1961; Goose Bay, Labrador, 1964; Units in Bomber Comd, 1959–69; RAF Staff Coll., Bracknell, 1970; PSO to DGEng (RAF), 1971–73; OC Eng. Wing, RAF Coningsby, 1973–75; OC No 23 Maintenance Unit, RAF Aldergrove, 1975–77; Group Captain (Plans), HQ RAF Support Command, 1977–79; MoD, 1979–81; Dep. Comdt, RAF Staff Coll., Bracknell, 1981–84; RCDS, 1984. *Recreations:* golf, model aircraft, sailing. *Address:* c/o National Westminster Bank, Farnborough, Hants. *Clubs:* Royal Air Force; Berkshire Golf, Trevose Golf.

ALDAM, Jeffery Heaton, CBE 1980; MC 1945; County Education Officer, Hampshire, 1973–83, retired; *b* 11 Nov. 1922; *s* of William and Clara Ellen Aldam; *m* 1950, Editha Hilary Mary (*née* Preece); two *s* two *d*. *Educ:* Chesterfield Grammar Sch.; Trinity Coll., Cambridge (MA); Harvard Univ. (AM). Served 13th/18th Royal Hussars (QMO), 1942–45. Admin. Asst, Asst Educn Officer, then Sen. Asst Educn Officer, Norfolk CC, 1949–56; Dep. County Educn Officer, NR Yorks CC, 1957–62; Chief Educn Officer, East Suffolk CC, 1962–71; County Educn Officer, (former) Hampshire CC, 1972–73. *Recreations:* reading, walking, gardening. *Address:* Derrymore, 71 Andover Road, Winchester, Hampshire SO22 6AU. *T:* Winchester 53594.

ALDENHAM, 6th Baron *cr* 1896, of Aldenham, Co. Hertford, **AND HUNSDON OF HUNSDON,** 4th Baron *cr* 1923, of Briggens, Co. Hertford; **Vicary Tyser Gibbs;** *b* 9 June 1948; *s* of 5th Baron Aldenham and of Mary Elizabeth, *o d* of late Walter Parkyns Tyser; *S* father, 1986; *m* 1980, Josephine Nicola, *er d* of John Richmond Fell, Lower Bourne, Farnham, Surrey; one *d*. *Educ:* Eton; Oriel College, Oxford. *Heir:* *b* Hon. George Henry Paul Gibbs [*b* 17 June 1950; *m* 1973, Janet Elizabeth, *d* of Harold Leonard Scott; two *s*]. *Address:* Aldenham Wood Lodge, Watling Street, Elstree, Herts WD6 3AA.

ALDER, Lucette, (Mrs Alan Alder); *see* Aldous, Lucette.

ALDER, Michael; Controller, English Regional Television, British Broadcasting Corporation, since 1977; *b* 3 Nov. 1928; *s* of Winifred Miller and late Thomas Alder; *m* 1955, Freda, *d* of late John and Doris Hall; two *d*. *Educ:* Ranelagh Sch., Bracknell, Berks; Rutherford Coll., Newcastle-upon-Tyne. Newcastle Evening Chronicle, 1947–59; BBC North-East: Chief News Asst, Newcastle; Area News Editor, Newcastle; Representative, NE England, 1959–69; Head of Regional Television Development, BBC, 1969–77. *Recreations:* gardening, fishing, walking, country pursuits. *Address:* Red Roofs, Bates Lane, Tanworth-in-Arden, Warwicks B94 5AR. *T:* Tanworth-in-Arden 2403.

ALDERSON, Brian Wouldhave; freelance editor and writer; Children's Books Editor, The Times, since 1967; *b* 19 Sept. 1930; *s* of John William Alderson and Helen Marjory (*née* Hogg), *m* 1953, Valerie Christine (*née* Wells); three *s* (and two *s* decd). *Educ:* Ackworth Sch.; University College of the South-West, Exeter (BA Hons). Work in the book trade, 1952–63; Tutor-librarian, East Herts Coll. of Further Educn, 1963–65; Sen. Lectr, (on Children's Literature and on the Book Trade), Polytechnic of N London, 1965–83. Visiting Professor: Univ. of Southern Mississippi, 1985; UCLA, 1986. Exhibition organiser: (with descriptive notes), Grimm Tales in England, British Library, 1985–86; (with full catalogue), Randolph Caldecott and the Art of the English Picture Book, 1986–87. Eleanor Farjeon Award, 1968. *Publications:* *translations:* Hürlimann, Three Centuries of Children's Books in Europe, 1967; Grimm, Popular Folk Tales, 1978; *edited:* The Juvenile Library, 1966–74; The Colour Fairy Books, by Andrew Lang, 1975–; Lear, a Book of Bosh, 1975; Children's Books in England, by F. J. Harvey Darton, 1982; Hans Christian Andersen and his Eventyr in England, 1982; Andersen and Drewsen, Christine's Picture Book, 1984. *Recreations:* bibliography, dale-walking. *Address:* 28 Victoria Road, Richmond, North Yorks DL10 4AS. *T:* Richmond 3648.

ALDERSON, John Cottingham, CBE 1981; QPM 1974; Chief Constable of Devon and Cornwall, 1973–82; Visiting Professor of Police Studies, University of Strathclyde, since 1983; *b* 28 May 1922; *e s* of late Ernest Cottingham Alderson and Elsie Lavinia Rose; *m* 1948, Irené Macmillan Stirling; one *s*. *Educ:* Barnsley Elem. Schs and Techn. College. Called to Bar, Middle Temple. British Meml Foundn Fellow, Australia, 1956; Extension Certif. in Criminology, Univ. of Leeds. CBIM. Highland LI, 1938–41 (Corp.); Army Phys. Trng Corps, N Africa and Italy, 1941–46 (Warrant Officer). West Riding Constabulary as Constable, 1946; Police Coll., 1954; Inspector, 1955; Sub-Divisional Comd, 1960; Sen. Comd Course, Police Coll., 1963–64; Dep. Chief Constable, Dorset, 1964–66; Metropolitan Police, Dep. Comdr (Admin and Ops), 1966; 2nd-in-comd No 3 Police District, 1967; Dep. Asst Comr (Trng), 1968; Comdt, Police Coll., 1970; Asst Comr (Personnel and Trng), 1973. Consultant on Human Rights to Council of Europe, 1981–. Member: BBC Gen. Adv. Council, 1971–78; Royal Humane Soc. Cttee, 1973; Pres., Royal Life-Saving Soc., 1974–78. Fellow Commoner, Corpus Christi Coll., Cambridge, 1982; Fellow, Inst. of Criminology, Cambridge, 1982; Gwilym Gibbon Res. Fellow, Nuffield Coll., Oxford, 1982–83. Contested (L) Teignbridge, Devon, 1983. Hon. LLD Exeter, 1979; Hon. DLitt Bradford, 1982. *Publications:* (contrib.) Encyclopedia of Crime and Criminals, 1960; (ed jtly) The Police We Deserve, 1973; Policing Freedom,

1979; Law and Disorder, 1984; Human Rights and the Police, 1984; articles in professional jls and newspapers. *Recreations:* reading, writing, keeping fit.

ALDERSON, Dr Michael Rowland; Chief Medical Statistician, Office of Population Censuses and Surveys, since 1981; *b* 8 June 1931; *s* of Christopher Rowland and Phyllis Maud Alderson; *m* 1956, Dorothy Carter; two *d*. *Educ:* Epsom Coll.; Guy's Hospital. MD; FFCM; FRCR; DPH etc. Prof. of Medical Information Science, Southampton Univ., 1970–75; Prof. of Epidemiology, Inst. of Cancer Research, 1975–81. *Publications:* Central Government Routine Health Statistics, 1974; An Introduction to Epidemiology, 1976, 2nd edn 1983; Health Surveys and Related Studies, 1979; International Mortality Statistics, 1981; Prevention of Cancer, 1982; Occupational Cancer, 1985. *Recreation:* sailing. *Address:* 8 Westgate Street, Southampton SO1 0AY. *T:* Southampton 31804.

ALDERTON, John; actor (stage, films, television); *b* Gainsborough, Lincs, 27 Nov. 1940; *s* of Gordon John Alderton and Ivy Handley; *m* 1st, Jill Browne (marr. diss.); 2nd, Pauline Collins, *qv*; two *s* one *d*. *Educ:* Kingston High Sch., Hull. *Stage:* 1st appearance (Rep.) Theatre Royal, York, in Badger's Green, 1961; cont. Rep.; 1st London appearance, Spring and Port Wine, Mermaid (later Apollo), 1965. Royal Shakespeare Company: Dutch Uncle, Aldwych, 1969; The Night I chased the Women with an Eel, Comedy, 1969; Punch and Judy Stories, Howff, 1973; Judies, Comedy, 1974; The Birthday Party, Shaw, 1975; Confusions (4 parts), Apollo, 1976; Rattle of a Simple Man, Savoy, 1980; Special Occasions, Ambassadors, 1983; The Maintenance Man, Comedy, 1986; *films:* (1962–): incl. Duffy, Hannibal Brooks, Zardoz, All Creatures Great and Small, Please Sir; *television:* series: Please Sir, No Honestly, My Wife Next Door, P. G. Wodehouse, The Upchat Line, Thomas and Sarah, Father's Day and various plays. *Address:* c/o Leading Players Management Ltd, 29–31 King's Road, SW3. *Club:* Garrick.

ALDINGTON, 1st Baron, *cr* 1962; **Toby (Austin Richard William) Low,** PC 1954; KCMG 1957; CBE 1945 (MBE 1944); DSO 1941; TD and clasp, 1950; DL; Warden, Winchester College, since 1979; Chairman, Leeds Castle Foundation, since 1984; Barrister-at-Law; *b* 25 May 1914; *s* of Col Stuart Low, DSO (killed at sea by enemy action, Dec. 1942), and of late Hon. Mrs Spear; *m* 1947, Araminta Bowman, *e d* of late Sir Harold MacMichael, GCMG, DSO; one *s* two *d*. *Educ:* Winchester; New Coll., Oxford (Hon. Fellow 1976). Called to the Bar, 1939. TA; 2nd Lieut 1934; Brig. BGS 5 Corps Italy, Aug. 1944–June 1945; served Greece, Crete, Egypt, Libya, Tunisia, Sicily, Italy, Austria (DSO, MBE, CBE, Croix de guerre avec palmes, Commander of Legion of Merit, USA); Hon. Col 288 LAA Regt RA (TA), 1947–59. MP (C) Blackpool North, 1945–62; Parliamentary Secretary, Ministry of Supply, 1951–54; Minister of State, Board of Trade, 1954–57; Dep. Chm., Cons. Party Organisation, Oct. 1959–63. Chm., GEC, 1964–68, Dep. Chm. 1968–84; Chairman: Grindlays Bank Ltd, 1964–76; Sun Alliance and London Insurance Co., 1971–85; Westland Aircraft, 1977–85 (Pres., 1985). Director: Lloyds Bank, 1967–85; Citicorp, 1969–83. Chairman: Port of London Authority, 1971–77; Jt Special Cttee on Ports Industry, 1972. Chm., Cttee of Management, Inst. of Neurology, 1962–80; Chairman: BBC Gen. Adv. Council, 1971–78; ISJC, 1986–. Fellow, Winchester Coll. DL Kent, 1973. *Recreation:* golf. *Heir:* *s* Hon. Charles Harold Stuart Low, *b* 22 June 1948. *Address:* Knoll Farm, Aldington, Kent. *T:* Aldington 292. *Clubs:* Beefsteak, Carlton.
See also Hon. P. J. S. Roberts.

ALDINGTON, Sir Geoffrey (William), KBE 1965 (OBE 1946); CMG 1958; HM Diplomatic Service, retired; *b* 1 June 1907; *s* of late Henry William Aldington; *m* 1932, Roberta Finch; two *d*. *Educ:* City of London School; Magdalen Coll., Oxford. Student Interpreter, China Consular Service, 1929; Vice-Consul (Grade II), China, 1931; Vice-Consul, Peking, 1931–33; Private Secretary to HM Minister, Peking, 1933–35; Foreign Office, 1936–37; Acting Consul, Chungking, 1937–39; Consul, Tsingtao, 1939–41; seconded to Min. of Information, 1943–45; Actg Consul-Gen., Hankow, 1945–46; Suptg Consul, Shanghai, 1946–47; Foreign Office, 1947–50; Political Adviser to Hong Kong Govt, 1950–53; Consul-Gen. Zagreb, Yugoslavia, 1954–56; Consul-General at Philadelphia, Pa, USA, 1956–61; HM Ambassador to Luxembourg, 1961–66; also Consul-General, Luxembourg, 1962–66. *Recreations:* riding, reading. *Address:* Rustlings, 4 Tudor Close, Barnmeadow Lane, Great Bookham, Surrey. *T:* Bookham 54088. *Clubs:* Hong Kong (Hong Kong); Racquet (Philadelphia, USA).
See also S. J. G. Semple.

ALDINGTON, John Norman, BSc, PhD; FRSC; FInstP; CEng; FIEE; Chairman, Royal Worcester Ltd, 1974–75 (Director, 1968–75); *b* 2 March 1905; *s* of Allen Aldington, Preston, Lancashire; *m* 1930, Edna, *d* of late John James Entwisle; one *s*. *Educ:* Balshaws Grammar Sch., Leyland; Harris Inst., Preston. Joined Siemens Electric Lamps and Supplies Ltd, 1923; Head of Laboratories, 1935; Dir of Research, 1948; Dir of the firm, 1948; Dir Alfred Graham & Co. Ltd, 1950; Man. Dir of Siemens Bros & Co. Ltd, 1955; former Man. Dir and Vice-Chm., AEI Ltd; former Director: LEW Ltd; Sub. Cables Ltd; Welwyn Electric Co. Ltd; Worcester Industrial Ceramics Ltd; Worcester Royal Porcelain Co. Ltd. Fellow and Past Pres., Illuminating Engrg Soc.; Mem. Amer. Illum. Engrg Soc., 1950; Chm. of Light Sources Secretariat, Internat. Commn on Illumination, 1945–54; Mem. various BSI Cttees. Part-time Lectr Harris Inst., Preston, 1928–38; Gov., Preston Grammar Sch., 1950–55; JP Duchy of Lancaster, 1953–55. MRI 1958. Leon Gaster Meml Award, IES, 1945 and 1947; Crompton Award, IEE, 1949; Gold Medal, IES, 1970. *Publications:* The High Current Density Mercury Vapour Arc, 1944 (thesis, London Univ. Library); numerous papers, particularly on light sources and kindred devices, and on high current discharges and xenon gas arc. *Recreations:* gardening and golf. *Address:* The Turn, Townside, Haddenham, Bucks HP17 8BG. *T:* Haddenham 291145. *Club:* Athenæum.

ALDISS, Brian Wilson; writer; critic; *b* 18 Aug. 1925; *s* of Stanley and Elizabeth May Aldiss; *m* 1965, Margaret Manson; one *s* one *d*, and one *s* one *d* by previous *m*. *Educ:* Framlingham Coll.; West Buckland School. Royal Signals, 1943–47; book-selling, 1947–56; writer, 1956–; Literary Editor, Oxford Mail, 1958–69. Pres., British Science Fiction Assoc., 1960–64. Editor, SF Horizons, 1964–. Chairman, Oxford Branch Conservation Soc., 1968–69; Vice Pres., The Stapledon Soc., 1975–; Jt Pres., European SF Cttees, 1976–79; Society of Authors: Mem., Cttee of Management, 1976–78, Chm., 1978; Chm., Cultural Exchanges Cttee, 1979–; Member: Arts Council Literature Panel, 1978–80; Internat. PEN, 1983–; Pres., World SF, 1982–84; Vice-Pres., H. G. Wells Soc., 1983–. Observer Book Award for Science Fiction, 1956; Ditmar Award for Best Contemporary Writer of Science Fiction, 1969; first James Blish Award, for SF criticism, 1977; Pilgrim Award, 1978; first Award for Distinguished Scholarship, Internat. Assoc. for the Fantastic in the Arts, Houston, 1986. *Publications:* The Brightfount Diaries, 1955; Space, Time and Nathaniel, 1957; Non-Stop, 1958 (Prix Jules Verne, 1977); Canopy of Time, 1959; The Male Response, 1961; Hothouse, 1962 (Hugo Award, 1961); Best Fantasy Stories, 1962; The Airs of Earth, 1963; The Dark Light Years, 1964; Introducing SF, 1964; Greybeard, 1964; Best SF Stories of Brian W. Aldiss, 1965; Earthworks, 1965; The Saliva Tree, 1966 (Nebula Award, 1965); Cities and Stones: A Traveller's Jugoslavia, 1966; An Age, 1967; Report on Probability A, 1968; Farewell, Fantastic Venus!, 1968; Intangibles Inc. and other Stories, 1969; A Brian Aldiss Omnibus, 1969; Barefoot in the Head, 1969; The Hand-Reared Boy, 1970; The Shape of Further Things, 1970; The Moment of Eclipse, 1971 (BSFA Award, 1972); A Soldier Erect, 1971; Brian Aldiss Omnibus II, 1971; Billion Year Spree: a history of science fiction, 1973 (Special BSFA Award, 1974; Eurocon Merit Award, 1976); Frankenstein Unbound, 1973; The Eighty-Minute Hour, 1974; (ed) Space Opera, 1974; (ed) Space Odysseys: an Anthology of Way-Back-When Futures, 1975; (ed) Hell's Cartographers, 1975; (ed) Evil Earths, 1975; Science Fiction Art: the fantasies of SF, 1975 (Ferrara Silver Comet, 1977); (ed with H. Harrison) Decade: the 1940s, 1976; (ed with H. Harrison) Decade: the 1950s, 1976; The Malacia Tapestry, 1976; (ed) Galactic Empires, vols 1 and 2, 1976; (ed with H. Harrison) The Year's Best Science Fiction No 9, 1976; Brothers of the Head, 1977; Last Orders, 1977; (ed with H. Harrison) Decade: the 1960's, 1977; A Rude Awakening, 1978; Enemies of the System, 1978; (ed) Perilous Planets, 1978; This World and Nearer Ones, 1979; New Arrivals, Old Encounters, 1979; Life in the West, 1980; Moreau's Other Island, 1980; Helliconia Spring, 1982 (BSFA Award, John W. Campbell Meml Award); Helliconia Summer, 1983; Seasons in Flight, 1984; Helliconia Winter, 1985; Helliconia Trilogy (boxed set of Helliconia Spring, Helliconia Summer, and Helliconia Winter), 1985; The Horatio Stubbs Saga, 1985; The Pale Shadow of Science, 1985; . . . And the Lurid Glare of the Comet, 1986. *Recreations:* fame, obscurity, trances. *Address:* Woodlands, Foxcombe Road, Boars Hill, Oxford OX1 5DL. *Clubs:* Groucho, Helen's.

ALDOUS, Alan Harold; Director of Sixth Form Studies, Longsands School, St Neots, since 1976; *b* 14 Nov. 1923; *o s* of George Arthur and Agnes Bertha Aldous; *m*; one *s* one *d*, and one step *s*. *Educ:* Ilford County High Sch. for Boys; Jesus Coll., Oxford (MA). Royal Signals and Royal West African Frontier Force, 1943–46. Oxford Univ., 1942 and 1946–49; Asst Master, St Dunstan's Coll., Catford, 1949–54; Asst Master, Merchant Taylors' Sch., Crosby, 1954–59; Headmaster: King's Sch., Pontefract, 1959–70; Leeds Grammar Sch., 1970–75. *Recreations:* music, walking. *Address:* Casterbridge, Madeley Court, Hemingford Grey, Huntingdon, Cambs PE18 9DF. *T:* St Ives 66153.

ALDOUS, Charles; QC 1985; *b* 3 June 1943; *s* of Guy Travers Aldous and Elizabeth Angela Aldous (*née* Paul); *m* 1969, Hermione Sara de Courcy-Ireland; one *s* two *d* (and one *d* decd). *Educ:* Harrow; University College London (LLB). Called to the Bar, Inner Temple, 1967. *Address:* Ravensfield Farm, Bures Hamlet, Suffolk. *Club:* Farmers'.
See also William Aldous.

ALDOUS, Lucette; Prima Ballerina, The Australian Ballet, since 1971; Master Teacher, Australian Ballet School, since 1979; Senior Adjudicator, National Eisteddfods, since 1979; *b* 26 Sept. 1938; *d* of Charles Fellows Aldous and Marie (*née* Rutherford); *m* 1972, Alan Alder; one *d*. *Educ:* Toronto Public Sch., NSW; Brisbane Public Sch., Qld; Randwick Girls' High Sch., NSW. Awarded Frances Scully Meml Schol. (Aust.) to study at Royal Ballet Sch., London, 1955; joined Ballet Rambert, 1957, Ballerina, 1958–63; Ballerina with: London Fest. Ballet, 1963–66; Royal Ballet, 1966–71. Rep. Australia, 1st Internat. Ballet Competition, Jackson, Miss, USA, 1979; Guest, Kirov Ballet and Ballet School, Leningrad, 1975–76. Guest appearances: Giselle, with John Gilpin, NY, 1968; Lisbon, 1969; with Rudolf Nureyev, in Don Quixote: Aust., 1970, NY, Hamburg and Marseilles, 1971; Carmen, Johannesburg, 1970; The Sleeping Beauty: E Berlin, 1970, Teheran, 1970, 1975; partnered Edward Villela at Expo '74, Spokane, USA. *Television:* title rôle, La Sylphide, with Fleming Flindt, BBC, 1960. *Films:* as Kitri, in Don Quixote, with Rudolf Nureyev and Robert Helpmann, Aust., 1972; The Turning Point, 1977. *Recreations:* music, reading, gardening, breeding Burmese cats.

ALDOUS, William; QC 1976; *b* 17 March 1936; *s* of Guy Travers Aldous, QC; *m* 1960, Gillian Frances Henson; one *s* two *d*. *Educ:* Harrow; Trinity Coll., Cambridge (MA). Barrister, Inner Temple, 1960, Bencher, 1985. Chm., Performing Rights Tribunal, 1986–. *Recreations:* hunting, tennis. *Address:* Layham Lodge, Layham, near Ipswich, Suffolk. *T:* Hadleigh 823143.
See also C. Aldous.

ALDRED, Cyril, FRSE 1978; *b* 19 Feb. 1914; 3rd *s* of late Frederick Aldred and Lilian Ethel (*née* Underwood); *m* 1938, Jessie Kennedy Morton; one *d*. *Educ:* Sloane Sch.; King's Coll. and Courtauld Art Inst., Univ. of London (BA). Asst. Keeper, Royal Scottish Museum, 1937; Scottish Educn Dept, 1939. Served War, RAF (Signals), 1942–46. Associate Curator, Dept of Egyptian Art, Metropolitan Museum of Art, New York, 1955–56; Mem. Cttee, Egypt Exploration Soc., 1959–76; Keeper, Dept of Art and Archaeology, Royal Scottish Museum, Edinburgh, 1961–74. *Publications:* The Development of Ancient Egyptian Art, 1952; The Egyptians, 1961, 2nd edn 1984; Egypt to the End of the Old Kingdom, 1965; Akhenaten, a New Study, 1968; Jewels of the Pharaohs, 1971; Akhenaten and Nefertiti, 1973; Tutankhamun, Craftsmanship in Gold in the Reign of the King, 1979; Egyptian Art in the Days of the Pharaohs, 1980; scripts for BBC programmes, Tutankhamun's Egypt, 1972, etc; chapters in: History of Technology; Cambridge Ancient History (3rd edn); Egypte (Univers des Formes); numerous articles on Ancient Egyptian art and archaeology in scientific periodicals. *Recreation:* gardening. *Address:* 4a Polwarth Terrace, Edinburgh EH11 1NE. *T:* 031–229 2845.

ALDRIDGE, Frederick Jesse; Member, Public Health Laboratory Service Board, 1977–83; Under-Secretary and Controller of Supply, Department of Health and Social Security, 1968–75; *b* 13 Oct. 1915; *s* of late Jesse and Clara Amelia Aldridge; *m* 1940, Grace Hetty Palser; two *d*. *Educ:* Westminster City Sch. Clerical Off., Air Min., 1933; Exec. Off., Min. of Health, 1935; RAF, 1940–46; Acct-General's Div., Min. of Health: Asst Acct-Gen., 1956; Dep. Acct-Gen., 1958; Asst Sec. for Finance and Dep. Acct-Gen., 1964; Asst Sec., Food, Health and Nutrition, also Civil Defence, 1966. *Recreation:* music. *Address:* High Trees, 17 Tanglewood Close, Croydon CR0 5HX. *T:* 01–656 3623.

ALDRIDGE, (Harold Edward) James; author; *b* 10 July 1918; *s* of William Thomas Aldridge and Edith Quayle Aldridge; *m* 1942, Dina Mitchnik; two *s*. With Herald and Sun, Melbourne, 1937–38; Daily Sketch, and Sunday Dispatch, London, 1939; subsequently Australian Newspaper Service and North American Newspaper Alliance (war correspondent), Finland, Norway, Middle East, Greece, USSR, until 1945; also correspondent for Time and Life, Teheran, 1944. Rhys Meml Award, 1945; Lenin Peace Prize, 1972. *Publications:* Signed With Their Honour, 1942; The Sea Eagle, 1944; Of Many Men, 1946; The Diplomat, 1950; The Hunter, 1951, Heroes of the Empty View, 1954; Underwater Hunting for Inexperienced Englishmen, 1955; I Wish He Would Not Die, 1958; Gold and Sand (short stories), 1960; The Last Exile, 1961; A Captive in the Land, 1962; The Statesman's Game, 1966; My Brother Tom, 1966; The Flying 19, 1966; (with Paul Strand) Living Egypt, 1969; Cairo: Biography of a City, 1970; A Sporting Proposition, 1973; The Marvellous Mongolian, 1974; Mockery in Arms, 1974; The Untouchable Juli, 1975; One Last Glimpse, 1977; Goodbye Un-America, 1979; The Broken Saddle, 1983; The True Story of Lilli Stubek, 1984. *Recreations:* trout fishing, etc. *Address:* c/o Curtis Brown, 162–168 Regent Street, W1R 5TA. *Club:* British Sub-Aqua.

ALDRIDGE, James; *see* Aldridge, Harold Edward James.

ALDRIDGE, Michael William ffolliott; actor; *b* 9 Sept. 1920; *s* of Dr Frederick James Aldridge and Kathleen M. M. Aldridge; *m* 1947, Kirsteen Rowntree; three *d*. *Educ:* Watford Grammar Sch.; Gresham's Sch., Holt, Norfolk. Served RAF, 1940–46 (Flight-

Lieut). First professional appearance in French without Tears, Palace Theatre, Watford, 1939; in rep. at Bristol, Blackpool, Sunderland, Sheffield, Bradford and Amersham, 1939–40; first London appearance in This Way to the Tomb, Garrick, 1946; toured with Arts Council Midland Theatre Co., 1946–48; title rôle in Othello, Nottingham, 1948, Embassy, 1949; with Birmingham Rep., 1949; Old Vic Co. at New Theatre, 1949–50: Love's Labour's Lost, She Stoops to Conquer, The Miser, Hamlet; with Arts Council Midland Theatre Co., 1950; Bristol Old Vic, 1951–52: title rôle in Macbeth, Two Gentlemen of Verona, Of Mice and Men; Chichester Festival, 1966–69, 1971–72. London appearances include: Escapade, St James's, Strand, 1953–54; Salad Days, Vaudeville, 1954; Free As Air, Savoy, 1957; Moon for the Misbegotten, Arts, 1960; Vanity Fair, Queen's, 1962; The Fighting Cock, Duke of York's, 1966; Heartbreak House, Lyric, 1967; The Cocktail Party, Wyndham's, Haymarket, 1968; The Magistrate, Cambridge, 1969; Bequest to the Nation, Haymarket, 1970; Reunion in Vienna, Piccadilly, 1972; Absurd Person Singular, Criterion, 1973; The Tempest, RSC at The Other Place, 1974; Jeeves, Her Majesty's, 1975; Lies, Albery, 1975; The Bed before Yesterday, Lyric, 1976; Rosmersholm, Haymarket, 1977; The Old Country, Queen's, 1978; Bedroom Farce, Nat. Theatre at The Prince of Wales, 1978; The Last of Mrs Cheyney, Cambridge, 1980; Noises Off, Lyric, Hammersmith and Savoy, 1982; The Biko Inquest, Riverside, 1984; Relatively Speaking, Greenwich, 1986. Films include, 1946–: Nothing Venture; Bank Holiday Luck; The North Sea Bus; Murder in the Cathedral; A Life for Ruth; Chimes at Midnight; The Public Eye; Bullshot; Turtle Diary; Mussolini; Clockwise; Murder by the Book; Shanghai Surprise. Television plays and serials include: The Man in Room 17; Happy and Glorious; Bleak House; Sense and Sensibility; Fall of Eagles; Love for Lydia; Tinker, Tailor, Soldier, Spy; Love in a Cold Climate; Voyage Round My Father; Spy Ship; Reilly; Under the Hammer; Charlie; Charters and Caldicote; Last of the Summer Wine; The Understanding. Mem., BAFTA. *Recreation:* sailing. *Address:* 11 Crooms Hill, Greenwich, SE10 8ER. *Club:* Little Ship.

ALDRIDGE, Trevor Martin; solicitor; Law Commissioner, since 1984; *b* 22 Dec. 1933; *s* of Dr Sidney and Isabel Aldridge; *m* 1966, Joanna, *d* of C. J. v. D. Edwards; one *s* one *d*. *Educ:* Frensham Heights School; Sorbonne; St John's College, Cambridge (MA). Partner in Bower Cotton & Bower, 1962–84. Mem., Conveyancing Standing Cttee, 1985–. Chm. of Governors, Frensham Heights School, 1977–. General editor, Property Law Bulletin, 1980–84. *Publications:* Boundaries, Walls and Fences, 1966, 5th edn 1986; Finding Your Facts, 1963; Directory of Registers and Records, 1963, 4th edn 1984; Service Agreements, 1964, 4th edn 1982; Rent Control and Leasehold Enfranchisement, 1965, 8th edn 1980; Betterment Levy, 1967; Letting Business Premises, 1971, 5th edn 1985; Your Home and the Law, 1975, 2nd edn 1979; (jtly) Managing Business Property, 1978; Criminal Law Act 1977, 1978; Guide to Enquiries of Local Authorities, 1978, 2nd edn 1982; Guide to Enquiries Before Contract, 1978; Guide to National Conditions of Sale, 1979, 2nd edn 1981; Leasehold Law, 1980; Housing Act, 1980, and as amended 1984, 2nd edn 1984; (ed) Powers of Attorney, 6th edn 1986; Guide to Law Society's Conditions of Sale, 1981, 2nd edn 1984; Questions of Law: Homes, 1982; Law of Flats, 1982; Practical Conveyancing Precedents, 1984. *Address:* Conquest House, 37/38 John Street, Theobalds Road, WC1N 2BQ. *T:* 01–242 0861. *Club:* United Oxford & Cambridge University.

ALDRIN, Dr Buzz; President, Research and Engineering Consultants Inc., since 1972; *b* Montclair, NJ, USA, 20 Jan. 1930; *s* of late Col Edwin E. Aldrin, USAF retd, Brielle, NJ, and Marion Aldrin (*née* Moon); two *s* one *d* of former marriage. *Educ:* Montclair High Sch., Montclair, NJ (grad.); US Mil. Academy, West Point, NY (BSc); Mass Inst. of Technology (DSc in Astronautics). Received wings (USAF), 1952. Served in Korea (66 combat missions) with 51st Fighter Interceptor Wing. Aerial Gunnery Instr, Nellis Air Force Base, Nevada; attended Sqdn Officers Sch., Air Univ., Maxwell Air Force Base, Alabama; Aide to Dean of Faculty, USAF Academy; Flt Comdr with 36th Tactical Fighter Wing, Bitburg, Germany. Subseq. assigned to Gemini Target Office of Air Force Space Systems Div., Los Angeles, Calif; later transf. to USAF Field Office, Manned Spacecraft Center. One of 3rd group of astronauts named by NASA, Oct. 1963; served as back up pilot, Gemini 9 Mission and prime pilot, Gemini 12 Mission (launched into space, with James Lovell, 11 Nov. 1966), 4 day 59 revolution flight which brought Gemini Program to successful close; he established a new record for extravehicular activity and obtained first pictures taken from space of an eclipse of the sun; also made a rendezvous with the previously launched Agena; later assigned to 2nd manned Apollo flight, as back-up command module pilot; Lunar Module Pilot, Apollo 11 rocket flight to the Moon; first lunar landing with Neil Armstrong, July 1969; left NASA to return to USAF as Commandant, Aerospace Res. Pilots Sch., Edwards Air Force Base, Calif, 1971; retired USAF 1972. Mem., Soc. of Experimental Test Pilots; FAIAA; Tau Beta Pi, Sigma Xi. Further honours include Presidential Medal of Freedom, 1969; Air Force DSM with Oak Leaf Cluster; Legion of Merit; Air Force DFC with Oak Leaf Cluster; Air Medal with 2 Oak Leaf Clusters; and NASA DSM, Exceptional Service Medal, and Group Achievement Award. Various hon. memberships and hon. doctorates. *Publication:* Return to Earth (autobiography), 1973. *Recreations:* athletics, scuba diving, etc.

ALDRIN, Dr Edwin E(ugene), Jr; *see* Aldrin, Dr Buzz.

ALEKSANDER, Prof. Igor, PhD; Professor of Information Technology Management, Computing Department, Imperial College of Science and Technology, University of London, since 1984; *b* 26 Jan. 1937. *Educ:* Marist Brothers' Coll., S Africa; Univ. of the Witwatersrand (BSc Eng); Univ. of London (PhD). Section Head of STC, Footscray, 1958–61; Lectr, Queen Mary Coll., Univ. of London, 1961–65; Reader in Electronics, Univ. of Kent, 1965–74; Prof. of Electronics and Head of Electrical Engrg Dept, Brunel Univ., 1974–84. *Publications:* An Introduction to Logic Circuit Theory, 1971; Automata Theory: an engineering approach, 1976; The Human Machine, 1978; Reinventing Man, 1983 (USA 1984); Designing Intelligent Systems, 1984; *c* 100 papers on computing and human modelling. *Recreations:* tennis, skiing, music, architecture. *Address:* c/o Department of Computing, Imperial College of Science and Technology, 180 Queen's Gate, SW7 2BZ. T: 01-589 5111, ext. 4985.

ALEPOUDELIS, Odysseus; *see* Elytis, Odysseus.

ALEXANDER, family name of **Baron Alexander of Potterhill,** of **Earl Alexander of Tunis,** and of **Earl of Caledon.**

ALEXANDER OF POTTERHILL, Baron *cr* 1974 (Life Peer), of Paisley; **William Picken Alexander,** Kt 1961; LHD, PhD, MEd, MA, BSc, FBPsS; General Secretary, Association of Education Committees (England, Wales, Northern Ireland, Isle of Man and Channel Islands), 1945–77; *b* 13 Dec. 1905; *y s* of Thomas and Joan Alexander; *m* 1949, Joan Mary, *d* of Robert and Margaret Williamson; one *s* (and one *s* decd). *Educ:* Paisley Grammar School; Glasgow Univ. Schoolmaster in Scotland, 1929–31; Asst Lectr in Education, Glasgow Univ., 1931–32; Rockefeller Research Fellow, 1932–33; Deputy Director of Education, Walthamstow, 1934–35; Director of Education, Margate, 1935–39, Sheffield, 1939–44. Joint Sec. to Management Panel of Burnham Committees and Associated Committees negotiating salaries of teachers, 1945–73. Hon. DLitt Leeds, 1977. *Publications:* Intelligence, Concrete and Abstract, 1935; The Educational Needs of Democracy, 1940; A Performance Scale for the Measurement of Technical Ability, 1947; A Parents' Guide to the Education Act, 1944, 1947; Education in England, 1953; Towards a new Education Act, 1969, etc. *Recreations:* golf and contract bridge. *Address:* 3 Moor Park Gardens, Pembroke Road, Moor Park, Northwood, Middlesex HA6 2LF. *T:* Northwood 21003. *Club:* Moor Park Golf (Herts).

ALEXANDER OF TUNIS, 2nd Earl *cr* 1952; **Shane William Desmond Alexander;** Viscount, 1946; Baron Rideau, 1952; Lieutenant Irish Guards, retired, 1958; Chairman, International Construction Group; Director: International Hospitals Group; Pathfinder Financial Corporation, Toronto; *b* 30 June 1935; *er s* of 1st Earl Alexander of Tunis, KG, PC, GCB, OM, GCMG, CSI, DSO, MC, and Lady Margaret Diana Bingham (Countess Alexander of Tunis), GBE, DStJ, DL (*d* 1977), *yr d* of 5th Earl of Lucan, PC, GCVO, KBE, CB; *S* father, 1969; *m* 1981, Hon. Davina Woodhouse (Lady-in-Waiting to Princess Margaret, 1975–), *y d* of 4th Baron Terrington, *qv*; two *d*. *Educ:* Ashbury Coll., Ottawa, Canada; Harrow. A Lord in Waiting (Govt Whip), 1974. Patron, British-Tunisian Soc. Liveryman, Mercers Company. *Heir:* *b* Hon. Brian James Alexander, *b* 31 July 1939. *Address:* 59 Wandsworth Common Westside, SW18 2ED. *T:* 01–874 4831. *Club:* MCC.

ALEXANDER, Sir Alexander Sandor, (Sir Alex), Kt 1974; Chairman, J. Lyons and Company, since 1979; Vice-Chairman, Allied-Lyons plc, since 1982; Director: Bain Dawes plc; Sir Alfred McAlpine plc; Tate & Lyle plc; Unigate plc; IBEC Inc. (USA); *b* 21 Nov. 1916; *m* 1946, Margaret Irma; two *s* two *d*. *Educ:* Charles Univ., Prague. Dir, 1954–69, Man. Dir and Chief Exec., 1967–69, Chm. 1969, Ross Group Ltd; Chm., Imperial Foods Ltd, 1969–79; Dir, Imperial Group Ltd (formerly Imperial Tobacco Group Ltd), 1969–79. Director: National Westminster Bank Ltd, South East Region, 1973–84; Ransomes, Sims & Jefferies plc, 1974–83; Dep. Chm., British United Trawlers, 1969–81. President: Processors and Growers Research Orgn, 1978–82; British Food Export Council, 1973–76; Member: Eastern Gas Bd, 1963–72; Agric. Econ. Develt Cttee, 1974–78; Governor: British Nutrition Foundn; Royal Ballet; Chm., Theatre Royal (Norwich) Trust Ltd, 1969–84; Trustee, 1975–, Vice Chm., 1978–, Glyndebourne Arts Trust; Member: National Theatre Develt Council; Court, UEA; Trustee, Charities Aid Foundn, 1979–; Friend of RCP, 1982–. FBIM; FRSA. High Sheriff, Norfolk, 1976. *Recreations:* tennis, shooting, painting, opera, ballet. *Address:* Westwick Hall, Westwick, Norwich. *T:* Swanton Abbot 664.

ALEXANDER, Anthony George Laurence; Director, Hanson Trust plc, since 1976; *b* 4 April 1938; *s* of George and Margaret Alexander; *m* 1962, Frances, *d* of Cyril Burdett; one *s* two *d*. *Educ:* St Edward's School, Oxford. FCA. Chm., subsids of Hanson Trust, incl. Imperial Group, London Brick Co, Butterley Brick Co., British Ever Ready. Underwriting Member of Lloyd's. *Recreation:* tennis. *Address:* Crafnant, Gregories Farm Lane, Beaconsfield, Bucks HP9 1HJ. *T:* Beaconsfield 2882.

ALEXANDER, Sir Charles G(undry), 2nd Bt *cr* 1945; MA, AIMarE; Chairman, Alexander Shipping Co. Ltd; *b* 5 May 1923; *s* of Sir Frank Alexander, 1st Bt, and Elsa Mary (*d* 1959), *d* of Sir Charles Collett, 1st Bt; *S* father 1959; *m* 1st, 1944, Mary Neale, *o c* of S. R. Richardson; one *s* one *d*; 2nd, 1979, Eileen Ann Stewart. *Educ:* Bishop's Stortford College; St John's College, Cambridge. Served War as Lieut (E), RN, 1943–46. Chm., Governors Care Ltd; Dep. Chm., Houlder Bros and Co. Ltd; Director: Furness-Houlder Insurance Ltd; Furness-Houlder (Reinsurance Services) Ltd; Inner London Region, National Westminster Bank Ltd; formerly Dir, Hull, Blyth & Co. Ltd (Chm., 1972–75). Chm., Bd of Governors, Bishop's Stortford College. Mem. Court of Common Council, 1969; Alderman (Bridge Ward), 1970–76. Master, Merchant Taylors' Co., 1981–82; Prime Warden, Shipwrights' Co., 1983–84. *Recreation:* farming. *Heir:* *s* Richard Alexander [*b* 1 Sept. 1947; *m* 1971, Lesley Jane, *d* of Frederick William Jordan, Bishop's Stortford; two *s*]. *Address:* 53 Leadenhall Street, EC3. *T:* 01–481 2020; Bells Farm, East Sutton, near Maidstone, Kent. *T:* 842410. *Club:* Royal Automobile.

ALEXANDER, Cherian; *see* Alexander, P. C.

ALEXANDER of Ballochmyle, Sir Claud Hagart-, 3rd Bt, *cr* 1886 of Ballochmyle; JP; Vice Lord-Lieutenant, Ayr and Arran, since 1983; *b* 6 Jan. 1927; *s* of late Wilfred Archibald Alexander (2nd *s* of 2nd Bt) and Mary Prudence, *d* of Guy Acheson; *S* grandfather, 1945; assumed additional surname of Hagart, 1949; *m* 1959, Hilda Etain, 2nd *d* of Miles Malcolm Acheson, Ganges, BC, Canada; two *s* two *d*. *Educ:* Sherborne; Corpus Christi Coll., Cambridge (BA 1948). MInstMC 1980. DL Ayrshire, 1973; JP Cumnock and Doon Valley, 1983. *Heir:* *s* Claud Hagart-Alexander, *b* 5 Nov. 1963. *Address:* Kingencleugh House, Mauchline, Ayrshire KA5 5JL. *T:* Mauchline 50217. *Club:* New (Edinburgh).

ALEXANDER, Sir Darnley (Arthur Raymond), Kt 1974; CBE 1963; CFR 1979; GCON 1983; Chairman, Nigerian Law Reform Commission, since 1979; *b* Castries, St Lucia, 28 Jan. 1920; *e s* of late Pamphile Joseph Alexander, MBE, and late Lucy Alexander; *m* 1943, Mildred Margaret King (*d* 1980); one *s* one *d*. *Educ:* St Mary's Coll., St Lucia; University Coll., London (LLB). Called to Bar, Middle Temple, 1942. Served in: legal service, Jamaica, WI, and Turks and Caicos Is, 1944–57; legal service, Western Nigeria, 1957–63; Solicitor-Gen. 1960; QC 1961; Judge, High Court of Lagos (later Lagos State), 1964–69; Chief Justice: South Eastern State of Nigeria, 1969–75; Fed. Repub. of Nigeria, 1975–79. Chm., Kiribati Constitutional Commn re status of Banabans. Member: Nigerian Body of Benchers (Past Chm. and Life Mem.); Nigerian Soc. of Internat. Law, 1968–; Nigerian Inst. of Internat. Affairs, 1979–. *Publications:* Report of Inquiry into Owegbe Cult, 1966; Report of Inquiry into Examination Leakages, 1969. *Recreations:* cricket, football, table-tennis, swimming, reading. *Address:* (office) Nigerian Law Reform Commission, Secretariat Complex, Ikoyi, PO Box 60008, Lagos, Nigeria; (home) 18 Osborne Road, Ikoyi, Lagos, Nigeria. *T:* 681080.

ALEXANDER, David; *see* Alexander, J. D.

ALEXANDER, Maj.-Gen. David Crichton, CB 1976; Commandant, Scottish Police College, since 1979; *b* 28 Nov. 1926; *s* of James Alexander and Margaret (*née* Craig); *m* 1957, Diana Joyce (Jane) (*née* Fisher); one *s* two *d* and one step *s*. *Educ:* Edinburgh Academy. Joined RM, 1944; East Indies Fleet; 45 Commando, Malaya, Malta, Canal Zone, 1951–54; Parade Adjt, Lympstone, 1954–57; Equerry and Acting Treasurer to Duke of Edinburgh, 1957–60; psc 1960; Directing Staff, Staff Coll., Camberley, 1962–65; 45 Commando (2IC), Aden, 1965–66; Staff of Chief of Defence Staff, incl. service with Sec. of State, 1966–69; CO 40 Commando, Singapore, 1969–70; Col GS to CGRM, 1970–73; ADC to the Queen, 1973–75; RCDS 1974; Comdr, Training Gp RM, 1975–77. Dir-Gen., English-Speaking Union, 1977–79. Governor, Corps of Commissionaires, and Mem., Admin. Bd, 1978–; Member: Civil Service Final Selection Bd, 1978–; MoD Police Review Cttee, 1985. Dir, Edinburgh Acad., 1980– (Chm., 1985–). Freeman, City of London; Liveryman, Painter Stainers' Co., 1978. *Recreations:* fishing, gardening, golf. *Address:* Tulliallan Castle, Kincardine, Alloa, Clackmannanshire FK1O 4BE. *Club:* Army and Navy.

ALEXANDER, Sir Desmond William Lionel C.; *see* Cable-Alexander.

ALEXANDER, Sir Douglas, 3rd Bt *cr* 1921; with Cowen & Co.; *b* 9 Sept. 1936; *s* of Lt-Comdr Archibald Gillespie Alexander (*d* 1978) (2nd *s* of 1st Bt), and of Margery Isabel, *d* of Arthur Brown Griffith; *S* uncle, 1983; *m* 1958, Marylon, *d* of Leonidas Collins Scatterday; two *s*. *Educ:* Rice Univ., Houston, Texas (MA 1961). PhD 1967 (Univ. of N Carolina). Formerly Assoc. Prof. and Chairman, French, State Univ. of New York at Albany. *Heir: s* Douglas Gillespie Alexander, *b* 24 July 1962. *Address:* 145 Main Street, Wickford, RI 02852, USA.

ALEXANDER, Henry Joachim, Dr phil, Dr jur Breslau; formerly Member, Conseil Fédéral, Fédération Internationale des Communautés d'Enfants, Trogen, 1960–83 (Secrétaire Général Adjoint, 1960–67; Chairman of UK Section, 1960–70; Vice-Pres., 1967–71); *b* 4 Jan. 1897; *s* of Bruno and Lisbeth Alexander-Katz; *m* 1st, 1925, Hilda (*née* Speyer) (*d* 1974); two *s*; 2nd, 1975, Amalia Cornelia (*née* Amato). *Educ:* Gymnasium Augustum Germany; Univs of Göttingen and Breslau. Member, Berlin Bar, 1925–37. Member, European Service of BBC, 1942–56; Vice-Chm. and Trustee, Assoc. of Broadcasting Staff, 1952–54 (Chm., Foreign Langs Panel, 1952–55). Chm., British Pestalozzi Children's Village Assoc., 1947–57; Chm. Pestalozzi Children's Village Trust, 1957–62 (Exec. Vice-Pres., 1962–63); Mem. Council, Pestalozzi Children's Village Foundation, Trogen, Switzerland, 1954–77; Mem. Exec. Cttee, Lifeline, an Internat. Refugee Organisation, 1965–72; Mem. Residential Care Assoc., 1965–, and Chm. of its Internat. Cttee, 1965–70. Hon. Mem., Mark Twain Soc., USA, 1977–. *Publication:* International Trade Mark Law, 1935. *Recreations:* music, hill walking. *Address:* Hildings, Pett, Hastings, East Sussex TN35 4JG. *T:* Pett 3055; Villa Hélios, Avenue des Amandiers, CH-1820 Montreux, Switzerland. *T:* Montreux 021. 631771.

ALEXANDER, Ian Douglas Gavin; a Recorder of the Crown Court, since 1982; *b* 10 April 1941; *s* of late Dr A. D. P. Alexander, MB ChB, and of Mrs D. Alexander; *m* 1969, Rosemary Kirkbride Richards; one *s* one *d*. *Educ:* Tonbridge; University College London (LLB). Called to Bar, Lincoln's Inn, 1964; Recorder, Midland and Oxford Circuit, 1982–. *Recreations:* horses, sailing, gardening. *Address:* 13 King's Bench Walk, Temple, EC4Y 7EN. *T:* 01–353 7204. *Club:* Naval and Military.

ALEXANDER, (John) David, DPhil; President, Pomona College, since 1969; American Secretary, Rhodes Scholarship Trust, since 1981; *b* 18 Oct. 1932; *s* of John David Alexander, Sr and Mary Agnes McKinnon; *m* 1956, Catharine Coleman; one *s* two *d*. *Educ:* Southwestern at Memphis (BA); Louisville Presbyterian Theological Seminary; Oxford University (DPhil). Instructor to Associate Prof., San Francisco Theol Seminary, 1957–64; Pres., Southwestern at Memphis, 1965–69. Trustee, Teachers Insurance and Annuity Assoc., NY, 1970–; Director: Great Western Financial Corp., Beverly Hills, 1973–; KCET (Community Supported TV of S Calif.), 1979–; Amer. Council on Educn, Washington DC, 1981–; Member: Nat. Panel on Academic Tenure, 1971–72; Assoc. of Amer. Med. Colls Panel on Gen. Professional Preparation of Physicians, 1981–84. Hon. LLD: Univ. of S California, 1970; Occidental Coll., 1970; Centre Coll. of Kentucky, 1971; Hon. LHD Loyola Marymount Univ., 1983. *Publications:* articles in Biblical studies; articles and chapters on higher educn in USA. *Recreations:* music, book collecting. *Address:* 345 North College Avenue, Claremont, Calif 91711, USA. *T:* 714/624 7848. *Clubs:* Century Association (NY); California (Los Angeles); Bohemian (San Francisco).

ALEXANDER, Sir (John) Lindsay, Kt 1975; MA; Deputy Chairman, Lloyds Bank PLC, since 1980 (Director since 1970); Deputy Chairman and Director, Lloyds Merchant Bank Holdings, since 1985; Director: British Petroleum Co. PLC, since 1975; Hawker Siddeley plc, since 1981; Wellington Underwriting Holdings Ltd, since 1986; Wellington Underwriting Agencies Ltd, since 1986; *b* 12 Sept. 1920; *e s* of Ernest Daniel Alexander and Florence Mary Mainsmith; *m* 1944, Maud Lilian, 2nd *d* of Oliver Ernest and Bridget Collard; two *s* one *d*. *Educ:* Alleyn's Sch.; Brasenose Coll., Oxford (Thomas Wall Schol.; Hon. Fellow 1977). Royal Engineers, 1940–45 (Capt.); served Middle East and Italy. Chm., The Ocean Steam Ship Co. Ltd, later Ocean Transport and Trading Ltd, 1971–80 (Man. Dir, 1955–71; Dir, 1955–86); Chm., Lloyds Bank Internat., 1980–85 (Dir, 1975–85; Dep. Chm., 1979–80); Director: Overseas Containers Holdings Ltd, 1971–82 (Chm., 1976–82); Jebsens Drilling PLC, 1980–86. Chairman: Liverpool Port Employers' Assoc., 1964–67; Cttee, European Nat. Shipowners' Assocs, 1971–73; Vice-Chm., Nat. Assoc. of Port Employers, 1965–69; President: Chamber of Shipping of UK, 1974–75 (Vice-Pres., 1973–74); Gen. Council, British Shipping Ltd, 1974–75. Hon. Mem., Master Mariners' Co., 1974–. FCIT (MInstT 1968); CBIM 1980 (FBIM 1972). JP Cheshire, 1965–75. Comdr, Royal Order of St Olav, Norway. *Recreations:* gardening, music, photography. *Address:* Lloyds Bank Plc, 71 Lombard Street, EC3P 3BS. *T:* 01–626 1500. *Club:* Brooks's.

ALEXANDER, Prof. John Malcolm; Emeritus Professor, University of Wales; Stocker Visiting Professor in Manufacturing, University of Ohio, 1985–June 1987; Visiting Professor, Universities of Reading and Surrey, since 1983; *b* 14 Oct. 1921; *s* of Robert Henry Alexander and Gladys Irene Lightfoot Alexander (*née* Domville); *m* 1946, Margaret, *d* of F. A. Ingram; two *s*. *Educ:* Ipswich Sch.; City and Guilds Coll. (Imperial Coll., London Univ.). DSc (Eng) London; PhD; FCGI; FICE; FIMechE; FIProdE; FIM; FEng; FRSA. Practical trng, Ransomes Sims & Jefferies Ltd, Ipswich, 1937–42; REME commn, 1942–47; res. in plasticity and applied mechanics, City and Guilds Coll., 1950–53; Head of Metal Deformation Section, Aluminium Labs Ltd, 1953–55; Head of Mech. Engrg Res. Labs and Nuclear Reactor Mechanical Design, English Electric, 1955–57; Reader in Plasticity, Univ. of London, 1957–63; Prof. of Engrg Plasticity, Univ. of London, 1963–69; Prof. of Applied Mechanics, Imp. Coll., Univ. of London, 1969–78; Prof. and Head of Dept of Mech. Engrg, University Coll. of Swansea, Univ. of Wales, 1978–83. Chm., Applied Mechanics Gp, IMechE, 1963–65; Mem., Collège Internationale Recherche et Production, 1965–; Vice-President: Inst. of Metals, 1968–71; Inst. of Sheet Metal Engrg, 1979–; Chm. Board of Studies in Civil and Mech. Engrg, Univ. of London, 1966–68. Governor: Reigate Grammar Sch., 1964–67; Ipswich Sch., 1977–. Chm., British Cold Forging Gp, 1973–79; Pres., Forming Gp, Collège International Recherche et Production, 1979–83; Engrg Adviser, Van Nostrand, 1964–70. Assessor, Sizewell 'B' Public Enquiry, 1983–. Freeman, City of London, 1976. Liveryman, Blacksmiths Co., 1976. Series Editor, Ellis Horwood Ltd, 1970–; Mem. Editorial Board: Jl Strain Analysis, 1965–71; Internat. Jl Mech. Sciences, 1968–; Internat. Jl Machine Tool Design and Research, 1973–; Metals Technology, 1976–; Mem. Adv. Bd, Jl Mech. Working Tech., 1976–. Joseph Bramah Medal, IMechE, 1970. *Publications:* Advanced Mechanics of Materials, Manufacturing Properties of Materials, 1963; Hydrostatic Extrusion, 1971; Strength of Materials, 1980; papers to Royal Soc., IMechE, Iron and Steel Inst., Inst. Metals, Metals Soc. *Recreations:* music, gardening, swimming. *Address:* Rowan Cottage, Furze Hill Road, Headley Down, Hants GU35 8NP. *T:* Headley Down 713212. *Club:* Army and Navy.

ALEXANDER, Jonathan James Graham, DPhil; FBA 1985; FSA 1981; Reader, History of Art Department, University of Manchester, since 1973; *b* 20 Aug. 1935; *s* of Arthur Ronald Brown and Frederica Emma Graham (who *m* 2nd, Boyd Alexander); *m* 1974, Mary Davey; one *s*. *Educ:* Magdalen Coll., Oxford (BA, MA, DPhil). Assistant, Dept of Western MSS, Bodleian Library, Oxford, 1963–71; Lecturer, History of Art Dept, Manchester Univ., 1971–73. Lyell Reader in Bibliography, Univ. of Oxford, 1982–83; Sen. Kress Fellow, Center for Adv. Study in Visual Arts, Nat. Gall. of Art, Washington DC, 1984–85; Sandars Reader in Bibliography, Cambridge Univ., 1984–85. *Publications:* (with Otto Pächt) Illuminated Manuscripts in the Bodleian Library, Oxford, 3 vols, 1966, 1970, 1973; (with A. C. de la Mare) Italian Illuminated Manuscripts in the Library of Major J. R. Abbey, 1969; Norman Illumination at Mont St Michel *c* 966–1100, 1970; The Master of Mary of Burgundy, A Book of Hours, 1970; Italian Renaissance Illuminations, 1977; Insular Manuscripts 6th-9th Century, 1978; The Decorated Letter, 1978; (with E. Temple) Illuminated Manuscripts in Oxford College Libraries, 1986; articles in Burlington Magazine, Arte Veneta, Pantheon, etc. *Recreations:* music, gardening. *Address:* 8 Pine Road, Didsbury, Manchester M20 0UY. *T:* 061–445 1025.

ALEXANDER, Sir Kenneth (John Wilson), Kt 1978; BSc (Econ.); FRSE 1978; Principal and Vice-Chancellor, Stirling University, 1981–86; *b* Edinburgh, 14 March 1922; *o s* of late William Wilson Alexander; *m* 1949, Angela-May, *d* of late Capt. G. H. Lane, RN; one *s* four *d*. *Educ:* George Heriot's Sch., Edinburgh; Sch. of Economics, Dundee. Research Asst, Univ. of Leeds, 1949–51; Lectr, Univ. of Sheffield, 1951–56; Lectr, Univ. of Aberdeen, 1957–62; Dean of Scottish Business Sch., 1973–75 (Chm., Acad. Exec. Cttee, 1972–73); Prof. of Econs, Strathclyde Univ., 1963–80, on leave of absence, 1976–80; Chm., Highlands and Islands Develt Bd, 1976–80. Umpire, N Derbyshire District Conciliation Bd, 1963; Mem. Adv. Cttee on University of the Air, 1965; Director: Fairfields (Glasgow) Ltd, 1966–68; Upper Clyde Shipbuilders Ltd, 1968–71; Chm., Govan Shipbuilders, 1974–76; Dir, Glasgow Chamber of Commerce, 1969–73; Economic Consultant to Sec. of State for Scotland, 1968–; Chm., Cttee on Adult Educn in Scotland, 1970–73; Mem. Exec. Cttee, 1968–, Dep. Chm. 1982–, Scottish Council (Develt and Industry); Member: (part-time) Scottish Transport Gp, 1969–76; SSRC, 1975–76; Scottish Develt Agency, 1975–86. Governor: Technical Change Centre, 1981–; Newbattle Abbey Coll., 1967–73; President: Section F, British Assoc., 1974; Saltire Soc., 1975–81; Scottish Section, Town and Country Planning, 1982–; Hon. Pres., The Highland Fund, 1983–; Trustee, Nat. Museums of Scotland, 1985–. CBIM 1980; FEIS 1983; FBEC(S) 1984. Hon. LLD: CNAA, 1976; Aberdeen, 1986; Dundee, 1986; DUniv: Stirling, 1977; Open 1985. *Publications:* The Economist in Business, 1967; Productivity Bargaining and the Reform of Industrial Relations, 1969; (with C. L. Jenkins) Fairfields, a study of industrial change, 1971; (ed) The Political Economy of Change, 1976; articles in Oxford Econ. Papers, Quarterly Jl of Econ., Scottish Jl of Pol. Econ., Economica, Yorkshire Bulletin Economics, and other jls. *Recreation:* Scottish antiquarianism. *Address:* 9 West Shore, Pittenweem, Fife KY10 2NV.

ALEXANDER, Sir Lindsay; *see* Alexander, Sir J. L.

ALEXANDER, Rt. Rev. Mervyn Alban Newman; *see* Clifton, Bishop of, (RC).

ALEXANDER, Michael Charles; writer; *b* 20 Nov. 1920; *s* of late Rear-Adm. Charles Otway Alexander and Antonia Geermans; *m* 1963, Sarah Wignall (marr. diss.); one *d*. *Educ:* Stowe; RMC, Sandhurst; Oflag IVC, Colditz. Served War: DCLI; 5 (Ski) Bn Scots Gds; 8 Commando (Layforce); HQ 13 Corps (GSO 3); Special Boat Section; (POW, 1942–44); 2nd SAS Regt; War Office (Civil Affairs). Intergovtl Cttee on Refugees, 1946; Editorial Dir, Common Ground Ltd, 1946–50. Located Firuzkoh, Central Afghanistan, 1952; Himalayan Hovercraft Expedn, 1972; Yucatan Straits Hovercraft Expedn, 1975; Upper Ganges Hovercraft Expedn, 1980. Dir, Acorn Productions Ltd, 1977–. Founded: Woburn Safari Service, 1977; Chelsea Wharf Restaurant, 1983. FZS, FRGS. Co-publisher, Wildlife magazine. *Publications:* The Privileged Nightmare (with Giles Romilly), 1952 (republ., as Hostages at Colditz, 1975); Offbeat in Asia, 1953; The Reluctant Legionnaire, 1955; The True Blue, 1957; Mrs Fraser on the Fatal Shore, 1972; Discovering the New World, 1976; Omai: Noble Savage, 1977; Queen Victoria's Maharajah, 1980. *Address:* 48 Eaton Place, SW1. *T:* 01–235 2724; Skelbo House, Dornoch, Sutherland. *T:* Golspie 3180.

ALEXANDER, Michael O'Donel Bjarne, CMG 1982; HM Diplomatic Service; Ambassador and UK Permanent Representative on the North Atlantic Council, Brussels, since 1986; *b* 19 June 1936; *s* of late Conel Hugh O'Donel Alexander, CMG, CBE, and Enid Constance Crichton Neate; *m* 1960, Traute Krohn; two *s* one *d*. *Educ:* Foyle Coll., Londonderry; Hall Sch., Hampstead; St Paul's Sch.; King's Coll., Cambridge (Schol.); Harkness Fellow (Yale and Berkeley) 1960–62. MA (Cantab), AM (Yale). Royal Navy, 1955–57. Entered HM Foreign (later Diplomatic) Service, 1962; Moscow, 1963–65; Office of Political Adviser, Singapore, 1965–68; FCO, 1968–72; Asst Private Sec. to Secretary of State (Rt Hon. Sir Alec Douglas-Home, MP, and Rt Hon. James Callaghan, MP) 1972–74; Counsellor (Conf. on Security and Co-operation in Europe) and later Head of Chancery, UK Mission, Geneva, 1974–77; Dep. Head, 1977–78, Head, 1978–79, Personnel Operations Dept, FCO; Private Sec. (Overseas Affairs) to the Prime Minister (Rt Hon. Margaret Thatcher, MP), 1979–81; Ambassador, Vienna, 1982–86; concurrently Hd of UK Delegn to the Negotiations on Mutual and Balanced Reduction of Forces and Armaments in Central Europe, 1985–86. Organised: Britain in Vienna Fest., 1986; Grosses Goldenes Ehrenzeichen (Wien), 1986. Former Public Schools', British Universities' and National Junior Foil Champion; fenced for Cambridge Univ., 1957–60 (Captain, 1959–60); English Internat., 1958; Silver Medallist (Epée Team) Olympic Games, 1960; Gold Medallist, US Championships, 1961; Captained England, 1963. Represented Cambridge in Field Events Match with Oxford, 1959, 1960. *Recreations:* reading history; watching or participating in sport of any kind. *Address:* c/o Foreign and Commonwealth Office, SW1. *Clubs:* Athenæum, Garrick, Epée, All England Fencing; Hawks (Cambridge).

ALEXANDER, Nell Haigh; President of Baptist Union, Great Britain and Ireland (first woman so appointed), 1978–79; *b* 24 Feb. 1915; *d* of William Henry and Grace Caroline Fowler; *m* 1938, Arthur Alexander; one *s*. *Educ:* Higher Grade (Central) Girls' Sch., Cambridge. Nat. Chm., Women's Work, Baptist Union, 1971–76; Representative for Europe, Baptist World Alliance (Women's Dept). *Recreations:* classical music, reading, theatre, church drama, poetry. *Address:* 86 Thornton Road, Cambridge. *T:* Cambridge 276368.

ALEXANDER, Sir Norman (Stanley), Kt 1966; CBE 1959. Professor of Physics: Raffles Coll., Singapore, 1936–49; Univ. of Malaya, Singapore, 1949–52; University Coll., Ibadan, Nigeria, 1952–60; Vice-Chancellor, Ahmadu Bello Univ., Nigeria, 1961–66.

ALEXANDER, Dr (Padimjarethalakkal) Cherian; High Commissioner for India to the Court of St James's, since 1985; *b* 10 March 1921; *m* 1942, Ackama Alexander; two *s* two *d*. *Educ:* India and Britain; MA (Hist. and Econ.); MLitt; DLitt. Indian Administrative Service, Kerela Cadre, 1948; Develt Comr, Small Scale Industries, 1960–63; Sen. Advr, Centre for Industrial Develt, UN HQ, NY, 1963–66; Chief, UN Project on Small Industries and Chief Advr to Govt of Iran, 1970–73; Develt Comr, Small Scale Industries, 1973–75; Sec., Foreign Trade, later Commerce Sec., 1975–78; Sen. Advr, later Exec. Dir and Asst Sec. Gen., Internat Trade Centre, UNCTAD-GATT, Geneva, 1978–81; Principal Sec. to Prime Minister of India, 1981–85. *Publications:* The Dutch in Malabar; Buddhism in Kerela; Industrial Estates in India. *Address:* Indian High Commission, India House, Aldwych, WC2B 4NA. *T:* 01–836 8484.

ALEXANDER, Maj.-Gen. Paul Donald, MBE 1968; Signal Officer in Chief (Army), since 1985; *b* 30 Nov. 1934; *s* of Donald Alexander and Alice Louisa Alexander (*née* Dunn); *m* 1958, Christine Winifred Marjorie Coakley; three *s. Educ:* Dudley Grammar Sch.; RMA Sandhurst; Staff Coll., Camberley; NDC; RCDS. Enlisted 1953; commissioned Royal Signals, 1955; served Hong Kong, E Africa, Germany; Comd 1st Div. Signal Regt, 1974–76; MoD, 1977–79; Comdr, Corps Royal Signals, 1st (Br) Corps, 1979–81; Dep. Mil. Sec. (B), 1982–85. *Recreations:* gardening, unstructured hedonism. *Address:* c/o Lloyds Bank, 6 Pall Mall, SW1. *Club:* Army and Navy.

ALEXANDER, Richard Thain; MP (C) Newark, since 1979; *b* 29 June 1934; *s* of Richard Rennie Alexander and Gladys Alexander; *m* 1966, Valerie Ann; one *s* one *d. Educ:* Dewsbury Grammar Sch., Yorks; University Coll. London (LLB Hons). Articled with Sir Francis Hill, Messrs Andrew & Co., Lincoln, 1957–60; Asst Solicitor, Messrs McKinnell, Ervin & Holmes, Scunthorpe, 1960–64; Sen. Partner, Messrs Jones, Alexander & Co., Retford, 1964–85, Consultant, 1986–. *Recreations:* tennis, bowls, horse riding, a little squash. *Address:* 28 Union Street, Retford, Notts. *Clubs:* Carlton; Newark Conservative; Retford Conservative.

ALEXANDER, Rear-Adm. Robert Love, CB 1964; DSO 1943; DSC 1944; *b* 29 April 1913; *o s* of Captain R. L. Alexander, Edinburgh; *m* 1936, Margaret Elizabeth, *o d* of late George Conrad Spring, and late Mrs Maurice House; one *s* three *d* (and one *d* decd). *Educ:* Merchiston Castle; Royal Naval College, Dartmouth. Joined RNC, 1927; Cadet HMS Repulse, 1930; Midshipman HMS Kent, 1931–33; Sub-Lieut, qualified in submarines, 1935. Served throughout War of 1939–45 in submarines; first command HMS H32, 1940; later commands: HMS Proteus, 1942; HMS Truculent, 1942–44; HMS Tuna, 1945. Second in command and in temp. command HMS Glory, Korean War, 1951–52; in command First Destroyer Squadron, 1957; Imperial Defence College, 1959; in command HMS Forth and 1st Submarine Squadron, 1960; Captain Submarines and Minesweepers, Mediterranean, and NATO Commander Submarines, Mediterranean, HMS Narvik, 1960–62. Vice Naval Deputy to the Supreme Allied Commander Europe, 1962–65. Lieut 1936; Comdr 1946; Capt. 1952; Rear-Adm. 1962; retd, 1965. *Address:* Tythe Barn, South Harting, Petersfield, Hants. *T:* Harting 505.

ALEXANDER, Robert Scott, QC 1973; QC (NSW) 1983; a Judge of the Courts of Appeal of Jersey and Guernsey, since 1985; *b* 5 Sept. 1936; *s* of late Samuel James and of Hannah May Alexander; *m*; two *s* one *d* (and one *s* decd). *Educ:* Brighton Coll.; King's Coll., Cambridge. BA 1959, MA 1963. Called to Bar, Middle Temple, 1961; Bencher, 1979; Vice Chm., 1984–85; Chm., 1985–86, of the Bar. Pres., King's Coll. Assoc., 1980–81. *Recreations:* tennis, gardening, going to the theatre. *Address:* 1 Brick Court, Temple, EC4. *T:* 01–583 0777; Weedon Lodge, Weedon, Aylesbury, Bucks. *T:* Aylesbury 641216. *Club:* Garrick.

ALEXANDER, Thomas John; Head of the Private Office of the Secretary General, OECD, Paris, since 1984; *b* 11 March 1940; *s* of late John Alexander and of Agnes Douglas Stewart (*née* Creedican); *m* 1961, Pamela Mason; two *s* one *d. Educ:* Royal High Sch., Edinburgh. Entered FO, 1958; MECAS, 1961; Third Sec. (Commercial), Kuwait, 1963; Asst Private Sec. to the Minister of State, FO, 1965; Second Sec. (Commercial), Tripoli, 1967; seconded to industry (ICI), 1970; Vice Consul (Commercial), Seattle, 1970; First Sec., FCO, 1974; special unpaid leave to act as Private Sec. to Sec.-Gen. of OECD, Paris, 1977–82; Counsellor and Head of Chancery, Khartoum, 1982–83; Dep Head of Planning,, OECD, 1984. *Recreations:* squash, tennis. *Address:* c/o OECD, 2 rue André Pascal, 75016 Paris, France.

ALEXANDER, Walter Ronald, CBE 1984; Chairman, Walter Alexander plc, since 1979 (Managing Director, 1973–79); *b* 6 April 1931; *s* of Walter Alexander and Katherine Mary Turnbull; *m* 1st, 1956, Rosemary Anne Sleigh (marr. diss. 1975); two *s* two *d*; 2nd, 1979, Mrs Lorna Elwes, *d* of Lydia Duchess of Bedford. *Educ:* Loretto Sch.; Cambridge Univ. (MA Hons). Chm. and Man. Dir, Tayforth Ltd, 1961–71; Chm., Scottish Automobile Co. Ltd, 1971–73. Director: Scotcros plc, 1965–82 (Chm., 1972–82); Investors Capital Trust plc, 1967–; Clydesdale Bank plc, 1971–; RIT and Northern plc (formerly Great Northern Investment Trust plc), 1973–84; Dawson Internat. plc, 1979–. Chm., Scottish Appeals Cttee, Police Dependants' Trust, 1974–81; Pres., Public Schs Golfing Soc., 1973–79; Chm., PGA, 1982–85; Governor, Loretto Sch., 1961–. Scottish Free Enterprise Award, 1977. *Recreation:* golf. *Address:* Ryland Lodge, Dunblane, Perthshire FK15 0HY. *T:* Dunblane 823351. *Clubs:* Royal and Ancient Golf (Captain, 1980–81); Hon. Company of Edinburgh Golfers; Prestwick Golf; Royal St George's Golf; Pine Valley Golf, Augusta National Golf (USA).

ALEXANDER, William Gemmell, MBE 1945; *b* 19 Aug. 1918; *s* of Harold Gemmell Alexander and Winifred Ada Alexander (*née* Stott); *m* 1945, Janet Rona Page Alexander (*née* Elias); four *s* one *d. Educ:* Tre Arddur Bay Sch.; Sedbergh Sch.; Oxford Univ. (MA). Served War of 1939–45 (despatches, war stars and clasps): Driver Mechanic, 2nd Lieut, Lieut, Capt., Maj.; served in France, S Africa, Eritrea, Egypt, Middle East, Sicily, Italy, Algeria, NW Europe. HM Overseas Civil Service, 1946–59: Gilbert and Ellice Is, 1946–51; Mauritius, 1951–55; Cyprus, 1955–59; Man., Cooperative Wholesale Soc., Agricultural Dept, 1960–63; Dir, Internat. Cooperative Alliance, 1963–68; Dir-Gen., RoSPA, 1968–74; County Road Safety Officer, W Yorks MCC, 1974–78; Chm., W. H. Stott & Co. Ltd, 1979–83 (Dir, 1968–83). Mem., BSI Quality Assurance Council, 1975–83. Clerk, Dent Parish Council, 1980–. AMBIM 1963. *Recreations:* all sports and long distance walking. *Address:* Cross House, Dent, Cumbria LA10 5TF. *T:* Dent 228. *Club:* Royal Commonwealth Society.

ALEXANDER-SINCLAIR of Freswick, Maj.-Gen. David Boyd, CB 1981; retired 1982; *b* 2 May 1927; *s* of late Comdr M. B. Alexander-Sinclair of Freswick, RN and late Avril N. Fergusson-Buchanan; *m* 1958, Ann Ruth, *d* of late Lt-Col Graeme Daglish; two *s* one *d. Educ:* Eton (King's Scholar). Commnd into Rifle Bde, 1946, served in Germany, Kenya, Cyprus; ADC to GOC South Malaya District and Maj.-Gen. Bde of Gurkhas, 1950–51; psc 1958; Bde Major, 6th Inf. Bde Gp, 1959–61; GSO2 (Dirg Staff) Staff Coll., 1963–65; comdg 3rd Bn Royal Green Jackets, 1967–69; MoD, 1965–67 and 1969–71; Comdr, 6th Armd Bde, 1971–73; Student, RCDS, 1974; GOC 1st Division, 1975–77; COS, UKLF, 1978–80; Comdt, Staff Coll., 1980–82. *Address:* c/o Midland Bank, 69 Pall Mall, SW1Y 5EY.

ALEXANDER-SINCLAIR, John Alexis Clifford Cerda, SMOM, FRSA, RMS; Chairman, Human Rights Trust, since 1974 (Founder and Chairman, 1969, Vice-Chairman, 1971–73); Vice-Chairman: Anti-Slavery Society and Committee for Indigenous People, since 1971 (Committee Member, since 1965); (also Founder) British Institute of Human Rights, since 1971; Vice President, International League for Animal Rights, Paris, 1986; Chairman: British League for Animal Rights; Art Registration Committee, since 1969; *b* 22 Feb. 1906; *s* of Col C. H. Alexander, Jacob's Horse, and Donna Lyta Alexander dei Marchesi della Cerda; *m* 1st, 1927, Baroness von Gottberg

(decd); one *d*; 2nd, 1933, Stella Tucker; one *s* one *d*; 3rd, 1950, Simonne de Rougemont (*née* Vion); 4th, 1965, Maureen Dover (*née* Wood); one step *s. Educ:* Charterhouse; Goettingen and Munich Univs. Entered HM Foreign Service, 1928; served in China as Vice-Consul and Consul; despatches (Admiralty) 1938; Founder and Mem., Chinese Industrial Co-operatives, 1940–41; Liaison Free French Headquarters, Far East, 1941 (POW Shanghai, 1942); served in Washington as 1st Sec. of Embassy, 1943; seconded to UNRRA, London and Paris, 1944 (Mem., Cabinet Particulier, French Minister Henri Frenay, Refugees, Deportees, and PoWs, Paris); CCG as Controller (Col) Economic Plans, 1945; 1st Sec. UK Delegation, UN, NY, 1946, 1947, 1948; Vice-Chm. UNICEF, 1946, 1947; Sec. Gen. UK Delegation Geneva Red Cross Conf., 1949; served UN, NY, 1950; Dir UN Office of High Comr for refugees, Geneva, 1951–52; transf. UN High Comr for Refugees Rep. (local rank Minister), Rome, 1953–55; European Dir (Paris), International Rescue Cttee, NY, 1957–58; UN Tech. Assistance Adviser to Min. of Finance, Govt of Thailand, Jan.-Feb. 1959, to Nat. Iranian Oil Co., Tehran, Iran, 1959–60; Head of Oil Industry Labour Re-deployment Unit, 1960; Manpower Expert, FAO (UN Special Fund) in the Rif, Morocco, 1961–62. Founder Mem., Hansard Soc. for Parliamentary Govt, 1944; Executive Sec. Liberal International, London, 1963–64; Hon. Campaign Dir, UK Cttee for Human Rights Year, 1967, 1968, 1969; Member: Cttee, Internat. Social Service, 1972; Cttee, League Against Cruel Sports, 1974–81; Dir, Animal Welfare Year, 1976; Vice-Pres., British Assoc. of Former UN Civil Servants, 1978–81. Exec. Chm., British Visual Artists Rights Soc., 1981–82; UK Consultant, Société de la Propriété Artistique Dessins et Modèles, 1981–83; Mem. Council, Design and Artists Copyright Soc., 1984–. Knight of Magistral Grace, British Assoc. of SMO Malta, 1957. Distinguished Service Award (Internat. Rescue Cttee), 1959. Life Member, Fellow 1965, Royal Soc. of Arts; Mem., Royal Soc. of Miniature Painters, Sculptors and Gravers, 1971; Hon. Mem. Exec. Cttee, UK Section, Association Internationale des Arts Plastiques et Graphiques, 1977–82. *Address:* 5 Aysgarth Road, Dulwich Village, SE21 7JR. *T:* 01–733 1666; The Clink, Goodings, Woodlands St Mary, Newbury RG16 7BD. *T:* Great Shefford 450; 56 Boulevard Richard Lenoir, 75011 Paris, France. *T:* Paris 4805 3588. *Club:* Athenæum.

ALFORD, Ven. John Richard; Archdeacon of Halifax, 1972–84, now Emeritus; *b* 21 June 1919; *s* of Walter John and Gertrude Ellen Alford. *Educ:* Fitzwilliam House, Cambridge (History Tri. Pts 1 and 2, BA 1941, MA 1947); Cuddesdon College, Oxford. Deacon 1943, priest 1944, Wakefield; Curate, St Paul, King Cross, Halifax, 1943–47; Curate, Wakefield Cathedral, 1947–50; Tutor, Wells Theological College, 1950–56; Priest Vicar, Wells Cathedral, 1950–56; Vice-Principal, The Queen's College, Birmingham, 1956–67; Exam. Chaplain to Bp of Kimberley and Kuruman, 1961–65; Domestic Chaplain, Director of Ordinands, and Exam. Chaplain to Bp of Chester, 1967–72; Vicar of Shotwick, Chester, 1967–72; Hon. Canon of Chester Cathedral, 1969–72, Emeritus, 1972; Canon Residentiary of Wakefield Cathedral, 1972–84, Emeritus 1985–; Examining Chaplain to Bp of Wakefield, 1972–84. Mem., General Synod of C of E, 1980–84; Vice-Pres., CEMS, 1980–86. *Recreations:* music, walking. *Address:* 3 Drummond Court, Leeds LS16 5QE. *Club:* Royal Over-Seas League.

ALFRED, (Arnold) Montague; Second Permanent Secretary, and Chief Executive, Property Services Agency, Department of the Environment, 1982–84; *b* 21 March 1925; *s* of Reuben Alfred and Bessie Alfred (*née* Arbesfield); *m* 1947, Sheila Jacqueline Gold; three *s. Educ:* Central Foundation Boys' Sch.; Imperial Coll., London; London Sch. of Economics. Head of Economics Dept, Courtaulds Ltd, 1953–69; Director, Nylon Div., Courtaulds Ltd, 1964–69; Dir, BPC Ltd, 1969–81; Chairman: BPC Publishing Ltd, 1971–81; Caxton Publishing Holdings Ltd, 1971–81. *Publications:* Discounted Cash Flow (jointly), 1965; Business Economics (jointly), 1968. Numerous articles in: Accountant, Textile Jl, Investment Analyst, etc. *Recreation:* active in Jewish community affairs. *Address:* c/o Institute of Directors, 168 Pall Mall, SW1Y 5ED.

ALFVÉN, Prof. Hannes Olof Gösta, PhD; Professor of Plasma Physics, Royal Institute of Technology, Stockholm, 1963–73; *b* Sweden, 30 May 1908; *s* of Johannes Alfvén and Anna-Clara Romanus; *m* 1935, Kerstin Erikson, *d* of Rolf E. and Maria Uddenberg. *Educ:* Univ. of Uppsala (PhD 1934). Prof. of Theory of Electricity, 1940–45 and of Electronics, 1945–63, Royal Inst. of Technology, Stockholm. Prof., Univ. of California at San Diego, 1967. Pres., Pugwash Confs on Science and World Affairs, 1967–72; Member: Bd of Dirs, Swedish Atomic Energy Co., 1956–68; Science Adv. Council of Swedish Govt, 1961–67. Member: Swedish Acad. of Sciences; several foreign acads incl. Royal Society, London, 1980, Acad. of Sciences of the USSR, Nat. Acad. of Sciences, Washington, DC. Hon. DSc Oxon, 1977. Awarded Gold Medal of Royal Astronomical Soc. (Gt Britain), 1967; Nobel Prize for Physics, 1970; Lomonosov Medal, 1971; Franklin Medal, 1971. *Publications:* Cosmical Electrodynamics, 1948; On the Origin of the Solar System, 1956; Cosmical Electrodynamics: Fundamental Principles (jointly), 1963; World-Antiworlds (Eng. trans.), 1966; (as Olof Johannesson) The Tale of the Big Computer (Eng. trans.), 1968; Atom, Man and the Universe (Eng. trans.), 1969; (with Kerstin Alfvén) M70–Living on the Third Planet, 1971; (with G. Arrhenius) Evolution of the Solar System NASA SP-345, 1976; Cosmic Plasma, 1981; papers in physics and astrophysics. *Address:* c/o Department of Plasma Physics, Royal Institute of Technology, S-100 44 Stockholm, Sweden; University of California, San Diego, EE & CS, C-014, La Jolla, Calif 92093, USA.

ALGAR, Claudius Randleson, JP; barrister-at-law; *b* 18 May 1900; *s* of Claudius G. Algar; *m* 1930, Constance, *d* of Edgar Tucker, Carmarthen; one *s. Educ:* Highgate School. Barrister-at-law, Inner Temple, 1925. Dep. Chm., Wilts QS, 1945–71. Member of the Corporation of London, 1930–48. JP Wiltshire, 1941. *Address:* Rye Hill, Longbridge Deverill, Warminster, Wilts. *T:* Maiden Bradley 316.

ALGOMA, Bishop of, since 1983; **Rt. Rev. Leslie Ernest Peterson;** *b* 4 Nov. 1928; *s* of late Ernest Victor Peterson and of Dorothy Blanche Peterson (*née* Marsh); *m* 1953, Yvonne Hazel Lawton; two *s* three *d. Educ:* Univ. of Western Ontario (BA 1952); Huron College (LTh 1954); Teachers' Coll., North Bay, Ont., 1970. Deacon 1954, priest 1955; Incumbent of All Saints', Coniston, Ont., 1954–59; St Peter's Elliot Lake, 1959–63; Rector, Christ Church, North Bay, 1963–78; Teacher, Marshall Park Elem. School, 1970–78; Rector, Trinity Church, Parry Sound, 1978–83; Coadjutor Bishop, June-Sept. 1983. *Recreations:* canoe tripping, gardening, skiing. *Address:* 134 Simpson Street, Sault Ste Marie, Ontario P6A 3V4, Canada. *T:* 705–256–7379, (office) 705–256–5061.

ALHEGELAN, Sheikh Faisal Abdul Aziz; Order of King Abdulaziz, Saudi Arabia; Saudi Arabian Ambassador to the United States of America, since 1979; *b* 7 Oct. 1929; *s* of Sheikh Abdulaziz Alhegelan and Fatima Al Eissa; *m* 1961, Nouha Tarazi; three *s. Educ:* Faculty of Law, Fouad Univ., Cairo. Min. of Foreign Affairs, 1952–54; Saudi Arabian Embassy, Washington, USA, 1954–58; Chief of Protocol, Jeddah, 1958–60; Polit. Adviser to the King, 1960–61; Ambassador to: Spain, 1961–68; Venezuela and Argentina (concurrently), 1968–75; Denmark, 1975–76; Court of St James's, 1976–79. Gran Cruz, Isabel la Catolica, Spain; Gran Cordon Orden del Libertador, Venezuela; Grande Official, Orden Rio Branco, Brazil. *Address:* Royal Embassy of Saudi Arabia, 1520 18th Street, NW, Washington, DC 20036, USA.

ALISON, Rt. Hon. Michael James Hugh; PC 1981; MP (C) Selby, since 1983 (Barkston Ash, 1964–83); *b* 27 June 1926; *m* 1958, Sylvia Mary Haigh; two *s* one *d. Educ:* Eton; Wadham Coll., Oxford. Coldstream Guards, 1944–48; Wadham Coll., Oxford, 1948–51; Lazard Bros & Co. Ltd, 1951–53; London Municipal Soc., 1954–58; Conservative Research Dept, 1958–64. Parly Under-Sec. of State, DHSS, 1970–74; Minister of State: Northern Ireland Office, 1979–81; Dept of Employment, 1981–83; PPS to Prime Minister, 1983–. *Address:* House of Commons, SW1A 0AA.

ALISON, William Andrew Greig, FLA; Director of Libraries, City of Glasgow, 1975–81; *b* 23 Oct. 1916; *m* 1942, Jessie Youngson Henderson; two *d. Educ:* Daniel Stewart's Coll., Edinburgh. Served War, Royal Air Force, 1940–46. Edinburgh Public Libraries, 1935–62: Assistant, 1935–46; Librarian, Fine Art Dept, 1946–55; Branch Librarian, 1955–61; Librarian, Scottish and Local History Depts, 1961–62; Glasgow City Libraries, 1962–81: Supt of District Libraries, 1962–64; Depute City Librarian, 1964–74; City Librarian, 1974–75. President: Scottish Library Assoc., 1975; Library Assoc., 1979 (also Mem. Council, 1979–82; Chm., Library Assoc. Publishing, 1981–82); Member: British Library Adv. Council, 1979–82; Nat. Library of Scotland Library Co-operation Cttee, 1974–81. British Council visits to: Zimbabwe, 1981; Bahrain, 1982; Syria, 1983. Church of Scotland elder and session clerk. Silver Jubilee Medal, 1977. *Recreations:* travel, philately. *Address:* St Mawgan, 103 Mossgiel Road, Glasgow G43 2BY. *T:* 041–632 6036.

AL-KHALIFA, Shaikh Abdul-Rahman Faris; Ambassador in the Ministry of Foreign Affairs, Bahrain, since 1984; *b* 24 Feb. 1942; *s* of Shaikh Faris bin Khalifa Al-Khalifa and Shaikha Latifa Rashid Al-Khalifa; *m* 1969, Shaikha Latifa Salman Al-Khalifa; one *s* four *d. Educ:* Bahrain; Univ. of Cairo (BSc Economics and Commercial Subjects). Member of the Ruling Family of the State of Bahrain. Ambassador to UK, 1980–84. *Address:* Ministry of Foreign Affairs, PO Box 547, Bahrain. *Clubs:* Royal Automobile; Wentworth Golf, Hampstead Golf.

ALLAIRE, Paul Arthur; President and Director, Xerox Corporation, PO Box 1600, Stamford, Connecticut, since 1986; *b* 21 July 1938; *s* of late Arthur E. Allaire and of Mrs G. P. Murphy; *m* 1963, Kathleen Buckley; one *s* one *d. Educ:* Worcester Polytechnic Inst., USA (BS Elect. Eng.); Carnegie-Mellon Univ., USA (MS Industrial Admin). Engineer, Univac, 1960–62; Project Manager, General Electric, 1962–64; Manager Financial Planning and Pricing, Xerox Corp., 1966–70; Financial Controller, Rank Xerox Ltd, 1970–73; Xerox Corporation: Dir, Internat. Finance, 1973–74; Dir, Internat. Ops, 1974–75; Rank Xerox Ltd: Chief Staff Officer, 1975–79; Dep. Man. Dir, 1979–80; Man. Dir, 1980–83; Sen. Vice-Pres., Xerox Corp., 1983–86. Bd Mem., American Chamber of Commerce, 1980–. *Recreations:* horse riding, tennis.

ALLAM, Peter John; Architect Principal in private practice of Peter Allam, Chartered Architect, Dollar, 1964–68, 1971–78 and since 1981; *b* 17 June 1927; *er s* of late Leslie Francis Allam and Annette Farquharson (*née* Lawson); *m* 1961, Pamela Mackie Haynes; two *d. Educ:* Royal High Sch., Edinburgh; Glasgow Sch. of Architecture. War service, 1944–48, Far East; commnd in Seaforth Highlanders, 1946. Architectural trng, 1948–53. Bahrain Petroleum Co., Engrg Div., 1954–55; Asst in private architectural practices, 1956–64; Partner in private practice of Haswell-Smith & Partners, Edinburgh, 1978–79; Director, Saltire Soc., 1968–70; Dir of Sales, Smith & Wellstood Ltd, Manfg Ironfounders, 1979–81. ARIBA 1964; FRIAS 1985 (Associate, 1964). *Recreations:* study and practice of conservation, both architectural and natural; music, riding, Rugby. *Address:* 4 Moir's Well, Dollar, Clackmannanshire FK14 7BQ. *T:* (home) Dollar 2973; (office) Dollar 2850.

ALLAN, Andrew Norman; Director of Programmes, Central Independent Television, since 1984; *b* 26 Sept. 1943; *s* of Andrew Allan and Elizabeth (*née* Davison); *m* 1978, Joanna Forrest; two *s* one *d*, and two *d* of a former marriage. *Educ:* Birmingham Univ. (BA). Presenter, ABC Television, 1965–66; Producer: Thames Television, 1966–69; ITN, 1970; Thames TV, 1971–75; Head of News, Thames TV, 1976–78; Tyne Tees Television: Dir of Progs, 1978–83; Dep. Man. Dir, 1982–83; Man. Dir, 1983–84. *Recreations:* reading, dining. *Address:* c/o Central Independent Television, Central House, Broad Street, Birmingham B1 2JP. *T:* 021–643 9898.

ALLAN, Sir Anthony James Allan H.; *see* Havelock-Allan.

ALLAN, (Charles) Lewis (Cuthbert), MA, CEng, FICE, FIEE, FBIM; Chairman, South of Scotland Electricity Board, 1967–73 (Deputy Chairman, 1964–67); Member, North of Scotland Hydro-Electric Board, 1967–73; *b* 22 July 1911; *s* of Charles W. Allan, Edinburgh, and Isabella H. Young; *m* 1938, Kathleen Mary Robinson, Chesterfield, Derbyshire; one *s* three *d. Educ:* Merchiston Castle School, Edinburgh; Pembroke College, Cambridge (Mechanical Sciences Tripos). Bruce Peebles & Co. Ltd, Edinburgh, 1933–35; Balfour Beatty & Co. Ltd, 1935–38; Central Electricity Board, 1938–41; Ipswich Corp. Electric Supply and Transport Dept, 1941–44; North of Scotland Hydro-Electric Board, 1944–63 (Chief Electrical and Mechanical Engineer, 1954–63). *Publications:* articles in the electrical technical press and for World Power Conference. *Recreations:* gardening, walking, fishing, piping, Church work. *Address:* Kil Modan, North Connel, Argyll PA37 1RE.

ALLAN, Colin Faulds, CB 1976; Chief Planning Inspector (Director of Planning Inspectorate), Department of the Environment, 1971–78, retired; *b* Newcastle upon Tyne, 1917; *s* of late Jack Stanley and Ruth Allan; *m* 1940, Aurea, 2nd *d* of Algernon Noble, Hexham; one *s* one *d. Educ:* Royal Grammar Sch., Newcastle upon Tyne; King's Coll. (Newcastle), Durham Univ. DipArch, ARIBA, DipTP (Distinction), FRTPI. Capt., RA, 1940–45; served in Iraq, India, Burma (despatches). Chief Asst to Dr Thomas Sharp, Planning Consultant, 1945–47; Area Planning Officer, Cumberland and Staffs CC, 1947–57; joined Housing and Planning Inspectorate, 1957; Chief Housing and Planning Inspector, DoE (formerly Min. of Housing and Local Govt), 1967–71. *Recreations:* walking, bird-watching, reading, eighteenth-century wineglasses. *Address:* Fieldfares, Chinthurst Lane, Shalford, Guildford, Surrey. *T:* Guildford 61528.

ALLAN, Sir Colin (Hamilton), KCMG 1977 (CMG 1968); OBE 1959; FRAI 1950; Her Majesty's Overseas Civil Service, retired; *b* 23 Oct. 1921; *yr s* of late John Calder Allan, Cambridge, NZ; *m* 1955, Betty Dorothy, *e d* of late A. C. Evans, Brisbane, Australia; three *s. Educ:* Hamilton High Sch., NZ; College House, Canterbury Univ., NZ; Magdalene College, Cambridge. Military Service, NZ, 1942–44. Cadet, Colonial Admin. Service, British Solomon Is, 1945; District Comr, Western Solomons, 1946; District Comr, Malaita, 1950; Special Lands Comr, 1953; Sen. Asst Sec., Western Pacific High Commn, 1957; Asst Resident Comr, New Hebrides, 1959; British Resident Comr, 1966–73; Governor and C-in-C, Seychelles, 1973–76, and Comr, British Indian Ocean Territory, 1973–76; Governor, Solomon Is, and High Comr for Western Pacific, 1976–78. Delegate: Seychelles Constitutional Conf., 1975, 1976; Solomon Is Constitutional Conf., 1977. Vis. Fellow, Australian Nat. Univ., Research Sch. of Pacific Studies, 1979; Vis. Lectr, Law Sch., Auckland Univ., 1981–. Member: Leprosy Trust Bd (NZ), 1980–; NZ Adv. Council, Province of Melanesia, 1982–. Commandeur, L'Ordre Nationale du Mérite (France), 1966. *Publications:* Land Tenure in the British Solomon Islands Protectorate, 1958; papers on colonial administration. *Recreations:* malacology,

reading The Times. *Address:* Glen Rowan, 17 Sale Street, Howick, Auckland, New Zealand. *Club:* Royal Commonwealth Society.

ALLAN, Diana Rosemary, (Mrs R. B. Allan); *see* Cotton, D. R.

ALLAN, Douglas; *see* Allan, J. D.

ALLAN, George Alexander, MA; Headmaster, Robert Gordon's College, Aberdeen, since 1978; *b* 3 Feb. 1936; *s* of William Allan and Janet Peters (*née* Watt); *m* 1962, Anne Violet Veevers; two *s. Educ:* Daniel Stewart's Coll., Edinburgh; Edinburgh Univ. (MA 1st Cl. Hons Classics; Bruce of Grangehill Scholar, 1957). Classics Master, Glasgow Acad., 1958–60; Daniel Stewart's College: Classics Master, 1960–63; Head of Classics, 1963–73; Housemaster, 1966–73; Schoolmaster Fellow, Corpus Christi Coll., Cambridge, 1972; Dep. Headmaster, Robert Gordon's Coll., 1973–77. Headmasters' Conference: Sec., Scottish Div., 1980–; Mem. Cttee, 1982, 1983; Mem., ISIS Scotland Cttee, 1984–; Governor, Welbeck Coll., 1980–. *Recreations:* golf, gardening, music. *Address:* 24 Woodend Road, Aberdeen AB2 6YH. *T:* Aberdeen 321733. *Clubs:* East India, Devonshire Sports and Public Schools; Royal Northern & University (Aberdeen).

ALLAN, Gordon Buchanan, TD 1950; CA; *b* 11 Aug. 1914; *s* of late Alexander Buchanan Allan, MIMechE, and Irene Lilian Allan, Glasgow; *m* 1971, Gwenda Jervis Davies, *d* of late John William and Elizabeth Davies, Porthcawl, Glam. *Educ:* Glasgow Academy; High Sch. of Glasgow; Glasgow Univ. Mem. Inst. Chartered Accountants (Scot.), 1937. Commissioned into Royal Signals (TA), 1938. Served War of 1939–45: DAAG, GHQ, India, 1945, (Major). Director: George Outram & Co. Ltd, 1960–75 (Dep. Man. Dir and Financial Dir, 1970–75); Holmes McDougall Ltd, 1966–72. Mem. Press Council, 1969–74. Vice-Pres., Scottish Daily Newspaper Soc., 1970, Pres. 1971–73; Dir, Glasgow Chamber of Commerce, 1971–75. Member: UK Newsprint Users' Cttee, 1972–75; Council, CBI, 1972–74; Finance Cttee, RIIA, 1975–77; Merchants' House of Glasgow, 1975–. Mem. Bd, Bield Housing Assoc. Ltd, 1978–. Trustee, Bield Housing Trust, 1975–. Governor, The Queen's College, Glasgow, 1976–. *Recreations:* music, golf. *Address:* 3 Winchester Court, Glasgow G12 0JN. *T:* 041–334 2353. *Club:* Royal Scottish Automobile (Glasgow).

ALLAN, Rt. Rev. Hugh James Pearson; *see* Keewatin, Bishop of.

ALLAN, Ian; Chairman, Ian Allan Group Ltd, since 1962; *b* 29 June 1922; *s* of George A. T. Allan, OBE, and Mary Louise (*née* Barnes); *m* 1947, Mollie Eileen (*née* Franklin); two *s. Educ:* St Paul's Sch. Joined Southern Railway Co., 1939. Founded Ian Allan Ltd, Publishers, 1945; other cos co-ordinated into Ian Allan Group Ltd, 1962. Chm., Dart Valley Light Railway PLC, 1976–. Governor, Christ's Hosp., 1944–, Almoner, 1980–; Chm., King Edward's Sch., Witley, 1983– (Governor, 1975–); Treas., Bridewell Royal Hosp. 1983–. Vice Pres., Transport Trust, 1979–; Mem., Transport Users Consultative Cttee for London, 1982–84. *Publications:* compiled and edited many books on railways and transport subjects, 1939–. *Recreations:* swimming, touring, miniature railways. *Address:* Terminal House, Shepperton TW17 8AS. *T:* Walton-on-Thames 228950; The Jetty, Middleton-on-Sea, Bognor Regis, W Sussex. *T:* Middleton-on-Sea 3378.

ALLAN, James Nicholas, CBE 1976; Ambassador to Mozambique, since 1986; *b* 22 May 1932; *s* of late Morris Edward Allan and Joan Bach; *m* 1961, Helena Susara Crouse; one *s* one *d. Educ:* Gresham's Sch.; London Sch. of Economics. HM Forces, 1950–53. Asst Principal, CRO, 1956–58; Third, later Second Sec., Cape Town/Pretoria, 1958–59; Private Sec. to Parly Under-Sec., 1959–61; First Secretary: Freetown, 1961–64; Nicosia, 1964; CRO, later FCO, 1964–68; Head of Chancery, Peking, 1969–71; Luxembourg, 1971–73; Counsellor, seconded to Northern Ireland Office, Belfast, 1973–75; Counsellor, FCO, 1976; Head of Overseas Inf. Dept., FCO, 1978–81 (Governor's Staff, Salisbury, Dec. 1979–March 1980); High Comr in Mauritius, 1981–85, concurrently Ambassador (non-resident) to the Comoros, 1984–85. *Address:* c/o Foreign and Commonwealth Office, SW1. *Club:* Athenæum.

ALLAN, Commissioner Janet Laurie; retired 1957; *b* 20 March 1892; *d* of Thomas Alexander Allan, chemist, Strathaven, Scotland. *Educ:* in Scotland. Entered Salvation Army Training Coll., 1911; commissioned as sergeant to the College, 1912; opened Salvation Army work in Castle Douglas, Scotland, 1913; returned to Training College as a Brigade Officer, 1915; Home Officer at Training Coll., 1918; with "Calypso" Party sailed to India (South Travancore, South India), 1921; returned to England, 1929, and appointed to slum and goodwill work in British Isles; returned to India; served in Travancore, Calcutta, and Eastern India; also Madras and Telegu country as Territorial Comdr; Territorial Comdr of Western India, 1951–54; Territorial Comdr of Southern India, 1954–57, Salvation Army. Leader Salvation Army Women's Social Work, Great Britain and Ireland, 1947; Comr, 1951. *Address:* Glebelands, 1 Grove Hill Road, SE5 8DF.

ALLAN, John Clifford, RCNC; Director, Manpower, Dockyards, 1975–79; *b* 3 Feb. 1920; *s* of James Arthur and Mary Alice Allan; *m* 1947, Dorothy Mary (*née* Dossett); two *d. Educ:* Royal Naval Coll., Greenwich. Entered Royal Corps of Naval Constructors, 1945; service at HM Dockyards: Portsmouth, Chatham, Devonport, Gibraltar, Singapore, 1950–75; Chief Constructor, Chief Executive Dockyard HQ, 1967–69, Asst Dir, 1969, Dir, 1975. *Recreations:* painting, tennis, squash (Pres., Lansdown Lawn Tennis & Squash Racquets Club). *Address:* New Morney, Lansdown Road, Bath, Avon BA1 5TD. *T:* Bath 315237.

ALLAN, (John) Douglas; Regional Procurator Fiscal for Lothians and Borders and Procurator Fiscal for Edinburgh, since 1983; *b* 2 Oct. 1941; *s* of Robert Taylor Allan and late Christina Helen Blythe Reid or Allan; *m* 1966, Helen Elizabeth Jean Aiton or Allan; one *s* one *d. Educ:* George Watson's Coll.; Edinburgh Univ. (BL); Napier Coll., Edinburgh (DMS); FBIM. Solicitor and Notary Public. Solicitor, 1963–67; Depute Procurator Fiscal, 1967–71; Sen. Legal Asst, Crown Office, 1971–76; Asst Procurator Fiscal, Glasgow, 1976–77; Sen. Asst Procurator Fiscal, Glasgow, 1978–79; Asst Solicitor, Crown Office, 1979–83. *Recreations:* youth work, church work, walking. *Address:* Minard, 80 Greenbank Crescent, Edinburgh EH10 5SW. *T:* 031-447 2593.

ALLAN, John Gray, CBE 1975; Legal Adviser and Solicitor to the Crown Estate Commissioners, 1961–77; *b* 10 Nov. 1915; *s* of late John Allan, CB, FSA, FBA, LLD, and Ida Mary (*née* Law). *Educ:* Charterhouse; Oriel College, Oxford. Called to Bar, Middle Temple, 1940. War Service, 1940–46: The Black Watch, GSO2 (War Office and Allied Land Headquarters, Melbourne), 1942–46. Legal Branch, Min. of Agriculture, Fisheries and Food, 1946–57. Deputy Legal Adviser, Crown Estate Office, 1957. *Recreations:* golf, bridge. *Address:* 5 Rheidol Terrace, N1. *T:* 01–226 7616. *Club:* Boodles.

ALLAN, Lewis; *see* Allan, C. L. C.

ALLAN, William Roderick Buchanan; Arts Consultant to United Technologies Corporation, since 1983, currently working with Tate Gallery, National Portrait Gallery and National Maritime Museum; *b* 11 Sept. 1945; *s* of James Buchanan Allan and Mildred Pattenden; *m* 1973, Gillian Gail Colgan; two *s. Educ:* Stowe; Trinity Coll., Cambridge (MA Hons History, 1970). Joined staff of The Connoisseur, 1972, Editor 1976–80;

Editorial Consultant to Ommific, 1980–83. Author of seven radio plays with nineteenth century historical themes. *Publications:* contrib. to several books dealing with British history; contrib. to History Today, The Connoisseur, and Antique Collector. *Recreations:* military history, cooking. *Address:* 54 South Western Road, St Margaret's, Twickenham, Mddx. *T:* 01–891 0974.

ALLANBRIDGE, Hon. Lord; William Ian Stewart; a Senator of the College of Justice in Scotland, since 1977; *b* 8 Nov. 1925; *s* of late John Stewart, FRIBA, and Mrs Maysie Shepherd Service or Stewart, Drimfearn, Bridge of Allan; *m* 1955, Naomi Joan Douglas, *d* of late Sir James Boyd Douglas, CBE, and of Lady Douglas, Barstibly, Castle Douglas; one *s* one *d*. *Educ:* Loretto; Glasgow and Edinburgh Univs. Sub-Lt, RNVR, 1944–46. Called to the Bar, 1951; QC (Scot.) 1965; Advocate-Depute, 1959–64; Mem., Criminal Injuries Compensation Bd, 1969–70; Home Advocate-Depute, 1970–72; Solicitor-General for Scotland, 1972–74; Temp. Sheriff-Principal of Dumfries and Galloway, Apr.-Dec. 1974. Mem., Criminal Injuries Compensation Bd, 1976–77. *Address:* 60 Northumberland Street, Edinburgh EH3 6JE. *T:* 031–556 2823. *Clubs:* New (Edinburgh); RNVR (Glasgow).

ALLANSON-WINN, family name of **Baron Headley.**

ALLARD, Sir Gordon (Laidlaw), Kt 1981; President, Royal Victorian Eye and Ear Hospital, 1964–80; *b* 7 Aug. 1909; *m* 1935, Cherry Singleton; one *s*. *Educ:* Scotch Coll., Melbourne. FCA; FCA (NZ). Joined Flack & Flack, later Price Waterhouse & Co., 1927; Partner, and a Sen. Partner, in Australia and NZ, 1942–74. Chm., Australian Motor Industries Ltd. Mem., Gen. Council, Inst. of Chartered Accountants in Australia, 1962–70 (Victorian Chm., 1962–64). *Recreations:* golf, tennis, gardening. *Address:* 4 St Martins Close, Kooyong, Vic 3144, Australia. *Clubs:* Melbourne, Australian (Melbourne); Royal Melbourne Golf, Frankston Golf.

ALLARD, General Jean Victor, CC (Canada) 1968; CBE 1946; DSO 1943 (Bars 1944, 1945); ED 1946; CD 1958; Chief of Canadian Defence Staff, 1966–69; Representative of the Province of Quebec in New York, Sept. 1969–June 1970; now engaged in business as a consultant in industrial promotion; *b* Nicolet, PQ, 12 June 1913; *s* of late Ernest Allard and Victorine Trudel; *m* 1939, Simone, *d* of Gustave Piche, OBE; two *d*. *Educ:* St Laurent Coll., Montreal; St Jerome Coll., Kitchener, Ont. Joined Three Rivers Regt, 1933; Capt., 1938; Major, 1939; War of 1939–45: Co. of London Yeomanry, 1940–41; Canadian Army Staff Coll., Kingston, 1941–42 (Instructor, 1942); 5th Canadian Armoured Div.; second in command: Régt de la Chaudière; Royal 22e Regt, 1943 (Italy); Lt-Col 1944; CO Royal 22e Regt; Brig. 1945; Comd 6th Canadian Infantry Brigade, 1945 (Holland); Military Attaché Canadian Embassy, Moscow, 1945–48; Comd Eastern Quebec Area, 1948–50; idc 1951; Vice Quarter-Master Gen., Canada, 1952; Comdr, 25th Canadian Infantry Brigade Group, in Korea, 1953; Comdr 3rd Canadian Infantry Brigade, 1954; Comd Eastern Quebec Area, 1956; Maj.-Gen. 1958; Vice Chief of the General Staff, Canada, 1958; Comdr 4th Division, BAOR, 1961–63 (first Canadian to command a British Div.); Maj.-Gen. Survival, Ottawa, 1963; Lt-Gen. 1964; Chief of Operational Readiness, Canada, 1964–65; Comdr, Mobile Command, Canada, Oct. 1965–June 1966; General, 1966; Col Comdt, 12 Regt Blindé du Canada; Col, Royal 22e Regt, 1985. Member: Royal Canadian Military Inst.; Royal 22e Regt Assoc.; La Régie du 22e; Royal Canadian Air Force Assoc.; Royal Canadian Naval Service Assoc.; Cercle Universitaire d'Ottawa; Chm. Bd of Governors, Ottawa Univ., 1966–69, Member Bd, 1969–. Hon. DSS Laval, 1958; Hon. LLD: Ottawa, 1959; St Thomas, 1966; St Mary's, Halifax, 1969; Hon. DScMil RMC Canada, 1970. FRSA. Bronze Lion (Netherlands), 1945; Légion d'Honneur and Croix de Guerre (France), 1945; Legion of Merit (US), 1954. Kt of Magistral Grace, Sovereign and Military Order of Malta, 1967. *Publication:* Mémoires, 1985. *Recreations:* golf, music, fishing, hunting. *Address:* 3265 Boulevard du Carmel, Trois-Rivieres, Quebec, Canada. *Clubs:* Quebec Garrison, KI-8–EB Golf; Maskety Fish and Game.

ALLARDICE, William Arthur Llewellyn; His Honour Judge Allardice; DL; a Circuit Judge since 1972 (Midland and Oxford Circuit); *b* 18 Dec. 1924; *s* of late W. C. Allardice, MD, FRCSEd, JP, and late Constance Winifred Allardice; *m* 1956, Jennifer Ann, *d* of late G. H. Jackson; one *s* one *d*. *Educ:* Stonyhurst Coll.; University Coll., Oxford (MA). Open Schol., Classics, 1942; joined Rifle Bde, 1943, commnd 1944; served with 52nd LI, Europe and Palestine, 1945; Oxford, 1946–48; called to Bar, Lincoln's Inn, 1950; practised Oxford Circuit, 1950–71. DL Staffs, 1980. *Recreations:* local history, matters equestrian. *Address:* c/o Courts Administrator, Stafford. *T:* Stafford 55219.

ALLASON, Lt-Col James Harry, OBE 1953; *b* 6 Sept. 1912; *s* of late Brigadier-General Walter Allason, DSO; *m* 1946, Nuala Elveen (marr. diss. 1974), *d* of late J. A. McArevey, Foxrock, Co. Dublin; two *s*. *Educ:* Haileybury; RMA, Woolwich. Commissioned RA, 1932; transferred 3rd DG, 1937; War Service India and Burma, 1939–44; retired 1953. Member Kensington Borough Council, 1956–65. Contested (C) Hackney Central, General Election, 1955; MP (C) Hemel Hempstead, 1959–Sept. 1974; PPS to Sec. of State for War, 1960–64. *Address:* 82 Ebury Mews, SW1. *T:* 01–730 1576. *Clubs:* White's; Royal Yacht Squadron.

ALLAUN, Frank; *b* 27 Feb. 1913; *s* of Harry and Hannah Allaun; *m* 1941, Lilian Ball; one *s* one *d*. *Educ:* Manchester Grammar Sch. BA (Com); ACA. Town Hall Correspondent, and later Industrial Correspondent, Manchester Evening News; Northern Industrial Correspondent, Daily Herald; Editor, Labour's Northern Voice, 1951–67. Mem., NUJ; formerly Mem. AEU and Shop Assistants' Union; Pres., Labour Action for Peace, 1965–; Vice-Pres., Campaign for Nuclear Disarmament, 1983–; helped organise first Aldermaston march. MP (Lab) East Salford, 1955–83; PPS to the Secretary of State for the Colonies, Oct. 1964–March 1965, resigned. Mem., Labour Party National Executive, 1967–83, Dep. Chm., 1977–78, Chm., 1978–79. *Publications:* Stop the H Bomb Race, 1959; Heartbreak Housing, 1966; Your Trade Union and You, 1950; No Place Like Home, 1972; The Wasted '30 Billions, 1975; Questions and Answers on Nuclear Weapons, 1981; numerous broadcasts. *Recreations:* walking, swimming. *Address:* 1 South Drive, Manchester M21 2DX.

ALLAWAY, Percy Albert, CBE 1973; FEng; Director, EMI Ltd, 1965–81; Chairman, EMI Electronics Ltd, 1968–81; Member, Executive Management Board, THORN EMI Ltd, 1980–81, Consultant, 1981–82; *b* 22 Aug. 1915; *s* of Albert Edward Allaway and Frances Beatrice (*née* Rogers); *m* 1959, Margaret Lilian Petyt. *Educ:* Southall Technical College. FEng 1980, FIProdE, FIERE, FIQA. Trained EMI Ltd, 1930–35, returned 1940. Man. Dir, 1961–81, Chm., 1969–81, EMI Electronics Ltd; Chairman: EMI-Varian Ltd, 1969–81; EMI-MEC Ltd, 1968–81; Director: Nuclear Enterprises Ltd, 1961–81; SE Labs (EMI) Ltd, 1967–81. Pres., EEA, 1969–70 (former Mem. Council). Chm., Defence Industries Quality Assurance Panel, 1971–78; Past Chm. and Hon. Mem., NCQR; Member: Nat. Electronics Council, 1965–80; Raby Cttee, 1968–69; Parly and Scientific Cttee, 1976–82; Pres., IERE, 1975; a Vice-Pres., and Mem. Council: Inst. of Industrial Managers; IQA; Member: Bd and Exec. Cttee, CEI, 1974–78 (Vice-Chm., 1979–80, Chm., 1980–81); Design Council, 1978–80; PO Engrg Adv. Cttee, 1977–81, British Telecom Engrg Adv. Cttee, 1981–82. Mem., Court and Council, Brunel Univ., 1976–82.

Liveryman, and Mem. Court, 1981–86, Worshipful Co. of Scientific Instrument Makers. FRSA. DTech (hc) Brunel, 1973. *Address:* Kroller, 54 Howards Wood Drive, Gerrards Cross, Bucks. *T:* Gerrards Cross 885028.

ALLCHIN, Rev. Canon Arthur Macdonald; Residentiary Canon of Canterbury Cathedral since 1973; *b* 20 April 1930; *s* of late Dr Frank Macdonald Allchin and Louise Maude Allchin. *Educ:* Westminster Sch.; Christ Church, Oxford (BLitt, MA); Cuddesdon Coll., Oxford. Curate, St Mary Abbots, Kensington, 1956–60; Librarian, Pusey House, Oxford, 1960–69; Visiting Lecturer: General Theological Seminary, NY, 1967 and 1968; Catholic Theological Faculty, Lyons, 1980; Trinity Inst., NY, 1983; Vis. Prof., Nashotah House, Wisconsin, 1984; Warden, Community of Sisters of Love of God, Oxford, 1967–. Editor, Sobornost, 1960–77; Jt Editor, Christian, 1975–80. Hon. DD: Bucharest Theol Inst., 1977; Nashotah House, 1985. *Publications:* The Silent Rebellion, 1958; The Spirit and the Word, 1963; (with J. Coulson) The Rediscovery of Newman, 1967; Ann Griffiths, 1976; The World is a Wedding, 1978; The Kingdom of Love and Knowledge, 1979; The Dynamic of Tradition, 1981; A Taste of Liberty, 1982; The Joy of All Creation, 1984; contrib. Studia Liturgica, Irenikon, Theology, Eastern Churches Review, Worship. *Recreations:* music, poetry, walking in hill country. *Address:* 12 The Precincts, Canterbury CT1 2EH. *T:* Canterbury (0227) 463060.
See also F. R. Allchin.

ALLCHIN, Frank Raymond, PhD; FBA 1981; Fellow of Churchill College, since 1963, and Reader in Indian Studies, since 1972, University of Cambridge; *b* 9 July 1923; *s* of Frank MacDonald Allchin and Louise Maude Wright; *m* 1951, Bridget Gordon; one *s* one *d*. *Educ:* Westminster Sch.; Regent Street Polytechnic; Sch. of Oriental and African Studies, London Univ. (BA, PhD 1954); MA Cantab. Lectr in Indian Archaeology, SOAS, 1954–59; Univ. Lectr in Indian Studies, Cambridge, 1959–72. Jt Dir, Cambridge Univ. (British) Archaeol Mission to Pakistan, 1975–. Treas., Ancient India and Iran Trust, 1978–; Vice Chm., British Assoc. for Conservation of Cultural Heritage of Sri Lanka, 1982–. Consultant: UNESCO, 1969, 1972, 1975; UNDP, 1971. Chm., Broads Tours, Wroxham, Ltd, 1975–86 (Dir, 1964–86). *Publications:* Piklihal Excavations, 1960; Utnur Excavations, 1961; Neolithic Cattle Keepers of South India, 1963; Kavitāvalī, 1964; The Petition to Rām, 1966; (with B. Allchin) Birth of Indian Civilization, 1968; (with N. Hammond) The Archaeology of Afghanistan, 1978; (with D. K. Chakrabarti) Sourcebook of Indian Archaeology, vol. 1, 1979; (with B. Allchin) The Rise of Civilization in India and Pakistan, 1982; contribs to learned journals. *Recreations:* gardening, brewing. *Address:* Westgate House, 3 Orwell Road, Barrington, Cambridge CB2 5SE. *T:* Cambridge 870494. *Club:* Royal Commonwealth Society.
See also Rev. Canon A. M. Allchin.

ALLCOCK, John Gladding Major, CB 1964; *b* 20 July 1905; *o s* of Rev. William Gladding Allcock, MA (TCD), and Ada Allcock (*née* Hall); *m* 1936, Eileen, *d* of Dr Ll. A. Baiss, OBE, Swanage, Dorset; one *s* one *d*. *Educ:* St Paul's School; Jesus College, Cambridge. Classical Tripos Cl. II in Pts I and II, BA 1927; MA 1931. Awarded Commonwealth Fund Fellowship, 1939. War Service in Admiralty, 1939–44. Asst Master: Exeter School, 1927–28; Liverpool College, 1928–35; HM Inspector of Schools, 1935–66; Divisional Inspector (NW Div.), 1949; Chief Inspector for Educational Developments, 1959–66, retired. *Recreations:* music, theatre, foreign travel. *Address:* Russet Cottage, Corfe Castle, Dorset. *T:* Corfe Castle 480574.

ALLCROFT, Sir Philip M.; see Magnus-Allcroft, Sir Philip.

ALLDAY, Coningsby, CBE 1971; BSc (Hons); Chairman and Chief Executive, British Nuclear Fuels Ltd, 1983–86 (Managing Director, 1971–83); Member, UKAEA, 1976–86; *b* 21 Nov. 1920; *s* of late Esca and Margaret Allday; *m* 1945, Iris Helena Adams; one *s* one *d*. *Educ:* Solihull Sch.; BSc (Hons) Chemistry, London. CEng, FIChemE, 1979. ICI, 1939–59; UKAEA, 1959–71: Chief Chemist, Technical Dir, Commercial Dir, Dep. Man. Dir. Dir, North Region, National Westminster Bank, 1985–. *Recreations:* gardening, music. *Address:* 54 Goughs Lane, Knutsford, Cheshire WA16 8QN.

ALLDIS, Air Cdre Cecil Anderson, CBE 1962; DFC 1941; AFC 1956; RAF (retd); *b* 28 Sept. 1918; 2nd *s* of John Henry and Margaret Wright Alldis, Birkenhead; *m* 1942, Jeanette Claire Tarrant, *d* of Albert Edward Collingwood and Aida Mary Tarrant, Johannesburg; no *c*. *Educ:* Birkenhead Institute; Emmanuel Coll., Cambridge (MA). Served War, 1939–45 (despatches, DFC): Pilot, Wing Comdr, RAF, Bomber Command. Asst Air Attaché, Moscow, 1947–49; Flying and Staff appts, RAF, 1949–59; Dir of Administrative Planning, Air Ministry, 1959–62; Air Attaché, Bonn, 1963–66. Retd from RAF and entered Home Civil Service, 1966; MoD, 1966–69; seconded to HM Diplomatic Service, 1969; Counsellor (Defence Supply), HM Embassy, Bonn, 1969–80; retired from Home Civil Service, 1980. In retirement, raises funds for Peter Le Marchant Trust for the Disabled. Sec. Gen., The Air League, 1982–. *Recreations:* golf, fishing. *Address:* Tudor Cottage, Oxshott Way, Cobham, Surrey. *T:* Cobham 66092. *Club:* Naval and Military.

ALLDIS, John; conductor; *b* 10 Aug. 1929; *s* of W. J. and N. Alldis; *m* 1960, Ursula Margaret Mason; two *s*. *Educ:* Felsted School; King's Coll., Cambridge (MA). ARCO. Formed John Alldis Choir, 1962; formed and conducted London Symphony Chorus, 1966–69; Conductor, London Philharmonic Choir, 1969–82; Joint Chief Conductor, Radio Denmark, 1971–77; Conductor, Groupe Vocal de France, 1979–. FGSM 1976; Fellow, Westminster Choir Coll., Princeton, NJ, 1978. Chevalier des Arts et des Lettres (France), 1984. *Address:* 3 Wool Road, Wimbledon, SW20 0HN. *T:* 01–946 4168.

ALLDRITT, Walter, JP; Regional Secretary, National Union of General and Municipal Workers, in Liverpool, North Wales, and Northern Ireland, 1970–81; *b* 4 July 1918; *s* of late Henry and Bridget Alldritt; *m* 1945, Mary Teresa, *d* of W. H. McGuinness; four *s* one *d*. *Educ:* St Francis de Sales; Liverpool University (WEA). Served with HM Forces, 1939–46. Trade Union Officer. MP (Lab) Scotland Div. of Liverpool, June 1964–Feb. 1971. Member various public bodies. Councillor 1955, JP 1958, Liverpool. *Address:* 104 Longmeadow Road, Knowsley, Prescot, Merseyside L34 0HT. *T:* 051–546 5703.

ALLEGRO, John Marco; author; *b* 17 Feb. 1923; *s* of late John Marco Allegro and Mabel Jessie (*née* Perry); *m* 1948, Joan Ruby Lawrence (marr. diss. 1985); one *s* one *d*. *Educ:* Wallington County Grammar Sch.; Univ. of Manchester. Royal Navy, 1941–46; Manchester Univ. 1947–52; BA 1st cl. Hons Oriental Studies, 1951; MA 1952; Bles Hebrew Prize, 1950; Scarborough Sen. Studentship, 1951–54; Leverhulme Research Award, 1958; Oxford Univ. (Magdalen), research in Hebrew dialects, 1952–53; University of Manchester: Lectureship in Comparative Semitic Philology and in Hebrew, 1954–62; Lectr in Old Testament and Intertestamental Studies, 1962–70. Brit. rep. on Internat. editing team for Dead Sea Scrolls, Jerusalem, 1953–; Adviser to Jordanian Govt on Dead Sea Scrolls, 1961–; Trustee and Hon. Sec. of Dead Sea Scrolls Fund, 1962–70. Organiser and leader of archaeological expedns to Jordan, 1959–. Popular lectr and broadcaster on archaeological subjects. TV films include: Dead Sea Scrolls, BBC, 1957; Search in the Kidron, BBC, 1963; The Mystery of the Dead Sea Scrolls, BBC; Physician, Heal Thyself, CBS. *Publications:* The Dead Sea Scrolls (Pelican), 1956 (revised edn 1964);

The People of the Dead Sea Scrolls, 1958; The Treasure of the Copper Scroll, 1960 (revised edn 1964); Search in the Desert, 1964; The Shapira Affair, 1964; Discoveries in the Judæan Desert, V, 1968; The Sacred Mushroom and the Cross, 1970; The End of a Road, 1970; The Chosen People, 1971; Lost Gods, 1977; The Dead Sea Scrolls and the Christian Myth, 1979; All Manner of Men, 1982; Physician, Heal Thyself..., 1985; articles in learned jls on Semitic philology. *Recreations:* fell walking, sketching. *Address:* 18 Wellbank, Sandbach, Crewe, Cheshire CW11 0EP. *T:* Crewe 761076. *Club:* Explorers' (New York).

See also Baron Croham.

ALLEN, family name of **Baron Allen of Abbeydale** and **Baron Croham.**

ALLEN OF ABBEYDALE, Baron *cr* 1976 (Life Peer), of the City of Sheffield; **Philip Allen,** GCB 1970 (KCB 1964; CB 1954); Member, Security Commission, since 1973; *b* 8 July 1912; *yr s* of late Arthur Allen and Louie Tipper, Sheffield; *m* 1938, Marjorie Brenda Coe. *Educ:* King Edward VII Sch., Sheffield; Queens' Coll., Cambridge (Whewell Schol. in Internat. Law, 1934; Hon. Fellow 1974). Entered Home Office, 1934; Offices of War Cabinet, 1943–44; Commonwealth Fellowship in USA, 1948–49; Deputy Chm. of Prison Commn for England and Wales, 1950–52; Asst Under Sec. of State, Home Office, 1952–55; Deputy Sec., Min. of Housing and Local Govt, 1955–60; Deputy Under-Sec. of State, Home Office, 1960–62; Second Sec., HM Treasury, 1963–66; Permanent Under-Sec. of State, Home Office, 1966–72. Chairman: Occupational Pensions Bd, 1973–78; Nat. Council of Social Service, 1973–77; Gaming Bd for GB, 1977–85 (Mem., 1975). Member Royal Commissions: on Standards of Conduct in Public Life, 1974–76; on Civil Liability and Compensation for Personal Injury, 1973–78; Mem., tribunal of inquiry into Crown Agents, 1978–82. Chief Counting Officer, EEC Referendum, 1975. *Address:* Holly Lodge, Englefield Green, Surrey TW20 0JP. *T:* Egham 32291.

ALLEN, Hon. Alfred Ernest, CMG 1973; JP; President, Associated Trustee Savings Banks of New Zealand, 1976–78 (Vice-President, 1974–76); Chairman, Blinded Servicemen's Trust Board, since 1961; *b* Onehunga, NZ, 20 May 1912; 4th *s* of Ernest Richard Allen and Harriet May Allen; *m* 1935, Nancy, 3rd *d* of Frederick Arthur Cutfield and Ethel Cutfield; one *s* three *d. Educ:* numerous primary schs; Auckland Grammar School. Farm hand, 1927; farming on own account from 1933. Served War of 1939–45, 24 Bn 2 NZEF, Middle East (Sgt-Major). MP Franklin, NZ, 1957–72; Junior Govt Whip, 1963–66; Chief Govt Whip, 1966–69; Chm. of Cttees and Deputy Speaker, 1969–71; Speaker, House of Representatives, 1972. Is a Freemason (Past Master). Mem., Auckland Electric Power Bd, 1948–77 (Chm., 1956, 1957 and 1958). Pres., Bd of Trustees, Auckland Savings Bank, 1973–75 (Vice-Pres., 1972–73). *Recreations:* bowls, horse racing; formerly Rugby football (Country Union Rep.), tennis. *Address:* 32 Carlton Crescent, Maraetai Beach, Auckland, New Zealand. *T:* Beachlands 6595. *Clubs:* Franklin (Pukekohe); Returned Servicemen's (Franklin); (Hon. Mem.) Bellamy's (Wellington).

ALLEN, Anthony Kenway, OBE 1946; **His Honour Judge Allen;** a Circuit Judge, since 1978; *b* 31 Oct. 1917; *s* of Charles Valentine Allen and Edith Kenway Allen; *m* 1975, Maureen Murtough. *Educ:* St George's Coll., Weybridge, Surrey; St John's Coll., Cambridge (BA Hons); Freiburg and Grenoble Univs. Served War, RAF Special Intelligence, 1939–45 (Wing Comdr). Called to the Bar, Inner Temple, 1947. *Recreations:* gardening, walking, music. *Address:* 73 Downswood, Epsom Downs, Surrey. *T:* Burgh Heath 50017.

ALLEN, Arnold Millman, CBE 1977; Chairman, UKAEA, 1984–86; *b* 30 Dec. 1924; *s* of Wilfrid Millman and Edith Muriel Allen; *m* 1947, Beatrice Mary Whitaker; three *s* one *d. Educ:* Hackney Downs Sec. Sch.; Peterhouse, Cambridge (Scholar). Entered HM Treasury, 1945; Private Sec. to Financial Secretary, 1951–52; Principal, HM Treasury, 1953–55; Private Sec. to Chm. of UKAEA (Lord Plowden), 1956–57; HM Treasury, 1958; Dir of Personnel and Admin., Development and Engineering Group (subseq. Reactor Group), UKAEA, 1959–63; Gen. Manager, British Waterways Bd, 1963–68, and Mem. of Bd 1965–68; UKAEA: Personnel Officer, 1968–69; Personnel and Programmes Officer, 1970; Secretary and Mem. for Administration, 1971; Mem. for Finance and Admin, 1976–84; Dep. Chm., 1981–84; Chief Exec., 1982–84. *Address:* Duntish Cottage, Duntish, Dorchester, Dorset. *T:* Buckland Newton 258. *Club:* Athenæum.

ALLEN, Dr Clabon Walter; Professor of Astronomy at University College, London University, 1951–72, now Emeritus Professor; *b* 28 Dec. 1904; *s* of J. B. Allen and A. H. Allen; *m* 1937, Rose M. Smellie; five *s. Educ:* Perth High School; University of Western Australia. DSc (WA), 1935. Assistant at Commonwealth Observatory, Canberra, 1926–51. Solar Eclipse Expeditions, 1936, 1940, 1954, 1955 and 1959; Hackett Research Studentship, 1935–37. *Publications:* Astrophysical Quantities, 1955, 3rd rev. edn 1973; Hiking from Early Canberra, 1977; papers in Monthly Notices of Royal Astronomical Soc., Astrophysical Jl, Memoirs of Commonwealth Observatory, etc. *Address:* 3 Norfolk Street, Red Hill, Canberra, ACT 2603, Australia.

ALLEN, Colin Mervyn Gordon, CBE 1978; General Manager, Covent Garden Market Authority, since 1967; *b* 17 April 1929; *s* of late Cecil G. Allen and late Gwendoline L. Allen (*née* Hutchinson); *m* 1953, Patricia, *d* of late William and Doris Seddon; two *s* one *d. Educ:* King Edward's Sch., Bath. BA Open, 1985. FInstPS. Naval Store Dept, Admiralty, 1948–56; National Coal Board: London HQ, 1956–59; Area Stores Officer, NE Div., 1959–64; Covent Garden Market Authority: Planning Officer, 1964–66; Asst Gen. Man., 1967. President: Assoc. of Wholesale Markets within Internat. Union of Local Authorities, 1972–78; IPS, 1982–83. Chm., Vauxhall Cross Amenity Trust, 1982–83. *Publications:* various papers on horticultural marketing and allied topics, and on supply and logistics matters. *Recreation:* archaeology. *Address:* 10 Whitecroft Way, Beckenham, Kent BR3 3AG. *T:* 01–650 0787.

ALLEN, Sir Denis; *see* Allen, Sir W. D.

ALLEN, Rev. Canon Derek William; Vicar of St Saviour and St Peter's, Eastbourne, since 1976; Prebendary of Heathfield, Chichester Cathedral, since 1984; *b* 2 Nov. 1925. *Educ:* Eastbourne College; Oriel College, Oxford. Curate of Christ the Saviour, Ealing, 1952–54. Tutor, 1954–56, Chaplain, 1956–60, St Stephen's House, Oxford. Asst Chaplain, Pembroke College, Oxford, 1955–60, Sub-Warden, King's College Hostel and Lecturer in Theology, King's College, London, 1960–62; Principal, St Stephen's House, Oxford, 1962–74; Warden: Community of St Mary the Virgin, Wantage, 1966–80; Community of Servants of the Cross, Lindfield, 1981–. Examining Chaplain to Bp of Chichester, 1980–. Mem. Gen. Synod, Church of England, 1985–. *Publications:* articles in: Theology, Church Quarterly Review, Internat. Rev. of Missions, Lambeth Essays on Unity, Sobornost. *Recreations:* music, poetry, bridge. *Address:* The Vicarage, Spencer Road, Eastbourne, Sussex BN21 4PA. *T:* 22317.

ALLEN, Prof. Deryck Norman de Garrs; Professor of Applied Mathematics in the University of Sheffield, 1955–80, now Emeritus; Warden of Ranmoor House, 1968–82; *b* 22 April 1918; *s* of Leonard Lincoln Allen and Dorothy Allen (*née* Asplin). *Educ:* King Edward VII School, Sheffield; Christ Church, Oxford. Messrs Rolls Royce, 1940; Research Asst to Sir Richard Southwell, FRS, 1941; Lectr in Applied Mathematics at Imperial Coll., London, 1945; Visiting Prof. in Dept of Mechanical Engineering, Massachusetts Inst. of Technology, 1949; Reader in Applied Mathematics at Imperial Coll. in Univ. of London, 1950. Pro-Vice-Chancellor, Sheffield Univ., 1966–70; Chm., Jt Matriculation Bd, 1973–76. *Publications:* Relaxation Methods, 1954 (US); papers on Applied Maths and Engineering Maths in: Proc. Royal Soc.; Philosophical Trans. of Royal Soc.; Quarterly Jl of Mechanics and Applied Maths; Jl of Instn of Civil Engineers. *Recreation:* travel. *Address:* 18 Storth Park, Fulwood Road, Sheffield S10 3QH. *T:* Sheffield 308751.

ALLEN, Donald George, CMG 1981; Deputy Parliamentary Commissioner for Administration (Ombudsman), since 1982, on transfer from HM Diplomatic Service; *b* 26 June 1930; *s* of Sidney George Allen and Doris Elsie (*née* Abercombie); *m* 1955, Sheila Isobel Bebbington; three *s. Educ:* Southall Grammar School. Foreign Office, 1948; HM Forces, 1949–51; FO, 1951–54; The Hague, 1954–57; 2nd Sec. (Commercial), La Paz, 1957–60; FO, 1961–65: 1st Sec. 1962; Asst Private Sec. to Lord Privy Seal, 1961–63 and to Minister without Portfolio, 1963–64; 1st Sec., Head of Chancery and Consul, Panama, 1966–69; FCO, 1969–72; Counsellor on secondment to NI Office, Belfast, 1972–74; Counsellor and Head of Chancery, UK Permanent Delegn to OECD, Paris, 1974–78; Inspector, 1978–80; Dir, Office of Parly Comr, 1980–82. *Recreations:* squash, tennis, golf. *Address:* Church House, Great Smith Street, SW1P 3BW; 99 Parkland Grove, Ashford, Mddx TW15 2JF. *T:* Ashford 55617. *Club:* Royal Automobile.

ALLEN, Fergus Hamilton, CB 1969; ScD, MA, MAI; First Civil Service Commissioner, Civil Service Department, 1974–81; *b* 3 Sept. 1921; *s* of Charles Winckworth Allen and Marjorie Helen, *d* of F. J. S. Budge; *m* 1947, Margaret Joan, *d* of Prof. M. J. Gorman; two *d. Educ:* Newtown Sch., Waterford; Trinity Coll., Dublin. ScD 1966. Asst Engineer, Sir Cyril Kirkpatrick and Partners, 1943–48; Port of London Authority, 1949–52; Asst Director, Hydraulics Research Station, DSIR, 1952–58; Dir of Hydraulics Research, DSIR, 1958–65; Chief Scientific Officer, Cabinet Office, 1965–69; Civil Service Comr, 1969–74; Scientific and Technological Advr, CSD, 1969–72. Consultant, Boyden Internat. Ltd, 1982–86. Instn Civil Engrs: Telford Gold Medal, 1958; Mem. Council, 1962–67, 1968–71. *Publications:* papers in technical journals; poems. *Address:* Dundrum, Wantage Road, Streatley, Berks RG8 9LB. *T:* Goring 873234. *Club:* Athenæum.

ALLEN, Francis Andrew; His Honour Judge Francis Allen; a Circuit Judge, since 1979; *b* 7 Dec. 1933; *s* of Andrew Eric Allen and Joan Elizabeth Allen; *m* 1961, Marjorie Pearce; one *s* three *d. Educ:* Solihull School; Merton College, Oxford. MA. 2nd Lieut, Highland Light Infantry, 1957; called to the Bar, Gray's Inn, 1958. A Recorder of the Crown Court, 1978–79. *Recreation:* walking. *Address:* 116 Oxford Road, Moseley, Birmingham B13 9SQ. *T:* 021–449 1270. *Club:* Mountain Bothies Association (Scottish Highlands).

ALLEN, Frank Graham, CB 1984; Clerk of the Journals, House of Commons, 1975–84; *b* 13 June 1920; *s* of Percy and Gertrude Allen; *m* 1947, Barbara Caulton; one *s* one *d. Educ:* Shrewsbury Sch. (Schol.); Keble Coll., Oxford (Exhibr, BA). 7th Bn Worcs Regt, 1940–46, India, 1942–44. Asst Clerk, House of Commons, 1946; Principal Clerk, 1973. Mem., House of Laity, Gen. Synod, 1970–80. Silver Jubilee Medal, 1977. *Address:* March Mount, Haddon Road, Chorleywood, Herts. *T:* Chorleywood 2709.

ALLEN, Prof. Sir Geoffrey, Kt 1979; PhD; FRS 1976; FInstP; Head of Research, Unilever PLC, since 1981; Director, Unilever PLC and NV, since 1982; *b* 29 Oct. 1928; *s* of John James and Marjorie Allen; *m* 1973, Valerie Frances Duckworth; one *d. Educ:* Clay Cross Tupton Hall Grammar Sch.; Univ. of Leeds (BSc, PhD). FInstP 1972; FPRI 1974. Postdoctoral Fellow, Nat. Res. Council, Canada, 1952–54; Lectr, Univ. of Manchester, 1955–65, Prof. of Chemical Physics, 1965–75; Prof. of Polymer Science, 1975–76, Prof. of Chemical Technology, 1976–81, Imperial Coll. of Science and Technology (Fellow, 1986); Vis. Fellow, Robinson Coll., Cambridge, 1980–. Mem., Science Research Council, 1976, Chm., 1977–81. Hon. MSc Manchester; DUniv Open, 1981; Hon. DSc: Durham, East Anglia, 1984; Bath, Bradford, Loughborough, 1985. *Publications:* papers on chemical physics of polymers in Trans Faraday Soc., Polymer. *Recreations:* walking, talking and eating. *Address:* 16 Burghley Road, Wimbledon, SW19 5BH. *T:* 01–947 7459.

ALLEN, Sir George Oswald Browning, Kt 1986; CBE 1962; TD 1945; *b* 31 July 1902; *s* of late Sir Walter M. Allen, KBE. *Educ:* Eton; Trinity College, Cambridge. GSO1, War Office, 1940–45. Member of London Stock Exchange, retired 1972. Cricket: Eton XI, 1919–21; Cambridge Univ., 1922–23; represented England in 25 Test Matches; Captain *v* India, 1936, *v* Australia, 1936–37, *v* West Indies, 1948; Chm. Selection Cttee, 1955–61; Chm. MCC cricket sub cttee, 1956–63; President, MCC, 1963–64; Treasurer, 1964–76; Mem., Cricket Council, 1968–82, resigned; Hon. Vice-Pres., Nat. Cricket Assoc., 1985. Legion of Merit (USA). *Recreations:* cricket, golf. *Address:* 4 Grove End Road, NW8. *T:* 01–286 4601. *Club:* White's.

ALLEN, Hamish McEwan, CB 1984; Head of Administration Department, House of Commons, 1981–85; *b* 7 Sept. 1920; *s* of late Ernest Frank Allen and Ada Florence Allen (*née* Weeks); *m* 1951, Peggy Joan Fifoot; one *s. Educ:* City of Bath Sch.; Portsmouth Southern Secondary Sch. Served RAF, 1941–46. Air Ministry: Clerical Officer, 1938; Exec. Officer, 1948; House of Commons: Asst Accountant, 1959; Dep. Accountant, 1962; Head of Estabs Office, 1968. *Address:* 124 Ridge Langley, South Croydon, Surrey CR2 0AS.

ALLEN, (Harold) Norman (Gwynne), CBE 1965; FEng; retired 1977; *b* 30 April 1912; *yr s* of Harold Gwynne Allen and Hilda Margaret Allen (*née* Langley), Bedford; *m* 1938, Marjorie Ellen (*née* Brown); one *s* three *d. Educ:* Westminster Sch.; Trinity Coll., Cambridge, BA 1933, MA 1936, Cantab; FEng 1979, FICE, FIMechE, FRINA, FIMarE, FIProdE. Engrg trng, John Samuel White & Co. Ltd, Cowes, John Brown & Co. Ltd, Clydebank, and in Merchant Navy, 1933–37; W. H. Allen Sons & Co. Ltd, Bedford: progressive staff appts, 1937–43; Dir 1943–77; Techn. Dir 1945–52; Jt Man. Dir 1952–; Dep. Chm. 1962–70; Chm. 1970–77; Amalgamated Power Engrg Ltd, Bedford: Techn. Dir 1968–70; Dep. Chm. 1970–77. Belliss & Morcom Ltd, Birmingham, 1968–77. Mem. Bedfordshire CC, 1947–50. Mem. Council: British Internal Combustion Engrg Res. Assoc., 1952–60 (Chm. 1953–54); British Hydromechanics Res. Assoc., 1947–59; IMechE, 1952–70 (Vice-Pres. 1959–65, Pres. 1965); Mem. Adv. Cttee, Nat. Engrg Lab., 1971–73 (Mem. Steering Cttee 1962–68); Mem. British Transport Commn Res. Adv. Council, 1958–60; Vice-Chm. of Council, Mander Coll., Bedford, 1958–74; Governor, Coll. of Aeronautics, Cranfield, 1955–69 (Vice-Chm. 1962–69); Charter Pro-Chancellor, Cranfield Inst. of Technology, 1969–75; Mem. Bd, Council of Engrg Instns, 1964–66; Mem. Exec. Bd, BSI, 1970–76. Provost, Buffalo Hunt of Manitoba, 1960. Dir, Son et Lumière, Woburn Abbey, 1957. Hon. DSc Bath, 1967; Hon. DSc Cranfield, 1977. *Publications:* papers in jls of IMarE, S African IMechE, Engrg Inst. Canada, IMechE. *Recreations:* sailing, gardening (FRHS), countryside (Mem. Nat. Trust), magic (Mem. Magic Circle). *Address:* 45 Berry Hill Crescent, Cirencester, Glos GL7 2HF. *Club:* Island Sailing.

ALLEN, Prof. Harry Cranbrook, MC 1944; Professor of American Studies, 1971–80, now Emeritus, and Dean of the School of English and American Studies, 1974–76, University of East Anglia; *b* 23 March 1917; *s* of Christopher Albert Allen and Margaret Enid (*née* Hebb); *m* 1947, Mary Kathleen Andrews; one *s* two *d*. *Educ:* Bedford School; Pembroke College, Oxford (Open Scholar; 1st cl. hons Modern History; MA). Elected Fellow, Commonwealth Fund of New York, 1939 (held Fellowship, Harvard Univ., Jan-Sept. 1946). Served War of 1939–45, with Hertfordshire and Dorsetshire Regts, in France and Germany (Major); comdt 43rd Division Educational Coll., June-Nov. 1945. Fellow and Tutor in Modern History, Lincoln College, Oxford, 1946–55; Commonwealth Fund Prof. of American History, University Coll., 1955–71, and Dir, Inst. of United States Studies, 1966–71, Univ. of London; Senior Research Fellow, Austr. Nat. Univ., Canberra, and Visiting Scholar, Univ. of California, Berkeley, 1953–54; Schouler Lecturer, The Johns Hopkins University, April 1956; American Studies Fellow, Commonwealth Fund of New York, 1957, at the University of Virginia; Vis. Mem., Inst. for Advanced Study, Princeton, NJ, 1959; Vis. Professor: Univ. of Rochester, New York, 1963; Univ. of Michigan, Ann Arbor, 1966. Member: Dartmouth Royal Naval College Review Cttee, 1958, Naval Education Adv. Cttee, 1960–66; Academic Planning Board, Univ. of Essex, 1962; Chm., British Assoc. for American Studies, 1974–77; Pres., European Assoc. for American Studies, 1976–80. *Publications:* Great Britain and the United States, 1955; Bush and Backwoods, 1959; The Anglo-American Relationship since 1783, 1960; The Anglo-American Predicament, 1960; The United States of America, 1964; Joint Editor: British Essays in American History, 1957; Contrast and Connection, 1976. *Recreation:* travel (when practicable). *Address:* 10 Lime Kiln Road, Tackley, Oxon OX5 3BW. *T:* Tackley 592. *Club:* Athenæum.

ALLEN, Janet Rosemary; Headmistress of Benenden School, Kent, 1976–85; *b* 11 April 1936; *d* of John Algernon Allen and Edna Mary Allen (*née* Orton). *Educ:* Cheltenham Ladies' Coll.; University Coll., Leicester; Hughes Hall, Cambridge. BA London 1958; CertEd Cambridge 1959. Asst Mistress, Howell's Sch., Denbigh, North Wales, 1959: Head of History Dept, 1961; in charge of First Year Sixth Form, 1968; Housemistress, 1968 and 1973–75. Member: E-SU Scholarship Selection Panel, 1977–85; South East ISIS Cttee, 1978–84; Boarding Schs Assoc. Cttee, 1980–83; GSA Educnl sub-cttee, 1983–85. Vice-President: Girls of the Realm Guild; Women's Career Foundn (incorporating Girls of the Realm Guild). *Recreations:* music, drama, dogwalking, swimming, reading. *Address:* 1 The Broadway, Alfriston, near Polegate, E Sussex BN26 5XL. *Club:* Royal Over-Seas League.

ALLEN, Prof. John Anthony, PhD, DSc; FIBiol; FRSE; Director, University Marine Biological Station, Millport, Isle of Cumbrae, since 1976; *s* of George Leonard John Allen and Dorothy Mary Allen; *m* 1st, 1952, Marion Ferguson Crow (marr. diss. 1983); one *s* one *d*; 2nd, 1983, Margaret Porteous Aitken. *Educ:* High Pavement Sch., Nottingham; London Univ. (PhD, DSc). FIBiol 1969; FRSE 1968 (Mem. Council, 1970–73). Served in Sherwood Foresters, 1945–46, and RAMC, 1946–48. Asst Lectr, Univ. of Glasgow, 1951–54; John Murray Student, Royal Soc., 1952–54; Lectr/Sen. Lectr in Zool., then Reader in Marine Biol., Univ. of Newcastle upon Tyne, 1954–76. Post Doctoral Fellow and Guest Investigator, Woods Hole Oceanographic Instn, USA, 1965–; Vis. Prof., Univ. of Washington, 1968, 1970, 1971; Royal Soc. Vis. Prof., Univ. of West Indies, 1976. Member: NERC, 1977–83 (Chm., Univ. Affairs Cttee, 1978–83); Council, Scottish Marine Biol Assoc., 1977–83; Council, Marine Biol Assoc. UK, 1981–83; Life Sciences Bd, CNAA, 1981–84; Nature Conservancy Council, 1982– (Chm., Adv. Cttee Sci., 1984–). Pres., Malacological Soc. of London, 1982–84. *Publications:* 80 papers on decapod crustacea and molluscs, and deep sea benthos, in learned jls. *Recreations:* travel, appreciation of gardens, pub-lunching. *Address:* Bellevue, Millport, Isle of Cumbrae, Scotland. *T:* Millport 530260.

ALLEN, Very Rev. John Edward; Provost of Wakefield, since 1982; *b* 9 June 1932; *s* of Rev. Canon Ronald and Mrs Isabel Allen; *m* 1957, Eleanor (*née* Prynne); one *s* three *d*. *Educ:* Rugby; University Coll., Oxford (MA); Fitzwilliam Coll., Cambridge (MA); Westcott House. Colonial Service, Kenya, 1957–63; Sales and Marketing, Kimberly-Clark Ltd, 1963–66; Theological College, 1966–68; Curate, Deal, Kent, 1968–71; Senior Chaplain to Univ. of Bristol and Vicar of St Paul's, Clifton, 1971–78; Vicar of Chippenham, Wilts, 1978–82. *Recreations:* walking, fishing and people. *Address:* The Cathedral Vicarage, Margaret Street, Wakefield, West Yorkshire WF1 2DQ. *T:* Wakefield 372402.

ALLEN, Prof. John Frank, FRS 1949; Professor of Natural Philosophy in the School of Physical Sciences, University of St Andrews, 1947–78, now Emeritus; *b* 16 May 1908; *s* of late Prof. Frank Allen, FRSC; *m* 1933, Elfriede Hiebert (marr. diss. 1951); one *s*. *Educ:* Public schools of Winnipeg, Canada. BA (University of Manitoba, 1928), MA (University of Toronto, 1930), PhD (University of Toronto, 1933). Bursar, Student and Fellow of National Research Council of Canada, 1930–33; Fellow of National Research Council of USA, 1933–35; Research Assistant, Royal Society Mond Laboratory, Cambridge, 1935–44; MA Cantab, 1936; Lecturer in Physics, Univ. of Cambridge and Fellow and Lecturer of St John's College, Cambridge, 1944–47. Hon. DSc: Manitoba, 1979; Heriot-Watt, 1984. *Publications:* numerous scientific papers and articles, mainly on experimental low temperature physics. *Recreations:* scientific cinefilms, golf. *Address:* 2 Shorehead, St Andrews, Fife. *T:* St Andrews 72717.

See also W. A. Allen.

ALLEN, Maj.-Gen. John Geoffrey Robyn, CB 1976; Lay Observer attached to Lord Chancellor's Department, 1979–85; *b* 19 Aug. 1923; *s* of R. A. Allen and Mrs Allen (*née* Youngman); *m* 1959, Ann Monica (*née* Morford); one *s* one *d*. *Educ:* Haileybury. Commissioned KRRC, 1942; trans. RTR, 1947; Bt Lt-Col, 1961; Lt-Col, CO 2 RTR, 1963; Mil. Asst (GSO1) to CGS, MoD, 1965; Brig., Comd 20 Armd Bde, 1967; IDC, 1970; Dir of Operational Requirements 3 (Army), MoD, 1971; Maj.-Gen., Dir-Gen., Fighting Vehicles and Engineer Equipment, MoD, 1973–74; Dir, RAC, 1974–76; Sen. Army Directing Staff, RCDS, 1976–78; retired 1979. Col Comdt, RTR, 1976–80; Hon. Colonel: Westminster Dragoons, 1982–; Royal Yeomanry, 1982–. Member: Adv. Cttee on Legal Aid, 1979–86; Booth Cttee on Procedure in Matrimonial Causes, 1982–85. *Recreation:* dinghy sailing. *Address:* Meadowleys, Charlton, Chichester, W Sussex PO18 0HU. *T:* Singleton 638. *Clubs:* Army and Navy; Bosham Sailing.

ALLEN, John Hunter, OBE 1978; company director; Mayor of Antrim, since 1973; *s* of John Allen and Jane Kerr Hunter; *m* 1952, Elizabeth Irwin Graham; three *d*. *Educ:* Larne Grammar Sch., NI; Orange's Acad., NI. Served RAF, pilot, 1942–47. Civil Service Excise, 1947–59; Proprietor: Ulster Farm Feeds Ltd, 1959–76; Antrim Feeds Ltd, 1959–76; Roadway Transport Ltd, 1959–; Aldergrove Farms Ltd, 1965–; A.B. Fuels, 1969–; Downtown Developments Ltd, 1975–; Allen Service Stns, 1977–; Century Supplies. Chm., NI Sports Council, 1977–84. Chm., Antrim Royal British Legion. *Recreations:* Rugby, sailing, boxing, tennis. *Address:* The Grange, Muckamore, Antrim, Co. Antrim. *T:* Antrim 62179. *Clubs:* Royal Air Force; Antrim Rugby (Pres.); Antrim Hockey (Pres.); Antrim Boxing (Pres.); Antrim Boat (Trustee); Muckamore Cricket (Life Member).

ALLEN, John Piers, OBE 1979; *b* 30 March 1912; *s* of Percy Allen and Marjorie Nash; *m* 1937; two *s*; *m* 1945; two *s* two *d*. *Educ:* Aldenham Sch. Old Vic Theatre, 1933–35; Victor Gollancz Ltd, 1936–37; London Theatre Studio, 1937–39; RNVR, 1940–45; Dir, Glyndebourne Children's Theatre, 1945–51; writer-producer, BBC, 1951–61; HM Inspector of Schs, 1961–72. Principal, Central School of Speech and Drama, 1972–78. Vis. Prof. of Drama, Westfield Coll., Univ. of London, 1979–83; Vis. Lectr, Centre for Arts, City Univ., 1979–83. Vice-Chm., British Theatre Assoc., 1978–83; Chairman: Accreditation Bd, Nat. Council of Drama Trng, 1979–83; Council of Dance Educn and Trng, 1982– (Chm., Accreditation Bd, 1979–82); Mem., CNAA Dance and Drama Panels, 1979–82. *Publications:* Going to the Theatre, 1949; Great Moments in the Theatre, 1949; Masters of British Drama, 1957; Masters of European Drama, 1962; Drama in Schools, 1978; Theatre in Europe, 1981; A History of the Theatre in Europe, 1983; (ed) Three Medieval Plays, 1956. *Address:* The Old Orchard, Lastingham, York YO6 6TQ. *T:* Lastingham 334.

ALLEN, Prof. John Robert Lawrence, DSc; FRS 1979; Professor of Geology, University of Reading, since 1972; *b* 25 Oct. 1932; *s* of George Eustace Allen and Alice Josephine (*née* Formby); *m* 1960, Jean Mary (*née* Wood); four *s* one *d*. *Educ:* St Philip's Grammar Sch., Birmingham; Univ. of Sheffield (BSc, DSc). Academic career in University of Reading, 1959–. FGS 1955. Lyell Medal, Geolog. Soc., 1980; David Linton Award, British Geomorphological Research Group, 1983. *Publications:* Current Ripples, 1968; Physical Processes of Sedimentation, 1970; Sedimentary Structures, 1982; Principles of Physical Sedimentology, 1985; numerous contribs to professional jls. *Recreations:* music, opera. *Address:* 17c Whiteknights Road, Reading RG1 5SY. *T:* Reading 64621.

ALLEN, Prof. Joseph Stanley; (first) Professor and Head of Department of Town and Country Planning, University of Newcastle upon Tyne (formerly King's College, Durham University), 1946–63 (developing first University Degree Course in Town and Country Planning); now Professor Emeritus; *b* 15 March 1898; *s* of late Harry Charles Allen and of Elizabeth S. Allen; *m* 1931, Guinevere Mary Aubrey Pugh (*d* 1974); one *s* one *d*; *m* 1977, Meryl, *d* of late Charles and Eveline Watts. *Educ:* Liverpool Collegiate School; Liverpool University; post-graduate study in USA. RIBA Athens Bursar. Lectr, Liverpool Univ., 1929–33; Head, Leeds School of Architecture, 1933–45; founded Leeds Sch. of Town and Country Planning, 1934. Vice-Chm. RIBA Bd of Architectural Education and Chm. Recognised Schools Cttee, 1943–45; Member of Council RIBA, 1943–50; Pres. Royal Town Planning Institute, 1959–60 (Vice-Pres. 1957–59). Architect and Town Planning Consultant for hospitals, churches, neighbourhood units, university and industrial undertakings, including: Develt Plan for Durham Univ.; Quadrangle, King's College, Newcastle; Courthouse, Chesterfield; Nat. Park Residential Study Centre, Maentwrog; Science Wing, Durham Univ. Consultant, Snowdonia National Park, 1957–74; Member, North of England Regional Advisory Committee, Forestry Commission, 1951–74; Member Diocesan Committees for Care of Churches: Ripon, Newcastle and York Dioceses. Hon. DLitt Heriot-Watt, 1978. *Publications:* (with R. H. Mattocks): Report and Plan for West Cumberland; Report and Plan for Accrington (Industry and Prudence), 1950. Founder-Editor, Planning Outlook (founded 1948); contrib. to professional journals on architecture and town and country planning. *Recreations:* motoring and walking in the countryside, music, arable farming studies and breeding Welsh ponies. *Address:* Bleach Green Farm, Ovingham, Northumberland. *T:* Prudhoe 32340.

ALLEN, Sir Kenneth; *see* Allen, Sir William Kenneth G.

ALLEN, Prof. Kenneth William; Professor of Nuclear Structure, since 1963, and Head of Department of Nuclear Physics, 1976–79 and 1982–85, University of Oxford; Fellow of Balliol College, since 1963, Estates Bursar, 1980–83; *b* 17 Nov. 1923; *m* 1947, Josephine E. Boreham; two *s*. *Educ:* Ilford County High School; London University (Drapers' Scholar); St Catharine's College, Cambridge University. PhD (Cantab) 1947. Physics Division, Atomic Energy of Canada, Chalk River, 1947–51; Leverhulme Research Fellow and Lecturer, Liverpool University, 1951–54; Deputy Chief Scientist, UKAEA, 1954–63. Mem., Nuclear Physics Bd, SRC, 1970–73. *Publications:* contribs to Nuclear Physics, Physical Review, Review of Scientific Instruments, Nature, etc. *Recreations:* music, chess. *Address:* Ridgeway, Lincombe Lane, Boars Hill, Oxford OX1 5DZ. *T:* Oxford 739327.

ALLEN, Mark Echalaz, CMG 1966; CVO 1961; HM Diplomatic Service, retired; *b* 19 March 1917; *s* of late Lancelot John Allen and Eleanor Mary (*née* Carlisle); *m* 1948, Elizabeth Joan, *d* of late Richard Hope Bowdler and Elsie (*née* Bryning); two *s* one *d* (and one *d* decd). *Educ:* Charterhouse; Christ Church, Oxford (MA). Appointed Asst Principal, Dominions Office, 1939. Served War of 1939–45 in Western Desert, Sicily and Italy. Dublin, 1945; Bombay, 1948; United Nations, New York, 1953; Madras, 1960; New Delhi, 1961; Diplomatic Service Inspector, 1964; Dep. Chief of Administration, DSAO, 1966; Minister (Econ. and Social Affairs), UK Mission to UN, New York, 1968; Ambassador to Zaïre and Burundi, 1971, and to Congo Republic, 1973; Permanent UK Rep. to Disarmament Conf., Geneva, 1974–77, retired from Diplomatic Service, 1977. Mem., Jt Inspection Unit, UN, 1978–84. *Address:* The Gate House, 65 Albion Street, Stratton, Cirencester, Glos.

ALLEN, Norman; *see* Allen, H. N. G.

ALLEN, Prof. Percival, FRS 1973; Professor of Geology, and Head of Geology Department, University of Reading, 1952–82; now Emeritus Professor; Director, Sedimentology Research Laboratory, 1965–82; *b* 15 March 1917; *s* of late Norman Williams Allen and Mildred Kathleen Hoad; British; *m* 1941, Frances Margaret Hepworth, BSc; three *s* one *d*. *Educ:* Brede Council Sch.; Rye Grammar School; University of Reading. BSc 1939, PhD 1943, Reading. Univ. Demonstrator, 1942–45, Univ. Asst Lectr, 1945–46, Reading; University Demonstrator, 1946–47, Univ. Lectr, 1947–52, Cambridge; Dean of Science Faculty, Reading, 1963–66. Vis. Prof., Univ. of Kuwait, 1970. Served War of 1939–45. In Royal Air Force, 1941–42. Sedgwick Prize, Univ. of Cambridge, 1952; Daniel Pidgeon Fund, Geological Soc. of London, 1944; Leverhulme Fellowships Research Grant, 1948, 1949. Hon. Member: American Soc. of Economic Paleontologists and Mineralogists; Bulgarian Geological Soc.; Geologists' Assoc.; Internat. Assoc. of Sedimentologists; For. Fellow, Indian Nat. Sci. Acad., 1979; Geological Soc. of London: Mem. Council, 1964–67; Lyell Medal, 1971; Pres., 1978–80; Royal Society: Mem. Council, 1977–79; a Vice-Pres., 1977–79; Chm., Expeditions Cttee, 1974–; British Nat. Cttee for Geology, 1982–; Sectional Cttee 5, 1983–. Council Mem., NERC, 1971–74 and Royal Soc. Assessor, 1977–80; Chm., vis. groups to depts in British Mus. (Nat. Hist.), 1975, and Univ. of Strathclyde, 1982; External Appraiser (Geol. Dept): Meml Univ., Newfoundland, 1968; Jadavpur Univ., 1977; Univ. of Western Ontario, 1982; Univ. of London, 1982; Univ. of Malaya, 1983; Adv. Panel, UNDP Project on Nile Delta, 1972–; UNESCO/UNDP Geology Consultant, India, 1976–77. Pres., Reading Geol. Soc., 1976–78. UK Editor, Sedimentology, 1961–67. Chm., Org. Cttees: VII Internat. Sedimentological Congress, 1967; first European Earth and Planetary Physics Colloquium, 1971; first Meeting European Geological Socs, 1975; UK Delegate to Internat. Union of Geol Sciences, Moscow, 1984. Sec.-Gen., Internat. Assoc.

Sedimentologists, 1967–71; Algerian Sahara Glacials Expedn, 1970; Sec., Philpots Quarry Ltd. *Publications:* papers in various scientific journals. *Recreations:* chess, natural history, gardening. *Address:* Orchard End, Hazeley Bottom, Hartley Wintney, Hants RG27 8LU.

ALLEN, Sir Peter (Christopher), Kt 1967; MA, BSc (Oxon); Advisory Director, New Perspective Fund, 1973–85; *b* Ashtead, Surrey, 8 Sept. 1905; *s* of late Sir Ernest King Allen and Florence Mary (*née* Gellatly); *m* 1st, 1931, Violet Sylvester Wingate-Saul (*d* 1951); two *d;* 2nd, 1952, Consuelo Maria Linares Rivas. *Educ:* Harrow; Trinity Coll., Oxford (Hon. Fellow 1969). Joined Brunner, Mond & Co., Ltd, 1928; Chm., Plastics Div. of ICI Ltd, 1948–51 (Man. Dir, 1942–48); Pres. and Chm., ICI of Canada Ltd, 1961–68; Chm., ICI Ltd, 1968–71 (Dir, 1951–63, a Dep. Chm., 1963–68); Dir, British Nylon Spinners Ltd, 1954–58; Pres., Canadian Industries Ltd, 1959–62, Chm., 1962–68; Director: Royal Trust Co., Canada, 1961–64; Bank of Montreal, 1968–75; BICC, 1971–81. Vice-President: Inst. of Manpower Studies, 1968–76; Manufacturing Chemists' Assoc., USA, 1961–62 (Dir, 1959–62); Mem. and Vice-Chairman: Council of Assoc. of Brit. Chem. Manufacturers, 1963–65; Bd of Dirs, Société de Chimie Industrielle, 1968; Chm., Chem. Ind. Assoc., 1966–67; President: Plastics Inst., 1950–52; Brit. Plastics Fedn, 1963–65; Univ. of Manchester Inst. of Sci. and Technology, 1968–71; Vice-Pres., British Assoc. for Commercial and Industrial Educn, 1969–; Mem. of Council, CBI, 1965–67. Chm., BNEC, 1970–71 (Mem., 1964–67; Chm., Cttee for Exports to Canada, 1964–67); Mem., British Overseas Trade Bd, 1972–75. Governor, Nat. Coll. of Rubber Technology, 1964–68; Member: Court, British Shippers' Council, 1968–70; Export Council for Europe, 1962–65; Overseas Development Inst. Council, 1963–64; Iron and Steel Holding and Realisation Agency, 1963–67; NEDC for Chemical Industry, 1964–67; Commonwealth Export Council, 1964–67; Industrial Policy Group, 1969–71. Pres., Transport Trust, 1967–. FBIM 1968; FInstD 1969; FRGS 1980. Hon. Member: Chemical Industries Assoc., 1968– (Pres., 1965–67; Mem. Council, 1967–68); Canadian Chemical Producers' Assoc., 1962–. Chm., Anglo-Spanish Soc., 1973–80. Trustee, Civic Trust, 1970–76. Governor, Harrow School, 1969–82. Freeman, City of London, 1978. Knight Grand Cross, Spanish Order of Civil Merit, 1981. *Publications:* The Railways of the Isle of Wight, 1928; Locomotives of Many Lands, 1954; On the Old Lines, 1957; (with P. B. Whitehouse) Narrow Gauge Railways of Europe, 1959; (with R. A. Wheeler) Steam on the Sierra, 1960; (with P. B. Whitehouse) Round the World on the Narrow Gauge, 1966; (with Consuelo Allen) The Curve of Earth's Shoulder, 1966; (with A. B. MacLeod) Rails in the Isle of Wight, 1967; Famous Fairways, 1968; Play the Best Courses, 1973; (with P. B. Whitehouse) Narrow Gauge the World Over, 1976; The 91 Before Lindbergh, 1985. *Recreations:* foreign travel, railways, golf, writing. *Address:* Telham Hill House, near Battle, E Sussex. *Clubs:* Carlton; Royal and Ancient; Royal Cinque Ports, Rye, Royal St George's; Oxford and Cambridge Golfing Soc.; Augusta National (Ga, USA); Pine Valley (NJ, USA).

ALLEN, Sir Richard (Hugh Sedley), KCMG 1960 (CMG 1953); retired; *b* 3 Feb. 1903; *s* of late Sir Hugh Allen, GCVO; *m* 1945, Juliet Home Thomson (*d* 1983); one step *s* (and one *s* decd). *Educ:* Royal Naval Colleges, Osborne and Dartmouth; New College, Oxford. Junior Asst Sec., Govt of Palestine, 1925–27. Entered Foreign Office and Diplomatic Service, 1927; Second Sec., 1932; First Sec., 1939; Counsellor, 1946; Minister, British Embassy, Buenos Aires, 1950–54; Minister to Guatemala, 1954–56; British Ambassador to Burma, 1956–62. *Publications:* Malaysia: Prospect and Retrospect, 1968; A Short Introduction to the History and Politics of Southeast Asia, 1970; Imperialism and Nationalism in the Fertile Crescent, 1974. *Recreation:* sailing. *Address:* 42 Somerstown, Chichester, Sussex PO19 4AL. *T:* Chichester 781182. *Clubs:* Athenæum; Royal Naval Sailing Association, Bosham and Itchenor Sailing.

ALLEN, Rowland Lancelot, CB 1968; Principal Assistant Treasury Solicitor, 1963–69, retired; *b* 17 Feb. 1908; *s* of Rowland Allen and Maud Annie Allen (*née* Bacon); *m* 1934, Elizabeth Ethel (*née* Lewis) (*d* 1982); two *s* one *d. Educ:* Eton College. Called to the Bar, Inner Temple, 1931; Public Trustee Office, 1934; Treasury Solicitor's Dept, 1940; Foreign Compensation Commission, 1950–53; Treasury Solicitor's Dept, 1953. *Recreation:* golf. *Address:* 12 Raeburn Court, St John's Hill, Woking, Surrey GU21 1QW. *T:* Woking 24326.

ALLEN, Thomas; singer; *b* 10 Sept. 1944; *s* of Thomas Boaz Allen and Florence Allen; *m* 1968, Margaret Holley; one *s. Educ:* Robert Richardson Grammar Sch., Ryhope; Royal College of Music. ARCM. Welsh Nat. Opera, 1969–72; Principal Baritone, Royal Opera, Covent Garden, 1972–78; appearances include: Glyndebourne Fest. Opera; English Opera Group; Paris Opera; Florence; Teatro Colon, Buenos Aires; Met. Opera, NY; Hamburg; BBC TV (The Gondoliers, The Marriage of Figaro); all major orchestras and various concert engagements abroad. Major rôles include: Figaro in Barber of Seville; Figaro and the Count in Marriage of Figaro; Paolo Albiani in Simon Boccanegra; Papageno in The Magic Flute; Billy Budd; Marcello in La Bohême; Belcore in l'Elisir d'Amore; Sid in Albert Herring; Tarquinius in Rape of Lucretia; Guglielmo in Così fan Tutte; Demetrius in A Midsummer Night's Dream; Valentin in Faust; Dr Falke in Die Fledermaus; King Arthur; The Count in Voice of Ariadne; Silvio in Pagliacci; Pelléas in Pelléas and Mélisande; Germont in La Traviata; title rôle in Don Giovanni; title rôle in Il ritorno d'Ulisse, and many others. Hon. MA Newcastle, 1984. *Recreations:* gardening, golf, sailing, reading, ornithology. *Address:* c/o John Coast, 1 Park Close, Knightsbridge, SW1X 7PQ.

ALLEN, Walter Ernest, author and literary journalist; *b* Birmingham, 23 Feb. 1911; 4th *s* of Charles Henry Allen and Annie Maria Thomas; *m* 1944, Peggy Yorke, 3rd *d* of Guy Lionel Joy and Dorothy Yorke Maundrell, Calne, Wilts; two *s* two *d. Educ:* King Edward's Grammar School, Aston, Birmingham; Birmingham University. Assistant Master, King Edward's Grammar School, Aston, Birmingham, 1934; Visiting Lecturer in English, State University of Iowa, USA, 1935; Features Editor, Cater's News Agency, Birmingham, 1935–37; Assistant Technical Officer, Wrought Light Alloys Development Assoc., 1943–45. Asst Literary Editor, New Statesman, 1959–60, Literary Editor, 1960–61. Margaret Pilcher Vis. Prof. of English, Coe Coll., Iowa, 1955–56; Visiting Professor of English: Vassar College, New York, 1963–64; Univ. of Kansas, 1967; Univ. of Washington, 1967; Prof. of English, New Univ. of Ulster, 1967–73; Berg Prof. of English, New York Univ., 1970–71; Vis. Prof. of English, Dalhousie Univ., Halifax, NS, 1973–74; C. P. Miles Prof. of English, Virginia Polytechnic Inst. and State Univ., 1974–75. FRSL. *Publications:* Innocence is Drowned, 1938; Blind Man's Ditch, 1939; Living Space, 1940; Rogue Elephant, 1946; The Black Country, 1946; Writers on Writing, 1948; Arnold Bennett, 1948; Reading a Novel, 1949; Dead Man Over All, 1950; The English Novel A Short Critical History, 1954; Six Great Novelists, 1955; All in a Lifetime, 1959; Tradition and Dream, 1964; George Eliot, 1964; The Urgent West: an Introduction to the Idea of the United States, 1969; Transatlantic Crossing: American visitors to Britain and British visitors to America in the nineteenth century, 1971; The Short Story in English, 1981; As I Walked Down New Grub Street, 1981. *Address:* 4B Alwyne Road, N1. *T:* 01-226 7085.

ALLEN, Walter John Gardener; Controller, Capital Taxes Office (formerly Estate Duty Office), Inland Revenue, 1974–78; *b* 8 Dec. 1916; *s* of late John Gardiner Allen and late Hester Lucy Allen, Deal, Kent; *m* 1944, Irene (*d* 1983), *d* of late John Joseph and Sarah Henderson, Lisburn, N Ireland; one *s* one *d. Educ:* Manwoods, Sandwich; London Univ. (LLB). Entered Inland Revenue, 1934. Served RAF, 1940–46 (Flying Officer). FGS 1982. *Recreations:* amateur geologist; gardening. *Address:* 43 The Chase, Eastcote, Pinner, Mddx HA5 1SH. *T:* 01-868 7101.

ALLEN, William Alexander, CBE 1980; RIBA; Chairman, Bickerdike Allen Partners, architects; *b* 29 June 1914; *s* of late Professor Frank Allen, FRSC; *m* 1938, Beatrice Mary Teresa Pearson; two *s* one *d. Educ:* public schools in Winnipeg; University of Manitoba. Royal Architectural Inst. of Canada Silver Medal, 1935. Univ. Gold Medal in Architecture, 1936. Appointed to Building Research Station, Watford, 1937; Chief Architect, Bldg Res. Stn, 1953–61; Principal of the Architectural Assoc. School of Architecture, 1961–66. Mem. Council RIBA, 1953–72, 1982– (Chm. various cttees); ARIBA 1937; FRIBA 1965; Chm., Fire Research Adv. Cttee, 1973–83, Visitor, 1983–; President: Institute of Acoustics, 1975–76; Ecclesiastic Arch. Assoc., 1980. Hon. Associate NZIA, 1965; Hon. Fellow, American Inst. Of Architects, 1984. Hon. LLD Manitoba, 1977. Commander, Ordem do Mérito, Portugal, 1972. *Publications:* (with R. Fitzmaurice) Sound Transmission in Buildings, 1939. Papers, etc, on scientific and technical aspects of architecture, professionalism, and modern architectural history and education. *Recreations:* writing, drawing, music. *Address:* 4 Ashley Close, Welwyn Garden City, Herts AL8 7LH. *T:* Welwyn Garden 324178. *Club:* Athenæum.

See also Prof. J. F. Allen.

ALLEN, Sir (William) Denis, GCMG 1969 (KCMG 1958; CMG 1950); CB 1955; HM Diplomatic Service, retired; *b* 24 Dec. 1910; *s* of John Allen; *m* 1939, Elizabeth Helen (*née* Watkin Williams); one *s. Educ:* Wanganui, New Zealand; Cambridge. HM Diplomatic Service, 1934–69; Deputy Commissioner General for South East Asia, 1959–62; Ambassador to Turkey, 1963–67; Dep. Under-Sec., Foreign Office (later FCO), 1967–69. *Address:* Stockland, Honiton, Devon.

ALLEN, Sir William (Guilford), Kt 1981; Chairman, family group of companies; *b* 22 April 1932; *s* of Sir William Guilford Allen, CBE, and Mona Maree Allen; *m* 1959, Elaine Therese Doyle; two *s* one *d. Educ:* Downlands Coll., Toowoomba, Qld. In grazing industry, Merino sheep; Principal, Historic Malvern Hills Registered Merino Stud; stud Shorthorn cattle breeder. Commercial broadcasting industry; Mem. Bd of Dirs, Qantas. Treasurer, Nat. Party, Qld. Councillor, Longreach Shire. Chm., Qld Transport and Technology Centre, 1984–. *Recreation:* aviation. *Address:* Toorak House, Hipwood Road, Hamilton, Brisbane, Qld 4007, Australia. *T:* Brisbane 2624111. *Clubs:* Brisbane, Tattersalls, Australian, Royal Queensland Golf, Longreach, Queensland Turf, Brisbane Amateur Turf (Brisbane); Royal Sydney Golf.

ALLEN, Sir (William) Kenneth (Gwynne), Kt 1961; DL; *b* 23 May 1907; *er s* of Harold Gwynne Allen and Hilda Allen, Bedford; *m* 1931, Eleanor Mary (*née* Eeles); one *s* one *d. Educ:* Westminster Sch.; Univ. of Neuchâtel, Switzerland. Started as engineering pupil, Harland & Wolff Ltd, Glasgow and Belfast; subsequently at W. H. Allen, Sons & Co. Ltd, Bedford; Dir, 1937–70, Man. Dir, 1946–70, Chm., 1955–70, W. H. Allen, Sons & Co. Ltd; Chm., Amalgamated Power Engineering, 1968–70; Director: Whessoe Ltd, 1954–65; Electrolux, 1970–78. Chm., Brit. Internal Combustion Engine Manufacturers' Assoc., 1955–57; Pres., British Engineers' Assoc., 1957–59 (now British Mechanical Engineering Fedn); Chm., BEAMA, 1959–61; Pres., Engineering Employers' Fedn, 1962–64; Chm., Labour and Social Affairs Cttee of CBI, 1965–67. FIMarE; MRINA; MIBritishE. Freeman of City of London. Liveryman, Worshipful Company of Shipwrights. Mem. Beds CC, 1945–55; High Sheriff Beds, 1958–59; DL Beds, 1978. *Address:* Manor Close, Aspley Guise, Milton Keynes, Bedfordshire MK17 8HZ. *T:* Milton Keynes 583161.

ALLEN, William Maurice; Executive Director, Bank of England, 1964–70; *b* 16 April 1908; *s* of David Allen. *Educ:* Dulwich College; London School of Economics. Army 1940–45. Asst Dir of Research, International Monetary Fund, 1947–49; Adviser, Bank of England, 1950–64. Fellow of Balliol Coll., Oxford, 1931–48; Visiting Fellow Nuffield Coll., Oxford, 1954–62. Hon. Fellow, LSE, 1963. Governor, LSE, 1951. *Address:* Bank of England, EC2. *Club:* Reform.

ALLEN, Maj.-Gen. William Maurice, CB 1983; FCIT, FIMI, FIPDM, FBIM, MInstPet; Director, Government Projects, Systems Development Corporation, Heidelberg, since 1985; *b* 29 May 1931; *s* of William James Allen and Elizabeth Jane Henrietta Allen; *m* 1955, Patricia Mary (*née* Fletcher); one *d* decd. *Educ:* Dunstable Sch. FCIT 1972; FIMI 1982; FIPDM 1982; FBIM 1983; MInstPet 1982. Commnd RASC, 1950; RCT, 1965; regtl and staff appts, Korea, Cyprus, Germany and UK; Student, Staff Coll., Camberley, 1961; Instructor, Staff Coll., Camberley and RMCS Shrivenham, 1968–70; Student, RCDS, 1976; Asst Comdt, RMA Sandhurst, 1979–81; Dir Gen. of Transport and Movements (Army), 1981–83. Dir of Educn and Trng, Burroughs Machines Ltd, 1983–85. Member, Council: IAM, 1982–85; NDTA, 1983–. Chm., Milton Keynes Information Technol. Trng Centre, 1983–85. Associate, St George's House. Freeman, City of London, 1981; Hon. Liveryman, Worshipful Co. of Carmen, 1981. *Recreations:* economics, trout fishing, squash, gardening, rough shooting. *Address:* c/o Royal Bank of Scotland, Holts Farnborough Branch, Lawrie House, 31–37 Victoria Road, Farnborough, Hants GU14 7PA. *Club:* Bristol Channel Yacht (Swansea).

ALLEN, Prof. William Sidney, MA, PhD (Cantab); FBA 1971; Professor of Comparative Philology in the University of Cambridge, 1955–82; Fellow of Trinity College, since 1955; *b* 18 March 1918; *er s* of late W. P. Allen and Ethel (*née* Pearce); *m* 1955, Aenea, *yr d* of late Rev. D. McCallum and Mrs McCallum, Invergordon. *Educ:* Christ's Hosp.; Trinity Coll., Cambridge (Classical Scholar); Porson Scholarship, 1939. War of 1939–45: RTR and General Staff (Int) (despatches). Lecturer in Phonetics, 1948–51, and in Comparative Linguistics, 1951–55, School of Oriental and African Studies, Univ. of London. Dialect research in India, 1952; Fellow of Rockefeller Foundation, USA, 1953; Brit. Council visitor, Univ. of W Indies, 1959. Linguistic Soc. of America's Professor, 1961; Collitz Professor, Linguistic Institute, USA, 1962; Ida Beam Lectr, Univ. of Iowa, 1983. Pres., Philological Soc., 1965–67. Hon. Fellow, Soc. for Cycladic Studies (Athens), 1977. Chm. Editorial Bd, CUP linguistic series, 1969–82; Editor, Lingua, 1963–85. *Publications:* Phonetics in Ancient India, 1953; On the Linguistic Study of Languages (inaugural lecture), 1957; Sandhi, 1962; Vox Latina, 1965; Vox Graeca, 1968; Accent and Rhythm, 1973; articles on general and comparative linguistics, phonetics, metrics and classical, Indian and Caucasian languages, Aegean cartography. *Address:* 24 Sherlock Road, Cambridge CB3 0HR. *T:* Cambridge 356739.

ALLEN, Woody; writer, actor, director; *b* Brooklyn, 1 Dec. 1935; *s* of Martin and Nettie Konigsberg; *m* 1966, Louise Lasser (marr. diss.). TV script writer, 1953–64, and appeared as a comedian in nightclubs and on TV shows. Sylvania Award, 1957. *Plays:* (writer) Don't Drink the Water, 1966; (writer and actor) Play It Again Sam, 1969 (filmed 1972). *Films:* (writer and actor) What's New Pussycat?, 1965; (actor) Casino Royale, 1967; (writer, actor and director): What's Up Tiger Lily?, 1966; Take the Money and Run, 1969; Bananas, 1971; Everything You Always Wanted to Know About Sex But Were Afraid to Ask, 1972; Sleeper, 1973; Love and Death, 1975; The Front, 1976; Annie Hall

(Academy Award), 1977; Manhattan, 1979; Stardust Memories, 1980; A Midsummer Night's Sex Comedy, 1982; Zelig, 1983; Broadway Danny Rose, 1984; (writer and director): Interiors, 1978; The Purple Rose of Cairo, 1985; Hannah and her Sisters, 1986. *Publications:* Getting Even, 1971; Without Feathers, 1975; Side Effects, 1981; contribs to New Yorker, etc.

ALLEN-JONES, Air Vice-Marshal John Ernest, CBE 1966; Director of RAF Legal Services, 1961–70, retired; *b* 13 Oct. 1909; *s* of Rev. John Allen-Jones, Llanyblodwel Vicarage, Oswestry; *m* 1st, 1937, Margaret Rix (*d* 1973), Sawbridgeworth; one *s* two *d*; 2nd, 1973, Diana Gibbons. *Educ:* Rugby; Worcester Coll., Oxford (MA). Solicitor (Honours), 1934; Partner with Vaudrey, Osborne & Mellor, Manchester. Joined RAF, 1939. Air Vice-Marshal, 1967. Gordon-Shepherd Memorial Prizeman, 1963. *Recreations:* tennis, bridge. *Address:* Hartfield, Duton Hill, Dunmow, Essex. *T:* Great Easton 554.

ALLENBY, family name of **Viscount Allenby.**

ALLENBY, 3rd Viscount *cr* 1919, of Megiddo and of Felixstowe; **Michael Jaffray Hynman Allenby;** Lieut-Colonel, The Royal Hussars; retired 1986; *b* 20 April 1931; *s* of 2nd Viscount Allenby and of Mary Lethbridge Allenby; *d* of Edward Champneys; *S* father, 1984; *m* 1965, Sara Margaret, *d* of Lt-Col Peter Milner Wiggin; one *s*. *Educ:* Eton; RMA Sandhurst. Commnd 2/Lieut 11th Hussars (PAO), 1951; served Malaya, 1953–56; ADC to Governor, Cyprus, 1957–58; Bde Major, 51 Brigade, Hong Kong, 1967–70; comd Royal Yeomanry (TA), 1974–77; GS01 Instructor, Nigerian Staff Coll., Kaduna, 1977–79. *Recreations:* horses, sailing. *Heir:* *s* Hon. Henry Jaffray Hynman Allenby, *b* 29 July 1968. *Club:* Cavalry and Guards.

ALLENBY, Rt. Rev. (David Howard) Nicholas; Assistant Bishop, Diocese of Worcester since 1968; *b* 28 Jan. 1909; *s* of late William Allenby; unmarried. *Educ:* Kelham Theological College. MA (Lambeth), 1957. Deacon, 1934; Priest, 1935. Curate of St Jude, West Derby, Liverpool, 1934–36; Tutor, Kelham Theological College and Public Preacher, Diocese of Southwell, 1936–44; Rector of Averham with Kelham, 1944–57; Mem., Southwell RDC, 1944–52; Proctor in Convocation, Southwell, 1950–57; Editor of Diocesan News and Southwell Review, 1950–55; Hon. Canon of Southwell, 1953–57, Canon Emeritus, 1957–62; Personal Chaplain to Bishop of Southwell, 1954–57; Rural Dean of Newark, 1955–57; Provincial of Society of Sacred Mission in Australia, 1957–62; Commissary, Melanesia, 1958–62; Warden of Community of Holy Name, City and Diocese of Melbourne, 1961–62; Bishop of Kuching, 1962–68; Commissary, Kuching, 1969. Chaplain, St Oswald's Almshouses, Worcester, 1973–84. *Publication:* Pray with the Church, 1937 (jointly). *Recreations:* reading, painting, cooking. *Address:* 16 Woodbine Road, Barbourne, Worcester WR1 3JB. *T:* Worcester 27980. *Club:* Royal Commonwealth Society.

ALLENDALE, 3rd Viscount, *cr* 1911; **Wentworth Hubert Charles Beaumont,** DL; Baron, 1906; *b* 12 Sept. 1922; *e s* of 2nd Viscount Allendale, KG, CB, CBE, MC, and Violet (*d* 1979), *d* of Sir Charles Seely, 2nd Bt; *S* father 1956; *m* 1948, Hon. Sarah Ismay, 2nd *d* of 1st Baron Ismay, KG, PC, GCB, CH, DSO; three *s*. *Educ:* Eton. RAFVR, 1940; Flight-Lieutenant 1943; ADC to Viceroy of India, 1946–47. DL Northumberland, 1961. *Heir:* *s* Hon. Wentworth Peter Ismay Beaumont [*b* 13 Nov. 1948; *m* 1975, Theresa Mary, *d* of F. A. More O'Ferrall; one *s* three *d*]. *Address:* Bywell Hall, Stocksfield on Tyne, Northumberland. *T:* Stocksfield 3169; Allenheads, Hexham, Northumberland. *T:* Allenheads 205. *Clubs:* Turf, White's; Northern Counties (Newcastle upon Tyne).
See also Earl of Carlisle.

ALLERTON, 3rd Baron of Chapel Allerton, *cr* 1902; **George William Lawies Jackson;** Squadron-Leader Auxiliary Air Force, retired; late Lieutenant Coldstream Guards; *b* 23 July 1903; *s* of 2nd Baron and Katherine Louisa (*d* 1956), *y d* of W. W. Wickham, JP, of Chestnut Grove, Boston Spa; *S* father, 1925; *m* 1st, 1926, Joyce (who obtained a divorce, 1934; *d* 1953), *o c* of late J. R. Hatfeild, Thorp Arch Hall, Yorks; (one *s* decd); 2nd, 1934, Mrs Hope Aline Whitelaw; 3rd, 1947, Anne, *er d* of late James Montagu, Skippetts, nr Basingstoke; (one *d* decd). *Educ:* Eton; RMC, Sandhurst. *Recreations:* shooting, golf. *Heir:* none. *Address:* Loddington House, Leicestershire LE7 9XE. *T:* Belton 220. *Clubs:* White's, Turf, Pratt's.

ALLERTON, Reginald John, CBE 1964; FRICS, FIH; retired 1963; *b* 20 June 1898; 3rd *s* of late Robert Sterry Allerton, Lowestoft, and Mary Maria (*née* Bailey); *m* 1924, Dorothy Rose Saunders; one *s*. *Educ:* Lowestoft Grammar School. Entered Local Government Service, 1915; on Active Service with RNVR, 1917–19. Various urban and borough appointments until 1926; Chief Architectural and Building Asst, Reading Borough Council, 1926–30; Estates Surveyor, City of Norwich, 1930–39; Housing Manager and Sec., City of Bristol, 1939–51; Housing Manager, City of Birmingham, 1951–54; Director of Housing to the London County Council, 1954–63. Pres., Inst. of Housing, 1949–50, 1960–61. Apptd (by Minister of Housing and Local Govt) as Vice-Pres., Surrey and Sussex Rent Assessment Panel, 1965–71. Served on Govt Cttees on Housing and Immigration, and Housing in Greater London (Sir Milner Holland Cttee); Founder Mem., Hanover Housing Assoc. *Publications:* many papers and lectures to professional societies and conferences dealing mainly with municipal housing work. *Recreation:* gardening. *Address:* 10 Mill Mead, Wendover, Bucks. *T:* Wendover 622691.

ALLEY, Ronald Edgar; Keeper of the Modern Collection, Tate Gallery, London, 1965–86; *b* 12 March 1926; *s* of late Edgar Thomas Alley; *m* 1955, Anthea Oswell (marr. diss.) (now painter and sculptor, as Anthea Alley); two *d*. *Educ:* Bristol Grammar School; Courtauld Institute of Art, London University. Tate Gallery staff as Asst Keeper II, 1951–54; Deputy Keeper, 1954–65. Member: Museum Board, Cecil Higgins Art Gallery, Bedford, 1957–; Art Cttee, Ulster Museum, Belfast, 1962–; Art Panel of Arts Council, 1963–70. *Publications:* Tate Gallery: Foreign Paintings, Drawings and Sculpture, 1959; Gauguin, 1962; William Scott, 1963; Ben Nicholson, 1963; Francis Bacon (with Sir John Rothenstein), 1964; British Painting since 1945, 1966; Picasso's "Three Dancers" 1967; Barbara Hepworth, 1968; Recent American Art, 1969; Abstract Expressionism, 1974; Catalogue of the Tate Gallery's Collection of Modern Art, other than works by British Artists, 1981. *Recreation:* ornithology. *Address:* 61 Deodar Road, SW15. *T:* 01–874 2016. *Club:* Institute of Contemporary Arts.

ALLEYNE, Rev. Sir John (Olpherts Campbell), 5th Bt *cr* 1769; Rector of Weeke, Diocese of Winchester, since 1975; *b* 18 Jan. 1928; *s* of Captain Sir John Meynell Alleyne, 4th Bt, DSO, DSC, RN, and Alice Violet (*d* 1985), *d* of late James Campbell; *S* father, 1983; *m* 1968, Honor, *d* of late William Albert Irwin, Belfast; one *s* one *d*. *Educ:* Eton; Jesus Coll., Cambridge (BA 1950, MA 1955). Deacon 1955, priest 1956; Curate, Southampton, 1955–58; Chaplain: Coventry Cathedral, 1958–62; Clare Coll., Cambridge, 1962–66; to Bishop of Bristol, 1966–68; Toc H Area Sec., SW England, 1968–71; Vicar of Speke, 1971–73, Rector, 1973–75. *Heir:* *s* Richard Meynell Alleyne, *b* 23 June 1972. *Address:* The Rectory, Cheriton Road, Winchester, Hants.

ALLFORD, David, CBE 1984; FRIBA; architect; Senior Partner, YRM Partnership, since 1975 (Partner since 1958); *b* 12 July 1927; *s* of Frank Allford and Martha Blanche Allford; *m* 1953, Margaret Beryl Roebuck; one *s* three *d*. *Educ:* High Storrs Grammar Sch., Sheffield; Univ. of Sheffield (BA Hons Architecture, 1952). FRIBA 1969. Served RAF, 1945–48. Joined Yorke Rosenberg Mardall, Architects (now YRM Partnership), 1952; Partner i/c architectural projects: schools, univs (principally Univ. of Warwick), Newcastle Airport, hosps and commercial projs in UK and overseas. Mem. Council, Architectural Assoc., 1970–71 and 1977–78. *Publications:* articles in architectural press and related jls. *Recreations:* drawing, painting, following Sheffield Wednesday Football Club. *Address:* 39 Belsize Road, NW6 4RX. *T:* 01–722 6724. *Clubs:* Arts, Danish.

ALLHUSEN, Major Derek Swithin, CVO 1984; DL; farmer; Standard Bearer, HM's Body Guard of Honourable Corps of Gentlemen at Arms, 1981–84; *b* 9 Jan. 1914; 2nd *s* of late Lt-Col F. H. Allhusen, CMG, DSO, Fulmer House, Fulmer, Bucks; *m* 1937, Hon. Claudia Violet Betterton, *yr d* of 1st and last Baron Rushcliffe, PC, GBE (*d* 1949); one *s* one *d* (and one *s* decd). *Educ:* Eton; Chillon Coll., Montreux, Switzerland; Trinity Coll., Cambridge. Lieut, 9th Queen's Royal Lancers, 1935. Served War of 1939–45: France, 1940 (wounded), North Africa, Italy (Silver Star Medal of USA, 1944); Major 1942; 2 i/c 1945–47; retired, 1949. One of HM's Body Guard of Hon. Corps of Gentlemen at Arms, 1963–84. Chm., Riding for the Disabled, Norwich and Dist. Gp, 1968– (Vice-Pres., Eastern Region); President: Royal Norfolk Agric. Assoc., 1974; Nat. Pony Soc., 1982; Cambridge Univ. Equestrian Club; Norfolk Schs Athletic Assoc.; Pres. elect, British Horse Soc., 1986 (Mem. Council, 1962–). Freeman, City of London; Hon. Yeoman, Worshipful Co. of Saddlers, 1969; Hon. Freeman, Worshipful Co. of Farriers. High Sheriff, 1958, DL 1969, Norfolk. *Recreations:* riding, shooting, skiing. Represented GB: Winter Pentathlon Olympic Games, 1948; Equestrianism European Championships Three-Day Event, 1957, 1959, 1965, 1967, 1969 (Winners of Team Championship, 1957, 1967, 1969); Olympic Games, Mexico, 1968 (Gold Medal, Team; Silver Medal, Individual); lent his horse Laurieston to British Olympic Equestrian Team, Munich, 1972 (individual and team Gold Medals). *Address:* Manor House, Claxton, Norwich, Norfolk. *T:* Thurton 228; Flat 1, 22 St James's Square, SW1. *T:* 01–839 3390. *Club:* Cavalry and Guards.

ALLIBONE, Thomas Edward, CBE 1960; DSc Sheffield; FRS 1948; FEng; External Professor of Electrical Engineering, University of Leeds, 1967–79, now Emeritus; Visiting Professor of Physics, City University, since 1971; also Robert Kitchin (Saddlers) Research Professor, since 1983, and first Frank Poynton Professor, Physics Department, since 1984, City University; *b* 11 Nov. 1903; *s* of Henry J. Allibone; *m* 1931, Dorothy Margery, LRAM, ARCM, *d* of Frederick Boulden, BSc, MEng, MIMechE; two *d*. *Educ:* Central Sch., Sheffield (Birley Scholar); Sheffield Univ. (Linley Scholar); Gonville and Caius Coll., Cambridge (Wollaston Scholar). PhD Sheffield; PhD Cantab. 1851 Exhibition Sen. Student, Cavendish Laboratory, Cambridge, 1926–30; i/c High-Voltage Laboratory, Metropolitan-Vickers Electrical Co., Manchester, 1930–46; Director: Res. Laboratory, AEI, Aldermaston, 1946–63; AEI (Woolwich) Ltd, 1948–63; Scientific Adviser, AEI, 1963; Chief Scientist, Central Electricity Generating Bd, 1963–70. Mem., British Mission on Atomic Energy, Berkeley, Calif, and Oakridge, Tenn, 1944–45; Visitor: BISRA, 1949–55; ASLIB, 1955–62. Lectures: Faraday, 1946, 1956; Royal Instn Christmas, 1959; Wm Menelaus, 1959; Bernard Price, 1959; Trotter Patterson, 1963; Fison Memorial, 1963; Royal Soc. Rutherford Memorial, 1964 and 1972; Baird Memorial, 1967; Melchett, 1970. President: Section A, British Assoc., 1958; EIBA, 1958–59; Inst. of Information Scientists, 1964–67. Vice-President: Inst. of Physics, 1948–52; Royal Instn, 1955–57, 1970–72. Chm., Res. Cttee, British Electrical and Allied Industries Res. Assoc., 1955–62. Member: Council, British Inst. of Radiology, 1935–38; Council, IEE, 1937–40, 1946–49, 1950–53; Cttee, Nat. Physical Laboratory, 1950–60; Govt Cttee on Copyright, 1951; DSIR (Mem., Industrial Grants Cttee, 1950–58); Council, Physical Soc., 1953–56; Council, Southern Electricity Bd, 1953–62; Adv. Council, Science Museum; Adv. Council, RMC; Adv. Court, AEA; Nuclear Safety Adv. Council, Min. of Power, 1959–. Trustee, British Museum, 1968–74. Governor, Downe House, 1959–69; Chm. Governors, Reading Technical Coll., 1959–68. Mem., Worshipful Co. of Broderers, 1967–. FInstP; Founder FEng; FIEE; Fellow, Amer. Inst. of Electrical Engineers. Hon. DSc: Reading, 1960; City, 1970; Hon. DEng Sheffield, 1969. Röntgen Medal, British Inst. of Radiology; Thornton and Cooper Hill Medals, IEE; Melchett Medal, Inst. of Fuel. *Publications:* The Release and Use of Nuclear Energy, 1961; Rutherford: Father of Nuclear Energy (Rutherford Lecture 1972), 1973; The Royal Society and its Dining Clubs, 1975; Lightning: the long spark, 1977; Cockcroft and the Atom, 1983; Metropolitan-Vickers Electrical Co. and the Cavendish Laboratory, 1984; papers on high voltage and transient electrical phenomena, fission and fusion. *Recreations:* photography, travel, gardening, philately. *Address:* York Cottage, Lovel Road, Winkfield, Windsor, Berks. *T:* Winkfield Row 884501.

ALLINSON, Sir Leonard; *see* Allinson, Sir W. L.

ALLINSON, Sir (Walter) Leonard, KCVO 1979 (MVO 1961); CMG 1976; HM Diplomatic Service, retired; *b* 1 May 1926; *o s* of Walter Allinson and Alice Frances Cassidy; *m* 1951, Margaret Patricia Watts; three *d* (of whom two are twins). *Educ:* Friern Barnet Grammar Sch.; Merton Coll., Oxford. First class in History, 1947; MA. Asst Principal, Ministry of Fuel and Power (Petroleum Div.), 1947–48; Asst Principal, later Principal, Min. of Education, 1948–58 (Asst Private Sec. to Minister, 1953–54); transf. CRO, 1958; First Sec. in Lahore and Karachi, 1960–62, Madras and New Delhi, 1963–66; Counsellor and Head of Political Affairs Dept, March 1968; Dep. Head, later Head, of Permanent Under Secretary's Dept, FCO, 1968–70; Counsellor and Head of Chancery, subsequently Deputy High Comr, Nairobi, 1970–73; RCDS, 1974; Diplomatic Service Inspectorate, 1975; Dep. High Comr and Minister, New Delhi, 1975–77; High Comr, Lusaka, 1978–80; Asst Under-Sec. of State (Africa), 1980–82; High Comr in Kenya and Ambassador to UN Environment Programme, 1982–86. Vice Pres., Royal African Soc., 1982–. *Address:* c/o National Westminster Bank, 6 Tothill Street, SW1. *Club:* Oriental.

ALLIOTT, Hon. Sir John (Downes), Kt 1986; **Hon. Mr Justice Alliott;** Judge of the High Court of Justice, Queen's Bench Division, since 1986; *b* 9 Jan. 1932; *er s* of late Alexander Clifford Alliott and Ena Kathleen Alliott (*née* Downes); *m* 1957, Patsy Jennifer, *d* of late Gordon Beckles Willson; two *s* one *d*. *Educ:* Charterhouse; Peterhouse, Cambridge (Schol., BA). Coldstream Guards, 1950–51; Peterhouse, 1951–54; called to Bar, Inner Temple, 1955, Bencher 1980; QC 1973. Dep. Chm., E Sussex QS, 1970–71; Recorder, 1972–86; Leader of the SE Circuit, 1983–86. Mem., Home Office Adv. Bd on Restricted Patients, 1983–86. *Recreations:* rural pursuits, France and Italy, military history. *Address:* Royal Courts of Justice, Strand, WC2.

ALLISON, Brian George; Group Executive Chairman, Business Intelligence Services Group, since 1985; *b* 4 April 1933; *s* of Donald Brian Allison and Edith Maud Allison (*née* Humphries); *m* 1958, Glennis Mary Taylor; one *s* one *d*. *Educ:* Hele's Sch., Exeter; University Coll. London (BSc Econ). FInstM 1981. Flying Officer, RAF, 1955–58. Economist Statistician, Shell-Mex & BP, 1958; Marketing Res. Manager, Spicers, 1958–64; Business Intelligence Services: Dir and Gen. Manager, 1964–69; Man. Dir and Dep. Chm., 1969–74; Chm. and Man. Dir, 1974–81; Chm. and Chief Exec., 1981–85. Dir, English China Clays, 1984–. Vis. Prof., Univ. of Surrey, 1976–. Mem., ESRC, 1986–. *Recreations:* tennis, travel, motoring, restoring historic properties. *Club:* Reform.

ALLISON, Charles Ralph, MA; Secretary, Lord Kitchener National Memorial Fund, 1968–83; Headmaster of Brentwood School, 1945–65; *b* 26 May 1903; *s* of Harry A. Allison, FCA, and Gertrude Wolfsberger; *m* 1930, Winifred Rita, *d* of A. C. Williams; two *s* one *d*. *Educ:* Caterham Sch.; University Coll., London; St Catharine's College, Cambridge (Exhibitioner). Assistant Master, Worksop College, 1928; Malvern College, 1929–36; English Tutor, Stowe School, 1936–38; Headmaster of Reigate Grammar School, 1938–40, and Alleyn's School, 1940–45. Formerly Mem. Cttee, Headmasters' Conf. (Vice-Chm. 1965). Governor: Sidney Perry Foundation (Chm.); Lindisfarne Coll., Ruabon, 1954–81; Brentwood Sch., 1970–85; Stowe Sch., 1965–80. Vice-Chm., Commonwealth Youth Exchange Cttee, 1970–72; Vice-Pres., Eastern Region, UNA, 1965–83. Mem., Nat. Commn for UNESCO, 1954–65; UK Delegate to Gen. Confs, 1958 and 1960. Member: Cttee, Governing Bodies' Assoc., 1972–79, 1980–83; Essex Education Cttee, 1967–74. Reader in the Parish of: St Mary's, Great Warley, 1967–83; St Alban, Tattenhall, 1985–. *Address:* Groom's Cottage, Chester Road, Tattenhall, Cheshire CH3 9AH. *T:* Tattenhall 70827. *Club:* East India, Devonshire, Sports and Public Schools.

ALLISON, Air Vice-Marshal Dennis; Director of Management and Support of Intelligence, Ministry of Defence, since 1985; *b* 15 Oct. 1932; *m* 1964, Rachel Anne Franks; one *s* four *d*. *Educ:* RAF Halton; RAF Coll., Cranwell. Commnd, 1954; No 87 Sqdn, 1955–58; cfs 1958; Flying Instructor and Coll. Adjt, RAF Coll., 1958–61; CO, RAF Sharjah, 1961–62; Indian Jt Services Staff Coll., 1965; MoD Central Staffs, 1968–70; ndc, 1973; MoD Central Staffs, 1973–74; CO, RAF Coningsby, 1974–76; Canadian Nat. Defence Coll., 1977; MoD Central Staffs, 1978–79; Comdt, Central Flying Sch., 1979–83; Dir of Training (Flying), MoD, 1983–84. *Recreations:* bridge, golf. *Address:* The Old Forge, Castle Bytham, Grantham, Lincs NG33 4RU. *T:* Castle Bytham 372. *Club:* Royal Air Force.

ALLISON, Rt. Rev. Oliver Claude, CBE 1971; Travelling Secretary, Sudan Church Association, since 1974; *b* Stafford, 1908; *s* of Rev. W. S. Allison. *Educ:* Dean Close School, Cheltenham; Queens' College and Ridley Hall, Cambridge. BA 1930; MA 1934. Deacon, 1932; Priest, 1933; Curate of Fulwood, 1932–36; Curate of St John, Boscombe, and Jt Sec. Winchester Dio. Council of Youth, 1936–38; CMS Miss. at Juba, Dio. Sudan, 1938–47; Asst Bp in the Sudan, 1948–53; Bishop in the Sudan, 1953–74. *Publications:* A Pilgrim Church's Progress, 1966; Through Fire and Water, 1976; Travelling Light, 1983. *Address:* 1 Gloucester Avenue, Bexhill-on-Sea, East Sussex TN40 2LA. *Club:* Royal Commonwealth Society.

ALLISON, Ralph Victor, CMG 1967; retired industrialist, Australia; *b* 20 Feb. 1900; *s* of late Albert John and Edith Victoria Allison; *m* 1923, Myrtle Ellen Birch; two *d*. *Educ:* public and night schools, Milang, SA. General Store, A. H. Landseer Ltd: Milang, 1916–19; Adelaide, 1919–26; R. J. Finlayson Ltd, Adelaide: Company Sec., 1926–39; Dir, 1939–64; Man. Dir, 1954–64; Chm. Dirs of subsidiaries, 1954–64. Mem. Council: Royal Agric. and Hort. Soc. of SA, 1937–72 (Exec. Mem. 8 yrs); SA Chamber of Manufactures, later Chamber of Commerce and Industry SA Inc. 1948– (now Hon. Mem.; (also Mem. Exec. Cttee); Pres., 1962, 1963); Mem. SA Dairy Bd, 1957. Pres. Aust. Chamber of Manufactures, 1964; Mem. Aust. Export Develt Council, 1964–68; Director, Australian Export Promotions Ltd and various other Australian cos until 1966. Mem., many Aust. Commonwealth Cttees. *Address:* c/o 12 First Street, Magill, SA 5072, Australia.

ALLISON, Roderick Stuart; Grade 3, Department of Employment, since 1977; *b* 28 Nov. 1936; *s* of Stuart Frew Allison and Poppy (*née* Hodges); *m* 1968, Anne Sergeant; one *s* one *d*. *Educ:* Manchester Grammar Sch.; Balliol Coll., Oxford. Entered Ministry of Labour, 1959; Private Sec. to Perm. Sec., 1963–64; Principal, 1964; Civil Service Dept, 1969–71; Asst Sec., 1971, Under Sec., 1977, Dept of Employment. *Recreations:* playing with children, music, sailing. *Address:* c/o Department of Employment, Caxton House, Tothill Street, SW1.

ALLISON, Ronald William Paul, CVO 1978; Managing Director, Ronald Allison & Associates Ltd, since 1978; Director of Corporate Affairs, Thames Television, since 1986; *b* 26 Jan. 1932; *o s* of Percy Allison and Dorothy (*née* Doyle); *m* 1956, Maureen Angela Macdonald; two *d*. *Educ:* Weymouth Grammar Sch.; Taunton's Sch., Southampton. Reporter, Hampshire Chronicle, 1952–57; Reporter, BBC, 1957–67; freelance broadcaster, 1968–69; special correspondent, BBC, 1969–73; Press Sec. to Queen, 1973–78; regular presenter and commentator, Thames TV, 1978–; Controller of Sport and Outside Broadcasts, Thames TV, 1980–85. *Publications:* Look Back in Wonder, 1968; The Queen, 1973; Charles, Prince of our Time, 1978; The Country Life Book of Britain in the Seventies, 1980. *Recreations:* photography, painting, watching football. *Address:* 36 Ormond Drive, Hampton, Mddx. *T:* 01–979 1912. *Clubs:* Royal Automobile; Stage Golf Soc.; Old Tauntonians (Southampton).
See also Sir E. G. Yarrow, Bt.

ALLISON, Rt. Rev. Sherard Falkner, MA, DD, LLD; *b* 19 Jan. 1907; *s* of Reverend W. S. Allison; *m* 1936, Ruth Hills; one *s* two *d* (and one *s* decd). *Educ:* Dean Close School, Cheltenham; Jesus Coll., Cambridge (Scholar); Ridley Hall, Cambridge. 1st Cl. Classical Tripos, Parts I and II; 2nd Class Theological Tripos, Part I and Jeremie Septuagint Prize; Curate of St James', Tunbridge Wells, 1931–34; Chaplain of Ridley Hall, Cambridge, and Examining Chaplain to Bishop of Bradford, 1934–36; Vicar of Rodbourne Cheney, Swindon, 1936–40; Vicar of Erith, 1940–45; Principal of Ridley Hall, Cambridge, 1945–50; Bishop of Chelmsford, 1951–61; Bishop of Winchester, and Prelate of the Most Noble Order of the Garter, 1961–74. Examining Chaplain to Bishop of Rochester, 1945, and to Bishop of Ely, 1947; Select Preacher: Univ. of Cambridge, 1946, 1955, 1962; Univ. of Oxford, 1953–55, 1963; Proctor in Convocation, Diocese of Ely, 1949. Hon. Fellow, Jesus College, Cambridge, 1963. DD, Lambeth, 1951; Hon. DD: Occidental Coll., Los Angeles, 1959; Wycliffe Coll., Toronto, 1959; Hon. STD, Church Divinity Sch. of the Pacific, 1959; Hon. LLD: Sheffield, 1960; Southampton, 1974. *Publication:* The Christian Life, 1938 (Joint). *Recreations:* sailing, water-colour sketching, bird watching, gardening. *Address:* Winton Lodge, Alde Lane, Aldeburgh, Suffolk.

ALLNUTT, Ian Peter, OBE; MA; Representative of the British Council in Mexico, 1973–77; *b* 26 April 1917; *s* of Col E. B. Allnutt, CBE, MC, and Joan C. Gainsford; *m* 1946, Doreen Louise Lenagan; four *d*. *Educ:* Imperial Service Coll., Windsor; Sidney Sussex Coll., Cambridge. HM Colonial Service, 1939–46, Nigeria, with break, 1940–45, for service in World War II, Nigeria Regt, RWAFF (despatches). British Council service in Peru, E Africa, Colombia, Argentina, Malta, London and Mexico, 1946–77. OBE 1976; Insignia of Aztec Eagle, 1975. *Recreations:* the arts, pre-Columbian civilisations, the Hispanic world. *Address:* Karen Cottage, Boulters Lane, Maidenhead, Berks SL6 8TJ. *T:* Maidenhead 20499. *Club:* Leander (Henley-on-Thames).

ALLOTT, Prof. Antony Nicolas, JP; Professor of African and Comparative Law, University of Buckingham, since 1987; *b* 30 June 1924; *s* of late Reginald William Allott and Dorothy Allott (*née* Dobson); *m* 1952, Anna Joan Sargant, *d* of Tom Sargant, *qv*, and Marie Černy; two *s* two *d*. *Educ:* Downside Sch.; New Coll., Oxford. Lieut Royal Northumberland Fusiliers and King's African Rifles, 1944–46. BA Oxon (1st class Hons Jurisprudence), 1948; PhD London 1954. Lecturer in African Law, School of Oriental and African Studies, London, 1948–60; Reader in African Law, 1960–64, Prof. of African Law, 1964–86, Univ. of London. Vis. Prof., Université de Paris I, 1984. Hon. Director, Africa Centre, 1963–66; Pres., African Studies Assoc. of UK, 1969–70 (past Hon. Treas.); Vice-Pres., Internat. African Law Assoc., 1967. Académicien associé, Académie Internat. de Droit Comparé, 1982–; Corresponding Mem., Académie Royale des Sciences d'Outre-Mer, Belgium, 1980. Vice-Chm., Governing Body, Plater Coll., Oxford; Govr, St Bartholomew's Hosp. Med. Sch. Member: Senate, Univ. of London, 1978–86; Council, Commonwealth Magistrates Assoc., 1972–; Chm., Mddx Magistrates' Cts Cttee, 1982–86. Chm., Barnet Petty Sessional Area, 1986. JP Middlesex 1969 (Chm., Gore Div., 1985–86). *Publications:* Essays in African Law, with special reference to the Law of Ghana, 1960; (ed) Judicial and Legal Systems in Africa, 1962, 2nd edn 1970; New Essays in African Law, 1970; The Limits of Law, 1980; (ed with G. Woodman) People's Law and State Law, 1985; articles in legal and other jls. *Recreations:* music, gardening, silviculture. *Address:* Department of Law, University of Buckingham, Buckingham MK18 1EG.
See also R. M. Allott, Prof. N. E. S. McIntosh.

ALLOTT, Air Cdre Molly Greenwood, CB 1975; *b* 28 Dec. 1918; *d* of late Gerald William Allott. *Educ:* Sheffield High Sch. for Girls (GPDST). Served War of 1939–45: joined WAAF, 1941; served in: Egypt, Singapore, Germany. Staff of AOC-in-C: RAF Germany, 1960–63; Fighter Command, 1963–66; Training Command, 1971–73; Dir, WRAF, 1973–76. ADC 1973–76; Nat. Chm., Girls' Venture Corps, 1977–82; Member: Council, Union Jack Club, 1977–; Main Grants Cttee, RAF Benevolent Fund, 1977–82. FBIM. *Recreations:* travel, decorative arts. *Address:* c/o Midland Bank, High Street, Lymington SO4 9ZP. *Clubs:* Royal Air Force, Royal Lymington Yacht.

ALLOTT, Robin Michael; Under-Secretary, Establishment Personnel Division, Departments of Industry and Trade, 1978–80; *b* 9 May 1926; *s* of Reginald William Allott and Dorothy (*née* Dobson). *Educ:* The Oratory Sch., Caversham; New Coll., Oxford; Sheffield Univ. Asst Principal, BoT, 1948; UK Delegn to OECD, Paris, 1952; Private Sec. to Sec. for Overseas Trade, 1953; Principal, Office for Scotland, Glasgow, 1954; UK Delegn to UN Conf. on Trade and Develt, Geneva, 1964; Asst Sec., BoT, 1965; Counsellor, UK Delegn to EEC, Brussels, 1971; sabbatical year, New Coll., Oxford, 1974–75; Dept of Industry (motor industry), 1975; Under-Sec., Dept of Trade, 1976. *Publication:* The Physical Foundation of Language, 1973. *Recreations:* studying the evolutionary relation of language, perception and action; computer programming. *Address:* 5 Fitzgerald Park, Seaford, East Sussex. *T:* Seaford 896022.
See also A. N. Allott.

ALLPORT, Denis Ivor; Chairman, 1979–85 and Chief Executive, 1977–85, Metal Box Ltd (Director, 1973–85, Managing Director, 1977–79, Deputy Chairman, 1979); *b* 20 Nov. 1922; *s* of late A. R. Allport and late E. M. Allport (*née* Mashman); *m* 1949, Diana (*née* Marler); two *s* one *d*. *Educ:* Highgate School. Served War, Indian Army, 1941–46; joined Metal Box Ltd, 1946; various appts in UK, Singapore and Pakistan; Man. Dir, Metal Box Co. of India, 1969–70; Director: Metal Box Overseas Ltd, 1970–74; Beecham Gp plc, 1981–; Marley plc, 1985–. Member: Nat. Enterprise Bd, 1980–83; NRDC, 1981–83. FBIM 1977. *Recreations:* golf, cricket. *Address:* Elm Place, Mumbery Hill, Wargrave, Reading, Berks RG10 8EE. *T:* Wargrave 3007. *Clubs:* MCC, Oriental.

ALLSOP, Peter Henry Bruce, CBE 1984; FRSA; FBIM; Chairman, Associated Book Publishers, since 1976; *b* 22 Aug. 1924; *s* of late Herbert Henry Allsop and of Elsie Hilpern (*née* Whitaker); *m* 1950, Patricia Elizabeth Kingwell Bown; two *s* one *d*. *Educ:* Haileybury; Caius Coll., Cambridge (MA). Called to Bar, Lincoln's Inn, 1948. Temp. Asst Principal, Air Min., 1944–48; Barrister in practice, 1948–50; Sweet & Maxwell: Editor, 1950–59; Dir, 1960–64; Man. Dir, 1965–73; Chm., 1974–80; Dir, Associated Book Publishers, 1963, Asst Man. Dir, 1965–67, Man. Dir, 1968–76. Dir, Yale University Press, 1981–84 (Trustee, 1984–). Mem. Council, Publishers Assoc., 1969–81 (Treasurer, 1973–75, 1979–81; Pres., 1975–77; Vice-Pres., 1977–78; Trustee, 1982–); Member: Printing and Publishing Industry Trng Bd, 1977–79; Publishers' Adv. Cttee, British Council, 1980–85; Publishers' Management Advisers, 1983–; Chairman: Teleordering Ltd, 1978–; Management Cttee Book House Training Centre, 1980–86; Dir, Woodard Schools (Western Div.) Ltd, 1985–. Chm., Social Security Appeal Tribunal, 1982– (Mem., 1979–82). Chm., Book Trade Benevolent Soc., 1986– (Trustee, 1976–85; Dir, 1985). Mem., St Albans City Council, 1955–68. Chm., Diocesan Adv. Cttee, Bath and Wells, 1985–. Mem. Council, King's Coll., Taunton, 1983–. Editor, later Editor-in-Chief: Current Law, 1952–; Criminal Law Review, 1954–. *Publications:* (ed) Bowstead's Law of Agency, 11th edn, 1951. *Recreations:* gardening, hill walking, theatre, farming. *Address:* Manor Farm, Charlton Mackrell, Somerton, Somerset. *T:* Charlton Mackrell 3650. *Clubs:* Garrick, Farmers'.

ALLSOPP, family name of **Baron Hindlip.**

ALLSOPP, Bruce; *see* Allsopp, H. B.

ALLSOPP, Prof. Cecil Benjamin, MA, PhD, DSc; FInstP; Professor of Physics Applied to Medicine, University of London at Guy's Hospital Medical School, 1953–70, now Emeritus; Consultant Physicist Emeritus to Guy's Hospital; *b* 2 Sept. 1904; *m* 1935, Ivy Kathleen Johns; one *s* one *d*. *Educ:* Emmanuel College, Cambridge; University of Frankfurt-am-Main. MA, Cambridge, 1930; PhD, Cambridge, 1932; DSc, London, 1951. Pres., British Institute of Radiology, 1963–64; Silvanus Thompson Memorial Lectr, 1965. *Publications:* Absorption Spectrophotometry (with F. Twyman, FRS), 1934. Papers in Proc. of the Royal Soc., Jl of the Chemical Soc., Trans of the Faraday Soc., British Journal of Radiology, British Journal of Experimental Pathology, Cancer Research, etc. *Address:* 40 Queen Edith's Way, Cambridge CB1 4PW.

ALLSOPP, (Harold) Bruce, BArch, DipCD, FSA, MRTPI; Chairman, Oriel Press Ltd, since 1962; *b* Oxford, 4 July 1912; *s* of Henry Allsopp and Elizabeth May Allsopp (*née* Robertson); *m* 1935, Florence Cyrilla Woodroffe, ARCA; two *s*. *Educ:* Manchester Grammar Sch.; Liverpool School of Architecture. BArch (1st Cl. Hons), Liverpool, 1933; Rome Finalist, 1934; Diploma in Civic Design 1935; ARIBA 1935; AMTPI 1936; FRIBA 1955; FSA 1968. Asst Architect in Chichester and London, 1934–35; Lecturer, Leeds Coll. of Art, 1935–40. War Service 1940–46, N Africa, Italy, Captain RE. Lecturer in Architecture, Univ. of Durham, 1946; Sen. Lecturer, 1955; Sen. Lecturer, Univ. of Newcastle upon Tyne, 1963, Dir of Architectural Studies, 1965–69; Sen. Lecturer in History of Architecture, 1969–73; Reader, 1973–77. Dir, Routledge & Kegan Paul Books Ltd, 1974–85. Chairman: Soc. of Architectural Historians of GB, 1959–65; Independent Publishers Guild, 1971–73; Master, Art Workers Guild, 1970; Pres., Northern Fedn of Art Socs, 1980–83. Presenter, TV films, including Fancy Gothic, 1974; The Bowes Museum, 1977; Country Houses and Landscape of Northumberland, 1979. *Publications:* Art and the Nature of Architecture, 1952; Decoration and Furniture, Vol. 1 1952, Vol. 2 1953; A General History of Architecture, 1955; Style in the Visual Arts, 1957; Possessed, 1959; The Future of the Arts, 1959; A History of Renaissance Architecture, 1959; The Naked Flame, 1962; Architecture, 1964; To Kill a King, 1965; A History of Classical Architecture, 1965; Historic Architecture of Newcastle upon Tyne, 1967; Civilization, the Next Stage, 1969; The Study of Architectural History, 1970; Modern Architecture of Northern England, 1970; Inigo Jones on Palladio, 1970; Romanesque Architecture, 1971; Ecological Morality, 1972; Towards a Humane Architecture, 1974; Return of the Pagan, 1974; Cecilia, 1975; Inigo Jones and the Lords A'Leaping, 1975; A Modern Theory of Architecture, 1977; Appeal to the Gods, 1980; Should Man Survive?, 1982; The Country Life Companion to British and European Architecture, 1985; Social Responsibility and the Responsible Society, 1985; Guide de l'Architecture, 1985; Larousse Guide to European Architecture, 1985; (with Ursula Clark): Architecture of France, 1963; Architecture of Italy, 1964; Architecture of England, 1964; Photography for Tourists, 1966; Historic Architecture of Northumberland, 1969; Historic Architecture of Northumberland and Newcastle, 1977; English Architecture, 1979; (with U. Clark and H. W. Booton): The Great Tradition of Western Architecture, 1966; articles in Encyclopedia Americana, Encyclopaedia Britannica, Jl of RSA, etc. *Recreations:* piano and harpsichord, gardening. *Address:* Woodburn, 3 Batt House Road, Stocksfield, Northumberland NE43 7QZ. *T:* Stocksfield 842323; Stocksfield Studio, Stocksfield, Northumberland NE43 7NA. *T:* Stocksfield 843065. *Clubs:* Athenæum, Arts.

ALLUM, Sarah Elizabeth Royle, (Mrs R. G. Allum); *see* Walker, S. E. R.

ALMENT, Sir (Edward) Anthony (John), Kt 1980; FRCOG; Consultant Obstetrician and Gynaecologist, Northampton, 1960–85, retired; *b* 3 Feb. 1922; *s* of Edward and Alice Alment; *m* 1946, Elizabeth Innes Bacon. *Educ:* Marlborough Coll.; St Bartholomew's Hosp. Med. Coll. MRCS, LRCP 1945; FRCOG 1967 (MRCOG 1951); FRCPI 1979; FRCGP 1982. Served RAFVR, 1947–48. Trng appointments: St Bartholomew's Hosp., 1945–46 and 1954–60; Norfolk and Norwich Hosp., 1948; Queen Charlotte's Hosp. and Chelsea Hosp. for Women, 1949–50; London Hosp., 1951–52. Royal Coll. of Obstetricians and Gynaecologists: Mem. Council, 1961–67; Hon. Sec., 1968–73; Pres., 1978–81. Chm., Cttee of Enquiry into Competence to Practise, 1973–76; Member: Oxford Reg. Hosp. Bd, 1968–74 (Chm., Med. Adv. Cttee, 1972–74); Oxford RHA, 1973–75; Central Midwives Bd, 1967–68; UK Central Council for Nursing, Midwifery and Health Visiting, 1980–83. Examiner: RCOG; Univs of Cambridge, Leeds and Dar-es-Salaam. Hon. Fellow, Amer. Assoc. of Obstetricians and Gynaecologists, 1973 (Joseph Price Oration, 1972); Hon. FRCPEd 1981; Hon. FRACOG 1984. Hon. DSc Leicester, 1982. *Publications:* Competence to Practise, 1976; contrib. to med. jls. *Recreations:* wine, fishing, engineering, church architecture. *Address:* Winston House, Boughton, Northampton NN2 8RR.

AL-NIMR, Nabih; Ambassador of Jordan to the Court of St James's, since 1985; *b* 26 Oct. 1931; *m* 1961, Rabab Al-Nimr; one *s* one *d*. *Educ:* Univ. of Alexandria. Attaché in Ankara, Karachi, Bonn, 1955–62; Third Sec., Tunisia, 1962–65; First Sec., London, 1967–71; Counsellor: Kuwait, 1971–73; Damascus, 1973–74; Ambassador to Syrian Arab Republic, 1974–78; Amb. to Fed. Rep. of Germany and non-resident Amb. to Sweden, Denmark, Norway, Luxembourg, 1978–81; Amb. to Tunisia and Perm. Rep. of Jordan to Arab League, 1981–85. Decorations from Jordan, Syria, Germany, Tunisia, Italy, Belgium, Ethiopia. *Address:* Embassy of the Hashemite Kingdom of Jordan, 6 Upper Phillimore Gardens, W8 7HB. *T:* 01–937 3685.

ALPHAND, Hervé; Grand Officier, Légion d'Honneur, 1968; *b* 1907; *s* of Charles Hervé and Jeanne Alphand; *m* 1958, Nicole Merenda (*d* 1979). *Educ:* Lycée Janson de Sailly; Ecole des Sciences Politiques. Inspector of Finances and Dir Dept of Treaties, Min. of Commerce, 1937–38; Financial Attaché to Embassy, Washington, 1940–41; Dir of Economic Affairs for French National Cttee in London, 1941–44; Director-General, Economic, Financial and Technical Affairs (Min. of Foreign Affairs), 1945; French Ambassador to OEEC; French Dep. to Atlantic Council, 1950, and Mem. NATO Perm. Council, 1952–54; Ambassador: to UN, 1955–56; to USA, 1956–65; Secretary-General, Min. of Foreign Affairs, France, 1965–73. *Publication:* L'étonnement d'être, 1978. *Address:* 122 rue de Grenelle, 75007 Paris, France.

ALPORT, family name of **Baron Alport.**

ALPORT, Baron, *cr* 1961, of Colchester (Life Peer); **Cuthbert James McCall Alport,** PC 1960; TD 1949; DL; *b* 22 March 1912; *o s* of late Prof. Arthur Cecil Alport, MD, FRCP, and of Janet, *y d* of James McCall, Dumfriesshire; *m* 1945, Rachel Cecilia (*d* 1983), *o d* of late Lt-Col R. C. Bingham, CVO, DSO, and late Dorothy Louisa Pratt; one *s* two *d*. *Educ:* Haileybury; Pembroke Coll., Cambridge. MA History and Law; Pres., Cambridge Union Society, 1935. Tutor Ashridge Coll., 1935–37. Barrister-at-Law, Middle Temple. Joined Artists Rifles, 1934. Served War of 1939–45: Hon. Lieut-Col; Director Conservative Political Centre, 1945–50. MP (C) Colchester division of Essex, 1950–61; Chairman Joint East and Central African Board, 1953–55; Governor, Charing Cross Hospital, 1954–55. Asst Postmaster-General, Dec. 1955–Jan. 1957; Parliamentary Under-Secretary of State, Commonwealth Relations Office, 1957–59; Minister of State, Commonwealth Relations Office, Oct. 1959–March 1961; British High Commissioner in the Federation of Rhodesia and Nyasaland, 1961–63; Mem. of Council of Europe, 1964–65; British Govt Representative to Rhodesia, June-July 1967. A Dep. Speaker, House of Lords, 1971–82, 1983–. Adviser to the Home Secretary, 1974–82. Chm., New Theatre Trust, 1970–83; Pres., Minories Art Gall., Colchester, 1978–. Life Governor, Haileybury Coll. Master, Skinners' Co., 1969–70, 1982–83. Pro-Chancellor, City Univ., 1972–79. Chm., Acad. Adv. Cttee, Gresham Coll., 1984–. High Steward of Colchester, 1967–; DL Essex 1974. Hon. DCL City Univ., 1979. *Publications:* Kingdoms in Partnership, 1937; Hope in Africa, 1952; The Sudden Assignment, 1965. *Address:* The Cross House, Layer de la Haye, Colchester, Essex. *T:* Layer de la Haye 217. *Clubs:* Pratt's, Farmers'.

AL-QARAGULI, Dr Wahbi Abdul Razaq Fattah; Ambassador of Iraq to Austria, since 1985; *b* Baghdad, 1929; *m* Mrs Suhaila Al-Khatib; two *s* one *d*. *Educ:* Univ. of Baghdad (BA Econs 1954); Univ. of Neuchâtel, Switzerland (PhD 1962). Dep. Perm. Rep., UN, Geneva, 1964–68; Counsellor: Algeria, 1968; China, 1970; Minister Plenipotentiary, Lebanon, 1972–76; Dep. Gen. Dir, Econs Dept, Min. of Foreign Affairs, Baghdad, 1977; Ambassador to Indonesia and (non-resident) to Australia, NZ, Singapore and PNG, 1977; Chief of Protocol, Presidential Palace, Baghdad, 1978; Ambassador: to Malaysia and (non-resident) to Philippines, 1980–82; to UK, 1982–85. *Address:* Iraqi Embassy, Johannes Gasse 26, A-1010 Vienna, Austria.

AL-SABAH, Shaikh Saud Nasir; Ambassador of Kuwait to the United States of America, and to Canada and Venezuela, since 1981; *b* 3 Oct. 1944; *m* 1962, Shaikha Awatif Al-Sabah; three *s* two *d*. Barrister-at-law, Gray's Inn. Entered Legal Dept, Min. of Foreign Affairs, Kuwait. Representative of Kuwait: to 6th Cttee of UN Gen. Assembly, 1969–74; to Seabed Cttee of UN, 1969–73; Vice-Chm., Delegn of Kuwait to Conf. of Law of the Sea, 1974–75; Rep. of Delegn to Conf. of Law of Treaties, 1969; Ambassador to the Ct of St James's, and to Norway, Sweden and Denmark, 1975–80. *Address:* Embassy of Kuwait, 2940 Tilden Street NW, Washington, DC 20008, USA.

AL SABBAGH, Salman Abdul Wahab; Ambassador of the State of Bahrain to the Court of St James's, since 1984; *b* 1932; *m* Mrs Sharifa Ahmed Abdulla. *Educ:* Western Elem. Sch.; Manama Secondary Sch.; Cairo Univ. (BA Accountancy). Chief Auditor, MoD, Kuwait, 1962–66; Accountant, Bank of Bahrain, Bahrain, 1967–69; Gen. Man., Agency of General Motors & Commodities, 1969–72; Min. of Foreign Affairs, Bahrain: posts held in Iraq, France and UK, 1972–84. *Address:* Embassy of the State of Bahrain, 98 Gloucester Road, SW7. *T:* 01–370 6213.

AL-SHAWI, Hisham Ibrahim; Ambassador of the Republic of Iraq to Austria, 1982–85; *b* Baghdad, 16 March 1931; *s* of Ibrahim Al-Shawi and Najia Al-Shawi; *m* 1966, Hadia Al-Atia; one *s* one *d*. *Educ:* Baghdad (High Sch. Certif., Lit. Section, 1948); Amer. Univ. of Beirut (BA with Distinction Pol. Science, 1952); Univ. of Oxford (MLitt Internat. Relations, 1956). Asst Prof. and Head of Dept of Politics, Univs of Baghdad and Al-Mustansyria, 1958–70; Dean, Coll. of Law and Politics, Mustansyria Univ., 1970–72; Ambassador, Min. of Foreign Affairs, 1972; Perm. Rep. at UN, Geneva, 1972; Minister of Higher Educn and Scientific Res., 1972–74; Minister of State, 1974–75; Minister of State for For. Affairs, 1975–76; Ambassador, Min. of For. Affairs, 1976–77; Perm. Rep. at UN, New York, 1977; Head, Diwan of Presidency of Republic, 1977–78; Ambassador, Min. of For. Affairs, 1978; Ambassador to UK, 1978–82. First President: Iraqi Political Science Assoc.; Iraqi UN Assoc.; Mem., UN Sub-Commn on Prevention of Racial Discrimination and Protection of Minorities, 1972–74; Rep. on Commn on Human Rights, 26th and 30th Sessions. Statue of Victory Personality of the Year, Centro Studi e Ricerche delle Nazioni, Parma, Italy, 1984. *Publications:* From the Essence of the Matter: a collection of articles, 1966; The Art of Negotiation, 1967; An Introduction in Political Science, 1967 (new edn 1978). *Recreations:* horse riding, hunting. *Address:* c/o Ministry of Foreign Affairs, Baghdad, Iraq. *Club:* Iraqi Hunting (Iraq).

ALSTEAD, Stanley, CBE 1960; MD, FRCP; Professor Emeritus, Regius Chair of Materia Medica, University of Glasgow; formerly Senior Visiting Physician, Stobhill Hospital, Glasgow; *b* 6 June 1905; *s* of late Robert Alstead, OBE, and Anne Alstead; *m* 1st, 1932, Nora (*d* 1980), 2nd *d* of late M. W. Sowden and late Nell Sowden; one *s*; 2nd, 1982, Dr Jessie, (Janet), McAlpine Pope. *Educ:* Wigan Grammar Sch.; Liverpool Univ. Held various appts in north of England, Glasgow and Inverness. Appointed Pollok Lecturer in Pharmacology, Univ. of Glasgow, 1932, and became interested in clinical aspects of subject; Regius Prof. of Materia Medica and Therapeutics, Univ. of Glasgow, 1948–70. Hon. Prof., Univ. of East Africa (Makerere University Coll.) and Hon. Physician to Kenyatta Nat. Hosp., Nairobi, Kenya, 1965–66. Served War of 1939–45, in RAMC as medical specialist to 5 CCS in Tunisia and Sicily, and in Belgium and Egypt as Officer in Charge of Med. Div. 67 Gen. Hosp. and 63 Gen. Hosp. with rank of Lt-Col (despatches). MD Liverpool (N. E. Roberts Prize); FRCP; FRCPGlas; FRCPE; FRSE. Pres. RFPSG (now RCPSGlas), 1956–58 (Hon. Fellow, 1979). Member: British Pharmacopœia Commn, 1953–57; Standing Jt Cttee on Classification of Proprietary Preparations; Commn. on Spiritual Healing (General Assembly of Church of Scotland). Jt Editor, Textbook of Medical Treatment. *Publications:* papers in med. jls on results of original research in clinical pharmacology. *Recreations:* gardening, music (violin) and reading poetry. *Address:* Glenholme, Glen Road, Dunblane, Perthshire. *T:* Dunblane 822466. *Clubs:* College (Glasgow), Royal Scottish Automobile (Glasgow).

ALSTON, (Arthur) Rex; freelance broadcaster and journalist with The Daily Telegraph; BBC Commentator, 1943–61, retired; *b* 2 July 1901; *e s* of late Arthur Fawssett Alston, Suffragan Bishop of Middleton, and late Mary Isabel Alston; *m* 1932, Elspeth (*d* 1985), *d* of late Sir Stewart Stockman and Lady Stockman; one *s* one *d*. *Educ:* Trent College; Clare College, Cambridge. Assistant Master, Bedford School, 1924–41. Joined BBC, Jan. 1942. *Publications:* Taking the Air, 1950; Over to Rex Alston, 1953; Test Commentary, 1956; Watching Cricket, 1962. *Recreations:* golf, gardening. *Address:* 15 Roding Close, Elmbridge Road, Cranleigh, Surrey GU6 8TE. *T:* Cranleigh 275731. *Clubs:* East India, Devonshire, Sports and Public Schools, MCC.

ALSTON, Rt. Rev. Mgr. Joseph Leo; Parish Priest, Sacred Heart Church, Ainsdale, Southport, since 1972; *b* 17 Dec. 1917; *s* of Benjamin Alston and Mary Elizabeth (*née* Moss). *Educ:* St Mary's School, Chorley; Upholland College, Wigan; English Coll., Rome; Christ's College, Cambridge. Priest, 1942; Licentiate in Theology, Gregorian Univ., Rome, 1942; BA (1st Cl. Hons Classics) Cantab 1945. Classics Master, Upholland Coll., Wigan, 1945–52, Headmaster, 1952–64; Rector, Venerable English Coll., Rome, 1964–71. Chm., Liverpool RC Ecumenism Commn, 1977–. *Recreation:* music. *Address:* 483 Liverpool Road, Ainsdale, Southport, Merseyside. *T:* Southport 77527.

ALSTON, Rex; *see* Alston, A. R.

ALSTON, Richard John William; Artistic Director, Ballet Rambert, since 1986 (Resident Choreographer, 1980–86); *b* 30 Oct. 1948; *s* of Gordon Walter Alston and Margot Alston (*née* Whitworth). *Educ:* Eton; Croydon Coll. of Art. Choreographed for London Contemporary Dance Theatre, 1970–72; founded Strider, 1972; worked in USA, 1975–77. Principal Ballets: Nowhere Slowly; Tiger Balm; Blue Schubert Fragments; Soft Verges; Rainbow Bandit; Doublework; Soda Lake; for Ballet Rambert: Bell High, 1980; Landscape, 1980; Rainbow Ripples, 1980; The Rite of Spring, 1981; Night Music, 1981; Apollo Distraught, 1982; Chicago Brass, 1983; Voices and Light Footsteps, Wildlife, 1984; Dangerous Liaisons, 1985; Java, 1985; Zansa, 1986. Created: The Kingdom of Pagodas, for Royal Danish Ballet, 1982; Midsummer, first work for Royal Ballet, 1983. *Recreations:* music, reading. *Address:* Ballet Rambert, 94 Chiswick High Road, W4 1SH. *T:* 01–995 4246.

ALSTON, Robert John; HM Diplomatic Service; Ambassador to Oman, since 1986; *b* 10 Feb. 1938; *s* of Arthur William Alston and Rita Alston; *m* 1969, Patricia Claire Essex; one *s* one *d*. *Educ:* Ardingly Coll.; New Coll., Oxford (BA Mod. Hist.). Third Sec., Kabul, 1963; Eastern Dept, FO, 1966; Head of Computer Study Team, FCO, 1969; First Sec. (Econ.), Paris, 1971; First Sec. and Head of Chancery, Tehran, 1974; Asst Head, Energy Science and Space Dept, FCO, 1977; Head, Joint Nuclear Unit, FCO, 1978; Political Counsellor, UK Delegn to NATO, 1981; Head, Defence Dept, FCO, 1984. *Recreations:* gardening, travel, music. *Address:* c/o Foreign and Commonwealth Office, King Charles Street, SW1A 2AH.

ALSTON, Dr Robin Carfrae; Consultant in Bibliography to the British Library, since 1977; Editor-in-Chief, 18th Century Short Title Catalogue, since 1978; Adviser to the Development and Systems Office, British Library Reference Division, since 1984; Editorial Director, The Nineteenth Century, series of microfiche texts 1801–1900, since 1985; *b* 29 Jan. 1933; *s* of Wilfred Louis Alston; *m* 1957, Joanna Dorothy Ormiston; two *s* one *d*. *Educ:* Rugby Sch.; Univs of British Columbia (BA), Oxford (MA), Toronto (MA) and London (PhD). Teaching Fellow, University Coll., Toronto, 1956–58; Lectr, New Brunswick Univ., 1958–60; Lectr in English Lit., Leeds Univ., 1964–76. David Murray Lectr, Univ. of Glasgow, 1983; Guest Lectr, Univ. of London, 1983, Sorbonne, 1984, Tokyo Symposium on micro-reproduction, 1984. Jt Editor, Leeds Studies in English and Leeds Texts and Monographs, 1965–72; Editor, Studies in Early Modern English, 1965–72; Jt Editor, The Direction Line, 1976–; Editor, Special Pubns, Bibliographical Soc., 1983–. Founder, Chm. and principal Editor, Scolar Press Ltd, 1966–72, Man. Dir, 1984–; Founder, Janus Press, devoted to original art prints, 1973. Member: Adv. Cttee, British Library, 1975–; Adv. Cttee, MLA of America for the Wing Project, 1980–; Adv.

Panel, Aust. Research Grants Cttee, 1983–. Member: Organising Cttee, 18th Century Short Title Catalogue, 1976–; Cttee, British Book Trade Index, 1984–. Mem. Council, Bibliographical Soc., 1967– (Vice-Pres., 1978–); Founding Mem. Council, Ilkley Literature Festival, 1973–. Consultant, Consortium of Univ. Research Libraries, 1985–86. Hon. FLA, 1986. Samuel Pepys Gold Medal, Ephemera Soc., 1984; Smithsonian Instn award, 1985. *Publications:* An Introduction to Old English, 1961 (rev. edn 1966); A Catalogue of Books relating to the English Language (1500–1800) in Swedish Libraries, 1965; English Language and Medieval English Literature: a Select Reading-List for Students, 1966; A Bibliography of the English Language from the Invention of Printing to the Year 1800: Vol. I, 1965; Vols V and VIII, 1966; Vols VII and IV, 1967; Vol. II, 1968; Vol. VI, 1969; Vol. III, 1970; Vol. IX, 1971; Vol. X, 1972; Vol. XI, 1978; Vol. XII, 1985; Alexander Gil's Logonomia Anglica (1619): a translation into Modern English, 1973; (jtly) The Works of William Bullokar, Vol. I, 1966; English Studies (rev. edn of Vol. III, Cambridge Bibl. Eng. Lit.), 1968; English Linguistics 1500–1800: a Collection of Texts in Facsimile (365 vols), 1967–72; European Linguistics 1500–1700: a Collection of Texts in Facsimile (12 vols), 1968–72; A Checklist of the works of Joseph Addison, 1976; Bibliography MARC and ESTC, 1978; Eighteenth-Century Subscription Lists, 1983; ESTC: the British Library Collections, 1983; numerous articles, printed lectures, reviews, etc. *Recreations:* music, photography. *Address:* Starveall, Aldworth, near Reading, Berks RG8 9TX.

ALSTON-ROBERTS-WEST, Lt-Col George Arthur; *see* West.

AL-TAJIR, Mohamed Mahdi; Ambassador of the United Arab Emirates to the Court of St James's, since 1972, and France, 1972–77; *b* 26 Dec. 1931; *m* 1956, Zohra Al-Tajir; five *s* one *d*. *Educ:* Al Tajir Sch., Bahrain; Preston Grammar Sch., Lancs, England. Dir, Dept of Port and Customs, Govt of Bahrain, 1955–63; Dir, Dept of HH the Ruler's Affairs and Petroleum Affairs, 1963–; Director: Nat. Bank of Dubai Ltd, 1963–; Dubai Petroleum Co., 1963–; Dubai Nat. Air Travel Agency, 1966–; Qatar-Dubai Currency Bd, 1965–73; United Arab Emirates Currency Bd, 1973–; Dubai Dry Dock Co., 1973–; Chm., S Eastern Dubai Drilling Co., 1968–. Hon. Citizen of State of Texas, USA, 1963. *Address:* Embassy of the United Arab Emirates, 30 Prince's Gate, SW7. *T:* 01–581 1281.

ALTAMONT, Earl of; Jeremy Ulick Browne; *b* 4 June 1939; *s* of 10th Marquess of Sligo, *qv*; *m* 1961, Jennifer June, *d* of Major Derek Cooper, Dunlewey, Co. Donegal, and Mrs C. Heber Percy, Pophleys, Radnage; five *d*. *Educ:* St Columba's College, Eire; Royal Agricultural College, Cirencester. *Address:* Westport House, Co. Mayo, Eire.

ALTHAUS, Nigel Frederick; Senior Broker to the Commissioners for the Reduction of the National Debt, since 1982; *b* 28 Sept. 1929; *er s* of Frederick Rudolph Althaus, CBE and Margaret Frances (*née* Twist); *m* 1958, Anne, *d* of P. G. Cardew; three *s* one *d*. *Educ:* Eton; Magdalen Coll., Oxford (Roberts Gawen Scholar; 2nd Cl. Lit. Hum. 1954). National Service, 60th Rifles, 1948–50. Joined Pember and Boyle (Stockbrokers), 1954; Partner, 1955–75, Sen. Partner, 1975–82; Sen. Partner, Mullens and Co., 1982–86. Mem., Stock Exchange, 1955–; Chm., Stock Exchange Benevolent Fund, 1975–82. Master, Skinners' Co., 1977–78; Chm. Governors, Skinners' Co. Sch. for Boys, Tunbridge Wells, 1982–. Chm., British Library of Tape Recordings for Hosp. Patients, 1975–. Queen Victoria's Rifles (TA), 1950–60; Hon. Col, 39 Signal Regt (TA), 1982–. *Publication:* (ed) British Government Securities in the Twentieth Century, 1976. *Recreations:* golf, shooting, music. *Address:* Bank of England, Threadneedle Street, EC2R 8AH. *T:* 01–601 4444. *Clubs:* Boodle's; Swinley Forest Golf (Ascot).

ALTHORP, Viscount; Charles Edward Maurice Spencer; *b* 20 May 1964; *s* and *heir* of 8th Earl Spencer, *qv*. *Educ:* Maidwell Hall; Eton College; Magdalen Coll., Oxford. Page of Honour to HM the Queen, 1977–79. *Address:* Althorp, Northampton NN7 4HG. *Club:* Buck's.

ALTMAN, Lionel Phillips, CBE 1979; Chairman and Chief Executive, Equity & General plc, since 1978; *b* 12 Sept. 1922; *s* of late Arnold Altman and Catherine Phillips; *m* 1977, Jan Mary (*née* Borrodell); two *d* (and one *s* by a previous marriage). *Educ:* University Coll. and Business Sch., also in Paris. FIMI; FInstM; MIPR. Served war, 1942–46, special intelligence duties, War Office and Political Intelligence Dept, FO (UK and Far East). Director: Carmo Holdings Ltd, 1947–63; Sears Holdings Motor Gp, 1963–72; Sears Finance, 1965–71; C. & W. Walker Holdings Ltd, 1974–77; H. P. Information plc, 1985–; Motor Agents Assoc. Ltd, 1986–; Chm. and Chief Exec., Pre-Divisional Investments Ltd, 1972–. Chm., Motor Industry Educnl Consultative Council Industry Working Party, producing Altman Report on recruitment and training, 1968. Mem., Nat. Council, Motor Agents Assoc., 1965– (Pres., 1975–77); Vice-Pres., and Mem. Council, Inst. of Motor Industry, 1970–78. Chairman: Publicity Club of London, 1961–62; Industry Taxation Panel, 1977–86; Member: Council, CBI, 1977–; CBI Industrial Policy Cttee, 1979–85; Dun & Bradstreet Industry Panel, 1982–. Freeman: City of London, 1973; City of Glasgow, 1974; Liveryman and former Hon. Treas., Coachmakers' and Coach Harness Makers' Co.; Burgess Guild Brother, Cordwainers' Co. *Publications:* articles and broadcasts. *Address:* (office) 66 Grosvenor Street, W1X 9DB. *T:* 01–493 3371; (home) The Cottage, Amersham Way, Little Chalfont, Bucks HP6 6SF.

ALTMAN, Robert; film director; *b* Kansas City, 20 Feb. 1925; *m* 3rd, Kathryn Altman; one *s* and one adopted *s* (and two *s* one *d* by previous marriages). *Educ:* Univ. of Missouri. Served US Army, 1943–47. Industrial film maker, Calvin Co., Kansas City, 1950–57. Television writer, producer and director, 1957–65. Films directed: That Cold Day in the Park, 1969; M*A*S*H*, 1970 (Grand Prix, Cannes, 1970); Brewster McCloud, 1971; McCabe and Mrs Miller, 1971; Images, 1972; The Long Goodbye, 1973; Thieves Like Us, 1974; California Split, 1974; Nashville, 1975; Buffalo Bill and the Indians, 1976; 3 Women, 1977; A Wedding, 1978; Quintet, 1979; A Perfect Couple, 1979; Health, 1979; Popeye, 1980; Come Back to the 5 & Dime Jimmy Dean, Jimmy Dean, 1982; Streamers, 1983; Fool for Love, 1986; directed and produced: Secret Honor, 1984; produced: Welcome to LA, 1977; The Late Show, 1977; Remember My Name, 1978; Rich Kids, 1979. *Address:* c/o Sandcastle 5 Productions, 128 Central Park South, New York City, NY 10019, USA.

ALTON, David Patrick; MP (L) Mossley Hill Division of Liverpool, since 1983 (Edge Hill Division, March 1979–1983); *b* 15 March 1951; *s* of Frederick and Bridget Alton. *Educ:* Edmund Campion Sch., Hornchurch; Christ's College of Education, Liverpool. Elected to Liverpool City Council as Britain's youngest City Councillor, 1972; CC, 1972–80; Deputy Leader of the Council and Housing Chairman, 1978; Vice-Pres., AMA, 1979–. MP (L) Liverpool, Edge Hill (by-election), with a 32 per cent swing, March 1979 (youngest member of that parliament); Liberal Party spokesman on: the environment and race relations, 1979–81; home affairs, 1981–82; Chief Whip, Liberal Party, 1985–. Mem., Select Cttee on the Environment, 1981–. Chm., Council for Educn in Commonwealth. Nat. Pres., Nat. League of Young Liberals, 1979; Pres., Liverpool Old People's Hostels Assoc. Trustee, Crisis at Christmas. *Recreations:* theatre, reading, walking. *Address:* 25 North Mossley Hill Road, Liverpool L18 8BL. *T:* 051–724 6106.

ALTON, Euan Beresford Seaton, MBE 1945; MC 1943; Under Secretary, Department of Health and Social Security, 1968–76; *b* 22 April 1919; *y s* of late William Lester St John Alton and Ellen Seaton Alton; *m* 1953, Diana Margaret Ede; one *s* one *d*. *Educ:* St Paul's Sch.; Magdalen Coll., Oxford. Served with Army, 1939–45; Major RA. Admin. Officer, Colonial Service and HM OCS, Gold Coast and Ghana, 1946–58; Admin. Officer, Class 1, 1957. Entered Civil Service as Asst Principal, Min. of Health, 1958; Principal, 1958; Asst Sec., 1961; Under Sec., 1968. *Recreations:* sailing, walking. *Address:* The Old School, Church Lane, Brantham, Manningtree, Essex CO11 1QA. *T:* Colchester 393419. *Clubs:* Cruising Association; Stour Sailing (Manningtree).

ALTRINCHAM, Barony of, *cr* 1945, of Tormarton; title disclaimed by 2nd Baron. *Heir to barony:* Hon. Anthony Ulick David Dundas Grigg [*b* 12 Jan. 1934; *m* 1965, Eliane de Miramon; two *s* one *d*].

ALUN-JONES, (John) Derek; Managing Director and Chief Executive, Ferranti plc, since 1975; *b* 6 June 1933; *s* of Thomas Alun-Jones, LLB and Madge Beatrice Edwards; *m* 1960, Gillian Palmer; two *s* three *d*. *Educ:* Lancing College; St Edmund Hall, Oxford (MA Hons Jurisp.). Philips Electrical, 1957–59; H. C. Stephens, 1959–60; Expandite, 1960–71 (Man. Dir, 1966–71); Man. Dir, Burmah Industrial Products, 1971–74; Director: Burmah Oil Trading, 1974–75; Royal Insurance, 1981–; Throgmorton Trust, 1978–84; SBAC, 1982–; Reed International PLC, 1984–; Guest Keen & Nettlefolds plc, 1986–. *Recreations:* shooting, fishing. *Address:* The Willows, Effingham Common, Surrey KT24 5JE. *T:* Bookham 58158.

ALVAREZ, Alfred; poet and author; *b* London, 1929; *s* of late Bertie Alvarez and Katie Alvarez (*née* Levy); *m* 1st, 1956, Ursula Barr (marr. diss. 1961); one *s*; 2nd, 1966, Anne Adams; one *s* one *d*. *Educ:* Oundle Sch.; Corpus Christi Coll., Oxford. BA (Oxon) 1952, MA 1956. Research Schol., CCC, Oxon, and Research Schol. of Goldsmiths' Company, 1952–53, 1954–55. Procter Visiting Fellowship, Princeton, 1953–54; Vis. Fellow of Rockefeller Foundn, USA, 1955–56, 1958; gave Christian Gauss Seminars in Criticism, Princeton, and was Lectr in Creative Writing, 1957–58; D. H. Lawrence Fellowship, New Mexico, 1958; Poetry Critic, The Observer, 1956–66. Visiting Professor: Brandeis Univ., 1960; New York State Univ., Buffalo, 1966. Vachel Lindsay Prize for Poetry (from Poetry, Chicago), 1961. *Publications:* The Shaping Spirit (US title, Stewards of Excellence), 1958; The School of Donne, 1961; The New Poetry (ed and introd), 1962; Under Pressure, 1965; Beyond All This Fiddle, 1968; Lost (poems), 1968; Penguin Modern Poets, No 18, 1970; Apparition (poems, with paintings by Charles Blackman), 1971; The Savage God, 1971; Beckett, 1973; Hers (novel), 1974; Hunt (novel), 1978; Autumn to Autumn and Selected Poems 1953–76, 1978; Life After Marriage, 1982; The Biggest Game in Town, 1983; Offshore, 1986. *Recreations:* rock-climbing, poker, music. *Address:* c/o Hodder & Stoughton, 47 Bedford Square, WC1. *Club:* Climbers'.

ALVAREZ, Prof. Luis W.; Professor of Physics, University of California, Berkeley, since 1945; *b* 13 June, 1911; *s* of late Dr Walter C. Alvarez and Harriet Smyth; *m* 1st, 1936, Geraldine Smithwick; one *s* one *d*; 2nd, 1958, Janet Landis; one *s* one *d*. *Educ:* University of Chicago. SB 1932, PhD 1936. Radiation Lab., Univ. of California, 1936–; MIT Radiation Lab., 1940–43; Metallurgical Lab., Univ. of Chicago, 1943–44; Los Alamos Sci. Lab., 1944–45; Associate Dir, Lawrence Rad. Lab., 1954–59. Pres., Amer. Physical Soc., 1969; Member: Nat. Acad. of Sciences; Nat. Acad. of Engineering; Am. Phil. Soc.; Am. Acad. of Arts and Sciences; Assoc. Mem., Institut d'Egypte. Awarded: Collier Trophy, 1946; John Scott Medal, 1953; US Medal for Merit, 1947; Einstein Medal, 1961; Pioneer Award, AIEEE, 1963; Nat. Medal of Science, 1964; Michelson Award, 1965; Nobel Prize in Physics, 1968. Nat. Inventors' Hall of Fame, 1978. Hon. ScD: Chicago, 1967; Carnegie-Mellon, 1968; Kenyon, 1969; Notre Dame, 1976; Ain Shams Univ., Cairo, 1979; Penn. Coll. of Optometry, 1982. *Publications:* more than 100 contributions to Physics Literature, largely in Nuclear Physics and High Energy Physics; many pubns developing evidence that mass extructions were caused by impacts of asteroids or comets; 40 US Patents, largely in Electronics and Optics. *Recreations:* flying, golf, music. *Address:* (business) Lawrence Berkeley Laboratory, University of California, 1 Cyclotron Road, Berkeley, Calif 94720, USA. *T:* 415–486 4400; (home) 131 Southampton Avenue, Berkeley, Calif 94707, USA. *T:* 415–525–0590. *Clubs:* Bohemian (San Francisco); Faculty (Berkeley); Miravista Golf (El Cerrito).

ALVES, Colin; General Secretary: General Synod Board of Education, since 1984; National Society for Promoting Religious Education, since 1984; *b* 19 April 1930; *s* of Donald Alexander Alves and Marjorie Alice (*née* Marsh); *m* 1953, Peggy (*née* Kember); two *s* one *d*. *Educ:* Christ's Hospital, Horsham; Worcester Coll., Oxford (MA). School teaching, 1952–59; Lectr, King Alfred's Coll., Winchester, 1959–68; Head of Dept, Brighton Coll. of Educn, 1968–74; Dir, RE Centre, St Gabriel's Coll., 1974–77; Colleges Officer, General Synod Bd of Educn, 1977–84. Mem., Durham Commn on RE, 1967–70; Chm., Schs Council RE Cttee, 1971–77; Sec., Assoc. of Voluntary Colls, 1978–84; Member: Adv. Cttee on Supply and Educn of Teachers, 1980–85; Nat. Adv. Body for Public Sector Higher Educn, 1983–; Voluntary Sector Consultative Council, 1984–. *Publications:* Religion and the Secondary School, 1968; The Christian in Education, 1972; The Question of Jesus, 1986; contrib. various symposia on RE. *Recreations:* music, walking, gardens. *Address:* 9 Park Road, Haywards Heath, Sussex RH16 4HY. *T:* Haywards Heath 454496. *Club:* United Oxford & Cambridge University.

ALVEY, John, CB 1980; FEng 1984; Managing Director, Development and Procurement, and Engineer-in-Chief, British Telecom, 1983–86; *b* 19 June 1925; *s* of George C. V. Alvey and Hilda E. Alvey (*née* Pellatt); *m* 1955, Celia Edmed Marson; three *s*. *Educ:* Reeds Sch.; London Univ.; BSc (Eng), DipNEC. FIEE. London Stock Exchange, to 1943. Royal Navy, 1943–46; Royal Naval Scientific Service, 1950; Head of Weapons Projects, Admiralty Surface Weapons Estabt, 1968–72; Dir-Gen. Electronics Radar, PE, MoD, 1972–73; Dir-Gen., Airborne Electronic Systems, PE, MoD, 1974–75; Dir, Admiralty Surface Weapons Estabt, 1976–77; Dep. Controller, R&D Estabts and Res. C, and Chief Scientist (RAF), MoD, 1977–80; Senior Dir, Technology, British Telecom, 1980–83. Hon. DSc City, 1984. *Recreations:* reading, Rugby, skiing, theatre going. *Address:* 9A St Omer Road, Guildford, Surrey. *T:* Guildford 63859.

ALVINGHAM, 2nd Baron, *cr* 1929, of Woodfold; **Maj.-Gen. Robert Guy Eardley Yerburgh,** CBE 1978 (OBE 1972); *b* 16 Dec. 1926; *s* of 1st Baron and Dorothea Gertrude (*d* 1927), *d* of late J. Eardley Yerburgh; *S* father 1955; *m* 1952, Beryl Elliott, *d* of late W. D. Williams; one *s* one *d*. *Educ:* Eton. Commissioned 1946, Coldstream Guards; served UK, Palestine, Farelf, British Guiana; Head of Staff, CDS, 1972–75; Dep. Dir, Army Staff Duties, 1975–78; Dir of Army Quartering, 1978–81, retired. *Heir:* *s* Captain Hon. Robert Richard Guy Yerburgh, 17th/21st Lancers, retired [*b* 10 Dec. 1956; *m* 1981, Vanessa, *yr d* of Captain Duncan Kirk; two *s*]. *Address:* Bix Hall, Henley-on-Thames, Oxfordshire.

AMALDI, Prof. Edoardo, PhD; Italian physicist; Professor of General Physics, University of Rome, since 1937; *b* Carpaneto, Piacenza, 5 Sept. 1908; *s* of Ugo Amaldi and Luisa Basini; *m* 1933, Ginestra Giovene; two *s* one *d*. *Educ:* Rome Univ. Dr of Physics, 1929. Sec.-Gen., European Org. for Nuclear Research, 1952–54; Pres., Internat. Union of Pure and Applied Physics, 1957–60; President: Istituto Nazionale di Fisica Nucleare, 1960–65; Council, CERN, 1970–71; Fellow: Acad. Naz. dei Lincei; Acad. Naz. dei XL; Foreign member: Royal Soc. of Sciences, Uppsala; Acad. of Sciences, USSR; Amer. Philos. Soc.; Amer. Acad. of Arts and Sciences; Nat. Acad. of Sciences, USA; Royal Acad., Netherlands; Acad. Leopoldina; Royal Instn of GB; Royal Society, London; Royal Acad. Sweden, 1968; Real Acad. Ciencias, Spain. Hon. DSc: Glasgow, 1973; Oxford, 1974. *Publications:* The production and slowing down of neutrons, 1959; contributor many papers on atomic, molecular and nuclear physics to learned jls. *Address:* Dipartimento di Fisica, Città Universitaria, Piazzale Aldo Moro 2, 00185 Rome, Italy; (home) Viale Parioli 50, 00197 Rome.

AMAN, family name of **Baron Marley.**

AMBARTSUMIAN, Victor; Hero of Socialist Labour (twice); Order of Lenin (five times); Order of Labour Red Banner (twice); President, Academy of Sciences of Armenian Soviet Socialist Republic, USSR, since 1947; *b* 18 Sept. 1908; *m* 1931, Vera Ambartsumian; two *s* two *d*. *Educ:* Univ. of Leningrad. Lecturer in Astronomy, 1931–34, Prof. of Astrophysics, 1934–44, Univ. of Leningrad; Prof. of Astrophysics, Univ. of Erevan, 1944–. Full Mem., Academy of Sciences of USSR, 1953–. Pres., Internat. Council of Scientific Unions, 1968–72. Hon. Dr of Science: Univs of Canberra, 1963; Paris, 1965; Liege, 1967; Prague, 1967; Torun, 1973; La Plata, 1974; Foreign Member of Academies of Science: Washington, Paris, Rome, Vienna, Berlin, Amsterdam, Copenhagen, Sofia, Stockholm, Boston, New York, New Delhi, Cordoba, Prague, Budapest; Foreign Member of Royal Society, London. *Publications:* Theoretical Astrophysics, 1953 (in Russian; trans. into German, English, Spanish, Chinese); about 100 papers in learned jls. Editor of jl, Astrofizika. *Address:* Academy of Sciences of Armenian SSR, Marshal Bagramian Avenue 24, Erevan, Armenia, USSR.

AMBLER, Eric, OBE 1981; novelist and screenwriter; *b* 28 June 1909; *s* of Alfred Percy and Amy Madeleine Ambler; *m* 1st, 1939, Louise Crombie; 2nd, 1958, Joan Harrison. *Educ:* Colfe's Grammar Sch.; London Univ. Apprenticeship in engineering, 1927–28; advertisement copywriter, 1929–35; professional writer, 1936–. Served War of 1939–45: RA, 1940; commissioned, 1941; served in Italy, 1943; Lt-Col, 1944; Asst Dir of Army Kinematography, War Office, 1944–46. US Bronze Star, 1946. Wrote and produced film, The October Man, 1947 and resumed writing career. Screenplays include: The Way Ahead, 1944; The October Man, 1947; The Passionate Friends, 1948; Highly Dangerous, 1950; The Magic Box, 1951; Gigolo and Gigolette, in Encore, 1952; The Card, 1952; Rough Shoot, 1953; The Cruel Sea, 1953; Lease of Life, 1954; The Purple Plain, 1954; Yangtse Incident, 1957; A Night to Remember, 1958; Wreck of the Mary Deare, 1959; Love Hate Love, 1970. *Publications:* The Dark Frontier, 1936; Uncommon Danger, 1937; Epitaph for a Spy, 1938; Cause for Alarm, 1938; The Mask of Dimitrios, 1939; Journey into Fear, 1940; Judgment on Deltchev, 1951; The Schirmer Inheritance, 1953; The Night-comers, 1956; Passage of Arms, 1959; The Light of Day, 1962; The Ability to Kill (essays), 1963; (ed and introd) To Catch a Spy, 1964; A Kind of Anger, 1964 (Edgar Allan Poe award, 1964); Dirty Story, 1967; The Intercom Conspiracy, 1969; The Levanter, 1972 (Golden Dagger award, 1973); Doctor Frigo, 1974 (MWA Grand Master award, 1975); Send No More Roses, 1977; The Care of Time, 1981; Here Lies (autobiog.), 1985; short stories, magazine and newspaper articles. *Address:* c/o Campbell Thomson & McLaughlin Ltd, 31 Newington Green, N16 9PU. *Clubs:* Garrick, Savile.

AMBLER, Harry, OBE 1963; QPM 1955; Chief Constable, City of Bradford Police, 1957–73; *b* 27 June 1908; *m* 1934, Kathleen Freda Muriel Mitchell; one *d*. *Educ:* Hanson Secondary Sch., Bradford; Oulton Sch., Liverpool. Joined City of Bradford Police as a Constable, 1930; Inspector, 1940; Staff Officer to HM Inspector of Constabulary, 1941–43; Superintendent, 1943; Asst and Dep. Chief Constable, 1952; Chief Constable, 1957. Hon. MA Bradford, 1973. Police Long Service and Good Conduct Medal, 1952; Coronation Medal, 1953. *Address:* 854 Leeds Road, Bramhope, near Leeds LS16 9ED. *T:* Leeds 673765.

AMBLER, John Doss; Chairman and Chief Executive Officer, Texaco Ltd, since 1982; *b* 24 July 1934; *m*; one *s* one *d*. *Educ:* Virginia Polytechnic Inst. (BSc Business Admin). Texaco Inc., USA: various assignments, Marketing Dept, Alexandra, Va, 1956–65; Dist Sales Manager, Harrisburg, Pa, 1965–67; Asst Divl Manager, Norfolk, Va, 1967–68; Staff Asst to Gen. Man. Marketing US, New York, 1968–72; various assignments, Chicago and New York, 1969–72; Gen. Man., Texaco Olie Maatschappij BV, Rotterdam, 1972–75; Man. Dir, Texaco Oil AB, Stockholm, 1975–77; Asst to Pres. of Texaco Inc., USA, 1977–80; Vice-Pres., Texaco Inc., USA, 1980–81; Pres., Texaco Europe, New York, 1981–82. *Recreations:* hunting, fishing, tennis, photography. *Address:* 1 Knightsbridge Green, SW1X 7QJ. *T:* 01–584 5000.

AMBO, Most Rev. George Somboba; *see* Papua New Guinea, Archbishop of.

AMBROSE, Prof. Edmund Jack, MA (Cantab); DSc (London); Professor of Cell Biology, University of London, Institute of Cancer Research, 1967–76, now Emeritus Professor; Staff of Chester Beatty Research Institute, Institute of Cancer Research: Royal Cancer Hospital since 1952; *b* 2 March 1914; *s* of Alderman Harry Edmund Ambrose and Kate (*née* Stanley); *m* 1943, Andrée (*née* Huck), Seine, France; one *s* one *d*. *Educ:* Perse Sch., Cambridge; Emmanuel Coll., Cambridge. Wartime research for Admiralty on infra-red detectors, 1940–45; subseq. research on structure of proteins using infra-red radiation at Courtauld Fundamental Research Laboratory. Formerly Convener of Brit. Soc. for Cell Biology. Formerly Special Adviser in Cancer to Govt of India at Tata Meml Centre, Bombay. Special Adviser in Leprosy, Foundn for Med. Res., Bombay, 1978– (awarded St Elizabeth Meml Medal, Order of St John, Paris, 1981 for leprosy work); Adviser, Regional Cancer Centre, Kerala, India, 1984–. Pres., Internat. Cell Tissue and Organ Culture Group. Research on structure of proteins, on structure of normal and cancer cells, and on characteristics of surface of cancer cells, cell biology and microbiology of leprosy, using labelled metabolites. *Publications:* Cell Electrophoresis, 1965; The Biology of Cancer, 1966, 2nd edn 1975; The Cancer Cell *in vitro*, 1967; (jtly) Cell Biology, 1970, rev. edn 1976; Nature of the Biological World, 1982; publications on Protein Structure and Cell Biology, in Proc. Royal Soc., biological jls. *Recreation:* sailing. *Address:* Institute of Cancer Research: Royal Cancer Hospital, Fulham Road, SW3 6BJ. *Clubs:* Chelsea Arts; Royal Bombay Yacht.

AMBROSE, James Walter Davy; Judge, Supreme Court Singapore, 1958–68; *b* 5 Dec. 1909; *s* of Samuel Ambrose; *m* 1945, Theresa Kamala Ambrose; no *c*. *Educ:* Free Sch., Penang; Oxford Univ. Asst Official Assignee, Singapore, 1936; Police Magistrate and Asst District Judge, Malacca, 1940; Registrar, Superior Court, Malacca, 1945; Dep. Public Prosecutor, 1946; Sen. Asst Registrar, Supreme Courts of Ipoh, Penang, and Kuala Lumpur, 1947–52; President, Sessions Court, Penang, 1953; Acting District Judge and First Magistrate, Singapore, 1955; Official Assignee, Public Trustee, and Comr of Estate Duties, Singapore 1957. *Address:* Block 10B, Apartment 04–06, Braddell Hill, Singapore 2057.

AMERS, Maj.-Gen. John Henry, OBE 1941; *b* 8 July 1904; *s* of John Amers; *m* 1st, 1933, Muriel Henrietta Ethel Haeberlin (*d* 1983); one *d*; 2nd, 1984, Mrs Nora Jessie Harding. *Educ:* Christ's Hospital; Royal Military Acad., Woolwich; Cambridge Univ. Commissioned 2nd Lieut into Royal Engineers, 1925. Served War of 1939–45, E Africa, Middle East and Italy. Col 1951; Brig. 1955; Maj.-Gen. 1958. Served HQ, BCOF, Japan, 1947–48; Chief Engineer, Salisbury Plain District, 1951–54; Deputy Director of Works, BAOR, 1955–57; Director of Fortification and Works, 1958–59; retired, 1959. *Address:* c/o Lloyds Bank, Cox's and King's Branch, 6 Pall Mall, SW1Y 5NH.

AMERY, Rt. Hon. Julian, PC 1960; MP (C) Brighton Pavilion since 1969; *b* 27 March 1919; *s* of late Rt Hon. Leopold Amery, PC, CH; *m* 1950, Lady Catherine, *d* of Earl of Stockton, *qv*; one *s* three *d*. *Educ:* Summerfields; Eton; Balliol Coll., Oxford. War Corresp. in Spanish Civil War, 1938–39; Attaché HM Legation, Belgrade, and on special missions in Bulgaria, Turkey, Roumania and Middle East, 1939–40; Sergeant in RAF, 1940–41; commissioned and transferred to army, 1941; on active service, Egypt, Palestine and Adriatic, 1941–42; liaison officer to Albanian resistance movement, 1944; served on staff of Gen. Carton de Wiart, VC, Mr Churchill's personal representative with Generalissimo Chiang Kai-Shek, 1945. Contested Preston in Conservative interest, July 1945; MP (C) Preston North, 1950–66; Delegate to Consultative Assembly of Council of Europe, 1950–53 and 1956. Member Round Table Conference on Malta, 1955. Parly Under-Sec. of State and Financial Sec., War Office, 1957–58; Parly Under-Sec. of State, Colonial Office, 1958–60; Sec. of State for Air, Oct. 1960–July 1962; Minister of Aviation, 1962–64; Minister of Public Building and Works, June-Oct. 1970; Minister for Housing and Construction, DoE, 1970–72; Minister of State, FCO, 1972–74. Pres., Horn of Africa and Aden Council, 1984–. Kt Comdr, Order of Phœnix, Greece; Grand Cordon, Order of Scanderbeg, Albania; Order of Oman, first class. *Publications:* Sons of the Eagle, 1948; The Life of Joseph Chamberlain: vol. IV, 1901–3: At the Height of his Power, 1951; vols V and VI, 1901–14: Joseph Chamberlain and the Tariff Reform Campaign, 1969; Approach March (autobiog.), 1973; articles in National Review, Nineteenth Century and Daily Telegraph. *Recreations:* ski-ing, mountaineering, travel. *Address:* 112 Eaton Square, SW1. *T:* 01–235 1543, 01–235 7409; Forest Farm House, Chelwood Gate, Sussex. *Clubs:* White's, Beefsteak, Carlton, Buck's.

AMES, Mrs Kenneth; *see* Gainham, S. R.

AMESS, David Anthony Andrew; MP (C) Basildon, since 1983; Director, Accountancy Aids Employment Agency, since 1981; *b* 26 March 1952; *s* of James Henry Valentine Amess and Maud Ethel Martin; *m* 1983, Julia Arnold. *Educ:* St Bonaventure's Grammar Sch.; Bournemouth Coll. of Technol. (BScEcon Hons 2.2., special subject Govt). Teacher, St John the Baptist Jun. Mixed Sch., Bethnal Green, 1970–71; Jun. Underwriter, Leslie & Godwin Agencies, 1974–77; Sen. Manager of temporary div., Accountancy Personnel, 1977–80; Consultant, Executemps, 1980–81. Dir, A&G Recruitment. Mem., Redbridge Council, 1982– (Vice Chm., Housing Cttee, 1982–). *Publications:* contrib. magazines and pamphlets. *Recreations:* socialising, popular music, animals, gardening, cricket, tennis. *Address:* 3 Fletchers, Basildon, Essex. *Clubs:* Carlton; Kingswood Squash and Racketball (Basildon).

AMHERST, family name of **Earl Amherst.**

AMHERST, 5th Earl, *cr* 1826; **Jeffery John Archer Amherst,** MC 1918; Baron Amherst of Montreal, 1788; Viscount Holmesdale, 1826; Major, late Coldstream Guards; Manager, External Affairs, BEA, 1946; later Director of Associated Companies, retd, Dec. 1966; Hon. Commission as Wing Commander, RAF, 1942; *b* 13 Dec. 1896; *e s* of 4th Earl and Hon. Eleanor Clementina St Aubyn (*d* 1960), *d* of 1st Baron St Levan; *S* father, 1927. *Educ:* Eton; RMC Sandhurst. Served European War, 1914–18, with Coldstream Guards (MC); placed on RARO 1921; recalled 1940, served Middle East, 1940–44. Reportorial Staff, New York Morning World, 1923–29; Commercial Air Pilot and General Manager Air Line Company, 1929–39; Asst Air Adviser to British Railways, 1945–46. Dir, BEA associated cos, 1946–66. *Publication:* Wandering Abroad (autobiog.), 1976. *Clubs:* Cavalry and Guards, Travellers', Pratt's, Garrick.

AMHERST OF HACKNEY, 4th Baron *cr* 1892; **William Hugh Amherst Cecil;** Director, E. A. Gibson Shipbrokers Ltd; *b* 28 Dec. 1940; *s* of 3rd Baron Amherst of Hackney, CBE, and of Margaret Eirene Clifton Brown, *d* of late Brig.-Gen. Howard Clifton Brown; *S* father, 1980; *m* 1965, Elisabeth, *d* of Hugh Humphrey Merriman, DSO, MC, TD, DL; one *s* one *d*. *Educ:* Eton. Heir: *s* Hon. Hugh William Amherst Cecil, *b* 17 July 1968. *Address:* Hazel Hall, Peaslake, Surrey. *Clubs:* Royal Yacht Squadron, Royal Ocean Racing.

AMIES, (Edwin) Hardy, CVO 1977; RDI 1964; FRSA 1965; Dressmaker by Appointment to HM The Queen; Director Hardy Amies Ltd, since 1946; Design Consultant to manufacturers in the UK, EEC, USA, Canada, Australia, New Zealand, Japan, and Korea; *b* 17 July 1909; *s* of late Herbert William Amies and Mary (*née* Hardy). *Educ:* Brentwood. Studied languages in France and Germany, 1927–30; trainee at W. & T. Avery Ltd, Birmingham, 1930–34; managing designer at Lachasse, Farm Street, W1, 1934–39. War Service, 1939–45: joined Intelligence Corps, 1939, becoming Lt-Col and head of Special Forces Mission to Belgium, 1944; founded dressmaking business, 1946. Chairman, Incorporated Society of London Fashion Designers, 1959–60 (Vice-Chm., 1954–56). Awards: Harper's Bazarr, 1962; Caswell-Massey, 1962, 1964, 1968; Ambassador Magazine, 1964; Sunday Times Special Award, 1965. Officier de l'Ordre de la Couronne (Belgium), 1946. *Publications:* Just So Far, 1954; ABC of Men's Fashion, 1964; Still Here, 1984. *Recreations:* lawn tennis, gardening, opera. *Address:* 29 Cornwall Gardens, SW7; Hardy Amies Ltd, 14 Savile Row, W1. *T:* 01–734 2436. *Clubs:* Queen's, Buck's.

AMIS, Kingsley, CBE 1981; author; *b* 16 April 1922; *o c* of William Robert and Rosa Amis; *m* 1st, 1948, Hilary Ann, *d* of Leonard Sidney and Margery Bardwell; two *s* one *d*; 2nd, 1965, Elizabeth Jane Howard, *qv* (marr. diss. 1983). *Educ:* City of London School; St John's, Oxford (Hon. Fellow, 1976). Served in Army, 1942–45. Lectr in English, University Coll. of Swansea, 1949–61 (Hon. Fellow, 1985); Fellow of Peterhouse, Cambridge, 1961–63. *Publications:* A Frame of Mind (verse), 1953; Lucky Jim (novel), 1954, filmed, 1957; That Uncertain Feeling (novel), 1955, filmed (Only Two Can Play), 1962, televised, 1986; A Case of Samples (verse), 1956; I Like it Here (novel), 1958; Take a Girl Like You (novel), 1960; New Maps of Hell (belles-lettres), 1960; My Enemy's Enemy (short stories), 1962; One Fat Englishman (novel), 1963; The James Bond Dossier (belles-lettres), 1965; The Egyptologists (novel), with Robert Conquest, 1965; The Anti-Death League (novel), 1966; A Look Round the Estate (poems), 1967; (as Robert Markham) Colonel Sun (novel), 1968; I Want it Now (novel), 1968; The Green Man (novel), 1969; What Became of Jane Austen? (belles-lettres), 1970; Girl, 20 (novel), 1971; On Drink, 1972; The Riverside Villas Murder (novel), 1973; Ending Up (novel), 1974; (ed) G. K. Chesterton selected stories, 1972; (ed) Tennyson, 1972; Rudyard Kipling and his World, 1975; The Alteration, 1976; (ed) Harold's Years, 1977; Jake's Thing (novel), 1978; (ed) The New Oxford Book of Light Verse, 1978; (ed) The Faber Popular Reciter, 1978; Collected Poems 1944–1979, 1979; Russian Hide-and-Seek (novel), 1980; Collected

Short Stories, 1980; (ed) The Golden Age of Science Fiction, 1981; Every Day Drinking, 1983; Stanley and the Women (novel), 1984; How's Your Glass?, 1984; The Old Devils (novel), 1986. *Recreations:* music, thrillers, television. *Address:* c/o Jonathan Clowes, 22 Prince Albert Road, NW1 7ST. *Club:* Garrick.

See also M. L. Amis.

AMIS, Martin Louis; author; special writer for The Observer, since 1980; *b* 25 Aug. 1949; *s* of Kingsley Amis, *qv* and Hilary Bardwell. *Educ:* various schools; Exeter Coll., Oxford (BA Hons 1st cl. in English). Fiction and Poetry Editor, TLS, 1974; Literary Editor, New Statesman, 1977–79. *Publications:* The Rachel Papers, 1973 (Somerset Maugham Award, 1974); Dead Babies, 1975; Success, 1978; Other People: a mystery story, 1981; Money, 1984; The Moronic Inferno and Other Visits to America, 1986. *Recreations:* tennis, chess, snooker. *Address:* c/o A. D. Peters, 10 Buckingham Street, WC2. *T:* 01–839 2556. *Club:* United Oxford & Cambridge University.

AMLOT, Roy Douglas; barrister; Senior Prosecuting Counsel to the Crown at the Central Criminal Court, since 1981; *b* 22 Sept. 1942; *s* of Douglas Lloyd Amlot and Ruby Luise Amlot; *m* 1969, Susan Margaret (*née* McDowell); two *s*. *Educ:* Dulwich Coll. Called to the Bar, Lincoln's Inn, 1963. Second Prosecuting Counsel to the Inland Revenue, Central Criminal Court and London Crown Courts, 1974; First Prosecuting Counsel to the Crown, Inner London Crown Court, 1975; Jun. Prosecuting Counsel to the Crown, Central Criminal Court, 1977. *Publication:* (ed) 11th edn, Phipson on Evidence. *Recreations:* skiing, squash, music. *Address:* 6 King's Bench Walk, Temple, EC4Y 7DR. *T:* 01–583 0410.

AMOORE, Rt. Rev. Frederick Andrew; Provincial Executive Officer, Church of the Province of South Africa, since 1982; *b* 6 June 1913; *s* of Harold Frederick Newnham Amoore and Emily Clara Amoore, Worthing; *m* 1948, Mary Dobson; three *s*. *Educ:* Worthing Boys' High Sch.; University of Leeds. BA (Hons Hist) Leeds, 1934. Curate of: Clapham, London, 1936; St Mary's, Port Elizabeth, S Africa, 1939; Rector of St Saviour's, E London, S Africa, 1945; Dean of St Albans Cathedral, Pretoria, 1950; Exec. Officer for Church of Province of S Africa, 1962–67; Bishop of Bloemfontein, 1967–82. *Recreations:* music, italic script. *Address:* Bishopscourt, Claremont, CP, 7700, South Africa. *Club:* City and Civil Service (Cape Town).

AMORY; *see* Heathcoat Amory and Heathcoat-Amory.

AMOS, Air Comdt Barbara Mary D.; *see* Ducat-Amos.

AMOS, Francis John Clarke, CBE 1973; BSc(Soc); DipArch, SPDip, ARIBA, PPRTPI; Chief Executive, Birmingham City Council, 1973–77; Senior Fellow, University of Birmingham, since 1977; *b* 10 Sept. 1924; *s* of late Frank Amos, FALPA (Director, H. J. Furlong & Sons, Ltd, London), and Alice Mary Amos; *m* 1956, Geraldine Mercy Sutton, MBE, JP, BSc (Econ), MRTPI; one *s* one *d* (and one *d* decd). *Educ:* Alleyns Sch., and Dulwich Coll., London; Sch. of Architecture, The Polytechnic, London (DipArch); Sch. of Planning and Regional Research, London (SPDip); LSE and Birkbeck Coll., Univ. of London (BSc(Soc)). Served War: Royal Corps of Signals, 1942–44; RIASC, 1944–47. Harlow Develt Corp, 1951; LCC, Planning Div., 1953–58; Min. of Housing and Local Govt, 1958–59 and 1962–63; Adviser to Imperial Ethiopian Govt, 1959–62; Liverpool Corp. City Planning Dept, 1962–74, Chief Planning Officer 1966–74; Chairman: Planning Sub-Cttee, Merseyside Area Land Use/Transportation Study, 1967–73; Working Gp, Educnl Objectives in Urban and Regional Planning, Centre for Environmental Studies, 1970–72. Consultant, Halcrow Fox and Associates, 1984–. Member: Exec. Cttee, Internat. Centre for Regional Planning and Develt, 1954–59; various Cttees, Liverpool Council of Social Services, 1965–72; Exec. Cttee, Town and Country Planning Summer Sch., 1969–70; Planning, Architecture and Bldg Studies Sub-Cttee, UGC, 1968–74; Community Work Gp of Calouste Gulbenkian Foundn, 1970–82; Constitution Cttee, Liverpool Community Relations Council, 1970–73; Planning and Transport Res. Adv. Council, DoE, 1971–77; Town and Country Planning Council and Exec. Cttee, 1972–74; Adv. Cttee, Bldg Res. Estabt, 1972–77 (Chm., Planning Cttee, 1972–80); SSRC Planning and Human Geography and Planning Cttees, 1972–76; Social Studies Sub-Cttee, UGC, 1974–76; W Midlands Economic Planning Council, 1974–77; Environmental Bd, DoE, 1975–78; Trustee, Community Projects Foundn, 1978–; Council of Management, Action Resource Centre, 1978–; Study Commn on Family, 1978–83; Arts Council Regional Cttee, 1979–; Exec. Cttee, Watt Cttee on Energy, 1980–; Planning Cttee, CNAA, 1980–83. Special Prof. of Planning Practice and Management, Univ. of Nottingham, 1979–. External Examiner in Planning: Univs of: Liverpool, 1967–70; Newcastle, 1968–71; Aston (Birmingham), 1970–71; Queen's (Belfast), 1972–74; Heriot-Watt, 1972–74; Nottingham, 1973–76; UCL 1975–77; Sheffield, 1979–82; Glasgow, 1979–82; Hong Kong, 1982–85; Polytechnics of: Leeds, 1967–68; Central London, 1967–70; Birmingham, 1975–; Liverpool, 1977–82. Since 1977, has acted as adviser to govts in aid programmes: Bangladesh (UN); Ghana (UN); Hong Kong (UK); India (ODA); Iraq; Tanzania (ODA); Turkey (OECD); Venezuela (IBRD); Kenya, Pakistan and Zimbabwe (UN); Iraq. Mem., County Exec. Cttee, Scout Assoc., 1977–. Mem., Court, Univ. of Nottingham, 1975–. Adviser to AMA Social Services Cttee, 1974–77; Chm., W Midlands Area, 1978–82, Mem. Nat. Exec., 1982–, Nat. Assoc. of CAB. Member: Jt Land Requirements Cttee, 1983–; Nuffield Inquiry into Town and Country Planning, 1984–. Pres., Royal Town Planning Inst., 1971–72 (AMTPI, 1955; Fellow 1967; Hon. Sec., 1979–); Architect RIBA, 1951. FRSA 1977. Freeman of City of London, 1968. *Publications:* Education for Planning (CES Report), 1973; various reports on Liverpool incl.: Annual Reviews of Plans, Study of Social Malaise; RTPI Report on Future of Planning, 1971, 1977; (part) City Centre Redevelopment; (part) Low Income Housing in the Developing World; articles on Planning and Management in Local Govt in various professional jls. *Recreations:* travel; unsystematic philately and unskilled building. *Address:* Grindstones, 20 Westfield Road, Edgbaston, Birmingham B15 3QG. *T:* 021–454 5661; The Coach House, Ashton Gifford Lane, Codford St Peter, Warminster, Wilts. *T:* Warminster 50610.

AMPLEFORTH, Abbot of; *see* Barry, Rt. Rev. N. P.

AMPTHILL, 4th Baron *cr* 1881; **Geoffrey Denis Erskine Russell,** CBE 1986; Deputy Chairman of Committees, since 1980, Deputy Speaker, since 1983, House of Lords; *b* 15 Oct. 1921; *s* of 3rd Baron Ampthill, CBE, and Christabel, Lady Ampthill (*d* 1976); *S* father, 1973; *m* 1st, 1946, Susan Mary (marr. diss. 1971), *d* of late Hon. Charles John Frederic Winn; two *s* one *d* (and one *s* decd); 2nd, 1972, Elisabeth Anne Marie, *d* of late Claude Henri Gustave Mallon. *Educ:* Stowe. Irish Guards, 1941–46; 2nd Lt 1941, Captain 1944. Gen. Manager, Fortnum and Mason, 1947–51; Chairman, New Providence Hotel Co. Ltd, 1951–64; Director: United Newspapers plc, 1981–; Dualvest plc, 1981–; Express Newspapers plc, 1985–. Managing Director of theatre owning and producing companies, 1953–81. Dir, Leeds Castle Foundn, 1980–82. *Heir: s* Hon. David Whitney Erskine Russell [*b* 27 May 1947; *m* 1980, April McKenzie Arbon, *y d* of Paul Arbon, New York; two *d*]. *Address:* 51 Sutherland Street, SW1V 4JX.

AMRITANAND, Rt. Rev. Joseph; Bishop of Calcutta, 1970–82; *b* Amritsar, 17 Feb. 1917; *m* 1943, Catherine Phillips; one *s* one *d*. *Educ:* District Board School, Toba Tek Singh, Punjab; Forman Christian Coll., Lahore, Punjab Univ. (BA); Bishop's College, Calcutta; Wycliffe Hall, Oxford. Deacon 1941, priest 1943; Missionary-in-charge of CMS Mission Field, Gojra, 1946–48; Bishop of Assam, 1949–62; Bishop of Lucknow, 1962–70; translated, after inauguration of Church of North India, Nov. 1970; first Bishop of Durgapur, 1972–74. *Address:* 2B Church Lane, Allahabad, UP 211002, India.

AMWELL, 2nd Baron *cr* 1947, of Islington; **Frederick Norman Montague;** *b* 6 Nov. 1912; *o s* of 1st Baron Amwell, CBE, and Constance (*d* 1964), *d* of James Craig; *S* father, 1966; *m* 1939, Kathleen Elizabeth Fountain; one *s* one *d*. *Educ:* Highbury Grammar School; Northampton Coll. of Technology. Aircraft Design Engineer (Apprenticeship in 1930), now retired. AFRAeS. *Heir: s* Hon. Keith Norman Montague, BSc, CEng, MICE, AMInstHE, FGS [*b* 1 April 1943; *m* 1970, Mary, *d* of Frank Palfreyman, Potters Bar, Herts; two *s*]. *Address:* 34 Halliford Road, Sunbury-on-Thames, Mddx. *T:* Sunbury-on-Thames 85413.

AMYOT, René, QC; barrister; Counsel, Jolin, Fournier & Associés; *b* Quebec City, 1 Nov. 1926; *s* of Omer Amyot and Caroline L'Espérance (*née* Barry); *m* 1954, Monique, *d* of Fernand Boutin; two *s* two *d*. *Educ:* Collège des Jésuites de Québec (BA 1946); Laval Univ. Law Sch. (LLL 1949); Harvard Univ. Grad. Sch. of Business Admin (MBA 1951). Called to Bar of Québec, 1949; QC Canada 1965. Joined Procter & Gamble, Montreal, 1951; Bouffard & Associates, Quebec, 1952. Chairman, Air Canada, 1981; Director: Imperial Life Assce Co. of Canada; Logistec Corp.; Rothmans of Pall Mall Can. Ltd; Société Immobilière du Canada (Vieux Port de Québec) Inc.; Dome Mines Ltd; Dome Petroleum Ltd; Gas Provincial du Nord de Québec Inc.; Champions Pipe Line Ltd; Sigma Mines Ltd; Davie Shipbuilding Ltd; Northern Quebec Finance Company. Dir, Council for Business and the Arts in Canada. Mem., Canadian Bar Assoc.; Governor, Canadian Tax Foundn; Mem. Cttee, Internat. Chamber. *Recreations:* skiing, swimming, tennis, farming. *Address:* Jolin, Fournier & Associés, Edifice Iberville Un, 1195 avenue Lavigerie, Suite 360, Sainte-Foy, Québec G1V 4N3, Canada.

ANCHORENA, Dr Manuel de; Argentine Ambassador to the Court of St James's, 1974–76; *b* 3 June 1933; *s* of Norberto de Anchorena and Ena Arrotea; *m* 1st, 1955, Elvira Peralta Martinez (*d* 1977); three *s* one *d*; 2nd, 1978, Anne Margaret Clifford. *Educ:* Univ. of Buenos Aires. Doctorate in Law, Buenos Aires, 1955. Landowner, politician, and historian. *Publications:* several articles contrib. to jl of Inst. of Historic Investigation, Argentina; articles on wild life and natural preservation. *Recreations:* polo, tennis, squash, fencing. *Address:* Estancia La Corona, Villanueva 7225, F.C. Roca, Provincia de Buenos Aires, Argentina. *Clubs:* Hurlingham, Royal Automobile; Circulo de Caza Mayor (Buenos Aires) (former Pres.).

ANCRAM, Earl of; Michael Andrew Foster Jude Kerr; MP (C) Edinburgh South, since 1979; Parliamentary Under Secretary of State, Scottish Office, since 1983; advocate; *b* 7 July 1945; *s* and *heir* of 12th Marquess of Lothian, *qv*; *m* 1975, Lady Jane Fitzalan-Howard, *y d* of 16th Duke of Norfolk, KG, PC, GCVO, GBE, TD, and of Lavinia Duchess of Norfolk, *qv*; two *d*. *Educ:* Ampleforth; Christ Church, Oxford (BA); Edinburgh Univ. (LLB). Advocate, Scottish Bar, 1970. MP (C) Berwickshire and East Lothian, Feb.-Sept. 1974; Chm., Cons. Party in Scotland, 1980–83 (Vice-Chm., 1975–80). Mem., Select Cttee on Energy, 1979–83. *Recreations:* ski-ing, photography, folksinging. *Address:* 6 Ainslie Place, Edinburgh; Monteviot, Jedburgh, Scotland. *T:* 031–226 3147. *Club:* Turf.

ANDERSEN, Valdemar Jens, CMG 1965; OBE 1960 (MBE 1955); VRD 1962; Resident Commissioner, Gilbert and Ellice Islands Colony, 1962–70, retired; *b* 21 March 1919; 2nd *s* of Max Andersen, Maraenui, NZ; *m* 1946, Alison Leone, 2nd *d* of G. A. Edmonds, Remuera, Auckland, NZ; one *s* one *d*. *Educ:* Napier Boys High Sch. NZ; Auckland University Coll. (BSc). Lieut, RNZNVR, 1940–46; Lieut, RANVR, 1947–62. British Solomon Islands Protectorate: Administrative Officer, 1947; Class A, Administrative Officer, 1954; Secretary Protectorate Affairs, 1958. *Recreations:* drama, gardening. *Address:* McKinney Road, Warkworth, New Zealand.

ANDERSON, family name of **Viscount Waverley.**

ANDERSON, Maj.-Gen. Alistair Andrew Gibson, CB 1980; *b* 26 Feb. 1927; *s* of Lt-Col John Gibson Anderson and Margaret Alice (*née* Scott); *m* 1953, Dr Margaret Grace Smith; one *s* two *d*. *Educ:* George Watson's Boys Coll., Edinburgh; University Coll. of SW of England, Exeter (Short Univ. Course, 1944); Staff Coll., Camberley; Jt Services Staff Coll., Latimer. Enlisted 1944; commnd Royal Corps of Signals, 1946; comd 18 Signal Regt, 1967–69; Defence Ops Centre, 1969–72; staff of Signal Officer-in-Chief, 1972–74; Comdt, Sch. of Signals, 1974–76; Signal Officer-in-Chief (Army), 1977–80, retired; Dir, Communications and Electronics Security Gp, GCHQ, 1980–85. Col Comdt, Royal Corps of Signals, 1980–86; Chm., Royal Signals Assoc. *Recreations:* hill walking, sailing, gardening. *Club:* Army and Navy.

See also Sir J. E. Anderson.

ANDERSON, Anthony John; QC 1982; Barrister; *b* 12 Sept. 1938; *s* of late A. Fraser Anderson and of Margaret Anderson; *m* 1970, Fenja Ragnhild Gunn. *Educ:* Harrow; Magdalen Coll., Oxford. MA. 2nd Lieut, The Gordon Highlanders, 1957–59. Called to the Bar, Inner Temple, 1964. *Recreation:* golf. *Address:* 2 Mitre Court Buildings, Temple, EC4Y 7BX. *T:* 01–583 1380; 33 Abinger Road, Bedford Park, W4. *T:* 01–994 2857. *Club:* Garrick.

ANDERSON, Dr Arthur John Ritchie, (Iain), CBE 1984; MA; MRCGP; General Medical and Hospital Practitioner, Trainer, since 1961; *b* 19 July 1933; *s* of Dr John Anderson and Dorothy Mary Anderson; *m* 1959, Janet Edith Norrish; two *s* one *d*. *Educ:* Bromsgrove Sch.; Downing Coll., Cambridge; St Mary's Hospital Medical Sch. MA, MB BChir (Cantab). MRCS; LRCP; DCH; DObstRCOG. Various hospital posts, 1958–61. Hemel Hempstead RDC, 1967–74, Vice-Chm., 1970–74; Councillor, Hertfordshire CC, 1973–, Vice-Chm., 1985– (Leader, 1977–83). Chm., Herts Police Authority, 1984–; Member: NW Thames Regional Health Authority, 1978–84; Regional Planning Council for South East, 1977–79. President, Hertfordshire Branch, BMA, 1973–74. Member, various governing bodies of primary, secondary, further and higher educn instns. FRSM 1984. *Publications:* numerous articles, mainly in periodicals. *Recreations:* writing, hockey, walking. *Address:* Leaside, Rucklers Lane, King's Langley, Herts WD4 9NQ. *T:* King's Langley 62884. *Club:* Herts 100.

ANDERSON, Campbell McCheyne; Managing Director, since 1985, and Chief Executive Officer, since 1986, Renison Gold Fields Consolidated; Director, Consolidated Gold Fields, since 1985; *b* 17 Sept. 1941; *s* of Allen Taylor Anderson and Ethel Catherine Rundle; *m* 1965, Sandra Maclean Harper; two *s* one *d*. *Educ:* The Armidale Sch., NSW, Aust.; Univ. of Sydney (BEcon). AASA. Trainee and General Administration, Boral Ltd, Australia, 1962–69; Gen. Manager/Man. Dir, Reef Oil NL, Australia, 1969–71; Asst Chief Representative, Burmah Oil Australia Ltd, 1972; Corporate Development, Burmah Oil Incorporated, New York, 1973; Corporate Development, 1974; Finance Director and Group Planning, Burmah Oil Trading Ltd, UK, 1975; Special Projects Dir, 1976,

Shipping Dir, 1978, Industrial Dir, 1979, Man. Dir, 1982–84, Burmah Oil Co. *Recreations:* golf, swimming, horse-racing, shooting. *Address:* 77 Drumalbyn Road, Bellevue Hill, Sydney, NSW 2023, Australia. *Clubs:* Oil Industries; Frilford Heath Golf; Australian; Royal Sydney Golf; Australian Jockey; Elanora Country (NSW).

ANDERSON, Carl David, PhD; Professor of Physics, California Institute of Technology, 1930–76, now Emeritus; Chairman, Division of Physics, Mathematics and Astronomy, 1962–70; *b* 3 Sept. 1905; *s* of Carl David Anderson and Emma Adolfina Ajaxson; *m* 1946, Lorraine Bergman; two *s. Educ:* California Institute of Technology. BS 1927, PhD 1930. War activities on projects, 1941–45; Presidential Certificate of Merit, 1945. Has conducted research on X-rays, gamma rays, cosmic rays, elementary particles, etc. Member: Nat. Acad. of Sciences; Amer. Philosoph. Soc.; Amer. Acad. of Arts and Sciences. Gold Medal, Amer. Inst., City of NY, 1935; Nobel prize in Physics, 1936; Elliott Cresson Medal of the Franklin Inst., 1937; John Ericsson Medal of Amer. Soc. of Swedish Engineers, 1960, etc. Holds hon. degrees. *Address:* California Institute of Technology, Pasadena, Calif 91109, USA.

ANDERSON, Rear-Adm. (Charles) Courtney, CB 1971; Flag Officer, Admiralty Interview Board, 1969–71, retired; *b* 8 Nov. 1916; *s* of late Lt-Col Charles Anderson, Australian Light Horse, and Mrs Constance Powell-Anderson, OBE, JP; *m* 1940, Pamela Ruth Miles; three *s. Educ:* RNC, Dartmouth. Joined RN, 1930. Served War of 1939–45: in command of Motor Torpedo Boats, Destroyers and Frigates. Naval Intelligence, 1946–49 and 1955–57; Commanded HMS Contest, 1949–51; Comdr, 1952; BJSM, Washington, 1953–55; Capt., 1959; Naval Attaché, Bonn, 1962–65; Director, Naval Recruiting, 1966–68; ADC to Queen, 1968; Rear-Adm., 1969. Editor, The Board Bulletin, 1971–78. *Publications:* The Drum Beats Still, 1951. Numerous articles and short stories. *Recreations:* gardening, do-it-yourself. *Address:* Bybrook Cottage, Bustlers Hill, Sherston, Malmesbury, Wilts SN16 0ND.

ANDERSON, Lt-Col Charles Groves Wright, VC 1942; MC; Member House of Representatives, for Hume, New South Wales, 1949–51 and 1955–61; grazier; *b* Capetown, South Africa, 12 Feb. 1897; *s* of A. G. W. Anderson; *m* 1931, Edith M. Tout (*d* 1984); two *s* two *d.* Served European War, 1914–18 (MC), KAR, E Africa. Served War of 1939–45 (VC, POW), 2nd AIF, Malaya. *Recreation:* motoring. *Address:* 119 Mugga Way, Canberra, ACT 2603, Australia.

ANDERSON, Courtney; *see* Anderson, (Charles) Courtney.

ANDERSON, Rev. David; Principal Lecturer in Religious Studies, Hertfordshire College of Higher Education (formerly Wall Hall College), Aldenham, Herts, 1974–84 (Senior Lecturer, 1970–74); *b* 30 Oct. 1919; *s* of William and Nancy Anderson, Newcastle upon Tyne; *m* 1953, Helen Finlay Robinson, 3rd *d* of Johnson and Eleanor Robinson, Whitley Bay, Northumberland; one *s* two *d. Educ:* Royal Grammar Sch. Newcastle upon Tyne; Selwyn Coll., Cambridge. Served in RA, 1940–42, Intelligence Corps, 1942–46, Lieut. Deacon, 1949, Priest, 1950; Curate of parish of St Gabriel, Sunderland, 1949–52; Tutor of St Aidan's Coll., Birkenhead, 1952–56; Warden of Melville Hall, Ibadan, Nigeria, 1956–58; Principal of: Immanuel Coll., Ibadan, Nigeria, 1958–62; Wycliffe Hall, Oxford, 1962–69. Examining Chaplain: to Bishop of Liverpool, 1969–75; to Bishop of St Albans, 1972–80. *Publications:* The Tragic Protest, 1969; Simone Weil, 1971; contrib: Religion and Modern Literature, 1975; William Golding: some critical considerations, 1978; The Passion of Man, 1980. *Recreations:* listening to music, hi-fi gramophones. *Address:* 1 Woodwaye, Watford, Herts WD1 4NN.

ANDERSON, David Colville, VRD 1947, and Clasp, 1958; QC (Scotland) 1957; *b* 8 Sept. 1916; *yr s* of late J. L. Anderson of Pittormie, Fife, solicitor and farmer, and late Etta Colville; *m* 1948, Juliet, *yr d* of late Hon. Lord Hill Watson, MC, LLD; two *s* one *d. Educ:* Trinity Coll., Glenalmond; Pembroke Coll., Oxford; Edinburgh Univ. BA (Hons) Oxford 1938; LLB (Distinction) 1946. Thow Scholar, Maclagan Prizeman, Dalgety Prizeman, Edinburgh Univ. Lecturer in Scots Law, Edinburgh Univ., 1947–60; Advocate, 1946; Standing Junior Counsel to Ministry of Works, 1954–55, and to War Office, 1955–57. Contested (C) Coatbridge and Airdrie, 1955, and East Dunbartonshire, 1959; MP (C) Dumfries, Dec. 1963–Sept. 1964. Solicitor-General for Scotland, 1960–64; Vice-Chairman, Commissioners of Northern Lighthouses, 1963–64; Hon. Sheriff-Substitute, Lothians and Peebles, 1965–; Chm., Industrial Tribunals (Scotland), 1971–72; Chief Reporter for Public Inquiries and Under Sec., Scottish Office, 1972–74. Joined RNVR, 1935. In VIII awarded Ashburton Shield, Bisley, 1933 (Trinity Coll., Glenalmond; schools event); Inter-Services XX at Bisley, 1936–38. Served War of 1939–45 in destroyers (despatches); Lieut 1940; Egerton Prizeman in Naval Gunnery, 1943; Gunnery Officer, Rosyth Escort Force, 1943–45; Norway, 1945; Lt-Comdr 1948. King Haakon VII Liberty Medal, 1946. *Relevant Play:* The Case of David Anderson QC by John Hale (Manchester, and Traverse Theatre, Edinburgh, 1980; Lyric Studio Hammersmith, 1981). *Address:* 8 Arboretum Road, Edinburgh EH3 5PD. *T:* 031-552 3003. *Club:* New (Edinburgh).

ANDERSON, David Fyfe, MD, ChB, FRCOG, FRCPGlas; Muirhead Professor of Obstetrics and Gynæcology, University of Glasgow, 1946–70, now Emeritus Professor; Obstetric Surgeon, Royal Maternity Hospital, Glasgow; Gynæcological Surgeon, Royal Infirmary, Glasgow; *b* 8 June 1904; *o s* of David Fyfe Anderson and Mary Ann Mackay, Viewfield, Strathaven, Lanarkshire; *m* 1945, Elizabeth Rose, 2nd *d* of W. F. McAusland, Wyndyknowe, Scotstounhill, Glasgow; three *s* one *d. Educ:* Strathaven Academy (Dux); High Sch. of Glasgow (Dux, Modern Side); Univ. of Glasgow (Gardiner Bursary); Johns Hopkins Univ. MB, ChB (Commendation), Univ. of Glasgow, 1926; McCunn Research Scholar, 1929–31; MRCOG 1932; FRFPSG 1935; MD (Hons) 1935; FRCOG 1940; Rockefeller Travelling Fellowship 1935–36; FRSM; FRCPGlas 1964; Fellow of Glasgow Obstetrical and Gynæcological Soc. and of Edinburgh Obstetrical Soc.; formerly Examiner to Central Midwives Board for Scotland; lately Professor of Midwifery and Diseases of Women at Anderson College of Medicine, Glasgow. Fellow, Ancient Monuments Soc. Freeman of City of Glasgow. Member of Incorporations of: Barbers, Bonnetmakers and Dyers, and Tailors (Ex-Deacon). OStJ 1973. *Publications:* medical papers and verse. *Address:* 55 Kingston Road, Bishopton, Renfrewshire PA7 5BA. *T:* Bishopton 862403.

ANDERSON, David Heywood, CMG 1982; HM Diplomatic Service; Legal Counsellor, Foreign and Commonwealth Office, since 1982; Barrister-at-Law; *b* 14 Sept. 1937; *s* of late Harry Anderson; *m* 1961, Jennifer Ratcliffe; one *s* one *d. Educ:* King James' Grammar Sch., Almondbury. LLB (Leeds); LLM (London). Called to Bar, Gray's Inn, 1963. Asst Legal Adviser, FCO, 1960–69; Legal Adviser, British Embassy, Bonn, 1969–72; Legal Counsellor, FCO, 1972–79; Legal Adviser, UK Mission to UN, NY, 1979–82. *Recreations:* reading, gardening. *Address:* c/o Foreign and Commonwealth Office, King Charles Street, SW1.

ANDERSON, David Munro; Chairman, E. D. & F. Man International Ltd, since 1986; *b* 15 Dec. 1937; *s* of Alexander Anderson and Jessica Anderson (*née* Vincent-Innes); *m* 1965, Veronica Jane (*née* Stevens); two *s* one *d. Educ:* Morrison's Academy, Perthshire; Strathallan, Perthshire. Commissioned Black Watch; served W Africa; tea production with James Finlay & Co., India, 1959–62; London Chamber of Commerce and Industry, 1962–63; joined E. D. & F. Man Ltd, 1963; formed Anderson Man Ltd, 1981; formed E. D. & F. Man International Ltd, 1985; Man. Dir, Commodity Analysis Ltd, 1968; numerous directorships. Chairman, formation cttees: Internat. Petroleum Exchange; Baltic Internat. Freight Futures Exchange (jtly); former Vice-Chm., London Commodity Exchange; Member: Securities and Investments Bd, 1986–87; Futures and Commodity Exchanges. *Recreations:* ski-ing, shooting. *Address:* The Old Rectory, Lamarsh, Bures, Suffolk. *T:* Bures 227271. *Club:* Caledonian.

ANDERSON, Brig. David William, CBE 1976 (OBE 1972); Chief Executive, Cumbernauld Development Corporation, since 1985; *b* 4 Jan. 1929; *s* of David Anderson and Frances Anderson; *m* 1954, Eileen Dorothy Scott; one *s* two *d. Educ:* St Cuthbert's Grammar Sch., Newcastle on Tyne; RMA, Sandhurst. Black Watch, 1946; RMA, Sandhurst, 1947; commnd HLI, 1948; served ME and Malaya; RHF, Staff Coll., Trucial Oman Scouts, Sch. of Inf., I RHF, Germany, and HQ NORTHAG, 1959–66; Instr, Staff Coll., 1967–69; CO I RHF, Scotland, N Ireland, Singapore, 1969–72; Colonel GS: MoD, 1972–73; HQ Dir of Inf., 1974; Comdr, 3 Inf. Bde, N Ireland, 1975–76; Comdt, Sch. of Infantry, 1976–79; Comdr, Highlands, 1979–81, Comdr 51 Highland Bde, 1982; ADC to the Queen, 1981–82. Chief Exec., NE Fife DC, 1982–85. Hon. Col, Aberdeen Univ. OTC, 1982–; Mem., Highland TA&VRA, 1984–. Chm., Fife Area Scout Council, 1985–86. Mem., St John Assoc., 1984–. Hon. Vice-Pres., Cumbernauld Br., Royal British Legion (Scotland), 1985–. *Recreations:* moving house, Scottish history. *Address:* c/o Royal Bank of Scotland, 1 Roadside, Cumbernauld G67 2SS.

ANDERSON, Prof. Declan John; Professor of Oral Biology, University of Bristol, 1966–85, now Professor Emeritus; *b* 20 June 1920; *s* of Arthur John Anderson and Katherine Mary Coffey; *m* 1947, Vivian Joy Dunkerton; four *s* three *d. Educ:* Christ's Hospital; Guy's Hospital Medical School, Univ. of London. BDS (London) 1942; LDSRCS 1943, BSc 1946, MSc 1947, PhD 1955. Prof. of Physiology, Univ. of Oregon, USA, 1957–58; Prof. of Physiology in Relation to Dentistry, Univ. of London, 1963–66. *Publications:* Physiology for Dental Students, 1952; scientific papers in professional jls. *Recreations:* silversmithing, forging, music. *Address:* Cornerstones, Church Lane, Islip, Oxford OX5 2TA.

ANDERSON, Donald; MP (Lab) Swansea East, since Oct. 1974; barrister-at-law; *b* 17 June 1939; *s* of David Robert Anderson and Eva (*née* Mathias); *m* 1963, Dr Dorothy Trotman, BSc, PhD; three *s. Educ:* Swansea Grammar Sch.; University Coll. of Swansea (Hon. Fellow, 1985). 1st cl. hons Modern History and Politics, Swansea, 1960. Barrister; called to Bar, Inner Temple, 1969. Member of HM Foreign Service, 1960–64: Foreign Office, 1960–63; 3rd Sec., British Embassy, Budapest, 1963–64; lectured in Dept of Political Theory and Govt, University Coll., Swansea, 1964–66. MP (Lab) Monmouth, 1966–70; Mem. Estimates Cttee, 1966–69; Vice-Chm., Welsh Labour Group, 1969–70; PPS to Min. of Defence (Administration), 1969–70; PPS to Attorney General, 1974–79; Chairman: Parly Lab. Party Environment Gp, 1974–; Welsh Lab. Gp, 1977–78; Select Cttee on Welsh Affairs, 1981–83 (Mem., 1980–83); opposition front-bench spokesman on foreign affairs, 1983–. Vice-Chm., Exec., IPU and CPA, 1985–; Vice-Pres., Assoc. of W European Parliamentarians for Action against Apartheid, 1984–. Councillor, Kensington and Chelsea, 1971–75. Pres., Gower Soc., 1976–78. Methodist local preacher. *Recreations:* church work, walking and talking. *Address:* House of Commons, SW1.

ANDERSON, Prof. Donald Thomas, AO 1986; PhD, DSc; FRS 1977; Challis Professor of Biology, University of Sydney, since 1984 (Professor of Biology, 1972–84); *b* 29 Dec. 1931; *s* of Thomas and Flora Anderson; *m* 1960, Joanne Trevathan (*née* Claridge). *Educ:* King's Coll., London Univ. DSc London, 1966; DSc Sydney, 1983. Lectr in Zoology, Sydney Univ., 1958–61; Sen. Lectr, 1962–66; Reader in Biology, 1967–71. Clarke Medal, Royal Soc. of NSW, 1979. *Publication:* Embryology and Phylogeny, of Annelids and Arthropods, 1973; papers in zool. jls. *Recreations:* gardening, photography. *Address:* 52 Spruson Street, Neutral Bay, NSW 2089, Australia. *T:* (home) 929.7583; (office) 692.2438.

ANDERSON, Prof. Ephraim Saul, CBE 1976; FRCP, FRS 1968; Director, Enteric Reference Laboratory, Public Health Laboratory Service, 1954–78; *b* 1911; *e s* of Benjamin and Ada Anderson, Newcastle upon Tyne; *m* 1959, Carol Jean (*née* Thompson) (marr. diss.); three *s. Educ:* Rutherford Coll., and King's Coll. Med. Sch. (Univ. of Durham), Newcastle upon Tyne. MB, BS 1934; MD Durham, 1953; Dip.Bact. London, 1948; Founder Fellow, Royal Coll. of Pathologists, 1963. GP, 1935–39; RAMC, 1940–46; Pathologist, 1943–46; Registrar in Bacteriology, Postgrad. Med. Sch., 1946–47; Staff, Enteric Reference Lab., 1947–52, Dep. Dir, 1952–54. WHO Fellow, 1953; FIBiol 1973; FRCP 1975. Chm., Internat. Fedn for Enteric Phage Typing of Internat. Union of Microbiol. Socs, 1966– (Jt Chm., 1958–66); Dir, Internat. Ref. Lab. for Enteric Phage Typing of Internat. Fedn for Enteric Phage Typing, 1954–78; Dir, Collab. Centre for Phage Typing and Resistance of Enterobacteria of WHO, 1960–78; Mem., WHO Expert Adv. Panel for Enteric Diseases. Vis. Prof., Sch. of Biol Sciences, Brunel Univ., 1973–77. Lectures: Scientific Basis of Medicine, British Postgrad. Med. Fedn, 1966; Almroth Wright, Wright-Fleming Inst. of Microbiol., 1967; Holme, UCH, 1970; Cutter, Sch. of Public Health, Harvard, 1972; Marjory Stephenson Meml, Soc. for Gen. Microbiol., 1975. Hon. DSc Newcastle, 1975. *Publications:* contrib. to: The Bacteriophages (Mark Adams), 1959; The World Problem of Salmonellosis (Van Oye), 1964; Ciba Symposium: Bacterial Episomes and Plasmids, 1969; numerous articles on bacteriophage typing and its genetic basis, microbial ecology, transferable drug resistance, its evolution, and epidemiology. *Recreations:* music, photography. *Address:* 10 Rosecroft Avenue, NW3 7QB.

ANDERSON, Eric; *see* Anderson, W. E. K.

ANDERSON, Sir Ferguson; *see* Anderson, Sir W. F.

ANDERSON, Dame Frances Margaret; *see* Anderson, Dame Judith.

ANDERSON, Rev. Prof. George Wishart, FRSE 1977; FBA 1972; Professor of Old Testament Literature and Theology, 1962–68, of Hebrew and Old Testament Studies, 1968–82, University of Edinburgh; *b* 25 Jan. 1913; *s* of George Anderson and Margaret Gordon Wishart; *m* 1st, 1941, Edith Joyce Marjorie Walter (decd); one *s* one *d*; 2nd, 1959, Anne Phyllis Walter. *Educ:* Arbroath High Sch.; Univs of St Andrews, Cambridge, Lund. United Coll., St Andrews: Harkness Scholar; MA 1st Cl. Hons Classics, 1935. Fitzwilliam House and Wesley House, Cambridge: 1st Cl. Theol Tripos Part I, 1937; 2nd Cl. Theol Tripos Part II, 1938; BA 1937; MA 1946. Asst Tutor, Richmond Coll., 1939–41. Chaplain, RAF, 1941–46; Tutor in OT Lang. and Lit., Handsworth Coll., 1946–56; Lecturer in OT Lit. and Theol., Univ. of St Andrews, 1956–58; Prof. of OT Studies, Univ. of Durham, 1958–62. Hon. Sec., Internat. Organization of Old Testament Scholars, 1953–71 (Pres., 1971–74); Mem. Editorial Bd of Vetus Testamentum, 1950–75; Editor, Book List of Soc. for OT Study, 1957–66; President, Soc. for OT Study, 1963; Hon. Sec. (Foreign Correspondence), Soc. for OT Study, 1964–74; Charles Ryder Smith Meml Lectr, 1964; Fernley-Hartley Lectr, 1969; Speaker's Lectr in Biblical Studies, Univ.

of Oxford, 1976–80; Henton Davies Lectr, 1977; A. S. Peake Meml Lectr, 1984. Hon. DD St Andrews, 1959; Hon. TeolD Lund, 1971. Burkitt Medal for Biblical Studies, British Acad., 1982. *Publications:* He That Cometh (trans. from Norwegian of S. Mowinckel), 1956; A Critical Introduction to the Old Testament, 1959; The Ras Shamra Discoveries and the Old Testament (trans. from Norwegian of A. S. Kapelrud, US 1963, UK 1965); The History and Religion of Israel, 1966; (ed) A Decade of Bible Bibliography, 1967; (ed) Tradition and Interpretation, 1979; articles in: The Old Testament and Modern Study (ed H. H. Rowley), 1951; The New Peake Commentary (ed M. Black and H. H. Rowley), 1962; The Cambridge History of the Bible, Vol. I (ed P. R. Ackroyd and C. F. Evans), 1970, and in various learned jls. *Recreations:* reading, music, walking. *Address:* 51 Fountainhall Road, Edinburgh EH9 2LH.

ANDERSON, Gordon Alexander, CA, FCMA; Partner, Arthur Young, Chartered Accountants (and predecessor firms), since 1958; *b* 9 Aug. 1931; *s* of Cecil Brown Anderson and Janet Davidson Bell; *m* 1958, Eirené Cochrane Howie Douglas; two *s* one *d. Educ:* High School of Glasgow. Qualified as Chartered Accountant, 1955; FCMA 1984. National Service, RN, 1955–57. Partner: Moores Carson & Watson, 1958 (subseq. McClelland Moores & Co., Arthur Young McClelland Moores & Co. and Arthur Young); McLintock Moores & Murray, 1963–69. Director: Bitmac Ltd, 1984–; High School of Glasgow Ltd, 1975–81; Mem., Scottish Milk Marketing Bd, 1979–85. Institute of Chartered Accountants of Scotland: Mem. Council, 1980–84; Vice-Pres., 1984–86; Pres., 1986–87. *Recreations:* golf, gardening, Rugby football. *Address:* (home) Ardwell, 41 Manse Road, Bearsden, Glasgow G61 3PN. *T:* 041–942 2803; (office) George House, 50 George Square, Glasgow G2 1RR. *T:* 041–552 4994. *Clubs:* Caledonian; Western (Glasgow); Glasgow Golf; Buchanan Castle Golf (Captain 1979–80).

ANDERSON, Rev. Hector David, LVO 1951; MA, BD; Chaplain to the Queen, 1955–77; *b* 16 Aug. 1906; *s* of Rev. David Anderson, LLD, Dublin; *m* 1931, Muriel Louise Peters; one *s. Educ:* The Abbey, Tipperary; Trinity Coll., Dublin. Schol. 1928, BA Mods 1929, MA 1932, BD 1949. Curate, Shirley, Croydon, 1930–33; St Michael's, Chester Square, SW1, 1933–39; CF, Sept. 1939–42; Domestic Chaplain to King George VI, 1942–52, to the Queen, 1952–55; Rector: Sandringham, 1942–55; Lutterworth, 1955–61; Swanage, 1961–69. Hon. Canon of Leicester, 1959–61. *Address:* Adare, The Hyde, Langton Matravers, Swanage, Dorset. *T:* Swanage 3206.

ANDERSON, H(ector) John, FRCP; Physician, St Thomas' Hospital, since 1948, Special Trustee since 1972; Physician, Lambeth Hospital, South Western Hospital and French Hospital; *b* Central Provinces, India, 5 Jan. 1915; *s* of H. J. Anderson; *m* 1st, 1940, Frances Pearce (marr. diss.), *er d* of Rev. W. P. Putt; one *s* one *d;* 2nd, 1956, Pauline Mary, *d* of A. Hammond; one *d. Educ:* Exeter Sch.; St Catharine's Coll., Cambridge; St Thomas' Hospital. MA, MB (Cantab), FRCP 1950. Medical Registrar and Res. Asst Physician, St Thomas' Hospital, 1941 and 1942. Hon. Lt-Col RAMC; served MEF, 1944–47. Kitchener Scholar; Mead Prizeman, St Thomas' Hospital; Murchison Scholar, RCP, 1942; Goulstonian Lectr, RCP, 1951; Examiner: MB London; Medicine, Conjoint Bd, London and England; RCP. Mem. AHA, Lambeth, Southwark, Lewisham Area (T). Member: Assoc. of Physicians of Gt Britain; Thoracic Soc.; FRSoc.Med. *Publications:* Brim of Day, 1944; contrib. to medical literature. *Address:* Churchill Clinic, 80 Lambeth Road, SE1. *T:* 01–928 5633; 102 Lambeth Road, SE1. *T:* 01–928 1533.

ANDERSON, Rev. Prof. Hugh, MA, BD, PhD, DD; Professor of New Testament Language, Literature and Theology, University of Edinburgh, 1966–85, now Professor Emeritus; *b* 18 May 1920; *s* of Hugh Anderson and Jeannie Muir; *m* 1945, Jean Goldie Torbit; one *s* one *d* (and one *s* decd). *Educ:* Galston Sch.; Kilmarnock Acad.; Univ. of Glasgow (MA (Hons Classics and Semitic Langs I), BD (Dist. New Testament); PhD); post-doctoral Fellow, Univs of Oxford and Heidelberg. Chaplain, Egypt and Palestine, 1945–46; Lectr in Old Testament, Univ. of Glasgow, 1946–51; Minister, Trinity Presb. Church, Glasgow, 1951–57; A. B. Bruce Lectr, Univ. of Glasgow, 1954–57; Prof. of Biblical Criticism, Duke Univ., N Carolina, 1957–66. Dir, Postgrad. Studies in Theology, Univ. of Edinburgh, 1968–72; Select Preacher, Oxford Univ., 1970; Haskell Lectr, Oberlin Coll., Ohio, 1971; McBride Vis. Prof. of Religion, Bryn Mawr Coll., Pa, 1974–75; Vis. Prof. of Religion, Meredith Coll., N Carolina, 1982; James A. Gray Lectr, 1982, Kenneth Willis Clark Meml Lectr, 1985, Duke Univ., N Carolina; Scholar-in-res., Florida Southern Coll., Lakeland, Fla, 1983; Warner Hall Lectr, St Andrews Presbyterian Coll., N Carolina, 1985. Convener of Ch. of Scotland's Special Commn on Priorities of Mission in 70s and 80s, 1969–71; Chm., Internat. Selection Council for Albert Schweitzer Internat. Prizes, 1972–. Hon. DD Glasgow, 1970. *Publications:* Psalms I-XLV, 1951; Historians of Israel, 1957; Jesus and Christian Origins, 1964; The Inter-Testamental Period in The Bible and History (ed W. Barclay), 1965; (ed with W. Barclay) The New Testament in Historical and Contemporary Perspective, 1965; Jesus, 1967; The Gospel of Mark, 1976; Commentary on 3 and 4 Maccabees: Doubleday Pseudepigrapha Vol., 1982; contribs to Religion in Life, Interpretation, Scottish Jl of Theology, Expos. Times. *Recreations:* golf, gardening, music. *Address:* 5 Comiston Springs Avenue, Edinburgh EH10 6NT. *T:* 031–447 1401. *Clubs:* Greek (Edinburgh); Luffness Golf (E Lothian).

ANDERSON, Iain; *see* Anderson, A. J. R.

ANDERSON, James Frazer Gillan, CBE 1979; JP, DL; Convener, Central Regional Council, Scotland, since 1974; *b* 25 March 1929; *m* 1956, May Harley; one *s* one *d. Educ:* Maddiston Primary Sch.; Graeme High Sch., Falkirk. Member: Stirling CC, 1958–75 (Convener, 1971–75); Central Regional Council, 1974–; Health and Safety Commission, 1974–80; Scottish Develt Agency, 1986–. OStJ. *Recreations:* gardening, walking. *Address:* 23 California Road, Maddiston, by Falkirk. *T:* Polmont 715875. *Club:* British Legion (Polmont).

ANDERSON, Prof. Sir (James) Norman (Dalrymple), Kt 1975; OBE (mil.) 1945 (MBE 1943); BA 1930, LLB 1931, MA 1934, LLD 1955 (Cantab); Hon. DD St Andrews 1974; FBA 1970; QC 1974; Professor of Oriental Laws in the University of London, 1954–75, now Emeritus Professor; Director of the Institute of Advanced Legal Studies in the University of London, 1959–76; *b* 29 Sept. 1908; *s* of late William Dalrymple Anderson; *m* 1933, Patricia Hope, *d* of A. Stock Givan; one *s* and two *d* decd. *Educ:* St Lawrence Coll., Ramsgate; Trinity Coll., Cambridge (Senior Scholar). 1st Class, Law Tripos Parts I and II (distinction in Part I); 1st Class LLB. Called to the Bar, Gray's Inn, 1965. Missionary, Egypt General Mission, 1932; served War of 1939–45 in Army as Arab Liaison Officer, Libyan Arab Force, 1940 (Capt.); Sec. for Sanusi Affairs, Civil Affairs Branch, GHQ, MEF, 1941 (Major); Sec. for Arab Affairs, 1943 (Lieut-Col); Political Sec., 1943; Chief Sec. (Col), 1944; Lectr in Islamic Law, Sch. of Oriental and African Studies, 1947; Reader in Oriental Laws in Univ. of London, 1951–53; Hd of Dept of Law, SOAS, 1953–71, now Hon. Fellow, SOAS; Dean of Faculty of Laws, Univ. of London, 1965–69. President, Soc. of Public Teachers of Law, 1968–69. Chm. UK Nat. Cttee of Comparative Law, 1957–59; Vice-Chm. Internat. African Law Assoc.; Visiting Prof., Princeton Univ. and New York Univ. Law Sch., 1958; Harvard Law Sch., 1966; Mem., Denning Cttee on Legal Education for Students from Africa, 1960. Conducted survey of application of Islamic Law in British African possessions for Colonial Office, 1950–51. President: BCMS, 1963–86; CPAS, 1974–86; Scripture Union, 1975–80; Victoria Inst., 1978–85. First Chairman, House of Laity in Gen. Synod of Church of England, 1970–79 (Mem., 1970–80; Mem. former Church Assembly, 1965–70); Anglican delegate to the World Council of Churches. Hon. LittD Wheaton Coll., 1980. Libyan Order of Istiqlal, Class II, 1959. *Publications:* Al-'Aql wa'l Iman (in Arabic), 1939; Islamic Law in Africa, 1954; Islamic Law in the Modern World, 1959; Into the World: The Need and Limits of Christian Involvement, 1968; Christianity: the witness of history, 1969; Christianity and Comparative Religion, 1970; Morality, Law and Grace (Forwood Lectures), 1972; A Lawyer among the Theologians, 1973; Law Reform in the Muslim World, 1976; Issues of Life and Death, 1976; Liberty, Law and Justice (Hamlyn Lectures), 1978; The Mystery of the Incarnation (Bishop John Prideaux Lectures), 1978; The Law of God and the Love of God, 1980; God's Word for God's World, 1981; The Teaching of Jesus, 1983; Christianity and World Religions: the challenge of pluralism, 1984; Jesus Christ: the witness of history, 1984; An Adopted Son (autobiog.), 1986; Editor: The World's Religions, 1950, 4th edn 1975; Changing Law in Developing Countries, 1963; Family Law in Asia and Africa, 1968; numerous articles in periodicals. *Address:* 9 Larchfield, Gough Way, Cambridge. *T:* Cambridge 358778. *Club:* Athenæum.

ANDERSON, Prof. John, MD, FRCP; Professor of Medicine, King's College Hospital Medical School, since 1964; *b* 11 Sept. 1921; *s* of James and Margaret Anderson; *m* 1952, Beatrice May Venner; three *s. Educ:* Durham Univ. BA Hons, Dunelm (Mod. Hist.) 1942; MB, BS Hons, 1950; BSc Hons, 1952 (Physiology); MA (Mod. Hist.), MD. Served War, Lt, RA (Field) (Ayrshire Yeomanry), 1940–45. MRC Fellow in Clin. Med., Univ. Coll. Hosp., London, 1952–55; Rockefeller Travelling Fellowship, 1956–57; Reader in Medicine, King's Coll. Hosp. Med. Sch., Med. Unit, 1962–65. Mem., Med. Research Soc. FRCP 1962; FBCS 1969; FIBiol 1977. *Publications:* A New Look at Medical Education, 1965; Information Processing of Medical Records, 1970; articles in Lancet and BMJ, on: nutron activation, medical computing, cancer, endocrinology, med. educn. *Recreations:* shooting, sailing, fishing. *Address:* 14 Styles Way, Park Langley, Beckenham, Kent. *T:* (office) 01–274 6222. *Club:* University (Durham).

ANDERSON, Prof. John Allan Dalrymple, TD 1967; DL; FRCGP; FFCM; MFOM; Professor of Community Medicine, University of London, at United Medical and Dental Schools (Guy's Campus), since 1975; *b* 16 June 1926; *s* of John Allan Anderson and Mary Winifred (*née* Lawson); *m* 1965, Mairead Mary MacLaren; three *d. Educ:* Loretto Sch.; Worcester Coll., Oxford (MA); Edinburgh Univ. (MD); London Univ. (DPH); DObstRCOG. Lectr in gen. practice, 1954–59, Dir, Industrial Survey Unit, 1960–63, Univ. of Edinburgh; Sen. Lectr, Social Medicine, LSHTM, 1963–69; Dir, Dept of Community Medicine, Guy's Hosp. Med. Sch., 1970–; Hon. Consultant Guy's Hosp., 1970–. Dir, Occupational Health Service, Lewisham and N Southwark HA, 1984–. Acad. Registrar, FCM, RCP, 1983–. OC London Scot. Co. 1/51 Highland Vols, TA, 1967–70; CO 221 Fd Amb. (TA), 1978–81; TA Col HQ Lond. Dist, 1981–84; Regtl Col Lond. Scot. Regt, 1983–. Elder, Ch. of Scotland, 1977–; Area Surg., SJAB, SW Lond., 1984–. DL Greater London, 1985; Rep. DL, Borough of Richmond, 1986. *Publications:* A New Look at Community Medicine, 1965; Self Medication, 1982; (with Dr R. Grahame) Bibliography of Low Back Pain, 1982; sci. papers on community and occupational med. and rheumatology. *Recreations:* hill walking, golf, bridge. *Address:* 24 Lytton Grove, Putney, SW15 2HB. *T:* 01–788 9420. *Clubs:* Hurlingham; New (Edinburgh).

ANDERSON, General Sir John (D'Arcy), GBE 1967 (CBE 1945); KCB 1961 (CB 1957); DSO 1940; *b* 23 Sept. 1908; *s* of late Major Reginald D'Arcy Anderson, RGA, and Norah Anderson (*née* Gracey), Ballyhossett, Downpatrick, Co. Down; *m* 1937, Elizabeth, *d* of late Augustus M. Walker. *Educ:* Winchester; New Coll., Oxford (MA). 2nd Lieut 5th Royal Inniskilling Dragoon Guards, 1929; served War of 1939–45, France, Middle East and Italy (wounded, despatches twice); GOC 11th Armoured Div., BAOR, 1955–56. Chief of Staff, Headquarters Northern Army Group and BAOR, 1956–58; Director, RAC, WO, 1958–59; Dir-Gen. of Military Training, 1959–61; DCIGS, 1961–63; Military Sec. to: Sec. of State for War, 1963–64; Min. of Defence, 1964–65. Commandant IDC, 1966–68; Col 5th Royal Inniskilling Dragoon Guards, 1962–67; Col Comdt, RAEC, 1964–70; Col Comdt, UDR, 1969–79 (Rep., 1969–77); Hon. Col: Oxford Univ. OTC, 1961–67; Queen's Univ., Belfast, OTC, 1964–75. ADC General to the Queen, 1966–68. Pro-Chancellor, QUB, 1969–80. Mem., Commonwealth War Graves Commn, 1963–71. Mem., Army Museums Ogilby Trust; Vice-Pres. Sandes Soldiers' and Airmen's Homes; Deputy Pres., ACF Assoc. (NI). DL Co. Down 1969–80, High Sheriff Co. Down 1974. Hon. LLD QUB, 1980. Grand Officer, Order of the Crown (Belgium), 1963. Grand Officer, Order of Leopold (Belgium), 1966. *Recreation:* painting. *Address:* 36 Whitelands House, Cheltenham Terrace, SW3 4QY. *T:* 01–730 1307. *Club:* Cavalry and Guards.

ANDERSON, Maj.-Gen. Sir John (Evelyn), KBE 1971 (CBE 1963); CEng, FIEE; CBIM; Executive Director, Europe Group, Armed Forces Communications and Electronics Association, since 1981; *b* 28 June 1916; *e s* of Lt-Col John Gibson Anderson, Christchurch, NZ, and Margaret (*née* Scott), Edinburgh; *m* 1944, Jean Isobel, *d* of Charles Tait, farmer, Aberdeenshire; one *s* one *d. Educ:* King's Sch., Rochester; RMA, Woolwich. Commissioned in Royal Signals, 1936; Lt-Col 1956; Col 1960; Brig. 1964; Maj.-Gen. 1967; Signal Officer in Chief (Army), MoD, 1967–69; ACDS (signals), 1969–72. Col Comdt, Royal Corps of Signals, 1969–74. Hon. Col 71st (Yeomanry) Signal Regt TAVR, 1969–76; Hon. Col Women's Transport Corps (FANY), 1970–76. Dir Gen., NATO Integrated Communications System Management Agency, 1977–81. *Recreation:* fishing. *Address:* The Beeches, Amport, Andover, Hampshire. *Clubs:* Army and Navy, Flyfishers'.
See also Maj.-Gen. A. A. G. Anderson.

ANDERSON, Prof. John Kinloch, FSA; Professor of Classical Archaeology, University of California, Berkeley, since 1958; *b* 3 Jan. 1924; *s* of late Sir James Anderson, KCIE, and of Lady Anderson; *m* 1954, Esperance, *d* of Guy Batham, Dunedin, NZ; one *s* two *d. Educ:* Trinity Coll., Glenalmond; Christ Church, Oxford (MA). Served War, in Black Watch (RHR) and Intelligence Corps, 1942–46 (final rank, Lieut). Student, British Sch. at Athens, 1949–52; Lecturer in Classics, Univ. of Otago, NZ, 1953–58. FSA 1976. *Publications:* Greek Vases in the Otago Museum, 1955; Ancient Greek Horsemanship, 1961; Military Theory and Practice in the Age of Xenophon, 1970; Xenophon, 1974; Hunting in the Ancient World, 1985; articles and reviews in Annual of British Sch. at Athens; Jl of Hellenic Studies, etc. *Recreations:* gardening, riding (Qualified Riding Mem., Calif Dressage Soc.). *Address:* 1020 Middlefield Road, Berkeley, California 94708, USA. *T:* Berkeley 841–5335.

ANDERSON, Sir John (Muir), Kt 1969; CMG 1957; Commissioner of State Savings Bank of Victoria, 1962–83, Chairman of Commissioners, 1967; *b* 14 Sept. 1914; *s* of John Weir Anderson; *m* 1949, Audrey Drayton Jamieson; one *s* one *d. Educ:* Brighton Grammar Sch.; Melbourne Univ. 2/6th Commando Co., 1941; Lieut, 1st Australian Parachute Bn, 1944; served SE Asia, 1941–45. Established John M. Anderson & Co. Pty Ltd, Manufacturers, Agents and Importers, 1951; Managing Director, King Oscar Fine Foods Pty Ltd. Pres. of Liberal and Country Party of Victoria, 1952–56 (Treasurer, 1957–61, 1978–80). Comr, Melbourne Harbour Trust, 1972–83. Trustee, Melbourne

Exhibn, 1960, Chm. of Trustees, 1968. *Recreations:* swimming, fishing. *Address:* 25 Cosham Street, Brighton, Vic 3186, Australia. *T:* 592–4790.

ANDERSON, Professor John Neil; (first) Professor of Dental Prosthetics, 1964–82 (now Emeritus), Dean of Dentistry, 1972–76, 1980–82, University of Dundee; *b* 11 Feb. 1922; *m* 1945, Mary G. Croll; one *s* one *d. Educ:* High Storrs Gram. Sch., Sheffield; Sheffield Univ. Asst Lectr, Sheffield Univ., 1945–46; Lectr, Durham Univ., 1946–48; Lectr, Birmingham Univ., 1948–52; Sen. Lectr, St Andrews Univ., 1952–64. External Examiner, Univs of Malaya, Baghdad, Newcastle upon Tyne, Bristol, Birmingham, Liverpool, RCSI. *Publications:* Anderson's Applied Dental Materials; (with R. Storer) Immediate and Replacement Dentures, 1966, 3rd edn, 1981; contribs to leading dental jls. *Recreations:* music, gardening, carpentry. *Address:* Wyndham, Derwent Drive, Baslow, Bakewell, Derbyshire.

ANDERSON, Prof. John Russell, CBE 1980; Professor of Pathology at the Western Infirmary, Glasgow University, 1967–83; *b* 31 May 1918; *s* of William Gregg Anderson and Mary Gordon Adam; *m* 1956, Audrey Margaret Shaw Wilson; two *s* two *d. Educ:* Worksop Coll.; St Andrews Univ. BSc (St Andrews) 1939, MB, ChB (St Andrews) 1942, MD (St Andrews) 1955; MRCP 1961; FRCPGlas 1965; FRCPath 1966; FRSE 1968. RAMC, 1944–47 (Emergency Commn). Lecturer and Senior Lecturer in Pathology, Glasgow Univ., 1947–65; George Holt Prof. of Pathology, Liverpool Univ., 1965–67. Rockefeller travelling fellowship in Medicine, at Rochester, NY, 1953–54. Pres., RCPath, 1978–81 (Vice-Pres., 1975). Hon. FRCPI, 1981. Hon. LLD Dundee, 1981. *Publications:* Autoimmunity, Clinical and Experimental (jtly), 1967; Muir's Textbook of Pathology (jtly), 9th edn 1972, 12th edn 1985; various papers on immunopathology in scientific jls. *Recreations:* squash, ski-ing, gardening. *Address:* Barnellan, Bardowie, Milngavie, Glasgow G62 6EZ.

ANDERSON, Prof. John Stuart, MA, PhD, MSc; FRS 1953; Professor of Inorganic Chemistry, Oxford University, 1963–75, now Emeritus; *b* 9 Jan. 1908; *m* 1935, Joan Taylor; one *s* three *d.* Formerly Dep. Chief Scientific Officer, Chemistry Div., Atomic Energy Research Establishment, Harwell, Berks; Prof. of Inorganic and Physical Chemistry and Head of the Dept of Chemistry, Univ. of Melbourne, Australia, 1954–59; Director of the National Chemical Laboratory (Department of Scientific and Industrial Research), Teddington, 1959–63. Pres., Dalton Div. of Chemical Soc., 1974–76. Hon. Fellow, Indian Acad. of Sciences, 1978. Hon. DSc Bath, 1979. Davy Medal, Royal Soc., 1973. *Address:* Research School of Chemistry, Australian National University, PO Box 4, Canberra, ACT 2600, Australia.

ANDERSON, Josephine, (Mrs Ande Anderson); *see* Barstow, J.

ANDERSON, Dame Judith, DBE 1960; **(Dame Frances Margaret Anderson);** Actress; *b* Adelaide, South Australia, 10 Feb. 1898; *d* of James Anderson Anderson and Jessie Saltmarsh; *m* 1937, Prof. B. H. Lehman (marr. diss. 1939); *m* 1946, Luther Greene (marr. diss. 1950). *Educ:* Norwood High Sch., South Australia. Started Theatre with Julius Knight; toured Australia and America, 1918; has played in: The Dove, 1925; Behold the Bridegroom, 1927; Strange Interlude, 1930; Mourning becomes Electra, 1931; Come of Age, 1934; The Old Maid, 1935; Hamlet, 1936; Macbeth (London), 1937; Family Portrait, 1939; Three Sisters, 1942; Medea (New York, 1947–48; toured America, 1948–49; Paris Internat. Drama Festival, 1955); The Seagull, Edin. Fest., 1960, Sept. at Old Vic; The Oresteia, 1966; Hamlet, 1970. *Films:* Rebecca, Edge of Darkness, Laura, King's Row, Spectre of the Rose, The Red House, Pursued, Tycoon, Cat on a Hot Tin Roof, Macbeth, Don't Bother to Knock, A Man Called Horse, Star Treck III; TV: The Chinese Prime Minister, 1974. *Recreation:* gardening.

ANDERSON, Julian Anthony; Under Secretary, Ministry of Agriculture, Fisheries and Food, since 1982; *b* 12 June 1938; *s* of Sir Kenneth Anderson, *qv; m* 1983, Penelope Ann Slocombe. *Educ:* King Alfred Sch.; Wadham Coll., Oxford (MA). Entered MAFF as Asst Principal, 1961; Asst Private Sec. to Minister of Agriculture, 1964–66; Principal, 1966; seconded to FCO, 1970–73; Asst Sec., MAFF, 1973; seconded as Minister (Food and Agriculture), UK Perm. Rep. to EEC, 1982–85. *Recreations:* music, sport, travel, photography, gardening, DIY. *Address:* c/o Ministry of Agriculture, Fisheries and Food, Whitehall Place, SW1. *T:* 01-233 3000. *Clubs:* United Oxford & Cambridge University, Civil Service.

ANDERSON, Sir Kenneth, KBE 1962 (CBE 1946); CB 1955; *b* 5 June 1906; *s* of Walter Anderson, Exmouth; *m* 1932, Helen Veronica Grose (*d* 1986); one *s* one *d. Educ:* Swindon Secondary Sch.; Wadham Coll., Oxford (MA). Entered India Office, 1928; Asst Sec., 1942; Dep. Financial Adviser to British Military Governor, Germany, 1947–48; Imperial Defence Coll., 1949; Under-Sec., HM Treasury, 1950–51; Dep. Director-General, 1954–66 and Comptroller and Accountant-General, 1952–66, GPO. Officer, Order of Orange-Nassau, 1947. *Address:* 7 Milton Close, N2 0QH. *T:* 01–455 8701. *Club:* United Oxford & Cambridge University.
See also J. A. Anderson.

ANDERSON, Hon. Sir Kevin (Victor), Kt 1980; Judge of the Supreme Court of Victoria, 1969–84; *b* 4 Sept. 1912; *s* of Robert Victor Anderson and Margaret Anderson (*née* Collins); *m* 1942, Claire Margaret Murphy; six *d. Educ:* Xavier Coll., Kew; Melbourne Univ. (LLB). Victorian Crown Law Dept, 1929–42: Courts Branch, 1929–35; Professional Asst, Crown Solicitor's Office, 1935–42; Lt, RAN, 1942–46; Victorian Bar, 1946–69; QC (Victoria) 1962. Chm., Bd of Inquiry into Scientology, 1963–65. Chm., Victorian Bar Council, 1966–67; Treasurer, Australian Law Council, 1966–68. Kt, Australian Assoc. of SMO of Malta, 1979. *Publications:* Stamp Duties in Victoria, 1949, 2nd edn 1968; joint author: Price Control, 1947; Landlord and Tenant Law, 1948, 3rd edn 1958; Victorian Licensing Law, 1952; Victoria Police Manual, 1956, 2nd edn 1969; Workers' Compensation, 1958, 2nd edn 1966; Fossil in the Sandstone: the Recollecting Judge, 1986; (ed) Victorian Law Reports, 1956–69. *Recreations:* yachting, woodworking. *Address:* 12 Power Avenue, Toorak, Victoria 3142, Australia. *T:* 03–202901. *Clubs:* Victoria Racing, Royal Automobile of Victoria, Celtic, Blairgowrie Yacht Squadron (all Melbourne).

ANDERSON, Lindsay (Gordon); film and theatre director; *b* 17 April 1923; 2nd *s* of late Maj.-Gen. A. V. Anderson and Estelle Bell Sleigh. *Educ:* Cheltenham Coll.; Wadham Coll., Oxford. Associate Artistic Director, Royal Court Theatre, 1969–75. Governor, British Film Institute, 1969–70. *Films include:* Wakefield Express, 1953; Thursday's Children (with Guy Brenton), 1954; O Dreamland, 1954; Every Day Except Christmas, 1957; This Sporting Life, 1963; The White Bus, 1966; Raz, Dwa, Trzy (The Singing Lesson), for Warsaw Documentary Studio, 1967; If . . . ., 1968 (Grand Prix, Cannes Fest., 1969); O Lucky Man!, 1973 (Film Critics' Guild award for best film of 1973); In Celebration, 1974; Britannia Hospital, 1982; If You Were There . . . , 1985. *Productions in theatre:* The Waiting of Lester Abbs, 1957; The Long and the Short and the Tall; Progress to the Park; Jazzetry; Serjeant Musgrave's Dance, 1959; The Lily White Boys; Billy Liar; Trials by Logue, 1960; The Fire-Raisers, 1961; The Diary of a Madman, 1963; Andorra, 1964; Julius Caesar, 1964; The Cherry Orchard, 1966, 1983; first Polish production of Inadmissible Evidence (Nie Do Obrony), Warsaw, 1966; In Celebration, 1969; The Contractor, 1969; Home (also NY), 1970; The Changing Room, 1973; The Farm, 1974; Life Class, 1974; What the Butler Saw, 1975; The Sea Gull, 1975; The Bed Before Yesterday, 1975; The Kingfisher, 1977 (NY, 1978); Alice's Boys, 1978; Early Days, 1980; Hamlet, 1981; The Holly and the Ivy, NY, 1982; The Playboy of the Western World, 1984; In Celebration, NY, 1984; Hamlet, Washington, DC, 1985. *Video plays:* Home, 1971; Look Back in Anger, NY, 1980. *Television play:* The Old Crowd, 1979. Editor, film quarterly, Sequence, 1947–51. *Publications:* Making a Film, 1952; About John Ford, 1981; contrib. to Declaration, 1957. *Address:* 9 Stirling Mansions, Canfield Gardens, NW6.

ANDERSON, Marian, (Mrs Orpheus H. Fisher); American contralto; *b* Philadelphia, Pa, 27 Feb. 1902; *m* 1943, Orpheus H. Fisher. *Educ:* Philadelphia; New York; Chicago; and in Europe. MusD Howard Univ., 1938. Singing career began in 1924; 1st prize at Lewisohn Stadium competition, New York, 1925. Has made numerous tours in the United States, Europe, Japan, Israel, India, Pakistan, Korea, etc. Ulrica in Verdi's The Masked Ball, Metropolitan Opera House, New York, 1955. US Delegate to UN, 1958. Has made many recordings. Holds numerous American and other hon. doctorates: Bok Award, 1940. Finnish decoration, 1940; Litteris et Artibus Medal, Sweden, 1952; Yukusho Medal, Japan, 1953; Gimbel Award, 1958; Gold Medal, US Inst. of Arts and Sciences, 1958; US Presidential Medal of Freedom, 1963; Congressional Gold Medal, 1978. *Publication:* My Lord, What a Morning, 1957. *Address:* Danbury, Conn 06810, USA.

ANDERSON, Brig. Hon. Dame Mary Mackenzie; *see* Pihl, Brig. Hon. Dame M. M.

ANDERSON, Vice Adm. Sir Neil (Dudley), KBE 1982 (CBE 1976); CB 1979; Chief of Defence Staff (NZ), 1980–83; *b* 5 April 1927; *s* of Eric Dudley Anderson and Margaret Evelyn (*née* Craig); *m* 1951, Barbara Lillias Romaine Wright; two *s. Educ:* Hastings High Sch.; BRNC. Joined RNZN, 1944; trng and sea service with RN, 1944–49; Korean War Service, 1950–51; qual. as navigation specialist; Navigator: HMS Vanguard, 1952–53; HMNZS Lachlan, 1954; HMS Saintes, 1958–59; Commanding Officer, HMNZS: Taranaki, 1961–62; Waikato, 1968–69; Philomel, 1969–70; Dep. Chief of Def. Staff, 1976–77; Chief of Naval Staff, 1977–80. Lieut 1949, Lt-Comdr 1957, Comdr 1960, Captain 1968, Cdre 1972, Rear Adm. 1977, Vice Adm. 1980. *Recreations:* golf, fishing. *Address:* 36 Beauchamp Street, Karori, Wellington, New Zealand. *T:* 766 257. *Club:* Wellington (Wellington, NZ).

ANDERSON, Sir Norman; *see* Anderson, Sir J. N. D.

ANDERSON, Prof. Philip Warren; Joseph Henry Professor of Physics, Princeton University, New Jersey, since 1975; Consulting Director, Physical Research Laboratory, Bell Telephone Laboratories, NJ, since 1976 (Member of Staff, 1949–76); *b* 13 Dec. 1923; *s* of Prof. H. W. Anderson and Mrs Elsie O. Anderson; *m* 1947, Joyce Gothwaite; one *d. Educ:* Harvard Univ. BS 1943; MA 1947; PhD 1949, Harvard. Naval Res. Lab., Washington, DC, 1943–45 (Chief Petty Officer, USN). Fulbright Lectr, Tokyo Univ., 1952–53; Overseas Fellow, Churchill Coll., Cambridge, 1961–62; Vis. Prof. of Theoretical Physics, Univ. of Cambridge, 1967–75, and Fellow of Jesus College, Cambridge, 1969–75, Hon. Fellow, 1978–; Cherwell-Simon Meml Lectureship, Oxford, 1979–80. Member: Amer. Acad. of Arts and Sciences, 1966; Nat. Acad. of Sciences, US, 1967; For. Mem., Royal Society, London, 1980; Foreign Associate, Accademia Lincei, Rome, 1985. Hon. FInstP, 1986. Hon. DSc Illinois, 1978. O. E. Buckley Prize, Amer. Phys. Soc., 1964; Dannie Heinemann Prize, Akad. Wiss. Göttingen, 1975; (jtly) Nobel Prize for Physics, 1977; Guthrie Medal, Inst. of Physics, 1978; Nat. Medal of Science, US, 1984. *Publications:* Concepts in Solids, 1963; Basic Notions of Condensed Matter Physics, 1984; numerous articles in scholarly jls. *Recreations:* go (Japanese game), rank sho-dan, walking. *Address:* 74 Aunt Molly Road, Hopewell, NJ 08525, USA.

ANDERSON, Reginald, CMG 1974; Chairman, A. B. Jay Ltd, since 1981; *b* 3 Nov. 1921; *s* of late Herbert Anderson and late Anne Mary (*née* Hicks); *m* 1945, Audrey Gabrielle Williams; two *d. Educ:* Palmers, Grays, Essex. Cabinet Office, 1938–40. Served War, RAF, Flt Lt, 1941–46. Ministry of: Supply, 1947–57; Supply Staff, Australia, 1957–59; Aviation, 1960–67; Counsellor, British Embassy, Washington, 1967–70; Asst Under-Sec. of State, 1970–76, Dep. Under-Sec. of State, 1976–81, MoD. *Recreations:* tennis, badminton, golf. *Address:* Reynosa, Heronway, Shenfield, Essex. *T:* Brentwood 213077. *Club:* Royal Air Force.

ANDERSON, Robert Bernerd; lawyer and statesman, United States; Chairman, Robert B. Anderson & Co. Ltd; *b* Burleson, Texas, 4 June 1910; *s* of Robert Lee Anderson and Elizabeth (*née* Haskew); *m* 1935, Ollie Mae Anderson; two *s. Educ:* Weatherford Coll., Texas; Univ. of Texas (LLB). Admitted to Texas Bar, and began law practice, Fort Worth, Texas, 1932; elected to Texas legislature, 1932; Asst Attorney-Gen., Texas, 1932; Prof. of Law, Univ. of Texas, 1933; State Tax Commr, Texas, 1934; Racing Commr, Texas, 1934; Member State Tax Board, 1934; Chm. and Executive Director, Texas Unemployment Commn, 1936; Gen. Counsel for the Waggoner Estate (oil and ranching), 1937–40 (Gen. Man., 1941–53). Secretary of US Navy, 1953–54; Dep. Secretary of Defense, 1954–55; Secretary of the Treasury, 1957–61. Chm., American Gas & Chemical Co. Ltd; Director: Intercontinental Trailsea Corp.; Gray and Co. Public Communications Internat.; Partner, Anderson & Pendleton. Mem. Texas Bar Assoc.; Associate of Bar of City of New York. *Address:* 535 Fifth Avenue, Suite 1004, New York, NY 10017, USA.

ANDERSON, Robert Geoffrey William; Director, National Museums of Scotland, since 1985; *b* 2 May 1944; *er s* of Herbert Patrick Anderson and Kathleen Diana Anderson (*née* Burns); *m* 1973, Margaret Elizabeth Callis Lea; two *s. Educ:* Woodhouse Sch., London; St John's Coll., Oxford (Casberd exhibitioner) (BSc, MA, DPhil). FRSC 1984; FSA 1986. Assistant Keeper: Royal Scottish Museum, 1970–75; Science Museum, 1975–78; Dep. Keeper, Wellcome Museum of History of Medicine, and Sec., Adv. Council, Science Museum, 1978–80; Keeper, Dept of Chemistry, Science Mus., 1980–84; Dir, Royal Scottish Mus., 1984–85. Sec., Royal Scottish Soc. of Arts, 1973–75; Mem. Council: Soc. for History of Alchemy and Chemistry, 1978–; Gp for Scientific, Technological and Medical Collections, 1979–83; British Soc. History of Science, 1981–84; Scottish Museums Council, 1984–; British Nat. Cttee for Hist. of Science, 1985–; Pres., Scientific Instrument Commn, IUHPS, 1982–. Member Editorial Board: Annals of Science, 1981–; Annali di Storia della Scienza, 1986–. Dexter Prize, Amer. Chemical Soc., 1986. *Publications:* The Mariner's Astrolabe, 1972; Edinburgh and Medicine, 1976; (ed) The Early Years of the Edinburgh Medical School, 1976; The Playfair Collection and the Teaching of Chemistry at the University of Edinburgh, 1978; (contrib.) The History of Technology, Vol. VI, ed T. I. Williams, 1978; Science in India, 1982. *Recreation:* books. *Address:* 11 Dryden Place, Edinburgh EH9 1RP. *T:* 031-667 8211. *Club:* Athenæum.

ANDERSON, Prof. Robert Henry; Joseph Levy Professor of Paediatric Cardiac Morphology, Cardiothoracic Institute, University of London, since 1979; *b* 4 April 1942; *s* of Henry Anderson and Doris Amy Anderson (*née* Callear); *m* 1966, Christine (*née* Ibbotson); one *s* one *d. Educ:* Wellington Grammar Sch., Shropshire; Manchester Univ.

BSc (Hons); MB ChB, MRCPath. House Officer, Professorial Surgical Unit, 1966, Medical Unit, 1967, Manchester Royal Infirmary; Asst Lectr in Anatomy, 1967–69, Lectr, 1969–73, Manchester Univ.; MRC Travelling Fellow, Dept of Cardiology, Univ. of Amsterdam, 1973–74; Cardiothoracic Institute, University of London: British Heart Foundn Sen. Res. Fellow and Sen. Lectr in Paediatrics, 1974–77; Joseph Levy Reader in Paediatric Cardiac Morphology, 1977–79. Hon. Prof. of Surgery, Univ. of N Carolina, USA, 1984; Vis. Prof., Univ. of Pittsburgh, Pa, 1985. Excerpta Medica Travel Award, 1977; British Heart Foundn Prize for Cardiovascular Research, 1984. Editor (European), Internat. Jl of Cardiology, 1985–. *Publications:* (ed jtly) Paediatric Cardiology, 1977, vol. 3, 1981, vol. 5, 1983, vol. 6, 1986; (with A. E. Becker) Cardiac Anatomy, 1980; (with E. A. Shinebourne) Current Paediatric Cardiology, 1980; (with A. E. Becker) Pathology of Congenital Heart Disease, 1981; (with M. J. Davies and A. E. Becker) Pathology of the Conduction Tissues, 1983; (jtly) Morphology of Congenital Heart Disease, 1983; (with A. E. Becker) Cardiac Pathology, 1984; (with G. A. H. Miller and M. L. Rigby) The Diagnosis of Congenital Heart Disease, 1985; (with B. R. Wilcox) Surgical Anatomy of the Heart, 1985; over 120 invited chapters in published books and over 230 papers in jls. *Recreations:* golf, tennis, music, wine. *Address:* 60 Earlsfield Road, SW18 3DN. *T:* 01-870 4368. *Club:* Roehampton.

ANDERSON, Robert (Woodruff); playwright; *b* NYC, 28 April 1917; *s* of James Hewston Anderson and Myra Esther (*née* Grigg); *m* 1st, 1940, Phyllis Stohl (*d* 1956); 2nd, 1959, Teresa Wright (marr. diss. 1978). *Educ:* Phillips Exeter Acad.; Harvard Univ. AB (*magna cum laude*) 1939, MA 1940. Served USNR, 1942–46 (Lt); won prize (sponsored by War Dept) for best play written by a serviceman, Come Marching Home, 1945, subseq. prod, Univ. of Iowa and Blackfriars Guild, NY. Rockefeller Fellowship, 1946; taught playwrighting, American Theatre Wing Professional Trng Prog., 1946–50; organized and taught Playwright's Unit, Actors Studio, 1955; Writer in Residence, Univ. of N Carolina, 1969; Faculty, Univ. of Iowa Writers' Workshop, 1976. Member: Playwrights Co., 1953–60; Bd of Governors, American Playwrights Theatre, 1963–; Council, Dramatists Guild, 1954– (Pres., 1971–73); New Dramatists Cttee, 1949– (Pres., 1955–57); Fac., Salzburg Seminar in American Studies, 1968; Vice-Pres., Authors' League of America; Chm., Harvard Bd of Overseers' Cttee to visit the Performing Arts, 1970–76. Wrote and adapted plays for TV and Radio, 1948–53. Elected to Theater Hall of Fame, 1980. *Plays:* Eden Rose, 1948; Love Revisited, 1952; Tea and Sympathy, 1953; All Summer Long, 1954; Silent Night, Lonely Night, 1959; The Days Between, 1965; You Know I Can't Hear You When the Water's Running (four short plays), 1967; I Never Sang For My Father, 1968; Solitaire/Double Solitaire, 1971; Free and Clear, 1981; The Kissing was Always the Best, 1984; *Screenplays:* Tea and Sympathy, 1956; Until They Sail, 1957; The Nun's Story, 1959; The Sand Pebbles, 1965; I Never Sang For My Father, 1970 (Writers Guild Award for Best Screenplay, 1971); The Patricia Neal Story, TV, 1981; *novels:* After, 1973; Getting Up and Going Home, 1978. *Recreations:* photography, tennis. *Address:* Roxbury, Conn 06783, USA. *Club:* Harvard (New York City).

ANDERSON, Roy Arnold; Chairman of the Board, Lockheed Corporation, since 1977; *b* Ripon, Calif, 15 Dec. 1920; *s* of Carl Gustav Anderson and Esther Marie Johnson; *m* 1948, Betty Leona Boehme; two *s* two *d*. *Educ:* Ripon Union High Sch.; Humphreys Sch. of Business; Stanford Univ. AB 1947; MBA 1949; Phi Beta Kappa; CPA. Served War, USNR, 1942–46 and 1950–52. Westinghouse Electric Corporation: Manager, Factory Accounting, 1952–56; Lockheed Missiles and Space Co.: Manager, Accounting and Finance, and Dir, Management Controls, 1956–65; Lockheed Georgia Co.: Dir of Finance, 1965–68; Lockheed Corporation: Asst Treas., 1968–69; Vice-Pres. and Controller, 1969–71; Sen. Vice-Pres., Finance, 1971–75; Vice-Chm. of Board, also Chief Financial and Admin. Officer, 1975–77. Director of cos in California. *Recreation:* tennis. *Address:* c/o Lockheed Corporation, PO Box 551, Burbank, California 91520, USA. *T:* (818) 847–6452; (office) 2555 N Hollywood Way, Burbank, California 91520, USA.

ANDERSON, Prof. Roy Malcolm, FRS 1986; Professor, since 1982, and Head of Department of Pure and Applied Biology, since 1984, Imperial College, London University; *b* 12 April 1947; *s* of James Anderson and Betty Watson-Weatherburn; *m* 1975, Dr Mary Joan Anderson. *Educ:* Duncombe Sch., Bengeo; Richard Hale Sch., Hertford; Imperial Coll., London (BSc, ARCS, PhD, DIC). CBiol, FIBiol. IBM Research Fellow, Univ. of Oxford, 1971–73; Lectr, King's Coll., London, 1973–77; Lectr, 1977–80, Reader, 1980–82, Imperial Coll. Zoological Soc. Scientific Medal, 1982; Huxley Meml Medal, 1983; Wright Meml Medal, 1986. *Publications:* (ed) Population Dynamics of Infectious Disease Agents: theory and applications, 1982; (ed jtly) Population Biology of Infectious Diseases, 1982. *Recreations:* hill walking, croquet, natural history, photography. *Address:* Ridgewood, Crampshaw Lane, Ashtead, Surrey KT21 2UJ. *T:* Ashtead 72767. *Club:* Athenæum.

ANDERSON, Thomas, CBE 1972; MD, FRCPE, FRCPGlas, FFCM; Henry Mechan Professor of Public Health, University of Glasgow, 1964–71, retired (Professor of Infectious Diseases, 1959–64); *b* 7 Dec. 1904; *e s* of Thomas Anderson and Mary (*née* Johnstone); *m* 1935, Helen Turner Massey (*d* 1974), one *s* three *d*. *Educ:* The High Sch. of Glasgow; Glasgow Univ. (MB, ChB 1928; MD, Hons and Bellahouston Gold Medal, 1945); MRCPE 1934; FRCPE 1940; FRCPGlas 1947. Dep. Phys., Ruchill Hosp., 1933–41; Phys. Supt, Knightswood Hosp., 1941–47; Sen. Lectr, subseq. Reader, Infectious Diseases, Glasgow Univ., 1947–59. Mem., Industrial Injuries Adv. Council, 1971–77. Formerly Consultant in Infectious Diseases to Western Region of Scotland. Founder, Scottish-Scandinavian Conf. on Infectious Disease. Hon. Member: Soc. for Study of Infectious Disease; Royal Medico-Chirurgical Soc., Glasgow; Swedish Med. Assoc.; Soc. for Social Med.; Section of Epidemiology and Preventive Med., RSM. Pres., Arran Heritage Museum, 1985–. *Publications:* various, on Infectious Diseases, in med. scientific jls. *Recreation:* bowls. *Address:* Braeside, Brodick, Isle of Arran KA27 8AF.

ANDERSON, Walter Charles, CBE 1968; Solicitor; General Secretary, National and Local Government Officers Association, 1957–73; Member, IBA, 1973–78; *b* 3 Dec. 1910; *s* of William Walter John Anderson and Mary Theresa McLoughlin; *m* 1941, Doris Jessie Deacon; two *s*. *Educ:* Bootle Grammar Sch. and Wigan Grammar Sch.; Liverpool Univ. (LLB). Articled Clerk, J. W. Wall & Co., Solicitors, Bootle, Liverpool, 1930–33; Asst Solicitor, Bootle, 1933–34; Dep. Town Clerk, Heywood, 1934–37; Asst Solicitor, Nalgo, 1937–41; Royal Air Force, 1941–45; Legal Officer, Nalgo, 1945–50; Dep. Gen. Sec., Nalgo, 1950–57; Mem., Gen. Council of TUC, 1965–73. Member: Fulton Cttee on Civil Service Recruitment, Structure, Management and Training, 1966–68; Nat. Insurance Adv. Cttee, 1970–74; Industrial Injuries Adv. Council, 1970–74; Nat. Inst. of Econ. and Social Res., 1970–76; Industrial Arbitration Bd, Workpeople's Rep., 1972; Royal Commn on Civil Liability and Compensation for Personal Injury, 1973–78. *Publication:* Simonds' Local Government Superannuation Act, 1937 (rev. and ed), 1947. *Recreations:* sport, gardening. *Address:* 1 The Comyns, Bushey, Watford WD2 1HN. *T:* 01–950 3708.

ANDERSON, (William) Eric (Kinloch), MA, BLitt, DLitt, FRSE; Headmaster of Eton College, since 1980; *b* 27 May 1936; *er s* of W. J. Kinloch Anderson, Edinburgh; *m* 1960, Poppy, *d* of W. M. Mason, Skipton; one *s* one *d*. *Educ:* George Watson's Coll.; Univ. of St Andrews (MA; Hon. DLitt); Balliol Coll., Oxford (BLitt). Asst Master: Fettes Coll., 1960–64, 1966–67; Gordonstoun, 1964–66; Housemaster, Arniston House, Fettes Coll., 1967–70; Headmaster: Abingdon Sch., 1970–75; Shrewsbury Sch., 1975–80. Pres., Edinburgh Sir Walter Scott Club, 1981. *Publications:* The Written Word, 1964; (ed) The Journal of Sir Walter Scott, 1972; articles and reviews. *Recreations:* golf, fishing. *Address:* Eton College, Windsor, Berks.

ANDERSON, Professor Sir (William) Ferguson, Kt 1974; OBE 1961; David Cargill Professor of Geriatric Medicine, University of Glasgow, 1965–79; *b* 8 April 1914; *s* of James Kirkwood Anderson, Capt. 7th Scottish Rifles (killed on active service Gaza 1917) and late Sarah Barr Anderson; *m* 1940, Margaret Battison Gebbie; one *s* two *d*. *Educ:* Merchiston Castle Sch.; Glasgow Academy; Glasgow Univ. (MB Hons 1936; MD Hons 1942, with Bellahouston Gold Medal). FRFPSG 1939 (now FRCPG); FRCPE 1961; FRCP 1964; FRCPI 1975; FRCP (C) 1976. Med. Registrar, Univ. Med. Clinic, 1939–41; Army Service, 1941–46, Major (Med. Specialist). Sen. Lectr, Dept of Materia Medica and Therapeutics, Univ. of Glasgow, and Asst Phys., Univ. Med. Clinic, Stobhill Hosp., Glasgow, 1946–49; Sen. Univ. Lectr, Medical Unit, also Hon. Cons. Phys., Cardiff Royal Infirmary, 1949–52; Physician in Geriatric Medicine, Stobhill Gen. Hosp., Adviser in Diseases of Old Age and Chronic Sickness, Western Reg. Hosp. Bd, Scotland, 1952–74. Mem., adv. panel on organization of medical care, WHO, 1973–83. Fogarty Internat. Scholar, Nat. Inst. on Aging, Bethesda, 1979. President: RCPGlas, 1974–76; British Geriatric Soc., 1975–78; BMA, 1977–78. Vice-President: Age Concern (Scotland); Abbeyfield Soc. Chairman, Scottish Retirement Council; Hon. Pres., Crossroads (Scotland) Care Attendant Schemes. Hon. Chairman: St Mungo's Old Folks' Club, Glasgow; European Clin. Sect., Internat. Assoc. Gerontology; Tenovus (Scotland). Member: Hanover Housing Assoc (Scotland); Turnberry Trust. Fellow, Australasian Coll. of Technologists, 1971; Hon. Fellow, Amer. Coll. of Physicians, 1980. St Mungo Prize, Glasgow, 1968; Brookdale Award, Gerontological Soc. of America, 1984. KStJ 1974. *Publications:* Practical Management of the Elderly, 1967, 4th edn (with Dr B. Williams) 1983; Current Achievements in Geriatrics (ed with Dr B. Isaacs), 1964; articles on Geriatric Medicine and Preventive aspects of Geriatrics in current med. jls. *Recreation:* walking. *Address:* Rodel, Moor Road, Strathblane, Glasgow G63 9EX. *T:* Blanefield 70862. *Clubs:* University Staff, Royal Scottish Automobile (Glasgow).

ANDERTON, (Cyril) James, CBE 1982; QPM 1977; Chief Constable, Greater Manchester Police Force, since 1976 (Deputy Chief Constable, 1975); *b* 24 May 1932; *o s* of late James Anderton and late Lucy Anderton (*née* Occleshaw); *m* 1955, Joan Baron; one *d*. *Educ:* St Matthew's Church Sch., Highfield; Wigan Grammar Sch. Certif. Criminology, Manchester Univ., 1960; Sen. Comd Course, Police Coll., 1967. Corps of Royal Mil. Police, 1950–53; Constable to Chief Inspector, Manchester City Police, 1953–67; Chief Supt, Cheshire Constab., 1967–68; Asst Chief Constable, Leicester and Rutland Constab., 1968–72; Asst to HM Chief Inspector of Constab. for England and Wales, Home Office, London, 1972–75; Dep. Chief Constable, Leics Constabulary, 1975. President: Manchester and Dist RSPCA, 1984– (Vice-Pres., 1981–84); Manchester Br., BIM, 1984–; British Coll. of Accordionists, 1984– (Chm. Governing Council, 1972–77; Vice-Pres., 1977–84); Leics Bn, Boys' Bde, 1972–76; Manchester NSPCC Jun. League, 1979–; Christian Police Assoc., 1979–81; Member: Manchester Adv. Bd, Salvation Army, 1977–; Exec. Cttee, Manchester NSPCC, 1979–; NW Regional Bd, BIM, 1985–; County Dir, St John Amb. Assoc., Greater Manchester, 1976–; Vice-President: Manchester YMCA, 1976–; Adelphi Lads' Club, Salford, 1979–; Sharp Street Ragged Sch., Manchester, 1982–; Manchester Schools Football Assoc., 1976–; Greater Manchester East Scout Council, 1977–; Greater Manchester Fedn of Boys' Clubs, 1984–; Hon. National Vice-Pres., The Boys' Bde, 1983–. Patron: NW Counties Schs ABA, 1980–; NW Campaign for Kidney Donors, 1983–; NW Eye Res. Trust, 1982–; N Manchester Hosp. Broadcasting Service, 1983–; Internat. Spinal Res. Trust (Greater Manchester Cttee), 1983–; Trustee, Piccadilly Radio Community Trust, 1983–. CBIM 1980; Hon. FBCA 1976; Hon. RNCM 1984. Member: RSCM; Corps of Royal Mil. Police Assoc.; National Geographical Soc.; St Andrew's Soc. of Manchester; Manchester Lit. and Phil. Soc. Mancunian of The Year, 1980. CStJ 1982 (OStJ 1978). Cross Pro Ecclesia et Pontifice, 1982. Chevalier de la Confrérie des Chevaliers du Tastevin, 1985. *Recreations:* home and family. *Address:* Greater Manchester Police Force, Police Headquarters, Chester House, Boyer Street, Manchester M16 0RE. *Clubs:* Royal Commonwealth Society, Special Forces, St John House.

ANDERTON, James, CBE 1966 (OBE 1956); CEng, MIMinE; *b* 3 Nov. 1904; *s* of Richard and Rebecca Anderton; *m* 1st, 1931, Margaret Asbridge (*d* 1945); no *c*; 2nd, 1949, Lucy Mackie; no *c*. *Educ:* Wigan and District Mining and Technical Coll. Manager of various collieries. On nationalisation of mining industry in 1947 became Asst Agent for a group of collieries in St Helens, Lancs; later made Prod. Man., St Helens Area, N Western Div.; Area Gen. Man., St Helens Area, 1949; Dep. Chm., Scottish Div., NCB, 1958. Chm., North Western Div., NCB, 1961–67. Dir, Gullick Ltd, Wigan, 1967–. Hon. MIMinE, 1968. Medal, Instn of Mining Engineers, 1965. Alfried Krupp von Bohlen und Halbach Prize for Energy Research, 1979. *Recreation:* golf. *Address:* The Knoll, Mere Road, Newton-le-Willows, Merseyside. *T:* Newton-le-Willows 5901.

ANDERTON, James; *see* Anderton, C. J.

ANDOVER, Viscount; Alexander Charles Michael Winston Robsahm Howard; *b* 17 Sept. 1974; *s* and *heir* of 21st Earl of Suffolk and Berkshire, *qv*.

ANDREAE-JONES, William Pearce; QC 1984; a Recorder of the Crown Court, since 1982; *b* 21 July 1942; *s* of Willie and Minnie Charlotte Andreae-Jones; *m* 1977, Anne Marie Cox; one *s*. *Educ:* Canford Sch.; Corpus Christi Coll., Cambridge (BA Hons). Called to the Bar, Inner Temple, 1965. *Address:* Vicar's Hill Lodge, Boldre, Lymington, Hants. *T:* Lymington 78404. *Clubs:* Royal Thames Yacht (Rear Cdre, 1981–84); Frewen (Oxford); Leander (Henley); Royal Lymington Yacht.

ANDRESKI, Prof. Stanislav Leonard; Professor of Sociology, University of Reading, 1964–84, now Emeritus; Professor of Comparative Sociology, Polish University in London, since 1982; *b* 18 May 1919; two *s* two *d*. *Educ:* Secondary sch. in Poznan, 1928–37, Univ. of Poznan (Faculty of Economics and Jurisprudence), 1938–39; London Sch. of Economics, 1942–43. Military service in Polish Army (with exception of academic year 1942–43), 1937–38 and 1939–47 (commissioned, 1944). Lectr in Sociology, Rhodes Univ., SA, 1947–53; Sen. Research Fellow in Anthropology, Manchester Univ., 1954–56; Lectr in Economics, Acton Technical Coll., London, 1956–57; Lectr in Management Studies, Brunel Coll. of Technology, London, 1957–60; Prof. of Sociology, Sch. of Social Sciences, Santiago, Chile, 1960–61; Sen. Res. Fellow, Nigerian Inst. of Social and Economic Research, Ibadan, Nigeria, 1962–64; Hd, Dept of Sociology, Univ. of Reading, 1964–82. Vis. Prof. of Sociology and Anthropology, City Coll., City Univ. of New York, 1968–69; Vis. Prof. of Sociology, Simon Frazer Univ., Vancouver, 1976–77. *Publications:* Military Organization and Society (Internat. Library of Sociology and Social Reconstruction), 1954 (2nd aug. edn, 1968, USA, 1968, paperback, 1969); Class Structure and Social Development (with Jan Ostaszewski and others), (London), 1964 (in Polish); Elements of Comparative Sociology (The Nature of Human Society Series), 1964, Spanish edn 1972;

The Uses of Comparative Sociology (American edn of the foregoing), 1965, paperback 1969; Parasitism and Subversion: the case of Latin America, 1966 (NY, 1967, rev. edn 1968, etc; Buenos Aires (in Spanish with a postscript), 1968; paperback edn, London, 1970); The African Predicament: a study in pathology of modernisation, 1968 (USA, 1969); Social Sciences as Sorcery, 1972, Spanish edn 1973, German edn 1974, French edn 1975, Italian edn 1977, Japanese edn 1982; Prospects of a Revolution in the USA, 1973; The Essential Comte, 1974; Reflections on Inequality, 1975; Max Weber's Insights and Errors, 1984; Editor: Herbert Spencer, Principles of Sociology, 1968; Herbert Spencer, Structure, Function and Evolution, 1970; Max Weber on Capitalism, Bureaucracy and Religion, 1983; contribs to: A Dictionary of the Social Sciences (UNESCO); A Dictionary of Sociology (ed D. Mitchell); Brit. Jl of Sociology; Japanese Jl of Sociology; The Nature of Fascism (ed S. Woolf); Science Jl, Man, European Jl of Sociology, Encounter, etc. *Recreations:* sailing, horse-riding. *Address:* Farriers, Village Green, Upper Basildon, Berkshire RG8 8LS. *T:* Upper Basildon 671318.

ANDREW, Rt. Rev. Agnellus Matthew, OFM; DD; (His Excellency the Right Reverend Agnellus Andrew); Bishop of Numana; Chairman, Communications Committee of the Episcopal Conference of England and Wales, since 1983; *b* 27 May 1908; *s* of Hugh Andrew and Mary Andrew (*née* Burns). *Educ:* Jesuit College, Garnet Hill; London Univ. Entered Franciscan Order, 1925; ordained priest, 1932; parish, missionary and retreat work, Manchester, 1932–55; Asst Chaplain, Manchester Univ., 1939–42. Began broadcasting career, 1942; Roman Catholic Adviser, BBC, 1946; attended BBC Staff College, 1946 and 1956; Assistant to Head of Religious Broadcasting, BBC, Director and Producer, 1955–67; Adviser to IBA, 1968–75; TV Commentator for many Papal and national occasions. President: Internat. Catholic Assoc. for Radio and Television (UNDA), 1968–80 (Life Pres. of Honour); Catholic Media Council, 1979–; Churches' Advisory Cttee for Local Broadcasting; Founder (1955) and Director, Nat. Catholic Radio and TV Centre, Hatch End, 1955–80, now Director Emeritus and Trustee; Exec. Head, Vatican Commn for Communication, 1980–83; Mem. Adv. Bd, Communications Dept, Gregorian Univ., Rome. DD, Gregorian Univ., Rome, 1980. *Publications:* numerous contribs to media and religious jls. *Recreation:* music (founded the Greyfriars Players, choral and orchestral society). *Address:* St Ninian's, Oakleigh Road, Hatch End, Middlesex. *Clubs:* BBC, KSC.

ANDREW, Dr Christopher Maurice, FRHistS; Fellow since 1967, and Senior Tutor since 1981, Corpus Christi College, Cambridge; *b* 23 July 1941; *s* of Maurice Viccars Andrew and Freda Mary (*née* Sandall); *m* 1962, Jennifer Ann Alicia Garratt; one *s* two *d*. *Educ:* Norwich Sch.; Corpus Christi Coll., Cambridge (MA, PhD). FRHistS 1976. Res. Fellow, Gonville and Caius Coll., Cambridge, 1965–67; Dir of Studies in History, Corpus Christi Coll., Cambridge, 1967–81; Univ. Lectr in History, 1972–. Ext. Examr in History, NUI, 1977–84. Specialist Adviser, H of C Select Cttee on Educn, Science and the Arts, 1982–83. Editor: The Historical Journal, 1976–85; Intelligence and National Security, 1986–. *Publications:* Théophile Delcasse and the making of the Entente Cordiale, 1968; The First World War: causes and consequences, 1970 (vol. 19 of Hamlyn History of the World); (with A. S. Kanya-Forstner) France Overseas: the First World War and the climax of French imperial expansion, 1981; (ed with Prof. D. Dilks) The Missing Dimension: governments and intelligence communities in the Twentieth Century, 1984; Secret Service: the making of the British Intelligence Community, 1985; Codebreaking and Signals Intelligence, 1985; broadcasts and articles on mod. history, Association football, secret intelligence, internat. relations. *Address:* 67 Grantchester Meadows, Cambridge CB3 9JL. *T:* Cambridge 353773.

ANDREW, Prof. Colin, FIMechE; Professor of Manufacturing Engineering, Cambridge University, since 1986; Managing Director, Bristol Technical Developments Ltd, since 1985; *b* 22 May 1934; *s* of Arnold Roy and Kathleen Andrew; *m* 1952, Ruth E. Probert; two *s* two *d*. *Educ:* Bristol Grammar Sch.; Christ's Coll., Cambridge Univ. MA; PhD. Res. Engr, Rolls-Royce, 1955–58; research, Cambridge, 1958–60; Develt Engr, James Archdale & Co., 1960–61; Bristol University: Lectr, 1961–68; Reader, 1968–71; Prof. of Applied Mechanics, 1971–82; Hon. Prof., 1982–85. Man. Dir, Flamgard Ltd, 1982–85. Chairman: Engrg Processes Cttee, SERC, 1981–83; Production Cttee, SERC, 1983–84; Mem., Technology Sub-Cttee, UGC, 1986–. *Publications:* (jtly) Creep Feed Grinding, 1985; papers in scientific jls. *Address:* 17 High Street, Orwell, Cambs. *T:* Cambridge 207662; Christ's College, Cambridge, CB2 3BU.

ANDREW, Prof. Edward Raymond, MA, PhD, ScD (Cambridge); FRS 1984; CPhys; FInstP; FRSE; Graduate Research Professor, University of Florida, since 1983; *b* Boston, Lincs, 27 June 1921; *o s* of late Edward Richard Andrew and Anne Andrew; *m* 1948, Mary Ralph Farnham (*decd* 1965); two *d*; *m* 1972, Eunice Tinning. *Educ:* Wellingborough Sch.; Christ's (Open Scholarship) and Pembroke Colls, Univ. of Cambridge. Scientific Officer, Royal Radar Establishment, Malvern, 1942–45; Cavendish Laboratory, Cambridge, 1945–48; Stokes Student, Pembroke Coll., Cambridge, 1947–49; Commonwealth Fund Fellow, Harvard Univ., 1948–49; Lectr in Natural Philosophy, Univ. of St Andrews, 1949–54; Prof. of Physics, University of Wales, Bangor, 1954–64; Lancashire-Spencer Prof. of Physics, 1964–83, and Dean of Faculty of Science, 1975–78, Univ. of Nottingham. Vis. Prof. of Physics, Univ. of Florida, 1969–70. President: Groupement Ampère, 1974–80 (Hon. Pres., 1980–); Internat. Soc. of Magnetic Resonance, 1984–; Chm., Standing Conf. of Profs of Physics, 1976–79; Mem. Council, European Physical Soc., 1976–79; Chm., British Radio Spectroscopy Gp, 1981–83 (Founder-Chm., 1956–59); Mem., Bd of Trustees, Soc. of Magnetic Resonance in Medicine, 1983–. Hon. DSc Univ. of Turku, 1980. Wellcome Medal and Prize, Royal Soc., 1984. Editor, Physics Reports, 1974–; Editor-in-Chief, Magnetic Resonance in Medicine, 1983–; Mem., Editorial Bd, Chemical Physics Letters, 1984–. *Publications:* Nuclear Magnetic Resonance, 1955; scientific papers in learned jls. *Recreation:* travel. *Address:* Department of Physics, University of Florida, 215 Williamson Hall, Gainesville, Florida 32611, USA.

ANDREW, Herbert Henry; QC 1982; **His Honour Judge Andrew;** a Circuit Judge, since 1984; *b* 26 July 1928; *s* of Herbert Henry Andrew and Nora Andrew (*née* Gough); *m* 1966, Annette Josephine Colbert; two *s* two *d*. *Educ:* Preston Grammar Sch.; Queens' Coll., Cambridge (BA). Called to the Bar, Gray's Inn, 1952; practised on Northern Circuit, 1953–84; a Recorder, 1978–84. *Recreation:* fell walking. *Address:* Peel House, 5/7 Harrington Street, Liverpool L2 9QA. *T:* 051–236 4321. *Club:* Liverpool Racquet.

ANDREW, Sir Robert (John), KCB 1986 (CB 1979); Permanent Under-Secretary of State, Northern Ireland Office, since 1984; *b* 25 Oct. 1928; *s* of late Robert Young Andrew; *m* 1963, Elizabeth, *d* of late Walter de Courcy Bayley; two *s*. *Educ:* King's College Sch., Wimbledon; Merton Coll., Oxford (MA). Intelligence Corps, 1947–49. Joined Civil Service, 1952: Asst Principal, War Office, Principal, 1957; Min. of Defence, 1963; Asst Sec., 1965; Defence Counsellor, UK Delegn to NATO, 1967–70. Private Sec. to Sec. of State for Defence, 1971–73; Under-Sec., CSD, 1973–75; Asst Under-Sec. of State, MoD, 1975–76; Dep. Under-Sec. of State, Home Office, 1976–83. Conservator of Wimbledon and Putney Commons. Governor, King's College Sch. *Recreations:* gardening, carpentry. *Address:* c/o Northern Ireland Office, Whitehall SW1A 2AZ. *Club:* United Oxford & Cambridge University.

ANDREW, Sydney Percy Smith, FRS 1976; FEng, FIChemE, MIMechE; ICI Senior Research Associate, Group Manager, Catalysts and Chemicals Research, 1963–76; *b* 16 May 1926; *s* of Harold C. Andrew and Kathleen M. (*née* Smith); *m* 1986, Ruth Harrison Kenyon (*née* Treanor). *Educ:* Barnard Castl Sch.; King's Coll., Durham Univ. (Open Schol.; BSc); Trinity Hall, Cambridge (Schol. and Prizeman; MA). Joined ICI Billingham Div., 1950; Chemical Engrg Res., 1951; Plant Engr, 1953; Section Manager: Reactor Res., 1955; Process Design, 1959. Chm., Res. Cttee, IChemE. Hon. DSc Leeds, 1979. *Publications:* Catalyst Handbook, 1970; various papers in chemical engrg, applied chemistry and plant physiology. *Recreations:* archaeology, ancient and medieval history. *Address:* 1 The Wynd, Stainton in Cleveland, Middlesbrough TS8 9BP. *T:* Middlesbrough 596348.

ANDREWES, Antony, MBE 1945; FBA 1957; Wykeham Professor of Ancient History, Oxford, 1953–77; Fellow of New College, Oxford, 1946–77, Hon. Fellow, since 1978; *b* 12 June 1910; *s* of late P. L. Andrewes; *m* 1938, Alison Blakeway (*née* Hope) (*d* 1983); two *d*. *Educ:* Winchester; New College, Oxford. Fellow of Pembroke Coll., Oxford, 1933–46. Intelligence Corps, 1941–45. Comdr of Order of Phœnix, Greece, 1978. *Publications:* (with R. Meiggs) revised edition of Sir George Hill's Sources for Greek History, 1951; The Greek Tyrants, 1955; The Greeks, 1967; (with K. J. Dover) Vol. IV of A. W. Gomme's Historical Commentary on Thucydides, 1970, Vol. V, 1981; articles in Classical Quarterly, etc. *Address:* 13 Manor Place, Oxford. *T:* Oxford 248807.

ANDREWES, Sir Christopher (Howard), Kt 1961; FRS 1939; Deputy Director, National Institute for Medical Research, 1952–June 1961 (Member of Scientific Staff from 1927) and in charge of World Influenza Centre (WHO) until June 1961; *b* 7 June 1896; *s* of late Sir Frederick William Andrewes, MD, FRS and Phyllis Mary Hamer; *m* 1927, Kathleen Helen Lamb (*d* 1984); three *s*. *Educ:* Highgate Sch.; St Bartholomew's Hospital. Surgeon Sub-Lt (RNVR), 1918–19; MRCS, LRCP, 1921, MB BS London (Univ. Gold Medal), 1921, MD London (Univ. Gold Medal), 1922, MRCP, 1923; FRCP, 1935; House Physician and Asst to Medical Unit St Bartholomew's Hospital, 1921–23 and 1925–26; Assistant Resident Physician, Hospital of the Rockefeller Institute, New York City, 1923–25; William Julius Mickle Fellowship, Univ. of London, 1931; Oliver-Sharpey Lectureship, Royal Coll. of Physicians, 1934; Bisset-Hawkins Medal, RCP, 1947; Stewart Prize, BMA, 1952; Robert Koch Gold Medal, 1979; Hon LLD Aberdeen 1963; Hon. MD Lund, 1968. *Publications:* Viruses of Vertebrates, 1964, 4th edn (with H. G. Pereira and P. Wildy) 1978; The Common Cold, 1965; Viruses and Evolution (Huxley lecture), 1966; Natural History of Viruses, 1967; The Lives of Wasps and Bees, 1969; Viruses and Cancer, 1970. *Recreation:* natural history, especially entomology. *Address:* Overchalke, Coombe Bissett, Salisbury, Wilts. *T:* Coombe Bissett 201.

ANDREWES, Edward David Eden; Deputy Chairman and Managing Director, Tube Investments Ltd, 1972–75; *b* Portmadoc, 4 Oct. 1909; *s* of Edward and Norah Andrewes; *m* 1935, Katherine Sheila (*d* 1984), *d* of Brig. W. B. G. Barne, CBE, DSO; one *s* two *d*. *Educ:* Repton Sch.; Oriel Coll., Oxford (BA). Admitted Solicitor, 1935. Joined Tube Investments Ltd, 1935. Former Dir, Maen Offeren Slate Quarry Co. Ltd. Trustee, Cheshire Foundn, 1976–80. Legion of Merit (USA). *Recreations:* gardening, hunting, shooting, fishing. *Address:* Stockton House, Worcester WR6 6UT. *T:* Eardiston 272. *Club:* Boodle's.

ANDREWS; *see* Burt-Andrews.

ANDREWS, David Roger Griffith, CBE 1981; Chairman, Gwion Ltd, since 1986; *b* 27 March 1933; *s* of C. H. R. Andrews and G. M. Andrews; *m* 1963, Dorothy Ann Campbell; two *s* one *d*. *Educ:* Abingdon Sch.; Pembroke Coll., Oxford (MA). ACMA, CBIM. Pirelli-General, 1956–59; Ford Motor Company, 1960–69: Controller: Product Engrg, 1965–66; Transmission and Chassis Div., 1967; European Sales Ops, 1967–69; Asst Controller, Ford of Europe, 1969; BLMC: Controller, 1970; Finance Dir, Austin Morris, 1971–72; Man. Dir, Power and Transmission Div., 1973–75; British Leyland Ltd: Man. Dir, Leyland International, 1975–77; Exec. Vice Chm., BL Ltd, 1977–82; Chm., Leyland Gp and Land Rover Gp, 1981–82; Chm. and Chief Exec., Land Rover-Leyland, 1982–86. Member: CBI Council, 1981–86; Exec. Cttee, SMMT, 1981–86; Open Univ. Visiting Cttee, 1982–85. FRSA. *Recreations:* reading, sailing. *Address:* Gainford, Mill Lane, Gerrards Cross, Bucks SL9 8BA. *T:* Gerrards Cross 884310.

ANDREWS, Derek Henry, CB 1984; CBE 1970; Deputy Secretary, Ministry of Agriculture, Fisheries and Food, since 1981; *b* 17 Feb. 1933; *s* of late Henry Andrews and Emma Jane Andrews; *m* 1956, Catharine May (*née* Childe) (*d* 1982); two *s* one *d*. *Educ:* LSE. BA (Hons) 1955. Ministry of Agriculture, Fisheries and Food: Asst Principal, 1957; Asst Private Sec. to Minister of Agriculture, Fisheries and Food, 1960–61; Principal, 1961; Asst Sec., 1968; Private Sec. to Prime Minister, 1966–70; Harvard Univ., USA, 1970–71; Under-Sec., 1973. *Address:* Ministry of Agriculture, Fisheries and Food, Whitehall Place, SW1.

ANDREWS, Éamonn, CBE; Television Compère; Broadcaster; Writer; *b* 19 Dec. 1922; *s* of William and Margaret Andrews; *m* 1951, Gráinne Bourke; one *s* two *d*. *Educ:* Irish Christian Brothers, Synge Street, Dublin. Radio Eireann broadcaster (boxing commentaries, general sports commentating, interview programmes, etc.), 1941–50; first broadcast for the BBC, 1950; first appeared on BBC Television, 1951; BBC programmes included: What's My Line?, This Is Your Life, Sports Report, Crackerjack, Playbox; also boxing commentaries, variety, interview and general sports programmes. Chm. Radio Eireann Statutory Authority, charged with establishment of television in Ireland, 1960–66; joined ABC Television, 1964, Thames Television, 1968; ITV programmes include: This Is Your Life, Today, Time for Business, Eamonn Andrews Show, Top of the World, What's My Line. Former All-Ireland Amateur Junior Boxing Champion (Middle Weight). Knight of St Gregory, 1964. CBE 1970. *Publications:* The Moon is Black (play), 1941; This Is My Life (autobiog.), 1963; Surprise of Your Life, 1978; articles for magazines and newspapers. *Recreations:* walking and talking. *Address:* Windsor House, Heathfield Gardens, Chiswick, W4 4ND. *Clubs:* Irish, Royal Automobile.

ANDREWS, Brig. George Lewis Williams, CBE 1960; DSO 1944; *b* 1 July 1910; *o s* of Captain C. G. W. Andrews, The Border Regt (killed in action, 1914) and of late Mrs Diana Gambier-Parry (*née* Norrington); *m* 1938, Marianne, *d* of late Carl Strindberg, Stockholm and late Fru Greta Winbergh (*née* Skjöldebrand); one *s*. *Educ:* Haileybury; Sandhurst. Commissioned 2nd Lieut, The Seaforth Highlanders, 1930; active service, Palestine, 1936. Served War of 1939–45; BEF, 1939, MEF, 1941–43, BLA, 1944–45; Comd 2nd Bn The Seaforth Highlanders, 1943–45. Comd 1st Bn Seaforth Highlanders, 1953–54; Comd 152nd Highland Infantry Brigade (TA), 1954–57; Assistant Commandant, RMA Sandhurst, 1957–60. Hon. Col, 2nd Bn 51st Highland Volunteers, 1975–79. Lieut-Col, 1953; Colonel, 1955; Hon. Brig., 1960; psc 1940; jssc 1948. Chevalier, Order of Leopold, Belgium, 1945; Croix de Guerre with palm, Belgium, 1945. *Address:* West Kingsteps, Nairn, Scotland. *T:* Nairn 53231.

ANDREWS, Lt-Col Harold Marcus E.; *see* Ervine-Andrews.

ANDREWS, Harry (Fleetwood), CBE 1966; Actor since 1933; *b* 10 Nov. 1911. *Educ:* Tonbridge; Wrekin Coll. With Liverpool Repertory, 1933–35. Played Horatio in

Hamlet, New York 1936; John Gielgud's Season, 1937; served War of 1939–45 (despatches); with Old Vic, 1945–49; Bolingbroke, Mirabel, Warwick in St Joan; Shakespeare Memorial Theatre; Wolsey, Macduff Brutus, Bolingbroke in Henry IV Pts I and II, 1949–51; Enobarbus, Buckingham, Kent, 1953; Othello, Claudius, 1956; Menenius in Coriolanus, 1959; Casanova in Camino Real, Phoenix, 1957; Henry VIII, Old Vic, 1958; Allenby in Ross, Haymarket, 1960; Rockhart in The Lizard on the Rock, Phoenix, 1962; Ekhart in Baal, Phoenix, 1963; Crampton in You Never Can Tell, Haymarket, 1966; Lear, Royal Court, 1971; Ivan in The Family, Haymarket, 1978; Serebryakov in Uncle Vanya, Haymarket, 1982; The General in A Patriot for Me, Haymarket, 1983, Los Angeles, 1984. Films: Red Beret, Helen of Troy, Alexander the Great, Hill in Korea, Moby Dick, St Joan, Dreyfus, Ice Cold in Alex, Solomon and Sheba, Question of Larceny, Circle of Deception, The Best of Enemies, The Inspector, Barabbas, Reach for Glory, Nine Hours to Rama, 55 Days at Peking, The Snout, The Best of Everything, The Hill, The Agony and the Ecstasy, The Sands of Kalahari, Modesty Blaise, The Deadly Affair, The Jokers, The Long Duel, A Dandy in Aspic, The Charge of The Light Brigade, The Night They Raided Minsky's, The Southern Star, The Seagull, A Nice Girl Like Me; Too Late The Hero; The Gaunt Woman; Entertaining Mr Sloan; I want what I want; Burke and Hare; Country Dance; Wuthering Heights; Nicholas and Alexandra; The Nightcomers; The Ruling Class; Man of La Mancha; Theatre of Blood; The Mackintosh Man; Man at the Top; Jacob and Esau; The Bluebird; Sky Riders; The Passover Plot; The Prince and the Pauper; Equus; The Four Feathers; Superman—the Movie; The Titanic; The Captain; The Curse of King Tutankhamen (Earl of Carnarvon); Mesmerised. Television: Leo Tolstoy; An Affair of Honour; Edward VII; Clayhanger series; The Garth People; Valley Forge; Two Gentle People, adapted from Graham Greene; A Question of Faith; A Question of Guilt; Constance Kent; Closing Ranks; 7 Dials Mystery; The Sound Machine; Tales of the Unexpected; A. J. Wentworth, BA; Lent; Tom Carrington in Dynasty; Inside Story; All Passion Spent. Recreations: cricket, tennis, sailing, gardening. Address: Church Farm Oast, Salehurst, Robertsbridge, E Sussex; Flat 2, 38 Alderney Street, SW1.

ANDREWS, Harry Thomson; Director, Welkom GM Co. (Anglo-American Corp. of South Africa); b Capetown, South Africa, 11 Dec. 1897; s of late H. Andrews, Capetown; m 1926, R. D. Williams, Pretoria. Educ: Observatory High Sch., Capetown; Marist Brothers' Coll., Capetown; Univ. of Pretoria. Served European War, 1917–19, in France, South African Signals, RE. Advocate, Supreme Court (Transvaal), 1927; Political Secretary South Africa House, London, 1930–35; Accredited Representative of Union of South Africa to League of Nations, Geneva, 1936–40; Asst Sec. for Defence, Pretoria; Under-Sec. for External Affairs, Pretoria; Head of South Africa Govt Supply Mission to USA, 1942–45; Ambassador of South Africa to USA, 1945–49; Permanent Representative of SA to United Nations, 1945–49; South African Ambassador to France, 1949–57; Minister to Switzerland, 1954–56. Member French-Commonwealth War Graves Commission, 1954–57. Vice-Pres., S Africa Foundn, 1977. Recreation: golf. Address: 214 Bretton Woods, Killarney, Johannesburg, 2193, S Africa. Clubs: Kimberley (Kimberley); Rand, Bryanston Country (Johannesburg); West Province Sports (Cape Town).

ANDREWS, James Roland Blake F.; see Fox-Andrews.

ANDREWS, John Hayward; Chairman, Sugar Board Queensland, since 1986; b 9 Nov. 1919; s of James Andrews and Florence Elizabeth Andrews; m 1947; one s one d (and one s decd). Educ: Univ. of Queensland (BEc). FIE(Aust); FAIM; DipT&CP; DipCE. Served Royal Aust. Engineers, 1940–45. Local Govt City Engineer, Wagga Wagga and Tamworth, NSW, 1946–60; Deputy Commissioner, Main Roads Dept, Queensland, 1961–78; Administrator, Gold Coast City, 1978–79; private practice, 1979–81; Agent-Gen. for Qld, 1981–84; Chm., Electoral Redistribution Commn for Qld, 1985–86. Dir, White Industries Ltd, 1986–. Recreations: golf, painting, walking. Address: 7/34 Sandford Street, St Lucia, Brisbane, Qld 4067, Australia. Clubs: Twin Towns Services (NSW); Indooroopilly Golf (Queensland).

ANDREWS, Air Vice-Marshal John Oliver, CB 1942; DSO 1917; MC; idc; b 20 July 1896; s of John Andrews, Waterloo, Lancs; m 1923, Bertha, d of Wilfred Bisdée, Hambrook, Glos; two s. Lieut Royal Scots; seconded RFC, 1914; served France, 1914–18; S Russia, 1919; India, 1920 (MC and bar, Montenegrin Silver Medal for bravery, DSO, despatches thrice); transferred to RAF, 1919; retired, 1945.

ANDREWS, Julie (Elizabeth); Actress; b 1 Oct. 1935; m 1st, Anthony J. Walton (marr. diss. 1968); one d; 2nd, 1969, Blake Edwards; one step s one step d, and two adopted d. Educ: Woodbrook Girls' Sch., Beckenham and private governess. Appeared in The Boy Friend, Broadway, New York, 1954; My Fair Lady: New York, 1956, London, 1958; Camelot, New York, 1960. Films: (Walt Disney) Mary Poppins, 1963 (Academy Award, 1964); Americanisation of Emily, 1964; Sound of Music, 1964; Hawaii, 1965; Torn Curtain, 1966; Thoroughly Modern Millie, 1966; Star, 1967; Darling Lili, 1970; The Tamarind Seed, 1973; "10", 1980; Little Miss Marker, 1980; S.O.B., 1981; Victor/Victoria, 1982; The Man Who Loved Women, 1983. TV: The Julie Andrews Hour, 1972–73. Publications: (as Julie Andrews Edwards) Mandy, 1972; Last of the Really Great Whangdoodles, 1973. Recreations: boating, ski-ing, riding.

ANDREWS, Prof. Kenneth Raymond, FBA 1986; Professor of History, University of Hull, since 1979, part-time since 1986; b 26 Aug. 1921; s of Arthur Walter and Marion Gertrude Andrews; m 1969, Ottilie Kalman, Olomouc, Czechoslovakia; two step s. Educ: Henry Thornton Sch., Clapham; King's College London (BA 1948, PhD 1951). Lectr, Univ. of Liverpool, 1963–64; Lectr and Sen. Lectr, Univ. of Hull, 1964–79; active research in English maritime history. Publications: English Privateering Voyages to the West Indies, 1959; Elizabethan Privateering, 1964; Drake's Voyages, 1967; The Last Voyage of Drake and Hawkins, 1972; The Spanish Caribbean, 1978; Trade, Plunder and Settlement, 1984; articles in learned jls. Recreations: chess, cookery, 20th century painting. Address: 8 Grange Drive, Cottingham, North Humberside HU16 5RE.

ANDREWS, Rev. Canon Leonard Martin, CVO 1946; MBE; MC 1917; Rector of Stoke Climsland, Cornwall, 1922–68; Chaplain to the Queen, 1952–69 (to King Edward VIII, 1936, and to King George VI, 1936–52); Hon. Canon of Truro since 1932; b 24 Sept. 1886. Educ: Queens' Coll., Cambridge. BA 1909; MA 1921; Deacon, 1909; Priest, 1910; Rector of Brewarrina, NSW, 1913–14; Vice-Principal Brotherhood of the Good Shepherd, NSW, 1914–15; Temp. CF, 1914–19; Chaplain at Khartoum, 1920–22; Rural Dean of Trigg Major, 1929–32. Publication: Canon's Folly, 1974. Address: Climsland, Downderry, Torpoint, Cornwall PL11 3LW.

ANDREWS, Raymond Denzil Anthony, MBE 1953; VRD 1960; Senior Partner, Andrews, Downie & Partners, Architects, since 1960; b 5 June 1925; s of Michael Joseph Andrews, BA, and Phylis Marie Andrews (née Crowley); m 1958, Gillian Whitlaw Small, BA; one s one d. Educ: Highgate Sch.; Christ's Coll., Cambridge; University Coll. London (DipArch, DipTP); Univ. of Michigan (MArch). RIBA. Lieut, Royal Marines, 1943–46; RM Reserve, 1948–68 (Major). King George VI Meml Fellow of English-Speaking Union of US, 1954–55; Chm., London Region, RIBA, 1968–72; Vice-Pres., RIBA, 1972–74, 1978–81; Chm., Festival of Architecture, 1984; Pres., Architectural Assoc., 1975–77. Civic Trust Award, 1971 and 1978; 1st Prize, Royal Mint Square Housing Competition,

GLC, 1974. Order of Al Rafadain (Iraq), 1956. Recreation: sailing. Address: 6 Addison Avenue, W11 4QR. T: 01–602 7701. Clubs: Bosham Sailing; RIBA Sailing (Cdre, 1983–86).

ANDREWS, Robert Graham M.; see Marshall-Andrews.

ANDREWS, Stuart Morrison; Head Master of Clifton College, since 1975; b 23 June 1932; s of William Hannaford Andrews and Eileen Elizabeth Andrews; m 1962, Marie Elizabeth van Wyk; two s. Educ: Newton Abbot Grammar Sch.; St Dunstan's Coll.; Sidney Sussex Coll., Cambridge (MA). Nat. service with Parachute Bde, 1952–53. Sen. History Master and Librarian, St Dunstan's Coll., 1956–60; Chief History Master and Librarian, Repton Sch., 1961–67; Head Master, Norwich Sch., 1967–75. Chm., Direct-grant Sub-cttee of Headmasters' Conf., 1974–75; Dep. Chm., Assisted Places Cttee, 1982–. Editor, Conference, 1972–82. Publications: Eighteenth-century Europe, 1965; Enlightened Despotism, 1967; Methodism and Society, 1970; articles in various historical jls. Recreations: walking, writing. Address: Headmaster's House, Clifton College, Bristol BS8 3HT. T: Bristol 735613. Clubs: East India, Devonshire, Sports and Public Schools; Clifton (Bristol).

ANDREWS, William Denys Cathcart, CBE 1980; WS; Partner, Shepherd & Wedderburn, WS, Edinburgh, since 1962; b 3 June 1931; s of Eugene Andrews and Agnes Armstrong; m 1955, May O'Beirne; two s two d. Educ: Girvan High Sch.; Worksop Coll.; Edinburgh Univ. (BL). Served RASC, 1950–52. Law Society of Scotland: Mem. Council, 1972–81; Vice Pres., 1977–78; Pres., 1978–79. Examr in Conveyancing, Edinburgh Univ., 1974–77. Pt-time Mem., Lands Tribunal for Scotland, 1980–. Recreation: gardening. Address: Hillend House, Lothianburn, Edinburgh EH10 4YS. T: 031–445 2767. Club: New (Edinburgh).

ANDRIESSEN, Dr Frans, (Franciscus H. J. J.), Kt, Order of Dutch Lion; Officer, Order of Orange-Nassau; LLD; Member, since 1981, Vice-President, since 1985, the European Commission (responsible for agriculture and fisheries, 1985, for agriculture and forestry, since 1986); b Utrecht, 2 April 1929; m; four c. Educ: Univ. of Utrecht (LLD). Served at Catholic Housing Institute, latterly as Director, 1954–72. Member: Provincial Estates of Utrecht, 1958–67; Lower House of the States-General, initially as specialist in housing matters, 1967–77; Chairman, KVP party in Lower House, 1971–77; Minister of Finance, 1977–80; Member, Upper House of States-General (Senate), 1980. Address: Commission of the European Communities, 200 rue de la Loi, 1049 Brussels, Belgium.

ANDRUS, Francis Sedley, LVO 1982; Beaumont Herald of Arms Extraordinary, since 1982; b 26 Feb. 1915; o s of late Brig.-Gen. Thomas Alchin Andrus, CMG, JP, and Alice Loveday (née Parr); unmarried. Educ: Wellington Coll.; St Peter's Hall (now Coll.), Oxford (MA). Entered College of Arms as Member of Staff, 1938; Bluemantle Pursuivant of Arms, 1970–72; Lancaster Herald of Arms, 1972–82. Address: 8 Oakwood Rise, Longfield, near Dartford, Kent DA3 7PA. T: Longfield 5424.

ANFINSEN, Dr Christian Boehmer; Professor of Biology, Johns Hopkins University, since 1982; b Monessen, Pa, 26 March 1916; s of Christian Boehmer Anfinsen and Sophie (née Rasmussen); m 1941, Florence Bernice Kenenger; one s two d; m 1979, Libby Esther Shulman. Educ: Swarthmore Coll. (BA); Univ. of Pennsylvania (MS); Harvard (PhD). Amer.-Scand. Foundn Fellow, Carlsberg Lab., Copenhagen, 1939; Sen. Cancer Res. Fellow, Nobel Inst. Medicine, Stockholm, 1947; Asst Prof. of Biological Chemistry, Harvard Medical Sch., 1948–50; Head of Lab. of Cellular Physiology and Metabolism, Nat. Heart Inst., Bethesda, Md, 1950–62; Prof. of Biochemistry, Harvard Med. Sch., 1962–63; Head of Lab. of Chem. Biol., Nat. Inst. of Arthritis, Metabolism and Digestive Diseases, Bethesda, 1963–82. Rockefeller Fellow, 1954–55; Guggenheim Fellow, Weizmann Inst., Rehovot, Israel, 1958. Mem., Bd of Governors, Weizmann Inst., Rehovot, 1960–. Member: Amer. Soc. of Biol Chemists (Pres., 1971–72); Amer. Acad. of Arts and Scis; Nat. Acad. of Scis; Royal Danish Acad.; Washington Acad. of Scis; Fedn Amer. Scientists (Vice-Chm., 1958–59, and 1974–75); Pontifical Acad., 1980. Hon. DSc: Swarthmore, 1965; Georgetown, 1967; Pennsylvania, 1973; NY Med. Coll., Gustavus Adolphus Coll., 1975; Brandeis, 1977; Providence Coll., 1978; Hon. MD Naples, 1982. (Jtly) Nobel Prize for Chemistry, 1972. Publication: The Molecular Basis of Evolution, 1959. Address: Department of Biology, Johns Hopkins University, Baltimore, Md 21218, USA.

ANFOM, Emmanuel E.; see Evans-Anfom.

ANGEL, Gerald Bernard Nathaniel Aylmer; Registrar of the Family Division of the High Court, since 1980; b 4 Nov. 1937; s of late Bernard Francis and Ethel Angel; m 1968, Lesley Susan Kemp; three s one d (and one s decd). Educ: St Mary's Sch., Nairobi. Served Kenya Regt, 1956–57. Called to Bar, Inner Temple, 1959; Advocate, Kenya, 1960–62; practice at Bar, 1962–80. Mem., Civil and Family Sub-Cttee, Judicial Studies Bd, 1985–. Publications: ed, Industrial Tribunals Reports, 1966–78. Recreations: reading, walking. Address: 9 Lancaster Avenue, SE27 9EL. T: 01–670 7184.

ANGELES, Victoria de los; see de los Angeles.

ANGELL-JAMES, John, CBE 1967; MD, FRCP, FRCS; Hon. Consulting Surgeon in Otolaryngology, United Bristol Hospitals, since 1966; b 23 Aug. 1901; s of Dr John Angell James, MRCS, LRCP and Emily Cormell (née Ashwin), Bristol; m 1930, Evelyn Miriam Everard, d of Francis Over and Ada Miriam Everard, Birmingham; one s two d. Educ: Bristol Grammar Sch.; Univ. of Bristol; London Hosp.; Guy's Hosp. MB ChB 1st Cl. Hons 1924, Bristol; MBBS London (Hons) 1924; MD 1927; FRCS 1928; FRCP 1965. Res. appts, 1924–28, Bristol and London; Hon. ENT Registrar, Bristol Royal Infirmary, 1928–29; Hon. ENT Surg., Bristol Children's Hosp., 1928–48; Cons. ENT Surg., 1948–66; Hon. Asst ENT Surg., later Hon. ENT Surg., Bristol Royal Infirmary, 1929–48; Clin. Tutor, Univ. of Bristol, 1928–55; Lectr and Head of Dept of Otolaryngology, 1955–66; Cons. ENT Surg., United Bristol Hosps, 1948–66. Lt-Col RAMC, 1942–46; Adviser in Otorhinolaryngol., MEF, 1945. Hunterian Prof., RCS, 1962; Semon Lectr in Laryngol., Univ. of London, 1965; James Yearsley Lectr, 1966; Sir William Wilde Meml Lectr, Irish Otolaryngol. Soc., 1966; Vis. Lectr, Univs of Toronto, Vermont, Cornell, Baylor and Chicago. Royal Soc. of Medicine: Former Fellow, Hon. FRSM 1976; Hon. Mem., Sections of Laryngol. (Pres., 1955) and otology. Member: SW Laryngolog. Assoc. (Chm. 1956); Brit. Medical Assoc. (Pres. Sect. of Otolaryngol., 1959; Chm. Bristol Div., 1966–67; Pres., Bath, Bristol and Som Br., 1968–69); Bristol Med.-Chirurg. Soc. (Pres. 1961); Visiting Assoc. of ENT Surgs of GB, 1948 (Pres. 1965–66); Brit. Assoc. of Otolaryngologists, 1942 (Pres. 1966–69); Collegium Oto-Rhino-Laryngologicum Amicitiae Sacrum, 1948 (Councillor, 1966–74; Pres., 1974); Barany Soc., Pres., Otolaryngological Res. Soc., 1978. Extern. Examr, Univ. of Manchester, 1964. Hon. Member: Irish Otolaryngol. Soc.; S Africa Soc. of Otolaryngol.; Corresp. Mem., Deutsche Gesellschaft für Hals-Nasen-Ohren-Heilkunde Kopf-und Hals-Chirurgie. Hon. FRCSE 1971; Jobson Horne Prize, BMA, 1962; Colles Medal, RCSI, 1963; Dalby Prize, RSM, 1963; W. J. Harrison Prize in Laryngology, RSM, 1968. President: Gloucester Soc., 1977; Colston Soc., 1983–84. Chm. Editorial Cttee, Clinical Otolaryngology. Publications: Chapters in: British Surgical Practice, 1951; Diseases of the Ear, Nose and Throat, 1952

(2nd edn 1966); Ultrasound as a diagnostic and surgical tool, 1964; Clinical Surgery, 1966; Ménière's Disease, 1969; Family Medical Guide, 1980; articles in learned jls in Eng., USA, Canada, Germany and Sweden. *Recreations:* farming; shooting. *Address:* Sundayshill House, Falfield, near Wotton-under-Edge, Glos GL12 8DQ; (consulting rooms) Litfield House, Clifton Down, Bristol BS8 3LS. *T:* Bristol 33483.

ANGLESEY, 7th Marquess of, *cr* 1815; **George Charles Henry Victor Paget;** Baron Paget, of Beau Desert, 1549; Earl of Uxbridge, 1784; Bt 1730; Lord-Lieutenant of Gwynedd, since 1983; *b* 8 Oct. 1922; *o s* of 6th Marquess of Anglesey, GCVO, and Lady Victoria Marjorie Harriet Manners (*d* 1946), *d* of 8th Duke of Rutland; *S* father, 1947; *m* 1948, Elizabeth Shirley Vaughan Morgan (*see* Marchioness of Anglesey); two *s* three *d*. *Educ:* Wixenford, Wokingham; Eton Coll. Major, RHG, 1946. Div. Dir, Wales, Nationwide Building Soc., 1973–. President: Anglesey Conservative Assoc., 1948–83; Nat. Museum of Wales, 1962–68; Friends of Friendless Churches, 1966–84; Ancient Monuments Soc., 1979–84. Treasurer, Danilo Dolci Trust (Britain), 1964–. Vice-Chm., Welsh Cttee, Nat. Trust, 1975–85; Member: Historic Buildings Council for Wales, 1953– (Chm., 1977–); Royal Fine Art Commn, 1965–71; Redundant Churches Fund, 1969–78; Royal Commn on Historical Manuscripts, 1984–; Council, Soc. of Army Historical Research; Trustee: Nat. Portrait Gall., 1979–; Nat. Heritage Memorial Fund, 1980–. Hon. Prof., UCW, 1986. FSA 1952; FRSL 1969; Hon. FRIBA, 1971; FRHistS, 1975. Cdre, Royal Welsh Yacht Club, 1948. Anglesey: CC, 1951–67; JP, 1959–68; DL, 1960, Vice-Lieut, 1960. Hon. Fellow, Royal Cambrian Acad. Lord of the Manor of Burton-upon-Trent; Freeman of the City of London. Hon. DLitt Wales, 1984. CStJ 1984. *Publications:* (ed) The Capel Letters, 1814–1817, 1955; One-Leg: the Life and Letters of 1st Marquess of Anglesey, 1961; (ed) Sergeant Pearman's Memoirs, 1968; (ed) Little Hodge, 1971; A History of the British Cavalry, 1816–1919, vol I, 1973, vol. II, 1975, vol. III, 1982, vol. IV, 1986. *Recreations:* gardening, music. *Heir:* *s* Earl of Uxbridge, *qv*. *Address:* Plâs-Newydd, Llanfairpwll, Anglesey. *T:* Llanfairpwll 714330.

ANGLESEY, Marchioness of; (Elizabeth) Shirley Vaughan Paget, DBE 1983 (CBE 1977); Chairman, Drama and Dance Advisory Committee, since 1981 and Member of Board, since 1985, British Council; *b* 4 Dec. 1924; *d* of late Charles Morgan and Hilda Vaughan (both novelists); *m* 1948, Marquess of Anglesey, *qv*; two *s* three *d*. *Educ:* Francis Holland Sch., London; St James', West Malvern; Kent Place Sch., USA. Personal Secretary to Gladwyn Jebb, FO, until marriage. Dep. Chm., Prince of Wales Cttee, 1970–80. Member: Civic Trust for Wales, 1967–76; Arts Council, 1972–81 (Chm., Welsh Arts Council, 1975–81); Royal Commn on Environmental Pollution, 1973–79; IBA, 1976–82; Museums and Galls Commn, 1981–; Radioactive Waste Management Adv. Cttee, 1981–; Chm., Nat. Federation of Women's Institutes, 1966–69; Vice-Chm., Govt Working Party on Methods of Sewage Disposal, 1969–70. Trustee, Pilgrim Trust, 1982–. Hon. LLD Wales, 1977. *Address:* Plâs-Newydd, Llanfairpwll, Gwynedd. *T:* Llanfairpwll 714330.
See also R. H. V. C. Morgan.

ANGLIN, Prof. Douglas (George); Professor of Political Science, Carleton University, Ottawa, Canada, since 1958; *b* Toronto, Canada, 16 Dec. 1923; *s* of George Chambers Anglin, MD, and Ruth Cecilia Cale, MD; *m* 1948, Mary Elizabeth Watson; two *d*. *Educ:* Toronto Univ.; Corpus Christi and Nuffield Colls, Oxford Univ. BA Toronto; MA, DPhil Oxon. Lieut, RCNVR, 1943–45. Asst (later Associate) Prof. of Polit. Sci. and Internat. Relations, Univ. of Manitoba, Winnipeg, 1951–58; Associate Prof. (later Prof.), Carleton Univ., 1958. Vice-Chancellor, Univ. of Zambia, Lusaka, Zambia, 1965–69; Associate Research Fellow, Nigerian Inst. of Social and Economic Research, Univ. of Ibadan, Ibadan, Nigeria, 1962–63; Research Associate, Center of Internat. Studies, Princeton Univ., 1969–70; Pres., Canadian Assoc. of African Studies, 1973–74. *Publications:* The St Pierre and Miquelon Affairs of 1941: a study in diplomacy in the North Atlantic quadrangle, 1966; Zambia's Foreign Policy: studies in diplomacy and dependence, 1979; edited jointly: Africa: Problems and Prospects 1961; Conflict and Change in Southern Africa, 1978; Canada, Scandinavia and Southern Africa, 1978; articles on Internat. and African affairs in a variety of learned jls. *Address:* Carleton University, Colonel By Drive, Ottawa, Ontario K1S 5B6, Canada.

ANGLIN, Eric Jack; HM Diplomatic Service, retired; Consul-General, Melbourne, 1979–83; *b* 9 Aug. 1923; *m* 1954, Patricia Farr; three *s*. Joined Foreign Service (subseq. Diplomatic Service), 1948; FO, 1948–52; HM Missions in: Damascus, 1952–56; Rangoon, 1956–59; Madrid, 1960–64; FO, 1964–67; La Paz, 1967–70; Khartoum, 1970–72; Inspector, Diplomatic Service, FCO, 1973–76; Buenos Aires, 1976–78; Chargé d'Affaires and Consul-Gen., Santiago, 1978–79. *Recreations:* auctions, lecturing. *Address:* Treetops, The Glade, Kingswood, Tadworth, Surrey KT20 6LH. *T:* Tadworth 832858.

ANGUS, Rev. (James Alexander) Keith, TD; Minister of Braemar and Crathie Parish Churches, since 1979; Domestic Chaplain to the Queen, since 1979; *b* 16 April 1929; *s* of late Rev. Walter C. S. Angus and late Margaret I. Stephen; *m* 1956, Alison Jane Daly; one *s* one *d*. *Educ:* High School of Dundee; Univ. of St Andrews (MA). National Service, Army, 1947–49; served with TA, 1950–76; Captain RA (TA), 1955; Chaplain to 5, KOSB (TA), 1957–67, to 154 Regt, RCT (V), 1967–76. Assistant Minister, The Cathedral, Glasgow, 1955–56; Minister: Hoddam Parish Church, 1956–67; Gourock Old Parish Church, 1967–79. Convener, Gen. Assembly's Cttee on Chaplains to HM Forces, 1981–85. *Recreations:* fishing, hill walking. *Address:* The Manse of Crathie, Crathie, near Ballater, Aberdeenshire AB3 5UL. *T:* Crathie 208. *Clubs:* New (Edinburgh); Royal Gourock Yacht.

ANGUS, Michael Richardson; Chairman, Unilever PLC, since 1986 (Director since 1970); Vice Chairman, Unilever NV, since 1986 (Director since 1970); *b* 5 May 1930; *s* of William Richardson Angus and Doris Margaret Breach; *m* 1952, Eileen Isabel May Elliott; two *s* one *d*. *Educ:* Marling Sch., Stroud, Glos; Bristol Univ. (BSc Hons). CBIM 1979. Served RAF, 1951–54. Unilever, 1954–: Marketing Dir, Thibaud Gibbs, Paris, 1962–65; Man. Dir, Res. Bureau, 1965–67; Sales Dir, Lever Brothers UK, 1967–70; Toilet Preparations Co-ordinator, 1970–76; Chemicals Co-ordinator, 1976–80; Regional Dir, N America, 1979–84; Chairman and Chief Exec. Officer: Unilever United States, Inc., New York, 1980–84; Lever Brothers Co., New York, 1980–84. Jt Chm., Netherlands-British Chamber of Commerce, 1984–; Internat. Counsellor, The Conference Board, 1984–. Vis. Fellow, Nuffield Coll., Oxford, 1986–. Trustee, Leverhulme Trust, 1984–. Governor, Ashridge Management Coll., 1974–; Mem. Court of Govs, LSE, 1985–. *Recreations:* countryside, wine, puzzles. *Address:* c/o Unilever PLC, PO Box 68, EC4P 4BQ. *T:* 01–822 5252. *Clubs:* University, Knickerbocker (New York).

ANNALY, 5th Baron *cr* 1863; **Luke Robert White;** Partner, W. Greenwell & Co., Members of London Stock Exchange; *b* 15 March 1927; *o s* of 4th Baron Annaly and Lady Annaly (formerly Lady Lavinia Spencer); *S* father, 1970; *m* 1st, 1953, Lady Marye Pepys (marr. diss. 1957; she *d* 1958); one *s*; 2nd, 1960, Jennifer Carey (marr. diss. 1967); two *d*; *m* 1984, Mrs Beverley Healy, *d* of William Maxwell; one step *d*. *Educ:* Eton. RAF, 1944–48; RAuxAF, 1948–51; Flying Officer (601 Sqdn). Livery, Haberdashers' Company; Freeman of City of London, 1953. *Recreations:* cricket, golf, theatre. *Heir:* *s* Hon. Luke Richard White [*b* 29 June 1954; *m* 1983, Caroline Nina, *yr d* of Col Robert Garnett, Hope Bowdler House, near Church Stretton. *Educ:* Eton; RMA Sandhurst. Commnd Royal Hussars, 1974–78, RARO]. *Address:* House of Lords, SW1A 0PW. *Clubs:* Turf, Royal Air Force, MCC; Hawks (Cambridge).

ANNAN, family name of **Baron Annan.**

ANNAN, Baron, *cr* 1965 (Life Peer); **Noël Gilroy Annan,** OBE 1946; Chairman, Board of Trustees, National Gallery, 1980–85 (Trustee, 1978–85); *b* 25 Dec. 1916; *s* of late James Gilroy Annan; *m* 1950, Gabriele, *d* of Louis Ferdinand Ullstein, Berlin; two *d*. *Educ:* Stowe Sch.; King's Coll., Cambridge (Exhibitioner and Scholar). Served War of 1939–45: WO, War Cabinet Offices, and Military Intelligence, 1940–44; France and Germany, 1944–46; GSO1, Political Div. of British Control Commn, 1945–46. University of Cambridge: Fellow of King's Coll., 1944–56, 1966; Asst Tutor, 1947; Lectr in Politics, 1948–66; Provost of King's Coll., 1956–66; Provost of University Coll., London, 1966–78; Vice-Chancellor, Univ. of London, 1978–81. Romanes Lectr, Oxford, 1965. Chairman: Departmental Cttee on Teaching of Russian in Schools, 1960; Academic Planning Bd, Univ. of Essex, 1965–70; Cttee on Future of Broadcasting, 1974–77, report published 1977. Member: Academic Adv. Cttee, Brunel Coll., 1966–73; Academic Planning Bd, Univ. of East Anglia, 1964–71; Public Schools Commn, 1966–70. Chm., Enquiry on the disturbances in Essex Univ. (report published 1974). Sen. Fellow Eton Coll., 1956–66. Governor: Stowe Sch., 1945–66; Queen Mary Coll., London, 1956–60. Trustee: Churchill Coll., 1958–76; British Museum, 1963–80. Dir, Royal Opera House, Covent Garden, 1967–78; Gulbenkian Foundation: Mem., Arts Cttee, 1957–64; Chm., Educn Cttee, 1971–76. FRHistS; Fellow, Berkeley Coll., Yale, 1963; Hon. Fellow, UCL, 1968; Emer. Fellow, Leverhulme Trust, 1984. For. Hon. Mem., Amer. Acad. of Arts and Sciences, 1973. Hon. DLitt: York, Ontario, 1966; New York, 1981; DUniv Essex, 1967; Hon. LLD Pennsylvania, 1980, Le Bas Prize, 1948; Diamond Jubilee Medal, Inst. of Linguists, 1971; Clerk Kerr Medal, Univ. of Calif, Berkeley, 1985. Comdr, Royal Order of King George I of the Hellenes (Greece), 1962. *Publications:* Leslie Stephen: his thought and character in relation to his time, 1951 (awarded James Tait Black Memorial Prize, 1951), rev. edn 1984; The Intellectual Aristocracy (in Studies in Social History, a tribute to G. M. Trevelyan, 1956); Kipling's Place in the History of Ideas (in Kipling's Mind and Art, 1964); The Curious Strength of Positivism in English Political Thought, 1959; Roxburgh of Stowe, 1965; articles in Victorian Studies and other periodicals. *Recreation:* writing English prose. *Address:* 16 St John's Wood Road, NW8 8RE. *Club:* Brooks's.

ANNAND, John Angus; Under Secretary, Welsh Office, 1975–85; *b* 13 May 1926; *s* of James Annand and Lilias Annand (*née* Smith); *m* 1971, Julia Dawn Hardman. *Educ:* Hillhead High Sch., Glasgow; Glasgow Univ. (MA, 1st Cl. Hons); Brasenose Coll., Oxford (MLitt). Lecturer: Univ. of Ceylon; Univ. of South Australia, 1951–53; Asst Dir, Civil Service Commn, 1953–57; Principal, 1957, Asst Sec., 1967, HM Treasury; Civil Service Dept, 1968; Welsh Office, 1971; Under Sec., Health and Social Work Dept, Welsh Office, 1975; Economic Policy Gp, 1978. Mem., GMC, 1986–. *Address:* 21 Fairwater Road, Llandaff, Cardiff CF5 2LD.

ANNAND, Richard Wallace, VC 1940; DL; Personnel Officer at Finchale Abbey Training Centre for the Disabled, near Durham, 1948–79; late Captain Durham Light Infantry (RARO); *b* 5 Nov. 1914; *s* of Lt-Comdr Wallace Moir Annand, Royal Naval Division (killed Gallipoli 1915), and late Dora Elizabeth Chapman, South Shields; *m* 1940, Shirley Osborne, JP 1957. *Educ:* Pocklington, East Yorks. Staff of National Provincial Bank, 1933–37; commissioned in RNVR 1933 (Tyne and London Divisions); transferred to Durham Light Infantry, Jan. 1938; served in France and Belgium, 1939–40 (wounded, VC). Invalided, Dec. 1948. Hon. Freeman Co. Borough of South Shields, 1940; Hon. Representative of The Officers' Assoc.; DL Co. of Durham, 1956. *Recreations:* Rugby football, golf; interest: general welfare of the deafened. *Address:* Springwell House, Whitesmocks, Durham City DH1 4LL. *Club:* County (Durham).

ANNANDALE AND HARTFELL, 11th Earl of, *cr* 1662 (S) with precedence to 1643; **Patrick Andrew Wentworth Hope Johnstone of Annandale and of that Ilk;** Earl of the territorial earldom of Annandale and Hartfell, and of the Lordship of Johnstone; Hereditary Steward of the Stewartry of Annandale; Hereditary Keeper of the Castle of Lochmaben; Chief of the Name and Arms of Johnstone; landowner; *b* 19 April 1941; *s* of Major Percy Wentworth Hope Johnstone of Annandale and of that Ilk, TD (*d* 1983) (*de jure* 10th Earl) and of Margaret Jane (now Margaret Countess of Annandale and Hartfell), *d* of Herbert William Francis Hunter-Arundell; claim to earldom admitted by Committee for Privileges, House of Lords, 1985; *m* 1969, Susan Josephine, *d* of late Col Walter John Macdonald Ross, CB, OBE, MC, TD, Netherhall, Castle Douglas; one *s* one *d*. *Educ:* Stowe School; RAC, Cirencester. Member: Dumfries CC, 1970–75; Dumfries and Galloway Regional Council, 1974–86; Scottish Valuation Advisory Council, 1983–85. Director: Bowring Members Agency, 1985–; Solway River Purification Bd, 1970–86; Chm., Royal Jubilee and Prince's Trusts for Dumfries and Galloway, 1984–. Underwriting Member of Lloyds, 1976–. *Recreations:* golf, shooting. *Heir:* *s* Lord Johnstone, *qv*. *Address:* Raehills, St Anns, Lockerbie, Dumfriesshire. *T:* Johnstonebridge 317. *Clubs:* Brooks's; Puffin's (Edinburgh).

ANNENBERG, Walter H., KBE (Hon.) 1976; US Ambassador to the Court of St James's, 1969–74; *b* 13 March 1908; *s* of M. L. Annenberg; *m* 1951, Leonore Cohn; one *d*. *Educ:* Peddie Sch.; Univ. of Pennsylvania. President, Triangle Publications Inc., Philadelphia, Pa; Publisher: Seventeen Magazine; TV Guide; Daily Racing Form. Medal of Freedom, 1986; holds foreign decorations. *Address:* Llanfair Road, Wynnewood, Pa 19096, USA; 250 King of Prussia Road, Radnor, Pa 19088, USA. *Clubs:* White's; Racquet, Rittenhouse (Philadelphia); Lyford Cay (Bahamas); National Press (Washington, DC); Swinley Forest Golf.

ANNESLEY, family name of **Earl Annesley** and **Viscount Valentia.**

ANNESLEY, 10th Earl *cr* 1789; **Patrick Annesley;** Baron Annesley, 1758; Viscount Glerawly, 1766; *b* 12 August 1924; *e s* of 9th Earl Annesley, and of Nora, *y d* of late Walter Harrison; *S* father, 1979; *m* 1947, Catherine, *d* of John Burgess, Edinburgh; four *d*. *Heir:* *b* Hon. Philip Harrison Annesley [*b* 29 March 1927; *m* 1951, Florence Eileen, *o d* of late John Arthur Johnston]. *Address:* 35 Spring Rise, Egham, Surrey.

ANNETT, David Maurice, MA; Headmaster of King's School, Worcester, 1959–79; *b* 27 April 1917; *s* of late M. W. Annett and Marguerite, *d* of Rev. W. M. Hobson; *m* 1953, Evelyn Rosemary, *d* of late W. M. Gordon, Headmaster of Wrekin Coll., and *widow* of R. E. Upcott; one *d* (one step-*s* two step-*d*). *Educ:* Haileybury Coll.; Queens' Coll., Cambridge. Head of Classical Dept at Oundle Sch., 1939–53, and Housemaster, 1948–53; Headmaster of Marling Sch., Stroud, 1953–59. Served with 27th Field Regt, RA, in India and Burma (Capt.), 1941–45. *Address:* The Old Shop, Whitbourne, Worcester WR6 5SR. *T:* Knightwick 21727.

ANNIGONI, Pietro, RP; Italian painter; artist in oil, tempera, etching and fresco; *b* Milan, 7 June 1910; *s* of Ricciardo Annigoni, engineer; *m* 1st, Anna Maggini (*d* 1969); one *s* one *d*; 2nd, 1976, Rosa Segreto. *Educ:* Accademia delle Belle Arti, Florence. Member of: Accademia di S Luca, Rome; Accademia delle Arti del Disegno, Florence; Academy of

Design, New York. Portraits exhibited: (at Nat. Portrait Gallery) The Queen, 1970; (at Royal Academy, London) The Queen (for the Fishmongers' Company), 1955, Dame Margot Fonteyn, 1956 (now at Nat. Portrait Gall.), The Duke of Edinburgh (for the Fishmongers' Company), 1957, Maharanee of Jaipur, 1958. Other works: Portrait of Princess Margaret, 1958; The Immaculate Heart of Mary, 1962; The Last Supper, fresco in San Michele Arcangelo, Ponte Buggianese, 1974–75; Glory of St Benedict, fresco at Montecassino, 1978; Scenes of St Benedict's life, fresco in dome of Montecassino Cathedral, 1980–81; Scenes of St Antony's life, frescoes in Basilica del Santo, Padova, 1981–82; Crucifix, Cathedral of Mirandola, 1983; Crucifix, Basilica del Santo, Padova, 1983; The Last Supper, fresco in Monastery of St Antony, Padua, 1984; St Antony preaching from the walnut tree, fresco in Basilica del Santo, Padova, 1985. Permanent collections showing his works include: Uffizi (Print Room), Florence; Galleria Arte Moderna, Milan; Frescoes: S Martino, Florence; Madonna del Consiglio, Pistoia; Basilica of S Lorenzo, Florence. Exhibitions include: Wildenstein Gall., London, 1954; Royal Academy, 1956; Wildenstein, NY, 1957; Galleries of Fedn of British Artists, 1961; retrospective exhbn, New York and San Francisco, 1969; Arts Unlimited Gall., London, 1971. Has also exhibited in Rome, Turin, Paris, Florence, Milan, etc. *Publication:* (autobiog.) An Artist's Life, 1977. *Address:* Borgo degli Albizi 8, 50122 Florence, Italy.

ANNING, Raymon Harry, CBE 1982; QPM 1975; Commissioner of Police, The Royal Hong Kong Police Force, since 1985; *b* 22 July 1930; *s* of Frederick Charles Anning and Doris Mabel Anning (*née* Wakefield); *m* 1949, Beryl Joan Boxall; one *s* one *d*. *Educ:* Richmond and East Sheen Grammar School. Army (East Surrey Regt and Royal Military Police), 1948–50. Metropolitan Police, 1952–79: Constable to Chief Supt, Divisions and Headquarters, 1952–69; Officer i/c Anguilla Police Unit, W Indies, 1969; Chief Supt i/c Discipline Office, New Scotland Yard, 1970–72; Commander i/c A 10 (Complaints Investigation) Branch, NSY, 1972–75; seconded to Hong Kong Govt, 1974; Dep. Asst Commissioner C (CID) Dept, 1975–78; Inspector of Metropolitan Police (Dep. Asst Comr), 1979; HM Inspector of Constabulary for England and Wales, 1979–83; Dep. Comr of Police, Hong Kong, 1983–85. Graduate of Nat. Exec. Inst., FBI Academy, Quantico, Virginia, USA, 1979. *Recreations:* walking, gardening. *Address:* Royal Hong Kong Police, Headquarters, Arsenal Street, Hong Kong. *Clubs:* Royal Over-Seas League; Royal Hong Kong Golf Club.

ANNIS, David, MD; FRCS; Science and Engineering Research Council Fellow, Institute of Medical and Dental Engineering, Liverpool University, since 1981; *b* 28 Feb. 1921; *s* of Harold and Gertrude Annis; *m* 1948, Nesta Roberts; three *s* one *d*. *Educ:* Manchester Grammar Sch.; Univ. of Liverpool. ChM 1953, MD 1959; FRCS 1946. Res. Fellow in Exptl Surgery, Mayo Clinic, Minn., 1949–51. Liverpool University: Sen. Lectr in Surgery, 1951–54; Dir of Studies, Surg. Sci., 1964–69; Dir, Bioengineering Unit, Dept of Surgery, 1969-85; Consultant Gen. Surgeon, Royal Liverpool Hosp., 1954–81. Member: Biomaterials Sub-Cttee, SRC, 1978–80; Physiolog. Systems and Disorders Bd, MRC, 1980–. Mem. Ct of Examrs, RCS, 1963–69; Examiner in Surgery, Univs of Leeds, Glasgow, Cardiff, Dundee, Liverpool and Lagos. Member, Editorial Committee: Bioengineering Jl, 1980–; British Jl of Surgery, 1965–80. *Publications:* contribs to: Wells and Kyle, Scientific Foundations of Surgery, 1967, 3rd edn 1982; Cuschieri, Moosa and Giles, Companion to Surgical Practice, 1982; papers on surgical and med. bioengrg subjects in learned jls. *Recreation:* countryside. *Address:* Little Hey, Dibbinsdale Road, Bromborough, Merseyside L63 0HQ. *T:* 051–334 3422.

ANNIS, Francesca; actress; *b* 1945. *Theatre:* Royal Shakespeare Company: Romeo and Juliet, 1976; Troilus and Cressida, 1976; Luciana in Comedy of Errors, 1976; Natalya in A Month in the Country, Nat. Theatre, 1981. *Films:* Penny Gold, 1972; Macbeth, 1973; Krull, 1983; Dune, 1984. *Television:* A Pin to see the Peepshow, 1973; Madame Bovary, 1975; Stronger than the Sun, 1977; The Ragazza, 1978; Lillie (series), 1978; Partners in Crime (series), 1983. *Address:* c/o Dennis Selinger, ICM, 388–396 Oxford Street, W1.

ANNIS, Philip Geoffrey Walter; Editor of series, The History of the Royal Regiment of Artillery, since 1986; *b* 7 Feb. 1936; *s* of Walter and Lilian Annis; *m* 1967, Olive, *d* of Mr & Mrs E. W. A. Scarlett; one *s*. *Educ:* Sale Grammar Sch.; Kelsick Grammar Sch., Ambleside; Manchester Univ. FSA 1973; FRHistS 1975. Served RA, 1957–59. Board of Inland Revenue, 1959–62. Joined National Maritime Museum, 1962; Head of Museum Services, 1971; Dep. Dir, 1979–86. Mem., British Commn, Internat. Commn for Maritime History, 1980–. *Publications:* Naval Swords, 1970; (with Comdr W. E. May) Swords For Sea Service, 1970; articles on the history of naval uniform. *Recreations:* gardening, walking. *Address:* The Royal Artillery Institution, Old Royal Military Academy, Woolwich, SE18 4DN. *T:* 01–856 5533.

ANOUILH, Jean; French dramatic author; *b* Bordeaux, 23 June 1910; *s* of François Anouilh and Marie-Magdeleine Soulue; *m* 1953, Nicole Lançon; one *s* two *d*. *Educ:* Collège Chaptal; Univ. of Paris. *Plays include:* L'Ermine, 1934 (prod Nottingham, 1955, as The Ermine); Y'avait un prisonnier, 1935; Le Voyageur sans bagages, 1937; Le Bal des Voleurs, 1938 (prod London, 1952, as Thieves' Carnival); La Sauvage, 1938 (prod London, 1957, as Restless Heart); Cavalcade d'Amour, 1941; Le Rendez-vous de Senlis, 1942: Léocadia, 1942 (prod London, 1954, as Time Remembered); Eurydice, 1942 (prod London as Point of Departure, 1950); Humulus le Muet (in collaboration with Jean Aurenche), 1945; Oreste, 1945; Antigone, 1946 (prod London, 1949); Jézébel, 1946; Roméo et Jeannette, 1946 (prod London, 1949, as Fading Mansion); Médée, 1946; L'Invitation au château, 1948 (prod London, 1950, 1968, as Ring Round the Moon); Ardèle ou la Marguerite, 1949; La Répétition, ou l'amour puni, 1950 (prod Edinburgh Festival 1957, and London, 1961); Colombe, 1950 (prod London, 1951); La Valse des toréadors, 1952 (prod London, 1956); L'Alouette, 1953 (prod London, 1955, as The Lark); Ornifle, 1955; L'Hurluberlu, 1958 (prod Chichester and London, 1966, as The Fighting Cock); La Foire d'Empoigne, 1960; Becket (prod London, 1961); La Grotte, 1961 (prod London, 1965, as The Cavern); Poor Bitos (prod London, 1963–64); Le Boulanger, la Boulangère et le Petit Mitson, 1968; Cher Antoine, 1969; Les Poissons Rouges, 1969; Ne Réveillez Pas, Madame, 1970; Tu étais si gentil quand tu étais petit, 1974; L'arrestation, 1975; Le Scénario, 1976; Chers Zoiseaux, 1976; Vive Henri IV, 1977; La Culotte, 1978; Le Nombril, 1981; Number One (prod London, 1984). *Films include:* Monsieur Vincent (awarded Grand Prix du Cinéma Français); Pattes blanches; Caprice de Caroline, etc. *Address:* c/o Les Editions de la Table Ronde, 40 rue du Bac, 75007 Paris, France.

ANSCOMBE, Gertrude Elizabeth Margaret, FBA 1967; Professor of Philosophy, University of Cambridge, 1970–86; Fellow, New Hall, Cambridge, 1970–86, Hon. Fellow, since 1986; *b* 1919; *d* of Allen Wells Anscombe and Gertrude Elizabeth Anscombe (*née* Thomas); *m* 1941, Prof. Peter Thomas Geach, *qv*; three *s* four *d*. *Educ:* Sydenham High Sch.; St Hugh's Coll., Oxford (Schol.); Newnham Coll., Cambridge. 2nd cl. Hon. Mods 1939, 1st cl. Greats 1941, Oxford. Research studentships, Oxford and Cambridge, 1941–44; research fellowships, Somerville Coll., Oxford, 1946–64; Fellow, Somerville Coll., 1964–70, Hon. Fellow, 1970–; Hon. Fellow, St Hugh's Coll., Oxford, 1972. Hon. Dr Laws Notre Dame Univ., 1986. For. Hon. Mem., Amer. Acad. of Arts and Sciences, 1979. Ehrenkreuz Pro Litteris et Artibus (Austria), 1978; Forschungspreis, Alexander von Humboldt Stiftung, 1983. *Publications:* Intention, 1957; An Introduction to Wittgenstein's Tractatus, 1959; (with Peter Geach) Three Philosophers, 1961; Collected Papers: 1, Parmenides to Wittgenstein, 2, Metaphysics and the Philosophy of Mind, 3, Ethics, Religion and Politics, 1981; translator and co-editor of posthumous works of Ludwig Wittgenstein. *Address:* New Hall, Cambridge.

ANSELL, Dr Barbara Mary, CBE 1982; Consultant Physician (Rheumatology), Wexham Park Hospital, Slough, since 1985; Head of Division of Rheumatology, Clinical Research Centre, Northwick Park Hospital, Harrow, since 1976; *b* 30 Aug. 1923; *m* A. H. Weston, MB, FRCGP. *Educ:* Kings High Sch. for Girls, Warwick; Birmingham Univ. (MD 1969). MRCP 1951, FRCP 1967. Consultant Physician (Rheumatol.), Canadian Red Cross Hosp., Taplow, 1962–85. Mem., Cttee for the Review of Medicines, 1979–82. Member: British Assoc. for Rheumatism and Rehabilitation (Mem. Council, 1978–81); Arthritis and Rheumatism Council (Member: Educn Cttee, 1961–77 (Chm., 1966–68); Scientific Co-ordinating Cttee, 1981–); RCP Cttee on Rheumatology, 1972–82; Warnock Cttee of Enquiry into Educn of Handicapped Children, 1975; Exec. Cttee, British League Against Rheumatism, 1976–; Standing Cttee, European League Against Rheumatism, 1979– (Chm., Cttee on Paedriatic Rheumatology, 1979–); Rheumatology Chm., RCP Cttee on Higher Med. Trng, 1977–79; Heberden Soc. (Pres., 1976). Hon. FRCS, 1984. Hon. Member: Amer. Coll. of Physicians; American, Australian, Finnish, French, German and South African Rheumatism Associations; Spanish Soc. of Rheumatology. Editor, Medicine, 1974, 1976, 1978–79. *Publications:* (ed) Clinics in Rheumatic Diseases, 1976; Chronic Ailments in Childhood, 1976; (ed jtly) Surgical Management of Juvenile Chronic Polyarthritis, 1978; Rheumatic Disorders in Childhood, 1980; Inflammatory Disorders of Muscle, 1984. *Recreations:* travelling, cooking. *Address:* Dumgoyne, Templewood Lane, Stoke Poges, Bucks SL2 4BG. *T:* Fulmer 2321; Flat 1, 27 Kings Road, W5. *T:* 01-997 1181. *Club:* Royal Society of Medicine.

ANSELL, Sir Michael Picton, Kt 1968; CBE 1951; DSO 1944; DL; First President/Chairman, British Equestrian Federation, 1972–76; Show Director, Royal International Horse Show, and Horse of the Year Show, 1949–75; *b* 26 March 1905; *s* of Lieut-Col G. K. Ansell and K. Cross; *m* 1st, 1936, Victoria Jacintha Fleetwood Fuller (*d* 1969); two *s* one *d*; 2nd, 1970, Eileen (*née* Stanton) (*d* 1971), *widow* of Maj.-Gen. Roger Evans, CB, MC. *Educ:* Wellington; RMC Sandhurst. Gazetted 5th Royal Inniskilling Dragoon Guards, 1924, Col, 1957–62. War of 1939–45: Lieut-Col to command 1st Lothian & Border Yeo., 1940 (severely wounded and prisoner, 1940); discharged disabled, 1944. Chairman: British Show Jumping Assoc., 1945–64, 1970–71 (Pres., 1964–66); (first) British Horse Soc. Council, 1963–72 (Hon. Dir, British Horse Soc., 1952–73). Yeoman, Worshipful Co. of Saddlers, 1963; Freeman: Worshipful Co. of Farriers, 1962, Worshipful Co. of Loriners, 1962. Mem. Council, St Dunstan's, 1958– (a Vice-Pres., 1970, Vice-Chm., 1975–77, Pres., 1977–86). DL 1966, High Sheriff 1967, Devon. Chevalier, Order of Leopold, Belgium, 1932; Commander's Cross, Order of Merit, German Federal Republic, 1975; Olympic Order, Silver, IOC, 1977. *Publications:* Soldier On (autobiog.), 1973; Riding High, 1974; Leopold, the Story of My Horse, 1980. *Recreations:* show jumping (International, 1931–39), polo International, fishing. *Address:* Pillhead House, Bideford, N Devon. *T:* Bideford 72574. *Club:* Cavalry and Guards.

ANSON, family name of **Earl of Lichfield.**

ANSON, Viscount; Thomas William Robert Hugh Anson; *b* 19 July 1978; *s* and *heir* of Earl of Lichfield, *qv*.

ANSON, Vice-Adm. Sir Edward (Rosebery), KCB 1984; FRAeS 1982; President and Chief Executive Officer, British Aerospace Inc., Washington, since 1986; *b* 11 May 1929; *s* of Ross Rosebery Anson and Ethel Jane (*née* Green); *m* 1960, Rosemary Anne Radcliffe; one *s* one *d*. *Educ:* Prince of Wales Sch., Nairobi, Kenya; BRNC, Dartmouth; Empire Test Pilots Sch., Farnborough (grad. 1957). Served, 1952–64: Naval Air Sqdns, and 700X and 700Z Flts (Blackburn Aircraft Ltd, 1959–61); comd HMS Eskimo, 1964–66; Commander (Air): RNAS Lossiemouth, 1967–68; HMS Eagle, 1969–70; comd Inter Service Hovercraft Trials Unit, 1971; Naval and Air Attaché, Tokyo and Seoul, 1972–74; comd HMS Juno and Captain F4, 1974–76; comd HMS Ark Royal, 1976–78; Flag Officer, Naval Air Command, 1979–82 C of S to C-in-C Fleet, 1982–84, retired. Exec. Dir, Sales, BAe Bristol Div., 1985–86. *Recreations:* walking, golf, tennis, photography. *Address:* c/o Lloyds Bank, High Street, Yeovil, Somerset.

ANSON, John, CB 1981; Deputy Secretary, HM Treasury, since 1977; *b* 3 Aug. 1930; *yr s* of Sir Edward Anson, 6th Bt, and of Dowager Lady Anson; *m* 1957, Myrica Fergie-Woods; two *s* two *d*. *Educ:* Winchester, Magdalene Coll., Cambridge. Served in HM Treasury, 1954–68; Financial Counsellor, British Embassy, Paris, 1968–71; Asst Sec., 1971–72, Under-Sec., 1972–74, Cabinet Office; Under-Sec., HM Treasury, 1974–77; Economic Minister, British Embassy, Washington, and UK Exec. Dir, IMF and World Bank, 1980–83. *Address:* c/o HM Treasury, Parliament Street, SW1P 3AG.
See also Sir Peter Anson, Bt.

ANSON, Malcolm Allinson; Chairman, Wessex Water Authority, since 1982; *b* 23 April 1924; *s* of Sir Wilfrid Anson, MBE, MC, and Dinah Anson (*née* Bourne); *m* 1950, Alison Lothian, *d* of late Sir Arthur Lothian, KCIE, CSI; three *s* one *d*. *Educ:* Winchester; Trinity College, Oxford (MA). War Service, Royal Horse Artillery, 1943–46. Joined Imperial Tobacco Co. (of GB & Ireland) Ltd, 1948; Dir, 1968; Dep. Chm., Imperial Gp Ltd, 1979–80, Chm. 1980–81. Director: Bristol Waterworks Co., 1981–82; Nat. Westminster Bank, 1981–85. Chairman: Bristol Assoc. of Youth Clubs, 1963–71; Endeavour Training, 1969–76; Cancer Help Centre, 1983–; Avon Enterprise Fund, 1984–. Dir, Oxford Univ. Business Summer Sch., 1966; Chm., Careers Adv. Bd, Bristol Univ., 1971–; Vice-Chm., Clifton Coll. Council, 1978–; Dir, Ullswater Outward Bound Mountain Sch., 1971–83. High Sheriff of Avon, 1977–78. Master, Society of Merchant Venturers, Bristol, 1979–80. *Recreations:* ski-ing, sailing, shooting, golf. *Address:* Hill Court, Congresbury, Bristol BS19 5AD. *T:* Yatton 832117. *Club:* Cavalry and Guards.

ANSON, Rear-Adm. Sir Peter, 7th Bt, *cr* 1831; CB 1974; CEng, FIERE; Chairman, Marconi Space Systems, since 1985 (Managing Director, 1984–85); *b* 31 July 1924; *er s* of Sir Edward R. Anson, 6th Bt, and Alison, *o d* of late Hugh Pollock; *S* father 1951; *m* 1955, Elizabeth Audrey, *o d* of late Rear-Adm. Sir Philip Clarke, KBE, CB, DSO; two *s* two *d*. *Educ:* RNC, Dartmouth. Joined RN 1938; Lieut 1944. Served War of 1939–45, HMS Prince of Wales, HMS Exeter. Lieut-Comdr, 1952; Comdr 1956. Commanding Officer, HMS Alert, 1957–58; Staff of RN Tactical Sch., Woolwich, 1959–61; Commanding Officer, HMS Broadsword, 1961–62; Captain, 1963; Director Weapons, Radio (Naval), 1965–66 (Dep. Director, 1963–65); CO HMS Naiad and Captain (D) Londonderry Squadron, 1966–68; Captain, HM Signal School, 1968–70; Commodore, Commander Naval Forces Gulf, 1970–72; ACDS (Signals), 1972–74, retired 1975. Divisional Manager, Satellites, Marconi Space and Defence Systems Ltd, 1977–84. Chm., UK Industrial Space Cttee, 1980–82. FIERE 1972. Mem., Inst. of Advanced Motorists. *Heir:* *s* Philip Roland Anson, *b* 4 Oct. 1957. *Address:* Rosefield, Rowledge, Farnham, Surrey. *T:* Frensham 2724. *Club:* Pratt's.
See also John Anson.

ANSTEE, Margaret Joan; Assistant Secretary-General of the United Nations (Department of Technical Co-operation for Development), New York, since 1978; Special Representative of the Secretary-General to Bolivia, since 1982 and for co-ordination of international assistance to Mexico following the earthquake, since Oct. 1985; *b* 25 June 1926; *d* of Edward Curtis Anstee and Anne Adaliza (*née* Mills). *Educ:* Chelmsford County High Sch. for Girls; Newnham Coll., Cambridge (MA; 1st cl. Hons, Mod. and Med. Langs Tripos); BSc(Econ) London. Lectr in Spanish, QUB, 1947–48; Third Sec., FO, 1948–52; Admin. Officer, UN Technical Assistance Bd, Manila, Philippines, 1952–54; Spanish Supervisor, Cambridge Univ., 1955–56; UN Technical Assistance Board: O i/c Bogotá, Colombia, 1956–57; Resident Rep., Uruguay, 1957–59; Resident Rep., UN Tech. Assistance Bd, Dir of Special Fund Progs, and Dir of UN Inf. Centre, Bolivia, 1960–65; Resident Rep., UNDP, Ethiopia, and UNDP Liaison Officer with UN Econ. Commn for Africa, 1965–67; Sen. Econ. Adviser, Prime Minister's Office, UK, 1967–68; Sen. Asst to Comr i/c Study of Capacity of UN Develt System, 1968–69; Resident Rep., UNDP, Morocco, 1969–72; Resident Rep., UNDP, Chile, and UNDP Liaison Officer with UN Econ. Commn for Latin America, 1972–74; Dep. to UN Under Sec.-Gen. i/c UN Relief Operation to Bangladesh, and Dep. Co-ordinator of UN Emergency Assistance to Zambia, June–Dec. 1973; United Nations Development Programme, New York: Dep. Asst Adminr, and Dep. Reg Dir for Latin America, 1974–76; Dir, Adminr's Unit for Special Assignments, Feb.–July 1976; Asst Dep. Adminr, July–Dec. 1976; Asst Adminr and Dir, Bureau for Prog. Policy and Evaluation, 1977–78. Chm., Adv. Gp on review of World Food Council, UN, 1985–86. Comdr, Order of Ouissam Alaouite, Morocco, 1972; Gran Cruz de Dama, Condor of the Andes, Bolivia, 1986. *Publications:* The Administration of International Development Aid, USA 1969; Gate of the Sun: a prospect of Bolivia, 1970 (USA 1971); (ed with R. K. A. Gardiner and C. Patterson) Africa and the World (Haile Selassie Prize Trust Symposium), 1970. *Recreations:* writing, gardening, hill-walking (preferably in the Andes), bird-watching, swimming. *Address:* Department of Technical Co-operation for Development, United Nations, Room DC1–1228, One United Nations Plaza, New York, NY 10017, USA. *T:* (212) 754–8366. *Club:* United Oxford & Cambridge University (Lady Associate Member).

ANSTEY, Edgar, MA, PhD; Deputy Chief Scientific Officer, Civil Service Department, and Head of Behavioural Sciences Research Division, 1969–77; *b* 5 March 1917; British; *s* of late Percy Lewis Anstey and Dr Vera Anstey; *m* 1939, Zoë Lilian Robertson; one *s*. *Educ:* Winchester Coll.; King's Coll, Cambridge. Assistant Principal, Dominions Office, 1938; Private Sec. to Duke of Devonshire, 1939. 2nd Lieut Dorset Regt, 1940; Major, War Office (DSP), 1941. Founder-Head of Civil Service Commission Research Unit, 1945; Principal, Home Office, 1951; Senior Principal Psychologist, Min. of Defence, 1958; Chief Psychologist, Civil Service Commn, 1964–69. Pres., N Cornwall Liberal Assoc., 1985–. *Publications:* Interviewing for the Selection of Staff (with Dr E. O. Mercer), 1956; Staff Reporting and Staff Development, 1961; Committees-How they work and how to work them, 1962; Psychological Tests, 1966; The Techniques of Interviewing, 1968; (with Dr C. A. Fletcher and Dr. J. Walker) Staff Appraisal and Development, 1976; An Introduction to Selection Interviewing, 1978; articles in Brit. Jl of Psychology, Occupational Psychology, etc. *Recreations:* fell-walking, surfing, golf, bridge. *Address:* Sandrock, Higher Tristram, Polzeath, Wadebridge, Cornwall PL27 6TF. *T:* Trebetherick 3324. *Club:* Royal Commonwealth Society.

ANSTEY, Edgar (Harold Macfarlane), OBE 1969; Documentary Film Producer, Lecturer and Critic; *b* 16 Feb. 1907; *s* of Percy Edgar Macfarlane Anstey and Kate Anstey (*née* Clowes); *m* 1949, Daphne Lilly, Canadian film-maker; one *s* one *d*. *Educ:* Watford Grammar Sch. Empire Marketing Board Film Unit, 1931; associated with Grierson group in develt of sociological and scientific documentaries, 1931–; organised Shell Film Unit, 1934; March of Time: London Dir of Productions, later Foreign Editor, NY, 1936–38. Produced wartime films for Ministries and Services, 1940–46. Film planning and prod. for BOAC, for oil industry in Venezuela and for CO in WI, 1946–49; rep. short films on Cinematograph Films Council, 1947–49; org. and acted as producer-in-charge, British Transport Films, 1949–74. Formerly film critic of The Spectator; regular mem., BBC Radio programme The Critics. Chairman: Brit. Film Acad., 1956; and again (with Soc. of Film and Television Arts), 1967; Pres., Internat. Scientific Film Assoc., 1961–63; Mem. Council RCA, 1963–74 (Sen. Fellow, 1970); led British cultural delegns to USSR, 1964, 1966; Pres., British Industrial and Scientific Film Assoc., 1974–81 (Chm., 1969–70); Chm., Children's Film Foundn Production Cttee, 1981–83; Governor, British Film Inst., 1965–75; Adjunct Prof., Temple Univ., 1982–. Hon. Fellow, British Kinematograph Soc., 1974. *Notable films include:* Housing Problems, 1935; Enough to Eat?, 1936; Journey into Spring, 1957 (British Film Acad. and Venice Award); Terminus, 1961 (British Film Acad. and Venice Award); Between the Tides, 1958 (Venice Award); Wild Wings, 1965 (Hollywood Oscar). *Publication:* The Development of Film Technique in Britain (Experiment in the Film), 1948. *Recreations:* formerly football, tennis and walking, now mental exercising with students of communications. *Address:* 6 Hurst Close, Hampstead Garden Suburb, NW11. *T:* 01–455 2385. *Club:* Savile.

ANSTEY, Brig. Sir John, Kt 1975; CBE 1946; TD; DL; President and Chairman, National Savings Committee, 1975–78 (a Vice-Chairman, 1968–75); retired as Chairman and Managing Director, John Player & Sons; Director, Imperial Tobacco Co., Ltd, 1949–67; *b* 3 Jan. 1907; *s* of late Major Alfred Anstey, Matford House, Exeter, Devon; *m* 1935, Elizabeth Mary, *d* of late William Garnett, Backwell, Somerset; one *s* one *d*. *Educ:* Clifton; Trinity Coll., Oxford. Served War of 1939–45: N Africa, France, SEAC (despatches); Lt-Col 1944; Brig. 1944. Mem. Council, Nottingham Univ. (Treasurer, 1979–81; Pro-Chancellor, 1982–); Member: (part-time) East Midlands Gas Board, 1968–72; Univ. Authorities Panel, 1979–82. Governor, Clifton Coll. Mem. Council, The Queen's Silver Jubilee Appeal, 1976. High Sheriff of Nottinghamshire, 1967; DL Notts 1970. Hon. LLD Nottingham, 1975. Legion of Honour; Croix de Guerre (France); Legion of Merit (USA). *Address:* West Wing, Norwood Park, Southwell, Notts NG25 0PB.

ANSTEY, Sidney Herbert; HM Diplomatic Service, retired; Consul-General, Atlanta, 1968–70; *b* 4 June 1910; *m* 1937, Winifred Mary Gray; three *s* one *d*. Foreign Office, 1940–49; Vice-Consul, Nantes, 1950; First Sec. and Consul, Port-au-Prince, 1951; Belgrade, 1952; Vienna, 1953; Dep. Finance Officer, Foreign Office, 1957; First Sec., Paris, 1960, Counsellor, 1963; Consul, Bilbao, 1965; Consul-Gen., Bilbao, 1966. *Address:* 17 Hambledon Hill, Epsom, Surrey. *T:* Epsom 25989.

ANSTRUTHER of that Ilk, Sir Ralph (Hugo), 7th Bt, *cr* 1694 (S), of Balcaskie, and 12th Bt *cr* 1700 (S), of Anstruther; KCVO 1976 (CVO 1967); MC 1943; DL; Hereditary Carver to the Queen; Equerry to the Queen Mother since 1959, also Treasurer, since 1961; *b* 13 June 1921; *o s* of late Capt. Robert Edward Anstruther, MC, The Black Watch, *o s* of 6th Bt; *S* grandfather, 1934, and cousin, Sir Windham Eric Francis Carmichael-Anstruther, 11th Bt, 1980. *Educ:* Eton; Magdalene Coll., Cambridge (BA). Major (retd), Coldstream Gds. Served Malaya, 1950 (despatches). Mem. Queen's Body Guard for Scotland (Royal Co. of Archers). DL Fife, 1960, Caithness-shire, 1965. *Heir: cousin,* Ian Fife Campbell Anstruther, Capt. late Royal Corps of Signals [*b* 11 May 1922; *m* 1st, 1951, Honor (marr. diss. 1963), *er d* of late Capt. Gerald Blake, MC; one *d*; 2nd, 1963, Susan Margaret Walker, *e d* of H. St J. B. Paten; two *s* three *d*]. *Address:* Balcaskie, Pittenweem, Fife; Watten, Caithness.

See also Sir T. D. Erskine.

ANSTRUTHER-GOUGH-CALTHORPE, Sir Euan (Hamilton), 3rd Bt *cr* 1929; Student; *b* 22 June 1966; *s* of Niall Hamilton Anstruther-Gough-Calthorpe (*d* 1970) and of Martha Rodman (who *m* 2nd, 1975, Charles C. Nicholson), *d* of Stuart Warren Don; *S* grandfather, 1985. *Educ:* Hawtreys, Savernake Forest; Harrow School; Royal Agricultural Coll., Cirencester. *Recreations:* shooting, sailing, tennis, fishing. *Heir: uncle* Michael Richard Anstruther-Gough-Calthorpe, ARICS, *b* 30 Oct. 1943. *Address:* Turners Green Farm, Elvetham, Hartley Wintney, Hants.

See also Sir J. N. Nicholson, Bt.

ANTCLIFFE, Kenneth Arthur; Director of Education, City of Liverpool, since 1975. *Address:* Education Offices, 14 Sir Thomas Street, Liverpool. *T:* 051–236 5480.

ANTHONY, Metropolitan, of Sourozh; Head of the Russian Orthodox Patriarchal Church in Great Britain and Ireland (Diocese of Sourozh); *né* André Borisovich Bloom; *b* Lausanne, Switzerland, 19 June 1914; *o c* of Boris Edwardovich Bloom (Russian Imperial Diplomatic Service) and Xenia Nikolaevna Scriabin (sister of the composer Alexander Scriabin). *Educ:* Lycée Condorcet and Sorbonne, Paris. Dr of Med., Sorbonne, 1943. Army service, med. corps French Army and Resistance, 1939–45. Gen. Practitioner, 1945–49. Took monastic vows, 1943; Priest, Russian Orthodox Church in Paris, 1948; Chaplain to Fellowship of St Alban and St Sergius, London, 1949–50; Vicar, Russian Orthodox Church of St Philip, London, 1950; apptd Hegumen, 1953, Archimandrite, 1956; consecrated Bishop of Sergievo, Suffragan Bishop, Exarchate of Western Europe, 1957; Archbishop of Sourozh, 1960, acting Exarch, 1962–65; Metropolitan of Sourozh and Exarch of the Patriarch of Moscow and All Russia in Western Europe, 1965–74. Member: Ecumenical Commn of Russian Orthodox Church; Central Cttee and Christian Medical Commn of World Council of Churches, 1968. Hulsean Preacher, Cambridge, 1972–73; Preacher, Lambeth Conf., 1978; Firth Lectures, Nottingham Univ., 1982; Eliot Lectures, Kent Univ., 1982; Constantinople Lecture, 1982. Médaille de Bronze de la Société d'encouragement au bien (France), 1945; Browning Award (for spreading of the Christian gospel), USA, 1974. Orders of: St Vladimir 1st Cl. (Russia), 1962; St Andrew (Ecumenical Patriarchate), 1963; St Sergius (Russia), 1977. Lambeth Cross, 1975. Hon. DD (Aberdeen), 1973. *Publications:* Living Prayer, 1965; School for Prayer, 1970; God and Man, 1971; Meditations on a Theme, 1972; Courage to Pray, 1973. *Address:* Russian Orthodox Cathedral, Ennismore Gardens, SW7. *T:* 01–584 0096.

ANTHONY, C. L.; *see* Smith, Dodie.

ANTHONY, Rt. Hon. Douglas; *see* Anthony, Rt Hon. J. D.

ANTHONY, Evelyn; author; *b* 3 July 1928; *d* of Henry Christian Stephens, inventor of the Dome Trainer in World War II, and Elizabeth (*née* Sharkey); *g g d* of Henry Stephens of Cholderton, Wilts, inventor of Stephens Ink; *m* 1955, Michael Ward-Thomas; four *s* two *d*. *Educ:* Convent of Sacred Heart, Roehampton. *Publications:* Imperial Highness, 1953; Curse Not the King, 1954; Far Fly the Eagles, 1955; Anne Boleyn, 1956 (US Literary Guild Award); Victoria, 1957 (US Literary Guild Award); Elizabeth, 1959; Charles the King, 1961; Clandara, 1963; The Heiress, 1964; Valentina, 1965; The Rendezvous, 1967; Anne of Austria, 1968; The Legend, 1969; The Assassin, 1970; The Tamarind Seed, 1971; The Poellenberg Inheritance, 1972; The Occupying Power, 1973 (Yorkshire Post Fiction Prize); The Malaspiga Exit, 1974; The Persian Ransom, 1975; The Silver Falcon, 1977; The Return, 1978; The Grave of Truth, 1979; The Defector, 1980; The Avenue of the Dead, 1981; Albatross, 1982; The Company of Saints, 1983; Voices on the Wind, 1984. *Recreations:* racing (National Hunt), riding, gardening, going to sale rooms, preferably Christie's. *Address:* Horham Hall, Thaxted, Essex.

ANTHONY, Rt. Hon. (John) Douglas, CH 1982; PC 1971; Chairman: Pan Australian Mining Ltd, since 1985; Westralian Iron Ore Associates Ltd, since 1985; Reef Link Pty Ltd, since 1986; Deputy Chairman, Resource Finance Associates, since 1986; *b* 31 Dec. 1929; *s* of late H. L. Anthony; *m* 1957, Margot Macdonald Budd; two *s* one *d*. *Educ:* Murwillumbah Primary and High Schs, The King's Sch., Parramatta; Queensland Agricultural Coll. (QDA). MP, Country Party, later National Party, Richmond, NSW, 1957–84, (Mem., Exec. Council, 1963–72, 1975–83). Minister for Interior, 1964; Minister for Primary Industry, 1967–71; Dep. Prime Minister and Minister for Trade and Industry, 1971–72; Minister for Overseas Trade, Minerals and Energy, Nov.-Dec. 1975; Dep. Prime Minister and Minister for Trade and Resources, 1975–83. Dep. Leader, Aust. Country Party, 1966–71; Leader, Nat. Country Party, later Nat. Party, 1971–84. Hon. LLD Victoria Univ. of Wellington, NZ, 1983. Council Gold Medal, Qld Agricl Coll., 1985. *Recreations:* golf, tennis, fishing, swimming. *Address:* Sunnymeadows, Murwillumbah, NSW 2484, Australia. *Clubs:* Union, Royal Sydney Golf (Sydney); Queensland (Brisbane).

ANTHONY, Sir Mobolaji B.; *see* Bank-Anthony.

ANTHONY, Ronald Desmond; Chief Inspector of Nuclear Installations, Health and Safety Executive, 1981–85; now Consultant; *b* 21 Nov. 1925; *s* of William Arthur Anthony and Olive Frances Anthony (*née* Buck); *m* 1948, Betty Margaret Croft; four *d*. *Educ:* Chislehurst and Sidcup Grammar School; City and Guilds Coll., Imperial Coll. of Science and Technology (BSc, ACGI). CEng, FIMechE, MRAeS. Vickers Armstrongs (Supermarine), 1950; Nuclear Power Plant Co., 1957; Inspectorate of Nuclear Installations, 1960; Deputy Chief Inspector, 1973; Dir, Safety Policy Div., 1977, Hazardous Installations Gp, 1981–82, Health and Safety Exec. *Publications:* papers in technical journals. *Recreations:* gardening, golf. *Address:* 3 Mereside, Orpington, Kent BR6 8ET. *T:* Farnborough (Kent) 57565.

ANTHONY, Vivian Stanley; Headmaster, Colfe's School, London, since 1976; *b* 5 May 1938; *s* of Captain and Mrs A. S. Anthony; *m* 1969, Rosamund Anne MacDermot Byrn; one *s* one *d*. *Educ:* Cardiff High Sch.; LSE (1st Div. 2nd Cl. Hons BSc Econ); Fitzwilliam Coll., Cambridge (DipEd); Merton Coll., Oxford (schoolmaster student). Asst Master, Leeds Grammar Sch., 1960–64; Asst Master and Housemaster, Tonbridge Sch., 1964–69; Lectr in Educn, Univ. of Leeds, 1969–71; Dep. Headmaster, The King's Sch., Macclesfield, 1971–76. Asst Examr, Econ. Hist., London Univ., 1964–71; Asst Examr, Econs, Oxford and Cambridge Bd, 1970–76, Chief Examr (Awarder), Econs, 1976–; Ext. Examr, Educn, Univs of Manchester, 1972–75, Birmingham, 1975–78, and Lancaster, 1977–79. Chm., Econs Assoc., 1974–77; Member: Schools Council Social Science Cttee, 1976–83; London Univ. Schs Examinations Cttee, 1981–85; Secondary Examinations Council Economics Panel, 1984–; CBI/Schools Panel, 1984; Court, Univ. Kent, 1985–. Sabbatical tour, US indep. schools, 1983. Elected Headmasters' Conf., 1980. *Publications:* Monopoly, 1968, 3rd edn 1976; Overseas Trade, 1969, 4th edn 1981; Banks and Markets, 1970, 3rd edn 1979; (contrib.) The Teaching of Economics in Secondary Schools, 1970; Objective Tests in A Level Economics, 1971, 2nd edn 1974; (contrib.) Curriculum Development in Secondary Schools, 1973; (contrib.) Control of the Economy, 1974; Objective Tests in

Introductory Economics, 1975, 3rd edn 1983; History of Rugby Football at Colfe's, 1980; US Independent Schools, 1984; (contrib.) Comparative Economics, in Teaching Economics, 1984; articles in Economics. *Recreations:* choral singing (Thomas Tallis Society, Dyfed Choir), Rugby football, squash, tennis. *Address:* Lincoln Lodge, Pines Road, Bickley, Kent BR1 2AA. *T:* 01–852 2283. *Clubs:* Athenæum, East India, Devonshire, Sports and Public Schools, Old Colfeians Association.

ANTICO, Sir Tristan, AC 1983; Kt 1973; Chairman and Managing Director, Pioneer Concrete Services Ltd; *b* 25 March 1923; *s* of Terribile Giovanni Antico and Erminia Bertin; *m* 1950, Dorothy Brigid Shields; three *s* four *d.* *Educ:* Sydney High Sch. Began career as Accountant; subseq. became Company Secretary, Melocco Bros; Founder of Pioneer Concrete Services Ltd. AC and Knighthood awarded for services to industry and the community. Comdr, Order of Star of Solidarity (Italy), 1967. *Recreations:* horse breeding and horse racing, swimming, tennis, yachting. *Address:* 161 Raglan Street, Mosman, NSW 2088, Australia. *T:* 969 4070. *Clubs:* Tattersall's, Australian Jockey, Sydney Turf, American National, Royal Sydney Yacht Squadron (Sydney); Manly Golf.

ANTON, Alexander Elder, CBE 1973; FRSE 1977; FBA 1972; *b* 1922; *m* 1949, Doris May Lawrence; one *s.* *Educ:* Aberdeen Univ. (MA, LLB with dist.). Solicitor, 1949; Lectr, Aberdeen, 1953–59; Prof. of Jurisprudence, Univ. of Glasgow, 1959–73. Hon. Vis. Prof., 1982–84, Hon. Prof., 1984, Aberdeen Univ. Mem., Scottish Law Commission, 1966–82. Literary Dir, Stair Soc., 1960–66. *Publications:* Private International Law, 1967; Civil Jurisdiction in Scotland, 1984; contribs to legal and historical jls. *Recreation:* hill walking. *Address:* 9 Baillieswells Terrace, Bieldside, Aberdeen AB1 9AR.

ANTONIO; *see* Ruiz Soler, Antonio.

ANTONIONI, Michelangelo; Film Director; *b* Ferrara, Italy, 29 Sept. 1912; *s* of Ismaele and Elisabetta Roncagli; *m* (marr. diss.). *Educ:* degree in Economics and Commerce, Univ. of Bologna. Formerly an Asst Dir, Film Critic to newspapers, and Script Writer. Films directed include: 8 documentaries, etc, 1943–50; subseq. long films: Cronaca di un Amore, 1950; one episode in Amore in Città, 1951; I Vinti, 1952; La Signora Senza Camelie, 1953; Le Amiche, 1955; Il Grido, 1957; L'Avventura, 1959–60; La Notte, 1961; L'Eclisse, 1962; Il Deserto Rosso, 1964; one episode in I Tre Volti, 1965; Blow-Up, 1967; Zabriskie Point, 1969; Chung Kuo-China, 1972; The Passenger, 1974; Il Mistero di Oberwald, 1979; Identificazione di una Donna, 1981. *Recreations:* collecting blown glass, tennis, ping-pong. *Address:* Via Vincenzo Tiberio 18, Rome, Italy.

ANTRIM, 14th Earl of, *cr* 1620; **Alexander Randal Mark McDonnell;** Viscount Dunluce; Keeper of Conservation, Tate Gallery, since 1975 (Restorer, 1965–75); *b* 3 Feb. 1935; *er s* of 13th Earl of Antrim, KBE, and Angela Christina (*d* 1984), *d* of Sir Mark Sykes, 6th Bt; *S* father, 1977 (but continues to be known as Viscount Dunluce); *m* 1963, Sarah Elizabeth Anne (marr. diss. 1974), 2nd *d* of St John Harmsworth; one *s* two *d*; *m* 1977, Elizabeth, *d* of late Michael Moses Sacher; one *d.* *Educ:* Downside; Christ Church, Oxford; Ruskin Sch. of Art. Restorer, the Ulster Museum, 1969–71. Dir, Ulster Television, 1982–. Mem., Exec. Cttee, City and Guilds Art School, 1983–. FRSA 1984. *Recreations:* painting, vintage cars. *Heir:* *s* Hon. Randal Alexander St John McDonnell, *b* 2 July 1967. *Address:* Glenarm Castle, Glenarm, Co. Antrim, N Ireland. *T:* Glenarm 229. *Club:* Beefsteak.

ANTROBUS, Sir Philip Coutts, 7th Bt, *cr* 1815; *b* 10 April 1908; *s* of late Geoffrey Edward Antrobus and Mary Atherstone, *d* of Hilton Barber, JP, Halesowen, Cradock, Cape Province; *S* cousin, 1968; *m* 1st, 1937, Dorothy Margaret Mary (*d* 1973), *d* of late Rev. W. G. Davis; two *s* one *d*; 2nd, 1975, Doris Primrose (*d* 1986), *widow* of Ralph Dawkins. Served War, 1939–45 (POW). *Heir:* *s* Edward Philip Antrobus [*b* 28 Sept. 1938; *m* 1966, Janet, *d* of Philip Sceales; one *s* two *d*]. *Address:* West Amesbury House, West Amesbury, near Salisbury, Wilts.

ANWAR, Mohamed Samih; Order of the Republic, 2nd Class (Egypt), 1958; Order of Merit, 1st Class (Egypt), 1968; *b* 10 Dec. 1924; *s* of Ahmed Fouad Anwar and Aziza Tewfik; *m* 1953, Omayma Soliman Hazza; one *s* one *d.* *Educ:* Cairo Univ. (Bachelor of Law, 1945). Min. of Justice, 1946–54; First Sec., Min. of Foreign Affairs, 1954; apptd to Egyptian Embassies in Moscow, 1957, and London, 1963; Ambassador to Kuwait, 1966; Under Sec., Min. of Foreign Affairs, 1968; Ambassador to Iran, 1970; Minister of State for Foreign Affairs, 1974; Ambassador to UK, 1975–79, to USSR, 1979–80. Order of Hamayon, 1st Cl. (Iran), 1974; Order of the Flag (Yugoslavia), 1970. *Recreations:* rowing, tennis. *Address:* Ministry of Foreign Affairs, Cairo, Egypt. *Clubs:* Royal Automobile, Hurlingham; Al Ahly (Cairo).

ANWYL, Shirley Anne, (Mrs R. H. C. Anwyl); *see* Ritchie, S. A.

ANWYL-DAVIES, Marcus John, MA, QC 1967; **His Honour Judge Anwyl-Davies;** a Circuit Judge, since 1972; *b* 11 July 1923; *s* of late Thomas Anwyl-Davies and of Kathleen Beryl Anwyl-Davies (*née* Oakshott); *m* 1st, 1954, Eva Hilda Elisabeth Paulson (marr. diss. 1974); one *s* one *d*; 2nd, 1983, Myrna Dashoff. *Educ:* Harrow Sch.; Christ Church, Oxford. Royal Artillery, including service with Hong Kong and Singapore RA, 1942–47 (despatches 1945). Called to Bar, Inner Temple, 1949. Legal Assessor, GMC and GDC, 1969–72; Liaison Judge to Herts Magistrates, 1972. Vice-Pres., Herts Magistrates' Assoc., 1975. Resident Judge, St Albans Crown Court, 1977–82. *Recreations:* farming, photography. *Club:* Reform.

ANYAOKU, Eleazar Chukwuemeka, (Emeka), CON 1982; Ndichie Chief Adazie of Obosi; Deputy Secretary-General of the Commonwealth (Political), 1978–83 and since 1984 (Assistant Secretary-General, 1975–77); *b* 18 Jan. 1933; *e s* of late Emmanuel Chukwuemeka Anyaoku, Ononukpo of Okpuno Ire, Obosi, Nigeria, and Cecilia Adiba (*née* Ogbogu); *m* 1962, Ebunola Olubunmi, *yr d* of late barrister Olusola Akanbi Solanke, of Abeokuta, Nigeria; three *s* one *d.* *Educ:* Merchants of Light Sch., Oba; Univ. of Ibadan (Schol.), Nigeria; courses in England and France.Exec. Asst, Commonwealth Develt Corp., in London and Lagos, 1959–62. Joined Nigerian Diplomatic Service, 1962; Mem. Nigerian Permanent Mission to the UN, New York, 1963–66; seconded to Commonwealth Secretariat as Asst Dir, 1966–71, and Dir, 1971–75, Internat. Affairs Div. Minister of External Affairs, Nigeria, Nov.-Dec. 1983. Served as Secretary: Review Cttee on Commonwealth inter-governmental organisations, June-Aug., 1966; Commonwealth Observer Team for Gibraltar Referendum, Aug.-Sept., 1967; Anguilla Commn, WI, Jan.-Sept. 1970. Vice-Pres., Royal Commonwealth Society, London, 1975– (Dep. Chm., 1972); Mem., Cttee of Management, London University's Inst. of Commonwealth Studies, 1972–; Chm., Africa Centre, London, 1977–82; Mem. Council, Overseas Develt Inst., 1979–. Mem., Governing Council, SCF, 1984–. *Recreations:* tennis, swimming, reading. *Address:* Commonwealth Secretariat, Marlborough House, Pall Mall, SW1. *T:* 01–839 3411; Orimili, Obosi, Anambra State, Nigeria. *Clubs:* Royal Commonwealth Society, Africa Centre, Travellers'; Metropolitan (Lagos).

AOTEAROA, Bishop of, since 1981; **Rt. Rev. Whakahuihui Vercoe,** MBE 1970; *b* 4 June 1928; *s* of Joseph and Wyness Vercoe; *m* 1951, Dorothy Eivers; three *s.* *Educ:* Torere Primary; Feilding Agricultural High School; College House Theological Coll.; Canterbury Univ. LTh 1985. Curate, St John's Church, Feilding, 1951–53; Priest-in-Charge, Wellington Pastorate, 1953–54; Pastor: Wairarapa, 1954–57; Rangitikei, 1957–61; Chaplain: Armed Forces, Malaya, 1961–64; Papakura Military Camp, 1964–65; ANZAC Brigade, Vietnam, 1968–69; Burnham Mil. Camp, 1965–71; Principal, Te Waipounamu Girls' School, 1971–76; Vicar: Ohinemutu Pastorate, 1976–78; Te Rohe o Whakaari, 1978–81; Archdeacon of Tairawhiti and Vicar-General to Bishopric of Aotearoa, 1978–81. *Recreations:* Rugby, golf, reading, tennis, cricket, fishing. *Address:* PO Box 146, Rotorua, New Zealand. *T:* (home) 479–241, (office) 86–093.

APEL, Dr Hans Eberhard; Social-democratic Member of Bundestag, since 1965 (Deputy-Chairman of Group, 1969–72); *b* Hamburg, 25 Feb. 1932; *m* 1956, Ingrid Schwingel; two *d.* *Educ:* Hamburg Univ. Diplom-Volkswirt, 1957, Dr.rer.pol, 1960. Apprentice in Hamburg export and import business, 1951–54; Sec., Socialist Group in European Parlt, 1958–61; Head of Economics, Finance and Transportation Dept of European Parlt, 1962–65. Chm., Bundestag Cttee on Transportation, 1969–72. Mem. Nat. Bd, Social-democratic Party (SPD), 1970–; Parly Sec. of State, Min. for Foreign Affairs, 1972–74; Federal Minister of Finance, 1974–78, of Defence, 1978–82. *Publications:* Edwin Cannan und seine Schüler (Doct. Thesis), 1961; Raumordnung der Bundesrepublik, in: Deutschland 1975, 1964; Europas neue Grenzen, 1964; Der deutsche Parlamentarismus, 1968; Bonn, den ..., Tagebuch eines Bundestagsabgeordneten, 1972. *Recreations:* sailing, soccer. *Address:* Bundeshaus, Görresstrasse 15, 5300 Bonn, Federal Republic of Germany.

APLEY, Alan Graham, FRCS; Editor, Journal of Bone and Joint Surgery, since 1983; *b* 10 Nov. 1914; *s* of Samuel Apley and Mary Tanis; *m* 1939, Janie Kandler; one *s* one *d.* *Educ:* Regent Street Polytechnic; University Coll. London; University College Hosp., London (MB BS); MRCS, LRCP 1938, FRCS 1941. Served RAMC, 1944–47. Cons. Surg., Rowley Bristow Orthopaedic Hosp., Pyrford, 1947; Dir of Accident and Emergency Centre, St Peter's Hosp., Chertsey, 1964; Hon. Dir, Dept of Orthopaedics, St Thomas' Hosp., London, 1972; Pres., Orthopaedic Sect., RSM, 1979. Mem. Council, 1973–85, Vice-Pres. 1984–85, RCS. *Publications:* System of Orthopaedics and Fractures, 1959, 6th edn 1982; (jtly) Replacement of the Knee, 1984; (jtly) Atlas of Skeletal Dysplasias, 1985; (ed) Recent Advances in Orthopaedics, 1969; (ed) Modern Trends in Orthopaedics, 1972; various articles in surg. jls. *Recreations:* music, ski-ing, travelling. *Address:* Singleton Lodge, West Byfleet, Surrey KT14 6PW. *T:* Byfleet 43353; (office) 01-405 7227.

APPEL, Karel Christian; Netherlands Artist (Painter); *b* 25 April 1921; *s* of Jan Appel and Johanna Chevallier. *Educ:* Royal Academy of Art, Amsterdam. Began career as artist in 1938. Has had one-man exhibitions in Europe and America including the following in London: Inst. of Contemporary Art, 1957; Gimpel Fils, 1959, 1960, 1964. UNESCO Prize, Venice Biennale, 1953; Lissone Prize, Italy, 1958; Acquisition Prize, Sao Paulo Biennale, Brazil, 1959; Graphique Internat. Prize, Ljubljana, Jugoslavia, 1959; Guggenheim National Prize, Holland, 1961; Guggenheim International Prize, 1961. *Publications:* Illustrations: De Blijde en Onvoorziene Week, by Hugo Claus, 1950; Atonaal, by Simon Vinkenoog, 1951; De Ronde Kant van de Aarde, by Hans Andreus, 1952; Het Bloed Stroomt Door, by Bert Schierbeek, 1954; Haine, by E. Looten, 1954; Cogne Ciel, by E. Looten, 1954; Rhapsodie de ma Nuit, by E. Looten, 1958; Unteilbare Teil, by André Frénaud, 1960; Een Dier Heeft een Mens Getekend, by B. Schierbeek, 1961.

APPLEBY, Brian John, QC 1971; a Recorder of the Crown Court, since 1972; *b* 25 Feb. 1930; *s* of Ernest Joel and Gertrude Appleby; *m* 1958, Rosa Helena (*née* Flitterman); one *s* one *d.* *Educ:* Uppingham; St John's Coll., Cambridge (BA). Called to Bar, Middle Temple, 1953; Bencher, 1980. Dep. Chm., Notts QS, 1970–71. Mem., Nottingham City Council, 1955–58 and 1960–63. District Referee, Nottinghamshire Wages Conciliation Board, NCB, 1980–. *Recreations:* watching good football (preferably Nottingham Forest: Mem. Club Cttee, 1965–82, Life Mem., 1982; Vice-Chm., 1972–75, Chm., 1975–78); swimming, reading and enjoying, when possible, company of wife and children. *Address:* The Poplars, Edwalton Village, Notts. *T:* Nottingham 232814.

APPLEBY, Maj.-Gen. David Stanley, CB 1979; MC 1943; TD 1950; Director of Army Legal Services, 1976–78, retired; *b* 4 Dec. 1918; *s* of Stanley Appleby and Mabel Dorothy Mary (*née* Dickson); *m* 1942, Prudence Marianne Chisholm; one *s* one *d* (and one *s* decd). *Educ:* St Peter's School. Barrister, Middle Temple, 1951. Rifleman, London Rifle Bde (TA), 1938; 2nd Lieut, Royal Fusiliers (TA), 1939; Army Legal Services, 1950–; Captain, 1950; Maj.-Gen. 1976. *Recreations:* sailing, military and other history. *Address:* Two Acres, Beechwood Lane, Burley, Ringwood, Hants. *Clubs:* Naval & Military; Island Sailing (Cowes).

APPLEBY, Douglas Edward Marrison; farmer and stockbreeder; retired as Managing Director, The Boots Co. Ltd; *b* 17 May 1929; *s* of late Robert Appleby, MSc and Muriel (*née* Surtees); *m* 1952, June (*née* Marrison), company director; one *s* one *d.* *Educ:* Durham Johnston Sch.; Univ. of Nottingham. BSc London, BSc Nottingham, 1950. Chartered Accountant, 1957. Commissioned, RAF, 1950–54. Moore, Stephens & Co., Chartered Accountants, London, 1954–57; Distillers Co. Ltd, 1957–58; Corn Products Co., NY, 1959–63; Wilkinson Sword Ltd, 1964–68; The Boots Co Ltd, 1968–81 (Finance Dir, 1968–72, Man. Dir, 1973–81). Regional Dir, Nat. Westminster Bank, 1979–; Chairman: John H. Mason Ltd, 1982–; Meadow Farm Produce plc, 1984–. Member Council: Inst. Chartered Accountants, 1971–75; Loughborough Univ., 1973–75; CBI, 1977–81. *Recreations:* Flat and National Hunt racing. *Address:* Pond Farm, Upper Broughton, Melton Mowbray, Leics; West Drums Farm, by Brechin, Angus.

APPLEBY, (Lesley) Elizabeth, (Mrs Michael Kenneth Collins), QC 1979; barrister-at-law; *b* 12 Aug. 1942; *o d* of Arthur Leslie Appleby and late Dorothy Evelyn Appleby (*née* Edwards); *m* 1978, Michael Kenneth Collins, OBE, BSc, MICE; one *s* one *d.* *Educ:* Dominican Convent, Brewood, Staffs; Wolverhampton Girls' High Sch.; Manchester Univ. (LLB Hons). Called to Bar, Gray's Inn, 1965 (Richardson Schol.); *ad eundem* Lincoln's Inn, 1975; in practice at Chancery Bar, 1966–; Member, Senate of Inns of Court and Bar, 1977–80, 1981–82. *Recreations:* sailing, swimming, music, golf, gardening. *Address:* 4/5 Gray's Inn Square, Gray's Inn, WC1R 5AY. *T:* 01–404 5252; 32 Pembroke Road, W8. *T:* 01–602 4141; The Glebe House, The Green, Chiddingfold, Surrey. *T:* Wormley 4671. *Club:* Royal Lymington Yacht.

APPLEBY, Malcolm Arthur; engraver designer; *b* 6 Jan. 1946; *s* of James William and Marjory Appleby. *Educ:* Haws Down County Secondary Modern School for Boys; Beckenham Sch. of Art; Ravensbourne Coll. of Art and Design; Central Sch. of Arts and Crafts; Sir John Cass Sch. of Art; Royal Coll. of Art. Set up trade, 1968; bought Crathes station, 1970; developed fresh approaches to engraving on silver, forging after engraving; works designed and executed include: engraving on Prince of Wales coronet; model of moon (subseq. gift to first moon astronauts); steel and gold cylinder box for Goldsmiths' Co.; steel, gold, ivory and silver chess set, 1977; 500th anniv. silver for London Assay Office; King George VI Diamond Stakes trophy, 1978; seal for the Board of Trustees. V & A; sporting guns, silver bowls, jewels, prints. Work in collections: Aberdeen Art Gallery; Royal Scottish Museum; Scottish Craft Collection; East Midlands Arts; British Museum; Goldsmiths' Co., V&A; Crafts Council; Contemporary Arts Soc.; Tower of

London Armouries. Mem., Crathes Drumoak Community Council (Chm., 1981). *Recreations:* work, walking, looking at garden, brown trout fishing (with a worm), drinking tea with friends, acting in pantomime, cat (Joan, a big bouncing tom), conservation matters, Scottish issues (supporter, NE Mountain Trust), breeding silver spangled Hamburg bantam hens. *Address:* Crathes Station, Banchory, Kincardineshire. *T:* Crathes 642.

APPLEBY, Dom Raphael; National Co-ordinator for RC Chaplains in Higher Education, since 1980; *b* 18 July 1931; *s* of Harold Thompson Appleby and Margaret Morgan. *Educ:* Downside; Christ's Coll., Cambridge (MA). Downside novitiate, 1951. Housemaster at Downside, 1962–75, Head Master, 1975–80. National Chaplain to Catholic Students' Council, 1974–; Diocesan Youth Chaplain, Clifton Diocese, 1983–. *Publication:* Dear Church, What's the Point?, 1984. *Recreations:* books, music. *Address:* Downside Abbey, Bath BA3 4RH.

APPLEBY, Robert, CBE 1969; Chairman, Black & Decker Ltd, 1956–75 (Managing Director, 1956–72); *b* 1913; *s* of Robert James Appleby; *m* 1957, Elisabeth Friederike (*d* 1975), *d* of Prof. Eidmann. *Educ:* Graham Sea Training and Engineering Sch., Scarborough. Dep. Chm., Black & Decker Manufacturing Co., Maryland, 1968–72. Mem., Post Office Bd, 1972–73. CEng, FIProdE; FBIM.

APPLETON, Rt. Rev. George, CMG 1972; MBE 1946; *b* 20 Feb. 1902; *s* of Thomas George and Lily Appleton; *m* 1929, Marjorie Alice (*d* 1980), *d* of Charles Samuel Barrett; one *s* two *d*. *Educ:* County Boys' School, Maidenhead; Selwyn Coll., Cambridge; St Augustine's Coll., Canterbury. BA Cantab 1924 (2nd Cl. Math. Trip. pt 1, 1st Cl. Theological Trip. pt I); MA 1929. Deacon, 1925; Priest, 1926. Curate, Stepney Parish Church, 1925–27; Missionary in charge SPG Mission, Irrawaddy Delta, 1927–33; Warden, Coll. of Holy Cross, Rangoon, 1933–41; Archdeacon of Rangoon, 1943–46; Director of Public Relations, Government of Burma, 1943–46; Vicar of Headstone, 1947–50; Sec., Conf. of Brit. Missionary Societies, 1950–57; Rector of St Botolph, Aldgate, 1957–62; Archdeacon of London and Canon of St Paul's Cathedral, 1962–63; Archbishop of Perth and Metropolitan of W Australia, 1963–69; Archbishop in Jerusalem and Metropolitan, 1969–74. Buber-Rosenzweig Medal, Council of Christians and Jews, 1975. *Publications:* John's Witness to Jesus, 1955; In His Name, 1956; Glad Encounter, 1959; On the Eightfold Path, 1961; Daily Prayer and Praise, 1962; Acts of Devotion, 1963; One Man's Prayers, 1967; Journey for a Soul, 1974; Jerusalem Prayers, 1974; The Word is the Seed, 1976; The Way of a Disciple, 1979; The Practice of Prayer, 1980; Glimpses of Faith, 1982; Praying with the Bible, 1982; Prayers from a Troubled Heart, 1983; The Quiet Heart, 1983; (ed) The Oxford Book of Prayer, 1985; The Heart of the Bible, 1986. *Address:* 112A St Mary's Road, Oxford OX4 1QF.

APPLEYARD, Leonard Vincent, CMG 1986; HM Diplomatic Service; Ambassador to Hungary, since 1986; *b* 2 Sept. 1938; *s* of Thomas William Appleyard; *m* 1964, Elizabeth Margaret West; two *d*. *Educ:* Read School, Drax, W Yorks; Queens' Coll., Cambridge (MA). Foreign Office, 1962; Third Secretary, Hong Kong, 1964; Second Secretary, Peking, 1966; Second, later First, Secretary, Foreign Office, 1969; First Secretary, Delhi, 1971, Moscow, 1975; HM Treasury, 1978; Financial Counsellor, Paris, 1979–82; Head of Economic Relations Dept, FCO, 1982–84; Principal Private Sec. to Sec. of State for Foreign and Commonwealth Affairs, 1984–86. *Recreations:* music, reading, tennis. *Address:* c/o Foreign and Commonwealth Office, SW1. *Club:* Brooks's.

APPLEYARD, Sir Raymond Kenelm, KBE 1986; PhD; Director-General for Information Market and Innovation, Commission of the European Communities, 1981–86; *b* 5 Oct. 1922; *s* of late Maj.-Gen. K. C. Appleyard, CBE, TD, DL, and Monica Mary Louis; *m* 1947, Joan Greenwood; one *s* two *d*. *Educ:* Rugby; Cambridge. BA 1943, MA 1948, PhD 1950. Instructor, Yale Univ., 1949–51; Fellow, Rockefeller Foundn, California Inst. of Technology, 1951–53; Research Officer, Atomic Energy of Canada Ltd, 1953–56; Sec., UN Scientific Cttee on effects of atomic radiation, 1956–61; Dir, Biology Div., Commn of European Atomic Energy Community, 1961–73; Dir-Gen. for Scientific and Tech. Information and Information Management, EEC Commn, 1973–80. Exec. Sec., European Molecular Biology Organisation, 1965–73; Sec., European Molecular Biology Conf., 1969–73. Hon. Dr.med Ulm, 1977. *Publications:* contribs to: Nature, Jl Gen. Microbiol., Genetics. *Recreations:* bridge, tennis, squash. *Club:* Athenæum.

ap ROBERT, Hywel Wyn Jones; His Honour Judge ap Robert; a Circuit Judge, since 1975, now Judge of Mid-Glamorgan and Neath and Port Talbot groups of County Courts; *b* 19 Nov. 1923; *s* of Rev. Robert John Jones, BA, BD and Mrs Jones (*née* Evans); *m* 1956, Elizabeth Davies; two *d*. *Educ:* Cardiff High Sch.; Corpus Christi Coll., Oxford (MA). War Service, FO and Intell. Corps. 1942–46, in Britain and India. Called to Bar, Middle Temple, 1950. A Recorder of the Crown Court, 1972–75; Stipendiary Magistrate, Cardiff, later S Glamorgan, 1972–75. Contested (Plaid Cymru) Cardiganshire, 1970. Hon. Mem., Gorsedd of the Bards, 1973. *Recreations:* Welsh literature, classical and modern languages. *Address:* Law Courts, Cardiff. *Club:* Cardiff and County (Cardiff).

APSLEY, Lord; Allen Christopher Bertram Bathurst; *b* 11 March 1961; *s* and *heir* of 8th Earl Bathurst, *qv*; *m* 1986, Hilary, *d* of John F. George, Weston Lodge Albury, Guildford. *Address:* Cirencester Park, Cirencester, Glos GL7 2BT.

APTHORP, John Dorrington; Executive Chairman, Bejam Group plc, since 1968; *b* 25 April 1935; *s* of Eric and Mildred Apthorp; *m* 1959, Jane Frances Arnold; three *s* one *d*. *Educ:* Aldenham School. FBIM 1977; FInstD 1978; FIGD 1981. Sub-Lieut RNVR, 1953–55. Family business, Appypak, 1956–68; started Bejam Group, 1968–. Guardian Young Business Man of Year, 1974. Councillor, London Bor. of Barnet, 1968–74. Liveryman, Butchers' Company, 1974–. Commandeur d'Honneur pour Commanderie du Bontemps de Medoc et des Graves, 1977. *Recreations:* shooting, wine. *Address:* The Field House, Newlands Avenue, Radlett, Herts WD7 8EL. *T:* Radlett 5201. *Clubs:* St Hubert's, Radlett Tennis and Squash (Pres., 1982–).

AQUILECCHIA, Prof. Giovanni; Professor of Italian, University of London, since 1970 (Bedford College, 1970–85; Royal Holloway and Bedford New College, since 1985); *b* Nettuno, Rome, 28 Nov. 1923; *s* of late Gen. Vincenzo Aquilecchia and Maria L. Filibeck; *m* 1951, Costantina M. Bacchetta (marr. diss. 1973); two *s* one *d*. *Educ:* Liceo T. Tasso, Rome; Univ. of Rome. Dott. Lett., 1946, Diploma of Perfezionamento in Filologia Moderna, 1948, Univ. of Rome. Asst in Italian, Univ. of Rome, 1946–49; Boursier du Gouvernement Français at Collège de France, Univ. of Paris, 1949–50; British Council Scholar, Warburg Inst., Univ. of London, 1950–51; Asst, Dept of Italian Studies, Univ. of Manchester, 1951–53; Asst Lectr in Italian, University Coll., London, 1953–55, Lectr, 1955–59; Libero Docente di Letteratura Italiana, Univ. of Rome, 1958–; Reader in Italian, Univ. of London, at University Coll., 1959–61; Prof. of Italian Lang. and Lit., Univ. of Manchester, 1961–70. Corr. Fellow, Arcadia, 1961; Vis. Prof., Univ. of Melbourne, 1983; Hon. Res. Fellow, UCL, 1984–. MA (Manchester) 1965. *Publications:* Giordano Bruno, 1971; Schede di italianistica, 1976; critical editions of: Giordano Bruno: La Cena de le Ceneri, 1955; Due Dialoghi sconosciuti, 1957; Dialoghi Italiani, 1958, repr. 1972, 1985; Praelectiones geometricæ e Ars deformationum, 1964; De la causa, principio et uno,

1973; Pietro Aretino: Sei Giornate, 1969, 2nd edn with Introduction, 1975, reprint 1980; Giovanni Villani: Cronica con le continuazioni di Matteo e Filippo, 1979; (co-editor) Collected essays on Italian Language and Literature, 1971; contrib.: Atti dell'Accad. Nazionale Lincei, Atti e Memorie dell'Arcadia, Bull. dell'Accad. della Crusca, Bull. John Rylands Library, Cultura Neolatina, Dizionario Biografico degli Italiani, Enciclopedia Dantesca, Encyclopædia Britannica, English Miscellany, Filologia e critica, Giornale storico della letteratura italiana, Lingua Nostra, Storia della cultura veneta, Studi Secenteschi, Studi Tassiani, etc. *Address:* Department of Italian, University College, Gower Street, WC1.

ARAIN, Shafiq; Minister without Portfolio, President's Office, and High Commissioner for Uganda to London, 1980–85; *b* 20 Nov. 1933; *s* of late Din Mohd Arain; *m* 1966, Maria Leana Godinho; one *s* two *d*. *Educ:* Government Sch., Kampala; Regent's Polytechnic, London; Nottingham Univ. MP (UPC), 1962–71; Member, E African Legislative Assembly, 1963–71; E African Minister for Common Market and Economic Affairs, later E African Minister for Communications, Research and Social Services; Chairman: Minimum Wages Commission, 1964; Statutory Commn on Cooperative Movement, 1967. Uganda's Delegate to UN General Assembly, 1965–66; Leader, Uganda Delegn to Canada and CPA Conf., Trinidad and Tobago, 1969. Member, Governing Council, Univ. of Dar es Salaam, 1967–68; Chm., Commonwealth Parly Assoc., Uganda Br., 1969–70. Pres., Uganda Cricket Assoc., 1968–69. Left for exile in London following coup in 1971; returned to Uganda, 1979; elections were held in Dec. 1980. *Recreations:* golf, walking, reading. *Address:* Blanton House, Kennel Avenue, Ascot, Berks SL5 7PB. *T:* Ascot 26660. *Clubs:* Uganda, Royal Commonwealth Society, Travellers'.

ARBER, Prof. Werner; Professor of Molecular Microbiology, Basle University, since 1971. Discovered restriction enzymes at Geneva in 1960's; Nobel Prize in Physiology or Medicine (jointly), 1978. *Address:* Department of Microbiology, Biozentrum der Universität Basel, 70 Klingelbergstrasse, CH 4056, Basel, Switzerland.

ARBUTHNOT, Andrew Robert Coghill; Missioner, London Healing Mission, since 1983; Director, Sun Alliance and London Insurance Ltd, since 1970; *b* 14 Jan. 1926; *s* of Robert Wemyss Muir Arbuthnot and Mary Arbuthnot (*née* Coghill); *m* 1952, Audrey Dutton-Barker; one *s* one *d*. *Educ:* Eton. Served 1944–47, Captain, Scots Guards, wounded. Dir, Arbuthnot Latham & Co. Ltd, 1953–82; Chm. and Chief Exec., Arbuthnot Latham Holdings, 1974–81; Chm., Arbuthnot Insurance Services, 1968–83. Contested (C) Houghton-le-Spring, 1959. Ordained Deacon, 1974; Priest, 1975. *Publication:* (with Audrey Arbuthnot) Love that Heals, 1986. *Recreations:* water colour painting, walking. *Address:* Monksfield House, Tilford, Farnham, Surrey GU10 2AL. *T:* Runfold 2233.

ARBUTHNOT, Sir John (Sinclair-Wemyss), 1st Bt *cr* 1964; MBE 1944; TD 1951; Chairman, Folkestone and District Water Co.; *b* 11 Feb. 1912; *s* of late Major K. W. Arbuthnot, the Seaforth Highlanders; *m* 1943, Margaret Jean, *yr d* of late Alexander G. Duff; two *s* three *d*. *Educ:* Eton; Trinity Coll., Cambridge. MA Hons in Nat. Sciences. Served throughout War of 1939–45, in RA, Major (wounded); Dep. Inspector of Shell, 1942–45; hon. pac 1944; TARO, 1948–62. Prospective Conservative candidate, Don Valley Div. of Yorks, 1934–35, Dunbartonshire, 1936–45, Dover Div. of Kent, 1945–50, contesting elections in 1935 and 1945. MP (C) Dover Div. of Kent, 1950–64; PPS to Parly Sec., Min. of Pensions, 1952–53, to Minister of Pensions, 1953–56, and to Minister of Health, 1956–57; a Chm. of Committees and a Temporary Chm. of the House, 1958–64; Second Church Estates Comr, 1962–64; Church Comr for England and Mem., Bd of Governors, 1962–77 (Dep Chm., Assets Cttee, 1966–77); Mem., Church Assembly and Gen. Synod of Church of England, 1955–75 (Panel of Chairmen, 1970–72); Trustee, Lambeth Palace Library, 1964–77; Chm., Archbp of Canterbury's Commn to inquire into the organisation of the Church by dioceses in London and the SE of England, 1965–67. Member: Crathorne Cttee on Sunday Observance, 1961–64; Hodson Commn on Synodical Government for the Church of England, 1964–66; Parliamentary Chm., Dock & Harbour Authorities Assoc., 1962–64; Member: Public Accounts Cttee, 1955–64; Standing Cttee, Ross Inst., 1951–62. Member Parliamentary Delegations: to the Iron and Steel Community, 1955; to West Africa, 1956; to USA, 1957; to The West Indies, 1958; to Zanzibar, Mauritius and Madagascar, 1961; Leader of Parliamentary Delegation to Bulgaria, 1963. A Vice Pres., Trustee Savings Banks Assoc., 1962–76; in business in tea industry concerned with India, Ceylon and the Cameroons, 1934–74; Chm., Estates & Agency Holdings Ltd, 1955–70; Joint Hon. Sec. Assoc. of British Chambers of Commerce, 1953–59. *Recreation:* gardening. *Heir:* *s* William Reierson Arbuthnot, *b* 2 Sept. 1950. *Address:* Poulton Manor, Ash, Canterbury, Kent CT3 2HW. *T:* Ash 812516. *Clubs:* Carlton, Royal Commonwealth Society.

ARBUTHNOT, Sir Keith Robert Charles, 8th Bt *cr* 1823, of Edinburgh; *b* 23 Sept. 1951; *s* of Sir Hugh Fitz-Gerald Arbuthnot, 7th Bt and Elizabeth Kathleen (*d* 1972), *d* of late Sqdn-Ldr G. G. A. Williams; *S* father, 1983; *m* 1982, Anne, *yr d* of Brig. Peter Moore; one *s*. *Educ:* Wellington; Univ. of Edinburgh. BSc (Soc. Sci.). *Heir:* *s* Robert Hugh Peter Arbuthnot, *b* 2 March 1986. *Address:* Whitebridge, Peebles, Peeblesshire.

ARBUTHNOTT, family name of **Viscount of Arbuthnott.**

ARBUTHNOTT, 16th Viscount of, *cr* 1641; **John Campbell Arbuthnott,** CBE 1986; DSC 1945; FRSE 1984; Lord-Lieutenant Grampian Region (Kincardineshire), since 1977; Lord High Commissioner to General Assembly, Church of Scotland, 1986; Director: Clydesdale Bank, since 1985 (Northern Area, 1975–85); Aberdeen and Northern Marts, since 1973; Chairman, Scottish Widows' Fund and Life Assurance Society, since 1984 (Director, since 1978); *b* 26 Oct. 1924; *e s* of 15th Viscount of Arbuthnott, CB, CBE, DSO, MC, and Ursula Collingwood; *S* father, 1966; *m* 1949, Mary Elizabeth Darley (*née* Oxley); one *s* one *d*. *Educ:* Fettes Coll.; Gonville and Caius Coll., Cambridge. Served RNVR (Fleet Air Arm), 1942–46; Near and Far East, British Pacific Fleet, 1945. Cambridge University, 1946–49 (Estate Management), MA 1967. Chartered Surveyor and Land Agent; Agricultural Land Service, 1949–55; Land Agent (Scotland), The Nature Conservancy, 1955–67; Member: Countryside Commn for Scotland, 1967–71; Aberdeen Univ. Court, 1978–84; Chm., Red Deer Commn, 1969–75; President: British Assoc. for Shooting and Conservation (formerly Wildfowlers Assoc. of GB and Ireland), 1973–; The Scottish Landowners' Fedn, 1974–79 (Convener, 1971–74); Royal Zool Soc. of Scotland, 1976–; Scottish Agricl Orgn Soc., 1980–83; RSGS, 1983–; Fedn of Agricl Co-operatives (UK) Ltd, 1983–; Dep. Chm., Nature Conservancy Council, 1980–85, Chm., Adv. Cttee for Scotland, 1980–85. FRSA. KStJ 1982, Prior of Scotland, OStJ, 1983. *Recreations:* countryside activities, historical research. *Heir:* *s* Master of Arbuthnott, *qv*. *Address:* Arbuthnott House, by Laurencekirk, Kincardineshire, Scotland. *T:* Inverbervie 61226. *Clubs:* Army and Navy, Farmers'; New (Edinburgh).

ARBUTHNOTT, Master of; Hon. John Keith Oxley Arbuthnott; *b* 18 July 1950; *s* and *heir* of 16th Viscount of Arbuthnott, *qv*; *m* 1974, Jill Mary, *er d* of Captain Colin Farquharson, *qv*; one *s* two *d*. *Educ:* Fettes College; Aberdeen Univ. *Address:* Kilternan, Arbuthnott, Laurencekirk, Kincardineshire AB3 1NA. *T:* Inverbervie 61203.

ARBUTHNOTT, Hugh James, CMG 1984; HM Diplomatic Service; Ambassador to Romania, since 1986; *b* 27 Dec. 1936; *m*; three *s*. Joined Foreign (subseq. Diplomatic) Service, 1960; 3rd Sec., Tehran, 1962–64; 2nd, later 1st Sec., FO, 1964–66; Private Sec., Minister of State for Foreign Affairs, 1966–68; Lagos, 1968–71; 1st Sec. (Head of Chancery), Tehran, 1971–74; Asst, later Head of European Integration Dept (External), FCO, 1974–77; Counsellor (Agric. and Econ.), Paris, 1978–80; Head of Chancery, Paris, 1980–83; Under Sec., Internat. Div., ODA, 1983–85. *Publication:* (ed with G. Edwards) Common Man's Guide to the Common Market, 1979. *Address:* c/o Foreign and Commonwealth Office, SW1A 2AH.

ARBUTHNOTT, Robert; with British Council; *b* 28 Sept. 1936; *s* of late Archibald Arbuthnott, MBE, ED, and of Barbara Joan (*née* Worters); *m* 1962, Sophie Robina (*née* Axford); one *s* two *d*. *Educ:* Sedbergh Sch. (scholar); Emmanuel Coll., Cambridge (exhibnr; BA Mod Langs, MA). Nat. service, 1955–57 (2nd Lieut The Black Watch RHR). British Council, 1960–: Karachi, 1960–62; Lahore, 1962–64; London, 1964–67; Representative, Nepal, 1967–72; London Inst. of Education, 1972–73; Representative, Malaysia, 1973–76; Director, Educational Contracts Dept, 1976–77; Controller, Personnel and Staff Recruitment Div., 1978–81; Representative, Germany, 1981–85. *Recreations:* music-making, the arts, sport. *Address:* Foundry Cottage, Foundry Lane, Haslemere, Surrey GU27 2QF. *T:* Haslemere 54528. *Club:* United Oxford & Cambridge University.

ARCHDALE, Sir Edward (Folmer), 3rd Bt, *cr* 1928; DSC 1943; Captain, RN, retired; *b* 8 Sept. 1921; *s* of Vice-Adm. Sir Nicholas Edward Archdale, 2nd Bt, CBE, and Gerda (*d* 1969), 2nd *d* of late F. C. Sievers, Copenhagen; *S* father 1955; *m* 1954, Elizabeth Ann Stewart (marr. diss. 1978), *d* of late Maj.-Gen. Wilfrid Boyd Fellowes Lukis, CBE; one *s* two *d*. *Educ:* Royal Naval Coll., Dartmouth. Joined Royal Navy, 1935; served War of 1939–45 (despatches, DSC). *Recreation:* civilization. *Heir:* *s* Nicholas Edward Archdale, *b* 2 Dec. 1965. *Address:* 19 Dermott Road, Comber, Co. Down BT23 5LG.

ARCHER, Albert, MBE 1980; Member, Royal Commission on Environmental Pollution, 1981–85; *b* 7 March 1915; *s* of Arthur Archer and Margaret Alice Norris; *m* 1st, 1939; two *s*; 2nd, 1975, Peggy, *widow* of John F. Marsh; two step *s*. *Educ:* Manchester Grammar Sch.; Manchester Coll. of Technology. Fellow, Instn of Environmental Health Officers, 1961. Chief Public Health Inspector, Bor. of Halesowen, 1943–73; City of Birmingham: Environmtl Protection Officer, 1973–75; Dep. City Environmtl Officer, 1975–76; City Environmtl Officer, 1976–80. Mem., govt working parties on air pollution. Pres., Inst. of Environmental Health Officers, 1979–83. *Publications:* articles on air pollution in technical jls. *Recreation:* watching cricket. *Address:* 8 Portland Drive, Stourbridge, West Midlands DY9 0SD. *T:* Hagley 883366.

ARCHER, Gen. Sir (Arthur) John, KCB 1976; OBE 1964; Chief Executive, Royal Hong Kong Jockey Club, 1980–86, retired; *b* 12 Feb. 1924; *s* of Alfred and Mildred Archer, Fakenham; *m* 1950, Cynthia Marie, *d* of Col Alexander and Eileen Allan, Swallowcliffe, Wilts; two *s*. *Educ:* King's Sch., Peterborough; St Catharine's Coll., Cambridge. Entered Army, 1943; commnd 1944; regular commn Dorset Regt, 1946; psc 1956; jssc 1959; GSO1 3rd Div., 1963–65; CO 1 Devon and Dorset Regt, 1965–67; Comdr Land Forces Gulf, 1968–69; idc 1970; Dir of Public Relations (Army), 1970–72; Comdr 2nd Div., 1972–74; Dir of Army Staff Duties, 1974–76; Comdr British Forces Hong Kong, 1976–78 and Lt-Gen. Brigade of Gurkhas, 1977–78; C-in-C, UKLF, 1978–79. CBIM. Col, Devonshire and Dorset Regt, 1977–79. Dir, Hongkong and Shanghai Banking Corp., 1981–. *Recreations:* light aviation and gliding. *Address:* 23 Rozel Manor, 48 Western Road, Poole, Dorset BH13 6EX. *T:* Poole 766270. *Clubs:* Army and Navy; Hong Kong.

ARCHER, Bruce; *see* Archer, L. B.

ARCHER, Sir Clyde Vernon Harcourt, Kt 1962; Judge of the Court of Appeal, Bahamas, 1971–75; *b* 12 Nov. 1904. *Educ:* Harrison Coll., Barbados; Cambridge Univ. Barrister-at-Law, Gray's Inn; clerk to the Attorney-General, Barbados, 1930; police magistrate Barbados, 1935; Judge, Bridgetown Petty Debt Court, 1938; Legal Draftsman, Trinidad and Tobago, 1944; Solicitor-General, Trinidad and Tobago, 1953; Puisne Judge, Trinidad and Tobago, 1954; Chief Justice of the Windward Islands and Leeward Islands, 1958; a Federal Justice, WI, 1958–62. *Publication:* (jointly) Revised Edition of the Laws of Barbados, 1944. *Address:* 40 Graeme Hall Terrace, Christchurch, Barbados.

ARCHER, Frank Joseph, RE 1960 (ARE 1940); RWS 1976 (ARWS 1972); ARCA 1937; Head of School of Fine Art, Kingston Polytechnic, Kingston upon Thames (formerly Kingston College of Art), 1962–73, retired; *b* 30 June 1912; *s* of Joseph and Alberta Archer; *m* 1939, Celia Cole; one *s* one *d*. *Educ:* Eastbourne Grammar Sch.; Eastbourne Sch. of Art; Royal Coll. of Art. ARCA 1937; Rome Scholar, Engraving, 1938; British Sch. at Rome, 1938. Paintings bought by numerous local authorities and private collectors. *Address:* 2 Owls Castle Cottages, Cottenden Road, Stonegate, Wadhurst, E Sussex. *T:* Ticehurst 200082.

ARCHER, Graham Robertson; HM Diplomatic Service; Counsellor, Pretoria, since 1982; *b* 4 July 1939; *s* of late Henry Robertson Archer and Winifred Archer; *m* 1963, Pauline Cowan; two *d*. *Educ:* Judd School, Tonbridge. Joined Commonwealth Relations Office, 1962; British High Commission, New Delhi, 1964; Vice Consul, Kuwait, 1966; CRO (later FCO), 1967; Second Secretary (Commercial), Washington, 1970; First Secretary: FCO, 1972; Wellington, NZ, 1975; FCO, 1979. *Recreations:* listening to music, gardening, hill walking. *Address:* c/o Foreign and Commonwealth Office, SW1; 218 Crown Avenue, Waterkloof, Pretoria, South Africa. *T:* 46–3811.

ARCHER, Mrs Jean Mary; Under-Secretary, Ministry of Agriculture, Fisheries and Food, 1973–86; *b* 24 Aug. 1932; *e d* of late Reginald R. and D. Jane Harvey, Braiseworth Hall, Tannington, Suffolk; *m* 1954, G. Michéal D. Archer, MB, BChir, FFARCS, *er s* of Maj.-Gen. G. T. L. Archer, CB; two *d*. *Educ:* Fleet House, Felixstowe; St Felix Sch., Southwold; Newnham Coll., Cambridge. MA Econs 1954. Asst Principal, Min. of Agriculture, 1954; Private Sec. to successive Perm. Secs, MAFF, 1956–59; Principal 1960; Sec., Reorganisation Commn for Eggs, 1967; Asst Sec. 1968; Under-Sec. i/c Food Policy Gp, MAFF, 1973; Under-Sec., Dept of Prices and Consumer Protection, 1974–76; returned to MAFF, as Under-Sec., Milk and Marketing Group, 1976; Under-Sec., Meat, Poultry and Eggs Div., 1980. *Recreations:* travel, music, tennis, watching sport, swimming administration (Team Man., Chelsea/Kensington Swimming Club; Hon. Sec., Swimmers' Parents' and Supporters' Assoc.). *Address:* 51 Sussex Street, SW1. *T:* 01–828 6296; Friary Cottage, Mendlesham, Suffolk. *T:* Mendlesham 395. *Club:* Hurlingham.
See also Sir A. J. D. McCowan.

ARCHER, Jeffrey Howard; politician and author; Deputy Chairman of the Conservative Party, since 1985; *b* 15 April 1940; *s* of William Archer and Lola Archer (*née* Cook); *m* 1966, Mary Weeden; two *s*. *Educ:* by my wife since leaving Wellington Sch., Somerset; Brasenose Coll., Oxford. Athletics Blues, 1963–65, Gymnastics Blue, 1963, Pres. OUAC 1965; ran for Great Britain (never fast enough); Oxford 100 yards record (9.6 sec.), 1966. Mem. GLC for Havering, 1966–70; MP (C) Louth, Dec. 1969–Sept. 1974. Mem. Exec., British Theatre Museum. Council Mem., Think British. Pres., Somerset AAA, 1973; Hon. Pres., Glasgow Univ. Dialectic Soc., 1984–. FRSA 1973. *Publications:* Not a Penny More, Not a Penny Less, 1975; Shall We Tell the President?, 1977; Kane and Abel, 1979 (televised, 1986); A Quiver Full of Arrows, 1980; The Prodigal Daughter, 1982; First Among Equals, 1984; A Matter of Honour, 1986. *Recreations:* theatre, watching Somerset play cricket (represented Somerset CCC in benefit match, 1981; Pres., Somerset Wyverns, 1983). *Address:* 93 Albert Embankment, SE1; The Old Vicarage, Grantchester. *Clubs:* MCC; Louth Working Men's.

ARCHER, Sir John; *see* Archer, Sir A. J.

ARCHER, John Francis Ashweek, QC 1975; a Recorder of the Crown Court since 1974; *b* 9 July 1925; *s* of late George Eric Archer, FRCSE, and late Frances Archer (*née* Ashweek); *m* 1960, Doris Mary Hennessey. *Educ:* Winchester Coll., 1938–43; New Coll., Oxford, 1947–49 (BA 1949). Served War of 1939–45, 1944–47; Lieut RA, 1948. Called to Bar, Inner Temple, 1950, Bencher, 1984. *Recreations:* motoring, bridge. *Address:* 22a Connaught Square, W2. *T:* 01–262 9406.

ARCHER, John Norman; Managing Director, International Tanker Owners Pollution Federation Ltd, 1979–86; *b* 27 Feb. 1921; *s* of late Clifford Banks Archer and Grace Archer; *m* 1st, 1952, Gladys Joy (*née* Barnes) (*d* 1985); one step *d*; 2nd, 1986, Mrs Anne L. M. Appleby (*née* Padwick). *Educ:* Wandsworth School. Served with RA, 1939–46 (Major). Entered Civil Service, Board of Educn, 1937; Asst Principal 1947, Principal 1949, Min. of Educn; attended Admin. Staff Coll., Henley, 1960; Asst Sec. (Joint Head, Architects and Buildings Br.), 1962; technical assistance assignments etc educn, Nigeria, Yugoslavia, Tunisia, 1961–63; Asst Sec., Treasury, O&M Div., 1964; Civil Service Department: Asst Sec., Management Services Development Div., 1968; Under-Sec., Management Services, 1970; Under-Sec., Marine Div., DTI, later Dept of Trade, 1972–79. Member: Cttee of Management, RNLI; Council, Marine Soc. Freeman, City of London, 1985; Liveryman, Shipwrights' Co., 1986–. *Recreations:* lawn tennis, bridge, watching cricket. *Address:* 46 St Mary Abbots Court, Warwick Gardens, W14 8RB. *T:* 01–603 5966. *Clubs:* All England Lawn Tennis, Hurlingham, MCC; Kent CC; Frinton Lawn Tennis.

ARCHER, Prof. (Leonard) Bruce, CBE 1976; DrRCA; CEng, MIMechE; Director of Research, Royal College of Art, since 1985; *b* 22 Nov. 1922; *s* of Leonard Castella Archer and Ivy Hilda Archer; *m* 1950, Joan Henrietta Allen; one *d*. *Educ:* Henry Thornton Sch., London; City Univ., London. MIED, ASIA(Ed). Served, Scots Guards, 1941–44. City Univ., 1946–50. Various posts in manufacturing industry, 1950–57; Lectr, Central Sch. of Art and Design, London, 1957–60; Guest Prof., Hochschule für Gestaltung, Ulm, 1960–61; Research Fellow, later Prof., Royal Coll. of Art, 1961–; Hd of Dept of Design Research, RCA, 1968–85. Various public appointments in design, educn and industrial and scientific policy, 1968–; Member: Design Council, 1972–80; Science Policy Foundn, 1979–; Council, Assoc. of Art Instns, 1980–; Chm., Confedn of Art and Design Assocs, 1981–. Director: Gore Projects Ltd, 1982–; Design Research Innovation Centre Ltd, 1982–86. *Publications:* varied, on the theory and practice of research, design, develt and educn. *Recreations:* music, the theatre. *Address:* 60 Jackson's Lane, N6 5SX. *T:* 01–725 5463.

ARCHER, Dr Mildred Agnes, (Mrs W. G. Archer), OBE 1979; in charge of Prints and Drawings Section, India Office Library, London, 1954–80; she has been engaged in cataloguing the Victoria and Albert Museum's 'Company' drawings and British drawings of India, since 1983; *b* 28 Dec. 1911; *d* of V. A. Bell, MBE; *m* 1934, William George Archer (*d* 1979); one *s* one *d*. *Educ:* St Hilda's College, Oxford (MA, DLitt 1978; Hon. Fellow 1978). Art historian (British period, India); resided India, 1934–47; revisited India (study tours), 1966, 1972, 1976, 1981–82, 1984. *Publications:* Patna Painting, 1947; (with W. G. Archer) Indian Painting for the British, 1955; Tippoo's Tiger, 1959; Natural History Drawings in the India Office Library, 1962; Indian Miniatures and Folk Paintings, 1967; Indian Architecture and the British, 1968; British Drawings in the India Office Library (2 vols), 1969; Indian Paintings from Court, Town and Village, 1970; Company Drawings in the India Office Library, 1972; Artist Adventurers in Eighteenth Century India, 1974; Indian Popular Painting, 1977; India and British Portraiture, 1770–1825, 1979; (with John Bastin) The Raffles Drawings in the India Office Library, 1979; Early Views of India, 1980; (with T. Falk) Indian Miniatures in the India Office Library, 1981; (with R. Lightbown) India Observed, 1982; articles in Country Life, Apollo, Connoisseur, History Today, Geographical Mag. *Recreations:* grandchildren, gardening, travel. *Address:* 18A Provost Road, Hampstead, NW3 4ST. *T:* 01–722 2713; 5 Frog Meadow, Dedham, Colchester, Essex. *T:* Colchester 323099.

ARCHER, Rt. Hon. Peter (Kingsley), PC 1977; QC 1971; MP (Lab) Warley West, since 1974 (Rowley Regis and Tipton, 1966–74); a Recorder of the Crown Court, since 1982; *b* 20 Nov. 1926; *s* of Cyril Kingsley Archer and May (*née* Baker); *m* 1954, Margaret Irene (*née* Smith); one *s*. *Educ:* Wednesbury Boys' High Sch.; LSE; University Coll., London (Fellow 1978). Called to Bar, Gray's Inn, 1952; Bencher, 1974; commenced practice, 1953. PPS to Attorney-Gen., 1967–70; Solicitor General, 1974–79; Opposition front bench spokesman on legal affairs, 1979–82, on trade, 1982–83, on N Ireland, 1983–. UK Deleg. to UN Gen. Assembly (Third Cttee), 1969. Chm., Amnesty International (British Section), 1971–74; Chm., Parly Gp for World Govt, 1970–74; Chm., Soc. of Labour Lawyers, 1971–74, 1979–; Vice-Chm., Anti-Slavery Soc., 1970–74; Mem., Exec. Cttee, Fabian Soc., 1974– (Chm., 1980–). *Publications:* The Queen's Courts, 1956; ed Social Welfare and the Citizen, 1957; Communism and the Law, 1963; (with Lord Reay) Freedom at Stake, 1966; Human Rights, 1969; (jtly) Purpose in Socialism, 1973; The Role of the Law Officers, 1978; contributions to: Trends in Social Welfare, 1965; Atkin's, Court Forms, 1965; The International Protection of Human Rights, 1967; Renewal, 1983; Fabian Centenary Essays, 1984. *Recreations:* music, writing, talking. *Address:* House of Commons, SW1A 0AA.

ARCHIBALD, Barony of, *cr* 1949, of Woodside, Glasgow; title disclaimed by 2nd Baron; *see under* Archibald, George Christopher.

ARCHIBALD, George Christopher, FRSC 1979; Professor of Economics, University of British Columbia, since 1970; *b* 30 Dec. 1926; *s* of 1st Baron Archibald, CBE, and Dorothy Holroyd Edwards (*d* 1960); *S* father, 1975, as 2nd Baron Archibald, but disclaimed his peerage for life; *m* 1st, 1951, Liliana Barou (marr. diss. 1965); 2nd, 1971, Daphne May Vincent. *Educ:* Phillips Exeter Academy, USA; King's Coll., Cambridge (MA); London Sch. of Economics (BSc Econ.). Served in Army, 1945–48, Captain RAEC. Formerly: Prof. of Economics, Univ. of Essex; Lectr in Economics, Otago Univ. and LSE; Leon Fellow, London Univ. Fellow, Econometric Soc., 1976. *Publications:* (ed) Theory of the Firm, 1971; (with R. G. Lipsey) Introduction to a Mathematical Treatment of Economics, 1973. *Address:* c/o Department of Economics, University of British Columbia, Vancouver, BC V6T 1Y2, Canada.

ARCHIBALD, Dr Harry Munro, CB 1976; MBE 1945; Deputy Chief Medical Officer (Deputy Secretary), Department of Health and Social Security, 1973–77; *b* 17 June 1915; *s* of James and Isabella Archibald; unmarried. *Educ:* Hillhead High Sch.; Univ. of Glasgow.

MB, ChB 1938; DPH 1956. War Service: RAMC, 1940–43; IMS/IAMC, 1943–46; Lt-Col; Italian Campaign (despatches). Colonial Medical Service, Nigeria, 1946–62: Senior Specialist (Malariologist), 1958; Principal Med. Officer, Prevent. Services, N Nigeria, 1960; Med. Officer, Min. of Health, 1962; Sen. Med. Off., 1964; Principal Med. Off., DHSS, 1970; Sen. Principal Med. Off., 1972. Mem. Bd, Public Health Laboratory Service, 1975–77. Fellow, Faculty of Community Medicine, 1973. *Recreation:* travel. *Address:* 1 Camborne House, Camborne Road, Sutton, Surrey. *T:* 01–643 1076. *Club:* Caledonian.

ARCHIBALD, Liliana; Director, Fenchurch Group International, since 1985; Managing Dirctor: Fenchurch Special Risks Ltd, since 1985; Fenchurch International Consultants, since 1985; International Affairs Adviser to Lloyd's, since 1981; Adviser to International Group of Protection & Indemnity Clubs, since 1980; *b* 25 May 1928; *d* of late Noah and Sophie Barou; *m* 1951, George Christopher Archibald (marr. diss. 1965). *Educ:* Kingsley Sch.; Geneva University. Univ. Lectr, Otago Univ., 1952–55; Director: Const & Co. Ltd, 1955–73; Credit Consultants Ltd, 1957–73; Adam Brothers Contingency Ltd, 1970–85; Head of Division (Credit Insurance and Export Credit), EEC, 1973–77; EEC Advr to Lloyd's and the British Insurance Brokers Assoc., 1978–85. Member of Lloyd's, 1973–. *Publications:* (trans. and ed) Peter the Great, 1958; (trans. and ed) Rise of the Romanovs, 1970; contrib. Bankers Magazine. *Recreations:* driving fast cars, ski-ing, gardening. *Address:* 21 Langland Gardens, NW3 6QE.

See also A. Kennaway.

ARCTIC, Bishop of The, since 1974; **Rt. Rev. John Reginald Sperry;** *b* 2 May 1924; *s* of William Reginald Sperry and Elsie Agnes (*née* Priest); *m* 1952, Elizabeth Maclaren; one *s* one *d* (and one *d* decd). *Educ:* St Augustine's Coll., Canterbury; King's Coll., Halifax (STh). Deacon, 1950; priest, 1951; St Andrew's Mission, Coppermine, NWT, 1950–69; Canon of All Saints' Cathedral, Aklavik, 1957–59; Archdeacon of Coppermine, 1959–69; Rector of St John's, Fort Smith, NWT, 1969–73; Rector of Holy Trinity, Yellowknife, NWT, 1974. Hon. DD; Coll. of Emmanuel, St Chad, 1974; Wycliffe Coll., Toronto, 1979. *Publications:* translations into Copper Eskimo: Canadian Book of Common Prayer (1962), 1969; Four Gospels and Acts of the Apostles, 1972. *Address:* 1 Dakota Court, Yellowknife, Northwest Territories, X1A 2A4, Canada. *T:* 403–873–6163.

ARCULUS, Sir Ronald, KCMG 1979 (CMG 1968); KCVO 1980; HM Diplomatic Service, retired; Director, Glaxo Holdings, since 1983; Consultant: Trusthouse Forte, since 1983; London and Continental Bankers Ltd, since 1985; Director of Appeals, King's Medical Research Trust, since 1984; *b* 11 Feb. 1923; *s* of late Cecil and Ethel L. Arculus; *m* 1953, Sheila Mary Faux; one *s* one *d*. *Educ:* Solihull; Exeter Coll., Oxford (MA). 4th Queen's Own Hussars (now Queen's Royal Irish Hussars), 1942–45 (Captain). Joined HM Diplomatic Service, 1947; FO, 1947; San Francisco, 1948; La Paz, 1950; FO, 1951; Ankara, 1953; FO, 1957; Washington, 1961; Counsellor, 1965; New York, 1965–68; IDC, 1969; Head of Science and Technology Dept, FCO, 1970–72; Minister (Economic), Paris, 1973–77; Ambassador and Permt Leader, UK Delegn to UN Conf. on Law of the Sea, 1977–79; Ambassador to Italy, 1979–83. Governor, British Institute, Florence, 1983–. FBIM 1984. Freeman, City of London, 1981. Kt Grand Cross, Order of Merit, Italy, 1980. *Recreations:* travel, music and fine arts. *Address:* 20 Kensington Court Gardens, W8 5QF. *Clubs:* Army and Navy, Hurlingham.

ARDAGH AND CLONMACNOISE, Bishop of, (RC), since 1983; **Most Rev. Colm O'Reilly;** *b* 11 Jan. 1935; *s* of John and Alicia O'Reilly. *Educ:* St Patrick's College, Maynooth. Pastoral work in parish ministry, 1960–83. Hon. DD Maynooth, 1983. *Address:* St Michael's, Longford, Ireland. *T:* Longford 46432.

ARDEE, Lord; John Anthony Brabazon; *b* 11 May 1941; *e s* of 14th Earl of Meath, *qv; m* 1973, Xenia Goudime; one *s* two *d*. *Educ:* Harrow. Page of Honour to the Queen, 1956–57. Served Grenadier Guards, 1959–62. *Heir: s* Hon. Anthony Jaques Brabazon, *b* 30 Jan. 1977. *Address:* Killruddery, Bray, Co. Wicklow, Ireland.

ARDEN, Rt. Rev. Donald Seymour, CBE 1981; Assistant Bishop of Willesden, since 1981, and voluntary assistant priest, St Alban's, North Harrow, since 1986; *b* 12 April 1916; *s* of Stanley and Winifred Arden; *m* 1962, Jane Grace Riddle; two *s*. *Educ:* St Peter's Coll., Adelaide; University of Leeds (BA); College of the Resurrection, Mirfield. Deacon, 1939; Priest, 1940. Curate of: St Catherine's, Hatcham, 1939–40; Nettleden with Potten End, 1941–43; Asst Priest, Pretoria African Mission, 1944–51; Director of Usuthu Mission, Swaziland, 1951–61; Bishop of Nyasaland, 1961 (name of diocese changed, when Nyasaland was granted independence, July 1964); Bishop of Malaŵi, 1964–71; of Southern Malaŵi, 1971–81; Archbishop of Central Africa, 1971–80; Priest-in-charge of St Margaret's, Uxbridge, 1981–86. *Publication:* Out of Africa Something New, 1976. *Recreations:* photography, farming. *Address:* 6 Frobisher Close, Pinner HA5 1NN. *T:* 01–866 6009.

ARDEN, John; playwright; *b* 26 Oct. 1930; *s* of C. A. Arden and A. E. Layland; *m* 1957, Margaretta Ruth D'Arcy; four *s* (and one *s* decd). *Educ:* Sedbergh Sch.; King's Coll., Cambridge; Edinburgh Coll. of Art. Plays produced include: All Fall Down, 1955; The Life of Man, 1956; The Waters of Babylon, 1957; Live Like Pigs, 1958; Serjeant Musgrave's Dance, 1959; Soldier, Soldier, 1960; Wet Fish, 1962; The Workhouse Donkey, 1963; Ironhand, 1963; Armstrong's Last Goodnight, 1964; Left-Handed Liberty, 1965; The True History of Squire Jonathan and his Unfortunate Treasure, 1968; The Bagman, 1970; Pearl, 1978; To Put It Frankly, 1979; Don Quixote, 1980; Garland for a Hoar Head, 1982; The Old Man Sleeps Alone, 1982; with Margaretta D'Arcy: The Business of Good Government, 1960; The Happy Haven, 1960; Ars Longa Vita Brevis, 1964; Friday's Hiding, 1966; The Royal Pardon, 1966; The Hero Rises Up, 1968; Island of the Mighty, 1972; The Ballygombeen Bequest, 1972; The Non-Stop Connolly Cycle, 1975; Vandaleur's Folly, 1978; The Little Gray Home in the West, 1978; The Manchester Enthusiasts, 1984. *Publications:* To Present the Pretence (essays), 1977; Silence Among the Weapons (novel), 1982. *Recreations:* antiquarianism, mythology. *Address:* c/o Margaret Ramsay Ltd, 14 Goodwin's Court, WC2.

ARDWICK, Baron cr 1970 (Life Peer), of Barnes; **John Cowburn Beavan;** Member of European Parliament, 1975–79; *b* 1910; *s* of late Silas Morgan Beavan and Alderman Emily Beavan, JP; *m* 1934, Gladys (*née* Jones); one *d*. *Educ:* Manchester Grammar Sch. Blackpool Times, 1927; Evening Chronicle, Manchester, 1928; Manchester Evening News, 1930; London staff, Manchester Evening News, 1933; News Editor, Manchester Evening News, Manchester, 1936; Asst Editor, Londoner's Diary, Evening Standard, and leader writer, 1940; News Editor and Chief Sub, Observer, 1942; Editor, Manchester Evening News, 1943; Dir, Manchester Guardian and Evening News Ltd, 1943–55; London Editor, Manchester Guardian, 1946–55; Asst Dir, Nuffield Foundation, 1955; Editor, Daily Herald, 1960–62; Political Adviser to the Daily Mirror Group, 1962–76; Mem. Editorial Bd, The Political Quarterly, 1978–; Chm., Press Freedom Cttee, Commonwealth Press Union, 1980–. Chm., Industrial Sponsors, 1975–. Hon. Sec., British Cttee, Internat. Press Inst., 1972–76. *Address:* 10 Chester Close, SW13. *T:* 01–789 3490. *Clubs:* Garrick, Roehampton.

ARGENT, Eric William, FCA; FCBSI; Director, Anglia Building Society, since 1978 (Joint General Manager, 1978–81); *b* 5 Sept. 1923; *s* of Eric George Argent and Florence Mary Argent; *m* 1949, Pauline Grant; two *d*. *Educ:* Chiswick Grammar Sch. FCA 1951. War Service, 1942–47. With City Chartered Accountants, 1940–42 and 1947–51; with London Banking House, Antony Gibbs & Sons Ltd, 1951–59; Hastings & Thanet Building Society, 1959–78: Sec. and Chief Accountant, 1962; Dep. Gen. Man., 1964; Gen. Man. and Sec., 1966; Dir and Gen. Man., 1976. *Recreations:* reading, gardening, travel. *Address:* Fairmount, 1 Carmel Close, Bexhill-on-Sea, East Sussex TN39 3SU. *T:* Cooden 2333.

ARGENT, Malcolm, CBE 1985; Secretary of British Telecommunications plc, since 1984; *b* 14 Aug. 1935; *s* of Leonard James and Winifred Hilda Argent; *m* 1961, Mary Patricia Addis Stimson (marr. diss. 1983); one *s* one *d*. *Educ:* Palmer's Sch., Grays, Essex. General Post Office, London Telecommunications Region: Exec. Officer, 1953–62; Higher Exec. Officer, 1962–66; Principal, PO Headquarters, 1966–70; Private Sec., Man. Dir, Telecommunications, 1970–74; Personnel Controller, External Telecommun. Exec., 1974–75; Dir, Chairman's Office, PO Central Headquarters, 1975–77; Dir, Eastern Telecommun. Region, 1977; Secretary: of the Post Office, 1978–81; of British Telecommunications Corp., 1981–84; Trustee, British Telecom Staff Superannuation Fund, 1981–. FBIM 1980. *Recreation:* tennis. *Address:* 4 Huskards, Fryerning, Ingatestone, Essex CM4 0HR.

ARGENTINA AND EASTERN SOUTH AMERICA, Bishop in, since 1975; **Rt. Rev. Richard Stanley Cutts;** *b* 17 Sept. 1919; *s* of Edward Stanley and Gabrielle Cutts; *m* 1960, Irene Adela Sack; one *s* three *d*. *Educ:* Felsted School, Essex. Asst Curate, SS Peter and Paul, Godalming, 1951–56; Director of St Cyprian's Mission, Etalaneni and Priest-in-Charge Nkandhla Chapelry, Zululand, 1957–63; Director, Kambula Mission District, 1963–65; Rector, St Mary's, Kuruman and Director, Kuruman Mission District, 1965–71; Archdeacon of Kuruman, 1969–71; Dean of Salisbury, Rhodesia, 1971–75. *Address:* 25 de Mayo 282, 1002 Buenos Aires, Argentina.

ARGOV, Shlomo; Ambassador of Israel to the Court of St James's, 1979–82; *b* 1929; *m* Hava Argov; one *s* two *d*. *Educ:* Georgetown Univ., USA (BSc Pol. Science); London School of Economics (Internat. Relns) (MSc Econ; Hon. Fellow, 1983). Israel Defence Force, 1947–50; Prime Minister's Office, Jerusalem, 1955–59; Consul General of Israel, Lagos, 1959–60; Counsellor, Accra, 1960–61; Consul, Consulate General of Israel, New York, 1961–64; Dep. Director, United States Div., Min. of Foreign Affairs, Jerusalem, 1965–68; Minister, Embassy of Israel, Washington, 1968–71; Ambassador of Israel, Mexico, 1971–74; Asst Dir Gen. (Dir of Israel Information Services), Min. of Foreign Affairs, Jerusalem, 1974–77; Ambassador of Israel, Netherlands, 1977–79. *Address:* 6 Hagdud Haivri, Jerusalem, Israel.

ARGYLE, Major Michael Victor, MC 1945; QC 1961; **His Honour Judge Argyle;** a Circuit Judge (formerly an Additional Judge of the Central Criminal Court), since 1970; *b* 31 Aug. 1915; *e s* of late Harold Victor Argyle and Elsie Marion, Repton, Derbyshire; *m* 1951, Ann Norah, *d* of late Charles Newton and V. Newton, later Mrs Jobson; three *d*. *Educ:* Shardlow Hall, Derbyshire; Westminster Sch.; Trinity Coll., Cambridge (MA). Served War of 1939–45: with 7th QO Hussars in India, ME and Italy (immediate MC), 1939–47. Called to Bar, Lincoln's Inn, 1938, Bencher, 1967, Treasurer, 1984; resumed practice at Bar, 1947 (Midland Circuit); Recorder of Northampton, 1962–65, of Birmingham, 1965–70; Dep. Chm., Holland QS, 1965–71; Lay Judge, Arches Court, Province of Canterbury, 1968–. General Elections, contested (C) Belper, 1950, and Loughborough, 1955. Master, Worshipful Co. of Makers of Playing Cards, 1984–85. *Publications:* (ed) Phipson on Evidence, 10th edn. *Recreations:* chess, boxing. *Address:* The Red House, Fiskerton, near Southwell, Notts. *Clubs:* Carlton, Cavalry and Guards, Kennel.

ARGYLL, 12th Duke of, *cr* 1701 (Scotland), 1892 (UK); **Ian Campbell;** Marquess of Lorne and Kintyre; Earl of Campbell and Cowal; Viscount Lochow and Glenyla; Baron Inveraray, Mull, Morvern, and Tiry, 1701; Baron Campbell, 1445; Earl of Argyll, 1457; Baron Lorne, 1470; Baron Kintyre, 1633 (Scotland); Baron Sundridge, 1766; Baron Hamilton of Hameldon, 1776; Bt 1627; 36th Baron and 46th Knight of Lochow; Celtic title, Mac Cailein Mhor, Chief of Clan Campbell (from Sir Colin Campbell, knighted 1280); Hereditary Master of the Royal Household, Scotland; Hereditary High Sheriff of the County of Argyll; Admiral of the Western Coast and Isles; Keeper of the Great Seal of Scotland and of the Castles of Dunstaffnage, Dunoon, and Carrick and Tarbert; *b* 28 Aug. 1937; *e s* of 11th Duke of Argyll, TD, and Louise (*d* 1970), *o d* of Henry Clews; *S* father, 1973; *m* 1964, Iona Mary, *d* of Captain Sir Ivar Colquhoun, *qv*; one *s* one *d*. *Educ:* Le Rosey, Switzerland; Glenalmond; McGill Univ., Montreal. Captain (retd) Argyll and Sutherland Highlanders. Member, Queen's Body Guard for Scotland, the Royal Company of Archers. Chm., Beim Bhuidhe Holdings; Director: S. Campbell & Son; Aberlour Glenlivet Distillery Co.; White Heather Distillers; Muir, MacKenzie & Co.; Cetec International; Visual Sound Programmes. Governor, Dollar Acad.; President: Royal Caledonian Schs; Argyll Scouts Assoc. Hon. Col, Argyll and Sutherland Highlanders Bn (ACF). KStJ 1975. *Heir: s* Marquess of Lorne, *qv*. *Address:* Inveraray Castle, Inveraray, Argyll PA32 8XF. *T:* Inveraray 2275. *Clubs:* White's; New (Edinburgh).

ARGYLL AND THE ISLES, Bishop of, since 1977; **Rt. Rev. George Kennedy Buchanan Henderson,** MBE 1974; *b* 5 Dec. 1921; *s* of George Buchanan Henderson and Anna Kennedy Butters; *m* 1950, Isobel Fergusson Bowman. *Educ:* Oban High School; University of Durham (BA, LTh). Assistant Curate, Christ Church, Glasgow, 1943–48; Priest in Charge, St Bride's, Nether Lochaber, 1948–50; Chaplain to Bishop of Argyll and The Isles, 1948–50; Rector, St Andrew's, Fort William, 1950–77; Canon, St John's Cathedral, Oban, 1960; Synod Clerk, 1964–73; Dean of Argyll and The Isles, 1973–77. JP of Inverness-shire, 1963–; Hon. Sheriff, 1971–; Provost of Fort William, 1962–75; Hon. Burgess of Fort William, 1973. *Address:* Bishop's House, Alma Road, Fort William, Inverness-shire PH33 6HD.

ARGYLL AND THE ISLES, Bishop of, (RC), since 1968; **Rt. Rev. Colin MacPherson;** *b* Lochboisdale, South Uist, 5 Aug. 1917; *e s* of Malcolm MacPherson and Mary MacPherson (*née* MacMillan). *Educ:* Lochboisdale School; Daliburgh H. G. School; Blairs Coll., Aberdeen; Pontificium Athenæum Urbanum, Rome. Bachelor of Philosophy 1936; Bachelor of Theology 1938; Licentiate of Theology 1940 (Rome). Assistant Priest, St Columba's Cathedral, Oban, 1940–42. Parish Priest: Knoydart, 1942–51; Eriskay, 1951–56; Benbecula, 1956–66; Fort William, 1966–68. Hon. LLD, Univ. of St Francis Xavier, Canada, 1974. *Address:* Bishop's House, Esplanade, Oban, Argyll. *T:* Oban 2010.

ARGYLL AND THE ISLES, Dean of; *see* Wilson, Very Rev. I. G. MacQ.

ARGYRIS, Prof. John, DScEng, DE Munich; FRS 1986; FRAeS 1955; Professor of Aeronautical Structures in the University of London, at Imperial College of Science and Technology, 1955–75, Visiting Professor 1975–78, now Emeritus Professor; Director, Institute for Computer Applications, Stuttgart, since 1984; *b* 19 Aug. 1916; *s* of Nicolas and Lucie Argyris; *m* 1953, Inga-Lisa (*née* Johansson); one *s*. *Educ:* 3rd Gymnasium, Athens; Technical Universities, Athens, Munich and Zurich. With J. Gollnow u. Son, Stettin, Research in Structures, 1937–39; Royal Aeronautical Soc., Research and Technical

Officer, 1943–49; Univ. of London, Imperial Coll. of Science and Technology, Dept of Aeronautics: Senior Lecturer, 1949; Reader in Theory of Aeronautical Structures, 1950; Hon. FIC 1985. Dir, Inst. for Statics and Dynamics, Stuttgart, 1959–84. Principal Editor, Jl of Computer Methods in Applied Mechanics and Engineering, 1972–. Hon. Professor: Northwestern Polytech. Univ., Xian, China, 1980; Tech. Univ. of Beijing, 1983; Qinghua Univ., Beijing, 1984. Corresp. Mem., Acad. of Scis, Athens, 1973; Life Mem., ASME, 1981; Hon. Life Mem., NY Acad. of Scis, 1983; Foreign Associate, US Nat. Acad. of Engrg, 1986. FAIAA 1983; FAAAS 1985; Hon. Fellow, Groupe pour l'Avancement des Méthodes Numériques de l'Ingénieur, Paris, 1974; Hon. FCGI 1976. Hon. Dott Ing Genoa; Hon. dr.tech Trondheim; Hon. Dr Ing Tech. Univ. of Hanover, 1983; Hon. Tek. Dr Univ. Linköping. Silver Medal, RAeS, 1971; Von Kármán Medal, ASCE, 1975; Copernicus Medal, Polish Acad. of Scis, 1979; Timoshenko Medal, ASME, 1981; I. B. Laskowitz Award with Gold Medal in Aerospace Engrg, NY Acad. of Scis, 1982; World Prize in Culture, and election as Personality of the Year 1984, Centro Studi e Ricerce delle Nazione, Acad. Italia, 1983; Royal Medal, Royal Soc., 1985. Gold Medal, Land Baden-Württemberg, 1980; Grand Cross of Merit, FRG, 1985. *Publications:* Handbook of Aeronautics, Vol. I, 1952: Energy Theorems and Structural Analysis, 1960; Modern Fuselage Analysis and the Elastic Aircraft, 1963; Recent Advances in Matrix Methods of Structural Analysis, 1964; Introduction into the Finite Element Method, vols I, II and III, 1986; articles and publications in Ingenieur Archiv, Reports and Memoranda of Aeronautical Research Council, Journal of Royal Aeronautical Society and Aircraft Engineering, CMAME, Jl of AIAA, etc; over 330 scientific publications. *Recreations:* reading, music, hiking, archæology. *Address:* Institute for Computer Applications, 27 Pfaffenwaldring, D-7000 Stuttgart 80, Federal Republic of Germany. *T:* 010–49711 6853594; c/o Department of Aeronautics, Imperial College, Prince Consort Road, SW7. *T:* 01–589 5111. *Club:* English-Speaking Union.

ARIAS, Dame Margot Fonteyn de, (Margot Fonteyn), DBE 1956 (CBE 1951); Prima Ballerina Assoluta; President of the Royal Academy of Dancing, since 1954; Chancellor of Durham University, since 1982; *b* 18 May 1919; *m* 1955, Roberto E. Arias, *qv*. Hon. degrees: LittD Leeds; DMus London and Oxon; LLD Cantab; DLitt Manchester; LLD Edinburgh. Benjamin Franklin Medal, RSA, 1974; Internat. Artist Award, Philippines, 1976; Hamburg Internat. Shakespeare Prize, 1977. Order of Finnish Lion, 1960; Order of Estacio de Sa, Brazil, 1973; Chevalier, Order of Merit of Duarte, Sanchez and Mella, Dominican Republic, 1975. *Publications:* Margot Fonteyn, 1975; A Dancer's World, 1978; The Magic of Dance, 1980 (BBC series, 1979); Pavlova Impressions, 1984. *Address:* c/o Royal Opera House, Covent Garden, WC2.

ARIAS, Roberto Emilio; *b* 1918; *s* of Dr Harmodio Arias (President of Panama, 1932–36) and Rosario Guardia de Arias; *m*; one *s* two *d*; *m* 1955, Margot Fonteyn (*see* Dame Margot Fonteyn de Arias). *Educ:* Peddie Sch., New Jersey, USA; St John's Coll., Cambridge. Called to the Bar, Panama, 1939; Fifth Circuit, Court of Appeals, US, 1941; Editor, El Panama-America, 1942–46; Counsellor to Panama Embassy, Chile, 1947; Publisher, La Hora, 1948–68; Delegate to UN Assembly, New York, 1953; Panamanian Ambassador to the Court of St James's, 1955–58, 1960–62; Elected Dep. to the Nat. Assembly of Panama, Oct. 1964–Sept. 1968. Paralyzed since June 1964, as result of gunshot wounds in political assassination attempt. *Address:* PO Box 6–1140, Eldorado, Panama, Republic of Panama.

ARIAS-SALGADO Y MONTALVO, Fernando; Director, International Legal Department, Ministry of Foreign Affairs, Spain, since 1983; Barrister-at-Law; *b* 3 May 1938; *s* of Gabriel Arias-Salgado y Cubas and Maria Montalvo Gutierrez; *m* 1969, Maria Isabel Garrigues Lopez-Chicheri; one *s* one *d*. *Educ:* Univ. of Madrid. Mem., Illustrious Coll. of Lawyers of Madrid. Entered Diplomatic Sch., 1963; Sec., Permanent Rep. of Spain to UN, 1966; Advr, UN Security Council, 1968–69; Asst Dir Gen., Promotion of Research, 1971, Asst Dir Gen., Internat. Co-operation, 1972, Min. of Educn and Science; Legal Advr (internat. matters), Legal Dept, Min. of Foreign Affairs, 1973; Counsellor, Spanish Delegn to Internat. Court of Justice, 1975; Tech. Sec. Gen., Min. of Foreign Affairs, 1976; Dir Gen., Radiotelevisión Española, 1977; Ambassador to the Court of St James's, 1981–83. Comendador: Orden de Isabel la Católica; Orden del Merito Civil; Orden de San Raimundo de Peñafort; Caballero, Orden de Carlos III. *Address:* Roncal 7, Madrid 2, Spain.

ARIE, Prof. Thomas Harry David, FRCPsych, FRCP, FFCM; Foundation Professor of Health Care of the Elderly, University of Nottingham, since 1977, and Hon. Consultant Psychiatrist, Nottingham Health Authority; *b* 9 Aug. 1933; *s* of late Dr O. M. Arie and Hedy (*née* Glaser); *m* 1963, Eleanor, MRCP, *yr d* of Sir Robert Aitken, *qv*; two *d* one *s*. *Educ:* Reading Sch.; Balliol Coll., Oxford (Open Exhibnr in Classics; 1st cl. Hons, Classical Mods; Leathersellers' Exhibn for Medicine); MA, BM 1960; DPM. Training, Radcliffe Infirmary and Maudsley and London Hosps; Consultant Psychiatrist, Goodmayes Hosp., 1969–77; Sen. Lectr in Social Medicine, London Hosp. Med. Coll.; Hon. Sen. Lectr in Psychiatry, UCH Med. Sch., London. Royal College of Psychiatrists: Vice-Pres., 1984–86; Chm., Specialist Section on Psychiatry of Old Age, 1981–86; Jt Cttee on Higher Psychiatric Training, 1978–84; Royal College of Physicians: Geriatrics Cttee; Examining Bd for Dipl. in Geriatric Medicine. Member: Standing Med. Adv. Cttee, DHSS, 1980–84; Cttee on Review of Medicines; Adv. Council, Centre for Policy on Ageing; Res. Cttee, Nat. Inst. for Social Work; Central Council for Educn and Trng in Social Work, 1975–81. Fotheringham Lectr, Univ. of Toronto, 1979; Vis. Prof., NZ Geriatrics Soc., 1980; Hon. Sec., Geriatric Psych. Section, World Psych. Assoc., 1983–. *Publications:* (ed) Health Care of the Elderly, 1981; (ed) Recent Advances in Psychogeriatrics, 1985; articles in med. jls and chapters in other people's books. *Address:* Department of Health Care of the Elderly, The Medical School, Queen's Medical Centre, Nottingham NG7 2UH. *T:* Nottingham 700111, 780608.

ARIFIN, Dr Sjahabuddin; Adviser to the Minister of Foreign Affairs, Indonesia; *b* 3 March 1928; *m* Siti Asiah; three *s*. *Educ:* Rechts- und Wirtschaftswissenschaftl. Fakultät, Universität Bern, Switzerland (Dr of Econs). Indonesian Embassy, Bern, Switzerland, 1951–57; Econ. Expert, Dept of Foreign Affairs, Jakarta, 1957–62; Lectr, Sch. of Econs, Pajajaran Univ., Bandung, 1960–62; Counsellor, Indonesian Embassy, Washington, USA, 1962–63; Ambassador to Iran, 1963–67; Dept of Foreign Affairs, Jakarta: Head of Directorate, Econ. Multilateral Co-operation, 1967–71; Dir Gen., Foreign Econ., Social and Cultural Relations, 1971–77; Sec. Gen., 1977–81; Ambassador to UK, 1981–85. *Recreations:* reading, walking, golf. *Address:* 10 Jalan Susukan, Kemang, Jakarta 12730, Indonesia. *T:* (021) 794398. *Club:* Jakarta Golf (Indonesia).

ARKELL, John Heward, CBE 1961; TD; MA; CBIM, FIPM; Director of Administration, BBC, 1960–70; *b* 20 May 1909; *s* of Rev. H. H. Arkell, MA, and Gertrude Mary Arkell; *m* 1st, 1940, Helen Birgit Huitfeldt; two *s* one *d*; 2nd, 1956, Meta Bachke Grundtvig (marr. diss.) one *s*. *Educ:* Dragon Sch.; Radley Coll.; Christ Church, Oxford (MA). Sir Max Michaelis (Investment) Trust, 1931–37. Asst Sec., CPRE, 1937–39, Mem. of Exec. Cttee, 1945–75, Vice-Chm., 1967–74, Vice-Pres., 1975–. Commissioned Territorial Officer, 1st Bn Queen's Westminsters, KRRC, 1939; Instructor, then Chief Instructor, Army Infantry Signalling Sch., 1940; served in BLA as special infantry signalling liaison officer, 1944; demobilised 1945, Major. Personnel Manager, J. Lyons, 1945–49; BBC: Controller, Staff Admin, 1949–58; Dir, Staff Admin, 1958–60. Director: The Boots Co. Ltd, 1970–79; UK Provident Instn, 1971–80; Sen. Associate, Kramer Internat. Ltd, 1980–86. Chm., Air Transport and Travel ITB, 1970–80. Lay Mem., Nat. Industrial Relations Ct, 1972–74. Lectr on indust. subjects; occasional indep. management consultancies include P&O and Coates Group of Cos (Dir, 1970–76). Founder, Exec. Pres. then Jt Pres., and former Gen. Hon. Sec., then Chm., Christ Church (Oxford) United Clubs (Community Centre, SE London), 1932–. Chm. Council, British Institute of Management, 1972–74 (Fellow, 1964–, now Companion; Vice-Chm., 1966–72; Chm. Exec. Cttee, 1966–69; Vice Pres., 1974–); Chm. BIM/CBI Educl Panel, 1971–72; Dir, BIM Foundn, 1976–81; Member Council: CBI, 1973–75; Industry for Management Educn, 1971–; Foundn for Management Educn, 1971–75; National Trust, 1971–84 (Chm., NT Council's Adv. Cttee on the Trust, its members and public, 1982–83); Adv. Council, Business Graduates Assoc., 1973–85; Action Resources Centre, 1975–; Chm., Cttee of British Council of Churches responsible for report on further educn of young people, 1960–61; Member: Finance Cttee, C of E Bd of Finance, 1960–68; CS Deptl Cttee to consider application of Fulton Report to Civil Service, 1968–70; Final Selection Bd, CS Commn, 1978–81. Trustee, Visnews, 1960–69; Vis. Fellow, Administrative Staff Coll., 1971–; Governor, Radley Coll., 1965–70; Chm., Radley Coll. War Meml Cttee, 1968–. Chm., Ringstead Bay Protection Soc., 1983–. FRSA. *Publications:* composer of light music; contrib. to jls on management and indust. subjects. *Recreations:* walking, swimming, music. *Address:* Pinnocks, Fawley, near Henley-on-Thames, Oxon RG9 6JH. *T:* Henley 573017; Glen Cottage, Ringstead Bay, Dorchester, Dorset. *T:* Warmwell 852686. *Clubs:* Savile; Leander.

ARKFELD, Most Rev. Leo; *see* Madang, Archbishop of, (RC).

ARLOTT, John; *see* Arlott, L. T. J.

ARLOTT, (Leslie Thomas) John, OBE 1970; wine and general writer, The Guardian; topographer; former broadcaster; *b* Basingstoke, 25 Feb. 1914; *s* of late William John and Nellie Jenvey Arlott; *m* 1st, Dawn Rees; one *s* (and one *s* decd); 2nd, Valerie France (*d* 1976); one *s* (one *d* decd); 3rd, 1977, Patricia Hoare. *Educ:* Queen Mary's Sch., Basingstoke. Clerk in Mental Hospital, 1930–34; Police (Detective, eventually Sergeant), 1934–45; Producer, BBC, 1945–50; General Instructor, BBC Staff Training School, 1951–53. Contested (L) Epping Division, Gen. Election, 1955 and 1959. President: Cricketers' Assoc., 1968–; Hampshire Schools Cricket Assoc., 1966–80. Hon. MA Southampton, 1973. Sports Journalist of 1979 (British Press Award); Sports Personality of 1980 (Soc. of Authors' Pye Radio Award); Sports Presenter of the Year, 1980 (TV and Radio Industries Club Award). DUniv. Open, 1981. *Publications:* (with G. R. Hamilton) Landmarks, 1943; Of Period and Place (poems), 1944; Clausentum (poems), 1945; First Time In America (anthology), 1949; Concerning Cricket, 1949; How to Watch Cricket, 1949, new edn, 1983; Maurice Tate, 1951; Concerning Soccer, 1952; (ed) Cricket (Pleasures of Life series), 1953; The Picture of Cricket, 1955; English Cheeses of the South and West, 1956; Jubilee History of Cricket, 1965; Vintage Summer, 1967; (with Sir Neville Cardus) The Noblest Game, 1969; Fred: portrait of a fast bowler, 1971; The Ashes, 1972; Island Camera: the Isles of Scilly in the photography of the Gibson family, 1973, repr. 1983; The Snuff Shop, 1974; (ed) The Oxford Companion to Sports and Games, 1975; (with Christopher Fielden) Burgundy, Vines and Wines, 1976; Krug: House of Champagne, 1977; (with Patrick Eagar) An Eye for Cricket, 1979; Jack Hobbs: a profile of The Master, 1981; A Word From Arlott (ed David Rayvern Allen), 1983; (ed) Wine, 1984; Arlott on Cricket, 1984; (with Patrick Eagar) Botham, 1985. *Recreations:* watching cricket, drinking wine, talking, sleeping, collecting aquatints, engraved glass, and wine artefacts. *Address:* c/o The Guardian, 119 Farringdon Road, EC1R 3ER. *Clubs:* National Liberal, MCC (Hon. Life Mem., 1980); Master's; Forty, Somerset CCC (Hon. Life Mem., 1982), Hampshire CCC (Hon. Life Mem., 1984).

ARMAGH, Archbishop of, and Primate of All Ireland, since 1986; **Most Rev. Robert Henry Alexander Eames;** *b* 27 April 1937; *s* pf William Edward and Mary Eleanor Thompson Eames; *m* 1966 Ann Christine Daly; two *s*. *Educ:* Belfast Royal Acad.; Methodist Coll., Belfast; Queen's Univ., Belfast (LLB (hons), PhD); Trinity Coll., Dublin. Research Scholar and Tutor, Faculty of Laws, QUB, 1960–63; Curate Assistant, Bangor Parish Church, 1963–66; Rector of St Dorothea's, Belfast, 1966–74; Examining Chaplain to Bishop of Down, 1973; Rector of St Mark's, Dundela, 1974–75; Bishop of Derry and Raphoe, 1975–80; Bishop of Down and Dromore, 1980–86. Irish Rep., 1984, Mem. Standing Cttee, 1985, ACC. Governor, Church Army, 1985. *Publications:* A Form of Worship for Teenagers, 1965; The Quiet Revolution—Irish Disestablishment, 1970; Through Suffering, 1973; Thinking through Lent, 1978; Through Lent, 1984; contribs to New Divinity, Irish Legal Quarterly, Criminal Law Review. The Furrow. *Address:* The See House, Cathedral Close, Armagh, Co. Armagh BT61 7EE.

ARMAGH, Archbishop of, (RC), and Primate of All Ireland, since 1977; **His Eminence Cardinal Tomás Séamus Ó Fiaich,** MRIA 1977; *b* Crossmaglen, 3 Nov. 1923; *s* of Patrick Fee and Annie Fee (*née* Caraher). *Educ:* Cregganduff Public Elem. School; St Patrick's Coll., Armagh; St Patrick's Coll., Maynooth; St Peter's Coll., Wexford; University Coll., Dublin; Catholic Univ. of Louvain. BA (Celtic Studies) 1943, MA (Early Irish History) 1950 (NUI); LicScHist 1952 (Louvain). Ordained, Wexford, 1948; Curate, Moy, Co. Tyrone, 1952–53; St Patrick's College, Maynooth: Lectr in Modern History, 1953–59; Prof. of Modern History, 1959–74; Pres., 1974–77. Cardinal, 1979. Chairman: Govt Commn on Restoration of the Irish Language, 1959–63; Irish Language Advisory Council, 1965–68; Pres., Soc. of Irish-speaking Priests, 1955–67; Treas., Catholic Record Soc. of Ireland, 1954–74; Pres., Irish Episcopal Conf., 1977–; Member: Congregation for Catholic Education and Congregation for the Clergy, and Secretariate for Christian Unity, Vatican, 1979–; Congregation for the Evangelisation of Peoples, 1984–; Congregation for Bishops, 1984–; Council for Public Affairs of the Church, 1984–. Editor, Jl of Armagh Historical Soc. and other jls. Hon. Doctorates: St Mary's, Notre Dame, Indiana and Thiel Coll., Greenville, Pa, 1979; Boston Coll. and College of St Thomas, St Paul, Minn, USA, 1981; NUI, 1984. *Publications:* Gaelscrínte i gCéin, 1960; Irish Cultural Influence in Europe, 1967; Imeacht na nIarlaí, 1972; Má Nuad, 1972; Art MacCumhaigh, 1973; St Columbanus in his own words, 1974; Oliver Plunkett: Ireland's New Saint, 1975; Aifreann Ceolta Tíre, 1977; Art Mac Bionaid, 1979. *Address:* Ara Coeli, Armagh, Ireland. *T:* Armagh 522045.

ARMAGH, Auxiliary Bishop of, (RC); *see* Lennon, Most Rev. J. G.

ARMAGH, Dean of; *see* Crooks, Very Rev. J. R. M.

ARMIDALE, Bishop of, since 1976; **Rt. Rev. Peter Chiswell;** *b* 18 Feb. 1934; *s* of Ernest and Florence Ruth Chiswell; *m* 1960, Betty Marie Craik; two *s* one *d*. *Educ:* Univ. of New South Wales (BE); Moore Theological College (BD London, Th. Schol.). Vicar of Bingara, 1961–68; Vicar of Gunnedah, 1968–76; Archdeacon of Tamworth, 1971–76. *Address:* Bishopscourt, Armidale, NSW 2350, Australia. *T:* 067–724555.

ARMITAGE, Edward, CB 1974; Comptroller-General, Patent Office and Industrial Property and Copyright Department, Department of Trade (formerly Trade and Industry), 1969–77; *b* 16 July 1917; *s* of Harry and Florence Armitage; *m* 1940, Marjorie Pope; one *s* two *d. Educ:* Huddersfield Coll.; St Catharine's Coll., Cambridge. Patent Office, BoT: Asst Examr 1939; Examr 1944; Sen. Examr 1949; Principal Examr 1960; Suptg Examr 1962; Asst Comptroller 1966. Governor, Centre d'Etudes Internationales de la Propriété Industrielle, Strasbourg, 1975–; Mem. Council, Common Law Inst. of Intellectual Property, 1981–. *Recreations:* tennis, bridge, gardening. *Address:* Lynwood, Lascot Hill, Wedmore, Somerset. *T:* Wedmore 712079.

See also Peter Armitage.

ARMITAGE, Maj.-Gen. Geoffrey Thomas Alexander, CBE 1968 (MBE 1945); *b* 5 July 1917; *s* of late Lt-Col H. G. P. Armitage and late Mary Madeline (*née* Drought); *m* 1949, Monica Wall Kent (*widow, née* Poat); one *s* one step *d. Educ:* Haileybury Coll.; RMA, Woolwich (Sword of Honour). Commissioned Royal Artillery, 1937. Served War of 1939–45 (despatches, MBE), BEF, Middle East, Italy, NW Europe. Transferred to Royal Dragoons (1st Dragoons), 1951, comd 1956–59; Instructor (GSO1), IDC, 1959–60; Col GS, War Office, 1960–62; Comdt RAC Centre, 1962–65; Chief of Staff, HQ1 (BR) Corps, 1966–68; Dir, Royal Armoured Corps, 1968–70; GOC Northumbrian Dist, 1970–72; retd 1973. Dir, CLA Game Fair, 1974–80. *Recreations:* writing, some field sports. *Address:* Clyffe, Tincleton, near Dorchester, Dorset. *Clubs:* Army and Navy, Kennel.

ARMITAGE, Henry St John Basil, CBE 1978 (OBE 1968); HM Diplomatic Service, retired; Middle East consultant; Director: Société Commissionaire et Financière, Geneva; SCF Finance Ltd, London; Honorary Secretary to British/Saudi Arabian Parliamentary Group; *b* 5 May 1924; *s* of Henry John Armitage and late Amelia Eleanor Armitage; *m* 1956, Jennifer Gerda Bruford, *d* of Prof. W. H. Bruford, *qv*; one *s* one *d. Educ:* St Bede's and Bradford Grammar Schs; Lincoln Christ's Hosp.; Trinity Coll., Cambridge. Served Army, 1943–49; Arab Legion, 1946; British Mil. Mission to Saudi Arabia, 1946–49. Mil. Adviser to Saudi Arabian Minister of Defence, 1949–51; Desert Locust Control, Kenya and Aden Protectorates, 1952; in mil. service of Sultan of Muscat and Oman in Oman and Dhofar, 1952–59; Resident Manager, Gen. Geophysical Co. (Houston), Libya, 1959–60; Oil Conslt, Astor Associates, Libya, 1960–61; Business conslt, Beirut, 1962; joined HM Diplomatic Service, 1962; First Secretary (Commercial): Baghdad, 1963–67; Beirut, 1967–68; First Sec., Jedda, 1968 and 1969–74; Chargé d'Affaires: Jedda, 1969 and 1973; Abu Dhabi, 1975, 1976 and 1977; Counsellor and Consul Gen. in charge British Embassy, Dubai. Mem., Editl Adv. Bd, 8 Days, 1978–79. *Recreations:* reading, travel. *Address:* The Old Vicarage, East Horrington, Wells, Somerset. *Club:* Travellers'.

ARMITAGE, John Vernon, PhD; Principal, College of St Hild and St Bede, Durham, since 1975; *b* 21 May 1932; *s* of Horace Armitage and Evelyn (*née* Hauton); *m* 1963, Sarah Catherine Clay; two *s. Educ:* Rothwell Grammar Sch., Yorks; UCL (BSc, PhD); Cuddesdon Coll., Oxford. Asst Master: Pontefract High Sch., 1956–58; Shrewsbury Sch., 1958–59; Lectr in Maths, Univ. of Durham, 1959–67; Sen. Lectr in Maths, King's Coll., London, 1967–70; Prof. of Mathematical Educn, Univ. of Nottingham, 1970–75; Special Prof., Nottingham Univ., 1976–79. Chm., Math. Instruction Sub-Cttee, Brit. Nat. Cttee for Maths, Royal Soc., 1975–78. *Publications:* A Companion to Advanced Mathematics (with H. B. Griffiths), 1969; papers on theory of numbers in various jls. *Recreations:* railways, cricket and most games inexpertly. *Address:* The Principal's House, Leazes Lane, Durham DH1 1TB. *T:* Durham 63741. *Club:* Athenæum.

ARMITAGE, Kenneth, CBE 1969; sculptor; *b* 18 July 1916; *m* 1940. Studied at Slade Sch., London, 1937–39. Served War of 1939–45 in the Army. Teacher of Sculpture, Bath Academy of Art, 1946–56. *One-man exhibitions:* Gimpel Fils, London, regularly 1952–; New York, 1954–58, the last at Paul Rosenberg & Co.; Marlborough Fine Art London, 1962, 1965; Arts Council Exhibn touring 10 English cities, 1972–73; Gall. Kasahara, Osaka, 1974, 1978 and Fuji Telecasting Gall., Tokyo, and Gal. Humanite, Nagoya; Stoke-on-Trent City Mus. and Art Gall., 1981; Sala Mendoza, Caracas, Venezuela, 1982; Taranman Gall., London, 1982; Retrospective Exhibn, Artcurial, Paris, 1985. Gregory Fellowship in sculpture, Leeds Univ., 1953–55; *Guest Artist:* Caracas, Venezuela, 1963; City of Berlin, 1967–69. *Work shown in:* Exhibn of Recent Sculpture in British Pavilion at 26th Venice Biennale, 1952; Internat. Open-Air Exhibns of sculpture in Antwerp, London, Sonsbeek, Varese, and Sydney; British Council Exhibns of sculpture since 1952, which have toured Denmark, Germany, Holland, Norway, Sweden, Switzerland, Canada, USA, and S America; New Decade Exhibn, Museum of Modern Art, New York, 1955; British Section of 4th Internat. São Paulo Biennial, Brazil, 1957; 5th Internat. Exhibn of Drawings and Engravings, Lugano, 1958 (prize-winner); British Pavilion at 29th Venice Biennale, 1958; Art since 1945, Kassel Exhibition, 1959; work in British Sculpture in the 'Sixties' exhibition, Tate Gallery, 1965; Internat. Open-air Exhibn, Hakone, Japan, 1969, 1971; 24 English Sculptors, Burlington House, 1971; Jubilee sculpture exhibn, Battersea Park, 1977. Work represented in: Victoria and Albert Museum, Tate Gallery; Museum of Modern Art, New York; Musée D'Art Moderne, Paris; Galleria Nazionale d' Arti Moderne, Rome; Hakone Open-Air Sculpture Museum, Japan, and other galleries throughout the world. *Address:* 22a Avonmore Road, W14 8RR. *T:* 01–603 5800.

ARMITAGE, Air Chief Marshal Sir Michael (John), KCB 1983; CBE 1975; Air Member for Supply and Organisation, Air Force Department, Ministry of Defence, since 1986; *b* 25 Aug. 1930; *m* 1955, Mary Mannion (marr. diss. 1969); three *s*; *m* 1970, Gretl Renate Steinig. *Educ:* Newport Grammar Sch., IW; Halton Apprentice; RAF Coll., Cranwell. psc 1965, jssc 1970, rcds 1975. Commnd 1953; flying and staff appts, incl. 28 Sqn, Hong Kong, and No 4 and No 1 Flying Trng Schools; Personal Staff Officer to Comdr 2ATAF, 1966; OC 17 Sqdn, 1967–70; Stn Comdr, RAF Luqa, Malta, 1972–74; Dir Forward Policy, Ministry of Defence (Air Force Dept), 1976–78; Dep. Comdr, RAF Germany, 1978–80; Senior RAF Mem., RCDS, 1980–81; Dir of Service Intelligence, 1982; Dep. Chief of Defence Staff (Intelligence), 1983–84; Chief of Defence Intelligence, 1985–86. *Publications:* (jtly) Air Power in the Nuclear Age, 1982; contrib. prof. jls. *Recreations:* military history, game shooting, reading. *Address:* c/o Lloyds Bank, 6 Pall Mall, SW1. *Club:* Royal Air Force.

ARMITAGE, Prof. Peter, CBE 1984; Professor of Biomathematics, and Fellow, St Peter's College, University of Oxford, since 1976; *b* 15 June 1924; *s* of Harry and Florence Armitage, Huddersfield; *m* 1947, Phyllis Enid Perry, London: one *s* two *d. Educ:* Huddersfield Coll.; Trinity Coll., Cambridge. Wrangler, 1947; MA Cambridge, 1952; PhD London, 1951; Ministry of Supply, 1943–45; National Physical Laboratory, 1945–46; Mem. Statistical Research Unit of Med. Research Council, London Sch. of Hygiene and Trop. Med., 1947–61; Prof. of Medical Statistics, Univ. of London, 1961–76. President: Biometric Soc., 1972–73; Royal Statistical Soc., 1982–84 (Hon. Sec., 1958–64); Mem., International Statistical Institute, 1961. Editor, Biometrics, 1980–84. *Publications:* Sequential Medical Trials, 1960, 2nd edn 1975; Statistical Methods in Medical Research, 1971; papers in statistical and medical journals. *Recreation:* music. *Address:* 71 High Street, Drayton, Abingdon, Oxon OX14 4JW. *T:* Abingdon 31763.

See also Edward Armitage.

ARMITAGE, Sir Robert (Perceval), KCMG 1954 (CMG 1951); MBE 1944; MA; *b* 21 Dec. 1906; *s* of late F. Armitage, CIE; *m* 1930, Gwladys Lyona, *d* of late Lt-Col H. M. Meyler, CBE, DSO, MC, Croix de Guerre; two *s. Educ:* Winchester; New Coll. District Officer, Kenya Colony, 1929; Sec. to Mem. for Agriculture and Natural Resources, 1945; Administrative Sec., 1947; Under Sec., Gold Coast, 1948; Financial Sec., 1948; Min. for Finance, Gold Coast, 1951–53; Governor and C-in-C, Cyprus, 1954–55; Governor of Nyasaland, 1956–61, retired. Trustee of the Beit Trust, 1963–. KStJ 1954. *Recreation:* gardening. *Address:* Suite 24, Great Maytham Hall, Rolvenden, Kent TN17 4NE. *T:* Cranbrook 241279. *Club:* Royal Commonwealth Society.

ARMITAGE, (William) Kenneth; *see* Armitage, Kenneth.

ARMOUR, Mary Nicol Neill, RSA 1958 (ARSA 1940); RSW 1956; RGI 1977 (Vice-President, 1982; Hon. President, 1983); Teacher of Still Life, Glasgow School of Art, 1952–62 (Hon. President, 1982); *b* 27 March 1902; *d* of William Steel; *m* 1927, William Armour, RSA, RSW, RGI (*d* 1979). *Educ:* Glasgow Sch. of Art. Has exhibited at Royal Academy, Royal Scottish Academy, Soc. of Scottish Artists, and Royal Glasgow Institute. Work in permanent collections: Glasgow Municipal Gallery; Edinburgh Corporation; Art Galleries of Aberdeen, Perth, Dundee, Newport, Paisley, Greenock and Victoria (Australia). Hon. Vice Pres., Paisley Inst., 1983; Hon. LLD Glasgow, 1980. *Recreations:* weaving, gardening. *Address:* 2 Gateside, Kilbarchan, Renfrewshire PA10 2LY. *T:* Kilbarchan 2873.

ARMSON, Rev. Canon John Moss; Principal, Edinburgh Theological College, since 1982; *b* 21 Dec. 1939; *s* of Arthur Eric Armson and Edith Isobel Moss. *Educ:* Wyggeston Sch.; Selwyn Coll., Cambridge (MA); St Andrews Univ. (PhD); College of the Resurrection, Mirfield. Curate, St John, Notting Hill, 1966; Chaplain and Fellow, Downing Coll., Cambridge, 1969; Chaplain, 1973–77, Vice-Principal, 1977–82, Westcott House, Cambridge. *Recreation:* gardening. *Address:* Edinburgh Theological College, Rosebery Crescent, EH12 5JT. *T:* 031–337 3838.

ARMSTRONG, 3rd Baron *cr* 1903, of Bamburgh and Cragside; **William Henry Cecil John Robin Watson-Armstrong;** *b* 6 March 1919; *s* of 2nd Baron Armstrong and Zaida Cecile (*d* 1978), *e d* of Cecil Drummond-Wolff; *S* father, 1972; *m* 1947, Baroness Maria-Teresa du Four Chiodelli Manzoni, *o c* of late Mme Ruegger (*see* Paul J. Ruegger); one adopted *s* one adopted *d. Educ:* Eton; Trinity College, Cambridge. An Underwriting Member of Lloyd's. Served War of 1939–45, Captain Scots Guards. *Heir:* none. *Address:* Bamburgh Castle, Northumberland. *Club:* Brooks's.

ARMSTRONG, Andrew Clarence Francis, CMG 1959; Permanent Secretary, Ministry of Mines and Power, Federation of Nigeria, retired; *b* 1 May 1907; *s* of E. R. C. Armstrong, FSA, MRIA, Keeper of Irish Antiquities and later Bluemantle Pursuivant, Herald's Coll., and Mary Frances, *d* of Sir Francis Cruise; *cousin* and *heir-pres.* to Sir Andrew St Clare Armstrong, 5th Bt, *qv*; *m* 1st, 1930, Phyllis Marguerite (*d* 1930), *e d* of Lt-Col H. Waithman, DSO; 2nd, 1932, Laurel May, *d* of late A. W. Stuart; one *s* (and one *s* decd). *Educ:* St Edmund's Coll., Old Hall, Ware; Christ's Coll., Cambridge; BA. Colonial Administrative Service: Western Pacific, 1929; Nigeria, 1940. *Recreation:* golf. *Address:* 15 Ravenscroft Road, Henley-on-Thames, Oxon. *T:* Henley-on-Thames 577635. *Clubs:* Phyllis Court, Temple Golf.

ARMSTRONG, Sir Andrew St Clare, 5th Bt *cr* 1841; *b* 20 Dec. 1912; *s* of Sir Nesbitt William Armstrong, 4th Bt, and Clarice Amy, *d* of John Carter Hodkinson, Maryborough, Victoria, Australia; *S* father 1953. *Educ:* Waitaki; Wellesley Coll. Served War of 1939–45 with RAE, 2nd AIF. *Heir: cousin* Andrew Clarence Francis Armstrong, *qv*.

ARMSTRONG, Anne Legendre; Member, Board of Directors: General Motors, and Halliburton Company, since 1977; Boise Cascade Corporation, since 1978; American Express, since 1983; Chairman, President's Foreign Intelligence Advisory Board, since 1981; *b* New Orleans, Louisiana, 27 Dec. 1927; *d* of Armant Legendre and Olive Martindale; *m* 1950, Tobin Armstrong; three *s* two *d. Educ:* Foxcroft Sch., Middleburg, Va; Vassar Coll., NY (BA). Deleg. Nat. Conventions, 1964, 1968 and 1972; Mem. Republican Nat. Cttee, 1968–73 (Co-Chm., 1971–73); Counselor to the President, with Cabinet rank, 1972–74; Ambassador to the Court of St James's, 1976–77. Co-Chm., Reagan/Bush Campaign, 1980. Lectr in Diplomacy, Chm. Adv. Bd, Vice-Chm. Exec. Bd, Center for Strategic and Internat. Studies, Georgetown Univ., 1977–. Dir, Atlantic Council, 1977–82; Member: Council on Foreign Relations, 1977–; Congressional Awards Bd, 1980–81; Chm. E-SU of the US, 1977–80. Trustee: Southern Methodist Univ., 1977–; Economic Club of NY, 1978–81; Guggenheim Foundn, 1980–84. Mem. President's Council, Tulane Univ., 1977–80; Citizen Regent, Smithsonian Instn, 1978–; Mem., Visiting Cttee, John F. Kennedy Sch. of Govt, Harvard Univ., 1978–82. Hon. Mem., City of London Br., Royal Soc. of St George, 1978; Mem. and Governor, Ditchley Foundn, 1977–. Phi Beta Kappa. Hon. LLD: Bristol, 1976; Washington and Lee, 1976; Williams Coll., 1977; St Mary's Univ., 1978; Tulane, 1978; Hon. LHD Mt Vernon Coll., 1978. Gold Medal, Nat. Inst. Social Scis, 1977. Josephine Meredith Langstaff Award, Nat. Soc. Daughters of British Empire in US, 1978; Republican Woman of the Year Award, 1979; Texan of the Year Award, 1981. *Address:* Armstrong Ranch, Armstrong, Texas 78338, USA. *Club:* Pilgrims (Washington, DC).

ARMSTRONG, Prof. Arthur Hilary, MA Cantab; FBA 1970; Emeritus Professor, University of Liverpool, since 1972; Visiting Professor of Classics and Philosophy, Dalhousie University, Halifax, Nova Scotia, 1972–83; *b* 13 Aug. 1909; *s* of the Rev. W. A. Armstrong and Mrs E. M. Armstrong (*née* Cripps); *m* 1933, Deborah, *d* of Alfred Wilson and Agnes Claudia Fox Pease; two *s* two *d* (and one *d* decd). *Educ:* Lancing Coll.; Jesus Coll., Cambridge. Asst Lectr in Classics, University Coll., Swansea, 1936–39; Professor of Classics, Royal University of Malta, Valletta, 1939–43; Classical VIth Form Master, Beaumont Coll., Old Windsor, Berks, 1943–46; Lectr in Latin, University Coll., Cardiff, 1946–50; Gladstone Professor of Greek, Univ. of Liverpool, 1950–72. Killam Sen. Fellow, Dalhousie Univ., 1970–71. *Publications:* The Architecture of the Intelligible Universe in the Philosophy of Plotinus, 1940, repr. 1967 (French trans. with new preface, 1984); An Introduction to Ancient Philosophy, 1947 (American edn, 1949, 4th edn, 1965, last repr. 1981); Plotinus, 1953 (American edn, 1963); Christian Faith and Greek Philosophy (with R. A. Markus), 1960 (American edn, 1964); Plotinus I–V (Loeb Classical Library), 1966–84; Cambridge History of Later Greek and Early Mediæval Philosophy (Editor and part author), 1967, repr. 1970; St Augustine and Christian Platonism, 1968; Plotinian and Christian Studies, 1979; contribs to Classical Qly, Jl Hellenic Studies, Jl Theological Studies, etc. *Recreations:* travel, gardening. *Address:* Minia, Livesey Road, Ludlow, Shropshire SY8 1EX. *T:* Ludlow 2854.

ARMSTRONG, Rt. Hon. Ernest, PC 1979; MP (Lab) North West Durham since 1964; *b* 12 Jan. 1915; *s* of John and Elizabeth Armstrong; *m* 1941, Hannah P. Lamb; one *s* one *d. Educ:* Wolsingham Grammar Sch. Schoolmaster, 1937–52; Headmaster, 1952–64. Chm., Sunderland Educn Cttee, 1960–65. Asst Govt Whip, 1967–69; Lord Comr, HM Treasury, 1969–70; an Opposition Whip, 1970–73; Parly Under-Sec. of State, DES, 1974–75, DoE, 1975–79; Dep. Chm., Ways and Means and Dep. Speaker, 1981–. Vice-

Pres., Methodist Conf., 1974–75. *Recreation:* walking. *Address:* Penny Well, Witton-le-Wear, Bishop Auckland, Co. Durham. *T:* Witton-le-Wear 397.

ARMSTRONG, Francis William, CB 1977; LVO 1953; *b* 11 July 1919; *s* of late W. T. Armstrong, Gravesend, Kent; *m* 1st, 1945, Brenda Gladys de Wardt (*d* 1967); one *d*; 2nd, 1969, Muriel Ernestine Hockaday, MBE. *Educ:* King's Sch., Rochester; Brasenose Coll., Oxford (Open Scholarship in Classics) (MA). Served War of 1939–45: RA (commissioned, 1940); Western Desert, India, Burma. Asst Principal, War Office, 1947; Private Sec. to Permanent Under-Sec., War Office, 1948–50; Principal Private Sec. to Sec. of State for War, 1957–60; Director of Finance, Metropolitan Police, 1968–69; Asst Under-Sec. of State, MoD, 1969–72; Under Sec., Cabinet Office, 1972–74; Dep. Sec., N Ireland Office, 1974–75; Dep. Sec., MoD, 1975–77, retired 1977. Comr, Royal Hospital, Chelsea, 1977–83. *Recreations:* walking, cricket, reading. *Address:* 7 Sandown Lodge, Avenue Road, Epsom, Surrey. *T:* Epsom 40951. *Clubs:* Royal Commonwealth Society, Kent CCC.

ARMSTRONG, Jack; *see* Armstrong, J. A.

ARMSTRONG, Rt. Rev. John, CB 1962; OBE 1942; Assistant Bishop in the Diocese of Exeter; *b* 4 Oct. 1905; *y s* of late John George and Emily Armstrong; *m* 1942, Diana Gwladys Prowse, *widow* of Lieut Geoffrey Vernon Prowse, and 2nd *d* of late Admiral Sir Geoffrey Layton, GBE, KCB, KCMG, DSO; one step *s*. *Educ:* Durham School and St Francis Coll., Nundah, Brisbane, Qld. LTh, 2nd Class Hons, Australian College of Theology, 1932. Ordained 1933; Mem. Community of Ascension, Goulburn, 1932–33; Curate, St Martin, Scarborough, 1933–35; Chaplain RN, HMS Victory, 1935; Courageous, 1936–39; 6th Destroyer Flotilla, 1939–41 (despatches 1940); RM Div., 1941–43; Commando Group, 1943–45; HMS Nelson, 1945; Sen. Naval Chaplain, Germany, 1946–48; Excellent, 1948–50; RM Barracks, Portsmouth, 1950–53; Indomitable, 1953; RN Rhine Sqdn, 1953–54; HMS Vanguard, 1954; Tyne, 1954; HM Dockyard, Malta, and Asst to Chaplain of the Fleet, Mediterranean, 1955–57; HMS Bermuda, 1957–59; RM Barracks, Portsmouth, 1959–60; Chaplain of the Fleet and Archdeacon of the Royal Navy, 1960–63; Bishop of Bermuda, 1963–68; Vicar of Yarcombe, Honiton, 1969–73. QHC, 1958–63. Life Mem., Guild of Freemen of City of London. *Address:* Foundry Farm, Yarcombe, Honiton, Devon EX14 9AZ. *T:* Chard 3332. *Club:* Naval and Military.

ARMSTRONG, John Anderson, CB 1980; OBE 1945; TD 1945; Master of the Court of Protection, 1970–82; *b* 5 May 1910; *s* of W. A. Armstrong; *m* 1938, Barbara, *d* of Rev. W. L. Gantz; two *d* (and one *s* decd). *Educ:* Wellington Coll.; Trinity Coll., Cambridge. BA 1931, MA 1943. Called to Bar, Lincoln's Inn, 1936. City of London Yeomanry, RHA(T), 1931–40. Served War: Lt-Col Comdg 73 Light AA Regt, 1940–45 (Normandy, 1944). Practice at Chancery Bar, 1946–70; Bencher, Lincoln's Inn, 1969. *Recreations:* gardening, walking, fishing, golf. *Address:* Dacre Cottage, Penrith, Cumbria CA11 0HL. *T:* Pooley Bridge 224. *Club:* Brooks's.

ARMSTRONG, John Archibald, (Jack), OC 1983; retired; Chief Executive Officer, 1973–82, and Chairman, 1974–82, Imperial Oil Ltd; *b* Dauphin, Manitoba, 24 March 1917. *Educ:* Univ. of Manitoba (BSc Geol.); Queen's Univ. at Kingston (BSc Chem. Engrg). Worked for short time with Geol Survey of Canada and in mining industry; joined Imperial Oil Ltd as geologist, Regina, 1940; appts as: exploration geophysicist, western Canada, and with affiliated cos in USA and S America; Asst Reg. Manager, Producing Dept, 1949; Asst Co-ordinator, Producing Dept of Standard Oil Co. (NJ), New York; Gen. Man., Imperial's Producing Dept, Toronto, 1960; Dir, 1961; Dir resp. for Marketing Ops, 1963–65; Exec. Vice-Pres., 1966, Pres. 1970, Chief Exec. officer, 1973, Chm., 1974. Director: Royal Bank of Canada; Export Develt Corp.; Finance Chm., Governor General's Canadian Study Conf.; Life Mem., Fraser Inst. Hon. LLD: Winnipeg, 1978; Calgary, 1980. *Address:* 1235 Bay Street, Suite 601, Toronto, Ont M5R 3K4, Canada.

ARMSTRONG, Most Rev. John Ward; *b* 30 Sept. 1915; *s* of John and Elizabeth Armstrong, Belfast; *m* 1941, Doris Winifred, *d* of William J. Harrison, PC and Florence Harrison, Dublin; two *s* two *d* (and one *d* decd). *Educ:* Belfast Royal Academy; Trinity College, Dublin, BA, Respondent, 1938; Toplady Memorial Prize, Past. Theol Pr. and Abp. King's Prize (2) 1937; Biblical Greek Prize and Downes Prize (1) 1938; 1st Class Hons Hebrew, 1936 and 1937; 1st Class Divinity Testimonium, 1938; BD 1945; MA 1957 (SC). Deacon, then Priest, All Saints, Grangegorman, 1938; Hon. Clerical Vicar, Christ Church Cathedral, 1939; Dean's Vicar, St Patrick's Cathedral, 1944; Prebend. of Tassagard, St Patrick's Cathedral, 1950; Rector of Christ Church, Leeson Park, 1951; Dean of St Patrick's Cathedral, Dublin, 1958–68; Bishop of Cashel and Emly, Waterford and Lismore, 1968–77 (when diocese reorganised), of Cashel, Waterford, Lismore, Ossory, Ferns and Leighlin (known as Bishop of Cashel and Ossory), 1977–80; Archbishop of Armagh and Primate of All Ireland, 1980–86. Wallace Lecturer, TCD, 1954–65; Dean of Residences, University College, Dublin, 1954–63. Vice-Pres. Boys' Brigade, 1963–73. Trustee, Nat. Library of Ireland, 1964–74; Member: British Council of Churches, 1966–80; Anglian Consultative Council, 1979–81. Hon. DD Trinity Coll. Dublin, 1981. *Publication:* contrib. to Church and Eucharist-an Ecumenical Study (ed Rev. M. Hurley, SJ), 1966. *Recreations:* carpentering and bird-watching. *Address:* 53 Greenlawns, Skerries, Co. Dublin. *T:* Dublin 490180. *Clubs:* Friendly Brothers of St Patrick, Kildare Street and University (Dublin).

ARMSTRONG, Leslie; *see* Twiggy.

ARMSTRONG, Neil A.; Chairman, CTA Inc., since 1982; formerly NASA Astronaut (Commander, Apollo 11 Rocket Flight to the Moon, 1969); *b* Wapakoneta, Ohio, USA, 5 Aug. 1930; *s* of Stephen and Viola Armstrong, Wapakoneta; *m* 1956, Janet Shearon, Evanston, Ill; two *s*. *Educ:* High Sch., Wapakoneta, Ohio; Univ. of Southern California (MS); Purdue Univ. (BSc). Pilot's licence obtained at age of 16. Served in Korea (78 combat missions) being a naval aviator, 1949–52. He joined NASA's Lewis Research Center, 1955 (then NACA Lewis Flight Propulsion Lab.) and later transf. to NASA High Speed Flight Station at Edwards Air Force Base, Calif, as an aeronautical research pilot for NACA and NASA, in this capacity, he performed as an X-15 project pilot, flying that aircraft to over 200,000 feet and approximately 4,000 miles per hour; other flight test work included piloting the X-1 rocket airplane, the F-100, F-101, F-102, F-104, F5D, B-47, the paraglider, and others; as pilot of the B-29 "drop" aircraft, he participated in the launches of over 100 rocket airplane flights. Selected as an astronaut by NASA, Sept. 1962; served as backup Command Pilot for Gemini 5 flight; as Command Pilot for Gemini 8 mission, launched 16 March 1966; he performed the first successful docking of 2 vehicles in space; served as backup Command Pilot for Gemini 11 mission; assigned as backup Comdr for Apollo VIII Flight, 1969; Dep. Associate Administrator of Aeronautics, NASA HQ, Washington, 1970–71; University Prof. of Aerospace Engrg, Univ. of Cincinnati, 1971–79; Chm., Cardwell International Ltd, 1980–82. Director: Cincinnati Gas and Electric Co.; Taft Broadcasting Co.; Eaton Corp.; Cincinnati Milacron; UAL Inc. Mem., Nat. Acad. of Engrg. Fellow, Soc. of Experimental Test Pilots; FRAeS. Honours include NASA Exceptional Service Medal, and AIAA Astronautics Award for 1966; RGS Gold Medal, 1970. Presidential Medal for Freedom, 1969. *Address:* CTA Inc., PO Box 7624, Charlottesville, Va 22906, USA.

ARMSTRONG, Robert George, CBE 1972; MC 1946; TD 1958; Deputy Director and Controller, Savings Bank, Department for National Savings, 1969–74, retired (Deputy Director and Controller, Post Office Savings Bank, 1964); *b* 26 Oct. 1913; *s* of late George William Armstrong; *m* 1947, Clara Christine Hyde; one *s* one *d*. *Educ:* Marylebone Grammar Sch.; University Coll., London. Post Office Engineering Dept, 1936–50. Served War of 1939–45, Royal Signals. Principal, PO Headquarters, 1950; Asst Sec., 1962; Dep. Dir of Savings, 1963; Under-Sec., 1972. *Address:* Barryleigh, Wheelers Lane, Brockham, Betchworth, Surrey. *T:* Betchworth 3217.

ARMSTRONG, Sir Robert (Temple), GCB 1983 (KCB 1978; CB 1974); CVO 1975; Secretary of the Cabinet, since 1979, Permanent Secretary to Management and Personnel Office, since 1981, and Head of the Home Civil Service, since 1983 (Joint Head, 1981–83); *b* 30 March 1927; *o s* of Sir Thomas (Henry Wait) Armstrong, *qv*; *m* 1st, 1953, Serena Mary Benedicta (marr. diss. 1985), *er d* of Sir Roger Chance, 3rd Bt, *qv*; two *d*; 2nd, 1985, Mary Patricia, *d* of late C. C. Carlow. *Educ:* Dragon Sch., Oxford; Eton; Christ Church, Oxford (Hon. Student 1985). Asst Principal, Treasury, 1950–55; Private Secretary to: Rt Hon. Reginald Maudling, MP (when Economic Sec. to Treasury), 1953–54; Rt Hon. R. A. Butler, CH, MP (when Chancellor of the Exchequer), 1954–55; Principal, Treasury, 1955–57; Sec., Radcliffe Cttee on Working of Monetary System, 1957–59; returned to Treasury as Principal, 1959–64; Sec., Armitage Cttee on Pay of Postmen, 1964; Asst Sec., Cabinet Office, 1964–66; Sec. of Kindersley Review Body on Doctors' and Dentists' Remuneration and of Franks Cttee on Pay of Higher Civil Service, 1964–66; Asst Sec., Treasury, 1967–68; Jt Princ. Private Sec. to Rt Hon. Roy Jenkins, MP (Chancellor of the Exchequer), 1968; Under Secretary (Home Finance), Treasury, 1968–70; Principal Private Sec. to Prime Minister, 1970–75; Dep. Sec., 1973; Dep. Under-Sec. of State, Home Office, 1975–77, Permt Under Sec. of State, 1977–79. Sec., Bd of Dirs, Royal Opera House, Covent Garden, 1968–; Member: Governing Body, RAM, 1975– (Hon. Fellow 1985); Council of Management, Royal Philharmonic Soc., 1975–; Rhodes Trust, 1975–. Fellow of Eton Coll., 1979–. *Recreation:* music. *Address:* Cabinet Office, SW1. *Clubs:* Athenæum, Brooks's.

ARMSTRONG, Sheila Ann; soprano; *b* 13 Aug. 1942. *Educ:* Hirst Park Girls' Sch., Ashington, Northumberland; Royal Academy of Music, London. Debut Sadler's Wells, 1965 Glyndebourne, 1966, Covent Garden, 1973. Sings all over Europe, Far East, N and S America; has made many recordings. K. Ferrier and Mozart Prize, 1965; Hon. RAM 1970, FRAM 1973. Hon. MA Newcastle, 1979. *Recreations:* interior decoration, collecting antique keys, swimming, driving.

ARMSTRONG, Dr Terence Edward; Founder Fellow, Clare Hall, since 1964, Vice-President, since 1985, and Reader in Arctic Studies, 1977–83, now Emeritus, Cambridge University; *b* 7 April 1920; *s* of Thomas Mandeville Emerson Armstrong and Jane Crawford (*née* Young); *m* 1943, Iris Decima Forbes; two *s* two *d*. *Educ:* Winchester; Magdalene Coll., Cambridge (BA 1941; MA 1947; PhD 1951). Served Army, 1940–46 (Intelligence Corps, parachutist, wounded at Arnhem). Scott Polar Research Institute: Res. Fellow in Russian, 1947–56; Asst Dir of Res. (Polar), 1956–77; Actg Dir, 1982–83; Tutor, Clare Hall, Cambridge, 1967–74. Extensive travel in Arctic and sub-Arctic, incl. voyage through NW Passage, 1954. US Nat. Sci. Foundn Sen. For. Scientist Fellowship, Univ. of Alaska, 1970. Jt Hon. Sec., Hakluyt Soc., 1965–. Hon. LLD McGill, 1963; Hon. DSc Alaska, 1980. Cuthbert Peek Award, RGS, 1954; Victoria Medal, RGS, 1978. *Publications:* The Northern Sea Route, 1952; Sea Ice North of the USSR, 1958; The Russians in the Arctic, 1958; Russian Settlement in the North, 1965; (ed) Yermak's Campaign in Siberia, 1975; (jtly) The Circumpolar North, 1978; contribs to jls on socio-economic problems of Arctic and sub-Arctic regions. *Recreations:* making music, walking, foreign travel. *Address:* Harston House, Harston, Cambridge CB2 5NH. *T:* Cambridge 870262.

ARMSTRONG, Sir Thomas Henry Wait, Kt 1958; MA, DMus; FRCM; Hon. FRCO, Hon. RAM; Principal, Royal Academy of Music, 1955–68; Organist of Christ Church, Oxford, 1933–55; Student of Christ Church, 1939–55; Student Emeritus, 1955; Hon. Student, 1981; Choragus of the University and University lecturer in music, 1937–54; Conductor of the Oxford Bach Choir and the Oxford Orchestral Society; Musical Director of the Balliol Concerts; Trustee, The Countess of Munster Musical Trust; *b* 15 June 1898; *o s* of A. E. Armstrong, Peterborough, Northants; *m* 1926, Hester (*d* 1982), 2nd *d* of late Rev. W. H. Draper; one *s* one *d*. *Educ:* Choir Sch., Chapel Royal, St James's; King's Sch., Peterborough; Keble Coll., Oxford; Royal Coll. of Music. Organist, Thorney Abbey, 1914; sub-organist, Peterborough Cathedral, 1915; Organ Scholar, Keble Coll., Oxford 1916, Hon. Fellow, 1955; served in RA, BEF, France, 1917–19; sub-organist, Manchester Cathedral, 1922; organist, St Peter's, Eaton Square, 1923; organist of Exeter Cathedral, 1928. Cramb Lectr in music, Univ. of Glasgow, 1949. Vice-President, Bruckner-Mahler Chorale, 1970. *Compositions:* various, the larger ones remain unpublished. *Publications:* include choral music, songs and church music, together with many occasional writings on music. *Address:* Slade Cottage, Newton Blossomville, near Turvey, Beds MK43 8AN. *T:* Turvey 329. *Club:* Garrick.

See also Sir R. T. Armstrong.

ARMSTRONG-JONES, family name of **Earl of Snowdon.**

ARMYTAGE, Sir (John) Martin, 9th Bt *cr* 1738, of Kirklees, Yorkshire; *b* 26 Feb. 1933; *s* of Sir John Lionel Armytage, 8th Bt, and of Evelyn Mary Jessamine, *d* of Edward Herbert Fox, Adbury Park, Newbury; *S* father, 1983. *Heir: cousin* Captain David George Armytage, CBE, RN [*b* 4 Sept. 1929; *m* 1954, Antonia Cosima, *er d* of Count Cosimo Diodono de Bosdari; two *s* one *d*]. *Address:* Halewell Close, Withington, Glos GL54 4BN. *T:* Withington 238. *Club:* Naval and Military.

ARMYTAGE, Prof. Walter Harry Green; Professor of Education, University of Sheffield, 1954–82, now Emeritus Professor; Gerald Read Professor of Education, Kent State University, Ohio, 1982–85; *b* 22 Nov. 1915; *e s* of Walter Green Armytage and Harriet Jane May Armytage; *m* 1948, Lucy Frances Horsfall; one *s*. *Educ:* Redruth County School; Downing Coll., Cambridge. 1st Cl. Hist. Trip. 1937, Cert. in Educ., 1938. History Master, Dronfield Grammar Sch., 1938–39; served War of 1939–45 (despatches); Captain, London Irish Rifles. Univ. of Sheffield: Lectr, 1946; Sen. Lectr, 1952; Pro-Vice-Chancellor, 1964–68. Visiting Lecturer: Univ. of Michigan, USA, 1955, 1959, 1961, 1963, 1975; Newcastle, NSW, 1977; Lectures: Ballard-Matthews, University Coll. of North Wales, 1973; Cantor, RSA, 1969; Hawkesley, IMechE, 1969; S. P. Thompson, IEE, 1972; Galton, Eugenics Soc., 1974; Clapton, Leeds Univ., 1979. Hon. DLitt: NUU, 1977; Hull, 1980. *Publications:* A. J. Mundella 1825–1897: The Liberal Background of the Labour Movement, 1951; Thomas Hughes: The Life of the Author of Tom Brown's Schooldays, 1953 (with E. C. Mack); Civic Universities: Aspects of a British Tradition, 1955; Sir Richard Gregory: his Life and Work, 1957; A Social History of Engineering, 1961; Heavens Below: Utopian Experiments in England, 1560–1960, 1962; Four Hundred Years of English Education, 1964; The Rise of the Technocrats, 1965; The

American Influence on English Education, 1967; Yesterday's Tomorrows: A Historical Survey of Future Societies, 1968; The French Influence on English Education, 1968; The German Influence on English Education, 1969; The Russian Influence on English Education, 1969. *Recreations:* walking, gardening. *Address:* 3 The Green, Totley, Sheffield, South Yorks. *T:* Sheffield 362515. *Clubs:* National Liberal; University Staff (Sheffield).

ARNDT, Ulrich Wolfgang, MA, PhD; FRS 1982; Member, Scientific Staff of Medical Research Council Laboratory of Molecular Biology, Cambridge, since 1962; *b* 23 April 1924; *o s* of E. J. and C. M. Arndt; *m* 1958, Valerie Howard, *e d* of late Maj.-Gen. F. C. Hilton-Sergeant, CB, CBE, QHP; three *d. Educ:* Dulwich Coll.; King Edward VI High Sch., Birmingham; Emmanuel Coll., Cambridge (MA, PhD). Metallurgy Dept, Birmingham Univ., 1948–49; Davy-Faraday Laboratory of Royal Instn, 1950–63; Dewar Fellow of Royal Instn, 1957–61; Univ. of Wisconsin, Madison, 1956; Institut Laue-Langevin, Grenoble, 1972–73. *Publications:* (with B. T. M. Willis) Single Crystal Diffractometry, 1966; (with A. J. Wonacott) The Rotation Method in Crystallography, 1977; papers in scientific jls. *Recreations:* walking, reading. *Address:* 28 Barrow Road, Cambridge CB2 2AS. *T:* Cambridge 350660.

ARNELL, Richard Anthony Sayer; Hon. FTCL; composer; conductor; film maker; Principal Lecturer, Trinity College of Music, since 1981 (Teacher of Composition, 1949–81); *b* 15 Sept. 1917; *s* of late Richard Sayer Arnell and of Helène Marie Sherf; *m* 1981, Audrey Millar Paul. *Educ:* The Hall, Hampstead; University Coll. Sch., NW3; Royal Coll. of Music. Music Consultant, BBC North American Service, 1943–46; Lectr, Royal Ballet Sch., 1958–59. Editor, The Composer, 1961–64; Chairman: Composers' Guild of GB, 1965, 1974–75; Young Musicians' Symph. Orch. Soc., 1973–75. Vis. Lectr (Fulbright Exchange), Bowdoin Coll., Maine, 1967–68; Vis. Prof. Hofstra Univ., New York, 1968–70. Music Dir and Board Mem., London Internat. Film Sch., 1975– (Chm., Film Sch. Trust, 1981–; Chm., Friends of LIFS, 1982–); Music Dir, Ram Filming Ltd, 1980–; Director: Organic Sounds Ltd, 1982–; A plus A Ltd, 1984–. Chm., Friends of TCM Junior Dept, 1986–. Composer of the Year 1966 (Music Teachers Assoc. Award). Compositions include: 5 symphonies; 2 concertos for violin; concerto for harpsichord; concerto for piano; 5 string quartets; 2 quintets; piano trio; piano works; songs; cantatas; organ works; music for string orchestra, wind ensembles, brass ensembles, song cycles; electronic music. *Opera:* Love in Transit; Moonflowers. *Ballet scores:* Punch and the Child, for Ballet Soc., NY, 1947; Harlequin in April, for Arts Council, 1951; The Great Detective, for Sadler's Wells Theatre Ballet, 1953; The Angels, for Royal Ballet, 1957; Giselle (Adam) re-orchestrated, for Ballet Rambert, 1965. *Film scores:* The Land, 1941; The Third Secret, 1963; The Visit, 1964; The Man Outside, 1966; Topsail Schooner, 1966; Bequest for a Village, 1969; Second Best, 1972; Stained Glass, 1973; Wires Over the Border, 1974; Black Panther, 1977; Antagonist, 1980; Dilemma, 1981; Doctor in the Sky, 1983; Toulouse Lautrec, 1984. *Other works:* Symphonic Portrait, Lord Byron, for Sir Thomas Beecham, 1953; Landscapes and Figures, for Sir Thomas Beecham, 1956; Petrified Princess, puppet operetta (libretto by Bryan Guinness), for BBC, 1959; Robert Flaherty, Impression for Radio Eireann, 1960; Musica Pacifica for Edward Benjamin, 1963; Festival Flourish, for Salvation Army, 1965; 2nd piano concerto, for RPO, 1967; Overture, Food of Love, for Portland Symph. Orch., 1968; My Ladye Greene Sleeves, for Hofstra Univ., 1968; Life Boat Voluntary, for RNLI, 1974; Call, for LPO, 1980; Ode to Beecham, for RPO, 1986. *Mixed media:* Nocturne: Prague, 1968; I Think of all Soft Limbs, for Canadian Broadcasting Corp., 1971; Astronaut One, 1973. *Address:* A plus A, 149A Shenley Road, Borehamwood, Herts. *Club:* Savage.

ARNOLD, Mrs Elliott; *see* Johns, Glynis.

ARNOLD, Rt. Rev. George Feversham, DD; *b* 30 Dec. 1914; *s* of Arnold Feversham and Elsie Mildred Arnold; *m* 1940, Mary Eleanor Sherman Holmes; one *s* one *d. Educ:* Univ. of King's Coll., Halifax, NS (LTh 1937, BD 1944); Dalhousie Univ. (BA 1935, MA 1938). Rector: Louisbourg, 1938–41; Mahone Bay, 1941–50; St John's, Fairview, 1950–53; Windsor, 1953–58; Clerical Sec. and Diocesan Registrar, 1958–67; Exam. Chaplain to Bishop of Nova Scotia, 1947–70; Hon. Canon of All Saints Cathedral, 1959–63, Canon, 1963–67; Bishop Suffragan of Nova Scotia, 1967–75, Bishop Coadjutor, May–Sept. 1975; Bishop of Nova Scotia, 1975–79. Hon. DD, King's Coll., Halifax, 1968. *Recreation:* yachting. *Address:* 56 Holmes Hill Road, Hantsport, NS B0P 1P0, Canada.

ARNOLD, Rt. Hon. Sir John Lewis, Kt 1972; PC 1979; President of Family Division, since 1979; a Judge in the Division, since 1972; *b* 6 May 1915; *s* of late A. L. Arnold and E. K. Arnold; *m* 1940, Alice Margaret Dorothea (*née* Cookson) (marr. diss., 1963); one *s* one *d; m* 1963, Florence Elizabeth, *d* of H. M. Hague, Montreal; one *s* two *d. Educ:* Wellington Coll.; abroad. Called to Bar, Middle Temple, 1937; served War of 1939–45 in Army (despatches, 1945); resumed practice at Bar, 1946; QC 1958; Chm. Bar Council, 1970–72, Chm., Plant Variety Rights Tribunal for proceedings in England and Wales, 1969–72. Hon. DLitt Reading, 1982. *Recreations:* cricket, travel. *Address:* Royal Courts of Justice, WC2.

ARNOLD, Very Rev. John Robert; Dean of Rochester, since 1978; *b* 1 Nov. 1933; *s* of John Stanley and Ivy Arnold; *m* 1963, Livia Anneliese Franke; one *s* two *d. Educ:* Christ's Hospital; Sidney Sussex Coll., Cambridge (MA); Westcott House Theol College. Curate of Holy Trinity, Millhouses, Sheffield, 1960–63; Sir Henry Stephenson Fellow, Univ. of Sheffield, 1962–63; Chaplain and Lectr, Univ. of Southampton, 1963–72; Secretary, Board for Mission and Unity, General Synod of the Church of England, 1972–78; Hon. Canon of Winchester Cathedral, 1974–78; Mem., General Synod, 1980–. Order of Saint Vladimir (Russian Orthodox Church), 1977. *Publications:* (trans.) Eucharistic Liturgy of Taizé, 1962; (contrib.) Hewitt, Strategist for the Spirit, 1985; contribs to Theology, Crucible. *Recreations:* music; European languages and literature. *Address:* The Deanery, The Precinct, Rochester, Kent ME1 1TG. *T:* Medway 44023. *Club:* Christ's Hospital.

ARNOLD, Rt. Rev. Keith Appleby; *see* Warwick, Bishop Suffragan of.

ARNOLD, Malcolm, CBE 1970; FRCM; composer; *b* 21 Oct. 1921; *s* of William and Annie Arnold, Northampton; *m*; two *s* one *d. Educ:* Royal Coll. of Music, London (Schol., 1938). FRCM 1983. Principal Trumpet, London Philharmonic Orchestra, 1941–44; served in the Army, 1944–45; Principal Trumpet, London Philharmonic Orchestra, 1945–48; Mendelssohn Schol. (study in Italy), 1948; Coronation Ballet, Homage to the Queen, performed Royal Opera House, 1953. Awarded Oscar for music for film Bridge on the River Kwai, 1957. Bard of the Cornish Gorsedd, 1969. Hon. DMus: Exeter, 1970; Durham, 1982; Leicester, 1984; Hon. RAM. *Publications:* symphonies: No 1, 1949; No 2, 1953; No 3, 1957; No 4, 1960; No 5, 1961; No 6, 1967; No 7, 1973; No 8, 1978; Symphony for Brass Instruments, 1979; *other works:* Beckus the Dandipratt, overture, 1943; Tam O'Shanter, overture, 1955; Peterloo, overture, 1967; eighteen concertos; five ballets; two one-act operas; two string quartets; brass quintet; vocal, choral and chamber music. *Recreations:* reading and foreign travel. *Club:* Savile.

ARNOLD, Dr Richard Bentham; Executive Vice-President, International Federation of Pharmaceutical Manufacturers' Associations, since 1984; *b* 29 Aug. 1932; *s* of George Benjamin and Alice Arnold; *m* 1956, Margaret Evelyn Racey; one *s* one *d. Educ:* Stamford

Sch.; King Edward VII Sch., King's Lynn; Nottingham Univ. BSc, PhD. Joined May & Baker Ltd, 1959; Commercial Manager, Pharmaceuticals Div., 1974–76; Dir Designate, 1976, Dir, 1977–83, Assoc. of British Pharmaceutical Industry. *Recreations:* golf, fishing, bird watching. *Address:* IFPMA Secretariat, 67 rue de St Jean, 1201 Geneva, Switzerland.

ARNOLD, Thomas Richard; MP (C) Hazel Grove, since Oct. 1974; *b* 25 Jan. 1947; *s* of Thomas Charles Arnold and Helen Breen; *m* 1984, Elizabeth Jane, *widow* of Robin Smithers. *Educ:* Bedales Sch.; Le Rosey, Geneva; Pembroke Coll., Oxford (MA). Theatre producer; publisher. Contested (C): Manchester Cheetham, 1970; Hazel Grove, Feb. 1974; PPS to Sec. of State for NI, 1979–81, to Lord Privy Seal, FCO, 1981–82. Vice-Chm., Conservative Party, 1983–. *Address:* House of Commons, SW1A 0AA. *T:* 01–219 4096. *Clubs:* Carlton, Royal Automobile.

ARNOLD, Vere Arbuthnot, CBE 1970; MC 1945; TD 1953; JP; DL; Chairman, Ross T. Smyth & Co. Ltd, 1957–80; *b* 23 May 1902; *s* of Rev. H. A. Arnold, Wolsingham Rectory, Co. Durham; *m* 1928, Joan Kathleen, *d* of C. J. Tully, Wairarapa, NZ; one *s* one *d. Educ:* Haileybury Coll.; Jesus Coll., Cambridge (BA). Ross T. Smyth & Co. Ltd, 1924, Director, 1931; Pres., Liverpool Corn Trade Association, 1947–48 and 1951–52. Chm., Runcorn Develt Corp., 1964–74. Served War of 1939–45 as Major (MC, TD). JP County of Chester, 1949; High Sheriff, Cheshire, 1958; DL Cheshire, 1969. *Recreations:* shooting, fishing. *Address:* Ardmore, Great Barrow, near Chester. *T:* Tarvin 40257.

ARNOLD-BAKER, Charles, OBE 1966; Deputy Eastern Traffic Commissioner, since 1978; Consultant Lecturer, since 1978, and Visiting Professor, since 1985, City University; Secretary, National Association of Local Councils, 1953–78; *b* 25 June 1918; *s* of Baron Albrecht v. Blumenthal and Alice Wilhelmine (*née* Hainsworth); *m* 1943, Edith (*née* Woods); one *s* one *d. Educ:* Winchester Coll.; Magdalen Coll., Oxford. BA 1940. Called to Bar, Inner Temple, 1948. Army (Private to Captain), 1940–46. Admty Bar, 1948–52; Mem., Royal Commn on Common Lands, 1955–58; Mem. European Cttee, Internat. Union of Local Authorities, 1960–78; a Deleg. to European Local Govt Assembly, Strasbourg, 1960–78. Gwylim Gibbons Award, Nuffield Coll., Oxford, 1959. King Haakon's Medal of Freedom (Norway), 1945. *Publications:* Norway (pamphlet), 1946; Everyman's Dictionary of Dates, 1954; Parish Administration, 1958; New Law and Practice of Parish Administration, 1966; The 5000 and the Power Tangle, 1967; The Local Government Act 1972, 1973; Local Council Administration, 1975, 2nd rev. edn 1981; The Local Government, Planning and Land Act 1980, 1981; Practical Law for Arts Administrators, 1983; The Five Thousand and the Living Constitution, 1986; many contribs to British and European local govt and legal jls. *Recreations:* travel, history, writing, music, cooking, journalism, wine and doing nothing. *Address:* Top Floor, 2 Paper Buildings, Inner Temple, EC4. *T:* 01–353 3490. *Club:* Union (Oxford).

ARNOTT, Sir Alexander John Maxwell, 6th Bt *cr* 1896, of Woodlands, Shandon, Co. Cork; *b* 18 Sept. 1975; *s* of Sir John Robert Alexander Arnott, 5th Bt, and of Ann Margaret, *d* of late T. A. Farrelly, Kilcar, Co. Cavan; *S* father, 1981. *Heir:* b Andrew John Eric Arnott, *b* 20 June 1978. *Address:* 11 Palmerston Road, Dublin 6, Ireland.

ARNOTT, Most Rev. Felix Raymond, CMG 1981; MA (Oxon); ThD; MACE; *b* Ipswich, Suffolk, 8 March 1911; *s* of late Richard Girling Arnott, Ipswich; *m* 1938, Anne Caroline, *d* of W. A. P. Lane, Kingston Gorse, Sussex; two *s* two *d. Educ:* Ipswich Sch.; Keble Coll., Oxford; Cuddesdon Theol Coll. Curate, Elland, Yorks, 1934–38; Exam. Chaplain, Bp of Wakefield, 1936–39; Vice-Prin., Cheshunt, 1938; Warden, St John's Coll., Brisbane, 1939–46; Warden, St Paul's Coll., Univ. of Sydney, 1946–63; Lectr i/c of Ecclesiastical History, Univ. of Sydney, 1951–63; a Co-Adjutor Bishop of Melbourne, 1963–70; Archbishop of Brisbane and Metropolitan of Queensland, 1970–80; Hon. Chaplain in Venice, 1980–85. Member: Monash Univ. Council, 1964–70; Anglican-Roman Catholic Internat. Cttee, 1969–81; Queensland Univ. Senate, 1971–80. Comr, Royal Commn on Human Relations, Australia, 1974–. A Founder of Blake Prize for Religious Art, 1951. *Publications:* The Anglican Via Media in the Seventeenth Century, 1948; contribs to learned jls. *Recreations:* walking, music. *Address:* 49 Westgate, Chichester, West Sussex PO19 3EZ. *Clubs:* Melbourne, Royal Automobile (Victoria); Australian (Sydney); Queensland (Brisbane).

ARNOTT, Sir Melville; *see* Arnott, Sir W. M.

ARNOTT, Prof. Struther, FRS 1985; Professor of Molecular Biology since 1970, and Vice-President for Research and Dean of the Graduate School, 1980–Sept. 1986, Purdue University; Principal, University of St Andrews, from Oct. 1986; *b* 25 Sept. 1934; *s* of Charles McCann and Christina Struthers Arnott; *m* 1970, Greta Maureen Edwards; two *s. Educ:* Hamilton Academy, Lanarkshire; Glasgow Univ. (BSc, PhD). King's College London: scientist, MRC Biophysics Research Unit, 1960–70; demonstrator in Physics, 1960–67; dir of postgraduate studies in Biophysics, 1967–70; Head, Dept of Biol Scis, Purdue Univ., 1975–80. Oxford University: Sen. Vis. Fellow, Jesus Coll., 1980–81; Nuffield Res. Fellow, Green Coll., 1985–86. *Publications:* papers in learned jls on structures of fibrous biopolymers and techniques for visualizing them. *Recreations:* bird watching, botanizing, gardening. *Address:* (until Oct. 1986) Green Knowe House, 421 Robinson Street, West Lafayette, Indiana 47906, USA. *T:* 317-743-9890; University House, St Andrews, Fife KY16 9AJ. *Club:* Athenæum.

ARNOTT, Sir (William) Melville, Kt 1971; TD (and clasps) 1944; MD; FRCP; FRCPE; FRSE, FRCPath; British Heart Foundation Professor of Cardiology, University of Birmingham, 1971–74, now Emeritus Professor of Medicine; Physician, United Birmingham Hospitals, 1946–74; Hon. Consultant Physician, Queen Elizabeth Hospital, Birmingham, since 1974; *b* 14 Jan. 1909; *s* of Rev. Henry and Jeanette Main Arnott; *m* 1938, Dorothy Eleanor, *er d* of G. F. S. Hill, Edinburgh; one *s. Educ:* George Watson's Coll., Edinburgh; Univ. of Edinburgh. MB, ChB (Hons), 1931, BSc (1st Cl. Hons Path.), 1934, MD (Gold Medal and Gunning Prize in Path.), 1937, Edinburgh; McCunn Res. Schol. in Path., 1933–35, Crichton Res. Schol. in Path., 1935, Shaw Macfie Lang Res. Fellow, 1936–38, Edinburgh. MD Birmingham, 1947. 2nd Lieut RA, 1929; TA 1929–39; War of 1939–45, served as specialist physician; five years foreign service (Siege of Tobruk; despatches, NW Europe); Lt-Col 1942. Asst Physician, Edinburgh Municipal Hosps, 1934–36; Hon. Asst Physician: Church of Scotland Deaconess Hosp., Edinburgh, 1938–46; Edinburgh Royal Infirmary, 1946. Dir, Post-grad. studies in Medicine, Edinburgh Univ., 1945–46; William Withering Prof. of Medicine, Univ. of Birmingham, 1946–71. Consultant Adviser in Research to W Midlands RHA, 1974–79. Associate Examr in Medicine, London Univ., 1948–49; Examr in Medicine, to Univs of Cambridge, 1950–56, London, 1951–54, Wales, 1954–57, Queen's, Belfast, 1956–59, Edinburgh, 1959–62, Leeds, 1959–62, St Andrews, 1961–63, Oxford, 1961–68, Newcastle, 1964–67, Manchester, 1964–67, Singapore, 1965, East Africa, 1965, Malaysia, 1973, NUI, 1975–77. Member: UGC, 1954–63; MRC, 1965–69; Council, University Coll. of Rhodesia, 1964–70; UGC Hong Kong, 1966–75; Home Office Cttee (Brodrick) on Death Registration and Coroners, 1965–71; Tropical Medicine Res. Bd, 1967–71. Dep. Pres., First Internat. Conf. on Med. Educn, 1953. Editor, Clinical Science, 1953–58. Member, Editorial Board: Brit. Jl of Social Medicine; Brit. Jl of Industrial Medicine and Cardiovascular Research. RCPE: Mem., 1933; Fellow, 1937; John Matheson Shaw Lectr,

1958; Cullen Prize, 1958. RCP: Mem., 1947; Fellow, 1951; Mem. Council, 1954–56; Oliver-Sharpey Lectr, 1955; Examr for Membership, 1957–66; Croonian Lectr, 1963; Censor, 1969–71; Sen. Vice-Pres., and Sen. Censor, 1973. Foundation Fellow, Royal Coll. of Pathologists. FRMedSoc 1929 (late Senior Pres.); Hon. FRCP(C), 1957; Hon. FACP, 1968 (Lilly Lectr, 1968). Member: Assoc. of Physicians; Physiological Soc.; Pathological Soc.; Med. Res. Soc.; Cardiac Soc.; Thoracic Soc.; Internat. Soc. of Internal Medicine. Sir Arthur Sims Commonwealth Trav. Prof. of Medicine, 1957. Lectures: Frederick Price, Trinity Coll., Dublin, 1959; Hall, Cardiac Soc. of Aust. and NZ, 1962; Henry Cohen, Hebrew Univ. of Jerusalem, 1964; Alexander Brown Meml, Univ. of Ibadan, 1972; John Snow, Soc. of Anaesthetists, 1973. President: Edinburgh Harveian Soc., 1955; British Lung Foundation, 1985–. Research: Originally into experimental path. of renal hypertension and peripheral vascular disease; at present, into physiology and path. of cardio-respiratory function. Hon. DSc: Edinburgh, 1975; Chinese Univ. of Hong Kong, 1983; Hon. LLD: Rhodesia, 1976; Dundee, 1976. Publications: some 50 scientific papers, principally in Lancet, Jl of Physiol., Jl of Path., Brit. Jl of Social Medicine, Edinburgh Med. Jl, etc. Recreation: travel. Address: 40 Carpenter Road, Edgbaston, Birmingham B15 2JJ. T: 021–440 2195. Club: Naval and Military.

ARONSOHN, Lotte Therese; see Newman, L. T.

ARONSON, Geoffrey Fraser, CB 1977; retired solicitor; Legal Adviser and Solicitor to Ministry of Agriculture, Fisheries and Food, to Forestry Commission, and to (EEC) Intervention Board for Agricultural Produce, 1974–79; b 17 April 1914; er s of late Victor Rees Aronson, CBE, KC, and Annie Elizabeth Aronson (née Fraser); m 1940, Marie Louise, e d of late George Stewart Rose-Innes; one s two d. Educ: Haileybury. Solicitor (Honours) 1936. Legal Dept, Min. of Agriculture and Fisheries, 1938; served War of 1939–45, Flying Control Officer, RAFVR; promoted Asst Solicitor, MAFF, 1960; Under-Sec. (Principal Asst Solicitor), 1971, when chiefly concerned with UK accession to EEC. Part-time consultant to Law Commn, 1979–84. Recreations: travel, gardening. Address: Cedars Cottage, 16 Church Street, Epsom, Surrey KT17 4QB. T: Epsom 22431; 30 Eastergate Green, Rustington, W Sussex. T: Rustington 775736. Clubs: Royal Commonwealth Society, Royal Automobile.

ARONSON, Hazel Josephine, (Mrs John A. Cosgrove); Sheriff of Lothian and Borders at Edinburgh, since 1983; b 12 Jan. 1946; d of late Moses Aron Aronson and Julia Tobias; m 1967, John Allan Cosgrove, dental surgeon; one s one d. Educ: Glasgow High Sch. for Girls; Univ. of Glasgow (LLB). Advocate at the Scottish Bar. Admitted to Fac. of Advocates, 1968; Standing Junior Counsel to Dept of Trade, 1977–79; Sheriff of Glasgow and Strathkelvin, 1979–83. Recreations: foreign travel, opera, walking, reading, cooking. Address: 14 Gordon Terrace, Edinburgh EH16 5QR. T: 031–667 8955.

ARRAN, 9th Earl of, cr 1762, of the Arran Islands, Co. Galway; **Arthur Desmond Colquhoun Gore;** Bt 1662; Viscount Sudley, Baron Saunders, 1758; Baron Sudley (UK), 1884; b 14 July 1938; er s of 8th Earl of Arran and of Fiona Bryde, er d of Sir Iain Colquhoun of Luss, 7th Bt, KT, DSO; S father, 1983; m 1974, Eleanor, er d of Bernard van Cutsem and Lady Margaret Fortescue; two d. Educ: Eton; Balliol College, Oxford. 2nd Lieutenant, 1st Bn Grenadier Guards (National Service). Asst Manager, Daily Mail, 1972–73; Man. Dir, Clark Nelson, 1973–74; Asst Gen. Manager Daily and Sunday Express, June-Nov. 1974. Co-Founder, Gore Publishing Ltd, 1980. Co-Chm., Children's Country Holidays Fund. Recreations: tennis, shooting, gardening, croquet. Address: Crocker End House, Nettlebed, Henley-on-Thames, Oxon. T: Nettlebed 641659. Clubs: Turf, Beefsteak.

ARRAU, Claudio; Concert Pianist; b Chillan, Chile, 6 Feb. 1903; American citizen, 1979; m; two s one d. Gave first recital at Santiago at age of 5; musical education in Europe financed by Chilean Govt; studied at Stern Konservatorie Berlin, under Martin Krause; won Liszt Prize 1919, 1920 (not awarded in 45 years), Schulhoff prize, Ibach prize (1917), and, in 1927, first place in Geneva International Piano Competition. Has appeared in US, Canada, England, France, Holland, Italy, Germany, Scandinavia, Russia, South America, Mexico, Cuba, Hawaii, South Africa, Australia, Israel, Japan, NZ, Iceland, Hong Kong, Singapore, Ceylon, New Delhi and Bombay. Chile has named two streets in his honour. Cycle performances include: all keyboard works of Bach in 12 recitals, Berlin, 1935; all Beethoven Sonatas, 8 recitals, Berlin, Buenos Aires, Santiago, NY and London; all Beethoven Sonatas, Diabelli Variations, (first BBC broadcast from London, 1952), all Beethoven, NY Season, 1953–54, 1962; renowned also for Chopin, Schumann, Brahms, Liszt, Debussy. Decorations from France, Germany, Mexico, Chile, Italy; International UNESCO Music Prize, 1983. Address: c/o ICM Artists Ltd, 40 West 57 Street, New York, NY 10019, USA.

ARRINDELL, Sir Clement Athelston, GCMG 1984; GCVO 1985; Kt 1982; QC; Governor-General, St Christopher and Nevis, since 1983 (Governor, St Kitts-Nevis, 1981–83); b Basseterre, 19 April 1931. Educ: private school; Basseterre Boys' Elementary Sch.; St Kitts-Nevis Grammar Sch. (Island Scholar). Called to the Bar, Lincoln's Inn, 1958. Post-grad. studies; in practice as barrister and solicitor, 1959–66; Acting Magistrate, 1964–66; Magistrate, 1966–71; Chief Magistrate, 1972–78; Judge, WI Associated States Supreme Court, 1978–81. Recreations: piano-playing, classical music, gardening. Address: Government House, Basseterre, St Christopher, West Indies. T: 2315.

ARROW, Kenneth Joseph; Professor of Economics and Operations Research, Stanford University, since 1979; b 23 Aug. 1921; s of Harry I. and Lillian Arrow; m 1947, Selma Schweitzer; two s. Educ: City College (BS in Social Science 1940); Columbia Univ. (MA 1941, PhD 1951). Captain, US AAF, 1942–46. Research Associate, Cowles Commn for Research in Economics, Univ. of Chicago, 1947–49; Actg Asst Prof., Associate Prof. and Prof. of Economics, Statistics and Operations Research, Stanford Univ., 1949–68; Prof. of Econs, later University Prof., Harvard Univ., 1968–79. Staff Mem., US Council of Economic Advisers, 1962. Consultant, The Rand Corp., 1948–. Fellow, Churchill Coll., Cambridge, 1963–64, 1970, 1973, 1986. Member: Inst. of Management Sciences (Pres., 1963); Nat. Acad. of Sciences; Amer. Inst. of Medicine; Amer. Philosoph. Soc.; Fellow: Econometric Soc. (Pres., 1956); Amer. Acad. of Arts and Sciences; Amer. Assoc. for Advancement of Science (Chm., Section K, 1982); Amer. Statistical Assoc.; Dist. Fellow: Amer. Econ. Assoc. (Pres., 1972); Western Econ. Assoc. (Pres., 1980–81); Corresp. Fellow, British Acad., 1976; Foreign Hon. Mem., Finnish Acad. of Sciences. John Bates Clark Medal, American Economic Assoc., 1957; Nobel Meml Prize in Economic Science, 1972; von Neumann Prize, 1986. Hon. LLD: Chicago, 1967; City Univ. of NY, 1972; Hon. Dr Soc. and Econ. Sciences, Vienna, 1971; Hon. ScD Columbia, 1973; Hon. DSocSci, Yale, 1974; Hon. Dr: Paris, 1974; Hebrew Univ. of Jerusalem, 1975; Helsinki, 1976; Aix-Marseille III, 1985; Hon. LittD Cambridge, 1985. Order of the Rising Sun (2nd class), Japan. Publications: Social Choice and Individual Values, 1951, 2nd edn 1963; (with S. Karlin and H. Scarf) Studies in the Mathematical Theory of Inventory and Production, 1958; (with M. Hoffenberg) A Time Series Analysis of Interindustry Demands, 1959; (with L. Hurwicz and H. Uzawa) Studies in Linear and Nonlinear Programming, 1959; Aspects of the Theory of Risk Bearing, 1965; (with M. Kurz) Public Investment and the Rate of Return, and Optimal Fiscal Policy, 1971; Essays in the Theory of Risk-Bearing,

1971; (with F. Hahn) General Competitive Analysis, 1972; The Limits of Organization, 1974; (with L. Hurwicz) Studies in Resource Allocation Processes, 1977; Collected Papers, Vols 1–6, 1984–86; 160 articles in jls and collective vols. Address: 4th Floor, Encina Hall, Stanford University, Calif 94305, USA.

ARROWSMITH, Sir Edwin (Porter), KCMG 1959 (CMG 1950); b 23 May 1909; s of late Edwin Arrowsmith and of Kathleen Eggleston Arrowsmith (née Porter); m 1936, Clondagh, e d of late Dr W. G. Connor; two d. Educ: Cheltenham Coll.; Trinity Coll., Oxford (MA). Assistant District Commissioner, Bechuanaland Protectorate, 1932; in various District posts, Bechuanaland Protectorate, 1933–38; Commissioner, Turks and Caicos Islands, BWI, 1940–46; Administrator, Dominica, BWI, 1946–52; Resident Commissioner, Basutoland, 1952–56; Governor and Commander-in-Chief, Falkland Islands, 1957–64, and High Commissioner, British Antarctic Territory, 1962–64; Dir of Overseas Services Resettlement Bureau, 1965–79. Mem. Council, St Dunstan's, 1965–. Vice-Pres., Royal Commonwealth Soc. for the Blind, 1985– (Chm., 1970–85). Pres., Freshwater Biol Assoc., 1977–83. Recreation: flyfishing. Address: 25 Rivermead Court, SW6 3RU. T: 01–736 4757. Clubs: Flyfishers', Hurlingham, Royal Commonwealth Society.

ARROWSMITH, Pat; pacifist and socialist; assistant editor at Amnesty International, since 1971; b 2 March 1930; d of late George Ernest Arrowsmith and late Margaret Vera (née Kingham); m Mr Gardner, 11 Aug. 1979, separated 11 Aug. 1979; lesbian partnership with Wendy Butlin, 1962–76. Educ: Farringtons; Stover Sch.; Cheltenham Ladies' Coll.; Newnham Coll., Cambridge (BA history); Univ. of Ohio; Liverpool Univ. (Cert. in Social Science). Has held many jobs, incl.: Community Organizer in Chicago, 1952–53; Cinema Usher, 1953–54; Social Caseworker, Liverpool Family Service Unit, 1954; Child Care Officer, 1955 and 1964; Nursing Asst, Deva Psychiatric Hosp., 1956–57; Reporter for Peace News, 1965; Gardener for Camden BC, 1966–68; Researcher for Soc. of Friends Race Relations Cttee, 1969–71; Case Worker for NCCL, 1971; and on farms, as waiter in cafes, in factories, as a toy demonstrator, as a 'temp' in numerous offices, as asst in children's home, as newspaper deliverer and sales agent, as cleaner, as bartender, and in a holiday camp. Organizer for Direct Action Cttee against Nuclear War, Cttee of 100 and Campaign for Nuclear Disarmament, 1958–68; gaoled 11 times as political prisoner, 1958–85 (adopted twice as Prisoner of Conscience by Amnesty International); awarded Holloway Prison Green Band, 1964; awarded Girl Crusaders knighthood, 1940. Contested: Fulham, 1966 (Radical Alliance) and 1970 (Hammersmith Stop the SE Asia War Cttee), on peace issues; Cardiff South East (Independent Socialist), 1979. Member: War Resisters' Internat.; Campaign for Nuclear Disarmament; Labour Party; TGWU. Publications: Jericho (novel), 1965; Somewhere Like This (novel), 1970; To Asia in Peace, 1972; The Colour of Six Schools, 1972; Breakout (poems and drawings from prison), 1975; On the Brink (anti-war poems with pictures), 1981; The Prisoner (novel), 1982; Thin Ice (anti-nuclear poems), 1984. Recreations: water colour painting (has held and contrib. exhibns), swimming, writing poetry. Address: 132c Middle Lane, N8. T: 01–340 2661.

ARTHINGTON-DAVY, Humphrey Augustine, LVO 1977; OBE 1965; HM Diplomatic Service, retired; High Commissioner to Tonga, 1973–80, and Western Samoa, 1973–77; b 1920. Educ: Eastbourne Coll.; Trinity Coll., Cambridge. Indian Army, 1941; Indian Political Service, 1946; Civil Service of Pakistan, 1947; CRO, 1958; British Representative in the Maldives, 1960; Deputy High Commissioner: Botswana, 1966; Mauritius, 1968; Tonga, 1970. Recreation: travel. Address: c/o Grindlays Bank, 13 St James's Square, SW1; PO Box 56, Nuku' Alofa, Tonga, South Pacific. Club: Naval and Military.

ARTHUR, family name of **Baron Glenarthur.**

ARTHUR, Allan James Vincent, MBE 1948; DL; Vice Lord-Lieutenant of Essex, 1978–85; b 16 Sept. 1915; s of late Col Sir Charles Arthur, MC, VD, and Lady (Dorothy Grace) Arthur; m 1940, Joan Deirdre Heape (marr. diss. 1948); m 1949, Dawn Rosemary Everil, d of Col F. C. Drake; two s two d. Educ: Rugby Sch.; Magdalene Coll., Cambridge (MA). Indian Civil Service (Punjab), 1938–47; Sub Divl Officer, Murree, Kasur; Dep. Comr, Attock, Multan; Sudan Political Service, 1948–54; District Comr, Khartoum, Shendi; Dep. Governor, Northern Province; J. V. Drake and Co. Ltd, Sugar Brokers, 1954–60; Woodhouse, Drake, and Carey Ltd, Commodity Merchants, 1960–75 (Chm., 1972–75). Member, Chelmsford Borough Council, 1973–79, Mayor, 1977–78; Governor: Chigwell Sch., 1972–82; Brentwood Sch., 1973–85; London Hosp. Med. Coll., 1956–74. Member: Bd of Visitors, HM Prison, Chelmsford, 1973–79; Council, Univ. of Essex, 1980–. Pres., Old Rugbeian Soc., 1982–84. High Sheriff of Essex, 1971–72; DL Essex, 1974. Publication: contrib. to The District Officer in India, 1930–47, 1980. Recreations: swimming, shooting, gardening. Address: Mount Maskall, Boreham, Chelmsford CM3 3HW. T: Chelmsford 467776. Clubs: Oriental; Hawks (Cambridge).

ARTHUR, Prof. Geoffrey Herbert; Emeritus Professor of Veterinary Surgery, University of Bristol, since 1980; b 6 March 1916; s of William Gwyn Arthur and Ethel Jessie Arthur; m 1948, Lorna Isabel Simpson; four s one d. Educ: Abersychan Secondary Sch.; Liverpool Univ. BVSc 1939; MRCVS 1939; MVSc 1945; DVSc 1957; FRCVS 1957. Lectr in Veterinary Medicine, Liverpool Univ., 1941–48; Reader in Veterinary Surgery, Royal Veterinary Coll., 1949–51; Reader in Veterinary Surgery and Obstetrics, Univ. of London, 1952–65; Prof. of Veterinary Obstetrics and Diseases of Reproduction, Univ. of London, 1965–73; Prof. and Head of Dept of Vet. Surgery, Bristol Univ., 1974–79. Examiner to Univs of Cambridge, Dublin, Edinburgh, Glasgow, Liverpool, London, Reading, Bristol and Ceylon. Visiting Professor: Univ. of Khartoum, 1964; Pahlavi Univ., 1976; Nairobi Univ., 1979; Clinical Prof., King Faisal Univ., Saudi Arabia, 1980–84. Publications: Wright's Veterinary Obstetrics (including Diseases of Reproduction, 3rd edn), 1964, 5th edn, as Veterinary Reproduction and Obstetrics, 1982; papers on medicine and reproduction in Veterinary Record, Veterinary Jl, Jl of Comparative Pathology, Jl Reprod. Fert., Equine Vet. Jl and Jl Small Animal Pract. (Editor). Recreations: observing natural phenomena and experimenting. Address: Fallodene, Stone Allerton, Axbridge, Som BS26 2NH.

ARTHUR, James Stanley, CMG 1977; HM Diplomatic Service, retired; British High Commissioner in Bridgetown, 1978–82, also British High Commissioner (non-resident) to Dominica, 1978–82, to St Lucia and St Vincent, 1979–82, to Grenada, 1980–82, to Antigua and Barbuda, 1981–82, and concurrently British Government Representative to West Indies Associated State of St Kitts-Nevis; retired 1983; b 3 Feb. 1923; s of Laurence and Catherine Arthur, Lerwick, Shetland; m 1950, Marion North; two s two d. Educ: Trinity Academy, Edinburgh; Liverpool Univ. (BSc). Scientific Civil Service, 1944–46; Asst Principal, Scottish Educn Dept, 1946; Min. of Educn/Dept of Educn and Science, 1947–66: Private Sec. to Parly Sec., 1948–50; Principal Private Sec. to Minister, 1960–62; Counsellor, FO, 1966; Nairobi, 1967–70; Dep. High Comr, Malta, 1970–73; High Comr, Suva, 1974–78, and first High Comr (non-resident), Republic of Nauru, 1977–78. Recreations: golf, music. Address: Moreton House, Longborough, Moreton-in-Marsh, Glos GL56 0QQ. T: Cotswold 30774. Club: Royal Commonwealth Society.

ARTHUR, Lt-Gen. Sir (John) Norman (Stewart), KCB 1985; General Officer Commanding Scotland and Governor of Edinburgh Castle, since 1985; *b* 6 March 1931; *s* of Col Evelyn Stewart Arthur and Mrs E. S. Arthur (*née* Burnett-Stuart); *m* 1960, Theresa Mary Hopkinson; one *s* one *d* (and one *s* decd). *Educ:* Eton Coll.; RMA, Sandhurst. rcds, jssc, psc. Commnd Royal Scots Greys, 1951; commanded: Royal Scots Dragoon Guards, 1972–74 (despatches, 1974); 7th Armoured Bde, 1976–77; GOC 3rd Armoured Div., 1980–82; Dir of Personal Services (Army), MoD, 1983–85. Col Comdt, Military Provost Staff Corps, 1983–; Col, The Royal Scots Dragoon Gds (Carabiniers and Greys), 1984–. Member: Royal Co. of Archers, Queen's Body Guard for Scotland; British Olympic Team, Equestrian Three-Day Event, 1960–. *Recreations:* field and country sports and pursuits, horsemanship, military history. *Address:* c/o Lloyds Bank, Cox's & King's Branch (Gds & Cav.), 6 Pall Mall, SW1Y 5NH. *Clubs:* Farmers'; Caledonian Hunt.

ARTHUR, John Rhys, DFC 1944; JP; **His Honour Judge Arthur;** a Circuit Judge, since 1975; *b* 29 April 1923; *s* of late John Morgan Arthur and Eleanor Arthur; *m* 1951, Joan Tremearne Pickering; two *s* one *d*. *Educ:* Mill Hill; Christ's Coll., Cambridge (MA). Commnd RAF, 1943, demobilised 1946. Cambridge, 1946–48; called to Bar, Inner Temple, 1949. Asst Recorder, Blackburn QS, 1970; Dep. Chm., Lancs County QS, 1970–71; a Recorder, 1972–75. JP Lancs 1970. *Address:* Orovales, Caldy, Wirral L48 1LP. *T:* 051–625 8624. *Clubs:* MCC, Old Millhillians; Athenæum (Liverpool).

ARTHUR, Lt-Gen. Sir Norman; *see* Arthur, Lt-Gen. Sir J. N. S.

ARTHUR, Peter Bernard; Deputy Chairman and Chairman of the Sub-Committees of Classification, Lloyd's Register of Shipping, 1976–84; *b* 29 Aug. 1923; *s* of Charles Frederick Bernard Arthur and Joan (*née* Dyer); *m* 1954, Irène Susy (*née* Schüpbach); one *s* two *d*. *Educ:* Oundle Sch. Commnd 1943; Mahratta LI, 1943–47 (mentioned in despatches, Italy, 1945); RA, 1947–53. Underwriting Mem. of Lloyd's, 1954–; Mem. Cttee, Lloyd's Register of Shipping, and Vice-Chm., Sub-Cttees of Classification, 1967. Dir, Bolton Steam Shipping Co. Ltd, 1958–84; Chairman: London Deep Sea Tramp Shipowners' Assoc., 1970–71; Deep Sea Tramp Sect., Chamber of Shipping of UK, 1972–73; Bolton Maritime Management Ltd, 1982–83. *Recreations:* golf, music, water colour painting, gardening. *Address:* Oak Lodge, Peter Avenue, Oxted, Surrey RH8 9LG. *T:* Oxted 2962. *Club:* Tandridge Golf.

ARTHUR, Rt. Rev. Robert Gordon; *b* 17 Aug. 1909; *s* of George Thomas Arthur and Mary Arthur; *m* Marie Olive Cavell Wheen; two *s* two *d*. *Educ:* Launceston and Devonport High Schs, Tasmania; Queen's Coll., Univ. of Melbourne. MA (Hons) 1932. Rector of: Berridale, NSW, 1950–53; St John's, Canberra, ACT, 1953–60; Wagga Wagga, NSW, 1960–61; Archdeacon of Canberra, 1953–60; Asst Bp of Canberra and Goulburn, 1956–61; Bishop of Grafton, NSW, 1961–73; Rector of St Philip's, Canberra, 1973–74; Priest-in-charge of Bratton, Wilts, 1975–78, and Rural Dean of Heytesbury, 1976–78; Hon. Asst Bishop of Sheffield, 1978–80. *Address:* 4 Berry Street, Downer, Canberra, ACT 2602, Australia.

ARTHUR, Sir Stephen (John), 6th Bt *cr* 1841, of Upper Canada; *b* 1 July 1953; *s* of Hon. Sir Basil Malcolm Arthur, 5th Bt, MP, and of Elizabeth Rita, *d* of late Alan Mervyn Wells; *S* father, 1985; *m* 1978, Carolyn Margaret, *d* of Burney Lawrence Daimond, Cairns, Queensland; one *s* two *d*. *Educ:* Timaru Boys' High School. *Recreations:* tennis, Rugby Union. *Heir: s* Benjamin Nathan Arthur, *b* 27 March 1979. *Address:* Grene Gables, No 3 RD, Seadown, Timaru, New Zealand. *T:* Timaru 47721.

ARTHURE, Humphrey George Edgar, CBE 1969; MD, FRCS, FRCOG; Consulting Obstetric and Gynæcological Surgeon: Charing Cross Hospital; Queen Charlotte's Hospital; Mount Vernon Hospital. MRCS, LRCP 1931; MB, BS 1933; FRCS 1935; MD London 1938; FRCOG 1950 (Hon. Sec. 1949–56; Vice-Pres. 1964–67); FRSM (Pres., Section of Obstetrics and Gynaecology, 1969); co-opted Mem. Council, RCS 1960; Pres., West London Medico-Chirurgical Soc., 1964; Formerly: Chm., Central Midwives Board, and Adviser, Obstetrics and Gynæcology, DHSS; Mem., Standing Maternity and Midwifery Advisory Cttee; Resident Obstetric Officer and Obstetrical Registrar, Charing Cross Hospital; Resident Medical Officer, Chelsea Hospital for Women. Served War of 1939–45, temp. Lt-Col, RAMC. *Publications:* Simpson Oration, 1972; (jtly) Sterilisation, 1976; contribs med. jls. *Address:* 12 Eyot Green, Chiswick Mall, W4 2PT. *T:* 01–994 7698.

ARTIS, Prof. Michael John; Professor of Economics, Manchester University, since 1975; *b* 29 June 1938; *s* of Cyril John and Violet Emily Artis; *m* 1st, 1961, Lilian Gregson (marr. diss. 1982); two *d*; 2nd, 1983, Shirley Knight. *Educ:* Baines Grammar Sch., Poulton-le-Fylde, Lancs; Magdalen Coll., Oxford. BA Hons (PPE) Oxon. Assistant Research Officer, Oxford Univ., 1959; Lectr in Economics, Adelaide Univ., 1964; Lectr and Sen. Lectr in Economics, Flinders Univ., 1966; Research Officer and Review Editor, Nat. Inst. of Economic and Social Research, London, 1967; Prof. of Applied Economics, Swansea Univ. Coll., 1972. *Publications:* Foundations of British Monetary Policy, 1964; (with M. K. Lewis) Monetary Control in the United Kingdom, 1981; Macroeconomics, 1984; (with S. Ostry) International Economic Policy Co-ordination, 1986; contribs on economics, economic policy to books and learned jls. *Recreations:* cycling, walking. *Address:* 76 Bexton Road, Knutsford, Cheshire WA16 0DX. *T:* Knutsford 3204.

ARTON, Major A. T. B.; *see* Bourne-Arton.

ARTRO MORRIS, John Evan; a Registrar of the Supreme Court, Family Division, since 1977; *b* 17 Feb. 1925; *s* of Tudor and Mabel Artro Morris; *m* 1961, Karin Ilse Alide Russell; two *s*. *Educ:* Liverpool Coll.; The Queen's Coll., Oxford. BA Oxon. Served RN, 1943–47. Called to the Bar, Middle Temple, 1952. *Recreations:* D-I-Y, Rugby (spectator), fishing. *Address:* 69 Gowan Avenue, SW6 6RH. *T:* 01-736 6492. *Club:* London Welsh RFC.

ARTUS, Ronald Edward; Group Chief Investment Manager, since 1979, an Executive Director, since 1984, Prudential Corporation PLC; Chief Investment Manager, since 1982, Deputy Chairman, since 1985, Prudential Assurance Co. Ltd, (Joint Secretary and Chief Investment Manager, 1975–82); Chairman: Prutec Ltd, since 1980; Prudential Portfolio Managers Ltd, since 1981; *b* 8 Oct 1931; *s* of late Ernest and of Doris Artus; *m* 1956, Brenda Margaret, *d* of late Sir Norman Touche, Bt, and Eva, Lady Touche (*née* Cameron); three *s* one *d*. *Educ:* Sir Thomas Rich's Sch., Gloucester; Magdalen Coll., Oxford (MA, 1st Cl. PPE). Joined Prudential, 1954; Head of Economic Intelligence Dept, 1958–71; Sen. Asst Investment Manager, 1971–73; Dep. Investment Manager, 1973–75; Secretary, 1979–84; Dir various cos, Prudential Gp. Director: Keyser Ullmann Holdings Ltd, 1972–80; Charterhouse Gp Ltd, 1980–82; Celltech Ltd, 1980–. Member: City Capital Markets Cttee, 1982–; Accounting Standards Cttee, 1982–86. Hon. Fellow, Soc. of Investment Analysts, 1980 (Mem. Council, 1964–76; Chm., 1973–75); FRSA. *Publications:* contrib. various jls on economic and investment matters. *Recreations:* music, collecting English watercolours. *Address:* 142 Holborn Bars, EC1N 2NH. *T:* 01–405 9222.

ARUNDEL AND BRIGHTON, Bishop of, (RC), since 1977; **Rt. Rev. Cormac Murphy-O'Connor;** *b* 24 Aug. 1932; *s* of late Dr P. G. Murphy-O'Connor and Ellen (*née* Cuddigan). *Educ:* Prior Park Coll., Bath; English Coll., Rome; Gregorian Univ. PhL, STL. Ordained Priest, 1956. Asst Priest, Portsmouth and Fareham, 1957–66; Sec. to Bp of Portsmouth, 1966–70; Parish Priest, Parish of the Immaculate Conception, Southampton, 1970–71; Rector, English College, Rome, 1971–77. Chairman: Bishops' Cttee for Europe, 1978–83; Cttee for Christian Unity, 1983–; Jt Chm., ARCIC-II, 1983–; Mem., Sacred Congregation for Catholic Educn, 1978–. *Recreations:* music, sport. *Address:* St Joseph's Hall, Storrington, Pulborough, Sussex RH20 4HE.

ARUNDEL AND SURREY, Earl of; Edward William Fitzalan-Howard; *b* 2 Dec. 1956; *s* and *heir* of 17th Duke of Norfolk, *qv*. *Educ:* Ampleforth Coll., Yorks; Lincoln Coll., Oxford. *Recreations:* ski-ing, motor-racing, shooting, farming. *Address:* Arundel Castle, Sussex. *T:* Arundel 882173; Carlton Towers, Yorks. *T:* Goole 860 243; Bacres House, Hambleden, Henley-on-Thames. *T:* Hambleden 350.

ARUNDELL; *see* Monckton-Arundell, family name of Viscount Galway.

ARUNDELL, Dennis Drew, OBE 1978; (formerly D. D. Arundel); actor, composer, producer, writer for theatre, radio, films and television, since 1926; *b* 22 July 1898; *s* of Arundel Drew Arundel and Rose Lucy Campbell. *Educ:* Tonbridge Sch.; St John's Coll., Cambridge. Lieut, RGA, 1917–19 (gassed, 1918). St John's Coll., 1919–29 (Sizarship, 1917; Strathcona Studentship, 1922); BA (Classics) 1922, MusB 1923, MA 1924. Fellow of St John's Coll., Cambridge, 1923–29; Lecturer in Music and English Drama, Deputy Organist St John's, 1924. First appeared on professional stage at Lyric, Hammersmith, 1926; subseq. joined Old Vic Company, playing Trofimov in A Month in the Country, Lucio in Measure for Measure, and has since taken many parts, inc. first Lord Peter Wimsey, Manningham in Gaslight; directed and composed music for plays in West End theatres, films, radio and television. Chief Producer, RCM Opera Sch., 1959–73 (Crees Lectr, RCM, 1970; FRCM 1969); Resident Opera Producer and Coach, Royal Northern Coll. of Music, Manchester, 1974. Chm., Internat. Jury of Singing, Jeunesses Musicales, Belgrade, 1972. As an opera director his work has been especially with Sadler's Wells and the BBC; producer of over 50 operas; translator of some 15 operas; arr. Purcell's Indian Queen for Opera da Camera, 1973; directed both operas and plays in Australia, 1956, 1975 and Finland, 1947, 1952, 1957 (scene from 1952 production of Hamlet inc. in centenary prog. of Helsinki Nat. Theatre, 1973). Lecture to Soc. of Theatre Research, 1971. *Publications:* Henry Purcell, 1927 (in German, 1929); (ed) King Arthur, Purcell Soc. edn, 1928; Dryden and Howard, 1929; The Critic at the Opera, 1957 (repr. NY, with subtitle Contemporary Comments on Opera in London over Three Centuries, 1980); The Story of Sadler's Wells, 1965 (new edn as The Story of Sadler's Wells, 1633–1977, 1978); Introduction to Le Nozze di Figaro and Cosi fan Tutte (Cassell Opera Guides), 1971; (ed) Congreve's Semele, 1925; (trans.) Morax and Honegger's King David, 1929; (trans.) Weinberger's Schwanda the Bagpiper, 1946; (trans.) Claudel's and Honegger's Jeanne d'Arc au Bûcher, 1939; (trans.) Monteverdi's Il Combattimento di Tancredi e Clorinda, 1974; Sibelius's Kullervo, 1974; various musical compositions and musical articles. *Recreation:* operatic research. *Address:* 21 Lloyd Square, WC1. *T:* 01–837 2942.

ARUNDELL, Brig. Sir Robert (Duncan Harris), KCMG 1950 (CMG 1947); OBE 1943; retired as Governor and Commander-in-Chief, Barbados (1953–59) (Acting Governor-General and C-in-C, The West Indies, 1959); Zanzibar Delimitation Commissioner, 1962; *b* Lifton, Devon, 22 July 1904; *s* of late C. H. Arundell; *m* 1929, Joan (*d* 1984), *d* of late Capt. J. A. Ingles, RN; one *s*. *Educ:* Blundell's Sch.; Brasenose Coll., Oxford. Colonial Administrative Service, Tanganyika Territory, 1927; seconded Colonial Office, 1935–37; Sec. Nyasaland Financial Commission, 1937–38; Tanganyika Territory, 1938–39; Assistant Chief Sec. Uganda, 1939; Army, Civil Affairs, 1941–45; served War of 1939–45 in Middle East and East Africa (despatches, OBE); Chief Civil Affairs Officer MEF (Brig.), 1944–45; British Resident Mem. in Washington of Caribbean Commission, 1946–47; Governor and C-in-C, Windward Islands, 1948–53. KStJ 1952. *Address:* Wakehill, Ilminster, Somerset TA19 0NR. *Club:* East India.

ARUP, Sir Ove (Nyquist), Kt 1971; CBE 1953; FEng, FICE, FIStructE, FSIAD, MICEI; MSocCE(France); Founder, Ove Arup Partnerships; *b* Newcastle upon Tyne, 16 April 1895; *s* of Jens Simon Johannes Arup and Mathilde B. Nyquist; *m* 1925, Ruth Sœrensen; one *s* two *d*. *Educ:* Preparatory Sch., Hamburg, Germany; Public Sch., Sorl; Univ. of Copenhagen, Denmark. MIngF (Medlem Ingenilr Forening), Copenhagen. Designer Christiani & Nielsen, GmbH, Hamburg, 1922–23, transf. to London 1923; Designer, 1923–25, Chief Designer, 1925–34, Christiani & Nielsen, Ltd, London; Director and Chief Designer, J. L. Kier & Co., Ltd, London, 1934–38; Consulting Engineer for: schools, flats, air raid shelters, industrial projects, marine work (Air Min.); Director: Arup Designs, Ltd; Arup & Arup, Ltd; Pipes, Ltd, 1938–45; Senior Partner: Ove Arup & Partners, Consulting Engineers, 1949; Arup Associates, 1963. Chm. Soc. of Danish Civil Engineers in Gt Britain and Ireland, 1955–59; Visiting Lectr, Harvard Univ., 1955; Alfred Bossom Lectr, RSA, 1970; Maitland Lecture, IStructE, 1968. RIBA Royal Gold Medal for Architecture for 1966; Gold Medal, IStructE, 1973. Hon. DSc: Durham, 1967; Heriot-Watt, 1976; City Univ., 1979; Hon. ScD East Anglia, 1968; Hon. Dr Tekniske Hojskole, Lyngby, Denmark, 1974. Fellow Amer. Concrete Inst., 1975. Commander (First Class), Order of the Dannebrog, 1975 (Chevalier, 1965). *Publications:* papers and articles in various technical jls. *Recreations:* music and reading. *Address:* 6 Fitzroy Park, Highgate, N6. *T:* 01–340 3388. *Clubs:* Athenæum; Danish.

ARVILL, Robert; *see* Boote, R. E.

ASAAD, Prof. Fikry Naguib M.; *see* Morcos-Asaad.

ASFA WOSSEN HAILE SELLASSIE, HIH Merd Azmatch; GCMG (Hon.) 1965; GCVO (Hon.) 1930; GBE (Hon.) 1932; Crown Prince of Ethiopia, since 1930; *b* 27 July 1916; *e s* and *heir* of late Emperor Haile Sellassie, KG, and Empress Menen; *m* 1st, Princess Wallatta Israel; one *d* decd; 2nd, Princess Madfariash Wark Abebe; one *s* three *d*. *Educ:* privately; Liverpool Univ. Governor of Wollo province; Mem., Crown Council. Fought in Italo-Ethiopian War, 1935–36. Grand Cross: Légion d'Honneur; Belgian Order of Leopold; Order of the Netherlands; Order of Rising Sun, Japan; Order of White Elephant, Siam. *Heir: s* Prince Zara Yacob, *b* 18 Aug. 1953.

ASH, Prof. Eric Albert, CBE 1983; FRS 1977; FEng 1978; Rector, Imperial College of Science and Technology, since 1985; *b* 31 Jan. 1928; *s* of Walter and Dorothea Ash; *m* 1954, Clare (*née* Babb); five *d*. *Educ:* University College Sch.; Imperial Coll. of Science and Technology. BSc(Eng), PhD, DSc; FCGI, DIC, FIEE; FIEEE; FInstP. Research Fellow: Stanford Univ., Calif, 1952–54; QMC, 1954–55; Res. Engr, Standard Telecommunication Laboratories Ltd, 1955–63; Sen. Lectr, 1963–65, Reader, 1965–67, Prof., 1967–85, Pender Prof. and Head of Dept, 1980–85, Dept of Electronic and Electrical Engrg, UCL (Hon. Fellow, 1985). Dep. Pres., IEE, 1985– (Vice-Pres., 1980–83); Member: Royal Soc. Cttees; Exec. Bd, Fellowship of Engrg, 1981–84. Sec., Royal Instn, 1984– (Vice Pres., 1980–82, Manager, 1980–84). Marconi International Fellowship, 1984. Faraday Medal, IEE, 1980;

Royal Medal, Royal Soc., 1986. *Publications:* patents; papers on topics in physical electronics in various engrg and physics jls. *Recreations:* music, skiing, swimming. *Address:* Imperial College, SW7 2AZ.

ASH, Maurice Anthony, BSc (Econ); Chairman of Council, Town and Country Planning Association, since 1983 (Chairman of Executive, 1969–83); *b* 31 Oct. 1917; *s* of Wilfred Cracroft and Beatrice Ash; *m* 1947, Ruth Whitney Elmhirst (*d* 1986); three *d* (one *s* decd). *Educ:* Gresham's Sch., Holt; LSE; Yale. Served War of 1939–45, armoured forces in Western Desert, Italy, Greece (despatches 1944). Mem., SW Regl Economic Planning Council, 1965–68; Chm., Green Alliance, 1978–83. Trustee, Dartington Hall, 1964– (Chm., 1972–84). Founder, Harlow Arts Trust. Mem., Henry Moore Foundn, 1980–. *Publications:* The Human Cloud, 1962; Who are the Progressives Now?, 1969; Regions of Tomorrow, 1969; A Guide to the Structure of London, 1972; Green Politics, 1980; articles on land use, education, international relations. *Recreation:* applying Wittgenstein. *Address:* Sharpham House, Ashprington, Totnes, Devon TQ9 7UT. *T:* Harbertonford 216. *Club:* Reform.

ASH, Raymond; former Director, Business Statistics Office, retired 1986; *b* 2 Jan. 1928; *s* of late Horace Ash and Gladys Ash; two *s* one *d*. *Educ:* Wolverhampton Grammar Sch. Civil Service, 1949–86: professional statistician and senior manager working on health, labour, overseas trade, and business statistics. *Publications:* contrib. learned jls. *Recreations:* country walks, tourism, historical studies. *Address:* 20 Taliesin Close, Rogerstone, Newport, Gwent NP1 0DD. *T:* Newport 895470.

ASH, Rear-Admiral Walter William Hector, CB 1962; WhSch; CEng; FIEE; *b* Portsmouth, Hants, 2 May 1906; *s* of Hector Sidney and Mabel Jessy Ash; *m* 1932, Louisa Adelaide Salt, Jarrow-on-Tyne; three *d*. *Educ:* City & Guilds Coll., Kensington; Royal Naval Coll., Greenwich. Whitworth Scholar, 1926; John Samuel Scholar, 1927. Asst Elect. Engr, Admiralty (submarine design), 1932–37; Elect. Engr, Admiralty (battleship design), 1937–39; Fleet Elect. Engr, Staff C-in-C Med., 1939–40; Supt Elect. Engr, Admiralty (supply and prod.), 1940–45; Supt Elect. Engr, HM Dockyard, Hong Kong, 1945–48; Supt Elect. Engr, Admiralty Engineering Lab., 1948–49; Comdr RN, HMS Montclare, 1950–51; Capt. RN, Admiralty (weapon control design), 1951–54; Capt. RN, Elect. Engr Manager, HM Dockyard, Devonport, 1954–58; Capt. RN, Ship Design Dept, Admiralty, 1959–60; Rear-Adm. 1960; subseq. Ship Dept Directorate, Admty, retd Aug. 1963. Vis. Lectr in electrical machinery design, RN Coll., Greenwich, 1934–37. Chairman IEE, SW Sub Centre, 1957–58. ADC to the Queen, 1958–60. *Recreations:* golf, music (piano and organ). *Address:* Saltash, 14 Beacon Drive, Highcliffe-on-Sea, Christchurch, Dorset BH23 5DH. *T:* Highcliffe 5261.

ASH, Rear-Adm. William Noel, CB 1977; LVO 1959; *b* 6 March 1921; *s* of late H. Arnold Ash, MRCS, LRCP; *m* 1951, Pamela, *d* of late Harry C. Davies, Hawkes Bay, NZ; one *s* one *d*. *Educ:* Merchant Taylors' School. Joined RN, 1938; HM Yacht Britannia, 1955–58; Captain 1965; Canadian NDC, 1965–66; Staff of SACLANT (NATO), 1966–69; Cabinet Office, 1969–71; comd HMS Ganges, 1971–73; Rear-Adm. 1974; Dir of Service Intelligence, 1974–77. Sec. Defence Press and Broadcasting Cttee, 1980–84. *Address:* c/o National Bank of New Zealand, PO Box 549, Papakura, New Zealand. *Club:* Royal Commonwealth Society.

ASHBEE, Paul; Archaeologist, University of East Anglia, 1969–83; *b* 23 June 1918; *s* of Lewis Ashbee and Hannah Mary Elizabeth Ashbee (*née* Brett); *m* 1952, Richmal Crompton Lamburn Disher; one *s* one *d*. *Educ:* sch. in Maidstone, Kent; Univ. of London; Univ. of Leicester (MA; DLitt 1984). Post-grad. Dip. Prehistoric Archaeology, London. Royal W Kent Regt and REME, 1939–46; Control Commn for Germany, 1946–49; Univ. of London, Univ. of Bristol (Redland Coll.), 1949–54; Asst Master and Head of History, Forest Hill Sch., 1954–68. Excavation of prehistoric sites, mostly barrows both long and round for then Min. of Works, 1949–; Co-dir with R. L. S. Bruce-Mitford of BM excavations at Sutton-Hoo, 1964–69; Mem., Sutton Hoo Research Cttee, 1982–. Mem. Council and Meetings Sec., Prehistoric Soc., 1960–74; Sec. (Wareham Earthwork), British Assoc. Sub-Cttee for Archaeological Field Experiment, 1961–; one-time Sec., Neolithic and Bronze Age Cttee, Council for British Archaeology; Mem. Royal Commn on Historical Monuments (England), 1975–85; Mem., Area Archaeological Adv. Cttee (DoE) for Norfolk and Suffolk, 1975–79. Pres., Cornwall Archæol Soc., 1976–80, Vice-Pres., 1980–84; Chm., Scolc Cttee for E Anglian Archaeology, 1979–84. FSA 1958. *Publications:* The Bronze Age Round Barrow in Britain, 1960; The Earthen Long Barrow in Britain, 1970, 2nd edn 1984; Ancient Scilly, 1974; The Ancient British, 1978; chapter in Sutton Hoo, Vol. I, 1976; numerous papers, articles and reviews in Archaeologia, Antiquaries Jl, Archaeological Jl, Proc. Prehistoric Soc., Antiquity, Cornish Archaeology, Arch. Cantiana, Proc. Dorset Arch. and Nat. Hist. Soc., Proc. Hants FC, Wilts Archaeol Magazine, Yorks Arch. Jl, etc. *Recreations:* East Anglia, historical architecture, bibliophilia, dog ownership. *Address:* The Old Rectory, Chedgrave, Norfolk NR14 6ND. *T:* Loddon 20595.

ASHBOURNE, 4th Baron *cr* 1885; **Edward Barry Greynville Gibson;** Lieut-Comdr RN, retired; investment marketing; *b* 28 Jan. 1933; *s* of 3rd Baron Ashbourne, CB, DSO, and of Reta Frances Manning, *e d* of E. M. Hazeland, Hong Kong; *S* father, 1983; *m* 1967, Yvonne Georgina, *d* of late Major Gordon William Ham; three *s*. *Educ:* Rugby. *Heir:* *s* Hon. Edward Charles D'Olier Gibson, *b* 31 Dec. 1967. *Address:* 107 Sussex Road, Petersfield, Hants.

ASHBROOK, 10th Viscount, *cr* 1751 (Ire.); **Desmond Llowarch Edward Flower,** KCVO 1977; MBE 1945; DL; Baron of Castle Durrow, 1733; Member of Council of Duchy of Lancaster, 1957–77; *b* 9 July 1905; *o s* of 9th Viscount and late Gladys, *d* of late Gen. Sir George Wentworth A. Higginson, GCB, GCVO; *S* father, 1936; *m* 1934, Elizabeth, *er d* of late Capt. John Egerton-Warburton, and of late Hon. Mrs Waters; two *s* one *d*. *Educ:* Eton; Balliol Coll., Oxford (BA 1927). Served War of 1939–45, RA. Formerly a Chartered Accountant. JP, 1946–67, DL 1949–, Vice-Lieutenant, 1961–67, Cheshire. *Heir:* *s* Hon. Michael Llowarch Warburton Flower [*b* 9 Dec. 1935; *m* 1971, Zoë Engleheart, *y d* of late F. H. A. Engleheart; two *s* one *d*]. *Address:* Woodlands, Arley, Northwich, Cheshire.

ASHBURNHAM, Captain Sir Denny Reginald, 12th Bt *cr* 1661; Captain South Staffordshire Regiment; *b* 24 March 1916; *o surv. s* of Sir Fleetwood Ashburnham, 11th Bt, and Elfrida, *d* of late James Kirkley, JP, Cleadon Park, Co. Durham; *S* father 1953; *m* 1946, Mary Frances, *d* of Major Robert Pascoe Mair, Wick, Udimore, Sussex; two *d* (one *s* decd). *Heir:* *g s* James Fleetwood Ashburnham, *b* 17 Dec. 1979. *Address:* Little Broomham, Guestling, Hastings, East Sussex.

ASHBURTON, 6th Baron, *cr* 1835; **Alexander Francis St Vincent Baring,** KG 1969; KCVO 1961; JP; DL; Lord Lieutenant and Custos Rotulorum, Hampshire and Isle of Wight, 1960–73 (Vice-Lieutenant, 1951–60); High Steward of Winchester, 1967–78; Receiver-General to the Duchy of Cornwall, 1961–74; *b* 7 April 1898; *o s* of 5th Baron and Hon. Mabel Edith Hood (*d* 1904), *d* of 4th Viscount Hood; *S* father, 1938; *m* 1924, Hon. Doris Mary Thérèse Harcourt (*d* 1981), *e d* of 1st Viscount Harcourt; two *s*. *Educ:* Eton; Royal Military Coll. Lieut The Greys, 1917–23; Flt-Lt AAF, 1939, retd as Group Captain, 1944. Director: Baring Brothers & Co. Ltd, 1962–68 (Managing Director, 1928–62); Alliance Assurance, 1932–68; Pressed Steel Co. Ltd, 1944–66; Mem. London Cttee, Hongkong & Shanghai Banking Corp., 1935–39. Treasurer, King Edward VII Hospital Fund for London, 1955–64, Governor, 1971–76; Trustee: King George's Jubilee Trust, 1949–68; Chantrey Bequest, 1963–81; St Cross Hospital of Noble Poverty, Winchester, 1961–81. Chm., Hampshire and IoW Police Authy, 1961–71. President: Hampshire and IoW Territorial Assoc., 1960–67 (Mem., 1951–60); Eastern Wessex Territorial Assoc., 1968–70. CC 1945, CA 1955, JP 1951, DL 1973, Hants. KStJ 1960. *Heir:* *s* Hon. Sir John Francis Harcourt Baring, *qv*. *Address:* Itchen Stoke House, Alresford, Hants SO24 0QU. *T:* Alresford 2479. *Clubs:* Lansdowne; Hampshire County (Winchester).

ASHBY, family name of **Baron Ashby.**

ASHBY, Baron *cr* 1973 (Life Peer), of Brandon, Suffolk; **Eric Ashby,** Kt 1956; FRS 1963; DSc London, MA Cantab; DIC; Chancellor, Queen's University, Belfast, 1970–83; Fellow of Clare College, Cambridge, 1958, Life Fellow since 1975; *b* 1904; *s* of Herbert Charles Ashby, Bromley, Kent, and Helena Chater; *m* 1931, Elizabeth Helen Farries, Castle-Douglas, Scotland; two *s*. *Educ:* City of London Sch.; Imperial Coll. of Science, Univ. of London; Univ. of Chicago. Demonstrator at Imperial Coll., 1926–29; Commonwealth Fund Fellow in Univ. of Chicago and Desert Laboratory of Carnegie Institution, 1929–31; Lectr, Imperial Coll. of Science, 1931–35; Reader in Botany, Bristol Univ., 1935–37; Prof. of Botany, Univ. of Sydney, Australia, 1938–46; Harrison Prof. of Botany and Dir of Botanical Labs, Univ. of Manchester, 1946–50; Pres. and Vice-Chancellor, Queen's Univ., Belfast, 1950–59; Master of Clare College, Cambridge, 1959–75; Vice-Chancellor, Univ. of Cambridge, 1967–69. Chm., Aust. National Research Council, 1940–42; Chm., Professorial Board, Univ. of Sydney, 1942–44; Mem., Power Alcohol Committee of Enquiry, 1940–41; conducted enquiry for Prime Minister into enlistment of scientific resources in war, 1942; Trustee, Aust. Museum, 1942–46; Dir, Scientific Liaison Bureau, 1942–43; Counsellor and Chargé d'Affaires at Australian Legation, Moscow, USSR, 1945–46; Member of: Advisory Council on Scientific Policy, 1950–53; Nuffield Provincial Hospitals Trust, 1951–59; Advisory Council on Scientific and Industrial Research, 1954–60; Chairman: Scientific Grants Cttee, DSIR, 1955–56; Postgraduate Grants Cttee, DSIR, 1956–60; Northern Ireland Adv. Council for Education, 1953–58; Adult Education Cttee, 1953–54; Cttee of Award of Commonwealth Fund, 1963–69 (Member, 1956–61); Royal Commn on Environmental Pollution, 1970–73; Member: Univ. Grants Cttee, 1959–67; Commonwealth Scholarship Commn, 1960–69; Council of Royal Soc., 1964–65; Governing Body, Sch. of Oriental and African Studies, Univ. of London, 1965–70; Chm., Commn for post-secondary and higher education in Nigeria, 1959–61; Chm., working party on pollution control in connection with UN conf. on the Environment, Stockholm, June 1972. Vice-Chm. Assoc. of Univs of Brit. Commonwealth, 1959–61; Pres., Brit. Assoc. for the Advancement of Science, 1963. Walgreen Prof., Michigan, 1975–77; Lectures: Godkin, Harvard Univ., 1964; Whidden, McMaster Univ., 1970; Bernal, Royal Soc., 1971; Prof-at-large, Cornell Univ., 1967–72; Trustee: Ciba Foundation, 1966–79; British Museum, 1969–77; Fellow: Imperial Coll. of Science; Davenport Coll., Yale Univ.; Hon. Fellow, Clare Hall; Hon. FRSE; Hon. FRIC. Hon. Foreign Mem., Amer. Acad. of Arts and Sciences. Hon. LLD: St Andrews; Aberdeen; Belfast; Rand; London; Wales; Columbia; Chicago; Michigan; Windsor; Western Australia; Manchester; Johns Hopkins; Liverpool; Hon. ScD Dublin; Hon. DSc: NUI; Univ. of Nigeria; Southampton; Hon. DLitt: W Ont; Sydney; Hon. DPhil Tech. Univ. Berlin; Hon. DCL East Anglia; Hon. DHL: Yale; Utah. Jephcott Medal, RSM, 1976. Order of Andrés Bello, first class, Venezuela, 1974. *Publications:* Environment and Plant Development, translated from German, 1931; German-English Botanical Terminology (with Elizabeth Helen Ashby), 1938; Food Shipment from Australia in Wartime; Challenge to Education, 1946; Scientist in Russia, 1947 (German trans., 1950); Technology and the Academics, 1958 (Japanese trans., 1963; Spanish trans, 1970); Community of Universities, 1963; African Universities and Western Tradition, 1964 (French trans. 1964); Universities: British, Indian, African (with Mary Anderson), 1966 (Spanish trans. 1972); Masters and Scholars, 1970; (with Mary Anderson) The Rise of the Student Estate, 1970; Any Person, Any Study, 1971; (with Mary Anderson) Portrait of Haldane, 1974; Reconciling Man with the Environment, 1978 (Spanish trans. 1981); (with Mary Anderson) The Politics of Clean Air, 1981. *Recreation:* chamber music. *Address:* Norman Cottage, Manor Road, Brandon, Suffolk IP27 0LG.

See also M. F. Ashby.

ASHBY, David Glynn; MP (C) North-West Leicestershire, since 1983; barrister; *b* 14 May 1940; *s* of Robert M. Ashby and Isobel A. Davidson; *m* 1965, Silvana Morena; one *d*. *Educ:* Royal Grammar Sch., High Wycombe; Bristol Univ. (LLB Hons). Called to the Bar, Gray's Inn, 1963; in practice on SE Circuit. Member: Hammersmith Bor. Council, 1968–71; for W Woolwich, GLC, 1977–81; ILEA, 1977–81. *Recreations:* gardening, skiing, music. *Address:* 29 Church Street, Appleby Magna, Leics; 132 West Hill, SW15 2UE. *Club:* Hurlingham.

ASHBY, Francis Dalton, OBE 1975; Director, National Counties Building Society, since 1980; *b* 20 Jan. 1920; *s* of late John Frederick Ashby and late Jessie Ashby; *m* 1948, Mollie Isabel Mitchell; one *s* two *d*. *Educ:* Watford Grammar Sch. Diploma in Govt Admin. War Service, Royal Signals, 1940–46: POW, Far East, 1942–45. National Debt Office: Exec. Officer, 1938; Asst Comptroller and Estabt Officer, 1966–76; Comptroller-General, 1976–80, retired. *Recreations:* dinghy sailing, walking. *Address:* Moorfield, Carpenters Wood Drive, Chorleywood, Herts.

ASHBY, Rt. Rev. Godfrey William Ernest Candler; Professor of Divinity, University of the Witwatersrand, Johannesburg, since 1985; *b* 6 Nov. 1930; *s* of William Candler Ashby and Vera Fane Ashby (*née* Hickey); *m* 1957, Valerie Hawtree; four *s* two *d*. *Educ:* King's School, Chester; King's Coll., London (BD, AKC, PhD). Deacon 1955, priest 1956; Assistant Curate: St Peter, St Helier, Morden, 1955–57; Clydesdale Mission, 1958; Priest-in-charge, St Mark's Mission, 1958–60; Subwarden, St Paul's Coll., Grahamstown, 1960–65; Rector of Alice and Lectr, Federal Theological Seminary, 1966–68; Sen. Lecturer, Old Testament and Hebrew, Rhodes Univ., Grahamstown, 1969–75; Assoc. Professor, 1974–75; Overseas Visiting Scholar, St John's Coll., Cambridge, 1975; Dean and Archdeacon, Cathedral of St Michael and St George, Grahamstown, 1976–80; Bishop of St John's (Transkei and S Africa), 1980–84. *Publications:* Theodoret of Cyrrhus as Exegete of the Old Testament, 1970; articles in theological jls. *Recreation:* ornithology. *Address:* Department of Religious Studies, University of Witwatersrand, 1 Jan Smuts Avenue, Johannesburg, 2001, S Africa.

ASHBY, Prof. Michael Farries, FRS 1979; Professor of Engineering Materials, University of Cambridge, since 1973; *b* 20 Nov. 1935; *s* of Lord Ashby, *qv*; *m* 1962, Maureen Ashby; two *s* one *d*. *Educ:* Campbell Coll., Belfast; Queens' Coll., Cambridge (BA, MA, PhD). Post-doctoral work, Cambridge, 1960–62; Asst, Univ. of Göttingen, 1962–65; Asst Prof., Harvard Univ., 1965–69; Prof. of Metallurgy, Harvard Univ., 1969–73. Mem., Akad. der Wissenschaften zu Göttingen, 1980–. Hon. MA Harvard, 1969. Editor,

Acta Metallurgica, 1974–. *Recreations:* music, design. *Address:* 51 Maids Causeway, Cambridge CB5 8DE. *T:* Cambridge 64741.

ASHCOMBE, 4th Baron, *cr* 1892; **Henry Edward Cubitt;** late RAF; Chairman, Cubitt Estates Ltd; *b* 31 March 1924; *er s* of 3rd Baron Ashcombe; *S* father, 1962; *m* 1955, Ghislaine (marr. diss. 1968), *o d* of Cornelius Willem Dresselhuys, Long Island, New York; *m* 1973, Hon. Virginia Carington, *yr d* of Baron Carrington, *qv*; *m* 1979, Mrs Elizabeth Dent-Brocklehurst. *Educ:* Eton. Served War of 1939–45, RAF. Consul-General in London for the Principality of Monaco, 1961–68. *Heir: cousin* (Mark) Robin Cubitt [*b* 13 June 1936; *m* 1962, Juliet Perpetua (marr. diss.), *d* of Edward Corbet Woodall, OBE; three *s*]. *Address:* Sudeley Castle, Winchcombe, Cheltenham, Glos. *Club:* White's.
See also Earl of Harrington.

ASHCROFT, David, TD 1957; MA Cantab; Headmaster, Cheltenham College, 1959–78; *b* 20 May 1920; *s* of late A. H. Ashcroft, DSO; *m* 1949, Joan Elizabeth Young; two *s* three *d*. *Educ:* Rugby Sch.; Gonville and Caius Coll., Cambridge. War Service, 1940–46 (despatches). Asst Master, Rossall Sch., 1946–50; Asst Master, Rugby Sch., 1950–59. *Address:* London House, Ashton Keynes, Swindon, Wilts. *T:* Cirencester 861319.

ASHCROFT, James Geoffrey; Deputy Under Secretary of State, Finance, Ministry of Defence, since 1985; *b* 19 May 1928; *s* of James Ashcroft and Elizabeth (*née* Fillingham); *m* 1953, Margery (*née* Barratt); one *s*. *Educ:* Cowley Sch., St Helens; Peterhouse, Cambridge. BA (Hons Hist.). Min. of Supply, 1950–59; Min. of Aviation, 1959–61, 1964–65; Min. of Defence, 1961–64, 1965–68, 1970–73; Inst. of Strategic Studies, 1968–70; Under-Sec., Pay Board, 1973–74; Asst Under Sec. of State, Management Services, PE, 1974–76; Asst Under Sec. of State, Gen. Finance, MoD, 1976–84. *Publications:* papers on international collaboration in military logistics. *Recreation:* golf. *Address:* 39 Hill Rise, Hinchley Wood, Esher, Surrey KT10 0AL. *T:* 01-398 5637.

ASHCROFT, Ven. Lawrence; retired as Archdeacon of Stow and Vicar of Burton-on-Stather (1954–62); *b* 1901; *s* of Lawrence Ashcroft; *m* 1927, Barbara Louise Casson; two *s* three *d*. *Educ:* University Coll., Durham; Lichfield Theological Coll. Deacon, 1926; Priest, 1927; Curate of Ulverston, 1926–29, of Egremont, 1929–30; District Sec., Brit. and Foreign Bible Society, 1930–33; Vicar of St Saviour's, Retford, 1934–40; Chaplain to the Forces (Emergency Commission), 1940–43; Rector of St Michael Stoke, Coventry, 1943; Rural Dean of Coventry, 1949; Hon. Canon of Coventry, 1952; Hon. Canon of Lincoln, 1954; Proctor in Convocation, Canterbury, 1955; Chaplain to High Sheriff of Lincolnshire, 1958, to British Embassy, Oslo, 1967, Luxembourg, 1968; Rector, St Philip's, Antigua, 1969, Manvers St Crispin, Toronto, 1970–79. Mem., Church Assembly, 1956–62. Governor, De Aston Grammar Sch., 1955–62; Founder and Chm., Brigg Church Sch., 1956–62. *Address:* c/o Lloyds Bank, St Helier, Jersey, Channel Islands.

ASHCROFT, Dame Peggy, (Edith Margaret Emily), DBE 1956 (CBE 1951); actress; Director, Royal Shakespeare Co., since 1968; *b* 22 Dec. 1907; *d* of William Worsley Ashcroft and Violet Maud Bernheim; *m* 1st, 1929, Rupert Hart-Davis (marr. diss.; he was knighted, 1967); 2nd, 1934, Theodore Komisarjevsky (marr. diss.); 3rd, 1940, Jeremy Hutchinson, QC, now Lord Hutchinson of Lullington (marr. diss., 1966); one *s* one *d*. *Educ:* Woodford Sch., Croydon; Central Sch. of Dramatic Art. Member of the Arts Council, 1962–64. Ashcroft Theatre, Croydon, named in her honour, 1962. First appeared as Margaret in Dear Brutus, Birmingham Repertory Theatre, 1926; parts include: Bessie in One Day More, Everyman, Eve in When Adam Delved, Wyndham's, 1927, Mary Bruin in The Land of Heart's Desire, Hester in The Silver Cord, 1928; Constance Neville in She Stoops to Conquer, Naomi in Jew Süss, 1929; Desdemona in Othello with Paul Robeson, 1930; Fanny in Sea Fever, 1931; Cleopatra, Imogen, Rosalind, etc, at Old Vic and Sadler's Wells, 1932; Juliet at New, 1935; Nina in The Seagull, New, 1936; Portia, Lady Teazle, and, Irina in Three Sisters, Queen's, 1937–38; Yeliena in White Guard and Viola, Phoenix, 1938–39; Cecily Cardew in The Importance of Being Earnest, 1939–40, and Dinah in Cousin Muriel, 1940, both at Globe; revival of Importance of Being Earnest, Phoenix, 1942; Catherine in The Dark River, Whitehall, 1943; Ophelia, Titania, Duchess of Malfi, Haymarket Repertory Season, 1944–45; Evelyn Holt in Edward my Son, His Majesty's, 1947; Catherine Sloper in The Heiress, Haymarket, 1949; Beatrice and Cordelia, Memorial Theatre, Stratford-on-Avon, 1950; Viola, Electra and Mistress Page, Old Vic, 1950–51; Hester Collyer in the Deep Blue Sea, Duchess, 1952; Cleopatra, Stratford-on-Avon and Princes, 1953; title-rôle, Hedda Gabler, Lyric, Hammersmith and Westminster, 1954; Beatrice in Much Ado About Nothing, Stratford Festival Company, 1955 (London, provinces and continental tour); Miss Madrigal in The Chalk Garden, Haymarket, 1956; Shen Te in The Good Woman of Setzuan, Royal Court, 1956; Rosalind, Imogen, Cymbeline, Stratford-on-Avon, 1957; Julia Rajk in Shadow of Heroes, Piccadilly, 1958; Stratford-on-Avon Season, 1960: Katharina in The Taming of the Shrew; Paulina in The Winter's Tale; The Hollow Crown, Aldwych, 1961; title rôle in The Duchess of Malfi, Aldwych, 1961; Emilia in Othello, Stratford-on-Avon, 1961, also Madame Ranevskaya in The Cherry Orchard, subseq. Aldwych; Margaret of Anjou in Henry VI and Margaret in Edward IV, also Margaret in Richard III, Stratford-on-Avon, 1963, Aldwych, 1964; Mme Arkadina in The Seagull, Queen's, 1964; Mother in Days in the Trees, Aldwych, 1966; Mrs Alving in Ghosts, 1967; A Delicate Balance, Aldwych, 1969; Beth in Landscape, Aldwych, 1969; Katharine of Aragon in Henry VIII, Stratford-on-Avon, 1969; The Plebeians Rehearse the Uprising, Aldwych, 1970; The Lovers of Viorne, Royal Court, 1971 (Evening Standard Best Actress award, 1972); All Over, Aldwych, 1972; Lloyd George Knew My Father, Savoy, 1972; Beth in Landscape, Flora in A Slight Ache, Ashcroft Theatre, foreign tour and Aldwych, 1973; The Hollow Crown, tour in US, 1973; John Gabriel Borkman, National, 1975; Happy Days, National, 1975, 1977; Old World, Aldwych, 1976; Watch on the Rhine, Edinburgh Fest. and National, 1980; Family Views, National, 1981; All's Well that Ends Well, Stratford-on-Avon, 1981, Barbican, 1982. Entered films 1933; subsequent films include: The Wandering Jew, The Thirty-nine Steps, The Nun's Story (played Mother Mathilde), Hullabaloo over Georgie and Bonnie's Pictures, 1979; Passage to India, 1985 (Oscar award; BAFTA award); Queen Victoria for BBC Radio, 1973; television: series include: Queen Mary in Edward and Mrs Simpson, ITV, 1978; The Jewel in the Crown, Granada, 1984 (BAFTA award); plays include: Caught on a Train, BBC2, 1980; Cream in My Coffee, LWT, 1980. King's Gold Medal, Norway, 1955; Special Award, British Theatre Assoc., 1982; Hon. DLitt: Oxford, 1961; Leicester, 1964; Warwick, 1974; Hon. DLit London, 1965; Hon LittD Cantab, 1972. Hon. Fellow, St Hugh's College, Oxford, 1964. Comdr, Order of St Olav, Norway, 1976. *Address:* Manor Lodge, Frognal Lane, NW3.

ASHCROFT, Philip Giles; Solicitor, British Telecommunications, since 1981; *b* 15 Nov. 1926; *s* of Edmund Samuel Ashcroft and Constance Ruth Ashcroft (*née* Giles); *m* 1st, 1968, Kathleen Margaret Senior (marr. diss. 1983); one *s*; 2nd, 1985, Valerie May Smith, *d* of late E. T. G. Smith. *Educ:* Royal Grammar Sch., Newcastle upon Tyne; Durham Univ. Admitted solicitor, 1951. Joined Treasury Solicitor's Dept, 1955; Asst Legal Adviser, Land Commn, 1967; Asst Treasury Solicitor, 1971; Under-Sec. (Legal), DTI, 1973; Legal Adviser, Dept of Energy, 1974–80; Dep. Solicitor to the Post Office, 1980–81. *Recreations:* reading, listening to music, walking. *Address:* 3 Julian Close, Woking, Surrey GU21 3HD. *T:* Woking 71383.

ASHDOWN, Jeremy John Dunham, (Paddy Ashdown); MP (L) Yeovil, since 1983; *b* 27 Feb. 1941; *s* of John W. R. D. Ashdown and Lois A. Ashdown; *m* 1961, Jane (*née* Courtenay); one *s* one *d*. *Educ:* Bedford Sch. Served RM, 1959–71: 41 and 42 Commandos; commanded 2 Special Boat Section; Captain RM; HM Diplomatic Service, 1st Sec., UK Mission to UN, Geneva, 1971–76; Commercial Manager's Dept, Westlands Gp, 1976–78; Sen. Manager, Morlands Ltd, 1978–81; employed by Dorset CC, 1982–83. Parly Spokesman for Trade and Industry, 1983–. *Recreations:* walking, gardening, wine making. *Address:* Vane Cottage, Norton sub Hamdon, Som TA14 6SG. *T:* Chiselborough 491. *Club:* National Liberal.

ASHE, Sir Derick (Rosslyn), KCMG 1978 (CMG 1966); HM Diplomatic Service, retired 1979; Ambassador and Permanent UK Representative to Disarmament Conference, Geneva, 1977–79 and Permanent Head of UK Delegation to UN Special Session on Disarmament, New York, 1977–78; *b* 20 Jan. 1919; *s* of late Frederick Allen Ashe and late Rosalind Ashe (*née* Mitchell); *m* 1957, Rissa Guinness, *d* of late Capt. Hon. Trevor Tempest Parker, DSC, Royal Navy and Mrs Parker; one *s* one *d*. *Educ:* Bradfield Coll.; Trinity Coll., Oxford. HM Forces, 1940–46 (despatches 1945). Second Sec., Berlin and Frankfurt-am-Main, 1947–49; Private Sec. to Permanent Under-Sec. of State for German Section of FO, 1950–53; First Sec., La Paz, 1953–55; FO, 1955–57; First Sec. (Information), Madrid, 1957–61; FO, 1961–62; Counsellor and Head of Chancery: Addis Ababa, 1962–64; Havana, 1964–66; Head of Security Dept, FCO (formerly FO), 1966–69; Minister, Tokyo, 1969–71; Ambassador to: Romania, 1972–75; Argentina, 1975–77. Knight of the Order of Orange-Nassau (with swords), 1945. *Recreations:* gardening, antiques. *Address:* Dalton House, Hurstbourne Tarrant, Andover, Hants. *T:* Hurstbourne Tarrant 276. *Clubs:* White's, Travellers', Beefsteak.

ASHE LINCOLN, Fredman; *see* Lincoln, F. A.

ASHERSON, Nehemiah, MA Cape; MB, BS London; FRCS, LRCP; FZS, etc; Fellow International College of Surgeons; Hon. Fellow Surgical Academy, Madrid; Associate, Royal Institute of Chemistry, 1919; Hon. Cons. Surgeon, The Royal National (Central London) Throat, Nose, and Ear Hospital (late Member of Board of Governors, 1948–49–50–58); late Hon. Secretary to the Medical Council; Lecturer to the Institute of Otology and Laryngology (Member Academic Board); Teacher in Oto-laryngology in the University of London; Consulting Surgeon for Diseases of the Ear, Nose, and Throat to the NE, NW and SE regional hospital boards, including the Queen Elizabeth Hospital for Children; FRSocMed (Hon. Fellow, former Pres., Section of Laryngology; Hon. Fellow, Member Council, Section History of Medicine; late Member Council Section Otology, and Library Committee); Trustee (Hon. Fellow, former Pres., Hunterian Society); formerly Hon. Treasurer, BMA, St Marylebone Division, and Mem. Ethical Cttee; Fellow and Hon. Librarian, late Councillor, Medical Society of London; *b* 1897; *s* of Isaac Asherson; *m*; one *s* one *d*. *Educ:* South African Coll.; Univ. of Cape Town (Entrance Scholar); University Coll. and Hospital, London; postgraduate study in speciality in London and Vienna. Medallist in Chemistry; exhibitioner at the BA examination; Jamieson Scholar at MA; Alexander Bruce Gold Medallist in Surgery and Liston Gold Medal in Surgical Pathology, University Coll. Hosp.; Geoffrey Duveen Travelling Scholar of the Univ. of London in Oto-rhino Laryngology; late Harker Smith Cancer (radium) Registrar and Casualty Surgical Officer at University Coll. Hosp.; Chief Asst to the Royal Ear Hosp., University Coll. Hosp.; Chief Asst to the Ear, Nose, and Throat Dept of the Bolingbroke Hosp., etc; Late: Ear Consultant to Army Medical Boards; Surgeon Emergency Medical Service, 1939–45; Consulting Surgeon to LCC and to the Charterhouse Rheumatism Clinic. Hunterian Prof., RCS, 1942. Mem. Royal Instn (Visitor, 1969–71). Mem., Apothecaries Soc. *Publications:* Diagnosis and Treatment of Foreign Bodies in the Upper Food and Respiratory Passages, 1932; Acute Otitis and Mastoiditis in General Practice, 1934; Chronic Ear Discharge (Otorrhœa) and its complications, 1936; Otogenic Cerebellar Abscess, Hunterian Lecture, 1942; Identification by Frontal Sinus Prints, 1965; The Deafness of Beethoven, 1965; Bibliography of G. J. Du Verney's Traité de l'Organe de l'Ouïe, 1683 (first scientific treatise on the ear), 1979; communications in Jl of Laryngology, of the Royal Society of Medicine, in The Lancet and in medical journals on subjects relating to the speciality. *Recreations:* numismatics, book collecting. *Address:* 21 Harley Street, W1. *T:* 01-580 3197; Green Shutters, East Preston, West Kingston, West Sussex. *Clubs:* Reform, Savage.

ASHFORD, (Albert) Reginald, CMG 1962; Assistant Secretary, Board of Customs and Excise, 1952–73; *b* 30 June 1914; *s* of Ernest Ashford; *m* 1946, Mary Anne Ross Davidson, *d* of Thomas Davidson; one *s*. *Educ:* Ealing Grammar Sch.; London Sch. of Economics. UK Delegate to and many times chm. of numerous internat. conferences on reduction of trade barriers and simplification of customs formalities, 1946–60. *Address:* 4 Tithe Green, Rustington, West Sussex. *T:* Rustington 776545.

ASHFORD, George Francis, OBE 1945; retired; *b* 5 July 1911; *s* of G. W. Ashford and L. M. Redfern; *m* 1950, Eleanor Vera Alexander; two *s*. *Educ:* Malvern Coll.; Trinity Hall, Cambridge; Birmingham Univ. Served War of 1939–45, Army, N Africa and Italy (despatches 1944). Distillers Co. Ltd, 1937–67: Solicitor, 1937; Legal Adviser, 1945; Dir, 1956; Management Cttee, 1963–67; Dir, BP Co. Ltd, 1967–73, Man. Dir, 1969–73; Dir, Albright & Wilson Ltd, 1973–79. Mem., Monopolies and Mergers Commn, 1973–80. Pres., British Plastics Fedn, 1966–67; Vice-President: Soc. of Chemical Industry, 1966–69; Chem. Ind. Assoc., 1967–70. Mem. Economic Policy Cttee for Chemical Industry, 1967–74; Chm., Working Party on Industrial Review, 1973. Organiser, Meals on Wheels, Woodley and Sonning, 1983–. *Recreation:* gardening. *Address:* The Old House, Sonning, Berks. *T:* Reading 692122.

ASHFORD, Ven. Percival Leonard; Vicar of Hambledon, Diocese of Portsmouth, since 1985; Chaplain to the Queen, since 1982; *b* 5 June 1927; *s* of late Edwin and Gwendoline Emily Ashford; *m* 1955, Dorothy Helen Harwood; two *s*. *Educ:* Kemp Welch Sch., Poole; Bristol Univ.; Tyndale Hall Theol Coll., Bristol. Asst Curate, St Philip and St James, Ilfracombe, 1954; Curate-in-Charge, Church of Good Shepherd, Aylesbury, 1956; Vicar, St Olaf's, Poughill, Bude, 1959; HM Prison Service: Asst Chaplain, Wormwood Scrubs, 1965; Chaplain: Risley Remand Centre, 1966; Durham, 1969; Wandsworth, 1971; Winchester, 1975; SW Reg. Chaplain of Prisons, 1977; Chaplain General of Prisons, 1981–85; Archdeacon to the Prison Service, 1982–85. Mem. Gen. Synod, C of E, 1985. Exam. Chaplain to Bishop of Portsmouth, 1986. *Recreations:* choral and classical music, reading, golf. *Address:* Hambledon Vicarage, Portsmouth, Hants PO7 6RT. *T:* Hambledon 717.

ASHFORD, Reginald; *see* Ashford, A. R.

ASHFORD, Air Vice-Marshal Ronald Gordon, CBE 1978; Chairman, Metropolitan Traffic Commissioners, since 1985; *b* 2 May 1931; *s* of Richard Ashford and Phyllis Lancaster; *m* 1966, Patricia Ann Turner; two *d*. *Educ:* Ilfracombe Grammar Sch.; Bristol Univ. (LLB). Joined RAF, 1952; qualified as Navigator, 1953; OC No 115 Squadron, 1971–72; OC RAF Finningley, 1976–77; RCDS, 1978; Air Cdre Intelligence, 1979–83; Comdr, Southern Maritime Air Region, 1983–84; Dir Gen., Personal Services (RAF),

MoD, 1984–85; retired. *Recreation:* golf. *Address:* Alborough Lodge, Packhorse Road, Gerrards Cross SL9 8JD. *Club:* Royal Air Force.

ASHFORD, William Stanton, OBE 1971; HM Diplomatic Service, retired; *b* 4 July 1924; *s* of Thomas and May Ashford; *m* 1957, Rosalind Anne Collett; two *s*. *Educ:* Winchester Coll.; Balliol Coll., Oxford. Served RAF, 1943–47; Air Ministry, 1948; Commonwealth Relations Office, 1961; Director of British Information Services, Sierra Leone, 1961, Ghana, 1962; Acting Consul-General, Tangier, 1965; Regional Information Officer, Bombay, 1966; Head of Chancery, British Government Office, Montreal, 1967; seconded to Northern Ireland Office, 1972; FCO, 1974; Consul-General, Adelaide, 1977; High Comr, Vanuatu, 1980–82. *Recreations:* music, backyard farming. *Address:* c/o Lloyds Bank, Fore Street, Bodmin, Cornwall PL31 2HP. *T:* Bodmin 3434.

ASHIOTIS, Costas; High Commissioner of Cyprus in London, 1966–79; Cyprus Ambassador to Denmark, Sweden, Norway and Malta, 1966–79; *b* 1908; *m*. *Educ:* Pancyprian Gymnasium, Nicosia; London Sch. of Economics. Journalist and editor; joined Govt Service, 1942; Asst Comr of Labour, 1948; Dir-Gen., Min. of Foreign Affairs, 1960. Mem. Cyprus delegns to UN and to internat. confs. Retired from Foreign Service, 1979. MBE 1952. *Publications:* Labour Conditions in Cyprus during the War Years, 1939–45; literary articles. *Address:* 16 Armenias Street, Nicosia (140), Cyprus.

ASHKENAZY, Vladimir; concert pianist; conductor; *b* Gorky, Russia, 6 July 1937; *m* 1961, Thorunn Johannsdottir, *d* of Johann Tryggvason, Iceland; two *s* three *d*. *Educ:* Central Musical Sch., Moscow; Conservatoire, Moscow. Studied under Sumbatyan; Lev Oborin class, 1955: grad 1960. Internat. Chopin Comp., Warsaw, at age of 17 (gained 2nd prize); won Queen Elizabeth Internat. Piano Comp., Brussels, at age of 18 (gold medal). Joint winner (with John Ogdon) of Tchaikovsky Piano Comp., Moscow, 1962. London debut with London Symph. Orch. under George Hurst, and subseq, solo recital, Festival Hall, 1963. Has played in many countries. Makes recordings. Hon. RAM 1972. Icelandic Order of the Falcon, 1971. *Publication:* (with Jasper Parrott) Beyond Frontiers, 1985. *Address:* Sonnenhof 4, 6004 Lucerne, Switzerland.

ASHLEY, Lord; Anthony Nils Christian Ashley-Cooper; *b* 24 June 1977; *s* and *heir* of Earl of Shaftesbury, *qv*.

ASHLEY, Bernard Albert, FSIAD; Chairman, Laura Ashley Ltd, since 1954 (Ashley, Mountney Ltd, 1954–68, name changed to Laura Ashley Ltd, 1968); *b* 11 Aug. 1926; *s* of Albert Ashley and Hilda Maud Ashley; *m* 1949, Laura Mountney (*d* 1985); two *s* two *d*. *Educ:* Whitgift Sch., Croydon, Surrey. Army commission, 1944; Royal Fusiliers, 1944–46, seconded 1 Gurkha Rifles, 1944–45. Incorporated Ashley, Mountney Ltd, 1954. Chm., Assoc. Laura Ashley Companies Overseas. *Recreations:* sailing, flying. *Address:* 43 rue Ducale, Brussels 1000, Belgium. *Clubs:* Royal Thames Yacht (Southampton), Army Sailing Association.

ASHLEY, Cedric, CBE 1984; PhD; Director, Motor Industry Research Association, since 1977; *b* 11 Nov. 1936; *s* of Ronald Ashley and Gladys Fincher; *m* 1st, 1960, Pamela Jane Turner (decd); one *s*; 2nd, 1965, (Marjorie) Vivien Gooch; one *s* one *d*. *Educ:* King Edward's Sch., Birmingham; Mech. Engrg Dept, Univ. of Birmingham (BSc 1958, PhD 1964). FIMechE 1978. Rolls-Royce Ltd, Derby, 1955–60; Univ. of Birmingham, 1960–73: ICI Res. Fellow, 1963; Lectr, 1966; Internat. Technical Dir, Bostrom Div., Universal Oil Products Ltd, 1973–77. Mem. and Chm. of internat. standards orgns, and BSI cttees and working groups, 1968–. Chairman: SEE, 1970–72; RAC Tech. Cttee, 1980–; Coordinating Gp of Res. Orgns, 1982–84 (Sec., 1984). Member: SMMT Technical Bds, 1977–; Board, Assoc. Ind. Contract Res. Orgns, 1977– (Pres., 1982–84); Coventry and District Engineering Employers Assoc., 1978–; Board, Automobile Div., IMechE, 1978–(Vice-Chm., 1985–); Court, Cranfield Inst. of Technol., 1977–; Engine and Vehicles Cttee, DTI, 1980–; Three-Dimensional Design Bd, CNAA, 1981–. FRSA 1983. Cementation Muffelite Award, SEE, 1968; Design Council Award, 1974. TA, 1959–68. *Publications:* (contrib.) Infrasound and Low Frequency Vibration, ed Tempest, 1976; papers on electro-hydraulics, vehicle ride, and effect of vibration and shock on man and buildings, in learned jls. *Recreations:* travel, reading. *Address:* The Old Rectory, Church Walk, Bilton, Rugby. *T:* Rugby 81677. *Clubs:* Royal Automobile, Anglo-Belgian.

ASHLEY, Rt. Hon. Jack, CH 1975; PC 1979; MP (Lab) Stoke-on-Trent, South, since 1966; *b* 6 Dec. 1922; *s* of John Ashley and Isabella Bridge; *m* 1951, Pauline Kay Crispin; three *d*. *Educ:* St Patrick's Elem. Sch., Widnes, Lancs; Ruskin Coll., Oxford; Gonville and Caius Coll., Cambridge. Labourer and cranedriver, 1936–46; Shop Steward Convener and Nat. Exec. Mem., Chemical Workers' Union, 1946; Scholarship, Ruskin Coll., 1946–48 and Caius Coll., 1948–51 (Chm. Cambridge Labour Club, 1950; Pres. Cambridge Union, 1951); BBC Radio Producer, 1951–57; Commonwealth Fund Fellow, 1955; BBC Senior Television Producer, 1957–66; Mem., General Advisory Council, BBC, 1967–69, 1970–74. Parliamentary Private Secretary to: Sec. of State for Econ. Affairs, 1967–68; Sec. of State, DHSS, 1974–76. Mem., Lab. Party Nat. Exec. Cttee, 1976–78. Founder and Pres., Hearing and Speech Trust, 1985–. Councillor, Borough of Widnes, 1945. *Publication:* Journey into Silence, 1973. *Address:* House of Commons, SW1A 0AA.

ASHLEY, Maurice Percy, CBE 1978; *b* 4 Sept. 1907; *s* of Sir Percy Ashley, KBE, and Lady Ashley (*née* Hayman); *m* 1935, Phyllis Mary Griffiths; one *s* one *d*. *Educ:* St Paul's Sch., London; New Coll., Oxford (History Scholar). 1st Class Hons Modern History; DPhil Oxon; DLitt Oxon, 1979. Historical Research Asst to Sir Winston Churchill, 1929–33; Editorial Staff, The Manchester Guardian, 1933–37; Editorial Staff, The Times, 1937–39; Editor, Britain Today, 1939–40. Served in Army, 1940–45 (Major, Intelligence Corps). Deputy Editor, The Listener, 1946–58, Editor, 1958–67; Research Fellow, Loughborough Univ. of Technology, 1968–70. Pres. Cromwell Association, 1961–77. *Publications include:* Financial and Commercial Policy under the Cromwellian Protectorate, 1934 (revised, 1962); Oliver Cromwell, 1937; Marlborough, 1939; Louis XIV and the Greatness of France, 1946; John Wildman: Plotter and Postmaster, 1947; Mr President, 1948; England in the Seventeenth Century, 1952, rev. edn, 1978; Cromwell's Generals, 1954; The Greatness of Oliver Cromwell, 1957 (revised 1967); Oliver Cromwell and the Puritan Revolution, 1958; Great Britain to 1688, 1961; The Stuarts in Love, 1963; Life in Stuart England, 1964; The Glorious Revolution of 1688, 1966 (revised, 1968); Churchill as Historian, 1968; A Golden Century, 1598–1715, 1969; (ed) Cromwell: great lives observed, 1969; Charles II: the man and the statesman, 1971; Oliver Cromwell and his World, 1972; The Life and Times of King John, 1972; The Life and Times of King William I, 1973; A History of Europe 1648–1815, 1973; The Age of Absolutism 1648–1775, 1974; A Concise History of the English Civil War, 1975; Rupert of the Rhine, 1976; General Monck, 1977; James II, 1978; The House of Stuart, 1980; The People of England: a short social and economic history, 1982. *Recreations:* bridge, gardening. *Address:* 34 Wood Lane, Ruislip, Mddx HA4 6EX. *T:* Ruislip 35993. *Club:* Reform.

ASHLEY-COOPER, family name of **Earl of Shaftesbury.**

ASHLEY-SMITH, Jonathan, PhD; Keeper, Department of Conservation, Victoria and Albert Museum, since 1977; *b* 25 Aug. 1946; *s* of Ewart Trist and Marian Tanfield Ashley-Smith; *m* 1967, Diane Louise (*née* Wagland); one *s* one *d*. *Educ:* Sutton Valence Public Sch.; Bristol Univ. (BSc (Hons), PhD). Post-doctoral research, Cambridge Univ., 1970–72; Victoria and Albert Museum, 1973–. Member: UK Inst. for Conservation, 1974– (Mem., Exec Cttee, 1978–; Vice-Chm., 1980–); Crafts Council, 1980–83; Conservation Cttee, Crafts Council, 1978–83; Council for Care of Churches Conservation Cttee, 1978–85; Board of Governors, London Coll. of Furniture, 1983–85; Chm., UK Inst. for Conservation, 1983–84. Scientific Editor, Science for Conservators (Crafts Council series), 1983–84. *Publications:* articles in learned jls on organometallic chemistry, spectroscopy and scientific examination of art objects. *Recreations:* loud music, good beer. *Address:* Victoria and Albert Museum, Exhibition Road, SW7 2RL. *T:* 01–589 6371.

ASHMOLE, Professor Bernard, CBE 1957; MC; MA, BLitt; Hon. FRIBA, FBA; FKC 1986; Hon. Fellow of Lincoln College, Oxford, 1980; Hon. Fellow, University College, London, 1974; Hon. Fellow, Hertford College, Oxford, 1961; *b* Ilford, 22 June 1894; 2nd *s* of late William Ashmole and Caroline Wharton Tiver; *m* 1920, Dorothy Irene, 2nd *d* of late Everard de Peyer, Newent Court, Glos; one *s* two *d*. *Educ:* Forest; privately; Hertford Coll., Oxford (Classical Scholar). 11th Royal Fusiliers, 1914–18; Captain (severely wounded, Somme, 1917). Craven Fellow, and Student of the British Schools at Athens and Rome, 1920–22; Asst Curator of Coins, Ashmolean Museum, 1923–25; Director of the British Sch. at Rome, 1925–28; Florence Bursar, RIBA, 1937; Hon. Member of the Archæological Institute of America, 1940; RAF 1940–45, Adjutant of 84 Sqdn in Greece, Iraq, Western Desert, Sumatra and India (despatches twice, Hellenic Flying Cross). Yates Professor of Archæology, University of London, 1929–48; Keeper of Greek and Roman Antiquities, British Museum, 1939–56; Lincoln Professor of Classical Archæology, Univ. of Oxford, 1956–61, and Fellow of Lincoln Coll., Oxford, 1956–80; Geddes-Harrower Professor of Greek Art and Archæology, Univ. of Aberdeen, 1961–63; Visiting Professor in Archæology, Univ. of Yale, 1964. Rhind Lectr, 1952; Myres Memorial Lectr, Oxford, 1961; Norton Lectr, Archæological Inst. of America, 1963; Wrightsman Lectr, New York, 1967. Hon. LLD Aberdeen, 1968. Hon. Fellow, Archaeol Soc. of Athens, 1978. Kenyon Medal, British Acad., 1979; Cassano Medal, Taranto, 1980. *Publications:* Catalogue of Ancient Marbles at Ince Blundell, 1929; Greek Sculpture and Painting (with Beazley), 1932, repr. 1966; The Ancient World (with Groenewegen-Frankfort), 1967; Olympia: sculptures of the temple of Zeus (with Yalouris and Frantz), 1967; Architect and Sculptor in Classical Greece, 1972; articles on Greek sculpture in the Journal of Hellenic Studies and other periodicals. *Address:* 5 Tweed Green, Peebles. *T:* Peebles 21154. *Club:* Athenæum.

ASHMOLE, (Harold) David; Senior Principal Dancer, Australian Ballet, since 1984; *b* 31 Oct. 1949; *s* of Richard Thomas Ashmole and Edith Ashmole. *Educ:* Sandye Place, Beds; Royal Ballet Sch. Solo Seal, Royal Acad. of Dancing; ARAD. Joined Royal Ballet Co., 1968; Soloist, 1972; Principal, 1975; transf. to Sadler's Wells Royal Ballet, 1976, Sen. Principal, 1978–84. Appeared in: Dame Alicia Markova's Master Classes, BBC Television, 1980; Maina Gielgud's Steps, Notes and Squeaks, Aberdeen Internat. Festival, 1981. Guest appearances with Scottish Ballet and in Japan, Germany, S Africa and France. *Classical ballets include:* La Bayadère, Coppélia, Daphnis and Chloe, Giselle, Nutcracker, Raymonda, The Seasons, Sleeping Beauty, Swan Lake, La Sylphide; *other ballets include:* (choreography by Ashton): Cinderella, The Two Pigeons, La Fille Mal Gardée, Les Rendezvous, The Dream, Lament of the Waves; (Balanchine): Apollo, Prodigal Son, Serenade, The Four Temperaments, Agon; (Béjart): Gaîté Parisienne, Webern Opus 5, Songs of a Wayfarer; (Bintley): Night Moves, Homage to Chopin, The Swan of Tuonela; (Cranko): Pineapple Poll, The Taming of the Shrew; (Darrell): The Tales of Hoffmann; (de Valois): Checkmate, The Rake's Progress; (Fokine): Les Sylphides, Petrushka; (Hynd): Papillon; (Lander): Etudes; (Lifar): Suite en Blanc; (MacMillan): Concerto, Elite Syncopations, Romeo and Juliet, Quartet; (Massine): La Boutique Fantasque; (Nijinska): Les Biches; (Nureyev): Don Quixote; (Robbins): Dances at a Gathering, Requiem Canticles, In the Night; (Seymour): Intimate Letters; (Samsova): Paquita; (Tetley): Gemini, Laborintus; (van Manen): Grosse Fugue, 5 Tangos; (Wright): Summertide. *Recreations:* Moorcroft pottery collection, gardening, shooting, fishing. *Address:* c/o Australian Ballet, 11 Mount Alexander Road, Flemington, Vic 3031, Australia.

ASHMORE, Dr Alick, CBE 1979; Director, Daresbury Laboratory, Science Research Council, 1970–81; *b* 7 Nov. 1920; *s* of Frank Owen Ashmore and Beatrice Maud Swindells; *m* 1947, Eileen Elsie Fuller; two *s* three *d*. *Educ:* King Edward VII Sch., Lytham; King's Coll., London. Experimental Officer, RRDE, Malvern, 1941–47; Lecturer in physics, University of Liverpool, 1947–59; Queen Mary Coll., London: Reader in experimental physics, 1960–64; Prof. of Nuclear Physics, 1964–70, also Head of Physics Dept, 1968–70. *Publications:* research publications on nuclear and elementary-particle physics in Proc. Phys. Soc., Nuclear Physics, Physical Review. *Recreations:* walking, camping. *Address:* Farnham House, Hesket Newmarket, Wigton, Cumbria CA7 8JG. *T:* Caldbeck 414.

ASHMORE, Admiral of the Fleet Sir Edward (Beckwith), GCB 1974 (KCB 1971; CB 1966); DSC 1942; Director, Racal Electronics plc, since 1978; *b* 11 Dec. 1919; *er s* of late Vice-Admiral L. H. Ashmore, CB, DSO and late Tamara Vasilevna Shutt, Petrograd; *m* 1942, Elizabeth Mary Doveton Sturdee, *d* of late Rear-Admiral Sir Lionel Sturdee, 2nd Bt, CBE; one *s* one *d* (and one *d* decd). *Educ:* RNC, Dartmouth. Served HMS Birmingham, Jupiter, Middleton, 1938–42; qualified in Signals, 1943; Staff of C-in-C Home Fleet, Flag Lieut, 4th Cruiser Sqdn, 1944–45; qualified Interpreter in Russian, 1946; Asst Naval Attaché, Moscow, 1946–47; Squadron Communications Officer, 3rd Aircraft Carrier Squadron, 1950; Commander 1950; comd HMS Alert, 1952–53; Captain 1955; Captain (F) 6th Frigate Sqdn, and CO HMS Blackpool, 1958; Director of Plans, Admiralty and Min. of Defence, 1960–62; Commander British Forces Caribbean Area, 1963–64; Rear-Adm., 1965; Asst Chief of the Defence Staff, Signals, 1965–67; Flag Officer, Second-in-Command, Far East Fleet, 1967–68; Vice-Adm. 1968; Vice-Chief, Naval Staff, 1969–71; Adm. 1970; C-in-C Western Fleet, Sept.-Oct. 1971; C-in-C, Fleet, 1971–74; Chief of Naval Staff and First Sea Lord, 1974–77; First and Principal Naval Aide-de-Camp to the Queen, 1974–77; CDS, Feb.-Aug. 1977. Governor, Suttons Hosp. in Charterhouse. *Recreations:* usual. *Address:* c/o National Westminster Bank plc, 26 Haymarket, SW1. *Club:* Naval and Military.

See also Vice-Adm. Sir P. W. B. Ashmore, Sir Francis Sykes, Bt.

ASHMORE, Vice-Adm. Sir Peter (William Beckwith), KCB 1972 (CB 1968); KCVO 1980 (MVO (4th Class) 1948); DSC 1942; Extra Equerry to the Queen, since 1952; *b* 4 Feb. 1921; *yr s* of late Vice-Adm. L. H. Ashmore, CB, DSO and late Tamara Vasilevna Schutt, Petrograd; *m* 1952, Patricia Moray Buller, *o d* of late Admiral Sir Henry Buller, GCVO, CB and of Lady Hermione Stuart; one *s* three *d*. *Educ:* Yardley Court; RN Coll., Dartmouth. Midshipman, 1939. Served War of 1939–45, principally in destroyers (despatches); Lieut, 1941; Equerry (temp.) to King George VI, 1946–48; Extra Equerry, 1948; Comdr, 1951; Captain, 1957; Deputy Director, RN Staff Coll., Greenwich, 1957; Captain (F) Dartmouth Training Squadron, 1960–61; Imperial Defence Coll.,

1962; Admiralty, Plans Division, 1963; Rear-Adm. 1966; Flag Officer, Admiralty Interview Board, 1966–67; Chief of Staff to C-in-C Western Fleet and to NATO C-in-C Eastern Atlantic, 1967–69; Vice-Adm. 1969; Chief of Allied Staff, NATO Naval HQ, S Europe, 1970–72, retired 1972. Master of HM's Household, 1973–86. *Recreations:* fishing, golf. *Address:* Netherdowns, Sundridge, near Sevenoaks, Kent TN14 6AR.

See also Adm. of the Fleet Sir E. B. Ashmore.

ASHMORE, Prof. Philip George; Professor of Physical Chemistry, The University of Manchester Institute of Science and Technology, 1963–81, now Professor Emeritus; *b* 5 May 1916; *m* 1943, Ann Elizabeth Scott; three *s* one *d*. *Educ:* Emmanuel Coll., Cambridge. Fellow, Asst Tutor and Dir of Studies of Natural Sciences, Emmanuel Coll., Cambridge, 1949–59; Lecturer in Physical Chem., Univ. of Cambridge, 1953–63; Fellow and Tutor to Advanced Students, Churchill Coll., Cambridge, 1959–63. Vice-Principal Acad. Affairs, UMIST, 1973, 1974. Course Consultant, Open Univ., 1981–. *Publications:* The Catalysis and Inhibition of Chemical Reactions, 1963; (ed) Reaction Kinetics, 1975; RIC Monographs for Teachers: No 5 and No 9; many papers in: TFS, International Symposium on Combustion, Jl of Catalysis. *Address:* 30 Queen Edith's Way, Cambridge CB1 4PN. *T:* Cambridge 248225.

ASHTON, family name of **Baron Ashton of Hyde.**

ASHTON OF HYDE, 3rd Baron *cr* 1911; **Thomas John Ashton,** TD; Director: Barclays Bank PLC and subsidiary companies; Barclays Merchant Bank Ltd; Barclays Bank of Canada; *b* 19 Nov. 1926; *s* of 2nd Baron Ashton of Hyde and of Marjorie Nell, *d* of late Hon. Marshall Jones Brooks; *S* father, 1983; *m* 1957, Pauline Trewlove, *er d* of late Lt-Col R. H. L. Brackenbury, OBE; two *s* two *d*. *Educ:* Eton; New Coll., Oxford (BA 1950, MA 1955). Sen. Exec. Local Dir, Barclays Bank, Manchester, 1968–81. Major retd, Royal Glos Hussars (TA). JP Oxon, 1965–68. *Heir:* *s* Hon. Thomas Henry Ashton, *b* 18 July 1958. *Address:* Fir Farm, Upper Slaughter, Bourton-on-the-Water GL54 2JR. *Club:* Boodle's.

ASHTON, Anthony Southcliffe; *b* 5 July 1916; *s* of late Prof. Thomas Southcliffe Ashton, FBA, and of Mrs Marion Hague Ashton; *m* 1939, Katharine Marion Louise Vivian; two *d*. *Educ:* Manchester Grammar Sch.; Hertford Coll., Oxford (MA). Economist, Export Credits Guarantee Dept, 1937. Served War of 1939–45, as driver and Lt-Col, RASC. Asst Financial Editor, Manchester Guardian, 1945; Dep. Asst Dir of Marketing, NCB, 1947; Manager, various depts of Vacuum Oil Co. (later Mobil Oil Co.), 1949; attended Advanced Management Programme, Harvard Business Sch., 1961; Treasurer, and later Finance Director, Esso Petroleum Co., 1961; Mem. Bd (Finance and Corporate Planning), Post Office Corp., 1970–73. Director: Tyzack and Partners Ltd, 1974–79; Provincial Insce Co., 1974–86. Member: Shipbuilding Industry Bd, 1967–71; Council of Manchester Business Sch., 1968–81; Dir, Oxford Univ. Business Summer Sch., 1974 (Mem., Steering Cttee, 1978–81). Trustee: PO Pension Fund, 1975–83; Tyzack Employee Trust, 1979–84; Dir, Exeter Trust, 1980–86 (Chm., 1982–86). Vice-Pres., Hertford Coll. Soc., 1977–. *Address:* Quarry Field, Stonewall Hill, Presteigne, Powys LD8 2HB. *T:* Presteigne 267447. *Club:* Army and Navy.

ASHTON, Sir Frederick (William Mallandaine), OM 1977; CH 1970; Kt 1962; CBE 1950; Founder-choreographer to the Royal Ballet (Principal Choreographer, 1933–70, and Director, 1963–70); *b* Guayaquil, Ecuador, 17 Sept. 1904; *s* of George Ashton and Georgiana Fulcher. *Educ:* The Dominican Fathers, Lima, Peru; Dover Coll., Dover. With Ballet Rambert, 1926–33, as dancer and choreographer; Ida Rubinstein Company, Paris, 1929–30. Best known ballets: Les Patineurs, Apparitions, Horoscope, Symphonic Variations, Façade, Wedding Bouquet, Scènes de Ballet, Cinderella (first English choreographer to do a 3–act ballet), Illuminations, Sylvia, Romeo and Juliet, Ondine, La Fille Mal Gardée, Les Deux Pigeons, Marguerite and Armand, The Dream, Sinfonietta, Jazz Calendar, Enigma Variations, Walk to the Paradise Garden, Birthday Offering, A Month in the Country, Rhapsody, Varii Capricci, etc. Film: The Tales of Beatrix Potter (choreography, and appeared as Mrs Tiggywinkle), 1971. Served in Royal Air Force during War as Flight Lieut. Queen Elizabeth II Coronation Award, Royal Academy of Dancing, 1959. Freedom of City of London, 1981. Hon. DLitt: Durham, 1962; East Anglia, 1967; Hon. DMus: London, 1970; Hull, 1971; Oxon, 1976. Legion of Honour (France), 1960; Order of Dannebrog (Denmark), 1964. *Relevant publications:* Frederick Ashton: a Choreographer and his Ballets, by Z. Dominic and J. S. Gilbert, 1971; Frederick Ashton and his Ballets, by David Vaughan, 1977. *Recreation:* dancing. *Address:* Royal Opera House, Covent Garden, WC2.

ASHTON, George Arthur, CEng; FIMechE; Chairman, Seamless Tubes Ltd, since 1983; *b* 27 Nov. 1921; *s* of Lewis and Mary Ashton; *m* 1st, 1948, Joan Rutter (decd); one *s*; 2nd, 1978, Pauline Jennifer Margett. *Educ:* Llanidloes Grammar Sch.; Birmingham Central Tech. Coll. Student Engrg Apprentice, Austin Motor Co., 1939–42. HM Forces, 1943–47 (Temp. Major, REME). Works Dir, Tubes Ltd, 1958; Tech. Dir, 1962, Dep. Man. Dir, 1966, TI Steel Tube Div.; Dir, Tube Investments, 1969; Man. Dir, Machine Div., 1974, Technical Dir and Business Area Chm., 1978–84, TI Group plc. Dir, A. Lee & Sons plc, 1981–. Dep. Chm., Steering Cttee, WINTECH, Welsh Develt Agency, 1984–. Pres., BISPA, 1974–75; Vice-Pres., MTIRA, 1986– (Chm. Council, 1982–86). FRSA 1981; CBIM. *Recreations:* gardening, walking. *Address:* Barn Cottage, Longford, Derby DE6 3DT. *T:* Great Cubley 561. *Club:* Naval and Military.

ASHTON, Joseph William; MP (Lab) Bassetlaw Division of Notts since Nov. 1968; journalist; *b* 9 Oct. 1933; *s* of Arthur and Nellie Ashton, Sheffield; *m* 1957, Margaret Patricia Lee; one *d*. *Educ:* High Storrs Grammar Sch.; Rotherham Technical Coll. Engineering Apprentice, 1949–54; RAF National Service, 1954–56; Cost Control Design Engineer, 1956–68; Sheffield City Councillor, 1962–69. PPS to Sec. of State for Energy, formerly Sec. of State for Industry, 1975–76; an Asst Govt Whip, 1976–77; Opposition Spokesman on Energy, 1979–81. Columnist for: Sheffield Star, 1970–75, 1979–80; Labour Weekly, 1971–82; Daily Star, 1979–. Columnist of the Year, What the Papers Say, Granada TV, 1984. *Publications:* Grass Roots, 1977; A Majority of One (stage play), 1981. *Recreations:* watching Sheffield Wednesday, reading, do-it-yourself, motoring, films, theatre. *Address:* 16 Ranmoor Park Road, Sheffield. *T:* Sheffield 301763. *Clubs:* Foundry Working Men's (Sheffield); Doncaster Road Working Men's (Langold); various Miners' Institutes, etc.

ASHTON, Kenneth Bruce; General Secretary, National Union of Journalists, 1977–85; *b* 9 Nov. 1925; *s* of late Harry Anstice Ashton and of Olive May Ashton; *m* 1955, Amy Anne, *d* of late John Baines Sidebotham and of Amy Sidebotham; four *s*. *Educ:* Latymer Upper School. Served Army, 1942–46. Reporter: Hampstead and Highgate Express, 1947–50; Devon and Somerset News, Mansfield Reporter, Sheffield Star, 1950–58; Sub-Editor, Sheffield Telegraph, Daily Express, London and Daily Mail, Manchester, 1958–75. Nat. Exec. Cttee Mem., NUJ, 1968–75, Pres., 1975, Regional Organiser, 1975–77. Member: TUC Printing Industries' Cttee, 1975—86; Printing and Publishers' Industry Training Bd, 1977–83; British Cttee, Journalists in Europe, 1980; Communications Adv. Cttee, UK Nat. Commn for Unesco, 1981–86; consultative Mem., Press Council, 1977–80. Deported from S Africa, Jan. 1981. *Recreation:* gliding. *Address:* 34 Manor Park Drive, North Harrow, Middx. *Clubs:* Manchester Press (Pres. 1971); Derbyshire and Lancashire Gliding.

ASHTON, Rt. Rev. Leonard (James), CB 1970; Bishop in Cyprus and The Gulf, 1976–83; Hon. Assistant Bishop, Diocese of Oxford, since 1984; Hon. Canon and Prebendary of St Botolph, Lincoln Cathedral, 1969–73, Canon Emeritus since 1973; *b* 27 June 1915; *s* of late Henry Ashton and Sarah Ashton (*née* Ing). *Educ:* Tyndale Hall, Bristol. Ordained, Chester, 1942; Curate, Cheadle, 1942–45; Chap. RAF, 1945–; N Wales, 1945; AHQ Malaya and Singapore, 1946; BC Air Forces, Japan, 1947–48; Halton, 1948–49; Feltwell, 1949–50; Chap. and Lectr, RAF Chap. Sch., Cheltenham, 1950–53; Sen. Chap., AHQ Iraq, 1954–55; RAF Coll., Cranwell, 1956–60; Br. Forces Arabian Peninsular and Mid. East Command, 1960–61; Asst Chap. Chief, Trng Commands, 1962–65; Res. Chap., St Clement Danes, Strand, 1965–69; Chaplain-in-Chief, (with relative rank of Air Vice-Marshal) RAF, and Archdeacon of RAF, 1969–73; QHC, 1967–73; Asst Bishop in Jerusalem, 1974–76; Episcopal Canon, St George's Cathedral, Jerusalem, 1976–83; Hon. Asst Bishop, Jerusalem and Middle East, 1983–84; Commissary for Bishop in Iran and Bishop in Jerusalem, 1984–. ChStJ 1976. *Recreations:* gardening, photography. *Address:* 60 Lowndes Avenue, Chesham, Bucks. *T:* Chesham 782952. *Clubs:* Royal Air Force, Royal Commonwealth Society.

ASHTON, Prof. Norman (Henry), CBE 1976; DSc (London); FRS 1971; FRCP, FRCS; FRCPath; Professor of Pathology, University of London, 1957–78, now Emeritus; Director, Department of Pathology, Institute of Ophthalmology, University of London, 1948–78; Consultant Pathologist, Moorfields Eye Hospital, 1948–78; *b* 11 Sept. 1913; 2nd *s* of Henry James and Margaret Ann Ashton. *Educ:* West Kensington Central Sch.; King's Coll. and Westminster Hosp. Med. Sch., Univ. of London. Westminster Hospital: Prize in Bacteriology, 1938; Editor Hosp. Gazette, 1939–40; House Surg., House Phys., Sen. Casualty Officer and RMO, 1939–41. Asst Pathologist, Princess Beatrice Hosp., 1939; Dir of Pathology, Kent and Canterbury Hosp., and Blood Transfusion Officer of East Kent, 1941. Lieut-Col RAMC, Asst Dir of Pathology and Officer i/c Central Pathological Lab., Middle East, 1946. Pathologist to the Gordon Hosp., 1947; Reader in Pathology, Univ. of London, 1953; Fellow in Residence, Johns Hopkins Hosp., Baltimore, 1953, and Visiting Prof. there, 1959. Emeritus Fellow, Leverhulme Trust. Vis. Research Fellow, Merton Coll., Oxford, 1980. Lectures: Walter Wright, 1959; Banting, 1960; Clapp (USA), 1964; Proctor (USA), 1965; Bradshaw (RCP), 1971; Montgomery, 1973; Foundn, Assoc. of Clinical Pathologists, 1985. Edward Nettleship Prize for Research in Ophthalmology, 1953; BMA Middlemore Prize, 1955; Proctor Medal for Research in Ophthalmology (USA), 1957; Doyne Medal (Oxford), 1960; William Julius Mickle Fellow, Univ. London, 1961; Bowman Medal, 1965; Donder's Medal, 1967; Wm Mackenzie Memorial Medal, 1967; Gonin Medal, 1978; 1st Jules Stein Award, USA, 1981; Francis Richardson Cross Medal, 1982. Chm., Fight for Sight Appeal; Trustee, Sir John Soane's Museum, 1977–82. Member, Board of Governors: Moorfields Eye Hosp., 1963–66 and 1975–78; Hosp. for Sick Children, Gt Ormond St, 1977–80; Royal Nat. Coll. for the Blind, 1977–; Member: Brit. Nat. Cttee for Prevention of Blindness, 1973–78; Royal Postgrad. Med. Sch. Council, 1977–80; Council, RCPath, 1963–66 and 1976–78 (Founder Fellow); Governing Body, Brit. Postgrad. Med. Fedn, 1967–82, and Cent. Acad. Council, 1957–78 (Chm., 1967–70); Council, RSM, 1971–79, and Exec. Cttee, 1976–81; Med. Adv. Bd, British Retinitis Pigmentosa Soc.; Pathological Soc. of Great Britain and Ireland; European Assoc. for Study of Diabetes; Chapter Gen. and Hosp. Cttee of St John; Oxford Ophthalmological Congress; Medical Art Soc.; Member, Cttee of Management: Inst. of Ophthalmology, 1953–78; Inst. of Child Health, 1960–65; Cardio-Thoracic Inst., 1972–78; Inst. of Rheumatology, 1973–77; Mem. Bd of Governors, Brendoncare Foundn, 1984–. President: Ophth. Sect., RSM, 1972–74; Assoc. of Clinical Pathologists, 1978–79; Ophth. Soc. of UK, 1979–81; Chm., Brit. Diab. Assoc. Cttee on Blindness in Diabetes, 1967–70. Fellow, Inst. of Ophthalmology. Hon. Life Mem., British Diabetic Association; Life Pres. European Ophth. Pathology Soc.; Pres. Brit. Div. Internat. Acad. of Pathology, 1962. Hon. Member: Assoc. for Eye Research; Hellenic Ophth. Soc.; British Div., Internat. Acad. of Pathology; Gonin Club. Hon. Fellow: RSocMed; Coll. of Physicians, Philadelphia; Amer. Acad. Ophthal. and Otolaryng. Mem. Ed. Bd, Brit. Jl Ophthalmology, 1963–78, and Jl Histopathology. FRSocMed; Master, Soc. of Apothecaries of London, 1984–85; Freeman, City of London. Hon. DSc Chicago. KStJ. *Publications:* contrib. to books and numerous scientific articles in Jl of Pathology and Bacteriology, Brit. Jl of Ophthalmology, and Amer. Jl of Ophthalmology. *Recreations:* painting, gardening. *Address:* 2 The Cloisters, Westminster Abbey, SW1. *T:* 01–222 4982. *Clubs:* Athenæum, Garrick.

ASHTON, Rev. Canon Patrick Thomas, LVO 1963; Chaplain to the Queen, since 1955; *b* 27 July 1916; *s* of Lieut-Col S. E. Ashton, OBE; *m* 1942, Mavis St Clair Brown, New Zealand; three *d* (one *s* decd). *Educ:* Stowe; Christ Church, Oxford (MA); Westcott House, Cambridge. Served War of 1939–45 as Captain, Oxfordshire Yeomanry; Curate, St Martin-in-the-Fields, 1947–51; Rector of All Saints, Clifton, Beds, 1951–55; Rector of Sandringham with West Newton and Appleton, and Domestic Chaplain to the Queen, 1955–70; Rector: Sandringham Gp of Eight Parishes, 1963–70; Swanborough Team of Parishes, 1970–73; Priest-in-charge of Avebury with Winterbourne Monkton and Berwick Bassett, 1974–77; Rector, Upper Kennet team of Parishes, 1975–77; a Canon of Salisbury Cathedral, 1975; Rural Dean of Marlborough, 1976–77. *Address:* Field Cottage, Bottlesford, Pewsey, Wilts. *T:* Woodborough 340.

ASHTON, Prof. Robert, PhD; Professor of English History, University of East Anglia, since 1963; *b* 21 July 1924; *s* of late Joseph and late Edith F. Ashton; *m* 1946, Margaret Alice Sedgwick; two *d*. *Educ:* Magdalen Coll. Sch., Oxford; University Coll., Southampton (1942–43, 1946–49); London Sch. of Economics (1949–52). BA 1st Cl. hons (London) 1949; PhD (London) 1953; Asst Lecturer in Economic History, Univ. of Nottingham, 1952; Lecturer, 1954; Senior Lecturer, 1961; Vis. Associate Prof. in History, Univ. of California, Berkeley, 1962–63; Prof. of English History, 1963, and Dean of Sch. of English Studies, 1964–67, Univ. of East Anglia. Vis. Fellow, All Souls Coll., Oxford, 1973–74 and 1987; James Ford Special Lectr in History, Oxford, 1982. FRHistS 1960 (Vice-Pres., 1983). *Publications:* The Crown and the Money Market, 1603–1640, 1960; Charles I and the City, in Essays in the Economic and Social History of Tudor and Stuart England in honour of R. H. Tawney (ed F. J. Fisher), 1961; James I by his Contemporaries, 1969; The Civil War and the Class Struggle, in The English Civil War and After 1642–1658 (ed R. H. Parry), 1970; The English Civil War: Conservatism and Revolution 1603–49, 1978; The City and the Court 1603–1643, 1979; Reformation and Revolution 1558–1660, 1984; articles in learned periodicals. *Recreations:* music, looking at old buildings, wine. *Address:* The Manor House, Brundall, Norwich NR13 5JY. *T:* Norwich 713368.

ASHTON, Roy; a Recorder of the Crown Court, since 1979; barrister-at-law; *b* 20 Oct. 1928; *s* of Charles and Lilian Ashton; *m* 1954, Brenda Alice Dales; one *s* one *d*. *Educ:* Boston Grammar Sch.; Nottingham Univ. (LLB Hons). National Service, Directorate of Legal Services, RAF, 1951–53. Called to the Bar, Lincoln's Inn, 1954. Dep. Chairman, Agricultural Land Tribunal, 1978–. *Recreations:* reading, chess, film collecting. *Address:* Pitsford House East, Manor Road, Pitsford, Northants. *Club:* Northampton and County.

ASHTON HILL, Norman, MBE (mil.) 1945; TD; Consultant, Ashton Hill Bond, Solicitors and Commissioners for Oaths, 1981 (Principal Partner, 1948–81); *b* 1 March 1918; *s* of Sydney and Marguerite Ashton Hill, Bewdley, Worcs; *m* 1971, Ireina Hilda Marie; (one *s* two *d* by former *m*). *Educ*: Uppingham Sch.; Birmingham Univ. (LLB Hons). Served War, 1939–45: commnd 2nd Lieut TA, 1939; BEF, BLA, BAOR; Staff Coll. (psc), mentioned in despatches; NW Europe War Crimes, 1945–46; Hon. Lt-Col, Royal Warwickshire Regt. Enrolled Gibraltar Bar, 1971. Chm., Radio Trent Ltd, 1973–79; Dir, 1971–78, Vice-Chm., 1972–78, Bonser Engrg Ltd. Director: Lunn Poly (formerly Sir Henry Lunn Ltd) (Vice-Chm., 1954–68); Eagle Aviation Ltd, and Cunard Eagle Airways Ltd and Group, 1952–68; North Midland Construction Plc, 1971–85; Morgan Housing Co. Ltd and Group, 1962–81; Derby Music Finance Ltd, 1978–84; Cooper & Roe Ltd, 1979–80. Chairman: Air Transport Cttee, ABCC, 1958–82 (a Vice-Pres. ABCC, 1977–); Air Transp. Cttee, ICC UK (formerly British National Chamber of Internat. Chamber of Commerce), 1970–; Air Transport Users Cttee, 1980–82 (Mem., 1976–82; Dep. Chm., 1978–79; Hon. Consultant, 1982–); Fedn of Air Transport Users Representatives in the Economic Community, 1982–. CRAeS 1980. NSPCC: Hon. Vice-Pres., and formerly Hon. Gen. and Cases Sec., Nottingham Br.; Mem. Central Exec. Cttee, 1955–80, Vice-Chm., 1974–80; Hon. Vice-Pres. Hon. Vice-Consul for Norway, Notts, 1955–80. Assistant, Glaziers Co., 1978–. FRSA. Kt (1st Cl.), Order of St Olav, Norway, 1972. *Recreations*: gardening, shooting, humanities. *Address*: Apartado 493, San Pedro de Alcantara, Málaga, Spain. *Club*: Royal Aero.

ASHTOWN, 6th Baron *cr* 1800; **Christopher Oliver Trench;** *b* 23 March 1931; *s* of Algernon Oliver Trench (*d* 1955) (*g g s* of 2nd Baron) and Muriel Dorothy (*d* 1954), *d* of Frank Thorne, Weston-super-Mare; *S* kinsman, 1979. *Recreation*: study of the philosophy of Gurdjeff and Ouspensky. *Heir*: cousin Sir Nigel Clive Cosby Trench, *qv. Address*: 131 Stinson Street, Hamilton, Ontario, Canada.

ASHWELL, Major Arthur Lindley, DSO 1916; OBE 1946; TD 1926; DL; late 8th Battalion Sherwood Foresters; *b* 19 Jan. 1886; *o s* of Arthur Thomas Ashwell, solicitor, Nottingham; *m* 1932, Sylvia Violet (*d* 1980), *widow* of Harold Gallatly, MC, and *d* of Philip Scratchley. *Educ*: Lambrook, Bracknell, Winchester Coll. Served European War, 1915 (wounded thrice, despatches, DSO). DL Notts, 1941. *Address*: Flat 3, 19 The Vale, SW3. *Clubs*: Naval and Military, Royal Automobile.

ASHWORTH, Prof. Graham William, CBE 1980; Professor of Urban Environmental Studies, University of Salford, since 1973; Director: University of Salford Environmental Institute, since 1978; CAMPUS (Campaign to promote University of Salford), since 1981; *b* 14 July 1935; *s* of Frederick William Ashworth and Ivy Alice Ashworth; *m* 1960, Gwyneth Mai Morgan-Jones; three *d. Educ*: Devonport High Sch., Plymouth; Univ. of Liverpool (Master of Civic Design, BArch). RIBA, PPRTPI, FRSA, MInstEnvSci, FBIM. LCC (Hook New Town Project), 1959–61; consultancy with Graeme Shankland, 1961–64; architect to Civic Trust, 1964–65; Dir, Civic Trust for North-West, 1965–73. Member: Skeffington Cttee on Public Participation in Planning, 1969; North-West Adv. Council of BBC, 1970–75 (Chm.); NW Economic Planning Council (and Sub-gp Chm.), 1968–79; Countryside Commn, 1974–77; Merseyside Urban Develt Corp., 1981–; (non-exec.) North Western Electricity Bd, 1985–. Governor, Northern Baptist Coll., 1966–82; Pres., Royal Town Planning Inst., 1973–74; Chairman: Exec. Cttee, Civic Trust for North-West, 1973–; Instn of Environmental Sciences, 1980–82. Member: Council, St George's House, Windsor, 1982–; Council, Baptist Union, 1983–. Editor, Internat. Jl of Environmental Educn, 1981–. *Publication*: An Encyclopædia of Planning, 1973. *Recreations*: gardening, painting, church and social work. *Address*: Manor Court Farm, Preston New Road, Samlesbury, Preston PR5 0UP. *Clubs*: Athenæum, National Liberal.

ASHWORTH, Sir Herbert, Kt 1972; Chairman: Nationwide Building Society, 1970–82 (Deputy-Chairman, 1968–70); Nationwide Housing Trust, since 1983; *b* 30 Jan. 1910; *s* of Joseph Hartley Ashworth; *m* 1936, Barbara Helen Mary, *d* of late Douglas D. Henderson; two *s* one *d. Educ*: Burnley Grammar Sch.; London Univ. (grad. econ. and law). General Manager, Portman Building Soc., 1938–50; General Manager, Co-operative Permanent Building Soc., 1950–61; Director and General Manager, Hallmark Securities Ltd, 1961–66. Dep. Chm., 1964–68, Chm., 1968–73, Housing Corp. Dir, The Builder Ltd, 1975–80. Chm., Surrey and W Sussex Agricl Wages Cttee, 1974–. Vice-President: Building Socs Assoc.; Building Socs Inst., Metropolitan Assoc. of Building Socs. *Publications*: Housing in Great Britain, 1951; Building Society Work Explained, (current edn), 1977; The Building Society Story, 1980. *Address*: 8 Tracery, Park Road, Banstead, Surrey SM7 3DD. *T*: Burgh Heath 52608.

ASHWORTH, Ian Edward; Circuit Administrator, Western Circuit, Lord Chancellor's Office (Under Secretary), since 1970; *b* 3 March 1930; *s* of William Holt and late Cicely Ashworth, Rochdale; *m* Pauline, *er d* of Maurice James Heddle, MBE, JP, and Gladys Heddle, Westliff-on-Sea; two *s* one *d. Educ*: Manchester Grammar Sch.; The Queen's Coll., Oxford (BCL, MA). Admitted Solicitor, 1956; FGA 1983. Asst Solicitor, Rochdale, 1956–58; Dep. Town Clerk, Dep. Clerk of Peace, Canterbury, 1958–63; Town Clerk, Clerk of Peace, Deal, 1963–66; Town Clerk, Rugby, 1966–70. *Recreations*: music, gemmology, gardening. *Address*: 5 St Hilary Close, Stoke Bishop, Bristol BS9 1DA. *T*: Bristol 685236. *Club*: United Oxford & Cambridge University.

ASHWORTH, James Louis, FIMechE, FIEE, ARTC (Salford); Full-Time Member for Operations, Central Electricity Generating Board, 1966–70, retired; *b* 7 March 1906; *s* of late James and late Janet Ashworth; *m* 1931 Clara Evelyn Arnold; one *s* two *d. Educ*: Stockport Grammar Sch.; Salford Royal Coll. of Technology. Apprenticeship with Mirrlees, Bickerton & Day Ltd, Stockport (Diesel Oil Engine Manufrs), 1924–29; Metro-Vickers Electrical Co. Ltd, 1929; Manchester Corp. Elec. Dept, Stuart Street Gen. Stn, 1930–32; Hull Corp. Elec. Dept, 1932–35; Halifax Corp. Elec. Dept, 1935–40; Mersey Power Co. Ltd, Runcorn, 1940–48; British Elec. Authority, N West: Chief Generation Engr (O), 1948–57; Dep. Divisional Controller, 1957–58; Central Elec. Gen. Bd, N West, Merseyside and N Wales Region: Dep. Regional Dir, 1958–62; Regional Dir, 1962–66. *Recreations*: gardening, photography, travel, reading. *Address*: Chase Cottage, 23 The Chase, Reigate, Surrey. *T*: Redhill 61279.

ASHWORTH, Brig. John Blackwood, CBE 1962; DSO 1944; DL; retired 1965; *b* 7 Dec. 1910; *s* of Lieut-Col H. S. Ashworth, Royal Sussex Regt (killed in action, 1917) and late Mrs E. M. Ashworth; *m* 1946, Eileen Patricia, *d* of late Major H. L. Gifford (Royal Ulster Rifles) and of Lady Gooch; one *d. Educ*: Wellington Coll.; RMC, Sandhurst. Commissioned Royal Sussex Regt, 1930; Instructor RMC, 1938; War of 1939–45 (despatches twice); OC Training Centre, 1942; OC 1/5 Queen's Royal Regt (wounded, DSO), 1944; GSO1, War Office, 1944; OC 4/5 Royal Sussex, 1945; OC 1st Royal Sussex, 1946; GSO1, Brit. Middle East Office, 1947; AMS War Office, 1948; OC 1st Royal Sussex, 1951; Comdt Joint Sch. of Chemical Warfare, 1954; Commander 133rd Inf. Bde (TA), 1957; Director of Military Training, War Office, 1959–62; Inspector of Boys' Training, War Office, 1962–65. ADC to the Queen, 1961–65. Col The Royal Sussex Regt, 1963–66; Dep. Col, The Queen's Regt (Royal Sussex), 1967–68. DL Sussex 1972.

OStJ 1950. Grand Officer, Order of House of Orange, 1967. *Address*: 16 Castlegate, New Brook Street, Ilkley, W Yorks LS29 8DF. *T*: Ilkley 602404.

ASHWORTH, Prof. John Michael, DSc; FIBiol; Vice-Chancellor, University of Salford, since 1981; Chairman, National Computing Centre, since 1983; *b* 27 Nov. 1938; *s* of late Jack Ashworth and late Constance Mary Ousman; *m* 1963, Ann Knight (*d* 1985); one *s* three *d. Educ*: West Buckland Sch., N Devon; Exeter Coll., Oxford (MA, DSc; Hon. Fellow, 1983); Leicester Univ. (PhD). FIBiol 1974. Dept of Biochemistry, Univ. of Leicester: Res. Demonstr, 1961–63; Lectr, 1963–71; Reader, 1971–73; Prof. of Biology, Univ. of Essex, 1974–79 (on secondment to Cabinet Office, 1976–79); Under-Sec., Cabinet Office, 1979–81 and Chief Scientist, Central Policy Review Staff, 1976–81. Harkness Fellow of Commonwealth Fund, NY, at Brandeis Univ. and Univ. of Calif, 1965–67. NEDO: Chm., Information Technology EDC, 1983–; Mem., Electronics EDC, 1983–. Chm., Nat. Accreditation Council for Certification Bodies, BSI, 1984–. Colworth Medal, Biochem. Soc., 1972. *Publications*: Cell Differentiation, 1972; (with J. Dee) The Slime Moulds, 1976; over 70 pubns in prof. jls on biochem., genet., cell biolog. and educnl topics. *Recreation*: windsurfing. *Address*: University of Salford, Salford M5 4WT.

ASHWORTH, Peter Anthony Frank; Director, Leeds Permanent Building Society, since 1971 (President, 1978); *b* 24 Aug. 1935; *s* of Peter Ormerod and Dorothy Christine Ashworth; *m* 1964, Elisabeth Crompton; one *s* one *d. Educ*: Leeds Grammar School. Articled to Hollis & Webb, Chartered Surveyors, Leeds (now Weatherall, Hollis & Gale), 1953–56; Partner, 1961–80. FRICS; ACIArb. *Recreations*: golf, gardening. *Address*: 4 Bridge Paddock, Collingham, Wetherby LS22 5BN. *T*: Collingham Bridge 72953. *Club*: Alwoodley Golf (Leeds).

ASHWORTH, Piers, QC 1973; a Recorder of the Crown Court, since 1974; *b* 27 May 1931; *s* of Tom and Mollie Ashworth; *m* 1st, 1959, Iolene Jennifer (marr. diss. 1978), *yr d* of W. G. Foxley; three *s* one *d*; 2nd, 1980, Elizabeth, *er d* of A. J. S. Aston. *Educ*: Christ's Hospital; Pembroke Coll., Cambridge (scholar). Commnd Royal Signals, 1951. BA (Cantab) 1955; Harmsworth Law Scholar, 1956; called to Bar, Middle Temple, 1956, Bencher, 1984; Midland and Oxford circuit. *Recreations*: sailing, squash, tennis, bridge. *Address*: 2 Harcourt Buildings, Temple, EC4Y 9DB. *T*: 01–583 9020.

ASHWORTH, Prof. William; Professor of Economic and Social History, University of Bristol, 1958–82, Pro-Vice-Chancellor, 1975–78; *b* 11 March 1920; *s* of Harold and Alice Ashworth; unmarried. *Educ*: Todmorden Grammar Sch.; London Sch. of Economics and Political Science. Served 1941–45, RAPC and REME. BSc (Econ.) 1946; PhD 1950. Research Assistant, London Sch. of Economics and Political Science, 1946–47; on staff of Cabinet Office (Historical Section), 1947–48; Assistant Lecturer and Lecturer in Economic History, London Sch. of Economics and Political Science, 1948–55; Reader in Economic History in the Univ. of London, 1955–58. Dean, Faculty of Social Sciences, Univ. of Bristol, 1968–70. *Publications*: A Short History of the International Economy, 1952 (revised 1962, 1975); Contracts and Finance (History of the Second World War: UK Civil Series), 1953; The Genesis of Modern British Town Planning, 1954; An Economic History of England, 1870–1939, 1960; History of the British Coal Industry: the nationalized industry 1946–1982, 1986; contributor to: London, Aspects of Change, ed by Centre for Urban Studies, 1964; Victoria County History of Essex, 1966; The Study of Economic History, ed N. B. Harte, 1971. Articles and reviews in Economic History Review and other jls. *Address*: Flat 14, Wells Court, Wells Promenade, Ilkley LS29 9LG. *T*: Ilkley 603157.

ASIMOV, Prof. Isaac, PhD; Professor of Biochemistry, University of Boston, since 1979; author; *b* 2 Jan. 1920; *s* of Judah Asimov and Anna Rachel (*née* Berman); *m* 1st, 1942, Gertrude Blugerman; one *s* one *d*; 2nd, 1973, Dr Janet Jeppson. *Educ*: Columbia Univ. (BS 1939, MA 1941, PhD 1948, all in chemistry). Joined faculty of Boston Univ. Sch. of Medicine, 1949; retd from academic labors, 1958, but retained title. First professional sale of short story, 1938; first book published, 1950; 300th book published, 1984. *Publications*: 340 books, including: I, Robot, 1950; The Human Body, 1963; Asimov's Guide to Shakespeare, 1970; Asimov's Guide to Science, 1972; Murder at the ABA, 1976; The Collapsing Universe, 1977; In Memory Yet Green (autobiog., vol. 1), 1979; A Choice of Catastrophes, 1979; In Joy Still Felt (autobiog., vol. 2), 1980; In the Beginning, 1981; Foundation's Edge, 1982; The Robots of Dawn, 1983; Asimov's New Guide to Science, 1984; Asimov's Guide to Halley's Comet, 1985; Robots and Empire, 1985. *Recreation*: a man's work is his play: my recreation is writing. *Address*: 10 West 66th Street, New York, NY 10023, USA. *T*: 212–362–1564.

ASIROGLU, Vahap; Turkish Ambassador to the Court of St James's, 1978–81; *b* Karamürsel, 1916; *m*; one *c. Educ*: Galatasaray High Sch.; Istanbul Univ. (Faculty of Law). Third Sec., Second Political Dept, Min. of Foreign Affairs, 1943–46; successively, Third, Second, First Sec., Turkish Embassy, Prague, 1946–51; First Sec., Dept of Internat. Economic Affairs, MFA, 1951–53; First Sec. and Counsellor, Turkish Perm. Mission to UN, 1953–59; Asst Dir Gen., Dept of Internat. Econ. Affairs, MFA, 1959–60; Asst Dir Gen. and Dir Gen., Personnel and Admin. Dept, MFA, 1960; Dir Gen., UN and Internat. Instns Dept, MFA, 1960–62; Asst Perm. Rep., Turkish Perm. Mission to UN, 1962–65; Turkish Ambassador: to Copenhagen, 1965–68; to Jakarta, 1968–71; Sec. Gen., Reg. Cooperation for Develt (a reg. org. between Turkey, Iran and Pakistan), 1971–74; Sen. Counsellor, MFA, 1974; Director General: Dept of Consular Affairs, MFA, 1974–75; Dept of Cultural Affairs, MFA, 1975–76; Asst Sec. Gen. for Inf. and Cultural Affairs, MFA, 1976. Mem., UN Human Rights Commn, 1953–56; Turkish Rep., ICAO Conf., Montreal, 1956–57; Head of Turkish Delegn, GATT Conf., Tokyo, 1959; Asst Chm., Conf. on Immunities and Diplomatic Relns, Vienna, 1961; Chm., Fifth Commn, UN Gen. Assembly, 1967.

ASKE, Rev. Sir Conan, 2nd Bt *cr* 1922; Assistant Curate of St John-in-Bedwardine, Worcester, 1972–80; *b* 22 April 1912; *s* of Sir Robert William Aske, 1st Bt, TD, QC, LLD, and Edith (*d* 1918), *d* of Sir Walter Herbert Cockerline; *S* father 1954; *m* 1st, 1948, Vera Faulkner (*d* 1960); 2nd, 1965, Rebecca, *d* of Hugh Grant, Wick, Caithness. *Educ*: Rugby; Balliol Coll., Oxford. TA, London Irish Rifles, 1939; served, 1939–49, with East York Regt, Sudan Defence Force, Somalia Gendarmerie. Major, Civil Affairs Officer, Reserved Area of Ethiopia and The Ogaden, 1949–51; Schoolmaster, Hillstone, Malvern, 1952–69; Asst Curate, Hagley, Stourbridge, 1970–72. *Heir*: *b* Robert Edward Aske [*b* 21 March 1915; *m* 1940, Joan Bingham, *o d* of Captain Bingham Ackerley, Cobham; one *s*]. *Address*: 167 Malvern Road, Worcester WR2 4NN. *T*: Worcester 422817.

ASKEW, Barry Reginald William; journalist, broadcaster and public relations consultant; *b* 13 Dec. 1936; *s* of late Reginald Ewart Askew and Jane Elizabeth Askew; *m* 1st, 1958, June Roberts (marr. diss. 1978), *d* of Vernon and late Betty Roberts; one *s* one *d*; 2nd, 1980, Deborah Parker, *d* of Harold and Enid Parker. *Educ*: Lady Manners Grammar Sch., Bakewell, Derbys. Trainee reporter upwards, Derbyshire Times, 1952–57; Reporter and sub-ed., Sheffield Telegraph, 1957–59; reporter, feature writer and broadcaster, Raymonds News Agency, Derby, 1959–61; Editor, Matlock Mercury, 1961–63; Industrial Correspondent, Asst Ed., Dep. Ed., Sheffield Telegraph, later Morning Telegraph, Sheffield, 1964–68; Associate Ed., The Star, Sheffield, 1968; Editor, 1968–81,

Dir, 1978–81, Lancashire Evening Post; Editor, News of the World, 1981. Presenter and anchor man: ITV, 1970–81; BBC Radio 4, 1971–72; BBC 1, 1972; BBC 2, 1972–76. Mem., Davies Cttee to reform hosp. complaints procedures in UK, 1971–73. Campaigning Journalist of 1971, IPC Nat. Press Awards; Journalist of 1977, British Press Awards; Crime Reporter of 1977, Witness Box Awards. *Recreations:* Rugby, chess, reading military history, golf. *Address:* The School House, Orton, near Penrith, Cumbria. *T:* Orton 434. *Club:* Preston Grasshoppers RF.

ASKEW, Bryan; Personnel Director, Samuel Smith Old Brewery (Tadcaster), since 1982; Chairman, Yorkshire Regional Health Authority, since 1983; *b* 18 Aug. 1930; *s* of John Pinkney Askew and Matilda Askew; *m* 1955, Millicent Rose Holder; two *d*. *Educ:* Wellfield Grammar Sch., Wingate, Co. Durham; Fitzwilliam Coll., Cambridge (MA Hons History). ICI Ltd, 1952–59; Consett Iron Co. Ltd (later part of British Steel Corporation), 1959–71; own consultancy, 1971–74; Samuel Smith Old Brewery (Tadcaster), 1974–. Member, Consett UDC, 1967–71; contested (C) General Elections: Penistone, 1964 and 1966; York, 1970. Mem., Duke of Edinburgh's Third Commonwealth Study Conf., Australia, 1968. Mem. Court, Univ. of Leeds, 1985–. *Recreations:* listening to music, reading, walking, particularly in Northumberland. *Address:* The Old Brewery, Tadcaster LS24 9SB. *T:* Tadcaster 832225.

ASKEW, John Marjoribanks Eskdale, CBE 1974; *b* 22 Sept. 1908; *o s* of late William Haggerston Askew, JP, Ladykirk, Berwicks, and Castle Hills, Berwick-on-Tweed; *m* 1st, 1933, Lady Susan Egerton (marr. diss., 1966), 4th *d* of 4th Earl of Ellesmere, MVO; one *s* one *d*; *m* 1976, Priscilla Anne, *e d* of late Algernon Ross-Farrow. *Educ:* Eton; Magdalene Coll., Cambridge (BA). Lieut 2 Bn Grenadier Guards, 1932; Capt. 1940; Major 1943; served NW Europe 1939–40 and 1944–45. Brigadier, Royal Company of Archers, Queen's Body Guard for Scotland. Convener: Berwicks CC, 1961; Border Regional Council, 1974–82. *Address:* Ladykirk, Berwicks. *T:* Berwick 82229; Castle Hills, Berwick-on-Tweed. *Clubs:* Boodle's; New (Edinburgh).
See also Baron Faringdon, Duke of Sutherland.

ASKEW, Rev. Canon Reginald James Albert; Principal of Salisbury and Wells Theological College since 1973; *b* 16 May 1928; *s* of late Paul Askew and Amy Wainwright; *m* 1953, Kate, *yr d* of late Rev. Henry Townsend Wigley; one *s* two *d*. *Educ:* Harrow; Corpus Christi Coll., Cambridge (MA); Lincoln Theological College. Curate of Highgate, 1957–61; Tutor and Chaplain of Wells Theol Coll., 1961–65, Vice-Principal 1966–69; Priest Vicar of Wells Cath., 1961–69; Vicar of Christ Church, Lancaster Gate, London, 1969–73; Canon of Salisbury Cathedral and Prebendary of Grantham Borealis, 1975–. *Publication:* The Tree of Noah, 1971. *Recreations:* music, gardening, cricket. *Address:* 19 The Close, Salisbury, Wilts. *T:* Salisbury 334223.

ASKONAS, Brigitte Alice, PhD; FRS 1973; Head of Division of Immunology, MRC, National Institute for Medical Research, London, since 1977; *b* 1 April 1923; *d* of late Charles F. Askonas and Rose Askonas. *Educ:* McGill Univ., Montreal (BSc, MSc); Cambridge Univ. (PhD). Research student, Sch. of Biochemistry, Univ. of Cambridge, 1949–52; Immunology Div., NIMR, 1953–; Dept of Bacteriology and Immunology, Harvard Med. Sch., Boston, 1961–62; Basel Inst. for Immunology, Basel, Switzerland, 1971–72. Hon. Member: Amer. Soc. of Immunology; Soc. française d'Immunologie. *Publications:* contrib. scientific papers to various biochemical and immunological jls and books. *Recreations:* art, travel. *Address:* 23 Hillside Gardens, N6 5SU. *T:* 01–348 6792.

ASKWITH, Hon. Betty Ellen, FRSL; *b* 26 June 1909; *o d* of late Baron Askwith, KCB, KC, LLD, and Lady Askwith, CBE; *m* 1950, Keith Miller Jones (*d* 1978). *Educ:* Lycée Français, London; North Foreland Lodge, Broadstairs. *Publications:* First Poems, 1928; If This Be Error, 1932; Poems, 1933; Green Corn, 1933; Erinna, 1937; Keats, 1940; The Admiral's Daughters, 1947; A Broken Engagement, 1950; The Blossoming Tree, 1954; The Tangled Web, 1960; A Step Out of Time, 1966; Lady Dilke, 1969; Two Victorian Families, 1971; The Lytteltons, 1975; A Victorian Young Lady, 1978; Piety and Wit: Harriet Countess Granville 1785–1862, 1982; (with Michael Russell) Crimean Courtship, 1985; with Theodora Benson: Lobster Quadrille, 1930; Seven Basketfuls, 1932; Foreigners, 1935; Muddling Through, 1936; How to Be Famous, 1937. *Translations:* The Tailor's Cake, 1947; A Hard Winter, 1947; Meeting, 1950. *Recreation:* reading Victorian novels. *Address:* 9/105 Onslow Square, SW7. *T:* 01–589 7126.

ASLIN, Elizabeth Mary; art historian; *b* 23 March 1923; *d* of Charles Herbert Aslin and Ethel Fawcett Aslin. *Educ:* various schools; Slade Sch. of Fine Art, Univ. of London. Res. Asst, Circulation Dept, V & A Museum, 1947; Asst Keeper i/c, Bethnal Green Museum, 1964–68; Asst Dir, V & A Museum, 1968–74; Keeper i/c, Bethnal Green Museum, 1974–81. Member: Victorian Soc.; Decorative Arts Soc. FRSA. *Publications:* Nineteenth Century English Furniture, 1962; The Aesthetic Movement: Prelude to Art Nouveau, 1969; E. W. Godwin, Furniture and Interior Decoration, 1986. *Recreations:* drawing, etching, travel. *Address:* 11 Fulmar Close, Hove, East Sussex BN3 6NW. *T:* Brighton 508467.

ASPEL, Michael Terence; broadcaster and writer; *b* 12 Jan. 1933; *s* of Edward and Violet Aspel; *m* 1st, 1957, Dian; two *s*; 2nd, 1962, Ann; twin *s* and *d*; 3rd 1977, Elizabeth; two *s* (and one *s* decd). *Educ:* Emanuel School. Tea boy, publishers, 1949–51. Nat. Service, KRRC and Para Regt, TA, 1951–53. Radio actor, 1954–57; television announcer, 1957–60, newsreader, 1960–68; freelance broadcaster, radio and TV, 1968–; occasional stage appearances. Pres., Stackpole Trust, 1985–; Vice-President: BLISS (Baby Life Support Systems), 1981–; ASBAH (Assoc. for Spina Bifida and Hydrocephalus), 1985–. Member: Equity, 1955–; Lord's Taverners; RYA. FZS. *Publications:* Polly Wants a Zebra (autobiog.), 1974; Hang On! (for children), 1982; (with Richard Hearsey) Child's Play, 1985; regular contribs to magazines. *Recreations:* water sports, theatre, cinema, eating, travel. *Address:* c/o Bagenal Harvey Organisation, 1A Cavendish Square, W1.

ASPELL, Col Gerald Laycock, TD (2 clasps); FCA; Vice Lord-Lieutenant of Leicestershire, since 1984; Deputy Chairman, Alliance and Leicester Building Society, 1985; *b* 10 April 1915; *s* of Samuel Frederick Aspell and Agnes Maude (*née* Laycock); *m* 1939, Mary Leeson Carroll, *d* of Rev. Ion Carroll, Cork; one *s* two *d*. *Educ:* Uppingham Sch. FCA 1938. Commnd 2nd Lieut, 4th Bn Leicestershire Regt, TA, 1933; served War of 1939–45 in UK and Burma, RE, RA, RAF; commanded 579 Light Anti-Aircraft Regt, RA (TA), 1946–51. Partner, Coopers & Lybrand, 1952–78; mem. of various nat. and local cttees of Inst. of Chartered Accountants during that time. Dir, 1964–85, Chm., 1978–85, Leicester Building Soc.; Local Dir, Eagle Star Insce Gp, 1949–84 (Chm., Midlands Bd, 1970–84). Chairman: Leicester and Dist Local Employment Cttee, then Leics Dist Manpower Cttee, 1971–79. Mem., Leicester Diocesan Bd of Finance, 1952–77. Civil Defence Controller, then Sub-Regl Dir CD, Leics, Rutland and Northants, 1956–65. Member: Leics and Rutland TAA, then E Midlands TAVRA, 1947–80 (Chm., Leics Cttee, 1969–80). Hon. Colonel: Royal Anglian Regt (Leics), 1972–79; Leics and Northants ACF, 1979–84. Grand Treasurer, United Grand Lodge of England, 1974–75. Trustee, Uppingham Sch., 1964– (Chm., 1977–). DL Leics, 1952. *Recreations:* cricket, tennis, squash, fishing, charitable involvements. *Address:* Laburnum House, Great Dalby, Melton Mowbray, Leics LE14 2HA. *T:* Melton Mowbray 63604. *Club:* Leicestershire (Leicester).

ASPIN, Norman, CMG 1968; HM Diplomatic Service, retired; Adviser and Secretary, East Africa Association, 1981–84; *b* 9 Nov. 1922; *s* of Thomas and Eleanor Aspin; *m* 1948, Elizabeth Irving; three *s*. *Educ:* Darwen Grammar Sch.; Durham Univ. (MA). War Service, 1942–45, Lieut RNVR. Demonstrator in Geography, Durham Univ., 1947–48; Asst Principal, Commonwealth Relations Office, 1948; served in India, 1948–51; Principal, Commonwealth Relations Office, 1952; served in Federation of Rhodesia and Nyasaland, 1954–57; British Deputy High Commissioner in Sierra Leone, 1961–63; Commonwealth Relations Office, 1963–65; British Embassy, Tel Aviv, 1966–69; IDC 1970; Head of Personnel Policy Dept, FCO, 1971–73; Under-Sec., FCO, 1973–76; Comr, British Indian Ocean Territory, 1976; British High Comr in Malta, 1976–79; Asst Under-Sec. of State, FCO, 1979–80. *Recreations:* sailing, tennis. *Address:* Mounsey Bank, Dacre, Cumbria CA11 0HL. *Club:* Naval.

ASPINALL, John Victor; Trustee, Howletts and Port Lympne Foundation, since 1984; Managing Director, Aspinall Holdings plc, since 1983; *b* 11 June 1926; *s* of late Col Robert Aspinall and of Mary, Lady Osborne; *m* 1st, 1956, Jane Gordon Hastings (marr. diss. 1966); one *s* one *d*; 2nd, 1966, Belinda Musker (marr. diss. 1972); 3rd, 1972, Lady Sarah Courage (*née* Curzon); one *s*. *Educ:* Rugby Sch.; Jesus Coll., Oxford. Howletts Zoo Park founded 1958; founded Clermont Club, 1962; Port Lympne Zoo Park founded 1973; Aspinall's Club founded 1978; Aspinall Curzon Club founded 1984. Won gaming case Crown *v* Aspinall, 1958. *Publications:* The Best of Friends, 1976, Amer. edn 1977, German edn 1978; contribs to Jl of Reproduction and Fertility, Ecologist. *Recreations:* wild animals, gambling. *Address:* 20 Curzon Street, W1Y 7AD. *T:* 01–629 4400.

ASPINALL, Wilfred; Parliamentary and Industrial Relations Consultant; Executive Director, Managerial, Professional & Staff Liaison Group, since 1978; Member: North Hertfordshire District Health Authority, since 1981; Hammersmith Special Health Authority, since 1981; Vice-President, Confédération International des Cadres (and Member Comité Directeur and CIC Bureau), since 1979; *b* 14 Sept. 1942; *s* of late Charles Aspinall and Elizabeth Aspinall; *m* 1973, Judith Mary, *d* of late Leonard James Pimlott and Kathleen Mary Pimlott; one *d*. *Educ:* Poynton Secondary Modern; Stockport Coll. for Further Educn. Staff, National Provincial Bank Ltd, 1960–69; Asst Gen. Sec., National Westminster Staff Assoc., 1969–75; Dep. Sec. (part-time), Council of Bank Staff Assocs, 1969–75; Mem., Banking Staff Council, 1970–77; Gen. Sec., Confedn of Bank Staff Assocs, 1975–79; Admin. Sec., Nationwide Bldg Soc. Staff Assoc., 1979; Gen. Sec., Halcrow Staff Assoc., 1979; Consultant: Nat. Unilever Managers Assoc., 1979–81; Royal Insurance Branch Managers Assoc., 1980–84. Mem., Professions Allied to Medicine, Whitley Management Negotiating Cttee, 1983–. *Recreations:* motoring, photography, fund raising for charity, social protection of individuals, travel—particularly to places of historical interest, social affairs and political history. *Address:* The Croft, Shillington Road, Pirton, Hitchin, Herts. *T:* Hitchin 712316; Tavistock House, Tavistock Square, WC1. *T:* 01–387 4499, 01–380 0472.

ASPINALL, William Briant Philip, OBE 1945; Headmaster, Queen's School, HQ Northern Army Group, Rheindahlen, 1960–72, retired; *b* 1912; *s* of William Pryce Aspinall and Ethel Eleanor (*née* Ravenscroft); *m* 1st, Aileen, *d* of Major R. FitzGerald; one *s*; 2nd, Phyllis, *d* of Leopold Hill. *Educ:* Royal Masonic Sch.; St John's Coll., Cambridge. Served War, GSO1 MI14, 1940–45. Headmaster, Sutton Valence Sch., 1950–53; Windsor Sch., Hamm, BAOR, 1953–58; King Richard Sch., Cyprus, 1959. *Recreations:* cricket, hockey, golf, etc. *Address:* 6 Cramptons, Mill Lane, Sissinghurst, Kent. *Clubs:* MCC; Rye Golf.

ASPINWALL, Jack Heywood; MP (C) Wansdyke, since 1983 (Kingswood, 1979–83); company director; *b* Feb. 1933; *m* Brenda Jean Aspinwall. *Educ:* Prescot Grammar School, Lancs; Marconi College, Chelmsford. Served RAF, 1949–56. Director, investment co. Mem., Avon County Council. Contested (L) Kingswood, Feb. and Oct. 1974. *Publication:* (comp.) Kindly Sit Down!: best after-dinner stories from both Houses of Parliament, 1983. *Address:* House of Commons, SW1A 0AA; 154 Bath Road, Willsbridge, Bristol.

ASPRAY, Rodney George, FCA; Chairman, Co-operative Bank, since 1986 (Director, since 1980); Chief Executive Officer, Norwest Cooperative Society, since 1969; *b* 1934. Secretary, Manchester and Salford Cooperative Society, 1965–69; Dir, Cooperative Wholesale Soc. Ltd, 1980–. Mem., Monopolies and Mergers Commn, 1975–81. FCA 1960. *Address:* Kambara, 4 Green Lane, Higher Poynton, Cheshire.

ASPREY, Algernon; independant artist and designer; *b* 2 June 1912; *s* of George Kenneth Asprey and Charlotte Esta Asprey; *m* 1939, Beatrice (*née* Bryant); one *s* two *d*. *Educ:* Bowden House Prep. Sch., Seaford; Charterhouse; Sch. of Art, Regent Street Polytechnic, London. Served War, 1940–46: commnd Scots Guards, Captain. Joined Asprey of Bond Street, 1933; with Aspreys, 1946–71, when own business, Algernon Asprey, formed; re-appointed Dir, Asprey & Co. Ltd, 1979–81; Chm., Algernon Asprey (Furnishing) Ltd, 1971–81. Chairman: Purchase Tax Cttee in post war years to disbandment; Guards Club, 1960–65. Pres., Bond Street Assoc., 1968–81 (Chm., 1965–68). Mem. Cttee, Friends of Royal Acad. Prime Warden, Worshipful Co. of Goldsmiths, 1977–78; Hon. Mem., Interior Decorators and Designers Assoc., 1983–. *Recreations:* painting, sailing, golf. *Address:* Magnolia Cottage, Upper House Lane, Shamley Green, Surrey GU5 0SX. *T:* Cranleigh 271502. *Club:* Buck's.

ASQUITH, family name of **Earl of Oxford and Asquith.**

ASQUITH, Viscount; Raymond Benedict Bartholomew Michael Asquith; HM Diplomatic Service; Foreign and Commonwealth Office, 1985; *b* 24 Aug. 1952; *er s* and *heir* of 2nd Earl of Oxford and Asquith, *qv*; *m* 1978, Mary Clare, *e d* of Francis Pollen; one *s* two *d*. *Educ:* Ampleforth; Balliol College, Oxford. FCO, 1980–83; First Sec., Moscow, 1983–85. *Heir:* *s* Hon. Mark Julian Asquith, *b* 13 May 1979. *Address:* Little Claveys, Mells, Frome, Somerset.

ASSHETON, family name of **Baron Clitheroe.**

ASTAIRE, Fred; actor, motion pictures; *b* 10 May 1899; *s* of F. E. Astaire and Ann Geilus; *m* 1933, Phyllis Livingston Potter (*d* 1954); two *s* one *d*; *m* 1980, Robyn Smith. *Educ:* private. Stage musical comedy-vaudeville until 1933, then motion pictures. First appearance in London, 1923, in Stop Flirting; American and English successes: Lady Be Good, Funny Face, The Band Waggon, Gay Divorce. *Films:* Flying Down to Rio, Top Hat, Roberta, Gay Divorce, Follow the Fleet, Swingtime, Shall We Dance?, Story of Vernon and Irene Castle, Holiday Inn, Ziegfeld Follies, Blue Skies, Easter Parade, The Barkleys of Broadway, Three Little Words, Let's Dance, Daddy Longlegs, Funny Face, Silk Stockings, On the Beach, The Pleasure of His Company, Finian's Rainbow, The Midas Run, A Run on Gold, The Towering Inferno, Un Taxi Mauve, Ghost Story. *Television Shows:* An Evening with Fred Astaire, 1958; Another Evening with Fred Astaire, 1959; Astaire Time, 1960; The Fred Astaire Show, 1968; Family Upside Down, 1978. *Publication:* Autobiography, Steps in Time, 1959. *Recreations:* golf, thoroughbred racing. *Address:* Beverly Hills, California 90210, USA. *Clubs:* Racquet and Tennis, The Brook, Lamb's (New York).

ASTAIRE, Jarvis Joseph; Deputy Chairman, Wembley Stadium, since 1984; Chairman, Viewsport Ltd, since 1964; *b* 6 Oct. 1923; *s* of Max and Esther Astaire; *m* 1st, 1948, Phyllis Oppenheim (*d* 1974); one *s* one *d*; 2nd, 1981, Nadine Hyman (*d* 1986). *Educ:* Kilburn Grammar Sch., London. Dir, Lewis & Burrows Ltd, 1957–60; Managing Director: Mappin & Webb Ltd, 1958–60; Hurst Park Syndicate, 1962–71; Director: Perthpoint Investments Ltd, 1959–70; Associated Suburban Properties Ltd, 1963–81; Anglo-Continental Investment & Finance Co. Ltd, 1964–75; William Hill Org., 1971–82; First Artists Prodns Inc. (USA), 1976–79; Technicolor Ltd, 1983–; Introduced into UK showing of sporting events on large screen in cinemas, 1964. Chm., Royal Free Hosp. and Med. Sch. Appeal Trust, 1974; Hon. Treas., London Fedn of Boys' Clubs, 1976–. Chm., Associated City Properties, 1981–. Chief Barker (Pres.), Variety Club of GB, 1983. *Recreations:* playing tennis, watching cricket and football. *Address:* 21 Cavendish Place, W1. *T:* 01–580 5927. *Clubs:* East India, MCC; Friars (USA).

ASTBURY, Norman Frederick, CBE 1968; MA, ScD Cantab; CEng, FIEE, CPhys, FInstP; Director, British Ceramic Research Association, 1960–73; *b* 1 Dec. 1908; *y c* of William and Clara Astbury, Normacot, Staffs; *m* 1933, Nora Enid (*d* 1979), *yr d* of William and Mary Wilkinson; three *s* one *d*. *Educ:* Longton High Sch.; St John's Coll., Cambridge (Scholar and Prizeman). National Physical Laboratory, 1929–39; HM Anti-Submarine Experimental Establishment, 1939–45; Dir of Research, J. Sankey & Sons Ltd and Guest, Keen & Nettlefold Ltd, 1945–49; Prof. of Applied Physics, NSW Univ. of Technology, 1949–51; Prof. of Physics, Univ. of Khartoum, 1951–56; Royal Aircraft Establishment, 1956–57; Dep. Dir of Research, Brit. Ceram. Research Assoc., 1957–60. Pres., Brit. Ceram. Soc., 1969; Member: Coun. Inst. of Physics and Phys. Soc., 1963–66; Nat. Coun. for Technological Awards, 1958–64; Coun. for Nat. Academic Awards, 1964–66; Inter-services Metallurgical Research Coun., 1962–64; Joint Services Non-metallic Materials Research Board, 1964–69; Chm. Cttee of Directors of Research Assocs, 1964–66; Vice-Pres., Parly and Sci. Cttee, 1965–68; Mem., Construction Res. Adv. Council, DoE (formerly MPBW), 1968–71. Hon. FICeram. FRSA. *Publications:* Industrial Magnetic Testing, 1952; Electrical Applied Physics, 1956; numerous papers in scientific jls. *Recreations:* music, model railways. *Address:* 85 Atlantic Way, Westward Ho!, Devon. *T:* Bideford 75482. *Clubs:* Athenæum; Federation (Stoke-on-Trent).

ASTELL HOHLER, Thomas Sidney, MC 1944; Director, King & Shaxson Plc, since 1946 (Chairman, 1965–84); Chairman of associated companies; *b* 1919; *s* of late Lt-Col Arthur Preston Hohler, DSO and late Mrs Stanley Barry, Long Crendon Manor, Bucks; granted name and arms of Astell in lieu of name and arms of Hohler, by Royal Licence, 1978; *m* 1952, Jacqueline, *d* of late Marquis de Jouffroy d'Abbans, Chateau d'Abbans, Doubs, France; one *d*. *Educ:* Eton. 2nd Lieut SRO Grenadier Guards, 1939; Major 1944; served in: France; N Africa, 1942; Italy, 1943–44. Director: Henry Sotheran Ltd; Britannia Internat. High Income Fund Ltd; CRC Balanced Growth Fund Ltd. Chm., London Discount Market Assoc., 1972. Liveryman, Grocers' Co., 1956. *Recreations:* farming, shooting. *Address:* Wolverton Park, Basingstoke, Hants RG26 5RU. *T:* Kingsclere 298200; 9 Kylestrome House, Cundy Street, SW1W 9JT. *T:* 01-730 9595. *Clubs:* Brooks's, City of London.

See also Earl of Erroll, H. A. F. Hohler.

ASTILL, Michael John; His Honour Judge Astill; a Circuit Judge, since 1984; *b* 31 Jan. 1938; *s* of Cyril Norman Astill and Winifred Astill; *m* 1968, Jean Elizabeth, *d* of Dr J. C. H. Mackenzie; three *s* one *d*. *Educ:* Blackfriars School, Laxton, Northants. Admitted solicitor, 1962; called to the Bar, Middle Temple, 1972; a Recorder, 1980–84. *Recreations:* music, gardening, sport. *Address:* Colborough House, Halstead, Tilton-on-the-Hill, Leics. *T:* Tilton 608.

ASTLEY, family name of **Baron Hastings.**

ASTLEY, Sir Francis Jacob Dugdale, 6th Bt, *cr* 1821; Head of Classics Department, The Atlantic College, St Donat's Castle, Glamorgan, 1962–69, retired; *b* 26 Oct. 1908; *s* of Rev. Anthony Aylmer Astley (6th *s* of 2nd Bt); *S* kinsman 1943; *m* 1934, Brita Margareta Josefina Nyström, Stockholm; one *d*. *Educ:* Marlborough; Trinity Coll., Oxford. Sen. Lectr, University Coll. of Ghana, 1948–61. *Heir:* none. *Address:* 16 Doulton Mews, Lymington Road, NW6 1XY. *T:* 01–435 9945.

ASTON, Bishop Suffragan of, since 1985; **Rt. Rev. Colin Ogilvie Buchanan;** *b* 9 Aug. 1934; *s* of late Prof. Robert Ogilvie Buchanan and of Kathleen Mary (*née* Parnell); *m* 1963, Diana Stephenie Gregory; two *d*. *Educ:* Whitgift Sch., S Croydon; Lincoln Coll., Oxford (BA, 2nd Cl. Lit. Hum., MA). Theological training at Tyndale Hall, Bristol, 1959–61; deacon, 1961; priest, 1962; Curate, Cheadle, Cheshire, 1961–64; joined staff of London Coll. of Divinity (now St John's Coll., Nottingham), 1964; posts held: Librarian, 1964–69; Registrar, 1969–74; Director of Studies, 1974–75; Vice-Principal, 1975–78; Principal, 1979–85; Hon. Canon of Southwell Minster, 1982–85. Member: Church of England Liturgical Commn, 1964–86; Doctrinal Commn, 1986–; General Synod of C of E, 1970–85; Assembly of British Council of Churches, 1971–80. *Publications:* (ed) Modern Anglican Liturgies 1958–1968, 1968; (ed) Further Anglican Liturgies 1968–1975, 1975; (jtly) Growing into Union, 1970; (ed jtly) Anglican Worship Today, 1980; (ed) Latest Anglican Liturgies 1976–1984, 1985; editor: Grove Booklets on Ministry and Worship, 1972–; Grove Liturgical Studies, 1975– (regular author in these series); News of Liturgy, 1975–; contrib. learned jls. *Recreations:* interested in electoral reform, sport, etc. *Address:* 60 Handsworth Wood Road, Birmingham B20 2DT. *T:* 021-554 5129.

ASTON, Archdeacon of; *see* Cooper, Ven. J. L.

ASTON, Sir Harold (George), Kt 1983; CBE 1976; Chairman, Bonds Coats Patons Ltd, since 1981 (Deputy Chairman, 1970–80); *b* Sydney, 13 March 1923; *s* of Harold John Aston and Annie Dorothea McKeown; *m* 1947, Joyce Thelma Smith; one *s* one *d*. *Educ:* Crown Street Boys' Sch., Sydney, Australia. Manager, Buckinghams Ltd, Sydney, 1948–55; Bonds Industries Ltd: Merchandising Manager, 1955–63; Gen. Man., 1963–67; Man. Dir, 1967–70; Director: Bonds Coats Patons Ltd (formerly Bonds Industries Ltd), 1963–; Manufacturers Mutual Insurance, 1982–; Downard-Pickfords Pty, 1983–; Australian Guarantee Corp. Ltd, 1983–; Australian Manufacturing Life Assce Ltd, 1984–. President: Textile Council of Australia, 1973–80 (Life Mem., 1984); Confedn of Aust. Industry, 1980–82; Vice Pres., Chamber of Manufacturers of NSW, 1979–80; Dep. Chm., National Cttee of Advance Australia, 1980–82. *Recreations:* bowls, swimming, walking, gardening. *Address:* 44 Greenway Drive, Pymble, NSW 2073, Australia. *T:* 449–3075. *Clubs:* American, Australian, Royal Sydney Yacht Squadron (Sydney); Concord Golf.

See also Sir William Aston.

ASTON, Prof. Peter George, DPhil; Professor of Music since 1974, Dean, School of Fine Arts and Music, 1981–84, University of East Anglia; *b* 5 Oct. 1938; *s* of late George William Aston and Elizabeth Oliver Smith; *m* 1960, Elaine Veronica Neale; one *s*. *Educ:* Tettenhall Coll.; Birmingham Sch. of Music (GBSM); Univ of York (DPhil); FTCL, ARCM. Lectr in Music, 1964–72, Sen. Lectr, 1972–74, Univ. of York. Dir, Tudor Consort, 1958–65; Conductor: English Baroque Ensemble, 1968–70; Aldeburgh Festival Singers, 1975–; Jt Artistic Dir, Norwich Fest. of Contemporary Church Music, 1981–; Chorus Master, Norfolk and Norwich Triennial Fest., 1982–. Chm., Eastern Arts Assoc. Music Panel, 1976–81; Pres., Trianon Music Gp, 1984–. Gen. Editor, UEA Recording Series, 1979–. FRSA 1980. *Compositions:* song cycles, chamber music, choral and orchestral works, church music, opera. *Publications:* George Jeffreys and the English Baroque, 1970; The Music of York Minster, 1972; Sound and Silence (jtly), 1970, German edn 1972, Italian edn 1979, Japanese edn 1982; (ed) The Collected Works of George Jeffreys, 3 vols, 1977; contrib. to internat. music jls. *Recreations:* Association football, cricket, bridge, chess. *Address:* University of East Anglia, Music Centre, School of Fine Arts and Music, University Plain, Norwich NR4 7TJ. *T:* Norwich 56161. *Club:* Athenæum.

ASTON, Hon. Sir William (John), KCMG 1970; JP; Speaker, House of Representatives, Australia, 1967–73; MP for Phillip, 1955–61, 1963–72; Chairman, Kolotex Holdings Ltd; Director, Neilson McCarthy & Partners; *b* 19 Sept. 1916; *s* of Harold John Aston and Dorothea (*née* McKeown); *m* 1941, Beatrice Delaney Burrett; one *s* two *d*. *Educ:* Randwick Boys' High School. Served War, 1939–45, AIF in New Guinea, Lieut. Mayor of Waverley, 1952–53. Dep. Govt Whip, 1959–61 and 1963–64; Chief Govt Whip, 1964–67; Trustee, Parlt Retiring Allowances, 1964–67; Mem. and Dep. Chm., Joint Select Cttee on New and Perm. Parlt House, 1965–72; Chairman: House of Reps Standing Orders Cttee, 1967–72; Joint House Cttee, 1967–72; Library Cttee, 1967–72; Joint Cttee on Broadcasting of Parly Proceedings, 1967–72; Jt Chm., Inter-Parliamentary Union (Commonwealth of Aust. Br.) and Commonwealth Parly Assoc. (Aust. Br.), 1967–72; Leader, Aust. Delegn to IPU Conf., Ottawa, 1964; Convenor and Chm., First Conf. of Aust. Presiding Officers, 1968; rep. Australia at: opening of Zambian Parlt Bldg; Funeral of Israeli Prime Minister Eshkol and IPU Symposium, Geneva, 1968; Conf. of Commonwealth Presiding Officers, Ottawa, 1969, New Delhi, 1971; opened Aust. House, Mt Scopus, Univ. of Israel, 1971; led Parly delegn to Turkey, Yugoslavia, UK and to Council of Europe, 1971. JP NSW 1954. Korean Order of Distinguished Service Merit (1st Class), 1969. *Recreations:* cricket, golf, football, fishing, bowls. *Address:* 55 Olola Avenue, Vaucluse, NSW 2030, Australia. *T:* 337–5992. *Clubs:* Royal Automobile of Australia (Sydney); Waverley Bowling, Royal Sydney Golf.

See also Sir H. G. Aston.

ASTOR, family name of **Viscount Astor** and **Baron Astor of Hever.**

ASTOR, 4th Viscount, *cr* 1917, of Hever Castle; Baron *cr* 1916; **William Waldorf Astor;** *b* 27 Dec. 1951; *s* of 3rd Viscount Astor; *S* father 1966; *m* 1976, Annabel Sheffield, *d* of T. Jones; two *s* one *d*. *Educ:* Eton Coll. *Heir:* *s* Hon. William Waldorf Astor, *b* 18 Jan. 1979. *Address:* Ginge Manor, Wantage, Oxon. *Clubs:* White's, Turf.

ASTOR OF HEVER, 3rd Baron *cr* 1956, of Hever Castle; **John Jacob Astor;** *b* 16 June 1946; *s* of 2nd Baron Astor of Hever and of Lady Irene Haig, *d* of Field Marshal 1st Earl Haig, KT, GCB, OM, GCVO, KCIE; *S* father, 1984; *m* 1970, Fiona Diana Lennox Harvey, *d* of Captain Roger Harvey; three *d*. *Educ:* Eton College. Lieut Life Guards, 1966–70, Malaysia, Hong Kong, Ulster. Director: Terres Blanches Services Sarl, 1975–; Valberg Plaza Sarl, 1977–82; Electro-Nucleonics, Inc., 1984–; Man. Dir, Honon et Cie, 1982–. *Heir:* *b* Hon. Philip Douglas Paul Astor, *b* 4 April 1959. *Address:* Les Greens, Cannes Marina, 06210 Mandelieu, France. *T:* (93) 49.05.64. *Club:* White's.

See also Hon. H. W. Astor, Hon. John Astor.

ASTOR, David Waldorf; farmer, since 1973; Chairman, Council for the Protection of Rural England, since 1983; *b* 9 Aug. 1943; *s* of late Michael Langhorne Astor and Barbara Mary (*née* McNeil); *m* 1968, Clare Pamela St John; two *s* two *d*. *Educ:* Eton Coll.; Harvard Univ. Short service comm in Royal Scots Greys, 1962–65. United Newspapers, 1970–72; Housing Corp., 1972–75; Head of Develt, National Th., 1976–77. Prospective Parly Candidate (SDP) for Plymouth Drake, 1985–. *Recreations:* walking, reading, cricket, ski-ing. *Address:* Bruern Grange, Milton under Wychwood, Oxford OX7 6HA. *T:* Shipton-under-Wychwood 830413. *Clubs:* Brook's, MCC.

ASTOR, Hon. (Francis) David (Langhorne); Editor of The Observer, 1948–75; Director, The Observer, 1976–81; *b* 5 March 1912; *s* of 2nd Viscount Astor and Nancy, Viscountess Astor, CH, MP (*d* 1964); *m* 1st, 1945, Melanie Hauser; one *d*; 2nd, 1952, Bridget Aphra Wreford; two *s* three *d*. *Educ:* Eton; Balliol, Oxford. Yorkshire Post, 1936. Served War of 1939–45, with Royal Marines, 1940–45. Foreign Editor of the Observer, 1946–48. Croix de Guerre, 1944. *Publication:* (with V. Yorke) Peace in the Middle East: super powers and security guarantees, 1978. *Address:* 9 Cavendish Avenue, St John's Wood, NW8 9JD. *T:* 01–286 0223; Manor House, Sutton Courtenay, Oxon. *T:* Abingdon 848221. *Club:* Athenæum.

ASTOR, Hon. Hugh Waldorf, JP; Director: Hambro's Bank; Winterbottom Trust Ltd; *b* 20 Nov. 1920; 2nd *s* of 1st Baron Astor of Hever; *m* 1950, Emily Lucy, *d* of Sir Alexander Kinloch, 12th Bt; two *s* three *d*. *Educ:* Eton; New Coll., Oxford. Served War of 1939–45; Intelligence Corps, Europe and SE Asia (Lieut-Col). Joined The Times as Asst Middle East Correspondent, 1947; elected to Board of The Times, 1956; Dep. Chm., 1959, resigned 1967 on merger with Sunday Times; Chm., The Times Book Co. Ltd, 1960, resigned 1967 on merger with Sunday Times. Chairman: Times Trust, 1967–82; Trust Houses Forte Council, 1971 (Mem. Council, 1962); Dep. Chm., Olympia Ltd, 1971–73. Dep. Chm., Middlesex Hosp., 1965–74; Chm., King Edward's Hospital Fund for London, 1983. Governor: Bradfield Coll.; Peabody Trust (Chm., Peabody Donation Fund, 1981); Hon. Treasurer: Franco-British Soc., 1969–76; Marine Biol Assoc. UK, 1968–78; has served on Council or governing body of: RNLI; RYA; RORC; Air League. Mem. Ct of Assts, Fishmongers' Co. (Prime Warden, 1976–77). In partnership with Sir William Dugdale participated in air races, London-Sydney 1969, London-Victoria 1971. JP Berks, 1953; High Sheriff of Berks, 1963. *Recreations:* sailing, flying, shooting, diving. *Address:* Folly Farm, Sulhamstead, Berks. *T:* Reading 302326; 14 Culross Street, W1. *T:* 01–629 4601. *Clubs:* Brooks's, Buck's, Pratt's; Royal Yacht Squadron, Royal Ocean Racing.

See also Baron Astor of Hever, Hon. John Astor.

ASTOR, Hon. John; *b* 26 Sept. 1923; 3rd *s* of 1st Baron Astor of Hever; *m* 1950, Diana Kathleen Drummond (*d* 1982); two *s* one *d*; *m* 1982, Penelope Eve Rolt (*née* Bradford). *Educ:* Summerfields, Hastings; Eton Coll. RAFVR, 1942–45. Berkshire County Council, 1953–74; Alderman, 1960; Chairman, Education Cttee, 1961–66. Vice-Chm., South Berkshire Conservative Assoc., 1958 until 1963, when adopted as candidate. MP (C) Newbury, 1964–Feb. 1974. *Recreations:* fishing, shooting. *Address:* Kirby House, Inkpen, Berks. *T:* Inkpen 284. *Clubs:* Buck's; Royal Yacht Squadron.

See also Baron Astor of Hever, Hon. H. W. Astor.

ASTOR, Major Hon. Sir John (Jacob), Kt 1978; MBE 1945; DL; Major, Life Guards; *b* 29 Aug. 1918; 4th *s* of 2nd Viscount Astor; *m* 1st, 1944, Ana Inez (marr. diss. 1972), *yr d* of Señor Dr Don Miguel Carcano, KCMG, KBE; one *s* one *d*; 2nd, 1976, Susan Sheppard (marr. diss. 1985), *d* of Major M. Eveleigh. *Educ:* Eton; New Coll., Oxford. Served War of 1939–45 (MBE, Legion of Honour, French Croix de Guerre). Contested (C) Sutton Div. of Plymouth, 1950; MP (C) Sutton Div. of Plymouth, 1951–Sept. 1959. PPS to

Financial Sec. of Treasury, 1951–52. Chairman: Governing Body of Nat. Inst. of Agricultural Engineering, 1963–68; Agric. Res. Council, 1968–78; NEDC for Agricultural Industry, 1978–83. Member: Horserace Totalisator Bd, 1962–68; Horserace Betting Levy Bd, 1976–80. Steward of Jockey Club, 1968–71 and 1983–85. DL 1962, JP, Cambs, 1960–74. *Address:* Hatley Park, Hatley St George, Sandy, Beds SG19 3HL. *T:* Gamlingay 50266. *Club:* White's.

ASTWOOD, Hon. Sir James (Rufus), Kt 1982; JP; Chief Justice of Bermuda, since 1977; *b* 4 Oct. 1923; *s* of late James Rufus Astwood, Sr, and Mabel Winifred Astwood; *m* 1952, Gloria Preston Norton; one *s* two *d. Educ:* Berkeley Inst., Bermuda; Univ. of Toronto, Canada. Called to the Bar, Gray's Inn, London, Feb. 1956, Hon. Bencher, 1985; admitted to practice at Jamaican Bar, Oct. 1956; joined Jamaican Legal Service, 1957; Dep. Clerk of Courts, 1957–58; Clerk of Courts, Jamaica, 1958–63; Stipendiary Magistrate and Judge of Grand Court, Cayman Islands (on secondment from Jamaica), 1958–59; Resident Magistrate, Jamaica, 1963–74; Puisne Judge, Jamaica, during 1971 and 1973; retd from Jamaican Legal Service, 1974. Sen. Magistrate, Bermuda, 1974–76; Solicitor General, 1976–77; Acting Attorney General, during 1976 and 1977; Acting Dep. Governor for a period in 1977. Has served on several cttees, tribunals and bds of enquiry, both in Bermuda and Jamaica. *Recreations:* golf, cricket, photography, reading, bridge, travel, cycling. *Address:* (home) Clifton, 8 Middle Road, Devonshire, Bermuda; (office) Chief Justice's Chambers, Supreme Court, Bermuda. *Clubs:* Kingston Cricket (Kingston, Jamaica); Castle Harbour Golf, Bermuda Senior Golfers Society, Royal Hamilton Amateur Dinghy, Coral Beach and Tennis, Mid Ocean (Bermuda).

ASTWOOD, Lt-Col Sir Jeffrey (Carlton), Kt 1972; CBE 1966; OBE (mil.) 1946; ED 1942; Speaker of House of Assembly, Bermuda, 1968–72, retired; *b* 5 Oct. 1907; *s* of late Jeffrey Burgess Astwood, Neston, Bermuda, and Lilian Maude (*née* Searles); *m* 1928, Hilda Elizabeth Kay (*née* Onions); one *s* one *d. Educ:* Saltus Grammar School, Bermuda. Served local TA, 1922–60; retired as Lt-Col, having commanded since 1943. House of Assembly, Bermuda, 1948–72; Minister of Agriculture, of Immigration and Labour, of Health; Member of Exec. Council; Dep. Speaker, 1957–68. Pres., Exec. Cttee, Sandys Grammar Sch., 1950–57 (Chm. Trustees, 1950–); Chm., St James' Church Vestry. President: Atlantic Investment and Development Co. Ltd; J. B. Astwood & Son Ltd; Belfield-in-Somerset Ltd; Brewer Distributors Ltd; Aberfeldy Nurseries Ltd. *Recreations:* theatre, horticulture. *Address:* Greenfield, Somerset, Bermuda. *T:* (business) Hamilton 1.1283; (home) Somerset 4.1729. 4.8180. *Clubs:* No 10; Royal Bermuda Yacht, Sandys Boat.

ATCHERLEY, Sir Harold Winter, Kt 1977; Chairman, Police Negotiating Board, since 1983 (Deputy Chairman, 1982); Member, Top Salaries Review Body, since 1971; *b* 30 Aug. 1918; *s* of L. W. Atcherley and Maude Lester (*née* Nash); *m* 1946, Anita Helen (*née* Leslie) (legal separation, 1978), *widow* of Sub Lt W. D. H. Eves, RN; one *s* two *d. Educ:* Gresham's Sch.; Heidelberg and Geneva Univs. Joined Royal Dutch Shell Gp, 1937. Served War: Queen's Westminster Rifles, 1939; commissioned Intelligence Corps, 1940; served 18th Infty Div., Singapore; PoW, 1942–45. Rejoined Royal Dutch Shell Gp, 1946; served Egypt, Lebanon, Syria, Argentina, Brazil, 1946–59. Personnel Co-ordinator, Royal Dutch Shell Group, 1964–70, retd. Recruitment Advisor to Ministry of Defence, 1970–71. Chm., Tyzack & Partners, 1979–85; Dir, British Home Stores Ltd, 1973–. Chm., Armed Forces Pay Review Body, 1971–82; Member: Nat. Staff Cttee for Nurses and Midwives, 1973–77; Cttee of Inquiry into Pay and Related Conditions of Service of Nurses, 1974; Cttee of Inquiry into Remuneration of Members of Local Authorities, 1977. Chm., Toynbee Hall, 1985– (Mem., Management Cttee, 1979–). Empress Leopoldina Medal (Brazil), 1958. *Recreations:* music, skiing, good food. *Address:* Conduit House, The Green, Long Melford, Suffolk. *T:* Sudbury 310897.

ATHA, Bernard Peter; Principal Lecturer in Business Studies, Huddersfield Technical College, since 1973; *b* 27 Aug. 1928; *s* of Horace Michael Atha and Mary Quinlan; unmarried. *Educ:* Leeds Modern Sch.; Leeds Univ. (LLB Hons). Barrister-at-law, Gray's Inn. Commn, RAF, 1950–52. Variety artist on stage; Mem. Equity; films and TV plays. Elected Leeds City Council, 1957; Chm., Leeds Social Services Cttee, 1984–; Leeds City representative, AMA Social Services Cttee; former Chairman: Watch Cttee; Leisure Services Cttee; Educn Cttee. Contested (Lab): Penrith and the Border, 1959; Pudsey, 1964. Pres., Leeds Co-op. Soc.; Chm., Leeds Playhouse; Director: Leeds Grand Theatre; Opera North. Member: Arts Council, 1979–82; Ministerial Working Party on Sport and Recreation, 1974; Vice-Chm., Sports Council, 1976–80; Chairman: Yorks and Humberside Reg. Sports Council, 1966–76; Nat. Water Sports Centre, 1978–84; UK Sports Assoc. for People with Mental Handicap; Yorks Dance Centre Trust; Red Ladder Theatre Co. Governor: Sports Aid Foundn; Further Educn Staff Coll. FRSA. *Recreations:* sport, the arts, travel. *Address:* 25 Moseley Wood Croft, Leeds 16, West Yorks. *T:* Leeds 672485.

ATHABASCA, Bishop of, since 1983; **Rt. Rev. Gary Frederick Woolsey;** *b* 16 March 1942; *s* of William and Doreen Woolsey; *m* 1967, Marie Elaine Tooker; two *s* two *d. Educ:* Univ. of Western Ontario (BA); Huron Coll., London, Ont. (BTh); Univ. of Manitoba (Teacher's Cert.). Deacon, 1967; Priest-pilot, Diocese of Keewatin, 1967–68; Rector: St Peter's, Big Trout Lake, Ont., 1968–72; St Mark's, Norway House, Manitoba, 1972–76; St Paul's, Churchill, Man., 1976–80; Program Director and Archdeacon of Keewatin, 1980–83. *Recreations:* fishing, hunting, boating, camping, photography, flying. *Address:* Box 279, Peace River, Alberta T0H 2X0, Canada. *T:* (home) (403) 624–5607, (office) (403) 624–2767.

ATHERTON, Alan Royle; Principal Establishment Officer, PSA, Department of the Environment, since 1982; *b* 25 April 1931; *s* of Harold Atherton and Hilda (*née* Royle); *m* 1959, Valerie Kemp; three *s* one *d. Educ:* Cowley Sch., St Helens; Sheffield Univ. (BSc (Hons Chem.)). ICI Ltd, 1955–58; DSIR: Sen. Scientific Officer, 1959–64, Private Sec. to Permanent Sec., 1960–64; Principal Sci. Officer, Road Res. Lab., 1964–65; Principal, Min. of Housing and Local Govt, 1965–70; Asst Sec., Ordnance Survey, 1970–74; Under-Sec., DoE, 1975–. *Recreation:* walking. *Address:* Riverside, East Mill, Fordingbridge, Hants SP6 2JS. *T:* Fordingbridge 52231. *Club:* Civil Service.

ATHERTON, David; Music Director, San Diego Symphony Orchestra, since 1980; Principal Guest Conductor, BBC Symphony Orchestra, since 1985; *b* 3 Jan. 1944; *s* of Robert and Lavinia Atherton; *m* 1970, Ann Gianetta Drake; one *s* two *d. Educ:* Cambridge Univ. (MA). LRAM, LTCL. Repetiteur, Royal Opera House, Covent Garden, 1967–68; Founder and Musical Dir, London Sinfonietta, 1967–73; Resident Conductor, Royal Opera House, 1968–79; Principal Conductor and Artistic Advr, 1980–83, Principal Guest Conductor, 1983–86, Royal Liverpool Philharmonic Orch.; Artistic Dir and Conductor: London Stravinsky Fest., 1979–82; Ravel/Varese Fest., 1983–84. Became youngest conductor in history of Henry Wood Promenade Concerts at Royal Albert Hall, and also at Royal Opera House, 1968; Royal Festival Hall debut, 1969; from 1970 performances in Europe, Middle East, Far East, Australasia, N America. Adapted and arranged Pandora by Roberto Gerhard for Royal Ballet, 1975. Conductor of the year award (Composers' Guild of GB), 1971; Edison award, 1973; Grand Prix du Disque award, 1977;

Koussevitzky Award, 1981; Internat. Record Critics Award, 1982; Prix Caecilia, 1982. *Publications:* (ed) The Complete Instrumental and Chamber Music of Arnold Schoenberg and Roberto Gerhard, 1973; (ed) Pandora and Don Quixote Suites by Roberto Gerhard, 1973; contrib., The Musical Companion, 1978, The New Grove Dictionary, 1981. *Recreations:* travel, squash, theatre. *Address:* c/o Harold Holt Ltd, 31 Sinclair Road, W14 0NS.

ATHERTON, James Bernard; Secretary-General, British Bankers' Association, since 1982; *b* 3 Dec. 1927; *s* of late James Atherton and Edith (*née* Atkinson); *m* 1953, Eileen Margaret Birch; two *s. Educ:* Alsop High Sch., Liverpool. Served RAF, 1946–48; Martins Bank, 1943–46 and 1948–69 (Asst Chief Accountant, 1966–69); Barclays Bank, 1969–82 (Chief Clearing Manager, 1969–73, Asst Gen. Manager, 1973–78, Divl Gen. Manager, 1978–82). *Recreations:* opera, gardening. *Address:* 29 Sloane Square, SW1W 8AB. *T:* 01–623 4001.

ATHOLL, 10th Duke of, *cr* 1703; **George Iain Murray;** DL; Lord Murray of Tullibardine, 1604; Earl of Tullibardine, Lord Gask and Balquhidder, 1606; Earl of Atholl, 1629; Marquess of Atholl, Viscount Balquhidder, Lord Balvenie, 1676; Marquess of Tullibardine, Earl of Strathtay, Earl of Strathardle, Viscount Glenalmond, Viscount Glenlyon, 1703—all in the peerage of Scotland; Representative Peer for Scotland in the House of Lords, 1958–63; *b* 19 June 1931; *s* of Lieut-Col George Anthony Murray, OBE, Scottish Horse (killed in action, Italy, 1945), and Hon. Mrs Angela Campbell-Preston, (*d* 1981), *d* of 2nd Viscount Cowdray (she *m* 2nd, 1950, Robert Campbell-Preston of Ardchattan, *qv*); *S* kinsman 1957. *Educ:* Eton; Christ Church, Oxford. Director: Westminster Press (Chm., 1974–); BPM Holdings, 1972–83; Pearson Longman Ltd, 1975–83. Convener, Scottish Landowners Fedn, 1976–79 (Vice-Convener, 1971–76); Chm., RNLI, 1979– (Dep. Chm., 1972–79); Member: Cttee on the Preparation of Legislation, 1973–75; Exec. Cttee, Nat. Trust for Scotland (Vice-Pres., 1977–); Red Deer Commn, 1969–83. DL Perth and Kinross, 1980. *Heir: cousin* Godfrey Pemberton Murray, DSO [*b* 13 June 1901; *m* 1934, Mary Isabel, *d* of Dr D. Brownlee; two *d*]. *Address:* Blair Castle, Blair Atholl, Perthshire. *T:* Blair Atholl 212; 31 Marlborough Hill, NW8. *Clubs:* Turf, White's; New (Edinburgh).

ATIYAH, Sir Michael (Francis), Kt 1983; MA, PhD Cantab; FRS 1962; FRSE 1985; Royal Society Research Professor, Mathematical Institute, Oxford, and Professorial Fellow of St Catherine's College, Oxford, since 1973; *b* 22 April 1929; *e s* of late Edward Atiyah and Jean Levens; *m* 1955, Lily Brown; three *s. Educ:* Victoria Coll., Egypt; Manchester Grammar Sch.; Trinity Coll., Cambridge. Research Fellow, Trinity Coll., Camb., 1954–58, Hon. Fellow, 1976; First Smith's Prize, 1954; Commonwealth Fund Fellow, 1955–56; Mem. Inst. for Advanced Study, Princeton, 1955–56, 1959–60, 1967–68; Asst Lectr in Mathematics, 1957–58, Lectr 1958–61, Univ. of Cambridge; Fellow Pembroke Coll., Cambridge, 1958–61 (Hon. Fellow, 1983); Reader in Mathematics, Univ. of Oxford, and Professorial Fellow of St Catherine's Coll., Oxford, 1961–63; Savilian Prof. of Geometry, and Fellow of New College, Oxford, 1963–69; Prof. of Mathematics, Inst. for Advanced Study, Princeton, NJ, 1969–72. Visiting Lecturer, Harvard, 1962–63 and 1964–65. Member: Exec. Cttee, Internat. Mathematical Union, 1966–74; SERC, 1984–; President: London Mathematical Soc., 1975–77; Mathematical Assoc., 1981–82. Foreign Member: Amer. Acad. of Arts and Scis; Swedish Royal Acad.; Leopoldina Acad.; Nat. Acad. of Scis, USA; Acad. des Sciences, France; Royal Irish Acad. Hon. DSc: Bonn, 1968; Warwick, 1969; Durham, 1979; St Andrew's, 1981; Dublin, 1983; Chicago, 1983; Edinburgh, 1984; Essex, 1985; London, 1985; Sussex, 1986; Hon. ScD Cantab, 1984. Fields Medal, Internat. Congress of Mathematicians, Moscow, 1966; Royal Medal, Royal Soc., 1968; De Morgan Medal, London Mathematical Soc., 1980; Antonio Feltrinelli Prize for mathematical sciences, Accademia Nazionale dei Lincei, Rome, 1981. *Publications:* papers in mathematical journals. *Recreation:* gardening. *Address:* Mathematical Institute, 24–29 St Giles, Oxford OX1 3LB. *T:* Oxford 54295; Shotover Mound, Headington, Oxford. *T:* Oxford 62359.

See also P. S. Atiyah.

ATIYAH, Prof. Patrick Selim, DCL; FBA 1978; Professor of English Law, Oxford University, since 1977; *b* 5 March 1931; *s* of Edward Atiyah and D. J. C. Levens; *m* 1951, Christine Best; four *s. Educ:* Woking County Grammar Sch. for Boys; Magdalen Coll., Oxford (MA 1957, DCL 1974). Called to the Bar, Inner Temple, 1956. Asst Lectr, LSE, 1954–55; Lectr, Univ. of Khartoum, 1955–59; Legal Asst, BoT, 1961–64; Fellow, New Coll., Oxford, 1964–69; Professor of Law: ANU, 1970–73; Warwick Univ., 1973–77; Visiting Professor: Univ of Texas, 1979; Harvard Law Sch., 1982–83; Duke Univ., 1985. Lectures: Lionel Cohen, Hebrew Univ., Jerusalem, 1980; Oliver Wendell Holmes, Harvard Law Sch., 1981; Cecil Wright Meml, Univ. of Toronto, 1983; Chorley, LSE, 1985. General Editor, Oxford Jl of Legal Studies. *Publications:* The Sale of Goods, 1957, 7th edn 1985; Introduction to the Law of Contract, 1961, 3rd edn 1981; Vicarious Liability, 1967; Accidents, Compensation and the Law, 1970, 3rd edn 1980; The Rise and Fall of Freedom of Contract, 1979; Promises, Morals and Law, 1981 (Swiney Prize, RSA/RSP, 1984); Law and Modern Society, 1983; articles in legal jls. *Recreations:* gardening, cooking. *Address:* St John's College, Oxford; 9 Sheepway Court, Iffley, Oxford. *T:* Oxford 717637.

See also Sir M. F. Atiyah.

ATKIN, Alec Field, CBE 1978; FEng, FIMechE, FRAeS; Managing Director, Marketing, Aircraft Group, British Aerospace, 1981–82, retired; Director, AWA (Consultancy) Ltd, since 1983; *b* 26 April 1925; *s* of Alec and Grace Atkin; *m* 1948, Nora Helen Darby (marr. diss. 1982); two *s* one *d; m* 1982, Wendy Atkin. *Educ:* Riley High Sch.; Hull Technical Coll. (DipAe); Hull Univ. (BSc Hons). FIMechE 1955; FRAeS 1952. English Electric Co., Preston: Aerodynamicist, 1950; Dep. Chief Aerodyn., 1954; Head of Exper. Aerodyns, 1957; Asst Chief Engr, then Proj. Manager, 1959; Warton Div., British Aircraft Corporation Ltd: Special Dir, 1964; Dir, 1970; Asst Man. Dir, 1973–75; Dep. Man. Dir, 1975–76; Man. Dir, 1976–77; Man. Dir (Mil.), Aircraft Gp of British Aerospace, and Chm., Warton, Kingston-Brough and Manchester Divs, 1978–81. FRSA. *Recreation:* sailing. *Address:* Les Fougères d'Icart, Icart Road, St Martin, Guernsey, Channel Islands.

ATKINS, Henry St J., DSc; President, University College, Cork, 1954–63, retired; *b* 19 March 1896; *s* of Patrick Atkins and Agnes Egan, Cork; *m* 1929, Agnes E. O'Regan (*d* 1960), MB, BCh; one *s* one *d. Educ:* Christian Brothers, North Monastery, Cork; University Coll., Cork. BSc (Math. Science) 1915; post-grad. scholar, MSc 1923. Prof. of Pure Maths, University Coll., Cork, 1936–54; Registrar, 1943–54. Hon. DSc 1955. MRIA 1957. *Recreations:* golf, fishing. *Address:* Knockrea Park, Cork. *T:* Cork 32448. *Clubs:* National University of Ireland; Cork City and County (Cork).

ATKINS, Rt. Hon. Sir Humphrey (Edward Gregory), KCMG 1983; PC 1973; MP (C) Spelthorne since 1970 (Merton and Morden, Surrey, 1955–70); *b* 12 Aug. 1922; *s* of late Capt. E. D. Atkins, Nyeri, Kenya Colony; *m* 1944, Margaret, *d* of Sir Robert Spencer-Nairn, 1st Bt; one *s* three *d. Educ:* Wellington Coll. Special entry cadetship, RN, 1940; Lieut RN, 1943; resigned, 1948. PPS to Civil Lord of the Admiralty, 1959–62; Hon.. Sec.

Conservative Parly Defence Cttee, 1965–67; Opposition Whip, 1967–70; Treasurer of HM Household and Dep. Chief Whip, 1970–73; Parly Sec. to the Treasury and Govt Chief Whip, 1973–74; Opposition Chief Whip, 1974–79; Secretary of State for N Ireland, 1979–81; Lord Privy Seal, 1981–82. Chm., Select Cttee on Defence, 1984–. Pres., Nat. Union of Conservative and Unionist Assocs, 1985–86. Underwriting Mem. of Lloyd's. Vice-Chm., Management Cttee, Outward Bound Trust, 1966–70. *Address:* House of Commons, SW1. *Club:* Brooks's.

ATKINS, John Spencer, DSO 1945; TD; DL; President, Atkins Brothers (Hosiery) Ltd; *b* 28 Oct. 1905; 3rd *s* of late Col E. C. Atkins, CB, DL; *m* 1936, Monica Lucy Standish; one *s* two *d. Educ:* Uppingham Sch. DL Leics 1946. *Address:* White House, Ullesthorpe, Lutterworth, Leics. *T:* Leire 209274. *Club:* Naval and Military.

ATKINS, Leonard B. W.; *see* Walsh Atkins.

ATKINS, Rt. Rev. Peter Geoffrey; *see* Waiapu, Bishop of.

ATKINS, Robert James; MP (C) South Ribble, since 1983 (Preston North, 1979–83); *b* 5 Feb. 1946; *s* of late Reginald Alfred and of Winifred Margaret Atkins; *m* 1969, Dulcie Mary (*née* Chaplin); one *s* one *d. Educ:* Highgate School. Councillor, London Borough of Haringey, 1968–77; Vice-Chm., Greater London Young Conservatives, 1969–70, 1971–72. Contested (C) Luton West, Feb. 1974 and Oct. 1974 general elections. PPS to Minister of State, DoI, then DTI, 1982–84, to Minister without Portfolio, 1984–85, to Sec. of State for Employment, 1985–. Vice-Chm., Cons. Aviation Cttee, 1979–82; Jt Sec., Cons. Defence Cttee, 1979–82. President: Cons. Trade Unionists, 1984–; Lancs Young Conservatives, 1984–86. *Publication:* (contrib.) Changing Gear, 1981. *Recreations:* wine, ecclesiology, cricket. *Address:* Manor House, Lancaster Road, Garstang, Lancs PR3 1JA. *T:* Garstang 2225. *Clubs:* MCC, Middlesex County Cricket, Lords and Commons Cricket, Lancashire County Cricket.

ATKINS, Ronald Henry; *b* Barry, Glam, 13 June 1916; *s* of Frank and Elizabeth Atkins; *m*; three *s* two *d. Educ:* Barry County Sch.; London Univ. (BA Hons). Teacher, 1949–66 (latterly Head, Eng. Dept, Halstead Sec. Sch.); Lectr, Accrington Coll. of Further Educn, 1970–74. Member: Braintree RDC, 1952–61; Preston Dist Council, 1974–76, 1980–. Contested (Lab) Lowestoft, 1964; MP (Lab) Preston North, 1966–70 and Feb. 1974–1979. *Recreations:* jazz, dancing, walking. *Address:* 38 James Street, Preston, Lancs. *T:* Preston 51910.

ATKINS, Sir William Sydney Albert, Kt 1976; CBE 1966; FEng, FICE, FIStructE; Chairman: W. S. Atkins & Partners, since 1951; W. S. Atkins & Partners (Ethiopia) Ltd, since 1963, W. S. Atkins & Associates Pty Ltd, since 1971; W. S. Atkins (Overseas Projects) Ltd, since 1973; W. S. Atkins International, since 1973; Sir William Atkins & Partners, since 1977; President, W. S. Atkins Group Consultants, since 1984 (Chairman, 1975–78); Hon. President, W. S. Atkins Group, since 1985 (Chairman, 1971–85); *b* 6 Feb. 1902; 2nd *s* of Robert Edward and Martha Atkins; *m* 1928, Elsie Jessie, *d* of Edward and Hilda Barrow, Hockley, Essex; two *d. Educ:* Coopers' Sch.; University Coll., London (BSc; Fellow, 1955). Chief Engr, Smith Walker Ltd, 1928; Founder and Man. Dir, London Ferro-Concrete Co. Ltd, 1935, Chm. 1937; Founder and Chm., R. E. Eagan Ltd, 1945; Founder and Sen. Partner, W. S. Atkins & Partners, 1938; Founder and Partner, Round Pond Nurseries, 1965. Mem. Council, London Chamber of Commerce. CInstMC; Hon. FInstW. Hon. Freeman, Borough of Epsom and Ewell. *Publications:* many technical papers. *Recreations:* gardening and horticultural research, swimming. *Address:* Chobham Place, Chobham, near Woking, Surrey GU24 8TN. *T:* Chobham 8867.

ATKINSON, Sir Alec; *see* Atkinson, Sir J. A.

ATKINSON, Prof. Anthony Barnes, FBA 1984; Professor of Economics, London School of Economics and Political Science, since Jan. 1980; *b* 4 Sept. 1944; *s* of Norman Joseph Atkinson and Esther Muriel Atkinson; *m* 1965, Judith Mary (*née* Mandeville); two *s* one *d. Educ:* Cranbrook Sch.; Churchill Coll., Cambridge (MA). Fellow, St John's Coll., Cambridge, 1967–71; Prof. of Econs, Univ. of Essex, 1971–76; Prof. and Hd of Dept of Political Economy, UCL, 1976–79. Vis. Prof. MIT, 1973. Mem., Royal Commn on Distribution of Income and Wealth, 1978–79. Fellow, Econometric Soc., 1975. Hon. Mem., Amer. Econ. Assoc., 1985. Editor, Jl of Public Economics, 1972–. *Publications:* Poverty in Britain and the Reform of Social Security, 1969; Unequal Shares, 1972; The Tax Credit Scheme, 1973; Economics of Inequality, 1975; (with A. J. Harrison) Distribution of Personal Wealth in Britain, 1978; (with J. E. Stiglitz) Lectures on Public Economics, 1980; Social Justice and Public Policy, 1982; (jtly) Parents and Children, 1983; articles in Rev. of Econ. Studies, Econ. Jl, Jl of Public Econs, Jl of Econ. Theory. *Address:* 33 Hurst Green, Brightlingsea, Colchester, Essex. *T:* Colchester 302253.

ATKINSON, Arthur Kingsley Hall, CB 1985; Chief Executive, Intervention Board for Agricultural Produce, 1980–86; *b* 24 Dec. 1926; *er s* of Arthur Hall Atkinson and Florence (*née* Gerrans). *Educ:* Priory Sch., Shrewsbury; Emmanuel Coll., Cambridge (MA). RAF, 1948; MAFF: Asst Principal 1950; Private Sec. 1953; Principal 1956; Asst Sec. 1965; Under Sec., 1973; Cabinet Office, 1976–78; MAFF, 1978–80. *Recreations:* travel, music, gardening.

ATKINSON, Prof. Bernard, FEng, FIChemE; Director, Brewing Research Foundation, since 1981; *b* 17 March 1936; *s* of late Thomas Atkinson and of Elizabeth Ann (*née* Wilcox); *m* 1957, Kathleen Mary Richardson; two *s. Educ:* Farnworth Grammar Sch.; Univ. of Birmingham (BSc); Univ. of Manchester Inst. of Science and Technology; PhD Univ. of Manchester. FEng 1980. Post-Doctoral Fellow and Asst Prof., Rice Univ., Houston, Texas, 1960–63; Lectr, Sen. Lectr in Chem. Engrg, and latterly Reader in Biochem. Engrg, University Coll. of Swansea, 1963–74; Prof. and Head of Dept of Chem. Engrg, UMIST, 1974–81; Vis. Prof., UMIST, 1981–. Editor, Biochemical Engineering Journal, 1983–. Senior Moulton Medal, IChemE, 1976; Gairn EEC Medal, Soc. of Engrs, 1985. *Publications:* Biochemical Reactors, 1974, trans. Japanese, Russian, Spanish; (with P. F. Cooper) Biological Fluidised Bed Treatment of Water and Waste Water, 1981; (with F. Mavituna) Biochemical Engineering and Biotechnology Handbook, 1982; (ed) Research and Innovation in the 1990s: the chemical engineering challenge, 1986; numerous contribs to chemical engrg and biochemical engrg jls. *Recreations:* cycling, sailing, walking. *Address:* Brewing Research Foundation, Lyttel Hall, Nutfield, Surrey RH1 4HX. *T:* Nutfield Ridge 2272; Little Mieders, Borers Arms Road, Copthorne, Crawley, West Sussex RH10 3LJ. *T:* Copthorne 713181.

ATKINSON, Colin Ronald Michael; Principal, Millfield Schools, Somerset, since 1986 (Headmaster, Millfield School, 1971–86, Acting Headmaster, 1969–70), Governor since 1977; *b* 23 July 1931; *s* of R. and E. Atkinson; *m* 1957, Shirley Angus; two *s* one *d. Educ:* Hummersknott, Darlington, Co. Durham; Durham Univ. (BA); Queen's Univ., Belfast (BA); Loughborough Coll. of Educn; MEd, Univ. of Bath, 1977. Served 5th Fusiliers (Northumberland) in Kenya, 1954–56. The Friends' School, Great Ayton, 1956–58; Haughton School, Darlington, 1958–60; Millfield, 1960–. West of England Hockey and Chief Divl coach, 1965–69; Founder and former Mem.: Nat. Hockey Coaching Cttee; Nat. Cricket Coaching Cttee, 1967–71; Chm., Phys. Educn Cttee of Schools Council, 1974–79; former Minister for Sport and Recreation's Nominee for SW Council for Sport and Recreation. Director: McArthur Steel Export Co.; HTV Ltd; Hillside Prop. Co.; C and D Co. Ltd; Hon. Dir, Millfield Enterprises Ltd. Chm., Edington Sch., Somerset. Member: TCCB (Chm., Discipline Cttee); Cricket Council of UK. President: Somerset CCC; Somerset Schools Cricket Assoc. *Publications:* An Experiment in Closed Circuit TV at Millfield School, 1970; various articles. *Recreations:* County Representation in five sports; Captain Somerset CCC XI, 1965–67 and County Hockey XI, 1963–65. *Address:* Millfield School, Street, Somerset. *T:* Street 42291. *Clubs:* East India, MCC, Free Foresters, I Zingari.

ATKINSON, David Anthony; MP (C) Bournemouth East, since Nov. 1977; *b* 24 March 1940; *s* of late Arthur Joseph Atkinson and of Joan Margaret Atkinson (*née* Zink); *m* 1968, Susan Nicola Pilsworth; one *s* one *d. Educ:* St George's Coll., Weybridge; Coll. of Automobile and Aeronautical Engrg, Chelsea. Diplomas in Auto. Engrg and Motor Industry Management. Member: Southend County Borough Council, 1969–72; Essex CC, 1973–78. Mem., Council of Europe, 1979–86. PPS to Rt Hon. Paul Channon, MP (Minister of State, Civil Service Dept, 1979–81, Minister for the Arts, 1981–83, Minister of State, DTI, 1983–86, Sec. of State for Trade and Industry, 1986–). Nat. Chm., Young Conservative Orgn, 1970–71; Pres., Christian Solidarity Internat. (UK), 1983– (Chm., 1979–83). *Recreations:* mountaineering, art and architecture, travel. *Address:* House of Commons, SW1.

ATKINSON, Air Marshal Sir David (William), KBE 1982; FFOM; FRCPE; FFCM; Director-General, Chest, Heart and Stroke Association, since 1985; Director-General, RAF Medical Services, 1981–84; *b* 29 Sept. 1924; *s* of late David William Atkinson and of Margaret Atkinson; *m* 1948, Mary (*née* Sowerby); one *s. Educ:* Edinburgh Univ. (MB, ChB 1948). DPH and DIH, London; FFCM 1976; MFOM 1978, FFOM 1983; FRCPE 1983. Joined RAF, 1949; med. officer appts, UK, Jordan and Egypt, 1949–63; Student, RAF Staff Coll., 1963–64; SMO, RAF Brüggen, Germany, 1964–67; Dep. PMO, HQ Air Support Comd, 1967–70; PMO, HQ Brit. Forces Gulf, Bahrain, 1970–71; OC RAF Hosp., Wegberg, Germany, 1971–73; Dir of Health and Research (RAF), 1974–78; QHP 1977–84; PMO, RAF Strike Command, 1978–81. *Publication:* (jtly) Double Crew Continuous Flying Operations: a study of aircrew sleep patterns, 1970. *Recreations:* walking, gardening, reading, looking at pictures. *Address:* 39 Brim Hill, N2. *Club:* Royal Air Force.

ATKINSON, Frank, OBE 1980; FSA; FMA; Director, Beamish North of England Open Air Museum, since 1970; *b* 13 April 1924; *s* of Ernest Atkinson and Elfrida (*née* Bedford); *m* 1953, Joan Peirson; three *s. Educ:* Holgate Grammar Sch., Barnsley; Sheffield Univ. (BSc). Director: Wakefield City Art Gall. and Mus., 1949; Halifax Museums, 1951; Bowes Mus. and Durham Co. Mus. Service, 1958. Member: Working Party on Preservation of Technolog. Material, 1970–71; Wright Cttee on Provincial Museums and Galls, 1971–73; Working Party of Standing Commn on Museums and Galls (Drew Report), 1975–78. Pres., Museums Assoc., 1974–75. Hon. MA Newcastle upon Tyne, 1971. *Publications:* Aspects of the 18th century Woollen and Worsted Trade, 1956; The Great Northern Coalfield, 1966, 3rd edn 1979; Industrial Archaeology of North East England, 1974; Life and Traditions in Northumberland and Durham, 1977, 2nd edn 1986; North East England: people at work 1860–1950, 1980; contribs to Trans Newcomen Soc., Procs of British Spel. Soc., Antiquaries Jl, Museums Jl, etc. *Recreations:* pot-holing (now only in retrospect), computer programming. *Address:* The Old Vicarage, Ovingham, Prudhoe, Northumberland NE42 6BW. *T:* Prudhoe 35445; (office) Stanley 231811.

ATKINSON, Sir Frederick John, (Sir Fred Atkinson), KCB 1979 (CB 1971); Hon. Fellow of Jesus College, Oxford, since 1979; *b* 7 Dec. 1919; *s* of George Edward Atkinson and of late Elizabeth Sabina Cooper; *m* 1947, Margaret Grace Gibson; two *d. Educ:* Dulwich Coll.; Jesus Coll., Oxford; Hon. Fellow, Jesus Coll., 1979. Lectr, Jesus and Trinity Colls, Oxford, 1947–49; Economic Section, Cabinet Office, 1949–51; British Embassy, Washington, 1952–54; HM Treasury, 1955–62; Economic Adviser, Foreign Office, 1962–63; HM Treasury, 1963–69 (Dep. Dir, Economic Section, Treasury, 1965–69); Controller, Economics and Statistics, Min. of Technology, 1970; Chief Econ. Adviser, DTI, 1970–73; an Asst Sec.-Gen., OECD, Paris, 1973–75; Dep. Sec. and Chief Econ. Advr, Dept of Energy, 1975–77; Chief Economic Adviser, HM Treasury, and Head of Govt Econ. Service, 1977–79. *Publication:* (with S. Hall) Oil and the British Economy, 1983. *Recreation:* reading. *Address:* 26 Lee Terrace, Blackheath, SE3. *T:* 01–852 1040; Tickner Cottage, Aldington, Kent. *T:* Aldington 514.

ATKINSON, Harry Hindmarsh, PhD; Under Secretary, Director Science, Science and Engineering Research Council, since 1983; *b* 5 Aug. 1929; *s* of late Harry Temple Atkinson and Constance Hindmarsh Atkinson (*née* Shields); *m* 1958, Anne Judith Barrett; two *s* one *d. Educ:* Nelson Coll., Nelson, NZ; Canterbury University Coll., NZ (BSc, sen. schol.; MSc (1st cl. Hons)), 1948–52. Asst Lectr, Physics, CUC, 1952–53; Research Asst, Cornell Univ., USA, 1954–55; Corpus Christi Coll. and Cavendish Laboratory, Cambridge Univ., 1955–58 (PhD); Sen. Research Fellow, AERE, Harwell, 1958–61; Head, General Physics Group, Rutherford Laboratory, 1961–69; Staff Chief Scientific Adviser, Cabinet Office, 1969–72; Dep. Chief Scientific Officer and Head of Astronomy, Space and Radio Division, SRC, 1972–78; Dir (Astronomy, Space and Radio, and Nuclear Physics), SRC later SERC, 1979–83. UK Deleg. to Council, ESA, 1974– (Vice Chm. of Council, 1981–84, Chm., 1984–); UK Member: EISCAT Council, 1976–; Bd, Anglo-Aust. Telescope, 1979–; Steering Cttee, Inst. Laue-Langevin, Grenoble (UK Delegate, 1983–; Chm. 1984); Council, European Synchrotron Radiation Facility (UK deleg., 1986–); Chm., Cttee on Netherlands/UK Astronomy Collaboration, 1981–. *Publications:* papers on various branches of physics. *Recreations:* sailing, walking, talking. *Address:* Smoke Acres, Faringdon Road, Abingdon OX14 1BD. *T:* Abingdon 20560. *Club:* Athenæum.

ATKINSON, Prof. James; Founder Director, Centre for Reformation Studies, Sheffield, since 1983; Professor of Biblical Studies, University of Sheffield, 1967–79, now Emeritus; *b* 27 April 1914; *s* of Nicholas Ridley Atkinson and Margaret (*née* Hindhaugh); *m* 1939, Laura Jean Nutley (decd); one *s* one *d. Educ:* Tynemouth High Sch.; Univ. of Durham. MA 1939, MLitt 1950 Durham; DrTheol, Münster, Germany, 1955. Curate, Newcastle upon Tyne, 1937; Precentor, Sheffield Cath., 1941; Vicar, Sheffield, 1944; Fellow, Univ. of Sheffield, 1951; Canon Theologian: Leicester, 1954–70; Sheffield, 1971–; Reader in Theology, Univ. of Hull, 1956; Vis. Prof., Chicago, 1966; Public Orator, Univ. of Sheffield, 1972–79; Consultant Prof. with Evangelical Anglican Res. Centre, Latimer House, Oxford, 1981–84. Examining Chaplain to: Bp of Leicester, 1968–79; Bp of Derby, 1978–. Member: Anglican-Roman Catholic Preparatory Commission, 1967–; Gen. Synod of Church of England, 1975–80; Marriage Commn, 1976–78. Pres., Soc. for Study of Theology, 1978–80; Mem., Acad. Internat. des Sciences Religieuses, 1980–. *Publications:* Library of Christian Classics, Vol. XVI, 1962; Rome and Reformation, 1965; Luther's Works, Vol. 44, 1966; Luther and the Birth of Protestantism, 1968; The Reformation, Paternoster Church History, Vol. 4, 1968 (trans. Spanish 1971, Italian 1983); The Trial of Luther, 1971; Martin Luther: Prophet to the Church Catholic, 1983; contribs to learned jls, also essays and parts of books. *Recreations:* gardening, music. *Address:* Leach House, Hathersage, Derbyshire. *T:* Hope Valley 50570; Centre for Reformation Studies, St George's Hall, Portobello, Sheffield S1 4DP. *T:* Sheffield 78555.

See also Sir Robert Atkinson.

ATKINSON, Sir John Alexander, (Sir Alec Atkinson), KCB 1978 (CB 1976); DFC 1943; Member, Panel of Chairmen, Civil Service Selection Board, since 1979; *b* 9 June 1919; *yr s* of late Rev. R. F. Atkinson and late Harriet Harrold Atkinson, BSc (*née* Lowdon); *m* 1945, Marguerite Louise Pearson; one *d. Educ:* Kingswood Sch.; Queen's Coll., Oxford. Served in RAF, 1939–45. Asst Prin., 1946, Prin., 1949, Min. of Nat. Insce; Cabinet Office, 1950–52; Prin. Private Sec. to Minister of Pensions and Nat. Insce, 1957–58; Asst Sec., 1958; Under-Sec., Min. of Social Security, later DHSS, 1966–73; Dep. Sec., DHSS, 1973–76, Second Perm. Sec., 1977–79. Mem., Occupational Pensions Bd, 1981–. Pres., Kingswood Assoc., 1983. *Address:* Bleak House, The Drive, Belmont, Sutton, Surrey. *T:* 01–642 6479. *Club:* United Oxford & Cambridge University.

ATKINSON, Sir (John) Kenneth, Kt 1953; retired as Chief Valuer, Valuation Office, Board of Inland Revenue (1951–66); *b* 21 May 1905; 2nd *s* of late James Oswald and Jane Atkinson, Liverpool; *m* 1930, Ellen Elsie Godwin Dod (*d* 1975); one *d. Educ:* The Leys, Cambridge. Joined Valuation Office, 1928; Deputy Chief Valuer, 1950. Fellow of the Royal Institution of Chartered Surveyors. *Recreation:* Rugby football. *Address:* 38 Clarence Road South, Weston-super-Mare, Avon BS23 4BW. *T:* Weston-super-Mare 23205.

ATKINSON, Sir Kenneth; *see* Atkinson, Sir J. K.

ATKINSON, Kenneth Neil, FIPM; Director of Youth Training, Manpower Services Commission, since 1983; *b* 4 April 1931; *s* of William Atkinson and Alice Reid. *Educ:* Kingussie High Sch., Inverness-shire. ARCM 1961; FIPM 1986. Various appts, Min. of Labour and Dept of Employment, 1948–67; Dep. Chief Conciliation Officer, Dept of Employment, 1968–72; Dir, Industry Trng Bd Relations, MSC, 1973–78; Manpower Services Dir, Scotland, 1979–82. *Recreations:* tennis, choral and solo singing, conducting. *Address:* 17 Graham Court, Sheffield S10 3DX. *T:* Sheffield 307983. *Club:* Royal Scottish Automobile (Glasgow).

ATKINSON, Leonard Allan, CMG 1963; *b* 6 Dec. 1906; *s* of L. Atkinson; *m* 1933, Annie R., *d* of A. E. Wells; one *s* two *d. Educ:* Wellington Coll. and Victoria Univ. of Wellington, New Zealand. Joined Customs Dept, 1924; Inspector, Public Service Commission, 1941–44; Sec., 1944–47; Asst Comr, 1947–54; Commission Member, 1954–58; Chm., 1958–62; Chm., State Services Commission, NZ, 1963–66. *Recreation:* bowls. *Address:* 181 The Parade, Island Bay, Wellington, NZ. *Club:* Wellington (NZ).

ATKINSON, Maj.-Gen. Sir Leonard Henry, KBE 1966 (OBE 1945); *b* 4 Dec. 1910; *s* of A. H. Atkinson; *m* 1939, Jean Eileen, *d* of C. A. Atchley, OBE; one *s* three *d. Educ:* Wellington Coll., Berks; University Coll., London (Fellow, 1977). BSc (Eng) 1932. Satchwell controls, GEC, 1932–36. Commnd in RAOC, 1936; transf. to REME, 1942; Comdr REME (Lieut-Col) Guards Armd Div. (NW Europe), 1943–45; DDEME (Col) Brit. Airborne Corps, India, 1945; Staff Coll., Quetta, 1945–46; served in Far East, UK and WO, 1946–50; JSSC, 1950–51; GSO1, REME Trg Centre, 1951–53; DDEME (Col) HQ 1st Corps (Germany), 1953–55; DDEME (Brig.). WO, 1956–58; Comdt (Brig.) REME Training Centre and Commander Berkshire Dist, 1958–63; Dir (Maj.-Gen.), Electrical and Mechanical Engineering, Army, 1963–66; Col Comdt, REME, 1967–72. Man. Dir, Harland Simon, 1970–72; Director: Harland Engineering, 1966–69; Simon Equipment, 1966–69; Weir Engineering Industries, 1970–74; United Gas Industries, 1972–76; C. & W. Walker Ltd, 1974–77; Bespoke Securities, 1974–82; Emray, 1978–85; Equity & General, 1985–. Chairman: Christopher Gold Associates, 1976–; DTI Cttee on Terotechnology, 1970–75; Council of Engineering Instns, 1974–75 (Vice-Chm., 1973); Technology Transfer Associates Ltd, 1980–; Vice Chm., Southern Regional Council for Further Educn, 1978–85. Member: Court of Bradford Univ., 1968–76; Court of Cranfield Inst. of Technology, 1975–77; Governor, Reading Coll. of Technology, 1968–85. FIMechE; FIEE; FIGasE; FIERE (past Pres.); FIMI; FRPSL; Hon. MIPlantE. Liveryman, 1966–, Upper Warden, 1986–87, Turners' Co. *Address:* Pound Cottage, Silchester, Reading, Berks. *T:* Basingstoke 881220. *Club:* Naval and Military.

ATKINSON, Leslie, CMG 1965; OBE 1961; Managing Director, Leslie Atkinson Pty Ltd, 1960; Member of Export Development Council, Sydney, 1959; *b* 11 Jan. 1913; *s* of J. Atkinson; *m* 1935, Ellen, *d* of J. Kinsey; one *s* one *d. Educ:* Wollongong Technical Sch. Controller, Nock and Kirby Ltd, 1943–49, Associate Dir, 1949–53; Dir and General Manager, Carr and Elliott, 1953–59. Pres., Sydney Junior Chamber of Commerce, 1946–47; Vice-Pres. and Hon. Treasurer, Sydney Chamber of Commerce, 1949–53, Pres., 1953–54, 1957–58; Vice-Pres., Associated Chambers of Commerce of the Commonwealth of Australia, 1956–57 (Pres., 1964–65). Mem. of Standing Cttee, NSW Methodist Conference, 1957–62. *Address:* 11 Kyle Parade, Kyle Bay, NSW 2221, Australia.

ATKINSON, Mary; *see under* Hardwick, Mollie.

ATKINSON, Michael William, CMG 1985; MBE 1970; HM Diplomatic Service; Ambassador to Ecuador, since 1985; *b* 11 April 1932; *m* 1963, Veronica Bobrovsky; two *s* one *d. Educ:* Purley County Grammar School; Queen's College, Oxford (BA Hons). Served FO, Vientiane, Buenos Aires, British Honduras, Madrid; FCO 1975; NATO Defence Coll., 1976; Counsellor, Budapest, 1977–80, Peking, 1980–82; Hd of Consular Dept, FCO, 1982–85. *Address:* c/o Foreign and Commonwealth Office, King Charles Street, SW1.

ATKINSON, Norman; MP (Lab) Tottenham, since 1964; *b* 25 March 1923; *s* of George Atkinson, Manchester; *m* 1948, Irene Parry. *Educ:* elementary and technical schs. Member of Manchester City Council, 1945–49. Chief Design Engineer, Manchester University, 1957–64. Contested (Lab) Wythenshawe, 1955, Altrincham and Sale, 1959. Treasurer, Labour Party, 1976–81. *Recreations:* walking, cricket, football. *Address:* House of Commons, SW1.

ATKINSON, Reay; *see* Atkinson, W. R.

ATKINSON, Prof. Richard John Copland, CBE 1979; MA; FSA 1946; Professor of Archaeology, University College, Cardiff, 1958–83, now Emeritus; *b* 22 Jan. 1920; *e s* of Roland Cecil Atkinson and Alice Noel Herbert Atkinson (*née* Wright); *m* 1st, 1942, Hester Renée Marguerite Cobb (*d* 1981); three *s*; 2nd, 1981, Judith Marion O'Kelly. *Educ:* Sherborne School; Magdalen College, Oxford. Asst Keeper, Department of Antiquities, Ashmolean Museum, Oxford, 1944–49; Lectr in Prehistoric Archæology, Univ. of Edinburgh, 1949–58; Dep. Principal, UC Cardiff, 1970–74. Member: Ancient Monuments Board for Wales, 1959–; Cttee of Enquiry into Arrangements for Protection of Field Monuments, 1966–68; Science-Based Archaeology Cttee, SRC, 1977–81 (UGC Assessor, SERC, 1981–); Royal Commission: on Ancient and Historical Monuments in Wales, 1963– (Chm., 1984–86); on Historical Monuments (England), 1968– (acting Chm., 1984); UGC, 1973–82 (Vice Chm., 1976–77; Chm., Arts Sub-cttee, 1978–82). Vice-President: Prehistoric Society, 1963–67; Council for British Archæology, 1970–73 (Hon. Sec., 1964–70); Dir, BBC Silbury Hill project, 1967–70; Chm., York Minster Excavation Cttee, 1975–. *Publications:* Field Archæology, 1946; Stonehenge, 1956; Stonehenge and Avebury, 1959; Archæology, History and Science, 1960; Stonehenge and Neighbouring Monuments, 1979; The Prehistoric Temples of Stonehenge and Avebury, 1980; articles in archæological journals. *Recreations:* archæology, wood-work and wine. *Address:* Warren House, Mountain Road, Pentyrch, Cardiff CF4 8QP. *Club:* United Oxford & Cambridge University.

ATKINSON, Sir Robert, Kt 1983; DSC 1941; RD 1947; FEng; Chairman: British Shipbuilders, 1980–84; Aurora Holdings, Sheffield, 1972–83; *b* 7 March 1916; *s* of Nicholas and Margaret Atkinson; *m* 1st, 1941, Joyce Forster (*d* 1973); one *s* one *d*; 2nd, 1977, Margaret Hazel Walker. *Educ:* London Univ. (BSc(Eng) Hons). MIMechE, CEng, FEng 1983. Served War 1939–45 (DSC 1941 and two Bars, 1st, 1943, 2nd, 1944, mentioned in Despatches, 1943). Managing Director: Wm Doxford, 1957–61; Tube Investments (Eng), 1961–67; Unicorn Industries, 1967–72; Dir, Stag Furniture Hldgs, 1973–. *Publications:* The Design and Operating Experience of an Ore Carrier Built Abroad, 1957; The Manufacture of Steel Crankshafts, 1960; Some Crankshaft Failures: Investigation into Causes and Remedies, 1960; technical papers. *Recreations:* salmon fishing, walking, gardening. *Address:* Southwood House, Itchen Abbas, Winchester, Hants SO21 1AT. *Club:* Royal Thames Yacht.

See also Prof. James Atkinson.

ATKINSON, Prof. Thomas, PhD; Professor and Head of Department of Mining Engineering, Nottingham University, since 1977; *b* 23 Jan. 1924; *s* of Thomas Bell and Elizabeth Atkinson; *m* 1948, Dorothy; one *d* (two *s* decd). *Educ:* Imperial Coll., London. DIC; CEng, FIMM, FIMinE, FIEE, FIMechE. FRSA. Served RN, 1942–46. Charlaw and Sacriston Collieries Ltd, Durham, 1938–42; NCB, 1946–49; Andrew Yule, India, 1949–53; KWPR, Australia, 1953–56; Mining Engr, Powell Duffryn Technical Services Ltd, 1956–68; Sen. Lectr, Imperial Coll., 1968–73; Head of Coal Mining Div., Shell Internat. Petroleum Maatschappij BV, Holland, 1973–77. Dir, British Mining Consultants Ltd, 1969–. Chm., Nat. Awards Tribunal, British Coal (formerly NCB), 1984–. *Publications:* contribs to Mining Engrg, Mineral Econs, Mine Electrics, etc. *Recreation:* painting. *Address:* 27 Kirk Lane, Ruddington, Nottingham NG11 6NN. *T:* Nottingham 842400. *Club:* Chaps.

ATKINSON, William Christopher; Stevenson Professor of Hispanic Studies in University of Glasgow, 1932–72; Director, Institute of Latin-American Studies, 1966–72; *b* Belfast, 9 Aug. 1902; *s* of Robert Joseph Atkinson; *m* 1928, Evelyn Lucy, *d* of C. F. Wakefield, Hampstead; one *s* three *d. Educ:* Univs of Belfast and Madrid. Lectr in Spanish at Armstrong Coll., Newcastle upon Tyne, 1926–32; Hon. Sec., Modern Humanities Research Assoc., 1929–36; Head of Spanish and Portuguese sections, Foreign Research and Press Service of Royal Institute of International Affairs, 1939–43; Visiting British Council Lecturer to Latin America, 1946, 1960, 1971; Hon. Prof. National Univ. of Colombia, 1946; Chm. 1st Scottish cultural delegation to USSR, 1954; Carnegie Research Fellow visiting US Univs, 1955; Member, Hispanic Society of America, 1955 (Corres. Mem., 1937); Rockefeller Fellow visiting Latin-American Univs, 1957; Visiting Prof. of Portuguese Studies, University Coll. of Rhodesia and Nyasaland, 1963. Commander, Order of Prince Henry the Navigator, Portugal, 1972. *Publications:* Spain, A Brief History, 1934; The Lusiads of Camoens, 1952; The Remarkable Life of Don Diego, 1958; A History of Spain and Portugal, 1960; The Conquest of New Granada, 1961; The Happy Captive, 1977; contributions to Encyclopædia Britannica, learned periodicals and reviews, and to composite works on Spanish and Portuguese studies. *Recreations:* travel and tramping. *Address:* 39 Manse Road, Bearsden, Glasgow. *T:* 041–942 0368.

ATKINSON, (William) Reay, CB 1985; FBCS; Under Secretary, 1978–86, and Regional Director, North Eastern Region, 1981–86, Department of Industry; *b* 15 March 1926; *s* of William Edwin Atkinson and Lena Marion (*née* Haselhurst); *m*; one *s* two *d*; *m* 1983, Rita Katherine (*née* Bunn). *Educ:* Gosforth Grammar Sch., Newcastle upon Tyne; King's Coll., Durham Univ.; Worcester Coll., Oxford. Served RNVR, 1943–46. Entered Civil Service as Inspector of Taxes, 1950; Principal, 1958, Asst. Sec., 1965; Secretaries Office, Inland Revenue, 1958–61 and 1962–69; Asst Sec., Royal Commn on the Press, 1961–62; Civil Service Dept, 1969; Under Sec., and Dir, Central Computer Agency, CSD, 1973–78. Dir, Hillcrest Holdings Ltd; Mem. Managing Cttee, Northern Rock Building Soc. Vice Pres., British Computer Soc. Gov., Newcastle-upon-Tyne Polytechnic. *Recreations:* fell walking, music. *Address:* High Dryburn, Garrigill, near Alston, Cumbria CA9 3EJ.

ATTALLAH, Naim Ibrahim; Book Publisher and Proprietor: Quartet Books, since 1976; The Women's Press, since 1977; Robin Clark, since 1980; Magazine Proprietor: The Literary Review, since 1981; (with Algy Cluff) Apollo, since 1984; The Wire, since 1984; Financial Director and Joint Managing Director, Asprey of Bond Street, since 1979; *b* 1 May 1931; *s* of Ibrahim and Genevieve Attallah; *m* 1957, Maria Attallah (*née* Nykolyn); one *s. Educ:* Battersea Polytechnic. Foreign Exchange Dealer, 1957; Financial Consultant, 1966; Dir of cos, 1969–. Launched Parfums Namara, Avant L'Amour and Après L'Amour, 1985. *Theatre:* co-presenter, Happy End, Lyric, 1975; presented and produced, The Beastly Beatitudes of Balthazar B, Duke of York's, 1981; co-prod, Trafford Tanzi, Mermaid, 1982; *films:* co-prod (with David Frost), The Slipper and the Rose, 1974–75; exec. producer, Brimstone and Treacle, 1982; also prod and presented TV docs. *Publications:* articles in The Literary Review. *Recreations:* classical music, opera, theatre, cinema, photography. *Address:* Namara House, 45–46 Poland Street, W1V 4AU. *T:* 01-439 6750. *Club:* Arts.

ATTENBOROUGH, Sir David (Frederick), Kt 1985; CBE 1974; FRS 1983; broadcaster and traveller; *b* 8 May 1926; *s* of late Frederick Levi Attenborough; *m* 1950, Jane Elizabeth Ebsworth Oriel; one *s* one *d. Educ:* Wyggeston Grammar Sch. for Boys, Leicester; Clare Coll., Cambridge (Hon. Fellow, 1980). Served in Royal Navy, 1947–49. Editorial Asst in an educational publishing house, 1949–52; joined BBC Television Service as trainee producer, 1952; undertook zoological and ethnographic filming expeditions to: Sierra Leone, 1954; British Guiana, 1955; Indonesia, 1956; New Guinea, 1957; Paraguay and Argentina, 1958; South West Pacific, 1959; Madagascar, 1960; Northern Territory of Australia, 1962; the Zambesi, 1964; Bali, 1969; Central New Guinea, 1971; Celebes, Borneo, Peru and Colombia, 1973; Mali, British Columbia, Iran, Solomon Islands, 1974; Nigeria, 1975; Controller, BBC-2, BBC Television Service, 1965–68; Dir of Programmes, Television, and Mem., Bd of Management, BBC, 1969–72. Writer and presenter, BBC series: Tribal Eye, 1976; Life on Earth, 1979; The Living Planet, 1984. Mem., Nature Conservancy Council, 1973–82. Trustee: WWF Internat., 1979–; British Museum, 1980–; Science Museum, 1984–. Corresp. Mem., Amer. Mus. Nat. Hist., 1985. Fellow, BAFTA 1980. Hon. Fellow: Manchester Polytechnic, 1976; UMIST, 1980. Special Award, SFTA, 1961; Silver Medal, Zool Soc. of London, 1966; Silver Medal, RTS, 1966; Desmond Davis Award, SFTA, 1970; Cherry Kearton Medal, RGS, 1972; Kalinga Prize, UNESCO, 1981; Washburn Award, Boston Mus. of Sci., 1983; Hopper Day Medal, Acad. of Natural Scis, Philadelphia, 1983; Founder's Gold Medal, RGS, 1985; Internat. Emmy Award, 1985. Hon. DLitt: Leicester, 1970; City, 1972; London, 1980; Birmingham, 1982; Hon. DSc: Liverpool, 1974; Heriot-Watt,

1978; Sussex, 1979; Bath, 1981; Ulster, Durham, 1982; Keele, 1986; Hon. LLD: Bristol, 1977; Glasgow, 1980; DUniv Open Univ., 1980; Hon. ScD Cambridge, 1984. Comdr of Golden Ark (Netherlands), 1983. *Publications:* Zoo Quest to Guiana, 1956; Zoo Quest for a Dragon, 1957; Zoo Quest in Paraguay, 1959; Quest in Paradise, 1960; Zoo Quest to Madagascar, 1961; Quest under Capricorn, 1963; The Tribal Eye, 1976; Life on Earth, 1979; The Living Planet, 1984, rev. edn 1985. *Recreations:* music, tribal art, natural history. *Address:* 5 Park Road, Richmond, Surrey.

See also Sir R. S. Attenborough.

ATTENBOROUGH, John Philip, CMG 1958; CBE 1953 (OBE 1946); retired; *b* 6 Nov. 1901; *s* of late Frederick Samuel and Edith Attenborough; *m* 1947, Lucie Blanche Woods, *y d* of late Rev. J. R. and Mrs Prenter and *widow* of late Dr P. P. Murphy; one step *s. Educ:* Manchester Grammar Sch.; Corpus Christi Coll., Oxford (MA). Superintendent of Education, Northern Nigeria, 1924–30; Lecturer and Senior Inspector, Education Dept, Palestine, 1930–37; Dir of Education, Aden, 1937–46; Deputy Dir of Education, Palestine, 1946–48; Asst Educational Adviser, Colonial Office, 1948; Dir of Education, Tanganyika, 1948–55; Mem. for Social Services, Tanganyika, 1955–57; Min. for Social Services, Tanganyika, 1957–58; Consultant: UNICEF, 1963–65; UNESCO, 1967; Devon, CC, 1961–68; Mem. SW Regional Hosp. Bd, 1965–71. Pres. Torbay Conservative Assoc., 1967–79. *Address:* 21 Thorncliff Close, Torquay, Devon. *T:* Torquay 27291.

ATTENBOROUGH, Peter John; Headmaster of Charterhouse, since 1982; *b* 4 April 1938; *m* 1967, Alexandra Deidre Campbell Page; one *s* one *d. Educ:* Christ's Hospital; Peterhouse, Cambridge. BA Classics 1960, MA 1964. Asst Master, Uppingham Sch., 1960–75 (Housemaster, Senior Classics Master); Asst Master, Starehe Boys' Centre, Nairobi, 1966–67; Headmaster, Sedbergh Sch., 1975–81. Freeman, City of London, 1965; Liveryman, Skinners' Co., 1978. *Address:* Charterhouse, Godalming, Surrey. *T:* Godalming 22589.

ATTENBOROUGH, Philip John; publisher; Chairman: Hodder & Stoughton Ltd and Hodder & Stoughton Holdings Ltd, since 1975; The Lancet Ltd, since 1977; *b* 3 June 1936; *er s* of John Attenborough, CBE, and Barbara (*née* Sandle); *m* 1963, Rosemary, *y d* of Dr W. B. Littler, *qv*; one *s* one *d. Educ:* Rugby; Trinity Coll., Oxford. Christmas postman (parcels), 1952–54; Nat. Service, Sergeant 68th Regt RA, Oswestry, 1956; lumberjack, Blind River, Ont, 1957; joined Hodder & Stoughton, 1957: Export Manager, 1960; Dir, 1963; Sales Dir, 1969. Dir, Book Tokens Ltd, 1985–. Publishers Association: Mem. Council, 1976– (Treasurer, 1981–82; Vice-Pres., 1982–83, 1985–86; Pres., 1983–85); Leader, delegns of Brit. publishers to China, 1978, to Bangladesh, India and Pakistan, 1986; Chm., Book Develt Council, 1977–79; Mem. British Council (Publishers Adv. Panel), 1977–. Liveryman, Skinners Co., 1970. *Recreations:* trout fishing, playing golf and tennis, watching cricket. *Address:* Coldhanger, Seal Chart, near Sevenoaks, Kent TN15 0EJ. *T:* Sevenoaks 61516. *Clubs:* Garrick, MCC; Kent CC, Rye Golf.

ATTENBOROUGH, Sir Richard (Samuel), Kt 1976; CBE 1967; actor, producer and director; *b* 29 Aug. 1923; *s* of late Frederick L. Attenborough; *m* 1945, Sheila Beryl Grant Sim; one *s* two *d. Educ:* Wyggeston Grammar Sch., Leicester. Leverhulme Schol. to Royal Acad. of Dramatic Art, 1941 (Bancroft Medal). First stage appearance as Richard Miller in Ah Wilderness, Intimate Theatre, Palmers Green, 1941. West End début as Ralph Berger in Awake and Sing, Arts Theatre, 1942; The Little Foxes, Piccadilly Theatre, 1942; Brighton Rock, Garrick, 1943. Joined RAF 1943; seconded to RAF Film Unit, 1944, and appeared in Journey Together; demobilised, 1946. Returned to Stage, Jan. 1949, in The Way Back (Home of the Brave), Westminster; To Dorothy, a Son, Savoy, 1950 (transf. to Garrick, 1951); Sweet Madness, Vaudeville, 1952; The Mousetrap, Ambassadors, 1952–54; Double Image, Savoy, 1956–57, St James's, 1957; The Rape of the Belt, Piccadilly, 1957–58. First film appearance in In Which We Serve, 1942; other film appearances include: School for Secrets, The Man Within, Dancing With Crime, Brighton Rock, London Belongs to Me, The Guinea Pig, The Lost People, Boys in Brown, Morning Departure, Hell is Sold Out, The Magic Box, Gift Horse, Father's Doing Fine, Eight O'Clock Walk, The Ship That Died of Shame, Private's Progress, The Baby and the Battleship, Brothers in Law, The Scamp, Dunkirk, The Man Upstairs, Sea of Sand, Danger Within, I'm All Right Jack, Jet Storm, SOS Pacific; The Angry Silence (also co-prod), 1959; The League of Gentlemen, 1960; Only Two Can Play, All Night Long, 1961; The Dock Brief, The Great Escape, 1962; Séance On a Wet Afternoon (also prod; Best actor, San Sebastian Film Fest. and British Film Acad.), The Third Secret, 1963; Guns at Batasi, 1964 (Best actor, British Film Acad.); The Flight of the Phœnix, 1965; The Sand Pebbles, Dr Dolittle, 1966 (both Hollywood Golden Globe); The Bliss of Mrs Blossom, 1967; Only When I Larf, 1968; The Last Grenade, A Severed Head, David Copperfield, Loot, 1969; 10 Rillington Place, 1970; Ten Little Indians, Rosebud, Brannigan, Conduct Unbecoming, 1974; The Chess Players, 1977; The Human Factor, 1979; produced: Whistle Down the Wind, 1961; The L-Shaped Room, 1962; directed: Oh! What a Lovely War, 1968 (16 Internat. Awards incl. Hollywood Golden Globe and SFTA UN Award); Young Winston, 1972 (Hollywood Golden Globe); A Bridge Too Far, 1976 (Evening News Best Drama Award); Magic, 1978; A Chorus Line, 1985; dir. and prod., Gandhi, 1980–81 (Hollywood Golden Globe, 8 Oscars). Formed: Beaver Films with Bryan Forbes, 1959; Allied Film Makers, 1960; Chm., Goldcrest Films, 1981–; Chm., Goldcrest Films & Television, 1985– (Dir, 1981–); Dep. Chm., Channel Four Television, 1980–; Chm., Capital Radio, 1973–. Member: British Actors' Equity Assoc. Council, 1949–73; Cinematograph Films Council, 1967–73; Arts Council of GB, 1970–73; Young Vic Bd, 1974–; Chairman: RADA, 1970– (Mem. Council, 1963–); Actor's Charitable Trust, 1956–; Combined Theatrical Charities, 1964–; Governor, Nat. Film Sch., 1970–81; Governor and Chm., BFI, 1982–; Vice-Pres., BAFTA (formerly SFTA), 1971– (Chm., 1969–70); Trustee, Tate Gall., 1976–82. Pres., Muscular Dystrophy Gp of GB, 1971– (Vice Pres., 1962–71). Dir, Chelsea Football Club, 1969–. Pro-Chancellor, Sussex Univ., 1970–. Fellow, BAFTA, 1983. Hon. DLitt: Leicester, 1970; Kent, 1981; Hon. DCL Newcastle, 1974. Padma Bhushan, 1983. *Publications:* In Search of Gandhi, 1982; (with Diana Carter) Richard Attenborough's Chorus Line, 1986. *Recreations:* listening to music, collecting paintings, watching football. *Address:* Old Friars, Richmond Green, Surrey. *Clubs:* Garrick, Beefsteak, Green Room.

See also Sir D. F. Attenborough.

ATTERTON, David Valentine, CBE 1981; PhD; FEng; FIM; Chairman, Foseco Minsep plc, since 1979; *b* 13 Feb. 1927; *s* of Frank Arthur Shepherd Atterton and Ella Constance (*née* Collins); *m* 1948, Sheila Ann McMahon; two *s* one *d. Educ:* Bishop Wordsworth's Sch., Salisbury; Peterhouse, Cambridge. MA, PhD Cantab. Post-doctorate research, Cambridge, 1950–52; joined Foundry Services Ltd, 1952; Managing Director: Foseco Ltd, 1966; Foseco Minsep Ltd, 1969. Dep. Chm., Associated Engineering plc, 1979– (Dir 1972–); Director: Investors in Industry plc (formerly Finance Corp. for Industry and FFI), 1974–; IMI plc, 1976–; Barclays Bank UK Ltd, 1982–84; Bank of England, 1984–; Barclays Bank, 1984–. Chm., NEDO Iron and Steel Sector Working Party, 1977–82; Member: Bd of Governors, United World Coll. of the Atlantic, 1968–85 (Chm., 1973–79); Adv. Council for Applied R&D, 1982–85; Pres., Birmingham Chamber of Commerce and Industry, 1974–75. *Publications:* numerous scientific papers in learned jls. *Recreations:* cartography, notaphilia, astronomy, photography. *Address:* The Doctors House, Doctors Hill, Tanworth in Arden, Warwicks B94 5AW. *T:* Tanworth in Arden 2423.

ATTLEE, family name of **Earl Attlee.**

ATTLEE, 2nd Earl, *cr* 1955; **Martin Richard Attlee;** Viscount Prestwood, 1955; *b* 10 Aug. 1927; *o s* of 1st Earl Attlee, KG, PC, OM, CH, FRS, and Violet Helen (*d* 1964), *d* of H. E. Millar; *S* father, 1967; *m* 1955, Anne Barbara, *er d* of late James Henderson, CBE, Bath, Somerset; one *s* one *d. Educ:* Millfield Coll.; Southampton University Coll. (now Southampton Univ.). MIPR 1964. Served in Merchant Navy, 1945–50. Active Mem. Hon. Artillery Company, 1951–55. Asst PRO, Southern Region, British Rail, 1970–76. Founder Mem., SDP, 1981; SDP spokesman on transport (excluding aviation), House of Lords, 1984–. *Publication:* Bluff Your Way in PR, 1971. *Recreations:* writing, DIY. *Heir: s* Viscount Prestwood, *qv. Address:* 1 Cadet Way, Church Crookham, Aldershot, Hants GU13 0UG. *T:* Aldershot 628007. *Club:* Pathfinders'.

ATTLEE, Air Vice-Marshal Donald Laurence, CB 1978; LVO 1964; fruit farmer, since 1977; *b* 2 Sept. 1922; *s* of Major Laurence Attlee; *m* 1952, Jane Hamilton Young; one *s* two *d. Educ:* Haileybury. Pilot trng in Canada, 1942–44; Flying Instructor, 1944–48; Staff, Trng Comd, 1949–52; 12 Sqdn, 1952–54; Air Ministry, Air Staff, 1954–55; RAF Staff Coll., 1956; 59 Sqdn, 1957–59; CO, The Queen's Flight (W/Cdr), 1960–63; HQ, RAF Germany, 1964–67; CO, RAF Brize Norton, 1968–69; IDC, 1970; MoD Policy Staff, 1971–72; Dir of RAF Recruiting, 1973–74; Air Cdre, Intell., 1974–75; AOA Trng Comd, 1975–77, retired. *Recreations:* genealogy, Do-it-Yourself, gardening. *Address:* Jerwoods, Culmstock, Cullompton, Devon. *T:* Hemycock 680317. *Club:* Royal Air Force.

ATTRIDGE, Elizabeth Ann Johnston, (Mrs John Attridge); Under Secretary, Emergencies, Food Quality and Pest Control, Ministry of Agriculture, Fisheries and Food, since 1985; *b* 26 Jan. 1934; *d* of late Rev. John Worthington Johnston, MA, CF, and Mary Isabel Giraud (*née* McFadden); *m* 1956, John Attridge; one *s. Educ:* Richmond Lodge Sch., Belfast; St Andrews Univ., Fife. Assistant Principal, Min. of Education, NI, 1955, reappointed on marriage (marriage bar), MAFF, London, 1956; assisted on Agriculture Acts, 1957 and 1958; Head Plant Health Br., 1963–66, Finance, 1966–69, External Relations (GATT) Br., 1969–72; Assistant Secretary: Animal Health I, 1972–75; Marketing Policy and Potatoes, 1975–78; Tropical Foods Div., 1978–83; Under Sec., European Community Group, 1983–85. Chairman, International Coffee Council, 1982–83. *Recreations:* collecting fabric, opera. *Address:* Croxley East, The Heath, Weybridge, Surrey. *T:* Weybridge 46218.

ATTWELL, Rt. Rev. Arthur Henry; *see* Sodor and Man, Bishop of.

ATTWOOD, Thomas Jaymril; Chairman, Cargill, Attwood and Thomas Ltd, Management Consultancy Group, since 1965; *b* 30 March 1931; *s* of George Frederick Attwood and Avril Sandys (*née* Cargill, NZ); *m* 1963, Lynette O. E. Lewis; one *s* one *d. Educ:* Haileybury and Imperial Service Coll.; RMA Sandhurst; Harvard Grad. Sch. of Business Admin; INSEAD, Fontainebleau. Pres., Internat. Consultants' Foundn, 1978–81. Conducted seminars for UN Secretariat, European Commn and World Council of Churches, 1970–80; presented papers to Eur. Top Management Symposium, Davos, Internat. Training Conf. and to World Public Relations Conf. Mem. Exec. Cttee, Brit. Management Training Export Council, 1978–85; Chm., Post Office Users National Council, 1982–83. Liveryman, Worshipful Company of Marketors, 1980. FIMC; FBIM. Mem., Richmond upon Thames Borough Council, 1969–71. *Publications:* (jtly) Bow Group pubn on United Nations, 1961; contrib. to reference books, incl. Systems Thinking, Innovation in Global Consultation, Handbook of Management Development, and Helping Across Cultures; articles on marketing, management and business topics. *Recreations:* travel, music, City of London, cricket. *Address:* 8 Teddington Park, Teddington, Mddx TW11 8DA. *T:* 01–977 8091. *Clubs:* City Livery, MCC, Lord's Taverners.

ATWELL, Sir John (William), Kt 1976; CBE 1970; FEng; FIMechE, FRSE; Chairman, Omega Software Ltd, 1982–84; *b* 24 Nov. 1911; *s* of William Atwell and Sarah Workman; *m* 1945, Dorothy Hendry Baxter, *d* of J. H. Baxter and Janet Muir; no *c. Educ:* Hyndland Secondary Sch., Glasgow; Royal Technical Coll., Glasgow (ARTC); Cambridge Univ. (MSc). General Management, Stewarts and Lloyds Ltd, 1939–54; Dir 1955–61, Man. Dir 1961–68, G. & J. Weir Ltd; Dir, The Weir Group Ltd, 1961–74, and Chm., Engineering Div., 1968–74; Mem., BRB (Scottish), 1975–81. Chm., Scottish Offshore Partnership, 1975–81; Director: Anderson Strathclyde Ltd, 1975–78; Govan Shipbuilders Ltd, 1975–79. Mem., Bd of Royal Ordnance Factories, 1974–79. Chm., Requirements Bd for Mechanical Engineering and Machine Tools, DTI, 1972–76. Member: University Grants Cttee, 1965–69; NEDC Mech. Eng Cttee, 1969–74; Court, Strathclyde Univ., 1967–83 (Chm., 1975–80); Council, RSE, 1974–85 (Treas., 1977–82; Pres., 1982–85); Exec. Cttee, Scottish Council of Develt and Industry, 1972–77; Adv. Council for Applied R&D, 1976–80; Scottish Hosps Res. Trust, 1972–84; Council, Scottish Business Sch., 1972–80. Vice-Pres., IMechE, 1966–73, Pres., 1973–74; Vice-Chm., 1977–78, Chm., 1978–79, CEI. Hon. LLD Strathclyde, 1973. *Recreation:* golf. *Address:* Elmfield, Buchanan Drive, Rutherglen, Glasgow. *T:* 041–647 1824. *Clubs:* New (Edinburgh); Western (Glasgow).

ATWILL, Sir (Milton) John (Napier), Kt 1979; Deputy Chairman: David Jones Ltd, since 1975 (Board Member, since 1971); D. J.'s Properties Ltd, since 1976; Chairman, Waugh & Josephson Holdings Ltd, since 1983 (Director, since 1965); Director: Bushells Holdings Ltd, since 1975; MEPC Australia Ltd, since 1980; *b* 16 Jan. 1926; *s* of Milton Spencer Atwill and Isabella Caroline Atwill; *m* 1955, Susan Playfair; two *d. Educ:* Cranbrook Sch., Sydney; Geelong Church of England Grammar Sch.; Jesus Coll., Cambridge (MA). Called to the Bar, Gray's Inn, 1953, NSW Bar, 1953. President, NSW Division, Liberal Party of Australia, 1970–75; Hon. Treas., 1968–69; Federal Pres., Liberal Party, 1975–82; Chm., Pacific Democrat Union, 1982; Vice-Chm., Internat. Democrat Union, 1983–. Dir, Austore Property Trust, 1986. Chm., United World Colls (Australia) Trust, 1985–. *Recreations:* cricket, tennis. *Address:* 5 Fullerton Street, Woollahra, NSW 2025, Australia. *T:* (02) 32 1570. *Clubs:* Australian, Union, Royal Sydney Golf, Melbourne.

AUBREY, John Melbourn, CBE 1979; consultant; *b* 5 March 1921; *s* of Melbourn Evans Aubrey and Edith Maria Aubrey; *m* 1949, Judith Christine Fairbairn; two *s* two *d* (and one *s* decd). *Educ:* St Paul's Sch.; Corpus Christi Coll., Cambridge (Mech. Sciences Tripos). FCIPA 1952. Armstrong Siddeley Motors Ltd, 1942–43; RE, 1943–47; Tootal Broadhurst Lee Co., 1947–49; Gill Jennings and Every, Chartered Patent Agents, 1949–55; Courtaulds Ltd, 1955–81, Consultant 1982–86. Chm., Baptist Insurance Co. Ltd, 1980– (Dir, 1971–); Mem. Council, Baptist Union of GB and Ireland, 1970–. *Recreations:* gardening, tennis, swimming, skiing. *Address:* 52 Kenilworth Road, Leamington Spa. *T:* Leamington Spa 24463. *Clubs:* United Oxford & Cambridge University, Ski of GB; Coventry Aeroplane.

AUBREY-FLETCHER, family name of **Baroness Braye.**

AUBREY-FLETCHER, Sir John (Henry Lancelot), 7th Bt *cr* 1782; a Recorder of the Crown Court, 1972–74; Metropolitan Magistrate, 1959–71; *b* 22 Aug. 1912; *s* of Major Sir Henry Aubrey-Fletcher, 6th Bt, CVO, DSO, and Mary Augusta (*d* 1963), *e d* of Rev. R. W. Chilton; *S* father, 1969; *m* 1939, Diana Fynvola, *d* of late Lieut-Col Arthur Egerton, Coldstream Guards, and late Mrs Robert Bruce; one *s* (one *d* decd). *Educ:* Eton; New Coll., Oxford. Called to Bar, 1937. Served War of 1939–45, Grenadier Guards, reaching rank of temp. Lieut-Col and leaving Army with rank of Hon. Major. Dep. Chm., Bucks Quarter Sessions, 1959–71. High Sheriff, Bucks, 1961. *Heir: s* Henry Egerton Aubrey-Fletcher [*b* 27 Nov. 1945; *m* 1976, Roberta Sara, *d* of Major Robert Buchanan, Blackpark Cottage, Evanton, Ross-shire, and Mrs Ogden White; three *s*]. *Address:* The Gate House, Chilton, Aylesbury, Bucks. *T:* Long Crendon 347.

AUCHINCLOSS, Louis Stanton; author; Partner, Hawkins Delafield and Wood, NYC, since 1957 (Associate, 1954–57); *b* NY, 27 Sept. 1917; *s* of J. H. Auchincloss and P. Stanton; *m* 1957, Adèle Lawrence; three *s*. *Educ:* Groton Sch.; Yale Univ.; Univ. of Virginia (LLB). Lieut USNR; served, 1941–45. Admitted to NY Bar, 1941; Associate Sullivan and Cromwell, 1941–51. Mem. Exec. Cttee, Assoc. of Bar of NY City. Pres., Museum of City of NY, 1967; Trustee, Josiah Macy Jr Foundn. Mem., Nat. Inst. of Arts and Letters. *Publications:* The Indifferent Children, 1947; The Injustice Collectors, 1950; Sybil, 1952; A Law for the Lion, 1953; The Romantic Egoists, 1954; The Great World and Timothy Colt, 1956; Venus in Sparta, 1958; Pursuit of the Prodigal, 1959; The House of Five Talents, 1960; Reflections of a Jacobite, 1961; Portrait in Brownstone, 1962; Powers of Attorney, 1963; The Rector of Justin, 1964; Pioneers and Caretakers, 1966; The Embezzler, 1966; Tales of Manhattan, 1967; A World of Profit, 1969; Second Chance: tales to two generations, 1970; Edith Wharton, 1972; I Come as a Thief, 1972; Richelieu, 1972; The Partners, 1974; A Writer's Capital, 1974; Reading Henry James, 1975; The Winthrop Covenant, 1976; The Dark Lady, 1977; The Country Cousin, 1978; The House of the Prophet, 1980; The Cat and the King, 1981; Watch Fires, 1982; Honourable Men, 1986; pamphlets on American writers. *Address:* 1111 Park Avenue, New York, NY 10028, USA; (office) 67 Wall Street, New York, NY 10005. *Club:* Century Association (NY).

AUCKLAND, 9th Baron (*cr* Irish Barony, 1789; British 1793); **Ian George Eden;** insurance consultant; Non-executive Director: C. J. Sims & Co. Ltd; George S. Hall & Co. Ltd; *b* 23 June 1926; *s* of 8th Baron Auckland; *S* father 1957; *m* 1954, Dorothy Margaret, *d* of H. J. Manser, Eastbourne; one *s* two *d*. *Educ:* Blundell's Sch. Royal Signals, 1945–48; 3/4 County of London Yeomanry (Sharpshooters) (TA), 1948–53. Underwriting Mem. of Lloyd's, 1956–64. Vice-Pres., Royal Society for Prevention of Accidents; Member: New Zealand Soc.; Anglo-Finnish Parly Gp. Pres., Surrey Co. Br., Royal British Legion. Master, Broderers' Co., 1967–68. Knight, 1st cl., White Rose (Finland), 1984. *Recreations:* music, theatre, tennis and walking. *Heir: s* Hon. Robert Ian Burnard Eden, *b* 25 July 1962. *Address:* Tudor Rose House, 30 Links Road, Ashtead, Surrey. *T:* Ashtead 74393. *Clubs:* City Livery, St Stephen's Constitutional.

AUCKLAND (Dio. Durham), **Archdeacon of;** *see* Hodgson, Ven. J. D.

AUCKLAND (NZ), Bishop of, since 1985; **Rt. Rev. Bruce Carlyle Gilberd;** *b* 22 April 1938; *s* of Carlyle Bond Gilberd and Dorothy Annie Gilberd; *m* 1963, Patricia Molly Tanton; two *s* one *d*. *Educ:* King's College, Auckland; Auckland Univ. (BSc); St John's Coll., Auckland (LTh Hons, STh). Deacon 1962, priest 1963, Auckland; Assistant Curate: Devonport, 1962–64; Ponsonby and Grey Lynn, 1965; Panmure, 1965–68; Vicar of Avondale, 1968–71. Trainee Industrial Chaplain, Tees-side Industrial Mission, and Asst Curate of Egglescliffe, 1971–73; visited industrial missions in UK and Europe. Director, Interchurch Trade and Industrial Mission, Wellington, 1973–79; founding Mem., Wellington Industrial Relations Soc.; Hon. Asst Curate, Lower Hutt 1973–77, Waiwhetu 1977–79; Lectr, St John's Coll., Auckland, 1980–85. Mem. Gen. Synod, NZ. Has travelled widely in UK, Europe, China, USA and S Africa. *Publication:* (ed) Christian Ministry: a definition, 1984. *Recreations:* fishing, surfing, sailing. *Address:* PO Box 37 023, Parnell, Auckland 1, New Zealand. *T:* 771 989.

AUCKLAND (NZ), Bishop of, (RC), since 1983; **Rt. Rev. Denis George Browne;** *b* 21 Sept. 1937; *s* of Neville John Browne and Catherine Anne Browne (*née* Moroney). *Educ:* Holy Name Seminary, Christchurch, NZ; Holy Cross College, Mosgiel, NZ. Assistant Priest: Gisborne, 1963–67; Papatoetoe, 1968–71; Remuera, 1972–74; Missionary in Tonga, 1975–77; Bishop of Rarotonga, 1977–83. Hon. DD. *Recreation:* golf. *Address:* Box 47–255, Auckland, New Zealand. *T:* 764–244.

AUCKLAND (NZ), Assistant Bishop of; *see* Buckle, Rt Rev. E. G.

AUDLAND, Christopher John, CMG 1973; Director-General for Energy, Commission of the European Communities, since 1981; *b* 7 July 1926; *s* of late Brig. Edward Gordon Audland, CB, CBE, MC, and Violet Mary, *d* of late Herbert Shepherd-Cross, MP; *m* 1955, Maura Daphne Sullivan; two *s* one *d*. *Educ:* Winchester Coll. RA, 1944–48 (Temp. Capt.). Entered Foreign (subseq. Diplomatic) Service, 1948; has served in: Bonn; British Representation to Council of Europe; Washington; UK Delegn to Common Market negotiations, Brussels, 1961–63; Buenos Aires; FCO, 1968–70; Counsellor (Head of Chancery), Bonn, 1970–73. Mem., UK Delegn to Four-Power Negotiations on Berlin, 1970–72; Dep. Sec. Gen., EEC, 1973–81. *Address:* (office) Commission des Communautés Européennes, 200 rue de la Loi, Bruxelles 1049, Belgium. *T:* Brussels 2351959; (home) 5 avenue des Lauriers, Brussels 1150, Belgium. *T:* Brussels 7313467. *Club:* United Oxford & Cambridge University.

AUDLEY, 25th Baron *cr* 1312–13; **Richard Michael Thomas Souter;** Director, Graham Miller & Co. Ltd, retired 1983; *b* 31 May 1914; *s* of Sir Charles Alexander Souter, KCIE, CSI (*d* 1958) and Lady Charlotte Dorothy Souter (*née* Jesson) (*d* 1958); *S* kinswoman, Baroness Audley (24th in line), 1973; *m* 1941, Pauline, *d* of D. L. Eskell; three *d*. *Educ:* Uppingham. Fellow, CILA. Military Service, 1939–46; Control Commission, Germany, 1946–50. Insurance Broker until 1955; Loss Adjuster, 1955–. *Recreations:* shooting, gardening. *Heir:* three co-heiresses. *Address:* Friendly Green, Cowden, near Edenbridge, Kent TN8 7DU. *T:* Cowden 682.

AUDLEY, Sir (George) Bernard, Kt 1985; Founder and Chairman, AGB Research PLC; *b* Stockton Brook, N Staffs, 24 April 1924; *s* of late Charles Bernard Audley and Millicent Claudia Audley; *m* 1950, Barbara, *d* of late Richard Arthur Heath; two *s* one *d*. *Educ:* Wolstanton Grammar Sch.; Corpus Christi Coll., Oxford (MA). Lieut, Kings Dragoon Guards, 1943–46. Asst Gen. Man., Hulton Press Ltd, 1949–57; Man. Dir, Television Audience Measurement Ltd, 1957–61; founded AGB Research, with Martin Maddan, MP, Dick Gapper, and Doug Brown, 1962. Chairman: Netherhall Trust, 1962–; Industry and Commerce Adv. Cttee, William and Mary Tercentenary Trust, 1985–; Arts Access, 1986–; President: EUROPANEL, 1966–70; Periodical Publishers Assoc., 1985–. Governor, Hong Kong Coll., 1984–. FRSA 1986. Freeman of City of London, 1978; Liveryman, Gold and Silver Wyre Drawers' Company, 1975–. *Recreations:* golf, reading, travel. *Address:* Capstone, Willenhall Avenue, New Barnet, Herts EN5 1JN. *T:* 01–449 2030; Le Collet du Puits, Montauroux, 83440 Fayence, France. *T:* (94) 765287. *Clubs:* City Livery, Toledo, MCC; Rye Golf, Hadley Wood Golf.

AUDLEY-CHARLES, Prof. Michael Geoffrey, PhD; Yates-Goldsmid Professor of Geology and Head of the Department of Geological Sciences, University College London, since 1982; *b* 10 Jan. 1935; *s* of Lawrence Geoffrey and Elsie Ada Audley-Charles; *m* 1965, Brenda Amy Cordeiro; one *s* one *d*. *Educ:* Royal Wanstead Sch.; Chelsea Polytechnic (BSc); Imperial Coll., London (PhD). Geologist with mining and petroleum cos, Canada and Australia, 1957–62; Imperial Coll. of Science and Technology, London: research in geology, 1962–67; Lectr in Geol., 1967–73; Reader in Geol., 1973–77; Prof. of Geol. and Head of Dept of Geol Sciences, Queen Mary Coll., London, 1977–82. *Publications:* geological papers dealing with stratigraphy of British Triassic, regional geol. of Indonesia and Crete and evolution of Gondwanaland, in learned jls. *Recreation:* gardening. *Address:* Shambrooks, Hurst Green, Etchingham, East Sussex TN19 7QT. *T:* Hurst Green 297.

AUDU, Dr Ishaya Shu'aibu, FRCPE; Minister of External Affairs, Federal Republic of Nigeria, 1979–83; *b* 1 March 1927; *s* of Malam Bulus Audu and Malama Rakiya Audu; *m* 1958, Victoria Abosede Ohiorhenuan; two *s* five *d*. *Educ:* Ibadan and London Univs. House Officer, Sen. House Officer, Registrar in Surgery, Medicine, Obstetrics and Gynæcology and Pædiatrics, King's Coll. Hosp., London and Univ. Coll. Hosp., Ibadan, 1954–58; postgrad. studies, UK, 1959–60; Specialist Physician, Pædiatrician to Govt of Northern Nigeria and Personal Physician to Premier of North Region Govt, 1960–62; Lectr to Associate Professorship in Pæds, Univ. of Lagos Med. Sch., 1962–66; Vis. Res. Associate Prof., Univ. of Rochester Med. Sch., NY, 1964–65; Dep. Chm., Lagos Univ. Teaching Hosp. Man. Bd and Mem. Council, Univ. Lagos Med. Coll., 1962–66; Mem. Senate, Lagos Univ., 1963–66; Vice-Chancellor, Ahmadu Bello Univ., 1966–1975; Prof. of Medicine, 1967–77; Sen. Medical Officer, Ashaka Cement Co. Ltd, 1977–79. Hon. LHD Ohio, 1968; Hon DSc Nigeria, 1971; Hon. LLD Ibadan, 1973; FMC (Pæd) Nigerian Med. Council; FRSocMed. *Publications:* contribs to learned jls. *Recreations:* walking, table tennis.

AUDUS, Prof. Leslie John, MA, PhD, ScD Cantab; FLS, FInstBiol; Hildred Carlile Professor of Botany, Bedford College, University of London, 1948–79; *b* 9 Dec. 1911; English; *m* 1938, Rowena Mabel Ferguson; two *d*. *Educ:* Downing Coll., Cambridge Univ. Downing Coll. Exhibitioner, 1929–31; Frank Smart Research Student (Cambridge Univ.), 1934–35; Lecturer in Botany, University Coll., Cardiff, 1935–40. Served War of 1939–45: RAFVR (Technical, Radar, Officer), 1940–46; PoW South Pacific, 1942–45. Scientific Officer, Agricultural Research Council, Unit of Soil Metabolism, Cardiff, 1946–47; Monsanto Lecturer in Plant Physiology, University Coll., Cardiff, 1948. Recorder, 1961–65, Pres., 1967–68, Section K, British Assoc. for the Advancement of Science. Vis. Prof. of Botany: Univ. of California, Berkeley, 1958; Univ. of Minnesota, Minneapolis, 1965; Vice-Pres. Linnean Soc. of London, 1959–60; Life Mem. New York Academy of Sciences, 1961. Editor, Journal Exp. Botany, 1965–74. *Publications:* Plant Growth Substances, 1953, 3rd edn 1972; (ed) The Physiology and Biochemistry of Herbicides, 1964; (ed) Herbicides: physiology, biochemistry and ecology, 1976; original research on plant respiration, hormones, responses to gravity, soil micro-biology in relation to pesticides, etc in Annals of Botany, New Phytologist, Nature, Journal of Experimental Botany, Weed Research, etc. *Recreations:* furniture construction and restoration, electronics, amateur radio. *Address:* 38 Belmont Lane, Stanmore, Middlesex HA7 2PT.

AUERBACH, Charlotte, PhD, DSc; FRS 1957; FRSE; Professor of Genetics in the University of Edinburgh (Institute of Animal Genetics), 1967, Emeritus 1969 (Lecturer, 1947–57; Reader, 1957–67). Has done pioneering work on the chemical induction of mutations. Hon. Mem., Genetics Soc., Japan, 1966; Foreign Mem., Kongelige Danske Videnskabernes Selskab, 1968; Foreign Associate, Nat. Acad. of Sciences, USA, 1970. Hon. Dr Leiden, 1975; Hon. ScD Dublin, 1977; Hon. ScD Cambridge, 1977. Darwin Medal, Royal Soc., 1976. *Publications:* Genetics in the Atomic Age, 1956; The Science of Genetics, 1961; Mutation Pt 1–Methods, 1962; Heredity, 1965; Mutation Research, 1976; papers in various genetical journals. *Address:* Institute of Animal Genetics, The University, West Mains Road, Edinburgh EH9 3JN.

AUERBACH, Frank Helmuth; painter, draughtsman; *b* 29 April 1931; *s* of Max Auerbach, lawyer, and Charlotte Norah Auerbach; *m* 1958, Julia Wolstenholme; one *s*. *Educ:* privately; St Martin's Sch. of Art; Royal Coll. of Art. *One-man exhibitions:* Beaux Arts Gallery, 1956, 1959, 1961, 1962, 1963; Marlborough Fine Art, 1965, 1967, 1971, 1974, 1977, 1983; Marlborough-Gerson, New York, 1969; Villiers, Sydney, Australia, 1972; Bergamini, Milan, 1973; Univ. of Essex, 1973; Mun. Gall. of Modern Art, Dublin, 1974; Marlborough, Zurich, 1976; Anthony D'Offay, London; Arts Council Retrospective, Hayward Gall., 1978; Edinburgh, 1978; Jacobson, NY, 1979; Marlborough, NY, 1982; Anne Berthoud, London, 1983. *Mixed exhibitions:* Carnegie International, Pittsburgh, 1958, 1962; Dunn International, Fredericton, 1963; Gulbenkian International, Tate Gallery, 1964; European Painting in the Seventies, USA, 1976; Annual Exhbn, part I, Hayward Gall., 1977; Westkunst, Cologne, 1981; Venice Biennale (Internat. Pavilion), 1982; Internat. Survey, Moma, NY, 1984; The Hard Won Image, Tate Gall., 1984; The British Show, Australia, 1985; *public collections:* Brit. Council; Brit. Museum; Tate Gallery, London; Metropolitan Museum, NY; Mus. of Modern Art, NY; National Gallery of Victoria, Melbourne; Nat. Galls of Australia, W Australia and NSW; Chrysler Museum, Provincetown, Mass; County Museum of LA, Calif; Cleveland Mus., Ohio; Univ. of Cincinnati; Aberdeen, Bedford, Bolton, Edinburgh, Hartlepool, Huddersfield, Hull, Leeds, Leicester, Manchester, Nottingham, Oldham, Rochdale, Sheffield, Southampton Galls; Arts Council, Contemporary Art Soc., etc. *Address:* c/o Marlborough Fine Art, 6 Albemarle Street, W1X 3HF.

AUGER, Pierre Victor, Grand Officer, Legion of Honour; retired as Director-General European Space Research Organisation (ESRO); Professor, Faculty of Sciences, University of Paris, since 1937; *b* 14 May 1899; *s* of Victor E. Auger, Prof., Univ. of Paris, and Eugénie Blanchet; *m* 1921, Suzanne Motteau; two *d*. *Educ:* Ecole Normale Supérieure, Paris; Univ. of Paris. Université de Paris (Faculté des Sciences): Asst 1927; Chef de Travaux, 1932; Maître de Conférences, 1937. Research Associate, Univ. of Chicago, 1941–43; Head of Physics Div., joint Anglo-Canadian research project on atomic energy, 1942–44; Dir of Higher Education, Min. of Education, France, 1945–48; Mem. exec. Board of UNESCO, 1946–48; Membre du comité de l'Energie Atomique, France, 1946–48; Dir, Natural Sciences Dept, UNESCO, 1948–59; Special Consultant, UNO and UNESCO, 1959–60; Chm., French Cttee on Space Research, 1960–62. Mem., French Academy of Sciences, 1977. Feltrinelli International Prize, 1961; Kalinga Internat. Prize, 1972; Gaede-Langmuir Award, 1979. FRSA. *Publications:* Rayons cosmiques, 1941; L'Homme microscopique, 1952; Current Trends in Scientific Research, 1961; scientific papers on physics (X-rays, neutrons, cosmic rays), 1923–; papers on philosophy of science, 1949–. *Address:* 12 rue Emile Faguet, 75014 Paris, France. *T:* 540 96 34.

AUGUSTINE, Fennis Lincoln; High Commissioner for Grenada in London, 1979–84; *b* 22 April 1932; *s* of late Mr Augustine and of Festina Joseph; *m* 1973, Oforiwa Augustine;

one *s* one *d*. *Educ:* London Univ. (LLB); Ruskin Coll., Oxford (Labour Studies). Called to the Bar, Inner Temple, 1972. *Recreations:* cricket, music. *Address:* c/o Augustine & Augustine Chambers, Lucas Street, St George's, Grenada.

AUKIN, David; Executive Director, National Theatre, since 1986; *b* 12 Feb. 1942; *s* of Charles and Regina Aukin; *m* 1969, Nancy Meckler, theatre director; two *s*. *Educ:* St Paul's Sch., London; St Edmund Hall, Oxford (BA). Admitted Solicitor, 1965. Literary Advr, Traverse Theatre Club, 1970–73; Administrator, Oxford Playhouse Co., 1974–75; Administrator, 1975–79, Dir, 1979–84, Hampstead Theatre; Dir, Leicester Haymarket Theatre, 1984–86. *Recreation:* golf. *Address:* c/o National Theatre, South Bank, SE1 9PX. *T:* 01–928 2033. *Clubs:* Garrick, Royal Automobile.

AULD, Alasdair Alpin, FMA; Director, Glasgow Museums and Art Galleries, since 1979; *b* 16 Nov. 1930; *s* of Herbert Bruce Auld and Janetta Isabel MacAlpine; *m* 1959, Mary Hendry Paul; one *s* one *d*. *Educ:* Shawlands Acad., Glasgow; Glasgow Sch. of Art (DA). FMA 1971. Glasgow Museums and Art Galleries: Asst Curator, 1956–72; Keeper of Fine Art, 1972–76; Depute Dir, 1976–79. Pres., Scottish Fedn of Museums and Art Galls, 1981–84. FRSA. *Publications:* catalogues; articles on museum subjects. *Recreations:* golf, travel. *Address:* 3 Dalziel Drive, Pollokshields, Glasgow G41 4JA. *T:* 041–427 1720. *Club:* Art (Glasgow).

AULD, Margaret Gibson, SRN, SCM; FRCN; MPhil; Chief Nursing Officer, Scottish Home and Health Department, since 1977; *b* 11 July 1932; *d* of Alexander John Sutton Auld and late Eleanor Margaret Ingram. *Educ:* Glasgow; Cardiff High Sch. for Girls; Radcliffe Infirm., Oxford (SRN 1953); St David's Hosp., Cardiff; Queen's Park Hosp., Blackburn (SCM 1954). Midwife Teacher's Dipl., 1962; Certif. of Nursing Admin, 1966, MPhil 1974, Edinburgh. Queen's Park Hosp., Blackburn, 1953–54; Staff Midwife, Cardiff Maternity Hosp., 1955, Sister, 1957; Sister, Queen Mary Hosp., Dunedin, NZ, 1959–60; Deptl Sister, Cardiff Maternity Hosp., 1960–66; Asst Matron, Simpson Meml Maternity Pavilion, Edinburgh, 1966–68, Matron, 1968–73; Actg Chief Reg. Nursing Officer, S-Eastern Reg. Hosp. Bd, Edinburgh, 1973; Chief Area Nursing Off., Borders Health Bd, 1973–76. Member: Cttee on Nursing (Briggs), 1970–72; Maternity Services Cttee, Integration of Maternity Work (Tennent Report), 1972–73; Gen. Nursing Council (Scotland), 1973–76; Central Midwives Bd (Scotland), 1972–76. FRCN 1981; CBIM 1983. *Recreations:* reading, music, entertaining. *Address:* Staddlestones, Belwood Road, Milton Bridge, Penicuik, Midlothian. *T:* Penicuik 72858. *Club:* University of Edinburgh Staff (Edinburgh).

AULD, Robin Ernest, QC 1975; a Recorder of the Crown Court, since 1977; *b* 19 July 1937; *s* of late Ernest Auld; *m* 1963, Catherine Eleanor Mary, *er d* of late David Henry Pritchard; one *s* one *d*. *Educ:* Brooklands Coll.; King's Coll., Univ. of London (LLB 1st cl. Hons, PhD). Called to Bar, Gray's Inn, 1959 (Macaskie Schol., Lord Justice Holker Sen. Schol.), Bencher, 1984; SE Circuit; in practice at English Bar, 1959–; called to N Ireland Bar, 1973; admitted to Bar, State of NY, 1984; called to Bar, State of NSW, Australia, 1985. Prosecuting Counsel to Dept of Trade, 1969–75; Legal Assessor, GMC and GDC, 1982–; Mem., Commn of Inquiry into Casino Gambling in the Bahamas, 1967; Chm., William Tyndale Schools' Inquiry, 1975–76; Dept of Trade Inspector, Ashbourne Investments Ltd, 1975–79; Chm., Home Office Cttee of Inquiry into Sunday and Late-Night Shopping, 1983–84. Master, Woolmen's Co., 1984–85. *Address:* Lamb Building, Temple, EC4Y 7AS. *T:* 01–353 6701. *Clubs:* Athenæum, City Livery.

AUST, Anthony Ivall; Legal Counsellor, Foreign and Commonwealth Office, since 1984; *b* 9 March 1942; *s* of Ivall George Aust and Jessie Anne Salmon; *m* 1969, Jacqueline Antoinette Thérèse Paris; two *d*. *Educ:* Wilson Central Sch., Reading; Stoneham Grammar Sch., Reading; London Sch. of Econs and Pol Science (LLB 1963, LLM 1967). Admitted Solicitor, 1967. Asst Legal Adviser, FCO (formerly CO), 1967–76; Legal Adviser, British Mil. Govt, Berlin, 1976–79; Asst Legal Adviser, FCO, 1979–84. *Recreations:* black and white photography, parlour games. *Address:* c/o Foreign and Commonwealth Office, SW1. *T:* 01-233 8713.

AUSTEN-SMITH, Air Marshal Sir Roy (David), KBE 1979; CB 1975; DFC 1953; retired; a Gentleman Usher to HM the Queen, since 1982; *b* 28 June 1924; *m* 1951, Ann (*née* Alderson); two *s*. *Educ:* Hurstpierpoint College. Pilot trng, Canada, 1943–44; 41 Sqn (2 TAF), 1945; 33 Sqdn, Malaya, 1950–53; Cranwell, 1953–56; 73 Sqdn, Cyprus, 1956–59; Air Min., 1960–63; 57 Sqdn, 1964–66; HQ 2 ATAF, 1966–68; CO, RAF Wattisham; MoD, 1970–72; AOC and Comdt, RAF Coll., Cranwell, 1972–75; SASO Near East Air Force, 1975–76; Comdr British Forces, Cyprus, AOC Air HQ Cyprus and Administrator, Sovereign Base Areas, Cyprus, 1976–78; Hd of British Defence Staff, Washington, and Defence Attaché, 1978–81. *Recreation:* golf. *Address:* c/o National Westminster Bank, Swanley, Kent. *Club:* Royal Air Force.

AUSTERBERRY, Ven. Sidney Denham; Archdeacon of Salop, 1959–79, now Archdeacon Emeritus; *b* 28 Oct. 1908; *s* of late Mr and Mrs H. Austerberry; *m* 1934, Eleanor Jane Naylor; two *s* two *d*. *Educ:* Hanley High Sch.; Egerton Hall, Manchester. Curate, Newcastle-under-Lyme Parish Church, 1931–38; Vicar of S Alkmund, Shrewsbury, 1938–52; Vicar of Brewood, 1952–59; Hon. Clerical Sec., Lichfield Diocesan Conf., 1954–70; Rural Dean of Penkridge, 1958–59; Vicar of Great Ness, 1959–77. Hon. Canon, Lichfield Cathedral, 1968–79. *Address:* 6 Honeysuckle Row, Sutton Park, Shrewsbury SY3 7TW. *T:* Shrewsbury 68080.

AUSTICK, David; Senior Partner, Austicks Bookshops, Leeds; Executive Chairman, Electoral Reform Society; *b* 8 March 1920; *m* 1944, Florence Elizabeth Lomath. Member: Leeds City Council (for W Hunslet), 1969–74; Leeds Metropolitan District Council (for Hunslet), 1974–75; W Yorkshire County Council (for Otley and Lower Wharfedale), 1974–79. MP (L) Ripon, July 1973–Feb. 1974; Contested (L) Ripon, 1974, (L) Cheadle, 1979, (L) Leeds, European Parlt, 1979. Member: Electoral Reform Soc.; European Movement; Fellowship of Reconciliation. *Address:* Austicks Bookshops, 29 Cookridge Street, Leeds LS1 3AN; 31 Cross Green, Otley, West Yorks; Electoral Reform Society, 6 Chancel Street, SE1 0UX. *Club:* National Liberal.

AUSTIN, Brian Patrick; HM Diplomatic Service; Counsellor, Foreign and Commonwealth Office, since 1984; *b* 18 March 1938; *s* of Edward William Austin and Winifred Alice Austin; *m* 1968, Augusta Francisca Maria Lina; one *s* one *d*. *Educ:* St Olave's Grammar Sch.; Clare Coll., Cambridge. National Service, 1956–58. Joined CRO, 1961; Central African Office, 1962; Lagos, 1963; The Hague, 1966; First Sec., FCO, 1969; Montreal, 1973; FCO, 1978; Dep. High Comr, Kaduna, 1981–84. *Recreation:* birdwatching. *Address:* c/o Foreign and Commonwealth Office, SW1A 2AH.

AUSTIN, Dr Colin François Lloyd, FBA 1983; Director of Studies in Classics and Fellow, Trinity Hall, Cambridge, since 1965; Lecturer in Classics, University of Cambridge, since 1973; *b* Melbourne, Australia, 26 July 1941; *s* of Prof. Lloyd James Austin, *qv*; *m* 1967, Mishtu Mazumdar, Calcutta, India; one *s* one *d*. *Educ:* Lycée Lakanal, Paris; Manchester Grammar Sch.; Jesus Coll., Cambridge (Scholar; MA 1965); Christ Church, Oxford (Sen. Scholar; MA, DPhil 1965); Freie Universität, West Berlin (Post-grad. Student). Univ. of Cambridge: John Stewart of Rannoch Scholar in Greek and Latin, 1960; Battie Scholar, Henry Arthur Thomas Scholar and Hallam Prize, 1961; Sir William Browne Medal for a Latin Epigram, 1961; Porson Prize, 1962; Prendergast Greek Student, 1962; Res. Fellow, Trinity Hall, 1965–69; Asst Univ. Lectr in Classics, 1969–72; Leverhulme Res. Fellow, 1979 and 1981. Treasurer: Jt Cttee, Greek and Roman Socs, London, 1983–; Cambridge Philological Soc., 1971–. *Publications:* De nouveaux fragments de l'Erechthée d'Euripide, 1967; Nova Fragmenta Euripidea, 1968; (with Prof. R. Kasser) Papyrus Bodmer XXV et XXVI, 2 vols, 1969; Menandri Aspis et Samia, 2 vols, 1969–70; Comicorum Graecorum Fragmenta in papyris reperta, 1973; (with Prof. R. Kassel) Poetae Comici Graeci: vol. IV, Aristophon—Crobylus, 1983, vol. III 2, Aristophanes, Testimonia et Fragmenta, 1984, vol. V, Damoxenus—Magnes, 1986; notes and reviews in classical periodicals. *Recreations:* cycling, philately, wine tasting. *Address:* 7 Park Terrace, Cambridge CB1 1JH. *T:* Cambridge 62732; Trinity Hall, Cambridge CB2 1TJ.

AUSTIN, Prof. Colin Russell; Charles Darwin Professor of Animal Embryology, and Fellow of Fitzwilliam College, University of Cambridge, 1967–81, now Professor Emeritus; *b* 12 Sept. 1914; *s* of Ernest Russell Austin and Linda Mabel King; *m* 1941, Patricia Constance Jack; two *s*. *Educ:* Univ. of Sydney, Australia (BVSc 1936; DSc 1954). Mem. Research Staff, CSIRO, Australia, 1938–54; Mem. Scientific Staff of MRC, UK, 1954–64; Editor, Jl of Reproduction and Fertility, 1959–64; Head of Genetic and Developmental Disorders Research Program, Delta Regional Primate Research Center, and Prof. of Embryology, Tulane Univ., New Orleans, 1964–67. Editor: Reproduction in Mammals, 1972–; Biological Reviews, 1981–84. Hon. Mem., Amer. Assoc. Anatomists, 1984. Marshall Medal, Soc. for Study of Fertility, 1981. *Publications:* The Mammalian Egg, 1961; Fertilization, 1965; Ultrastructure of Fertilization, 1968; numerous research papers. *Recreations:* gardening, swimming, squash. *Address:* 47 Dixon Road, Buderim, Qld 4556, Australia.

AUSTIN, Hon. Jacob, (Jack), PC (Canada) 1981; QC (Canada) 1970; Member of the Senate, Canadian Parliament, since 1975; *b* 2 March 1932; *s* of Morris Austin and Clara Edith (*née* Chetner); *m* (marr. diss.); three *d*; *m* 1978, Natalie Veiner Freeman. *Educ:* Univ. of British Columbia (BA, LLB); Harvard Univ. (LLM). Barrister and Solicitor, BC and Yukon Territory. Asst Prof. of Law, Univ. of Brit. Columbia, 1955–58; practising lawyer, Vancouver, BC, 1958–63; Exec. Asst to Minister of Northern Affairs and Nat. Resources, 1963–65; contested (Liberal) Vancouver-Kingsway, Can. Federal Election, 1965; practising lawyer, Vancouver, BC, 1966–70; Dep. Minister, Dept of Energy, Mines and Resources, Ottawa, 1970–74; Principal Sec. to Prime Minister, Ottawa, May 1974–Aug. 1975; Minister of State, 1981–82; Minister of State for Social Develt, responsible for Canada Develt Investment Corp., 1982–84; Chm., Ministerial Sub-Cttee on Broadcasting and Cultural Affairs, 1982–84. Pres., Internat. Div., Bank of British Columbia, 1985–86. *Publications:* articles on law and public affairs in Canadian Bar Rev., Amer. Soc. of Internat. Law and other publns. *Recreations:* sailing, tennis, reading, theatre. *Address:* Suite 304, 140 Wellington Street, The Senate, Ottawa, Ontario K1A 0A4, Canada. *T:* (613) 992–1437. *Clubs:* Rideau (Ottawa); Cercle Universitaire d'Ottawa; University Club of Vancouver (Vancouver, BC); Metropolitan (NY).

AUSTIN, Professor Lloyd James; FBA 1968; Emeritus Fellow of Jesus College, Cambridge; Emeritus Drapers Professor of French; *b* 4 Nov. 1915; *s* of late J. W. A. Austin and late Mrs J. E. Austin (*née* Tymms), Melbourne, Australia; *m* 1939, Jeanne Françoise Guérin, Rouen, France; three *s* one *d*. *Educ:* Melbourne Church of England Grammar Sch.; Univ. of Melbourne; Univ. of Paris. French Government Scholar, Paris, 1937–40; Lecturer in French, Univ. of Melbourne, 1940–42. Active Service as Lieut (Special Branch) RANVR, SW Pacific area, 1942–45. Lecturer in French, Univ. of Melbourne, 1945–47; Lecturer in French, Univ. of St Andrews, 1947–51; Research work in Paris, 1951–55; Fellow of Jesus Coll., Cambridge, 1955–56, 1961–80; Professor of Modern French Literature, Univ. of Manchester, 1956–61; Lecturer in French, Univ. of Cambridge, 1961–66, Reader, 1966–67, Drapers Prof. of French, 1967–80; Librarian, Jesus Coll., Cambridge, 1965–68, 1972–73. Herbert F. Johnson Visiting Prof., Inst. for Research in the Humanities, Univ. of Wisconsin, 1962–63; Mem., Editorial Bd, French Studies, 1964–80, Gen. Editor, 1967–80, Mem. Adv. Bd, 1980–; Pres., Assoc. Internat. des Etudes Françaises, 1969–72 (Vice-Pres., 1966–69). Hon. FAHA 1985; Hon. Member: Soc. for French Studies, 1980–; Société d'Histoire Littéraire de la France, 1980; Mem., Acad. Royale de Langue et de Littérature Françaises de Belgique, 1980. Docteur *hc* Paris-Sorbonne, 1973. Prix Henri Mondor, Acad. française, 1981; Prix internat. des amitiés françaises, Soc. des Poètes français, 1982. Chevalier de l'Ordre des Arts et des Lettres, 1971; Officier de l'Ordre National du Mérite, 1976. *Publications:* Paul Bourget, 1940; Paul Valéry: Le Cimetière marin, 1954; L'Univers poétique de Baudelaire, 1956; ed (with E. Vinaver and G. Rees) Studies in Modern French Literature, presented to P. Mansell-Jones, 1961; ed (with H. Mondor) Les Gossips de Mallarmé, 1962; ed (with H. Mondor) Stéphane Mallarmé: Correspondance (1871–1898), 11 vols, 1965–85; (ed) Baudelaire: L'Art romantique, 1968; (contrib.) The Symbolist Movement in the Literature of European Languages, 1982; contrib. to French Studies, Modern Languages, Modern Language Review, Forum for Modern Language Studies, Bulletin of the John Rylands Library, Mercure de France, Nouvelle Revue Française, Revue des Sciences Humaines, Revue d'Histoire littéraire de la France, Revue de littérature comparée, Romanic Review, Studi francesi, Synthèses, Revue de l'Université de Bruxelles, L'Esprit créateur, Comparative Literature Studies, Wingspread Lectures in the Humanities, Encyclopædia Britannica, Yale French Studies, Meanjin Quarterly, Australian Jl for French Studies, AUMLA, Quadrant, etc. *Recreations:* watching cricket, tennis, looking at pictures, listening to music, travel. *Address:* 2 Park Lodge, Park Terrace, Cambridge CB1 1JJ. *T:* 359630; Jesus College, Cambridge.

See also C. F. L. Austin.

AUSTIN, Dame (Mary) Valerie (Hall), DBE 1979 (OBE 1952); JP; *b* London, 29 July 1900; *d* of Admiral Percival Henry Hall Thompson, CB, CMG, RN, and Helen Sydney Hall Thompson (*née* Deacon); *m* 1925, Ronald Albert Austin, MC; one *s*. *Educ:* Marsden College, New Zealand. Travelled with father, etc, to Australia, New Zealand, Malta, England; married Australia; lived on land at Eilyer, Mortlake, Vic. Vice Pres., Liberal Party, Victoria, 1947–76; Hon. Life Member: Red Cross, Australia, 1979 (Mem., 1936–); Victoria League; Victorian Family Council. Coronation Medal, 1953. *Address:* 255 Domain Road, South Yarra, Victoria 3141, Australia. *Clubs:* Alexandra (Melbourne); Barwon Heads Golf.

AUSTIN, Vice-Adm. Sir Peter (Murray), KCB 1976; Chairman, Special Training Services, since 1985; Director, Avanova International Consultants, since 1980; *b* 16 April 1921; *er s* of late Vice-Adm. Sir Francis Austin, KBE, CB, and late Lady (Marjorie) Austin (*née* Barker); *m* 1959, Josephine Rhoda Ann Shutte-Smith; three *s* one *d*. *Educ:* RNC, Dartmouth. Cadet, Dartmouth, 1935. Served War of 1939–45: at sea in HMS Cornwall, 1939–40; destroyers, 1941–45. Qualif. as pilot in FAA, 1946; served in 807 Sqdn, 1947–49; CO 736 Sqdn, 1950–52; grad. from RAF Flying Coll., Manby, 1953; comd 850 Sqdn in HMAS Sydney, incl. Korea, 1953–54; Lt-Cmdr (Flying), HMS Bulwark, 1954–56; Comdr (Air), RNAS Brawdy, 1956–58; Comdr (Air), HMS Eagle, 1958–59;

Captain, 1961; Captain F7 in HMS Lynx, 1963–65; CO, RNAS Brawdy, 1965–67; Staff of SACLANT, 1967–69; comd aircraft carrier, HMS Hermes, 1969–70; Rear-Adm., 1971; Asst Chief of Naval Staff (Ops and Air), 1971–73; Flag Officer, Naval Air Comd, 1973–76, retired; Vice-Adm., 1974. Operations Dir, Mersey Docks and Harbour Co., 1976–80. CBIM. *Recreations:* golf, ski-ing, squash, sailing, caravanning. *Address:* Dolphin Cottage, 93 The Parade, West Kirby, Wirral LA8 0RR.

AUSTIN, Richard, FRCM; Professor, 1946–76, Director of Opera, 1955–76, Royal College of Music; *b* 26 Dec. 1903; *s* of Frederic and Amy Austin; *m* 1935, Leily, *y d* of Col Wilfred Howell, CBE, DSO. *Educ:* Gresham's Sch., Holt; RCM; Munich. Conductor, Carl Rosa Opera Co., 1929; Musical Dir of the Bournemouth Corporation, 1934–40; Music Advisor Northern Command, 1941–45; Music Dir, New Era Concert Soc., 1947–57. Guest Conductor: Sadler's Wells, London and provincial orchestras, Holland, Belgium, Germany, Spain, Sweden, Switzerland, Finland, Yugoslavia, Czechoslovakia, Cuba, Mexico, South Africa, South America and USA. *Recreations:* squash, tennis. *Address:* Stubbles, Ashampstead, Berks. *T:* Compton 565. *Club:* Savage.

AUSTIN, Dame Valerie; *see* Austin, Dame M. V. H.

AUSTIN, Sir William (Ronald), 4th Bt *cr* 1894; *b* 20 July 1900; *s* of Sir William Michael Byron Austin, 2nd Bt, and Violet Irene (*d* 1962), *d* of Alexander Fraser, Westerfield House, near Ipswich; *S* brother, 1981; *m* 1st, 1926, Dorothy Mary (*d* 1957), *d* of late L. A. Bidwell, FRCS; two *s*; 2nd, 1958, Mary Helen Farrell. *Heir:* *s* Michael Trescawen Austin [*b* 27 Aug. 1927; *m* 1951, Bridget Dorothea Patricia, *d* of late Francis Farrell; three *d*]. *Address:* Creagan, Appin, Argyll. *T:* Appin 213.

AUSTRALIA, Primate of; *see* Brisbane, Archbishop of.

AUSTRALIA, North-West, Bishop of, since 1981; **Rt. Rev. Gerald Bruce Muston;** *b* 19 Jan. 1927; 3rd *s* of Stanley John and Emily Ruth Muston; *m* 1951, Laurel Wright; one *s* one *d*. *Educ:* N Sydney Chatswood High School; Moore Theological College, Sydney. ThL (Aust. Coll. of Theology). Rector, Wallerawang, NSW, 1951–53; Editorial Secretary, Church Missionary Society (Aust.), 1953–58; Rector, Tweed Heads, NSW, 1958–61; Vicar, Essendon, Vic, 1961–67; Rural Dean of Essendon, 1963–67; Rector of Darwin, NT, and Archdeacon of Northern Territory, 1967–69; Federal Secretary, Bush Church Aid Society of Aust., 1969–71; Bishop Coadjutor, dio. Melbourne (Bishop of the Western Region), 1971–81. *Recreations:* golf, reading. *Address:* Bishop's House, 11 Mark Way, Tarcoola, Geraldton, WA 6530, Australia. *Club:* Melbourne (Melbourne).

AUSTWICK, Prof. Kenneth, JP; Professor of Education, Bath University, since 1966; *b* 26 May 1927; *s* of Harry and Beatrice Austwick; *m* 1956, Gillian Griffin; one *s* one *d*. *Educ:* Morecambe Grammar Sch.; Sheffield Univ. BSc Maths, DipEd, MSc, PhD Sheffield. Fellow, Royal Statistical Soc.; FRSA. Schoolmaster, Bromsgrove, Frome and Nottingham, 1950–59; Lectr/Sen. Lectr, Sheffield Univ., 1959–65; Dep. Dir, Inst. of Educn, Reading Univ., 1965–66; Pro-Vice-Chancellor, Bath Univ., 1972–75. Vis. Lecturer: Univ. of BC, 1963; Univ. of Michigan, 1963; Univ. of Wits., 1967. Consultant, OECD, 1965; Adviser, Home Office, 1967–81; Chm., Nat. Savings SW Regional Educn, 1975–78. JP Bath 1970. *Publications:* Logarithms, 1962; Equations and Graphs, 1963; (ed) Teaching Machines and Programming, 1964; (ed) Aspects of Educational Technology, 1972; Maths at Work, 1985; articles and contribs on maths teaching and educnl technology. *Recreations:* gardening, wine making. *Address:* Brook House, Combe Hay, near Bath. *T:* Combe Down 832541. *Club:* Royal Commonwealth Society.

AUTY, Richard Mossop, CBE 1978 (OBE 1968); retired British Council officer; *b* 29 Jan. 1920; *s* of Rev. Thomas Richard Auty and Mrs Edith Blanche Auty (*née* Mossop); *m* 1st, 1944, Noreen Collins (marr. diss. 1949); one *d*; 2nd, 1956, (Anne) Marguerite Marie Poncet; one *s* one *d*. *Educ:* Hanley High Sch.; LSE, Univ. of London. Planning Br., Min. of Agriculture and Fisheries, 1942–46; Bureau of Current Affairs, 1946–49; Lectr, Goldsmiths' Coll. and Morley Coll., 1947–49; British Council, 1949–80: Lectr, Milan, 1949–57; Head, Overseas Students Centre, London, 1957–61; Reg. Rep., S India, 1961–65; Cultural Attaché, Brit. Embassy, Budapest, 1965–68; Director: S Asia Dept, 1968–70; Personnel Dept, 1970–72; Controller, European Div., 1972–76; Rep., France, and Cultural Counsellor, British Embassy, Paris, 1976–80. *Recreations:* literature, theatre, cinema. *Address:* 4 Thurlow Road, NW3. *T:* 01–435 8982.

AVEBURY, 4th Baron *cr* 1900; **Eric Reginald Lubbock;** Bt 1806; *b* 29 Sept. 1928; *s* of Hon. Maurice Fox Pitt Lubbock (6th *s* of 1st Baron) (*d* 1957), and Hon. Mary Katherine Adelaide Stanley (*d* 1981), *d* of 5th Baron Stanley of Alderley; *S* cousin, 1971; *m* 1953, Kina Maria (marr. diss. 1983) (*see* Lady Avebury); two *s* one *d*; 2nd, 1985, Lindsay Stewart; one *s*. *Educ:* Upper Canada Coll.; Harrow Sch.; Balliol Coll., Oxford (BA Engineering; boxing blue). Welsh Guards (Gdsman, 2nd Lieut), 1949–51; Rolls Royce Ltd, 1951–56; Grad. Apprentice; Export Sales Dept; Tech. Assistant to Foundry Manager. Management Consultant: Production Engineering Ltd, 1953–60; Charterhouse Group Ltd, 1960. MP (L) Orpington, 1962–70; Liberal Whip in House of Commons, 1963–70. Consultant, Morgan-Grampian Ltd, 1970–; Chm., Cell Information Systems Ltd, 1986–; Dir, C. L. Projects Ltd. President: Data Processing Management Assoc., 1972–75; Fluoridation Soc., 1972–84; Conservation Soc., 1973–83. Member: Council, Inst. of Race Relations, 1972–74; Royal Commn on Standards of Conduct in Public Life, 1974–76. Pres., London Bach Soc. and Steinitz Bach Players, 1984–. MIMechE. *Recreations:* listening to music, reading. *Heir:* *s* Hon. Lyulph Ambrose Jonathan Lubbock [*b* 15 June 1954; *m* 1977, Susan (*née* MacDonald); one *s* one *d*]. *Address:* House of Lords, SW1.

AVEBURY, Lady; Kina-Maria Lubbock, (Kina Lady Avebury); Sociologist, Department of Psychiatry, London Hospital Medical College, since 1983; *b* 2 Sept. 1934; *d* of late Count Joseph O'Kelly de Gallagh and of Mrs M. Bruce; *m* 1953, 4th Baron Avebury, *qv* (marr. diss. 1983); two *s* one *d*. *Educ:* Convent of the Sacred Heart, Tunbridge Wells; Goldsmiths' College (BScSoc Hons) and LSE, Univ. of London. Lectr, Royal Coll. of Nursing, 1970–74; campaign organizer, European Movement, 1975; Asst Dir, Nat. Assoc. for Mental Health, 1976–82; Chairman: Nat. Marriage Guidance Council, 1975–82; Family Service Units, 1984–; Avebury Working Party, 1982–84 (produced Code of Practice for Residential Care for DHSS). JP Kent, 1974–79. *Publications:* Volunteers in Mental Health, 1985; articles on mental health and related social policy. *Recreations:* painting, opera, cooking.

AVELING, Alan John, CB 1986; Under Secretary, Director of Home Regional Services, Property Services Agency, Department of the Environment, since 1980; *b* 4 Jan. 1928; *s* of late Herbert Ashley Aveling and Ethel Aveling; *m* 1960, Stella May Reed; one *s* one *d*. *Educ:* Fletton Grammar Sch.; Rugby Technical Coll. CEng; FIEE, FIMechE, FCIBSE. Air Min. Works Dir, Newmarket, 1951–52; RAF Airfield Construction, 2nd Allied Tactical Air Force, 1952–55; Air Min. HQ, 1955–61; Sen. Engr, War Office Works Dept, 1961–63; BAOR Services, Germany, MPBW, 1963–66; Directorate Personnel, MPBW, 1966–67; Superintending Engr, Overseas Defence and FCO Services, 1967–72; Reg. Works Officer, later Regional Dir, British Forces, Germany, PSA/DoE, 1972–76; Dir of Estate Management Overseas, 1976–78; Dir Eastern Region, PSA/DoE, 1978–80. *Recreations:* aviculture, skiing. *Address:* Running Hook, Peaslake, Guildford, Surrey. *T:* Shere 2499. *Club:* Royal Air Force.

AVERY, Gillian Elise, (Mrs A. O. J. Cockshut); writer; *b* 1926; *d* of Norman and Grace Avery; *m* 1952, A. O. J. Cockshut; one *d*. *Educ:* Dunottar Sch., Reigate. *Publications: children's fiction:* The Warden's Niece, 1957; Trespassers at Charlcote, 1958; James without Thomas, 1959; The Elephant War, 1960; To Tame a Sister, 1961; The Greatest Gresham, 1962; The Peacock House, 1963; The Italian Spring, 1964; The Call of the Valley, 1966; A Likely Lad (Guardian Award, 1972), 1971; Huck and her Time Machine, 1977; *adult fiction:* The Lost Railway, 1980; Onlookers, 1983; *non-fiction:* 19th Century Children: heroes and heroines in English children's stories (with Angela Bull), 1965; Victorian People in Life and Literature, 1970; The Echoing Green: memories of Regency and Victorian youth, 1974; Childhood's Pattern, 1975. Ed, Gollancz revivals of early children's books, 1967–70, and anthologies of stories and extracts from early children's books. *Recreations:* walking, growing vegetables, cooking. *Address:* 32 Charlbury Road, Oxford.

AVERY, James Royle, (Roy Avery); Headmaster, Bristol Grammar School, 1975–86; *b* 7 Dec. 1925; *s* of Charles James Avery and Dorothy May Avery; *m* 1954, Marjorie Louise (*née* Smith); one *s* one *d*. *Educ:* Queen Elizabeth's Hosp., Bristol; Magdalen Coll., Oxford; Bristol Univ. MA Oxon, CertifEd Bristol; FRSA. Asst History Master, Bristol Grammar Sch., 1951–59; Sen. History Master, Haberdashers' Aske's Sch. at Hampstead, then Elstree, 1960–65; Head Master, Harrow County Boys' Sch., 1965–75. *Publications:* The Story of Aldenham House, 1961; The Elstree Murder, 1962; contrib. Dictionary of World History, 1973; articles, reviews in educnl jls. *Recreations:* ecumenical movement, American studies and international affairs, sport, theatre, music, walking. *Address:* First Floor Flat, 4 Rockleaze, Sneyd Park, Bristol.

AVERY, Percy Leonard; Chairman, staff side, Civil Service National Whitley Council, 1977–80; General Secretary, Association of Government Supervisors and Radio Officers, 1951–79; *b* 10 March 1915; *s* of Percy James Avery and Frances Elisabeth Avery; *m* 1940, Joan Mahala Breakspear; one *s* one *d* (and one *d* decd). *Educ:* Woolwich Polytechnic. Served War: Navigator, RAF Bomber Comd, 1941–45; Flt Lieut. Exec. Sec., Internat. Fedn of Air Traffic Electronics Assoc., 1972–79. Member: Kent Area Health Authority, 1973–79; MoD Management Review Body, 1975–76; Civil Service Pay Rev. Board, 1978–79; CS Deptl Whitley Councils (various), 1949–77. Dir of Admin, British Karate Bd, 1979–82; Dir, Internat. Amateur Karate Fedn, 1983–; Treasurer: English Karate Council, 1981–82; European Amateur Karate Fedn, 1982–. Governor, Ruskin Coll; Mem., Kent Age Concern, 1980–83. *Recreations:* athletics, Rugby, music, gardening. *Address:* High Ridge, Tower Hill, Williton, Somerset. *T:* Williton 32238.

AVERY, Roy; *see* Avery, J. R.

AVERY JONES, Sir Francis, Kt 1970; CBE 1966; FRCP; retired; Consulting Physician, Gastroenterological Department, Central Middlesex Hospital (Physician, 1940–74); Consulting Gastroenterologist: St Mark's Hospital (Consultant, 1948–78); Royal Navy (Consultant, 1950–78); Hon. Consulting Physician, St Bartholomew's Hospital, 1978; *b* 31 May 1910; *s* of Francis Samuel and Marion Rosa Jones; *m* 1st, 1934, Dorothea Pfirter (*d* 1983); one *s*; 2nd, 1983, K. Joan Edmunds. *Educ:* Sir John Leman Sch., Beccles; St Bartholomew's Hosp. Baly Research Scholarship, St Bart's, 1936; Julius Mickle Fellowship, University of London, 1952. Goulstonian Lecturer, Royal College of Physicians, 1947; Lumleian Lectr, RCP; Nuffield Lectr in Australia, 1952; First Memorial Lectr, Amer. Gastroenterological Assoc., 1954; Croonian Lectr, RCP, 1969; Harveian Orator, RCP, 1980. Formerly Examiner: RCP; Univ. of London; Univ. of Leeds. Chairman: Emergency Bed Service, 1967–72; Med. Records Cttee, Dept of Health and Social Security; Medical Adv. Cttee, British Council, 1973–79; Member: Med. Sub-cttee, UGC, 1966–71; Brent and Harrow AHA, 1975–78; Dep. Chm., Management Cttee, King Edward VII Hosp. Fund, 1976–79; Mem. Council, Surrey Univ., 1975–. Pres., United Services Section, RSM, 1974–75 (formerly Pres., section of Proctology); 2nd Vice-Pres., RCP, 1972–73; President: Medical Soc. of London, 1977–78; Medical Artists Assoc., 1980–; British Digestive Foundn, 1981–. Editor of Gut, 1965–70. Hon. FRCS 1981; Hon. FACP 1985; Hon. Mem., Amer., Canadian, French, Scandinavian and Australian Gastroenterological Assocs. Master, Worshipful Co. of Barbers, 1977–78. Hon. MD Melbourne, 1952; DUniv Surrey, 1980. Ambuj Nath Bose Prize, RCP, 1971; Moxon Medal, RCP, 1978; Fothergillian Gold Medal, Med. Soc., 1980; Henry L. Bockus Medal, World Orgn of Gastroenterology, 1982. *Publications:* Clinical Gastroenterology (jt author), 2nd edn 1967; Editor of Modern Trends in Gastroenterology First and Second Series, 1952 and 1958; many articles on Gastroenterology in the Medical Press. *Recreation:* water-side gardening. *Address:* Mill House, Nutbourne, Pulborough, West Sussex. *T:* West Chiltington 3314. *Club:* Athenæum.

See also J. F. Avery Jones.

AVERY JONES, John Francis, FTII; Senior Partner, Speechly Bircham, since 1985; *b* 5 April 1940; *s* of Sir Francis Avery Jones, *qv*. *Educ:* Rugby Sch.; Trinity Coll., Cambridge (MA, LLM). Solicitor, 1966; Partner in Bircham & Co., 1970. Member: Meade Cttee, 1975–77; Keith Cttee, 1980–84. Pres., Inst. of Taxation, 1980–82; Chm., Law Soc.'s Revenue Law Cttee, 1983–. Mem. Bd of Governors, Voluntary Hosp. of St Bartholomew, 1984–; Chm., Addington Soc., 1985–. Master, Co. of Barbers, 1985–86. Jt Editor, British Tax Review, 1974–; Mem. Editl Bd, Simon's Taxes, 1977–. *Publications:* (ed) Tax Havens and Measures Against Tax Avoidance and Evasion in the EEC, 1974; (gen. ed) Encyclopedia of VAT (loose leaf), 1972; numerous articles on tax. *Recreations:* music, particularly opera. *Address:* 7 Cleveland Gardens, W2 6HA. *T:* 01–258 1960. *Club:* Athenæum.

AVGHERINOS, George, QC 1982; *b* Poti, Georgia, Caucasus, 6 Jan. 1906; *s* of Homer and Eftichia Avgherinos; *m* 1944, Beatrice Eleanor, *d* of Oscar and Mabel Siewert; one *s*. *Educ:* St Paul's School; Brasenose Coll., Oxford. MA, BCL. Served RAF, 1941–46, Administration. Harmsworth Scholarship, Middle Temple, 1929; called to the Bar, Middle Temple, 1932; Barstow Scholarship, 1932; Bencher, Middle Temple, 1964. *Publications:* (ed jtly) Landlord and Tenant Act 1927, 3rd edn 1949; (jtly) Leasehold Property (Temporary Provisions) Act 1951, 1951; (jtly) Housing Repairs and Rents Act 1954, 1954; (ed jtly) Rent and Mortgage Interest Restrictions, 23rd edn, 1956. *Recreations:* music, braille. *Address:* Flat 5, 1 Linden Gardens, W2 4HA.

AVNER, Yehuda; Ambassador of Israel to the Court of St James's, since 1983; *b* 30 Dec. 1928; *m* Miriam Avner; one *s* three *d*. *Educ:* High School, Manchester. Editor of publications, Jewish Agency, Jerusalem, 1956–64; Editor of Political Publications, Min. of Foreign Affairs, and Asst to Prime Minister Levi Eshkol, 1964–67; Consul, New York, 1967–68; First Sec. then Counsellor, Washington, 1968–72; Dir of Foreign Press Bureau, Foreign Ministry, and Asst to PM Golda Meir, 1972–74; seconded to PM's Bureau, and Adviser to PM Yitzhak Rabin, 1974–77; Adviser to PM Menachem Begin, 1977–83. *Publication:* The Young Inheritors: a portrait of Israeli youth, 1982. *Address:* 2 Palace Green, W8. *T:* 01–937 8050.

AVONSIDE, Rt. Hon. Lord; Ian Hamilton Shearer, PC 1962; a Senator of the College of Justice in Scotland, 1964–84; *b* 6 Nov. 1914; *s* of Andrew Shearer, OBE, and Jessie Macdonald; *m* 1st, 1942; one *s* one *d;* 2nd, 1954, Janet Sutherland Murray (*see* Lady Avonside). *Educ:* Dunfermline High Sch.; Glasgow Univ.; Edinburgh Univ. MA Glasgow, 1934; LLB Edinburgh, 1937. Admitted to Faculty of Advocates, 1938; QC (Scotland) 1952. Served War of 1939–45, RA; Major; released 1946, Emerg. R of O. Standing Counsel: to Customs and Excise, Bd of Trade and Min. of Labour, 1947–49; to Inland Revenue, 1949–51; to City of Edinburgh Assessor, 1949–51; Junior Legal Assessor to City of Edinburgh, 1951; Sheriff of Renfrew and Argyll, 1960–62; Lord Advocate, 1962–64. Mem., Lands Valuation Court, 1964 (Chm., 1975–84). Chm. Nat. Health Service Tribunal, Scotland, 1954–62; Mem. Scottish Cttee of Coun. on Tribunals, 1958–62; Chm. Scottish Valuation Advisory Coun., 1965–68; Mem., Scottish Univs Cttee of the Privy Council, 1971–. Pres., Stair Soc., 1975–. *Publications:* Purves on Licensing Laws, 1947; Acta Dominorum Concilii et Sessionis, 1951. *Recreations:* golf, gardening. *Address:* The Mill House, Samuelston, East Lothian. *T:* Haddington 2396. *Club:* New (Edinburgh).

AVONSIDE, Lady; Janet Sutherland Shearer, OBE 1958; Scottish Governor, BBC, 1971–76; *b* 31 May 1917; *d* of William Murray, MB, ChB, and Janet Harley Watson; *m* 1954, Ian Hamilton Shearer, Rt Hon. Lord Avonside, *qv. Educ:* St Columba's Sch., Kilmacolm; Erlenhaus, Baden Baden; Univ. of Edinburgh. LLB, Dip. of Social Science. Asst Labour Officer (Scot.), Min. of Supply, 1941–45; Sec. (Scot.), King George's Fund for Sailors, 1945–53; Hon. Sec. (Scot.), Federal Union and United Europe, 1945–64; Scottish Delegate: Congress of Europe, 1947; Council of Europe, Strasburg, 1949. Contested (C), elections: Maryhill, Glasgow, 1950; Dundee East, 1951; Leith, 1955. Lectr in Social Studies, Dept of Educational Studies, Univ. of Edinburgh, 1962–70. *Recreation:* gardening. *Address:* The Mill House, Samuelston, East Lothian, Scotland. *T:* Haddington 2396. *Clubs:* Caledonian (Associate Mem.); New (Edinburgh).

AWAD, Muhammad Hadi; Ambassador of The People's Democratic Republic of Yemen to Tunisia and Permanent Representative to The Arab League, since 1980; *b* 5 May 1934; Yemeni; *m* 1956, Adla; one *s* three *d. Educ:* Murray House Coll. of Educn. DipEd, Certif. Social Anthrop. Edinburgh. Teacher, 1953–59; Educn Officer, 1960–62; Chief Inspector of Schs, 1963–65; Vice-Principal, As-Shaab Coll., 1965–67; Perm. Rep. to Arab League, Ambassador to UAR and non-resident Ambassador to Sudan, Lebanon, Libya and Iraq, 1968–70; Perm. Sec., Min. of For. Affairs, 1970–73; Ambassador to London, 1973–80, to Sweden and Spain, 1974–80, to Denmark, Portugal and the Netherlands, 1975–80. *Recreation:* photography. *Address:* Embassy of The People's Democratic Republic of Yemen, Tunis, Tunisia.

AWAK, Shehu, OFR 1981; High Commissioner for Nigeria in the UK, 1981–84; *b* Awak, 14 May 1932; *m* 1953, A'ishatu Shehu Awak; four *s* seven *d. Educ:* Nigerian Coll.; Manchester Univ. (DCPA 1966); London Sch. of Economics. ASTC IV, Zaria, 1961. Nigerian Foreign Service: Admin. Officer, 1961–70; actg Perm. Sec., 1970–73; Perm. Sec., 1973–78; Sec. to Mil. Govt, 1978–79, and Head of CS, 1978–81, Bauchi State. *Recreations:* table tennis, walking, gaming.

AWDRY, Daniel (Edmund), TD; DL; *b* 10 Sept. 1924; *s* of late Col Edmund Portman Awdry, MC, TD, DL, Coters, Chippenham, Wilts, and Mrs Evelyn Daphne Alexandra Awdry, JP (formerly French); *m* 1950, Elizabeth Cattley; three *d. Educ:* Winchester Coll. RAC, OCTU, Sandhurst, 1943–44 (Belt of Honour). Served with 10th Hussars as Lieut, Italy, 1944–45; ADC to GOC 56th London Div., Italy, 1945; Royal Wilts Yeo., 1947–62; Major and Sqdn Comdr, 1955–62. Qualified Solicitor, 1950. Mayor of Chippenham, 1958–59; Pres., Southern Boroughs Assoc., 1959–60. MP (C) Chippenham, Wilts, Nov. 1962–1979; PPS to Minister of State, Board of Trade, Jan.-Oct. 1964; PPS to Solicitor-Gen., 1973–74. Director: BET Omnibus Services, 1966–80; Sheepbridge Engineering, 1968–79; Rediffusion Ltd, 1973–85; Colonial Mutual Life Assurance Ltd, 1974–. DL Wilts, 1979. *Recreations:* cricket (Mem. Free Foresters and Butterflies), chess. *Address:* Old Manor, Beanacre, near Melksham, Wilts. *T:* Melksham 702315.

AXELROD, Julius, PhD; Guest Researcher, Laboratory of Cell Biology, since 1984, Chief, Section on Pharmacology, Laboratory of Clinical Science, 1955–84 (Acting Chief, Jan.-Oct. 1955), National Institute of Mental Health, USA; Laboratory of Cell Biology, since 1984; *b* NYC, 30 May 1912; *s* of Isadore Axelrod, Michaliev, Poland, and Molly Liechtling, Striej, Poland (formerly Austria); *m* 1938, Sally (*née* Taub); two *s. Educ:* George Washington Univ., Wash., DC (PhD); New York Univ. (MA); New York City Coll. (BS). Lab. Asst. Dept Bacteriology, NY Univ. Med. Sch., 1933–35; Chemist, Lab. Industrial Hygiene, 1935–46; Res. Associate, Third NY Univ.; Research Div., Goldwater Memorial Hosp., 1946–49; Nat. Heart Inst., NIH: Associate Chemist, Section on Chem. Pharmacology, 1949–50; Chemist, 1950–53; Sen. Chemist, 1953–55. Jt Nobel Prize for Physiology-Medicine, 1970; Mem., Nat. Academy of Sciences, 1971; Fellow, Amer. Acad. of Arts and Sciences; Senior Mem., Amer. Inst. of Medicine, 1979. Foreign Member: Royal Society, 1979; Deutsche Akademie der Naturforscher, 1984. Hon. LLD: George Washington, 1971; College City, NY, 1972; Hon. DSc: Chicago, 1966; Med. Coll., Wisconsin, 1971; New York, 1971; Pennsylvania Coll. of Med., 1973; Doctor *hc* Panama, 1972; DPhil *hc:* Ripon Coll., 1984; Tel Aviv Univ., 1984. Winner of 15 awards; holds 23 hon. lectureships; Member: 13 editorial boards; 5 Sci. Adv. Cttees. *Publications:* (with Richard J. Wurtman and Douglas E. Kelly) The Pineal, 1968; numerous original papers and contribs to jls in Biochem., Pharmacol. and Physiology. *Recreations:* reading and listening to music. *Address:* 10401 Grosvenor Place, Rockville, Maryland 20852, USA. *T:* (301) 493–6376.

AXFORD, David Norman, PhD, CEng, FIEE; Director of Services, Meteorological Office, since 1984; *b* 14 June 1934; *s* of Norman Axford and Joy Alicia Axford (*née* Williams); *m* 1st, 1962, Elizabeth Anne (*née* Stiles) (marr. diss. 1980); one *s* two *d;* 2nd, 1980, Diana Rosemary Joan (*née* Bufton); three step *s* one step *d. Educ:* Merchant Taylors' School, Sandy Lodge; Plymouth Coll.; St John's Coll., Cambridge (Baylis Open Scholarship in Maths; BA 1956, MA 1960, PhD (Met.) 1972); MSc (Electronics) Southampton 1963; FIEE 1982. Entered Met. Office, 1958; Flying Officer, RAF, 1958–60; Meteorological Office: Forecasting and Research, 1962–68; Met. Research Flight, and Radiosondes, 1968–76; Operational Instrumentation, 1976–80; Telecommunications, 1980–82; Dep. Dir, Observational Services, 1982–84. Mem. Council and Hon. Gen. Sec., Roy. Met. Soc., 1983–; Pres., N Atlantic Observing Stations (NAOS) Bd, 1983–86; L. G. Groves 2nd Meml Prize for Met., 1970. *Publications:* papers in learned jls on met. and aspects of met. instrumentation in GB and USA. *Recreations:* home and garden, music, travel, good food. *Address:* Rudgewick Cottage, Binfield Heath, Henley-on-Thames, Oxon RG9 4JY. *T:* Henley 574423. *Club:* Phyllis Court (Henley-on-Thames).

AXFORD, Dr William Ian, FRS 1986; Director, Max Planck Institut für Aeronomie, Katlenburg-Lindau, West Germany, since 1985; *b* 2 Jan. 1933; *s* of John Edgar Axford and May Victoria Axford; *m* 1955, Catherine Joy; two *s* two *d. Educ:* Univ. of Canterbury, NZ (MSc Hons, ME Dist.); Univ. of Manchester (PhD); Univ. of Cambridge. NZ Defence Science Corps, 1957–63; seconded to Defence Res. Bd, Ottawa, 1960–62; Associate Prof. of Astronomy, 1963–66, Prof. of Astronomy, 1966–67, Cornell Univ., Ithaca, NY; Prof. of Physics and Applied Physics, Univ. of Calif at San Diego, 1967–74; Dir, Max-Planck-Institut für Aeronomie, Lindau, W Germany, 1974–82; Vice-Chancellor, Victoria Univ. of Wellington, NZ, 1982–85. Hon. Prof., Göttingen Univ., 1978–; Appleton Meml Lectr, URSI, 1969. Fellow, Amer. Geophysical Union, 1971; ARAS 1981; For. Associate, US Nat. Acad. of Scis, 1983; Mem., Internat. Acad. of Astronautics, 1985. Space Science Award, AIAA, 1970; John Adam Fleming Medal, Amer. Geophysical Union, 1972. *Publications:* about 170 articles in scientific jls on aspects of space physics and astrophysics. *Address:* Max Planck Institut für Aeronomie, Postfach 20, D-3411 Katlenburg-Lindau, West Germany. *T:* 5556–41414; 2 Gladstone Road, Napier, New Zealand. *T:* 70–52188. *Club:* Wellington (Wellington).

AXISA, John Francis, MBE 1950; *b* 20 Nov. 1906; *s* of late Emmanuel Axisa and Vincenzina (*née* Micallef); *m* 1939, Ariadne Cachia; three *s* one *d. Educ:* St Paul's Sch., Malta and privately. Joined Malta Civil Service, 1927; Dir of Emigration, 1947–56; Dir of Technical Education, 1956–59; Dir of Emigration, Labour and Social Welfare, 1959–60; Under-Sec., 1960–61; Commissioner-Gen. for Malta in London, 1961–64; Malta's first High Commissioner on Malta's Independence, 1964–69; Ambassador of Malta to: France, 1966–69; Fed. Republic of Germany, 1967–69; Libya, 1966–68; Belgium, 1967–68; Netherlands, 1968–69. *Recreations:* carpentry, fishing, reading. *Address:* Godolphin, San Anton, Attard, Malta, GC. *Club:* Union (Malta).

AXTON, Henry Stuart, FCA; Chairman, Brixton Estate plc, since 1983; *b* 6 May 1923; *s* of Wilfrid George Axton and Mary Louise Laver; *m* 1947, Constance Mary Godefroy; one *d. Educ:* Rock Ferry. RMC, Sandhurst, commissioned 1942; served: N Africa, Royal Tank Regt, NW Europe, Fife and Forfar Yeo.; wounded three times, invalided out, 1945. Articles, G. E. Holt & Son; Chartered Accountant 1948. Treas., United Sheffield Hosps and other hosp. appts, 1948–55; Company Sec., Midland Assurance, 1955–61; Brixton Estate, 1961–: Man. Dir, 1964–83; Dep. Chm., 1971–83; Chm., Investment Cos in Australia, Belgium, France, Germany, Switzerland, USA. Pres., British Property Fedn, 1984–86 (Mem. Council, 1974–; Vice-Pres., 1983–84). Mem., Audit Commn, 1986–. Chairman: Council, St George's Hosp. Med. Sch., 1977– (Mem., 1969–; Dep. Chm. 1974–77); St George's New Hosp. Bldg Cttee, 1972– (Mem., 1969–); Nuffield Hosps, 1976– (Governor, 1968–; Dep. Chm. 1975–76); Medical Centre, 1973–82 (Governor, 1970–82); Mem., Chichester HA, 1985–; Governor: BUPA, 1969–80; St George's Hosp., 1970–74, Special Trustee, 1974–77. Dir, Chichester Cathedral Works Organisation, 1985–. *Recreations:* sailing, music. *Address:* Hook Place, Aldingbourne, near Chichester, Sussex PO20 6TS. *T:* Eastergate 2291. *Clubs:* Royal Thames Yacht, Royal Ocean Racing.

AXWORTHY, Geoffrey (John); Artistic Director of Sherman Theatre, University College, Cardiff, since 1970; *b* Plymouth, England, 10 Aug. 1923; *s* of William Henry Axworthy and Gladys Elizabeth Kingcombe; *m* 1st, 1951, Irene Dickinson (*d* 1976); two *s* one *d;* 2nd, 1977, Caroline Griffiths; one *s* one *d. Educ:* Exeter Coll., Oxford (MA). On staff of: Univ. of Baghdad 1951–56; Univ. of Ibadan, Nigeria, 1956–67. First Director, Univ. of Ibadan Sch. of Drama, 1962–67. Principal, Central School of Speech and Drama, London, 1967–70. Founded Univ. of Ibadan Travelling Theatre, 1961. *Address:* 22 The Walk, West Grove, Cardiff CF2 3AF. *T:* Cardiff 490696.

AYALA, Jaime Z. de; *see* Zobel de Ayala.

AYCKBOURN, Alan; playwright; Artistic Director, Stephen Joseph Theatre-in-the-Round, Scarborough; Associate Director, National Theatre, since 1986; *b* 12 April 1939; *s* of Horace Ayckbourn and Irene Maude (*née* Worley); *m* 1959, Christine Helen (*née* Roland); two *s. Educ:* Haileybury. Worked in repertory as Stage Manager/Actor at Edinburgh, Worthing, Leatherhead, Oxford, and with late Stephen Joseph's Theatre-in-the-Round Co., at Scarborough. Founder Mem., Victoria Theatre, Stoke-on-Trent, 1962. BBC Radio Drama Producer, Leeds, 1964–70. Has written numerous full-length plays, mainly for Theatre-in-the-Round Co., 1959–. London productions: Mr Whatnot, Arts, 1964; Relatively Speaking, Duke of York's, 1967, Greenwich, 1986 (televised 1969); How the Other Half Loves, Lyric, 1970; Time and Time Again, Comedy, 1972 (televised 1976); Absurd Person Singular, Criterion, 1973 (Evening Standard Drama Award, Best Comedy, 1973) (televised, 1985); The Norman Conquests (Trilogy), Globe, 1974 (Evening Standard Drama Award, Best Play; Variety Club of GB Award; Plays and Players Award) (televised, 1977); Jeeves (musical, with Andrew Lloyd Webber), Her Majesty's, 1975; Absent Friends, Garrick, 1975 (televised, 1985); Confusions, Apollo, 1976; Bedroom Farce, Nat. Theatre, 1977 (televised 1980); Just Between Ourselves, Queen's, 1977 (Evening Standard Drama Award, Best Play) (televised, 1978); Ten Times Table, Globe, 1978; Joking Apart, Globe, 1979 (Plays and Players Award); Sisterly Feelings, Nat. Theatre, 1980; Taking Steps, Lyric, 1980; Suburban Strains (musical with Paul Todd), Round House, 1981; Season's Greetings, Apollo, 1982; Way Upstream, Nat. Theatre, 1982; Making Tracks (musical with Paul Todd), Greenwich, 1983; Intimate Exchanges, Ambassadors, 1984; A Chorus of Disapproval, Nat. Theatre, 1985 (Standard Drama Award, Best Comedy; Olivier Award, Best Comedy; Drama Award, Best Comedy, 1985), transf. Lyric, 1986; Woman in Mind, Vaudeville, 1986; Scarborough: It Could Be Any One of Us, 1983. Plays directed, Nat. Theatre: Tons of Money, 1986. Hon. DLitt Hull, 1981. *Publications:* The Norman Conquests, 1975; Three Plays (Absurd Person Singular, Absent Friends, Bedroom Farce), 1977; Joking Apart and Other Plays (Just Between Ourselves, Ten Times Table), 1979; Sisterly Feelings, and Taking Steps, 1981. *Recreations:* music, reading, cricket, films. *Address:* c/o Margaret Ramsay Ltd, 14a Goodwin's Court, St Martin's Lane, WC2N 4LL. *T:* 01–240 0691. *Club:* Garrick.

AYER, Sir Alfred (Jules), Kt 1970; FBA 1952; Wykeham Professor of Logic in the University of Oxford, and Fellow of New College, Oxford, 1959–78, Hon. Fellow, 1980; Fellow of Wolfson College, Oxford, 1978–83; *b* 29 Oct. 1910; *s* of late Jules Louis Cyprien Ayer; *m* 1st, 1932, Grace Isabel Renée Lees; one *s* one *d;* 2nd, 1960, Alberta Constance Chapman, (Dee Wells) (marr. diss. 1983); one *s;* 3rd, 1983, Vanessa Mary Addison Lawson (*née* Salmon) (*d* 1985). *Educ:* Eton Coll. (scholar); Christ Church, Oxford (scholar; Hon. Student, 1979). 1st class Lit. Hum. 1932; MA 1936; Lecturer in Philosophy at Christ Church, 1932–35; Research Student, 1935–44; Fellow of Wadham Coll., Oxford, 1944–46, Hon. Fellow, 1957; Dean, 1945–46; Grote Professor of the Philosophy of Mind and Logic, 1946–59, and Dean of the Arts Faculty, UCL, 1950–52, Univ. of London; Hon. Fellow, UCL, 1979. Visiting Prof. at: NY Univ., 1948–49; City Coll., New York, 1961–62; Surrey Univ., 1978–84; Lectures: William James, Harvard, 1970; John Dewey, Columbia, 1970; Gifford, St Andrews, 1972–73; Montgomery Fellow, Dartmouth Coll., 1982–83. Mem., Central Advisory Council for Education, 1963–66; President: Independent (formerly Agnostics) Adoption Soc., 1965–85; Humanist Assoc., 1965–70; Modern Languages Assoc., 1966–67; Internat. Inst. of Philosophy, 1968–71. Chm., Booker Prize Cttee, 1978. Hon. Mem. Amer. Acad. of Arts and Sciences 1963; For. Mem., Royal Danish Acad. of Sciences and Letters, 1976. Dr *hc* Univ. of Brussels, 1962; Hon. DLitt: East Anglia, 1972; London, 1978; Trent, Ontario, 1980; Durham, 1986; Hon. DHL Bard Coll., 1983. Chevalier de la Légion d'Honneur, 1977; Order of Cyril and Methodius, 1st cl. (Bulgaria), 1977. Enlisted in Welsh Guards, 1940; commissioned, 1940; Capt. 1943. Attaché at HM Embassy, Paris, 1945. *Publications:* Language, Truth and Logic, 1936 (revised edn 1946); The Foundations of Empirical Knowledge, 1940; Thinking and Meaning (Inaugural Lecture), 1947; (ed with Raymond Winch) British Empirical Philosophers, 1952; Philosophical Essays, 1954; The Problem of Knowledge, 1956; (ed) Logical Positivism, 1959; Privacy (British Academy lecture), 1960; Philosophy and Language (Inaugural lecture), 1960; The Concept of a Person and Other Essays, 1963; Man as a Subject for Science (Auguste Comte Lecture), 1964; The Origins of Pragmatism, 1968; (ed) The Humanist Outlook, 1968; Metaphysics and Common Sense, 1969; Russell and Moore: the analytical heritage, 1971; Probability and Evidence, 1972; Russell, 1972; Bertrand Russell as a Philosopher (British Acad. Lecture), 1973; The Central Questions of Philosophy, 1974; Part of my Life, 1977; Perception and Identity (Festschrift with reply to critics), 1979; Hume, 1980; Philosophy in the Twentieth Century, 1982; More of my Life, 1984; Freedom and Morality and Other Essays, 1984; Wittgenstein, 1985; Voltaire, 1986; articles in philos. and lit. jls. *Address:* 51 York Street, W1H 1PU. *T:* 01–402 0235. *Clubs:* Athenæum, Beefsteak, Garrick.

AYERS, John Gilbert; Keeper, Far Eastern Department, Victoria and Albert Museum, 1970–82; *b* 27 July 1922; *s* of H. W. Ayers, CB, CBE; *m* 1957, Bridget Elspeth Jacqualine Fanshawe; one *s* two *d. Educ:* St Paul's Sch.; St Edmund Hall, Oxford. Served in RAF, 1941–46 (Sgt). Asst Keeper, Dept of Ceramics, Victoria and Albert Museum, 1950, Dep. Keeper 1963. Pres., Oriental Ceramic Soc., 1984–. *Publications:* The Seligman Collection of Oriental Art, II, 1964; The Baur Collection: Chinese Ceramics, I-IV, 1968–74, Japanese Ceramics, 1982; (with R. J. Charleston) The James A. de Rothschild Collection: Meissen and Oriental Porcelain, 1971; Oriental Ceramics, The World's Great Collections: Victoria and Albert Museum, 1975; (with J. Rawson) Chinese Jade throughout the Ages, exhbn catalogue, 1975; (with D. Howard) China for the West, 2 vols, 1978; (with D. Howard) Masterpieces of Chinese Export Porcelain, 1980; Oriental Art in the Victoria and Albert Museum, 1983; (ed) Chinese Ceramics in the Topkapi Saray Museum, Istanbul, 3 vols, 1986. *Address:* 3 Bedford Gardens, W8 7ED. *T:* 01–229–5168.

AYKROYD, Sir Cecil William, 2nd Bt, *cr* 1929; *b* 23 April 1905; *e s* of Sir Frederic Alfred Aykroyd, 1st Bt and late Lily May, *e d* of Sir James Roberts, 1st Bt, LLD, of Strathallan Castle, Perthshire, and Fairlight Hall, near Hastings; *S* father 1949; unmarried. *Educ:* Charterhouse; Jesus Coll., Cambridge. BA 1926. Dir, Nat. Provincial Bank Ltd, 1958–69 (Dir Bradford and District Bd, 1946–69). *Recreations:* fishing and shooting. *Heir: nephew* James Alexander Frederic Aykroyd [*b* 6 Sept. 1943; *m* 1973, Jennifer, *d* of Frederick William Marshall; two *d*]. *Address:* Birstwith Hall, near Harrogate, North Yorks. *T:* Harrogate 770250.

AYKROYD, Sir William Miles, 3rd Bt *cr* 1920; MC 1944; *b* 24 Aug. 1923; *s* of Sir Alfred Hammond Aykroyd, 2nd Bt, and Sylvia Ambler Aykroyd (*née* Walker), *widow* of Lieut-Col Foster Newton Thorne; *S* father, 1965. *Educ:* Charterhouse. Served in 5th Royal Inniskilling Dragoon Guards, Lieut, 1943–47. Dir, Hardy Amies Ltd, 1950–69. *Heir: cousin* Michael David Aykroyd [*b* 14 June 1928; *m* 1952, Oenone Gillian Diana, *o d* of Donald George Cowling, MBE; one *s* three *d*]. *Address:* Buckland Newton Place, Dorchester, Dorset. *T:* Buckland Newton 259. *Club:* Boodle's.

AYLEN, Rear-Adm. Ian Gerald, CB 1962; OBE 1946; DSC 1942; CEng; FIMechE; *b* 12 Oct. 1910; *s* of late Commander A. E. Aylen, RN and Mrs S. C. M. Aylen; *m* 1937, Alice Brough Maltby; one *s* two *d. Educ:* Blundell's, Tiverton. RNE Coll., Keyham, 1929–33; served in HMS Rodney; Curacoa; Galatea, 1939–40; Kelvin, 1940–42; 30 Assault Unit, 1945; Cossack; Fleet Engineer Officer, Home Fleet, 1957–58; CO HMS Thunderer, RNE Coll., 1958–60; Rear-Admiral, 1960; Admiral Superintendent, HM Dockyard, Rosyth, 1960–63; Dep. Sec., Instn Mechanical Engineers, 1963–65; Asst Sec., Council of Engineering Instns, 1966–71, retired 1971. *Address:* Tracey Mill Barn, Honiton, Devon.

AYLEN, Walter Stafford; QC 1983; a Recorder, since 1985; *b* 21 May 1937; *s* of late Rt Rev. Charles Arthur William Aylen and Elisabeth Margaret Anna (*née* Hills); *m* 1967, Peggy Elizabeth Lainé Woodford; three *d. Educ:* Summer Fields Sch.; Winchester Coll. (schol.); New Coll., Oxford (schol., sen. schol.; BCL; MA). Commnd 2nd Lieut KRRC, 1956–57. Called to the Bar, Middle Temple, 1962; Asst Recorder, 1982. Bishop's Commissioned Assistant, Christian Stewardship Dept, Dio. of Southwark, 1970–. *Recreations:* reading novels (especially his wife's), theatre, music. *Address:* 27 Gauden Road, SW4 6LR. *T:* 01–622 7871; 2 Garden Court, Temple, EC4Y 9BL. *T:* 01–353 4741.

AYLESFORD, 11th Earl of; **Charles Ian Finch-Knightley,** JP; Baron Guernsey, 1703; Lord-Lieutenant of West Midlands, since 1974; *b* 2 Nov. 1918; *er s* of 10th Earl of Aylesford; *S* father, 1958; *m* 1946, Margaret Rosemary Tyer; one *s* two *d. Educ:* Oundle. Lieut RSF, 1939; Captain Black Watch, 1947. Regional Dir, Birmingham and W Midlands Bd, Lloyds Bank, 1982–. Mem., Water Space Amenity Commn, 1973–83. County Comr for Scouts, 1949–74, Patron 1974–. JP 1948, DL 1954, Vice-Lieutenant 1964–74, Warwicks. KStJ 1974. *Recreations:* wild life and nature conservation. *Heir: s* Lord Guernsey, *qv. Address:* Packington Old Hall, Coventry, West Midlands CV7 7HG. *T:* (home) Meriden 23273; (office) Meriden 22274. *Club:* Warwickshire CC (President, 1980–).

AYLESTONE, Baron *cr* 1967 (Life Peer), of Aylestone; **Herbert William Bowden;** PC 1962; CH 1975; CBE 1953; Chairman, Independent Broadcasting Authority (formerly Independent Television Authority), 1967–75; *b* 20 Jan. 1905; *m* 1928, Louisa Grace, *d* of William Brown, Cardiff; one *d*. RAF, 1941–45. MP (Lab) S Leicester, 1945–50, S-W Div. of Leicester, 1950–67. PPS to Postmaster-Gen., 1947–49; Asst Govt Whip, 1949–50; a Lord Comr of the Treasury, 1950–51; Dep. Chief Oppn Whip, 1951–55; Chief Oppn Whip, 1955–64; Lord Pres. of the Council and Leader of the House of Commons, 1964–66; Secretary of State for Commonwealth Affairs, 1966–67; joined SDP, 1981; Dep. Speaker, House of Lords. *Address:* c/o House of Lords, SW1.

AYLING, Peter William, BSc, CEng, FRINA; Secretary, Royal Institution of Naval Architects, since 1967; *b* 25 Sept. 1925; *s* of late William Frank and Edith Louise Ayling; *m* 1949, Sheila Bargery; two *s* two *d. Educ:* Royal Dockyard Sch., Portsmouth; King's Coll., Univ. of Durham (BSc). Shipwright apprentice, HM Dockyard, Portsmouth, 1942–47; King's Coll., Univ. of Durham, 1947–50; Research and Principal Research Officer, British Ship Research Assoc., London, 1950–65; Principal Scientific Officer, Ship Div., Nat. Physical Laboratory, Feltham (now British Maritime Technology Ltd), 1965–67. *Publications:* papers on ship strength and vibration, Trans RINA, NECInst and IESS. *Recreations:* music, gardening, walking, motoring. *Address:* Royal Institution of Naval Architects, 10 Upper Belgrave Street, SW1X 8BQ. *T:* 01–235 4622; (home) Oakmead, School Road, Camelsdale, Haslemere, Surrey. *T:* Haslemere 4474.

AYLING, Air Vice-Marshal Richard Cecil, CB 1965; CBE 1961 (OBE 1948); Adjudicator, Immigration Appeals, since 1970; *b* 7 June 1916; *s* of A. C. Ayling, LDS, Norwood, London; *m* 1st, 1941, Patricia Doreen Wright (*d* 1966); one *s* one *d*; 2nd, 1971, Virginia, *d* of Col Frank Davis, Northwood; two *d. Educ:* Dulwich Coll. No 3(F) Sqdn, 1936–39. Served RNZAF, 1940–43; Comd No 51 Sqdn (Bomber Comd), 1944; Station Comdr, Bomber Comd, 1944–45; Staff Coll., 1945. Staff of Central Bomber Estabt, 1946–48; Air Staff (Plans) Far East, 1948–50; Air Min. (OR1 and Dep. Dir Policy Air Staff), 1951–54; Station Comdr, Bomber Comd, 1954–58; Asst Chief of Defence Staff, Min. of Defence, 1958–59; Dir of Organisation (Estabts), Air Min., 1960–61; SASO, Flying Training Command, 1962–65; Min. of Defence, 1965–66; AOA, RAF Air Support (formerly Transport) Comd, 1966–69; retd, 1969. *Recreations:* ski-ing, sailing, gardening. *Address:* Buckler's Spring, Buckler's Hard, Beaulieu, Hants. *T:* Buckler's Hard 204. *Clubs:* various yacht clubs and sailing associations.

AYLMER, family name of **Baron Aylmer.**

AYLMER, 13th Baron *cr* 1718; **Michael Anthony Aylmer;** Bt 1662; *b* 27 March 1923; *s* of Christopher Aylmer (*d* 1955) and Marjorie (*d* 1981), *d* of Percival Ellison Barber, surgeon, Sheffield; *S* cousin, 1982; *m* 1950, Countess Maddalena Sofia, *d* of late Count Arbeno Attems, Aiello del Friuli, Italy; one *s* one *d. Educ:* privately and Trinity Hall, Cambridge (Exhibnr, MA, LLM). Admitted a solicitor, 1948. Employed in Legal Dept of Equity & Law Life Assurance Society plc, 1951 until retirement, 1983. *Recreations:* reading and music. *Heir: s* Hon. (Anthony) Julian Aylmer, *b* 10 Dec. 1951. *Address:* 42 Brampton Grove, NW4 4AQ. *T:* 01–202 8300.

AYLMER, Sir Fenton Gerald, 15th Bt, *cr* 1622; *b* 12 March 1901; *s* of Sir Gerald Evans-Freke Aylmer, 14th Bt, and Mabel Howard, *d* of late Hon. J. K. Ward, MLC, Province of Quebec; *S* father, 1939; *m* 1928, Rosalind Boultbee, *d* of J. Percival Bell, Hamilton, Ont; one *s* one *d. Educ:* Lower Canada Coll., Montreal; Bishop's Coll. Sch., Lennoxville. *Heir: s* Richard John Aylmer [*b* 23 April 1937; *m* 1962, Lise Demers; one *s* one *d*]. *Address:* 29 Church Hill, Westmount, Quebec H3Y 2Z8, Canada.

AYLMER, Dr Gerald Edward, FBA 1976; Master of St Peter's College, Oxford, since 1978; *b* 30 April 1926; *s* of late Captain E. A. Aylmer, RN, and Mrs G. P. Aylmer (*née* Evans); *m* 1955, Ursula Nixon; one *s* one *d. Educ:* Winchester; Balliol Coll., Oxford (MA, DPhil). Served RN, 1944–47. Jane Eliza Proctor Vis. Fellow, Princeton Univ., NJ, USA, 1950–51; Jun. Res. Fellow, Balliol Coll., Oxford, 1951–54; Asst Lectr in History, Univ. of Manchester, 1954–57, Lectr, 1957–62; Prof. of History and Head of Dept of History, Univ. of York, 1963–78. Vis. Mem., Inst. for Advanced Study, Princeton, 1975. Mem., Royal Commn on Historical Manuscripts, 1978–. Pres., RHistS, 1984–. Mem., Editorial Bd, History of Parliament, 1969–. *Publications:* The King's Servants, 1961 (2nd edn 1974); (ed) The Diary of William Lawrence, 1962; The Struggle for the Constitution, 1963 (5th edn 1975); (ed) The Interregnum, 1972 (2nd edn 1974); The State's Servants, 1973; (ed) The Levellers in the English Revolution, 1975; (ed with Reginald Cant) A History of York Minster, 1978; Rebellion or Revolution?: England 1640–1660, 1986; articles and revs in learned jls. *Address:* Canal House, St Peter's College, Oxford OX1 2DL. *T:* Oxford 248436, 240554.

AYOUB, John Edward Moussa, FRCS; Consulting Surgeon, Moorfields Eye Hospital, since 1973 (Surgeon, 1950–73); Consulting Ophthalmic Surgeon, London Hospital, since 1973 (Surgeon, 1947–73); Consulting Ophthalmic Surgeon, Royal Masonic Hospital, since 1973 (Consultant, 1967–73); Consulting Ophthalmic Surgeon, Royal Navy; *b* 7 Sept. 1908; British; *m* 1939, Madeleine Marion Coniston Martin; one *s* one *d. Educ:* St Paul's Sch.; Lincoln Coll., Oxford; St Thomas' Hospital. BM, BCh Oxon 1933; FRCS 1935. Fellow, and past Vice-Pres. Section of Ophthalmology, RSM; Past Mem. Council, Faculty of Ophthalmologists (Vice-Pres., 1959–). Served War of 1939–45, Surg. Lieut-Comdr RNVR, specialist in ophthalmology. Visiting consultant ophthalmologist to Western Memorial Hosp., Newfoundland, 1974–. Chm., Alderney Branch Cttee, RNLI, 1983–86. *Publications:* contributions to medical journals. *Recreation:* gardening. *Address:* 2 Clarendon Road, Boston Spa, near Wetherby, West Yorks LS23 6NG. *Clubs:* Leander; Royal Cruising.

AYRES, Gillian, OBE 1986; ARA 1982; painter, artist; *b* 3 Feb. 1930; *d* of Stephen and Florence Ayres; *m* (marr. diss.); two *s. Educ:* St Paul's Girls' Sch.; Camberwell Sch. of Art. Student, 1946–50; taught, 1959–81 (incl. Sen. Lectr, St Martin's Sch. of Art, and Head of Painting, Winchester Sch. of Art, 1978–81). One-woman Exhibitions include: Gallery One, 1956; Redfern Gall., 1958; Moulton Gall., 1960 and 1962; Kasmin Gall., 1965, 1966 and 1969; William Darby Gall., 1976; Women's Internat. Centre, New York, 1976; Knoedler Gall., 1979 and 1982; Mus. of Mod. Art, Oxford, 1981; retrospective exhibn, Serpentine Gall., 1983; also exhibited: Redfern Gall., 1957; 1st Paris Biennale, 1959; Hayward Gall., 1971; Hayward Annual Exhibn, 1974 and 1980; Silver Jubilee Exhibn, RA, 1977; Knoedler Gall., NY, 1985. Works in public collections: Tate Gall.; Mus. of Mod. Art, NY; Olinda Mus., Brazil; Gulbenkian Foundn, Lisbon; V&A Mus.; British Council. Prize winner: Tokyo Biennale, 1963; John Moores 2nd Prize, 1982; Major Arts Council Bursary, 1979. *Recreation:* gardening. *Address:* The Old Rectory, Llaniestyn, Pwllheli, Gwynedd, N Wales. *T:* Bottwnog 262.

AYRTON, Norman Walter; international theatre and opera director; *b* London, 25 Sept. 1924. Served War of 1939–45, RNVR. Trained as an actor at Old Vic Theatre School under Michael Saint Denis, 1947–48; joined Old Vic Company, 1948; repertory experience at Farnham and Oxford, 1949–50; on staff of Old Vic Sch., 1949–52; rejoined Old Vic Company for 1951 Festival Season; opened own teaching studio, 1952; began dramatic coaching for Royal Opera House, Covent Garden, 1953; apptd Asst Principal of London Academy of Music and Dramatic Art, 1954; taught at Shakespeare Festival, Stratford, Ont, and Royal Shakespeare Theatre, Stratford-upon-Avon, 1959–62; apptd GHQ Drama Adviser to Girl Guide Movement, 1960–74; Principal, LAMDA, 1966–72; Dean, World Shakespeare Study Centre, Bankside, 1972; Acad. Chm., Brit. Amer. Drama Acad., Regent's Coll., London, 1986–. *Director:* Artaxerxes, for Handel Opera Soc., Camden Festival, 1963; La Traviata, Covent Garden, 1963; Manon, Covent Garden, 1964; Sutherland-Williamson Grand Opera Season, in Australia, 1965; Twelfth Night at Dallas Theatre Center, Texas, 1967; The Way of the World, NY, 1976; Lakmé, Sydney Opera House, 1976; Der Rosenkavalier, Sydney Opera House, 1983; *Guest Director:* Australian Council for Arts, Sydney and Brisbane, 1973; Loeb Drama Center, Harvard (and teacher), 1974; Faculty, Juillard Sch., NY, 1974–85; Melbourne Theatre Co., 1974–; Nat. Inst. of Dramatic Art, Sydney, 1974; Vancouver Opera Assoc., 1975–; Sydney Opera House, 1976–81, 1983; Williamstown Festival, USA, 1977; Hartford Stage Co. and Amer. Stage Fest., 1978–; Missouri Rep. Theatre, 1980–81; Nat. Opera Studio, London, 1980–81; Spoleto Fest., USA, 1984; Resident Stage Director: Amer. Opera Center, NY, 1981–85. *Recreations:* reading, music, travel. *Address:* 40A Birchington Road, NW6.

AZIKIWE, Rt. Hon. Nnamdi, GCFR 1980; PC 1960; LLD, DLitt, MA, MSc; Ndichie Chief Owelle of Onitsha, 1973; Leader, Nigeria People's Party, since 1979; (First) President of the Federal Republic of Nigeria, 1963–66; Governor-General and Commander-in-Chief of Nigeria, 1960–63; *b* Zungeru, Northern Nigeria, 16 Nov. 1904; *s* of Obededom Chukwuemeka and Rachel Chinwe Azikiwe; *m* 1936, Flora Ogbenyeanu Ogoegbunam, *d* of Chief Ogoegbunam, the Adazia of Onitsha (Ndichie Chief); three *s* one *d. Educ:* CMS Central Sch., Onitsha; Methodist Boys' High Sch., Lagos; Storer Coll., Harpers Ferry, W Va, USA; Howard Univ., Washington, DC; Lincoln Univ., Pa; Univ. of Pennsylvania. Overseas Fellow, Inst. Journalists, London, 1962 (Mem., 1933–). Editor-in-Chief, African Morning Post, Accra, 1934–37; Editor-in-Chief, West African Pilot,

1937–45; Correspondent for Associated Negro Press, 1944–47; Gen. Sec., Nat. Council of Nigeria and the Cameroons, 1944–46 (Pres., 1946–60); Correspondent for Reuter's, 1944–46; Chm. African Continental Bank Ltd, 1944–53. MLC Nigeria, 1947–51; Mem. Foot Commission for Nigerianisation of Civil Service, 1948. Leader of Opposition in the Western House of Assembly, 1952–53; Mem. Eastern House of Assembly, 1954–59; MHR 1954; Minister, Eastern Nigeria, 1954–57; Leader, Educational Missions to UK and USA, for establishment of Univ. of Nigeria, 1955 and 1959; Premier of Eastern Nigeria, 1954–59; Pres., Exec. Council of Govt of E Nigeria, 1957–59; President of Senate of Federation, Jan–Nov. 1960. NPP Candidate, Presidential Election, 1979. Mem., Council of State, 1979–83. Ndichie Chief Ozizani Obi of Onitsha, 1963–72. Chm., Provisional Council of Univ. of Nigeria, 1960–61; Chancellor of Univ. of Nigeria, 1961–66, of Univ. of Lagos, 1970–76. Jt Pres., Anti-Slavery Soc. for Human Rights, London, 1970– (Vice-Pres., 1966–69). (Life) FREconS; (Life) FRAI; (Life) Mem. British Association for Advancement of Science; Member: American Soc. of International Law; American Anthropological Assoc. Pres. numerous sporting assocs and boards, 1940–60; Mem., Nigerian Olympic Cttee, 1950–60. Hon. DCL Liberia, 1969; Hon. DSc Lagos, 1972. KStJ 1960–66. *Publications:* Liberia in World Politics, 1934; Renascent Africa, 1937; The African in Ancient and Mediaeval History, 1938; Land Tenure in Northern Nigeria, 1942; Political Blueprint of Nigeria, 1943; Economic Reconstruction of Nigeria, 1943; Economic Rehabilitation of Eastern Nigeria, 1955; Zik: a selection of speeches, 1961; Meditations: a collection of poems, 1965; My Odyssey, 1971; Military Revolution in Nigeria, 1972; Dialogue on a New Capital for Nigeria, 1974; Treasury of West African Poetry; Democracy with Military Vigilance, 1974; Onitsha Market Crisis, 1975; Civil War Soliloquies: further collection of poems, 1976; Ideology for Nigeria, 1978. *Recreations:* athletics, boxing, cricket, soccer, swimming, tennis, reading. *Address:* Onuiyi Haven, PO Box 7, Nsukka, Nigeria.

AZIZ, Suhail Ibne; international management consultant, since 1981; *b* Bangladesh (then India), 3 Oct. 1937; permanently resident in England, since 1966; *s* of Azizur Rahman and Lutfunnessa Khatoon; *m* 1960, Elizabeth Ann Pyne, Dartmouth, Devon; two *d*. *Educ:* Govt High Sec. Sch., Sylhet; Murarichand Coll., Dacca Univ., Sylhet (Intermed. in Science, 1954); Jt Services Pre-Cadet Trng Sch., Quetta; Cadet Trng Sch., PNS Himalaya, Karachi; BRNC, Dartmouth (Actg Sub-Lieut 1958); (mature student) Kingston upon Thames Polytechnic and Trent Polytech., Nottingham (Dipl. in Man. Studies, 1970); (ext. student) London Univ. (BScEcon Hons 1972); (internal student) Birkbeck Coll., London Univ., (MScEcon 1976). FBIM; MIMC 1986. Sub-Lieut and Lieut, Pakistan Navy Destroyers/Mine Sweeper (Exec. Br.), 1954–61. Personnel and indust. relations: Unilever (Pakistan); Royal Air Force; Commn on Indust. Relations, London; Ford Motor Co. (GB); Mars Ltd, 1963–78; Dir of Gen. Services Div., CRE, 1978–81. Leading Mem., Bangladesh Movement in UK, 1971. Member: Exec., Standing Conf. of Asian Orgs in UK, 1972–; N Metropol. Conciliation Cttee, Race Relations Bd, 1971–74; Exec., Post Conf. Constituent Cttee, Black People in Britain—the Way Forward, 1975–76; Adv. Cttee to Gulbenkian Foundn on Area Resource Centre and Community Support Forum, 1976–81; Exec., Nottingham and Dist Community Relations Council, 1975–78; Dept of Employment Race Relations Employment Adv. Gp, 1977–78; BBC Asian programme Adv. Cttee, 1977–81; Industrial Tribunals, 1977–; Exec., Nat. Org. of African, Asian and Caribbean Peoples, 1976–77; Home Sec.'s Standing Adv. Council on Race Relations, 1976–78; Steering Cttee, Asian Support Forum, 1984–86; Jt Consultative Cttee with Ethnic Minorities, Merton BC, 1985–; Chm., Jalalabad Overseas Orgn in UK, 1983–; Pres., London Boroughs Bangladesh Assoc., 1984–; Jt Convenor and Founder Mem., Bangladesh Community Support Forum, 1984–. Mem., Labour Econ. Finance Taxation Assoc., 1973–80; Institute of Management Consultants: Chm., Third World Specialist Gp, 1984–; Treasurer, London Reg., 1985–. Jt Trustee, United Action-Bangladesh Relief Fund, 1971–; Trustee, Brixton Neighbourhood Assoc., 1979–82. Deeply interested in community and race relations and believes profoundly that future health of Brit. society depends on achieving good race relations. *Recreations:* travelling, seeing places of historical interest, meeting people, reading (*eg* political economy). *Address:* 126 St Julian's Farm Road, West Norwood, SE27 0RR. *Clubs:* Royal Air Force; Sudan (Khartoum).

AZNAM, Raja Tan Sri bin Raja Haji Ahmad; Malaysian High Commissioner in London, 1979–82; *b* Taiping, 21 Jan. 1928; *s* of Raja Haji Ahmad and Hajjah Zainab; *m* 1954, Tengku Puan Sri Zailah Btd T. Zakaria; one *s* two *d*. *Educ:* King Edward VII Coll., Taiping; Malay Coll., Kuala Kangsar; Univ. of Malaya in Singapore. Joined Malayan Civil Service 1953, Foreign Service 1956; Second Sec., Bangkok, 1957; First Sec., Cairo, 1960–62; Principal Asst Sec., Min. of Foreign Affairs, 1962–65; Dep. Perm. Rep to UN, 1965–68; High Comr in India, 1968–71; Ambassador to Japan, 1971–74, to USSR, Bulgaria, Hungary, Mongolia, Poland and Romania, 1974–77, to France, Morocco, Portugal and Spain, 1977–79. *Recreations:* reading, golf. *Address:* c/o Ministry of Foreign Affairs, Wismaputre, Kuala Lumpur, Malaysia.

B

BABCOCK, Horace Welcome; Director, Mount Wilson and Palomar Observatories, 1964–78, retired; *b* 13 Sept. 1912; *s* of Harold D. Babcock and Mary G. (*née* Henderson); *m* 1st, 1940; one *s* one *d*; 2nd, 1958, Elizabeth M. Aubrey; one *s*. *Educ:* California Institute of Technology (BS); Univ. of California (PhD). Instructor, Yerkes and McDonald Observatories, 1939–41; Radiation Laboratory, Mass Inst. of Tech., 1941–42; Calif Inst. of Tech., 1942–45; Staff Mem., Mount Wilson Observatory, 1946–51; Astronomer, Mount Wilson and Palomar Observatories, 1951–80, Asst Dir, 1957–63, Associate Dir, 1963–64. Constructed Las Campanas Observatory, Chile, of Carnegie Instn, Washington, 1968. Elected to: National Acad. of Sciences, 1954 (Councillor, 1973–76); American Acad. of Arts and Sciences, 1959; American Philosophical Soc., 1966; Corres. Mem., Société Royale des Sciences de Liège, 1968; Associate, Royal Astronomical Soc., 1969; Member: American Astronomical Soc.; Astronomical Soc. of the Pacific; Internat. Astronomical Union. Hon. DSc Univ. of Newcastle upon Tyne, 1965. US Navy Bureau of Ordnance Development Award, 1945; Eddington Gold Medal, RAS, 1958; Henry Draper Medal of the National Acad. of Sciences, 1957; Bruce Medal, Astronomical Soc. of the Pacific, 1969; Gold Medal, RAS, 1970. *Publications:* scientific papers in Astrophysical Jl, Publications of the Astronomical Soc. of the Pacific, Jl of Optical Soc. of America, etc, primarily on magnetic fields of the stars and sun, astrophysics, diffraction gratings, and astronomical instruments. *Address:* Mount Wilson and Las Campanas Observatories, Carnegie Institution of Washington, 813 Santa Barbara Street, Pasadena, California 91101, USA. *T:* (213) 577–1122.

BABER, Ernest George; Judge of the Supreme Court of Hong Kong, 1973–86; *b* 18 July 1924; *s* of late Walter Averette Baber and Kate Marion (*née* Pratt); *m* 1960, Dr Flora Marion, *y d* of late Dr Raymond Bisset Smith and Mrs Jean Gemmell Bisset Smith (*née* Howie); one *s* two *d*. *Educ:* Brentwood; Emmanuel Coll., Cambridge (MA, LLB). Served RN, 1942–47 (Lieut (S)). Called to Bar, Lincoln's Inn, 1951. Resident Magistrate, Uganda, 1954–62; Magistrate and President of Tenancy Tribunal, Hong Kong, 1962; Senior Magistrate, 1963–67; District Judge, 1967–73. *Recreations:* children, music, walking. *Address:* 18 Cumnor Hill, Oxford OX2 9NA. *Club:* Naval.

BABINGTON, Anthony Patrick; His Honour Judge Babington; a Circuit Judge, since 1972; *b* 4 April 1920; 2nd *s* of late Oscar John Gilmore Babington, MAI, AMICE, Monkstown, Co. Cork. *Educ:* Reading Sch. Served with Royal Ulster Rifles and Dorset Regt, 1939–45 (wounded twice); Croix de Guerre with Gold Star (France), 1944. Called to the Bar, Middle Temple, 1948; Bencher, 1977; South Eastern Circuit; Prosecuting Counsel to Post Office, SE Circuit (South), 1959–64; Metropolitan Stipendiary Magistrate, 1964–72. Mem., Home Office Working Party on Bail, 1971–73. Mem., Nat. Exec. Cttee, Internat. PEN English Centre, 1979–. *Publications:* No Memorial, 1954; The Power to Silence, 1968; A House in Bow Street, 1969; The English Bastille, 1971; The Only Liberty, 1975; For the Sake of Example, 1983. *Recreations:* music, theatre, reading. *Address:* 3 Gledhow Gardens, South Kensington, SW5 0BL. *T:* 01–373 4014; Thydon Cottage, Chilham, near Canterbury, Kent. *T:* Canterbury 730300. *Clubs:* Garrick, Special Forces.

BABINGTON, Robert John, DSC 1943; QC (NI) 1965; **His Honour Judge Babington;** appointed County Court Judge for Fermanagh and Tyrone, 1978; *b* 9 April 1920; *s* of David Louis James Babington and Alice Marie (*née* McClintock); *m* 1952, Elizabeth Bryanna Marguerite Alton, *d* of Dr E. H. Alton, Provost of Trinity College, Dublin; two *s* one *d*. *Educ:* St Columba's Coll., Rathfarnham, Dublin; Trinity Coll., Dublin (BA). Called to the Bar, Inn of Court of NI, 1947. MP North Down, Stormont, 1968–72. *Recreations:* golf, bird-watching. *Address:* Royal Courts of Justice, Chichester Street, Belfast BT1 3JF. *Clubs:* Special Forces; Tyrone County (Omagh); Fermanagh County (Enniskillen); Royal Belfast Golf.

BABINGTON, William, CBE 1972; QFSM 1969; Chief Officer, Kent County Fire Brigade, 1966–76, retired; *b* 23 Dec. 1916; *s* of William and Annie Babington; *m* 1940, Marjorie Perdue Le Seelleur; one *d*. *Educ:* King Edward's Grammar Sch., Birmingham. Addtl Supt of Police, Assam, India, 1942–44; Instructor, Fire Service Coll., 1951–53; Divl Officer, Hampshire Fire Service, 1954–59; Asst Chief Officer, Suffolk and Ipswich Fire Service, 1959–62; Dep. Chief Officer, Lancashire Fire Brigade, 1962–66. *Recreations:* sailing, travel. *Address:* Alpine Cottage, Grouville, Jersey, CI. *T:* Jersey 52737.

BACHE, Andrew Philip Foley; HM Diplomatic Service; Counsellor, Ankara, since 1985; *b* 29 Dec. 1939; *s* of late Robert Philip Sidney Bache, OBE and of Jessie Bache; *m* 1963, Shân Headley; two *s* one *d*. *Educ:* Shrewsbury Sch.; Emmanuel Coll., Cambridge (MA). Joined HM Diplomatic Service, 1963; 3rd Sec., Nicosia, 1964–66; Treasury Centre for Admin. Studies, 1966; 2nd Sec., Sofia, 1966–68; FCO, 1968–71; 1st Sec., Lagos, 1971–74; FCO, 1974–78; 1st Sec. (Commercial), Vienna, 1978–81; Counsellor and Hd of Chancery, Tokyo, 1981–85. *Recreations:* diverse, including history, ornithology, fine arts, squash, tennis, cricket and logging. *Address:* c/o Foreign and Commonwealth Office, King Charles Street, SW1. *Clubs:* Royal Commonwealth Society, MCC.

BACK, Mrs J. H.; *see* Harrison, Kathleen.

BACK, Kenneth John Campbell, AO 1984; MSc, PhD; Executive Director, International Development Program of Australian Universities and Colleges Ltd, since 1986; *b* 13 Aug. 1925; *s* of J. L. Back; *m* 1950, Patricia, *d* of R. O. Cummings; two *d*. *Educ:* Sydney High Sch.; Sydney Univ. (MSc); Univ. of Queensland (PhD). Res. Bacteriologist, Davis Gelatine (Aust.) Pty Ltd, 1947–49; Queensland University: Lectr in Bacteriology, 1950–56; Sen. Lectr in Microbiology, 1957–61; Actg Prof. of Microbiology, 1962; Warden, University Coll. of Townsville, Queensland, 1963–70; Vice-Chancellor, James Cook Univ. of N Queensland, 1970–85. Chm., Standing Cttee, Australian Univs Internat. Develt Prog. (formerly Australian-Asian Univs Co-operation Scheme), 1977–85. Hon. DSc Queensland, 1982. *Publications:* papers on microbiological metabolism. *Recreations:* golf, bridge, sailing. *Address:* International Development Program of Australian Universities and Colleges Ltd, GPO Box 2006, Canberra, ACT 2601, Australia; 13 Steinwedel Street, Farrer, ACT 2607, Australia. *Club:* Commonwealth (Canberra).

BACK, Patrick, QC 1970; a Recorder of the Crown Court, since 1972; *b* 23 Aug. 1917; *s* of late Ivor Back, FRCS, and Barbara Back (*née* Nash). *Educ:* Marlborough; Trinity Hall, Cambridge. Captain, 14th Punjab Regt, 1941–46. Called to Bar, 1940; Bencher, Gray's Inn, 1978. Commenced practice, Western Circuit, 1948, Leader, 1984–; Dep. Chm., Devon QS, 1968. *Recreation:* fly-fishing. *Address:* Paddock Edge, Broadwindsor, Dorset. *T:* Broadwindsor 644; 3 Paper Buildings, Temple, EC4; Flat 3, Marquess House, 74 Marquess Road, N1. *T:* 01–226 0991.

BACK, Ronald Eric George, CBE 1985; Managing Director, National Networks, and Corporate Director, British Telecom, since 1983; *b* 20 April 1926; *s* of George Ernest Back and Margery A. (*née* Stupples); *m* 1949, Beryl Gladys Clark. *Educ:* Ashford Grammar School; Northampton Polytechnic. CEng; FIEE. Joined Post Office as engineering trainee, 1942; Asst Engineer on plant protection, 1949; Exec. Engineer, civil engineering projects, 1951–60; Sen. Exec. Engineer, microwave link provision, 1960–65; Asst Staff Engineer and Staff Engineer, Satellite Earth Station design and provision, 1965–72; Dep. Dir Engineering, Network Planning, 1972–76; Dir, Service Dept, 1976–79; Sen. Dir, Network, 1979–82; Asst Man. Dir, Nat. Network, 1982–83. *Recreations:* breeding and exhibiting Airedale terriers (International Judge). *Address:* High Oaks, Lamberhurst, Kent TN3 8EP. *T:* Lamberhurst 890317. *Club:* Reform.

BACKETT, Prof. Edward Maurice; Foundation Professor of Community Health, University of Nottingham, 1969–81, now Professor Emeritus; *b* 12 Jan. 1916; *o s* of late Frederick and Louisa Backett; *m* 1940, Shirley Paul-Thompson; one *s* two *d*. *Educ:* University Coll., London; Westminster Hospital. Operational Research with RAF; Nuffield Fellow in Social Medicine; Research Worker, Medical Research Council; Lecturer, Queen's Univ., Belfast; Senior Lecturer, Guy's Hospital and London Sch. of Hygiene and Tropical Medicine; Prof. and Head of Dept of Public Health and Social Medicine, Univ. of Aberdeen, 1958–69. Hon. Mem., Internat. Epidemiol Assoc., 1984. *Publications:* The Risk Approach to Health Care, 1984; papers in scientific journals. *Recreations:* swimming, walking, sailing. *Address:* Lidstones, South Town, Dartmouth, Devon TQ6 9BU. *T:* Dartmouth 3788.

BACKHOUSE, Jonathan; retired; *b* 16 March 1907; 2nd *s* of late Lieut-Col M. R. C. Backhouse, DSO, TD, and of Olive Backhouse; *m* 1934, Alice Joan Woodroffe (*d* 1984), two *s* one *d*. *Educ:* RNC Dartmouth. Served War of 1939–45, Royal Artillery. Merchant Bank, 1924–28; Stock Exchange, 1928–50; Merchant Bank, 1950–70. *Recreations:* shooting, etc. *Address:* Breewood Hall, Great Horkesley, Colchester, Essex. *T:* Colchester 271260. *Club:* Royal Thames Yacht.

BACKHOUSE, Sir Jonathan Roger, 4th Bt, *cr* 1901; formerly Managing Director, W. H. Freeman & Co. Ltd, Publishers; *b* 30 Dec. 1939; *s* of Major Sir John Edmund Backhouse, 3rd Bt, MC, and Jean Marie Frances, *d* of Lieut-Col G. R. V. Hume-Gore, MC, The Gordon Highlanders; *S* father, 1944. *Educ:* Oxford. *Heir: b* Oliver Richard Backhouse [*b* 18 July 1941; *m* 1970, Gillian Irene, *o d* of L. W. Lincoln, Northwood, Middx]. *Address:* c/o Lloyds Bank, 39 Piccadilly, W1.

BACKHOUSE, Roger Bainbridge; QC 1984; *b* 8 March 1938; *s* of Leslie Bainbridge Backhouse and Jean Backhouse; *m* 1962, Elizabeth Constance, *d* of Comdr J. A. Lowe, DSO, DSC; two *s* one *d*. *Educ:* Liverpool Coll.; Trinity Hall, Cambridge (History Tripos parts I & II). Nat. Service, RAF, 1956–58 (Pilot Officer). Worked in family business, 1961–62; Schoolmaster, 1962–64; called to the Bar, Middle Temple, 1965. *Recreations:* shooting, golf, opera. *Address:* Preston House, Colebrook Street, Winchester, Hants SO23 9LH. *T:* Winchester 63053; (chambers) 2 King's Bench Walk, Temple, EC4Y 7AE. *Clubs:* Royal Air Force; Hampshire (Winchester).

BACON, family name of **Baroness Bacon.**

BACON, Baroness *cr* 1970 (Life Peer), of Leeds and Normanton; **Alice Martha Bacon,** PC 1966; CBE 1953; DL; *d* of late County Councillor B. Bacon, miner. *Educ:* Elementary Schs, Normanton, Yorks; Normanton Girls' High Sch.; Stockwell Training Coll.; external student of London Univ. Subsequently schoolmistress. MP (Lab) NE Leeds, 1945–55, SE Leeds, 1955–70; Minister of State: Home Office, 1964–67; Dept of Educn and Science, 1967–70. Mem. National Executive Cttee of Labour Party, 1941–70; Chm., Labour Party, 1950–51. DL W Yorkshire 1974. Hon. LLD Leeds, 1972. *Address:* 53 Snydale Road, Normanton, West Yorks WF6 1NY. *T:* Wakefield 893229.

BACON, Francis, artist; *b* Dublin, 28 Oct. 1909; English parents. Self-taught. Exhibited furniture and rugs of his own design, Queensbury Mews studio, 1929; began painting; destroyed nearly all earlier works, 1941–44; rep. GB with Ben Nicholson and Lucien Freud, 27th Venice Biennale, 1954. *One-man exhibitions:* Hanover Gall., London, 1949, 1950, 1951, 1952 (after travelling in S Africa and Kenya), 1954, 1957, 1959; Durlacher Bros, NY 1953; ICA, 1955; Galerie Rive Droite, Paris, 1957; Galleria Galatea, Turin, 1958, 1970; Marlborough Fine Art Gall., London, 1960, 1963, 1965, 1967, 1983, 1985; Tate Gall., 1962 (retrospective), 1985 (retrospective); Solomon R. Guggenheim Mus., NY, 1963 (retrospective); Kunstverein, Hamburg, 1965 (retrospective); Galerie Maeght, Paris, 1966, 1984; Oberes Schloss, Siegen, 1967; Marlborough Gall., NY, 1968, 1980,

1984; Grand Palais, Paris, 1971 (retrospective); Metrop. Mus. of Art, NY, 1975; Galerie Claude Bernard, Paris, 1977; Mus. de Arte Moderno, Mexico, 1977; Fundación Juan March, 1978; Nat. Mus. of Modern Art, Tokyo, 1983 (retrospective). *Travelling exhibitions:* Mannheim, Turin, Zürich, Amsterdam, 1963; Chicago, 1963; Hamburg, Stockholm, Dublin, 1965; Düsseldorf, 1972; Caracas, 1977; Barcelona, 1978; Kyoto, Nagoya, 1983; Stuttgart, Berlin, 1986. *Important works include:* triptychs: Three Studies for Figures at the Base of a Crucifixion, 1944; Three Studies for a Crucifixion, 1962; Three Figures in a Room, 1964; Crucifixion, 1965; Sweeney Agonistes, 1967; Oresteia of Aeschylus, 1981; single oils: Painting, 1946; Study after Velasquez's portrait of Pope Innocent X, 1953; Two Figures, 1953; Study for portrait of Van Gogh VI, 1957; Portrait of Isabel Rawsthorne standing in a street in Soho, 1967; Landscape, 1978; Jet of Water, 1979; Study of the Human Body, 1982. Paintings acquired by: Tate Gall., Arts Council; Aberdeen, Belfast and Leeds Museums; Nat. Galls of Adelaide and Canberra; Museums in Berlin, Bochum, Düsseldorf, Hamburg, Hanover, Mannheim, Munich and Stuttgart; CNAC, Paris; MOMA, NY; Amsterdam, Rotterdam, Stockholm etc. Rubens Prize, 1967; Prize, Carnegie Inst., Pittsburgh, 1967. *Address:* c/o Marlborough Fine Art, 6 Albemarle Street, W1X 4BY.

BACON, Francis Thomas, OBE 1967; FRS 1973; FEng 1976; consultant on fuel cells, retired; *b* 21 Dec. 1904; 2nd *s* of T. W. Bacon, Ramsden Hall, Billericay; *m* 1934, Barbara Winifred, *y d* of G. K. Papillon, Manor House, Barrasford; one *s* one *d* (and one *s* decd). *Educ:* Eton Coll.; Trinity Coll., Cambridge. CEng, MIMechE 1947. With C. A. Parsons & Co. Ltd, Newcastle-on-Tyne, 1925–40 (i/c production of silvered glass reflectors, 1935–39); experimental work on hydrogen/oxygen fuel cell at King's Coll., London, for Merz & McLellan, 1940–41; Temp. Exper. Off. at HM Anti-Submarine Experimental Estbt, Fairlie, 1941–46; exper. work on hydrogen/oxygen fuel cell at Cambridge Univ., 1946–56 (for ERA); Consultant to: NRDC on fuel cells at Marshall of Cambridge Ltd, 1956–62; Energy Conversion Ltd, Basingstoke, 1962–71; Fuel Cells Ltd, AERE, 1971–72; Johnson Matthey PLC, 1984–. British Assoc. Lecture, 1971; Bruno Breyer Meml Lecture and Medal, Royal Aust. Chem. Inst., 1976. S. G. Brown Award and Medal (Royal Soc.), 1965; British Silver Medal (RAeS), 1969; Churchill Gold Medal, Soc. of Engineers, 1972; Melchett Medal, Inst. of Fuel, 1972; Vittorio de Nora Diamond Shamrock Award and Prize, Electrochemical Soc. Inc., 1978. Hon. FSE, 1972. Hon. DSc Newcastle upon Tyne, 1980. *Publications:* chapter 5 in Fuel Cells (ed G. J. Young), 1960; chapter 4 in Fuel Cells (ed W. Mitchell), 1963; papers on fuel cells for World Power Conf., Royal Instn, Nature, two UN Confs, Amer. Inst. of Chem. Eng., Inst. of Fuel, Electrochimica Acta, Royal Soc., 5th World Hydrogen Energy Conf. *Recreations:* hill walking, music, photography, gardening. *Address:* Trees, 34 High Street, Little Shelford, Cambridge CB2 5ES. *T:* Cambridge 843116. *Club:* Athenæum.

BACON, Prof. George Edward, MA, ScD Cantab, PhD London; Professor of Physics, University of Sheffield, 1963–81, now Emeritus; *b* 5 Dec. 1917; *s* of late George H. Bacon and Lilian A. Bacon, Derby; *m* 1945, Enid Trigg; one *s* one *d*. *Educ:* Derby Sch.; Emmanuel Coll., Cambridge (Open and Sen. Schol.); CPhys. Air Ministry, Telecommunications Research Estabt, 1939–46. Dep. Chief Scientific Officer, AERE, Harwell, 1946–63; Dean, Faculty of Pure Science, Sheffield Univ., 1969–71. FInstP. *Publications:* Neutron Diffraction, 1955; Applications of Neutron Diffraction in Chemistry, 1963; X-ray and Neutron Diffraction, 1966; Neutron Physics, 1969; Neutron Scattering in Chemistry, 1977; The Architecture of Solids, 1981; many scientific pubns on X-ray and neutron crystallographic studies in Proc. Royal Society, Acta Cryst., etc. *Recreations:* gardening, photography, travel. *Address:* Windrush Way, Guiting Power, Cheltenham GL54 5US.

BACON, Jennifer Helen; Under Secretary and Director of Adult (formerly Occupational) Training, Manpower Services Commission, since 1982; *b* 16 April 1945; *d* of Dr Lionel James Bacon and Joyce Bacon (*née* Chapman). *Educ:* Bedales Sch., Petersfield; New Hall, Cambridge (BA Hons 1st cl.). Joined Civil Service as Asst Principal, Min. of Labour, 1967; Private Sec. to Minister of State for Employment, 1971–72; Principal, 1972–78, worked on health and safety and industrial relations legislation; Principal Private Sec. to Sec. of State for Employment, 1977–78; Asst Sec., Controller of Trng Services, MSC, 1978–80; sabbatical, travelling in Latin America, 1980–81; Asst Sec., Machinery of Govt Div., CSD, later MPO, 1981–82. *Recreations:* classical music especially opera, travelling, walking. *Address:* 87 Northchurch Road, N1 3NU. *T:* 01–359 4689.

BACON, Sir Nicholas (Hickman Ponsonby), 14th Bt of Redgrave, *cr* 1611, and 15th Bt of Mildenhall, *cr* 1627; Premier Baronet of England; *b* 17 May 1953; *s* of Sir Edmund Castell Bacon, 13th and 14th Bt, KG, KBE, TD and of Priscilla Dora, *d* of Col Sir Charles Edward Ponsonby, 1st Bt, TD; *S* father, 1982; *m* 1981, Susan, *d* of Raymond Dinnis, Edenbridge, Kent; two *s*. *Educ:* Eton; Dundee Univ. (MA). Barrister-at-law, Gray's Inn. A Page of Honour to the Queen, 1966–69. *Heir: s* Henry Hickman Bacon, *b* 23 April 1984. *Address:* Raveningham Hall, Norfolk NR14 6NS. *Club:* Pratt's.

BACON, Sir Ranulph Robert Maunsell, Kt 1966; KPM 1953; Consultant, International Intelligence Inc., USA, since 1981 (Director, 1970–81); *b* 6 Aug. 1906; *s* of late Arthur Ranulph and Hester Mary (*née* Ayles), Westgate-on-Sea; *m* 1932, Alfreda Violet (*née* Annett) (*d* 1984); one *d* decd. *Educ:* Tonbridge Sch; Queens' Coll., Cambridge (BA). Joined Metropolitan Police, 1928; Metropolitan Police Coll., 1935 (Baton of Honour); seconded to Provost Service, 1940; Capt. 1940, Major 1941, Lieut-Col 1941; all service was in Middle East; Dep. Provost Marshal, Ninth Army, 1942; seconded to Colonial Police Service, 1943; Dep. Inspector-Gen., 1943, Inspector-Gen., 1944–47, Ceylon Police; Chief Constable of Devon, 1947–61; Asst Comr, Met. Police, 1961–66; Dep. Comr New Scotland Yard, 1966. Dir, Securicor Ltd, 1966–81. Mem., Gaming Board, 1968–75. President: Gun Trade Assoc., 1972–77; Shooting Sports Trust, 1972–77. CStJ 1964. *Address:* 3 Royal Court, 8 King's Gardens, Hove, Sussex BN3 2PF. *T:* Brighton 732396. *Club:* United Oxford & Cambridge University.

BACON, Sir Sidney (Charles), Kt 1977; CB 1971; BSc(Eng); FEng, FIMechE, FIProdE, FTP; Managing Director, Royal Ordnance Factories, 1972–79; Deputy Chairman, Royal Ordnance Factories Board, 1972–79; *b* 11 Feb. 1919; *s* of Charles and Alice Bacon. *Educ:* Woolwich Polytechnic; London Univ. Military Service, 1943–48, Capt. REME. Royal Arsenal, Woolwich, 1933–58; Regional Supt of Inspection, N Midland Region, 1958–60; Asst Dir, ROF, Nottingham, 1960–61; Director, ROF: Leeds, 1961–62; Woolwich, 1962–63; Birtley, 1965; idc, 1964; Dir of Ordnance Factories, Weapons and Fighting Vehicles, 1965–66; Dep. Controller, ROFs, 1966–69; Controller, ROFs, 1969–72. Dir, Short Brothers Ltd, 1980–. Pres., IProdE, 1979. *Recreations:* golf, listening to music. *Address:* 228 Erith Road, Bexleyheath, Kent. *Club:* Shooters Hill Golf.

BADCOCK, Maj.-Gen. John Michael Watson, CB 1976; MBE 1969; DL; Chairman, S. W. Mount & Sons, since 1982; *b* 10 Nov. 1922; *s* of late R. D. Badcock, MC, JP and Mrs J. D. Badcock; *m* 1948, Gillian Pauline (*née* Attfield); one *s* two *d*. *Educ:* Sherborne Sch.; Worcester Coll., Oxford. Enlisted in ranks (Army), 1941; commnd Royal Corps of Signals, 1942; war service UK and BAOR; Ceylon, 1945–47; served in UK, Persian Gulf, BAOR and Cyprus; Comdr 2 Inf. Bde and Dep. Constable of Dover Castle, 1968–71; Dep. Mil. Sec., 1971–72; Dir of Manning (Army), 1972–74; Defence Advr and Head of British Defence Liaison Staff, Canberra, 1974–77; retired. psc, jssc, idc. Col Comdt, Royal Signals, 1974–80 and 1982–; Master of Signals, 1982–; Hon. Col, 31 (London) Signal Regt (Volunteers), 1978–83. Chm., SE TA&VRA, 1979–85. Chief Appeals Officer, CRC, 1978–82. DL Kent, 1980. *Recreations:* Rugby football, cricket, hockey, most field sports less horsemanship. *Address:* Autumn Lodge, Stodmarsh Road, Canterbury CT4 5RH. *T:* Canterbury 66360. *Club:* Army and Navy.

BADDELEY, Sir John (Wolsey Beresford), 4th Bt *cr* 1922; Financial Controller, Wines and Spirits Division, Whitbread & Co., since 1983; *b* 27 Jan. 1938; *s* of Sir John Beresford Baddeley, 3rd Bt, and of Nancy Winifred, *d* of late Thomas Wolsey; *S* father, 1979; *m* 1962, Sara Rosalind Crofts; three *d*. *Educ:* Bradfield College, Berks. FCA. Qualified as Chartered Accountant, 1961; Deloitte Haskins & Sells, 1961–65; Baddeley Bros (London) Ltd, 1966–69; Burmah Oil Co. Ltd, 1969–70; Court Line Ltd, 1971–73; Babcock & Wilcox, 1973–77; Spillers International Ltd, 1978–79. *Recreations:* inland waterways, tennis, squash. *Heir: cousin* Mark David Baddeley, *b* 10 May 1921. *Address:* 41 School Hill, Storrington, Sussex. *T:* Storrington 2423.

BADDELEY, Very Rev. William Pye, BA; Dean Emeritus of Brisbane, 1981; *b* 20 March 1914; *s* of W. H. Clinton-Baddeley and Louise Bourdin, Shropshire; *m* 1947, Mary Frances Shirley, *d* of Col E. R. C. Wyatt, CBE, DSO; one *d*. *Educ:* Durham Univ.; St Chad's Coll., Durham; Cuddesdon Coll., Oxford. Deacon, 1941; Priest, 1942; Curate of St Luke, Camberwell, 1941–44; St Anne, Wandsworth, 1944–46; St Stephen, Bournemouth, 1946–49; Vicar of St Pancras (with St James and Christ Church from 1954), 1949–58; Dean of Brisbane, 1958–67; Rector of St James's, Piccadilly, 1967–80; RD of Westminster (St Margaret's), 1974–79; Commissary to: Archbishop of Brisbane, 1967–; Bishop of Wangaratta, 1970–; Archbishop of Papua New Guinea, 1972–80; Bishop of Newcastle, NSW, 1976–. Member: London Diocesan Synod, 1970–80; Bishop of London's Council, 1975–80. Chaplain: Elizabeth Garrett Anderson Hospital, London, 1949–59; St Luke's Hostel, 1952–54; Qld Univ. Anglican Soc., 1960–64; St Martin's Hosp., Brisbane, 1960; London Companions of St Francis, 1968–80; Lord Mayor of Westminster, 1968–69 and 1974–75; Actors' Church Union, 1968–70; Royal Acad. of Arts, 1968–80; Vis. Chaplain, Westminster Abbey, 1980–. Hon. Chaplain to: Archbishop of Brisbane (Diocesan Chaplain, 1963–67); Union Soc. of Westminster, 1972–80. President: Brisbane Repertory Theatre, 1961–64; Qld Univ. Dramatic Soc., 1961–67; Qld Ballet Co., 1962–67; Dir, Australian Elizabethan Theatre Trust, 1963–67; Mem. Council of Management, Friends of Royal Academy, 1978–; Chairman: Diocesan Radio and Television Council, 1961–67; weekly television Panel "Round Table", 1962–66; monthly television Panel "What Do YOU Think", 1960–67; Pres., Connard and Seckford Players, 1984–. Governor: Burlington Sch., 1967–76; Archbishop Tenison's Sch., 1967–80; Chairman: Assoc. for Promoting Retreats, 1967–80; Malcolm Sargent Cancer Fund for Children, 1968–; Cttee for Commonwealth Citizens in China, 1970–73; Mem. Council, Metropolitan Hosp. Sunday Fund, 1968–78; Vice-Pres., Cancer Relief Appeal, 1977–. Life Governor of Thomas Coram Foundation, 1955–. Mem. Chapter-Gen., OStJ, 1974–. ChStJ 1971 (SBStJ 1959). *Recreations:* theatre, music, photography. *Address:* Cumberland House, Woodbridge, Suffolk IP12 4AH. *T:* Woodbridge 4104. *Clubs:* East India, Carlton, Arts.

BADDILEY, Prof. Sir James, Kt 1977; PhD, DSc; FRS 1961; FRSE 1962; Professor of Chemical Microbiology, 1977–83, now Emeritus, and Director, Microbiological Chemistry Research Laboratory, 1975–83, University of Newcastle upon Tyne; SERC Senior Research Fellow, and Fellow of Pembroke College, University of Cambridge, 1981–85, now Emeritus; *b* 15 May 1918; *s* of late James Baddiley and Ivy Logan Cato; *m* 1944, Hazel Mary, *yr d* of Wesley Wilfrid Townsend and Ann Rayner Townsend (*née* Kilner); one *s*. *Educ:* Manchester Grammar Sch.; Manchester University (BSc 1941, PhD 1944, DSc 1953; Sir Clement Royds Meml Schol., 1942, Beyer Fellow, 1943–44); MA Cantab 1981. Imperial Chemical Industries Fellow, University of Cambridge, 1945–49; Swedish Medical Research Council Fellow, Wenner-Grens Institute for Cell Biology, Stockholm, 1947–49; Mem. of Staff, Dept of Biochemistry, Lister Institute of Preventive Medicine, London, 1949–55; Rockefeller Fellowship, Mass. Gen. Hosp., Harvard Med. Sch., 1954; Prof. of Organic Chem., King's Coll., Univ. of Durham, 1955–77 (later Univ. of Newcastle upon Tyne); Head of Sch. of Chemistry, Newcastle upon Tyne Univ., 1968–78. Member: Council, Chemical Soc., 1962–65; Cttee, Biochemical Soc., 1964–67; Council, Soc. of Gen. Microbiol., 1973–75; Council, SERC (formerly SRC), 1979–81 (Mem., Enzyme Chem. and Technol Cttee, 1972–75, Biol Scis Cttee, 1976–79; Mem., Science Bd, 1979–81); Council, Royal Soc., 1977–79; Editorial Boards, Biochemical Preparations, 1960–70, Biochimica et Biophysica Acta, 1970–77. Karl Folkers Vis. Prof. in Biochem., Illinois Univ., 1962; Tilden Lectr, Chem. Soc., 1959; Special Vis. Lectr, Dept of Microbiology, Temple Univ., Pa, 1966; Leeuwenhoek Lectr, Royal Society, 1967; Pedler Lectr, Chem. Soc., 1978; Endowment Lectr, Bose Inst., Calcutta, 1980. Hon. Mem., Amer. Soc. Biol Chem. Hon. DSc Heriot Watt, 1979; Bath, 1986. Meldola Medal, RIC, 1947; Corday-Morgan Medal, Chem. Soc., 1952; Davy Medal, Royal Soc., 1974. *Publications:* numerous in Journal of the Chemical Society, Nature, Biochemical Journal, etc; articles in various microbiological and biochemical reviews. *Recreations:* photography, music. *Address:* Hill Top Cottage, Hildersham, Cambridge CB1 6DA. *T:* Cambridge 893055; Department of Biochemistry, University of Cambridge, Tennis Court Road, Cambridge CB2 1QW. *T:* Cambridge 51781.

BADEN-POWELL, family name of **Baron Baden-Powell.**

BADEN-POWELL, 3rd Baron, *cr* 1929, of Gilwell; **Robert Crause Baden-Powell;** Bt, *cr* 1922; Vice-President, Scout Association, since 1982 (Member of Council, since 1965); *b* 15 Oct. 1936; *s* of 2nd Baron and Carine Crause Baden-Powell (*née* Boardman); *S* father, 1962; *m* 1963, Patience Hélène Mary Batty (*see* Lady Baden-Powell). *Educ:* Bryanston (Blandford). Chief Scouts Comr, 1965–82; Pres., West Yorks Scout Council, 1972–; Mem. Cttee, Scout Assoc. Council, 1972–78. *Recreations:* model making, breeding Quarter Horses. *Heir: b* Hon. David Michael Baden-Powell [*b* 11 Dec. 1940; *m* 1966, Joan Phillips, *d* of H. W. Berryman, Melbourne, Australia; three *s*]. *Address:* Grove Heath Farm, Ripley, Woking, Surrey GU23 6ES. *T:* Guildford 224262.

BADEN-POWELL, Lady; Patience Hélène Mary Baden-Powell, CBE 1986; Chief Commissioner, The Girl Guides Association, 1980–85; President, Commonwealth Youth Exchange Council, 1982–86; *b* 27 Oct. 1936; *d* of Mr and Mrs D. M. Batty, Zimbabwe; *m* 1963, Baron Baden-Powell, *qv*. *Educ:* St Peter's Diocesan Sch., Bulawayo. Internat. Comr, Girl Guides Assoc., 1975–79. Director: Laurentian Holding Company; Trident Life; Imperial Life (UK), 1985–. Pres., Surrey Council for Voluntary Youth Services. Patron: National Playbus Assoc.; Woodlarks Camp Site for the Disabled; Surrey Antiques Fair. *Address:* Grove Heath Farm, Ripley, Woking, Surrey GU23 6ES. *T:* Guildford 224262.

BADENOCH, Alec William, MA, MD, ChM, FRCS; *b* 23 June 1903; *s* of late John Alexander Badenoch, chartered accountant, Banff; *m* 1942, Jean McKinnell, MB, ChB (Edinburgh), *d* of late Alexander Brunton; two *s* (and one *s* decd). *Educ:* Banff Academy;

Aberdeen Univ. Pres. Student Representation Council of Scotland, 1926. Served RAFVR, 1937–45, as Temp. Wing Comdr, i/c Surgical Divs, RAF Hosps Rauceby, Wroughton and St Athan; Surgeon: Royal Hosp. of St Bartholomew, 1947–68; St Peter's Hosp. for Stone and other Urological Diseases, 1946–68; Visiting Urologist: Royal Masonic Hosp., 1950–70; King Edward VII's Hosp. for Officers, 1947–77; Visiting Professor: Cairo, 1962; Dallas, Texas, 1967; Guest Lectr, Amer. Urological Assoc., 1968; Hon. Civilian Consultant in Urology to RAF. Hunterian Prof., RCS, 1948; Hon. Fellow, British Assoc. of Urological Surgeons (Pres., 1968–69; St Peter's Medal, 1974); Hon. FRSocMed (Hon. Treasurer 1971–76, Hon. Mem. and Past Pres. Section of Urology); Hon. Fellow, Hunterian Soc. (Pres. 1949, Vice-Pres. and Orator, 1957); Chm., Editorial Bd, British Jl of Urology, 1969–72 (Treasurer, 1961–67); Member: BMA (Vice-Pres. Section of Urology, 1955); Internat. Soc. of Urology (Treas. London Congress, 1964, British Delegate, 1966–74; Hon. Fellow); (Founder Mem.) Cttee of Management, European Soc. of Urology, 1972; Council, RCS, 1963–71 (Patron, 1975); GMC, 1966–71; GDC, 1969–71. Mem., Bd of Governors, St Peter's Hosp. Gp, 1948–73; Chm., Management Cttee, Inst. of Urology, 1968–72. Hon. Mem. Peruvian, American and French Urological Assocs; Corresp. Mem., Mexican Urological Assoc. and Amer. Assoc. of Genito Urinary Surgeons. Founding Jt Editor, European JL of Urology, 1974–78. *Publications:* Manual of Urology, 1953, 2nd edn 1974; contrib. to British Surgery, Modern Operative Surgery, and Modern Trends in Urology. Articles in scientific jls. *Recreations:* gardening, music, swimming. *Address:* 123 Harley Street, W1N 1HE. *T:* 01–935 3881; Church Hayes, Lea, Malmesbury, Wilts. *T:* Malmesbury 2289. *Club:* Royal Air Force.

BADENOCH, Sir John, Kt 1984; DM; FRCP, FRCPE; Consultant Physician, Oxford District Health Authority (Teaching); University Lecturer in Medicine, and Fellow of Merton College, Oxford University; *b* 8 March 1920; *s* of William Minty Badenoch, MB, and Ann Dyer Badenoch (*née* Coutts); *m* 1944, Anne Newnham, *d* of Prof. Lancelot Forster; two *s* two *d*. *Educ:* Rugby Sch.; Oriel College, Oxford. MA; DM 1952; FRCP 1959; FRCPE 1982. Rockefeller Med. Studentship, Cornell Univ. Med. Coll., 1941. Res. Asst, Nuffield Dept of Clin. Medicine, Oxford, 1949–56; Dir, Clin. Studies, Univ. of Oxford, 1954–65. Former Mem., Board of Governors of United Oxford Hosps; Mem. Board, Oxford AHA(T), 1974–; Mem., GMC, 1984–. Royal College of Physicians: Pro-Censor and Censor, 1972–73; Sen. Censor and Sen. Vice-Pres., 1975–76; Goulstonian Lectr, 1960; Lumleian Lectr, 1977. Examiner in Medicine at various times for the Universities of: Oxford, Cambridge, Manchester, QUB and NUI. Member: Assoc. of Physicians of GB and Ireland; Med. Res. Soc.; British Soc. of Haematology; British Soc. of Gastroenterology. Liveryman, Soc. of Apothecaries. *Publications:* (ed jtly) Recent Advances in Gastroenterology, 1965, 2nd edn 1972; various papers in the field of gastroenterology and medicine. *Recreations:* reading, walking, natural history. *Address:* 21 Hartley Court, 84 Woodstock Road, Oxford OX2 7PF.

BADGE, Peter Gilmour Noto; a Metropolitan Stipendiary Magistrate, since 1975; Chairman, Inner London Juvenile Panel, since 1979; Deputy Circuit Judge, since 1979; a Recorder of the Crown Court, since 1980; *b* 20 Nov. 1931; *s* of late Ernest Desmond Badge, LDS and Marie Benson Badge (*née* Clough); *m* 1956, Mary Rose Noble; four *d*. *Educ:* Univ. of Liverpool (LLB). National Service, 1956–58: RNVR, lower deck and commnd; UK, ME and FE; RNR, 1958–62. Solicitor, 1956; Mem., Solicitor's Dept, New Scotland Yard, 1958–61; Asst Solicitor and later Partner, 1961–75, Notary Public 1964–75, Kidd, Rapinet, Badge & Co.; Clerk to Justices, Petty Sessional Div. of Marlow, 1967–74; Lectr in Magisterial Law, Bucks Magistrates Courts Cttee, 1968–72; Sen. Solicitor to Comr and Detention Appeals Tribunal, NI, 1973–75. Member: Cttee on Criminal Law, Law Soc., 1971–79; Lord Chancellor's Adv. Cttee for Inner London; Magisterial Cttee, Judicial Studies Bd. Contested (L) Windsor and Maidenhead, 1964. *Recreations:* skiing, coracles, music. *Address:* Thames Magistrates' Court, Aylward Street, E1.

BADGER, Sir Geoffrey Malcolm, Kt 1979; AO 1975; PhD, DSc; FRSC, FRACI, FACE, FAIM, FTS, FAA; Chairman, Australian Science and Technology Council, 1977–82; *b* 10 Oct. 1916; *s* of J. McD. Badger; *m* 1941, Edith Maud, *d* of Henry Chevis. *Educ:* Geelong Coll.; Gordon Inst. of Technology; Univs of Melbourne, London (PhD), Glasgow (DSc). Instructor Lieut, RN, 1943–46. Finney-Howell Research Fellow, London, 1940–41; Research Chemist, ICI, 1941–43; Research Fellow, Glasgow, 1946–49. Univ. of Adelaide: Sen. Lectr, 1949–51; Reader, 1951–54; Prof. of Organic Chemistry, 1955–64, now Emeritus Professor; Dep. Vice-Chancellor, 1966–67; Vice-Chancellor, 1967–77; Res. Professor, 1977–79. Mem. Executive, CSIRO, 1964–65. President: Aust. Acad. of Science, 1974–78; Aust. and NZ Assoc. for Advancement of Science, 1979–80. DUniv Adelaide. *Publications:* Structures and Reactions of Aromatic Compounds, 1954; Chemistry of Heterocyclic Compounds, 1961; The Chemical Basis of Carcinogenic Activity, 1962; Aromatic Character and Aromaticity, 1969; (ed) Captain Cook, 1970; numerous papers in Jl Chem. Soc. etc. *Address:* 1 Anna Court, West Lakes, SA 5021, Australia. *T:* (08) 49–4594. *Club:* Adelaide (Adelaide).

BADHAM, Douglas George, CBE 1975; JP; HM Lord-Lieutenant for Mid Glamorgan, since 1985; company director; Chairman: T. T. Pascoe, since 1983; Economic Forestry Group PLC, since 1981 (Director, since 1978); Powell Duffryn Wagon Co. since 1965; Hamell (West) Ltd, since 1968; Member, Welsh Development Agency, since 1978 (Deputy Chairman, 1980–84); *b* 1 Dec. 1914; *s* of late David Badham, JP; *m* 1939, Doreen Spencer Phillips; two *d*. *Educ:* Leys Sch., Cambridge. CA. Exec. Director: Powell Duffryn Gp, 1938–69; Pascoe Hldgs, 1983–; Alignrite, 1984–; T. H. Crouch, 1984–; World Trade Centre Wales, 1984–. Chm., Nat. Health Service Staff Commn, 1972–75; Member: Wales and the Marches Telecommunications Bd, 1973–80; British Gas Corp., 1974–83; Forestry Commn, S Wales Reg. Adv. Cttee, 1946–76 (Chm., 1973–76); Western Region Adv. Bd, BR, 1977–82; Welsh Council (Chm., Industry and Planning Panel), 1971–80; Nature Conservancy Council Adv. Cttee for Wales; Council, UWIST, 1975–80; Develt Corp. for Wales, 1965–83 (Chm., 1971–80). JP Glamorgan, 1962; DL, 1975–82, High Sheriff, 1976, Lieut, 1982, Mid Glamorgan. *Recreations:* forestry, trout breeding. *Address:* Plas Watford, Caerphilly, Mid Glamorgan CF8 1NE. *T:* Caerphilly 882094. *Clubs:* Royal Automobile; Cardiff and County (Cardiff).

BADHAM, Leonard; Vice Chairman, J. Lyons & Company Ltd, since 1984; Director, Allied-Lyons PLC (formerly Allied Breweries), since 1978; *b* 10 June 1923; *s* of John Randall Badham and Emily Louise Badham; *m* 1944, Joyce Rose Lowrie; two *d*. *Educ:* Wandsworth Grammar Sch. Commnd E Surrey Regt, 1943; Royal W Kent Regt, 5th Indian Div., 1944–46; SO II Stats, Burma Comd, 1946–47. J. Lyons & Co. Ltd: Management Trainee, 1939; Main Bd, 1965; Chief Comptroller, 1965; Tech. and Commercial Co-ordinator, 1967; Exec. Dir, Finance and Admin, 1970; Asst Gp Man. Dir, 1971; Dep. Gp Man. Dir, 1975; Man Dir, 1977. FHCIMA; CBIM. *Recreations:* bridge, gardening. *Address:* 26 Vicarage Drive, East Sheen, SW14 8RX. *T:* 01–876 4373.

BADIAN, Ernst, FBA 1965; Professor of History, since 1971, John Moors Cabot Professor, since 1982, Harvard University; *b* 8 Aug. 1925; *s* of Joseph Badian and Sally (*née* Horinger), Vienna (later Christchurch, NZ); *m* 1950, Nathlie Anne (*née* Wimsett); one *s* one *d*. *Educ:* Christchurch Boys' High Sch.; Canterbury Univ. Coll., Christchurch, NZ;

University Coll., Oxford (Chancellor's Prize for Latin Prose, 1950; Craven Fellow, 1950; Conington Prize, 1959). MA (1st cl. hons), NZ, 1946; LitD, Victoria, NZ, 1962. BA (1st cl. hons Lit. Hum.) Oxon, 1950; MA 1954; DPhil 1956. Asst Lectr in Classics, Victoria University Coll., Wellington, 1947–48; Rome Scholar in Classics, British Sch. at Rome, 1950–52; Asst Lectr in Classics and Ancient History, Univ. of Sheffield, 1952–54; Lectr in Classics, Univ. of Durham, 1954–65; Prof. of Ancient History, Univ. of Leeds, 1965–69; Prof. of Classics and History, State Univ. of NY at Buffalo, 1969–71. John Simon Guggenheim Fellow, 1985. Vis. Professor: Univs of Oregon, Washington and California (Los Angeles), 1961; Univ. of S Africa, 1965, 1973; Harvard, 1967; State Univ. of NY (Buffalo), 1967–68; Heidelberg, 1973; Univ. of California (Sather Prof.), 1976; Univ. of Colorado, 1978; Univ. of Tel-Aviv, 1981; Martin Classical Lectr, Oberlin Coll., 1978; lecturing visits to Australia, Canada, France, Germany, Holland, Israel, Italy, NZ, Rhodesia, Switzerland, and S Africa. Fellow, Amer. Acad. of Arts and Sciences, 1974; Corresponding Member: Austrian Acad. of Scis, 1975; German Archaeol Inst., 1981; Foreign Mem., Finnish Acad. of Sci. and Letters, 1985. Hon. Mem., Soc. for Promotion of Roman Studies, 1983. Editor, Amer. Jl of Ancient History. *Publications:* Foreign Clientelae (264–70 BC), 1958; Studies in Greek and Roman History, 1964; Polybius (The Great Histories Series), 1966; Roman Imperialism in the Late Republic, 1967 (2nd edn 1968); Publicans and Sinners, 1972; contribs to Artemis-Lexikon, Encyc. Britannica, Oxf. Class. Dictionary and to classical and historical journals. *Recreations:* travelling, reading. *Address:* Department of History, Harvard University, Cambridge, Mass 02138, USA.

BADMIN, Stanley Roy, RE 1935 (ARE 1931); (Hon. retired 1965); RWS 1939 (ARWS 1932); ARCA 1927; *b* Sydenham, 18 April 1906; 2nd *s* of Charles James and Margaret Badmin, Somersetshire; *m* 1st, 1929; one *s* one *d*; 2nd, 1950, Mrs Rosaline Flew, *widow* of Dr R. Flew; one *d* one step-*d*. *Educ:* private tutor; Royal College of Art. One man exhibitions: Twenty One Gall., London, 1930; Fine Art Soc., 1933, 1937; MacDonald's Gall., NY, 1936; Leicester Gall., 1955; Worthing Art Gall., 1967; (retrospective), Chris Beetles Gall., London, 1985; works bought by Liverpool, Manchester, Huddersfield, Bradford, Birmingham, V & A Museum, Chicago Inst. of Art, South London Galleries, Newport, Ashmolean, Worthing, Boston Museum, London Museum, NY Metropolitan Museum, etc. *Publications:* Etched Plates; Autolithoed Educational books; Village and Town, Trees in Britain and Farm Crops in Britain; colour prints; illustrations to: British Countryside in Colour; Trees for Town & Country and Famous Trees; Shell Guide to Trees and Shrubs; The Seasons (by Ralph Wightman); Trees of Britain (Sunday Times); Readers' Digest Publications; Royles Publications. *Recreations:* painting and gardening. *Address:* Streamfield, Bignor, Pulborough, West Sussex RH20 1PQ. *T:* Sutton (Sussex) 229.

BAELZ, Very Rev. Peter Richard; Dean of Durham, since 1980; *b* 27 July 1923; 3rd *s* of Eberhard and Dora Baelz; *m* 1950, Anne Thelma Cleall-Harding; three *s*. *Educ:* Dulwich Coll.; Cambridge Univ. BA 1944, MA 1948, BD 1971; DD Oxon 1979. Asst Curate: Bournville, 1947–50; Sherborne, 1950–52; Asst Chap. Ripon Hall, Oxford, 1952–53; Rector of Wishaw, Birmingham, 1953–56; Vicar of Bournville, 1956–60; Fellow and Dean, Jesus Coll., Cambridge, 1960–72; University Lectr in Divinity, Cambridge, 1966–72; Canon of Christ Church and Regius Prof. of Moral and Pastoral Theology, Univ. of Oxford, 1972–79. Hulsean Lectr, 1965–66; Bampton Lectr, 1974. *Publications:* Prayer and Providence, 1968; Christian Theology and Metaphysics, 1968; The Forgotten Dream, 1975; Ethics and Belief, 1977; Does God Answer Prayer?, 1982; contributor to: Traditional Virtues Reassessed, 1964; Faith, Fact and Fantasy, 1964; The Phenomenon of Christian Belief, 1970; Christianity and Change, 1971; Christ, Faith and History, 1972; Is Christianity Credible?, 1981; God Incarnate: story and belief, 1981; edited and contributed to: Choices in Childlessness, 1982; Perspectives on Economics, 1984; Ministers of the Kingdom, 1985. *Recreations:* walking, motoring. *Address:* The Deanery, Durham DH1 3EQ. *T:* Durham 47500.

BAER, Jack Mervyn Frank; Managing Director, Hazlitt, Gooden & Fox, since 1973; *b* 29 Aug. 1924; *yr s* of late Frank and Alix Baer; *m* 1st, 1952, Jean St Clair (marr. diss. 1969; she *d* 1973), *o c* of late L. F. St Clair and Evelyn Synnott; one *d*; 2nd, 1970, Diana Downes Baillieu, *yr d* of Aubrey Clare Robinson and Mollie Panter-Downes, *qv*; two step *d*. *Educ:* Bryanston; Slade Sch. of Fine Art, University Coll., London. Served RAF (Combined Ops), 1942–46. Joined Hazlitt Gallery as Partner, 1948, Man. Dir, 1957, Chm. 1960–82. Chm., Fine Arts and Antiques Export Adv. Cttee to Dept of Trade, 1971–73 (Vice-Chm., 1969–71). Pres., Fine Art Provident Institution, 1972–75. Chm., Soc. of London Art Dealers, 1977–80 (Vice Chm. 1974–77). *Publications:* numerous exhibition catalogues; articles in various jls. *Recreation:* drawing. *Address:* 9 Phillimore Terrace, W8. *T:* 01–937 6899. *Clubs:* Brooks's, Buck's, Beefsteak.

BAGGE, Sir John (Alfred Picton), 6th Bt *cr* 1867; ED; DL; *b* 27 Oct. 1914; *e s* of Sir Picton Bagge, 5th Bt, CMG, and Olive Muriel Mary (*d* 1965), *d* of late Samuel Mendel; *S* father, 1967; *m* 1939, Elizabeth Helena (Lena), *d* of late Daniel James Davies, CBE, Comr for Newfoundland in London; three *s* three *d*. *Educ:* Eton and abroad. Served Inns of Court Regt, 1936–39; commnd into Cheshire Yeo., 1939; served War of 1939–45, Palestine, Sudan, Liberation Campaign of Ethiopia; Major 1941; GSO 2, Brit. Mil. Mission to Ethiopia, 1941–44; GSO 2, HQ, E Africa Comd Liaison with French, 1944; Mil. Asst to Brit. Comdr Allied Control Commn for Bulgaria, 1944–45; GSO 2, War Office, 1945. KStJ 1975; Chm. Council of St John in Norfolk, 1969–80. Vice-Chm., W Norfolk DC, 1973–76, Chm., 1976–77; High Sheriff of Norfolk, 1977; DL Norfolk, 1978. *Recreations:* shooting, ski-ing and water ski-ing. *Heir:* *s* (John) Jeremy (Picton) Bagge [*b* 21 June 1945; *m* 1979, Sarah, *d* of late James Armstrong; two *s* one *d*. Chartered Accountant, 1968]. *Address:* Stradsett Hall, Kings Lynn, Norfolk. *T:* Fincham 215. *Club:* Allsorts (Norfolk).

BAGGLEY, Charles David Aubrey, CBE 1980; MA; Headmaster of Bolton School, 1966–83; *b* 1 Feb. 1923; *s* of A. C. and M. Baggley, Bradford, Yorks; *m* 1st, 1949, Marjorie Asquith Wood (marr. diss. 1983), *d* of M. H. Wood, Harrogate; one *s* one *d*; 2nd, 1983, Julia Hazel Yorke, *d* of S. Morris, Sonning-on-Thames. *Educ:* Bradford Grammar Sch.; King's Coll., Cambridge (1942 and 1945–47) (Exhibitioner in Classics, Scholar in History; Class I, Part II of Historical Tripos, 1947; BA 1947, MA 1952). Temp. Sub. Lieut, RNVR, 1942–45. History Master, Clifton Coll., 1947–50; Head of History Side, Dulwich Coll., 1950–57; Headmaster, King Edward VII Sch., Lytham, 1957–66. Chm., HMC, 1978. Schools Liaison Advr, Salford Univ., 1983–. Mem., Bolton Civic Trust. Gov., Giggleswick School. FRSA. *Recreations:* walking, gardening, reading. *Address:* Martin's Farm, Broadhead, Turton, Bolton, Lancs BL7 0JQ. *T:* Turton 852568.

BAGIER, Gordon Alexander Thomas; MP (Lab) Sunderland South since 1964; *b* 7 July 1924; *m* 1949, Violet Sinclair; two *s* two *d*. *Educ:* Pendower Secondary Technical Sch., Newcastle upon Tyne. Signals Inspector, British Railways; Pres., Yorks District Council, NUR, 1962–64. Mem. of Keighley Borough Council, 1956–60; Mem. of Sowerby Bridge Urban Council, 1962–65. PPS to Home Secretary, 1968–69. Chm., Select Cttee on Transport, 1985–. *Address:* House of Commons, SW1A 0AA; Rahana, Whickham Highway, Dunston, Gateshead, Tyne and Wear NE11 9QH.

BAGNALL, Frank Colin, CBE 1950; Commercial Director, Imperial Chemical Industries Ltd, 1965–70, also Finance Director, 1967–68; Director, African Explosives and Chemical Industries Ltd, 1965–70; *b* 6 Nov. 1909; *s* of late Francis Edward Bagnall, OBE and Edith Bagnall; *m* 1st, 1933, Ethel Hope Robertson (killed in an air raid, by enemy action, 1941), Blechingley; 2nd, Rona Rooker Roberts (marr. diss.), Belmont, Mill Hill; one *s* one *d*; 3rd, Christine Bagnall, Westhill, Ledbury. *Educ:* Repton; Brasenose Coll., Oxford (MA); Dept of Business Administration, London Sch. of Economics. ICI Ltd, 1932–38; Urwick, Orr and Partners, 1938–40. War Office, 1940–42; Man. Dir, British Nylon Spinners, 1944–64; Non-Exec. Dir, ICI, 1964; Dir, Richard Thomas & Baldwins, 1964–67. Mem., Oxford Univ. Appts Cttee, 1948–69; Governor, Ashridge Coll., 1958–70; Chm. Regular Forces Resettlement Cttee for Wales, 1958–68. Chm. Wales Business Training Cttee, 1946–49; Founder Mem., BIM (Mem. Council, 1949–52); Dir Oxford Univ. Business Summer Sch., 1954; Mem. Govt Cttee of Enquiry into Electricity Supply Industry, 1954–55; Chm. SW Reg. Council, FBI, 1956–57; Mem. Air Transport Licensing Bd, 1960–64; Chm. Man-Made Fibres Producers Cttee, 1961–65; Vice-Pres. British Man-Made Fibres Fedn, 1965–70 (Chm. 1963–65); Pres. Textile Inst., 1964–65. Pres., UC of S Wales and Monmouthshire, 1963–68 (Hon. Fellow and Life Governor). Hon. LLD, Wales, 1969. OStJ. *Address:* Vermont, Budleigh Salterton, Devon. *T:* Budleigh Salterton 3068. *Club:* Boodle's.

See also R. M. Bagnall.

BAGNALL, Kenneth Reginald, QC 1973; QC (Hong Kong) 1983; *b* 26 Nov. 1927; *s* of Reginald and Elizabeth Bagnall; *m* 1st, 1955, Margaret Edith Wall; one *s* one *d*; 2nd, 1963, Rosemary Hearn; one *s* one *d*. *Educ:* King Edward VI Sch., Birmingham; Univ. of Birmingham. LLB (Hons). Yardley Scholar. Served Royal Air Force; Pilot Officer, 1947, Flt Lt, 1948. Called to the Bar, Gray's Inn, 1950; a Dep. Judge of Crown Court, 1975–83. Co-founder, 1980, Chm., 1980–82, and Life Govr, 1983, Anglo-American Real Property Inst. Mem., Crafts Council, 1982–85; Co-founder, Bagnall Gall., Crafts Council, 1982. Mem., Inst. of Dirs. Freeman, City and Corp. of London, 1972; Freeman and Liveryman, Barber-Surgeons' Co., 1972. *Publications:* Guide to Business Tenancies, 1956; Atkins Court Forms and Precedents (Town Planning), 1973; (with K. Lewison) Development Land Tax, 1978; Judicial Review, 1985. *Recreations:* yachting, motoring, travel. *Address:* 11 King's Bench Walk, Temple, EC4Y 7EQ. *T:* 01–353 2484.

BAGNALL, Gen. Sir Nigel (Thomas), GCB 1985 (KCB 1981); CVO 1978; MC 1950 and Bar 1953; Chief of the General Staff, since 1985; Aide-de-Camp General to the Queen, since 1985; *b* 10 Feb. 1927; *s* of Lt-Col Harry Stephen Bagnall and Marjory May Bagnall; *m* 1959, Anna Caroline Church; two *d*. *Educ:* Wellington Coll. Joined Army, 1945; commnd Green Howards, 1946; Palestine, 1946–48, 6th Airborne Div.; Malaya, 1949–53, Green Howards; GSO1 (Intell.), Dir of Borneo Ops, 1966–67; comd 4/7 Royal Dragoon Guards, NI and BAOR, 1967–69; Sen. Directing Staff (Army), Jt Services Staff Coll., 1970; comd Royal Armoured Corps HQ 1 (Br.) Corps, 1970–72; Defence Fellow, Balliol Coll., Oxford, 1972–73; Sec., Chief of Staff Cttee, 1973–75; GOC 4th Div., 1975–77; ACDS (Policy), MoD, 1978–80; Comdr, 1 (Br.) Corps, 1980–83; C-in-C BAOR and Comdr, Northern Army Gp, 1983–85. Col Comdt, APTC, 1981–, RAC, 1985–. Hon. Fellow, Balliol Coll., Oxford, 1986. *Recreations:* country pursuits. *Address:* Ministry of Defence, Main Building, Whitehall, SW1; c/o Royal Bank of Scotland, Kirkland House, SW1.

BAGNALL, Richard Maurice, MBE 1945; Deputy Chairman, Tube Investments Ltd, 1976–81, Managing Director, 1974–81, Director, 1969–81; *b* 20 Nov. 1917; *s* of late Francis Edward Bagnall, OBE and Edith Bagnall; *m* 1946, Irene Pickford; one *s* one *d*. *Educ:* Repton. Served War, 1939–45: RA, Shropshire Yeomanry, 1939–43 (despatches); Bde Major, 6 AGRA Italy, 1943–45. Joined Tube Investments Ltd, 1937. Chm., Round Oak Steel Works Ltd, 1976–81 (Dir, 1974–81). Governor, King's Sch., Worcester, 1977–81. Bronze Star, USA, 1945. *Recreations:* golf, gardening, photography. *Address:* Vila da Chypre, Carvoeiro, 8400 Lagoa, Algarve, Portugal. *Club:* MCC.

See also F. C. Bagnall.

BAGNOLD, Brig. Ralph Alger, OBE 1941; FRS 1944; Consultant on movement of sediments by wind and water, since 1956; Fellow of Imperial College, University of London, since 1971; *b* 3 April 1896; *s* of late Col A. H. Bagnold, CB, CMG; *m* 1946, Dorothy Alice, *d* of late A. E. Plank; one *s* one *d*. *Educ:* Malvern College; Royal Military Academy, Woolwich; Gonville and Caius Coll., Cambridge. Commission RE, 1915; Capt, 1918; transferred Royal Corps of Signals, 1920; Major, 1927; retired, 1935. Served European War, Western Front, 1915–18 (despatches); North-West Frontier of India, 1930 (despatches). Organised and led numerous explorations in Libyan Desert and elsewhere, 1925–32; Founder's Medal of Royal Geographical Soc., 1935. Called up, 1939. Raised and commanded Long Range Desert Group in Middle East, 1940–41 (despatches); Deputy Signal-Officer-in-Chief, Middle East, 1943–44; released from Army Service, 1944. G. K. Warren Prize, US Acad. of Sciences, 1969; Penrose Medal, Geolog. Soc. of America, 1970; Wollaston Medal, Geolog. Soc. of London, 1971; Sorby Medal, Internat. Assoc. of Sedimentologists, 1978. *Publications:* Libyan Sands, 1935; Physics of Blown Sand and Desert Dunes, 1941; papers, etc, on deserts, hydraulics, beach formation, and random distributions. *Recreations:* exploration, research. *Address:* 7 Manor Way, Blackheath, SE3 9EF. *T:* 01–852 1210.

BAGOT, family name of **Baron Bagot.**

BAGOT, 9th Baron *cr* 1780; **Heneage Charles Bagot;** Bt 1627; *b* 11 June 1914; *s* of Charles Frederick Heneage Bagot (*d* 1939) (4th *s* of *g s* of 1st Baron) and of Alice Lorina, *d* of Thomas Farr; *S* half-brother, 1979; *m* 1939, Muriel Patricia Moore, *y d* of late Maxwell James Moore Boyle; one *s* one *d*. *Educ:* Harrow. Formerly Major, 6th Gurkha Rifles. *Recreations:* shooting, skiing, sailing. *Heir: s* Hon. Charles Hugh Shaun Bagot, *b* 23 Feb. 1944. *Address:* c/o House of Lords, SW1. *Clubs:* Army and Navy, Alpine Ski; Himalayan.

BAILEY, family name of **Baron Glanusk.**

BAILEY, Sir Alan Marshall, KCB 1986 (CB 1982); Permanent Secretary, Department of Transport, since 1986; *b* 26 June 1931; *s* of John Marshall Bailey and Muriel May Bailey; *m* 1st, 1959, Stella Mary Scott (marr. diss. 1981); three *s*; 2nd, 1981, Shirley Jane Barrett. *Educ:* Bedford Sch.; St John's and Merton Colls, Oxford (MA, BPhil). Harmsworth Senior Scholarship, 1954; Harkness Commonwealth Fellowship, USA, 1963–64. Principal Private Sec. to Chancellor of the Exchequer, 1971–73; Under-Sec., HM Treasury, 1973–78, Dep. Sec., 1978–83 (Central Policy Review Staff, Cabinet Office, 1981–82), 2nd Perm. Sec., 1983–85. *Address:* 11 Park Row, SE10. *T:* 01–858 3015.

BAILEY, Sir Brian (Harry), Kt 1983; OBE 1976; JP; Chairman: Health Education Council, since 1983; Television South West Ltd, since 1980; Director, Oracle Teletext Ltd, since 1983; *b* 25 March 1923; *s* of Harry Bailey and Lilian (*née* Pulfer); *m* 1948, Nina Olive Sylvia (*née* Saunders); two *d*. *Educ:* Lowestoft Grammar Sch. RAF, 1941–45. SW Dist Organisation Officer, NALGO, 1951–82; South Western Reg. Sec., TUC, 1968–81. Chm., South Western RHA, 1975–82; Member: Somerset CC, 1966–84; SW Econ. Planning Council, 1969–79; Central Health Services Council, 1978–80; MRC, 1978–86; Adv. Cttee on Severn Barrage, Dept of Energy, 1978–81; Business Educn Council, 1980–84; NHS Management Inquiry Team, 1983–84. Advr to Home Sec. under Prevention of Terrorism (Temp. Provisions) Act 1984, 1984–. Vice-Chm., BBC Radio Bristol Adv. Council, 1971–78; Member: BBC West Reg. Adv. Council, 1973–78; Council, ITCA, 1982–86; South and West Adv. Bd, Legal and General Assurance Soc. Ltd, 1985–. Director: Channel Four, 1985–; Independent Television Publications Ltd, 1985–; Western Orchestral Soc. Ltd, 1982–. JP Somerset, 1964. *Recreations:* football, cricket and tennis (watching), music, fishing and golf (playing). *Address:* Runnerstones, 32 Stonegallows, Taunton, Somerset TA1 5JP. *T:* Taunton 46265. *Club:* Wyvern (Taunton).

BAILEY, D(avid) R(oy) Shackleton, LittD; FBA 1958; Pope Professor of the Latin Language and Literature, Harvard University, since 1982; *b* 10 Dec. 1917; *y s* of late Rev. J. H. Shackleton Bailey, DD, and Rosamund Maud (*née* Giles); *m* 1967, Hilary Ann (marr. diss. 1974), *d* of Leonard Sidney and Margery Bardwell. *Educ:* Lancaster Royal Grammar Sch.; Gonville and Caius Coll., Cambridge. Fellow of Gonville and Caius Coll., 1944–55, Praelector, 1954–55; Fellow and Dir of Studies in Classics, Jesus Coll., Cambridge, 1955–64; Visiting Lecturer in Classics, Harvard Coll., 1963; Fellow and Dep. Bursar, Gonville and Caius Coll., 1964; Senior Bursar 1965–68; Univ. Lectr in Tibetan, 1948–68; Prof. of Latin, Univ. of Michigan, 1968–74; Prof. of Greek and Latin, Harvard Univ., 1975–82. Andrew V. V. Raymond Vis. Prof., State Univ. of NY at Buffalo, 1973–74; Vis. Fellow of Peterhouse, Cambridge, 1980–81; Nat. Endowment of Humanities Fellowship, 1980–81. Mem., Amer. Philosophical Soc., 1977. Fellow, Amer. Acad. of Arts and Sciences, 1979. Editor, Harvard Studies in Classical Philology, 1978–84. Hon. LittD Dublin, 1984. Charles J. Goodwin Award of Merit, Amer. Philol Assoc., 1978; Kenyon Medal, British Acad., 1985. *Publications:* The Śatapañcāśatka of Mātrceta, 1951; Propertiana, 1956; Towards a Text of Cicero, *ad Atticum,* 1960; Ciceronis Epistulae ad Atticum IX-XVI, 1961; Cicero's Letters to Atticus, Vols I and II, 1965; Vol. V, 1966, Vol. VI, 1967, Vols III and IV, 1968, Vol. VII, 1970; Cicero, 1971; Two Studies in Roman Nomenclature, 1976; Cicero: *Epistulae ad Familiares,* 2 vols, 1977; (trans.) Cicero's Letters to Atticus, 1978; (trans.) Cicero's Letters to his Friends, 2 Vols, 1978; Towards a Text of *Anthologia Latina,* 1979; Selected Letters of Cicero, 1980; Cicero: *Epistulae ad Q. Fratrem et M. Brutum,* 1981; Profile of Horace, 1982; Anthologia Latina, I.1, 1982; Horatius, 1985; Cicero: Philippics, 1986; articles in Classical and Orientalist periodicals. *Recreation:* cats. *Address:* Department of Classics, Harvard University, Cambridge, Mass 02138, USA.

BAILEY, David Royston, FRPS, FSIAD; photographer, film director; *b* 2 Jan. 1938; *s* of William Bailey and Agnes (*née* Green); *m* 1st, 1960, Rosemary Bramble; 2nd, 1967, Catherine Deneuve; 3rd, 1975, Marie Helvin (marr. diss. 1985). *Educ:* self taught. FRPS 1972; FSIAD 1975. Photographer for Vogue, 1959–; Dir of television commercials, 1966–, Dir of documentaries, 1968–. Exhibitions: Nat. Portrait Gall., 1971; one-man retrospective, V&A, 1983; Internat. Centre of Photograph, NY, 1984; Photographs from the Sudan, ICA and tour, 1985. *Publications:* Box of Pinups, 1964; Goodbye Baby and Amen, 1969; Warhol, 1974; Beady Minces, 1974; Papua New Guinea, 1975; Mixed Moments, 1976; Trouble and Strife, 1980; David Bailey's London NW1, 1982; Black and White Memories, 1983; Nudes 1981–84, 1984; Imagine, 1985. *Recreations:* aviculture, photography, travelling, painting. *Address:* c/o R. Montgomery & Partners, 5–6 Portland Mews, D'Arblay Street, W1.

BAILEY, Dennis, RDI 1980; ARCA; graphic designer and illustrator, since 1957; *b* 20 Jan. 1931; *s* of Leonard Charles Bailey and Ethel Louise Funnell; *m* 1985, Nicola Anne Roberts; one *d*. *Educ:* West Tarring Sec. Mod. Sch.; West Sussex Sch. of Art, Worthing; Royal College of Art. Asst Editor, Graphis magazine, Zürich, 1956; free-lance graphic design and illustrator, London, 1957–60; Vis. Lectr in Typography, Central Sch. of Art, 1959–60; worked on film projects, advertising and art direction, Paris, 1961–64; Art Dir, Town magazine, London, 1964–66; graphic design, illustration and design cons. practice, London, 1967–; Lectr in graphic design, Chelsea Sch. of Art, 1970–81. *Clients and work include:* Economist Newspaper: covers and typographic advisor; Architectural Assoc.: art dir of magazine AA Files; Arts Council of GB: design of exhibn catalogues and posters for Dada and Surrealism Reviewed, 1978, Picasso's Picassos, 1981, Renoir, 1985, Torres-Garcia, 1985, Le Corbusier, 1987; Royal Academy: catalogue and graphics for Pompeii AD 79, 1977, graphics and publicity for The Genius of Venice, 1984; Imperial War Mus.: graphics for Cabinet War Rooms, Whitehall, 1984; Olivetti: design of graphics for Leonardo da Vinci's The Last Supper exhibn, 1983; design of business print for Cons. Gold Fields, Ultramar, London Merchant Securities. Drawings and illustrations in Economist, Esquire, Harpers Bazaar (USA), Harpers and Queen, Listener, Nova, Observer, Olympia (Paris), Town; book jackets and covers for Jonathan Cape and Penguin Books. *Address:* 115 Crawford Street, W1H 1AG. *T:* 01–935 6415.

BAILEY, Sir Derrick Thomas Louis, 3rd Bt, *cr* 1919; DFC; *b* 15 Aug. 1918; 2nd *s* of Sir Abe Bailey, 1st Bt, KCMG; *S* half-brother, 1946; *m* 1st, 1946, Katharine Nancy Stormonth Darling; four *s* one *d*; 2nd, 1980, Mrs Jean Roscoe. *Educ:* Winchester. Engaged in farming. *Recreations:* all sports, all games. *Heir: s* John Richard Bailey [*b* 11 June 1947; *m* 1977, Jane, *o d* of John Pearson Gregory; one *s* one *d*]. *Address:* Lappingford, Worminghall, Aylesbury, Bucks; Bluestones, Alderney, CI. *Club:* Rand (Johannesburg).

BAILEY, His Honour Desmond Patrick; a Circuit Judge (formerly Judge of County Courts), 1965–79; *b* 6 May 1907; 3rd *s* of Alfred John Bailey, Bowdon, Cheshire, and of Ethel Ellis Johnson; unmarried. *Educ:* Brighton Coll.; Queens' Coll., Cambridge (BA, LLB). Called to Bar, Inner Temple, 1931. Northern Circuit. Served War of 1939–45: Rifle Brigade, Lancashire Fusiliers, Special Operations Executive, North Africa, Italy (Major). Recorder of Carlisle, 1963–65. *Recreations:* cricket, fishing, gardening. *Address:* Chaseley, Bowdon, Cheshire. *T:* 061–928 0059. *Club:* St James's (Manchester).

BAILEY, Air Vice-Marshal Dudley Graham, CB 1979; CBE 1970; Deputy Managing Director, Services Sound and Vision (formerly Services Kinema) Corporation, since 1980; *b* 12 Sept. 1924; *s* of P. J. Bailey and D. M. Bailey (*née* Taylor); *m* 1948, Dorothy Barbara Lovelace-Hunt; two *d*. Pilot trng, Canada, 1943–45; Intell. Officer, Air HQ Italy, 1946–47 and HQ 23 Gp, 1948–49; Berlin Airlift, 1949; Flt Comdr No 50 and 61 Sqdns, Lincolns, 1950–52; exchange duties, USAF, B-36 aircraft, 1952–54, Canberra Sqdn: Flt Comdr, 1955; Sqdn Comdr, 1956; Air Min., 1956–58; psc (m) 1959; OC No 57 (Victor) Sqdn, 1960–62; Air Warfare course, Manby, 1962; Wing Comdr Ops, HQ Air Forces Middle East, 1963–65; MoD Central Staffs, 1965–66; MoD (Air) Directorate of Air Staff Plans, 1966–68; OC RAF Wildenrath, 1968–70; Sen. Personnel Staff Officer, HQ Strike Comd, 1970–71; Royal Coll. of Defence Studies, 1972; Dir of Personnel (Air), RAF, 1972–74; SASO, RAF Germany, 1974–75; Dep. Comdr, RAF Germany, 1975–76; Dir Gen., Personal Services (RAF), MoD, 1976–80, retired. *Address:* Firs Corner, Abbotswood, Speen, Bucks. *T:* Hampden Row 462. *Club:* Royal Air Force.

BAILEY, Eric; Director, Plymouth Polytechnic, 1970–74, retired; *b* 2 Nov. 1913; *s* of Enoch Whittaker Bailey, Overton Hall, Sandbach, Cheshire; *m* 1942, Dorothy Margaret Laing, Stockport; one *s* one *d*. *Educ:* King's Sch., Macclesfield; Manchester Univ. BSc

Hons; CEng, FRIC, MIChemE; DipEd. Lectr, Stockport Coll. of Technology, 1936–41; Industrial Chemist, 1941–45; Lectr, Enfield Coll. of Technology, 1945–46; Vice-Principal, Technical Coll., Worksop, 1946–51; Principal: Walker Technical Coll., Oakengates, Salop, 1951–59; Plymouth Coll. of Technology, 1959–69. *Recreations:* putting colour into gardens, photography, pursuing leisure and voluntary activities. *Address:* 3 St Bridget Avenue, Crownhill, Plymouth, Devon. *T:* Plymouth 771426. *Club:* Rotary (Plymouth).

BAILEY, Harold, CMG 1960; Under-Secretary, Department of Trade and Industry, 1970–74, retired; *b* 26 Feb. 1914; *yr s* of late John Bailey and Elizabeth Watson, Preston, Lancashire; *m* 1946, Rosemary Margaret, *d* of Harold and Irene Brown, Shotesham St Mary, Norfolk; two *s* one *d*. *Educ:* Preston Grammar Sch.; Christ Church, Oxford. Asst Principal Air Ministry, 1937; Principal, Min. of Aircraft Production, 1942; Served, Royal Air Force, 1942–45; Private Sec. to Minister of Supply and Aircraft Production, 1945–47; Asst Sec., 1947; Min. of Supply Rep. and Adviser (Defence Supplies) to UK High Comr, Ottawa, 1953–55; Under-Secretary: Ministry of Supply, 1957; BoT, 1958; British Senior Trade Comr in India, and Economic Adviser to the British High Comr, 1958–63. *Address:* Hollies, Hurstbourne Tarrant, Hants. *T:* Hurstbourne Tarrant 976482.

BAILEY, Sir Harold (Walter), Kt 1960; FBA 1944; MA, W Aust.; MA, DPhil Oxon; Professor of Sanskrit, Cambridge Univ., 1936–67, Professor Emeritus, 1967; *b* Devizes, Wilts, 16 Dec. 1899. Was Lecturer in Iranian Studies at Sch. of Oriental Studies. Member of: Danish Academy, 1946; Norwegian Academy, 1947; Kungl. Vitterhets Historie och Antikvitets Akademien, Stockholm, 1948; Governing Body, SOAS, Univ. of London, 1946–70; L'Institut de France, Associé étranger, Académie des Inscriptions et Belles-Lettres, 1968. President: Philological Soc., 1948–52; Royal Asiatic Society, 1964–67 (Gold Medal, RAS, 1972); Soc. for Afghan Studies, 1972–79; Soc. of Mithraic Studies (1971), 1975–; Council, Corpus inscriptionum iranicarum, 1985–; Chm., Anglo-Mongolian Soc., 1979–81. Chm., Ancient India and Iran Trust, 1981–. FAHA 1971; Hon. Fellow: SOAS, London Univ., 1963–; Queens' Coll., Cambridge, 1967; St Catherine's Coll., Oxford, 1976. Hon. Mem., Bhandarkar Oriental Res. Inst., Poona, 1968. Hon. DLitt: W Aust., 1963; ANU, 1970; Oxon, 1976; Hon. DD Manchester, 1979. *Publications:* in Bulletin of Sch. of Oriental Studies, Journal of Royal Asiatic Soc., Zeitschrift der Deutschen Morgenländischen Gesellschaft, etc. Codices Khotanenses, 1938; Zoroastrian Problems in the Ninth Century Books, 1943, 2nd edn 1971; Khotanese Texts I, 1945; Khotanese Buddhist Texts, 1951; Indoscythian Studies, Khotanese Texts II, 1953; III, 1956; IV, 1961; V, 1963; VI, 1967; VII, 1985; Corpus inscriptionum iranicarum, Saka Documents, Portfolios I-IV, 1960–67; Saka Documents, text volume, 1968; Dictionary of Khotan Saka, 1979; Bibliotheka Persica: the culture of the Sakas in ancient Iranian Khotan, 1982. *Address:* Queens' College, Cambridge.

BAILEY, Jack Arthur; Secretary, MCC, since 1974; Secretary, International Cricket Conference, since 1974; *b* 22 June 1930; *s* of Horace Arthur and Elsie Winifred Bailey; *m* 1957, Julianne Mary Squier; one *s* two *d*. *Educ:* Christ's Hospital; University Coll., Oxford (BA). Asst Master, Bedford Sch., 1958–60; Reed Paper Group, 1960–67; Rugby Football Correspondent, Sunday Telegraph, 1962–74; Asst Sec., MCC, 1967–74. *Recreations:* cricket (played for Essex and for Oxford Univ.), golf. *Address:* 20 Elm Tree Road, NW8. *T:* 01–286 6246. *Clubs:* Wig and Pen, MCC; Vincent's (Oxford).

BAILEY, John; *see* Bailey, W. J. J.

BAILEY, John Bilsland, CB 1982; HM Procurator General and Treasury Solicitor, since 1984; *b* 5 Nov. 1928; *o s* of late Walter Bailey and Ethel Edith Bailey, FRAM (who *m* 2nd, Sir Thomas George Spencer); *m* 1952, Marion Rosemary (*née* Carroll); two *s* one *d*. *Educ:* Eltham Coll.; University Coll., London (LLB). Solicitor of Supreme Court. Legal Asst, Office of HM Treasury Solicitor, 1957; Sen. Legal Asst, 1962; Asst Treasury Solicitor, 1971; Principal Asst Treasury Solicitor, 1973; Under-Sec. (Legal), Dept of HM Procurator General and Treasury Solicitor, 1973–77; Legal Dir, Office of Fair Trading, 1977–79; Dep. Treasury Solicitor, 1979–84. *Recreations:* walking, reading, listening to music. *Address:* Sherwood Cottage, West Meon, Hampshire. *T:* West Meon 354; 01–834 1376. *Club:* Reform.

BAILEY, John Everett Creighton, CBE 1947; Executive Chairman, Difco Laboratories (UK) Ltd, 1970–75; Chairman and Managing Director, Baird & Tatlock Group of Cos, 1941–69; *b* 2 Nov. 1905; *s* of late John Edred Bailey and late Violet Constance Masters; *m* 1928, Hilda Anne Jones (*d* 1982); one *s* four *d*. *Educ:* Brentwood Sch. Peat Marwick Mitchell & Co., 1925–31; Director: Derbyshire Stone Ltd, 1959–69; Tarmac Derby Ltd, 1969–70; G. D. Searle & Co., 1969–70, and other companies. Mem., Admlty Chemical Adv. Panel, 1940–50; Pres. Scientific Instrument Manufacturers Assoc., 1945–50; Chm. Brit. Laboratory Ware Assoc., 1950–52, Pres., 1974–83; Chm. Brit. Sci. Instr. Research Assoc., 1952–64 (Pres. 1964–71), first Companion, SIRA Inst.; Mem., Grand Council FBI, 1945–58; Mem. BoT Exhibns Adv. Cttee, 1957–65, and Census of Production Adv. Cttee, 1960–68. Formerly Special Member, Prices and Incomes Board. Master, 1957–58 and 1974–75, Worshipful Co. of Scientific Instrument Makers; Master, Worshipful Co. of Needlemakers, 1981–83; Freeman of City of London. Fellow, Inst. of Export; MRI; FBIM. *Recreation:* golf. *Address:* Wayford Manor, Wayford, Crewkerne, Somerset. *Club:* Athenæum.

BAILEY, Ven. Jonathan Sansbury; Archdeacon of Southend, since 1982; Bishop's Officer for Industry and Commerce, diocese of Chelmsford, since 1982; *b* 24 Feb. 1940; *s* of Walter Eric and Audrey Sansbury Bailey; *m* 1965, Susan Mary Bennett-Jones; three *s*. *Educ:* Quarry Bank High School, Liverpool; Trinity College, Cambridge (MA). Assistant Curate: Sutton, St Helens, Lancs, 1965–68; St Paul, Warrington, 1968–71; Warden, Marrick Priory Residential Youth Training Centre, 1971–76; Vicar of Wetherby, Yorks, 1976–82. *Address:* 144 Alexandra Road, Southend-on-Sea SS1 1HB. *T:* Southend 345175.

BAILEY, Norman Stanley, CBE 1977; operatic and concert baritone; *b* Birmingham, 23 March 1933; *s* of late Stanley and Agnes Bailey; *m* 1957, Doreen Simpson (marr. diss. 1983); two *s* one *d*; *m* 1985, Kristine Ciesinski. *Educ:* Rhodes Univ., S Africa; Vienna State Academy. BMus; Performer's and Teacher's Licentiate in Singing; Diplomas, opera, lieder, oratorio. Principal baritone, Sadler's Wells Opera, 1967–71; regular engagements at world's major opera houses and festivals, including: La Scala, Milan; Royal Opera House, Covent Garden; Bayreuth Wagner Festival (first British Hans Sachs in Meistersinger, 1969); Vienna State Opera (first British Wanderer in Siegfried, 1976); Metropolitan Opera, NY; Paris Opera; Edinburgh Festival; Hamburg State Opera; Munich State Opera. BBC Television performances in Falstaff, La Traviata, The Flying Dutchman, Macbeth. Recordings include The Ring (Goodall); Meistersinger and Der Fliegende Holländer (Solti); Walküre (Klemperer), among others. Hon. RAM, 1981; Hon. DMus, 1986. *Recreations:* Mem., Baha'i world community; chess, notaphily, golf, microcomputing. *Address:* c/o Music International, 13 Ardilaun Road, Highbury, N5 2QR.

BAILEY, Patrick Edward Robert; Director, Dan-Air Associated Services, since 1985; *b* 16 Feb. 1925; *s* of late Edward Bailey and Mary Elizabeth Bailey; *m* 1947, Rowena Evelyn Nichols; two *s* three *d*. *Educ:* Clapham Coll.; St Joseph's Coll., Mark Cross; LSE. BSc(Econ). MIPM; FCIT 1971 (Mem. Council, 1982–85). RAPC and RAEC (Captain), 1943–48; Labour Management, Min. of Supply and Army Department: ROF Glascoed, 1951–54; RAE Farnborough, 1954–58; RSAF Enfield, 1958–59; ROF Radway Green, 1959–61; ROFs Woolwich, 1961–66. British Airports Authority: Dep. Personnel Dir, 1966; Personnel Dir, 1970; Airport Services Dir, 1974; Dir, Gatwick and Stansted Airports, 1977–85. Chm. Trustees, British Airports Authority Superannuation Scheme, 1975–86. Mem., Air Transport and Travel Industry Trng Bd, 1971–76; Mem. Bd, Internat. Civil Airports Assoc., 1974–77. *Address:* 17 Lucastes Lane, Haywards Heath, W Sussex. *Club:* Reform.

BAILEY, Paul (christened **Peter Harry**); freelance writer, since 1967; *b* 16 Feb. 1937; *s* of Arthur Oswald Bailey and Helen Maud Burgess. *Educ:* Sir Walter St John's Sch., London; Central School of Speech and Drama. Actor, 1956–64: appeared in first productions of Ann Jellicoe's The Sport of My Mad Mother, 1958, and John Osborne's and Anthony Creighton's Epitaph for George Dillon, 1958. Literary Fellow at Univ. of Newcastle and Univ. of Durham, 1972–74; Bicentennial Fellowship, 1976; Visiting Lectr in English Literature, North Dakota State Univ., 1977–79. FRSL, 1982–84. E. M. Forster Award, 1974; George Orwell Meml Prize, 1978, for broadcast essay The Limitations of Despair. *Publications:* At the Jerusalem, 1967 (Somerset Maugham Award, 1968; Arts Council Prize, 1968); Trespasses, 1970; A Distant Likeness, 1973; Peter Smart's Confessions, 1977; Old Soldiers, 1980; An English Madam, 1982; Gabriel's Lament, 1986; contribs to Observer, TLS. *Recreations:* visiting churches, opera, watching tennis. *Address:* 79 Davisville Road, W12 9SH. *T:* 01–749 2279.

BAILEY, Reginald Bertram, CBE 1976; Member, Employers' Panel, Industrial Tribunals in England and Wales, 1977–85; *b* 15 July 1916; *s* of late George Bertram Bailey and Elizabeth Bailey, Ilford; *m* 1942, Phyllis Joan Firman; one *s* one *d*. *Educ:* Owen's School. Served War of 1939–45: RAPC, 1940–42; RE, 1942–46 (Captain). Entered Post Office as Exec. Officer, 1935; Higher Exec. Officer, 1947; Sen. Exec. Officer, 1948; Principal, 1950; Instructor, Management Trng Centre, 1957; Staff Controller, SW Region, 1958; Comdt, Management Trng Centre, 1962; Asst Sec., 1965; Dir, Wales and the Marches Postal Region, 1967; Dir, South-Eastern Postal Region, 1970–76. *Recreations:* walking, gardening, philately, old railway timetables. *Address:* 21 Preston Paddock, Rustington, Littlehampton, West Sussex BN16 2AA. *T:* Rustington 72451.

BAILEY, Sir Richard (John), Kt 1984; CBE 1977; Chairman, Royal Doulton Ltd, since 1980; Chairman, Royal Crown Derby Porcelain Co., since 1983; *b* 8 July 1923; *s* of Philip Bailey and Doris Margaret (*née* Freebody); *m* 1945, Marcia Rachel Cureton Webb; one *s* three *d*. *Educ:* Newcastle; Shrewsbury. FICeram 1955 (Founder Fellow). Served RN 1942–46 (Lieut). Trainee Manager, Ridgways (Bedford) Works, 1946–50; Doulton Fine China: Asst to Gen. Manager, 1950–55; Technical Dir, 1955–63; Man. Dir, 1963–72; Dir, Doulton & Co., 1967–82; Man. Dir, Royal Doulton Tableware, 1972–80; Dir of subsidiary cos. Dir, Central Independent Television plc, 1986– (Dir, 1981–, Chm., 1986–, W Midlands Regl Bd). Mem., Ceramic Industry Training Bd, 1967–70; Dir, W Midlands Industrial Develt Assoc., 1983–; President: BCMF, 1973–74 (Mem., 1961–84, Chm., 1969–84, Wages Adv. Cttee); British Ceramic Soc., 1980–81; Chairman: British Ceramic Research Ltd, 1982–83; North Staffs Business Initiative, 1981–. MUniv Keele, 1983. FRSA 1977. *Recreations:* golf, walking, gardening. *Address:* Royal Doulton Ltd, Minton House, London Road, Stoke-on-Trent ST4 7QD; Lea Cottage, School Lane, Aston, near Pipe Gate, Market Drayton, Salop TF9 4JD. *Club:* Army and Navy.

BAILEY, Ronald William, CMG 1961; HM Diplomatic Service, retired; *b* 14 June 1917; *o s* of William Staveley and May Eveline Bailey, Southampton; *m* 1946, Joan Hassall, *d* of late A. E. Gray, JP, Stoke-on-Trent; one *s* one *d*. *Educ:* King Edward VI Sch., Southampton; Trinity Hall, Cambridge (Wootton Isaacson Scholar in Spanish). Probationer Vice-Consul, Beirut, 1939–41; HM Vice-Consul, Alexandria, 1941–45; Asst Oriental Sec., British Embassy, Cairo, 1945–48; Foreign Office, 1948–49; 1st Sec., British Legation, Beirut, 1949–52 (acted as Chargé d'Affaires, 1949, 1950 and 1951); 1st Sec., British Embassy, Washington, 1952–55; Counsellor, Washington, 1955–57; Khartoum, 1957–60 (acted as Chargé d'Affaires in each of these years); Chargé d'Affaires, Taiz, 1960–62; Consul-Gen., Gothenburg, 1963–65; Minister, British Embassy, Baghdad, 1965–67; Ambassador to Bolivia, 1967–71; Ambassador to Morocco, 1971–75. Mem. Council, Anglo-Arab Assoc., 1978–85. Vice-Pres., Soc. for Protection of Animals in N Africa; Chm., Black Down Cttee, Nat. Trust; Vice-Pres., British-Moroccan Soc. *Recreations:* walking, photography, gardening. *Address:* Redwood, Tennyson's Lane, Haslemere, Surrey. *T:* Haslemere 2800. *Club:* Oriental.

BAILEY, Sir Stanley Ernest, Kt 1986; CBE 1980; QPM 1975; DL; Chief Constable of Northumbria, since 1975; Regional Police Commander, No 1 Home Defence Region; *b* 30 Sept. 1926; *m* 1954, Marguerita Dorothea Whitbread. Joined Metropolitan Police, 1947; Asst Chief Constable, Staffs, 1966; Dir, Police Res., Home Office, 1970–72; Dep. Chief Constable, Staffs, 1973–75. Mem., IACP (Chairman: Adv. Cttee on Internat. Policy, 1984–; Europ. Sub-Cttee, 1984–); Pres., ACPO, England, Wales & NI, 1985–86 (Vice-Pres., 1984–85). Chairman: Cttee on Burglar Alarms, BSI, 1975–; cttees and working parties on crime prevention, intruder alarms, criminal intelligence, computer privacy, and physical stress in police work. DL Tyne and Wear, 1986. OStJ 1981. *Recreations:* gardening, travel. *Address:* Police HQ, Ponteland, Newcastle-upon-Tyne NE20 0BL.

BAILEY, Thomas Aubrey, MBE 1959; Director, Peter Cox Ltd, Building Restoration Specialists (Member of SGB Group of Cos), 1970–76; *b* 20 Jan. 1912; *o s* of late Thomas Edward Bailey and Emma Bailey; *m* 1944, Joan Woodman, *d* of late John Woodman Hooper; one *s*. *Educ:* Adams' Grammar Sch., Newport, Shropshire; Regent Street Polytechnic Sch. of Architecture. Entered HM Office of Works, Ancient Monuments Br., 1935; Asst Architect, 1945–49; Architect, London and E Anglia, 1949–54; Sen. Architect in charge Ancient Monuments Br., Eng., Wales and Overseas, Min. of Public Building and Works, 1954–69; Architectural Adv. to Oxford Historic Bldgs Fund, 1963–69. Served on various cttees on stone decay and preservation; seconded to Sir Giles G. Scott, OM, RA, for Rebuilding of House of Commons, 1944–49. *Principal works:* Direction of MPBW Survey for Oxford Historic Bldg Appeal, 1957–62 and Cambridge Appeal, 1963; re-erection of fallen Trilithons at Stonehenge, 1958–64; Conservation of Claudian Aqueduct and Aurelian Wall, Brit. Embassy at Rome, 1957–69; etc. Resigned professional membership of RIBA and ARCUK, to enter specialised Bldg Industry, 1969. Mem. Conservation Cttee, for Council for Places of Worship, 1968; Mem. Council, Ancient Monuments Soc., 1970–. FSA 1957; FRSA 1969; Fellow of Faculty of Bldg, 1970. Freeman of City of London, 1967; Freeman and Liveryman, Worshipful Company of Masons, 1973. Hon. MA Oxon, 1963. *Publications:* (jointly) The Claudian Aqueduct in the Grounds of the British Embassy, Rome, 1966; many technical reports on conservation of Historic Monuments. *Recreations:* music, photography, travel, motoring. *Address:* 32 Anne Boleyn's Walk, Cheam, Sutton, Surrey SM3 8DF. *T:* 01–642 3185. *Club:* City Livery.

BAILEY, Wilfrid; Chairman, Southern Gas Region (formerly Southern Gas Board), 1969–75; Chartered Accountant; *b* 9 March 1910; *s* of late Harry Bailey and Martha

Bailey (née Pighills); m 1934, Vera (née Manchester); two s one d. Educ: Keighley Grammar Sch. Borough Treasurer, Bexley BC, 1945–47; Chief Financial Officer, Crawley Development Corp., 1947–49; Gas Council: Chief Accountant, 1949–58; Secretary, 1958–61; Dep. Chm., Southern Gas Bd, 1961–69. FCA 1935; CBIM. Recreations: cricket, motoring, music, photography, gardening. Address: (home) Bramble Way, Clease Way, Compton Down, near Winchester. T: Twyford 713382.

BAILEY, (William) John (Joseph); journalist; b 11 June 1940; s of Ernest Robert Bailey and Josephine Smith; m 1963, Maureen Anne, d of James Gibbs Neenan and Marjorie Dorema Wrigglesworth; five s three d. Educ: St Joseph's, Stanford-le-Hope, Essex; Campion Hall, Jamaica; St George's Coll., Kingston, Jamaica; St Chad's Coll., Wolverhampton. Reporter: Southend Standard, Essex, and Essex and Thurrock Gazette, 1960–63; Northern Daily Mail, 1963–64; Chief Reporter, Billingham and Stockton Express, 1964–72; Sub-Editor, Mail, Hartlepool, 1972–75; Features Editor, Echo, Sunderland, 1975–. Member: Press Council, 1974–80; Complaints Cttee, 1974–76, 1977–; Cttee for Evidence to Royal Commission on Press, 1975–76; Gen. Purposes Cttee, 1976–77; Secretariat Cttee, 1976–. Nat. Union of Journalists: Mem., Nat. Exec. Council, 1966–82; Vice-Pres., 1972–73; Pres., 1973–74; Gen. Treasurer, 1975–83. Provincial Journalist of the Year (jtly with Carol Roberton), British Press Awards, 1977 (commended, 1979). Address: 225 Park Road, Hartlepool, Cleveland TS26 9NG. T: Hartlepool 264577. Clubs: Press (Glasgow); Press (Newcastle).

BAILIE, Rt. Hon. Robin John, PC (N Ire) 1971; Solicitor of the Supreme Court of Judicature, Northern Ireland, since 1961; b 6 March 1937; m 1961, Margaret F. (née Boggs); one s three d. Educ: Rainey Endowed Sch. Magherafelt, Co. Londonderry; The Queen's Univ. of Belfast (LLB). MP (N Ire) for Newtonabbey, 1969–72; Minister of Commerce, Govt of NI, 1971–72. Chm., Fine Wine Wholesalers; Director: Goodyear Tyre & Rubber Co. (GB); United Dominions Trust (Carplant). Recreations: wine drinking, ski-ing, squash, golf, tennis. Address: 39a Malone Park, Belfast. T: Belfast 668085; 1 Thurloe Close, SW7. T: 01–581 4898.

BAILLIE, family name of Baron Burton.

BAILLIE, Alastair Turner; HM Diplomatic Service; Governor of Anguilla, since 1983; b 24 Dec. 1932; s of late Archibald Turner Baillie and Margaret Pinkerton Baillie; m 1st, 1965, Wilma Noreen Armstrong (marr. diss. 1974); one s; 2nd, 1977, Irena Maria Gregor; one step s one step d. Educ: Dame Allan's Sch., Newcastle upon Tyne; Christ's Coll., Cambridge (BA). National Service, commissioned Queen's Own Cameron Highlanders, 1951–53. HMOCS: North Borneo, subseq. Sabah, Malaysia, 1957–67; joined HM Diplomatic Service, 1967; FCO, 1967–73; Consul (Commercial), Karachi, 1973–77; First Sec. and Head of Chancery, Manila, 1977–80; Counsellor, Addis Ababa, 1980–81; Counsellor (Commercial), Caracas, 1981–83. Recreations: sport, reading, travelling. Address: c/o Foreign and Commonwealth Office, SW1A 2AH. Club: Royal Commonwealth Society.

BAILLIE, Sir Gawaine George Hope, 7th Bt, of Polkemmet, cr 1823; b 8 March 1934; s of Sir Adrian Baillie, 6th Bt, and Hon. Olive Cecilia (d 1974), d of 1st Baron Queenborough, GBE; S father, 1947; m 1966, Margot, d of Senator Louis Beaubien, Montreal; one s one d. Heir: s Adrian Louis Baillie, b 26 March 1973. Address: Freechase, Warninglid, Sussex.

BAILLIE, Ian Fowler, CMG 1966; OBE 1962; Director, The Thistle Foundation, Edinburgh, 1970–81; b 16 Feb. 1921; s of late Very Rev. Principal John Baillie, CH, DLitt, DD, LLD and Florence Jewel (née Fowler); m 1951, Sheila Barbour (née Mathewson); two s one d. Educ: Edinburgh Acad,; Corpus Christi Coll., Oxford (MA). War service, British and Indian Armies, 1941–46. HM Overseas Civil Service (formerly Colonial Service), 1946–66: Admin. Officer (District Comr), Gold Coast, 1946–54; Registrar of Co-operative Socs and Chief Marketing Officer, Aden, 1955; Protectorate Financial Sec., Aden, 1959; Dep. British Agent, Aden, 1962; Brit. Agent and Asst High Comr, Aden, 1963; Dir, Aden Airways 1959–66; Sen. Research Associate and Administrative Officer, Agricultural Adjustment Unit, Dept of Agricultural Economics, Univ. of Newcastle upon Tyne, 1966–69. Publication: (ed with S. J. Sheehy) Irish Agriculture in a Changing World, 1971. Recreation: angling. Address: 4 Grange Loan Gardens, Edinburgh EH9 2EB. T: 031–667 2647.

BAILLIE, Prof. John, MA, CA; Johnstone-Smith Professor of Accountancy, University of Glasgow, since 1983; Partner, KMG Thomson McLintock (where, in terms of his University appointment, he continues to practise); b 7 Oct. 1944; s of Arthur and Agnes Baillie; m 1972, Annette Alexander; one s one d. Educ: Whitehill Sch. CA 1967 (Gold Medal and Distinction in final exams). Partner, Thomson McLintock & Co., later KMG Thomson McLintock, 1978–. Mem. various technical and professional affairs cttees, Inst. of Chartered Accountants of Scotland. Hon. MA Glasgow, 1983. Publications: Systems of Profit Measurement, 1985; Consolidated Accounts and the Seventh Directive, 1985; technical and professional papers; contribs to Accountants' Magazine and other professional jls. Recreations: keeping fit, reading, music, golf. Address: The Glen, Glencairn Road, Kilmacolm, Renfrewshire. T: Kilmacolm 3254. Clubs: Western, Royal Scottish Automobile (Glasgow).

BAILLIE, John Strachan, CBE 1965; b 1896; s of William T. Baillie, Belfast; m 1926, Eileen Mary, d of Saxon J. Payne. Educ: Queen's Univ., Belfast (BComSc). Joined Harland and Wolff, Belfast, 1913, and (apart from service in RN, 1914–18) was with Co. throughout his career; transf. to Co.'s London Office, 1924; Asst Sec., Harland & Wolff, Belfast, 1937; London Manager, 1945; Dir 1947; Dep. Chm. 1958; Chm. 1962–65; Dir, Short Brothers & Harland Ltd, 1948–67; Dep. Chm. Brown Bros & Co. Ltd, 1962–67. Liveryman, Worshipful Co. of Shipwrights. Commander: Order of St Olav (Norway), 1960; Dannebrog (Denmark) 1964. Address: Merrydown, 12 Aldersey Road, Guildford, Surrey GU1 2ES.

BAILLIE, William James Laidlaw, RSA 1979 (ARSA 1968); PRSW 1974 (RSW 1963); painter; Senior Lecturer in Drawing and Painting, Edinburgh College of Art, since 1968; Treasurer, Royal Scottish Academy, since 1980; b 19 April 1923; s of James and Helen Baillie; m 1961, Helen Gillon; one s two d. Educ: Dunfermline High Sch.; Edinburgh College of Art (Andrew Grant Schol., 1941–50; Dip. Drawing and Painting 1950). Studies interrupted by war service with Royal Corps of Signals, mainly in Far East, 1942–47. Taught in Edinburgh schools, 1951–60; Mem., Teaching Staff, Edin. College of Art, 1960–; Visiting Tutor, National Gallery of Canada Summer Sch., near Ottawa, 1955. Exhibits at Gall. 10, London, but mostly in Scotland, mainly at Scottish Gall., Edinburgh; first retrospective exhibn in Kirkcaldy Art Gallery, 1977. Recreations: music, travel. Address: 6A Esslemont Road, Edinburgh EH16 5PX. T: 031–667 1538.

BAILLIE-HAMILTON, family name of Earl of Haddington.

BAILLIEU, family name of Baron Baillieu.

BAILLIEU, 3rd Baron cr 1953, of Sefton, Australia and Parkwood, Surrey; James William Latham Baillieu; Associate Director, Rothschild Australia Ltd, since 1985; b 16 Nov. 1950; s of 2nd Baron Baillieu and Anne Bayliss, d of Leslie William Page, Southport, Queensland; S father, 1973; m 1974, Cornelia Masters Ladd (marr. diss.), d of W. Ladd; one s. Educ: Radley College; Monash Univ., Melbourne (BEc 1977). Short Service Commission, Coldstream Guards, 1970–73. Manager Asst, Banque Nationale de Paris, Melbourne, 1980; Rothschild Australia Ltd: Manager, 1983; Sen. Manager, 1984. Heir: s Hon. Robert Latham Baillieu, b 2 Feb. 1979. Address: c/o Mutual Trust Pty Ltd, 360 Collins Street, Melbourne, Victoria 3000, Australia. Club: Boodle's.

BAILLIEU, Colin Clive; Member: Monopolies and Mergers Commission, since 1984; Council of Lloyd's, since 1983; b 2 July 1930; s of Ian Baillieu and Joanna Baillieu (née Brinton); m 1st, 1955, Diana Robinson (marr. diss. 1968); two d; 2nd, 1968, Renata Richter; two s. Educ: Dragon Sch.; Eton. Commissioned Coldstream Guards, 1949. Local newspaper, Evening Standard, 1951–52; British Metal Corp., 1952–58; British Aluminium, 1958–60; Monsanto Fibres, 1960–66; Arthur Sanderson, 1966–68; Ultrasonic Machines, 1968–76. Contested (C) Rossendale, Lancs, 1964 and 1966. Recreations: skiing, tennis, teaching boys to play polo, theology, 17th Century history Address: Hoyle Farm, Heyshott, Midhurst, West Sussex GU29 0DY. T: Graffham 230. Clubs: Travellers', Beefsteak, MCC.

BAIN, Andrew David, FRSE 1980; Group Economic Adviser, Midland Bank, since 1984; b 21 March 1936; s of Hugh Bain and Kathleen Eadie; m 1960, Anneliese Minna Frieda Kroggel; three s. Educ: Glasgow Academy; Christ's Coll., Cambridge. PhD Cantab 1963. Junior Res. Officer, Dept of Applied Econs, Cambridge Univ., 1958–60; Res. Fellow, Christ's Coll., Cambridge, 1960; Instructor, Cowles Foundn, Yale Univ., 1960–61; Lectr, Cambridge, 1961–66; Fellow, Corpus Christi Coll., Cambridge, 1962; on secondment to Bank of England, 1965–67; Prof. of Econs, 1967–70, Esmee Fairbairn Prof. of Econs of Finance and Investment, 1970–77, Univ. of Stirling; Walton Prof. of Monetary and Financial Econs, Univ. of Strathclyde, 1977–84. Member: Cttee to Review the Functioning of Financial Institutions, 1977–80; (part-time) Monopolies and Mergers Commn, 1981–82. Publications: The Growth of Television Ownership in the United Kingdom (monograph), 1964; The Control of the Money Supply, 1970; Company Financing in the UK, 1975; The Economics of the Financial System, 1981; articles on demand analysis, monetary policy and other subjects. Address: 552 Ben Jonson House, Barbican, EC2. Club: Reform.

BAIN, Cyril William Curtis, MC; DM Oxford; FRCP; Hon. Consulting Physician, Harrogate General Hospital; Past President BMA; b Thornfield, Heaton Mersey, near Manchester, 5 June 1895; e s of late William Bain, MD, FRCP, and Ellen, d of late John Curtis, Rose Leigh, Heaton Chapel, near Manchester; m 1930, Diana Alice, y d of late Lt-Col H R. Pease, and ggd of late Joseph Robinson Pease, Hesslewood, near Hull; two s one d (and one s decd). Educ: Bilton Grange, near Rugby; Wellington Coll.; Christ Church, Oxford; St Thomas's Hospital, London. Served European War, 1914–18; gazetted to the Duke of Wellington's Regt 29 August 1914; Captain, 1916; Major, 1918; served in Machine Gun Corps (despatches, MC); active service in France and Flanders, 1915–17; retired, 1918; Extra-ordinary member of the Cardiac Society. Publications: Recent Advances in Cardiology (with C. F. T. East), 5th edn, 1959; Incomplete Bundle Branch Block; Bilateral Bundle Branch Block; The Oesophageal Lead; Clinical Value of Unipolar Chest and Limb Leads, etc. Address: Beechwood Private Hotel, Carbis Bay, St Ives, Cornwall. T: Penzance 795170.

BAIN, Douglas John; Director, J. & P. Coats Ltd, 1968–83; b 9 July 1924; s of Alexander Gillan Bain and Fanny Heaford; m 1946, Jean Wallace Fairbairn; three d. Educ: Pollokshields Secondary School; Royal Technical Coll. (now Strathclyde Univ.), Glasgow (DRTC). ATI. Royal Tech. Coll., 1941–43 and 1948–51. RAF, 1943–48. J. & P. Coats Ltd, 1951–83: graduate trainee, 1951–55; overseas management, 1955–60; central management, 1960–68; Director, 1968–83; seconded to Scottish Office (Scottish Econ. Planning Dept) as Under Sec., 1979–82. Industrial Advr to Sec. of State for Scotland, 1983–85. Recreations: golf, walking, geology, flying. Address: 49 Bimbadeen Crescent, Yallambie, Melbourne, Vic 3085, Australia.

BAIN, Prof. George Sayers, DPhil; Professor of Industrial Relations, University of Warwick, since 1979; b 24 Feb. 1939; s of George Alexander Bain and Margaret Ioleen Bamford; m 1962, Carol Lynne Ogden White; one s one d. Educ: Univ. of Manitoba (BA Hons 1961, MA 1964); Oxford Univ. (DPhil 1968). Lectr in Econs, Univ. of Manitoba, 1962–63; Res. Fellow, Nuffield Coll., Oxford, 1966–69; Frank Thomas Prof. of Indust. Relations, UMIST, 1969–70; Dep. Dir, 1970–74, Dir, 1974–81, SSRC Industrial Relations Res. Unit, Univ. of Warwick. Member: Res. Staff, Royal Commn on Trade Unions and Employers' Assocs (Donovan Commn), 1966–67; Mech. Engrg Econ. Develt Cttee, NEDO, 1974–76; Cttee of Inquiry on Indust. Democracy, Dept of Trade (Chm., Lord Bullock), 1975–76; Res. Staff, Canadian Task Force on Labour Relations, 1968. Consultant, NBPI, 1967–69; acted as Consultant to Dept of Employment, and to the Manitoba and Canada Depts of Labour; frequently acts as arbitrator and mediator in indust. disputes. Publications: Trade Union Growth and Recognition, 1967; The Growth of White-Collar Unionism, 1970; (jtly) The Reform of Collective Bargaining at Plant and Company Level, 1971; (jtly) Social Stratification and Trade Unionism, 1973; (jtly) Union Growth and the Business Cycle, 1976; (jtly) A Bibliography of British Industrial Relations, 1979; (jtly) Profiles of Union Growth, 1980; (ed) Industrial Relations in Britain, 1983; (jtly) A Bibliography of British Industrial Relations 1971–1979, 1985; contrib. prof. and learned jls. Recreation: ice skating. Address: 7 Northumberland Road, Leamington Spa CV32 6HE. T: Leamington Spa 24050.

BAIN, Iain Andrew; Editor, The Geographical Magazine, since 1981; b 25 Feb. 1949; s of Alistair I. R. Bain and Jean R. Forrest; m 1974, Maureen Beattie; three d. Educ: Nairn Acad.; Univ. of Aberdeen (MA). Research, Univ. of Durham, 1971–74; Sub-editor, 1974, Asst Editor, 1980, The Geographical Magazine. Publications: Mountains and People, 1982; Water on the Land, 1983; Mountains and Earth Movements, 1984; various articles. Recreations: reading, walking, photography, allotment gardening. Address: 14 Weirdale Avenue, Whetstone, N20. T: 01–361 0491. Club: Geographical.

BAIN, John Taylor, CBE 1975; JP; Director of Education, Glasgow, 1968–75; Lay Observer (Solicitors Act) in Scotland, 1977–83; b 9 May 1912; m; one s two d. Educ: St Andrews Univ. (BSc, MA); Edinburgh Univ. (BEd). War Service, RAF (Technical Br.). Entered educational administration in 1947. JP Glasgow, 1971. Recreation: golf. Address: 20 Kensington Court, Glasgow G12 9NX. T: 041–339 2939. Club: Royal Scottish Automobile.

BAIN, Margaret Anne; see Ewing, M. A.

BAINBRIDGE, Beryl, FRSL; actress, writer; b 21 Nov. 1934; d of Richard Bainbridge and Winifred Baines; m 1954, Austin Davies (marr. diss.); one s two d. Educ: Merchant Taylors' Sch., Liverpool; Arts Educational Schools, Ltd, Tring. FRSL 1978. Hon. LittD Liverpool, 1986. Plays: Tiptoe Through the Tulips, 1976; The Warrior's Return, 1977;

Its a Lovely Day Tomorrow, 1977; Journal of Bridget Hitler, 1981; Somewhere More Central (TV), 1981. *Publications:* A Weekend with Claud, 1967, revd edn 1981; Another Part of the Wood, 1968, rev. edn 1979; Harriet Said . . ., 1972; The Dressmaker, 1973; The Bottle Factory Outing, 1974 (Guardian Fiction Award); Sweet William, 1975 (film, 1980); A Quiet Life, 1976; Injury Time, 1977 (Whitbread Award); Young Adolf, 1978; Winter Garden, 1980; English Journey, 1984; Watson's Apology, 1984; Mum and Mr Armitage, 1985; Forever England, 1986 (TV series, 1986). *Recreations:* painting, sleeping. *Address:* 42 Albert Street, NW1 7NU. *T:* 01–387 3113.

BAINBRIDGE, Cyril; Assistant Managing Editor, The Times, since 1982; author and journalist; *b* 15 Nov. 1928; *o s* of late Arthur Herman Bainbridge and of Edith Bainbridge; *m* 1952, Barbara Hannah (*née* Crook); one *s* two *d. Educ:* privately (Negus Coll., Bradford). Served Army, staff of CGS, WO, 1947–49. Entered journalism as Reporter, Bingley Guardian, 1944–45; Telegraph and Argus, and Yorkshire Observer, Bradford, 1945–54; Press Assoc., 1954–63; joined The Times, 1963; Asst News Editor, 1967; Dep. News Editor, 1967–69; Regional News Editor, 1969–77; Managing News Editor, 1977–82. Vice-Pres., 1977–78, Pres., 1978–79, Inst. of Journalists; Member: Press Council, 1980–; Nat. Council for Trng of Journalists, 1983–. Mem. Editorial Adv. Bd, Thomson Foundn, 1983–. *Publications:* Taught With Care: a Century of Church Schooling, 1974; The Brontës and their Country, 1978; Brass Triumphant, 1980; North Yorkshire and North Humberside, 1984; (ed) One Hundred Years of Journalism, 1984. *Recreations:* reading, brass bands, collecting old bookmarks. *Address:* 98 Mayfield Avenue, North Finchley, N12 9JE. *T:* 01–445 4178. *Club:* Press.

BAINBRIDGE, Maj.-Gen. Henry, CB 1948; CBE 1944; psc; retired; late Corps of Royal Engineers; *b* 1903. 2nd Lieut Royal Engineers, 1923. Served War of 1939–45, 1939–44 (despatches twice, CBE). Dir of Man-power Planning, War Office, 1949–52; Dep. QMG, War Office, 1952–55, retired 1955. *Address:* Brizlee, Hoe Lane, Peaslake, Surrey GU5 9SW.

BAINES, Anthony Cuthbert, DLitt; FBA 1980; *b* 6 Oct. 1912; *s* of Cuthbert Edward Baines and Margaret Clemency Lane Poole; *m* 1960, Patricia Margaret Stammers. *Educ:* Westminster Sch. (KS); Christ Church Oxford; Royal College of Music. BA 1933, MA 1970, DLitt 1977, Oxon. Member, London Philharmonic Orchestra, 1935–39, 1946–49. Commissioned Royal Tank Regt, 1940–45. Associate Conductor, International Ballet Co., 1950–53; Member, Music Staff: Uppingham Sch., 1954–65; Dean Close Sch., 1965–70; Curator, Bate Collection of Historical Wind Instruments, Oxford Univ., 1970–80, retired. Fellow, University Coll., Oxford, 1974–80, retired. Editor, Galpin Society Jl, 1956–63 and 1970–. *Publications:* Woodwind Instruments and their History, 1957, 5th edn 1977; Bagpipes, 1960, 4th edn 1979; ed and contrib. Musical Instruments through the Ages, 1961, 6th edn 1978; Victoria and Albert Museum, Catalogue of Musical Instruments, vol. II, Non-Keyboard, 1968; European and American Musical Instruments, 1966, 2nd edn 1981; Brass Instruments, their History and Development, 1976, 3rd edn 1980. *Recreations:* folk music, wild birds. *Address:* 8 Lynette Avenue, SW4 9HD. *T:* 01–673 8389.

BAINES, Sir George G.; *see* Grenfell-Baines.

BAINES, Prof. John Robert, MA, DPhil; Professor of Egyptology, Oxford University and Fellow of Queen's College, Oxford, since 1976; *b* 17 March 1946; *o s* of late Edward Russell Baines and of Dora Margaret Jean (*née* O'Brien); *m* 1971, Jennifer Christine Ann, *e d* of S. T. Smith; one *s* one *d. Educ:* Winchester Coll.; New Coll., Linacre Coll., Worcester Coll., Oxford (BA 1967, MA, DPhil 1976). Lectr in Egyptology, Univ. of Durham, 1970–75; Laycock Student, Worcester Coll., Oxford, 1973–75; Vis. Prof., Univ. of Arizona, 1982; Fellow, Humboldt-Stiftung, 1982. *Publications:* (trans. and ed) H. Schäfer, Principles of Egyptian Art, 1974; (with J. Málek) Atlas of Ancient Egypt, 1980; (trans. and ed) E. Hornung, Conceptions of God in Ancient Egypt, 1982; Fecundity Figures, 1985; articles in Acta Orientalia, American Anthropologist, Art History, Jl Egypt. Archaeol., Man, Orientalia, Studien altägypt. Kultur, etc. *Address:* The Queen's College, Oxford OX1 4AW.

BAINS, Lawrence Arthur, CBE 1983; FCII; DL; Director: Bains Brothers Ltd; Crowland Leasings Ltd; Bains Finance Management Ltd, and associated companies; Chairman, Haringey District Health Authority, since 1982; *b* 11 May 1920; *s* of late Arthur Bains and Mabel (*née* Payn); *m* 1954, Margaret, *d* of late Sir William and Lady Grimshaw; two *s* one *d. Educ:* Stationers' Company's School. Served War, 1939–46: Middlesex Yeomanry, 1939; N Africa, 1940; POW, 1942, escaped, 1943. Member of Lloyd's. Hornsey Borough Council: Mem., 1949–65; Dep. Leader, 1958–64; Mayor, 1964–65; Council, London Borough of Haringey: Mem., 1964–74; Finance Chm., 1968–71; Greater London Council: Chm., 1977–78; Mem. for Hornsey/Haringey, 1967–81; Chm., South Area Planning Bd, 1970–73; Dep. Leader, Housing Policy Cttee, 1979–81; Chm., GLC/Tower Hamlets Jt Management Cttee, 1979–81; Mem., Lee Valley Regional Park Authority, 1968–81 (Chm., 1980–81). Liveryman, Worshipful Co. of Basketmakers. DL Greater London, 1978 (Rep. DL for Borough of Barnet, 1983). *Recreation:* riding. *Address:* Crowland Lodge, 100 Galley Lane, Arkley, Barnet EN5 4AL. *T:* 01–440 3499. *Clubs:* City Livery, United Wards.

BAINS, Malcolm Arnold; JP, DL; Clerk of the Kent County Council and Clerk to the Lieutenancy of Kent, 1970–74; *b* 12 Sept. 1921; *s* of Herbert Bains, Newcastle-upon-Tyne; *m* 1st, 1942, Winifred Agnes Davies (marr. diss. 1961); three *s*; 2nd, 1968, Margaret Hunter. *Educ:* Hymers Coll.; Durham Univ. (LLB (Hons)); Solicitor. Commnd as Pilot in RAF, 1942–46. Solicitor with Taunton and Sunderland and with Notts and Hants County Councils, 1946–55; Dep. Clerk of Hants County Council and Dep. Clerk of the Peace, 1955–60; Dep. Clerk of Kent County Council, 1960–70; Chm., Working Group which advised Secretary of State for Environment on future management of Local Authorities, 1971–73. Chm., Local Govt Review Bd of Victoria, 1978–79. Fellow, ANU and Advr to NSW Govt, 1977–78. Head of Norfolk Island Public Service, 1979–82. FRSA 1976. DL Kent 1976; JP Norfolk Is, 1980. *Publications:* The Bains Report, 1972; Principles and Processes of Management for New Local Authorities, 1974; Management Reform in English Local Government, 1978. *Recreations:* swimming, walking, travel. *Address:* 77 Langham Road, Teddington, Middlesex; PO Box 244, Norfolk Island, 2899, via Australia.

BAIRD, Charles Fitz; Chairman and Chief Executive Officer, Inco Ltd, since 1980; *b* 4 Sept. 1922; *s* of George White and Julia (Fitz) Baird; *m* 1947, Norma Adele White; two *s* two *d. Educ:* Middlebury Coll. (BA); New York Univ. (Grad. Sch. of Bus. Admin); Harvard Univ. (Advanced Management Program). Standard Oil Co. (NJ), now Exxon, 1948–65: Dep. European Financial Rep., London, 1955–58; Asst Treas., 1958–62; Dir, Esso Standard SA Française, 1962–65; Asst Sec., Financial Man., US Navy, 1965–67, Under Secretary, 1967–69; Internat. Nickel Co. of Canada Ltd (Inco Ltd): Vice Pres. Finance, 1969–72, Sen. Vice Pres., 1972–76; Dir, 1974–; Vice Chm., 1976–77; Pres., 1977–80. Director: Bank of Montreal, 1975–; ICI Americas Inc., 1978–; Aetna Life and Casualty Co., 1981–. Dir, Conf. Bd of Canada. Member: Business Council on National Issues; Ontario Business Adv. Council; British North-American Cttee; Council on Foreign Relations; Can. Inst. of Mining and Metallurgy; Canadian American Cttee.

Governor, Olympic Trust of Canada. Hon. LLD Bucknell Univ. 1976. US Navy Distinguished Civilian Service Award, 1969. *Recreations:* tennis, platform tennis, golf. *Address:* Inco Ltd, 1 First Canadian Place, Toronto, Ontario M5X 1C4, Canada. *T:* (416) 361–7720. *Clubs:* Toronto, Queen's, Rosedale Golf, Badminton and Racquet (Toronto); The Links (New York City); Chevy Chase (Washington, DC).

BAIRD, Sir David Charles, 5th Bt of Newbyth, *cr* 1809; *b* 6 July 1912; *s* of late William Arthur Baird, of Lennoxlove, and Lady Hersey Baird; *S* uncle, 1941. *Educ:* Eton; Cambridge. *Heir: b* Robert Walter Stuart Baird [*b* 5 March 1914; *m* 1st, 1938, Maxine Christine (marr. diss. 1960), *o c* of Rupert Darrell, New York; one *s*; 2nd, 1960, Maria Florine Viscart; one *d*]. *Address:* 33A Lygon Road, Newington, Edinburgh EH16 5QD.

BAIRD, Sir Dugald, Kt 1959; MD, FRCOG, Hon. FRCPGlas, BSc, DPH; Belding Scholar, Association for Aid to Crippled Children, New York, 1966–71; Regius Professor of Midwifery in the University of Aberdeen, 1937–65, retired; formerly Obstetrician-in-Chief, Aberdeen Maternity Hospital and Visiting Gynæcologist, Aberdeen Royal Infirmary and Hon. Director, Obstetric Medicine Research Unit, Medical Research Council; *b* 16 Nov. 1899; *er s* of David Baird, MA, Gourock, Renfrewshire; *m* 1928, May Tennent, CBE (*d* 1983); two *s* two *d. Educ:* Greenock Acad.; University of Glasgow; University of Strasbourg. Formerly with Glasgow Royal Maternity and Women's Hosp., Glasgow Royal Infirmary, and Glasgow Royal Cancer Hosp. Hon. FRCOG, 1986. Freedom of City of Aberdeen, 1966. Hon. LLD: Glasgow, 1959; Aberdeen, 1966; Hon. DSc: Manchester, 1962; Wales, 1966; Hon. DCL, Newcastle; DUniv Stirling, 1974. *Publications:* various papers on obstetrical and gynæcological subjects. *Recreation:* golf. *Address:* Manor House, Boswall Road, Edinburgh.

BAIRD, Lt-Gen. Sir James (Parlane), KBE 1973; MD, FRCP, FRCPEd; Medical Adviser, National Advice Centre for Postgraduate Education, 1977–84; *b* 12 May 1915; *s* of Rev. David Baird and Sara Kathleen Black; *m* 1948, Anne Patricia Anderson; one *s* one *d. Educ:* Bathgate Academy; Univ. of Edinburgh. FRCPEd 1952, MD 1958, FRCP 1959. Commissioned, RAMC, 1939; Lt-Col 1956; Prof. of Military Medicine, Royal Army Medical Coll., 1965; Cons. Physician, BAOR, 1967; Dir of Medicine and Consulting Physician to the Army, 1969–71; Comdt and Dir of Studies, Royal Army Med. Coll., 1971–73; Dir Gen., Army Medical Services, 1973–77. QHP 1969. QHA (Pakistan), 1982. *Publications:* Tropical Diseases Supplement to Principles and Practice of Medicine, 1968; (contrib.) The Oxford Companion to Medicine, 1986. *Recreation:* golf. *Address:* 30 Stonehills Court, College Road, Dulwich, SE21 7LZ. *T:* 01–693 2735. *Club:* West Sussex Golf.

BAIRD, Sir James Richard Gardiner, 10th Bt *cr* 1695; MC 1945; *b* 12 July 1913; *er s* of Captain William Frank Gardiner Baird (killed in action 1914) (2nd *s* of 8th Bt) and Violet Mary (*d* 1947), *d* of late Richard Benyon Croft; *S* uncle, Sir James Hozier Gardiner Baird, 9th Bt, 1966; *m* 1941, Mabel Ann (Gay), *d* of A. Algernon Gill; two *s* one *d. Educ:* Eton. Served War of 1939–45. Lieut, Royal Artillery, 1940; Captain, Kent Yeomanry, 1944. *Recreation:* shooting. *Heir: s* James Andrew Gardiner Baird [*b* 2 May 1946; *m* 1984, Jean Margaret, *yr d* of Brig. Sir Ian Jardine, 4th Bt; one *s. Educ:* Eton]. *Address:* The Old Vicarage, Arreton, Isle of Wight. *T:* Isle of Wight 525814. *Club:* Naval and Military.

BAIRD, Joyce Elizabeth Leslie; Joint General Secretary, Assistant Masters and Mistresses Association, since 1978; *b* 8 Dec. 1929; *d* of Dr J. C. H. Baird and Mrs J. E. Baird. *Educ:* The Abbey School, Reading; Newnham College, Cambridge (MA); secretarial training. Secretary to Sir Austin Robinson and editorial assistant, Royal Economic Soc., 1952–60; Senior Geography Mistress, Hertfordshire and Essex High School, Bishop's Stortford, 1961–77 (Dep. Head, 1973–75). President: Assoc. of Assistant Mistresses, 1976–77; Internat. Fedn of Secondary Teachers, 1981–85. *Recreations:* walking, thinking about gardening, travel. *Address:* 26 Fulbrooke Road, Cambridge CB3 9EE. *T:* Cambridge 354909; 103 Clare Court, Judd Street, WC1H 9QP. *T:* 01–837 5822. *Club:* University Women's.

BAIRD, Vice-Adm. Sir Thomas (Henry Eustace), KCB 1980; DL; *b* Canterbury, Kent, 17 May 1924; *s* of Geoffrey Henry and Helen Jane Baird; *m* 1953, Angela Florence Ann Paul, Symington, Ayrshire; one *s* one *d. Educ:* RNC, Dartmouth. Served HM Ships: Trinidad, in support of convoys to Russia, 1941, Midshipman; Bermuda, Russian convoys and landings in N Africa, and Orwell, Russian convoys and Atlantic escort force, 1942; Howe, E Indies, 1943, Sub-Lt; Rapid, E Indies, 1944 until VJ Day, Lieut; St James, Home Fleet, 1946; Ganges, Ratings' New Entry Trng, 1948; Plucky, Exec. Officer, mine clearance in Mediterranean, 1950; Lt Comdr 1952; Veryan Bay, Exec. Officer, W Indies and Falkland Is., 1953; O-in-C, Petty Officers' Leadership Sch., Malta, 1954; Exec. Officer, HMS Whirlwind, Home Fleet and Med., for Suez Op., 1956; Comd, HMS Acute, Dartmouth Trng Sqdn, 1958; Comdr 1959; Comd, HMS Ulysses, Home Fleet, 1960; Staff, C-in-C, Home Fleet, Northwood, 1961; Exec. Officer, Jt Anti-Sub. Sch., Londonderry, 1963; EO, HMS Bulwark, Far East, 1965; Ch. Staff Officer to Cdre, Naval Drafting, 1966; Captain 1967; Dep. Dir, Naval Equipment, Adm., Bath, 1967; Captain: Mine Countermeasures; Fishery Protection and HMS Lochinvar (comd), 1969; Comd, HMS Glamorgan, Far East, W Indies, S Amer., Med., and UK Waters, 1971; Captain of the Fleet, 1973; Rear Adm. 1976; Chief of Staff to C-in-C Naval Home Comd, 1976–77; Dir Gen., Naval Personal Services, 1978–79; Vice-Adm. 1979; Flag Officer Scotland and NI, 1979–82. DL Ayr and Arran, 1982. *Recreations:* cricket, golf, shooting, fishing. *Address:* Craigrethill, Symington, Ayrshire KA1 5QN. *Clubs:* Army and Navy; Prestwick Golf (Prestwick).

BAIRD, Dr Thomas Terence, CB 1977; Chief Medical Officer, Department of Health and Social Services, Northern Ireland, 1972–78, retired; *b* 31 May 1916; *s* of Thomas Baird, Archdeacon of Derry, and Hildegarde Nolan; *m* 1st, 1940, Joan Crosbie; two *d*; 2nd, 1982, Mary Wilson Powell. *Educ:* Haileybury Coll.; Queen's Univ. of Belfast. MB, BCh, BAO, 1939; DPH, 1947; FFCM (RCP), 1972; MRCPI 1973, FRCPI 1975; MRCPEd 1975; FFCM Ireland (Founder Fellow), 1977. Ho. Surg./Ho. Phys., North Lonsdale Hosp., Barrow-in-Furness, 1939–40. Served War, RNVR, 1940–46. Queen's Univ. of Belfast, DPH course, 1946–47. Berks CC: Asst MO, 1947–49; Dep. County MO and Dep. Principal Sch. MO, 1949–54. Welsh Bd of Health: MO, 1954–57; Sen. MO, 1957–62; Min. of Health and Local Govt, Northern Ireland: PMO, 1962–64; Dep. Chief MO, 1964–68; Min. of Health and Social Services, NI, Sen. Dep. Chief MO, 1968–72. Chairman: NI Med. Manpower Adv. Cttee; NI Adv. Cttee on infant mortality and handicaps. Member: GMC, 1973–79; Faculty of Medicine, QUB; NI Council for Postgrad. Med. Educn; Bd, Faculty of Community Medicine, RCPI. Chief Surgeon for Wales, St John Ambulance Bde, 1959–62. QHP 1974–77. CStJ 1959. *Publications:* (jtly) Infection in Hospital—a code of practice, 1971; papers in various learned jls. *Recreations:* fishing, forestry. *Address:* 2 Kensington Road, Belfast BT5 6NF. *T:* Belfast 798020; Port-a-Chapel, Greencastle, Co. Donegal. *T:* Greencastle 38. *Club:* Carlton.

BAIRD, William; Under Secretary, Scottish Home and Health Department, since 1978; *b* 13 Oct. 1927; *s* of Peter and Christina Baird, Airdrie; *m* 1954, Anne Templeton Macfarlane; two *d. Educ:* Airdrie Academy; Glasgow Univ. Entered Scottish Home Dept, 1952; Private Sec. to Perm. Under-Sec. of State, Scottish Office, 1957; Principal, Scottish

Educn Dept, 1958–63; Private Sec. to Minister of State and successive Secs of State for Scotland, 1963–65; Asst Sec., Scottish Educn Dept, 1965–66; Dept of Agriculture and Fisheries for Scotland, 1966–71; Scottish Office Finance Div., 1971–73; Registrar General for Scotland, 1973–78. *Address:* 18 Lygon Road, Edinburgh EH16 5QB. *T:* 031-667 3054. *Club:* Royal Commonwealth Society.

BAIRSTO, Air Marshal Sir Peter (Edward), KBE 1981 (CBE 1973); CB 1980; AFC 1957; Military Aviation Adviser, Ferranti Defence Systems Ltd, Edinburgh, since 1984; *b* 3 Aug. 1926; *s* of late Arthur Bairsto and Beatrice (*née* Lewis); *m* 1947, Kathleen (*née* Clarbour); two *s* one *d. Educ:* Rhyl Grammar Sch. Pilot, FAA, 1944–46; 1946–62: FO RAF Regt, Palestine, Aden Protectorate; Flying Instr; Fighter Pilot, Fighter Comd and Near East; Flight Comdr, 43 Sqdn, and Leader, RAF Aerobatic Team; Sqdn Comdr, 66 Sqdn; RAF Staff Coll.; Wing Comdr, Flying, Nicosia, 1963–64; Op. Requirements, MoD, 1965–67; JSSC Latimer, 1967; Instr, RAF Staff Coll., 1968–70; Stn Comdr, RAF Honington, 1971–73; Dir, Op. Requirements, MoD, 1974–77; AOC Training Units, Support Command, 1977–79; Comdr, Northern Maritime Air Region, 1979–81; Dep. C-in-C, Strike Command, 1981–84. Vice-Chm. (Air), Highland TAVRA, 1982–. Mem., Scottish Sports Council, 1985–. HM Comr, Queen Victoria Sch., Dunblane, 1984–; Chm. Management Bd, RAF Benevolent Fund Home, Alastrean House, Tarland, 1984–. Queen's Commendation for Valuable Services in the Air, 1955 and 1960. CBIM. *Recreations:* golf, fishing, shooting, gardening. *Address:* Lucklaw House, Logie, by Cupar, Fife. *T:* Balmullo 870546. *Clubs:* Royal Air Force; New (Edinburgh); Royal and Ancient Golf, New Golf (St Andrews).

BAKER, Prof. Alan, FRS 1973; Professor of Pure Mathematics, University of Cambridge, since 1974; Fellow of Trinity College, Cambridge, since 1964; *b* 19 Aug. 1939; *o c* of Barnet and Bessie Baker. *Educ:* Stratford Grammar Sch.; University Coll. London; Trinity Coll., Cambridge. BSc (London); MA, PhD (Cantab). Mem., Dept of Mathematics, UCL, 1964–65 and Fellow, UCL, 1979; Research Fellow, 1964–68, and Dir of Studies in Mathematics, 1968–74, Trinity Coll., Cambridge; Mem., Dept of Pure Maths and Math. Statistics, Univ. of Cambridge, 1966–; Reader in Theory of Numbers, 1972–74. Visiting Professor: Univs of Michigan and Colorado, 1969; Stanford Univ., 1974; Mem., Inst. for Advanced Study, Princeton, 1970; First Turán Lectr, J. Bolyai Math. Soc. Hungary, 1978. For. Fellow, Indian Nat. Sci. Acad., 1980. Fields Medal, Internat. Congress of Mathematicians, Nice, 1970; Adams Prize of Univ. of Cambridge, 1971–72. *Publications:* Transcendental Number Theory, 1975; (ed jtly) Transcendence Theory: advances and applications, 1977; A Concise Introduction to the Theory of Numbers, 1984; papers in various mathematical jls. *Recreations:* hiking, travel. *Address:* Trinity College, Cambridge. *T:* Cambridge 338400.

BAKER, Alex Anthony, CBE 1973; MD, MRCP, DPM; FRCPsych; Consultant Psychiatrist with special interest in the elderly to Gloucestershire Clinical Area, 1973–77, retired; *b* 22 March 1922; *m* 1944; two *s* two *d. Educ:* St Mary's Hosp. Med. Sch. Consultant Psychiatrist: Banstead Hosp., 1955; Mother and Baby Unit, Downview Hosp., 1958; St Mary Abbotts Hosp., 1967; Medical Administrator, Banstead Hosp., 1964; sometime Consultant to WHO; Sen. Principal Medical Officer, Dept of Health, 1968; Dir, NHS Hospital Adv. Service, 1969–73. *Publications:* (jtly) Psychiatric Services and Architecture, 1958; (jtly) Social Psychiatry; Psychiatric Disorders in Obstetrics, 1967; Comprehensive Psychiatric Care, 1976; chapters in sundry books; papers in numerous jls on research, psychiatric treatment, organisation of psychiatric services, etc. *Address:* Pineholm, High Close, Bovey Tracey, Devon.

BAKER, Alexander Shelley, CB 1977; OBE 1958; DFC 1944; Assistant Under Secretary of State, Home Office, 1973–77, retired; *b* 5 June 1915; *s* of late Rev. William Shelley Baker and Mrs Winifred Baker, Staines and Stratford E15; *m* 1944, Cynthia, 2nd *d* of late Charles Mould, Great Easton, Leics; two *d. Educ:* West Ham Secondary School. Served RAF, 1939–65 (despatches, 1944; 2 citations French Croix de Guerre); comd Nos 4, 16, 37 and 224 Sqdns and RAF North Front Gibraltar; retd as Group Captain. Principal, Home Office, 1965; Asst Sec., 1969–73. Reader, Church of England. *Recreations:* gardening, bridge. *Address:* High View, Foxearth, near Sudbury, Suffolk. *T:* Sudbury 72548. *Club:* Royal Air Force.

BAKER, Allan; *see* Baker, J. F. A.

BAKER, Sir (Allan) Ivor, Kt 1972; CBE 1944; JP; DL; Chairman, Baker Perkins Holdings Ltd, 1944–75; *b* 2 June 1908; *s* of late Allan Richard Baker; *m* 1935, Josephine, *d* of late A. M. Harley, KC; three *s* one *d. Educ:* Bootham, York; King's Coll., Cambridge; Harvard, USA. Baker Perkins: Student apprentice, 1931; Director, 1935–; Jt Man. Dir., 1942–67; Chm., 1944–75. British Engineers' Assoc.: Mem. Council, 1943–68; Pres., 1960–61; Director: Lloyds Bank Ltd, 1973–79; Lloyds Bank Eastern Region, 1953–73 (Chm., 1973–79); Mitchell Construction Holdings Ltd, 1963–85. Member: Economic Planning Council for East Anglia, 1965–69; Peterborough Development Corp., 1968–78. JP 1954; High Sheriff, 1968–69, DL 1973, Cambridgeshire. *Recreations:* golf, gardening. *Address:* 214 Thorpe Road, Peterborough PE3 6LW. *T:* Peterborough 262437.

BAKER, Ann Maureen, (Mrs D. R. Baker); *see* Jenner, A. M.

BAKER, Anthony Baxter, CBE 1983; JP; Regional Administrator, Northern Regional Health Authority, 1973–83; *b* 12 June 1923; *s* of late Anthony Thurlbeck Baker and Robina Frances Jane (*née* Baxter); *m* 1st, 1946, Mary Margherita Patterson (*d* 1978); one *s* three *d*; 2nd, 1981, Judith Margaret Ayers, JP. *Educ:* Tynemouth High Sch.; Durham Univ. DPA; FHA. RAFVR, UK, Canada and Iceland, 1942–46. Admin. Asst, later Dep. Sec., SE Northumberland HMC, 1949–60; Asst Sec., later Principal Asst Sec., Newcastle Regional Hosp. Bd, 1960–73. JP Tynemouth 1965; former Chm., North Tyneside PSD. *Recreations:* Rugby football (PP Percy Park RFC; PP Northumberland RFU), golf. *Address:* 59 Broadway, Tynemouth, North Shields NE30 2LJ. *T:* North Shields 574660.

BAKER, Anthony Castelli, LVO 1980; MBE 1975; HM Diplomatic Service, retired; *b* 27 Dec. 1921; *s* of late Alfred Guy Baker and of Luciana (*née* Castelli). *Educ:* Merchant Taylors' Sch., Northwood, Mddx. Served War: munitions worker, 1940–41; volunteered for RAFVR and served in UK, ME and Italy, 1941–46 (Flt Lieut). Joined HM Diplomatic Service, 1946, served in Rome and Paris, 1946–50, Third Sec., Prague, 1951; Hamburg, 1953; Vice-Consul, Milan, 1954; Third, later Second Sec., Athens, 1959; Second Sec., Beirut, 1963; First Sec., Cairo, 1965; Naples, 1968; Turin, 1970; First Sec. Commercial, Calcutta, 1972; Consul, Montreal, 1975; First Sec. Commercial, Port of Spain, 1976; Consul, Genoa, 1979–81. Officer, Order of Merit (Italy), 1980. *Recreations:* tennis, watching cricket, travelling, jazz music. *Address:* c/o Flat 2, 44 Elsworthy Road, NW3 3BU; Box 91, La Bisbal, Gerona, Spain. *Clubs:* Royal Air Force, MCC; Gloucestershire CC.

BAKER, Arthur John, CBE 1981; Principal, Brockenhurst Tertiary College (formerly Brockenhurst Grammar School, then Brockenhurst Sixth Form College), since 1969; *b* 29 Nov. 1928; *s* of Arthur Reginald and Ruth Baker; *m* 1953, June Henrietta Dunham; one *s* two *d. Educ:* Southampton Univ. (BSc; DipEd). Mathematics Master, Hampton Grammar Sch., 1952–55; Dep. Head, Sunbury Grammar Sch., 1955–61; Headmaster, Christchurch Grammar Sch., 1961–69. *Recreations:* walking, gardening. *Address:* 93 New Forest Drive, Brockenhurst, Hampshire SO42 7QT. *T:* Lymington 23138.

BAKER, Cecil John; Chairman: Hunting Gate Group Ltd, since 1980; Alliance and Leicester Building Society (formerly Alliance Building Society), since 1981; *b* 2 Sept. 1915; *s* of late Frederick William Baker and Mildred Beatrice Palmer; *m* 1st, 1942, Kathleen Cecilia Henning (marr. diss. 1965); one *s*; 2nd, 1971, Joan Beatrice Barnes; one *d. Educ:* Whitgift Sch.; LSE (LLB 1939; BSc(Econ) 1949); Inst. of Actuaries. FIA 1948; ACII 1937. Sec., Insurance Inst. of London, 1945–49; Investment Manager, London Assurance, 1950–64; Investment Consultant, Hambros Bank Ltd, 1964–74; Chairman: Pension Fund Property Unit Trust, 1966–86; Charities Property Unit Trust, 1967–; Agricl Property Unit Trust for Pension Funds and Charities, 1976–; Victory Insurance Holdings Ltd, 1979–85; British American Property Unit Trust, 1982–; United Real Property Trust plc, 1983– (Dir, 1982–); Director: Hampton Gold Mining Areas plc, 1972–85; Abbey Life Group plc, 1985–. *Recreations:* golf, travel. *Address:* 73 Brook Street, W1Y 1YE. *T:* 01-499 7191.

BAKER, Charles A.; *see* Arnold-Baker.

BAKER, Derek; *see* Baker, L. G. D.

BAKER, Douglas Robert Pelham, FCA; Chairman, Touche Ross & Co., Chartered Accountants, since 1984; *b* 21 May 1929. With Touche Ross & Co., 1945–47 and 1949–. Royal Naval Service, 1947–49. *Address:* Touche Ross & Co., Hill House, 1 Little New Street, EC4A 3TR. *T:* 01-353 8011.

BAKER, Hon. Francis Edward N.; *see* Noel-Baker.

BAKER, Francis Eustace, CBE 1984 (OBE 1979); Governor and Commander-in-Chief, St Helena and Dependencies, since 1984; *b* 19 April 1933; *s* of Stephen and Jessica Wilhelmina Baker; *m* 1957, Constance Anne Shilling; two *s* two *d. Educ:* Borden Grammar Sch.; New Coll., Oxford (MA). Nat. Service, RN, 1955–57 (Sub Lieut). Admin. Officer, HMOCS, 1957; Solomon Is, 1958–63; farming, 1963–67; Admin. Officer, Condominium of New Hebrides, 1967–79; Chief Sec. to Falkland Is Govt, 1979–83. Silver Jubilee Medal, 1977. *Recreations:* swimming, reading, farming, interesting motor cars. *Address:* Plantation House, St Helena; Dark Orchard, Primrose Lane, Bredgar, near Sittingbourne, Kent ME9 8EH. *T:* Wormshill 295.

BAKER, Geoffrey, QC 1970; **His Honour Judge Geoffrey Baker;** a Circuit Judge, since 1978; *b* 5 April 1925; *er s* of late Sidney and Cecilia Baker, Bradford; *m* 1948, Sheila (*née* Hill); two *s* one *d. Educ:* Bradford Grammar Sch.; Leeds Univ.; LLB (Hons). Called to Bar, Inner Temple, 1947. Recorder: of Pontefract, 1967–71; of Sunderland, 1971; a Recorder of the Crown Court, 1972–78. Pres., Leeds and WR Medico-Legal Soc., 1984–85 (Mem. Cttee, 1980–). Chm., Standing Council, Convocation of Leeds Univ., 1986– (Mem. 1980–); Member: Adv. Cttee on Law, Leeds Univ., 1983–; Court, Leeds Univ., 1984–; Pres., Leeds Univ. Law Graduates' Assoc., 1981–. *Recreations:* gardening, painting, photography. *Address:* c/o Courts Administrator, CMA House, King Street, Leeds LS1 2HW.

BAKER, Geoffrey Hunter, CMG 1962; HM Diplomatic Service, retired; *b* 4 Aug. 1916; *s* of late Thomas Evelyn Baker and Gladys Beatrice Baker (*née* Marsh); *m* 1963, Anita Wägeler; one *d. Educ:* Haberdashers' Aske's Hampstead Sch.; Royal Masonic Sch., Bushey, Herts; Gonville and Caius Coll., Cambridge (Scholar). Joined Consular Service, 1938; Vice-Consul at Hamburg, 1938, Danzig, 1939, Bergen, 1939; captured by German forces there, April 1940; Vice-Consul, Basra, 1942, Jedda, 1942; Foreign Office, 1945–47; First Sec., Rangoon, 1947–51, Tehran, 1951–52; FO, 1953–54; NATO Def. Coll., Paris, 1954; Consul-Gen., Hanoi, 1954–56; UK Delegation, UN, Nov. 1956–March 1957; Cabinet Office, 1957–60; UK Delegation to the European Free Trade Association, Geneva, 1960–66; Consul-General, Munich, 1966–71, Zagreb, 1971–74. Order of Merit (Bavaria), 1971. *Recreations:* tennis, sailing, reading, and listening to music. *Address:* 10 Leigh Road, Highfield, Southampton SO2 1EF. *Clubs:* United Oxford & Cambridge University; Cambridge University Cruising (Cambridge).

BAKER, George William, CBE 1977 (OBE 1971); VRD 1952 (Clasp 1979); HM Diplomatic Service, retired; *b* 7 July 1917; *e s* of late George William Baker and of Lilian Turnbull Baker; *m* 1942, Audrey Martha Elizabeth, *e d* of Harry and Martha Day; two *d. Educ:* Chigwell Sch.; Hertford Coll., Oxford (Colonial Service Second Devonshire Course). London Div., RNVR, 1937–62; served War, RN, 1939–45. Colonial Admin. Service, Tanganyika, 1946–62: Asst Colonial Attaché, Washington (incl. service in UK Delegn to Trusteeship Council at UN), 1957; Defence Sec., Tanganyika, 1959; Head of Tanganyika Govt Information Dept, 1959–62; retd after Tanganyika Independence, 1962. Joined CRO, 1962; First Sec. (Information) and Dir of British Inf. Services, British High Commn, Freetown, 1962–65; served in FCO (Consular and Defence Depts), 1965–69; First Sec. and Head of Chancery, Kinshasa, 1969–72; Dep. British Govt Rep., St Vincent and Grenada, Windward Is, 1972–74; British Commissioner, Port Moresby, Papua New Guinea, 1974–75, High Comr to Papua New Guinea, 1975–77. Mem., E Sussex Cttee, VSO, 1984– (Chm., 1980–84). A Vice-Pres., Royal African Soc., 1973–; Hon. Mem. and Foreign Affairs Advr, Scientific Exploration Soc. Chm., Heathfield Cttee, Sussex Housing Assoc. for Aged, 1979–84; Chm., Waldron Br., Wealden Cons. Assoc. and Vice-Chm., Constituency Political Cttee, 1983–84. Mem. Guild of Freemen of City of London, 1980–; Freeman, City of London, 1980; Liveryman, Clockmakers' Co., 1984– (Mem., 1981–). Mem., Queenhithe Ward Club, City of London. Member: Exeter Flotilla; Hertford Soc. *Publications:* official booklets and contribs to learned jls. *Recreations:* photography, fishing, sailing, climbing, tennis, Rugby Union, cricket, flying, clock and cabinet-making. *Address:* Crosswinds, Coreway, Sidford, Sidmouth, Devon EX10 9SD. *T:* Sidmouth 78845. *Club:* MCC.

See also Baron Coleridge.

BAKER, Gordon Meldrum; HM Diplomatic Service; Counsellor, Head of Chancery and Consul-General, Santiago, since 1986; *b* 4 July 1941; *o s* of Walter John Ralph Gordon Baker and Kathleen Margaret Henrietta Dawe Baker (*née* Meldrum); *m* 1978, Sheila Mary Megson. *Educ:* St Andrew's Sch., Bawdrip, near Bridgwater. MSc Bradford 1976. Lord Chancellor's Dept, 1959–66; transf. to HM Diplomatic Service, 1966; Commonwealth Office, 1966–68; FO (later FCO), 1968–69; Lagos, 1969–72; First Sec., FCO, 1973–75 (Resident Clerk, 1974–75); sabbatical at Postgrad. Sch. of Studies in Industrial Technol., Univ. of Bradford, 1975–76; FCO, 1976–78 (Res. Clerk, 1976–78); First Sec. (Chancery/Information), subseq. First Sec., Head of Chancery and Consul, Brasilia, 1978–81; Asst Head, Mexico and Central America Dept, FCO, 1982–84; Counsellor, 1984; on secondment to British Aerospace, 1984–86. *Recreations:* walking, watching birds, amateur dramatics, browsing. *Address:* c/o Foreign and Commonwealth Office, SW1A 2AH.

BAKER, Howard Henry, Jr; Senior Partner, Vinson and Elkins, and Baker, Worthington, Crossley, Stansberry & Woolf, law firms; *b* 15 Nov. 1925; *s* of Howard H. Baker and Dora Ladd; *m* 1951, Joy Dirksen; one *s* one *d. Educ:* McCallie Sch.; Tulane Univ.; Univ.

of Tennessee (LLB 1949). Served USN, 1943–46. Director: AT & T; Gannett Co. Inc.; MCA. Former Chm. of Bd, First Nat. Bank, Oneida, Tenn. US Senate: Senator from Tennessee 1967–85; Minority Leader, 1977–81; Majority Leader, 1981–85; former Co-Chm., Senate Select Cttee on Presidential Campaign Activities, and mem. other Senate cttees. Member: Adv. Bd, Merrill Lynch; Trustees Bd, Mayo Clinic. Mem., Amer. Bar Assoc. Presidential Medal of Freedom, 1984. *Address:* Huntsville, Tenn 37756, USA.

BAKER, Sir Humphrey D. B. S.; *see* Sherston-Baker.

BAKER, Maj.-Gen. Ian Helstrip, CBE 1977 (MBE 1965); rcds, psc; Secretary, University College London, since 1982; *b* 26 Nov. 1927; *s* of late Henry Hubert Baker and Mary Clare Baker (*née* Coles); *m* 1956, Susan Anne, *d* of Major Henry Osmond Lock, York House, Dorchester, Dorset; one *s* one *d* (and one *s* decd). *Educ:* St Peter's Sch., York; St Edmund Hall, Oxford; RMA, Sandhurst. Commnd 2nd Lieut, RA, 1948; 10th Fd Regt RA, 1949–51; Lieut 1950; 2nd Regt RHA, 1951–53; Capt. 1953; RAC Centre, 1953–55; transf. RTR, 1955; 4th Royal Tank Regt, 1955–57; HQ 10th Inf. Bde, 1957–58; Staff Coll., 1959; Major 1960; DAAG HQ 17 Gurkha Div., Malaya and Singapore, 1960–62; OC Parachute Sqdn RAC (C Sqdn 2nd Royal Tank Regt), 1962–65; Instr Staff Coll., Camberley, and Bt Lt-Col, 1965; GSO1 and Asst Sec., Chiefs of Staff Cttee, MoD, 1966–67; Lt-Col 1966; CO, 1st Royal Tank Regt, UK and BAOR, 1967–69; Col 1970; Col, RTR, 1970–71; Brig. 1972; Comdr, 7th Armoured Bde, BAOR, 1972–74; RCDS, 1974; Brig. Gen. Staff, HQ UKLF, 1975–77; Service Fellow, St Catharine's Coll., Cambridge, 1977; Maj.-Gen., 1978; Asst Chief of Gen. Staff 1978–80; GOC, NE District, 1980–82. Member: Army Combat Develt Cttee, MoD, 1975–80; MoD Op. Requirements Cttee, 1978–80; Hd, UK Delegn, NATO talks on weapons and equipment policy, 1978–80. Col Comdt, Royal Tank Regt, 1981–86. Mem., Internat. Cttee of UK Univ. Administrators, 1984–. Hon. Pres., Medical and Dental Students Soc., UCL, 1983–. Governor, Welbeck Coll., 1980–82. *Publications:* contribs to service and university papers and journals. *Recreations:* skiing, sailing, outdoor pursuits. *Address:* University College London, Gower Street, WC1. *T:* 01–387 7050; Owen's Farm, Hook, Hants. *T:* Hook 2524. *Club:* Athenæum.

BAKER, Sir Ivor; *see* Baker, Sir A. I.

BAKER, James Addison, III; Secretary of the US Treasury, since 1985; *b* 28 April 1930; *s* of James A. Baker, Jr and Bonner Means Baker; *m* 1973, Susan Garrett; eight *c*. *Educ:* Princeton Univ. (BA); Univ. of Texas at Austin (law degree). Served US Marine Corps, 1952–54. Practised law, firm of Andrews, Kurth, Campbell and Jones, Houston, Texas, 1957–75, 1977–81. Under Sec. of Commerce, US Govt, 1975; National Chairman: President Ford's re-elecn campaign, 1976; George Bush for President Cttee, 1979–80; Dep. Dir, Reagan–Bush Transition and Sen. Advr to 1980 Reagan–Bush Cttee, 1980–Jan. 1981; Chief of Staff to US President, 1981–85. Numerous hon. degrees. *Recreations:* hunting, fishing, tennis, golf. *Address:* Department of the Treasury, 1500 Pennsylvania Avenue, NW, Washington, DC 20220, USA. *T:* 202/566–2000. *Clubs:* numerous social, civic and paternal.

BAKER, Dame Janet (Abbott), DBE 1976 (CBE 1970); professional singer; *b* 21 Aug. 1933; *d* of Robert Abbott Baker and May (*née* Pollard); *m* 1957, James Keith Shelley. *Educ:* The College for Girls, York; Wintringham, Grimsby. Mem., Munster Trust. Pres., RSAMD, 1983–. Daily Mail Kathleen Ferrier Award, 1956; Queen's Prize, Royal College of Music, 1959; Shakespeare Prize, Hamburg, 1971; Copenhagen Sonning Prize, 1979. Hon. DMus: Birmingham, 1968; Leicester, 1974; London, 1974; Hull, 1975; Oxon, 1975; Leeds, 1980; Lancaster, 1983; York, 1984; Hon. MusD Cantab, 1984; Hon. LLD Aberdeen, 1980; Hon. DLitt Bradford, 1983. Hon. Fellow: St Anne's Coll., Oxford, 1975; Downing Coll., Cambridge, 1985. FRSA 1979. *Publication:* Full Circle (autobiog.), 1982. *Recreations:* reading, tennis, walking. *Address:* c/o Ibbs & Tillett Ltd, 450–452 Edgware Road, W2 1EG.

BAKER, John Arnold, DL; **His Honour Judge Baker**; a Circuit Judge, since 1973; *b* Calcutta, 5 Nov. 1925; *s* of late William Sydney Baker, MC and Hilda Dora Baker (*née* Swiss); *m* 1954, Edith Muriel Joy Heward; two *d*. *Educ:* Plymouth Coll.; Wellington Sch., Somerset; Wadham Coll., Oxford (MA, BCL). Treas., Oxford Union, 1948. Admitted Solicitor, 1951; called to Bar, Gray's Inn, 1960. A Recorder, 1972–73. Chm., Nat. League of Young Liberals, 1952–53; contested (L): Richmond, 1959 and 1964; Dorking, 1970; Vice-Pres., Liberal Party, 1968–69; Chm., Liberal Party Exec., 1969–70. DL Surrey, 1986. *Recreations:* music, boating. *Address:* 1 Rosemont Road, Richmond, Surrey. *T:* 01–940 6983.

BAKER, Rt. Rev. John Austin; *see* Salisbury, Bishop of.

BAKER, John B.; *see* Brayne-Baker.

BAKER, John Burkett, QC 1975; **His Honour Judge J. Burkett Baker**; a Circuit Judge, since 1978; *b* 17 Sept. 1931; *s* of Philip and Grace Baker; *m* 1955, Margaret Mary Smeaton; three *s* seven *d*. *Educ:* Finchley Catholic Grammar Sch.; White Fathers, Bishops Waltham; UC Exeter. LLB London. RAF, 1955–58. Called to Bar, Gray's Inn, 1957; practised from 1958. Prosecuting Counsel to Dept of Health and Social Security, 1969–75; Dep. Chm., Shropshire QS, 1970–71; a Recorder of the Crown Court, 1972–78. Marriage Counsellor, Catholic Marriage Adv. Council (Chm., 1981–83); Pres., Barnet, Haringey and Hertsmere Marriage Guidance Council, 1982–. Governor: Bedford Coll., London, 1983–85; Holy Family Convent, Enfield, 1984–. Papal Cross Pro Ecclesia et Pontifice, 1986. *Address:* 43 The Ridgeway, Enfield, Mddx EN2 8PD.

BAKER, (John Frederic) Allan, CB 1957; FEng; Ministry of Transport, retired; *b* 5 Oct. 1903; *s* of late H. J. Baker; *m* 1927, Nancy Elizabeth Wells; one *d* (and one *s* decd). *Educ:* St Paul's Sch. After Local Authority experience in Middlesex, 1922–, joined Ministry of Transport, 1929, serving in Exeter, Bedford, Nottingham and London; apptd Divisional Road Engineer for Wales and Mon, at Cardiff, 1947, and Dep. Chief Engineer at Headquarters, 1953; Chief Engineer and Dir of Highway Engineering, 1954–65. Member: Road Research Board, 1954–65; London Roads Cttee, 1959; Traffic Signs Cttee, 1963; Cons. Adviser to Automobile Assoc., 1965–69. Past Chm., Road Engrg Industry Cttee of BSI; Vice-Pres., Internat. Exec. Cttee of Permanent Internat. Assoc. of Road Congresses, 1960–72 and Pres. d'Honneur, Brit. Nat. Cttee. Mem. Council, ICE, 1956–61, 1962–67. Founder Fellow, Fellowship of Engineering, 1976; Hon. FIMunE; Hon. FInstHE; Hon. FICE. Viva Shield and Gold Medal, Worshipful Co. of Carmen, (for pioneering the British Motorway system), 1967. *Address:* 36 Imber Close, Ember Lane, Esher, Surrey. *T:* 01–398 3331.

See also B. D. Dance.

BAKER, John Hamilton, LLD; FBA 1984; Reader in English Legal History, Cambridge University, since 1983; Fellow of St Catharine's College, since 1971; *b* 10 April 1944; *s* of Kenneth Lee Vincent Baker, QPM and Marjorie (*née* Bagshaw); *m* 1968, Veronica Margaret, *d* of Rev. W. S. Lloyd; two *d*. *Educ:* King Edward VI Grammar School, Chelmsford; UCL (LLB 1965 (Andrews Medal), PhD 1968); MA Cantab 1971, LLD 1984, Yorke Prize, 1975. FRHistS 1980. Called to the Bar, Inner Temple, 1966, *aeg* Gray's Inn, 1978. Asst Lectr, Faculty of Laws, UCL, 1965–67, Lectr, 1967–71; Cambridge University: Librarian, Squire Law Library, 1971–73; Univ. Lectr in Law, 1973–83; Junior Proctor, 1980–81. Vis. Prof., European Univ. Inst., Florence, 1979; Vis. Lectr, Harvard Law Sch., 1982; Mellon Senior Res. Fellow, H. E. Huntington Lib., San Marino, Calif., 1983; Ford Special Lectr, Oxford Univ., 1984. Jt Literary Dir, Selden Soc., 1981–. Ames Prize, Harvard, 1985. *Publications:* An Introduction to English Legal History, 1971, 2nd edn 1979; English Legal Manuscripts, vol. I, 1975, vol. II, 1978; The Reports of Sir John Spelman, 1977–78; (ed) Legal Records and the Historian, 1978; Manual of Law French, 1979; The Order of Serjeants at Law, 1984; English Legal Manuscripts in the USA, 1985; The Legal Profession and the Common Law, 1986; articles in legal and hist. jls. *Address:* 75 Hurst Park Avenue, Cambridge CB4 2AB. *T:* Cambridge 62251; St Catharine's College, Cambridge CB2 1RL. *T:* Cambridge 338300.

BAKER, John William; Joint Managing Director, Central Electricity Generating Board, since 1986 (Member, since 1980); *b* 5 Dec. 1937; *s* of Reginald and Wilhelmina Baker; *m* 1st, 1962, Pauline (*née* Moore); one *s*; 2nd, 1976, Gillian (*née* Bullen). *Educ:* Harrow Weald County Grammar Sch.; Oriel Coll., Oxford. Served Army, 1959–61. MoT, 1961–70; DoE, 1970–74; Dep. Chief Exec., Housing Corp., 1974–78; Sec., CEGB, 1979–80. *Recreations:* tennis, squash, bridge, music, theatre. *Address:* Central Electricity Generating Board, Sudbury House, 15 Newgate Street, EC1A 7AU. *T:* 01–634 7039.

BAKER, Sir Joseph; *see* Baker, Sir S. J.

BAKER, Rt. Hon. Kenneth (Wilfred); PC 1984; MP (C) Mole Valley, since 1983 (St Marylebone, Oct. 1970–1983); Secretary of State for Education and Science, since 1986; *b* 3 Nov. 1934; *s* of late W. M. Baker, OBE and of Mrs Baker (*née* Harries); *m* 1963, Mary Elizabeth Gray-Muir; one *s* two *d*. *Educ:* St Paul's Sch.; Magdalen Coll., Oxford. Nat. Service, 1953–55: Lieut in Gunners, N Africa; Artillery Instructor to Libyan Army. Oxford, 1955–58 (Sec. of Union). Served Twickenham Borough Council, 1960–62. Contested (C): Poplar, 1964; Acton, 1966; MP (C) Acton, March 1968–70. Parly Sec., CSD, 1972–74; PPS to Leader of Opposition, 1974–75; Minister of State and Minister for Information Technology, DTI, 1981–84; a Minister for Local Govt, DoE, 1984–85; Sec. of State for the Environment, 1985–86. Mem., Public Accounts Cttee, 1969–70. Mem. Exec., 1922 Cttee. Chm., Hansard Soc., 1978–81. Sec. Gen., UN Conf. of Parliamentarians on World Population and Development, 1978. *Publications:* I Have No Gun But I Can Spit, 1980; (ed) London Lines, 1982, 1984. *Recreation:* collecting books. *Address:* House of Commons, SW1. *Clubs:* Athenæum, Carlton.

BAKER, Prof. (Leonard Graham) Derek, MA, BLitt; Professor of History, University of Texas, since 1986; *b* 21 April 1931; *s* of Leonard and late Phoebe Caroline Baker; *m* 1970, Jean Dorothy Johnston; one *s* one *d*. *Educ:* Christ's Hospital; Oriel Coll., Oxford (1st Class Hons Modern History 1955, MA, BLitt). Captain, Royal Signals, 1950–52. Senior History Master, The Leys School, 1956–66; Lecturer in Medieval History, Univ. of Edinburgh, 1966–79; Headmaster, Christ's Hosp., 1979–85. Editor, Ecclesiastical History Soc., 1969; Pres., British Sub-Commission, Commission Internationale d'Histoire Ecclésiastique Comparée, 1971. FRHistS 1969. *Publications:* Portraits and Documents, Vol. 1 1967, Vol. 2 1969; Partnership in Excellence, 1974; (ed) Studies in Church History, 7–17, 1970–80 (subsidia 1–2, 1978–79); numerous articles in historical jls. *Recreations:* singing; climbing, mountaineering, pot-holing, camping; good company; food and wine; travel. *Address:* 5 Allendale, Southwater, Horsham, Sussex RH13 7UE; 30 Dick Place, Edinburgh EH9 2JB. *T:* 031–667 5920. *Clubs:* National Liberal; Leander (Henley-on-Thames).

BAKER, Mark Alexander Wyndham; Secretary, United Kingdom Atomic Energy Authority, since 1986; *b* 19 June 1940; *s* of late Lt-Comdr Alexander Arthur Wyndham Baker, RN and Renée Gavrelle Stenson (*née* Macnaghten); *m* 1964, Meriel, *yr d* of Capt. Hugh Chetwynd-Talbot, MBE and Cynthia Chetwynd-Talbot; one *s* one *d*. *Educ:* Prince Edward Sch., Salisbury, S Rhodesia; University Coll. of Rhodesia & Nyasaland (Beit Schol.; BA London); Christ Church, Oxford (Rhodes Schol.; MA). United Kingdom Atomic Energy Authority, 1964–: Sec., 1976–78, Gen. Sec., 1978–81, AERE, Harwell; Dir of Personnel and Admin, Northern Div., 1981–84; Authority Personnel Officer, 1984–86. *Recreations:* gardening, squash, walking, words. *Address:* The Old School, Fyfield, Abingdon, Oxon OX13 5LR. *T:* Frilford Heath 390724. *Clubs:* United Oxford & Cambridge University; Antrobus Dining (Cheshire).

BAKER, Martyn Murray; Under Secretary, Regional Director, North Western Region, Department of Trade and Industry, since 1986; *b* 10 March 1944; *s* of Norman and Constance Baker; *m* 1970, Rosemary Caroline Holdich. *Educ:* Dulwich Coll.; Pembroke Coll., Oxford (MA). Asst Principal, Min. of Aviation, 1965–67; Asst Private Sec. to Minister of State, Min. of Technology, 1968–69; Private Sec. to Parly Under Secs of State, Min. of Technology, Min. of Aviation Supply, and DTI, 1969–71; Principal 1971; Principal Private Sec. to Sec. of State for Trade, 1977–78; Asst Sec., Dept of Trade, 1978; Counsellor, Civil Aviation and Shipping, Washington, 1978–82; Asst Sec., Air Div., 1982–85, Projects and Export Policy Div., 1985–86, DTI. Mem., Export Guarantees Advisory Council, 1985–. *Address:* Department of Trade and Industry, Manchester M1 4BA.

BAKER, Maurice S.; Managing Director, F. W. Woolworth & Co. Ltd, 1967–71, retired; *b* 27 Jan. 1911; *s* of Sidney B. Baker and Ellen Elizabeth (*née* Airey); *m* 1st, 1935, Helen Johnstone (*née* Tweedie) (*d* 1977); one *s*; 2nd, 1978, Kirsten Randine (*née* Haugen). *Educ:* Lowestoft Grammar School. Trainee Manager, F. W. Woolworth & Co. Ltd, 1928; RAOC, 1940–46 (Major); rejoined company; Dir 1962. Officer, Legion of Merit (US), 1945. *Recreation:* bowls (Pres., 1975, Hon. Life Mem., 1983, Surrey County Bowling Assoc.). *Address:* Ness Point, 7a Woodcote Park Avenue, Purley, CR2 3ND. *T:* 01–660 3718.

BAKER, Michael John David; a Recorder of the Crown Court, since 1980; *b* 17 April 1934; *s* of late Ernest Bowden Baker and of Dulcie Baker; *m* 1958, Edna Harriet Lane; one *s* one *d*. *Educ:* Trinity Sch. of John Whitgift; Bristol Univ. (LLB Hons). Admitted solicitor, 1957. Flying Officer, RAF, 1957–60. Joined firm of Glanvilles, Wells & Way, Solicitors, Portsmouth, 1960; Partner, 1963–. Coroner, S Hampshire, 1973– (Asst Dep. Coroner, 1971; Dep. Coroner, 1972). Pres., Southern Coroners Soc., 1975–76; Mem. Council, Coroners Soc. of England and Wales, 1979–. *Recreations:* walking, tennis and cricket (playing and watching), the theatre, music (particularly choral singing). *Address:* The Drift, Park Crescent, Emsworth, Hants PO10 7NT. *T:* Emsworth 372748. *Clubs:* Law Society; Emsworth Sailing; Waterlooville Rotary.

BAKER, Nicholas Brian; MP (C) North Dorset, since 1979; *b* 23 Nov. 1938; *m* 1970, Penelope Carol d'Abo; one *s* one *d*. *Educ:* Clifton Coll.; Exeter Coll., Oxford (MA). Partner in Frere Cholmeley, solicitors, WC2, 1973–. PPS to Min. of State for the Armed Forces, 1981–83, for Defence Procurement, MoD, 1983–84, to Sec. of State for Defence, MoD, 1984–86. *Publication:* Better Company: proposals for company law reform (Bow Gp), 1973. *Recreations:* squash, music, English countryside. *Address:* House of Commons, SW1. *Clubs:* Wimborne Conservative, Blandford Constitutional.

BAKER, Paul Vivian; His Honour Judge Paul Baker; a Circuit Judge, since 1983; *b* 27 March 1923; *er s* of Vivian Cyril Baker and Maud Lydia Baker; *m* 1957, Stella Paterson Eadie, *d* of William Eadie, MD; one *s* one *d*. *Educ:* City of London Sch.; University Coll., Oxford (BCL, MA). Called to Bar, Lincoln's Inn, 1950, Bencher, 1979; QC 1972. Editor, Law Quarterly Review, 1971–. *Recreations:* music, gardening. *Address:* 9 Old Square, Lincoln's Inn, WC2A 3SR. *T:* 01–242 2633. *Clubs:* Athenæum, Authors'.

BAKER, Prof. Peter Frederick, ScD; FRS 1976; FKC 1985; Halliburton Professor and Head of Department of Physiology, King's College, London, since 1975; *b* 11 March 1939; *s* of F. T. Baker and D. E. Skelton; *m* 1966, Phyllis Light; one *s* three *d*. *Educ:* Lincoln Sch.; Emmanuel Coll., Cambridge (Scholar; BA Natural Sciences Tripos, Cl. 1, 1960; PhD 1964; ScD 1980). FIBiol 1976. Univ. of Cambridge: Demonstrator in Physiol., 1963–66; Lectr in Physiol., 1966–74; Fellow, Emmanuel Coll., Cambridge, 1962–74. Mem., AFRC, 1986–. Mem., Univ. of London Senate, 1982–. Guest Investigator, Rockefeller Univ., NY, 1964. G. L. Brown Lectr, Physiological Soc., 1977. Scientific Medal, Zool Soc. of London, 1975; Wander Prize, Switzerland, 1981. *Publications:* Calcium Movement in Excitable Cells (with H. Reuter), 1975; The Squid Axon, 1984; papers on cell physiol. in Jl of Physiol. and other sci. jls. *Recreation:* natural history. *Address:* Meadow Cottage, Bourn, Cambridge. *T:* Caxton 212.

BAKER, Peter Maxwell; QC 1974; **His Honour Judge Peter Baker;** a Circuit Judge, since 1983; *b* 26 March 1930; *s* of late Harold Baker and of Rose Baker; *m* 1954, Jacqueline Mary Marshall; three *d*. *Educ:* King Edward VII Sch., Sheffield; Exeter Coll., Oxford. MA Oxon. Called to Bar, Gray's Inn, 1956 (Holker Senior Exhibitioner); Junior, NE Circuit, 1960; a Recorder of the Crown Court, 1972–83. *Recreations:* yachting, music, watching others garden. *Address:* 28 Snaithing Lane, Sheffield S10 3LG. *Club:* Sheffield (Sheffield).

BAKER, Richard Douglas James, OBE 1976; RD 1979; broadcaster and author; *b* Willesden, London, 15 June 1925; *s* of Albert and Jane Isobel Baker; *m* 1961, Margaret Celia Martin; two *s*. *Educ:* Kilburn Grammar Sch.; Peterhouse, Cambridge (MA). Served War, Royal Navy, 1943–46. Actor, 1948; Teacher, 1949; Third Programme Announcer, 1950–53; BBC TV Newsreader, 1954–82; Commentator for State Occasion Outside Broadcasts, 1967–70; TV Introductions to Promenade Concerts, 1960–; Panellist on BBC2's Face the Music, 1966–79; Presenter, Omnibus, BBC TV, 1983; on Radio 4: Presenter of Start the Week with Richard Baker, 1970–; These You Have Loved, 1972–77; Baker's Dozen, 1978–; Rollercoaster, 1984; on Radio 2: Presenter of Melodies for You, 1986–. Columnist, Now! Magazine, 1979–80. Dir, Youth and Music; Mem., Exec. Cttee, Friends of Covent Garden; Governor, NYO of GB, 1985–. TV Newscaster of the Year (Radio Industries Club), 1972, 1974, 1979; BBC Radio Personality of the Year (Variety Club of GB), 1984. FRSA. Hon. FLCM 1974; Hon. LLD: Strathclyde, 1979; Aberdeen, 1983. *Publications:* Here is the News (broadcasts), 1966; The Terror of Tobermory, 1972; The Magic of Music, 1975; Dry Ginger, 1977; Richard Baker's Music Guide, 1979; Mozart, 1982. *Recreations:* gardening, the gramophone. *Address:* c/o Bagenal Harvey Organisation, 1A Cavendish Square, W1M 9HA. *T:* 01–637 5541 (Agent). *Club:* Garrick.

BAKER, Richard Hugh; HM Diplomatic Service; Deputy High Commissioner, Ottawa, since 1982; *b* 22 Oct. 1935; *s* of Hugh Cuthbert Baker and Muriel Lovenda Baker (*née* Owens); *m* 1963, Patricia Marianne Haigh Thomas; one *s* three *d*. *Educ:* Marlborough Coll.; New Coll., Oxford. Army (2nd Lieut RA), 1954–56. Plebiscite Officer, UN Plebiscite, S Cameroons, 1960–61; joined Diplomatic Service, 1962; 3rd, later 2nd, then 1st Sec., Addis Ababa, 1963–66; Foreign Office, 1967; Private Sec. to Permanent Under-Sec. of State, Foreign Office (later FCO), 1967–70; 1st Sec. and Head of Chancery, Warsaw, 1970–72; FCO, 1973–76; RCDS 1977; Econ. and Financial Counsellor, and Dep. Head, UK Perm. Delegn to OECD, Paris, 1978–82. *Recreations:* music, painting, wind-surfing. *Address:* c/o Foreign and Commonwealth Office, SW1.

BAKER, Scott; *see* Baker, T. S. G.

BAKER, Sir (Stanislaus) Joseph, Kt 1958; CB 1947; retired as Receiver for the Metropolitan Police District and Courts (1952–60); *b* 7 March 1898; *s* of Henry G. Baker, Liverpool; *m* 1920, Eleonora White (*d* 1981); one *d* (and one *d* decd). *Educ:* St Francis Xavier Sch.; Liverpool Univ. BSc 1919, Hons 1920. Served European War, 1914–18, RE 1915–17; Royal Artillery, 1917–18. Local Government Board for Ireland, 1920; Chief Sec.'s Office, Dublin Castle, 1922; Irish Office, 1922; Home Office, 1924; Sec. to Privy Council Cttee on question of contributions to Imperial Funds from the Islands of Jersey, Guernsey and Man, 1925. Asst Under-Sec. of State, Home Office, 1941–52. Chairman: National Police Fund Advisory Council, 1946–52; Police Regional Services Cttee, 1945–48; Police Common Services Cttee, 1948–52; Mem. Board of Governors of Police Coll., 1947–52. Chm., Kenya Police Commission, 1953. *Address:* Camplehaye Hotel, Lamerton, Tavistock, Devon PL19 8QD. *T:* Tavistock 2702.

BAKER, Stephen; Managing Director, British Electricity International, since 1978; *b* 27 March 1926; *s* of late Arthur and Nancy Baker; *m* 1950, Margaret Julia Wright; one *s* two *d*. *Educ:* Epsom Coll.; Clare Coll., Cambridge (MA). FIMechE. Engr Officer, RN, 1944–47; Apprentice, Davy United Engineering Co. Ltd, 1947–49; Works Engr, John Baker & Bessemer Ltd, 1949–51; Davy United Engrg Co. Ltd, 1951: Dir of Prodn, 1960; Gen. Man., 1961; Dir, Davy Ashmore Ltd, 1963; Dir of Ops, Davy-Ashmore Engrg Ltd, 1964; Chm. and Chief Exec. of Davy United Engrg Co. Ltd, Ashmore Benson Pease Ltd and Loewy Robertson Engrg Co. Ltd, 1968; Man. Dir, Kearney & Trecker Ltd, 1970; Co-ordinator of Industrial Advrs, Depts of Trade and Industry, 1974–78. *Recreations:* shooting, gardening. *Address:* Flat 3, Arundel Court, Jubilee Place, SW1.

BAKER, Very Rev. Thomas George Adames, MA; Dean of Worcester, 1975–86, retired; *b* 22 Dec. 1920; *s* of late Walter and Marion Baker, Southampton; unmarried. *Educ:* King Edward VI Sch., Southampton; Exeter Coll., Oxford; Lincoln Theological Coll. Curate of All Saints, King's Heath, Birmingham, 1944–47; Vicar of St James, Edgbaston, 1947–54; Sub-Warden of Lincoln Theological Coll., 1954–60; Principal of Wells Theological College and Prebendary of Combe II in Wells Cathedral, 1960–71; Archdeacon of Bath, 1971–75. Canon Theologian of Leicester Cathedral, 1959–66. Select Preacher, Univ. of Cambridge, 1963, Univ. of Oxford, 1973. Recognised Teacher, Bristol Univ., 1969–74. *Publications:* What is the New Testament?, 1969; Questioning Worship, 1977. *Recreation:* music. *Address:* 2 Brooklyn Road, Bath.

BAKER, (Thomas) Scott (Gillespie); QC 1978; a Recorder of the Crown Court, since 1976; *b* 10 Dec. 1937; *s* of late Rt Hon. Sir George Baker, PC, OBE; *m* 1973, Margaret Joy Strange; two *s* one *d*. *Educ:* Haileybury; Brasenose Coll., Oxford. Called to the Bar, Middle Temple, 1961 (Astbury Schol.), Bencher 1985; Midland and Oxford Circuit. Mem. Senate, Inns of Court, 1977–84. Mem., Govt Cttee of Inquiry into Human Fertilisation (Warnock Cttee), 1982–84. Mem., Chorleywood UDC, 1965–68. *Recreations:* golf, fishing. *Address:* Highlands, Woodrow, near Amersham, Bucks HP7 0QG. *T:* Amersham 7068. 1 Crown Office Row, Temple, EC4Y 7HH. *T:* 01–353 1801. *Clubs:* Caledonian, MCC; Denham Golf.

BAKER, Willfred Harold Kerton, TD; *b* 6 Jan. 1920; *o s* of late W. H. Baker; *m* 1st, 1945, Kathleen Helen Sloan (*née* Murray Bisset); one *s* two *d*; 2nd, Jean Gordon Scott (*née* Skinner). *Educ:* Hardye's Sch.; Edinburgh Univ.; Cornell Univ., USA. Joined TA, and served War of 1939–45 (Major). Edinburgh Univ. (BSc Agriculture), 1946–49. MP (C) Banffshire, 1964–Feb. 1974. *Recreations:* golf, fishing, philately. *Address:* Ashdown, 42 Southfield Avenue, Paignton, South Devon TQ3 1LH. *T:* Paignton 550861.

BAKER, Rt. Rev. William Scott, MA; Assistant Bishop, Diocese of Liverpool, since 1968; *b* 22 June 1902; *s* of late Rev. Canon William Wing Carew Baker, Vicar of Southill, Beds; unmarried. *Educ:* King's Coll. Choir Sch., Cambridge; Aldenham; King's Coll., Cambridge; Cuddesdon. Deacon, 1925; Priest, 1927; Chaplain of King's Coll., Cambridge, and Asst Curate of St Giles with St Peter's Church, Cambridge, 1925–32; Vicar of St John The Baptist's, Newcastle on Tyne, 1932–43; Examining Chaplain to Bishop of Wakefield, 1928–32; to Bishop of Newcastle, 1941–43; Proctor in Convocation for Diocese of Newcastle, 1943; Bishop of Zanzibar and Dar-es-Salaam, 1943–65, of Zanzibar and Tanga, 1965–68; Lectr, St Katherine's Coll., Liverpool, 1968–75. *Publication:* (contributor) The Parish Communion, 1937. *Address:* 11 Woolacombe Road, Liverpool L16 9JG. *T:* 051–722 5035.

BAKER, Wilson, FRS 1946; FRSC; BSc, MSc, PhD, DSc (Manchester); MA (Oxon.); retired; Alfred Capper Pass Professor of Organic Chemistry, University of Bristol, 1945–65 (Dean of the Faculty of Science, 1948–51; Emeritus Professor, University of Bristol, 1965); *b* 24 Jan. 1900; *yr s* of Harry and Mary Baker, Runcorn, Cheshire; *m* 1927, Juliet Elizabeth, *d* of Henry and Julia R. Glaisyer, Birmingham; one *s* two *d*. *Educ:* Liverpool Coll. Upper Sch.; Victoria Univ. of Manchester (Mercer Schol., Baeyer Fellow and Dalton Scholar). Asst Lecturer in Chemistry, Univ. of Manchester, 1924–27; Tutor in Chemistry, Dalton Hall, Manchester, 1926–27; Univ. Lecturer and Demonstrator in Chemistry, Univ. of Oxford, 1927–44; Fellow and Praelector in Chemistry, The Queen's Coll., Oxford, 1937–44. Vice-Pres. of the Chemical Society, 1957–60. *Publications:* numerous original papers on organic chemistry, dealing chiefly with the synthesis of natural products, the development of synthetical processes, compounds of abnormal aromatic type, organic inclusion compounds, and the preparation of large-ring compounds, and the chemistry of penicillin, published mainly in Journal of the Chemical Society; (with T. W. J. Taylor) 2nd Edition of Professor N. V. Sidgwick's The Organic Chemistry of Nitrogen, 1937. *Recreations:* walking, gardening, music, mineralogy. *Address:* Lane's End, 54 Church Road, Winscombe, Avon. *T:* Winscombe 3112.

BAKER-BATES, Merrick Stuart; HM Diplomatic Service; Deputy High Commissioner and Counsellor (Commercial/Economic), Kuala Lumpur, since 1986; *b* 22 July 1939; *s* of late E. T. Baker-Bates, MD, FRCP, and of Norah Stuart (*née* Kirkham); *m* 1963, Chrystal Jacqueline Goodacre; one *s* one *d*. *Educ:* Shrewsbury Sch.; Hertford Coll., Oxford (MA); College of Europe, Bruges. Journalist, Brussels, 1962–63; entered HM Diplomatic Service, 1963; 3rd, later 2nd Sec., Tokyo, 1963–68; 1st Secretary: FCO, 1968–73; (Inf.), Washington, 1973–76; (Commercial), Tokyo, 1976–79; Counsellor (Commercial), Tokyo, 1979–82. Dir, Cornes & Co., Tokyo, 1982–85; Representative Dir, Gestetner Ltd (Japan), 1982–85. *Recreations:* photography, Japanese fencing, cycling. *Address:* c/o Foreign and Commonwealth Office, SW1A 2AH; Highfield House East, Creaton, Northampton NN6 8NT. *Clubs:* Brooks's; Tokyo (Tokyo).

BAKER-CARR, Air Marshal Sir John (Darcy), KBE 1962 (CBE 1951); CB 1957; AFC 1944; Controller of Engineering and Equipment, Air Ministry, 1962–64, retired; *b* 13 January 1906; *s* of late Brigadier-General C. D. Baker-Carr, CMG, DSO and Sarah Quinan; *m* 1934, Margery Dallas; no *c*. *Educ:* England and USA. Entered RAF as Pilot Officer, 1929; No 32 Fighter Sqdn 1930, Flying Officer; Flying Boats at home and overseas, 1931; Armament Specialist Course, 1934; Flight-Lieut; Armament and Air Staff appts, 1935–38; Sqdn Ldr, 1938; Armament Research and Development, 1939–45 (AFC); Wing Comdr, 1940; Gp Captain, 1942; Central Fighter Estab., 1946–47; Dep. Dir Postings, Air Min., 1947–48; Air Cdre, 1948; Dir of Armament Research and Development, Min. of Supply, 1948–51 (CBE); idc 1952; Comdt RAF, St Athan, 1953–56; Senior Technical Staff Officer, HQ Fighter Command, RAF, 1956–59; Air Vice-Marshal, 1957; Air Officer Commanding, No 41 Group, Maintenance Command, 1959–61; Air Marshal, 1962. *Recreations:* sailing and carpentry. *Address:* Thatchwell Cottage, King's Somborne, Hants. *Club:* Royal Air Force Yacht (Hamble, Hants).

BAKER WILBRAHAM, Sir Richard, 8th Bt *cr* 1776; Director: J. Henry Schroder Wagg & Co. Ltd, since 1969; Ashdown Investment Trust, since 1973; Westpool Investment Trust, since 1974; Brixton Estate, since 1985; *b* 5 Feb. 1934; *s* of Sir Randle Baker Wilbraham, 7th Bt, and Betty Ann, CBE (*d* 1975), *d* of W. Matt Torrens; *S* father, 1980; *m* 1962, Anne Christine Peto, *d* of late Charles Peto Bennett, OBE; one *s* three *d*. *Educ:* Harrow. Welsh Guards, 1952–54. J. Henry Schroder Wagg & Co. Ltd, 1954–. Director: The Really Useful Group plc, 1985; Charles Barker Group, 1986–. Trustee, Grosvenor Estate, 1981–. Governor, Harrow Sch., 1982–. *Recreations:* field sports. *Heir:* *s* Randle Baker Wilbraham, *b* 28 May 1963. *Address:* 41 Carlyle Square, SW3 6HA. *T:* 01–352 5069; Rode Hall, Scholar Green, Cheshire. *T:* Alsager 3237. *Clubs:* Brooks's, Pratt's.

BAKEWELL, Joan Dawson; broadcaster and writer; Arts Correspondent to BBC Television, since 1981; *b* 16 April 1933; *d* of John Rowlands and Rose Bland; *m* 1st, 1955, Michael Bakewell (marr. diss. 1972); one *s* one *d*; 2nd, 1975, Jack Emery. *Educ:* Stockport High Sch. for Girls; Newnham Coll., Cambridge (BA History and Econs). *BBC Television incl:* Meeting Point, 1964; The Second Sex, 1964; Late Night Line Up, 1965–72; The Youthful Eye, 1968; Moviemakers at the National Film Theatre, 1971; Film 72, and Film 73, 1972–73; For the Sake of Appearance, Where is Your God?, Who Cares?, and The Affirmative Way (series), 1973; Holiday '74, '75, '76, '77 and '78 (series); What's it all About? (2 series) and Time Running Out (series), 1974; The Shakespeare Business, The Brontë Business, and Generation to Generation (series), 1976; My Day with the Children, 1977; The Moving Line, 1979; Arts UK: OK?, 1980. *ITV incl.* Sunday Break, 1962; Home at 4.30, 1964; (writer and producer) Thank You, Ron (documentary), 1974; Fairest Fortune and Edinburgh Festival Report, 1974; Reports Action (4 series), 1976–78. *Radio:* Away from it All, 1978–79, PM, 1979–. *Theatre.* Brontës: The Private Faces, Edinburgh Fest., 1979. *Publications:* (with Nicholas Garnham) The New Priesthood: British television today, 1970; (with John Drummond) A Fine and Private Place, 1977; The Complete Traveller, 1977; journalism for Punch, Radio Times; Television Critic of The Times, 1978–81. *Recreations:* theatre, travel, talk. *Address:* c/o A. D. Peters & Co. Ltd, 10 Buckingham Street, WC2N 6BU. *T:* 01–839 2556.

BALCAZAR-MONZON, Dr Gustavo; Gran Cruz, Order of Boyaca, Colombia; Orden del Mérito Militar, General José Maria Córdoba, Colombia; Ciudades Confederadas Gran Cauca, Colombia; Senator of the Republic of Colombia, since 1962; *b* 10 Aug. 1927; *m* 1952, Bolivia Ramos de Balcázar; two *d*. *Educ:* Universidad Javeriana, Bogotá, Colombia (Dr in Econ. and Jurid. Sciences). Municipal Civil Judge, Cali, 1949–51; Attorney of the City of Cali, 1951–52. Member, House of Representatives, 1958–62, President, 1960; Governor of the Valle, 1962–64; Minister of Agriculture, 1964–65; President of the

Senate, 1975; President Designate of the Republic, 1978–80; Colombian Ambassador to the Court of St James's, 1979–81. Member, Liberal Party Nat. Governing Body, 1970–71, 1974–77 and 1978; a Director of the Liberal Party, 1978. *Publications:* La Ciudad, el Urbanismo y el Impuesto de Valorización (The City, Urban Planning and the Tax for Increase in Value), 1950; La Reforma Tributaria de 1960 (The Tax Reform of 1960), 1961; several articles for the press. *Recreation:* apiculture. *Address:* Calle 10 Norte 9AN-10, Cali, Colombia; Senado de la Républica, Capitolio Nacional, Bogotá, Colombia. *Clubs:* Royal Automobile, Travellers'; Les Ambassadeurs.

BALCHIN, John Alfred; General Manager, Stevenage Development Corporation, 1969–76, retired; *b* 8 Aug. 1914; *er s* of Alfred and Florence Balchin; *m* 1940, Elsie Dormer (*d* 1982); one *s* two *d*. *Educ:* Sir Walter St John's Sch., Battersea; Sir John Cass Coll., City of London. DPA (London), DMA, FCIS, FIH. LCC Clerk's Dept, 1932–38; civil defence co-ordination work, 1938–45; to Housing Dept, 1946–65; Principal Clerk, 1952; Asst Dir (Finance), 1960; Asst Dir (Housing Management), 1963; Sen. Asst Dir of Housing, GLC, 1965–69. Assoc. Sen. Lectr, for Housing Management and Administration, Brunel Univ., 1969–71. Member: Housing Services Adv. Gp, DoE, 1976–80; North British Housing Assoc., 1976–. *Publications:* Housing: programming and development of estates, 1971, revd edn 1978; Housing Management: history, principles and practice, 1972; Housing Studies, 1st series, 1979, 2nd series, 1980, revd edn 1981; First New Town: an autobiography of the Stevenage Development Corporation, 1980. *Address:* Westwards, Perran Downs, Goldsithney, Cornwall TR20 9HL. *T:* Penzance 710449.

BALCHIN, Robert George Alexander, KStJ 1984; Director-General, St John Ambulance, since 1984; *b* 1942; *s* of late Leonard George and Elizabeth Balchin; *m* 1970, Jennifer, BA (Mus), ACP, *d* of Bernard Kevin Kinlay, Cape Town; twin *s*. *Educ:* Bec Sch.; Univs of London and Hull. MEd, Adv. DipEd; FCP. Asst Master, Chinthurst Sch., 1964–68; Hd of English Dept, Ewell Sch., 1968–69; Res., Univ. of Hull Inst. of Educn, 1969–71; Headmaster, Hill Sch., Westerham, 1972–80; Company Director; Nat. Schs Advr, St John Amb., 1979–82, Asst Dir-Gen., 1982–84. Standing Conf. on Sch. Sci. and Technol., 1976–79; Treasurer: Coll. of Preceptors, 1979–; Catch 'em Young Project Trust, 1984–; Chm./Founder, Campaign for a Gen. Teaching Council, 1981–; Editorial Bd, Education Today; Member: Surrey CC, 1981–85 (Mem., Educn and Social Services Cttees); Centre for Policy Studies, 1982; Lecture Sec., Heraldry Soc., 1982–; Trustee, Adeline Genée Th., 1982–; Gov., Oxted County Sch., 1985–. Vice-Pres., Lambeth Cons. Assoc., 1976–81; Treas., E Surrey Cons. Assoc., 1982–85; Cons. Party Dep. Area Treas., 1983–. Hon. Mem. CGLI, 1983. Hon. DPhil Northland Open Univ., Canada, 1985. Freeman, Goldsmiths' Co., 1980. *Publications:* Emergency Aid in Schools, 1984; New Money, 1985. *Address:* New Place, Lingfield, Surrey RH7 6EF. *T:* Lingfield (Surrey) 834543; 7 Ashley Court, Westminster, SW1. *Clubs:* Athenæum, Carlton, St Stephen's Constitutional.

BALCHIN, Prof. William George Victor, MA, PhD; FKC; FRGS, FRMetS; Emeritus Professor of Geography in the University of Wales (Swansea), 1978 (Professor of Geography, 1954–78); *b* 20 June 1916; *s* of Victor Balchin and Ellen Winifred Gertrude Chapple; *m* 1939, Lily Kettlewood; one *s* one *d* (and one *d* decd). *Educ:* Aldershot County High Sch. (State Scholar and County Major Scholar, 1934); St Catharine's Coll., Cambridge (1st Cl. Pt I Geographical Tripos, 1936; College Prize for Geography, 1936; BA 1937; MA 1941). PhD KCL 1951; FKC 1984. FRGS 1937; FRMetS 1945. Jun. Demonstrator in Geog., Univ. of Cambridge, 1937–39 (Geomorphologist on Spitsbergen Expedn, 1938); Hydrographic Officer, Hydrographic Dept, Admiralty, 1939–45 (also part-time Lectr for Univ. of Bristol Regional Cttee on Educn and WEA Tutor and Lectr); Lectr in Geog., KCL, 1945–54 (Geomorphologist on US Sonora-Mohave Desert Expedn, 1952); University Coll. of Swansea, Univ. of Wales: Head, Dept of Geog., 1954–78; Dean, Faculty of Pure and Applied Science, 1959–61; Vice-Principal, 1964–66 and 1970–73. Leverhulme Emeritus Fellow, 1982. Royal Geographical Society: Open Essay Prize, 1936; Gill Meml Award, 1954; Mem. Council, 1962–65, 1975–82, 1984–; Chm., Educn Cttee, 1974–; Vice-Pres., 1978–82; Chm., Ordnance Survey Cons. Cttee for Educn, 1983–. Geographical Association: Hon. Annual Conf. Organiser, 1950–54; Mem. Council, 1950–81; Trustee, 1954–77; Pres., 1971; Hon. Mem., 1980. Pres., Section E (Geog.), BAAS, 1972. Member: Met. Res. Cttee, MoD, 1963–69; British Nat. Cttee for Cartography, 1961–71 and 1976–79, for Geography, 1964–70 and 1976–78. Treasurer, Second Land Utilisation Survey of Britain, 1961–; Chm., Land Decade Educnl Council, 1978–83. Mem., Nature Conservancy Cttee for Wales, 1959–68; Vice-Pres., Glam Co. Naturalists' Trust, 1961–80. Mem., Hydrology Cttee, ICE, 1962–76. Member, Court of Governors: Nat. Mus. of Wales, 1966–74; UCW, Swansea, 1980–; Mem. Council, St David's UC, 1968–80. *Publications:* (ed) Geography and Man (3 vols), 1947; (with A. W. Richards) Climatic and Weather Exercises, 1949; (with A. W. Richards) Practical and Experimental Geography, 1952; Cornwall (The Making of the English Landscape Series), 1954; (ed and contrib.) Geography: an outline for the intending student, 1970; (ed and contrib.) Swansea and its Region, 1971; (ed and contrib.) Living History of Britain, 1981; Concern for Geography, 1981; The Cornish Landscape, 1983; over 150 res. papers, articles and contribs on geomorphology, climatology, hydrology, econ. geography and cartography in learned jls. *Recreations:* travel, writing. *Address:* 10 Low Wood Rise, Ben Rydding, Ilkley, West Yorks LS29 8AZ. *T:* Ilkley 600768. *Clubs:* Royal Commonwealth Society, Geographical.

BALCOMBE, Rt. Hon. Sir (Alfred) John, Kt 1977; PC 1985; **Rt. Hon. Lord Justice Balcombe;** a Lord Justice of Appeal, since 1985; *b* 29 Sept. 1925; *er s* of late Edwin Kesteven Balcombe; *m* 1950, Jacqueline Rosemary, *yr d* of late Julian Cowan; two *s* one *d*. *Educ:* Winchester (schol.); New Coll., Oxford (exhibnr). Served, 1943–47: Royal Signals; commnd 1945. BA 1949 (1st class Hons Jurisprudence), MA 1950. Called to Bar, Lincoln's Inn, 1950, Bencher 1977; QC 1969; practised at Chancery Bar, 1951–77; Judge of the High Court of Justice, Family Div., 1977–85; Judge of the Employment Appeal Tribunal, 1983–85. Mem., Gen. Council of the Bar, 1967–71. Chm., London Marriage Guidance Council, 1982–. Master, Worshipful Company of Tin Plate Workers, 1971–72. *Publications:* Exempt Private Companies, 1953; (ed) Estoppel, in Halsbury's Laws of England, 4th edn. *Address:* Royal Courts of Justice, Strand, WC2A 2LL. *Club:* Garrick.

BALCOMBE, Frederick James, Lord Mayor of Manchester, 1974–75, Deputy Lord Mayor, 1975–76; *b* 17 Dec. 1911; *s* of late Sidney and late Agnes Balcombe; *m* 1st, 1936, Clarice (*née* Cassel) (*d* 1949); two *s* (and two *c* decd); 2nd, 1956, Rhoda (*née* Jaffe); one *d*. *Educ:* St Anthony's RC Sch., Forest Gate; West Ham Secondary Central Sch., Stratford, London. Served War of 1939–45, RAF (commnd). Chm., family co. of insurance loss assessors. President: Manchester and District Fedn of Community Assocs, 1962–78; Manchester and District Allotments Council, 1963–78; Higher Blackley Community Assoc., 1963–78; Vice-President: Blackley Prize Band, 1964–; formerly Mem. Cttee and Hon. Treas., Crumpsall Hosp., 1964–70, League of Friends, 1966–; connected with 199th Manchester Scout Gp. Mem. Manchester City Council, Crumpsall Ward, subseq. St Peter's Ward, Collegiate Church Ward, 1958–82; served as Chm. Central Purchasing Cttee, 1964–67, Gen. and Parly (now Policy), Markets, 1958–82, Airports, 1971–82 (Chm.), Parks, 1958–67, and Finance, 1964–73, Cttees (Dep. Chm.). Chm., Manchester Internat. Airport, 1975–79. Mem., Airport Owners' Assoc., 1979–. Founder, Hillel House, Manchester Univ, 1958 (Hon. Sec., 1958–68, now Sen. Life Vice-Pres.); Chm. of Governors, Coll. of Building, Manchester, 1964–67; Mem. Council, BBC Radio Manchester, 1970–76; Mem. Council, Manchester and Salford Police Authority, 1968–74; Mem., AMC Rating Cttee, 1973–74. Mem., Bd of Deputies of British Jews, 1956–64; Mem., Council, Manchester and Salford Jews, 1958– (Exec. Mem., 1963–68); Founder Mem., Manchester Jewish Blind Soc., 1956– (Hon. Sec. 13 years, now Vice-Pres.); Adjutant, Jewish Lads' Brigade and Club, Manchester, 1946–49, Chm. 1972–78; Governor, King David Schs, Manchester, 1954–84; Vice-Pres., Fedn of Boys' Clubs, 1969–; President: Manchester Cttee, Central British Fund, 1969–; RAFA Manchester South, 1981–84; Manchester City Swimming Club, 1981–. Founder Mem., Variety Club of Israel, 1972; Barker of Variety Club, 1970– (Chm. Manchester Cttee, 1976). JP Manchester, 1967–82. Mem. Jewish Faith. Life long blood donor. *Recreations:* family, communal endeavour, swimming, walking. *Address:* 16 Spath Road, Didsbury, Manchester M20 8GA. *T:* 061–434 2555; (office) 061–941 6231.

BALCOMBE, Rt. Hon. Sir John; *see* Balcombe, Rt. Hon. Sir A. J.

BALCON, Dr Raphael, MD; FRCP, FACC; Consultant Cardiologist, National Heart and Chest Hospitals, London Chest Hospital, since 1970; *b* 26 Aug. 1936; *s* of Henry and Rhoda Balcon; *m* 1959, Elizabeth Ann Henry; one *d*. *Educ:* King's Coll., London; King's Coll. Hosp. Med. Sch. (MB, BS 1960, MD 1969). LRCP, MRCS 1960, MRCP 1965, FRCP 1977; FACC 1973. House Phys., Med. Unit, KCH, 1960; House Surg., KCH, Dulwich, 1960; House Phys., London Chest Hosp., 1961; Sen. House Officer, St Stephen's Hosp., 1962; Public Health Fellow in Cardiology, Wayne State Univ. Med. Sch., USA, 1963; British Heart Foundn Fellow, Dept of Cardiol., KCH, 1964, Med. Registrar 1965; Registrar, then Sen. Registrar, National Heart Hosp., 1966–70. Dean, Cardiothoracic Inst., 1976–80. Hon. Treasurer, British Cardiac Soc. *Publications:* contrib. books on cardiological subjects; papers in BMJ, Lancet, Brit. Heart Jl, Amer. Jl of Cardiol., Circulation, Eur. Jl of Cardiol., Acta Medica Scandinavica. *Recreations:* ski-ing, tennis, mountain walking. *Address:* 68 Gloucester Crescent, NW1 7EG. *T:* 01–267 2212.

BALDERSTONE, Sir James (Schofield), Kt 1983; company director and grazier; Chairman: Broken Hill Proprietary Co. Ltd, since 1984 (Director, since 1971); Stanbroke Pastoral Co., since 1982 (Managing Director, 1964–81); Victorian Branch Board, AMP Society, since 1984 (Director, since 1962); *b* 2 May 1921; *s* of James Schofield and Mary Essendon Balderstone; *m* 1946, Mary Henrietta Tyree; two *s* two *d*. *Educ:* Scotch College, Melbourne. Service with RANR, WWII, 1940–45. General Manager for Aust., Thos Borthwick & Sons, 1953–67; Chm., Squatting Investment Co., 1966–73; Director: Commercial Bank of Australia, 1970–81; Westpac Banking Corp. (after merger), 1981–84; NW Shelf Develt Pty, 1976–83; Woodside Petroleum, 1976–83; ICI (Australia), 1981–84; Principal, Board, AMP Soc., 1979–; Chase AMP Bank, 1985–. Founding Chm., Australian Meat Exporters' Fed. Council, 1963–64; Member: Australian Meat Bd, 1964–67; Export Develt Council, 1968–71. Pres., Inst. of Public Affairs, 1981–84; Chm., Commonwealth Govt's Working Gp on Agricl Policy: Issues and Options for the 1980s, 1981–82. DUniv Newcastle, NSW, 1985. *Recreations:* farming, reading, watching sport. *Address:* 115 Mont Albert Road, Canterbury, Victoria 3126, Australia. *T:* 03–836–3137. *Clubs:* Australian, Melbourne (Melbourne); Union (Sydney); Queensland (Brisbane).

BALDOCK, John Markham, VRD 1949; Lieutenant Commander RNVR 1948; Chairman Lenscrete Ltd, 1949; Director CIBA-GEIGY (UK) Ltd; *b* 19 Nov. 1915; *s* of late Captain W. P. Baldock, and Mrs H. Chalcraft; *m* 1949, Pauline Ruth Gauntlett; two *s*. *Educ:* Rugby Sch.; Balliol Coll., Oxford. Agric. degree, 1937. Served War of 1939–45, with Royal Navy, Atlantic, Mediterranean, Indian Ocean; Russian convoys, 1942–43. Lloyds, EC3, 1945. Joined Board of Lenscrete, 1946. MP (C) Harborough Div. of Leics, 1950–Sept. 1959, retd, also as Parl. Private Sec. to Rt Hon. D. Ormsby Gore (Minister of State, Foreign Office). Founder, Hollycombe steam collection and steam fair. *Recreations:* country life, sailing, steam engines, industrial archæology, theatre. *Address:* Hollycombe House, Liphook, Hants. *T:* Liphook 723233; 17 Aylesford Street, SW1; *T:* 01–821 8759. *Club:* Farmers'.

BALDRY, Antony Brian, (Tony); MP (C) Banbury, since 1983; barrister; *b* 10 July 1950; *e s* of Peter Edward Baldry and Oina (*née* Paterson); *m* 1979, Catherine Elizabeth, 2nd *d* of Captain James Weir, RN and Elizabeth Weir; one *s* one *d*. *Educ:* Leighton Park Sch., Reading; Univ. of Sussex (BA, LLB). Called to the Bar, Lincoln's Inn, 1975; practising barrister on Oxford and Midland Circuit. Director: New Opportunity Press, 1975–; Newpoint Publishing Gp, 1983–. Contested (C) Thurrock, 1979; PPS to Minister of State for Foreign and Commonwealth Affairs, 1986–. Mem., Parly Select Cttee on Employment, 1983–. Joined Sussex Yeomanry, 1971; TA Officer, staff of Force Artillery Officer, ACE Mobile Force (Land). Robert Schuman Silver Medal, Stiftung FVS Hamburg, 1978. *Recreations:* walking in the country, reading historical biography, gardening, cricket, beagling. *Address:* Mullions, Wroxton St Mary, near Banbury, Oxon OX15 6QQ. *T:* Wroxton St Mary 686; House of Commons, SW1A 0AA. *Clubs:* Carlton; Brass Monkey; Banbury Conservative.

BALDRY, Prof. Harold Caparne; Emeritus Professor of Classics, University of Southampton; *b* 4 March 1907; *s* of William and Gertrude Mary Baldry, Nottingham; *m* 1934, Carina Hetley (*née* Pearson) (*d* 1985); one *s* two *d*. *Educ:* Nottingham High Sch.; Trinity Hall, Cambridge (Warr Schol., MA). Editor Cambridge Review, 1931. Educational Staff, Trinity Hall, Cambridge, 1931–34; Asst Lecturer in Classics, University Coll. of Swansea, 1934–35; Univ. of Cape Town: Lecturer in Classics, 1936–48, Prof. of Classics, 1948–54; Univ. of Southampton: Prof. of Classics, 1954–72; Dean of Faculty of Arts, 1959–62; Dep. Vice-Chancellor, 1963–66; Public Orator, 1959–67. Chm., Council of University Classical Depts, 1969–72; Pres., Orbilian Soc., 1970; Vice-Pres., Classical Assoc., 1972–; Mem., Arts Council of GB, 1973–78 (Chm. Regional Cttee, 1975–78); Chm., Southern Arts Assoc., 1972–74. Hon. DLitt Southampton, 1975. *Publications:* The Classics in the Modern World (an Inaugural Lecture), 1949; Greek Literature for the Modern Reader, 1951; Ancient Utopias (an Inaugural Lecture), 1956; The Unity of Mankind in Greek Thought, 1965; Ancient Greek Literature in its Living Context, 1968; The Greek Tragic Theatre, 1971; The Case for the Arts, 1981; articles and reviews in classical journals. *Address:* 19 Uplands Way, Southampton SO2 1QW. *T:* Southampton 555290.

BALDRY, Jack Thomas; Director, Purchasing and Supplies, Post Office, 1969–72; *b* 5 Oct. 1911; *s* of late John and Ellen Baldry; *m* 1936, Ruby Berenice (*née* Frost); three *d*. *Educ:* Framlingham Coll. Post Office: Asst Traffic Supt, 1930; Asst Surveyor, 1935; Asst Princ., 1940; Princ., 1947 (Private Sec. to PMG, 1950–53); Asst Sec., 1953; Dep. Dir, External Telecommunications, 1960; Dir of Personnel, 1967. *Recreations:* tennis, farming, foreign travel. *Address:* Bruisyard Road, Badingham, Woodbridge IP13 8NA. *T:* Badingham 331.

BALDRY, Tony; *see* Baldry, A. B.

BALDWIN, family name of **Earl Baldwin of Bewdley.**

BALDWIN OF BEWDLEY, 4th Earl *cr* 1937; **Edward Alfred Alexander Baldwin;** Viscount Corvedale, 1937; *b* 3 Jan. 1938; *o s* of 3rd Earl Baldwin of Bewdley and Joan Elspeth, *y d* of late C. Alexander Tomes, New York, USA; *S* father, 1976; *m* 1970, Sarah MacMurray, *er d* of Evan James, *qv*; three *s*. *Educ:* Eton; Trinity Coll., Cambridge (MA). *Heir: s* Viscount Corvedale, *qv*. *Address:* Manor Farm House, Upper Wolvercote, Oxford OX2 8AJ.

BALDWIN, Captain George Clifton, CBE 1966; DSC 1941 and Bar 1944; RN (retd); Member: Press Council, 1973–78; Press Council Appointments Commission, since 1978; *b* 17 Jan. 1921; *s* of late George and late Louisa Baldwin; *m* 1947, Hasle Mary MacMahon; three *s*. *Educ:* Sleaford Grammar Sch., Lincs; Hitchin Grammar Sch., Herts. Served War: joined RN, 1939, and trained as Pilot in Fleet Air Arm; in comd: 807 Sqdn, 1943; No 4 Naval Fighter Wing, 1944–45. Qual. at Empire Test Pilots' Sch., 1946; in comd, 800 Sqdn, 1952; Captain, RN, 1958; in comd, RN Air Station, Lossiemouth, 1961–62; IDC course, 1963; Dir, Naval Air Warfare, MoD, 1964–66; in comd, RN Air Station, Yeovilton, 1966–68; ADC, 1967; retd, 1968. Mem., Royal United Services Inst., 1968. Chm., Fleet Air Arm Officers' Assoc., 1973–78. *Publications:* articles in: Air Pictorial, Navy International, Embassy, etc. *Recreations:* gardening, tennis, swimming. *Address:* Three Greens, Level Mare Lane, Eastergate, Chichester, West Sussex. *T:* (home) Eastergate 3040; (office) Chichester 782559. *Club:* Naval and Military.

BALDWIN, Prof. Jack Edward, PhD; FRS 1978; Waynflete Professor of Chemistry and Fellow of Magdalen College, University of Oxford, since 1978; *b* 8 Aug. 1938; *s* of Frederick Charles Baldwin and Olive Frances Headland; *m* 1977, Christine Louise, *d* of William B. Franchi. *Educ:* Lewes County Grammar Sch.; Imperial Coll., London Univ. (BSc, DIC, PhD). ARCS. Asst Lectr in Chem., Imperial Coll., 1963, Lectr, 1966; Asst Prof. of Chem., Pa State Univ., 1967, Associate Prof., 1969; Associate Prof. of Chem., MIT, 1970, Prof., 1972; Daniell Prof. of Chem., King's Coll., London, 1972; Prof. of Chem., MIT, 1972–78. Chemical Society: Tilden Lectr, 1979; Simonsen Lectr, 1982; Corday Morgan Medal and Prize, 1975; Award in Synthetic Chemistry, 1979. Priestley Lectr, USA, 1984; Pacific West Coast Lectr, USA, 1984; Monsanto Lectr, USA, 1985; Musselmann Lectr, USA, 1985; Atlantic Coast Lectr, USA, 1986. Paul Karrer Medal, Zürich, 1985. *Publications:* res. pubns in Jl of Amer. Chem. Soc., Jl of Chem. Soc., Tetrahedron. *Address:* Dyson Perrins Laboratory, South Parks Road, Oxford OX1 3QY.

BALDWIN, James (Arthur); Author; *b* Harlem, New York City, 2 Aug. 1924; *s* of David and Berdis Emma Baldwin. *Educ:* DeWitt Clinton High Sch., New York. Various non-literary jobs, 1942–45. Moved to Paris, 1948; lived in Europe until 1956. Active in civil rights movement in USA. Saxton Fellow, 1945; Rosenwald Fellow, 1948; Guggenheim Fellow, 1954; Nat. Inst. of Arts and Letters Award, and Partisan Review Fellow, 1956. Mem. Nat. Inst. of Arts and Letters, 1964. Martin Luther King Jr Award, City Coll. of Univ. of NY, 1978. DLitt, Univ. of British Columbia, 1963. *Publications: novels:* Go Tell It on the Mountain, 1953; Giovanni's Room, 1956; Another Country, 1962; Going to Meet the Man, 1965; Tell Me How Long the Train's Been Gone, 1968; If Beale Street Could Talk, 1974; Little Man, Little Man (with Yoran Cazac), 1975; The Devil Finds Work, 1976; Just Above my Head, 1979; *essays:* Notes of a Native Son, 1955; Nobody Knows My Name, 1961; The Fire Next Time, 1963; Nothing Personal (with Richard Avedon), 1964; No Name in the Street, 1971; (with Margaret Mead) A Rap on Race, 1971; (with Nikki Giovanni) A Dialogue, 1975; Evidence of Things not Seen, 1983; The Price of the Ticket, 1985; *plays:* The Amen Corner, 1955 (prod Saville, London, 1965); Blues for Mr Charlie, 1964; One Day when I was Lost, 1972; The Woman at the Well, 1972; essays and short stories in many jls and anthologies, 1946–.

BALDWIN, John, OBE 1978; National Secretary, Amalgamated Engineering Union (formerly Amalgamated Union of Engineering Workers) Workers/Construction Section, since 1976; *b* 16 Aug. 1923; *s* of Stephen John Baldwin and Elizabeth (*née* Hutchinson); *m* 1945, Grace May Florence (*née* Wilson); two *d*. *Educ:* Laindon High Road Sen. Sch., Essex. Boy service, RN, HMS Ganges, 1938; returned to civilian life, 1948; Steel Erector, CEU, 1950; played active part as Shop Steward and Site Convenor; elected full-time official, 1957; Asst Gen. Sec., AUEW/Construction Sect., 1969–76. Chm., Mechanical Handling Sector Working Party of NEDO; Member: Engrg Construction EDC, 1975–; Construction Equipment and Mobile Cranes Sector Working Party of NEDO; National Jt Council for the Engrg Construction Industry. Prominent Mem., Labour Party, 1962–. *Recreations:* most sports. *Address:* 7 Ridge Langley, Sanderstead, South Croydon, Surrey. *T:* 01-651 1643.

BALDWIN, Maj.-Gen. Peter Alan Charles; Deputy Director, Radio, Independent Broadcasting Authority, since 1979; *b* 19 Feb. 1927; *s* of Alec Baldwin and Anne Dance; *m* 1st, 1953, Judith Elizabeth Mace; 2nd, 1982, Gail J. Roberts. *Educ:* King Edward VI Grammar Sch., Chelmsford. Enlisted 1942; commnd R Signals 1947; early service included Berlin, 1948–49 (during airlift), and Korean War, 1950; Staff Coll., 1960; JSSC, 1964; Borneo operations (despatches, 1967); Directing Staff, Staff Coll., 1967–69; Comdr, 13 Signal Regt, BAOR, 1969–71; Sec. for Studies, NATO Defence Coll., 1971–74; Comdr, 2 Signal Group, 1974–76; ACOS Jt Exercises Div., Allied Forces Central Europe, 1976–77; Maj.-Gen. and Chief Signal Officer, BAOR, 1977–79. *Recreations:* tennis, cricket, music, theatre. *Address:* c/o Lloyds Bank, 6 Pall Mall, SW1. *Club:* Army and Navy.

BALDWIN, Sir Peter (Robert), KCB 1977 (CB 1973); MA; Chairman, SE Thames Regional Health Authority, since 1983; *b* 10 Nov. 1922; *s* of Charles Baldwin and Katie Baldwin (*née* Field); *m* 1951, Margaret Helen Moar; two *s*. *Educ:* City of London Sch.; Corpus Christi Coll., Oxford (Hon. Fellow, 1980). Foreign Office, 1942–45; Gen. Register Office, 1948–54; HM Treasury, 1954–62; Cabinet Office, 1962–64; HM Treasury, 1964–76; Principal Private Sec. to Chancellor of Exchequer, July 1966–Jan. 1968; Under-Sec., HM Treasury, 1968–72; Dep. Sec., HM Treasury, 1972–76; Second Permanent Sec., DoE, 1976; Permanent Sec., Dept of Transport, 1976–82. Dir, Mitchell Cotts, 1983–; Mem. Bd, Public Finance Foundation, 1984–. Chairman: PHAB, 1982– (Vice-Chm., 1981); Rural Village Develt Foundn, 1983–85 (Vice-Chm., 1985–); Community Transport, 1985–; President: Disability Action Westminster, 1986– (Chm., 1983–86); Hearing Dogs for the Deaf, 1986– (Chm., 1983–86); Vice-President: RNID, 1983–; Disabled Drivers Motoring Club, 1985–. Member: Royal Soc. of Arts, 1985– (Mem. Council, 1982–) (FRSA); Cttee, AA, 1983–. Life Vice-Pres., Civil Service Sports Council, 1982– (Chm., 1978–82; Vice-Chm., 1974–78). Chm., St Catherine's Home and Sch., Ventnor, 1961–78. Governor, Eltham Coll., 1984–85. FCIT; Hon. FIHE. *Recreations:* painting, watching cricket. *Address:* 123 Alderney Street, SW1V 4HE. *T:* 01-821 7157. *Club:* Reform.

BALES, Kenneth Frederick; Regional General Manager, West Midlands Regional Health Authority, since 1984; *b* 2 March 1931; *s* of Frederick Charles Bales and Deborah Alice Bales; *m* 1958, Margaret Hazel Austin; two *s* one *d*. *Educ:* Buckhurst Hill Grammar Sch.; LSE; Univ. of Manchester. BScSoc; DipSocAdmin. Hosp. Sec., Newhall & Hesketh Park Hosps, 1958–62; Regional Trng Officer, Birmingham Regional Hosp. Bd, 1962–65; Regional Staff Officer, Birmingham Regional Staff Cttee, 1965–68; Group Sec., W Birmingham HMC, 1968–73; Regional Administrator, W Midlands RHA, 1973–84. Associate, Inst. Health Service Management. *Recreations:* painting, sport. *Address:* 25 South Road, West Hagley, West Midlands DY9 0JT. *T:* Hagley 882550.

BALFE, Richard Andrew; Member (Lab) London South Inner, European Parliament, since 1979, and Labour spokesman on human rights, and the Third World; Director, Royal Arsenal Co-operative Society and associated companies, 1978–85 (Political Secretary, 1973–79); *b* 14 May 1944; *s* of Dr Richard J. Balfe and Mrs Dorothy L. Balfe (*née* de Cann); *m* Susan Jane Honeyford; one *s* by a previous marriage. *Educ:* Brook Secondary Sch., Sheffield; LSE (BSc Hons 1971). Fellow Royal Statistical Soc., 1972. Res. Officer, Finer Cttee on One Parent Families, 1970–73. Parly Candidate (Labour), Paddington South, 1970. Mem., GLC for Southwark/Dulwich, 1973–77; Chairman: Thamesmead New Town Cttee, 1973–75; GLC Housing Cttee, 1975–77. Member: Exec. Cttee, Fabian Soc., 1981–82; London Labour Party Exec., 1973– (Chair Policy Cttee, 1983–). Member: Ct of Governors, LSE, 1973–; RIIA, 1982–. *Publications:* Housing: a new Socialist perspective, 1976; Role and Problems of the Co-operative Movement in the 1980s (with Tony Banks), 1977. *Recreations:* collecting books and pamphlets on political and social history topics, music. *Address:* 132 Powis Street, London SE18 6JN. *T:* (office) 01–855 2128. *Clubs:* Reform; Peckham Labour; Sheffield Trades and Labour, Lewisham Labour.

BALFOUR, family name of **Earl of Balfour** and **Barons Balfour of Inchrye, Kinross** and **Riverdale.**

BALFOUR, 4th Earl of, *cr* 1922; **Gerald Arthur James Balfour;** Viscount Traprain 1922; JP; *b* 23 Dec. 1925; *er s* of 3rd Earl of Balfour and Jean (*d* 1981), 4th *d* of late Rev. Canon J. J. Cooke-Yarborough; *S* father, 1968; *m* 1956, Natasha Georgina, *d* of late Captain George Anton. *Educ:* Eton; HMS Conway. Holds Master Mariner's certificate. Mem., E Lothian CC, 1960–75. JP East Lothian, 1970. Mem., Internat. Assoc. of Cape Horners, 1960. *Heir: cousin* Eustace Arthur Goschen Balfour [*b* 26 May 1921; *m* 1st, 1946, Anne, *d* of late Major Victor Yule; two *s*; 2nd, 1971, Mrs Paula Cuene-Grandidier]. *Address:* The Tower, Whittingehame, Haddington, Scotland. *Club:* English-Speaking Union.

BALFOUR OF BURLEIGH, Lord *cr* 1607 (*de facto* 8th Lord, 12th but for the Attainder); **Robert Bruce,** CEng, FIEE; Director: Bank of Scotland, since 1968 (Deputy Governor, 1977); Scottish Investment Trust, since 1971; Tarmac plc, since 1981; Chairman, Federation of Scottish Bank Employers, since 1977; President, Friends of Vellore, since 1973; Treasurer, Royal Scottish Corporation, since 1967; *b* 6 Jan. 1927; *e s* of 11th Lord Balfour of Burleigh and Dorothy (*d* 1976), *d* of late R. H. Done; *S* father, 1967; *m* 1971, Mrs Jennifer Brittain-Catlin, *d* of late E. S. Manasseh; two *d*. Served RN, 1945–48, as Ldg Radio Electrician's Mate. Joined English Electric Co. Ltd, 1951; graduate apprentice, 1951–52; Asst Foreman, Heavy Electrical Plant Dept, Stafford Works, 1952–54; Asst Superintendent, Heavy Electrical Plant Dept, Netherton Works, Liverpool, 1954–57; Manager, English Electric Co. of India (Pvt) Ltd, Madras, 1957–60; Dir and Gen. Manager, English Electric Co. India Ltd, 1960–64; Dep. Gen. Manager, English Electric Co. Ltd, Netherton, Liverpool, 1964–65, Gen. Manager 1965–66; Dir and Gen. Manager, D. Napier & Son Ltd, 1966–68; Chm., Viking Oil Ltd, 1971–80. Chairman: Scottish Arts Council, 1971–80; NBL Scotland, 1982–. Mem., British Rail Scotland regl bd, 1982–. Forestry Comr, 1971–74. Hon. FRIAS, 1982. *Recreations:* music, climbing, woodwork. *Heir: d* Hon. Victoria Bruce, *b* 7 May 1973. *Address:* Brucefield, Clackmannan FK10 3QF.

See also G. J. D. Bruce.

BALFOUR OF INCHRYE, 1st Baron *cr* 1945, of Shefford; **Harold Harington Balfour,** PC 1941; MC and Bar; *b* 1 Nov. 1897; *s* of Col N. H. Balfour, OBE, Belton, Camberley, Surrey; *m* 1st, 1921, Diana Blanche (marr. diss. 1946; she *d* 1982), *d* of Sir Robert G. Harvey, 2nd Bt; one *s*; 2nd, 1947, Mary Ainslie Profumo, *d* of late Baron Profumo, KC, and of Baroness Profumo; one *d*. *Educ:* Chilverton Elms, Dover; RN Coll., Osborne. Joined 60th Rifles, 1914; attached RFC 1915; served European War, 1914–18 (MC and bar); RAF 1918–23; journalism and business since 1923; contested (C) Stratford, West Ham, 1924; MP (C) Isle of Thanet, 1929–45; Parly Under-Sec. of State for Air, 1938–44; Minister Resident in West Africa, 1944–45. President, Federation Chambers of Commerce of the British Empire, 1946–49; President, Commonwealth and Empire Industries Association, 1956–60; Part-time Member, Board of BEA, 1955–66; Chairman, BEA Helicopters Ltd, 1964–66. *Publications:* An Airman Marches, 1935; Wings over Westminster, 1973; Folk, Fish and Fun, 1978. *Recreation:* fishing. *Heir: s* Hon. Ian Balfour [*b* 21 Dec. 1924; *m* 1953, Josephine Maria Jane, *d* of late Mr and of the Hon. Mrs Morogh Bernard, Shankill, Co. Dublin; one *d*]. *Address:* End House, St Mary Abbot's Place, W8 6LS. *T:* 01–603 6231. *Club:* Carlton.

See also J. D. Profumo.

BALFOUR, David, CBE 1960; DPhil; FIL; retired diplomat; free-lance conference interpreter; *b* London, 20 Jan. 1903; *s* of Reginald Balfour and Charlotte Warre Cornish; *m* 1948, Louise Fitzherbert; one *d*. *Educ:* Oratory Sch., Edgbaston; and at Angers, Prague, Salzburg, Rome, Athens. Graduate of Oriental Institute, Rome, and of Athens Univ. (1940); DPhil (Oxon), 1978. On staff of the Institute of English Studies, Athens, 1939–41. Served War of 1939–45 in Army, 1941–43, GSO II, GHQ, Middle East Forces (despatches). Entered HM Foreign Service, 1943, established 1946; served Cairo, Athens, Foreign Office, Tel Aviv (Oriental Sec., 1949–50), Smyrna (Consul-Gen., 1951–55), Genoa (Consul-Gen., 1955–60), and Geneva (Consul-Gen., 1960–63); Interpreter and Translator, FO, 1963–68; retd 1968. Mem., Internat. Assoc. of Conf. Interpreters, 1969. *Recreations:* theology, byzantinology (especially 14th and 15th century). *Publications:* critical editions of unedited works of Symeon of Thessalonica, 1979 and 1981, of Gregory of Sinai, 1982, of Gregory Palamas and of John of Karpathos, 1986; The Palamas/Gregoras Debate of 1355 (16th Internat. Byzantine Congress), 1982. *Address:* The Old Mill, Kingsclere, Hants. *T:* Kingsclere 298610.

BALFOUR, David Mathers, CBE 1970; MA; CEng, MICE; Director, R. M. Douglas Construction Ltd, 1975–83; Chairman, Balfour, Beatty & Co. Ltd, 1971–74 (Managing Director, 1966–72); *b* 11 Jan. 1910; *s* of late George Balfour, MP and Margaret (*née* Mathers); *m* 1938, Elisabeth, *d* of John Murdoch Beddall; two *s* one *d*. *Educ:* Shrewsbury Sch.; Pembroke Coll., Cambridge (MA). Served War of 1939–45, Lt-Col RE. Joined Balfour, Beatty & Co. Ltd, as Civil Engineer, 1930 (Dir, 1942); Chairman: Power Securities Corporation Ltd, 1971–74; Balfour Kilpatrick Ltd, 1971–72 (Dir, 1971–75); Exec. Dir, British Insulated Callender's Cables Ltd, 1970–72. Chm., Export Gp for the Constructional Industries, 1963–65; Vice-Pres., Fedn of Civil Engineering Contractors (Chm. 1966–67). *Recreations:* golf, shooting. *Address:* Little Garnstone Manor, Seal, Sevenoaks, Kent. *T:* Sevenoaks 61221. *Clubs:* East India, Devonshire, Sports and Public Schools; Rye Golf (Rye); Wildernesse Golf (Sevenoaks).

BALFOUR, (Elizabeth) Jean, CBE 1981; FRSE 1980; FRSA 1981; FICFor; JP; Chairman, Countryside Commission for Scotland, 1972–82; *b* 4 Nov. 1927; 2nd *d* of late

Maj.-Gen. Sir James Syme Drew, KBE, CB, DSO, MC, and late Victoria Maxwell of Munches; *m* 1950, John Charles Balfour, *qv*; three *s. Educ*: Edinburgh Univ. (BSc). Partner, Balbirnie Home Farms; Dir, A. & J. Bowen & Co. Ltd. Pres., Royal Scottish Forestry Soc., 1969–71; Mem., Fife CC, 1958–70; Chm., Fife County and City and Royal Burgh of Dunfermline Joint Probation Cttee, 1967–69; Governor, East of Scotland Coll. of Agriculture, 1958–, Vice Pres. 1982–; Member: Scottish Agric. Develt Council, 1972–77; Verney Working Party on Management of National Resources, 1971–72; Nature Conservancy Council, 1973–80; Oil Develt Council, 1973–78; Council, Scottish Agricultural Coll., 1974–; Scottish Economic Council, 1978–83; Cttee of Enquiry into handling of Geographic Information, 1985–; Vice-Chm., Scottish Wildlife Trust, 1968–72; Chm., Regional Adv. Cttee, East (Scotland) Conservancy, Forestry Commn, 1976–85. Hon. Vice-Pres., Scottish YHA, 1983–. Mem. Court, St Andrews Univ., 1983. JP Fife, 1963. FRZSScot 1983. Hon. DSc St Andrews, 1977. *Recreations*: hill walking, fishing, painting, exploring arctic vegetation, shooting. *Address*: Kirkforthar House, Markinch, Fife KY7 6LS. *T*: Glenrothes 752233; Scourie, by Lairg, Sutherland. *Clubs*: Farmers', Royal Commonwealth Society; (Assoc. Mem.) New (Edinburgh).

BALFOUR, Rear-Adm. George Ian Mackintosh, CB 1962; DSC 1943; *b* 14 Jan. 1912; *yr s* of late Dr T. Stevenson Balfour, Chard, Som, and Mrs Balfour; *m* 1939, Pamela Carlyle Forrester, *y d* of late Major Hugh C. C. Forrester, DL, JP, Tullibody House, Cambus, and late Mrs Forrester; two *s* one *d. Educ*: Royal Naval Coll., Dartmouth. Served in China, 1930–32; South Africa, 1935–37. Commanded Destroyers for most of War of 1939–45, on various stations. Mediterranean, 1948, Far East, 1949–50, USA 1951–53, Captain (D) 2nd Destroyer Flotilla, 1956–58; Dir of Officer Appointments, 1958–59; Senior Naval Mem., Imperial Defence Coll., 1960–63; retired list, 1963. Chief Appeals Officer, Cancer Res. Campaign, 1963–77. *Address*: Westover, Farnham Lane, Haslemere, Surrey. *T*: 3876.

BALFOUR, Rear-Adm. Hugh Maxwell, LVO 1974; Commander, Sultan of Oman's Navy, since 1985; *b* 29 April 1933; *s* of Ronald Hugh Balfour and Ann Smith; *m* 1958, Sheila Ann Weldon; one *s* two *d. Educ*: Ardvreck; Crieff; Kelly College, Tavistock. Joined RN 1951; qualified as Signal Officer, 1959; Commanded HM Ships Sheraton, Phoebe, Whitby and Fifth Destroyer Squadron in HMS Exeter, to 1985 (Exec. Officer, HM Yacht Britannia, 1972–74). *Recreations*: sailing, shooting, gardening. *Club*: Naval and Military.

BALFOUR, Jean; *see* Balfour, E. J.

BALFOUR, John Charles, OBE 1978; MC 1943; JP; DL; Chairman, Fife Area Health Board, since 1983 (Member since 1981); *b* 28 July 1919; *s* of late Brig. E. W. S. Balfour, CVO, DSO, OBE, MC, and Lady Ruth Balfour, CBE; *m* 1950, (Elizabeth) Jean Drew (*see* (Elizabeth) Jean Balfour); three *s. Educ*: Eton Coll.; Trinity Coll., Cambridge (BA). Served war, Royal Artillery, 1939–45 (Major), N Africa and Europe. Member, Royal Company of Archers, Queen's Body Guard for Scotland, 1949–. Member: Inter-departmental Cttee on Children and Young Persons, Scotland (Chm., Lord Kilbrandon), 1961–64; Scottish Council on Crime, 1972–75; Chairman: Children's Panel, Fife County, 1970–75, Fife Region 1975–77; Scottish Assoc. of Youth Clubs, 1968–79. JP 1957, DL 1958, Fife. *Recreations*: shooting, fishing. *Address*: Kirkforthar House, Markinch, Glenrothes, Fife KY7 6LS. *T*: Glenrothes 752233. *Club*: New (Edinburgh).

See also P. E. G. Balfour.

BALFOUR, Hon. Mark Robin; Chairman: Finglands Services Ltd, since 1981; Light Trades House Ltd, since 1973; *b* 16 July 1927; *s* and *heir* of 2nd Baron Riverdale, *qv*; *m* 1959, Susan Ann Phillips; one *s* two *d. Educ*: Aysgarth Sch., Yorks; Lisgar Collegiate, Ottawa, Canada; Trinity Coll. Sch., Port Hope, Ont; Millfield Sch.; Rotherham Technical Coll. (Intermediate Cert. in Metallurgy). Served RN, 1944–47. Arthur Balfour & Co. Ltd: Trainee, 1948; Sales Rep., 1952; Dir, 1955; Manager, London Office, Home and Export, 1957; Asst Man. Dir, 1959; negotiated merger with Darwins Group Ltd, 1960; Man. Dir, Balfour Darwins Ltd, 1961, Chm. 1971–75; initiated formation of Sheffield Rolling Mills Ltd (consortium of BSC, James Neill subsid., Balfour Darwins Ltd subsid.), 1969, Chm. 1970–74; non-exec. Dir, Special Steels Div., BSC, 1971–73; negotiated sale of private sector interests in Sheffield Rolling Mills Ltd to BSC, 1973; Dir, Overseas Ops, Edgar Allen Balfour Ltd (formed by merger of Balfour Darwins Ltd and Edgar Allen Ltd), 1975–79. British Independent Steel Producers' Association: Mem., Exec. Cttee, 1969–75; Mem., Product Group (Special Steels), 1962–75 (Chm., 1970–71); Mem., Steelmakers' Cttee, 1970–75. Pres., National Fedn of Engineers' Tool Manufrs, 1974–76; Member: EDC for Machine Tools, 1976–78; Council, Fedn of British Hand Tool Manufrs, 1972–77; Econs and Management Cttee, Iron and Steel Inst., 1970–75; Iron and Steel Industry Regional Trng Bd, 1964–68; Sheffield and Dist Br. Cttee, Inst. of Dirs, 1969–77; Council, Sheffield Chamber of Commerce, 1959– (Pres., 1978); Australian British Trade Assoc. Council, BOTB, 1975–; ANZ Trade Adv. Cttee, BOTB, 1975–. Chm., Ashdell Schs Trust, 1985–. Master, Cutlers' Co. of Hallamshire, 1969–70; Mem., Worshipful Co. of Blacksmiths, 1972–; Freeman, City of London, 1972. High Sheriff, S Yorks, 1986–87. Vice-Consul for Finland in Sheffield, 1962–; Order of the Lion, Finland, 1975. Silver Jubilee Medal, 1977. *Recreations*: fishing, shooting. *Address*: Fairways, Saltergate, Bamford, Derbyshire S30 2BE. *T*: Hope Valley 51314. *Club*: The Club (Sheffield).

BALFOUR, Michael John; Assistant Director, Bank of England, 1980–85; *b* 17 Oct. 1925; *s* of Duncan and Jeanne Germaine Balfour; *m* 1951, Mary Campbell Penney, *d* of Maj.-Gen. Sir (William) Ronald Campbell Penney, KBE, CB, DSO, MC; two *s* one *d* (and *e s* decd). *Educ*: Eton Coll.; Christ Church, Oxford (MA Hons Modern Languages 1949). War service, RAF, 1944–47. Entered Bank of England, 1950: Senior Adviser, European affairs, 1973, Chief Adviser, 1976. Alternate Director, Bank for International Settlements, 1972–85; Member, EEC Monetary Cttee, 1974–85. Director, Balgonie Estates Ltd, 1955–. *Recreations*: music, textiles, tennis, boat-building, etc. *Address*: Harrietfield, Kelso, Roxburghshire TD5 7SY. *T*: Kelso 24825; 17 Shrewsbury Mews, W2 5PN. *T*: 01-229 8013.

BALFOUR, Nancy, OBE 1965; President, Contemporary Art Society, since 1984 (Chairman, 1976–82); Chairman, Art Services Grants, since 1982; *b* 1911; *d* of Alexander Balfour and Ruth Macfarland Balfour. *Educ*: Wycombe Abbey Sch.; Lady Margaret Hall, Oxford (MA). Foreign Office Research Dept, 1941–45; BBC N American Service, 1945–48; Economist Newspaper, 1948–72: Asst Editor with responsibility for American Survey, 1954–72; Fellow, Inst. of Politics, Kennedy Sch. of Govt, Harvard Univ., 1973–74. Member: Council, RIIA, 1963–84; Bd, British–American Arts Assoc., 1980–; Hon. Treasurer, Contemporary Art Soc., 1971–76; Vice-Chm., Crafts Council, 1983–85 (Mem., 1980–85). FRSA 1985. *Recreations*: sightseeing, ancient and modern; viewing work by living artists. *Address*: 36E Eaton Square, SW1W 9DH. *T*: 01-235 7874. *Club*: Arts.

BALFOUR, Neil Roxburgh; Managing Director, York & Equity Trust plc (formerly York Trust Ltd), since 1983; Chairman: Yorkshire General Unit Trust, since 1985; York Mount Group, since 1986; *b* 12 Aug. 1944; *s* of Archibald Roxburgh Balfour and Lilian

Helen Cooper; *m* 1st, 1969, HRH Princess Elizabeth of Yugoslavia; one *s*; 2nd, 1978, Serena Mary Churchill Russell; one *s* one *d. Educ*: Ampleforth Coll., Yorks; University Coll., Oxford Univ. (BA History); called to the Bar, Middle Temple, 1969. Baring Brothers & Co., 1968–74; European Banking Co. Ltd, 1974–83 (Exec. Dir, 1980–83). Mem. (C) N Yorks, European Parlt, 1979–84. *Publication*: Paul of Yugoslavia (biography), 1980. *Recreations*: bridge, golf, tennis, shooting, fishing. *Address*: Studley Royal, near Ripon, North Yorkshire. *T*: Ripon 2535. *Clubs*: Turf, Pratt's; Royal St George's (Sandwich).

BALFOUR, Peter Edward Gerald, CBE 1984; Chairman: National Commercial & Glyn's, since 1984; Charterhouse plc, since 1985; a Vice-Chairman, Royal Bank of Scotland, since 1985 (Director, since 1971); Director, Royal Bank of Scotland Group, since 1978; *b* 9 July 1921; *y s* of late Brig. Edward William Sturgis Balfour, CVO, DSO, OBE, MC and Lady Ruth Balfour, CBE, MB; *m* 1st, 1948, Grizelda Davina Roberta Ogilvy (marr. diss. 1967); two *s* one *d*; 2nd, 1968, Diana Rosemary Wainman; one *s* one *d. Educ*: Eton College. Scots Guards, 1940–54. Joined Wm McEwan & Co. Ltd, 1954; Chm. and Chief Exec., Scottish & Newcastle Breweries, 1970–83. Director: British Assets Trust Ltd; Edinburgh American Assets Trust, 1962– (Chm., 1978–); First Charlotte Assets Trust (Chm., 1981–). Chm., Scottish Council for Develt and Industry, 1978–85. Mem., Hansard Soc. Commn on Electoral Reform, 1975–76. *Address*: Scadlaw House, Humbie, East Lothian. *T*: Humbie 252. *Clubs*: Cavalry and Guards; New (Edinburgh).

See also J. C. Balfour.

BALFOUR, Raymond Lewis, LVO 1965; HM Diplomatic Service, retired; Counsellor, Kuwait, 1979–83; *b* 23 April 1923; *s* of Henry James Balfour and Vera Alice (*née* Dunford); *m* 1975, Vanda Gaye Crompton. RMA Sandhurst, 1942; commnd RAC; served with IV Queen's Own Hussars, 1942–47. Diplomatic Service, 1947–; served at Munich, Beirut, Gdansk (Poland), Baghdad, Khartoum, Geneva, Damascus; Counsellor, Tripoli, 1976–79. Order of the Blue Nile, Sudan, 1965. *Recreations*: travel, gardening. *Address*: 25 Chenery Drive, Sprowston, Norwich, Norfolk NR7 8RR. *Clubs*: Royal Commonwealth Society, Players Theatre.

BALFOUR, Richard Creighton, MBE 1945; retired; *b* 3 Feb. 1916; *s* of Donald Creighton Balfour and Muriel Fonçeca; *m* 1943, Adela Rosemary Welch; two *s. Educ*: St Edward's Sch., Oxford (Pres., Sch. Soc., 1985–86). FIB. Joined Bank of England, 1935; Agent, Leeds, 1961–65; Deputy Chief Cashier, 1965–70; Chief Accountant, 1970–75. Dir, Datasaab Ltd, 1975–81. Naval Service, Lt-Comdr RNVR, 1939–46. President: Royal National Rose Soc., 1973 and 1974; World Fedn of Rose Socs, 1983–85 (Vice-Pres. for Europe, 1981–83); Chm., Classification Cttee, 1981–); Chairman: 1976—The Year of the Rose; Internat. Rose Conf., Oxford, 1976; organiser and designer of the British Garden at Montreal Floralies, 1980. Liveryman, Worshipful Co. of Gardeners; Freeman, City of London. DHM 1974. *Publications*: articles and photographs in Rose Annual and many horticultural magazines. *Recreations*: roses, gardening, photography, dancing, sea floating, collecting rocks and hat pins, travel, watching sport. *Address*: Albion House, Little Waltham, Chelmsford, Essex CM3 3LA. *T*: Chelmsford 360410.

BALFOUR, Sir Robert George Victor FitzGeorge; *see* FitzGeorge-Balfour.

BALFOUR-PAUL, (Hugh) Glencairn, CMG 1968; HM Diplomatic Service, retired; Director General, Middle East Association, 1978–79; Research Fellow, University of Exeter, since 1979; *b* 23 Sept. 1917; *s* of late Lt-Col J. W. Balfour Paul, DSO; *m* 1st, 1950, Margaret Clare Ogilvy (*d* 1971); one *s* three *d*; 2nd, 1974, Janet Alison Scott; one *s* one *d. Educ*: Sedbergh; Magdalen Coll., Oxford. Served War of 1939–45, Sudan Defence Force. Sudan Political Service, Blue Nile and Darfur, 1946–54; joined Foreign Office, 1955; Santiago, 1957; Beirut, 1960; Counsellor, Dubai, 1964; Dep. Political Resident, Persian Gulf, 1966; Counsellor, FO, attached St Antony's Coll., Oxford, 1968; Ambassador to Iraq, 1969–71; Ambassador to Jordan, 1972–75; Ambassador to Tunisia, 1975–77. *Recreations*: archaeology, modern poetry, carpentry. *Address*: Bradridge House, Diptford, Totnes, Devon. *T*: South Brent 3165.

BALGONIE, Lord; David Alexander Leslie Melville; Director, Wood Conversion Ltd, since 1984; *b* 26 Jan. 1954; *s* and *heir* of Earl of Leven and Melville, *qv; m* 1981, Julia Clare, *yr d* of Col I. R. Critchley, Lindores, Muthill, Perthshire; one *s. Educ*: Eton. Captain Queen's Own Highlanders (GSM for N Ireland); RARO 1979. *Heir: s* Hon. Alexander Ian Leslie Melville, *b* 29 Nov. 1984. *Address*: 3 Bradbourne Street, SW6 3TF.

BALKWILL, Bryan Havell; conductor; Professor of Conducting, Indiana University, Bloomington, since 1977; *b* 2 July 1922; *s* of Arthur William Balkwill and Dorothy Silver Balkwill (*née* Wright); *m* 1949, Susan Elizabeth Roberts; one *s* one *d. Educ*: Merchant Taylors' Sch.; Royal Academy of Music. Asst Conductor, New London Opera Co., 1947–48; Associate Conductor, Internat. Ballet, 1948–49; Musical Director and Principal Conductor, London Festival Ballet, 1950–52; Music staff and subseq. Associate Conductor, Glyndebourne Opera, 1950–58; Musical Dir, Arts Council 'Opera For All', 1953–63; Resident Conductor, Royal Opera House, Covent Garden, 1959–65; Musical Director: Welsh Nat. Opera Company, 1963–67; Sadler's Wells Opera, 1966–69; free-lance opera and concert conducting in N America, Europe and GB, 1970–. Guest Conductor: Royal Opera House, Covent Garden, English Nat. Opera, Glyndebourne, Wexford Festival, Aldeburgh, RPO, LPO, BBC. Mem. Royal Philharmonic Society; FRAM. *Recreation*: open air. *Address*: 8 The Green, Wimbledon Common, SW19 5AZ. *T*: 01–947 4250.

BALL, Alan Hugh; Deputy Chairman, Lonrho Ltd, since 1982 and Director of associated companies (Chairman and Joint Managing Director, 1961–72; Executive Deputy Chairman, 1972–78); *b* 8 June 1924; *s* of late Sir George Joseph Ball, KBE and Mary Caroline Ball; *m* 1948, Eleanor Katharine Turner; two *s* one *d. Educ*: Eton. KRRC, 1943–47. Lonrho Ltd and associated cos, 1947–. *Recreations*: fishing, shooting. *Address*: The Old Mill, Ramsbury, Marlborough, Wilts. *T*: Marlborough 20266.

BALL, Air Marshal Sir Alfred (Henry Wynne), KCB 1976 (CB 1967); DSO 1943; DFC 1942; Hon. Air Commodore, No 2624 (County of Oxford) Royal Auxiliary Air Force Regiment Squadron, since 1984; Vice-Chairman (Air), Council of Territorial, Auxiliary and Volunteer Reserve Associations, 1979–84; *b* 18 Jan. 1921; *s* of Captain J. A. E. Ball, MC, BA, BE; *m* 1942, Nan McDonald; three *s* one *d. Educ*: Campbell Coll., Belfast; RAF Coll., Cranwell; idc, jssc, psc, pfc. Served War of 1939–45 (Despatches twice; US Air Medal 1943); Sqdn Ldr 1942; Wing Comdr 1944; air operations, Lysanders, Spitfires, Mosquitoes; commanded: 4 Photo. Reconn. Unit; 682, 542, 540 and 13 Photo. Reconn. Sqdns in N Africa, UK, France and Middle East; E Africa, 1947; Bomber Comd, 1952; Gp Captain, Operations, BJSM, Washington, 1959; Comdr, Honington V Bomber Base, 1963–64; Air Cdre, Air Officer, Administration, Aden, 1965; IDC, 1967; Dir of Operations, (RAF), MoD, 1967–68; Air Vice-Marshal, 1968; ACOS, Automatic Data Processing Div., SHAPE, 1968–71; Dir-Gen. Organisation (RAF), 1971–75; Air Marshal, 1975; UK Rep., Perm. Mil. Deputies Gp, Cento, 1975–77; Dep. C-in-C, RAF Strike Command, 1977–79, retired 1979. Mil. Affairs Advr, Internat. Computers Ltd, 1979–83. Hon. Mem. British Computer Soc., 1974. *Recreations*: golf, bridge. *Address:* Tarshyne, Lambridge Wood Road, Henley-on-Thames, Oxon. *Clubs:* Royal Air Force; Phyllis Court (Henley-on-Thames); Huntercombe.

BALL, Anthony George, MBE 1986; FInstM; Chairman: Tony Ball Associates Ltd, since 1983; Tony Ball Consultants Ltd, since 1983; Geoff Howe & Associates Ltd, since 1983; Deputy Chairman, Lumley Warranty Services Ltd, since 1985; Director: Lumley Insurance Ltd, since 1983; LIC Management Ltd, since 1983; Midas Holdings Ltd, since 1983; Autoclenz Ltd, since 1983; Customer Concern Ltd, since 1986; Harry Ball (Bridgwater) Ltd, since 1960; *b* 14 Nov. 1934; *s* of Harry Ball and Mary Irene Ball, Bridgwater; *m* 1957, Ruth Parry Davies; two *s* one *d*. *Educ:* Dr Morgan's Grammar Sch., Bridgwater. FIMI, ACIArb. Indentured engineering apprentice, Austin Motor Co., 1950–55; management trainee, 1955–57; sales representative, 1957–59; UK sales executive, 1959–62; responsible for launch of Mini, 1959; Commercial Vehicle Sales Manager, 1962–64, Car Sales Manager, 1964–66, Austin Motor Co.; Sales and Marketing Exec., British Motor Corp., 1966–67; Chm. and Man. Dir, Barlow Rand UK Motor Gp, 1967–78; Managing Director: Barlow Rand Ford, S Africa, 1971–73; Barlow Rand European Operations, 1973–78; Barlow Handling Ltd, 1975–78; returned to British Leyland as Man. Dir, Overseas Trading Operations, 1978; Director: Leyland Australia, Leyland S Africa, Leyland Kenya and all BL African subsids; Dep. Man. Dir, Austin Morris Ltd, 1979; Chm. and Man. Dir, BL Europe & Overseas, 1979–82; Director, 1979–82: BL Cars Ltd (World Sales Chief, 1979–82); Austin Morris Ltd; Rover Triumph Ltd; Jaguar Rover Triumph Inc. (USA); Dir, Jaguar Cars Ltd, 1981–82; responsible for: conducting BL's Buy British campaign and launch of the Austin Metro in 1980; staging General Motors' UK dealer launch of Vauxhall Astra, 1984, and Vauxhall Belmont range, 1985. Chm., Nuffield Press, 1978–80. Ch. Exec. and Gp Man. Dir, Henlys plc, 1982–83. Apptd special Mktg Advr to Sec. of State for Energy, 1984–; responsible for staging Nat. Energy Management Confs and Exhibns, 1985 and 86. Lectr, public and after dinner speaker; TV and radio broadcasts on motoring, marketing and industrial subjects include: The Money Programme, Today, Top Gear, Going Places, World in Action, Focus, World at One, Gloria Hunniford show; documentaries Moving the Metal, The Edwardes Years; panellist, BBC, Any Questions, Start the Week. Mason Meml Lecture, Birmingham Univ., 1983. Governor, N Worcs Coll., 1984–. Freeman of City of London, 1980; Liveryman: Worshipful Co. of Coach Makers and Coach Harness Makers, 1980; Worshipful Co. of Carmen, 1982. Fellowship of Inst. of Marketing awarded 1981, for launch of the Metro and services to Brit. Motor Industry; Hon. Mem. CGLI, 1982, for services to technical and vocational educn; Prince Philip Medal, CGLI, 1984, for outstanding contribution to the motor industry. *Publications:* contribs to numerous industrial, management and marketing jls. *Recreations:* theatre, British military history, golf, gliding, good humour. *Address:* Blythe House, Bidford-on-Avon, Warwickshire B50 4BY. *T:* Bidford-on-Avon 778015. *Club:* Oriental.

BALL, Arthur Beresford, OBE 1973; HM Diplomatic Service, retired; Consul-General, Perth, Western Australia, 1978–80; *b* 15 Aug. 1923; *s* of Charles Henry and Lilian Ball; *m* 1961, June Stella Luckett; one *s* two *d*. *Educ:* Bede Collegiate Boys' Sch., Sunderland; Univ. of E Anglia. Joined HM Diplomatic Service, 1949: Bahrain, 1949; Tripoli, 1950; Middle East Centre for Arab Studies, 1952; Ramullah, 1953; Damascus, 1954; Foreign Office, 1957; Kuwait, 1959; HM Consul, New Orleans, 1963; Jedda, 1965; FO, 1967; São Paulo, 1969; Lisbon, 1972; Ankara, 1975. *Recreations:* sailing, ice skating, historical studies. *Address:* 15 Eccles Road, Holt, Norfolk NR25 6HJ.

BALL, Sir Charles (Irwin), 4th Bt *cr* 1911; *b* 12 Jan. 1924; *s* of Sir Nigel Gresley Ball, 3rd Bt, and of Florine Isabel, *d* of late Col Herbert Edwardes Irwin; *S* father, 1978; *m* 1950, Alison Mary Bentley (marr. diss. 1983); one *s* one *d*. *Educ:* Sherborne Sch. FCA 1960. Served RA, 1942–47. Chartered Accountant, 1950; Peat, Marwick, Mitchell & Co., 1950–54; joined Robert, Benson, Lonsdale & Co. Ltd (now Kleinwort, Benson Ltd), 1954; Director: Kleinwort, Benson Ltd, 1964–76 (Vice-Chm., 1974–76); Kleinwort, Benson, Lonsdale Ltd, 1974–76; Cadbury Schweppes Ltd, 1971–76; Chubb & Son Ltd, 1971–76; Sun Alliance and London Insurance Ltd, 1971–83; Telephone Rentals plc, 1971– (Vice-Chm., 1978–81, Chm., 1981–); Tunnel Holdings Ltd, 1976–82; Barclays Bank Ltd, 1976–77 (Chm., Barclays Merchant Bank Ltd, 1976–77); Rockware Group plc, 1978–84; Peachey Property Corporation plc, 1978– (Chm., 1981–); British Transport Docks Bd, 1971–82; Associated British Ports Holdings (Dep.-Chm., 1982–). Liveryman, 1960, Mem. Ct of Assts, 1979–, Master, 1985, Clockmakers' Co. *Heir:* *s* Richard Bentley Ball, *b* 29 Jan. 1953. *Address:* Appletree Cottage, Heath Lane, Ewshot, near Farnham, Surrey GU10 5AW. *T:* Aldershot 850208.

BALL, Christopher John Elinger, MA; Warden, Keble College, Oxford, since 1980; Chairman, Board of National Advisory Body for Public Sector Higher Education in England, since 1982; *b* 22 April 1935; *er s* of late Laurence Elinger Ball, OBE, and Christine Florence Mary Ball (*née* Howe); *m* 1958, Wendy Ruth Colyer, *d* of Cecil Frederick Colyer and Ruth Colyer (*née* Reddaway); three *s* three *d*. *Educ:* St George's School, Harpenden; Merton College, Oxford (Harmsworth Scholar 1959). 1st Cl. English Language and Literature, 1959; Dipl. in Comparative Philology, 1962; MA Oxon, 1963. 2nd Lieut, Parachute Regt, 1955–56. Lectr in English Language, Merton Coll., Oxford, 1960–61; Lectr in Comparative Linguistics, Sch. of Oriental and African Studies (Univ. of London), 1961–64; Fellow and Tutor in English Language, Lincoln Coll., Oxford, 1964–79 (Sen. Tutor and Tutor for Admissions, 1971–72; Bursar, 1972–79; Hon. Fellow, 1981). Sec., Linguistics Assoc. of GB, 1964–67; Pres., Oxford Assoc. of University Teachers, 1968–70; Publications Sec., Philological Soc., 1969–75; Chairman: Oxford Univ. English Bd, 1977–79; Jt Standing Cttee for Linguistics, 1979–82; Conf. of Colls Fees Cttee, 1979–85; Hebdomadal Council, 1985–; Member: General Bd of the Faculties, 1979–82; CNAA, 1982– (Chm., English Studies Bd, 1973–80, Linguistics Bd, 1977–82); BTEC, 1984–; IT Skills Shortages Cttee (Butcher Cttee), 1984–85; CBI IT Skills Agency, 1985–. Mem. Editl Bd, Oxford Rev. of Education, 1984–. *Publications:* Fitness for Purpose, 1985; various contributions to philological, linguistic and educational jls. *Address:* Keble College, Oxford. *T:* Oxford 59201. *Club:* United Oxford & Cambridge University.

BALL, Denis William, MBE 1971; industrial consultant; Headmaster of Kelly College, 1972–85; *b* 20 Oct. 1928; *er s* of William Charles Thomas and Dora Adelaide Ball, Eastbourne; *m* 1972, Marja Tellervo Lumijärvi, *er d* of Osmo Kullervo and Leila Tellervo Lumijärvi, Toijala, Finland; two *s* one *d*. *Educ:* Brunswick Sch.; Tonbridge Sch. (Scholar); Brasenose Coll., Oxford (MA). Asst Master, The King's Sch., Canterbury, 1953–72 (Housemaster, 1954–72). Sub-Lt, RNR, 1953; Lieut 1954; Lt-Comdr 1958. Trustee, Tavistock Sch., 1972–85; Vice-Chm. of Governors, St Michael's Sch., Tawstock Court, 1974– (Headmaster during interregnum, 1986); Mem., Political and PR Sub-Cttee, HMC, 1979–84. *Recreations:* Elizabethan history, cryptography, literary and mathematical puzzles, cricket, real tennis, squash (played for Oxford Univ. and Kent), golf. *Address:* Ickham Hall, Ickham, Canterbury, Kent CT3 1QT. *Clubs:* East India, Devonshire, Sports and Public Schools, MCC.

BALL, Sir George Thomas T.; *see* Thalben-Ball.

BALL, Dr Harold William; Keeper of Palæontology, British Museum (Natural History), 1966–86; *b* 11 July 1926; *s* of Harold Ball and Florence (*née* Harris); *m* 1955, Patricia Mary (*née* Silvester); two *s* two *d*. *Educ:* Yardley Gram. Sch.; Birmingham Univ. BSc 1947, PhD 1949, Birmingham. Geologist, Nyasaland Geological Survey, 1949–51; Asst Lectr in Geology, King's Coll., London, 1951–54; Dept of Palæontology, British Museum (Nat. Hist.), 1954–86: Dep. Keeper, 1965; Keeper, 1966. Adrian Vis. Fellow, Univ. of Leicester, 1972–77. Sec., 1968–72, Vice-Pres., 1972–73, 1984–86, Geological Soc. of London; Pres., 1981–84, Vice-Pres., 1984–86, Soc. for the History of Natural History. Wollaston Fund, Geological Soc. of London, 1965. *Publications:* papers on the stratigraphy of the Old Red Sandstone and on the palæontology of the Antarctic in several scientific jls. *Recreations:* music, wine, gardening. *Address:* Wilderbrook, Dormans Park, East Grinstead, West Sussex. *T:* Dormans Park 426.

BALL, Sir James; *see* Ball, Sir R. J.

BALL, Prof. John Geoffrey, CEng; consultant metallurgist; Senior Research Fellow, Imperial College, University of London, since 1980, Professor of Metallurgy, 1956–80, now Emeritus; Head of Metallurgy Department, 1957–79; *b* 27 Sept. 1916; *s* of late I. H. Ball and late Mrs E. M. Ball; *m* 1941, Joan C. M., *d* of late Arthur Wiltshire, JP, Bournemouth. *Educ:* Wellington (Salop) High Sch.; Univ. of Birmingham. British Welding Res. Assoc., 1941–49; Sen. Metallurgist, 1945–49; AERE, Harwell, 1949–56; Head of Reactor Metallurgy, 1953–56. Min. of Tech. Visitor to British Non-Ferrous Metals Res. Assoc., 1962–72. Dean, Royal Sch. of Mines, Imperial Coll., 1962–65 and 1971–74; Dean, Faculty of Engineering, Univ. of London, 1970–74. Chairman: Res. Bd, 1964–74, and Mem. of Council Br. Welding Res. Assoc., 1964–81; Engrg Physics Sub-Cttee, Aeronautical Res. Council, 1964–68; Metallurgy Bd, CNAA, 1965–71; Metallurgy and Materials Cttee and Univ. Science and Technology Bd, SRC, 1967–70; Engrg Bd, SRC, 1969–71; Manpower Utilisation Working Party, 1967–69; Mem., Light Water Reactor Pressure Vessel Study Gp, Dept of Energy, 1974–77. Consultant on Materials, SERC, 1983–84. President: Inst. of Welding, 1965–66; Instn of Metallurgists, 1966–67 (Mem. Council 1951–56, 1958–70); Member: Council, Br. Nuclear Forum, 1964–71; Manpower Resources Cttee, 1965–; Council, Inst. of Metals, 1965; Council, Iron and Steel Inst., 1965; Council, City Univ., 1966–; Brain Drain Cttee, 1966–67; Public Enquiry into loss of "Sea Gem", 1967; Materials and Structures Cttee, 1967–70; Technology Sub-Cttee of UGC, 1968–73; Chartered Engineer Section Bd, CEI, 1978–83; Mem., Group IV Exec. Cttee, Engineering Council, 1983–. Governor, Sir John Cass Coll., 1958–67. Hon. ARSM 1961. Brooker Medal, Welding Inst., 1979; Freedom of Inst. and Distinguished Service Award, Indian Inst. of Technology, Delhi, 1985. *Recreations:* gardening, painting, travel. *Address:* 3 Sylvan Close, Limpsfield, Surrey RH8 0DX. *T:* Oxted 3511.

BALL, Rev. Kenneth Vernon James, MA; *b* 10 July 1906; *s* of Vernon Arthur and Eveline Ball, Brighton; *m* 1939, Isabella Jane Armstrong, MB, ChB, *d* of Archibald Armstrong, JP, and Eleanor Elsie Armstrong, Strachur, Argyll; one *s* one *d*. *Educ:* The College, Swindon; Jesus Coll., Oxford; Wycliffe Hall, Oxford. Acting Headmaster, Busoga High Sch., Uganda, 1930–32; Curate, St Paul, Bedminster, 1932–35; Curate, Temple or Holy Cross Church, Bristol, 1935–38; Vicar, St Barnabas, Bristol, 1938–42; Vicar, St Leonard, Redfield, Bristol, 1942–47; Bishop of Liverpool's Special Service Staff, 1947–50; Vicar, St Nicholas, and Chap. St Bartholomew's Hosp., Rochester, 1950–59; Oriel Canon of Rochester Cath., 1955–59; Vicar of Leatherhead, Surrey, 1959–70; Rector of Piddlehinton, Dorset, 1970–72; retd. *Publication:* Spiritual Approach to Marriage Preparation, 1948. *Recreation:* singing. *Address:* Manormead Nursing Home, Tilford Road, Hindhead, Surrey. *T:* Hindhead 4044.

BALL, Rt. Rev. Michael Thomas; *see* Jarrow, Bishop Suffragan of.

BALL, Rt. Rev. Peter John; *see* Lewes, Bishop Suffragan of.

BALL, Rev. Canon Peter William; Residentiary Canon of St Paul's Cathedral, since 1984; *b* 17 Jan. 1930; *s* of Leonard Wevell Ball and Dorothy Mary Ball; *m* 1956, Angela Jane Dunlop; one *s* two *d*. *Educ:* Aldenham School; Worcester Coll., Oxford (MA); Cuddesdon Coll., Oxford. Asst Curate, All Saints, Poplar, 1955; Vicar, The Ascension, Wembley, 1961; Rector, St Nicholas, Shepperton, 1968; Area Dean of Spelthorne, 1972–83; Prebendary of St Paul's Cathedral, 1976. *Publications:* Journey into Faith, 1984. *Recreations:* gardening, walking, music. *Address:* 1 Amen Court, EC4M 7BU. *T:* 01–248 1817.

BALL, Robert Edward, CB 1977; MBE 1946; Chief Master of the Supreme Court of Judicature (Chancery Division), 1969–79 (Master, 1954–68); *b* 8 March 1911; *s* of James Ball, LLB, Purley, Surrey, and Mabel Louise (*née* Laver); *m* 1935, Edith Margaret Barbara, *d* of late Dr Patrick Edward Campbell; one *s* two *d* (and one *s* decd). *Educ:* Westminster Sch.; Lycée de Vendôme, France; Germany; London Univ. (LLB). Law Soc.'s Studentship, 1929. Admitted Solicitor, 1933; junior partner, James Ball & Son, 1933–46; served War, 1939–46; commissioned in Queen's Royal Regt, 1940; served KORR and in various staff appts, England, France and India; AA & QMG, Madras; released with rank of Lt-Col, 1946; formed practice of Potts and Ball, Chester and London, with Henry Potts, 1946. Mem. Council, Teilhard Centre for the Future of Man, 1971–; Dep. Chm., Friends of Friendless Churches, 1984–. Formerly: Hon. Sec., Chester and North Wales Incorp. Law Soc.; Chm. Chester Insurance Tribunal, etc. *Publications:* The Law and the Cloud of Unknowing, 1976; The Crown, The Sages and Supreme Morality, 1983; contrib. to Study Notes of the Inst. of Moralogy, Chiba, Japan. *Recreations:* history, oriental studies, gardening. *Address:* 62 Stanstead Road, Caterham, Surrey. *T:* Caterham 43675. *Club:* Athenæum.

BALL, Prof. Sir (Robert) James, Kt 1984; MA, PhD; Professor of Economics, London Business School, since 1965; Chairman, Legal & General Group, since 1980; Director, IBM UK Holdings Ltd, since 1979; Economic Adviser, Touche Ross & Co., since 1984; *b* 15 July 1933; *s* of Arnold James Hector Ball; *m* 1st, 1954, Patricia Mary Hart Davies (marr. diss. 1970); one *s* three *d* (and one *d* decd); 2nd, 1970, Lindsay Jackson (*née* Wonnacott); one step *s*. *Educ:* St Marylebone Grammar Sch.; The Queen's College, Oxford; Styring Schol.; George Webb Medley Junior Schol. (Univ. Prizeman), 1956. BA 1957 (First cl. Hons PPE), MA 1960; PhD Univ. of Pennsylvania, 1973. RAF 1952–54 (Pilot-Officer, Navigator). Research Officer, Oxford University Inst. of Statistics, 1957–58; IBM Fellow, Univ. of Pennsylvania, 1958–60; Lectr, Manchester Univ., 1960, Sen. Lectr, 1963–65; London Business School: Governor, 1969–84; Dep. Principal, 1971–72; Principal, 1972–84. Director: Ogilvy and Mather Ltd, 1969–71; Economic Models Ltd, 1971–72; Barclays Bank Trust Co., 1973–86. Part-time Mem., Nat. Freight Corporation, 1973–77; Dir, Tube Investments, 1974–84. Member: Cttee to Review National Savings (Page Cttee), 1971–73; Economics Cttee of SSRC, 1971–74; Cttee on Social Forecasting, SSRC, 1971–72; Cttee of Enquiry into Electricity Supply Industry (Plowden Cttee), 1974–75; Chm., Treasury Cttee on Policy Optimisation, 1976–78. Governor, NIESR, 1973–. Member Council: REconS, 1973–79; BIM, 1974–82 (Chm., Economic and Social Affairs Cttee, 1979–82); British–N American Cttee, 1985–. Fellow, Econometric Soc., 1973; CBIM 1974; FIAM 1985. *Publications:* An Econometric Model of the United Kingdom, 1961; Inflation and the Theory of Money, 1964; (ed) Inflation, 1969; (ed) The International Linkage of National Economic Models, 1972; Money and Employment,

1982; (with M. Albert) Toward European Economic Recovery in the 1980s (report to European Parliament), 1984; articles in professional jls. *Recreations:* fishing, chess. *Address:* London Business School, Sussex Place, Regent's Park, NW1 4SA. *T:* 01–262 5050; Timbers, 8 Winchester Close, Esher, Surrey KT10 8QH. *Club:* Royal Dart Yacht.

BALLANTYNE, Colin Sandergrove, CMG 1971; photographer and director; Chairman, Performing Arts Collection of South Australia, since 1980; *b* 12 July 1908; *s* of James Fergusson Ballantyne, Adelaide; *m* 1934, Gwenneth Martha Osborne Richmond; one *s* two *d*. *Educ:* Adelaide High School. Directed: cycle Shakespeare plays, 1948–52; 100 contemporary plays, 1948–78; five major productions Adelaide Festival of Arts, 1960–68. Dir, Sheridan Theatre, 1962–72. Chm. Bd of Governors, State Theatre Co., 1972–78; Pres., Arts Council of Australia (SA), 1974–77 (Federal Dir, 1966–74). Hon. FIAP 1971. *Publications:* (plays) Harvest, 1936; The Ice-Cream Cart, 1962; Between Gunshots, 1964 (also Pacific Rape, unpublished). *Address:* 77 Kingston Terrace, North Adelaide, SA 5006, Australia. *T:* Adelaide 267 1138.

BALLARAT, Bishop of, since 1975; **Rt. Rev. John Hazlewood;** *b* 19 May 1924; *s* of George Harold Egerton Hazlewood and Anne Winnifred Edeson; *m* 1961, Dr Shirley Shevill; two *s*. *Educ:* Nelson Coll., New Zealand; King's Coll., Cambridge (BA 1948, MA 1952); Cuddesdon Coll., Oxford. Deacon 1949, priest 1950, Southwark; Asst Curate: SS Michael and All Angels, Camberwell, 1949–50, 1953–55; St Jude, Randwick, Sydney, 1950–51; Holy Trinity, Dubbo, NSW, 1951–53; Vice-Principal, St Francis Coll., Brisbane, 1955–60; Asst Lectr in Ecclesiastical History, Univ. of Queensland, 1959–60; Dean of Rockhampton, Qld, 1960–68; Dean of Perth, WA, 1968–75. Chaplain to Victorian Br., Order of St Lazarus of Jerusalem, 1984–. Mem., Soc. of Holy Cross (SSC), 1985–. *Recreations:* travelling, music, gardening, reading, theatre, art. *Address:* Bishopscourt, 454 Wendouree Parade, Ballarat, Victoria 3350, Australia. *T:* 053–392370. *Clubs:* Melbourne, Naval and Military, Royal Automobile of Victoria (Melbourne); Ballarat.

BALLARAT, Bishop of, (RC), since 1971; **Most Rev. Ronald Austin Mulkearns,** DD, DCL; *b* 11 Nov. 1930. *Educ:* De La Salle Coll., Malvern; Corpus Christi Coll., Werribee; Pontifical Lateran Univ., Rome. Ordained, 1956; Coadjutor Bishop, 1968–71. *Address:* 1444 Sturt Street, Ballarat, Victoria 3350, Australia.

BALLARD, Prof. Clifford Frederick; Professor Emeritus in Orthodontics, University of London; Hon. Consultant, Eastman Dental Hospital, London; *b* 26 June 1910; *s* of Frederick John Ballard and Eliza Susannah (*née* Wilkinson); *m* 1937, Muriel Mabel Burling; one *s* one *d*. *Educ:* Kilburn Grammar Sch.; Charing Cross Hosp. and Royal Dental Hospital. LDS 1934; MRCS, LRCP 1940. Hd of Dept of Orthodontics, Inst. of Dental Surgery, British Post-Grad. Med. Fedn, Univ. of London, 1948–72; Prof. of Orthodontics, London Univ., 1956–72; Dental Surgeon, Victoria Hosp. for Children, SW3, 1948–64, Tooting, 1964–71. Pres. of Brit. Soc. for the Study of Orthodontics, 1957, Senior Vice-Pres., 1963, 1964; Mem. Council of Odontological Section of Royal Society Med., 1954–56, 1959–62 (Sec., 1957, Vice-Pres., 1969–72); Mem. Board, Faculty of Dental Surgery. RCS, 1966–74. FDS 1949; Diploma in Orthodontics, 1954 (RCS); FFDRCS Ire., 1964. Charles Tomes Lectr, RCS, 1966; Northcroft Memorial Lectr, Brit. Soc. for Study of Orthocorties, 1967. Hon. Life Mem., British Dental Assoc., 1982; Hon. Member: British Soc. for Study of Orthodontics; Israel Orthodontic Soc.; NZ Orthodontic Soc.; European Orthodontic Soc.; Membre d'Honneur, Société Française d'Orthopédie Dento-faciale. Colyer Gold Medal, RCS, 1975. *Publications:* numerous contributions to learned journals, 1948–. *Recreations:* golf, gardening. *Address:* Winnards Perch, Ridge, Wareham, Dorset BH20 5BQ. *T:* Wareham 3346.

BALLARD, Geoffrey Horace, CBE 1978; JP; Managing Director: G. H. Ballard (Farms) Ltd, since 1968; G. H. Ballard (Leasing) Ltd, since 1968; Chairman, MSF Ltd, since 1984; Vice-Chairman, NFU Mutual Insurance Society Ltd, since 1982; *b* 21 May 1927; *s* of Horace and Mary Catherine Ballard; *m* 1948, Dorothy Sheila Bache (*d* 1979); two *s* one *d*; *m* 1983, Anne Ballard. *Educ:* Hanley Castle Grammar Sch. Farming with father at Home Farm, Abberley, 1943; Maesllwch Castle Estates: Cowman, 1947, Bailiff, 1948; in partnership with father and brother at Home Farm, 1950; farming, on own account, at Old Yates Farm, Abberley, 1953; Nuffield Farming Schol. to USA, 1965. Chm., W Midlands Reg. panel for Agric., 1972–80. Chm., Worcestershire County NFU, 1967. JP 1967–. *Recreations:* sailing, shooting. *Address:* Orchard House, Abberley, Worcester WR6 6AT. *T:* Great Witley 307. *Clubs:* Farmers'; Dale Sailing (Dyfed); Astley and District Farmers Discussion (Worcs).

BALLARD, James Graham; novelist and short story writer; *b* 15 Nov. 1930; *s* of James Ballard and Edna Ballard (*née* Johnstone); *m* 1954, Helen Mary Matthews (*d* 1964); one *s* two *d*. *Educ:* Leys School, Cambridge; King's College, Cambridge. *Publications:* The Drowned World, 1963; The 4–Dimensional Nightmare, 1963 (re-issued as The Voices of Time, 1985); The Terminal Beach, 1964; The Drought, 1965; The Crystal World, 1966; The Disaster Area, 1967; The Atrocity Exhibition, 1970; Crash, 1973; Vermilion Sands, 1973; Concrete Island, 1974; High Rise, 1975; Low-Flying Aircraft, 1976; The Unlimited Dream Company, 1979; Myths of the Near Future, 1982; Empire of the Sun, 1984. *Address:* 36 Old Charlton Road, Shepperton, Middlesex. *T:* Walton-on-Thames 225692.

BALLARD, Ronald Alfred; Head of Technical Services of the Central Computers and Telecommunications Agency, HM Treasury (formerly Civil Service Department), 1980–85, now Consultant; *b* 17 Feb. 1925; *s* of Joseph William and Ivy Amy Ballard; *m* 1948, Eileen Margaret Edwards; one *d*. *Educ:* Univ. of Birmingham (BSc (Hons) Physics). National Service, RN, 1945–47. Admiralty Surface Weapons Establishment, Portsmouth: Scientific Officer, then Sen. Scientific Officer, Research and Development Seaborne Radar Systems, 1948–55; Application of Computers to Naval Comd and Control Systems, 1955–69; PSO, 1960, responsibilities for Action Data Automation (ADA), on HMS Eagle and destroyers; SPSO, to Head Computer Systems and Techniques in Civil Service Dept (Central Computers Agency in 1972), 1969; Head of Central Computers Facility, 1972–76; DCSO, to Head Technical Services Div. of Central Computers Agency, 1977; CSO(B), 1980–85. *Address:* Central Computer and Telecommunications Agency, Riverwalk House, 157–161 Millbank, SW1P 4RT.

BALLENTYNE, Donald Francis, CMG 1985; HM Diplomatic Service; Consul-General, Los Angeles, since 1985; *b* 5 May 1929; *s* of late Henry Q. Ballentyne and Frances R. MacLaren; *m* 1950, Elizabeth Heywood, *d* of Leslie A. Heywood; one *s* one *d*. *Educ:* Haberdashers' Aske's Hatcham Sch. FO, 1950–53; Berne and Ankara, 1953–56; Consul: Munich, 1957; Stanleyville, 1961; Cape Town, 1962; First Secretary: Luxembourg, 1965–69, Havana, 1969–72; FCO, 1972–74; Counsellor (Commercial), The Hague, 1974–78, Bonn, 1978–81; Counsellor, E Berlin, 1982–84. *Recreation:* sailing. *Address:* c/o Foreign and Commonwealth Office, SW1.

BALLESTEROS, Severiano; golfer; *b* Santander, Spain, 9 April 1957. Professional golfer, 1974–; won Spanish Young Professional title, 1974; Open Champion, Lytham St Anne's, 1979, St Andrews, 1984; won US Masters, 1980, 1983; World Matchplay Champion, Wentworth, 1981, 1982, 1984, 1985; numerous other titles in Europe, USA, Australasia; Mem. Ryder Cup team, 1979, 1983, 1985. *Address:* c/o Jorge de Ceballos, Fairway SA, Fernandez de la Hoz 57 1/4, 28003 Madrid, Spain.

BALLS, Alastair Gordon; Regional Director, Departments of the Environment and Transport (Northern Region), since 1984; *b* 18 March 1944; *s* of Dr Ernest George Balls and Mrs Elspeth Russell Balls; *m* 1978, Beryl May Nichol; one *s* one *d*. *Educ:* Hamilton Acad.; Univ. of St Andrews (MA); Univ. of Manchester (MA). Economist: Treasury, Govt of Tanzania, 1966–68; Min. of Transport, UK, 1969–74; Sec., Adv. Cttee on Channel Tunnel, 1974–75; Sen. Econ. Adviser, HM Treasury, 1976–79; Asst Sec., Dept of Environment, 1979–83. *Recreations:* sailing, cycling, walking, camping in the company of my family. *Address:* Departments of the Environment and Transport, Wellbar House, Gallowgate, Newcastle upon Tyne NE1 4TD.

BALME, Prof. David Mowbray, CMG 1955; DSO 1943; DFC 1943; MA; Professor of Classics, Queen Mary College, London University, 1964–78, retired; *b* 8 Sept. 1912; *s* of late Harold Balme, OBE, MD, FRCS; *m* 1936, Beatrice Margaret Rice; four *s* one *d*. *Educ:* Marlborough; Clare Coll., Cambridge. Res. Student, Clare Coll. and Univ. of Halle, Germany, 1934–36; Lecturer, Reading Univ., 1936–37; Research Fellow, Clare Coll., Cambridge, 1937–40; Fellow of Jesus Coll., 1940. Served with No 207 (Bomber) Squadron, 1943; Comd Nos 227 and 49 Squadrons, 1945. Tutor of Jesus Coll., 1945–47; Senior Tutor, 1947–48; University Lecturer in Classics, 1947–48; Principal, University College of Ghana, 1948–57; Reader in Classics, Queen Mary Coll., London, 1957–64. Vis. Prof., Princeton Univ., 1973. Hon. LLD Lincoln, Pa, 1955; Hon. LittD Ghana, 1970. Editor, Phronesis, 1965–70. *Publications:* Aristotle's De Partibus Animalium, I, 1972; articles in classical journals on Greek Philosophy. *Recreations:* music, foxhunting. *Address:* Gumley, near Market Harborough, Leics. *T:* Kibworth 2762.

BALMER, Sir Joseph (Reginald), Kt 1965; JP; Retired Insurance Official; *b* 22 Sept. 1899; *s* of Joseph Balmer; *m* 1927, Dora, *d* of A. Johnson; no *c*. *Educ:* King Edward's Grammar Sch., Birmingham. North British and Mercantile Insurance Co. Ltd, 1916–60; National Chairman Guild of Insurance Officials, 1943–47. Pres. Birmingham Borough Labour Party, 1946–54; elected to Birmingham City Council, 1945, 1949, 1952; Alderman 1952–74; Chairman Finance Cttee, 1955–64; Lord Mayor of Birmingham, 1954–55; Hon. Alderman, 1974; City Magistrate, 1956. Hon. Life Mem. Court, Birmingham Univ.; formerly Governor, King Edward VI Schs, Birmingham; Member or ex-member various cttees. Served European War, 1914–18, overseas with RASC and Somerset Light Infantry. *Recreations:* gardening, woodwork and reading. *Address:* 26 Stechford Lane, Ward End, Birmingham B8 2AN. *T:* 021–783 3198.

BALMFORTH, Ven. Anthony James; Archdeacon of Bristol, since 1979; *b* 3 Sept. 1926; *s* of Joseph Henry and Daisy Florence Balmforth; *m* 1952, Eileen Julia, *d* of James Raymond and Kitty Anne Evans; one *s* two *d*. *Educ:* Sebright School, Wolverley; Brasenose Coll., Oxford (BA 1950, MA 1951); Lincoln Theological Coll. Army service, 1944–48. Deacon 1952, priest 1953, dio. Southwell; Curate of Mansfield, 1952–55; Vicar of Skegby, Notts, 1955–61; Vicar of St John's, Kidderminster, Worcs, 1961–65; Rector of St Nicolas, King's Norton, Birmingham, 1965–79; Hon. Canon of Birmingham Cathedral, 1975–79; RD of King's Norton, 1973–79; Examining Chaplain to: Bishop of Birmingham, 1978–79; Bishop of Bristol, 1981–. Hon. Canon of Bristol Cathedral, 1979–. *Recreations:* cricket, gardening. *Address:* 10 Great Brockeridge, Westbury-on-Trym, Bristol BS9 3TY. *T:* Bristol 622438.

BALNIEL, Lord; Anthony Robert Lindsay; *b* 24 Nov. 1958; *s* and *heir* of 29th Earl of Crawford and 12th of Balcarres, *qv*. *Educ:* Eton Coll.; Univ. of Edinburgh. *Address:* 82 Onslow Gardens, SW7.

BALSTON, Antony Francis; His Honour Judge Balston; a Circuit Judge, since 1985; *b* 18 Jan. 1939; *s* of Comdr E. F. Balston, DSO, RN, and D. B. L. Balston (*née* Ferrers); *m* 1966, Anne Marie Judith Ball; two *s* one *d*. *Educ:* Downside; Christ's Coll., Cambridge (MA). Served Royal Navy, 1957–59; Univ. of Cambridge, 1959–62; admitted Solicitor, 1966. Partner, Herington Willings & Penry Davey, Solicitors, Hastings, 1967–85; a Recorder of the Crown Court, 1980–85; Hon. Recorder, Hastings, 1984–. *Recreation:* gardening. *Address:* Elmside, Northiam, Rye, East Sussex TN31 6NS. *T:* Northiam 2270.

BALTIMORE, Prof. David, PhD; Professor of Biology, Massachusetts Institute of Technology, since 1972; Director, Whitehead Institute, since 1982; *b* New York, 7 March 1938; *s* of Richard and Gertrude Baltimore; *m* 1968, Alice Huang; one *d*. *Educ:* Swarthmore Coll.; Rockefeller Univ. Postdoctoral Fellow, MIT, 1963–64; Albert Einstein Coll. of Med., NY, 1964–65; Research Associate, Salk Inst., La Jolla, Calif, 1965–68; Associate Prof., 1968–72, Amer. Cancer Soc. Prof. of Microbiol., 1973–83, MIT. FAAAS 1980. Member: Nat. Acad. of Scis, 1974; Amer. Acad. of Arts and Scis, 1974; Pontifical Acad. of Scis, 1978. Eli Lilly Award in Microbiology and Immunology, 1971; US Steel Foundn Award in Molecular Biology, 1974; (jtly) Nobel Prize for Physiology or Medicine, 1975. *Address:* Whitehead Institute for Biomedical Research, 9 Cambridge Center, Cambridge, Mass 02142, USA.

BAMBERG, Harold Rolf, CBE 1968; Chairman, Bamberg Group Ltd and other companies, including Eagle Aircraft Services Ltd, Eagle Beechcraft Ltd and Eagle Aerotech; *b* 17 Nov. 1923; *m* 1957, June Winifred Clarke; one *s* two *d* (and one *s* one *d* of a former marriage). *Educ:* Fleet Sch.; William Ellis Sch., Hampstead. FRSA. *Recreations:* polo, shooting, bloodstock breeding. *Address:* Harewood Park, Sunninghill, Berks.

BAMBOROUGH, John Bernard; Principal of Linacre College, Oxford, since 1962; Pro-Vice-Chancellor, Oxford University, since 1966; *b* 3 Jan. 1921; *s* of John George Bamborough; *m* 1947, Anne, *d* of Olav Indrehus, Indrehus, Norway; one *s* one *d*. *Educ:* Haberdashers' Aske's Hampstead Sch. (Scholar); New College, Oxford (Scholar). 1st Class, English Language and Literature, 1941; MA 1946. Service in RN, 1941–46 (in Coastal Forces as Lieut RNVR; afterwards as Educ. Officer with rank of Instructor Lieut, RN). Junior Lectr, New Coll., Oxford, 1946; Fellow and Tutor, Wadham Coll., Oxford, 1947–62 (Dean, 1947–54; Domestic Bursar, 1954–56; Sen. Tutor, 1957–61); Univ. Lectr in English, 1951–62; Mem. Hebdomadal Council, Oxford Univ., 1961–79. Hon. Fellow, New Coll., Oxford, 1967. Editor, Review of English Studies, 1964–78. *Publications:* The Little World of Man, 1952; Ben Jonson, 1959; (ed) Pope's Life of Ward, 1961; Jonson's Volpone, 1963; The Alchemist, 1967; Ben Jonson, 1970. *Address:* 40 St Giles', Oxford. *T:* 59886. *Club:* United Oxford & Cambridge University.

BAMFIELD, Clifford, CB 1981; Member, Civil Service Commission Panel of Selection Board Chairmen, since 1982; Official Side Member, Civil Service Appeal Board, since 1982; *b* 21 March 1922; *s* of G. H. Bamfield. *Educ:* Wintringham Grammar Sch., Grimsby; Manchester Business Sch., 1966. Served War, RNVR, 1941–46. Customs and Excise: Exec. Officer, 1946; Private Sec. to Chm., 1959–61; Principal, 1961; Asst Sec., 1967; Under Sec., Comr and Dir of Estabs, 1973; Under Sec., CSD, 1974–80. *Address:* 15 The Linkway, Sutton, Surrey SM2 5SE. *T:* 01–642 5377. *Club:* Army and Navy.

BAMFORD, Alan George, CBE 1985; Principal, Homerton College, Cambridge, since 1985; *b* 12 July 1930; *s* of James Ross and Margaret Emily Bamford; *m* 1954, Joan

Margaret, *e d* of Arthur W. Vint; four *s. Educ:* Prescot Grammar School; Borough Road College, London; Liverpool University (DipEd, MEd); MA Cantab; Cert. Ed. London. Teacher and Dep. Headmaster, Lancashire primary schs, 1952–62; Lectr in Primary Educn, Liverpool Univ., 1962–63; Sen. Lectr in Educn, Chester Coll., 1963–66; Principal Lectr and Head of Educn Dept, St Katharine's Coll., Liverpool, 1966–71; Principal, Westhill Coll., Birmingham, 1971–85. Pres., Birmingham Council of Christian Educn, 1972–74, Vice-Pres., 1974–; Vice-Pres., Colls of Educn Christian Union, 1965–, Pres., 1966–67, 1972–73; Chm., Birmingham Assoc. of Youth Clubs, 1972–85, Vice-Pres., 1985–; Trustee, Invest in Youth Trust, 1973–79; Member: Standing Conf. on Studies in Educn, 1974– (Exec. Cttee and Editl Bd, 1978–, Sec., 1982–84); Council of Nat. Youth Bureau, 1974–80 (Exec. Cttee, 1978–80); Adv. Cttee on religious broadcasts, BBC Radio Birmingham, 1972–80; Educn Cttee, Free Church Fed. Council, 1978–; BCC Standing Cttee on Theol Educn, 1979–82; Council, British and Foreign School Soc., 1979–85; Exec. Cttee, Assoc. of Voluntary Colls, 1979–86; Chairman: Colls Cttee, NATFHE, 1981–82; Central Register and Clearing House Cttee, 1981–82 (Mem. Council of Management, 1982–). Governor, London Bible Coll., 1981–. JP Birmingham 1977–85. FRSA. Hon. MA Birmingham, 1982. *Publications:* articles on educn and church-related subjects. *Recreations:* travel, photography. *Address:* Principal's House, Homerton College, Cambridge CB2 2PH. *T:* Cambridge 245931. *Club:* Royal Commonwealth Society.

BAMFORD, Anthony Paul; Chairman and Managing Director, J. C. Bamford Group, since 1976; *b* 23 Oct. 1945; *s* of Joseph Cyril Bamford, *qv*; *m* 1974, Carole Gray Whitt; two *s* one *d. Educ:* Ampleforth Coll.; Grenoble Univ. Joined JCB on shop floor, 1962; led company's only takeover so far, Chaseside Engineering, 1968; launched JCB's French company and received a Young Exporter of the Year award for the achievement, 1972. Young Businessman of the Year, 1979. High Sheriff, Staffs, 1985–86. *Recreations:* riding, farming. *Address:* c/o J. C. Bamford Excavators Ltd, Rocester, Uttoxeter, Staffs ST14 5JP. *T:* Rocester 590312. *Clubs:* Pratt's, British Racing Drivers'.

BAMFORD, Prof. Clement Henry, FRS 1964; MA, PhD, ScD Cantab; CChem, FRSC; Honorary Senior Fellow, Institute of Medical and Dental Bioengineering, University of Liverpool, since 1980; Campbell Brown Professor of Industrial Chemistry, University of Liverpool, 1962–80, now Emeritus Professor; *b* 10 Oct. 1912; *s* of Frederic Jesse Bamford and Catherine Mary Bamford (*née* Shelley), Stafford; *m* 1938, Daphne Ailsa Stephan, BSc Sydney, PhD Cantab, of Sydney, Australia; one *s* one *d. Educ:* St Patrick's and King Edward VI Schs, Stafford; Trinity Coll., Cambridge (Senior Scholar). Fellow, Trinity Coll., Cambridge, 1937; Dir of Studies in Chemistry, Emmanuel Coll., Cambridge, 1937. Joined Special Operations Executive, 1941; joined Fundamental Research Laboratory of Messrs Courtaulds Ltd, at Maidenhead, 1945; head of laboratory, 1947–62; Liverpool University: Dean, Faculty of Science, 1965–68; Pro-Vice-Chancellor, 1972–75. Member: Council, Chem. Soc., 1972–75; Council, Soc. Chem. Ind., 1974–75. Pres., British Assoc. Section B (Chemistry), 1975–76; Vice-Pres., 1977–81, Pres., 1981–85, Macromolecular Div., Internat. Union of Pure and Applied Chemistry. Vis. Professor: Kyoto Univ., 1977; Univ. of NSW, 1981. Mem. Edit. Bd, Polymer, 1958–. Hon. DSc Bradford, 1980. Meldola Medal, Royal Inst. of Chemistry, 1941; Macromolecules and Polymers Award, Chemical Soc., 1977. *Publications:* Synthetic Polypeptides (with A. Elliott and W. E. Hanby), 1956; The Kinetics of Vinyl Polymerization by Radical Mechanisms (with W. G. Barb, A. D. Jenkins and P. F. Onyon), 1958; (ed with late C. F. H. Tipper and R. G. Compton) Comprehensive Chemical Kinetics, 25 vols, 1969–85; papers on physical chemistry and polymer science in learned journals. *Recreations:* music, especially violin playing, hill walking, gardening. *Address:* Broom Bank, Tower Road, Prenton, Birkenhead, Merseyside L42 8LH. *T:* 051–608 3979.

BAMFORD, Joseph Cyril, CBE 1969; formerly Chairman and Managing Director: J. C. Bamford Excavators Ltd; JCB Farms Ltd; JCB Research Ltd; JCB Sales Ltd; JCB Service; JCB Earthmovers Ltd; *b* 21 June 1916; *m* 1941, Marjorie Griffin; two *s. Educ:* St John's, Alton, Staffs; Stonyhurst Coll. Founded J. C. Bamford Excavators Ltd, 1945; more than seventy per cent of total production now goes to export market. Hon. DTech Loughborough Univ. of Technol., 1983. *Recreations:* yacht designing, landscaping, landscape gardening. *Address:* 16 Rue de Bourg, CH 1003 Lausanne, Switzerland.

See also A. P. Bamford.

BAMFORD, Louis Neville Jules; Legal Executive with Margetts & Ritchie, Solicitors, Birmingham, since 1960; *b* 2 July 1932; *s* of Neville Barnes Bamford and Elise Marie Bamford; unmarried. *Educ:* local schools in Birmingham. Elected Mem. (Lab) Birmingham CC, 1971 (Mem., Airport Police Cttee); elected Birmingham DC, 1974 (Mem., Land and Finance Cttees); elected W Midlands CC: Chm., 1981–82; Chm., Legal and Parly Cttee, 1974–77; formerly Member: Police Cttee and No 4 Dist Police Authorities Cttee; Finance, Fire, and Personnel and Admin Cttees. *Recreations:* football, cricket, reading, music (classical and jazz). *Address:* 20 Westbourne House, Farcroft Avenue, Handsworth, Birmingham B21 8AE.

BAMPFYLDE, family name of **Baron Poltimore.**

BANANA, Rev. the Hon. Dr Canaan Sodindo; President of Zimbabwe, since 1980; *b* Esiphezini, Matabeleland, 5 March 1936; *s* of Aaron and Jese Banana; *m* 1961, Janet Mbuyazwe; three *s* one *d. Educ:* Mzinyati Mission; Tegwani Trng Inst.; Epworth Theol Coll., Salisbury; Kansai Industrial Centre, Japan; Wesley Theol Seminary, Washington, DC; Univ. of S Africa. Dip. in Urban and Industrial Mission, Kansai, 1970; MTS Hons, Wesley Theol Seminary, 1974; BA Hons Univ. of SA, 1980. Methodist Minister and Manager of Schools: Wankie Area, 1963–64; Plumtree Area, 1965–66 (Sch. Chaplain, Tegwani High Sch.); Methodist Minister, Fort Viet Area, 1967–68; Methodist Minister, Bulawayo and Chm., Bulaway Council of Churches, 1969–70; with Mambo Press as Promotion Officer for Moto, Catholic newspaper, 1971; Founder Mem. and first Vice Pres., ANC, Zimbabwe, 1971–73; ANC Rep. in N America and UN, 1973–75; Chaplain, American Univ., 1974–75; Publicity Sec., People's Movement Internal Co-ordinating Cttee (ZANU-PF), 1976–77; Reg. Co-ordinator, Matabeleland N and S Provinces, 1979–80. Chm., Southern Africa Contact Gp, 1970–73; Mem., Adv. Cttee, WCC, 1970–80. Hon. LLD: Amer. Univ., 1981; Univ. of Zimbabwe, 1983. *Publications:* The Zimbabwe Exodus, 1974; The Gospel According to the Ghetto, 1974, 3rd edn 1980; The Woman of my Imagination, 1980 (also in Ndebele and Shona versions); Theology of Promise, 1982; various articles. *Recreations:* tennis, table tennis; soccer (player, referee and coach); volley ball (umpire); music. *Address:* State House, Box 368, Harare, Zimbabwe. *T:* Harare 26666.

BANBURY, family name of **Baron Banbury of Southam.**

BANBURY OF SOUTHAM, 3rd Baron *cr* 1924, of Southam; **Charles William Banbury;** Bt 1902; *b* 29 July 1953; *s* of 2nd Baron Banbury of Southam and of Hilda Ruth, *d* of late A. H. R. Carr; *S* father, 1981; *m* 1984, Lucinda Trehearne. *Educ:* Eton College. *Heir:* none. *Address:* The Mill, Fossebridge, Glos.

BANBURY, (Frederick Harold) Frith; Theatrical director, producer and actor; *b* 4 May 1912; *s* of Rear-Adm. Frederick Arthur Frith Banbury and Winifred (*née* Fink); unmarried. *Educ:* Stowe Sch.; Hertford Coll., Oxford; Royal Academy of Dramatic Art. First stage appearance in "If I Were You", Shaftesbury Theatre, 1933; for next 14 years appeared both in London and Provinces in every branch of theatre from Shakespeare to revue. Appearances included: Hamlet, New Theatre, 1934; Goodness How Sad, Vaudeville, 1938; (revue) New Faces, Comedy, 1939; Uncle Vanya, Westminster, 1943; Jacobowsky and the Colonel, Piccadilly, 1945; Caste, Duke of York's, 1947. During this time he also appeared in numerous films including The Life and Death of Colonel Blimp and The History of Mr Polly, and also on the television screen. Since 1947 he has devoted his time to production and direction, starting with Dark Summer at Lyric, Hammersmith (later transferred St Martin's), 1947; subseq. many, in both London and New York, including The Holly and the Ivy, Duchess, 1950; Waters of the Moon, Haymarket, 1951; The Deep Blue Sea, Duchess, 1951, and Morosco, New York, 1952; A Question of Fact, Piccadilly, 1953; Marching Song, St Martin's, 1954; Love's Labour's Lost, Old Vic, 1954; The Diary of Anne Frank, Phoenix, 1956; A Dead Secret, Piccadilly, 1957; Flowering Cherry, Haymarket, 1957, and Lyceum, New York, 1959; A Touch of the Sun, Saville, 1958; The Ring of Truth, Savoy, 1959; The Tiger and the Horse, Queen's, 1960; The Wings of the Dove, Lyric, 1963; The Right Honourable Gentleman, Billy Rose, New York, 1965; Howards End, New, 1967; Dear Octopus, Haymarket, 1967; Enter A Free Man, St Martin's, 1968; A Day In the Death of Joe Egg, Cameri Theatre, Tel Aviv, 1968; Le Valet, Théâtre de la Renaissance, Paris, 1968; On the Rocks, Dublin Theatre Festival, 1969; My Darling Daisy, Lyric, 1970; The Winslow Boy, New, 1970; Captain Brassbound's Conversion, Cambridge, 1971; Reunion in Vienna, Chichester Festival, 1971, Piccadilly, 1972; The Day After the Fair, Lyric, 1972, Shubert, Los Angeles, 1973; Glasstown, Westminster, 1973; Ardèle, Queen's, 1975; On Approval, Canada and SA, 1976, Vaudeville, 1977; directed in Australia, Kenya, USA, 1978–79; Motherdear, Ambassadors, 1980; Dear Liar, Mermaid, 1982; The Aspern Papers, Haymarket, 1984; The Corn is Green, Old Vic, 1985. *Recreation:* playing the piano.

BANBURY, Frith; *see* Banbury, Frederick Harold F.

BANCROFT, family name of **Baron Bancroft.**

BANCROFT, Baron *cr* 1982 (Life Peer), of Coatham in the county of Cleveland; **Ian Powell Bancroft,** GCB 1979 (KCB 1975; CB 1971); Head of the Home Civil Service and Permanent Secretary to the Civil Service Department, 1978, retired Nov. 1981; *b* 23 Dec. 1922; *s* of A. E. and L. Bancroft; *m* 1950, Jean Swaine; two *s* one *d. Educ:* Coatham Sch.; Balliol Coll., Oxford (Scholar; Hon. Fellow 1981). Served Rifle Brigade, 1942–45. Entered Treasury, 1947; Private Secretary: to Sir Henry Wilson Smith, 1948–50; to Chancellor of the Exchequer, 1953–55, to Lord Privy Seal, 1955–57; Cabinet Office, 1957–59; Principal Private Sec. to successive Chancellors of the Exchequer, 1964–66; Under-Sec., HM Treasury, 1966–68, Civil Service Dept, 1968–70; Dep. Sec., Dir Gen. of Organization and Establishments, DoE, 1970–72; a Comr of Customs and Excise, and Dep. Chm. of Bd, 1972–73; Second Permanent Sec., CSD, 1973–75; Permanent Sec., DoE, 1975–77. Mem., Adv. Council on Public Records, 1983–. A Vice-Chm., Sun Life Assce Soc. plc, 1986– (Dir, 1983–); Director: Rugby Portland Cement Plc, 1982–; Bass Plc, 1982–; Grindlays Bank plc, 1983–85; ANZ Holdings (UK) plc, 1985–; Coral Social Clubs Ltd, 1984–; Bass Leisure Ltd, 1984–. Vis. Fellow, Nuffield Coll., Oxford, 1973–81; Chm. Council, Mansfield Coll., Oxford, 1981–. Chm., Royal Hosp. and Home for Incurables, 1984–; Governor, Cranleigh Sch., 1983–. *Address:* 13 Putney Heath Lane, SW15 3JG. *T:* 01–789 6971. *Club:* United Oxford & Cambridge University.

BAND, Robert Murray Niven, MC 1944; QC 1974; **His Honour Judge Band;** a Circuit Judge, since 1978; *b* 23 Nov. 1919; *s* of Robert Niven Band and Agnes Jane Band; *m* 1948, Nancy Margery Redhead; two *d. Educ:* Trinity Coll., Glenalmond; Hertford Coll., Oxford (MA). Served in Royal Artillery, 1940–46. Called to the Bar, Inner Temple, 1947; Junior Treasury Counsel in Probate Matters, 1972–74; Chm. Family Law Bar Assoc., 1972–74; a Recorder of the Crown Court, 1977–78. Chm., St Teresa's Hosp., Wimbledon, 1969–83. *Recreations:* the countryside, gardens, old buildings, treen. *Address:* Well Farm, Banstead, Surrey. *T:* Burgh Heath 52288.

BAND, Thomas Mollison; Director, Historic Buildings and Monuments, Scottish Development Department, since 1984; *b* 28 March 1934; *s* of late Robert Boyce Band and of Elizabeth Band; *m* 1959, Jean McKenzie Brien; one *s* two *d. Educ:* Perth Academy. National Service, RAF, 1952–54. Joined Civil Service, 1954; Principal, BoT, 1969; Sen. Principal, 1973; Scottish Econ. Planning Dept, 1975, Asst Sec., 1976; Scottish Development Dept, 1978; Scottish Office, Finance, 1981. *Recreations:* skiing, gardening, beating. *Address:* Heathfield, Pitcairngreen, Perthshire. *T:* Almondbank 403. *Club:* Royal Commonwealth Society.

BANDA, Hastings Kamuzu, MD, **(His Excellency Ngwazi Dr H. Kamuzu Banda);** President of Malaŵi since 1966, Life President, 1971; Chancellor, University of Malaŵi, since 1965; Life President, Malaŵi Congress Party; *b* Nyasaland, 1905. *Educ:* Meharry Medical Coll., Nashville, USA (MD); Universities of Glasgow and Edinburgh. Further degrees: BSc, MB, ChB, LRCSE; and several hon. degrees awarded later. Practised medicine in Liverpool and on Tyneside during War of 1939–45 and in London, 1945–53. Returned to Africa, 1953, and practised in Gold Coast. Took over leadership of Nyasaland African Congress in Blantyre, 1958, and became Pres.-Gen.; was imprisoned for political reasons, 1959; unconditionally released, 1960; Minister of Natural Resources and Local Government, Nyasaland, 1961–63; Prime Minister of Malaŵi (formerly Nyasaland), 1963–66. *Address:* Office of the President, Lilongwe, Malaŵi.

BANDARANAIKE, Mrs Sirimavo; President, Sri Lanka Freedom Party, since 1960; Member of Parliament of Sri Lanka, 1960–80; Prime Minister of Sri Lanka (Ceylon until 1972), 1960–65, and 1970–77, also Minister of Defence and Foreign Affairs, of Planning and Economic Affairs, and of Plan Implementation; *b* 17 April 1916; *d* of Barnes Ratwatte, Ratemahatmaya of Ratnapura Dist, Mem. of Ceylon Senate; *m* 1940, Solomon West Ridgeway Dias Bandaranaike (*d* 1959), Prime Minister of Ceylon, 1956–59; one *s* two *d. Educ:* Ratnapura Ferguson Sch.; St Bridget's Convent, Colombo. Assisted S. W. R. D. Bandaranaike in political career. Campaigned for Sri Lanka Freedom Party in election campaigns, March and July 1960. Formerly Pres. and Treasurer, Lanka Mahila Samiti. Prime Minister of Ceylon, also Minister of Defence and External Affairs, 1960–65; Minister of Information and Broadcasting, 1964–65; Leader of the Opposition, 1965–70. Chm., Non Aligned Movt, 1976–77. Ceres Medal, FAO, 1977. *Address:* Horagolla, Nittambuwa, Sri Lanka.

BANERJEE, Rabindra Nath, CSI 1946; CIE 1938; Chairman, Union Public Service Commission, India, 1949–55, retired; *b* 1 Feb 1895; *s* of late Haradhan Banerjee; *m* Manisha (*d* 1953) *d* of late Lieut-Col Upendra Nath Mukerjee, IMS; one *s* (one *d* decd). *Educ:* Calcutta Univ. (MA 1915); Emmanuel Coll., Cambridge (BA 1918). Entered Indian Civil Service, 1920; Registrar Co-operative Societies and Dir Of Industries, Central Provinces and Berar, 1929–33; Vice-Chm. Provincial Banking Enquiry Cttee, 1929; Sec. to Govt, Central Provinces and Berar, Revenue Dept, 1933; Sec. to Govt, CP and Berar, Local Self-Government Dept, 1936; Mem. CP and Berar Legislative Council, 1929–36; Sec. to the Governor, CP and Berar, 1937; Commissioner, 1941; Commissioner of Food

Supply, 1943; Sec. to Govt of India, Commonwealth Relations Dept and Min. of Home Affairs, 1944–48. Mem. Council of State (India), 1944, 1945, 1947; MLA (India), 1946. Mem. of Cttee of Experts of International Labour Organisation, 1956–58. *Address:* 175 Jor Bagh, New Delhi 110003, India. *T:* 611219.

BANGHAM, Alec Douglas, MD; FRS 1977; retired; Research Worker, Agricultural Research Council, Institute of Animal Physiology, Babraham, 1952–82 and Head, Biophysics Unit, 1971–82; *b* 10 Nov. 1921; *s* of Dr Donald Hugh and Edith Bangham; *m* 1943, Rosalind Barbara Reiss; three *s* one *d.* *Educ:* Bryanston Sch.; UCL and UCH Med. Sch. (MD). Captain, RAMC, 1946–48. Lectr, Dept of Exper. Pathology, UCH, 1949–52; Principal Scientific Officer, 1952–63, Senior Principal Scientific Officer (Merit Award), 1963–82, ARC, Babraham. Fellow, UCL, 1981–. *Publications:* contrib. Nature, Biochim. Biophys. Acta, and Methods in Membrane Biol. *Recreations:* horticulture, photographic arts, sailing. *Address:* 17 High Green, Great Shelford, Cambridge. *T:* Cambridge 843192.

BANGOR, 7th Viscount *cr* 1781; **Edward Henry Harold Ward;** Baron, 1770; freelance journalist (as Edward Ward); *b* 5 Nov. 1905; *s* of 6th Viscount Bangor, PC (Northern Ireland), OBE and Agnes Elizabeth (*d* 1972), 3rd *d* of late Dacre Hamilton of Cornacassa, Monaghan; *S* father, 1950; *m* 1st, 1933, Elizabeth (who obtained a divorce, 1937), *e d* of T. Balfour, Wrockwardine Hall, Wellington, Salop; 2nd, 1937, Mary Kathleen (marr. diss. 1947), *d* of W. Middleton, Shanghai; 3rd, 1947, Leila Mary (marr. diss. 1951; she died, 1959), *d* of David R. Heaton, Brookfield, Crownhill, S Devon; one *s*; 4th, 1951, Mrs Marjorie Alice Simpson, *d* of late Peter Banks, St Leonards-on-Sea; one *s* one *d.* *Educ:* Harrow; RMA, Woolwich. Formerly Reuter's correspondent in China and the Far East; BBC War Correspondent in Finland, 1939–40, ME, 1940–41, and Foreign Correspondent all over world, 1946–60. *Publications:* 1940 Despatches from Finland, 1946; Give Me Air, 1946; Chinese Crackers, 1957; The New Eldorado, 1957; Oil is Where They Find It, 1959; Sahara Story, 1962; Number One Boy, 1969; I've Lived like a Lord, 1970. With his wife, Marjorie Ward: Europe on Record, 1950; The US and Us 1951; Danger is Our Business, 1955. *Heir: s* Hon. William Maxwell David Ward [*b* 9 Aug. 1948; *m* 1976, Mrs Sarah Bradford; one *s*]. *Address:* 59 Cadogan Square, SW1. *T:* 01–235 3202. *Clubs:* Savile, Garrick.

BANGOR, Bishop of, since 1983; **Rt. Rev. John Cledan Mears;** *b* 8 Sept. 1922; *s* of Joseph and Anna Lloyd Mears; *m* 1949, Enid Margaret; one *s* one *d.* *Educ:* Univ. of Wales, Aberystwyth (BA Philosophy 1943); Wycliffe Hall, Oxford; St Deiniol's Library, Hawarden. MA Wales 1948 (research, Blaise Pascal). Deacon 1947, priest 1948, St Asaph; Curate: Mostyn, 1947–49; Rhosllannerchrugog, 1949–55; Vicar of Cwm, 1955–58; Lecturer, St Michael's Coll., Llandaff and Univ. of Wales, Cardiff, 1959–73; Chaplain, 1959–67; Sub-warden, 1967–73; Vicar of St Mark's, Gabalfa, Cardiff, 1973–82. Examining Chaplain, 1960–73; Hon. Canon of Llandaff Cathedral, 1981–82; Sec. of Governing Body, Church in Wales, 1977–82. *Publications:* reviews in Theology, articles in Efrydiau Athronyddol, Diwynyddiaeth, and Barn. *Recreations:* hiking, mountaineering. *Address:* Ty'r Esgob, Bangor, Gwynedd LL57 2SS. *T:* Bangor 362895.

BANGOR, Dean of; *see* Rees, Very Rev. J. I.

BANHAM, Mrs Belinda Joan, CBE 1977; JP; Member, Kensington and Chelsea and Westminster Family Practitioner Committee, since 1977 (Chairman, 1979–85); Co-ordinator, funding of Medical Research and Development, St Mary's Hospital Special Trustees, since 1986; *d* of Col Charles Unwin and Winifred Unwin; *m* 1939, Terence Middlecott Banham; two *s* two *d.* *Educ:* privately; West Bank Sch.; Brussels. BSc (Hons) London; Dip. Social Studies London. SRN. Ward and Departmental Sister, Theatre Sister, Night Sister, 1939–51; work in theory and practice on aspects of social deviance/deprivation, 1954–67; Member, SW Regional Hosp. Board, 1965–74; Chairman: Cornwall and Isles of Scilly HMC, 1967–74; Cornwall and Isles of Scilly AHA, 1974–77; Paddington and N Kensington HA, 1981–86. Director, then Hon. Director, Disabled Living Foundn, 1977–83, a Vice-Chm., 1984–. Member, MRC, 1980–; Chairman: Standing Cttee on Use of Medical Records for Research (MRC), 1982–; KIDS, 1983– (Mem., 1977–); Trustee, Wytham Hall, 1985–; special interest: social deprivation, social deviance, use of operational research in Health Service Management, and resource allocation. JP Cornwall, 1972. *Publication:* (jtly) (paper) Systems Science in Health Care (NATO Conf., Paris, 1977). *Recreations:* tennis, botany, gardening, theatre. *Address:* Ponsmaen, St Feock, Truro, Cornwall TR3 6QG. *T:* Truro 862 275; 81 Vandon Court, Petty France, SW1. *T:* 01–222 1414.

See also J. M. M. Banham.

BANHAM, John Michael Middlecott; Controller, Audit Commission for Local Authorities in England and Wales, since 1983; *b* 22 Aug. 1940; *s* of Terence Middlecott Banham, FRCS and Belinda Joan Banham, *qv*; *m* 1965, Frances Barbara Molyneux Favell; one *s* two *d.* *Educ:* Charterhouse; Queens' Coll., Cambridge (Foundn Schol.; BA 1st cl. in Natural Scis, 1962). Asst Principal, HM Foreign Service, 1962–64; Dir of Marketing, Wallcoverings Div., Reed International, 1965–69; McKinsey & Co. Inc., 1969–: Associate, 1969–75; Principal, 1975–80; Dir, 1980–83. Dir (non-exec.), English China Clays, 1985–. Mem. Council, BIM, 1985–. *Publications:* Future of the British Car Industry, 1975; Realizing the Promise of a National Health Service, 1977; numerous reports for Audit Commn on different aspects of local govt, 1984–. *Recreations:* ground clearing, cliff walking in W Cornwall, ocean sailing. *Address:* Upper Woolhampton, Berks; Penberth, St Buryan, near Penzance, Cornwall. *Clubs:* Travellers', Oriental.

BANHAM, Prof. (Peter) Reyner; Professor of Art History, University of California at Santa Cruz, since 1980; *b* 2 March 1922; *m* 1946, Mary Mullett; one *s* one *d.* *Educ:* King Edward VI Sch., Norwich; Courtauld Institute of Art, London. BA 1952, PhD 1958. Bristol Aeroplane Co., 1939–45. Editorial Staff, Architectural Review, 1952–64; Sen. Lectr, University Coll., London, 1964, Reader in Architecture, 1967, Prof. of History of Architecture, 1969–76. Chm., Dept of Design Studies, State Univ. of NY at Buffalo, NY, 1976–80. Research Fellow, Graham Foundation (Chicago), 1964–66; Bannister Fletcher Vis. Prof., UCL, 1982. Mem., Architect-Selection Panel, J. Paul Getty Trust, 1983–84. Architectural Advr, Brooklyn Mus., 1985–86. Jury Mem., Pirelli-Bicocca redevelt competition, Milan, 1986. Hon. FRIBA, 1983. Hon. DLitt East Anglia, 1986. Prix Jean Tschumi, 1975; AIA Honor Award, 1984. *Publications:* Theory and Design in the First Machine Age, 1960; Guide to Modern Architecture, 1962; The New Brutalism, 1966; Architecture of the Well-tempered Environment, 1969; Los Angeles, 1971; (ed) The Aspen Papers, 1974; The Age of the Masters: a Personal View of Architecture, 1975; Megastructure, 1976; Design by Choice, 1981; Scenes in America Deserta, 1982; A Concrete Atlantis, 1986. *Recreations:* indistinguishable from daily interests in architecture and design. *Address:* Porter College, University of California at Santa Cruz, Santa Cruz, Calif 95064, USA.

BANISTER, Stephen Michael Alvin; Secretary, British and Foreign School Society, since 1978; Director, Taylor and Francis Ltd, since 1978; Editor, Transport Reviews, since 1981; *b* 7 Oct. 1918; *s* of late Harry Banister and Idwen Banister (*née* Thomas); *m* 1944, Rachel Joan Rawlence; four *s.* *Educ:* Eton; King's Coll., Cambridge (MA). With Foreign Office, 1939–45; Home Guard (Major, 1944). Asst Principal, Min. of Civil Aviation, 1946; Principal, 1947; Private Sec. to six successive Ministers of Transport and Civil Aviation, 1950–56; Asst Sec., Min. of Transport and BoT, 1956–70; Under Sec., DoE, 1970–76, Dept of Transport, 1976–78. UK Shipping Delegate, UNCTAD, 1964. Mem., Nat. Insurance Tribunal, Kingston upon Thames, 1979–85. *Compositions:* (amateur) for singers, including Bluebeard. *Recreations:* countryside, walking, singing (particularly in opera); formerly cricket (Cambridge Crusader); played for CU *v* Australians, 1938. *Address:* Bramshaw, Lower Farm Road, Effingham, Surrey KT24 5JJ. *T:* Bookham 52778.

BANK-ANTHONY, Sir Mobolaji, KBE 1963 (OBE 1956); Company Director, Lagos, Nigeria; *b* 11 June 1907; *e s* of Alfred Bank-Anthony and Rabiatu Aleshinloye Williams, Lagos; *m* 1935, Olamide Adeshigbin. *Educ:* Methodist Boys' High Sch., Lagos; CMS Gram. Sch., Lagos; Ijebu-Ode Gram. Sch. Postal Clerk in Nigerian P & T Dept, 1924; course in Palm Oil cultivation methods, in England, 1931–33, when returned Nigeria, and gradually built up extensive business, opening stores in many parts of Lagos; Dir of some leading local companies. Fellow of Royal Commonwealth Society; FRSA, FInstD. Stella della Solidarieta (Italy), 1957. *Recreations:* working, reading, newspapers, dancing. *Address:* Executive House, 2a Oil Mill Street, Lagos, Nigeria. *T:* Lagos 24660, 24669; Fountainpen House, 29 Okotie-Eboh Street, Ikoyi, Lagos, Nigeria. *T:* Lagos 21900 and 21363. *Clubs:* Royal Automobile (London); Rotary, Metropolitan, Island, Lagos Race, Lagos Motor, Lagos Amateur Cricket, Yoruba Tennis, Skal, Lodge Academic (Lagos).

BANKS, family name of **Baron Banks.**

BANKS, Baron *cr* 1974 (Life Peer), of Kenton in Greater London; **Desmond Anderson Harvie Banks,** CBE 1972; President, Liberal European Action Group, since 1971; *b* 23 Oct. 1918; *s* of James Harvie Banks, OBE and Sheena Muriel Watt; *m* 1948, Barbara Wells; two *s.* *Educ:* Alpha Prep. Sch.; University College Sch. Served with KRRC and RA, 1939–46, Middle East and Italy (Major); Chief Public Relations Officer to Allied Mil. Govt, Trieste, 1946. Joined Canada Life Assce Co., subseq. Life Assoc. of Scotland; life assce broker from 1959; Director: Tweddle French & Co. (Life & Pensions Consultants) Ltd, 1973–82; Lincoln Consultants Ltd, 1982–. Liberal Party: Pres., 1968–69; Chm. Exec., 1961–63 and 1969–70; Dir of Policy Promotion, 1972–74; Chm. Res. Cttee, 1966; Hon. Sec., Home Counties Liberal Fedn, 1960–61; Chairman: Working Party on Machinery of Govt, 1971–74; Liberal Summer Sch. Cttee, 1979–; Member: For. Affairs Panel, 1961– (now Vice-Chm.); Social Security Panel, 1961–; Hon. Sec., Liberal Candidates Assoc., 1947–52; contested (L): Harrow East, 1950; St Ives, 1955; SW Herts, 1959. Vice-Chm., Liberal Party Standing Cttee, 1973–79; Dep. Liberal Whip, House of Lords, 1977–83; Liberal spokesman on social services, 1977–83; Vice-Chairman: European Atlantic Gp, 1979–85; British Council, European Movement, 1979–. Elder, United Reformed Church. *Publications:* Clyde Steamers, 1947, 2nd edn 1951; numerous political pamphlets. *Recreations:* pursuing interest in Gilbert and Sullivan opera and in Clyde river steamers; reading. *Address:* Lincoln House, The Lincolns, Little Kingshill, Great Missenden, Bucks HP16 0EH. *T:* Great Missenden 6164. *Club:* National Liberal (President, 1981–).

BANKS, Alan George; HM Diplomatic Service, retired; *b* 7 April 1911; *s* of George Arthur Banks and Sarah Napthen; *m* 1946, Joyce Frances Telford Yates; two *s.* *Educ:* Preston Gram. Sch. Served in HM Forces, 1939–43; at Consulate-Gen., Dakar, 1943–45; Actg Consul, Warsaw, 1945–48; HM Vice-Consul: Bordeaux, 1948–50; Istanbul, 1950–52; Zagreb, 1952–55; FO, 1955–58; HM Consul, Split, 1958–60; 1st Sec. and Consul, Madrid, 1960–62; 1st Sec., FO, 1962–67; Consul-General, Alexandria, 1967–71. *Recreations:* classical music, gardening, photography. *Address:* Ferney Field, Parkgate Road, Newdigate, Dorking, Surrey. *T:* Newdigate 434. *Club:* MCC.

BANKS, A(rthur) Leslie, MA Cantab; MD London; FRCP; DPH; Barrister-at-Law (Lincoln's Inn); Professor of Human Ecology, Cambridge, 1949–71, now Emeritus; Fellow, Gonville and Caius College; *b* 12 Jan. 1904; *o s* of late A. C. and E. M. F. Banks; *m* 1933, Eileen Mary (*d* 1967), *d* of Sidney Barrett, Arkley, Herts; two *s.* *Educ:* Friern Barnet Gram. Sch.; Middlesex Hospital and Medical Sch. Resident hospital appointments, including house-surgeon, resident officer to special depts and acting Registrar, Middlesex Hosp., 1926–28; Locum tenens and asst in general practice, Asst Medical Officer, Gen. Post Office, EC1, 1928–34; Divisional Medical Officer, Public Health Dept, LCC (duties included special public health enquiries and slum clearance), 1934–37; Min. of Health, 1937–49; seconded as Medical Officer of Health to City of Newcastle, 1946. Formerly Principal Medical Officer, Min. of Health. Member: GMC, 1957–70; WHO Expert Advisory Panel on Organisation of Med. Care, 1972–76; Hon. Society of Lincoln's Inn; Middlesex Hosp. Club. FRSocMed. First Viscount Bennett Prize, Lincoln's Inn, for essay on Jurisdiction of Judicial Cttee of Privy Council. *Publications:* Social Aspects of Disease, 1953; (ed) Development of Tropical and Sub-tropical Countries, 1954; Health and Hygiene, 1957; (with J. A. Hislop) Art of Administration, 1961; private and official papers on medical and social subjects. *Address:* 4 Heycroft, Eynsham, Oxford. *T:* Oxford 880791.

BANKS, Colin; Founder Partner, Banks and Miles, graphic designers, London, since 1958; *b* 16 Jan. 1932; *s* of William James Banks and late Ida Jenny (*née* Hood); *m* 1961, Caroline Grigson, PhD; one *s* (one *d* decd). Prodn Editor (with John Miles) of Which? and other Consumers' Assoc. magazines, 1964–. Design Consultant to: Zool Soc., 1962–82; British Council, 1968–83; E Midlands Arts Assoc., 1974–77; English National Opera, 1975–76; Direct Election Campaign, European Parlt, 1978, 1984; (new visual identity for) Post Office: Royal Mail, Telecommunications, etc, 1972–; British Telecom., 1980; US Govt Social Marketing Project, Family Planning in Indonesia, 1985–. Designer/Design Adviser to: City and Guilds; Commn for Racial Equality; London Transp.; SERC; Central Clearing Banks; other instns and commercial cos. Exhibitions: London, Amsterdam, Glasgow, Brussels, Kyoto. Vice-Pres., SIAD, 1974–76. Mem. Council, Design and Industries Assoc. Manager, Blackheath Sch. of Art, 1981–. Lectured in Europe, India, Japan, SE Asia, USA. FRSA. Heinrick Mann Medals for art editorship, Cambridge History series, 1971. *Publications:* Social Communication, 1979; contrib. jls, London, Budapest, Copenhagen and USA. *Recreation:* India. *Address:* 1 Tranquil Vale, Blackheath, SE3 0BU. *T:* 01–318 1131; Little Town Farmhouse, Wilts. *Clubs:* Arts; Double Crown, Wynkyn de Worde.

BANKS, Frank David, FCA; Chairman, H. Berkeley (Holdings) Ltd, since 1984; *b* 11 April 1933; *s* of Samuel and Elizabeth Banks; *m* 1st, 1955, Catherine Jacob; one *s* two *d*; 2nd, 1967, Sonia Gay Coleman; one *d.* *Educ:* Liverpool Collegiate Sch.; Carnegie Mellon Univ. (PFE). British Oxygen Co. Ltd, 1957–58; Imperial Chemical Industries Ltd, 1959–62; English Electric Co. Ltd, 1963–68; Finance Dir, Platt International Ltd, 1969–71; Industrial Advr, DTI, 1972–73; Constructors John Brown Ltd, 1974–80; Man. Dir, Agribusiness Div., Tate & Lyle Ltd, 1981–83. *Recreations:* music, history. *Address:* Town House, Ightham, Sevenoaks, Kent TN15 9HH.

BANKS, Mrs Gillian Theresa; Director, Health Authority Finance, Department of Health and Social Security, since 1985; *b* 7 Feb. 1933; *d* of Percy and Enid Brimblecombe; *m* 1960, John Anthony Gorst Banks; one *s* two *d.* *Educ:* Walthamstow Hall Sch.,

Sevenoaks; Lady Margaret Hall, Oxford (BA). Asst Principal, Colonial Office, 1955; Principal, Treasury, 1966; Asst Sec., DHSS, 1972, Under Sec. 1981. *Recreation:* hill walking. *Address:* 16 Chalcot Square, NW1 8YA. *T:* 01–722 3962.

BANKS, John, FEng, FIEE; Chairman, Adacom 3270 Communications Ltd; Director: St James Capital Venture Fund; Surface Electronics Ltd; *b* 2 Dec. 1920; *s* of John Banks and Jane Dewhurst; *m* 1943, Nancy Olive Yates; two *s*. *Educ:* Univ. of Liverpool (BEng Hons, Elec. Engrg). FEng 1983; FIEE 1959. Chief Engr, Power Cables Div., BICC, 1956–67; Divl Dir and Gen Man., Supertension Cables Div., BICC, 1968–74; Exec. Dir, 1975–78, Chm., 1978–84, BICC Research and Engineering Ltd; Exec. Dir, BICC, 1979. Pres., IEE, 1982–83. *Recreations:* golf, swimming, music and the arts. *Address:* Flat B1 Marine Gate, Marine Drive, Brighton BN2 5TQ. *T:* Brighton 690756. *Club:* Wimbledon Golf.

BANKS, Lynne Reid; writer; *b* 1929; *d* of Dr James Reid-Banks and Muriel (Pat) (*née* Alexander); *m* Chaim Stephenson, sculptor; three *s*. *Educ:* schooling mainly in Canada; RADA. Actress, 1949–54; reporter for ITN, 1955–62; English teacher in kibbutz in Western Galilee, Israel, 1963–71; full-time writer, 1971–; writing includes plays for stage, television and radio. *Publications: plays:* It Never Rains, 1954; All in a Row, 1956; The Killer Dies Twice, 1956; Already, It's Tomorrow, 1962; *fiction:* The L-Shaped Room, 1960 (trans. 10 langs; filmed 1962); An End to Running, 1962 (trans. 2 langs); Children at the Gate, 1968; The Backward Shadow, 1970; Two is Lonely, 1974; Defy the Wilderness, 1981; The Warning Bell, 1984; Casualties, 1986; *biographical fiction:* Dark Quartet: the story of the Brontes, 1976 (Yorks Arts Lit. Award, 1977); Path to the Silent Country: Charlotte Bronte's years of fame, 1977; *history:* Letters to my Israeli Sons, 1979; Torn Country, USA 1982; *for young adults:* One More River, 1973; Sarah and After, 1975; My Darling Villain, 1977 (trans. 3 langs); The Writing on the Wall, 1981; *for children:* The Adventures of King Midas, 1976; The Farthest-Away Mountain, 1977; I, Houdini, 1978; The Indian in the Cupboard, 1980 (trans. 6 langs) (Pacific NW Choice Award, 1984; Calif. Young Readers Medal, 1985); Maura's Angel, 1984; The Fairy Rebel, 1985; Return of the Indian, 1986; short stories; articles in The Times, the Guardian, Sunday Telegraph, the Observer, TES, Jewish Chronicle, Spectator, and in overseas periodicals. *Recreations:* theatre, gardening. *Address:* c/o Watson, Little Ltd, Suite 8, 26 Charing Cross Road, WC2H 0DG. *T:* 01–836 5880.

BANKS, Sir Maurice (Alfred Lister), Kt 1971; *b* 11 Aug. 1901; *s* of Alfred Banks, FRCS and Elizabeth Maud (*née* Davey); *m* 1933, Ruth Hall, Philadelphia, USA; one *s* two *d*. *Educ:* Westminster Sch.; Manchester Univ., Coll. of Technology. BSc Tech., FRIC, MIChemE. Coal Research Fellowship under DSIR, 1923; joined Anglo Persian Oil Co., 1924. British Petroleum: a Man. Dir, 1960; a Dep. Chm., 1965; retd from BP, 1967. Chairman: Adv. Council on Calibration for Min. of Technology, 1965–66; Adv. Cttee on Hovercraft for Min. of Technology, 1967–68; Chairman BoT Departmental Cttee to enquire into Patent Law and Procedure, 1967–70; Chm., Laird Gp Ltd, 1970–75. *Recreations:* golf, gardening. *Address:* Beech Coppice, Kingswood, Surrey. *T:* Mogador 832270. *Clubs:* Athenæum; Walton Heath Golf.

BANKS, Richard Alford, CBE 1965; *b* 11 July 1902; *s* of William Hartland Banks, Hergest Croft, Kington, Hereford; *m* 1st, 1937, Lilian Jean (*d* 1974), *d* of Dr R. R. Walker, Presteigne, Radnorshire; two *s* one *d*; 2nd, 1976, Rosamund Gould. *Educ:* Rugby; Trinity Coll., Cambridge (BA). Dir of Imperial Chemical Industries Ltd, 1952–64; Chm. of the Industrial Training Council, 1962–64; Mem., Water Resources Bd, 1964–74. Veitch Meml Medal, RHS, 1983. JP Hereford, 1963–73. *Recreations:* arboriculture, gardening and travel. *Address:* Ridgebourne, Kington, Herefordshire.

BANKS, Robert George; MP (C) Harrogate, since Feb. 1974; *b* 18 Jan. 1937; *s* of late George Walmsley Banks, MBE, and of Olive Beryl Banks (*née* Tyler); *m* 1967, Diana Margaret Payne Crawfurd; four *s* one *d* (of whom one *s* one *d* are twins). *Educ:* Haileybury. Lt-Comdr RNR. Jt Founder Dir, Antocks Lairn Ltd, 1963–67. Member of Lloyd's. Mem., Alcohol Educn and Res. Council, 1982–. Mem., Paddington BC, 1959–65. PPS to Minister of State and to Under-Sec. of State, FCO, 1979–82. Member: Council of Europe, 1977–81; WEU, 1977–81; N Atlantic Assembly, 1981–. Jt Sec., Cons. Defence Cttee, 1976–79; Vice-Chm., All-Party Tourism Gp, 1979–; Chm., All-Party Anglo-Sudan Gp, 1982– (Sec., 1978–82); Mem., Select Cttee on Foreign Affairs (and its Overseas Develt Sub-Cttee), 1982–83. Introd Licensing (Alcohol Educn and Res.) Act, 1981. Reports: for Mil. Cttee of WEU, Report on Nuclear, Biol. and Chem. Protection, adopted by WEU Assembly April 1980; North Atlantic Assembly document, The Technology of Military Space Systems, 1982; New Jobs from Pleasure, report on tourism, 1985. *Publications:* (jtly) Britain's Home Defence Gamble (pamphlet), 1979; committee reports. *Recreations:* travel, farming, architecture. *Address:* House of Commons, SW1A 0AA.

BANKS, Tony; MP (Lab) Newham North West, since 1983. *Educ:* York Univ. (BA); London School of Economics. Former trade union research worker; Head of Research, AUEW, 1969–75; an Asst Gen. Sec., Assoc. of Broadcasting and Allied Staffs, 1976–83. Political Advr to Minister for Overseas Develt, 1975. Joined Labour Party, 1963; Greater London Council: Mem. for Hammersmith, 1970–77, for Tooting, 1981–86; Chairman: Gen. Purposes Cttee, 1970–77; Arts and Recreation Cttee, 1981–83; GLC, 1985–86. Contested (Lab): E Grinstead, 1970; Newcastle upon Tyne N, Oct. 1974; Watford, 1979. Mem., Nat. Theatre Bd, 1981–85. *Address:* House of Commons, SW1A 0AA.

BANKS, Captain William Eric, CBE 1943; DSC; RN retired; *b* 17 July 1900; *er s* of late Walter Banks; *m* 1937, Audrey Steel; two *s*. *Educ:* University Coll. Sch. Joined Navy in 1918; retired list, 1952. *Address:* 2 College Yard, Gloucester. *Club:* Naval and Military.

BANKS, William Hartley; Member, West Yorkshire County Council, 1977–86 (Chairman, 1982–83); *b* 5 July 1909; *s* of Hartley and Edith Banks; *m* 1935, Elsie Kendrew; four *s* one *d* (and one *s* decd). *Educ:* Holbeck Technical Sch. Entered local politics, 1947; Mem., Divl Educn Exec., 1948; Mem., Rothwell UDC, 1959–74 (Chm., 1972–73); Chairman: Sch. Governors, Rothwell, 1964–68; Rothwell Primary Schs, 1974–; Rothwell Secondary Schs, 1982–. Sec., Rothwell and Dist Civic Soc., 1974–77; President: Rothwell Athletic Club, 1974– (Treasurer, 1951–74); Rothwell Cricket Club, 1960–; Chm., Rothwell Gateway Club, 1980–; Leader, Rothwell Windmill Youth Club, 1950–55. *Recreations:* classical music, most sports. *Address:* 8 Spibey Crescent, Rothwell, Leeds LS26 0NR.

BANNENBERG, Jon, RDI 1978; AMRINA; *b* Australia, 8 July 1929; *s* of Henryk and Kay Bannenberg; *m* 1960, Beaupré Robinson; two *s*. *Educ:* Canterbury High Sch., Sydney; Sydney Conservatorium of Music. RDI (Motor Yacht Design) 1978. Designed: 'Siècle d'Elégance' Exhibn, Louvre, Paris, 1959; CINOA Exhibn, V&A Museum, London, 1960; Motor and Sail Boat Designs include: Queen Elizabeth 2, 1967; Tiawana, Tamahine, 1968; Carinthia V, Anemos II, 1969; Benedic, 1970; Carinthia VI, Arjuna, Aetos, 1971; Blue Lady, Yellowbird, Firebird, Heron 21, 1972; Stilvi, Pegasus III, 1973; My Gail, Xiphas, Mediterranean Sky, 1974; Boule Dogue, Southern Breeze, 1975; Solitaire, 1976; Majestic, 1977; Rodis Island, Nabila, Cimba, 1979; My Gail II, Nahema, 1981; Acajou, Azteca, Paraiso Bobbara, Three Y's, 1983; My Gail III, Cedar Sea, Shirley B, Highlander, Sterling One, Oceanfast, Garuda, 1985. Member, RYA. *Recreations:* running, swimming, sailing, music, Polynesian and Pacific history. *Address:* 35 Carlyle Square, Chelsea, SW3. *T:* 01–352 6129; 6 Burnsall Street, SW3 3ST. *T:* 01–352 8444.

BANNER, Mrs Delmar; *see* Vasconcellos, J. de.

BANNER, Sir George Knowles H.; *see* Harmood-Banner.

BANNERMAN, Lt-Col Sir Donald Arthur Gordon, 13th Bt, *cr* 1682; *b* 2 July 1899; *s* of Lt-Col Sir Arthur D'Arcy Gordon Bannerman, KCVO, CIE, 12th Bt and of late Virginia Emilie Bannerman; *S* father 1955; *m* 1932, Barbara Charlotte, *d* of late Lieut-Col A. Cameron, OBE, IMS; two *s* twin *d*. *Educ:* Harrow; Royal Military Coll., Sandhurst; commissioned into Queen's Own Cameron Highlanders, 1918; served in N Russian Campaign, 1919; 1st Class Interpreter (Russian), 1925; served with 1st and 2nd Bns of his Regt in Egypt and India, 1931–34 and 1936–39; served War of 1939–45: with 4th Indian Div. and in MEF, 1940–43; in NW Europe, 1945, attached to US 9th Army, in closing stages of fighting, and then for 3 yrs with Control Commission as Senior Control Officer; retired from Army as Lieut-Col, 1947. On staff of Gordonstoun Sch., 1948–52, of Fettes Coll., 1952–69. *Publications:* Bannerman of Elsick: a short family history, 1975; Random Recollections, 1980. *Recreations:* gardening, walking, reading. *Heir: s* Alexander Patrick Bannerman [*b* 5 May 1933; *m* 1977, Joan Mary Wilcox]. *Address:* 11 Learmonth Place, Edinburgh EH4 1AX. *T:* 031–332 1076.

BANNISTER, Grace, OBE 1984; JP; Lord Mayor of Belfast, 1981–82; *d* of William H. Collim and Grace (*née* Johnston); *m* 1948, John Bannister; one *d*. *Educ:* Park Parade Sch. Belfast County Borough Council, later City Council: Councillor, 1965–85; Dep. Lord Mayor, 1975–77; High Sheriff, 1979; Chm., Parks and Cemeteries Cttee, 1969–72 (Dep. Chm., 1966–69, 1972–73); Dep. Chm., Parks and Recreation Cttee, 1973–78; Chm., Parks Cttee, 1978–85; Member: Improvement, Educn, Town Planning and Traffic Special Cttees, 1965–73; Gen. Purposes Cttee, 1969–73; Gen. Purposes and Finance Cttee, 1978–81; Leisure Centres/Services Cttee, 1976–81. Member: Belfast, Holywood and Castlereagh Jt Bd, 1969–73; Belfast Educn and Library Area Board, 1973–81. JP Belfast, 1965. *Recreations:* welfare, community work, knitting, pottery, music, school management committees. *Address:* 34 Grand Parade, Belfast BT5 5HH. *T:* Belfast 57879.

BANNISTER, Sir Roger (Gilbert), Kt 1975; CBE 1955; DM (Oxon); FRCP; Master of Pembroke College, Oxford, since 1985; Consultant Physician, National Hospital for Nervous Diseases, Queen Square, WC1; Hon. Consultant Neurologist: St Mary's Hospital, W2 (formerly Consultant Physician); Western Ophthalmic Hospital, NW1; Oxford Regional and District Health Authorities; Chairman, Hon. Consultants, King Edward VII Convalescent Home for Officers, Osborne; *b* 23 March 1929; *s* of late Ralph and of Alice Bannister, Harrow; *m* 1955, Moyra Elver, *d* of late Per Jacobsson, Chairman IMF; two *s* two *d*. *Educ:* City of Bath Boys' Sch.; University Coll. Sch., London; Exeter and Merton Colls, Oxford; St Mary's Hospital Medical Sch., London. Amelia Jackson Studentship, Exeter Coll., Oxford, 1947; BA (hons) Physiology, Junior Demonstrator in Physiology, Harmsworth Senior Scholar, Merton Coll., Oxford, 1950; Open and State Schol., St Mary's Hosp., 1951; MSc Thesis in Physiology, 1952; MRCS, LRCP, 1954; BM, BCh Oxford, 1954; DM Oxford, 1963. William Hyde Award for research relating physical education to medicine; MRCP 1957. Junior Medical Specialist, RAMC, 1958; Radcliffe Travelling Fellowship from UC, Oxford, at Harvard, USA, 1962–63. Chm., Medical Cttee, St Mary's Hosp., 1983–85; Vice-Pres., St Mary's Hosp. Med. Sch., 1985–. President: National Fitness Panel, NABC, 1956–59; Alzheimer's Disease Soc., 1982–84. Mem. Council, King George's Jubilee Trust, 1961–67; Pres., Sussex Assoc. of Youth Clubs, 1972–79; Chm., Res. Cttee, Adv. Sports Council, 1965–71; Mem., Min. of Health Adv. Cttee on Drug Dependence, 1967–70; Chm., Sports Council, 1971–74; Pres., Internat. Council for Sport and Physical Recreation, 1976–83. Mem., Management Cttee, 1979–84, Council, 1984–, King Edward's Hosp. Fund for London; Trustee, King George VI and Queen Elizabeth Foundn of St Catharine's, Cumberland Lodge, Windsor, 1985–; Governor, Atlantic Coll., 1985–. Saville Lectr, West End Hosp., London, 1970; Chadwick Trust Lectr, 1972; George Cecil Clarke Lectr, Univ. of Nottingham, 1982. Winner Oxford *v* Cambridge Mile, 1947–50; Pres. OUAC, 1948; Capt. Oxford & Cambridge Combined American Team, 1949; Finalist, Olympic Games, Helsinki, 1952; British Mile Champion, 1951, 1953, 1954; World Record for One Mile, 1954; British Empire Mile title and record, 1954; European 1500 metres title and record, 1954. Hon. FUMIST, 1974; Hon. Fellow, Exeter Coll., Oxford, 1979. Hon. LLD Liverpool, 1972; Hon. DLitt Sheffield, 1978; Hon. Doctorates: Univ. of Jyvaskyla, Finland; Univ. Bath, 1984; Univ. Rochester, NY, 1985. Hans-Heinrich Siegbert Prize, 1977. *Publications:* First Four Minutes, 1955; (ed) Brain's Clinical Neurology, 3rd edn 1969 to 6th edn 1985; (ed) Autonomic Failure, 1983; papers on physiology of exercise, heat illness and neurological subjects. *Address:* Master's Lodgings, Pembroke College, Oxford. *T:* Oxford 242271; 7 Pembroke Court, South Edwardes Square, W8. *Clubs:* Athenæum, United Oxford & Cambridge University; Vincent's (Oxford).

BANNON, John Kernan, ISO 1969; Director of Services, Meteorological Office, 1973–76; *b* 26 April 1916; *s* of Frederick J. Bannon, Clerk in Holy Orders and Eveline Bannon, Muckamore, NI; *m* 1947, Pauline Mary Roch Thomas, Pembroke; one *s* one *d*. *Educ:* Royal Sch., Armagh; Emmanuel Coll., Cambridge (Braithwaite Batty Scholar). BA (Wrangler) 1938. Technical Officer, Meteorological Office, 1938; commnd RAFVR, 1943–46 (Temp. Sqdn Ldr); Met. Office, 1946–76; idc 1963. *Publications:* some official scientific works; articles in meteorological jls. *Recreations:* walking, gardening. *Address:* 18 Courtenay Drive, Emmer Green, Reading RG4 8XH. *T:* Reading 473696.

BANTOCK, Prof. Geoffrey Herman; Emeritus Professor of Education, University of Leicester, 1975; *b* 12 Oct. 1914; *s* of Herman S. and Annie Bantock; *m* 1950, Dorothy Jean Pick; no *c*. *Educ:* Wallasey Grammar Sch.; Emmanuel Coll., Cambridge. BA 1936, MA 1942, Cantab. Taught in grammar schs, training coll.; Lectr in Educn, University Coll. of Leicester, 1950–54; Reader in Educn, University Coll., Leicester, later Univ. of Leicester, 1954–64; Prof. of Educn, 1964–75; Leverhulme Emeritus Fellow, 1976–78. Vis. Prof., Monash Univ., Melbourne, 1971. Book Prize (for best book on educn published in 1984), Standing Conf. on Studies in Educn. *Publications:* Freedom and Authority in Education, 1952 (2nd edn 1965); L. H. Myers: a critical study, 1956; Education in an Industrial Society, 1963 (2nd edn 1973); Education and Values, 1965; Education, Culture and the Emotions, 1967; Education, Culture and Industrialization, 1968; T. S. Eliot and Education, 1969 (paperback 1970); Studies in the History of Educational Theory: Vol. I, Artifice and Nature 1350–1765, 1980, Vol. II, The Minds and the Masses 1760–1980, 1984; Dilemmas of the Curriculum, 1980; The Parochialism of the Present, 1981. *Recreations:* music, art, foreign travel. *Address:* c/o The University, Leicester.

BANTOCK, John Leonard; Assistant Under Secretary of State, Home Office Police Department, 1980–84; *b* 21 Oct. 1927; *s* of Edward Bantock and Agnes Bantock; *m* 1947, Maureen McKinney; two *s*. *Educ:* Colfe's Sch., SE13; King George V Sch., Southport, Lancs; LSE, London Univ. (LLB 1951). Unilever Ltd, 1943–45; Army, 1945–48 (Staff Captain); Colonial Office, 1951–52; Inland Revenue, 1952–69; Secretariat, Royal Commn on Constitution, 1969–73; Cabinet Office, 1973–76; Sec., Cttee of Privy Counsellors on

Recruitment of Mercenaries, 1976; Asst Under Sec. of State, Home Office Radio Regulatory Dept, 1976–79 (Head, UK Delegn, World Admin. Radio Conf., 1979). *Club:* MCC.

BANTON, Prof. Michael Parker; JP; PhD, DSc; Professor of Sociology, since 1965, and Pro-Vice-Chancellor since 1985, University of Bristol; *b* 8 Sept. 1926; *s* of Francis Clive Banton and Kathleen Blanche (*née* Parkes); *m* 1952, Rut Marianne (*née* Jacobson), Luleå; two *s* two *d. Educ:* King Edward's Sch., Birmingham; London Sch. of Economics. BSc Econ. 1950; PhD 1954; DSc 1964. Midn, then Sub-Lieut RNVR, 1945–47. Asst, then Lecturer, then Reader, in Social Anthropology, University of Edinburgh, 1950–65; Dir, SSRC Res. Unit on Ethnic Relations, 1970–78; Visiting Professor: MIT, 1962–63; Wayne State Univ., Detroit, 1971; Univ. of Delaware, 1976; ANU, 1981; Duke Univ., 1982. Editor, Sociology, 1966–69. Pres., Section N, 1969–70 and Section H, 1958–86, BAAS; Mem., Vetenskapssocieteten, Lund, Sweden, 1972; Member: Royal Commn on Criminal Procedure, 1978–80; Royal Commn on Bermuda, 1978; UK National Commn for UNESCO, 1963–66 and 1980–85; UN Cttee for the Elimination of Racial Discrimination; SW Regl Hosp. Board, 1966–70. JP Bristol, 1966. FRSA 1981. *Publications:* The Coloured Quarter, 1955; West African City, 1957; White and Coloured, 1959; The Policeman in the Community, 1964; Roles, 1965; Race Relations, 1967; Racial Minorities, 1972; Police-Community Relations, 1973; (with J. Harwood) The Race Concept, 1975; The Idea of Race, 1977; Racial and Ethnic Competition, 1983; Promoting Racial Harmony, 1985; Investigating Robbery, 1985. *Address:* The Court House, Llanvair Discoed, Gwent NP6 6LX. *T:* Penhow 400208.

BANWELL, Derick Frank, CBE 1978; Chairman: BCAR (Homes) Ltd, since 1979; BCAR (Housing) Ltd, since 1979; *b* 19 July 1919; *s* of Frank Edward Banwell; *m* 1945, Rose Kathleen Worby; two *s* one *d. Educ:* Kent Coll., Canterbury. Admitted as Solicitor, 1947; Asst Solicitor, Southend-on-Sea Co. Borough Coun., 1947–48; Sen. Asst Solicitor, Rochdale Co. Borough Coun., 1948–51; Chief Common Law Solicitor, City of Sheffield, 1951–56; Sen. Asst Solicitor, 1956–59, Asst Town Clerk, 1959–60, Southend-on-Sea Co. Borough Coun.; Dep. Town Clerk and Dep. Clerk of the Peace, Swansea Co. Borough Council, 1960–64; Gen. Manager, Runcorn Develt Corp., 1964–78. Sec., Church Bldgs Cttee, United Reformed Church, 1978–85. *Recreations:* history, music, model railways. *Address:* 57 Broad Street, Canterbury, Kent.

BÁNYÁSZ, Dr Rezső; Order of Merit for Labour, 1955, 1984; State Secretary, and Chairman, Information Office of Hungarian Government, since 1984; *b* 9 Jan. 1931; *m* 1951, Irén Horváth; two *s. Educ:* Univ. of Budapest. Foreign Editor, "Magyar Ifjuság" (Hungarian Youth) daily, "Népszava" (People's Voice) daily, 1950–61; entered Min. of Foreign Affairs, 1961; First Sec., Press Attaché, Stockholm, 1962–68; Counsellor and Dep. Head of Press Dept, Budapest, 1968–70, Head of Press Dept, 1970–72; Sen. Counsellor and Dep. Perm. Rep. of Hungary to UN, NY, 1972–76; Vice-Chm., Hungarian Delegn to Belgrade Meeting of CSCE, 1977; Head, Press Dept, 1978–81; Ambassador to London, 1981–84. Commenda da Orden do Infante D. Henrique (Portugal), 1979. *Recreation:* gardening. *Address:* Information Office, 1–3 Kossuth Square, Budapest, Hungary.

BARBACK, Ronald Henry; Consultant, Confederation of British Industry, since 1981; *b* 31 Oct. 1919; *s* of late Harry Barback and Winifred Florence (*née* Norris); *m* 1950, Sylvia Chambers; one *s* one *d. Educ:* Woodside Sch., Glasgow; Univ. Coll., Nottingham (BScEcon); Queen's and Nuffield Colls, Oxford (MLitt). Asst Lectr in Econs, Univ. of Nottingham, 1946–48; Lectr in Econs, subseq. Sen. Lectr, Canberra University Coll., Australia, 1949–56; Univ. of Ibadan (formerly University Coll., Ibadan): Prof. of Econs and Social Studies, 1956–63; Dean, Faculty of Arts, 1958–59; Dean, Faculty of Econs and Social Studies, 1959–63; Dir, Nigerian (formerly W African) Inst. of Social and Econ. Res., 1956–63; Sen. Res. Fellow, Econ. Res. Inst., Dublin, 1963–64; Prof. of Econs, TCD, 1964–65; Univ. of Hull: Prof. of Econs, 1965–76; Dean, Faculty of Social Sciences and Law, 1966–69; Head, Dept of Econs and Commerce, 1971–74. Dep. Econ. Dir and Head, Econ. Res., CBI, 1977–81. Nigeria: Mem., Ibadan Univ. Hosp. Bd of Management, 1958–63; Mem., Jt Econ. Planning Cttee, Fedn of Nigeria, 1959–61; Sole Arbitrator, Trade Disputes in Ports and Railways, 1958; Chm., Fed. Govt Cttee to advise on fostering a share market, 1959. UK Official Delegate, FAO meeting on investment in fisheries, 1970; Mem., FAO mission to Sri Lanka, 1975. Consultant, Div. of Fisheries, Europ. Commn Directorate-Gen. of Agriculture, 1974. Commonwealth Scholarships Commn Adviser on Econs, 1971–76; Mem., Schools Council Social Sciences Cttee, 1971–80; Chm., Schs Council Econs and Business Studies Syllabus Steering Gp, 1975–77. Member: Hull and Dist Local Employment Cttee, 1966–73; N Humberside Dist Manpower Cttee, 1973–76; CNAA Business and Management Studies Bd, 1978–81, Economics Bd, 1982–; Ct, Brunel Univ., 1979–; Editorial Bd, Bull. of Economic Research (formerly Yorks Bull. of Social and Economic Research), 1965–76 (Jt Editor, 1966–67); Editorial Adv. Bd, Applied Economics, 1969–80. Editor, Humberside Statistical Bull., nos 1–3, 1974, 1975, 1977. Specialist adviser, House of Lords Select Cttee on the European Communities, 1980–. *Publications:* (contrib.) The Commonwealth in the World Today, ed J. Eppstein, 1956; (ed with Prof. Sir Douglas Copland) The Conflict of Expansion and Stability, 1957; (contrib.) The Commonwealth and Europe (EIU), 1960; The Pricing of Manufactures, 1964; (contrib.) Insurance Markets of the World, ed M. Grossmann 1964; (contrib.) Webster's New World Companion to English and American Literature, 1973; Forms of Co-operation in the British Fishing Industry, 1976; (with M. Breimer and A. F. Haug) Development of the East Coast Fisheries of Sri Lanka, 1976; contrib. New Internat. Encyc., FAO Fisheries Reports, and jls. *Recreations:* walking, music. *Address:* 14a Calverley Park Gardens, Tunbridge Wells, Kent TN1 2JN. *T:* Tunbridge Wells 33290. *Club:* Royal Commonwealth Society.

BARBARA, Agatha; President of the Republic of Malta, since 1982; *b* 11 March 1923. *Educ:* Government Grammar School. School teacher, 1945; entered politics, 1946; first woman Member of Parliament, 1947; became first woman Minister, in Labour Govt, 1955, as Minister of Education; also Minister of Educn, 1971–74; Minister of Labour, Culture, and Welfare, 1974–81. Was Acting Prime Minister on various occasions, and elected President of the Republic, 16 Feb. 1982. Hon. Academician, Accademia Universale A. Magno, Prato, Italy; Hon. PhD Univ. of Beijing, China. Stara Planina, 1st cl. with ribbon (Bulgaria), 1983; Order of National Flag 1st Class (Democratic People's Republic of Korea). *Recreations:* philately, classical and modern music. *Address:* The Palace, San Anton, Republic of Malta. *T:* 40354.

BARBARITO, Most Rev. Luigi, DD, JCD; Titular Archbishop of Fiorentino; Apostolic Pro-Nuncio to the Court of St James's, since 1986; *b* Atripalda, Avellino, Italy, 19 April 1922; *s* of Vincenzo Barbarito and Alfonsina Armerini. *Educ:* Pontifical Seminary, Benevento, Italy; Gregorian Univ., Rome (JCD); Papal Diplomatic Academy, Rome (Diploma). Priest, 1944; served Diocese of Avellino, 1944–52; entered Diplomatic Service of Holy See, 1953; Sec., Apostolic Delegn, Australia, 1953–59; Secretariat of State of Vatican (Council for Public Affairs of the Church), 1959–67; Counsellor, Apostolic Nunciature, Paris, 1967–69; Archbishop and Papal Nuncio to Haiti and Delegate to the Antilles, 1969–75; Pro-Nuncio to Senegal, Bourkina Fasso, Niger, Mali, Mauretania, Cape Verde Is and Guinea Bissau, 1975–78; Apostolic Pro-Nuncio to Australia, 1978–86.

Mem., Mexican Acad. of Internat. Law. Grand Cross, National Order of Haiti, 1975; Grand Cross, Order of the Lion (Senegal), 1978; Knight Commander, Order of Merit (Italy), 1966, (Portugal), 1967. *Recreations:* music, walking, snooker. *Address:* Apostolic Nunciature, 54 Parkside, Wimbledon, SW19 5NF. *T:* 01–946 1410.

BARBER, family name of **Baron Barber.**

BARBER, Baron *cr* 1974 (Life Peer), of Wentbridge; **Anthony Perrinott Lysberg Barber,** PC 1963; TD; Chairman, Standard Chartered Bank plc, since 1974; a Government Director, British Petroleum, since 1979; *b* 4 July 1920; *s* of John Barber, CBE, Doncaster; *m* 1950, Jean Patricia (*d* 1983), *d* of Milton Asquith, Wentbridge, Yorks; two *d. Educ:* Retford Grammar Sch.; Oriel Coll., Oxford Univ. (PPE, MA) (Hon. Fellow 1971). Served War of 1939–45: commnd in Army (Dunkirk); seconded to RAF as pilot, 1940–45 (despatches; prisoner of war, 1942–45, took Law Degree with 1st Class Hons while POW, escaped from Poland, prisoner of the Russians). Barrister-at-law, Inner Temple, 1948 (Inner Temple Scholarship). MP (C): Doncaster, 1951–64; Altrincham and Sale, Feb. 1965–Sept. 1974; PPS to the Under-Sec. of State for Air, 1952–55; Asst Whip, 1955–57; a Lord Comr of the Treasury, 1957–58; PPS to the Prime Minister, 1958–59; Economic Sec. to the Treasury, 1959–62; Financial Sec. to the Treasury, 1962–63; Minister of Health and Mem. of the Cabinet, 1963–64; Chancellor of the Duchy of Lancaster, June-July 1970; Chancellor of the Exchequer, 1970–74. Chm., Conservative Party Organisation, 1967–70. Mem., Falkland Islands Inquiry (Franks Cttee), 1982. Chm. Council, Westminster Med. Sch., 1975–84. *Address:* Standard Chartered Bank plc, 38 Bishopsgate, EC2N 4DE. *T:* 01–280 7001. *Club:* Carlton.

See also N. J. L. Barber.

BARBER, Sir Derek (Coates), Kt 1984; Environment Consultant to Humberts, Chartered Surveyors, since 1972; Chairman, Countryside Commission, since 1981; *b* 17 June 1918; *s* of Thomas Smith-Barber and Elsie Coates; 1st marr. diss. 1981; *m* 2nd, 1983, Rosemary Jennifer Brougham, *o d* of late Lt-Comdr Randolph Brougham Pearson, RN, and of Hilary Diana Mackinlay Pearson (*née* Bennett). *Educ:* Royal Agricl Coll., Cirencester (MRAC; Gold Medal, Practical Agriculture). Served War: invalided, Armed Forces, 1942. Farmed in Glos Cotswolds; Mem., Cheltenham Rural District Council, 1948–52; Dist Adv. Officer, National Agricl Adv. Service, MAFF, 1946–57; County Agricl Advisor, Glos, 1957–72; MAFF Assessor: Pilkington Cttee on Agric. Educ., 1966; Agric. and Hort. Trng Bd, 1968. Chm., BBC's Central Agricl Adv. Cttee, 1974–80 (*ex officio* Mem., BBC's Gen. Adv. Council, 1972–80). Royal Soc. for Protection of Birds: Mem., 1970–75, Chm., 1976–81, Council; Chm., Educn Cttee, 1972–75; Vice-Pres., 1982; Pres., Glos Naturalists' Soc., 1981–; Founder Mem., 1969, Farming and Wildlife Adv. Gp of landowning, farming and wildlife conservation bodies; Member: Ordnance Survey Adv. Bd, 1982–85; Bd, RURAL Council, 1983–; Bd, Centre for Environmental and Econ. Develt, 1984–; Centre for Agricl Strategy, 1985–; Dep. Chm., Bd, Groundwork Foundn, 1985–. Associate Mem., Guild of Agricl Journalists, 1981. Hon. FRASE, 1986. First Recipient, Summers Trophy for services to agric. in practice or science, 1955; Bledisloe Gold Medal for Distinguished Service to UK Agriculture, 1967; RSPB Gold Medal for services to bird protection, 1982. Silver Jubilee Medal, 1977. Editor, Humberts Commentary, 1973–; Spec. Correspondent, Waitaki NZR Times, 1982–. *Publications:* (with Keith Dexter) Farming for Profits, 1961, 2nd edn 1967; (with J. G. S. and Frances Donaldson) Farming in Britain Today, 1969, 2nd edn 1972; (ed) Farming with Wildlife, 1971; A History of Humberts, 1980; contrib. farming and wildlife conservation jls. *Recreations:* birds, wildlife conservation, farming, hill walking. *Address:* The Manor Farm, Stanley Pontlarge, Winchcombe, Glos GL54 5HD. *T:* Cheltenham 602394. *Club:* Farmers'.

BARBER, Hon. Sir (Edward Hamilton) Esler, Kt 1976; Puisne Judge, Supreme Court of Victoria, Australia, 1965–77; *b* Hamilton, Vic., 26 July 1905; *s* of late Rev. John Andrew Barber and Maggie Rorke; *m* 1954, Constance, *d* of Captain C. W. Palmer; one *s* one *d. Educ:* Hamilton Coll., Victoria; Scots Coll., Sydney; Scotch Coll., Melbourne; Melbourne Univ. Barrister-at-law, 1929; QC (Vic.) 1955, Tas. 1956; Judge, County Court, Vic., 1957–65; Actg Judge, 1964–65. Chm., Royal Commn into Failure of King's Bridge, 1962–63; Dep. Chm. Parole Bd, Vic., Nov. 1969–77; Mem. Council of Legal Educn, 1968–77; Chm., Royal Commn into West Gate Bridge Disaster, 1970–71; Chm., Bd of Inquiry into causes and origins of bush and grass fires in Vic. during Jan.-Feb. 1977, 1977–. *Publications:* articles on Matrimonial Law, incl. Divorce—the Changing Law, 1968. *Address:* 1 St George's Court, Toorak, Vic 3142, Australia. *T:* 24–5104. *Club:* Australian (Melbourne).

BARBER, Hon. Sir Esler; see Barber, Hon. Sir E. H. E.

BARBER, Frank; Partner, Morgan, Fentiman & Barber, since 1968; Deputy Chairman of Lloyd's, 1983, 1984; *b* 5 July 1923; *s* of S. Barber and F. K. Seath; *m* 1945, Gertrude Kathleen Carson; one *s* one *d* (and one *s* decd). *Educ:* West Norwood Central School. Pilot, RAFVR, 1942–46; Underwriter, Lloyd's syndicate, Frank Barber & others, 1962–81; Member: Cttee of Lloyd's, 1977–80 and 1982–85. Council of Lloyd's, 1983–85; Dep. Chm., Lloyd's Underwriters' Non-Marine Assoc., 1971, Chm., 1972; Dep. Chm., British Insurers' European Cttee, 1983. *Recreations:* music, walking, sailing. *Address:* Godden House, Godden Green, Sevenoaks, Kent. *Club:* Royal Thames Yacht.

BARBER, Dr James Peden, JP; Master, Hatfield College, Durham, since 1980; *b* 6 Nov. 1931; *s* of John and Carrie Barber; *m* 1955, Margaret June (*née* McCormac); three *s* one *d. Educ:* Liverpool Inst. High Sch.; Pembroke Coll., Cambridge (MA, PhD); The Queen's Coll., Oxford. Served RAF, 1950–52 (Pilot Officer). Colonial Service, Uganda: Dist Officer, subseq. Asst Sec. to Prime Minister and Clerk to the Cabinet, 1956–63; Lectr, Univ. of NSW, Australia, 1963–65; Lectr in Govt, Univ. of Exeter, 1965–69 (seconded to University Coll. of Rhodesia, 1965–67); Prof. of Political Science, Open Univ., 1969–80. Mem. RIIA; Part-time Dir, Chatham House study, Southern Africa in Conflict, 1979–81. Mem., Amnesty International. Vice-Pres., Durham Univ. Soc. of Fellows, 1985–; Pres., Durham Univ. Hockey Club. JP Bedford, 1977–80. *Publications:* Rhodesia: the road to rebellion, 1967; Imperial Frontier, 1968; South Africa's Foreign Policy, 1973; European Community: vision and reality, 1974; The Nature of Foreign Policy, 1975; Who Makes British Foreign Policy?, 1977; The West and South Africa, 1982; The Uneasy Relationship: Britain and South Africa, 1983. *Recreations:* choral music, all kinds of sport, walking the dog. *Address:* Kingsgate House, Bow Lane, Durham DH1 3ER. *T:* Durham 48651. *Club:* Royal Commonwealth Society.

BARBER, Rear-Adm. John L.; see Lee-Barber.

BARBER, John Norman Romney; Company chairman; *s* of George Ernest and Gladys Eleanor Barber; *m* 1941, Babette Chalu; one *s. Educ:* Westcliff. Served with Army, 1939–46 (Capt.). Min. of Supply, 1946–55 (Princ.). Joined Ford Motor Co. Ltd, 1955, Finance Dir, 1962; Chm., Ford Motor Credit Co. Ltd, 1963; Dir, Henry Ford & Son Ltd, Cork, 1963; Dir Autolite Motor Products Ltd, 1963; Finance Dir, AEI Ltd, 1965; Chm., Telephone Cables Ltd, 1967; Dir of Finance and Planning, 1968–71, Dep. Man. Dir, 1971–73, Dep. Chm. and Man. Dir, 1973–75, British Leyland Motor Corp. Ltd;

Chairman, 1973–75: British Leyland International Ltd; Leyland Innocenti, SpA; Leyland Motor Corp. of Australia Ltd; Director: Leyland España SA; Automóviles de Turismo Hispano Ingleses SA; NZ Motor Corp. Ltd; British Leyland Motors Inc.; Metalurgica de Santa Ana SA; Chairman: Pullmaflex International Ltd, 1976–79; Aberhurst Ltd, 1976–; A. C. Edwards Engineering Ltd, 1976–81; Cox & Kings Financial Services Ltd, 1980–; C & K Executive Search Ltd, 1980–; C & K Consulting Group Ltd, 1982–; C & K Marketing Ltd, 1982–; Director: Acrow plc, 1977–; Good Relations Group plc, 1979–; Amalgamated Metal Corp. Ltd, 1980–81; Spear & Jackson International plc, 1980–; Twinprint Ltd, 1981–; Economists Advisory Group Ltd, 1981–; UK Investments Ltd, 1985–; Deputy Chairman: Cox & Kings Ltd, 1980–81; John E. Wiltshier Group Ltd, 1980– (Dir, 1979–). Mem., Royal Commn on Medical Educn, 1965–68; Chm., Adv. Cttee to BoT on Investment Grants, 1967–68; Mem., Adv. Council for Energy Conservation, 1974–75. Vice Pres., SMMT, 1974–76. CBIM; Mem. Council BIM, 1967–71. *Publications:* papers on management subjects in various jls. *Recreations:* motor sport, forestry, photography. *Address:* High Walls, Claremont Drive, Esher, Surrey KT10 9LU. *Clubs:* British Automobile Racing, British Racing and Sports Car.

BARBER, Prof. Michael, FRS 1985; Professor of Physical Chemistry, University of Manchester Institute of Science and Technology, since 1985; *b* 3 Nov. 1934; *s* of Joseph and Alice Anne Barber; *m* 1958, Joan (*née* Gaskell); one *s* two *d*. *Educ:* Manchester Grammar Sch.; The Queen's Coll., Oxford (DPhil). Joined AEI Scientific Apparatus Dept, Trafford Park, Manchester, 1961; Hon. Lectr, Chemistry Dept, Univ. of Manchester, 1970–73; Lectr 1973, Reader 1977, Chem. Dept, UMIST. Royal Soc. of Chemistry: Perkin Elmer Award and Medal for analytical science and instrumentation, 1979; Strock Medal and Award for Applied Spectroscopy, 1983. *Recreations:* lacrosse; organist and choirmaster of St Michael and All Angels, Wythenshawe. *Address:* Chemistry Department, UMIST, PO Box 88, Sackville Street, Manchester M60 1QD. *T:* 061-236 3311; (home) 29 New Forest Road, Manchester M23 9JT. *T:* 061-962 5881.

BARBER, Nicholas Charles Faithorn; Group Managing Director, Ocean Transport & Trading plc, since 1986 (Director since 1980); *b* 7 Sept. 1940; *s* of Bertram Harold and Nancy Lorraine Barber; *m* 1966, Sheena Macrae Graham; two *s* one *d*. *Educ:* Ludgrove Sch.; Shrewsbury Sch.; Wadham Coll., Oxford (MA); Columbia Univ., New York, 1969–71 (MBA). Lectr, Marlboro Coll., Vermont, USA, 1963–64; joined Ocean Transport and Trading, 1964; Divl Dir, NEB, 1977–79. Mem., NW Industrial Develt Bd, 1982–85; Trustee, Nat. Museums and Galls of Merseyside, 1986–. Governor, Shrewsbury Sch., 1983–; Mem. Council, Liverpool Univ., 1985–; Dir, Liverpool Playhouse, 1982–. *Recreations:* hill-walking, cricket. *Address:* Burners Cottage, Rowley Lane, Wexham, Stoke Poges, Bucks SL3 6PD. *Clubs:* MCC; Liverpool Racquet.

BARBER, Noël John Lysberg; author; *b* 9 Sept. 1909; *s* of John Barber, CBE, and Danish-born 'Musse' Barber (*née* Lysberg); *m* 1st, 1938, Helen Whichello, in Singapore; 2nd, 1954, Countess de Feo of Florence; one *s* one *d*. *Educ:* erratically, briefly, terminated by attack of lockjaw at age of fourteen. After unsuccessful attempts to write books and articles, became professional journalist in the 1930s with Yorkshire Post group, then Daily Express, Manchester; after travelling world by tramp steamer, became editor, Malaya Tribune, Singapore, 1937–38; travels in China, Siberia, Russia, 1938–39; Editor, Overseas Daily Mail, London, 1940. RAF navigator, 1942–45. Légion d'Honneur, 1945. Editor and Man. Dir, Continental Daily Mail, Paris, 1945–53; paintings exhibited at Salon d'Hiver, Paris, 1950–53; Foreign Correspondent, Daily Mail, 1953–65; wounded, Morocco, during French N African war, 1954; wounded, Hungarian Uprising, 1956; first Briton to reach South Pole since Captain Scott, 1957. Organized and appeared in Assignment Unknown, series of TV documentary travelogues, 1959–60; Foreign Manager, then Syndication Manager and Dir, Associated Newspapers Ltd, 1962–73. Ridder of Danneborg, Denmark, 1948. Jordanian Order of Merit, 1961. *Publications:* (after 19 full-length books had been rejected) Newspaper Reporting, 1936; How Strong is America, 1941; The Menace of Japan, 1942; Trans-Siberian, 1943; Prisoner of War, 1944; Fires of Spring, 1952; Strangers in the Sun, 1952; Distant Places, 1956; A Handful of Ashes, 1957; The White Desert, 1958; From the Land of Lost Content, 1960; Life with Titina, 1961; Conversations with Painters, 1964; The Black Hole of Calcutta, 1965; Sinister Twilight, the Fall of Singapore, 1968; The War of the Running Dogs, 1971; Lords of the Golden Horn, 1973; Seven Days of Freedom, 1974; The Week France Fell, 1976; The Natives were Friendly, an autobiography, 1977, revd edn 1985; The Singapore Story, 1979; The Fall of Shanghai, 1979; *Juveniles:* Adventures at Both Poles, 1958; Let's Visit the USA, 1960; *Novels:* Tanamera, 1981; A Farewell to France, 1983; A Woman of Cairo, 1984; The Other Side of Paradise, 1986; *In partnership:* Hitler's Last Hope (with Ernest Phillips), 1942; Cities (with Rupert Croft-Cooke), 1946; An Island to Oneself (with Tom Neale), 1966. *Recreations:* writing, music, painting, travel, tennis, bridge, watching cricket. *Address:* 312a King's Road, SW3. *Clubs:* Savage, Savile, International Lawn Tennis of Great Britain.

See also Baron Barber.

BARBER, Ven. Paul Everard; Archdeacon of Surrey, since 1980; Hon. Canon of Guildford, since 1980; *b* 16 Sept. 1935; *s* of Cecil Arthur and Mollie Barber; *m* 1959, Patricia Jayne Walford; two *s* two *d* (and one *s* decd). *Educ:* Sherborne School; St John's Coll., Cambridge (BA 1958, MA 1966); Wells Theological College. Deacon 1960, priest 1961, dio. Guildford; Curate of St Francis, Westborough, 1960–66; Vicar: Camberley with Yorktown, 1966–73; St Thomas-on-The Bourne, Farnham, 1973–80; Rural Dean of Farnham, 1974–79. General Synod, 1979–85; Member, Council of College of Preachers, 1969–. *Recreations:* diocesan clergy cricket, theatre. *Address:* Tarawera, 71 Boundstone Road, Rowledge, Farnham, Surrey GU10 4AT. *T:* Frensham 3987.

BARBER, Col Sir William (Francis), 2nd Bt *cr* 1960; TD; JP; *b* 20 Nov. 1905; *yr* and *o* surv. *s* of Sir (Thomas) Philip Barber, 1st Bt, DSO, TD, JP, DL, and of Beatrice Mary (*d* 1962), *d* of Lieut-Col W. Ingersoll Merritt; *S* father, 1961; *m* 1st, 1936, Diana Constance (marr. diss. 1978; she *d* 1984), *d* of late Lieut-Col Thomas Owen Lloyd, CMG, Minard Castle, Argyll; one *s* one *d*; 2nd, 1978, Jean Marie, *widow* of Dr H. C. Nott, Adelaide, S Australia. *Educ:* Eton Coll. South Nottinghamshire Hussars Yeomanry (Commnd, 1924). Royal Horse Artillery; served in Palestine, Egypt, North Africa, NW Europe; Lieut-Col 1947. Hon. Col, South Nottinghamshire Hussars Yeomanry, 1961–66. JP Notts, 1952; High Sheriff, Notts, 1964. *Heir:* *s* (Thomas) David Barber [*b* 18 Nov. 1937; *m* 1st, 1972, Amanda Mary (*née* Rabone) (marr. diss. 1976), *widow* of Maj. Michael Healing; one *s*; 2nd, 1978, Jeannine Mary Boyle, *d* of Captain T. J. Gurney; one *s* one *d*]. *Address:* Lamb Close, Eastwood, Notts; Dunmaglass, Aberarder, Invernessshire.

BARBER, Prof. William Joseph, Hon. OBE 1981; Professor of Economics, Wesleyan University, Middletown, Conn, USA, since 1965; *b* 13 Jan. 1925; *s* of Ward Barber; *m* 1955, Sheila Mary Marr; three *s*. *Educ:* Harvard Univ. (AB); Balliol Coll., Oxford. BA, 1st Cl. Hons, 1951, MA 1955; DPhil (Nuffield Coll.) 1958. Served War, US Army, 1943–46. Lectr in Econs, Balliol Coll., Oxford, 1956; Dept of Economics, Wesleyan Univ., USA, 1957– (Asst Prof., 1957–61; Associate Prof., 1961–65; Prof., 1965–; Andrews Prof., 1972–). Research Associate: Oxford Univ. Inst. of Economics and Statistics, 1962–63; Twentieth Century Fund, South Asian Study, 1961–62. Amer. Sec., Rhodes Scholarship Trust, 1970–80. *Publications:* The Economy of British Central Africa, 1961; A History of Economic Thought, 1967; contributor to Asian Drama: an inquiry into the poverty of nations (with Gunnar Myrdal and others), 1968; British Economic Thought and India 1600–1858, 1975; (jtly) Exhortation and Controls: the search for a wage-price policy, 1975; Energy Policy in Perspective, 1981; From New Era to New Deal: Herbert Hoover, the economists, and American economic policy 1921–1933, 1985; contribs to professional jls. *Address:* 306 Pine Street, Middletown, Conn, USA. *T:* 203–346–2612.

BARBIERI, Margaret Elizabeth; Senior Principal, Sadler's Wells Royal Ballet, since 1974; *b* 2 March 1947; *d* of Ettore Barbieri and Lea Barbieri; *m* 1983, Iain Webb, soloist SWRB. *Educ:* Convent High Sch., Durban, S Africa. Trained with Iris Manning and Brownie Sutton, S Africa; Royal Ballet Sen. Sch., 1963; joined Royal Ballet, 1965; Principal, 1970. Gypsy Girl, Two Pigeons, 1966; 1st Giselle, Covent Garden, 1968; 1st Sleeping Beauty, Leeds, 1969; 1st Swan Lake, Frankfurt, 1977, Covent Garden, 1983; 1st Romeo and Juliet, Covent Garden, 1979; 1st Sleeping Beauty, Covent Garden, 1985. Other roles with Royal Ballet: La Fille mal Gardée, Two Pigeons, The Dream, Façade, Wedding Bouquet, Rendezvous (Ashton); Lady and the Fool, Card Game, Pineapple Poll (Cranko); The Invitation, Solitaire, (Summer) The Four Seasons (MacMillan); Checkmate, The Rake's Progress (de Valois); Grosse Fugue, Tilt (van Manen); Lilac Garden (Tudor); Fête Etrange (Howard); Grand Tour (Layton); Summer Garden (Hynd); Game Piano (Thorpe), 1978; Cinderella (Killar), 1978; Cinderella (Rodrigues), 1979; Papillon, The Taming of the Shrew, 1980; Coppélia, Les Sylphides, Raymonda Act III, Spectre de la Rose; La Vivandière, 1982; Petrushka, 1984. Roles created: Knight Errant (Tudor), 1968; From Waking Sleep (Drew), 1970; Ante-Room (Cauley), 1971; Oscar Wilde (Layton), 1972; Sacred Circles and The Sword (Drew), 1973; The Entertainers (Killar), 1974; Charlotte Brontë (Hynd), 1974; Summertide (Wright), 1977; Metamorphosis (Bintley), 1984; Flowers of the Forest (Bintley), 1985; The Wand of Youth (Corder), 1985. Recreated: Pavlova's Dragonfly Solo, 1977; The Dying Swan, produced by Dame Alicia Markova after Fokine, 1985. Travelled with Royal Ballet to Australia, Canada, Egypt, Far East, France, Germany, Greece, Holland, Israel, Italy, New Zealand, Portugal, Spain, Switzerland, Yugoslavia, India and North and South America; guest appearances, USA, Germany, S Africa, France, Norway, Czechoslovakia. TV Appearances in: Spectre de la Rose; Grosse Fugue; Giselle; Coppelia; Checkmate; Markova master classes. *Recreations:* music (classical), theatre, gardening. *Address:* Chiswick.

BARBOUR, Very Rev. Prof. Robert Alexander Stewart, MC 1945; Professor of New Testament Exegesis, University of Aberdeen, 1971–82; Master of Christ's College, Aberdeen, 1977–82; Chaplain-in-Ordinary to the Queen, since 1976; Dean of the Chapel Royal in Scotland, since 1981; Prelate of the Priory of Scotland of the Order of St John, since 1977; *b* 11 May 1921; *s* of George Freeland Barbour and Helen Victoria (*née* Hepburne-Scott); *m* 1950, Margaret Isobel Pigot; three *s* one *d*. *Educ:* Rugby Sch.; Balliol Coll., Oxford (MA 1946); Univ. of St Andrews (BD 1952); Yale Univ. (STM 1953). Sec., Edinburgh Christian Council for Overseas Students, 1953–55; Lectr and Sen. Lectr in NT Lang., Lit. and Theol., Univ. of Edinburgh, 1955–71. Hensley Henson Lectr, Univ. of Oxford, 1983–84. Moderator, Gen. Assembly of Church of Scotland, 1979–80. Chm., Scottish Churches' Council, 1982–. Hon. Sec., Studiorum Novi Testamenti Societas, 1970–77. Chm. Governors, Rannoch Sch., 1973–79. Hon. DD St Andrews, 1979. *Publications:* The Scottish Horse 1939–45, 1950; Traditio-Historical Criticism of the Gospels, 1972; What is the Church for?, 1973; articles in various jls. *Recreations:* music, walking, forestry. *Address:* Fincastle, Pitlochry, Perthshire PH16 5RJ. *T:* Pitlochry 3209. *Club:* New (Edinburgh).

BARBOUR, Walworth; US Ambassador to Israel, 1961–73; *b* 4 June 1908; *s* of Samuel Lewis Barbour and Clara Hammond; unmarried. *Educ:* Harvard Coll. USA. Vice Consul, Naples, 1932; Athens, 1933; Baghdad, 1936; Sofia, 1939; Dip. Sec., Cairo, 1941; Athens, 1944; Dept of State, Washington, 1945–49; Minister, Moscow, 1949–51; Dept of State, Washington, 1951–55; Deputy Asst Sec. of State for European Affairs, 1954–55; American Minister, London, 1955–61. Hon. Fellow, Weizmann Inst. of Sci., 1970. Hon. PhD: Tel Aviv, 1971; Hebrew Univ. of Jerusalem, 1972; Hon. LLD Dropsie, Pa, 1973. *Recreation:* golf. *Address:* 14 Grapevine Road, Gloucester, Mass 01930, USA. *Clubs:* American; Swinley Forest (Surrey); Chevy Chase (Md, USA).

BARBOZA, Mario G.; *see* Gibson-Barboza.

BARCLAY, Alexander, CBE 1957; ARCS, FRSC; Keeper, Department of Chemistry and Photography, Science Museum, S Kensington, 1938–59; retired; *b* 25 July 1896; *o s* of late Alexander Barclay; *m* 1921, Irene Margaret (*d* 1973), *y d* of late Frank Carrington Falkner, Wisbech. *Educ:* Berkhamsted Sch.; Royal College of Science. Served European War with Special Gas Brigade, RE, 1916–17; invalided, 1917; Postal Censorship Research Dept, 1918; entered Science Museum, 1921; Asst Keeper, 1930; Board of Education, 1940 and 1943; Postal Censorship, 1944–45. Hon. Member Royal Photographic Soc.; Mem. of Nat. Film Library Cttee, British Film Institute, 1938–55. *Publications:* Official Handbooks to the Chemistry Collections, Science Museum, 1927–37; various papers in scientific journals. *Address:* Towers End, Walberswick, Southwold, Suffolk. *T:* Southwold 722146.

BARCLAY, Christopher Francis Robert, CMG 1967; *b* 8 June 1919; *s* of late Captain Robert Barclay, RA (retired) and late Annie Douglas Dowdeswell Barclay (*née* Davidson); *m* 1st, 1950, Clare Justice Troutbeck (marr. diss., 1962); two *s* one *d*; 2nd, 1962, Diana Elizabeth Goodman; one *s* one *d*. *Educ:* Eton Coll.; Magdalen Coll., Oxford (MA). 2nd Lieut The Rifle Bde, 1940; Capt. 1942; Major 1943; served in Middle East; Political Officer, Northern Iraq, 1945; Brit. Embassy, Baghdad, 1946. Foreign Office, 1946; Second Sec., British Embassy, Cairo, 1947; First Sec., Foreign Office, 1950; Brit. Embassy, Bonn, 1953; FO, 1956; Regional Information Officer, Beirut, 1960; FO, 1961; Counsellor and Head of Information Research Dept, 1962–66; Head of Personnel Dept (Training and General), FCO, 1967–69; Asst Sec., CSD, 1969–73, DoE, 1973–76; Sec., Govt Hospitality Fund, 1976–80. Mem. Council, City Univ., 1976–84. Master, Saddlers' Co., 1983–84. FRSA 1984. *Recreations:* fishing, gardening. *Address:* Croft Edge, Painswick, Glos. *T:* Painswick 812232. *Club:* Army and Navy.

BARCLAY, Sir Colville Herbert Sanford, 14th Bt, *cr* 1668; Painter; *b* 7 May 1913; *s* of late Rt Hon. Sir Colville Adrian de Rune Barclay, 3rd *s* of 11th Bt, and Sarita Enriqueta, *d* of late Herbert Ward; *S* uncle, 1930; *m* 1949, Rosamond Grant Renton Elliott; three *s*. *Educ:* Eton, Trinity Coll., Oxford. Third Sec., Diplomatic Service, 1937–41; enlisted in Navy, Nov. 1941; Sub-Lieut RNVR 1942; Lieut 1943; Lieut Commander 1945; demobilised, 1946. Exhibitor: Royal Academy, RBA, London Group, Bradford City and Brighton Art Galleries. Chm. Royal London Homoeopathic Hospital, 1970–74 (Vice-Chm., 1961–65; Chm., League of Friends, 1974–84). *Publications:* Crete: checklist of the vascular plants, 1986; articles in botanical jls. *Recreations:* gardening, plant-hunting. *Heir:* *s* Robert Colraine Barclay [*b* 12 Feb. 1950; *m* 1980, Lucilia Saboia, *y d* of Carlos Saboia de Albuquerque, Rio de Janeiro; one *s* one *d*]. *Address:* Pitshill, Petworth, West Sussex. *T:* Lodsworth 341. *Club:* Naval.

BARCLAY, Hugh Maben; Clerk of Private Bills, House of Commons, since 1982; *b* 20 Feb. 1927; *s* of late William Barclay, FRCS, and late Mary Barclay; *m* 1956, Hilda

Johnston; one *s* one *d*. *Educ:* Fettes Coll., Edinburgh (exhbnr); Gonville and Caius Coll., Cambridge (schol.). Served Royal Artillery, 1948. House of Commons: Asst Clerk, 1950; Sen. Clerk, 1955; Dep. Principal Clerk, 1967; Principal Clerk, 1976; Clerk of Standing Cttees, 1976. *Address:* 37 Stockwell Green, SW9. *T:* 01–274 7375.

BARCLAY, Peter Maurice, CBE 1984; Partner, Beachcrofts, Solicitors, since 1974; *b* 6 March 1926; *s* of George Ronald Barclay and Josephine (*née* Lambert); *m* 1953, Elizabeth Mary Wright; one *s* two *d*. *Educ:* Bryanston Sch.; Magdalene Coll., Cambridge (MA). Served RNVR, 1944–46. Admitted Solicitor, 1952; Senior Partner, Beachcroft & Co., 1964–74. Chairman: Ctte on Roles and Tasks of Social Workers, 1981–82; Social Security Adv. Cttee, 1984–. Chairman: National Inst. for Social Work, 1973–85; St Pancras Housing Assoc., 1983–. Trustee, Joseph Rowntree Memorial Trust, 1972–; Governor, Bryanston Sch., 1972–. *Recreations:* gardening, painting, golf. *Address:* 100 Fetter Lane, EC4A 1BN. *T:* 01–242 1011.

BARCLAY, Sir Roderick (Edward), GCVO 1966 (KCVO 1957; CVO 1953); KCMG 1955 (CMG 1948); HM Diplomatic Service, retired; *b* 22 Feb. 1909; *s* of late J. Gurney Barclay and Gillian (*née* Birkbeck); *m* 1934, Jean Cecil, *d* of late Sir Hugh Gladstone; one *s* three *d*. *Educ:* Harrow; Trinity Coll., Cambridge. Entered Diplomatic Service, 1932. Served at HM Embassies at Brussels, Paris, Washington and in FO; Counsellor in FO 1946; Principal Private Sec. to Sec. of State for Foreign Affairs, 1949–51; Asst Under-Sec. of State, 1951; Dep. Under-Sec. of State, 1953–56; HM Ambassador to Denmark, 1956–60; Adviser on European Trade Questions, Foreign Office, and Dep. Under-Sec. of State for Foreign Affairs, 1960–63; Ambassador to Belgium, 1963–69. Director: Slough Estates, 1969–84; Barclays Bank SA, 1969–79 (Chm., 1970–74); Barclays Bank Internat., 1971–77; Banque de Bruxelles, 1971–77. Knight Grand Cross of the Dannebrog (Denmark) and of the Couronne (Belgium). *Publication:* Ernest Bevin and the Foreign Office 1932–69, 1975; contrib. Country Life, etc. *Recreations:* shooting, fishing. *Address:* Great White End, Latimer, Bucks HP5 1UJ. *T:* Little Chalfont 2050. *Club:* Brooks's.
See also A. E Palmer.

BARCLAY, Yvonne Fay, (Mrs William Barclay); *see* Minton, Y. F.

BARCROFT, Prof. Henry, FRS 1953; MA; MD; FRCP; Professor of Physiology, St Thomas's Hospital Medical School, London, 1948–71, Emeritus since 1971; a Wellcome Trustee, 1966–75; *b* 18 Oct. 1904; *s* of late Sir Joseph Barcroft, CBE, FRS; *m* 1933, Bridget Mary, *d* of late A. S. Ramsey; three *s* one *d*. *Educ:* Marlborough Coll.; King's Coll. Cambridge; Exhibitioner, 1923. Natural Science Tripos Class I, Parts I and II; Harold Fry and George Henry Lewes studentships at Cambridge, 1927–29; Gedge Prize, 1930; Harmsworth Scholar, St Mary's Hospital, London, 1929–32; Lectr in Physiology, University Coll., London, 1932–35; Dunville Prof. of Physiology, Queen's Univ., Belfast, 1935–48. Arris and Gale Lectr, RCS, 1945; Bertram Louis Abrahams Lectr, RCP, 1960; Robert Campbell Meml Orator, Ulster Med. Soc., 1975; Bayliss-Starling Meml Lectr, Physiological Soc., 1976; Vis. Prof., Univ. of Adelaide, 1963. Chairman: Editorial Bd, Monographs of Physiological Soc., 1957–65; Research Defence Soc., 1968–71, Sec. 1972–77, Vice-Pres., 1978–. Hon. Member: Academic Adv. Cttee, Loughborough Coll. of Technology, 1964–66; Société Française d'Angiologie; Japanese Coll. of Angiology; Czechoslovak Med. Soc. J. E. Purkinje. Hon. DSc Univ. Western Australia, 1963; Hon. MD Leopold-Franzens Univ., Innsbruck, 1969; Hon. DSc QUB, 1975. Pro meritis médaille in silver, Karl Franzens Univ., Graz. *Publications:* (with H. J. C. Swan) Sympathetic Control of Human Blood Vessels, 1953; papers in the Journal of Physiology. *Recreations:* sailing and golf. *Address:* 73 Erskine Hill, NW11 6EY. *T:* 01–458 1066. *Club:* Athenæum.

BARD, Dr Basil Joseph Asher, CBE 1968; Chairman: Xtec Ltd, since 1983 (Director, since 1981); ProMicro Ltd, since 1985; Director: Interflex Structural Coatings Ltd, since 1984; Scanning Technology Ltd, since 1984; *b* London, 20 Aug. 1914; *s* of late Abram Isaac Bard and Anita Bard; *m* 1942, Ena Dora Birk; three *s*. *Educ:* Owen's Sch.; RCS (Imperial Coll.). BSc(Chem.), ARCS 1934, DIC (Chem. Engrg and Fuel Technology) 1935, PhD (Chem. Constitution of Coal) 1936, London; Bar Finals (1st cl. hons) and Studentship, Coun. of Legal Educn, 1937; called to Bar, Gray's Inn (Birkenhead and William Shaw Schol.), 1938. Practised at Bar, 1938–39; Legal Dept, Coal Commn, 1939–41; Explosives Prodn Dept, Min. of Supply, 1941–43; Materials Dept, Min. of Aircraft Production, 1943–45; Depts of Industrial Res., Educn, Design, etc, FBI, 1945–49; NRDC, 1950–74; in turn, Commercial Man., Techn. Dir, Exec. Dir, and Chief Exec., Dept of Applied Science; Mem., NRDC, 1956–73, Man. Dir, 1971–73; Exec. Dir, First National Finance Corp., 1974–76; Chm., Birmingham Mint Ltd, 1977–81. Dir, Allied Insulators Ltd, 1975–77; Chm., NPM Gp, 1977–83. Founder and Chm., 1968, subsequently Vice-Pres., UK Licensing Execs Soc. (awarded Gold Medal 1973). Consultant to UNIDO, 1972–74; Hon. Treasurer, Foundn for Sci. and Technol., 1984– (Mem. Council, 1982–); has served on various Govt Cttees. Pres., Jewish Meml Council, 1982–; Vice-Pres., Anglo-Jewish Assoc., 1983– (Pres., 1977–83). *Publications:* (ed) Industry and Research, 1947; (ed) The Patent System, 1975; various articles on science, technology, patents, industry, commerce and their inter-relationships. *Recreations:* music, bridge, chess, social life. *Address:* 23 Mourne House, Maresfield Gardens, Hampstead, NW3 5SL. *T:* 01–435 5340; c/o 1/3 Canfield Place, NW6. *T:* 01–328 8183. Club: Athenæum.

BARDEEN, Prof. John; Professor of Physics and Electrical Engineering, University of Illinois, 1951–75, now Emeritus; *b* Madison, Wisconsin, 23 May 1908; *s* of Dr Charles R. Bardeen and Althea Bardeen (*née* Harmer); *m* 1938, Jane Maxwell; two *s* one *d*. *Educ:* Univ. of Wisconsin; Princeton Univ. BS 1928, MS 1929, Univ. of Wisconsin; PhD 1936, Princeton Univ. Geophysicist, Gulf Research and Development Corp., Pittsburgh, Pa, 1930–33; Junior Fellow, Soc. of Fellows, Harvard Univ., 1935–38; Asst Prof. of Physics, Univ. of Minnesota, 1938–41; Physicist, Naval Ordnance Laboratory, Washington, DC, 1941–45; Research Physicist, Bell Telephone Laboratories, Murray Hill, NJ, 1945–51. Foreign Member: Royal Soc., 1973; Indian Nat. Sci. Acad., 1976; Japan Acad., 1977; Acad. of Sci., USSR, 1982. Holds hon. doctorates. Nobel Prize for Physics: (with W. H. Brattain and W. Shockley), 1956; (with L. N. Cooper and J. R. Schrieffer), 1972; National Medal of Science, 1965; Presidential Medal of Freedom, 1977. *Publications:* articles on solid state physics, including semi-conductors, metals, superconductivity in Physical Review and other periodicals and books. *Address:* 337 Loomis Laboratory, 1110 W Green Street, Urbana, Ill 61801, USA; 55 Greencroft, Champaign, Illinois 61821, USA. *T:* Champaign 352–6497.

BARDEN, Prof. Laing, PhD, DSc; FICE; Director, Newcastle upon Tyne Polytechnic, since 1978; *b* 29 Aug. 1931; *s* of Alfred Eversfield Barden and Edna (*née* Laing); *m* 1956, Nancy Carr; two *s* one *d*. *Educ:* Washington Grammar Sch.; Durham Univ. (BSc, MSc). R. T. James & Partners, 1954–59. Liverpool Univ., 1959–62 (PhD); Manchester Univ., 1962–69 (DSc); Strathclyde Univ., 1969–74; Newcastle Polytechnic, 1974–. Director: Newcastle Technology Centre Ltd; Microelectronics Applications Res. Inst. Ltd; Tyne and Wear Enterprise Trust Ltd. *Publications:* contribs to Geotechnique, Proc. ICE, Jl Amer. Soc. CE, Qly Jl Eng. Geol. *Recreations:* cricket, soccer, snooker. *Address:* 7 Westfarm Road, Cleadon, Tyne and Wear SR6 7UG. *T:* Boldon 362317. *Clubs:* National Liberal; Mid Boldon (Boldon).

BARDER, Brian Leon; HM Diplomatic Service; Ambassador to Poland, since 1986; *b* 20 June 1934; *s* of Harry and Vivien Barder; *m* 1958, Jane Maureen Cornwell; one *s* two *d*. *Educ:* Sherborne; St Catharine's Coll., Cambridge (BA). 2nd Lieut, 7 Royal Tank Regt, 1952–54. Colonial Office, 1957; Private Sec. to Permanent Under-Sec., 1960–61; HM Diplomatic Service, 1965; First Secretary, UK Mission to UN, 1964–68; FCO, 1968–70; First Sec. and Press Attaché, Moscow, 1971–73; Counsellor and Head of Chancery, British High Commn, Canberra, 1973–77; Canadian Nat. Defence Coll., Kingston, Ontario, 1977–78; Head of Central and Southern, later Southern African Dept, FCO, 1978–82; Ambassador to Ethiopia, 1982–86. *Address:* c/o Foreign and Commonwealth Office, SW1A 2AH. *Clubs:* United Oxford & Cambridge University, Royal Commonwealth Society.

BARDSLEY, Andrew Tromlow; JP; Principal, Westgate Development Consultancy; Chairman, Holbank Securities Ltd; *b* 7 Dec. 1927; *o s* of Andrew and Gladys Ada Bardsley; *m* 1954, June Patricia (*née* Ford); one *s* one *d*. *Educ:* Ashton-under-Lyne Grammar Sch.; Manchester Coll. of Art. CEng, FICE. Royal Navy, 1947–49. Entered Local Govt (Municipal Engrg), 1950; various appts leading to Borough Engr and Surveyor, Worksop MB, 1962–69; Director of Technical Services: Corby New Town, 1969–71; Luton CBC, 1971–73; Gen. Manager and Chief Exec., Harlow Develt Corp., 1973–80. JP Essex, 1975. *Publications:* papers on engrg and associated matters incl. housing and town centre re-development. *Recreations:* golf, music, gardening, most spectator sports. *Address:* 5A Northgate End, Bishops Stortford, Herts. *T:* Bishops Stortford 53804.

BARDSLEY, Rt. Rev. Cuthbert Killick Norman, CBE 1952; DD 1957; *b* 28 March 1907; *yr s* of late Canon J. U. N. Bardsley and Mabel Killick; *m* 1972, Ellen Mitchell. *Educ:* Eton; New Coll., Oxford. Curate of All Hallows, Barking by the Tower, 1932–34; Rector of Woolwich, 1940–44; Provost of Southwark Cathedral, 1944–47. Suffragan Bishop of Croydon, 1947–56; Bishop of Coventry, 1956–76. Hon. Canon in Canterbury Cathedral, 1948–56; Archbishop of Canterbury's Episcopal Representative with the three Armed Forces, 1948–56; Hon. Chaplain Siemens Bros, 1943–46; Proctor in Convocation, 1945–46. Select Preacher, University of Cambridge, 1958. ChStJ 1976. Hon. DLitt Warwick Univ., 1976. *Publications:* Bishop's Move, 1952; Sundry Times, Sundry Places, 1962; Him We Declare, 1967; I Believe in Mission, 1970. *Recreations:* golf, sketching. *Address:* Grey Walls, Berkeley Road, Cirencester, Gloucestershire GL7 1TY.

BARENBOIM, Daniel; pianist and conductor; Musical Director, Orchestre de Paris, since 1975; *b* Buenos Aires, 15 Nov. 1942; *s* of Enrique Barenboim and Aida Barenboim (*née* Schuster); *m* 1967, Jacqueline du Pré, *qv*. *Educ:* Santa Cecilia Acad., Rome; studied with his father; coached by Edwin Fischer, Nadia Boulanger, and Igor Markevitch. Debut as pianist with: Israel Philharmonic Orchestra, 1953; Royal Philharmonic Orchestra, 1956; Berlin Philharmonic Orchestra, 1963; NY Philharmonic Orchestra, 1964; tours include: Australia, North and South America, Far East; regular appearances at Bayreuth, Edinburgh, Lucerne, Prague and Salzburg Festivals. Many recordings as conductor and pianist. Beethoven Medal, 1958; Paderewski Medal, 1963; subsequently other awards. *Address:* c/o Harold Holt Ltd, 31 Sinclair Road, W14 0NS.

BARFETT, Ven. Thomas; Archdeacon of Hereford and Canon Residentiary of Hereford Cathedral, 1977–82, now Emeritus; Prebendary of Colwall and Treasurer, 1977–82; Chaplain to the Queen, 1975–86; *b* 2 Oct. 1916; *s* of Rev. Thomas Clarence Fairchild Barfett and Dr Mary Deborah Barfett, LRCP, LRCS, MA; *m* 1945, Edna, *d* of Robert Toy; one *s* one *d*. *Educ:* St John's Sch., Leatherhead; Keble Coll., Oxford (BA 1938; MA 1942); Wells Theol Coll. Ordained deacon, Portsmouth, 1939; priest, 1940; Curate: Christ Church, Gosport, 1939–44; St Francis of Assisi, Gladstone Park, London, 1944–47; St Andrew Undershaft with St Mary Axe, City of London, 1947–49; Asst Sec., London Diocesan Council for Youth, 1944–49; Vicar, St Paul, Penzance, dio. of Truro, 1949–55; Rector of Falmouth, 1955–77; Officiating Chaplain, 1102 Marine Craft Unit, RAF, 1957–75; Sec., Truro Diocesan Conf., 1952–67; Proctor in Convocation, dio. of Truro, 1958–76; Hon. Canon, Truro, 1964–77. Chm., House of Clergy, and Vice-Pres., Truro Diocesan Synod, 1970–76; Mem., Gen. Synod, 1977–82. Chaplain to lay Sheriff, City of London, 1976–77. Church Comr, 1975–82; Mem. C of E Central Bd of Finance, 1969–77, Pensions Board, 1973–86. Freeman, City of London, 1973; Freeman and Liveryman, Scriveners Co., 1976. Sub ChStJ, 1971 (Asst ChStJ, 1963). Silver Jubilee Medal, 1977. *Publication:* Trebarfoote: a Cornish family, 1975. *Recreations:* heraldry, genealogy. *Address:* Treberveth, 57 Falmouth Road, Truro, Cornwall TR1 2HL. *T:* Truro 73726. *Club:* United Oxford & Cambridge University.

BARFORD, Sir Leonard, Kt 1967; Deputy Chairman, Horserace Totalisator Board, 1974–77 (Member, 1973–77); Chief Inspector of Taxes, Board of Inland Revenue, 1964–73; Commissioner of Inland Revenue, 1970–73; *b* 1 Aug. 1908; *s* of William and Ada Barford, Finsbury Park; *m* 1939, Betty Edna Crichton, Plymouth; two *s*. *Educ:* Dame Alice Owen's Sch.; St Catharine's Coll., Cambridge Univ. (Exhibitioner in History). Asst Inspector of Taxes, 1930; Administrative Staff Coll., Henley, 1948; President, Assoc. of HM Inspectors of Taxes, 1951–53; Principal Inspector of Taxes, 1953; Senior Principal Inspector of Taxes, 1957; Deputy Chief Inspector, 1960. *Publication:* (jointly) Essay on Management in Tax Offices, 1950. *Recreations:* badminton, tennis, chess, bridge. *Address:* Harley House, 79 Sutton Road, Seaford, East Sussex. *T:* Seaford 893364. *Club:* Civil Service.

BARING, family name of **Baron Ashburton,** of **Earl of Cromer,** of **Baron Howick of Glendale,** of **Baron Northbrook,** and of **Baron Revelstoke.**

BARING, Sir Charles Christian, 2nd Bt, *cr* 1911; JP; *b* 16 Dec. 1898; *s* of Sir Godfrey Baring, 1st Bt, KBE, DL, and Eva Hermione Mackintosh of Mackintosh (*d* 1934); *S* father 1957; *m* 1948, Jeanette (Jan), (*d* 1985), *d* of Henry Charles Daykin. *Educ:* Eton. Served European War: Lieut Coldstream Guards, 1917–18 (severely wounded); War of 1939–45: Major Coldstream Guards, 1940–45; Political Warfare Executive, 1943–44; Staff, AFHQ, Italy, War Office, 1944–45. Attaché, HM Legation, Warsaw, 1922–23; Cunard White Star Ltd, 1933–36; HM Prison Service, 1936–38; Probation Officer: West London Magistrates' Court, 1938–40; Central Criminal Court, 1945–46; Inspector, Probation Branch Home Office, 1946–49; Colonial Service: Warden of Prisons, Bermuda, 1949–53. Member, Cttee of Management, RNLI (Vice-Pres., 1972). JP Isle of Wight County, 1956; DL Co. Southampton subseq. IoW, 1962–84; Chm. of Justices, IoW Petty Sessional Div., 1962–70. *Recreations:* golf, swimming, walking. *Heir: nephew* (Charles) Peter Baring [*b* 24 May 1939; *m* 1st, 1964, Sarah (marr. diss. 1974), *d* of late Col William Gill Withycombe; two *d*; 2nd, 1976, Susannah Jane, *d* of Dr W. E. Smith; two *d*]. *Address:* Springvale Hotel, Seaview, Isle of Wight.

BARING, Hon. Sir John (Francis Harcourt), Kt 1983; CVO 1980; Chairman: Barings plc, since 1985; Baring Brothers & Co. Ltd, since 1974 (a Managing Director, 1955–74); Receiver-General of Duchy of Cornwall, since 1974; Director, Bank of England, since 1983; *b* 2 Nov. 1928; *er s* and *heir* of 6th Baron Ashburton, *qv*; *m* 1955, Susan Mary

Renwick (marr. diss. 1984), *e d* of 1st Baron Renwick, KBE, and Mrs John Ormiston; two *s* two *d*. *Educ*: Eton (Fellow, 1982); Trinity Coll., Oxford (MA). Director: Trafford Park Estates Ltd, 1964–77; Pye Holdings Ltd, 1966–79; Outwich Ltd, Johannesburg, 1967–77; Dep. Chm., Royal Insurance Co. Ltd, 1975–82 (Dir, 1964–82); Chm., Outwich Investment Trust Ltd, 1968–; Director: Dunlop Holdings Ltd, 1981–84; British Petroleum, 1982–. Vice-Pres., British Bankers' Assoc., 1977–81; Pres., Overseas Bankers' Club, 1977–78. Chm., Accepting Houses Cttee, 1977–81; Chm., Cttee on Finance for Industry, NEDC, 1980–. Mem., British Transport Docks Bd, 1966–71; Mem. Council, CBI, 1976–80 (Mem. President's Cttee, 1976–79). Rhodes Trustee, 1970; Trustee, Nat. Gall., 1981–. Hon. Fellow, Hertford Coll., Oxford, 1976. *Address*: Lake House, Northington, Alresford, Hants SO24 9TG. *T*: Alresford 4293; Flat 7, 34 Bryanston Square, W1H 7LQ. *Clubs*: Pratt's, Flyfishers'.

BARING, Sir Mark, KCVO 1980 (CVO 1970); JP; General Commissioner for Income Tax, since 1966; Executive Chairman, King Edward VII's Hospital for Officers, since 1969; *b* 9 June 1916; *yr s* of late Hon. Windham Baring and Lady Gweneth Cavendish, 3rd *d* of 8th Earl of Bessborough; *m* 1949, Victoria Winifred Russell, *d* of late Col R. E. M. Russell, CVO, CBE, DSO; two *d*. *Educ*: Eton Coll.; Trinity Coll., Cambridge. Served War of 1939–45, Grenadier Guards; in Italy and UK; Mil. Liaison Officer HM Embassy, Rome, 1945–46 (Major 1945); retd 1946. Man. Dir, Seccombe Marshall and Campion Ltd, Discount Brokers, 1950–76. JP, Inner Area of London, 1963. Treasurer, Inst. of Urology, 1969–74; Mem. Bd of Governors, St Peter's Hosp., 1970–74; Governor, The Peabody Trust, 1971; Mem. Council, Baring Foundn, 1975–; Chm., Assoc. of Independent Hosps; Pres., St Marylebone Housing Assoc., 1956–77. High Sheriff, Greater London, 1976–77. *Recreations*: tennis, bridge. *Address*: 18 Thurloe Square, SW7. *T*: 01–589 8485. *Clubs*: Brooks's, White's.

BARING, Nicholas Hugo; Chairman, Baring Investment Management Holdings Ltd, since 1986; Director, Barings plc; *b* 2 Jan. 1934; *er s* of late Francis Anthony Baring (killed in action, 1940) and of Lady Rose Baring, *qv*; *m* 1972, Elizabeth Diana, *d* of late Brig. Charles Crawfurd; three *s*. *Educ*: Eton (King's Schol.); Magdalene Coll., Cambridge (exhibnr, BA). Nat. service, 2nd Lieut Coldstream Guards, 1952–54. ADC to Governor of Kenya, 1957–58; joined Baring Brothers, 1958; Man. Dir, Baring Brothers & Co., 1963–86; Director: Commercial Union, 1968– (Vice-Chm., 1978–83; Dep. Chm., 1983–); Swaziland Settlement, 1963–; Witan Investment Co., 1968–. National Trust: Mem. Exec. Cttee, 1965–69 and 1979–; Mem. Council, 1978–; Chm., Finance Cttee, 1980– (Mem., 1969–); Mem., Royal Opera House Trust, 1982–85; Chm., City Capital Markets Cttee, 1983–. *Address*: 8 Bishopsgate, EC2N 4AE. *T*: 01–283 8833. *Club*: Brooks's.

BARING, Lady Rose (Gwendolen Louisa), DCVO 1972 (CVO 1964); Extra Woman of the Bedchamber to the Queen, since 1973; *b* 23 May 1909; *er d* of 12th Earl of Antrim and of Margaret, *y d* of late Rt Hon. J. G. Talbot; *m* 1933, Francis Anthony Baring (killed in action, 1940); two *s* one *d*. Woman of the Bedchamber to the Queen, 1953–73. *Address*: 43 Pembroke Square, W8.

　　See also N. H. Baring.

BARK, Evelyn (Elizabeth Patricia), CMG 1967; OBE 1952; retired as Director International Affairs Department of British Red Cross (1950–66); *b* 26 Dec. 1900; *e d* of late Frederick William Bark. *Educ*: privately. On staff of Swedish Match Co. (at home and abroad) until 1939, when joined British Red Cross. Served War, 1939–44, VAD (Stars: of 1939–45, of France, and of Germany; Defence Medal, and War Medal, 1939–45). Foreign Relations Officer, 1944–48. Commissioner, NW Europe, 1948–49; Foreign Relations and Relief Adviser, 1950 (title later changed to Dir International Affairs). Serving Sister of St John's, 1953; British Red Cross Certificate First Class, 1966. *Publication*: No Time to Kill, 1960. *Recreations*: reading, music, nordic languages. *Address*: c/o 15 Holly Hill Drive, Banstead, Surrey.

BARKE, James Allen; Director: Falcon Engineering Co., since 1972; D.B. Holdings; *b* 16 April 1903; *s* of James E. Barke and Emma Livsey; *m* 1st, 1937, Doris Marian Bayne (*d* 1952); two *s* one *d*; 2nd, 1953, Marguerite Amy Sutcliffe (*née* Williams) (*d* 1968); one step *d*. *Educ*: Birley Street Central Sch.; Manchester Coll. of Technology. Mather & Platt and general engineering experience, 1922–32; joined Ford Motor Co., 1932; Buyer, Purchase Dept, 1939; Chief Buyer (Tractors), 1947; Manager, Leamington Foundry, 1948; Executive Dir and General Manager, Briggs Motor Bodies Ltd, 1953; Ford Motor Co.: Dir, Product Divs, 1959; Asst Man. Dir, 1961; Man. Dir, 1962; Chief Exec. Officer and Man. Dir, 1963; Vice-Chm., 1965–68; Dir, De La Rue Company Ltd, 1970–73. *Recreations*: golf, rock climbing, walking, reading. *Address*: Thurlestone, Mill Green, Ingatestone, Essex. *Club*: Oriental.

BARKER, family name of **Baroness Trumpington.**

BARKER, Alan; *see* Barker, William A.

BARKER, Sir Alwyn (Bowman), Kt 1969; CMG 1962; BSc, BE; CEng, FIEAust; Chairman, Kelvinator Australia Ltd, 1967–80 (Managing Director, 1952–67); *b* 5 Aug. 1900; *s* of late A. J. Barker, Mt Barker, South Australia; *m* 1926, Isabel Barron Lucas, *d* of late Sir Edward Lucas; one *d* (one *s* decd). *Educ*: St Peter's Coll., Adelaide; Geelong C of E Grammar Sch.; Univ. of Adelaide. British Thomson Houston Co. Ltd, England, 1923–24; Hudson Motor Car Co., Detroit, 1924–25; Production Manager, Holden's Motor Body Builders Ltd, Adelaide, 1925–30; Works Manager, Kelvinator Aust. Ltd, Adelaide, 1931–40; Gen. Man., Chrysler Aust. Ltd, Adelaide, 1940–52; Chm., Municipal Tramways Trust SA, 1953–68; Life mem., Australian Mineral Foundn; Dir, public companies. Mem. Faculty of Engineering, Univ. of Adelaide, 1937–66 (Lectr in Industrial Engineering, 1929–53). Chm., Industrial Develt Adv. Council, 1968–70; Fellow, Internat. Acad. of Management; Member: Manufacturing Industries Adv. Council, 1958–72; Res. and Develt Adv. Cttee, 1967–72. Hon. Fellow Australian Inst. of Management (Federal Pres., 1952–53, 1959–61; Pres. Adelaide Div., 1952–54); Pres., Australian Council, Inst. of Prodn Engrs, 1970–72. John Storey Meml Medal, 1965; Jack Finlay Nat. Award, 1964. *Publications*: Three Presidential Addresses, 1954; William Queale Memorial Lecture, 1965. *Recreations*: pastoral. *Address*: 51 Hackney Road, Hackney, SA 5069, Australia. *T*: 42.2838. *Club*: Adelaide.

BARKER, Anthony; QC 1985; a Recorder, since 1985; *b* 10 Jan. 1944; *s* of Robert Herbert Barker and Ellen Doreen Barker; *m* 1st, 1969, Judith Ann Stevens (marr. diss. 1980); two *d*; 2nd, 1983, Mrs Valerie Ann Ellis; one step *s*. *Educ*: Newcastle-under-Lyme High Sch.; Clare Coll., Cambridge (BA Hons). Called to the Bar, Middle Temple, 1966. Asst Recorder, 1981. *Recreations*: gardening, walking, music. *Address*: Hilderstone House, Hilderstone, near Stone, Staffs. *T*: Hilderstone 331.

BARKER, Arthur Vincent, CBE 1974 (OBE 1955); FCIT; Scottish Chartered Accountant; financial planning consultant; *b* 10 Nov. 1911; *e s* of late Arthur and Susannah Mary Barker; *m* 1936, Dorothy Drew; one *d*. *Educ*: Whitley and Monkseaton High Sch.; London Sch. of Economics. Qual. as CA, 1934; with Price Waterhouse & Co., 1934–35; with NAAFI in Middle East and UK, 1935–62 (Jt Gen. Man., 1955). Asst Gen.

Man., Southern Region, British Railways, and Mem., Southern Railway Bd, 1962; Asst Gen. Man., London Midland Region, British Railways, and Mem., LMR Bd, 1965; Chairman: Shipping and Internat. Services Div., British Railways, 1968–69; British Rail Hovercraft, 1970–71; British Transport Hotels Ltd, 1968–74; Mem., British Railways Bd, 1968–74. *Recreation*: fly-fishing. *Address*: 25 West Mount, The Mount, Guildford, Surrey GU2 5HL. *T*: Guildford 39524.

BARKER, Audrey Lilian; writer; *b* 13 April 1918; *d* of Harry and Elsie Barker. *Educ*: County secondary schools in Beckenham, Kent and Wallington, Surrey. Editorial office, Amalgamated Press, 1936; Publisher's reader, Cresset Press, 1947; BBC, 1949–78. Atlantic Award in Literature, 1946; Somerset Maugham Award, 1947; Cheltenham Festival of Literature Award, 1963; SE Arts Creative Book Award, 1981. FRSL 1970; Mem. Exec. Cttee, PEN, 1981–85; Member Panel of Judges: Katherine Mansfield Prize, 1984; Macmillan Silver Pen Award for Fiction, 1986. *Publications: collected stories*: Innocents, 1947; Novelette, 1951; Lost Upon the Roundabouts, 1964; Femina Real, 1971; Life Stories, 1981; No Word of Love, 1985; *novels*: Apology for a Hero, 1950; The Joy-Ride, 1963; A Case Examined, 1965; The Middling, 1967; John Brown's Body, 1969 (shortlisted for Booker Prize, 1969); A Source of Embarrassment, 1974; A Heavy Feather, 1978; Relative Successes, 1984. *Address*: 103 Harrow Road, Carshalton, Surrey.

BARKER, Barry, MBE 1960; FCIS; Secretary and Chief Executive, Institute of Chartered Secretaries and Administrators (formerly Chartered Institute of Secretaries), since 1976; *b* 1929; *s* of late Francis Walter Barker and of Amy Barker; *m* 1954, Dr Vira Dubash; two *s*. *Educ*: Ipswich Sch.; Trinity Coll., Oxford (MA Class. Greats). FBIM. Secretary: Bombay Chamber of Commerce and Industry, 1956–62; The Metal Box Co. of India Ltd, 1962–67. Dir, Shipbuilding Industry Bd, 1967–71; Consultant at Dept of Industry, 1972; Sec., Pye Holdings Ltd, 1972–76. Member: BTEC, 1985–86; DES/MSC Wkg Gp to Review Vocational Qualifications, 1985–86; Bd of Management, Young Vic Co., 1984–; Court, Cranfield Inst. of Technology, 1984–. *Recreations*: the theatre and the arts. *Address*: 29 Darwin Court, Gloucester Avenue, NW1 7BG. *T*: 01–485 4608. *Club*: Oriental.

BARKER, Brian John; a Recorder of the Crown Court, since 1985; *b* 15 Jan. 1945; *s* of William Barker and Irene Barker (*née* Gillow); *m* 1977, Anne Judith Rafferty; three *d* (and one *d* decd). *Educ*: Strode's School, Egham; Univ. of Birmingham (LLB); Univ. of Kansas (MA). Called to the Bar, Gray's Inn, 1969. *Recreations*: gardening, golf. *Address*: Queen Elizabeth Building, Temple, EC4Y 9BS. *T*: 01–583 5766. *Club*: Royal Mid-Surrey Golf.

BARKER, Rt. Rev. Clifford Conder; *see* Selby, Bishop Suffragan of.

BARKER, David, QC 1976; a Recorder of the Crown Court, since 1974; *b* 13 April 1932; *s* of Frederick Barker and Amy Evelyn Barker; *m* 1957, Diana Mary Vinson Barker (*née* Duckworth); one *s* three *d*. *Educ*: Sir John Deane's Grammar Sch., Northwich; University Coll., London; Univ. of Michigan. 1st cl. hons LLB London; LLM Michigan. RAF, 1956–59. Called to Bar, Inner Temple, 1954, Bencher, 1985; practised Midland and Oxford Circuit; Mem., Senate of Inns of Court and the Bar, 1981–84. Contested (Lab) Runcorn, 1955. *Recreations*: gardening, walking, sailing. *Address*: Nanhill, Woodhouse Eaves, Leics. *T*: Woodhouse Eaves 890224; Francis Taylor Building, Temple, EC4. *T*: 01–353 7768. *Club*: Northampton and County (Northampton).

BARKER, Prof. David (Faubert), MA, DPhil, DSc; Professor of Zoology, University of Durham, since 1962; *b* 18 Feb. 1922; *s* of Faubert and Doreen Barker; *m* 1st, 1945, Kathleen Mary Frances Pocock; three *s* two *d*; 2nd, 1978, Patricia Margaret Drake; one *s* one *d*. *Educ*: Bryanston Sch.; Magdalen Coll., Oxford. DSc 1972. Senior Demy of Magdalen Coll., 1946; Leverhulme Research Scholar, Royal Coll. of Surgeons, 1946; Demonstrator in Zoology and Comparative Anatomy, Oxford, 1947; DPhil 1948; Rolleston Prizeman, 1948; Prof. of Zoology, Univ. of Hong Kong, 1950–62; led scientific expeditions to Tunisia, 1950, North Borneo, 1952; Dean of Faculty of Science, Hong Kong, 1959–60; Public Orator, Hong Kong, 1961; Sir Derman Christopherson Fellow, Durham Univ. Research Foundn, 1984–85. *Publications*: (Founder) Editor, Hong Kong Univ. Fisheries Journal, 1954–60; Editor, Symposium on Muscle Receptors, 1962; scientific papers, mostly on muscle innervation. *Address*: Department of Zoology, Science Laboratories, South Road, Durham. *T*: Durham 64971.

BARKER, Dennis Albert; Hon. Mr Justice Barker; Justice of Appeal, Hong Kong, since 1981; *b* 9 June 1926; *s* of J. W. and R. E. Barker; *m* 1st, 1949, Daphne (*née* Ruffle) (marr. diss. 1984); one *s* one *d* (and one *d* decd); 2nd, 1984, Deirdre (*née* Rendall-Day). *Educ*: Nottingham High Sch.; The Queen's Coll. Oxford (Jodrell Schol.). Flying Officer, RAFVR, 1944–47. 1st cl. hons (Jurisprudence), Oxon, 1949; 1st cl. Certif. of Honour and Studentship, Bar Finals, 1950; Harmsworth Law Schol., 1950; Eldon Law Schol., 1950; called to the Bar, Middle Temple, 1950, Bencher, 1975. Mem. Midland Circuit; Dep. Chm., Bucks QS, 1963–71; QC 1968; a Recorder of the Crown Court, 1972–79. Former Mem., Criminal Injuries Compensation Bd. *Recreations*: golf, flying, music. *Address*: Supreme Court, Hong Kong. *Clubs*: Hong Kong, Sheko Country (Hong Kong); Ashridge Golf (Bucks).

BARKER, Edward, OBE 1966; QPM 1961; Chief Constable of Sheffield and Rotherham Constabulary, 1967–72; *b* 1 Nov. 1909; *s* of George and Gertrude Barker; *m* 1935, Clare Garth; one *d*. *Educ*: The Grammar School, Malton. Joined Preston Borough Police, 1931; transf. Lancs Constabulary, 1938; Inspector/Chief Inspector, Comdt of Constabulary Trng Sch., 1946–51; Supt 1954; Vis. Lectr to Bermuda Police, 1955; Chief Supt 1956; Asst Comdt, Police Coll., Bramshill, 1956–57; Chief Constable: Bolton Borough Police, 1957; Sheffield City Police, 1964. Police Long Service and Good Conduct Medal, 1953. SBStJ. *Recreations*: golf, gardening, watching field sports. *Address*: 21 Woodstock Road, Aberdeen. *T*: Aberdeen 38484. *Clubs*: Royal Over-Seas League; Deeside Golf.

BARKER, Eric Leslie; Author and Entertainer; *b* 20 Feb. 1912; *s* of Charles and Maude Barker; *m* 1936, Pearl Hackney; one *d*. *Educ*: Whitgift Sch. Character actor Birmingham, Oxford and Croydon Repertory Theatres, 1932–33; Comedian, also sketch and lyric writer, Charlot revues, Windmill, and Prince of Wales Theatre, 1933–38. Author and star of radio series: Howdyfolks, 1939–40; Navy Mixture, 1944–45; Merry-Go-Round, 1945–49, Just Fancy, 1950–62; Passing Parade, 1957; Barker's Folly, 1958; Law and Disorder, 1960. Lieut RNVR, 1940–45. Author and star of television series: Eric Barker Half Hour, 1952–55; Absolutely Barkers, 1963. *Films*: Brothers-in-Law (British Film Acad. Award); Clean Sweep; Blue Murder at St Trinians; Happy Is The Bride; Carry on, Sergeant; Eye Spy; Bachelor of Hearts; Right, Left and Centre; Carry on, Constable; Dentist in the Chair; Raising the Wind; The Fast Lady; Those Magnificent Men in their Flying Machines; Doctor in Clover; Maroc 7. *Publications*: short stories, 3 novels, 1931–33; The Watch Hunt, 1931; Day Gone By, 1932; Steady Barker (Autobiog.), 1956; Golden Gimmick, 1958. *Recreations*: antiques, photography, gardening, history, cricket, swimming. *Address*: c/o Lloyds Bank, Faversham, Kent.

BARKER, George Granville; writer; *b* 26 Feb. 1913; *s* of George Barker and Marion Frances Barker (*née* Taaffe); *m* 1964, Elspeth Langlands. *Educ*: Marlborough Road London County Council Sch., Chelsea. Prof. of English Literature at Imperial Tohoku Univ.,

Japan, 1939; visited America, 1940; returned to England, 1943; lived in Rome, 1960–65. Arts Fellow York Univ., 1966–67; Vis. Prof., Florida Internat. Univ., 1974. *Publications:* Thirty Preliminary Poems, 1933; Alanna Autumnal, 1933; Poems, 1935; Janus, 1935; Calamiterror, 1937; Lament and Triumph, 1940; Eros in Dogma, 1944; News of the World, 1950; The Dead Seagull, 1950; The True Confession of George Barker, 1950; A Vision of Beasts and Gods, 1954; Collected Poems, 1930–55, 1957; The True Confession of George Barker, Book II, 1957; Two Plays, 1958; The View from a Blind I, 1962; Dreams of a Summer Night, 1966; The Golden Chains, 1968; Essays, 1970; Runes & Rhymes & Tunes & Chimes, 1970; To Aylsham Fair, 1970; At Thurgarton Church, 1970; Poems of Places and People, 1971; The Alphabetical Zoo, 1972; In Memory of David Archer, 1973; Dialogues etc, 1976; Villa Stellar, 1978; Anno Domini, 1983. *Address:* Bintry House, Itteringham, Aylsham, Norfolk. *T:* Saxthorpe 240.

BARKER, Dr Graeme William Walter, FSA; Senior Lecturer in Prehistory and Archaeology, Sheffield University, since 1981; Director of the British School at Rome, since 1984 (on secondment); *b* 23 Oct. 1946; *s* of Reginald Walter Barker and Kathleen (*née* Walton); *m* 1976, Sarah Miranda Buchanan; one *s* one *d. Educ:* Alleyn's Sch., Dulwich; St John's Coll., Cambridge (Henry Arthur Thomas Schol., 1965–67; MA, PhD). FSA 1979. Rome Schol. in Classical Studies, British Sch. at Rome, 1969–71; Lectr in Prehist. and Archaeol., Sheffield Univ., 1972–81. Dir, Molise survey and excavation project, S Italy, 1974–78; Co-Dir, UNESCO Libyan Valleys Survey, 1979–. *Publications:* Landscape and Society: Prehistoric Central Italy, 1981, Italian edn 1984; (with R. Hodges) Archaeology and Italian Society, 1981; Prehistoric Communities in Northern England, 1981; (jtly) La Casatico di Marcaria, 1983; (jtly) Cyrenaica in Classical Antiquity, 1984; Prehistoric Farming in Europe, 1985; (with C. S. Gamble) Beyond Domestication in Prehistoric Europe: Investigations in Subsistence Archaeology and Social Complexity, 1985; contribs, esp. on archaeol survey, archaeozool. and ancient agric., to learned jls. *Recreations:* bell ringing, hill walking and climbing, small scale sheep farming. *Address:* British School at Rome, Via Gramsci 61, 00197 Rome, Italy. *T:* Rome 873424; Oaker Farm, Edale Road, Hope, Derbyshire S30 2RF.

BARKER, Harold; retired; Keeper, Department of Conservation and Technical Services, British Museum, 1975–79; Member: Council for Care of Churches, 1976–81; Crafts Council, 1979–80; *b* 15 Feb. 1919; *s* of William Frampton Barker and Lily (*née* Pack); *m* 1942, Everilda Alice Whittle; one *s* one *d. Educ:* City Secondary Sch., Sheffield; Sheffield Univ. (BSc). Experimental Asst, 1940, Experimental Officer, 1942, Chemical Inspectorate, Min. of Supply; British Museum: Experimental Officer, Research Lab., 1947; Sen. Experimental Officer, 1953; Chief Experimental Officer, 1960; Principal Scientific Officer, 1966; Acting Keeper, 1975. *Publications:* papers on radiocarbon dating and scientific examination of antiquities in various jls. *Recreations:* music, walking, cinematography. *Address:* 27 Westbourne Park, Falsgrave, Scarborough, N Yorks YO12 4AS. *T:* Scarborough 370967.

BARKER, Sir Harry Heaton, KBE 1978 (CBE 1972; OBE 1964); JP; New Zealand Journalist; chairman various organisations; *b* Nelson, NZ, 18 July 1898; *s* of J. H. Barker; *m* 1926, Anita (MBE), *d* of H. Greaves; no *c. Educ:* Wellington and Auckland; New Plymouth Boys' High Sch. Served NZEF, 1917–19. Entered journalism, working with NZ Herald and country newspapers, 1916–17, 1919–23; Gisborne Herald: joined, 1923; sub-editor, 1926; Leader Writer, Associate Editor, 1930; Editor, 1935–43, resigned. Mayor of Gisborne, 1950; re-elected, 1953, 1956, 1959, 1962, 1965, 1968, 1971, 1974. Contested Gisborne seat, 1943, 1946. Member: Cook Hospital Board, 1944–71; King George V Health Camps Federation Board, 1953–69; Exec., Dist Roads Council, 1953–78; East Coast Planning Council, 1972–77. Chairman: Barrington Miller Educnl Trust, 1950–77; Gisborne Airport Cttee, 1958–77; cttee organising nat. celebration, Cook Bicentenary celebration, 1969. Executive, NZ Municipalities Assoc., and Dir, Municipalities Insurance Co., 1959–69. Knighted for services to the City of Gisborne, NZ, and local government. *Publications:* To-Days and Yesterdays, 1978; political articles. *Recreations:* reading, writing, gardening. *Address:* 218 Harris Street, Gisborne, New Zealand. *T:* 76405. *Club:* Victoria League.

BARKER, John Francis Holroyd, CB 1984; Cabinet Office; *b* 3 Feb. 1925; *s* of Rev. C.H. Barker and B.A. Barker (*née* Bullivant); *m* 1954, Felicity Ann (*née* Martindale); three *d. Educ:* King Edward's School, Stourbridge; Oriel College, Oxford. RNVR, 1943–46. Director of Music, Abingdon School, 1950–54; War Office/Ministry of Defence, 1954–85. *Recreation:* music. *Address:* c/o Coutts & Co., 440 Strand, WC2. *Club:* Athenæum.

BARKER, Air Vice-Marshal John Lindsay, CB 1963; CBE 1946; DFC 1945; RAF (Retired); *b* 12 Nov. 1910; *s* of Abraham Cockroft Barker and Lilian Alice (*née* Woods); *m* 1948, Eleanor Margaret Hannah; one *s. Educ:* Trent Coll., Derbys; Brasenose Coll., Oxford. Called to the Bar, Middle Temple, 1947. RAFO, 1930, RAF, 1933. Served War of 1939–45: France, 1939–40; N Africa, 1942–44; Bomber Command, 1944–45; Far East, 1945–48; Egypt, 1950–53; Air Attaché, Rome, 1955–58; Cmdr Royal Ceylon Air Force, 1958–63. Air Vice-Marshal, 1959. Retd, 1963. Order of Merit, Italy, 1958. *Recreations:* golf, photography, sailing. *Address:* Ravensbourne, Ravensbourne Lane, Stoke Fleming, Dartmouth, Devon TQ6 0QR. *Club:* Royal Air Force.

BARKER, John Michael Adrian; His Honour Judge Barker; a Circuit Judge, since 1979; *b* 4 Nov. 1932; *s* of Robert Henry Barker and Annie Robson Barker (*née* Charlton); *m* 1971, Gillian Marsha (*née* Greenstone). *Educ:* Marist Coll., Hull Univs of Sheffield and Hull. BSc, LLB. Called to Bar, Middle Temple, 1959. Schoolmaster, Stonyhurst Coll., 1957–59; Lectr in Law, Univ. of Hull, 1960–63. A Recorder of the Crown Court, 1974–79. Mem., Hull CC, 1965–71. *Publications:* articles in Conveyancer and Property Lawyer, Solicitors' Jl and Solicitor. *Recreations:* music, cricket. *Address:* 2 Harcourt Buildings, Temple, EC4. *Club:* Lansdowne.

BARKER, Rear-Adm. John Perronet, CB 1985; Chief of Staff to Commander-in-Chief, Naval Home Command, 1983–85; RN retired, 1986; *b* 24 June 1930; *s* of late Gilbert Barker and Dorothy G. Barker (*née* Moore); *m* 1955, Priscilla, *d* of late Sir William Christie, KCIE, CSI, MC; two *s. Educ:* Edgbaston Prep. Sch., Birmingham; Nautical Coll., Pangbourne; BRNC, Dartmouth. Entered RN, 1948; served, 1949–72: HMS King George V, Glory, Condor, Ceres, Lagos, Hampshire and Centurion; staff of C-in-C Home Fleet, of C-in-C Nore and of Comdr British Navy Staff, Washington; sec. to ACNS (OR), MoD (Navy), to Flag Officer 2FEF, and to Flag Officer Plymouth; Sec. to Controller of the Navy, 1972–76; Student, RCDS, 1977; Dir, Fleet Supply Duties, MoD (Navy), 1978–80; Cdre, HMS Centurion, 1980–83. Liveryman, Worshipful Co. of Shipwrights, 1983. *Recreations:* sailing, gardening. *Address:* c/o Lloyds Bank, 125 Colmore Row, Birmingham B3 3AD. *Clubs:* Royal Yacht Squadron (Cowes); Royal Naval Sailing Association (Portsmouth); Midland Sailing (Birmingham); Hill Head Sailing (Fareham); Royal Lymington Yacht.

BARKER, Nicolas John; Deputy Keeper, British Library, since 1976; Editor, Book Collector, since 1965; *b* 6 Dec. 1932; *s* of Sir Ernest Barker, FBA, and Olivia Stuart Horner; *m* 1962, Joanna Mary Sophia Nyda Cotton; two *s* three *d. Educ:* Westminster Sch.; New Coll., Oxford (MA). With Bailliere, Tindall & Cox, 1959 and Rupert Hart-Davis, 1959; Asst Keeper, National Portrait Gallery, 1964; with Macmillan & Co. Ltd, 1965; with OUP, 1976. President: Amici Thomae Mori, 1978–; Double Crown Club, 1980–81; Bibliographical Soc., 1981–85; Member: Publication Bd of Dirs, RNIB, 1969–; London Library Cttee, 1971–; BBC and ITV Appeals Adv. Cttee, 1977–; Nat. Trust Arts Panel, 1979–; Trustee, The Pilgrim Trust, 1977–; Chm., Laurence Sterne Trust, 1984–. *Publications:* The Publications of the Roxburghe Club, 1962; The Printer and the Poet, 1970; Stanley Morison, 1972; (ed) Essays and Papers of A. N. L. Munby, 1977; (ed) The Early Life of James McBey: an autobiography, 1883–1911, 1977; Bibliotheca Lindesiana, 1977; The Oxford University Press and the Spread of Learning 1478–1978, 1978; (with John Collins) A Sequel to an Enquiry, 1983; Aldus Manutius and the Development of Greek Script and Type, 1985. *Address:* 22 Clarendon Road, W11. *T:* 01–727 4340. *Clubs:* Garrick, Beefsteak.

BARKER, Paul; writer and broadcaster; Social Policy Editor, Sunday Telegraph, since 1986; Visiting Fellow, Centre for Analysis of Social Policy, University of Bath, since 1986; *b* 24 Aug. 1935; *s* of Donald and Marion Barker; *m* 1960, Sally, *e d* of James and Marion Huddleston; three *s* one *d. Educ:* Hebden Bridge Grammar Sch.; Calder High Sch.; Brasenose Coll., Oxford (Hulme Exhibr), MA. Intell. Corps (commn), 1953–55. Lecteur, Ecole Normale Supérieure, Paris, 1958–59; The Times, 1959–63; New Society, staff writer, 1964; The Economist, 1964–65; New Society: Assistant Editor, 1965–68; Editor, 1968–86. *Publications:* (ed) A Sociological Portrait, 1972; (ed) One for Sorrow, Two for Joy, 1972; (ed) The Social Sciences Today, 1975; (ed) Arts in Society, 1977; (ed) The Other Britain, 1982; (ed) Founders of the Welfare State, 1985. *Recreation:* driving along an empty motorway to a baroque church, with the radio on. *Address:* 15 Dartmouth Park Avenue, NW5. *T:* 01–485 8861.

BARKER, Richard Philip; Headmaster, Sevenoaks School, since 1981; *b* 17 July 1939; *s* of late Philip Watson Barker and Helen May Barker; *m* 1966, Imogen Margaret Harris; two *s* one *d. Educ:* Repton; Trinity Coll., Cambridge (MA 1962); Bristol Univ. (Cert. Ed. 1963). Head of Geography, Bedales Sch., 1963–65; Dir, A level business studies project, 1966–73; Lectr, Inst. of Education, London Univ., 1973–74; Housemaster, Marlborough Coll., 1973–81. *Publications:* (ed) Understanding Business Series, 1976–86. *Recreations:* fishing, sailing, travelling. *Address:* Headmaster's House, Sevenoaks School, Kent TN13 1HU. *T:* Sevenoaks 455133.

BARKER, Ronald Hugh, PhD, BSc; CEng, FIEE, FIMechE; Deputy Director, Royal Armament Research and Development Establishment, 1965–75, retired; *b* 28 Oct. 1915; *s* of E. W. Barker and L. A. Taylor; *m* 1943, W. E. Hunt; two *s. Educ:* University of Hull. Physicist, Standard Telephones and Cables, 1938–41; Ministry of Supply, 1941–59; Dep. Dir, Central Electricity Research Laboratories, 1959–62; Technical Dir, The Pullin Group Ltd, 1962–65. *Publications:* various, on servomechanisms and control systems. *Address:* Cró Madra, St Monica's Road, Kingswood, Surrey KT20 6HA. *T:* Burgh Heath 55489.

BARKER, Ronnie, (Ronald William George Barker), OBE 1978; actor; *b* 25 Sept. 1929; *s* of Leonard and Edith Barker; *m* 1957, Joy Tubb; two *s* one *d. Educ:* Oxford High Sch. Started acting career, Aylesbury Rep. Co., 1948. *Plays (West End):* Mourning Becomes Electra, 1955; Summertime, 1955; Listen to the Wind, 1955; Double Image, 1956; Camino Real, 1957; Lysistrata, 1958; Irma la Douce, 1958; Platanov, 1960; On the Brighter Side, 1961; Midsummer Night's Dream, 1962; Real Inspector Hound, 1968; The Two Ronnies, Palladium, 1978. *Films include:* Robin and Marian, 1975; Picnic, 1975; Porridge, 1979. *Television: series:* Seven Faces of Jim, 1965; Frost Report, 1966–67; Hark at Barker, 1968–69; Six Dates with Barker, 1970; The Two Ronnies, 10 series, 1971–; Porridge, 1974, 1975, 1976, 1977; Open All Hours, 1976, 1981, 1982; Going Straight, 1978. *Awards:* Variety Club, 1969, 1974, 1980; SFTA, 1971; Radio Industries Club, 1973, 1974, 1977, 1981; Water Rats, 1975; British Acad. Award, 1975, 1977, 1978; Royal Television Society's award for outstanding creative achievement, 1975; Sun Awards, 1975, 1977. *Publications:* Book of Bathing Beauties, 1974; Book of Boudoir Beauties, 1975; It's Goodnight From Him, 1976; Sauce, 1977; Gentlemen's Relish, 1979; Sugar and Spice, 1981; Ooh-la-la!, 1983; Pebbles on the Beach, 1985; A Pennyworth of Art, 1986. *Recreations:* writing song lyrics, collecting postcards.

BARKER, Susan Vera; *see* Cooper, Susie.

BARKER, Prof. Theodore Cardwell, PhD, FRHistS; Professor of Economic History, University of London, 1976–83, now Emeritus; *b* 19 July 1923; *s* of Norman Humphrey Barker and Louie Nettleton Barker; *m* 1955, Joy Marie (Judith) Pierce. *Educ:* Cowley Sch., St Helens; Jesus Coll., Oxford (MA); Manchester Univ. (PhD). FRHistS 1963. Econ. History staff, LSE, 1953–64; first Prof. of Econ. and Social Hist., Univ. of Kent at Canterbury, 1964–76. Pres., Econ. Hist. Soc., 1986– (Hon. Sec., 1960–86); Vice-Pres., Internat. Historical Congress, 1986– (Chm., British Nato Cttee, 1978–); Chairman: Management Cttee, Inst. of Historical Res., London Univ., 1977–; Hist. Bd, CNAA, 1977–81; Management Cttee, London Univ. Business History Unit, 1979–86; Debrett's Business History Research Ltd, 1984–; Oral Hist. Soc., 1973–76. Mem. Council, RHistS, 1967–70 and 1974–77. *Publications:* A Merseyside Town in the Industrial Revolution (with J. R. Harris), 1954; A History of the Girdlers Company, 1957; Pilkington Brothers and the Glass Industry, 1960; (with R. H. Campbell, Peter Mathias and B. S. Yamey) Business History, 1960, 2nd edn 1970; (with R. M. Robbins) A History of London Transport: Vol. I, 1963, Vol. II, 1974; (ed with J. C. McKenzie and John Yudkin) Our Changing Fare: two hundred years of British food habits, 1966; (with B. W. E. Alford) A History of the Worshipful Company of Carpenters, 1968; (ed) The Long March of Everyman, 1974; (with M. J. Hatcher) A History of British Pewter, 1974; (with C. I. Savage) An Economic History of Transport, 1975; The Glassmakers, 1977; The Transport Contractors of Rye, 1982; (ed with Michael Drake) The Population Factor, 1982. *Recreations:* walking, motoring. *Address:* Minsen Dane, Brogdale Road, Faversham, Kent ME13 8YA. *T:* Faversham 3523. *Club:* Reform.

BARKER, Thomas Christopher; HM Diplomatic Service, retired; Curator, Scottish National War Memorial, Edinburgh; *b* 28 June 1928; *s* of Rowland Francis Barker and Kathleen Maude Barker (*née* Welch); *m* 1960, Griselda Helen Cormack; two *s* one *d. Educ:* Uppingham (Schol.); New Coll., Oxford (Schol.). MA, Lit Hum, 1952. 2nd Lt, 1st Bn, The Worcestershire Regt, 1947–48. HM Foreign (now Diplomatic) Service, 1952; Third Sec., Paris, 1953–55; Second Sec., Baghdad, 1955–58; FO, 1958–62; First Sec., Head of Chancery and Consul, Mexico City, 1962–67; FO, 1967–69; Counsellor and Head of Chancery, Caracas, 1969–71; FCO, 1971–75; seconded as Under Sec., NI Office, Belfast, 1976. *Address:* Abdic House, Grange of Lindores, Fife KY14 6HX. *T:* Newburgh 40286.

BARKER, Timothy Gwynne; Head of Corporate Finance Division, Kleinwort, Benson Ltd, 1986 (Director, since 1973); *b* 8 April 1940; *s* of Frank Richard Peter Barker and Hon. Olwen Gwynne (*née* Philipps); *m* 1964, Philippa Rachel Mary Thursby-Pelham; one *s* one *d. Educ:* Eton Coll.; McGill Univ., Montreal; Jesus Coll., Cambridge (MA). Director-General: City Panel on Take-overs and Mergers, 1984–85; Council for the Securities Industry, 1984–85. *Address:* 20 Fenchurch Street, EC3P 3DB. *T:* 01-623 8000.

BARKER, Sir William, KCMG 1967 (CMG 1958); OBE 1949; Bowes Professor of Russian, University of Liverpool, 1969–76, now retired; *b* 19 July 1909; *s* of Alfred Barker; *m* 1939, Margaret Beirne; one *s* one *d*. *Educ:* Universities of Liverpool and Prague. Employed in Foreign Office, 1943; First Sec., Prague, 1945; Foreign Service Officer, Grade 7, Senior Branch of Foreign Service, 1946; Chargé d'Affaires, Prague, 1947; transferred Moscow, Aug. 1947; granted rank of Counsellor, Dec. 1948; Grade 6, 1950; Counsellor, Oslo, 1951, also Chargé d'Affaires; Consul-Gen., Boston, Mass, Sept. 1954; Counsellor, Washington, 1955; Minister, Moscow, 1960–63; Fellow, Center for Internat. Affairs, Harvard Univ., 1963–64. Asst Under-Sec. of State, FO, 1965–66; British Ambassador to Czechoslovakia, 1966–68. *Address:* 53 Eshe Road North, Liverpool L23 8UE.

BARKER, (William) Alan; Head Master, University College School, Hampstead, 1975–82, retired through ill-health; *b* 1 Oct. 1923; 2nd *s* of late T. L. Barker, Edinburgh and Beaconsfield and late I. N. Barker, Salisbury, Zimbabwe; *m* 1954, Jean Alys (*see* Baroness Trumpington); one *s*. *Educ:* Rossall Sch.; Jesus Coll., Cambridge (scholar). Lieut Royal Artillery, 69 (WR) Field Regt, NW Europe; wounded, 1944. 1st cl. Hons Hist. Tripos Pt I, 1946, Pt II, 1947; BA 1946, MA 1948. Part-time Lectr, WEA (Eastern Region), 1946-47; Asst Master, Eton Coll., 1947–53; Commonwealth Fund Fellow, Yale Univ., 1951–52, MA (Yale) 1952. Fellow Queens' Coll., Cambridge, and Dir Studies in History, 1953–55; Asst Master, Eton Coll., 1955–58; Headmaster, The Leys School, 1958–75. Governor, Sandwich County Sec. Sch.; Life Governor, Rossall Sch.; Mem. Eton UDC, 1956–59; Councillor, Cambs and I of Ely, 1959–70, Alderman 1970–74. Select Preacher, Oxford Univ., 1966; Paul M. Angle Meml Lectr, Chicago, 1978. Patron, Sandwich Local History Soc., 1964–. *Publications:* (jt) A General History of England 1688–1950, 2 vols, 1952, 1953; Religion and Politics (1558–1642), 1957; The Civil War in America, 1961, repr. US 1974, UK 1977; (contrib.) The Rebirth of Britain, 1964. *Recreations:* bridge, American history, accumulating books and dust.*Address:* Luckboat House, 52 King Street, Sandwich, Kent CT13 9BL. *T:* Sandwich 613007; 25 Laxford House, Cundy Street, SW1. *T:* 01–730 4016. *Clubs:* Pitt (Cambridge); Elizabethan (Yale); Royal St George's Golf (Sandwich).

BARKING, Area Bishop of; Rt. Rev. James William Roxburgh; appointed Bishop Suffragan of Barking, 1983; *b* 5 July 1921; *s* of James Thomas and Margaret Roxburgh; *m* 1949, Marjorie Winifred (*née* Hipkiss); one *s* one *d*. *Educ:* Whitgift School; St Catharine's Coll., Cambridge (MA); Wycliffe Hall, Oxford. Deacon 1944, priest 1945; Curate: Christ Church and Holy Trinity, Folkestone, 1944–47; Handsworth, Birmingham, 1947–50; Vicar: S Matthew, Bootle, 1950–56; Drypool, Hull, 1956–65; Barking, 1965–77; Archdeacon of Colchester, 1977–83. Canon of Chelmsford, 1972–77. Pro-Prolocutor, Convocation of Canterbury, 1977–83. Pres. Barking Rotary Club, 1976–77. *Recreations:* travel, philately. *Address:* Barking Lodge, 28A Connaught Avenue, Loughton, Essex IG10 4DS. *T:* 01–508 6680.

BARKLEY, Rev. Prof. John Montieth; retired; Principal, Union Theological College, Belfast, 1978–81; *b* 16 Oct. 1910; *s* of Rev. Robert James Barkley, BD, and Mary Monteith; *m* 1936, Irene Graham Anderson; one *d*. *Educ:* Magee Univ. Coll. Derry; Trinity Coll., Dublin; The Presbyterian Coll., Belfast. BA 1934, MA 1941, BD 1944, PhD 1946, DD 1949, Trinity Coll., Dublin; BA 1952, MA 1953, Queen's Univ., Belfast. Thompson Memorial Prizeman in Philosophy, 1934; Larmour Memorial Exhibitioner in Theology, 1944; Paul Memorial Prizeman in History, 1953; Carey Lecturer, 1954–56; Lecturer in Ecclesiastical History, Queen's Univ., Belfast, 1951–54; Prof. in Ecclesiastical Hist., 1954–79, Vice-Principal, 1964–76, Principal, 1976–78, Presbyterian Coll., Belfast, until amalgamated with Magee Coll. to form Union Theological Coll. FRHistS. Ordained, Drumreagh Presbyterian Church, 1935; installed in II Ballybay and Rockcorry, 1939; installed in Cooke Centenary, Belfast, 1949. *Publications:* Handbook on Evangelical Christianity and Romanism, 1949; Presbyterianism, 1951; Westminster Formularies in Irish Presbyterianism, 1956; History of the Presbyterian Church in Ireland, 1959; Weltkirchenlexikon (arts), 1960; History of the Sabbath School Society for Ireland, 1961; The Eldership in Irish Presbyterianism; The Baptism of Infants, 1963; The Presbyterian Orphan Society, 1966; Worship of the Reformed Church, 1966; St Enoch's 1872–1972, 1972; (ed) Handbook to Church Hymnary, 3rd edn, 1979; articles in Scottish Journal of Theology, Verbum Caro, Biblical Theology, Dictionary of Worship. *Recreations:* bowls, golf. *Address:* 14 Clonallon Park, Belfast BT4 2BZ.

BARKSHIRE, John; *see* Barkshire, R. R. St J.

BARKSHIRE, Robert Hugh, CBE 1968; *b* 24 Oct. 1909; *yr s* of late Lt-Col Charles Robert Barkshire, OBE; *m* 1934, Emily Blunt, *er d* of A. S. Blunt, Bedford; one *s*. *Educ:* King's Sch., Bruton. Bank of England, 1927–55: Private Sec. to the Governor (C. F. Cobbold, later Lord Cobbold), 1949–53; Sec. to Cttee of London Clearing Bankers, British Bankers' Assoc., Bankers' Clearing House, and Mem., various inter-Bank Cttees, 1955–70; Hon. Sec., Meetings of Officers of European Bankers' Assocs, 1959–72; Gen. Comr of Income Tax for City of London, 1969–78; Governor, NIESR, 1970–78. FIB 1960. Freeman, City of London. *Address:* The Boat House, Fowey, Cornwall PL23 1BH. *T:* Fowey 3389. *Clubs:* Royal Thames Yacht; Royal Fowey Yacht.

See also R. R. St J. Barkshire.

BARKSHIRE, Robert Renny St John, (John), TD; JP; Chairman: Mercantile House Holdings plc, since 1972; International Commodities Clearing House Ltd, since 1986; Deputy Chairman, Extel Group, since 1986; *b* 31 Aug. 1935; *s* of Robert Hugh Barkshire, *qv*; *m* 1960, Margaret Elizabeth Robinson; two *s* one *d*. *Educ:* Bedford School. AIB. Served Duke of Wellington's Regt, 2nd Lt, 1953–55; HAC, 1955–74 (CO, 1970–72; Regtl Col, 1972–74). Joined Cater Ryder & Co., 1955, Jt Man. Dir, 1963–72. Non-exec. Dir, Extel Gp PLC, 1979–; Chm., Financial Futures Wkg Pty, 1980, later LIFFE Steering Cttee, 1981–82; Dir, LIFFE, 1982– (Chm., 1982–85); Mem., Adv. Bd, Internat. Monetary Market Div., Chicago Mercantile Exchange, 1981–84. Gen. Comr for Income Tax, City of London, 1981–. Chairman: Reserve Forces Assoc., 1983–; Sussex TA Cttee, 1983–85; Chm., SE TAVR Assoc., 1985–; Dep. Chm., TA Sport Bd, 1983– (Mem., 1979–). Fin. Advisor, Victory Services Club, 1981–; Dir, Officers' Pensions Soc. Investment Co. Ltd, 1982–. Mem., Chiddingly Parish Council, 1979–; Chm., Chiddingly & Dist Royal British Legion, 1982–; Treas., Chiddingly PCC, 1976–. Governor: Harpur Trust, 1984– (Chm., Bedford Sch. Cttee, 1984–); Eastbourne Coll., 1980 (Vice Chm., 1983–); Roedean Sch., 1984–. Freeman, City of London, 1973; Liveryman, Worshipful Co. of Farmers, 1981. JP Lewes, 1980. *Recreations:* sailing, shooting. *Address:* Highlands, Chiddingly, near Lewes, East Sussex BN8 6HB. *T:* Chiddingly 872355. *Clubs:* City of London, Cavalry and Guards; MCC; Royal Fowey Yacht (Cornwall).

BARKWORTH, Peter Wynn; actor, since 1948; *b* 14 Jan. 1929; *s* of Walter Wynn Barkworth and Irene May Barkworth. *Educ:* Stockport Sch.; Royal Academy of Dramatic Art. Folkestone and Sheffield Repertory Cos, 1948–51. West End plays include: A Woman of No Importance, Savoy, 1953; Roar Like a Dove, Phoenix, 1957–60; The School for Scandal, Haymarket, 1962; Crown Matrimonial, Haymarket, 1972; Donkeys' Years, Globe, 1976; Can You Hear Me at the Back?, Piccadilly, 1979; A Coat of Varnish, Haymarket, 1982. Television serials: The Power Game, 1966; Manhunt, 1969; Telford's Change, 1979; Winston Churchill: the wilderness years, 1981; The Price, 1985; Late Starter, 1985; The Gospel According to St Matthew, 1986. Film: Champions, 1984. Awards: Best Actor, BAFTA, 1974 and 1977; Royal TV Soc. and Broadcasting Press Guild, 1977 (both 1977 awards for Professional Foul). *Publications:* About Acting, 1980; First Houses, 1983; More About Acting, 1984. *Recreations:*walking, gardening, music, looking at paintings. *Address:* 47 Flask Walk, NW3 1HH. *T:* 01–794 4591. *Clubs:* Garrick, British Academy of Film and Television Arts.

BARLEY, Prof. Maurice Willmore, MA; Professor of Archaeology, University of Nottingham, 1971–74, now Emeritus; *b* 19 Aug. 1909; *s* of late Levi Baldwin and Alice Barley, Lincoln; *m* 1934, Diana, *e d* of late A. E. Morgan; two *s* one *d*. *Educ:* Lincoln Sch.; Reading Univ. (BA). Asst Lectr, UC Hull, 1935–40; Mins of Information and Labour, 1940–45; Adult Educn Dept, Nottingham, 1946–62; Classics Dept, Nottingham, 1962–74. Sec. 1954–64, Pres. 1964–67, Council for British Archaeology; Vice-Pres., Soc. of Antiquaries, 1965–68; Mem. Royal Commn Hist. Monuments, 1966–76. FSA. *Publications:* Lincolnshire and the Fens, 1952 (repr. 1972); The English Farmhouse and Cottage, 1961; The House and Home, 1963 (repr. 1971); Guide to British Topographical Collections, 1974; The Plans and Topography of Medieval Towns in England and Wales, 1975; European Towns, their Archaeology and early History, 1977; Houses and History, 1986; contrib. Agrarian History of England vols IV and V, Antiquaries Jl and other learned jls. *Address:* 60 Park Road, Chilwell, Nottingham NG9 4DD. *T:* Nottingham 257501.

BARLOW, Sir Christopher Hilaro, 7th Bt, *cr* 1803; architect; *b* 1 Dec. 1929; *s* of Sir Richard Barlow, 6th Bt, AFC, and Rosamund Sylvia, *d* of late F. S. Anderton (she *m* 2nd, 1950, Rev. Leonard Haslet Morrison, MA); *S* father, 1946; *m* 1952, J. C. de M. Audley, *e d* of late J. E. Audley, Cheshire; one *s* two *d* (and one *s* decd). *Educ:* Eton; McGill Univ., Montreal. BArch. MRAIC. Past Pres., Newfoundland Architects' Assoc. Lt Governor's Silver Medal, 1953. *Heir:* *s* Crispian John Edmund Audley Barlow, Inspector, Royal Hong Kong Police, [*b* 20 April 1958; *m* 1981, Anne Waiching Siu]. *Address:* 18 Winter Avenue, St John's, Newfoundland.

BARLOW, David John; Controller, Public Affairs, BBC, since 1986; *b* 20 Oct. 1937; *s* of Ralph and Joan Barlow; *m* 1981, Sanchia Béatrice Oppenheimer; one *d*, and three *s* of previous marr. *Educ:* Leighton Park Sch.; The Queen's Coll., Oxford; Leeds Univ. MA, DipEd (Oxon); DipESL (Leeds). British Council, 1962–63; BBC, 1963–: Producer, African Service; Schools Broadcasting, 1965–67; Programme Organiser, Hindi, Tamil, Nepali and Bengali Service, 1967–70; Further Educn Radio, 1970–71; UNESCO, British Council Consultancies, 1970–73; Head of Liaison Internat. Relations, 1974–76; Chief Asst Regions, 1977–79; Gen. Sec., ITCA, 1980–81; BBC: Sec., 1981–84; Controller, Public Affairs and Internat. Relations, 1984–86. *Recreations:* photography, bird watching, mountain walking, book collecting. *Address:* 1 St Joseph Close, Olney, Bucks. *T:* Bedford 712960. *Club:* English-Speaking Union.

BARLOW, Donald Spiers Monteagle, MS London; FRCS; Consulting Surgeon: Hospitals for Diseases of the Chest, since 1971 (Consultant Surgeon 1947–71); Southend Group of Hospitals, since 1970 (Consultant Surgeon 1936–70); Luton Group of Hospitals, since 1970 (Consultant Surgeon 1940–70); Italian Hospital, since 1970 (Hon. Consultant Thoracic Surgeon 1955–70); Penrose-May Surgical Tutor to the Royal College of Surgeons of England, since 1969 (Surgical Tutor, 1962–69); *b* 4 July 1905; *s* of late Leonard Barlow, MIEE, and Katharine Barlow; *m* 1934, Violet Elizabeth (*née* Maciver); one *s* three *d* (and one *d* decd). *Educ:* Whitgift Sch.; University Coll. Hospital and Medical Sch. MRCS, LRCP 1927; MB, BS London 1928; MS London 1930; FRCS 1930. Formerly: RMO, Wimbledon Hosp., 1927; House Phys., UCH, 1928; House Surg., UCH, 1929; Ho. Surg., Norfolk and Norwich Hosp., 1930–31; Resident Asst Surg., West London Hosp., 1931–35; Surg. Registrar London Lock Hosp., 1936; Research work at UCL, 1936–37; Hon. Surg., St John's Hosp., Lewisham, 1937–47; Cons. Thoracic Surg., LCC, 1945–48. Teacher, 1964–67, Lectr, 1967–71, Inst. of Diseases of the Chest, Univ. of London. Chm., S Beds Div., BMA, 1971–72. Coronation Medal, 1953. *Publications:* contribs to: Progress of Clinical Surgery, 1960 (ed Rodney Smith); Operative Surgery, 2nd edn 1969 (ed Rob and Smith). Many publications in learned jls mostly concerning diseases of oesophagus, chest and abdomen. Also 3 reports (Ceylon Govt White Papers), 1952, 1954, 1967. *Recreations:* golf (Captain, Harpenden Golf Club, 1971–72, Pres., 1976–79), painting. *Address:* Deacons Field, High Elms, Harpenden, Herts. *T:* Harpenden 3400.

See also Prof. H. E. M. Barlow, Michael Miller.

BARLOW, Prof. Frank, MA, DPhil; FBA 1970; FRSL 1971; Professor of History and Head of Department, University of Exeter, 1953–76, now Emeritus Professor; *b* 19 April 1911; *e s* of Percy Hawthorn and Margaret Julia Barlow; *m* 1936, Moira Stella Brigid Garvey; two *s*. *Educ:* Newcastle High Sch.; St John's Coll., Oxford. Open Schol., St John's Coll., Oxford, 1929; 1st Cl. Hons Sch. of Modern History, 1933; Bryce Student, 1933; Oxford Senior Student, 1934.; BLitt, 1934; Fereday Fellow, St John's Coll., Oxford, 1935–38; DPhil 1937. Asst Lecturer, University Coll., London, 1936–40; War service in the Army, 1941–46, commissioned into Intelligence Corps, demobilised as Major; Lecturer 1946, Reader 1949, Dep. Vice-Chancellor, 1961–63, Public Orator, 1974–76, University of Exeter. Hon. DLitt Exon, 1981. *Publications:* The Letters of Arnulf of Lisieux, 1939; Durham Annals and Documents of the Thirteenth Century, 1945; Durham Jurisdictional Peculiars, 1950; The Feudal Kingdom of England, 1955; (ed and trans.) The Life of King Edward the Confessor, 1962; The English Church, 1000–1066, 1963; William I and the Norman Conquest, 1965; Edward the Confessor, 1970; (with Martin Biddle, Olof von Feilitzen and D. J. Keene) Winchester in the Early Middle Ages, 1976; The English Church 1066–1154, 1979; The Norman Conquest and Beyond (selected papers), 1983; William Rufus, 1983; Thomas Becket, 1986. *Recreation:* gardening. *Address:* Middle Court Hall, Kenton, Exeter. *T:* Starcross 890438.

BARLOW, Sir (George) William, Kt 1977; BSc Tech, FEng, FIMechE, FIEE; Chairman and Chief Executive, BICC, since 1984 (Director, since 1980); Director, THORN EMI, since 1980; *b* 8 June 1924; *s* of Albert Edward and Annice Barlow; *m* 1948, Elaine Mary Atherton (*née* Adamson); one *s* one *d*. *Educ:* Manchester Grammar Sch.; Manchester Univ. (Kitchener Schol., Louis Atkinson Schol.; BSc Tech. 1st cl. Hons Elec. Engrg, 1944). Served as Elec. Lt, RNVR, 1944–47. Various appts, The English Electric Co. Ltd (in Spain, 1952–55, Canada, 1958–62); Gen. Manager, Liverpool and Netherton, 1964–67; Managing Director: English Electric Domestic Appliance Co. Ltd, 1965–67; English Electric Computers Ltd, 1967–68. Gp Chief Exec., 1969–77, Chm., 1971–77, Ransome Hoffman Pollard Ltd. Chm., Post Office, 1977–80, organized separation of Post Office and British Telecom, 1980. Member: Industrial Develt Adv. Bd, 1972–79; Electronics EDC, 1981–83; Council, IEE, 1969–72 (Vice-Pres., 1978–80, Dep. Pres., 1983–84); Council, IMechE, 1971–74; National Electronics Council, 1982–; President: IWM, 1976–77; BEAMA, 1986–; Vice Pres., Fellowship of Engrg, 1985–; Chm., Ferrous Foundries Adv. Cttee, 1975–78; Vice Pres., City and Guilds of London Inst., 1982–. Chm., Design Council, 1980–86. Governor, London Business Sch., 1979–. Freeman, City of London; Liveryman, Worshipful Company of Glaziers; Master, Worshipful Company of

Engineers, 1986–87 (Warden, 1985–86). CBIM 1971. Hon. FUMIST, 1978; Hon. DSc: Cranfield, 1979; Bath, 1986. *Recreation:* golf. *Address:* BICC, Devonshire House, Mayfair Place, W1X 5FH. *Clubs:* Army and Navy, Brooks's; Hampstead Golf, Royal Birkdale Golf.

BARLOW, Prof. Harold Everard Monteagle, BSc (Eng.) London, PhD (Sci.), London; FRS 1961; FEng; FIEEE; FIEE; MIMechE; Emeritus Professor of Electrical Engineering, University College, London (Pender Professor, 1950–67); *b* Highbury, 15 Nov. 1899; *s* of late Leonard Barlow, MIEE, and Katharine Monteagle, Glasgow; *m* 1931, Janet Hastings, *d* of the late Rev. J. Hastings Eastwood, BA; three *s* one *d. Educ:* Wallington Grammar School; City & Guilds Engineering College; University College, London. FEng 1976. Sub-Lieut. RNVR 1917–19; Student at University College, London, 1919–23; Practical engineering training with East Surrey Ironworks and Barlow & Young Ltd, 1923–25; Member of Academic Staff, Faculty of Engineering, UCL, 1925–67 (absent from University on War Service, Sept. 1939–Oct. 1945). Joined staff of Telecommunications Research Establishment, Air Ministry, to deal with Radar development, Sept. 1939; Superintendent, Radio Dept, RAE, 1943–45. Fellow of University College, 1946, Prof. of Elec. Engineering, 1945–50; Dean of Engineering Faculty, and Mem. UCL Cttee, 1949, 1961. Mem. of: Radar and Signals Advisory Bd, Min. of Supply, 1947; Scientific Advisory Council, Min. of Supply, 1949; Radio Research Bd, DSIR, 1948 and 1960; London Regional Advisory Council and of Academic Bd for Higher Technological Educn, 1952–67; Academic Council, Univ. of London, 1953–55; BBC Scientific Advisory Committee, 1953–76; Governor, Woolwich Polytechnic, 1948; Dir, Marconi Instruments, 1963. Member of Council of IEE, 1955–58 and 1960–; awarded Kelvin Premium, J. J. Thomson Premium, Oliver Lodge and Fleming Premium of IEE; Faraday Medal, 1967; Mem. Council, IERE, 1973–76. FCGI 1969. For. Mem., Polish Acad. of Science, 1966; Hon. Mem., Japanese Inst. of Electronics and Communications Engineers, 1973; For. Associate, US Nat. Acad. of Engineering, 1979. Chm., British Nat. Cttee for Radio Science, 1968; Mem., Nat. Electronics Council, 1969–. Dellinger Gold Medal, Internat. Radio Union, 1969; Harold Hartley Medal, Inst. of Measurement and Control, 1973; Mervin J. Kelly Award, IEEE, 1975; Microwave Career Award, IEEE, 1985. Hon. DSc Heriot-Watt, 1971; Hon. DEng Sheffield, 1973. *Publications:* Micro-waves and Wave-guides, 1947; (with A. L. Cullen) Micro-Wave Measurements, 1950; (with J. Brown) Radio Surface Waves, 1962; many scientific papers. *Recreations:* sailing, walking, reading. *Address:* 13 Hookfield, Epsom, Surrey. *T:* Epsom 21586; University College, Gower Street, WC1. *T:* 01–387 7050. *Club:* Athenæum.
See also D. S. M. Barlow.

BARLOW, Prof. Horace Basil, FRS 1969; Royal Society Research Professor, Physiological Laboratory, Cambridge University, since 1973; *b* 8 Dec. 1921; *s* of Sir (James) Alan (Noel) Barlow, 2nd Bt, GCB, KBE (*d* 1968), and of Nora Barlow (*née* Darwin); *m* 1st, 1954, Ruthala (marr. diss., 1970), *d* of Dr M. H. Salaman, *qv;* four *d;* 2nd, 1980, Miranda, *d* of John Weston Smith. *Educ:* Winchester; Trinity Coll., Cambridge. Research Fellow, Trinity Coll., 1950–54, Lectr, King's Coll., Cambridge, 1954–64. Demonstrator and Asst Dir of Research, Physiological Lab., Cambridge, 1954–64; Prof. of Physiological Optics and Physiology, Univ. of Calif, Berkeley, 1964–73. *Publications:* several, on neurophysiology of vision in Jl of Physiology, and elsewhere. *Address:* Physiological Laboratory, Cambridge CB2 3EG.
See also Sir T. E. Barlow, Bt.

BARLOW, Sir John (Kemp), 3rd Bt *cr* 1907, of Bradwall Hall, Sandbach; merchant banker and farmer; Chairman: Thomas Barlow and Bro. Ltd; Barlow Services Ltd; Majedie Investments plc; Director of other companies; *b* 22 April 1934; *s* of Sir John Denman Barlow, 2nd Bt and Hon. Diana Helen (*d* 1986), *d* of 1st Baron Rochdale, CB and *sister* of Viscount Rochdale, *qv; S* father, 1986; *m* 1962, Susan, *er d* of Col Sir Andrew Horsbrugh-Porter, *qv;* four *s. Educ:* Winchester; Trinity Coll., Cambridge (BA 1956). Chm., Rubber Growers' Assoc., 1974. High Sheriff, Cheshire, 1979. *Recreations:* steeplechasing, hunting, shooting. *Heir: s* John William Marshall Barlow, *b* 12 March 1964. *Address:* Bulkeley Grange, Malpas, Cheshire. *Clubs:* Brooks's, City of London, Jockey.

BARLOW, Roy Oxspring; solicitor; a Recorder of the Crown Court, since 1975; *b* 13 Feb. 1927; *s* of George and Clarice Barlow; *m* 1957, Kathleen Mary Roberts; two *s* one *d. Educ:* King Edward VII Sch., Sheffield; Queen's Coll., Oxford; Sheffield Univ. (LLB). Local Government, 1952–62; solicitor in private practice, 1962–. *Recreations:* farming, walking, reading. *Address:* The Cottage, Oxton Rakes, Barlow, Sheffield S18 5TH. *T:* Sheffield 890652.

BARLOW, Thomas Bradwall; merchant banker; director of rubber, insurance and other public companies; Joint Senior Consultant in Thomas Barlow & Bro. Ltd, London and Manchester; *b* 7 March 1900; 2nd *s* of Sir John Emmott Barlow, 1st Bt; *m* 1943, Elizabeth Margaret, *d* of Hon. B. G. Sackville-West; one *s* one *d.* Chairman: Br. Assoc. of Straits Merchants, 1937; Rubber Trade Assoc., 1942–43; Rubber Growers' Assoc., 1945–46; British Assoc. of Malaysia, 1965; Highlands & Lowlands Para Rubber Co. Ltd; Chersonese (F.M.S.) Estates Ltd. Farming. *Recreations:* hunting, steeplechasing, and travelling. *Address:* Thornby House, Northampton. *T:* Northampton 740214. *Clubs:* Brooks's, City of London, Hurlingham.

BARLOW, Sir Thomas (Erasmus), 3rd Bt *cr* 1902; DSC 1945; DL; *b* 23 Jan. 1914; *s* of Sir Alan Barlow, 2nd Bt, GCB, KBE, and of Nora, *d* of late Sir Horace Darwin, KBE; *S* father, 1968; *m* 1955, Isabel, *d* of late Dr T. M. Body, Middlesbrough, Yorks; two *s* two *d. Educ:* Winchester College. Entered RN as cadet, 1932; qualified Submarines, 1937; served in Submarines in Atlantic, Mediterranean, Indian Ocean and Far East during War of 1939–45; Naval Staff Course, 1946; Joint Services Staff Course, 1947, Commander, 1950. British Joint Services Mission, Washington, 1950–53; Captain 1954; Imperial Defence Coll., 1957; Chief Staff Officer to Flag Officer Submarines, 1960–62; Commodore, HMS Drake, Devonport, 1962–64; retired, 1964. Actively concerned in Wildlife and Countryside Conservation: Royal Soc. for Nature Conservation; Berks, Bucks and Oxfordshire Naturalists' Trust; Charles Darwin Foundn for Galapogos Is. DL Bucks, 1977. *Recreations:* bird watching, the countryside. *Heir: s* James Alan Barlow, *b* 10 July 1956. *Address:* 45 Shepherds Hill, Highgate, N6 5QJ. *T:* 01–340 9653. *Clubs:* Athenæum, Savile.
See also Prof. H. B Barlow.

BARLOW, Sir William; *see* Barlow, Sir G. W.

BARLTROP, Roger Arnold Rowlandson, CVO 1982; HM Diplomatic Service; High Commissioner to Fiji and (non-resident) to Republic of Nauru and to Tuvalu, since 1982; *b* 19 Jan. 1930; *s* of late Ernest William Barltrop, CMG, CBE, DSO, and Ethel Alice Lucy Barltrop (*née* Baker); *m* 1962, Penelope Pierrepont Dalton; two *s* two *d. Educ:* Solihull Sch.; Leeds Grammar Sch.; Exeter Coll., Oxford. BA (Hons). Served RN, 1949–50, RNVR/RNR, 1950–64 (Lt-Comdr 1962). Asst Principal, CRO, 1954–56; Second Sec., New Delhi, 1956–57; Private Sec. to Parly Under-Sec. of State and Minister of State, CRO, 1957–60; First Sec., E Nigeria, 1960–62; Actg Dep. High Comr, W Nigeria, 1962; First Sec., Salisbury, Rhodesia, 1962–65; CO and FO, later FCO, 1965–69; First Sec. and Head of Chancery, Ankara, 1969–70; Dep. British Govt Rep., WI Associated States, 1971–73; Counsellor and Head of Chancery, Addis Ababa, 1973–77; Head of Commonwealth Coordination Dept, FCO, 1978–82. *Recreations:* sailing, genealogy, opera. *Address:* c/o Foreign and Commonwealth Office, SW1A 2AH. *Clubs:* Royal Commonwealth Society; Fiji, Royal Suva Yacht (Suva).

BARNA, Prof. Tibor, CBE 1974; Professor of Economics, University of Sussex, 1962–82, Professor Emeritus 1984; Member, Monopolies and Mergers Commission, 1963–78; *b* 1919. *Educ:* London School of Economics. Lecturer, London School of Economics, 1944; Official Fellow, Nuffield College, Oxford, 1947; senior posts in UN Economic Commission for Europe, 1949; Assistant Director, National Institute of Economic and Social Research, London, 1955. *Publications:* Redistribution of Income through Public Finance in 1937, 1945; Investment and Growth Policies in British Industrial Firms, 1962; Agriculture towards the Year 2000, 1979; European Process Plant Industry, 1981; papers in Jl Royal Statistical Soc., Economic Jl, European Econ. Review. *Address:* Beanacre, Westmeston, Hassocks, West Sussex. *T:* Hassocks 2384.

BARNARD, 11th Baron, *cr* 1698; **Harry John Neville Vane,** TD 1960; Landowner; Lord-Lieutenant and Custos Rotulorum of County Durham, since 1970; *b* 21 Sept. 1923; *er s* of 10th Baron Barnard, CMG, OBE, MC, TD, and Sylvia Mary, *d* of Herbert Straker; *S* father, 1964; *m* 1952, Lady Davina Mary Cecil, DStJ, *e d* of 6th Marquess of Exeter, KCMG; one *s* four *d. Educ:* Eton. Served War of 1939–45, RAFVR, 1942–46 (Flying Officer, 1945). Northumberland Hussars (TA), 1948–66; Lt-Col Commanding, 1964–66. Vice-Pres., N of England TA&VRA, 1970 and 1977–, Pres., 1974–77. Hon. Col, 7 Bn The Light Infantry, 1979–. County Councillor, Durham, 1952–61. Member: Durham Co. AEC, 1953–72 (Chm., 1970–72); N Regional Panel, MAFF, 1972–76; CLA Council, 1950–80; Dir, NE Housing Assoc., 1964–77; Mem. Council, BRCS, 1982–85; President: Durham Co. Br., BRCS, 1969–; Farmway Ltd, 1965–; Durham Co. Br., CLA, 1965–; Durham Co. St John Council, 1971–; Durham Co. Scout Assoc., 1972–; Durham and Cleveland Co. Br. RBL, 1973–; Durham Co. Conservation Trust, 1984–. DL Durham, 1956, Vice-Lieutenant, 1969–70; JP Durham, 1961. Joint Master of Zetland Hounds, 1963–65. KStJ 1971. *Heir: s* Hon. Henry Francis Cecil Vane, *b* 11 March 1959. *Address:* (seat and office) Raby Castle, PO Box 50, Staindrop, Darlington, Co. Durham DL2 3AY. *T:* Staindrop 60751; (residence) Selaby, Gainford, Darlington, Co. Durham DL2 3HF. *T:* Darlington 730206. *Clubs:* Brooks's; Durham County (Durham); Northern Counties (Newcastle upon Tyne).

BARNARD, Sir (Arthur) Thomas, Kt 1958; CB 1954; OBE 1946; Director-General of Inspection, Ministry of Supply, 1956–58, retired; *b* 28 Sept. 1893; *s* of late Arthur Barnard; *m* 1921, Grace (*d* 1986), *d* of William Magerkorth, Belvedere, Kent. *Educ:* Erith Technical Coll. Is a Chartered Civil Engineer. Chief Superintendent, Royal Ordnance Factories, Woolwich, 1951–55; Dep. Dir-Gen., Royal Ordnance Factories, Adelphi, London, 1955–56. *Address:* Kentmere, 26 Heathfield, Chislehurst, Kent BR7 6AE.

BARNARD, Prof. Christiaan Neethling, MD, MMed, PhD; Professor of Surgical Science, Cape Town University, 1968–83, Professor Emeritus, 1984; Senior Consultant and Scientist in Residence, Oklahoma Heart Centre, Baptist Medical Centre; *b* 8 Nov. 1922; *s* of Adam Hendrik Barnard and Maria Elizabeth Barnard (*née* De Swart); *m* 1st, 1948, Aletta Gertruida Louw (marr. diss. 1970); one *d* (one *s* decd); 2nd, 1970, Barbara Maria Zoellner (marr. diss. 1982); two *s. Educ:* Beaufort West High Sch.; Univs of Cape Town and Minnesota. MB, ChB 1946, MD 1953, Cape Town; MS, PhD 1958, Minnesota. Private practice, Ceres, CP, 1948–51; Sen. Resident MO, City Hosp., Cape Town, 1951–53; subseq. Registrar, Groote Schuur Hosp.; Registrar, Surgery Dept, Cape Town Univ.; Charles Adams Meml Schol. and Dazian Foundn Bursary for study in USA; US Public Health Grant for further res. in cardiac surgery; Specialist Cardio-Thoracic Surgeon, Lectr and Dir of Surg. Res., Cape Town Univ. and Groote Schuur Hosp., 1958; Head of Cardio-Thoracic Surgery, Cape Town Univ. Teaching Hosps, 1961; Assoc. Prof., Cape Town Univ., 1962. Oppenheimer Meml Trust Bursary for overseas study, 1960. Performed world's first human heart transplant operation, 3 Dec. 1967, and world's first double-heart transplant, 25 Nov. 1974. Holds numerous hon. doctorates, foreign orders and awards, hon. citizenships and freedoms, medallions, etc; Dag Hammarskjöld Internat. Prize and Peace Prize, Kennedy Foundn Award, Milan Internat. Prize for Science, etc; hon. fellow or member various colleges, societies, etc. FACS 1963; Fellow NY Cardiological Soc. 1965; FACC 1967. *Publications:* (with V. Schrire) Surgery of Common Congenital Cardiac Malformations, 1968; One Life, 1969; Heart Attack: You Don't Have to Die, 1971; The Unwanted, 1974; South Africa: Sharp Dissection, 1977; In The Night Season, 1977; Best Medicine, 1979; Good Life—Good Death, 1980; (jtly) The Arthritis Handbook, 1984; numerous contribs to med. jls. *Recreations:* viticulture, ornithology, farming. *Address:* PO Box 988, Cape Town 8000, Republic of South Africa.

BARNARD, Prof. Eric Albert, PhD; FRS 1981; Director, MRC Molecular Neurobiology Unit, Cambridge, since 1985; *b* 2 July 1927; *m* 1956, Penelope J. Hennessy; two *s* two *d. Educ:* Davenant Foundn Sch.; King's Coll., London. BSc, PhD 1956. King's College, London: Nuffield Foundn Fellow, 1956–59; Asst Lectr, 1959–60; Lectr, 1960–64. State University of New York at Buffalo: Associate Prof. of Biochemical Pharmacol., 1964–65; Prof. of Biochemistry, 1965–76; Head of Biochemistry Dept, 1969–76; Imperial College of Science and Technology, London: Rank Prof. of Physiol Biochemistry, 1976–85; Chm., Div. of Life Sciences, 1977–85; Head, Dept of Biochem., 1979–85. Rockefeller Fellow, Univ. of Calif, Berkeley, 1960–61; Guggenheim Fellow, MRC Lab. of Molecular Biol., Cambridge, 1971. Vis. Prof., Univ. of Marburg, Germany, 1965; Vis. Scientist, Inst. Pasteur, France, 1973. Member: Amer. Soc. Biol Chemists; Internat. Soc. Neurochem; Committee Member: MRC; CNRS. Josiah Macy Faculty Scholar Award, USA, 1975; Medal of Polish Acad. of Scis, 1980; Ciba Medal and Prize, 1985. *Publications:* editor of five scientific books; mem., editorial bds of four scientific jls; numerous papers in learned jls. *Recreation:* the pursuit of good claret. *Address:* MRC Molecular Neurobiology Unit, MRC Centre, University of Cambridge, Hills Road, Cambridge CB2 2QH. *T:* Cambridge 245133.

BARNARD, Surg. Rear Adm. Ernest Edward Peter, DPhil; FFCM; Surgeon Rear Admiral, Operational Medical Services, 1982–84; retired 1984; *b* 22 Feb. 1927; *s* of Lionel Edward Barnard and Ernestine (*née* Lethbridge); *m* 1955, Dr Joan Barnard (*née* Gunn); one *s* one *d. Educ:* schools in England and Australia; Univ. of Adelaide; St Mary's Hosp., Univ. of London (MB, BS 1955); St John's Coll., Univ. of Oxford (student, 1966–68; DPhil 1969). MRCS, LRCP 1955; MFOM 1979; FFCM 1980. After house appts, joined RN, 1956; served, 1957–76: HMS Bulwark, Reclaim and Dolphin; RN Physiol Lab.; RN Med. Sch.; Inst. of Naval Medicine; Dept of Med. Dir Gen. (Naval); exchange service with US Navy at Naval Med. Res. Inst., Bethesda, Md, 1976–78; Inst. of Naval Medicine, 1978–80; QHP 1980–84; Dep. Med. Dir Gen. (Naval), 1980–82; Surgeon Rear-Adm., Inst. of Naval Medicine, and Dean of Naval Medicine, 1982. FRSM 1962. *Publications:* papers on underwater medicine and physiology. *Recreations:* gardening, literature, photography. *Address:* c/o Barclays Bank, 12 The Square, Wickham, Hants PO17 5JQ.

BARNARD, Prof. George Alfred, MA, DSc; Emeritus Professor of Mathematics, University of Essex; statistical consultant to various organisations; *b* 23 Sept. 1915; *s* of Frederick C. and Ethel C. Barnard; *m* 1st, 1942, Helen J. B. Davies; three *s*; 2nd, 1949, Mary M. L. Jones; one *s. Educ:* Sir George Monoux Grammar Sch., Walthamstow; St John's Coll., Cambridge. Math. Trip., Pt III, 1936, Res. Studentship, St John's Coll., spent at Grad. Sch. Princeton, NJ, USA, 1937–39. Plessey Co., Ilford, as Math. Consultant, 1940–42; Ministry of Supply Adv. Unit, 1942–45; Maths Dept, Imperial Coll., London: Lectr, 1945–47; Reader in Math. Statistics, 1948–54, Professor, 1954–66; Prof. of Mathematics, Univ. of Essex, 1966–75; Prof. of Statistics, Univ. of Waterloo, 1975–81. Visiting Professor: Yale, 1966; Univ. of Waterloo, 1972–73; Univ. of Nottingham, 1975–77. Member: UGC, 1967–72; Computer Bd, 1970–72; SSRC, 1971–74. Royal Statistical Society: Council Mem. and Vice-Pres., 1952, 1962, Pres. 1971–72 (Chm. Res. Sect., 1958; Guy Medal in Silver, 1958, in Gold, 1975); Mem. Internat. Statistical Inst., 1952; Statistical Adviser, Brit. Standards Instn (with Prof. E. S. Pearson), 1954; Chm. Inst. of Statisticians, 1960–62; President: Operational Res. Soc., 1962–64; Inst. of Mathematics and its Applications, 1970–71; Fellow: Amer. Statistical Assoc.; Inst. of Mathematical Statistics; Amer. Assoc. for Advancement of Science. *Publications:* (ed) The Foundations of Statistical Inference, 1962; papers in Jl Royal Statistical Society; Technometrics; Biometrika. *Recreations:* viola playing, boating. *Address:* Mill House, Hurst Green, Brightlingsea, Essex. *T:* Brightlingsea 2388.
See also D. E. C. Wedderburn.

BARNARD, Captain Sir George (Edward), Kt 1968; Deputy Master of Trinity House, 1961–72; *b* 11 Aug. 1907; 2nd *s* of Michael and Alice Louise Barnard; *m* 1940, Barbara Emma Hughes (*d* 1976); one *s.* Apprenticed at sea, 1922; 1st Command, Blue Star Line, 1945. Elder Brother of Trinity House, 1958–. Trustee, Nat. Maritime Museum, 1967–74; Treasurer, Internat. Assoc. of Lighthouse Authorities, 1961–72; Hon. Sec., King George's Fund for Sailors, 1967–75; first Chm., Nautical Inst., 1972–73, Pres., 1973–75, Fellow, 1975; former Mem. Cttee of Management, RNLI. FRSA 1969. *Address:* Warden, Station Road, Much Hadham, Herts SG10 6AX. *T:* Much Hadham 3133.

BARNARD, Sir Joseph (Brian), Kt 1986; JP; Chairman, National Union of Conservative and Unionist Associations, Yorkshire Area, since 1983; *b* 22 Jan. 1928; *s* of Joseph Ernest Barnard and Elizabeth Loudon (*née* Constantine); *m* 1959, Suzanne Hamilton Bray; three *s* (incl. twins). *Educ:* Bramcote School, Scarborough; Sedbergh School. Served Army, 1946–48, commissioned KRRC. Director: Joseph Constantine Steamship Line, 1952–66; Teesside Warehousing Co., 1966–. Farms at East Harlsey. Chairman: NE Electricity Cons. Council, N Yorks Dist Cttee, 1986–; Governors, Ingleby Arncliffe C of E Primary School, 1979–; Patron and churchwarden, St Oswald's, E Harlsey. JP Northallerton, 1973; Chm., Allertonshire PSD, 1981–; Mem., N Yorks Magistrates' Courts Cttee, 1981–. *Recreations:* walking, shooting, gardening. *Address:* Harlsey Hall, Northallerton, N Yorks DL6 2BL. *T:* Northallerton 82203. *Club:* Carlton.

BARNARD, Hon. Lance Herbert, AO 1979; retired; Director, Office of Australian War Graves, Department of Veterans' Affairs, Commonwealth of Australia, 1981–83; *b* 1 May 1919; *s* of Hon. H. C. Barnard and M. M. Barnard (*née* McKenzie); *m* 2nd, 1962, Jill Denise Carstairs, *d* of Senator H. G. J. Cant; one *s* two *d* (and one *d* decd); also one *d* by a former marriage. *Educ:* Launceston Technical Coll. Served War, overseas, AIF 9th Div., 1940. Formerly teacher, Tasmanian Educn Dept. Elected to House of Representatives as Member for Bass, 1954, 1955, 1958, 1961, 1963, 1966, 1969, 1972, 1974. From Dec. 1972: Minister of Defence, Navy, Army, Air, Supply, Postmaster-Gen., Labour and National Service, Immigration, Social Services, Repatriation, Health, Primary Industry, National Development, and of the Interior. Dep. Leader, Federal Parliamentary Labor Party, 1967–72; Deputy Prime Minister, 1973–74; Minister for Defence (Navy, Army, Air and Supply), 1973–75. Australian Ambassador to Sweden, Norway and Finland, 1975–78. Captain, Aust. Cadet Corps, post War of 1939–45. State Pres., Tasmanian Br., Aust. Labor Party; Tasmanian deleg., Federal Exec., Aust. Labor Party. *Publication:* Labor's Defence Policy, 1969. *Recreation:* gardening. *Address:* 6 Bertland Court, Launceston, Tasmania 7250, Australia.

BARNARD, Sir Thomas; *see* Barnard, Sir A. T.

BARNEBY, Lt-Col Henry Habington, TD 1946; retired from HM Forces 1955; Vice Lord-Lieutenant of Hereford and Worcester, 1974–77; *b* 19 June 1909; *er s* of Richard Hicks Barneby, Longworth Hall, Hereford; *m* 1st, 1935, Evelyn Georgina Heywood; 2nd, 1944, Angela Margaret Campbell (*d* 1979); four *s* one *d* (and one *s* decd). *Educ:* Radley Coll.; RMC Sandhurst. QALAS 1939. 2nd Lieut KSLI 1929, retd 1935; Lieut Hereford Regt TA 1936; commanded: Hereford Regt (TA), 1945–46; Hereford LI (TA), 1947–51; Jamaica Bn, 1951–53; regranted commn in KSLI as Major, 1947; retd 1955. Mem., Herefordshire T&AFA, 1955–68; Mem., W Midlands T&AVR, 1968–77. Member: Hereford RDC, 1955–67 (Chm., 1964–67); Dore and Bredwardine RDC, 1966–73; S Herefordshire RDC, 1973–76. DL Herefordshire 1958–83, Vice Lieut, 1973–74, High Sheriff 1972; JP Hereford County PSD, 1957–79 (Chm., 1977–79). *Address:* Llanerch-y-Coed, Dorstone, Herefordshire HR3 6AG. *T:* Clifford 215.

BARNES, family name of **Baron Gorell.**

BARNES, Adrian Francis Patrick; Remembrancer of the City of London, since 1986; *b* 25 Jan. 1943; *s* of Francis Walter Ibbetson Barnes, *qv* and Heather Katherine (*née* Tamplin); *m* 1980, Sally Eve Whatley; one *s* one *d. Educ:* St Paul's School; MA City of London Polytechnic 1981. Called to the Bar, Gray's Inn, 1973; Solicitor's Dept, DTI, 1975; Dep. Remembrancer, Corp. of London, 1982. *Address:* Guildhall, EC2P 2EJ. *T:* 01–606 3030.

BARNES, Alan Robert, CBE 1976; JP; Headmaster, Ruffwood School, Kirkby, Liverpool, since 1959; *b* 9 Aug. 1927; *s* of Arthur Barnes and Ida Barnes; *m* 1951, Pearl Muriel Boughton; one *s* (and one *s* decd). *Educ:* Enfield Grammar Sch.; Queens' Coll., Cambridge (MA). National Service, RAEC. Wallington County Grammar Sch., 1951–55; Churchfields Sch., West Bromwich, 1955–59. Pres., Headmasters' Assoc., 1974, Treas., 1975–77; Chm., Jt Four Secondary Assocs, 1978; Treas., Secondary Heads Assoc., 1978–82; Vice-Chm., British Educn Management and Admin Soc., 1980–82, Chm. 1982–84. JP Knowsley, Merseyside, 1967. *Publications:* (contrib.) Going Comprehensive (ed Halsall), 1970; (contrib.) Management and Headship in the Secondary School (ed Jennings), 1978; contrib. to: HMA Rev., Education, BEMAS Jl. *Recreations:* bridge, cricket. *Address:* 16 Oaktree Road, St Helens, Merseyside. *T:* St Helens 28073.

BARNES, Dame (Alice) Josephine (Mary Taylor), (Dame Josephine Warren), DBE 1974; FRCP, FRCS, FRCOG; Consulting Obstetrician and Gynaecologist, Charing Cross Hospital and Elizabeth Garrett Anderson Hospital; President, Women's National Cancer Control Campaign, since 1974 (Chairman 1969–72; Vice-President, 1972–74); *b* 18 Aug. 1912; *er d* of late Rev. Walter W. Barnes, MA(Oxon), and Alice Mary Ibbetson, FRCO, ARCM; *m* 1942, Sir Brian Warren, *qv* (marr. diss. 1964); one *s* two *d. Educ:* Oxford High Sch.; Lady Margaret Hall, Oxford (Hon. Fellow, 1980); University College Hosp. Med. Sch. 1st class Hons Physiology, Oxford, BA 1934, MA, BM, BCh 1937, DM

1941. University College Hospital: Goldschmid Scholar; Aitchison Scholar; Tuke Silver Medal; Fellowes Silver Medal; F. T. Roberts Prize; Suckling Prize. Various appointments at UCH, Samaritan Hosp., Queen Charlotte's Hosp., and Radcliffe Infirmary, Oxford; Dep. Academic Head, Obstetric Unit, UCH, 1947–52; Surgeon, Marie Curie Hosp., 1947–67. Medical Women's Federation: Hon. Sec., 1951–57; Pres., London Assoc., 1958–60; Pres., 1966–67. Royal Society of Medicine: Mem. Council, 1949–50; Pres., Sect. of Obstetrics and Gynaecology, 1972–73; Hon. Editor, Sect. of Obstetrics, 1951–71. President: W London Medico-Chirurgical Soc., 1969–70; Nat. Assoc. of Family Planning Doctors, 1976–; Obstetric Physiotherapists Assoc., 1976–; BMA, 1979–80 (Pres.-elect, 1978–79); Union Professionnelle Internationale de Gynécologie et d'Obstétrique, 1977–79; Royal Medical Benevolent Fund, 1982–. Examiner in Obstetrics and Gynaecology: Univ. of London; RCOG; Examining Bd in England, Queen's Univ., Belfast; Univ. of Oxford; Univ. of Kampala; Univ. of Ibadan; Univ. of Maiduguri. Member: Council, Med. Defence Union, 1961–82, Vice-Pres. 1982–; Royal Commn on Med. Educn, 1965–68; Council, RCOG, 1965–71 (Jun. Vice-Pres., 1972–74, Sen. Vice-Pres., 1974–75); MRC Cttee on Analgesia in Midwifery; Min. of Health Med. Manpower Cttee; Medico-Legal Soc.; Population Investigation Cttee, Eugenics Soc.; Cttee on the Working of the Abortion Act, 1971–73; Standing Med. Adv. Cttee, DHSS, 1976–80; Council, Advertising Standards Authority, 1980–; DHSS Inquiry into Human Fertilisation and Embryology, 1982–84; Vice-Pres., Nat. Union of Townswomen's Guilds, 1979–82; Pres., Nat. Assoc. of Family Planning Nurses, 1980–. Mem. of Honour, French Gynaecological Soc., 1945; Hon. Member: Italian Soc. of Obstetrics and Gynaecology, 1979; Nigerian Soc. of Gynaecology and Obstetrics, 1981; Corresp. Mem., Royal Belgian Soc. of Obstetricians and Gynaecologists, 1949. Governor: Charing Cross Hosp.; Chelsea Coll. of Science and Technology, 1958–85; Member Council: Benenden Sch.; Bedford Coll., 1976–85; King's Coll., London, 1985– (FKC 1985); Mem. Court of Patrons, RCOG, 1984. Lectures: Fawcett, Bedford Coll., 1969; Rhys-Williams, Nat. Birthday Trust, 1970; Winston Churchill Meml, Postgrad. Med. Centre, Canterbury, 1971; Bartholomew Mosse, Rotunda Hosp., Dublin, 1975; Simpson Oration, RCOG, 1977; Annual, Liverpool Med. Instn, 1979; Sophia, Univ. of Newcastle upon Tyne, 1980; Ann Horler, Newcastle upon Tyne, 1984. Hon. FRCPI 1977; Hon. Fellow, Edinburgh Obstetrical Soc., 1980. Hon. MD: Liverpool, 1979; Southampton, 1981; Hon. DSc Leicester, 1980. Commandeur du Bontemps de Médoc et des Graves, 1966. *Publications:* Gynaecological Histology, 1948; The Care of the Expectant Mother, 1954; Lecture Notes on Gynaecology, 1966; (ed, jtly) Scientific Foundations of Obstetrics and Gynaecology, 1970; Essentials of Family Planning, 1976; numerous contribs to med. jls, etc. *Recreations:* music, gastronomy, motoring, foreign travel; formerly hockey (Oxford Univ. Women's Hockey XI, 1932, 1933, 1934). *Address:* 8 Aubrey Walk, W8 7JG. *T:* 01–727 9832.
See also F. W. I. Barnes, M. G. J. Neary.

BARNES, Clive Alexander, CBE 1975; Associate Editor and Chief Drama and Dance Critic, New York Post, since 1977; *b* London, 13 May 1927; *s* of Arthur Lionel Barnes and Freda Marguerite Garratt; *m* 1958, Patricia Winckley; one *s* one *d. Educ:* King's Coll., London; St Catherine's Coll., Oxford. Served RAF, 1946–48. Admin. Officer, Town Planning Dept, LCC, 1952–61; concurrently freelance journalist; Chief Dance Critic, The Times, 1961–65; Exec. Editor, Dance and Dancers, Music and Musicians, and Plays and Players, 1961–65; a London Correspondent, New York Times, 1963–65, Dance Critic, 1965–77, Drama Critic (weekdays only), 1967–77; a NY correspondent, The Times, 1970–. Knight of the Order of Dannebrog (Denmark), 1972. *Publications:* Ballet in Britain since the War, 1953; (ed, with others) Ballet Here and Now, 1961; Frederick Ashton and his Ballets, 1961; Dance Scene, USA (commentary), 1967; (ed with J. Gassner) Best American Plays, 6th series, 1963–67, 1971, and 7th series, 1974; (ed) New York Times Directory of the Theatre, 1973; Nureyev, 1983; contribs to jls, inc. Punch, The New Statesman, The Spectator, The New Republic. *Recreations:* eating, drinking, walking, theatregoing. *Club:* Century (NY).

BARNES, Rev. Cyril Arthur; *b* 10 Jan. 1926; *s* of Reginald William and Mary Adeline Barnes; *m* 1951, Patricia Patience Allen. *Educ:* Penistone Grammar School; Edinburgh Theological Coll. King's Own Scottish Borderers, 1944–47. Curate, St John's, Aberdeen, 1950–53; Rector, St John's, Forres, 1953–55; Priest-in-Charge, Wentbridge, Yorks, 1955–58; Vicar, St Bartholomew's, Ripponden with St John's, Rishworth, 1958–67, also St John's, Thorpe, 1966–67; Rector, Christ Church, Huntly with St Marnan's, Aberchirder, 1967–84, also Holy Trinity, Keith, 1974–84; Canon of Inverness Cathedral, 1971–80; Synod Clerk, 1977–80; Dean of Moray, Ross and Caithness, 1980–84. *Recreations:* gardening, do-it-yourself. *Address:* Tillytarmont Cottage, Bridge of Isla, Huntly, Aberdeenshire AB5 4SP.

BARNES, Daniel Sennett, CBE 1977; CEng, FIEE; HQ Director, British Aerospace PLC, since 1986; Chairman, Berkshire and Oxfordshire Manpower Board, since 1983; *b* 13 Sept. 1924; *s* of Paula Sennett Barnes and John Daniel Barnes; *m* 1955, Jean A. Steadman; one *s. Educ:* Dulwich Coll.; Battersea Polytechnic (BScEng, 1st Cl. Hons). Apprenticeship at Philips, 1941–46; served REME, 1946–48; Battersea Polytechnic, 1948–51; Sperry Gyroscope, 1951–82: Dir of Engineering, 1962–68; Manager, Defence Systems, 1968–70; Gen. Manager, 1970–71; Man. Dir, 1971–82; Man. Dir, Electronic Systems and Equipment Div., British Aerospace PLC (formerly Sperry Gyroscope), 1982–85; Director: Sperry Ltd UK, 1971–82; Sperry AG Switzerland, 1979–83. Pres., Electronic Engrg Assoc., 1981–82. *Recreations:* sailing, joinery, music and ballet, gardening.

BARNES, David Michael William, QC 1981; a Recorder, since 1985; *b* 16 July 1943; *s* of David Charles Barnes and Florence Maud Barnes; *m* 1970, Susan Dorothy Turner; three *s. Educ:* Monmouth Sch.; Wadham Coll., Oxford. Called to Bar, Middle Temple, 1965. Hon. Research Fellow, Lady Margaret Hall, Oxford, 1979. *Publications:* Leasehold Reform Act 1967, 1967; Hill and Redman's Law of Landlord and Tenant, 15th edn 1970–17th edn 1982. *Recreations:* walking, crime fiction. *Address:* 21 Frank Dixon Way, SE21 7ET.

BARNES, Sir Denis (Charles), KCB 1967 (CB 1964); Director: Glynwed Ltd; General Accident, Fire & Life Assurance Corporation, 1976–85; President, Manpower Society, since 1976; *b* 15 Dec. 1914; *s* of Frederick Charles Barnes; *m* 1938, Patricia Abercrombie. *Educ:* Hulme Gram. Sch., Manchester; Merton Coll., Oxford. Chambers Postmaster, Merton Coll., Oxford, 1933–37. BA, 1st Cl. Mod. History, 1936; PPE 1937. Entered Min. of Labour, 1937; Private Sec. to Minister of Labour, 1945–47; Dep. Sec., Min. of Labour, 1963, Permanent Sec. 1966; Permanent Sec., Dept of Employment, 1968–73; Chairman: Manpower Services Commn, 1974–76; Member: Council, Manchester Business Sch., 1975; Council, Zoological Soc. of London, 1978–81. FIPM 1974. Commonwealth Fellowship, 1953. *Publication:* Governments and Trade Unions, 1980. *Address:* The Old Inn, 30 The Street, Wittersham, Kent. *T:* Wittersham 528. *Club:* Savile.

BARNES, Edward Campbell; independent television producer/director and television consultant; Head of Children's Programmes, BBC Television, 1978–86; *b* 8 Oct. 1928; *s* of Hubert Turnbull Barnes and Annie Mabel Barnes; *m* 1950, Dorothy Smith; one *s* two *d. Educ:* Wigan Coll. British Forces Network, Vienna, 1946–49; stage management, provincial and West End theatre, 1949–55; BBC Television: studio management,

1955–62; Producer, Blue Peter, 1962–70; Dep. Head of Children's Progs, 1970–78, incl.: original Editor, John Craven's Newsround; Producer: Blue Peter Royal Safari with Princess Anne; 6 series of Blue Peter Special Assignments. Mem. Bd, Children's Film and Television Foundn Ltd, 1983–. *Publications:* 19 Blue Peter Books and 8 Blue Peter Mini Books, 1964–79; 6 Blue Peter Special Assignment Books, 1973–75; Blue Peter Royal Safari, 1971; Petra: a dog for everyone, 1977; numerous articles for nat. press. *Recreations:* cricket, ballet, opera, walking. *Club:* BAFTA.

BARNES, Eric Cecil, CMG 1954; Colonial Administrative Service; Provincial Commissioner, Nyasaland, 1949–55, retired; *b* 1899; *m* 1950, Isabel Margaret Lesley, MBE, *d* of late Mrs Isabel Wauchope; one *s* one *d*. *Educ:* Bishop Cotton's Sch., Simla; Bedford Sch. and Cadet Coll., Quetta, India. Indian Army, 1917–23; Administrative Service, Nyasaland, 1925. Deputy Provincial Commissioner, 1946. *Address:* 9 Riverdale Close, Fordingbridge, Hants. *T:* Fordingbridge 53860.

BARNES, Hon. Eric Charles; Hon. Mr Justice Barnes; High Court Judge, Hong Kong, since 1981; *b* 12 Sept. 1924; *m* 1st, Estelle Fay Barnes (*née* Darnell); four *s* one *d*; 2nd, 1978, Judianna Wai Ling Barnes (*née* Chang); one *s* one *d*. *Educ:* Univ. of Queensland (LLB). *Recreations:* tennis, racing (horse), sports. *Address:* 2B Eastview, 3 Cox's Road, Kowloon, Hong Kong. *T:* 3–679221. *Clubs:* United Services Recreation, Kowloon Cricket, Royal Hong Kong Jockey (Hong Kong); Tattersall's (Brisbane).

BARNES, Sir (Ernest) John (Ward), KCMG 1974; MBE (mil.) 1946; HM Diplomatic Service, retired; *b* 22 June 1917; *er s* of Rt Rev. Ernest William Barnes, 3rd Bishop of Birmingham, and Adelaide, *d* of Sir Adolphus Ward, Master of Peterhouse, Cambridge; *m* 1948, Cynthia Margaret Ray (JP E Sussex), *d* of Sir Herbert Stewart, CIE, *qv;* two *s* three *d*. *Educ:* Dragon Sch., Oxford; Winchester; Trinity Coll., Cambridge. Classical Tripos, Pts I and II, Class I; Porson Scholar, 1939. Royal Artillery, 1939–46 (Lt-Col, MBE, US Bronze Star). HM Foreign Service, 1946; served Washington, Beirut, Bonn and Harvard Univ. (Center for International Affairs); Ambassador to Israel, 1969–72; Ambassador to the Netherlands, 1972–77. Director: Alliance Investment Co., 1977–; Whiteaway Laidlaw Ltd, 1979–. Chairman: Sussex Rural Community Council, 1982–; Governors, Hurstpierpoint Coll., 1983–. Member: Chichester Diocesan Synod, 1978–; Council, Sussex Univ., 1981–85 (Vice-Chm. 1982–84). *Publication:* Ahead of his Age, 1979. *Address:* Hampton Lodge, Hurstpierpoint, Sussex; 20 Thurloe Place Mews, SW7. *Clubs:* Athenæum, Beefsteak, Brooks's; MCC.

BARNES, Francis Walter Ibbetson; a full-time Chairman, Industrial Tribunals, since 1976; *b* 10 May 1914; *s* of late Rev. Walter W. Barnes, MA (Oxon) and Alice Mary Ibbetson, FRCO, ARCM; *m* 1st, 1941, Heather Katherine (marr. diss. 1953), *d* of Frank Tamplin; two *s*; 2nd, 1955, Sonia Nina (Nina Walker, pianist), *d* of late Harold Higginbottom; two *s* one *d*. *Educ:* Dragon Sch., Oxford; Mill Hill Sch.; Balliol Coll., Oxford. BA Jurisprudence (Hons), Oxford, 1937; MA 1967. Called to Bar, Inner Temple, 1938. Profumo Prize, Inner Temple, 1939. Served War, 1939–46 in Army (Middlesex Regt) and Home Office and Military Fire Services; Sen. Company Officer NFS and Capt. comdg military Fire Fighting Co. on BLA; later Staff Capt., JAG (War Crimes Section). Functioned as Judge Advocate and Prosecutor in various trials of war criminals in Germany. Recorder of Smethwick, 1964–66; Dep. Chm., Oxfordshire QS, 1965–71; Recorder of Warley, 1966–71, Hon. Recorder, 1972; a Recorder of the Crown Court, 1972–76. Life Governor, Mill Hill Sch., 1939–; Mem., Dame Henrietta Barnett Bd (Educl Trust), 1951–. Elected to Bar Council, 1961. Bar Council's rep. (observer) on Cons. cttee of Lawyers of the Common Market countries, 1962–71; contrib. to Common Market Law Review. Union Internat. des Avocats: Mem. Council, 1964–; Rapporteur Général at Vienna Congress, 1967; Rapporteur National at Paris Congress, 1971. *Recreations:* music, gardening, motoring. *Address:* Office of Industrial Tribunals, Renslade House, Bonhay Road, Exeter EX4 3BX; 83 St George's Drive, Ickenham, Mddx. *T:* Ruislip 72532; Southernhay, Diptford, S Devon.

See also A. F. P. Barnes, Dame A. J. M. T. Barnes.

BARNES, James Edwin; Under-Secretary, Small Firms and Regional Development Grants, Department of Industry, 1974–75; retired; *b* 23 Nov. 1917; *s* of James Barnes and Kate (*née* Davies); *m* 1943, Gloria Parkinson; two *s* one *d*. *Educ:* King Edward VI Sch., Nuneaton. Joined Civil Service as Executive Officer, War Office, 1936; Higher Executive Officer, Min. of Supply, 1942; Sen. Exec. Officer 1945, Principal, 1946, Asst Sec. 1952; Under-Secretary: Min. of Aviation, 1964–66; BoT, 1966–70; DTI, 1970–74. Coronation Medal, 1953. *Address:* La Blythe, Bartholomew Street, Hythe, Kent CT21 5BY. *T:* Hythe 60336.

BARNES, James Frederick, CB 1982; Deputy Chief Scientific Adviser, and Head of Profession for the Science Group, Ministry of Defence, since 1986; *b* 8 March 1932; *s* of Wilfred and Doris M. Barnes; *m* 1957, Dorothy Jean Drew; one *s* two *d*. *Educ:* Taunton's Sch., Southampton; Queen's Coll., Oxford. BA 1953, MA 1957; CEng, FIMechE, FRAeS. Bristol Aeroplane Co. (Engine Div.), 1953; Min. of Supply, Nat. Gas Turbine Estabt: Sci. Officer 1955; Sen. Sci. Off. 1957; Principal Sci. Off. 1962; Sen. Principal Sci. Off. (Individual Merit) 1965; Min. of Aviation Supply, Asst Dir, Engine R&D, 1970; seconded to HM Diplomatic Service, Counsellor (Science and Technology), British Embassy, Washington, 1972; Under-Sec., MoD, 1974; Dir Gen. Res. (C), MoD (Procurement Exec.), 1974–77; Dep. Dir (Weapons), RAE, 1978–79; Dep. Chief Scientific Adviser (Projs), MoD, 1979–82; Dep. Controller, Establishments Resources and Personnel, MoD, 1982–84; Dep. Controller, Estabts and Res., MoD, 1984–86. Mem., Council on Christian Approaches to Defence and Disarmament, 1980–; Lay Member: Guildford Diocesan Synod, 1978–84; Winchester Diocesan Synod, 1985–; Churchwarden, All Saints', Farringdon, 1985–. James Clayton Fund Prize, IMechE, 1964. *Publications:* contrib. books and learned jls on mech. engrg, esp. gas turbine technology, heat transfer and stress analysis. *Recreation:* making things. *Address:* Ministry of Defence, Main Building, Whitehall, SW1A 2HB. *Club:* Athenæum.

BARNES, Sir James George, Kt 1976; MBE (mil.) 1946; JP; Mayor of Dunedin, New Zealand, 1968–77; sharebroker; *b* Dunedin, NZ, 1908; *s* of Richard R. Barnes; *m* 1938, Elsie, *d* of James D. Clark; one *d*. *Educ:* King Edward Technical High Sch. Served War, RNZAF 75 Sqdn, 1940–46 (POW, 1942–45). Mem., Dunedin City Council, 1947–53 and 1959–80 (Dep. Mayor 1951–53 and 1959–68); MP, 1951–57. Exec. Mem.: Otago Peninsula Trust; NZ Fedn for the Blind; Chm., Bd of Ocean Beach Domain. Past Pres., Otago Savings Bank. Chm. or Dir, Sch. Bds and Youth orgs. NZ mile champion, 1932; NZ Cross Country Champion, 1933; Manager NZ Empire Games Team, 1950; Asst Man., NZ Olympic Team, 1956; Past Pres., NZ AAA; Mem. Otago AAA; Mem. NZ Trotting Conf. (Pres., 1979–80); Sen. Vice Pres., Aust. Trotting Council, 1977–80; Exec. Mem., World Trotting Congress, 1980; Past Pres., Forbury Park Trotting Club. CStJ 1979. *Recreations:* golf, trotting. *Address:* 35 Cliffs Road, Dunedin, New Zealand; PO Box 221, Dunedin.

BARNES, Sir John; *see* Barnes, Sir E. J. W.

BARNES, John Alfred; Director-General, City and Guilds of London Institute, since 1985; *b* 29 April 1930; *s* of John Joseph and Margaret Carr Barnes; *m* 1954, Ivy May (*née* Walker); two *d*. *Educ:* Bede Boys Grammar Sch., Sunderland; Durham Univ. (MA, BSc, MEd). Teacher, Grangefield Grammar Sch., Stockton-on-Tees, 1953–57; Asst Educn Officer, Barnsley, 1957–61; Dep. Dir, then Dir of Educn, City of Wakefield, 1963–68; Chief Educn Officer, City of Salford, 1968–84. Mem. Council, Assoc. of Colls of Further and Higher Educn, 1976–82 (Chm. 1980–81); Chairman: Northern Examining Assoc., 1979–82; Associated Lancs Schs Examg Bd, 1972–84; Member: Associated Examg Bd, Nat. Exams Bd for Supervisory Studies, 1985–; Further Educn Unit Management Bd, 1986–; YTS Certification Bd, 1986–; various ind. trng bds, 1969–78, and MSC cttees, 1978–84; Nat. Exec. Cttee, Soc. of Educn Officers, 1979–84; Sec., Assoc. of Educn Officers, 1977–84; Treas., NFER, 1979–84; Pres., Educnl Develt Assoc., 1980–85. *Publications:* occasional papers in educnl press. *Recreations:* cultural activities, foreign travel. *Address:* 37 Woodfield Park, Amersham, Bucks HP6 5QM. *T:* Amersham 6120. *Clubs:* Athenæum, Rotary.

BARNES, Prof. John Arundel, DSC 1944; FBA 1981; Fellow of Churchill College, Cambridge, since 1969; Visiting Fellow, Department of Sociology, Research School of Social Sciences, Australian National University, since 1985; *b* Reading, 9 Sept. 1918; *s* of T. D. and M. G. Barnes, Bath; *m* 1942, Helen Frances, *d* of Charles Bastable; three *s* one *d*. *Educ:* Christ's Hosp.; St John's Coll., Cambridge; Balliol Coll., Oxford. Fellow, St John's Coll., Cambridge, 1950–53; Simon Research Fellow, Manchester Univ., 1951–53; Reader in Anthropology, London Univ., 1954–56; Prof. of Anthropology, Sydney Univ., 1956–58; Prof. of Anthropology, Inst. of Advanced Studies, ANU, Canberra, 1958–69; Overseas Fellow, Churchill Coll., Cambridge, 1965–66; Prof. of Sociology, Univ. of Cambridge, 1969–82, now Emeritus. *Publications:* Marriage in a Changing Society, 1951; Politics in a Changing Society, 1954; Inquest on the Murngin, 1967; Sociology in Cambridge, 1970; Three Styles in the Study of Kinship, 1971; Social Networks, 1972; The Ethics of Inquiry in Social Science, 1977; Who Should Know What?, 1979. *Address:* Department of Sociology, Research School of Social Sciences, Australian National University, GPO Box 4, Canberra, ACT 2601, Australia.

BARNES, Dame Josephine; *see* Barnes, Dame A. J. M. T.

BARNES, Sir Kenneth, KCB 1977 (CB 1970); Permanent Secretary, Department of Employment, 1976–82; *b* 26 Aug. 1922; *s* of Arthur and Doris Barnes, Accrington, Lancs; *m* 1948, Barbara Ainsworth; one *s* two *d*. *Educ:* Accrington Grammar Sch.; Balliol Coll., Oxford. Entered Ministry of Labour, 1948; Asst Sec., 1963; Under-Sec., Cabinet Office, 1966–68; Dep. Sec., Dept of Employment, 1968–75. *Address:* 49 Cockshot Road, Reigate, Surrey. *T:* Reigate 45237.

BARNES, Kenneth James, CBE 1969 (MBE 1964); Advisor (Finance), Directorate General for Development, Commission of the European Communities, since 1982; *b* 8 May 1930; *s* of late Thomas Arthur Barnes and Ethel Maude Barnes; *m* 1st, 1953, Lesley Dawn Grummett Wright (*d* 1976); two *s* one *d*; 2nd, 1981, Anna Elisabeth Gustaf Maria Vanoorlé. *Educ:* Dover Coll.; St Catharine's Coll., Cambridge (Crabtree exhibnr; MA); London Univ. Pilot Officer, RAF, 1949–50; Flying Officer, RAFVR, 1950–53. Administrative Officer, HMOCS Eastern Nigeria, 1954–60; Asst Sec., Min. of Finance, Malaŵi, 1960–64, Sen. Asst Sec., 1965, Dep. Sec., 1966, Permanent Sec., 1967–71; Asst Sec., British Steel Corp., 1971–73; EEC: Principal Administrator, Directorate-Gen. for Develt, 1973–75; Head of Div. for Ind. Co-operation, Trade Promotion and Regional Co-operation, 1976–78; Hd of Div. for Caribbean, Indian and Pacific Oceans, 1979–80; Advr (Political), 1981–82. *Recreations:* reading, esp. history, listening to music, mediaeval fortifications. *Address:* Commission of the European Communities, 200 rue de la Loi, B1049 Brussels, Belgium. *T:* (office) Brussels 2355970; (home) 767 28 55.

BARNES, Michael Cecil John; Director, United Kingdom Immigrants' Advisory Service, since 1984; *b* 22 Sept. 1932; *s* of late Major C. H. R. Barnes, OBE and of Katherine Louise (*née* Kennedy); *m* 1962, Anne Mason; one *s* one *d*. *Educ:* Malvern; Corpus Christi Coll., Oxford. MP (Lab) Brentford and Chiswick, 1966–Feb. 1974; an Opposition Spokesman on food and food prices, 1970–71; Chairman: Parly Labour Party Social Security Group, 1969–70; ASTMS Parly Cttee, 1970–71; Jt Hon. Sec., Labour Cttee for Europe, 1969–71; Mem., Public Accounts Cttee, 1967–74. Contested (Lab): Wycombe, 1964; Brentford and Isleworth, Feb. 1974; Mem. Labour Party, 1957–79; helped form SDP, 1981; rejoined Labour Party, 1983–. Chm., Electricity Consumers' Council, 1977–83. Member: Council of Management, War on Want, 1972–77; Nat. Consumer Council, 1975–80; Arts Council Trng Cttee, 1977–83; Energy Commn, 1977–79; Internat. Cttee of Nat. Council for Voluntary Organisations, 1977–83; Advertising Standards Authority, 1979–85; Direct Mail Services Standards Bd, 1983–86; Data Protection Tribunal, 1985–; Chairman: UK Adv. Cttee on EEC Action Against Poverty Programme, 1975–76; Notting Hill Social Council, 1976–79; West London Fair Housing Gp Ltd, 1980–; Vice Chm., Bangabandhu Soc., 1980–; Organising Secretary: Gulbenkian Foundn Drama Trng Inquiry, 1974–75; Music Trng Inquiry, 1976–77; Sec., Nat. Council for Drama Trng, 1976–84; Chm., Hounslow Arts Trust, 1974–82; Trustee, Project Hand Trust, 1974–77; Governor, Internat. Musicians Seminar, Prussia Cove, 1978–81. *Recreations:* lawn tennis, walking, swimming, reading. *Address:* 45 Ladbroke Grove, W11. *T:* 01–727 2533.

BARNES, Peter; dramatist; *b* 10 Jan. 1931; *s* of Frederick and Martha Barnes; *m* 1958, Charlotte (*née* Beck). *Educ:* Stroud Grammar Sch. 1st Play, Sclerosis, 1965. Adapted and co-directed: Wedekind's Lulu, 1970; The Bewitched, 1974; adapted and directed: Feydeau's The Purging, 1976; Wedekind's The Singer, 1976; Jonson's Bartholomew Fair, 1978; Marston's Antonio, 1979; Wedekind's The Devil Himself, 1980; adapted Jonson's The Devil is an Ass, 1977; directed: For All Those Who Get Despondent, 1977; Laughter!, 1978; Somersaults, 1981; Barnes' People One, 1982; Barnes' People Two, 1984; Red Noses, 1985; Barnes' People Three, 1986. John Whiting Award, 1968; Evening Standard Award, 1969; Laurence Olivier Award for Best Play, 1985. *Publications:* The Ruling Class, 1969; Leonardo's Last Supper, 1970; Noonday Demons, 1970; Lulu, 1971; The Bewitched, 1974; The Frontiers of Farce, 1976; Laughter!, 1978; The Collected Plays, 1981; Barnes' People Two, 1984; Red Noses, 1985. *Address:* 7 Archery Close, Connaught Street, W2 2BE. *T:* 01–262 9205.

BARNES, Peter Robert, CB 1982; Deputy Director of Public Prosecutions, 1977–82; *b* 1 Feb. 1921; *s* of Robert Stanley Barnes and Marguerite (*née* Dunkels); *m* 1955, Pauline Belinda Hannen; two *s* one *d*. *Educ:* Eton Coll.; Trinity Coll., Cambridge (BA). Called to Bar, Inner Temple, 1947. Dir. of Public Prosecutions: Legal Asst, 1951; Sen. Legal Asst, 1958; Asst Solicitor, 1970; Asst Director, 1974; Principal Asst Dir, 1977. Pres., Video Appeals Cttee, 1985–. *Recreations:* golf, bridge, conjuring. *Address:* The Old Vicarage, Church Lane, Witley, Surrey GU8 5PN.

BARNES, Dr Robert Sandford; Chairman, Robert S. Barnes Consultants Ltd, since 1978; Principal, Queen Elizabeth College, Kensington, London University, 1978–85, Fellow, 1985; *b* 8 July 1924; *s* of William Edward and Ada Elsie Barnes (*née* Sutherst); *m* 1952, Julia Frances Marriott Grant; one *s* three *d*. *Educ:* Univ. of Manchester. BSc Hons

1948, MSc 1959, DSc 1962. Radar Research, Admiralty Signals Estab., Witley, Surrey, 1944–47; AERE, Harwell: Metallurgical Research, 1948–62; Head of Irradiation Branch, 1962–65; Vis. Scientist, The Science Center, N Amer. Aviation Co., Calif, 1965; Head of Metallurgy Div., AERE, Harwell, 1966–68; Dep. Dir, BISRA, 1968–69; Dir, BISRA, 1969–70; Dir R&D, British Steel Corp., 1970–75; Chief Scientist, BSC, 1975–78. Technical Adviser: Bd of BOC Ltd, 1978–79; Bd of BOC International Ltd, 1979–81; Bd of New Ventures Secretariat, 1978–80. Chm., Ruthner Continuous Crop Systems Ltd, 1976–78. Member: CBI Res. and Technol. Cttee, 1968–75; Adv. Council on R&D for Iron and Steel, 1970–75; European Industrial Res. Management Assoc., 1970 (Vice-Pres., 1974–78); Parly and Scientific Cttee, 1970–80, 1983–85; Council, Welding Inst., 1970–75; Council, Instn of Metallurgists, 1970–75 and 1979–85 (Vice Pres., 1979); Sen. Vice Pres., 1982; Pres., 1983–85); Council, Metals Soc., 1974–80, 1982–85 (Chairman: Coordinating Cttee, 1976–78, Executive Cttee, 1976–80); Steering Gp, 1983–84, Council, 1985–, Exec. Cttee, 1985–, Inst of Metals; Chm., Combined Operations Working Party, 1980–81; Materials Science and Technology Cttee, SRC, 1975–79; Chm., European Nuclear Steel-making Club, 1973–76; UK Representative: Commn de la Recherche Technique Sidérurgique, 1972–78; Conseil d'Association Européenne pour la Promotion de la Recherche Technique en Sidérurgie, 1972–78; Adv. Council on Energy Conservation, Industry Group, 1977–78; Council, Backpain Assoc., 1979–. Hon. Mem. Council, Iron and Steel Inst., 1969–73. Governor, Sheffield Polytechnic, 1968–72; Member: Court of Univ. of Surrey, 1968–80; Collegiate Council, Univ. of London, 1978–85; Jt Finance and Gen. Purposes Cttee, Univ. of London, 1978–85; Senate, Univ. of London, 1980–85; Member Council: King's Coll. London, 1982–85; Chelsea Coll., 1983–85; Bd Mem., CSTI, 1984–. Lectures: Hatfield Meml, Iron and Steel Inst., 1973; John Player, IMechE, 1976. Freeman, City of London, 1984; Liveryman, Worshipful Co. of Engrs, 1985. Rosenhain Medallist, Inst. of Metals, 1964. FInstP 1961, FIM 1965, FRSA 1976, FKC 1985. CEng 1977. *Publications*: chapters in specialist books of science; scientific papers in various learned jls. *Recreations*: yachting, gardening. *Address*: Pigeon Forge, Daneshill, The Hockering, Woking, Surrey GU22 7HQ. *T*: Woking 61529. *Clubs*: Athenæum, Cruising Association.

BARNES, Roland, CBE 1970; BSc, MB, ChB, FRCS, FRCSE, FRCSGlas; Professor of Orthopaedic Surgery, University of Glasgow, 1959–72, now Professor Emeritus; *b* 21 May 1907; *y s* of Benjamin Barnes and Mary Ann Bridge, Accrington, Lancs.; *m* 1938, Mary Mills Buckley; one *s* two *d. Educ*: University of Manchester. BSc 1927; MB, ChB 1930; Medical and Surgical Clinical prizes. Usual resident appointments; Resident Surgical Officer, Manchester Royal Infirmary, 1934–35; Dickinson Travelling Scholar, Univ. of Manchester, 1935–36; visited orthopaedic clinics in USA; Fellow, Hospital for Ruptured and Crippled, New York. Chief Asst to Sir Harry Platt, Bt, Orthopaedic Department, Royal Infirmary, Manchester, 1937–39; Surgeon in Charge of Orthopædic and Peripheral Nerve Injury Centre, EMS Hospital, Winwick, Lancs, 1940–43. Past Pres., British Orthopædic Assoc.; Hon. Mem. French, Finnish, German and S African Orthopædic Assocs; Corresp. Mem. Amer. Orthopædic Assoc. *Publications*: papers on injuries of the peripheral nerves and spine, fractures of neck of femur, and on tumours of bone. *Recreation*: gardening. *Address*: 35 Boclair Road, Bearsden, Glasgow. *T*: 041–942 2699.

BARNES, Rt. Hon. Sally O.; *see* Oppenheim-Barnes.

BARNES, Timothy Paul; QC 1986; *b* 23 April 1944; *s* of Arthur Morley Barnes and Valerie Enid Mary Barnes; *m* 1969, Patricia Margaret Gale; one *s* three *d. Educ*: Bradfield Coll., Berkshire; Christ's Coll., Cambridge (MA). Called to Bar, Gray's Inn, 1968, Hilbery Exhibn; practises Midland and Oxford Circuit; Asst Recorder, 1983. *Recreations*: gardening, hockey. *Address*: The White House, Crooms Hill, SE10 8HH. *T*: 01–858 1185. *Club*: MCC.

BARNES, Sir William Lethbridge G.; *see* Gorell Barnes.

BARNES, Prof. Winston Herbert Frederick, MA (Oxon); Professor Emeritus, Universities of Manchester and Liverpool; *b* 30 May 1909; *er s* of Frederick Charles and Martha Lilley Barnes; *m* 1938, Sarah (*d* 1985), *d* of late Thomas David Davies; two *d. Educ*: Manchester Grammar Sch.; Corpus Christi Coll., Oxford (Hugh Oldham Scholar, Haigh Scholar). 1st Cl., Classical Hon. Mods. 1930; 1st Cl., Lit. Hum. 1932; John Locke Scholar in Mental Philosophy, Oxford, 1932; Sen. Demy, Magdalen Coll., Oxford, 1933–34. Asst Lecturer in Philosophy, 1936–39; Lecturer 1939–41, Univ. of Liverpool; served in RAFVR, 1941–42, Temporary Principal, Ministry of Supply, 1942–45; Prof of Philosophy, Univ. of Durham (Durham Colls) 1945–59; Prof. of Moral Philosophy, Univ. of Edinburgh, 1959–63, Gifford Lectr in Natural Theology, 1968–69, 1969–70; Vice-Chancellor, Univ. of Liverpool, 1963–69; Vis. Prof. of Philosophy, Univ. of Auckland, NZ, 1970; Sir Samuel Hall Prof. of Philosophy, Manchester Univ., 1970–73. Pres., Mind Assoc., 1948. Mem. Planning Bd, Independent Univ., 1970–73; Mem. Council, University Coll. at Buckingham, 1973–78 (Hon. Fellow, 1979–83). Hon. DCL Durham, 1964; Hon. DLitt Buckingham, 1983. *Publications*: The Philosophical Predicament, 1950; contributions to Mind, Philosophy, Aristotelian Society Proceedings. *Recreations*: walking, swimming. *Address*: 7 Great Stuart Street, Edinburgh EH3 7TP. *T*: 031–226 3158.

BARNETT, family name of **Baron Barnett.**

BARNETT, Baron *cr* 1983 (Life Peer), of Heywood and Royton in Greater Manchester; **Joel Barnett;** PC 1975; JP; chairman and director of a number of companies; Vice-Chairman, Board of Governors, BBC, since 1986; *b* 14 Oct. 1923; *s* of Louis and Ettie Barnett, both of Manchester; *m* 1949, Lilian Goldstone; one *d. Educ*: Derby Street Jewish Sch.; Manchester Central High Sch. Certified accountant. Served RASC and British Military Govt in Germany. Mem. of Prestwich, Lancs, Borough Council, 1956–59; JP Lancs 1960; Hon. Treas. Manchester Fabian Society, 1953–65. Contested (Lab) Runcorn Div. of Cheshire, Oct. 1959; MP (Lab) Heywood and Royton Div., Lancs, 1964–83. Member: Public Accounts Cttee, 1965–71 (Chm., 1979–83); Public Expenditure Cttee, 1971–74; Select Cttee on Tax Credits, 1973–74; Chm. Parly Labour Party Economic and Finance Group, 1967–70 and 1972–74 (Vice-Chm., 1966–67); Opposition Spokesman on Treasury matters, 1970–74; Chief Sec. to the Treasury, 1974–79 (Cabinet Mem., 1977–79); Opposition spokesman on the Treasury in House of Lords, 1983–. Hon. Visiting Fellow, Univ. of Strathclyde, 1980–. Chm., British Screen Finance Ltd (formerly British Screen Finance Consortium), 1985–. Trustee, V&A Museum, 1984–. Mem., Hallé Cttee, 1982–. Hon. LLD Strathclyde, 1983. *Publication*: Inside the Treasury, 1982. *Recreations*: walking, conversation and reading; good food. *Address*: Flat 92, 24 John Islip Street, SW1; 7 Hillingdon Road, Whitefield, Manchester M25 7QQ.

BARNETT, Christopher John Anthony; QC 1983; a Recorder of the Crown Court, since 1982; *b* 18 May 1936; *s* of Richard Adrian Barnett and Phyllis Barnett (*née* Cartwright); *m* 1959, Sylvia Marieliese (*née* Pritt); two *s* one *d. Educ*: Repton Sch., Derbyshire; College of Law, London. Called to the Bar, Gray's Inn, 1965. District Officer (Kikuyu Guard) and Kenya Government Service, 1955–60; a District Officer in HM Overseas Civil Service, serving in Kenya, 1960–62; in practice as barrister, 1965–.

Recreations: cricket, tennis. *Address:* 4 Paper Buildings, Temple, EC4Y 7EX. *T:* 01–583 7765. *Club:* Norfolk (Norwich).

BARNETT, Colin Michael; industrial consultant, since 1985; Regional Secretary, North-West Regional Council of the Trades Union Congress, 1976–85; Divisional Officer, North-West Division of the National Union of Public Employees, 1971–84; *b* 27 Aug. 1929; *s* of Arthur Barnett and Kathleen Mary Barnett; *m* 1st, 1953, Margaret Barnett (marr. diss. 1980); one *s* one *d*; 2nd, 1982, Hilary Carolyn Hodge, PhD; one *s* one *d. Educ:* St Michael's Elem. Sch., Southfields; Wandsworth Grammar Sch.; London Sch. of Econs and Polit. Science; WEA classes. Area Officer, NUPE, 1959, Asst Divl Officer 1961. Chm. Gp H, Duke of Edinburgh Conf. on Industry and Society, 1974. Secretary: NW Peace Council, 1979–; NW Cttee against Racism, 1980–. Chm., MSC Area Bd, Gtr Manchester and Lancaster, 1978–83. Member: Merseyside District Manpower Bd, 1983–; Industrial Tribunal, Manchester, 1974–. Debt and Industrial Advr, St Helens CAB, 1984–; Marriage Guidance Counsellor, 1984–. Organised: People's March for Jobs, 1981; (jtly) People's March for Jobs, 1983. Employment Advr, This is Your Right, Granada TV, 1970–. Governor, William Temple Foundn, 1980–. *Recreations:* walking, reading, promotion of socialism. *Address:* 14 Elm Grove, Eccleston Park, Prescot, Merseyside L34 2AX. *T:* 051–426 4045.

BARNETT, Correlli (Douglas); author; Keeper of the Churchill Archives Centre, and a Fellow, Churchill College, Cambridge, since 1977; *b* 28 June 1927; *s* of D. A. Barnett; *m* 1950, Ruth Murby; two *d. Educ:* Trinity Sch., Croydon; Exeter Coll., Oxford. Second class hons, Mod. Hist. with Mil. Hist. and the Theory of War as a special subject; MA 1954. Intell. Corps, 1945–48. North Thames Gas Bd, 1952–57; Public Relations, 1957–63. Vice-Pres., E Arts Assoc., 1978– (Chm. Literature Panel, and Mem. Exec. Cttee, 1972–78); Pres., East Anglian Writers; Member: Council, Royal Utd Services Inst. for Defence Studies, 1973–85; Cttee, London Library, 1977–79 and 1982–84. Leverhulme Res. Fellowship, 1976; apptd Lectr in Defence Studies, Univ. of Cambridge, 1980; resigned in order to devote more time to writing, 1983. Winston Churchill Meml Lectr, Switzerland, 1982. FRSL; FRHistS. *Publications:* The Hump Organisation, 1957; The Channel Tunnel (with Humphrey Slater), 1958; The Desert Generals, 1960, new enlarged edn, 1983; The Swordbearers, 1963; Britain and Her Army, 1970 (RSL award, 1971); The Collapse of British Power, 1972; Marlborough, 1974; Bonaparte, 1978; The Great War, 1979; The Audit of War, 1986; (historical consultant and writer to) BBC Television series: The Great War, 1963–64; The Lost Peace, 1965–66; The Commanders, 1972–73; reviews Mil. Hist. for The Sunday Telegraph; contrib. to: The Promise of Greatness (a symposium on the Great War), 1968; Governing Elites (a symposium), 1969; Decisive Battles of the Twentieth Century, 1976; The War Lords, 1976; The Economic System in the UK, 1985; Education for Capability, 1986. *Recreations:* gardening, interior decorating, idling, eating, mole-hunting. *Address:* Catbridge House, East Carleton, Norwich. *T:* Mulbarton 410.

BARNETT, Air Chief Marshal Sir Denis Hensley Fulton, GCB 1964 (KCB 1957; CB 1956); CBE 1945; DFC 1940; RAF, retired; Member for Weapons Research and Development, Atomic Energy Authority, 1965–72; *b* 11 Feb. 1906; *y s* of late Sir Louis Edward Barnett; *m* 1939, Pamela, *y d* of late Sir Allan John Grant; one *s* two *d. Educ:* Christ's Coll., NZ; Clare Coll., Cambridge (BA 1929, MA 1935). Perm. Commn, RAF, 1929; Flt Lieut, 1934; Sqdn Ldr 1938; comd 84 Sqdn, Shaibah, 1938. Served War of 1939–45; Sqdn Comdr, Stn Comdr and G/C Ops, Bomber Comd, 1939–44; Dep. Dir Bomber Ops, Air Min., 1944; Dep. SASO at HQ Bomber Comd, 1945; Actg Wing Cdr, 1940; Gp Capt., 1941; Air Cdre, 1945; Dir of Ops at Air Min., 1945–46; Air Staff, India, 1946–47; Jt Services Staff Coll., 1948; Comdt Central Bomber Estabt, 1949; Dir of Ops Air Min., 1950–52; idc, 1952; Representative of UK Chiefs of Staff at HQ, UN Command, Tokyo, 1952–54; AOC, No. 205 Group, Middle East Air Force, 1954–56; Commandant, RAF Staff Coll., Bracknell, 1956; Commander Allied Air Task Force, Near East, 1956; Air Secretary, Air Ministry, 1957–59; AOC-in-C, RAF Transport Command, 1959–62; Air Officer Commanding-in-Chief, RAF Near East; Commander, British Forces Cyprus, and Administrator of the Sovereign Base Areas, 1962–64; Subst. Air Commodore, 1950; Air Vice-Marshal, 1953; Air Marshal, 1959; Air Chief Marshal, 1962. Comdr, US Legion of Merit, 1954; French Légion d'Honneur (Commandeur) and Croix de Guerre, 1958. *Recreation:* fishing. *Address:* River House, Rushall, Pewsey, Wilts SN9 6EN. *Club:* Army and Navy.
See also J. S Peel.

BARNETT, Guy; *see* Barnett, N. G.

BARNETT, Joseph Anthony, CBE 1983 (OBE 1975); Representative, British Council, Tokyo, since 1983; *b* 19 Dec. 1931; *s* of Joseph Edward Barnett and Helen Johnson; *m* 1960, Carolina Johnson Rice; one *s* one *d. Educ:* St Albans Sch.; Pembroke Coll., Cambridge (BA (Hons) English and Psychology); Edinburgh Univ. (Diploma in Applied Linguistics). Served Army, 1950–51 (2nd Lieut). Teaching, Aylesford House, St Albans, 1954–55; Unilever Ltd, 1955–58; apptd British Council, 1958; Asst Educn Officer, Dacca, Pakistan, 1958; trng at Sch. of Applied Linguistics, Edinburgh Univ., 1960; Educn Officer, Dacca, 1961; seconded to Inst. of Educn, London Univ., 1963; Head, English Language Teaching Inst., London, 1964; Dir of Studies, Regional Inst. of English, Bangalore, India, 1968; Representative, Ethiopia, 1971; Controller, English Language Teaching Div., 1975; Representative, Brazil, 1978–82. *Publications:* (jtly) Getting on in English, 1960; Success with English (language laboratory materials), Books 1–3, 1966–69. *Recreation:* sport (tennis, cricket, riding). *Address:* The Thatch, Stebbing Green, Dunmow, Essex. *T:* Stebbing 352. *Club:* Athenæum.

BARNETT, Kenneth Thomas, CB 1979; Director, Abbey Data Systems Ltd, since 1984; *b* 12 Jan. 1921; *yr s* of late Frederick Charles Barnett and Ethel Barnett (*née* Powell); *m* 1943, Emily May Lovering; one *d. Educ:* Howard Gardens High Sch., Cardiff. Entered Civil Service (Min. of Transport), 1937; Sea Transport Office, Port Said, 1951–54; Asst Sec., 1965; Under-Sec., Cabinet Office (on secondment), 1971–73; Under-Sec., DoE, 1970–76, Dep. Sec., 1976–80. *Recreations:* gardening, watching Rugby football. *Address:* The Stone House, Frith End, Bordon, Hants. *T:* Bordon 2856.

BARNETT, (Nicolas) Guy; MP (Lab) Greenwich, since July 1971; *b* 23 Aug. 1928; *s* of late B. G. Barnett; *m* 1967, Daphne Anne, *d* of Geoffrey William Hortin, JP; one *s* one *d. Educ:* Highgate; St Edmund Hall, Oxford. Teacher: Queen Elizabeth Gram. Sch., 1953–59; Friends Sch., Kamusinga, Kenya, 1960–61. Famine Relief Sec., Christian Council of Kenya, 1962; on staff VSO, 1966–69; Chief Educn Officer, Commonwealth Inst., 1969–71. Contested (Lab) NR Yorks (Scarborough and Whitby Div.), 1959; MP (Lab) S Dorset Div., Nov. 1962–Sept. 1964; PPS to Minister for Local Govt and Planning, 1974–75; Parly Under-Sec. of State, DoE, 1976–79; junior opposition spokesman on overseas development, 1980–81; on European and Community affairs, 1981–82; opposition spokesman on overseas development, 1982–83; Jt Sec., Parly Gp on Overseas Develt, 1984–; Member: Parly Select Cttee on Race Relations and Immigration, 1972–74; Public Accts Cttee, 1975; Exec. Cttee, UK Br., CPA, 1982– (Jt Hon. Treas., 1985–). Mem., European Parlt, 1975–76. Parly Adviser, Soc. of Civil Servants, 1973–76. Member:

Gen. Adv. Council of BBC, 1973–76; Bd, Christian Aid, 1984–. Chm., UK Chapter, Soc. for Internat. Develt, 1983–. Governor, Inst. of Develt Studies, 1984–; Trustee, Nat. Maritime Museum, 1974–76; Chm. of Trustees, Greenwich Fest., 1984–. *Publication:* By the Lake, 1964. *Recreations:* music, walking. *Address:* 32 Westcombe Park Road, SE3. *Club:* Royal Commonwealth Society.

BARNETT, Sir Oliver (Charles), Kt 1968; CBE 1954 (OBE 1946); QC 1956; *b* 7 Feb. 1907; *er s* of Charles Frederick Robert Barnett, 2nd Lieut Gloucestershire Regt (TA) (killed in action, 1915), and late Cicely Frances Barnett (*née* Cornish); *m* 1945, Joan, *o surv c* of Capt. W. H. Eve, 13th Hussars (killed in action, 1917), *o s* of late Rt Hon. Sir Harry Trelawney Eve, a Judge of the High Court. *Educ:* Eton. Called to Bar, Middle Temple, 1928; Bencher, Middle Temple, 1964, Oxford Circuit; Central Criminal Court Sessions; Dep. Chm., Somerset QS, 1967–71. Dir of Public Prosecutions Office, 1931; Legal Asst, Judge Advocate General's Office, 1934; Second Deputy Judge Advocate, 1937; First Deputy Judge Advocate, 1938; RAF, 1939–47 (OBE); Wing Comdr (RAFVR); Asst Judge Advocate Gen. (RAF), 1942–47; Asst Judge Advocate Gen. (Army and RAF), 1947–54; Deputy Judge Advocate Gen. (Army and RAF) BAOR, BTA and 2nd TAF, 1953–54; Vice Judge Advocate Gen., 1955–62; Judge Advocate Gen., 1963–68. *Address:* The Almonry, Stogumber, Taunton, Somerset. *T:* Stogumber 291. *Clubs:* Brooks's, Pratt's.

BARNETT, William Evans; QC 1984; barrister; a Recorder of the Crown Court, since 1981; *b* 10 March 1937; *s* of late Alec Barnett and Esmé (*née* Leon); *m* 1976, Lucinda Jane Gilbert, MA, ARCM, JP; two *s. Educ:* Repton; Keble Coll., Oxford (BA Jurisprudence, 1961; MA 1965). National Service, RCS, 1956–58. Called to the Bar, Inner Temple, 1962; Major Scholarship, Inner Temple, 1962. Mem., Personal Injuries Litigation Procedure Wkg Pty, 1976–78. *Recreations:* golf, photography, gardening. *Address:* Carleon, 55 Croham Manor Road, South Croydon, Surrey CR2 7BJ. *T:* 01–688 9559; 12 King's Bench Walk, Temple, EC4Y 7EL. *T:* 01–583 0811. *Club:* Addington Golf.

BARNEWALL, family name of **Baron Trimlestown.**

BARNEWALL, Sir Reginald Robert, 13th Bt, *cr* 1622; cattle breeder and orchardist at Mount Tamborine; *b* 1 Oct 1924; *o s* of Sir Reginald J. Barnewall, 12th Bt and of Jessie Ellen, *d* of John Fry; *S* father 1961; *m* 1st, 1946, Elsie Muriel (*d* 1962), *d* of Thomas Matthews-Frederick, Brisbane; three *d* (one *s* decd); 2nd, 1962, Maureen Ellen, *d* of William Joseph Daly, South Caulfield, Vic; one *s. Educ:* Xavier Coll., Melbourne. Served War of 1939–45, overseas with Australian Imperial Forces. Served with Citizen Military Forces Unit, Royal Australian Armoured Corps, 1948–56. Managing Dir, Southern Airlines Ltd of Melbourne, 1953–58; Operation Manager, Polynesian Airlines, Apia, Western Samoa, 1958–62; Managing Dir, Orchid Beach (Fraser Island) Pty Ltd, 1962–71; Dir, Island Airways Pty Ltd, Pialba, Qld, 1964–68; owner and operator, Coastal-Air Co. (Qld), 1971–76; Dir and Vice-Chm., J. Roy Stevens Pty Ltd, to 1975. *Heir: s* Peter Joseph Barnewall, *b* 26 Oct. 1963. *Address:* Mount Tamborine, Queensland 4272, Australia. *Clubs:* United Service (Brisbane); RSL (Surfers Paradise).

BARNSLEY, Alan Gabriel; *see* Fielding, Gabriel.

BARNSLEY, Thomas Edward, OBE 1975; FCA; a Managing Director, Tube Investments Ltd, 1974–82; *b* 1 Sept. 1919; *s* of Alfred E. Barnsley and Ada F. Nightingale; *m* 1947, Margaret Gwyneth Llewellin; one *s* one *d. Educ:* Wednesbury Boys' High Sch. ACMA. Friends' Ambulance Unit, 1940–45. Price Waterhouse Peat & Co., South America, 1948–49; Asst Sec., 1958–62, Group Financial Controller, 1962–65, Tube Investments Ltd; Chm. and Man. Dir, Raleigh Industries Ltd, 1968–74; Dir., HP Bulmer Holdings, 1980–. Chm., Nat. Industrial Cttee, Nat. Savings Movement, 1975–78. *Recreations:* gardening, cycling. *Address:* Old Rectory, Cossington, near Leicester LE7 8UU. *T:* Sileby 2623.

BARNSLEY, (William) Edward, CBE 1945; Designer and maker of furniture and building woodwork; Adviser in woodwork design, Loughborough Training College, 1938–65; Consultant in Furniture Design to Rural Industries Bureau, 1945–60; *b* 7 Feb. 1900; *s* of Sidney Howard Barnsley, Sapperton, Cirencester; *m* 1925, Tatiana, *d* of late Dr Harry Kellgren; one *s* one *d. Educ:* Bedales. Retrospective exhibition, 60 Years of Designing and Making, at Fine Arts Society Gallery, London, and then at Holburne of Menstrie Museum, Bath, 1982. Work includes Throne and Prie-Dieu for Archbishop, Canterbury Cathedral; practically all work still in private or public use; examples in V & A Museum and Melbourne Art Gall., Australia. *Address:* Froxfield, Petersfield, Hants. *T:* Hawkley 233.

BARNSTAPLE, Archdeacon of; *see* Herniman, Ven. R. G.

BARODA, Maharaja of; *see* Gaekwad, Lt-Col F. P.

BARON, Alexander; Writer; *b* 4 Dec. 1917; *s* of Barnet Baron and Fanny Levinson; *m* 1960, Delores Salzedo; one *s. Educ:* Hackney Downs Sch., London. Asst Editor, The Tribune, 1938–39. Served War of 1939–45, Army. Editor, New Theatre, 1946–49. *Publications: novels:* From the City, From the Plough, 1948; There's No Home, 1950; Rosie Hogarth, 1951; With Hope, Farewell, 1952; The Human Kind, 1953; The Golden Princess, 1954; Queen of the East, 1956; Seeing Life, 1958; The Lowlife, 1963; Strip Jack Naked, 1966; King Dido, 1969; The In-Between Time, 1971; Gentle Folk, 1976; Franco is Dying, 1977; also film scripts and television plays. *Address:* 30 Cranbourne Gardens, NW11. *T:* 01–455 8352. *Club:* PEN.

BARON, Colin; Director General, Research (General) and Assistant Chief Scientific Adviser (Research), Ministry of Defence, 1977–81; *b* 20 May 1921; *s* of John Henry Baron and Dorothy May (*née* Crumpler); *m* 1961, Anita Veronica Hale; one *s* one *d* by former marriage. *Educ:* Carlton Grammar Sch., Bradford; Univ. of Leeds (BSc Hons 1941, MSc 1947). Scientific Civil Service, 1941–81; Royal Radar Estabt, Malvern: radar trials and res., 1941–57; weapon systems assessment, 1957–66; RAE, Farnborough: Head, Weapons Res. Gp, 1966–70; Head, Avionics Dept, 1970–74; Head, Flt Systems Dept, 1974–76; Dir Gen., Weapons Res., MoD, 1976–77. *Publications:* contribs to Jl IEE and Jl Applied Physics. *Recreations:* gardening, badminton, economics. *Address:* Tanglewood, Vicarage Lane, The Bourne, Farnham, Surrey. *T:* Farnham 721433. *Club:* Civil Service.

BARR, A. W. Cleeve, CBE 1972; retired 1977; *b* 1910; *s* of Albert John Barr and Ellen (*née* Cleeve); *m* 1st, 1935, Edith M. Edwards, BA (*d* 1965); one *s* one *d* (and one *s* decd); 2nd, 1966, Mrs Mary W. Harley (*widow*). *Educ:* Borlase, Marlow; Liverpool Univ. Private offices (Charles Holden and Paul Mauger); Herts CC (schools) and LCC (housing). Dep. Housing Architect, LCC, 1956–57; Development Architect, Ministry of Education, 1957–58; Chief Architect, Min. of Housing and Local Govt, 1959–64. Dir, Nat. Building Agency, 1964–77 (Man. Dir, 1967–77); Dir, Nat. Building Agency Film Unit, 1977–80; Vice-Pres., UK Housing Trust, 1981–. Hon. Sec. RIBA, 1963–65. *Recreations:* ceramics, sculpture. *Address:* 72 Eastwick Road, Walton-on-Thames, Surrey KT12 5AR.

BARR, David; a Metropolitan Stipendiary Magistrate, since 1976; *b* Glasgow, 15 Oct. 1925; *s* of late Walter and of Betty Barr; *m* 1960, Ruth Weitzman; one *s* one *d. Educ:*

Haberdashers' Aske's Hampstead Sch.; Brookline High Sch., Boston, USA; Edinburgh Univ.; University Coll., London (LLB). Royal Navy, 1943–47. Solicitor, 1953; private practice, 1953–76 (Partner, Pritchard Englefield & Tobin). JP Inner London Area, 1963–76; Chm., Inner London Juvenile Panel, 1969–76; Dep. Chm., N Westminster PSD, 1968–76. Manager, Finnart House Sch., Weybridge, 1955–81, Trustee 1973–. *Recreations:* book collecting, bridge. *Address:* Highbury Corner Magistrates' Court, Holloway Road, N7. *Clubs:* Garrick, MCC.

BARR, Ian; Chairman, Post Office Scotland (formerly Scottish Postal Board), since 1984; Board Member, National Girobank Scotland, since 1984; *b* 6 April 1927; *s* of late Peter McAlpine Barr and Isobel Baillie; *m* 1951, Gertrud Karla, *d* of late August Otto Odefey, Schleswig-Holstein; two *d. Educ:* Boroughmuir High Sch., Edinburgh. Post Office: Asst Postal Controller, N Western Region, 1955; Inspector of Postal Services, 1957; Asst Controller, Planning, 1962; Principal, 1966. Mem., CS Selection Bd, 1966–71; Post Office: Asst Sec., 1971; Regional Dir, Eastern Region, 1976; Dir, Bldgs, Mechanisation and Transport, 1978; Dir, Estates Exec., 1981–84. Chairman: PO National Arts Cttee, 1976–; Scottish Cttee, Assoc. for Business Sponsorship of the Arts, 1986; CEPT (Bâtiments), 1982–86; Member: British Materials Handling Board, 1978–81; Scottish Council, CBI, 1984–. Convenor, Fest. and Performing Arts Cttee, Saltire Soc., 1986. *Recreations:* composing serial music, writing esoteric poetry, reading epistemology, practising solipsism. *Address:* West Port House, 102 West Port, Edinburgh EH3 9HS.

BARR, Rev. Prof. James, MA, BD, DD; FBA 1969; Regius Professor of Hebrew, Oxford University, and Student of Christ Church, since 1978; *b* 20 March 1924; *s* of Rev. Prof. Allan Barr, DD; *m* 1950, Jane J. S. Hepburn, MA; two *s* one *d. Educ:* Daniel Stewart's Coll., Edinburgh; Edinburgh Univ. (MA 1948, BD 1951); MA 1976, BD DD 1981, Oxon. Served War of 1939–45 as pilot in RNVR (Fleet Air Arm), 1942–45. Minister of Church of Scotland, Tiberias, Israel, 1951–53; Prof. of New Testament Literature and Exegesis, Presbyterian Coll., Montreal, 1953–55; Prof. of Old Testament Literature and Theology, Edinburgh Univ., 1955–61; Prof. of Old Testament Literature and Theology, Princeton Theological Seminary, 1961–65; Prof. of Semitic Languages and Literatures, Manchester Univ., 1965–76; Oriel Prof. of the Interpretation of Holy Scripture, and Fellow of Oriel Coll., Oxford Univ., 1976–78 (Hon. Fellow, 1980). Visiting Professor: Hebrew Univ., Jerusalem, 1973; Chicago Univ., 1975, 1981; Strasbourg Univ., 1975–76; Brown Univ., Providence, RI, 1985; Univ. of Otago, NZ, 1986; lectured in Princeton Univ., 1962–63; in Union Theol. Seminary, New York, 1963; Lectures: Currie, Austin Theol. Seminary, Texas, 1964; Cadbury, Birmingham Univ., 1969; Croall, Edinburgh Univ., 1970; Grinfield, on the Septuagint, Oxford Univ., 1974–78; Firth, Nottingham Univ., 1978; Sprunt, Richmond, Va, 1982; Sanderson, Ormond Coll., Melbourne, 1982; Faculty, Cardiff, 1986; Schweich, British Acad., 1986; Guggenheim Memorial Fellowship for study in biblical semantics, 1965. Mem., Inst. for Advanced Study, Princeton, NJ, 1985. Editor: Jl of Semitic Studies, 1965–76; Oxford Hebrew Dictionary, 1974–80. President: Soc. for OT Studies, 1973; British Assoc. for Jewish Studies, 1978. FRAS 1969. Hon. Fellow, SOAS, 1975. Hon. DD: Knox Coll., Toronto, 1964; Dubuque, 1974; St Andrews, 1974; Edinburgh, 1983; Hon. DTheol Univ. of South Africa, 1986; Hon. MA Manchester, 1969. Corresp. Mem., Göttingen Acad. of Sciences, 1976; Mem., Norwegian Acad. of Science and Letters, 1977; Hon. Mem., Soc. of Biblical Lit. (USA), 1983. *Publications:* The Semantics of Biblical Language, 1961; Biblical Words for Time, 1962; Old and New in Interpretation, 1966; Comparative Philology and the Text of the Old Testament, 1968; The Bible in the Modern World, 1973; Fundamentalism, 1977; The Typology of Literalism, 1979; Explorations in Theology 7: The Scope and Authority of the Bible, 1980; Holy Scripture: Canon, Authority, Criticism, 1983; Escaping from Fundamentalism, 1984; articles in Semitic and biblical journals. *Recreation:* bird watching. *Address:* 6 Fitzherbert Close, Iffley, Oxford OX4 4EN. *T:* Oxford 772741; 11 Résidence Galawa, Quai Nord-Est, 34340 Marseillan (Hérault), France.

BARR, Kenneth Glen; Sheriff of South Strathclyde, Dumfries and Galloway at Dumfries, since 1976; *b* 20 Jan. 1941; *o s* of Rev. Gavin Barr and Mrs Catherine McLellan Barr (*née* McGhie); *m* 1970, Susanne Crichton Keir. *Educ:* Ardrossan Acad.; Royal High Sch.; Edinburgh Univ. (MA, LLB). Admitted to Faculty of Advocates, 1964. *Address:* Sheriff Court House, Dumfries DG1 2AN.

BARR, Prof. Murray Llewellyn, OC (Canada) 1968; FRS 1972; Professor of Anatomy, University of Western Ontario, 1949–79, now Emeritus Professor; *b* 20 June 1908; Canadian; *m* 1934, Ruth Vivian King; three *s* one *d. Educ:* Univ. of Western Ontario (BA, MD, MSc). FRSC 1958; FRCP(C) 1964; FACP 1965; FRCOG 1972. Served War of 1939–45 as MO, RCAF (Wing Comdr). Univ. of Western Ontario: Instructor in Anatomy, 1936–45; Associate Prof. of Anatomy, 1945–49 (Chm., Dept of Anatomy, 1951–67). Hon. Degrees: LLD Queen's, 1963; LLD Toronto, 1964; Drmed Basel, 1966; LLD Alberta, 1967; LLD Dalhousie, 1968; LLD Saskatchewan, 1973; DSc Western Ontario, 1974. *Publications:* The Human Nervous System: an anatomical viewpoint, 1972, 4th edn (with J. A. Kiernan) 1983; A Century of Medicine at Western, 1977; numerous scientific papers. *Address:* 452 Old Wonderland Road, London, Ontario, Canada N6K 3R2. *T:* (519) 471–5618. *Club:* Harvey (London, Ont.).

BARR, His Honour Judge Reginald Alfred; a Circuit Judge (formerly Judge of County Courts), since 1970; *b* 21 Nov. 1920; *s* of Alfred Charles Barr; *m* 1946, Elaine, 2nd *d* of James William Charles O'Bala Morris, Llanstephan, Carmarthenshire. *Educ:* Christ's Hospital; Trinity Coll., Oxford (MA). Served War, 1941–46, Middle East and Burma. Called to Bar, Middle Temple, 1954; Standing Counsel to Registrar of Restrictive Trading Agreements, 1962–70. Mem. Review Bd for Govt Contracts, 1969–70. *Address:* 42 Bathurst Mews, Hyde Park, W2. *T:* 01–262 5731.

BARR, William Greig, DL; Rector, Exeter College, Oxford, 1972–82; *b* 10 June 1917; *s* of late William S. Barr, Glasgow; *m* 1954, Helen Georgopoulos; two *s. Educ:* Sedbergh Sch.; Magdalen Coll., Oxford. Stanhope Prize, 1938; 1st cl., Hon. Sch. of Modern History, 1939. Served War, 1939–45: Lt-Col., Royal Devon Yeomanry. Fellow of Exeter Coll., Oxford, 1945–72; Sub-Rector, 1947–54; Sen. Tutor, 1960–66; Hon. Fellow, 1982. Lectr in Modern History, Univ. of Oxford, 1949–72. Hon. Treas., Oxford Univ. Rugby Football Club, 1948–73; Jun. Proctor, 1951–52. A Rhodes Trustee, 1975–. Visiting Prof. of Hist., Univ. of South Carolina, 1968. Governor: Brighton Coll.; Sedbergh Sch.; Trustee, Uppingham Sch. DL Oxon 1974. *Address:* 24 Northmoor Road, Oxford. *T:* Oxford 58253.

BARR YOUNG, Gavin Neil; a Recorder of the Crown Court, since 1979; *b* 14 Aug. 1939; *s* of Dr James Barr Young and Elsie Barr Young (*née* Hodgkinson); *m* 1969, Barbara Elizabeth Breckon; two *d. Educ:* Loretto Sch., Musselburgh; Leeds Univ. (LLB). Called to the Bar, Gray's Inn, 1963; Member, North Eastern Circuit, 1964– (North Eastern Circuit Junior, 1968). *Recreations:* gardening, music, sailing. *Address:* 2 Park Square, Leeds LS1 2NE. *T:* Leeds 433277; 4 Paper Buildings, Temple, EC4. *T:* 01–353 8408.

BARRACK, William Sample, Jr; Senior Vice-President, Texaco Inc., NY, since 1983; *b* 26 July 1929; *s* of William Sample Barrack and Edna Mae Henderson; *m* 1953, Evelyn

Irene Ball; one *s* one *d*. *Educ:* Pittsburgh Univ. BSc (Engr) 1950. FInstPet 1981. Comdr, USN, 1950–53. Joined Texaco Inc., 1953; marketing and management positions in USA, 1953–67; in Europe, 1967–71; Vice-President: in NY, 1971–80; Marketing Dept, Europe, 1971–76; Producing Dept, Eastern Hemisphere, 1976–77; Personnel and Corporate Services Dept, 1977–80; Chm. and Chief Exec., Texaco Ltd, London, 1980–82. Director: Caltex Petroleum Corp.; Texaco Philanthropic Foundn. Governor, Foreign Policy Assoc.; Mem., US Naval War College Foundn; Trustee, Manhattanville College. *Address:* Texaco Inc., 2000 Westchester Avenue, White Plains, New York, NY 10650, USA. *Clubs:* Woodway Country; Ox Ridge Hunt; Ida Lewis Yacht; North Sea (Belgium).

BARRACLOUGH, Air Chief Marshal Sir John, KCB 1970 (CB 1969); CBE 1961; DFC 1942; AFC 1941; FRSA, FIPM, FBIM, MIPR; Gentleman Usher to the Sword of State, since 1980; Vice-Chairman, Commonwealth War Graves Commission, 1981–86 (Commissioner 1974–86); Vice-Chairman Editorial Board, NATO's Sixteen Nations, 1981–86 (Editorial Director, 1978–81); *b* 2 May 1918; *s* of late Horatio and Marguerite Maude Barraclough; *m* 1946, Maureen (*née* McCormack), niece of George Noble, Count Plunkett; one *d*. *Educ:* Cranbrook Sch. Service Artists' Rifles, 1935–38. Commissioned RAF, 1938. Air Vice-Marshal, 1964; Air Marshal, 1970; Air Chief Marshal, 1973. Served Near, Middle and Far East; first single-engined jet flight to S Africa, 1957. On staffs of Central Flying Sch. and IDC, 1949–54; Station Commander, RAF Biggin Hill and Middleton St George, 1954–58; Dir of Public Relations, Air Ministry, 1961–64; AOC No 19 Group, and NATO Air Comdr, Central Sub-Area, Eastern Atlantic Comd, 1964–67; Harvard Business Sch., 1967; AOA, Bomber Command, 1967–68; AOA, Strike Comd, 1968–70; Vice-Chief of Defence Staff, 1970–72; Air Secretary, 1972–74; Comdt, Royal Coll. of Defence Studies, 1974–76, retired. Hon. Air Cdre, No 3 (County of Devon) Maritime HQ Unit, 1979–, Hon. Inspector-Gen., 1984–, RAuxAF. Mem., RAF Training and Educn Adv. Bd, 1976–79; Vice Chm., Air League Council, 1977–81; Vice-Chm., British Export Finance Adv. Council, 1982–; Chm., RUSI Council, 1977–80, Vice-Pres., 1980–; Pres., West Devon Area, St John Ambulance, 1977–85. OStJ 1985. Past Pres., RAF Modern Pentathlon Assoc. *Publications:* (jtly) The Third World War, 1978; contrib. to The Third World War: The Untold Story, 1982; contribs to professional jls. *Recreations:* sailing, country pursuits. *Address:* c/o Barclays Bank, 11 Newgate Street, EC1. *Clubs:* Boodle's, Royal Air Force; Royal Western Yacht.

BARRACLOUGH, Sir Kenneth (James Priestley), Kt 1978; CBE 1967 (OBE 1945); TD; JP; Chief Metropolitan Magistrate 1975–78, retired; *b* 1907; *s* of Herbert Barraclough, Leeds; *m* 1931, Gladys Evelyn, *d* of Charles Henderson, Liverpool and Rio de Janeiro; two *s* one *d*. *Educ:* Oundle Sch.; Clare Coll., Cambridge. Barrister, Middle Temple, 1929 (Master of the Bench, 1975), North Eastern Circuit; Inns of Court Regt, TA, 1938; Col 1945. HQ, 21st Army Group (despatches). Metropolitan Magistrate, 1954; Dep. Chm. Appeals Cttee, Hampshire QS, 1957–62; Chm., HO Poisons Board, 1958–76. Member: Adv. Cttee on Drug Dependence, 1966–70; Adv. Council on the Misuse of Drugs, 1972–73; Medicines Commn, 1969–75. JP Hampshire, 1957. *Address:* 18 Fitzroy Road, Fleet, Hants.

BARRAN, Sir David Haven, Kt 1971; Chairman, Midland Bank Ltd, 1980–82 (Deputy Chairman, 1975–80); *b* 23 May 1912; *s* of Sir John Barran, 2nd Bt and Alice Margarita (*née* Parks); *m* 1944, Jane Lechmere Macaskie; four *s* three *d*. *Educ:* Winchester; Trinity Coll., Cambridge. BA 1934. Joined Asiatic Petroleum Co., 1934; served in Egypt, Palestine, Sudan, India, 1935–46. Pres., Asiatic Petroleum Corp., New York, 1958; Managing Dir, Royal Dutch/Shell Group, 1961–72; Chm., Shell Oil Co., 1970–72; Director: Shell Transport and Trading Co. Ltd, 1961–83 (Dep. Chm., 1964–67; Chm., 1967–72; Man. Dir, 1964–73); General Accident Insurance; BICC; Glaxo Hldgs. Chairman: CBI Cttee on Inflation Accounting, 1973–74; Adv. Cttee on Appt of Advertising Agents, 1975–78 (Mem., 1973–78); Ct of Governors, Administrative Staff Coll., 1971–76; Governor, Centre for Environmental Studies, 1972–75. Comdr, Order of Oranje Nassau, 1971; Comdr, Order of Merit, Fed. Repub. of Germany, 1980. *Recreations:* gardening, shooting, embroidery (Pres., Embroiderers' Guild, 1982–). *Address:* 36 Kensington Square, W8. *T:* 01–937 5664; Brent Eleigh Hall, Suffolk. *T:* Lavenham 247202. *Club:* River (New York).

BARRAN, Sir John (Napoleon Ruthven), 4th Bt *cr* 1895; Head of Information Technology, Central Office of Information, since 1985; *b* 14 Feb. 1934; *s* of Sir John Leighton Barran, 3rd Bt, and Hon. Alison Mary (*d* 1973), 3rd *d* of 9th Baron Ruthven, CB, CMG, DSO; *S* father, 1974; *m* 1965, Jane Margaret, *d* of Sir Stanley Hooker, CBE, FRS; one *s* one *d*. *Educ:* Heatherdown Sch., Ascot; Winchester Coll. National Service, 1952–54, Lieut, 5th Roy. Inniskilling Dragoon Guards; served Canal Zone. Asst Account Executive: Dorland Advertising Ltd, 1956–58; Masius & Fergusson Advertising Ltd, 1958–61; Account Executive, Ogilvy, Benson & Mather (New York) Inc., 1961–63; Overseas TV News Service, COI, 1964; First Sec. (Information), British High Commission, Ottawa, 1965–67; Central Office of Information: Home Documentary Film Section, 1967–72; Overseas TV and Film News Services, 1972–75; TV Commercials and Fillers Unit, 1975–78; Head of Viewdata Unit, 1978–85. Mem. Council, Videotex Industry Assoc. *Recreations:* entertaining, gardening. *Heir: s* John Ruthven Barran, *b* 10 Nov. 1971. *Address:* 17 St Leonard's Terrace, SW3. *T:* 01–730 2801; The Hermitage, East Bergholt, Suffolk.

BARRASS, Gordon Stephen; HM Diplomatic Service; Counsellor on secondment to Ministry of Defence, since 1984; *b* 5 Aug. 1940; *s* of James and Mary Barrass; *m* 1965, Alice Cecile Oberg (*d* 1984). *Educ:* Hertford Grammar Sch.; LSE (BSc (Econs)); SOAS (postgrad.). FCO, 1965–67; Chinese Language student, Hong Kong Univ., 1967–69; in Office of HM Chargé d'Affaires, Peking, 1970–72; Cultural Exchange Dept, FCO, 1972–74; UKMIS Geneva, 1974–78; Planning Staff, FCO, 1979–82; RCDS, 1983. *Recreations:* people, Chinese and Western art, opera, travel, books. *Address:* c/o Foreign and Commonwealth Office, SW1A 2AH. *T:* 01–218 3051. *Club:* Athenæum.

BARRATT, Francis Russell, CB 1975; Director, Amdahl (UK), since 1983; Member, Review Board for Government Contracts, since 1984; *b* 16 Nov. 1924; *s* of Frederick Russell Barratt; *m* 1st, 1949, Janet Mary Sherborne (marr. diss. 1978); three *s*; 2nd, 1979, Josephine Norah Harrison (*née* McCririck). *Educ:* Durban High Sch., SA; Clifton; University Coll., Oxford. War Service, 1943–46; Captain, Intelligence Corps, 1946. Asst Principal, HM Treasury, 1949; Principal, 1953; First Sec., UK High Commission, Karachi, 1956–58; Asst Sec., 1962, Under Sec., 1968, Dep. Sec., 1973–82, HM Treasury. *Recreations:* reading, golf, music. *Address:* 8 Arlington Avenue, N1. *T:* 01–359 1747. *Club:* Athenæum.

BARRATT, Gilbert Alexander; Master of the Supreme Court, Chancery Division, since 1980; *b* 1930; *s* of Arthur Walter Barratt and Frances Erskine Barratt (*née* Scott); *m* 1964, Fiona MacDermott; one *s* one *d*. *Educ:* Winchester; New Coll., Oxford. BA Modern History. Qualified as Solicitor, 1957; Partner: Stitt & Co., 1960–63; Thicknesse & Hull, 1963–67; Lee Bolton & Lee, 1967–78; Winckworth & Pemberton, 1978–80. *Recreation:* travel. *Address:* The Old School, Clungunford, Craven Arms, Shropshire. *Club:* Travellers'.

BARRATT, Herbert George Harold, OBE 1966; General Secretary, Confederation of Shipbuilding and Engineering Unions, 1957–70; *b* 12 Jan. 1905; *m* 1926; one *s* three *d*. *Educ:* Vicarage Street Church of England Sch., Nuneaton. Nuneaton Borough Councillor, 1945–47; Mem. Nat. Cttee AEU, 1943–48; Delegate to USSR, 1946. Chm. Nuneaton Labour Party, 1944–46; Coventry Dist. Cttee AEU, 1943–49; Shop Steward Convener, Daimler Motors, 1940–49; Appeals Board Assessor during war years; Nat. Insurance Tribunal Assessor; elected Nat. Organiser AEU, 1949–57. Formerly Member: Gas Adv. Council; Shipbuilding and Ship repairing Council; Nat. Adv. Council for the Motor Manufacturing Industry; Motor Industry Joint Labour Council; British Railways Productivity Council; Econ. Develt Cttee for Mech. Engrg Industry; Econ. Develt Cttee for Electrical Engrg Industry; Econ. Develt Cttee for Motor Manufacturing Industry; Industrial Training Board, Engrg; Industrial Training Board, Shipbuilding; British Productivity team to Swedish Shipyards, 1959; visited German Federal Railways, 1960; Exchange Leader Scheme visitor to USA, 1961; Vice-Chm., Sub-Cttee on Programme and Planning, Metal Trades Cttee, ILO, Geneva, 1965. *Recreation:* gardening. *Address:* 15 Danesmead, Grovehurst, near Sittingbourne, Kent.

BARRATT, Sir Lawrence (Arthur), (Sir Lawrie Barratt), Kt 1982; FCIS; Chairman and Managing Director, Barratt Developments plc, and subsidiary companies, since 1962; *b* Newcastle, 14 Nov. 1927; *m* 1st, 1951 (marr. diss. 1984); two *s*; 2nd, 1984, Mary Sheila (*née* Brierley). Founded Barratt Developments, as a private co., 1958. *Recreations:* golf, shooting, sailing. *Address:* Barratt Developments, Wingrove House, Ponteland Road, Newcastle upon Tyne NE5 3DP.

BARRATT, Michael Fieldhouse; communications consultant; broadcaster on radio and television; Chairman: Commercial Video Ltd, since 1981; Michael Barratt Ltd, since 1977; Director: United Media Finance Ltd, since 1981; Travel and Leisure Communications Ltd, since 1982; *b* 3 Jan. 1928; *s* of late Wallace Milner Barratt and Doris Barratt; *m* 1st, 1952, Joan Francesca Warner (marr. diss.); three *s* three *d*; 2nd, 1977, Dilys Jane Morgan; two *s* one *d*. *Educ:* Rossall and Paisley Grammar Sch. Entered journalism, Kemsley Newspapers, 1944; Editor, Nigerian Citizen, 1956; *television:* Reporter, Panorama, 1963; Presenter: 24 Hours, 1965–69; Nationwide, 1969–77; Songs of Praise, 1977–82; Reporting London, 1983–; *radio:* Question-Master, Gardeners' Question Time, 1973–79. Mem. Cttee, Yorks and Humberside Develt Assoc., 1975. Rector, Aberdeen Univ., 1973. Hon. LLD Aberdeen, 1975. FRHS. *Publications:* Michael Barratt, 1973; Michael Barratt's Down-to-Earth Gardening Book, 1974; Michael Barratt's Complete Gardening Book, 1977; Golf with Tony Jacklin, 1978. *Recreations:* golf, cricket, listening. *Address:* 108 Cromwell Road, SW7 4ES. *T:* 01–370 4391. *Club:* Lord's Taverners.

BARRATT, Prof. Michael George; Professor of Mathematics, Northwestern University, Illinois, since 1974; *b* 26 Jan. 1927; *e s* of George Bernard Barratt and Marjorie Holloway Barratt (*née* Oldham); *m* 1952, Jenepher Hudson; one *s* four *d*. *Educ:* Stationers' Company's Sch.; Magdalen Coll., Oxford. Junior Lecturer, Oxford Univ., 1950–52; Fellow, Magdalen Coll., Oxford, 1952–56; Lectr, Brasenose Coll., Oxford, 1955–59; Sen. Lectr and Reader, 1959–63, Prof. of Pure Maths, 1964–74, Manchester Univ. Vis. Prof., Chicago Univ., 1963–64. *Publications:* papers in mathematical jls. *Address:* Department of Mathematics, Northwestern University, Lunt Building, Evanston, Ill 60201, USA.

BARRATT, Richard Stanley, CBE 1981; QPM 1974; HM Inspector of Constabulary, since 1978; *b* 11 Aug. 1928; *s* of Richard Barratt and Mona Barratt; *m* 1952, Sarah Elizabeth Hale; one *s* two *d*. *Educ:* Saltley Grammar Sch., Birmingham. CBIM. Birmingham City Police (Constable to Chief Inspector), 1949–65; Dir, Home Office Crime Prevention Centre, Stafford, 1963; seconded to Home Office (Res. and Develt), 1964; Sen. Comd Course, Police Coll., 1964; Supt, Cheshire Constab., 1965, Chief Supt, 1966; Asst Chief Constable, Manchester City Police, 1967; Asst Chief Constable, Manchester and Salford Police, 1968, Dep. Chief Constable, 1972; Dep. Chief Constable, Greater Manchester Police, 1974; Chief Constable, S Yorks Police, 1975–78. OStJ 1978. *Recreations:* reading, gardening. *Address:* Loddon House, Basing View, Basingstoke, Hants RG21 2JT. *T:* Basingstoke 51106.

BARRATT-BOYES, Sir Brian (Gerald), KBE 1971 (CBE 1966); Surgeon-in-Charge, Cardio-Thoracic Surgical Unit, Greenlane Hospital, Auckland, since 1964; Hon. Senior Cardio Thoracic Surgeon, Mater Misericordiae Hospital, Auckland, since 1966; *b* 13 Jan. 1924; *s* of Gerald Cave Boyes and Edna Myrtle Boyes (*née* Barratt); *m* 1949, Norma Margaret Thompson (marr. diss. 1986); five *s*; *m* 1986, Sara Rose Monester. *Educ:* Wellington Coll.; Univ. of Otago. MB, ChB 1946; FRACS 1952; FACS 1960; ChM 1962. Lectr in Anatomy, Otago Univ. Med. Sch., 1947; House Surg. and Registrar, Wellington Hosp., 1948–50; Surgical Registrar and Pathology Registrar, Palmerston North Hosp., 1950–52; Fellow in Cardio-Thoracic Surgery, Mayo Clinic, USA, 1953–55; Nuffield Trav. Fellowship UK (Bristol Univ.), 1956; Sen. Cardio-Thoracic Surg., Greenlane Hosp., 1957. Hon. Prof. of Surgery, Auckland Univ., 1971. R. T. Hall Prize for Distinguished Cardiac Surgery in Austr. and NZ, 1966. FRSNZ 1970. Hon. FACS 1977; Hon. FRCS 1985. Hon. DSc, 1985. *Publications:* Heart Disease in Infancy: diagnosis and surgical treatment, 1973; (jtly) Cardiac Surgery, 1986; numerous in med. jls throughout the world. *Recreations:* farming, trout fishing. *Address:* Greenhills, Main Road, Waiwera, New Zealand; (consulting rooms) 102 Remuera Road, Auckland 5. *T:* 500176. *Club:* Northern (Auckland).

BARRAULT, Jean-Louis; Officer of the Legion of Honour; actor, director, producer; Director: Odéon-Théâtre de France, 1959–68; Théâtre des Nations, Paris, 1965–67, and since 1971; *b* Vésinet, France, 8 Sept. 1910; *m* Madeleine Renaud, *qv*. *Educ:* public sch., Paris; Collège Chaptal. Taught at Collège Chaptal, 1931; Atelier Dramatic Sch. and Theatre (schol.), 1931–35; formed experimental theatrical company. Served War of 1939–40. With Comédie-Française as producer-director, 1940–46. At instigation of French Govt formed company with Madeleine Renaud, Marigny Theatre. Has appeared at Venice; Edinburgh Festival, 1948, 1957 and 1985; St James's Theatre, London, 1951; Palace Theatre, London, 1956, etc.; produced Duel of Angels, Apollo, 1958; World Theatre Season, Aldwych, 1965, 1968; toured Western Europe, S America, Canada, and US. Films include: Les Beaux Jours, Hélène, Les Perles de la couronne, La Symphonie fantastique, Les Enfants du Paradis, D'Hommes à hommes, Versailles, Chappaqua, Le Puritain, La route de Varennes. *Publications:* Une Troupe et ses auteurs, 1950; Reflections on the Theatre (autobiography), 1951; Rabelais, 1971 (prod, Paris 1968–69, tours in Japan and USA, 1969, London 1971); Memories for Tomorrow: the memoirs of Jean-Louis Barrault, 1974; articles in theatrical publications. *Address:* 18 avenue du Président Wilson, 75116 Paris, France.

BARRE, Raymond; Chevalier de la Légion d'Honneur, Chevalier de l'Ordre National du Mérite agricole, Officier des Palmes Académiques; Grand Croix de l'Ordre National du Mérite, 1977; Député from Rhône, French National Assembly; *b* Saint-Denis, Réunion, 12 April 1924; *s* of René Barre and Charlotte Déramond; *m* 1954, Eve Hegedüs; two *s*. *Educ:* Lycée Leconte-de-Lisle, Saint-Denis-de-la-Réunion; Faculté de Droit, Paris; Institut d'Etudes Politiques, Paris. Professor at Faculté de Droit et des Sciences Economiques: Caen,

1950; Paris (Chair of Political Economy), 1963–; Professor at Institut d'Etudes Politiques, Paris, 1961–. Director of Cabinet of Mr J.-M. Jeanneney (Minister of Industry), 1959–62; Member: Cttee of Experts (Comité Lorain) studying financing of investments in France, 1963–64; Gen. Cttee on Economy and Financing of Fifth Plan, 1966; Vice-Chm., Commn of European Communities (responsible for Economic and Financial Affairs), 1967–72; Minister of Foreign Trade, Jan. 1976; Prime Minister, Aug. 1976–1981; elected to National Assembly, from Rhône, 1978. Mem. Gen. Council, Banque de France, 1973; Chm. Cttee for studying Housing Financing Reform, 1975–76. *Publication*: Economie Politique, 1955, and 1974. *Address*: 4–6 avenue Emile-Acollas, 75007 Paris, France.

BARRER, Prof. Richard Maling, FRS 1956; PhD Cantab; DSc (NZ); ScD Cantab; FRSC (FRIC 1939); Hon. ARCS, 1959; Senior Research Fellow, Imperial College of Science and Technology, since 1977; Professor of Physical Chemistry, Imperial College of Science and Technology, University of London, 1954–77, now Emeritus; Head of Department of Chemistry, 1955–76; *b* 16 June 1910; *s* of T. R. Barrer, 103 Renall Street, Masterton, New Zealand; *m* 1939, Helen Frances Yule, Invercargill, NZ; one *s* three *d*. *Educ*: Canterbury University Coll., NZ (MSc); Clare Coll., Cambridge (1851 Exhibition Scholar). PhD Cantab, 1935; DSc NZ, 1937; ScD Cantab, 1948. Major Research Student, 1935–37, Research Fellow, 1937–39, Clare Coll.; Head of Chemistry Dept, Technical Coll., Bradford, 1939–46; Reader in Chemistry, London Univ., 1946–49; Prof. of Chemistry, Aberdeen Univ., 1949–54. Dean, Royal Coll. of Science, 1964–66. Member Council: Faraday Soc., 1952–55; Chemical Soc., 1956–59, 1974–77; Royal Institute of Chemistry, 1961–64; Soc. of Chemical Industry, 1965–68. Governor, Chelsea Coll. of Sci. and Technol., 1960–81. Hon. ARCS 1959; Hon. FRSNZ 1965; Hon. DSc: Bradford, 1967; Aberdeen, 1983. *Publications*: Diffusion in and through Solids, 1941; Zeolites and Clay Minerals as Sorbents and Molecular Sieves, 1978; Hydrothermal Chemistry of Zeolites, 1982; research papers in British and foreign scientific journals. *Recreations*: tennis and interest in athletics. Full Blue for cross-country running, 1934. *Address*: Flossmoor, Orpington Road, Chislehurst, Kent. *Clubs*: Hawks (Cambridge); Achilles.

BARRETT, (Arthur) Michael, PhD; FIBiol; Vice-Chancellor, University of Buckingham, since Jan. 1985; *b* 1 April 1932; *s* of Arthur Cowley Barrett and late Doris Annie Barrett; *m* 1960, Patricia Lillian Harris; one *s* one *d*. *Educ*: Cheltenham Grammar Sch.; Sch. of Pharmacy, Univ. of London (BPharm 1st Cl. Hons, PhD). Cleveland, Ohio, Rotary Foundn Fellow, Western Reserve Univ., 1956–57; Asst Lectr in Pharmacology, 1958–59, Lectr, 1959–61, Sch. of Pharmacy, London Univ.; Res. Pharmacologist, Pharmaceuticals Div., ICI Ltd, 1961–70; Head of Pharmacology, Organon Internat. BV, 1970; Prof. and Hd of Dept of Pharmacology, 1970–84, Pro Vice Chancellor, 1979–81, Leeds Univ. Chm., Leeds Eastern Health Authority, 1981–84; Vice-Chm., Kirklees AHA, 1978–79 (Mem., 1974–79); Mem., Gen. Sales List Cttee, Medicines Commn, DHSS, 1971–74; Assessor to Inquiry on LD50 Test, Home Office, 1977–79. Sec. Gen., Internat. Union for Pharmacology, 1981–; Member: British Pharmacol Soc., 1963– (Meetings Sec., 1977–79; Gen. Sec., 1980–82); Soc. for Endocrinology, 1959–. Mem. Bd Governors, RAC, Cirencester, 1985; Chm. Trustees, Lorch Foundn, 1986. FIBiol 1984; FRSA 1985. *Publications*: The Pharmacology of Beta-adrenoceptor blockade, 1975; papers in pharmacol and endocrinol jls. *Recreations*: models, gardening, music. *Address*: Willowbank, University of Buckingham, Buckingham MK18 1EG. *T*: Buckingham 814080.

BARRETT, Rev. Prof. Charles Kingsley, DD; FBA 1961; Professor of Divinity, Durham University, 1958–82; *b* 4 May 1917; *s* of Rev. F. Barrett and Clara (*née* Seed); *m* 1944, Margaret E. Heap, Calverley, Yorks; one *s* one *d*. *Educ*: Shebbear Coll.; Pembroke Coll., Cambridge; Wesley House, Cambridge. DD Cantab, 1956. Asst Tutor, Wesley Coll., Headingley, 1942; Methodist Minister, Darlington, 1943; Lecturer in Theology, Durham Univ., 1945. Lectures: Hewett, USA, 1961; Shaffer, Yale, 1965; Delitzsch, Münster, 1967; Cato, Australia, 1969; Tate-Willson, Dallas, 1975; McMartin, Ottawa, 1976; Sanderson, Melbourne, and West-Watson, Christchurch, NZ, 1983; Alexander Robertson Lectr, Univ. of Glasgow, 1984; Woodruff Vis. Prof., Emory Univ., Atlanta, 1986. Vice-Pres., British and Foreign Bible Soc.; Pres., Studiorum Novi Testamenti Societas, 1973; Hon. Mem., Soc. of Biblical Literature, USA. Hon. DD: Hull, 1970; Aberdeen, 1972; Hon. DrTheol Hamburg, 1981; Burkitt Medal for Biblical Studies, 1966. *Publications*: The Holy Spirit and the Gospel Tradition, 1947; The Gospel according to St John, 1955, 2nd edn 1978; The New Testament Background: Selected Documents, 1956; Biblical Preaching and Biblical Scholarship, 1957; The Epistle to the Romans, 1957; Westcott as Commentator, 1959; Yesterday, Today and Forever: The New Testament Problem, 1959; Luke the Historian in Recent Study, 1961; From First Adam to Last, 1962; The Pastoral Epistles, 1963; Reading Through Romans, 1963; History and Faith: the Story of the Passion, 1967; Jesus and the Gospel Tradition, 1967; The First Epistle to the Corinthians, 1968; The Signs of an Apostle, 1970; Das Johannesevangelium und das Judentum, 1970; The Prologue of St John's Gospel, 1971; New Testament Essays, 1972; The Second Epistle to the Corinthians, 1973; The Fourth Gospel and Judaism, 1975; (ed) Donum Gentilicium, 1978; Essays on Paul, 1982; Essays on John, 1982; Freedom and Obligation, 1985; Church, Ministry and Sacraments in the New Testament, 1985; contributions to learned journals and symposia in Britain, the Continent, Australia and USA. *Address*: 8 Princes Street, Durham DH1 4RP. *T*: Durham 61340.

BARRETT, David; broadcaster, writer and political commentator on national and provincial media, since 1985; Premier and Minister of Finance, Province of British Columbia, Canada, 1972–75; *b* Vancouver, 2 Oct. 1930; *s* of Samuel Barrett and Rose (*née* Hyatt); father a business man in East Vancouver, after war service; *m* 1953, Shirley Hackman, West Vancouver; two *s* one *d*. *Educ*: Britannia High Sch., Vancouver; Seattle Univ.; St Louis Univ. BA(Phil) Seattle, 1953; Master of Social Work, St Louis, 1956. Personnel and Staff Trng Officer, Haney Correctional Inst., 1957–59; also gained experience in a variety of jobs. Elected: MLA for Dewdney, Sept. 1960 and 1963; to re-distributed riding of Coquitlam 1966, 1969 and 1972; Vancouver East, by-election 1976, 1979; New Democratic Party Leader, June 1970–84 (first Social Democratic Govt in history of Province); Leader, Official Opposition, British Columbia, 1970–72 and 1975–84. Dr of Laws, *hc*, St Louis Univ., 1974; Hon. DPhil Simon Fraser Univ., BC, 1986. *Address*: 1179 Monro Street, Victoria, British Columbia, Canada.

BARRETT, Lt-Gen. Sir David William S.; *see* Scott-Barrett.

BARRETT, Denis Everett; a Special Commissioner of Income Tax, 1967–71; *b* 7 Jan. 1911; *o s* of late Walter Everett Barrett, London, and Julia Barrett (*née* MacCarthy), Cork; *m* 1947, Eilish (*d* 1974), *y d* of late William and Margaret Phelan, Co. Laois; one *s* two *d*. *Educ*: Wimbledon Coll.; London Univ. Entered Inland Revenue Dept, 1930; Asst Sec., 1948. *Address*: c/o The Pump House, Bone Mill Lane, Enborne, Newbury, Berks RG15 0EU.

BARRETT, Sir Dennis Charles T.; *see* Titchener-Barrett.

BARRETT, Edmond Fox, OBE 1981; HM Diplomatic Service; Consul-General, Bilbao, since 1981; *b* 24 Aug. 1928; *s* of late Edmond Henry Barrett and Ellen Mary Barrett (*née* Fox); *m* 1959, Catherine Wendy Howard (*née* Slater). *Educ*: St Brendan's Coll., Bristol. Dominions Office, 1946; Royal Navy, 1947–49; CRO, 1949–50; Karachi, 1950–52;

New Delhi, 1952–54; CRO, 1954–55; Admiralty, 1955–60; Foreign Office, 1960–63; Bucharest, 1963–65; Rio de Janeiro, 1965–68; Boston, 1968–70; Mexico City, 1971–73; FCO, 1973–76; Santo Domingo, 1976–79; Tehran, 1979–81. *Recreations*: reading, golf, gardening. *Address*: c/o Foreign and Commonwealth Office, SW1. *Club*: Royal Commonwealth Society.

BARRETT, Ernest; Chairman: Henry Barrett & Sons Ltd, since 1982 (Joint Managing Director, 1968–85); Steel Stockholding Division, Henry Barrett & Sons Ltd, 1967–85; Henry Lindsay Ltd, since 1974; *b* 8 April 1917; *s* of Ernest Barrett and Marian Conyers; *m* 1940, Eileen Maria Peel; one *d*. *Educ*: Charterhouse. Joined Henry Barrett & Sons Ltd, Bradford, 1934. Served War, RA, and commissioned, 1940; served in Mediterranean Theatre, with 1st Army, 1943–46 (despatches, 1944); Major 1945. Apptd Dir, Henry Barrett & Sons Ltd, 1946. Pres., Nat. Assoc. of Steel Stockholders, 1977–79 (Chm., Yorks Assoc., 1964–66; Vice-Pres., 1975–77); Pres., Engineering Industries Assoc., 1971 (Chm. Yorks Region, 1960–65; Vice-Pres. of Assoc., 1965–71). *Recreations*: badminton, gardening. *Address*: West Ghyll, Victoria Avenue, Ilkley, W Yorks. *T*: Ilkley 609294.

BARRETT, Jack Wheeler, CBE 1971; PhD; FEng; CChem; FIC; Chairman, Cole Group plc, 1979–86 (Director, 1978); *b* 13 June 1912; *s* of John Samuel Barrett, Cheltenham; *m* 1935, Muriel Audley Read; two *s* two *d*. *Educ*: Cheltenham Grammar Sch.; Imperial Coll., Univ. of London. BSc, PhD, CChem, FRSC, FEng, FIChemE. Chief Chemist, London Essence Co. Ltd, 1936–41; joined Monsanto Chemicals Ltd, 1941; Dir of Research, 1955–71; Dir, Monsanto Ltd, 1955–78; Chm., Info-line Ltd, 1976–80. President: IChemE, 1971–72; Chem. Soc., 1974–75; IInfSc, 1976–79; ICSU Abstracting Bd, 1974–77; Chm., Chemical Divl Council, BSI, 1973–79; Mem., British Library Bd, 1973–79. *Publications*: articles in Jl Chem. Soc., Chemistry and Industry, Jl ASLIB, Chemistry in Britain. *Recreation*: gardening. *Address*: 195 Latymer Court, Hammersmith Road, W6 7JQ. *T*: 01–748 7080; West Manor House, Bourton-on-the-Water, Cheltenham, Glos GL54 2AP. *T*: Bourton-on-the-Water 20296. *Club*: Athenæum.

BARRETT, Prof. Michael; *see* Barrett, Prof. A. M.

BARRETT, Stephen Jeremy, CMG 1982; HM Diplomatic Service; Ambassador to Czechoslovakia, since 1985; *b* 4 Dec. 1931; *s* of late W. P. Barrett and Dorothy Barrett; *m* 1958, Alison Mary Irvine; three *s*. *Educ*: Westminster Sch.; Christ Church, Oxford (MA). FO, 1955–57; 3rd, later 2nd Sec., Political Office with Middle East Forces, Cyprus, 1957–59; Berlin, 1959–62; 1st Sec., FO, 1962–65; Head of Chancery, Helsinki, 1965–68; 1st Sec., FCO, 1968–72; Counsellor and Head of Chancery, Prague, 1972–74; Head of SW European Dept, FCO, later Principal Private Sec. to Foreign and Commonwealth Sec., 1975; Head of Science and Technology Dept, FCO, 1976–77; Fellow, Center for Internat. Affairs, Harvard, 1977–78; Counsellor, Ankara, 1978–81; Head of British Interests Section, Tehran, 1981; Asst Under-Sec. of State, FCO, 1981–84. *Recreations*: climbing small mountains, reading. *Address*: c/o Foreign and Commonwealth Office, SW1. *Clubs*: Travellers', Keene Valley Country.

BARRETT, William Spencer, FBA 1965; Fellow of Keble College, Oxford, 1952–81 and Tutor in Classics, 1939–81; Hon. Fellow, 1981; Reader in Greek Literature, University of Oxford, 1966–81; *b* 29 May 1914; *o s* of William Barrett and Sarah Jessie Barrett (*née* Robbins); *m* 1939, Georgina Margaret Elizabeth, *e d* of William and Alma Georgina Annie Hill; one *s* one *d*. *Educ*: Derby Sch; Christ Church, Oxford (Scholar). Ireland and Craven Schol. 1933; 1st Class Classical Hon. Mods, 1934; Gaisford Prize for Greek Verse, 1934; de Paravicini Schol., 1934; 1st Class Lit. Hum., 1937; Derby Schol., 1937; Charles Oldham Prize, 1938. Lectr, Christ Church, Oxford, 1938–39; Lectr, Keble Coll. 1939–52; Librarian, 1946–66; Univ. Lectr in Greek Literature, 1947–66; Sub Warden, Keble Coll., 1968–76. Temp. Civilian Officer, Admty (Naval Intelligence Div.), 1942–45. *Publications*: (ed) Euripides, Hippolytos, 1964; Sophocles, Niobe (in Papyrus Fragments of Sophocles, ed R. Carden), 1974; articles in learned jls. *Address*: 8 The Avenue, Clifton, Bristol BS8 3HE. *T*: Bristol 743321.

BARRETT-LENNARD, Rev. Sir Hugh (Dacre), 6th Bt *cr* 1801; Priest, London Oratory; *b* 27 June 1917; *s* of Sir Fiennes Cecil Arthur Barrett-Lennard (*d* 1963) and Winifrede Mignon (*d* 1969), *d* of Alfred Berlyn; *S* cousin, 1977. *Educ*: Radley College, Berks; Pontifical Beda College, Rome. Teaching, 1936. Served War of 1939–45, NW Europe (despatches); enlisted London Scottish, Jan. 1940; commissioned 2nd Lt, Oct. 1940; Captain Essex Regt, 1945. Entered Brompton Oratory, 1946; ordained Priest in Rome, 1950. *Recreations*: on Isle of Eigg, Hebrides. *Heir*: cousin Richard Fynes Barrett-Lennard, *b* 6 April 1941. *Address*: The Oratory, South Kensington, SW7 2RW. *T*: 01–589 4811.

BARRIE, Derek Stiven Maxwelton, OBE 1969 (MBE 1945); FCIT; *b* 8 Aug. 1907; *s* of John Stiven Carruthers Barrie and Dorothea Barrie; *m* 1936, Kathleen Myrra Collins; one *s* one *d*. *Educ*: Apsley House, Clifton; Tonbridge Sch. London and provincial journalism (Daily Graphic, Allied Newspapers, etc), reporter and sub-editor, 1924–32; joined LMS Railway, 1932; on return from war service, rejoined LMS, 1946; PRO Railway Exec., 1948; Chief PRO British Transport Commn, 1956; Asst Sec.-Gen., BTC, 1958; Asst Gen. Man., York, 1961; Chm., British Railways (Eastern) Bd, and Gen. Man., British Railways Eastern Region, 1968–70. Mem. Council, Inst. of Transport, 1968. Served with Royal Engineers, 1941–46; Hon. Col 74 Movement Control Regt, RE and RCT, 1961–67; Major, Engr. and Rly Staff Corps (T & AVR), 1967, Lt-Col 1968–73. Bronze Star Medal (US), 1945. OStJ 1968. *Publications*: A Regional History of the Railways of Great Britain, vol. 12, South Wales, 1980; numerous railway historical books and monographs; contribs various transport jls, 1928–. *Recreations*: railways, authorship, country life. *Address*: 1 Norman Close, Castlegate, Pickering, N Yorks YO18 7AZ. *T*: Pickering 73580.

BARRIE, Herbert, MD, FRCP; Consultant Paediatrician, Charing Cross Hospital, since 1966; Physician in charge, since 1984; *b* 9 Oct. 1927; *m* 1963, Dinah Barrie, MB, BS, FRCPath; one *s* one *d*. *Educ*: Wallington County Grammar School; University College and Med. Sch., London. MB, BS 1950; MD 1952; MRCP 1957, FRCP 1972. Registrar, Hosp. for Sick Children, Gt Ormond St, 1955–57; Research Fellow, Harvard Univ., Children's Med. Center, 1957; Sen. Registrar and Sen. Lectr, Dept of Paediatrics, St Thomas' Hosp., 1959–65; Consultant Paediatrician: Moor House Sch. for Speech Disorders, 1968–74; St Teresa's Hosp., Wimbledon; Parkside Hosp., Wimbledon; New Victoria Hosp., Kingston. Vis. Prof., Downstate Univ. Med. Center, NY, 1976. Member: London Med. Soc.; British Paediatric Assoc.; British Assoc. of Perinatal Paediatrics; Neonatal Soc.; Perinatal Visiting Club; BMA. Member, Editorial Board: Midwife; Health Visitor and Community Nurse; Maternity and Mothercraft. *Publications*: numerous contribs to books and jls on paediatric and neonatal topics, esp. resuscitation of newborn and neonatal special care. *Recreations*: tennis, writing, wishful thinking. *Address*: 3 Burghley Avenue, New Malden, Surrey KT3 4SW. *T*: 01–942 2836.

BARRIE, Sir Walter, Kt 1958; Chairman of Lloyd's, 1953, 1954, 1957, 1958; Director: Jos. W. Hobbs Ltd; Westminster Bank Ltd, 1958–68; Ulster Bank, 1964–72; *b* 31 May 1901; *y s* of late Right Hon. H. T. Barrie, MP, DL, JP, and late Katie Barrie; *m* 1927,

Noele Margaret (*d* 1968), *d* of G. J. Furness, JP; one *s* (and one *s* decd). *Educ:* Coleraine; Merchiston Castle, Edinburgh; Gonville and Caius Coll., Cambridge. Entered Lloyd's, 1926; first served on Cttee of Lloyd's, 1946; Deputy-Chm. of Lloyd's, 1951, 1952. Lloyd's Gold Medal, 1958. Pres., Insurance Inst. of London, 1955–56; Vice-Pres., Chartered Insurance Inst., 1957, 1958, 1959, Dep. Pres. 1961. Pres. 1962–63. *Recreation:* golf. *Address:* Compton Elms, Pinkneys Green, Maidenhead, Berks SL6 6NR. *T:* Maidenhead 27151.

BARRINGTON, family name of **Viscount Barrington.**

BARRINGTON, 11th Viscount *cr* 1720; **Patrick William Daines Barrington;** Baron Barrington, 1720; Baron Shute (UK) 1880 (sits as Baron Shute); *b* 29 Oct. 1908; *s* of Hon. Walter Bernard Louis Barrington (*d* 1959); *S* uncle, 1960. *Educ:* Eton; Magdalen Coll., Oxford (BA). Called to the Bar, Inner Temple, 1940. Late 2nd Lieut, RA. Formerly Hon. Attaché, HBM's Embassy, Berlin, and sometime in Foreign Office. *Heir:* none.

BARRINGTON, Sir Alexander (Fitzwilliam Croker), 7th Bt *cr* 1831; retired; *b* 19 Nov. 1909; *s* of Sir Charles Burton Barrington, 5th Bt, and Mary Rose (*d* 1943), *d* of Sir Henry Hickman Bacon, 10th and 11th Bt; *S* brother, 1980. *Educ:* Castle Park, Dalkey, Co. Dublin; Shrewsbury School; Christ Church, Oxford. Director of various private companies, 1932–39. Served in Army as Captain, Intelligence Corps, 1939–42; prisoner of war, Singapore and Thailand, 1942–45. Book publishers' executive, editor and production manager, 1946–72. *Recreations:* gardening, travel, Viennese music. *Heir: cousin* John William Barrington, Major retd, Royal Irish Fusiliers [*b* 20 Oct. 1917; *m* 1948, Annie Wetten (decd); two *s* one *d*]. *Address:* 11 Tedworth Square, SW3 4DU.

BARRINGTON, Sir Kenneth (Charles Peto), Kt 1973; *b* 27 Aug. 1911; *er s* of C. W. Barrington; *m* 1938, Eileen Doris Stone; one *d*. *Educ:* St Paul's School. FCA. Joined Morgan Grenfell & Co. Ltd, Merchant Bankers, 1929; Naval Service, 1939–46; Chartered Accountant, 1952; Director: Morgan Grenfell & Co. Ltd, 1961–76; Morgan Grenfell Holdings Ltd, 1971–76 (Mem., Internat. Adv. Council, 1980–83); English & New York Trust plc, 1967–84; Ultramar plc, 1970–83.

BARRINGTON, Nicholas John, CMG 1982; CVO 1975; HM Diplomatic Service; Assistant Under-Secretary of State (Public Departments), Foreign and Commonwealth Office, since 1984; *b* 23 July 1934; *s* of late Eric Alan Barrington and Mildred (*née* Bill). *Educ:* Repton; Clare Coll., Cambridge (MA 1957). HM Forces, RA, 1952–54. Joined Diplomatic Service, 1957; Tehran (language student), 1958; Oriental Sec., Kabul, 1959; FO, 1961; 2nd Sec., UK Delegn to European Communities, Brussels, 1963; 1st Sec., Rawalpindi, 1965; FO, 1967; Private Sec. to Permanent Under Sec., Commonwealth Office, April 1968; Asst Private Sec. to Foreign and Commonwealth Sec., Oct. 1968; Head of Chancery, Tokyo, 1972–75 (promoted Counsellor and for a period apptd Chargé d'Affaires, Hanoi, 1973); Head of Guidance and Information Policy (subsequently Information Policy) Dept, FCO, 1976–78; Counsellor, Cairo, 1978–81; Minister and Head of British Interests Section, Tehran, 1981–83; Supernumary Ambassador attached to UK Mission to UN, NY, for Gen. Assembly, autumn 1983; Co-ordinator for London Econ. Summit, 1984. FRSA 1984. 3rd Cl., Order of the Sacred Treasure, Japan, 1975. *Recreations:* theatre, drawing, tennis, prosopography. *Address:* c/o Foreign and Commonwealth Office, King Charles Street, SW1; 33 Gilmerton Court, Trumpington, Cambridge. *Clubs:* Athenæum, Royal Commonwealth Society.

BARRINGTON-WARD, Rt. Rev. Simon; *see* Coventry, Bishop of.

BARRITT, Sir David (Thurlow), Kt 1969; BSc, FEng, FIChemE; Chairman, Cammell Laird, 1971–79; *b* 17 Oct. 1903; *er s* of late David Webster Barritt and Rachel Barritt; *m* 1931, Hilda Marshall Creyke; one *s*. *Educ:* High Sch., Newcastle-under-Lyme, Staffs; N Staffs Polytechnic. Chairman: Simon Engineering Ltd, 1963–70; Twyfords Holdings Ltd, 1969–71; Davy International, 1970–73. Chm. Govs, The Newcastle-under-Lyme Endowed Schs, Newcastle, Staffs, 1962–72. SFInstE; Vice-Pres., IChemE 1974. MUniv Keele, 1981. *Publications:* papers in technical jls. *Recreations:* golf, music, gardening, photography. *Address:* 7 Castle Rise, Prestbury, Cheshire SK10 4UR. *T:* Prestbury 829716.

BARRITT, Rev. Dr Gordon Emerson, OBE 1979; Principal, National Children's Home, 1969–86; President of the Methodist Conference, 1984–85; *b* 30 Sept. 1920; *s* of Norman and Doris Barritt; *m* 1947, Joan Mary Alway; two *s* one *d*. *Educ:* William Hulme's Grammar Sch., Manchester; Manchester Univ.; Cambridge Univ. (Wesley House and Fitzwilliam Coll.). Served War, RAF, 1942–45 (despatches). Methodist Minister: Kempston Methodist Church, Bedford, 1947–52; Westlands Methodist Church, Newcastle-under-Lyme, 1952–57; Chaplain, Univ. of Keele, 1953–57. Treasurer, 1969–86, Chm., 1970–72, Nat. Council of Voluntary Child Care Organisations; Member: Home Office Adv. Council on Child Care, 1968–71; Nat. Children's Bureau; Brit. Assoc. of Social Workers; Internat. Union for Child Welfare; UK and Internat. Cttees; Chm., Social Studies Cttee, Selly Oak Colls, Birmingham. DUniv Keele, 1985. *Publications:* The Edgworth Story, 1972; (ed) Many Pieces—One Aim, 1975; (ed) Family Life, 1979; Residential Care, 1979; contrib.: Caring for Children, 1969; Giving Our Best, 1982. *Recreations:* music, do-it-yourself. *Address:* 10 Cadogan Gardens, Grange Park, N21 1ER. *T:* 01–360 8687.

BARRON, Derek Donald; Chairman and Chief Executive, Ford Motor Co. Ltd, since 1986; *b* 7 June 1929; *s* of Donald Frederick James Barron and Hettie Barbara Barron; *m* 1963, Rosemary Ingrid Brian; two *s*. *Educ:* Beckenham Grammar School; University College London (Intermediate LLB). Joined Ford Motor Co. Sales, 1951; Tractor Group, 1961; Tractor Manager, Ford Italiana 1963; Marketing Associate, Ford Motor Co. USA, 1970; Gen. Sales Manager, Overseas Markets, 1971; Man. Dir, Ford Italiana, 1973; Group Dir, Southern European Sales, Ford of Europe, 1977; Sales and Marketing Dir, Ford Brazil, 1979; Vice-Pres., Ford Motor de Venezuela, 1982; Dir-Vice-Pres., Operations, Ford Brazil, 1985. *Recreation:* sailing. *Address:* c/o Ford Motor Co. Ltd, Eagle Way, Brentwood, Essex CM13 3BW. *T:* Brentwood 253000.

BARRON, Sir Donald (James), Kt 1972; DL; Chairman, Midland Bank plc, 1982–April 1987 (Director, since 1972; Vice-Chairman, 1981–82); *b* 17 March 1921; *o s* of Albert Gibson Barron and Elizabeth Macdonald, Edinburgh; *m* 1956, Gillian Mary, *o d* of John Saville, York; three *s* two *d*. *Educ:* George Heriot's Sch., Edinburgh; Edinburgh Univ. (BCom). Member, Inst. Chartered Accountants of Scotland. Joined Rowntree Mackintosh Ltd, 1952; Dir, 1961; Vice-Chm., 1965; Chm., 1966–81. Dep. Chm., CLCB, 1983–85; Chm., Cttee of London and Scottish Bankers, 1985–. Director: Investors in Industry Gp plc, 1980–; Canada Life Assurance Co. of GB Ltd, 1980–; Canada Life Unit Trust Managers Ltd, 1980–; Canada Life Assurance Co., Toronto, 1980–; Clydesdale Bank, 1986–. Dir, BIM Foundn, 1977–80 and Mem. Council, BIM, 1978–80; Trustee, Joseph Rowntree Memorial Trust, 1966–73, 1975– (Chm., 1981–); Treasurer, 1966–72, a Pro-Chancellor, 1982–, York Univ.; Member: Council of CBI, 1966–81 (Chm., CBI Educn Foundn, 1981–85); SSRC, 1971–72; UGC, 1972–81; Council, PSI, 1978–; Council, Inst. of Chartered Accountants of Scotland, 1980–81; NEDC, 1983–85. Governor, London Business Sch., 1982. DL N Yorks (formerly WR Yorks and City of York), 1971. Hon. doctorates: Loughborough, 1982; Heriot-Watt, 1983; CNAA, 1983; Edinburgh, 1984; Nottingham 1985. *Recreations:* golf, tennis, gardening. *Address:* Greenfield, Sim Balk Lane, Bishopthorpe, York YO2 1QH. *T:* York 705675. *Clubs:* Athenæum; Yorkshire (York).

BARRON, Douglas Shield, CIE 1945; Chairman, Godfrey Phillips, India, Ltd, retired 1973; *b* 18 March 1904; *s* of Thomas Barron; *m* 1934, Doris Katherine (*d* 1970), *o d* of late Henry Deakin; no *c*. *Educ:* Holgate Grammar Sch.; Corpus Christi Coll., Cambridge. Joined Indian Civil Service, 1926; retired, 1948. *Address:* Sundial Cottage, Cross Lanes, Mockbeggar, Ringwood, Hants BH24 3NQ. *T:* Ringwood 3885. *Club:* Bombay Yacht.

BARRON, Iann Marchant; Chief Strategic Officer, Inmos International plc, since 1984 (Director since 1978); Managing Director, Inmos Ltd, since 1981; *b* 16 June 1936; *s* of William A. Barron and Lilian E. Barron; *m* 1961, Jacqueline R. Almond; two *s* two *d*. *Educ:* University College School; Christ's College, Cambridge (exhibitioner; MA). Elliott Automation, 1961–65; Managing Director: Computer Technology Ltd, 1965–72; Microcomputer Analysis Ltd, 1973–78. Vis. Prof., Westfield Coll., London, 1976–78; Vis. Indust. Prof., Bristol Univ., 1985–; Vis. Fellow: QMC, 1976; Science Policy Res. Unit, 1977–78. *Publications:* The Future with Microelectronics (with Ray Curnow), 1977; technical papers. *Address:* Barrow Court, Barrow Gurney, Avon.

BARRON, Prof. John Penrose, MA, DPhil, FSA; Director of Institute of Classical Studies, University of London, since 1984, and Professor of Greek Language and Literature, King's College London, since 1971; *b* 27 Apr. 1934; *s* of George Barron and Minnie Leslie Marks; *m* 1962, Caroline Mary, *d* of late W. D. Hogarth, OBE; two *d*. *Educ:* Clifton Coll.; Balliol Coll., Oxford (Hon. Exhibnr). 1st Cl., Class. Hon. Mods, 1955; Lit. Hum., 1957; MA 1960, DPhil 1961; Thomas Whitcombe Greene Prizeman, 1955, and Scholar, 1957; Barclay Head Prizeman, 1959; Cromer Prize, British Academy, 1965. Asst Lectr in Latin, Bedford Coll., 1959–61, and Lectr, 1961–64; Lectr in Archaeology, University Coll. London, 1964–67; Reader in Archaeology and Numismatics, Univ. of London, 1967–71; Head of Dept of Classics, KCL, 1972–84; Dean, Faculty of Arts, Univ. of London, 1976–80; Mem. Senate, 1977–81, Mem. Academic Council, 1977–81; Public Orator, 1978–81. Vis. Mem., Inst. for Advanced Study, Princeton, 1973. Blegen Distinguished Vis. Res. Prof., Vassar Coll., NY, 1981; T. B. L. Webster Vis. Prof., Stanford Univ., 1986. *Publications:* Greek Sculpture, 1965 (new and rev. edn 1981); Silver Coins of Samos, 1966; articles in Classical Quarterly, Jl of Hellenic Studies, Bulletin of Inst. of Classical Studies, etc. *Recreations:* travel, gardens. *Address:* Institute of Classical Studies, 31–34 Gordon Square, WC1H 0PY. *T:* 01–387 7696. *Club:* Athenæum.

BARRON, Kevin John; MP (Lab) Rother Valley, since 1983; *b* 26 Oct. 1946; *s* of Richard Barron; *m* 1969; one *s* two *d*. *Educ:* Maltby Hall Secondary Modern Sch.; Ruskin Coll., Oxford. NCB, 1962–83. PPS to Leader of the Opposition, 1985–. Pres., Rotherham and Dist TUC. *Address:* House of Commons, SW1A 0AA.

BARRON, Rt. Rev. Patrick Harold Falkiner; *b* 13 Nov. 1911; *s* of Albert Harold and Mary Isabel Barron; *m* 1942, Kathleen May Larter; two *s* one *d*. *Educ:* King Edward VII Sch., Johannesburg; Leeds Univ. (BA); College of the Resurrection, Mirfield. Curate: Holy Redeemer, Clerkenwell, London, 1938–40; Boksburg, S Africa, 1940–41; CF (S African), 1941–46; Rector: Zeerust, S Africa, 1946–50; Potchefstroom, 1950–51; Blyvooruitzicht, 1951–55. St Cyprian's Mission, Johannesburg, 1956–59; Archdeacon of Germiston, 1957–58; Dean of Johannesburg, 1959–64; Bishop Suffragan of Cape Town, 1965–66; Bishop of George, 1966–77. *Recreation:* gardening. *Address:* E37 Edingight, Queen Road, Rondebosch, 7700, South Africa. *T:* 69.1820.

BARRON, (Thomas) Robert, CBE 1980; FCIT; Member, British Railways Board, 1978–81; *b* 27 Dec. 1918; *s* of late Robert and Florence May Barron; *m* 1942, Constance Lilian Bolter; one *s* three *d*. *Educ:* Dame Allan's Sch., Newcastle-on-Tyne; King's Coll., Durham Univ. BA 1st class Hons (Econ.). Served RA and 1st Airborne Div., 1940–46. Joined LNER as Traffic Apprentice, 1946; Asst Gen. Manager, London Midland Region, 1966, Western Region, 1967; British Railways Board: Dir Management Staff, 1970; Controller of Corporate Planning, 1972; Dir of Planning and Investment, 1977. Exec. Dir, Channel Tunnel, 1981–82. Mem., NW Economic Planning Council, 1965–67. *Recreations:* music, fishing, watching sport. *Address:* 8 Pigeonwick, Harpenden, Herts. *T:* Harpenden 62792.

BARRONS, John Lawson; Vice-Chairman: Northern Press Ltd, since 1986; Northumberland Gazette Ltd, since 1986; *b* 10 Oct. 1932; *s* of late William Cowper Barrons, MBE and Amy Marie Barrons (*née* Lawson); *m* 1957, Caroline Anne, *d* of late George Edward Foster; three *s*. *Educ:* Caterham Sch. Nat. Service, 1st Bn Northamptonshire Regt, 1952–54. Journalist, UK and USA, 1950–57; Gen. Manager, Nuneaton Observer, 1957; Managing Editor, Northampton Chronicle & Echo, 1959; Gen. Manager, Edinburgh Evening News, 1961; Gen. Manager, 1965–76, Man. Dir, 1976–85, Westminster Press. Director: Pearson Longman, 1979–83; Stephen Austin Newspapers, 1986–; President: Westminster (Florida) Inc., 1980–85; Westminster (Jacksonville) Inc., 1982–85. Dir, Evening Newspaper Advertising Bureau, 1978–81 (Chm. 1979–80); Founder Dir, Reg. Newspaper Advertising Bureau, 1980– (Chm. 1982–84); Dir, The Press Association Ltd, 1985–86; Chm., Printing Industry Res. Assoc., 1983–85 (Mem. Council, 1978, a Vice-Chm., 1979–83); Mem. Bd of Management, Internat. Electronic Publishing Res. Centre, 1981–85. Member, Council: Newspaper Soc., 1975– (Pres., 1981–82; Hon. Vice-Pres., 1983–); CPU, 1970–86. *Recreations:* walking, fishing. *Address:* 24 Carlingford Road, Hampstead, NW3 1RX. *Club:* Flyfishers'.

BARROW, Rt. Hon. Errol Walton, PC 1969; QC 1979; MP (Democratic Labour Party), Barbados; Prime Minister of Barbados, since 1986; *b* 21 Jan. 1920; *s* of late Reginald Grant Barrow, LTh, DD, and of Ruth Barrow (*née* O'Neal); *m* 1945, Carolyn Plaskett; one *s* one *d*. *Educ:* Harrison Coll., Barbados; LSE (BSc); Hon. Fellow 1975. Royal Air Force, 1940–47. Barrister, Lincoln's Inn, 1949. Elected House of Assembly, Barbados, 1951; Minister of Finance, 1961–76; Premier, 1961; Prime Minister, 1966–76. Founder Mem., Democratic Labour Party, 1955, Chm. 1958–76. Hon. LLD: McGill, 1966; Sussex. *Publications:* What Canada Can Do for the West Indies, 1964; Democracy and Development, 1979. *Recreations:* sailing, flying, diving, tennis. *Address:* Office of the Prime Minister, Bay Street, Bridgetown, Barbados, W Indies; PO Box 125, Bridgetown, Barbados.

BARROW, Prof. Geoffrey Wallis Steuart, FBA 1976; Sir William Fraser Professor of Scottish History and Palæography, University of Edinburgh, since 1979; *b* Headingley, Leeds, 28 Nov. 1924; *s* of late Charles Embleton Barrow and Marjorie, *d* of Donald Stuart; *m* 1951, Heather Elizabeth, *d* of James McLeish Lownie; one *s* one *d*. *Educ:* St Edward's Sch., Oxford; Inverness Royal Acad.; St Andrews Univ.; Pembroke Coll., Oxford. FRSE 1977. Lecturer in History, University Coll., London, 1950–61; Prof. of Mediaeval Hist., King's Coll., Univ. of Durham, later Univ. of Newcastle upon Tyne, 1961–74; Prof. of Scottish History, Univ. of St Andrews, 1974–79. Mem., Royal Commn on Historical MSS, 1984–. Ford's Lectr, Univ. of Oxford, 1977; Rhind Lectr, Soc. of Antiquaries of Scotland, 1985. *Publications:* Feudal Britain, 1956; Acts of Malcolm IV, King of Scots, 1960; Robert Bruce and the Community of the Realm of Scotland, 1965;

Acts of William I, King of Scots, 1971; Kingdom of the Scots, 1973; (ed) The Scottish Tradition, 1974; The Anglo-Norman Era in Scottish History, 1980; Kingship and Unity, 1981; contrib. Scottish Historical Review, etc. *Recreation:* hill walking. *Address:* University of Edinburgh, Edinburgh EH8 9JY.

BARROW, John Frederick; HM Diplomatic Service, retired; *b* 28 Dec. 1918; *s* of Frederick William and Caroline Barrow; *m* 1947, Mary Roberta Young; two *d. Educ:* King Edward VII Sch., King's Lynn. Home Civil Service, 1936–39; war service in British and Indian Armies, 1939–46 (Major); rejoined Home Civil Service, 1946; Treasury, 1952–62; FCO, 1962; service overseas at Delhi, Kuala Lumpur, Jesselton, Prague, Washington, Hong Kong; retired as Counsellor, 1977. *Address:* 135 Alphonse Circle, Port Charlotte, Fla 33952, USA; 3 Tomkyns, Hillside Street, Hythe, Kent.

BARROW, Captain Michael Ernest, DSO 1982; RN; Clerk to the Worshipful Company of Haberdashers, since 1983; *b* 21 May 1932; *s* of late Captain Guy Runciman Barrow, OBE, RN and Barbara Barrow; *m* 1962, Judith Ann (*née* Cooper); two *s* one *d. Educ:* Wellesley House; RNC, Dartmouth. FNI; FBIM. Served in HM Ships: Devonshire, Liverpool (trng, 1950–52); Agincourt, Euryalus, 1952–53; HM Yacht Britannia, 1954–56; Camperdown, 1958–59; Flag Lt to Cdre Hong Kong, 1956–58; commanded: Caunton, 1960; Laleston, 1961–62; Mohawk, 1963–64; Torquay, 1967–69; Diomede, 1973–75; Glamorgan, 1980–83; RN Staff Course, 1966; Staff Flag Officer, Malta, 1970–71; Comdr RNC, Dartmouth, 1971–73; Dep. Dir, Recruiting, 1975–77; Asst Chief of Staff (Ops) to Comdr, Allied Naval Forces Southern Europe, Naples, 1978–80; ADC to the Queen, 1982–83; retired 1983. Gentleman Usher to Her Majesty, 1984–. *Recreations:* sailing, skiing, gardening, do-it-yourself. *Address:* Heathfield, Shear Hill, Petersfield, Hampshire GU31 4BB. *T:* Petersfield 64198. *Clubs:* Royal Naval Sailing; Royal Naval Ski.

BARROW, Captain Sir Richard John Uniacke, 6th Bt *cr* 1835; *b* 2 Aug. 1933; *s* of Sir Wilfrid John Wilson Croker Barrow, 5th Bt and (Gwladys) Patricia (*née* Uniacke); *S* father 1960; *m* 1961, Alison Kate (marr. diss. 1974), *yr d* of late Capt. Russell Grenfell, RN, and of Mrs Lindsay-Young; one *s* two *d. Educ:* Abbey Sch., Ramsgate; Beaumont Coll., Old Windsor. Commnd 2nd Lieut Irish Guards, 1952; served: Germany, 1952–53; Egypt, 1953–56; Cyprus, 1958; Germany, 1959–60; retired, 1960; joined International Computers and Tabulators Ltd; resigned 1973. *Heir: s* Anthony John Grenfell Barrow, *b* 24 May 1962.

BARROWCLOUGH, Anthony Richard, QC 1974; Parliamentary Commissioner for Administration, and Health Service Commissioner for England, Wales and Scotland,since 1985; *b* 24 June 1924; *m* 1949, Mary Agnes Pery-Knox-Gore; one *s* one *d. Educ:* Stowe; New Coll., Oxford. Served RNVR, 1943–46 (Sub-Lieut and later Lieut). Called to the Bar, Inner Temple, 1949, Bencher 1982; Recorder, 1972–84. Part-time Member, Monopolies Commn, 1966–69; Mem., Council on Tribunals (and Mem., Scottish Cttee), 1985–. *Recreation:* country pursuits. *Address:* 60 Ladbroke Grove, W11; The Old Vicarage, Winsford, near Minehead, Somerset.

BARRY, Daniel; Permanent Secretary, Department of the Environment for Northern Ireland, since 1983; *b* 4 March 1928; *s* of William John Graham Barry and Sarah (*née* Wilkinson); *m* 1951, Florence (*née* Matier); two *s* one *d. Educ:* Belfast Mercantile Coll. FCIS, FSCA, FIHT. Local Government Officer with various NI Councils, 1944–68; Town Clerk, Carrickfergus Borough Council, 1968–73; Asst Sec. (Roads), Dept of the Environment for NI, 1973–76, Dep. Sec., 1976–80; Dep. Sec., Dept of Educn for NI, 1980–83. *Recreations:* golf, gardening, tobacco producing, wine making.

BARRY, (Donald Angus) Philip, CBE 1980 (OBE 1969); HM Chief Inspector of Prisons for Scotland, 1981–85; *b* 16 Sept. 1920; *s* of John and Dorothy Barry; *m* 1942, Margaret Orr; five *s* one *d. Educ:* The Abbey Sch., Fort Augustus. Army Service, 1939–46: Captain Gordon Highlanders, 51st (Highland) Div., N Africa, Sicily. Family Business, 1946–82, Man. Dir, 1964–82. Cruz de Caballero del Orden de Isabel La Católica (Spain), 1980. *Address:* c/o Bank of Scotland, 28 Bernard Street, Edinburgh EH6 6QD. *Club:* University Staff (Edinburgh).

BARRY, Sir Edward; *see* Barry, Sir L. E. A. T.

BARRY, Edward Norman, CB 1981; Under Secretary, Northern Ireland Office, 1979–81, retired 1981; *b* 22 Feb. 1920; *s* of Samuel and Matilda (*née* Legge); *m* 1952, Inez Anna (*née* Elliott); one *s* two *d. Educ:* Bangor Grammar Sch. Northern Ireland Civil Service: Department of Finance: Establishment Div., 1940–51; Works Div., 1951–60; Treasury Div., 1960–67; Establishment Officer, 1967–72; Min. of Home Affairs, 1972–74; Asst Sec., N Ireland Office, 1974–79. *Recreations:* golf, Irish Football Association Ltd (Hon. Treasurer). *Address:* Allied Irish Banks Ltd, 697/703 Upper Newtownards Road, Dundonald, Belfast.

BARRY, James Edward; Stipendiary Magistrate for South Yorkshire, since 1985; a Recorder of the Crown Court, since 1985; *b* 27 May 1938; *s* of James Douglas Barry and Margaret Elizabeth (*née* Thornton); *m* 1963, Pauline Pratt; three *s. Educ:* Merchant Taylors' Sch., Crosby; Brasenose Coll., Oxford (schol.; MA Jurisp.). Called to the Bar, Inner Temple, 1963; in practice, NE Circuit, 1963–85. *Recreations:* reading, domestic pursuits. *Address:* Law Courts, Doncaster, S Yorks DN1 3HT.

BARRY, Sir (Lawrence) Edward (Anthony Tress), 5th Bt *cr* 1899; Baron de Barry in Portugal *cr* 1876; *b* 1 Nov. 1939; *s* of Sir Rupert Rodney Francis Tress Barry, 4th Bt, MBE, and Diana Madeline (*d* 1948), *o d* of R. O'Brien Thompson; *S* father, 1977; *m* 1968, Fenella Hoult; one *s* one *d. Educ:* Haileybury. Formerly Captain, Grenadier Guards. *Heir: s* William Rupert Philip Tress Barry, *b* 13 Dec. 1973. *Address:* 3 Sunnyside Cottages, Warehorne Road, Ham Street, Kent. *T:* Ham Street 2454.

BARRY, Michael, (James Barry Jackson); OBE 1956; Principal, London Academy of Music and Dramatic Art, 1973–78, retired; *b* 15 May 1910; *s* of A. G. and Helen Jackson; *m* 1st, 1934, Judith Gick (marr. diss. 1947); one *d*; 2nd, 1948, Rosemary Corbett (*d* 1968); one *d*; 3rd, 1973, Pamela Corbett. Studied farming and horticulture in Glos and Herts. Studied for theatre at RADA (Baliol Holloway Award, Best Diploma Performance, 1930) and subsequently as actor, stage-manager, designer and producer at the Northampton, Birmingham, Hull and Croydon Repertory Theatres before working in London. Appointed BBC television producer, 1938. Served Royal Marine Brigade, Landing-Craft and as AMS, RM Office, 1939–45 (Major); Producer and writer, BBC television drama and documentary, 1946–51 (Programmes included: The Silence of the Sea, I Want to Be a Doctor, Promise of Tomorrow, The Passionate Pilgrim, Shout Aloud Salvation); Head of Drama, BBC Television, 1952–61; Programme Controller, Irish Television, 1961–63; prod The Wars of the Roses (TV), 1966; Prof. of Drama and Dept Head, Stanford Univ., Calif, 1968–72. Literary Adviser, Council of Repertory Theatres, 1964–67; Dir, Manchester Royal Exchange Theatre (formerly 1969 Theatre), 1972–85. Member: Drama Panel, Arts Council, 1955–68; Council, RADA, 1966–69; Nat. Council Drama Training, 1976–78; Governing Body, Wimbledon Sch. of Art, 1976–78. Desmond Davis Award, SFTA, 1961. *Publication:* (selected) The Television Playwright, 1960. *Address:* 11 Marlborough Mews, Marlborough Street, Brighton, East Sussex BN1 2EG.

BARRY, Rt. Rev. (Noel) Patrick, OSB; Abbot of Ampleforth, since 1984; *b* 6 Dec. 1917; 2nd *s* of Dr T. St J. Barry, Wallasey, Cheshire. *Educ:* Ampleforth Coll.; St Benet's Hall, Oxford. Housemaster, Ampleforth Coll., 1954–64, Headmaster 1964–79. First Asst to Abbot Pres. of English Benedictine Congregation, 1985–. Chairman: Conference of Catholic Colleges, 1973–75; HMC, 1975. *Address:* Ampleforth Abbey, York. *T:* Ampleforth 421.

BARRY, Peter; TD (FG) Cork South Central; Minister for Foreign Affairs, Ireland, since 1982; *b* Cork, 10 Aug. 1928; *s* of Anthony Barry and Rita Costello; *m* 1958, Margaret O'Mullane; four *s* two *d. Educ:* Christian Brothers' Coll., Cork. Alderman of Cork Corp., 1967–73; Lord Mayor of Cork, 1970–71. TD: Cork City SE, 1969–82; Cork South Central, 1982–; opposition spokesman on labour and public services, 1972–73; Minister for: Transport and Power, 1973–76; Education, 1976–77; opposition spokesman on finance and economic affairs, 1977–81; Minister for the Environment, 1981–82; opposition spokesman on the environment, 1982. Dep. Leader of Fine Gael Party, 1979–; Chm., Nat. Exec. *Address:* Sherwood, Blackrock, Co. Cork; Department of Foreign Affairs, 80 St Stephen's Green, Dublin 2. *T:* Dublin 780822.

BARRY, Philip; *see* Barry, D. A. P.

BARRY, Sir Philip Stuart M.; *see* Milner-Barry.

BARRY, Maj.-Gen. Richard Hugh, CB 1962; CBE 1953 (OBE 1943); retired; *b* 9 Nov. 1908; *s* of Lieut-Col Alfred Percival Barry and Helen Charlotte (*née* Stephens); *m* 1st, 1940, Rosalind Joyce Evans (*d* 1973); one *s* two *d*; 2nd, 1975, Elizabeth Lucia Middleton. *Educ:* Winchester; Sandhurst. 2nd Lieut Somerset LI, 1929; Staff Coll., Camberley, Capt., 1938; served War of 1939–45; BEF, SOE, AFHQ, Algiers. Military Attaché, Stockholm, 1947; Deputy Chief of Staff Western Europe Land Forces, 1948; Dir, Standing Group, NATO, 1952; Chief of Staff, HQ British Troops in Egypt, 1954–56; Imperial Defence Coll., 1957; Standing Group Representative, North Atlantic Council, 1959–62; retired, 1962. Maj.-Gen. 1959. Africa Star, 1943; 1939–45 Star; Defence, Victory Medals, 1945. *Recreation:* hunting. *Address:* Little Place, Farringdon, Alton, Hants GU34 3EH. *T:* Tisted 216. *Club:* Army and Navy.

BARSTOW, Josephine, (Mrs Ande Anderson), CBE 1985; opera singer, free-lance since 1971; *b* Sheffield, 27 Sept. 1940; *m* 1969, Ande Anderson; no *c. Educ:* Birmingham Univ. (BA). Debut with Opera for All, 1964; studied at London Opera Centre, 1965–66; Opera for All, 1966; Glyndebourne Chorus, 1967; Sadler's Wells Contract Principal, 1967–68, sang Cherubino, Euridice, Violetta; *Welsh Nat. Opera:* Contract Principal, 1968–70, sang Violetta, Countess, Fiordiligi, Mimi, Amelia, Simon Boccanegra; Don Carlos, 1973; Jenufa, 1975; Peter Grimes, 1978, 1983; Tatyana in Onegin, 1980; Tosca, 1985; *Covent Garden:* Denise, world première, Tippett's The Knot Garden, 1970 (recorded 1974); Falstaff, 1975; Salome, 1982; Santuzza, 1982; *Glyndebourne:* Lady Macbeth (for TV), 1972; Idomeneo, 1974; Fidelio, 1981; *Coliseum:* Der Rosenkavalier, 1975, 1984; Salome, 1975; Don Carlos, 1976; Tosca, 1976; Forza del Destino, 1978; Aida, 1979; Fidelio, 1980; Arabella, 1980; The Flying Dutchman, La Bohème, 1982; The Valkyrie, 1983; Don Giovanni, 1985; has sung all parts in Hoffman, Emilia Marty (Makropulos Case), Natasha (War and Peace) and Traviata, ENO; Alice in Falstaff, Aix-en-Provence Festival, 1971; Nitocris in Belshazzar, Geneva, 1972; Jeanne, British première, Penderecki's The Devils, 1973; Marguerite, world première, Crosse's The Story of Vasco, 1974; Fidelio, Jenufa, Scottish Opera, 1977; Gayle, world première, Tippett's The Ice Break, 1977; US debut as Lady Macbeth, Miami, 1977; Musetta in La Bohème, NY Met., 1977; Salome, Staatsoper, East Berlin, 1979 (Critics Prize); Abigaille in Nabucco, Miami, 1981; debut in Chicago as Lady Macbeth, 1981; new prod. of Jenufa, Cologne, 1981; Salome, San Francisco, 1982; La Voix Humaine and Pagliacci, Chicago, 1982; The Makropulos Case (in Italian), Florence, 1983; Gutrune, Bayreuth, 1983; Die Fledermaus, San Francisco, 1984; Peter Grimes, 1984, La Traviata, 1985, Houston; sings in other opera houses in USA, Canada and Europe. Fidelio medal, Assoc. of Internat. Opera Directors, 1985. *Recreation:* farm which she runs with her husband (they raise cattle and have horses for riding; she also breeds pure-bred Arabian horses). *Address:* c/o John Coast, 1 Park Close, Knightsbridge, SW1X 7PQ.

BARSTOW, Stan; writer; *b* 28 June 1928; *s* of Wilfred Barstow and Elsie Gosnay; *m* 1951, Constance Mary Kershaw; one *s* one *d. Educ:* Ossett Grammar Sch. Employed in Engineering Industry, 1944–62, mainly as Draughtsman. Best British Dramatisation, Writers' Guild of GB, 1974; Royal TV Soc. Writers' Award, 1975. Hon. Fellow, Bretton Coll., 1985. Hon. MA Open Univ., 1982. *Television:* dramatisations: A Raging Calm, 1974; South Riding, 1974; Joby, 1975; The Cost of Loving, 1977; Travellers, 1978; A Kind of Loving (from A Kind of Loving, The Watchers on the Shore, The Right True End), 1982; A Brother's Tale, 1983; *Publications:* A Kind of Loving, 1960; The Desperadoes, 1961; Ask Me Tomorrow, 1962; Joby, 1964; The Watchers on the Shore, 1966; A Raging Calm, 1968; A Season with Eros, 1971; The Right True End, 1976; A Brother's Tale, 1980; A Kind of Loving: The Vic Brown Trilogy, 1982; The Glad Eye, 1984; Just You Wait and See, 1986; *plays:* Listen for the Trains, Love, 1970; Joby (TV script), 1977; An Enemy of the People (ad. Ibsen), 1978; The Human Element, and Albert's Part (TV scripts), 1984; (with Alfred Bradley): Ask Me Tomorrow, 1966; A Kind of Loving, 1970; Stringer's Last Stand, 1972. *Address:* Goring House, Goring Park Avenue, Ossett, West Yorks. *T:* Wakefield 273362.

BART, A. S.; *see* Schwarz-Bart.

BART, Lionel; composer, lyricist and playwright; *b* 1 Aug. 1930. Wrote lyrics for Lock Up Your Daughters, 1959; music and lyrics for Fings Ain't Wot They Used T'be, 1959; music, lyrics and book for Oliver!, 1960; music, lyrics and direction of Blitz!, 1962; music and lyrics of Maggie May, 1964; music of Lionel, 1977. Has also written several film scores and many individual hit songs. *Films:* Serious Charge; In the Nick; Heart of a Man; Let's Get Married; Light up the Sky; The Tommy Steele Story; The Duke Wore Jeans; Tommy the Toreador; Sparrers Can't Sing; From Russia with Love; Man in the Middle; Oliver; The Optimists. Ivor Novello Awards as a song writer: three in 1957; four in 1959; two in 1960. Variety Club Silver Heart as Show Business Personality of the Year, 1960. Broadway, USA; Tony (Antoinette Perry) Award, etc (for Oliver!), best composer and lyricist, 1962. *Address:* c/o Patricia Macnaughton, MLR, 200 Fulham Road, SW10. *T:* 01–351 5442.

BARTELL, Lt-Col (Hon.) Kenneth George William, CBE 1977; FIB; Past President, British Chambers of Commerce in Continental Europe; Past President (twice) and Honorary Vice-President, British Chamber of Commerce, France; *b* 5 Dec. 1914; *s* of William Richard Aust Bartell and Daisy Florence (*née* Kendall); *m* 1955, Lucie Adèle George. *Educ:* Cooper's Company's Sch. BCom London. Westminster Bank Ltd, London, 1933. Served war, RAOC: France, 1939–40, Egypt and Middle East, 1940–46 (despatches twice); demobilised Hon. Lt-Col. Westminster Bank Ltd, London, 1946–49; Westminster Foreign Bank Ltd: Paris, 1950–51; Lyons, 1952–53; Bordeaux, 1954–55; Manager, State

Commercial Bank, Rangoon, Burma, 1955–59; Man., then Chief Man., Westminster Foreign Bank, Paris, 1960–74; Gen. Man., Internat. Westminster Bank Ltd, France, 1974–76, retired. Freeman: Coopers' Co., 1981; City of London, 1981. *Recreations:* swimming, bridge. *Address:* 5 avenue Saint-Honoré-d'Eylau, Paris 75116, France. *T:* (1) 45 53 69 48. *Clubs:* Army and Navy, Royal Automobile; Cercle de l'Union Interalliée (Paris).

BARTLE, Ronald David; a Metropolitan Stipendiary Magistrate since 1972; a Deputy Circuit Judge, since 1975; *b* 14 April 1929; *s* of Rev. George Clement Bartle and Winifred Marie Bartle; *m* 1st, 1963; one *s* one *d*; 2nd, 1981, Hisako (*née* Yagi). *Educ:* St John's Sch., Leatherhead; Jesus Coll., Cambridge (MA). Nat. Service, 1947–49 (Army Athletic Colours). Called to Bar, Lincoln's Inn, 1954. Contested (C) Islington North, 1958 and 1959. A Chm., Inner London Juvenile Courts, 1975–79. Liveryman, Basketmaker's Co., 1976. Freeman, City of London, 1976 (Mem., Guild of Freemen, 1979); Mem., Royal Soc. of St George. *Publications:* Introduction to Shipping Law, 1958; The Police Officer in Court, 1984; Crime and the New Magistrate, 1985. *Recreations:* music, reading, swimming. *Address:* Bow Street Magistrates' Court, WC2E 7AS. *Clubs:* Garrick, Lansdowne.

BARTLEET, Rt. Rev. David Henry; *see* Tonbridge, Bishop Suffragan of.

BARTLES-SMITH, Ven. Douglas Leslie; Archdeacon of Southwark, since 1985; *b* 3 June 1937; *s* of Leslie Charles and Muriel Rose Bartles-Smith; *m* 1967, Patricia Ann Coburn; two *s* one *d*. *Educ:* Shrewsbury School; St Edmund Hall, Oxford (MA); Wells Theol Coll. Curate of St Stephen's, Rochester Row, SW1, 1963–68; Curate-in-charge, St Michael and All Angels with Emmanuel and All Souls, Camberwell, 1968–72; Vicar, 1972–75; Vicar of St Luke, Battersea, 1975–85; RD of Battersea, 1981–85. *Publication:* (co-author) Urban Ghetto, 1976. *Recreations:* Shrewsbury Town Football Club, reading, walking, travel. *Address:* 1a Dog Kennel Hill, East Dulwich, SE22 8AA. *T:* 01–274 6767.

BARTLETT, Charles; *see* Bartlett, Harold Charles.

BARTLETT, Sir David; *see* Bartlett, Sir H. D. H.

BARTLETT, George Robert; QC 1986; *b* 22 Oct. 1944; *s* of Commander H. V. Bartlett, RN and Angela (*née* Webster); *m* 1972, Dr Clare Virginia, *y d* of G. C. Fortin; three *s*. *Educ:* Tonbridge Sch.; Trinity Coll., Oxford (MA). Called to the Bar, Middle Temple, 1966. *Recreations:* cricket and other games. *Address:* 2 Mitre Court Buildings, Temple, EC4Y 7BX. *T:* 01–583 1380.

BARTLETT, (Harold) Charles, ARCA 1949; RE 1961 (ARE 1950); RWS 1970 (ARWS 1959); painter and printmaker; *b* Grimsby, 23 Sept. 1921; *s* of Charles Henry and Frances Kate Bartlett; *m*; one *s*. *Educ:* Eastbourne Grammar Sch.; Eastbourne Sch. of Art; Royal College of Art. First one man exhibition in London, 1960. *Recreations:* music, sailing. *Address:* St Andrews, Fingringhoe, near Colchester, Essex. *T:* Rowhedge 406.

BARTLETT, Sir (Henry) David (Hardington), 3rd Bt *cr* 1913; MBE (mil.) 1943; *b* 18 March 1912; *s* of Hardington Arthur Bartlett (*d* 1920) (2nd *s* of 1st Bt) and Irene (*d* 1974), *d* of Prof. Henry Robinson; *S* brother, 1985; *m* 1st, 1936, Kathlene Rosamond Stanbury (marr. diss. 1974); three *s*; 2nd, 1974, Joyce Lillian Odell (*d* 1982); one adopted *d*; 3rd, 1982, Jeanne Margaret Esther Brewer. *Educ:* Stowe; Corpus Christi Coll., Cambridge. Successes in fencing: British Amateur Men's Champion, 1934 and 1935; Mem., British Olympic Team, Berlin, 1936. War service with TA; passed War Gunnery Staff Course; Lt-Col RA, retired rank Hon. Major. *Recreations:* gardening, cooking, playing with soldiers. *Heir:* *s* John Hardington Bartlett [*b* 15 March 1938; *m* 1971, Elizabeth Joyce, *d* of George Raine; two *s*]. *Address:* Brockley Place, Brockley, Bury St Edmunds, Suffolk IP29 4AG. *T:* Bury St Edmunds 830473.

BARTLETT, Henry Francis, CMG 1975; OBE 1964; Executive Officer, Utah Foundation, Brisbane, since 1976; painter; HM Diplomatic Service, retired; *b* 8 March 1916; *s* of F. V. S. and A. G. Bartlett, London; *m* 1940, A. D. Roy. *Educ:* St Paul's Sch.; Queen's Coll., Oxford; Ruskin Sch. of Drawing; Univ. of California (Commonwealth Fellow). Min. of Inf., 1940–45; Paris, 1944–47; Vice-Consul Lyons, 1948–49; FO, 1949–50; Vice-Consul, Szczecin, 1950; Second, later First, Sec., Warsaw, 1951–53; FO, 1953–55; First Sec. (Commercial), Caracas, 1955–60; First Sec. (Inf.), Mexico City, 1960–63; Consul, Khorramshahr, 1964–67; Dep. High Comr, Brisbane, 1967–69; Counsellor, Manila, 1969–72 (Chargé d'Affaires, 1971); Ambassador to Paraguay, 1972–75. Hon. Prof., Nat. Univ. of Asunción, 1975. Exhibitions of painting: Paris, 1947; London, 1950; Caracas, 1957, 1959; Mexico City, 1962; Brisbane, 1969, 1978, 1981, 1983, 1985. Represented: Commonwealth Art Bank; Queensland and S Aust. State Galleries; Brisbane Colleges of Advanced Educn. Trustee: Queensland Art Gallery, 1977–; Qld Cultural Centre Trust, 1980–. *Address:* c/o Utah Foundation, PO Box 279, Brisbane, Qld 4001, Australia; 14 Bowen Place, 341 Bowen Terrace, New Farm, Qld 4005, Australia.

BARTLETT, Maj.-Gen. John Leonard, CB 1985; Paymaster-in-Chief and Inspector of Army Pay Services, 1983–86, retired; *b* 17 Aug. 1926; *s* of late F. Bartlett and E. Bartlett; *m* 1952, Pauline (*née* Waite); two *s*. *Educ:* Holt Grammar Sch., Liverpool. MBCS, FBIM, jssc, psc, pfc. Commissioned Royal Army Pay Corps, 1946; served Hong Kong, Singapore, BAOR, War Office, Washington, Malta, Libya, HQ MELF, 1966–67 (despatches 1968); Staff Pmr and O i/c FBPO Berlin, 1968–69; GSO1 (Secretary) NATO Mil. Agency for Standardisation, 1969–71; Comd Pmr, Hong Kong, 1972–74; Col GS, MoD (ADP Coord.), 1974–76; Chief Pmr ADP and Station Comdr, Worthy Down, 1976–79; Chief Pmr, BAOR, 1980–82. Freeman, City of London, 1984. *Recreation:* golf. *Address:* c/o Lloyds Bank, The Square, Wickham, Hants PO17 5JQ. *Clubs:* Royal Commonwealth Society, Lansdowne.

BARTLETT, John Vernon, CBE 1976; MA; FEng, FICE, FASCE, FIE Aust.; Consulting Engineer; Chairman, Mott, Hay & Anderson; *b* 18 June 1927; *s* of late Vernon F. Bartlett and Olga Bartlett (*née* Testrup); *m* 1951, Gillian, *d* of late Philip Hoffmann, Sturmer Hall, Essex; four *s*. *Educ:* Stowe; Trinity Coll., Cambridge. Served 9th Airborne Squadron, RE, 1946–48; Engineer and Railway Staff Corps, TA, 1978; Lt-Col 1982. Engineer with John Mowlem & Co. Ltd, 1951–57; joined staff of Mott, Hay & Anderson, 1957; Partner, 1966–. Pres., ICE, 1983–84 (Vice-Pres., 1979–82; Mem. Council, 1974–77); Chm., British Tunnelling Soc., 1977–79. Telford Gold Medal, (jointly) 1971, 1973; S. G. Brown Medal, Royal Soc., 1973. FRSA 1975. Mem. Council, Fellowship of Engrg, 1982–86. *Publications:* Tunnels: Planning Design and Construction (with T. M. Megaw), vol. 1, 1981, vol. 2, 1982; contrib. various papers to ICE, ASCE, etc. *Recreation:* sailing. *Address:* c/o Mott, Hay & Anderson, 20/26 Wellesley Road, Croydon, Surrey CR9 2UL. *T:* 01–686 5041. *Clubs:* St Stephen's Constitutional; Hawks (Cambridge); Harlequin Football; Royal Engineers Yacht.

BARTLETT, Prof. Maurice Stevenson, FRS 1961; MA Cambridge, DSc London; Professor of Bio-mathematics in the University of Oxford, 1967–75, now Emeritus; *b* 18 June 1910; *s* of W. S. Bartlett, Scrooby; *m* 1957, Sheila, *d* of C. E. Chapman; one *d*. *Educ:* Latymer Upper Sch.; Queens' Coll., Cambridge. Wrangler, 1932; Rayleigh Prize, 1934. Asst Lectr in Statistics, University Coll., London, 1933–34; Statistician, Imperial Chemical Industries, Ltd, 1934–38; Lectr in Mathematics, Univ. of Cambridge, 1938–47. National Service, Min. of Supply, 1940–45. Visiting Prof. of Mathematical Statistics, Univ. of North Carolina, 1946; Prof. of Mathematical Statistics, Univ. of Manchester, 1947–60; Prof. of Statistics, Univ. of London (University Coll.), 1960–67. Mem. Internat. Statistical Institute, 1949, Hon. Mem., 1980; President: Manchester Statistical Soc., 1959–60; Biometric Soc. (Brit. Reg.), 1964–66; Internat. Assoc. Statistics Phys. Sci., 1965–67; Royal Statistical Society, 1966–67. Hon. DSc: Chicago, 1966; Hull, 1976. Gold Medal, Royal Statistical Soc., 1969; Weldon Prize and Medal, Oxford, 1971. *Publications:* An Introduction to Stochastic Processes, 1955; Stochastic Population Models in Ecology and Epidemiology, 1960; Essays in Probability and Statistics, 1962; Probability, Statistics and Time, 1975; Statistical Analysis of Spatial Pattern 1976; papers on statistical and biometrical theory and methodology. *Address:* Priory Orchard, Priory Avenue, Totnes, Devon TQ9 5HR.

BARTLETT, Prof. Neil, FRS 1973; FRSC; Professor of Chemistry, University of California, Berkeley, since 1969, and Principal Investigator, Materials and Molecular Research Division, Lawrence Berkeley Laboratory, since 1969; *b* Newcastle upon Tyne, 15 Sept. 1932; *s* of Norman Bartlett and Ann Willins Bartlett (*née* Voak), both of Newcastle upon Tyne; *m* 1957, Christina I., *d* of J. W. F. Cross, Guisborough, Yorks; three *s* one *d*. *Educ:* Heaton Grammar Sch., Newcastle upon Tyne; King's Coll., Univ. of Durham, Newcastle upon Tyne. BSc 1954, PhD 1958. Senior Chemistry Master, The Duke's Sch., Alnwick, Northumberland, 1957–58; Mem. Faculty (Dept of Chemistry), Univ. of British Columbia, 1958–66; Prof. of Chemistry, Princeton Univ., and Scientist, Bell Telephone Laboratories, Murray Hill, NJ, USA, 1966–69. For. Associate, Nat. Acad. of Sciences, USA, 1979. Member: Deutsche Akademie der Naturforscher Leopoldina, 1969; Der Akademie der Wissenschaften in Göttingen, 1977; Amer. Chem. Soc., Amer. Soc. for Advancement of Science, etc. Sigma Xi. Visiting Miller Prof., Univ. of Calif, Berkeley, 1967–68; Brotherton Vis. Prof., Univ. of Leeds, 1981, etc. Erskine Fellow, Univ. of Canterbury, NZ, 1983; Vis. Fellow, All Souls, Oxford, 1984. Hon. DSc: Univ. of Waterloo, Canada, 1968; Colby Coll., Maine, USA, 1972; Univ. of Newcastle, 1981; Dr *hc* Univ. of Bordeaux, 1976. Fellow: Amer. Acad. of Arts and Scis, 1977; Chem. Inst. of Canada; Chem. Soc. (London). Corday-Morgan Medal and Prize of Chem. Soc., 1962; Robert A. Welch Award, 1976; Medal of Inst. Jožef Stefan, Ljubljana, 1980; W. H. Nichols Medal, NY Section, ACS, 1983; various overseas awards and prizes, 1965–. *Publications:* The Chemistry of the Monatomic Gases, 1975; scientific papers to: Jl of Chem. Soc., Inorganic Chem., etc; Mem. various editorial advisory bds in Gt Britain, France and USA. *Recreations:* water colour painting; walking in high country; gardening. *Address:* 6 Oak Drive, Orinda, Calif 94563, USA; Chemistry Department, University of California, Berkeley, Calif 94720, USA. *T:* (business) (415) 642–7259.

BARTON, Anne; *see* Barton, B. A.

BARTON, Prof. (Barbara) Anne, PhD; Professor of English, Cambridge University, since 1984; Fellow of Trinity College, Cambridge, since 1986; *b* 9 May 1933; *d* of Oscar Charles Roesen and Blanche Godfrey Williams; *m* 1st, 1957, William Harvey Righter; 2nd, 1969, John Bernard Adie Barton, *qv*. *Educ:* Bryn Mawr College, USA. BA 1954 (*summa cum laude*); PhD Cantab 1960. Lectr in History of Art, Ithaca Coll., NY, 1958–59; Girton College, Cambridge: Rosalind Lady Carlisle Research Fellow, 1960–62; Official Fellow in English, 1962–72; Dir of Studies in English, 1963–72; Univ. Asst Lectr, later Univ. Lectr in English, Cambridge, 1962–72; Hildred Carlile Prof. of English and Head of Dept, Bedford Coll., London, 1972–74; Fellow and Tutor in English, New Coll., Oxford and CUF Lectr, 1974–84. Lectures: British Acad. Chatterton, 1967; Alexander Meml, Univ. Coll., Toronto, 1983; Hon. Fellow, Shakespeare Inst., Univ. of Birmingham, 1982; Member Editorial Advisory Boards: Shakespeare Survey, 1972–; Shakespeare Quarterly, 1981–; Studies in English Literature, 1976–. *Publications:* Shakespeare and the Idea of the Play, 1962, 4th edn 1977, trans. Japanese 1982; Ben Jonson, Dramatist, 1984; essays and studies in learned jls. *Recreations:* opera, fine arts, travel. *Address:* Trinity College, Cambridge.

BARTON, Sir Charles Newton, Kt 1974; OBE; ED; BE; Hon. FIEAust; FAIM; FTS 1978; Chairman: Port of Brisbane Authority, 1977–79; Queensland Local Government Grants Commission, 1977–79; *b* 5 July 1907; *s* of J. Barton, Maryborough, Qld; *m* 1935, Enid, *d* of W. Wetherell. *Educ:* Maryborough Boys' Grammar Sch.; Queensland Univ. (BE Civil). Consulting Engr, Mackay, 1935–59; Comr of Main Roads, Qld, 1960–68; Co-ordinator-Gen., Qld, 1969–76. Served War, AIF, 1940–41; 2/15th Bn (PW), Europe, 1941–45. CO, 31 Bn, CMF, 1948–52, 42 Bn, 1952–57; Hon. Col, Kennedy Regt, 1958–60; Aust. Cadet Corps, N Comd, 1962–66; Qld Univ. Regt, 1966–73. Peter Nicol Russel Medal, 1978. *Recreations:* gardening, fishing. *Address:* 78 Jilba Street, Indooroopilly, Queensland 4068, Australia. *Clubs:* Queensland, Johnsonian, United Service, Mackay (all in Qld).

BARTON, Sir Derek Harold Richard, Kt 1972; FRS 1954; FRSE 1956; Professor of Chemistry, Texas A and M University, since 1985; *b* 8 Sept. 1918; *s* of William Thomas and Maude Henrietta Barton; *m* 1st, 1944, Jeanne Kate Wilkins; one *s*; 2nd, 1969, Christiane Cognet. *Educ:* Tonbridge Sch.; Imperial Coll., Univ. of London (Fellow, 1980). BSc Hons (1st Class) 1940; Hofmann Prizeman; PhD (Organic Chemistry) 1942; DSc London 1949. Research Chemist: on Govt project, 1942–44. Albright and Wilson, Birmingham, 1944–45; Asst Lectr, Dept of Chemistry, Imperial Coll., 1945–46, ICI Research Fellow, 1946–49; Visiting Lectr in Chemistry of Natural Products, Harvard Univ., USA, 1949–50; Reader in Organic Chemistry, Birkbeck Coll., 1950, Prof. of Organic Chemistry, 1953–55; Regius Prof. of Chemistry, Glasgow Univ., 1955–57; Prof. of Organic Chem., 1957–70, Hofmann Prof. of Organic Chem., 1970–78, Imperial Coll.; Emeritus Prof. of Organic Chem., Univ. of London, 1978. Arthur D. Little Vis. Prof., MIT, 1958; Karl Folkers Vis. Prof., Univs of Illinois and Wisconsin, 1959; Cecil H. and Ida Green Vis. Prof., Univ. of British Columbia, 1977; Firth Vis. Prof. in Chemistry, Univ. of Sheffield, 1978. Lectures: Tilden, Chem. Soc., 1952; Max Tischler, Harvard Univ., 1956; First Simonsen Memorial, Chem. Soc., 1958; Falk-Plaut, Columbia Univ., 1961; Aub, Harvard Med. Sch., 1962; Renaud, Michigan State Univ., 1962; Inaugural 3 M's, Univ. of Western Ontario, 1962; 3 M's, Univ. of Minnesota, 1963; Hugo Müller, Chem. Soc., 1963; Pedler, Chem. Soc., 1967; Sandin, Univ. of Alberta, 1969; Robert Robinson, Chem. Soc., London, 1970; Bakerian, Royal Society, 1970; Bose Endowment, Bose Inst., Calcutta, 1972; Stieglitz, Chicago Univ., 1974; Bachmann, Michigan, 1975; Woodward, Yale, 1975; First Smissman, Kansas, 1976; Benjamin Rush and Priestley, Pennsylvania State Univ., 1977; Romanes, Edinburgh, 1979; (first) Hirst, St Andrews Univ., 1980. President: Section B, British Assoc. for the Advancement of Science, 1969; Organic Chemistry Div., Internat. Union of Pure and Applied Chemistry, 1969; Perkin Div., Chem. Soc., 1971; Pres., Chem. Soc., 1973–74. Mem., Council for Scientific Policy, 1965–68. Hon. Member: Sociedad Quimica de Mexico, 1969; Belgian Chem. Soc., 1970; Chilean Chem. Soc., 1970; Polish Chem. Soc., 1970; Pharmaceutical Soc. of Japan, 1970; Royal Acad. Exact Scis, Madrid, 1971; Acad. of Pharmaceutical Scis, USA, 1971; Danish

Acad. Scis, 1972; Argentinian Acad. Scis, 1973; Societa Italiana per il Progresso delle Scienze, 1976; Chem. Soc. of Japan, 1982; Corresp. Mem., Argentinian Chem. Soc., 1970; Foreign Member: Acad. das Ciencias de Lisboa, 1971; Academia Nazionale dei Lincei, Rome, 1975; Foreign Hon. Mem. American Academy of Arts and Sciences, 1960; Foreign Associate: Nat. Acad. of Sciences, USA, 1970; l'Académie des Sciences, Institute de France, 1978. Hon. Fellow: Deutsche Akad. der Naturforscher Leopoldina, 1967; Birkbeck Coll., 1970; ACS Centennial Foreign Fellow, 1976; Hon. FRSC 1985. Hon. DSc: Montpellier Univ., 1962; Dublin, 1964; St Andrews, Columbia NYC, 1970; Coimbra, 1971; Oxon, Manchester, 1972; South Africa, 1973; City, 1975; Hon. Dr: La Laguna, 1975; Univ. of Western Virginia, 1975; Univs of Valencia, Sheffield, Western Ontario, Metz, 1979. Harrison Memorial Prize, Chem. Soc., 1948; First Corday-Morgan Medallist, Chemical Soc., 1951; Fritzsche Medal, Amer. Chem. Soc., 1956; First Roger Adams Medal, Amer. Chem. Soc., 1959; Davy Medal, Royal Society, 1961; Nobel Prize for Chemistry (jointly), 1969; First award in Natural Product Chemistry, Chem. Soc. of London, 1971; Longstaff Medal, Chem. Soc., 1972; B. C. Law Gold Medal, Indian Assoc. for Cultivation of Science, 1972; Medal, Soc. of Cosmetic Chem. of GB, 1972; Royal Medal, Royal Soc., 1972; Second Centennial of Priestly Chemistry Award, Amer. Chem. Soc., 1974; Medal of Union of Sci. Workers, Bulgaria, 1978; Univ. of Sofia Medal, 1978; Acad. of Scis, Bulgaria Medal, 1978; Copley Medal, Royal Soc., 1980; Hanbury Meml Medal, PSGB, 1981. Order of the Rising Sun (2nd class), Japan, 1972; Officier, Légion d'Honneur, 1986 (Chevalier, 1974). *Publications:* numerous, in Journal of Chemical Society. *Address:* Department of Chemistry, Texas A and M University, College Station, Texas 77843–3255, USA.

BARTON, Maj.-Gen. Eric Walter, CB 1983; MBE 1966; BSc, FBIM, FRGS; Director, Caravan Club Ltd, since 1984; *b* 27 April 1928; *s* of Reginald John Barton and Dorothy (*née* Bradfield); *m* 1963 (marr. diss. 1983); two *s*; *m* 1984, Mrs Pamela Clare Frimann, *d* of late Reginald D. Mason and of Doris Mason, Winchelsea. *Educ:* St Clement Danes Sch., London; Royal Military Coll. of Science (BScEng 1955). Dip. in Photogrammetry, UCL, 1960. FBIM 1979; FRGS 1979. Commnd RE, 1948; served Mid East, 1948–50; Arab Legion, 1951–52; seconded to Dir, Overseas Surveys, E Africa, 1957–59; Sen. Instr, Sch. of Mil. Survey, 1961–63; OC 13 Fd Survey Sqdn, Aden, 1965–67; Dir, Surveys and Prodn, Ordnance Survey, 1977–80; Dir of Mil. Survey, 1980–84. Major 1961, Lt-Col 1967, Col 1972, Brig. 1976, Maj.-Gen. 1980. Col Comdt, RE, 1982–; Hon. Col 135 Field Survey Sqn RE (V) TA, 1984–. Chm., Field Survey Assoc., 1984–86; Member: Council, Photogrammetric Soc., 1979–82; Nat. Cttee for Photogrammetry, 1979–84; Council, RGS, 1980–83; Nat. Cttee for Geography, 1981–84. *Recreations:* swimming, water sports, ski-ing, numismatics. *Address:* c/o Barclays Bank, 50 Jewry Street, Winchester, Hants. *Clubs:* Army and Navy, Geographical.

BARTON, Maj.-Gen. Francis Christopher, CB 1966; CBE 1964; *b* 17 Jan. 1916; *s* of Rev. John Bernard Barton, Elphinstone House, Hastings; *m* 1939, Olivia Mary Darroll-Smith; two *d*. *Educ:* Haileybury Coll. 2nd Lieut, Royal Marines, 1934; Lieut-Col, 1956; Brig., 1961; Maj.-Gen., 1964. Comd 45 Commando, RM, 1958–60; Comd 3 Commando Brigade, RM, 1962–63; Comdt, Joint Warfare Establishment, Old Sarum, 1964–66; retired, 1966. Voluntary Help Organiser, Royal Victoria Hospitals, Bournemouth, 1967–80; Chm., Standing Conf., Voluntary Help Organisers, 1971–72. *Address:* Moorcroft, Blissford, Fordingbridge, Hants.

BARTON, John Bernard Adie, CBE 1981; Associate Director, Royal Shakespeare Company, since 1964; *b* 26 Nov. 1928; *s* of late Sir Harold Montague Barton and Joyce Wale; *m* 1968, Anne Righter (*see* B. A. Barton). *Educ:* Eton Coll.; King's Coll., Cambridge (BA, MA). Fellow, King's Coll., Cambridge, 1954–60 (Lay Dean, 1956–59). Joined Royal Shakespeare Company, 1960; Associate Dir, 1964. Has adapted texts and directed or co-directed many plays for Royal Shakespeare Company, including: The Taming of the Shrew, 1960; The Hollow Crown, 1961; The Art of Seduction, 1962; The Wars of the Roses, 1963–64; Henry IV, Parts I and II, and Henry V, 1964–66; Love's Labour's Lost, 1965; Coriolanus and All's Well That Ends Well, 1967; Julius Caesar and Troilus and Cressida, 1968; Twelfth Night and When Thou Art King, 1969; Measure for Measure and The Tempest, 1970; Richard II, Henry V, and Othello, 1971; Richard II, 1973; King John, Cymbeline, and Dr Faustus, 1974; Perkin Warbeck, 1975; Much Ado About Nothing, The Winter's Tale, and Troilus and Cressida, 1976; A Midsummer Night's Dream, Pillars of the Community, 1977; The Way of the World, The Merchant of Venice, Love's Labour's Lost, 1978; The Greeks, 1979; Hamlet, 1980; The Merchant of Venice, Titus Andronicus and The Two Gentlemen of Verona, 1981; La Ronde, 1982; Life's a Dream, 1983; The Devils, 1984; Waste, Dream Play, 1985; The Rover, 1986. Directed: The School for Scandal, Haymarket, 1983, Duke of York's, 1983; The Vikings at Helgeland, Den Nationale Scene, Bergen, 1983. Wrote and presented Playing Shakespeare, LWT, 1982, Channel 4, 1984; narrated Morte d'Arthur, BBC2, 1984. *Publications:* The Hollow Crown, 1962 (and 1971); The Wars of the Roses, 1970. *Recreations:* travel, chess, work. *Address:* 14 DeWalden Court, 85 New Cavendish Street, W1. *T:* 01-580 6196.

BARTON, Margaret, LRAM; writer; *b* 1897; *y d* of Thomas Lloyd Barton and Fanny Roberta Isaacs. *Educ:* St Paul's Girls' Sch.; Royal Academy of Music. *Publications:* Tunbridge Wells, 1937; Garrick, 1948; (with Sir Osbert Sitwell) Sober Truth, 1930; Victoriana, 1931; Brighton, 1935. *Address:* 8 Penywern Road, SW5.

BARTON-CHAPPLE, Dorothy, (Mrs Derek Barton-Chapple); *see* Tutin, Dorothy.

BARTOSIK, Rear-Adm. Josef C., CB 1968; DSC 1943; *b* 20 July 1917; *m* 1st, 1943, Cynthia Pamela Bowman; three *s* one *d*; 2nd, 1969, Jeannine Scott (*née* Bridgeman). Joined Polish Navy, 1935; served in Polish destroyers under British operational control, 1939–46; transf. to RN, 1948; commanded: HMS Comus, 1955–56; HMS Scarborough and 5th Frigate Sqn, 1960–61; HMS Seahawk (RN Air Station Culdrose), 1962–63, HMS London, 1964–65; Rear-Adm. 1966; Asst Chief of Naval Staff (Ops), 1966–68; retired 1968. Coordinating Dir, European Jt Org., Australia Europe Container Service and Australia NZ Europe Container Service, 1969–81, retired 1981. *Recreation:* outdoor activities. *Address:* 33 Cheval Place, SW7.

BARTTELOT, Lt-Col Sir Brian Walter de Stopham, 5th Bt, *cr* 1875; OBE 1983; psc; Coldstream Guards; General Staff Officer 1, HQ BAOR, since 1985; *b* 17 July 1941; *s* of Lt-Col Sir Walter de Stopham Barttelot, 4th Bt, and Sara Patricia (who *m* 2nd, 1965, Comdr James Barttelot, RN retd), *d* of late Lieut-Col H. V. Ravenscroft; *S* father, 1944; *m* 1969, Hon. Mary Angela Fiona Weld Forester, *y d* of 7th Baron Forester, and of Marie Louise Priscilla, CStJ, *d* of Sir Herbert Perrott, 6th Bt, CH, CB; four *d*. *Educ:* Eton; RMA, Sandhurst. Temp. Equerry to HM the Queen, 1970–71; Camberley Staff Coll., 1974; GSO2, Army Staff Duties Directorate, MoD, 1975–76; Second in comd, 2nd Bn, Coldstream Guards, 1977–78; Mil. Sec. to Maj.-Gen. comdg London Dist and Household Div., 1978–81; GSO1, MoD, 1981–82; CO 1st Bn Coldstream Gds, 1982–85. Liveryman, Gunmakers' Co., 1981. *Heir:* *b* Robin Ravenscroft Barttelot, *b* 15 Dec. 1943. *Address:* Keepers, Stopham, Pulborough, W Sussex RH20 1EB. *Clubs:* Cavalry and Guards, Pratt's, Farmers', Buck's.

BARWELL, David John Frank; HM Diplomatic Service; Counsellor, Paris, since 1985; *b* 12 Oct. 1938; *s* of James Howard and Helen Mary Barwell; *m* 1968, Christine Sarah Carter; one *s*. *Educ:* Lancing College; Trinity College, Oxford; Institut des Hautes Etudes Internationales, Geneva. FCO, 1965; served: Aden, 1967; Baghdad, 1968; Bahrain, 1971; Cairo, 1973; FCO, 1976; Nicosia, 1982. *Recreations:* gardening, singing. *Address:* c/o Foreign and Commonwealth Office, SW1. *Club:* Cerle de l'Union Interalliée (Paris).

BARWICK, David Robert, CBE 1976; QC 1977; Governor of British Virgin Islands, since 1982; *b* 20 Oct. 1927; *s* of Jack Barwick and Kathleen Barwick (*née* Gould); *m* 1951, Margaret (*née* Funnell); one *s* two *d*. *Educ:* Christchurch Boys' High Sch.; Univ. of New Zealand (LLB). Barrister and Solicitor of the Supreme Court of New Zealand. Private practice, NZ, 1953–56; Asst Attorney-General, Judicial Comr, British Solomon Islands, 1956–62; Judge of the High Court of Western Pacific, Gilbert and Ellice Islands, 1962–67; Parliamentary Draftsman, Solicitor-General, Secretary for Justice, Actg Attorney-General, Malaŵi, 1967–76; Attorney-General: Solomon Islands, 1976; Cayman Islands, 1976–82. *Recreations:* painting, conchology, music, golf. *Address:* Government House, Tortola, British Virgin Islands. *T:* 43400. *Club:* Royal Commonwealth Society.

BARWICK, Rt. Hon. Sir Garfield (Edward John), AK 1981; GCMG 1965; Kt 1953; PC 1964; QC (Australia); Chief Justice of Australia, 1964–81; *b* 22 June 1903; *s* of late Jabez Edward Barwick and Lilian Grace Ellicott; *m* 1929, Norma Mountier Symons; one *s* one *d*. *Educ:* Fort Street Boys' High Sch., Sydney; University of Sydney, BA 1923; LLB (Hons) 1926; Hon. LLD Sydney, 1972. New South Wales Bar, 1927; KC 1941; Victorian Bar, 1945; KC (Vic) 1945; Queensland Bar, 1958; QC Queensland, 1958. Practised extensively in all jurisdictions: Supreme Court, High Court of Australia and Privy Council. Pres. NSW Bar Assoc., 1950–52 and 1955–56; Attorney-Gen. Commonwealth of Australia, Dec. 1958–Feb. 1964; Minister for External Affairs, Dec. 1961–April 1964. Judge ad hoc, Internat. Court of Justice, 1973–74. President: Law Council of Australia, 1952–54; Australian Inst. of Internat. Affairs, 1972–83. Hon. Bencher, Lincoln's Inn, 1964. Leader: Australian Delegation, SEATO Council, Bangkok, 1961, Paris, 1963; UN Delegation, 1960, 1962–64; Australian Delegation to ECAFE, Manila, 1963; Australian Delegation, ANZUS, Canberra, 1962, Wellington, 1963. Chancellor, Macquarie Univ., 1967–78. Pres., NSW Inst. for Deaf and Blind Children, 1976–. *Recreations:* fishing, yachting. *Address:* 71 The Cotswolds, Curagul and Bobbin Head Roads, North Turramurra, NSW 2074, Australia. *Clubs:* Australian (Sydney); Royal Yacht Squadron; Royal Sydney Yacht Squadron; Hon. Member: Pioneers' (Australasian); Tattersalls; City Tattersalls; Middle Harbour Yacht.

BARYSHNIKOV, Mikhail; Artistic Director, since 1980, and Principal Dancer, 1974–78 and since 1980, American Ballet Theater; *b* 28 Jan. 1948; *s* of Nicolai Baryshnikov and Alexandra (*née* Kisselov). *Educ:* Ballet Sch. of Riga, Latvia; Kirov Ballet Sch., Leningrad. Soloist, Kirov Ballet Co., 1969–74; Principal Dancer, NY City Ballet, 1978–79. Guest Artist, 1974–, with: Royal Ballet; National Ballet of Canada; Hamburg Ballet; Ballet Victoria, Aust.; Stuttgart Ballet; Alvin Ailey Dance Co., and Eliot Feld Ballet, New York; Spoleto Festival. Repertoire includes: Shadowplay (Tudor); Le Jeune Homme et la Morte (Petit); Sacré du Printemps (Tetley); Prodigal Son, Apollo, Theme and Variations (Balanchine); Afternoon of a Faun (Robbins); Romeo and Juliet, Wild Boy (MacMillan); Configurations (Choo San Goh); Les Patineurs, A Month in the Country (Ashton); Spectre de la Rose, Le Pavillon d'Armide, Petrouchka (Fokine); Santa Fe Saga (Feld); La Sylphide, La Bayadère, Coppélia, La Fille mal gardée (Bournonville); Swan Lake (Sergeyev and Bruhn); The Nutcracker, Don Quixote (own choreography). Works created: Medea (Butler), 1975; Push Comes to Shove, and, Once More Frank (Tharp), Connotations on Hamlet (Neumeier), Pas de Duke (Ailey), Other Dances (Robbins), 1976; Variations on America (Feld), 1977; Rubies (Balanchine), Opus Nineteen (Robbins), 1979; Rhapsody (Ashton), 1980. Gold Medal: Varna Competition, Bulgaria, 1966; 1st Internat. Ballet Comp., Moscow, 1968 (also awarded Nijinsky Prize by Paris Acad. of Dance); Dance Magazine Award, NYC, 1978. *Films:* The Turning Point, 1978; White Nights, 1986. *Publication:* (with Charles Engell France, photographs by Martha Swope) Baryshnikov at Work, 1976. *Recreation:* fishing. *Address:* c/o Edgar Vincent Associates, 145 East 52nd Street, Suite 804, New York, NY 10023, USA. *T:* (212) 752–3020.

BARZEL, Dr Rainer C.; Member of the Bundestag, Federal Republic of Germany, since 1957; *b* 20 June 1924; *s* of Dr Candidus Barzel, Senior Asst Master, and Maria Barzel. *Educ:* studied Jurisprudence and Political Economy, Univ. of Cologne (Referendar, Dr jur.). With Govt of North Rhine-Westphalia, 1949–56; Federal Minister in the Adenauer Govt, for all-German affairs, Dec. 1962–Oct. 1963; Chairman: Cttee on Economic Affairs, German Fed. Parlt, 1977–79; Cttee on Foreign Affairs, 1980–82; Fed. Minister for Inter-German Affairs, 1982–83; Pres. of Bundestag, 1983–84. Coordinator for German-French cooperation, Feb.-Dec. 1980. Chm., CDU, 1971–73 and Chm., CDU/CSU Group in German Federal Parlt, 1964–73. Pres., German-French Inst., 1980–83. *Publications:* (all publ. in Germany): Die geistigen Grundlagen der politischen Parteien, 1947; Die deutschen Parteien, 1952; Gesichtspunkte eines Deutschen, 1968; Es ist noch nicht zu spät, 1976; Auf dem Drahtseil, 1978; Das Formular, 1979; Unterwegs—Woher und wohin, 1982. *Recreation:* skating. *Address:* Bundeshaus, 5300 Bonn, Germany.

BARZUN, Jacques; University Professor Emeritus, Columbia University; *b* 30 Nov. 1907; *s* of Henri Barzun and Anna-Rose Martin; *m* 1936, Mariana Lowell (*d* 1979); two *s* one *d*; *m* 1980, Marguerite Davenport. *Educ:* Lycée Janson de Sailly; Columbia Univ. Instructor in History, Columbia Univ., 1929; Research Fellow, American Council of Learned Socs, 1933–34; Columbia University: Asst Prof., 1938; Associate Prof., 1942; Prof. of History, 1945–75; University Prof., 1967; Dean of Grad. Faculties, 1955–58; Dean of Faculties and Provost, 1958–67. Director: American Friends of Cambridge Univ.; Council for Basic Educn; Peabody Inst.; NY Soc. Library; Mem. Adv. Council, Univ. Coll. at Buckingham. Membre Associé de l'Académie Delphinale, Grenoble, 1952; Member: Amer. Acad. of Arts and Letters, USA (President, 1972–75, 1977–79); Amer. Acad. of Arts and Sciences; American Historical Assoc.; Amer. Philos. Soc.; FRSA, USA (Benjamin Franklin Fellow). Seth Low Prof. of History, Columbia Univ., 1960; Extraordinary Fellow, Churchill Coll., Cambridge, 1961–. Literary Advisor, Charles Scribner's Sons Ltd, 1975–; Mem. Bd of Editors, Encyclopaedia Britannica, 1962–. Chevalier de la Légion d'Honneur. *Publications:* The French Race: Theories of its Origins, 1932; Race: A Study in Superstition, 1937 (revd, 1965); Of Human Freedom, 1939 (revd, 1964); Darwin, Marx, Wagner, 1941 (revd, 1958); Teacher in America, 1945 (revd, 1981); Berlioz and the Romantic Century, 1950 (4th edn 1982); Pleasures of Music, 1951, rev. edn 1977; Selected Letters of Byron, 1953 (2nd edn 1957); Nouvelles Lettres de Berlioz, 1954, 2nd edn 1974; God's Country and Mine, 1954; Music in American Life, 1956; The Energies of Art, 1956; The Modern Researcher (with Henry F. Graff), 1957, 4th edn 1985; The House of Intellect, 1959 (2nd edn 1961); Classic, Romantic and Modern, 1961; Science: The Glorious Entertainment, 1964; (ed) Follett's Modern American Usage, 1967; The American University, 1968 (2nd edn 1970); (with W. H. Taylor) A Catalogue of Crime, 1971, rev. edn 1973; On Writing, Editing and Publishing, 1971; Berlioz's Evenings with the Orchestra, 1956, 2nd edn 1973; The Use and Abuse of Art, 1974; Clio and the Doctors, 1974; Simple and Direct, 1975; Critical Questions,

1982; A Stroll with William James, 1983; contrib. to leading US journals. *Address:* Charles Scribner's Sons, 115 Fifth Avenue, New York, NY 10003, USA. *T:* 486–4041. *Clubs:* Athenæum, Authors'; Century (New York).

BASARAH, Air Chief Marshal Saleh; Indonesian Ambassador to the Court of St James's, 1978–81; *b* 14 Aug. 1928; *m* 1955, Sartini Kartina; two *s* three *d. Educ:* Air Force Staff and Command College. Sqdn Comdr, 1960; AO for Operation No 001 Trng Wing, 1963; Actg Wing Comdr, CO Wing, No 001 Trng Wing, 1964–66; Dir of Operation Air HQ, 1966–68; Comdr, Fifth Regional Air Comd, 1966–69; Comdr, Air Force Special Troop Comd, 1967–69; Asst CoS for Operation, 1969–70; CoS, Deptl Affairs, Dept of Defence and Security, 1970–73; CoS of Air Force, 1973–77. 11 Medals and Satya Lencana Orders of Merit. *Recreations:* golf, soccer, boxing. *Address:* c/o Department of Defence, Jakarta, Indonesia.

BASHFORD, Humphrey John Charles, MA; Headmaster, Hessle High School, 1964–81, retired; *b* 5 Oct. 1920; *s* of late Sir Henry Bashford, MD, FRCP, and late Margaret Eveline Sutton; *m* 1942, Alyson Margaret Liddle; two *s* three *d. Educ:* Sherborne Sch.; Clare Coll., Cambridge. MA Cambridge 1950. Served War of 1939–45: commissioned 2nd Bn Oxford Bucks LI, 1941; GSO3 HQ Airborne Corps 1944–46. Senior History Master, Leys Sch., Cambridge, 1947; Part-time Tutor, WEA, 1950; Headmaster, Wellingborough Sch., 1956–64. *Recreations:* gardening, fly-fishing. *Address:* 16 Main Street, Hotham, York.

BASING, 5th Baron *cr* 1887; **Neil Lutley Sclater-Booth;** *b* 16 Jan. 1939; *s* of 4th Baron Basing and Jeannette (*d* 1957), *d* of late Neil Bruce MacKelvie, New York; *S* father, 1983; *m* 1967, Patricia Ann, *d* of late George Bryan Whitfield, New Haven, Conn; two *s. Educ:* Eton; Harvard Univ. (BA). *Heir: s* Hon. Stuart Whitfield Sclater-Booth, *b* 18 Dec. 1969. *Address:* 112 East 74th Street, New York, NY 10021, USA.

BASINGSTOKE, Bishop Suffragan of, since 1977; **Rt. Rev. Michael Richard John Manktelow;** Residentiary Canon of Winchester Cathedral, since 1977; *b* 23 Sept. 1927; *s* of late Sir Richard Manktelow, KBE, CB, and late Helen Manktelow; *m* 1966, Rosamund Mann; three *d. Educ:* Whitgift School, Croydon; Christ's Coll., Cambridge (MA 1952); Chichester Theological Coll. Deacon 1953, priest 1954, Lincoln; Asst Curate of Boston, Lincs, 1953–57; Chaplain of Christ's Coll., Cambridge, 1957–61; Chaplain of Lincoln Theological Coll., 1961–64, Sub-Warden, 1964–66; Vicar of Knaresborough, 1966–73; Rural Dean of Harrogate, 1972–77; Vicar of St Wilfrid's, Harrogate, 1973–77; Hon. Canon of Ripon Cathedral, 1975–77. President: Anglican and Eastern Churches Assoc., 1980–; Assoc. for Promoting Retreats, 1982–. *Publication:* Forbes Robinson: Disciple of Love, 1961. *Recreations:* music, walking. *Address:* 1 The Close, Winchester, Hants SO23 9LS. *T:* Winchester 69374.

BASINGSTOKE, Archdeacon of; *see* Nash, Ven. T. G.

BASINSKI, Zbigniew Stanislaw, OC 1985; DPhil, DSc; FRS 1980; FRSC; Principal Research Officer and Head of Materials Physics (Division of Physics), National Research Council of Canada; *b* Wolkowysk, Poland, 28 April 1928; *s* of Antoni Basinski and Maria Zofia Anna Hilferding Basinska; *m* 1952, Sylvia Joy Pugh; two *s. Educ:* Lyceum of Krzemieniec, Poland; Polish Army Cadet Sch., Camp Barbara, Palestine, 1943–47; Univ. of Oxford (BSc, MA, DPhil, DSc). Research Asst, Univ. of Oxford, 1951–54; Staff Member, Dept of Mech. Engrg (Cryogenic Lab.), Massachusetts Inst. of Technol., 1954–56; Nat. Res. Council of Canada, 1956–. Ford Distinguished Vis. Prof., Carnegie Inst. of Technol., Pittsburgh, USA, 1964–65; Commonwealth Vis. Prof., Univ. of Oxford, Fellow of Wolfson Coll., Oxford, 1969–70; Adjunct Prof., Carleton Univ., Ottawa, 1975–77, 1981–; Overseas Fellow, Churchill Coll., Cambridge, 1980–81. *Publications:* many original research papers, mainly related to crystal defects and the mechanical properties of metals, in learned jls. *Recreations:* computer design, the stock market, winemaking, general reading. *Address:* 108 Delong Drive, Gloucester, Ontario K1J 7E1, Canada. *T:* (613) 7468227. *Clubs:* Oxford Union, Halifax House (Oxford).

BASNETT, David; General Secretary: General and Municipal Workers' Union, 1973; General, Municipal, Boilermakers and Allied Trades Union, 1982; retired 1986; *b* 9 Feb. 1924; British; *m* 1956, Kathleen Joan Molyneaux; two *s. Educ:* Quarry Bank High School, Liverpool. Served War of 1939–45, RAF. Trade Union Official, 1948; Nat. Industrial Officer, GMWU, 1960–72. Mem. TUC General Council, 1966–86 (Chm., 1977–78): Chairman: Trade Union Adv. Cttee to OECD, 1983–86; TULV, 1979–85. Pres., Unity Trust, 1984–86. Numerous committees of enquiry including: Royal Commission on Penal Reform; Commission on the Constitution, 1969–71; Royal Commn on the Press, 1974–77. Mem., NEDC, 1973–86; Mem., National Enterprise Bd, 1975–79 (and of Organising Cttee, 1975). *Address:* Windrush, St John's Avenue, Leatherhead, Surrey. *T:* Leatherhead 372216.

BASOV, Prof. Nikolai Gennadievich; Orders of Lenin, 1967, 1969, 1972, 1975, 1982; Hero of Socialist Labour, 1969, 1982; Physicist, USSR; Member of the Praesidium of the Academy of Sciences of USSR, since 1967; Deputy of USSR Supreme Soviet, since 1974; Member of the Praesidium of the USSR Supreme Soviet, since 1982; Director of the P. N. Lebedev Physical Institute, Moscow, since 1973 (Vice-Director, 1958–72), also Head of the Laboratory of Quantum Radiophysics; Professor, Moscow Institute of Physical Engineers; *b* 1922; *s* of Prof. Gennady Fedorovich Basov and Zinaida Andreevna Molchanova; *m* 1950, Ksenia Tikhonovna Nazarova Basova; two *s. Educ:* secondary; Kiev Military-medical Sch.; Institute of Physical Engineers, Moscow. Joined the P. N. Lebedev Physical Institute, 1948. Pres., All-Union Soc., Znanie, 1978; Vice-Pres., WFSW, 1983 (Vice-Pres., Exec. Council, 1976). Editor: Priroda (Nature), Popular Sciences Magazine; Soviet Jl of Quantum Electronics. Corresponding Mem. USSR Acad. of Sciences, 1962; Academician, 1966. Fellow, Optical Soc. of America, 1974 (Mem. 1972); Member: Acad. of Sciences of GDR, 1967; German Acad. of Natural Scis, Leopoldina, 1971; Bulgarian Acad. of Scis, 1974; Swedish Royal Acad. of Engineering Sciences, 1975; Polish Acad. of Scis, 1977; Czechoslovakian Acad. of Scis, 1977 (Gold Medal, 1975). Hon. Dr: Polish Mil.-Tech. Acad., 1972; Jena Univ., 1974; Prague Polytechnic Inst., 1975; Pavia Univ., 1977; Madrid Polytechnic Univ., 1985. Awarded Lenin Prize, 1959; Nobel Prize for Physics (jointly with Prof. A. M. Prokhorov of the P. N. Lebedev Physical Institute, Moscow, and Prof. C. H. Townes of MIT Cambridge, Mass, USA), 1964; A. Volta gold medal, Italian Physical Soc., 1977. *Address:* P. N. Lebedev Physical Institute, Academy of Sciences of the USSR, Lenin Prospekt 53, Moscow, USSR.

BASS, Harry Godfrey Mitchell, CMG 1972; HM Diplomatic Service, retired; *b* 26 Aug. 1914; *s* of late Rev. Arthur Edward Bass and Mildred Bass; *m* 1948, Monica Mary, *d* of late Rev. H. F. Burroughs (and eponym of the orchid *Oncidium flexuosum* x *Rodriguezia fragrans*); two *s* one *d. Educ:* Marlborough Coll.; Gonville and Caius Coll., Cambridge; St John's Coll., Oxford (BA (Oxon) 1937, MA (Cantab) 1940). British Museum, Dept of Egyptian and Assyrian Antiquities, 1939; Admiralty, 1940; Dominions Office, 1946; Asst Sec., Office of UK High Commissioner, Australia, 1948–51; Mem. of Secretariat, Commonwealth Economic Conference, 1952 and Meeting of Commonwealth Prime Ministers, 1953; Counsellor, Office of UK High Commissioner, Calcutta, 1954–57; Dep. UK High Commissioner, Federation of Rhodesia and Nyasaland, 1959–61; British Minister (Pretoria and Cape Town) in the Republic of S Africa, 1961–62; seconded to Central African Office, 1963–64; British Dep. High Commissioner, Ibadan, 1965–67; Head of Consular Dept, FCO, 1967–70; High Comr in Lesotho, 1970–73. Chapter Clerk, St George's Chapel, Windsor, 1974–77. Silver Jubilee Medal, 1977. *Recreations:* birdwatching, walking. *Address:* Tyler's Mead, Reepham, Norfolk NR10 4LA.

See also Baron Crofton.

BASS, Rear-Adm. Paul Eric, CB 1981; CEng, FIMechE, MIMarE; *b* 7 March 1925; *s* of C. H. P. Bass, Ipswich; *m* 1948, Audrey Bruce Tomlinson; one *s. Educ:* Northgate School, Ipswich; Royal Naval Engineering Coll., Keyham. Served as Midshipman in HM Ships Cambrian, Mauritius, Premier and Rodney; Lieut in Belfast, Phoebe and Implacable; Lt Comdr in Ulysses; Comdr in Lion and Tiger; Naval Staff Course, 1962; Captain, Weapons Trials, 1969–72; NATO Defense Course, 1972–73; Asst Chief of Staff (Intelligence), SACLANT, 1973–75; Dir, Naval Manning and Training (Engineering), 1975–78; Flag Officer, Portsmouth and Port Admiral, Portsmouth, 1979–81, retired 1981. *Recreations:* sailing, fishing, golf. *Address:* c/o National Westminster Bank, 68 Palmerston Road, Southsea, Hants PO5 3PN. *Clubs:* Royal Yacht Squadron; Royal Naval Sailing Association; Royal Naval and Royal Albert Yacht (Portsmouth).

BASSET, Bryan Ronald; Chairman, Royal Ordnance plc, since 1985; *b* 29 Oct, 1932; *s* of late Ronald Lambart Basset and of Lady Elizabeth Basset, CVO, *d* of 7th Earl of Dartmouth; *m* 1960, Lady Carey Elizabeth Coke, *d* of 5th Earl of Leicester; three *s. Educ:* Eton; RMA Sandhurst. Captain, Scots Guards, 1952–57. Stockbroker, Toronto, Canada, 1957–59; Panmure Gordon & Co., Stockbrokers, 1959–72; Managing Director, Philip Hill Investment Trust, 1972–85. *Recreations:* farming, shooting, fishing. *Address:* 10 Stack House, Cundy Street, SW1. *T:* 01–730 2785; Quarles, Wells-next-the-Sea, Norfolk. *T:* Fakenham 738105. *Clubs:* White's, Pratt's.

BASSETT, Douglas Anthony; Director, National Museum of Wales, 1977–86; *b* 11 Aug. 1927; *s* of Hugh Bassett and Annie Jane Bassett; *m* 1955, Elizabeth Menna Roberts; three *d. Educ:* Llanelli Boys' Grammar Sch.; University Coll. of Wales, Aberystwyth. Asst Lectr and Lectr, Dept of Geology, Glasgow Univ., 1952–59; Keeper, Dept of Geology, Nat. Museum of Wales, 1959–77. Member: Water Resources Bd, 1965–73; Nature Conservancy Council (and Chm., Adv. Cttee for Wales), 1973–85; Secretary of State for Wales, Celtic Sea Adv. Cttee, 1974–79; Ordnance Survey Rev. Cttee, 1978–79; Founder Mem. and first Chm., Assoc. of Teachers of Geology, 1967–68; Chm., Royal Soc. Cttee on History of Geology, 1972–82. Dir, Nat. Welsh-American Foundn, 1980–. Hon. Professorial Fellow, University Coll., Cardiff, 1977. Aberconway Medal, Institn of Geologists, 1985. Mem. White Order of Bards of GB, 1979; Officier de l'Ordre des Arts et des Lettres (received from Min. of Culture, Paris), 1983. *Publications:* Bibliography and Index of Geology and Allied Sciences for Wales and the Welsh Borders, 1897–1958, 1961; A Source-book of Geological, Geomorphological and Soil Maps for Wales and the Welsh Borders (1800–1966), 1967; contribs to various geological, museum and historical jls. *Recreations:* bibliography, chronology. *Address:* 4 Romilly Road, Cardiff CF5 1FH.

BASTEN, Sir Henry (Bolton), Kt 1966; CMG 1947; MA Oxon and Adelaide; retired, 1982; University of Adelaide, 1953–67, Vice-Chancellor, 1958–67. Formerly Chairman and General Manager, Singapore & Penang Harbour Boards. Investigated conditions in Australian ports for Commonwealth Government, 1951–52, report published, 1952. Chm., Aust. Univs Commn, 1968–71; Foundn Chm., Council, Australian Inst. of Marine Science, 1972–77. Hon. DLitt Flinders Univ. (S Australia), 1967. *Address:* 13 Holmes Crescent, Campbell, ACT 2601, Australia.

BASTIN, Prof. John Andrew, MA, PhD; FRAS; Professor, since 1971, and Head of Department of Physics, 1975–80, Queen Mary College, London University; *b* 3 Jan. 1929; *s* of Lucy and Arthur Bastin; *m* 1959, Wendy Susan Jacobsen; one *s* one *d. Educ:* George Monoux Grammar Sch., London; Corpus Christi Coll., Oxford. MA, PhD. Univ. of Ibadan, Nigeria, 1952–56; Univ. of Reading, 1956–59; Queen Mary Coll., Univ. of London, 1959–. Initiated a group in far infrared astronomy at Queen Mary College, 1960–70. *Publications:* papers on far infrared astronomy and lunar evolution. *Recreations:* English water colours, architecture, Renaissance and Baroque music, tennis, skiing. *Address:* 27 Endwell Road, SE4 2NE.

BATCHELOR, Prof. George Keith, FRS 1957; Emeritus Professor of Applied Mathematics, University of Cambridge, 1983; *b* Melbourne, 8 March 1920; *s* of George Conybere Batchelor and Ivy Constance Batchelor (*née* Berneye); *m* 1944, Wilma Maud Rätz, MBE; three *d. Educ:* Essendon and Melbourne High Schs; Univ. of Melbourne. BSc 1940, MSc 1941, Melbourne; PhD 1948, Adams Prize, 1951, Univ. of Cambridge. Research Officer, Aeronautical Research Laboratory, Melbourne, 1940–44; Fellow of Trinity Coll., Cambridge, 1947–; Lectr, Univ. of Cambridge, 1948–59, Reader in Fluid Dynamics, 1959–64, and Head of Dept of Applied Mathematics and Theoretical Physics, 1959–83; Prof. of Applied Maths, Univ. of Cambridge, 1964–83. Chairman: European Mechanics Cttee, 1965–; Nat Cttee for Theoretical and Applied Mechanics, 1967–72. Editor, Cambridge Monographs on Mechanics and Applied Mathematics, 1953–; Editor, Journal of Fluid Mechanics, 1956–. Mem. Council, Royal Soc., 1986–; Mem., Royal Soc. of Sciences, Uppsala, 1972. Foreign Hon. Member: Amer. Acad. of Arts and Scis, 1959; Polish Acad. of Scis, 1974; French Acad. of Sci., 1984. Dr *hc*: Univ. of Grenoble, 1959; Tech. Univ. of Denmark, 1974; McGill Univ., 1986. *Publications:* The Theory of Homogeneous Turbulence, 1953; An Introduction to Fluid Dynamics, 1967; (ed) The Scientific Papers of G. I. Taylor, vol. 1, 1958, vol. 2, 1960, vol. 3, 1963, vol. 4, 1971; papers on fluid mechanics and its applications in scientific jls. *Address:* Cobbers, Conduit Head Road, Cambridge. *T:* Cambridge 356387.

BATCHELOR, Sir Ivor (Ralph Campbell), Kt 1981; CBE 1976; FRCPE, DPM, FRSE, FRCPsych; Professor of Psychiatry, University of Dundee, 1967–82, now Emeritus Professor; *b* 29 Nov. 1916; *s* of Ralph C. L. Batchelor, FRCSE, FRCPE, and Muriel (*née* Shaw); *m* 1941, Honor Wallace Williamson; one *s* three *d. Educ:* Edinburgh Academy; Edinburgh Univ. MB ChB. FRCPsych 1971 (Hon. 1984). RAFVR, 1941–46; Sqdn Ldr, Comd Neuro-psychiatrist, CMF. Asst Phys. and Dep. Phys. Supt, Royal Edinburgh Hosp., and Sen. Lectr in Psychiatry, Univ. of Edinburgh, 1947–56; Phys. Supt, Dundee Royal Mental Hosp., 1956–62; Prof. of Psychiatry, Univ. of St Andrews, 1962–67. Member: Gen. Nursing Council for Scotland (Chm. Educn Cttee), 1964–71; Standing Med. Adv. Cttee, Scot., 1967–74; Adv. Cttee on Med. Research, Scotland, 1969–73; Scottish Council for Postgraduate Med. Educn, 1970–79; Chief Scientist Cttee, Scotland, 1973–82. Mem., Med. Services Review (Porritt) Cttee, 1958–62; Chm., Cttee on Staffing Mental Deficiency Hosps, 1967–70; Member: Cttee on Nursing (Briggs Cttee), 1970–72; Cttee on the Working of the Abortion Act (Lane Cttee), 1971–74; MRC (Chm. Clinical Research Bd, 1973–74, Chm. Neuro-Sciences Bd, 1974–75), 1972–76; MRC Health Services Res. Panel, 1981–82; Royal Commn on the Nat. Health Service, 1976–79; Indep. Sci. Cttee on Smoking and Health, 1980–86; UK Central Council for Nursing, Midwifery and Health Visiting, 1980–83; Scottish Hosp. Endowments Res. Trust, 1984–. Chm. Trustees, Orchar Art Gall., Dundee, 1980–. *Publications:* Aviation Neuro-Psychiatry, 1945;

Henderson and Gillespie's Textbook of Psychiatry, 8th edn 1956 and subseq. edns to 10th edn 1969; contribs to med. jls. *Address:* 55 Hepburn Gardens, St Andrews, Fife KY16 9LS. *T:* St Andrews 73130. *Club:* Athenæum.

BATCHELOR, Prof. (John) Richard; Professor of Immunology, Royal Postgraduate Medical School, Hammersmith Hospital, since 1979; *b* 4 Oct. 1931; *s* of B. W. Batchelor, CBE and Mrs C. E. Batchelor; *m* 1955, Moira Ann (*née* McLellan); two *s* two *d*. *Educ:* Marlborough Coll.; Emmanuel Coll., Cambridge; Guy's Hospital, London. MB, BChir Cantab, 1955; MD Cantab 1965. Nat. Service, RAMC, 1957–59; Dept of Pathology, Guy's Hospital: Res. Fellow, 1959–61; Lectr and Sen. Lectr, 1961–67. Prof. of Transplantation Research, RCS, 1967; Dir, McIndoe Res. Unit, Queen Victoria Hosp., East Grinstead, 1967–78. Mem. Court, Skinners' Company. Hon. Sec., then Vice-Pres. (E Hemisphere), Transplantation Soc., 1976–80; Member Council, Nat. Kidney Res. Fund, 1979–. European Editor, Transplantation, 1964–. *Publications:* scientific articles upon tissue transplantation research in various special jls. *Recreations:* sailing; tennis; walking. *Address:* Little Ambrook, Nursery Road, Walton-on-the-Hill, Tadworth, Surrey. *T:* Tadworth 2028. *Clubs:* Brooks's, Queen's, Royal Society of Medicine.

BATCHELOR, John Stanley, FRCS; Orthopaedic Surgeon, Guy's Hospital, 1946–70, retired; *b* 4 Dec. 1905; *s* of Dr Ferdinand Stanley Batchelor and Florence Batchelor; *m* 1934, Marjorie Blanche Elvina Rudkin; two *s* one *d*. *Educ:* Christ's Coll., Christchurch, NZ; Otago Univ.; Guy's Hospital. MRCS, LRCP 1931; FRCS 1934. Pres., Section of Orthopaedics, RSocMed, 1958–59; British Orthopaedic Assoc.: Hon. Treas. 1960–65; Hon. Sec. 1964; Vice-Pres. 1967–68; Pres. 1970–72. *Publications:* contribs to med. jls. *Recreations:* golf, walking, antiques.

BATCHELOR, Richard; *see* Batchelor, J. R.

BATE, Ven. Alban F., MA; DCnL; Archdeacon of St John, 1949–63, retired; Rector of St Paul's Church, St John, New Brunswick, 1936–63, retired; *b* 12 May 1893; *s* of Rev. William John Bate and Alice C. McMullen; *m* 1919, Norah F. Warburton, Charlottetown, PEI; two *s* five *d*. *Educ:* Rothesay Collegiate Sch.; Dalhousie, Superior Sch.; University of King's Coll., Nova Scotia, (made Hon. Fellow 1939), BA, 1914; Divinity Testamur, 1916; MA, 1918; Deacon, 1916; Priest, 1917; Curate of Cathedral, Fredericton, 1916–19; Asst at Parish Church, Fredericton, 1919–20; Rector of Fredericton 1920–36 and Archdeacon of Fredericton, 1932–36; Canon of Christ Church Cathedral, Fredericton, 1946; Chaplain of the Legislature of Province of New Brunswick, 1925–35; Chaplain 7th Machine Gun Bn, 1927–36; Chaplain, St George's Soc., 1939–42; Pres. Rotary Club of Fredericton, 1928–29; Saint John, 1941–42. DCnL (King's Univ. Halifax) 1955. *Recreation:* gardening. *Address:* 351 Charlotte Street West, Saint John, NB E2M 1Y7, Canada. *Clubs:* Rotary, Canadian (St John, NB).

BATE, Sir David (Lindsay), KBE 1978 (CBE 1968); Chief Judge, Benue and Plateau States of Nigeria, 1975–77; Senior Puisne Judge, High Court of Justice, Northern States of Nigeria, 1968–75 (Puisne Judge 1957–68); *b* 3 March 1916; *m* 1948, Thadeen June, *d* of late R. F. O'Donnell Peet; two *s*. *Educ:* Marlborough; Trinity Coll., Cambridge. Called to Bar, Inner Temple, 1938. Commissioned, Royal Artillery, 1939 and served, Royal Artillery, 1939–46. Entered Colonial Legal Service, 1947; Crown Counsel, Nigeria, 1947–52; Senior Crown Counsel, Nigeria, 1952–54; Senior Crown Counsel, Northern Nigeria 1954–56; Solicitor-Gen., Northern Nigeria, 1956. *Recreations:* shooting, fishing. *Address:* 4029 Lanchaster Road, RR2, Duncan, British Columbia, Canada.

BATE, Sir (Walter) Edwin, Kt 1969; OBE 1955; Barrister, Solicitor and Notary Public, Hastings, New Zealand, since 1927; *b* 12 March 1901; *s* of Peter and Florence Eleanor Bate; *m* 1925, Louise Jordan; two *s* one *d*. *Educ:* Victoria Univ., Wellington. LLM (first class hons), 1922. Admitted Barrister and Solicitor, 1922; practised: Taumarunui, NZ, 1923; Hastings, NZ, 1927. Mayor, City of Hastings, NZ, 1953–59; Chm., Hawke Bay Hosp. Bd, 1941–74; Pres., Hosp. Bds Assoc. of NZ, 1953–74; Pres., Associated Trustee Savings Banks of NZ, 1968 and 1969. OStJ 1961. Grand Master of Freemasons in NZ, 1972–74. *Recreations:* fishing, gardening. *Address:* PO Box 749, Hastings, New Zealand. *T:* 777448.

BATE, Prof. Walter Jackson; Kingsley Porter University Professor, Harvard University, since 1980; *b* 23 May 1918; *s* of William George Bate. *Educ:* Harvard Univ. AB 1939, PhD 1942. Harvard University: Associate Prof. of English, 1949–55; Prof. of English, 1955–62; Chm., Dept of English, 1955–62; Abbott Lawrence Lowell Prof. of the Humanities, 1962–80. Corresp. Fellow, British Acad., 1978. Member: Amer. Acad. of Arts and Sciences; Amer. Philosophical Soc.; Cambridge Scientific Soc. Christian Gauss Award, 1956, 1964, 1970; Pulitzer Prize for Biography, 1964, 1978; Nat. Book Award, 1978; Nat. Book Critics Award, 1978. *Publications:* Stylistic Development of Keats, 1945; From Classic to Romantic, 1946; Criticism: The Major Texts, 1952; The Achievement of Samuel Johnson, 1955; Prefaces to Criticism, 1959; Yale Edition of Samuel Johnson, Vol. II, 1963, Vols III–V, 1969; John Keats, 1963; Coleridge, 1968; The Burden of the Past and The English Poet, 1971; Samuel Johnson, 1977; (ed) Coleridge, *Biographia Literaria,* 1982; (ed) British and American Poets: Chaucer to the present, 1985. *Recreation:* farming. *Address:* 3 Warren House, Cambridge, Mass, USA. *Club:* Saturday (Boston, Mass).

BATE, Maj.-Gen. William, CB 1974; OBE 1963; DL; Secretary to the Council of TAVR Associations, 1975–86 (Deputy Secretary, 1973–75); *b* 6 June 1920; *s* of S. Bate, Warrington; *m* 1946, Veronica Mary Josephine (*née* Quinn); two *s* two *d*. Commnd, 1941; war service in Burma, 1941–46 (despatches); Senior Instructor, RASC Officers Sch., 1947–50; Co. Comd 7th and 11th Armoured Divs, 1951–53; psc 1954; DAA&QMG Q (Ops), WO, 1955–57; jssc 1957; Admin. Staff Coll., Henley, 1958; Directing Staff, Staff Coll., Camberley, 1958–60; AA&QMG, Ops and Plans, HQ BAOR, 1961–63; CO, 2 Div. Column, BAOR, 1963–65; Col GS, Staff Coll., Camberley, 1965–67; Brig. Q (Maint.), MoD, 1967–68; ADC to the Queen, 1969; idc 1969; Dir of Admin. Planning (Army), 1970; Dir of Movements (Army), MoD, 1971–73. Col Comdt, 1974–86, Rep. Col Comdt, 1986–, RCT; Hon. Col, 163 Movement Control Regt, RCT(V), TAVR, 1974–79. FCIT 1967. DL Surrey, 1980. *Recreations:* cricket, tennis. *Address:* Netherbury, Belton Road, Camberley, Surrey. *T:* Camberley 63529. *Clubs:* East India, Devonshire, Sports and Public Schools, MCC.

BATE, Dame Zara (Kate), DBE 1968; *b* 10 March; *d* of Sidney Herbert Dickens; *m* 1st, 1935, Captain James Fell; three *s*; 2nd, 1946, Rt Hon. Harold Edward Holt, PC, CH (*d* 1967), Prime Minister of Australia; 3rd, 1969, Hon. Henry Jefferson Percival Bate, MHR. *Educ:* Ruyton and Toorak Coll. Director: John Stafford & Co.; Colebrook Estates. Chm. Bd, St Laurent, Melbourne. Hon. Dr Lit and Hum, Ewha Women's Univ., Seoul, Korea, 1967. Coronation Medal, 1953. *Recreations:* tennis, reading, spear fishing. *Address:* 58 Monaco Street, Florida Gardens, Gold Coast, Qld, Australia.

BATE-SMITH, Dr Edgar Charles, CBE 1963; FLS 1959; Hon. FIFST; ScD; Director, Low Temperature Research Station, Cambridge, 1947–65, retired; *b* 24 Aug. 1900; *s* of Albert Edward Smith and Avis Ellen Jenkinson; *m* 1933, Margaret Elizabeth Bate Hardy (*d* 1982); one *s*. *Educ:* Wellingborough Sch.; Manchester Univ.; Gonville and Caius Coll.,

Cambridge. Mem., Soc. of Chemical Industry Food Group Cttee, 1939–41, 1956–60; (Jubilee Memorial Lectr, 1962–63); formerly Mem. Council, Inst. of Food Science and Technology; Pres., Cambridge Philosophical Soc., 1953–55; Chm., Phytochemical Soc. (formerly Plant Phenolics Group), 1958–60. *Publications:* Food Science (with T. N. Morris), 1952. Papers in scientific jls on post-mortem physiology of muscle, chemistry and taxonomy of plants. *Recreations:* plants and animals; sketching. *Address:* c/o Institute of Animal Physiology, Babraham, Cambridge.

BATELY, Prof. Janet Margaret, (Mrs L. J. Summers); Professor of English Language and Medieval Literature, King's College, University of London, since 1977; *b* 3 April 1932; *d* of late Alfred William Bately and of Dorothy Maud Bately (*née* Willis); *m* 1964, Leslie John Summers, sculptor; one *s*. *Educ:* Greenhead High Sch., Huddersfield; Westcliff High Sch. for Girls; Somerville Coll., Oxford (Shaw Lefevre Scholar). BA 1st cl. hons English 1954, Dip. in Comparative Philology (with distinction) 1956, MA 1958; FKC 1986. Asst Lectr in English, Birkbeck Coll., Univ. of London, 1955–58, Lectr, 1958–69, Reader, 1970–76. Sir Israel Gollancz Meml Lectr, British Acad., 1978. Member: Council, EETS, 1981–; Exec. Cttee, Fontes Anglo-Saxonici (formerly Sources of Anglo-Saxon Literature), 1985–; Adv. Cttee, Internat. Soc. of Anglo-Saxonists, 1986–. Governor, Cranleigh Sch., 1982–. *Publications:* The Old English Orosius, 1980; The Literary Prose of King Alfred's Reign: Translation or Transformation, 1980; (ed) The Anglo-Saxon Chronicle: MS.A, 1986; contribs to: England Before the Conquest, 1971; Saints, Scholars and Heroes (ed M. H. King and W. M. Stevens), 1979; Five Hundred Years of Words and Sounds (ed E. G. Stanley and Douglas Grey), 1983; Learning and Literature in Anglo-Saxon England (ed M. Lapidge and H. Gneuss), 1985; Leeds Studies in English, Eichstatter Beitrage, Medium Aevum, Rev. of English Studies, Anglia, English Studies, Essays and Studies, Classica et Mediaevalia, Scriptorium, Studies in Philology, Mediev. Arch., Notes and Queries, Archaeologia, Anglo-Saxon England, The Dickensian, Jl Soc. of Archivists. *Recreations:* music, gardening. *Address:* 86 Cawdor Crescent, W7 2DD. *T:* 01–567 0486.

BATEMAN, Sir Cecil (Joseph), KBE 1967 (MBE 1944); Chairman, G. Heyn & Sons Ltd, since 1971; Director: Nationwide Building Society, 1970–84; Allied Irish Banks, 1970–80; Allied Irish Investment Bank Ltd, 1971–80; *b* 6 Jan. 1910; *s* of Samuel and Annie Bateman; *m* 1938, Doris M. Simpson; one *s* one *d*. *Educ:* Queen's Univ., Belfast. Served War of 1939–45, Royal Artillery (Major). Entered NI Civil Service, Nov. 1927. Dir of Establishments, Min. of Finance, 1958–63; Sec. to Cabinet and Clerk of Privy Council of N Ireland, 1963–65; Permanent Sec., Min. of Finance, and Head of Northern Ireland Civil Service, 1965–70. *Recreations:* golf, reading. *Address:* 26 Schomberg Park, Belfast BT4 2HH. *T:* Belfast 63484. *Club:* Shandon Park Golf.

BATEMAN, Sir Charles Harold, KCMG 1950 (CMG 1937); MC; *b* Portsmouth, 4 Jan. 1892; *s* of late Charles Bateman; *m* 1940, Bridget Mary, *d* of late Michael Kavanagh, Co. Wicklow. *Educ:* London Univ. (BA); Sorbonne, Paris. Served European War, 1914–18, with 2nd London Regt (Royal Fusiliers), Gallipoli and France; Royal Artillery, France and Belgium (MC, twice wounded); entered Diplomatic Service, 1920; Third Sec., Santiago, Chile; Foreign Office, 1924; First Sec., 1929; transferred Bagdad, 1932; Acting Counsellor, 1935; Counsellor, Lisbon, 1937; Minister at Cairo, 1938; transferred Foreign Office, 1940; Minister to Mexico, 1941–44, Ambassador, 1944–47; Asst Under Sec., Foreign Office, 1948–50; British Ambassador to Poland, 1950–52; retired, 1952. *Address:* Amesbury Abbey, Amesbury, Wiltshire.

BATEMAN, Sir Geoffrey (Hirst), Kt 1972; FRCS; Surgeon, Ear, Nose and Throat Department, St Thomas' Hospital, London, 1939–71; *b* 24 Oct. 1906; *s* of Dr William Hirst Bateman, JP, Rochdale, Lancs; *m* 1931, Margaret, *d* of Sir Samuel Turner, Rochdale; three *s* one *d*. *Educ:* Epsom Coll.; University Coll., Oxford. Theodore Williams Schol. in Anat., Oxford Univ., 1926; BA Oxon, Hons sch. Physiol., 1927; Epsom schol. to King's Coll. Hosp., 1927; BM, BCh Oxon, 1930; FRCS, 1933; George Herbert Hunt Trav. Schol., Oxford Univ., 1933. RAFVR, Wing Comdr, 1939–45. Mem., Bd Governors, St Thomas' Hosp., 1948; Mem. Collegium Otolaryngologica Amicitiæ Sacrum, 1949; Hon. Corr. Mem. Amer. Laryngological Assoc., 1960; Past Mem. Council, RCS; Editor, Jl of Laryngology and Otology, 1961–77; Formerly Hon. Cons. on Oto-rhino-laryngology to the Army; Cons. Adviser in Otolaryngology, Dept of Health and Social Security. Pres., British Assoc. of Otolaryngologists, 1970–71 (Vice-Pres., 1967–70). Hon. FRSM 1978. *Publications:* Diseases of the Nose and Throat (Asst Editor to V. E. Negus, 6th edn), 1955; contributor various jls, etc. *Recreations:* golf, fishing. *Address:* Thorney, Graffham, Petworth, West Sussex GU28 0QA. *T:* Graffham 314.

See also Sir R. M. Bateman.

BATEMAN, Leslie Clifford, CMG 1965; FRS 1968; Secretary-General, International Rubber Study Group, 1976–83; *b* 21 March 1915; *s* of Charles Samuel Bateman; *m* 1st, 1945, Marie Louise Pakes (*d* 1967); two *s*; 2nd, 1973, Mrs Eileen Joyce Jones (*née* Henwood); one step *s* one step *d*. *Educ:* Bishopshalt Sch., Uxbridge; University Coll., London. BSc, 1st cl. Hons Chem., 1935; PhD and Ramsey Memorial Medal, 1938; DSc 1955; Fellow, 1974. Oriel Coll., 1940–41; Chemist, Natural Rubber Producers Research Assoc., 1941–53; Dir of Research, 1953–62; Controller of Rubber Res., Malaysia, 1962–74; Chm., Internat. Rubber R&D Board, 1962–74. Mem., Malaysian Govt Task Force on Rubber Industry, 1983. Hon. DSc: Malaya, 1968; Aston, 1972. Colwyn Medal, 1963, and Jubilee Foundn Lectr, 1971, Inst. of Rubber Industry. Hon. PSM, Malaysia, 1974. *Publications:* (ed and contrib.) The Chemistry and Physics of Rubber-like Substances, 1963; numerous scientific papers in Jl Chem. Soc., etc, and articles on technical-economic status of natural rubber and its developments. *Recreations:* cricket, golf and other outdoor pursuits. *Address:* 3 Palmerston Close, Welwyn Garden City, Herts. *T:* Welwyn Garden 322391.

BATEMAN, Mary-Rose Christine, MA; Headmistress, Perse School for Girls, Cambridge, since 1980; *b* 16 March 1935; *d* of Comdr G. A. Bateman, RN, and Mrs G. A. Bateman. *Educ:* The Abbey, Malvern Wells, Worcs; St Anne's Coll., Oxford (MA); CertEd Cambridge. Assistant English Mistress: Westonbirt Sch., Tetbury, Glos, 1957–60; Ashford Sch., Kent, 1960–61; Lady Eleanor Holles Sch., Mddx, 1961–64; Head of English Department: Westonbirt Sch., Glos, 1964–69; Brighton and Hove High Sch., GPDST, 1969–71; Headmistress, Berkhamsted School for Girls, Herts, 1971–80. *Address:* 27 Leys Road, Cambridge CB4 2AR. *T:* Cambridge 315373.

BATEMAN, Sir Ralph (Melton), KBE 1975; MA Oxon; Chairman, Stothert and Pitt, 1977–85; Vice-President, Confederation of British Industry, since 1976 (Deputy President, 1973–74, President, 1974–76); *b* 15 May 1910; 3rd *s* of William Hirst Bateman, MB, BCh, and of Ethel Jane Bateman, Rochdale, Lancs; *m* 1935, Barbara Yvonne, 2nd *d* of Herbert Percy Litton and Grace Vera Litton, Heywood, Lancs; two *s* two *d*. *Educ:* Epsom Coll.; University Coll., Oxford. Turner & Newall Ltd: joined as management trainee, 1931; held various directorships in Group, 1942–76; Dir, 1957; Dep. Chm., 1959; Chm., 1967–76. Mem., NEDC, 1973–76. Mem. Council, Manchester Business Sch., 1972–76; Vice-Pres., Ashridge Management Coll.; Chm. of Council, University Coll. at Buckingham, 1976–79; Member Court: Manchester Univ.; Salford Univ. FCIS, CBIM; FRSA 1970. Hon. Fellow, UMIST, 1977. Hon. DSc: Salford, 1969; Buckingham, 1983.

Recreations: family and social affairs. *Address:* 2 Bollin Court, Macclesfield Road, Wilmslow, Cheshire. *T:* Wilmslow 530437.
See also Sir G. H. Bateman.

BATEMAN, Richard George Saumarez La T.; *see* La Trobe-Bateman.

BATES, Alan (Arthur); actor; *b* 17 Feb. 1934; *m* 1970, Victoria Ward; twin *s. Educ:* Herbert Strutt Grammar Sch., Belper, Derbyshire; RADA. *Theatre:* English Stage Co. (Royal Court Theatre, London): The Mulberry Bush; Cards of Identity; Look Back in Anger; The Country Wife; In Celebration; London (West End): Long Day's Journey into Night; The Caretaker; The Four Seasons; Hamlet; Butley, London and NY (Evening Standard Best Actor award, 1972; Antoinette Perry Best Actor award, 1973); Poor Richard, NY; Richard III and The Merry Wives of Windsor, Stratford, Ont.; Venice Preserved, Bristol Old Vic; Taming of the Shrew, Stratford-on-Avon, 1973; Life Class, 1974; Otherwise Engaged, Queen's, 1975 (Variety Club of GB Best Stage Actor award, 1975); The Seagull, Duke of York's, 1976; Stage Struck, Vaudeville, 1979; A Patriot for Me, Chichester, Haymarket, 1983, transf. Ahmanson, LA (Variety Club of GB Best Stage Actor award, 1983); Victoria Station, and One for the Road, Lyric Studio, 1984; The Dance of Death, Riverside Studios, Hammersmith, 1985; Yonadab, NT, 1985. *Films:* The Entertainer, Whistle Down the Wind, A Kind of Loving, The Running Man, The Caretaker, Zorba the Greek, Nothing but the Best, Georgie Girl, King of Hearts, Far from the Madding Crowd, The Fixer (Oscar nomination), Women in Love, The Three Sisters (National Theatre Co.), A Day in the Death of Joe Egg, The Go-Between, Second Best (also prod.), Impossible Object, Butley, In Celebration, Royal Flash, An Unmarried Woman, The Shout, The Rose, Nijinsky, Quartet, The Return of the Soldier, The Wicked Lady. *Television:* various plays; Plaintiff and Defendant, Two Sundays, The Collection, 1977; The Mayor of Casterbridge, 1978; Very Like a Whale, The Trespasser, 1980; A Voyage Round my Father, Separate Tables, An Englishman Abroad, 1983 (BAFTA Best TV Actor award, 1984); Dr Fisher of Geneva, 1984. *Recreations:* swimming, squash, driving, riding, water skiing, reading. *Address:* c/o Chatto & Linnit, Prince of Wales Theatre, Coventry Street, W1.

BATES, Alfred; researcher and presenter since 1980, and an assistant producer since 1983, BBC Television; *b* 8 June 1944; *s* of Norman and Alice Bates; single. *Educ:* Stretford Grammar Sch. for Boys; Manchester Univ. (BSc); Corpus Christi Coll., Cambridge. Lectr in Maths, De La Salle Coll. of Educn, Middleton, 1967–74. MP (Lab) Bebington and Ellesmere Port, Feb. 1974–1979; PPS to Minister of State for Social Security, 1974–76; Asst Govt Whip, 1976–79; a Lord Comr, HM Treasury, 1979. *Recreation:* cricket umpiring. *Address:* 116 Jackson Street, Stretford, Manchester M32 8BB.

BATES, Allan Frederick, CMG 1958; BA (Hons); *b* 15 July 1911; *s* of John Frederick Lawes and Ethel Hannah Bates; *m* 1937, Ena Edith, *d* of John Richard Boxall; three *s. Educ:* Woolwich Central Sch.; London Univ. Qualified as Certified Accountant, 1938; practised in London, 1938–44. Joined Colonial Service (now Overseas Civil Service), 1944; Deputy Comptroller Inland Revenue, Cyprus, 1944–48; Comptroller Inland Revenue, Cyprus, 1948–52; Financial Secretary: Cyprus, 1952–60; Mauritius, 1960–64; Man. Dir, Develt Bank of Mauritius, 1964–70; Financial Advr (IMF) to Govt of Bahamas, 1971–75; Budget Advr (IMF) to Govt of Lesotho, 1975–76. Accounts Adviser, British Exec. Service Overseas, to Govt of Belize, 1982. Fellow Inst. of Taxation 1950; Mem., Inst. of Directors. *Recreations:* painting, carving. *Address:* 5 Redford Avenue, Coulsdon, Surrey. *T:* 01–660 7421. *Club:* Royal Commonwealth Society.

BATES, Sir Darrell; *see* Bates, Sir J. D.

BATES, Air Vice-Marshal David Frank, CB 1983; RAF retired; *b* 10 April 1928; *s* of late S. F. Bates, MusB, FRCO, and N. A. Bates (*née* Story); *m* 1954, Margaret Winifred (*née* Biles); one *s* one *d. Educ:* Warwick Sch.; RAF Coll., Cranwell. Commnd, 1950; served Egypt, Innsworth, UKSLS Australia, HQ Transport Comd, RAF Technical Coll., Staff Coll., Lyneham, El Adem, Staff Coll., Jt Services Staff Coll., Innsworth, and RCDS, 1950–73; Stn Comdr, Uxbridge, 1974–75; Dir of Personnel Ground, 1975–76; Dir of Personnel Management (ADP), 1976–79; AOA, RAF Support Comd, 1979–82. Bursar, Warwick Sch., 1983–85. Pres., Adastrian Cricket Club, 1977–82. *Recreations:* cricket, most sports, gardening, model railways. *Clubs:* Royal Air Force, MCC.

BATES, Prof. Sir David (Robert), Kt 1978; MSc; DSc; FRS 1955; MRIA; *b* Omagh, Co. Tyrone, N Ireland, 18 Nov. 1916; *s* of late Walter Vivian Bates and of Mary Olive Bates; *m* 1956, Barbara Bailey Morris; one *s* one *d. Educ:* Royal Belfast Academical Institution; Queen's Univ., Belfast; University Coll., London. Engaged at Admiralty Research Laboratory, 1939–41, and at Mine Design Department, 1941–45; Lecturer in Mathematics, University Coll., London, 1945–50; Consultant at US Naval Ordnance Test Station, Inyokern, Calif., 1950; Reader in Physics, University Coll., London, 1951; Queen's Univ., Belfast: Prof. of Applied Mathematics, 1951–68; Prof. of Theoretical Physics, 1968–74; Research Prof., 1976–82, now Emeritus; Smithsonian Regent's Fellow, Center for Astrophysics, Cambridge, Mass, Vis. Scholar in Atmospheric Scis, Harvard Univ., 1982–83. Chm., Adv. Bd Postgrad. Awards, NI Dept of Educn, 1974–82; Mem., UGC Working Party on Higher Educn in NI, 1983–. Vice-Pres., RIA, 1976–77; Chapman Meml Lectr, Univ. of Colorado, 1973; Kistiakowsky Lectr, Harvard Univ., 1983; Hon. Pres., Sanibel Symposium, Florida, 1983. Vice-Pres., Alliance Party of NI, 1971–. Mem., Internat. Acad. Astronautics, 1961; Hon. Foreign Mem., Amer. Acad. of Arts and Scis, 1974; Associate Mem., Royal Acad., Belgium, 1979; Foreign Associate, Nat. Acad. of Scis, USA, 1984. Hon. DSc: Ulster, 1972; NUI, 1975; York (Ontario), 1983; QUB, 1984; Hon. ScD Dublin, 1979; Hon. LLD Glasgow, 1979; DUniv: York, 1983; Stirling, 1986. Hughes Medal, Royal Soc., 1970; Chree Medal, Inst. Physics, 1973; Gold Medal, Royal Astron. Soc., 1977. *Publications:* papers in geophysical and physical journals. Editor-in-Chief, Planetary and Space Science; (ed with B. Bederson) Advances in Atomic and Molecular Physics. *Recreations:* reading and listening to radio. *Address:* 1 Newforge Grange, Belfast BT9 5QB. *T:* Belfast 665640.

BATES, Sir Dawson; *see* Bates, Sir J. D.

BATES, Maj.-Gen. Sir (Edward) John (Hunter), KBE 1969 (OBE 1952); CB 1965; MC 1944; Director, Thomson Regional Newspapers, 1969–77; *b* 5 Dec. 1911; *s* of Ernest Bates, FRIBA; *m* 1947, Sheila Ann Norman; two *s* two *d. Educ:* Wellington Coll.; Corpus Christi Coll., Cambridge. BA 1933; MA 1963. Commissioned, 1932; Pre-war service in UK and Malaya; War Service in Africa, Middle East, Sicily, Italy and Greece; Senior Army Instructor, JSSC, 1954–57; Student, IDC, 1958; CRA, 2 Div., 1959; CCRA 1 (British) Corps, 1960–61; Dir, RA, War Office, 1961–64; Comdt of RMCS, 1964–67; Dir, Royal Defence Acad., 1967–68. Special Comr, Duke of York's Royal Military Sch., 1972–. Col Comdt, RA 1966–76. Mem. Ct of Assts, 1972–, Warden, 1977, Master, 1979, Worshipful Co. of Haberdashers. Chm., RUSI, 1976–78. *Recreation:* fishing. *Address:* Chaffenden, Frensham Road, Rolvenden Layne, Cranbrook, Kent. *T:* Cranbrook 241536. *Clubs:* Army and Navy; Rye Golf.
See also Hon. Sir J. D. Waite.

BATES, Eric; Chairman, Midlands Electricity Board, 1969–72; *b* 1 Nov. 1908; *s* of late John Boon Bates and late Edith Anne Bates; *m* 1933, Beatrice, *d* of late William Henry Herapath and late Beatrice Herapath; one *s* two *d.* Trained Ilford Elec. Dept.; Asst, County of London Elec. Supply Co., 1929–32; Consumers' Engr: West Kent Electric Co., 1933–36; Isle of Thanet Elec. Supply Co., 1937–42; Elec. Engr, Kennedy & Donkin, 1942–44; Consumers' Engr, Luton Elec. Dept, 1944–48; Sect. Head, Eastern Elec. Bd, 1948–49; Dep. Chief Commercial Officer, Eastern Elec. Bd, 1949–57; North Eastern Electricity Board: Chief Commercial Officer, 1957–62; Dep. Chm., 1962–67; Chm., 1967–69. *Publications:* contribs to Proc. IEE. *Recreation:* golf. *Address:* 24 Grange Road, Broadstairs, Kent.

BATES, Sir Geoffrey Voltelin, 5th Bt, *cr* 1880; MC 1942; *b* 2 Oct. 1921; *s* of Major Cecil Robert Bates, DSO, MC (3rd *s* of 2nd Bt) and Hylda, *d* of Sir James Heath, 1st Bt; *S* uncle, 1946; *m* 1st, 1945, Kitty Kendall Lane (*d* 1956); two *s*; 2nd, 1957, Olivia Gwyneth Zoë (*d* 1969) *d* of Capt. Hon. R. O. FitzRoy (later 2nd Viscount Daventry); one *d* (and one *d* decd); 3rd, 1971, Mrs Juliet Eleanor Hugolyn Whitelocke-Winter, *widow* of Edward Colin Winter and *d* of late Comdr G. C. A. Whitelocke, RN retd, and Mrs S. H. Whitelocke. *Educ:* Radley. High Sheriff, Flintshire, 1969. *Recreations:* hunting, shooting, fishing. *Heir:* *s* Edward Robert Bates, *b* 4 July 1946. *Address:* Gyrn Castle, Llanasa, near Holywell, Clwyd. *T:* Prestatyn 3500. *Club:* Army and Navy.

BATES, Rt. Rev. Gordon; *see* Whitby, Bishop Suffragan of.

BATES, James P. M.; *see* Martin-Bates.

BATES, Maj.-Gen. Sir John; *see* Bates, Maj.-Gen. Sir E. J. H.

BATES, Sir John (David), Kt 1969; CBE 1962; VRD; Australian Consul-General in New York, 1970–73; *b* 1 March 1904; *s* of H. W. Bates, Plymouth, Devon; *m* 1930, Phyllis Helen Muller; one *s. Educ:* Plymouth. Joined sea staff of Orient Line, 1925; transf. to shore staff, in Australia, 1929; RANVR, 1932–57, Comdr; Gen. Manager in Australia of Orient Line, 1954–60; Dep. Chm., P & O Lines of Australia, 1960–67; Chm., Hon. Bd of Australian Nat. Travel Assoc., 1956–67; Chm. Australian Tourist Commn, 1967–69. Federal Pres., Navy League of Australia, 1950–56; Trustee, Art Gallery of NSW, 1962–70; Lay Member, Trade Practices Tribunal, 1968–70. *Recreations:* reading, walking. *Address:* 35 Mainsail Avenue, St Huberts Island, NSW 2256, Australia. *Club:* Union (Sydney).

BATES, Sir (John) Dawson, 2nd Bt, *cr* 1937; MC 1943; Regional Director of the National Trust, retired 1981; *b* 21 Sept. 1921; *o s* of Sir (Richard) Dawson Bates, 1st Bt, PC, and Muriel (*d* 1972), *d* of late Sir Charles Cleland, KBE, MVO, LLD; *S* father, 1949; *m* 1953, Mary Murray, *o d* of late Lieut-Col Joseph M. Hoult, Norton Place, Lincoln; two *s* one *d. Educ:* Winchester; Balliol. BA 1949. FRICS. Served War of 1939–45, Major, Rifle Brigade (MC). *Heir:* *s* Richard Dawson Hoult Bates, *b* 12 May 1956. *Address:* Butleigh House, Butleigh, Glastonbury, Somerset.

BATES, Sir (Julian) Darrell, Kt 1966; CMG 1956; CVO 1954; *b* 10 Nov. 1913; *y s* of late E. Stuart Bates; *m* 1944, Susan Evelyn June Sinclair; two *s* one *d. Educ:* Sevenoaks Sch.; Keble Coll., Oxford. Entered Colonial Service, Tanganyika Territory, 1936; served King's African Rifles (despatches), 1940–43; seconded Colonial Office, 1944–46; Officer Administering the Government, Seychelles, 1950–51; Deputy Chief Secretary, Somaliland Protectorate, 1951–53; Colonial Sec., Gibraltar, 1953–64, Permanent Sec., 1964–68. *Publications:* A Fly Switch from the Sultan, 1961; The Shell at My Ear, 1961; The Mango and the Palm, 1962; A Longing for Quails, 1964; Susie, 1964; A Gust of Plumes, 1972; The Companion Guide to Devon and Cornwall, 1976; The Abyssinian Difficulty, 1979; The Fashoda Incident of 1898, 1984. *Address:* Mellinpons, St Buryan, Cornwall. *Club:* Travellers'.

BATES, Merrick Stuart B.; *see* Baker-Bates.

BATES, Peter Edward Gascoigne; Director, General Technology Systems Ltd, since 1986; *b* 6 Aug. 1924; *s* of James Edward Bates and Esmé Grace Gascoigne Bates (*née* Roy); *m* 1947, Jean Irene Hearn, *d* of late Brig. W. Campbell Grant; two *s* one *d. Educ:* Kingston Grammar Sch.; School of Oriental and African Studies, Univ. of London; Lincoln Coll., Oxford. Served War, Intelligence Corps, SEAC and Japan, 1943–46; Captain 1945. Malayan CS, 1947–55; Rolls-Royce, Aero Engine Div., 1955–57; Bristol Aircraft (later British Aircraft Corp.), 1957–64, Special Director, 1963; joined Plessey Co., 1964: Gen. Man., Plessey Radar, 1967–71; Man. Dir, Radar Div., 1971–76; Dep. Chm., Plessey Electronic Systems Ltd, 1976–86. Member: CBI Overseas Cttee, 1981–86; BOTB, 1984–. Member: Council, Electronic Engrg Assoc., 1973–86 (Pres. 1976); Council, SBAC, 1978–86 (Pres. 1983–84); Pres., AECMA, 1985–86. *Recreations:* golf, gardening, theatre, reading history and biography. *Address:* 12 Lindisfarne Road, Wimbledon, SW20 0NW. *T:* 01–946 0345. *Clubs:* Army and Navy, Roehampton; Royal Wimbledon Golf.

BATES, Ralph; *b* Swindon, Wilts, 3 Nov. 1899; *s* of Henry Roy and Mabel Stevens Bates; *m* 1940, Eve Salzman; one *s. Educ:* Swindon and North Wilts. Secondary Sch. After service in 16th Queen's Royal West Surreys, 1917–19, worked in Great Western Railway Factory at Swindon; in Spain, 1930–37; took active part in Republican politics in Spain; began literary career in 1933 as consequence of unemployment; Capt. in the Spanish Loyalist Army and in the International Brigade, Madrid sector, 1936–37; lecture tour in USA 1937–38; one year resident in Mexico, 1938–39; Adjunct Prof. of Literature, New York Univ. 1948–68, now Professor Emeritus of Literature. *Publications:* Sierra, 1933; Lean Men, 1934; Schubert, 1934, The Olive Field, 1936; Rainbow Fish, 1937; The Miraculous Horde, 1939; The Fields of Paradise, 1941; The Undiscoverables, 1942; The Journey to the Sandalwood Forest, 1947; The Dolphin in the Wood, 1949. *Recreations:* small boating, music. *Address:* 37 Washington Square West, New York, NY 10011, USA. *T:* (212) 254–4149.

BATES, Stewart Taverner, QC 1970; a Recorder of the Crown Court, since 1981; *b* 17 Dec. 1926; *s* of John Bates, Greenock; *m* 1950, Anne Patricia, *d* of David West, Pinner; two *s* four *d. Educ:* Univs of Glasgow and St Andrews; Corpus Christi Coll., Oxford. Called to Bar, Middle Temple, 1954, Bencher, 1975; Mem. Bar Council, 1962–66. Chm., Barristers' Benevolent Assoc., 1983–; Member: Goodman Cttee on Charity Law and Voluntary Organisations, 1976; Cttee of Management, Inst. of Urology, Univ. of London, 1978–; Chm., St Peter's Hosp. Special Cttee, 1986. *Recreations:* theatre, sailing, ski-ing. *Address:* The Grange, Horsington, Templecombe, Somerset BA8 0EF. *T:* Templecombe 70521. *Club:* Garrick.

BATES, William Stanley, CMG 1971; HM Diplomatic Service, retired; *b* 7 Sept. 1920; *m* 1970, Suzanne Elston. *Educ:* Christ's Hospital; Corpus Christi Coll., Cambridge. Asst Principal, Colonial Office, 1948; Principal, 1951; Commonwealth Relations Office, 1956; Canberra, 1956–59; Asst Sec., 1962. British Deputy High Commissioner, Northern Nigeria, 1963–65; Imperial Defence Coll., 1966; Head of Communications Dept, FCO, 1967–70; High Comr in Guyana, 1970–75; Ambassador to Korea, 1975–80. *Address:* 3 Houndean Close, Lewes, East Sussex BN7 1EZ.

BATESON; *see* de Yarburgh-Bateson, family name of Baron Deramore.

BATESON, Andrew James, QC 1971; *b* 29 June 1925; *m* 1954, Janette Mary Poupart (*d* 1970); one *s* three *d*. *Educ:* Eton. Called to the Bar, Middle Temple, 1951; Bencher, 1977. *Recreations:* shooting, fishing, gardening. *Address:* 10 South Square, Gray's Inn, Holborn, WC1; Bracken House, Beechwood Avenue, Weybridge, Surrey. *Clubs:* Garrick; Flyfishers'.

BATESON, Prof. Paul Patrick Gordon, FRS 1983; Director of Sub-Department of Animal Behaviour since 1976, and Professor of Ethology since 1984, University of Cambridge; Professorial Fellow of King's College, Cambridge, since 1984 (Fellow, 1964–84); *b* 31 March 1938; *s* of Richard Gordon Bateson and Sölvi Helene Berg; *m* 1963, Dusha Matthews; two *d*. *Educ:* Westminster Sch.; King's Coll., Cambridge (BA 1960, PhD 1963, MA 1965, ScD 1977). Harkness Fellow, Stanford Univ. Medical Centre, Calif, 1963–65; Sen. Asst in Res., Sub-Dept of Animal Behaviour, Univ. of Cambridge, 1965–69; Lectr in Zoology, Univ. of Cambridge, 1969–78; Reader in Animal Behaviour, 1978–84. Pres., Assoc. for the Study of Animal Behaviour, 1977–80. Scientific Medal, Zool Soc. of London, 1976. *Publications:* (ed with P. H. Klopfer) Perspectives in Ethology, Vols 1–6, 1973–85; (ed with R. A. Hinde) Growing Points in Ethology, 1976; (ed) Mate Choice, 1983; (contrib.) Defended to Death, 1983; (with Paul Martin) Measuring Behaviour, 1986. *Recreations:* cooking and dreaming. *Address:* 37 Panton Street, Cambridge CB2 1HL. *T:* Cambridge 62977.

BATH, 6th Marquess of, *cr* 1789; **Henry Frederick Thynne,** Bt 1641; Viscount Weymouth and Baron Thynne, 1682; Major Royal Wiltshire Yeomanry; JP; *b* 26 Jan. 1905; *o surv. s* of 5th Marquess, KG, PC, CB and Violet Caroline (*d* 1928), *d* of Sir Charles Mordaunt, 10th Bt; *S* father, 1946; *m* 1st, 1927, Hon. Daphne (marr. diss., 1953; she *m* 2nd, 1953, Major A. W. Fielding, DSO), *er d* of 4th Baron Vivian, DSO; two *s* one *d* (and one *s* decd); 2nd, 1953, Mrs Virginia Penelope Tennant, *d* of late Alan L. R. Parsons; one *d*. *Educ:* Harrow; Christ Church, Oxford. MP (U) Frome Division, Som., 1931–35. Served War of 1939–45 (wounded). Chm., Football Pools Panel, 1967–87. Life-long interest in forestry; Longleat has some of the best private woodland in the country. *Heir:* *s* Viscount Weymouth, *qv*. *Address:* Job's Mill, Warminster, Wilts BA12 8BB. *T:* Warminster 2279; Longleat, Warminster, Wilts. *Club:* White's.

See also Duke of Beaufort.

BATH and WELLS, Bishop of, since 1975; **Rt. Rev. John Monier Bickersteth;** Clerk of the Closet to the Queen, since 1979; *b* 6 Sept. 1921; *yr s* of late Rev. Canon Edward Monier Bickersteth, OBE; *m* 1955, Rosemary, *yr d* of late Edward and Muriel Cleveland-Stevens, Gaines, Oxted; three *s* one *d*. *Educ:* Rugby; Christ Church, Oxford; Wells Theol College. MA Oxon 1953. Captain, Buffs and Royal Artillery, 1941–46. Priest, 1951; Curate, St Matthew, Moorfields, Bristol, 1950–54; Vicar, St John's, Hurst Green, Oxted, 1954–62; St Stephen's, Chatham, 1962–70; Hon. Canon of Rochester, 1968–70; Bishop Suffragan of Warrington, 1970–75. A C of E delegate to 4th Assembly, WCC, 1968. Chaplain and Sub-Prelate OStJ, 1977. Chairman: Royal Sch. of Church Music, 1977–; Bible Reading Fellowship, 1978–; Vice Chm., Central Bd of Finance of Church of England, 1981–84. Mem., Marlborough Coll. Council, 1980–. Freeman of the City of London, 1979. Entered H of L, 1981. *Recreations:* country pursuits, calligraphy. *Address:* The Palace, Wells, Somerset. *T:* Wells 72341. *Club:* Royal Commonwealth Society.

BATH, Archdeacon of; *see* Burgess, Ven. J. E.

BATH, Alan Alfred; Director, Education and Training, Commission of the European Communities, 1973–80; *b* 3 May 1924; *s* of Alfred Edward Bath and Doris Ellen Lawson; *m* 1946, Joy Roselle Thornton (*d* 1979), *d* of George Jeune, St Saviour, Jersey; one *s* two *d*. *Educ:* Frays Coll., Uxbridge; Queen's Univ., Belfast (BSc Econ). RAF, 1942–46. Asst Lectr in Econs, QUB, 1950–53; Admin. Officer, Assoc. of Univs of British Commonwealth, 1953–58; Imperial Coll., Univ. of London, 1958–62 (Develt Sec., 1960–62); Sec., Cttee of Vice-Chancellors and Principals of Univs of UK, 1964–73; Sec., UK Nat. Delegn to Council of Europe Cttee for Higher Educn and Research, 1969–73. *Publication:* A Survey of the Work of the Winston Churchill Memorial Trust, 1985. *Recreations:* music, sailing, gardening. *Address:* 12 Voltaire, Ennerdale Road, Kew Gardens, Surrey TW9 3PQ. *T:* 01–940 6577. *Club:* Athenæum.

BATHER, Elizabeth Constance, OBE 1946; retired as Chief Superintendent Metropolitan (Women) Police, (1946–60); *b* 11 Oct. 1904; *d* of late Rev. Arthur George Bather, MA, and Lilian Dundas Firth, Winchester. *Educ:* St Swithuns Sch., Winchester. Mem. Hampshire County Council, 1937–46. Served in WAAF, 1939–45; Group Officer, 1944–45. JP Winchester, 1937–46; Councillor, Hartley Witney and Hart DCs, 1967–76. *Address:* 8 South Ridge, Odiham, Basingstoke RG25 1NG.

BATHO, Sir Maurice Benjamin, 2nd Bt, *cr* 1928; Chairman and Managing Director, Ridgley (Huntingdon) Ltd and associated companies; *b* 14 Jan. 1910; *o* surv. *s* of Sir Charles Albert Batho, 1st Bt, and Bessie (*d* 1961), 4th *d* of Benjamin Parker, Oulton Broad, Suffolk; *S* father, 1938; *m* 1934, Antoinette, *o d* of Baron d'Udekem d'Acoz, Ghent; two *s* two *d*. *Educ:* Uppingham; Belgium. Served War of 1939–45: Lt-Col, KRRC. Jt Sub-Dir, Syrian Wheat Collection Scheme of Spears Mission, 1943; Adviser on Cereals Collection, Min. of Finance of Imp. Iranian Govt, 1944; Dep. Dir, Rice Procurement, Bengal, 1945; Managing Dir, Reed Paper & Board Sales Ltd, 1959, resigned 1965; formerly Director: Reed Paper & Board (UK) Ltd; London Paper Mills Co. Ltd; Empire Paper Mills Ltd; Reed Board Mills (Colthorp) Ltd; Reed Brookgate Ltd. *Recreation:* golf. *Heir:* *s* Peter Ghislain Batho [*b* 9 Dec. 1939; *m* 1966, Lucille Mary, *d* of Wilfrid F. Williamson; three *s*]. *Address:* Carlton Hall, Saxmundham, Suffolk. *T:* 2505. *Clubs:* Naval and Military, St Stephen's Constitutional.

BATHO, Walter James Scott; Regional Director and Chairman of the Regional Board for the Eastern Region, Departments of the Environment and Transport, 1983–85; *b* 13 Nov. 1925; *er s* of Walter Scott Batho and Isabella Laidlaw Batho (*née* Common); *m* 1951, Barbara Kingsford; two *s* two *d*. *Educ:* Epsom County Grammar Sch.; Univ. of Edinburgh (MA Eng. Lit. and Lang.). Served War, RNVR, 1943–46. Air Min., 1950–53; WO, 1953–63 (Private Sec. to Perm. Under Sec. of State, 1956–57); MPBW, 1963–70; DoE, 1970–85, Under Sec., 1979–85. *Recreations:* singing, reading, gardening. *Address:* Bushpease, Grays Lane, Ashtead, Surrey KT21 1BU. *T:* Ashtead 73471. *Club:* Naval.

BATHURST, family name of **Earl Bathurst** and **Viscount Bledisloe.**

BATHURST, 8th Earl, *cr* 1772; **Henry Allen John Bathurst,** DL; Baron Bathurst of Battlesden, Bedfordshire, 1712; Baron Apsley of Apsley, Sussex, 1771; Earl Bathurst of Bathurst, Sussex, 1772; Capt. Royal Gloucestershire Hussars (TA); TARO, 1959; *b* 1 May 1927; *s* of late Lord Apsley, DSO, MC, MP (killed on active service, 1942), and late Lady Apsley, CBE; *g s* of 7th Earl; *S* grandfather, 1943; *m* 1st 1959, Judith Mary (marr. diss. 1977), *d* of Mr and Mrs A. C. Nelson, Springfield House, Foulridge, Lancs; two *s* one *d*; 2nd, 1978, Gloria, *widow* of David Rutherston and *o d* of Harold Edward Clarry, Vancouver, BC. *Educ:* Ridley Coll., Canada; Eton; Christ Church, Oxford, 1948–49. Late Lieut 10th Royal Hussars (PWO). Capt., Royal Glos. Hussars, TA, 1949–57. Hon. Sec. Agricultural Cttee (Conservative), House of Lords, 1957; a Lord-in-Waiting, 1957–61; Joint Parliamentary Under-Sec. of State, Home Office, 1961–July 1962. Governor, Royal Agricultural Coll.; Pres. Glos Branch CPRE. DL County of Gloucester, 1960. Chancellor, Primrose League, 1959–61. Member: CLA Council, 1965 (Chm., Glos Branch of CLA, 1968–71); Timber Growers' Organisation (TGO) Council, 1966; President: Royal Forestry Soc., 1976–78; InstSMM, 1982–; Assoc. of Professional Foresters, 1983. *Heir:* *s* Lord Apsley, *qv*. *Address:* Cirencester Park, Cirencester, Glos GL7 2BT. *T:* Cirencester 3135. *Club:* White's.

BATHURST (NSW), Bishop of, since 1981; **Rt. Rev. Howell Arthur John Witt;** *b* 12 July 1920; *s* of Thomas Leyshon Witt and Harriet Jane Witt; *m* 1949, Gertrude Doreen Edwards; three *s* two *d*. *Educ:* Newport Sec. Sch.; Leeds Univ.; Coll. of the Resurrection, Mirfield. Deacon 1944; Priest 1945. Asst Curate of: Usk, Mon, 1944–47; St George's, Camberwell, 1948–49; Chaplain, Woomera, S Australia, 1949–54; Rector, St Mary Magdalene's, Adelaide, 1954–57; Priest in charge of Elizabeth, 1957–65; Missioner of St Peter's Coll. Mission, 1954–65; Bishop of North-West Australia, 1965–81. *Publication:* Bush Bishop (autobiography), 1980. *Recreations:* Rugby football coaching; script writing. *Address:* Bishopscourt, Bathurst, NSW 2795, Australia. *Club:* Public Schools (Adelaide).

BATHURST, Vice-Adm. (David) Benjamin; Chief of Fleet Support, since 1986; *b* 27 May 1936; *s* of late Group Captain Peter Bathurst, RAF and Lady Ann Bathurst; *m* 1959, Sarah Peto; one *s* three *d*. *Educ:* Eton College; Britannia RN College, Dartmouth. Joined RN, 1953; qualified as Pilot, 1960, as Helicopter Instructor, 1964; Fleet Air Arm appts incl. 2 years' exchange with RAN, 723 and 725 Sqdns; Senior Pilot, 820 Naval Air Sqdn; CO 819 Naval Air Sqdn; HMS Norfolk, 1971; Naval Staff, 1973; CO, HMS Ariadne, 1975; Naval Asst to First Sea Lord, 1976; Captain, 5th Frigate Sqdn, HMS Minerva, 1978; RCDS 1981; Dir of Naval Air Warfare, 1982; Flag Officer, Second Flotilla, 1983–85; Dir.-Gen., Naval Manpower and Training, 1985–86. Freeman, Guild of Air Pilots and Navigators. *Recreations:* gardening, shooting, fishing. *Address:* c/o Coutts and Co., 440 Strand, WC2. *Clubs:* Army and Navy, MCC.

BATHURST, Sir Frederick Peter Methuen Hervey-, 6th Bt, *cr* 1818; *b* 26 Jan. 1903; *s* of Sir Frederick Edward William Hervey-Bathurst, 5th Bt, DSO and Hon. Moira O'Brien, 2nd *d* of 14th Baron Inchiquin; *S* father 1956; *m* 1st, 1933, Maureen (marr. diss. 1956), *d* of Charles Gordon, Boveridge Park, Salisbury; one *s* one *d*; 2nd, 1958, Mrs Cornelia Shepard Riker, *widow* of Dr John Lawrence Riker, Rumson, NJ, USA. *Educ:* Eton. Served War of 1939–45, Capt. Grenadier Guards. *Recreations:* sailing, riding, skiing, flying. *Heir:* *s* Frederick John Charles Gordon Hervey-Bathurst [*b* 23 April 1934; *m* 1957, Caroline Myrtle, *d* of Lieut-Col Sir William Starkey, 2nd Bt, and late Irene Myrtle Francklin; one *s* two *d*]. *Address:* Bellevue Avenue, Rumson, New Jersey 07760, USA. *T:* 842–0791. *Clubs:* Cavalry and Guards, Royal Ocean Racing.

See also Sir J. F. Portal, Bt.

BATHURST, Joan Caroline, (Lady Bathurst); *see* Petrie, J. C.

BATHURST, Sir Maurice (Edward), Kt 1984; CMG 1953; CBE 1947; QC 1964; Judge, Arbitral Tribunal and Mixed Commission for the Agreement on German External Debts, since 1977; *b* 2 Dec. 1913; *o s* of late Edward John James Bathurst and Annie Mary Bathurst; *m* 1941, Dorothy (marr. diss. 1963), *d* of late W. S. Stevens, LDS, RCS; one *s*; *m* 1968, Joan Caroline Petrie, *qv*. *Educ:* Haberdashers' Aske's, Hatcham; King's Coll., London; Gonville and Caius Coll., Cambridge; Columbia Univ. LLB, First Class Hons. (London), 1937; University Law Schol. (London), 1937; Post-Grad. Research Studentship (London), 1938; Bartle Frere Exhibitioner (Camb.), 1939; Tutorial Fellow (Chicago), 1939; Special Fellow (Columbia), 1940; LLM (Columbia), 1941; Hon. DCL (Sacred Heart, NB), 1946; PhD (Camb.), 1949; LLD (London), 1966. Solicitor of Supreme Court, 1938–56. Called to Bar, Gray's Inn, 1957; Master of the Bench, 1970; Master of the Library, 1978–81. Legal Adviser, British Information Services, USA, 1941–43; Legal Adviser, British Embassy, Washington, 1943–46 (First Sec., 1944; Counsellor, 1946); Legal Member, UK Delegation to United Nations, 1946–48; UK Representative, Legal Advisory Cttee, Atomic Energy Commission, 1946–48; Legal Adviser to British Chm., Bipartite Control Office, Frankfurt, 1949; Dep. Legal Adviser, CCG, 1949–51; Legal Adviser, UK High Commn, Germany, 1951–55; Judge, Supreme Court, British Zone, Germany, 1953–55; Legal Adviser, British Embassy, Bonn, 1955–57; British Judge, Arbitral Commn, Germany, 1968–69. Mem. UK Delegations to UNRRA; United Nations San Francisco Conference; Bermuda Civil Aviation Conference; PICAO; Washington Financial Talks; UN Gen. Assembly; FAO; WHO; Internat. Tin Study Group; UK-US Double Taxation Treaty Negotiations; London Nine-Power Conf.; Paris Conf. on W Eur. Union; NATO Status of Forces Conf., Bonn. Internat. Vice-Pres. UN League of Lawyers; Vice Pres., Brit. Inst. of International and Comparative Law; a Pres. of Arbitral Tribunals, Internat. Telecommunications Satellite Orgn, 1974–78. Member: Panel of Arbitrators, Internat. Centre for Settlement of Investment Disputes; UK Cttee, UNICEF, 1959–84; Ct of Assistants, Haberdashers' Co. (Fourth Warden, 1973–74; Second Warden, 1978–79; First Warden, 1979–80; Master, 1980–81); Editorial Cttee, British Yearbook of International Law; *ad eundem*, Inner Temple; Gen. Council of the Bar, 1970–71; Senate of Inns of Court, 1971–73; Council of Legal Educn, 1971–79; Senate of the Inns of Court and the Bar, 1974–77. Hon. Vis. Prof. in Internat. Law, King's Coll., London, 1967–77; Hon. Fellow, King's Coll., London. Chm. Governors, Haberdashers' Aske's Hatcham Schools, 1972–80. Pres., British Insurance Law Assoc., 1971–75. Freeman of the City of London and of the City of Bathurst, NB. *Publications:* Germany and the North Atlantic Community: A Legal Survey (with J. L. Simpson), 1956; (ed, jtly) Legal Problems of an Enlarged European Community, 1972; notes and articles in legal jls, etc., British and American. *Recreation:* theatre. *Address:* Airlie, The Highlands, East Horsley, Surrey KT24 5BG. *T:* East Horsley 3269. *Club:* Garrick.

BATHURST NORMAN, George Alfred; His Honour Judge Bathurst Norman; a Circuit Judge, since 1986; *b* 15 Jan. 1939; *s* of Charles Phipps Bathurst Norman and Hon. Doreen Albinia de Burgh Norman (*née* Gibbs); *m* 1973, Susan Elizabeth Ball; one *s* one *d*. *Educ:* Harrow Sch.; Magdalen Coll., Oxford (BA). Called to the Bar, Inner Temple, 1961; SE Circuit, 1962; Dep. Circuit Judge, 1975; a Metropolitan Stipendiary Magistrate, 1981–86; a Recorder, 1986. Mem., Home Office Working Party on Coroners Rules, 1976–81. Mem., Gen. Council of the Bar, 1968–70. *Recreations:* wildlife, ornithology, cricket, travel. *Address:* 3 Hare Court, Temple, EC4. *Club:* MCC.

BATISTE, Spencer Lee; MP (C) Elmet, since 1983; solicitor in private practice, since 1970; *b* 5 June 1945; *m* 1969, Susan Elizabeth (*née* Atkin); one *s* one *d*. *Educ:* Carmel Coll.; Sorbonne, Paris; Cambridge Univ. (MA). PPS to Min. of State for Industry and IT, 1985–. Mem., Select Cttee on Energy, 1985; Sec., Cons. Backbench Space Cttee, 1983–85. Chm., Yorks Cons. Trade Unionists, 1984–. Vice-Chm., Small Business Bureau, 1983–. Law Clerk to the Guardians of the Standard of Wrought Plate within the Town of Sheffield, 1973–. Mem. Council, Univ. of Sheffield, 1982–. *Recreations:* gardening, reading, photography, stamp collecting, competitive debating (six British Jun. Chamber National Awards). *Address:* House of Commons, SW1A 0AA. *Club:* The Club (Sheffield).

BATLEY, John Geoffrey, CEng; Secretary, British Railways Board, since 1984; *b* 21 May 1930; *s* of John William and Doris Batley; *m* 1953, Cicely Anne Pindar; one *s* one *d*. *Educ:* Keighley Grammar School. MICE, MCIT. British Rail: trained and qualified as a chartered engineer in NE Region, 1947–53; Asst Divl Engr, Leeds, 1962; Management Services Officer, BR HQ, London, 1965; Dep. Principal, British Transport Staff Coll., Woking, 1970; Divl Manager, Leeds, 1976; Dep. Chief Secretary, BRB, London, 1982. *Recreations:* walking, golf, gardening. *Address:* Wentworth Cottage, Old Lodge Hill, Ilkley, West Yorkshire LS29 0BB. *T:* Ilkley 601396. *Club:* Savile.

BATSFORD, Sir Brian (Caldwell Cook), Kt 1974; painter; *b* 18 Dec. 1910; *s* of late Arthur Caldwell Cook, Gerrards Cross, Bucks; assumed mother's maiden name of Batsford by Deed Poll 1946; *m* 1945, Joan (Wendy), *o d* of late Norman Cunliffe, DSc, of Oxford; two *d. Educ:* Repton Sch.; Central Sch. of Arts and Crafts. Dip., Paris Exhibn, 1935. Joined B. T. Batsford Ltd, Booksellers and Publishers, 1928; Chairman, 1952–74; President, 1974–77. As Brian Cook, illustrated topographical books; designed over 100 book jackets, and posters for LNER and British Travel and Holidays Assoc. Lectured in Canada under auspices Canadian National Council of Education, 1935, 1937; lectured in Scandinavia and Baltic States under auspices of British Council, 1940. Hon. Sec. Empire Youth Sunday Cttee, 1938; Chm. Youth City Cttee of Enquiry, 1939. RAF, 1941–46. Contested Chelmsford Div. of Essex for Nat. Govt, 1945; MP (C) Ealing South, 1958–Feb. 1974; PPS to Minister of Works, 1959–60; Asst Govt Whip, 1962–64; Opposition Deputy Chief Whip, 1964–67. Chairman: Adv. Cttee on Works of Art in House of Commons, 1970; House of Commons Library Cttee, 1970–74. Alderman, GLC, and Parly Rep. of GLC Majority Party, 1967–70; co-opted Mem., GLC Arts and Recreation Cttee, 1970–72. Pres., London Appreciation Soc., 1955. FRSA 1955, Mem. Council, 1967, Treasurer, 1971–73; Chm., RSA, 1973–75, Vice-Pres., 1975; SGA 1933; FSIAD 1971 (MSIA 1936). Mem., Post Office Stamp Adv. Cttee, 1967–80. Pres., Old Reptonian Soc., 1973; Mem., Governing Body, Repton Sch., 1973. Vice-Pres., Questors' Theatre, Ealing, 1978; Pres., Rye Conservation Soc., 1983– (Chm., 1978–83). Hon. RI 1985. *Recreations:* painting (two paintings included in Arts Council Exhibn, Landscape in Britain 1850–1950, Hayward Gall., 1983), gardening. *Address:* Lamb House, Rye, Sussex. *T:* Rye 223763. *Clubs:* Pratt's, Royal Air Force.

BATT, Reginald Joseph Alexander; barrister; a Recorder of the Crown Court, since 1982; *b* 22 July 1920; *o s* of late Benjamin and Alice Harriett Batt; *m* 1951, Mary Margaret (*née* Canning), actress; one *d. Educ:* local authority schs; privately. Called to the Bar, Inner Temple, 1952. *Publications:* articles on law of real property and on landlord and tenant. *Recreations:* walking, tennis, antiques, music. *Address:* 6 King's Bench Walk, Temple, EC4Y 7DR. *T:* 01–583 0410.

BATTEN, Jean Gardner, CBE 1936; *b* 1909; *d* of Capt. F. H. Batten, Dental Surg., Auckland, New Zealand. *Educ:* Cleveland House Coll., Auckland, NZ. Gained Private pilot's licence at London Aeroplane Club, 1930; commercial pilot's licence London, 1932; solo flight England-Australia (women's record) May 1934; solo flight Australia-England (first woman to complete return flight), April 1935; solo flight England-Argentina (first woman to make solo flight across South Atlantic Ocean to South America), Nov. 1935; world records established: England-Brazil 61 hrs 15 mins; fastest crossing of South Atlantic Ocean by air 13 hrs 15 mins; solo flight England-New Zealand 11 days 45 mins, Oct. 1936; first direct flight from England to Auckland, NZ; solo record England-Australia 5 days 21 hrs; record flight across Tasman Sea, Australia-New Zealand, 9hrs 29 mins; record solo flight Australia-England, 5 days 18 hrs 15 mins, Oct. 1937. Jean Batten Archive estbd RAF Museum, Hendon, 1972; Museum issued 13,000 Jean Batten Commemorative Covers which were flown over route to New Zealand by British Airways to mark 40th anniversary of first direct flight, 1976; 1981 Airliner of Britannia Airways named 'Jean Batten'. Invited to visit Auckland, NZ by Mus. of Transport and Technology to open new Pavilion, 1977. Officer of the Order of the Southern Cross, Brazil; Chevalier of the Legion of Honour, France; awarded Britannia Trophy, Royal Aero Club, 1935 and 1936; Harmon Trophy awarded by international vote, 1935, 1936 and 1937; Johnston Memorial Air Navigation Trophy, 1935; Challenge Trophy (USA), Women's International Association of Aeronautics, 1934, 1935 and 1936; Segrave Trophy, 1936; Coupe de Sibour, 1937; gold medals: Fédération Aéronautique Internationale; Royal Aero Club, Aero Club de France, Belgian Royal Aero Club, Académie des Sports, Royal Swedish Aero Club, Ligue International des Aviateurs, Aero Club of Argentine, Royal Danish Aeronautical Society, Royal Norwegian Aero Club, Aero Club of Finland. City of Paris Medal, 1971. Liveryman, Guild of Air Pilots and Air Navigators, 1978. Freeman, City of London, 1978. *Publication:* My Life, 1938, repr. as Alone in the Sky, 1979. *Recreations:* walking, swimming, music.

BATTEN, John Charles, MD, FRCP; Physician to the Queen, since 1974 (Physician to HM Royal Household, 1970–74), and Head of HM Medical Household, since 1982; Physician: Brompton Hospital, since 1959; King Edward VII Hospital for Officers, since 1968; King Edward VII Hospital, Midhurst, since 1969; Hon. Physician to: St Dunstan's, since 1960; St George's Hospital, since 1980; Chief Medical Referee, Confederation Life Assoc. of Canada, since 1974 (Deputy Chief Medical Referee, 1958–74); *b* 11 March 1924; *s* of late Raymond Wallis Batten, JP and Gladys (*née* Charles); *m* 1950, Anne Mary Margaret, *d* of late John Oriel, CBE, MC; one *s* two *d* (and one *d* decd). *Educ:* Mill Hill School; St Bartholomew's Medical School. MB, BS 1946 London Univ.; MRCP 1950; MD London 1951; FRCP 1964. Junior appts, St George's Hosp. and Brompton Hosp., 1946–58. Surgeon Captain, Royal Horse Guards, 1947–49. Physician, St George's Hospital, 1958–79. Dorothy Temple Cross Research Fellow, Cornell Univ. Medical Coll., New York, 1954–55. Examiner in Medicine, London Univ., 1968; Marc Daniels Lectr, RCP, 1969; Croonian Lectr, RCP, 1983. Member: Board of Governors, Brompton Hosp., 1966–69; St George's Hosp. Medical School Council, 1969; Management Cttee, King Edward VII Hosp. Fund; Council, RSocMed, 1970; Royal College of Physicians: Censor, 1977–78; Senior Censor, 1980–81; Vice-Pres., 1980–81. *Publications:* contributions to medical books and journals. *Recreations:* music and sailing. *Address:* 7 Lion Gate Gardens, Richmond, Surrey. *T:* 01–940 3282.

BATTEN, Mark Wilfrid, RBA 1962; FRBS 1952 (ARBS 1950); Sculptor, direct carver in stone; *s* of Edward Batten; *m* 1933, Elsie May Owston Thorneloe (*d* 1961); one *d. Educ:* Chelsea Sch. of Art. Commenced to experiment individually with stone carving, 1927; exhibited only drawings and paintings until 1934; combined experiment in sculpture with learning craft of stone carving mainly in granite mason's yards in Cornwall; first exhibited sculpture, 1936; FRSA 1936. Collaborated with Eric Gill, 1939; first exhibited sculpture at Royal Academy, 1939. War service in Life Guards, 1940–45. Exhibited Paris Salon, 1949, and thereafter frequently at RA and many sculpture exhibitions in Paris, London and provincial cities. Many commissions for stone sculptures on public buildings; works in museums and art galleries. President, RBS 1956–61; Council, 1953–; Council, RBA, 1964–. Société des Artistes Français: Gold Medal for Sculpture, 1977 (Silver Medal, 1952); Associate, 1970. Hon. Mem. National Sculpture Soc. of the USA, 1956; Syracuse Univ., USA, estab. Mark Batten Manuscripts Collection, 1965, also Wichita State Univ., 1971. *Publications:* Stone Sculpture by Direct Carving, 1957; Direct Carving in Stone, 1966; articles in art magazines. *Recreations:* country life, travel, contemplation of other men's sculptures. *Address:* Christian's River Studio, Dallington, Heathfield, East Sussex TN21 9NX. *Club:* Chelsea Arts.

BATTERBURY, Paul Tracy Shepherd, TD 1972 (2 bars); **His Honour Judge Batterbury;** a Circuit Judge, since 1983; *b* 25 Jan. 1934; only *s* of late Hugh Basil John Batterbury and of Inez Batterbury; *m* 1962, Sheila Margaret, *d* of John Watson; one *s* one *d. Educ:* St Olave's Grammar Sch., Southwark; Univ. of Bristol (LLB). Served RAF, 1952–55, TA, 1959–85 (Major, RA). Called to Bar, Inner Temple, 1959; practising barrister, 1959–83; Dep. Circuit Judge, 1975–79; a Recorder of the Crown Court, 1979–83. Councillor: Chislehurst and Sidcup UDC, 1960–62; London Borough of Greenwich, 1968–71 (Chm., Housing Cttee, 1970–71). *Recreations:* photography, walking, caravanning. *Address:* 3 Hare Court, Temple, EC4Y 7BJ. *T:* 01–583 4555.

BATTERSBY, Prof. Alan Rushton, MSc, PhD, DSc, ScD; FRS 1966; Professor of Organic Chemistry, University of Cambridge, since 1969; Fellow of St Catharine's College, Cambridge; Director, FBC Ltd; *b* Leigh, 4 March 1925; *s* of William and Hilda Battersby; *m* 1949, Margaret Ruth, *d* of Thomas and Annie Hart, Whaley Bridge, Cheshire; two *s. Educ:* Grammar Sch., Leigh; Univ. of Manchester (Mercer and Woodiwis Schol.); Univ. of St Andrews. MSc Manchester; PhD St Andrews; DSc Bristol; ScD Cantab. Asst Lectr in Chemistry, Univ. of St Andrews, 1948–53; Commonwealth Fund Fellow at Rockefeller Inst., NY, 1950–51 and at Univ. of Illinois, 1951–52; Lectr in Chemistry, Univ. of Bristol, 1954–62; Prof. of Organic Chemistry, Univ. of Liverpool, 1962–69. Mem. Council, Royal Soc., 1973–75. Mem. Deutsche Akademie der Naturforscher Leopoldina, 1967. Pres., Bürgenstock Conf., 1976. Chm., Exec. Council, Ciba Foundn, 1983–. Lectures: Treat Johnson, Yale, 1969; Pacific Coast, USA, 1971; Karl Folkers, Wisconsin, 1972; N-E Coast, USA, 1974; Andrews, NSW, 1975; Middle Rhine, 1976; Tishler, Harvard, 1978; August Wilhelm von Hoffmann, Ges. Deutscher Chem., 1979; Pedler, Chem. Soc., 1980–81; Rennebohm, Wisconsin, 1981; Kharasch, Chicago, 1982; Baker, Cornell, 1984; Visiting Professor: Cornell Univ., 1969; Virginia Univ., 1971; Tohoku Univ., Japan, 1974; ANU, 1975; Technion, Israel, 1977; Univ. of Canterbury, NZ, 1980. Chemical Society: Corday-Morgan Medal, 1959; Tilden Medal and Lectr, 1963; Hügo Müller Medal and Lectr, 1972; Flintoff Medal, 1975; Award in Natural Product Chemistry, 1978; Longstaff Medal, 1984. Paul Karrer Medal and Lectr, Univ. Zürich, 1977; Davy Medal, 1977, Royal Medal, 1984, Royal Soc.; Roger Adams Award in Organic Chemistry, ACS, 1983; Havinga Medal, Holland, 1984. Hon. LLD St Andrews, 1977; Hon. DSc: Rockefeller Univ., USA, 1977; Sheffield, 1986. *Publications:* papers in chemical jls, particularly Jl Chem. Soc. *Recreations:* music, camping, sailing, fly fishing, gardening. *Address:* University Chemical Laboratory, Lensfield Road, Cambridge CB2 1EW. *T:* Cambridge 66499.

BATTERSBY, Robert Christopher, MBE 1971; Member (C) Humberside, European Parliament, since 1979; *b* 14 Dec. 1924; *s* of late Major Robert Luther Battersby, MM, RFA, late Indian Army, and Dorothea Gladys (*née* Middleton); *m* 1st, 1949, June Scriven (marr. diss.); one *d*; 2nd, 1955, Marjorie Bispham; two *s* one *d. Educ:* Firth Park Grammar Sch., Sheffield; Edinburgh Univ. (Gen. Sciences); Fitzwilliam House, Cambridge; Sorbonne; Toulouse Univ. BA Cantab (Hons Russian and Modern Greek) 1950; Cert. of Educn 1952; MA Cantab 1954; Cert. de Langue française, Toulouse, 1953; FIL 1958. Served Royal Artillery (Field) and Intelligence Corps, 1942–47 (Italian Campaign, Greece and Crete 1944, Central and Western Macedonia 1945–47); TA to 1952; Lieut RARO. With Dowsett Gp of shipbuilding and civil engrg cos on major distant water trawler and pre-stressed concrete plant export contracts, 1953–63; Manager, Eastern Trade Dept, Glacier Metal Co. Ltd, 1963–66; Sales Dir, Associated Engrg Export Services Ltd, 1966–71; Sales Dir, GKN Contractors Ltd, 1971–73. Responsible for negotiating and installing USSR, Polish, Czechoslovak and Romanian plain bearing industries, Polish diesel engine component industry, and several other metallurgical and machining plants in E Europe; Export, Financial and Commercial Adviser to various UK and USA cos. Mem. CBI and Soc. of British Engrs delegns to China, Poland, Yugoslavia and Singapore. Mem. Exec. Council, Russo-British Chamber of Commerce, and of London Chamber of Commerce Russian and Polish sections, 1968–73; Adviser to E European Trade Council, 1969–71. Principal Administrator: Credit and Investments Directorate-Gen., EEC Commn, Luxembourg, 1973–75; Agriculture Directorate-Gen., 1975–76; Fisheries Directorate-Gen., Brussels, 1976–79; Mem., first EEC Vice-Presidential delegn to Poland, 1977. European Parliament: Mem., Agriculture and Budgetary Control Cttees, 1979; Chm., Fisheries Working Gp, 1979–84; Vice-Chairman: Fisheries Sub-Cttee, 1984–; Budgetary Control, 1984–; Vice-Pres., Eur. Parlt Delegn to China, 1981 and 1984–. Vice Pres., Yorkshire and Humberside Develt Assoc., 1980–. Occasional lectr at Farnham Castle on East/West trade, and in Poland and USSR on automotive component manufg technology; broadcaster. Member: RIIA; Royal Belgian Inst. for Foreign Affairs; Anglo-Hellenic Soc.; Belgian section, E-SU; British Cons. Assoc., Brussels; European Democrat Forum; Cons. Foreign Affairs Forum; European Atlantic Gp. Silver Medal for European Merit, Luxembourg, 1981. FBIM 1982. *Publications:* works in English and Russian on distant water trawler operation; articles on fishing technology, shipbuilding and East/West trade; translations from Greek, Russian and other languages. *Recreations:* politics, European and Oriental languages, history, opera, music, rowing, travel. *Address:* West Cross, Rockshaw Road, Merstham, Surrey RH1 3BZ. *T:* Merstham 3783; 16 New Walkergate, Beverley, N Humberside. *Club:* Carlton.

BATTISCOMBE, Christopher Charles Richard; HM Diplomatic Service; Counsellor, Foreign and Commonwealth Office, since 1986; *b* 27 April 1940; *s* of Lt-Col Christopher Robert Battiscombe and late Karin Sigrid (*née* Timberg); *m* 1972, Brigid Melita Theresa Lunn; one *s* one *d. Educ:* Wellington Coll.; New Coll., Oxford (BA Greats). Entered FO, 1963; ME Centre for Arabic Studies, Shemlan, Lebanon, 1963–65; Third/Second Sec., Kuwait, 1965–68; FCO, 1968–71; First Secretary: UK Delegn, OECD, Paris, 1971–74; UK Mission to UN, New York, 1974–78; Asst Head, Eastern European and Soviet Dept, FCO, 1978–80; Commercial Counsellor: Cairo, 1981–84; Paris, 1984–86. *Recreations:* golf, skiing, tennis. *Address:* 8 Gayton Road, NW3. *T:* 01–794 8778. *Club:* Moor Park Golf (Rickmansworth, Herts).

BATTISCOMBE, Mrs (Esther) Georgina, BA; FRSL 1964; author; *b* 21 Nov. 1905; *d* of late George Harwood, MP, Master Cotton Spinner, Bolton, Lancs, and Ellen Hopkinson, *d* of Sir Alfred Hopkinson, KC, MP, First Vice-Chancellor of Manchester Univ.; *m* 1932, Lt-Col Christopher Francis Battiscombe, OBE, FSA (*d* 1964), Grenadier Guards, one *d. Educ:* St Michael's Sch., Oxford; Lady Margaret Hall, Oxford. *Publications:* Charlotte Mary Yonge, 1943; Two on Safari, 1946; English Picnics, 1949; Mrs Gladstone, 1956; John Keble (James Tait Black Memorial Prize for best biography of year), 1963; Christina Rossetti (Writers and their Work), 1965; ed, with M. Laski, A Chaplet for Charlotte Yonge, 1965; Queen Alexandra, 1969; Shaftesbury, 1974; Reluctant Pioneer: The Life of Elizabeth Wordsworth, 1978; Christina Rossetti: a divided life, 1981; The Spencers of Althorp, 1984. *Recreation:* looking at churches. *Address:* 40 Phyllis Court Drive, Henley-on-Thames, Oxfordshire RG9 2HO. *T:* Henley 574830.

BATTISHILL, Anthony Michael William; Chairman, Board of Inland Revenue, since 1986 (Deputy Chairman, 1985); *b* 5 July 1937; *s* of William George Battishill and Kathleen Rose Bishop; *m* 1961, Heather Frances Lawes; one *d. Educ:* Taunton Sch.; Hele's Sch., Exeter; London Sch. of Economics. BSc (Econs). 2nd Lieut, RAEC, 1958–60. Inland

Revenue, 1960–63; HM Treasury, 1963–65; Inland Revenue, 1965–76, Asst Sec., 1970; Central Policy Review Staff, 1976–77; Principal Private Sec. to Chancellor of the Exchequer, HM Treasury, 1977–80; Under Sec., HM Treasury, 1980–82, 1983–85, Inland Revenue, 1982–83. *Recreations:* gardening, walking. *Address:* The Board Room, Somerset House, WC2R 1LB. *T:* 01–438 7711.

BATTY, Peter Wright; television and film producer, director and writer; Chief Executive, Peter Batty Productions, since 1970; *b* 18 June 1931; *s* of Ernest Faulkner Batty and late Gladys Victoria Wright; *m* 1959, Anne Elizabeth Stringer; two *s* one *d. Educ:* Bede Grammar Sch., Sunderland; Queen's Coll., Oxford. Feature-writer, Financial Times, 1954–56; freelance journalist, 1956–58; Producer, BBC TV, 1958–64: mem. original Tonight team, other prodns incl. The Quiet Revolution, The Big Freeze, The Katanga Affair, Sons of the Navvy Man; Editor, Tonight, 1963–64; Exec. Producer and Associate Head of Factual Programming, ATV, 1964–68: prodns incl. The Fall and Rise of the House of Krupp (Grand Prix for Documentary, Venice Film Fest., 1965; Silver Dove, Leipzig Film Fest., 1965), The Road to Suez, The Suez Affair, Vietnam Fly-in, Battle for the Desert; freelance work for BBC TV and ITV, 1968–. Progs dir., prod and scripted incl. The Plutocrats, The Aristocrats, Battle for Cassino, Battle for the Bulge, Birth of the Bomb, Farouk: last of the Pharaohs, Operation Barbarossa, Superspy, Sunderland's Pride and Passion, A Rothschild and his Red Gold, Search for the Super, Spy Extraordinary, Story of Wine, World of Television, The Rise and Rise of Laura Ashley, The Gospel According to St Michael, Battle for Warsaw, Battle for Dien Bien Phu, Nuclear Nightmares, A Turn Up in a Million, Il Poverello, Swindle!, The Algerian War, Fonteyn and Nureyev, and The Divided Union; prod and scripted 6 episodes World at War series. *Publication:* The House of Krupp, 1966. *Recreations:* walking, reading, listening to music. *Address:* Claremont House, Renfrew Road, Kingston, Surrey. *T:* 01–942 6304. *Club:* White Elephant.

BATTY, Mrs Ronald; *see* Foyle, C. A. L.

BATTY, Sir William (Bradshaw), Kt 1973; TD 1946; Chairman, Ford Motor Co. Ltd, 1972–75, retired (Managing Director, 1968–73); *b* 15 May 1913; *s* of Rowland and Nellie Batty; *m* 1946, Jean Ella Brice; one *s* one *d* (and one *s* decd). *Educ:* Hulme Grammar Sch., Manchester. Served War of 1939–45, RASC (Lt-Col). Apprentice toolmaker, Ford Motor Co. Ltd, Trafford Park, Manchester, 1930; Co. trainee, 1933; Press liaison, Advertising Dept, 1936; Service Dept, 1937; Tractor Sales Dept, 1945; Asst Man., Tractor Dept, 1948; Man., Tractor and Implement Product Planning, 1953; Man., Tractor Div., 1955; Gen. Man., Tractor Gp, 1961; Dir, Tractor Gp, 1963; Dir, Car and Truck Gp, 1964; Exec. Dir, 1963–75. Chairman: Ford Motor Credit Co. Ltd, 1968 (Dir, 1963–); Automotive Finance Ltd, 1970–75; Director: Henry Ford & Son Ltd, Cork, 1965–75; Ford Lusitana SARL, Portugal, 1973–75. Mem., Engineering Industries Council, 1975–76. Pres., SMMT, 1975–76. Hon. LLD Manchester, 1976. FBIM. *Recreations:* golf, sailing, gardening. *Address:* Glenhaven Cottage, Riverside Road West, Newton Ferrers, South Devon. *Club:* Royal Western Yacht.

BATTYE, Maj.-Gen. (Retd) Stuart Hedley Molesworth, CB 1960; *b* 21 June 1907; *s* of late Lieut-Col W. R. Battye, DSO, MS, LRCP, Chev. de Legion d'Honneur, CStJ, and late M. St G. Molesworth; *m* 1940, Evelyn Désirée, *d* of late Capt. G. B. Hartford, DSO and bar, RN; one *s* two *d. Educ:* Marlborough Coll.; RMA, Woolwich; Cambridge Univ. (MA). Commissioned 2nd Lieut, RE, 1927; served with Bengal Sappers and Miners, India, 1930–44 (NW Frontier Campaign, 1930–31); Iraq, 1941–42; India, 1942–44; 21 Army Group, BLA, 1945–47; MELF, 1952–55; War Office, 1955; Dir of Movements, the War Office, 1958–61; Dir, Council for Small Industries in Rural Areas (formerly Rural Industries Bureau), 1963–73. FRSA 1963. *Publications:* contrib. to Blackwood's and RE Journal. *Recreations:* fishing, painting. *Club:* Army and Navy.
See also Baron Hankey.

BAUDOUX, Most Rev. Maurice, STD, PhD, DèsL; *b* Belgium, 1902. *Educ:* Prud'homme convent, Saskatchewan; St Boniface College, Manitoba; St Joseph's Seminary, Alberta; Grand Seminary, Quebec. Priest, 1929; Curate then Pastor, Prud'homme, Sask; Domestic Prelate, 1944; First Bishop of Saint Paul in Alberta, 1948; Coadjutor-Archbishop of Saint Boniface, 1952; Archbishop of St Boniface, 1955–74. *Address:* c/o Archbishop's Residence, 151 Cathedral Avenue, St Boniface, Manitoba R2H 0H6, Canada.

BAUER, family name of **Baron Bauer.**

BAUER, Baron *cr* 1982 (Life Peer), of Market Ward in the City of Cambridge; **Peter Thomas Bauer,** MA; DSc; FBA; Professor of Economics (with special reference to economic development and under-developed countries) in the University of London, at the London School of Economics, 1960–83, now Emeritus Professor of Economics; Fellow of Gonville and Caius College, Cambridge, 1946–60, and since 1968; *b* 6 Nov. 1915; unmarried. *Educ:* Scholae Piae, Budapest; Gonville and Caius Coll., Cambridge. Reader in Agricultural Economics, University of London, 1947–48; University Lecturer in Economics, Cambridge Univ., 1948–56; Smuts Reader in Commonwealth Studies, Cambridge Univ., 1956–60. *Publications:* The Rubber Industry, 1948; West African Trade, 1954; The Economics of Under-developed Countries (with B. S. Yamey), 1957; Economic Analysis and Policy in Under-developed Countries, 1958; Indian Economic Policy and Development, 1961; (with B. S. Yamey) Markets, Market Control and Marketing Reform, 1968; Dissent on Development, 1972; Aspects of Nigerian Development, 1974; Equality, the Third World and Economic Delusion, 1981; Reality and Rhetoric: studies in the economics of development, 1984; articles on economic subjects. *Address:* House of Lords, Westminster, SW1. *Club:* Garrick.

BAUGH, John Trevor; Director General of Supplies and Transport (Naval), Ministry of Defence, since 1986; *b* 24 Sept. 1932; *s* of late Thomas Harold Baugh and of Nellie Baugh (*née* Machin); *m* 1st, 1956, Pauline Andrews (decd); three *s*; 2nd, 1981, Noreen Rita Rosemary Sykes; two step *s. Educ:* Queen Elizabeth's Hospital, Bristol. MCIT 1956. Asst Naval Store Officer, Devonport, 1953; Dep. Naval Store Officer, Admiralty, 1959; Armament Supply Officer, Alexandria, 1966; Principal, MoD, Bath, 1970; Supt, RN Store Depot, Copenacre, 1974; Asst Sec., MoD (Navy), 1976, Exec. Dir, 1979; MoD (Army), 1983, Asst Under Sec. of State 1985. *Recreations:* bridge, golf. *Address:* c/o Ministry of Defence, Ensleigh, Bath. *T:* Bath 67707. *Club:* Bath Golf.

BAUGHEN, Rt. Rev. Michael Alfred; *see* Chester, Bishop of.

BAUM, Prof. Michael, ChM; FRCS; Professor of Surgery, King's College Hospital Medical School, London, since 1980; *b* 31 May 1937; *s* of Isidor and Mary Baum; *m* 1965, Judith (*née* Marcus); one *s* two *d. Educ:* Univ. of Birmingham (MB, ChB; ChM). FRCS 1965. Lecturer in Surgery, King's College Hosp., 1969–72; Research Fellow, Univ. of Pittsburgh, USA, 1971–72; Reader in Surgery, Welsh National Sch. of Medicine, Cardiff, 1972–78; Hon. Cons. Surgeon, King's College Hosp., 1978–80. *Publications:* Breast Cancer—The Facts, 1981; multiple pubns on breast cancer, cancer therapy, cancer biology and the philosophy of science. *Recreations:* painting, theatre, reading, philosophizing. *Address:* 22 Red Post Hill, SE24 9JQ. *T:* 01–733 6229. *Club:* Royal Society of Medicine.

BAVERSTOCK, Donald Leighton; Executive Producer, Television, BBC Manchester, 1975–77; *b* 18 Jan. 1924; *s* of Thomas Philip Baverstock and Sarah Ann; *m* 1957, Gillian Mary, *d* of late Mrs Kenneth Darrell Waters (Enid Blyton); one *s* two *d.* (and one *s* decd). *Educ:* Canton High Sch., Cardiff; Christ Church, Oxford (MA). Served with RAF, 1943–46; completed tour of operations Bomber Command, 1944; Instructor, Navigation, 1944–46. History Master, Wellington Coll., 1949. Producer, BBC General Overseas Service, 1950–54; Producer, BBC Television Service, 1954–57; Editor, Tonight Programme, 1957–61; Asst Controller, Television Programmes, BBC, 1961–63; Chief of Programmes BBC TV (1), 1963–65; Partner, Jay, Baverstock, Milne & Co., 1965–67; Dir of Programmes, Yorkshire TV, 1967–73; Man. Dir, Granada Video Ltd, 1974–75. *Address:* Low Hall, Middleton, Ilkley, Yorks. *T:* Ilkley 608037.

BAVIN, Alfred Robert Walter, CB 1966; Deputy Secretary, Department of Health and Social Security, 1968–73 (Ministry of Health, 1966–68); *b* 4 April 1917; *s* of late Alfred and late Annie Bavin; *m* 1947, Helen Mansfield; one *s* three *d. Educ:* Christ's Hosp.; Balliol Coll., Oxford. 1st cl. Hon. Mods 1937; 1st cl. Lit. Hum. 1939. Min. of Health, Asst Principal, 1939, Principal, 1946; Cabinet Office, 1948–50; Min. of Health, Principal Private Sec. to Minister, 1951; Asst Sec. 1952; Under-Sec. 1960. Nuffield Home Civil Service Travelling Fellowship, 1956. *Address:* 7 First Avenue, Felpham, Bognor Regis, W Sussex. *T:* Middleton-on-Sea 3073. *Clubs:* Athenæum, MCC.

BAVIN, Rt. Rev. Timothy John; *see* Portsmouth, Bishop of.

BAWDEN, Prof. Charles Roskelly, FBA; Professor of Mongolian, University of London, 1970–84, now Emeritus Professor; *b* 22 April 1924; *s* of George Charles Bawden and Eleanor Alice Adelaide Bawden (*née* Russell); *m* 1949, Jean Barham Johnson; three *s* one *d. Educ:* Weymouth Grammar School; Peterhouse, Cambridge (MA, PhD, Dipl. in Oriental Languages). War Service, RNVR, 1943–46. Asst Principal, German Section, Foreign Office, 1948–49; Lectr in Mongolian, SOAS, 1955; Reader in Mongolian, 1962, and Prof., 1970, Univ. of London; Head of Dept of Far East, SOAS, 1970–84; Pro-Director, SOAS, 1982–84. FBA 1971–80, 1985; Mem. corresp., Soc. Finno-Ougrienne 1975. *Publications:* The Mongol Chronicle Altan Tobči, 1955; The Jebtsundamba Khutukhtus of Urga, 1961; The Modern History of Mongolia, 1968; The Chester Beatty Library: a catalogue of the Mongolian Collection, 1969; Shamans Lamas and Evangelicals: the English missionaries in Siberia, 1985; articles and reviews in SOAS Bull., Central Asiatic Jl, Zentralasiatische Studien and other periodicals. *Address:* c/o School of Oriental and African Studies, University of London, Malet Street, WC1E 7HP.

BAWDEN, Edward, CBE 1946; RA 1956 (ARA 1947); RDI 1949; Painter and Designer; Draughtsman; formerly a Tutor in the School of Graphic Design, Royal College of Art; *b* Braintree, Essex, 1903; *m* 1932, Charlotte (*d* 1970), *d* of Robert Epton, Lincoln; one *s* one *d. Educ:* Cambridge Sch. of Art; Royal Coll. of Art. As an Official War Artist he travelled in Middle East, 1940–45; visited Canada during 1949 and 1950 as a guest instructor at Banff Sch. of Fine Arts, Alberta. His work is represented in the Tate Gallery, London, and by water-colour drawings in several London, Dominion and provincial galleries; exhibitions at: Leicester Galleries, 1938, 1949, 1952; Zwemmer Gallery, 1934, 1963; Fine Art Soc., 1968, 1975, 1978, 1979; Fitzwilliam Museum, 1978; Imperial War Museum, 1983. Printmaker and graphic designer. He has designed and cut blocks for a series of wallpapers printed by Messrs Cole & Son, and has painted mural decorations for the SS Orcades and SS Oronsay, also for Lion and Unicorn Pavilion on South Bank site of Festival of Brtain. Trustee of Tate Gallery, 1951–58. Hon. Dr RCA; DUniv Essex; Hon. RE; *Illustrated books include:* The Histories of Herodotus, Salammbô, Tales of Troy and Greece, The Arabs, Life in an English Village. *Relevant publications:* Edward Bawden, by J. M. Richards (Penguin Modern Painters); Edward Bawden, by Robert Harling (English Masters of Black and White); Edward Bawden: A Book of Cuts, 1978; Edward Bawden, by Douglas Percy Bliss, 1979. *Address:* 2 Park Lane, Saffron Walden, Essex CB10 1DA.

BAWDEN, Nina Mary, (Mrs A. S. Kark), MA; FRSL; JP; novelist; *b* 19 Jan. 1925; *d* of Charles and Ellalaine Ursula May Mabey; *m* 1st, 1946, Henry Walton Bawden; one *s* (and one *s* decd); 2nd, 1954, Austen Steven Kark, *qv*; one *d. Educ:* Ilford County High Sch.; Somerville Coll., Oxford (BA). Asst, Town and Country Planning Assoc., 1946–47. JP Surrey, 1968. Mem., ALCS. Pres., Soc. of Women Writers and Journalists. *Publications: novels:* Who Calls the Tune, 1953; The Odd Flamingo, 1954; Change Here for Babylon, 1955; Devil by the Sea, 1958, 2nd edn 1972 (abridged for children, 1976); The Solitary Child, 1956; Just Like a Lady, 1960; In Honour Bound, 1961; Tortoise by Candlelight, 1963; Under the Skin, 1964; A Little Love, a Little Learning, 1965; A Woman of My Age, 1967; The Grain of Truth, 1969; The Birds on the Trees, 1970; Anna Apparent, 1972; George beneath a Paper Moon, 1974; Afternoon of a Good Woman, 1976 (Yorkshire Post Novel of the Year, 1976); Familiar Passions, 1979; Walking Naked, 1981; The Ice House, 1983; *for children:* The Secret Passage; On the Run; The White Horse Gang; The Witch's Daughter; A Handful of Thieves; The Runaway Summer; Squib; Carrie's War; The Peppermint Pig (Guardian award, 1976); Rebel on a Rock, 1978; The Robbers, 1979; Kept in the Dark, 1982; The Finding, 1985; Princess Alice, 1985. *Recreations:* travelling, reading, garden croquet. *Address:* 22 Noel Road, N1. *T:* 01–226 2839. *Clubs:* Lansdowne; Ski Club of Great Britain, PEN, Society of Authors.

BAWN, Cecil Edwin Henry, CBE 1956; FRS 1952; BSc, PhD; Brunner Professor of Physical Chemistry in the University of Liverpool, 1969–Dec. 1973, now Emeritus (Grant-Brunner Professor of Inorganic and Physical Chemistry, 1948–69); *b* 6 Nov. 1908; British; *m* 1934, Winifred Mabel Jackson; two *s* one *d. Educ:* Cotham Grammar Sch., Bristol. Graduated, Univ. of Bristol, 1929; PhD in Chemistry (Bristol), 1932; Asst Lectr in Chemistry, Univ. of Manchester, 1931–34; Lectr in Chemistry, 1934–38; Lectr in Physical Chemistry, Univ. of Bristol, 1938–45; Reader in Physical Chemistry, 1945–49. During War of 1939–45 was in charge of a Physico-Chemical Section in Armament Research Dept, Min. of Supply. Mem., Univ. Grants Cttee, 1965–74. Swinburne Gold Medal, 1966. Hon. DSc: Bradford, 1966; Birmingham, 1968; Bristol, 1974. *Publications:* The Chemistry of High Polymers, 1948; papers in chemical journals. *Address:* Springfields, Stoodleigh, near Tiverton, Devon EX16 9PT. *T:* Oakford 220.

BAXANDALL, David Kighley, CBE 1959; Director of National Galleries of Scotland, 1952–70; *b* 11 Oct. 1905; *m* 1931, Isobel, *d* of Canon D. J. Thomas; one *s* twin *d. Educ:* King's Coll. Sch., Wimbledon; King's Coll., University of London. Asst Keeper, 1929–39, and Keeper of the Department of Art, 1939–41, National Museum of Wales. Served in RAF, 1941–45. Dir of Manchester City Art Galleries, 1945–52. *Publications:* Ben Nicholson, 1962; numerous articles, gallery handbooks, catalogues and broadcast talks. *Address:* 24 Guardian Court, Ferrers Street, Hereford HR1 2LP. *T:* Hereford 57881.
See also M. D. K. Baxandall.

BAXANDALL, Prof. Michael David Kighley, FBA 1982; Professor of the History of the Classical Tradition, Warburg Institute, University of London, since 1981 (Reader, 1973–81); *b* 18 Aug. 1933; *o s* of David Baxandall, *qv*; *m* 1963, Katharina Simon; one *s* one *d. Educ:* Manchester Grammar Sch.; Downing Coll., Cambridge (MA); Univs of Pavia and Munich. Jun. Res. Fellow, Warburg Inst., 1959–61; Asst Keeper, Dept of Architecture and Sculpture, Victoria and Albert Museum, 1961–65; Lectr in Renaissance

Studies, Warburg Inst., 1965–73; Slade Prof. of Fine Art, Univ. of Oxford, 1974–75. *Publications:* Giotto and the Orators, 1971; Painting and Experience in Fifteenth-Century Italy, 1972; South German Sculpture 1480–1530 in the Victoria and Albert Museum, 1974; The Limewood Sculptors of Renaissance Germany, 1980; Patterns of Intention, 1985. *Address:* The Warburg Institute, Woburn Square, WC1H 0AB.

BAXENDELL, Sir Peter (Brian), Kt 1981; CBE 1972; FEng 1978; FIC 1983; Director: Shell Transport and Trading Co., since 1973 (Chairman, 1979–85); Inchcape PLC, since 1986; Chairman, Hawker Siddeley Group PLC, since 1986 (Director, since 1984; Deputy Chairman, Jan.–April 1986); *b* 28 Feb. 1925; *s* of Lesley Wilfred Edward Baxendell and Evelyn Mary Baxendell (*née* Gaskin); *m* 1949, Rosemary (*née* Lacey); two *s* two *d*. *Educ:* St Francis Xavier's, Liverpool; Royal School of Mines, London (ARSM, BSc; FIC 1983). Joined Royal Dutch/Shell Group, 1946; Petroleum Engr in Egypt, 1947, and Venezuela, 1950; Techn. Dir, Shell-BP Nigeria, 1963; Head of SE Asia Div., London, 1966; Man. Dir, Shell-BP Nigeria, 1969; Man. Dir, 1973–75, Chm., 1974–79, Shell UK; Man. Dir, 1973, Chm., Cttee of Man. Dirs, 1982–85, Royal Dutch/Shell Gp of Cos; Chm., Shell Canada Ltd, 1980–85; Dir, Shell Oil Co., USA, 1982–85. Mem., UGC, 1983–. Hon. DSc Heriot-Watt 1982. Commander, Order of Orange–Nassau, 1985. *Publications:* articles on petroleum engrg subjects in scientific jls. *Recreations:* tennis, fishing. *Address:* Shell Centre, SE1 7NA. *T:* 01–934 2772.

BAXTER, Prof. Alexander Duncan, CEng; Research Consultant, since 1970; Director, de Havilland Engine Co. Ltd, 1958–63; Chief Executive Rocket Division and Nuclear Power Group, de Havilland Engine Co. Ltd, 1957–63; *b* 17 June 1908; *e s* of Robert Alexander and Mary Violet Baxter; *m* 1933, Florence Kathleen McClean; one *s* two *d*. *Educ:* Liverpool Institute High Sch.; Liverpool Univ. BEng (1st Cl. Hons MechEng) 1930; MEng 1933. Post-graduate pupil with Daimler Company, 1930–34; commissioned in RAFO, 1930–38; Research Engineer with Instn. of Automobile Engrs, 1934–35; Scientific Officer at RAE, Farnborough, 1935; engaged on aircraft propulsion and gas turbine research until 1947; Supt, Rocket Propulsion, RAE, 1947–50; Prof. of Aircraft Propulsion, Coll. of Aeronautics, Cranfield, 1950–57; Dep. Principal, Cranfield, 1954–57; Sen. Exec., Bristol Siddeley Engines Ltd, 1963–68, Bristol Engine Div. of Rolls Royce Ltd, 1968–70. Mem. Council: InstMechE, 1955–57; RAeS, 1953–70 (Vice-Pres, 1962–66, Pres., 1966–67). Served as member of many educnl bodies, incl.: jt Cttee on Higher Nat. Certificate in Engrg; RAF Educn Adv. Cttee; Aeronautical Board, CNAA; Board of CEI, 1962–69; various Govt advisory cttees. Member of Court: Univ. of Bristol; Cranfield Inst. of Technology. Hon. DSc Cranfield Inst. of Technology, 1980. FIMechE, FRAeS, FInstPet, Fellow, British Interplanetary Soc. *Publications:* various reports in government R & M series; papers in Proc. Instn Mech. Engineers and RAeS. *Recreations:* do-it-yourself, grandchildren, cine photography. *Address:* Glebe Cottage, Pucklechurch, Glos. *T:* Abson 2204.

BAXTER, Jeremy Richard; Assistant Director, Nationalised Industries' Chairmen's Group, since 1984; *b* 20 Jan. 1929; *s* of late Andrew Paterson Baxter and late Ann Winifred Baxter; *m* 1965, Faith Elizabeth Graham; two *s* one *d*. *Educ:* Sedbergh Sch.; St John's Coll., Cambridge (BA Class. Tripos). Asst Principal, Post Office, 1952; Asst Private Sec. to Postmaster-Gen., 1956; Private Sec. to Asst Postmaster-Gen., 1957; Principal, Post Office, 1958; Principal, Treasury, 1964; Asst Sec., Post Office, 1967; Dir, Postal Personnel, 1971; Dir of Personnel, European Commn, 1973–81; Sec., Post Office, 1982–84. *Recreations:* sailing, gardening. *Address:* Spring Grove Farm, Mursley, Milton Keynes MK17 0SA. *Club:* Travellers'.

BAXTER, John Lawson; *b* 25 Nov. 1939; *s* of John Lawson Baxter and Enid Maud Taggart; *m* 1967; three *s*. *Educ:* Trinity Coll., Dublin; Queen's Univ., Belfast; BA, BComm, LLB; LLM Tulane Univ., New Orleans. Solicitor. Mem. (U) N Ireland Assembly, for N Antrim, 1973–75; Minister of Information, N Ireland Executive, 1974. Chm. (part-time), Industrial Tribunals (NI), 1980–83; Mem., Northern Health and Social Services Board, 1982–. *Recreations:* golf, fishing. *Address:* Beardiville, Cloyfin, Coleraine, N Ireland. *T:* Bushmills 31552.

BAXTER, Prof. Sir (John) Philip, KBE 1965 (OBE 1945); CMG 1959; PhD, FAA, FTS; Chairman, Sydney Opera House Trust, 1968–75; *b* 7 May 1905; *s* of John and Mary Netta Baxter; *m* 1931, Lilian May Baxter (*née* Thatcher); three *s* one *d*. *Educ:* University of Birmingham. BSc 1925, PhD 1928. University of Birmingham. Research Dir, ICI General Chemicals Ltd and Dir, Thorium Ltd, until 1949; Prof. Chem. Eng, NSW University of Technology, 1950; Vice-Chancellor, Univ. of NSW, 1953–69. Chm, Australian Atomic Energy Commn, 1957–72. Fellow: Aust. Acad. of Science; Aust. Acad. of Technological Sciences. FRACI; MIE(Aust). Hon. LLD Montreal, 1958; Hon. DSc: Newcastle, Queensland; NSW; Hon. DTech Loughborough, 1969. *Address:* 1 Kelso Street, Enfield, NSW 2136, Australia. *T:* 7474261.

BAXTER, John Walter, CBE 1974; Consultant, G. Maunsell & Partners (Partner, 1955, Senior Partner, 1959–80); *b* 4 June 1917; *s* of late J. G. Baxter and late D. L. Baxter (*née* Phelps); *m* 1941, Jessie, *d* of late T. Pimblott; one *d*. *Educ:* Westminster City Sch.; City and Guilds Engrg College. BSc(Eng), FCGI, FEng, FICE, FRSA. Civil Engineer: Trussed Concrete Steel Co. Ltd, 1936–41; Shell Refining Co. Ltd, 1941–52; Maunsell Posford & Pavry, 1952–55. President: ICE, 1976–77 (Vice-Pres., 1973–76, Mem. Council, 1963–68 and 1970–79); Smeatonian Soc. of Civil Engrs, 1986; Vice-Chm., ACE, 1979–80, Chm., 1980–81. *Publications:* contrib. Proc. ICE. *Address:* The Down Side, Itchen Abbas, Hants.

BAXTER, Prof. Sir Philip; *see* Baxter, Prof. Sir J. P.

BAXTER, Raymond Frederic, FRSA; broadcaster and writer; *b* 25 Jan. 1922; *s* of Frederick Garfield Baxter and Rosina Baxter (*née* Rivers); *m* 1945, Sylvia Kathryn (*née* Johnson), Boston, Mass; one *s* one *d*. *Educ:* Ilford County High Sch. Joined RAF, 1940; flew Spitfires with 65, 93 and 602 Sqdns, in UK, Med. and Europe. Entered Forces Broadcasting in Cairo, still as serving officer, 1945; civilian deputy Dir BFN BBC, 1947–49; subseq. short attachment West Region and finally joined Outside Broadcast Dept, London; with BBC until 1966; Dir, Motoring Publicity, BMC, 1967–68. Member Cttee of Management: RNLI, 1979–; Air League, 1980–85. Hon. Freeman, City of London, 1978; Liveryman, GAPAN, 1983. Hon. Admiral, Assoc. of Dunkirk Little Ships, 1982–. *Publications:* (with James Burke and Michael Latham) Tomorrow's World, Vol. 1, 1970, Vol. 2, 1971; Farnborough Commentary, 1980; film commentaries, articles and reports on motoring and aviation subjects, etc. *Recreations:* motoring, riding, boating. *Address:* The Green Cottage, Wargrave Road, Henley-on-Thames, Oxon RG9 3HX. *T:* Henley-on-Thames 571081. *Clubs:* British Racing Drivers, Eccentric, etc.

BAXTER, Prof. Rodney James, FRS 1982; FAA 1977; Professor in the Department of Theoretical Physics, Research School of Physical Sciences, Australian National University, since 1981; *b* 8 Feb. 1940; *s* of Thomas James Baxter and Florence A. Baxter; *m* 1968, Elizabeth Phillips; one *s* one *d*. *Educ:* Bancroft's Sch., Essex; Trinity Coll., Cambridge; Australian National Univ. Reservoir Engineer, Iraq Petroleum Co., 1964–65; Research Fellow, ANU, 1965–68; Asst Prof., Mathematics Dept, Massachusetts Inst. of Technology, 1968–70; Fellow, ANU, 1970–81. Pawsey Medal, Aust. Acad. of Science, 1975; Boltzmann Medal, IUPAP, 1980. *Publications:* Exactly Solved Models in Statistical Mechanics, 1982; contribs to Proc. Royal Soc., Jl of Physics A, Physical Rev., Statistical Physics, Annals of Physics. *Recreation:* theatre. *Address:* Theoretical Physics IAS, Australian National University, Canberra, ACT 2601, Australia. *T:* (062) 492968.

BAXTER, Roger George, PhD; FRAS, FRSA; Headmaster of Sedbergh School, since 1982; *b* 21 April 1940; *s* of Rev. Benjamin George Baxter and Gweneth Muriel Baxter (*née* Causer); *m* 1967, Dorothy Ann Cook; one *s* one *d*. *Educ:* Handsworth Grammar Sch., Birmingham; Univ. of Sheffield (BSc, PhD). Junior Research Fellow, Univ. of Sheffield, 1965–66, Lectr, Dept of Applied Mathematics, 1966–70; Asst Mathematics Master, Winchester Coll., 1970–81, Under Master, 1976–81. Governor: Bramcote Sch., Scarborough, 1982–; Hurworth Hse Sch., Darlington, 1982–; Cathedral Choir Sch., Ripon, 1984–. Mowden Hall Sch., Northumberland, 1984–. HMC Academic Policy Cttee, 1985–. *Publications:* various papers on numerical studies in magnetoplasma diffusion with applications to the F-2 layer of the ionosphere. *Recreations:* opera, music, cooking. *Address:* Birksholme, Sedbergh, Cumbria LA10 5HQ. *T:* Sedbergh 20491.

BAXTER, Walter; author; *b* 1915. *Educ:* St Lawrence, Ramsgate; Trinity Hall, Cambridge. Worked in the City, 1936–39; served War of 1939–45, with KOYLI in Burma; afterwards, in India, ADC to General Slim, and on Staff of a Corps HQ during re-conquest of Burma. After completion of first novel, returned to India to work temporarily on a mission. *Publications:* Look Down in Mercy, 1951; The Image and The Search, 1953. *Address:* 119 Old Brompton Road, SW7.

BAXTER, William T., BCom Edinburgh; Professor of Accounting, London School of Economics, 1947–73, Hon. Fellow 1980; *b* 27 July 1906; *s* of W. M. Baxter and Margaret Threipland; *m* 1st, 1940, Marjorie Allanson (*d* 1971); one *s* one *d*; 2nd, 1973, Leena-Kaisa Laitakari-Kaila. *Educ:* George Watson's Coll.; Univ. of Edinburgh. Chartered Accountant (Edinburgh), 1930; Commonwealth Fund Fellow, 1931, at Harvard Univ.; Lectr in Accounting, Univ. of Edinburgh, 1934; Prof. of Accounting, Univ. of Cape Town, 1937. Hon. DLitt: Kent at Canterbury, 1974; Heriot-Watt, 1976; Hon. DSc Buckingham, 1983; Hon. DSc(Econ) Hull, 1977. *Publications:* Income Tax for Professional Students, 1936; The House of Hancock, 1945; Depreciation, 1971; Accounting Values and Inflation, 1975; Collected Papers on Accounting, 1979; Inflation Accounting, 1984. *Address:* 1 The Ridgeway, NW11. *T:* 01–455 6810.

BAYDA, Hon. Edward Dmytro; Chief Justice of Saskatchewan, since 1981; *b* 9 Sept. 1931; *s* of Dmytro A. Bayda and Mary Bilinski; *m* 1953, Marie-Thérèse Yvonne Gagnè; one *s* five *d*. *Educ:* Univ. of Saskatchewan (BA 1951, LLB 1953). Called to the Bar, Saskatchewan, 1954; QC (Sask) 1966. Judge, Court of Queen's Bench, 1972; Justice, Court of Appeal, 1974. KM 1975. *Address:* (home) 9 Turnbull Place, Regina, Sask S4S 4H2, Canada. *T:* 586–2126; (chambers) Court House, 2425 Victoria Avenue, Regina, Sask S4P 3V7. *T:* 787–5415.

BAYLEY, Gordon Vernon, CBE 1976; FIA, FIMA, FSS, CBIM; Chairman, Swiss Reinsurance Co. (UK) Ltd, since 1985; Director: National Provident Institution, since 1970; TR Industrial and General Trust PLC, since 1983; *b* 25 July 1920; *s* of late Capt. Vernon Bayley, King's Regt, and Mrs Gladys Maud Bayley; *m* 1945, Miriam Allenby, *d* of late Frederick Walter Ellis and Miriam Ellis, Eastbourne; one *s* two *d*. *Educ:* Abingdon. Joined HM Forces, 1940; commissioned Royal Artillery, Major 1945. Asst Actuary, Equitable Life Assurance Soc., 1949; Partner, Duncan C. Fraser and Co. (Actuaries), 1954–57; National Provident Institution: Assistant Sec., 1957, Joint Sec. 1959; Gen. Manager and Actuary 1964–85. Mem., Occupational Pensions Bd, 1973–74. Mem., Cttee to Review the Functioning of Financial Institutions, 1977–80. Institute of Actuaries: Fellow, 1946; Hon. Sec., 1960–62; Vice-Pres., 1964–67; Pres., 1974–76; Chm., Life Offices Assoc., 1969–70 (Dep. Chm., 1967–68). Chm., Bd of Governors, Abingdon Sch., 1979–83. *Publications:* contribs to Jl Inst. Actuaries, Jl Royal Statistical Soc. *Recreations:* tennis, ski-ing, sailing. *Address:* The Old Manor, Witley, Surrey. *T:* Wormley 2301. *Clubs:* Athenæum, English Speaking Union; Island Sailing; Sea View Yacht.

BAYLEY, Prof. John Oliver; Warton Professor of English Literature, and Fellow of St Catherine's College, University of Oxford, since 1974; *b* 27 March 1925; *s* of F. J. Bayley; *m* 1956, Jean Iris Murdoch, *qv*. *Educ:* Eton; New Coll., Oxford. 1st cl. hons English Oxon 1950. Served in Army, 1943–47. Mem., St Antony's and Magdalen Colls, Oxford, 1951–55; Fellow and Tutor in English, New Coll., Oxford, 1955–74. *Publications:* In Another Country (novel), 1954; The Romantic Survival: A Study in Poetic Evolution, 1956; The Characters of Love, 1961; Tolstoy and the Novel, 1966; Pushkin: A Comparative Commentary, 1971; The Uses of Division: unity and disharmony in literature, 1976; An Essay on Hardy, 1978; Shakespeare and Tragedy, 1981.

BAYLEY, Mrs John Oliver; *see* Murdoch, J. I.

BAYLEY, Lt-Comdr Oscar Stewart Morris, RN retd; *b* 15 April 1926; *s* of late Rev. J. H. S. Bayley; *m* Pamela Margaret Harrison (one *s* one *d* by a former marriage). *Educ:* St John's Sch., Leatherhead; King James's Grammar Sch., Knaresborough. Called to Bar, Lincoln's Inn, 1959. Entered RN, 1944: Ceylon, 1956–58; Supply Off., HMS Narvik and Sqdn Supply Off., 5th Submarine Div., 1960–62; Sec. to Comdr British Forces Caribbean Area, 1962–65; retd from RN at own request, 1966. Legal Asst (Unfair Competition), The Distillers Co. Ltd, 1966–68; Clerk, Fishmongers' Co., 1968–73. Director: Anglers Co-operative Assoc. Trustee Co. Ltd; Seed Oysters (UK) Ltd. Clerk to Governors of Gresham's Sch., Holt; Hon. Sec., Salmon and Trout Assoc. and of Shellfish Assoc. of Great Britain; Vice-Chm., National Anglers' Council; Secretary: Atlantic Salmon Research Trust; City and Guilds of London Art Sch. Ltd, 1968–73; Nat. Assoc. of Pension Funds Investment Protection Cttee, 1974–75. Dir and Chief Sec., The Royal Life Saving Soc., 1976–78; Accountant, Hawker Siddeley Group, 1978–81, John Lewis Partnership, 1981–82. *Address:* 244 Bexley Lane, Sidcup, Kent DA14 4JG.

BAYLEY, Peter Charles; Emeritus Professor, University of St Andrews; *b* 25 Jan. 1921; *y s* of late William Charles Abell Bayley and Irene (*née* Heath); *m* 1951, Patience (marr. diss. 1980), *d* of late Sir George (Norman) Clark, and Lady Clark; one *s* two *d*. *Educ:* Crypt Sch., Gloucester; University Coll., Oxford (Sidgwick Exhibnr; MA 1st Cl. Hons English, 1947). Served RA and Intell. Corps, India, 1941–45. Jun. Fellow, University Coll., Oxon, 1947; Fellow and Praelector in English, 1949–72 (at various times Domestic Bursar, Tutor for Admissions, Librarian, Editor of University Coll. Record); Univ. Lectr in English, 1952–72; Proctor, 1957–58; Oxford Univ. Corresp., The Times, 1960–63; Master of Collingwood Coll. and Lectr, Dept of Engish, Univ. of Durham, 1971–78; Berry Prof. and Head of Dept of English, Univ. of St Andrews, 1978–85. Vis. Reader, Birla Inst., Pilani, Rajasthan, India, 1966; Vis. Lectr, Yale Univ., and Robert Bates Vis. Fellow, Jonathan Edwards Coll., 1970; Brown Distinguished Vis. Prof., Univ. of the South, Sewanee, Tenn, 1978. *Publications:* Edmund Spenser, Prince of Poets, 1971; 'Casebook' on Spenser's The Faerie Queene, 1977; Poems of Milton, 1982; An ABC of Shakespeare, 1985; edited: Spenser, The Faerie Queene: Book II, 1965; Book I, 1966; Loves and Deaths: short stories by 19th century novelists, 1972. *Address:* 63 Oxford Street, Woodstock, Oxford OX7 1TJ.

BAYLEY, Prof. Peter James; Drapers Professor of French, since 1985, and Fellow of Gonville and Caius College, since 1971, Cambridge University; *b* 20 Nov. 1944; *s* of John Henry Bayley and Margaret Burness, Portreath, Cornwall. *Educ:* Redruth County Grammar Sch.; Emmanuel Coll., Cambridge (Kitchener Schol., 1963–66; 1st cl. Hons Mod. and Med. Langs Tripos, 1964 and 1966; MA 1970; PhD 1971); Ecole Normale Supérieure, Paris (French Govt Schol., 1967–68). Cambridge University: Fellow of Emmanuel Coll., 1969–71; Coll. Lectr, Gonville and Caius Coll., 1971–85; Tutor, 1973–79; Praelector Rhetoricus, 1980–86; Univ. Asst Lectr in French, 1974–78; Univ. Lectr, 1978–85 (Actg Head, Dept of French, 1983–85). *Publications:* French Pulpit Oratory 1598–1650, 1980; (ed with D. Coleman) The Equilibrium of Wit: essays for Odette de Mourgues, 1982; (ed) Selected Sermons of the French Baroque, 1983; contributions to: Critique et création littéraires en France (ed Fumaroli), 1977; Bossuet: la Prédication au XVIIe siècle (ed Collinet and Goyet), 1980; Cambridge Rev., Dix-Septième Siècle, French Studies, Mod. Lang. Rev., etc. *Recreations:* Spain, cooking and wine-tasting, music, English ecclesiastical history. *Address:* Gonville and Caius College, Cambridge CB2 1TA. *T:* Cambridge 332439. *Club:* Reform.

BAYLIS, Clifford Henry, CB 1971; Clerk, The Worshipful Company of Shipwrights, 1977–86; *b* 20 March 1915; *s* of late Arthur Charles and Caroline Jane Baylis, Alcester, Warwicks; *m* 1st, Phyllis Mary Clark; two *s*; 2nd, Margaret A. Hawkins. *Educ:* Alcester Grammar Sch.; Keble Coll., Oxford. Harrods Ltd, 1937–39. Served with HM Forces, 1940–46: Major RASC. Principal, Board of Trade, 1947; Asst Sec., UK Trade Commissioner, Bombay, 1955; Export Credits Guarantee Dept, 1963–66; Under-Sec., Board of Trade, 1966–67; Under-Sec., Min. of Technology, 1967–69; Controller, HM Stationery Office, and Queen's Printer of Acts of Parlt, 1969–74; Dir, Shipbuilders' and Repairers' Nat. Assoc., 1974–77. *Address:* 38 Cleaver Street, SE11 4DP. *T:* 01–587 0817. *Club:* City Livery.

BAYLIS, Rear-Adm. Robert Goodwin, CB 1984; OBE 1963; CEng; FIEE; Principal Consultant, Reliability Consultants Ltd, since 1984; *b* 29 Nov. 1925; *s* of Harold Goodwin Baylis and Evelyn May (*née* Whitworth); *m* 1949, Joyce Rosemary Churchill; two *s* one *d. Educ:* Highgate Sch.; Edinburgh Univ.; Loughborough Coll.; RN Engrg Coll.; Trinity Coll., Cambridge. MA Cantab. MRAeS. Joined Royal Navy, 1943; various appts at sea in Far East and Home Fleet and ashore in research and develt and trng establishments; Staff of C-in-C, S Atlantic and S America, 1958; British Navy Staff, Washington, and Special Projects (Polaris), 1964; Defence Fellow, Southampton Univ., 1969; Staff of Vice Chief of Defence Staff, 1979; President, Ordnance Board, 1981–84. Comdr 1961, Captain 1970, Rear-Adm. 1979. Mem. Council, IEE, 1984–86. *Recreations:* tennis, sailing. *Address:* Broadwaters, 4 Cliff Road, Still Head, Fareham, Hants PO14 3JS. *Club:* Owls.

BAYLISS, Frederic Joseph; Accountant General, Department of Employment, 1977–86; *b* 15 April 1926; *s* of Gordon and Gertrude Bayliss; *m* 1948, Mary Provost; two *d. Educ:* Ashby de la Zouch Grammar Sch.; Hertford Coll., Oxford. PhD Nottingham 1960. RAF, 1944–47. Tutor in Economics, Oxford Univ. Tutorial Classes Cttee, 1950–57; Lectr in Industrial Relations, Dept of Adult Education, Univ. of Nottingham, 1957–65; Industrial Relations Advr, NBPI, 1965–69; Asst Sec., CIR, 1969–71; Sen. Economic Advr, Dept of Employment, 1971–73; Under Sec., Pay Board, 1973–74; Sec., Royal Commn on the Distribution of Income and Wealth, 1974–77. *Publications:* British Wages Councils, 1962; The Standard of Living, 1965. *Recreations:* gardening, walking. *Address:* 11 Deena Close, Queens Drive, W3 0HR. *T:* 01–992 1126. *Club:* Reform.

BAYLISS, Sir Noel (Stanley), Kt 1979; CBE 1960; PhD, FRACI, FAA; Professor of Chemistry, University of Western Australia, 1938–71, Emeritus Professor, 1972; *b* 19 Dec. 1906; *s* of Henry Bayliss and Nelly Stothers; *m* 1933, Nellie Elise Banks; two *s. Educ:* Queen's Coll., Univ. of Melbourne (BSc 1927); Lincoln Coll., Oxford (BA 1930); Univ. of Calif, Berkeley (PhD 1933). FRACI 1942; FAA 1954. Victorian Rhodes Scholar, 1927–30; Commonwealth Fund (Harkness) Fellow, Univ. of Calif, 1930–33; Sen. Lectr in Chem., Univ. of Melbourne, 1933–37. Chm., Murdoch Univ. Planning Bd, 1970–73; Member: Australian Univs Commn, 1959–70; Hong Kong Univ. and Polytech. Grants Cttee, 1966–73. Hon. FACE 1965; Hon. DSc Univ. of WA, 1968; Hon. DUniv Murdoch Univ., 1975. *Publications:* over 70 original papers in scientific jls. *Recreations:* golf, music. *Address:* 104 Thomas Street, Nedlands, WA 6009, Australia. *T:* (09) 386 1453. *Clubs:* Royal Perth Yacht, Nedlands Golf (WA).

BAYLISS, Sir Richard (Ian Samuel), KCVO 1978; MD, FRCP; Physician to the Queen, 1970–81, and Head of HM Medical Household, 1973–81; Consultant Physician, King Edward VII's Hospital for Officers, since 1964; Consulting Physician, Westminster Hospital, since 1981; Assistant Director, Royal College of Physicians Research Unit; *b* 2 Jan. 1917; *o s* of late Frederick William Bayliss, Tettenhall, and late Muryel Anne Bayliss; *m* 1st, 1941, Margaret Joan Hardman (marr. diss. 1956); one *s* one *d*; 2nd, 1957, Constance Ellen, *d* of Wilbur J. Frey, Connecticut; two *d*; 3rd, 1979, Marina Rankin, *widow* of Charles Rankin. *Educ:* Rugby; Clare Coll., Cambridge (Hon. Fellow, 1983); St Thomas' Hosp., London. MB, BChir Cambridge 1941; MRCS, LRCP 1941; MRCP 1942; MD Cambridge 1946; FRCP 1956. Casualty Officer, Ho.-Phys., Registrar, Resident Asst Phys., St Thomas' Hosp.; Off. i/c Med. Div., RAMC, India; Sen. Med. Registrar and Tutor, Hammersmith Hosp.; Rockefeller Fellow in Medicine, Columbia Univ., New York, 1950–51; Lectr in Medicine and Physician, Postgrad. Med. Sch. of London; Dean, Westminster Med. Sch., 1960–64; Physician to HM Household, 1964–70; Consultant Physician: Westminster Hosp., 1954–81; King Edward VII Hosp., Midhurst, 1973–82; Civilian Consultant in Medicine, RN, 1975–82. Hon. Sec., Assoc. of Physicians, 1958–63, Cttee 1965–68, Pres., 1980–81; Pres., Section of Endocrinology, RSM, 1966–68; Examr in Medicine, Cambridge and Oxford Univs; Examr, MRCP. Member: Bd of Governors, Westminster Hosp., 1960–64, 1967–74; Council, Westminster Med. Sch., 1960–75; Soc. for Endocrinology (Council, 1956–60); Brit. Cardiac Soc., 1952; Council, RCP, 1968–71 (Second Vice-Pres., 1983–84); Bd of Advrs, Merck Inst. of Therapeutic Res., 1972–76. Med. Dir, Swiss Reinsurance Co. (UK), 1968–85; Director: Private Patients Plan, 1979–; JS Pathology plc, 1984–; Hon. Med. Adviser, Nuffield Nursing Home Trust, 1981–. Harveian Orator, RCP, 1983. *Publications:* Thyroid Disease: the facts, 1982; Practical Procedures in Clinical Medicine, 3rd edn; various, in med. jls and textbooks, on endocrine, metabolic and cardiac diseases. *Recreations:* ski-ing, music. *Address:* 6 Harley Street, W1N 1AA. *T:* 01–935 2071; Flat 7, 61 Onslow Square, SW7. *T:* 01–589 3087. *Club:* Garrick.

BAYLY, Vice-Adm. Sir Patrick (Uniacke), KBE 1968; CB 1965; DSC 1944, and 2 bars, 1944, 1951; Director, The Maritime Trust, since 1971; *b* 4 Aug. 1914; *s* of late Lancelot F. S. Bayly, Nenagh, Eire; *m* 1945, Moy Gourlay Jardine, *d* of Robert Gourlay Jardine, Newtonmearns, Scotland; two *d. Educ:* Aravon, Bray, Co. Wicklow; RN Coll., Dartmouth, Midshipman, 1932; Sub-Lieut, 1934; Lieut, 1935; South Africa, 1936; China station, 1938; Combined operations, 1941–44, including Sicily and Salerno; Lieut-Comdr 1944; HMS Mauritius, 1946; Comdr 1948, Naval Staff, 1948; Korean War, 1952–53, in HMS Alacrity and Constance; Captain 1954, Naval Staff; Imperial Defence Coll., 1957; Capt. (D) 6th Destroyer Sqdn, 1958; Staff of SACLANT, Norfolk, Va, 1960; Chief of Staff, Mediterranean, 1962; Rear-Admiral, 1963; Flag Officer, Sea Training, 1963; Adm. Pres., RN Coll., Greenwich, 1965–67; Chief of Staff, COMNAVSOUTH, Malta,

1967–70; retd, 1970. Vice-Adm. 1967. US Legion of Merit, 1951. *Recreation:* golf. *Address:* Dunning House, Liphook, Hants.

BAYNE, John; Advocate; Sheriff of Glasgow and Strathkelvin, 1975–79; Sheriff (formerly Sheriff-Substitute) of Lanarkshire at Glasgow, 1959–74. *Address:* Winsford, 7 Milrig Road, Rutherglen G73 2NQ.

BAYNE, Nicholas Peter, CMG 1984; HM Diplomatic Service; Ambassador and UK Permanent Representative to OECD, Paris, since 1985; *b* 15 Feb. 1937; *s* of late Captain Ronald Bayne, RN and of Elisabeth Ashcroft; *m* 1961, Diana Wilde; three *s. Educ:* Eton Coll.; Christ Church, Oxford (MA, DPhil). Entered Diplomatic Service, 1961; served at British Embassies in Manila, 1963–66, and Bonn, 1969–72; seconded to HM Treasury, 1974–75; Financial Counsellor, Paris, 1975–79; Head of Financial, later Economic Relations, Dept, FCO, 1979–82; attached to RIIA, 1982–83; Ambassador to Zaire, 1983–84, also accredited to the Congo, Rwanda and Burundi, 1984; seconded to CSSB, 1985. *Publication:* (with R. D. Putnam) Hanging Together: the Seven-Power Summits, 1984. *Recreations:* reading, sightseeing. *Address:* c/o Foreign and Commonwealth Office, King Charles Street, SW1. *Club:* Travellers'.

BAYNE-POWELL, Robert Lane, CB 1981; Senior Registrar of the Family Division, High Court of Justice, 1976–82, retired (Registrar, 1964–76); *b* 10 Oct. 1910; 2nd *s* of William Maurice and Rosamond Alicia Bayne-Powell; *m* 1938, Nancy Geraldine (*d* 1979), *d* of late Lt-Col J. L. Philips, DSO; one *s* two *d. Educ:* Charterhouse; Trinity Coll., Cambridge (BA). Called to Bar, Middle Temple, 1935; Mem., Senate of Inns of Court and the Bar, 1978–81. Served War of 1939–45, Intell. Corps; Major 1944; Allied Commn for Austria, 1945. Mem., Reviewing Cttee on Export of Works of Art, 1975–81; Hon. Keeper of the Miniatures, Fitzwilliam Museum, Cambridge, 1980–. *Publications:* (special editor) Williams and Mortimer on Executors and Probate, 1970; Catalogue of Miniatures in the Fitzwilliam Museum, Cambridge, 1985. *Recreations:* gardening, miniature collecting, wine-tasting. *Address:* The Mount, Borough Green, Sevenoaks, Kent. *T:* Borough Green 882045. *Club:* Athenæum.

BAYNES, Sir John (Christopher Malcolm), 7th Bt *cr* 1801; Lt-Col retd; Joint Proprietor, Lake Vyrnwy Hotel; *b* 24 April 1928; *s* of Sir Rory Malcolm Stuart Baynes, 6th Bt and Ethel Audrey (*d* 1947), *d* of late Edward Giles, CIE; *S* father, 1979; *m* 1955, Shirley Maxwell, *o d* of late Robert Allan Dodds; four *s. Educ:* Sedbergh School; RMA Sandhurst; Edinburgh Univ. (MSc). Commissioned Cameronians (Scottish Rifles), 1949; served Malaya, 1950–53 (despatches); Aden, 1966; Defence Fellow, Edinburgh Univ., 1968–69; comd 52 Lowland Volunteers (TAVR), 1969–72; retired, 1972. Order of the Sword, 1st Class (Sweden), 1965. *Publications:* Morale, 1967, new edn 1986; The Jacobite Rising of 1715, 1970; History of the Cameronians, Vol. IV, 1971; The Soldier in Modern Society, 1971; contribs to RUSI Jl, Purnell's History of First World War, and other military jls. *Recreations:* shooting, fishing, golf. *Heir:* *s* Christopher Rory Baynes, *b* 11 May 1956. *Address:* The Cottage, Lake Vyrnwy Hotel, via Oswestry, Salop SY10 0LY. *T:* Llanwddyn 244. *Club:* Army and Navy.

BAYNES, Pauline Diana, (Mrs F. O. Gasch); designer and book illustrator; *b* 9 Sept 1922; *d* of Frederick William Wilberforce Baynes, CIE and Jessie Harriet Maud Cunningham; *m* 1961, Fritz Otto Gasch. *Educ:* Beaufront Sch., Camberley; Farnham Sch. of Art; Slade Sch. of Art. MSIA 1951. Mem., Women's Internat. Art Club, 1938. Voluntary worker, Camouflage Develt and Trng Centre, RE, 1940–42; Hydrographic Dept, Admty, 1942–45. Designed world's largest crewel embroidery, Plymouth Congregational Church, Minneapolis, 1970. Kate Greenaway Medal, Library Assoc., 1968. *Publications: illustrated:* Farmer Giles of Ham, and subseq. books and posters by J. R. R. Tolkien, 1949; The Lion, the Witch and the Wardrobe, and subseq. Narnia books by C. S. Lewis, 1950; The Arabian Nights, 1957; The Puffin Book of Nursery Rhymes by Iona and Peter Opie, 1963; Recipes from an Old Farmhouse by Alison Uttley, 1966; Dictionary of Chivalry, 1968; Snail and Caterpillar, 1972; A Companion to World Mythology, 1979; The Enchanted Horse, 1981; Frog and Shrew, 1981; The Song of the Three Holy Children, 1986; All Things Bright and Beautiful, 1986; The Story of Daniel by George MacBeth, 1986; numerous other children's books, etc.; *written and illustrated:* Victoria and the Golden Bird, 1948; How Dog Began, 1985. *Recreation:* going for walks with dogs. *Address:* Rock Barn Cottage, Dockenfield, Farnham, Surrey. *T:* Headley Down 713306.

BAYNHAM, Dr Alexander Christopher; Director, Royal Signals and Radar Establishment, Malvern, 1984–86; *b* 22 Dec. 1935; *s* of Alexander Baynham and Dulcie Rowena Rees; *m* 1961, Eileen May Wilson; two *s* one *d. Educ:* Marling Sch.; Reading Univ. (BSc); Warwick Univ. (PhD); Royal Coll. of Defence Studies (rcds). Joined Royal Signals and Radar Estab., Malvern, 1955; rejoined, 1961 (univ. studies, 1958–61); Head, Optics and Electronics Gp, 1976; RCDS, 1978; Scientific Adviser to Asst Chief Adviser on Projects, 1979; Dep. Dir, 1980–83. *Publications:* Plasma Effects in Semi-conductors, 1971; assorted papers in Jl of Physics, Jl of Applied Physics and in Proc. Phys. Soc. *Recreations:* church activities, music. *Address:* c/o Royal Signals and Radar Establishment, St Andrews Road, Great Malvern, Worcs WR14 3PS.

BAYÜLKEN, Ümit Halûk; Secretary-General, Presidency of the Turkish Republic, since 1977; *b* 7 July 1921; *s* of Staff Officer H. Hüsnü Bayülken and Mrs Melek Bayülken; *m* 1952, Mrs Valihe Salci; one *s* one *d. Educ:* Lycée of Haydarpasa, Istanbul; Faculty of Political Science (Diplomatic Sect.), Univ. of Ankara. Joined Min. of For. Affairs, 1944; 3rd Sec., 2nd Political Dept; served in Private Cabinet of Sec.-Gen.; mil. service as reserve Officer, 1945–47; Vice-Consul, Frankfurt-on-Main, 1947–49; 1st Sec., Bonn, 1950–51; Dir of Middle East Sect., Ankara, 1951–53; Mem. Turkish Delegn to UN 7th Gen. Assembly, 1952; Political Adviser, 1953–56, Counsellor, 1956–59, Turkish Perm. Mission to UN; rep. Turkey at London Jt Cttee on Cyprus, 1959–60; Dir-Gen., Policy Planning Gp, Min. of Foreign Affairs, 1960–63; Minister Plenipotentiary, 1963; Dep. Sec.-Gen. for Polit. Affairs, 1963–64; Sec.-Gen. with rank of Ambassador, 1964–66; Ambassador to London, 1966–69, to United Nations, 1969–71; Minister of Foreign Affairs, 1971–74; Secretary-General, Cento, 1975–77. Mem., Turkish Delegns to 8th-13th, 16th-20th Gen. Assemblies of UN; rep. Turkey at internat. confrs, 1953–66; Leader of Turkish Delegn: at meeting of For. Ministers, 2nd Afro-Asian Conf., Algiers, 1965. Univ. of Ankara: Mem., Inst. of Internat. Relations; Lectr, Faculty of Polit. Scis, 1963–66. Hon. Gov., Sch. of Oriental and African Studies, London. Isabel la Catolica (Spain), 1964; Grand Cross of Merit (Germany), 1965; Hon. GCVO, 1967; Sitara-i-Pakistan (Pakistan), 1970; Star, Order One (Jordan), 1972; Sirdar-i-Ali (Afghanistan), 1972. *Publications:* lectures, articles, studies and essays on subject of minorities, Cyprus, principles of foreign policy, internat. relations and disputes. *Recreations:* music, painting, reading. *Address:* Cumhurbaskanligi Genel Sekreteri, Ankara, Turkey. *Clubs:* Hurlingham, Travellers', Royal Automobile.

BAZALGETTE, Rear-Adm. Derek Willoughby, CB 1976; Independent Inquiry Inspector, since 1983; *b* 22 July 1924; *yr s* of late H. L. Bazalgette; *m* 1947, Angela Hilda Vera, *d* of late Sir Henry Hinchliffe, JP, DL; four *d. Educ:* RNC Dartmouth. Served War of 1939–45; specialised in Gunnery, 1949; HMS Centaur, 1952–54; HMS Birmingham, 1956–58; SO 108th Minesweeping Sqdn and in comd HMS Houghton, 1958–59; HMS

Centaur, 1963–65; Dep. Dir Naval Ops, 1965–67; comd HMS Aurora, 1967–68; idc 1969; Chief Staff Officer to Comdr British Forces Hong Kong, 1970–72; comd HMS Bulwark, 1972–74; Admiral President, RNC Greenwich, 1974–76; Comdr 1958; Captain 1965; Rear-Adm. 1974. ADC 1974. HQ Comr for Water Activities, Scout Assoc., 1976; Principal, Netley Waterside House, 1977–83. Lay Canon, Portsmouth Cathedral, 1984–; Mem., General Synod, 1985–. Governor, Corp. of Sons of the Clergy, 1982. Liveryman, Shipwrights' Co., 1986. Freeman, City of London, 1976. *Address:* The Glebe House, Newtown, Fareham, Hants. *Club:* Lansdowne.

BAZIN, Germain René Michel; Officier, Légion d'Honneur; Commandeur des Arts et des Lettres; Conservateur en chef honoraire du Musée du Louvre, since 1971; Professeur honoraire à L'Ecole du Louvre, since 1971; Conservateur de musée Condé, Chantilly, since 1983; Research Professor Emeritus, York University, Toronto; Membre de l'Institut, 1975; *b* Paris, 1907; *s* of Charles Bazin, Industrialist and engineer of Ecole Centrale de Paris, and J. Laurence Mounier-Pouthot; *m* 1947, Countess Heller de Bielotzerkowka. *Educ:* Ste Croix de Neuilly; Ste Croix d'Orléans; Collège de Pontlevoy; Sorbonne. D ès L; Lic. en Droit; Dipl. Ecole du Louvre. Served French Infantry (Capt.), 1939–45. Prof., Univ. Libre de Bruxelles, since 1934; joined staff of Louvre, 1937; Conservateur en chef du Musée du Louvre, 1951–71; Professeur de muséologie, Ecole du Louvre, 1942–71; lecturer and writer; responsible for more than 30 exhibitions of paintings in France and elsewhere; his books are translated into English, German, Spanish, Italian, Japanese, Portuguese, Yugoslav, Hebrew, Swedish, Dutch, Rumanian, Czech, Danish. Corresponding Mem. of many Academies. Grand Officier, Ordre Léopold, Belgium; Grand Officier, Couronne, Belgium; Commandeur, Mérite, République d'Italie; Officier: Ordre de Santiago, Portugal; Star of the North, Sweden; Cruzeiro do Sul, Brazil, etc. Dr *hc:* Univ. of Rio de Janiero; Villanova, Pa, Univ. *Publications:* Mont St Michel, 1933; Le Louvre, 1935, rev. edn 1980; Les primitifs français, 1937; La peinture italienne aux XIVe et XVe siècles, 1938; Memling, 1939; De David à Cézanne, 1941; Fra Angelico, 1941; Corot, 1942; Le crépuscule des images, 1946; L'Epoque impressioniste, 1947; Les grands maîtres de la peinture hollandaise, 1950; Histoire générale de l'art, 1951; L'Architecture religieuse baroque au Brésil, 1956–58; Trésors de la peinture au Louvre, 1957; Musée de l'Ermitage: écoles étrangères, 1957; Trésors de l'impressionisme au Louvre, 1958; A gallery of Flowers, 1960; Baroque and Rococo, 1964; Message de l'absolu, 1964; Aleijadinho, 1963; Francesco Messina, 1966; Le Temps des Musées, 1967; La Scultura francese, 1968; Destins du baroque, 1968; La peinture d'avant garde, 1969; Le Monde de la sculpture, 1972 (trans. as Sculpture in the World, 1968); Manet, 1972; Langage des styles, 1976; Les Palais de la Foi, 1980; L'Univers impressioniste, 1981; Les fleurs vues par les peintres, 1984; numerous articles in principal reviews and French periodicals and foreign art journals of Europe and America. *Recreations:* rowing, swimming. *Address:* 4 avenue Raymond Poincaré, 75019 Paris, France. *Clubs:* Army and Navy, Carlton, East India, Devonshire, Sports and Public Schools; Cercle de l'Union, Fondateur de la Maison de l'Amérique Latine (Paris).

BAZIRE, Rev. Canon Reginald Victor; Archdeacon and Borough Dean of Wandsworth, 1973–75; an Honorary Canon of Southwark, 1959–67 and since 1975; *b* 30 Jan. 1900; *s* of Alfred Arsène Bazire and Edith Mary (*née* Reynolds); *m* 1927, Eileen Crewsdon Brown; two *s. Educ:* Christ's Hospital. Missionary, China Inland Mission, 1922–45; Vicar, St Barnabas, Clapham Common, 1949–67; Rural Dean of Battersea, 1953–66; Archdeacon of Southwark, 1967–73. Proctor in convocation: 1959–64, 1970–. *Address:* 7 Grosvenor Park, Bath BA1 6BL. *T:* Bath 317100.

BAZLEY, Rt. Rev. Colin Frederick; *see* Chile, Bishop of.

BAZLEY, Sir Thomas Stafford, 3rd Bt, *cr* 1869; *b* 5 Oct. 1907; *s* of Captain Gardner Sebastian Bazley, DL, *o s* of 2nd Bt (*d* 1911) and Ruth Evelyn (*d* 1962), *d* of late Sir E. S. Howard (she *m* 2nd, Comdr F. C. Cadogan, RN, retd; he *d* 1970); *S* grandfather, 1919; *m* 1945, Carmen, *o d* of late J. Tulla; three *s* two *d. Educ:* Harrow; Magdalen Coll., Oxford. *Heir:* *s* Thomas John Sebastian Bazley, *b* 31 Aug. 1948. *Address:* Eastleach Folly, near Hatherop, Cirencester, Glos. *T:* Cirencester 75333.

See also H. A. Abel Smith.

BB; *see* Watkins-Pitchford, D. J.

BEACH; *see* Hicks-Beach, family name of Earl St Aldwyn.

BEACH, Gen. Sir (William Gerald) Hugh, GBE 1980 (OBE 1966); KCB 1976; MC 1944; Chief Royal Engineer, since 1982; Member, Security Commission, since 1982; Director, Council for Arms Control, since 1986; *b* 20 May 1923; *s* of late Maj.-Gen. W. H. Beach, CB, CMG, DSO; *m* 1951, Estelle Mary (*née* Henry); three *s* one *d. Educ:* Winchester; Peterhouse, Cambridge (MA; Hon. Fellow 1982). Active service in France, 1944 and Java, 1946; comd: 4 Field Sqn, 1956–57; Cambridge Univ. OTC, 1961–63; 2 Div. RE, 1965–67; 12 Inf. Bde, 1969–70; Defence Fellow, Edinburgh Univ. (MSc), 1971; Dir, Army Staff Duties, MoD, 1971–74; Comdt, Staff Coll., Camberley, 1974–75; Dep. C-in-C, UKLF, 1976–77; Master-Gen. of the Ordnance, 1977–81; Warden, St George's House, Windsor Castle, 1981–86. Vice Lord-Lieut for Greater London, 1981–86. Kermit Roosevelt Vis. Lectr to US Armed Forces, 1977; Mountbatten Lectr, Edinburgh Univ., 1981; Gallipoli Meml Lectr, 1985; Wilfred Fish Meml Lectr, GDC, 1986. Colonel Commandant: REME, 1976–81; RPC, 1976–80; RE, 1977–; Hon. Colonel, Cambridge Univ. OTC, TAVR, 1977–; Chm., CCF Assoc., 1981–; Chm., MoD Study Gp on Censorship, 1983. CBIM; FRSA. *Publications: chapters on:* nuclear weapons in the defence of North-West Europe, in Unholy Warfare (ed Martin and Mullen), 1983; where does the nuclear-free path lead, in The Cross and the Bomb (ed Francis Bridger), 1983; disarmament and security in Europe, in Armed Peace (ed O'Connor Howe), 1984; military implications of 'No First Use', in Dropping the Bomb (ed John Gladwin), 1985. *Recreations:* sailing, ski-ing. *Address:* The Ropeway, Beaulieu, Hants. *T:* Beaulieu 612269. *Clubs:* Farmers'; Royal Lymington Yacht.

BEACH, Surgeon Rear-Adm. William Vincent, CB 1962; OBE 1949; MRCS; LRCP; FRCSE; Retd; *b* 22 Nov. 1903; *yr s* of late William Henry Beach; *m* 1931, Daphne Muriel, *yr d* of late Eustace Ackworth Joseph, ICS; two *d. Educ:* Seaford Coll.; Guy's Hospital, London. Joined RN Medical Service, 1928. Served War of 1939–45 as Surgical specialist in Hospital ships, Atlantic and Pacific Fleets. Surgical Registrar, Royal Victoria Infirmary, Newcastle upon Tyne; Senior Specialist in Surgery, RN Hospitals, Chatham, Haslar, Malta, Portland; Senior Medical Officer, RN Hospital, Malta; Medical Officer i/c RN Hospital, Portland; Sen. Medical Officer, Surgical Division, RN Hospital, Haslar; Medical Officer in charge of Royal Naval Hospital, Chatham, and Command MO on staff of C-in-C the Nore Command, 1960–61; MO i/c RN Hospital, Malta, and on staff of C-in-C, Mediterranean and as Medical Adviser to C-in-C, Allied Forces, Mediterranean, 1961–63. Surg. Rear-Admiral, 1960. QHS 1960. Senior Surgeon i/c Shaw Savill Passenger Liners, 1966–75. Fellow, Assoc. of Surgeons of Great Britain and Ireland, 1947, Senior Fellow, 1963. *Publications:* Urgent Surgery of the Hand, 1940; Inguinal Hernia—a new operation, 1946; The Treatment of Burns, 1950. *Recreations:* shooting, fishing. *Address:* Cherrytree Cottage, Easton, Winchester. *T:* Itchen Abbas 222. *Club:* Naval and Military.

BEACHAM, Prof. Arthur, OBE 1961; MA, PhD; Deputy Vice-Chancellor, Murdoch University, Western Australia, 1976–79 (Acting Vice-Chancellor, 1977–78); *b* 27 July 1913; *s* of William Walter and Maud Elizabeth Beacham; *m* 1938, Margaret Doreen Moseley (*d* 1979); one *s* one *d. Educ:* Pontywaun Grammar Sch.; University Coll. of Wales (BA 1935); Univ. of Liverpool (MA 1937); PhD Belfast 1941. Jevons Res. Student, Univ. of Liverpool, 1935–36; Leon Res. Fellow, Univ. of London, 1942–43; Lectr in Economics, Queen's Univ. of Belfast, 1938–45; Sen. Lectr, University Coll. of Wales, 1945–47; Prof. of Indust. Relations, University Coll., Cardiff, 1947–51; Prof. of Economics, University Coll. of Wales, Aberystwyth, 1951–63; Vice-Chancellor, Univ. of Otago, Dunedin, New Zealand, 1964–66; Gonner Prof. of Applied Econs, Liverpool Univ., 1966–75. Chairman: Mid-Wales Industrial Develt Assoc., 1957–63; Post Office Arbitration Tribunal, 1972–73; Member: Advisory Council for Education (Wales), 1949–52; Transp. Consultative Cttee for Wales, 1948–63 (Chm. 1961–63); Central Transp. Consultative Cttee, 1961–63; Economics Cttee of DSIR, 1961–63; North West Economic Planning Council, 1966–74; Merseyside Passenger Transport Authority, 1969–71; Council, Royal Economic Soc., 1970–74. Chm., Cttees on Care of Intellectually Handicapped, Australia, 1982–; Dir, Superannuation Scheme for Aust. Univs, 1982–83. Hon. LLD Otago, 1969; Hon. DUniv Murdoch, 1982. *Publications:* Economics of Industrial Organisation, 1948 (5th edn 1970); Industries in Welsh Country Towns, 1950. Articles in Econ. Jl, Quarterly Jl of Economics, Oxford Econ. Papers, etc. *Recreations:* golf, gardening. *Address:* 10 Mannersley Street, Carindale, Qld 4152, Australia. *T:* 398 6524. *Club:* Cricketers' (Qld).

BEACHCROFT, Thomas Owen; Author; Chief Overseas Publicity Officer, BBC, 1941–61; *b* 3 Sept. 1902; *s* of Dr R. O. Beachcroft, Dir of Music at Clifton Coll., and Nina Cooke, Beckley Grove, Oxfordshire; *m* 1926, Marjorie Evelyn Taylor (*d* 1978); one *d. Educ:* Clifton Coll.; Balliol Coll., Oxford. Scholarship, Balliol. Joined BBC 1924; subsequently in Messrs. Unilevers Advertising Service; rejoined BBC 1941. *Publications: fiction:* A Young Man in a Hurry, 1934; You Must Break Out Sometimes, 1936; The Man Who Started Clean, 1937; The Parents Left Alone, 1940; Collected Stories, 1946; Asking for Trouble, 1948; Malice Bites Back, 1948; A Thorn in The Heart, 1952; Goodbye Aunt Hesther, 1955; *non-fiction:* (with Lowes Luard) Just Cats, 1936; Calling All Nations, 1942; British Broadcasting, 1946 (booklets about BBC); The English Short Story, 1964; The Modest Art, 1968; (with W. Emms) Five Hide Village: a history of Datchworth, 1984; contributor of short stories and literary criticism to numerous publications throughout world, and to BBC. Gen. Editor British Council series Writers and their Work, 1949–54. *Recreations:* the arts in general; formerly track and cross-country running (represented Oxford against Cambridge at mile and half-mile). *Address:* 3 Worcester Court, Worcester Road, Clifton, Bristol BS8 3JL. *Club:* United Oxford & Cambridge University.

BEADLE, Prof. George Wells; President Emeritus and Professor of Biology Emeritus, University of Chicago; *b* Wahoo, Nebraska, 22 Oct. 1903; *s* of Chauncey E. Beadle and Hattie Albro; *m* 1st, 1928, Marion Cecile Hill (marr. diss., 1953); one *s*; 2nd, 1953, Muriel McClure Barnett; one step *s. Educ:* Univ. of Nebraska; Cornell Univ. BS 1926, MS 1927, Nebraska; MA Oxford, 1958; PhD Cornell, 1931. Teaching Asst, Cornell, 1926–27; Experimentalist, 1927–31; National Research Fellow, Calif. Institute of Technology, 1931–33; Research Fellow and Instructor, Calif. Institute of Technology, 1933–35; Guest Investigator, Institut de Biologie Physico-Chimique, Paris, 1935; Asst Prof. of Genetics, Harvard Univ., 1936–37; Prof. of Biology, Stanford Univ., 1937–46; Prof. of Biology and Chm. of the Division of Biology, California Institute of Technology, 1946–60, Acting Dean of Faculty, 1960–61; Univ. of Chicago: Pres., 1961–68, Emeritus, 1969. Trustee and Prof. of Biology, 1961–68; William E. Wrather Distinguished Service Prof., 1969–75. Research interests: genetics, cytology and origin of Indian corn (Zea); genetics and development of the fruit fly Drosophila; biochemical genetics of the bread mould Neurospora. Hon. Trustee, Univ. of Chicago, 1971–. Hon. DSc: Yale, 1947; Nebraska, 1949; Northwestern, 1952; Rutgers, 1954; Kenyon Coll., 1955; Wesleyan Univ., 1956; Oxford Univ., 1959; Birmingham Univ., 1959; Pomona Coll., 1961; Lake Forest Coll., 1962; Univ. of Rochester, Univ. of Illinois, 1963; Brown Univ., Kansas State Univ., Univ. of Pennsylvania, 1964; Wabash Coll., 1966; Syracuse, 1967; Loyola, 1970; Eureka Coll., 1972; Butler Univ., 1973; Hon. PhD: Gustavus Adolphus Coll.; Indiana State Univ., 1976; Hon. LLD: UCLA, 1962; Univ. of Miami, Brandeis Univ., 1963; Johns Hopkins Univ., Beloit Coll., 1966; Michigan, 1969; Hon. DHL: Jewish Theological Seminary of America, 1966; DePaul Univ., 1969; Univ. of Chicago, 1969; Canisius Coll., 1969; Knox Coll., 1969; Roosevelt Univ., 1971; Carroll Coll., 1971; DPubSer, Ohio Northern Univ., 1970. Pres., Chicago Horticultural Soc., 1968–71; Trustee: Museum of Sci. and Industry, Chicago, 1967–68; Nutrition Foundn, 1969–73. Member: Twelfth Internat. Congress of Genetics (Hon. Pres.), 1968; National Academy of Sciences (Mem. Council, 1969–72); American Philosophical Soc.; Amer. Assoc. of Adv. Sci. (Pres., 1946); Amer. Acad. of Arts and Sciences; Genetics Soc. of America (Pres., 1955); President's Sci. Adv. Cttee, 1960; Genetics Soc. (Gt Britain); Indian Soc. of Genetics and Plant Breeding; Inst. Lombardo di Scienze E Lettre; Sigma Xi. Hon. Member: Japan Acad.; Phi Beta Kappa. Royal Danish Academy of Sciences; Foreign Member: Royal Society 1960; Indian Nat. Science Acad. Lasker Award, American Public Health Association, 1950; Emil Christian Hansen Prize (Denmark), 1953; Albert Einstein Commemorative Award in Science, 1958; Nobel Prize for Medicine (jointly), 1958; National Award, American Cancer Soc., 1959; Kimber Genetics Award, National Academy of Sciences, 1959; Priestley Memorial Award, 1967; Donald Forsha Jones Award, 1972; (with Muriel B. Beadle) Edison Award for Best science book for youth, 1967. George Eastman Visiting Professor, University of Oxford, 1958–59. Trustee Pomona Coll., 1958–61. *Publications:* An Introduction to Genetics (with A. H. Sturtevant), 1939; Genetics and Modern Biology, 1963; The Language of Life (with Muriel Beadle), 1966. Technical articles in Cytology and Genetics. *Address:* 900 East Harrison Avenue, Apt D33, Pomona, Calif 91767, USA.

BEAGLEY, Thomas Lorne, CB 1973; President, European Society of Transport Institutes, since 1984; Member, Dover Harbour Board, since 1980; *b* 2 Jan. 1919; *s* of late Captain T. G. Beagley, Royal Montreal Regt; *m* 1942, Heather Blanche Osmond; two *s* one *d. Educ:* Bristol Grammar Sch.; Worcester Coll., Oxford (MA). Served War: 2nd Lieut, Northamptonshire Regt, 1940; Lt-Col, AQMG (Movements), AFHQ, Italy, 1945. Joined Min. of Transport, 1946; Cabinet Office, 1951–52; Min of Defence, 1952–54; UK Delegn to NATO, 1954–57; UK Shipping Rep, Far East, 1960–63; Asst Under-Sec. of State, Dept of Economic Affairs, 1966–68; Under-Sec., Min. of Transport, 1968–71; Dep. Sec., Transport Industries, DoE, 1972–76; Dep. Chief Exec., PSA, 1976–79. Mem., Nat. Ports Council, 1979–81. FCIT, 1972 (Pres., 1977; Hon. Sec.); Hon. FIRTE 1979. *Recreations:* golf, galleries, gardening. *Address:* 3 Sheen Common Drive, Richmond, Surrey. *T:* 01–876 1216. *Clubs:* Travellers'; Richmond Golf, St Enodoc Golf.

BEAL, Anthony Ridley; Chairman: Heinemann Educational Books, 1979–85; Heinemann International, 1984–85; Managing Director, Heinemann Educational Books (International), 1979–85; *b* 28 Feb. 1925; *s* of Harold and Nesta Beal; *m* 1958, Rosemary Jean Howarth; three *d. Educ:* Haberdashers' Aske's Hampstead School; Downing College, Cambridge (scholar); 1st class English Tripos 1948. RN, 1943–46; Lectr in English,

Eastbourne Training Coll., 1949; joined William Heinemann, 1949; Dep. Man. Dir, Heinemann Educational Books, 1962–73, Man. Dir, 1973–79; Dir, Heinemann Group of Publishers, 1973–85; Chairman: Heinemann Publishers (NZ), 1980–85; Heinemann Publishers Australia Pty, 1981–85. Chm., Educational Publishers' Council, 1980–83 (Vice-Chm., 1978–80); Mem. Council, Publishers' Assoc., 1982–86. *Publications:* D. H. Lawrence: Selected Literary Criticism, 1956; D. H. Lawrence, 1961; contribs to books on literature, education and publishing. *Recreations:* reading maps, travelling, thinking while gardening. *Address:* 24 Loom Lane, Radlett, Herts. *T:* Radlett 4567. *Club:* Garrick.

BEAL, Rt. Rev. Robert George; *see* Wangaratta, Bishop of.

BEALE, Anthony John; Solicitor and Legal Adviser, Welsh Office, since 1980; Under Secretary (Legal), Welsh Office, since 1983; *b* 16 March 1932, *o s* of late Edgar Beale and Victoria Beale; *m* 1969, Helen Margaret Owen-Jones; one *s* one *d. Educ:* Hitchin Grammar Sch.; King's Coll. London (LLB; AKC). Solicitor of the Supreme Court, 1956. Legal Asst, 1960, Sen. Legal Asst, 1966, Min. of Housing and Local Govt and Min. of Health; Consultant, Council of Europe, 1973; Asst Solicitor, DoE 1974. LRPS. *Recreations:* photography, golf, collecting old cheques. *Address:* Welsh Office, Cathays Park, Cardiff CF1 3NQ. *T:* Cardiff 825111.

BEALE, Edward; *see* Beale, T. E.

BEALE, Prof. Geoffrey Herbert, MBE 1947; FRS 1959; PhD; Royal Society Research Professor, Edinburgh University, 1963–78; *b* 11 June 1913; *s* of Herbert Walter and Elsie Beale; *m* 1949, Betty Brydon McCallum (marr. diss. 1969); three *s. Educ:* Sutton County Sch.; Imperial Coll. of Science, London. Scientific Research Worker, John Innes Horticultural Institution, London, 1935–40. Served in HM Forces (1941–46). Research worker, department of Genetics, Carnegie Institute, Cold Spring Harbor, New York, 1947; Rockefeller Fellow, Indiana Univ., 1947–48; Lecturer, Dept of Animal Genetics, 1948–59, Reader in Animal Genetics, 1959–63, Edinburgh Univ. Research Worker (part-time), Chulalongkorn Univ., Bangkok, 1976–. *Publications:* The Genetics of Paramecium aurelia, 1954; (with Jonathan Knowles) Extranuclear Genetics, 1978. *Address:* 23 Royal Terrace, Edinburgh EH7 5AH. *T:* 557 1329.

BEALE, Josiah Edward Michael; lately Assistant Secretary, Department of Trade and Industry; *s* of late Mr and Mrs J. E. Beale, Upminster, Essex; *m* 1958, Jean Margaret McDonald; two *d* (and one *d* decd). *Educ:* Brentwood Sch.; Jesus Coll., Cambridge. UK Shipping Adviser, Singapore, 1968–71. Assistant Secretary, Monopolies and Mergers Commission, 1978–81. *Address:* 43 Shenfield Road, Brentwood, Essex.

BEALE, (Thomas) Edward, CBE 1966; JP; Chairman, Beale's Ltd; *b* 5 March 1904; *s* of late Thomas Henderson Beale, London; *m* Beatrice May (*d* 1986), *d* of William Steele McLaughlin, JP, Enniskillen; one *s. Educ:* City of London Sch. Mem. Bd, British Travel Assoc., 1950–70, Dep. Chm. 1965–70. Vice-Pres. and Fellow, Hotel and Catering Inst., 1949–71; Chm., Caterers' Assoc. of Gt Britain, 1949–52; Pres., Internat. Ho-Re-Ca (Union of Nat. Hotel, Restaurant & Caterers Assocs), 1954–64. Chm., Treasury Cttee of Enquiry, House of Commons Refreshment Dept, 1951. Master, Worshipful Co. of Bakers, 1955. Mem., Islington Borough Council, 1931–34; JP Inner London, 1950 (Chm. EC Div., Inner London Magistrates, 1970–73). FRSH 1957; FRSA 1968. Médaille d'Argent de Paris, 1960. *Recreation:* arboriculture. *Address:* West Lodge Park, Hadley Wood, Herts. *Club:* Carlton.

BEALE, Sir William (Francis), Kt 1956; OBE 1945; *b* 27 Jan. 1908; *y s* of late George and Elizabeth Beale, Potterspury Lodge, Northants; *m* 1934, Dèva Zaloudek; one *s* one *d. Educ:* Downside Sch., Pembroke Coll., Cambridge. Joined Green's Stores (Ilford) Ltd, Dir, 1929–63 (Chm., 1950–63). Navy, Army and Air Force Institutes, UK, 1940–41, Dir, 1949–61 (Chm. 1953–61). EFI, GHQ West Africa, 1942–43; EFI, 21st Army Gp, 1944–46. *Recreations:* hunting, shooting; formerly Rugby football (Eastern Counties Cap, 1932). *Address:* The Old Rectory, Woodborough, Pewsey, Wilts. *Club:* Army and Navy.

BEALES, Prof. Derek Edward Dawson, PhD; FRHistS; Professor of Modern History, University of Cambridge, since 1980; Fellow of Sidney Sussex College, Cambridge, since 1958; *b* 12 June 1931; *s* of late Edward Beales and of Dorothy Kathleen Beales (*née* Dawson); *m* 1964, Sara Jean (*née* Ledbury); one *s* one *d. Educ:* Bishop's Stortford Coll.; Sidney Sussex Coll., Cambridge (MA, PhD). Sidney Sussex College: Research Fellow, 1955–58; Tutor, 1961–70; Vice-Master, 1973–75; University Asst Lectr, Cambridge, 1962–65; Lectr, 1965–80. Vis. Lectr, Harvard Univ., 1965; Chairman, Faculty Board of History, Cambridge, 1979–81. Mem. Council, RHistS, 1984–. Editor, Historical Journal, 1971–75. *Publications:* England and Italy 1859–60, 1961; From Castlereagh to Gladstone, 1969; The Risorgimento and the Unification of Italy, 1971; History and Biography, 1981; (ed with Geoffrey Best) History, Society and the Churches, 1985; Joseph II: in the shadow of Maria Theresa 1741–80, 1986; articles in learned jls. *Recreations:* playing keyboard instruments and bridge, walking, not gardening. *Address:* Sidney Sussex College, Cambridge. *T:* Cambridge 61501.

BEALES, Hugh Lancelot; Reader in Economic History in University of London, 1931–56; *b* 18 Feb. 1889; 3rd *s* of Rev. W. Beales; *m*; two *s* one *d. Educ:* Kingswood Sch., Bath; University of Manchester. Lecturer in Economic History, University of Sheffield, 1919–26; Lecturer in Economic History, University of London (London Sch. of Economics), 1926–31. Visiting Prof., Columbia Univ., 1954–55, Harvard Univ., 1956, University of Washington, 1959, USA. Editorial Adviser, Penguin and Pelican Books, to 1945; Ed. of Agenda, a journal of reconstruction issued by London Sch. of Economics to 1945; mem. of Editorial Bd of Political Quarterly; Editor, Kingswood Books on Social History. Mem. of CS Arbitration Tribunal, 1955–65. Hon. Fellow, LSE, 1971. Hon. DLitt: Exeter, 1969; Sheffield, 1971; Hon. DrRCA, 1974. *Publications:* Industrial Revolution, 1929; Early English Socialists, 1932; Making of Social Policy (Hobhouse Lecture), 1945, etc. Contributor to Economic History Review and various periodicals. *Address:* 16 Denman Drive, NW11. *T:* 01–455 4091.

BEALEY, Prof. Frank William; Professor of Politics, University of Aberdeen, since 1964; *b* Bilston, Staffs, 31 Aug. 1922; *er s* of Ernest Bealey and Nora (*née* Hampton), both of Netherton, Dudley; *m* 1960, Sheila Hurst; one *s* two *d. Educ:* Hill Street Elem. Sch.; King Edward VI Grammar Sch., Stourbridge; London Sch. of Economics. Seaman in RN, 1941–46; Student, LSE, 1946–48; Finnish Govt Scholar, 1948–49; Research Asst for Passfield Trust, 1950–51; Extra-Mural Lectr, University of Manchester (Burnley Area), 1951–52; Lectr, University of Keele, 1952–64. Vis. Fellow, Yale, 1980. *Publications:* (with Henry Pelling) Labour and Politics, 1958, 2nd edn 1982; (with J. Blondel and W. P. McCann) Constituency Politics, 1965; The Social and Political Thought of the British Labour Party, 1970; The Post Office Engineering Union, 1976; (with John Sewel) The Politics of Independence, 1981; articles in academic jls. *Recreations:* reading poetry, eating and drinking, watching football and cricket, darts. *Address:* 355 Clifton Road, Aberdeen. *T:* Aberdeen 44689. *Club:* Economicals Association Football and Cricket.

BEAM, Jacob D.; US Ambassador to USSR, 1969–73; *b* Princeton, NJ, 24 March 1908; *s* of Jacob Newton Beam and Mary Prince; *m* 1952, Margaret Glassford; one *s. Educ:* Kent Sch., USA; Princeton Univ. (BA 1929); Cambridge Univ., England (1929–30). Vice-Consul, Geneva, 1931–34; Third Sec., Berlin, 1934–40; Second Sec., London, 1941–45; Asst Political Adviser, HQ, US Forces, Germany, 1945–47; Chief of Central European Div., Dept of State, 1947–49; Counsellor and Consul-Gen., US Embassy, Djakarta, 1949–51; Actg US Rep., UN Commn for Indonesia, 1951; Counsellor, Belgrade, 1951–52; Minister-Counsellor, US Embassy, Moscow, 1952–53 (actg head); Dep. Asst Sec. of State, 1953–57; US Ambassador to Poland, 1957–61; Asst Dir, Internat. Relations Bureau, Arms Control and Disarmament Agency, USA, 1962–66; US Ambassador to Czechoslovakia, 1966–68. Chm., US Delegn to Internat. Telecomm. Union Plenipotentiary Conf., Malaga, 1973. Dir, Radio Free Europe, 1974–. LLB *hc* Princeton, 1970. *Publication:* Multiple Exposure, 1978. *Address:* 3129 'O' Street NW, Washington, DC 20007, USA. *Club:* Metropolitan (Washington, DC).

BEAMENT, Sir James (William Longman), Kt 1980; ScD; FRS 1964; Drapers' Professor of Agriculture and Head of the Department of Applied Biology, University of Cambridge, since 1969; Vice-President, Queens' College, Cambridge, since 1981; *b* 17 Nov. 1921; *o c* of late T. Beament, Crewkerne, Somerset; *m* 1962, Juliet, *y d* of late Prof. Sir Ernest Barker, Cambridge; two *s. Educ:* Crewkerne Grammar Sch.; Queens' Coll., Cambridge; London Sch. of Tropical Medicine. Exhibitioner, Queens' Coll., 1941; BA 1943; MA 1946; PhD London 1945; ScD Cantab 1960. Research Officer with Agricultural Research Council, Cambridge, 1946; Univ. Lectr, and Fellow and Tutor of Queens' Coll., Cambridge, 1961; Reader in Insect Physiology, 1966. Member: Adv. Bd for the Res. Councils, 1977; NERC, 1970–83 (Chm., 1977–80). Mem., Composers' Guild of Great Britain, 1967. Scientific Medal of Zoological Soc., 1963. *Publications:* many papers on insect physiology in scientific journals; Editor of several review volumes. *Recreations:* acoustics, playing the double-bass. *Address:* 19 Sedley Taylor Road, Cambridge CB2 2PW. *T:* 246045; Queens' College, Cambridge CB3 9ET. *T:* 335511. *Clubs:* Farmers'; Amateur Dramatic (Cambridge).

BEAMISH, family name of **Baron Chelwood.**

BEAMISH, Adrian John; HM Diplomatic Service; Head of Falkland Islands Department, Foreign and Commonwealth Office, since 1985; *b* 21 Jan. 1939; *s* of Thomas Charles Constantine Beamish and Josephine Mary (*née* Lee); *m* 1965, Caroline Lipscomb; two *d. Educ:* Christian Brothers' Coll., Cork; Prior Park Coll., Bath; Christ's Coll., Cambridge (BA); Università per gli Stranieri, Perugia. Third, later Second Secretary, Tehran, 1963–66; Foreign Office, 1966–69; First Sec., UK Delegn, OECD, Paris, 1970–73; New Delhi, 1973–76; FCO, 1976–78; Counsellor, Dep. Head, Personnel Operations Dept, FCO, 1978–80; Counsellor (Economic), Bonn, 1981–85. *Recreations:* people, books, plants. *Address:* c/o Foreign and Commonwealth Office, SW1.

BEAMISH, Air Vice-Marshal Cecil Howard, CB 1970; FDSRCS; Director of Dental Services, Royal Air Force, 1969–73; *b* 31 March 1915; *s* of Frank George Beamish, Coleraine; *m* 1955, Frances Elizabeth Sarah Goucher; two *s. Educ:* Coleraine Acad.; Queen's Univ., Belfast. Joined Royal Air Force, 1936; Group Capt., 1958; Air Cdre, 1968; Air Vice-Marshal, 1969. QHDS 1969–73. *Recreations:* Rugby football, golf, squash. *Address:* East Keal Manor, Spilsby, Lincs.

BEAMONT, Wing Comdr Roland Prosper, CBE 1969 (OBE 1953); DSO 1943, Bar 1944; DFC 1941, Bar 1943; DFC (US) 1946; FRAeS; author, aviation consultant; *b* 10 Aug. 1920; *s* of Lieut-Col E. C. Beamont and Dorothy Mary (*née* Haynes); *m* 1946, Patricia Raworth; three *d. Educ:* Eastbourne Coll. Commissioned in RAF, 1939; served War of 1939–45, Fighter Command, RAF, BEF, Battle of Britain (despatches), Battle of France and Germany. Attached as Test Pilot to Hawker Aircraft Ltd during rest periods, in 1941–42 and 1943–44; Experimental Test Pilot, Gloster Aircraft Co. Ltd, 1946; Chief Test Pilot, English Electric Co., 1947–61; Special Dir and Dep. Chief Test Pilot, BAC, 1961–64; Director and Manager, Flight Operations, BAC Preston, later British Aerospace, Warton Division, 1965–78; Dir of Flight Operations, Panavia, 1971–79. Events while Chief Test Pilot, English Electric Co. Ltd: 1st British pilot to fly at speed of sound (in USA), May 1948; 1st Flight of Britain's 1st jet bomber (the Canberra), May 1949; holder of Atlantic Record, Belfast-Gander, 4 hours 18 mins. Aug. 1951 and 1st two-way Atlantic Record, Belfast-Gander-Belfast, 10 hrs 4 mins Aug. 1952 (in a Canberra); first flight of P1, 1954 (Britain's first fully supersonic fighter); first British pilot in British aircraft to fly faster than sound in level flight, 1954, and first to fly at twice the speed of sound, Nov. 1958; first flight of Lightning supersonic all-weather fighter, 1957; first flight of TSR2, Sept. 1964 (Britain's first supersonic bomber). Britannia Trophy for 1953; Derry and Richards Memorial Medal, 1955; R. P. Alston Memorial Medal, RAeS, 1960; British Silver Medal for Aeronautics, 1965. Pres., Popular Flying Assoc., 1979–84. Master Pilot and Liveryman, Guild of Air Pilots. Hon. Fellow, Soc. of Experimental Testpilots, USA, 1985. DL Lancashire 1977–81. *Publications:* Phoenix into Ashes, 1968; Typhoon and Tempest at War, 1975; Testing Years, 1980; English Electric Canberra, 1984; English Electric P1 Lightning, 1985; Fighter Test Pilot, 1986. *Recreation:* fishing. *Address:* Cross Cottage, Pentridge, Salisbury, Wilts SP5 5QX. *Club:* Royal Air Force.

BEAN, Basil, CBE 1985; Director-General, National House Building Council, since 1985; Member, British Waterways Board; *b* 2 July 1931; *s* of Walter Bean and Alice Louise Bean; *m* 1956, Janet Mary Brown; one *d. Educ:* Archbishop Holgate Sch., York. Mem. CIPFA. York City, 1948–53; West Bromwich Borough, 1953–56; Sutton London Bor., 1957–62; Skelmersdale Develt Corp., 1962–66; Havering London Bor., 1967–69; Northampton Develt Corp., 1969–80 (Gen. Manager, 1977–80); Chief Exec., Merseyside Develt Corp., 1980–85; overseas consultancies. *Publications:* financial and technical papers. *Recreations:* reading, walking, travel. *Address:* The Forge, Manor Farm, Church Lane, Princes Risborough, Bucks. *T:* Princes Risborough 6133. *Clubs:* Royal Commonwealth Society; Northampton and County (Northampton).

BEAN, Hugh (Cecil), CBE 1970; violinist (freelance); Professor of Violin, Royal College of Music, since 1954; *b* 22 Sept. 1929; *s* of Cecil Walter Claude Bean and Gertrude Alice Chapman; *m* 1963, Mary Dorothy Harrow; one *d. Educ:* Beckenham Grammar Sch. Studied privately, and at RCM, London (principal prize for violin) with Albert Sammons, 1938–57; Boise Trav. Schol., 1952; at Brussels Conservatoire with André Gertler (double premier prix for solo and chamber music playing), 1952–53. National Service, Gren. Gds, 1949–51. Formerly Leader of Harvey Phillips String Orch. and Dennis Brain Chamber Orch.; Leader of Philharmonia and New Philharmonia Orch., 1957–67; Associate Leader, BBC Symph. Orch., 1967–69. Member: Bean-Parkhouse Duo; Music Gp of London. Has made solo commercial records, and has performed as soloist with many major orchestras. Hon. ARCM 1961, FRCM 1968. *Recreations:* design and construction of flying model aircraft; steam-driven passenger hauling model railways; gramophone record collection. *Address:* Rosemary Cottage, 30 Stone Park Avenue, Beckenham, Kent. *T:* 01–650 8774.

BEAN, Rev. Canon John Victor; Vicar, St Mary, Cowes, IoW, since 1966, and Priest-in-charge, All Saints, Gurnard, IoW, since 1978; Chaplain to the Queen, since 1980; *b* 1 Dec. 1925; *s* of Albert Victor and Eleanor Ethel Bean; *m* 1955, Nancy Evelyn Evans; two *s* one *d* (and one *d* died in infancy). *Educ:* local schools; Grammar Sch., Gt Yarmouth; Downing Coll., Cambridge (MA); Salisbury Theological Coll., 1948. Served War,

RNVR, 1944–46; returned to Cambridge, 1946–48. Assistant Curate: St James, Milton, Portsmouth, 1950–55; St Peter and St Paul, Fareham, 1955–59; Vicar, St Helen's, IoW, 1959–66. Rural Dean of West Wight, 1968–73; Clergy Proctor for Diocese of Portsmouth, 1973–80; Hon. Canon, Portsmouth Cathedral, 1970–. *Recreations:* photography, boat-watching. *Address:* The Vicarage, Church Road, Cowes, Isle of Wight PO31 8HA. *T:* Cowes 292509. *Clubs:* Island Sailing (Cowes); Gurnard Sailing (Gurnard).

BEAN, Leonard, CMG 1964; MBE 1945; MA; Secretary, Southern Gas Region, 1966–79, retired; *b* 19 Sept. 1914; *s* of late Harry Bean, Bradford, Yorks, and late Agnes Sherwood Beattie, Worcester; *m* 1938, Nancy Winifred, *d* of Robert John Neilson, Dunedin, NZ; one *d. Educ:* Canterbury Coll., NZ; Queens' Coll., Cambridge. Served War of 1939–45: Major, 2nd NZ Div. (despatches, MBE). Entered Colonial Service, N Rhodesia, 1945; Provincial Comr, 1959; Perm. Sec. (Native Affairs), 1961; acted as Minister for Native Affairs and Natural Resources in periods, 1961–64; Permanent Secretary: to Prime Minister, 1964; also to President, 1964. Adviser to President, Zambia, 1964–66. *Recreations:* golf, gardening. *Address:* Squirrels Gate, 20 Ashley Park, Ringwood, Hants BH24 2HA. *T:* Ringwood 5262. *Clubs:* MCC; Bramshaw Golf.

BEAN, Robert E.; *b* 5 Sept. 1935. *Educ:* Rochester Mathematical Sch.; Medway Coll. of Technol. MIOB; AMBIM. Polytechnic Lectr. Joined Labour Party, 1950. Mem., Chatham Borough Council, 1958–74; formerly Member: Fabian Soc.; Co-operative party. MP (Lab) Rochester and Chatham, Oct. 1974–1979. Contested (Lab): Gillingham, 1970; Thanet East, Feb. 1974; Rochester and Chatham, 1979; Medway, 1983. Mem., Medway Borough Council, 1974–76. *Address:* 22 Horsted Way, Rochester, Kent ME1 2XY. *T:* Medway 42689.

BEAR, Leslie William, CBE 1972; Editor of Official Report (Hansard), House of Commons, 1954–72; *b* 16 June 1911; *s* of William Herbert Bear, Falkenham, Suffolk; *m* 1st, 1932, Betsy Sobels (*d* 1934), Lisse, Holland; 2nd, 1936, Annelise Gross (*d* 1979), Trier, Germany; two *s. Educ:* Gregg Sch., Ipswich. Served War, 1943–44, Royal Air Force. Mem. of Official Reporting Staff, League of Nations, Geneva, 1930–36; joined Official Report (Hansard), House of Commons, 1936; Asst Ed., 1951. *Recreations:* ski-ing, gardening, chess. *Address:* Medleys, Ufford, Woodbridge, Suffolk. *T:* Eyke 358.

BEARD, Allan Geoffrey, CB 1979, Under Secretary, Department of Health and Social Security, 1968–79 (Ministry of Social Security 1966–68); *b* 18 Oct. 1919; *s* of late Major Henry Thomas Beard and Florence Mercy Beard; *m* 1945, Helen McDonagh; one *d. Educ:* Ormskirk Grammar Sch. Clerical Officer, Air Min., 1936; Exec. Off., Higher Exec. Off., Asst Principal, Assistance Board, 1938–47; Army Service, 1940–46 (Capt., RE); Principal, Nat. Assistance Board, 1950; Asst Sec., 1962. Hon. Treasurer, Motability, 1985. *Recreations:* music, gardening, do-it-yourself. *Address:* 51 Rectory Park, Sanderstead, Surrey CR2 9JR. *T:* 01–657 4197. *Club:* Royal Automobile.

BEARD, (Christopher) Nigel; Senior Consultant, Imperial Chemical Industries Ltd, since 1979; *b* 10 Oct. 1936; *o s* of Albert Leonard Beard, Castleford, Yorks, and Irene (*née* Bowes); *m* 1969, Jennifer Anne, *d* of T. B. Cotton, Guildford, Surrey; one *s* one *d. Educ:* Castleford Grammar Sch., Yorks; University Coll. London. BSc Hons, Special Physics. Asst Mathematics Master, Tadcaster Grammar Sch., Yorks, 1958–59; Physicist with English Electric Atomic Power Div., working on design of Hinckley Point Nuclear Power Station, 1959–61; Market Researcher, Esso Petroleum Co., assessing future UK Energy demands and market for oil, 1961. MoD: Scientific Officer, later Principal Scientific Officer, in Defence Operational Analysis Estabt (engaged in analysis of central defence policy and investment issues), 1961–68, and Supt of Studies pertaining to Land Ops; responsible for policy and investment studies related to Defence of Europe and strategic movement of the Army, Dec. 1968–72; Chief Planner, Strategy, GLC, 1973–74; Dir, London Docklands Develt Team, 1974–79. Mem., SW Thames RHA, 1978–; Mem. Bd, Royal Marsden Hosp., 1982–. Contested (Lab): Woking, 1979; Portsmouth N, 1983. FRSA. *Publication:* The Practical Use of Linear Programming in Planning and Analysis, 1974 (HMSO). *Recreations:* reading, walking, sailing, the theatre. *Address:* Lanquhart, The Ridgway, Pyrford, Woking, Surrey. *T:* Byfleet 48630.

BEARD, Derek, CBE 1979; Assistant Director General, British Council, since 1984; *b* 16 May 1930; *s* of Walter Beard and Lily Beard (*née* Mellors); *m* 1st, 1953, Ruth Davies (marr. diss. 1966); two *s*; 2nd, 1966, Renate Else, *d* of late W. E. Kautz, Berlin and Mecklenburg; two *s. Educ:* Hulme Grammar Sch., Oldham; Brasenose Coll., Oxford (MA, DipEd). Stand Grammar Sch., Whitefield, 1954–56; HMOCS, Nyasaland, 1956–59; Asst Educn Officer, WR Yorks, 1959–61; Sen. Asst, Oxfordshire, 1961–63; British Council, Pakistan, 1963–65; Producer, BBC Overseas Educnl Recordings Unit, 1965–66; Dir, Appts, Services Dept, British Council, 1966–70; Dep. Rep., India, 1970–73; Controller, Educn and Science Div., British Council, 1973–77; Rep. in Germany, 1977–81, Belgium, 1981–84. *Publications:* articles on educn and cultural relns. *Recreations:* sculpture, music, travel. *Address:* British Council, 10 Spring Gardens, SW1A 2BN. *Clubs:* Anglo-Belgian, Institute of Directors.

BEARD, Nigel; *see* Beard, C. N.

BEARD, Paul, OBE 1952; FRAM; FGSM; Professor of Violin, Guildhall School of Music, retired 1968; *b* 4 Aug. 1901; *m* 1925, Joyce Cass-Smith; one *s* one *d. Educ:* Birmingham Oratory and St Philip's. Began violin playing at 4, being taught by father; first public appearance at 6; studied as Scholarship holder at RAM; appointed ARAM, 1921, and FRAM 1939; Principal 1st Violin of following Orchestras: City of Birmingham and Spa, Scarborough, 1920–32; National of Wales, 1929; London Philharmonic, 1932–36; BBC Symphony Orchestra, 1936–62. *Recreations:* golf, gardening. *Address:* 84 Downs Wood, Epsom Downs, Surrey. *T:* Burgh Heath 50759.

BEARD, Paul Michael; a Recorder of Crown Courts since 1972; Chairman, Medical Appeal Tribunal, Nottingham, since 1984; Barrister-at-Law; *b* 21 May 1930; *s* of late Harold Beard, Sheffield; *m* 1959, Rhoda Margaret, *er d* of late James Henry Asquith, Morley, Yorks; one *s* one *d. Educ:* The City Grammar Sch., Sheffield; King's Coll., London. LLB (Hons). Commissioned RASC, 1949; served BAOR (Berlin), 1949–50. Called to Bar, Gray's Inn, 1955; North-Eastern Circuit. Contested (C): Huddersfield East, 1959; Oldham East, 1966; Wigan, Feb. and Oct. 1974; Doncaster, 1979; Chm., Brightside Conservative Assoc., 1961–68. *Recreations:* reading, walking. *Address:* Flowerdale, Church Street, East Markham, near Newark, Notts NG22 0SA. *T:* Tuxford 870074; 42 Bank Street, Sheffield S1 1EE. *T:* Sheffield 751223. *Club:* Sheffield (Sheffield).

BEARDMORE, Prof. John Alec, CBiol, FIBiol; Professor of Genetics, University College of Swansea, since 1966; *b* 1 May 1930; *s* of George Edward Beardmore and Anne Jean (*née* Warrington); *m* 1953, Anne Patricia Wallace; three *s* one *d* (and one *s* decd). *Educ:* Burton on Trent Grammar Sch.; Birmingham Central Tech. Coll.; Univ. of Sheffield. BSc (1st Cl. Botany) 1953, PhD (Genetics) 1956. Research Demonstrator, Dept of Botany, Univ. of Sheffield, 1954–56; Commonwealth Fund Fellow, Columbia Univ., 1956–58; Vis. Asst Prof. in Plant Breeding, Cornell Univ., 1958; Lectr in Genetics, Univ. of Sheffield, 1958–61; Prof. of Genetics and Dir, Genetics Inst., Univ. of Groningen, 1961–66; Nat. Science Foundn Senior Foreign Fellow, Pennsylvania State Univ., 1966; Dean of Science, University Coll. of Swansea, 1974–76, Vice-Principal, 1977–80, Dir, Inst. of Marine Studies, 1983–. Member: NERC Aquatic Life Scis Cttee, 1982– (Chm., 1984–); CNAA: Life Scis Cttee, 1979–85; Cttee for Science, 1985–; Bd, Council of Sci. and Technology Insts, 1983–85 (Chm., 1984–85); Council, Eugenics Soc., 1980– (Chm., Res. Cttee, 1979–); British Nat. Cttee for Biology, 1983–; Vice-Pres., Inst. of Biol., 1985– (Mem. Council, 1976–79; Hon. Sec., 1980–85); UK rep., Council of European Communities Biologists Assoc., 1980–. FRSA. Darwin Lectr, 1984. Univ. of Helsinki Medal, 1980. *Publications:* (ed with B. Battaglia) Marine Organisms: genetics ecology and evolution, 1977; articles on evolutionary genetics, human genetics and biological educn. *Recreations:* bridge, fell walking, sailing. *Address:* 153 Derwen Fawr Road, Swansea SA2 8ED. *T:* Swansea 206232. *Club:* Athenæum.

BEARDS, Paul Francis Richmond; *b* 1 Dec. 1916; *s* of late Dr Clifford Beards and Dorothy (*née* Richmond); *m* 1950, Margaret Elizabeth, *y d* of late V. R. Aronson, CBE, KC; one *s* one *d. Educ:* Marlborough; Queen's Coll., Oxford (Open Scholar; 1st cl. hons Mod. Hist.). Entered Admin. Class of Home Civil Service, 1938; Asst Princ., War Office; served in Army, 1940–44; Principal War Office, 1945; Asst Private Sec. to successive Prime Ministers, 1945–48; Princ. Private Sec. to successive Secs of State for War, 1951–54; Asst Sec., 1954; Imp. Def. Coll., 1961; Asst Under-Sec. of State, MoD, 1964–69; Comr for Administration and Finance, Forestry Commn, 1969; retd, 1970. Coronation Medal, 1953. *Recreations:* fishing, gardening, archæology. *Address:* Thrale Cottage, Budleigh Salterton, Devon EX9 6EA. *T:* Budleigh Salterton 2084. *Club:* Royal Commonwealth Society.

BEARDSWORTH, Maj.-Gen. Simon John, CB 1984; Company Executive, Air-Log Ltd, since 1984; *b* 18 April 1929; *s* of late Captain (S) Stanley Thomas Beardsworth, RN and Pearl Sylvia Emma (Biddy) Beardsworth (*née* Blake); *m* 1954, Barbara Bingham Turner; three *s. Educ:* RC Sch. of St Edmund's Coll., Ware; RMA Sandhurst; RMCS. BSc; FBIM. Commissioned Royal Tank Regt, 1949; Regtl service, staff training and staff appts, 1950–69; CO 1st RTR, 1970–72; Project Manager, Future Main Battle Tank, 1973–77; Student, Royal Naval War College, 1977; Dir of Projects, Armoured Fighting Vehicles, 1977–80; Dep. Comdt, RMCS, 1980–81; Vice Master Gen. of the Ordnance, 1981–84, retired. *Recreations:* game shooting, Pony Club Tetrathlon, horses, amateur dramatics, contemplating authorship. *Address:* c/o Lloyds Bank, Chard, Somerset. *Club:* Army and Navy.

BEARE, Robin Lyell Blin, MB, BS; FRCS; Hon. Consultant Plastic Surgeon: Queen Victoria Hospital, East Grinstead, since 1960; Brighton General Hospital and Brighton and Lewes Group of Hospitals, since 1960; Hon. Consulting Plastic Surgeon, St Mary's Hospital, London, since 1976 (Consultant Plastic Surgeon, 1959–76); *b* 31 July 1922; *s* of late Stanley Samuel Beare, OBE, FRCS, and late Cecil Mary Guise Beare (*née* Lyell); *m* 1947, Iris Bick; two *s* two *d. Educ:* Radley (scholar). Middlesex Hosp. Medical Sch. MB, BS (Hons) 1952 (dist. Surg.); FRCS (Eng) 1955. Served with RAF Bomber Command (Aircrew) 1940–46. Formerly Ho. Surg., Casualty Officer, Asst Pathologist and Surgical Registrar, The Middlesex Hosp., 1952–56. Surg. Registrar, Plastic Surgery and Jaw Injuries Centre, Queen Victoria Hosp., East Grinstead, 1957–60. Examr in gen. surgery for FRCS, 1972–78. Fellow Assoc. of Surgeons of Gt Britain and Ireland; Fellow Royal Society Med.; Mem. Brit. Assoc. of Plastic Surgeons; Mem. of Bd of Trustees, McIndoe Memorial Research Unit, E Grinstead; Hon. Mem. Société Française de Chirurgie Plastique et Reconstructive. *Publications:* various on surgical problems in BMJ, Amer. Jl of Surgery, etc. *Recreations:* fishing, shooting. *Address:* 149 Harley Street, W1N 2DE. *T:* 01–935 4444; Scraggs Farm, Cowden, Kent. *T:* Cowden 386.

BEARN, Prof. Alexander Gordon, MD; FRCP, FRCPEd, FACP; Senior Vice President, Medical and Scientific Affairs, Merck Sharp and Dohme International since 1979; Professor of Medicine, Cornell University Medical College, since 1966 (Stanton Griffis Distinguished Medical Professor, 1976–79); Attending Physician, The New York Hospital, since 1966; *b* 29 March 1923; *s* of E. G. Bearn, CB, CBE; *m* 1952, Margaret, *d* of Clarence Slocum, Fanwood, NJ, USA; one *s* one *d. Educ:* Epsom Coll.; Guy's Hosp., London. Postgraduate Medical Sch. of London, 1949–51. Rockefeller Univ., 1951–66; Hon. Research Asst, University Coll. (Galton Laboratory), 1959–60; Prof. and Sen. Physician, Rockefeller Univ., 1964–66, Vis. and Adjunct Prof. 1966–; Chm., Dept of Medicine, Cornell Univ. Med. Coll., 1966–77; Physician-in-Chief, NY Hosp., 1966–77. Woodrow Wilson Foundn Vis. Fellow, 1979–80. Trustee, Rockefeller Univ.; Dir, Josiah Macy Jr Foundn. Mem. Editorial Bd, several scientific and med. jls. Lectures: Lowell, Harvard, 1958; Medical Research Soc., 1969; Lilly, RCP, 1973; Harvey, 1975; Lettsomian, Med. Soc., 1976. Macy Faculty Scholar Award, 1974–75. Alfred Benzon Prize, Denmark, 1979. Member: Nat. Acad. Science; Amer. Philosophical Soc.; Foreign Mem., Norwegian Acad. Science and Letters. Docteur *hc* Paris, 1975. *Publications:* articles on human genetics and liver disease, 1950–; (Co-Editor) Progress in Medical Genetics, Vol. 2, 1962–; (Associate Editor) Cecil and Loeb: Textbook of Medicine. *Recreations:* biography, collecting mulls, travel. *Address:* 1225 Park Avenue, New York, NY 10028, USA. *T:* 534–2495. *Clubs:* Grolier, Knickerbocker, Century (NY).

BEARNE, Air Vice-Marshal Guy, CB 1956; *b* 5 Nov. 1908; *y s* of late Lieut-Col L. C. Bearne, DSO, AM; *m* 1933, Aileen Cartwright, *e d* of late H. J. Randall, Hove; one *s* two *d.* Commissioned RAF, 1929; served in various Bomber Sqdns, 1930–33; specialist armament course, 1933; armament duties, 1934–44; Bomber Command, 1944–45 (despatches twice); Staff Officer i/c Administration, RAF Malaya, 1946; Joint Services Staff Coll., 1947; Dep. Dir Organisation (Projects), 1947–49; Command of Central Gunnery Sch., 1949–51; SASO, Rhodesian Air Training Gp, 1951–52; AOC Rhodesian Air Training Gp, 1953; Dir of Organisation (Establishments), Air Ministry, 1954–56; Air Officer in Charge of Administration, Technical Training Command, 1956–61; retd, 1961. *Recreation:* golf. *Address:* 2 Mill Close, Hill Deverill, Warminster, Wilts BA12 7EE. *T:* Warminster 40533.

BEARSTED, 3rd Viscount, *cr* 1925, of Maidstone; **Marcus Richard Samuel,** TD 1945; DL; Baron, *cr* 1921; Bt *cr* 1903; Chairman: 1928 Investment Trust Ltd, 1948–82; Samuel Properties Ltd and subsidiary companies, 1961–82; Hill Samuel & Co. (Jersey) Ltd, 1962–80; Negit SA, Luxembourg, 1966–82; Director: Hill Samuel Group Ltd, 1933–79 (formerly Chairman); Sun Alliance & London Insurance Group, 1949–80; Lloyds Bank Ltd and subsidiary companies, 1963–80; *b* 1 June 1909; *e s* of 2nd Viscount and Dorothea (*d* 1949), *e d* of late E. Montefiore Micholls; *S* father 1948; *m* 1st, 1947, Elizabeth Heather (marr. diss. 1966), *er d* of G. Firmston-Williams; one *d* (and one *d* decd); 2nd, 1968, Mrs Jean Agnew Somerville (*d* 1978), *d* of R. A. Wallace. *Educ:* Eton; New Coll., Oxford. Served War of 1939–45, Warwicks Yeomanry (Major), Middle East, Italy (wounded). Chm., Warwicks Hunt, 1960–69. Trustee and Chm. of Whitechapel Art Gallery, 1949–73. Chm., Bearsted Meml Hosp., 1948–; President: Jewish Home and Hosp. at Tottenham, 1948–; St Mary's Hosp. Med. Sch., 1964–80; Dep. Chm., St Mary's Hosp., Paddington, 1958–74; Vice-Chm., Tottenham Gp HMC, 1949–74; Board Member: Eastman Dental Hosp., 1970–75; Kensington, Chelsea and Westminster AHA, 1973–77; St John's Hosp. for Diseases of the Skin, 1975–78. Pres., Nat. Soc. for Epileptics, Chalfont Colony, 1960–; Jt Pres., Barkingside Jewish Youth Centre, 1969–. DL Warwicks, 1950.

Recreation: tapestry. *Heir:* *b* Hon. Peter Montefiore Samuel, *qv.* *Address:* 3 Netherton Grove, SW10 9TQ. *T:* 01–730 2026; Upton House, Banbury, Oxon OX15 6HT. *T:* Edgehill 242. *Club:* White's.

BEASLEY, John T.; *see* Telford Beasley.

BEASLEY, Michael Charles, IPFA, FCA, FCCA; County Treasurer, Royal County of Berkshire, since 1970; *b* 20 July 1924; *y s* of late William Isaac Beasley and Mary Gladys (*née* Williams), Ipswich, Suffolk; *m* 1955, Jean Anita Mary, *o d* of late Reginald John Webber and of Margaret Dorothy (*née* Rees), Penarth, S Glamorgan; one *s.* *Educ:* Northgate Grammar Sch., Ipswich. BScEcon London. Treasurer's Dept, East Suffolk County Council, 1940–48; served Royal Navy, 1943–46; Treasurer's Dept, Staffordshire CC, 1948–51; Educn Accountant, Glamorgan CC, 1951–54; Asst County Treasurer, Nottinghamshire CC, 1954–61; Dep. County Treasurer, Royal County of Berkshire, 1961–70. Examiner, CIPFA, 1963–66; Financial Adviser, Assoc. of County Councils and former County Councils Assoc., 1971–; Hon. Treasurer, Soc. of County Treasurers, 1984– (Hon. Sec., 1972–80, Vice-Pres., 1980–81, Pres., 1981–82); Mem., Treasury Cttee on Local Authority Borrowing, 1972–; Member Council: Local Authorities Mutual Investment Trust, 1974–75; RIPA, 1976–82. *Publications:* contribs to jls on local govt finance and computers. *Recreations:* pottering and pondering. *Address:* Greenacre, Hyde End Road, Spencers Wood, Berkshire RG7 1BU. *T:* Reading 883868.

BEASLEY, Prof. William Gerald, CBE 1980; BA, PhD; FRHistS; FBA 1967; Professor of the History of the Far East, University of London, 1954–83; Head of Japan Research Centre, School of Oriental and African Studies, 1978–83; *b* 1919; *m* 1955, Hazel Polwin; one *s.* *Educ:* Magdalen Coll. Sch., Brackley; University Coll., London. Served War, 1940–46, RNVR. Lecturer, Sch. of Oriental and African Studies, University of London, 1947. Mem., 1961–68, British Chm., 1964–68, Anglo-Japanese Mixed Cultural Commn. Vice-Pres., British Acad., 1974–75, Treasurer, 1975–79. Hon. Mem., Japan Acad., 1984. Hon. DLitt Hong Kong, 1978. Order of the Rising Sun (Third Class), Japan, 1983. *Publications:* Great Britain and the opening of Japan, 1951; Select Documents on Japanese foreign policy, 1853–1868, 1955; The Modern History of Japan, 1963; The Meiji Restoration, 1972. *Address:* 172 Hampton Road, Twickenham TW2 5NJ.

BEASLEY-MURRAY, George Raymond, DD, PhD; Senior Professor of New Testament Interpretation, Southern Baptist Theological Seminary, Louisville, Kentucky, since 1980; *b* 10 Oct. 1916; *s* of George Alfred Beasley; *m* 1942, Ruth Weston; three *s* one *d.* *Educ:* City of Leicester Boys' Sch.; Spurgeon's Coll. and King's Coll., London; Jesus Coll., Cambridge (MA). BD 1941, MTh 1945, PhD 1952, DD 1964, London; DD McMaster, Canada, 1973. Baptist Minister, Ilford, Essex, 1941–48; Cambridge, 1948–50; New Testament Lectr, Spurgeon's Coll., 1950–56; New Testament Prof., Baptist Theological Coll., Rüschlikon, Zürich, 1956–58; Principal, Spurgeon's Coll., 1958–73; Buchanan-Harrison Prof. of New Testament Interpretation, Southern Baptist Theol Seminary, Louisville, Ky, 1973–80. Pres., Baptist Union of Great Britain and Ireland, 1968–69. *Publications:* Christ is Alive, 1947; Jesus and the Future, 1956; Preaching the Gospel from the Gospels, 1956; A Commentary on Mark Thirteen, 1957; Baptism in the New Testament, 1962; The Resurrection of Jesus Christ, 1964; Baptism Today and Tomorrow, 1966; Commentary on 2 Corinthians (Broadman Commentary), 1971; The Book of Revelation (New Century Bible), 1974; The Coming of God, 1983; Jesus and the Kingdom of God, 1986. *Recreation:* music. *Address:* 193 Croydon Road, Beckenham, Kent BR3 3QH.

BEATON, Arthur Charles, CMG 1954; Assistant Area General Manager, North Staffs Area, West Midlands Division, National Coal Board, 1955–61; National Coal Board Civil Defence Organiser, 1961, retired 1967; *b* 22 Aug. 1904; *s* of Samuel and Alice Ellen Beaton; *m* 1935, Jessie, *d* of Albert and Sarah Burrow; one *s* one *d.* *Educ:* Leeds Grammar Sch.; Keble Coll., Oxford. BA Litt. Hum. (Oxon), 1927; MA (Oxon), 1935. Sudan Political Service, 1927; District Comr, 1937; Dep. Gov., Equatoria, 1947; Dir, Local Govt Branch, 1950; Dep. Civil Sec., 1952; Actg Civil Sec., 1953; Permanent Under Sec. Ministry of the Interior, Sudan Government, 1954. 4th Class, Order of the Nile, 1941. *Publications:* Handbook, Equatoria Province, 1952. Articles in Sudan Notes and Records on anthropological subjects. *Recreations:* gardening, reading. *Address:* Barr Cottage, Clubhouse Lane, Waltham Chase, Southampton, Hampshire SO3 2NN. *T:* Bishop's Waltham 4680.

BEATON, Surg. Rear-Adm. Douglas Murdo, CB 1960; OBE 1940; retired as Medical Officer in Charge, RN Hospital, Plymouth, and Command Medical Officer, Plymouth Command (1957–60); *b* 27 May 1901; *s* of late Murdo Duncan Beaton, Kishorn, Ross-shire; *m* 1929, Violet, 2nd *d* of late David R. Oswald, MD, Kinross, Scotland; one *s* one *d.* *Educ:* Bristol Grammar Sch.; Edinburgh, Royal Colleges LDS 1923; LRCPE, LRCSE, LRFPS (Glas), 1924; Surg. Lieut Royal Navy, 1924; Surg. Comdr, 1936; Surg. Capt., 1948; Surg. Rear-Adm., 1957. Asst to Medical Dir-Gen., 1944–46; Medical Officer in Charge, HMHS Maine, 1947–48; MO i/c RN Sick Quarters, Shotley, 1949–51; Senior Medical Officer, Medical Section, RN Hospital, Plymouth, 1951–54; Asst to Medical Dir-Gen., Admiralty, 1954–57. QHP 1956–60; KStJ 1979. *Recreations:* golf, gardening, sailing. *Address:* Ardarroch, Auchterarder, Perthshire. *T:* Auchterarder 2329.

BEATON, Chief Superintendent James Wallace, GC 1974; Chief Superintendent, Metropolitan Police, since 1985; *b* St Fergus, Aberdeenshire, 16 Feb. 1943; *s* of J. A. Beaton and B. McDonald; *m* 1965, Anne C. Ballantyne; two *d.* *Educ:* Peterhead Acad., Aberdeenshire. Joined Metropolitan Police, 1962: Notting Hill, 1962–66; Sergeant, Harrow Road, 1966–71; Station Sergeant, Wembley, 1971–73; Royalty Protection Officer, 'A' Division, 1973; Police Officer to The Princess Anne, 1973–79; Police Inspector, 1974; Chief Inspector, 1979; Superintendent, 1983. Director's Honor Award, US Secret Service, 1974. *Recreations:* reading, keeping fit. *Address:* 12 Embry Way, Stanmore, Mddx HA7 3AZ. *T:* 01–954 5054.

BEATON, John Angus, CB 1975; solicitor; Director, Scottish Courts Administration, 1974–75 (Deputy Director, 1972–74); *b* 24 July 1909; *s* of Murdoch Beaton, TD, ISO, Inverness, and Barbara Mackenzie Beaton (*née* Rose); *m* 1942, Margaret Florence McWilliam; two *s* one *d.* *Educ:* Inverness Royal Acad.; Edinburgh Univ. (BL). Scottish Office: Sen. Legal Asst, 1947; Asst Solicitor, 1960; Deputy Solicitor, 1966–72. Vice-Pres., 1960–63 and Hon. Mem., 1963–, Instn of Professional Civil Servants. *Publications:* Glossary of Scottish Legal Terms, 1980, 1986; Scots Law Terms and Expressions, 1982; articles in the Stair Memorial and Green's Encycls of Scots Law and in legal jls. *Recreations:* reading, golf, fishing. *Address:* 2 Dryden Place, Edinburgh EH9 1RP. *T:* 031–667 3198. *Clubs:* Edinburgh University Staff (Edinburgh); Gullane Golf (East Lothian); New Golf (St Andrews).

BEATTIE, Hon. Sir Alexander (Craig), Kt 1973; **Hon. Mr Justice Beattie;** President, The Eryldene Trust, since 1983; *b* 24 Jan. 1912; *e s* of Edmund Douglas and Amie Louisa Beattie; *m* 1st, 1944, Joyce Pearl Alder (*d* 1977); two *s*; 2nd, 1978, Joyce Elizabeth de Groot. *Educ:* Fort Street High Sch., Sydney; Univ. of Sydney (BA, LLB; Hon. LLD). Admitted to NSW Bar, 1936. Served War of 1939–45: Captain, 2nd AIF, Royal Australian Armoured Corps, New Guinea and Borneo. Pres., Industrial Commn of NSW, 1966–81 (Mem., 1955). Trustee, Royal Botanic Gardens and Govt Domain, Sydney, 1976–82, Chm. 1980–82. *Recreations:* gardening, bowls. *Club:* Australian (Sydney).

BEATTIE, Anne Heather; *see* Steel, A. H.

BEATTIE, Prof. Arthur James, FRSE 1957; Professor of Greek at Edinburgh University, 1951–81; Dean of the Faculty of Arts, 1963–65; *b* 28 June 1914, *e s* of Arthur John Rait Beattie. *Educ:* Montrose Academy; Aberdeen Univ.; Sidney Sussex Coll., Cambridge. Wilson Travelling Fellowship, Aberdeen, 1938–40. Served War, 1940–45; RA 1940–41; Int. Corps, 1941–45; Major GS02; despatches, 1945. Fellow and Coll. Lectr, Sidney Sussex Coll., 1946–51; Faculty Asst Lectr and Univ. Lectr in Classics, Cambridge, 1946–51. Chm. Governors, Morrison's Acad., Crieff, 1962–75; Governor, Sedbergh Sch., 1967–78. Comdr, Royal Order of the Phœnix (Greece), 1966. *Publications:* articles contributed to classical jls. *Recreations:* walking, bird-watching. *Club:* New (Edinburgh).

BEATTIE, Charles Noel, QC 1962; *b* 4 Nov. 1912; *s* of Michael William Beattie and Edith Beattie (*née* Lickfold); *m*; one *s* three *d.* *Educ:* Lewes Grammar Sch. LLB (London). Admitted a solicitor, 1938. Served War of 1939–45 (despatches), Capt. RASC. Called to the Bar, Lincoln's Inn, 1946; Bencher 1971. *Address:* 24 Old Buildings, Lincoln's Inn, WC2A 3UJ. *T:* 01–242 2744.

BEATTIE, Colin Panton, MA, MB, ChB, DPH; FRCPath; Professor of Bacteriology, University of Sheffield, 1946–67; now Emeritus Professor; *b* 11 Sept. 1902; *s* of James Beattie, MA, and Eleanor Anne Beattie; *m* 1937, May Hamilton Christison, BA, PhD; no *c.* *Educ:* Fettes Coll., Edinburgh; University of Edinburgh. House appointments in Royal Infirmary, Edinburgh, and Royal Northern Infirmary, Inverness, 1928–30; Asst in Bacteriology Dept., University of Edinburgh, 1930–32; Rockefeller Travelling Fellow, 1932–33; Lecturer in Bacteriology Dept, University of Edinburgh, 1933–37; Prof. of Bacteriology in The Royal Faculty of Medicine of Iraq and Dir of Govt Bacteriology Laboratory, Baghdad, 1937–46. *Publications:* various papers on bacteriological and parasitological subjects. *Recreation:* gardening. *Address:* 391a Fulwood Road, Sheffield S10 3GE. *T:* Sheffield 302158.

BEATTIE, David; HM Diplomatic Service; Head of Energy, Science and Space Department, Foreign and Commonwealth Office, since 1985; *b* 5 March 1938; *s* of George William David Beattie and Norna Alice (*née* Nicolson); *m* 1966, Ulla Marita Alha, *d* of Allan Alha and Britta-Maja (*née* Tuominen), Helsinki, Finland; two *d.* *Educ:* Merchant Taylors' Sch., Crosby; Lincoln Coll., Oxford (BA 1964, MA 1967). National Service, Royal Navy, 1957–59; Sub-Lieut RNR, 1959; Lieut RNR 1962–67. Entered HM Foreign (now Diplomatic) Service, 1963; FO, 1963–64; Moscow, 1964–66; FO, 1966–70; Nicosia, 1970–74; FCO, 1974–78; Counsellor, later Dep. Head, UK Delegn to Negotiations on Mutual Reduction of Forces and Armaments and Associated Measures in Central Europe, Vienna, 1978–82; Counsellor (Commercial), Moscow, 1982–85. *Recreations:* diplomacy, bridge, walking, history of the House of Stuart. *Address:* c/o Foreign and Commonwealth Office, SW1A 2AH. *Club:* Travellers'.

BEATTIE, Hon. Sir David (Stuart), GCMG 1980; GCVO 1981; QSO 1985; Governor-General of New Zealand, 1980–85; *b* Sydney, Australia, 29 Feb. 1924; *s* of Joseph Nesbitt Beattie; *m* 1950, Norma Macdonald, QSO, *d* of John Macdonald; three *s* four *d.* *Educ:* Dilworth Sch.; Univ. of Auckland (LLB). Served War of 1939–45, Naval Officer. Barrister and Solicitor; President Auckland Dist Law Soc., 1964; QC 1965; Judge of Supreme Court, 1969–80; Chairman, Royal Commission on the Courts, 1977–78. Chairman: Sir Winston Churchill Memorial Trust Board, 1975–80; Trustees, NZ Sports Foundn, 1977–80. Hon. LLD Auckland, 1983. *Publications:* legal articles. *Address:* 18 Golf Road, Heretaunga, Wellington, New Zealand.

BEATTIE, Thomas Brunton, CMG 1981; OBE 1968; HM Diplomatic Service, retired 1982; *b* 17 March 1924; *s* of Joseph William Beattie and Jessie Dewar (*née* Brunton), Rutherglen; *m* 1st, 1956, Paula Rahkola (marr. diss. 1981); one *d*; 2nd, 1982, Josephine Marion Collins. *Educ:* Rutherglen Acad.; Pembroke Coll., Cambridge. MA. Served RAF, 1943–47. Jt Press Reading Service, British Embassy, Moscow, 1947; Finnish Secretariat, British Legation, Helsinki, 1951; FO, 1954; Second Sec., Madrid, 1956; FO, 1960; First Sec., Athens, 1964; First Sec., later Counsellor, FCO, 1969; Counsellor, Rome, 1977, FCO 1981. *Recreations:* hill walking, local Scottish history, music. *Address:* Cairnside, Kirkland of Glencairn, Moniaive, Dumfriesshire DG3 4HD. *Clubs:* Carlton; Royal Scottish Automobile (Glasgow).

BEATTIE, William John Hunt Montgomery, MA Cantab; MD, FRCS, FRCOG, FRCGP; Consultant Gynæcologist and Obstetric Surgeon, St Bartholomew's Hospital; Gynæcologist: Leatherhead Hospital; Florence Nightingale Hospital; retired. *Educ:* Cambridge Univ.; London Univ. MRCS; LRCP 1927; BCh (Cantab) 1928; FRCS 1929; MB 1930; MD 1933; FRCOG 1942; Examiner: Central Midwives' Board; Univs. of Oxford, Cambridge and London (Obst. and Gynæcol.); Conjoint Board (Midwifery and Gynæcol.). *Publications:* (jt) Diseases of Women by Ten Teachers, 1941; articles in medical journals. *Address:* Ivy Cottage, Reigate Heath, Surrey.

BEATTY, 3rd Earl *cr* 1919; **David Beatty;** Viscount Borodale of Wexford, Baron Beatty of the North Sea and of Brooksby, 1919; *b* 21 Nov. 1946; *s* of 2nd Earl Beatty, DSC, and Dorothy Rita, *d* of late M. J. Furey, New Orleans, USA; *S* father, 1972; *m* 1971, Ann (marr. diss. 1982), *d* of A. Please, Wokingham; one *s.* *Educ:* Eton. *Heir:* *s* Viscount Borodale, *qv.* *Address:* c/o House of Lords, SW1A 0PW.

BEAUCHAMP, Sir Christopher Radstock Proctor-, 9th Bt *cr* 1744; solicitor with Gilbert H. Stephens & Sons, Exeter; *b* 30 Jan. 1935; *s* of Rev. Sir Ivor Cuthbert Proctor-Beauchamp, 8th Bt, and Caroline Muriel, *d* of late Frank Densham; *S* father, 1971; *m* 1965, Rosalind Emily Margot, 3rd *d* of G. P. Wainwright, St Leonards-on-Sea; two *s* one *d.* *Educ:* Rugby; Trinity College, Cambridge (MA). *Heir:* *s* Charles Barclay Proctor-Beauchamp, *b* 7 July 1969. *Address:* The White House, Harpford, near Sidmouth, East Devon.

BEAUCLERK, family name of **Duke of St Albans.**

BEAUFORT, 11th Duke of, *cr* 1682; **David Robert Somerset;** Earl of Worcester, 1514; Marquess of Worcester, 1642; Chairman, Marlborough Fine Art Ltd, since 1977; *b* 23 Feb. 1928; *s* of late Captain Henry Robert Somers Fitzroy de Vere Somerset, DSO (*d* 1965) (*g g s* of 8th Duke) and late Bettine Violet Somerset (*née* Malcolm) (*d* 1973); *S* cousin, 1984; *m* 1950, Lady Caroline Jane Thynne, *d* of Marquess of Bath, *qv*; three *s* one *d.* *Educ:* Eton. Formerly Lieutenant, Coldstream Guards. *Heir:* *s* Marquess of Worcester, *qv.* *Address:* Badminton, Avon GL9 1DB.

BEAUMAN, Wing Commander Eric Bentley; Librarian, Royal United Service Institution, 1952–57; *b* 7 Feb. 1891; *yr s* of late Bentley Martin Beauman; *m* 1940, Katharine Burgoyne, MA, *yr d* of late F. W. Jones; one *s.* *Educ:* Malvern Coll.; Geneva Univ.; Royal Aero Flying Certificate, 1913; served European war, 1914–18: commnd RNAS Aug. 1914; Anti-Submarine patrols, Home and Aegean; Home Defence and flying instruction: comd seaplane stations at Dundee and Newhaven (despatches). Major, RAF 1918; psa 1922–23 (first course of RAF Staff College); psc 1929–30; instructor at RAF Staff Coll., 1932–33; retd, 1938; Air Ministry, 1938–51. War of 1939–45; RAF liaison officer with BBC. Expeditions: Mount Kamet, Himalaya, 1931; Coast Range of British Columbia, 1934 (paper to RGS on Coast Range Crossing); climbed the Matterhorn 5 times. Pres. Alpine Ski Club, 1933–35, Hon. Mem., 1978–; Hon. Librarian, Alpine Club, 1947–58. Vice-Pres. RAF Mountaineering Assoc. 1951–; Chm., Touring and Mountaineering Cttee of Ski Club of Gt Britain, 1952–54. Broadcasts on many occasions. *Publications:* compiled: Winged Words, 1941 (Book Soc. Choice); The Airmen Speak, 1941; (with Cecil Day Lewis) compiled: We Speak from the Air, 1942; Over to You, 1943; chapters in: Living Dangerously, 1936; Travellers' Tales, 1945; The Boys' Country Book, 1955; contributor to: The Second Cuckoo; The Way to Lords; The Times, Guardian, Sunday Times, The Field, The Listener, National Review, The Geographical Magazine, Alpine Jl, RUSI Jl, British Ski Year Book, Dictionary of National Biography, Encyclopædia Britannica. *Recreations:* writing, reading, gardening. *Address:* 59 Chester Row, SW1W 8JL. *T:* 01–730 9038. *Clubs:* Alpine (elected 1920), Royal Air Force.

BEAUMONT, family name of **Viscount Allendale** and **Baron Beaumont of Whitley.**

BEAUMONT OF WHITLEY, Baron *cr* 1967 (Life Peer), of Child's Hill; **Rev. Timothy Wentworth Beaumont,** MA (Oxon); priest and writer; Parish Priest, St Philip and All Saints, North Sheen, and St Luke, Richmond, since 1986; *b* 22 Nov. 1928; *o s* of Major and Hon. Mrs M. W. Beaumont; *m* 1955, Mary Rose Wauchope; one *s* two *d* (and one *s* decd). *Educ:* Gordonstoun; Christ Church, Oxford; Westcott House, Cambridge. Asst Chaplain, St John's Cathedral, Hong Kong, 1955–57; Vicar, Christ Church Kowloon Tong, Hong Kong, 1957–59; Hon. Curate, St Stephen's Rochester Row, London, 1960–63; resigned orders, 1973; resumed orders, 1984. Editor: Prism, 1960–63 and 1964; New Outlook, 1964, 1972–74; Chm., Studio Vista Books Ltd, 1963–68; Proprietor of New Christian, 1965–70. Food Columnist, Illustrated London News, 1976–80. Asst Dir (Public Affairs), Make Children Happy, 1977–78; Co-ordinator, The Green Alliance, 1978–80. Liberal Party Organisation: Jt Hon. Treas., 1962–63; Chm., Liberal Publications Dept, 1963–64; Head of Org., 1965–66; Chm., Liberal Party's Org. Cttee, 1966; Chm., Liberal Party, 1967–68; Pres., Liberal Party, 1969–70; Vice-Chm., Liberal Party Exec. and Dir, Policy Promotion, 1980–83; Liberal spokesman on education and the arts, House of Lords, 1968–78, 1980–; Alternate Mem., Assemblies of Council of Europe and WEU, 1973–77, Leader of Liberal Delegn, 1977–78, Vice-Chm., Liberal Gp, 1977–78. Pres., British Fedn of Film Socs, 1973–79. Chairman: Albany Trust, 1969–71; Inst. of Res. into Mental and Multiple Handicap, 1971–73; Exit, 1980–81. Mem., Exec. Cttee, British Council, 1974–78. Mem. Exec., Church Action on Poverty, 1983–85. *Publications:* (ed) Modern Religious Verse, 1965; ed and contrib., The Liberal Cookbook, 1972; (ed) New Christian Reader, 1974; (ed) The Selective Ego: the diaries of James Agate, 1976. *Address:* 70 Marksbury Avenue, Richmond, Surrey.

BEAUMONT, Bill; *see* Beaumont, W. B.

BEAUMONT, Christopher Hubert; a Recorder of the Crown Court, since 1981; *b* 10 Feb. 1926; *s* of Hubert and Beatrix Beaumont; *m* 1st, 1959, Catherine Sanders Clark (*d* 1971); two *s*; 2nd, 1972, Sara Patricia Magee; one *d*. *Educ:* West Monmouth Sch., Pontypool; Balliol Coll., Oxford (MA). Served RN, 1944–47 (Sub-Lieut RNVR). Called to Bar, Middle Temple, 1950. Asst Dep. Coroner, Inner West London, 1963–81. Dep. Chairman, Agricultural Land Tribunal, Eastern Area, 1979–. *Publications:* Law Relating to Sheriffs, 1968; Town and Country Planning Act 1968, 1969; Housing Act 1969, 1969; Town and Country Planning Acts 1971 and 1972, 1973; (with W. G. Nutley) Land Compensation Act 1973, 1973; (with W. G. Nutley) Community Land Act 1975, 1976. *Address:* Rose Cottage, Lower Eashing, Godalming, Surrey GU7 2QG. *T:* Godalming 6316; 2 Harcourt Buildings, Temple, EC4Y 9DB. *T:* 01–353 8415.

BEAUMONT, Sir George Howland Francis, 12th Bt, *cr* 1661; late Lieutenant 60th Rifles; *b* 24 Sept. 1924; *s* of 11th Bt and Renée Muriel, 2nd *d* of late Maj.-Gen. Sir Edward Northey, GCMG, CB; *S* father 1933; *m* 1949, Barbara Singleton (marr. annulled, 1951); *m* 1963, Henrietta Anne (marr. diss. 1986), *d* of late Dr A. Waymouth and Mrs J. Rodwell, Riverside Cottage, Donnington, Berks; twin *d*. *Educ:* Stowe Sch. *Address:* The Corner House, Manor Court, Stretton-on-Fosse, near Moreton-in-Marsh, Glos. *T:* Shipston-on-Stour 62845. *Club:* Lansdowne.

BEAUMONT, His Honour Herbert Christopher, MBE 1948; a Circuit Judge, 1972–85; temporary Resident Judge, Cyprus, 1986; *b* 3 June 1912; *s* of late Gerald Beaumont, MC and bar, and Gwendolene Beaumont (*née* Haworth); *m* 1940, Helen Margaret Gordon Smail, *d* of William Mitchell Smail; one *s* two *d*. *Educ:* Uppingham Sch.; Worcester Coll., Oxford. Indian Civil and Political Services, 1936–48; Foreign Office, 1948–52. Called to the Bar, Inner Temple, 1951; Metropolitan Magistrate, 1962–72. Chm. of the London Juvenile Courts, 1964; Dep. Chm., North Riding QS, 1966–71. Mem., Parole Bd, 1974–76. *Recreations:* travel in Europe, bridge. *Address:* Minskip Lodge, Boroughbridge, Yorks. *T:* Boroughbridge 2365. *Clubs:* Brooks's; Yorkshire (York).

See also G. M. Waller.

BEAUMONT, (John) Michael; Seigneur of Sark since 1974; *b* 20 Dec. 1927; *s* of late Lionel (Buster) Beaumont and Enid Beaumont (*née* Ripley); *m* 1956, Diana (*née* La Trobe-Bateman); two *s*. *Educ:* Loughborough Coll. (DLC). Aircraft Design Engr, 1952–70; Chief Techn. Engr, Beagle Aircraft, 1969–70; Design Engr, BAC GW Div., 1970–75. *Recreations:* theatre, music, gardening. *Heir: s* Christopher Beaumont, Captain RE, *b* 4 Feb. 1957. *Address:* La Seigneurie, Sark. *T:* Sark 2017.

BEAUMONT, Sir Richard Ashton, KCMG 1965 (CMG 1955); OBE 1949; HM Diplomatic Service, retired; Chairman, Arab-British Chamber of Commerce, since 1980; *b* 29 Dec. 1912; *s* of A. R. Beaumont, FRCS, Uppingham, and Evelyn Frances (*née* Rendle); *m* 1942, Alou (*d* 1985), *d* of M. Camran, Istanbul; one *d*. *Educ:* Repton; Oriel Coll., Oxford. Joined HM Consular Service, 1936; posted Lebanon and Syria, 1936–41. Served War, 1941–44. Returned to Foreign Office, 1944; served in London, Iraq, Venezuela; Imperial Defence Coll., 1958; Head of Arabian Department, Foreign Office, 1959; Ambassador: to Morocco, 1961–65; to Iraq, 1965–67; Dep. Under-Sec. of State, FO, 1967–69; Ambassador to the Arab Republic of Egypt, 1969–72. Dir-Gen., Middle East Assoc., 1973–77; Chairman: Arab British Centre, 1976–77; Anglo-Arab Assoc., 1979–. Governor, SOAS, 1973–78. Trustee, Thomson Foundn, 1974–. *Recreation:* golf. *Address:* 14 Cadogan Square, SW1X 0JU. *Club:* United Oxford & Cambridge University.

BEAUMONT, William Anderson, CB 1986; OBE (mil.) 1961; AE 1953; Speaker's Secretary, House of Commons, since 1982; *b* 30 Oct. 1924; *s* of late William Lionel Beaumont and of Mrs E. Taverner; *m* 1946, Kythé, *d* of late Major K. G. Mackenzie, Victoria, BC; one *d*. *Educ:* Terrington Hall, York; Cranleigh Sch. (Entrance Exhibnr); Christ Church, Oxford (MA, DipEd). Served RAF, Navigator, 1942–47, 355 Sqdn, 232 Sqdn, SEAC (Flt Lt); RAuxAF 3507 (Co. of Somerset) FCU, 1948–54; 3609 (W Riding) FCU, 1954–61 (Wing Comdr CO, 1958–61); Observer Comdr, No 18 (Leeds) Gp, Royal Observer Corps, 1962–75 (ROC Medal 1975). Asst Master, Bristol Grammar Sch., 1951–54; Beaumont and Smith Ltd, Pudsey, 1954–66 (Man. Dir, 1958–66); Henry Mason (Shipley) Ltd (Man. Dir, 1966–76); Principal, Welsh Office, 1976–79; Asst Sec., Welsh Office, 1979–82. FRSA 1977. *Recreations:* inland waterways, reluctant gardening, walking. *Address:* Kelowna, St Hilary, S Glamorgan CF7 7DP. *T:* Cowbridge 3251. *Clubs:* Royal Air Force; United Services Mess (Cardiff); Maison des Ailes (Brussels).

BEAUMONT, William Blackledge, (Bill), OBE 1982; Rugby Union footballer, retired; sports broadcaster and writer; Director, J. Blackledge & Son Ltd, since 1981; *b* 9 March 1952; *s* of Ronald Walton Beaumont and Joyce Beaumont; *m* 1977, Hilary Jane Seed; one *s*. *Educ:* Ellesmere Coll., Shropshire. Joined family textile business, 1971. First played Rugby Union for England, 1975; 34 caps (20 caps as Captain); Mem., British Lions, NZ tour, 1977; Captain, British Lions, S Africa tour, 1980; played for Lancashire Barbarians, retd 1982. *Publications:* Thanks to Rugby 1982; Bill Beaumont's Tackle Rugby, 1983; Bill Beaumont's Sporting Year Book, 1984. *Recreations:* tennis, golf, water-skiing. *Address:* Alderley, 113 Liverpool Road, Longton, Preston, Lancs PR4 5AA. *Clubs:* East India, MCC; Fylde Rugby Union Football; Royal Lytham St Anne's Golf.

BEAUMONT-DARK, Anthony Michael; MP (C) Birmingham, Selly Oak, since 1979; investment analyst; *b* Birmingham, 11 Oct. 1932; *s* of Leonard Cecil Dark; *m* 1959, Sheelagh Irene, *d* of R. Cassey; one *s* one *d*. *Educ:* Birmingham Coll. of Arts and Crafts; Birmingham Univ. Mem., Birmingham Stock Exchange, 1958–; Consultant, Smith, Keen, Cutler, 1958– (Partner, 1959–85); Director: Wigham Poland (Midlands) Ltd, 1960–; Nat. Exhibition Centre Ltd, 1971–73; Cope Allman Internat. Ltd, 1972–; Birmid Qualcast PLC, 1983–; Birmingham Executive Airways (Chm., 1983–86). Mem., Central Housing Adv. Cttee, DoE, 1970–76. Member: Birmingham City Council, 1956–67 (Alderman, 1967–74, Hon. Alderman, 1976); W Midlands CC, 1973– (Chm., Finance Cttee, 1977–). Contested (C) Birmingham, Aston, 1959, 1964. Mem., Treasury and Civil Service Select Cttee, 1979–. Governor: Aston Univ., 1980–; Birmingham Univ., 1984–. Trustee, Birmingham Copec Housing Trust, 1975–. *Address:* House of Commons, SW1; 124 Lady Byron Lane, Copt Heath, Solihull, Birmingham B93 9BA. *Club:* Carlton.

BEAUREPAIRE, Dame Beryl (Edith), DBE 1981 (OBE 1975); *b* 24 Sept. 1923; *d* of late E. L. Bedggood; *m* 1946, Ian Francis Beaurepaire, *qv*; two *s*. *Educ:* Fintona Girls' Sch., Balwyn, Victoria; Univ. of Melbourne. ASO, WAAAF, 1942–45. Mem. Nat. Exec., YWCA Australia, 1969–77. Liberal Party of Australia: Chm., Victorian Women's Sect., 1973–76; Chm., Federal Women's Sect., 1974–76; Vice-Pres., Victorian Div., 1976–; Convenor, Nat. Women's Adv. Council, Australia, 1978–82. Member: Council, Australian War Memorial, 1982– (Chm., 1985–); Australian Children's Television Foundation Bd, 1982–. Chm., Bd of Management, Fintona Girls' Sch., 1973–. Jubilee Medal, 1977. *Recreations:* golf, swimming. *Address:* 124 Powlett Street, East Melbourne, Vic 3002, Australia. *T:* 419 2996. *Clubs:* Alexandra (Melbourne); Peninsula Country Golf (Frankston).

BEAUREPAIRE, Ian Francis, CMG 1967; Director, Pacific Dunlop Ltd (formerly Dunlop Olympic Ltd), since 1980; Chairman, Olex Ltd, since 1973; *b* 14 Sept. 1922; *s* of late Sir Frank and Lady Beaurepaire; *m* 1946, Beryl Edith Bedggood (*see* Dame Beryl Beaurepaire); two *s*. *Educ:* Carey Grammar Sch., Scotch Coll., Melbourne; Royal Melbourne Inst. of Technology. Served RAAF (Flying Officer), 1942–45. Man. Dir, Beaurepaire Tyre Service Pty Ltd, 1953–55; Gen. Man., The Olympic Tyre & Rubber Co. Pty Ltd, 1955–61; Chm., 1959–78, Man. Dir, 1959–75, Chief Exec., 1975–78, Exec. Chm., 1978–80, Olympic Consolidated Industries Ltd. Mem., Melbourne Underground Rail Loop Authority, 1971–83, Chm., 1981–83. Member: Melbourne City Council, 1956–75 (Lord Mayor of Melbourne, 1965–67); Management Cttee of Royal Victorian Eye and Ear Hosp., 1966– (Pres., 1982–). *Recreations:* golf, grazing. *Address:* GPO Box 1492N, Melbourne, Victoria 3001, Australia. *Clubs:* Athenæum, Naval and Military, Melbourne (Melbourne); Peninsula Country Golf (Frankston).

BEAVAN, family name of **Baron Ardwick.**

BEAVEN, John Lewis, CMG 1986; CVO 1983 (MVO 1974); HM Diplomatic Service; Consul-General, San Francisco, since 1982; *b* 30 July 1930; *s* of Charles and Margaret Beaven; *m* 1960, Jane Beeson (marr. diss.); one *s* one *d*; *m* 1975, Jean McComb Campbell. *Educ:* Newport (Gwent) High Sch. BoT, 1946; RAF, 1948–50; Asst Trade Comr, British High Commn, Karachi, 1956–60; Second Secretary (Commercial), British High Commn, Freetown, 1961–64; First Secretary (Commercial): British High Commn, Nicosia, 1964–66; Nairobi, 1966–68; FCO, 1969–72; Head of Chancery, British Embassy, Jakarta, 1972–74; Counsellor (Economic and Commercial), British High Commn, Lagos, 1975–77; Dep. Consul General and Dir, British Trade Develt Office, NY, 1978–82. *Recreations:* music, needlepoint, walking. *Address:* c/o Foreign and Commonwealth Office, SW1; Scannell Road, Ghent, NY 12075, USA. *T:* 518.392.2152. *Club:* Brook (New York).

BEAVERBROOK, 3rd Baron *cr* 1917, of Beaverbrook, New Brunswick, and of Cherkley, Surrey; **Maxwell William Humphrey Aitken;** Bt 1916; a Lord in Waiting (Government Whip), since 1986; Director of Ventech Ltd, since 1983; Chairman, Beaverbrook Foundation, since 1985; *b* 29 Dec. 1951; *s* of Sir (John William) Max Aitken, 2nd Bt, DSO, DFC, and of Violet, *d* of Sir Humphrey de Trafford, 4th Bt, MC; *S* to disclaimed barony of father, 1985; *m* 1974, Susan Angela More O'Ferrall; two *s* two *d*. *Educ:* Charterhouse; Pembroke Coll., Cambridge. Beaverbrook Newspapers Ltd, 1973–77; Trustee, Beaverbrook Foundation, 1974–. *Recreations:* yachting, antique motor cars. *Heir: s* Hon. Maxwell Francis Aitken, *b* 17 March 1977. *Address:* Denchworth Manor, Wantage, Oxfordshire. *T:* West Hanney 303. *Clubs:* White's; Royal Yacht Squadron.

BEAVIS, David, CBE 1976; retired; Chairman, West Midlands Gas Region (formerly West Midlands Gas Board), 1968–77; Part-time Member, British Gas Corporation, 1973–77; *b* 12 Dec. 1913; *s* of David Beavis; *m* 1946, Vera, *d* of F. C. Todd; one *s* one *d*. *Educ:* Whitehill Secondary Sch.; Royal Technical Coll., Glasgow (now Strathclyde Univ.). Dep. Engineer and Manager, Helensburgh Town Council Gas Dept, 1935–41; Asst Engineer, Camb. Univ. and Town Gas Light Co., 1942–47; Dep. Engineer and Manager, Edin. Corp. Gas Dept, 1947–49; Divisional Gen. Man. Edin. and SE Div., and subseq. Area Manager, Scottish Gas Bd, 1949–64; Mem. Scottish Gas Bd, 1962–64; Dep. Chm., Eastern Gas Bd, 1964–68. President: Scottish Assoc. of Gas Managers, 1960–61; IGasE, 1967. *Publications:* technical papers presented to Engineering Instns. *Recreations:* technological education, golf, sailing. *Address:* 1 Sandal Rise, Solihull, West Midlands. *T:* 021–704 1819.

BEAVIS, Air Chief Marshal Sir Michael (Gordon), KCB 1981; CBE 1977 (OBE 1969); AFC 1962; Deputy Commander-in-Chief, Allied Forces Central Europe, 1984–86, retired; *b* 13 Aug. 1929; *s* of Walter Erle Beavis and Mary Ann (*née* Sarjantson); *m* 1950, Joy Marion (*née* Jones); one *s* one *d*. *Educ:* Kilburn Grammar School. Joined RAF 1947; commnd 1949; served Fighter Comd Squadrons 1950–54, RNZAF 1954–56; flew Vulcan aircraft, Bomber Comd, 1958–62; Staff Coll., 1963; MoD, 1964–66; OC No 10

Squadron (VC10s), 1966–68; Group Captain Flying, Akrotiri, Cyprus, 1968–71; Asst Dir, Defence Policy, MoD, 1971–73; RCDS, 1974; RAF Germany, 1975–77 (SASO 1976–77); Dir Gen. RAF Training, 1977–80; Comdt, RAF Staff Coll, 1980–81; AOC-in-C, RAF Support Comd, 1981–84. CBIM. Freeman, City of London, 1980; Liveryman, GAPAN, 1983. *Recreation:* golf. *Address:* c/o Lloyds Bank, 202 High Street, Lincoln. *Club:* Royal Air Force.

BEAZER, Brian Cyril; Chairman and Chief Executive, C. H. Beazer (Holdings) PLC, since 1983; *b* 22 Feb. 1935; *s* of late Cyril Henry George Beazer and of Ada Vera Beazer; *m* 1958, Patricia (*née* White); one *d*. *Educ:* Wells Cathedral School. Joined C.H. Beazer, 1958; Man. Dir, 1968; apptd Chm. and Chief Exec. on death of his father in 1983. *Recreations:* walking, reading. *Address:* The Weavers House, Castle Combe, Wiltshire SN14 7HX.

BEAZLEY, Christopher John Pridham; Member (C) Cornwall and Plymouth, European Parliament, since 1984; *b* 5 Sept. 1952; *s* of Peter George Beazley, *qv*. *Educ:* Shrewsbury, Bristol Univ. Formerly Nuffield Research Fellow, School of European Studies, Sussex Univ. Vice Chm., Lewes and Eastbourne branch, European Movement, 1980; Wealden DC, 1979–83. *Address:* The Grange, Devoran, near Truro, Cornwall TR3 6PF. *Club:* Oriental.

BEAZLEY, Hon. Kim Christian; MP (ALP) Swan, Perth, Australia, since 1980; Minister of State for Defence, since 1984; *b* 14 Dec. 1948; *s* of Hon. Kim Edward Beazley and Betty Beazley; *m* 1974, Mary, *d* of Hon. Sir Shane Paltridge, KBE; two *d*. *Educ:* Univ. of Western Australia (MA); Oxford Univ. (Rhodes Scholar; MPhil). Tutor in Social and Political Theory, Murdoch Univ., WA, 1976–79, Lectr 1980. Minister of State for Aviation, and Minister Assisting the Minister for Defence, 1983–84; Special Minister of State, 1983–84. *Publication:* (with I. Clark) The Politics of Intrusion: the Super-Powers in the Indian Ocean, 1979. *Recreations:* swimming, reading. *Address:* Parliament House, Canberra, ACT 2600, Australia. *T:* (062) 73 3955.

BEAZLEY, Peter George; Member (C) Bedfordshire South, European Parliament, since 1984 (Bedfordshire, 1979–84); Vice-Chairman, Economic and Monetary Affairs and Industrial Policy Committee, European Parliament, since 1984; *b* 9 June 1922; *s* of Thomas Alfred and Agnes Alice Mary Beazley; *m* 1945, Joyce Marion Sulman; one *s* two *d* (and one *d* decd). *Educ:* Highgate Sch.; St John Baptist Coll., Oxford. 2nd Cl. Final Hons PPE, MA Oxon. Captain, Rifle Brigade, served in N Africa, Italy, Austria, 1942–47. Joined ICI, 1947; served in UK, Portugal, Germany, Belgium and S Africa as Manager, Gen. Manager, Divl Bd Dir, Vice Chm. and Man. Dir of associated cos, 1948–77; retd from ICI 1978. Member: European Democratic Gp Bureau, 1982–83; European Parlt Portuguese Parlt Jt delegn, 1979–84; European Parlt Japanese delegn, 1985. MRI; Mem., RIIA (Res. Fellow 1977–78). *Publication:* The Role of Western Technology Transfer in the Development of the Soviet Union's Chemical Industry (with V. Sobeslavsky), 1979. *Recreations:* golf, gardening. *Address:* Rest Harrow, 14 The Combe, Ratton, Eastbourne, East Sussex BN20 9DB. *T:* Eastbourne 504460; 4 Bridgewater Court, Little Gaddesden, Herts. *T:* Little Gaddesden 3548. *Club:* Oriental.
See also C. J. P. Beazley.

BECHER, Major Sir William Fane Wrixon-, 5th Bt, *cr* 1831; MC 1943; Temp. Major, Rifle Brigade (SRO); *b* 7 Sept. 1915; *o s* of Sir Eustace W. W. W. Becher, 4th Bt, and Hon. Constance Gough-Calthorpe, *d* of 6th Baron Calthorpe; *S* father, 1934; *m* 1st, 1946, Vanda (marr. diss. 1960; she *m* 1962, Rear-Adm. Viscount Kelburn, later 9th Earl of Glasgow), *d* of 4th Baron Vivian; one *s* one *d*; 2nd, 1960, Hon. Mrs Yvonne Mostyn. *Educ:* Harrow; Magdalene Coll., Cambridge. Served War of 1939–45; Western Desert and Tunisian Campaigns, 1940–43 (MC, wounded twice; taken prisoner at battle of Sidi Rezegh, Nov. 1941, and escaped); Italian Campaign, 1944; ADC to FM Lord Wilson, Supreme Allied Comdr Mediterranean. Lloyd's Underwriter, 1950. Member: British Boxing Bd of Control, 1961–82; Nat. Playing Fields Assoc., 1953–65 (Pres., Wiltshire Branch, NPFA, 1950–56). *Recreations:* golf and cricket (played cricket for Sussex, 1939, captained Wiltshire, 1949–53). *Heir: s* John William Michael Wrixon-Becher, *b* 29 Sept. 1950. *Address:* 16 Wilton Place, SW1; 37 Clabon Mews, SW1. *Clubs:* MCC, White's, Royal Green Jackets; I Zingari.

BECK, Prof. Arnold Hugh William, BSc (Eng), MA; Professor of Engineering, 1966–83, Head of Electrical Division, 1971–81, University of Cambridge, now Emeritus Professor; Life Fellow of Corpus Christi College, Cambridge, since 1983 (Fellow, 1962); Fellow of University College, London, since 1979; *y s* of Major Hugh Beck and Diana L. Beck; *m* 1947, Katharine Monica, *y d* of S. K. Ratcliffe; no *c*. *Educ:* Gresham's Sch., Holt; University Coll., London. Research Engr, Henry Hughes & Sons, 1937–41; seconded to Admty Signal Estab., 1941–45; Standard Telephones & Cables, 1947–58; Lectr, Cambridge Univ., 1958–64; Reader in Electrical Engrg, 1964–66. FIEEE 1959. *Publications:* Velocity Modulated Thermionic Tubes, 1948; Thermionic Valves, 1953; Space-charge Waves, 1958; Words and Waves, 1967; (with H. Ahmed) Introduction to Physical Electronics, 1968; Handbook of Vacuum Physics, Vol. 2, Parts 5 and 6, 1968; Statistical Mechanics, Fluctuations and Noise, 1976; papers in Jl IEE, Inst. Radio Engrs, etc. *Address:* 18 Earl Street, Cambridge. *T:* Cambridge 62997.

BECK, Rev. Brian Edgar, MA; Secretary of the Methodist Conference, since 1984; *b* 27 Sept. 1933; *o s* of A. G. and C. A. Beck; *m* 1958, Margaret Ludlow; three *d*. *Educ:* City of London School; Corpus Christi College, Cambridge (1st Cl. Classical Tripos pts 1 and 2); Wesley House, Cambridge (1st Cl. Theol. Tripos pt 2). BA 1955, MA 1959. Ordained Methodist Minister, 1960; Asst Tutor, Handsworth Coll., 1957–59; E Suffolk Circuit Minister, 1959–62; St Paul's United Theological Coll., Limuru, Kenya, 1962–68; Tutor, Wesley House, Cambridge, 1968–80, Principal 1980–84. Sec., E African Church Union Consultation Worship and Liturgy Cttee, 1963–68; Mem., World Methodist Council, 1966–71, 1981–; Co-Chm., Oxford Inst. of Methodist Theol. Studies, 1976–. Fernley-Hartley Lectr, 1978. *Publications:* (contrib.) Christian Belief, a Catholic-Methodist statement, 1970; (contrib.) Unity the Next Step? (ed P. Morgan), 1972; Reading the New Testament Today, 1977; (contrib.) Suffering and Martyrdom in the New Testament (ed Horbury and McNeile), 1981; articles in NT Studies, Epworth Review. *Recreations:* walking, jogging, DIY. *Address:* 1 Central Buildings, SW1H 9NH; 76 Beaumont Road, Purley, Croydon, Surrey CR2 2EG. *T:* 01–645 9162.

BECK, Sir Edgar (Charles), Kt 1975; CBE 1967; MA; FEng 1977; Chairman, John Mowlem & Company Ltd, 1961–79, President, since 1981; *b* 11 May 1911; *s* of Edgar Bee Beck and Nellie Stollard Beck (*née* Osborne); *m* 1933, Mary Agnes Sorapure (marr. diss. 1972); three *s* two *d*; *m* 1972, Anne Teresa Corbould. *Educ:* Lancing Coll.; Jesus Coll., Cambridge (MA). Joined John Mowlem & Co. Ltd as Engineer, 1933: Dir 1940; Man. Dir 1958. Director: Scaffolding Great Britain Ltd, 1942–85 (Chm., 1958–78); Builders' Accident Insce Ltd, 1959, Dep. Chm., 1969; Mem., ECGD Adv. Council, 1964–69; President, Fedn of Civil Engrg Contractors, 1971–75 (Chm., 1958–59); Chairman: Export Gp for the Constructional Industries, 1959–63; Brit. Hosps Export Council, 1964–75. Under-writing Mem. of Lloyd's, 1955–. FEng; FICE. *Recreations:* golf, salmon fishing. *Address:* 13 Eaton Place, SW1. *T:* 01–235 7455. *Clubs:* Buck's; Swinley Forest Golf.

BECK, James Henry John; Director of Industries and Farms, Prison Department, Home Office, 1976–80; *b* 5 April 1920; *s* of James Henry and Elizabeth Kate Beck; *m* 1942, Doris Peacock; two *d*. *Educ:* Polytechnic Secondary Sch., Regent Street, W1. Entered Home Office as Clerical Officer, 1937; HM Forces, 1939; returned to Home Office as Executive Officer, 1946; Higher Exec. Officer, 1950; Sen. Exec. Officer, 1958; Principal, 1963; Asst Sec., 1968. *Address:* Scarlet Oaks, Ridgway, Pyrford, Woking, Surrey GU22 8PN. *T:* Byfleet 46064.

BECK, Prof. (John) Swanson; FRSE 1984; Professor of Pathology, University of Dundee, since 1971; Consultant Pathologist, Tayside Health Board, since 1974; *b* 22 Aug. 1928; *s* of late Dr John Beck and Mary (*née* Barbour); *m* 1960, Marion Tudhope Paterson; one *s* one *d*. *Educ:* Glasgow Acad.; Univ. of Glasgow. BSc, MB, ChB, MD, FRCPG, FRCPE, FRCPath. Lectr in Pathology, Univ. of Glasgow, 1958–63; Sen. Lectr in Pathology, Univ. of Aberdeen, 1963–71. Consultant Pathologist: N Eastern Regional Hosp. Bd, 1963–71; Eastern Regional Hosp. Bd, 1971–74. Chairman: Breast Tumour Panel, MRC, 1979–; Biomedical Res. Cttee, SHHD, 1983– (Mem. 1975–79). Member: Cell Biology and Disorders Bd, MRC, 1978–82; Health Services Res. Panel, MRC, 1981–82; Chief Scientist's Cttee, SHHD, 1983–; Tayside Health Bd, 1983–. *Publications:* various papers in Jl of Pathology and other medical and scientific jls. *Recreations:* walking, gardening, sailing. *Address:* 598 Perth Road, Dundee DD2 1QA. *T:* Dundee 57298. *Club:* Royal Commonwealth Society.

BECK, (Richard) Theodore, FRIBA, FSA, FRSA, MRTPI; architect; *b* 11 March 1905; *s* of Alfred Charles Beck and Grace Sophia Beck (*née* Reading); *m* 1950, Margaret Beryl Page; one *s* one *d*. *Educ:* Haileybury; Architectural Association Sch. Past Mem. Council, Royal Archaeological Inst.; Past Master: Broderers Company; Barber-Surgeons Company; Parish Clerks Co.; Mem. Court of Common Council, Corporation of London, 1963–82; Dep., Ward of Farringdon Within, 1978–82; Sheriff, City of London, 1969–70; former Dep. Chm., Central Criminal Court Extension Cttee. Former Dep. Governor, the Hon. the Irish Soc.; Chm., Governors, City of London Sch., 1971–75, Dep. Chm., 1976; Chm., Schools Cttee, Corporation of London, 1977, Dep. Chm., 1978. Former Governor: Bridewell Royal Hosp.; King Edward's Sch., Witley; Christ's Hospital (Aldermanic Almoner); Reeves Foundn. Vicary Lectr, 1969; Prestonian Lectr, 1975. *Publication:* The Cutting Edge: early history of the surgeons of London, 1975. *Recreations:* gardening, archaeology. *Address:* Blundens House, Upper Froyle, Alton, Hants. *T:* Bentley 23147. *Clubs:* East India, Devonshire, Sports and Public Schools, City Livery.

BECK, (Rudolph) Rolf, (Baron Rolf Beck); Chairman and Managing Director of Slip and Molyslip Group of Companies since 1939; *b* 25 March 1914; *s* of Baron Dr Otto Beck (famous industrialist and politician in Austrian and Hungarian Empire; also special Envoy and Representative in Switzerland of Emperor Franz Josef of Austria during 1914–18 War) and Baroness Margaret Beck; *m* 1st, 1944, Elizabeth Lesley Brenchley (marr. diss.), *d* of Captain Fletcher, RN; one *s*; 2nd, 1979, Countess Mariana von Rosen, *d* of Count and Countess Mörner, Bjorksund, Sweden. *Educ:* Theresanium Mil. Acad.; Univs of Geneva, Lausanne, Vienna. Degrees in Engrg and Chem. Whilst still at univ. took up racing and rally driving seriously in a Skoda car; became well known amateur driver, 1935; came to London as rep. of Skoda works to make Skoda cars in UK with 51 per cent British parts and labour and 49 per cent Czechoslovakian parts; outbreak of war ended this develt, 1938; founded Slip Products Ltd, 1939; discovered Milex (petrol economiser), 1940, and Dieslip (fuel additive of interest to the Admty and Min. of War Transport); apptd Adviser on gas producer research, 1940; acted as export adviser to Rolls Royce and toured USA twice. Formed cos: Slip Products and Engrg, Slip Trading and Shipping also Slip Auto Sales and Engrg, 1948–49. Invented for automobiles or oil drilling: Molyslip (lubricant); Copaslip (compound), 1959. Founded: Slip Internat. Ltd; Molyslip Trading, 1961; Molyslip Holdings, 1964; Molyslip Chemicals Ltd, 1967; Molytex Internat., 1970; on 1 Nov. 1980 a 50/50 company formed between Molyslip Holdings Ltd and Jet-Lube Lubricants Ltd, Maidenhead, called Molyslip Internat. Sales Ltd. Introduced additives: Multiglide and Molyglide, 1972; invented Molyslip 2001 (a metal treatment to be added to oil which considerably reduces engine wear, petrol and oil consumption, water and oil temps), 1984. Fellow of Scientific Exploration Soc.; FZS. *Recreations:* skiing, water skiing, shooting, sailing. *Heir: s* Stephen Rolf Beck, *b* 2 Dec. 1948. *Address:* 62 Bishops Mansions, Bishops Park Road, SW6. *T:* 01–731 3021; Cap Davia, Marine de Davia, Ile Rousse, Corsica. *T:* Ile Rousse 600.625. *Clubs:* Royal Automobile; Royal Scottish Automobile; Royal Harwich Yacht; West Mersey Yacht; Hurlingham; Union Interalliée (Paris); Princeton (NY).

BECK, Swanson; *see* Beck, J. S.

BECKE, Mrs Shirley Cameron, OBE 1974; QPM 1972; Vice-Chairman, 1976–83 and Regional Administrator, London Region, 1974–79, Women's Royal Voluntary Service, retired; *b* 29 April 1917; *er d* of late George L. Jennings, AMIGasE and Marion Jennings; *m* 1954, Rev. Justice Becke, MBE, TD, FCA; no *c*. *Educ:* privately; Ealing Co. Gram. Sch. Trained in Gas Engineering, 1935–40. Joined Metropolitan Police as Constable, 1941; served in various ranks; Woman Commander, 1969–74. OStJ 1975. *Recreations:* reading, keeping cats. *Address:* 51 St Pancras, Chichester, Sussex PO19 4LT. *T:* Chichester 784295.

BECKE, Lt-Col William Hugh Adamson, CMG 1964; DSO 1945; *b* 24 Sept. 1916; *er s* of late Brig.-Gen. J. H. W. Becke, CMG, DSO, AFC, and late Mrs A. P. Becke (*née* Adamson); *m* 1945, Mary Catherine, 3rd *d* of late Major G. M. Richmond, Kincairney, Murthly, Perthshire. *Educ:* Charterhouse; RMC Sandhurst. Commissioned in The Sherwood Foresters, 1937. British Military Mission to Greece, 1949–52; Asst Military Adviser to the High Commissioner for the UK in Pakistan, 1957–59; Military Attaché, Djakarta, 1962–64; retd 1966. Private Sec. and Comptroller to Governor of Victoria, 1969–74; Personnel Officer, Gas and Fuel Corp. of Vic, 1974–82. *Address:* 3 Chambers Street, South Yarra, Vic 3141, Australia. *Clubs:* Army and Navy; Melbourne, Victoria Racing (Melbourne).

BECKERMAN, Wilfred, PhD, DPhil; Fellow of Balliol College, Oxford, since 1975; Reader in Economics, Oxford University, since 1978; *b* 19 May 1925; *s* of Morris and Mathilda Beckerman; *m* 1952, Nicole Geneviève Ritter (*d* 1979); one *s* two *d*. *Educ:* Ealing County Sch.; Trinity Coll., Cambridge (MA, PhD); MA, DPhil Oxon. RNVR, 1943–46. Trinity Coll., Cambridge, 1946–50; Lecturer in Economics, Univ. of Nottingham, 1950–52; OEEC and OECD, Paris, 1952–61; National Inst. of Economic and Social Research, 1962–63. Fellow of Balliol Coll., Oxford, 1964–69; Prof. of Political Economy, Univ. of London, and Head of Dept of Political Economy, UCL, 1969–75; The Economic Adviser to the Pres. of the Board of Trade (leave of absence from Balliol), 1967–69. Mem., Royal Commn on Environmental Pollution, 1970–73. Mem. Exec. Cttee, NIESR, 1973–. Elie Halévy Vis. Prof. Institut d'Etudes Politiques, Paris, 1977; Resident Scholar, Woodrow Wilson Internat. Center for Scholars, Washington, DC, 1982. Consultant: World Bank; OECD; ILO. Pres., Section F (Economics), BAAS, 1978. *Publications:* The British Economy in 1975 (with associates), 1965; International

Comparisons of Real Incomes, 1966; An Introduction to National Income Analysis, 1968; (ed and contrib.) The Labour Government's Economic Record, 1972; In Defence of Economic Growth, 1974; Measures of Leisure, Equality and Welfare, 1978; (ed and contrib.) Slow Growth in Britain: causes and consequences, 1979; Poverty and the Impact of Income Maintenance Programmes, 1979; (with S. Clark) Poverty and the Impact of Social Security in Britain since 1961, 1982; (ed and contrib.) Wage Rigidity and Unemployment, 1986; articles in Economic Jl, Economica, Econometrica, Review of Economic Studies, Review of Economics and Statistics, etc. *Recreations:* various. *Address:* Balliol College, Oxford OX1 3BJ. *T:* Oxford 244784.

BECKETT, family name of **Baron Grimthorpe.**

BECKETT, Prof. Arnold Heyworth, OBE 1983; Professor of Pharmacy, Chelsea College (University of London), 1959–85, now Emeritus; *b* 12 Feb. 1920; *m* 1st, 1942, Miriam Eunice Webster; one *s* one *d*; 2nd, Susan Yvonne Harris. *Educ:* Baines Grammar Sch., Poulton-le-Fylde; Sch. of Pharmacy and Birkbeck Coll., University of London, FPS 1942; BSc 1947; PhD 1950; DSc London, 1959. Head, Dept of Pharmacy, Chelsea Coll. of Sci. and Technology, 1959–79. Member: Med. Commn, Internat. Olympic Cttee, 1968–; British Olympic Assoc. Med. Commn; Chm., Bd of Pharmaceutical Sciences, Fédération Internat. Pharmaceutique, 1960–80; Pres., Pharmaceutical Soc. of GB, 1981– (Mem. Council, 1965–). Vis. Prof. to Univs, USA and Canada. Examr in Pharmaceut. Chem., Univs in UK, Nigeria, Ghana, Singapore. Pereira Medal, 1942; STAS Medal, Belg. Chem. Soc., 1962; Hanbury Meml Medal, 1974; Charter Gold Medal, 1977; Mem. of Olympic Order, Silver Medal, 1980. Hon. DSc: Heriot-Watt Univ., 1976; Univ. of Uppsala, 1977. *Publications:* (co-author) Practical Pharmaceutical Chemistry, 1962; Part 1, 3rd edn, 1975, Part 2, 3rd edn, 1976; founder Co-editor, Jl of Medicinal Chemistry; research contribs to jls. *Recreations:* travel, sport, photography. *Address:* 16 Crestbrook Avenue, Palmers Green, N13.

BECKETT, Bruce Probart, FRIBA, FRTPI, FRIAS, FCIOB; Partner and Chairman, Hutchison Locke & Monk, Chartered Architects, Planners and Landscape Architects, since 1984; Chairman, Helm Securities Ltd, since 1985; *b* 7 June 1924; *s* of J. D. L. Beckett and Florence Theresa (*née* Probart); *m* 1957, Jean McDonald; two *s* three *d* (incl. twin *s* and *d*). *Educ:* Rondebosch Boys' High Sch., Cape Town; Univ. of Cape Town (BArch with distinction, 1950); University Coll. London (Diploma in Town Planning, 1963). Active Service SA Navy, 1943; Midshipman, 1943; Sub-Lieut, 1944; seconded RN, 1944; Lieut, 1946. ARIBA 1950, FRIBA 1968; FRIAS 1968. Mem. Inst. S African Architects, 1950; FRTPI (AMTPI 1966); FCIOB 1979. Private practice in S Africa, 1952–59, London, 1960. Sen. Architect, War Office, 1961; Superintending Grade Arch., Directorate-Gen. of Res. and Development, 1963–67; Chief Architect, 1967–84 and Dir of Bldg, 1978–84, Scottish Office, retd. Dep. Leader, Timber Trade Mission to Canada, 1964. A Vice-Pres., RIBA, 1972–73, 1975–76, 1976–77; Hon. Librarian, 1976–78. Sec. of State for Scotland's nominee on ARCUK, 1970–85, RIBA nominee, 1985–; Member Council: EAA, 1970–78; RIAS, 1971–78, 1984–; RIBA, 1972–78; Member: Sec. of State for Environment's Construction and Housing Res. Adv. Council, 1968–79; Building Res. Estabt Adv. Cttees in England and Scotland, 1970–84; York Adv. Cttee for continuing educn for building profession, 1975–80. Assessor to Scottish Cttee of Design Council, 1974–84; Civic Trust Assessor, 1985–. *Publications:* papers on industrialised building, contract procedure, etc, in various jls; HMSO publications on Scottish housing, educational and health buildings. *Recreations:* sailing, walking. *Address:* Summerfield, Vines Cross Road, Horam, near Heathfield, East Sussex TN21 0HE; (office) 9 St Colme Street, Edinburgh EH3 6AA. *T:* 031–225 5078. *Clubs:* Arts; New (Edinburgh); Western Province Sports (Kelvin Grove, Cape Town).

BECKETT, Maj.-Gen. Denis Arthur, CB 1971; DSO 1944; OBE 1960; *b* 19 May 1917; *o s* of late Archibald Beckett, Woodford Green, Essex; *m* 1946, Elizabeth (marr. diss. 1974), *er d* of late Col Guy Edwards, Upper Slaughter, Glos; one *s*; *m* 1978, Nancy Ann Hitt. *Educ:* Forest Sch.; Chard Sch. Joined Hon. Artillery Co., 1939; commnd into Essex Regt, 1940; served in W Africa, Middle East, Italy and Greece, 1940–45; DAA & QMG and Bde Major, Parachute Bdes, 1948–50; Instructor, RMA Sandhurst, 1951–53; Staff Coll., Camberley, 1953–56; Second in Comd 3rd Bn Para. Regt, 1956–58; comd 2nd Bn Para. Regt, 1958–60; jssc 1960–61; comd 19 Bde, 1961–63; idc 1964; DAG, BAOR, 1965–66; Chief of Staff, Far East Land Forces, 1966–68; Dir of Personal Services (Army), 1968–71, retired 1971. *Address:* 12 Wellington House, Eton Road, NW3. *Clubs:* Army and Navy, Lansdowne.

BECKETT, Maj.-Gen. Edwin Horace Alexander, MBE 1974; Chief of Staff, HQ BAOR, since 1985; *b* 16 May 1937; *s* of William Alexander Beckett and Doris Beckett; *m* 1963, Micaela Elizabeth Benedicta, *d* of Col Sir Edward Malet, Bt, *qv*; three *s* one *d*. *Educ:* Henry Fanshawe School; RMA Sandhurst; ndc, psc, sq. Commissioned 1957 West Yorks Regt; regtl service in Aden (despatches 1968), Gibraltar, Germany and N Ireland; DAA&QMG 11 Armd Brigade, 1972–74; CO 1 PWO, 1976–78 (despatches 1977); GSO1 (DS) Staff Coll., 1979; Comdt Junior Div., Staff Coll., 1980; Comdr UKMF and 6 Field Force, 1981; Comdr UKMF, 1 Inf. Brigade and Tidworth Garrison, 1982; Director: Concepts, MoD, 1983–84; Army Plans and Programmes, MoD, 1984–85. *Recreations:* fishing, picture framing, farming for fun. *Address:* Lloyds Bank, Cox's & King's Branch, 6 Pall Mall, SW1. *Club:* Naval and Military.

BECKETT, Prof. James Camlin, MA; Professor of Irish History, Queen's University of Belfast, 1958–75; *b* 8 Feb. 1912; 3rd *s* of Alfred Beckett and Frances Lucy Bushell. *Educ:* Royal Belfast Academical Instn; Queen's Univ., Belfast. History Master, Belfast Royal Academy, 1934; Lectr in Modern History, Queen's Univ., Belfast, 1945, Reader in Modern History, 1952. Fellow Commoner, Peterhouse, Cambridge, 1955–56; Cummings Lectr, McGill Univ., Montreal, 1976; Mellon Prof., Tulane Univ., New Orleans, 1977; Member: Irish Manuscripts Commn, 1959; Royal Commission on Historical Manuscripts, 1960. Hon. DLitt New Univ. of Ulster, 1979; Hon. DLit Queen's Univ. of Belfast, 1980. FRHistS; MRIA. *Publications:* Protestant Dissent in Ireland, 1687–1780, 1948; Short History of Ireland, 1952; (ed with T. W. Moody) Ulster since 1800: a Political and Economic Survey, 1954; (ed with T. W. Moody) Ulster since 1800: a Social Survey, 1957; (with T. W. Moody) Queen's Belfast, 1845–1949, 1959; The Making of Modern Ireland 1603–1923, 1966; (ed with R. E. Glasscock) Belfast: the Origin and Growth of an Industrial City, 1966; (ed) Historical Studies VII, 1969; Confrontations, 1973; The Anglo-Irish Tradition, 1976; contrib. The Ulster Debate, 1972; articles, reviews, etc., in English Hist. Rev., History, Irish Hist. Studies and other jls. *Recreations:* chess, walking. *Address:* 19 Wellington Park Terrace, Belfast, N Ireland BT9 6DR. *Club:* Ulster Reform (Belfast).

BECKETT, John Angus, CB 1965; CMG 1956; MA; Chairman, Davy Offshore Modules Ltd, since 1984; Director, Total Oil Marine Ltd, since 1979; *b* 6 July 1909; *s* of late John Beckett, BA; *m* 1935, Una Joan, *yr d* of late George Henry Wright; one *s* two *d*. *Educ:* privately; Sidney Sussex Coll., Cambridge. BA 2nd Cl. Hons (Geog. Tripos); Mem., Cambridge Iceland Expedition, 1932. Schoolmaster, 1933–40; entered Civil Service, 1940; Principal Private Sec. to Minister of Fuel and Power, 1946–47; Asst Sec., Min. of Fuel and Power, 1947–59; Under-Sec., 1959 (Gas Div., 1959–64, Petroleum Div., 1964–72) Min. of Power, Min. of Technology, DTI; retired 1972. Chm., Petroleum Cttee of OEEC, 1948–50, 1955–59, 1965–72; Petroleum Attaché, British Embassy, Washington, 1950–53. Chm., Press Offshore Gp (formerly William Press Production Systems), 1972–83. *Publication:* Iceland Adventure, 1934. *Recreations:* rowing, Rugby football, administration. *Address:* Tyle Cottage, Needlesbank, Godstone, Surrey RH9 8LN. *T:* Godstone 842295. *Clubs:* St Stephen's Constitutional; Arctic (Cambridge).

BECKETT, John Michael; Chairman and Chief Executive, Woolworth Holdings plc, 1982–86; *b* 22 June 1929; *yr s* of H. N. Beckett, MBE, and C. L. Beckett; *m* 1955, Joan Mary, *o d* of Percy and F. M. Rogerson; five *d*. *Educ:* Wolverhampton Grammar Sch.; Magdalen Coll., Oxford (BA 1953, MA 1957). Nat. Service and Reg. Commn RA, 1947–50; TA 1950–60. Called to Bar, Gray's Inn, 1954. Bar, 1954–55; Tootal Ltd, 1955–58; Tarmac Ltd, 1958–75; Dir, 1963–82 (non-exec., 1975–82); Chief Exec., British Sugar Corp. Ltd, 1975–82. Dir, Johnson Matthey, 1985–86. Hon. MIQ; FRSA; CBIM. *Club:* Naval and Military.

See also Sir T. N. Beckett.

BECKETT, Margaret M., (Mrs L. A. Beckett); MP (Lab) Derby South, since 1983; *b* Jan. 1943; *d* of Cyril and Winifred Jackson; *m* 1979, Lionel A. Beckett. *Educ:* Notre Dame High Sch., Norwich; Manchester Coll. of Sci. and Technol. Formerly: student apprentice, AEI, Manchester; exptl officer, Manchester Univ.; Labour Party res. asst; political adviser, Minister for Overseas Develt, 1974; Principal Researcher, Granada TV, 1979–83. Contested (Lab) Lincoln, Feb. 1974; MP (Lab) Lincoln, Oct. 1974–1979; PPS to Minister for Overseas Develt, 1974–75; Asst Govt Whip, 1975–76; Parly Under-Sec. of State, DES, 1976–79; Opposition front bench spokesman on health and social security, 1984–. Mem. NEC, Labour Party, 1980–81, 1985–. *Address:* Rose Cottage, 102 Village Street, Old Normanton, Derby.

BECKETT, Sir Martyn Gervase, 2nd Bt, *cr* 1921; MC 1945; RIBA; Architect; *b* 6 Nov. 1918; *s* of Hon. Sir Gervase Beckett, 1st Bt, and Lady Marjorie Beckett (*d* 1964), *e d* of 5th Earl of Warwick; *S* father, 1937; *m* 1941, Hon. Priscilla Brett, *y d* of 3rd Viscount Esher, GBE; two *s* one *d*. *Educ:* Eton; Trinity Coll., Cambridge. Enlisted in Green Howards, 1939; commnd Welsh Guards, 1940; served War of 1939–45 (MC); Lieut (temp. Captain). DipArch 1951, ARIBA 1952. Built or reconstructed several country houses and housing estates, hotels, libraries etc; works to various scheduled buildings and for National Trust. Architect to King's College Chapel, Cambridge, 1960– (internal alterations and renovations to the Chapel, 1968); Cons. Architect to: Savoy Hotel Gp, 1981–; Temple Bar Trust, 1983–; Ampleforth Coll., 1984; Gordonstoun, 1954–58. Exhibited: RA, London, provinces; one man exhibn, Clarges Gall., 1980 and 1983. Trustee: The Wallace Collection, 1972– (Chm. 1976–); British Museum, 1978–; CPRE Trust, 1983–; Chm., Yorkshire Regional Cttee, Nat. Trust, 1980–85; Member: N York Moor Nat. Park Cttee, 1972–78; Council of Management, Chatsworth House Trust, 1981; President: Ryedale Br., CPRE, 1964–; Friends of York Art Gall., 1970–83. Council, RSPB, 1985–. FRSA 1982; FAMS 1955. *Recreations:* painting, photography, piano. *Heir: s* Richard Gervase Beckett [*b* 27 March 1944; *m* 1976, Elizabeth, *d* of Major Hugo and Lady Caroline Waterhouse; three *d*]. *Address:* 3 St Albans Grove, W8. *T:* 01–937 7834; Kirkdale Farm, Nawton, Yorks. *Clubs:* Brooks's, MCC.

BECKETT, Noel George Stanley; HM Diplomatic Service, retired; *b* 3 Dec. 1916; *s* of Captain J. R. Beckett, MC, and Ethel Barker; *m* 1948, Huguette Laure Charlotte Voos (*d* 1982); one *s* two *d*. *Educ:* Peterhouse, Cambridge. MA Hons Cantab 1938, BScEcon Hons London 1961. Mem., Inst. of Linguists. British Embassy, Paris, 1946; UK Commercial Rep., Frankfurt and Cologne, 1949; Lima, 1956; Bonn, 1959; British Embassy, Addis Ababa, 1963 and liaison officer with Econ. Commn for Africa; Sec., European Conf. on Satellite Communications, FO, 1965; British Embassy, Beirut, 1968; Consul-Gen., Casablanca, 1973–76. *Recreations:* painting, art studies, photography, reading, travel. *Address:* The Second House, South Drive, Dorking, Surrey. *T:* Dorking 882665. *Club:* Royal Commonwealth Society.

BECKETT, Samuel, CLit 1984; author and playwright; *b* Dublin, 1906. *Educ:* Portora Royal School; Trinity Coll., Dublin (MA). Lectr in English, Ecole Normale Supérieure, Paris, 1928–30; Lectr in French, Trinity Coll., Dublin, 1930–32; from 1932 has lived mostly in France, in Paris since 1937. Nobel Prize for Literature, 1969. *Publications: verse:* Whoroscope, 1930; Echo's Bones, 1935; Collected Poems in English and French, 1977; Collected Poems 1930–1978, 1984; *prose:* Collected Shorter Prose 1945–1980, 1984; *novels:* Murphy, 1938; Watt, 1944; Molloy, 1951 (Eng. trans. 1956); Malone meurt, 1952 (Eng. trans. Malone Dies, 1956); L'Innommable, 1953 (Eng. trans. 1960); Comment c'est, 1961 (Eng. trans. 1964); Imagination Dead Imagine, 1966 (trans. from French by author); First Love, 1973; Mercier and Camier, 1974; Company, 1980; Ill Seen Ill Said, 1982; *short stories:* More Pricks than Kicks, 1934; Nouvelles et textes pour rien, 1955; Le Dépeupleur, 1971 (Eng. trans., The Lost Ones, 1972); Four Novellas, 1977; *plays:* En attendant Godot, 1952 (Eng. trans. Waiting for Godot, 1954); Fin de Partie, 1957 (Eng. trans. End Game); Krapp's Last Tape, 1959; La Dernière Bande, 1961; Happy Days, 1961; Play, 1963; Film, 1972; Breath and Other Short Plays, 1972; Not I, 1973; Collected Shorter Plays of Samuel Beckett, 1984; *radio plays:* All that Fall, 1957; Embers, 1959; Cascando, 1964; *TV plays:* Ghost Trio and . . . But the Clouds . . . , 1977. *Address:* c/o Faber & Faber Ltd, 3 Queen Square, WC1.

BECKETT, Sir Terence (Norman), Kt 1978; CBE 1974; FEng; Director General, Confederation of British Industry, 1980–86; *b* 13 Dec. 1923; *s* of late Horace Norman Beckett, MBE and late Clarice Lillian (*née* Allsop); *m* 1950, Sylvia Gladys Asprey; one *d*. *Educ:* London Sch. of Econs. BScEcon, FIMechE, CBIM, FIMI. Captain REME, British Army (UK, India, Malaya), 1945–48; RARO, 1949–62. Company Trainee, Ford Motor Co. Ltd, 1950; Asst in office of Dep. Chm. and Man. Dir, 1951; Man., Styling, Briggs Motor Bodies Ltd (Ford subsid.), 1954; Admin Man., Engrg, Briggs, 1955; Manager: Product Staff, 1955; Product Planning Staff, 1961 (responsible for Cortina, Transit Van, 'D' series truck); Marketing Staff, 1963; Dir, Car Div., 1964; Exec. Dir, Ford Motor Co. Ltd, 1966 and Dir of Sales, 1968; Vice-Pres., European and Overseas Sales Ops, Ford of Europe Inc., 1969; Man. Dir and Chief Exec., 1974–80 and Chm., 1976–80, Ford Motor Co. Ltd; Chm., Ford Motor Credit Co. Ltd, 1976–80; Director: ICI, 1976–80, Automotive Finance Ltd, 1974–77. Member: NEDC, 1980–; Engineering Industries Council, 1975–80; BIM Council, 1976–77; CBI Council, 1976–80; Grand Council, Motor and Cycle Trades Benevolent Fund (BEN), 1976–80; SMMT Council and Exec. Cttee, 1974–80; Council, Automobile Div., IMechE, 1979–80; Vice Pres. and Hon. Fellow, Inst. of the Motor Industry, 1974–80; Vice-Pres., Conference on Schs, Sci. and Technol., 1979–80; Chm., Governing Body, London Business Sch., 1980–86; Member Court: Cranfield Inst. of Technology, 1977–82; Univ. of Essex, 1985; Governor, Nat. Inst. of Econ. and Social Res., 1978–; Governor and Mem. Court, LSE, 1978–; Mem. Court of Assts, Worshipful Co. of Engineers, 1983–. Patron: MSC Award Scheme for Disabled People, 1979–80; AIESEC, 1985. Lectures: Stamp, London Univ., 1982; Pfizer, Kent at Canterbury Univ., 1983. Hon. Fellow, Sidney Sussex Coll., Cambridge, 1981; Hon. DSc: Cranfield, 1977; Heriot-Watt, 1981; Hon. DSc (Econ.) London, 1982. FRSA

1984. Hambro Businessman of the Year, 1978; BIM Gold Medal, 1980. *Recreations:* ornithology, music. *Address:* c/o Barclays Bank plc, Goodmayes Road, Goodmayes, Ilford, Essex. *Club:* Athenæum.
See also J. M. Beckett.

BECKETT, Veronica Evelyn, (Mrs A. J. Sutherland); *see* Sutherland, V. E.

BECKETT, William Cartwright, CB 1978; LLM; Solicitor to the Corporation of Lloyd's, since 1985; *b* 21 Sept. 1929; *s* of late William Beckett and Emily (*née* Cartwright); *m* 1st, 1956, Marjorie Jean Hoskin; two *s*; 2nd, 1974, Lesley Margaret Furlonger. *Educ:* Salford Grammar Sch.; Manchester Univ. (LLB 1950, LLM 1952). Called to Bar, Middle Temple, 1952. Joined Treasury Solicitor's Dept, 1956; Board of Trade, 1965; Asst Solicitor, DEP, 1969; Under-Sec., DTI, 1972; Dep.-Sec. 1977; Legal Secretary, Law Officers' Dept, 1975–80; Solicitor, DTI, 1980–84. *Recreations:* music, golf. *Address:* Park House, Bradwell, near Braintree, Essex. *T:* Braintree 61109. *Club:* Reform.

BECKINGHAM, Prof. Charles Fraser, FBA 1983; Professor of Islamic Studies, University of London, 1965–81, now Emeritus; International Director, Fontes Historiae Africanae Project, Union Académique Internationale, since 1986; *b* 18 Feb. 1914; *o c* of Arthur Beckingham, ARBA and Alice Beckingham, Houghton, Hunts; *m* 1946, Margery (*d* 1966), *o d* of John Ansell; one *d*. *Educ:* Grammar Sch., Huntingdon; Queens' Coll., Cambridge (scholar, Members' English prizeman, 1934). Dept of Printed Books, British Museum, 1936–46. Seconded to military and naval Intelligence, 1942–46. Foreign Office (GCHQ), 1946–51; Lectr in Islamic History, Manchester Univ., 1951–55; Sen. Lectr, 1955–58; Prof. of Islamic Studies, 1958–65. Pres., Hakluyt Soc., 1969–72; Treas., Royal Asiatic Soc., 1964–67, Pres., 1967–70, 1976–79, Hon. Fellow, Sri Lanka Branch, 1978. Chm., St Marylebone Soc., 1980–84. Jt Editor, 1961–64, Editor, 1965, Jl of Semitic Studies; Editor, Jl of RAS, 1984–. *Publications:* contribs to Admiralty Handbook of Western Arabia, 1946; (with G. W. B. Huntingford) Some Records of Ethiopia, 1954; Introduction to Atlas of the Arab World and Middle East, 1960; (with G. W. B. Huntingford) A True Relation of the Prester John of the Indies, 1961; Bruce's Travels (ed and selected), 1964; The Achievements of Prester John, 1966; (ed) Islam, in, Religion in the Middle East (ed A. J. Arberry), 1969; (with E. Ullendorff) The Hebrew Letters of Prester John, 1982; Between Islam and Christendom, 1983; (ed) The Itinerário of Jerónimo Lobo, 1984; articles in learned jls. *Address:* 56 Queen Anne Street, W1M 9LA. *Club:* Travellers'.

BECKLAKE, Dr Ernest John Stephen; Keeper, Department of Engineering, Science Museum, since 1985; *b* 24 June 1943; *s* of Ernest and Evelyn Becklake; *m* 1965, Susan Elizabeth (*née* Buckle), BSc; two *s*. *Educ:* Bideford Grammar Sch.; Exeter Univ. (BSc, PhD). Engr, EMI Electronics, Wells, 1967–69; Post-Doctoral Fellow, Victoria Univ., BC, Canada, 1969–70; Sen. Scientist, Marconi Space and Def. Systems, Frimley, 1970–72; Science Museum: Asst Keeper, Dept of Earth and Space Sciences, 1972–80; Keeper, Dept of Elect. Engrg, Communications and Circulation, 1980–85. *Publications:* Man and the Moon, 1980; (series editor) Exploration and Discovery, 1980–; technical pubns in Electronics Letters, Jl of Physics D, Jl of British Interplanetary Soc., and Spaceflight. *Recreations:* gardening, golf, rugby. *Address:* Tree Wood, Robin Hood Lane, Sutton Green, Guildford, Surrey. *T:* Woking 66931. *Club:* Puttenham Golf.

BECKMAN, Michael David, QC 1976; *b* 6 April 1932; *s* of Nathan and Esther Beckman; *m* 1966, Sheryl Robin (*née* Kyle) (marr. diss.); two *d*. *Educ:* King's Coll., London (LLB (Hons)). Called to the Bar, Lincoln's Inn, 1954. *Recreations:* various. *Address:* Bullards, Widford, Herts. *T:* Much Hadham 2669; (chambers) 19 Old Buildings, Lincoln's Inn, WC2; 3 East Pallants, Chichester. *Club:* Tennis de Talloires.

BECKWITH, John Gordon, FBA 1974; FSA 1968; Keeper, Department of Architecture and Sculpture, Victoria and Albert Museum, 1974–79; *b* 2 Dec. 1918; *s* of late John Frederick Beckwith. *Educ:* Ampleforth Coll., York; Exeter Coll., Oxford (Loscombe Richards Exhibnr; Amelia Jackson Student). MA. Served with The Duke of Wellington's Regt, 1939–45. Victoria and Albert Museum: Asst Keeper, Dept of Textiles, 1948; Asst Keeper, Dept of Architecture and Sculpture, 1955, Dep. Keeper, 1958. Vis. Fellow of Harvard Univ. at Dumbarton Oaks Res. Library and Collection, Washington, DC, 1950–51; Visiting Professor: at Harvard Univ. (Fogg Museum of Art), 1964; at Univ. of Missouri, Columbia, Mo, 1968–69; Slade Prof. of Fine Art, Oxford Univ., 1978–79. Reynolds-Stephens Meml Lecture, RBS, 1965. Mem., Centre International des Etudes des Textils Anciens at Lyon, 1953–. *Publications:* The Andrews Diptych, 1958; Coptic Textiles, 1959; Caskets from Cordoba, 1960; The Art of Constantinople, 1961; The Veroli Casket, 1962; Coptic Sculpture, 1963; The Basilewsky Situla, 1963; Early Medieval Art, 1964; The Adoration of the Magi in Whalebone, 1966; Early Christian and Byzantine Art, Pelican History of Art, 1970; Ivory Carvings in Early Medieval England, 1972; Catalogue of Exhibition, Ivory Carvings in Early Medieval England 700–1200, 1974; contrib. Art Bulletin, Burlington Magazine, etc. *Recreation:* music. *Address:* Flat 12, 77 Ladbroke Grove, W11 2PF. *T:* 01–727 7277.

BECTIVE, Earl of; Thomas Michael Ronald Christopher Taylour; *b* 10 Feb. 1959; *s* and *heir* of 6th Marquis of Headfort, *qv*. *Educ:* Harrow; RAC Cirencester. *Address:* Horsley Hall, Eccleshall, Stafford. *Clubs:* Lansdowne; Royal Dublin Society (Dublin).

BEDBROOK, Sir George (Montario), Kt 1978; OBE 1963; FRCS; FRACS; Senior Surgeon, Spinal Unit, Royal Perth Hospital and Royal Perth Rehabilitation Hospital, since 1972; *b* 8 Nov. 1921; *s* of Arthur Bedbrook and Ethel (*née* Prince); *m* 1946, Jessie Violet (*née* Page); two *s* three *d*. *Educ:* University High Sch., Melbourne; Medical Sch., Univ. of Melbourne (MB BS (Hons) 1944, J. P. Ryan Schol. in Surgery, MS 1950). FRACS 1950; FRCS (England) 1951; DPRM (Sydney) 1970. Resident MO, Royal Melb. Hosp., Vic, 1944–45; Lectr in Anatomy, Univ. of Melb., Vic, 1946–50; Resident MO, Nat. Orthopaedic Hosp., London, 1951; Registrar, Orthopaedic Dept, Croydon Gp Hosps, 1951–53; private practice in Perth, WA; Mem. Orthopaedic Dept, Royal Perth Hosp., 1953; began Paraplegic Service, Royal Perth Hosp., 1954; Head, Dept of Paraplegia, Royal Perth Rehabilitation Hosp., 1954–72, resigned; Chm., Dept of Orthopaedic Surgery, Royal Perth Hosp. and Royal Perth Rehabilitation Hosp., 1965–79, Sen. Orthopaedic Consultant, 1979–82. Past Vice Chm., Nat. Adv. Council for the Handicapped; Past Vice-Pres., Australian Council for the Rehabilitation of the Disabled (ACROD); Past Pres., Internat. Med. Soc. of Paraplegia; Chm., W Australian Cttee, Internat. Year of Disabled Persons, 1981. Hon. FRCSE 1981; Hon. MD, WA, 1973; Hon. DTech WA Inst. of Technol., 1984. OStJ 1972. *Publications:* Care and Management of Spinal Cord Injuries, 1981; Lifetime Care of the Paraplegic Patient, 1985; numerous (114) papers and contribs to medical and scientific jls, espec. relating to spinal injuries with paraplegia. *Recreations:* reading, music, travel, sports for the disabled. *Address:* (home) 29 Ulster Road, Floreat Park, WA 6014, Australia. *T:* 387.3582; (office) 13 Colin Grove, West Perth, WA 6005, Australia. *T:* 321.7543.

BEDBROOK, Jack Harry, CEng, FRINA; FBIM; RCNC; Managing Director, HM Dockyard, Devonport, 1979–84; *b* 8 Aug. 1924; *s* of Harry Bedbrook and Emma Bedbrook; *m* 1963, Janet Bedbrook; three *d*. *Educ:* Technical Coll., Portsmouth; RNC, Greenwich. Dir Gen. Ships Dept, Admiralty, 1946–51; Asst Constructor, Devonport, 1951–54; Dockyard Dept, Bath, 1954–56; Constructor, Gibraltar Dockyard, 1956–58; Admiralty Exptl Works, Haslar, 1958–62; Dir Gen. Ships Dept, 1962–65; Chief Constructor, Portsmouth, 1965–71; Project Manager, Rosyth, 1971–74; Prodn Dir, Devonport, 1974–77; Man. Dir, HM Dockyard, Rosyth, 1977–79. *Recreations:* badminton, sailing, gardening, music. *Address:* Laxtons, Cargreen Saltash, Cornwall. *T:* Saltash 4519.

BEDDALL, Hugh Richard Muir; Chairman, Muir Beddall & Co. Ltd, since 1964; Member of Lloyd's; *b* 20 May 1922; *s* of Herbert Muir Beddall and Jennie Beddall (*née* Fowler); *m* 1946, Monique Henriette (*née* Haefliger); three *s* one *d*. *Educ:* Stowe; Ecole de Commerce, Neuchatel, Switzerland. Employee of Muir Beddall & Co., 1939–41. Served War of 1939–45; Royal Marines, 2nd Lieut, 1941; subseq. Captain A Troop 45 RM Commando and No 1 Commando Bde HQ; demob., 1946. Employee, Muir Beddall, Mise & Cie, Paris, 1946–47; returned as employee of Muir Beddall & Co. Ltd, 1947; Dir, 1949; Dep. Chm., 1960; Chm., 1964. FCII. Dir, Muir Beddall Mise & Cie, Paris. *Recreations:* shooting, fishing, racing. *Address:* Iver Lodge, Iver, Bucks. *T:* Iver 653007. *Clubs:* Buck's, East India, Devonshire, Sports and Public Schools; Denham Golf.

BEDDINGTON, Charles Richard; Metropolitan Magistrate, 1963–80; *b* 22 Aug. 1911; *s* of late Charles Beddington, Inner Temple, and Stella (*née* de Goldschmidt); *m* 1939, Debbie, *d* of late Frederick Appleby Holt; two *s* one *d*. *Educ:* Eton (scholar); Balliol Coll., Oxford. Barrister, Inner Temple, 1934. Joined TA, 1939; served RA, 1939–45, Major. Practised at the Bar in London and on SE Circuit. Mem. Mental Health Review Tribunal (SE Metropolitan Area), 1960–63. *Recreations:* swimming, French country life. *Address:* Rosehill, Cuckfield, Sussex RH17 5EU. *T:* Haywards Heath 454063; 1 Temple Gardens, Temple, EC4.

BEDDINGTON, Nadine Dagmar, MBE 1982; architect in own practice, since 1967; *d* of Frank Maurice Beddington and Mathilde Beddington. *Educ:* New Hall; Regent Polytechnic Sch. of Architecture. FRIBA (ARIBA 1940); FSIAD; FRSA; FAMS. Asst in central and local govt, 1940–45; asst in private practice, 1945–55; Chief Architect to Freeman Hardy Willis/Trueform, 1957–67. Vice-Chm., Architects in Industry Group, 1965–67; Mem., RIBA Council, 1969–72, 1975–79; Vice-Pres., RIBA, 1971–72; Mem., ARCUK, 1969–; Chm., Camberwell Soc., 1970–77. Silver Jubilee Medal, 1977. *Publications:* Design for Shopping Centres, 1982; articles on shops, shopping centres, building maintenance, building legislation. *Recreations:* reading, riding, people, music, travel, dogs. *Address:* 17 Champion Grove, SE5 8BN; (office) 60 Welbeck Street, W1M 7HB. *T:* 01–486 7348/9. *Clubs:* Reform; Brixton and District Dog Training (Vice Chm.).

BEDDOE, Jack Eglinton, CB 1971; Chief Executive, Severn Trent Water Authority, 1974–77; *b* 6 June 1914; *s* of Percy Beddoe and Mabel Ellen Hook; *m* 1st, 1940, Audrey Alison Emelie (*d* 1954); two *s* one *d*; 2nd, 1957, Edith Rosina Gillanders. *Educ:* Hitchin Grammar Sch.; Magdalene Coll., Cambridge. Entered Ministry of Health, 1936; Principal Private Sec. to Minister of Health, 1948–51; to Minister of Housing and Local Government, 1951–53; Asst Sec., 1953; Under-Sec., Ministry of Housing and Local Government, 1961–65; Asst Under-Sec. of State, Dept of Economic Affairs, 1965–66; Chm., SE Planning Board, during 1966; Under-Sec., Min. of Housing and Local Govt, later DoE, 1966–74. *Address:* 32 Northfield End, Henley, Oxfordshire.

BEDDOES, Air Vice-Marshal John Geoffrey Genior, CB 1981; FRAeS; aviation consultant; Director, Colechurch (UK) Ltd, since 1983; *b* 21 May 1925; *s* of Algernon Geoffrey Beddoes and Lucy Isobel (*née* Collier); *m* 1948, Betty Morris Kendrick; three *s*. *Educ:* Wirral Grammar Sch., Bebington, Cheshire. Pilot training in Rhodesia and Egypt, 1943–45; No 114 Sqdn, Italy and Aden, Bostons and Mosquitos, 1945–46; No 30 Sqdn, Abingdon and Berlin Airlift, Dakotas, 1947–49; Central Flying Sch., 1949; Flying Instr, RAF Coll., Cranwell and Central Flying Sch., 1950–55; Flight Comdr, No 57 Sqdn, Canberras, 1955; Air Ministry, 1956–57; Flying Coll., 1958; Flt Comdr No 57 Sqdn, Victor Mk 1, 1959–61; sc Bracknell, 1962; OC No 139 (Jamaica) Sqdn, Victor Mk 2, 1963–64; Wing Comdr Ops HQ No 3 Gp, 1965–67; Directing Staff Coll. of Air Warfare, 1968–69; OC RAF Laarbruch, 1969–71; MoD Dep. Dir, Operational Requirements, 1971–73; HQ 2 ATAF Asst COS Offensive Operations, 1974–75; MoD Director of Operational Requirements, 1975–78; Dir Gen. Aircraft (2), MoD PE, 1978–80; retired RAF, 1981. FBIM. *Recreations:* music, cricket, DIY, golf, gardening. *Address:* White Stables, Stow Bedon, Norfolk NR17 1HP. *T:* Caston 524. *Clubs:* Royal Air Force, MCC.

BEDFORD, 13th Duke of, *cr* 1694; **John Robert Russell;** Marquess of Tavistock, 1694; Earl of Bedford, 1550; Baron Russell of Chenies, 1540; Baron Russell of Thornhaugh, 1603; Baron Howland of Streatham, 1695; *b* 24 May 1917; *er s* of 12th Duke and Louisa Crommelin Roberta (*d* 1960), *y d* of Robert Jowitt Whitwell; *S* father 1953; *m* 1st, 1939, Clare Gwendolen Hollway, *née* Bridgman (*d* 1945); two *s*; 2nd, Lydia (marr. diss., 1960), *widow* of Capt. Ian de Hoghton Lyle, 3rd *d* of 3rd Baron Churston and late Duchess of Leinster; one *s*; 3rd, 1960, Mme Nicole Milinaire, *d* of Paul Schneider. Coldstream Guards, 1939; invalided out, 1940. *Publications:* A Silver-Plated Spoon, 1959; (with G. Mikes) Book of Snobs, 1965; The Flying Duchess, 1968; (with G. Mikes) How to Run a Stately Home, 1971. *Heir: s* Marquess of Tavistock, *qv*. *Address:* Château de Les Ligures, 2 rue Honoré Labande, Monte Carlo, MC 98000, Monaco. *Clubs:* Brooks's, Pratt's.

BEDFORD, Bishop Suffragan of, since 1981; **Rt. Rev. David John Farmbrough;** *b* 4 May 1929; 2nd *s* of late Charles Septimus and late Ida Mabel Farmbrough; *m* 1955, Angela Priscilla Hill; one *s* three *d*. *Educ:* Bedford Sch.; Lincoln Coll., Oxford (BA 1951, MA 1953); Westcott House, Cambridge, 1951–53. Deacon, 1953, priest, 1954; Curate of Bishop's Hatfield, 1953–57; Priest-in-charge, St John's, Hatfield, 1957–63; Vicar of Bishop's Stortford, 1963–74; Rural Dean of Bishop's Stortford, 1973–74; Archdeacon of St Albans, 1974–81. Mem., Gen. Synod, 1972–81. *Publications:* In Wonder, Love and Praise, 1966; Belonging, Believing, Doing, 1971. *Recreations:* sailing, gardening. *Address:* 168 Kimbolton Road, Bedford MK41 8DN. *T:* Bedford 57551.

BEDFORD, Archdeacon of; *see* Bourke, Ven. M.

BEDFORD, Alfred William, (Bill), OBE 1961; AFC 1945; FRAeS; Aerospace consultant, since 1986; *b* 18 Nov. 1920; *m* 1941, Mary Averill; one *s*. *Educ:* Loughborough College School, Leics. Electrical engineering apprenticeship, Blackburn Starling & Co. Ltd. RAF 1940–51: served Fighter Sqdns, 605 (County of Warwick) Sqdn, 1941; 135 Sqdn, 1941–44; 65 Sqdn, 1945. Qualified Flying Instructor, Upavon, 1945, and Instructor, Instrument Rating Examiner, until 1949; Graduate Empire Flying School all-weather course. Awarded King's Commendation, 1949; Graduate and Tutor, Empire Test Pilots' School, 1949–50; Test Pilot, RAE Farnborough, 1950–51; Experimental Test Pilot, Hawker Aircraft Ltd, 1951–56; Chief Test Pilot, Hawker Aircraft Ltd, 1956–63; Chief Test Pilot (Dunsfold); Hawker Siddeley Aviation Ltd, 1963–67; Sales Man., Hawker Siddeley Aviation, 1968–78; British Aerospace: Divisional Mktg Manager, 1978–83; Regional Exec., SE Asia, 1983–86. London-Rome and return world speed records, 1956. Made initial flight, Oct. 1960, on the Hawker P1127 (the World's first VTOL strike fighter), followed by first jet V/STOL operations of such an aircraft from an Aircraft

Carrier (HMS Ark Royal) on 8 Feb. 1963; Harrier first flight, Aug. 1966. Holder Gliding Internat. Gold 'C' with two diamonds; held British and UK national gliding records of 257 miles and altitude of 21,340 ft (19,120 ft gain of height); awarded BGA trophies: de Havilland (twice), Manio, and Wakefield, 1950–51. Approved Air Registration Bd glider test pilot. Chm. and founder Mem., Test Pilots' Group, RAeS, 1964–66. Member SBAC Test Pilots' Soc., 1956–67. Member Society of Experimental Test Pilots. RAeS Alston Memorial Medal, 1959; Guild of Air Pilots and Air Navigators Derry Richards Memorial Medal, 1959–60; Segrave Trophy, 1963; Britannia Trophy, 1964; Air League Founders Medal, 1967. First Class Wings, Indonesian Air Force, for services to the Republic, 1982. *Recreations:* squash, sail-plane flying. *Address:* The Chequers, West End Lane, Esher, Surrey. *T:* Esher 62285. *Clubs:* Royal Air Force; Esher Squash.

BEDFORD, David; Associate Visiting Composer to Gordonstoun, since 1983; *b* 4 Aug. 1937; *s* of Leslie Herbert Bedford, *qv; m* 1st, 1958, Maureen Parsonage; two *d;* 2nd, 1969, Susan Pilgrim; two *d. Educ:* Lancing College; Royal Acad. of Music; Trinity Coll. London (LTCL). Guy's Hosp. porter, 1956; teacher, Whitefield Sch., Hendon, 1965; teacher, 1968–80, and composer-in-residence, 1969–81, Queen's Coll., London. ARAM. Mem. Exec. Cttee, Soc. for the Promotion of New Music, 1982–. Numerous compositions, many commissioned by major London orchestras and BBC; numerous recordings. *Recreations:* squash, table tennis, cricket, astronomy, ancient history, philosophy. *Address:* 39 Shakespeare Road, Mill Hill, NW7 4BA. *T:* 01–959 3165. *Clubs:* Ridgeway Table Tennis, Mill Hill Squash.
  See also S. J. R. Bedford.

BEDFORD, Eric, CB 1959; CVO 1953; Chief Architect, Ministry of Works, 1952–70 (Chief Architect, Directorate General of Works, Ministry of Public Building and Works, 1963–70). ARIBA 1933; Grissell Gold Medal of Royal Institute of British Architects, 1934. Was responsible for Ministry of Works decorations for the Coronation, 1953.

BEDFORD, Leslie Herbert, CBE 1956 (OBE 1942); retired as Director of Engineering, Guided Weapons Division, British Aircraft Corporation Ltd, 1968; *b* 23 June 1900; *s* of Herbert Bedford; *m* 1928, Lesley Florence Keitley Duff; three *s. Educ:* City and Guilds Engineering Coll., London (BSc); King's Coll., Cambridge (MA). Standard Telephones & Cables Ltd, 1924–31; Dir Research, A. C. Cossor Ltd, 1931–47; Chief TV Engr, Marconi's Wireless Telegraph Co. Ltd, 1947–48. Chief Engineer, GW Div., The English Electric Aviation Ltd, 1948–59; Dir, 1959–60. Mem., Council for Scientific and Industrial Research, 1961–. CEng, FCGI, FIERE, FIEE, FRAeS. Silver Medal (RAeS), 1963; Gold Medal, Société d'Encouragement pour la Recherche et l'Invention, 1967; Faraday Medal, 1968; Achievement Award, Scientific Instrument Makers' Co., 1980. *Publications:* Articles in: Proc. Phys. Soc., Jl BritIRE, Jl RSA, Jl RAeS, Jl IEE, Wireless Engineer, Electronic and Radio Engineer, Electronic Technology. *Recreations:* music, sailing. *Address:* 29 Holly Park, N3 3JB.
  See also D. Bedford, S. J. R. Bedford.

BEDFORD, Steuart John Rudolf; freelance conductor; Co-Artistic Director, English Music Theatre Co. since 1976; Artistic Director, English Sinfonia, since 1981; *b* 31 July 1939; *s* of L. H. Bedford, *qv; m* 1st, 1969, Norma Burrowes, *qv;* 2nd, 1980, Celia, *er d* of Mr and Mrs G. R. Harding; two *d. Educ:* Lancing Coll., Sussex; Royal Acad. of Music. Fellow, RCO; FRAM; BA. Artistic Dir, Aldeburgh Festival, 1974; Royal Acad. of Music, 1965; English Opera Gp, now English Music Theatre, 1967–. Debut at Metropolitan, NY, 1974 (Death in Venice); new prodn of The Marriage of Figaro, 1975. Has conducted regularly with English Opera Gp and Welsh National Opera; also at Royal Opera House, Covent Garden (operas incl. Owen Wingrave and Death in Venice, by Benjamin Britten, and Cosi Fan Tutte); also in Santa Fe, Buenos Aires, France, Belgium, Holland, Canada, Vienna, etc. *Recreations:* golf, gardening. *Address:* c/o Harrison Parrott Ltd, 12 Penzance Place, W11 4PA.
  See also D. Bedford.

BEDFORD, Sybille, OBE 1981; author; *b* 16 March 1911; *d* of Maximilian von Schoenebeck and Elizabeth Bernard; *m* 1935, Walter Bedford. *Educ:* privately, in Italy, England and France. Career in writing and literary journalism. Vice-Pres., PEN, 1979. FRSL. *Publications:* The Sudden View, A Visit to Don Otavio, 1953, new edn 1982; A Legacy, 1956, 6th edn 1984, televised 1975; The Best We Can Do (The Trial of Dr Adams), 1958; The Faces of Justice, 1961; A Favourite of the Gods, 1962, new edn 1984; A Compass Error, 1968, new edn 1984; Aldous Huxley, a Biography, Vol I, 1973, Vol II, 1974. *Recreations:* wine, reading, travel. *Address:* c/o Messrs Coutts, 1 Old Park Lane, W1Y 4BS. *Clubs:* PEN, Sloane.

BEDINGFELD; *see* Paston-Bedingfeld.

BEDINGFIELD, Christopher Ohl Macredie, TD 1968; QC 1976; a Recorder of the Crown Court, since 1972; *b* 2 June 1935; *s* of late Norman Macredie Bedingfield, Nantygroes, Radnorshire and of Mrs Macredie Bedingfield. *Educ:* Rugby; University Coll., Oxford (MA). Called to Bar, Gray's Inn, 1957; Wales and Chester Circuit. Commnd 2 Mon R; NS 24th Regt; Staff Captain TA, 1960–64; Coy Comdr 4 RWF, 1964–69; Lt-Col TAVR, 1973–76, Co. Comdt Denbigh and Flint ACF 1973, Clwyd ACF 1974–76 (resigned on appt as QC). *Recreations:* riding, squash. *Address:* 5 Essex Court, Temple, EC4. *T:* 01–353 2440; (residence) Nantygroes, near Knighton, Powys. *T:* Whitton 220. *Clubs:* Reform; Bristol Channel Yacht (Swansea).

BEDSER, Alec Victor, CBE 1982 (OBE 1964); PR Consultant; *b* 4 July 1918; twin *s* of late Arthur and of Florence Beatrice Bedser. *Educ:* Monument Hill Secondary Sch., Woking. Served with RAF in UK, France (BEF), N Africa, Sicily, Italy, Austria, 1939–46. Joined Surrey County Cricket Club, as Professional, 1938; awarded Surrey CCC and England caps, 1946, 1st Test Match v India, created record by taking 22 wickets in first two Tests; toured Australia as Member of MCC team, 1946–47, 1950–51, 1954–55; toured S Africa with MCC, 1948–49; held record of most number of Test wickets (236), since beaten, 1953; took 100th wicket against Australia (first English bowler since 1914 to do this), 1953; Asst Man. to Duke of Norfolk on MCC tour to Australia, 1962–63; Manager: MCC team to Australia, 1974–75; England team tour of Australia and India, 1979–80; Member: England Cricket Selection Cttee, 1961–85 (Chm., 1968–81); MCC Cttee, 1982–85. Founded own company (office equipment and supplies) with Eric Bedser, 1955. Freeman, City of London, 1968; Mem., Guild of Master Cleaners, 1981–. *Publications:* (with E. A. Bedser) Our Cricket Story, 1951; Bowling, 1952; (with E. A. Bedser) Following On, 1954; Cricket Choice, 1981; (with Alex Bannister) Twin Ambitions (autobiog.), 1986. *Recreations:* cricket, golf. *Address:* c/o Brengreen Holdings Ltd, 61 Cheapside, EC2. *Clubs:* MCC (Hon. Life), East India, Devonshire, Sports and Public Schools, Eccentric; Surrey County Cricket (Vice-Pres.); West Hill Golf.

BEEBY, Clarence Edward, CMG 1956; PhD; International Consultant and Director Emeritus, New Zealand Council for Educational Research, since 1969; *b* 16 June 1902; *s* of Anthony and Alice Beeby; *m* 1926, Beatrice Eleanor, *d* of Charles Newnham; one *s* one *d. Educ:* Christchurch Boys' High Sch.; Canterbury Coll., University of NZ (MA); University Coll., London; University of Manchester (PhD). Lectr in Philosophy and Education, Canterbury Univ. Coll., University of NZ, 1923–34; Dir, NZ Council for Educational Research, 1934–38; Asst Dir of Education, Education Dept, NZ, 1938–40; Dir of Education, NZ, 1940–60 (leave of absence to act as Asst Dir-Gen. of UNESCO, Paris, 1948–49); NZ Ambassador to France, 1960–63; Research Fellow, Harvard Univ., 1963–67; Commonwealth Visiting Prof., Univ. of London, 1967–68; Consultant: to Australian Govt in Papua and New Guinea, 1969; to Ford Foundn in Indonesia, 1970–77; to UNDP in Malaysia, 1976; to World Bank, Washington, DC, 1983; External Consultant to Univ. of Papua New Guinea, 1982. Leader of NZ Delegs to Gen. Confs of UNESCO, 1946, 1947, 1950, 1953, 1954, 1956, 1958, 1960, 1962. Hon. Counsellor of UNESCO, 1950; Mem., Exec. Bd, UNESCO, 1960–63 (Chm., Exec. Bd, 1963–64); Mem., Council of Consultant Fellows, Internat. Inst. for Educnl Planning, Paris, 1971–77. For. associate, US Nat. Acad. of Educn, 1981. Hon. Fellow, NZ Educnl Inst., 1971. Hon. LLD Otago, 1969; Hon. LittD Wellington, 1970. Mackie Medal, ANZAAS, 1971. Grand Cross, Order of St Gregory, 1964. *Publications:* The Intermediate Schools of New Zealand, 1938; (with W. Thomas and M. H. Oram) Entrance to the University, 1939; The Quality of Education in Developing Countries, 1966; (ed) Qualitative Aspects of Educational Planning, 1969; Assessment of Indonesian Education: a guide in planning, 1978; articles in educational periodicals. *Recreations:* gardening, fishing, cabinet-making. *Address:* 73 Barnard Street, Wellington N2, New Zealand.

BEEBY, George Harry, CBE 1974; PhD, BSc; CEng, FIChemE, CChem, FRSC; Chairman, Inveresk Research Foundation, 1977–84; *b* 9 Sept. 1902; *s* of George Beeby and Lucy Beeby (*née* Monk); *m* 1929, Helen Elizabeth Edwards; one *d. Educ:* Loughborough Grammar Sch.; Loughborough Coll. BSc Hons 1922; PhD 1924, London Univ. Various appts in rubber and chemical industries, 1924–84; Chm., Thorium Ltd and Radiochemical Centre (later Amersham Internat.), 1949–57; Divisional Chm., ICI, 1954–57; Chm., British Titan Ltd, 1957–69. Chairman: EDC for Chemical Industry, 1964–67; Nat. Sulphuric Acid Assoc., 1963–65; British Standards Instn, 1967–70 (Dep. Pres. 1970–73). Pres., Soc. of Chemical Industry, 1970–72 (Vice-Pres., 1966–69); Vice-Pres., RoSPA, 1969–84; Hon. Mem., Chemical Industries Assoc. Member: Robens Cttee on Safety and Health at Work, 1970–72; Parly and Sci. Cttee, 1971–83; Windeyer Cttee on lead poisoning, 1972. FRSA 1969. Hon. DTech Loughborough Univ. of Technology, 1969. Soc. of Chemical Industry Medal, 1973. *Publications:* contribs to various jls on industrial safety, industrial economics and business administration. *Recreations:* golf, racing. *Address:* The Laurels, Sandy Drive, Cobham, Surrey. *T:* Oxshott 2346. *Club:* Royal Automobile.

BEECH, Patrick Mervyn, CBE 1970; Controller, English Regions, BBC, 1969–72, retired; *b* 31 Oct. 1912; *s* of Howard Worcester Mervyn Beech and Stella Patrick Campbell; *m* 1st, 1935, Sigrid Gunnel Christenson (*d* 1959); two *d;* 2nd, 1960, Merle-Mary Barnes; one *d. Educ:* Stowe; Exeter Coll., Oxford. Joined BBC as Producer, West Region, 1935; News Editor, West Region, 1945; Asst Head of programmes, West Region, 1954; Controller, Midland Region, 1964–69. *Recreations:* photography, music, theatre. *Address:* Mill Bank, Cradley, near Malvern, Worcs. *T:* Ridgway Cross 234.

BEECHAM, Jeremy Hugh; Member, Newcastle upon Tyne City Council, since 1967, Leader since 1977; Partner, Allan Henderson Beecham & Peacock, since 1968; *b* 17 Nov. 1944; *s* of Laurence and Florence Beecham; *m* 1968, Brenda Elizabeth (*née* Woolf); one *s* one *d. Educ:* Royal Grammar Sch., Newcastle upon Tyne; University Coll., Oxford (First Cl. Hons Jurisprudence; MA). Chm., OU Labour Club, 1964. Admitted Solicitor, 1968. Newcastle upon Tyne City Council: Chairman: Social Services Cttee, 1973–77; Chm., Policy and Resources Cttee, 1977–; Finance Cttee, 1979–85; Dep. Chm., AMA, 1984–; Vice Chm., Northern Regl Councils Assoc., 1986–. Member: RTPI Working Party on Public Participation in Planning, 1980–82; Historic Bldgs and Monuments Commn for England, 1983–; Local and Regional Govt Sub-Cttee, Labour Party NEC, 1971–83; Labour Party NEC/Shadow Cabinet Wkg Pty on Future of Local Govt, 1984–; Participant, Königswinter Conf., 1986. Contested (Lab) Tynemouth, 1970. *Recreations:* reading, history, music, very amateur photography, the Northumbrian countryside. *Address:* 39 The Drive, Gosforth, Newcastle upon Tyne NE3 4AJ. *T:* Tyneside 2851888. *Club:* Manors Social (Newcastle upon Tyne).

BEECHAM, John Stratford Roland; *S* father as 4th Bt (*cr* 1914), 1982, but has declined to prove his claim and does not use the title. *Heir: b* Robert Adrian Beecham [*b* 6 Jan. 1942; *m* 1969, Daphne Mattinson; one *s* one *d*].

BEECHER, Most Rev. Leonard James, CMG 1961; ARCS, MA, DD; *b* 21 May 1906; *er s* of Robert Paul and Charlotte Beecher; *m* 1930, Gladys Sybil Bazett (*d* 1982), *yr d* of late Canon Harry and Mrs Mary Leakey; two *s* one *d. Educ:* St Olave's Grammar Sch., Southwark; Imperial Coll. and London Day Trg Coll., University of London. ARCS 1926; BSc 1927; MA (London) 1937. DD Lambeth, 1962. Asst Master, Alliance High Sch., Kikuyu, Kenya, 1927–30; Missionary, Church Missionary Soc., Diocese of Mombasa, 1930–57; Unofficial Mem. of Legislative Council, Colony of Kenya, representing African interests, 1943–47; MEC of the Colony of Kenya, 1947–52; Asst Bishop of Mombasa, Kenya Colony, 1950–53; Archdeacon and Canon of the Diocese, 1945–53; Bishop of Mombasa, 1953–64; Archbishop of East Africa, 1960–70; Bishop of Nairobi, 1964–70; Archbishop Emeritus, 1970. *Publications:* (with G. S. B. Beecher) A Kikuyu-English Dictionary, 1933; translator of parts of the Kikuyu Old Testament, 1939–49; Editor, Kenya Church Review, 1941–50. *Recreations:* recorded music, bird-watching, photography. *Address:* PO Box 21066, Nairobi, Kenya. *T:* Nairobi 567485.

BEEDHAM, Brian James; Foreign Editor, The Economist; *b* 12 Jan. 1928; *s* of James Victor Beedham and Nina Beedham (*née* Zambra); *m* 1960, Ruth Barbara Zollikofer. *Educ:* Leeds Grammar Sch.; The Queen's Coll., Oxford. RA, 1950–52. Asst Editor, Yorkshire Post, 1952–55; The Economist, 1955–, Washington correspondent, 1958–61. Commonwealth Fellowship, 1956–57. Fellow, Royal Geographical Society. *Recreations:* hillwalking, music, Kipling and Wodehouse. *Address:* 9 Hillside, SW19. *T:* 01–946 4454. *Club:* Travellers'.

BEELEY, Sir Harold, KCMG 1961 (CMG 1953); CBE 1946; *b* 15 Feb. 1909; *s* of Frank Arthur Beeley; *m* 1st, 1933, Millicent Mary Chinn (marr. diss., 1953); two *d;* 2nd, 1958, Mrs Patricia Karen Brett-Smith; one *d. Educ:* Highgate; Queen's Coll., Oxford. 1st Cl in Modern History, 1930. Asst Lectr in Modern History, Sheffield Univ., 1930–31; University Coll., London, 1931–35; Junior Research Fellow and Lecturer, Queen's Coll., Oxford, 1935–38; Lecturer in Charge of History Dept, University Coll., Leicester, 1938–39. Mem. of wartime organisation of Royal Institute of International Affairs, and subsequently of Foreign Office Research Dept, 1939–45. Mem. of Secretariat of San Francisco Conf. and of Preparatory Commission of UN, 1945; Sec. of Anglo-American Cttee of Enquiry on Palestine, 1946. Entered Foreign Service, 1946; Counsellor of Embassy, Copenhagen, 1949–50; Baghdad, 1950–53; Washington, 1953–55; Ambassador to Saudi Arabia, during 1955; Asst Under-Sec., Foreign Office, 1956–58; Dep. UK Representative to UN, New York, 1958–61; UK Representative, Disarmament Conf., Geneva, 1964–67; Ambassador to the United Arab Republic, 1961–64, 1967–69. Lectr in History, Queen Mary Coll., Univ. of London, 1969–75. Pres., Egypt Exploration Soc.,

1969–; Chairman: World of Islam Festival Trust, 1973–; Egyptian-British Chamber of Commerce, 1981–. Chm., Ibis Securities Ltd, 1979–. *Address:* 38 Slaidburn Street, SW10. *Club:* Reform.

BEER, Prof. (Anthony) Stafford; International Consultant and Adviser in Cybernetics to Ernst and Whinney (Canada); Director, Metapraxis Ltd (UK); Visiting Professor of Cybernetics at Manchester University (Business School), since 1969, also Adjunct Professor of Statistics and Operations Research at Pennsylvania University (Wharton School), 1972–81, and of Social Systems Sciences since 1981; *b* London, 25 Sept. 1926; *er s* of late William John and of Doris Ethel Beer; *m* 1st, 1947, Cynthia Margaret Hannaway; four *s* one *d*; 2nd, 1968, Sallie Steadman (*née* Child); one *s* two *d*. *Educ:* Whitgift Sch.; University Coll., London. MBA Manchester. Lieut, 9th Gurkha Rifles 1945; Captain, Royal Fusiliers 1947. Man. of Operational Res. and Prodn Controller, S. Fox & Co., 1949–56; Head of Op. Res. and Cybernetics, United Steel, 1956–61; Man. Dir, SIGMA Science in General Management Ltd and Dir, Metra International, 1961–66; Develt Dir, International Publishing Corp.; Dir, International Data Highways Ltd; Chm., Computaprint Ltd, 1966–69. Vis. Prof. of Gen. Systems, Open Univ., 1970–71; Scientific Dir, Project Cybersyn, Chile, 1971–73. Ex-Pres., Operational Res. Soc.; Ex-Pres., Soc. for Gen. Systems Res. (USA); Pres., World Orgn of Gen. Systems and Cybernetics, 1981–; Mem. UK Automation Council, 1957–69; Mem. Gen. Adv. Council of BBC, 1961–69. Governor, Internat. Council for Computer Communication, 1979–. Hon. Chm., The Stafford Beer Foundn, 1986–. Silver Medal, Royal Swedish Acad. for Engrg Scis, 1958; Lanchester Prize (USA) for Ops Res., 1966; McCulloch Award (USA) for Cybernetics, 1970; Wiener Meml Gold Medal for Cybernetics, World Orgn of Gen. Systems and Cybernetics, 1984. *Publications:* Cybernetics and Management, 1959; Decision and Control, 1966; Management Science, 1967; Brain of the Firm, 1972 (new edn, 1981); Designing Freedom, 1974; Platform for Change, 1975; Transit (poems), 1977, extended edn 1983; The Heart of Enterprise, 1979; Diagnosing the System, for organizations, 1985; Pebbles to Computers: the thread, 1986; chapters in numerous other books. *Recreations:* spinning, painting, poetry, classics, staying put. *Address:* Cwarel Isaf, Pont Creuddyn, Lampeter, Dyfed, Wales SA48 8PG; 34 Palmerston Square, Toronto, Ontario M6G 2S7, Canada. *Club:* Athenæum.

See also I. D. S. Beer.

BEER, Ian David Stafford, MA; JP; Head Master of Harrow, since 1981; *b* 28 April 1931; *s* of late William Beer and Doris Ethel Beer; *m* 1960, Angela Felce, *d* of Col E. S. G. Howard, MC, RA; two *s* one *d*. *Educ:* Whitgift Sch.; St Catharine's Coll., Cambridge (Exhibitioner). E-SU Scholar, 1968. Second Lieut in 1st Bn Royal Fusiliers, 1950. House Master, Marlborough Coll., Wilts, 1957–61; Head Master: Ellesmere Coll., Salop, 1961–69; Lancing Coll., Sussex, 1969–81. Chairman: HMC Academic Cttee, 1977–79; HMC, 1980. Governor, Whitgift Sch., 1986–. Chm. Editorial Bd, Rugby Post (formerly Rugby World), 1977–. JP Shropshire, 1963–69, JP W Sussex, 1970–81, JP Mddx, 1981–. *Recreations:* Rugby Football Union Cttee (Mem. Exec. Cttee, 1984–) (formerly: played Rugby for England; CURFC (Capt.), Harlequins, Old Whitgiftians), swimming, reading, zoology, meeting people. *Address:* Peel House, Football Lane, Harrow-on-the-Hill, Mddx. *Clubs:* East India, Devonshire, Sports and Public Schools; Hawks (Cambridge).

See also A. S. Beer.

BEER, James Edmund; Director: Short Loan and Mortgage Co. Ltd, since 1978; Short Loan (Leasing) Ltd, since 1979; London Financial Futures Co. Ltd, since 1982; *b* 17 March 1931; *s* of Edmund Huxtable Beer and Gwendoline Kate Beer; *m* 1953, Barbara Mollie (*née* Tunley); two *s* one *d*. *Educ:* Torquay Grammar School. IPFA, FRVA, MBCS, MBIM. Torquay Borough Council, 1951–54; Chatham, 1954–56; Wolverhampton, 1956–58; Doncaster, 1958–60; Chief Accountant, Bedford, 1960–62; Asst Borough Treas., Croydon, 1963–65; Dep. Treas., Leeds, 1965; Chief Financial Officer, Leeds, 1968; Dir of Finance, Leeds City Council, 1973–78. Mem. Local Govt Financial Exec., CIPFA, 1974–78; Financial Adviser to AMA, 1974–78; Treas., Soc. of Metropolitan Treasurers, 1974–78; Member: LAMSAC Computer Panel, 1972–78; Yorks and Humberside Develt Assoc. London Section, 1970–; Past Examr, CIPFA; Adviser on Rate Support Grant, AMA, 1974–78; Treas., Leeds Grand Theatre & Opera House Ltd, 1974–78; Governor, Leeds Musical Festival, 1979–84. Freeman, City of London, 1972; Liveryman, Basketmakers Co., 1982. *Publications:* contrib. professional jls. *Recreations:* golf, theatre, swimming, Rugby (past playing mem., Torquay Athletic RUFC). *Address:* 48 High Ash Avenue, Alwoodley, Leeds LS17 8RG. *T:* Leeds 683907. *Clubs:* Gresham, City Livery.

BEÉR, Prof. János Miklós, DSc, PhD, FEng; Professor of Chemical and Fuel Engineering, Massachusetts Institute of Technology (MIT), since 1976; Programme Director for Combustion, MIT Energy Laboratory, since 1976; *b* Budapest, 27 Feb. 1923; *s* of Sándor Beér and Gizella Trismai; *m* 1944, Marta Gabriella Csató. *Educ:* Berzsenyi Dániel Gymnasium, Budapest; Univ. of Budapest (Dipl-Ing 1950). PhD (Sheffield), 1960, DSc(Tech) Sheffield, 1967. Heat Research Inst., Budapest: Research Officer, 1949–52; Head, Combustion Dept, 1952–56; Princ. Lectr (part-time), University of Budapest, 1953–56; Research Engr, Babcock & Wilcox Ltd, Renfrew, 1957; Research Bursar, University of Sheffield, 1957–60; Head, Research Stn, Internat. Flame Research Foundn, Ijmuiden, Holland, 1960–63; Prof., Dept of Fuel Science, Pa State Univ., 1963–65; Newton Drew Prof. of Chemical Engrg and Fuel Technology and Head of Dept, Univ. of Sheffield, 1965–76; Dean, Faculty of Engineering, Univ. of Sheffield, 1973–75. Member: Adv. Council on R&D for Fuel and Power, DTI, later Dept of Energy, 1973–76; Adv. Bd, Safety in Mines Research, Dept of Energy, 1974–76; Clean Air Council, DoE, 1974–76; Bd of Directors, The Combustion Inst., Pittsburgh, USA, 1974–; Mem., Adv. Cttee, Italian Nat. Res. Council, 1974–. Gen. Superintendent of Research, Internat. Flame Research Foundn, 1971–. Australian Commonwealth Vis. Fellow, 1972; Fellow ASME, 1978 (Moody Award, 1964); FEng 1979. Melchett Medal, Inst. Energy, London, 1985. Editor, Fuel and Energy Science Monograph Series, 1966–. *Publications:* (with N. Chigier) Combustion Aerodynamics, 1972; (ed with M. W. Thring) Industrial Flames, 1972; (ed with H. B. Palmer) Developments in Combustion Science and Technology, 1974; (ed with N. Afgan) Heat Transfer in Flames, 1975; contribs to Nature, Combustion and Flame, Basic Engrg Jl, Amer. Soc. Mech. Engrg, Jl Inst. F, ZVDI, Internat. Gas Wärme, Proc. Internat. Symposia on Combustion, etc. *Recreations:* swimming, rowing, reading, music. *Address:* Department of Chemical Engineering, Massachusetts Institute of Technology, Cambridge, Mass 02139, USA. *T:* 617–253–6661.

BEER, Mrs Nellie, OBE 1957; JP; DL; Member of Manchester City Council, 1937–72 (Alderman 1964–72; Lord Mayor of Manchester, 1966); *b* 22 April 1900; *d* of Arthur Robinson and Nelly Laurie Robinson (*née* Hewitt); *m* 1927, Robert Beer (*d* 1977); one *d*. *Educ:* Ardwick Higher Grade Sch. Hon. MA Univ. of Manchester, 1978. JP Manchester, 1942; DL Lancs, 1970.

BEER, Patricia, (Mrs J. D. Parsons); freelance writer; *b* 4 Nov. 1924; *yr d* of Andrew William and Harriet Beer, Exmouth, Devon; *m* 1964, John Damien Parsons. *Educ:* Exmouth Grammar Sch.; Exeter Univ. (BA, 1st cl. Hons English); St Hugh's Coll., Oxford (BLitt). Lecturer: in English, Univ. of Padua, 1947–49; British Inst., Rome, 1949–51; Goldsmiths' Coll., Univ. of London, 1962–68. *Publications: poetry:* Loss of the Magyar, 1959; The Survivors, 1963; Just Like The Resurrection, 1967; The Estuary, 1971; (ed) New Poems 1975, 1975; Driving West, 1975; (ed jtly) New Poetry 2, 1976; Selected Poems, 1980; The Lie of the Land, 1983; *novel:* Moon's Ottery, 1978; *non-fiction:* Wessex, 1985; *autobiog.:* Mrs Beer's House, 1968; *criticism:* Reader, I Married Him, 1974; contrib. The Listener, London Review of Books. *Recreations:* travelling, cooking. *Address:* Tiphayes, Up Ottery, near Honiton, Devon. *T:* Up Ottery 255.

BEER, Prof. Stafford; *see* Beer, Prof. A. S.

BEERLING, John William; Controller, BBC Radio 1, since 1985; *b* 12 April 1937; *s* of Raymond Starr and May Elizabeth Julia Beerling; *m* 1959, Carol Ann Reynolds; one *s* one *d*. *Educ:* Sir Roger Manwood's Grammar Sch., Sandwich, Kent. National Service, RAF, wireless fitter, 1955–57. Joined BBC, 1957; Studio Manager, 1958; Producer, 1962; Head of Radio 1 Programmes, 1983. *Publication:* Emperor Rosko's D. J. Handbook, 1976. *Recreations:* photography, fishing. *Address:* (office) Room 228, Egton House, Portland Place, W1A 1AA.

BEESLEY, Mrs Alec M.; *see* Smith, Dodie.

BEESLEY, Ian Blake; Partner, Price Waterhouse, since 1986; *b* 11 July 1942; *s* of Frank and Catherine Beesley; *m* 1st, 1964, Birgitte (*née* Smith) (marr. diss. 1982); 2nd, 1983, Elizabeth (*née* Wigley); one *d*. *Educ:* Manchester Grammar School; St Edmund Hall, Oxford (PPE). MA; Cert. in Statistics. Central Statistical Office, 1964–76; Chief Statistician, HM Treasury, 1976–78; Dep. Head, Unit supporting Lord Rayner, PM's adviser on efficiency, 1981–83; Under Sec. and Official Head of PM's Efficiency Unit, 1983–86. Alternate Mem., Jarratt Cttee on efficiency in universities, 1984–85; Mem., Croham Cttee to review function and operation of UGC. *Publications:* Policy analysis and evaluation in British Government (RIPA seminary papers), 1983; contribs to Jl Royal Statistical Soc. *Address:* c/o Price Waterhouse, 1 London Bridge, SE1 9QL.

BEESLEY, Prof. Michael Edwin, CBE 1985; PhD; Professor of Economics, London Business School, since 1965; Chairman, Institute of Public Sector Management, London Business School, since 1983 (Director, 1978–83); *b* 3 July 1924; *s* of late Edwin S. and Kathleen D. Beesley; *m* 1947, Eileen Eleanor Yard; three *s* two *d*. *Educ:* King Edward's Grammar Sch., Five Ways, Birmingham; Univ. of Birmingham (BCom Div. 1, 1945; PhD 1951). Lectr in Commerce, Univ. of Birmingham, 1951–60; Rees Jeffreys Res. Fellow, LSE, 1961–64; Sir Ernest Cassel Reader in Econs, with special ref. to transport, Univ. of London tenable at LSE, 1964–65. Vis. Associate Prof., Univ. of Pennsylvania, 1959–60; Vis. Prof., Harvard Univ., 1974; Vis. Prof. and Commonwealth Fellow: Univ. of BC, 1968; Macquarie Univ., Sydney, 1979–80. Dir, Transmark Ltd, 1979–. Chief Econ. Adviser, Min. of Transport, 1964–68; Special Adviser, Treasury and CS Cttee, Nationalised Industry Financing, 1981; formerly Member: Cttee on Road Pricing (Smeed Cttee); Cttee on Transport in London; Cttee on Transport Planning (Lady Sharp Cttee); Urban Motorways Inter-Deptl Cttee; Standing Adv. Cttee on Trunk Road Assessment (Sir George Leitch Cttee). Managing Editor, Jl of Transport Economics and Policy, 1975–. *Publications:* Urban Transport: studies in economic policy, 1973; (co-ed with D. C. Hague) Britain in the Common Market: a new business opportunity, 1974; (ed) Productivity and Amenity: achieving a social balance, 1974; (ed) Industrial Relations in a Changing World, 1975; (with T. C. Evans) Corporate Social Responsibility: a reassessment, 1978; Liberalisation of the Use of British Telecommunications Network: an independent economic enquiry, 1981. *Recreations:* music, table tennis, golf. *Address:* 59 Canons Drive, Edgware, Mddx HA8 7RG. *T:* 01–952 1320. *Club:* Reform.

BEESON, Prof. Paul Bruce, Hon. KBE 1973; FRCP; Professor of Medicine, University of Washington, 1974–82, now Emeritus; *b* 18 Oct. 1908; *s* of John Bradley Beeson, Livingston, Mont; *m* 1942, Barbara Neal, *d* of Ray C. Neal, Buffalo, NY; two *s* one *d*. *Educ:* Univ. of Washington, McGill Univ. Med. Sch. MD, CM, 1933. Intern, Hosp. of Univ. of Pa, 1933–35; Gen. practice of medicine, Wooster, Ohio, 1935–37; Asst Rockefeller Inst., 1937–39; Chief Med. Resident, Peter Bent Brigham Hosp., 1939–40; Instructor in Med., Havard Med. Sch., and Chief Phys., American Red Cross-Harvard Field Hosp. Unit, Salisbury, 1940–42; Asst and Assoc. Prof. of Med., Emory Med. Sch., 1942–46; Prof. of Med. Emory Med. Sch., 1946–52; Prof. of Med. and Chm. Dept of Med., Yale Univ., 1952–65; Nuffield Prof. of Clinical Med., Oxford Univ., and Fellow of Magdalen Coll., 1965–74, Hon. Fellow, 1975; Hon. Fellow RSM, 1976. Vis. Investigator, Wright-Fleming Inst., St Mary's Hosp., 1958–59. Pres., Assoc. Amer. Physicians, 1967; Master, Amer. Coll. of Physicians, 1970. Phillips Award, Amer. Coll. Physicians, 1975; Flexner Award, Assoc. Amer. Med. Colls, 1977. *Alumnus Summa Laude Dignatus*, Univ. of Washington, 1968; Hon. DSc: Emory Univ., 1968; McGill Univ., 1971; Yale Univ., 1975; Albany Med. Coll., 1975; Ohio Med. Coll., 1979. *Publications:* (ed jtly) The Oxford Companion to Medicine, 1986; edited: Cecil-Loeb Textbook of Medicine, 1959–82; Yale Journal Biology and Medicine, 1959–65; Journal Amer. Geriatric Soc., 1981–84; numerous scientific publications relating to infectious disease, pathogenesis of fever, pyelonephritis and mechanism of eosinophilia. *Address:* 21013 NE 122nd Street, Redmond, Washington 98053, USA.

BEESON, Very Rev. Trevor Randall; Dean of Winchester, since 1987; *b* 2 March 1926; *s* of late Arthur William and Matilda Beeson; *m* 1950, Josephine Grace Cope; two *d*. *Educ:* King's Coll., London (AKC 1950); St Boniface Coll., Warminster. RAF Met Office, 1944–47. Deacon, 1951; Priest, 1952; Curate, Leadgate, Co. Durham, 1951–54; Priest-in-charge and subseq. Vicar of St Chad, Stockton-on-Tees, 1954–65; Curate of St Martin-in-the-Fields, London, 1965–71; Vicar of Ware, Herts, 1971–76; Canon of Westminster, 1976–87; Treasurer, Westminster, 1978–82; Rector of St Margaret's, Westminster, 1982–87; Chaplain to Speaker of House of Commons, 1982–87. Chaplain of St Bride's, Fleet Street, 1967–84. Gen. Sec., Parish and People, 1962–64; Editor, New Christian, and Man. Dir, Prism Publications Ltd, 1965–70; European Corresp. of The Christian Century (Chicago), 1970–83; Chm., SCM Press Ltd, 1978–. Hon. MA (Lambeth) 1976. *Publications:* New Area Mission, 1963; (jtly) Worship in a United Church, 1964; An Eye for an Ear, 1972; The Church of England in Crisis, 1973; Discretion and Valour: religious conditions in Russia and Eastern Europe, 1974; Britain Today and Tomorrow, 1978; Westminster Abbey, 1981; A Vision of Hope: the churches and change in Latin America, 1984. *Recreations:* cricket, gardening. *Address:* The Deanery, The Close, Winchester, Hants SO23 9LS.

BEESTON, Prof. Alfred Felix Landon, MA, DPhil; FBA 1965; Laudian Professor of Arabic, Oxford, 1956–78; Emeritus Fellow, St John's College, Oxford, 1978 (Fellow, 1955–78); *b* 1911; *o s* of Herbert Arthur Beeston and Edith Mary Landon. *Educ:* Westminster Sch.; Christ Church, Oxford. James Mew Arabic Scholarship, Oxford, 1934; MA (Oxford), 1936; DPhil (Oxford), 1937. Asst in Dept of Oriental Books, Bodleian Library, Oxford, 1935–40; Sub-Librarian and Keeper of Oriental Books, Bodleian Library, 1946–55. Mem., Governing Body, SOAS, Univ. of London, 1980–84 (Hon. Fellow 1980). *Publications:* Baiḍāwī's Commentary on Sūrah 12, 1963; Written Arabic, 1968; The Arabic Language Today, 1970; Selections from the Poetry of Baššār, 1977; Samples of Arabic Prose, 1977; The 'Epistle on Singing Girls' of Jāḥiz, 1980; Sabaic Grammar, 1984; many articles. *Address:* St John's College, Oxford OX1 3JP.

BEETHAM, Marshal of the Royal Air Force Sir Michael (James), GCB 1978 (KCB 1976); CBE 1967; DFC 1944; AFC 1960; FRAeS; Chief of the Air Staff, 1977–82; Air ADC to the Queen, 1977–82; Chairman, GEC (formerly Marconi) Avionics Ltd, since 1986 (Director, since 1984); *b* 17 May 1923; *s* of Major G. C. Beetham, MC; *m* 1956, Patricia Elizabeth Lane; one *s* one *d*. *Educ:* St Marylebone Grammar School. Joined RAF, 1941; pilot trng, 1941–42; commnd 1942; Bomber Comd: 50, 57 and 35 Sqdns, 1943–46; HQ Staff, 1947–49; 82 (Recce) Sqdn, E Africa, 1949–51; psa 1952; Air Min. (Directorate Operational Requirements), 1953–56; CO 214 (Valiant) Sqdn Marham, 1958–60; Gp Captain Ops, HQ Bomber Comd, 1962–64; CO RAF Khormaksar, Aden, 1964–66; idc 1967; Dir Ops (RAF), MoD, 1968–70; Comdt, RAF Staff Coll., 1970–72; ACOS (Plans and Policy), SHAPE, 1972–75; Dep. C-in-C, Strike Command, 1975–76; C-in-C RAF Germany, and Comdr, 2nd Tactical Allied Air Force, 1976–77. Dir, Brixton Estate PLC, 1983–. Chm., Trustees, RAF Museum, 1983–. FRSA 1979; FRAeS 1982. *Recreations:* golf, tennis. *Address:* Lloyds Bank, Cox's & King's Branch, 6 Pall Mall, SW1. *Clubs:* Royal Air Force; Royal West Norfolk Golf.

BEETHAM, Roger Campbell, LVO 1976; HM Diplomatic Service; Head of Maritime, Aviation and Environment Department, Foreign and Commonwealth Office, since 1985; *b* 22 Nov. 1937; *s* of Henry Campbell and Mary Beetham; *m* 1965, Judith Mary Yorwerth Rees. *Educ:* Peter Symonds Sch., Winchester; Brasenose Coll., Oxford (MA). Entered HM Diplomatic Service, 1960; FO, 1960–62; UK Delegation to Disarmament Conference, Geneva, 1962–65; Washington, 1965–68; News Dept, FCO, 1969–72; Head of Chancery, Helsinki, 1972–76; FCO, 1976; seconded to European Commission, Brussels, as Spokesman of the President, Rt Hon. Roy Jenkins, 1977–80; Counsellor (Econ. and Commercial), New Delhi, 1981–85. Order of the White Rose of Finland, 1976. *Recreations:* oenology, cooking, travel. *Address:* c/o Foreign and Commonwealth Office, SW1; 64 Beaulieu Avenue, SE26. *Club:* Travellers'.

BEEVOR, John Grosvenor, OBE 1945; *b* 1 March 1905; *s* of Henry Beevor, Newark-on-Trent, Notts; *m* 1st, 1933, Carinthia Jane (marr. diss., 1956), *d* of Aubrey and Caroline Waterfield, Aulla, Italy; three *s*; 2nd, 1957, Mary Christine Grepe. *Educ:* Winchester; New Coll., Oxford. Solicitor, 1931–53, Slaughter and May, London, EC2. Served HM Army, 1939–45, RA and SOE. Adviser to British Delegation to Marshall Plan Conf., Paris, 1947; Mem. Lord Chancellor's Cttee on Private Internat. Law, 1952–53; Man. Dir, Commonwealth Development Finance Co. Ltd, 1954–56; Vice-Pres., Internat. Finance Corp., Washington, DC, 1956–64. Chairman: Doulton & Co., 1966–75; Tilbury Contracting Group, 1966–76; Lafarge Organisation Ltd, 1966–76; Director: Lafarge SA, 1969–80; Williams & Glyn's Bank Ltd, 1970–75; Glaxo Holdings Ltd, 1965–75. Member Councils: The Officers' Assoc.; Overseas Develt Inst. *Publications:* The Effective Board, a Chairman's View, 1975; SOE, Recollections and Reflections, 1981. *Address:* 161 Fulham Road, Chelsea, SW3 6SN. *T:* 01–581 8386.

BEEVOR, Miles; retired Solicitor and Director of Companies; *b* 8 March 1900; 2nd *s* of Rowland Beevor; *m* 1st, 1924, Margaret Florence Platt (*d* 1934); one *s* (and one *d* decd); 2nd, 1935, Sybil Gilliat; two *s* one *d*. *Educ:* Winchester (Scholar); New Coll., Oxford (Scholar), BA 1921. Admitted a Solicitor, 1925. Served European War, 1914–18, in Army (RE Officer Cadet Battalion), 1918; War of 1939–45, RAFVR (Flt-Lieut Admin. and Special Duties Br.), 1941–43. Chief Legal Adviser, LNER, 1943–47; Actg Chief General Manager, LNER, 1947; Chief Sec. and Legal Adviser, British Transport Commission, 1947–51; Managing Dir, Brush Electrical Engineering Co. Ltd (which became The Brush Group Ltd), 1952–56; Deputy Chm. and Joint Managing Dir, 1956–57. *Address:* 44 Mill Lane, Welwyn, Herts. *T:* Welwyn 5103.

BEEVOR, Sir Thomas Agnew, 7th Bt, *cr* 1784; *b* 6 Jan. 1929; *s* of Comdr Sir Thomas Beevor, 6th Bt, and Edith Margaret Agnew (who *m* 2nd, 1944, Rear-Adm. R. A. Currie, *qv*, and *d* 1985); *S* father 1943; *m* 1st, 1957, Barbara Clare (marr. diss., 1965), *y d* of Capt. R. L. B. Cunliffe, RN (retd); one *s* two *d*; 2nd, 1966, Carola, *d* of His Honour J. B. Herbert, MC; 3rd, 1976, Mrs Sally Bouwens, White Hall, Saham Toney, Norfolk. *Heir: s* Thomas Hugh Cunliffe Beevor, *b* 1 Oct. 1962. *Address:* Hargham Hall, Norwich.

BEEZLEY, Frederick Ernest; His Honour Judge Beezley; a Circuit Judge, since 1976; *b* 30 Jan. 1921; *s* of Frederick William Beezley and Lilian Isabel (*née* Markham); *m* 1969, Sylvia Ruth (*née* Locke). *Educ:* Acton County Sch. Served War, Royal Signals, Combined Operations, 1940–46. Called to Bar, Gray's Inn, 1947. *Recreation:* sea angling. *Address:* c/o The Crown Court, Shirehall, Norwich. *T:* Norwich 29859.

BEGG, Rt. Rev. Ian Forbes, MA, DD; *b* 12 Feb. 1910; *e s* of Rev. John Smith Begg and Elizabeth Macintyre; *m* 1949, Lillie Taylor Paterson. *Educ:* Aberdeen Grammar Sch.; Aberdeen Univ.; Westcott House, Cambridge. Deacon 1933; Priest 1934. Curate, St Paul's, Prince's Park, Liverpool, 1933–35; Priest-in-Charge of St Ninian's Episcopal Church, Seaton, Aberdeen, 1935–73; Dean, United Diocese of Aberdeen and Orkney, 1969–73; Bishop of Aberdeen and Orkney, 1973–77; permission to officiate in Diocese, 1978; Canon of St Andrew's Cathedral, Aberdeen, 1965. Chm., Church Guest Houses' Assoc., 1969–. Hon. DD Aberdeen, 1971. *Recreations:* fishing, gardening. *Address:* 430 King Street, Aberdeen. *T:* Aberdeen 632169.

BEGG, Dr Sir Neil (Colquhoun), KBE 1986 (OBE 1973); Director of Medical Services, Royal New Zealand Plunket Society, 1956–76, retired; *b* 13 April 1915; *s* of Charles Mackie Begg, CB, CMG, Croix de Guerre, and Lillian Helen Lawrence Begg; *m* 1942, Margaret Milne MacLean; two *s* two *d*. *Educ:* John McGlashan Coll., Dunedin, NZ; Otago Univ. Med. Sch. (MB ChB 1940); postgrad. paediatrics, London and Edinburgh, 1947–48. DCH, MRCP London, MRCPE. Served 2 NZ Expedn Force, 1942–46, Med. Corps, ME and Italy. Paediatrician, Dunedin Public Hosp., 1949–56. Chm., NZ Historic Places Trust, 1978–86. Hon. FRCPE 1958, Hon. FRCP 1977. *Publications:* Dusky Bay (with A. C. Begg), 1966; (with A. C. Begg) James Cook and New Zealand, 1969; Child and his Family, 1970, 8th edn 1975; (with A. C. Begg) Port Preservation, 1973; (with A. C. Begg) The World of John Boultbee, 1979; contribs to NZ Med. Jl. *Recreation:* trout fishing. *Address:* 86 Newington Avenue, Dunedin, New Zealand. *T:* 772–089.

BEGG, Robert William, CBE 1977; MA; CA; FRSA; Consultant, Mann Judd Gordon, Chartered Accountants, Glasgow, since 1986 (Partner, 1951–86); *b* 19 Feb. 1922; *s* of late David Begg, CA, FFA, and of Elizabeth Young Thomson; *m* 1948, Sheena Margaret Boyd; two *s*. *Educ:* Greenock Acad.; Glasgow Univ. (MA 1942). Served Royal Navy, 1942–46, Lieut RNVR (despatches). Institute of Chartered Accountants of Scotland: Member, 1948; Examining Bd, 1952–58; Public Relations Cttee, 1968–74; Pres., Benevolent Assoc., 1973–75; Mem. Glasgow Univ. General Council Business Cttee, 1973–76; Hon. Treasurer: Royal Philosophical Soc. of Glasgow, 1952–62; Royal Glasgow Inst. of Fine Arts, 1975–; Mem. Bd of Governors, Glasgow School of Art, 1955–77, Chm., 1970–76; Assessor, Glasgow Univ. Court, 1986–; Trustee, RIAS Hill House Trust, 1977–82; Bd of Trustees, National Galleries of Scotland, 1974–, Chm., 1980–; Mem. Council, National Trust for Scotland, 1984– (Mem. Exec. Cttee, 1985–). *Recreation:* painting. *Address:* 142 St Vincent Street, Glasgow G2 5LD. *T:* 041–221 6991; (home) 3 Colquhoun Drive, Bearsden, Glasgow G61 4NQ. *T:* 041–942 2436. *Clubs:* Art (Glasgow); New (Edinburgh).

BEGG, Admiral of the Fleet Sir Varyl (Cargill), GCB 1965 (KCB 1962; CB 1959); DSO 1952; DSC 1941; Governor and Commander-in-Chief of Gibraltar, 1969–73; *b* 1 Oct. 1908; *s* of Francis Cargill Begg and Muriel Clare Robinson; *m* 1943, Rosemary Cowan, CStJ; two *s*. *Educ:* St Andrews Sch., Eastbourne; Malvern Coll. Entered RN, special entry, 1926; Qualified Gunnery Officer, 1933; HMS Glasgow, 1939–40; HMS Warspite, 1940–43; Comdr Dec. 1942; Capt. 1947; commanded HM Gunnery Sch., Chatham, 1948–50; 8th Destroyer Flotilla, 1950–52; HMS Excellent, 1952–54; HMS Triumph, 1955–56; idc 1954; Rear-Adm. 1957; Chief of Staff to C-in-C Portsmouth 1957–58; Flag Officer Commanding Fifth Cruiser Squadron and Flag Officer Second-in-Command, Far East Station, 1958–60; Vice-Adm. 1960; a Lord Commissioner of the Admiralty and Vice-Chief of Naval Staff, 1961–63; Admiral, 1963; C-in-C, British Forces in the Far East, and UK Military Adviser to SEATO, 1963–65; C-in-C, Portsmouth, and Allied C-in-C, Channel, 1965–66; Chief of Naval Staff and First Sea Lord, 1966–68. KStJ 1969. PMN 1966. *Recreations:* fishing, gardening. *Address:* Copyhold Cottage, Chilbolton, Stockbridge, Hants. *Club:* Army and Navy.

BEGGS, Roy; MP (UU) East Antrim, since 1983 (resigned seat Dec. 1985 in protest against Anglo-Irish Agreement; re-elected Jan. 1986); *b* 20 Feb. 1936; *s* of John Beggs; *m* 1959, Wilma Lorimer; two *s* two *d*. *Educ:* Ballyclare High Sch.; Stranmillis Trng Coll. (Certificate/Diploma in Educn). Teacher, 1957–78, Vice-Principal, 1978–83, Larne High Sch. Mem., 1973–, Vice-Chm., 1981–, NE Educn and Library Bd; Pres., Assoc. of Educn and Liby Bds, NI, 1984–85 (Vice-Pres., 1983–84). Mem., Larne Borough Council, 1973–; Mayor of Larne, 1978–83; Mem. for N Antrim, NI Assembly, 1982–86. Mem., Public Accounts Cttee, 1984–. *Address:* House of Commons, SW1; 9 Carnduff Road, Ballyvernstown, Larne, Co. Antrim. *T:* Larne 73258.

BEGIN, Menachem, MJr; Prime Minister, State of Israel, 1977–83; *b* Brest-Litovsk, Poland, 16 Aug. 1913; *s* of Ze'ev-Dov and Hassia Begin; *m* 1939, Aliza Arnold (*d* 1982); one *s* two *d*. *Educ:* Mizrachi Hebrew Sch.; Polish Gymnasium (High Sch.); Univ. of Warsaw (MJr). Belonged to Hashomer Hatza'ir scout movement as a boy, joining Betar, the Zionist Youth Movement, when 16; head of Organization Dept of Betar for Poland, 1932; also delegated to Czechoslovakia to head movement there; returned to Poland, 1937, and after spell of imprisonment for leading demonstration against British policy in Eretz Israel became head of the movement in Poland, 1939. On outbreak of World War II, arrested by Russian NKVD and later confined in concentration camps in Siberia, 1941–42; subseq. released under Stalin-Sikorski agreement; joined Polish Army, 1942, his brigade being posted to Eretz Israel; after demobilization assumed comd of IZL, the National Military Organization, directing from underground headquarters operations against the British; met members of UN Inquiry Cttee and foreign press, secretly, to explain his movement's outlook. After estabt of State of Israel, 1948, he and his colleagues founded the Herut Movement and he headed that party's list of candidates for the Knesset; has been a member of the Knesset since the first elections; on eve of Six Day War, 1 June 1967, joined Govt of Nat. Unity, serving as Minister without Portfolio, until Aug. 1970; presented his Coalition to the Knesset, June 1977, winning necessary vote of confidence to become Prime Minister; re-elected Prime Minister following nat. elections, June 1981. Nobel Peace Prize (jtly, with Mohamed Anwar El-Sadat), 1978. *Publications:* White Nights (describing his wartime experience in Europe); The Revolt, trans. several languages; numerous articles. *Address:* Herut Movement Headquarters, Beit Jabotinsky, 38 King George Street, Tel Aviv, Israel.

BEHNE, Edmond Rowlands, CMG 1974; Managing Director, Pioneer Sugar Mills Ltd, Queensland, 1952–76; *b* 20 Nov. 1906; *s* of late Edmund Behne; *m* 1932, Grace Elizabeth Ricketts; two *s* one *d*. *Educ:* Bendigo Sch. of Mines; Brisbane Boys' Coll.; Univ. of Queensland. BSc and MSc (App.); ARACI. Bureau of Sugar Experiment Stations, 1930–48 (Director, 1947); Pioneer Sugar Mills Ltd, 1948–80. *Recreation:* bowls. *Address:* Craigston, 217 Wickham Terrace, Brisbane, Qld 4000, Australia. *T:* 221–5657. *Clubs:* Queensland, Johnsonian (both in Brisbane).

BEHR, Norman Isaac, FRICS; Valuer Member, London Rent Assessment Panel, since 1983; *b* 28 Sept. 1922; *s* of Moses and Sarah Behr; *m* 1950, Anne Laurette Hilton. *Educ:* Haberdashers' Aske's Sch.; College of Estate Management. Chartered Surveyor. Articled, De Groot & Co., 1939–42; served War, RAOC, REME, 1942–46; joined Valuation Office, 1948; District Valuer and Valuation Officer, Westminster, 1965–67, City of London, 1967–70; Superintending Valuer, 1970; Asst Chief Valuer, 1977; Dep. Chief Valuer (Rating), 1981–83. First Prize, Chartered Auctioneers and Estate Agents Inst., 1941; Wainwright Prize, Royal Instn of Chartered Surveyors, 1950. *Recreations:* opera, cooking, computers. *Address:* 43 Netherhall Gardens, NW3 5RL. *T:* 01–435 9391.

BEHRMAN, Simon, FRCP; Hon. Consultant Emeritus in Neurology, Guy's Health District; Consulting Physician, Moorfields, Eye Hospital; formerly Consulting Neurologist: Regional Neurosurgical Centre, Brook Hospital; Lewisham, Dulwich, St Giles', St Francis', St Leonard's, Bromley and Farnborough Hospitals; *s* of late Leopold Behrman; *m* 1940, Dorothy, *d* of late Charles Engelbert; two *s* two *d*. *Educ:* University Coll. and St Bartholomew's Hosp., London. BSc (Hons) London. 1925; MRCS Eng. 1928; MRCP London 1932. Member: Assoc. of British Neurologists; Ophthalmological Soc. of UK; Academic Bd of Inst of Ophthalmology, University of London; FRSocMed. House Physician and Registrar, Hosp. for Nervous Diseases, Maida Vale, 1930–33; Registrar: Nat. Hosp., Queen Square, 1934–38; Dept of Nervous Diseases, Guy's Hosp., 1935–45. *Publications:* articles on neurology and neuro-ophthalmology. *Address:* 33 Harley Street, W1. *T:* 01–580 3388; The Dower House, Oxney, St Margaret's-at-Cliffe, Kent. *T:* Dover 852161.

BEILL, Air Vice-Marshal Alfred, CB 1986; Director General of Supply (RAF) , since 1984; *b* 14 Feb. 1931; *s* of late Group Captain Robert Beill, CBE, DFC and of Sophie Beill; *m* 1953, Vyvian Mary Crowhurst Archer; four *d*. *Educ:* Rossall Sch.; RAF Coll., Cranwell. FCIT 1980; FBIM 1976; FInstPS 1985. Commnd RAF, 1952; served, 1952–64: RAF Marham, Stafford and Fauld; HQ Air Forces ME, Aden; RAF Supply Control Centre, Hendon; student, RAF Staff Coll., Andover, 1964; HQ FEAF, Singapore, 1965–67; student, JSSC, Latimer, 1968; OC Supply and Movements Sqdn, RAF Scampton, 1968–69, HQ Maintenance Comd, 1969–70; DS JSSC (later NDC), 1970–73; Comd Supply Officer, HQ NEAF, Cyprus, 1973–75; Dir of Engrg and Supply Policy (RAF), 1976–78; student, RCDS, 1978; Dir of Movements (RAF), 1979–82; Dir of Supply Policy and Logistics Plans (RAF), 1982–84. ADC to the Queen, 1974–75. Pres., RAF Swimming Assoc., 1982–. *Address:* c/o Lloyds Bank, Cox's & King's Branch, 6 Pall Mall, SW1Y 5NH. *Club:* Royal Air Force.

BEISHON, (Ronald) John, DPhil, CEng; seconded as Acting Director, 1985, Permanent Director, since 1986, Polytechnic of North London; *b* 10 Nov. 1930; *s* of Arthur and Irene Beishon; *m* 1955, Gwenda Jean Solway; two *s* two *d*. *Educ:* Battersea Polytechnic; Univ. of London (BSc); Univ. of Birmingham; Univ. of Oxford (DPhil). MIM, MWeldI. National Service, RASC, 1951–53; Technical Officer, ICI Ltd, 1954–58; Section Leader, BICC Ltd, 1958–61; Sen. Res. Asst, Oxford Univ., 1961–64; Lectr, Bristol Univ., 1964–68; Reader, Sussex Univ., 1968–71; Professor of Systems, Open Univ., 1971–80;

Dir, Poly. of South Bank, 1980–85. FRSA. *Publications:* (ed with G. Peters) Systems Behaviour, 1973, 2nd edn 1976; articles in various jls. *Recreation:* squash. *Address:* 421 Ditchling Road, Brighton, Sussex BN1 6XB. *T:* Brighton 552100. *Club:* Wig and Pen.

BEIT, Sir Alfred Lane, 2nd Bt, *cr* 1924; Trustee of the Beit Trust; Trustee of Beit Fellowships for scientific research; *b* London, 19 Jan. 1903; *o* surv. *s* of 1st Bt and Lilian (*d* 1946), *d* of late T. L. Carter, New Orleans, USA; *S* father, 1930; *m* 1939. Clementine, 2nd *d* of late Major the Hon. Clement Mitford, DSO and Lady Helen Nutting. *Educ:* Eton; Christ Church, Oxford. Contested West Islington in LCC election 1928; South-East St Pancras (C) in general election, 1929; MP (U) St Pancras South-East, 1931–45. Pres., Wexford Fest. Opera; Mem., Board of Governors and Guardians, Nat. Gallery of Ireland. Hon. LLD Nat. Univ. of Ireland, 1979. *Heir:* none. *Address:* Russborough, Blessington, Co. Wicklow, Eire; Gordon's Bay, CP, S Africa. *Clubs:* Brooks's, Carlton; Kildare Street and University (Dublin); Civil Service (Cape Town); Muthaiga (Nairobi).

BEITH, Alan James; MP (L) Berwick-upon-Tweed since Nov. 1973; Deputy Leader, Liberal Party, since 1985; spokesman on Parliamentary and Constitutional Affairs, since 1983 and on Foreign Affairs, since 1985; *b* 20 April 1943; *o s* of James and Joan Beith, Poynton, Ches; *m* 1965, Barbara Jean Ward; one *s* one *d*. *Educ:* King's Sch., Macclesfield; Balliol and Nuffield Colls, Oxford. BLitt, MA Oxon. Lectr, Dept of Politics, Univ. of Newcastle upon Tyne, 1966–73. Vice-Chm., Northumberland Assoc. of Parish Councils, 1970–71 and 1972–73; Jt Chm., Assoc. of Councillors, 1974–79; Member: Gen. Adv. Council of BBC, 1974–84; Hexham RDC, 1969–74; Corbridge Parish Council, 1970–74; Tynedale District Council, 1973–74; BBC NE Regional Adv. Council, 1971–74; NE Transport Users' Consultative Cttee, 1970–74. Mem., House of Commons Commn, 1979–; UK Rep. to Council of Europe and WEU, 1976–84. Liberal Chief Whip, 1976–85; spokesman on Educn, 1977–83. Methodist Local Preacher. *Publications:* The Case for the Liberal Party and the Alliance, 1983; chapter in The British General Election of 1964, ed Butler and King, 1965; articles in Public Administration Bull., Policy and Politics, Parliamentary Affairs, New Society, Local Government Chronicle, Parish Councils Review, etc. *Recreations:* walking, music, looking at old buildings. *Address:* West End Cottage, Whittingham, Alnwick, Northumberland. *T:* Whittingham 313. *Clubs:* National Liberal; Union Society (Oxford); Shilbottle Working Men's (Alnwick).

BEITH, Sir John, KCMG 1969 (CMG 1959); HM Diplomatic Service, retired; *b* 4 April 1914; *s* of late William Beith and Margaret Stanley, Toowoomba, Qld; *m* 1949, Diana Gregory-Hood, *d* of Sir John Little Gilmour, 2nd Bt; one *s* one *d* (and one *d* decd), (one step *s* one step *d*). *Educ:* Eton; King's Coll., Cambridge. Entered Diplomatic Service, 1937, and served in FO until 1940; 3rd Sec., Athens, 1940–41; 2nd Sec., Buenos Aires, 1941–45; served Foreign Office, 1945–49; Head of UK Permanent Delegation to the UN at Geneva, 1950–53; Head of Chancery at Prague, 1953–54; Counsellor, 1954; Counsellor and Head of Chancery, British Embassy, Paris, 1954–59; Head of Levant Dept, FO, 1959–61; Head of North and East African Dept, Foreign Office, 1961–63; Ambassador to Israel, 1963–65; an Asst Sec.-Gen., NATO, 1966–67; Asst Under-Sec. of State, FO, 1967–69; Ambassador to Belgium, 1969–74. *Recreations:* music, racing, tennis. *Address:* Dean Farm House, Winchester. *T:* Sparsholt 326. *Clubs:* White's, Anglo-Belgian.

BEITH, John William, CBE 1972; Director Special Duties, Massey Ferguson Holdings Ltd, 1971–74, retired; *b* 13 Jan. 1909; *s* of John William Beith and Ana Theresia (*née* Denk); *m* 1931, Dorothy (*née* Causbrook); two *s*. *Educ:* Spain, Chile, Germany; Llandovery Coll., S Wales. Joined Massey Harris (now Massey Ferguson), 1927, London; occupied senior exec. positions in Argentina, Canada, France and UK; Vice-Pres., Canadian parent co., 1963; Chm., Massey Ferguson (UK) Ltd, 1970. Pres., Agricl Engrs Assoc. Ltd, 1970. *Recreations:* ancient and contemporary history; follower of Rugby; swimming. *Address:* Torre Blanca, Cala Serena, Cala d'Or, Mallorca. *T:* Baleares 657830. *Club:* Oriental.

BÉJART, Maurice (Jean); choreographer; Director, Twentieth Century Ballet Company, since 1959; *b* 1 Jan. 1927; *s* of Gaston and Germaine Berger. *Educ:* Lycée de Marseilles. Début as ballet dancer with Marseilles Opéra, 1945; International Ballet, 1949–50; Royal Opera, Stockholm, 1951–52; co-founded Les Ballets de l'Etoile, later Ballet-Théâtre de Paris, 1954 (Dir, 1954–59); Dir of Ballet, Théâtre Royal de la Monnaie, Brussels, 1959; Dir, Mudra sch., 1972–. Grand Prix National de la Musique, 1970; Prix Erasme de la danse, 1974. Chevalier des Arts et des Lettres. Principal works include: La Belle au Boa, Symphonie pour un homme seul, 1955; Orphée, 1958; Le sacre du printemps, 1960; The Tales of Hoffman, 1962; The Merry Widow, 1963; The Damnation of Faust, 1964; Ode à la joie (Beethoven's 9th Symphony), Romeo and Juliet, 1966; Messe pour le temps présent, 1967; Firebird, 1970; Nijinsky: clown de Dieu, Stimmung, 1972; Le Marteau sans Maître, La Traviata, 1973; Pli selon Pli, Notre Faust, 1976; Rhapsodie, Ah vous dirai-je Mamam?, 1977; Gaîté Parisienne, 1980; The Magic Flute, La Muette, Les Uns et Les Autres (film), Light, 1981; Don Giovanni, Wien, Wien, nur du Allein, 1982; Thalassa: Mare Nostrum, Salome, 1983. *Publications:* Mathilde, ou le temps perdu (novel), 1963; La Reine Verte (play), 1963; L'autre chant de la danse, 1974. *Address:* Ballet du XXe Siècle, Théâtre de la Monnaie, 4 Rue Léopold, Brussels, Belgium.

BEKER, Prof. Henry Joseph, PhD; Director-in-Charge, Racal-Guardata Ltd, since 1986; Visiting Professor of Information Technology, Royal Holloway and Bedford New College (formerly Royal Holloway College), University of London, since 1984; *b* 22 Dec. 1951; *s* of Jozef and Mary Beker; *m* 1976, Mary Louise (*née* Keilthy); one *d*. *Educ:* Kilburn Grammar Sch.; Univ. of London (BSc Maths 1973, PhD 1976); Open Univ. (BA 1982). CEng, MIEE, 1984; MIS, 1977; AFIMA, 1978. Sen. Res. Asst, Dept of Statistics, University Coll. of Swansea, 1976–77; Principal Mathematician, Racal-Comsec Ltd, 1977–80, Chief Mathematician, 1980–83; Dir of Research, Racal Research Ltd, 1983–85; Dir of Systems, Racal-Chubb Security Systems Ltd, 1985–86. Vis. Prof. of IT, Westfield Coll., Univ. of London, 1983–84. FRSA. *Publications:* Cipher Systems, 1982; Secure Speech Communications, 1985. *Recreations:* music, reading, travel. *Address:* Richmond Court, 309 Fleet Road, Fleet, Hants GU13 8BU. *T:* Fleet 622144.

BEKOE, Dr Daniel Adzei; Director, UNESCO Regional Office for Science and Technology for Africa, since 1983; Member, Pontifical Academy of Sciences, since 1983; *b* 7 Dec. 1928; *s* of Aristocles Silvanus Adzete Bekoe and Jessie Nadu (*née* Awuletey); *m* 1958, Theresa Victoria Anyisaa Annan (marr. diss. 1983); three *s* (and one *s* decd). *Educ:* Achimota Sch.; University Coll. of Gold Coast (BSc London); Univ. of Oxford (DPhil). Jun. Res. Asst, Univ. of Calif, LA, 1957–58; Univ. of Ghana (formerly University Coll. of Ghana): Lectr, 1958–63; Sen. Lectr, 1963–65; Associate Prof., 1965–74; Prof. of Chemistry, 1974–83; Vice-Chancellor, 1976–83. Sabbatical year, Univ. of Calif, LA, 1962–63; Vis. Associate Prof., Univ. of Ibadan, 1966–67. Member: UN Univ. Council, 1980–83; UN Adv. Cttee on Science and Technology for Develt, 1980–82. Pres., ICSU, 1980–83. *Publications:* articles on molecular structures in crystallographic and chemical jls; gen. articles in Proc. Ghana Acad. of Arts and Sciences. *Recreations:* music, swimming, walking. *Address:* UNESCO Regional Office for Science and Technology for Africa, PO Box 30592, Bruce House, Standard Street, Nairobi, Kenya. *T:* Nairobi 25861, 25868.

BELAM, Noël Stephen; Under-Secretary, Department of Industry, 1975–79, retired; *b* 19 Jan. 1920; *s* of Dr Francis Arthur Belam and Hilda Mary Belam; *m* 1948, Anne Coaker; one *s* one *d*. *Educ:* Cranleigh Sch.; St Edmund Hall, Oxford (MA). Royal Artillery (T/Captain), 1940–46. Board of Trade, 1947; Trade Comr, Karachi, 1955–58; Private Sec. to successive Ministers of State, BoT, 1961–63; Asst Sec., 1963; Principal Trade Comr, Vancouver, 1963–67; Board of Trade: Regional Controller NW Region, 1967–70; Asst Sec., London, 1970–75; Under Sec., 1975. *Recreations:* fishing, Dartmoor ponies. *Address:* Fore Stoke Farm, Holne, Newton Abbot, Devon TQ13 7SS. *T:* Poundsgate 394.

BELCH, Alexander Ross, CBE 1972; FRSE 1977; FRINA; CBIM; Chairman: Jebsens Travel Ltd, since 1981; Lithgow Hotels Ltd, since 1983; Irvine Development Corporation, since 1985; Deputy Chairman, Jebsens Drilling plc, since 1980; *b* 13 Dec. 1920; *s* of Alexander Belch, CBE, and Agnes Wright Ross; *m* 1947, Janette Finnie Murdoch; four *d*. *Educ:* Morrison's Acad., Crieff, Perthshire; Glasgow Univ. (BSc Naval Arch. 1st Cl. Hons). Lithgows Ltd: Dir and Gen. Manager, 1954–59; Asst Man. Dir, 1959–64; Man. Dir, 1964–69; Scott Lithgow Ltd: Man. Dir, 1969–80; Chm., 1978–80; Director: Lithgows Ltd, 1972–; Jebsens (UK) Ltd, and various other Jebsen Gp cos, 1973–; YARD Ltd, 1980–; Kongsberg Ltd, 1983–; J. H. Carruthers & Co. Ltd, 1983–; Gault Armstrong and Kemble (Holdings), 1984–; Inverclyde Enterprise Trust Ltd, 1984–; Data-Ship (UK), 1984–. Chm., Mining Machinery Sector Working Pty, NEDO, 1983–. Pres., Shipbuilders and Repairers Nat. Assoc., 1974–76. Chm., Council of Trustees, Scottish Maritime Museum, 1983–. CBIM 1981. Hon. LLD Strathclyde, 1978. *Address:* Altnacraig, Lyle Road, Greenock, Renfrewshire. *T:* Greenock 21124.

BELCHER, John Rashleigh, MS 1946; FRCS 1942; Consultant Thoracic Surgeon, NE Metropolitan Regional Hospital Board, since 1950; Surgeon, London Chest Hospital, since 1951; Thoracic Surgeon, Middlesex Hospital, since 1955; *b* 11 Jan. 1917; *s* of late Dr Ormonde Rashleigh Belcher, Liverpool; *m* 1940, Jacqueline Mary, *d* of late C. P. Phillips; two *s* one *d*. *Educ:* Epsom Coll.; St Thomas' Hosp. MB 1939; FRCS 1942; MS 1946; Resident appointments at St Thomas' Hospital, 1939–40. RAF, 1940–46: Medical Service; general duties and surgical specialist; Squadron Leader. Resident and Asst posts at St Thomas', Brompton, London Chest, and Middlesex Hosps; followed by consultant appointments; co-editor, Brit. Jl of Diseases of the Chest. Pres., Assoc. of Thoracic Surgeons, 1980; Member: Thoracic Soc.; Cardiac Soc.; Amer. Coll. of Chest Physicians. Toured: for British Council, Far East 1969, Cyprus and Greece 1973; for FCO, Indonesia 1971, Bolivia 1975; Yugoslavia 1977. Hunterian Prof., RCS, 1979. *Publications:* Thoracic Surgical Management, 1953; chapters in standard text-books; papers in British and foreign medical journals. *Recreations:* golf, ski-ing, photography. *Address:* 23 Hornton Court, Hornton Street, W8 7RT. *T:* 01–937 7006.

BELCHER, Ronald Harry, CMG 1958; Under-Secretary, Ministry of Overseas Development, 1965–75; *b* 5 Jan 1916; *s* of Harry Albert Belcher; *m* 1948, Hildegarde (*née* Hellyer-Jones); one *s*. *Educ:* Christ's Hosp., Horsham; Jesus Coll., Cambridge; Brasenose Coll., Oxford. BA (Hons Classics) Cantab 1937; Dipl. Class. Arch. Cantab 1938; BA Oxon 1938. Indian Civil Service, Punjab, 1939–48; Commonwealth Relations Office, 1948–65; seconded to Foreign Office for service in British Embassy, Washington, 1951–53; Private Sec., 1953–54; Asst Sec., 1954; Deputy High Commissioner for the UK in S Africa, 1956–59; Asst Under Sec. of State, CRO, 1960–61; British Dep. High Comr, Delhi, 1961–65. *Address:* Fieldview, Lower Road, Fetcham, Surrey. *Club:* Royal Commonwealth Society.

BELDAM, Hon. Sir (Alexander) Roy (Asplan), Kt 1981; **Hon. Mr Justice Beldam;** a Judge of the High Court of Justice, Queen's Bench Division, since 1981; Chairman of the Law Commission, since 1985; *b* 29 March 1925; *s* of George William Beldam and Margaret Frew Shettle (formerly Beldam, *née* Underwood); *m* 1953, Elisabeth Bryant Farr; two *s* one *d*. *Educ:* Oundle Sch.; Brasenose Coll., Oxford. Sub-Lt, RNVR Air Branch, 1943–46. Called to Bar, Inner Temple, 1950; Bencher, 1977; QC 1969; a Recorder of the Crown Court, 1972–81; Presiding Judge, Wales and Chester Circuit, Jan.–Oct. 1985. *Recreations:* sailing, cricket, naval history. *Address:* Royal Courts of Justice, Strand, WC2.

BELFAST, Earl of; Arthur Patrick Chichester; banker; *b* 9 May 1952; *s* and *heir* of 7th Marquess of Donegall, *qv*. *Educ:* Harrow. Coldstream Guards. *Recreations:* hunting, shooting, fishing. *Address:* Dunbrody Park, Arthurstown, Co. Wexford, Eire.

BELFRAGE, Leif Axel Lorentz, GBE (Hon.), 1956; former Swedish Ambassador; *b* 1 Feb. 1910; *s* of J. K. E. Belfrage and G. U. E. Löfgren; *m* 1937, Greta Jering; one *s* three *d*. *Educ:* Stockholm University. Law degree, 1933. Practised law at Stockholm Magistrates Court; joined Min. of Commerce, 1937; Dir, Swedish Clearing Office, 1940; Dir, wartime Swedish Trade Commn, 1943–45; entered Swedish Diplomatic Service, as Head of Section in Commercial Dept, 1945; Commercial Counsellor. Swedish Embassy, Washington, 1946; Head of Commercial Dept, FO, Stockholm, 1949–53; Dep. Under-Sec. of State, FO, 1953; Perm. Under-Sec. of State, FO, 1956; Ambassador to Court of St James's, 1967–72; Ambassador and Head of Swedish Delegn to OECD and UNESCO, 1972–76. Internat. Advr, PKbanken, Stockholm, 1976–. Grand Cross, Order of North Star (Sweden). *Address:* Sturegatan 14, 11436 Stockholm, Sweden.

BELHAM, David Ernest, CB 1975; Principal Assistant Solicitor (Under Secretary), Department of Employment, 1970–77, retired; *b* 9 Aug. 1914; *s* of Ernest George Belham and Grace Belham (*née* Firth); *m* 1938, Eunice Monica (*née* Vine); two *s* two *d*. *Educ:* Whitgift Sch.; Law Society's Sch. of Law. Solicitor (Hons), 1937. Private practice, 1937–39. Served War, RAFVR, 1940–46. Entered Solicitor's Department, Min. of Labour, 1946; Asst Solicitor, 1962. *Address:* 26 The Chase, Findon, Worthing, W Sussex BN14 0TT. *T:* Findon 3771.

BELHAVEN and STENTON, 13th Lord, *cr* 1647; **Robert Anthony Carmichael Hamilton;** farming; *b* 27 Feb. 1927; *o s* of 12th Lord; *S* father, 1961; *m* 1st, 1952, Elizabeth Ann, *d* of late Col A. H. Moseley, Warrawee, NSW; one *s* one *d*; 2nd, 1973, Rosemary Lady Mactaggart (marr. diss. 1986), *o d* of Sir Herbert Williams, 1st Bt, MP; one *d* (adopted). *Educ:* Eton. Commissioned, The Cameronians, 1947. *Recreation:* cooking. *Heir:* *s* Master of Belhaven, *qv*. *Address:* 16 Broadwater Down, Tunbridge Wells, Kent; 701 Nelson House, Dolphin Square, SW1. *Club:* Army and Navy.

BELHAVEN, Master of; Hon. Frederick Carmichael Arthur Hamilton; *b* 27 Sept. 1953; *s* of 13th Lord Belhaven and Stenton, *qv*; *m* 1981, Elizabeth Anne, *d* of S. V. Tredinnick, Wisborough Green, Sussex; two *s*. *Educ:* Eton. *Address:* 11 Markham Square, SW3.

BELL, Alexander Gilmour; Chief Reporter for Public Inquiries, Scottish Office, since 1979; *b* 11 March 1933; *s* of Edward and Daisy Bell; *m* 1966, Mary Chisholm; four *s*. *Educ:* Hutchesons' Grammar Sch.; Glasgow Univ. (BL). Admitted Solicitor, 1954. After commercial experience in Far East and in private practice, entered Scottish Office, as Legal Officer, 1967; Dep. Chief Reporter, 1973. *Recreations:* casual outdoor pursuits, choral music. *Address:* Woodend, Haddington, East Lothian EH41 4PE. *T:* Haddington 3514.

BELL, Alistair Watson; His Honour Judge Bell; a Circuit Judge, since 1978; *b* Edinburgh, 31 March 1930; *s* of Albert William Bell and Alice Elizabeth Watson; *m* 1957, Patricia Margaret Seed; one *s* two *d*. *Educ:* Lanark Grammar Sch.; George Watson's Coll.; Univs of Edinburgh (MA) and Oxford (MA, BCL). 2nd Lieut RASC, 1955. Called to Bar, Middle Temple, 1955; Harmsworth Scholar, 1956; entered practice, Northern Circuit, 1957; a Recorder of the Crown Court, 1972–78. Contested (L) Chorley, 1964 and Westmorland, 1966. *Recreation:* hill walking, with or without golf clubs. *Club:* Reform (Manchester).

BELL, Andrew Montgomery; Sheriff of Glasgow and Strathkelvin, since 1984; *b* 21 Feb. 1940; *s* of James Montgomery Bell and Mary Bell (*née* Cavaye), Edinburgh; *m* 1969, Ann Margaret Robinson; one *s* one *d*. *Educ:* Royal High Sch., Edinburgh; Univ. of Edinburgh (BL). Solicitor, 1961–74; called to Bar, 1975; Sheriff of S Strathclyde, Dumfries and Galloway at Hamilton, 1979–84. *Address:* 5 York Road, Trinity, Edinburgh EH5 3EJ. *T:* 031–552 3859.

BELL, Archibald Angus, QC (Scot.) 1961; Sheriff of Glasgow and Strathkelvin (formerly Lanark) at Glasgow, since 1973; *b* 13 April 1923; *o s* of James Dunlop Bell, Solicitor, Ayrshire, and Katherine Rachel Gordon Miller; *m* 1949, Dorothy, *d* of Dr Pollok Donald, Edinburgh, and Mrs Dorothy Donald; two *s*. *Educ:* The Leys Sch., Cambridge; Univ. of St Andrews; Univ. of Glasgow. Served War, Royal Navy, 1941–45; Sub-Lieut RNVR. MA, St Andrews, 1947; LLB, Glasgow, 1949; admitted to Faculty of Advocates, 1949; Reporter, Court of Session Cases, 1952–55. Contested (C and U) Maryhill Div. of Glasgow, Gen. Elec., 1955. Standing Junior Counsel in Scotland: to Board of Trade, 1955–57; to War Dept, 1957–61. Pres., Scottish Cricket Union, 1975. *Recreations:* watching the sun rise, getting fun out of games. Formerly: hockey and cricket blue, St Andrews, and Pres. UAU and Dramatic Soc. *Clubs:* Royal Scots (Edinburgh); MCC; Royal and Ancient (St Andrews); RNVR (Scotland).

BELL, Arthur; *see* Bell, E. A.

BELL, (Charles) Trevor; General Secretary, Colliery Officials and Staffs Area of the National Union of Mineworkers, since 1979; Member, National Executive Committee of the National Union of Mineworkers, since 1979; *b* 22 Sept. 1927; *s* of Charles and Annie Bell; *m* 1974, Patricia Ann Tappin. *Educ:* state schools; Technical Coll. (City and Guilds Engrg); Coleg Harlech, N Wales (Trades Union scholarship, 1955). Craftsman in coal mining industry, 1941. Mem., Labour Party, 1946–. *Recreations:* gardening, sport. *Address:* Wakefield, West Yorks WF2 6SH. *T:* Wakefield 363228. *Clubs:* Pontefract Labour; Painthorpe Country.

BELL, Sir Charles (William), Kt 1980; CBE 1968; Chairman of Coats Patons Ltd, 1967–75; *b* 4 June 1907; *s* of Herbert James Bell and Bertha Alice Bell (*née* Jones), Pen-y-Ffordd, Flintshire; *m* 1931, Eileen, *d* of Edwin James Hannaford, Eastham, Cheshire; three *s*. *Educ:* Chester City Grammar Sch.; Selwyn Coll., Cambridge (Open Exhibr). Joined Coats Patons Ltd, 1930; Dir, Central Agency Ltd (subsid. co.), 1934; Dir, J. & P. Coats Ltd, (Subsid. Co.), 1947; Man. Dir, J. & P. Coats Ltd, 1961; Dir, Coats Patons Ltd, 1961. Dep. Chm., and Nat. Treasurer, Scottish Conservative and Unionist Party, 1971–81. *Recreations:* shooting, fishing, golf. *Address:* The White Cottage, 19 Lennox Drive East, Helensburgh, Dunbartonshire. *T:* Helensburgh 4973. *Clubs:* Royal and Ancient (St Andrews); Royal Northern Yacht; Helensburgh Golf.

BELL, Dr Donald Atkinson, CEng; Director, National Engineering Laboratory, East Kilbride, since 1983; *b* 28 May 1941; *s* of Robert Hamilton Bell and late Gladys Mildred Bell; *m* 1967, Joyce Louisa Godber; two *s*. *Educ:* Royal Belfast Academical Instn; Queen's Univ., Belfast (BSc); Southampton Univ. (PhD). MIEE; MBCS. National Physical Lab., 1966–77; Dept of Industry, 1978–82. *Address:* National Engineering Laboratory, East Kilbride, Glasgow G75 0QU. *T:* East Kilbride 20222.

BELL, Donald L.; *see* Lynden-Bell.

BELL, Prof. Donald Munro; international concert and opera artist; freelance; Associate Professor of Music, Calgary University, since 1982; *b* 19 June 1934; one *s*. *Educ:* South Burnaby High Sch., BC, Canada. Made Wigmore Hall Debut, 1958; since then has sung at Bayreuth Wagner Festival, 1958, 1959, 1960; Lucerne and Berlin Festivals, 1959; Philadelphia and New York debuts with Eugene Ormandy, 1959; Israel, 1962; Russia Recital Tour, 1963; Glyndebourne Festival, 1963, 1973, 1974, 1982; with Deutsche Oper am Rhein, Düsseldorf, 1964–66; Scottish National Opera, 1974; Scottish Opera, 1978; Basler Kammer Orchestre, 1978; Australian Tour (Musica Viva), 1980. Prof. and Head of Vocal Dept, Ottawa Univ., 1979–82. Now has Opera Workshop at Univ. of Calgary. Dir, Alberta Br., Nat. Opera Assoc. Mem., NATS. Has made recordings. Arnold Bax Medal, 1955. *Address:* University of Calgary, Faculty of Fine Arts, Department of Music, 1500 University Drive NW, Calgary, Alberta T2N 1N4, Canada.

BELL, Douglas Maurice, CBE 1972; Chairman and Chief Executive, Tioxide Group Ltd (formerly British Titan Ltd), 1973–78; Chairman, Tinsley Wire Industries Group, since 1981 (Director, since 1978); *b* Shanghai, China, 15 April 1914; *s* of Alexander Dunlop Bell; *m* 1947, Elizabeth Mary Edelsten; one *s* two *d*. *Educ:* The Edinburgh Academy; St Andrews Univ. War Dept, Chemist, Woolwich Arsenal, 1936. Imperial Chemical Industries: Dyestuffs Div., 1937–42; Regional Sales Manager, 1946–53; Billingham Dir, 1953; Billingham Man. Dir, 1955–57; Heavy Organic Chemicals Managing Dir, 1958–61; Chm. of European Council, Imperial Chemical Industries Ltd, 1960–65; Chief Executive, ICI (Europa) Ltd, 1965–72. Director: British Titan Products Ltd, 1968–78; Tioxide Australia Pty Ltd, 1973–78; Tioxide of Canada Ltd, 1973–78; Tioxide SA, 1973–78; Titanio SA, 1973–78. Hon. Dir, NV Bekaert SA, 1979–. FBIM 1974; FRSA 1976; Soc. of Chemical Industry: Vice-Pres., 1975–76; Pres., 1976–78; Mem. Council, Chemical Industry Assoc., 1973–78. Member, Governing Board: British Sch. of Brussels, 1971–; Maison de la Chemie Française, 1972–. Hon. FIChemE, 1977. Hon. LLD St Andrews, 1977. Comendador de Numero de la Orden de Merito Civil (Spain), 1967; Commandeur, Ordre de Léopold II (Belgium), 1973. *Recreations:* sports and gardens. *Address:* Stocks Cottage, Church Street, West Chiltington, Sussex. *T:* West Chiltington 2284. *Clubs:* Anglo-Belgian; Cercle Royal Gaulois (Brussels); Royal Waterloo Golf, West Sussex Golf.

BELL, Edith Alice, OBE 1981; Chief Nursing Officer, Welsh Office, 1972–81; *b* 14 Sept. 1919; *d* of George and Alice Bell. *Educ:* Girls' Grammar Sch., Lancaster. SRN University Hosp., Leeds; SCM St Luke's Hosp., Bradford; Cert. Royal Medico Psychological Assoc., Westwood Hosp., Bradford; Registered Nurse, Mentally Subnormal, Aston Hall, Derby. Ward Sister, Aston Hall Hosp., Derby, 1941–43; Asst Matron, Royal Albert Hosp., Lancaster, 1943–46; Dep. Matron, Darenth Park Hosp., Dartford, 1946–48; Gp Matron, Fountain Gp HMC, London, 1948–60; Management Services Officer, SE RHB, Scotland, 1960–63; Chief Regional Nursing Officer, E Anglian RHB, 1963–72. WHO Fellowship, 1951. Past Member: Gen. Nursing Council, England and Wales; Nat. Council of Nurses; Standing Nursing Adv. Cttee; Services Cttee, Internat. Council of Nurses; Jt Bd, Clinical Nursing Studies; Council, Queen's Inst. of Dist Nursing Service; SW Metrop. RHB: Nursing, Research and Trng Cttees. Chairman: Mental Nurses Cttee; Jt Organizations; Reg. Nursing Officers Gp; Royal Coll. of Nursing Br. Mem., NHS Reorganization Steering Cttee. Hon. Sec., Mental Hosp. Matrons Assoc.; Pres., Inst. of Religion and Medicine. *Publications:* contribs to professional jls. *Recreations:* reading, travel, gardening, supporting ecumenical activities. *Address:* Tyla Teg, 51 Farmdale Road, Newlands, Lancaster LA1 4JB.

BELL, (Edward) Percy, OBE 1974; Member for Newham South, Greater London Council, 1973–81 (for Newham, 1964–73); *b* 3 April 1902; *m* 1932, Ethel Mary Bell. *Educ:* Rutherford Coll., Newcastle upon Tyne; King's Coll., London. Teacher in the service of West Ham County Borough, 1922–64; Headmaster, Shipman County Secondary School, West Ham, 1951–64. Chairman: Planning Cttee of GLC, 1973–74; Town Development Cttee, 1974–75; Docklands Jt Cttee, 1974–77. *Recreations:* foreign travel; local and national social history. *Address:* 151c Ham Park Road, E7 9LE. *T:* (private) 01–472 8897.

BELL, (Ernest) Arthur, PhD; FLS, CChem, FRSC; Director, Royal Botanic Gardens, Kew, since 1981; *b* 20 June 1926; *s* of Albert Bell and Rachel Enid (*née* Williams), Gosforth, Northumberland; *m* 1952, Jean Swinton Ogilvie; two *s* one *d*. *Educ:* Dame Allan's Sch., Newcastle upon Tyne; Univ. of Durham (King's Coll., Newcastle upon Tyne) BSc; Trinity Coll., Univ. of Dublin (MA, PhD). CChem, FRIC (now FRSC) 1961. Res. Chemist, ICI, Billingham, 1946; Demonstr and holder of Sarah Purser Med. Res. Award, TCD, 1947; Asst to Prof. of Biochem., TCD, 1949; Lectr in Biochem., KCL, 1953; Reader in Biochem., Univ. of London, 1964–68; Prof. of Botany, Univ. of Texas, 1968; Prof. of Biology, London Univ., and Hd of Dept of Plant Scis, KCL, 1972–81; FKC 1982. Sen. Foreign Scientist Fellow, Nat. Sci. Foundn, USA, and Vis. Prof. of Biol., Univ. of Kansas, 1966; Vis. Professor: Univ. of Sierra Leone, 1977; KCL, 1982–; Univ. of Reading, 1982–; Vis. Commonwealth Fellow, Australia, 1980. Hon. Botanical Adviser, Commonwealth War Graves Commn, 1983–. Pres., Section K (Plant Biol.), BAAS, 1985–86; Vice Pres., Linnean Soc., 1983–85 (Mem. Council, 1980–85); Mem. Council, RHS, 1985–. *Publications:* contribs on plant biochem., chemotaxonomy, and chem. ecology to Phytochemistry, and Biochem. Jl. *Recreations:* walking, travel. *Address:* Royal Botanic Gardens, Kew, Richmond, Surrey. *Club:* Athenæum.

BELL, Sir Ewart; *see* Bell, Sir W. E.

BELL, Prof. Frank, DSc, PhD; FRSC; FRSE; Professor of Chemistry, Heriot-Watt University (formerly College), Edinburgh, 1950–66 (now Emeritus); *b* 24 Dec. 1904; *o s* of Thomas Bell, Derby; *m* 1930, May Perryman; one *s* one *d*. *Educ:* Crypt Grammar Sch., Glos; Queen Mary Coll., University of London. Head of Science Dept, Blackburn Tech. Coll. 1935–41; Principal, Lancaster Tech. Coll., 1941–46; Prof. of Chemistry, Belfast Coll. of Tech., 1947–50. *Publications:* original papers mainly in Journal of Chemical Soc. *Recreations:* numismatics, walking and field-club activities (Past Pres., Cotteswold Naturalists' Field Club; Past Pres., Edinburgh Natural History Soc.). *Address:* Hilcot, Finchcroft Lane, Prestbury, Cheltenham, Glos.

BELL, Sir Gawain (Westray), KCMG 1957; CBE 1955 (MBE mil. 1942); Secretary-General, South Pacific Commission, 1966–70; *b* 21 Jan. 1909; *s* of late William Westray Bell; *m* 1945, Silvia, *d* of Major Adrian Cornwell-Clyne; three *d*. *Educ:* Winchester; Hertford Coll., Oxford. Sudan Political Service, 1931; seconded to the Government of Palestine, 1938 (attached Palestine Police, DSP). 2nd Lt TA, 1929–32; Military Service in Middle East, 1941–45; Kaimakam (Col): Arab Legion, 1942–45; RARO, 1949–59. District Comr, Sudan Political Service, 1945–49; Dep. Sudan Agent, Cairo, 1949–51; Dep. Civil Sec., Sudan Government, 1953–54; Permanent Under-Sec., Ministry of the Interior, 1954–55; HM Political Agent, Kuwait, 1955–57; Governor, Northern Nigeria, 1957–62; Sec Gen., Council for Middle East Trade, 1963–64; engaged, with Sir Ralph Hone, as Constitutional Adviser to Govt of Fedn of S Arabia, 1965–66. Various missions to Arab world, 1970–. Vice-President: LEPRA, 1984– (Chm. Exec. Cttee, 1972–84); Anglo-Jordanian Soc., 1985–. Member: Governing Body, SOAS, London Univ., 1971–81; part-time Chm., CS Selection Bds, 1972–77; Chapter Gen., Order of St John, 1964–66, 1970– (KStJ 1958). Order of Independence 3rd Class (Trans Jordan), 1944. *Publication:* Shadows on the Sand, 1984. *Recreations:* walking, riding, shooting, rifle shooting (Capt. Oxford Univ., 1931; shot for Sudan). *Address:* Hidcote Bartrim Manor, Chipping Campden, Glos. *T:* Mickleton 305. *Club:* Army and Navy.

BELL, George Douglas Hutton, CBE 1965; FRS 1965; PhD; Director, Plant Breeding Institute, Cambridge, 1947–71, retired; a Vice President, Royal Society, 1976–78; *b* 18 Oct. 1905; *er s* of George Henry and Lilian Mary Matilda Bell; *m* 1934, Eileen Gertrude Wright; two *d*. *Educ:* Bishop Gore's Grammar Sch., Swansea; Univ. Coll. of North Wales, Bangor (BSc 1928); University of Cambridge. PhD 1931. Research Officer, Plant Breeding Inst., 1931; University Demonstrator, Cambridge, 1933, Lectr, 1944; Fellow of Selwyn Coll., Cambridge, 1944–54, Hon. Fellow, 1965. Research Medal, Royal Agricultural Soc. of England, 1956; Royal Society Mullard Medal, 1967. Hon. DSc: Reading Univ., 1968; Univ. Wales, 1968; Liverpool Univ., 1970; Hon. ScD Cambridge, 1978. Massey-Ferguson National Award, 1973. *Publications:* Cultivated Plants of the Farm, 1948; The Breeding of Barley Varieties in Barley and Malt, 1962; Cereal Breeding in Vistas in Botany, Vol. II, 1963; Phylogeny of Temperate Cereals in Crop Plant Evolution, 1965; papers on barley and breeding in Jl of Agricultural Science, etc. *Recreations:* natural history; theatre, music. *Address:* 6 Worts Causeway, Cambridge CB1 4RL. *T:* Cambridge 247449.

BELL, Prof. George Howard, MD; FRCPGlas 1946; FRSE 1947; Symers Professor of Physiology in the University of Dundee (formerly Queen's College, Dundee), 1947–75, now Emeritus; Dean of The Faculty of Medicine, 1954–56 and 1963; *b* 24 Jan. 1905; *m* 1934, Isabella Margaret Thomson, MB, ChB; two *s*. *Educ:* Ayr Academy; Glasgow Univ. BSc 1929; MB (Hons) 1930; MD (Hons) 1943. House Physician, Royal Hosp. for Sick Children, 1930; Asst Lecturer in Physiology Dept, University of Glasgow, 1931–34; Lecturer in Physiology: Univ. of Bristol, 1934–35; Univ. of Glasgow, 1935–47. Mem. Physiological Soc., 1934–, and Sec., 1949–54; Mem. Inter-University Council for Higher Education Overseas, 1957–75; Mem. Eastern Regional Hospital Board, 1957–67 (Vice-Chm., 1966–67); Gen. Dental Council Visitor, 1960–62; Comr, Royal University of Malta, 1962–70. Hon. Fellow, Accademia Anatomico-Chirurgica, Perugia, 1959. *Publications:* (with D. Emslie Smith and C. R. Paterson) Textbook of Physiology, 10th edn, 1980; papers in Journal of Physiology, Journal of Endocrinology, Lancet, etc. *Address:* Duntulm, 80 Grove Road, Broughty Ferry, Dundee DD5 1LB. *T:* Dundee 78724.

BELL, Sir (George) Raymond, KCMG 1973; CB 1967; Vice-President, European Investment Bank, 1973–78, retired; Hon. Vice-President, European Investment Bank, 1978; *b* 13 March 1916; *e s* of late William Bell and Christabel Bell (*née* Appleton); *m* 1944, Joan Elizabeth, *o d* of late W. G. Coltham and Christina Coltham; two *s* two *d*. *Educ:* Bradford Grammar Sch.; St John's Coll., Cambridge (Scholar). Entered Civil Service, Assistant Principal, 1938; Min. of Health, 1938; transf. Treasury, 1939; served War 1941–44, Royal Navy (Lieut RNVR). Principal, Civil Service, 1945; Asst Sec., 1951; Under-Sec., 1960; Dep. Sec., 1966; Dep. Sec. HM Treasury, 1966–72. Sec. (Finance), Office of HM High Commissioner for the UK in Canada, 1945–48; Counsellor, UK

Permanent Delegn to OEEC/NATO, Paris, 1953–56; Principal Private Sec. to Chancellor of Exchequer, 1958–60. Mem. UK Delegation to Brussels Conference, 1961–62 and 1970–72. *Recreations:* music, reading, travel. *Address:* Quartier des Bories, Aouste-sur-Sye, 26400 Crest, Drôme, France. *T:* (75) 25 26 94. *Club:* Athenæum.

BELL, Griffin B.; Attorney-General, USA, 1977–79; *b* Americus, Georgia, 31 Oct. 1918; *s* of A. C. Bell and Thelma Pilcher; *m* 1943, Mary Foy Powell; one *s. Educ:* Southwestern Coll., Ga; Mercer Univ. (LLB *cum laude* 1948, LLD 1967). Served AUS, 1941–46, reaching rank of Major. Admitted to Georgia Bar, 1947; practice in Savannah and Rome, 1947–53. Partner in King and Spalding, Atlanta, 1953–59, 1976–77, 1979–, Managing Partner, 1959–61; United States Judge, 5th Circuit, 1961–76. Chairman: Atlanta Commn on Crime and Delinquency, 1965–66; CSCE, 1980. Mem., Vis. Cttee, Law Sch., Vanderbilt Univ.; Trustee, Mercer Univ.; Member: Amer. Law Inst.; Amer. Coll. of Trial Lawyers (Pres., 1985–). *Address:* 145 15th Street, Atlanta, Georgia 30361, USA.

BELL, Ian Wright, CBE 1964; HM Diplomatic Service, retired; *b* Radlett, Herts, 21 Aug. 1913; *s* of late T. H. D. Bell; *m* 1940, Winifred Mary Ruth Waterfield, *y d* of late E. H. Waterfield, ICS; three *s. Educ:* Canford Sch.; St Peter's Hall, Oxford. Vice-Consul: Valparaiso, 1938; Montevideo, 1940; Foreign Office, 1946; First Sec., 1947; First Sec., Addis Ababa, 1949, Chargé d'Affaires, 1949, 1950, 1952 and 1953; Consul, Innsbruck, 1953; First Sec., Prague, 1954, Chargé d'Affaires, 1954 and 1956; Counsellor and Consul-Gen., Jedda, 1956; Counsellor and Official Sec., UK High Commission, Canberra, 1957; HM Consul-Gen., Lyons, 1960–65; Ambassador, Santo Domingo, 1965–69; Consul-Gen., Stuttgart, 1969–73. FRSA; FRGS. *Publications:* The Scarlet Flower (Poems), 1947; The Dominican Republic, 1981; reviews and articles in various periodicals. *Recreations:* painting, drama, music, walking. *Address:* Liveras House, Broadford, Skye. *Club:* Athenæum.

BELL, Very Rev. John, MM 1917; Dean Emeritus of Perth, WA; Dean, 1953–59, retired; *b* 11 Nov. 1898; *s* of Thomas and Isabella McCracken Bell; unmarried. *Educ:* Gair Sch., Dumfriesshire; privately; St John's Coll., Perth, WA. Deacon, 1926, Priest, 1928; Curate of Christ Church, Claremont, 1926–29; Rector of S Perth, 1929–32; Priest-in-Charge of Claremont, 1933, Rector, 1933–43; Canon of St George's Cathedral, Perth, 1938–44; Org. Sec. (for NSW) Austr. Bd of Missions, 1943–46; Dean of Armidale, 1946–48; Exam. Chap. to Bp of Armidale, 1946–48; Rector of Oddington with Adlestrop, Dio. Gloucester, 1948–52. *Publications:* This Way Peace, 1939; Many Coloured Glass, 1943; Facing the Week, 1947; For Comfort and Courage, 1958. *Recreation:* travel. *Address:* 22/8 Darley Street, South Perth, Western Australia 6151. *T:* 367–4434. *Club:* Weld (Perth, WA).

BELL, Rear-Adm. John Anthony, CB 1977; Hon. Research Fellow, Exeter University, since 1986; Director, Naval Education Service, 1975–78; Chief Naval Instructor Officer, 1978–79; *b* 25 Nov. 1924; *s* of Mathew Bell, Dundee, and Mary Ann Ellen Bell (*née* Goss), London; *m* 1946, Eileen Joan Woodman; three *d. Educ:* St Ignatius Coll., Stamford Hill; London Univ. BA, BSc, LLB. Barrister, Gray's Inn, 1970. RM 1943–45; Schoolmaster, RN, Instr Lt, Courses, Reserve Fleet, service with RAN, 1945–52; HMS Implacable, Theseus, Admiralty, HMS Excellent, 1952–59; HMS Centaur, RN Staff Course, Staff of SACLANT, USA, Directing Staff, RN Staff Course, Western Fleet, 1959–69; Naval Educn Service, Dir, Dept of Naval Oceanography and Meteorology, 1969–75; Instr Captain 1969, Rear-Adm. 1975. Educn Sec. of the BBC, 1979–83; Dep. Chairman: Police Complaints Bd, 1983–85; (Discipline), Police Complaints Authority, 1985–86; BEC Educn Cttee, 1975–79; C&G Policy Cttee, 1975–79; TEC, 1976–79; Cert. of Extended Educn Cttee, DES, 1978–79. Governor, SOAS, 1975–79; Vice-Chm., Court of Governors, City of London Polytechnic, 1984–; Pres., Area 2, RN Assoc. and SCC, Gravesend, 1982–84; Vice-Pres., United Services Catholic Assoc., 1979–; Nat. Vice-Pres., RN Assoc., 1983. Chm., Kent EC Cttee, 1982–84. *Recreations:* swimming, wines, travelling, France.

BELL, John Geoffrey Y.; *see* Yates-Bell.

BELL, Sir John Lowthian, 5th Bt *cr* 1885; *b* 14 June 1960; *s* of Sir Hugh Francis Bell, 4th Bt and of Lady Bell (Mary Howson, MB, ChB, *d* of late George Howson, The Hyde, Hambledon); *S* father, 1970; *m* 1985, Venetia, *d* of J. A. Perry, Taunton. *Recreations:* shooting, fishing. *Heir:* *b* David Hugh Bell, *b* 8 Oct. 1961. *Address:* Hollins House, East Rounton, Northallerton, N Yorks.

BELL, Dr John Stewart, FRS 1972; Physicist, CERN, Geneva, since 1960; *b* 28 July 1928; *s* of John Bell and Annie (*née* Brownlee); *m* 1954, Mary Ross. *Educ:* Technical High Sch., Belfast; Queen's Univ., Belfast (BSc); Univ of Birmingham (PhD). AERE Harwell, 1949–60. *Publications:* various papers on electromagnetic, nuclear, elementary particle, and quantum theory. *Address:* CERN, 1211 Geneva 23, Switzerland.

BELL, Joseph, CBE 1953; Chief Constable, City of Manchester, 1943–58, retired; *b* 15 July 1899; *s* of late Joseph Bell; *m* 1926, Edith (*d* 1980), *d* of late Matthew Adamson; one *s* (one *d* decd). *Educ:* Alderman Wood Sch., Stanley, Co. Durham. Royal Naval Volunteer Reserve, 1917–19. Newcastle on Tyne City Police, 1919–33; Chief Constable, Hastings, 1933–41; Asst Chief Constable, Manchester, 1941–43. *Address:* Norwood, 246 Windlehurst Road, Marple, Cheshire.

BELL, Joseph Denis Milburn; Chairman, North Western Electricity Board, 1976–85; *b* 2 Sept. 1920; *s* of John Bell, BEM, and Ann Bell; *m* 1949, Wilhelmina Maxwell Miller; one *s* one *d. Educ:* Bishop Auckland Grammar Sch.; St Edmund Hall, Oxford (MA). Served War, RAF, 1941–45. Contested (Lab) Canterbury, 1945. Lectr in Modern Econ. History, Univ. of Glasgow, 1946; National Coal Board: Indust. Relations Dept, 1954; Dep. Indust. Relations Dir, Durham Div., 1963; Electricity Council: Statistical Officer, Indust. Relations Dept, 1966; Dep. Indust. Relations Adviser (Negotiating), 1967; Indust. Relations Adviser, 1972. *Publications:* Industrial Unionism: a critical analysis, 1949 (repr. in Trade Unions: selected readings, ed W. E. J. McCarthy, 1972); (contrib.) The Scottish Economy (ed A. K. Cairncross), 1953; (contrib.) The System of Industrial Relations in Great Britain (ed A. Flanders and H. A. Clegg), 1954; (contrib.) The Lessons of Public Enterprise (ed M. Shanks), 1963. *Address:* Rossways, Broad Lane, Hale, Altrincham, Cheshire. *T:* 061–980 4451. *Club:* United Oxford & Cambridge University.

BELL, Prof. Kathleen Myra, CBE 1978; Professor of Social Studies in the University of Newcastle upon Tyne, 1971–83, now Professor Emeritus; *b* 6 March 1920; *d* of late Walter Petty and late Myra Petty; *m* 1945, Rev. Jack Martin Bell; one *s* one *d. Educ:* St Joseph's Coll., Bradford; Univ. of Manchester (Prize in Public Admin. 1940). Asst Personnel Officer, later Trng Officer, Min. of Supply ROF, 1942–45; Tutor and Lectr in Univ. Depts of Extra-Mural Studies, 1945–63; University of Newcastle upon Tyne: Lectr in Social Studies, 1963–67; Sen. Tutor, 1967–69; Sen. Lectr, 1969–71. Member: Lord Chancellor's Council on Tribunals, 1963–81 (Ch. person, Cttee on Functions of the Council, 1977–81); Social Admin. Cttee of Jt Univ. Council for Public and Social Admin., 1965–83; BBC Programmes Complaints Commn, 1978–81; Academic Adviser (apptd by Govt Chief Scientist) to DHSS Social Security Res. Policy Cttee, 1976–83; Expert Adviser to OECD Directorate for Social Affairs and Educn, for their project, Role of Women in the Economy, 1976–77; Mem., AHA for N Tyneside, 1974–77; Mem., Davies Cttee on Hosp. Complaints Procedure, 1971–73; Member Editorial Board: Jl of Social Policy, 1971–78; Jl of Social Welfare Law, 1977–. *Publications:* Tribunals in the Social Services, 1969; Disequilibrium in Welfare, 1973; Research Study on Supplementary Benefit Appeal Tribunals—Review of Main Findings, Conclusions and Recommendations, 1975; The Functions of the Council on Tribunals, 1980; various papers in Jl of Social Policy, Econ. and Social Admin, and other jls. *Address:* 57 Great King Street, Edinburgh EH3 6RP.

BELL, Leslie Gladstone, CEng, FRINA; RCNC; Director of Naval Ship Production, Ministry of Defence, 1977–79, retired; *b* 20 Oct. 1919; *s* of late John Gladstone Bell and Jessie Gray Bell (*née* Quigley); *m* 1963, Adriana Agatha Jacoba van den Berg; one *s* one *d. Educ:* Portsmouth Dockyard Tech. Coll.; Royal Naval Engineering Coll., Keyham; Royal Naval Coll., Greenwich. Staff Constructor Cdr, Home Fleet, 1953–56; Aircraft Carrier Design, 1956–59; Chief Constructor, Weapon Development, 1959–67; IDC, 1968; Asst Dir, Submarine Design, 1969–72; Director, Submarine Project Team, 1972–77. *Recreations:* gardening, golf, music. *Address:* Haytor, Old Midford Road, Bath, Avon. *T:* Bath 833357. *Club:* Bath Golf.

BELL, Martin; Washington Correspondent, BBC TV News, since 1978; *b* 31 Aug. 1938; *s* of late Adrian Hanbury Bell and of Marjorie H. Bell; *m* 1971, Nelly Lucienne Gourdon; two *d*; *m* 1985, Rebecca D. Sobel. *Educ:* The Leys Sch., Cambridge; King's Coll., Cambridge (MA). Reporter, BBC TV News, 1965–77; Diplomatic Correspondent, BBC TV News, 1977–78. Royal Television Society Reporter of the Year, 1977. *Address:* c/o BBC, 2030 M Street NW, Suite 607, Washington, DC 20036, USA. *T:* 202–223–2050.

BELL, Martin George Henry: Senior Partner, Ashurst Morris Crisp, since 1986; *b* 16 Jan. 1935; *s* of Leonard George Bell and Phyllis Bell (*née* Green); *m* 1965, Shirley Wrightson; two *s. Educ:* Charterhouse. Admitted Solicitor, 1961. Joined Ashurst Morris Crisp, 1961; Partner, 1963. *Recreations:* walking, riding. *Address:* Mulberry, Woodbury Hill, Loughton, Essex IG10 1JB. *T:* 01–508 1188.

BELL, Michael John Vincent; Director General of Management Audit, Ministry of Defence, since 1984; *b* 9 Sept. 1941; *e s* of C. R. V. Bell, OBE and Jane Bell, MBE; *m* 1983, Mary Shippen, *o d* of late J. W. Shippen and Mrs Margaret Shippen; one *s. Educ:* Winchester Coll.; Magdalen Coll., Oxford (BA Lit. Hum.). Res. Associate, Inst. for Strategic Studies, 1964; Ministry of Defence: Asst Principal, 1965; Principal, 1969; Asst Sec., 1975; on loan to HM Treasury, 1977–79; Asst Under Sec. of State (Resources and Programmes), 1982–84. *Recreations:* motorcycling, military history. *Address:* Ministry of Defence, Whitehall, SW1A 2HB. *T:* 01–218 4096.

BELL, Percy; see Bell, E. P.

BELL, Prof. Peter Robert; Emeritus Professor of Botany, University of London; *b* 18 Feb. 1920; *s* of Andrew and Mabel Bell; *m* 1952, Elizabeth Harrison; two *s. Educ:* Simon Langton School, Canterbury; Christ's Coll., Cambridge (MA 1949). University College London: Asst Lecturer in Botany, 1946; Lectr in Botany, 1949; Reader in Botany, 1967; Prof. of Botany, 1967; Quain Prof. of Botany and Head of Dept of Botany and Microbiol., 1978–85. Visiting Professor: Univ. of California, Berkeley, 1966–67; Univ. of Delhi, India, 1970. British Council Distinguished Visitor, NZ, 1976; many other visits overseas, including exploration of Ecuadorian Andes. Vice-Pres., Linnean Soc., 1962–65; Mem. Biological Sciences Cttee, 1974–79 (Chm. Panel 1, 1977–79), SRC. *Publications:* Darwin's Biological Work, Some Aspects Reconsidered, 1959; (with C. F. Woodcock) The Diversity of Green Plants, 1968, 3rd edn 1983; (trans., with D. E. Coombe) Strasburger's Textbook of Botany, 8th English edn, 1976; scientific papers on botanical topics, particularly reproductive cells of land plants. *Recreation:* mountains. *Address:* 13 Granville Road, Barnet, Herts EN5 4DU. *T:* 01–449 9331.

BELL, Prof. Peter Robert Frank, MD; FRCS, FRCSGlas; Professor of Surgery, University of Leicester, since 1974; *b* 12 June 1938; *s* of Frank and Ruby Bell; *m* 1961, Anne Jennings; one *s* two *d. Educ:* Univ. of Sheffield (MB, ChB Hons 1961; MD 1969). FRCS 1965; FRCSGlas 1968. Postgrad. surg. career in Sheffield hosps, 1961–65; Lectr in Surgery, Univ. of Glasgow, 1965–68; Sir Henry Wellcome Travelling Fellow, Univ. of Colorado, 1968–69; Consultant Surgeon and Sen. Lectr, Western Infirm., Glasgow, 1969–74. Pres., Surgical Res. Soc., 1986–. *Publications:* Surgical Aspects of Haemodialysis, 1974, 2nd edn 1983; Operative Arterial Surgery, 1982; pubns on vascular disease, transplantation and cancer in med. and surg. jls. *Recreations:* horticulture, oil painting, tennis. *Address:* Department of Surgery, Clinical Sciences Building, PO Box 65, Royal Infirmary, Leicester. *Club:* Leicestershire (Leicester).

BELL, Prof. Quentin (Claudian Stephen), FRSA; FRSL; Emeritus Professor of the History and Theory of Art, Sussex University; painter, sculptor, potter, author, art critic; *b* 19 Aug. 1910; 2nd *s* of late Clive Bell and Vanessa Stephen; *m* 1952, Anne Olivier Popham; one *s* two *d. Educ:* Leighton Park. Exhibitions, 1935, 1947, 1949, 1972, 1977, 1981, 1982, 1986. Political warfare executive, 1941–43. Lectr in Art Education, King's Coll., Newcastle, 1952; Senior Lecturer, 1956; Prof. of Fine Art, University of Leeds, 1962–67 (Head of Dept of Fine Art, 1959); Slade Professor of Fine Art, Oxford Univ., 1964–65; Ferens Prof. of Fine Art, University of Hull, 1965–66; Prof. of History and Theory of Art, Sussex Univ., 1967–75. Commissioned Sculpture for Univ. of Leeds. MA Dunelm, 1957. Regular contributor to Listener, 1951–. *Publications:* On Human Finery, 1947, rev. edn 1976; Those Impossible English (with Helmut Gernsheim), 1951; Roger Montané, 1961; The Schools of Design, 1963; Ruskin, 1963; Victorian Artists, 1967; Bloomsbury, 1968; Virginia Woolf, a Biography, 2 vols, 1972 (James Tait Black Meml Prize; Duff Cooper Meml Prize); A New and Noble School, 1982; Techniques of Terracotta, 1983; The Brandon Papers (novel), 1985. *Address:* 81 Heighton Street, Firle, Sussex BN8 6NZ. *T:* Glynde 201. *Club:* Reform.

BELL, Sir Raymond; *see* Bell, Sir G. R.

BELL, Robert Donald Murray, CB 1966; *b* 8 Oct. 1916; *s* of Robert William and Mary Caroline Bell; *m* 1941, Karin Anna Smith; one *s* one *d. Educ:* Christ's Hosp.; Clare Coll., Cambridge. First Class Honours, Natural Sciences Tripos (Physics), 1938. Joined Scottish Office, 1938. War of 1939–45: Royal Artillery, 1940–45 (Mil. Coll. of Science, Bury, 1943). Principal, Scottish Home Dept, 1946; Private Sec. to Sec. of State for Scotland, 1947–50; Under-Secretary in Scottish Depts, 1959–76. *Address:* Smeaton House, Inveresk, Musselburgh, Midlothian. *T:* 031–665 2940.

BELL, Prof. Robert Edward, CC (Canada) 1971; FRS 1965; FRSC 1955; Emeritus Professor of Physics, McGill University, Montreal, since 1983; *b* 29 Nov. 1918; *s* of Edward Richardson Bell and Edith E. Rich, British Columbia; *m* 1947, Jeanne Atkinson; one *d. Educ:* Univ. of British Columbia (BA 1939, MA 1941); McGill Univ. (PhD 1948). Wartime Radar development, Nat. Research Council, Ottawa, 1941–45; Sen. Research Officer, Chalk River Nuclear Laboratories, 1946–56; McGill University: seconded to Foster Radiation Lab., 1952–56; Assoc. Prof. of Physics, 1956–60; Dir, Foster Radiation Lab., 1960–69; Vice-Dean for Physical Scis, 1964–67; Dean, Fac. of Grad. Studies and Research, 1969–70; Rutherford Prof. of Physics, 1960–83; Principal and Vice-Chancellor,

1970–79; Dir, Arts, Sciences and Technol. Centre, Vancouver, 1983–85. Visiting scientist, Copenhagen Univ. Inst. for Theoretical Physics, under Niels Bohr, 1958–59. President: Royal Society of Canada, 1978–81 (Sec., Section III (Science), 1962–64); Canadian Assoc. of Physicists, 1965–66. Fellow, American Physical Soc. Hon. DSc: Univ. of New Brunswick, 1971; Université Laval, 1973; Université de Montréal, 1976; Univ. of BC, 1978; McMaster Univ., McGill Univ., 1979; Carleton Univ., 1980; Hon. LLD: Univ. of Toronto, 1971; Concordia Univ., 1979; Hon. DCL Bishop's Univ., 1976. *Publications:* contribs to books: Annual Reviews of Nuclear Science, 1954; Beta and Gamma Ray Spectroscopy, 1955; Alpha, Beta and Gamma Ray Spectroscopy, 1964; papers on nuclear physics and allied topics in scientific jls. *Address:* 822 Tsawwassen Beach, Delta, BC V4M 2J3, Canada. *T:* (604) 943–0667.

BELL, Rodger, QC 1982; a Recorder of the Crown Court, since 1980; *b* 13 Sept. 1939; *s* of John Thornton Bell and Edith Bell; *m* 1969, Sylvia Claire Tatton Brown; one *s* three *d*. *Educ:* Brentwood Sch.; Brasenose Coll., Oxford (BA). Called to the Bar, Middle Temple, 1963. Legal Mem., Mental Health Review Tribunals, 1983–. *Recreation:* running. *Address:* 14 Castello Avenue, SW15 6EA. *T:* 01–788 3857.

BELL, Dr Ronald Leslie, CEng, FIM, FInstP, FIAgrE; Director-General, Agricultural Development and Advisory Service, and Chief Scientific Adviser, Ministry of Agriculture, Fisheries and Food, since 1984; *b* 12 Sept. 1929; *s* of Thomas William Alexander Bell and Annie (*née* Mapleston); *m* 1954, Eleanor Joy (*née* Lancaster); one *s* two *d*. *Educ:* The City School, Lincoln; Univ. of Birmingham (BSc, PhD). Research Fellow, Royal Radar Estabt, Malvern, 1954–57; Imperial College, Univ. of London: Lectr in Metallurgy, 1957–62; Reader in Metallurgy, 1962–65; University of Southampton: Prof. of Engrg Materials, 1965–77; Head of Dept of Mech. Engrg, 1968; Dean of Faculty of Engrg and Applied Scis, 1970–72; Dep. Vice Chancellor, 1972–76; Dir, NIAE, 1977–84. Vis. Prof., Cranfield Inst. of Technology, 1979–. Pres., British Crop Protection Council, 1985–; Member: AFRC, 1984–; Council, RASE, 1984–. Hon. DSc Southampton, 1985. *Publications:* papers in learned jls dealing with twinning and brittle fracture of metals, grain boundary sliding and creep in metals, dislocations in semi-conductors, agricultural engineering. *Recreations:* jogging, music, Association football, gardening. *Address:* 3 Old Garden Court, Mount Pleasant, St Albans AL3 4RQ *Club:* Farmers'.

BELL, Ronald Percy, MA; FRS 1944; FRSE 1968; FRSC; Professor of Chemistry, University of Stirling, 1967–75, now Emeritus; Hon. Research Professor of Chemistry, University of Leeds, 1976–82; *b* 1907; *e s* of E. A. Bell, Maidenhead; *m* 1931, Margery Mary West; one *s*. *Educ:* County Boys' Sch., Maidenhead; Balliol Coll., Oxford. Bedford Lecturer in Physical Chemistry, Balliol Coll., 1932; Fellow of Balliol Coll., 1933 (Vice-Master, 1965); Hon. Fellow, 1967; Univ. Lecturer and Demonstrator, Oxford Univ., 1938; Univ. Reader, Oxford Univ., 1955. George Fisher Baker Lectr, Cornell Univ., 1958; Nat. Science Foundn Fellow, Brown Univ., 1964; Visiting Professor: Weizmann Inst. of Sci., Israel, 1973; Tech. Univ. of Denmark, Lyngby, 1976. President: Faraday Soc., 1956; Chemistry Section, British Assoc. Meeting, Durham, 1970; Vice-Pres. Chemical Soc., 1958 (Tilden Lectureship 1941; Liversidge Lectureship, 1973–74; Spiers Meml Lectureship, 1975). Foreign Mem. Royal Danish Acad. of Arts and Sciences, 1962; Foreign Associate, Nat. Acad. of Sciences, USA, 1972; Foreign Hon. Mem., Amer. Acad. of Arts and Scis, 1974. Hon. LLD Illinois Inst. of Techn., 1965; Hon. DTech, Tech. Univ. of Denmark, 1969; Hon. DSc Kent, 1974; Hon. DUniv. Stirling, 1977. Leverhulme Emeritus Fellow, 1976. Meldola Medal, Inst. of Chemistry, 1936; Chem. Soc. Award in Kinetics and Mechanism, 1974. *Publications:* Acid-Base Catalysis, 1941; Acids and Bases, 1952, 2nd edn 1969; The Proton in Chemistry, 1959, 2nd edn 1973; The Tunnel Effect in Chemistry, 1980; papers in scientific journals. *Address:* Flat 5, Park Villa Court, Roundhay, Leeds LS8 1EB. *T:* Leeds 664236; Bowderbeck, Buttermere, Cumbria. *T:* Buttermere 226.

BELL, Stewart Edward; QC (Scot.) 1982; Sheriff Principal of Grampian, Highland and Islands, since 1983; *b* 4 Aug. 1919; *yr s* of late Charles Edward Bell, shipowner, and Rosalind Stewart; *m* 1st, 1948, Isla (*d* 1983), 2nd *d* of late James Spencer and Adeline Kelly; three *d*; 2nd, 1985, Mavis Kydd, *d* of late A. St Clair Jameson, WS, and *widow* of Sheriff R. R. Kydd; two step *d*. *Educ:* Kelvinside Academy, Glasgow; Trinity Hall, Cambridge; Glasgow Univ. Trinity Hall, 1937–39 and 1946 (MA Cantab); Glasgow Univ., 1946–48 (LLB). Commissioned, Loyal Regt, 1939; served with 2nd Bn in Singapore and Malaya, 1940–42 (wounded, POW in Singapore and Korea, 1942–45). Admitted Advocate, 1948; practised: in Malacca, Malaya as Advocate and Solicitor, 1949–51; at Scottish Bar, 1951–61; Sheriff of Lanarks at Glasgow, later of Glasgow and Strathkelvin, 1961–82. *Recreation:* Highland bagpipe (Hon. Pipe-major, The Royal Scottish Pipers' Soc., 1975–77). *Address:* The Castle, Inverness IV2 3EG. *T:* Inverness 230782; The Little House, Thurlow Road, Nairn IV12 4HJ. *T:* Nairn 52131. *Clubs:* Western (Glasgow); Royal Northern and University (Aberdeen).

BELL, Stuart; MP (Lab) Middlesbrough, since 1983; barrister; *b* High Spen, Co. Durham, 16 May 1938; *s* of Ernest and Margaret Rose Bell; *m* 1st, 1960, Margaret, *d* of Mary Bruce; one *s* one *d*; 2nd, 1980, Margaret, *d* of Edward and Mary Allan; one *s*. *Educ:* Hookergate Grammar Sch. Formerly colliery clerk, newspaper reporter, typist and novelist. Called to the Bar, Gray's Inn, 1970. Conseil Juridique and Internat. Lawyer, Paris, 1970–77. Member: Newcastle City Council, 1980–83 (Mem., Finance, Health and Environment, Arts and Recreation Cttees; Chm., Youth and Community Cttee; Vice-Chm., Educn Cttee); Educn Cttee, AMA; Council of Local Educn Authorities; Newcastle AHA (T). Contested (Lab) Hexham, 1979. PPS to Dep. Leader of Opposition, Rt Hon. Roy Hattersley, 1983–; Opposition front bench spokesman on NI, 1984–. Member: Fabian Soc.; Soc. of Lab. Lawyers; GMBATU. *Publications:* novels: Paris 69, 1973; Days That Used To Be, 1975; How to Abolish the Lords (Fabian Tract), 1981; Valuation for United States Customs Purposes, 1981. *Recreation:* writing short stories. *Address:* 38 The Avenue, Linthorpe, Middlesbrough TS5 6PD.

BELL, Timothy John Leigh; Group Chief Executive, Lowe Howard Spink & Bell PLC (formerly Lowe Howard Spink Campbell Ewald), since 1985; *b* 18 Oct. 1941; *s* of Arthur Leigh Bell and Greta Mary Bell (*née* Findlay). *Educ:* Queen Elizabeth's Grammar Sch., Barnet, Herts. FIPA. ABC Television, 1959–61; Colman Prentis & Varley, 1961–63; Hobson Bates, 1963–66; Geers Gross, 1966–70; Saatchi & Saatchi, 1970–85. *Address:* Frognal Cottage, 102 Frognal, NW3 6XU. *T:* 01–584 5033. *Clubs:* Marks, Harry's Bar.

BELL, Trevor; see Bell, C. T.

BELL, Rev. Vicars (Walker), MBE 1964; author; Vicar of Clawton, and Rector of Tetcott with Luffincott, 1966–78; formerly Lecturer; *b* 24 Jan. 1904; *s* of W. A. Bell, Edinburgh; *m* 1926, Dorothy Carley. *Educ:* Radnor Sch., Redhill; Reigate Grammar Sch.; Goldsmiths' Coll., King's Coll., Univ. of London. Asst master at Horley Boys' Council Sch., 1925; Headmaster: Spaldwick Council Sch., 1926; Little Gaddesden C of E Sch., 1929–63. *Publications:* Little Gaddesden: the story of an English Parish, 1949; Death Under the Stars, 1949; The Dodo, 1950; Two by Day and One by Night, 1950; Death has Two Doors, 1950; This Way Home, 1951; Death Darkens Council, 1952; On Learning the English Tongue, 1953; Death and the Night Watches, 1954; To Meet Mr

Ellis, 1956; Death Walks by the River, 1959; That Night, a play for the Nativity, 1959; Orlando and Rosalind, three tales, 1960; Steep Ways and Narrow, 1963; The Flying Cat, 1964; (ed) Prayers for Every Day, 1965. *Address:* 20 Watts Road, Tavistock, Devon.

BELL, Walter (Fancourt), CMG 1967; *b* 7 Nov. 1909; *s* of Canon George Fancourt Bell; *m* 1948, Katharine Spaatz, Washington, DC, USA; no *c*. *Educ:* Tonbridge Sch. Barrister, Inner Temple. Vice-Consul (Acting): New York, 1935–40; Mexico City, 1940–41; New York, 1941–42; Foreign Office, London, 1942–45; 1st Sec., Brit. Embassy, Washington, DC, 1946–48; attached E Africa High Commn, Nairobi, Kenya, 1949–52; 1st Sec., Brit. High Commn, New Delhi, 1952–55; attached War Office, London, 1956–57; Adviser, Federal Govt, W Indies, 1957–60; attached Govt of Kenya, 1961–63; Counsellor, British High Commn, Nairobi, Kenya, 1963–67. US Medal of Freedom with Bronze Palm, 1946. *Recreation:* walking. *Address:* 6 Onslow Square, SW7. *Club:* Travellers'.

BELL, William Archibald Ottley Juxon; Chairman, Heritage of London Trust, since 1980; Member, London Advisory Committee, English Heritage, since 1986; *b* 7 July 1919; *s* of Maj. William Archibald Juxon Bell and Mary Isabel Maude Bell (*née* Ottley); *m* 1947, Belinda Mary (*née* Dawson); three *s* three *d*. *Educ:* Eton; Trinity College, Oxford (MA(Hist.)). Temp. Captain, Welsh Guards, 1940–45. Entered HM Foreign Service, 1945; Political Private Sec. to Sir Terence Shone, UK High Comr in India, 1946–47; Sec. to Exec. Dirs, British S Africa Co., 1947–50; Partner and Dir, King & Shaxson Ltd (Billbrokers), 1950–. Mem., for Chelsea, GLC and ILEA, 1970–86. Chairman: Diocesan Bd of Finance for Oxon, 1973–76; Historic Bldgs Cttee, 1977–81; Mem., UK Cttee for European Architectural Heritage Year, 1973–75. High Sheriff, Oxon, 1978–79. *Recreations:* shooting, golf, music. *Address:* Cottisford House, near Brackley, Northants. *T:* Finmere 247; Langcliffe Hall, Settle, N Yorks. *T:* Settle 2556; 165 Cranmer Court, SW3. *T:* 01–589 1033. *Clubs:* White's, Pratt's.

BELL, William Bradshaw; Member for South Antrim, Northern Ireland Assembly, 1982–86; Lord Mayor of Belfast, 1979–80; *b* 9 Oct. 1935; *s* of Robert Bell and Mary Ann Bell; *m* 1969, Leona Maxwell; one *s* three *d*. *Educ:* Fane Street Primary School, Belfast; Grosvenor High School, Belfast. Mem. for N Belfast, NI Constitutional Convention, 1975–76; Mem., Belfast City Council, 1976–85 (Unionist spokesman on housing 1976–79). Former Dep. Chm., Finance and Personnel Cttee, NI Assembly. *Recreations:* music, motoring, gardening.

BELL, William Edwin, CBE 1980; Chairman, Enterprise Oil plc, since 1984; *b* 4 Aug. 1926; *s* of late Cuthbert Edwin Bell and Winifred Mary Bell (*née* Simpson); *m* 1952, Angela Josephine Vaughan; two *s* two *d*. *Educ:* Birmingham University (BSc Civil Eng.); Royal School of Mines, Imperial College. Joined Royal Dutch Shell Group, 1948; tech. and managerial appts, Venezuela, USA, Kuwait, Indonesia; Shell International Petroleum Co. (Middle East Coordination), 1965–73; Gen. Man., Shell UK Exploration and Production and Dir, Shell UK, 1973; Man. Dir, Shell UK, 1976–79; Middle East Regional Coordinator and Dir, Shell International Petroleum Co., 1980–84, retired; non-exec. Dir, Costain Group, 1982–. Mem., Offshore Energy Technology Bd, 1985–. Pres., UK Offshore Operators Assoc., 1975–76. *Publications:* contribs to internat. tech. jls, papers on offshore oil industry develts. *Recreations:* golf, sailing. *Address:* Fordcombe Manor, near Tunbridge Wells, Kent. *Clubs:* Nevill Golf; Chichester Yacht.

BELL, Sir (William) Ewart, KCB 1982 (CB 1978); Head of Northern Ireland Civil Service, 1979–84 and Second Permanent Secretary, Northern Ireland Office, 1981–84, retired; Director, Ulster Bank Ltd, since 1985; *b* 13 Nov. 1924; *s* of late Rev. Dr Frederick G. Bell and late Margaret Jane Ewart; *m* 1957, Kathleen Ross Boucher; two *d*. *Educ:* Methodist Coll., Belfast; Wadham Coll., Oxford (MA). Asst Master, Cheltenham Coll., 1946–48; Northern Ireland Civil Service, 1948–84; Min. of Health and Local Govt, 1948–52; Min. (later Dept) of Commerce, 1952–76; Asst Sec., 1963–70; Dep. Sec., 1970–73; Sec., 1973–76; Permanent Sec., Dept of Finance, 1976–79. Hon. Treas., QUB, 1985–. Pres., Irish RFU, 1986–87. *Recreations:* gardening, golf, Rugby football (Irish Rugby International, 1953).

BELL, Sir William H. D. M.; see Morrison-Bell.

BELL, William Lewis, CMG 1970; MBE 1945; retired; Information Officer, University of Oxford, 1977–84; *b* 31 Dec. 1919; *s* of Frederick Robinson Bell and Kate Harper Bell (*née* Lewis); *m* 1943, Margaret Giles; one *s* one *d*. *Educ:* Hymers Coll., Hull; Oriel Coll., Oxford. Served The Gloucestershire Regt (Major), 1940–46. Colonial Administrative Service, Uganda, 1946–63: Dep. Sec. to the Treasury, 1956–58; Perm. Sec., Min. of Social Services, 1958–63; Fellow, Economic Develt Inst., World Bank, 1958. Chm., Uganda National Parks, 1962; Pres., Uganda Sports Union, 1961–62. Director, Cox & Danks Ltd (Metal Industries Group), 1963–64. Sec. to the Governors, Westfield Coll., Univ. of London, 1964–65; Head of British Develt Div. in the Caribbean, ODA, 1966–72; UK Dir, Caribbean Develt Bank, 1970–72; Dir-Gen., Technical Educn and Training Org. for Overseas Countries, 1972–77. *Recreations:* cricket, writing, Caribbeana. *Address:* Greystones, Stanton St John, Oxon. *Club:* MCC.

BELL, William Rupert Graham, CB 1978; Under Secretary, Department of Industry, 1975–80; *b* 29 May 1920; *m* 1950, Molly Bolton; two *d*. *Educ:* Bradford Grammar Sch.; St John's Coll., Cambridge (Scholar). Served Royal Artillery, 1940–45 (despatches). Asst Principal, Min. of Fuel and Power, 1948; Principal, 1949; Asst Sec., 1959; Under-Sec., Min. of Power, 1966–70, DTI, 1970–72; Deputy Principal, Civil Service Coll., 1972–75. Imperial Defence Coll., 1965. *Address:* 47 Chiswick Staithe, Hartington Road, W4 3TP. *T:* 01–994 2545.

BELL DAVIES, Vice-Adm. Sir Lancelot (Richard), KBE 1977; Chairman, Sea Cadet Council, since 1983; *b* 18 Feb. 1926; *s* of late Vice-Adm. R. Bell Davies, VC, CB, DSO, AFC, and Mrs Bell Davies, Lee on Solent, Hants; *m* 1949, Emmeline Joan (*née* Molengraaff), Wassenaar, Holland; one *s* two *d*. *Educ:* Boxgrove Preparatory Sch., Guildford; RN Coll., Dartmouth. War of 1939–45: Midshipman, HMS Norfolk, 1943 (Scharnhorst sunk); joined Submarines, 1944. First Command, HMS Subtle, 1953; subseq. commands: HMS Explorer, 1955; Comdr, HMS Leander, 1962; Captain: HMS Forth, also SM7, 1967, and HMS Bulwark, 1972; Rear-Adm., 1973. Ministry of Defence Posts: (Comdr) Naval Staff, 1960; (Captain) Naval Asst to Controller, 1964; Director of Naval Warfare, 1969; Comdr, British Naval Staff, Washington, and UK Rep. to Saclant, 1973–75; Supreme Allied Commander Atlantic's Rep. in Europe, 1975–78; Comdt, Nato Defence Coll., Rome, 1978–81. CBIM (FBIM 1977). *Recreations:* sailing, skiing, gardening. *Address:* Holly Hill Lodge, Barnes Lane, Sarisbury Green, Southampton. *T:* Locks Heath 3131. *Clubs:* Naval and Military, Royal Yacht Squadron, Royal Naval Sailing Association.

BELLAIRS, Prof. Angus d'Albini; Emeritus Professor of Vertebrate Morphology in the University of London, at St Mary's Hospital Medical School, 1982 (Professor, 1970); *b* 11 Jan. 1918; *s* of late Nigel Bellairs and Kathleen Bellairs (*née* Niblett); *m* 1949 (Madeline) Ruth (PhD, Professor of Embryology at UCL), *d* of Trevor Morgan; one *d*. *Educ:* Stowe Sch.; Queens' Coll., Cambridge (MA); University Coll. Hosp., London. DSc London, MRCS, LRCP. Served War, RAMC, 1942–46; Major, Operational Research, SE Asia, 1944–46. Lectr in Anat. and Dental Anat., London Hosp. Med. Coll., 1946–51; Lectr in

Anat., Univ. of Cambridge, 1951–53; St Mary's Hosp. Med. Sch.: Reader in Anatomy, 1953–66, in Embryology, 1966–70. Vis. Prof. of Zoology, Kuwait Univ., 1970. Scientific Fellow and Hon. Cons. Herpetologist, Zoological Soc. of London; FLS 1941; FIBiol 1974. *Publications:* Reptiles, 1957 (4th edition with J. Attridge, 1975); The World of Reptiles (with Richard Carrington), 1966; The Life of Reptiles, 1969; contribs to zoological literature, mainly on reptiles. *Recreations:* natural history (especially reptiles and cats), modern fiction, military history. *Address:* 7 Champion Grove, SE5. *T:* 01–274 1834.

BELLAK, John George; Chairman: Severn-Trent Water Authority, since 1983; Sutcliffe, Speakman PLC, since 1986; *b* 19 Nov. 1930; *m* 1960, Mary Prudence Marshall; three *s* one *d. Educ:* Uppingham; Clare College, Cambridge. MA (Economics). Sales and Marketing Dir, Royal Doulton, 1968–80, Man. Dir, 1980–83; Chairman: Royal Crown Derby, 1972–83; Lawleys Ltd, 1972–83. President: British Ceramic Manufacturers' Fedn, 1982–83; Fedn of European Porcelain and Earthenware Manufacturers, 1982–83. Mem., Grand Council, CBI, 1984–. Mem. Court, Keele Univ., 1984–. *Recreations:* ornithology, field sports, reading. *Address:* Tittensor Chase, Staffs ST12 9HH. *Club:* Carlton.

BELLAMY, Rear-Adm. Albert John, CB 1968; OBE 1956; Deputy Director, Polytechnic of the South Bank, 1970–80; *b* Upton-on-Severn, 26 Feb. 1915; *s* of late A. E. Bellamy and late Mrs A. E. Bellamy; *m* 1942, Dorothy Joan Lawson; one *s* one *d. Educ:* Hanley Castle Grammar Sch.; Downing Coll., Cambridge (Buchanan Exhibitioner). 1st cl. hons Pts I and II, Math. tripos. Asst master, Berkhamsted Sch., 1936–39. Joined RN, 1939, as Instructor Lieut; Fleet Instr and Meteorological Officer, America and WI, 1948–50 (HMS Glasgow); Instr Comdr, 1950; Headmaster, RN Schs, Malta, 1951–54; HMS Ark Royal, 1955–56; Dean of the College, RN Engineering Coll., Manadon, Plymouth, 1956–60; Instr Capt., 1958; staff of Dir, Naval Educn Service, 1960–63; Dir of Studies, RN Electrical, Weapons and Radio Engineering Sch., HMS Collingwood, 1963–65; Instr Rear-Adm., 1965; Dir, Naval Educn Service and Hd of Instructor Branch, MoD, 1965–70. *Recreations:* gardening, show jumping (BSJA representative for Dorset). *Address:* The Cottage, Kington Magna, Gillingham, Dorset. *T:* East Stour 668.

BELLAMY, Alexander (William); retired; Senior Legal Assistant, Council on Tribunals, 1967–76 (temporary Legal Assistant, 1963–67); *b* Aug. 1909; *m* 1931, Lena Marie Lauga Massy. *Educ:* Mill Hill Sch.; Clare Coll., Cambridge. Called to Bar, Gray's Inn, 1934; practised at Bar, London, 1934–38; Magistrate, Straits Settlements and FMS, 1938; seconded as District Magistrate, Gold Coast, 1942; legal staff, Malaya Planning Unit, WO, 1944; Crown Counsel, Singapore, 1946; District Judge (Civil), Singapore, 1948; District Judge and 1st Magistrate, Singapore, 1952; actg Puisne Judge, Fed. of Malaya, 1953–54; Puisne Judge, Supreme Court, Nigeria, 1955; Actg Chief Justice, High Court of Lagos and Southern Cameroons, 1959, 1960; Actg Chief Justice, High Court of Lagos, 1961; a Judge of High Court of Lagos and Southern Cameroons, 1955–62. *Address:* 212 Collingwood House, Dolphin Square, SW1.

BELLAMY, Basil Edmund, CB 1971; Under-Secretary, Department of Trade and Industry (formerly Board of Trade), 1965–74; *b* 9 Feb. 1914; *s* of William Henry and Mary Bellamy; *m* 1943, Sheila Mary Dolan; one *d. Educ:* Whitgift Sch. Joined Board of Trade, 1932; Asst Dir, Min. of War Transport, 1943; Asst Sec., Min. of Transport, 1951; Under-Sec., 1963–65. Joint Services Staff Coll., 1950; Imperial Defence Coll., 1957. *Address:* 52 Denmark Road, Wimbledon, SW19 4PQ.

BELLAMY, Christopher William; QC 1986; *b* 25 April 1946; *s* of late William Albert Bellamy, TD, MRCS, LRCP and of Vyvienne Hilda Bellamy; *m* 1975, Maria-Elizabeth Vogelaar-Hoffmann (marr. diss. 1982). *Educ:* Tonbridge Sch.; Brasenose Coll., Oxford. Called to the Bar, Middle Temple, 1968. *Publication:* (with G. Child) Common Market Law of Competition, 1973, 3rd edn 1987. *Recreations:* history, walking. *Address:* Gray's Inn Chambers, Gray's Inn, WC1R 5JA. *T:* 01–405 7211.

BELLAMY, David James, PhD; FLS; FIBiol; botanist; writer and broadcaster; *b* 18 Jan. 1933; *s* of Thomas Bellamy and Winifred (*née* Green); *m* 1959, Rosemary Froy; two *s* three *d. Educ:* London University: Chelsea Coll. of Science and Technology (BSc); Bedford Coll. (PhD). Lectr, then Sen. Lectr, Dept of Botany, Univ. of Durham, 1960–80; Hon. Prof. of Adult and Continuing Educn, 1980–82. Founder Dir, Conservation Foundn; Trustee: WWF, 1985–; Living Landscape Trust, 1985–; President: WATCH, 1982–83; YHA, 1983–; Governor, Repton Sch., 1983–. Chief I Spy, 1983. Presenter and script writer for television and radio programmes, BBC and ITV; programmes include Longest Running Show on Earth, 1985; main series: Life in our Sea, 1970; Bellamy on Botany, 1973; Bellamy's Britain, 1975; Bellamy's Europe, 1977; Botanic Man, 1979; Up a Gum Tree, 1980; Backyard Safari, 1981; The Great Seasons, 1982; Bellamy's New World, 1983; You Can't See The Wood, 1984; Discovery, 1985; Seaside Safari, 1985; End of the Rainbow Show, 1985; Bellamy's Bugle, 1986; Turning the Tide, 1986; The End of the Rainbow Show, 1986. DUniv Open 1984. *Publications:* Peatlands, 1974; Bellamy on Botany, 1974; Bellamy's Britain, 1975; Bellamy's Europe, 1977; Life Giving Sea, 1977; Botanic Man, 1978; Half of Paradise, 1979; The Great Seasons, 1981; Backyard Safari, 1981; Discovering the Countryside with David Bellamy: vols I and II, 1982, vols III and IV, 1983; The Mouse Book, 1983; Bellamy's New World, 1983; The Queen's Hidden Garden, 1984; Turning the Tide, 1986; The Vanishing Bogs of Ireland, 1986. *Recreations:* children, ballet. *Address:* Mill House, Bedburn, Bishop Auckland, Co. Durham.

BELLAMY, Prof. Edmund Henry, MA, PhD; Professor of Physics in the University of London, Westfield College, 1960–84; *b* 8 April 1923; *s* of Herbert Bellamy and Nellie (*née* Ablett); *m* 1946, Joan Roberts; three *s. Educ:* Quarry Bank Sch., Liverpool; King's Coll., Cambridge. Lectr in Natural Philosophy, Univ. of Glasgow, 1951–59, Sen. Lectr, 1959–60. Mem., Nuclear Physics Board of Science Research Council, 1965–66. Visiting Professor: Univ. of Stanford, 1966–67; Univ. of Pisa, 1985–86. *Publications:* numerous scientific papers in Proc. Phys. Soc. and other journals. *Recreations:* skiing, squash, travel, football, golf. *Address:* 134 Main Road, Long Harborough, Oxford OX7 2JY. *T:* Freeland 882227.

BELLAMY, (Kenneth) Rex; Tennis Correspondent, The Times, since 1967; *b* 15 Sept. 1928; *s* of Sampson Bellamy and Kathleen May Bellamy; *m* 1951, Hilda O'Shea; one step *d. Educ:* Yeovil; Woodhouse Grammar Sch., Sheffield. National Service, RA and RASC, 1946–49. Sports and Feature Writer, Sheffield Telegraph, 1944–46 and 1949–53; Sports Writer: Birmingham Gazette, 1953–56; The Times, 1956–. Member: Inst. of Journalists; Lawn Tennis Writers' Assoc.; National Trust; Ramblers' Assoc. Internat. Tennis-writing Awards: 5 from Assoc. of Tennis Professionals, 1975–79 (award discontinued); 2 from Women's Tennis Assoc., 1977–78. *Publications:* Teach Yourself Squash (jtly), 1968; The Tennis Set, 1972; The Story of Squash, 1978; The Peak District Companion, 1981; Walking the Tops, 1984; Game, Set and Deadline, 1986. *Recreations:* hill-walking, squash. *Address:* 8 Guillards Oak, Midhurst, W Sussex GU29 9JZ. *Club:* Jesters (Hon. Mem.).

BELLEW, family name of **Baron Bellew.**

BELLEW; *see* Grattan-Bellew.

BELLEW, 7th Baron *cr* 1848; **James Bryan Bellew;** Bt 1688; *b* 5 Jan. 1920; *s* of 6th Baron Bellew, MC, and Jeanie Ellen Agnes (*d* 1973), *d* of late James Ormsby Jameson; *S* father, 1981; *m* 1st, 1942, Mary Elizabeth (*d* 1978), *d* of Rev. Edward Eustace Hill; two *s* one *d*; 2nd, 1978, Gwendoline, formerly wife of Major P. Hall and *d* of late Charles Redmond Clayton-Daubeny. Served War of 1939–45, Irish Guards (Captain). *Heir: s* Hon. Bryan Edward Bellew [*b* 19 March 1943; *m* 1968, Rosemary Sarah, *d* of Major Reginald Kilner Brasier Hitchcock; two *s*]. *Address:* Barmeath Castle, County Louth, S Ireland; 24 Dartmouth Place, W4; Burgage House, Sheep Street, Stow on the Wold, Glos.

BELLEW, Hon. Sir George (Rothe), KCB 1961; KCVO 1953 (CVO 1950; MVO 1935); Kt 1950; FSA 1948; Secretary of the Order of the Garter, 1961–74, Garter Principal King of Arms, 1950–61; Genealogist of the Order of the Bath, 1950–61; Genealogist Order of St John, 1951–61; Knight Principal of Imperial Society of Knights Bachelor, 1957–62 (Deputy Knight Principal, 1962–71); Inspector of Regimental Colours, 1957–61; *b* 13 Dec. 1899; *s* of late Hon. Richard Bellew and Gwendoline, *d* of William R. J. Fitzherbert Herbert-Huddleston of Clytha; *m* 1935, Ursula Kennard, *e d* of late Anders Eric Knös Cull, Warfield House, Bracknell; one *s. Educ:* Wellington Coll.; Christ Church, Oxford. Served War of 1939–45: Squadron Leader RAFVR, 1940–45 (despatches). Formerly Portcullis Pursuivant of Arms; Somerset Herald, 1926–50, and Registrar of the Coll. of Arms, 1935–46. KStJ 1951 (Mem. Chapter Gen., 1951–). *Address:* The Grange, Farnham, Surrey.

BELLINGER, Sir Robert (Ian), GBE 1967; Kt 1964; Chairman: Kinloch (PM) Ltd, 1946–75; National Savings Committee, 1970–75, and President, 1972–75; Director, Rank Organisation, 1971–83; *b* Tetbury, Glos, 10 March 1910; *s* of David Morgan Bellinger, Cardiganshire, and Jane Ballantine Deans, Edinburgh; *m* 1962, Christiane Marie Louise Janssens, Brussels; one *s* one *d. Educ:* Church of England sch. Elected Court of Common Council, 1953; Chm. City of London Freemen's Sch., 1957; Alderman for Ward of Cheap, 1958; Sheriff, City of London, 1962–63; Lord Mayor of London, 1966–67; one of HM Lieutenants, City of London, 1976–. Chairman: Panel for Civil Service Manpower Review, 1968–71; Adv. Cttee on Magistracy, City of London, 1968–76; Licensing Cttee, City of London; Finance Cttee, BBC; Governor, BBC, 1968–71; Trustee, St Paul's Cathedral Trust, 1977–; Dir, Arsenal Football Club. Chairman: Anglo-Danish Soc., 1976–83; Danish Trade Adv. Bd, 1979–82. Past Master, Broderers' Company; Liveryman, Fletchers' Company. Hon. DSc City Univ., 1966. Gentleman Usher of the Purple Rod, Order of the British Empire, 1969–85. KStJ 1966; Commandeur, Ordre de Léopold, cl. III (Belgium), 1963; Comdr, Royal Order of the Phoenix (Greece), 1963; Officier, Ordre de la Valeur Camerounaise (Cameroons), 1963; Knight Comdr of the Order of Dannebrog (Denmark), 1977. *Recreations:* tennis, football, music, motoring. *Address:* Penn Wood, Fulmer, Bucks. *T:* Fulmer 2029. *Club:* City Livery.

BELLINGHAM, Henry Campbell; MP (C) Norfolk North West, since 1983; *b* 29 March 1955; *s* of late Henry Bellingham. *Educ:* Eton; Magdalene Coll., Cambridge (BA 1977). Called to the Bar, Middle Temple, 1978. Partner in family farming and property co.; Mem. of Lloyd's; Founder W Norfolk Small Business Bureau, 1982; Mem. Exec., Nat. Small Business Bureau, 1982–. Sec., Cons. Parly Smaller Businesses Cttee, 1983–; Jt Sec., Cons. NI Cttee, 1983–. *Address:* House of Commons, SW1A 0AA; Congham Lodge, King's Lynn, Norfolk. *Clubs:* White's, Pratt's.

BELLINGHAM, Sir Noel (Peter Roger), 7th Bt (2nd creation) *cr* 1796; accountant; *b* 4 Sept. 1943; *s* of Sir Roger Carroll Patrick Stephen Bellingham, 6th Bt, and of Mary, *d* of late William Norman; *S* father, 1973; *m* 1977, Jane, *d* of late Edwin William and of Joan Taylor, Sale, Cheshire. *Heir: b* Anthony Edward Norman Bellingham, *b* 24 March 1947. *Address:* 20 Davenport Park Road, Davenport, Stockport, Cheshire. *T:* 061–483 7168. *Club:* 64 Society (Cheshire).

BELLIS, Bertram Thomas; Headmaster, The Leys School, Cambridge, 1975–86; *b* 4 May 1927; *s* of Rev. Thomas J. Bellis and Mary A. Bellis; *m* 1952, Joan Healey; two *s. Educ:* Kingswood Sch., Bath; St John's Coll., Cambridge (Exhibr in Maths, MA). Rossall Sch., 1951–55; Highgate Sch., 1955–65; Headmaster, Daniel Stewart's Coll., 1965–72; Principal, Daniel Stewart's and Melville Coll., 1972–75. Chm., Scottish Educn Dept Cttee on Computers and the Schools (reports, 1969 and 1972); Member: Council, Inst. of Math., 1975–79; Educational Research Bd, SSRC, 1975–80. Governor: Queenswood Sch., 1980–; St John's Coll. Sch., 1981–. Pres., Mathematical Assoc., 1971–72. Schoolmaster Fellow, Balliol Coll., Oxford, 1963; FIMA 1964; FRSE 1972. *Recreation:* fell walking. *Address:* 33 Oxford Road, Cambridge CB4 3PH.

BELLIS, John Herbert; Chairman of Industrial Tribunals, Manchester Region, since 1984; *b* 11 April 1930; *s* of Thomas and Jane Bellis; *m* 1961, Sheila Helen McNeil Ford; two *s* one *d. Educ:* Friars Grammar Sch., Bangor; Liverpool Univ. (LLB). Admitted Solicitor, 1953. National Service, 1953–55. In practice as solicitor on own account, Penmaenmawr, N Wales, 1958–84. Parly Cand. (L) Conway, Caernarvonshire, 1959. *Recreations:* golf, walking, gardening. *Address:* 148 Grove Lane, Cheadle Hulme, Cheadle, Cheshire SK8 7NH. *T:* 061–439 7582.

BELLOW, family name of **Baron Bellwin.**

BELLOW, Saul; American writer; *b* 10 June 1915; *s* of Abraham and Liza Gordon Bellow; *m* Alexandra (*née* Bagdasar); three *s. Educ:* Univ. of Chicago: Northwestern Univ. Nobel Prize for Literature, 1976; Malaparté Prize for Literature, Italy, 1984. Hon. DLitt, Northwestern Univ., 1962. Commander, Legion of Honour (France), 1983; Commander, Order of Arts and Letters (France), 1985 (Croix de Chevalier, 1968). *Publications:* Dangling Man, 1944 (reissued 1972); The Victim, 1947; The Adventures of Augie March, 1953 (National Book Award, 1954); Seize the Day, 1956; Henderson the Rain King, 1959; Herzog, 1964 (National Book Award, Internat. Literary Prize, 1965); Mosby's Memoirs and Other Stories, 1969; Mr Sammler's Planet, 1970 (National Book Award, 1970); Humboldt's Gift, 1975 (Pulitzer Prize 1976); To Jerusalem and Back, 1976; The Dean's December, 1982; (short stories) Him with His Foot in His Mouth, 1984. *Address:* University of Chicago, Chicago, Ill 60637, USA.

BELLOWS, James Gilbert; Executive Producer, ABC-TV News, since 1983; *b* 12 Nov. 1922; *s* of Lyman Hubbard Bellows and Dorothy Gilbert Bellows; *m* 1950, Marian Raines (decd); three *d*; *m* 1964, Maggie Savoy (decd); *m* 1971, Keven Ryan; one *d. Educ:* Kenyon Coll. (BA, LLB). Columbus (Ga) Ledger, 1947; News Editor Atlanta (Ga) Jl, 1950–57; Asst Editor, Detroit (Mich.) Free Press, 1957–58; Managing Editor Miami (Fla) News, 1958–61; Exec. Editor (News Ops), NY Herald Tribune, 1961–62; Editor, 1962–66; associate Editor, Los Angeles Times, 1966–75; Editor: Washington Star, 1975–78; Los Angeles Herald Examiner, 1979–82; Managing Editor, Entertainment Tonight (TV show), 1982–83. Member: Kenyon Review Adv. Bd; Amer. Soc. of Newspaper Editors. *Address:* 54E 66 Street, New York, NY 10021, USA. *Club:* Bel-Air Country (Los Angeles).

BELLWIN, Baron *cr* 1979 (Life Peer), of the City of Leeds; **Irwin Norman Bellow;** JP; *b* 7 Feb. 1923; *s* of Abraham and Leah Bellow; *m* 1948, Doreen Barbara Saperia; one *s* two *d*. *Educ:* Lovell Road; Leeds Grammar School; Leeds Univ. LLB. Leader, Leeds City Council, 1975–79; Vice-Chm. Assoc. of Metropolitan Authorities, 1978–79. Parly Under Sec. of State, DoE, 1979–Jan. 1983; Minister of State, 1983–84. Mem., Commn for New Towns, 1985–; Vice-Pres., Internat. New Towns Assoc. Non-executive Director: Taylor Woodrow, 1985–; London and Continental Advertising (Hldgs), 1985–. JP Leeds, 1969. *Recreation:* golf. *Address:* Woodside Lodge, Ling Lane, Scarcroft, Leeds LS14 3HX. *T:* Leeds 892908. *Club:* Moor Allerton Golf (Club Pres.).

BELMORE, 8th Earl of, *cr* 1797; **John Armar Lowry-Corry;** Baron Belmore, 1781; Viscount Belmore, 1789; *b* 4 Sept. 1951; *s* of 7th Earl of Belmore and Gloria Anthea, *d* of late Herbert Bryant Harker, Melbourne, Australia; *S* father 1960; *m* 1984, Lady Mary Meade, *d* of Earl of Clanwilliam, *qv*; one *s*. *Educ:* Lancing; Royal Agricultural Coll., Cirencester. *Heir:* *s* Viscount Corry, *qv*. *Recreation:* conservation. *Address:* Castle Coole, Enniskillen, Co. Fermanagh, N Ireland. *T:* Enniskillen 22368/24255. *Club:* Kildare Street and University (Dublin).

BELOFF, family name of **Baron Beloff.**

BELOFF, Baron *cr* 1981 (Life Peer), of Wolvercote in the County of Oxfordshire; **Max Beloff;** Kt 1980; MA, DLitt (Oxon); FBA 1973; FRHistS; FRSA; *b* 2 July 1913; *er s* of late Simon and Mary Beloff; *m* 1938, Helen Dobrin; two *s*. *Educ:* St Paul's Sch.; Corpus Christi Coll., Oxford (Scholar). Gibbs Schol. in Mod. Hist., 1934; 1st Cl. Hons, School of Modern History, 1935; Senior Demy, Magdalen Coll., Oxford, 1935. Junior Research Fellow, Corpus Christi Coll., 1937; Asst Lecturer in History, Manchester Univ., 1939–46; Nuffield Reader in Comparative Study of Institutions, Oxford Univ., 1946–56; Fellow of Nuffield Coll., 1947–57; Gladstone Prof. of Govt and Public Admin, Oxford Univ., 1957–74, now Professor Emeritus, and Fellow, All Souls Coll., 1957–74, Emeritus Fellow, 1980–; Supernumerary Fellow, St Antony's Coll., Oxford, 1975–84; Principal, University Coll. at Buckingham, 1974–79. War of 1939–45, Royal Corps of Signals, 1940–41. Governor, Haifa Univ.; Ex-Trustee and Ex-Librarian, Oxford Union Soc. Hon. LLD Pittsburgh, USA, 1962; Hon. DCL, Bishop's Univ. Canada, 1976; Hon. DLitt Bowdoin Coll., USA, 1976; Hon. DrUniv. Aix-Marseille III, 1978. *Publications:* Public Order and Popular Disturbances, 1660–1714, 1938; The Foreign Policy of Soviet Russia, Vol. 1, 1947, Vol. 2, 1949; Thomas Jefferson and American Democracy, 1948; Soviet Policy in the Far East, 1944–51, 1953; The Age of Absolutism, 1660–1815, 1954; Foreign Policy and the Democratic Process, 1955; Europe and the Europeans, 1957; The Great Powers, 1959; The American Federal Government, 1959; New Dimensions in Foreign Policy, 1961; The United States and the Unity of Europe, 1963; The Balance of Power, 1967; The Future of British Foreign Policy, 1969; Imperial Sunset, vol. 1, 1969; The Intellectual in Politics, 1970; (with G. R. Peele) The Government of the United Kingdom, 1980, 2nd edn 1985; Wars and Welfare 1914–1945, 1984; edited: The Federalist, 1948; Mankind and his Story, 1948; The Debate on the American Revolution, 1949; On the Track of Tyranny, 1959; (jtly) L'Europe du XIXe et XXe siècle, 1960–67; (with V. Vale) American Political Institutions in the 1970's, 1975; articles in English, French, Italian and American journals. *Recreation:* watching cricket. *Address:* c/o House of Lords, SW1. *T:* 01–219 6669. *Club:* Reform.

See also Hon. Michael Beloff.

BELOFF, Hon. Michael Jacob, MA; QC 1981; barrister and writer; a Recorder, since 1985; *b* 19 April 1942; *s* of Baron Beloff, *qv*; *m* 1969, Judith Mary Arkinstall; one *s* one *d*. *Educ:* Dragon Sch., Oxford; Eton Coll. (King's Schol.; Captain of Sch. 1960); Magdalen Coll., Oxford (Demy; H. W. C. Davis Prizeman, 1962; BA Hist. (1st cl.) 1963, Law 1965; MA 1967). Pres., Oxford Union Soc., 1962; Oxford Union tour of USA, 1964. Called to the Bar, Gray's Inn, 1967 (Gerald Moody Schol., 1963; Atkin Schol., 1967). Lectr in Law, Trinity Coll., Oxford, 1965–66. Legal Correspondent: New Society, 1969–79; The Observer, 1979–81. Chm., Administrative Law Bar Assoc., 1986–; Mem., Bingham Law Reform Cttee on Discovery of Documents and Disclosure, 1982–. Hon. Mem., Internat. Athletes' Club. *Publications:* A Short Walk on the Campus (with J. Aitken), 1966; The Plateglass Universities, 1968; The Sex Discrimination Act, 1976; Halsbury's Laws of England (contribution on time), 1983; contrib. Encounter, Minerva, Irish Jurist, Political Qly, etc. *Recreation:* running marathons. *Address:* 58 Park Town, Oxford OX2 6SJ; Flat 6, 38/9 Redcliffe Road, SW10 9NJ; 4–5 Gray's Inn Square, Gray's Inn, WC1R 5AY. *T:* 01–404 5252. *Clubs:* Reform; Vincent's (Oxford).

BELOFF, Nora; author and journalist; *b* 24 Jan. 1919. *Educ:* King Alfred Sch.; Lady Margaret Hall, Oxford. BA Hons History 1940. Polit. Intell. Dept, FO, 1941–44; British Embassy, Paris, 1944–45; reporter, Reuters News Agency, 1945–46; Paris corresp., The Economist, 1946–48; Observer corresp., Paris, Washington, Moscow, Brussels etc, 1948–78; political correspondent, 1964–76, roving correspondent, 1976–78. *Publications:* The General Says No, 1963; The Transit of Britain, 1973; Freedom under Foot, 1976; No Travel like Russian Travel, 1979 (US, as Inside the Soviet Empire: myth and reality, 1980); Tito's Flawed Legacy: Yugoslavia and the West 1939–1984, 1985. *Address:* 11 Belsize Road, NW6 4RX. *T:* 01–586 0378.

BELPER, 4th Baron *cr* 1856; **Alexander Ronald George Strutt;** formerly Major, Coldstream Guards; *b* 23 April 1912; *s* of 3rd Baron and Hon. Eva Isabel Mary Bruce, 2nd *d* of 2nd Baron Aberdare (she *m* 2nd, 6th Earl of Rosebery); *S* father 1956; *m* 1940, Zara Sophie Kathleen Mary (marr. diss. 1949), *y d* of Sir Harry Mainwaring, 5th Bt; one *s*. *Educ:* Harrow. Served War with Coldstream Guards, 1939–44 (wounded). *Heir:* *s* Hon. Richard Henry Strutt [*b* 24 Oct. 1941; *m* 1966, Jennifer Vivian, *d* of late Capt. Peter Winser and of Mrs James Whitaker; one *s* one *d*; *m* 1980, Judith Mary de Jonge, *d* of Mr and Mrs James Twynam, Kitemore House, Faringdon, Oxon]. *Address:* Kingston Hall, Nottingham.

BELSKY, Franta; sculptor; *b* Brno, 6 April 1921; *s* of Joseph Belsky, economist; *m* Margaret Owen (cartoonist Belsky). *Educ:* Acad. of Fine Arts, Prague; Royal Coll. of Art, London. ARCA, Hons Dip. 1950. Served War as gunner (France, 1940; Normandy, 1944; various decorations). Taught in art schs, 1950–55. FRBS (Mem. Council); Pres., Soc. of Portrait Sculptors, 1963–68; Governor, St Martin's Sch. of Art, 1967–. Work in Nat. Portrait Gall. and collections in Europe and USA, for numerous co. councils, industrial, shipping and private cos and educn authorities: Paratroop Memorial, Prague, 1947; Lt-Col Peniakoff (Popski), Ravenna, 1952; statue of Cecil Rhodes, 8′, Bulawayo, 1953; groups: Constellation, Colchester, 1953; Lesson, LCC housing develt, 1957–58; Triga, Knightsbridge, 1958; Joy-ride, Stevenage New Town Centre, 1958; Astronomer Herschel Memorial, 18′, Slough, 1969; Oracle, 18′, Temple Way House, Bristol, 1975 (RBS Sir Otto Beit Medal, 1976); Totem, 32′, Manchester Arndale Centre, 1975 (RBS Sir Otto Beit Medal, 1978); fountains: European Shell Centre, 30′, South Bank; Four Seasons, 17′, Yate; reliefs: Epicentre, Doncaster City Centre, 1965; Key West, Slough, 1966; Radiation, St Luke's Hosp., Guildford; BR and P & O ships; 1978 Jean Masson Davidson Award for Dist. in Portrait Sculpture; portraits include: Queen Mother, Birmingham Univ., 1962; Prince Philip, 1979 and HM the Queen, 1981, Nat. Portrait Gall.; Prince Andrew, 1963 and 1984; statue of Sir Winston Churchill for Churchill Meml and Library in US, Fulton, Missouri, and bust in Churchill Archives, Cambridge, 1971; Harry S. Truman, Presidential Library, Independence, Mo and H. S. T. Dam, Osage River, Mo; Adm. Cunningham, Trafalgar Square, 1969; Lord Cottesloe, Nat. Theatre; Mountbatten Meml, Horse Guards Parade, 1983; Adm. Lord Lewin, HMS Dryad, 1985. Queen Mother 80th Birthday Crown coin. *Publications:* illus. and contrib. various books and jls. *Recreations:* ski-ing, gardening, amateur archaeology. *Address:* 12 Pembroke Studios, W8 6HX.

BELSTEAD, 2nd Baron, *cr* 1938; **John Julian Ganzoni;** Bt 1929; PC 1983; JP; Minister of State, Ministry of Agriculture, Fisheries and Food, since 1983; *b* 30 Sept. 1932; *o s* of 1st Baron Belstead and Gwendolen Gertrude Turner (*d* 1962); *S* father, 1958. *Educ:* Eton; Christ Church, Oxford. MA 1961. Parliamentary Under-Secretary of State: DES, 1970–73; NI Office, 1973–74; Home Office, 1979–82; Minister of State, FCO, 1982–83. Chm., Assoc. of Governing Bodies of Public Schools, 1974–79. JP Borough of Ipswich, 1962; DL Suffolk, 1979. *Heir:* none. *Address:* The Old Rectory, Great Bealings, near Woodbridge, Suffolk. *T:* Grundisburgh 278. *Clubs:* All England Lawn Tennis (Wimbledon); MCC.

BELTRAM, Geoffrey; Under-Secretary, Department of Health and Social Security, 1973–81; *b* 7 April 1921; *s* of George and Beatrice Dorothy Beltram; *m* 1945, Audrey Mary (*née* Harkett); one *s* one *d*. *Educ:* Dame Alice Owen's School. Tax Officer, Inland Revenue, 1938; served in RAF, 1941–46; Exec. Officer and Higher Exec. Officer, Min. of Town and Country Planning, 1947–51; Asst Principal, Nat. Assistance Bd, 1951–55; Principal 1955–63; Asst Sec. 1963–73 (NAB 1963–66, Min. of Social Security 1966–68, DHSS 1968–73). Vis. Res. Associate, LSE, 1981–84. *Publication:* Testing the Safety Net: a study of the Supplementary Benefit scheme, 1984. *Recreations:* literature, listening to music, opera, ballet, walking, tennis, swimming.

BEN-TOVIM, Atarah, (Mrs Douglas Boyd), MBE 1980 (for services to children's music); Founder and Artistic Director, Children's Concert Centre, since 1975; *b* 1 Oct. 1940; *d* of Tsvi Ben-Tovim and Gladys Ben-Tovim; *m* 1976, Douglas Boyd; one *d*. *Educ:* Royal Acad. of Music, London. ARAM 1967. Principal Flautist, Royal Liverpool Philharmonic Orchestra, 1962–75. Founder and Trustee, Ben Tovim Children's Music Centre Trust, 1978–. *Publications:* Atarah's Book (autobiog.), 1976, 2nd edn 1979; Atarah's Band Kits (14 published), 1978–; Children and Music, 1979; (jtly) The Right Instrument For Your Child, 1985; You Can Make Music!, 1986. *Recreations:* music, writing, France and the Mediterranean. *Address:* c/o Watson Little Ltd, Suite 8, 26 Charing Cross Road, WC2H 0DG. *T:* 01–836 5860.

BENABDELJALIL, Mohamed-Mehdi; Ambassador of the Kingdom of Morocco to the Court of St James's, since 1981; *b* 12 Jan. 1930; *m* 1962, Mrs Kinza Abdelkhalek Torres; two *s* one *d*. *Educ:* Imperial Coll., Rabat, Morocco; Faculty of Law, Univ. of Paris; Inst. for Internat. Studies, and Inst. for Polit. Studies, Paris. Formerly: Head of Cabinet of Minister i/c Negotiations; Head of Cabinet of Minister of Interior; Head, Dept of Mines and Geology; Under-Sec. of State for Indust. Prodn and Mining; Gen. Sec., Min. of National Economy; Dir Gen., Bureau des Etudes et des Participations Industrielles; successively Ambassador in Bonn and Tehran (with accreditation to Turkey and Afghanistan); law practice, Casablanca, 1973–80. Grand Cross: West Germany; Lebanon; Iran. *Recreations:* sport, hunting. *Address:* Embassy of the Kingdom of Morocco, 49 Queen's Gate Gardens, SW7 5NE. *T:* 01–581 5004.

BENACERRAF, Prof. Baruj; Fabyan Professor of Comparative Pathology and Chairman of the Department of Pathology, Harvard Medical School, since 1970; President, Dana-Farber Cancer Institute, Boston, since 1980; *b* 29 Oct. 1920; *m* 1943, Annette Dreyfus; one *d*. *Educ:* Lycée Janson, Paris (BèsL 1940); Columbia Univ. (BS 1942); Medical Coll. of Virginia (MD 1945). Served US Army, 1946–48. Intern, Queens Gen. Hosp., NY, 1945–46; Res. Fellow, Dept of Micro-biol., Coll. of Physicians and Surgeons, Columbia Univ., 1948–49; Chargé de Recherches, CNRS, Hôpital Broussais, Paris, 1950–56; New York University School of Medicine: Asst Prof. of Pathol., 1956–58; Assoc. Prof. of Pathol., 1958–60; Prof. of Pathol., 1960–68; Chief, Lab. of Immunol., Nat. Inst. of Allergy and Infectious Diseases, NIH, Bethesda, 1968–70. Scientific Advr, WHO; Chm., Scientific Adv. Cttee, Centre d'Immunologie de Marseille, CNRS-INSERM; Member: Immunology A Study Sect., NIH, 1965–69; Adv. Council, National Inst. of Allergy and Infectious Disease, 1985–; Scientific Adv. Cttee, Basel Inst. of Immunology, 1985–; Member Scientific Advisory Board: Trudeau Foundn, 1970–76; Mass Gen. Hosp., 1971–74. Associate Editor: Amer. Jl of Pathology; Jl of Exptl Medicine. President: Amer. Assoc. of Immunologists, 1973–74; Fedn of Amer. Socs for Exptl Biol., 1974–75; Internat. Union of Immunol Socs, 1980–83. Fellow, Amer. Acad. of Arts and Scis, 1972. Member: Nat. Acad. of Scis, 1973; Nat. Inst. of Med., 1981; Amer. Assoc. of Pathologists and Bacteriologists; Amer. Soc. for Exptl Pathol.; Soc. of Exptl Biol. and Medicine; British Assoc. for Immunol.; French Soc. of Biol Chem.; Harvey Soc.; NY Acad. of Scis. Lectures: R. E. Dyer, NIH, 1969; Harvey, 1971, 1972; J. S. Blumenthal, Univ. of Minnesota, 1980. Hon. MD Geneva, 1980; Hon. DSc: Virginia Commonwealth Univ., 1981; NY Univ., 1981; Columbia Univ., 1985. Rabbi Shai Shacknai Lectr and Prize, Hebrew Univ. of Jerusalem, 1974; T. Duckett Jones Meml Award, Helen Hay Whitney Foundn, 1976; Waterford Biomedical Science Award, 1980; (jtly) Nobel Prize for Physiology or Medicine, 1980; Rous-Whipple Award, Amer. Assoc. of Pathologists, 1985. *Publications:* (with D. Katz) Immunological Tolerance, 1974; Immunogenetics and Immunodeficiency, 1975; (with D. Katz) The Role of Products of the Histocompatibility Gene Complex in Immune Responses, 1976; Textbook of Immunology, 1979; 550 articles in professional journals. *Recreations:* music, art collecting. *Address:* Department of Pathology, Harvard Medical School, 25 Shattuck Street, Boston, Mass 02115, USA. *T:* 617.732.1971.

BENARROCH, Heather Mary, (Mrs E. J. Benarroch); *see* Harper, Heather.

BENAUD, Richard, OBE 1961; international sports consultant, journalist and media representative; BBC and Channel Nine Network television commentator, since 1960; *b* 6 Oct. 1930; *s* of Louis Richard Benaud and Irene Benaud; *m* 1967, Daphne Elizabeth Surfleet; two *s* by previous marr. *Educ:* Parramatta High Sch. Captain, Australian Cricket Team, 28 Tests, played for Australia 63 Tests, Tours to England, 1953, 1956, 1961. *Publications:* Way of Cricket, 1960; Tale of Two Tests, 1962; Spin Me a Spinner, 1963; The New Champions, 1965; Willow Patterns, 1972; Benaud on Reflection, 1984. *Recreation:* golf. *Address:* 19/178 Beach Street, Coogee, NSW 2034, Australia. *T:* Sydney 665–6464.

BENCE, Cyril Raymond; *b* 26 Nov. 1902; *s* of Harris Bryant Bence; *m* 1st, 1926, Florence Maud Bowler (*d* 1974); one *s* one *d*; 2nd, 1975, Mrs I. N. Hall (*née* Lewis). *Educ:* Pontywaen Sch.; Newport High Sch., Mon. Apprenticed to Ashworth Son & Co. Ltd of Dock Street, Newport, Mon, Weighing Machine Manufacturers; moved to Birmingham, 1937. Member of National Union of Scalemakers; Mem. of AEU; Mem. of Birmingham Trades Council, 1942–45; Pres. Witton Branch AEU. Contested (Lab) Handsworth Div. of Birmingham, at Gen. Elections of 1945 and 1950, and Bye-election Nov. 1950; MP (Lab) Dunbartonshire East, 1951–70. *Address:* Leda, Sweethay Close, Staplehay, Taunton, Som.

See also V. L. Pearl.

BENDALL, David Vere, CMG 1967; MBE 1945; HM Diplomatic Service, retired; Chairman: Banque Morgan Grenfell en Suisse, since 1981 (Morgan Grenfell Switzerland SA, 1974–81); Morgan Grenfell Italia spa, since 1982; Director, Morgan Grenfell France sa, since 1986; Chairman, Banca Nazionale del Lavoro (UK) Ltd, since 1986; Deputy Chairman, Avon Cosmetics Ltd, since 1979; *b* 27 Feb. 1920; *s* of John Manley Bendall; *m* 1941, Eve Stephanie Merrilees Galpin; one *d. Educ*: Winchester; King's Coll., Cambridge (BA). Served Grenadier Guards, 1940–46. Third Sec., Allied Force HQ, Caserta, 1946; Rome, 1947; FO, 1949; First Sec., Santiago, 1952; FO, 1955; seconded to NATO Secretariat, Paris 1957; FO, 1960; NATO Secretariat, Paris as Dep. Head, Economic and Finance Div. and Special Advisor on Defence Policy, 1962; Counsellor, 1962; Counsellor, Washington, 1965–69; Asst Under-Sec. of State for Western Europe, 1969–71. Chm., Morgan Grenfell Internat. Ltd, 1979–85; Dir, Morgan Grenfell (Holdings) Ltd, 1971–85; Member: Morgan Grenfell Internat. Adv. Council, 1986–; London Adv. Bd, Banque de l'Indochine et de Suez, 1974–. Chm., British Red Cross Soc., 1980–85 (Vice-Chm., 1979–80). CStJ 1985. *Recreations:* golf, tennis, shooting, languages. *Address:* 3 Eaton Terrace Mews, SW1. *T:* 01–730 4229; Ashbocking Hall, near Ipswich, Suffolk. *T:* Helmingham 262. *Club:* Boodle's.

BENDALL, Dr Eve Rosemarie Duffield; Chief Executive Officer, English National Board for Nursing, Midwifery and Health Visiting, since 1981; *b* 7 Aug. 1927; *d* of Col F. W. D. Bendall, CMG, MA, and Mrs M. L. Bendall, LRAM, ARCM. *Educ:* Malvern Girls' Coll.; London Univ. (MA, PhD); Royal Free Hosp. (SRN). Ward Sister, Dorset County Hosp., 1953–55; Night Supt, Manchester Babies' Hosp., 1955–56; Nurse Tutor: United Sheffield Hosps Sch. of Nursing, 1958–61; St George's Hosp., London, 1961–63; Principal, Sch. of Nursing, Hosp. for Sick Children, Gt Ormond Street, 1963–69. Registrar, GNC, 1973–77. *Publications:* (jtly) Basic Nursing, 1963, 3rd edn 1970; (jtly) A Guide to Medical and Surgical Nursing, 1965, 2nd edn 1970; (jtly) A History of the General Nursing Council, 1969; So You Passed, Nurse (research), 1975. *Recreations:* gardening, breeding Jersey cows. *Address:* c/o English National Board for Nursing, Midwifery and Health Visiting, Victory House, 170 Tottenham Court Road, W1P 0HA.

BENDALL, Vivian Walter Hough; MP (C) Ilford North, since March 1978; surveyor and valuer; *b* 14 Dec. 1938; *s* of late Cecil Aubrey Bendall and Olive Alvina Bendall (*née* Hough); *m* 1969, Ann Rosalind (*née* Jarvis). *Educ:* Coombe Hill House, Croydon; Broad Green Coll., Croydon. LRVA 1976, MRSH 1965. Mem. Croydon Council, 1964–78; Mem. GLC, 1970–73; Chm., Greater London Young Conservatives, 1967–68. Backbench Committees: Vice-Chm., Transport Cttee, 1982–83; Sec., Foreign and Commonwealth Affairs Cttee, 1981–84; Vice-Chm., Employment Cttee, 1984– (Jt Sec. 1981–84); Former Member: Central Council for Care of the Elderly; South Eastern Area Reg. Assoc. for the Blind; Mem., Dr Barnardo's New Mossford Home Fund Raising Cttee. Contested (C) Hertford and Stevenage, Feb. and Oct. 1974. *Recreation:* cricket. *Address:* (business) 25 Brighton Road, South Croydon, Surrey CR2 6EA. *T:* 01–688 0341. *Clubs:* Carlton; Essex County Cricket.

BENDER, Prof. Arnold Eric; Emeritus Professor, University of London; Professor of Nutrition and Dietetics, University of London and Head of Department of Food Science and Nutrition, Queen Elizabeth College, 1978–83 (Professor of Nutrition, 1971–78); *b* 24 July 1918; *s* of Isadore and Rose Bender; *m* 1941, Deborah Swift; two *s. Educ:* Liverpool Inst. High Sch.; Univ. of Liverpool (BSc Hons); Univ. of Sheffield (PhD). FRSH, FIFST. Research, Pharmaceutical Industry, 1940–45 and 1950–54; Res. Fellow, National Inst. of Radiotherapy, Sheffield, 1945–47; Lectr, Univ. of Sheffield, 1947–49; Research, Food Industry, 1954–64; Teaching and Research, Univ. of London, 1965–83. Department of Health and Social Security: Gp Sec. of Working Party on Protein Requirements, 1963; Mem., Sub-cttee on Protein Requirements, 1967; Mem., Cttee on Toxic Chemicals in Food and the Environment, 1976–83; Mem., Cttee on Med. Aspects of Food Policy, 1978–85; Chm., Panel on Novel Foods, 1980–85. Ministry of Agriculture, Fisheries and Food: Mem., Cttee on Dietetic Foods, 1969–73 and on Composition of Foods, 1975–77; Mem., Adv. Cttee on Irradiated and Novel Foods, 1981–85 and on Naturally Occurring Toxic Substances in Foods, 1983–. Society of Chemical Industry: Mem. Council, 1982–85; Food Group: Hon. Sec., 1955–60; Chm., 1979–80; Vice-Chm., 1980–82; Chm., Nutrition Panel, 1960–63 and 1976–78. Royal Society of Health: Mem. Council, 1974–; Chm., Examinations Cttee, 1983–85; Chm., Conf. and Meetings Cttee, 1985–86; Chm., Food and Nutrition Gp, 1968–70 (Vice Chm., 1967–68). Member: Royal Soc. British Nat. Cttee for Biochem., 1963–69, for Nutritional Scis, 1976–; Eur. Cttee for Co-operation in Sci. and Technol. (COST 91), 1980–83 (Chm., Nutrition Sub-cttee, 1982–83); Cttee on Protein Quality Evaluation, ARC, 1955–66; Sector D Res. Cttee, CNAA, 1982–; Vice-Pres., Internat. Union of Food Sci. and Technol., 1983–87 (Mem. Exec., 1978–83). Hon. Treasurer, UK Nutrition Soc., 1962–67; Hon. Sec., UK Council for Food Sci. and Technol., 1964–77. Hon. DSc Univ. Complutense, Madrid. Mem. Editorial Board: Jl of Human Nutrition; Jl of Science of Food and Agriculture; Jl of Food Technol.; British Jl of Nutrition. *Publications:* Dictionary of Nutrition and Food Technology, 1960, 5th edn 1982, Japanese edn 1965, Arabic edn 1985; Nutrition and Dietetic Foods, 1967, 2nd edn 1973; Value of Food, 1970, 3rd edn 1979, Spanish edn 1972; Facts of Food, 1975, Polish edn 1979; Food Processing and Nutrition, 1978, Japanese edn 1978; The Pocket Guide to Calories and Nutrition, 1979, 2nd edn 1986, Dutch, US, Italian and Spanish edns, 1981; Nutrition for Medical Students, 1982; Health or Hoax?, 1985; Food Tables, 1986; research papers and review articles in Brit. Jl of Nutrition, Biochem. Jl, BMJ, Jl Human Nutrition, Jl Science Food and Agric., and other professional jls, and reports. *Recreations:* writing, gardening, lecturing. *Address:* 2 Willow Vale, Fetcham, Leatherhead, Surrey KT22 9TE. *T:* Bookham 54702.

BENDIGO, Bishop of, since 1975; **Rt. Rev. Oliver Spencer Heyward;** *b* Launceston, Tasmania, 16 March 1926; *s* of Harold and Vera Heyward; *m* 1952, Peggy Butcher; four *s. Educ:* Church Gram. Sch., Launceston; Univ. of Tasmania (BA Hons 1949); Oriel Coll., Univ. of Oxford (BA 1953, MA 1956); Cuddesdon Coll., Oxford. RAAF, 1944–46. Rhodes Scholar, 1949. Deacon 1953, priest 1954, dio. Chichester; Asst Curate, St Peter's, Brighton, 1953–56; Rector of Sorell, Tasmania, 1956–60; Rector of Richmond, Tasmania, 1960–62; Precentor, St David's Cathedral, Hobart, 1962–63; Warden, Christ Coll., Univ. of Tasmania, 1963–74. Pres., Bendigo Coll. of Advanced Educn, 1976–86; Comr, Victorian Post-Secondary Educn Commn, 1982–. *Recreation:* gardening. *Address:* 8 Myers Street, Bendigo, Vic 3550, Australia.

BENEDICTUS, David Henry; writer and director for stage, television and radio; Commissioning Editor, Drama Series, Channel 4 TV, since 1984; *b* 16 Sept. 1938; *s* of Henry Jules Benedictus and Kathleen Constance (*née* Ricardo); *m* 1971, Yvonne Daphne Antrobus; one *s* one *d. Educ:* Stone House, Broadstairs; Eton College; Balliol College, Oxford (BA English); State Univ. of Iowa. News and current affairs, BBC Radio, 1961; Drama Director, BBC TV, 1962; Story Editor, Wednesday Play and Festival Series, BBC, 1965; Thames TV Trainee Director, at Bristol Old Vic, 1968; Asst Dir, RSC, Aldwych, 1970; Judith E. Wilson Vis. Fellow, Cambridge, and Fellow Commoner, Churchill Coll., Cambridge, 1981–82. Writer in Residence: Sutton Library, Surrey, 1975; Bitterne Library, Southampton, 1983–84; Kibbutz Gezer, Israel, 1978. Antiques corresp., Standard,

1977–80; reviewer for books, stage, films, records, for major newspapers and magazines. Member: BAFTA; Amnesty International; Writers' Guild. *Publications:* The Fourth of June, 1962; You're a Big Boy Now, 1963; This Animal is Mischievous, 1965; Hump, or Bone by Bone Alive, 1967; The Guru and the Golf Club, 1969; A World of Windows, 1971; The Rabbi's Wife, 1976; Junk, how and where to buy beautiful things at next to nothing prices, 1976; A Twentieth Century Man, 1978; The Antique Collector's Guide, 1980; Lloyd George (from Elaine Morgan's screenplay), 1981; Whose Life is it Anyway? (from Brian Clarke's screenplay), 1981; Who Killed the Prince Consort?, 1982; Local Hero (from Bill Forsyth's screenplay), 1983; The Essential London Guide, 1984; Floating Down to Camelot, 1985; The Streets of London, 1986; The Absolutely Essential London Guide, 1986. *Recreations:* chess, tennis, squash, cricket, auctions, table tennis, piano playing, horse racing, eating. *Address:* 19 Oxford Road, Teddington, Middlesex. *T:* 01–977 4715.

BENEDIKTSSON, Einar, MA; Commander, Order of the Falcon, Iceland, 1973; Ambassador of Iceland to the Court of St James's, since 1982; concurrently Ambassador to The Netherlands, Nigeria and Ireland; *b* Reykjavik, 30 April 1931; *s* of Stefan M. Benediktsson and Sigridur Oddsdóttir; *m* 1956, Elsa Petursdóttir; three *s* two *d. Educ:* Colgate Univ., NY; Fletcher Sch. of Law and Diplomacy, Mass; London Sch. of Econs and Pol. Science; Inst. des Etudes Européennes, Turin. With OEEC, 1956–60; Head of Section, Mins of Econ. Affairs and Commerce, 1960–64, and Min. of For. Affairs, 1964; Counsellor, Paris, 1964–68; Head of Section, Min. of For. Affairs, 1968–70; Perm. Rep. to Internat. Orgns, Geneva, 1970–76; Chm., EFTA Council, 1975; Ambassador to France (also accredited to Spain and Portugal, and Perm. Rep. to OECD and UNESCO, 1976–82). Holds foreign decorations. *Address:* Icelandic Embassy, 1 Eaton Terrace, SW1W 8EY. *T:* 01–730 5131; 101 Park Street, W1Y 3FB. *T:* 01–629 8660.

BENGOUGH, Sir Piers (Henry George), KCVO 1986; OBE 1973; Her Majesty's Representative, Ascot, since 1982; *b* 24 May 1929; *s* of Nigel and Alice Bengough; *m* 1952, Bridget Shirley Adams; two *s. Educ:* Eton. Commnd 10th Royal Hussars (PWO), 1948; commanded Royal Hussars (PWO), 1971–73, retired. Formerly amateur rider; wins incl. Grand Military Gold Cup (4 times). Member: Jockey Club, 1965– (Steward, 1974–77); Horserace Betting Levy Board, 1978–81; Director: Cheltenham Steeplechase Co., 1977–; Hereford Racecourse Co., 1974–; Ludlow Race Club, 1979–; Chm., Compensation Fund for Jockeys, 1981–. Hon. Col The Royal Hussars (PWO), 1983–. *Recreations:* shooting, fishing. *Address:* Great House, Canon Pyon, Herefordshire. *Clubs:* Cavalry and Guards, Pratt's.

BENJAMIN, Prof. Bernard; Professor of Actuarial Science, The City University, London, 1973–75; now Visiting Professor; *b* 8 March 1910; *s* of Joseph and Lucy Benjamin, London; *m* 1937, May Pate, Horham, Suffolk; two *d. Educ:* Colfe Grammar Sch.; Sir John Cass Coll. (London University). BSc (Hons); PhD London. LCC, 1928; statistician Public Health Dept, 1940; served War, 1943–46, RAF; statistician, General Register Office, 1952; Chief Statistician, 1954; Dir of Statistics, Ministry of Health, 1963–65; Dir of Research and Intelligence, GLC, 1965–70; Dir of Statistical Studies, CS College, 1970–73; Hon. Cons. in Med. Stats to Army, 1966. Chm., Statistics Users Council (formerly Standing Cttee of Statistics Users), 1971–. Fellow: Inst. of Actuaries (a Vice-Pres. 1963; Pres., 1966–68; Gold Medal, 1975); Royal Statistical Soc. (Pres. 1970–71; Guy Medal in Gold, 1986); Eugenics Soc. (Pres., 1982–; Galton Lectr, 1981). Hon. DSc City Univ., London, 1981. Internat. Insurance Prize of Italy, 1985. *Publications:* Social and Economic Factors in Mortality, 1965; Health and Vital Statistics, 1968; Demographic Analysis, 1969; The Population Census, 1970; (with H. W. Haycocks) The Analysis of Mortality and Other Actuarial Statistics, 1971; Statistics in Urban Administration, 1976; (ed) Medical Records, 1977; General Insurance, 1977; (with J. H. Pollard) The Analysis of Mortality and Other Actuarial Statistics, 1980; numerous medical and population statistical papers and contribs to Jl of Royal Statistical Society and Jl of Inst. of Actuaries. *Recreations:* gardening, painting (both kinds). *Address:* 4 Mount Lodge, 53A Shepherds Hill, Highgate, N6 5QP. *Club:* Athenæum.

BENJAMIN, Brooke; *see* Benjamin, T. B.

BENJAMIN, Louis; Chief Executive, Stoll Moss Theatres Ltd, since 1981 (The London Palladium, Theatre Royal, Drury Lane, Victoria Palace, Apollo, Her Majesty's, Lyric, Globe, and Queen's); *b* 17 Oct. 1922; *s* of Benjamin and Harriet Benjamin; *m* 1954, Vera Doreen Ketteman; two *d. Educ:* Highbury County Sec. Sch. Served Second World War: RAC, India, Burma and Singapore. Joined Moss Empires Ltd, 1937; entered theatrical management as Second Asst Manager, London Palladium, 1945; Asst Man., then Box Office Man., Victoria Palace, 1948; Gen. Man., Winter Gardens, Morecambe, 1953; Pye Records: Sales Controller, 1959; Gen. Man., 1962; Man. Dir, 1963; Chm., Pye Records Gp, 1975–80; a Jt Man. Dir, ATV Corp., 1975; Mem., Exec. Bd, Associated Communications Corp., 1982–; Director: ATV Music Ltd, 1962–; Bermans & Nathans Ltd, 1973–84; Precision Records & Tapes Ltd, 1982–; Precision Video Ltd, 1983–. Entertainment Artistes Benevolent Fund: Vice-Pres., 1971–82; Life Governor, 1982–; Presenter of Royal Variety Perf., annually, 1979–, and of Children's Royal Variety Perf., 1981 and 1982. Companion, Grand Order of Water Rats; Mem., Exec. Cttee, Variety Club of GB. *Address:* Cranbourn Mansions, Cranbourn Street, WC2H 7AG. *T:* 01–437 2274.

BENJAMIN, Pauline, (Mrs Joseph Benjamin); *see* Crabbe, Pauline.

BENJAMIN, Dr Ralph, CB 1980; DSc, PhD, BSc, FCGI, FEng, FIEE, FIERE; Head of Communications Techniques, SHAPE Technical Centre, The Hague, since 1982; *b* 17 Nov. 1922; *s* of Charles Benjamin and Claire Benjamin (*née* Stern); *m* 1951, Kathleen Ruth Bull, BA; two *s. Educ:* in Germany and Switzerland; St Oswald's Coll., Ellesmere; Imperial Coll. of Science and Technology, London. DSc(Eng) London, 1970; FEng 1983; FCGI 1982. Joined Royal Naval Scientific Service, 1944; Senior Scientific Officer, 1949; Principal Scientific Officer, 1952; Senior Principal Scientific Officer (Special Merit), 1955; Deputy Chief Scientific Officer (Special Merit), 1960; Head of Research and Deputy Chief Scientist, Admiralty Surface Weapons Establishment, 1961; Dir and Chief Scientist, Admiralty Underwater Weapons Estab., 1964–71, and Dir, Underwater Weapons R&D (Navy), 1965–71; Chief Scientist, GCHQ, 1971–82. Hon. consultant: Univ. of Illinois; US Office of Naval Research, 1956; IEE Marconi Premium, 1964; IERE Heinrich Hertz Premium, 1980, 1983; Council Mem., Brit. Acoustical Soc., 1971; Vis. Prof., Dept of Electrical and Electronic Engineering, Univ. of Surrey, 1973–80. *Publications:* Modulation, Resolution and Signal Processing for Radar Sonar and Related Systems, 1966; contribs to various advisory cttees, working parties, symposia, etc; articles in Jls of Inst. of Electrical and Electronic Engrs, Instn of Electrical Engineers and Inst. of Electronic and Radio Engineers, etc. *Recreations:* work, mountaineering, ski-ing, swimming, sailing, sub-aqua (qualified naval diving officer), canoeing, judo (black belt). *Address:* c/o SHAPE Technical Centre, PO Box 174, 2501 The Hague, Netherlands. *Club:* Athenæum.

BENJAMIN, Prof. (Thomas) Brooke, MEng, MA, PhD; FRS 1966; Sedleian Professor of Natural Philosophy, and Fellow of The Queen's College, University of Oxford, since 1979; *b* 15 April 1929; *s* of Thomas Joseph Benjamin and Ethel Mary Benjamin (*née* Brooke); *m* 1st, 1956, Helen Gilda-Marie Rakower Ginsburg (marr. diss. 1974); one *s* two *d*; 2nd, 1978, Natalia Marie-Thérèse Court; one *d. Educ:* Wallasey Grammar Sch.; University of Liverpool; Yale Univ. (USA); University of Cambridge. BEng (Liverpool) 1950; MEng. (Yale) 1952; PhD (Cantab) 1955; MA (Oxon) 1979. Fellow of King's Coll., Cambridge, 1955–64; Asst Dir of Research, University of Cambridge, 1958–67; Reader in Hydrodynamics, Univ. of Cambridge, 1967–70; Prof. of Maths, and Dir, Fluid Mechanics Res. Inst., Essex Univ., 1970–78. Visiting Professor: Univ. of Wisconsin, 1980–81; Univ. of Houston, 1985; Univ. of Calif, Berkeley, 1986. Chairman: Mathematics Cttee, SRC, 1975–78; Jt Royal Soc./IMA Mathematical Educn Cttee, 1979–85. Editor, Journal of Fluid Mechanics, 1960–65; Consultant to English Electric Co., 1956–67. William Hopkins Prize, Cambridge Philosophical Soc., 1969. *Publications:* various papers on theoretical and experimental fluid mechanics. *Recreation:* music. *Address:* Mathematical Institute, 24–29 St Giles, Oxford OX1 3LB. *T:* Oxford 54295; 8 Hernes Road, Oxford OX2 7PU. *T:* Oxford 54439.

BENN, Anthony, OBE 1945; *b* 7 Oct. 1912; *s* of late Francis Hamilton Benn and Arta Clara Benn (*née* Boal); *m* 1943, Maureen Lillian Kathleen Benn (*née* Denbigh); two *s* four *d. Educ:* Harrow; Christ Church, Oxford (Scholar). Oxford Univ. Cricket XI, 1935. Price & Pierce Ltd, 1935 (Director, 1947, Chm., 1956–72). Joined Surrey and Sussex Yeomanry, 1936. Served War of 1939–45 (OBE): Staff Coll., 1942; Instructor, Middle East Staff Coll., 1943. Comdr, Order of the Lion of Finland, 1958. *Recreation:* travel.

BENN, Edward, CMG 1981; Minister (Defence Equipment), British Embassy, Washington, 1978–82, retired; *b* 8 May 1922; *s* of John Henry Benn and Alice (*née* Taylor); *m* 1947, Joan Taylor; one *d. Educ:* High Storrs Grammar Sch., Sheffield; Sheffield Univ. (BEng; 1st Cl. Hons Civil Engrg; Mappin Medal, 1943). Operational Research with Army, 1943–48; India and Burma, 1944–46 (Major); entered War Office, 1948; tank research, Supt Special Studies, and later Dep. Dir, Army Op. Res. Estabt, 1961; Asst Sci. Adviser to SACEUR, Paris, 1962–65; Dep. Chief Sci. Adviser, Home Office, 1966–68; Dir, Defence Policy, MoD, 1968–75; Under Sec. and Dep. Chief Scientist (RAF), MoD, 1975–78. *Recreation:* golf. *Address:* 37 Woodham Waye, Woking, Surrey GU21 5SJ. *Clubs:* MCC; West Byfleet Golf.

BENN, Edward Glanvill; Life President, Benn Brothers plc, Publishers, since 1976, Chairman, 1945–75; *b* 1905; 2nd *s* of late Sir Ernest Benn, 2nd Bt, CBE; *m* 1931, Beatrice Catherine, MBE, *d* of Claude Newbald; one *s* one *d. Educ:* Harrow; Clare Coll., Cambridge. Served War of 1939–45, East Surrey Regt, 1940–45; Brigade Major, 138 Infantry Brigade, Italy, 1944 (despatches). Council Member: Nat. Advertising Benevolent Soc., 1937–61 (Trustee, 1951–80, and Pres. 1961–62); Advertising Assoc., 1951–67 (Hon. Treasurer 1960–65); Commonwealth Press Union, 1956– (Hon. Treasurer 1967–77, Hon. Life Mem. 1975; Astor Award, 1982); Vice Pres., Readers' Pension Cttee, 1950–; Life Vice Pres., Newspaper Press Fund, 1965– (Appeals Pres. 1971); Chm., Advertising Advisory Cttee, Independent Television Authority, 1959–64 (Mackintosh medal, 1967); Dir., Exchange Telegraph Co. Ltd, 1960–72 (Chm. 1969–72); Pres., Periodical Publishers Assoc., 1976–78. Master, Stationers' Company, 1977. *Address:* Crescent Cottage, Aldeburgh, Suffolk IP15 5HW.
See also Sir J. J. Benn.

BENN, Sir (James) Jonathan, 4th Bt *cr* 1914; Chairman and Chief Executive, Reed Paper & Board (UK) Ltd, since 1977; Chief Executive, European Paper Group, Reed International PLC, since 1982; *b* 27 July 1933; *s* of Sir John Andrews Benn, 3rd Bt, and of Hon. Ursula Lady Benn, *o d* of 1st Baron Hankey, PC, GCB, GCMG, GCVO, FRS; *S* father, 1984; *m* 1960, Jennifer Mary, *e d* of Dr Wilfred Howells; one *s* one *d. Educ:* Harrow; Clare College, Cambridge (MA). Various positions with Reed International PLC (formerly A. E. Reed & Co.), 1957–; Director, Reed Paper & Board (UK) Ltd, 1971, Managing Dir 1976; Director, Reed Group Ltd, 1976. Pres., British Paper and Board Industries Fedn, 1985. *Recreations:* golf, skiing, music. *Heir: s* Robert Ernest Benn [*b* 17 Oct. 1963; *m* 1985, Sheila Margaret, 2nd *d* of Dr Alastair Blain]. *Address:* Fielden Lodge, Ightham, Kent TN15 9AN.
See also E. G. Benn, T. J. Benn.

BENN, John Meriton, CB 1969; Pro-Chancellor, Queen's University, Belfast, since 1979, Senator, since 1973; *b* 16 July 1908; *s* of late Ernest and Emily Louise Benn, Burnley; *m* 1933, Valentine Rosemary, *d* of late William Seward, Hanwell; two *d. Educ:* Burnley Gram. Sch.; Christ's Coll., Cambridge (Scholar; Modern Languages Tripos, 1st Cl. Hons French, 2nd Cl. Hons German). Asst Master, Exeter Sch., 1931–34; Lektor, Halle Univ., Germany, 1934; Asst Master, Regent Street Polytechnic Secondary Sch., 1935; Inspector of Schs., Ministry of Education for Northern Ireland, 1935–44; Principal, 1944–51; Asst Sec., 1951–59; Senior Asst Sec., 1959–64; Permanent Sec., 1964–69; NI Comr for Complaints, 1969–73; Parly Comr for Administration, NI, 1972–73. Chm., NI Schools Exams Council, 1974–81. Hon. LLD QUB, 1972. *Publication:* Practical French Proses, 1935. *Recreations:* gardening, bell-ringing, amateur dramatics. *Address:* 7 Tudor Oaks, Holywood, Co. Down BT18 0PA. *T:* Holywood 2817.

BENN, Sir Jonathan; *see* Benn, Sir J. J.

BENN, Captain Sir Patrick (Ion Hamilton), 2nd Bt *cr* 1920; Captain, Reserve of Officers, late Duke of Cornwall's Light Infantry; Major, Norfolk Army Cadet Force, 1960; *b* 26 Feb. 1922; *o s* of late Col Ion Bridges Hamilton Benn, JP (*o s* of 1st Bt), Broad Farm, Rollesby, Gt Yarmouth, and late Theresa Dorothy, *d* of late Major F. H. Blacker, Johnstown, Co. Kildare; *S* grandfather, 1961; *m* 1959, Edel Jørgine, *d* of late Col W. S. Løbach, formerly of The Royal Norwegian Army, Andenes, Vesteraalen; one *s* one *d* (both adopted). *Educ:* Rugby. Served War of 1939–45 (despatches); North Africa, Italy, Greece, 1941–45; Capt. 1943; served Korea, 1951–52; retd, 1955. *Recreations:* shooting, fishing. *Address:* Rollesby Hall, Great Yarmouth, Norfolk NR29 5DT. *T:* Great Yarmouth 740313.

BENN, Timothy John; Chairman: Timothy Benn Publishing Ltd, since 1983; Bouverie Publishing Co. Ltd (Publisher, UK Press Gazette), since 1983; South Eastern Magazines Ltd (Publisher, Kent Life, Sussex Life, Surrey Life, Business in Kent), since 1983; Buckley Press Ltd, since 1984 (Publisher, Post Magazine and Insurance Monitor, Re-insurance, Insurance Week, Policy Holder, The Aquarist); Director, Media Catalogues Ltd; *b* 27 Oct. 1936; *yr s* of Sir John Andrews Benn, 3rd Bt, and of Hon. Ursula Helen Alers Hankey. *Educ:* Harrow; Clare Coll., Cambridge (MA); Princeton Univ., USA; Harvard Business Sch., USA (National Marketing Council Course; Scholarship Award). FInstM. Benn Brothers Ltd: Board Member, 1961–82; Managing Director, 1972–82; Dep. Chm., 1976–81; Chm., Benn Brothers plc, 1981–82; Ernest Benn: Board Member, 1967–82; Managing Director, 1973–82; Chairman and Managing Director, 1974–82. *Publication:* The (Almost) Compleat Angler, 1985. *Recreations:* fishing, flytying, writing, toymaking. *Address:* 244 Temple Chambers, Temple Avenue, EC4Y 0DT. *T:* 01–583 6463. *Club:* Flyfishers'.
See also Sir J. J. Benn.

BENN, Rt. Hon. Tony; PC 1964; MP (Lab) Chesterfield, since March 1984; *b* 3 April 1925; *er surv. s* of 1st Viscount Stansgate, DSO, DFC, PC, former Labour MP (*d* 1960);

having unsuccessfully attempted to renounce his right of succession, 1955 and 1960, won a bye-election in May 1961 only to be prevented from taking seat; instigated Act to make disclaimer possible, and disclaimed title for life, 1963; *m* 1949, Caroline Middleton De Camp, MA; three *s* one *d.* Served: RAFVR, 1943–45; RNVR, 1945–46. Joined Labour Party, 1943; Mem., NEC, 1959–60, 1962– (Chm., 1971–72). MP (Lab) Bristol SE, Nov. 1950–1960 and Aug. 1963–1983; Postmaster-Gen., 1964–66, recommended establishment of GPO as public corp. and founded Giro; Minister of Technology, 1966–70, assumed responsibility for Min. of Aviation, 1967 and Min. of Power, 1969; opposition spokesman on Trade and Industry, 1970–74; Sec. of State for Industry and Minister for Posts and Telecommunications, 1974–75; Sec. of State for Energy, 1975–79. Contested (Lab) Bristol East, 1983. *Publications:* The Privy Council as a Second Chamber, 1957; The Regeneration of Britain, 1964; The New Politics, 1970; Speeches, 1974; Arguments for Socialism, 1979; Arguments for Democracy, 1981; (ed) Writings on the Wall: a radical and socialist anthology 1215–1984, 1984; numerous pamphlets. *Address:* House of Commons, SW1A 0AA.

BENNER, Patrick, CB 1975; Deputy Secretary, Department of Health and Social Security, 1976–84; *b* 26 May 1923; *s* of Henry Grey and Gwendolen Benner; *m* 1952, Joan Christabel Draper; two *d. Educ:* Ipswich Sch.; University Coll., Oxford. Entered Min. of Health as Asst Princ., 1949; Princ., 1951; Princ. Private Sec. to Minister, 1955; Asst Sec., 1958; Under-Sec., Min. of Health, 1967–68, DHSS 1968–72; Dep. Sec., Cabinet Office, 1972–76. *Address:* 44 Ormond Crescent, Hampton, Mddx TW12 2TH. *T:* 01–979 1099. *Club:* Royal Commonwealth Society.

BENNET, family name of **Earl of Tankerville.**

BENNETT, Alan; dramatist and actor; *b* 9 May 1934; *s* of Walter Bennett and Lilian Mary Peel; unmarried. *Educ:* Leeds Modern Sch.; Exeter Coll., Oxford. BA Modern History, 1957. Jun. Lectr, Modern History, Magdalen Coll., Oxford, 1960–62. Co-author and actor, Beyond the Fringe, Royal Lyceum, Edinburgh, 1960, Fortune, London, 1961 and Golden, NY, 1962; author and actor: On the Margin (TV series), 1966; Forty Years On, Apollo, 1968; *stage plays:* Getting On, Queen's, 1971; Habeas Corpus, Lyric, 1973; The Old Country, Queen's, 1977; Enjoy, Vaudeville, 1980; *BBC TV films:* A Day Out, 1972; Sunset Across the Bay, 1975; *TV Plays for LWT,* 1978–79: Doris and Doreen; The Old Crowd; Me! I'm Afraid of Virginia Woolf; All Day on the Sands; Afternoon Off; One Fine Day; *BBC TV plays:* A Little Outing, A Visit from Miss Prothero, 1977; Intensive Care, Say Something Happened, Our Winnie, Marks, A Woman of No Importance, Rolling Home; An Englishman Abroad, 1983; The Insurance Man, 1986; *feature film:* A Private Function, 1984. *Publications:* (with Cook, Miller and Moore) Beyond the Fringe, 1962; Forty Years On, 1969; Getting On, 1972; Habeas Corpus, 1973; The Old Country, 1978; Enjoy, 1980; Office Suite, 1981; Objects of Affection, 1982; A Private Function, 1984; The Writer in Disguise, 1985. *Address:* c/o A. D. Peters, 10 Buckingham Street, WC2N 6BU. *T:* 01–839 2556.

BENNETT, (Albert) Edward; Director, Health and Safety Directorate, Commission of the European Communities, since 1981; *b* 11 Sept. 1931; *s* of Albert Edward and Frances Ann Bennett; *m* 1957, Jean Louise Paston-Cooper; two *s. Educ:* University Coll. Sch., Hampstead; London Hosp. Med. Coll. MB BS London; FFCM 1972, FFOM 1984. Surgeon Lieut, RN, 1957–60; Senior Lectr, Dept of Clinical Epidemiology and Social Medicine, St. Thomas's Hosp. Med. Sch., 1964–70; Dir, Health Services Evaluation Gp, Univ. of Oxford, 1970–77; Prof. and Head of Dept of Clinical Epidemiology and Social Medicine, St George's Hosp. Med. Sch., Univ. of London, 1974–81. Hon. Editor, Internat. Jl of Epidemiology, 1977–81. *Publications:* Questionnaires in Medicine, 1975; (ed) Communications between Doctors and Patients, 1976; (ed) Recent Advances in Community Medicine, 1978; numerous sci. reports and contribs on epidemiology of chronic disease and evaluation of health services. *Recreations:* cinema, browsing. *Address:* Résidence Cascade, Rue du Scheid, Rameldange, L6996 Luxembourg. *T:* 34 82 29. *Club:* Athenæum.

BENNETT, Albert Joseph, CBE 1966; Secretary, National Health Service Staff Commission, 1972–75; Vice-Chairman, Paddington and North Kensington Health Authority, 1982–85; *b* 9 April 1913; *er s* of late Albert James Bennett and late Alice Bennett, Stourbridge, Worcs; unmarried. *Educ:* King Edward VI Sch., Stourbridge; St John's Coll., Cambridge (MA) Mathematical Tripos (Wrangler). Admin. Officer, LCC, 1936–39; Central Midwives Board: Asst Sec., 1939–45; Sec., 1945–47; Instructor Lieut, later Lt-Comdr, RN, 1940–45; Sec., NW Met. Regional Hosp. Bd, 1947–65; Principal Officer, NHS Nat. Staff Cttee, 1965–72; Under-Sec., DHSS, 1972–75, seconded as Sec., NHS Staff Commn. Member: Nat. Selection Cttee for Recruitment of Trainee Hospital Admin. Staff, 1955–64; Cttee of Inquiry into the Recruitment, Training and Promotion of Admin. and Clerical Staff in Hospital Service, 1962–63; Adv. Cttee on Hospital Engineers Training, 1967–72; Admin. Training Cttee, Cttee of Vice-Chancellors and Principals, 1970–72; Kensington and Chelsea and Westminster AHA(T), 1977–82, and Family Practitioner Cttee, 1977–85. *Recreations:* walking, gardening. *Address:* 19 Garson House, Gloucester Terrace, W2 3DG. *T:* 01–262 8311.

BENNETT, Alexander; *see* Bennett, F. O. A. G.

BENNETT, Andrew Francis; MP (Lab) Denton and Reddish, since 1983 (Stockport North, Feb. 1974–1983); Teacher; *b* Manchester, 9 March 1939; *m*; two *s* one *d. Educ:* Birmingham Univ. (BSocSc). Joined Labour Party, 1957; Member, Oldham Borough Council, 1964–74. Member, National Union of Teachers. Contested (Lab) Knutsford, 1970; an Opposition spokesperson on educn, 1983–. Interested especially in social services and education. *Recreations:* photography, walking, climbing. *Address:* 28 Brownsville Road, Stockport SK4 4PF; House of Commons, SW1A 0AA.

BENNETT, Charles John Michael, CBE 1974; FCA; Partner in Barton, Mayhew & Co., Chartered Accountants, 1937–71; *b* 29 June 1906; *e s* of late Hon. Sir Charles Alan Bennett and Constance Radeglance, *d* of Major John Nathaniel Still; *m* 1931, Audrey Thompson; two *d. Educ:* Clifton Coll.; Trinity Coll., Cambridge. Served with HM Forces, 1939–45. Member: Electricity Supply Companies Commn, 1959, in Hong Kong; Fiji Sugar Inquiry Commn, 1961; Commn of Inquiry (Sugar Industry) 1962, in Mauritius; Commn of Inquiry into Banana Industry of St Lucia, 1963; Commn of Inquiry (Chm.) into Sugar Industry and Agriculture of Antigua, 1965; Commn of Enquiry into Sugar Industry of Guyana, 1967; Cttee of Enquiry into the pricing of certain contracts for the overhaul of aero-engines by Bristol Siddeley Engines Ltd. Mem. of Council, Institute of Chartered Accountants, 1963–69. Part-time Mem., Commonwealth Development Corp., 1965–73; Dep. Chm. 1970–71, 1972–73; Independent Mem., NEDC for Chemical Industry, and Chm., Pharmaceuticals Working Party, 1969. Mem., E Anglian Regional Cttee of Nat. Trust, 1971–81. *Recreations:* golf, fishing. *Address:* 15 St Olave's Court, St Petersburgh Place, W2 4JY. *T:* 01–229 9554. *Clubs:* Oriental; Royal West Norfolk Golf; Denham Golf.
See also R. H. Cooke.

BENNETT, Sir Charles (Moihi), Kt 1975; DSO 1943; company director; President, New Zealand Labour Party, 1972–76; *b* 27 July 1913; *s* of Rt Rev. Frederick August Bennett, Bishop of Aotearoa, 1928–50, and Rangioue Bennett; *m* 1947, Elizabeth May Stewart. *Educ:* Univ. of New Zealand; Exeter Coll., Oxford. MA, DipSocSci, DipEd. Director of Maori Welfare, 1954–57; High Comr for New Zealand to Fedn of Malaya, 1959–63; Asst Sec., Dept of Maori Affairs, 1963–69. Mem., NZ Prisons Parole Bd, 1974–76. Hon. LLD Canterbury Univ. of NZ, 1973. Hon. Kt PMN (Malaysia), 1963. *Address:* Maketu, Bay of Plenty, New Zealand. *T:* Te Puke (NZ) 32010. *Club:* Officers' (Wellington).

See also Rt Rev. M. A. Bennett.

BENNETT, Edward; *see* Bennett, A. E.

BENNETT, Air Vice-Marshal Erik Peter, CB 1984; Commander, Sultan of Oman's Air Force, since 1974; *b* 3 Sept. 1928; *s* of Robert Francis and Anne Myra Bennett. *Educ:* The King's Hospital, Dublin. Air Adviser to King Hussein, 1961–62; RAF Staff College, 1963; Jt Services Staff Coll., 1968; RAF Coll. of Air Warfare, 1971. Order of Istiqlal (Jordan), 1960; Order of Oman, 1980; Order of Sultan Qaboos (Oman), 1985. *Recreations:* reading, riding, sailing. *Address:* PO Box 1722, Seeb, Sultanate of Oman. *Club:* Royal Air Force.

BENNETT, Rt. Hon. Sir Frederic (Mackarness), Kt 1964; PC 1985; MP (C) Torbay, since 1974 (Reading N, 1951–55; Torquay, Dec. 1955–1974); *b* 2 Dec. 1918; 2nd *s* of late Sir Ernest Bennett and of Lady (Marguerite) Bennett; *m* 1945, Marion Patricia, *e d* of Cecil Burnham, OBE, FRCSE. *Educ:* Westminster. Served War of 1939–45, enlisted Middx Yeo., 1939; commissioned RA, 1940; commended for gallantry, 1941; Military Experimental Officer in Petroleum Warfare Dept, 1943–46, when released with rank of Major. TA&VRA, 1973–83. Called to English Bar, Lincoln's Inn, 1946, Southern Rhodesian Bar, 1947. Observer, Greek Communist War, 1947–49; Diplomatic correspondent, Birmingham Post, 1950–52. Contested (C) Burslem, 1945, Ladywood Div. of Birmingham, 1950. PPS: to Under-Sec. of State, Home Office, 1953–55, to Minister of Supply, 1956–57, to Paymaster-Gen., 1957–59, and to Pres. of Bd of Trade, 1959–61. Chm. Exec. Cttee, CPA Gen. Council, 1971–73; Leader, UK Delegation and Chm., Council of Europe and WEU Assemblies, 1979–; Chm., Europ. Democratic Political Gp Council of Europe and CD, ED & RPR Federated Gp, WEU. Director: Kleinwort Benson Europe SA; BCCI (Hong Kong); Squibb A/S; Commercial Union Assurance Co. Ltd, West End and Exeter Bds; Arawak Trust (Caymans) Ltd; Gibraltar Building Soc.; Gulf Banking and Trust Corp. Ltd (Caymans); Lord of the Manor of Mawddwy. Freeman, City of London, 1984. Hon. Dr of Law Istanbul, 1984. Comdr, Order of Phœnix, Greece, 1963; (Sithari) Star of Pakistan, 1st cl., 1964; Commander, Polonia Restituta, Poland, 1977, Grand Commander's Cross, 1984; Order of Al-Istiqlal, 1st cl., Jordan, 1980; Comdr, Order of Isabel la Católica, Spain, 1982; Order of Hilal-i-Quaid-i-Azam, Pakistan, 1983. *Publications:* Speaking Frankly, 1960; Detente and Security in Europe, 1976; China and European Security, 1978; The Near and Middle East and Western European Security, 1979, 2nd edn 1980; Impact of Individual and Corporate Incentives on Productivity and Standard of Living, 1980; Fear is the Key; Reds under the Bed, or the Enemy at the Gate—and Within, 1979, 3rd edn 1982. *Recreations:* shooting, fishing, yachting. *Address:* Cwmllecoediog, Aberangell, Powys; Kingswear Castle, Kingswear, South Devon; House of Commons SW1A 0AA; 2 Stone Buildings, Lincoln's Inn, WC2. *T:* 01–219 3403. *Club:* Carlton.

BENNETT, (Frederick Onslow) Alexander (Godwyn), TD; Chairman: Whitbread & Co. Ltd, 1972–77; Whitbread Investment Co. Ltd, since 1977; *b* 21 Dec. 1913; *s* of Alfred Bennett, banker and Marjorie Muir Bremner; *m* 1942, Rosemary, *d* of Sir Malcolm Perks, 2nd Bt, and of Neysa Gilbert (*née* Cheney); one *s* four *d*. *Educ:* Winchester Coll.; Trinity Coll., Cambridge (BA). Commnd 2nd Bn London Rifle Bde TA, 1938; Lt-Col 1944, GS01 SHAEF and 21 Army Gp (despatches). Joined Whitbread & Co. Ltd, 1935: Man. Dir, 1949; Dep. Chm., 1958; Chief Exec., 1967–75. Master, Brewers' Company, 1963–64; Chm., Brewers' Soc., 1972–74. US Bronze Star, 1944. *Recreations:* garden and countryside, music. *Address:* Grove House, Selling, Faversham, Kent ME13 9RN. *T:* Selling 250. *Club:* MCC.

BENNETT, Harry Graham, QC 1968; **His Honour Judge Bennett;** a Circuit Judge, since 1972; *b* 19 Sept. 1921; *s* of Ernest and Alice Mary Bennett, Cleckheaton, Yorks. *Educ:* Whitcliffe Mount Grammar Sch., Cleckheaton; King's Coll., London. Royal Artillery, 1943–47. Called to Bar, Gray's Inn, 1948. Recorder: Doncaster, 1966–68; York, 1968–71; Crown Court, 1972; Dep. Chm., ER of Yorks QS, 1964–71. Chm., Agricl Land Tribunal (N Area), 1967–72. *Address:* c/o Leeds Crown Court, Leeds LS2 7DG. *Club:* Leeds (Leeds).

BENNETT, Sir Hubert, Kt 1970; FRIBA; Architect in private practice; Architect to UNESCO Headquarters, Paris, since 1980; former Architect to the Greater London Council (formerly London County Council) and Superintending Architect of Metropolitan Buildings, 1956–71; *b* 4 Sept. 1909; *s* of late Arthur Bennett and Eleanor Bennett; *m* 1938, Louise F. C. Aldred; three *d*. *Educ:* Victoria University, Manchester, School of Architecture. Asst Lecturer, Leeds School of Architecture, 1933–35; Asst Lecturer, Regent Street Polytechnic Sch. of Architecture, 1935–40; Superintending Architect (Lands), War Dept, 1940–43; Borough Architect, Southampton, 1943–45; County Architect, W Riding of Yorks, 1945–56. Exec. Dir, English Property Corp. Ltd, 1971–79. Mem. of Council, RIBA, 1952–55, 1957–62, 1965–66, 1967–69; Hon. Treas., RIBA, 1959–62; Pres., W Yorks Soc. of Architects, 1954–66; Chm., Technical Panel, Standing Conf. on London Regional Planning, 1962–64; Member: Building Res. Bd, 1959–66; Timber Res. and Develt Assoc. Adv. Panel, 1965–68; Housing Study Mission from Britain to Canada, 1968. Dir, Help the Aged Housing Assoc. (UK) Ltd. Prof., Univ of NSW, 1973. Architect for the Hyde Park Corner-Marble Arch Improvement Scheme, Crystal Palace Recreational Centre and South Bank Arts Centre; Consulting Architect, Guest Palace for the Sultan of Oman, Muscat, 1982. RIBA Assessor, South Bank Competition, Vauxhall Cross, 1981; Assessor, City Polytechnic of Hong Kong, 1982–83. RIBA: Silver Medallist for Measured Drawings (Hon. Mention), 1932; Arthur Cates Prize, 1933; Sir John Soane Medallist, 1934; Neale Bursar, 1936; Godwin and Wimperis Bursar, 1948; RIBA London Architecture Bronze Medal, 1959; RIBA Bronze Medal, 1968. Royal Society of Arts Medal, 1934; Rome Scholarship Special Award, 1936; Min. of Housing and Local Govt Housing Medal, 1954, 1963, 1964, 1966, 1968; Civic Trust Awards; Sir Patrick Abercrombie Award (for planning project Thamesmead), Internat. Union of Architects, 1969; Fritz Schumacher Prize, 1970. Hon. Member: Architects in Industry Group; Inst. of Architects of Czechoslovakia; Soc. of Architects of Venezuela. *Address:* Shepherds Close, Munstead Park, Godalming, Surrey GU8 4AR. *T:* Godalming 28828.

BENNETT, Jill; actress; *b* Penang, SS, 24 Dec. 1931; *d* of Randle and Nora Bennett; *m* 1st, 1962, Willis Hall, *qv* (marr. diss., 1965); 2nd, 1968, John Osborne, *qv* (marr. diss. 1977). *Educ:* Tortington Park; Priors Field. Stratford-upon-Avon, 1949–50. First London appearance in Captain Carvallo, St James's Theatre, 1950; Iras in Anthony and Cleopatra, and Caesar and Cleopatra (Olivier Season), St James's, 1951; Helen Elliot in Night of the Ball, New, 1955; Masha in The Seagull, Saville, 1956; Sarah Stanham in The Touch of Fear, Aldwych, 1956; Isabelle in Dinner with the Family, New, 1957; Penelope in Last Day in Dream Land, Lyric, Hammersmith, 1959; Feemy Evans and Lavinia in Shaw double bill, Mermaid, 1961; Estelle in In Camera, Oxford Playhouse, 1962; Ophelia in Castle in Sweden, Piccadilly, 1962; Hilary and Elizabeth in double bill of Squat Betty and The Sponge Room, Royal Court, 1962; The Countess in A Patriot for Me, Royal Court, 1965; Anna Bowers in A Lily of Little India, St Martin's, 1965; Katrina in The Storm, and Imogen Parrott in Trelawney of the Wells, National, 1966; Pamela in Time Present, Royal Court (and later) Duke of York's, 1968 (won Evening Standard Award and Variety Club's Best Actress Award); Anna in Three Months Gone, Royal Court and Duchess, 1970; West of Suez, Royal Court and Cambridge, 1971; Hedda Gabler, Royal Court, 1972; Leslie in The Letter, Palace, Watford, 1973; Amanda in Private Lives, Globe, 1973; The End of Me Old Cigar, Greenwich, 1975; Loot, Royal Court, 1975; Watch It Come Down, National, 1976; Separate Tables, Apollo, 1977; The Aspern Papers, Chichester, 1978; The Eagle has Two Heads, The Man Who Came to Dinner, Chichester, 1979; Hamlet, Royal Court, 1980; The Little Foxes, Nottingham Playhouse, 1981; Dance of Death, Royal Exchange, Manchester, 1983. *Films include:* Lust for Life; The Nanny; The Criminal; The Charge of the Light Brigade; Inadmissible Evidence; Julius Caesar (Calpurnia); I Want What I Want; Quilp; Full Circle; For Your Eyes Only; Britannia Hospital; Country; The Aerodrome; Lady Jane. TV series: Poor Little Rich Girls, 1984; Paradise Postponed, 1986; numerous TV appearances in classical works, etc. *Publication:* (with Suzanne Goodwin) Godfrey, A Special Time Remembered, 1983. *Recreations:* riding, water ski-ing, ski-ing, looking at paintings. *Address:* 15 Golden Square, W1.

BENNETT, Joan; Actress (films and plays); *b* 27 Feb. 1910; *d* of Richard Bennett and Adrienne Morrison; *m* 1st, 1926, John Fox (marr. diss., 1928; he *d* 1963); one *d*; 2nd, 1932, Gene Markey (marr. diss., 1936; he *d* 1980); one *d*; 3rd, 1940, Walter Wanger (marr. diss., at Juarez, Mexico, 1965; he *d* 1968); two *d*; *m* 1978, David Wilde. *Educ:* St Margaret's Sch., Waterbury, Conn.; Mlle Lataple's, Versailles, France. *Films include:* (first film) Bulldog Drummond, 1929; Three Live Ghosts; Disraeli; Little Women; Pursuit of Happiness; Private Worlds; The Man in the Iron Mask; Margin for Error; Woman in the Window; Man Hunt; Scarlet Street; Father of the Bride. *Plays include:* (first play) Jarnegan, 1928; Bell, Book and Candle; We're no Angels; Love Me Little; Butterflies are Free; Never too Late, Prince of Wales Theatre, London, 1963. Has appeared on Television: (series) Too Young to go Steady; Dark Shadows. *Publication:* The Bennett Playbill (with Lois Kibbee), 1970. *Recreation:* interior decorating. *Address:* 67 Chase Road, Scarsdale North, NY 10583, USA.

BENNETT, John, MBE 1945; HM Senior Chief Inspector of Schools for Scotland, 1969–73; *b* 14 Nov. 1912; *m* 1940, Johanne R. McAlpine, MA; two *s* one *d*. *Educ:* Edinburgh Univ. MA (first class hons) 1934. Schoolmaster until 1951. Served War of 1939–45: Capt. REME, 79 Armd Div., 1940–46. HM Inspector of Schools, 1951. *Recreations:* mathematics, golf, bridge. *Address:* 35 Cadzow Drive, Cambuslang, Glasgow G72 8NF. *T:* 041–641 1058.

BENNETT, John Sloman, CMG 1955; *b* 22 Nov. 1914; *y s* of late Ralph Bennett, FRCVS, and Constance Elkington; *m* 1955, Mary Fisher (*see* Mrs. M. L. S. Bennett). *Educ:* Royal Liberty Sch., Romford; Magdalene Coll., Cambridge (Schol.). 1st cl. historical tripos, 1935. Entered Colonial Office, 1936; seconded to Office of Minister of State in Middle East, 1941–45; Asst Sec., Colonial Office, 1946; Imperial Defence College, 1953; served Commonwealth Office, subsequently FCO, after merger of Colonial Office in 1966; retired 1976. *Address:* Rock Cottage, Thursley, Surrey. *Club:* United Oxford & Cambridge University.

BENNETT, Rt. Rev. Manu Augustus, CMG 1981; DD; *b* 10 Feb. 1916; *s* of Rt Rev. F. A. Bennett, Bishop of Aotearoa, 1928–50, and Alice Rangioue Bennett; *m* 1944, Kathleen Clark; one *d*. *Educ:* Victoria Univ. Coll., Univ. of Hawaii. BSc 1954. Deacon, 1939; Priest, 1940; Vicar of Tauranga, Te Puke Maori District, Dio. Waiapu, 1940–44; Chaplain to 2 NZEF, 1944–46; Pastor of Rangitikei South-Manawatu Pastorate, Dio. Wellington, 1946–52; Asst Vicar of Church of Holy Nativity, Honolulu, 1953–54; Pastor of Wellington Pastorate, 1952–57; Vicar of Ohinemutu Pastorate, Waikato, 1964–68; Bishop of Aotearoa, 1968–81. Nat. Council of Churches Chaplain, Dept of Justice. Hon. DD Jackson Coll., 1964. *Address:* PO Box 115, Te Puke, New Zealand.

See also Sir C. M. Bennett.

BENNETT, Mrs Mary Letitia Somerville, MA; Principal, St Hilda's College, Oxford, 1965–80, Hon. Fellow 1980; Pro-Vice-Chancellor, Oxford University, 1979–80; *b* 9 Jan. 1913; *o c* of Rt Hon. H. A. L. Fisher, OM, and Lettice Ilbert; *m* 1955, John Sloman Bennett, *qv*. *Educ:* Oxford High Sch.; Somerville Coll. (Schol.); 2nd Cl. Mods, 1st Cl. Lit. Hum.; Hon. Fellow, 1977. Jt Broadcasting Cttee, 1940–41; Transcription Service of BBC, 1941–45; Colonial Office, 1945–56. Mem., Hebdomodal Council, Oxford Univ., 1973–79. Hon. Sec., Society for the Promotion of Roman Studies, 1960–85. *Address:* Rock Cottage, Thursley, Surrey; 25A Alma Place, Oxford OX4 1JW. *Club:* University Women's.

BENNETT, Patrick, QC 1969; a Recorder of the Crown Court, since 1972; *b* 12 Jan. 1924; *s* of Michael Bennett; *m* 1951, Lyle Reta Pope; two *d*. *Educ:* Bablake Sch., Coventry; Magdalen Coll., Oxford. State Scholar, 1941, MA, BCL 1949. Served RNVR, 1943–46, Sub Lt. Called to Bar, Gray's Inn, 1949, Bencher 1976, Master of Students, 1980; Asst Recorder, Coventry, 1969–71; Dep. Chm., Lindsey QS, 1970–71. Mem., Mental Health Act Commn, 1984–86. Fellow: Internat. Soc. of Barristers; Nat. Inst. of Advocacy. *Publication:* Assessment of Damages in Personal Injury and Fatal Accidents, 1980. *Recreations:* food, flying. *Address:* (home) 22 Wynnstay Gardens, W8. *T:* 01–937 2110; 233 rue Nationale, Boulogne sur Mer, France. *T:* 21 91 33 39; (professional) 2 Crown Office Row, Temple, EC4. *T:* 01–236 9337. *Clubs:* Hurlingham; Spartan Flying (Denham).

BENNETT, Peter Ward, OBE; Chairman, W. H. Smith & Son Holdings Ltd, 1977–82. Dir, Watt Gp of Canada. Member: Prince of Wales' Adv. Gp on Disability; Council, Riding for the Disabled Assoc. *Address:* Dene House, Littledene, Glynde, Lewes, Sussex BN8 6LB.

BENNETT, Philip Hugh Penberthy, CBE 1972; FRIBA; FCIArb; Consultant, T. P. Bennett & Son, architects, since 1980 (Partner, 1948–80, Senior Partner, 1967–80); *b* 14 April 1919; *o s* of late Sir Thomas Penberthy Bennett, KBE, FRIBA, and late Mary Langdon Edis; *m* 1943, Jeanne Heal; one *s* one *d*. *Educ:* Highgate Sch.; Emmanuel Coll., Cambridge (MA). Lieut (G) RNVR, 1940–46. Principal works: town centres at Bootle and Stratford (London); head offices for Norwich Union Insce Socs, Ford Motor Co. and other commercial cos; dept stores for United Africa Co. in Ghana and Nigeria, Bentalls (Kingston) and Fenwicks (Newcastle); extensions to Middlesex Hosp.; hostel for Internat. Students Trust; Cunard Internat. Hotel; flats for local authorities and private developers; buildings for airfield and dock develt. Chm., Building Regulations Adv. Cttee (DoE), 1965–77; former RIBA rep. on Jt Contracts Tribunal (Chm. 1973–78) and Nat. Jt

Consultative Cttee (Chm. 1970); Mem. other cttees of RIBA and NEDO; Governor: Sch. of Building, 1952–72; Vauxhall Coll. of Further Educn, 1972–77; Member: Home Office Deptl Cttee enquiring into Fire Service, 1967–70; Adv. Council for Energy Conservation, 1974–76. *Publications:* Architectural Practice and Procedure, 1981; chapter on building, in Britain 1984, 1963; articles in Building, Financial Times, etc. *Recreations:* travel, drawing, theatre. *Address:* Grey Walls, Park Lane, Aldeburgh, Suffolk. *T:* Aldeburgh 2766.

BENNETT, Gen. Sir Phillip (Harvey), AC 1985 (AO 1981); KBE 1983; DSO 1969; Chief of the Defence Force, Australia, since 1984; *b* 27 Dec. 1928; *m* 1955, Margaret Heywood; two *s* one *d. Educ:* Perth Modern Sch.; Royal Mil. Coll.; jssc, rcds, psc (Aust.). Served, 1950–56: 3rd Bn RAR, Korea (despatches), Sch. of Infantry (Instr), 25 Cdn Bde, Korea, Pacific Is Regt, PNG, and 16th Bn Cameron Highlanders of WA; Commando training, Royal Marines, England, Malta and Cyprus, 1957–58; OC 2 Commando Co., Melb., 1958–61; Aust. Staff Coll., 1961–62; Sen. Instr, then Chief Instr, Officer Cadet Sch., Portsea, 1962–65; AAG Directorate of Personal Services, AHQ, 1965–67; Co 1 RAR, 1967–69 (served Vietnam; DSO); Exchange Instr, Jt Services Staff Coll., England, 1969–71; COL Directorate of Co-ordination and Organization, AHQ, 1971–74; COS HQ Fd Force Comd, 1974–76; RCDS, England, 1976; Comdr 1st Div., 1977–79; Asst Chief of Def. Force Staff, 1979–82; Chief of General Staff, 1982–84. *Recreations:* sailing, golf. *Address:* Department of Defence, Russell Offices, Canberra, ACT 2600, Australia. *T:* 652858. *Clubs:* United Services (Brisbane); University House, Commonwealth (Canberra).

BENNETT, Ralph Featherstone; *b* 3 Dec. 1923; *o s* of late Mr and Mrs Ralph J. P. Bennett, Plymouth, Devon; *m* 1948, Delia Marie, *o d* of late Mr and Mrs J. E. Baxter, Franklyns, Plymouth; two *s* two *d. Educ:* Plympton Grammar Sch.; Plymouth Technical Coll. Articled pupil to City of Plymouth Transport Manager, 1940–43; Techn. Asst, Plymouth City Transp., 1943–54; Michelin Tyre Co., 1954–55; Dep. Gen. Man., City of Plymouth Transp. Dept, 1955–58; Gen. Manager: Gt Yarmouth Transp. Dept, 1958–60; Bolton Transp. Dept, 1960–65; Manchester City Transp., 1965–68; London Transport Executive (formerly London Transport Board): Mem., 1968–71; Dep. Chm., 1971–78; Chief Exec., 1975–78; Chairman: London Transport Executive, 1978–80; London Transport International, 1976–80. Pres., Confedn of Road Passenger Transport, 1977–78; Vice-President: Internat. Union of Public Transport, 1978–81; CIT, 1979–82. CEng; FIMechE; FCIT; FRSA. *Address:* Buffers, Green Lane, Yelverton, South Devon. *T:* Yelverton 2153. *Club:* National Liberal.

BENNETT, Sir Reginald (Frederick Brittain), Kt 1979; VRD 1944; MA Oxon; BM, BCh., 1942; LMSSA 1937; DPM 1948; Grand Officer, Italian Order of Merit, 1977; company director and wine consultant; formerly psychiatrist; *b* 22 July 1911; *e s* of late Samuel Robert Bennett and Gertrude (*née* Brittain); *m* 1947, Henrietta, *d* of Capt. H. B. Crane, CBE, RN; one *s* three *d. Educ:* Winchester Coll.; New College, Oxford. Oxford Univ. Air Squadron, 1931–34; RNVR, 1934–46; Fleet Air Arm, Medical Officer and Pilot; torpedoed twice. St George's Hosp., SW1, 1934–37; Maudsley Hosp., SE5, 1947–49. MP(C) Gosport and Fareham, 1950–74, Fareham, 1974–79; PPS to Rt Hon. Iain Macleod, MP, 1956–63; Chairman: House of Commons Catering Sub-Cttee, 1970–74, 1976–79; Anglo-Italian Parly Gp, 1971–79 (Hon. Sec. 1961–71); Parly and Scientific Cttee, 1959–62. Vice-Pres., Franco-British Parly Relations Cttee, 1973–79; Mem. Council, Internat. Inst. of Human Nutrition, 1975–. Helmsman: Shamrock V, 1934–35; Evaine, 1936–38; Olympic Games (reserve), 1936; in British-American Cup Team, 1949 and 1953 in USA; various trophies since. Chairman: Amateur Yacht Research Soc., 1972–; World Sailing Speed Record Cttee, RYA, 1980–. Hon. Lieut-Col, Georgia Militia, 1960; Hon. Citizen: of Atlanta, Ga, 1960; Port-St Louis-du-Rhône, France, 1986. Commandeur du Bontemps-Médoc, 1959; Chevalier du Tastevin, 1970; Galant de la Verte Marennes; Chevalier de St Etienne, Alsace, 1971; Chevalier Bretvin (Muscadet), 1973; Legato del Chianti, 1983. *Publications:* articles on wine, medicine, psychiatry, politics and yacht racing. *Recreations:* sailing, painting, foreign travel, basking in the sun, avoiding exercise. *Address:* 30 Strand-on-the-Green, W4. *Clubs:* White's; Imperial Poona Yacht (Cdre); Wykehamist Sailing (Cdre); Seaview Buffs, etc.

BENNETT, Richard Rodney, CBE 1977; composer; Member of General Council, Performing Right Society, since 1975; *b* 29 March 1936; *s* of H. Rodney and Joan Esther Bennett. *Educ:* Leighton Park Sch., Reading; Royal Academy of Music. Works performed, 1953–, at many Festivals in Europe, S Africa, USA, Canada, Australia, etc. Has written music for numerous films including: Indiscreet; The Devil's Disciple; Only Two Can Play; The Wrong Arm of the Law; Heavens Above; Billy Liar; One Way Pendulum; The Nanny; Far from the Madding Crowd; Billion Dollar Brain; Secret Ceremony; The Buttercup Chain; Figures in a Landscape; Nicholas and Alexandra; Lady Caroline Lamb; Voices; Murder on the Orient Express (SFTA award, 1975; Academy Award Nomination, 1975; Ivor Novello award, PRS, 1976); Permission to Kill; Equus (BAFTA Nomination, 1978); Sherlock Holmes in New York; L'Imprecateur; The Brinks Job; Yanks (BAFTA Nomination, 1980); Return of the Soldier; also the music for Television series, Hereward the Wake; The Christians. Commissioned to write 2 full-length operas for Sadler's Wells: The Mines of Sulphur, 1965, A Penny for a Song, 1968; commnd to write opera for Covent Garden: Victory, 1970; (children's opera) All the King's Men, 1969; Guitar Concerto, 1970; Spells (choral work), 1975. *Publications include:* chamber music, orchestral music, educational music, song cycles, etc; articles for periodicals, about music. *Recreations:* cinema, modern jazz. *Address:* c/o Mrs Keys, London Management, Regent House, 235 Regent Street, W1.

BENNETT, Rev. Robin; Vice-Principal, Clapham Battersea Adult Education Institute, since 1986; *b* 6 Nov. 1934; *s* of Arthur James Bennett, Major RA, and Alice Edith Bennett, Kesgrave, Ipswich; *m* 1962, Patricia Ann Lloyd, Hall Green, Birmingham; one *s* one *d. Educ:* Northgate Grammar School, Ipswich; St. John's Coll., Univ. of Durham (BA); Queen's Coll., and Univ. of Birmingham (Dip Th). Assistant Curate: Prittlewell, 1960–63; St Andrew with St Martin, Plaistow, 1963–65; Vicar, St Cedd, Canning Town, 1965–72; Rector of Loughton, 1972–75; Director, Oxford Inst. for Church and Society, 1975–77; Principal, Aston Training Scheme, 1977–82; Adult Education Officer, Gen. Synod Bd of Education, 1982–85; Archdeacon of Dudley and Dir of Lay Ministerial Develt and Training. Diocese of Worcester, 1985–86. *Recreations:* golf, travel, opera, caravanning, BMX clubs, steam, West Ham United. *Address:* 6 Edgeley Road, SW4. *T:* 01–622 2965.

BENNETT, Ronald Alistair, CBE 1986; QC (Scotland) 1959; Vice-President for Scotland, Value Added Tax Tribunals, since 1977; *b* 11 Dec. 1922; *s* of Arthur George Bennett, MC and Edythe Sutherland; *m* 1950, Margret Magnusson, *d* of Sigursteinn Magnusson, Icelandic Consul-Gen. for Scotland; three *s* three *d. Educ:* Edinburgh Academy; Edinburgh Univ.; Balliol Coll., Oxford. MA, LLB Univ. of Edinburgh, 1942; Muirhead and Dalgety Prizes for Civil Law, 1942. Lieut, 79th (Scottish Horse) Medium Regt RA, 1943–45; Capt. attached RAOC, India and Japan, 1945–46. Called to Scottish Bar, 1947; Vans Dunlop Schol. in Scots Law and Conveyancing, 1948; Standing Counsel to Min. of Labour and National Service, 1957–59; Sheriff-Principal: of Roxburgh, Berwick and Selkirk, 1971–74; of S Strathclyde, Dumfries and Galloway, 1981–82; of N

Strathclyde, 1982–83. Lectr in Mercantile Law: Edinburgh Univ., 1956–68; Heriot-Watt Univ., 1968–75. Chairman: Med. Appeal Tribunals (Scotland), 1971–; Agricultural Wages Bd for Scotland, 1973–; Local Govt Boundaries Commn for Scotland, 1974–; Northern Lighthouse Bd, April-Sept. 1974; Industrial Tribunals, (Scotland), 1977–; War Pension Tribunals, 1984–. Arbiter, Motor Insurers' Bureau appeals, 1975–; Mem., Scottish Medical Practices Cttee, 1976–. *Publications:* Bennett's Company Law, 2nd edn, 1950; Fraser's Rent Acts in Scotland, 2nd edn 1952; Editor: Scottish Current Law and Scots Law Times Sheriff Court Reports, 1948–74; Court of Session Reports, 1976–. *Recreations:* swimming, reading, music, gardening. *Address:* Laxamyri, 46 Cammo Road, Barnton, Edinburgh EH4 8AP. *T:* 031–339 6111. *Club:* New (Edinburgh).

BENNETT, Sir Ronald (Wilfred Murdoch), 3rd Bt, *cr* 1929; *b* 25 March 1930; *o s* of Sir Wilfred Bennett, 2nd Bt, and Marion Agnes, OBE (*d* 1985), *d* of late James Somervell, Sorn Castle, Ayrshire, and step *d* of late Edwin Sandys Dawes; *S* father 1952; *m* 1st, 1953, Rose-Marie Audrey Patricia, *o d* of Major A. L. J. H. Aubépin, France and Co. Mayo, Ireland; two *d*; 2nd, 1968, Anne, *d* of late Leslie George Tooker; *m* 3rd. *Educ:* Wellington Coll.; Trinity Coll., Oxford. *Heir:* cousin Mark Edward Francis Bennett, *b* 5 April 1960. *Clubs:* Kampala, Uganda (Kampala).

BENNETT, Roy Grissell, CMG 1971; Chairman, Maclaine Watson & Co. Ltd, London and Singapore, 1970–72 (Director, 1958–72), retired; Chairman: Pilkington (South East Asia) Private Ltd, since 1972; Beder International and Beder Malaysia, since 1972; *b* 21 Nov. 1917. *Educ:* RMC Sandhurst. Served War of 1939–45, 17th/21st Lancers (Major). Joined J. H. Vavasseur & Co. Ltd, Penang, 1946; Director, 1949; joined Maclaine, Watson & Co. Ltd, Singapore 1952, Dir London Board 1958, Man. Dir, Eastern interests, 1960; Chm. and Man. Dir, London and Singapore, 1970–72; Director, Fibreglass Pilkington Ltd (Chm.), and other cos; retired from Singapore Internat. Chamber of Commerce (Chm. 1967–70); Singapore Chamber of Commerce Rubber Assoc. (Chm. 1960–72); Rubber Assoc. of Singapore (past Chm., Dep. Chm. 1966–72); Chm. Council, Singapore Anti-Tuberculosis Assoc., 1962–; Founder and Governor, United World Coll., SE Asia, 1972– (Chm. Governors, 1972–79); Chm., Racehorse Spelling Station, Cameron Highlands, Malaysia, 1976–; Founder Chm., Riding for Disabled Assoc. of Singapore, 1982–85 (Mem. Cttee, 1982–); Patron, Nat. Kidney Foundn. MInstD. *Recreations:* economics, commercial, polo, racing, shooting, swimming, photography, motoring, safaris, camping, gardening, zoology, boating, reading, travelling, people especially of the East, social welfare. *Address:* Beder International, PO Box 49, Bukit Panjang, Singapore 9168; 22 Jalan Perdana, Johore Bharu 80300, Malaysia. *T:* Johore Bharu (07) 224505; (UK) Dorking 889414. *Clubs:* Cavalry and Guards; Tanglin, British, Turf (Dep. Chm.), Polo (Patron; Past Chm.) (Singapore), Turf, Polo (Penang).

BENNETT, William John, OBE 1946; LLD; retired 1977; Consultant, Iron Ore Company of Canada, Montreal; Chairman, C. D. Howe Institute; Director: Canadian Reynolds Metals Co. Ltd; Eldorado Nuclear Ltd; Peterson, Howell & Heather Canada Inc.; *b* 3 Nov. 1911; *s* of Carl Edward Bennett and Mary Agnes Downey; *m* 1936, Elizabeth Josephine Palleck; three *s* four *d. Educ:* University of Toronto (BA Hons). Private Sec., Minister of Transport, 1935–39; Chief Exec. Asst to Minister of Munitions and Supply, 1939–46; President: Atomic Energy of Canada Ltd, 1953–58; Canadian British Aluminium Co. Ltd, 1958–60. Eldorado Mining & Refining Ltd, 1946–58. Hon. LLD, Toronto Univ., 1955; Hon. Dr of Science, St Francis Xavier Univ., Antigonish, NS, 1956; Hon Dr of Laws, University of Ottawa, 1957. *Recreations:* ski-ing, music. *Address:* 1321 Sherbrooke Street West, Apt F41, Montreal, Quebec H3G 1J4, Canada. *Club:* Mount Royal (Montreal).

BENNETT, Hon. William Richards, PC (Can.); Premier of British Columbia, 1975–86; *b* 1932; *y s* of late Hon. William Andrew Cecil Bennett, PC (Can.) and of Annie Elizabeth May Richards; *m* Audrey; four *s.* Began a business career. Elected MP for Okanagan South (succeeding to a constituency which had been held by his father), 1973; Leader of Social Credit Group in Provincial House, 1973; formed Social Credit Govt after election of Dec. 1975. *Address:* c/o Provincial House of Legislature, Victoria, BC V8V 4R3, Canada.

BENNEY, (Adrian) Gerald (Sallis), RDI 1971; goldsmith and silversmith; Professor of Silversmithing and Jewellery, Royal College of Art, 1974–83; *b* 21 April 1930; *s* of late Ernest Alfred Benney and Aileen Mary Benney, *m* 1957, Janet Edwards; three *s* one *d. Educ:* Brighton Grammar Sch.; Brighton Coll. of Art (Nat. Dip. in Art); RCA (DesRCA). FSIAD 1975. Estabd 1st workshop, Whitfield Place, London, 1955; Consultant Designer, Viners Ltd, 1957–69; began designing and making Reading civic plate, 1963; discovered technique of texturing on silver, 1964; moved workshop to Bankside, London, 1969; began prodn of Beenham Enamels, 1970. Holds Royal Warrants of Appt to the Queen, the Duke of Edinburgh, Queen Elizabeth the Queen Mother and the Prince of Wales. Member: Govt's Craft Adv. Cttee, 1972–77; UK Atomic Energy Ceramics Centre Adv. Cttee, 1979–83; British Hallmarking Council, 1983–. Metalwork Design Advisor to Indian Govt (UP State), 1977–78; Chm., Govt of India Hallmarking Survey, 1981; Export Advisor and Designer to Royal Selangor Pewter Co., Kuala Lumpur, 1986–. Liveryman, Worshipful Co. of Goldsmiths, 1964; Major Exhibn, Worshipful Co. of Goldsmiths, 1973. Hon. MA Leicester, 1963. Freeman, Borough of Reading, 1984. *Recreations:* walking, oil painting, landscape gardening. *Address:* Beenham House, Beenham, Berks RG7 5LJ. *T:* Reading 744370. *Club:* Arts.

BENNION, Francis Alan Roscoe; barrister, writer and lecturer; *b* 2 Jan. 1923; *o s* of Thomas Roscoe Bennion, Liverpool; *m* 1st, 1951, Barbara Elisabeth Braendle (separated 1971, marr. diss. 1975); three *d*; 2nd, 1977, Mary Field. *Educ:* John Lyon's, Harrow; Balliol Coll., Oxford. Pilot, RAFVR, 1941–46. Gibbs Law Scholar, Oxford, 1948. Called to Bar, Middle Temple, 1951 (Harmsworth Scholar). Lectr and Tutor in Law, St Edmund Hall, Oxford, 1951–53; Office of Parly Counsel, 1953–65, and 1973–75; Dep. Parly Counsel, 1964; Parly Counsel, 1973–75; seconded to Govt of Pakistan to advise on drafting of new Constitution, 1956; seconded to Govt of Ghana to advise on legislation and drafting Constitution converting the country into a Republic, 1959–61. Sec., RICS, 1965–68; Governor, College of Estate Management, 1965–68. Co-founder and first Chm., Professional Assoc. of Teachers, 1968–72; Founder: Statute Law Soc., 1968 (Chm., 1978–79); Freedom Under Law, 1971; Dicey Trust, 1973; Towards One World, 1979; founder and first Chm., World of Property Housing Trust (later Sanctuary Housing Assoc.), 1968–72; Co-founder, Areopagitica Educnl Trust, 1979. *Publications:* Constitutional Law of Ghana, 1962; Professional Ethics: The Consultant Professions and their Code, 1969; Tangling with the Law, 1970; Consumer Credit Control, 1976–; Consumer Credit Act Manual, 1978, 3rd edn 1986; Statute Law, 1980, 2nd edn 1983; Statutory Interpretation, 1984; articles and contribs to books on legal and other subjects. *Recreation:* creation. *Address:* 4–5 Gray's Inn Square, WC1R 5AY. *T:* 01–404 5252. *Club:* MCC.

BENNISON, Dr (Robert) John, FRCGP; medical practitioner; Principal in General Practice, Hatfield Broad Oak, Essex, since 1959; *b* 4 Feb. 1928; *s* of John Jennings Bennison and Agnes Bennison; *m* 1952, Kathleen Mary Underwood, MB, BChir, MA; two *s* three *d. Educ:* Sedbergh Sch.; Corpus Christi Coll., Cambridge (MB, BChir 1951; MA 1953); London Hosp. Med. Coll. DObstRCOG 1957; FRCGP 1972 (MRCGP 1961). Served Med. Br., RAF, 1952–54. General medical practice, 1957–. Associate Adviser in Gen. Practice, NE Thames Region, 1975–79; Mem., English National Bd for Nursing, Midwifery and Health Visiting, 1983–. Royal Coll. of General Practitioners: Mem. Council, 1975–84 (Vice-Chm., 1982–83); Chm., Educn Cttee, 1978–81. Med. Editor, Well Being, Channel 4, 1982–85. *Publications:* chapters in med. textbooks; papers in med. jls. *Recreations:* music, drama, wine, France, making things. *Address:* Eden End, Hatfield Broad Oak, near Bishop's Stortford, Herts CM22 7HD. *T:* Hatfield Broad Oak 245.

BENNITT, Mortimer Wilmot; Secretary, Islington Society, since 1984; *b* 28 Aug. 1910; *s* of Rev. F. W. and Honoria Bennitt. *Educ:* Charterhouse; Trinity Coll., Oxford. Entered Office of Works, 1934; Private Sec. to Sir Philip Sassoon, 1937–38. Served War of 1939–45: RAF, 1943–45. Under Sec., 1951; Dep. Dir, Land Commn, 1967–71; retired 1971. Chairman: Little Theatre Guild of Gt Britain, 1959–60; Tavistock Repertory Company, London, 1975–77. Patron of St Mary's, Bletchley. *Publication:* Guide to Canonbury Tower, 1980. *Recreation:* travel. *Address:* 3/5 Highbury Grove, N5. *T:* 01–226 5937. *Clubs:* United Oxford & Cambridge University, Tower Theatre.

BENSON, family name of **Baron Benson.**

BENSON, Baron *cr* 1981 (Life Peer), of Drovers in the County of W Sussex; **Henry Alexander Benson,** GBE 1971 (CBE 1946); Kt 1964; FCA; Partner, Coopers and Lybrand (formerly Cooper Brothers & Co.), Chartered Accountants, 1934–75; Adviser to the Governor of the Bank of England, 1975–83; *b* 2 Aug. 1909; *s* of Alexander Stanley Benson and Florence Mary (*née* Cooper); *m* 1939, Anne Virginia Macleod; two *s* one *d. Educ:* Johannesburg, South Africa. ACA (Hons) 1932; FCA 1939. Commissioned Grenadier Guards, 1940–45; seconded from Army to Min. of Supply to advise on reorganisation of accounts of Royal Ordnance Factories, 1943–44, and in Dec. 1943 apptd Dir Ordnance Factories, to carry out reorganisation; apptd Controller of Building Materials, Min. of Works, 1945; Special appt to advise Minister of Health on housing production, 1945, and subseq. other appts, also Mem. Cttee (Wilson Cttee) to review work done on, and to make recommendations for further research into, processes for transformation of coal into oil, chemicals and gas, 1959–60. Mem., Crawley Development Corp., 1947–50; Mem., Royal Ordnance Factories Board, 1952–56; Dep. Chm. Advisory Cttee (Fleck Cttee) to consider organisation of National Coal Board, 1953–55. Dir Hudson's Bay Co., 1953–62 (Dep. Governor 1955–62); Director: Finance Corporation for Industry Ltd, 1953–79; Industrial and Commercial Finance Corp., 1974–79; Hawker Siddeley Gp, 1975–81; Council, Institute of Chartered Accountants, 1956–75 (Pres., 1966); Mem. Advisory Cttee on Legal Aid, 1956–60; Mem. Tribunal under Prevention of Fraud (Investments) Act 1939, 1957–75; Mem. Special Advisory Cttee to examine structure, finance and working of organisations controlled by British Transport Commission, 1960; apptd by Minister of Commerce, N Ireland, to investigate position of railways; to make recommendations about their future, and to report on effect which recommendations will have on transport system of Ulster Transport Authority, 1961; apptd Chm. of a Cttee to examine possible economies in the shipping and ancillary services engaged in meat, dairy products and fruit trades of New Zealand, 1962; Mem. Cttee apptd by Chancellor of the Exchequer to investigate practical effects of introduction of a turnover tax, 1963. Chm., Royal Commn on Legal Services, 1976–79. Joint Comr to advise on integration of Nat. Assoc. of Brit. Manufrs, FBI, Brit. Employers' Confed., and on formation of a Nat. Industrial Organisation (CBI), 1963; Joint Inspector, Bd of Trade, to investigate affairs of Rolls Razor Ltd, 1964; Indep. Chm. of British Iron & Steel Fedn Development Co-ordinating Cttee, 1966; Indep. Chm., Internat. Accounting Standards Cttee (IASC), 1973–76; Dir, Finance for Industry Ltd, 1974–79; Member: Permanent Jt Hops Cttee, 1967–74; Dockyard Policy Bd, 1970–75; NCB team of inquiry into Bd's purchasing procedures, 1973; CBI Company Affairs Cttee, 1972; City Liaison Cttee, 1974–75; Chm., Exec. Cttee of Accountants' Jt Disciplinary Scheme to review cases involving public concern, 1979–; Vice-Pres., Union Européene des Experts Comptables économiques et financiers (UEC), 1969; Member: Cttee to enquire into admin and organisation of MoD; Cttee on Fraud Trials (Roskill Cttee), 1984–85. Apptd by Nat. Trust as Chm. of adv. cttee to review management, organisation and responsibilities of Nat. Trust, 1967; apptd by Jt Turf Authorities as Chm. of The Racing Industry Cttee of Inquiry to make detailed study of financial structure and requirements of racing industry, 1967. Treasurer, Open Univ., 1975–79. Trustee, Times Trust, 1967–81. Hon. Bencher, Inner Temple, 1983; Freeman, City of London, 1986. Distinguished Service Award, Univ. of Hartford, 1977; Mem., Accounting Hall of Fame, Ohio State Univ., 1984; Founding Societies' Centenary Award, ICA, 1984. *Recreations:* shooting, golf, sailing. *Address:* 9 Durward House, 31 Kensington Court, W8 5BH. *T:* 01–937 4850. *Clubs:* Brooks's, Jockey; Royal Yacht Squadron.

BENSON, Sir Arthur (Edward Trevor), GCMG 1959 (KCMG 1954; CMG 1952); *b* 21 Dec. 1907; *s* of late Rev. Arthur H. Trevor Benson, Vicar of Ilam, Staffs, formerly of Castle Connell, Co. Limerick and of St Saviour's, Johannesburg, and Emily Maud Malcolmson, Woodlock, Portlaw, Co. Waterford, late of Hanson Mount, Ashbourne, Derbyshire; *m* 1933, Daphne Mary Joyce, *d* of late E. H. M. Fynn, Serui, near Hartley, S Rhodesia; two *d. Educ:* Wolverhampton Sch.; Exeter Coll., Oxford. Colonial Administrative Service; Cadet, N Rhodesia, 1932; seconded to Colonial Office, 1939; to Prime Minister's Office, 1940–42; to Cabinet Office, 1942–43; to Colonial Office, 1943–44; Northern Rhodesia, 1944–46; Administrative Sec., Uganda, 1946–49; Chief Sec., Central African Council, 1949–51; Chief Sec. to Govt of Nigeria, 1951–54; Governor of Northern Rhodesia, 1954–59. Hon. Fellow, Exeter Coll., Oxford, 1963. JP Devon, 1962–66. KStJ 1954. *Recreation:* fishing. *Address:* Otter Hill, Tipton St John, Sidmouth EX10 0AJ.

BENSON, Christopher John, FRICS; Vice-Chairman since 1977, Managing Director since 1976, MEPC plc; Chairman, London Docklands Development Corporation, since 1984; *b* 20 July 1933; *s* of Charles Woodburn Benson and Catherine Clara (*née* Bishton); *m* 1960, Margaret Josephine, OBE, JP, *d* of Ernest Jefferies Bundy; two *s. Educ:* Worcester Cathedral King's Sch.; Thames Nautical Trng Coll., HMS Worcester. FRICS. Director: MEPC plc, 1974–; House of Fraser plc, 1982–. Underwriting Mem. of Lloyd's, 1979–; Member: Investment Cttee, British Petroleum Pension Trust, 1979–84. Pres., British Property Fedn, 1981–83; Mem., Property Adv. Gp, 1982–. Dir, Royal Opera House, 1984–. Chairman: Westminster Christmas Appeal; Civic Trust, 1985– (Trustee, 1983–). Mem. Council, Marlborough Coll., 1982–. Hon. Bencher, Middle Temple, 1984. Freeman: City of London, 1975; Co. of Watermen and Lightermen, 1985; Liveryman: Worshipful Co. of Gold and Silver Wyre Drawers, 1975; Guild of Air Pilots and Air Navigators, 1981. *Recreations:* farming, aviation. *Address:* Pauls Dene House, Castle Road, Salisbury, Wilts SP1 3RY. *T:* Salisbury 22187. *Clubs:* Naval, Royal Automobile, City Livery, MCC.

BENSON, Prof. Frank Atkinson, BEng, MEng (Liverpool); PhD, DEng (Sheffield); FIEE, FIEEE; DL; Professor and Head of Department of Electronic and Electrical Engineering, University of Sheffield, since 1967; Pro-Vice Chancellor, 1972–76; *b* 21 Nov. 1921; *s* of late John and Selina Benson; *m* 1950, Kathleen May Paskell; two *s. Educ:* Ulverston Grammar Sch.; Univ. of Liverpool. Mem. research staff, Admty Signal Estab., Witley, 1943–46; Asst Lectr in Electrical Engrg, University of Liverpool, 1946–49; Lectr 1949–59, Sen. Lectr 1959–61, in Electrical Engrg, University of Sheffield; Reader in Electronics, University of Sheffield, 1961–67. DL South Yorks, 1979. *Publications:* Voltage Stabilizers, 1950; Electrical Engineering Problems with Solutions, 1954; Voltage Stabilized Supplies, 1957; Problems in Electronics with Solutions, 1958; Electric Circuit Theory, 1959; Voltage Stabilization, 1965; Electric Circuit Problems with Solutions, 1967; Millimetre and Submillimetre Waves, 1969; many papers on microwaves, gas discharges and voltage stabilization in learned jls. *Address:* 64 Grove Road, Sheffield S7 2GZ. *T:* Sheffield 363493.

BENSON, (Harry) Peter (Neville), CBE 1982; MC 1945; FCA; Chairman, Davy Corporation PLC, 1982–85; *b* 10 Feb. 1917; *s* of Harry Leedham Benson and Iolanthe Benson; *m* 1948, Margaret Young Brackenridge; two *s* one *d. Educ:* Cheltenham Coll. FCA 1946. Served War, S Staffs Regt, 1939–45 (Major; MC). Moore Stephens, 1946–48; John Mowlem, 1948–51; Dir, 1951–54, Man. Dir, 1954–57, Waring & Gillow; Dir, APV Co., 1957–66; Man. Dir, 1966–77, Chm., 1977–82, APV Holdings. Director: Rolls Royce Motors, 1971–80; Vickers Ltd, 1980–82. *Recreation:* golf. *Address:* The Gate House, Little Chesters, Nursery Road, Walton-on-the-Hill, Tadworth, Surrey KT20 7TX. *T:* Tadworth 3767. *Clubs:* Naval and Military; Walton Heath Golf.

BENSON, Horace Burford; *b* 3 April 1904; *s* of Augustus W. Benson and Lucy M. (*née* Jarrett); *m* 1930, Marthe Lanier; one *s* one *d.* Called to Bar, Gray's Inn, 1936; practised as Barrister, Seychelles Islands, 1936–46; District Magistrate, Ghana, 1946; Puisne Judge, Ghana, 1952–57; retired, 1957. Temp. Magistrate, Basutoland, 1958–60; Puisne Judge, Basutoland, Bechuanaland Protectorate and Swaziland, 1960–61; Chief Justice, Basutoland (now Lesotho), 1965; Puisne Judge, Malawi, 1967–69. *Recreations:* bowls, bridge. *Address:* c/o Barclays Bank, 8 Tulse Hill, SE27.

BENSON, James; Vice-Chairman, Ogilvy & Mather International Inc., since 1971; *b* 17 July 1925; *s* of Henry Herbert Benson and Olive Benson (*née* Hutchinson); *m* 1950, Honoria Margaret Hurley; one *d. Educ:* Bromley Grammar Sch., Kent; Emmanuel Coll., Cambridge (MA). Manager, Res. and Promotion, Kemsley Newspapers, 1948–58; Dir, Mather & Crowther, 1959–65; Man. Dir, 1966–69, Chm., 1970–71 and 1975–78, Ogilvy & Mather Ltd. *Publications:* Above Us The Waves, 1953; The Admiralty Regrets, 1956; Will Not We Fear, 1961; The Broken Column, 1966. *Recreations:* swimming, walking, fishing, reading. *Address:* 580 Park Avenue, New York, NY 10021, USA.

BENSON, Jeffrey; *see* Benson, W. J.

BENSON, Jeremy Henry, OBE 1984; architect in private practice, (Benson & Benson F/ARIBA), since 1954; *b* 25 June 1925; *s* of late Guy Holford Benson and Lady Violet Benson; *m* 1951, Patricia Stewart; two *s* three *d. Educ:* Eton; Architectural Assoc. (AADipl.); FRIBA. Royal Engineers, 1944–47. Pres., Georgian Gp, 1985– (Mem., Exec. Cttee, 1967–85; Chm., 1980–85); Vice-Chairman: Soc. for Protection of Ancient Buildings, 1971– (Mem. Exec. Cttee, 1959–); Joint Cttee of SPAB, GG, Victorian Soc., Civic Trust and Ancient Monuments Soc., 1972– (Mem., 1968–), and Chm. of its Tax Group; Member: Forestry Commn's Westonbirt Adv. Cttee, 1969–; Historic Buildings Council for England, 1974–84; Historic Buildings and Monuments Commn for England, 1983– (Chm., Gardens Cttee, 1985–); Adv. Cttee on Trees in the Royal Parks, 1977–80. *Recreation:* gardening. *Address:* Walpole House, Chiswick Mall, W4 2PS. *T:* 01–994 1611; Field Barn, Taddington, Temple Guiting, Cheltenham, Glos. *T:* Stanton 228. *Club:* Brooks's.

BENSON, Peter; *see* Benson, H. P. N.

BENSON, Maj.-Gen. Peter Herbert, CBE 1974 (MBE 1954); Member of Panel of Independent Inspectors, Planning Inspectorate, Departments of Environment and Transport, since 1981; *b* 27 Oct. 1923; *s* of Herbert Kamerer Benson and Edith Doris Benson; *m* 1949, Diana Betty Ashmore; one *s* one *d.* Joined Army, 1944; commnd into S Wales Borderers, 1945; transf. to RASC, 1948, and Royal Corps of Transport, 1965; served, Palestine, Cyprus, Malaya and Singapore (three times), Borneo, Africa and Australia; Comdr, 15 Air Despatch Regt, 1966–68; GSO1 (DS) Staff Coll., Camberley, and Australian Staff Coll., 1968–70; Col Q (Movements), MoD (Army), 1971–72; Comdr, 2 Transport Gp RCT (Logistic Support Force), 1972–73. Comdr, ANZUK Support Gp Singapore, Sen. British Officer Singapore, and Leader, UK Jt Services Planning Team, 1973–74; Chief Transport and Movements Officer, BAOR, 1974–76; Dir Gen. of Transport and Movements (Army) (formerly Transport Officer in Chief (Army)), MoD, 1976–78. Chm., Grants Cttee, Army Benevolent Fund. Col Comdt, RCT, 1978–. Chm., Abbeyfield Soc., Beaminster. Liveryman, Co. of Carmen. *Recreations:* golf, fly-fishing, photography.

BENSON, (William) Jeffrey, FIB; Director, since 1975 and a Deputy Chairman since 1983, National Westminster Bank plc; *b* 15 July 1922; *s* of Herbert Benson and Lilian (*née* Goodson); *m* 1947, Audrey Winifred Parsons; two *s. Educ:* West Leeds High Sch. FIB 1976. Served War, RAF, 1941–46. Joined National Provincial Bank Ltd, 1939; Asst Gen. Manager, 1965–68; National Westminster Bank: Reg. Exec. Dir, 1968–73; Gen. Man., Management Services Div., 1973–75; Dep. Chief Exec., 1975–77; Gp Chief Exec., 1978–82. Vice Chm., 600 Group, 1985– (Dir, 1983–); Chm., Export Guarantees Adv. Council, 1982–; Pres., Inst. of Bankers, 1983–85. *Recreations:* golf, swimming. *Address:* Auben, Spencer Walk, The Drive, Rickmansworth, Herts. *T:* Rickmansworth 78260. *Club:* Clifton (Bristol).

BENTALL, Hugh Henry, MB; FRCS; Emeritus Professor of Cardiac Surgery, Royal Postgraduate Medical School of London, 1985; Hon. Consulting Cardiac Surgeon, Hammersmith Hospital, since 1985 (Professor, 1965–85); *b* 28 April 1920; *s* of late Henry Bentall and Lilian Alice Greeno; *m* 1944, Jean, *d* of late Hugh Cameron Wilson, MD, FRCS; three *s* one *d. Educ:* Seaford Coll., Sussex; Medical Sch. of St Bartholomew's Hospital, London. RNVR, Surg Lieut, 1945–47. Consultant Thoracic Surgeon, Hammersmith Hosp., 1955; Lecturer in Thoracic Surgery, Postgraduate Medical Sch., London, 1959; Reader, 1962–65. Order of Yugoslav Flag with Gold Leaves, 1984. *Publications:* books and papers on surgical subjects. *Recreations:* sailing, antique horology. *Address:* Royal Postgraduate Medical School of London, Ducane Road, W12. *T:* 01–743 2030. *Clubs:* Cruising Association; Royal Naval Sailing Association (Portsmouth); Royal Air Force Yacht (Hamble).

BENTALL, (Leonard Edward) Rowan, DL; President, Bentalls PLC, since 1978 (Chairman, 1968–78 and Managing Director, 1963–78); *b* 27 Nov. 1911; *yr s* of late Leonard H. Bentall and Mrs Bentall; *m* 1937, Adelia Elizabeth (*d* 1986), *yr d* of late David Hawes and Mrs Hawes; three *s* two *d. Educ:* Aldro Sch.; Eastbourne Coll. Joined family business, 1930. Served War of 1939–45: joined East Surrey Regt, 1940; commissioned, Royal Welch Fusiliers, 1941; served Middle East, N Africa, Sicily, Italy, France, Belgium, Holland, 231 (Malta) Inf. Bde; now Hon. Captain, Royal Welch Fusiliers. Bentalls: Dep. Chm., 1950; Merchandise Dir, 1946–63. Pres., Surrey Br., Inst. of Directors, 1979–84.

Trustee, New Victoria Hosp., Kingston upon Thames; Mem. Nat. Exec. Cttee, Forces Help Soc. and Lord Roberts Workshops, 1984–. Freeman of City of London, 1972. Pres., Steadfast Sea Cadet Corps. FRSA. DL, Greater London 1977, Rep. for Kingston-upon-Thames 1979–84. Cavaliere, Order Al Merito della Repubblica Italiana, 1971. *Publication:* My Store of Memories, 1974. *Recreations:* gardening, ornithology. *Address:* Hill House, Broughton, near Stockbridge, Hants. *Club:* Royal Automobile.

BENTHALL, Sir (Arthur) Paul, KBE 1950; FLS; Medal, Internationales Burgen Institut, 1978; *b* 25 Jan. 1902; *s* of Rev. Charles Francis Benthall and Annie Theodosia Benthall; *m* 1932, Mary Lucy, *d* of John A. Pringle, Horam, Sussex; four *s*. *Educ:* Eton; Christ Church, Oxford. Joined Bird & Co. and F. W. Heilgers & Co., Calcutta, 1924; partner (later dir) of both firms, 1934–53; Pres., Bengal Chamber of Commerce, and of Assoc. Chambers of Commerce of India, 1948 and 1950; Mem. Central Board, Imperial Bank of India, 1948 and 1950–53; Chm. All India Board of Technical Studies in Commerce and Business Administration, 1950–53; Pres. Royal Agri-Horticultural Society of India, 1945–47; Pres., UK Citizens' Assoc. (India), 1952. Chairman: Bird & Co. (London) Ltd, 1953–73; Amalgamated Metal Corporation Ltd, 1959–72; Director: Chartered Bank, 1953–72; Royal Insurance Co. and Associated Cos, 1953–72. Trustee: Victoria Meml, Calcutta, 1950–53; Gandhi Meml Fund, India, 1948–63; Vice Chm., Indo-British Historical Soc., Madras, 1985–. Certified blind, 1985. *Publication:* The Trees of Calcutta, 1946. *Address:* Benthall Hall, Broseley, Salop. *T:* Telford 882254. *Clubs:* Oriental, Landsowne.
See also J. C. M. Benthall.

BENTHALL, Jonathan Charles Mackenzie; Director, Royal Anthropological Institute, since 1974; *b* Calcutta, 12 Sept. 1941; *s* of Sir Arthur Paul Benthall, *qv*; *m* 1975, Zamira, *d* of Sir Yehudi Menuhin, *qv*; two *s* one step *s*. *Educ:* Eton (KS); King's Coll., Cambridge (MA). Sec., Inst. of Contemporary Arts, 1971–73. Member: UK Child Care Cttee, 1981–, Overseas Cttee, 1985–, SCF; Assoc. of Social Anthropologists, 1983. Chevalier de l'Ordre des Arts et des Lettres (France), 1973. *Publications:* Science and Technology in Art Today, 1972; The Body Electric: patterns of western industrial culture, 1976; (ed) Ecology: the Shaping Enquiry, 1972; (ed) The Limits of Human Nature, 1973; (ed jtly) The Body as a Medium of Expression, 1975. *Recreations:* listening to music, swimming, gardening. *Address:* 212 Hammersmith Grove, W6 7HG. *Club.* Athenæum.

BENTHALL, Sir Paul; *see* Benthall, Sir A. P.

BENTHAM, Prof. Richard Walker; Professor of Petroleum and Mineral Law, and Director of the Centre for Petroleum and Mineral Law Studies, University of Dundee, since 1983; *b* 26 June 1930; *s* of Richard Hardy Bentham and Ellen Walker (*née* Fisher); *m* 1956, Stella Winifred Matthews; one *d*. *Educ:* Campbell Coll., Belfast; Trinity Coll., Dublin (BA, LLB). Called to the Bar, Middle Temple, 1955. Lecturer in Law: Univ. of Tasmania, 1955–57; Univ. of Sydney, 1957–61; Legal Dept, The British Petroleum Co. PLC, 1961–83 (Dep. Legal Advisor, 1979–83). FRSA 1986. *Publications:* articles in learned jls in UK and overseas. *Recreations:* cricket, military history, military modelling. *Address:* West Bryans, 87 Dundee Road, West Ferry, Dundee DD5 1LZ. *T:* Dundee 77100.

BENTINCK; *see* Cavendish-Bentinck, family name of Duke of Portland.

BENTLEY, Rt. Rev. David Edward; *see* Lynn, Bishop Suffragan of.

BENTLEY, David Ronald; QC 1984; a Recorder, since 1985; *b* 24 Feb. 1942; *s* of Edgar Norman and Hilda Bentley; *m* 1978, Christine Elizabeth Stewart; one *s*. *Educ:* King Edward VII Sch., Sheffield; University Coll. London. LLB (Hons) 1963; LLM and Brigid Cotter Prize, London Univ., 1979. Called to the Bar, Gray's Inn, 1969 (Macaskie Scholar). In practice at the bar, 1969–. *Recreations:* legal history, wildlife, dogs, soccer, cinema. *Address:* 311 Ecclesall Road South, Sheffield.

BENTLEY, Ven. Frank William Henry; Archdeacon of Worcester and Canon Residentiary of Worcester Cathedral, since 1984; *b* 4 March 1934; *s* of Nowell and May Bentley; *m* 1st, 1957, Muriel Bland (*d* 1958); one *s*; 2nd, 1960, Yvonne Wilson; two *s* one *d*. *Educ:* Yeovil School; King's College London (AKC). Deacon 1958, priest 1959; Curate at Shepton Mallet, 1958–62; Rector of Kingsdon with Podymore Milton and Curate-in-charge, Yeovilton, 1962–66; Rector of Babcary, 1964–66; Vicar of Wiveliscombe, 1966–76; Rural Dean of Tone, 1973–76; Vicar of St John-in-Bedwardine, Worcester, 1976–84; Rural Dean of Martley and Worcester West, 1979–84. Hon. Canon of Worcester Cathedral, 1981. *Recreations:* gardening, countryside. *Address:* 7 College Yard, Worcester WR1 2LA. *T:* Worcester 25046.

BENTLEY, Rev. Canon Geoffrey Bryan; Canon of Windsor, 1957–82; Hon. Canon, since 1982; *b* 16 July 1909; *s* of late Henry Bentley; *m* 1938, Nina Mary, *d* of late George Coombe Williams, Clerk; two *s* two *d*. *Educ:* Uppingham Sch.; King's Coll., Cambridge (Scholar); Cuddesdon Coll., Oxford. BA and Carus Greek Testament Prize, 1932; MA 1935. Ordained, 1933; Asst Curate, St Cuthbert's, Copnor, 1933–35; Tutor of Scholae Cancellarii, Lincoln, 1935–38; Lecturer, 1938–52; Priest Vicar of Lincoln Cathedral and Chaplain of Lincoln County Hosp., 1938–52; Proctor in Convocation, 1945–55; Rector of Milton Abbot with Dunterton, Dio. Exeter, 1952–57; Examg Chap. to Bp of Exeter, 1952–74; Commissary to Bp of SW Tanganyika, 1952–61; Canon of Windsor, 1957, Precentor, 1958–69, 1970–73, 1977, President, May-Dec. 1962, Feb.-July 1971 and Aug.-Nov. 1976, Steward 1969, 1975–76; Mem., Archbp's Group on Reform of Divorce Law, 1964; William Jones Golden Lectr., 1965; Scott Holland Lectr., 1966. *Publications:* The Resurrection of the Bible, 1940; Catholic Design for Living, 1940; Reform of the Ecclesiastical Law, 1944; God and Venus, 1964; Dominance or Dialogue?, 1965. *Address:* 5 The Cloisters, Windsor Castle, Berks SL4 1NJ. *T:* Windsor 863001. *Club:* National Liberal.

BENTLEY, Prof. George, FRCS; Professor of Orthopaedic Surgery, Institute of Orthopaedics, University of London, since 1982; *b* 19 Jan. 1936; *s* of George and Doris Bentley; *m* 1960, Ann Gillian Hutchings; two *s* one *d*. *Educ:* Rotherham Grammar Sch.; Sheffield Univ. (MB, ChB, ChM), FRCS 1964. House Surgeon, Sheffield Royal Infirmary, 1959–61; Lectr in Anatomy, Birmingham Univ., 1961–62; Surg. Registrar, Sheffield Royal Infirm., 1963–65; Sen. Registrar in Orthopaedics, Nuffield Orthopaedic Centre and Radcliffe Infirm., Oxford, 1967–69; Instructor in Orth., Univ. of Pittsburgh, USA, 1969–70; Lectr, 1970–71, Sen. Lectr and Reader in Orth., 1971–76, Univ. of Oxford; Prof. of Orth. and Accident Surgery, Univ. of Liverpool, 1976–82. *Publications:* (ed) 3rd edn vols I and II, Rob and Smith Operative Surgery—Orthopaedics, 1979; (ed) Mercer's Orthopaedic Surgery, 8th edn, 1983; papers on arthritis, accident surgery and scoliosis in leading med. and surg. jls. *Recreations:* tennis, music. *Address:* Institute of Orthopaedics, University Department of Orthopaedic Surgery, The Middlesex Hospital, Mortimer Street, W1N 8AA. *T:* 01–631 0560.

BENTLEY, John Ransome; Director, Wordnet International PLC, since 1983; *b* 19 Feb. 1940; *m* 1st, 1960 (marr. diss. 1969); one *s* one *d*; 2nd, 1982, Katherine Susan (marr. diss. 1986), *d* of Gerald Percy and the Marchioness of Bute. *Educ:* Harrow Sch. Chairman: Bardsey PLC, 1980–81; Intervision Video (Holdings) PLC, 1980–82. *Recreation:* living.

BENTLEY, Sir William, KCMG 1985 (CMG 1977); HM Diplomatic Service; Ambassador to Norway, since 1983; *b* 15 Feb. 1927; *s* of Lawrence and Elsie Jane Bentley; *m* 1950, Karen Ellen Christensen; two *s* three *d*. *Educ:* Bury High Sch.; Manchester Univ.; Wadham Coll., Oxford (1st cl. Mod. Hist.); Coll. of Europe, Bruges. HM Foreign (later Diplomatic) Service, 1952; 3rd (later 2nd) Sec., Tokyo, 1952–57; United Nations Dept, Foreign Office, 1957–60; 1st Sec., UK Mission to United Nations, 1960–63; Far Eastern Dept, FO, 1963–65; Head of Chancery, Kuala Lumpur, 1965–69; Dep. Comr-Gen., British Pavilion, Expo 70, Osaka, 1969–70; Counsellor, Belgrade, 1970–73; Head of Permanent Under-Sec.'s Dept, FCO, 1973–74; Head of Far Eastern Dept, FCO, 1974–76; Ambassador to the Philippines, 1976–81; High Comr in Malaysia, 1981–83. *Recreations:* golf, skiing, fishing, shooting. *Address:* c/o Foreign and Commonwealth Office, SW1; Oak Cottage, Oak Lane, Crickhowell, Breconshire. *Clubs:* Brooks's; Roehampton.

BENTON, Kenneth Carter, CMG 1966; *b* 4 March 1909; *s* of William Alfred Benton and Amy Adeline Benton (*née* Kirton); *m* 1938, Peggie, *d* of Maj.-Gen. C. E. Pollock, CB, CBE, DSO; one *s* one step *s* (and one step *s* decd). *Educ:* Wolverhampton Sch.; London Univ. Teaching and studying languages in Florence and Vienna, 1930–37; employed British Legation, Vienna, 1937–38; Vice-Consul, Riga, 1938–40; 2nd Sec., British Embassy, Madrid, 1941–43; 2nd, later 1st Sec., Rome, 1944–48; FO, 1948–50; 1st Sec., Rome, 1950–53; 1st Sec., Madrid, 1953–56; FO, 1956–62; 1st Sec. and Consul, Lima, 1963–64; FO, 1964–66; Counsellor, Rio de Janeiro, 1966–68; retd from Diplomatic Service, 1968. *Publications:* Twenty-fourth Level, 1969; Sole Agent, 1970; Spy in Chancery, 1972; Craig and the Jaguar, 1973; Craig and the Tunisian Tangle, 1974; Death on the Appian Way, 1974; Craig and the Midas Touch, 1975; A Single Monstrous Act, 1976; The Red Hen Conspiracy, 1977; Ward of Caesar, 1986; as James Kirton: Time for Murder, 1985; Greek Fire, 1985. *Recreations:* writing, enamelling. *Address:* 2 Jubilee Terrace, Chichester, West Sussex PO19 1XL. *T:* Chichester 787148. *Club:* Detection.

BENTON, Peter Faulkner, MA, CBIM; Chairman, European Practice, Nolan, Norton & Co., since 1984; Director: Singer and Friedlander, since 1983; Tandata Holdings plc, since 1983; The Turing Institute, since 1985; Chairman, Enfield District Health Authority, since 1986; *b* 6 Oct. 1934; *s* of late S. F. Benton and Mrs H. D. Benton; *m* 1959, Ruth, *d* of late R. S. Cobb, MC, and Mrs J. P. Cobb; two *s* three *d*. *Educ:* Oundle; Queens' Coll., Cambridge (MA Nat. Sciences). 2nd Lieut RE, 1953–55. Unilever Ltd, 1958–60; Shell Chemicals Ltd, 1960–63; Berger Jenson and Nicholson Ltd, 1963–64; McKinsey & Co. Inc., London and Chicago, 1964–71; Gallaher Ltd, 1971, Dir, 1973–77; Man. Dir, Post Office Telecommunications, 1978–81; Dep. Chm., British Telecom, 1981–83. Chairman: Saunders Valve Ltd, 1972–77; Mono Pumps Group, 1976–77. Chm., Heating, Ventilating, Air Conditioning and Refrigerating Equipment Sector Working Party, NEDO, 1976–79; Member: Electronics Industry EDC, 1980–83; Econ. and Financial Policy Cttee, CBI, 1979–83; Special Adviser to EEC, 1983–84. Vice-Pres., British Mech. Engrg Confedn, 1974–77. Chairman: Ditchley Conf. on Inf. Technol., 1982; Financial Times Conf., World Electronics, 1983. Royal Signals Instn Lectr, London, 1980. Pres., Highgate Literary and Scientific Instn, 1981–. Chm., N London Hospice Gp, 1985–. Trustee, Molecule Club Theatre. *Recreations:* reading, fishing, golf, gardening, looking at buildings. *Address:* Northgate House, Highgate Hill, N6 5HD. *T:* 01–341 1133. *Clubs:* United Oxford & Cambridge University, The Pilgrims; Highgate Golf.

BENTON JONES, Sir Simon W. F.; *see* Jones.

BENYON, Thomas Yates; Director of various companies; Chairman, Association of Lloyd's Members, since 1983; *b* 13 Aug. 1942; *s* of late Thomas Yates Benyon and Joan Ida Walters; *m* 1968, Olivia Jane (*née* Scott Plummer); two *s* two *d*. *Educ:* Wellington Sch., Somerset; RMA Sandhurst. Lieut, Scots Guards, 1963–67. Insurance Broker, 1967–71; Director of various companies, 1971–: commodity broking, leasing, banking. Councillor, Aylesbury Vale DC, 1976–79. Contested (C): Huyton, Feb. 1974; Haringey (Wood Green), Oct. 1974; MP (C) Abingdon, 1979–83; Vice Chm., Health and Social Services Cttee, 1982–83; Mem., Social Services Select Cttee, 1980–83. Vice-Pres., Guidepost Trust (charity for mentally sick), 1978–. *Recreation:* hunting. *Address:* Old Rectory, Adstock, near Winslow, Bucks. *Clubs:* Brooks's, Pratt's.

BENYON, William Richard, DL; MP (C) Milton Keynes, since 1983 (Buckingham, 1970–83); *b* 17 Jan. 1930; *e s* of late Vice-Adm. R. Benyon, CB, CBE, and of Mrs. Benyon, The Lambdens, Beenham, Berkshire; *m* Elizabeth Ann Hallifax; two *s* three *d*. *Educ:* Royal Naval Coll., Dartmouth. Royal Navy, 1947–56; Courtaulds Ltd, 1956–64; Farmer, 1964–. PPS to Minister of Housing and Construction, 1972–74; Conservative Whip, 1974–76. Mem., Berks CC, 1964–74; JP 1962–78, DL 1970, Berks. *Address:* Englefield House, Englefield, near Reading, Berkshire. *T:* Reading 302221. *Clubs:* Boodle's, Pratt's.

BERE, Rennie Montague, CMG 1957; retired; *b* 28 Nov. 1907; *s* of late Rev. M. A. Bere; *m* 1936, Anne Maree Barber; no *c*. *Educ:* Marlborough Coll.; Selwyn Coll., Cambridge (MA). Colonial Administrative Service, Uganda, 1930–55; Asst District Officer, 1930; District Officer, 1942; Provincial Commissioner, 1951–55. Commandant, Polish Refugee Settlements, 1943–44; Dir and Chief Warden, Uganda National Parks, 1955–60; Pres., Cornwall Naturalists' Trust, 1967–70. *Publications:* The Wild Mammals of Uganda, 1961; The African Elephant, 1966; Wild Animals in an African National Park, 1966; The Way to the Mountains of the Moon, 1966; Birds in an African National Park, 1969; Antelopes, 1970; Wildlife in Cornwall, 1971; Crocodile's Eggs for Supper, 1973; The Mammals of East and Central Africa, 1975; (with B. D. Stamp) The Book of Bude and Stratton, 1980; The Nature of Cornwall, 1982; articles (chiefly of mountaineering and wild life and anthropological interest) in Alpine Jl, Uganda Jl, Oryx, Animals, etc. *Recreations:* mountaineering; game and bird watching; cricket. *Address:* West Cottage, Bude Haven, Bude, Cornwall. *T:* Bude 2082. *Clubs:* Alpine, Royal Commonwealth Society; Uganda Kobs (past Pres.).

BERESFORD, family name of **Baron Decies** and **Marquess of Waterford.**

BERESFORD, Prof. Maurice Warwick, FBA 1985; Professor of Economic History, University of Leeds, 1959–85, now Emeritus; *b* 6 Feb. 1920; *s* of late H. B. Beresford and Mrs N. E. Beresford. *Educ:* Boldmere and Green Lane Elementary Schs; Bishop Vesey's Grammar Sch., Sutton Coldfield; Jesus Coll., Cambridge. Historical Tripos, Pt I class I, 1940, Pt II class I, 1941; MA 1945. On Staff of Birmingham Univ. Settlement, 1941–42; Sub-warden, Percival Guildhouse, Rugby, 1942–43; Warden, 1943–48; University of Leeds: Lecturer, 1948–55; Reader, 1955–59; Dean, 1958–60; Chm., Sch. of Economic Studies, 1965–68, 1971–72, 1981–83; Chm. of Faculty Bd, 1968–70. Harrison Vis. Prof. of History, Coll. of William and Mary, Virginia, 1975–76. Chairman: Yorks Citizens' Advice Bureaux Cttee, 1963–69; Parole Review Cttee, Leeds Prison, 1970–; Northern Area Inst. for Study and Treatment of Delinquency, 1973–78; Co-opted Mem., City of Leeds Probation Cttee, 1972–78; SSRC, Economic and Social History Cttee, 1972–75. Minister's nominee, Yorkshire Dales National Park Cttee, 1964–71; Member: Consumer Council, 1966–71; Hearing Aids Council, 1969–71; Royal Commn on Historical Monuments (England), 1979–. Hon. DLitt: Loughborough, 1984; Hull, 1986. *Publications:* The Leeds Chambers of Commerce, 1951; The Lost Villages of England, 1954, rev. edn 1983; History on the Ground, 1957, rev. edn 1984; (with J. K. S. St Joseph) Medieval

England: an Aerial Survey, 1958, rev. edn 1979; Time and Place, 1962; New Towns of the Middle Ages, 1967; (Ed, with G. R. J. Jones) Leeds and Its Region, 1967; (with J. G. Hurst) Deserted Medieval Villages, 1971; (with H. P. R. Finberg) English Medieval Boroughs, 1973; (with B. J. Barber) The West Riding County Council 1889–1974, 1979; Walks Round Red Brick, 1980; Time and Place: collected essays, 1985; contribs to Economic History Review, Agricultural History Review, Medieval Archaeology, etc. *Recreations:* music, theatre, maps, delinquency. *Address:* 6 Claremont Avenue, Leeds LS3 1AT. *T:* Leeds 454563.

BERESFORD, Meg; General Secretary, Campaign for Nuclear Disarmament, since 1985; *b* 5 Sept. 1937; *d* of Tristram Beresford and Anne Beresford; *m* 1959, William Tanner; two *s*. *Educ:* Sherborne School for Girls; Seale Hayne Agricultural Coll., Newton Abbot; Univ. of Warwick. Community worker, Leamington Spa; Organising Sec., European Nuclear Disarmament, 1981–83. *Publications:* contributor to End Jl, Sanity. *Recreations:* walking, reading, camping, music. *Address:* Campaign for Nuclear Disarmament, 22–24 Underwood Street, N1 7JG. *T:* 01–250 4010.

BERESFORD-PEIRSE, Sir Henry Grant de la Poer, 6th Bt *cr* 1814; *b* 7 Feb. 1933; *s* of Sir Henry Campbell de la Poer Beresford-Peirse, 5th Bt, CB, and of Margaret, *d* of Frank Morison Seafield Grant, Knockie, Inverness-shire; *S* father, 1972; *m* 1966, Jadranka, *d* of Ivan Njerš, Zagreb, Yugoslavia; two *s*. *Heir: s* Henry Njerš de la Poer Beresford-Peirse, *b* 25 March 1969.

BERESFORD-WEST, Michael Charles; QC 1975; a Recorder of the Crown Court, 1975–83; *b* 3 June 1928; *s* of Arthur Charles and Ida Dagmar West; *m* 1956, Patricia Eileen Beresford (marr. diss.); two *s* one *d*. *Educ:* St Peter's, Southbourne; Portsmouth Grammar Sch.; Brasenose Coll., Oxford (MA). Nat. Service, Intell. Corps, Middle East, SIME. Called to Bar, Lincoln's Inn, 1952, Inner Temple, 1980; Western Circuit, 1953–65; SE Circuit, 1965; a Chm., Independent Schools Tribunal and Tribunal (Children's Act 1948), 1974–80. *Recreations:* swimming, lawn tennis, music, golf. *Address:* 1 Gray's Inn Square, WC1R 5AG. *T:* 01–404 5416. *Clubs:* MCC (1951–80); Hampshire Hogs Cricket; Nomads; Aldeburgh Yacht; Aldeburgh Golf.

BERG, Rev. John J.; *see* Johansen-Berg.

BERG, Prof. Paul, PhD; Willson Professor of Biochemistry, Stanford University School of Medicine, since 1970; *b* New York, 30 June 1926; *m* Mildred Levy; one *s*. *Educ:* Pennsylvania State Univ. (BS); Western Reserve Univ. (PhD). Pre-doctoral and post-doctoral med. research, 1950–54; scholar in cancer research, American Cancer Soc., Washington Univ., 1954; Asst to Associate Prof. of Microbiology, Washington Univ., 1955–59; Stanford Univ. Sch. of Medicine: Associate Prof. of Biochem., 1959–60; Prof., Dept of Biochem., 1960, Chm. 1969–74; Non-resident Fellow, Salk Inst., 1973–. Editor, Biochemical and Biophysical Res. Communications, 1959–68; Member: NIH Study, Sect. on Physiol Chem.; Editorial Bd, Jl of Molecular Biology, 1966–69; Bd of Sci. Advisors, Jane Coffin Childs Foundn for Med. Res.; Adv. Bds to Nat. Insts of Health, Amer. Cancer Soc., Nat. Sci. Foundn, MIT and Harvard, 1970–80; Council, Nat. Acad. of Scis, 1979. Former Pres., Amer. Soc. of Biological Chemists; Foreign Member: Japan Biochem. Soc., 1978–; French Acad. of Scis, 1981–. Lectures: Harvey, 1972; Lynen, 1977; Weizmann Inst., 1977; Univ. of Pittsburgh, 1978; Priestly, Pennsylvania State Univ., 1978; Shell, Univ. of California at Davis, 1978; Dreyfus, Northwestern Univ., 1979; Jesup, Columbian Univ., 1980; Karl-August-Förster, Univ. of Mainz, 1980; David Rivett Meml, CSIR, Melb., 1980. Hon. DSc: Rochester and Yale Univs, 1978; numerous awards include: Nat. Acad. of Scis, 1966, 1974; Amer. Acad. of Arts and Scis, 1966; Henry J. Kaiser, Stanford Univ. Sch. of Med., 1969, 1972; Dist. Alumnus, Pennsylvania State Univ.; V. D. Mattia Prize of Roche Inst. for Molec. Biol., 1972; Gairdner Foundn Award, Nobel Prize in Chemistry, New York Acad. of Scis and Albert Lasker Med. Res. awards, 1980; National Medal of Science, 1983. *Publications:* many scientific articles and reviews. *Address:* Stanford University Medical Center, Stanford, California 94305, USA.

BERGANZA, Teresa; singer (mezzo-soprano); *b* Madrid, Spain; *d* of Guillermo and Maria Ascension Berganza; *m*; three *c*. Début in Aix-en-Provence, 1957; début in England, Glyndebourne, 1958; appeared at Glyndebourne, 1959; Royal Opera House, Covent Garden, 1959, 1960, 1963, 1964, 1976, 1977, 1979, 1981, 1984, 1985; Royal Festival Hall, 1960, 1961, 1962, 1967, 1971; appears regularly in Vienna, Milan, Aix-en-Provence, Holland, Japan, Edinburgh, Paris, Israel, America. Prizes: Lucretia Arana; Nacional Lírica, Spain; Lily Pons, 1976; Acad. Nat. du Disque Lyrique; USA record award; Harriet Cohen Internat. Music Award, 1974. Charles Cross (6 times); Grand Cross, Isabel la Católica, Spain; Gran Cruz al Mérito en las Bellas Artes, Spain; Commandeur, l'Ordre des Arts et des Lettres, France. *Publication:* Flor de Soledad y Silencio, 1984. *Recreations:* music, books, the arts. *Address:* San Lorenzo del Escorial, Madrid, Spain. *T:* 34–1–890.48.06.

BERGEL, Prof. Franz, FRS 1959; DPhil. Nat. (Freiburg), PhD (London), DSc (London), CChem, FRSC, FIBiol; Professor Emeritus of Chemistry, University of London; Member, Institute of Cancer Research: Royal Cancer Hospital; *b* Vienna, 13 Feb. 1900; *s* of Moritz Martin Bergel and Barbara Betty Spitz; *m* 1939, Phyllis Thomas. *Educ:* Universities of Vienna and Freiburg im Breisgau. Head of Dept of Medical Chemistry, Inst. Chem., 1927–33, and Privatdoz., Univ. of Freiburg, 1929–33; research worker: Med. Chem. Dept, Univ. of Edinburgh, 1933–36; Lister Inst. of Preventive Med., Dept of Biochemistry, 1936–38; Dir of Research, Roche Products Ltd, Welwyn Garden City, 1938–52; Head, Chemistry Dept, Chester Beatty Res. Inst., 1952–66; Dean, Inst. Cancer Research, 1963–66. Hon. Lectr, Pharmacology Dept, Faculty of Medical Sciences. University Coll., London 1946–73; Consultant: Harvard Med. Sch. and Children's Cancer Research Foundn (now Sidney Farber Cancer Inst.), Boston, Mass, 1959–60, 1967–73; FRSM; FRSA 1957 (Life Mem., 1967–); Member: Soc. Chem. Ind.; Biochem. Soc.; Amer. Assoc. Adv. Sci. (Fellow); Brit. Pharm. Soc. Inst. of Cancer Research, Sutton, named their new library Bergel Library, 1980. *Publications:* Chemistry of Enzymes in Cancer, 1961; All about Drugs, 1970; Today's Carcinochemotherapy, 1970; Alexander Haddow (biographical memoir), 1977; papers and reviews in chemical, biochemical and pharmacological journals. *Recreation:* sketching. *Address:* Magnolia Cottage, Bel Royal, St Lawrence, Jersey, CI. *T:* Jersey 33688.

BERGER, John; author and art critic; *b* London, 5 Nov. 1926; *s* of late S. J. D. Berger, OBE, MC, and Mrs Miriam Berger (*née* Branson). *Educ:* Central Sch. of Art; Chelsea Sch. of Art. Began career as a painter and teacher of drawing; exhibited at Wildenstein, Redfern and Leicester Galls, London. Art Critic: Tribune; New Statesman. Numerous TV appearances, incl.: Monitor; two series for Granada TV. Scenario: (with Alain Tanner) La Salamandre; Le Milieu du Monde; Jonas (New York Critics Prize for Best Scenario of Year, 1976). George Orwell Meml Prize, 1977. *Publications: fiction:* A Painter of Our Time, 1958; The Foot of Clive, 1962; Corker's Freedom, 1964; G (Booker Prize, James Tait Black Meml Prize), 1972; Pig Earth, 1979; *theatre:* (with Nella Bielski) Question of Geography, 1984 (staged Marseilles, 1984 and Paris, 1986); *non-fiction:* Marcel Frishman, 1958; Permanent Red, 1960; The Success and Failure of Picasso, 1965; (with J. Mohr) A Fortunate Man: the story of a country doctor, 1967; Art and Revolution, Moments of Cubism and Other Essays, 1969; The Look of Things, Ways of Seeing, 1972; The Seventh Man, 1975 (Prize for Best Reportage, Union of Journalists and Writers, Paris, 1977); About Looking, 1980; (with J. Mohr) Another Way of Telling, 1982; And Our Faces, My Heart, Brief as Photos, 1984; The White Bird, 1985 (USA, as The Sense of Sight, 1985); *translations:* (with A. Bostock): Poems on the Theatre, by B. Brecht, 1960; Return to My Native Land, by Aime Cesaire, 1969; (with Lisa Appignanesi) Oranges for the Son of Alexander Levy, by Nella Bielski, 1982. *Address:* Quincy, Mieussy, 74440 Taninges France.

BERGER, Vice-Adm. Sir Peter (Egerton Capel), KCB 1979; MVO 1960; DSC 1949; MA; Bursar and Fellow, Selwyn College, Cambridge, since 1981; *b* 11 Feb. 1925; *s* of late Capel Colquhoun Berger and Winifred Violet Berger (*née* Levett-Scrivener); *m* 1956, June Kathleen Pigou; three *d*. *Educ:* Harrow Sch. MA Cantab 1984. Served War of 1939–45: entered RN as a Cadet, 1943; Normandy and South of France landings in HMS Ajax, 1944; Sub-Lt, 1945; Lieut, 1946; Yangtse Incident, HMS Amethyst, 1949; Lt-Comdr, 1953; Comdr, 1956; Fleet Navigating Officer, Home Fleet, 1956–58; Navigating Officer, HM Yacht Britannia, 1958–60; Commanded HMS Torquay, 1962–64; Captain, 1964; Defence, Naval and Military Attaché, The Hague, 1964–66; commanded HMS Phoebe, 1966–68; Commodore, Clyde, 1971–73; Rear-Adm., 1973; Asst Chief of Naval Staff (Policy), 1973–75; COS to C-in-C Fleet, 1976–78; Flag Officer Plymouth, Port Admiral Devonport, Comdr Central Sub Area Eastern Atlantic and Comdr Plymouth Sub Area Channel, 1979–81, retired 1981. *Recreations:* shooting, fishing, history. *Address:* Linton End House, Linton Road, Balsham, Cambs CB1 6HA. *T:* Cambridge 892959.

BERGERSEN, Dr Fraser John, FRS 1981; FAA 1985; Chief Research Scientist, Division of Plant Industry, CSIRO, Canberra, since 1972; *b* 26 May 1929; *s* of Victor E. and Arabel H. Bergersen; *m* 1952, Gladys Irene Heather; two *s* one *d*. *Educ:* Univ. of Otago, New Zealand (BSc, MSc (Hons)); Univ. of New Zealand (DSc 1962). Bacteriology Dept, Univ. of Otago, 1952–54; Div. of Plant Industry, CSIRO, Canberra, Aust., 1954–, currently engaged full-time in scientific research in microbiology, with special reference to symbiotic nitrogen fixation in legume root-nodules. David Rivett Medal, CSIRO Officers' Assoc. 1968. *Publications:* Methods for Evaluating Biological Nitrogen Fixation, 1980; Root Nodules of Legumes: structure and functions, 1982; one hundred and twenty articles and chapters in scientific journals and books. *Recreations:* music, gardening. *Address:* CSIRO Division of Plant Industry, GPO Box 1600, Canberra City, ACT 2601, Australia. *T:* (062) 465098, (home) (062) 477413.

BERGMAN, (Ernst) Ingmar; Swedish film producer; Director, Royal Dramatic Theatre, Stockholm; director of productions on television; *b* Uppsala, 14 July 1918; *s* of a Chaplain to the Royal Court at Stockholm; *m* 1971, Mrs Ingrid von Rosen; (eight *c* by previous marriages). *Educ:*Stockholm Univ. Producer, Royal Theatre, Stockholm, 1940–42; Producer and script-writer, Swedish Film Co., 1940–44; Theatre Director: Helsingborg, 1944–46; Gothenburg, 1946–49; Malmo, 1952–1959. Produced: Hedda Gabler, Cambridge, 1970; Show, 1971; King Lear, 1985. Films (British titles) produced include: Torment, 1943; Crisis, 1945; Port of Call, 1948; Summer Interlude, 1950; Waiting Women, 1952; Summer with Monika, 1952; Sawdust and Tinsel, 1953; A Lesson in Love, 1953; Journey into Autumn, 1954; Smiles of a Summer Night, 1955; The Seventh Seal, 1956–57; Wild Strawberries, 1957; So Close to Life, 1957; The Face, 1958; The Virgin Spring, 1960 (shown Edinburgh Fest., 1960); The Devil's Eye, 1961 (shown Edinburgh Fest., 1961); Through a Glass Darkly, 1961; Winter Light, 1962; The Silence, 1963; Now About all these Women, 1964 (first film in colour); Persona, 1967; Hour of the Wolf, 1968; Shame, 1968; The Rite, 1969; The Passion, 1970; The Fâro Document, 1970 (first documentary, shown Vienna Fest., 1980); The Touch, 1971; Cries and Whispers, 1972 (NY Film Critics Best Film Award, 1972); Scenes from a Marriage, 1974 (BBC TV Series, 1975; published, 1975); Face to Face, 1976 (BBC TV Series, 1979); The Serpent's Egg, 1977; Autumn Sonata, 1978; From the Life of the Marionettes, 1981; Fanny and Alexander, 1983. Has gained several international awards and prizes for films; Goethe Prize, 1976; Great Gold Medal, Swedish Acad. of Letters, 1977. *Publication:* Four Stories, 1977.

BERGMAN, Ingmar; *see* Bergman, E. I.

BERGONZI, Prof. Bernard, FRSL; Professor of English, University of Warwick, since 1971; *b* 13 April 1929; *s* of late Carlo and Louisa Bergonzi; *m* 1960, Gabriel Wall (*d* 1984); one *s* two *d*. *Educ:* Wadham Coll., Oxford (BLitt, MA). Asst Lectr in English, Manchester Univ., 1959–62, Lectr, 1962–66; Sen. Lectr, Univ. of Warwick, 1966–71, Pro-Vice-Chancellor, 1979–82. Vis. Lectr, Brandeis Univ., 1964–65; Vis. Prof., Stanford Univ., 1982. FRSL 1984. *Publications:* Descartes and the Animals (verse), 1954; The Early H. G. Wells, 1961; Heroes' Twilight, 1965; The Situation of the Novel, 1970; Anthony Powell, 1971; T. S. Eliot, 1972; The Turn of a Century, 1973; Gerard Manley Hopkins, 1977; Reading the Thirties, 1978; Years (verse), 1979; The Roman Persuasion (novel), 1981; The Myth of Modernism and Twentieth Century Literature, 1986. *Recreations:* conversation, looking at pictures and buildings. *Address:* Department of English, University of Warwick, Coventry CV4 7AL. *T:* Coventry 24011.

BERGSTRÖM, Prof. Sune, MD; Swedish biochemist; *b* 10 Jan. 1916; *s* of Sverker Bergström and Wera (*née* Wistrand). *Educ:* Karolinska Inst (MD 1944, DMedSci 1944). Squibb Inst., USA, 1941–42; Med. Nobel Inst., Stockholm, 1942–46; Basle Univ., 1946–47; Prof. of Biochemistry, Lund Univ., 1947–58; Prof at Karolinska Inst, 1958–80, Dean of Med. Faculty, 1963–66, Rector, 1969–77. Consultant to WHO. Chm., Board, Nobel Foundn, 1975– (and Chm., Adv. Council, Med. Research, 1977–82). Member: Swedish Acad. of Scis; Swedish Acad. of Engineering; Amer. Acad. of Arts and Scis; Nat. Acad. of Scis, USA; Acad. of Sci., USSR; Acad. of Med. Scis, USSR; Papal Acad. of Sci.; Hon. Mem., Amer. Soc. of Biol. Chemists. Albert Lasker Basic Med. Research Award, 1977; (jtly) Nobel Prize for Physiology or Medicine, 1982. *Publications:* papers on heparin, autoxidation, bile acids and chlorestrol, prostaglandins. *Address:* c/o Karolinska Institutet, Solnavägen 1, PO Box 60400, 10401 Stockholm, Sweden.

BERIO, Luciano; composer; *b* 24 Oct. 1925; *s* of Ernesto Berio and Ada dal Fiume; *m* 1st, 1950, Cathy Berberian (marr. diss. 1964); one *d*; 2nd, 1964, Susan Oyama (marr. diss 1971); one *s* one *d*; 3rd, 1977, Talia Pecker; two *s*. *Educ:* Liceo Classico, Oneglia; Conservatorio G. Verdi, Milan. Hon. degree in Composition, City Univ., London, 1979. Works include: Differences, 1958; Epifanie, 1959–63; Circles, 1960; Passaggio, 1962; Laborintus II, 1965; Sinfonia, 1968; Concerto for 2 pianos, 1972; Opera, 1969–74; Sequenzas for solo instruments, and for female voice; A-Ronne for five actors, 1974–75; Coro for chorus and orchestra, 1975–76; La Ritirata Notturna di Madrid, 1975; Ritorno degli Snovidenia, 1977; La Vera Storia, 1981; Un Re in Ascolto, 1983; Voci, 1984. *Address:* Il Colombaio, Radicondoli (Siena), Italy.

BERIOZOVA, Svetlana; Ballerina; *b* 24 Sept. 1932; *d* of Nicolas and Maria Beriozoff (Russian); *m* 1959, Mohammed Masud Khan (marr. diss. 1974). *Educ:* New York, USA. Joined Grand Ballet de Monte Carlo, 1947; Metropolitan Ballet, 1948–49; Sadler's Wells Theatre Ballet, 1950–52; Sadler's Wells Ballet (now The Royal Ballet), 1952. Has created leading rôles in Designs for Strings (Taras), Fanciulla delle Rose (Staff), Trumpet Concerto (Balanchine), Pastorale (Cranko), The Shadow (Cranko), Rinaldo and Armida (Ashton),

The Prince of the Pagodas (Cranko), Antigone (Cranko), Baiser de la Fée (MacMillan), Diversions (MacMillan), Persephone (Ashton), Images of Love (MacMillan). Classical Roles: Le Lac des Cygnes, The Sleeping Beauty, Giselle, Coppélia, Sylvia, Cinderella. Other rôles currently danced: Les Sylphides, The Firebird, The Lady and Fool, Checkmate, Fête Etrange, Ondine, Nutcracker. Has danced with The Royal Ballet in USA, France, Italy, Australia, S Africa, Russia, and as guest ballerina in Belgrade, Granada, Milan (La Scala), Stuttgart, Bombay, Nervi, Helsinki, Paris, Vienna, New Zealand, Zurich. Played the Princess in The Soldier's Tale (film), 1966. Has frequently appeared on television. *Relevant publications:* Svetlana Beriosova (by C. Swinson), 1956, Svetlana Beriosova (by A. H. Franks), 1958. *Recreation:* the arts. *Address:* 10 Palliser Court, Palliser Rd, W14.

BERISAVLJEVIĆ, Živan; Member of the Presidency of the Provincial Committee of the League of Communists of Vojvodina, since 1981; *b* 19 Sept. 1935; *s* of Rajko and Ljubica Prodanović; *m* 1963, Slobodanka Koledin; two *d. Educ:* Belgrade Univ. Held leading political functions in Youth League of Socialist Republic of Serbia, 1955–62; Editor-in-Chief, Gledista magazine, 1962–65; held scientific, cultural, educational and press positions, Central Cttee of League of Communists of Serbia, 1962–67; Sec. for Educn, Science and Culture, Serbia, 1967–71; Official of Assembly, Serbia, 1971–72; Advr to Fed. Sec., 1972–74, Asst Fed. Sec., i/c press, information and cultural affairs, 1974–77, Yugoslav Fed. Secretariat for Foreign Affairs. Mem., Commn for Information and Propaganda, Exec. Cttee of Presidency of League of Communists of Yugoslavia, 1972–77; Yugoslav Ambassador to London, 1977–81; Mem., Cttee for Internat. Relations of Central Cttee of League of Communists of Yugoslavia, 1982–. Formerly: Mem. Council, Museum of Contemporary Art, Belgrade; Mem. Federal Cttees for Information, and for Science and Culture. Pres., Univ. of Novi Sad, 1981–. Several decorations. *Publications:* Democratisation of Society and the League of Communists, 1967; Cultural Action, 1972; Education between the Past and Future, 1973; many articles and papers in journals and newspapers. *Recreations:* tennis, football, walking. *Address:* Bulevar Marsala Tita 20, Novi Sad, Yugoslavia.

BERKELEY, Baroness (17th in line); (*cr* 1421; called out of abeyance, 1967); **Mary Lalle Foley-Berkeley;** *b* 9 Oct. 1905; *e d* of Col Frank Wigram Foley, CBE, DSO (*d* 1949), Royal Berks Regt, and Eva Mary Fitzhardinge, Baroness Berkeley; *S* mother, Baroness Berkeley (16th in line) (*d* 1964). *Heiress presumptive: sister* Hon. Cynthia Ella [*b* 31 Jan. 1909; *m* 1937, Brig. Ernest Adolphus Leopold Gueterbock (*d* 1984); one *s*]. *Address:* Pickade Cottage, Great Kimble, Aylesbury, Bucks. *T:* Princes Risborough 3051.

BERKELEY, (Augustus Fitzhardinge) Maurice, CB 1975; MA; Chief Registrar of The High Court in Bankruptcy, 1966–75; Registrar of The Companies Court, 1957–75 and Clerk of the Restrictive Practices Court, 1965–75; *b* 26 Feb. 1903; *s* of late Dr Augustus Frederic Millard Berkeley and Anna Louisa Berkeley; *m* 1st, 1931, Elaine Emily (*d* 1985), *d* of Adin Simmonds; no *c*; 2nd, 1985, Margaret Mary Thérèse, *d* of Edward Cyril Arthur Crookes. *Educ:* Aldenham Sch.; Pembroke Coll., Cambridge. Called to the Bar, Inner Temple, 1927. Served War of 1939–45, in The Welch Regiment, 1940–45; Temp. Lieut-Col; AAG, AG3d, War Office. Junior Counsel in Chancery Matters to Ministry of Agriculture, Fisheries and Food, The Commissioners of Crown Lands and the Forestry Commissioners, 1956–57. Bar Council, 1955–57. *Recreations:* watching cricket, travel, theatre, reading. *Address:* 3 Dr Johnson's Buildings, Inner Temple, EC4. *T:* 01–353 2448; 10 Dover House, Abbey Park, Beckenham, Kent BR3 1QB. *T:* 01–650 4634; 11 Boyes Croft, White Street, Great Dunmow, Essex CM6 3AY. *T:* Great Dunmow 3709. *Club:* Garrick.

See also F. G. Berkeley.

BERKELEY, Frederic George; Master of the Supreme Court (Taxing Office), since 1971; *b* 21 Dec. 1919; *s* of late Dr Augustus Frederic Millard Berkeley and Anna Louisa Berkeley; *m* 1964, Gillian Eugenie Louise Depreux; one *s* two *d* and one step *s. Educ:* Aldenham Sch.; Pembroke Coll., Cambridge (MA). Admitted Solicitor, 1948. Served War of 1939–45, Leics Regt, Normandy (wounded); Major; DADAWS Allied Land Forces SE Asia, 1945–46. Partner in Lewis & Lewis (from 1964 Penningtons and Lewis & Lewis), 1951–70. Mem. No 1 (London) Legal Aid Area Cttee (later No 14), 1954–70, Vice-Chm. 1964–70, Chm. 1970. General Editor and contributor, Butterworth's Costs Service, 1984–. *Recreations:* reading, travel, gardening. *Address:* Tyrells End Farm, Eversholt, Milton Keynes MK17 9DS. *T:* Ridgmont 308.

See also A. F. M. Berkeley.

BERKELEY, Humphry John; writer and broadcaster; Director, Sharon Allen Leukaemia Trust, since 1984; *b* 21 Feb. 1926; *s* of late Reginald Berkeley, author and playwright, former MP (L), and Mrs Hildegarde Tinne. *Educ:* Dragon Sch., Oxford; Malvern; Pembroke Coll., Cambridge (Exhibitioner); BA 1947, MA 1963; Pres., Cambridge Union, 1948; Chm., Cambridge Univ. Conservative Assoc., 1948. Held various appointments at Conservative Political Centre, 1949–56; Dir Gen., UK Council of European Movement, 1956–57; Chairman of Coningsby Club, 1952–55; Hon. Sec., Carlton Club Political Cttee, 1954–59. MP (C) Lancaster, 1959–66; Member, British Parly Delegn to Council of Europe and Council of WEU, 1963–66; personal representative of Colonial Secretary in constitutional talks in Seychelles, 1965; Hon. Sec., Cons. Parly West Africa Cttee, 1959–64; Hon. Sec., UN Parly Gp, 1962–64; joined Labour Party July 1970; contested (Lab) N Fylde, Oct. 1974; joined SDP, 1981. Director: Caspair Ltd; Island Developments Ltd. Mem., Prince Philip's Cttee on Overseas Volunteers, 1966–70; Chm., UNA of GB and NI, 1966–70; Vice-Chm, Nat. Coordinating Cttee for 25th Anniversary of UN, 1970; Mem., UK Nat. Commn for Unesco, 1966–71. Patron, Internat. Centre for Child Studies, 1984–. Hon. Treasurer, Howard League for Penal Reform, 1965–71; Mem. Governing Body, Inst. for Study of Internat. Relations, Sussex Univ., 1969–. *Publications:* The Power of the Prime Minister, 1968; Crossing the Floor, 1972; The Life and Death of Rochester Sneath, 1974; The Odyssey of Enoch: a political memoir, 1977; The Myth that will not Die: the formation of the National Government 1931, 1978. *Address:* 3 Pages Yard, Church Street, Chiswick, W4 2PA. *Club:* Savile.

BERKELEY, Sir Lennox (Randal), Kt 1974; CBE 1957; composer; President Emeritus, Cheltenham Festival of Music, since 1984 (President, 1977–83); *b* 12 May 1903; *o s* of Capt. Hastings George Fitzhardinge Berkeley, RN, and Aline Carla (*née* Harris); *m* 1946, Elizabeth Freda Bernstein; three *s. Educ:* Gresham's Sch., Holt; Merton Coll., Oxford. BA Oxford, 1926; Hon. DMus Oxford, 1970. Studied music in Paris under Nadia Boulanger, 1927–32. Returned to London, 1935; on staff of BBC Music Dept, 1942–45. Composition Professor, Royal Acad. of Music, 1946–68. Hon. Prof. of Music, Keele Univ., 1976–. Pres. of Honour, Performing Right Soc., 1975–83; Pres., Composers' Guild of Great Britain, 1975–. Vice-President: Bach Choir, 1978–; Western Orchestral Soc., 1978–; Cttee, Internat. Soc. of Authors and Composers, 1980–82. Hon. Mem., Amer. Acad. and Inst. of Arts and Letters, 1980; Associate, Académie Royale, Belgium, 1983. Hon. Fellow, Merton Coll., Oxford, 1974. Hon. DMus: City, 1983; Royal Northern Coll. of Music, 1976; Awarded Collard Fellowship in Music, 1946; Cobbett Medal 1962; Ordre de Mérite Culturel, Monaco, 1967; KSG 1973. Composer of the Year, Composers' Guild of GB, 1973. *Compositions include: symphony orchestra:* four symphonies; Divertimento; piano concerto; Concerto for Two Pianos; Flute Concerto; Suite: A Winter's Tale; Voices of the Night; orchestration of Poulenc's Flute Sonata; *chamber orchestra:* Violin Concerto; Partita; Windsor Variations; Dialogue for cello and chamber orchestra; Sinfonia Concertante for oboe and orchestra; *string orchestra:* Serenade; Antiphon; Suite; *vocal/choral music:* Four Poems of St Teresa of Avila for contralto and strings; Stabat Mater for soloists and ensemble; Missa Brevis; Batter My Heart for soprano, choir and chamber orchestra; Four Ronsard Sonnets for tenor and orchestra; Signs in the Dark for choir and strings; Magnificat for choir and orchestra; Three Latin Motets; Hymn for Shakespeare's Birthday; The Hill of the Graces; Judica Me; *chamber music:* many chamber works, including four string quartets; String Trio; Trio for horn, violin and piano; Sextet for clarinet, horn and string quartet; Oboe Quartet; Quintet for wind and piano; various piano works; many songs; *opera:* Nelson; A Dinner Engagement; Ruth; Castaway. *Recreations:* reading, walking. *Address:* 8 Warwick Avenue, W2.

BERKELEY, Maurice; *see* Berkeley, A. F. M.

BERKELEY MILNE, Alexander; *see* Milne, A. B.

BERKHOUWER, Cornelis; Chevalier, Order of the Netherlands Lion 1966; Commander, Order of Orange–Nassau, 1979; Member, European Parliament, 1963–84, elected Member, 1979–84; *b* Alkmaar, Holland, 19 March 1919; *m* 1966, Michelle Martel; one *s. Educ:* Amsterdam Univ. Dr of Law 1946. Barrister, High Court of Amsterdam, 1942. Pres., European Parliament, 1973–75, Vice-Pres., 1975–79. Grand Cross of Merit (Italy), 1974; Grand Cross of Merit (Spain), 1981. *Publications:* Conversion of Void Legal Acts (thesis), 1946; Medical Responsibilities, 1951; Civil Responsibility for Illegal Publicity, 1954. *Recreations:* tennis, ancient literature, swimming, bibliothèque, vinothèque, chess. *Address:* 56 Stationsweg, Heiloo, Netherlands. *Clubs:* National Liberal; de Witte (The Hague); Cercle Gaulois (Brussels).

BERKSON, David Mayer; a Recorder of the Crown Court, since 1978; Deputy Judge Advocate, since 1984; *b* 8 Sept. 1934; *s* of Louis Berkson and Regina Berkson (*née* Globe); *m* 1961, Pamela Anne (*née* Thwaite); one *d. Educ:* Birkenhead School. Called to the Bar, Gray's Inn, 1957. *Recreation:* caravanning. *Address:* Etchingham Park Road, N3. *Clubs:* Athenæum (Liverpool); Border and County (Carlisle).

BERLIN, Irving; author and composer; *b* Russia, 11 May 1888; *s* of Moses Baline and Leah Lipkin; brought to USA, 1893; *m* 1st, 1913, Dorothy Goetz (*d* 1913); 2nd, 1926, Ellin, *d* of Clarence H. Mackay, NY; three *d. Educ:* public schools, NY City, for two years only. First song published, Marie From Sunny Italy, 1907; first complete Broadway score, Watch Your Step, 1914; Music Box Revue, 1921–24; Ziegfeld Follies, 1919, 1920, 1927. Pres. Irving Berlin Music Corp. Served as Sergt Infantry at Camp Upton, LI. Hon. Degrees, Bucknell, Temple, and Fordham Univs; Medal of Merit for This Is The Army; awarded a special Gold Medal by Congress for God Bless America; Legion of Honour, France. Has composed about 800 songs, including: Alexander's Ragtime Band; Oh, How I Hate To Get Up In the Morning; When I Lost You; A Pretty Girl Is Like A Melody; Say It With Music; Always; Remember; Blue Skies; Easter Parade; Heat Wave; Isn't This A Lovely Day; Top Hat, White Tie and Tails; I've Got My Love To Keep Me Warm; White Christmas; This Is The Army, Mr Jones; Anything You Can Do; Doin' What Comes Natur'lly; The Girl That I Marry; There's No Business Like Show Business. Musicals (several of which have been filmed) include: As Thousands Cheer; Face The Music; Louisiana Purchase; Annie Get Your Gun; Miss Liberty; Call Me Madam; Mr President. US Medal of Freedom, 1977. *Address:* Irving Berlin Music Corp., 1290 Avenue of the Americas, New York City, USA. *Clubs:* Lambs, Friars.

BERLIN, Sir Isaiah, OM 1971; Kt 1957; CBE 1946; FBA 1957; MA; President of the British Academy, 1974–78; Fellow of All Souls College, Oxford; *b* 6 June 1909; *s* of Mendel and Marie Berlin; *m* 1956, Aline, *d* of Pierre de Gunzbourg. *Educ:* St Paul's Sch.; Corpus Christi Coll., Oxford. Lectr in Philosophy, New Coll., Oxford, 1932; Fellow: All Souls, 1932–38; New Coll., 1938–50; war service with Min. of Information, in New York, 1941–42, at HM Embassy in Washington, 1942–46, HM Embassy, Moscow, Sept. 1945–Jan. 1946; Fellow, All Souls Coll., Oxford, 1950–66, 1975–; Chichele Prof. of Social and Pol Theory, Oxford Univ., 1957–67; Pres., Wolfson Coll., Oxford 1966–Mar. 1975, Hon. Fellow, 1975. Mem. Cttee of Awards: Commonwealth (Harkness) Fellowships, 1960–64; Kennedy Scholarships, 1967–. Vice-Pres., British Academy, 1959–61; Pres. Aristotelian Soc., 1963–64. Mem., Academic Adv. Cttee., Univ. of Sussex, 1963–66. Visiting Professor: Harvard Univ., 1949, 1951, 1953, 1962; Bryn Mawr Coll., 1952; Chicago Univ., 1955; Princeton Univ., 1965; ANU, Canberra, 1975; Prof. of Humanities, City Univ. of NY, 1966–71. Lectures: Northcliffe, UCL, 1953; Mellon, Nat. Gall. of Art, Washington, DC, 1965; Danz, Washington Univ., 1971. Foreign Member: American Academy of Arts and Sciences; American Academy-Institute of Arts and Letters; American Philosophical Soc. Member, Board of Directors, Royal Opera House, Covent Garden, 1954–65, 1974–; a Trustee, Nat. Gall., 1975–85. Hon. Pres., British Friends of the Univ. of Jerusalem. Hon. doctorates of the following universities: Hull, 1965; Glasgow, 1967; E Anglia, 1967; Brandeis (USA), 1967; Columbia, 1968; Cambridge, 1970; London, 1971; Jerusalem, 1971; Liverpool, 1972; Tel Aviv, 1973; Harvard, 1979; Sussex, 1979; Johns Hopkins, 1981; Northwestern, 1981; NY, 1982; Duke, 1983; City, NY, 1983. Hon. Fellow: Corpus Christi Coll., Oxford; Wolfson Coll., Cambridge. Erasmus Prize (jtly), 1983. *Publications:* Karl Marx, 1939, 4th edn 1978; Translation of First Love by I. S. Turgenev, 1950; The Hedgehog and the Fox, 1953, 4th edn 1979; Historical Inevitability, 1954; The Age of Enlightenment, 1956; Moses Hess, 1958; Two Concepts of Liberty, 1959; Mr Churchill in 1940, 1964; Four Essays on Liberty, 1969; Fathers and Children, 1972; Vico and Herder, 1976; Russian Thinkers, 1978; Concepts and Categories, 1978; Against the Current, 1979; Personal Impressions, 1980; translation of A Month in the Country by I. S. Turgenev, 1980. *Address:* All Souls College, Oxford. *Clubs:* Athenæum, Brooks's, Garrick; Century (New York).

BERMAN, Edward David, (ED Berman), MBE 1979; social entrepreneur, playwright, theatre director and producer; educationalist; Founder and Artistic Director, Inter-Action, since 1968; *b* 8 March 1941; 2nd *s* of Jack Berman and Ida (*née* Webber); naturalized British citizen, 1976. *Educ:* Harvard (BA Hons); Exeter Coll., Oxford (Rhodes Schol.); Dept of Educnl Studies, Oxford (1978–). *Plays:* 8 produced since 1966; *director: theatre:* (premières) *inter alia* Dirty Linen (London and Broadway), 1976, and The Dogg's Troupe (15 minute) Hamlet, (ed) by Tom Stoppard, 1976 (also filmed, 1976); The Irish Hebrew Lesson, 1978 and Samson and Delilah, 1978, by Wolf Mankowitz; Dogg's Hamlet, Cahoot's Macbeth, 1979, by Tom Stoppard; *producer: theatre:* 125 stage premières for adults and 170 new plays for children, London, 1967–83; *maker of films:* (educational) The Head, 1971; Two Weeker, 1972; Farm in the City, 1977; Marx for Beginners Cartoon (co-prod., voice dir), 1978; *actor:* over 1200 performances as Prof. Dogg, Otto Première Check, Super Santa. Editor: 18 community arts, action and constructive leisure handbooks, 1972–; 2 anthologies of plays, 1976–78. Trustee and Founder, Inter-Action Trust, 1968; Director and Founder: Ambiance Lunch-Hour Th. Club, 1968; Prof. Dogg's Troupe for Children, 1968; Labrys Trust, 1969; Inter-Action Advisory Service, 1970; Infilms, 1970; The Almost Free Th., 1971; Inprint Publishing Unit, 1972; City Farm 1, 1972; Alternative Education Project, 1973–84; Inter-Action Trust Ltd, 1974; Town and

Country Inter-Action (Milton Keynes) Ltd, 1975; Ambiance Inter-Action Inc., 1976; Talacre Centre Ltd, 1977; Co-Founder: Inter-Action Housing Trust Ltd, 1970; NUBS, Neighbourhood Use of Bldgs and Space; Community Design Centre, 1974; Beginners Books Ltd, 1978; Inter-Action Housing Co-operative, 1978. Founder, Artistic Dir, BARC, British Amer. Rep. Co., 1978. Devised: Inter-Action Creative Game Method, 1967; Super Santa, Father Xmas Union, 1967–82; Chairman: Save Piccadilly Campaign, 1971–80; Talacre Action Gp, 1972; Nat. Assoc. of Arts Centres, 1975–79; Dir, Islington Bus Co., 1974–76; Treas., Fair Play for Children Campaign, 1975–77; Founder: City Farm Movement, 1976; WAC—Weekend Arts Coll., 1979; co-founder: Sport-Space, 1976; FUSION—London and Commonwealth Youth Ensemble, 1981. Founder and Co-Director: Internat. Inst. for Social Enterprise, 1980; Country Wings, 1981; OPS, Occupation Preparation Systems, 1982; Options Training Ltd, 1983; Interactive Software Arts Ltd; Social Property Developments Ltd; Software Village Ltd; Whole Health Centres, 1983; East London Radio Riverside Ltd; Radio Docklands Ltd, 1985. Special Adviser on inner city matters to Sec. of State for the Environment, 1982–83. As community artist: created 17 formats for participatory theatre, 1968–85; Community Media Van, 1973; Community Cameos, 1977–83; MIY—Make It Yourself, 1978; RIY—Raise It Yourself, 1981. *Publications:* Prof. R. L. Dogg's Zoo's Who I and II, 1975; Make a Real Job of It, Breaks for Young Bands, 1985. *Recreations:* solitude, conversation, work, music. *Address:* Inter-Action Trust, Royal Victoria Dock, E16 1BT. *T:* 01–511 0414.

BERMAN, Franklin Delow, CMG 1986; Legal Counsellor, Foreign and Commonwealth Office, since 1985; *b* 23 Dec. 1939; *s* of Joshua Zelic Berman and Gertrude (*née* Levin); *m* 1964, Christine Mary Lawler; two *s* three *d. Educ:* Rondebosch Boys' High Sch., Cape Town; Univ. of Cape Town; Wadham and Nuffield Colls, Oxford. BA, BSc Cape Town; MA Oxford. Rhodes Scholar, 1961; called to Bar (Middle Temple), 1966. HM Diplomatic Service, 1965: Asst Legal Adviser, FO, 1965; Legal Adviser: British Military Govt, Berlin, 1971; British Embassy, Bonn, 1972; Legal Counsellor, FCO, 1974; Counsellor and Legal Adviser, UK Mission to UN, NY, 1982. Chm., Diplomatic Service Assoc., 1979–82. *Recreations:* walking, reading, music, choral singing. *Address:* c/o Foreign and Commonwealth Office, SW1. *T:* 01–233 3000. *Club:* United Oxford & Cambridge University.

BERMAN, Lawrence Sam, CB 1975; consultant; *b* 15 May 1928; *yr s* of Jack and Violet Berman; *m* 1954, Kathleen D. Lewis; one *s* one *d. Educ:* St Clement Danes Grammar Sch.; London Sch. of Economics. BSc (Econ) 1st cl. hons 1947; MSc (Econ) 1950. Res. Asst, LSE, 1947; Nuffield Coll., Oxford, 1948; Econ. Commn for Europe, 1949; Central Statistical Office: Asst Statistician 1952; Statistician 1955; Chief Statistician 1964; Asst Dir 1968; Dir of Statistics, Depts of Industry and Trade, 1972–83. Statistical Advr, Caribbean Tourism R & D Centre, Barbados, 1984–85. Editor, National Income Blue Book, 1954–60; Member: Council, Royal Statistical Soc., 1970–74 (Vice-Pres., 1973–74); Council Internat. Assoc. for Research in Income and Wealth, 1980–85; ISI. *Publications:* Caribbean Tourism Statistical Reports; articles and papers in Jl of Royal Statistical Soc., Economica, Economic Trends, Statistical News, etc. *Recreations:* travel, theatre, collecting sugar tongs and bow ties. *Address:* 10 Carlton Close, Edgware, Mddx. *T:* 01–958 6938.

BERMANT, Chaim Icyk; author, since 1966; *b* 26 Feb. 1929; *s* of Azriel Bermant and Feiga (*née* Daets); *m* 1962, Judy Weil; two *s* two *d. Educ:* Queen's Park Sch., Glasgow; Glasgow Yeshiva; Glasgow Univ. (MA Hons; MLitt); London School of Economics (MScEcon). School-master, 1955–57; Economist, 1957–58; Television script writer, 1958–61; Journalist, 1961–66. *Publications:* Jericho Sleep Alone, 1964; Berl Make Tea, 1965; Ben Preserve Us, 1965; Diary of an Old Man, 1966; Israel, 1967; Swinging in the Rain, 1967; Troubled Eden, 1969; The Cousinhood, 1971; Here Endeth the Lesson, 1969; Now Dowager, 1971; Roses are Blooming in Picardy, 1972; The Last Supper, 1973; The Walled Garden, 1974; Point of Arrival, 1975; The Second Mrs Whitberg, 1976; Coming Home, 1976 (Wingate-Jewish Chronicle Book Award); The Squire of Bor Shachor, 1977; The Jews, 1978; Now Newman was Old, 1978; Belshazzar, 1979; (with Dr M. Weitzman) Ebla, 1979; The Patriarch, 1981; On the Other Hand, 1982; The House of Women, 1983; Dancing Bear, 1984; What's the Joke, 1986. *Recreations:* walking, sermon-tasting. *Address:* c/o Gillon Aitken, 17 South Eaton Place, SW1W 9ER. *T:* 01–730 8716.

BERMINGHAM, Gerald Edward; MP (Lab) St Helens South, since 1983; *b* Dublin, 20 Aug. 1940; *s* of late Patrick Xavier Bermingham and of Eva Terescena Bermingham; *m* 1st, 1964, Joan (marr. diss.); two *s*; 2nd, 1978, Judith. *Educ:* Cotton College, N Staffs; Wellingborough Grammar School; Sheffield University. LLB Hons. Admitted Solicitor, 1967; called to the Bar, Gray's Inn, 1985. Councillor, Sheffield City Council, 1975–79, 1980–82. Contested (Lab) SE Derbyshire, 1979. *Recreations:* sport, reading, TV. *Address:* 10 Devonshire Drive, Sheffield S17 3PJ; 51B Junction Lane, St Helens, Merseyside WA9 3JN. *T:* St Helens 810083.

BERMUDA, Bishop of, since 1984; **Rt. Rev. Christopher Charles Luxmoore;** Dean of Bermuda Cathedral since 1984; *b* 9 April 1926; *s* of Rev. William Cyril Luxmoore and Constance Evelyn Luxmoore; *m* 1955, Judith, *d* of late Canon Verney Johnstone; four *s* one *d. Educ:* Sedbergh School, Yorks; Trinity Coll., Cambridge; Chichester Theol Coll. Deacon 1952, priest 1953; Asst Curate, St John the Baptist, Newcastle upon Tyne, 1952–55; Priest-in-Charge, St Bede's Ecclesiastical Dist, Newsham, 1955–57; Vicar of Newsham, 1957–58; Rector of Sangre Grande, Trinidad, 1958–66; Vicar of Headingley, Leeds, 1967–81; Proctor in Convocation and Mem. Gen. Synod, 1975–81; Hon. Canon of Ripon Cathedral, 1980–81; Precentor and Canon Residentiary of Chichester Cathedral, 1981–84. Commissary for Bishop of Trinidad and Tobago, 1968–84. *Recreations:* music, church history, winemaking. *Address:* Bishop's Lodge, PO Box 769, Hamilton, Bermuda. *T:* Bermuda 22967.

BERNAL-PEREIRA, Gen. Waldo; Bolivian Orders of: Merito Aeronautico; Guerrilleros Lanza; Merito Naval; Constancia Militar; Merito Aeronautico Civil; La Gran Orden de la Educación (Colombia); US Legion of Merit; Commander-in-Chief, Bolivian Air Force, since 1980; *b* 5 Dec. 1934; *s* of Romulo Bernal and Amalia Pereira; *m* Maria Antonieta Arze; three *s. Educ:* German Coll., Oruro, Bolivia; Military Aviation Coll.; Pilotage Course, USA; grad. as Pilot in Reese AFB, USA, 1958; Modern Meteorological Techniques Course at Chanute AFB, USA; Squadron Comd Course, Air Force Univ., Maxwell AFB, USA; Diploma, Comd and Mil. Staff, Buenos Aires, Argentina; Diploma Top Grade Nat. Studies, La Paz, Bolivia. Pilot Instructor, Air Force Mil. Coll., 1958; Pilot, Mil. Air Transport, 1959; Head of Operations, Aerial Fighter Gp, 1964; Head of Mil. Aeronaut. Polytechnic, 1966; Chief of Dept III, Aerial Comd Ops, 1970; Comdr, Air Transport Gp, 1972; Comdr, Mil. Aviation Coll., 1973; Head of Presidential COS, 1974; Minister of State for Education and Culture, Aug. 1974–Nov. 1976; Air Attaché, Bolivian Embassy, Washington, 1977; Comdr, Mil. Aviation Coll., 1978; Ambassador to Court of St James's, 1979–80. *Recreation:* tennis. *Address:* Avenida Julio C. Patiño No 665, Calacoto, Casilla No 345, La Paz, Bolivia; Comando General de la Fuerza Aérea Boliviana, Avenida Montes No 734, La Paz, Bolivia.

BERNARD, Sir Dallas (Edmund), 2nd Bt *cr* 1954; Chairman: National & Foreign Securities Trust Ltd, since 1981; Thames Trust Ltd, since 1983; Director: Dreyfus Intercontinental Investment Fund NV, since 1970; Italian International Bank Plc, since 1978; Dreyfus Dollar International Fund Inc., since 1982; *b* 14 Dec. 1926; *o s* of Sir Dallas Gerald Mercer Bernard, 1st Bt, and Betty (*d* 1980), *e d* of late Sir Charles Addis, KCMG; *S* father, 1975; *m* 1st, 1959 (marr. diss. 1979); three *d*; 2nd, 1979, Mrs Monica Montford, *d* of late James Edward Hudson; one *d. Educ:* Eton Coll.; Corpus Christi Coll., Oxford (MA). FCIS. Director: Morgan Grenfell (Holdings) Ltd, 1972–79; Morgan Grenfell & Co. Ltd, 1964–77; Dominion Securities Ltd, Toronto, 1968–79. Mem. Monopolies and Mergers Commn, 1973–79. *Heir:* none. *Address:* 7 Cresswell Gardens, SW5 0BJ. *T:* 01–373 9412. *Club:* Brooks's.

BERNARD, Joan Constance, MA, BD; FKC; Principal of Trevelyan College, University of Durham, and Honorary Lecturer in Theology, 1966–79; *b* 6 April 1918; *d* of late Adm. Vivian Henry Gerald Bernard, CB, and Eileen Mary Bernard. *Educ:* Ascham Sch., Sydney, NSW; St Anne's Coll., Oxford Univ. (BA Lit. Hum. 1940, MA 1943); King's Coll., London (BD 1961). War Service, ATS, 1940–46; AA Comd, 1940–44; SO Air Def. Div., SHAEF, 1944–45 (mentioned in despatches 1945); Special Projectile Ops Gp, July-Nov. 1945. Dep. Admin. Officer, NCB, 1946–50; Asst Sec., Educn, Music and Drama, NFWI, 1950–57; full-time student, 1957–61; Warden, Canterbury Hall, Univ. of London, and part-time Lectr, Dept of Theol., KCL, 1962–65; FKC 1976. Mem., Ordination Candidates' Cttee, ACCM, 1972–; Examining Chaplain to Bishop of Southwark, 1984–. Governor: Godolphin Sch., Salisbury, 1980–; St Saviour's Sch., Southwark, 1981–85. FRSA 1984. *Recreations:* music (assisted John Tobin in Handel research for many years); mountaineering, photography. *Address:* 89 Rennie Court, Upper Ground, SE1 9NZ.

BERNERS, Baroness (15th in line) *cr* 1455; **Vera Ruby Williams;** *b* 25 Dec. 1901; *d* of late Hon. Rupert Tyrwhitt, Major RA (5th *s* of Emma Harriet, Baroness Berners) and of Louise I. F. (*née* Wells); *S* cousin, 1950; *m* 1927, Harold Williams, Colonial Civil Service; two *d. Educ:* Ladies' Coll., Eastbourne; St Agnes' Sch., East Grinstead. *Co-heiresses: d* Hon. Mrs Michael Kirkham [*b* (Pamela Vivian Williams) 30 Sept. 1929; *m* 1952; two *s* one *d*]; and *d* Hon. Mrs Kelvin Pollock [*b* (Rosemary Tyrwhitt Williams) 20 July 1931; *m* 1959; two *s*]. *Address:* Ashwellthorpe, Charlton Lane, Cheltenham, Glos. *T:* Cheltenham 519595.

BERNEY, Sir Julian (Reedham Stuart), 11th Bt *cr* 1620; *b* 26 Sept. 1952; *s* of Lieut John Reedham Erskine Berney (killed on active service in Korea, 1952), Royal Norfolk Regt, and of Hon. Jean Davina, *d* of 1st Viscount Stuart of Findhorn, PC, CH, MVO, MC; *S* grandfather, 1975; *m* 1976, Sheena Mary, *yr d* of Ralph Day and Ann Gordon Day; one *s* one *d. Educ:* Wellington Coll.; North-East London Polytechnic. ARICS. *Recreation:* sailing. *Heir: s* William Reedham John Berney, *b* 29 June 1980. *Address:* Reeds House, 40 London Road, Maldon, Essex CM9 6HE. *T:* Maldon 53420. *Club:* Royal Ocean Racing.

BERNSTEIN, family name of **Baron Bernstein.**

BERNSTEIN, Baron *cr* 1969 (Life Peer), of Leigh; **Sidney Lewis Bernstein,** LLD; President, Granada Group PLC, since 1979, Chairman, 1934–79 (Granada Television, Granada Theatres, Granada TV Rental, Granada Motorway Services, Novello & Co.); *b* 30 Jan. 1899; *s* of Alexander and Jane Bernstein; *m* Sandra, *d* of Charles and Charlotte Malone, Toronto; one *s* two *d.* A founder, Film Society, 1924. Mem., Mddx CC, 1925–31. Films Adviser, Min. of Inf., 1940–45; Liaison, British Embassy, Washington, 1942; Chief, Film Section, AFHQ N Africa, 1942–43; Chief, Film Section, SHAEF, 1943–45. Lectr on Film and Internat. Affairs, New York Univ. and Yale. Mem., Resources for Learning Cons. Cttee, Nuffield Foundn, 1965–72. Governor, Sevenoaks Sch., 1964–74. Fellow, BFI, 1984. *Address:* 36 Golden Square, W1R 4AH; Coppings Farm, Leigh, Tonbridge, Kent TN11 8PN. *Club:* Garrick.

BERNSTEIN, Alexander; Chairman, Granada Group plc, since 1979; *b* 15 March 1936; *s* of late Cecil Bernstein and of Myra Ella, *d* of Lesser and Rachel Lesser; *m* 1962, Vanessa Anne, *d* of Alwyn and Winifred Mills; one *s* one *d. Educ:* Stowe Sch.; St John's Coll., Cambridge. Chairman: Granada TV Rental Ltd, 1977– (Man. Dir, 1964–68); Granada Theatres, 1985–; Granada Motorway Services, 1985–; Director: Granada TV Ltd, 1970– (Jt Man. Dir, 1971–75; Dep. Chm., 1975–79); Barranquilla Investments, 1975–; Waddington Galleries, 1966–; Trustee: Civic Trust for the North-West, 1964–; Granada Foundn, 1968–. Chm., Royal Exchange Theatre, 1983– (Dep. Chm., 1980–83). Member of Court: Univ. of Salford, 1976–; Univ. of Manchester, 1983–. Hon. DLitt Salford 1981. *Recreations:* modern art, ski-ing. *Address:* 36 Golden Square, W1R 4AH.

BERNSTEIN, Prof. Basil Bernard; Karl Mannheim Professor of Sociology of Education, since 1979, Head of Sociological Research Unit, since 1963, University of London; *b* 1 Nov. 1924; *s* of Percival and Julia Bernstein; *m* 1955, Marion Black; two *s. Educ:* LSE (BScEcon); UCL (PhD). Teacher, City Day Coll., Shoreditch, 1954–60; Hon. Research Asst, UCL, 1960–62; Sen. Lectr, Sociology of Educn, Univ. of London Inst. of Educn, 1963; Reader in Sociology of Educn, 1965; Prof., 1967. Hon. DLitt Leicester, 1974; Fil H Dr Univ. of Lund, 1980; DUniv Open, 1983. *Publications:* Class Codes and Control, Vol. I 1971 (2nd edn 1974), Vol. II 1973, Vol. III 1975, revd edn 1977; (with W. Brandis) Selection and Control, 1974. *Recreations:* music, painting, conversation, etc. *Address:* 90 Farquhar Road, Dulwich, SE19 1LT. *T:* 01–670 6411.

BERNSTEIN, Ingeborg, (Inge); a Recorder of the Crown Court, since 1978; *b* 24 Feb. 1931; *d* of Sarah and Eli Bernstein; *m* 1967, Eric Geoffrey Goldrein; one *s* one *d. Educ:* Peterborough County School; St Edmund's College, Liverpool; Liverpool University. Called to the Bar, Inner Temple, 1952; practice on Northern Circuit. Chm., Mental Health Review Tribunal; Mem., Mental Health Act Commn, 1984–. *Recreations:* children and domesticity. *Address:* 54 Castle Street, Liverpool L2 7LQ. *T:* 051–236 4421.

BERNSTEIN, Leonard; conductor, composer, pianist, lecturer; *b* Lawrence, Mass, 25 Aug. 1918; *s* of Samuel J. and Jennie (Resnick) Bernstein; *m* 1951, Felicia Montealegre Cohn (*d* 1978); one *s* two *d. Educ:* Boston Latin Sch.; Harvard Univ.; Curtis Inst. of Music. Asst to Koussevitzky, Berkshire Music Center, 1942, Head of Conducting Dept, 1951–56; Asst Conductor, NY Philharmonic Orch., 1943–44; Conductor, NYC Symphony, 1945–48; Musical Adviser, Israel Philharmonic Orch., 1948–49; Prof. of Music, Brandeis Univ., 1951–56; Charles Eliot Norton Prof. of Poetry, Harvard Univ., 1973–74; co-conductor (with Dimitri Mitropoulos), NY Philharmonic Orch., 1957–58; Music Dir, NY Philharmonic Orch., 1958–69, now Laureate Conductor; Pres., English Bach Festival, 1977–. Has conducted all major orchestras of US and Europe in annual tours, 1944–; has toured N and S America, Europe, Near East, USSR and Japan with NY Philharmonic Orch. Holds decorations from: France, Italy, Finland, Chile and Austria. *Works include:* Clarinet Sonata, 1942; Symphony, No 1, Jeremiah, 1942; Song Cycle (I Hate Music), 1943; Seven Anniversaries for Piano, 1943; Fancy Free, 1944; Hashkivenu, 1945; Facsimile, 1946; Five Pieces for Brass Instruments, 1947; Four Anniversaries for Piano, 1948; Symphony, No 2, The Age of Anxiety, 1949; Song Cycle (La Bonne Cuisine), 1949; songs, Afterthought and Silhouette, 1951; Trouble in Tahiti (one-act opera), 1952; Serenade (after Plato's Symposium) for violin solo, with string orch. and percussion, 1954; Symphony, No 3, Kaddish, 1963; Five Anniversaries for Piano, 1964; Chichester Psalms (a choral work with orchestra), 1965; Mass, a theatre piece for singers, players and dancers, 1971; Score for ballet, Dybbuk, 1974; Suite No 1 from Dybbuk, 1975; Seven Dances from Dybbuk, 1975; Songfest, 1977; A Quiet Place (opera), 1983; scores for Broadway musicals including: On the Town, 1944, Wonderful Town, 1953, Candide, 1956, West Side Story, 1957; Score for Film, On the Waterfront, 1954. Has received Hon. Degrees from universities and colleges. *Publications:* The Joy of Music, 1959; Leonard Bernstein's Young People's Concerts for Reading and Listening, 1962; The Infinite Variety of Music, 1966; The Unanswered Question, 1973; Findings, 1982. *Address:* Amberson Productions, 1414 Avenue of the Americas, New York, NY 10019, USA.

BERNSTEIN, Ronald Harold, DFC 1944; QC 1969; FCIArb; a Recorder of the Crown Court, since 1974; *b* 18 Aug. 1918; *s* of late Mark and Fanny Bernstein; *m* 1955, Judy, *d* of David Levi, MS, and Vera Levi; three *s* one *d*. *Educ:* Swansea Grammar Sch.; Balliol Coll., Oxford. BA (Jurisprudence) 1939; FCIArb 1982. Served in RA, 1939–46, and in 654 Air OP Sqdn, RAF, 1942–46. Commanded 661 Air OP Sqdn, RAuxAF, 1954–56. Called to the Bar, Middle Temple, 1948, Bencher, 1975–. Mem., Gen. Council of the Bar, 1965–69; Mem., Law Commn Working Party on the Law of Landlord and Tenant, 1966–. Pres., Highgate Soc., 1983–. *Publications:* (jointly) The Restrictive Trade Practices Act, 1956; Handbook of Rent Review, 1981; (Joint Editor) Foa, Landlord and Tenant, 8th edn, 1957. *Address:* (professional) Temple Chambers, Temple Avenue, EC4Y 0HP. *T:* 01–353 9353; *T:* (home) 01–340 9933. *Club:* Athenæum.

BERRAGAN, Maj.-Gen. Gerald Brian; Director General of Ordnance Services, since 1985; *b* 2 May 1933; *s* of William James and Marion Beatrice Berragan; *m* 1956, Anne Helen Kelly; three *s*. Commissioned REME 1954; attached 7th Hussars, Hong Kong, 1954–55; transf. RAOC 1956; served UK, Belgium, Germany and with 44 Para Bde (TA); Staff College, 1966; Nat. Defence Coll., 1972–73; Comdr RAOC 3 Div., 1973–76; AQMG HQ N Ireland, 1976–78; HQ DGOS, 1978–80; Comdt Central Ordnance Depot, Chilwell, 1980–82; Sen. Management Course, Henley, 1982; Comdt COD Bicester, 1982–83; Dir, Supply Ops (Army), 1983–85; Sen. Internat. Defence Management Course, USA, 1985. Chm., Army Gliding Assoc. FBIM. *Recreations:* offshore sailing, tennis. *Address:* c/o Ministry of Defence, Portway, Monxton Road, Andover, Hants SP11 8HT. *Clubs:* Athenæum, Army and Navy.

BERRIDGE, (Donald) Roy, CBE 1981; FEng; Chairman, South of Scotland Electricity Board, 1977–82 (Deputy Chairman, 1974–77); Director, Howden Group, since 1982; *b* 24 March 1922; *s* of Alfred Leonard Berridge and Pattie Annie Elizabeth (*née* Holloway); *m* 1945, Marie (*née* Kinder); one *d*. *Educ:* King's Sch., Peterborough; Leicester Coll. of Art and Technology. FEng 1979; FIMechE 1962. Taylor, Taylor & Hobson Ltd, Leicester, 1940; James Gordon & Co., 1946; British Electricity Authority, 1948; seconded to AERE, Harwell, 1952; Reactor Design Engr, CEGB, 1962; Chief Generation Design Engr, 1964–70; Dir-Gen., Gen. Develt Constr. Div., CEGB, 1970–72; Dir of Engrg, SSEB, 1972–74. Member: N of Scotland Hydro-Electric Bd, 1977–82; Scottish Economic Council, 1977–83; CBI (Scottish Council), 1977–83. FRSA. *Address:* East Gate, Chapel Square, Deddington, Oxford.

BERRIDGE, Dr Michael John, FRS 1984; Senior Principal Scientific Officer, Agricultural and Food Research Council, since 1981; Fellow of Trinity College, Cambridge, since 1972; *b* 22 Oct. 1938; *s* of George Kirton Berridge and Stella Elaine Hards; *m* 1965, Susan Graham Winter; one *s* one *d*. *Educ:* University Coll. of Rhodesia and Nyasaland (BSc); Univ. of Cambridge (PhD). Post-doctoral Fellow: Univ. of Virginia, 1965–66; Case Western Reserve Univ., Cleveland, Ohio, 1966–69; Mem., AFRC Unit of Insect Neurophysiology and Pharmacology, Dept of Zoology, Univ. of Cambridge, 1969–. *Publications:* papers in Jl Exptl Biol., Biochem. Jl and Nature. *Recreations:* golf, gardening. *Address:* 13 Home Close, Histon, Cambridge CB4 4JL. *T:* Histon 2416.

BERRIEDALE, Lord; Alexander James Richard Sinclair; *b* 26 March 1981; *s* and *heir* of Earl of Caithness, *qv*.

BERRILL, Sir Kenneth, KCB 1971; Chairman, Securities and Investment Board, since 1985; *b* 28 Aug. 1920; *m* 1st, 1941, Brenda West (marr. diss.); one *s*; 2nd, 1950, June Phillips (marr. diss.); one *s* one *d*; 3rd, 1977, Jane Marris. *Educ:* London Sch. of Economics; Trinity Coll., Cambridge. BSc(Econ) London; MA Cantab, 1949. Served War, 1939–45, REME. Economic Adviser to Turkey, Guyana, Cameroons, OECD, and World Bank. Univ. Lectr in Economics, Cambridge, 1949–69, Rockefeller Fellowship Stanford and Harvard Univs, 1951–52; Fellow and Bursar, St Catharine's Coll., Cambridge, 1949–62, Hon. Fellow, 1974; Prof., MIT, 1962; Fellow and First Bursar, King's Coll., Cambridge, 1962–69, Hon. Fellow, 1973; HM Treasury Special Adviser (Public Expenditure), 1967–69; Chm., UGC, 1969–73; Head of Govt Econ. Service and Chief Economic Advr, HM Treasury, 1973–74; Head of Central Policy Review Staff, Cabinet Office, 1974–80; Chm., Vickers da Costa Ltd and Vickers da Costa & Co. Hong Kong Ltd, 1981–85. Member: Council for Scientific Policy, 1969–72; Adv. Bd for Research Councils, 1972–77; Adv. Council for Applied R&D, 1977–80; Brit. Nat. Commn for UNESCO, 1967–70; Inter-Univ. Council, 1969–73; UGC, Univ. of S Pacific, 1972–; Council, Royal Economic Soc., 1972–; Adv. Bd, RCDS, 1974–80; Review Bd for Govt Contracts, 1981–85; (Nominated), Governing Council, Lloyd's, 1983–. Governor: Administrative Staff Coll., Henley, 1969–84; Overseas Develt Inst., 1969–73; Mem. Council, Salford Univ., 1981–84; Pro Chancellor, Open Univ., 1983–. Cambridge City Cllr, 1963–67. Deputy Chairman: General Funds Investment Trust, 1982–85; Robert Horne Group plc, 1982–; Director: Investing in Success Investment Trust, 1965–67; Ionian Bank, 1969–73; Dep. Chm., Universities' Superannuation Scheme, 1981–85. Hon. Fellow: LSE, 1970; Chelsea Coll., London, 1973. Hon. LLD: Cambridge, 1974; Bath, 1974; East Anglia, 1975; Leicester, 1975; DUniv Open, 1974; Hon. DTech Loughborough, 1974; Hon DSc Aston, 1974. Jephcott Lectr and Medallist, 1978; Stamp Meml Lectr, 1980. *Recreations:* ski-ing, sailing. *Address:* Salt Hill, Bridle Way, Grantchester, Cambs CB3 9NY. *T:* Cambridge 840335; Securities and Investment Board, 3 Royal Exchange Buildings, EC3V 3NL. *T:* 01–283 2474. *Clubs:* Climbers (Hon. Mem.); Himalayan; Cambridge Alpine.

BERRILL, Prof. Norman John, PhD, DSc; FRS 1952; FRSC; FAAAS; lately Strathcona Professor of Zoology, McGill University, Montreal; *b* 28 April 1903. *Educ:* Bristol Gram. Sch., Somerset, England; Bristol Univ.; London Univ. BSc Bristol; PhD, DSc London. FRSC 1936; FAAAS 1979. *Publications:* The Tunicata, 1951; The Living Tide, 1951; Journey into Wonder, 1953; Sex and the Nature of Things, 1954; The Origin of Vertebrates, 1955; Man's Emerging Mind, 1955; You and the Universe, 1958; Growth, Development and Pattern, 1962; Biology in Action, 1966; Worlds Apart, 1966; Life of the Oceans, 1967; The Person in the Womb, 1968; Developmental Biology, 1971; Development, 1976. *Address:* 410 Swarthmore Avenue, Swarthmore, Pa 19081, USA.

BERRIMAN, David, FIB; CBIM; Chairman: North East Thames Regional Health Authority, since 1984; Bunzl Textile Holdings Ltd, since 1981 (Deputy Chairman, 1980); Director (non-executive): Cable and Wireless plc, since 1975; Guinness Mahon & Co. Ltd, since 1973 (Executive Director, 1973–85); Satellite Television plc, since 1981 (Chairman, 1981–85); Bahrein Telecommunications Corporation, since 1982; Britannia Building Society, since 1983; Malcrest Advertising Ltd, since 1983; Solent Cablevision Ltd, since 1983; Ashenden Enterprises Ltd, since 1983; *b* 20 May 1928; *s* of late Algernon Edward Berriman, OBE and late Enid Kathleen Berriman (*née* Sutcliffe); *m* 1st, 1955, Margaret Lloyd (*née* Owen) (marr. diss. 1970); two *s*; 2nd, 1971, Shirley Elizabeth (*née* Wright). *Educ:* Winchester; New Coll., Oxford (MA, Dip. Econ. and Pol. Sc.); Harvard Business Sch. PMD course, 1961. First National City Bank of New York, 1952–56; Ford Motor Co. Ltd, 1956–60; AEI Hotpoint, 1960–63; Gen. Manager, United Leasing Corporation Ltd, 1963–64; Morgan Grenfell & Co. Ltd: Manager, 1964; Dir, 1968–73. Chm., Lewisham and N Southwark DHA, 1981–84. Member: Bd of Trade's Interim Action Cttee for the Film Industry, 1977–85; Govt review body on Harland and Wolff diversification, 1980; British Screen Adv. Council, 1985–. Director: British Screen Finance Ltd, 1985–; Nat. Film Develt Fund, 1985–. Governor, Nat. Film and Television School, 1977–. Chm., MacIntyre Foundation (for mentally handicapped), 1986– (Governor, 1972; Chm., MacIntyre, 1978–); Member, Council: Internat. Hosp. Fedn, 1985–86; King Edward's Hosp. Fund for London, 1985–. *Recreations:* golf, lawn tennis. *Address:* North East Thames Regional Health Authority, 40 Eastbourne Terrace, W2 3QR. *Clubs:* Royal Automobile, International Lawn Tennis; Wilderness Golf (Sevenoaks); Royal St George's Golf; Le Touquet Golf.

BERRY, family name of **Viscount Camrose, Baron Hartwell** and **Viscount Kemsley.**

BERRY, Anthony Arthur; Chairman, Berry Bros & Rudd Ltd, 1965–85; *b* 16 March 1915; *s* of Francis L. Berry and Amy Marie (*née* Freeman); *m* 1953, Sonia Alice, *d* of Sir Harold Graham-Hodgson, KCVO; one *s* one *d*. *Educ:* Charterhouse; Trinity Hall, Cambridge. Served War, RNVR, 1939–45, incl. 2¼ yrs in the Mediterranean. Joined the wine trade on leaving Cambridge, 1936; rejoined family firm of Berry Bros & Rudd on completion of war service; Dir, 1946–. Worshipful Co. of Vintners: Liveryman, 1946; Mem. Court, 1972–; Master, 1980–81. *Recreations:* golf, walking. *Address:* 4 Cavendish Crescent, Bath, Avon BA1 2UG. *T:* Bath 22669. *Clubs:* Boodle's, MCC; Saintsbury; Bath and County (Bath); Royal Wimbledon Golf; Royal St George's Golf (Sandwich).

BERRY, Cicely Frances, (Mrs H. D. Moore), OBE 1985; Voice Director, Royal Shakespeare Co., since 1969; *b* 17 May 1926; *d* of Cecil and Frances Berry; *m* 1951, Harry Dent Moore (*d* 1978); two *s* one *d*. *Educ:* Eothen Sch., Caterham, Surrey; Central Sch. of Speech and Drama, London. Teacher, Central Sch. of Speech and Drama, 1948–68; 4-week Voice Workshops: Nat. Repertory Co. of Delhi, 1980; Directors and Actors in Australia (org. by Aust. Council), 1983; Directors, Actors, Teachers in China, Chinese Min. of Culture, 1984. Patron of Northumberland and Leicester Youth Theatres. *Publications:* Voice and the Actor, 1973, 6th edn 1986; Your Voice and How to Use it Successfully, 1975, 4th edn 1985.

BERRY, Prof. Colin Leonard, FRCPath; Professor of Morbid Anatomy, University of London, at The London Hospital Medical College, since 1976; *b* 28 Sept. 1937; *s* of Ronald Leonard Berry and Peggy-Caroline (*née* Benson); *m* 1960, Yvonne Waters; two *s*. *Educ:* privately; Charing Cross Hosp. Med. Sch. (MB, BS; Governors' Clinical Gold Medal, Llewellyn Schol., Pierera Prize in Clinical Subjects, Steadman Prize in Path.); trained in Histopath., Charing Cross Hosp., 1962–64. MD, PhD (London). Lectr and Sen. Lectr, Inst. of Child Health, London, 1964–70; Reader in Pathology, Guy's Hosp. Med. Sch., 1970–76; Gillson Scholar, Worshipful Soc. of Apothecaries, 1967–68 and 1970–72; Arris and Gail Lectr, RCS, 1973. Mem., Toxicology Review Panel, WHO, 1976–84; Chm., Cttee on Dental and Surgical Materials, 1982–(Vice-Chm., 1979–82); Pres., Developmental Path. Soc., 1976–79; Hon. Sec., ACP, 1982–85 (Meetings Sec., 1979–82); Chm., Scientific Sub-Cttee on Pesticides, MAFF, 1984–; Member: Adv. Cttee on Pesticides, MAFF/DHSS, 1982–; Scientific Adv. Commn on Pesticides, EEC, 1981–; Cttee on Toxicity of Chemicals in Food, Consumer Products and the Environment, 1982–. Asst Registrar, RCPath, 1981–84. *Publications:* Teratology: trends and applications, 1975; Paediatric Pathology, 1981; contrib. Cardiac Pathology (Pomerance and Davies), 1975, and to other texts; numerous publns in LJl of Path., Circulation Res. and other path. jls. *Recreations:* sailing, fishing, pond building. *Address:* 1 College Gardens, Dulwich SE21 7BE. *T:* 01–299 0066. *Clubs:* Reform; Tollesbury Cruising (Essex).

BERRY, Prof. Francis; Emeritus Professor of English Language and Literature, Royal Holloway College, University of London, since 1980; President, South West of England Shakespeare Trust, since 1985; *b* 23 March 1915; *s* of James Berry and Mary Augusta Jane Berry (*née* Ivens); *m* 1st, 1947, Nancy Melloney (*d* 1967), *d* of Cecil Newton Graham; one *s* one *d*; 2nd, 1970, Patricia, *d* of John Gordon Thomson (marr. diss. 1975); 3rd, 1979, Eileen, *d* of Eric Charles Lear. *Educ:* Hereford Cathedral Sch.; Dean Close Sch.; University Coll., Exeter. BA London (1st cl. hons); MA Exeter. Solicitor's articled clerk, 1931; University Coll., Exeter, 1937. War Service, 1939–46. University Coll., Exeter, 1946; successively Asst Lectr, Lectr, Sen. Lectr, Reader in English Literature, and Prof. of English Literature, Univ. of Sheffield, 1947–70; Prof. of English Lang. and Lit., Royal Holloway Coll., Univ. of London, 1970–80. Visiting Lecturer: Carleton Coll., Minn, USA, 1951–52; University Coll. of the West Indies, Jamaica, 1957; W.P. Ker Lectr, Glasgow, 1979; Lectr for British Council: in India, 1966–67; tour of univs in Japan, 1983; Vis. Fellow, ANU, Canberra, 1979; Vis. Prof. of English, Univ. of Malaŵi, 1980–81. FRSL 1968. *Publications:* Gospel of Fire, 1933; Snake in the Moon, 1936; The Iron Christ, 1938; Fall of a Tower, 1942; Murdock and Other Poems, 1947; The Galloping Centaur, 1952, 2nd edn 1970; Herbert Read, 1953, 2nd edn 1961; An Anthology of Medieval Poems (ed), 1954; Poets' Grammar: time, tense and mood in poetry, 1958, 2nd edn, 1974; Morant Bay and other poems, 1961; Poetry and the Physical Voice, 1962; The Shakespeare Inset, 1965, 2nd edn 1971; Ghosts of Greenland, 1967; John Masefield: the Narrative Poet, 1968; (ed) Essays and Studies for the English Association, 1969; Thoughts on Poetic Time, 1972; I Tell of Greenland (novel), 1977; From the Red Fort: new and selected poems, 1984; contributor: Essays in Criticism; BBC Radio Three, ABC, etc. *Recreations:* following first-class cricket, chess, travel, gardening. *Address:* 4 Eastgate Street, Winchester, Hants SO23 8EB. *T:* Winchester 54439.

BERRY, Dr James William; Director of Scientific and Technical Intelligence, since 1982; *b* 5 Oct. 1931; *s* of Arthur Harold Berry and Mary Margaret Berry; *m* 1960, Monica Joan Hill; three *d*. *Educ:* St Mary's Coll., Blackburn; Municipal Technical Coll., Blackburn, Manchester Univ. (BSc); Leeds Univ. (PhD); CEng, FIEE. Royal Signals and Radar Estab., Malvern, 1956–60; Admiralty Surface Weapons Estab., Portsdown, 1960–76 (Head of Computer Div., 1972–76); Dir of Long Range Surveillance and Comd and Control Projs, MoD (PE), 1976–79; Dir Gen. Strategic Electronic Systems, MoD (PE), 1979–82. *Recreations:* music, walking, bird watching. *Address:* c/o Ministry of Defence, Northumberland Avenue, WC2N 5AP. *Club:* Civil Service.

BERRY, John, CBE 1968; MA (Cantab); PhD (St Andrews); FRSE 1936; DL; Consultant on Water Impoundment Biology; Conservation and Fisheries Adviser to: North of Scotland Hydro-Electric Board, since 1968; South of Scotland Electricity Board, since 1973; Consultant Ecologist to Scottish Landowners' Federation, since 1984; *b* Edinburgh, 5 Aug. 1907; *o s* of late William Berry, OBE, DL, Tayfield, Newport, Fife; *m* 1936, Hon. Bride Fremantle, MA (Cantab), 3rd *d* of 3rd Baron Cottesloe, CB; two *s* one *d*. *Educ:* Eton; Trinity Coll., Cambridge. BA 1929 (Zoo. Chem. Phys. Pt I and Law Pt II); MA

1933; PhD 1935; Salmon research, Fishery Bd for Scotland, 1930–31; Biological Research Station, University Coll., Southampton, Research Officer, 1932–36 and Dir, 1937–39. Press Censor for Scotland, 1940–44; Biologist and Information Officer, North of Scotland Hydro-Electric Bd, 1944–49; Dir of Nature Conservation in Scotland, 1949–67. Chm., Interdepartmental Salmon Res. Gp (UK and Ireland), 1971–82; Dir, British Pavilion, Expo '71, Budapest. Mem., Scottish Marine Biology Assoc., 1947–71 (RSE rep., Exec. Cttee, 1947; Mem Council, 1948–54, 1957–66). Pres. 1954–56, Vice-Pres. 1956–60, and Mem., 1966–72, Commn on Ecology, Internat. Union for Conservation of Natural Resources; UK rep., Exec. Bd, Internat. Wildfowl Research Bureau, 1963–72; Vice-President: RZS Scotland, 1959–82 (Hon. Life Fellow and Hon. Vice-Pres., 1982); Scottish Wildlife Trust; Vice-Pres. and Mem. Council, Wildfowl Trust, 1969– (Hon. Life Fellow, 1983). Mem. Court, Dundee Univ., and Delegate to Commonwealth Univs Congress, 1970–78. Hon. LLD Dundee, 1970. DL Fife, 1969. *Publications:* The Status and Distribution of Wild Geese and Wild Duck in Scotland, 1939; various papers and articles on fresh-water fisheries, hydro-electric development and ornithology. *Recreations:* wild geese, music. *Address:* Tayfield, Newport-on-Tay, Fife DD6 8HA. *T:* Newport-on-Tay 543118. *Club:* New (Edinburgh).

BERRY, Col Hon. Julian, OBE (mil.) 1959; Vice Lord-Lieutenant of Hampshire, since 1983; *b* 24 May 1920; *y s* of 1st Viscount Camrose and Mary Agnes (*née* Corns); *m* 1946, Denise, *d* of Major Leslie Rowan Thomson; one *s* one *d*. *Educ:* Eton. 2nd Lieut, Royal Horse Guards (The Blues), 1939; served War, Middle East and Italy; Captain, 1943; Major, 1945; Lt-Col Commanding Royal Horse Guards, 1958–60; Col Comdg Household Cavalry and Silver Stick in Waiting, 1960–64; retired, 1964. JP 1966, DL 1974, Hants. Bronze Star Medal, USA, 1945. *Recreations:* racing and shooting. *Address:* Old Rectory, Tunworth, Basingstoke, Hants. *T:* Basingstoke 471436. *Clubs:* White's, Jockey (Steward 1970–72); Royal Yacht Squadron.

See also Viscount Camrose, Baron Hartwell.

BERRY, Michael Francis; Director of Robert Fleming & Co. Ltd, Merchant Bankers, 1937–77; *b* 17 Oct. 1906; *e s* of C. Seager Berry and Constance, *d* of Rev. D. C. Cochrane; *m* 1939, Prudence, *d* of C. G. Atha, Haverbrack House, Milnthorpe; one *d*. *Educ:* Eton; Hertford Coll., Oxford. Entered City, 1929; served War of 1939–45, Royal Artillery. A Crown Estate Commissioner, 1956–65. High Sheriff Northants 1973. *Publications:* A History of the Puckeridge Hunt, 1950; (with C. M. Floyd) A History of the Eton College Hunt 1857–1968, 1969. *Recreations:* hunting, farming. *Address:* Benefield House, near Peterborough PE8 5AF. *T:* Benefield 219. *Club:* Boodle's.

BERRY, Very Rev. Peter Austin; Provost of Birmingham, since 1986; *b* 27 April 1935; *s* of Austin James Berry and Phyllis Evelyn Berry. *Educ:* Solihull Sch.; Keble Coll., Oxford (MA, English and Theol.); St Stephen's House, Oxford. Intelligence Corps, 1954–56. Ordained deacon, 1962, priest, 1963; Chaplain to Bishop of Coventry, 1963–70; Midlands Regl Officer, Community Relations Commn, 1970–73; Canon Residentiary, Coventry Cathedral, 1973–77; Vice-Provost of Coventry, 1977–85. *Recreations:* music, theatre, architecture. *Address:* Birmingham Cathedral, Colmore Row, Birmingham B3 2QB. *T:* 021–236 6323; 16 Pebble Mill Road, Edgbaston, Birmingham B5 7SA; The Round House, Ilmington, Compton Scorpion, Warwicks.

BERRY, Rt. Rev. Robert Edward Fraser; *see* Kootenay, Bishop of.

BERRY, Prof. Robert James, FRSE 1981; FIBiol; Professor of Genetics in the University of London, since 1974; *b* 26 Oct. 1934; *o s* of Albert Edward James Berry and Nellie (*née* Hodgson); *m* 1958, Anne Caroline Elliott, *d* of Charles Elliott and Evelyn Le Cornu; one *s* two *d*. *Educ:* Shrewsbury Sch.; Caius Coll., Cambridge (MA); University Coll. London (PhD; DSc 1976). Lectr, subseq. Reader, then Prof., in Genetics, at Royal Free Hospital Sch. of Medicine, 1962–78; Prof. of Genetics at University Coll. London, 1978–. Member: Board of Social Responsibility of the General Synod, 1976–; Natural Environment Research Council, 1981–; President, Linnean Soc., 1982–85; Chm., Research Scientists' Christian Fellowship, 1968–. Trustee, Merseyside Museums and Galleries, 1986–. Governor, Monkton Combe Sch., 1979–. *Publications:* Teach Yourself Genetics, 1965, 3rd edn 1977; Adam and the Ape, 1975; Inheritance and Natural History, 1977; (jtly) Natural History of Shetland, 1980; ed, Biology of the House Mouse, 1981; Neo-Darwinism, 1982; ed, Evolution in the Galapagos, 1984; (jtly) Free to be Different, 1984; Natural History of Orkney, 1985. *Recreations:* hill-walking (especially Munros), recovering. *Address:* Department of Zoology, University College London, Gower Street, WC1E 6BT. *T:* 01–387 7050.

BERRY, Dr Robert Langley Page, CBE 1979; Chairman, 1968–78, Deputy Chairman, 1978–79, Alcoa of Great Britain Ltd; *b* 22 Nov. 1918; *s* of Wilfred Arthur and Mabel Grace Berry; *m* 1946, Eleanor Joyce (*née* Cramp); one *s* one *d*. *Educ:* Sir Thomas Rich's Sch., Gloucester; Birmingham Univ. (BSc (Hons), PhD). Served war, Royal Engrs, 1939–45. ICI Metals Div., 1951–66, Director, 1960–66; Man. Dir, Impalco, 1966–68. Non-Exec. Dir, Royal Mint, 1981–86. Dir, Nat. Anti-Waste Prog., 1976–80. President: Inst. of Metals, 1973; Aluminium Fedn, 1974. *Publications:* several, in scientific jls. *Recreations:* fly-fishing, gardening. *Address:* Waterloo Cottage, Waterloo Lane, Fairford, Glos GL7 4BP. *T:* Cirencester 712038. *Club:* Army and Navy.

BERRY, Air Cdre Ronald, CBE 1965 (OBE 1946); DSO 1943; DFC 1940 and Bar, 1943; RAF retired; Director of Control Operations, Board of Trade, 1965–68; *b* 3 May 1917; *s* of W. Berry, Hull; *m* 1940, Nancy Watson, Hessle, near Hull; one *d*. *Educ:* Hull Technical Coll. VR Pilot, Brough Flying Sch., 1937–39; 603 F Sqdn, Turnhouse/Hornchurch, 1939–41 (Battle of Britain); Sqdn Ldr, and CO 81 F Sqdn, North Africa, 1942; Wing Comdr, and CO 322 F Wing, North Africa, 1942–43; Camberley Army Staff Coll., 1944; CO, RAF Acklington, 1945–46; jssc 1955; various operational appts in Fighter and Bomber Comd; V Sqdn, 1957–59; Group Capt., Air Min. and HQ Bomber Comd, 1959. *Recreations:* motoring, gardening, flying. *Address:* Aldrian, Mereview Avenue, Hornsea, N Humberside HU18 1RR.

BERTHOIN, Georges Paul; Médaille militaire, Croix de Guerre, Médaille de la Résistance avec Rosette, France, 1945; Executive Member of the Trilateral Commission (Japan, N America, W Europe), since 1973, Chairman, since 1975; Honorary International Chairman, the European Movement, since 1981 (Chairman, 1978–81); *b* Nérac, France, 17 May 1925; *s* of Jean Berthoin and Germaine Mourgnot; *m* 1st, 1950, Ann White Whittlesey; four *d*; 2nd, 1965, Pamela Jenkins; two *s*. *Educ:* Grenoble Univ.; École Sciences Politiques, Paris; Harvard Univ. Licencié ès Lettres (Philosophie), Licencié en Droit, Laureate for Economics (Grenoble). Lectr, McGill Univ., Montreal, 1948; Private Sec. to French Minister of Finance, 1948–50; Head of Staff of Superprefect of Alsace-Lorraine-Champagne, 1950–52. Joined High Authority of European Coal and Steel Community, and then Principal Private Sec. to its Pres. (Jean Monnet), 1952–53–55. Dep. Chief Rep. of ECSC in UK, 1956–67; Chargé d'Affaires for Commission of the European Communities (ECSC Euratom-Common Market), 1968; Principal Adviser to the Commission, and its Dep. Chief Rep. in London, 1969–70, Chief Representative, 1971–73. *Recreations:* art, theatre, walking, collecting objects. *Address:* 67 Avenue Niel, 75017 Paris, France.

BERTHON, Vice-Adm. Sir Stephen (Ferrier), KCB 1980; *b* 24 Aug. 1922; *s* of late Rear-Adm. C. P. Berthon, CBE and Mrs C. P. Berthon (*née* Ferrier); *m* 1948, Elizabeth Leigh-Bennett; two *s* two *d*. *Educ:* Old Malthouse, Swanage; RNC Dartmouth. Served War of 1939–45 at sea, Mediterranean, Atlantic, Russia; spec. communications, 1945–46; Flag Lieut Singapore, 1946–48; submarines, 1949–51; East Indies Flagship, 1951–52; HMS Mercury, 1952–54; Staff of Flag Officer Aircraft Carriers, 1954–56; Fleet Communications Officer Mediterranean, 1957–59; jssc 1959; Comdr HMS Mercury, 1959–61; Jt Planning Staff, 1961–64; Naval Attaché, Australia, 1964–66; Dir of Defence Policy, MoD, 1968–71; Cdre HMS Drake, 1971–73; Flag Officer Medway and Port Adm. Chatham, 1974–76; Asst Chief of Naval Staff (Op. Req.), 1976–78; Dep. Chief of Defence Staff (Operational Requirements), 1978–81; retired 1981. Jt MFH, Avon Vale Hunt, 1981–84. *Recreations:* hunting, riding, gardening, walking, painting. *Club:* Army and Navy.

BERTHOUD, Sir Eric Alfred, KCMG 1954 (CMG 1945); DL; MA; retired from HM Foreign Service, 1960; *b* 10 Dec. 1900; 2nd *s* of late Alfred E. Berthoud and Helene Berthoud; *m* 1927, Ruth Tilston, *d* of Sir Charles Bright, FRSE; two *s* two *d* (and one *s* decd). *Educ:* Gresham's Sch., Holt; Magdalen Coll., Oxford; MA. Demy; Hons in Natural Science; Goldsmith's Exhibnr. Anglo-Austrian Bank Ltd, London, 1922–26; Anglo-Iranian Oil Co. (BP) Ltd, 1926–39; served as board mem. in France, Holland and Germany, war time mandate, 1939–44, denial of oil to Axis. Commercial Sec. to HM Legation, Bucharest, 1939–41; Mem. British military and econ. mission to Soviet Union, 1941–42; Asst Sec., Min. of Fuel and Power (Petroleum Div.), 1942–44; Minister of State's Office, Cairo, 1942–43; Dir Economic Div., Allied Commission for Austria (British Element), 1944–46; Under-Sec., Petroleum Div., Min. of Fuel and Power, 1946–48; Asst Under-Sec., FO, 1948–52; HM Ambassador to Denmark, 1952–56, to Poland, 1956–60. Jt Chairman: International Cttee setting up OEEC in Paris, 1948; Anglo-Polish Round Table Confs, 1963–70. Chm. (part-time) Civil Service Selection Bd, 1963–68. Pres., Colchester Constituency Liberal Assoc., 1974–76. Member: Council, 1962–73, and Court, Essex Univ.; Council, SSEES, London Univ., 1964–76. Mem. Internat. Council and Governor, Atlantic College, 1962–. Mem., Bd of Visitors, Chelmsford Prison, 1960–75; Pres. (formerly Chm.), Katherine Low Settlement, Battersea; Vice Chm., Sue Ryder Foundn, 1970–72. DL Essex, 1969–. Knight Comdr's Cross with star, Order of Polonia Restituta, 1965; Commander's Order of Merit with Star (Poland), 1985. *Recreation:* international relations. *Address:* Gosfield Hall, Halstead, Essex CO9 1SF. *T:* Halstead 473844. *Club:* Brooks's.

See also Sir M. S. Berthoud, R. G. Pentney.

BERTHOUD, Sir Martin (Seymour), KCVO 1985; CMG 1985; HM Diplomatic Service; High Commissioner in Trinidad and Tobago, since 1985; *b* 20 Aug. 1931; *s* of Sir Eric Berthoud, *qv*; *m* 1960, Marguerite Joan Richarda Phayre; three *s* one *d*. *Educ:* Rugby Sch.; Magdalen Coll., Oxford (BA). Served with British Embassies in: Tehran, 1956–58; Manila, 1961–64; Pretoria/Cape Town, 1967–71; Tehran, 1971–73; Counsellor, Helsinki, 1974–77; Inspector, HM Diplomatic Service, 1977–79; Head of N. American Dept, FCO, 1979–81; Consul-General, Sydney, 1982–85. Commander, Order of the Lion, Finland, 1976. *Recreations:* squash, tennis, food and wine, photography, bird-watching. *Address:* c/o Foreign and Commonwealth Office, SW1A 2AH. *Club:* United Oxford & Cambridge University.

BERTIE, family name of **Earl of Lindsey and Abingdon.**

BERTRAM, Dr Christoph; Diplomatic Correspondent, Die Zeit; *b* 3 Sept. 1937; German national; *m* 1st, 1967, Renate Edith Bergemann (marr. diss. 1980); 2nd, 1980, Ragnhild Lindemann; two *s* one *d*. *Educ:* Free Univ. Berlin and Bonn Univ. (law); Institut d'Etudes Politiques, Paris (political science). Dr of Law 1967. Joined Internat. Inst. for Strategic Studies as Research Associate, 1967, Asst Dir, 1969–74, Dir, 1974–82; Mem. Planning Staff, West German Min. of Defence, 1969–70. *Publications:* (with Alastair Buchan *et al.*) Europe's Futures—Europe's Choices, 1969; Mutual Force Reductions in Europe: the political aspects, 1972; (ed, with Johan J. Holst) New Strategic Factors in the North Atlantic, 1977; Arms Control and Technological Change, 1979. *Recreations:* clocks, sailing. *Address:* Die Zeit, Pressehaus, Speersort, 2000 Hamburg 1, West Germany. *Club:* Garrick.

BERTRAM, (Cicely) Kate, MA; PhD; JP; President, Lucy Cavendish College, Cambridge, 1970–79 (Tutor, 1965–70; Hon. Fellow, 1982); *b* 8 July 1912; *d* of late Sir Harry Ralph Ricardo, FRS; *m* 1939, Dr George Colin Lawder Bertram (Fellow and formerly Senior Tutor of St John's Coll., Cambridge); four *s*. *Educ:* Hayes Court, Kent; Newnham Coll., Cambridge. MA, PhD (Cantab), 1940. Jarrow Research Studentship, Girton Coll., Cambridge, 1937–40. Mem. Colonial Office Nutrition Survey, in Nyasaland, 1939; Adviser on Freshwater Fisheries to Govt of Palestine, 1940–43. Mem. Council, New Hall, Cambridge, 1954–66; Associate of Newnham Coll. FLS. JP: Co. Cambridge, and Isle of Ely, 1959; W Sussex, 1981. *Publications:* 2 Crown Agents' Reports on African Fisheries, 1939 and 1942; papers on African Fish, in zoological jls; papers and articles on Sirenia (with G.C.L. Bertram). *Recreations:* foreign travel, gardening. *Address:* Ricardo's, Graffham, near Petworth, Sussex. *T:* Graffham 205. *Club:* English-Speaking Union.

BERTRAM, Prof. Douglas Somerville; Professor of Medical Entomology and Director of Department of Entomology, London School of Hygiene and Tropical Medicine, 1956–76, now Emeritus; *b* 21 Dec. 1913; *s* of William R. J. Bertram and Katherine Arathoon Macaskill, Glasgow, Scotland; *m* 1st, 1947, Louisa Menzies MacKellar (*d* 1956); two *d*; 2nd, 1973, Muriel Elizabeth (*née* Maas), *widow* of W. M. Drury. *Educ:* Hillhead High Sch., Glasgow; Univ. of Glasgow. 1st cl. hons BSc (Zoology), 1935, PhD 1940, DSc 1964, Glasgow Univ.; FIBiol; Strang-Steel Scholar, Glasgow Univ., 1935–36. Demonstrator, Dept of Zoology, Glasgow Univ., 1936–38; Lectr, Liverpool Sch. of Tropical Medicine, 1938–40, and 1946–48; Reader in Entomology, London Sch. of Hygiene and Tropical Medicine, 1948–56. Hon. Treas., Royal Society of Tropical Medicine and Hygiene, 1960–73. Overseas work in East and West Africa, India and Ceylon, Central and South America periodically. Served War of 1939–45: Lieut to Major, Royal Army Medical Corps, Middle East, POW Germany, Army Sch. of Health Staff, 1945–46. *Publications:* scientific papers in Annals of Trop. Medicine and Parasitology, Transactions Royal Society Tropical Medicine and Hygiene, Adv. Parasitology, Bulletin WHO, etc. *Recreations:* gardening, painting, travel. *Club:* Royal Commonwealth Society.

BERTRAM, Kate; *see* Bertram, C. K.

BERTRAM, Robert David Darney; Partner, Dundas & Wilson, Clerks to the Signet, Edinburgh, since 1969; *b* 6 Oct. 1941; *s* of late D. N. S. Bertram; *m* 1967, Patricia Joan Laithwaite; two *s*. *Educ:* Edinburgh Academy; Oxford Univ. (MA); Edinburgh Univ. (LLB (Hons), Berriedale Keith Prize). An Assistant Solicitor, Linklaters & Paines, London, 1968–69. Associate, Institute of Taxation, 1970 (Mem., Technical Cttee, 1986–); Examiner, Law Society of Scotland, 1972–75; Member: Scottish Law Commn, 1978–86; (part-time), VAT Tribunal, Scotland, 1984–. Non-exec. Dir, The Weir Group plc, 1983–. *Publications:* contribs to professional jls. *Address:* 25 Charlotte Square, Edinburgh EH2 4EZ. *T:* 031–225 1234. *Clubs:* Scottish Arts, Edinburgh University Staff.

BESCH, Anthony John Elwyn; opera and theatre director, since 1950; *b* 5 Feb. 1924; *s* of Roy Cressy Frederick Besch and late Anne Gwendolen Besch. *Educ:* Rossall Sch., Lancs; Worcester Coll., Oxford (MA). Dir, opera and theatre, 1950–: Royal Opera House, Covent Garden; Glyndebourne Opera; English Nat. Opera, London Coliseum; Scottish Opera; New Opera Co., London; Handel Opera Soc.; Edinburgh Festival; Wexford Festival; Deutsche Oper, Berlin; Royal Netherlands Opera; Théâtre de la Monnaie, Brussels; Teatro Colon, Buenos Aires; New York City Opera; San Francisco Opera; Canadian Opera Co.; Nat. Arts Centre, Canada; Australian Opera; State Opera, S Australia; Victoria State Opera. *Recreation:* gardening. *Address:* 19 Church Lane, Aston Rowant, Oxfordshire. *Club:* Garrick.

BESLEY, Christopher; a Metropolitan Magistrate since 1964; *b* 18 April 1916; *s* of late C. A. Besley, Tiverton; *m* 1947, Pamela, *d* of Dr W. E. David, Sydney, Australia; four *s* two *d*. *Educ:* King's Coll., Wimbledon; King's Coll., London. Barrister, Gray's Inn, 1938. Served War of 1939–45, Devon Regt. *Address:* Queen Elizabeth Building, Temple, EC4; 15 Belvedere Avenue, SW19. *T:* 01–946 2184.

BESSBOROUGH, 10th Earl of, *cr* 1739, Earl (UK), *cr* 1937; **Frederick Edward Neuflize Ponsonby;** DL; Baron of Bessborough; Viscount Duncannon, 1723; Baron Ponsonby, 1749; Baron Duncannon (UK), 1834; Chairman, Stansted Park Foundation, since 1984; *b* 29 March 1913; *s* of 9th Earl of Bessborough, PC, GCMG, and Roberte de Neuflize, GCStJ (*d* 1979), *d* of late Baron Jean de Neuflize; *S* father, 1956; *m* 1948, Mary, *d* of Charles A. Munn, USA; one *d*. *Educ:* Eton; Trinity Coll., Cambridge (MA). Contested W Div. Islington (Nat. Govt), 1935. Joined Sussex Yeomanry (TA), 1936; Sec., League of Nations High Commission for Refugees, 1936–39. Served War of 1939–45, France, Flanders and Dunkirk; ADC to Comdr, Canadian Corps; Experimental Officer (Capt.) Tank Gunnery; GSO2 (liaison) in West and North Africa; Second and subsequently First Sec., British Embassy, Paris, 1944–49. Formerly: with Robert Benson, Lonsdale and Co. Ltd and Overseas Adviser to Pye Gp of Cos; Director: High Definition Films; Associated Broadcasting Development Co. Ltd; ATV; Glyndebourne Arts Trust; English Stage Co. Ltd; Southdown Radio Ltd; Chm., Inst. for Educnl TV. Chm. of Governors, British Soc. for Internat. Understanding, 1951–71; Chairman: International Atlantic Cttee, 1952–55; European Atlantic Group, 1954–61. Mem. of UK Parly Delegn to USSR, 1960. Parly Sec. for Science, Oct. 1963; Jt Parly Under-Sec. of State for Educn and Science, 1964; Cons. front bench spokesman on Science, Technology, Power, Foreign and Commonwealth Affairs, 1964–70; Minister of State, Min. of Technology, June-Oct. 1970. Dep. Chm., Metrication Board, 1969–70; Chm., Cttee of Inquiry into the Res. Assocs, 1972–73. Lectures throughout world on British sci. and ind.; Member: Parly and Scientific Cttee (Vice-Pres.); European Parliament, 1972–79 (Vice-Pres., 1973–76; Dep. Leader, European Cons. Gp, 1972–77; Mem. Cttees on Budgets, Energy, Research and Technology); House of Lords Select Cttees on European Communities and Science and Technology, 1979–85; led missions to People's Republic of China, 1977, 1984. President: SE Assoc. of Building Socs; Men of the Trees; Chichester Cons. Assoc.; Chichester Festival Theatre Trust; British Theatre Assoc. Chm. of Governors, Dulwich Coll., 1972–73. DL West Sussex, 1977. OStJ; Chevalier Legion of Honour; MRI; FRGS. *Plays and publications:* Nebuchadnezzar (with Muriel Jenkins), 1939; The Four Men (after H. Belloc), 1951; Like Stars Appearing, 1953; The Noon is Night, 1954; Darker the Sky, 1955; Triptych, 1957; A Place in the Forest, 1958; Return to the Forest, 1962; (with Clive Aslet) Enchanted Forest, 1984; articles, reviews. *Heir pres.: c* Arthur Mountifort Longfield Ponsonby [*b* 11 Dec. 1912; *m* 1939, Patricia (*d* 1952), *d* of Col Fitzhugh Lee Minnigerode, Va, USA; one *s* one *d*; *m* 1956, Princess Anne Marie Galitzine (marr. diss., 1963), *d* of late Baron Sir Rudolph Slatin Pasha; *m* 1963, Madeleine, *d* of Maj.-Gen. Laurence Grand, CB, CIE, CBE; two *s*]. *Address:* 4 Westminster Gardens, SW1. *T:* 01–828 5959; Stansted Park, Rowland's Castle, Hants. *T:* Rowlands Castle 2223. *Clubs:* Turf, Garrick, Beefsteak, Roxburghe.

See also Lady M. B. M. Browne.

BESSEY, Gordon Scott, CBE 1968; *b* 20 Oct. 1910; *s* of late Edward Emerson and Mabel Bessey, Great Yarmouth; *m* 1937, Cynthia (JP 1966), *d* of late William and Mary Bird, Oxford; one *s* three *d*. *Educ:* Heath Sch., Halifax; St Edmund Hall, Oxford. BA 1932, Dip Ed 1933, MA 1937. Teaching: Keighley and Cheltenham, 1933–37; Admin. Asst, Surrey, 1937–39; Asst, later Dep. Educn Officer, Norfolk, 1939–45; Dep. Educn Officer, Somerset, 1945–49. Mem., Youth Service Development Council, 1960–67; Chm., Working Party on part-time training of Youth Leaders, 1961–62; Pres., Assoc. of Chief Educn Officers, 1963; Treas., Soc. of Educn Officers, 1971–74; Chairman: Educnl Adv. Council of IBA (formerly ITA), 1970–74; County Educn Officers' Soc., 1969–70; Dir of Educn, Cumberland, 1949–74, Cumbria, 1974–75. Chairman: East Cumbria Community Health Council, 1974–79; Assoc. of Community Health Councils in England and Wales, 1977–79; Voluntary Action, Cumbria, 1975–84. Hon. DCL Newcastle upon Tyne, 1970. *Recreations:* fishing, golf, fell-walking, ornithology. *Address:* 8 St George's Crescent, Carlisle. *T:* Carlisle 22253. *Club:* Border and County (Carlisle).

BEST, family name of **Baron Wynford.**

BEST, Alfred Charles, CBE 1962 (OBE 1953); DSc (Wales); Director of Services, Meteorological Office, 1960–66; *b* 7 March 1904; *s* of late Charles William Best, Barry, Glam; *m* 1932, Renée Margaret, *d* of late John Laughton Parry, Blaina, Mon; two *s*. *Educ:* Barry Grammar Sch.; University Coll., Cardiff. Professional Asst, Meteorological Office, 1926; appointments: Shoeburyness, 1926; Porton, 1928; Air Min., 1933; Malta, 1936; Larkhill, 1939; Air Min., 1940; Wing Comdr RAFVR, ACSEA, 1945; Air Min., 1945; Research, 1945–54; Meteorological Office Services, 1955–66. *Publications:* Physics in Meteorology, 1957; meteorological papers in jls. *Recreation:* photography. *Address:* 10 Flintgrove, Bracknell, Berks. *T:* Bracknell 421772.

BEST, Edward Wallace, CMG 1971; JP; Deputy Chairman, Melbourne and Metropolitan Board of Works, 1975–79; *b* 11 Sept. 1917; *s* of Edward Lewis Best and Mary Best (*née* Wallace); *m* 1940, Joan Winifred Ramsay; three *d*. *Educ:* Trinity Grammar Sch. and Wesley Coll., Melbourne. Served War 6 years with AIF; 3½ years PoW (Lieut). Elected to Melbourne City Council, 1960; Lord Mayor of Melbourne, 1969–71; has served on numerous cttees: Electric Supply, Finance, Civic Square Bldg, Victoria Market Redevelopment Cttees; Melbourne and Metropolitan Bd of Works Finance and Publicity Cttee; Sidney Myer Music Bowl, 1967– (Chm. 1969); Victorian Olympic Park Cttee of Management, 1967–; Chm., Sports and Recreation Council to Victoria State Govt; Trustee for Olympic Park (Exec. Mem. on Vic. Olympic Cttee which applied for 1956 Melbourne Olympic Games; Mem. Publicity and Pentathlon Cttees at Melbourne Games); Chm., Exhibn Buildings, 1973–75; Melbourne Moomba Festival, 1969– (Pres. 1969–71); Lord Mayor's Holiday Camp, 1969– (Chm. 1969–71); associated 25 years with Lord Mayor's Fund, in an adv. capacity, for appeals; Mem. Cttee: Royal Agricultural Soc. Council, 1970–; Equestrian Fedn of Australia, 1965–75; Moonee Valley Racing Club, 1975–. Visited Edinburgh, Commonwealth Games, 1970 to present Melbourne's application for 1974 Commonwealth Games; Victorian Chm., 1972 Aust. Olympic Appeal, 1971–72; 1974 Commonwealth Games Appeal; Pres., XXth World Congress of Sports Medicine; Chm., Victorian Olympic Council, 1970–75. *Recreations:* racing,

hunting, farming; athletics (rep. Australia at 1938 Empire Games; former Victorian champion sprinter). *Address:* 670 Orrong Road, Toorak, Vic 3142, Australia. *Clubs:* Australian, Bendigo Jockey, Melbourne Cricket, Moonee Valley Racing, Victorian Amateur Turf, Victoria Racing, Royal Automobile Club of Victoria.

BEST, Prof. Ernest; Professor of Divinity and Biblical Criticism, University of Glasgow, 1974–82, now Professor Emeritus; Dean of the Faculty of Divinity, 1978–80; *b* 23 May 1917; *s* of John and Louisa Elizabeth Best; *m* 1949, Sarah Elizabeth Kingston; two *d*. *Educ:* Methodist Coll., Belfast; Queen's Univ., Belfast (BA, MA, BD, PhD); Presbyterian Coll., Belfast. Asst Minister, First Bangor Presbyterian Church, 1943–49; Minister, Caledon and Minterburn Presbyt. Churches, 1949–63; Lectr (temp.), Presbyt. Coll., Belfast, 1953–54; Guest Prof., Austin Presbyt. Theol Seminary, Texas, 1955–57; Lectr in Biblical Lit. and Theol., St Andrews Univ., 1963–74 (Sen. Lectr 1971–74). Lectures: Nils W. Lund, Chicago, 1978; Manson Meml, Manchester Univ., 1978; Sprunt, Richmond, Virginia, 1985; Ethel M. Wood, London Univ., 1986. Vis. Prof. of New Testament Studies, Knox Coll., Dunedin, NZ, 1983; Vis. Fellow, Univ. of Otago, 1983. Jt Editor, Biblical Theology, 1962–72; Associate Editor, Irish Biblical Studies, 1978–. *Publications:* One Body in Christ, 1955; The Temptation and the Passion, 1965; The Letter of Paul to the Romans, 1967; 1 Peter, 1971; 1 and 2 Thessalonians, 1972; From Text to Sermon, 1977; Text and Interpretation (ed jtly), 1979; Following Jesus, 1981; Mark: the Gospel as story, 1983; 2 Corinthians, 1986; Disciples and Discipleship, 1986; contrib. Biblica, Ecumenical Review, Expository Times, Interpretation, Jl Theol Studies, New Testament Studies, Novum Testamentum, Scottish Jl Theology, Catholic Biblical Qly, Zeit. neu. test. Wiss. *Recreations:* vegetable growing, golf. *Address:* 13 Newmill Gardens, St Andrews, Fife KY16 8RY.

BEST, Dr Geoffrey Francis Andrew; Academic Visitor, Department of International Relations, London School of Economics, since 1983; *b* 20 Nov. 1928; *s* of Frederick Ebenezer Best and Catherine Sarah Vanderbrook (*née* Bultz); *m* 1955, Gwenllyan Marigold Davies; two *s* one *d*. *Educ:* St Paul's Sch.; Trinity Coll., Cambridge (MA, PhD). Army (RAEC), 1946–47; Choate Fellow, Harvard Univ., 1954–55; Fellow of Trinity Hall and Asst Lectr, Cambridge Univ., 1955–61; Lectr, Edinburgh Univ., 1961–66; Sir Richard Lodge Prof. of History, Edinburgh Univ., 1966–74; Prof. of History, Sch. of European Studies, 1974–82, Dean, 1980–82, Univ. of Sussex. Vis. Prof., Chicago Univ., 1964; Visiting Fellow: All Souls Coll., Oxford, 1969–70; ANU, 1984; Fellow, Woodrow Wilson Internat. Centre, Washington, DC, 1978–79. Lees Knowles Lectr, Cambridge, 1970; Joanne Goodman Lectr, Univ. of Western Ontario, 1981. Mem. Council, British Red Cross Soc., 1981–84, Hon. Consultant, 1985–. Jt Editor, Victorian Studies, 1958–68; Editor, War and Society Newsletter, 1973–82. FRHistS 1977. *Publications:* Temporal Pillars, 1964; Shaftesbury, 1964; Bishop Westcott and the Miners, 1968; Mid-Victorian Britain, 1971; (ed) Church's Oxford Movement, 1971; (jt ed) War, Economy and the Military Mind, 1976; Humanity in Warfare, 1980; War and Society in Revolutionary Europe, 1982; Honour Among Men and Nations, 1982; Nuremberg and After: the continuing history of war crimes and crimes against humanity, 1984; (ed jtly) History, Society and the Churches, 1985; contrib. various jls. *Recreations:* music, walking, Victorian arts and architecture. *Address:* 12 Florence Street, Islington, N1 2DX.

BEST, Giles Bernard; His Honour Judge Best; a Circuit Judge, since 1975; *b* 19 Oct. 1925; *yr s* of late Hon. James William Best, OBE. *Educ:* Wellington Coll.; Jesus Coll., Oxford. Called to Bar, Inner Temple, 1951; Dep. Chm., Dorset QS, 1967–71; a Recorder, 1972–75. *Recreations:* walking, fishing, shooting. *Address:* Pitcombe, Little Bredy, Dorset.

BEST, Keith (Lander), TD; MP (C) Ynys Môn, since 1983 (Anglesey, 1979–83); *b* 10 June 1949; *s* of late Peter Edwin Wilson Best and of Margaret Louisa Best. *Educ:* Brighton Coll.; Keble Coll., Oxford (BA (Hons) Jurisprudence; MA). Assistant Master, Summerfields Sch., Oxford, 1967; called to the Bar, Inner Temple, 1971; Lectr in Law, 1973. Served: 289 Parachute Battery, RHA (V), 1970–76; with RM on HMS Bulwark, 1976; Naval Gunfire Liaison Officer with Commando Forces (Major). Councillor, Brighton Borough Council (Chm. Lands Cttee, Housing Cttee), 1976–80. PPS to Sec. of State for Wales, 1981–84. Chm., All Party Alcohol Policy and Services Gp; Mem., Select Cttee on Welsh Affairs. Chairman: Bow Gp Defence Cttee; British Cttee for Vietnamese Refugees; Internat. Council of Parliamentarians' Global Action; Member: UN Disarmament Cttee; Young Conservative Nat. Adv. Cttee, 1978. Mem. Cttee, Assoc. of Lloyd's Mems. Founder Member: Two Piers Housing Co-operative, 1977–; Brighton Housing Trust, 1976–; school manager, Downs County First Sch. and Downs Middle Sch., 1976–. *Publications:* Write Your Own Will, 1978 (paperback); The Right Way to Prove a Will, 1980 (paperback); contrib. District Councils Rev. *Recreations:* parachuting, walking, photography, travel. *Address:* House of Commons, SW1. *T:* 01–219 4118. *Clubs:* Town House Royal Artillery Mess (Woolwich); Holyhead Conservative.

BEST, Richard Radford, MBE 1977; HM Diplomatic Service; Deputy High Commissioner, Kaduna, since 1984; *b* 28 July 1933; *s* of Charles and Frances Best (*née* Raymond); *m* 1st, 1957, Elizabeth Vera Wait (*d* 1968); two *d*; 2nd, 1969, Mary Hill (*née* Wait); one *s*. *Educ:* Worthing High Sch.; University Coll. London (BA Hons). Home Office, 1957–66; HM Diplomatic Service, 1966–: served Lusaka, 1969–72; Stockholm, 1972–76; New Delhi, 1979–83. BBC 'Brain of Britain', 1966. *Recreations:* cricket watching, gardening. *Address:* c/o Foreign and Commonwealth Office, SW1A 2AH. *Club:* Royal Over-Seas League.

BEST, Richard Stuart; Director, National Federation of Housing Associations, since 1973; *b* 22 June 1945; *s* of Walter Stuart Best, DL, JP and Frances Mary Chignell; *m* 1st, 1970, Ima Akpan (marr. diss. 1976); one *s* one *d*; 2nd, 1978, Belinda Janie Tremayne Stemp; one *s* one *d*. *Educ:* Shrewsbury School; University of Nottingham (BA). British Churches Housing Trust, 1968–73 (Dir, 1971–73). Trustee, Sutton Housing Trust, 1971–84 (Dep. Chm., 1983–84); Chm., Omnium Central Housing Assoc., 1978–80; Committee Member: UK Housing Trust, 1976–; Sutton Hastoe Housing Assoc. and other Housing Assocs, 1982–; Board Member: Anchor Housing Assoc., 1985–; Guardian Housing Assoc., 1985–. Sec., Duke of Edinburgh's Inquiry into British Housing, 1984–. *Publication:* Rural Housing: problems and solutions, 1981. *Recreation:* photography. *Address:* 19 Chiddingstone Street, Parsons Green, SW6 3TQ. *T:* 01–736 3960. *Club:* Travellers'.

BEST-SHAW, Sir John (Michael Robert), 10th Bt *cr* 1665; retired; *b* 28 Sept. 1924; *s* of Sir John James Kenward Best-Shaw, 9th Bt, Commander RN, and Elizabeth Mary Theodora (*d* 1986), *e d* of Sir Robert Hughes, 12th Bt; *S* father, 1984; *m* 1960, Jane Gordon, *d* of A. G. Guthrie; two *s* one *d* (and one *s* decd). *Educ:* Lancing; Hertford Coll., Oxford (MA); Avery Hill Coll., London (Teachers' Cert.). Captain Royal West Kent Regt, 1943–47. Royal Fedn of Malaya Police, 1950–58; church work, 1958–71; teaching, 1972–82. *Recreations:* gardening, wine and beer making. *Heir: s* Thomas Joshua Best-Shaw, *b* 7 March 1965. *Address:* The Stone House, Boxley, Maidstone, Kent ME14 3DJ. *T:* Maidstone 57524. *Club:* Royal Commonwealth Society.

BESTERMAN, Edwin Melville Mack, MD, MA, Cantab; FRCP; FACC; Honorary Consultant Cardiologist: Department of Medicine, University of the West Indies, since

1985; St Mary's Hospital, London, since 1985; Paddington Green Children's Hospital, since 1985; Hon. Consultant Physician, Department of Medicine, Hammersmith Hospital, since 1981; *b* 4 May 1924; *s* of late Theodore Deodatus Nathaniel Besterman and Evelyn, *y d* of Arthur Mack, NY; *m* 1978, Perri Marjorie Burrowes, *d* of R. Burrowes, Kingston, Jamaica, WI; four *s* by previous marriage. *Educ:* Stowe Sch.; Trinity Coll., Cambridge; Guy's Hospital. BA (Cantab) 1943 (1st cl. hons Physiology); MB, BChir 1947; MRCP 1949; MD 1955 (Raymond Horton Smith Prize); FRCP 1967. Out-patient Officer, Guy's Hosp., 1947; House Physician, Post-graduate Medical Sch., Hammersmith, 1948; Registrar, Special Unit for Juvenile Rheumatism, Canadian Red Cross Memorial Hosp., Taplow, Berks, 1949–52; First Asst (Lectr), Inst of Cardiology and Nat. Heart Hosp., 1953–56; Sen. Registrar, Middlesex Hosp., 1956–62; Consultant Cardiologist: St Mary's Hosp., London, 1962–85; Paddington Green Children's Hosp., 1972–85. Member: Brit. Cardiac Soc.; Faculty of History of Medicine and Pharmacy; British Pacing Group. *Publications:* contribs to Paul Wood, Diseases of the Heart and Circulation, 3rd edn, 1968; articles on phonocardiography, pulmonary hypertension, atherosclerosis, blood platelet function, lipid fractions and drug trials in angina and hypertension in Brit. Heart Jl, Brit. Med. Jl, Lancet, Circulation, Atherosclerosis Research, etc. *Recreations:* photography, gardening, fishing, tennis, dogs. *Address:* PO Box 340, Stony Hill, Kingston 9, Jamaica, West Indies. *Club:* Liguanea.

BESTOR, Arthur (Eugene); Professor of History, University of Washington, 1962–76, now Emeritus; *b* 20 Sept. 1908; *s* of Arthur Eugene and Jeanette Louise Lemon Bestor; *m* 1st, 1931, Dorothea Nolte (marr. diss.); 2nd, 1939, Anne Carr (*d* 1948); two *s*; 3rd, 1949, Dorothy Alden Koch; one *s*. *Educ:* Yale Univ. PhB 1930; PhD 1938. Yale University: Instructor in English, 1930–31; Instructor in History, 1934–36; Teachers Coll., Columbia University: Associate in History, 1936–37; Asst Prof. of History, 1937–42; Stanford University: Asst Prof. of Humanities, 1942–45; Associate Prof. of History, 1945–46; Lectr in American History, Univ. of Wisconsin, 1947; University of Illinois: Associate Prof. of History, 1947–51; Prof. of History, 1951–62. Harold Vyvyan Harmsworth Prof. of American History, Oxford, 1956–57; Fulbright Vis. Prof., University of Tokyo, 1967. Editor-in-chief, Chautauquan Daily, Chautauqua, NY, 1931–33. Fellow, Newberry Library, Chicago, Ill., 1946; John Simon Guggenheim Memorial Fellow, 1953–54, 1961–62. President: Ill. State Historical Soc., 1954–55; Council for Basic Education, 1956–57; Pacific Coast Branch, Amer. Historical Assoc., 1976. MA (Oxon) by decree, 1956; LLD Lincoln Univ. (Pa), 1959. John Addison Porter Prize, Yale Univ., 1938; Albert J. Beveridge Award, Amer. Historical Assoc., 1946. *Publications:* Chautauqua Publications, 1934; David Jacks of Monterey, 1945; Education and Reform at New Harmony, 1948; Backwoods Utopias, 1950, 2nd edn 1970; Educational Wastelands, 1953, 2nd edn 1985; The Restoration of Learning, 1955; State Sovereignty and Slavery (in Jl Ill State Historical Soc.), 1961; The American Civil War as a Constitutional Crisis (in Amer. Historical Review), 1964; Separation of Powers in the Realm of Foreign Affairs (in Seton Hall Law Review), 1974; Respective Roles of Senate and President in the Making and Abrogation of Treaties (in Washington Law Review), 1979; jointly: Problems in American History, 1952, 3rd edn 1966; Three Presidents and Their Books, 1955; The Heritage of the Middle West, 1958; Education in the Age of Science, 1959; Interpreting and Teaching American History, 1961; The American Territorial System, 1973; contribs to Amer. Hist. Review, Jl of Hist. of Ideas, William and Mary Quarterly, Encounter, Procs Amer. Philosophical Soc., American Scholar, Daedalus, Washington Law Review, New England Quarterly, Jl of Southern History, Harvard Educational Review, New Republic, Scientific Monthly, School and Society. *Recreations:* photography, walking. *Address:* Department of History, DP-20, Smith Hall, University of Washington, Seattle, Washington 98195, USA; (home) 4553 55th Avenue NE, Seattle, Washington, 98105, USA. *Club:* Elizabethan (New Haven).

BESWICK, Baron, *cr* 1964 (Life Peer); **Frank Beswick,** PC 1968; JP; Chairman, British Aerospace, 1976–80 (Chairman, Organising Committee, 1975–76); *b* 1912; *m* Dora, *d* of Edward Plumb; one *s* one *d*. Joined RAF, 1940; Transport Command (KCVSA). MP (Lab Co-op.) Uxbridge Div. of Middlesex, 1945–Oct. 1959. PPS to Under-Sec. of State for Air, 1946–49; Parly Sec., Min. of Civil Aviation, 1950–Oct. 1951. UK Govt Observer, Bikini Tests, 1946; Delegate UN General Assembly, 1946. Formerly: Chm., Parly Labour Party Civil Aviation Sub-Cttee; Chm., Co-operative Party Parly Group; a Lord-in-Waiting, 1965; Parly Under-Sec. of State in CO, 1965–67; Captain, Hon. Corps of Gentlemen at Arms, and Govt Chief Whip, House of Lords, 1967–70, Chief Opposition Whip, 1970–74; Minister of State for Industry, and Deputy Leader, House of Lords, 1974–75. Special Adviser to Chm., British Aircraft Corp., 1970–74. Chm. Supervisory Bd, Airbus Industrie, 1978–80. Pres., British Air Line Pilots Assoc., 1978–82 (Vice-Pres., 1965–77). Companion, RAeS, 1978. FRSA 1979. JP Co. of London, 1963. Hon. DSc Cranfield, 1981. *Address:* 27 Margin Drive, SW19.

BESWICK, John Reginald, CBE 1973; FCIArb; FBIM; *b* 16 Aug. 1919; *s* of Malcolm Holland Beswick and Edythe Beswick (*née* Bednall); *m* 1943, Nadine Caruth Moore Pryde; one *s* two *d*. *Educ:* Manchester Grammar Sch.; Rossall Sch.; Trinity College, Cambridge (MA). Sub-Lt RNVR, 1940–42: anti submarine trawlers, N and S Atlantic; Lt RNVR, 1942–46: submarines, home waters and Far East. Called to Bar, Lincoln's Inn, 1947. Practised at Chancery Bar, 1947–51. Sec., Mullard Ltd, 1951–62; Jt Sec., Philips Electrical Industries Ltd, 1953–62; Dir, Mullard Equipment Ltd, 1955–62; Dir, Soc. of Motor Manufrs & Traders Ltd, 1963–79; Dir-Gen., British Ports Assoc., 1980–83; Dir, Mersey Docks and Harbour Co., 1984–. Member: CBI Council, 1965–79; Council, Inst. of Advanced Motorists, 1966–76. UK delegate, Bureau Permanent International des Constructeurs d'Automobiles, 1966–79. FCIArb 1978. FRSA 1954; FBIM 1982. Asst, Worshipful Co. of Coachmakers, 1973–79. *Recreations:* golf, fly-fishing, reading. *Address:* White House, Redhill, near Buntingford, Herts SG9 0TG. *T:* Broadfield 256. *Clubs:* Naval and Military; Hampstead Golf.

BETHE, Prof. Hans Albrecht, PhD; Professor of Theoretical Physics, Cornell University, 1937–75, now Professor Emeritus; *b* Strassburg, Germany, 2 July 1906; *m* 1939, Rose Ewald; one *s* one *d*. *Educ:* Goethe Gymnasium, Frankfurt on Main; Univs of Frankfurt and Munich. PhD Munich, 1928. Instructor in Theoretical Physics, Univs of Frankfurt, Stuttgart, Munich and Tübingen, 1928–33; Lectr, Univs of Manchester and Bristol, England, 1933–35; Asst Prof., Cornell Univ., Ithaca, 1935–37. Dir, Theoretical Physics Div. of Los Alamos Atomic Scientific Laboratory, 1943–46. Sabbatic leave to Cambridge Univ., academic year, 1955–56. Mem., President's Science Adv. Cttee, 1956–59. Member: Nat. Acad. Sciences; Amer. Physical Soc.; Amer. Astron. Soc.; For. Mem., Royal Society. Holds hon. doctorates in Science. US Medal of Merit, 1946; Planck Medal, German Physical Soc., 1955; Eddington Medal, Royal Astronomical Soc., 1961; Enrico Fermi Award, US Atomic Energy Commn, 1961; Nobel Prize for Physics, 1967. *Publications:* (jt author) Elementary Nuclear Theory, 1947; Mesons and Fields, 1955; Quantum Mechanics of One- and Two-Electron Atoms, 1957; Intermediate Quantum Mechanics, 1964; contributions to: Handbuch der Physik, 1933, 1954; Reviews of Mod. Physics, 1936–37; Physical Review. *Address:* Laboratory of Nuclear Studies, Cornell University, Ithaca, NY 14853, USA.

BETHEL, David Percival, CBE 1983; Director, Leicester Polytechnic, since 1973; *b* Bath, 7 Dec. 1923; *m* 1943, Margaret Elizabeth, *d* of late Alexander Wrigglesworth; one *s* one *d*. *Educ:* King Edward VII Sch., Bath; Crypt Grammar Sch., Glos; West of England Coll. of Art; Bristol Univ., 1946–51; NDD, ATD, FRSA, FSAE, FSIAD, ARWA. Served with RN, Far East, 1943–45. Lectr, Stafford Coll. of Art, 1951–56; Deputy Principal, Coventry Coll. of Art, 1956–65; Principal, Coventry Coll. of Art, 1965–69; Dep. Dir, Leicester Polytechnic, 1969–73. Pres., Nat. Soc. for Art Educn, 1965–66; Member: Nat. Adv. Cttee for Art Educn, 1965–71; Jt Summerson Coldstream Cttee, 1968–70; The Design Council, 1980–; Nat. Adv. Bd for Local Authority Higher Educn, 1983–; Chairman: CNAA Cttee for Art and Design (and Research Degrees Sub-Cttee), 1975–81; Cttee of Dirs of Polytechnics, 1978–80; Vice-Chm., Inter-Univs and Polytechnics Council for Higher Educn Overseas. Sometime Design Consultant to Massey Ferguson, Van Heusen, Monotype Corp., etc. British Council Adviser to Hong Kong Govt, 1971–; Chm., UGC/NAB Town & Country Planning Courses Cttee, 1985–86; Member: Hong Kong UPGC, 1982–; World Council, INSEA; Council of Europe; Chairman: Cyril Wood Meml Trust; Leicester Haymarket Theatre, 1979–85. Paintings and prints in Glos. Libraries, Stafford Art Gallery, Coventry, RWA, private collections. Mem., Worshipful Co. of Frame-Work Knitters. Aust. Commonwealth Travelling Fellowship, 1979. Hon. LLD Leicester, 1982. *Recreations:* travel; study of art, design, architecture; archæology and music. *Address:* Leicester Polytechnic, PO Box 143, Leicester LE1 9BH. *Club:* Athenæum.

BETHEL, Martin; QC 1983; a Recorder of the Crown Court, since 1979; *b* 12 March 1943; *o s* of late Rev. Ralph Bethel and of Enid Bethel; *m* 1974, Kathryn Denby; two *s* one *d*. *Educ:* Kingswood Sch.; Fitzwilliam Coll., Cambridge (MA, LLM). Called to the Bar, Inner Temple, 1965; North-Eastern Circuit (Circuit Junior, 1969). *Recreations:* family, music, travel, skiing, golf. *Address:* (chambers) Pearl Chambers, 22 East Parade, Leeds LS1 5BU. *T:* Leeds 452702.

BETHELL, family name of **Barons Bethell** and **Westbury.**

BETHELL, 4th Baron *cr* 1922, of Romford; **Nicholas William Bethell;** Bt 1911; Member (C) European Parliament, since 1975, elected Member for London North-West, since 1979; free-lance writer; *b* 19 July 1938; *s* of Hon. William Gladstone Bethell (*d* 1964) (3rd *s* of 1st Baron), and of Ann Margaret Bethell (*née* Barlow, now Don); *S* kinsman, 1967; *m* 1964, Cecilia Mary (marr. diss. 1971, she *d* 1977), *er d* of Prof. A. M. Honeyman, *qv*; two *s*. *Educ:* Harrow; Pembroke Coll., Cambridge. On editorial staff of Times Literary Supplement, 1962–64; a Script Editor in BBC Radio Drama, 1964–67. A Lord in Waiting (Govt Whip, House of Lords), June 1970–Jan. 1971. Chm., Friends of Cyprus, 1981–; Vice-Chm., European Parlt Human Rights Sub-Cttee, 1984–. *Publications:* Gomulka: his Poland and his Communism, 1969; The War Hitler Won, 1972; The Last Secret, 1974; Russia Besieged, 1977; The Palestine Triangle, 1979; The Great Betrayal, 1984; *translations:* Six Plays, by Slawomir Mrozek, 1967; Elegy to John Donne, by Joseph Brodsky, 1967; Cancer Ward, by A. Solzhenitsyn, 1968; The Love Girl and the Innocent, by A. Solzhenitsyn, 1969; The Ascent of Mount Fuji, by Chingiz Aitmatov, 1975; dramatic works for radio and TV; occasional journalism. *Recreations:* poker, cricket. *Heir:* *s* Hon. James Nicholas Bethell [*b* 1 Oct. 1967. *Educ:* Harrow]. *Address:* 73 Sussex Square, W2 2SS. *T:* 01–402 6877. *Clubs:* Garrick, Pratt's.

BETHELL, Maj.-Gen. Donald Andrew Douglas Jardine; Warden, Sackville College, since 1981; *b* 6 Feb. 1921; *e s* of D. L. Bethell, Stourbridge, near Birmingham, and L. K. Bethell; *m* 1946, Pamela Mary Woosnam; two *s*. *Educ:* Sherborne Sch., Dorset. Commnd RA, 1940; Regimental Service, 1940–47; Staff and Regimental appts, 1947–66; CRA, 3rd Div., 1966–68; Dep. Commandant, Staff Coll., 1969–72; Pres., Regular Commissions Bd, 1972–75. Col Comdt, RA, 1978–83. *Recreations:* sailing, fishing, golf, shooting. *Address:* Sackville College, East Grinstead, W Sussex. *T:* East Grinstead 26561; Yacht Acquest. *Club:* Royal Cruising.

BETHELL, Richard Anthony; Lord-Lieutenant of Humberside, since 1983; *b* 22 March 1922; *s* of late William Adrian Bethell and Cicely Bethell (*née* Cotterell); *m* 1945, Lady Jane Pleydell-Bouverie, *d* of 7th Earl of Radnor, KG, KCVO; two *s* two *d*. *Educ:* Eton. JP, ER Yorks, 1950; DL 1975, High Sheriff 1976–77, Vice Lord-Lieutenant 1980–83, Humberside. *Address:* Rise Park, Hull HU11 5BL. *T:* Skirlaugh 62241.

BETHUNE, Sir Alexander Maitland Sharp, 10th Bt (NS), *cr* 1683; retired; Director: Copytec Services Ltd, 1964–86; Contoura Photocopying Ltd, 1952–86; *b* 28 March 1909; *o s* of late Alexander Bethune, JP, DL, of Blebo, Cupar, 9th Bt of Scotscraig, and Elisabeth Constance Carnegie (*d* 1935), 3rd *d* of Frederick Lewis Maitland Heriot of Ramornie, Fife; *S* father, 1917; *m* 1955, Ruth Mary, *d* of J. H. Hayes; one *d*. *Educ:* Eton; Magdalene Coll., Cambridge. *Recreations:* golf, nature. *Address:* 21 Victoria Grove, W8 5RW.

BETHUNE, Hon. Sir (Walter) Angus, Kt 1979; pastoralist; *b* 10 Sept. 1908; *s* of Frank Pogson Bethune and Laura Eileen Bethune; *m* 1936, Alexandra P., *d* of P. A. Pritchard; one *s* one *d*. *Educ:* Hutchin's Sch., Hobart; Launceston Church of England Grammar Sch. Served War, RAAF Air Crew, Middle East, 1940–43. Member, Hamilton Municipal Council, 1936–56, resigned (Dep. Warden, 1955–56). MHA, Wilmot, Tasmania, 1946–75, resigned; Leader of Opposition, 1960–69; Premier and Treasurer, Tasmania, 1969–72. Leader of Liberal Party, 1960–72, resigned. President: Clarendon Children's Homes, 1977–83; St John's Ambulance Brigade (Tasmania), 1979–86. OStJ 1982. *Address:* Dunrobin, Ouse, Tasmania 7461, Australia. *Clubs:* Tasmanian; Naval, Military and Air Force; Royal Autocar of Tasmania.

BETT, Michael, MA; Managing Director Local Communications Services Division, British Telecommunications, since 1985; *b* 18 Jan. 1935; *s* of Arthur Bett, OBE and Nina Daniells; *m* 1959, Christine Angela Reid; one *s* two *d*. *Educ:* St Michael's Coll.; Aldenham Sch.; Pembroke Coll., Cambridge. FIPM, CBIM. Dir, Industrial Relations, Engrg Employers' Fedn, 1970–72; Personnel Dir, General Electric Co. Ltd, 1972–77; Dir of Personnel, BBC, 1977–81; Bd Mem. for Personnel, 1981–84, Corporate Dir, Personnel and Corporate Services, 1984–85, BT. Member: Pay Bd, 1973–74; Training Levy Exemption Referee, 1975–82; Civil Service Arbitration Tribunal, 1977–83; Cttee of Inquiry into UK Prison Services, 1978–79; Cttee of Inquiry into Water Service Dispute, 1983; NHS Management Inquiry, 1983; Armed Forces Pay Review Body, 1983–; Civil Service Coll. Adv. Council, 1983–; MSC, 1985–. Member: Court and Council, Cranfield Inst. of Technology; Council, Inst. Manpower Studies. Governor, Forest Sch., Snaresbrook, 1984–. Mem., RTS. FRSA. *Recreations:* television and radio, theatre, cooking, gardening. *Address:* The Spinney, Lodge Road, Bromley, Kent. *T:* 01–460 2846.

BETTLEY, F(rancis) Ray, TD 1945; MD; FRCP; Physician for Diseases of the Skin, Middlesex Hospital, London, 1946–74, now Emeritus; Physician, St John's Hospital for Diseases of the Skin, London, 1947–74, now Emeritus; formerly Dean, Institute of Dermatology, British Postgraduate Medical Federation; Lieutenant-Colonel RAMC, TARO; *b* 18 Aug. 1909; *yr s* of late Francis James Bettley; *m* 1951, Jean Rogers, 2nd *d* of late Archibald Barnet McIntyre; one *s* (one *d* decd), and one adopted *d*. *Educ:* Whitgift Sch., Croydon; University Coll., London; University Coll. Hosp. Medically qualified, 1932; MD 1935; FRCP 1948. Gazetted RAMC TA, 1932; Resident House-appointments, 1932–33; Radcliffe-Crocker Student (Vienna, Strasbourg), 1936; Hon. Dermatologist to

Cardiff Royal Infirmary, 1937; various military hosps in UK and Middle East, 1939–44; Dermatologist and Venereologist, E Africa Comd, 1944–45. Malcolm Morris Lectr, 1959 and 1970; Watson Smith Lectr (RCP), 1960; Emeritus Mem., and former Pres., Brit. Assoc. of Dermatologists; Hon. or Corresp. Mem. of dermatological assocs of Belgium, Denmark, France, Holland, India, Israel, Poland, USA, Venezuela. *Publications:* Skin Diseases in General Practice, 1949; Editor, British Jl of Dermatology, 1949–59; medical papers in various medical jls. *Recreation:* painting. *Address:* Friary House, St Michael's Road, Winchester, Hants. *Club:* Athenæum.

BETTRIDGE, Brig John Bryan, CBE 1983; Principal, Civil Defence College, since 1984; *b* 16 Aug. 1932; *s* of Henry George Bettridge and Dorothy Bettridge; *m* 1959, one *s* one *d. Educ:* Eastbourne Grammar School. Commissioned RA, 1951; regimental duty, 3 RHA and 52 Locating Regt, 1952–59; Instructor, RMA Sandhurst, 1959–61; Student, Staff Coll., Camberley, 1962; War Office, 1964–66; Bty Comd, 1 RHA, 1968–70; Comd, 3 RHA, 1973–75, Hong Kong; Chief Instructor, Tactics, RSA, 1976; Comd RA 2 Div., 1977–78; RCDS 1979; Dep. Comdt, Staff Coll., 1980–82; Comdt, RSA Larkhill, 1983–84. *Recreations:* golf, carpentry. *Address:* Cherry Garth, Main Street, Bishopthorpe, York YO2 1RB. *T:* York 704270.

BETTS, Alan Osborn, PhD, MA, BSc, MRCVS; Principal and Dean, The Royal Veterinary College, since 1970, and Deputy Vice-Chancellor, since 1984, University of London; *b* 11 March 1927; *s* of A. O. and D. S. A. Betts; *m* 1952, Joan M. Battersby; one *s* one *d. Educ:* Royal Veterinary Coll.; Magdalene Coll., Cambridge. Asst in Gen. Practice, 1949; Animal Health Trust Research Scholar, 1950–52; Demonstrator, Univ. of Cambridge, 1952–56; Commonwealth Fund Fellow, Cornell Univ., USA, 1955–56; University Lectr, Cambridge, 1956–64; Prof. of Veterinary Microbiology and Parasitology, Univ. of London, 1964–70. Leverhulme Vis. Fellow, Graduate Sch. of Admin, Univ. of Calif, Davis, 1982. Vice-Chm., Governing Body of Wye Coll., 1976–; University of London: Chairman: Collegiate Council, 1981–84; Cttee of Management, Audiovisual Centre, 1981–; Mem. Court, 1983–. Treasurer: BVA, 1967–70; RCVS, 1978–81. Member: Brit. Pharmacopoeia Commn, 1978– (Chm., Cttee 'N', 1978–); EEC Adv. Cttee on Veterinary Trng, 1980– (Chm., Working Party, 1984–). Governor, Imperial Cancer Research Fund. Dalrymple-Champneys Cup and Medal of BVA, 1978. *Publications:* Viral and Rickettsial Infections of Animals, 1967; papers in microbiological and veterinary jls. *Recreations:* travel, gliding. *Address:* The Royal Veterinary College, Royal College Street, NW1 0TU. *T:* 01–387 2898; Lower Boycott, Stowe, Buckingham. *T:* Buckingham 813287. *Club:* Athenæum.

BETTS, Air Vice-Marshal (Charles) Stephen, CBE 1963; MA; Head of Control and Inspection Division, Agency for the Control of Armaments, WEU, Paris, 1974–84; *b* 8 April 1919; *s* of H. C. Betts, Nuneaton; *m* 1st, 1943, Pauline Mary (deceased), *d* of Lt-Col P. Heath; two *d*; 2nd, 1964, Margaret Doreen, *d* of Col W. H. Young, DSO. *Educ:* King Edward's Sch., Nuneaton; Sidney Sussex Coll., Cambridge. Joined RAF 1941; Air Cdre 1966; Asst Comdt (Eng.), RAF Coll., Cranwell, 1971–72; Air Vice-Marshal 1972; AOC No 24 Group, RAF, 1972–73, retired 1974. *Recreations:* travel, music. *Address:* Cranford, Weston Road, Bath BA1 2XX. *T:* Bath 310995; Le Moulin de Bourgeade, Bourg-du-Bost, 24600 Riberac, France. *T:* (53) 90.96.93. *Club:* Royal Air Force.

BETTS, Lily Edna Minerva, (Mrs John Betts); *see* Mackie, L. E. M.

BETTS, Rt. Rev. Stanley Woodley, CBE 1967; *b* 23 March 1912; *yr s* of Hubert Woodley and Lillian Esther Betts. *Educ:* Perse Sch.; Jesus Coll., Cambridge (MA 1937); Ridley Hall, Cambridge. Curate of St Paul's Cheltenham, 1935–38; Chaplain, RAF, 1938–47 (despatches); Sen. Chaplain of BAFO, Germany, 1946–47; Comdt, RAF Chaplains' Sch., Dowdeswell Court, 1947; Chaplain, Clare Coll., Cambridge, 1947–49; Chaplain, Cambridge Pastorate, 1947–56; Proctor in Convocation, 1952–59; Vicar of Holy Trinity Cambridge, 1949–56; Exam. Chaplain to Bishop of Southwell, 1947–56; Select Preacher to University of Cambridge, 1955; Suffragan Bishop of Maidstone, 1956–66; Archbishop of Canterbury's Episcopal Representative with the three Armed Forces, 1956–66; Dean of Rochester, 1966–77. Chm., Bd of the Church Army, 1970–80; Vice-President: Lee Abbey, 1977–; Wadhurst Coll., 1984– (Chm. Council 1976–84). *Address:* 2 King's Houses, Old Pevensey, Sussex. *T:* Eastbourne 762421. *Club:* National.

BETTS, Stephen; *see* Betts, C. S.

BEVAN, family name of **Baroness Lee of Asheridge.**

BEVAN, (Andrew) David Gilroy; MP (C) Yardley (Birmingham), since 1979; Principal, A. Gilroy Bevan, Incorporated Valuers & Surveyors; *b* 10 April 1928; *s* of Rev. Thomas John Bevan and Norah Gilroy Bevan; *m* 1967, Cynthia Ann Villiers Boulstridge; one *s* three *d. Educ:* Woodrough's Sch., Moseley; King Edward VI Sch., Birmingham. Served on Birmingham City Council and later W Midlands County Council, 1959–81; past Mem., Finance and Gen. Purposes Cttee, and Policy and Priorities Cttee; past Chm., City Transport Cttee, W Midlands PTA and Transport and Highways Cttee. Member, House of Commons Committees: Select Cttee on Transport, 1983–; All Party Leisure and Recreation Industry (Jt Chm., 1979–); Urban Affairs and New Towns (Jt Hon. Sec., 1980–); Tourism (Chm., 1984–). FIAA&S 1962 (Past Chm., W Midlands Br.); FRVA 1971; FSVA 1968 (Past Chm., W Midlands Br.); FFB 1972; FCIA 1954; MRSH 1957. *Recreations:* gardening, walking. *Address:* The Cottage, 12 Wentworth Road, Four Oaks Park, Sutton Coldfield, West Midlands B74 2SG. *T:* (home) 021–308 3292; (business) 021–308 6319. *Club:* Carlton.
See also P. G. Bevan.

BEVAN, Cecil Wilfrid Luscombe, CBE 1965; Principal, 1966–Sept. 1987, and Hon. Fellow, since 1982, University College, Cardiff; *b* 2 April 1920; *s* of Benjamin Cecil Bevan and Maud Luscombe; *m* 1st, 1944, Elizabeth Bondfield (*d* 1984), *d* of Henry Dale Bondfield; four *s*; 2nd, 1984, Dr Beatrice Avalos. *Educ:* University Coll. of Wales, Aberystwyth; University Coll., London. BSc Wales 1940; PhD London 1949; FRSC (FRIC 1957); DSc London 1971. Served Royal Welch Fusiliers and Nigeria Regt, 1940–46 (despatches). Univ. of Exeter, 1949–53; Prof. and Head of Dept of Chemistry, Univ. of Ibadan, 1953–66, Vice Principal and Dep. Vice-Chancellor, 1960–64; Vice-Chancellor, Univ. of Wales, 1973–75 and 1981–83. Member: Tropical Products Inst. Adv. Cttee, 1971–77; Council, University of Cape Coast, Ghana, 1967–74; Welsh Council, 1968–71; Chm., Conciliation Cttee of Wales and SW Race Rel. Bd, 1968–72; Governor Welbeck Coll.; Prof. Associé Univ. de Strasbourg, 1965. Fellow UCL, 1969. Hon. DSc, Univ. of Ibadan, 1973 (Palmes Académiques, 1986). *Publications:* papers, mainly in Jl of Chemical Soc., 1951–. *Recreation:* labouring. *Address:* University College, Cathays Park, Cardiff; (from Sept. 1987) Flat 7b, The Cathedral Green, Llandaff, Cardiff CF5 2EB. *Clubs:* Athenæum, Royal Commonwealth Society; Cardiff and County.

BEVAN, Rear-Adm. Christopher Martin, CB 1978; Under Treasurer Gray's Inn, since 1980; *b* London, 22 Jan. 1923; *s* of Humphrey C. Bevan and Mary F. Bevan (*née* Mackenzie); *m* 1948, Patricia C. Bedford; one *s* three *d. Educ:* Stowe Sch., Bucks; Victoria Univ., Wellington, NZ. Trooper in Canterbury Yeoman Cavalry (NZ Mounted Rifles), 1941; joined RN as Ord. Seaman, 1942; served remainder of 1939–45 war, Mediterranean

and N Atlantic; commissioned 1943; Comdr 1958; Captain 1967; Supt Weapons and Radio, Dockyard Dept, MoD (Navy), 1967–70; Asst Dir, Weapons Equipment (Surface), later, Captain Surface Weapons Acceptance, Weapons Dept, MoD (Navy), 1970–73; Dir, Naval Officer Appts (Engrs), 1973–76; ADC to the Queen, 1976; Rear-Adm. 1976; Flag Officer Medway and Port Adm. Chatham, 1976–78. *Recreations:* photography, theatre, music, gardening. *Address:* c/o Messrs C. Hoare and Co., 37 Fleet Street, EC4P 4DQ.

BEVAN, David Gilroy; *see* Bevan, A. D. G.

BEVAN, (Edward) Julian; a Senior Prosecuting Counsel at the Central Criminal Court, since 1985, *b* 23 Oct. 1940; *m* 1966, Bronwen Mary Windsor Lewis; two *s* two *d. Educ:* Eton. Called to the Bar, Gray's Inn, 1962; Standing Counsel for the Inland Revenue, 1974; Jun. Prosecuting Counsel, Central Criminal Court, 1977. *Address:* 30 Halsey Street, SW3. *T:* 01–584 1316. *Clubs:* White's, Garrick.

BEVAN, Prof. Hugh Keith; JP; Professor of Law, University of Hull, since 1969; *b* 8 Oct. 1922; *s* of Thomas Edward Bevan and Marjorie Avril Bevan (*née* Trick); *m* 1950, Mary Harris; one *s* one *d. Educ:* Neath Grammar Sch.; University Coll. of Wales, Aberystwyth. LLB 1949, LLM 1966. Called to the Bar, Middle Temple, 1959. Served RA, 1943–46. University of Hull: Lectr in Law, 1950–61; Sen. Lectr in Law, 1961–69; Pro Vice-Chancellor, 1979–82. Chm., Rent Assessment Cttees, 1982–. JP Kingston-upon-Hull, 1972 (Chm. of Bench, 1984–). *Publications:* Source Book of Family Law (with P. R. H. Webb), 1964; Law Relating to Children, 1973; (with M. L. Parry) The Children Act 1975, 1978; numerous articles. *Recreations:* music, golf. *Address:* Faculty of Law, University of Hull, Cottingham Road, Hull HU6 7RX. *T:* Hull 46311 ext. 7736.

BEVAN, John Stuart; Secretary, National Advisory Body for Public Sector (formerly Local Authority) Higher Education, since 1982; *b* 19 Nov. 1935; *s* of Frank Oakland and Ruth Mary Bevan; *m* 1960, Patricia Vera Beatrice (*née* Joyce); two *s* two *d. Educ:* Eggar's Grammar Sch.; Jesus Coll., Oxford; S Bartholomew's Hosp. Med. Coll. MA, MSc; FInstP. Health Physicist, UK Atomic Energy Authority, 1960–62; Lectr, then Sen. Lectr in Physics, Polytechnic of the South Bank (previously Borough Polytechnic), 1962–73; Inner London Education Authority: Asst Educn Officer, then Sen. Asst Educn Officer, 1973–76; Dep. Educn Officer, 1977–79; Dir of Educn, 1979–82. Former Member, National Executive Committees: Nat. Union of Teachers; Assoc. of Teachers in Technical Instns (Pres., 1972–73). *Publications:* occasional papers in the educnl press. *Recreations:* Scouting (Asst Comr, Kent), mountaineering. *Address:* 4 Woodland Way, Bidborough, Tunbridge Wells, Kent TN4 0UX. *T:* Tunbridge Wells 27461.

BEVAN, Julian; *see* Bevan, E. J.

BEVAN, Rt. Rev. Kenneth Graham; Assistant Bishop, Diocese of Wakefield, 1968–77; *b* 27 Sept. 1898; *s* of late Rev. James Alfred Bevan, MA; *m* 1927, Jocelyn Duncan Barber; three *d. Educ:* The Grammar Sch., Great Yarmouth; London Coll. of Divinity. Deacon, 1923; Priest, 1924; Curate of Holy Trinity, Tunbridge Wells, 1923–25; Missionary, Diocese of Western China, 1925–36, Diocese of Eastern Szechwan, 1936–40; Bishop of Eastern Szechwan, 1940–50; Vicar of Woolhope, 1951–66; Rural Dean, Hereford (South), 1955–66; Prebendary de Moreton et Whaddon, Hereford Cathedral, 1956–66; Master of Archbishop Holgate's Hosp., Wakefield, 1966–77. *Address:* Grimston Court, Hull Road, York YO1 5LE.

BEVAN, Leonard; HM Diplomatic Service, retired; *b* 16 Nov. 1926; *s* of Richard (Dick) and Sarah Bevan; *m* 1st, 1953, Muriel Anne Bridger (*d* 1979); 2nd, 1981, Jeanette Elfreda Phillips. *Educ:* Swansea and Gowerton Grammar Schs; UCW, Aberystwyth (BA Hons). RAF, 1948–50. BoT, 1950 (Private Sec. to Parly Sec., 1952–54); UK Trade Comr: Karachi, 1954; Kuala Lumpur, 1957; Principal British Trade Comr and Econ. Adviser to High Comr, Accra, 1959; Nairobi, 1964; Commonwealth Office (later FCO), 1968; Counsellor (Econ. and Commercial), Canberra, 1970; Head, SW Pacific Dept, FCO, 1974; Counsellor (Economic), Brasilia, 1976–79. *Recreations:* bird spotting, clock repairing and restoring, flower gardening. *Address:* Waun Wen, Abercastle Road, Trefin, Dyfed. *T:* Croesgoch 570 and 490.

BEVAN, Sir Martyn Evan E.; *see* Evans-Bevan.

BEVAN, Michael Guy Molesworth; Lord Lieutenant of Cambridgeshire, since 1985; *b* 23 Aug. 1926; *s* of late Temple Percy Molesworth Bevan and Amy Florence Bevan (*née* Briscoe); *m* 1948, Mary Brocklebank; three *s* one *d. Educ:* Eton College. Grenadier Guards, 1944–47. Joined City of London company, 1948; Director, Briscoes Ltd, Walford Maritime Hldgs Ltd, 1953–85; farmer, 1957–. Governor, Papworth Village Settlement, 1962–, Chm., 1980–. Syndic, Fitzwilliam Mus. 1985–. KStJ 1986. *Recreations:* classical music, cricket, bridge. *Address:* Longstowe Hall, Longstowe, Cambridge CB3 7UH. *T:* Caxton 203.

BEVAN, Nicolas; Assistant Under Secretary of State (Defence Staff), Ministry of Defence, since 1986; *b* 8 March 1942; *s* of late Roger Bevan, BM, and Diana Mary Bevan (*née* Freeman); *m* 1982, Helen Christine, *d* of N. A. Berry. *Educ:* Westminster Sch.; Corpus Christi Coll., Oxford (MA LitHum). Ministry of Defence: Asst Principal, 1964; Principal, 1969; Private Sec. to Chief of Air Staff, 1970–73; Cabinet Office, 1973–75; Asst Sec., 1976; RCDS 1981; Asst Under Sec. of State (Gen. Finance), 1985–86. *Recreation:* gardening. *Address:* c/o Ministry of Defence, SW1. *Club:* Royal Commonwealth Society.

BEVAN, Prof. Peter Gilroy, CBE 1983; MB, ChB; FRCS; Consultant Surgeon, Dudley Road Hospital, Birmingham, since 1958; Professor of Surgery and Postgraduate Medical Education, University of Birmingham, since 1981; *b* 13 Dec. 1922; *s* of Rev. Thomas John Bevan and Norah (*née* Gilroy); *m* 1949, Patricia Joan (*née* Laurie) (*d* 1985); one *s* one *d. Educ:* King Edward VI High Sch., Birmingham; Univ. of Birmingham Medical Sch. (MB, ChB 1946; ChM 1958). LRCP MRCS 1946, FRCS 1952; FRCSI 1984. Served RAMC, BAOR, 1947–49 (Captain). Demonstrator in Anatomy, Univ. of Birmingham, 1949–51; Resident Surgical Officer, Birmingham Children's Hosp., 1954–55; Lectr in Surgery and Sen. Surgical Registrar, Queen Elizabeth Hosp., Birmingham, 1954–58; WHO Vis. Prof. of Surgery to Burma, 1969; Director, Board of Graduate Clinical Studies, Univ. of Birmingham, 1978–. Mem. Council, RCS, 1971–83, Vice-Pres., 1980–82; Founder Chm., W Midlands Oncology Assoc., 1974–79; Vice-Pres., Brit. Assoc. of Surgical Oncology, 1975–78; President: Pancreatic Soc. of Gt Britain, 1977. British Inst. of Surgical Technologists, 1980–; Assoc. of Surgeons of Gt Britain and Ireland, 1984–85 (Fellow, 1960–; Mem. Council, 1975–). EEC: UK representative: on Monospecialist Section of Surgery, 1975–84; on Adv. Cttee on Medical Trng, 1980–85. Civil Consultant Advr in Gen. Surgery to RN, 1983–. Chm., Adv. Cttee of Deans, 1986–. *Publications:* Reconstructive Procedures in Surgery, 1982; various surgical papers in BMJ, Brit. Jl Surgery, Lancet, Annals of RCS. *Recreations:* inland waterways, golf, photography. *Address:* 10 Russell Road, Moseley, Birmingham B13 8RD. *T:* 021–449 3055. *Club:* Edgbaston Golf (Birmingham).
See also A. D. G. Bevan.

BEVAN, Richard Thomas, MD; FRCP; Chief Medical Officer, Welsh Office, 1965–77, retired; *b* 13 Jan. 1914; *s* of T. Bevan, Bridgend; *m* 1940, Dr Beryl Bevan (*née* Badham) (*d* 1986); two *s* one *d*. *Educ:* Welsh Nat. Sch. of Medicine. MB, BCh 1939; DPH 1941; MD 1955; FRCP; FFCM. Resident Medical Officer, St David's Hosp., Cardiff; RAF, 1941–46; Lecturer, Welsh Nat. Sch. of Medicine, 1946–68; Deputy County MO, Glamorgan CC, 1948–62. QHP 1974–77. *Address:* 40 Richard Cooper Road, Shenstone, near Lichfield. *T:* Shenstone 481 070.

BEVAN, Sir Timothy (Hugh), Kt 1984; Chairman, Barclays Bank PLC, 1981–May 1987; Director, The Union Discount Company of London Ltd, since 1975; *b* 24 May 1927; *y s* of late Hugh Bevan and Pleasance (*née* Scrutton); *m* 1952, Pamela, *e d* of late Norman Smith and late Margaret Smith; two *s* two *d*. *Educ:* Eton. Lieut Welsh Guards. Called to Bar, 1950. Joined Barclays Bank Ltd, 1950; Vice-Chm., 1968–73; Dep. Chm., 1973–81; Chm., Barclays Bank UK Management Ltd, 1972–80. Chm., Cttee of London Clearing Bankers, 1983–85. Mem., Institut International d'Etudes Bancaires. *Recreations:* sailing, gardening. *Address:* c/o Barclays Bank PLC, 54 Lombard Street, EC3P 3AH. *Clubs:* Cavalry and Guards, Royal Ocean Racing; Royal Yacht Squadron.

BEVAN, Rear-Adm. Timothy Michael, CB 1986; Assistant Chief of the Defence Staff (Intelligence), since 1984; *b* 7 April 1931; *s* of Thomas Richard and Margaret Richmond Bevan; *m* 1970, Sarah Knight; three *s*. *Educ:* Eton College. psc(n), jssc. Entered RN, 1949; commanded: HMS Decoy, 1966; HMS Caprice, 1967–68; HMS Minerva, 1971–72; HMS Ariadne, 1976–78; HMS Ariadne, and Captain of 8th Frigate Sqdn, 1980–82; Britannia Royal Naval Coll., 1982–84. *Address:* c/o Ministry of Defence, Whitehall, SW1. *Club:* Brooks's.

BEVAN, Walter Harold, CBE 1977; FCIS; Chairman, Gateshead District Health Authority (formerly of Gateshead Area Health Authority), 1977–84; *b* 22 May 1916; *s* of late Walter Bevan and Sarah (*née* Grainger); *m* 1958, Patricia Edna Sadler, *d* of late Sir Sadler Forster, CBE, DCL; twin *s* and *d*. *Educ:* Gateshead Sec. Sch. FCIS 1961. 5th Bn Royal Northumberland Fusiliers, TA, 1938–42; served War: commissioned RA; Arakan campaign, Burma, with 81st W African Div., 1942–46; 4/5 Bn Royal Northumberland Fusiliers, TA, 1947–52. Asst to Sec., North Eastern Trading Estates Ltd, 1937, Chief Accountant 1956; English Industrial Estates Corporation: Chief Accountant, 1960; Sec., 1966; Finance Dir and Sec., 1973; Chief Exec. and Chm., Management Bd, 1974–79. Governor, Gateshead Technical Coll., 1971–81. *Publications:* articles on industrial estates and distribution of industry. *Recreations:* public and voluntary services, angling, reading. *Address:* Cornerways, Lyndhurst Grove, Low Fell, Gateshead NE9 6AX. *T:* Low Fell 876827.

BEVERIDGE, Prof. Gordon Smith Grieve, FRSE; FEng 1984; FIChemE; President and Vice-Chancellor, The Queen's University of Belfast, since 1986; *b* 28 Nov. 1933; *s* of late Victor Beattie Beveridge and Elizabeth Fairbairn Beveridge (*née* Grieve); *m* 1963, Geertruida Hillegonda Johanna Bruyn; two *s* one *d*. *Educ:* Inverness Royal Academy; Univ. of Glasgow (BSc, 1st Cl. Hons Chem. Engrg); Royal College of Science and Technology, Glasgow (ARCST 1st Cl. Hons Chem. Engrg); Univ. of Edinburgh (PhD). Asst Lectr, Univ. of Edinburgh, 1956–60; post-doctoral Harkness Fellow of Commonwealth Fund, New York, at Univ. of Minnesota, 1960–62; Vis. Prof., Univ. of Texas, 1962–64; Lectr, Univ. of Edinburgh and Heriot-Watt Univ., 1962–67; Sen. Lectr/Reader, Heriot-Watt Univ., 1967–71; Prof. of Chem. Engrg and Head of Dept of Chem. and Process Engrg, Univ. of Strathclyde, Glasgow, 1971–86. Consultant to industry. Institution of Chemical Engineers: Fellow, 1969–; Vice-Pres., 1979–81, 1983–84, Pres., 1984–85; Exec. Cttee, 1981–86; Hon. Librarian, 1977–84; Member: Council, 1975–76, 1977–; Careers Cttee, 1965–73; Research Cttee, 1973–79; Engrg Practice Cttee, 1977–84; Sen. Academics Cttee, 1967–86; Technical Responses Bd, 1979–84; Scottish Branch: Sec., 1963–71; Vice-Chm., 1972–74; Chm., 1974–76. Society of Chemical Industry, London: Mem. Council, 1978–; Vice-Pres., 1985–86; Chm. of W of Scotland Section, 1978–86. Council of Engineering Institutions (Scotland): Member, 1977–82; Vice-Chm., 1979–80; Chm., 1980–81; Organiser of 1981 Exhibn, Engineering in the '80s, Edinburgh. Council for National Academic Awards: Chemical, Instrumentation and Systems Engrg Bd, 1976–81: Vice-Chm., 1979–81; Engineering Bd, 1981–84. Science and Engineering Research Council (formerly Science Research Council), various committees: 1973–76, 1980–83; Mem., Engrg Bd; Chm., Process Engrg Cttee (formerly Chemical Engrg Cttee), 1983–86. Engineering Council: Mem., 1981–; Vice-Chm., 1984–85; Chm., Standing Cttee for Professional Instns, 1982–. NEDO: Mem., Chemicals EDC, 1983–; Chm., Petrochemicals Sector Wkg Gp, 1983–. Chm., Cremer and Warner Gp, 1985–. Associate Editor, Computers and Chemical Engineering, 1974–. *Publications:* Optimization - theory and practice (with R. S. Schechter), 1970; multiple pubns in learned jls. *Recreations:* Scottish and Dutch history, Marlburian war-games, family golf, hill-walking. *Address:* The Office of the Vice-Chancellor, The Queen's University of Belfast, Belfast, Northern Ireland BT7 1NN. *T:* Belfast 245133. *Club:* Caledonian.

BEVERIDGE, John Caldwell, QC 1979; Recorder, Western Circuit, since 1975; *b* 26 Sept. 1937; *s* of William Ian Beardmore Beveridge, *qv*; *m* 1972, Frances Ann Clunes Grant Martineau. *Educ:* privately; Jesus Coll., Cambridge (MA, LLB). Called to the Bar, Inner Temple, 1963, Bencher, 1985; Western Circuit; called to the Bar, NSW, 1975, QC (NSW), 1980. Partner, Beveridge & Forwood, Zurich. Conservative Mem., Westminster City Council, 1968–72. Freeman, City of London. Jt Master, Westmeath Foxhounds, 1976–79. *Recreations:* hunting, shooting, travelling. *Address:* 5 St James's Chambers, Ryder Street, SW1Y 6QA. *T:* 01–839 2660. *Clubs:* Brooks's, Turf.

BEVERIDGE, William Ian Beardmore, MA, ScD Cantab; DVSc Sydney; Professor of Animal Pathology, Cambridge, 1947–75; Emeritus Fellow of Jesus College; *b* 1908; *s* of J. W. C. and Ada Beveridge; *m* 1935, Patricia, *d* of Rev. E. C. Thomson; one *s*. *Educ:* Cranbrook Sch., Sydney; St Paul's Coll., University of Sydney. ScD Cantab 1974. Research bacteriologist, McMaster Animal Health Laboratory, Sydney, 1931–37; Commonwealth Fund Service Fellow at Rockefeller Inst. and at Washington, 1938–39; Walter and Eliza Hall Inst. for Medical Research, Melbourne, 1941–46; Visiting Worker, Pasteur Inst., Paris, 1946–47; Vis. Prof., Ohio State Univ., 1953; Guest Lectr, Norwegian Veterinary Sch., 1955; first Wesley W. Spink Lectr on Comparative Medicine, Minnesota, 1971. Consultant: WHO, Geneva, 1964–79; Bureau of Animal Health, Canberra, 1979–84; Vis. Fellow, John Curtin Sch. of Med. Res., ANU, Canberra, 1979–84, Fellow, University House, 1980–85. Chm. Permanent Cttee of the World Veterinary Assoc., 1957–75. DVM (*hc*) Hanover, 1963; Hon. Associate RCVS, 1963; Life Fellow, Aust. Vet. Assoc., 1963; Hon. Member: British Veterinary Assoc., 1970; Amer. Vet. Med. Assoc., 1973; World Veterinary Congresses, 1975; Univ. House, Canberra, 1986; Hon. Foreign Mem., Académie Royale de Médicine de Belgique, 1970; Foundation Fellow, Aust. Coll. Vet. Scientists, 1971; Mem., German Acad. for Scientific Research, Leopoldina, 1974; Hon. Dip., Hungarian Microbiological Assoc., Budapest, 1976. Karl F. Meyer Goldheaded Cane Award, 1971; Gamgee Gold Medal, World Vet. Assoc., 1975; Medal of Honour, French Nat. Cttee of World Vet. Assoc., 1976. *Publications:* The Art of Scientific Investigation, 1950; Frontiers in Comparative Medicine, 1972; Influenza: the last great plague, 1977; Seeds of Discovery, 1980; Viral Diseases of Farm Livestock, 1981; Bacterial Diseases of Cattle, Sheep and Goats, 1983; articles on infectious diseases of man and domestic animals and comparative medicine, in scientific jls. *Recreations:* bush-walking, skiing. *Address:* 5 Bellevue Road, Wentworth Falls, Blue Mts, NSW 2782, Australia. *T:* (047) 571606.

See also J C. Beveridge.

BEVERLEY, Maj.-Gen. Henry York La Roche, OBE 1979; Major General Training Reserve and Special Forces Royal Marines, since 1986; *b* 25 Oct. 1935; *s* of Vice-Adm. Sir York Beverley, KBE, CB, and Lady Beverley; *m* 1963, Sally Ann Maclean; two *d*. *Educ:* Wellington College. DS Staff Coll., 1976–78; CO 42 Cdo RM, 1978–80; Comdt CTC RM, 1980–82; Director RM Personnel, MoD, 1983–84; Comd 3 Cdo Bde RM, 1984–86. *Recreations:* cricket, golf, skiing. *Club:* Army and Navy.

BEVERTON, Prof. Raymond John Heaphy, CBE 1968; FRS 1975; FIBiol 1973; Professor of Fisheries Science, Department of Applied Biology, University of Wales Institute of Science and Technology, since 1984; *b* 29 Aug. 1922; *s* of Edgar John Beverton and Dorothy Sybil Mary Beverton; *m* 1947, Kathleen Edith Marner; three *d*. *Educ:* Forest Sch., Snaresbrook; Downing Coll., Cambridge (MA). Cambridge, 1940–42 and 1946–47. Joined Fisheries Research Lab. (MAFF), 1947; Dep. Dir, Fisheries Res., 1959–65; Sec., NERC, 1965–80. Sen. Res. Fellow, Univ. of Bristol, engaged on study of change and adaptation in scientific res. careers, 1981–82; Prog. Integrator, Internat. Fedn of Insts for Advanced Study, 1982–84; Hon. Professorial Fellow, UWIST, 1982–84. Hon. posts during research career: Chm., Comparative Fishing Cttee of ICES, 1957–62; Chm., Res. and Statistics Cttee of Internat. Commn for Northwest Atlantic Fisheries, 1960–63. Member: MAFF Fisheries R & D Bd, 1972–79; NRPB, 1976–80. Head of UK delegn to Intergovernmental Oceanographic Commn, 1981–84; Vis. Lectr in fish population dynamics, Univ. of Southampton, 1982–. Chm., Nat. Scis Adv. Cttee for UNESCO, 1984–85. Pres., Fisheries Soc. of British Isles; Vice-Pres., Freshwater Biological Assoc., 1980–; Mem. Council, Scottish Marine Biol. Assoc., 1984–; Trustee, World Wildlife Fund UK, 1983–85. Editor, Jl ICES, 1983–. *Publications:* (with S. J. Holt) On the Dynamics of Exploited Fish Populations, 1957; (with G. W. D. Findlay) Funding and Policy for Research in the Natural Sciences (in The Future of Research, ed. Geoffrey Oldham), 1982; papers on mathematical basis of fish population dynamics, theory and practice of fisheries conservation and various fisheries research topics. *Recreations:* fishing, sailing, golf, music. *Address:* Montana, Old Roman Road, Langstone, Gwent.

BEVINGTON, Eric Raymond, CMG 1961; *b* 23 Jan. 1914; *s* of late R. Bevington and N. E. Bevington (*née* Sutton); *m* 1939, Enid Mary Selina (*née* Homer); one *s* one *d*. *Educ:* Monkton Combe Sch.; Loughborough Coll.; Queens' Coll., Cambridge. CEng, MIMechE. Cadet, HM Overseas Service, Gilbert and Ellice Islands, 1937; District Officer, Fiji, 1942; Sec., Commn of Enquiry into Cost of Living Allowances, Nigeria, 1945–46; Admin. Officer Cl I, Fiji, 1950; Asst Col Sec. (Devel), Fiji, 1951; Develt Comr, Brunei, 1954; Financial Sec., Fiji, 1958–61, Development Commissioner, 1962–63; Mem., Executive Council, Fiji, 1958–63; Senior Project Engineer, Wrigh Rain Ltd, 1964–67; Appeals Inspector, Min. of Housing and Local Govt, 1967–70; Sen. Housing and Planning Inspector, DoE, 1970–78. Mem., New Forest DC, 1979–83. *Recreations:* golf, sailing, zymurgy. *Address:* Holmans Cottage, Bisterne Close, Burley, Hants. *T:* Burley 3316.

BEVINS, Rt. Hon. John Reginald, PC 1959; *b* 20 Aug. 1908; *e s* of John Milton and Grace Eveline Bevins, Liverpool; *m* 1933, Mary Leonora Jones; three *s*. *Educ:* Dovedale Road and Liverpool Collegiate Schs. Served War of 1939–45; gunner, 1940; Major, RASC, 1944; MEF and Europe. Mem. Liverpool City Council, 1935–50. Contested West Toxteth Div., 1945, and Edge Hill (bye-election), 1947; MP (C) Toxteth Div. of Liverpool, 1950–64; PPS to the Minister of Housing and Local Government, 1951–53; Parliamentary Sec., Ministry of Works, 1953–57, Ministry of Housing and Local Govt, 1957–59; Postmaster-General, 1959–64. *Publication:* The Greasy Pole, 1965. *Address:* 37 Queen's Drive, Liverpool L18 2DT. *T:* 051–722 8484.

See also K. M. Bevins.

BEVINS, Kenneth Milton, CBE 1973; TD 1951; Director: Royal Insurance plc, since 1970; British Aerospace plc, since 1981; *b* 2 Nov. 1918; *yr s* of late John Milton Bevins and Grace Eveline Bevins, Liverpool; *m* 1st, 1940, Joan Harding (*d* 1969); two *d*; 2nd, 1971, Diana B. Sellers, *y d* of Godfrey J. Sellers, Keighley. *Educ:* Liverpool Collegiate Sch. Joined Royal Insurance Co. Ltd, 1937. Served War, 1939–46: 136 Field Regt, RA, incl. with 14th Army in Burma, 1943–46 (Major). Sec., Royal Insurance Co. Ltd, 1957; Gen. Manager, 1963; Dep. Chief Gen. Manager, 1966; Chief Gen. Manager, 1970–80; Director: Trade Indemnity Co. Ltd, 1970–80 (Chm., 1975–80); Mutual & Federal Insurance Co. Ltd, 1971–80. Dir, Fire Protection Assoc., 1963–77 (Chm., 1966–68). Member: Jt Fire Research Organisation Steering Cttee, 1966–68; Home Secretary's Standing Cttee on Crime Prevention, 1967–73; Exec. Cttee, City Communications Centre, 1976–80; Bd, British Aerospace, 1980–81; Govt Cttee to review structure, functions and status of ECGD, 1983–84. Chm., British Insurance Assoc., 1971–73 (Dep. Chm., 1967–71). *Address:* Linton, The Drive, Sevenoaks, Kent. *T:* Sevenoaks 456909. *Clubs:* Oriental, Army and Navy.

See also Rt Hon. J R. Bevins.

BEWES, Rev. Richard Thomas; Rector, All Souls Church, Langham Place, since 1983; *b* 1 Dec. 1934; *s* of Cecil and Sylvia Bewes; *m* 1964, Elisabeth Ingrid Jaques; two *s* one *d*. *Educ:* Marlborough Sch.; Emmanuel Coll., Cambridge (MA); Ridley Hall, Cambridge. Deacon, 1959; priest, 1960; Curate of Christ Church, Beckenham, 1959–65; Vicar: St Peter's, Harold Wood, 1965–74; Emmanuel, Northwood, 1974–83. *Publications:* God in Ward 12, 1973; Advantage Mr Christian, 1975; Talking about Prayer, 1979; The Pocket Handbook of Christian Truth, 1981; John Wesley's England, 1981; The Church Reaches Out, 1981; The Church Overcomes, 1983; On The Way, 1984; Quest for Truth, 1985; Quest for Life, 1985; The Church Marches On, 1986; When God Surprises, 1986. *Recreations:* tennis, photography, audio-visual production. *Address:* 2 All Souls Place, W1N 3DB. *T:* 01–580 6029.

BEWICK, Herbert; barrister; *b* 4 April 1911; *s* of late James Dicker and Elizabeth Jane Bewick. *Educ:* Whitehill Secondary Sch., Glasgow; Royal Grammar Sch., Newcastle upon Tyne; St Catharine's Coll., Cambridge. Called to Bar, Gray's Inn, 1935. Recorder of Pontefract, 1961–67. Chm. of Industrial Tribunal (Newcastle upon Tyne), 1967–72. *Address:* 51 Westgate Road, Newcastle upon Tyne NE1 1SS. *T:* Newcastle 320541; 27 Mitchell Avenue, Jesmond, Newcastle upon Tyne NE2 3JY. *T:* Tyneside 2811138.

BEWICKE-COPLEY, family name of **Baron Cromwell.**

BEWLEY, Edward de Beauvoir; Hon. Mr Justice Bewley; Judge of the High Court of Hong Kong, since 1980; *b* 12 March 1931; *s* of Harold de Beauvoir Bewley and Phyllis Frances Cowdy; *m* 1956, Sheelagh Alice Brown; one *s*; *m* 1968, Mary Gwenefer Jones; three *d*. *Educ:* Shrewsbury School; Trinity College, Dublin. BA, LLB; Barrister at Law. Administrative Officer, Northern Rhodesia, 1956–59; English Bar, 1960–61; Resident Magistrate, Nyasaland, 1961–64; Magistrate, Hong Kong, 1964–76, District Judge, 1976–80. *Recreations:* golf, skiing, squash, reading, music. *Address:* 11 Mansfield Road,

The Peak, Hong Kong. *T:* 5–8496111. *Clubs:* Hong Kong; Royal Irish Yacht (Dun Laoghaire), Royal Hong Kong Golf, Kowloon Cricket.

BEWLEY, Thomas Henry, MA; MD; PRCPsych; FRCPI; Consultant Psychiatrist, Tooting Bec and St Thomas' Hospitals, since 1961; *b* 8 July 1926; *s* of Geoffrey Bewley and Victoria Jane Wilson; *m* 1955, Beulah Knox; one *s* four *d*. *Educ:* St Columba's College, Dublin; Trinity College, Dublin University. MA, MD. Qualified TCD, 1950; trained St Patrick's Hosp., Dublin, Maudsley Hosp., Univ. of Cincinnati. Member: Standing Adv. Cttee on Drug Dependence, 1966–71; Adv. Council on Misuse of Drugs, 1972–84; Consultant Adviser on Drug Dependence to DHSS, 1972–81; Consultant, WHO, 1969–78. Pres., RCPsych, 1984–87 (Dean, 1977–82); Jt Co-founder and Mem. Council, Inst. for Study of Drug Dependence, 1967–. *Publications:* Handbook for Inceptors and Trainees in Psychiatry, 1976, 2nd edn 1980; papers on drug dependence, medical manpower and side effects of drugs. *Address:* 11 Garrads Road, SW16 1JU. *T:* 01–769 1703. *Club:* London Chapter of Irish Georgian Society.

BEXON, Roger, CBE 1985; Chairman, Laporte Industries (Holdings), since 1986; Managing Director, British Petroleum Co. Ltd, 1981–86, and Deputy Chairman, 1983–86; *b* 11 April 1926; *s* of late Macalister Bexon, CBE, and Nora Hope Bexon (*née* Jenner); *m* 1952, Lois Loughran Walling; one *s* one *d*. *Educ:* Denstone Coll. (schol.); St John's Coll., Oxford (MA); Tulsa Univ. (MS). Geologist and petroleum engineer with Trinidad Petroleum Development Co. Ltd, 1946–57; management positions with British Petroleum Co., E Africa, 1958–59; Libya, 1959–60; Trinidad, 1961–64; London, 1964–66; Manager, North Sea Operations, 1966–68; General Manager, Libya, 1968–70; Regional Coordinator, Middle East, London, 1971–73; Gen. Manager, Exploration and Production, London, 1973–76; Managing Director, BP Exploration Co. Ltd, London, 1976–77; Director: Standard Oil Co., 1982–86 (Dir and Sen. Vice Pres., 1977–80); BP Canada Inc., 1983–; BICC, 1985–; Laporte Industries, 1985–. *Publications:* general and technical contribs to internat. jls on oil and energy matters. *Recreations:* reading, golf, Times crossword puzzles. *Address:* c/o Laporte Industries (Holdings), Hanover House, 14 Hanover Square, W1R 0BE.

BEYFUS, Drusilla Norman; writer, editor, broadcaster; *d* of Norman Beyfus and Florence Noel Barker; *m* 1956, Milton Shulman, *qv*; one *s* two *d*. *Educ:* Royal Naval Sch; Channing Sch. Woman's Editor, Sunday Express, 1950; columnist, Daily Express, 1952–55; Associate Editor, Queen magazine, 1956; Home Editor, The Observer, 1963; Associate Editor, Daily Telegraph magazine, 1966; Editor, Brides and Setting Up Home magazine, 1972–79; Associate Editor, Vogue magazine, 1979–. TV and radio appearances, incl. Call My Bluff and talks programmes. *Publications:* (with Anne Edwards) Lady Behave, 1956 (rev. edn 1969); The English Marriage, 1968; The Brides Book, 1981; contrib. to Sunday Times, Punch, New Statesman. *Recreations:* walking, modern art, cooking. *Address:* 51G Eaton Square, SW1. *T:* 01–235 7162.

BEYNON, Ernest Geoffrey; Joint General Secretary, Assistant Masters and Mistresses Association, since 1979; *b* 4 Oct. 1926; *s* of late Frank William George and of Frances Alice Pretoria Beynon; *m* 1956, Denise Gwendoline Rees; two *s* one *d*. *Educ:* Borden Grammar Sch., Kent; Univ. of Bristol, 1944–47, 1949–50 (BSc (Hons Maths) 1947, CertEd 1950). National Service, Royal Artillery, 1947–49. Mathematics Master, Thornbury Grammar Sch., Glos, 1950–56; Mathematics Master and Sixth Form Master, St George Grammar Sch., Bristol, 1956–64; Asst Sec., Assistant Masters Assoc., 1964–78. Hon. FCP, 1985. *Publications:* many reports/pamphlets for AMA, incl. The Middle School System, Mixed Ability Teaching, Selection for Admission to a University. *Recreations:* family, work, canal boating, walking, books. *Address:* (office) 7 Northumberland Street, WC2N 5DA. *T:* 01–930 6441; (home) 3 Templewood, Welwyn Garden City, Herts AL8 7HT. *T:* Welwyn Garden 321380. *Club:* Royal Commonwealth Society.

BEYNON, Sir Granville; *see* Beynon, Sir W. J. G.

BEYNON, Ven. James Royston; Archdeacon of Winchester, 1962–73, now Emeritus; *b* 16 Sept. 1907; *s* of James Samuel and Catherine Beynon; *m* 1933, Mildred Maud Fromings (*d* 1986); four *d*. *Educ:* St Augustine's Coll., Canterbury. LTh Durham. Ordained, 1931; Chaplain, Indian Eccl. Estabt, 1933; Senior Chaplain: Peshawar, 1941; Quetta, 1943; Archdeacon of Lahore, 1946–48; Vicar of Twyford, Winchester, 1948–73; Rural Dean of Winchester, 1958–62. Hon. CF, 1945. *Address:* 1511 Geary Avenue, London, Ontario, Canada.

BEYNON, Prof. John David Emrys, CEng, FIEE, FIERE; Professor of Electrical Engineering, since 1979, Pro Vice Chancellor, since 1983, University of Surrey; *b* 11 March 1939; *s* of John Emrys and Elvira Beynon; *m* 1964, Hazel Janet Hurley; two *s* one *d*. *Educ:* Univ. of Wales (BSc); Univ. of Southampton (MSc, PhD). FIERE 1977; FIEE 1978. Scientific Officer, Radio Res. Station, Slough, 1962–64; Univ. of Southampton: Lectr, Sen. Lectr and Reader, 1964–77; Prof. of Electronics, UWIST, Cardiff, 1977–79; Head of Dept of Electronic and Elec. Engrg, Univ. of Surrey, 1979–83. Vis. Prof., Carleton Univ., Ottawa, 1975; Cons. to various cos, Govt estabts and Adviser to British Council, 1964–. Member: Accreditation Cttee, IEE, 1983–; Adv. Cttee on Engrg and Technology, British Council, 1983–; Technology Sub-Cttee, UGC, 1984–; Nat. Electronics Council, 1985–. Engrg Professors' Conference: Chm. 1985– (Hon. Sec. 1982–84, Vice-Chm. 1984–85). FRSA 1982. *Publications:* Charge-Coupled Devices and Their Applications (with D. R. Lamb), 1980; papers on plasma physics, semiconductor devices and integrated circuits, and engrg educn. *Recreations:* music, photography, travel. *Address:* University of Surrey, Guildford, Surrey GU2 5XH. *T:* Guildford 571281.

BEYNON, Prof. John Herbert, DSc; FRS 1971; Royal Society Research Professor, University College Swansea, University of Wales, since 1974; *b* 29 Dec. 1923; British; *m* 1947, Yvonne Lilian (*née* Fryer); no *c*. *Educ:* UC Swansea, Univ. of Wales. BSc (1st cl. hons Physics); DSc; CPhys; FInstP; CChem; FRSC. Experimental Officer, Min. of Supply, Tank Armament Research, 1943–47; ICI Ltd (Organics Div.), 1947–74; Associate Research Man. i/c Physical Chemistry, 1962–70; Sen. Res. Associate, 1965–74. Hon. Professorial Fellow, and Lectr in Chemistry, UC Swansea, 1967–74; Prof. of Chemistry, Purdue Univ., Indiana, 1969–75; Associate Prof. of Molecular Sciences, Univ. of Warwick, 1972–74, 1983–; Vis. Prof., Univ. of Essex, 1973–74, 1982–; Hon. Prof., Univ. of Warwick, 1977–. *Publications:* Mass Spectrometry and its Applications in Organic Chemistry, 1960; Mass and Abundance Tables for use in Mass Spectrometry, 1963; The Mass Spectra of Organic Molecules, 1968; Table of Ion Energies for metastable transitions in mass spectrometry, 1970; Metastable Ions, 1973; An Introduction to Mass Spectrometry, 1981; Current Topics in Mass Spectrometry and Chemical Kinetics, 1982; Application of Transition State Theory to Unimolecular Reactions, 1983; papers in Proc. Royal Soc., Nature, Jl Sci. Inst., Jl Applied Physics, Chem. Soc., JACS, Trans Faraday Soc., Int. Jl Mass Spectrom. and Ion Physics, Org. Mass Spectrom., Anal. Chem., etc. *Recreations:* photography, golf. *Address:* Royal Society Research Unit, University College Swansea, Singleton Park, Swansea SA2 8PP. *T:* Swansea 295298; 17 Coltshill Drive, Mumbles, Swansea SA3 4SN. *T:* Swansea 68718. *Club:* Athenæum.

BEYNON, Timothy George, MA; FRGS 1983; Headmaster, The Leys School, Cambridge, since 1986; *b* 13 Jan. 1939; *s* of George Beynon and Fona I. Beynon; *m* 1973, Sally Jane Wilson; two *d*. *Educ:* Swansea Grammar Sch.; King's Coll., Cambridge (MA). City of London Sch., 1962–63; Merchant Taylors' Sch., 1963–78; Headmaster, Denstone Coll., 1978–86. *Recreations:* ornithology, fishing, shooting, sport, music, expeditions. *Address:* The Leys School, Cambridge CB2 2AD.

BEYNON, Prof. Sir (William John) Granville, Kt 1976; CBE 1959; PhD, DSc; FRS 1973; Professor and Head of Department of Physics, University College of Wales, Aberystwyth, 1958–81, now Emeritus; *b* 24 May 1914; *s* of William and Mary Beynon; *m* 1942, Megan Medi, *d* of Arthur and Margaret James; two *s* one *d*. *Educ:* Gowerton Grammar Sch.; University Coll., Swansea. Scientific Officer, later Senior Scientific Officer, National Physical Laboratory, 1938–46; Lecturer, later Senior Lecturer in Physics, University Coll. of Swansea, 1946–58. Mem., SRC, 1976–80. Mem., Schools Council, 1965–76; Pres., 1972–75, Hon. Pres., 1981–, URSI; Hon. Professorial Fellow, UC Swansea, 1981–; Hon. DSc Leicester, 1981. *Publications:* (ed) Solar Eclipses and the Ionosphere, 1956; (ed) Proceedings Mixed Commission on the Ionosphere, 1948–58; numerous publications in scientific jls. *Recreations:* music, cricket, tennis, Rugby. *Address:* Caebryn, Caergôg, Aberystwyth. *T:* Aberystwyth 3947; Bryn Eithin, 103 Dunvant Road, Swansea. *T:* Swansea 23585.

BHASKAR, Prof. Krishan Nath; Professor of Accountancy and Finance, University of East Anglia, Norwich, since 1978; *b* 9 Oct. 1945; *s* of Dr Ragu Nath Bhaskar and Mrs Kamla Bhaskar (*née* Dora Skill); *m* 1977, Fenella Mary (*née* McCann); one *s* one *d*. *Educ:* St Paul's Sch., London; London Sch. of Econs and Pol. Science (BSc Econ 1st Cl. Hons, MSc Econ). Lectr, LSE, 1968–70; Lectr in Accounting, Univ. of Bristol, 1970–78. *Publications:* (with D. Murray) Macroeconomic Systems, 1976; Building Financial Models: a simulation approach, 1978; Manual to Building Financial Models, 1978; The Future of the UK Motor Industry, 1979; The Future of the World Motor Industry, 1980; (with M. J. R. Shave) Computer Science Applied to Business Systems, 1982; The UK and European Motor Industry: analysis and future prospects, 1983; (jtly) Financial Modelling with a Microcomputer, 1984; (with R. J. Housden) Management Information Systems and Data Processing for the Management Accountant, 1985; (with B. C. Williams) The Impact of Microprocessors on the Small Practice, 1985; A Fireside Chat on Databases for Accountants, 1985; Quality and the Japanese Motor Industry: lessons for the West?, 1986; *reports:* A Research Report on the Future of the UK and European Motor Industry, 1984; (with G. R. Kaye) Financial Planning with Personal Computers, Vol. 1, 1985, Vol. 2, 1986; State Aid to the European Motor Industry, 1985; Demand Growth: a boost for employment?, 1985; Japanese Automotive Strategies: a European and US perspective, 1986. *Address:* School of Information Systems, University of East Anglia, Norwich NR4 7TJ. *T:* Norwich 56161, ext. 2314.

BIBBY, Benjamin; *see* Bibby, J. B.

BIBBY, Dr Cyril; *b* 1914; *s* of William and Elizabeth Jane Bibby, Liverpool; *m* 1936, Frances (Florence Mabel) Hirst, Mddx; two *s* two *d*. *Educ:* Liverpool Collegiate Sch.; Queens' Coll., Cambridge. Open Major Scholar in natural sciences, 1932; Coll. Prizeman, 1933; Icelandic expedn, 1934; BACantab, 1935. Physics and Chemistry Master, Oulton Sch., Liverpool, 1935–38; Scientific research, Univ. of Liverpool, 1935–40; MACantab, 1939; Sen. Biology Master, Chesterfield Grammar Sch., 1938–40; MSc Liverpool, 1940. Educn Officer to Brit. Social Hygiene Council and then Central Council for Health Educn, 1941–46; Tutor in Biol. (becoming Co-ordinator of Sciences and Sec. to Academic Bd), Coll. of S Mark and S John, London, 1946–59; educational and other research, 1947–59; Principal, Kingston upon Hull Coll. of Educn, 1959–76; Pro-Dir, Hull Coll. of Higher Educn, 1976–78. Visiting Prof., Univ. of Illinois, 1950; PhD London, 1955; Silver Medal of RSA, 1956. Visiting Lecturer at several Univs in USA (also investigatory visits for US Nat. Science Foundn, 1962). Delegate to many internat. congresses, etc., 1947–64. At various periods, Mem. Executive of: Internat. Union of Family Organisations; Fraternité Mondiale; Assoc. of Teachers in Colls and Depts of Educn; Council of Christians and Jews; Eugenics Soc., Nat. Foundn for Educl Research; Soc. for Research into Higher Educn; School Broadcasting Council of UK, etc. Many political activities. FLS, 1942; FRSA, 1954. *Publications:* Evolution of Man and His Culture, 1938; Heredity, Eugenics and Social Progress, 1939; Experimental Human Biology, 1942; Simple Experiments in Biology, 1943; Sex Education, 1944; How Life is Handed On, 1946; Healthy and Happy, 1948; Story of Birth, 1949; Healthy Day, 1949; Active Human Biology, 1950; Health Education, 1951; Healthy People, 1954; Human Body, 1955; Education in Racial and Intergroup Relations, 1957; T. H. Huxley, 1959; Race, Prejudice and Education, 1959; The First Fifty Years, 1964; Essence of T. H. Huxley, 1968; Biology of Mankind, 1968; T. H. Huxley on Education, 1971; Scientist Extraordinary, 1972; The Art of the Limerick, 1978; Verse Offerings, 1986; papers in various scientific, health, educnl, political, sociological and gen. lit. jls. *Recreations:* reading, writing, walking, sun-bathing, film, theatre, music, travel. *Address:* 11 Beech Grove, Beverley Road, Hull.

BIBBY, Sir Derek (James), 2nd Bt *cr* 1959, of Tarporley, Co. Palatine of Chester; MC 1945; Chairman, Bibby Line Ltd, since 1969; *b* 29 June 1922; *s* of Major Sir (Arthur) Harold Bibby, 1st Bt, DSO, DL, LLD, and of Marjorie, *d* of Charles J. Williamson; *S* father, 1986; *m* 1961, Christine Maud, *d* of late Rt Rev. F. J. Okell, MA, DD, Bishop of Stockport; four *s* one *d*. *Educ:* Rugby; Trinity Coll., Oxford (MA). Served War, Army, 1942–46. *Recreations:* shooting, gardening. *Heir:* *s* Michael James Bibby, *b* 2 Aug. 1963. *Address:* Willaston Grange, Willaston, South Wirral L64 2UN. *T:* 051–327 4913. *Club:* Royal Commonwealth Society.

BIBBY, (John) Benjamin; Director, since 1961, Chairman, 1970–78, J. Bibby & Sons PLC; *b* 19 April 1929; *s* of late J. P. and D. D. Bibby; *m* 1956, Susan Lindsay Paterson; two *s* one *d*. *Educ:* Oundle Sch.; St Catharine's Coll., Cambridge (MA). Called to the Bar, Gray's Inn, 1981. Has held various positions in J. Bibby & Sons PLC, 1953–. Mem. Council, Univ. of Liverpool, 1978–81; Mem. Exec. Cttee, West Kirby Residential Sch., 1978–. Chm., Nat. Squib Class Owners' Assoc., 1983– (Mem. Cttee, 1982–). JP Liverpool 1975–81. *Publication:* (with C. L. Bibby) A Miller's Tale, 1978. *Recreations:* sailing, gardening. *Address:* Kirby Mount, Warwick Drive, West Kirby, Wirral, Merseyside. *T:* 051–625 8071. *Clubs:* Liverpool Racquet; West Kirby Sailing; Royal Mersey Yacht; Royal Anglesey Yacht.

BICESTER, 3rd Baron *cr* 1938, of Tusmore; **Angus Edward Vivian Smith;** *b* 20 Feb. 1932; *s* of Lt-Col Hon. Stephen Edward Vivian Smith (*d* 1952) (2nd *s* of 1st Baron) and Elenor Anderson, *d* of Edward S. Hewitt, New York City; *S* uncle, 1968. *Educ:* Eton. *Heir:* *b* Hugh Charles Vivian Smith, *b* 8 Nov. 1934.

BICK, Martin James M.; *see* Moore-Bick.

BICKERSTETH, Rt. Rev. John Monier; *see* Bath and Wells, Bishop of.

BICKERTON, Frank Donald, CBE 1966; Director General, Central Office of Information, 1971–74; *b* 22 June 1917; *s* of F. M. Bickerton and A. A. Hibbert; *m* 1945, Linda Russell; two *s*. *Educ:* Liverpool Collegiate Sch. Min. of Health, in Public Relations

Div., 1935–40. Served War, RNVR, 1940–45. Min. of National Insurance (later Min. of Pensions and Nat. Insurance), 1946–61: initially Asst Press Officer and in charge of Information Div., 1952–61; Chief Information Officer, Min. of Transport, 1961–68; Controller (Home), COI, 1968–71. *Recreations:* walking, gardening. *Address:* 6 Diana Close, Granville Rise, Totland, Isle of Wight.

BICKFORD, James David Prydeaux; HM Diplomatic Service; Legal Counsellor, Foreign and Commonwealth Office, since 1984; *b* 28 July 1940; *s* of William A. J. P. Bickford and late Muriel Bickford (*née* Smythe); *m* 1965, Carolyn Jane, *d* of late Major W. A. R. Sumner, RHA; three *s*. *Educ:* Downside; Law Society's College of Law, London. Admitted to Roll of Solicitors, 1963; Solicitor of the Supreme Court. In practice, J. J. Newcombe, Solicitors, Okehampton, 1963–69; Crown Counsel and Legal Advr to Govt of Turks and Caicos Islands, BWI, 1969–71; Asst Legal Advr, FCO, 1971–79 and 1982–84; Legal Advr, British Mil. Govt, Berlin, 1979–82. Mem., Panel of Legal Experts, Internat. Telecommunications Satellite Orgn, 1985–; Chm., Assembly of Internat. Maritime Satellite Orgn, 1985–. *Publication:* Land Dealings Simplified in the Turks and Caicos Islands, 1971. *Recreations:* the family, sailing, fishing. *Address:* c/o Foreign and Commonwealth Office, SW1.

BICKFORD SMITH, John Roger, TD 1950; Senior Master of Supreme Court, Queen's Bench Division, and Queen's Remembrancer, since 1983 (Master, since 1967); *b* 31 Oct. 1915; *er s* of late Leonard W. Bickford Smith, Camborne, Cornwall, For. Man., ICI, and Anny Grete (*née* Huth); *m* 1st, 1939, Cecilia Judge Heath (marr. diss.), *er d* of W. W. Heath, Leicester; two *s*; 2nd, 1972, Baronin Joaise Miranda et Omnes Sancti von Kirchberg-Hohenheim. *Educ:* Eton (King's Schol.); Hertford Coll., Oxford (Schol.). BA 1937; MA 1952. Commnd in Duke of Cornwall's LI (TA), 1939; served 1939–46: UK, India, Burma and Germany; AJAG (Major), 1942; Lieut-Col 1944. Called to Bar, Inner Temple, 1942, Bencher, 1985. Practised at Common Law Bar in London and on Midland Circuit, 1946–67. *Publications:* The Crown Proceedings Act 1947, 1948; various contribs to legal pubns. *Recreation:* foreign travel. *Address:* Royal Courts of Justice, WC2. *Club:* Garrick.

BICKNELL, Mrs Christine Betty, CBE 1986; MA (Oxon); Chairman, Victoria Health Authority, 1982–85; *b* 23 Dec. 1919; *er d* of Walter Edward and Olive Isabelle Reynolds; *m* 1960, Claud Bicknell, *qv*. *Educ:* St Martin-in-the-Fields High Sch. for Girls; Somerville Coll., Oxford (Exhibr). BA 1941. Board of Trade, 1941–60; Northern Regional Officer, Min. of Land and Natural Resources, 1965–67. Chairman: Prudhoe and Monkton HMC, 1966–70; Leavesden HMC, 1971–74; Kensington and Chelsea and Westminster AHA (T), 1973–77; Member: Newcastle RHB, 1961–70, and NW Metrop. RHB, 1971–74; Nat. Whitley Council for Nurses and Midwives, 1962–70; Northern Econ. Planning Bd, 1965–67; Bd of Governors, Royal Vic. Infirm., Newcastle upon Tyne, 1965–70 and St Bartholomew's Hosp., 1971–74; Chm., CSSB, 1970–86; Member: Industrial Tribunals, 1977–86; Newspaper Panel, Monopolies Commn, 1973–83; British Library Board, 1979–82; Pres., Hosp. Domestic Administrators' Assoc., 1970–74. *Recreations:* gardening, mountains, hill walking, sailing. *Address:* Aikrigg End Cottage, Burneside Road, Kendal LA9 6DZ. *Clubs:* Alpine, United Oxford & Cambridge University.

BICKNELL, Claud, OBE 1946; a Law Commissioner, 1970–75; a part-time Chairman of Industrial Tribunals, 1975–83; *b* Rowlands Gill, near Newcastle upon Tyne, 15 June 1910; 2nd *s* of Raymond Bicknell and Phillis Bicknell (*née* Lovibond); *m* 1st, 1934, Esther Irene (*d* 1958), *e d* of Kenneth Bell; one *s* two *d* (one *d* decd); 2nd, 1960, Christine Betty Reynolds (*see* C. B. Bicknell). *Educ:* Oundle Sch.; Queens' Coll., Cambridge. MA 1935. Pres., Cambridge Univ. Mountaineering Club, 1930–31. Admitted as a solicitor, 1934; Asst Solicitor, 1934–39, and partner, 1939–70, in firm of Stanton, Atkinson & Bird, Newcastle upon Tyne. Dir, Northern Corporation Ltd, 1939–53. Auxiliary Fire Service, Newcastle upon Tyne, 1939–41; Nat. Fire Service, 1941–45; Sen. Fire Staff Officer, Home Office, 1943–45. Mem. Planning Bd, Lake District Nat. Park, 1951–70 (Chm., Development Control Cttee, 1957–70). Pres., Newcastle upon Tyne Incorp. Law Soc., 1969. *Recreation:* mountains. *Address:* Aikrigg End Cottage, Burneside Road, Kendal LA9 6DZ. *Clubs:* Garrick, Alpine.

See also Sir J. R. Shelley, Bt.

BIDDLE, Martin, FBA 1985; FSA, FRHistS; Director, Winchester Research Unit, since 1968; Lecturer of The House, Christ Church, Oxford, since 1983; *b* 4 June 1937; *s* of Reginald Samuel Biddle and Gwladys Florence Biddle (*née* Baker); *m* 1966, Birthe, *d* of Landsretssagfører Axel Th. and Anni Kjølbye of Sønderborg, Denmark; two *d* (and two *d* by previous marr.). *Educ:* Merchant Taylors' Sch., Northwood; Pembroke Coll., Cambridge (MA 1965); MA Oxon 1967; MA Pennsylvania 1977. FSA 1964; FRHistS 1970; MIFA 1984. Second Lieut, 4 RTR, 1956; 1 Indep. Sqn, RTR, Berlin, 1956–57. Asst Inspector of Ancient Monuments, MPBW, 1961–63; Lectr in Medieval Archaeology, Univ. of Exeter, 1963–67; Vis. Fellow, All Souls Coll., Oxford, 1967–68; Dir, University Museum, and Prof. of Anthropology and of History of Art, Univ. of Pennsylvania, 1977–81. Directed excavations: Nonsuch Palace, 1959–60; Winchester, 1961–71; Repton (with wife), 1974–; St Alban's Abbey (with wife), 1978, 1982–84. Chm., Rescue, Trust for British Archaeology, 1971–75. Mem., Royal Commn on Historical Monuments for England, 1984–. General Editor, Winchester Studies, 1976–. (With Birthe Biddle) Frend Medal, Soc. of Antiquaries, 1986. *Publications:* (with C. Heighway) The Future of London's Past, 1973; (with F. Barlow and others) Winchester in the Early Middle Ages, 1976; (with H.M. Colvin, J. Summerson and others) The History of the King's Works, vol. iv, pt 2, 1982; papers on archaeological, historical and art-historical subjects in learned jls. *Recreations:* travel, esp. Hellenic travel, reading. *Address:* 19 Hamilton Road, Oxford OX2 7PY. *T:* Oxford 513056; Christ Church, Oxford OX1 1DP. *T:* Oxford 242353. *Club:* Athenæum.

BIDDULPH, family name of **Baron Biddulph.**

BIDDULPH, 4th Baron *cr* 1903; **Robert Michael Christian Biddulph;** *b* 6 Jan. 1931; *s* of 3rd Baron Biddulph and Lady Amy Louise Agar (*d* 1983), *d* of 4th Earl of Normanton; *S* father, 1972; *m* 1958, Lady Mary Maitland, *d* of Viscount Maitland (killed in action, 1943) and *g d* of 15th Earl of Lauderdale; two *s* one *d*. *Educ:* Canford; RMA, Sandhurst. Lt 16/5 The Queen's Royal Lancers, retd. *Recreations:* shooting, fishing. *Heir:* *s* Hon. Anthony Nicholas Colin Maitland Biddulph, *b* 8 April 1959. *Address:* Makerstoun, Kelso, Roxburghshire, Scotland. *Club:* New (Edinburgh).

BIDDULPH, Constance; *see* Holt, C.

BIDDULPH, Sir Stuart (Royden), 10th Bt *cr* 1664; retired grazier; *b* 24 June 1908; *s* of Sir Francis Henry Biddulph, 9th Bt, and Janet (*d* 1956), *d* of Walter Bain Hannah, Brisbane; *S* father, 1980; *m* 1939, Muriel Margaret, 3rd *d* of Angus Harkness, Hamley Bridge, S Australia; one *s* two *d*. *Educ:* Brisbane Grammar School. *Recreation:* gliding. *Heir:* *s* Ian D'Olier Biddulph [*b* 28 Feb. 1940; *m* 1967, Margaret Eleanor, *o d* of late John Gablonski; one *s* two *d*]. *Address:* 119 Watson Street, Charleville, Queensland 4470, Australia.

BIDE, Sir Austin (Ernest), Kt 1980; Hon. President, Glaxo Holdings plc, since 1985 (Chief Executive, 1973–80; Chairman, 1973–85); non-executive Chairman, BL plc, 1982–86 (Deputy Chairman, 1980–82; Director, 1977–86); *b* 11 Sept. 1915; *o s* of late Ernest Arthur Bide and Eliza Bide (*née* Young); *m* 1941, Irene (*née* Ward); three *d*. *Educ:* County Sch., Acton; Univ. of London. 1st cl. hons BSc Chemistry; FRSC, CChem. Govt Chemist's Dept, 1932–40; Research Chemist, Glaxo, 1940: i/c Chemical Develt and Intellectual Property, 1944–54; Dep. Sec., 1954–59; Sec., 1959–65; Dir, 1963–71; Dep. Chm., 1971–73; Dir, J. Lyons & Co. Ltd, 1977–78. Chm., QCA Ltd, 1985–. Member: Review Body, UGC, 1985–; MRC, 1986–; Working Party on Biotechnology (under auspices of ACARD/ABRD and Royal Soc.) (Report 1980); Adv. Cttee on Industry to the Vice-Chancellors and Principals of UK Univs, 1984–; Chm., Information Technology 1986 Cttee, 1986. Member: Adv. Council, Inst. of Biotechnological Studies, 1985–; Adam Smith Inst., 1985–; Council, Inst. of Manpower Studies, 1985–; Chm., Visiting Cttee, Open Univ., 1982–. Confederation of British Industry: Member: Council, 1974–85; President's Cttee, 1983–86; Chm., Res. and Technol. Cttee, 1977–86; British Institute of Management: CBIM (FBIM 1972); Mem. Council, 1976–; Chm., Finance Cttee, 1976–79; Dir, BIM Foundn, 1977–79. Mem. Court, British Shippers Council, 1984–. Trustee, British Motor Industry Heritage Trust, 1983–86. Chm., Salisbury Cathedral Appeal Cttee. Mem. Council, Imperial Soc. of Knights Bachelor, 1980–. Hon. FIChemE 1983; Hon. FIIM 1983 (Vice-Pres., 1983); Hon. Fellow, Inst. Biotechnological Studies 1985. Hon. DSc QUB, 1986. Gold Medal, BIM, 1983. *Publications:* papers in learned jls on organic chemical subjects. *Recreations:* fishing, handicrafts. *Address:* Clarges House, 6–12 Clarges Street, W1Y 8DH. *Club:* Hurlingham.

BIDGOOD, John Claude, MIEx; Chairman: Anglo-Dominion Finance Co. Ltd; Anglo-Dominion Construction Co. Ltd; Anglo-Dominion Trading Co. Ltd; *b* 12 May 1914; *s* of late Edward Charles Bidgood, Leeds; *m* 1945, Sheila Nancy Walker-Wood; one *s* two *d*. *Educ:* London Choir Sch.; Woodhouse Technical Sch. Served early part of War of 1939–45 as Pilot RAF. Mem. Leeds City Council, 1947–55 (late Chm. Works Cttee and City Architects Cttee); contested (C) N E Leeds, 1950, 1951; MP (C) Bury and Radcliffe, 1955–64; PPS to Joint Parly Secs, Min. of Pensions and Nat. Insurance, 1957–58; Mem. Parly Select Cttee on Estimates, 1958–64. Director: Bidgood Holdings Ltd; Edward Bidgood & Co. Ltd; Bidgood Larsson Ltd; Wright & Summerhill Ltd; R. Horsfield & Co. Ltd; Constructional Erection Ltd; Bidgood Larsson (Iraq) Ltd; Chm., Yorks Assoc. for the Disabled, 1950–58; Member: Inst. of Export; Leeds and Bradford Joint Aerodrome Cttee, 1951–55; W Riding Rating Valuation Court, 1955. Gen. Comr of Income Tax. Councillor, Chapeltown Corporation, 1976–. Governor, Bury Grammar Schs, 1955. Freeman, City of London; Liveryman and Mem., Worshipful Co. of Horners. *Recreations:* music, travel. *Address:* The Old Joinery, Walton, near Wetherby, W Yorks LS23 7DQ. *T:* Boston Spa 844028. *Clubs:* City Livery, Naval and Military; Leeds (Leeds).

BIDSTRUP, (Patricia) Lesley, MD, FRCP, FRACP; Member, Medical Appeals Tribunal, since 1970; *b* 24 Oct. 1916; *d* of Clarence Leslie Bidstrup, Chemical Works Manager, South Australia, and Kathleen Helena Bidstrup (*née* O'Brien); *m* 1952, Ronald Frank Guymer, TD, MD, FRCP, FRCS, DPH, DIH; one step *s* one step *d*. *Educ:* Kadina High Sch. and Walford House, Adelaide, SA. MB, BS (Adel.) 1939; MD (Adel.) 1958; FRACP 1954; FRCP (Lond.) 1964. Resident Ho. Phys. and Registrar, Royal Adelaide Hosp., SA, 1939–41. Hon. Capt., AAMC, 1942–45. MO, UNRRA, Glyn-Hughes Hosp., Belsen, 1945–46. General practice: Acting Hon. Asst Phys., Royal Adelaide Hosp.; Tutor in Med., St Mark's Coll., Adelaide, and in Univ. of Adelaide Med. Sch.; Lectr in Med., Univ. of Adelaide Dental Faculty, 1942–45; Asst, Dept for Research in Industrial Medicine, MRC, 1947–58; Clinical Asst (Hon.), Chest Dept, St Thomas' Hosp., 1958–78. Private consulting concerned mainly with industrial medicine, 1958–. Mem., Scientific Sub-Cttee on Poisonous Substances used in Agriculture and Food Storage, 1956–58; Corr. Mem., Amer. Acad. of Occupational Medicine. Visiting Lectr, TUC Centenary Inst. of Occupational Health; Examiner for Diploma in Industrial Health: Conjoint Bd, 1965–71, 1980–82; Society of Apothecaries, 1970–76; External Examiner for Diploma in Industrial Health, Dundee, 1980–82. Mem., Industrial Injuries Adv. Council, 1970–83. Mayoress, Royal Borough of Kingston-upon-Thames, 1959, 1960. *Publications:* The Toxicity of Mercury and its Compounds, 1964; chapters in: Cancer Progress, 1960; The Prevention of Cancer, 1967; Clinical Aspects of Inhaled Particles, 1972; contribs to Brit. Jl Indust. Med., Lancet, BMJ, Proc. Royal Soc. Med., ILO Encyclopaedia on Industrial Diseases. *Recreations:* people, theatre, music. *Address:* 11 Sloane Terrace Mansions, Sloane Terrace, SW1X 9DG. *T:* 01–730 8720.

BIDWELL, Hugh Charles Philip; Chairman, Ellis, Son & Vidler, since 1986; *b* 1 Nov. 1934; *s* of Edward and Elisabeth Bidwell; *m* 1962, Jenifer Webb; two *s* one *d*. *Educ:* Stonyhurst College, Director: Viota Foods, 1962–70; Robertson Foods, 1968–70; Chm., Pearce Duff, 1970–85. Pres., British Food Export Council, 1980–; Mem., Food From Britain Council, 1983–; Dep. Pres., Food and Drink Fedn., 1985–. Alderman, Billingsgate Ward, 1979–; Sheriff of the City of London, 1986–87. Master, Grocers' Co., 1984–85. *Recreations:* golf, fishing. *Address:* Waterlane Farm, Bovingdon, Herts HP3 0NA. *T:* Hemel Hempstead 832179. *Clubs:* Boodle's, City of London, MCC; Denham Golf, Royal St George's.

BIDWELL, Sydney James; MP (Lab) Ealing, Southall, since 1974 (Southall, 1966–74); *b* Southall, 14 Jan. 1917; *s* of late Herbert Emmett Bidwell; *m* 1941; one *s* one *d*. *Educ:* Elementary sch., evening classes and trade union study. Railway worker; Tutor and Organiser, Nat. Council of Labour Colls. Mem., TGWU. TUC Reg. Educn Officer, London, 1963–66. Mem., Southall Bor. Council, 1951–55. Contested (Lab): E Herts, 1959; Herts SW, 1964. Former Mem., Parly Select Cttee on Race Relations and Immigration, 1968–79; Mem., Select Cttee on Transport, 1979–. *Publications:* Red White and Black Book on Race-Relations, 1976; The Turban Victory, 1977; articles on TU and Labour history. *Recreations:* soccer, painting, cartooning. *Address:* House of Commons, SW1.

BIERICH, Marcus; Chairman, Board of Management, Robert Bosch GmbH, Stuttgart, since 1984; *b* 29 April 1926. *Educ:* Univs of Münster and Hamburg (PhD 1951; studies in mathematics, science and philosophy). Bankhaus Delbrück Schickler & Co., 1956–61; Director 1961–67, Mem. Bd of Management 1967–80, Mannesmann AG, Düsseldorf; Mem. Bd of Management, Allianz Versicherungs-AG, München, 1980–84. Hon. Dr.rer.oec Univ. of Bochum, 1977. *Address:* Robert Bosch GmbH, Postfach 50, 7000 Stuttgart 1, Federal Republic of Germany. *T:* 0711/811–6101.

BIFFEN, Rt. Hon. (William) John, PC 1979; MP (C) Shropshire North, since 1983 (Oswestry Division of Salop, Nov. 1961–1983); Leader of the House of Commons, since 1982 and Lord Privy Seal, since 1983; *b* 3 Nov. 1930; *s* of Victor W. Biffen; *m* 1979, Mrs Sarah Wood (*née* Drew); one step *s* one step *d*. *Educ:* Dr Morgan's Sch., Bridgwater; Jesus Coll., Cambridge (BA). Worked in Tube Investments Ltd, 1953–60; Economist Intelligence Unit, 1960–61. Chief Sec. to the Treasury, 1979–81; Sec. of State for Trade, 1981–82; Lord Pres. of the Council, 1982–83. *Address:* c/o House of Commons, SW1.

BIGGAM, Robin Adair; Managing Director, BICC plc, since 1986; *b* 8 July 1938; *s* of Thomas and Eileen Biggam; *m* 1962, Elizabeth McArthur McDougall; one *s* two *d*. *Educ:*

Lanark Grammar Sch. Chartered accountant. Peat Marwick Mitchell, 1960–63; ICI, 1964–81; Director: ICL, 1981–84; Dunlop Holdings plc, 1984–85; Non Executive Director: Chloride Group plc, 1985–; Abbey Life Gp, 1985–. *Recreations*: golf, swimming, gardening. *Address*: Devonshire House, Mayfair Place, W1X 5FH. *T*: 01–629 6622. *Club*: Harpenden Common Golf.

BIGGAR, (Walter) Andrew, CBE 1980 (OBE 1967); MC 1945; FRAgS; farming since 1956; *b* 6 March 1915; *s* of Walter Biggar and Margaret Sproat; *m* 1945, Patricia Mary Irving Elliot; one *s* one *d*. *Educ*: Sedbergh Sch., Cumbria; Edinburgh Univ. (BScAgric). FRAgS 1969. Commnd Royal Signals, 1938; War Service, 51st Highland Div., 1939–46; POW, Germany, 1940–45. Rowett Res. Inst., 1935–54. Director and Trustee: Scottish Soc. for Research in Plant Breeding, 1958–; Animal Diseases Res. Assoc., 1966–. Member: Farm Animals Welfare Adv. Cttee, 1967–77; ARC, 1969–80; Scottish Agricultural Develt Council, 1971–82; JCO Consultative Bd, 1980–84; Chm., Animals Bd, JCO, 1973–80. Dir, Caledonian Produce (Holdings), 1969–. Governor: St Margaret's Sch., Edinburgh, 1960–81; Grassland Res. Inst., 1962–81; Scottish Crop Res. Inst., 1980–83. *Recreation*: photography. *Address*: Magdalenehall, St Boswells, Roxburghshire. *T*: St Boswells 3741. *Club*: Farmers'.

BIGGART, Thomas Norman, CBE 1984; WS; Partner, Biggart Baillie & Gifford, WS, Solicitors, Glasgow and Edinburgh, since 1959; *b* 24 Jan. 1930; *o s* of Andrew Stevenson Biggart, JP and Marjorie Scott Biggart; *m* 1956, Eileen Jean Anne Gemmell; one *s* one *d*. *Educ*: Morrisons Acad., Crieff; Glasgow Univ. (MA 1951, LLB 1954). Served RN, 1954–56 (Sub-Lt RNVR). Law Society of Scotland: Mem. Council, 1977–86; Vice-Pres., 1981–82; Pres., 1982–83. Pres., Business Archives Council, Scotland, 1977–86. Member: Exec. Cttee, Scottish Council (Development and Industry), 1984–; Scottish Tertiary Educn Adv. Council, 1984–; Scottish Records Adv. Council, 1985–. Director: Clydesdale Bank, 1985–; New Scotland Insurance Gp. Hon. Mem., American Bar Assoc., 1982. OStJ 1968. *Recreations*: golf, hill walking. *Address*: Gailes, Kilmacolm, Renfrewshire PA13 4LZ. *T*: Kilmacolm 2645. *Clubs*: Royal Scottish Automobile, The Western (Glasgow).

BIGGS; *see* Ewart-Biggs.

BIGGS, Brig. Michael Worthington, CBE 1962 (OBE 1944); MA; MICE; *b* 16 Sept. 1911; *s* of late Lt-Col Charles William Biggs, OBE, Cheltenham and late Winifred Jesse Bell Biggs (*née* Dickinson); *m* 1940, Katharine Mary, *d* of late Sir Walter Harragin, CMG, QC, Colonial Legal Service, and Lady Harragin; two *d*. *Educ*: Cheltenham Coll.; RMA Woolwich; Pembroke Coll., Cambridge. MA (Cantab) 1966; MICE 1967. 2nd Lieut RE, 1931; served War of 1939–45, E Africa, Abyssinia (Bde Major), and Burma (GSO1 and CRE); Lt-Col 1942; Col 1954; Mil. Adviser to High Comr, Australia, 1954–57; Brig. 1960; Chief of Staff, E Africa Comd, 1960–62; Dir of Quartering (Army), MoD, 1963–66; retd, 1966. Group Building Exec., Forte's (Holdings) Ltd, 1966–67; Manager, Hatfield and Welwyn Garden City, Commn for New Towns, 1967–78. Member: Council, TCPA; Exec. Cttee, Hertfordshire Soc.; Chm., Herts Bldg Preservation Trust, 1978–86. Pres., KAR and EAF Officers' Dinner Club. Freeman, City of London, 1985. *Recreations*: golf, gardening (FRHS). *Address*: Strawyards, High Street, Kimpton, Herts. *T*: Kimpton 823498. *Club*: Army and Navy.

BIGGS, Sir Norman (Parris), Kt 1977; Director, Banco de Bilbao, since 1981; *b* 23 Dec. 1907; *s* of John Gordon Biggs and Mary Sharpe Dickson; *m* 1936, Peggy Helena Stammwitz; two *s* one *d*. *Educ*: John Watson's Sch., Edinburgh. Bank of England, 1927–46; Dir, Kleinwort Sons & Co. Ltd, 1946–52; Esso Petroleum Company, Ltd: Dir, 1952–66, Chm., 1968–72; Chairman: Williams & Glyn's Bank Ltd, 1972–76; United International Bank Ltd, 1970–79; Deputy Chairman: National and Commercial Banking Gp Ltd, 1974–76; Privatbanken Ltd, 1980–83; Director: Royal Bank of Scotland, 1974–76; Gillett Bros Discount Co. Ltd, 1963–77. Mem., Bullock Cttee on Industrial Democracy, 1976. *Recreations*: sailing, travel. *Address*: Northbrooks, Danworth Lane, Hurstpierpoint, Sussex. *T*: Hurstpierpoint 832022.

BIGGS, Peter Martin, PhD, DSc; FRS 1976; Director, of Animal Disease Research, Agricultural and Food Research Council, since 1986; *b* 13 Aug. 1926; *s* of Ronald Biggs and Cécile Biggs (*née* Player); *m* 1950, Alison Janet Molteno; two *s* one *d*. *Educ*: Bedales Sch.; Cambridge Sch., USA; Queen's Univ., Belfast; Royal Veterinary Coll., Univ. of London (BSc 1953, DSc 1975); Univ. of Bristol (PhD 1958). FRCVS, FRCPath, FIBiol, CBiol. Served RAF, 1944–48; Research Asst, Univ. of Bristol, 1953–55, Lectr, 1955–59; Houghton Poultry Research Station: Head of Leukosis Experimental Unit, 1959–74; Dep. Dir, 1971–74; Dir, 1974–86. Vis. Prof. of Veterinary Microbiology, RVC, Univ. of London, 1982–. Sir William Dick Meml Lectr, Univ. of Edinburgh, 1974; E.H.W. Wilmott Guest Lectr, Univ. of Bristol, 1977. Hon. DVM Ludwig-Maximilians Univ., 1976; Tom Newman Meml Award, 1964; J. T. Edwards Meml Medal, 1969; Dalrymple-Champneys Cup and Medal, 1973; Bledisloe Veterinary Award, 1977; Jozsef Marek Meml Medal, Vet. Univ. of Budapest, 1979. *Publications*: scientific papers on viruses and infectious disease. *Recreations*: music making, boating. *Address*: Willows, London Road, St Ives, Huntingdon, Cambridgeshire PE17 4ES. *T*: St Ives 63471.

BIGGS-DAVISON, Sir John (Alec), Kt 1981; MP (C) Epping Forest, since 1974 (Chigwell, 1955–74 (as Ind C 1957–58)); *b* 7 June 1918; *s* of late Major John Norman Biggs-Davison, RGA, retd; *m* 1948, Pamela Mary, 2nd *d* of late Ralph Hodder-Williams, MC; two *s* four *d*. *Educ*: Clifton (scholar); Magdalen Coll., Oxford (exhibitioner, MA). Royal Marines, 1939, Lieut 1940; served in RM Brigade and RM Division. Indian Civil Service: Asst Comr, 1942; Forward Liaison Officer, Cox's Bazar, 1943–44; Sub-Divisional Officer, Pindi Gheb, 1946; Political Asst and Comdt, Border Military Police, subsequently Dep. Comr, Dera Ghazi Khan, during and after transfer of Power to Dominion of Pakistan, 1947; retired from Pakistan Administrative Service, 1948. Conservative Research Dept, 1950–55; Sec., Brit. Conservative Delegn to Council of Europe, 1952, 1953. Contested (C) Coventry South, 1951. Co-founder Pakistan Soc., 1951. Indep. Observer of Malta Referendum, 1956. Mem. Parly Delegations: West Africa, 1956; Guernsey, 1961; Austria, 1964; France, 1965; Canada (Inter-Parly Union Conf.), 1965; Malawi, 1968; Tunisia, Gibraltar, 1969; Portugal, 1973; Cyprus, 1979; Canada, 1984. Vice-Pres., Franco-British Parly Relations Cttee; Chairman: British-Pakistan Parly Gp; Cons. Parly NI Cttee; Vice-Chm., Cons. Parly Foreign and Commonwealth Affairs Cttee. An Opposition Front Bench spokesman on NI, 1976–78. Mem., Parly Assembly, Council of Europe and WEU, 1984–86. Mem. Exec., Cons. and Unionist Members (1922) Cttee. Governor, Clifton Coll., 1972. *Publications*: George Wyndham, 1951; Tory Lives, 1952; The Uncertain Ally, 1957; The Walls of Europe, 1962; Portuguese Guinea: Nailing a Lie, 1970; Africa: Hope Deferred, 1972; The Hand is Red, 1974; Rock Firm for the Union, 1979; The Cross of St Patrick, 1985; contribs to many periodicals. *Recreations*: reading, riding, tennis, walking (Gold Medal London-Brighton Pacesetters' Walk, 1963), took part in parliamentary parachute jump, 1980. *Address*: House of Commons, SW1. *Clubs*: Carlton, Special Forces, Oxford Union Society.

BIGHAM, family name of **Viscount Mersey** and of **Lady Nairne.**

BIGNALL, John Reginald, FRCP; Physician, Brompton Hospital, 1957–79; *b* 14 Oct. 1913; *s* of Walter and Nellie Bignall; *m* 1939, Ruth Thirtle; one *s* three *d*. *Educ*: Nottingham High Sch.; St John's Coll. Cambridge; London Hospital. MA 1938; MD 1947; FRCP 1961. Served in RAMC, 1941–46, Middle East and Mediterranean (Major).

BIKANER, Maharaja of; Dr Karni Singhji Bahadur; *b* 21 April 1924; *e s* of late Lt-Gen. HH Maharaja Sri Sadul Singhji Bahadur of Bikaner, GCSI, GCIE, CVO; *S* father as Maharaja of Bikaner, 1950; *m* 1944, Princess Sushila Kumari, *d* of Maharawal Shri Sir Lakshman Singh Bahadur of Dungapur, *qv*; one *s* two *d*. *Educ*: St Stephen's Coll., Delhi; St Xavier's Coll., Bombay. BA (Hons) (History and Politics); PhD (thesis) Bombay Univ., 1964. Visited Middle East War Front in Nov. 1941 with his grandfather, Maharaja Sri Ganga Singhji Bahadur. Insignia Grand Commander: Order of Vikram Star (Bikaner), Order of Sadul Star (Bikaner), Order of Star of Honour (Bikaner); Africa Star; War Medal; India Service Medal; Arjun Award for Shooting, 1961. Has travelled extensively in Europe, Egypt, USA, Mexico, Honolulu and Far East, etc. Elected to House of People (Parliament of India) as an Independent, 1952; re-elected for 2nd and 3rd terms; elected 4th time, 1967, with largest margin (193,816) in the country; elected 5th time, 1971; left Parliament, 1977; served on various consultative cttees of different ministries. Member: Asiatic Soc. of India; Bombay Natural History Soc. *Publications*: The Relations of the House of Bikaner with the Central Powers 1465–1949, 1974; From Rome to Moscow, 1982 (memoirs). *Recreations*: tennis; shooting (National Champion in clay pigeon traps and skeet for many years; rep. India, clay pigeon shooting, Olympic Games: Rome, 1960, Pre-Olympics, Tokyo, 1963, Tokyo, 1964 (Captain), Mexico, 1968, Munich, 1972, Moscow, 1980; World Shooting Championships: Oslo, 1961; Cairo (Captain), 1962 (2nd in world after tie for 1st place); Wiesbaden, 1966 (Captain); Bologna, 1967; San Sebastian, Spain, 1969; Asian Shooting Championships: Tokyo, 1967; Seoul, 1971 (Captain, Gold Medal); won Clay Pigeon Welsh Grand Prix, 1981, 1984, N Wales Cup, 1981 and NW England Cup, 1981, 1984; Asian Games, Tehran, 1974 (Silver Medal); Kuala Lumpur 1975 (Silver Medal; mem. Indian team which won Team Clay Pigeon Silver Medal, Delhi Asiad, 1982); golf; flying (qualified for private pilot's licence); cricket; mechanics; photography; oil painting. *Address*: Lallgargh Palace, Bikaner, Rajasthan, India. *Clubs*: Clay Pigeon Shooting Assoc., Essex (Hon. Life Vice-Pres.); Willingdon Sports, Cricket Club of India, Bombay Flying, Bombay Presidency Golf, Western India Automobile Association (Bombay); Delhi Golf (Delhi); National Sports Club of India (in all 4 cities).

BILBY, Prof. Bruce Alexander, BA, PhD; FRS 1977; Consultant; Professor of the Theory of Materials, University of Sheffield, 1966–84, now Emeritus; *b* 3 Sept. 1922; *e s* of late George Alexander Bilby and Dorothy Jean (*née* Telfer); *m* 1st, 1946, Hazel Joyce (*née* Casken); two *s* one *d*; 2nd, 1966, Lorette Wendela (*née* Thomas); two *s*. *Educ*: Dover Grammar Sch.; Peterhouse, Cambridge (BA); Univ. of Birmingham (PhD). Admiralty, 1943–46. Research, Birmingham, 1946–51; Univ. of Sheffield: Royal Soc. Sorby Res. Fellow, 1951–57; J. H. Andrew Res. Fellow, 1957–58; Reader in Theoretical Metallurgy, 1958–62, Prof., 1962–66. Has made contributions to theory of dislocations and its application to the deformation, transformation and fracture of metallic crystals. Rosenhain Medal, 1963. *Publications*: contribs to learned jls. *Recreation*: sailing. *Address*: 32 Devonshire Road, Totley, Sheffield S17 3ND. *T*: Sheffield 361086; Department of Mechanical Engineering, The University, Mappin Street, Sheffield S1 3JD. *T*: Sheffield 78555.

BILL, Commander Robert, DSO 1940; FRICS; FRGS; RN, retired 1955; Consultant, retired 1975; *b* 1 April 1910; *s* of late R. W. Bill, Penn, Staffs; *m* 1st, 1933, Peggy Shaw (marr. diss. 1952), *d* of late Comdr A. R. S. Warden, AM, RN (retd), Paignton, Devon; 2nd, 1952, Wendy Jean (*d* 1962), *d* of late C. P. Booth, Hampstead, NW2; one *s* one *d*; 3rd, 1965, Mrs Nancy Elizabeth Johnson (*d* 1973), *d* of late Major Arthur Edward Phillips, DSO, MFH, Mompesson House, Salisbury; 4th, 1975, Gillian Ruth, 2nd *d* of late Dr Geoffrey Clarke, and *g d* of late Sir William Clarke of Chatteris. *Educ*: RNC, Dartmouth and Greenwich. Specialised in Hydrographic Survey, 1931, and in Electronic Distance Measurement, 1956; Special Director, Vickers Instruments Ltd, 1956–65; Dir and Man. Dir, Tellurometer (UK) Ltd, 1960–66. Lectures and papers on survey by trilateration, UK and Europe. Mem., Chichester DC, 1982–85. Manby Premium, ICE, 1962. *Address*: Shieling Cottage, North Street, Petworth, West Sussex. *T*: Petworth 42357.

BILLETT, Paul Rodney, CB 1981; *b* 19 Feb. 1921; *s* of late Arthur William and Grace Hilda Billett; *m* 1st, 1945, Muriel Gwendoline Marsh (*d* 1977); one *s*; 2nd, 1985, Eileen May Nourse. *Educ*: Commonweal and College Grammar Schools, Swindon. Entered Exchequer and Audit Dept, 1939. Served RASC, 1941–46. Deputy Secretary, Exchequer and Audit Dept, 1975–81 (retired). *Address*: Wynthorpe, Cornsland, Brentwood, Essex CM14 4JL. *T*: Brentwood 224830.

BILLING, Melvin George, CMG 1961; retired as Provincial Commissioner, Provincial Administration, Northern Rhodesia (1951–62); *b* 24 June 1906; *s* of Stuart Morrison Billing and Gertrude Roswell Billing; *m* 1934, Kathleen Jane, *d* of late A. N. Brand; no *c*. *Educ*: Dulwich Coll.; Worcester Coll., Oxford. Provincial Administration, Northern Rhodesia: Cadet, 1930; District Officer, 1932; Grade II, 1942; Grade I, 1946; Senior, 1950. *Recreations*: bowls, photography. *Address*: Formosa Garden Village, Box 416, Plettenberg Bay, Cape 6600, S Africa. *Club*: Royal Commonwealth Society.

BILLINGHAM, Prof. Rupert Everett, MA, DPhil, DSc Oxon; FRS 1961; Professor and Chairman, Department of Cell Biology and Anatomy, Southwestern Medical School, University of Texas Health Science Center at Dallas, since 1971; *b* 15 Oct. 1921; *o s* of Albert Everett and Helen Louise Billingham, Oxford; *m* 1951, Jean Mary Morpeth; two *s* one *d*. *Educ*: City of Oxford High Sch.; Oriel Coll., Oxford. Served 1942–46, as Lieut RNVR. Asst Lectr, later Lectr in Zoology, University of Birmingham, 1947; Junior Research Fellow, British Empire Cancer Campaign, 1950; Intermediate Research Fellow, Brit. Emp. Cancer Campaign, 1953; Hon. Res. Asst, later Res. Associate, Dept of Zoology, University Coll., London, 1951; Wistar Prof. of Zoology, Univ. of Pennsylvania, USA, and Mem. of Wistar Institute of Anatomy and Biology, Philadelphia, 1957; Prof. and Chm., Dept of Medical Genetics, Univ. of Pennsylvania Med. Sch., Pa, 1965–71. Member: Allergy and Immunology Study Section, Nat. Insts of Health, US Public Health Service, 1958–62; Transplantation and Immunology Cttee, Nat. Insts of Health, 1968–70, 1971–73; Scientific Adv. Cttee, Massachusetts General Hospital, 1976–79; Nat. Allergy and Infectious Diseases Council, Nat. Insts of Health, 1980–83; Sigma Xi College of Nat. Lecturers, 1981–83; President: Transplantation Soc., 1974; Internat. Soc. for Immunology of Reproduction, 1983–86. Fellow, New York Acad. of Sciences, 1962; Fellow, Amer. Acad. of Arts and Sciences, 1965; Alvarenga Prize, Coll. Physicians, Philadelphia, 1963; Herman Beerman Lecture, Soc. for Investigative Dermatology, 1963; Hon. Award Medal, American Assoc. of Plastic Surgeons, 1964; AOA Honor Med. Soc., 1974; Lectures: I. S. Ravdin, Amer. College of Surgeons, 1964; *Sigma Xi*, Yale, 1965; Nat. Insts of Health, 1965; J. W. Jenkinson Meml, Oxford, 1965–66; Harvey, NY, 1966; Kinyoun, Nat. Inst. of Allergy and Infectious Diseases, 1979; Dist. Guest, Soc. for Gyn. Investigation, 1982. Adair Award, Amer. Gynecological Soc., 1971. Hon. DSc, Trinity Coll., Hartford, Conn, USA. *Publications*: The Immunobiology of Transplantation (with W. K. Silvers), 1971; The Immunobiology of Mammalian Reproduction (with A. E. Beer) 1976; contribs to scien. jls on biology of skin, immunology of tissue transplantation and immunology of manmalian reproduction. *Recreations:* woodwork, gardening. *Address:* Department of Cell Biology and Anatomy, University of Texas Health Science Center, 5323 Harry Hines Boulevard, Dallas, Texas 75235, USA; (home) 6181 Preston Haven Drive, Dallas, Texas 75230, USA. *T:* (214) 661–9895.

BILLINGTON, Kevin; film, theatre and television director; *b* 12 June 1934; *s* of Richard and Margaret Billington; *m* 1967, Lady Rachel Mary Pakenham (*see* Lady Rachel Billington); two *s* two *d*. *Educ:* Bryanston Sch.; Queens' Coll., Cambridge (BA). Film dir, BBC prog., Tonight, 1960–63; documentary film dir, BBC, 1963–67; films include: A Sort of Paradise; Many Mexicos; The Mexican Attitude; Twilight of Empire; Mary McCarthy's Paris; These Humble Shores; Matador; A Few Castles in Spain; The English Cardinal; A Socialist Childhood; Madison Avenue, USA; ATV documentary, All The Queen's Men. Feature Film Director: Interlude, 1967; The Rise and Rise of Michael Rimmer, 1969; The Light at the Edge of the World, 1970; Voices, 1974; Reflections, 1984. Television Director: And No One Can Save Her, 1973; Once Upon a Time is Now (documentary), 1978; The Music Will Never Stop (documentary), 1979; Henry VIII, 1979; The Jail Diary of Albie Sachs, 1980; The Good Soldier, 1981; Outside Edge, 1982; The Sonnets of William Shakespeare, 1984. Theatre Director: Find Your Way Home, 1970; Me, 1973; The Birthday Party, 1974; The Caretaker, 1975; Bloody Neighbours, 1975; Emigrés, 1976; The Homecoming, 1978; Quartermaine's Terms, 1982; The Deliberate Death of a Polish Priest, 1985; The Philanthropist, 1986. Screenwriters' Guild Award, 1966 and 1967; Guild of TV Producers and Directors Award, 1966 and 1967. *Address:* 30 Addison Avenue, W11 4QP. *Club:* Garrick.

BILLINGTON, Michael; Drama Critic of The Guardian, since 1971; *b* 16 Nov. 1939; *s* of Alfred Billington and Patricia (*née* Bradshaw); *m* 1978, Jeanine Bradlaugh. *Educ:* Warwick Sch.; St Catherine's Coll., Oxford (BA). Trained as journalist with Liverpool Daily Post and Echo, 1961–62; Public Liaison Officer and Director for Lincoln Theatre Co., 1962–64; reviewed plays, films and television for The Times, 1965–71. Film Critic: Birmingham Post, 1968–78; Illustrated London News, 1968–81; London Arts Correspondent, New York Times, 1978–. Contributor to numerous radio and television Arts programmes, incl. Kaleidoscope, Critics' Forum, The Book Programme, Arena. Presenter, The Billington Interview and Theatre Call, BBC World Service. Prof. of Drama, Colorado Coll., 1981. IPC Critic of the Year, 1974. *Publications:* The Modern Actor, 1974; How Tickled I Am, 1977; (ed) The Performing Arts, 1980; The Guinness Book of Theatre Facts and Feats, 1982; Alan Ayckbourn, 1983. *Recreations:* work, travel, cricket. *Address:* 15 Hearne Road, W4 3NJ. *T:* 01–995 0455. *Club:* Critics' Circle.

BILLINGTON, Lady Rachel (Mary); writer; *b* 11 May 1942; *d* of 7th Earl of Longford, *qv*, and Countess of Longford, *qv*; *m* 1967, Kevin Billington, *qv*; two *s* two *d*. *Educ:* London Univ. (BA English). Work includes: short stories; four BBC radio plays; two BBC TV plays, Don't be Silly, 1979, Life After Death, 1981. Reviewer: Financial Times; BBC Radio (Kaleidoscope); etc. *Publications:* All Things Nice, 1969; The Big Dipper, 1970; Lilacs out of the Dead Land, 1971; Cock Robin, 1973; Beautiful, 1974; A Painted Devil, 1975; A Woman's Age, 1979; Rosanna and the Wizard-Robot (for children), 1981; Occasion of Sin, 1982; The First Christmas (for children), 1983; Star-Time (for children), 1984; The Garish Day, 1985. *Recreation:* children. *Address:* 30 Addison Avenue, W11 4QP. *Clubs:* Society of Authors, PEN.

BILLOT, Barbara Kathleen; Deputy Director (Under-Secretary), Department for National Savings, 1974–80; *b* 26 May 1920; *d* of Alfred Billot and Agnes Billot (*née* Hiner). *Educ:* Petersfield County High Sch. for Girls. Post Office Savings Bank: Clerical Officer 1938; Exec. Off. 1939; Higher Exec. Off. 1946; Sen. Exec. Off. 1953; Chief Exec. Off. 1957; Principal, Post Office Headquarters, 1960; Sen. Chief Exec. Off., PO Savings Dept, 1961; Principal Exec. Off. (Estabt Off.), 1969; Asst Sec., Dept for Nat. Savings, 1971. *Recreations:* reading, theatre-going. *Address:* 6 Springbank, Chichester, W Sussex PO19 4BX.

BILNEY, Air Vice-Marshal Christopher Neil Hope, CB 1949; CBE 1946 (OBE 1940); RAF, retired; *b* 26 Oct. 1898; *s* of late William A. and late Maud H. Bilney, Fir Grange, Weybridge, Surrey; *m* 1926, Nellie G. Perren (*d* 1983); two *d*. *Educ:* Tonbridge Sch. Joined RNAS, 1917; commissioned 1917; served European War, 1914–18, N Sea and Middle East (despatches); Flt-Lieut RAF, 1926; India, 1925–30 (despatches); Sqdn Leader, 1935, serving at Air Ministry; Wing Comdr, 1939; served War of 1939–45: Boscombe Down, 1939; MAP, 1940–41; Group Capt, 1941; Air Cdre, Vice-Pres. Ordnance Board, 1942; HQ Bomber Comd as Comd Armament Officer, 1944 (despatches); AOC No. 25 Group, 1945 (CBE); Air Ministry, Dir Technical Training, 1947–49 (CB); Air Officer i/c Administration, HQ Maintenance Comd, 1949–51; Dir-Gen. of Technical Services (1), Air Ministry, 1951–52; Pres. Ordnance Board, Ministry of Supply, 1953–54; retd 1954. Took up scouting: District Comr, Andover, 1954; County Comr, Hampshire, 1960–67; awarded Silver Acorn for good service by Chief Scout. *Recreations:* shooting, gardening. *Address:* Old Parsonage Cottage, Hatchet Lane, Cranbourne, Windsor Forest, Berks.

bin YEOP, Tan Sri Abdul Aziz, Al-Haj; PSM (Malaysia); Hon. GCVO 1972; Member, Malaysian Parliament; Partner in legal firm, Aziz and Mazlan, Advocates and Solicitors, 1966–71, and since 1973; *b* 5 Oct. 1916; *m* 1942, Puan Sri Hamidah Aziz; six *s* three *d*. *Educ:* King Edward VII Sch., Perak, Malaysia. Malay Administrative Service, 1937; called to Bar, Lincoln's Inn, 1950; Malayan Civil Service, 1951; First Asst State Sec., Perak 1954; London Univ. (course in Community Development), 1955. Permanent Sec., Min. of Agriculture, 1958–62; Dep. Sec., Malaysian Affairs Div., Prime Minister's Dept, 1962–64; Permanent Sec., Min. of Education, 1964–66. Chm. and Dir of firms in Malaysia, 1966–71. High Comr for Malaysia in London, 1971–73. First Chm., Bd of Governors of BERNAMA (Malaysia's National News Agency), 1967–71; Chairman: Council, Universiti Teknologi, Malaysia, 1974– (Pro-chancellor, 1977–80); Majlis Amanah Raayat, Malaysia, 1975–. *Recreations:* walking, reading, fishing. *Address:* c/o Aziz and Mazlan, 17 Jalan Klyne, Kuala Lumpur, Malaysia.

BINCHY, Daniel A.; Senior Professor, Dublin Institute for Advanced Studies, 1950–75; *b* 3 June 1900. *Educ:* Clongowes Wood Coll.; University Coll., Dublin; Munich, Berlin, Paris and The Hague. MA (NUI and Oxford); Dr Phil (Munich). Prof. of Jurisprudence and Legal History, University Coll., Dublin, 1925–45; Senior Research Fellow, Corpus Christi Coll., Oxford, 1945–50, Hon. Fellow, 1971. Envoy Extraordinary and Minister Plenipotentiary for the Irish Free State to Germany, 1929–32. Mem. Council, Royal Irish Academy, 1926, Vice-Pres., 1945. Rhys Lectr, British Academy, 1943; Lowell Lectr, Boston, 1954; Visiting Prof. of Celtic, Harvard Univ., 1962–63; Gregynog Lectr, Univ. of Wales, 1966; O'Donnell Lectr, Oxford, 1967–68. DLitt (*hc*): Dublin, 1956; Wales, 1963; Belfast, 1973; NUI, 1973; DèsL (*hc*) Rennes, 1971. Corresp. Mem., Norwegian Instituttet for Sammenlignende Kulturforsking, 1960; For. Mem., Amer. Acad. of Arts and Sciences, 1962; Corresp. Fellow, British Acad., 1976. *Publications:* Church and State in Fascist Italy, 1941, repr. 1970; Crith gablach, An Early Irish Legal Tract, 1940, repr. 1970; Celtic and Anglo-Saxon Kingship, 1970; Corpus Juris Hibernici, 6 vols., 1979; papers on Old Irish law; various articles in Irish, English, and German reviews. *Address:* Lisnagree, Castleknock, Co. Dublin. *Club:* United Service (Dublin).

BING, Sir Rudolf (Franz Joseph), KBE 1971 (CBE 1956); General Manager, Metropolitan Opera, New York, 1950–72; Distinguished Professor, Brooklyn College, City University of New York, 1972–75; Director Columbia Artists Management, since 1973; *b* Vienna, 9 Jan. 1902; *m* 1929, Nina (*née* Schelemskaja). *Educ:* Vienna. Hessian State Theatre, Darmstadt, 1928–30; Civic Opera, Berlin-Charlottenburg, 1930–33. Gen. Manager, Glyndebourne Opera, 1935–49; Artistic Director, Edinburgh Festival, 1947–49. Holds hon. doctorates in music and in letters, from the US. Légion d'Honneur, 1958; Comdr's Cross of Order of Merit, Federal Republic of Germany, 1958; Grand Silver Medal of Honour, Republic of Austria, 1959; Comdr, Order of Merit, Republic of Italy, 1959, Grand Officer, 1970. *Publication:* 5000 Nights at the Opera, 1972. *Address:* Essex House, 160 Central Park South, New York, NY 10019, USA.

BINGHAM, family name of **Baron Clanmorris** and of **Earl of Lucan.**

BINGHAM, Lord; George Charles Bingham; *b* 21 Sept. 1967; *s* and *heir* of 7th Earl of Lucan, *qv*.

BINGHAM, Caroline Margery Conyers; professional writer; *b* 7 Feb. 1938; *o d* of Cedric and Muriel Worsdell; *m* 1958, Andrew Bingham (marr. diss. 1972); one *d*. *Educ:* Mount Sch., York; Convent de la Sagesse, Newcastle upon Tyne; Cheltenham Ladies' Coll.; Univ. of Bristol (BA Hons History). *Publications:* The Making of a King: the early years of James VI and I, 1968 (USA 1969); James V, King of Scots, 1971; (contrib.) The Scottish Nation: a history of the Scots from Independence to Union, 1972; The Life and Times of Edward II, 1973; The Stewart Kingdom of Scotland, 1371–1603, 1974 (USA 1974); The Kings and Queens of Scotland, 1976 (USA 1976); The Crowned Lions: the Early Plantagenet Kings, 1978; James VI of Scotland, 1979; The Voice of the Lion (verse anthology), 1980; James I of England, 1981; Land of the Scots: a short history, 1983. *Address:* 199 Prince of Wales Road, NW5 3QB. *T:* 01–267 2931.

BINGHAM, Hon. Charlotte Mary Thérèse; playwright and novelist; *b* 29 June 1942; *d* of Baron Clanmorris, *qv*; *m* 1964, Terence Brady, *qv*; one *s* one *d*. *Educ:* The Priory, Haywards Heath; Sorbonne. TV series with Terence Brady: Boy Meets Girl; Take Three Girls; Upstairs Downstairs; Away From It All; Play for Today; No—Honestly; Yes—Honestly; Pig in the Middle; Thomas and Sarah; The Complete Lack of Charm of the Bourgeoisie; Nanny; Oh Madeline! (USA TV); Father Matthew's Daughter; A View of Meadows Green; TV film, Love With a Perfect Stranger, 1986; stage: (contrib.) The Sloane Ranger Revue, 1985. *Publications:* Coronet among the Weeds, 1963; Lucinda, 1965; Coronet among the Grass, 1972; Belgravia, 1983; Country Life, 1984; At Home, 1986. With Terence Brady: Victoria, 1972; Rose's Story, 1973; Victoria and Company, 1974; Yes—Honestly, 1977. *Recreations:* horses, watching others garden. *Address:* c/o A. D. Peters, Literary Agent, 10 Buckingham Street, WC2N 6BU.

BINGHAM, James; Chairman, Greater Manchester County Council, 1980–81 (Member, 1974–81); *b* 29 June 1916; *s* of James and Beatrice Bingham; *m* 1940, Jessie Noden. *Educ:* Manchester Central Grammar Sch.; Alsager Teacher Trng Coll.; Manchester Univ. (BSc (Hons) Geology, 1983). Insurance agent, 1938–39. Served War: RA from 1940; commnd 1943; in Eighth Army in N Africa, Italy, Austria; attained rank of Captain. Teacher in local schools, 1946–52; Headmaster: Eccles Parish Sch., 1952–59; St Paul's C of E Sch., Walkden, 1959–78, retired. Worsley UDC: Mem., 1962, 1965–73; last Chm., 1973–74; Chm., Recreation and Arts Cttee, GMC, 1977–80, and mem. other cttees. Member: NW Arts; Royal Exchange Theatre Trust; Hallé Concerts Soc. Cttee; NW Tourist Bd. *Recreations:* geology, keen golfer, cutting and polishing stones, fell walking. *Address:* 30 Ryecroft Lane, Worsley, Manchester M28 4PN. *T:* 061–794 3885.

BINGHAM, John; *see* Clanmorris, 7th Baron.

BINGHAM, John, FRS 1977; Deputy Chief Scientific Officer at the Plant Breeding Institute, Cambridge, since 1981; *b* 19 June 1930. SPSO, Plant Breeding Inst., Cambridge, to 1981. Has researched in plant breeding, culminating in production of improved, highly successful winter wheat varieties for British agriculture. Mullard Medal of Royal Society, 1975. *Address:* 25 Stansgate Avenue, Cambridge CB2 2QZ. *T:* Cambridge 247737; Plant Breeding Institute, Maris Lane, Trumpington, Cambridge CB2 2LQ. *T:* Trumpington 2411.

BINGHAM, Richard Martin, TD 1949; QC 1958; **His Honour Judge Bingham;** a Circuit Judge, since 1972; *b* 26 Oct. 1915; *s* of late John and Dorothy Ann Bingham; *m* 1949, Elinor Stephenson; one *d*. *Educ:* Harrow; Clare Coll., Cambridge. Called to Bar, Inner Temple, 1940; Bencher, 1964; joined Northern Circuit, 1946; Recorder of Oldham, 1960–71; Judge of Appeal, IoM, 1965–72. Served with 59th Med. Regt, RA (TA), 1937–46 and 1947–49: Major from 1945; Campaigns, Dunkirk and NW Europe (despatches, 1944). Mem. of Liverpool City Council, 1946–49. MP (C) Garston Division of Liverpool, Dec. 1957–March 1966. Member: HO Departmental Cttee on Coroners, 1965; Royal Commn Assizes and Quarter Sessions, 1966. *Publications:* Cases on Negligence, 1st edn 1961, 3rd edn 1978; Cases and Statutes on Crime, 1980. *Address:* Hook End, Gayton, Merseyside L60 3SR. *T:* 051–342 5793. *Clubs:* Royal Automobile; Royal Liverpool Golf.

BINGHAM, Rt. Hon. Sir Thomas (Henry), Kt 1980; PC 1986; **Rt. Hon. Lord Justice Bingham;** a Lord Justice of Appeal, since 1986; *b* 13 Oct. 1933; *o s* of late Dr T. H. Bingham and of Dr C. Bingham, Reigate; *m* 1963, Elizabeth, *o d* of late Peter Loxley; two *s* one *d*. *Educ:* Sedbergh; Balliol Coll., Oxford (MA). Royal Ulster Rifles, 1952–54 (2nd Lt); London Irish Rifles (TA) 1954–59. Univ. of Oxford: Gibbs Schol. in Mod. Hist., 1956; 1st cl. Hons, Mod. Hist., 1957. Eldon Law Schol., 1957; Arden Schol., Gray's Inn, 1959; Cert. of Honour, Bar Finals, 1959; called to Bar, Gray's Inn, 1959; Bencher, 1979. Standing Jun. Counsel to Dept of Employment, 1968–72; QC 1972; a Recorder of the Crown Court, 1975–80; Judge of the High Court of Justice, Queen's Bench Div., 1980–86. Leader, Investigation into the supply of petroleum and petroleum products to Rhodesia, 1977–78. Mem., Lord Chancellor's Law Reform Cttee; Chm., Council of Legal Educn, 1982–. Governor: Sedbergh, 1978–; Atlantic Coll., 1984–. Special Trustee, St Mary's Hosp., 1985–. Fellow, Winchester, 1983–. *Publication:* Chitty on Contracts, (Asst Editor) 22nd edn, 1961. *Recreations:* walking, theatre. *Address:* Royal Courts of Justice, Strand, WC2.

BINGLEY, Juliet Martin, (Lady Bingley); Senior Social Worker, City Corporation Social Services, based at St Mark's Hospital, EC1, since 1973; *b* 18 July 1925; *d* of Mary Kate Vick and Reginald Vick, OBE, MCh, FRCS; *m* 1948, Adm. Sir Alexander Noel Campbell Bingley, GCB, OBE (*d* 1972); one *s* two *d*. *Educ:* King Alfred School, Hampstead; London Sch. of Economics. Associated Mem., Inst. of Medical Social Workers. Social Worker, St Bartholomew's Hosp., 1945–48. Chm., Nat. Assoc. of Mental Health, 1979–84; Mem., Working Seminar, Royal Coll. of Medicine, 1984. CStJ 1962. Companion of Honour, Republic of Malta, 1976. *Recreations:* music, gardening, reading, theatre, moving furniture, collecting Staffordshire figures, lawn mowing. *Address:* Hoddesdonbury Farm, Hoddesdon, Herts. *T:* Hoddesdon 463238.

BINNEY, H(arry) A(ugustus) Roy, CB 1950; UN Adviser on Standards to Government of Cyprus, 1974–77; Adviser, International, British Standards Institution, 1972–73 (Director-General, BSI, 1951–70; Director-General, International, BSI, 1971–72); *b* 18 May 1907; *s* of Harry Augustus Binney, Churston, Devon; *m* 1944, Barbara Poole (*d* 1975); three *s* one *d* (and one *d* decd). *Educ:* Royal Dockyard Sch., Devonport; London Univ. BSc(Eng). Entered Board of Trade, 1929, Under-Sec. 1947–51. Chm., Standardization Cttee, European Productivity Agency, 1953–58; first Chm., Exec. Cttee, ISO, 1967–69 (Mem. Council, ISO, 1951–72, Vice-Pres., 1964–69); Chm., Cttee for European Standardization (CEN), 1963–65; Chm., ISO/CERTICO, 1970–73. Member: Gen. Bd, and Exec. Cttee, Nat. Physical Laboratory, 1957–63. Hon. Life Fellow, Standards Engrg Soc. of America; Hon. Life Mem., American Soc. for Testing and Materials. FKC; FRSA. *Recreation:* gardening. *Address:* Hambutts Orchard, Edge Lane, Painswick, Glos GL6 6UW.

BINNEY, Marcus Hugh Crofton, OBE 1983; writer; President, SAVE Britain's Heritage, since 1984 (Chairman, 1975–84); *s* of late Lt-Col Francis Crofton Simms, MC and of Sonia, *d* of Rear-Adm. Sir William Marcus Charles Beresford-Whyte, KCB, CMG (she *m* 2nd, Sir George Binney, DSO); *m* 1st, 1966, Hon. Sara Anne Vanneck (marr. diss. 1976), *e d* of 6th Baron Huntingfield; 2nd, 1981, Anne Carolyn, *d* of Dr T. H. Hills, Merstham, Surrey; two *s. Educ:* Magdalene Coll., Cambridge (BA 1966). Architectural writer, 1968–77, Architectural Editor, 1977–84, Editor, 1984–86, Country Life. Sec., UK Cttee, Internat. Council on Monuments and Sites, 1972–81; Dir, Rly Heritage Trust, 1985–. *Publications:* (with Peter Burman): Change and Decay: the future of our churches, 1977; Chapels and Churches: who cares?, 1977; (with Max Hanna) Preservation Pays, 1978; (ed jtly) Railway Architecture, 1979; (ed jtly) Our Past Before Us, 1981; (with Kit Martin) The Country House: to be or not to be, 1982; (with Max Hanna) Preserve and Prosper, 1983; Sir Robert Taylor, 1984; Our Vanishing Heritage, 1984; contributor to: Satanic Mills, 1979; Elysian Gardens, 1979; Lost Houses of Scotland, 1980; Taking the Plunge, 1982; SAVE Gibraltar's Heritage, 1982; Vanishing Houses of England, 1983; (contrib.) Time Gentlemen Please, 1983. *Address:* 21 Cambridge Street, SW1.

BINNIE, Alfred Maurice, FRS 1960; FEng 1976; Fellow of Trinity College (1944) and University Reader Emeritus in Engineering, Cambridge; *b* 6 Feb. 1901; *s* of late David Carr Binnie. *Educ:* Weymouth Coll.; Queens' Coll., Cambridge. Jun. Research Engineer, Bridge Stress Cttee, 1923–25; Demonstrator and Lectr, Engrg Lab., Oxford, 1925–44; Rhodes Travelling Fellow, 1932–33; Lectr, New Coll., Oxford, 1933–44; Univ. Lectr, 1944–54, Reader in Engrg, 1954–68, Engrg Lab., Cambridge; Sen. Research Fellow, California Inst. of Technology, 1951–52; Scott Visiting Fellow, Ormond Coll., Univ. of Melbourne, 1966; Vis. Scholar, Univ. of California, Berkeley, 1967–68. FIMechE 1937; FICE 1947. *Publications:* articles in scientific and engrg jls. *Recreation:* mountaineering. *Address:* Trinity College, Cambridge CB2 1TQ. *T:* 358201. *Club:* Alpine.

BINNIE, David Stark, OBE 1979; FCIT; FInstM; FBIM; railway and rapid transport consultant; *b* 2 June 1922; *s* of Walter Archibald Binnie and Helen (*née* Baxter), Bonkle, Lanarkshire; *m* 1947, Leslie Archibald; one *s* one *d. Educ:* Wishaw High School. British Railways: Gen. and Signalling Asst to Gen. Manager Scottish Region, 1955; Asst District Operating Supt 1961, District Operating Supt 1963, Glasgow North; Divisional Movements Manager, Glasgow Div., 1965; Movements Manager, Scottish Region, 1967; Divisional Manager, SE Div., Southern Region, 1969; Asst Gen. Manager, Southern Region, 1970, Gen. Manager, 1972; Exec. Dir, Freight, BR Board, 1974–76; Gen. Manager, BR, London Midland Region, 1977–80. Lt-Col Engineer and Railway Staff Corps, RE (T&AVR). OStJ. *Recreation:* Dartmoor and Highland life. *Address:* Above Ways, Lower Knowle Road, Lustleigh, Devon. *T:* Lustleigh 386.

BINNIE, Geoffrey Morse, FRS 1975; FEng 1976; Consultant to Binnie & Partners, 1973–83; *b* 13 Nov. 1908; *s* of William Eames Binnie and Ethel Morse; *m* 1st, 1932, Yanka Paryczko (*d* 1964); one *s* one *d*; 2nd, 1964, Elspeth Maud Cicely Thompson. *Educ:* Charterhouse; Trinity Hall, Cambridge (MA); Zurich Univ. FICE, FIWE, FASCE, FGS. Served War of 1939–45, RE (Major). Asst Engr, Gorge Dam, Hong Kong, 1933–37; Chief Asst, Eye Brook Reservoir, Northants, 1937–39; Partner, Binnie & Partners, 1939, resumed practice, 1945; responsible for design and supervision of construction of several water supplies in UK; Sen. Partner 1956–72, resp. for design and supervision of constr. of major projects abroad incl. Dokan dam, Iraq, completed 1960 and Mangla project, W Pakistan, compl. 1970. Chm., Panel advising on design and constr. of 2500 MW Peace River Hydro-electric project, BC, 1962–68. Chief Technical Supervisor, Poechos Dam, Peru, 1972–76; Chm., Advisory Board for Mornos dam, Greece, 1975–76; Chm., Chadwick Trust, 1980–83; Mem., Severn Barrage Cttee, 1978–81; Pres., JInstE, 1955; Vice-Pres., ICE, 1970–72; Fellow Imperial Coll. 1972. Telford Gold Medal, 1968; (1st) Smeaton Gold Medal, 1974. *Publications:* Early Victorian Water Engineers, 1981; techn. articles on engrg subjects, papers for World Power Conf., Internat. Commn on Large Dams and ICE. *Recreation:* engineering history. *Address:* St Michael's Lodge, Benenden, Cranbrook, Kent TN17 4EZ. *T:* Cranbrook 240498. *Club:* Athenæum.

BINNING, Lord; George Edmund Baldred Baillie-Hamilton; *b* 27 Dec. 1985; *s* and heir of Earl of Haddington, *qv.*

BINNING, Kenneth George Henry, CMG 1976; Director of Government Relations, NEI International, since 1983; *b* 5 Jan. 1928; *o s* of late Henry and Hilda Binning; *m* 1953, Pamela Dorothy, *o d* of A. E. and D. G. Pronger; three *s* one *d. Educ:* Bristol Grammar Sch.; Balliol Coll., Oxford. Joined Home Civil Service, 1950; Nat. Service, 1950–52; HM Treasury, 1952–58; Private Sec. to Financial Sec., 1956–57; AEA, 1958–65; seconded to Min. of Technology, 1965; rejoined Civil Service, 1968; Dir-Gen. Concorde, 1972–76 and Under-Sec., DTI later Dept of Industry, 1972–83. Mem., BSC, 1980–83. *Recreations:* music, gardening. *Address:* 12 Kemerton Road, Beckenham, Kent. *T:* 01–650 0273. *Club:* Reform.

BINNS, David John; General Manager, Warrington and Runcorn Development Corporation, since 1981; *b* 12 April 1929; *s* of Henry Norman Binns, OBE and Ivy Mary Binns; *m* 1957, Jean Margaret Evans; one *s* (one *d* decd). *Educ:* Fleetwood Grammar Sch.; Rossall Sch.; Sheffield Univ. LLB 1951. Solicitor 1954. Articled Clerk, Sheffield City Council, 1949; Asst Solicitor, Warrington County Borough Council, 1954; Dep. Town Clerk, Warrington County Borough Council, 1958; Gen. Manager, Warrington Develt Corp., 1969–81. *Recreations:* walking, gardening, music. *Address:* 4 Cedarways, Appleton, Warrington, Cheshire WA4 5EW. *T:* Warrington 62169. *Club:* Warrington (Warrington).

BINNS, Edward Ussher Elliott E.; *see* Elliott-Binns.

BINNS, Geoffrey John; His Honour Judge Binns; a Circuit Judge, since 1980; *b* 12 Oct. 1930; *s* of Rev. Robert Arthur Geoffrey Binns and Elizabeth Marguerite Binns; *m* 1964, Elizabeth Anne Poole Askew. *Educ:* Perse Sch.; Jesus Coll., Cambridge (MA). Admitted solicitor, 1956; Partner, Fraser, Woodgate & Beall, Wisbech, 1958–80; a

Recorder of the Crown Court, 1977–80. Chm., N Cambs Hosp. Management Cttee, 1970–74; Member: E Anglian Reg. Hosp. Bd, 1972–74; E Anglian RHA, 1974–76; Panel of Chairmen, Cambridge Univ. Ct of Discipline, 1976–80. Registrar, Archdeaconry of Wisbech, 1972–80. *Publication:* Contributing Ed., Butterworths' County Court Precedents and Pleadings, 1985. *Recreations:* golf, gardening. *Address:* c/o Crown Court, Shirehouse, Market Avenue, Norwich. *T:* Norwich 629859. *Club:* Norfolk (Norwich).

BINNS, Surgeon Rear-Adm. George Augustus, CB 1975; ophthalmic medical practitioner; *b* 23 Jan. 1918; *s* of Dr Cuthbert C. H. Binns and Julia Binns (*née* Frommel); *m* 1949, Joan Whitaker; one *s* two *d. Educ:* Repton Sch.; St Bartholemew's Hosp. MRCS, LRCP, DO. Casualty House Surgeon, Luton and Dunstable Hosp., 1942. Served War of 1939–45: joined RNVR, Dec. 1942. Served as Specialist in Ophthalmology, 1952, and promoted to Sen. Specialist in Ophthalmology, 1962; subseq. Admiralty Medical Bd, HMS Excellent, and RN Hosp., Gibraltar; MO in Charge, RN Hosp., Plymouth, and Command MO, 1972–75. QHS 1972–75. FRSocMed; Member: BMA, 1942–; Southern Ophthalmological Soc., 1959–; Council, Medical Eye Centre (formerly NOTB) Assoc., 1983–; Faculty of Opthalmologists, 1984; Medical Soc. of London, 1986; Pres., Farnham Br., RN Assoc. Chm., Grayshott Hort. Soc. CStJ 1972. *Recreations:* photography, house and garden maintenance, brewing, wine making, listening to music. *Address:* Netherseal, Hindhead Road, Haslemere, Surrey GU27 3PJ. *T:* Haslemere 4281. *Clubs:* Naval and Military; Fountain.

BINNS, Professor Howard Reed, CMG 1958; OBE 1948; MA (Cantab), BSc (Edin), MRCVS; *b* 3 Aug. 1909; *s* of Cuthbert Evelyn Binns and Edith Mildred Edwards; *m* 1935, Katharine Vroom Lawson; one *s* one *d. Educ:* Bootham Sch., York; St John's Coll., Cambridge; Royal (Dick) Veterinary Coll.; Edinburgh Univ. Veterinary Officer, Nyasaland, 1935–39; Veterinary Research Officer, Palestine, 1940–41; Senior Veterinary Research Officer, Palestine, 1941–47; Dep. Dir of Veterinary Services, Palestine, 1947–48; Director, East African Veterinary Research Organization, 1950–67 (Principal Scientific Officer, EAVRO, 1948–50); Dir, Centre for Internat. Programs, and Prof. of Veterinary Microbiology, Univ. of Guelph, 1969–75; Vis. Prof., Univ. of Guelph, 1975–80; Vis. Lectr on animal diseases exotic to N America, US Dept of Agriculture, 1980, 1983; Vis. Lectr, Animal Path. Divn, Canada Dept of Agric., 1981, 1982; Consultant to Internat. Develt Res. Centre, Ottawa, 1976, 1978; Vis. Prof., Univ. of Saskatchewan, 1980; Vis. Lectr, US Univs, 1980–83. Scientific missions to: USA and Canada, 1939; Syria and the Lebanon, 1945; India, 1946; USA, 1947; South Africa, 1949; Australia, 1960; USA and Germany, 1966; West Indies and S America, 1970; West Africa, 1971; India, 1973; Kenya, 1975, 1976; Carnegie Corp. Grant, 1956; Rockefeller Foundn Grants, 1966, 1970; Commonwealth Foundn Grant, 1971. Consultant to US Nat. Acad. of Sciences, on animal science in tropical Africa, 1959. Mem. Scientific Council for Africa, 1961–65 (Assoc. Mem., 1955–61). Hon. Prof. of Vet. Science in Univ. of East Africa. *Publications:* contribs to scientific jls. *Recreations:* travel, reading, gardening. *Address:* San Diego, Torreguadiaro, Cadiz Province, Spain.

BINNS, Kenneth Johnstone, CMG 1960; Under-Treasurer and Commissioner of State Taxes, Government of Tasmania, 1952–76; *b* New South Wales, Australia, 3 June 1912; *s* of late Kenneth Binns, CBE; *m* 1940, Nancy H. Mackenzie; no *c. Educ:* Melbourne Church of England Grammar Sch.; Queen's Coll., Univ. of Melbourne (MA, BCom); Harvard Univ., USA. First Canberra Scholarship, 1930; Fellow, Commonwealth Fund of NY, 1950. Tasmanian Treasury, 1942–76; Dep. Chm., Tasmanian Govt Insurance Office, 1970–82. Mem., State Library Bd of Tasmania, 1942–80. Fiscal Review Comr to Federal Republic of Nigeria, 1964; with IMF as Adviser to Minister of Finance, Indonesia, 1969. Dir, Comalco Aluminium (Bell Bay) Ltd, 1960–80. Member: State Grants Commn, 1976–80; Retirement Benefits Trust, 1976–82; Launceston Savings Bank Adv. Bd, 1976–83. First Life Mem., Tasmanian Branch, Australian Economic Soc., 1985. *Publications:* Federal-State Financial Relations, Canada and Australia, 1948; Social Credit in Alberta, 1947; various government reports; articles in Economic Record. *Recreations:* fishing, reading. *Address:* 3 Ellington Road, Sandy Bay, Tasmania 7005, Australia. *T:* 25 1863. *Clubs:* Athenæum, Tasmanian, Hobart.

BINNS, Malcolm; concert pianist; *b* 29 Jan. 1936; *s* of Douglas and May Binns. *Educ:* Bradford Grammar Sch.; Royal Coll. of Music (ARCM, Chappell Gold Medal, Medal of Worshipful Co. of Musicians). London début, 1957; Henry Wood Proms début, 1960; Royal Festival Hall début, 1961; Festival Hall appearances in London Philharmonic Orchestra International series, 1969–; concerts at Aldeburgh Festival, Leeds Festival, Three Choirs Festival (1975) and Canterbury Festival; regular appearances at Promenade concerts and broadcasts for BBC Radio. First complete recording of Beethoven piano sonatas on original instruments, 1980. *Recreation:* collecting antique gramophone records. *Address:* 233 Court Road, Orpington, Kent. *T:* Orpington 31056.

BINNS, St John, MBE 1977; JP; Member, West Yorkshire County Council, 1974–86 (Chairman, 1984–85); *b* 25 July 1914; *s* of John William and Lena Binns; *m* 1938, Gwendoline, *e d* of Fred and Minnie Clough; one *s. Educ:* Holbeck Junior Technical School. Amalgamated Union of Engineering Workers: Leeds District Pres., 1948, Sec., 1953; Divisional Organiser, 1970. Councillor, Leeds City Council, 1956 (Chm., Civic Catering, Plans, Licensing, Fire Cttees); Alderman, 1972; W Yorks Metropolitan County Council: Chm., Leeds Area Cttee, 1976; Chm., Personnel Cttee and Chief Whip, 1981–84. JP Leeds, 1959. *Recreation:* gardening. *Address:* 146 West Park Drive (West), Roundhay, Leeds LS8 2DA.

BINNY, John Anthony Francis; *b* 13 Dec. 1911. *Educ:* Wellington College. Supplementary Reserve of Officers, 15th/19th The King's Royal Hussars, 1936. Served War of 1939–45, France and Burma (despatches). *Address:* Byways, Pound Lane, Burley, Ringwood, Hampshire. *Clubs:* Cavalry and Guards, White's, MCC.

BINTLEY, David Julian; Resident Choreographer and Principal Dancer with Sadler's Wells Royal Ballet, since 1985; *b* 17 Sept. 1957; *s* of David Bintley and Glenys Bintley (*née* Ellinthorpe); *m* 1981, Jennifer Catherine Ursula Mills; one *s. Educ:* Holme Valley Grammar School. Royal Ballet School, 1974; Sadler's Wells Royal Ballet, 1976; first professional choreography, The Outsider, 1978; youngest choreographer to work at the Royal Opera House, for production of Adieu, 1980; first three act ballet, The Swan of Tuonela, 1982; Company Choreographer, Sadler's Wells Royal Ballet, 1983–85. Evening Standard Award for Ballet, for Choros and Consort Lessons, both 1983; Laurence Olivier Award for Petrushka, 1984.

BIOBAKU, Dr Saburi Oladeni, CMG 1961; MA, PhD; Research historian and management consultant; Research Professor and Director, Institute of African Studies, University of Ibadan, 1976–83; *b* 16 June 1918; *s* of late Chief S. O. Biobaku, Aré of Iddo, Abeokuta; *m* 1949, Muhabat Folasade, *d* of Alhaji L. B. Agusto, barrister-at-law, Lagos; one *s. Educ:* Govt Coll., Ibadan; Higher Coll., Yaba; University Coll., Exeter; Trinity Coll., Cambridge. BA London, 1945, BA Cantab, 1947, MA 1951; PhD London, 1951. Education Officer, Nigeria, 1947–53; Registrar, University Coll., Ibadan, 1953–57; Dir, Yoruba Historical Research Scheme, 1956–; Sec. to Premier and Executive Council, Western Nigeria, 1957–61; Pro-Vice-Chancellor, Univ. of Ife, Nigeria, 1961–65; Vice-

Chancellor, Univ. of Lagos, 1965–72; Chairman, Management Consultant Services Ltd, Lagos, 1972–76, 1983–. Created: Aré of Iddo, Abeokuta, 1958; Agbakin of Igbore, 1972; Maye of Ife, 1980; Baapitan of Egbaland, 1980. *Publications:* The Origin of the Yoruba, 1955; The Egba and Their Neighbours, 1842–1872, 1957; contribs to Africa, jl of Nigerian Historical Soc., Odu (Joint Ed.), etc. *Recreations:* soccer, tennis, badminton, swimming, walking. *Address:* PO Box 7741, Lagos, Nigeria. *T:* (home) 961430. *Clubs:* Metropolitan (Lagos); Dining (Ibadan).

BIRCH, Alexander Hope, CMG 1970; OBE 1961; HM Diplomatic Service, retired; *b* 19 Jan. 1913; *s* of Denys Goldney and Lucy Helen Booth Birch; *m* 1st, 1940, Honor Pengelley (marr. diss., 1948); 2nd, 1953, Joan Hastings-Hungerford (*d* 1982); no *c. Educ:* St Catherine's and St Mark's Colls, Alexandria, and privately. Appointed to: HM Embassy, Cairo, 1937; Addis Ababa, 1942; Moscow, 1946; Budapest, 1947; Tel-Aviv, 1949; Second Sec. (Inf.), Baghdad, 1950, First Sec. and Consul, Seoul, 1951, and Djakarta, 1954; First Sec. (Commercial), Khartoum, 1956, and Paris, 1961; Counsellor (Commercial), Paris, 1962, and Baghdad, 1965; Counsellor (Economic and Commercial), Accra, 1967–70; Dep. High Comr, Perth, WA, 1970–73; Administrative Adviser to Premier of Antigua, 1973–75. *Recreations:* international affairs, reading, walking. *Address:* Woodrow, Edgehill Road, Clevedon, Avon BS21 7BZ.

BIRCH, Prof. Anthony Harold, PhD; Professor of Political Science, University of Victoria, British Columbia, since 1977; *b* 17 Feb. 1924; *o s* of late Frederick Harold Birch and of Rosalind Dorothy Birch; *m* 1953, Dorothy Madeleine Overton, Bayport, New York; one *s* one *d. Educ:* The William Ellis Sch.; University Coll., Nottingham; London Sch. of Economics. BSc (Econ) London, with 1st cl. hons, 1945; PhD London, 1951. Asst Principal, Board of Trade, 1945–47; University of Manchester: Asst Lectr in Govt, 1947–51; Lectr, 1951–58; Senior Lectr in Government, 1958–61; Prof. of Political Studies, Univ. of Hull, 1961–70; Prof. of Political Sci., Exeter Univ., 1970–77. Commonwealth Fund Fellow at Harvard Univ. and University of Chicago, 1951–52. Consultant to Government of Western Region of Nigeria, 1956–58. Vis. Prof. Tufts Univ., 1968. Vice-Pres., Internat. Political Sci. Assoc., 1976–79; Life Vice-Pres., UK Political Studies Assoc., 1976– (Chm., 1972–75). *Publications:* Federalism, Finance and Social Legislation, 1955; Small-Town Politics, 1959; Representative and Responsible Government, 1964; The British System of Government, 1967, 7th edn 1986; Representation, 1971; Political Integration and Disintegration in the British Isles, 1977; articles in various journals. *Recreation:* sailing. *Address:* Department of Political Science, University of Victoria, PO Box 1700, Victoria, BC, Canada V8W 2Y2.

BIRCH, Prof. Arthur John, CMG 1979; DPhil (Oxon); FRS 1958; PAA, FRACI; Professor of Organic Chemistry, Australian National University, 1970–80, now Emeritus Professor and University Fellow; *b* 3 Aug. 1915; *s* of Arthur Spencer and Lily Birch; *m* 1948, Jessie Williams; three *s* two *d. Educ:* Sydney Technical High Sch.; Sydney Univ. MA Oxon 1981; MSc: Sydney, 1939; Manchester, 1957. Scholar of the Royal Commission for the Exhibition of 1851, Oxford, 1938–41; Research Fellow, Oxford, 1941–45; ICI Research Fellow, Oxford, 1945–48; Smithson Fellow of the Royal Society, Cambridge, 1949–52; Prof. of Organic Chemistry, University of Sydney, 1952–55; Prof. of Organic Chemistry, Manchester Univ., 1955–67; Dean, Research Sch. of Chemistry, ANU, Canberra, 1967–70, 1973–76; Newton Abraham Prof. of Organic Chemistry, Univ. of Oxford, 1980–81. Treas., Australian Acad. Science, 1969–73, Pres., 1982–; Pres., RACI, 1978. Chairman: Ind. Enquiry into CSIRO, 1976–; Aust. Marine Sciences and Technologies Adv. Cttee, 1978–81. Foreign Mem., USSR Acad. of Science, 1976. Hon. FRCS 1980. Hon. DSc: Sydney, 1977; Manchester, 1982; Monash, 1982. Davy Medal, Royal Soc., 1972. *Publications:* How Chemistry Works, 1950; about 400 original scientific communications, chiefly in Journal of Chemical Soc. and Australian Journal of Chemistry. *Address:* Department of Chemistry, Australian National University, PO Box 4, Canberra, ACT 2600, Australia.

BIRCH, Prof. Bryan John, FRS 1972; Professor of Arithmetic, University of Oxford, since 1985; Professorial Fellow of Brasenose College, Oxford, since 1985 (Fellow since 1966); *b* 25 Sept. 1931; *s* of Arthur Jack and Mary Edith Birch; *m* 1961, Gina Margaret Christ; two *s* one *d. Educ:* Shrewsbury Sch.; Trinity Coll., Cambridge (MA, PhD). Harkness Fellow, Princeton, 1957–58; Fellow: Trinity Coll., Cambridge, 1956–60; Churchill Coll., Cambridge, 1960–62; Sen. Lectr, later Reader, Univ. of Manchester, 1962–65; Reader in Mathematics, Univ. of Oxford, 1966–85. *Publications:* articles in learned jls, mainly on number theory; various editorships. *Recreations:* gardening (theoretical), music (passive). *Address:* Green Cottage, Boars Hill, Oxford OX1 5DQ. *T:* Oxford 735367; Mathematical Institute, 25–29 St Giles, Oxford. *T:* Oxford 54295.

BIRCH, Dennis Arthur, CBE 1977; DL; Councillor, West Midlands County Council, 1974–77; *b* 11 Feb. 1925; *s* of George Howard and Leah Birch; *m* 1948, Mary Therese Lyons; one *d. Educ:* Wolverhampton Municipal Grammar Sch. Wolverhampton County Borough Council: elected, 1952; served, 1952–74; Alderman, 1970–73; Mayor, 1973–74; Leader, 1967–73. Elected (following Local Govt reorganisation) Chm. West Midlands CC, 1974–76. DL West Midlands, 1979. MInstM. *Address:* 3 Tern Close, Wolverhampton Road East, Wolverhampton WV4 6AU. *T:* Sedgley 3837.

BIRCH, Frank Stanley Heath; Town Clerk and Chief Executive, Croydon, since 1982; *b* 8 Feb. 1939; *s* of late John Stanley Birch, CEng and Phyllis Edna Birch (*née* Heath), BA; *m* 1963, Diana Jacqueline Davies, BA; one *d. Educ:* Weston-super-Mare Grammar Sch. for Boys; Univ. of Wales (BA); Univ. of Birmingham (Inst. of Local Govt Studies). IPFA; MBIM. Entered local govt service, 1962; various appts, City Treasurer and Controller's Dept, Cardiff, 1962–69; Chief Internal Auditor, Dudley, 1969–73; Asst County Treasurer, 1973–74, Asst Chief Exec., 1974–76, W Midlands CC; Chief Exec., Lewisham, 1976–82. Hon. Clerk, Gen. Purposes Cttee, 1982–; Principal Grants Advr, 1983–86, London Boroughs Assoc.; Sec., London Co-ordinating Cttee, 1985–86. Dir, Croydon Business Venture Ltd, 1983–. Freeman, City of London, 1980. FRSA 1980. *Publications:* various articles on public admin and local govt management. *Recreations:* music, walking, caravanning, the countryside. *Address:* Town Clerk's Office, Taberner House, Croydon CR9 3JS. *T:* 01–686 4433.

BIRCH, John Allan; HM Diplomatic Service; Ambassador and Deputy Permanent Representative to United Nations, New York, since 1986; *b* 24 May 1935; *s* of late C. Allan Birch, MD, FRCP; *m* 1960, Primula Haselden; three *s* one *d. Educ:* Leighton Park Sch.; Corpus Christi Coll., Cambridge (MA). Served HM Forces, Middlesex Regt, 1954–56. Joined HM Foreign Service, 1959; served: Paris, 1960–63; Singapore, 1963–64; Bucharest, 1965–68; Geneva, 1968–70; Kabul, 1973–76; Royal Coll. of Defence Studies, 1977; Comprehensive Test Ban Treaty Negotiations, Geneva, 1977–80; Counsellor, Budapest, 1980–83; Hd of East European Dept, FCO, 1983–86. *Recreations:* tennis, skiing. *Address:* c/o Foreign and Commonwealth Office, SW1; 185 Emery Hill Street, SW1. *T:* 01–828 1746. *Club:* Athenæum.

BIRCH, John Anthony, MA; FRCM, PRCO(CHM), LRAM; Organist and Director of the Choir, Temple Church, since 1982; University Organist, University of Sussex, since 1967; Professor, Royal College of Music, since 1959; Organist: to the Royal Choral Society, since 1966; of the Royal Philharmonic Orchestra, since 1983; Curator-Organist, Royal Albert Hall, since 1984; *b* 9 July 1929; *s* of late Charles Aylmer Birch, Leek, Staffs; unmarried. *Educ:* Trent Coll.; Royal Coll. of Music (ARCM). Organist and Choirmaster, St Thomas's Church, Regent Street, London, 1950–53; Accompanist to St Michael's Singers, 1952–58; Organist and Choirmaster, All Saints Church, Margaret Street, London, 1953–58; Sub-Organist, HM Chapels Royal, 1957–58; Organist and Master of the Choristers, Chichester Cathedral, 1958–80. With the Cathedral Organists of Salisbury and Winchester re-established the Southern Cathedrals Festival, 1960; Musical Advr, Chichester Festival Theatre, 1962–80; Choirmaster, Bishop Otter Coll., Chichester, 1963–69. Rep., 1950–66, and Man. Dir, 1966–73, C. A. Birch Ltd, Staffs. Accompanist, Royal Choral Soc., 1965–70; Examr to Associated Bd, Royal Schs of Music, 1958–77; Vis. Lectr in Music, Univ. of Sussex, 1971–83. Special Comr, Royal Sch. of Church Music; Royal College of Organists: Mem. Council, 1964–; Pres., 1984–. Fellow, Corp. of SS Mary and Nicolas (Woodard Schs) 1973–; Governor: Hurstpierpoint Coll., 1974–; St Catherine's, Bramley, 1981–. Has made concert appearances in France, Belgium, Germany, Switzerland, Netherlands, Spain, Scandinavia and Far East; recital tours: Canada and US, 1966 and 1967, Australia and NZ, 1969, S Africa, 1978. Hon. MA Sussex, 1971. *Address:* 14 Spencer Walk, Putney, SW15 1PL. *T:* 01–789 6022. *Club:* Garrick.

BIRCH, Peter Gibbs; Chief Executive, Abbey National Building Society, since 1984; *b* 4 Dec. 1937; *m* 1962, Gillian (*née* Benge); three *s* one *d. Educ:* Allhallows Sch., Devon. Royal West Kent Regt, 1957–58 (2nd Lieut). Nestlé Co., 1958–65; Sales Manager, Gillette, 1965; Gen. Sales Manager, Gillette Australia, 1969; Man. Dir, Gillette, NZ, 1971; Gen. Manager, Gillette, SE Asia, 1973; Gp Gen. Manager, Gillette, Africa, ME, Eastern Europe, 1975; Man. Dir, Gillette UK, 1981. Dir, Abbey Nat. Building Soc., 1984–. *Recreations:* active holidays, swimming. *Address:* Cherry Croft, 6 Broad Highway, Cobham, Surrey KT11 2RP. *T:* Cobham 62655.

BIRCH, Philip Thomas; Deputy Chairman and Director, Piccadilly Radio, since 1973 (Founding Managing Director, 1973–83); *b* 23 April 1927; *s* of Thomas Stephen Birch and Ivy May Birch (*née* Bunyard); *m* 1979, Shiona Nelson Hawkins; four *s* one *d. Educ:* Beckenham Grammar Sch. Commnd Queen's Own Royal W Kent Regt, BAOR, 1945–47. Space Buyer, Notley Advertising, 1948–49; Media and Account Dir, J. Walter Thompson Co., 1950–64; Founding Man. Dir, Radio London, 1964–68; Head of Broadcasting, Associated Newspapers Gp, 1969–73. Founding Chairman: Associated Indep. Radio Services, 1973–81; AIRC Pension Trust, 1974–83; Chm., Assoc. of Indep. Radio Contractors Ltd, 1976; Founding Chm., Indep. Radio Sales, 1981–; Director: Associated Indep. Radio Gp, 1973–83; Indep. Radio News, 1983. *Recreations:* aviation, sailing, travel. *Address:* Piccadilly Radio, Piccadilly Plaza, Manchester M1 4AW. *T:* 061–236 9913. *Club:* St James (Manchester).

BIRCH, Reginald; Chairman, Communist Party of Britain (Marxist Leninist), since 1968; Member, General Council of the TUC, 1975–79; Member, Executive Council, AUEW, 1966–79; *b* 7 June 1914; *s* of Charles and Anne Birch; *m* 1942, Dorothy; three *s. Educ:* St Augustine's Elementary Sch., Kilburn. Apprentice toolmaker, 1929; at trade (toolmaker), until 1960. Divisional Organiser, AEU, 1960–66. Mem., Energy Commn, 1977–79. *Recreations:* swimming, growing herbs. *Address:* 29 Langley Park, NW7. *T:* 01–959 7058.

BIRCH, Robert Edward Thomas, CBE 1979; Director General, Federation Against Copyright Theft, 1982–85; *b* 9 May 1917; *s* of late Robert Birch and Edith Birch; *m* 1946, Laura Pia Busini; two *d. Educ:* Dulwich Coll. Served RA, 1940–46; Africa, Italy, NW Europe; Major. Admitted solicitor, 1942; joined Solicitors' Dept, New Scotland Yard, 1946; Dep. Solicitor, 1968; Solicitor, 1976–82. *Recreations:* swimming, travel. *Address:* c/o FACT Ltd, St Margarets House, 19–23 Wells Street, W1P 3FP.

BIRCH, Robin Arthur; Under Secretary, Department of Health and Social Security, since 1982; *b* 12 Oct. 1939; *s* of Arthur and Olive Birch; *m* 1962, Jane Marion Irvine Sturdy; two *s. Educ:* King Henry VIII Sch., Coventry; Christ Church, Oxford (Marjoribanks Scholar, 1957; Craven Scholar, 1959; MA). Entered Min. of Health as Asst Principal, 1961; Private Sec. to Charles Loughlin, MP (Parly Sec.), 1965–66; Principal, 1966; seconded to: Interdeptl Social Work Gp, 1969–70; Home Office, 1970–72; Asst Sec., DHSS, 1973; Chm., Working Party on Manpower and Trng for Social Services, 1974–76; Principal Private Sec. to Rt Hon. Norman St John-Stevas, MP (Leader of the House of Commons), 1980–81; Asst Auditor Gen., Nat. Audit Office, 1984–86, on secondment. Hon. Sec., Friends of Christ Church Cathedral, Oxford, 1978–. *Recreations:* family and friends; travel by train and bicycle; music, mainly before 1809; byways of classical antiquity; model railway. *Address:* Department of Health and Social Security, Alexander Fleming House, SE1.

BIRCH, Roger, QPM 1980; FBIM; Chief Constable, Sussex Police, since 1983; *b* 27 Sept. 1930; *s* of John Edward Lawrence Birch and Ruby Birch; *m* 1954, Jeanne Margaret Head; one *s. Educ:* King's Coll., Taunton. Cadet, Royal Naval Coll., Dartmouth, 1949–50; Pilot Officer, RAF, 1950–52. Devon Constabulary, 1954–72: Constable, uniform and CID; then through ranks to Chief Supt: Asst Chief Constable, Mid-Anglia Constab., 1972–74; Dep. Chief Constable, Kent Constab., 1974–78; Chief Constable, Warwickshire Constab., 1978–83. Part-time Lectr, Univ. of Cambridge Bd of Extra-Mural Studies, 1973–. Dir, Police Extended Interviews, 1983–; Chm., Traffic Cttee, Assoc. of Chief Police Officers, 1983–86; Trustee: Police Dependants' Trust, 1981–; Police Gurney Fund, 1983–. Mem., St John Ambulance Council, Sussex, 1986–. UK Vice-Pres., Royal Life Saving Soc., 1985– (Chm., SE Region, 1983–). Mem. Council, IAM, 1984–. *Publications:* articles on criminal intelligence, breath measuring instruments and on the urban environment, in learned jls. *Recreations:* swimming, music. *Address:* Police Headquarters, Malling House, Lewes, East Sussex BN7 2DZ. *T:* Lewes 475432. *Clubs:* Royal Air Force, Royal Automobile.

BIRCH, William, PhD; Director, Bristol Polytechnic, 1975–86; *b* 24 Nov. 1925; *s* of Frederick Arthur and Maude Olive Birch; *m* 1950, Mary Vine Stammers; one *s* one *d. Educ:* Ranelagh Sch.; Univ. of Reading. BA 1949, PhD 1957. Royal Navy, 1943–46, Sub-Lt RNVR. Lectr, Univ. of Bristol, 1950–60; Prof. of Geography, Grad. Sch. of Geog., Clark Univ., Worcester, Mass, USA, 1960–63; Prof., and Chm. of Dept of Geog., Univ. of Toronto, Canada, 1963–67; Prof., and Head of Dept of Geog., Univ. of Leeds, 1967–75. Pres., Inst. of British Geographers, 1976–77; Chm., Cttee of Directors of Polytechnics, 1982–84. Mem., ESRC, 1985–. *Publications:* The Isle of Man: a study in economic geography, 1964; contribs on higher educn policy and on geography and planning, Trans Inst. Brit. Geographers, Geog. Jl, Economic Geog., Annals Assoc. Amer. Geographers, Jl Environmental Management, etc. *Recreations:* sailing, squash, travel, gardening, pottery. *Address:* 13 Richmond Park Road, Clifton, Bristol BS8 3AS. *T:* 39719.

BIRCHALL, Prof. James Derek, FRS 1982; FRSC; ICI Senior Research Associate, Mond Division, since 1975; *b* 7 Oct. 1930; *s* of David Birchall and Dora Mary Birchall; *m* 1956, Pauline Mary Jones; two *s*. Joined ICI, 1957; Research Leader, 1965; Research Associate, 1970. Visiting Professor: Univ. of Surrey, 1976–; MIT, 1984–; Prof. Associate, Brunel Univ., 1983–. Industrial Fellow, Wolfson Coll., Oxford, 1977–79. Lectures: John D. Rose Meml, SCI, 1983; Mellor Meml, Inst. of Ceramics, 1984; Hurter Meml, SCI, Univ. of

Liverpool, 1986. *Publications:* A Classification of Fire Hazards, 1952, 2nd edn 1961; contribs to various encyclopedias and to learned jls, *ie* Nature, on inorganic chemistry and materials science. *Recreations:* old books, new cars. *Address:* Braeside, Stable Lane, Mouldsworth, Chester CH3 8AN. *T:* Manley 320.

BIRCHENOUGH, (John) Michael, BSc, PhD; Visiting Professor, School of Education, Open University, since 1986; Research Fellow, School of Education, University of Bristol, since 1983; Chief Inspector, Inner London Education Authority, 1973–83; *b* 17 Jan. 1923; *s* of John Buckley Birchenough and Elsie Birchenough; *m* 1945, Enid Humphries; two *s*. *Educ:* Ashford Grammar Sch., Kent; Chiswick County Sch.; London Univ. Chemist, May & Baker Ltd, 1943–45; teaching posts, 1946–60; HM Inspector of Schools, 1960; Staff Inspector, 1966; Chief Inspector, 1968–72. Pres., Educn Section, BAAS Annual Meeting, Stirling, 1974. *Publications:* contribs to Jl of Chem. Soc. and other scientific jls. *Address:* 28 London Lane, Great Paxton, Huntingdon, Cambs PE19 4RH.

BIRD, Rev. Dr Anthony Peter; General Medical Practitioner, since 1979; Principal of The Queen's College, Edgbaston, Birmingham, 1974–79; *b* 2 March 1931; *s* of late Albert Harry Bird and of Noel Whitehouse Bird; *m* 1962, Sabine Boehmig; two *s* one *d*. *Educ:* St John's Coll., Oxford (BA LitHum, BA Theol, MA); Birmingham Univ. (MB, ChB, 1970). Deacon, 1957; Priest, 1958; Curate of St Mary's, Stafford, 1957–60; Chaplain, then Vice-Principal of Cuddesdon Theological Coll., 1960–64. General Medical Practitioner, 1972–73. Member: Home Office Policy Adv. Cttee on Sexual Offences, 1976–80; Parole Board, 1977–80. *Publication:* The Search for Health: a response from the inner city, 1981. *Recreations:* water, walking, music—J. S. Bach, innovation in primary health care. *Address:* 93 Bournbrook Road, Birmingham B29 7BX.

BIRD, James Gurth, MBE 1945; TD 1951; *b* 30 Jan. 1909; *s* of Charles Harold Bird and Alice Jane Bird (*née* Kirtland); *m* 1940, Phyllis Ellis Pownall; one *s* two *d*. *Educ:* King William's Coll., Isle of Man (Scholar); St Catharine's Coll., Cambridge (exhibnr). Classical Tripos Pts I and II, BA 1931, MA 1933. Asst Master, Rossall Sch., 1931–33; Asst Master and House Master, Denstone Coll., 1933–47 (interrupted by War Service); Head Master, William Hulme's Grammar Sch., Manchester, 1947–74. FRSA. *Recreations:* golf, gardening. *Address:* Ty Deryn, Ravenspoint Road, Trearddur Bay, Holyhead, Gwynedd LL65 2AX.

BIRD, Michael Gwynne, CBE 1985; Chairman, Massey-Ferguson Holdings Ltd, since 1980; *b* 16 Aug. 1921; *s* of Edward Gwynne Bird, Chaplain, RN, and Brenda Bird (*née* Rumney); *m* 1944, Frances Yvonne Townley; one *s* two *d*. *Educ:* Harrow Sch.; St Catharine's Coll., Cambridge. Served war: commnd, Rifle Bde, 1941; demobilised (Major), 1946. Colonial Service (Administration), Malawi, 1948–54; called to the Bar, Inner Temple, 1955; joined Massey-Ferguson, 1955; Director, Legal Services, Massey-Ferguson Ltd, 1977; Chm., Perkins Engines Group, 1980; Vice-Pres., Massey-Ferguson Ltd, and Chm. European Corp., 1982–. *Address:* Broad Oak, Clive Road, Esher, Surrey. *T:* Esher 66241. *Clubs:* Oriental, MCC.

BIRD, Michael James; Chairman of Industrial Tribunal, Bristol, since 1984; *b* 11 Nov. 1935; *s* of Walter Garfield and Ireen Bird; *m* 1963, Susan Harris; three *d*. *Educ:* Lewis Sch., Pengam; King's Coll., Univ. of London (LLB Hons). Solicitor (Hons) 1961. Assistant solicitor, 1961–62; Partner, T. S. Edwards & Son, 1962–67, Sen. Partner, 1967–84. Deputy Registrar of County and High Court, 1976–77; Chairman of Industrial Tribunal, Cardiff (part-time), 1977–83. Chm., Gwent Italian Soc., 1978– (Sec., 1976–78); Member: Royal Life Saving Soc., 1976– (President's Commendation, 1984); Amateur Swimming Assoc. (Advanced Teacher, 1981–). *Recreations:* water sports, opera. *Address:* 17 Allt-yr-yn Avenue, Newport, Gwent NP9 5DA. *T:* Newport 52000.

BIRD, Sir Richard Dawnay M.; *see* Martin-Bird.

BIRD, Sir Richard (Geoffrey Chapman), 4th Bt *cr* 1922; *b* 3 Nov. 1935; *er* surv. *s* of Sir Donald Bird, 3rd Bt, and of Anne Rowena (*d* 1969), *d* of late Charles Chapman; *S* father, 1963; *m* 1st, 1957, Gillian Frances (*d* 1966), *d* of Bernard Haggett, Solihull; two *s* four *d*; 2nd, 1968, Helen Patricia, *d* of Frank Beaumont, Pontefract; two *d*. *Educ:* Beaumont. *Heir:* *s* John Andrew Bird, *b* 19 Jan. 1964. *Address:* 39 Ashleigh Road, Solihull, W Midlands B91 1AF.

BIRD, Richard Herries, CB 1983; Deputy Secretary, Department of Education and Science, since 1980; *b* 8 June 1932; *s* of late Edgar Bird and Armorel (*née* Dudley Scott); *m* 1963, Valerie, *d* of Edward and Mary Sanderson; two *d*. *Educ:* Winchester Coll.; Clare Coll., Cambridge. Min. of Transport and Civil Aviation, 1955; Private Sec. to Permanent Sec., 1958–60; Principal, 1960, Asst Sec., 1966, Min. of Transport; Principal Private Sec. to Minister of Transport, 1966–67; CSD 1969; DoE 1971; DES 1973, Under Sec. 1975. *Address:* High Beech, 53 Kippington Road, Sevenoaks, Kent TN13 2LL. *T:* Sevenoaks 456777.

BIRD, Rt. Hon. Vere Cornwall, PC 1982; Prime Minister of Antigua and Barbuda, since 1981; *b* 7 Dec. 1910. *Educ:* St John's Boys' School, Antigua; Salvation Army Training School, Trinidad. Founder Mem. Exec., Antigua Trades and Labour Union, 1939 (Pres., 1943–67); Member: Antigua Legislative Council, 1945; Antigua Exec. Council, 1946 (Cttee Chm., 1951–56, land reform); Ministry of Trade and Production, 1956–60; first Chief Minister, 1960–67, first Premier, 1967–71; re-elected to Parlt, 1976, 1980; Leader, Antigua Labour Party. *Address:* Office of the Prime Minister, St John's, Antigua, West Indies.

BIRD-WILSON, Air Vice-Marshal Harold Arthur Cooper, CBE 1962; DSO 1945; DFC 1940 and Bar 1943; AFC 1946 and Bar 1955; *b* 20 Nov. 1919; *m* 1942, Audrey Wallace; one *s* one *d*. *Educ:* Liverpool Coll. Joined RAF, Nov. 1937; No 17 Fighter Sqdn, Kenley, 1938. Served War of 1939–45 (France, Dunkirk, Battle of Britain): Flt Comdr No 234 Sqdn, 1941; Sqdn Comdr Nos 152 and 66, 1942 (despatches); Wing Leader, No 83 Gp, 1943; Comd and Gen. Staff Sch., Fort Leavenworth, Kansas, USA, 1944; Wing Leader, Harrowbeer, Spitfire Wing and then Bentwater Mustang Wing, 1944–45; CO, Jet Conversion Unit, 1945–46; CO, Air Fighting Development Sqdn, CFE, 1946–47; Op. Staff, HQ, MEAF, 1948; RAF Staff Coll., Bracknell, 1949; Personal Staff Officer to C-in-C, MEAF, 1949–50; RAF Flying Coll., Manby, 1951; OC Tactics, CFE, 1952 54; Staff, BJSM, Washington, USA, 1954–57; Staff, Air Sec. Dept., Air Min., 1957–59; CO, RAF Coltishall, 1959–61; Staff Intell., Air Min., 1961–63; AOC and Comdt, CFS, 1963–65; AOC Hong Kong, 1965–67; Dir of Flying (Research and Develt), Min. of Technology, 1967–70; AOC No 23 Gp, 1970–73; Comdr, S Maritime Air Region, RAF, 1973–74, retired. BAC, Saudi Arabia, then British Aerospace, 1974–84, retired. Czechoslovak Medal of Merit 1st class, 1945; Dutch DFC, 1945.

BIRDSALL, Derek Walter, RDI; AGI; FSIAD; freelance graphic designer; *b* 1 Aug. 1934; *s* of Frederick Birdsall and Hilda Birdsall (*née* Smith); *m* 1954, Shirley Thompson; three *s* one *d*. *Educ:* King's Sch., Pontefract, Yorks; Wakefield Coll. of Art, Yorks; Central Sch. of Arts and Crafts, London (NDD). National Service, RAOC Printing Unit, Cyprus, 1955–57. Lectr in Typographical Design, London Coll. of Printing, 1959–61; freelance graphic designer, working from his studio in Covent Garden, 1961–. Has broadcast on TV and radio on design subjects and his work; catalogue designs for major museums in UK and USA have won many awards. Mem., AGI, 1968–; FSIAD 1964; RDI 1982. *Publications:* (with C. H. O'D. Alexander) Fischer *v* Spassky, 1972; (with C. H. O'D. Alexander) A Book of Chess, 1974; (with Carlo M. Cippola) The Technology of Man—a visual history, 1978. *Recreations:* chess, poker. *Address:* 9 Compton Terrace, Islington, N1 2UD. *T:* 01-226 8057. *Club:* Seven Dials.

BIRDSALL, Mrs Doris, CBE 1985; Lord Mayor of Bradford Metropolitan District, 1975–76; *b* 20 July 1915; *d* of Fred and Violet Ratcliffe; *m* 1940, James Birdsall; one *s* one *d*. *Educ:* Hanson Girls' Grammar School. Mem. Bradford City Council, 1958, Chm. of Educn Cttee, 1972–74; Mem. Bradford Univ. Council, 1963–. Hon. MA Bradford, 1975; Hon. LHD Lesley Coll., Mass, 1976. *Address:* 24 Baildon Road, Baildon, Bradford, West Yorks. *T:* Bradford 596251.

BIRDWOOD, family name of **Baron Birdwood.**

BIRDWOOD, 3rd Baron *cr* 1938, of Anzac and of Totnes; **Mark William Ogilvie Birdwood;** Bt 1919; Director, Wrightson Wood Ltd; *b* 23 Nov. 1938; *s* of 2nd Baron Birdwood, MVO, and of Vere Lady Birdwood, CVO; *S* father, 1962; *m* 1963, Judith Helen, *e d* of R. Seymour Roberts, Newton Aycliffe, Darlington, Co. Durham; one *d*. *Educ:* Radley Coll.; Trinity Coll., Cambridge. Liveryman, Glaziers' Co. *Address:* 5 Holbein Mews, SW1; Russell House, Broadway, Worcs. *Club:* Brooks's.

BIRK, family name of **Baroness Birk.**

BIRK, Baroness *cr* 1967 (Life Peer), of Regent's Park in Greater London; **Alma Birk,** JP; journalist; *d* of late Barnett and Alice Wilson; *m* Ellis Birk; one *s* one *d*. *Educ:* South Hampstead High Sch.; LSE. BSc Econ (Hons) London. Leader of Labour Group, Finchley Borough Council, 1950–53; contested (Lab): Ruislip-Northwood, 1950; Portsmouth West, 1951, 1955. Baroness in Waiting (Govt Whip), March-Oct. 1974; Parly Under-Sec. of State, DoE, 1974–79; Minister of State, Privy Council Office, 1979. Associate Editor, Nova, 1965–69. Dir, New Shakespeare Co. Ltd, 1979–. Formerly Lectr and Prison Visitor, Holloway Prison. Mem., Youth Service Develt Council, 1967–71; Chm., Health Educn Council, 1969–72; President: Assoc. of Art Instns, 1984–; Craft Arts Design Assoc.,1984–; Vice-President: AMA, 1982–; Council for Children's Welfare, 1968–75; H. G. Wells Soc., 1967–; Stamford Hill Associated Clubs, 1967–70; Redbridge Jewish Youth Centre, 1970–; Playboard, 1984–; Member: Fabian Soc., 1946– (Sec., Fabian Soc. Res. Cttee on Marriage and Divorce, 1951–52); Howard League for Penal Reform, 1948– (Exec., 1980–); Hendon Group Hosp. Management Cttee, 1951–59; Panel, London Pregnancy Adv. Service, 1968–; RCOG working party on the unplanned pregnancy, 1969–72; Exec., Council of Christians and Jews, 1971–77; Hon. Cttee, Albany Trust; Ct of Governors, LSE, 1971–; Council, British Museum Soc., 1979–; Council, RSA, 1983–; Adv. Cttee on Service Candidates, 1984–; All-party Penal Affairs Gp, 1983–; Council, Georgian Gp, 1985; Chm. Arts Sub-Cttee, Holocaust Meml Cttee, 1979–. Trustee: Yorkshire Sculpture Park, 1980–; Health Promotion Res. Trust, 1983–; Stress Syndrome Foundn, 1983–; Governor: BFI, 1981–; Mander Mitchenson Theatre Collection, 1981–. FRSA 1980. JP Highgate, 1952. *Publications:* pamphlets, articles. *Recreations:* travelling, theatre, reading, talking. *Address:* 3 Wells Rise, NW8 7LH.

BIRKENHEAD, Bishop Suffragan of, since 1974; **Rt. Rev. Ronald Brown;** *b* 7 Aug. 1926; *s* of Fred and Ellen Brown; *m* 1951, Joyce Hymers; one *s* one *d*. *Educ:* Kirkham Grammar Sch.; Durham Univ. (BA, DipTh). Vicar of Whittle-le-Woods, 1956; Vicar of St Thomas, Halliwell, Bolton, 1961; Rector and Rural Dean of Ashton-under-Lyne, 1970. *Recreations:* antiques and golf. *Address:* Trafford House, Queen's Park, Chester CH4 7AX. *T:* Chester 675895. *Club:* National Liberal.

BIRKETT, family name of **Baron Birkett.**

BIRKETT, 2nd Baron *cr* 1958, of Ulverston; **Michael Birkett;** film producer since 1961; *b* 22 Oct. 1929; *s* of 1st Baron Birkett, PC and Ruth Birkett (*née* Nilsson, she *d* 1969); *S* father, 1962; *m* 1st, 1960, Junia Crawford (*d* 1973); 2nd, 1978, Gloria Taylor; one *s*. *Educ:* Stowe; Trinity Coll., Cambridge. Asst Dir at Ealing Studios and Ealing Films, 1953–59; Asst Dir, 1959–61, on films including: The Mark; The Innocents; Billy Budd; Associate Producer: Some People, 1961–62; Modesty Blaise, 1965; Producer: The Caretaker, 1962; Marat/Sade, 1966; A Midsummer Night's Dream, 1967; King Lear, 1968–69; Director: The Launching and The Soldier's Tale, 1963; Overture and Beginners, the More Man Understands, 1964; Outward Bound, 1971. Dep. Dir, National Theatre, 1975–77; Consultant to Nat. Theatre on films, TV and sponsorship, 1977–79; Dir for Recreation and Arts, GLC, 1979–86. A Vice-Pres., British Board of Film Classification, 1985–. Master, Curriers' Co., 1975–76. *Recreations:* music, printing, horticulture, ballet. *Heir:* *s* Hon. Thomas Birkett, *b* 25 July 1982. *Address:* House of Lords, SW1.

BIRKETT, George William Alfred, CBE 1960; CEng, FIEE, FIMechE; Director of Weapons Production, Ministry of Defence (Naval), 1965–70, retired; *b* 16 June 1908; *m* 1939, Doris Lillian Prince; one *s*. *Educ:* Portsmouth Municipal College. Portsmouth Dockyard, 1929; Techn. Officer, HM Signal Sch., 1938; Prin. Scientific Officer, RNSS, 1946; Sen. Prin. Production Engr, Admty Production Pool, 1953; Supt of Production Pool, Admty, 1956. *Recreation:* sailing. *Address:* 81 Ferndale, Inhurst Wood, Waterlooville, Portsmouth, Hants. *T:* Waterlooville 52695.

BIRKIN, Sir John (Christian William), 6th Bt *cr* 1905, of Ruddington Grange, Notts; with BBC Television, since 1977; *b* 2 July 1953; *s* of Sir Charles Lloyd Birkin, 5th Bt and Janet (*d* 1983), *d* of Peter Johnson; *S* father, 1985. *Educ:* Eton; Trinity Coll., Dublin; London Film School. *Heir:* *cousin* Geoffrey Ivor Birkin, TD, *b* 17 Nov. 1911. *Address:* 23 St Luke's Street, Chelsea, SW3 3RP. *T:* 01-351 4810.

BIRKIN, John Derek, TD 1965; Chief Executive and Deputy Chairman, Rio Tinto-Zinc Corporation PLC, since 1985; *b* 30 Sept 1929; *s* of Noah and Rebecca Birkin; *m* 1952, Sadie Smith; one *s* one *d*. *Educ:* Hemsworth Grammar Sch. Managing Director: Velmar Ltd, 1966–67; Nairn Williamson Ltd, 1967–70; Tunnel Holdings Ltd, 1970–75; Chm. and Man. Dir, Tunnel Holdings, 1975–82; Dir, Rio Tinto-Zinc Corp., 1982–, Dep. Chief Exec., 1983–85. Director: Smiths Industries, 1977–84; British Gas Corp., 1982–85; George Wimpey, 1984–; CRA Ltd (Australia), 1985–; Rio Algom Ltd (Canada), 1985–; RTZ Metals Ltd, 1985–; RTZ Oil & Gas Ltd, 1985–; RTZ Pillar Ltd, 1985–; The Merchants Trust PLC, 1986–. Mem. Council, Industrial Soc., 1985–. *Recreations:* opera, Rugby, cricket. *Address:* (office) 6 St James's Square, SW1Y 4LD.

BIRKINSHAW, Prof. John Howard, DSc; FRSC; retired as Professor of Biochemistry and Head of Department of Biochemistry, London School of Hygiene and Tropical Medicine, University of London (1956–62), now Emeritus; *b* 8 Oct. 1894; *s* of John Thomas and Madeline Birkinshaw, Garforth, near Leeds; *m* 1929, Elizabeth Goodwin Guthrie, Ardrossan, Ayrshire; one *s* one *d*. *Educ:* Leeds Modern Sch.; Leeds Univ. War service, 1915, West Yorks Regt and Machine Gun Corps (POW); demobilised, 1919. BSc Hons 1920, MSc 1921, DSc 1929, Leeds. Research Biochemist to Nobel's Explosives Co. (later ICI), 1920–30; Research Asst to Prof. Raistrick, London Sch. of Hygiene and

Tropical Medicine, 1931; Senior Lecturer, 1938; Reader, 1945. *Publications:* about 60 scientific papers in Biochemical Journal, Philos. Trans. Royal Society, etc. *Recreation:* photography. *Address:* 87 Barrow Point Avenue, Pinner, Mddx. *T:* 01–866 4784.

BIRKMYRE, Sir Henry, 2nd Bt *cr* 1921, of Dalmunzie; *b* 24 March 1898; *er s* of Sir Archibald Birkmyre, 1st Bt and Anne, *e d* of Capt. James Black; *S* father, 1935; *m* 1922, Doris Gertrude, *er d* of late Col H. Austen Smith, CIE; one *s* one *d*. *Educ:* Wellington. War Service in France with RFA, 1917. *Heir: s* Archibald Birkmyre [*b* 12 Feb. 1923; *m* 1953, Gillian Mary, *o d* of Eric Downes, OBE; one *s* two *d*]. *Recreation:* golf. *Address:* 11 Crittles Court, Wadhurst, E Sussex TN5 6BY. *T:* Wadhurst 3486.

BIRKS, Dr Jack, CBE 1975; FEng 1978; Chairman: LAE Energy (formerly Schroder Energy) Inc., since 1981; Charterhouse Petroleum plc, since 1982; British Maritime Technology, since 1985; London American Energy NV, since 1986; Director: George Wimpey PLC, since 1982; Jebsens Drilling plc, since 1982; Petrofina (UK) Ltd, since 1986; Mountain Petroleum Ltd, since 1986; *b* 1 Jan. 1920; *s* of late Herbert Horace Birks and of Ann Birks; *m* 1948, Vere Elizabeth Burrell-Davis; two *s* two *d*. *Educ:* Ecclesfield Grammar Sch.; Univ. of Leeds (BSc, PhD). Served with REME, Europe and India, 1941–46 (despatches, Captain). Exploration Research Div., Anglo Iranian Oil Co., 1948–57; Man., Petroleum Engrg Research, BP Research Centre, Sunbury, 1957–59; Vice-Pres. Exploration, BP North America, NY, 1959–62; various techn. and managerial appts, subseq. Dir and Gen. Man., Iranian Oil Exploration & Producing Co., Teheran and Masjid-i-Sulaiman, 1962–70; Gen. Man., Exploration and Production Dept, British Petroleum Co. Ltd, London, 1970–72; Technical Dir, BP Trading Ltd, and Dep. Chm., BP Trading Exec. Cttee, 1972–77; a Man. Dir, British Petroleum, 1978–82; Chairman: BP Coal, 1981–82; Selection Trust, 1981–82; BP Minerals International, 1981–82; NMI Ltd, 1982–85. Member: SRC, 1976–80; Meteorological Cttee, 1977–82; Adv. Council on R&D, Dept of Energy, 1978–82; Offshore Energy Technology Bd, Dept of Energy, 1978–82. President: Soc. for Underwater Technology, 1974; Pipeline Industries Guild, 1979–81; Inst. of Petroleum, 1984–. Hon. LLD Aberdeen, 1981; DU Surrey, 1981. *Publications:* contribs to technical internat. oil jls, sci. papers on oilfields develts and North Sea oil. *Recreations:* tennis, cricket, golf. *Address:* 1A Alwyne Road, Canonbury, N1 2HH. *T:* 01–226 4905; High Silver, High Street, Holt, Norfolk NR25 6BN. *T:* Holt 2847. *Club:* Athenæum.

BIRKS, Michael; His Honour Judge Birks; a Circuit Judge, since 1983; *b* 21 May 1920; *s* of late Falconer Moffat Birks, CBE, and Monica Katherine Lushington (*née* Mellor); *m* 1947, Ann Ethne, *d* of Captain Henry Stafford Morgan; one *d*. *Educ:* Oundle; Trinity Coll., Cambridge. Commissioned 22nd Dragoons, 1941; attached Indian Army, 1942, invalided out, 1943. Admitted Solicitor, 1946; Assistant Registrar: Chancery Div., High Court, 1953–60; Newcastle upon Tyne group of County Courts, 1960–61; Registrar: Birkenhead gp of County Courts, 1961–66; W London County Court, 1966–83; a Recorder of the Crown Court, 1979–83. Adv. Editor, Atkins Court Forms, 1966–; Jt Editor, County Court Practice, 1976–83. Mem. County Court Rule Cttee, 1980–83. *Publications:* Gentlemen of the Law, 1960; Small Claims in the County Court, 1973; Enforcing Money Judgments in the County Court, 1980; contributed titles: County Courts and Interpleader (part), 4th edn Halsbury's Laws of England; Judgments and Orders (part), References and Inquiries (part), Service (part), and Transfer (part), County Courts Atkins Court Forms; contribs to legal jls. *Recreations:* sailing, painting. *Address:* c/o South Eastern Circuit Office, New Cavendish House, 18 Maltravers Street, WC2R 3EU.

BIRKS, Prof. Peter Brian Herrenden; Professor of Civil Law, Edinburgh University, since 1981; *b* 3 Oct. 1941; *e s* of Dr Peter Herrenden Birks and Mary (*née* Morgan); *m* 1984, Jacqueline S. Berrington (*née* Stimpson). *Educ:* Trinity Coll., Oxford (MA); University Coll., London (LLM). Lectr in Laws, UCL, 1966–71; Law Fellow, Brasenose Coll., Oxford, 1971–81. *Publications:* Introduction to the Law of Restitution, 1985; articles on Roman law, legal history and restitution. *Address:* Flat 12, 3 Forrest Hill, Edinburgh EH1 2QL. *T:* 031–225 2429; 8 Cobden Crescent, Oxford OX1 4LJ. *T:* Oxford 727170.

BIRLEY, Anthony Addison, CB 1979; Clerk of Public Bills, House of Commons, 1973–82, retired; *b* 28 Nov. 1920; *s* of Charles Fair Birley and Eileen Mia Rouse; *m* 1951, Jane Mary Ruggles-Brise; two *d*. *Educ:* Winchester (exhibnr); Christ Church, Oxford (MA). Served War in RA (Ayrshire Yeomanry), 1940–45, in North Africa and Italian campaigns (wounded). Asst Clerk, House of Commons, 1948; Clerk of Standing Cttees, 1970. *Recreations:* gardening, walking, racing. *Address:* Holtom House, Paxford, Chipping Campden, Glos. *T:* Paxford 318. *Club:* Army and Navy.

BIRLEY, Derek; Vice-Chancellor, University of Ulster, since 1984; *b* 31 May 1926; *s* of late Sydney John and late Margaret Birley; *m* 1948, Margery Duckworth; two *s*. *Educ:* Hemsworth Grammar Sch.; Queens' Coll., Cambridge; Manchester Univ. BA 1950, MA 1954, Cantab. Royal Artillery, 1944–48; Schoolmaster, Queen Elizabeth Grammar Sch., Wakefield, 1952–55; Admin. Asst, Leeds Educn Cttee, 1955–59; Asst Educn Officer: Dorset, 1959–61; Lancs, 1961–64; Dep. Dir of Educn, Liverpool, 1964–70; Rector, Ulster Polytechnic, 1970–84. *Publications:* The Education Officer and his World, 1970; (with Anne Dufton) An Equal Chance, 1971; Planning and Education, 1972; The Willow Wand, 1979. *Recreations:* books, cricket, jazz. *Address:* Knocktarna, 195 Mountsandel Road, Coleraine, Co. Londonderry BT52 1TA.

BIRLEY, Prof. Eric, MBE 1943; FSA 1931; FBA 1969; Professor of Roman-British History and Archæology, University of Durham, 1956–71, now Professor Emeritus; *b* 12 Jan. 1906; *y s* of J. Harold Birley; *m* 1934, Margaret Isabel, *d* of Rev. James Goodlet; two *s*. *Educ:* Clifton Coll.; Brasenose Coll., Oxford. Lecturer, University of Durham, 1931; Reader, 1943. War of 1939–45: Military Intelligence, Lt-Col, GSO1 Military Intelligence Research Section; Chief of German Military Document Section, War Dept. Vice-Master, Hatfield Coll., Durham, 1947–49, Master, 1949–56; first Dean of Faculty of Social Sciences, Univ. of Durham, 1968–70. President: Soc. of Antiquaries of Newcastle upon Tyne, 1957–59; Cumberland and Westmorland Antiquarian and Archaeological Soc., 1957–60; Architectural and Archæological Soc. of Durham and Northumberland, 1959–63; Member: German Archæological Inst.; Ancient Monuments Board for England, 1966–76; Hon. Member, Gesellschaft Pro Vindonissa (Switzerland); Hon. FSAScot, 1980; Chm., Vindolanda Trust, 1970–; Hon. Life Pres., Internat. Congress of Roman Frontier Studies, 1974. Hon. Dr Phil Freiburg i Br, 1970; Hon. DLitt Leicester, 1971; Dr *hc* Heidelberg, 1986. Polonia Restituta, 1944; Legion of Merit, 1947. *Publications:* The Centenary Pilgrimage of Hadrian's Wall, 1949; Roman Britain and the Roman Army, 1953; (ed) The Congress of Roman Frontier Studies 1949, 1952; Research on Hadrian's Wall, 1961; (jt ed) Roman Frontier Studies 1969, 1974; Fifty-one Ballades, 1980; numerous papers on Roman Britain and on the Roman army, excavation reports, etc. *Recreation:* archæology. *Address:* Carvoran House, Greenhead, Carlisle CA6 7JB. *T:* Gilsland 594.

BIRLEY, James Leatham Tennant, FRCP, FRCPsych, DPM; Consultant Psychiatrist, Bethlem Royal and Maudsley Hospitals, since 1969; Dean, Royal College of Psychiatrists, 1982–July 1987; *b* 31 May 1928; *s* of late Dr James Leatham Birley and Margaret Edith (*née* Tennant); *m* 1954, Julia Davies; one *s* three *d*. *Educ:* Winchester Coll.; University Coll., Oxford; St Thomas' Hosp., London. Maudsley Hospital: Registrar, 1960; Sen. Registrar, 1963; Mem. Scientific Staff, MRC Social Psychiatry Research Unit, 1965; Dean, Inst. of Psychiatry, SE5, 1971–82. *Publications:* contribs to scientific jls. *Recreations:* music, gardening. *Address:* 133 Sydenham Hill, SE26 6LW.

BIRLEY, Michael Pellew, MA (Oxon); Housemaster, 1970–80, Assistant Master, 1980–84, Marlborough College; *b* 7 Nov. 1920; *s* of late Norman Pellew Birley, DSO, MC, and of Eileen Alice Morgan; *m* 1949, Ann Grover (*née* Street); two *s* two *d*. *Educ:* Marlborough Coll.; Wadham Coll., Oxford. 1st class Classical Honour Moderations, 1940; 1st class *Litterae Humaniores,* 1947; MA 1946. Served War of 1939–45 with the Royal Fusiliers; joined up, Sept. 1940; commissioned, April 1941; abroad, 1942–45 (despatches); demobilised, Jan. 1946. Taught Classics: Shrewsbury Sch., 1948–50; Eton Coll., 1950–56; Headmaster, Eastbourne College, 1956–70. Member Council: Ardingly Coll., 1981–; Marlborough Coll., 1985–. Fellow, Woodard Corp., 1983–. *Recreations:* sailing, gardening, wine-making. *Address:* Long Summers, Cross Lane, Marlborough, Wilts.

BIRMINGHAM, Archbishop of, (RC), since 1982; **Most Rev. Maurice Noël Léon Couve de Murville;** *b* 27 June 1929; *s* of Noël Couve de Murville and Marie, *d* of Sir Louis Souchon. *Educ:* Downside School; Trinity Coll., Cambridge (MA); STL (Institut Catholique, Paris); MPhil (Sch. of Oriental and African Studies, Univ. of London). Priest, 1957; Curate, St Anselm's, Dartford, 1957–60; Priest-in-Charge, St Francis, Moulsecoomb, 1961–64; Catholic Chaplain: Univ. of Sussex, 1961–77; Univ. of Cambridge, 1977–82. *Publications:* (with Philip Jenkins) Catholic Cambridge, 1983; John Milner 1752–1826, 1986. *Recreations:* walking, gardening, local history. *Address:* 57 Mearse Lane, Barnt Green, Birmingham B45 8HJ. *T:* 021–445 1467.

BIRMINGHAM, Bishop of, 1978–1 April 1987; **Rt. Rev. Hugh William Montefiore,** MA, BD; *b* 12 May 1920; *s* of late Charles Sebag-Montefiore, OBE, and Muriel Alice Ruth Sebag-Montefiore; *m* 1945, Elisabeth Mary Macdonald Paton, *d* of late Rev. William Paton, DD, and Mrs Grace Paton; three *d*. *Educ:* Rugby Sch.; St John's Coll., Oxford (Hon. Fellow, 1981). Served during war, 1940–45; Capt. RA (Royal Bucks Yeo). Deacon 1949, priest 1950. Curate, St George's, Jesmond, Newcastle, 1949–51; Chaplain and Tutor, Westcott House, Cambridge, 1951–53; Vice-Principal, 1953–54; Examining Chaplain: to Bishop of Newcastle, 1953–70; to Bishop of Worcester, 1957–60; to Bishop of Coventry, 1957–70; to Bishop of Blackburn, 1966–70; Fellow and Dean of Gonville and Caius Coll., 1954–63; Lectr in New Testament, Univ. of Cambridge, 1959–63; Vicar of Great Saint Mary's, Cambridge, 1963–70; Canon Theologian of Coventry, 1959–70; Hon. Canon of Ely, 1969–70; Bishop Suffragan of Kingston-upon-Thames, 1970–78. Mem., Archbishops' Commn on Christian Doctrine, 1967–76; Chm., General Synod Bd for Social Responsibility, 1983–. Chm., Indep. Commn on Transport, 1973. Hon. DD: Aberdeen, 1976; Birmingham, 1985. *Publications:* (contrib.) The Historic Episcopate and the Fullness of the Church, 1954; To Help You To Pray, 1957; (contrib.) Soundings, 1962; Josephus and the New Testament, 1962; (with H. E. W. Turner) Thomas and the Evangelists, 1962; Beyond Reasonable Doubt, 1963; (contrib.) God, Sex and War, 1963; Awkward Questions on Christian Love, 1964; A Commentary on the Epistle to the Hebrews, 1964; Truth to Tell, 1966; (ed) We Must Love One Another Or Die, 1966; (contrib.) The Responsible Church, 1966; Remarriage and Mixed Marriage, 1967; (contrib.) Journeys in Belief, 1968; (ed) Sermons From Great St Mary's, 1968; My Confirmation Notebook, 1968; The Question Mark, 1969; Can Man Survive, 1970; (ed) More Sermons From Great St Mary's, 1971; Doom or Deliverance?, 1972; (ed) Changing Directions, 1974; (ed) Man and Nature, 1976; Apocalypse, 1976; (ed) Nuclear Crisis, 1977; (ed) Yes to Women Priests, 1978; Taking our Past into our Future, 1978; Paul the Apostle, 1981; Jesus Across the Centuries, 1983; The Probability of God, 1985; So Near And Yet So Far, 1986; contribs to New Testament and Theological jls. *Address:* Bishop's Croft, Birmingham, W Midlands B17 0BG. *T:* 021–427 2062. *Club:* Royal Commonwealth Society.

See also Rev. Canon D. M. Paton, Ven. M. J. M. Paton, Prof. Sir W. D. M. Paton.

BIRMINGHAM, Auxiliary Bishops of, (RC); *see* Cleary, Rt Rev. Joseph; McCartie, Rt Rev. P. L.

BIRMINGHAM, Provost of; *see* Berry, Very Rev. P. A.

BIRMINGHAM, Archdeacon of; *see* Duncan, Ven. J. F.

BIRT, John; Director of Programmes, London Weekend Television, since 1982; *b* 10 Dec. 1944; *s* of Leo Vincent Birt and Ida Birt; *m* 1965, Jane Frances (*née* Lake); one *s* one *d*. *Educ:* St Mary's Coll., Liverpool; St Catherine's Coll., Oxford (MA). Producer, Nice Time, 1968–69; Joint Editor, World in Action, 1969–70; Producer, The Frost Programme, 1971–72; Executive Producer, Weekend World, 1972–74; Head of Current Affairs, LWT, 1974–77; Co-Producer, The Nixon Interviews, 1977; Controller of Features and Current Affairs, LWT, 1977–81. Member: Wilton Park Academic Council, 1980–83; Media Law Gp, 1983–; Broadcasting Research Unit: Mem., Working Party on the new Technologies, 1981–83; Mem., Exec. Cttee, 1983–. *Publications:* various articles in newspapers and journals. *Recreation:* walking. *Address:* c/o London Weekend Television, SE1. *T:* 01–261 3434.

BIRT, Prof. (Lindsay) Michael, AO 1986; CBE 1980; Vice-Chancellor, University of New South Wales, since 1981; *b* 18 Jan. 1932; *s* of Robert Birt and Florence Elizabeth Chapman; *m* 1959, Avis Jennypher Tapfield; two *s*. *Educ:* Melbourne Boys' High Sch.; Univ. of Melbourne; Univ. of Oxford. BAgrSc, BSc and PhD (Melb), DPhil (Oxon). Univ. of Melbourne: Lectr in Biochemistry, 1960–63, Sen. Lectr in Biochem., 1964; Sen. Lectr in Biochem., Univ. of Sheffield, 1964–67; Foundn Prof. of Biochemistry, ANU, 1967–73; Vice-Chancellor designate, Wollongong Univ. Coll., Nov. 1973; Vice-Chancellor, Univ. of Wollongong, 1975–81; Emer. Prof., ANU, 1974. Hon. DLitt Wollongong, 1981. *Publication:* Biochemistry of the Tissues (with W. Bartley and P. Banks), 1968 (London), 1970 (Germany, as Biochemie), 1972 (Japan). *Recreations:* music, reading. *Address:* University of New South Wales, PO Box 1, Kensington, NSW 2033, Australia. *T:* (02)-697–2884. *Clubs:* Union (Sydney); Melbourne Cricket, Sydney Cricket.

BIRT, Ven. Canon William Raymond; Assistant Rector of West Woodhay; *b* 25 Aug. 1911; *s* of Rev. Douglas Birt, Rector of Leconfield with Scorborough, and Dorothy Birt; *m* 1936, Marie Louise Jeaffreson; one *s* two *d*. *Educ:* Christ's Hospital; Ely Theological Coll. Journalist until 1940. Major, 22nd Dragoons (RAC), 1941–46 (despatches). Publisher, 1946–55. Deacon, 1956; priest, 1957; Curate, Caversham, 1956–59; Vicar, St George, Newbury, 1959–71; Rector of West Woodhay, 1971–81; Rural Dean of Newbury, 1969–73; Archdeacon of Berkshire, 1973–77; Hon. Canon of Christ Church Cathedral, Oxford, 1980; Archdeacon Emeritus, Diocese of Oxford, 1985. *Recreations:* gardens and gardening. *Address:* West Woodhay Rectory, Newbury, Berkshire RG15 0BL. *T:* Inkpen 359.

BIRTWISTLE, Maj.-Gen. Archibald Cull, CB 1983; CBE 1976 (OBE 1971); Signal Officer in Chief (Army), 1980–83, retired; *b* 19 Aug. 1927; *s* of Walter Edwin Birtwistle and Eila Louise Cull; *m* 1956, Sylvia Elleray; two *s* one *d. Educ:* Sir John Deane's Grammar School, Northwich; St John's Coll., Cambridge (MA Mech. Sciences). CEng, MIEE. Commissioned, Royal Signals, 1949; served: Korea (despatches, 1952); UK; BAOR; CCR Sigs 1 (Br) Corps, 1973–75; Dep. Comdt, RMCS, 1975–79; Chief Signal Officer, BAOR, 1979–80. Col Comdt, Royal Corps of Signals, 1983–; Hon. Col, Durham and South Tyne ACF, 1983–. *Recreations:* all sports, especially Rugby (former Chairman, Army Rugby Union), soccer and cricket; gardening. *Address:* c/o National Westminster Bank PLC, 97 High Street, Northallerton, North Yorks DL7 8PS. *T:* (home) Northallerton 2685.

BIRTWISTLE, Harrison; composer; an Associate Director, National Theatre, since 1975; *b* 1934; *m* Sheila; three *s. Educ:* Royal Manchester Coll. of Music; RAM. Dir of Music, Cranborne Chase Sch., 1962–65. Vis. Fellow, Princeton Univ., 1966–68; Cornell Vis. Prof. of Music, Swarthmore Coll., 1973; Vis. Slee Prof., State Univ. of NY at Buffalo, 1974–75. *Publications:* Refrains and Choruses, 1957; Monody for Corpus Christi, 1959; Précis, 1959; The World is Discovered, 1960; Chorales, 1962, 1963; Entre'actes and Sappho Fragments, 1964; Three Movements with Fanfares, 1964; Tragoedia, 1965; Ring a Dumb Carillon, 1965; Carmen Paschale, 1965; The Mark of the Goat, 1965, 1966; The Visions of Francesco Petrarca, 1966; Verses, 1966; Punch and Judy, 1966–67 (opera); Three Lessons in a Frame, 1967; Linoii, 1968; Nomos, 1968; Verses for Ensembles, 1969; Down by the Greenwood Side, 1969; Hoquetus David (arr. of Machaut), 1969; Cantata, 1969; Ut Hermita Solvs, 1969; Medusa, 1969–70; Prologue, 1970; Nenia on the Death of Orpheus, 1970; An Imaginary Landscape, 1971; Meridian, 1971; The Fields of Sorrow, 1971; Chronometer, 1971; Epilogue—Full Fathom Five, 1972; Tombeau, 1972; The Triumph of Time, 1972; La Plage: eight arias of remembrance, 1972; Dinah and Nick's Love Song, 1972; Chanson de Geste, 1973; The World is Discovered, 1973; Grimethorpe Aria, 1973; 5 Chorale Preludes from Bach, 1973; Chorales from a Toyshop, 1973; Interludes from a Tragedy, 1973; The Mask of Orpheus, 1973–84 (opera); Melencolia I, 1975; Pulse Field, Bow Down, Silbury Air, 1977; For O, for O, the Hobby-horse is forgot, 1977; Carmen Arcardiae Mechanicae Perpetuum, 1978; agm, 1979; On the Sheer Threshold of the Night, 1980; Quintet, 1981; Pulse Sampler, 1981; Deowa, 1983; Yan Tan Tetherer, 1984; Still Movement, 1984; Secret Theatre, 1984; Songs by Myself, 1984. *Address:* c/o Allied Artists Agency, 42 Montpelier Square, SW7 1JZ.

BISCHOFF, Winfried Franz Wilhelm, (Win); Group Chief Executive, Schroders plc, since 1984 (Director, since 1983); Chairman, J. Henry Schroder Wagg & Co. Ltd, since 1983 (Director, since 1978); *b* 10 May 1941; *s* of Paul Helmut Bischoff and Hildegard (*née* Kühne); *m* 1972, Rosemary Elizabeth, *d* of Hon. Leslie Leathers; two *s. Educ:* Marist Brothers, Inanda, Johannesburg, S Africa; Univ. of the Witwatersrand, Johannesburg (BCom). Man. Dir, Schroders & Chartered Ltd, Hong Kong, 1971–82. *Recreations:* opera, music, golf. *Address:* 28 Bloomfield Terrace, SW1W 8PQ. *Clubs:* Hurlingham; Woking Golf.

BISCOE, Rear-Adm. Alec Julian T.; *see* Tyndale-Biscoe.

BISCOE, Prof. Timothy John; Jodrell Professor of Physiology, University College London, since 1979; *b* 28 April 1932; *s* of late Rev. W. H. Biscoe and Mrs M. G. Biscoe; *m* 1955, Daphne Miriam (*née* Gurton); one *s* two *d. Educ:* Latymer Upper School; The London Hospital Medical College. BSc (Hons) Physiology, 1953; MB, BS 1957; FRCP 1983. London Hospital, 1957–58; RAMC Short Service Commission, 1958–62; Physiologist, CDEE, Porton Down, 1959–62; ARC Inst. of Animal Physiology, Babraham, 1962–65; Res. Fellow in Physiology, John Curtin Sch. of Med. Res., Canberra, 1965–66; Associate Res. Physiologist, Cardiovascular Res. Inst., UC Medical Center, San Francisco, 1966–68; University of Bristol: Res. Associate, Dept of Physiology, 1968–70; 2nd Chair of Physiology, 1970–79; Head of Dept of Physiology, 1975–79. Hon. Secretary: Physiological Soc., 1977–82; Research Defence Soc., 1983–. Mem. Council, Harveian Soc., 1983–. *Publications:* papers on neurophysiology in Journal of Physiology, etc. *Recreations:* looking, listening, reading. *Address:* Department of Physiology, University College London, Gower Street, WC1E 6BT. *T:* 01–387 7050.

BISHOP, Alan Henry; Principal Establishment Officer, Scottish Office, since 1984; *b* 12 Sept. 1929; *s* of Robert Bishop and May Watson; *m* 1959, Marjorie Anne Conlan; one *s* one *d. Educ:* George Heriot's Sch., Edinburgh; Edinburgh Univ. (MA 1st Cl. Hons Econ. Science, 1951, 2nd Cl. Hons History, 1952). Served RAF Educn Br., 1952–54. Asst Principal, Dept of Agric. for Scotland, 1954; Private Sec. to Parly Under-Secs of State, 1958–59; Principal, 1959; First Sec., Food and Agric., Copenhagen and The Hague, 1963–66; Asst Sec., Scottish Develt Dept, 1968; Asst Sec., Commn on the Constitution, 1969–73; Asst Under-Sec. of State, Scottish Office, 1980–84. *Recreation:* contract bridge (Pres., Scottish Bridge Union, 1979–80). *Address:* 10 Wester Coates Avenue, Edinburgh EH12 5LS. *T:* 031–337 2163. *Clubs:* Royal Commonwealth Society; Melville (Edinburgh).

BISHOP, Ann, ScD; FRS 1959; *b* 19 Dec. 1899; *o d* of late James Kimberly and Ellen Bishop. *Educ:* Manchester High Sch. for Girls; Manchester Univ.; Cambridge Univ. BSc 1921, DSc 1932, Manchester; PhD 1926, ScD 1941, Cambridge. Hon. Research Fellow, Manchester Univ., 1925–26; Research Asst, Medical Research Council, 1926–29; Beit Memorial Research Fellow, 1929–32; Yarrow Fellow of Girton Coll., Cambridge, 1932–37; Research Fellow of Girton Coll., Cambridge, 1937–66, Life Fellow, 1966; Mem., MRC Staff, 1937–42; Director, MRC Chemotherapy Research Unit at the Molteno Inst., Univ. of Cambridge, 1942–64. *Publications:* articles on the biology of Protozoa, and chemotherapy, published in Scientific Journals. *Address:* 47 Sherlock Close, Cambridge CB3 0HP.

BISHOP, Dr Arthur Clive; Deputy Director, British Museum (Natural History), since 1982, and Keeper of Mineralogy since 1975; *b* 9 July 1930; *s* of late Charles Henry Bishop and Hilda (*née* Clowes); *m* 1962, Helen (*née* Bennison); one *d. Educ:* Wolstanton County Grammar Sch., Newcastle, Staffs; King's Coll., Univ. of London (FKC 1985). BSc 1951, PhD 1954. Geologist, HM Geological Survey, 1954; served RAF Educn Br., 1955–57; Lectr in Geology, Queen Mary Coll., Univ. of London, 1958; Principal Sci. Officer, British Museum (Natural History), 1969, Deputy Keeper 1972. Geological Society: Daniel Pidgeon Fund, 1958; Murchison Fund, 1970; Vice-Pres., 1977–78; Mineralogical Society: Gen. Sec., 1965–72; Vice-Pres., 1973–74; Pres., 1986–; Pres., Geologists' Assoc., 1978–80; Vice-Pres., Inst. of Science Technology, 1973–82. Mem. d'honneur, La Société Jersiaise, 1983. *Publications:* An Outline of Crystal Morphology, 1967; (with W. R. Hamilton and A. R. Woolley) Hamlyn Guide to Minerals, Rocks and Fossils, 1974; papers in various jls, mainly on geology of Channel Is and Brittany, and on dioritic rocks. *Recreations:* drawing and painting. *Address:* British Museum (Natural History), Cromwell Road, SW7 5BD. *T:* 01–589 6323.

BISHOP, Rt. Rev. Clifford Leofric Purdy, *b* 1908; *s* of Rev. E. J. Bishop; *m* 1949, Ivy Winifred Adams. *Educ:* St John's, Leatherhead; Christ's Coll., Cambridge (MA); Lincoln Theological Coll. Deacon 1932; Priest, 1933; Curacies, 1932–41; Vicar, St Geo.,

Camberwell, 1941–49; Rural Dean, 1943–49; Curate-in-charge, All Saints, Newington, 1944–47; Rector of: Blakeney, 1949–53 (Rural Dean of Walsingham, 1951–53); Bishop Wearmouth, 1953–62 (Rural Dean of Wearmouth and Surrogate, 1953–62); Hon. Canon of Durham, 1958–62; Bishop Suffragan of Malmesbury, 1962–73; Canon of Bristol, 1962–73. *Address:* Rectory Cottage, Cley-next-Sea, Holt, Norfolk. *T:* Cley 740250.

BISHOP, Detta; *see* O'Cathain, D.

BISHOP, Sir Frederick (Arthur), Kt 1975; CB 1960; CVO 1957; Director-General of the National Trust, 1971–75; *b* 4 Dec. 1915; *o s* of A. J. Bishop, Bristol; *m* 1940, Elizabeth Finlay Stevenson; two *s* one *d. Educ:* Colston's Hospital, Bristol. LLB (London). Inland Revenue, 1934. Served in RAF and Air Transport Auxiliary, 1942–46. Ministry of Food, 1947, where Principal Private Secretary to Ministers, 1949–52; Asst Secretary, Cabinet Office, 1953–55; Principal Private Secretary to the Prime Minister, 1956–59; Deputy Secretary: of the Cabinet, 1959–61; Min. of Agriculture, Fisheries and Food, 1961–64; Perm. Sec., Min. of Lands and Natural Resources, 1964–65, resigned. Chm., Home Grown Timber Advisory Cttee, 1966–73; Member: BBC Gen. Adv. Council, 1971–75; Crafts Adv. Council, 1973–75. Director: S. Pearson & Son Ltd, 1965–70; Pearson Longman, 1970–77; English China Clays Ltd, 1975–86; Devon and Cornwall Bd, Lloyds Bank, 1976–86. *Address:* 18 Tower Park, Fowey, Cornwall PL23 1JB.

BISHOP, George Robert, DPhil; FRSE; FInstP; Director General, Ispra Establishment, Joint Research Centre, European Commission, Ispra, Italy, since 1983 (Director, 1982–83); *b* 16 Jan. 1927; *s* of George William Bishop and Lilian Elizabeth Garrod; *m* 1952, Adriana Giuseppina, *d* of Luigi Caberlotto and Giselda Mazzariol; two *s* one *d. Educ:* Christ Church, Oxford (MA, DPhil). ICI Research Fellow, Univ. of Oxford, 1951; Research Fellow, St Antony's Coll., Oxford, 1952; Chercheur, Ecole Normale Supérieure, Paris, 1954; Ingénieur-Physicien, Laboratoire de l'Accelerateur Linéaire, ENS, Orsay, 1958; Prof., Faculté des Sciences, Univ. de Paris, 1962; Kelvin Prof. of Natural Philosophy, Univ. of Glasgow, 1964–76; Dir, Dept of Natural and Physical Sciences, JRC, Ispra, 1974–82. Hon. DSc, Strathclyde, 1979. *Publications:* Handbuch der Physik, Band XLII, 1957; β and X-Ray Spectroscopy, 1960; Nuclear Structure and Electromagnetic Interactions, 1965; numerous papers in learned jls on nuclear and high energy physics. *Recreations:* literature, music, swimming, tennis, gardening, travel. *Address:* via Santa Caterina 12, Leggiuno, Varese, Italy. *T:* (0332) 647 913.

BISHOP, Sir George (Sidney), Kt 1975; CB 1958; OBE 1947; Director, Booker McConnell Ltd, 1961–82 (Vice-Chairman, 1970–71, Chairman, 1972–79); Director: Barclays Bank International, 1972–83; Barclays Bank Ltd, 1974–83; Ranks Hovis McDougall, 1976–84; International Basic Economy Corporation, USA, 1980–83; *b* 15 Oct. 1913; *o s* of late J. and M. Bishop; *m* 1940, Marjorie Woodruff (marr. diss. 1961); one *d*; *m* 1961, Una Padel. *Educ:* Ashton-in-Makerfield Grammar Sch.; London Sch. of Economics. Social service work in distressed areas, 1935–38; SW Durham Survey, 1939; Ministry of Food, 1940; Private Secretary to Minister of Food, 1945–49; Under-Secretary, Ministry of Agriculture, Fisheries and Food, 1949–59, Dep. Secretary, 1959–61. Chm., Bookers Agricultural Holdings Ltd, 1964–70; Director: Nigerian Sugar Co. Ltd, 1966–70; Agricultural Mortgage Corp. Ltd, 1973–79. Chairman: Internat. Sugar Council, 1957; West India Cttee, 1969–71 (Pres., 1977–); Industry Co-operative Programme, 1976–78; Council, Overseas Develt Inst., 1977–84; Vice-Chm., Internat. Wheat Council, 1959; Member: Panel for Civil Service Manpower Review, 1968–70; Royal Commn on the Press, 1974–77; Council, CBI, 1973–80; Dir, Industry Council for Develt, USA (Chm., 1979); Governor, Nat. Inst. for Economic and Social Research, 1968–. President: RGS, 1983– (Mem. Council, 1980–; Hon. Fellow 1980; a Vice Pres., 1981); Britain-Nepal Soc., 1979–; Mem., Management Cttee, Mount Everest Foundn, 1980– (Vice Chm. 1982; Chm. 1983). *Recreations:* mountaineering, motoring, photography. *Address:* Brenva, Eghams Wood Road, Beaconsfield, Bucks. *T:* Beaconsfield 3096. *Clubs:* Reform, Travellers', Himalayan, Alpine, Royal Geographical Society, MCC.

BISHOP, Rev. Hugh William Fletcher; Licensed to officiate, Diocese of London; *b* 17 May 1907; *e s* of John and Mary Bishop, Haughton House, Shifnal, Shropshire. *Educ:* Malvern Coll.; Keble Coll., Oxford (MA). Cuddesdon Coll., Oxford, 1932–33; Deacon, 1933; Priest, 1934. Curate of St Michael's, Workington, 1933–35; Curate of Cuddesdon and Lectr, Cuddesdon, 1935–37. Mem., Community of the Resurrection, Mirfield, (taking name of Hugh), 1940–74; Chaplain to the Forces (EC), 1940–45 (POW, 1942–45); Warden, Hostel of the Resurrection, Leeds, 1946–49; Guardian of Novices, Mirfield, 1949–52; Principal of the College, 1956–65; Father Superior of the Community of the Resurrection, 1965–74, released from the Community of the Resurrection, 1974. *Publications:* The Passion Drama, 1955; The Easter Drama, 1958; Life is for Loving, 1961; (contrib. to) Mirfield Essays in Christian Belief, 1962; The Man for Us, 1968. *Address:* 6 Evelyn Mansions, Carlisle Place, SW1P 1NH. *T:* 01–828 0564.

BISHOP, James Drew; Editor of the Illustrated London News, since 1971; Director, Illustrated London News & Sketch Ltd, since 1973; Editorial Director, Natural World, since 1981; *b* 18 June 1929; *s* of late Sir Patrick Bishop, MBE, MP, and Vera Drew; *m* 1959, Brenda Pearson; two *s. Educ:* Haileybury; Corpus Christi Coll., Cambridge. Reporter, Northampton Chronicle & Echo, 1953; joined editorial staff of The Times, 1954; Foreign Correspondent, 1957–64; Foreign News Editor, 1964–66; Features Editor, 1966–70. Dir, International Thomson Publishing Ltd, 1980–85. Contributor of American section of Annual Register, 1960–, Mem. Adv. Bd, 1970–. *Publications:* A Social History of Edwardian Britain, 1977; Social History of the First World War, 1982; (with Oliver Woods) The Story of The Times, 1983; (ed) The Illustrated Counties of England, 1985. *Recreations:* reading, walking, looking and listening. *Address:* (home) 11 Willow Road, NW3 1TJ. *T:* 01–435 4403; (office) 20 Upper Ground, SE1 9PJ. *T:* 01–928 6969. *Clubs:* United Oxford & Cambridge University, MCC.

BISHOP, Dr John Edward; Principal Lecturer, Tutor in Organ and Head of Admissions, Birmingham School of Music, since 1979; *b* 23 Feb. 1935; *s* of late Reginald John Bishop and of Eva Bishop (*née* Lucas). *Educ:* Cotham Sch., Bristol; St John's Coll., Cambridge (Exhibr); Reading and Edinburgh Univs. MA, MusB Cantab; DMus Edin.; FRCO (CHM); ADCM. John Stewart of Rannoch Schol. (Univ. prize) 1954. Organist and Asst Dir of Music, Worksop Coll., Notts, 1958–69; Dir of Music, Worksop Coll., 1969–73; Birmingham School of Music: Dir of Studies, 1973–74; Sen. Lectr, 1974–79. Hon. Director of Music: Cotham Parish Church, Bristol, 1976–; St Paul's Church, Birmingham, 1986–; Dir, Bristol Highbury Singers, 1978–; Organ recitalist (incl. many broadcasts) and choral conductor, accompanist, examiner, adjudicator and reviewer, 1960–. Former Pres., Sheffield, Birmingham and Bristol Organists' Assocs. *Publications:* various articles on history and practice of church music and 19th century organ design. *Recreations:* walking, ecclesiology, savouring the countryside, cities and towns, railways, architecture. *Address:* 98 High Kingsdown, Bristol BS2 8ER. *T:* Bristol 423373.

BISHOP, Dame (Margaret) Joyce, DBE 1963 (CBE 1953); MA Oxon; Head Mistress of The Godolphin and Latymer School, Hammersmith, W6, 1935–63, retired; *b* 28 July 1896; 2nd *d* of Charles Benjamin and Amy Bishop. *Educ:* Edgbaston High Sch., Birmingham; Lady Margaret Hall, Oxford. English Mistress, Hertfordshire and Essex

High Sch., 1918–24; Head Mistress, Holly Lodge High Sch., Smethwick, Staffs, 1924–35. Member Working Party set up by Minister of Education to enquire into Recruitment of Women to Teaching Profession, 1947. President, Association of Head Mistresses, 1950–52. Member: Secondary School Examinations Council, 1950–62; University Grants Cttee, 1961–63; Council for Professions Supplementary to Medicine, 1961–70; TV Research Cttee set up by Home Secretary, 1963–69. Chairman, Joint Cttee of the Four Secondary Associations, 1956–58. FKC 1973. *Recreations:* listening to cassettes and radio, the theatre. *Address:* 22 Malbrook Road, Putney, SW15. *T:* 01–788 5862.

BISHOP, Michael David, CBE 1986; Chairman, British Midland Holdings Ltd, since 1978; Chairman and Managing Director, British Midland Airways Ltd, its subsidiary and associated cos, since 1978; Chairman: Manx Airlines, since 1982; Loganair, since 1983; *b* 10 Feb. 1942; *s* of Clive Leonard Bishop and Lilian Bishop (*née* Frost). *Educ:* Mill Hill School. Joined Mercury Airlines, Manchester, 1963; British Midland Airways Ltd: Manchester, 1964–69; General Manager and Director, 1969–72; Managing Director, 1972–. Member: E Midlands Electricity Bd, 1980–83; E Midlands Reg. Bd, Central Indep. Television, 1981–. *Recreation:* music. *Address:* Donington Hall, Castle Donington, near Derby DE7 2SB. *T:* Derby 810741. *Club:* St James's (Manchester).

BISHOP, Prof. Peter Orlebar, AO 1986; DSc; FRS 1977; FAA; Professor Emeritus, and Visiting Fellow, Department of Behavioural Biology, Research School of Biological Sciences, since 1983, Australian National University; *b* 14 June 1917; *s* of Ernest John Hunter Bishop and Mildred Alice Havelock Bishop (*née* Vidal); *m* 1942, Hilare Louise Holmes; one *s* two *d*. *Educ:* Barker Coll., Hornsby; Univ. of Sydney (MB, BS, DSc). Neurol Registrar, Royal Prince Alfred Hosp., Sydney, 1941–42; Surgeon Lieut, RANR, 1942–46; Fellow, Postgrad. Cttee in Medicine (Sydney Univ.) at Nat. Hosp., Queen Square, London, 1946–47 and Dept Anatomy, UCL, 1947–50; Sydney University: Res. Fellow, Dept Surgery, 1950–51; Sen. Lectr, 1951–54, Reader, 1954–55, Prof. and Head, Dept Physiology, 1955–67; Prof. and Head of Dept of Physiology, John Curtin School of Medical Res., ANU, 1967–82. Visiting Professor: Japan Soc. for Promotion of Science, 1974, 1982; Katholieke Universiteit Leuven, Belgium, 1984–85; Guest Prof., Zürich Univ., 1985; Vis. Fellow, St John's Coll., Cambridge, Jan.–Oct. 1986. FAA 1967; Fellow: Aust. Postgrad. Fedn in Medicine, 1969; Nat. Vision Res. Inst. of Australia, 1983. Hon. Member: Neurosurgical Soc. of Aust., 1970; Ophthalmol Soc. of NZ, 1973; Aust. Assoc. of Neurologists, 1977; Australian Neuroscience Soc., 1986. Hon. MD Sydney, 1983. *Publications:* contribs on physiological optics and visual neurophysiology. *Recreation:* bushwalking. *Address:* Department of Physiology, John Curtin School of Medical Research, Australian National University, Canberra City, ACT 2601, Australia; 93 Arthur Circle, Forrest, ACT 2603, Australia.

BISHOP, Prof. Richard Evelyn Donohue, CBE 1979; FRS 1980, FEng 1977, FIMechE, FRINA, MRAeS; Vice-Chancellor and Principal, Brunel University, since 1981; Fellow of University College London, since 1964; *b* London, 1 Jan. 1925; *s* of Rev. Dr N. R. Bishop; *m* 1949, Jean Paterson, London; one *s* one *d*. *Educ:* The Roan Sch., Greenwich. RNVR, 1943–46. University Coll., London, 1946–49 (DSc Eng); Commonwealth Fund Fellow in Stanford Univ., California, 1949–51 (MS, PhD). Sen. Scientific Officer, Ministry of Supply, 1951–52; Cambridge Univ.: Demonstrator, 1952; Fellow of Pembroke Coll., 1954; University Lecturer in Engineering, 1955 (MA, ScD); Kennedy Prof. of Mechanical Engrg, Univ. of London, 1957–81. Vis. Prof., Massachusetts Institute of Technology, Summer, 1959; Vis. Lectr, National Science Foundation, USA, Spring, 1961; John Orr Meml Lectr, S Africa, 1971; C. Gelderman Foundn Vis. Prof., Technical Univ., Delft, 1976. Member of Council, Instn of Mechanical Engineers, 1961–64, 1969–70; President, British Acoustical Soc., 1966–68; Hon. Member Royal Corps of Naval Constructors, 1968; Originator of Greenwich Forum, 1973. Mem. Senate, London Univ., 1980–81. Hon. Fellow, Portsmouth Polytechnic, 1982. George Stephenson Res. Prize, IMechE, 1959; Thomas Hawksley Gold Medal, IMechE, 1965; Silver Medal of Skoda Works, 1967; Křižík Gold Medal, Acad. Sci. CSSR, 1969; Rayleigh Gold Medal, Brit. Acoustical Soc., 1972; Clayton Prize, IMechE, 1972; RINA Bronze Medals, 1975, 1977. *Publications:* (with D. C. Johnson) Vibration Analysis Tables, 1956; (with D. C. Johnson) The Mechanics of Vibration, 1960; (with G. M. L. Gladwell and S. Michaelson) The Matrix Analysis of Vibration, 1965; Vibration, 1965; (with W. G. Price) Probabilistic Theory of Ship Dynamics, 1974; (with W. G. Price) Hydroelasticity of Ships, 1979; (with B. R. Clayton) Mechanics of Marine Vehicles, 1982; many scientific papers. *Recreation:* sailing. *Address:* Brunel University, Uxbridge, Middlesex UB8 3PH. *Club:* Royal Naval and Royal Albert Yacht (Portsmouth) (Chm., 1979–82).

BISHOP, Ronald Eric, CBE 1946; FRAeS; Deputy Managing Director, de Havilland Aircraft Co. Ltd, 1958–64; Design Director, de Havilland Aircraft Co. Ltd, Hatfield, 1946–64; *b* 1903. Joined de Havilland Aircraft Co. Ltd, as an apprentice, 1921; entered Drawing Office; appointed in charge, 1936. Responsible for following designs: Flamingo, Mosquito, Hornet, Vampire, Dove, Venom, Heron, DH 108, DH 110, Comet Jet Airliner. Gold Medal, RAeS, 1964.

BISHOP, Stanley Victor, MC 1944; management consultant; Director, Britarge Ltd, since 1979; *b* 11 May 1916; *s* of George Stanley Bishop, MA; *m* 1946, Dorothy Primrose Dodds, Berwick-upon-Tweed; two *s* one *d*. *Educ:* Leeds. Articled to Beevers & Adgie, Leeds; CA 1937. Served War of 1939–45: enlisted London Scottish (TA), 1938; commissioned, West Yorkshire Regt, 1940; served overseas, 1940–45, Middle East, India and Burma (MC) (Hon. Major). Joined Albert E. Reed and Co. Ltd, 1946; Brush Group, 1951; Massey Ferguson Ltd, 1959–79; Perkins Diesel Engine Group, 1963. Man. Dir, British Printing Corp., 1966–70; Chm. and Dir various cos, 1970–73; Dir, Massey-Ferguson Europe Ltd, 1973–79. Has lectured to British Institute of Management, Institute of Chartered Accountants, Oxford Business Summer School, etc. *Publication:* Business Planning and Control, 1966. *Recreations:* golf, swimming, pottering. *Address:* Halidon, Rogers Lane, Ettington, Stratford-upon-Avon, Warwicks CV37 7SX. *Club:* Army and Navy.

BISHOP, Stephen; *see* Bishop-Kovacevich.

BISHOP, Terence Alan Martyn, FBA 1971; *b* 1907; *s* of Cosby Martyn Bishop. *Educ:* Christ's Hospital; Keble Coll., Oxford. 2nd Mods, 1928; 2nd Hist. 1930; BA 1931, MA 1947. *Publications:* books and articles on palaeography, etc, incl.: Facsimiles of English Royal Writs to AD 1100 (with P. Chaplais), 1957; Scriptores Regis, 1961; (ed) Umbrae Codicum Occidentalium (Vol. 10), 1966 (Holland); English Caroline Minuscule, 1971. *Address:* 16 Highbury Road, Wimbledon, SW19 7PR.

BISHOP, Instructor Rear-Adm. Sir William (Alfred), KBE 1955 (OBE 1941); CB 1950; MA; Director of Naval Education Service, 1948–56, retired; *b* 29 May 1899; *s* of late Alfred Bishop, Purley, Surrey; *m* 1929, Stella Margaret Macfarlane, MBE (*d* 1985); no *c*. *Educ:* Whitgift Sch.; Corpus Christi, Cambridge. 2nd Lieut, RE Signals, 1918; Cambridge 1919. Entered RN as Instructor Lieut, 1922; Instructor Lieut-Comdr, 1928; Instructor Comdr, 1936; Instructor Captain, 1945; Instructor Rear-Adm., 1951. Chief Naval Meteorological Officer, South Atlantic Station, 1939; Asst Director of Naval Meteorological Service, 1944; Dep. Director of Education Dept, 1947. Naval ADC to the King, 1950. Retired Sept. 1956. *Address:* Myrtle Cottage, Burlawn, Wadebridge, Cornwall PL27 7LD. *T:* Wadebridge 2773.

BISHOP, Rev. William Fletcher; *see* Bishop, Rev. H.W.F.

BISHOP-KOVACEVICH, Stephen; pianist; *b* 17 Oct. 1940. *Educ:* studied under Lev Shorr and Myra Hess. Solo and orchestral debut, San Francisco, USA 1951; London debut, Nov. 1961. Concert tours: in England, Europe and USA, with many of the world's leading orchestras, incl. New York Philharmonic, Los Angeles Philharmonic, Israel Philharmonic, Amsterdam Concertgebouw, London Symphony, London Philharmonic, and BBC Symphony. Has appeared at Edinburgh, Bath, Berlin and San Sebastian Festivals. Gave 1st performance of Richard Rodney Bennett's Piano Concerto, 1969 (this work is dedicated to and has been recorded by him, under Alexander Gibson). Performed all Mozart Piano concertos, 1969–71. Edison Award for his recording of Bartok's 2nd Piano Concerto and Stravinsky's Piano Concerto, with BBC Symphony Orchestra, under Colin Davis. *Recreations:* snooker, chess, films, tennis. *Address:* c/o Harrison-Parrott Ltd, 12 Penzance Place, W11 4PA. *T:* 01–229 9166.

BISS, Godfrey Charles D'Arcy; retired as Senior Partner, Ashurst, Morris, Crisp & Co., Solicitors, 1977; *b* 2 Sept. 1909; *s* of Gerald Biss and Sarah Ann Coutts Allan; *m* 1946, Margaret Jean Ellis; two *s*. *Educ:* St Paul's Sch. (Scholar); Worcester Coll., Oxford (Exhibitioner). 1st Class Jurisprudence, 1932. Solicitor, 1935; Partner in Ashurst, Morris, Crisp & Co., 1947. Royal Artillery, 1940–46; Staff Capt. RA, 23rd Indian Div. Chairman: The Fairey Company Ltd, 1958–70; UKO International (formerly UK Optical & Industrial Holdings Ltd), 1958–78; Director: Siebe Gorman & Co. Ltd, 1963–81; Trafalgar House Ltd, to 1981; International Press Centre Ltd. *Recreations:* gardening, racing. *Address:* Spring Bank, Back Street, Thornborough, Buckingham MK18 2DH. *T:* Buckingham 2157.

BISSELL, Claude Thomas, CC 1969; MA, PhD; FRSC 1957; Professor, University of Toronto, since 1971 (President of the University, 1958–71); *b* 10 Feb. 1916; *m* 1945, Christina Flora Gray; one *d*. *Educ:* University of Toronto; Cornell Univ. BA 1936, MA 1937, Toronto; PhD Cornell, 1940. Instructor in English, Cornell, 1938–41; Lecturer in English, Cornell, 1938–41; Lecturer in English, Toronto, 1941–42. Canadian Army, 1942–46; demobilised as Capt. University of Toronto: Asst Prof. of English, 1947–51; Assoc. Prof. of English, 1951–56; Prof. of English, 1962; Asst to Pres., 1948–52; Vice-Pres., 1952–56; Dean in Residence, University Coll., 1946–56; Pres., Carleton Univ., Ottawa, 1956–58; Chm., The Canada Council, 1960–62. President, Nat. Conference of Canadian Universities and Colleges, 1962–; Chairman, Canadian Universities Foundation, 1962–; President, World University Service of Canada, 1962–63. Visiting Prof. of Canadian Studies, Harvard, 1967–68. Aggrey-Fraser-Guggisberg Meml Lectr, Ghana Univ., 1976. Hon. DLitt: Manitoba, 1958; W Ontario, 1971; Lethbridge, 1972; Leeds, 1976; Toronto, 1977; Hon. LLD: McGill, 1958; Queen's, 1959; New Brunswick, 1959; Carleton, 1960; Montreal, 1960; The St Lawrence, 1962; British Columbia, 1962; Michigan, 1963; Columbia, 1965; Laval, 1966; Prince of Wales Coll., 1967; Windsor, 1968; St Andrews, 1972. *Publications:* (ed) University College, A Portrait, 1853–1953, 1953; (ed) Canada's Crisis in Higher Education, 1957; (ed) Our Living Tradition, 1957; (ed) Great Canadian Writing, 1966; The Strength of the University, 1968; Halfway up Parnassus, 1974; The Humanities in the University, 1977; The Young Vincent Massey, 1981; number of articles on literary subjects in Canadian and American jls. *Address:* 229 Erskine Avenue, Toronto, Ontario, Canada. *Clubs:* Arts and Letters, York (Toronto); Cercle Universitaire (Ottawa).

BISZTYGA, Jan; Officer's Cross of the Order of Polonia Restituta 1970; Order of Merit 1973; Ideology Department, Polish United Workers' Party; *b* 19 Jan. 1933; *s* of Kazimierz Biszytyga; *m* 1956, Otylia; one *s*. *Educ:* Jagiellonian Univ. (MSc Biochemistry). Asst Professor, Jagiellonian Univ., Cracow, 1954–57; political youth movement, 1956–59; Min. for Foreign Affairs, 1959–63; Attaché, New Delhi, 1963–64; Min. for Foreign Affairs, 1964–69; Head of Planning Dept, Min. for Foreign Affairs, 1969–71; Dep. Foreign Minister, 1972–75; Ambassador in Athens, 1975–78, to UK, 1978–81. *Recreations:* game shooting, fishing, history. *Address:* Komitet Centralny PZPR, ul. Nowy Świat 6, 00–497 Warsaw, Poland. *Club:* Travellers'.

BJARNASON, Sigurdur; Commander with Star, Order of the Icelandic Falcon, 1950; Hon. Emblem, Foundation of the Icelandic Republic, 1944; Ambassador of Iceland (stationed in Reykjavik) to India and other West Asian countries, since 1982; *b* 18 Dec. 1915; *s* of Bjarni Sigurdsson and Björg Bjornsdóttir; *m* 1956, Ólöf Pálsdóttir, sculptress; one *s* one *d*. *Educ:* Univ. of Iceland (Law); Univ. of Cambridge (Internat. and Company Law). Editor of weekly newspaper, 1942–47; Political Editor, Morgunbladid, 1947–56, Editor in Chief, 1956–70. Mem. Icelandic Parlt (Althing), 1942–70; Pres. Lower House, 1949–56 and 1963–70; Chm. Cttee of Foreign Affairs, 1963–70. Mem. govt and municipal cttees, including Pres. Municipal Council of Isfajördur, 1946–50; Mem. Council of State Radio of Iceland, 1947–70, Chm. 1959 and Vice-Chm. 1960–70. Pres. Icelandic Sect. of Soc. for Inter-scandinavian Understanding, 1965–70. Member Nordic Council, 1952–59 and 1963–70; Vice-Pres., 1952–56 and 1959; Pres., 1965 and 1970. Delegate of Iceland to UN Gen. Assembly, 1960, 1961 and 1962; Mem. Cultural Cttee of Nordic Countries, 1954–70. Mem. Icelandic Cttee on territorial rights, 1957–58. Ambassador to: Denmark, Turkey, 1970–76; Ireland, 1970–82; China, 1973–76; UK, The Netherlands and Nigeria, 1976–82. Commander of the Finnish Lion, 1958; Commander, Order of the Vasa (Sweden), 1958; Grand Cross: Order of Dannebrog (Denmark), 1970; Order of Orange-Nassau (Netherlands), 1982. *Publications:* articles for foreign periodicals, especially within the field of culture and Scandinavian co-operation. *Recreations:* fishing, bird watching. *Address:* Útsalir, Seltjarnarnes, Iceland.

BJELKE-PETERSEN, Hon. Sir Johannes, KCMG 1984; MLA; Premier of Queensland, since 1968; *b* Dannevirke, NZ, 13 Jan. 1911; *s* of late C. G. Bjelke-Petersen, Denmark; *m* 1952, Florence Isabel (elected as Senator for Queensland in Commonwealth Parliament, 1981), *d* of J. P. Gilmour; one *s* three *d*. *Educ:* Taabinga Valley Sch.; corresp. courses, and privately. MLA National Party (formerly Country Party): for Nanango, 1947–50; for Barambah, 1950–. Minister for Works and Housing, Qld, 1963–68. *Address:* (office) Premier's Department, George Street, Brisbane, Queensland 4000, Australia; (home) Bethany, Kingaroy, Queensland 4610.

BJÖRNSSON, Henrik Sveinsson, KBE (Hon.) 1963; Icelandic diplomat, retired; Ambassador to Belgium, Luxembourg and Greece, concurrently accredited to European Economic Community, and Permanent Icelandic Representative to NATO, 1979–84; *b* 2 Sept. 1914; *s* of Sveinn Björnsson (late President of Iceland) and Georgia Hoff-Hansen; *m* 1941, Gróa Torfhildur Jónsdóttir; one *s* two *d*. *Educ:* Reykjavik Grammar Sch.; Univ. of Iceland. Graduated in Law, 1939. Entered Foreign Service, 1939; served in Copenhagen, Washington, DC, Oslo, Paris and Revkjavik; Secretary to President of Iceland, 1952–56; Secretary-General of Min. of Foreign Affairs, Iceland, 1956–61; Ambassador to: the Court of St James's, 1961–65, also to Royal Netherlands Court, and Minister to Spain and Portugal, 1961–65; Belgium and Permanent Representative to NATO, 1965–67, France, Luxembourg, Yugoslavia, 1965–76, UAR and Ethiopia, 1971–76, and concurrently

Permanent Rep. to Council of Europe, 1968–70, and OECD and UNESCO, 1965–76; Permt Under Secretary, Ministry for Foreign Affairs, 1976–79. Kt Comdr of the Order of the Icelandic Falcon, 1963. Holds various foreign decorations. *Address:* Sjafnargata 4, Reykjavik, Iceland.

BLACHE-FRASER, Louis Nathaniel, HBM 1971; CMG 1959; Chairman, Insurance Brokers West Indies Ltd; Director: George Wimpey (Caribbean) Ltd; Trinidad Building and Loan Association; *b* 19 Feb. 1904; *s* of late Winford and Emma Blache-Fraser, Trinidad; *m* 1941, Gwenyth, *d* of George Kent, Grenada; two *s* one *d* (and one *d* decd). *Educ:* Queen's Royal Coll., Trinidad. Joined Trinidad and Tobago Government Service, 1924; Dep. Accountant-General, 1947; Accountant-General, 1948; Dep. Financial Secretary, 1952; Financial Secretary, 1953; Financial Secretary, The West Indies, 1956–60; Chairman, Public Service Commission of The West Indies, 1961–62. Asst Sec., Alstons Ltd, 1962–65, Sec., 1965–70. Past Pres., Trinidad Chamber of Commerce. *Address:* 14 Coblentz Gardens, St Ann's, Trinidad. *Clubs:* Queen's Park Cricket, Harvard Sports (Trinidad).

BLACK, Alastair Kenneth Lamond; DL; Under Sheriff of Greater London, since 1974; Clerk, Bowyers' Company, since 1985; *b* 14 Dec. 1929; *s* of Kenneth Black and Althea Joan Black; *m* 1955, Elizabeth Jane, *d* of Sir Henry Darlington, KCB, CMG, TD; one *s* two *d*. *Educ:* Sherborne Sch.; Law Soc. Coll. of Law. Admitted solicitor, 1953. Nat. Service, Intelligence Corps, 1953–55, Lieut. Partner in Messrs Burchell & Ruston, Solicitors, 1953–. Dep. Sheriff, Co. of London, then Greater London, 1953–74; DL Greater London, 1978. Mem. Council, Shrievalty Assoc., 1985–; Vice-Pres., Under Sheriffs Assoc., 1985–. Member: House of Laity, Gen. Synod, 1982–; Dioceses Commn, 1986–; Lay Reader, 1983–. *Publications:* contributions to: Halsbury's Laws of England, 4th edn, vols 25, 1978, and 42, 1983; Atkin's Court Forms, 3rd edn, vols 19, 1972 (rev. edn 1985), 22, 1968, and 36, 1977; Enforcement of a Judgement, 7th edn, 1986. *Recreations:* horseracing, gardening, travel. *Address:* South Lodge, Effingham, Surrey KT24 5QE. *T:* Bookham 52862.

BLACK, Archibald Niel; Professor of Engineering, University of Southampton, 1968–72, retired; *b* 10 June 1912; *s* of late Steuart Gladstone Black, Glenormiston, Victoria, Australia, and Isabella McCance (*née* Moat); *m* 1940, Cynthia Mary Stradling; one *s* two *d*. *Educ:* Farnborough Sch.; Eton Coll.; Trinity Coll., Cambridge. 1st cl. hons with distinction in Applied Mechanics in Mech. Sciences Tripos, Cambridge, 1934; MA 1938. Lectr and Demonstrator in Engrg Science, Oxford Univ., 1935; Donald Pollock Reader in Engrg Science, Oxford Univ., 1945–50; Prof. of Mech. Engrg, Southampton Univ., 1950–67. Dep. Chm., Universities Central Council on Admissions, 1964–72. Hon. DSc Southampton, 1975. *Publications:* (with K. Adlard Coles) North Biscay Pilot, 1970, revd edn 1977; papers in Proc. Royal Soc. and technical jls. *Recreation:* sailing. *Address:* Little Pensbury, Compton Street, Compton, Winchester, Hants SO21 2AS. *T:* Twyford 712360. *Club:* Royal Ocean Racing.

BLACK, Barrington; a Metropolitan Stipendiary Magistrate, since 1984; *b* 16 Aug. 1932; *s* of Louis and Millicent Black; *m* 1962, Diana Black (*née* Heller), JP; two *s* two *d*. *Educ:* Roundhay Sch.; Leeds Univ. (Pres. of Union, 1952; Vice-Pres., NUS, 1953–54; LLB). Admitted Solicitor, 1956. Served Army, 1956–58, commnd RASC. Partner, Walker, Morris & Coles, 1958–69; Sen. Partner, Barrington Black, Austin & Co., 1969–84. Mem. Court and Council, Leeds Univ., 1979–84. Councillor, Harrogate Bor. Council, 1964–67; contested (L) Harrogate, 1964. Contributor, Calendar (Yorkshire TV), and Look North and Panorama (BBC), 1959–84. Mem., British Acad. of Forensic Science. *Publications:* contrib. Sunday Telegraph Magazine on legal topics. *Recreations:* ski-bobbing, opera, music. *Address:* c/o Bow Street Magistrates' Court, WC2. *Clubs:* Sloane, Ronnie Scott's.

BLACK, Sir Cyril (Wilson), Kt 1959; JP; *b* 1902; *s* of Robert Wilson Black, JP, and Annie Louise Black (*née* North); *m* 1930, Dorothy Joyce, *d* of Thomas Birkett, Wigston Hall, Leicester; one *s* two *d*. *Educ:* King's College Sch. Chartered Surveyor, FRICS; Chairman: Temperance Permanent Building Soc., 1939–73; Beaumont Properties Ltd, 1933–80; London Shop Property Trust Ltd, 1951–79; M. F. North Ltd, 1948–81, and other companies. JP County of London, 1942; Member Wimbledon Borough Council, 1942–65; Mayor, 1945–46, 1946–47; Alderman, 1942–65; Member, London Borough of Merton Council, 1965–78; Mayor, 1965–66; Member Surrey County Council, 1943–65; County Alderman, 1952–65, and Chm., 1956–59; MP (C) Wimbledon, 1950–70. DL Surrey, 1957–66; DL Greater London, 1966–. Governor of King's College Sch., Wimbledon Coll., Ursuline Convent Sch., Wimbledon, and other Schools. Freedom of City of London, 1943; Freedom of Wimbledon, 1957. Hon. Mem., Houses of Parliament Christian Fellowship; Patron: Wimbledon Youth Cttee; Wimbledon Community Assoc.; Member: SW Metrop. Regional Hospital Board, 1959–62; Baptist Union Council (Pres., 1970–71); Free Church Federal Council; Vice-President: Girls' Bde, 1969– (Hon. Treasurer, 1939–69); Boys' Bde, (Hon. Treasurer, 1962–69). Pres., United Nations Association (London Region), 1964–65. *Recreations:* public work, music, reading. *Address:* Rosewall, Calonne Road, Wimbledon, SW19. *T:* 01-946 2588. *Club:* Carlton.

BLACK, Sir David; *see* Black, Sir R. D.

BLACK, Sir Douglas (Andrew Kilgour), Kt 1973; MD, FRCP; Professor of Medicine, Manchester University and Physician, Manchester Royal Infirmary, 1959–77, now Emeritus; Chief Scientist, Department of Health and Social Security, 1973–77; *b* 29 May 1913; *s* of late Rev. Walter Kilgour Black and Mary Jane Crichton; *m* 1948, Mollie Thorn; one *s* two *d*. *Educ:* Forfar Academy; St Andrews Univ. BSc 1933; MB, ChB 1936; MD 1940; MRCP 1939; FRCP 1952; FACP, FRACP, FRCPGlas, 1978; FRCPath, FRCPI, FRCPE, 1979; FRCPsych, 1982; FRCGP, FRCOG, FFCM, 1983; FFOM 1984. MRC Research Fellow, 1938–40; Beit Memorial Research Fellow, 1940–42. Major RAMC, 1942–46. Lecturer, then Reader, in Medicine, Manchester Univ., 1946–58. Horder Travelling Fellow, 1967; Sir Arthur Sims Commonwealth Travelling Prof., 1971; Rock Carling Fellow, 1984. Lectures: Goulstonian, RCP, 1953; Bradshaw, RCP, 1965; Lumleian, RCP, 1970; Harben, RIPH&H, 1973; Crookshank, RCR, 1976; Harveian Orator, RCP, 1977; Maurice Bloch, Glasgow, 1979; Linacre, St John's Coll., Cambridge, 1980; Lloyd Roberts, RSM, 1980. Secretary, Manchester Medical Soc., 1957–59. Member: Medical Research Council, 1966–70 and 1971–77 (Chm., Clinical Res. Bd, 1971–73); Assoc. of Physicians; Medical Research Soc.; Renal Assoc., etc. President: RCP, 1977–83; Section X, British Assoc., 1977; Medical Protection Soc., 1982–85; BMA, 1984–85. Trustee, 1968–77, Chm., 1977–83, Smith Kline & French Foundn. Chm., Research Working Group on Inequalities in Health, 1977–80. Hon. DSc: St Andrews, 1972; Manchester, 1978; Leicester, 1980; Hon. LLD Birmingham, 1984; Hon. MD Sheffield, 1984. *Publications:* Sodium Metabolism in Health and Disease, 1952; Essentials of Fluid Balance, 4th edn, 1967; The Logic of Medicine, 1968; (ed) Renal Disease, 4th edn, 1979; An Anthology of False Antitheses (Rock Carling Lecture), 1984; Invitation to Medicine, 1987; contributions to various medical journals. *Recreations:* reading and writing. *Address:* The Old Forge, Duchess Close, Whitchurch-on-Thames, near Reading, RG8 7EN. *T:* Pangbourne 4693. *Club:* Athenæum.

BLACK, Eugene R(obert); Banker, United States; Chairman: Blackwell Land Co. Inc.; Scandinavian Securities Corp.; Director, Warner Communications; *b* Atlanta, Ga, USA, 1 May 1898; *s* of Eugene R. Black and Gussie Grady; *m* 1st, 1918, Elizabeth Blalock (decd); one *s* one *d*; 2nd, 1930, Susette Heath; one *s*. *Educ:* Univ. of Georgia. Atlanta Office, Harris, Forbes & Co. (NY Investment Bankers), 1919; Manager, Atlanta Office, Chase-Harris, Forbes Corp., in charge of Atlanta, New Orleans, Houston and Dallas offices, 1933; Chase National Bank of the City of NY: 2nd Vice-Pres., 1933; Vice-Pres., 1937; Senior Vice-Pres., 1949, resigned. US Executive Director, Internat. Bank for Reconstruction and Development, 1947–49, President, 1949–53. Consultant and Dir, Chase Manhattan Bank, 1963–70; Consultant, American Express Co., 1970–78. Special Adviser to President Johnson on SE Asia development, 1965–69; Trustee, Corporate Property Investors, and other financial trusteeships. Medal of Freedom (US), 1969. Holds numerous hon. doctorates and has been decorated by many countries. *Publications:* The Diplomacy of Economic Development, 1963 (trans. other languages); Alternative in Southeast Asia, 1969. *Recreations:* golf, fishing; student of William Shakespeare. *Address:* 178 Columbia Heights, Brooklyn, New York 11201. *Clubs:* Athenæum (London, England); Lotos, River (New York); International (Washington, DC); National Golf Links of America (Southampton, NY), etc.

BLACK, Air Vice-Marshal George Philip, OBE 1967; AFC 1962 (Bar 1971); FBIM; Deputy Chief of Staff (Operations), Headquarters Allied Air Forces Central Europe, since 1984; *b* 10 July 1932; *s* of William and Elizabeth Black; *m* 1954, Ella Ruddiman (*née* Walker); two *s*. *Educ:* Hilton Acad., Aberdeen. Joined RAF, 1950; flying trng in Canada, 1951; served, 1952–64: fighter pilot; carrier pilot (on exchange to FAA); Flying Instr; HQ Fighter Comd; commanded No 111 (Fighter) Sqdn, 1964–66; Mem., Lightning Aerobatic Team, 1965; commanded Lightning Operational Conversion Unit, 1967–69; commanded No 5 (Fighter) Sqdn, 1969–70 (Huddleston Trophy); JSSC, 1970; Air Plans, MoD, 1971–72; Stn Comdr, RAF Wildenwrath, and Harrier Field Force Comdr, RAF Germany, 1972–74; Gp Captain Ops HQ 38 Gp, 1974–76; RCDS, 1977; Gp Captain Ops HQ 11 (Fighter) Gp, 1978–80; Comdr Allied Air Defence Sector One, 1980–83; Comdt ROC, 1983–84. Air ADC to the Queen, 1981–83. FBIM 1977. *Recreations:* philately, military aviation history, railways. *Address:* c/o Lloyds Bank, 6 Pall Mall, SW1Y 5NH. *Clubs:* Royal Air Force; Wolseley and Morris Vintage Cars.

BLACK, Prof. Gordon; CPhys; Professor of Computation, Faculty of Technology, University of Manchester, since 1964; Member, National Electronics Council, since 1967; *b* 30 July 1923; *s* of Martin Black and Gladys (*née* Lee), Whitehaven, Cumbria; *m* 1953, Brenda Janette, *y d* of H. Josiah Balsom, London; two *s* two *d*. *Educ:* Workington Grammar Sch.; Hatfield Coll., Durham Univ.; Imperial Coll., London Univ. BSc Durham, 1945; MSc Manchester, 1968; PhD, DIC London, 1954; FInstP 1952; FBCS 1968. Physicist, British Scientific Instrument Research Assoc., 1946–56. UKAEA, 1956–66; Principal Sci. Officer, 1956–58; Senior Principal Sci. Officer, 1958–60; Dep. Chief Sci. Officer, 1960–64. Dir, Nat. Computing Centre, 1965–69; Dir, Univ. of Manchester Regional Computing Centre, 1969–83. Dir, Internat. Computers Ltd, 1976–84. Chm., Computer Policy Cttee, Vickers Ltd, 1977–79. Governor, Huddersfield Polytechnic, 1974–80. UN Consultant, 1983–. *Publications:* scientific papers in learned jls (physics and computers). *Recreations:* piano playing; listening to piano players; old clocks. *Address:* University of Manchester Institute of Science and Technology, Sackville Street, Manchester. *T:* 061–236 3311; Ennerdale, 24 Marlfield Road, Hale Barns, Altrincham, Cheshire WA15 0SQ. *T:* 061–980 4644. *Club:* Athenæum.

BLACK, Sir Hermann David, Kt 1974; AC 1986; Chancellor of the University of Sydney, New South Wales, Australia, since 1970; Fellow, University of Sydney, since 1949; Part-time Lecturer in Economics and Education; also a radio commentator on economics and international affairs, in Australia; *b* 1905. Former Economic Adviser to the Treasury, NSW; former Pres., Economic Soc. of Australia and NZ; Pres., Australian Instn of Internat. Affairs. Hon. DLitt Univ. of Newcastle, NSW. *Address:* University of Sydney, Sydney, New South Wales 2006, Australia; 99 Roseville Avenue, Roseville, NSW 2069, Australia.

BLACK, Iain James, QC 1971; a Recorder of the Crown Court, since 1972; Called to the Bar, Gray's Inn, 1947, Bencher, 1985; Dep. Chm., Staffs QS, 1965–71. Member: Criminal Injuries Compensation Bd, 1975–; Mental Health Review Tribunal, 1984–. *Address:* 3 Fountain Court, Steelhouse Lane, Birmingham B4 6DR. *T:* 021–236 5854; 3 Pump Court, Temple, EC4. *T:* 01–353 0711.

BLACK, James Walter, QC 1979; a Recorder of the Crown Court, since 1976; *b* 8 Feb. 1941; *s* of Dr James Black and Mrs Clementine M. Black (*née* Robb); *m* 1st, 1964, Jane Marie Keyden; two *s* one *d*; 2nd, 1985, Diana Marjorie Day (*née* Harris); one *d*. *Educ:* Harecroft Hall, Gosforth, Cumbria; Trinity Coll., Glenalmond, Perthshire; St Catharine's Coll., Cambridge (MA). Called to the Bar, Middle Temple, 1964. *Recreations:* fishing, sailing, golf. *Address:* Guildhall Chambers, 23 Broad Street, Bristol BS1 2HG. *T:* Bristol 273366. *Clubs:* Beaufort (Bristol); Royal Scottish Automobile (Glasgow), Royal Dornoch Golf.

BLACK, Sir James (Whyte), Kt 1981; FRCP; FRS 1976; Professor of Analytical Pharmacology, King's College Hospital Medical School, University of London, since 1984; *b* 14 June 1924. *Educ:* Beath High Sch., Cowdenbeath; Univ. of St Andrews (MB, ChB). Asst Lectr in Physiology, Univ. of St Andrews, 1946; Lectr in Physiology, Univ. of Malaya, 1947–50; Sen. Lectr, Univ. of Glasgow Vet. Sch., 1950–58; ICI Pharmaceuticals Ltd, 1958–64; Head of Biological Res. and Dep. Res. Dir, Smith, Kline & French, Welwyn Garden City, 1964–73; Prof. and Head of Dept of Pharmacology, University College, London, 1973–77; Dir of Therapeutic Research, Wellcome Res. Labs, 1978–84. Mem., British Pharmacological Soc., 1961–. Hon. FRSE 1986. Mullard Award, Royal Soc., 1978. *Address:* Analytical Pharmacology Unit, Rayne Institute, 123 Coldharbour Lane, SE5 9NU. *T:* 01–274 7437.

BLACK, Vice-Adm. John Jeremy, DSO 1982; MBE 1963; Stia Negara Brunei 1963; Deputy Chief of Defence Staff (Systems), since 1986; *b* 1932; *s* of Alan H. Black and G. Black; *m* 1958, Alison Pamela Barber; two *s* one *d*. *Educ:* Royal Naval College, Dartmouth (entered 1946). Korean War and Malayan Emergency, 1951–52; qualified in gunnery, 1958; commanded HM Ships: Fiskerton, 1960–62 (Brunei Rebellion, 1962); Decoy, 1969 (Comdr 1969, Captain 1974); Fife, 1977; RCDS 1979; Director of Naval Operational Requirements, Naval Staff, 1980–81; commanded HMS Invincible (Falklands), 1982–83; Flag Officer, First Flotilla, 1983–84; ACNS (Policy), Oct-Dec. 1984; ACNS, 1985–86. *Recreations:* sailing, history. *Club:* Royal Commonwealth Society.

BLACK, John Newman, CEng, FICE, FIMarE; FRGS; Deputy Chairman, 1985–86, Chief Executive, 1982–86, and Board Member, 1978–86, Port of London Authority; *b* 29 Sept. 1925; *s* of late John Black and late Janet Black (*née* Hamilton); *m* 1952, Euphemia Isabella Elizabeth Thomson; two *d*. *Educ:* Cumberland and Medway Technical Colls. Civil and marine engrg naval stations and dockyards, UK and abroad, incl. Singapore, Hong Kong, Colombo, Gibraltar and Orkney Isles, 1941–64; joined PLA as Civil Engr, 1964; Planning and Construction, Tilbury Docks, 1964–66; Planning Manager, 1967;

seconded to Thames Estuary Devel t Co. Ltd, for work on Maplin Airport/Seaport Scheme, 1969; Asst Dir Planning, PLA, 1970; Director: Maplin, 1972; Tilbury Docks, 1974; all London Docks, 1977; Man. Dir, 1978–81. Dep. Chm., PLA (Met. Terminals) Ltd, 1974; Director: PLACON Ltd (PLA's cons. subsid. co.), 1972; Orsett Depot Ltd, 1974; Port Documentation Services Ltd (Chm.), 1978; Chairman: Thames Riparian Housing Assoc., 1974; PLA Group Property Holdings, 1984. Member: Exec. Council, British Ports Assoc., 1982–; Exec. Cttee, Nat. Assoc. of Port Employers, 1982– (Vice-Chm., 1984–); British Nat. Cttee, Permt Internat. Assoc. of Navigation Congresses, 1981–; London Maritime Assoc., 1975; Council, ICHCA Internat., 1985–; Nat. Exec. Cttee, ICHCA (UK), 1985–; PLA Representative: Internat. Assoc. of Ports and Harbours; Council, RGS. Co-Adviser to Indian Govt on port ops and potential, 1968; lectures: for UN, Alexandria, 1975; for ESCAP (UN), Bangkok, 1983. FInstPet. Freeman: City of London, 1977; Watermen and Lightermen of River Thames, 1977. *Publications:* numerous articles and papers in Geographical Jl, Civil Engr and other learned jls. *Recreations:* shooting, fishing. *Address:* Westdene Cottage, Tanyard Hill, Shorne, near Gravesend, Kent DA12 3EN. *T:* Shorne 3111.

BLACK, John Nicholson, MA, DPhil, DSc, FRSE; Director and Secretary, The Wolfson Foundation, since 1981; *b* 28 June 1922; *e s* of Harold Black, MD, FRCP, and Margaret Frances Black (*née* Nicholson); *m* 1st, 1952, Mary Denise Webb (*d* 1966); one *s* one *d*; 2nd, 1967, Wendy Marjorie Waterston; two *s. Educ:* Rugby Sch.; Exeter Coll., Oxford. MA 1952, DPhil 1952, Oxford; DSc 1965, Adelaide; FRSE 1965. Served War, RAF, 1942–46. Oxford Univ., 1946–49; BA Hons Cl. 1 (Agri.) 1949; Agricl Research Council Studentship, 1949–52; Lectr, Sen. Lectr, Reader, Univ. of Adelaide (Waite Agricl Research Inst.), 1952–63; André Mayer Fellowship (FAO), 1958; Prof. of Forestry and Natural Resources, Univ. of Edinburgh, 1963–71; Principal, Bedford Coll., Univ. of London, 1971–81. Mem., Nat. Environment Research Council, 1968–74. Chm., Donizetti Soc., 1984–. *Publications:* The Dominion of Man, 1970; Donizetti's Operas in Naples, 1983; The Italian Romantic Libretto, 1984; papers on: ecological subjects in scientific jls; Italian opera libretti. *Recreation:* music. *Address:* Westholm, Orchehill Avenue, Gerrards Cross, Bucks SL9 8QE.

BLACK, Prof. Joseph, CBE 1980; PhD; FEng, FIMechE, FRAeS; Professor of Engineering, University of Bath, 1960–85, Head of School of Engineering, 1960–70 and 1973–85; Science and Engineering Research Council/Design Council Engineering Design Co-ordinator, since 1985; *b* 25 Jan. 1921; *s* of Alexander Black and Hettie Black; *m* 1946, Margaret Susan Hewitt; three *s* one *d. Educ:* Royal Belfast Academical Instn; QUB (BScEng, MSc). PhD Bristol; FRAeS 1961, FIMechE 1964, FEng 1981. Scientific Officer, RAE, 1941–44; Res. Fellow, QUB, 1944–45; Aerodynamicist, de Havilland Aircraft, 1945–46; Lectr/Sen. Lectr in Engrg, Univ. of Bristol, 1946–59. Gillette Fellow, USA, 1963. Pro-Vice-Chancellor, Univ. of Bath, 1970–73. Member: UGC, 1964–74 (Chm. Educnl Technol. Cttee); (founder) Council for Educnl Technol., 1974–; A/M Cttee, SRC, 1975–79; Design Council, 1977–82 (Chm. Engrg Components Awards 1976, Engrg Products Awards 1977); Mech. Engrg and Machine Tool Requirement Bd, DoI, 1979–81. Silver Jubilee Medal, 1977. *Publications:* Introduction to Aerodynamic Compressibility, 1950; contrib. aeronaut. and mech. engrg jls (UK and Europe). *Recreations:* photography, antiquarian books, silversmithing. *Address:* 20 Summerhill Road, Bath BA1 2UR. *T:* Bath 23970. *Club:* Athenæum.

BLACK, Kenneth Oscar, MA, MD Cantab, FRCP, BChir, MRCS; Consulting Physician, St Bartholomew's Hospital; *b* 10 Nov. 1910; *s* of late George Barnard Black, Scarborough; *m* 1959, Virginia, *d* of Herbert Lees, Petersham, Surrey; two *d. Educ:* Bootham Sch., York; King's Coll., Cambridge (1st Class Nat. Science Tripos part 1, Senior Exhibitioner); St Bartholomew's Hospital, London. Demonstrator of Physiology and Medical Chief Asst, St Bartholomew's Hospital; Physician, St Bartholomew's Hospital, 1946. MB, BChir 1937; MRCP 1937; MD 1942; FRCP 1946. War service temp. Lt-Col RAMC; served W Africa and India as Medical Specialist and OC Medical Div. Mem., Assoc. of Physicians; Fellow Royal Society Medicine. Examiner in Medicine: University of London, 1953; Soc. of Apothecaries, 1957; for MRCP London, 1967. *Publications:* contributions to journals and textbooks on diabetes and other medical topics. *Recreation:* natural history. *Address:* 28 Palmeira Avenue, Hove, East Sussex BN3 3GB.

BLACK, Margaret McLeod; Head Mistress, Bradford Girls' Grammar School, 1955–75; *b* 1 May 1912; *d* of James Black and Elizabeth Malcolm. *Educ:* Kelso High Sch.; Edinburgh Univ. (MA). Classics Mistress, Lancaster Girls' Grammar Sch., 1936–44, and Manchester High Sch. for Girls, 1944–50; Head Mistress, Great Yarmouth Girls' High Sch., 1950–55. President: Leeds Branch of Classical Assoc., 1963–65; Joint Assoc. of Classical Teachers, 1967–69; Yorkshire Divl Union of Soroptimist Clubs, 1968–69. *Recreation:* music. *Address:* 37 Marton Road, Gargrave, Skipton, N Yorks BD23 0BN. *T:* Gargrave 311. *Club:* Royal Over-Seas League.

BLACK, Rev. Prof. Matthew, DD, DLitt, DTheol, LLD; FRSE; FBA 1955; Professor of Divinity and Biblical Criticism, and Principal of St Mary's College, University of St Andrews, 1954–78; now Emeritus Professor; Dean of the Faculty of Divinity, 1963–67; *b* 3 Sept. 1908; *s* of late James and Helen Black, Kilmarnock, Ayrshire; *m* 1938, Ethel M., *d* of late Lt-Comdr A. H. Hall, Royal Indian Navy; one *s* one *d. Educ:* Kilmarnock Academy; Glasgow Univ. Glasgow: 1st cl. hons MA Classics, 1930; 2nd cl. hons Mental Philosophy, 1931; BD with distinction in Old Testament, 1934; DLitt 1944; Dr Phil Bonn, 1937. Hon. DTheol Münster, 1960; Hon. LLD St Andrews, 1980; Hon. DD: Glasgow, 1954; Cambridge, 1965; Queen's, Ontario, 1967. Buchanan Prize, Moral Philosophy, 1929; Caird Scholar, Classics, 1930; Crombie Scholar, Biblical Criticism, 1933 (St Andrews award); Brown Downie Fellow, 1934; Maxwell Forsyth Fellow and Kerr Travelling Scholarship, Trinity Coll., Glasgow, 1934. Asst to Prof. of Hebrew, Glasgow, 1935–37; Warden of Church of Scotland Students' Residence, 1936–37; Asst Lecturer in Semitic Languages and Literatures, University of Manchester, 1937–39; Bruce Lectr, Trinity Coll., Glasgow, 1940; Lectr in Hebrew and Biblical Criticism, Univ. of Aberdeen, 1939–42; Minister of Dunbarney, Church of Scotland, 1942–47; Officiating CF, Bridge of Earn, 1943–47; Lecturer in New Testament Language and Literature, Leeds Univ., 1947–52; Prof. of Biblical Criticism and Biblical Antiquities, University of Edinburgh, 1952–54. Chm., Adv. Cttee of Peshitta Project of Univ. of Leiden, 1968–78. Morse Lectr, 1956 and De Hoyt Lectr, 1963, Union Theological Seminary, NY; Thomas Burns Lectr, Otago, 1967. Pres., Soc. for Old Testament Study, 1968. FRSE 1977. Pres., SNTS, 1970–71; Corresp. Mem., Göttingen Akademie der Wissenschaften, 1957; Mem., Royal Soc. of Scis, Uppsala, 1979; Hon. Member: Amer. Soc. of Biblical Exegesis, 1958; American Bible Soc., 1966. British Academy Burkitt Medal for Biblical Studies, 1962. *Publications:* Rituale Melchitarum (Stuttgart), 1938; An Aramaic Approach to the Gospels and Acts, 3rd edn, 1967 (Die Muttersprache Jesu, 1982); A Christian Palestinian Syriac Horologion, Texts and Studies, Contributions to Patristic Literature, New Series, Vol. I, 1954; The Scrolls and Christian Origins, 1961, repr. 1983; General and New Testament Editor, Peake's Commentary on the Bible (revised edn, 1962); Bible Societies' edn of the Greek New Testament (Stuttgart), 1966; (Jt Editor) In Memoriam Paul Kahle (Berlin), 1968; (Editor and contributor) The Scrolls and Christianity, 1968; (with A. M. Denis)

Apocalypsis Henochi Graece Fragmenta Pseudepigraphorum, 1970; Commentary on Romans, 1973; (ed with William A. Smalley) On Language, Religion and Culture, in honor Eugene A. Nida, 1974; (organising Editor) The History of the Jewish People in the Age of Jesus Christ, vol. I, ed by G. Vermes and F. Millar, 1973, vol. II, ed jtly with G. Vermes and F. Millar, 1979; vol. III 1, 2, ed by G. Vermes, F. Millar and M. Goodman, 1986; (jtly) The Book of Enoch or I Enoch, 1985; Editor, New Testament Studies, to 1977; articles in learned journals. *Address:* St Michael's, 40 Buchanan Gardens, St Andrews, Fife. *Clubs:* Athenæum; Royal and Ancient (Hon. Chaplain).

BLACK, Prof. Paul Joseph, OBE 1983; PhD; Professor of Science Education University of London, since 1976; Head of Centre for Educational Studies, King's College London, since 1985 (Director, 1976–85, Centre for Science and Mathematics Education, Chelsea College, University of London, which merged with King's College, 1985); *b* 10 Sept. 1930; *s* of Walter and Susie Black; *m* 1957, Mary Elaine Weston; four *s* one *d. Educ:* Rhyl Grammar Sch.; Univ. of Manchester (BSc); Univ. of Cambridge (PhD). Royal Society John Jaffé Studentship, 1953–56. Univ. of Birmingham: Lectr in Physics, 1956–66; Reader in Crystal Physics, 1966–74; Prof. of Physics (Science Education), 1974–76; Dean, Faculty of Educn, Univ. of London, 1978–82. Vice-Pres., Royal Instn of Great Britain, 1983–85; Mem., School Curriculum Develt Cttee, 1984–. Pres., Groupe Internat. de la Recherche sur l'Enseignement de la Physique, 1984–; Hon. Pres., Assoc. for Science Educn, 1986. Bragg Medal, Inst. of Physics, 1973. Kt of St Gregory, 1973. *Publications:* (jtly) Nuffield Advanced Physics Project, 1972; (contrib.) Higher Education Learning Project Books, 1977; papers in Crystallography, Physics and Science Education Jls. *Address:* 16 Wilton Crescent, SW19 3QZ. *T:* 01–542 4178.

BLACK, Peter Blair, JP; Senior Partner, P. Blair Black & Partners, since 1948; *b* 22 April 1917; *s* of Peter Blair Black and Cissie Crawford Samuel; *m* 1952, Mary Madeleine Hilly, Philadelphia; one *s* three *d. Educ:* Sir Walter St John's, Battersea; Bearsden Acad.; Sch. of Building. CC 1949, Alderman 1961, Middlesex; Mem., GLC, 1963–86, Chm., 1970–71, Leader, Recreation and Community Services Policy Gp, 1977–81; motivator of Thames Barrier project; Chm., Cons. Group, GLC, 1982. Chm., Thames Water Authority, 1973–78; Pres., Pure Rivers Soc., 1976–. Leader: GLC group to Moscow and Leningrad, 1971; British delegn to Washington, Potomac/Thames River Conf., 1977; Mem. internat. team to Tokyo, Metropolitan Clean Air Conf., 1971. Frequent performer on TV and radio. Former Member: Thames Conservancy Bd; Metrop. Water Bd; Jager Cttee on Sewage Disposal; PLA; Council, Nat. Fedn of Housing Socs; Founder Chm., Omnium Housing Assoc., 1962; Chm., 1972, Pres., 1983, Abbeyfield, London Region. JP Thames Div., 1961. *Recreations:* small boats and fishing. *Address:* 101A Limmer Lane, Felpham, Sussex. *T:* Middleton-on-Sea 2054. *Clubs:* Middleton Sports; Sewers Synonymous (Dir).

BLACK, Prof. Robert; Professor of Scots Law, University of Edinburgh, since 1981; *b* 12 June 1947; *s* of James Little Black and Jeannie Findlay Lyon. *Educ:* Lockerbie Acad.; Dumfries Acad.; Edinburgh Univ. (LLB); McGill Univ., Montreal (LLM); Lord Pres. Cooper Meml Prize, Univ. of Edinburgh, 1968; Vans Dunlop Scholarship, Univ. of Edinburgh, 1968; Commonwealth Scholarship, Commonwealth Scholarship Commn, 1968. Advocate, 1972; Lectr in Scots Law, Univ. of Edinburgh, 1972–75; Sen. Legal Officer, Scottish Law Commn, 1975–78; in practice at Scottish Bar, 1978–81; Temp. Sheriff, 1981–. Dep. Gen. Editor, The Laws of Scotland: Stair Memorial Encyclopaedia, 1981–. *Publications:* An Introduction to Written Pleading, 1982; Civil Jurisdiction: the new rules, 1983; articles in UK and S African legal jls. *Recreation:* baiting sociologists. *Address:* 6/4 Glenogle Road, Edinburgh EH3 5HW. *T:* 031–557 3571. *Clubs:* Sloane; Scottish Arts (Edinburgh).

BLACK, Sir Robert (Brown), GCMG 1962 (KCMG 1955; CMG 1953); OBE 1949 (MBE (mil.) 1948); *b* 3 June 1906; *s* of late Robert and Catherine Black, formerly of Blair Lodge, Polmont, Stirlingshire; *m* 1937, (Elsie) Anne Stevenson, CStJ (*d* 1986); two *d. Educ:* George Watson's Coll.; Edinburgh Univ. Colonial Administrative Service, 1930; served in Malaya, Trinidad, N Borneo, Hong Kong. Served War of 1939–45, commissioned in Intelligence Corps, 1942; 43 Special Military Mission; POW Japan, 1942–45. Colonial Secretary, Hong Kong, 1952–55; Governor and C-in-C: Singapore, 1955–57; Hong Kong, 1958–64. Chancellor: Hong Kong Univ., 1958–64; Chinese University of Hong Kong, 1963–64. Mem., Commonwealth War Graves Commn, 1964–82. Chm., Clerical, Medical and General Life Assurance Soc., 1975–78. Chm., Internat. Social Service of GB, 1965–73, Pres., 1973–82. LLD (*hc*): Univ. of Hong Kong; Chinese Univ. of Hong Kong. KStJ. Grand Cross Order of Merit, Peru. *Recreations:* walking, fishing. *Address:* Mapletons House, Ashampstead Common, near Reading, Berks RG8 8QN. *Club:* East India, Devonshire, Sports and Public Schools.

BLACK, Sir (Robert) David, 3rd Bt *cr* 1922; *b* 29 March 1929; *s* of Sir Robert Andrew Stransham Black, 2nd Bt, ED, and Ivy (*d* 1980), *d* of late Brig.-Gen. Sir Samuel Wilson, GCMG, KCB, KBE; *S* father, 1979; *m* 1st, 1953, Rosemary Diana (marr. diss. 1972), *d* of Sir Rupert John Hardy, 4th Bt; two *d* (and one *d* decd); 2nd, 1973, Dorothy Maureen, *d* of Major Charles R. Eustace Radclyffe and *widow* of A. R. D. Pilkington. *Educ:* Eton. Lieut, Royal Horse Guards, 1949; Captain 1953; Major 1960; retired, 1961. Served with Berkshire and Westminster Dragoons, TA, 1964–67, and Berkshire Territorials, TAVR III, 1967–69; Vice-Chm., Berkshire and Eastern Wessex TAVRA, 1985. Joint Master, Garth and South Berks Foxhounds, 1965–73. *Recreations:* hunting, shooting, stalking and fishing. *Heir:* none. *Address:* Elvendon Priory, Goring, near Reading, Berks. *T:* Goring-on-Thames 872160; Shurrery Lodge, Shebster, Thurso, Caithness. *T:* Reay 252. *Club:* Cavalry and Guards.

BLACK, Prof. Robert Denis Collison, FBA 1974; Professor of Economics, and Head of Department of Economics, Queen's University Belfast, 1962–85, now Emeritus; *b* 11 June 1922; *s* of William Robert Black and Rose Anna Mary (*née* Reid), Dublin; *m* 1953, Frances Mary, *o d* of William F. and Mary Weatherup, Belfast; one *s* one *d. Educ:* Sandford Park Sch.; Trinity Coll., Dublin (Hon. Fellow, 1982). BA 1941, BComm 1941, PhD 1943, MA 1945. Dep. for Prof. of Polit. Economy, Trinity Coll., Dublin, 1943–45; Asst Lectr in Economics, Queen's Univ., Belfast, 1945–46, Lectr, 1946–58, Sen. Lectr, 1958–61, Reader, 1961–62. Rockefeller Post-doctoral Fellow, Princeton Univ., 1950–51; Visiting Prof. of Economics, Yale Univ., 1964–65; Dean of Faculty of Economics and Social Sciences, QUB, 1967–70; Pro-Vice-Chancellor, 1971–75. President: Statistical & Social Inquiry Soc. of Ireland, 1983–86; Section F, BAAS, 1984–85. MRIA 1974. *Publications:* Centenary History of the Statistical Society of Ireland, 1947; Economic Thought and the Irish Question 1817–1870, 1960; Catalogue of Economic Pamphlets 1750–1900, 1969; Papers and Correspondence of William Stanley Jevons, Vol. I, 1972, Vol. II, 1973, Vols III–VI, 1977, Vol. VII, 1981; articles in Economic Jl, Economica, Oxford Econ. Papers, Econ. History Review, etc. *Recreations:* travel, music. *Address:* Queen's University, Belfast, Northern Ireland BT7 1NN. *T:* Belfast 245133.

BLACK, Sheila (Psyche); OBE 1986; Feature Writer; Director, MAI plc (formerly Mills and Allen International), since 1976; *b* 6 May 1920; *d* of Clement Johnston Black, CA, and Mildred Beryl Black; *m* 1st, 1939, Geoffrey Davien, Sculptor (marr. diss. 1951); one *d* (one *s* decd); 2nd, 1951, L. A. Lee Howard (from whom she obtained a divorce, 1973).

Educ: Dorset; Switzerland; RADA. Actress, until outbreak of War of 1939–45, she became Asst to production manager of an electrical engineering factory. Post-war, in advertising; then in journalism, from the mid-fifties; Woman's Editor, Financial Times, 1959–72; Chm., Interflex Data Systems (UK) Ltd, 1975–83. Features writer for The Director, Financial Weekly, Punch, Mediaworld, and many newspapers and magazines. Chairman: Nat. Gas Consumers' Council, 1981–86; Gas Consumers' Council, 1986–; Dir, Money Management Council, 1985–; Member: Furniture Develt Council, 1967–70; Liquor Licensing Laws Special Cttee, 1971–72; (part-time) Price Commn, 1973–77; Nat. Consumer Council, 1981–. Mem. Council, Inst. of Directors, 1975–. *Publications:* The Black Book, 1976; Mirabelle: cuisine de qualité et tradition, 1979; The Reluctant Money Minder, 1980. *Recreations:* horticulture in London, grandchildren, football. *Address:* c/o National Westminster Bank, 104 Tottenham Court Road, W1P 0EN.

BLACKBURN, Bishop of, since 1982; **Rt. Rev. David Stewart Cross;** *b* 4 April 1928; *s* of Charles Stewart and Constance Muriel Cross; *m* 1954, Mary Margaret Workman Colquhoun; one *s* two *d*. *Educ:* Trinity Coll., Dublin (MA 1956). Deacon 1954, priest 1955; Curate of Hexham, 1954–57; on staff of Cathedral and Abbey Church of St Alban, St Albans, Herts, 1957–63; Precentor, 1960–63; Curate of St Ambrose, Chorlton-on-Medlock and Asst Chaplain to Manchester Univ., 1963–67; BBC Producer in religious broadcasting, 1968–76 (Religious Broadcasting Assistant, BBC North, 1968–71, then Religious Broadcasting Organiser, Manchester Network Production Centre, 1971–76); Bishop Suffragan of Doncaster, 1976–82; Chairman: Local Radio Council, BBC Radio Sheffield, 1980–82; Churches Adv. Cttee on Local Broadcasting, 1980–83; British Churches' Cttee for Channel Four, 1981–85. Chm., Sandford St Martin Trust, 1986–. *Recreations:* photography, making music and exchanging puns. *Address:* Bishop's House, Ribchester Road, Blackburn, Lancs BB1 9EF.

BLACKBURN, Archdeacon of; *see* Robinson, Ven. W. D.

BLACKBURN, Provost of; *see* Jackson, Very Rev. Lawrence.

BLACKBURN, Anthony; *see* Blackburn, D. A. J.

BLACKBURN, Captain (David) Anthony (James), LVO 1978; RN; Ministry of Defence (Navy), 1981–83 and since 1984; *b* 18 Jan. 1945; *s* of late Lieut J. Blackburn, DSC, RN, and late Mrs M. J. G. Pickering-Pick; *m* 1973, Elizabeth Barstow; three *d*. *Educ:* Taunton Sch. RNC Dartmouth, 1963; HMS Kirkliston (in comd), 1972–73; Equerry-in-Waiting to the Duke of Edinburgh, 1976–78; Exec. Officer, HMS Antrim, 1978–81; Comdr, HMS Birmingham, 1983–84. *Address:* Rillet Cottage, Selborne, Alton, Hants GU34 3LH. *T:* Selborne 385. *Club:* Royal Cruising.

BLACKBURN, Fred; *b* 29 July 1902; *s* of Richley and Mary Blackburn, Mellor; *m* 1930, Marion, *d* of Walter W. and Hannah Fildes, Manchester; two *s*. *Educ:* Queen Elizabeth's Grammar Sch., Blackburn; St John's Coll., Battersea; Manchester Univ. Teacher. MP (Lab) Stalybridge and Hyde Div. of Cheshire, 1951–70, retired 1970. *Publications:* The Regional Council; Local Government Reform; George Tomlinson. *Address:* 114 Knutsford Road, Wilmslow, Cheshire. *T:* Wilmslow 523142.

BLACKBURN, Guy, MBE 1944; MChir, FRCS; Consultant Surgeon Emeritus, Guy's Hospital; *b* 20 Nov. 1911; *s* of Dr A. E. Blackburn, Beckenham; *m* 1953, Joan, *d* of Arthur Bowen, Pontycymmer, Wales; one *d* (and one *s* by a previous marriage). *Educ:* Rugby; Clare Coll., Cambridge (MA). MRCS, LRCP 1935; MB, BChir 1935; FRCS 1937; MChir 1941. House appointments, St Bartholomew's Hospital, 1935–37; Brackenbury Scholar in Surgery, 1935; Demonstrator of Anatomy and Chief Asst in Surgery, 1938–39; Military Service, 1942–46; Lt-Col i/c Surgical Div., 1945–46; served in N Africa and Italy. Hunterian Prof., RCS, 1946; late Examiner in Surgery, Univs of Cambridge and London; Member Court of Examiners, RCS, 1962–68. Hon. Visiting Surgeon, Johns Hopkins Hospital, Baltimore, USA, 1957; President, Medical Society of London, 1964–65. Hon. Consulting Surgeon, British Army at Home, 1967–76. Pres., Assoc. of Surgeons of GB and Ireland, 1976–77. Master, Soc. of Apothecaries, 1980–81. *Publications:* (co-ed) A Textbook of Surgery, 1958; (co-ed) Field Surgery Pocket Book, 1981; various publications in medical jls and books. *Address:* 4 Holly Lodge Gardens, N6 6AA. *T:* 01–340 9071. *Clubs:* Garrick, Royal Automobile.

BLACKBURN, John; QC 1984; barrister; *b* 13 Nov. 1945; *s* of Harry and Violet Blackburn; *m* 1st, 1970, Alison Nield (marr. diss. 1978); 2nd, 1979, Elizabeth Parker; one *s*. *Educ:* Rugby Sch.; Worcester Coll., Oxford (Scholar, 1967; Gibbs Prize in Law, 1967). Called to the Bar, Middle Temple, 1969 (Astbury Law Scholar). Practising barrister, 1970–. *Recreations:* cricket, golf, paintings, wine. *Address:* 22 Old Buildings, Lincoln's Inn, WC2. *T:* 01–404 0102.

BLACKBURN, John Graham, PhD; MP (C) Dudley West, since May 1979; *b* 2 Sept. 1933; *s* of Charles Frederick Blackburn and Grace Blackburn; *m* 1958, Marjorie (*née* Thompson); one *s* one *d*. *Educ:* Liverpool Collegiate Sch.; Liverpool Univ.; Berlin Univ. (PhD). Staff/Sgt, Special Investigation Br., Royal Military Police, 1949–53; D/Sgt, Liverpool Police, 1953–65; National Sales Manager with an Internat. Public Engrg Gp, 1965–79; Sales Dir, Solway Engrg Co. Ltd, 1965–. Member, Wolverhampton Council, 1970–80. Member: Post Office Users National Council, 1972–80; Council of Europe, 1983–85. Sec., Cons. Parly Cttee for Arts and Heritage, 1980–; Mem., Home Affairs Select Cttee, 1980–83. Mem., Ecclesiastical Council, 1979–. Freeman: City of London, 1980; City of Tel Aviv, 1981. FInstM 1979; FISE 1975; FInstMSM 1976; FRSA 1984. *Recreation:* keen yachtsman. *Address:* 129 Canterbury Road, Penn, Wolverhampton WV4 4EQ. *T:* Wolverhampton 36222. *Clubs:* Wolverhampton and Bilston Athletic (Vice-President); Traeth Coch Yacht (Executive Member).

BLACKBURN, Michael John, FCA; Managing Partner, Touche Ross & Co., since 1984; *b* 25 Oct. 1930; *s* of Francis and Ann Blackburn; *m* 1955, Maureen (*née* Dale); one *s* two *d*. *Educ:* Kingston Grammar Sch. Joined Touche Ross, 1954; Partner, 1960. *Recreations:* horse racing, gardening. *Address:* Hill House, 1 Little New Street, EC4A 3TR. *T:* 01–353 8011. *Club:* City of London.

BLACKBURN, Michael Scott; His Honour Judge Blackburn; a Circuit Judge, since 1986; *b* 16 Jan. 1936; *m* 1961, Vivienne (*née* Smith); one *s* one *d*. *Educ:* Dame Allen's Sch., Newcastle upon Tyne; William Hulme's Grammar Sch., Manchester; Keble Coll., Oxford (MA). Recorder, 1981–86. President, Manchester Law Society, 1979–80; Chairman, North Western Legal Services Cttee, 1981–85. *Recreations:* squash rackets, hill walking, fishing. *Address:* 123 Deansgate, Manchester M3 2BU. *T:* 061–832 3000. *Clubs:* Lansdowne; Northern Lawn Tennis (Manchester).

BLACKBURN, Hon. Sir Richard (Arthur), Kt 1983; OBE (mil.) 1965; Chief Justice, Supreme Court of the Australian Capital Territory, 1977–85; Judge, Federal Court of Australia, 1977–85; *b* 26 July 1918; *s* of late Brig. Arthur Seaforth Blackburn, VC, CMG, CBE, and Rose Ada (*née* Kelly); *m* 1951, Bryony Helen, *d* of H. H. Dutton; one *s* one *d*. *Educ:* St Peter's Coll., Adelaide; St Mark's Coll., Univ. of Adelaide (BA; Hon. Fellow, 1986); Magdalen Coll., Oxford (BA, BCL; Rhodes Schol. for SA, 1940). Served War, AIF, 1940–45. Called to the Bar, Inner Temple, 1949; Bonython Prof. of Law, Adelaide Univ., 1950–57; in private practice, Adelaide, 1957–66; Judge: NT Supreme Ct, 1966–71; ACT Supreme Ct, 1971–77. Pro-Chancellor, ANU, 1977–84, Chancellor, 1984–. Lt-Col, Adelaide Univ. Regt, 1954–57; Col, 1st Bn Royal SA Regt, 1962–65; Hon. ADC to Governor-Gen. of Australia, 1965–66. Patron, Order of St John, ACT, 1981–; KStJ 1985 (CStJ 1982). *Address:* 29 Custance Street, Farrer, ACT 2607, Australia. *T:* 86–3915.

BLACKBURN, Ronald Henry Albert; a Planning Appeals Commissioner for Northern Ireland, since 1980; *b* 9 Feb. 1924; *s* of late Sidney James and Ellen Margaret Selina Blackburn; *m* 1950, Annabell Hunter; two *s*. *Educ:* Royal Belfast Academical Institution; Univ. of London (LLB (Hons)). Intelligence Service, 1943; Dept of the Foreign Office, 1944–46. Parly Reporting Staff (N Ire.), 1946–52; Second Clerk Asst, Parlt of N Ire., 1952–62; Clerk Asst, 1962–71; Clerk of the Parliaments, 1971–73; Clerk to NI Assembly, 1973–79; Clerk to NI Constitutional Convention, 1975–76. *Recreations:* golf, gardening. *Address:* Trelawn, Jordanstown Road, Newtownabbey, Co. Antrim, N Ireland. *T:* Whiteabbey 62035.

BLACKBURNE, Rt. Rev. Hugh Charles; *b* 4 June 1912; *s* of late Very Rev. Harry William Blackburne; *m* 1944, Doris Freda, *widow* of Pilot Officer H. L. N. Davis; two *s* one *d*. *Educ:* Marlborough; Clare Coll., Cambridge (MA); Westcott House, Cambridge. Deacon, 1937; Priest, 1938; Curate of Almondbury, Yorks, 1937–39. Chaplain to the Forces, 1939–47; served with 1st Guards Bde, 11th Armoured Div., HQ Anti-Aircraft Comd, and as Chaplain, RMC, Sandhurst. Rector, Milton, Hants, 1947–53; Vicar, St Mary's, Harrow, 1953–61. Rector of the Hilborough Group, 1961–72; Vicar of Ranworth and Chaplain for the Norfolk Broads, 1972–77; Hon. Canon of Norwich, 1965–77; Chaplain to the Queen, 1962–77. Bishop Suffragan of Thetford, 1977–80. *Recreations:* sailing, bird-watching. *Address:* 39 Northgate, Beccles, Suffolk NR34 9AU.

BLACKER, Gen. Sir Cecil (Hugh), GCB 1975 (KCB 1969; CB 1967); OBE 1960; MC 1944; Adjutant-General, Ministry of Defence (Army), 1973–76, retired; ADC (General) to the Queen, 1974–76; *b* 4 June 1916; *s* of Col Norman Valentine Blacker and Olive Georgina (*née* Hope); *m* 1947, Felicity Mary, *widow* of Major J. Rew and *d* of Major I. Buxton, DSO; two *s*. *Educ:* Wellington Coll. Joined 5th Royal Inniskilling Dragoon Guards, 1936; Commanded 23rd Hussars, 1945; Instructor, Staff Coll., Camberley, 1951–54; Commanded 5th Royal Inniskilling Dragoon Guards, 1955–57; Military Asst to CIGS, 1958–60; Asst Commandant, RMA, Sandhurst, 1960–62; Commander, 39 Infantry Brigade Group, 1962–64; GOC 3rd Div., 1964–66; Dir, Army Staff Duties, MoD, 1966–69; GOC-in-C Northern Command, 1969–70; Vice-Chief of the General Staff, 1970–73. Colonel Commandant: RMP, 1971–76; APTC, 1971–76; Col, 5th Royal Inniskilling Dragoon Guards, 1972–81. Member: Jockey Club, 1954– (Dep. Sen. Steward, 1984–); Horserace Betting Levy Bd, 1981–84; President: BSJA, 1976–80; BEF, 1980–84. *Publications:* The Story of Workboy, 1960; Soldier in the Saddle, 1963. *Recreations:* painting; amateur steeplechase rider, 1947–54; represented GB in World Modern Pentathlon Championships, 1951; represented GB in Showjumping, 1959–61. *Address:* Whitchurch House, Whitchurch, Aylesbury, Bucks.

BLACKER, Captain Derek Charles, RN; Director of Personnel, Orion Royal Bank Ltd, since 1984; *b* 19 May 1929; *s* of Charles Edward Blacker and Alexandra May Farrant; *m* 1952, Brenda Mary Getgood; one *s* one *d*. *Educ:* County Sch., Isleworth; King's Coll., Univ. of London (BSc Hons 1950). Entered RN, 1950; specialisations: navigation, meteorology, oceanography; HMS Birmingham, HMS Albion, BRNC Dartmouth, HMS Hermes, 1956–69; Comdr 1965; NATO Commands: SACLANT, 1969; CINCHAN, 1972; SACEUR, 1974; Captain 1975; Dir of Public Relations (RN), 1977–79; Bd Pres., Admiralty Interview Bd, 1980; staff of C-in-C, Naval Home Comd, 1980–81; Dir of Naval Oceanography and Meteorology, MoD, 1981–84. *Recreations:* music, tennis, fishing, shooting. *Address:* Chapel Hill, Brettenham, Ipswich, Suffolk IP7 7PG. *T:* Bildeston 740385. *Club:* Army and Navy.

BLACKER, Norman; Chairman, British Gas North Eastern, since 1985; *b* 22 May 1938; *s* of Cyril Norman Blacker and Agnes Margaret Blacker; *m* 1961, Jennifer Mary Anderson. *Educ:* Wolverton Grammar School. IPFA; CIGasE; CBIM. British Gas Corporation: Dir of Finance, Northern Reg., 1976–80; Dir of Finance, 1980–84; Chm., N Eastern Region, 1985. *Address:* British Gas Corporation, North Eastern Region, New York Road, Leeds LS2 7PE. *T:* Leeds 436291.

BLACKETT, Sir George (William), 10th Bt *cr* 1673; *b* 26 April 1906; *s* of Sir Hugh Douglas Blackett, 8th Bt, and Helen Katherine (*d* 1943), *d* of late George Lowther; *S* brother, 1968; *m* 1st, 1933, Euphemia Cicely (*d* 1960), *d* of late Major Nicholas Robinson; 2nd, 1964, Daphne Laing, *d* of late Major Guy Laing Bradley, TD, Hexham, Northumberland. Served with Shropshire Yeomanry and CMP, 1939–45. *Recreations:* hunting, forestry, farming. *Heir:* *b* Major Francis Hugh Blackett [*b* 16 Oct. 1907; *m* 1950, Elizabeth Eily Barrie (*d* 1982), 2nd *d* of late Howard Dennison; two *s* two *d*]. *Address:* Colwyn, Corbridge, Northumberland. *T:* Corbridge 2252. *Club:* English-Speaking Union.

BLACKETT-ORD, Andrew James; His Honour Vice-Chancellor Blackett-Ord; a Circuit Judge since 1972; Vice-Chancellor, County Palatine of Lancaster, since 1973; Member, Council of Duchy of Lancaster, since 1973; *b* 21 Aug. 1921; 2nd *s* of late John Reginald Blackett-Ord, Whitfield, Northumberland; *m* 1945, Rosemary Bovill; three *s* one *d*. *Educ:* Eton; New Coll., Oxford (MA). Scots Guards, 1943–46; called to Bar, 1947, Bencher, Lincoln's Inn, 1985; County Court Judge, 1971. Chancellor, dio. of Newcastle-upon-Tyne, 1971–. *Recreations:* reading, shooting. *Address:* Helbeck Hall, Brough, Kirkby Stephen, Cumbria. *T:* Brough 323. *Clubs:* Garrick, Lansdowne.

BLACKFORD, 4th Baron *cr* 1935; **William Keith Mason;** Bt 1918; *b* 27 March 1962; *s* of 3rd Baron Blackford, DFC, and of Sarah, *d* of Sir Shirley Worthington-Evans, 2nd Bt; *S* father, 1977. *Educ:* Harrow School. *Address:* 17 The Gateways, Sprimont Place, SW3.

BLACKHAM, Rear-Adm. Joseph Leslie, CB 1965; DL; *b* 29 Feb. 1912; *s* of Dr Walter Charles Blackham, Birmingham, and Margaret Eva Blackham (*née* Bavin); *m* 1938, Coreen Shelford Skinner, *er d* of Paym. Captain W. S. Skinner, CBE, RN; one *s* one *d*. *Educ:* West House Sch., Edgbaston; RNC Dartmouth. Specialised in Navigation; served war of 1939–45; JSSC 1950; Comdr, RNC Greenwich, 1953–54; Captain 1954; Admty, 1955–57; Sen. Officer, Reserve Fleet at Plymouth, 1957–59; Admty Naval Staff, 1959–61; Cdre. Supt, HM Dockyard, Singapore, 1962–63; Rear-Adm. 1963; Admiral Supt, HM Dockyard, Portsmouth, 1964–66; retired. Mem., IoW Hosp. Management Cttee, 1968–74; Vice-Chm., IoW AHA 1974–82; Chm., Family Practitioners Cttee, IoW, 1974–85; Mem., Bd of Visitors, HM Prison, Parkhurst, 1967–82 (Chm., 1974–77). CC Isle of Wight, 1967–77 (Chm., 1975–77); DL Hants and IoW, 1970–; High Sheriff, IoW, 1975. Mentioned in despatches for service in Korea, 1951. *Address:* Trinity Cottage, Love Lane, Bembridge, Isle of Wight PO35 5NH. *T:* Bembridge 874386.

BLACKLOCK, Captain Ronald William, CBE 1944; DSC 1917; RN (retired); *b* 21 June 1889; *s* of late J. H. Blacklock, JP, Overthorpe, Banbury; *m* 1920, Aline Frances Anstell (*d* 1975); one *s*. *Educ:* Preparatory Sch.; HMS Britannia. Midshipman, 1906. Specialised in Submarines in 1910. Served European War in Submarines (despatches twice, DSC); Captain 1931; retd owing to ill-health, 1938; War of 1939–45, Director of Welfare Services, Admiralty. *Address:* The Edinburgh Private Clinic, 19 Drumsheugh Gardens, Edinburgh EH3 7RN. *Clubs:* Naval and Military; Royal Yacht Squadron.

BLACKMAN, Sir Frank (Milton), KA 1985; KCVO 1985 (CVO 1975); OBE 1969 (MBE 1964); Cabinet Secretary of Barbados, 1966–86, and Head of the Civil Service, Barbados, 1981–86; *b* 31 July 1926; *s* of late A. Milton Blackman and Winnifred Blackman (*née* Pile); *m* 1958, Edith Mary Knight; one *s*. *Educ:* Wesley Hall Boys' Sch., Barbados; Harrison Coll., Barbados. Clerical Officer, Colonial Secretary's Office, 1944–56; Sec., Public Service Commn, 1956–57; Asst. Sec., Colonial Sec.'s Office, 1957; Cabinet Office/Premier's Office, 1958–66: Clerk of the Legislative Council, 1958–64; Perm. Sec./ Cabinet Sec., 1966–86. *Recreation:* gardening. *Address:* Rendezvous Hill, Christ Church, Barbados. *T:* 427–3463.

BLACKMAN, Gilbert Albert Waller, CBE 1978 (OBE 1973); FEng, FIMechE, FInstE; CBIM; Deputy Chairman and Production Managing Director, Central Electricity Generating Board, since 1986 (Member, since 1977); *b* 28 July 1925; *s* of Ernest Albert Cecil Blackman and Amy Blackman; *m* 1948, Lilian Rosay. *Educ:* Wanstead County High Sch.; Wandsworth Tech. Coll. (CEng, FIMechE 1967). FInstF 1964. Trainee Engr, London Div., Brit. Electricity Authority, 1948–50; various appts in power stns, 1950–63; Central Electricity Generating Board: Stn Supt, Belvedere, 1963–64; Asst Reg. Dir, E Midlands Div., 1964–67; Asst Reg. Dir, Midlands Reg., 1967–70; Dir of Generation, Midlands Reg., 1970–75; Dir Gen., N Eastern Reg., 1975–77. *Recreations:* shooting, photography, walking. *Address:* Gryphon Lodge, 15 Norton Park, St Mary's Hill, Sunninghill, Berks. *T:* Ascot 24374.

See also L. C. F. Blackman.

BLACKMAN, Dr Lionel Cyril Francis; Director, British American Tobacco Co. Ltd, 1980–84 (General Manager, Group Research and Development, 1978–80); *b* 12 Sept. 1930; *s* of Ernest Albert Cecil Blackman and Amy McBain; *m* 1955, Susan Hazel Peachey (marr. diss. 1983); one *s* one *d*. *Educ:* Wanstead High Sch.; Queen Mary Coll., London. BSc 1952; PhD 1955. Scientific Officer, then Senior Research Fellow, RN Scientific Service, 1954–57; ICI Research Fellow, then Lectr in Chemical Physics of Solids, Imperial Coll., London, 1957–60; Asst Dir (London), then Dir, Chemical Research Div., BR, 1961–64; Dir of Basic Research, then Dir Gen., British Coal Utilisation Research Assoc., 1964–71; Director: Fibreglass Ltd (subsid. of Pilkington Bros Ltd), 1971–78; Compocem Ltd, 1975–78; Cemfil Corp. (US), 1975–78; Vice-Pres., Cementos y Fibras SA (Spain), 1976–78. CEng; CChem; FRSC; DIC; SFInstE. *Publications:* (ed) Modern Aspects of Graphite Technology, 1970; papers in various scientific and technical jls on dropwise condensation of steam, ferrites, sintering of oxides, graphite and its crystal compounds, glass surface coatings, glass reinforced cement. *Recreations:* gardening, music, wine. *Address:* Griffin House, Knowl Hill, The Hockering, Woking, Surrey GU22 7HL. *T:* Woking 66328. *Club:* Athenæum.

See also G. A. W. Blackman.

BLACKMAN, Raymond Victor Bernard, MBE 1970; CEng, FIMarE, FRINA; Editor of Jane's Fighting Ships, 1949–50 to 1972–73 editions; Author and Journalist; *b* 29 June 1910; *e s* of late Leo Albert Martin Blackman and late Laura Gertrude, *e d* of Albert Thomas; *m* 1935, Alma Theresa Joyce, *y d* of late Francis Richard Hannah; one *s* one *d*. *Educ:* Southern Grammar Sch., Portsmouth. Contrib. to general and technical press, and associated with Jane's Fighting Ships since 1930; Naval Correspondent, Hampshire Telegraph and Post, 1936–46, Sunday Times, 1946–56. Served Royal Navy, 1926–36 and War of 1939–45, HMS Vernon, Mine Design Dept, Admiralty. Member of The Press Gang. Broadcaster on naval topics. *Publications:* Modern World Book of Ships, 1951; The World's Warships, 1955, 1960, 1963, 1969; Ships of the Royal Navy, 1973; contrib. to The Statesman's Year Book, The Diplomatist, Encyclopædia Britannica Book of the Year, Warships and Navies 1973, The Motor Ship, The Engineer, Navy, Lloyd's List, etc. *Recreations:* seagoing, foreign travel, philately. *Address:* 72 The Brow, Widley, Portsmouth, Hants PO7 5DA. *T:* Cosham 376837. *Clubs:* Anchorites; Press; Royal Naval and Royal Albert Yacht (Portsmouth).

BLACKMUN, Harry A(ndrew); Associate Justice, United States Supreme Court, since 1970; *b* Nashville, Illinois, 12 Nov. 1908; *s* of late Corwin Manning Blackmun and of Theo Huegely (*née* Reuter); *m* 1941, Dorothy E. Clark; three *d*. *Educ:* Harvard Univ.; Harvard Law Sch. AB, LLB. Admitted to Minnesota Bar, 1932; private legal practice with Dorsey, Colman, Barker, Scott & Barber, Minneapolis, 1934–50: Associate, 1934–38; Jun. Partner, 1939–42; General Partner, 1943–50; Instructor: St Paul Coll. of Law, 1935–41; Univ. of Minnesota Law Sch., 1945–47; Resident Counsel, Mayo Clinic, Rochester, 1950–59; Judge, US Ct of Appeals, 8th Circuit, 1959–70. Member: American Bar Assoc.; Amer. Judicature Soc.; Minnesota State Bar Assoc.; 3rd Judicial Dist (Minn) Bar Assoc.; Olmsted Co. (Minn) Bar Assoc.; Judicial Conf. Adv. Cttee on Judicial Activities, 1969–79; Rep. of Judicial Br., Nat. Historical Pubns and Records Commn, 1975–82; Mem., Bd of Mems, Mayo Assoc. Rochester, 1953–60; Bd of Dirs and Exec. Cttee, Rochester Methodist Hosp., 1954–70; Trustee: Hamline Univ., St Paul, 1964–70; William Mitchell Coll. of Law, St Paul, 1959–74. Chm. Faculty, Salzburg Seminar in Amer. Studies (Law), 1977; Co-moderator, Seminar on Justice, Society and the Individual, Aspen Inst., 1979–85; participant, Franco-Amer. Colloquium on Human Rights, Paris, 1979. Hon. LLD: De Pauw Univ., 1971; Hamline Univ., 1971; Ohio Wesleyan Univ., 1971; Morningside Coll., 1972; Wilson Coll., 1972; Dickinson Sch. of Law, 1973; Drake Univ., 1975; Southern Illinois Univ., 1976; Pepperdine Univ., 1976; Emory Univ., 1976; Rensselaer Polytech. Inst., 1979; Nebraska Univ., 1983; New York Law Sch., 1983; McGeorge Sch. of Law, 1984; Vermont Law Sch., 1985; Dartmouth Coll., 1985; Hon. DLitt. Dickinson Sch. of Law, 1983; Hon. DPS Ohio Northern Univ., 1973; Hon. DHL: Oklahoma City, 1976; Massachusetts Sch. of Professional Psychology, 1984. *Publications:* contrib. legal and medical jls. *Recreations:* gardening, reading, music. *Address:* Supreme Court Building, 1 First Street NE, Washington, DC 20543, USA. *Club:* Cosmos (Washington, DC).

BLACKSHAW, Alan, VRD 1970; business consultant and author; Consultant Director, Strategy International Ltd, since 1980; *b* 7 April 1933; *s* of late Frederick William and Elsie Blackshaw; *m* 1st, 1956, Jane Elizabeth Turner (marr. diss. 1983); one *d*; 2nd, 1984, Dr Elspeth Paterson Martin, *d* of late Rev. Gavin C. Martin and Agnes Martin; one *s*. *Educ:* Merchant Taylors' Sch., Crosby; Wadham Coll., Oxford (MA). Royal Marines (commnd), 1954–56. Entered Home Civil Service, Min. of Power, 1956; 1st Sec., UK Delegn to OECD, Paris, 1965–66; Principal Private Sec. to Minister of Power, 1967–69; with Charterhouse Gp on loan, 1972–73; Dept of Energy: Under Sec., 1974; Offshore Supplies Office, 1974–78 (Dir-Gen., 1977–78); Coal Div., 1978–79. Member: Offshore Energy Technol. Bd, 1977–78; Ship and Marine Technol. Requirements Bd, 1977–78. Libel damages against Daily Telegraph (upheld in Ct of Appeal, 1983) and Daily Mail, 1981. Pres., Oxford Univ. Mountaineering Club, 1953–54; Alpine Club: Editor, Alpine Jl, 1968–70; Vice-Pres., 1979–81; British Mountaineering Council: Pres., 1973–76; Patron, 1979–; Chairman: Standing Adv. Cttee on Mountain Trng Policy, 1980–86; Nat. Centre for Mountain Activities, Plas y Brenin, 1986–; Mem., Mountaineering Cttee UIAA, 1985–; Leader, British Alpine Ski Traverse, 1972; Ski Club of Great Britain: Vice-Pres., 1977–80, 1983–85; Pery Medal, 1977; Pres., Eagle Ski Club, 1979–81; British Ski Federation: Vice-Pres., 1983–84; Chm., 1984–. Freeman, City of London. FRGS; FInstPet. *Publication:* Mountaineering, 1965, 3rd revision 1975. *Recreations:* mountaineering and ski-ing. *Address:* 4 St George's Square, SW1V 2HP. *T:* 01–821 8720. *Club:* Royal Scottish Automobile.

BLACKSHAW, William Simon; Headmaster of Brighton College, 1971–Aug. 1987; *b* 28 Oct. 1930; *s* of late C. B. Blackshaw, sometime Housemaster, Cranleigh School and of Kathleen Mary (who *m* 1965, Sir Thomas McAlpine, 4th Bt); *m* 1956, Elizabeth Anne Evans; two *s* one *d*. *Educ:* Sherborne Sch.; Hertford Coll., Oxford. 2nd cl. hons Mod. Langs. Repton School: Asst Master, 1955–71; Head of Modern Languages Dept, 1961–66; Housemaster, 1966–71. *Publication:* Regardez! Racontez!, 1971. *Recreations:* philately, painting, cricket, golf. *Address:* Squash Court, The Green, Rottingdean, Sussex.

BLACKSTONE, Dr Tessa Ann Vosper, PhD; Master, Birkbeck College, from Sept. 1987; Deputy Education Officer (Resources), Inner London Education Authority, 1983–87; *b* 27 Sept. 1942; *d* of Geoffrey Vaughan Blackstone and Joanna Blackstone; *m* 1963, Tom Evans (marr. diss.); one *s* one *d*. *Educ:* Ware Grammar Sch.; London School of Economics (BScSoc, PhD). Associate Lectr, Enfield Coll., 1965–66; Asst Lectr, then Lectr, Dept of Social Administration, LSE, 1966–75; Adviser, Central Policy Review Staff, Cabinet Office, 1975–78; Prof. of Educnl Admin, Univ. of London Inst. of Educn, 1978–83. Fellow, Centre for Studies in Social Policy, 1972–74. *Publications:* Students in Conflict (jtly), 1970; A Fair Start, 1971; Education and Day Care for Young Children in Need, 1973; The Academic Labour Market (jtly), 1974; Social Policy and Administration in Britain, 1975; Disadvantage and Education (jtly), 1982; Educational Policy and Educational Inequality (jtly), 1982; Response to Adversity (jtly), 1983; Testing Children (jtly), 1983. *Address:* 11 Grazebrook Road, N16 0HU. *T:* 01–802 1132.

BLACKWELL, Sir Basil (Davenport), Kt 1983; FEng; Chief Executive, 1974–85, and Chairman, 1985, Westland PLC (Vice-Chairman, 1974–84, Deputy Chairman, 1984); retired; *b* Whitkirk, Yorks, 8 Feb. 1922; *s* of late Alfred Blackwell and late Mrs H. Lloyd; *m* 1948, Betty Meggs, *d* of late Engr Captain Meggs, RN; one *d*. *Educ:* Leeds Grammar Sch.; St John's Coll., Cambridge (MA; Hughes Prize); London Univ. (BScEng). FIMechE; FRAeS (Gold Medal, 1982); CBIM. Sci. Officer, Admiralty, 1942; Rolls-Royce Ltd, 1945; Engine Div., Bristol Aeroplane Co. Ltd, 1949; Bristol Siddeley Engines Ltd: Dep. Chief Engr, 1959; Sales Dir, 1963; Man. Dir, Small Engine Div., 1965 (subseq. Small Engines Div. of Rolls-Royce Ltd). Commercial Dir, Westland Aircraft Ltd, later Westland PLC, 1970; Westland Helicopters Ltd: Man. Dir, 1972; Chm., 1976–85; Chairman: British Hovercraft Corp., 1979–85; Normalair-Garrett Ltd, 1979–85. Member Council: BIM; CBI; NDIC; SBAC (Vice-Pres., 1978; Pres., 1979 and 1980; Dep. Pres., 1980); EEF (Vice-Pres., 1983–85). Pres., AECMA, 1984–85 and Président d'honneur. Hon. DSc, Bath Univ., 1984. *Publications:* contrib. professional jls. *Recreations:* gardens and gardening. *Address:* High Newland, Newland Garden, Sherborne, Dorset DT9 3AF. *T:* Sherborne 813516. *Club:* United Oxford & Cambridge University.

BLACKWELL, Prof. Donald Eustace, MA, PhD; Savilian Professor of Astronomy, University of Oxford, and Fellow of New College, Oxford, since 1960; *b* 27 May 1921; *s* of John Blackwell and Ethel Bowe; *m* 1951, Nora Louise Carlton; two *s* two *d*. *Educ:* Merchant Taylors' Sch.; Sandy Lodge; Sidney Sussex Coll., Cambridge. Isaac Newton Student, University of Cambridge, 1947; Stokes Student, Pembroke Coll., Cambridge, 1948; Asst Director, Solar Physics Observatory, Cambridge, 1950–60. Various Astronomical Expeditions: Sudan, 1952; Fiji, 1955; Bolivia, 1958 and 1961; Canada, 1963; Manuae Island, 1965. Pres., RAS, 1973–75. *Publications:* papers in astronomical journals. *Address:* Department of Astrophysics, South Parks Road, Oxford.

BLACKWELL, Julian, (Toby); Chairman, The Blackwell Group Ltd, since 1980; *b* 10 Jan. 1929; *s* of Sir Basil Henry Blackwell and late Marion Christine, *d* of John Soans; *m* 1953, Jennifer Jocelyn Darley Wykeham; two *s* one *d*. *Educ:* Winchester; Trinity Coll., Oxford. Served 5th RTR, 1947–49; 21st SAS (TA), 1950–59. Dir and Chm., various Blackwell companies, 1956–. Chm. Council, ASLIB, 1966–68 (Vice-Pres., 1982); Mem., Library and Inf. Services Council, 1981–84; Co-founder and Chm., Mail Users' Assoc., 1975–78; Pres., Booksellers' Assoc., 1980–82. *Recreations:* sawing firewood, sailing. *Address:* c/o 50 Broad Street, Oxford OX1 3BQ. *T:* Oxford 244944. *Clubs:* Athenæum; Royal Yacht Squadron; Leander (Henley); Royal Southern Yacht (Southampton).

BLACKWOOD, HAMILTON-TEMPLE-; family name of **Marquess of Dufferin.**

BLACKWOOD, Sir Francis (George), 7th Bt *cr* 1814; Retired Chemical Engineer; now in private practice as a Consulting Engineer; *b* 20 May 1916; *s* of Captain Maurice Baldwin Raymond Blackwood, DSO, RN (*d* 1941) (3rd *s* of 4th Bt) and Dorothea (*d* 1967), *d* of Hon. G. Bertrand Edwards, Sydney, NSW; *S* cousin, 1979; *m* 1941, Margaret Alice, *d* of Hector Kirkpatrick, Lindfield, NSW; two *s* one *d*. *Educ:* Knox Grammar School; Sydney Technical Coll. (ASTC). ARACI, FIEAust. Worked in the chemical industry, mainly for Union Carbide, Australia Ltd (formerly Timbrol Ltd) as a design engineer, 1936–78. *Recreations:* community service and domestic. *Heir:* *s* John Francis Blackwood, architect [*b* 18 Oct. 1944; *m* 1971, Kay Greenhill; one *s* one *d*]. *Address:* 408 Bobbin Head Road, North Turramurra, NSW 2074, Australia. *T:* 44 5189. *Clubs:* Royal Automobile of Australia, Rotary.

BLACKWOOD, Wing Comdr George Douglas; Chairman, William Blackwood & Sons Ltd, publishers and printers, 1948–83; Editor of Blackwood's Magazine, and Managing Director of William Blackwood & Sons Ltd, 1948–76; *b* 11 Oct. 1909; *e s* of late James H. Blackwood and *g g g s* of Wm Blackwood, founder of Blackwood's Magazine; *m* 1936, Phyllis Marion, *y d* of late Sir John Caulcutt, KCMG; one *s* one *d*. *Educ:* Eton; Clare Coll., Cambridge. Short Service Commission in RAF, 1932–38; re-joined 1939. Formed first Czech Fighter Squadron, 1940–41; Battle of Britain (despatches); commanded Czech Wing of Royal Air Force 2nd TAF, 1944 (despatches); retired 1945. Czech War Cross, 1940; Czech Military Medal 1st class, 1944. *Recreations:* countryside activities. *Address:* Airhouse, Oxton, Berwickshire. *T:* Oxton 225.

BLACKWOOD, Prof. William; Professor of Neuropathology, University of London, at The Institute of Neurology, The National Hospital, Queen Square, 1958–76, now Professor Emeritus; *b* 13 March 1911; *m* 1940, Cynthia Gledstone; one *s* one *d*. *Educ:* Cheltenham Coll.; Edinburgh Univ. MB, ChB Edinburgh 1934; FRCSEd 1938; FRCPEd 1961; FRCPath (FCPath 1963). Pathologist, Scottish Mental Hospitals Laboratory; Neuropathologist, Edinburgh Royal Infirmary, and Municipal Hospitals, 1939; Senior Lecturer in Neuropathology, University of Edinburgh, 1945; Asst Pathologist, 1947, Pathologist, 1949, The National Hospital, Queen Square, London. *Publications:* Atlas of

Neuropathology, 1949; (ed jtly) Greenfield's Neuropathology, 3rd edn, 1976. *Address:* 71 Seal Hollow Road, Sevenoaks, Kent. *T:* Sevenoaks 454345.

BLADES, family name of **Baron Ebbisham.**

BLAIKLEY, Robert Marcel; HM Diplomatic Service, retired; *b* 1 Oct. 1916; *s* of late Alexander John Blaikley and late Adelaide Blaikley (*née* Miller); *m* 1942, Alice Mary Duncan; one *s* one *d. Educ:* Christ's Coll., Finchley; St John's Coll., Cambridge. Served HM Forces, 1940–46. Inland Revenue, 1946–48; General Register Office, 1948–65, Asst Secretary, 1958; transferred to Diplomatic Service as Counsellor, 1965; on loan to Colonial Office, 1965–66; Head of Aviation and Telecommunications Dept, CO, 1966–68; Counsellor, Jamaica, 1968–71, Ghana, 1971–73. *Recreations:* walking, growing shrubs. *Address:* 17 Chestnut Grove, Upper Westwood, Bradford-on-Avon, Wilts.

BLAIR, Sir Alastair Campbell, KCVO 1969 (CVO 1953); TD 1950; WS; JP; *b* 16 Jan. 1908; 2nd *s* of late William Blair, WS, and late Emelia Mylne Campbell; *m* 1933, Catriona Hatchard, *o d* of late Dr William Basil Orr; four *s. Educ:* Cargilfield; Charterhouse; Clare Coll., Cambridge (BA); Edinburgh Univ. (LLB). Writer to the Signet, 1932; retired 1977 as Partner, Dundas & Wilson, CS. RA (TA) 1939; served 1939–45 (despatches); Secretary, Queen's Body Guard for Scotland, Royal Company of Archers, 1946–59; appointed Captain 1982; retired 1984. Purse Bearer to The Lord High Commissioner to the General Assembly of the Church of Scotland, 1961–69. JP Edinburgh, 1954. *Recreations:* archery, curling, golf, shooting. *Address:* 7 Abbotsford Court, Colinton Road, Edinburgh EH10 5EH. *T:* 031-447 3095. *Club:* New (Edinburgh).
See also M. C. Blair.

BLAIR, Anthony Charles Lynton, (Tony); MP (Lab) Sedgefield, since 1983; *b* 6 May 1953; *s* of Leo Charles Lynton Blair and late Hazel Blair; *m* 1980, Cherie Booth; two *s. Educ:* Durham Choristers School; Fettes College, Edinburgh; St John's College, Oxford. Called to the Bar, Lincoln's Inn, 1976. *Address:* Myrobella, Trimdon Station, Co. Durham. *T:* Hartlepool 882202; (office) 01-219 5059, 01-219 4456. *Clubs:* Trimdon Colliery and Deaf Hill Working Men's, Trimdon Village Working Men's, Fishburn Working Men's.

BLAIR, Lt-Gen. Sir Chandos, KCVO 1972; OBE 1962; MC 1941 and bar, 1944; GOC Scotland and Governor of Edinburgh Castle, 1972–76; *b* 25 Feb. 1919; *s* of Brig.-Gen. Arthur Blair and Elizabeth Mary (*née* Hoskyns); *m* 1947, Audrey Mary Travers; one *s* one *d. Educ:* Harrow; Sandhurst. Commnd into Seaforth Highlanders, 1939; comd 4 KAR, Uganda, 1959–61; comd 39 Bde, Radfan and N. Ireland. GOC 2nd Division, BAOR, 1968–70; Defence Services Secretary, MoD, 1970–72. Col Comdt, Scottish Div., 1972–76; Col, Queen's Own Highlanders, 1975–83. *Recreations:* golf, fishing, shooting, hunting. *Address:* c/o Royal Bank of Scotland, 44 Brompton Road, SW3. *Club:* Naval and Military.

BLAIR, Charles Neil Molesworth, CMG 1962; OBE (mil.) 1948; Lt-Col; *b* 22 Oct. 1910; *o s* of late Col J. M. Blair, CMG, CBE, DSO, Glenfoot, Tillicoultry, Scotland; *m* 1938, Elizabeth Dorothea, *d* of late Lord Justice Luxmoore, PC; one *d* (one *s* decd). *Educ:* Stowe; RMC Sandhurst. 2nd Lieut The Black Watch, 1930. Served War of 1939–45 in Europe, North Africa and Sicily; Instructor, Army Staff Coll., 1941 and 1944; commanded 1st Black Watch, 1943. Retired from Army on account of war wounds, 1951. Attached FO, 1951–67. *Address:* c/o Lloyds Bank, 6 Pall Mall, SW1Y 5NH. *Club:* Army and Navy.

BLAIR, Claude; FSA 1956; Keeper, Department of Metalwork, Victoria and Albert Museum, 1972–82; *b* 30 Nov. 1922; *s* of William Henry Murray Blair and Lilian Wearing; *m* 1952, Joan Mary Greville Drinkwater; one *s. Educ:* William Hulme's Grammar Sch., Manchester; Manchester Univ. (MA). Served War, Army (Captain RA), 1942–46. Manchester Univ., 1946–51; Asst, Tower of London Armouries, 1951–56; Asst Keeper of Metalwork, V&A, 1956–66; Dep. Keeper, 1966–72. Hon. Editor, Jl of the Arms and Armour Soc., 1953–77. Consultant to Christie's, 1983–; Member: Redundant Churches Fund, 1982–; Exec. Cttee, Council for the Care of Churches, 1983–; Arch. Adv. Panel, Westminster Abbey, 1979–. Hon. Pres., Meyrick Soc.; Hon. Vice-President: Soc. for Study of Church Monuments, 1984– (Hon. Pres., 1978–84); Monumental Brass Soc. Hon. Freeman, Cutlers' Co. Liveryman: Goldsmiths' Co.; Armourers and Brasiers' Co. Medal of Museo Militar, Barcelona, 1969. *Publications:* European Armour, 1958 (2nd edn, 1972); European and American Arms, 1962; The Silvered Armour of Henry VIII, 1965; Pistols of the World, 1968; Three Presentation Swords in the Victoria and Albert Museum, 1972; The James A. de Rothschild Collection: Arms, Armour and Miscellaneous Metalwork, 1974; (ed) Pollard's History of Firearms, 1983; numerous articles and reviews in Archaeological Jl, Jl of Arms and Armour Soc., Connoisseur, Waffen-und Kostümkunde, etc. *Recreations:* travel, looking at churches, listening to music. *Address:* 90 Links Road, Ashtead, Surrey KT21 2HW. *T:* Ashtead 75532. *Club:* Anglo-Polish.

BLAIR, Sir Edward Thomas H.; *see* Hunter-Blair.

BLAIR, George William S.; *see* Scott Blair.

BLAIR, Prof. Gordon Purves, PhD, DSc; FEng 1982; FIMechE, FSAE; Professor of Mechanical Engineering since 1976, Head of the Department of Mechanical and Industrial Engineering since 1982, Dean of Faculty of Engineering, since 1985, Queen's University of Belfast; *b* 29 April 1937; *s* of Gordon Blair and Mary Helen Jones Blair; *m* 1964, Norma Margaret Millar; two *d. Educ:* Queen's Univ. of Belfast (BSc; PhD 1962; DSc 1978). CEng, FIMechE 1977; FSAE 1979. Asst Prof., New Mexico State Univ., 1962–64; Queen's Univ. of Belfast: Lectr, 1964–71; Sen. Lectr, 1971–73; Reader, 1973–76. *Publications:* wide pubn in IMechE and SAE Jls on design and develt of internal combustion engines. *Recreations:* golf, fishing. *Address:* 9 Ben Madigan Park South, Newtownabbey, N Ireland BT36 7PX. *T:* Belfast 773280. *Clubs:* Cairndhu Golf; Royal Portrush Golf.

BLAIR, Rt. Rev. James Douglas, CBE 1975; *b* 22 Jan. 1906; *s* of Rev. A. A. Blair; unmarried. *Educ:* Marlborough; Keble Coll., Oxford; Cuddesdon Coll. 2nd class Lit. Hum., 1928. Deacon, Penistone, Yorks, 1929; Priest, 1930; Oxford Mission Brotherhood of the Epiphany, Calcutta, 1932–; Asst Bishop of Calcutta, with charge of East Bengal, 1951; Bishop of East Bengal, 1956; title of diocese changed to Dacca, 1960; retired as Bishop of Dacca, 1975. *Recreation:* walking. *Address.* Oxford Mission, Barisha, Calcutta 700008, India.

BLAIR, Michael Campbell; Circuit Administrator, Midland and Oxford Circuit, since 1982; *b* 26 Aug. 1941; *s* of Sir Alastair Blair, *qv*; *m* 1966, Halldóra Isabel (*née* Tunnard); one *s. Educ:* Rugby Sch.; Clare Coll., Cambridge (MA, LLM); Yale Univ., USA (Mellon Fellow; MA). Called to the Bar, Middle Temple, 1965 (Harmsworth Law Scholar). Lord Chancellor's Dept, 1966–: Private Sec. to the Lord Chancellor, 1968–71; Sec., Law Reform Cttee, 1977–79; Under-Sec., 1982. Cabinet Office Management Programme, 1986. *Publications:* Sale of Goods Act 1979, 1980; legal articles in Modern Law Rev., Lancet, New Law Jl, Civil Justice Qly. *Address:* Wootton House, 34 Brook Street, Warwick CV34 4BL. *T:* Warwick 491774; 3 Burbage Road, SE24 9HJ. *T:* 01-274 7614. *Club:* Athenæum.

BLAIR, Thomas Alexander, QC (NI) 1958; Chief Social Security (formerly National Insurance) Commissioner (Northern Ireland), 1969–83; *b* 12 Dec. 1916; *s* of late John Blair and of Wilhelmina Whitla Blair (*née* Downey); *m* 1947, Ida Irvine Moore; two *s* one *d. Educ:* Royal Belfast Academical Instn; Queen's Univ. Belfast (BA, LLB). Served War, in Royal Navy, 1940–46 (commissioned, 1941). Called to Bar of N Ireland, 1946. Chairman: Wages Councils; War Pensions Appeal Tribunal. Sen. Crown Counsel for Co. Tyrone; Mem. Departmental Cttee on Legal Aid. Apptd Dep. Nat. Insurance Umpire, 1959; Pres., Industrial Tribunals (NI), 1967–69; Chief Nat. Insurance Commissioner (NI), 1969. *Recreation:* golf. *Address:* Lilac Cottage, Bowden, Melrose, Roxburghshire TD6 0SS. *T:* St Boswells 23680.

BLAIR, Tony; *see* Blair, A. C. L.

BLAIR-CUNYNGHAME, Sir James (Ogilvy), Kt 1976; OBE 1945 (MBE 1943); Chairman, The Royal Bank of Scotland Group plc, 1968–78, Director 1968–82; *b* 28 Feb. 1913; 2nd *s* of late Edwin Blair-Cunynghame and Anne Tod, both of Edinburgh. *Educ:* Sedbergh Sch.; King's Coll., Cambridge (MA). Elected Fellow, St Catharine's Coll., 1939. Served War of 1939–45 (MBE, OBE); RA and Intelligence, Mediterranean and Europe, Lt-Col 1944. FO, 1946–47; Chief Personnel Officer, BOAC, 1947–55; Dir-Gen. of Staff, National Coal Board, 1955–57; Mem. for Staff of Nat. Coal Bd, 1957–59; part-time Mem., Pay Board, 1973–74. Chairman: Royal Bank of Scotland, 1971–76 (Dir, 1960–82); Williams & Glyn's Bank, 1976–78 (Dir, 1969–82); Dep. Chm., Provincial Insurance, 1979–85; Dir, Scottish Mortgage and Trust, 1967–83. Member: Scottish Economic Council, 1965–74; Exec. Cttee Scottish Council Develt and Industry; Council of Industry for Management Educn; Ct of Governors London Sch. of Economics and Political Science; Council Industrial Soc.; Governor, Sedbergh Sch. FBIM; CIPM. Mem., Queen's Body Guard for Scotland. Hon. LLD St Andrews, 1965; Hon. DSc (Soc. Sci.) Edinburgh, 1969. Hon. FRCSEd 1978; FIB 1977. *Publications:* various articles on aspects of personnel management and the economy. *Recreation:* fishing. *Address:* Broomfield, Moniaive, Thornhill, Dumfriesshire. *T:* Moniaive 217. *Clubs:* Savile, Flyfishers'; New, Scottish Arts (Edinburgh).

BLAIR-KERR, Sir William Alexander, (Sir Alastair Blair-Kerr), Kt 1973; President of the Court of Appeal for Bermuda, since 1979; Member, Court of Appeal for Gibraltar, since 1982; *b* 1 Dec. 1911; *s* of William Alexander Milne Kerr and Annie Kerr (*née* Blair), Dunblane, Perthshire, Scotland; *m* 1942, Esther Margaret Fowler Wright; one *s* one *d. Educ:* McLaren High Sch., Callander; Edinburgh Univ. (MA, LLB). Solicitor in Scotland, 1939; Advocate (Scots Bar), 1951. Advocate and Solicitor, Singapore, 1939–41; Straits Settlements Volunteer Force, 1941–42; escaped from Singapore, 1942; Indian Army: Staff Capt. "A" Bombay Dist. HQ, 1942–43; DAAG 107 Line of Communication area HQ, Poona, 1943–44; British Army: GSO2, War Office, 1944–45; SO1 Judicial, BMA Malaya, 1945–46. Colonial Legal Service (HM Overseas Service): Hong Kong: Magistrate, 1946–48; Crown Counsel, 1949; Pres. Tenancy Tribunal, 1950; Crown Counsel, 1951–53; Sen. Crown Counsel, 1953–59; District Judge, 1959–61; Puisne Judge, Supreme Court, 1961–71; Sen. Puisne Judge, Supreme Court, 1971–73; Pres., Court of Appeal for the Bahamas, 1978–80; sometime Actg Chief Justice of Hong Kong. Pres., various Commns of Inquiry. *Recreations:* golf, walking, music. *Address:* Gairn, Kinbuck, Dunblane, Perthshire FK15 0NQ. *T:* Dunblane 823377. *Club:* Royal Over-Seas League.

BLAIR-OLIPHANT, Air Vice-Marshal David Nigel Kington, CB 1966; OBE 1945; *b* 22 Dec. 1911; *y s* of Col P. L. K. Blair-Oliphant, DSO, Ardblair Castle, Blairgowrie, Perthshire, and Laura Geraldine Bodenham; *m* 1942, Helen Nathalie Donald (*d* 1983), *yr d* of Sir John Donald, KCIE; one *s* (and one *s* and one *d* decd). *Educ:* Harrow; Trinity Hall, Cambridge (BA). Joined RAF, 1934; Middle East and European Campaigns, 1939–45; RAF Staff Coll., 1945–48; Group Capt. 1949; Air Cdre 1958; Director, Weapons Engineering, Air Ministry, 1958–60; British Defence Staffs, Washington, 1960–63; Acting Air Vice-Marshal, 1963; Pres., Ordnance Board, 1965–66; Air Vice-Marshal, 1966. *Address:* 9 Northfield Road, Sherfield-on-Lodon, Basingstoke, Hants. *Clubs:* Royal Air Force.

BLAIS, Hon. Jean Jacques, PC (Can.) 1976; QC (Can.) 1978; Member of Law Firm, Nicholls & Blais; Lecturer in Private International Law, University of Ottawa; *b* 27 June 1940; *m* 1968, Maureen Ahearn; two *s* one *d. Educ:* Secondary Sch., Sturgeon Falls; Univ. of Ottawa (BA, LLB). Professional lawyer. MP (L) Nipissing, Ontario, 1972, re-elected 1974, 1979, 1980; defeated Sept. 1984; Parliamentary Sec. to Pres. of Privy Council, 1975; Post Master General, 1976; Solicitor General, 1978; Minister of Supply and Services, and Receiver General, 1980; Minister of Nat. Defence, 1983–84. Mem., Security and Intelligence Review Cttee, 1984–. *Recreations:* squash, skiing, swimming. *Address:* (office) 10th Floor, 1000 Sparks Street, Ottawa, Ontario K1P 5B7, Canada. *T:* 238–8300.

BLAIZE, Rt. Hon. Herbert; PC 1986; Prime Minister of Grenada, since 1984. Chief Minister of Grenada, 1960–61, 1962–67; insurance business, 1979–83; Leader, New National Party, 1984–. *Address:* Office of the Prime Minister, St George's, Grenada.

BLAKE, family name of **Baron Blake.**

BLAKE, Baron *cr* 1971 (Life Peer), of Braydeston, Norfolk; **Robert Norman William Blake,** FBA 1967; JP; Provost of The Queen's College, Oxford, since 1968; Pro-Vice-Chancellor, Oxford University, since 1971; Editor, Dictionary of National Biography, since 1980; *b* 23 Dec. 1916; *er s* of William Joseph Blake and Norah Lindley Daynes, Brundall, Norfolk; *m* 1953, Patricia Mary, *e d* of Thomas Richard Waters, Great Plumstead, Norfolk; three *d. Educ:* King Edward VI Sch., Norwich; Magdalen Coll., Oxford (MA), 1st Cl. Final Honour Sch. of Modern Greats, 1938; Eldon Law Scholar, 1938. Served War of 1939–45; Royal Artillery; North African campaign, 1942; POW in Italy, 1942–44; escaped, 1944; despatches, 1944. Lectr in Politics, Christ Church, Oxford, 1946–47; Student and Tutor in Politics, Christ Church, 1947–68, Emeritus Student, 1969; Censor, 1950–55; Senior Proctor, 1959–60; Ford's Lectr in English History for 1967–68; Mem., Hebdomadal Council, 1959–81. Member: Royal Commn on Historical Manuscripts, 1975– (Chm., 1982–); Bd of Trustees, BM, 1978–; Bd, Channel 4, 1983–. Chm., Hansard Soc. Commn on Electoral Reform, 1975–76; Pres., Electoral Reform Soc., 1986–. Mem. (Conservative) Oxford City Council, 1957–64. Governor of Norwich Sch., of Trent and Malvern Colls, and of St Edward's Sch., Oxford; Rhodes Trustee, 1971 (Chm., 1983–). Prime Warden, Dyers' Co., 1976–77. Hon. Student, Christ Church, Oxford, 1977. Hon. DLitt: Glasgow, 1972; East Anglia, 1983. *Publications:* The Private Papers of Douglas Haig, 1952; The Unknown Prime Minister (Life of Andrew Bonar Law), 1955; Disraeli, 1966; The Conservative Party from Peel to Churchill, 1970, 2nd edn, The Conservative Party from Peel to Thatcher, 1985; The Office of Prime Minister, 1975; (ed with John Patten) The Conservative Opportunity, 1976; A History of Rhodesia, 1977; Disraeli's Grand Tour, 1982; (ed) The English World, 1982, The Decline of Power 1915–1964, 1985. *Address:* The Queen's College, Oxford; Riverview House, Brundall, Norfolk. *Clubs:* Beefsteak, Brooks's, Pratt's, United Oxford & Cambridge University; Vincent's (Oxford); Norfolk County.

BLAKE, Sir Alfred (Lapthorn), KCVO 1979 (CVO 1975); MC 1945; Director, The Duke of Edinburgh's Award Scheme, 1967–78; Consultant with Blake Lapthorn, Solicitors, Portsmouth and area, since 1985 (Partner, 1949–85, Senior Partner, 1983–85); *b* 6 Oct. 1915; *s* of late Leonard Nicholson Blake and Nora Woodfall Blake (*née* Lapthorn); *m* 1st, 1940, Beatrice Grace Nellthorp (*d* 1967); two *s*; 2nd, 1969, Mrs Alison Kelsey Dick, Boston, Mass, USA. *Educ:* Dauntsey's Sch. LLB (London), 1938. Qual. Solicitor and Notary Public, 1938. Royal Marines Officer, 1939–45: Bde Major 2 Commando Bde, 1944; Lieut-Col comdg 45 (RM) Commando and Holding Operational Commando, 1945 (despatches). Mem., Portsmouth CC, 1950–67 (Past Chm., Portsmouth Educn Cttee); Lord Mayor of Portsmouth, 1958–59. Mem., Youth Service Development Coun., 1960–66; Pres., Portsmouth Youth Activities Cttee, 1976–. Lay Canon, Portsmouth Cathedral, 1962–72. Hon. Fellow, Portsmouth Polytechnic, 1981. *Recreation:* golf. *Address:* 1 Kitnocks Cottages, Wickham Road, Curdridge, Southampton SO3 2HG. *T:* Botley 2281. *Clubs:* Royal Commonwealth Society; Royal Naval and Royal Albert Yacht (Portsmouth).

BLAKE, Charles Henry, CB 1966; a Commissioner of Customs and Excise, 1968–72; European Adviser, British American Tobacco Co., 1972–76; *b* 29 Nov. 1912; *s* of Henry and Lily Blake, Westbury on Trym, Bristol; *m* 1938, M. Jayne McKinney (*d* 1974), *d* of James and Ellen McKinney, Castle Finn, Co. Donegal; three *d. Educ:* Cotham Grammar Sch.; Jesus Coll., Cambridge (Major Scholar). Administrative Class, Home Civil Service, 1936; HM Customs and Excise: Princ., 1941; Asst Sec., 1948; Comr and Sec., 1957–64; Asst Under-Sec. of State, Air Force Dept, MoD, 1964–68. *Recreation:* gardens. *Address:* 33 Grenville Court, Chorleywood, Herts. *T:* Chorleywood 3795. *Clubs:* United Oxford & Cambridge University; Moor Park.

BLAKE, Prof. Christopher, FRSE; Bonar Professor of Applied Economics, University of Dundee, since 1974; *b* 28 April 1926; *s* of George Blake and Eliza Blake; *m* 1951, Elizabeth McIntyre; two *s* two *d. Educ:* Dollar Academy; St Andrews Univ. MA St Andrews 1950, PhD St Andrews 1965. Served in Royal Navy, 1944–47. Teaching posts, Bowdoin Coll., Maine, and Princeton Univ., 1951–53; Asst, Edinburgh Univ., 1953–55; Stewarts & Lloyds Ltd, 1955–60; Lectr and Sen. Lectr, Univ. of St Andrews, 1960–67; Sen. Lectr and Prof. of Economics, Univ. of Dundee, 1967–74. Dir, Alliance Trust plc, 1974–; Chm., William Low & Co. plc, 1985– (Dir, 1980–). Member: Council for Applied Science in Scotland, 1978–; Royal Commn on Envtl Pollution, 1980–86; *Publications:* articles in economic and other jls. *Recreation:* golf. *Address:* Westlea, Wardlaw Gardens, St Andrews, Fife KY16 9DW. *T:* St Andrews 75564. *Clubs:* Royal Commonwealth Society; New (Edinburgh); Royal and Ancient (St Andrews).

BLAKE, Prof. David Leonard; Professor of Music, University of York, since 1976; *b* 2 Sept. 1936; *s* of Leonard Blake and Dorothy Blake; *m* 1960, Rita Muir; two *s* one *d. Educ:* Latymer Upper School; Gonville and Caius College, Cambridge (BA 1960, MA 1963); Deutsche Akademie der Künste, Berlin, GDR. School teacher: Ealing Grammar Sch., 1961–62; Northwood Secondary Sch., 1962–63; University of York: Granada Arts Fellow, 1963–64; Lectr in Music, 1964; Sen. Lectr, 1971–76. *Recordings:* Violin concerto: In Praise of Krishna; Variations for Piano; The Almanack. *Publications* include: It's a Small War (musical for schools), 1963; Chamber Symphony, 1981; Lumina (cantata for soprano, baritone, chorus and orch.), 1969; Metamorphoses for large orch., 1978; Nonet for wind, 1979; The Bones of Chuang Tzu (Chang Heng) (cantata for baritone and piano), 1976; In Praise of Krishna: Bengali lyrics, 1976; String Quartet No 2, 1977; Violin Concerto, 1979; Toussaint (opera), 1977; From the Mattress Grave (song cycle), 1981; Cassation for wind, 1982; Clarinet Quintet, 1983. *Recreations:* conservation (mills etc), political debate. *Address:* Mill Gill, Askrigg, near Leyburn, North Yorks DL8 3HR. *T:* Wensleydale 50364.

BLAKE, Sir Francis Michael, 3rd Bt *cr* 1907; *b* 11 July 1943; *o s* of Sir F. Edward C. Blake, 2nd Bt and Olive Mary (*d* 1946) *d* of Charles Liddell Simpson; *S* father, 1950; *m* 1968, Joan Ashbridge, *d* of F. C. A. Miller; two *s. Educ:* Rugby. *Heir: s* Francis Julian Blake, *b* 17 Feb. 1971. *Address:* The Dower House, Tillmouth Park, Cornhill-on-Tweed, Northumberland TD12 4UR. *T:* Coldstream 2443.

BLAKE, (Henry) Vincent; marketing consultant; Secretary, Glassfibre Reinforced Cement Association, 1977–86; *b* 7 Dec. 1912; *s* of Arthur Vincent Blake and Alice Mabel (*née* Kerr); *m* 1938, Marie Isobel Todd; one *s. Educ:* King Edward's High Sch., Birmingham. Pupil apprentice, Chance Brothers, Lighthouse Engineers, Birmingham, 1931–34; subseq. Asst Sales Manager, 1937 and Sales Manager there, of Austinlite Ltd, 1945; Textile Marketing Manager, Fibreglass Ltd, 1951; Commercial Manager: Glass Yarns and Deeside Fabrics Ltd, 1960; BTR Industries Ltd, Glass and Resin Div., 1962–63, Plastics Group, 1963–66; Gen. Manager, Indulex Engineering Co. Ltd, 1966–71. Mem. Council and Chm., Reinforced Plastics Gp, British Plastics Fedn, 1959. Mem. Council, Royal Yachting Assoc., 1980– (Vice-Chm., Thames Valley Region, 1979–). *Publications:* articles in technical jls on reinforced plastics. *Recreations:* sailing, motoring, reading, and talking about reinforced plastics. *Address:* Farthings End, Dukes Ride, Gerrards Cross, Bucks. *T:* Gerrards Cross 882606. *Club:* Datchet Water Sailing (Hon. Life Mem.), Cookham Reach Sailing (Hon. Life Mem.), Pwllheli Sailing.

BLAKE, John Clifford, CB 1958; *b* 12 July 1901; *s* of late Alfred Harold and Ada Blake, Prestwich, Lancs; *m* 1928, Mary Lilian Rothwell; one *s* two *d. Educ:* Manchester Grammar Sch.; Queen's Coll., Oxford (MA). Admitted solicitor, 1927. Ministry of Health Solicitor's Dept, 1929; Solicitor and Legal Adviser to Ministries of Health and Housing and Local Government, and to Registrar Gen., 1957–65; Mem., Treasurer and Jt Exec. Sec., Anglican-Methodist Unity Commn, 1965–69; Vice-Pres., Methodist Conference, 1968. *Recreations:* music, especially organ and choral. *Address:* 3 Clifton Court, 297 Clifton Drive South, St Anne's on Sea, Lancs FY8 1HN. *T:* St Anne's 728365.

BLAKE, John William, CBE 1972; Professor of History, New University of Ulster, 1972–77, now Emeritus; *b* 7 Dec. 1911; *s* of Robert Gay Blake and Beatrice Mary Blake (*née* Tucket); *m* 1938, Eileen Florence Lord; two *s* one *d. Educ:* Kilburn Grammar Sch.; King's Coll., London (MA). Inglis Student and Derby Scholar, 1933–34; QUB: Asst Lectr, 1934; Lectr, 1944; Sen. Lectr, 1945; served War of 1939–45 in Civil Defence and as Offical War Historian to NI Govt; Prof. of History, Univ. of Keele (until 1962 University Coll. of N Staffs), 1950–64; Acting Principal of University Coll. of N Staffs, 1954–56; Vice-Chancellor, Univ. of Botswana, Lesotho and Swaziland (formerly Basutoland, Bechuanaland Protectorate and Swaziland), 1964–71. Vis. Prof., Univ. of North Carolina at Asheville, 1979. Mem. Staffs Co. Educn Cttee, 1955–61; Mem. Inter-Univ. Council for Higher Educn Overseas, 1955–64; FRHistS. Hon. Fellow, Hist. Soc., Ghana. Hon. DLitt: Keele 1971; Botswana, Lesotho and Swaziland, 1971. *Publications:* European Beginnings in West Africa, 1937; Europeans in West Africa, 2 vols 1942; Official War History of Northern Ireland, 1956; West Africa: Quest for God and Gold, 1977; contribs to historical jls. *Recreations:* gardening, philately. *Address:* Greystones, Northside, Shadforth, Co. Durham.

BLAKE, Mary Netterville, MA; Headmistress, Manchester High School for Girls, 1975–83; *b* 12 Sept. 1922; *d* of John Netterville Blake and Agnes Barr Blake. *Educ:* Howell's Sch., Denbigh; St Anne's Coll., Oxford (MA). Asst Mistress, The Mount Sch., York, 1945–48; Head of Geography Dept, King's High Sch., Warwick, 1948–56; Associate Gen. Sec., Student Christian Movement in Schools, 1956–60; Head Mistress, Selby Grammar Sch., 1960–75. Pres., Assoc. of Headmistresses, 1976–77; first Pres., Secondary Heads Assoc., 1978. *Address:* 2A Hartington Road, Bramhall, Stockport SK7 2DZ. *T:* 061–439 5165.

BLAKE, Peter Thomas, CBE 1983; RA 1980 (ARA 1974); ARCA; painter; *b* 25 June 1932; *s* of Kenneth William Blake; *m* 1963, Jann Haworth (marr. diss. 1982); now lives with Chrissy Wilson; two *d. Educ:* Gravesend Tech. Coll.; Gravesend Sch. of Art; RCA. Works exhibited: ICA, 1958, 1960; Guggenheim Competition, 1958; Cambridge, 1959; RA, 1960; Musée d'Art Moderne, Paris, 1968; Waddington Galls, 1970, 1972 and 1979; Stedlijk Mus., Amsterdam, 1973; Kunstverein, Hamburg, 1973; Gemeentemuseum, Arnhem, 1974; Palais des Beaux-Arts, Brussels, 1974; Galleria Documenta, Turin, 1982; retrospective exhibn, Tate Gall., 1983; works in public collections: Trinity Coll., Cambridge; Carlisle City Gall.; Tate Gall.; Arts Council of GB; Mus. of Modern Art, NY; V & A Mus.; Mus. Boymans-van Beuningen, Rotterdam; Calouste Gulbenkian Foundn, London; RCA; Whitworth Art Gall., Univ. of Manchester; Baltimore Mus. of Art, Md; *Publications:* illustrations for: Oxford Illustrated Old Testament, 1968; Roger McGough, Summer with Monica, 1978; cover illustration, Arden Shakespeare: Othello, 1980; Anthony and Cleopatra, 1980; Timon of Athens, 1980; contribs to: Times Educnl Supp.; Ark; Graphis 70; World of Art; Architectural Rev.; House and Garden; Painter and Sculptor. *Recreations:* sculpture, wining and dining, going to rock and roll concerts, boxing and wrestling matches; living well is the best revenge. *Address:* c/o Waddington Galleries Ltd, 2 Cork Street, W1X 1PA.

BLAKE, Quentin Saxby, RDI; freelance artist and illustrator, since 1957; Head of Department of Illustration, 1978–86, Senior Visiting Tutor, since 1986, Royal College of Art (Tutor, 1965, Senior Tutor, 1977); *b* 16 Dec. 1932; *s* of William Blake and Evelyn Blake. *Educ:* Downing Coll., Cambridge (MA). FSIAD. Exhibns of watercolour drawings, Workshop Gallery: Invitation to the Dance, 1972; Runners and Riders, 1973; Creature Comforts, 1974; Water Music, 1976; Retrospective exhibn of illustration work, Nat. Theatre, 1984. *Publications:* (author and illustrator) for children: Patrick, 1968; Jack and Nancy, 1969; Angelo, 1970; Snuff, 1973; The Adventures of Lester, 1977; (ed and illus.) Custard and Company, by Ogden Nash, 1979; Mr Magnolia, 1980 (Fedn of Children's Bk Gps Award; Kate Greenaway Medal, 1981); Quentin Blake's Nursery Rhyme Book, 1983; The Story of the Dancing Frog, 1984; (illustrator) for children: Russell Hoban, How Tom Beat Captain Najork and his Hired Sportsmen, 1974 (Whitbread Lit. Award, 1975; Hans Andersen Honour Book, 1975); Russell Hoban, A Near Thing for Captain Najork, 1976; Andrew Lloyd Webber and Tim Rice, Joseph and the Amazing Technicolour Dreamcoat, 1982; Russell Hoban, The Rain Door, 1986; Roald Dahl: The Enormous Crocodile, 1978; The Twits, 1980; George's Marvellous Medicine, 1981; Revolting Rhymes, 1982; The BFG, 1982; The Witches, 1983; Dirty Beasts, 1984; The Giraffe and the Pelly and Me, 1985; books by John Yeoman, Joan Aiken, Clement Freud, Sid Fleischman, Michael Rosen, Sylvia Plath, Margaret Mahy and Dr Seuss; (illustrator) for adults: Aristophanes, The Birds, 1971; Lewis Caroll, The Hunting of the Snark, 1976; Stella Gibbons, Cold Comfort Farm, 1977; Evelyn Waugh, Black Mischief, 1980, Scoop, 1981; George Orwell, Animal Farm, 1984. *Address:* 30 Bramham Gardens, SW5 0HF. *T:* 01–373 7464.

BLAKE, Sir Richard; *see* Blake, Sir T. R. V.

BLAKE, Richard Frederick William; Editor, Whitaker's Almanack, since 1981; *b* 9 April 1948; *s* of late Frederick William Blake and of Doris Margaret Blake; *m* 1973, Christine Vaughan; one *d. Educ:* Archbishop Tenison's Grammar School. Joined J. Whitaker & Sons, Ltd (Whitaker's Almanack Dept), 1966; apptd Asst Editor of Whitaker's Almanack, 1974. *Recreations:* music, sport. *Address:* 118 Warren Drive, Elm Park, Hornchurch, Essex.

BLAKE, Sir (Thomas) Richard (Valentine), 17th Bt *cr* 1622, of Menlough; Director: Sir Richard Blake & Associates Ltd; City Chase Ltd; Sales Manager, R & B Trading, Fontwell, Sussex; *b* 7 Jan. 1942; *s* of Sir Ulick Temple Blake, 16th Bt, and late Elizabeth Gordon (she *m* 1965, Vice-Adm. E. Longley-Cook, CB, CBE, DSO); *S* father, 1963; *m* 1976, Mrs Jacqueline Hankey; *m* 1982, Bertice Reading (marr. diss. 1986). *Educ:* Bradfield Coll., Berks. Member, Standing Council of Baronets. *Recreations:* shooting; Royal Naval Reserve. *Heir: kinsman* Anthony Teilo Bruce Blake, *b* 5 May 1951. *Address:* 1 City Chase, The Needlemakers, Chichester, Sussex. *T:* Eastergate 2118. *Club:* Chequers (Bognor Regis).

BLAKE, Vincent; *see* Blake, H. V.

BLAKELY, Colin George Edward; actor and director since 1957; *b* 23 Sept. 1930; *s* of Victor Charles and Dorothy Margaret Ashmore Blakely; *m* 1961, Margaret Elsa Whiting; three *s. Educ:* Sedbergh School. Manager, Athletic Stores Ltd, Belfast, 1948–57; 1st prof. acting job, Children's Touring Theatre (Gwent), 1957; Group Theatre, Belfast, 1957–59; Cock a Doodle Dandy, Royal Court, 1959; Moon for the Misbegotten, Arts, 1960; The Naming of Murderers Rock, Royal Court, 1960; entered TV and films (Saturday Night and Sunday Morning), 1960–61; Hastings, in Richard III, and Touchstone, in As You Like It, Royal Shakespeare Co., Stratford, 1961; subseq. various films, TV, etc; Nat. Theatre, 1963–68: Pizarro, in Royal Hunt of the Sun; Captain Boyle, in Juno and the Paycock; Proctor, in Crucible; Philoctetes, in Philoctetes; Kite, in Recruiting Officer; Volpone, in Volpone; Hobson, in Hobson's Choice; Captain Shot-over, in Heartbreak House; Astrov, in Uncle Vanya, and Schmidt, in Fire Raisers, Royal Court; Torvald, in A Doll's House, Criterion, 1973; Vukhow, in Judgement, Royal Court, 1976; Dysart, in Equus, Albery, 1976; Dennis, in Just Between Ourselves, Queen's, 1977; Filumena, Lyric, 1977; Enjoy, Vaudeville, 1980; All My Sons, Wyndham's, 1981; Lovers Dancing, Albery, 1983; One for the Road, Duchess, 1985; Daffyd, in Chorus of Disapproval, Nat. Theatre, then Lyric, 1986. *Principal films* include: This Sporting Life; Decline and Fall; Watson, in The Private Life of Sherlock Holmes; The National Health; It Shouldn't Happen to a Vet; The Pink Panther Strikes Again; Equus; Dogs of War; Evil under the Sun; The Little World of Don Camillo; *TV appearances* include: Christ, in Son of Man; Peer Gynt, in Peer Gynt; Antony, in Antony and Cleopatra; Stalin, in The Red Monarch; Landscape, 1983; title rôle in The Father, 1985; The Dumb Waiter, 1985; Operation Julie, 1985; The Birthday Party, 1986. *Recreations:* piano, painting, sketching, golf. *Address:* c/o Leading Artists, 60 St James's Street, SW1. *T:* 01–491 4400.

BLAKEMORE, Alan, CBE 1976; Town Clerk and Chief Executive (formerly Town Clerk), Croydon, 1963–82; *b* 17 May 1919; *s* of late John William and Mary Blakemore, Salford; *m* 1956, José Margaret Cavill; two *s. Educ:* North Manchester School. Solicitor, 1943. Articled to Town Clerk, Salford, 1936; RASC (TA), 1939; Army service to 1946; released with hon. rank Lt-Col; Asst Solicitor, Salford, 1946–48; Deputy Town Clerk: Wigan, 1948–52; Bolton, 1952–57; Town Clerk, Stockport, 1957–63; Officer Adviser: AMC, 1965–74; AMA, 1974–82. Hon. Clerk, General Purposes Cttee, London Boroughs Assoc., 1971–82; Consultant, 1982–. Member: DHSS Housing Benefits Rev. Cttee,

1984–85; London Residuary Body, 1985–. Hon. Freeman, London Bor. of Croydon, 1982. *Address:* Chaseley, 4 Waterfield Drive, Warlingham, Surrey CR3 9HP. *T:* Upper Warlingham 4249. *Club:* Royal Over-Seas League.

BLAKEMORE, Prof. Colin Brian; Waynflete Professor of Physiology, Oxford University, since 1979; Fellow of Magdalen College, since 1979; *b* 1 June 1944; *s* of Cedric Norman Blakemore and Beryl Ann Smith; *m* 1965, Andrée Elizabeth Washbourne; three *d. Educ:* King Henry VIII Sch., Coventry; Corpus Christi Coll., Cambridge (Smyth Scholar; BA 1965, MA 1969); Univ. of Calif, Berkeley (PhD 1968). Harkness Fellow, Neurosensory Lab., Univ. of Calif, Berkeley, 1965–68; Cambridge University: Fellow and Dir of Medical Studies, Downing Coll., 1971–79; Univ. Demonstr in Physiol., 1968–72; Univ. Lectr in Physiol., 1972–79; Leverhulme Fellow, 1974–75. Royal Soc. Locke Res. Fellow, 1976–79. Chm., Neurobiology and Mental Health Bd Grants Cttee, MRC, 1977–79. Vis. Professor: NY Univ., 1970; MIT, 1971; Royal Soc. Study Visit, Keio Univ., Tokyo, 1974; Lethaby Prof., RCA, 1978; Storer Vis. Lectr, Univ. of Calif, Davis, 1980; Vis. Scientist, Salk Inst., 1982, 1983; Macallum Vis. Lectr, Univ. of Toronto, 1984. Hon. Pres., World Cultural Council, 1983–. Member: Central Council, Internat. Brain Res. Org., 1973–; BBC Science Consultative Group, 1975–79. BBC Reith Lectr, 1976; Lectures: Aubrey Lewis, Inst. of Psych., 1979; Lord Charnwood, Amer. Acad. of Optometry, 1980; Vickers, Neonatal Soc., 1981; Kershman, Eastern Assoc. of Electroencephalographers, NY, 1981; Harveian, Harveian Soc. of London, 1982; Christmas, Royal Instn, 1982; Earl Grey Meml, Newcastle Univ., 1982; George Frederic Still, BPA, 1983; Edridge-Green, RCS, 1984; Cyril Leslie Oakley Meml, Leeds Univ., 1984; Plenary, European Neuroscience Assoc., 1984; Mac Keith Meml, Brit. Paediatric Neurology Assoc., 1985; Faculty of Science, RHC, 1985; Halliburton, KCL, 1986; Cairns Meml, 1986; Betram Louis Abrahams, RCP, 1986. Robert Bing Prize, Swiss Acad. of Med. Sciences, 1975; Richardson Cross Medal, S Western Opthalmol Soc., 1978; Copeman Medal, Corpus Christi Coll., Cambridge, 1976; Man of the Year, Royal Assoc. for Disability and Rehabilitation, 1978; Phi Beta Kappa Award in Sci., 1978; John Locke Medal, Apothecaries' Soc., 1983; Prix du Docteur Robert Netter, Acad. Nat. de Médecine, Paris, 1984; Cairns Medal, 1986. *Publications:* Handbook of Psychobiology (with M. S. Gazzaniga), 1975; Mechanics of the Mind, 1977; (with S. A. Greenfield) Mind Waves, 1986; res. reports in Jl of Physiol., Brit. Med. Bull., Nature, etc. *Recreation:* wasting time. *Address:* University Laboratory of Physiology, Parks Road, Oxford OX1 3PT.

BLAKEMORE, Michael Howell; freelance director; *b* Sydney, NSW, 18 June 1928; *s* of Conrad Blakemore and late Una Mary Blakemore (*née* Litchfield); *m* 1960, Shirley (*née* Bush); one *s*; lives with Tanya McCallin; two *d. Educ:* The King's Sch., NSW; Sydney Univ.; Royal Academy of Dramatic Art. Actor with Birmingham Rep. Theatre, Shakespeare Memorial Theatre, etc, 1952–66; Co-dir, Glasgow Citizens Theatre (1st prod., The Investigation), 1966–68; Associate Artistic Dir, Nat. Theatre, 1971–76. Dir, Players, NY, 1978. Resident Dir, Lyric Theatre, Hammersmith, 1980. Best Dir, London Critics, 1972. *Productions include:* A Day in the Death of Joe Egg, 1967; Arturo Ui, 1969; Forget-me-not Lane, 1971; Design for Living, 1973; Knuckle, 1974; Separate Tables, 1976; Privates on Parade, 1977; Candida, 1977; All My Sons, 1981; Benefactors, 1984, NY, 1986; Made in Bangkok, 1986; *National Theatre:* The National Health, 1969; Long Day's Journey Into Night, 1971; The Front Page, Macbeth, 1972; The Cherry Orchard, 1973; Plunder, 1976; *Lyric Theatre, Hammersmith:* Make and Break, 1980 (his opening production); Travelling North, 1980; The Wild Duck, 1980; Noises off, 1982 (transf. to Savoy, 1982, NY, 1983). *Films:* A Personal History of the Australian Surf, 1981; Privates on Parade, 1983. *Publication:* Next Season, 1969 (novel). *Recreation:* surfing. *Address:* 11a St Martin's Almshouses, Bayham Street, NW1. *T:* 01-267 3952.

BLAKENEY, Hon. Allan Emrys; PC (Canada) 1982; Leader of the Opposition, Saskatchewan, since 1982; Member of Legislative Assembly, Saskatchewan, since 1960; *b* Bridgewater, NS, 7 Sept. 1925; *m* 1st, 1950, Mary Elizabeth (Molly) Schwartz (*d* 1957), Halifax, NS; one *s* one *d*; 2nd, 1959, Anne Gorham, Halifax; one *s* one *d. Educ:* Dalhousie Univ. (BA, LLB); Queen's Coll., Oxford (MA). Univ. Medal for Achievement in Coll. of Law, Dalhousie; Rhodes Schol. Sec. and Legal Adviser, Saskatchewan Crown Corps, 1950; Chm., Saskatchewan Securities Commn, 1955–58; private law practice, 1958–60 and 1964–70. Formerly Minister of Educn, Provincial Treas. and Health Minister; Chm., Wascana Centre Authority, 1962–64; Opposition Financial Critic, 1964–70; Dep. Leader, 1967–70; Federal New Democratic Party President, 1969–71; Saskatchewan NDP Leader and Leader of Opposition, 1970; Premier, 1971–82. Formerly Dir and Vice-Pres., Sherwood Co-op. and Sherwood Credit Union. Hon. DCL Mount Allison, 1980; Hon. LLD Dalhousie, 1981. *Recreations:* reading, swimming, formerly ice hockey and badminton. *Address:* Office of the Leader of the Opposition, Legislative Building, Regina, Saskatchewan S4S 0B3, Canada.

BLAKENEY, Frederick Joseph, CBE 1968; Australian diplomat, retired 1978; *b* Sydney, NSW, 2 July 1913; *s* of Frederick Joseph Blakeney, Sydney; *m* 1943, Marjorie, *d* of John Martin, NSW; one *d. Educ:* Marist Darlinghurst and Mittagong; Univ. of Sydney. AMF, 1940–41; RAAF Flt Lieut (Navigator), 1942–45. Teaching Fellow, Univ. of Sydney, 1946; Dept of External Affairs, Canberra, 1946; 2nd Sec. and 1st Sec., Austr. Embassy, Paris, 1947; 1st Sec., then Chargé d'Affaires, Austr. Embassy, Moscow, 1949–51; Dept of Ext. Affairs, Canberra, 1952–53; Counsellor, Austr. Embassy, Washington, 1953–56; Minister to Vietnam and Laos, 1957–59, and to Cambodia, 1957; Asst Sec. (S and SE Asia), Dept of Ext. Affairs, Canberra, 1959–62; Australian Ambassador to Federal Republic of Germany, 1962–68; Australian Ambassador to USSR, 1968–71; First Asst Sec. (Defence), Dept of Foreign Affairs, Canberra, 1972–74; Australian Ambassador to the Netherlands, 1974–77; Australian Ambassador and Perm. Rep. to the UN, Geneva, 1977–78. *Address:* 19 Grey Street, Deakin, Canberra, ACT, Australia.

BLAKENHAM, 2nd Viscount *cr* 1963, of Little Blakenham; **Michael John Hare;** Chairman, since 1983, Managing Director, since 1986, Pearson plc; *b* 25 Jan. 1938; *s* of 1st Viscount Blakenham, PC, OBE, VMH, and of Hon. Beryl Nancy Pearson, *d* of 2nd Viscount Cowdray; *S* father, 1982; *m* 1965, Marcia Persephone, *d* of Hon. Alan Hare, *qv*; one *s* two *d. Educ:* Eton College; Harvard Univ. (AB Econ.). Life Guards, 1956–57; English Electric, 1958; Harvard, 1959–61; Lazard Brothers, 1961–63; Standard Industrial Group, 1963–71; Royal Doulton, 1972–77; Pearson, 1977– (Man. Dir, 1978–83); Chm., The Financial Times; Dir, Lazard Bros. Chm., Royal Soc. for Protection of Birds. *Address:* 17th Floor, Millbank Tower, SW1P 4QZ. *T:* 01–828 9020.

BLAKER, George Blaker, CMG 1963; Under-Secretary, HM Treasury, 1955–63, and Department of Education and Science, 1963–71 retired; *b* Simla, India, 30 Sept. 1912; *m* 1938, Richenda Dorothy Buxton; one *d. Educ:* Eton; Trinity Coll., Cambridge. Private Sec. to Ministers of State in the Middle East, 1941–43; Cabinet Office, 1943; Private Sec. to Sec. of War Cabinet, 1944; Principal Private Sec. to Minister of Production and Presidents of the Board of Trade, 1945–47; accompanied Cabinet Mission to India, 1946; Sec. of UK Trade Mission to China, 1946; HM Treasury, 1947; UK Treasury Representative in India, Ceylon and Burma, 1957–63. Pres., Surrey Trust for Nature Conservation, 1969–80. Hon. Sec., Scientific and Medical Network, 1973–. Gold Medal, Royal Soc. for the Protection of Birds, 1934. *Address:* Lake House, Ockley, Surrey RH5 5NS.

BLAKER, Sir John, 3rd Bt *cr* 1919; *b* 22 March 1935; *s* of Sir Reginald Blaker, 2nd Bt, TD, and of Sheila Kellas, *d* of Dr Alexander Cran; *S* father, 1975; *m* 1st, 1960, Catherine Ann (marr. diss. 1965), *d* of late F. J. Thorold; 2nd, 1968, Elizabeth Katherine, *d* of late Col John Tinsley Russell, DSO. *Address:* Stantons Farm, East Chiltington, near Lewes, East Sussex.

BLAKER, Nathaniel Robert, QC 1972; DL; **His Honour Judge Blaker;** a Circuit Judge, since 1976; *b* 31 Jan. 1921; *s* of Major Herbert Harry Blaker and Annie Muriel Blaker (*née* Atkinson); *m* 1951, Celia Margaret, *o d* of W. Hedley, DSO, KC, and Mrs Hedley; two *d. Educ:* Winchester; University College, Oxford (MA). Royal Signals, 1940–47. Called to the Bar, Inner Temple, 1948; Bencher, 1971. Dep. Chm., Dorset QS, 1970; a Recorder of the Crown Court, 1972–76. Wine Treasurer, Western Circuit, 1964–76. DL Hants, 1985. *Address:* 2 Culver Road, Winchester, Hants. *T:* Winchester 69826.

BLAKER, Rt. Hon. Sir Peter (Allan Renshaw), KCMG 1983; PC 1983; MA; MP (C) Blackpool South, since 1964; *b* Hong Kong, 4 Oct. 1922; *s* of late Cedric Blaker, CBE, MC; *m* 1953, Jennifer, *d* of late Sir Pierson Dixon, GCMG, CB; one *s* two *d. Educ:* Shrewsbury; Trinity Coll., Toronto (BA, 1st class, Classics); New Coll., Oxford (MA). Served 1942–46: Argyll and Sutherland Highlanders of Canada (Capt., wounded). Admitted a Solicitor, 1948. New Coll., Oxford, 1949–52; 1st Class, Jurisprudence, Pass degree in PPE. Pres. Oxford Union. Called to Bar, Lincoln's Inn, 1952. Admitted to HM Foreign Service, 1953; HM Embassy, Phnom Penh, 1955–57; UK High Commn, Ottawa, 1957–60; FO, 1960–62; Private Sec. to Minister of State for Foreign Affairs, 1962–64. Attended Disarmament Conf., Geneva; UN Gen. Assembly, 1962 and 1963; signing of Nuclear Test Ban Treaty, Moscow, 1963. An Opposition Whip, 1966–67; PPS to Chancellor of Exchequer, 1970–72; Parliamentary Under-Secretary of State: (Army), MoD, 1972–74; FCO, 1974; Minister of State: FCO, 1979–81; for the Armed Forces, MoD, 1981–83. Joint Secretary: Conservative Party Foreign Affairs Cttee, 1965–66; Trade Cttee, 1967–70; Exec. Cttee of 1922 Cttee, 1967–70; Vice-Chm., All-Party Tourism Cttee, 1974–79; Mem., Select Cttee on Conduct of Members, 1976–77; Chairman: Hong Kong Parly Gp, 1970–72, 1983–; Cons. For. and Commonwealth Affairs Cttee, 1983– (Vice-Chm., 1974–79); Mem. Exec. Cttee, British-American Parly Gp, 1975–79; Hon. Sec., Franco-BritishParly Relations Cttee, 1975–79. Chm., Bd, Royal Ordnance Factories, 1972–74; Chm. Governors, Welbeck Coll., 1972–74; Mem. Council: Chatham House, 1977–79, 1986–; Council for Arms Control, 1983–; Freedom Assoc., 1984–; Vice-Chairman: Peace Through NATO, 1983–; GB-USSR Assoc., 1983– (Mem. Council, 1974–79); Vice-Pres., Cons. Foreign and Commonwealth Council, 1983–; Governor, Atlantic Inst., 1978–79; Trustee, Inst. for Negotiation and Conciliation, 1984–. Chm., World Trading and Shipping (Europe) Ltd, 1986–; Consultant, The English Trust Group plc, 1986–. *Address:* c/o House of Commons, SW1A 0AA.

BLAKEWAY, John Denys; HM Diplomatic Service, retired; *b* 27 May 1918; *s* of late Sir Denys Blakeway, CIE; *m* 1946, Jasmine Iremonger; one *s* two *d. Educ:* Rugby (Schol.); Magdalen Coll., Oxford (Schol., MA). British and Indian Army, 1939–46 (wounded). Joined Foreign (subseq. Diplomatic) Service, 1946; served Sofia, Lyons, Athens (twice), Tripoli, FO (twice), Bologna, Rome, Ibadan, The Hague; Consul-Gen., Istanbul, 1975–78. *Recreation:* viticulture. *Address:* Row Farm, Zeals, Warminster, Wilts. *T:* Bourton (Dorset) 840209.

BLAKISTON, Sir Ferguson Arthur James, 9th Bt *cr* 1763; farmer; *b* 19 Feb. 1963; *er s* of Sir Arthur Norman Hunter Blakiston, 8th Bt, and Mary Ferguson (*d* 1982), *d* of late Alfred Ernest Gillingham, Cave, S Canterbury, NZ; *S* father, 1977. *Educ:* Lincoln Coll., NZ (Diploma in Agriculture 1983). *Heir: b* Norman John Balfour Blakiston, Stock and Station Agent, *b* 7 April 1964. *Address:* 28 McKenzie Street, Geraldine, S Canterbury, New Zealand.

BLAKSTAD, Michael Björn; Chairman and Chief Executive, Workhouse Productions Ltd, since 1984; Chairman: Filmscreen International Ltd, since 1984; Friday Productions Ltd, since 1984; Joint Chief Executive, Videodisc Co., since 1984; *b* 18 April 1940; *s* of Clifford and Alice Blakstad; *m* 1965, Patricia Marilyn Wotherspoon; one *s* twin *d. Educ:* Ampleforth Coll.; Oriel Coll., Oxford (MA Lit. Hum.). General trainee, BBC, 1962–68; Producer, Yorkshire Television, 1968–71; freelance TV producer, 1971–74; Programme Editor, BBC, 1974–80; Dir of Programmes, TV South, 1980–84. Founder and Managing Director, Blackrod, 1980 (Chm., 1981–84). Awards include: Radio Industries Club, 1975, 1977, 1979; RTS, 1976; BAFTA/Shell Prize, 1976; BIM/John Player, 1976; Nyon, 1978. Hon. MSc Salford, 1983; FRSA; MRI. *Publications:* The Risk Business, 1979; Tomorrow's World looks to the Eighties, 1979. *Recreations:* golf, writing. *Address:* The Tudor House, Workhouse Lane, East Meon, Hants. *Club:* Reform.

BLAMEY, Norman Charles, RA 1975 (ARA 1970); Senior Lecturer, Chelsea School of Art, London, 1963–79; *b* 16 Dec. 1914; *s* of Charles H. Blamey and Ada Blamey (*née* Beacham); *m* 1948, Margaret (*née* Kelly); one *s. Educ:* Holloway Sch., London; Sch. of Art, The Polytechnic, Regent Street, London. ROI 1952; Hon. ROI 1974. Exhibited at: RA, RHA, ROI, RBA, NEAC, and provincial galleries; *mural decorations in:* Anglican Church of St Luke, Leagrave, Beds, 1956; Lutheran Church of St Andrew, Ruislip Manor, Middx, 1964; *works in permanent collections:* Municipal Gall., Port Elizabeth, S Africa; Beaverbrook Gall., Fredericton, NB; Beecroft Art Gall., Southend-on-Sea; Towner Art Gall., Eastbourne; Preston Art Gall.; Pennsylvania State Univ. Mus of Art; La Salle Coll., Pa; V & A Museum; Tate Gall.; Chantry Bequest purchase, 1972, 1985; *portraits include:* Mrs Alison Munro, Dr Harry Pitt, Rev. Dennis Nineham, Sir Cyril Clarke, Prof. Graham Higman, Rt Hon. Bernard Weatherill, Speaker of H of C, Sir Alec Merrison, FRS. Works in private collections in UK and USA. RA Summer Exhibitions: Rowney Bicentenary Award, 1983; Charles Wollaston Award, 1984. *Recreation:* walking. *Address:* 39 Lyncroft Gardens, NW6. *T:* 01–435 9250.

BLAMIRE, Roger Victor; veterinary consultant; Director of Veterinary Field Services, Ministry of Agriculture, Fisheries and Food, 1979–83; *b* 9 July 1923; *s* of Thomas Victor Blamire and Anetta Elizabeth (*née* Lawson); *m* 1947, Catherine Maisie Ellis Davidson; two *d. Educ:* Kendal Sch.; Royal (Dick) Veterinary Coll., Edinburgh. MRCVS, DVSM. RAVC, 1945–48 (Captain); served India, Burma and Malaya. MAF, 1949; Asst Vet. Officer, City of London, 1949; Dep. Chief Advr on Meat Inspection, MOF, 1952; Dep. Dir, Vet. Field Services, MAFF, 1968. Hon. FRSH, 1979. *Recreations:* walking, gardening, listening to music. *Address:* 4 Mandeville Drive, Surbiton, Surrey KT6 5DT. *T:* 01–398 4773.

BLAMIRE-BROWN, John, DL; County Clerk and Chief Executive, Staffordshire County Council, 1973–78; *b* 16 April 1915; *s* of Rev. F. J. Blamire Brown, MA; *m* 1945, Joyce Olivia Pearson; two *s. Educ:* Cheam Sch.; St Edmund's Sch., Canterbury. Solicitor 1937. Served War of 1939–45, Royal Marines (Captain). Asst Solicitor, Wednesbury, 1937; West Bromwich, 1946; Staffs CC, 1948; Deputy Clerk of County Council and of

Peace, 1962; Clerk, Staffs CC, 1972; Clerk to Lieutenancy, 1972–78; Sec., Staffs Probation and After Care Cttee; Hon. Sec., W Mids Planning Authorities Conf., 1972–78. Dep. Chm., Manpower Services Commn Area Board, Staffs, Salop, W Midlands (North), 1978–. Mem. Council, Beth Johnson Foundn, 1978–; Governor, Newcastle-under-Lyme Endowed Schools, 1978–; Chm., St Giles Home Ltd, 1979–. DL Staffs, 1974. *Recreations:* beagling, gardening. *Address:* The Mount, Codsall Wood, Wolverhampton, West Midlands. *T:* Codsall 2044.

BLANCH, family name of **Baron Blanch.**

BLANCH, Baron *cr* 1983 (Life Peer), of Bishopthorpe in the county of North Yorkshire; **Rt. Rev. and Rt. Hon. Stuart Yarworth Blanch,** PC 1975; *b* 1918; *s* of late William Edwin and of Elizabeth Blanch; *m* 1943, Brenda Gertrude, *d* of late William Arthur Coyte; one *s* four *d*. *Educ:* Alleyns Sch., Dulwich; Oxford (BA 1st cl. Theo. 1948, MA 1952). Employee of Law Fire Insurance Soc. Ltd, 1936–40; Navigator in RAF, 1940–46; St Catherine's Coll., Oxford, 1946–49 (Hon. Fellow, 1975); Curate of Highfield, Oxford, 1949–52; Vicar of Eynsham, Oxon, 1952–57; Tutor and Vice-Principal of Wycliffe Hall, Oxford, 1957–60 (Chm. 1967–); Oriel Canon of Rochester and Warden of Rochester Theological Coll., 1960–66; Bishop of Liverpool, 1966–75; Archbishop of York, 1975–83. Sub-Prelate, OStJ, 1975–. Hon. Fellow, St Peter's Coll., Oxford, 1983. Hon. LLD Liverpool, 1975; Hon. DD: Hull, 1977; Wycliffe Coll., Toronto, 1979; Manchester, 1984; DUniv York, 1979. *Publications:* The World Our Orphanage, 1972; For All Mankind, 1976; The Christian Militant, 1978; The Burning Bush, 1978; The Trumpet in the Morning, 1979; The Ten Commandments, 1981; Living by Faith, 1983; Way of Blessedness, 1985. *Recreations:* squash, walking, music. *Address:* Little Garth, Church Street, Bloxham, Oxfordshire. *Club:* Royal Commonwealth Society.

BLANCH, Mrs Lesley, (Madame Gary); FRSL; author; *b* 1907; *m* 2nd, 1945, Romain Gary Kacew (Romain Gary) (marr. diss. 1962; he *d* 1980). *Educ:* by reading, and listening to conversation of elders and betters. FRSL 1969. *Publications:* The Wilder Shores of Love (biog.), 1954; Round the World in Eighty Dishes (cookery), 1956; The Game of Hearts (biog.), 1956; The Sabres of Paradise (biog.), 1960; Under a Lilac Bleeding Star (travels), 1963; The Nine Tiger Man (fict.), 1965; Journey into the Mind's Eye (autobiog.), 1968; Pavilions of the Heart (biog.), 1974; Pierre Loti: portrait of an escapist (biog.), 1983. *Recreations:* travel, opera, acquiring useless objects, animal welfare, gardening. *Address:* Roquebrune Village, 06190 Roquebrune-Cap-Martin, France. *Club:* Taharir (formerly Mahommed Ali) (Cairo).

BLANCHARD, Francis; Director-General, International Labour Office, Geneva, since 1974; *b* Paris, 21 July 1916; *m* 1940, Marie-Claire Boué; two *s*. *Educ:* Univ. of Paris. French Home Office; Internat. Organisation for Refugees, Geneva, 1947–51; Internat. Labour Office, Geneva, 1951–, Asst Dir-Gen., 1956–68, Dep. Dir-Gen., 1968–74. *Recreations:* ski-ing, hunting, riding. *Address* (office) International Labour Office, 4 chemin des Morillons, Geneva, Switzerland. *T:* 99.61.11; (home) Prébailly, 01170 Gex, France. *T:* 41–51–70 Gex.

BLANCO WHITE, Thomas Anthony, QC 1969; *b* 19 Jan. 1915; *s* of late G. R. Blanco White, QC, and Amber Blanco White, OBE; *m* 1950, Anne Katherine Ironside-Smith; two *s* one *d*. *Educ:* Gresham's Sch.; Trinity Coll., Cambridge. Called to Bar, Lincoln's Inn, 1937, Bencher 1977. Served RAFVR, 1940–46. *Publications:* Patents for Inventions, 1950, 1955, 1962, 1974, 1983, etc. *Recreations:* gardening, photography. *Address:* Francis Taylor Building, EC4.

BLAND, (Francis) Christopher (Buchan); Chairman: LWT (Holdings), since 1984; Century Hutchinson Group, since 1984; Director, National Provident Institution, since 1978; *b* 29 May 1938; *e s* of James Franklin MacMahon Bland and Jess Buchan Bland (*née* Brodie); *m* 1981, Jennifer Mary, Viscountess Enfield, *er d* of late Rt Hon. W. M. May, PC, FCA, MP, and of Mrs May, Mertoun Hall, Holywood, Co. Down; one *s* and two step *s* two step *d*. *Educ:* Sedbergh; The Queen's Coll., Oxford (Hastings Exhibnr). 2nd Lieut, 5th Royal Inniskilling Dragoon Guards, 1956–58; Lieut, North Irish Horse (TA), 1958–69. Dir, NI Finance Corp., 1972–76; Dep. Chm., IBA, 1972–80; Chm., Sir Joseph Causton & Sons, 1977–85. Mem. GLC, for Lewisham, 1967–70; Chm., ILEA Schs Sub-Cttee, 1970; Mem. Burnham Cttee, 1970; Chm., Bow Group, 1969–70; Editor, Crossbow, 1971–72; Chairman: NHS Rev. Gp on Nat. Trng Council and Nat. Staff Cttees, 1982; Hammersmith Special Health Authority, 1982–. Governor, Prendergast Girls Grammar Sch. and Woolwich Polytechnic, 1968–70; Mem. Council: RPMS, 1982–; St Mary's Med Sch., 1984–. *Publication:* Bow Group pamphlet on Commonwealth Immigration. *Recreations:* fishing, skiing; formerly: Captain, OU Fencing Team, 1961; Captain, OU Modern Pentathlon Team, 1959–60; Mem. Irish Olympic Fencing Team, 1960. *Address:* Abbots Worthy House, Abbots Worthy, Winchester, Hants. *T:* Winchester 881333; 10 Catherine Place, SW1E 6HF. *T:* 01–834 0021. *Club:* Beefsteak.

BLAND, Sir Henry (Armand), Kt 1965; CBE 1957; FRSA; *b* 28 Dec. 1909; *s* of Emeritus Prof. F. A. Bland, CMG, and Elizabeth Bates Jacobs; *m* 1933, Rosamund, *d* of John Nickal; two *d* (and one *d* decd). *Educ:* Sydney High Sch.; Univ. of Sydney. LLB (Hons) 1932. Admitted Solicitor Supreme Court of NSW, 1935. Entered NSW Public Service, 1927; Alderman, Ryde (NSW) Municipal Council, 1937–39; Acting Agent-Gen. for NSW in London, 1940–41; Adviser on Civil Defence to NSW and Commonwealth Govts, 1941; Princ. Asst to Dir-Gen. of Manpower, 1941–45; Asst Sec., First Asst Sec., 1946–51, Sec. 1952–67, Dept of Labour and National Service; Sec., Dept of Defence, Australia, 1967–70. Leader, Austr. Govt Delegns to Confs: 1948, 1953, 1957, 1960, 1962, 1963, 1964, 1966; Austr. Govt Rep. on the Governing Body of ILO, 1963–67; Adviser on industrial relations to Singapore Govt, 1958. Bd of Inquiry into Victorian Land Transport System, 1971; Chairman: Cttee on Administrative Discretions, 1972–73; Bd of Inquiry into Victorian Public Service, 1973–75; Commonwealth Admin. Rev. Cttee, 1976; ABC, 1976; Arbitrator between Aust. Nat. Railways and Tasmanian Govt, 1978. Chm. and Dir of numerous cos, 1970–. *Address:* 27 Charlton Close, Bowral, NSW 2576, Australia. *T:* (048) 613320. *Clubs:* Athenæum (Melbourne); Bowral Golf.

BLAND, Lt-Col Sir Simon (Claud Michael), KCVO 1982 (CVO 1973; MVO 1967); Comptroller, Private Secretary and Equerry to Princess Alice Duchess of Gloucester and the Duke and Duchess of Gloucester, since 1972; *b* 4 Dec. 1923; *s* of late Sir Nevile Bland, KCMG, KCVO; *m* 1954, Olivia, *d* of late Major William Blackett; one *s* three *d*. *Educ:* Eton College. Served War of 1939–45, Scots Guards, in Italy; BJSM, Washington, 1948–49; 2nd Bn, Scots Guards, Malaya, 1949–51; Asst Mil. Adviser at UK High Commn, Karachi, 1959–60; Comptroller and Asst Private Sec. to late Duke of Gloucester, 1961–74 and Private Sec. to late Prince William, 1968–72. Dir, West End Bd, Commercial Union. CStJ 1978. *Recreation:* shooting. *Address:* Tower Flat, Kensington Palace, W8 4PY. *T:* 01–937 6374; Gabriels Manor, Edenbridge, Kent. *T:* Edenbridge 862340. *Club:* Buck's.

BLANDFORD, Marquess of; Charles James Spencer-Churchill; on agricultural course at Royal Agricultural College, Cirencester; *b* 24 Nov. 1955; *e s* and *heir* of 11th Duke of Marlborough, *qv*. *Educ:* Pinewood; Harrow. *Address:* Blenheim Palace, Woodstock, Oxon; 35 Redcliffe Road, SW10. *Clubs:* Turf, Tramp's, Annabel's; Racquet and Tennis (New York).

BLANDFORD, Eric George, CBE 1967; formerly a Judge of the Supreme Court of Aden; *b* 10 March 1916; *s* of George and Eva Blanche Blandford; *m* 1940, Marjorie Georgina Crane; one *s*. *Educ:* Bristol Grammar Sch. Admitted Solicitor Supreme Court, England, 1939; LLB (London) 1939. War Service, 1939–46 (despatches): India, Burma, Malaya; rank on release Temp. Major RA. Solicitor in London, 1946–51; Asst Comr of Lands, Gold Coast, 1951; Dist Magistrate, Gold Coast, 1952; called to the Bar, Inner Temple, 1955; Chief Registrar, Supreme Court, Gold Coast, 1956; Registrar of High Court of Northern Rhodesia, 1958; Judge, Supreme Court of Aden, 1961–68; Dep. Asst Registrar of Criminal Appeals, 1968–78; Asst Registrar of Criminal Appeals, Royal Courts of Justice, 1978–81. Chm. Aden Municipality Inquiry Commn, 1962. *Publication:* Civil Procedure Rules of Court, Aden, 1967. *Recreations:* country pursuits. *Address:* Boot Lane, Dinton, Bucks HP17 8UJ. *Club:* Royal Commonwealth Society.

BLANDFORD, Heinz Hermann, CBE 1981; Vice-Chairman, since 1982, and Fellow, 1973, Royal Postgraduate Medical School, Hammersmith Hospital (Hon. Treasurer, 1964–82); Vice-Chairman, School of Pharmacy, London University, since 1979 (Member Council and Hon. Treasurer since 1975); *b* Berlin, Germany, 28 Aug. 1908; *s* of late Judge Richard Blumenfeld and Hedwig Kersten; *m* 1933, Hilde Kleczewer; one *s* one *d*. *Educ:* Augusta Gymnasium; (classical scholar) Univs of Berlin and Hamburg. Controller of continental cos in ceramic, pharmaceutical, iron and steel industries, 1933–39. Chm., Ulvir Ltd and various cos, 1936–76. Pioneered synthesis, manufacture and use of Liquid Fertilisers in the UK, 1945–60. Founded (Mem. Bd of Trustees), Blandford Trust for advancement of health and prevention and relief of sickness by med. research and teaching. British Postgraduate Medical Federation: Mem. Governing Body, 1969–; Hon. Treas., 1969–84; Chm., 1977–79, Dep. Chm., 1980–85; Member: Management Cttee, Inst. of Ophthalmology, Moorfields, 1974–; Court of Governors, LSHTM, 1982–; Governor, London House for Overseas Graduates, 1977–80. Member: Org. Cttee, 6th World Congress of Cardiology, London, 1971; Board of Governors: Hammersmith and St Mark's Hospitals, 1972–74. *Recreations:* farming, gardening. *Address:* Holtsmere End, Redbourn, Herts. *T:* Redbourn 2206. *Club:* Farmers'.

BLANDY, Prof. John Peter, MA, DM, MCh, FRCS, FACS; Consultant Surgeon: The London Hospital, since 1964; St Peter's Hospital for the Stone, since 1969; Professor of Urology, University of London, since 1969; *b* 11 Sept. 1927; *s* of late Sir E. Nicolas Blandy, KCIE, CSI, ICS and Dorothy Kathleen (*née* Marshall); *m* 1953, Anne, *d* of Hugh Mathias, FRCS, Tenby; four *d*. *Educ:* Clifton Coll.; Balliol Coll., Oxford; London Hosp. Med. Coll. BM, BCh 1951; MA 1953; FRCS 1956; DM 1963; MCh 1963; FACS 1980. House Phys. and House Surg., London Hosp., 1952; RAMC, 1953–55; Surgical Registrar and Lectr in Surgery, London Hosp., 1956–60; exchange Fellow, Presbyterian St Luke's Hosp., Chicago, 1960–61; Sen. Lectr, London Hosp., 1961; Resident Surgical Officer, St Paul's Hosp., 1963–64. Member: BMA; RSM; Council, RCS, 1982– (Hunterian Prof., 1964); Internat. Soc. Pædiatric Urol. Surg.; Internat. Soc. of Urological Surgeons; British Assoc. Urological Surgeons (Pres., 1984); Fellow, Assoc. of Surgeons. Hon. Fellow: Urological Soc. of Australasia, 1973; Mexican Coll. of Urology, 1974. Maurice Davidson Award, Fellowship of Postgrad. Med., 1980; St Peter's Medal, 1982. *Publications:* (with A. D. Dayan and H. F. Hope-Stone) Tumours of the Testicle, 1970; Transurethral Resection, 1971; (ed) Urology, 1976; Lecture Notes on Urology, 1976; Operative Urology, 1978; papers in surgical and urological jls. *Recreation:* painting. *Address:* The London Hospital, Whitechapel, E1. *T:* 01–247 5454.

BLANK, Maurice Victor; Chairman and Chief Executive, Charterhouse Bank Ltd, since 1985; Chief Executive, Charterhouse plc, since 1985; *b* 9 Nov. 1942; *s* of Joseph Blank and Ruth Blank (*née* Levey); *m* 1977, Sylvia Helen (*née* Richford); two *s* one *d*. *Educ:* Stockport Grammar Sch.; St Catherine's Coll., Oxford (MA). Solicitor of the Supreme Court. Joined Clifford-Turner as articled clerk, 1964: Solicitor, 1966; Partner, 1969; Dir, and Head of Corporate Finance, Charterhouse Bank, 1981. *Publication:* (jtly) Weinberg and Blank on Take-Overs and Mergers, 4th edn 1979. *Recreations:* family, cricket, tennis, theatre. *Address:* 1 Paternoster Row, St Paul's, EC4M 7DH. *T:* 01–248 4000.

BLANKENHORN, Herbert, GCVO (Hon.) 1965; Member and Vice-President, Executive Board, UNESCO, 1970–76; *b* 15 Dec. 1904; *s* of Erich Blankenhorn; *m* 1944, Gisela Krug; two *s* two *d*. *Educ:* Gymnasiums in Strasbourg, Berlin, and Karlsruhe; Universities of Munich, London, Heidelberg and Paris. Entered Foreign Service, 1929; served in: Athens, 1932–35; Washington, 1935–39; Helsinki, 1940; Berne, 1940–43; Foreign Office, Berlin (Protocol Section), 1943–45; Dep. Sec.-Gen., Zonal Advisory Council, Hamburg, 1946–48; Sec.-Gen. Christian Democratic Party (British Zone), 1948; Private Sec. to President of Parliamentary Council, Bonn (Dr Adenauer), 1948–49; Political Dir, Foreign Office, 1950–55; German Ambassador: to NATO, 1955–58; to France, 1958–63; to Italy, 1963–65; to London, 1965–70. *Publication:* (political memoirs) Verständnis und Verständigung, 1980. *Address:* 7847 Badenweiler, Hintere Au 2, Germany.

BLANKS, Howard John; Under-Secretary, Highways Policy and Programme, Department of Transport, since 1985; *b* 16 June 1932; *s* of Lionel and Hilda Blanks; *m* 1958, Judith Ann (*née* Hughes). *Educ:* Barking Abbey Sch.; Keble Coll., Oxford (BA 1st Cl. Hons Music). National Service, RAF (Pilot), 1956–58. Air Traffic Control Officer, Min. of Aviation, 1958–64; Principal, Min. of Aviation (later Min. of Technology and Aviation Supply), 1964–71; Private Sec. to Chief Executive, Min. of Defence (Procurement Executive), 1972; Assistant Secretary: MoD, 1972–75; Cabinet Office, 1975–77; Dept of Trade, 1977–79; Under-Secretary, Head of Civil Aviation Policy Div., Dept of Trade (subseq. Transport), 1980–85. *Recreations:* music, travel. *Address:* Withinlee, Hedgehog Lane, Haslemere, Surrey GU27 2PJ. *T:* Haslemere 52468.

BLANTYRE, Archbishop of, (RC), since 1968; **Most Rev. James Chiona;** *b* 1924. *Educ:* Nankhunda Minor Seminary, Malaŵi; Kachebere Major Seminary, Malaŵi. Priest, 1954; Asst Parish Priest, 1954–57; Prof., Nankhunda Minor Seminary, 1957–60; study of Pastoral Sociology, Rome, 1961–62; Asst Parish Priest, 1962–65; Auxiliary Bishop of Blantyre and Titular Bishop of Bacanaria, 1965; Vicar Capitular of Archdiocese of Blantyre, 1967. *Recreation:* music. *Address:* Archbishop's House, PO Box 385, Blantyre, Malaŵi. *T:* (10)633516.

BLASCHKO, Hermann Karl Felix, MD, FRS 1962; Emeritus Reader in Biochemical Pharmacology, Oxford University, and Emeritus Fellow, Linacre College, Oxford, since 1967; *b* Berlin, 4 Jan. 1900; *o s* of late Prof. Alfred Blaschko, MD and late Johanna Litthauer; *m* 1944, Mary Douglas Black, *d* of late John Robert Black, Yelverton, S Devon; no *c*. *Educ:* Universities of Berlin, Freiburg im Breisgau and Göttingen. MD Freiburg; PhD Cambridge; MA Oxon. Research Asst to late Prof. O. Meyerhof at Berlin-Dahlem and Heidelberg at various periods, 1925–32; University Asst in Physiology, Univ. of Jena, 1928–29; worked at UCL, 1929–30 and 1933–34; Physiological Lab., Cambridge Univ., 1934–44; came to Oxford, 1944. Visiting Professor: Yale Univ., 1967–68; Upstate Medical Center, Syracuse, NY, 1968; RCS, 1968–73; Univ. of Pennsylvania, 1969; Univ.

of Bergen, Norway, 1969–70. Hon. Prof., Faculty of Medicine, Heidelberg, 1966. Member of Editorial Board of: Pharmacological Reviews, 1957–64; British Journal of Pharmacology and Chemotherapy, 1959–65; Journal of Physiology, 1965–72; Neuropharmacology, 1962–72; Naunyn-Schmiedebergs Arch. Exp. Pharmak., 1966; Molecular Pharmacol., 1966–77. Mem. Neuropharmacology Panel, International Brain Research Organisation (IBRO). Hon. FRSocMed, 1978; Hon. Member: British Pharmacological Soc., 1979; Hungarian Pharm. Soc., 1979; Physiological Soc., 1980; Berliner Medizinische Ges., 1980; Corresp. Mem., German Pharmacolog. Soc. Schmiedeberg Plakette, 1972; Hon. Pres., Internat. Catecholamine Symposium, Göteborg, 1983. First Thudichum Lectr and Medallist, London, 1974; Aschoff Lectr, Freiburg, 1974. Hon. MD: Berlin (Free Univ.), 1966; Bern, 1984. *Publications:* numerous papers in scientific publications. *Address:* Department of Pharmacology, South Parks Road, Oxford OX1 3QT; 24 Park Town, Oxford OX2 6SH.

BLASHFORD-SNELL, Col John Nicholas, MBE 1969; on staff of Ministry of Defence, since 1983; *b* 22 Oct. 1936; *s* of late Rev. Prebendary Leland John Blashford Snell and Gwendolen Ives Sadler; *m* 1960, Judith Frances (*née* Sherman); two *d. Educ:* Victoria Coll., Jersey, CI; RMA, Sandhurst. Commissioned Royal Engineers, 1957; 33 Indep. Fd Sqdn RE Cyprus, 1958–61; comd Operation Aphrodite (Expedition) Cyprus, 1959–61; Instructor: Junior Leaders Regt RE, 1962–63; RMA Sandhurst, 1963–66; Adjt 3rd Div. Engineers, 1966–67; comd Great Abbai Expedn (Blue Nile), 1968; sc RMCS Shrivenham and Camberley, 1968–69; comd Dahlak Quest Expedn, 1969–70; GSO2 MoD, 1970–72; comd British Trans-Americas Expedn, 1971–72; OC 48 Fd Sqdn RE, service in Belize, Oman, Ulster, 1972–74; comd Zaire River Expedn, 1974–75; CO Junior Leaders Regt RE, 1976–78; Dir of Operations, Operation Drake, 1977–81; on staff (GSO1), MoD, 1978–82; in command, The Fort George Volunteers, 1982–83. Operations Dir, Operation Raleigh, 1982–. Hon. Chm., Scientific Exploration Soc., 1969–. Freeman, City of Hereford, 1984. Hon. DSc Durham, 1986. Darien Medal (Colombia), 1972. *Publications:* Weapons and Tactics (with Tom Wintringham), 1970; (with Richard Snailham) The Expedition Organiser's Guide, 1970, 2nd edn 1976; Where the Trails Run Out, 1974; In the Steps of Stanley, 1975, 2nd edn 1975; (with A. Ballantine) Expeditions the Experts' Way, 1977, 2nd edn 1978; A Taste for Adventure, 1978; Operation Drake, 1981; Mysteries: Encounters with the Unexplained, 1983. *Recreations:* motoring, shooting, underwater diving, stamp collecting. *Address:* c/o Lloyds Bank, 9 Broad Street, St Helier, Jersey, CI. *Clubs:* Royal Automobile, Little Ship, Wig and Pen; Explorers' (New York) (Chm., British Chapter).

BLATCHLY, John Marcus, MA, PhD; FSA 1975; Headmaster, Ipswich School, since 1972; *b* 7 Oct. 1932; *s* of late Alfred Ernest Blatchly and of Edith Selina Blatchly (*née* Giddings); *m* 1955, Pamela Winifred, JP, *d* of late Major and Mrs L. J. Smith; one *s* one *d. Educ:* Sutton Grammar Sch., Surrey; Christ's Coll., Cambridge (Natural Scis Triposes; BA, MA, PhD). Instr Lieut RN, 1954–57. Asst Master and Head of Science Dept: King's Sch., Bruton, 1957–62; Eastbourne Coll., 1962–66; Charterhouse, 1966–72 (PhD awarded 1967 publication of work carried out with Royal Society grants at these three schools). Pres., Suffolk Inst. of Archaeology and History, 1975–; Trustee, five county and town conservation trusts in Suffolk; Hon. Custodian, Ipswich Old Town Library, 1982–. *Publications:* Organic Reactions, vol. 19, 1972 (jtly, with J. F. W. McOmie); The Topographers of Suffolk, 1976, 4th edn 1981; (with Peter Eden) Isaac Johnson of Woodbridge, 1979; Eighty Ipswich Portraits, 1980; (ed) Davy's Suffolk Journal, 1983; many papers in chemical, educnl, archaeological and antiquarian jls. *Recreations:* opera, chamber music, books. *Address:* Headmaster's House, Ipswich School, Suffolk IP1 3QY. *T:* Ipswich 59941.

BLATHERWICK, David Elliott Spiby, OBE 1973; HM Diplomatic Service; Head of Chancery, UK Mission to the United Nations, New York; *b* 13 July 1941; *s* of Edward S. Blatherwick; *m* 1964, (Margaret) Clare Crompton; one *s* one *d. Educ:* Lincoln Sch.; Wadham Coll., Oxford. Entered FO, 1964; Second Sec., Kuwait, 1968; First Sec., Dublin, 1970; FCO, 1973; Head of Chancery, Cairo, 1977; seconded to Northern Ireland Office as Head of Pol Affairs Dept, Belfast, 1981; Hd Energy, Science and Space Dept, FCO, 1983; sabbatical leave at Stanford Univ., Calif, 1985–86. *Recreations:* sailing, walking. *Address:* c/o Foreign and Commonwealth Office, King Charles Street, SW1A 2AH.

BLAXTER, Sir Kenneth (Lyon), Kt 1977; FRS 1967; FRSE 1965; Director, 1965–82, Rowett Research Institute, Bucksburn, Aberdeen, and Consultant Director, Commonwealth Bureau of Nutrition; Honorary Research Associate, Rowett Research Institute, since 1982; *b* 19 June 1919; *s* of Gaspard Culling Blaxter and Charlotte Ellen Blaxter; *m* 1957, Mildred Lillington Hall; two *s* one *d. Educ:* City of Norwich Sch.; University of Reading; University of Illinois. BSc(Agric.), PhD, DSc, NDA (Hons). Scientific Officer, Nat. Inst. for Research in Dairying, 1939–40 and 1941–44. Served RA, 1940–41. Research Officer, Ministry of Agriculture Veterinary Laboratory, 1944–46; Commonwealth Fellow, University of Ill, 1946–47; Head of Dept of Nutrition, Hannah Inst., Ayr, Scotland, 1948–65. Vis. Prof., Univ. of Newcastle, 1982–. Chm., Individual Merit Promotion Panel, MPO, Cabinet Office. President: British Soc. of Animal Production, 1970–71; Nutrition Soc., 1974; RSE, 1979–82; Inst. of Biology, 1986–. For. Mem., Lenin Acad. of Agric. Sciences, 1970. Hon. DSc: QUB, 1974; Leeds, 1977; Newcastle, 1984; Hon. LLD Aberdeen, 1981; Hon. DAgric Agricl Univ., Norway, 1975; Hon. MRCVS, 1978. Thomas Baxter Prize and Gold Medal, 1960; Gold Medal, RASE, 1964; Wooldridge Gold Medal, British Vet. Assoc., 1973; De Laval Medal, Royal Swedish Acad. Engrg Scis, 1976; Messel Medal, Soc. of Chem. Industry, 1976; Keith Medal and Prize, RSE, 1977; Massey-Ferguson Award, 1977; Wolf Foundn Internat. Prize, 1979. *Publications:* Energy Metabolism of Ruminants, 1962; Energy Metabolism, 1965; People, Food and Resources, 1986; scientific papers in Jl Endocrinology, Jl Agricultural Science, British Jl Nutrition, Research in Veterinary Science, etc. *Recreation:* painting. *Address:* Stradbroke Hall, Stradbroke, near Eye, Suffolk. *Club:* Farmers'.

BLAYNEY, Elizabeth Carmel, (Eily Blayney); Head of Library and Records Department and Departmental Record Officer, Foreign and Commonwealth Office, 1977–85, retired; *b* 19 July 1925; *d* of William Blayney, MRCS, LRCP, Medical Practitioner (previously County Inspector, RIC) of Harrold, Beds, and Mary Henrietta (*née* Beveridge). *Educ:* St Mary's Convent, Shaftesbury; The Triangle, S Molton Street. Chartered Librarian. Served War, WTS(FANY) in UK, India and Ceylon (Force 136), 1944–46. Library Asst, Hampstead Borough Libraries, 1947–50; Assistant Librarian: RSA, 1950–52; CO/CRO Jt Library, CRO, 1953; Head of Printed Library, FO, 1959–68; Librarian i/c, ODM, 1968–69; Librarian, FCO, 1969–77. *Address:* 6 Bamville Wood, East Common, Harpenden, Herts AL5 1AP. *T:* Harenden 5067.

BLEACKLEY, David, CMG 1979; DPhil; Head, Overseas Division, and Assistant Director, Institute of Geological Sciences, 1975–80; *b* 1 Feb. 1919; *s* of Alfred Mason and Hilda Gertrude Bleackley; *m* 1st, 1945, Peggy Florence Chill (*d* 1966); one *s* one *d*; 2nd, 1973, Patricia Clavell Strakosch (*née* Hore); two step *s* one step *d. Educ:* City of Oxford Sch.; The Queen's Coll., Oxford (BA 1939, MA 1942, DPhil 1960). Served War, Royal Engineers, 1939–45. Geologist: Shell Oil Co., 1946–50; Geological Survey, British Guiana, 1954–57, Dep. Dir, 1957–60; Overseas Geological Surveys, 1960–65; Dep. Head, Overseas Div., Inst. of Geological Sciences, 1965–75. FIMM 1969; FGS 1943. *Publications:* papers in various jls. *Recreations:* walking, shooting. *Address:* Well Farm, Dagnall, near Berkhamsted, Herts HP4 1QU. *T:* Little Gaddesden 3232.

BLEAKLEY, Rt. Hon. David Wylie, CBE 1984; PC (NI) 1971; Chief Executive, Irish Council of Churches, since 1980; *b* 11 Jan. 1925; *s* of John Wesley Bleakley and Sarah Bleakley (*née* Wylie); *m* 1949, Winifred Wason; three *s. Educ:* Ruskin Coll., Oxford; Queen's Univ., Belfast. MA, DipEconPolSci (Oxon). Belfast Shipyard, 1940–46; Oxford and Queen's Univ., 1946–51; Tutor in Social Studies, 1951–55; Principal, Belfast Further Educn Centre, 1955–58; Lectr in Industrial Relations, Kivukoni Coll., Dar-es-Salaam, 1967–69; Head of Dept of Economics and Political Studies, Methodist Coll., Belfast, 1969–79. MP (Lab) Victoria, Belfast, Parliament of N Ireland, 1958–65; contested: (Lab) East Belfast, General Elections, 1970, Feb. and Oct. 1974. Minister of Community Relations, Govt of NI, March-Sept. 1971; Member (NILP), E Belfast: NI Assembly, 1973–75; NI Constitutional Convention, 1975–76. Mem., Cttee of Inquiry on Police, 1978. Chm., NI Standing Adv. Commn on Human Rights, 1980–84. Irish Deleg. to Anglican Consultative Council, 1976; Deleg. to World Council of Churches; Pres., Church Missionary Soc., 1983–; WEA and Open Univ. tutor; Vis. Sen. Lectr in Peace Studies, Univ. of Bradford, 1974–. Hon. MA Open, 1975. *Publications:* Ulster since 1800: regional history symposium, 1958; Young Ulster and Religion in the Sixties, 1964; Peace in Ulster, 1972; Faulkner: a biography, 1974; Saidie Patterson, Irish Peacemaker, 1980; In Place of Work, 1981; The Shadow and Substance, 1983; Beyond Work—Free to Be, 1985; regular contribs to BBC and to press on community relations and industrial studies. *Address:* 8 Thornhill, Bangor, Co. Down, Northern Ireland BT19 1RD. *T:* Bangor 454898.

BLEANEY, Prof. Brebis, CBE 1965; FRS 1950; MA, DPhil; Warren Research Fellow, Royal Society, 1977–80, Leverhulme Emeritus Fellow, 1980–82; Fellow, 1957–77, Senior Research Fellow, 1977–82, Wadham College, Oxford, now Emeritus Fellow; Dr Lee's Professor of Experimental Philosophy, University of Oxford, 1957–77, now Emeritus Professor; *b* 6 June 1915; *m* 1949, Betty Isabelle Plumpton; one *s* one *d. Educ:* Westminster City Sch.; St John's Coll., Oxford. Lecturer in Physics at Balliol Coll., Oxford, 1947–50. Research Fellow, Harvard Univ. and Mass Institute of Technology, 1949. University Demonstrator and Lectr in Physics, Univ. of Oxford, 1945–57; Fellow and Lectr in Physics, St John's Coll., Oxford, 1947–57; Tutor, 1950–57; Hon. Fellow, 1968. Visiting Prof. in Physics in Columbia Univ., 1956–57; Harkins Lectr, Chicago Univ., 1957; Kelvin Lectr, Instn Electrical Engineers, 1962; Morris Loeb Lectr, Harvard Univ., 1981; Cherwell Simon Meml Lectr, Oxford Univ., 1981–82; John and Abigail Van Vleck Lectr, Univ. of Minnesota, 1985; Visiting Professor: Univ. of California, Berkeley, 1961; Univ. of Pittsburgh, 1962–63; Manitoba, 1968; La Plata, Argentina, 1971; Amer. Univ. in Cairo, 1978; Univ. of NSW, 1981. Mem. Council for Scientific and Industrial Res., 1960–62; Chm., British Radiofrequency Spectroscopy Gp, 1983–85. FRSA 1971. Corr. Mem. Acad. of Sciences, Inst. of France, 1974, Associé Etranger, 1978; For. Hon. Mem., Amer. Acad. of Arts and Scis, 1978. Charles Vernon Boys Prize, Physical Soc., 1952; Hughes Medal, Royal Society, 1962; ISMAR Prize, Internat. Soc. for Magnetic Resonance, 1983; Holweck Medal and Prize, Inst. of Physics and Société Française de Physique, 1984. *Publications:* (with B. I. Bleaney) Electricity and Magnetism, 1957, 3rd edn, 1976; (with A. Abragam) Electron Paramagnetic Resonance, 1970; various papers in Proceedings of the Royal Society and Proceedings of the Physical Society, etc. *Recreations:* music and tennis. *Address:* Clarendon Laboratory, Parks Road, Oxford OX1 3PU.

BLEASDALE, Alan; playwright and novelist, since 1975; *b* 23 March 1946; *s* of George and Margaret Bleasdale; *m* 1970, Julia Moses; two *s* one *d. Educ:* St Aloysius RC Jun. Sch., Huyton; Wade Deacon Grammar Sch., Widnes; Padgate Teachers Trng Coll. (Teacher's Cert.). Schoolteacher, 1967–75. BAFTA Writers Award, 1982; RTS Writer of the Year, 1982. *Publications:* Scully, 1975; Who's been sleeping in my bed, 1977; No more sitting on the Old School Bench, 1979; Boys from the Blackstuff, 1982 (televised; Broadcasting Press Guild Television Award for Best Series, 1982); Are you lonesome tonight?, 1985 (Best Musical, London Standard Drama Awards, 1985); No Surrender (film script), 1986; Having a Ball, 1986; It's a Madhouse, 1986; The Monocled Mutineer, 1986 (televised 1986). *Recreations:* a lifelong personal study of hypochondria and anxiety attacks; watching our winderful children grow; avoiding bookshops, cinema screens and television sets; wishing I was still a sportsman, woman or person. *Address:* c/o Harvey Unna & Stephen Durbridge Ltd, 24 Pottery Lane, Holland Park, W11 4LZ. *T:* 01-727 1346.

BLEASDALE, Cyril, FCIT; General Manager, British Rail London Midland Region, since 1986; *b* 8 July 1934; *s* of Frederick and Alice Bleasdale; *m* 1970, Catherine; two *d.* MBIM; Stanford Univ., Calif (Exec. Programme). Man. Dir, Freightliner Ltd, 1975–82; Dir, Inter City British Rail, 1982–86. FRSA. *Recreations:* music, fitness. *Address:* Stanier House, 10 Holliday Street, Birmingham, B1 1TG.

BLEASE, family name of **Baron Blease.**

BLEASE, Baron *cr* 1978 (Life Peer), of Cromac in the City of Belfast; **William John Blease,** JP; *b* 28 May 1914; *e s* of late William and Sarah Blease; *m* 1939, Sarah Evelyn Caldwell; three *s* one *d. Educ:* elementary and technical schs; Nat. Council of Labour Colls; WEA. Retail Provision Trade (apprentice), 1929; Retail Grocery Asst (Branch Manager), 1928–40; Clerk, Belfast Shipyard, 1940–45; Branch Manager, Co-operative Soc., Belfast, 1945–59; Divl Councillor, Union of Shop Distributive Workers, 1948–59; NI Officer, 1959–75, Exec. Consultant, 1975–76, Irish Congress of Trade Unions; Divl Chm. and Nat. Exec. Mem., Nat. Council of Labour Colls, 1948–61; Exec. Mem., NI Labour Party (Dep. Chm., 1957–58); Labour Party Spokesman in House of Lords, on N Ireland, 1979–82; Trade Union Side Sec., NI CS Industrial Jt Council, 1975–77. Member: NI Economic Council, 1964–75; Review Body on Local Govt, NI, 1970–71; Review Body on Ind. Relations, NI, 1970–73; Working Party on Discrimination in Employment, NI, 1972–73; NI Trng Res. Cttee, 1966–80; NI Regional Adv. Bd, BIM, 1971–80; NUU Vocational Guidance Council, 1974–83; Ind. Appeals Tribunals, 1974–76; Local Govt Appeals Tribunal, 1974–83; Irish Council of Churches Working Party, 1974–; IBA, 1974–79; Standing Adv. Commn on Human Rights, NI, 1977–79; Police Complaints Bd, 1977–80; Conciliation Panel, Ind. Relations Agency, 1978–; Security Appeal Bd, NI SC Commn, 1979–; Chm., Public Service Order Cttee, 1979–80; Rapporteur, EEC Cross Border Communications Study on Londonderry/Donegal, 1978; President: NI Assoc., NACRO, 1982–85; NI Hospice, 1981–85; E Belfast Access Council for Disabled, 1982–; NI Widows Assoc., 1985–. Trustee, Belfast Charitable Trust for Integrated Educn, 1984–. Ford Foundn Travel Award, USA, 1959. Hon. Res. Fellow, Univ. of Ulster, 1976–83; Jt Hon. Res. Fellow, TCD, 1976–79. Hon. FBIM 1981 (MBIM 1960). JP Belfast, 1976–. Hon. DLitt New Univ. of Ulster, 1972; Hon. LLD QUB, 1982. *Publication:* Encyclopaedia of Labour Law, vol. 1: The Trade Union Movement in Northern Ireland, 1983. *Recreation:* reading. *Address:* 30 Clonaver Crescent North, Belfast BT4 2FD.

BLECH, Harry, CBE 1984 (OBE 1962); Hon. RAM, 1963; Musical Director, Haydn-Mozart Society, and Founder and Conductor, London Mozart Players, 1949–84; *b* 2 March 1910; British; *m* 1935, Enid Marion Lessing (*d* 1977); one *s* two *d*; *m* 1957, Marion

Manley, pianist; one *s* three *d*. *Educ:* Central London Foundation; Trinity Coll. of Music (Fellow); Manchester Coll. of Music (Fellow). Violin soloist, 1928–30; joined BBC Symphony Orchestra, 1930–36. Responsible for formation of: Blech Quartet, 1933–50; London Wind Players, 1942 (conductor); London Mozart Players, 1949 (Conductor Laureate); Haydn-Mozart Soc., 1949; London Mozart Choir, 1952. Dir of Chamber Orchestra, RAM, 1961–65. FRSA. *Address:* The Owls, 70 Leopold Road, Wimbledon, SW19 7JQ.

BLEDISLOE, 3rd Viscount *cr* 1935; **Christopher Hiley Ludlow Bathurst,** QC 1978; *b* 24 June 1934; *s* of 2nd Viscount Bledisloe, QC, and of Joan Isobel Krishaber; *S* father, 1979; *m* 1962, Elizabeth Mary (marr. diss. 1986), 2nd *d* of Sir Edward Thompson, *qv*; two *s* one *d*. *Educ:* Eton; Trinity Coll., Oxford. Called to the Bar, Gray's Inn, 1959. *Heir:* *s* Hon. Rupert Edward Ludlow Bathurst, *b* 13 March 1964. *Address:* Lydney Park, Glos GL15 6BT. *T:* Dean 42566; Fountain Court, Temple, EC4Y 9DH. *T:* 01–353 7356.

BLEEHEN, Prof. Norman Montague; Cancer Research Campaign Professor of Clinical Oncology and Hon. Director of MRC Unit of Clinical Oncology and Radiotherapeutics, since 1975, and Director, Radiotherapeutics, and Oncology Centre, since 1984, University of Cambridge; Fellow of St John's College, Cambridge, since 1976; *b* 24 Feb. 1930; *s* of Solomon and Lena Bleehen; *m* 1969, Tirza, *d* of Alex and Jenny Loeb. *Educ:* Manchester Grammar Sch.; Haberdashers' Aske's Sch.; Exeter Coll., Oxford (Francis Gotch medal, 1953); Middlesex Hosp. Med. School. BA 1951, BSc 1953, MA 1954, BM, BCh 1955, Oxon; MRCP 1957, FRCP 1973; FRCR 1964; DMRT 1962. MRC Res. Student, Biochem. Dept, Oxford, 1951; house appts: Middlesex Hosp., 1955–56; Hammersmith Hosp., 1957; Asst Med. Specialist Army, Hanover, 1957; Med. Specialist Army, Berlin, 1959 (Captain); Jun. Lectr in Medicine, Dept of Regius Prof. of Medicine, Oxford, 1959–60; Registrar and Sen. Registrar in Radiotherapy, Middlesex Hosp. Med. Sch., 1961–66; Lilly Res. Fellow, Stanford Univ., 1966–67; Locum Consultant, Middlesex Hosp., 1967–69; Prof. of Radiotherapy, Middlesex Hosp. Med. Sch., 1969–75. Consultant advr to CMO, DHSS, for radiation oncology, 1986–. Simon Lectr, RCR, 1986. Member: Jt MRC/CRC Cttee for jtly supported insts, 1971–74; Coordinating Cttee for Cancer Res., 1973–79; Council, Imperial Cancer Res. Fund, 1973–; Council, Brit. Inst. of Radiology, 1974–77; Sci. Cttee, Cancer Res. Campaign, 1976–; MRC Cell Bd, 1980–84; UICC Fellowships Cttee, 1983–; Council, European Organisation for Treatment of Cancer, 1983–; Vice-Pres., Bd of Dirs, Internat. Assoc. for Study of Lung Cancer, 1980–82; Pres., Internat. Soc. of Radiation Oncology, 1985–; Chairman: MRC Lung Cancer Wkg Party, 1973–; MRC Brain Tumour Wkg Party, 1978–; MRC Cancer Therapy Cttee, 1972–; British Assoc. for Cancer Res., 1976–79; Soc. for Comparative Oncology, 1983–86. Hon. FACR 1984. Roentgen Prize, British Inst. of Radiology, 1986. *Publications:* (ed jtly) Radiation Therapy Planning, 1983; (Scientific Editor) British Medical Bulletin 24/1, The Scientific Basis of Radiotherapy, 1973; various on medicine, biochemistry cancer and radiotherapy. *Recreations:* gardening, television. *Address:* 21 Bentley Road, Cambridge CB2 2AW. *T:* Cambridge 354320. *Club:* Athenæum.

BLELLOCH, John Niall Henderson, CB 1983; Second Permanent Under-Secretary of State, Ministry of Defence, since 1984; *b* 24 Oct. 1930; *s* of late Ian William Blelloch, CMG and Leila Mary Henderson; *m* 1958, Pamela, *d* of late James B. Blair and E. M. Blair; one *s* (and one *s* decd). *Educ:* Fettes Coll.; Gonville and Caius Coll., Cambridge (BA). Nat. Service, RA, 1949–51 (commnd 1950). Asst Principal, War Office, 1954; Private Sec. to successive Parly Under Secs of State, 1956–58; Principal, 1958; MoD, 1964–80; London Business Sch. (EDP 3), 1967; Asst Sec., 1968; RCDS, 1974; Asst Under-Sec. of State (Air), Procurement Exec., 1976; Asst Under-Sec. of State, Defence Staff, 1979; Dep. Sec., NI Office, 1980–82; Dep. Under-Sec of State (Policy and Programmes), MoD, 1982–84. *Recreations:* golf, squash, skiing, learning the piano. *Address:* c/o Bank of Scotland, 57/60 Haymarket, SW1. *Clubs:* Roehampton; Royal Mid-Surrey Golf.

BLENKINSOP, Dorothy; Regional Nursing Officer, Northern Regional Health Authority, since 1973; *b* 15 Nov. 1931; *d* of late Joseph Henry Blenkinsop, BEM, and Thelma Irene (*née* Bishop). *Educ:* South Shields Grammar Sch. for Girls. MA Dunelm 1978. SRN 1953; SCM 1954; Health Visitors Cert. 1962. Ward Sister, Royal Victoria Infirm., Newcastle upon Tyne, 1955–61; Health Visitor, South Shields, 1962–64; Dep. Matron, Gen. Hosp., South Shields, 1964–67; Durham Hosp. Management Cttee: Principal Nurse, Durham City Hosps, 1967–69; Principal Nursing Officer (Top), 1969–71; Chief Nursing Officer, 1971–73. Mem. Methodist Church (Circuit Steward, 1968–82; Sunday School Teacher). *Publications:* (with E. G. Nelson): Changing the System, 1972; Managing the System, 1976; articles in nursing press. *Recreation:* gardening. *Address:* 143 Temple Park Road, South Shields, Tyne and Wear. *T:* South Shields 561429.

BLENNERHASSETT, Francis Alfred, QC 1965; **His Honour Judge Blennerhassett;** a Circuit Judge, since 1978; *b* 7 July 1916; 2nd *s* of John and Annie Elizabeth Blennerhassett; *m* 1948, Betty Muriel Bray; two *d*. *Educ:* Solihull Sch. Served War of 1939–45 RA and Royal Warwicks Regt, Britain and East Africa (Captain). Called to Bar, Middle Temple, 1946; Bencher, 1971; Oxford Circuit. Dep. Chm., Staffordshire QS, 1963–71; Recorder of New Windsor, 1965–71; a Recorder of the Crown Court, 1972–78; Hon. Recorder of New Windsor, 1972–76; Hon. Recorder of Windsor and Maidenhead, 1976–. Legal Assessor to GMC and Dental Council, 1971–78; Chm., Govt Cttee on Drinking and Driving, 1975–76; Mem., Parole Bd, 1981–83. *Recreation:* golf. *Address:* Manor Cottage, Hampton in Arden, Warwickshire. *T:* Hampton in Arden 2660. *Club:* Copt Heath Golf.

BLENNERHASSETT, Sir (Marmaduke) Adrian (Francis William), 7th Bt, *cr* 1809; *b* 25 May 1940; *s* of Lieut Sir Marmaduke Blennerhassett, 6th Bt, RNVR (killed in action, 1940), and Gwenfra (*d* 1956), *d* of Judge Harrington-Morgan, Churchtown, Co. Kerry, and of Mrs Douglas Campbell; *S* father 1940; *m* 1972, Carolyn Margaret, *yr d* of late Gilbert Brown; one *s* one *d*. *Educ:* Michael Hall, Forest Row; McGill Univ.; Imperial Coll., Univ. of London (MSc); Cranfield Business Sch. (MBA). *Recreations:* flying (private pilot's licence), ocean racing (sailing), ski-ing. *Heir:* *s* Charles Henry Marmaduke Blennerhassett, *b* 18 July 1975. *Address:* 41 Park Road, Chiswick, W4. *Club:* Royal Ocean Racing.

BLESSLEY, Kenneth Harry, CBE 1974 (MBE 1945); ED; Valuer and Estates Surveyor, Greater London Council, 1964–77; *b* 28 Feb. 1914; *s* of Victor Henry le Blond Blessley and Ellen Mary Blessley; *m* 1946, Gwendeline MacRae; two *s*. *Educ:* Haberdashers' Aske's Hampstead Sch.; St Catharine's Coll., Cambridge (MA); Coll. of Estate Management. FRICS. Private practice, West End and London suburbs. Served War of 1939–45, TA Royal Engrs, Persia, Middle East, Sicily, Italy (despatches 1942 and 1944). Sen. Property Adviser, Public Trustee, 1946–50; Dep. County Valuer, Mddx CC, 1950–53; County Valuer, Mddx CC, 1953–65. Mem. Urban Motorways Cttee, 1970–72; Chm., Covent Garden Officers' Steering Gp, 1970–77; Chm., Thamesmead Officers' Steering Gp, 1971–76; Pres., Assoc. of Local Authority Valuers and Estate Surveyors, 1962 and 1972; Mem. Gen. Council, RICS, 1972–78, Pres., Gen. Practice Div., 1976–77. Pres., Old Haberdashers' Assoc., 1963 (Pres. RFC, 1966–68). *Publications:* numerous articles and papers on compensation, property valuation and development. *Recreations:* music, drama, sport, motoring. *Address:* 99 Maplehurst Road, Summersdale, Chichester, West Sussex. *T:* Chichester 528188.

BLEWETT, Maj.-Gen. Robert Sidney, OBE 1974; Commander Medical, HQ BAOR, since 1985; *b* 5 Aug. 1931; *s* of late Sidney Blewett and Phylis Ann Norah (*née* Hamilton); *m* 1958, Elizabeth Maud Lewis; one *s* one *d*. *Educ:* Truro Sch.; Middlesex Hosp. Med. Sch., Univ. of London. MB BS; MFCM; D(Obst)RCOG; DTM&H. Ho. Surg. and Ho. Phys., W Kent Gen. Hosp., 1955–56. Regtl MO Caribbean Area, 1956–59; Asst Dir of Med. Servs, HQ 53 Welsh Div., 1961–62; Regtl MO 2/2 Gurkha Rifles, 1963–65 (GSMs Brunei, Borneo, Malay Peninsula; mentioned in despatches); D(Obst)RCOG Trainee, BMH Singapore, 1965–66; OC 11 Field Dressing Station, 1966–67; psc 1968; Asst Comdt Royal Army Med. Coll., 1969–71; Commanding Officer: 15 Field Ambulance, 1971–73; BMH Munster, 1973–75; Asst Dir of Med. Servs, HQ 4 Div., 1975–76; Asst Dir Gen. Army Med. Directorate 3/Adjt Gen. 3, 1977–79; CO Cambridge Mil. Hosp., 1979–80; Dep. Comdr Medical, HQ BAOR, 1980–83; Comdr Medical, HQ 1st British Corps, 1983–84; Asst Surg. Gen. (Ops & Plans), MoD (Defence Med. Services Directorate), 1984–85. OStJ 1984. Chadwick Meml Prize, UCL, 1980. Rhodesia Medal, 1979; Zimbabwe Independence Medal, 1980; Commendation, Comdr Monitoring Force, Rhodesia, 1980. *Recreations:* garden, joinery, tennis. *Address:* c/o Coutts & Co., 23 Hanover Square, W1A 4YE.

BLEWITT, Major Shane Gabriel Basil, LVO 1981; Deputy Keeper of the Privy Purse, since 1985 (Assistant Keeper, 1975–85); *b* 25 March 1935; *s* of late Col Basil Blewitt; *m* 1969, Julia Morrogh-Bernard, *widow* of Major John Morrogh-Bernard, Irish Guards, and *d* of Mr Robert Calvert; one *s* one *d* (and one step *s* one step *d*). *Educ:* Ampleforth Coll.; Christ Church, Oxford (MA Hons Mod. Languages). Served Irish Guards, 1956–74; Antony Gibbs and Sons, 1974. *Recreations:* gardening, shooting. *Address:* South Corner House, Duncton, near Petworth, West Sussex. *T:* Petworth 42143. *Club:* White's.

BLIGH, family name of **Earl of Darnley.**

BLIN-STOYLE, Prof. Roger John, FRS 1976; Professor of Theoretical Physics, University of Sussex, since 1962; Chairman, School Curriculum Development Committee, since 1983; *b* 24 Dec. 1924; *s* of Cuthbert Basil St John Blin-Stoyle and Ada Mary (*née* Nash); *m* 1949, Audrey Elizabeth Balmford; one *s* one *d*. *Educ:* Alderman Newton's Boys' Sch., Leicester; Wadham Coll., Oxford (Scholar). MA, DPhil Oxon; FInstP; ARCM. Served Royal Signals, 1943–46 (Lieut). Pressed Steel Co. Res. Fellow, Oxford Univ., 1951–53; Lectr in Math. Physics, Birmingham Univ., 1953–54; Sen. Res. Officer in Theoret. Physics, Oxford Univ., 1952–62; Fellow and Lectr in Physics, Wadham Coll., Oxford, 1956–62; Vis. Associate Prof. of Physics, MIT, 1959–60; Vis. Prof. of Physics, Univ. of Calif, La Jolla, 1960; Sussex University: Dean, Sch. of Math. and Phys. Sciences, 1962–68; Pro-Vice-Chancellor, 1965–67; Dep. Vice-Chancellor, 1970–72; Pro-Vice-Chancellor (Science), 1977–79. Member: Royal Greenwich Observatory Cttee, 1966–70; Nuclear Physics Bd, SRC, later SERC, 1967–70, 1982–84; Council, Royal Soc., 1982–83. Rutherford Medal and Prize, IPPS, 1976. Editor: Reports on Progress in Physics, 1977–82; Student Physics Series, 1983–. *Publications:* Theories of Nuclear Moments, 1957; Fundamental Interactions and the Nucleus, 1973; papers on nuclear and elementary particle physics in scientific jls. *Recreation:* making music. *Address:* 14 Hill Road, Lewes, E Sussex BN7 1DB. *T:* Lewes 473640.

BLISHEN, Anthony Owen, OBE 1968; HM Diplomatic Service; Counsellor, Foreign and Commonwealth Office, since 1981; *b* 16 April 1932; *s* of Henry Charles Adolphus Blishen and Joan Cecile Blishen (*née* Blakeney); *m* 1963, Sarah Anne Joscelyne; three *s* one *d*. *Educ:* Clayesmore Sch., Dorset; SOAS, London Univ. Commnd Royal Hampshire Regt, 1951; Lt 1st Bn: BAOR, 1953; Malaya, 1953–55; Captain, GSO3 HQ 18 Inf. Bde, Malaya, 1955–56; attached HQ Land Forces, Hong Kong (language trng), 1957–59; GSO3 HQ Far East Land Forces, Singapore, 1960–62; FO, 1963–65; First Sec. and Consul, Peking, 1965–67; First Sec., FCO, 1968–70; Chargé d'Affaires (ad interim), Ulan Bator, 1970; Trade Comr (China trade), Hong Kong, 1971–73; First Sec., FCO, 1973–77; First Sec., 1977–78, Counsellor, 1978–81, Tokyo. *Recreations:* Renaissance music, oriental languages. *Address:* c/o Foreign and Commonwealth Office, SW1A 2AH.

BLISHEN, Edward; author; *b* 29 April 1920; *s* of William George Blishen and Elizabeth Anne (*née* Pye); *m* 1948, Nancy Smith; two *s*. *Educ:* Queen Elizabeth's Grammar Sch., Barnet. Weekly Newspaper reporter, 1937–40; agricultural worker, 1941–46. Teaching: Prep. Schoolmaster, 1946–49; Secondary Modern School Teacher, 1950–59. Carnegie Medal, 1970; Soc. of Authors Travelling Scholarship, 1979. *Publications:* Roaring Boys, 1955; This Right Soft Lot, 1969; (with Leon Garfield) The God Beneath the Sea, 1970; (with Leon Garfield) The Golden Shadow, 1972; *autobiography:* A Cackhanded War, 1972; Uncommon Entrance, 1974; Sorry, Dad, 1978; A Nest of Teachers, 1980; Shaky Relations, 1981 (J. R. Ackerley Prize); Lizzie Pye, 1982; Donkey Work, 1983; A Second Skin, 1984; The Outside Contributor, 1986; *edited:* Junior Pears Encyclopaedia, 1961–; Oxford Miscellanies, 1964–69; Blond Encyclopaedia of Education, 1969; The School that I'd Like, 1969; The Thorny Paradise, 1975; *compiled:* Oxford Book of Poetry for Children, 1964; Come Reading, 1967. *Recreations:* walking, photography, listening to music. *Address:* 12 Bartrams Lane, Hadley Wood, Barnet EN4 0EH. *T:* 01–449 3252.

BLISS, Christopher John Emile, PhD; Nuffield Reader in International Economics, Oxford University, and Fellow of Nuffield College, since 1977; *b* 17 Feb. 1940; *s* of John Llewlyn Bliss and Patricia Paula (*née* Dubern); *m* 1983, Ghada (*née* Saqf El Hait); one *s* two *d* by previous marr. *Educ:* Finchley Catholic Grammar Sch.; King's Coll., Cambridge (BA 1962, MA 1964, PhD 1966). Fellow of Christ's Coll., Cambridge, 1965–71; Asst Lectr, 1965–67, and Lectr, 1967–71, Cambridge Univ.; Prof. of Econs, Univ. of Essex, 1971–77. Fellow, Econometric Soc., 1978. Editor or Asst Editor, Rev. of Econ. Studies, 1967–71. Dir, General Funds Investment Trust Ltd, 1980–. *Publications:* Capital Theory and the Distribution of Income, 1975; (with N. H. Stern) Palanpur: the economy of an Indian village, 1982; papers and reviews in learned jls. *Recreation:* gratification of the higher appetites. *Address:* Nuffield College, Oxford OX1 1NF. *T:* Oxford 248014.

BLISS, John Cordeux, QPM; retired as Deputy Assistant Commissioner, Metropolitan Police, 1971 (seconded as National Co-ordinator of Regional Crime Squads of England and Wales from inception, 1964–71); *b* 16 March 1914; *s* of late Herbert Francis Bliss and Ida Muriel (*née* Hays); *m* 1947, Elizabeth Mary, *d* of Charles Gordon Howard; one *s* two *d*. *Educ:* Haileybury Coll. Metropolitan Police Coll., Hendon, 1936–37. Served in RAF, 1941–45, Flt Lt, 227 Sqdn, MEF. Various ranks of Criminal Investigation Dept of Metropolitan Police, 1946–62; seconded as Dir of Criminal Law at Police Coll., Bramshill, 1962–63; Dep. Comdr, 1963–64. Barrister, Middle Temple, 1954. Mem., Parole Bd, 1973–76 and 1978–81. Liveryman, Merchant Taylors' Company. Churchill Memorial Trust Fellowship, 1967; Queen's Police Medal, 1969. *Recreations:* squash rackets, hillwalking; but mostly gardening; formerly: Rugby football, tennis. *Address:* Foxhanger Down, Hurtmore, Godalming, Surrey. *T:* Godalming 22487. *Club:* Royal Air Force.

BLISS, Kathleen Mary, (Mrs Rupert Bliss), MA Cantab 1934; Lecturer in Religious Studies, University of Sussex, 1967–72; *b* 5 July 1908; *née* Moore; *m* 1932, Rev. Rupert

Bliss; three d. *Educ:* Girton Coll., Cambridge. Educational work in India, 1932–39; Editor, the Christian Newsletter, 1945–49; organized Christian-humanist debate, BBC, 1951–55; Studies of education in industry, 1956–57; General Sec., Church of England Board of Education, 1958–66. Member of Public Schools Commn, 1967–70. Hon. DD (Aberdeen), 1949. Select Preacher before the Univ. of Cambridge, 1967. *Publications:* The Service and Status of Women in the Churches, 1951; We the People, 1963; The Future of Religion, 1969. *Address:* 26B Ellerdale Road, Hampstead, NW3 6BB.

BLISS, Mrs Rupert; see Bliss, K. M.

BLISSETT, Alfreda Rose; see Hodgson, A. R.

BLIX, Hans, PhD, LLD; Director General, International Atomic Energy Agency, since 1981; *b* 28 June 1928; *s* of Gunnar Blix and Hertha Blix (*née* Wiberg); *m* 1962, Eva Margareta Kettis; two *s. Educ:* Univ. of Uppsala; Columbia Univ.; Univ. of Cambridge (PhD); Stockholm Univ. (LLD). Associate Prof. in International Law, 1960; Ministry of Foreign Affairs, Stockholm: Legal Adviser, 1963–76; Under-Secretary of State, in charge of internat. development co-operation, 1976; Minister for Foreign Affairs, 1978; Under-Secretary of State, in charge of internat. development co-operation, 1979. Member: Sweden's delegn to UN General Assembly, 1961–81; Swedish delegn to Conference on Disarmament in Geneva, 1962–78. *Publications:* Treaty Making Power, 1959; Statsmyndigheternas Internationella Förbindelser, 1964; Sovereignty, Aggression and Neutrality, 1970; The Treaty-Maker's Handbook, 1974. *Recreations:* skiing, hiking. *Address:* International Atomic Energy Agency, POB 100, A-1400 Vienna, Austria. *T:* 2360, ext. 1111.

BLOCH, Prof. Konrad E.; Higgins Professor of Biochemistry, Harvard University, since 1954; *b* 21 Jan. 1912; *s* of Frederick D. Bloch and Hedwig (*née* Striemer); *m* 1941, Lore Teutsch; one *s* one *d. Educ:* Technische Hochschule, Munich; Columbia Univ., New York. MA Oxon 1982. Instructor and Research Associate, Columbia Univ., 1939–46; Univ. of Chicago: Asst Prof., 1946–48; Associate Prof., 1948–50; Prof., 1950–54. Newton-Abraham Vis. Prof., and Fellow of Lincoln Coll., Oxford, 1982. Nobel Prize for Medicine (jointly), 1964. *Publications:* Lipide Metabolism, 1961; numerous papers in biochemical journals. *Address:* 16 Moon Hill Road, Lexington, Mass 02173, USA. *T:* (617) 862–9076; Department of Chemistry, Harvard University, 12 Oxford Street, Cambridge, Mass 02138, USA.

BLOCH, Dame Merle Florence; see Park, Dame Merle F.

BLOCK, Maj.-Gen. Adam Johnstone Cheyne, CB 1962; CBE 1959 (OBE 1951); DSO 1945; *b* 13 June 1908; *s* of late Col Arthur Hugh Block, RA; *m* 1945, Pauline Bingham, *d* of late Col Norman Kennedy, CBE, DSO, TD, DL, Doonholm, Ayr; two *d* (and one *d* decd). *Educ:* Blundell's; RMA Woolwich. 2nd Lieut RA 1928; served War of 1939–45 (France, UK, N Africa and Italy); CO 24th Field Regt, RA, 1943–45. GSO1, RA and AMS, GHQ, 1945–47; AQMG and GSO1 Trg AA Comd, 1947–50; Lieut-Col, 1950; Senior Directing Staff (Army). Joint Services Staff College, 1950–53; Col, 1953; CRA 6 Armd Div., 1953; Comdt, School of Artillery, Larkhill, 1956; Maj.-Gen. 1959; GOC Troops, Malta, 1959–62; retd. Chief Information Officer to General Synod (formerly Church Assembly), 1965–72. Mem. Basingstoke DC, 1973–75. Col Comdt, Royal Regt of Artillery, 1965–73. *Recreations:* all country pursuits. *Address:* St Cross House, Whitchurch, Hants. *T:* Whitchurch 2344.

BLOCK, Brig. David Arthur Kennedy William, CBE 1961; DSO 1945; MC 1943; retired; *b* 13 June 1908; *s* of late Col Arthur Hugh Block; *m* 1949, Elizabeth Grace (*d* 1975), *e d* of late Lieut-Col E. G. Troyte-Bullock, CMG, Zeals House, Wiltshire, and widow of Major G. E. Sebag-Montefiore, D'Anvers House, Culworth, near Banbury; no *c. Educ:* Blundell's; RMA, Woolwich. Served War of 1939–45 (despatches, MC, DSO); CO 152nd (Ayrshire Yeomanry) Field Regt, RA, 1943–45. CO 2nd Regt RHA, 1950–53; CRA, 7th Armoured Div., 1954–57; Comd 18th Trg Bde, RA, 1958–61; retired, 1961. ADC to the Queen, 1959. *Recreations:* hunting, shooting, golf. *Address:* Benville Manor Lodge, Corscombe, Dorchester, Dorset DT2 0NW. *T:* Corscombe 205. *Club:* Army and Navy.

BLOEMBERGEN, Prof. Nicolaas; Gerhard Gade University Professor, Harvard University, since 1980; *b* 11 March 1920; *m* 1950, Huberta Deliana Brink; one *s* two *d. Educ:* Univ. of Utrecht (BA, MA); Univ. of Leiden (PhD). Research Associate, Leiden, 1947–48; Harvard University: Associate Prof., 1951; Gordon McKay Prof. of Applied Physics, 1957; Rumford Prof. of Physics, 1974. (Jtly) Nobel Prize in Physics, 1981. *Publications:* Nuclear Magnetic Relaxation, 1948 (New York 1961); Nonlinear Optics, 1965, 4th printing, 1982; over 250 papers in scientific jls. *Address:* Pierce Hall, Harvard University, Cambridge, Mass 02138, USA. *T:* (617) 495–3336.

BLOEMFONTEIN, Bishop of, since 1982; **Rt. Rev. Thomas Shaun Stanage;** *b* 6 April 1932; *s* of Robert and Edith Clarice Stanage. *Educ:* King James I Grammar Sch., Bishop Auckland; Univ. of Oxford (MA, Hons Theology, 1956). Curate, St Faith, Great Crosby, 1958–61; Minister of Conventional District of St Andrews, Orford, 1961–63; Vicar, St Andrew, Orford, 1963–70; Rector, All Saints, Somerset West, 1970–75; Dean of Kimberley, 1975–78; Bishop Suffragan of Johannesburg, 1978–82. Liaison Chaplain to Missions to Seamen, Southern Africa. Hon. DD, 1986. *Recreations:* flying (private pilot); music (organ, violin and piano). *Address:* Bishop's House, 16 York Road, Bloemfontein, 9301, S Africa. *T:* (051) 314351. *Club:* Bloemfontein.

BLOFELD, John Christopher Calthorpe, QC 1975; **His Honour Judge Blofeld;** a Circuit Judge, since 1982; *b* 11 July 1932; *s* of late T. R. C. Blofeld, CBE; *m* 1961, Judith Anne, *er d* of Alan Mohun and Mrs James Mitchell; two *s* one *d. Educ:* Eton; King's Coll., Cambridge. Called to Bar, Lincoln's Inn, 1956; a Recorder of the Crown Court, 1975–82. Inspector, Dept of Trade, 1979–81. Chancellor, Dio. St Edmundsbury and Ipswich, 1973. *Recreations:* cricket, gardening. *Address:* Hoveton Green, Wroxham, Norfolk. *Club:* Boodle's.

BLOIS, Sir Charles (Nicholas Gervase), 11th Bt, *cr* 1686; farming since 1965; *b* 25 Dec. 1939; *s* of Sir Gervase Ralph Edmund Blois, 10th Bt and Mrs Audrey Winifred Blois (*née* Johnson); *S* father, 1968; *m* 1967, Celia Helen Mary Pritchett; one *s* one *d. Educ:* Harrow; Trinity Coll., Dublin; Royal Agricultural Coll., Cirencester. Australia, 1963–65. *Recreations:* yachting, shooting. *Heir: s* Andrew Charles David Blois, *b* 7 Feb. 1971. *Address:* Red House, Westleton, Saxmundham, Suffolk. *T:* Westleton 200. *Clubs:* Cruising Association; Ocean Cruising.

BLOKH, Alexandre, PhD, (pen-name **Jean Blot**); writer, since 1956; International Secretary, PEN Club, since 1982; *b* Moscow, 31 March 1923; *s* of Arnold Blokh, man of letters, and Anne (*née* Berlinrote); *m* 1956, Nadia Ermolaiev. *Educ:* Bromsgrove Public Sch., Worcester; Univ. of Paris (PhD Law, PhD Letters). International Civil Servant, United Nations, 1947–62: New York, until 1956; Geneva, 1958–62; Director, Arts and Letters, UNESCO, Paris, 1962–81. Critic, arts and letters, in reviews: Arche, Preuves, NRF. Prix des Critiques, 1972; Prix Valéry Larbaud, 1977; Prix Cazes, 1982. *Publications:*

novels: Le Soleil de Cavouri, 1956; Les Enfants de New York, 1959; Obscur Ennemi, 1961; Les Illusions Nocturnes, 1964; La Jeune Géante, 1969; La Difficulté d'aimer, 1971; Les Cosmopolites, 1976; Gris du Ciel, 1981; La Montagne Sainte, 1984; *essays:* Marguerite Yourcenar; Ossip Mandelstan; Là où tu iras; Sporade; Ivan Goutchorov. *Address:* 34 Square Montsouris, 75014 Paris. *T:* 589 34 16; 38 King Street, WC2. *T:* 01–379 7939.

BLOM-COOPER, Louis Jacques, QC 1970; *b* 27 March 1926; *s* of Alfred Blom-Cooper and Ella Flesseman, Rotterdam; *m* 1952 (marr. diss. 1970); two *s* one *d; m* 1970, Jane Elizabeth, *e d* of Maurice and Helen Smither, Woodbridge, Suffolk; one *s* two *d. Educ:* Port Regis Prep. Sch.; Seaford Coll.; King's Coll., London; Municipal Univ. of Amsterdam; Fitzwilliam Coll., Cambridge. LLB London, 1952; Dr Juris Amsterdam, 1954. HM Army, 1944–47: Capt., E Yorks Regt. Called to Bar, Middle Temple, 1952; Bencher, 1978. Mem., Home Secretary's Adv. Council on the Penal System, 1966–78. Chm., Panel of Inquiry into circumstances surrounding the death of Jasmine Beckford, 1985. Vice-Pres., Howard League for Penal Reform, 1984– (Chm., 1973–84). Chm., BBC London Local Radio Adv. Council, 1970–73. Jt Dir, Legal Res. Unit, Bedford Coll., Univ. of London, 1967–82; Vis. Prof., QMC, London Univ., 1983–. Trustee, Scott Trust (The Guardian Newspaper), 1982–. Joint Editor, Common Market Law Reports. JP Inner London, 1966–79 (transf. City of London, 1969). FRSA 1984. *Publications:* Bankruptcy in Private International Law, 1954; The Law as Literature, 1962; The A6 Murder (A Semblance of Truth), 1963; (with T. P. Morris) A Calendar of Murder, 1964; Language of the Law, 1965; (with O. R. McGregor and Colin Gibson) Separated Spouses, 1970; (with G. Drewry) Final Appeal: a study of the House of Lords in its judicial capacity, 1972; (ed) Progress in Penal Reform, 1975; (ed with G. Drewry) Law and Morality, 1976; contrib. to Modern Law Review, Brit. Jl of Criminology, Brit. Jl of Sociology. *Recreations:* watching and reporting on Association football, reading, music, writing, broadcasting. *Address:* 25 Richmond Crescent, N1 0LY. *T:* 01–607 8045; Glebe House, Montgomery, Powys. *T:* Montgomery 458; Goldsmith Building, EC4Y 7BL. *T:* 01–353 6802. *Clubs:* Athenæum, MCC.

BLOMEFIELD, Sir Charles; see Blomefield, Sir T. C. P.

BLOMEFIELD, Peregrine Maitland; His Honour Judge Blomefield; a Circuit Judge (formerly County Court Judge), since 1969; *b* 25 Oct. 1917; 2nd *s* of Lt-Col Wilmot Blomefield, OBE; *m* 1941, Angela Catherine, *d* of Major Geoffrey Hugh Shenley Crofton, Heytesbury, Wilts; one *s. Educ:* Repton Sch.; Trinity Coll., Oxford (MA). Royal Signals, 1940–46 (Captain). Called to the Bar, Middle Temple, 1947, Bencher, 1967; Oxford Circuit; Recorder of Burton-on-Trent, 1969; Dep. Chm., Berkshire QS, 1967–71. *Address:* c/o Middle Temple Treasury, Middle Temple Lane, EC4Y 9AT.

BLOMEFIELD, Sir (Thomas) Charles (Peregrine), 6th Bt *cr* 1807; Fine Art Dealer; *b* 24 July 1948; *s* of Sir Thomas Edward Peregrine Blomefield, 5th Bt, and of Ginette, Lady Blomefield; *S* father, 1984; *m* 1975, Georgina Geraldine, *d* of Commander C. E. Over, Lugger End, Portscatho, Cornwall; one *s* two *d. Educ:* Wellington Coll., Berks; Mansfield Coll., Oxford. Christie's, 1970–75; Wildenstein and Co., 1975–76; Director, Lidchi Art Gallery, Johannesburg, 1976–78; Man. Director, Charles Blomefield and Co., 1980–; Dir, Thomas Heneage and Co. Ltd, 1982–; Dir, Fleetwood-Hesketh Ltd, 1982–. *Recreations:* travel, listening to music. *Heir: s* Thomas William Peregrine Blomefield, *b* 16 July 1983. *Address:* Clapton Manor, Cheltenham, Glos GL54 2LG. *T:* Cotswold 20255.

BLOMFIELD, Brig. John Reginald, OBE 1957; MC 1944; *b* 10 Jan. 1916; *s* of late Douglas John Blomfield, CIE, and Coralie, *d* of F. H. Tucker, Indian Police; *m* 1939, Patricia Mary McKim; two *d. Educ:* Clifton Coll.; RMA, Woolwich; Peterhouse, Cambridge (MA). Commissioned Royal Engineers, 1936; Lt-Col 1955; Col 1961; Brig. 1965. Retired as Dep. Director, Military Engineering Experimental Establishment, 1969. New Towns Commn Manager, Hemel Hempstead, 1969–78. MBIM 1966. *Recreations:* cruising, ocean racing. *Address:* 9 Armstrong Close, Brockenhurst, Hants. *Clubs:* Royal Ocean Racing; Royal Lymington Yacht.

BLONDEL, Prof. Jean Fernand Pierre; Professor of Political Science, European University Institute, Florence, since 1985; *b* Toulon, France, 26 Oct. 1929; *s* of Fernand Blondel and Marie Blondel (*née* Santelli); *m* 1st, 1954, Michèle (*née* Hadet) (marr. diss. 1979); two *d*; 2nd, 1982, Mrs Theresa Martineau. *Educ:* Collège Saint Louis de Gonzague and Lycée Henri IV, Paris; Institut d'Etudes Politiques and Faculté de Droit, Paris; St Antony's Coll., Oxford. Asst Lectr, then Lectr in Govt, Univ. of Keele, 1958–63; Vis. ACLS Fellow, Yale Univ., 1963–64; Prof. of Government, 1964–84, and Dean, Sch. of Comparative Studies, 1967–69, Univ. of Essex; Vis. Prof., Carleton Univ., Canada, 1969–70; Vis. Schol., Russell Sage Foundn, NY, 1984–85. Exec. Dir, European Consortium for Political Res., 1970–79. *Publications:* Voters, Parties and Leaders, 1963; (jtly) Constituency Politics, 1964; (jtly) Public Administration in France, 1965; An Introduction to Comparative Government, 1969; (jtly) Workbook for Comparative Government, 1972; Comparing Political Systems, 1972; Comparative Legislatures, 1973; The Government of France, 1974; Thinking Politically, 1976; Political Parties, 1978; World Leaders, 1980; The Discipline of Politics, 1981; The Organisation of Governments, 1982; (jtly) Comparative Politics, 1984; Government Ministers in the Contemporary World, 1985; articles in: Political Studies, Parliamentary Affairs, Public Administration, Revue Française de Science Politique, etc. *Recreation:* holidays in Provence. *Address:* 308 Fulham Road, SW10. *T:* 01–351 1526; c/o European University Institute, S Domenico di Fiesole, I-50016 Florence, Italy; 9 rue Général de Partouneaux, Mourillon, Toulon, France.

BLOOD, (Peter) Bindon; Chairman, Industrial Market Research Ltd, since 1984; *b* 24 Sept. 1920; *o s* of Brig. William Edmunds Robarts Blood, CBE, MC, Croix de Guerre, and Eva Gwendoline (*née* Harrison); *m* 1953, Elizabeth Ann, *d* of Harold Drummond Hillier, MC; one *s* one *d. Educ:* Imperial Service Coll., Windsor. Family public works and civil engineering business, 1938–41; served Royal Engineers, 1941–46 (despatches 1944); Engineering Div., Forestry Commn, 1946–48; regular commn, RE, 1948; Second i/c, RE Officer Training Unit, 1948–51; Staff Coll., Camberley, 1951; Sec., Army Bd, NATO Mil. Agency for Standardisation, 1952–53; invalided from service, 1953. Intelligence Co-ordination Staff, FO, 1953–58; Founder and formerly Managing Director: Isora Integrated Ceilings Ltd; Clean Room Construction Ltd; Mitchel and King (Sales) Ltd; Dep. Chm. and Group Marketing Dir, King Group; Institute of Marketing: Dir of Marketing Services, 1971; Dir-Gen., 1972–84. Chm. of Governors, Berks Coll. of Art and Design, 1981–. FRSA, FInstM. *Recreations:* photography, furniture restoration, travel, music, local community activities. *Address:* The Malt Cottage, School Lane, Cookham Village, Berks SL6 9QN. *T:* Bourne End 25319.

BLOOM, André Borisovich; see Anthony, Metropolitan.

BLOOM, Charles; a Recorder of the Crown Court, since 1983; *b* 6 Nov. 1940; *s* of Abraham Barnett Bloom and Freda Bloom (*née* Craft); *m* 1967, Janice Rachelle Goldberg; one *s* one *d. Educ:* Manchester Central Grammar School; Manchester University. LLB Hons 1962. Called to the Bar, Gray's Inn, 1963; practised on Northern Circuit, 1963–. Chairman: Medical Appeal Tribunals, 1979–; Vaccine Damage Tribunal, 1979–

Recreations: tennis, chess, theatre. *Address:* 28 St John Street, Manchester. *T:* 061–834 8418.

BLOOM, Claire; *b* London, 15 Feb. 1931; *d* of late Edward Bloom and of Elizabeth Bloom; *m* 1st, 1959, Rod Steiger (marr. diss. 1969); one *d*; 2nd, 1969. *Educ:* Badminton, Bristol; America and privately. First work in England, BBC, 1946. Stratford: Ophelia, Lady Blanche (King John), Perdita, 1948; The Damask Cheek, Lyric, Hammersmith, 1949; The Lady's Not For Burning, Globe, 1949; Ring Round the Moon, Globe, 1949–50. Old Vic: 1952–53: Romeo and Juliet; 1953: Merchant of Venice; 1954: Hamlet, All's Well, Coriolanus, Twelfth Night, Tempest; 1956: Romeo and Juliet (London, and N American tour). Cordelia, in Stratford Festival Company, 1955 (London, provinces and continental tour); Duel of Angels, Apollo, 1958; Rashomon, NY, 1959; Altona, Royal Court, 1961; The Trojan Women, Spoleto Festival, 1963; Ivanov, Phoenix, 1965; A Doll's House, NY, 1971; Hedda Gabler, 1971; Vivat! Vivat Regina!, NY, 1971; A Doll's House, Criterion, 1973 (filmed 1973); A Streetcar Named Desire, Piccadilly, 1974; Rosmersholm, Haymarket, 1977; The Cherry Orchard, Chichester Fest., 1981; These are Women, a portrait of Shakespeare's heroines, US tour, 1981–82. First film, Blind Goddess, 1947; *films include:* Limelight; The Man Between; Richard III; Alexander the Great; The Brothers Karamazov; The Buccaneers; Look Back in Anger; Three Moves to Freedom; The Brothers Grimm; The Chapman Report; The Haunting; 80,000 Suspects; Alta Infedelta; Il Maestro di Vigevano; The Outrage; The Spy Who Came in From The Cold; Charly; Three into Two won't go; A Severed Head; Red Sky at Morning; Islands In The Stream; The Clash of the Titans, 1979; Always, 1984. First appearance on television programmes, 1952, since when she has had frequent successes on TV in the US; In Praise of Love, 1975; *Television:* BBC: A Legacy, 1975; The Ghost Writer, 1983; Shadowlands, 1985 (BAFTA award Best TV Actress); Time and the Conways, 1985; Oedipus the King, 1986; BBC Shakespeare: Katharine in Henry VIII, 1979; Gertrude in Hamlet, 1980; the Queen in Cymbeline, Lady Constance in King John, 1983; ITV series: Brideshead Revisited, 1981. *Publication:* Limelight and After (autobiog.), 1982. *Recreations:* ballet, reading. *Address:* c/o James Sharkey, 15 Golden Square, W1.

BLOOM, G(eorge) Cromarty, CBE 1974; Director, Cablevision (Wellingborough) Ltd; *b* 8 June 1910; *s* of late George Highfield Bloom and Jessie Bloom (*née* Cromarty); *m* 1st, 1940, Patricia Suzanne Ramplin (*d* 1957); two *s*; 2nd, 1961, Sheila Louise Curran; one *s*. *Educ:* Australia and China, privately; Keble Coll., Oxford. With Reuters, 1933–60. Gen. Manager and Chief Exec., The Press Assoc. Ltd, 1961–75; Dep. Chm., London Broadcasting Co., 1976–81; Jt Chm., Independent Radio Sales Ltd, 1979–83; Dir, Selkirk Communications Ltd, 1976–84. Vice-Chm., Internat. Press Telecommunications Council, 1971–75; Vice-Pres., Alliance Européenne des Agences de Presse, 1971–75; Chm., CPU Telecommunications Cttee, 1973–77. *Address:* 1 Tivoli Court, Tivoli Road, Cheltenham GL50 2TD. *T:* Cheltenham 39413.

BLOOM, Ronald; HM Diplomatic Service, retired; free-lance political/commercial consultant; Director: Trefoil Associates, since 1982; Cavendish Richards & Co., since 1983; Eastech Services Co. Ltd (Hong Kong), since 1984; Lesta-Group AG, since 1985; *b* 21 Jan. 1926; *s* of John Bloom and Marjorie Bloom (*née* Barker); *m* 1956, Shirley Evelyn Edge; one *s* two *d*. *Educ:* inadequately. HM Forces, DLI, E Yorks Regt, 1943–57. Joined HM Diplomatic Service, 1958; Hong Kong, 1958–61; Singapore, 1961–63; FO, 1963–65; Zomba, 1965–67; FO, 1967–69; Kuala Lumpur, 1969–71; Singapore, 1971–74; Counsellor, FO, 1974–81. *Publications:* reviews in Man (Royal Anthropol Inst.), occasional articles on uniforms and model soldiers. *Address:* The Old House, Deep Street, Prestbury, Glos. *T:* Cheltenham 44141; Lesta-Group AG, 50 Pall Mall, SW1. *T:* 01–839 1030. *Club:* Brooks's.

BLOOMFIELD, Barry Cambray, MA, FLA; Director, Collection Development, Humanities and Social Sciences, British Library, since 1985; *b* 1 June 1931; *s* of Clifford Wilson Bloomfield and Eileen Elizabeth (*née* Cambray); *m* 1958, Valerie Jean Philpot. *Educ:* East Ham Grammar Sch.; University College of the South-West, Exeter; University Coll. London; Birkbeck Coll., London. Served in Intelligence Corps, Malaya, 1952–54. Assistant, National Central Library, 1955; Librarian, College of S Mark and S John, Chelsea, 1956–61; Asst Librarian, London Sch. of Economics, 1961–63; Dep. Librarian, 1963–72, Librarian, 1972–78, School of Oriental and African Studies; Dir, India Office Library and Records, British Library (formerly FCO), 1978–85 and concurrently Keeper, Dept of Oriental MSS and Printed Bks, British Library, 1983–85. Chm., SCONUL Group of Orientalist Libraries, 1975–80; Vice-Pres., Bibliographical Soc., 1979–; Member: Council, Royal Asiatic Soc., 1980–84; British Assoc. for Cemeteries in S Asia, 1980–; Exec. Cttee, Friends of the Nat. Libraries, 1981–. Vis. Professor, Univ. of Florida, 1963; Vis. Fellow, Univ. of Hawaii, 1977. *Publications:* New Verse in the '30s, 1960; W. H. Auden: a bibliography, 1964, 2nd edn 1972; ed, Autobiography of Sir J. P. Kay Shuttleworth, 1964; ed, (with V. J. Bloomfield, J. D. Pearson) Theses on Africa, 1964; ed, Theses on Asia, 1967; ed, The Acquisition and Provision of Foreign Books by National and University Libraries in the UK, 1972; An Author Index to Selected British 'Little' Magazines, 1976; Philip Larkin: a bibliography 1933–1976, 1979; (ed) Middle East Studies and Libraries, 1980; numerous articles in library and bibliog. jls. *Recreations:* reading, music. *Address:* Brambling, 24 Oxenturn Road, Wye, Kent TN25 5BE. *T:* Wye 813038. *Club:* Royal Commonwealth Society.

BLOOMFIELD, Hon. Sir John (Stoughton), Kt 1967; QC (Victoria) 1965; LLB; Member for Malvern, Legislative Assembly, Victoria, 1953–70, retired; *b* 9 Oct. 1901; *s* of Arthur Stoughton Bloomfield, Chartered Accountant, Melbourne, and Ada Victoria Bloomfield; *m* 1931, Beatrice Madge, *d* of W. H. Taylor, Overnewton, Sydenham, Victoria; one *s* one *d*. *Educ:* Geelong Grammar Sch.; Trinity Coll., Melbourne Univ. Served AIF, 1940–45; Lieut-Col retired. Solicitor, 1927–45; called to Victorian Bar, 1945. Government of Victoria: Minister of Labour and Industry and of Electrical Undertakings, 1955–56; Minister of Education, 1956–67. Mem. Council, University of Melbourne, 1956–70. *Publications:* Company Law Amendments, 1939; Screens and Gowns: Some Aspects of University Education Overseas, 1963; articles in professional journals. *Recreation:* painting. *Address:* 1/22 Mercer Road, Armadale, Victoria 3143, Australia. *T:* 20–2947. *Clubs:* Melbourne, Naval and Military (Melbourne).

BLOOMFIELD, Kenneth Percy, CB 1982; Head of Northern Ireland Civil Service, and Second Permanent Under Secretary of State, Northern Ireland Office, since 1984; *b* 15 April 1931; *o c* of Harry Percy Bloomfield and Doris Bloomfield, Belfast; *m* 1960, Mary Elizabeth Ramsey; one *s* one *d*. *Educ:* Royal Belfast Academical Instn; St Peter's Coll., Oxford (MA). Min. of Finance, N Ireland, 1952–56; Private Sec. to Ministers of Finance, 1956–60; Dep. Dir, British Industrial Develt Office, NY, 1960–63; Asst and later Dep. Sec. to Cabinet, NI, 1963–72; Under-Sec., Northern Ireland Office, 1972–73; Sec. to Northern Ireland Executive, Jan.-May 1974; Permanent Secretary: Office of the Executive, NI, 1974–75; Dept of Housing, Local Govt and Planning, NI, 1975–76; Dept of the Environment, NI, 1976–81; Dept of Commerce, NI, 1981–82; Dept of Economic Develt, 1982–84. Governor, Royal Belfast Academical Instn. *Recreations:* reading history and biography, swimming. *Address:* Stormont Castle, Belfast BT4 3ST. *T:* Belfast 63011.

BLOSSE, Sir Richard Hely L.; *see* Lynch-Blosse.

BLOT, Jean; *see* Blokh, A.

BLOUNT, Bertie Kennedy, CB 1957; DrPhilNat; CChem, FRSC; *b* 1 April 1907; *s* of late Col G. P. C. Blount, DSO, and late Bridget Constance, *d* of Maj.-Gen. J. F. Bally, CVO; unmarried. *Educ:* Malvern Coll.; Trinity Coll., Oxford (MA 1932, BSc 1929); Univ. of Frankfurt (DrPhilNat 1931). Ramsay Memorial Fellow, 1931; 1851 Senior Student, 1933; Dean of St Peter's Hall, Oxford, 1933–37; Messrs Glaxo Laboratories Ltd: Head of Chemical Research Laboratory, 1937; Principal Technical Executive, 1938–40. Served Army (Intelligence Corps), War of 1939–45; Capt. 1940; Major 1942; Col 1945. Asst Director of Research, The Wellcome Foundation, 1947; Director of Research Branch, Control Commission for Germany, 1948, and subsequently also Chief of Research Div. of Military Security Board; Director of Scientific Intelligence, Min. of Defence, 1950–52; Dep. Secretary, DSIR, 1952; Min. of Technology, 1964; retired 1966. Chairman Steering Cttees: Torry Res. Station and Forest Products Res. Lab., 1958–66; Lab. of the Govt Chemist, 1962–66; Building Res. Station, Joint Fire Res. Organisation, Hydraulics Res. Stat., Water Pollution Res. Lab., Warren Spring Lab., 1965–66. Member Exec. Cttee, British Council, 1957–66. Royal Society of Arts: Armstrong Lecturer, 1955; Cantor Lecturer, 1963. Member Parry Cttee to review Latin American Studies in British Universities, 1962; Pres., Exec. Cttee, Internat. Inst. of Refrigeration, 1963–71, Hon. Pres. 1971; Hon. Member: (British) Inst. of Refrigeration, 1971; Max-Planck-Ges. zur Förderung der Wissenschaften, 1984. Golden doctorate, Frankfurt Univ., 1982. *Publications:* papers in scientific and other journals. *Recreations:* travel, walking, gardening. *Address:* Tarrant Rushton House, Blandford, Dorset. *T:* Blandford 52256. *Club:* Athenæum.

BLOUNT, Sir Walter (Edward Alpin), 12th Bt *cr* 1642; DSC 1943 and two Bars 1945; farmer; *b* 31 Oct. 1917; *s* of Sir Edward Robert Blount, 11th Bt, and Violet Ellen (*d* 1969), *d* of Alpin Grant Fowler; *S* father, 1978; *m* 1954, Eileen Audrey, *d* of late Hugh B. Carritt; one *d*. *Educ:* Beaumont College; Sidney Sussex Coll., Cambridge (MA). Served RN, 1939–47. Qualified as Solicitor, 1950; practised Gold Coast, West Africa, 1950–52; London and Cambridge, 1952–76; Consultant, London, 1976. Farmer, Tilkhurst, East Grinstead, Sussex, 1978–. Lloyd's Underwriter. *Recreation:* sailing. *Heir:* none. *Address:* 19 St Anns Terrace, St John's Wood, NW8. *T:* 01–722 0802; Regent House, Seaview, IoW. *Clubs:* Bembridge Sailing, Seaview Yacht, Cambridge Cruising, RNVR Sailing, Law Society Yacht, Island Sailing.

BLOW, Prof. David Mervyn, FRS 1972; Professor of Biophysics at Imperial College, University of London, since 1977 (Dean of the Royal College of Science, 1981–84); *b* 27 June 1931; *s* of Rev. Edward Mervyn and Dorothy Laura Blow; *m* 1955, Mavis Sears; one *s* one *d*. *Educ:* Kingswood Sch.; Corpus Christi Coll., Cambridge (MA, PhD). FInstP. Fulbright Scholar, Nat. Inst. of Health, Bethesda, Md, and MIT, 1957–59; MRC Unit for Study of Molecular Biological Systems, Cambridge, 1959–62; MRC Lab. of Molecular Biology, Cambridge, 1962–77; College Lectr and Fellow, Trinity Coll., Cambridge, 1968–77. Pres., British Crystallographic Assoc., 1984–. Biochem. Soc. CIBA Medal, 1967; Charles Léopold Meyer Prize, 1979. *Publications:* papers and reviews in scientific jls. *Recreations:* hill walking, sailing. *Address:* Blackett Laboratory, Imperial College of Science and Technology, University of London, SW7 2BZ.

BLOW, Joyce, (Mrs Anthony Darlington), FIPR; FBIM; Director: Cadogan Management Ltd, since 1985; Money Management Council, since 1986; Chairman, Mail Order Publishers' Authority, since 1986; *b* 4 May 1929; *d* of late Walter Blow and Phyllis (*née* Grainger); *m* 1974, Lt-Col J. A. B. Darlington, RE retd. *Educ:* Bell Baxter Sch., Cupar, Fife; Edinburgh Univ. (MA Hons). FIPR 1964. John Lewis Partnership, 1951–52; FBI, 1952–53; Press Officer, Council of Indust. Design, 1953–63; Publicity and Advertising Manager, Heal & Son Ltd, 1963–65; entered Civil Service on first regular recruitment of direct entry Principals from business and industry: BoT, 1965–67; Monopolies Commn (gen. enquiry into restrictive practices in supply of prof. services), 1967–70; DTI, 1970, Asst Sec. 1972; Dept of Prices and Consumer Protection, 1974–77; Under-Secretary: OFT, 1977–80; DTI, 1980–84. Vice-Pres., Inst. of Trading Standards Admin, 1985–; Founder Mem. and Past Pres. Assoc. of Women in Public Relations. Freeman, City of London. *Recreations:* music, particularly opera; travel. *Address:* 17 Fentiman Road, SW8 1LD. *T:* 01–735 4023; 9 Crouchfield Close, Seaford, E Sussex. *Clubs:* Reform, Arts.

BLOW, Sandra, RA 1978 (ARA 1971); *b* 14 Sept. 1925; *d* of Jack and Lily Blow. *Educ:* St Martin's School of Art; Royal Academy Sch.; Accademia di Belle Arti, Rome. Tutor, Painting School, Royal Coll. of Art, 1960–75. *One-man Exhibitions:* Gimpel Fils, 1952, 1954, 1960, 1962; Saidenburg Gallery, NY, 1957; New Art Centre, London, 1966, 1968, 1971, 1973. Represented in group exhibitions in Britain (including British Painting 74, Hayward Gall.), USA, Italy, Denmark, France. Won British Section of Internat. Guggenheim Award, 1960; 2nd prize, John Moore's Liverpool Exhibition, 1961; Arts Council Purchase Award, 1965–66. *Official Purchases:* Peter Stuyvesant Foundation; Nuffield Foundation; Arts Council of Great Britain; Arts Council of N Ireland; Walker Art Gallery, Liverpool; Allbright Knox Art Gallery, Buffalo, NY; Museum of Modern Art, NY; Tate Gallery; Gulbenkian Foundation; Min. of Public Building and Works; Contemp. Art Society; silk screen prints: Victoria and Albert Museum; Fitzwilliam Museum, Cambridge; City of Leeds Art Gall.; Graves Art Gall., Sheffield; painting purchased for liner Queen Elizabeth II. *Address:* 12 Sydney Close, SW3. *T:* 01–589 8610.

BLOY, Rt. Rev. Francis Eric Irving, DD, STD; *b* Birchington, Isle of Thanet, Kent, England, 17 Dec. 1904; *s* of Rev. Francis Joseph Field Bloy and Alice Mary (*née* Poynter); *m* 1929, Frances Forbes Cox, Alexandria, Va; no *c*. *Educ:* University of Missouri (BA); Georgetown Univ. of Foreign Service; Virginia Theological Seminary (BD). Rector, All Saints Ch., Reisterstown, Maryland, 1929–33; Assoc. Rector, St James-by-the-Sea, La Jolla, Calif, 1933–35, Rector, 1935–37; Dean, St Paul's Cathedral, Los Angeles, Calif, 1937–48; Bishop of Los Angeles, 1948–73. DD: Ch. Divinity Sch. of the Pacific, Berkeley, Calif, 1942; Occidental Coll., Los Angeles, 1953; Va Theol Sem., 1953; STD: Ch. Divinity Sch. of the Pacific, 1948; Univ. of S Calif, 1955. Pres., Church Federation of Los Angeles, 1946–47; Pres., Univ. Religious Conf., 1956; Hon. Chm. Bd of Trustees, Good Samaritan Hosp.; Mem. Town Hall. *Address:* 3919 Starland Drive, Flintridge, Calif 91011, USA. *Club:* California (Los Angeles).

BLUCK, Duncan Robert Yorke, OBE 1984; Chairman: British Tourist Authority, since 1984; English Tourist Board, since 1984; Kent Economic Development Board, since 1986; Director, John Swire & Sons, since 1984; *b* 19 March 1927; *s* of Thomas Edward Bluck and Ida Bluck; *m* 1952, Stella Wardlaw Murdoch; one *s* three *d*. *Educ:* Taunton Sch. RNVR, 1944–47. Joined John Swire & Sons, 1948; Dir, 1964–, Chief Exec., 1971–84, Chm., 1980–84, Cathay Pacific Airways; Chairman: John Swire & Sons (HK) Ltd, 1980–84; Swire Pacific Ltd, 1980–84. Chm., Hongkong Tourist Assoc., 1981–84. Governor, Marlborough House Sch., 1986–. *Recreations:* sailing, tennis. *Address:* Elfords, Hawkhurst, Kent TN18 4RP. *T:* Hawkhurst 2153. *Clubs:* Brooks's; Hongkong, Sheko (Hongkong).

BLUCKE, Air Vice-Marshal Robert Stewart, CB 1946; CBE 1945; DSO 1943; AFC 1936, Bar 1941; RAF, retired; *b* 22 June 1897; *s* of late Rev. R. S. K. Blucke, Monxton Rectory, Andover, Hants; *m* 1926, Nancy, *d* of late Frank Wilson, Auckland, NZ; one *d* (one *s* decd). *Educ:* Malvern Coll. Dorset Regt and RFC, 1915–18; Mesopotamia, 1916–18; Royal Air Force, 1922; India, 1927–32; Test Pilot Royal Aircraft Establishment, Farnborough, 1933–37; Air Ministry, 1938–42; served in Bomber Comd, 1942–46; AOC No 1 Group RAF, 1945; SASO, AHQ, India, 1947; AOA, Technical Trg Comd, 1947–49; AOA, Far East Air Force, 1949–50; AOC Malaya, 1951; AOC-in-C Transport Comd, 1952; retired 1952. General Manager, National Assoc. for Employment of Regular Sailors, Soldiers and Airmen, 1952–65. *Address:* Flat 3, Melrose House, South View Road, Crowborough, East Sussex. *T:* Crowborough 61638. *Club:* Royal Air Force.

BLUE, Rabbi Lionel; Convener of the Bethdin (Ecclesiastical Court) of the Reform Synagogues of Great Britain, since 1971; Lecturer, Leo Baeck College, since 1967; *b* 6 Feb. 1930; *s* of Harry and Hetty Blue. *Educ:* Balliol Coll., Oxford (MA History); University Coll. London (BA Semitics); Leo Baeck Coll., London (Rabbinical Dip). Ordained Rabbi, 1960; Minister to Settlement Synagogue and Middlesex New Synagogue, 1960–63; European Dir, World Union for Progressive Judaism, 1963–66; Co-Editor, Forms of Prayer, 1967–; broadcaster, 1967–; Feature Writer, The Standard, 1985–. *Publications:* To Heaven with Scribes and Pharisees, 1975; (jtly) A Taste of Heaven, 1977; (ed jtly) Forms of Prayer (Sabath and Daily), 1977; A Backdoor to Heaven, 1979, revd edn 1985; (ed jtly) Forms of Prayer (Days of Awe), 1985; Bright Blue, 1985; (jtly) Simply Divine, 1985; Kitchen Blues, 1985; Bolts from the Blue, 1986. *Recreations:* window shopping, package holidays, monasteries, cooking. *Address:* 80 East End Road, N3 2SY. *T:* 01–349 2568.

BLUGLASS, Prof. Robert Saul, MD, FRCPsych; Professor of Forensic Psychiatry, University of Birmingham, since 1979 (Regional Postgraduate Clinical Tutor in Forensic Psychiatry, since 1967); *b* 22 Sept. 1930; *s* of Henry Bluglass and Fay (*née* Griew); *m* 1962, Jean Margaret Kerry (*née* Montgomery); one *s* one *d*. *Educ:* Warwick Sch., Warwick; Univ. of St Andrews (MB, ChB 1957, MD 1967). DPM 1962; FRCPsych 1976 (MRCPsych 1971). Formerly, Sen. Registrar in Psych., Royal Dundee Liff Hosp. and Maryfield Hosp., Dundee; Consultant in For. Psych., W Midlands RHA and the Home Office, 1967–; Consultant i/c Midland Centre for For. Psych., All Saints Hosp., Birmingham, 1967–; Hon. Lectr in For. Psych., Univ. of Birmingham, 1968–75, Sen. Clin. Lectr in For. Psych., 1975–79; Jt Dir, Midland Inst. of For. Medicine, 1975–; Clinical Dir, Reaside Clinic, Birmingham, 1986–. Dep. Reginal Advr in Psychiatry, W Midlands RHA, 1985–; Specialist Advr, H of C Select Cttee on Social Services, 1985–. Member: Adv. Cttee on Alcoholism, DHSS, 1975–80; Adv. Council on Probation, Home Office, 1974–77; Mental Health Act Commn, 1983–85; Forensic Psych. Res. Liaison Gp, DHSS. Royal College of Psychiatrists: Mem., Ct of Electors, 1976–79; Mem. Council, 1973–76, 1976–78, 1980–86, 1986–; Vice-Pres., 1983–85; Chm., For. Psych. Specialist Section, 1978–82. FRSocMed 1975; Past Pres., Sect. of Psych., Birmingham Med. Inst.; Mem., Brit. Acad. of For. Sciences. Baron ver Heyden de Lancey Law Prize, RSocMed, 1983. *Publications:* Psychiatry, The Law and The Offender, 1980; A Guide to the Mental Health Act 1983, 1983; (ed with Prof. Sir Martin Roth) Psychiatry, Human Rights and the Law, 1985; articles in Brit. Jl of Hosp. Med., BMJ, and Med., Science and the Law. *Recreations:* water-colour painting, cooking, gardening, swimming. *Address:* Midland Centre for Forensic Psychiatry, All Saints Hospital, Birmingham B18 5SD.

BLUMBERG, Prof. Baruch Samuel, MD, PhD; Associate Director for Clinical Research, Fox Chase Cancer Center, since 1964; University Professor of Medicine and Anthropology, University of Pennsylvania, since 1970; Clinical Professor, Department of Epidemiology, University of Washington School of Public Health, since 1983; *b* 28 July 1925; *s* of Meyer Blumberg and Ida Blumberg; *m* 1954, Jean Liebesman Blumberg; two *s* two *d*. *Educ:* Union Coll. (BS Physics, 1946); Columbia University Coll. of Physicians and Surgeons (MD 1951); Balliol Coll., Oxford Univ. (PhD Biol Sciences, 1957); FRCP 1984. US Navy, 1943–46 (Lieut JG). US Public Health Service (rank of med. dir, col), and Chief, Geographic Medicine and Genetics Sect., Nat. Insts. of Health, Bethesda, Md, 1957–64. George Eastman Vis. Prof., Oxford Univ., 1983–84. Mem. Nat. Acad. of Sciences, Washington, DC. Hon. Fellow, Balliol Coll., Oxford, 1977. Hon. DSc: Univ. of Pittsburgh, 1977; Union Coll., Schenectady, NY, 1977; Med. Coll. of Pa, 1977; Dickinson Coll., Carlisle, Pa, 1977; Hahnemann Med. Coll., Philadelphia, Pa, 1977; Dr *hc* Univ. of Paris VII, 1978. (Jt) Nobel Prize in Physiology or Medicine, 1976. *Publications:* (ed) Genetic Polymorphisms and Geographic Variations in Disease, 1961; (ed jtly) Medical Clinics of North America: new developments in medicine, 1970; (ed jtly) Hepatitis B: the virus, the disease and the vaccine, 1984; *chapters in:* McGraw-Hill Encyclopedia of Science and Technology Yearbook, 1962; The Genetics of Migrant and Isolate Populations, ed E. Goldschmidt, 1963; Hemoglobin: its precursors and metabolites, ed F. W. Sunderman and F. W. Sunderman, Jr, 1964; McGraw-Hill Yearbook of Science and Technology, 1970; (also co-author chapter) Viral Hepatitis and Blood Transfusion, ed G. N. Vyas and others, 1972; Hematology, ed W. J. Williams and others, 1972; Progress in Liver Disease, Vol. IV, ed H. Popper and F. Schaffner, 1972; Australia Antigen, ed J. E. Prier and H. Friedman, 1973; Drugs and the Liver, ed. W. Gerok and K. Sickinger, 1975 (Germany); (*jtly*) *chapters in:* Progress in Medical Genetics, ed A. G. Steinberg and A. G. Bearn, 1965 (also London); Viruses Affecting Man and Animals, ed M. Sanders and M. Schaeffer, 1971; Perspectives in Virology, 1971; Transmissable Disease and Blood Transfusion, ed T. J. Greenwalt and G. A. Jamieson, 1975; Physiological Anthropology, ed A. Damon, 1975; Hepatite a Virus B et Hemodialyse, 1975 (Paris); Onco-Developmental Gene Expression, 1976; contrib. symposia; over 360 articles in scientific jls. *Recreations:* squash, canoeing, middle distance running, cattle raising. *Address:* Fox Chase Cancer Research, Philadelphia, Pa 19111, USA. *T:* 215–728–2203. *Clubs:* Explorers (NY); Provincetown Yacht (Provincetown, Mass); Chesapeake and Ohio Canal Association.

BLUMENTHAL, W(erner) Michael, PhD; Chairman, since 1981, and Chief Executive Officer, since 1980, Burroughs Corporation; *b* Germany, 3 Jan. 1926. *Educ:* Univ. of California at Berkeley; Princeton Univ. Went to USA, 1947; naturalised, 1952. Research Associate, Princeton Univ; Vice-Pres., Dir, Crown Cork Internat. Corp., 1957–61. Dep. Asst Sec. of State for Econ. Affairs, Dept of State, 1961–63; Dep. Special Rep. of the President (with rank Ambassador) for Trade Negotiations, 1963–67. Pres., Bendix Internat., 1967–70; Bendix Corp.: Dir, 1967–77; Vice-Chm., 1970–71; Pres. and Chief Operating Officer, 1971–72; Chm. and Chief Exec. Officer, 1972–77; US Secretary of the Treasury, 1977–79; Vice Chm., Burroughs Corp., 1980. Director: Burroughs Tenneco, Inc.; Chemical NY Corp.; Chemical Bank; Pillsbury Co.; Member: Business Council; Business Roundtable; Amer. Economic Assoc.; Board of Directors: Detroit Renaissance, Inc.; New Detroit Inc.; Economic Club of Detroit; Vice-Pres., Mem. Bd of Dirs and Exec. Cttee, Utd Foundn of Detroit. Mem. Exec. Bd, Detroit Area Council, Boy Scouts of America. Trustee, Rockefeller Foundn. *Address:* Burroughs Corporation, Burroughs Place, Detroit, Michigan 48232, USA.

BLUMFIELD, Clifford William, OBE 1976; Director, Dounreay Nuclear Power Development Establishment, since 1975, and Deputy Managing Director, Northern Division, UKAEA, since 1985; *b* 18 May 1922. *Educ:* Ipswich Boys' Central Sch. CEng, FIMechE, FINucE. With Reavell & Co. Ltd, 1938–44; served REME, 1944–47 (Major); Min. of Supply, Harwell, 1947–54; UKAEA, Harwell, 1954–58; Atomic Energy Estabt, Winfrith, 1958–68 (Group Leader, Design Gp, and Head of Gen. Ops and Tech. Div.); Asst Dir, Ops and Engineering, later Dep. Dir, Dounreay, 1968–75. *Address:* UKAEA, Dounreay Nuclear Power Development Establishment, Thurso, Caithness KW14 7TZ.

BLUMGART, Prof. Leslie Harold, MD; FRCS, FRCSE, FRCSGlas; Professor of Surgery, University of Bern, Switzerland, since 1986; *b* 7 Dec. 1931, of S African parentage; *m* 1955, Pearl Marie Navias (decd); *m* 1968, Sarah Raybould Bowen; two *s* two *d*. *Educ:* Jeppe High Sch., Johannesburg, SA; Univ. of Witwatersrand (BDS); Univ. of Sheffield (MB, ChB Hons; MD 1969). Prize Medal, Clin. Med. and Surg.; Ashby-de-la-Zouche Prize, Surg., Med., Obst. and Gynaecol. FRCS 1966, FRCSGlas 1973, FRCSE 1976. General dental practice, Durban, SA, 1954–59; Sen. Surgical Registrar, Nottingham Gen. Hosp. and Sheffield Royal Infirmary, 1966–70; Sen. Lectr and Dep. Dir, Dept of Surgery, Welsh Nat. Sch. of Med., also Hon. Cons. Surg., Cardiff Royal Inf., 1970–72; St Mungo Prof. of Surgery, Univ. of Glasgow, and Hon. Cons. Surg., Glasgow Royal Inf., 1972–79; Prof. of Surgery, Royal Postgrad. Sch. of London and Dir of Surgery, Hammersmith Hosp., 1979–86. Moynihan Fellow, Assoc. of Surgs of Gt Brit. and Ire., 1972; Mayne Vis. Prof., Univ. of Queensland, Brisbane, 1976; Vis. Prof., Univ. of Lund, Sweden, 1977; Nimmo Vis. Prof., Adelaide Univ., 1982; Purvis Oration, 1974; President's Oration, Soc. for Surgery of Aliment. Tract, Toronto, 1977; Honyman Gillespie Lecture, Univ. of Edinburgh, 1978; Walton Lecture, RCPGlas, 1984; Monsarrat Lect., Univ. of Liverpool, 1985; Legg Meml Lect., KCH, 1985. One time examiner in Surgery: Univs of: Cambridge; Hong Kong; Edinburgh. Member: BMA, 1963–; Assoc. of Surgs of Gt Brit. and Ire., 1971–; Surgical Research Soc., 1971–; Brit. Assoc. of Surgical Oncology, 1976–; Brit. Soc. of Gastroenterology, 1972–; Internat. Biliary Assoc.; Editorial Cttee, Brit. Jl of Surgery, 1973–; Hon. Mem., Soc. for Surgery of Aliment. Tract, USA, 1977. Order of Prasidda, Prabala-Gorkha-Dakshin Bahu, Nepal, 1984. *Publications:* (ed with A. C. Kennedy), Essentials of Medicine and Surgery for Dental Students, 3rd edn 1977, 4th edn 1982; (ed) The Biliary Tract, 1982; chapters in: Recent Advances in Surgery, 1973, 1980; Abdominal Operations, 1974, 1980; Liver and Biliary Disease, 1979; Operative Surgery—Abdomen, 4th edn 1983; Surgical Gastroenterology, 1984; Advances in Surgery, 1975; Textbook of Surgical Physiology, 1977; Hepatotrophic Factors, 1978; Clinics in Gastroenterology, 1978; papers, mainly on liver, biliary and pancreatic surgery and hepatic pathophysiology, in med. and surgical jls. *Recreations:* water colour painting, wood carving. *Address:* 12 Glebe Road, Barnes, SW13 0EA. *T:* 01–878 3752.

BLUNDELL, Commandant Daphne Mary, CB 1972; Director, WRNS, 1970–73; *b* 19 Aug. 1916. *Educ:* St Helen's Sch., Northwood; Bedford Coll., London. Worked for LCC as Child Care Organiser. Joined WRNS, Nov. 1942; commnd 1943; served in Orkneys, Ceylon, E Africa; Malta, 1954–56; Staff of Flag Officer Naval Air Comd, 1964–67; Staff of C-in-C Portsmouth, 1967–69; Supt WRNS Training and Drafting, 1969–70. Supt 1967; Comdt 1970, retd 1973; Hon. ADC to the Queen, 1970–73. Governor, St Helen's Sch., Northwood. *Address:* 15 Northbrook Drive, Northwood, Mddx HA6 2YU.

BLUNDELL, Sir Michael, KBE 1962 (MBE 1943); *b* 7 April 1907; *s* of Alfred Herbert Blundell and Amelia Woodward Blundell (*née* Richardson); *m* 1946, Geraldine Lötte Robarts (*d* 1983); one *d*. *Educ:* Wellington Coll. Settled in Kenya as farmer, 1925. 2nd Lieut, RE, 1940; Major, 1940; Lieut-Col, 1941; Col, 1944; served Abyssinian campaign and SEAC. Commissioner, European Settlement, 1946–47; MLC, Rift Valley Constituency, Kenya, 1948–63; Leader European Members, 1952–54; Minister on Emergency War Council, Kenya, 1954–55; Minister of Agriculture, Kenya, 1955–59 and April 1961–June 1963; Leader of New Kenya Group, 1959–63. Chairman: Pyrethrum Board of Kenya, 1949–54; Egerton Agricultural Coll., 1962–72; EA Breweries Ltd, 1964–77; Uganda Breweries Ltd, 1965–76; Dir, Barclays Bank of Kenya Ltd, 1968–82. Chm., Kenya Soc. for the Blind, 1977–81. Freeman, Goldsmiths' Co., 1950; Hon. Col, 3rd KAR, 1955–61; Judge, Guernsey cattle, RASE, 1977. *Publications:* So Rough a Wind, 1964; The Wild Flowers of Kenya, 1982. *Recreations:* gardening, music, 18th century English porcelain. *Address:* Box 30181, Nairobi, Kenya. *T:* Nairobi 512278. *Clubs:* Brooks's; Muthaiga (Nairobi).

BLUNDELL, Prof. Thomas Leon, FRS 1984; Professor of Crystallography, Birkbeck College, University of London, since 1976; *b* 7 July 1942; *s* of Horace Leon Blundell and Marjorie Blundell; one *s*. *Educ:* Steyning Grammar Sch.; Brasenose Coll., Oxford (BA, DPhil). Postdoctoral Res. Fellow, Laboratory of Molecular Biophysics, Oxford Univ., 1967–72; Jun. Res. Fellow, Linacre Coll., Oxford, 1968–70; Lectr, Biological Scis, Sussex Univ., 1973–76. Director, International Sch. of Crystallography, 1981–; Chm., Biological Scis Cttee, SERC, and Mem. Science Bd, 1983–; Mem. Council, AFRC, 1985–. Lectures: Plenary, Internat. Congress of Crystallography, 1969 and 1978; Gerhardt Schmidt, Weizman Inst., Israel, 1983; Plenary, Europ. Cryst. Meeting, 1983; Ferdinand Springer, Fedn of Europ. Biochemical Socs, 1984. Councillor, Oxford CBC, 1970–73 (Chm. Planning Cttee, 1972–73). Governor, Birkbeck Coll., 1985–. Alcon Award for Dist. Work in Vision Research, 1985. Jt Editor, Progress in Biophysics and Molecular Biology, 1979–. *Publications:* Protein Crystallography, 1976; papers in Jl of Molecular Biology, Nature, European Jl of Biochemistry, etc. *Recreations:* playing jazz, listening to opera, walking, local politics. *Address:* 1 Asmara Road, NW2 3SS. *T:* 01–794 6085.

BLUNDEN, George; Deputy Governor, Bank of England, since 1986 (Executive Director, 1976–84, Non-Executive Director, 1984–85); *b* 31 Dec. 1922; *s* of late George Blunden and Florence Holder; *m* 1949, Anne, *d* of late G. J. E. and of Phyllis Bulford; two *s* one *d*. *Educ:* City of London Sch.; University Coll., Oxford (MA). Royal Sussex Regt, 1941–45. Bank of England, 1947–55; IMF, 1955–58; Bank of England: rejoined 1958; on staff of Monopolies Commn, 1968; Dep. Chief Cashier, 1968–73; Chief of Management Services, 1973–74; Head of Banking Supervision, 1974–76. Jt Dep. Chm., Leopold Joseph Hldgs, 1984–85; Director: Eagle Star Hldgs, 1984–85; Portals Hldgs, 1984–; Grindlays Hldgs, 1984–85. Chm., Group of Ten Cttees, BIS, Basle, on Banking Regulations and Supervisory Practices, 1974–77, on Payments Systems, 1981–83. Chm., Dovedale Almshouses Trust, 1984–85 (Hon. Treasurer, 1973–79); Treasurer, UK Friends of Insead, 1979–84. Chm. Governors, St Peter's Gp of Hosps, 1978–82; Chm., St Peter's Hosps Special Trustees, 1982–; Chm., Inst. of Urology, 1982– (Hon. Treasurer, 1975–78); Mem. Council, Imperial Cancer Res. Fund, 1981–. Mem., Family Welfare Assoc., 1984–85; Chm., Samuel Lewis Housing Trust, 1985 (Trustee, 1980–85); Trustee, St Peter's Trust for Kidney Res., 1971–; Mem. Exec. Cttee, Nat. Assoc. of Almshouses, 1984–85; Vice-Pres., Opportunities for the Disabled, 1980–. Member: Court, Mermaid Theatre Trust, 1979–84; Governing Body, London Business Sch., 1982–84; Council: Oxford Centre for Management Studies, 1983–85; RCM, 1983–. *Address:* Bank of England, Threadneedle Street, EC2R 8AH. *Clubs:* Reform, MCC.

BLUNDEN, Sir Philip (Overington), 7th Bt *cr* 1766, of Castle Blunden, Kilkenny; artist and art restorer; *b* 27 Jan. 1922; *s* of Sir John Blunden, 5th Bt and Phyllis Dorothy (*d* 1967), *d* of Philip Crampton Creaghe; *S* brother, 1985; *m* 1945, Jeannette Francesca

Alexandra, *e d* of Captain D. Macdonald, RNR; two *s* one *d. Educ*: Repton. Served RN, 1941–46 (1939–45 Star, Atlantic Star, Defence Medal). Estate Manager, Castle Blunden, 1947–60; engaged in marketing of industrial protective coatings, 1962–83; in art and art restoration, 1976–. *Recreations*: fishing, field sports, swimming, tennis, reading. *Heir: s* Hubert Chisholm Blunden, *b* 9 Aug. 1948. *Address*: 68 Ashgrove, Fortunestown, Tallaght, Co. Dublin. *T*: Dublin 520435. *Club*: Royal Dublin Society (Life Mem.).

BLUNKETT, David; Leader of Sheffield City Council, since 1980; *b* 6 June 1947; *m*; three *c. Educ*: night sch. and day release, Shrewsbury Coll. of Technol. and Richmond Coll. of Further Educn, Sheffield; Nat. Cert. in Business Studies, E Midlands Gas Bd; Sheffield Univ. (BA Hons Pol Theory and Instns); Huddersfield Holly Bank Coll. of Educn (Tech.) (PGCFE). Tutor in Industrial Relns, Barnsley Coll. of Technol., 1984–. Elected to Sheffield City Council at age of 22; Chm., Family and Community Services Cttee, 1976–80; Dep. Chm., AMA, 1984–. Joined Labour Party at age of 16; Mem., Labour Party NEC, 1983–; Chm., Labour Party Cttee on Local govt, 1984–. Prospective parly cand. (Lab), Sheffield Brightside, 1985–. *Publications*: (jtly) Local Enterprise and Workers' Plans, 1981; (jtly) Building from the Bottom: the Sheffield Experience, 1983. *Address*: 190 Main Street, Grenoside, Sheffield S30 3PR.

BLUNT, Christopher Evelyn, OBE 1945; FBA 1965; retired; *b* 16 July 1904; 2nd *s* of Rev. A. S. V. Blunt and Hilda Violet Blunt; *m* 1930, Elisabeth Rachel Bazley (*d* 1980); one *s* two *d. Educ*: Marlborough (Foundation Scholar). Entered merchant banking firm of Higginson & Co., 1924; partner, 1947; executive director of successor companies, 1950–64. Served War, 1939–46; 52 AA (TA) Regt; GHQ (Gen. Staff), BEF (despatches), Home Forces, 21 Army Group; SHAEF; retired 1946 (Col). FSA 1936; President: British Numismatic Soc., 1946–50; Royal Numismatic Soc., 1956–61; Wilts Arch. Soc., 1970–74; Soc. of Medieval Archaeol., 1978–80. Medals of Royal, British and Amer. Numismatic Socs. Officer Legion of Merit (USA), 1945. *Publications*: The Coinage of Athelstan, 1974; (with M. M. Archibald) Catalogue of Anglo-Saxon Coins in the British Museum 924–c 973, 1986; contributions to Numismatic Chronicle, British Numismatic Journal, Archæologia, etc. *Recreation*: numismatics. *Address*: Ramsbury Hill, Ramsbury, Marlborough, Wilts. *T*: Marlborough 20358. *Clubs*: Travellers', Pratt's.

BLUNT, Sir David Richard Reginald Harvey, 12th Bt *cr* 1720; *b* 8 Nov. 1938; *s* of Sir Richard David Harvey Blunt, 11th Bt and Elisabeth Malvine Ernestine, *d* of Comdr F. M. Fransen Van de Putte, Royal Netherlands Navy (retd); *S* father, 1975; *m* 1969, Sonia Tudor Rosemary (*née* Day); one *d. Heir: kinsman*: Robin Anthony Blunt, CEng, MIMechE [*b* 23 Nov. 1926; *m* 1st, 1949, Sheila Stuart (marr. diss. 1962), *d* of C. Stuart Brindley; one *s*; 2nd, 1962, June Elizabeth, *d* of Charles Wigginton; one *s*].

BLUNT, Maj.-Gen. Peter, CB 1978; MBE 1955; GM 1959; Chairman, since 1983 and Managing Director, since 1980, Angex Limited; Director, Associated Newspaper Holdings, since 1984; *b* 18 Aug. 1923; *s* of A. G. Blunt and M. Blunt; *m* 1949, Adrienne, *o d* of Gen. T. W. Richardson; three *s*. Joined Army aged 14 yrs, 1937; commnd Royal Fusiliers; served Duke of Cornwall's LI and Royal Scots Fusiliers, until 1946; foreign service, 1946–49; Staff Coll., 1957; Jt Services Staff Coll., 1963; RCDS, 1972; comd 26 Regt, Bridging, 1965; GSO 1 Def. Plans, FARELF, 1968; Comdr RCT 1 Corps, 1970; Dep. Transport Officer-in-Chief (Army), later Transp. Off.-in-Chief, 1973; Asst Chief of Personnel and Logistics (Army), MoD, 1977–78; Asst Chief of Defence Staff (Personnel and Logistics), MoD, 1978–79. Man. Dir, Earls Court Ltd, 1979–80; Exec. Vice-Chm., Brompton and Kensington Special Catering Co. Ltd, 1979–80; Jt Man. Dir, Angex-Watson, 1980–83. Col Comdt, RCT, 1974–. Specially apptd Comr, Royal Hosp., Chelsea, 1979. Liveryman, Co. of Carmen, 1973. *Recreation*: fishing. *Address*: Greenbank, Bracknell Lane, Hartley Wintney, Hants. *T*: Hartley Wintney 2313. *Club*: Army and Navy.

BLUNT, Wilfrid Jasper Walter; Curator of the Watts Gallery, Compton, 1959–85, now Emeritus; *b* 19 July 1901; *s* of late Rev. Arthur Stanley Vaughan Blunt and Hilda Violet Master. *Educ*: Marlborough Coll.; Worcester Coll., Oxford; Royal College of Art. Art Master, Haileybury Coll., 1923–38; Drawing Master, Eton Coll., 1938–59. ARCA (London) 1923. Introduced into the Public Schs the craft of pottery (Haileybury, 1927) and Italic handwriting (Eton, 1940). FLS 1969. *Publications*: The Haileybury Buildings, 1936; Desert Hawk, 1947; The Art of Botanical Illustration, 1950; Tulipomania, 1950; Black Sunrise, 1951; Sweet Roman Hand, 1952; Japanese Colour Prints, 1952; Georg Dionysius Ehret, 1953; Pietro's Pilgrimage, 1953; Sebastiano, 1956; Great Flower Books (with Sacheverell Sitwell and Patrick Synge), 1956; A Persian Spring, 1957; Lady Muriel, 1962; Of Flowers and a Village, 1963; Cockerell, 1964; Omar, 1966; Isfahan, 1966; John Christie of Glyndebourne, 1968; The Dream King, 1970; The Compleat Naturalist, 1971; The Golden Road to Samarkand, 1973; On Wings of Song, 1974; 'England's Michelangelo', 1975; The Ark in the Park, 1976; Splendours of Islam, 1976; In for a Penny: a prospect of Kew Gardens, 1978; (with Sandra Raphael) The Illustrated Herbal, 1979; Married to a Single Life: autobiography 1901–1938, 1983; Slow on the Feather: autobiography 1938–1959, 1986. *Recreations*: writing, formerly singing and travel. *Address*: The Curator's House, The Watts Gallery, Compton, near Guildford, Surrey. *T*: Guildford 810437.

BLYE, Douglas William Alfred, CMG 1979; OBE 1973; Economic and Financial Adviser, Government of Dubai; *b* 15 Dec. 1924; *s* of William Blye and Ethel Attwood; *m* 1955, Juanita Buckley. *Educ*: King's Road Sch., Herne Bay; Maidstone Polytechnic. ACMA. Served War, RAF, 1941–46. Various commercial and industrial appts in UK, 1947–55; Govt of Fedn of Malaya, 1955–58; Hong Kong Govt, 1958–85: Sec. for Monetary Affairs, Hong Kong, 1977–85. *Recreations*: squash, tennis. *Address*: HH The Ruler's Court, PO Box 12848, Dubai. *T*: Dubai 422883.

BLYTH, family name of **Baron Blyth.**

BLYTH, 4th Baron *cr* 1907; **Anthony Audley Rupert Blyth;** Bt 1895; *b* 3 June 1931; *er s* of 3rd Baron Blyth and Edna Myrtle (*d* 1952), *d* of Ernest Lewis, Wellington, NZ; *S* father, 1977; *m* 1st, 1954, Elizabeth Dorothea (marr. diss., 1962), *d* of R. T. Sparrow, Vancouver, BC; one *s* two *d*; 2nd, 1963, Oonagh Elizabeth Ann, *yr d* of late William Henry Conway, Dublin; one *s* one *d. Educ*: St Columba's College, Dublin. *Heir: s* Hon. Riley Audley John Blyth, *b* 4 March 1955. *Address*: Blythwood Estate, Athenry, Co. Galway.

BLYTH, Charles, (Chay Blyth), CBE 1972; BEM; Managing Director, British Clippers Ltd; Director, Sailing Ventures (Hampshire) Ltd, since 1969; *b* 14 May 1940; *s* of Robert and Jessie Blyth; *m* 1962, Maureen Margaret Morris; one *d. Educ*: Hawick High School. HM Forces, Para. Regt, 1958–67. Cadbury Schweppes, 1968–69. Rowed North Atlantic with Captain John Ridgway, June-Sept. 1966; circumnavigated the world westwards solo in yacht British Steel, 1970–71; circumnavigated the world eastwards with crew in yacht Great Britain II, 1973–74; Atlantic sailing record, Cape Verde to Antigua, 1977; won Round Britain Race in yacht Great Britain IV, 1978 (crew Robert James); won The Observer/Europe 1 doublehanded transatlantic race in record time, 1981 (crew Robert James). *Publications*: A Fighting Chance, 1966; Innocent Aboard, 1968; The Impossible Voyage, 1971; Theirs is the Glory, 1974. *Recreations*: sailing, horse-riding, hunting.

Address: Penquite Farm, Rosecraddoc, Liskeard, Cornwall PL14 5AQ. *Clubs*: Royal Southern Yacht, Royal Western Yacht.

BLYTH, Sir James, Kt 1985; Managing Director, The Plessey Co. plc, since 1986; *b* 8 May 1940; *s* of Daniel Blyth and Jane Power Carlton; *m* 1967, Pamela Anne Campbell Dixon; one *d* (one *s* decd). *Educ*: Spiers Sch.; Glasgow Univ. (MA Hons). Mobil Oil Co., 1963–69; General Foods Ltd, 1969–71; Mars Ltd, 1971–74; Director and General Manager: Lucas Batteries Ltd, 1974–77; Lucas Aerospace Ltd, 1977–81; Dir, Joseph Lucas Ltd, 1977–81; Head of Defence Sales, MoD, 1981–85; Man. Dir, Plessey Electronic Systems, 1985–86. Non-exec. Dir, Imperial Gp PLC, 1984–86. Mem. Council, SBAC, 1977–81, 1986–. Liveryman, Coachmakers' and Coach Harness Makers' Co. *Recreations*: ski-ing, tennis, paintings, theatre. *Clubs*: East India, Queen's.

BLYTH, John Douglas Morrison, CMG 1981; HM Diplomatic Service, retired; *b* 23 July 1924; *s* of late William Naismith Blyth and Jean (*née* Morrison); *m* 1st, 1949, Gabrielle Elodie (*née* Belloc) (*d* 1971); three *s* two *d*; 2nd, 1973, Lucy Anne (*née* Alcock); one *s* one *d. Educ*: Christ's Coll.; Lincoln Coll., Oxford (MA); Downing Coll., Cambridge (MA). Served War, RNVR, 1942–46. Editor, The Polar Record (publd by Scott Polar Res. Inst., Cambridge), 1949–54; joined FO, 1954; served: Geneva, 1955; Athens, 1959; Leopoldville, 1963; Accra, 1964; FO, 1966; Athens, 1968; FCO, 1972; Vienna, 1974; FCO, 1977. Pres., Hélène Heroys Literary Foundn, 1975–. Hon. Sec., Suffolk Preservation Soc., 1985–. *Publications*: articles in The Polar Record. *Recreations*: gardening, military history, enjoying wine. *Address*: Crownland Hall, Walsham-le-Willows, Suffolk IP31 3BU. *T*: Walsham-le-Willows 369. *Club*: Naval and Military.

BLYTHE, James Forbes, TD 1946; **His Honour Judge Blythe;** a Circuit Judge, since 1978; Solicitor; *b* Coventry, 11 July 1917; *s* of J. F. Blythe; *m* 1949, Margaret, *d* of P. D. Kinsey; two *d. Educ*: Wrekin Coll.; Birmingham Univ. (LLB). Commissioned TA, Royal Warwickshire Regt, 1936–53 (Major); served War of 1939–45 with BEF in France (Dunkirk), 1939–40; Central Mediterranean Force (Tunisia, Sicily, Corsica, S France and Austria), 1942–45; Air Liaison Officer GSO II (Ops) with RAF (Despatches). Admitted solicitor, 1947; private practitioner in partnership in Coventry and Leamington Spa, 1948. HM Deputy Coroner for City of Coventry and Northern Dist of Warwickshire, 1954–64; HM Coroner for City of Coventry, 1964–78; a Recorder of the Crown Court, 1972–78. Pres., Warwicks Law Soc., 1978–79. *Recreations*: shooting, sailing; past player and Sec. Coventry Football Club (RU). *Address*: Hazlewood, Upper Ladyes' Hill, Kenilworth, Warwickshire. *T*: Kenilworth 54168. *Clubs*: Army and Navy; Drapers (Coventry); Tennis Court (Leamington Spa).

BLYTHE, Rex Arnold; Under-Secretary, Board of Inland Revenue, 1981–86, retired; *b* 11 Nov. 1928; *s* of late Sydney Arnold Blythe and Florence Blythe (*née* Jones); *m* 1953, Rachel Ann Best; one *s* two *d. Educ*: Bradford Grammar Sch.; Trinity Coll., Cambridge (BA Classics). Entered Inland Revenue as Inspector of Taxes, 1953; Sen. Inspector, 1962; Principal Inspector, 1968; Asst Sec., 1974. *Recreations*: golf, photography, walking. *Address*: 32 Townsend Lane, Harpenden, Herts AL5 2QS. *T*: Harpenden 5833. *Club*: MCC.

BLYTON, family name of **Baron Blyton.**

BLYTON, Baron, *cr* 1964 (Life Peer); **William Reid Blyton;** *b* 2 May 1899; *s* of late Charles H. Blyton, retired labourer, and Hannah A. Blyton; *m* 1919, Jane B. Ord; three *d. Educ*: Elementary Education Holy Trinity Sch. and Dean Road Sch., South Shields. Served in HM Submarines in European War, 1914–18. Chm., Harton Miners' Lodge, Durham Miners' Assoc., 1928–41, Sec., 1941–45; Mem., Durham Miners' Exec. Cttee, 1930–32, 1942–43. Chm. South Shields Labour Party, 1928–29, 1931–32; Councillor, S Shields Borough Council, 1936–45; Chm. of South Shields Education Cttee, 1943, and of South Shields Electrical Cttee, 1937–40; MP (Lab) Houghton-le-Spring Div. of County Durham, 1945–64; late PPS to Ministry of Civil Aviation; resigned, 1949. Chm. High Sch. Governors and Chm. Secondary and Technical Cttee of South Shields. *Address*: 139 Brockley Avenue, South Shields, Tyne and Wear; Dylan Hotel, 14 Devonshire Terrace, W2.

BOAG, Prof. John Wilson; Professor of Physics as Applied to Medicine, University of London, Institute of Cancer Research, 1965–76, now Emeritus; *b* Elgin, Scotland, 20 June 1911; *s* of John and Margaret A. Boag; *m* 1938, Isabel Petrie; no *c. Educ*: Universities of Glasgow, Cambridge and Braunschweig. Engineer, British Thomson Houston Co., Rugby, 1936–41; Physicist, Medical Research Council, 1941–52; Visiting Scientist, National Bureau of Standards, Washington, DC, 1953–54; Physicist, British Empire Cancer Campaign, Mount Vernon Hospital, 1954–64; Royal Society (Leverhulme) Visiting Prof. to Poland, 1964. President: Hosp. Physicists' Assoc., 1959; Assoc. for Radiation Res. (UK), 1972–74; Internat. Assoc. for Radiation Res., 1970–74; British Inst. of Radiology, 1975–76. L. H. Gray Medal, ICRU, 1973; Barclay Medal, BIR, 1975. *Publications*: papers on radiation dosimetry, statistics, radiation chemistry, radiodiagnosis. *Address*: Flat 1, 40 Overton Road, Sutton, Surrey.

BOAL, John Graham; a Recorder of the Crown Court, since 1985; Senior Prosecuting Counsel to the Crown, Central Criminal Court, since 1985; *b* 24 Oct. 1943; *s* of late Surg. Captain Jackson Graham Boal, RN, and Dorothy Kenley Boal; *m* 1978, Elizabeth Mary East; one *s. Educ*: Eastbourne Coll.; King's Coll. London (LLB). Called to the Bar, Gray's Inn, 1966; Junior Treasury Counsel, 1977–85. *Recreations*: theatre, sport. *Address*: Queen Elizabeth Building, Temple, EC4Y 9BS. *Clubs*: Garrick, MCC; Royal Wimbledon Golf.

BOAM, Maj.-Gen. Thomas Anthony, CBE 1978 (OBE 1973); Commander, British Forces Hong Kong, and Major-General, Brigade of Gurkhas, 1985–Aug. 1987; *b* 14 Feb. 1932; *s* of late Lt-Col T. S. Boam, OBE, and of Mrs Boam; *m* 1961, Penelope Christine Mary Roberts; one *s* two *d. Educ*: Bradfield Coll.; RMA Sandhurst. Commissioned Scots Guards, 1952; Canal Zone, Egypt (with 1SG), 1952–54; GSO3, MO4 War Office, 1959–61; psc 1962; Kenya (with 2SG), 1963–64; DAA&QMG 4GDS Bde, 1964–65; Malaysia (with 1SG), 1966–67; BM 4GDS Bde, 1967–69; GSO1 (DS) Staff Coll., Camberley, 1970–71; CO 2SG, 1972–74; RCDS 1974–75; Comd BAAT Nigeria, 1976–78; BGS (Trg) HQ UKLF, 1978; Dep. Comdr and COS Hong Kong, 1979–81; Hd of British Defence Staff Washington, Mil. Attaché, 1981–83 and Defence Attaché, 1981–84. *Recreations*: shooting, fishing, gardening, sport. *Address*: c/o Barclays Bank, 23 Euston Road, NW1 2SB. *Club*: MCC.

BOARDMAN, family name of **Baron Boardman.**

BOARDMAN, Baron *cr* 1980 (Life Peer), of Welford in the County of Northamptonshire; **Thomas Gray Boardman,** MC 1944; TD 1952; DL; Chairman, National Westminster Bank, since 1983 (Director, since 1979; Chairman, Eastern Region, 1979–83); Director, MEPC PLC, since 1980; *b* 12 Jan. 1919; *s* of John Clayton Boardman, late of Daventry, and Janet Boardman, formerly Houston; *m* 1948, Norah Mary Deirdre, *widow* of John Henry Chaworth-Musters, Annesley Park, Nottingham, and *d* of Hubert Vincent Gough; two *s* one *d. Educ*: Bromsgrove. Served Northants Yeomanry, 1939–45 and subsequently; Commanding Northants Yeomanry, 1956. Qualified as a Solicitor, 1947. MP (C) Leicester

SW, Nov. 1967–74, Leicester South Feb.–Sept. 1974; Minister for Industry, DTI, 1972–74; Chief Sec. to Treasury, 1974. Jt Hon. Treas., Cons. Party, 1981–82. Chairman: Chamberlain Phipps Ltd, 1958–72; The Steetly Co. Ltd, 1978–83 (Dir, 1975–83); Dir, Allied Breweries Ltd, 1968–72 and 1974–77 (Vice-Chm., 1975–76). Pres., Assoc. of British Chambers of Commerce, 1977–80. Mem., Exec. Assoc. of Cons. Peers, 1981–84. DL Northants, 1977–, High Sheriff, Northants, 1979. *Recreation*: riding. *Address*: 29 Tufton Court, Tufton Street, SW1P 3QH. *T*: 01–222 6793; The Manor House, Welford, Northampton. *T*: Welford 235. *Club*: Cavalry and Guards.

See also Baron Ellenborough.

BOARDMAN, Harold; *b* 12 June 1907; *m* 1936, Winifred May, *d* of Jesse Thorlby, Derbys; one *d*. *Educ*: Bolton and Derby. Formerly Trade Union Official. Joined Labour party, 1924; formerly Chm., Derby Labour Party; for 3 yrs Mem. Derby Town Council. MP (Lab) Leigh, 1945–79; PPS to Ministry of Labour, 1947–51. ILO Confs in Geneva, 1947, 1949, 1950, and San Francisco, 1948; Delegate to Council of Europe, 1960, 1961. Former Exec. Mem., NW Industrial Develt Assoc., from 1946. *Address*: 18 Norris Road, Brooklands, Sale, Manchester.

BOARDMAN, Prof. John, FSA 1957, FBA 1969; Lincoln Professor of Classical Archaeology and Art, and Fellow of Lincoln College, University of Oxford, since 1978; *b* 20 Aug. 1927; *s* of Frederick Archibald Boardman; *m* 1952, Sheila Joan Lyndon Stanford; one *s* one *d*. *Educ*: Chigwell Sch.; Magdalene Coll., Cambridge (BA 1948, MA 1951, Walston Student, 1948–50; Cromer Greek Prize, 1959; Hon. Fellow 1984). 2nd Lt, Intell. Corps, 1950–52. Asst Dir, British Sch. at Athens, 1952–55; Asst Keeper, Ashmolean Museum, Oxford, 1955–59; Reader in Classical Archaeology, Univ. of Oxford, 1959–78; Fellow of Merton Coll., Oxford, 1963–78, Hon. Fellow, 1978. Geddes-Harrower Prof., Aberdeen Univ., 1974. Editor: Journal of Hellenic Studies, 1958–65; Lexicon Iconographicum, 1972–. Conducted excavations on Chios, 1953–55, and at Tocra in Libya, 1964–65. Delegate, OUP, 1979. Corr. Fellow, Bavarian Acad. of Scis, 1969; Fellow, Inst. of Etruscan Studies, Florence, 1983; Foreign Member: Royal Danish Acad., 1979; Acad. des Inscriptions et Belles Lettres, Institut de France, 1985. Hon. MRIA, 1986. *Publications*: Cretan Collection in Oxford, 1961; Date of the Knossos Tablets, 1963; Island Gems, 1963; Greek Overseas, 1964, rev. edn 1980; Greek Art, 1964, rev. edns 1973, 1984; Excavations at Tocra, vol. I 1966, vol. II 1973; Pre-Classical, 1967, repr. 1978; Greek Emporio, 1967; Engraved Gems, 1968; Archaic Greek Gems, 1968; Greek Gems and Finger Rings, 1970; (with D. Kurtz) Greek Burial Customs, 1971; Athenian Black Figure Vases, 1974; Athenian Red Figure Vases, 1975; Intaglios and Rings, 1975; Corpus Vasorum, Oxford, vol. 3, 1975; Greek Sculpture, Archaic Period, 1978; (with M. Robertson) Corpus Vasorum, Castle Ashby, 1978; (with M. L. Vollenweider) Catalogue of Engraved Gems, Ashmolean Museum, 1978; (with D. Scarisbrick) Harari Collection of Finger Rings, 1978; (with E. La Rocca) Eros in Greece, 1978; Escarabeos de Piedra de Ibiza, 1984; La Ceramica Antica, 1984; Greek Sculpture, Classical Period, 1985; (with D. Finn) The Parthenon and its Sculptures, 1985; (jtly) The Oxford Dictionary of the Classical World, 1986; articles in jls. *Address*: 11 Park Street, Woodstock, Oxford. *T*: Woodstock 811259. *Club*: Athenæum.

BOARDMAN, Sir Kenneth (Ormrod), Kt 1981; DL; Chairman, Boardman Securities Ltd, since 1952; Founder Chairman, Planned Giving Ltd, since 1959; *b* 18 May 1914; *s* of Edgar Nicholas Boardman and Emily Boardman; *m* 1939, Lucy Stafford; one *s* two *d*. *Educ*: St Peter's Sch., Swinton, Lancs. Trooper, Duke of Lancaster's Own Yeomanry, 1932–33; served War 1939–45, Major RA, 1942–46. Chm., K. O. Boardman Internat. Ltd, 1954–78. Hon. Treasurer, NW Area of Conservative Party, 1977–84; Member: Nat. Union of Cons. and Unionist Assocs, 1975–84 (Patron NW Area, 1984–); NW Industrial Council, 1967–84; several Cons. constituency offices 1984. Pres., Manchester E Euro Constituency, 1984–. Dist Chm., NSPCC 100th Anniv. Appeal, 1984; Pres., Stockport & Dist NSPCC, 1985–; Appeals Chm., John Charnley Trust, 1985–; Patron, Hallé 125th Anniv. Appeal, 1984. Chm., Stockport Parish Church Restoration Fund, 1974–. Liveryman, Farriers Co., 1965–. *Recreations*: gardening, reading and writing, horse racing. *Address*: Clarendon House, Carrwood Road, Bramhall, Cheshire SK7 3LR. *Clubs*: St James's, (Manchester); Royal Anglesey Yacht (Beaumaris).

BOARDMAN, Norman Keith, PhD, ScD; FRS 1978; FAA; Chairman and Chief Executive, Commonwealth Scientific and Industrial Research Organization, since 1985; *b* 16 Aug. 1926; *s* of William Robert Boardman and Margaret Boardman; *m* 1952, Mary Clayton Shepherd; two *s* five *d*. *Educ*: Melbourne Univ. (BSc 1946, MSc 1949); St John's Coll., Cambridge (PhD 1954, ScD 1974). FAA 1972. ICI Fellow, Cambridge, 1953–55; Fulbright Scholar, Univ. of Calif, LA, 1964–66. Res. Officer, Wool Res. Section, CSIRO, 1949–51; CSIRO Div. of Plant Industry: Sen. Res. Scientist, 1956; Principal Res. Scientist, 1961; Sen. Prin. Res. Scientist, 1966; Chief Res. Scientist, 1968; Mem. Exec., CSIRO, 1977–85. Member: Aust. Res. Grants Cttee, 1971–75; Council, ANU, 1979–; Bd, Aust. Centre for Internat. Agricl Research, 1982–; Nat. Water Research Council, 1982–85. Pres., Aust. Biochem. Soc., 1976–78; Treas., Aust. Acad. of Sci, 1978–81. Corresp. Mem., Amer. Soc. of Plant Physiologists. David Syme Res. Prize, Melbourne Univ., 1967; Lemberg Medal, Aust. Biochem. Soc., 1969. *Publications*: scientific papers on plant biochemistry, partic. photosynthesis and structure, function and biogenesis of chloroplasts. *Recreations*: reading, tennis, listening to music. *Address*: 6 Somers Crescent, Forrest, ACT 2603, Australia. *T*: (062) 95–1746. *Club*: Commonwealth (Canberra).

BOAS, Leslie, OBE 1961; HM Diplomatic Service, retired; *b* Buenos Aires, Argentine, 25 Feb. 1912; *s* of late Gustavus Thomas Boas and late Flora Shield McDonald; *m* 1st, 1944, Margaret Ann Jackson (marr. diss. 1951); one *s*; 2nd, 1951, Patricia Faye Fenning (*d* 1972); 3rd, 1972, Natalie K. Prado (*née* Kitchen). *Educ*: Spain; Gibraltar; Granada University. In business, 1933–39. Joined Coldstream Guards, 1940; commissioned in Royal Ulster Rifles, 1940; invalided out of Army as result of injuries, 1944. Joined Latin American Section of BBC, 1944. Apptd Temp. Press Attaché, Panama, 1946; Temp. First Sec. (Inf.), Bogotá, 1948; Temp. First Sec. (Inf.), Caracas, 1952; estab. as a Permanent First Sec., 1959; Regional Inf. Counsellor, Caracas, 1962–69; Chargé d'Affaires, Panama, April–May 1964; Ambassador to Santo Domingo, 1969–72. Dir, Secretariat of British Bicentennial Liaison Cttee of FCO, 1973–75. *Recreations*: golf, chess, Latin American studies. *Address*: c/o The Royal Bank of Scotland, 97 New Bond Street, W1Y 0EU. *Clubs*: Bucks; Jockey (Bogotá, Colombia).

BOASE, Martin; Chairman, Boase Massimi Pollitt plc, since 1977 (Joint Chairman, 1977–79); *b* 14 July 1932; *s* of Prof. Alan Martin Boase and Elizabeth Grizelle Boase; *m* 1st, 1960, Terry Ann Moir (marr. diss. 1971); one *s* one *d*; 2nd, 1974, Pauline Valerie Brownrigg; one *s* one *d*. *Educ*: Bedales Sch.; Rendcomb Coll.; New Coll., Oxford. MA; FIPA 1976. Executive, The London Press Exchange, Ltd, 1958–60; Pritchard Wood and Partners, Ltd: Manager, 1961–65; Dir, then Dep. Man. Dir, 1965–68; Founding Partner and Joint Man. Dir, The Boase Massimi Pollitt Partnership, Ltd, 1968. *Recreation*: the Turf. *Address*: 104 Hamilton Terrace, NW8. *T*: 01–286 7821; Brook House, North Stoke, Oxon. *T*: Wallingford 37606.

BOATENG, Prof. Ernest Amano, GM 1968; Environmental and Educational Consultant; Executive Chairman, Environmental Protection Council, Ghana, 1973–81, now retired; *b* 30 Nov. 1920; 2nd *s* of Rev. Christian Robert Boateng and Adelaide Akonobea, Aburi, Ghana; *m* 1955, Evelyn Kensema Danso, *e d* of late Rev. Robert Opong Danso, and of Victoria Danso, Aburi; four *d*. *Educ*: Achimota Coll.; St Peter's Hall, Oxford (Gold Coast Govt Schol.). Henry Oliver Beckit Meml Prize, 1949; BA (Geog.) 1949, MA 1953, MLitt 1954. UC Ghana: Lectr in Geography, 1950–57; Sen. Lectr, 1958–61; Prof. of Geography, 1961–73; Dean, Faculty of Social Studies, 1962–69; Principal, 1969–71, Vice-Chancellor, 1971–73, Univ. of Cape Coast, Ghana. Vis. Asst Prof., Univ. of Pittsburgh and UCLA, 1960–61. Pres., Ghana Geographical Assoc., 1959–69; Foundn Fellow, Ghana Acad. of Arts and Sciences (Sec. 1959–62, Pres., 1973–76); Mem., Unesco Internat. Adv. Cttee on Humid Tropics Research, 1961–63; Mem., Scientific Council for Africa, 1963–; Mem., Nat. Planning Commn of Ghana, 1961–64; Smuts Vis. Fellow, Univ. of Cambridge, 1965–66; Vis. Prof., Univ. of Pittsburgh, 1966; Deleg., UN Conf. on geographical names, Geneva, 1967; Mem., Council for Scientific and Industrial Research, Ghana, 1967–75; Dir, Ghana Nat. Atlas Project, 1965–77; Chm., Geographical Cttee, Ghana 1970 population census; Member: Nat. Economic Planning Council of Ghana, 1974–78; Chm., Land Use Planning Cttee of Ghana, 1978–79; Pres., Governing Council of UNEP, 1979, Senior Consultant, 1980–; Member: Constituent Assembly for drafting constitution for third Republic of Ghana, 1978–79; Presidential Task Force on Investments, Ghana, 1980; Nat. Council for Higher Educn, 1975–82; Chm., W African Exams Council, 1977–85. Pres., Ghana Wildlife Soc., 1974–. Alternate Leader, Ghana Delegn to UN Conf., Vancouver, 1976. Hon. Mem., Ghana Inst. of Planners, 1984. FRSA 1973. Hon. DLitt Ghana, 1979. Nat. Book Award, Ghana, 1978. *Publications*: A Geography of Ghana, 1959; (contrib.) Developing Countries of the World, 1968; (contrib.) Population Growth and Economic Development in Africa, 1972; Independence and Nation Building in Africa, 1973; A Political Geography of Africa, 1978; African Unity: the dream and the reality (J. B. Danquah Memorial Lectures 1978), 1979; various pamphlets, Britannica and other encyclopaedia articles and articles in geographical and other jls and reference works. *Recreations*: photography, gardening. *Address*: Environmental Consultancy Services, PO Box 84, Trade Fair Site, Accra, Ghana. *T*: Accra 77875; (home) 3 Aviation Road, Airport Residential Area, Accra, Ghana.

BOATENG, Paul Yaw; solicitor; *b* 14 June 1951; *s* of Eleanor and Kwaku Boateng; *m* 1980, Janet Alleyne; one *s* three *d*. *Educ*: Ghana Internat. Sch.; Accra Acad.; Apsley Grammar Sch.; Bristol Univ. (LLB Hons); Coll. of Law. Admitted Solicitor, 1976; Solicitor, Paddington Law Centre, 1976–79; Solicitor and Partner, B. M. Birnberg and Co., 1979–. Legal Advr, Scrap Sus Campaign, 1977–81. Greater London Council: Mem. (Lab) for Walthamstow, 1981–86; Chm., Police Cttee, 1981–86; Vice-Chm., Ethnic Minorities Cttee, GLC, 1981–86. Contested (Lab) Hertfordshire W, 1983; Prospective Parly Cand. (Lab.), Brent South, 1985–. Chairman: Afro-Caribbean Educn Resource Project, 1978–; Westminster CRC, 1979–81; Vice-Pres., Waltham Forest CRC, 1981–. Member: NEC Lab. Party Sub-Cttee on Human Rights, 1979–83; Lab. Party Jt Cttee on Crime and Policing, 1984–; Home Sec.'s Adv. Council on Race Relations, 1981–86; WCC Commn on prog. to combat racism, 1984–; Police Training Council, 1981–85; Exec., NCCL, 1980–86. Chm. Governors, Priory Park Sch., 1978–84; Governor, Police Staff Coll., Bramshill, 1981–84. Mem. Bd, ENO, 1984–. Broadcaster. *Recreations*: escapist. *Clubs*: Mangrove; Black and White Café (Bristol).

BOCK, Prof. Claus Victor, MA, DrPhil; Professor of German Language and Literature, Westfield College, University of London, 1969–84, now Emeritus; Hon. Research Fellow, Westfield College, 1984; *b* Hamburg, 7 May 1926; *o s* of Frederick Bock, merchant and manufacturer, and Margot (*née* Meyerhof). *Educ*: Quaker Sch., Eerde, Holland; Univs of Amsterdam, Manchester, Basle. DrPhil (insigni cum laude) Basle 1955. Asst Lectr in German, Univ. of Manchester, 1956–58; University of London: Lectr, Queen Mary Coll., 1958–69; Reader in German Lang. and Lit., 1964; Chm., Bd of Studies in Germanic Langs and Lit., 1970–73; Hon. Dir, Inst. of Germanic Studies, 1973–81; Dean, Fac. of Arts, 1980–84; Mem., Senate, 1981–83; Mem., Acad. Council, 1981–83; Mem., Central Research Fund (A), 1981–84. Mem. Council, English Goethe Soc., 1965–; Chm., Stichting Castum Peregrini, 1981– (Mem., 1971–). Hon. Pres., Assoc. of Teachers of German, 1973–75. Mem., Maatschappij der Nederlandse Letteren, 1977. Mem. Editl Bd, Bithell Series of Dissertations, 1978–84. Officer, Order of Merit (FRG), 1984. *Publications*: Deutsche erfahren Holland 1725–1925, 1956; Q. Kuhlmann als Dichter, 1957; ed (with Margot Ruben) K. Wolfskehl Ges. Werke, 1960; ed (with G. F. Senior) Goethe the Critic, 1960; Pente Pigadia und die Tagebücher des Clement Harris, 1962; ed (with L. Helbing) Fr. Gundolf Briefwechsel mit H. Steiner und E. R. Curtius, 1963; Wort-Konkordanz zur Dichtung Stefan Georges, 1964; ed (with L. Helbing) Fr. Gundolf Briefe Neue Folge, 1965; A Tower of Ivory?, 1970; (with L. Helbing and K. Kluncker) Stefan George: Dokumente seiner Wirkung, 1974; (ed) London German Studies, 1980; (with K. Kluncker) Wolfgang Cordan: Jahre der Freundschaft, 1982; Untergetaucht unter Freunden, 1985; articles in English and foreign jls and collections. *Recreation*: foreign travel. *Address*: Westfield College, Kidderpore Avenue, NW3 7ST. *T*: 01–435 7141; 8 Heath Drive, NW3 7SN. *T*: 01–435 8598.

BOCKETT, Herbert Leslie, CMG 1961; Member, Shipping Industry Tribunal, since 1972; Professional Accountant, and Member New Zealand Society of Accountants; *b* 29 June 1905; *s* of C. F. Bockett and L. M. Bockett (*née* Bridger); *m* 1932, Constance Olive Ramsay; two *d*. *Educ*: Dilworth Sch.; Seddon Memorial Technical Coll. Joined NZ Public Service, 1921; Accountant, Unemployment Board, 1934; Asst Director: Social Security Dept, 1939; National Service Dept, 1940; Controller of Man-power, 1942; Dir of National Service, 1944; Sec. of Labour, New Zealand, 1947–64; retd Dec. 1964. Chm., Workers' Compensation Bd, NZ, 1960–75. *Recreation*: bowls. *Address*: 189 The Parade, Island Bay, Wellington, NZ. *T*: 838–549.

BODDIE, Donald Raikes; Consultant in Public Affairs, since 1975; *b* 27 June 1917; *o s* of William Henry and Violet May Boddie; *m* 1941, Barbara Stuart Strong; one *s*. *Educ*: Colston's Sch., Bristol. Joined: London Star, 1942–47; Natal Mercury, Durban, 1947–52; London Evening News, 1953 (held various exec. posts, to Dep. Editor, 1966 and Editor, 1972–74); Dir, Harmsworth Publications Ltd, 1973–74; Vice-Chm., Evening News Ltd, 1974. *Recreations*: travel, theatre, cinematography. *Address*: 87 Regent Street, W1. *T*: 01–439 6992.

BODDINGTON, Ewart Agnew, JP; Chairman, Boddingtons Breweries PLC, since 1970; *b* 7 April 1927; *m* 1954, Vine Anne Clayton; two *s* one *d*. *Educ*: Stowe Sch., Buckingham; Trinity Coll., Cambridge (MA). Jt Man. Dir, Boddingtons', 1957, Man. Dir, 1980. Dir, Northern Bd, National Westminster Bank, 1977–. Pres., Inst. of Brewing, 1972–74; Chm., Brewers' Soc., 1984–85; Mem., Brewers' Co., 1980–. JP Macclesfield, 1959; High Sheriff of Cheshire, 1978–79. Hon. MA Manchester, 1977. *Recreations*: shooting, golf, fishing, music. *Address*: Fanshawe Brook Farm, Henbury, Macclesfield. *T*: Marton Heath 387.

BODDINGTON, Lewis, CBE 1956; *b* 13 Nov. 1907; *s* of James and Anne Boddington; *m* 1936, Morfydd, *d* of William Murray; no *c*. *Educ*: Lewis' Sch., Pengam; City of Cardiff Technical Coll.; University Coll. of S Wales and Monmouthshire. Pupil Engineer, Fraser & Chalmers Engineering Works, Erith, 1928–31; Asst to Major H. N. Wylie, 1931–36;

Royal Aircraft Establishment, 1936; Head of Catapult Section, 1938; Supt of Design Offices, 1942–45; Head of Naval Aircraft Dept, 1945–51; Asst Dir (R&D) Naval, Min. of Supply, 1951–53; Dir Aircraft R&D (RN), 1953–59; Dir-Gen., Aircraft R&D, 1959–60; Dir and Consultant, Westland Aircraft, 1961–72. Medal of Freedom of USA (Bronze Palm), 1958. *Address:* Flat 5 Bermuda Court, 20 Winn Road, Southampton SO2 1WT.

BODDY, Jack Richard, MBE 1973; JP; Group Secretary, Agricultural and Allied Workers Trade Group, Transport and General Workers Union, since 1982 (General Secretary, National Union of Agricultural and Allied Workers, 1978–82); *b* 23 Aug. 1922; *s* of Percy James Boddy and Lucy May Boddy, JP; *m* 1943, Muriel Lilian (*née* Webb); three *s* one *d*. *Educ:* City of Norwich Sch. Agricultural worker, 1939; farm foreman, 1943. District Organiser: Lincolnshire NUAAW, 1953; Norfolk NUAAW, 1960. Mem., TUC Gen. Council, 1978–83. Leader, Workers' side, Agricl Wages Bd, 1978–. Member: Agricl Cttee, EDC, 1978–; Economic and Social Cttee, EEC, 1980; Food and Drink Cttee, EDC, 1984–; Industrial Injuries Adv. Cttee, DHSS. Freeman, City of Norwich. JP Swaffham, 1947. *Recreation:* caravanning. *Address:* (home) 36 Station Street, Swaffham, Norfolk. *T:* Swaffham 22916; (office) 308 Gray's Inn Road, WC1X 8DS. *T:* 01–278 7801.

BODEN, Edward Arthur; retired; Agent-General for Saskatchewan, Canada, 1973–77; *b* 13 Nov. 1911; *s* of English and Welsh parents; *m* 1939, Helen Harriet Saunders; one *s* one *d*. *Educ:* Cutknife, Saskatchewan, Canada. Born and raised on a Saskatchewan farm and actively farmed until 1949, retaining interest in farm until 1973. Royal Canadian Mounted Police, 1937–39. Saskatchewan Wheat Pool and Canadian Fedn of Agriculture, 1939–73; held several active positions in these organisations and retired, as 1st Vice-Pres., 1973; in this field acted on various provincial and national govtl bds and cttees; Advr to Saskatchewan Dept of Industry and Commerce, 1977–78; policy Advr, Dept of Agriculture, and Co-ordinator of Sask's 75th Anniv. Celebration for Agricl features 1980, 1979–81; with others, rep. Canada at internat. agricultural confs in different parts of the world. Sen. Counsellor, Provincial Sen. Citizens' Council, 1982–. *Recreations:* boxing, hunting. *Address:* Box 988, Battleford, Saskatchewan S0M 0E0, Canada.

BODEN, Leonard, RP; FRSA; portrait painter; *b* Greenock, Scotland, 1911; *s* of John Boden; *m* Margaret Tulloch (portrait painter, as Margaret Boden, PS, FRSA); one *d*. *Educ:* Sedbergh; Sch. of Art, Glasgow; Heatherley Sch. of Art, London. *Official portraits* include: HM Queen Elizabeth II; HRH The Prince Philip, Duke of Edinburgh; HM Queen Elizabeth the Queen Mother; HRH The Prince of Wales; The Princess Royal; HH Pope Pius XII; Field Marshals Lord Milne and Lord Slim, Margaret Thatcher, and many others. Vice-President: Artists' Gen. Benevolent Instn; St Ives Soc. of Artists; Governor, Christ's Hospital. Freeman, City of London; Liveryman, Painter-Stainers Co. Gold Medal, Paris Salon. *Work reproduced in:* The Connoisseur, The Artist, Fine Art Prints. *Address:* 36 Arden Road, N3 3AN. *T:* 01–346 5706. *Clubs:* Savage, Chelsea Arts.

BODEN, Prof. Margaret Ann, PhD; FBA 1983; Professor of Philosophy and Psychology, University of Sussex, since 1980; *b* 26 Nov. 1936; *d* of late Leonard Forbes Boden, OBE, LLB and Violet Dorothy Dawson; *m* 1967, John Raymond Spiers (marr. diss. 1981); one *s* one *d*. *Educ:* City of London Sch. for Girls; Newnham Coll., Cambridge (Major schol.; MA); Harvard Grad. Sch. (Harkness Fellow; AM, PhD). Asst Lectr, then Lectr, in Philosophy, Birmingham Univ., 1959–65; Sussex University: Lectr, 1965–72; Reader, 1972–80. Vis. Scientist, Yale Univ., 1979. Co-founder, Dir, 1968–85, Sec., 1968–79, Harvester Press. *Publications:* Purposive Explanation in Psychology, 1972; Artificial Intelligence and Natural Man, 1977; Piaget, 1979; Minds and Mechanisms, 1981; General Editor: Explorations in Cognitive Science; Harvester Studies in Cognitive Science; Harvester Studies in Philosophy; contribs to philosophical and psychological jls. *Recreations:* dress-making, dreaming about the South Pacific. *Address:* c/o Cognitive Studies Programme, University of Sussex, Brighton BN1 9QN. *T:* Brighton 606755. *Club:* Reform.

BODEN, Thomas Bennion, OBE 1978; JP; Deputy President, National Farmers' Union of England and Wales, 1979; an authority on structural reform in farming; *b* 23 Oct. 1915; *s* of late Harry Bertram Boden and Florence Nellie Mosley; *m* 1939, Dorothy Eileen Ball; one *s* two *d*. *Educ:* Alleynes Grammar Sch., Uttoxeter; Nottingham Univ. BSc course up to final year, when moved into farming on death of father, 1937; became involved in agricultural politics through NFU, 1948; office holder of NFU, 1977. Chm., EEC Adv. Cttee on Questions of Agricl Structure Policy. JP Staffs 1957. *Publications:* articles on agricultural taxation, farm structures in EEC, farm finance, young new entrants into farming. *Recreations:* cricket, tennis, swimming, hockey. *Address:* Denstone Hall, Denstone, Uttoxeter, Staffs. *T:* Rocester 590243. *Clubs:* Farmers', NFU.

BODGER; *see* Steele-Bodger.

BODILLY, Sir Jocelyn, Kt 1969; VRD; Chairman, Industrial Tribunals for London, 1976–86, retired; Chief Justice of the Western Pacific, 1965–75; *b* 1913; *m* 1st, 1936, Phyllis Maureen (*d* 1963), *d* of Thomas Cooper Gotch, ARA; 2nd, 1964, Marjorie, *d* of Walter Fogg. *Educ:* Munro Coll., Jamaica; Schloss Schule, Baden; Wadham Coll., Oxford. Called to Bar, Inner Temple, 1937; engaged in private practice until War; Royal Navy until 1946; RNVR, 1937–56 (Lt-Comdr (S)); Lt-Comdr, RNR, Hong Kong, 1961–65. High Court Judge, Sudan, 1946–55; Crown Counsel, Hong Kong, 1955, Principal Crown Counsel, 1961–65. *Address:* Myrtle Cottage, St Peters Hill, Newlyn, Penzance, Cornwall. *Club:* Royal Ocean Racing.

BODMER, Sir Walter (Fred), Kt 1986; FRS 1974; FRCPath 1984; Director of Research, Imperial Cancer Research Fund, since 1979; *b* 10 Jan. 1936; *s* of Dr Ernest Julius and Sylvia Emily Bodmer; *m* 1956, Julia Gwynaeth Pilkington; two *s* one *d*. *Educ:* Manchester Grammar Sch.; Clare Coll., Cambridge. BA 1956, MA, PhD 1959, Cambridge. Research Fellow 1958–61, Official Fellow 1961, Clare Coll., Cambridge; Demonstrator in Genetics, Univ. of Cambridge, 1960–62; Asst Prof. 1962–66, Associate Prof. 1966–68, Prof. 1968–70, Dept of Genetics, Stanford Univ.; Prof. of Genetics, Univ. of Oxford, 1970–79. Member: BBC Gen. Adv. Council, 1981–; Chm., BBC Sci. Consultative Gp, 1981–; Council, Internat. Union Against Cancer, 1982–; Adv. Bd for Res. Councils, 1983–; Vice-Pres., Royal Instn, 1981–82. Trustee: BM (Natural History), 1983–; Sir John Soane's Mus., 1983–. Pres., Royal Statistical Soc., 1984–85 (Vice-Pres., 1983–84). For. Associate, US Nat. Acad. of Scis, 1981; For. Hon. Mem., Amer. Acad. Arts and Scis, 1972; Hon. Mem., Amer. Assoc. of Immunologists. Hon. Fellow, Keble Coll Oxford, 1982; Hon. FRCP 1985; Hon. FRCS 1986. William Allan Meml Award, Amer. Soc. Human Genetics, 1980; Conway Evans Prize, RCP/Royal Soc., 1982; Rabbi Shai Shacknai Meml Prize Lectr, 1983; John Alexander Meml Prize and Lectureship, Univ. of Pennsylvania Med. Sch., 1984; Rose Payne Dist. Scientists Lectureship, Amer. Soc. for Histocompatibility and Immunogenetics, 1985; Bernal Lectr, Royal Soc., 1986. *Publications:* The Genetics of Human Populations (with L. L. Cavalli-Sforza), 1971; (with A. Jones) Our Future Inheritance: choice or chance?, 1974; (with L. L. Cavalli-Sforza) Genetics, Evolution and Man, 1976; research papers in genetical, statistical and mathematical jls, etc. *Recreations:* playing the piano, riding, swimming. *Address:* Imperial Cancer Research Fund, Lincoln's Inn Fields, WC2. *T:* 01–242 0200. *Club:* Athenæum.

BODMIN, Archdeacon of; *see* Temple, Ven. G. F.

BODY, Sir Richard (Bernard Frank Stewart), Kt 1986; MP (C) Holland with Boston, since 1966; *b* 18 May 1927; *s* of Lieut-Col Bernard Richard Body, formerly of Hyde End, Shinfield, Berks; *m* 1959, Marion, *d* of late Major H. Graham, OBE; one *s* one *d*. Called to the Bar, Middle Temple, 1949. Underwriting Mem. of Lloyd's. Contested (C) Rotherham, 1950; Abertillery bye-election, 1950; Leek, 1951; MP (C) Billericay Div., Essex, 1955–Sept. 1959. Member: Jt Select Cttee on Consolidation of Law, 1975–; Commons Select Cttee on Agric., 1979– (Chm., 1986–); Chm., Open Seas Forum, 1971–; Pres., Cobden Club, 1981–. Jt Chm., Council, Get Britain Out referendum campaign, 1975. Vice-Pres., Small Farmers' Assoc., 1985–. *Publications:* The Architect and the Law, 1954; (contrib.) Destiny or Delusion, 1971; (ed jtly) Freedom and Stability in the World Economy, 1976; Agriculture: The Triumph and the Shame, 1982; Farming in the Clouds, 1984. *Address:* Jewell's Farm, Stanford Dingley, near Reading, Berks. *T:* Reading 744295. *Clubs:* Carlton, Reform, Farmers'.

BOEGNER, Jean-Marc; Commandeur, Légion d'Honneur; Commandeur, Ordre National du Mérite; Ambassadeur de France, 1973; *b* 3 July 1913; *s* of Marc and Jeanne Boegner; *m* 1945, Odilie de Moustier; three *d*. *Educ:* Lycée Janson-de-Sailly; Ecole Libre des Sciences Politiques; Paris University (LèsL). Joined French diplomatic service, 1939; Attaché: Berlin, 1939; Ankara, 1940; Beirut, 1941; Counsellor: Stockholm, 1945; The Hague, 1947; Ministry of Foreign Affairs, Paris, 1952–58; Counsellor to Charles de Gaulle, 1958–59; Ambassador to Tunisia, 1959–60; Permanent Representative of France: to EEC, 1961–72; to OECD, 1975–78. *Publication:* Le Marché commun de Six à Neuf, 1974. *Address:* 19 rue de Lille, 75007 Paris, France.

BOERMA, Addeke Hendrik; Director-General, Food and Agriculture Organisation of the United Nations, 1968–75; *b* 3 April 1912; *m* 1953, Dinah Johnston; five *d*. *Educ:* Agricultural Univ., Wageningen. Netherlands Farmers' Organisation, 1935–38; Ministry of Agriculture of the Netherlands, 1938–45; Commissioner for Foreign Agricultural Relations, 1946; FAO positions: Regional Representative for Europe, 1948–51; Dir, Economics Div., 1951–58; Head of Programme and Budgetary Service, 1958–62; Asst Dir-Gen., 1960; Exec. Dir, World Food Programme, 1962–67. Holds Hon. Degrees from Univs in USA, Netherlands, Belgium, Hungary, Canada, Italy and Greece. Wateler Peace Prize, Carnegie Foundn, The Hague, 1976. Comdr, Netherlands Order of Lion; Commander, Order of Leopold II, Belgium; Officer, Ordre Mérite Agricole, France; Cavaliere di Gran Croce (Italy). *Address:* Prinz Eugenstrasse 44/10, 1040 Vienna, Austria.

BOEVEY, Sir Thomas (Michael Blake) C.; *see* Crawley-Boevey.

BOGARDE, Dirk; *see* Van den Bogaerde, D. N.

BOGDANOV, Michael; an Associate Director of the National Theatre of Great Britain, since 1980; Joint Artistic Director, English Shakespeare Company, since 1986; *b* 15 Dec. 1938; *s* of Francis Benzion Bogdin and Rhoda Rees Bogdin; *m* 1966, Patsy Ann Warwick; two *s* one *d*. *Educ:* Lower School of John Lyon, Harrow; Univ. of Dublin Trinity Coll. (MA); Univs of the Sorbonne, and Munich. Writer, with Terence Brady, ATV series, Broad and Narrow, 1965; Producer/Director with Telefis Eireann, 1966–68; opening production of Theatre Upstairs, Royal Court, A Comedy of the Changing Years, 1969; The Bourgeois Gentilhomme, Oxford Playhouse, 1969; Asst Dir, Royal Shakespeare Theatre Co., 1970–71; Associate Dir, Peter Brook's A Midsummer Night's Dream, Stratford 1970, New York 1971, World Tour 1972; Dir, Two Gentlemen of Verona, São Paulo, Brazil, 1971; Associate to Jean Louis Barrault, Rabelais, 1971; Associate Director: Tyneside Th. Co., 1971–73; Haymarket Th., Leicester; Director: Phoenix Th., Leicester, 1973–77; Young Vic Th., London, 1978–80; Directed: The Taming of the Shrew, RSC, Stratford 1978, London 1979 (SWET Dir of the Year award, 1979); The Seagull, Toho Th. Co., Tokyo, 1980; Shadow of a Gunman, RSC, 1980; The Knight of the Burning Pestle, RSC, 1981; Hamlet, Dublin, 1983; Romeo and Juliet, Tokyo, 1983, RSC, 1986; The Mayor of Zalamea, Washington, 1984; Measure for Measure, Stratford, Ont., 1985; Mutiny (musical), 1985; Donnerstag aus Licht, Royal Opera House, 1985; National Theatre productions: Sir Gawain and the Green Knight, The Hunchback of Notre Dame, 1977–78; The Romans in Britain, Hiawatha, 1980; One Woman Plays, The Mayor of Zalamea, The Hypochondriac, 1981; Uncle Vanya, The Spanish Tragedy, 1982; Lorenzaccio, 1983; You Can't Take it With You, 1983; Strider, 1984. Deviser and Presenter, Shakespeare Lives, TV series, 1983. Co-author, plays, adaptations and children's theatre pieces. *Recreations:* cricket, football, music, farmhouse in Wales. *Address:* c/o The National Theatre, SE1.

BOGDANOVICH, Peter; film director, writer, actor; *b* Kingston, NY, 30 July; *s* of Borislav Bogdanovich and Herma Robinson; *m* 1st, 1962, Polly Platt (marr. diss. 1970); two *d*; 2nd, 1971, Cybill Shepherd (marr. diss. 1978). *Educ:* Collegiate Sch., New York; Stella Adler Theatre Studio. Owner, Saticoy Productions Inc., 1968–; Co-Founder, Directors Co., 1972, Copa de Oro Productions, 1973–; Owner Moon Pictures, 1981–; Gen. Partner, Bogdanovich Film Partners, 1982; Member: Dirs Guild of America; Writers' Guild of America; Acad. of Motion Picture Arts and Sciences. *Theatre:* Actor, Amer. Shakespeare Fest., 1956, NY Shakespeare Fest., 1958; Dir and producer, off-Broadway: The Big Knife, 1959; Camino Real, Ten Little Indians, Rocket to the Moon, 1961; Once in a Lifetime, 1964. *Films include:* The Wild Angels (2nd-Unit Dir, co-writer, actor) 1966; Targets (dir, co-writer, prod., actor), 1968; The Last Picture Show (dir, co-writer), 1971 (NY Film Critics' Award, British Acad. Award); Directed by John Ford (dir, writer, prod.), 1971; What's Up, Doc? (dir, co-writer, prod.), 1972 (Writers' Guild of America Award); Paper Moon (dir, prod., co-writer), 1973 (Silver Shell Award, Spain); Daisy Miller (dir, co-writer, prod.), 1974 (Brussels Festival Award); At Long Last Love (dir, writer, prod.), 1975; Nickelodeon (dir, co-writer), 1976; Saint Jack (dir, co-writer, actor), 1979 (Critics' Prize, Venice Festival); They All Laughed (dir, writer), 1981; Mask (dir). *Publications:* The Cinema of Orson Welles, 1961; The Cinema of Howard Hawks, 1962; The Cinema of Alfred Hitchcock, 1963; John Ford, 1968; Fritz Lang in America, 1969; Allan Dwan: the last pioneer, 1971; Pieces of Time (Picture Shows in UK): Peter Bogdanovich on the Movies 1973–74; The Killing of the Unicorn: Dorothy Ruth Stratten, 1960–1980, a Memoir, 1983; articles in Esquire, New York Times, Village Voice, Cahiers du Cinema, Los Angeles Times, New York Magazine, Vogue, Variety etc. *Address:* c/o CPK, 2040 Avenue of the Stars, Century City, Calif 90067, USA.

BOGGIS-ROLFE, Hume, CB 1971; CBE 1962; farmer; *b* 20 Oct. 1911; *s* of Douglass Horace Boggis-Rolfe and Maria Maud (*née* Bailey); *m* 1941, Anne Dorothea, *e d* of Capt. Eric Noble, Henley-on-Thames; two *s* one *d*. *Educ:* Westminster Sch.; Freiburg Univ.; Trinity Coll., Cambridge. Called to Bar, Middle Temple, 1935. Army, Intelligence Corps, 1939–46 (Lieut-Col). Private Sec. to Lord Chancellor, 1949–50; Asst Solicitor in Lord Chancellor's Office, 1951–65; Sec. to Law Commn, 1965–68; Deputy Clerk of the Crown in Chancery, and Asst Perm. Sec. to Lord Chancellor, 1968–75, and Deputy Secretary, Lord Chancellor's Office, 1970–75. Master, Merchant Taylors' Co., 1971–72. Chm.,

Friends of the Elderly and Gentlefolks' Help, 1977–84. *Recreations:* gardening, travelling. *Address:* 22 Victoria Square, SW1W 0RB. *T:* 01–834 2676; The Grange, Wormingford, Colchester, Essex. *T:* Bures 227303. *Club:* Athenæum.

BOGIE, David Wilson; Sheriff of Grampian, Highland and Islands at Aberdeen and Stonehaven, since 1985; *b* 17 July 1946; *o s* of late Robert T. Bogie, Edinburgh; *m* 1983, Lady Lucinda Mackay, *o d* of Earl of Inchcape, *qv. Educ:* George Watson's Coll.; Edinburgh Univ. (LLB); Balliol Coll., Oxford (MA). FSAScot. Admitted to Faculty of Advocates, 1972; Temp. Sheriff, 1981. *Recreations:* architecture, heraldry, antiquities. *Address:* 50 Whitehall Road, Aberdeen AB2 4PR. *Clubs:* New, Puffin's (Edinburgh); Royal Northern and University (Aberdeen).

BOGLE, David Blyth, CBE 1967; formerly Senior Partner, Lindsays, WS, Edinburgh; Member of Council on Tribunals, 1958–70, and Chairman of Scottish Committee, 1962–70; *b* 22 Jan. 1903; *s* of late Very Rev. Andrew Nisbet Bogle, DD and Helen Milne Bogle; *m* 1955, Ruth Agnes Thorley. *Educ:* George Watson's Coll., Edinburgh; Edinburgh Univ. (LLB). Writer to the Signet, 1927. Commissioned in the Queen's Own Cameron Highlanders, 1940, and served in UK and Middle East, 1942–45; demobilised, with rank of Major, 1945. *Address:* 3 Belgrave Crescent, Edinburgh. *T:* 031–332 0047. *Club:* New (Edinburgh).

BOHAN, William Joseph; Assistant Under Secretary of State, Criminal Department, Home Office, since 1979; *b* 10 April 1929; *s* of John and Josephine Bohan; *m* 1955, Brenda Skevington; one *c* (and one *c* decd). *Educ:* Finchley Catholic Grammar Sch.; Cardinal Vaughan Sch., Kensington; King's Coll., Cambridge (Chancellor's Classical Medallist, 1952). Home Office: Asst Principal, 1952; Principal, 1958; Sec., Cttee on Immigration Appeals, 1966–67; Asst Sec., 1967. *Recreations:* languages and literature, walking. *Address:* c/o Home Office, SW1. *T:* 01–213 4083.

BOHM, Prof. David (Joseph), PhD; Professor of Theoretical Physics, Birkbeck College, University of London, 1961–83, now Emeritus; *b* 20 Dec. 1917; *s* of Samuel and Freda Bohm; *m* 1956, Sarah Woolfson; no *c. Educ:* Pennsylvania State Coll. (BS); University of Calif (PhD). Research Physicist, University of Calif, Radiation Laboratory, 1943–47; Asst Prof., Princeton Univ., 1947–51; Prof., University de São Paulo, Brazil, 1951–55; Prof., Technion, Haifa, Israel, 1955–57; Research Fellow, Bristol Univ., 1957–61. *Publications:* Quantum Theory, 1951; Causality and Chance in Modern Physics, 1957; Special Theory of Relativity, 1965; Fragmentation and Wholeness, 1976; Wholeness and Order: cosmos and consciousness, 1979; Wholeness and the Implicate Order, 1980; various papers in Physical Review, Nuovo Cimento, Progress of Theoretical Physics, British Jl for Philosophy of Science, etc, inc. papers on Implicate Order and A New Mode of Description in Physics. *Recreations:* walking, conversation, music (listener), art (viewer). *Address:* c/o Physics Department, Birkbeck College, Malet Street, WC1.

BOHR, Prof. Aage Niels, DSc, DrPhil; physicist, Denmark; Professor of Physics, University of Copenhagen, since 1956; *b* Copenhagen, 19 June 1922; *s* of late Prof. Niels Bohr and Margrethe Nlrlund; *m* 1st, Marietta Bettina (*née* Soffer) (*d* 1978); two *s* one *d*; 2nd, 1981, Bente, *d* of late Chief Physician Johannes Meyer and Lone (*née* Rubow) and *widow* of Morten Scharff. *Educ:* Univ. of Copenhagen. Jun. Scientific Officer, Dept of Scientific and Industrial Research, London, 1943–45; Research Asst, Inst. for Theoretical Physics, Univ. of Copenhagen, 1946; Dir, Niels Bohr Inst. (formerly Inst. for Theoretical Physics), 1963–70. Bd Mem., Nordita, 1958–74, Dir, 1975–81. Member: Royal Danish Acad. of Science, 1955–; Royal Physiolog. Soc., Sweden, 1959–; Royal Norwegian Acad. of Sciences, 1962–; Acad. of Tech. Sciences, Copenhagen, 1963–; Amer. Phil. Soc., 1965–; Amer. Acad. of Arts and Sciences, 1965–; Nat. Acad. of Sciences, USA, 1971–; Royal Swedish Acad. of Sciences, 1974–; Yugoslavia Acad. of Sciences, 1976–; Pontificia Academia Scientiarum, 1978–; Norwegian Acad. of Sciences, 1979–; Polish Acad. of Sciences, 1980–; Finska Vetenskups-Societeten, 1980–; Deutsche Akademie der Naturforscher Leopoldina, 1981–. Awards: Dannie Heineman Prize, 1960; Pius XI Medal, 1963; Atoms for Peace Award, 1969; H. C. Ørsted Medal, 1970; Rutherford Medal, 1972; John Price Wetherill Medal, 1974; (jointly) Nobel Prize for Physics, 1975; Ole Rømer Medal, 1976. Dr *hc*: Manchester, 1961; Oslo, 1969; Heidelberg, 1971; Trondheim, 1972; Uppsala, 1975. *Publications:* Rotational States of Atomic Nuclei, 1954; (with Ben R. Mottelson) Nuclear Structure, vol. I, 1969, vol. II 1975. *Address:* Strandgade 34, 1st Floor, 1401 Copenhagen K, Denmark.

BOHUSZ-SZYSZKO, Dame Cicely (Mary Strode); *see* Saunders, Dame C. M. S.

BOILEAU, Sir Guy (Francis), 8th Bt *cr* 1838; Company Director; *b* 23 Feb. 1935; *s* of Sir Edmond Charles Boileau, 7th Bt, and of Marjorie Lyle, *d* of Claude Monteath D'Arcy; *S* father, 1980; *m* 1962, Judith Frances, *d* of George Conrad Hannan; two *s* three *d. Educ:* Xavier College, Melbourne; Royal Military Coll., Duntroon, Australia. Lieut, Aust. Staff Corps, 1956; Platoon Comdr, 3rd Bn, Royal Aust. Regt, Malaysia, 1957–58; Observer, UN Mil. Observer Gp in India and Pakistan, 1959–60; Instructor, Aust. Army Training Team, Vietnam, 1963–64; attached US Dept of Defence, Washington, DC, 1966–68; Security Adviser, Dept of the Administrator, Territory of Papua-New Guinea, 1970–71; CO, Army Intelligence Centre, 1972–74; Directing Staff (Instructor), Aust. Staff Coll., 1975–76; SO1 Personnel, HQ Third Mil. Dist, 1979. *Recreations:* tennis, boating, fishing. *Heir: s* Nicolas Edmond George Boileau, *b* 17 Nov. 1964. *Address:* 14 Faircroft Avenue, Glen Iris, Victoria 3146, Australia. *T:* (03) 20 8273. *Club:* The Heroes (Toorak, Victoria).

BOJAXHIU, Agnes Gonxha; *see* Teresa, Mother.

BOK, Derek; President, Harvard University, since 1971, Professor of Law, since 1961; *b* 22 March 1930, Bryn Mawr, Pa; *s* of late Curtis and of Margaret Plummer Bok (now Mrs William S. Kiskadden); *m* 1955, Sissela Ann Myrdal, *d* of Karl Gunnar and Alva Myrdal, *qqv*; one *s* two *d. Educ:* Stanford Univ., BA; Harvard Univ., JD; Inst. of Political Science, Univ. of Paris (Fulbright Scholar); George Washington Univ., MA in Economics. Served AUS, 1956–58. Asst Prof. of Law, Harvard Univ., 1958–61, Dean of Law Sch., 1968–71. *Publications:* The First Three Years of the Schuman Plan, 1955; (ed with Archibald Cox) Cases and Materials on Labor Law, 5th edn 1962, 6th edn 1965, 7th edn 1969, 8th edn 1977; (with John Dunlop) Labor and the American Community, 1970; Beyond the Ivory Tower, 1982. *Recreations:* gardening, tennis, skiing. *Address:* Office of the President, Harvard University, Cambridge, Mass 02138, USA.

BOKSENBERG, Prof. Alexander, PhD; FRS 1978; Director, Royal Greenwich Observatory, since 1981; *b* 18 March 1936; *s* of Julius Boksenberg and Ernestina Steinberg; *m* 1960, Adella Coren; one *s* one *d. Educ:* Stationers' Co.'s Sch.; Univ. of London (BSc, PhD). Dept of Physics and Astronomy, University Coll. London: SRC Res. Asst, 1960–65; Lectr in Physics, 1965–75; Head of Optical and Ultraviolet Astronomy Res. Group, 1969–81; Reader in Physics, 1975–78; SRC Sen. Fellow, 1976–81; Prof. of Physics, 1978–81; Visiting Professor: Dept of Physics and Astronomy, UCL, 1981–; Astronomy Centre, Univ. of Sussex, 1981–. FRSA 1984. Freeman, Clockmakers' Co., 1984. Dr *hc*, l'Observatoire de Paris, 1982. *Publications:* contrib. learned jls. *Address:* Herstmonceux Castle, Hailsham, East Sussex BN27 1RP. *T:* Herstmonceux 833171.

BOLAM, James; actor; *b* Sunderland, 16 June 1938; *s* of Robert Alfred Bolam and Marion Alice Bolam (*née* Drury). *Educ:* Bede Grammar Sch., Sunderland; Bemrose Sch., Derby. First stage appearance, The Kitchen, Royal Court, 1959; later plays include: Events While Guarding the Bofors Gun, Hampstead, 1966; In Celebration, Royal Court, 1969; Veterans, Royal Court, 1972; Treats, Royal Court, 1976; Who Killed 'Agatha' Christie?, Ambassadors, 1978; King Lear (title rôle), Young Vic, 1981; Run for Your Wife!, Criterion, 1983; Arms and the Man, Cambridge. *Films:* Straight on till Morning, Crucible of Terror, Otley, A Kind of Loving, Half a Sixpence, Murder Most Foul, The Likely Lads, In Celebration, Whatever Happened to the Likely Lads?, The Great Question. *Television series:* The Likely Lads; Whatever Happened to the Likely Lads?; When the Boat Comes In; The Limbo Connection (Armchair Thriller Series); Only When I Laugh; The Beiderbecke Affair; Room at the Bottom; also As You Like It, Macbeth, in BBC Shakespeare. *Address:* c/o Barry Burnett Organisation Ltd, Suite 42–43, Grafton House, 2–3 Golden Square, W1.

BOLAND, Bridget; author; *b* 13 March 1913; *d* of late John Boland. *Educ:* Sacred Heart Convent, Roehampton; Oxford Univ. (BA 1935). Screenwriter 1937–; numerous films. Served War, 1941–46, in ATS; Senior Comdr. Stage plays: Abca Play Unit productions, 1946; Cockpit, 1948; The Damascus Blade, 1950; Temple Folly, 1952; The Return, 1953; The Prisoner, 1954 (adapted film version, 1955); Gordon, 1961; The Zodiac in the Establishment, 1963; Time out of Mind, 1970. *Publications: novels:* The Wild Geese, 1938; Portrait of a Lady in Love, 1942; Caterina, 1975; *non-fiction:* (with M. Boland) Old Wives' Lore for Gardeners, 1976; Gardener's Magic and Other Old Wives' Lore, 1977; At My Mother's Knee, 1978; The Lisle Letters: an abridgement, 1983 (ed by Muriel St Clare Byrne; selected and arranged by Bridget Boland). *Address:* Bolands, Hewshott Lane, Liphook, Hants.

BOLAND, John Anthony; Public Trustee, since 1980; *b* 23 Jan. 1931; *s* of late Daniel Boland, MBE, and Hannah Boland (*née* Barton), Dublin; *m* 1972, Ann, *d* of James C. Doyle and Maureen Doyle, Fermoy, Co. Cork. *Educ:* Castleknock Coll.; Xavier Sch.; Christian Brothers, Synge Street; Trinity Coll., Dublin (MA, LLB). Called to the Bar, Middle Temple, 1956; called to Irish Bar, 1967. Joined Public Trustee Office, 1956; Chief Administrative Officer, 1974–79; Asst Public Trustee, 1979–80. Hon. Member, College Historical Soc., TCD; Trustee of Trinity College Dublin (Univ. of Dublin) Trust; Chairman: TCD Assoc., London, 1982–85; London Cttee, Irish Sch. of Ecumenics; Hon. Treasurer, Family Res. Trust, 1971–80. *Recreations:* travel, reading, walking. *Address:* Stewart House, Kingsway, WC2B 6JX. *T:* 01–405 4300. *Club:* Kildare Street and University (Dublin).

BOLES, Sir Jeremy John Fortescue, 3rd Bt, *cr* 1922; *b* 9 Jan. 1932; *s* of Sir Gerald Fortescue Boles, 2nd Bt, and Violet Blanche (*d* 1974), *er d* of late Major Hall Parlby, Manadon, Crown Hill, S Devon; *S* father 1945; *m* 1st, 1955, Dorothy Jane (marr. diss. 1970), *yr d* of James Alexander Worswick; two *s* one *d*; 2nd, 1970, Elisabeth Gildroy, *yr d* of Edward Phillip Shaw; one *d*; 3rd, 1982, Marigold Aspey (*née* Seckington). *Heir: s* Richard Fortescue Boles, *b* 12 Dec. 1958.

BOLES, Sir John Dennis, (Sir Jack), Kt 1983; MBE 1960; Director General of the National Trust, 1975–83; *b* 25 June 1925; *s* of late Comdr Geoffrey Coleridge Boles and Hilda Frances (*née* Crofton); *m* 1st, 1953, Benita (*née* Wormald) (*d* 1969); two *s* three *d*; 2nd, 1971, Lady Anne Hermione, *d* of 12th Earl Waldegrave, *qv. Educ:* Winchester Coll. Rifle Brigade, 1943–46. Colonial Administrative Service (later Overseas Civil Service), North Borneo (now Sabah), 1948–64; Asst Sec., National Trust, 1965, Sec., 1968; Mem., Devon and Cornwall Regl Cttee, Nat. Trust, 1985. Dir, Devon and Cornwall Bd, Lloyds Bank plc, 1984–. Trustee, Ernest Cook Trust. *Address:* Rydon House, Talaton, near Exeter, Devon EX5 2RP. *Club:* Army and Navy.

BOLINGBROKE, 7th Viscount *cr* 1712, **AND ST JOHN,** 8th Viscount *cr* 1716; **Kenneth Oliver Musgrove St John;** Bt 1611; Baron St John of Lydiard Tregoze, 1712; Baron St John of Battersea, 1716; *b* 22 March 1927; *s* of Geoffrey Robert St John, MC (*d* 1972) and Katherine Mary (*d* 1958), *d* of late A. S. J. Musgrave; *S* cousin, 1974; *m* 1st, 1953, Patricia Mary McKenna (marr. diss. 1972); one *s*; 2nd, 1972, Jainey Anne McRae; two *s. Educ:* Eton; Geneva Univ. Chairman, A&P Gp of Cos, 1958–75; Director: Shaw Savill Holidays Pty Ltd; Bolingbroke and Partners Ltd; Wata Investment Inc., Panama. Pres., Travel Agents Assoc. of NZ, 1966–68; Dir, World Assoc. of Travel Agencies, 1966–75; Chm., Aust. Council of Tour Wholesalers, 1972–75. Fellow, Aust. Inst. of Travel; Mem., NZ Inst. of Travel. *Recreations:* golf, cricket, tennis, history. *Heir: s* Hon. Henry Fitzroy St John, *b* 18 May 1957. *Address:* 25 Andover Street, Christchurch, New Zealand. *Club:* Christchurch (Christchurch, NZ).

BOLITHO, Major Simon Edward, MC 1945; JP; Director: Barclays Bank, 1959–86; English China Clays, 1963–86; Vice-Lord-Lieutenant of Cornwall, since 1970; *b* 13 March 1916; *s* of late Lieut-Col Sir Edward Bolitho, KBE, CB, DSO; *m* 1953, Elizabeth Margaret, *d* of late Rear-Adm. G. H. Creswell, CB, DSO, DSC; two *s* two *d. Educ:* Royal Naval Coll., Dartmouth; RMC Sandhurst. Grenadier Guards, 1936–49; Lt-Col, DCLI, 1957–60. Hon. Air Cdre, No 2625 (Co. of Cornwall) RAuxAF Regt Sqdn, 1984–. DL Cornwall, 1964; High Sheriff of Cornwall, 1956–57; JP 1959; CC 1953–67. *Recreations:* shooting, fishing, hunting, sailing, gardening. *Address:* Trengwainton, Penzance, Cornwall. *T:* Penzance 63106. *Clubs:* Pratt's, MCC; Royal Yacht Squadron.

BOLLAND, Sir Edwin, KCMG 1981 (CMG 1971); HM Diplomatic Service, retired; Ambassador to Yugoslavia, 1980–82; *b* 20 Oct. 1922; *m* 1948, Winifred Mellor; one *s* three *d* (and one *s* decd). *Educ:* Morley Grammar Sch.; University Coll., Oxford. Served in Armed Forces, 1942–45. Foreign Office, 1947; Head of Far Eastern Dept, FO, 1965–67; Counsellor, Washington, 1967–71; St Antony's Coll., Oxford, 1971–72; Ambassador to Bulgaria, 1973–76; Head of British delegn to Negotiations on MBFR, 1976–80. *Recreations:* walking, gardening. *Address:* Lord's Spring Cottage, Godden Green, Sevenoaks, Kent. *T:* Sevenoaks 61105.

BOLLAND, Group Captain Guy Alfred, CBE 1943; Chief Intelligence Officer, BJSM (AFS), Washington, USA, 1956–59, retired; *b* 5 Nov. 1909; 3rd *s* of late Capt. L. W. Bolland; *m* 1935, Sylvia Marguerite, 2nd *d* of late Oswald Duke, Cambridge; one *s* three *d. Educ:* Gilbert Hannam Sch., Sussex. Commissioned RAF, 1930. Served in Iraq and Home Squadrons. Served War of 1939–45: commanded 217 Squadron during attacks on French ports, 1940; North African Operations, 1943 (despatches, CBE). *Recreation:* golf. *Address:* The Oaks, Shaftesbury Road, Woking, Surrey. *T:* Woking 60548.

BOLLAND, John; His Honour Judge Bolland; a Circuit Judge since 1974; *b* 30 March 1920; *s* of late Dominic Gerald Bolland and Gladys Bolland; *m* 1947, Audrey Jean Toyne (*née* Pearson); one *s* one step *s* one step *d. Educ:* Malvern Coll.; Trinity Hall, Cambridge (BA). Commnd Royal Warwicks Regt, 1939; 2nd Bn 6th Gurkha Rifles, 1941–46. Called to Bar, Middle Temple, 1948. *Recreations:* cricket, Rugby, golf, theatre. *Address:* 11 Firle Road, North Lancing, Sussex BN15 0NY. *T:* Lancing 755337.

BOLLERS, Hon. Sir Harold (Brodie Smith), Kt 1969; Chief Justice of Guyana, 1966–81; *b* 5 Feb. 1915; *s* of late John Bollers; *m* 1st, 1951, Irene Mahadeo (*d* 1965); two *s* one *d*; 2nd, 1968, Eileen Hanoman; one *s*. *Educ:* Queen's Coll., Guyana; King's Coll., London; Middle Temple. Called to the Bar, Feb. 1938; Magistrate, Guyana, 1946, Senior Magistrate, 1959; Puisne Judge, Guyana, 1960. *Recreations:* reading, walking. *Address:* c/o Chief Justice's Residence, 245 Vlissengen Road, Georgetown, Guyana. *T:* 5204. *Club:* Royal Commonwealth Society.

BOLSOVER, George Henry, CBE 1970 (OBE 1947); Director, School of Slavonic and East European Studies, University of London, 1947–76; *b* 18 Nov. 1910; *yr s* of Ernest and Mary Bolsover; *m* 1939, Stephanie Kállai; one *d*. *Educ:* Leigh Grammar Sch.; Univ. of Liverpool; Univ. of London. BA 1931, MA (Liverpool), 1932, PhD (London), 1933. Univ. of Birmingham, Resident Tutor in Adult Education in Worcs, 1937–38; Asst Lectr in Modern European History, Univ. of Manchester, 1938–43; Attaché and First Sec., HM Embassy, Moscow, 1943–47; Mem. of Editorial Board, Slavonic and East European Review, 1947–63, and Chm., 1958–63; Member: UGC Sub-Cttee on Oriental, African, Slavonic and East European Studies, 1961–71; Treasury Cttee for Studentships in Foreign Languages and Cultures, 1948–58; Inst. of Historical Res. Cttee, 1948–75; Adv. Cttee on Educn of Poles in Gt Britain, 1948–67; Ct of Govs of London Sch. of Economics and Political Science, 1955–77; Council and Exec. Cttee of St Bartholomew's Med. Coll., 1962–76; Council of Royal Dental Hosp. London Sch. of Dental Surgery, 1966–77; Min. of Educn Cttee on Teaching of Russian, 1960–62; Senior Treasurer of University of London Union, 1958–77; Chm., Tutorial Classes Cttee of Council for Extra-Mural Studies of Univ. of London, 1965–76; Chm., Council for Extra-Mural Studies, 1968–76; Mem., 1951–, Treas., 1966–72, British Nat. Historical Cttee; Mem. Governing Body, GB/East Europe Centre, 1967–78; Governor, Northwood Coll. for Girls, 1963–. *Publications:* essays in: Essays presented to Sir Lewis Namier, 1956, Transactions of Royal Historical Society, 1957; articles in English Historical Review, Journal of Modern History, Slavonic and East European Review, International Affairs, etc. *Recreations:* music, travel. *Address:* 7 Devonshire Road, Hatch End, Mddx HA5 4LY. *T:* 01–428 4282.

BOLT, Rear-Adm. Arthur Seymour, CB 1958; DSO 1951; DSC 1940 and bar 1941; *b* 26 Nov. 1907; *s* of Charles W. Bolt, Alverstoke, Hants; *m* 1933, Evelyn Mary June, *d* of Robert Ellis, Wakefield, Yorks; four *d*. *Educ:* Nautical Coll., Pangbourne; RN Coll., Dartmouth. Joined RN, 1923. Served War of 1939–45; HMS Glorious and Warspite (DSC and Bar), and at Admiralty. Capt. HMS Theseus (Korea), 1949–51; Dir Naval Air Warfare, Admty, 1951–53; Chief of Staff to Flag Officer Air (Home), 1954–56; Dep. Controller of Military Aircraft, Min. of Supply, 1957–60; retd. Capt. 1947; Rear-Adm. 1956. *Recreations:* tennis, squash, sailing. *Address:* 12 Mount Boone Way, Dartmouth, Devon. *T:* Dartmouth 3448. *Clubs:* Royal Naval and Royal Albert Yacht (Portsmouth); Royal Naval Sailing Association; Royal Dart Yacht.

BOLT, Air Marshal Sir Richard (Bruce), KBE 1979 (CBE 1973); CB 1977; DFC 1945; AFC 1959; Chairman, Pacific Aerospace Corp. of New Zealand, since 1982; *b* 16 July 1923; *s* of George Bruce Bolt and Mary (*née* Best); *m* 1946, June Catherine South; one *s* one *d*. *Educ:* Nelson Coll., NZ. Began service with RNZAF in mid 1942; served during 2nd World War in RAF Bomber Command (Pathfinder Force); Chief of Air Staff, NZ, 1974–76; Chief of Defence Staff, NZ, 1976–80. *Recreations:* fly fishing, golf. *Address:* 12 Monaghan Avenue, Karori, Wellington, NZ. *Club:* Wellington (Wellington, NZ).

BOLT, Robert Oxton, CBE 1972; playwright; *b* 15 Aug. 1924; *s* of Ralph Bolt and Leah Binnion; *m* 1st, 1949, Celia Ann Roberts (marr. diss., 1967); one *s* two *d*; 2nd, 1967, Sarah Miles (marr. diss. 1976); one *s*; 3rd, 1980, Ann Zane (marr. diss. 1985). *Educ:* Manchester Grammar Sch. Left sch., 1941; Sun Life Assurance Office, Manchester, 1942; Manchester Univ., 1943; RAF and Army, 1943–46; Manchester Univ., 1946–49; Exeter Univ., 1949–50; teaching, 1950–58; English teacher, Millfield Sch., 1952–58. Hon. LLD Exeter, 1977. *Plays:* The Critic and the Heart, Oxford Playhouse, 1957; Flowering Cherry, Haymarket, 1958; A Man for All Seasons, Globe, 1960 (filmed 1967); The Tiger and The Horse, Queen's, 1960; Gentle Jack, Queen's, 1963; The Thwarting of Baron Bolligrew, 1966; Vivat! Vivat Regina!, Piccadilly, 1970; State of Revolution, Nat. Theatre, 1977; *screenplays:* Lawrence of Arabia, 1962; Dr Zhivago, 1965 (Academy Award); Man for all Seasons, 1967 (Academy Award); Ryan's Daughter, 1970; Lady Caroline Lamb, 1972 (also dir.); The Bounty, 1984; The Mission, 1986; TV and radio plays. *Address:* c/o Margaret Ramsay Ltd, 14a Goodwins Court, St Martin's Lane, WC2. *Club:* The Spares (Somerset) (Hon. Life Mem.).

BOLTE, Hon. Sir Henry (Edward), GCMG 1972 (KCMG 1966); Premier and Treasurer of the State of Victoria, Australia, 1955–72; *b* Skipton, Victoria, 20 May 1908; *s* of J. H. Bolte; *m* 1934, Edith Lilian Elder (Dame Edith Bolte, DBE) (*d* 1986). *Educ:* Skipton State Sch.; Ballarat C of E Grammar Sch. Grazier, with sheep property near Meredith in western district of Victoria. Entered Parliament, 1947; MLA for Hampden, 1947–73; Minister of: Water Supply and Mines, 1948–50; Soil Conservation, 1949–50; Water Supply and Soil Conservation, 1950; Leader of Liberal Party (formerly Liberal and Country Party), 1953–72 (Dep. Leader, Nov. 1950–53). Freedom, City of Melbourne, 1975. Hon. LLD: Melbourne Univ., 1965; Monash Univ., 1967. *Recreations:* golf, shooting, turf. *Address:* Kialla, Meredith, Victoria 3333, Australia. *Clubs:* Australian, Athenæum (Melbourne); Geelong (Geelong).

BOLTON, 7th Baron, *cr* 1797; **Richard William Algar Orde-Powlett;** *b* 11 July 1929; *s* of 6th Baron Bolton; *S* father, 1963; *m* 1st, 1951, Hon. Christine Helena Weld Forester (marr. diss.), *e d* of 7th Baron Forester, and of Marie Louise Priscilla, CStJ, *d* of Sir Herbert Perrott, 6th Bt, CH, CB; two *s* one *d*; 2nd, 1981, Masha Anne, *d* of Major F. E. Hudson, Winterfield House, Hornby, Bedale, Yorks. *Educ:* Eton; Trinity Coll., Cambridge (BA). Chairman, Richmond Div., Conservative Assoc., 1957–60; Chairman Yorkshire Div., Royal Forestry Soc., 1962–64; Member Council, Timber Growers' Organization. Director: Yorkshire Insurance Co., 1964–70; General Accident Life Assurance Ltd, 1970–. JP, North Riding of Yorkshire, 1957–80. FRICS. *Recreations:* shooting, fishing. *Heir: s* Hon. Harry Algar Nigel Orde-Powlett [*b* 14 Feb. 1954; *m* 1977, Philippa, *d* of Major P. L. Tapply; two *s*]. *Address:* Park House, Wensley, Leyburn, North Yorkshire. *T:* Wensleydale 22464. *Clubs:* White's; Central African Deep Sea Fishing.

BOLTON, Bishop Suffragan of, since 1984; **Rt. Rev. David George Galliford;** *b* 20 June 1925; *s* of Alfred Edward Bruce and Amy Doris Galliford; *m* 1954, Enid May Drax (*d* 1983); one *d*. *Educ:* Bede Coll., Sunderland; Clare Coll., Cambridge (Organ Scholar 1942, BA 1949, MA 1951); Westcott House, Cambridge. Served 5th Royal Inniskilling Dragoon Guards, 1943–47. Curate of St John Newland, Hull, 1951–54; Minor Canon of Windsor, 1954–56; Vicar of St Oswald, Middlesbrough, 1956–61; Rector of Bolton Percy and Diocesan Training Officer, 1961–70; Canon of York Minster, 1969; Canon Residentiary and Treasurer of York Minster, 1970–75; Bishop Suffragan of Hulme, 1975–84. *Publications:* God and Christian Caring, 1973; Pastor's Post, 1975; (ed) Diocese in Mission, 1968. *Recreations:* pottery, music, painting in oils. *Address:* 4 Sandfield Drive, Lostock, Bolton, Lancs BL6 4DU. *T:* Bolton 43400. *Clubs:* Royal Over-Seas League; Manchester.

BOLTON, Archdeacon of; *see* Brison, Ven. W. S.

BOLTON, Group Captain David; Director, Royal United Services Institute for Defence Studies, since 1981; *b* 15 April 1932; *o s* of late George Edward and Florence May Bolton; *m* 1955, Betty Patricia Simmonds; three *d*. *Educ:* Bede Grammar Sch., Sunderland. Entered RAF as National Serviceman; commnd RAF Regt, 1953; subsequent service in Egypt, Jordan, Singapore, Aden, Cyprus, Malta and Germany; RAF Staff Coll., 1969; National Def. Coll., 1972; Central Planning Staff, MoD, 1973–75; OC 33 Wing RAF Regt, 1975–77; Comdt RAF Regt Depot, Catterick, 1977–80; retd 1980; Dep. Dir and Dir of Studies, RUSI, 1980–81. Member: RUSI Council, 1973–79; IISS, 1964–; RIIA, 1975–; Council, British Atlantic Cttee, 1981–. Hon. Steward, Westminster Abbey, 1981–. Mem. Editl Bd, Brassey's Yearbook, 1982–; Gen. Editor, RUSI-Macmillan Defence Studies, 1983–. Trench Gascoigne Essay Prize, RUSI, 1972. *Publications:* contrib. learned jls. *Recreations:* music, theatre, jogging, work. *Address:* Royal United Services Institute for Defence Studies, Whitehall, SW1A 2ET. *T:* 01–930 5854. *Club:* Royal Air Force.

BOLTON, Eric James; Senior Chief Inspector of Schools, Department of Education and Science, since 1983; *b* 11 Jan. 1935; *s* of late James and Lilian Bolton; *m* 1960, Ann Gregory; one *s* twin *d*. *Educ:* Wigan Grammar Sch.; Chester Coll.; Lancaster Univ. MA. English teacher at secondary schs, 1957–68; Lectr, Chorley Teacher Training Coll., 1968–70; Inspector of Schs, Croydon, 1970–73; HM Inspector of Schs, 1973–79; Staff Inspector (Educnl Disadvantage), 1979–81; Chief Inspector of Schools, DES, 1981–83. *Publications:* Verse Writing in Schools, 1964; various articles in educnl jls. *Recreations:* reading, music and opera, fly fishing.

BOLTON, Sir Frederic (Bernard), Kt 1976; MC; FIMarE; Chairman, The Bolton Group, since 1953; Chairman or Director of other companies (subsidiaries); Chairman: Dover Harbour Board, since 1983 (Member, 1957–62 and since 1980); British Ports Association, since 1985; *b* 9 March 1921; *s* of late Louis Hamilton Bolton and late Beryl Dyer; *m* 1st, 1950, Valerie Margaret Barwick (*d* 1970); two *s*; 2nd, 1971, Vanessa Mary Anne Robarts; two *s* two *d*. *Educ:* Rugby. Served War, with Welsh Guards, 1940–46 (MC 1945, Italy); Northants Yeomanry, 1952–56. Member: Lloyd's, 1945–; Baltic Exchange, 1946–. Chm., Atlantic Steam Nav. Co. & Subs, 1960–71; Dir, B.P. Tanker Co., 1968–82; Mem., Brit. Rail Shipping & Int. Services Bd, 1970–82 (now Sealink UK Ltd). Pres., Chamber of Shipping of UK, 1966; Mem., Lloyd's Register of Shipping Gen. Cttee, 1961–; Chm., Ship & Marine Technol. Requirements Bd, 1977–81; Member: PLA, 1964–71; Nat. Ports Council, 1967–74; President: Inst. of Marine Engineers, 1968–69 and 1969–70; British Shipping Fedn, 1972–75; Internat. Shipping Fedn, 1973–82; Gen. Council of British Shipping, 1975–76; British Maritime League, 1985–. Hon. FNI. Grafton Hunt: Jt Master, 1956–67, Chm., 1967–72. *Recreations:* country sports. *Address:* Pudlicote, near Charlbury, Oxon OX7 3HX. *Club:* City of London.

BOLTON, Prof. Geoffrey Curgenven, DPhil; Professor of History, Murdoch University, 1973–82, and since 1985; *b* 5 Nov. 1931; *s* of Frank and Winifred Bolton, Perth, W Australia; *m* 1958, (Ann) Carol Grattan; two *s*. *Educ:* North Perth State Sch.; Wesley Coll., Perth; Univ. of Western Australia; Balliol Coll., Oxford, (DPhil). FRHistS 1967; FAHA 1974; FASSA 1976. Res. Fellow, ANU, 1957–62; Sen. Lectr, Monash Univ., 1962–65; Prof. of Modern Hist., Univ. of Western Australia, 1966–73; Pro-Vice-Chancellor, Murdoch Univ., 1973–76; Prof. of Australian Studies, Univ. of London, 1982–85. Mem. Council, Australian Nat. Maritime Museum, Sydney, 1985–. FRSA. *Publications:* Alexander Forrest, 1958; A Thousand Miles Away, 1963; The Passing of the Irish Act of Union, 1966; Dick Boyer, 1967; A Fine Country to Starve In, 1972; Spoils and Spoilers: Australians Make Their Environment, 1981; articles in learned jls. *Recreation:* sleep. *Address:* 6 Melvista Avenue, Claremont, WA 6010, Australia. *Clubs:* Athenæum, Royal Commonwealth Society.

BOLTON, John, CB 1985; consulting engineer and arbitrator, since 1986; *b* 30 Dec. 1925; *s* of John and Elizabeth Ann Bolton, Great Harwood, Lancs; *m* 1950, Nell Hartley Mount, *d* of John and Kathleen Mount; three *d*. *Educ:* Blackburn Coll. of Technology and Art. LLB (Hons) London; CEng, FICE, FIMechE, FInstE, FCIArb. Mech. Engrg Apprentice, Bristol Aeroplane Co. Ltd; Civil Engrg Pupil, Courtaulds Ltd; subseq. with English Electric Co. Ltd and NW Gas Board. Entered Health Service as Group Engr, W Manchester HMC, 1954; subseq. Chief Engr to Board of Govs of United Liverpool Hosps, Dep. Regional Engr to Leeds Regional Hosp. Board and Regional Engr to E Anglian Regional Hosp. Board; Chief Engr, 1969–77, Chief Works Officer and Dir Gen. of Works, 1977–86, DHSS. Part-time lectr in building and engrg subjects, 1948–55, Principal, 1955–59, Irlam Evening Inst., Manchester. Liveryman, Co. of Fanmakers. President: CIBSE, 1983–84 (Vice-Pres., 1981–83; Hon. FCIBSE); IHospE, 1985 (Hon. FIHospE); Hon. FIPHE. *Publications:* contribs to: British Hosps Export Council Yearbooks, 1973, 1974, 1975; The Efficient Use of Energy, 1975; papers to internat. confs and to British learned societies; technical articles in various jls. *Recreations:* theatre, music, reading, gardening, swimming. *Address:* Allsprings House, High Street, Little Shelford, Cambs. *T:* Cambridge 842591.

BOLTON, John Eveleigh, CBE 1972; DSC 1945; DL; Chairman and Managing Director, Growth Capital Ltd, since 1968; Chairman: Hall Bolton Estates Ltd; Atesmo Ltd; Riverview Investments Ltd; Director: NCR Co. Ltd; Alphameric PLC; Black & Decker Group Inc.; Black & Decker Holdings Inc.; Black & Decker Investment Co.; Black & Decker Corp.; Plasmec PLC; Dawson International plc; Johnson Wax Ltd; Redland plc; County Sound plc; President, Development Capital Group Ltd, since 1984; *b* 17 Oct. 1920; *s* of late Ernest and Edith Mary Bolton; *m* 1948, Gabrielle Healey Hall, *d* of late Joseph and Minnie Hall; one *s* one *d*. *Educ:* Ilkley Sch.; Wolverhampton Sch.; Trinity Coll., Cambridge (Cassel Travelling Schol., 1948; BA Hons Econs 1948, MA 1953); Harvard Business School (Baker Schol., 1949; MBA with dist., 1950). Articled pupil to Chartered Acct, 1937–40; intermed. exam. of Inst. of Chartered Accts, 1940. Served War of 1939–45 (DSC): Destroyers, Lt RNVR, 1940–46. Research for Harvard in British Industry, 1950–51; Finance Dir, Solartron Laboratory Instruments Ltd, Kingston-upon-Thames, 1951–53 (Chm., 1953); Chm. and Man. Dir: Solartron Engineering Ltd, 1952; The Solartron Electronic Group Ltd, Thames Ditton and subseq. Farnborough, Hants, 1954–63 (Dep. Chm., 1963–65). A Gen. Comr of Income Tax, 1964–. British Institute of Management: Chm. Council, 1964–66; Bowie Medal 1969; CBIM; Life Vice-Pres.; Pres., Engrg Industries Assoc., 1981–84; Chm. and Founder Subscriber: Advanced Management Programmes Internat. Trust; Foundn for Management Educn; Business Grads Assoc.; Dir, Management Publications Ltd, 1966–73 (Chm., 1969); Mem. Exec. Cttee, AA; Hon. Treasurer, Surrey Univ., 1975–82 (Past Chm.); Member: Sub-Cttee on Business Management Studies, UGC; Council of Industry for Management Educn; Harvard Business Sch. Vis. Cttee, 1962–75; Adv. Cttee on Industry, Cttee of Vice-Chancellors, 1984–; Business Educn Forum, 1969–74. Mem. Org. Cttee, World Research Hospital. Member: UK Automation Council, 1964–65; Adv. Cttee for Management Efficiency in NHS, 1964–65; Cttee for Exports to New Zealand, 1965–68; Adv. Cttee, Queen's Award to Industry, 1972–; Council, Inst. of Dirs; Chm., Economic Develt Cttee for the Rubber Industry, 1965–68; Vice-Chm., Royal Commn on Local Govt in England, 1966–69; Chm., Committee of Inquiry on Small Firms, 1969–71. Trustee, Small Business Research Trust. Life FRSA. DL Surrey, 1974; High

Sheriff of Surrey, 1980–81. DUniv Surrey, 1982. *Publications:* articles in newspapers and journals; various radio and TV broadcasts on industrial topics. *Recreations:* shooting, swimming, gardening, opera, antiques. *Address:* Brook Place, Chobham, Woking, Surrey. *T:* Chobham 8157. *Clubs:* Harvard Club of London; Philippics (Surrey).

BOMBAY, Archbishop of, (RC), since 1978; **Most Rev. Simon Ignatius Pimenta;** *b* 1 March 1920; *s* of late Joseph Anthony Pimenta and Rosie E. Pimenta. *Educ:* St Xavier's Coll., Bombay (BA with Maths); Propaganda Univ., Rome (Degree in Canon Law). Secretary at Archbishop's House, Bombay, 1954; also Vice-Chancellor and Defensor Vinculi; Vice Rector of Cathedral, 1960; Visiting Prof. of Liturgy, Bombay Seminary, 1960–65; Rector of Cathedral and Episcopal Vicar for Liturgy and Pastoral Formation of Junior Clergy, 1967; Rector of Seminary, 1971; Auxiliary Bishop, 1971; Coadjutor Archbishop with right of succession, 1977. Pres., Catholic Bishops' Conf. of India, 1982. *Publications:* (edited) The Catholic Directory of Bombay, 1960 and 1964 edns; Circulars and Officials of the Archdiocese of Bombay, 3 vols; booklet on the Cathedral of the Holy Name. *Address:* Archbishop's House, 21 Nathalal Parekh Marg, Bombay 400039, India. *T:* 2021093, 2021193, 2021293.

BOMFORD, Nicholas Raymond, MA; Headmaster of Uppingham School, since 1982; *b* 27 Jan. 1939; *s* of late Ernest Raymond Bomford and of Patricia Clive Bomford (*née* Brooke), JP; *m* 1966, Gillian Mary Reynolds; two *d. Educ:* Kelly Coll.; Trinity Coll., Oxford (MA, Mod. History). Teaching appts, 1960–64; Lectr in History and Contemp. Affairs, BRNC, Dartmouth, 1964–66, Sen. Lectr, 1966–68; Wellington Coll., 1968–76 (Housemaster, 1973–76); Headmaster, Monmouth Sch., 1977–82. Chm., Jt Standing Cttee, HMC/IAPS, 1986–. Mem. Navy Records Soc. (Councillor, 1967–70, 1973–76, 1984–). *Publications:* Documents in World History, 1914–70, 1973; (contrib.) Dictionary of World History, 1973. *Recreations:* shooting (Captain OURC, 1959–60; England VIII (Elcho match), 1960), fishing, gardening, music, enjoying Welsh border country. *Address:* Uppingham School, Rutland LE15 9QE.

BOMPAS, Donald George, CMG 1966; Secretary, United Medical and Dental Schools of Guy's and St Thomas's Hospitals, 1984–86; *b* 20 Nov. 1920; *yr s* of Rev. E. Anstie Bompas; *m* 1946, Freda Vice, *y d* of F. M. Smithyman, Malawi; one *s* one *d. Educ:* Merchant Taylors' Sch., Northwood; Oriel Coll., Oxford. MA Oxon, 1947. Overseas Audit Service, 1942–66, retired; Nyasaland, 1942–47; Singapore, 1947–48; Malaya (now Malaysia), 1948–66; Deputy Auditor-General, 1957–60; Auditor-General, Malaysia (formerly Malaya), 1960–66. Dep. Sec., Guy's Hosp. Med. and Dental Schools, 1966–69, Sec., 1969–82; Dep. Sec., United Med. Schools, 1982–83. Chm., Univ. of London Purchasing Gp, 1976–82. Mem. Exec., Federated Pension Schemes, 1979–86. Liveryman, Merchant Taylors' Co., 1951. JMN (Hon.) Malaya, 1961. *Address:* 8 Birchwood Road, Petts Wood, Kent. *T:* Orpington 21661. *Club:* Royal Commonwealth Society.

BON, Christoph Rudolf; Partner, Chamberlin Powell & Bon, since 1952; *b* 1 Sept. 1921; *s* of Rudolf Bon and Nelly Fischbacher. *Educ:* Cantonal Gymnasium, Zürich; Swiss Federal Inst. of Technology, Zürich (DipArch ETH 1946). Prof. Holford's Office–Master Plan for City of London, 1946; Studio BBPR, Milan, 1949–50; teaching at Kingston Sch. of Art, 1950–52; Founder Partner, Chamberlin Powell & Bon, 1952. Work includes: Golden Lane Estate; Expansion of Leeds Univ.; schools, housing and commercial buildings; New Hall, Cambridge; Barbican. *Address:* The Mill House, Sonning on Thames, Berks. *T:* (office) 01–352 2841.

BONALLACK, Michael Francis, OBE 1971; Secretary, Royal and Ancient Golf Club of St Andrews, since 1983; *b* 31 Dec. 1934; *s* of Sir Richard (Frank) Bonallack, *qv; m* 1958, Angela Ward; one *s* three *d. Educ:* Chigwell; Haileybury ISC. National Service, 1953–55 (1st Lieut, RASC). Joined family business, Bonallack and Sons Ltd, later Freight Bonallack Ltd, 1955; Director, 1962–74; Dir, Buckley Investments, 1976–84. Chairman: Golf Foundn, 1977–83; Professional Golfers' Assoc., 1976–82; Pres., English Golf Union, 1982. *Recreation:* golf (British Amateur Champion, 1961, 1965, 1968, 1969, 1970; English Amateur Champion, 1962–63, 1965–67 and 1968; Captain, British Walker Cup Team, 1971; Bobby Jones Award for distinguished sportsmanship in golf, 1972). *Address:* c/o Royal and Ancient Golf Club, St Andrews, Fife. *T:* St Andrews 72112. *Clubs:* Golfers'; Chantilly (France); Pine Valley (USA).

BONALLACK, Sir Richard (Frank), Kt 1963; CBE 1955 (OBE (mil.) 1944); MIMechE; Director, Freight Bonallack Ltd; *b* 2 June 1904; *s* of Francis and Ada Bonallack; *m* 1930, Winifred Evelyn Mary Esplen; two *s* one *d. Educ:* Haileybury. War service in TA, 1939–45; transferred to TA Reserve, 1946, with rank of Colonel. Pres., Freight Bonallack Ltd, 1974– (Chm., 1971–74 and formerly of Bonallack and Sons Ltd, 1953–71); Chm., Freight Container Section, SMMT, 1967–83; Mem., Basildon Development Corporation, 1962–77. *Recreation:* golf. *Address:* 4 The Willows, Thorpe Bay, Southend on Sea, Essex SS1 3SH. *T:* Southend 588180.
See also M. F. Bonallack.

BONAR, Sir Herbert (Vernon), Kt 1967; CBE 1946; Chairman, 1949–74, and Managing Director, 1938–73, The Low & Bonar Group Ltd; retired 1974; *b* 26 Feb. 1907; *s* of George Bonar and Julia (*née* Seehusen); *m* 1935, Marjory (*née* East); two *s. Educ:* Fettes Coll.; Brasenose Coll., Oxford (BA). Joined Low & Bonar Ltd, 1929; Director, 1934; Managing Director, 1938; Chairman and Managing Director, 1949. Jute Control, 1939–46; Jute Controller, 1942–46. Trustee, WWF, UK, 1974–80 (Vice Pres. 1981). Hon. LLD: St Andrews, 1955; Birmingham, 1974; Dundee, 1985. Comdr, Order of the Golden Ark, Netherlands, 1974. *Recreations:* golf, fishing, photography, wild life preservation. *Address:* St Kitts, Albany Road, Broughty Ferry, Dundee, Angus. *T:* Dundee 79947. *Clubs:* Blairgowrie Golf; Panmure Golf.

BOND, Alan, AO 1984; Executive Chairman, Bond Corporation Holdings Ltd, since 1969; *b* 22 April 1938; *s* of Frank and Kathleen Bond; *m* 1956, Eileen Teresa Hughes; two *s* two *d. Educ:* Perivale Sch., Ealing, UK; Fremantle Boys' Sch., W Australia. Chairman, Bond Corporation Holdings Ltd, founded 1969; interests in property, brewing, electronic media, oil and gas, minerals, retailing, airships. Syndicate Head, America's Cup Challenge 1983 Ltd; Australia II Winners of 1983 America's Cup Challenge, following three previous attempts: 1974 Southern Cross, 1977 Australia, 1980 Australia. Australian of the Year, 1977. *Recreation:* yachting. *Address:* Dalkeith, Western Australia. *Clubs:* Royal Ocean Racing; Young Presidents Organisation, American National, Royal Perth Yacht, Cruising Yacht, Western Australian Turf (WA).

BOND, Arthur, CBE 1972; Chairman, Yorkshire Electricity Board, 1962–71; *b* 19 July 1907; *s* of Rev. A. and Mrs Anne Bond, Darwen, Lancs; *m* 1935, Nora Wadsworth; one *s* one *d. Educ:* Darwen Grammar Sch. Solicitor to Cleethorpes Corporation, 1930; Dep. Town Clerk, Luton, 1935; Town Clerk: Macclesfield, 1938; Stockport, 1944; Secretary, Eastern Electricity Board, 1948; Dep. Chairman, Yorkshire Electricity Board, 1952. Solicitor, Legal Member, RTPI; Comp. IEE; CBIM. Hon. Life Mem., Furniture History Soc. *Address:* 5 Linton Road, Wetherby, West Yorks. *T:* Wetherby 62847.

BOND, Rt. Rev. (Charles) Derek; *see* Bradwell, Area Bishop of.

BOND, Edward; playwright and director; *b* 18 July 1934; *m* 1971, Elisabeth Pablé. Northern Arts Literary Fellow, 1977–79. Hon. DLitt Yale, 1977. George Devine Award, 1968; John Whiting Award, 1968. *Opera Libretti:* We Come to the River (music by Hans Werner Henze), 1976; The English Cat (music by Hans Werner Henze), 1983; *ballet libretto:* Orpheus, 1982; *translations:* Chekhov, The Three Sisters, 1967; Wedekind, Spring Awakening, 1974. *Publications:* (plays): Saved, 1965; Narrow Road to the Deep North, 1968; Early Morning, 1968; The Pope's Wedding, 1971; Passion, 1971; Black Mass, 1971; Lear, 1972; The Sea, 1973; Bingo, 1974; The Fool, 1976; A-A-merica! (Grandma Faust, and The Swing), 1976; Stone, 1976; The Woman, 1978; The Bundle, 1978; Theatre Poems and Songs, 1978; The Worlds and The Activist Papers, 1980; Restoration, 1981; Summer: a play for Europe, 1982; Derek, 1983; Human Cannon, 1984; The War Plays (part 1, Red Black and Ignorant; part 2, The Tin Can People; part 3, Great Peace), 1985. *Recreation:* the study of physics, because in physics the problems of human motives do not have to be considered. *Address:* c/o Margaret Ramsay, 14A Goodwins Court, St Martin's Lane, WC2N 4LL.

BOND, Prof. George, FRS 1972; Hooker Professor of Botany, University of Glasgow, 1973–76, now Emeritus Professor (Titular Professor, 1965–73); *b* 21 Feb. 1906; *m* 1st, 1931, Gwendolyne Kirkbride (*d* 1960); one *s* one *d* (and one *s* decd); 2nd, 1961, Mary Catherine McCormick; two *s. Educ:* The Brunts Sch., Mansfield; UC Nottingham. BSc, PhD, DSc, FIBiol. Asst Lectr, Dept of Botany, Univ. of Glasgow, 1927; subseq. Lectr, then Reader. Technical Officer, Min. of Food, Dehydration Div., 1942–45. *Publications:* articles in various learned jls on symbiotic fixation of nitrogen. *Recreations:* gardening, church music, draughtsmanship, cricket and tennis. *Address:* 23 Westland Drive, Glasgow G14 9NY. *T:* 041–959 4201.

BOND, Maj.-Gen. George Alexander, CB 1956; CBE 1953 (OBE 1942); late RASC; *b* 31 Dec. 1901; *s* of late Alexander Maxwell Bond, Dover; *m* 1929, Dora Margaret, *d* of late H. A. Gray; two *s. Educ:* Dover Grammar Sch.; RMC. Served War of 1939–45 (despatches, OBE); Brig. 1948; Director of Supplies and Transport, BAOR, 1950–53; DDST, Southern Command, 1953–54; Maj.-Gen. 1955; Inspector RASC, War Office, 1954–57; Dir, Supplies and Transport, 1957, retd. Col Comdt, RASC, 1960–65; Col Comdt, Royal Corps of Transport, 1965–66. *Address:* Coldharbour Hall, Rake, Liss, Hants GU33 7JQ.

BOND, Maj.-Gen. Henry Mark Garneys, JP; Vice Lord-Lieutenant of Dorset, since 1984; *b* 1 June 1922; *s* of W. R. G. Bond, Tyneham, Dorset; unmarried. *Educ:* Eton. Enlisted as Rifleman, 1940; commnd in Rifle Bde, 1941; served Middle East and Italy; seconded to Parachute Regt, 1947–50; ADC to Field Marshal Viscount Montgomery of Alamein, 1950–52; psc 1953; served in Kenya, Malaya, Cyprus and Borneo; Comd Rifle Bde in Cyprus and Borneo, 1964–66; Comd 12th Inf. Bde, 1967–68; idc 1969; Dir of Defence Operational Plans and Asst Chief of Defence Staff (Ops), 1970–72; retd 1972. Pres., Dorset Natural History and Archaeological Soc., 1972–75; Chairman: Dorset Br., CPRE, 1975–78; Dorset Community Council, 1978–81; Dorset Policy Authy, 1980–. Mem., Dorset CC, 1973–85 (Vice-Chm., 1981–85). JP Dorset, 1972, High Sheriff of Dorset, 1977, DL Dorset, 1977. Chm., Governors of Milton Abbey Sch., 1979–. *Recreations:* forestry, reading. *Address:* Moigne Combe, Dorchester, Dorset. *T:* Warmwell 852265. *Club:* Boodle's.

BOND, Sir Kenneth (Raymond Boyden), Kt 1977; Vice-Chairman, General Electric Company plc, since 1985 (Financial Director, 1962–66; Deputy Managing Director, 1966–85); *b* 1 Feb. 1920; *s* of late James Edwin and Gertrude Deplidge Bond; *m* 1958, Jennifer Margaret, *d* of late Sir Cecil and Lady Crabbe; three *s* three *d. Educ:* Selhurst Grammar School. Served TA, Europe and Middle East, 1939–46. FCA 1960 (Mem. 1949). Partner, Cooper & Cooper, Chartered Accountants, 1954–57; Dir, Radio & Allied Industries Ltd, 1957–62. Member: Industrial Develt Adv. Bd, 1972–77; Cttee to Review the Functioning of Financial Instns, 1977–80; Audit Commn, 1983–86; Civil Justice Rev. Adv. Cttee, 1985–. *Recreation:* golf. *Address:* White Gables, Austenwood Common, Gerrards Cross, Bucks. *T:* Gerrards Cross 883513. *Club:* Addington Golf.

BOND, Michael; author; *b* 13 Jan. 1926; *s* of Norman Robert and Frances Mary Bond; *m* 1950, Brenda Mary Johnson (marr. diss. 1981); one *s* one *d; m* 1981, Susan Marfrey Rogers. *Educ:* Presentation College, Reading. RAF and Army, 1943–47; BBC Cameraman, 1947–66, full-time author from 1966. Paddington TV series, 1976. *Publications: for children:* A Bear Called Paddington, 1958; More About Paddington, 1959; Paddington Helps Out, 1960; Paddington Abroad, 1961; Paddington at Large, 1962; Paddington Marches On, 1964; Paddington at Work, 1966; Here Comes Thursday, 1966; Thursday Rides Again, 1968; Paddington Goes to Town, 1968; Thursday Ahoy, 1969; Parsley's Tail, 1969; Parsley's Good Deed, 1969; Parsley's Problem Present, 1970; Parsley's Last Stand, 1970; Paddington Takes the Air, 1970; Thursday in Paris, 1970; Michael Bond's Book of Bears, 1971; Michael Bond's Book of Mice, 1972; The Day the Animals Went on Strike, 1972; Paddington Bear, 1972; Paddington's Garden, 1972; Parsley the Lion, 1972; Parsley Parade, 1972; The Tales of Olga da Polga, 1972; Olga Meets her Match, 1973; Paddington's Blue Peter Story Book, 1973; Paddington at the Circus, 1973; Paddington Goes Shopping, 1973; Paddington at the Sea-side, 1974; Paddington at the Tower, 1974; Paddington on Top, 1974; Windmill, 1975; How to make Flying Things, 1975; Eight Olga Readers, 1975; Paddington's Loose End Book, 1976; Paddington's Party Book, 1976; Olga Carries On, 1976; Paddington's Pop-up Book, 1977; Paddington Takes the Test, 1979; Paddington's Cartoon Book, 1979; J. D. Polson and the Liberty-Head Dime, 1980; J. D. Polson and the Dillogate Affair, 1981; Paddington on Screen, 1981; Olga Takes Charge, 1982; The Caravan Puppets, 1983; Paddington at the Zoo, 1984; Paddington and the Knickerbocker Rainbow, 1984; Paddington's Painting Exhibition, 1985; Paddington at the Fair, 1985; Oliver the Greedy Elephant, 1985; Paddington at the Palace, 1986; Paddington Minds the House, 1986; with Karen Bond: Paddington Posts a Letter, 1986; Paddington at the Airport, 1986; *for adults:* Monsieur Pamplemousse, 1983; Monsieur Pamplemousse and the Secret Mission, 1984; Monsieur Pamplemousse on the Spot, 1986; Monsieur Pamplemousse Takes the Cure, 1987; The Pleasures of Paris, 1987. *Recreations:* photography, travel, cars, wine. *Address:* 22 Maida Avenue, W2 1SR. *T:* 01–262 4280. *Club:* Wig and Pen.

BOND-WILLIAMS, Noel Ignace, CBE 1979; Director, National Exhibition Centre Ltd, since 1970; *b* 7 Nov. 1914; *s* of late W. H. Williams, Birmingham; *m* 1939, Mary Gwendoline Tomey; one *s* two *d. Educ:* Oundle Sch.; Birmingham Univ. (BSc). FIM, FBIM. Pres. Guild of Undergrads 1936–37, Pres. Guild of Grads 1947, Birmingham Univ. Various appts in metal industry; Director: Enfield Rolling Mills Ltd, 1957–65; Delta Metal Co. Ltd, 1967–77; Vice-Chm., 1978–79, Chm., 1979–83, Remploy Ltd; Dir, 1972–85, and Vice-Chm., 1979–85, Lucas (Industries) Ltd. Industrial Adviser, DEA, 1965–67. Pres., Birmingham Chamber of Commerce, 1969. Member: Commn on Industrial Relations, 1971–74; Price Commn, 1977 79. Mem. Council, Industrial Soc., 1947–78; Pres., Brit. Non-ferrous Metals Fedn, 1974–75. Pro-Chancellor, Univ. of Aston in Birmingham, 1970–81. Hon. DSc Aston, 1975. *Publications:* papers and articles on relationships between people in industry. *Recreation:* sailing. *Address:* Courtyard House,

High Street, Lymington, Hants SO4 9AH. *T:* Lymington 72593. *Clubs:* Metallics; Royal Ocean Racing, Royal Cruising, Royal Lymington Yacht.

BONDI, Prof. Sir Hermann, KCB 1973; FRS 1959; FRAS; Master of Churchill College, Cambridge, since 1983; Professor of Mathematics, King's College, London, since 1954 (titular since 1971, emeritus since 1985); *b* Vienna, 1 Nov. 1919; *s* of late Samuel and Helene Bondi, New York; *m* 1947, Christine M. Stockman, *d* of late H. W. Stockman, CBE; two *s* three *d. Educ:* Realgymnasium, Vienna; Trinity Coll., Cambridge (MA). Temporary Experimental Officer, Admiralty, 1942–45; Fellow Trinity Coll., Cambridge, 1943–49, and 1952–54; Asst Lecturer, Mathematics, Cambridge, 1945–48; University Lecturer, Mathematics, Cambridge, 1948–54. Dir-Gen., ESRO, 1967–71; Chief Scientific Advr, MoD, 1971–77; Chief Scientist, Dept of Energy, 1977–80; Chm. and Chief Exec., NERC, 1980–84. Research Associate, Cornell Univ., 1951; Lecturer, Harvard Coll. Observatory, 1953; Lowell Lecturer, Boston, Mass, 1953; Visiting Prof. Cornell Univ., 1960; Halley Lecturer, Oxford, 1962; Tarner Lectr, Cambridge, 1965; Lees-Knowles Lectr, Cambridge, 1974. Chairman: Space Cttee, MoD, 1964–65; Nat. Cttee for Astronomy, 1963–67; Adv. Council on Energy Conservation, 1980–82; IFIAS 1984–. Secretary, Royal Astronomical Soc., 1956–64; Mem., SRC, 1973–80. President: Inst. of Mathematics and its Applications, 1974–75; British Humanist Assoc.; Assoc. of British Science Writers, 1981–85; Soc. for Res. into Higher Educn, 1981–; Assoc. for Science Educn, 1982; Hydrographic Soc., 1985–; Rationalist Press Assoc., 1982–. Member: Science Policy Foundn; Mem., Ct, London Univ., 1963–67. FKC 1968. Hon. DSc: Sussex 1974; Bath 1974; Surrey 1974; York 1980; Southampton 1981; Salford, 1982; Birmingham, 1984; St Andrews, 1985. Hon. FIEE 1979. Einstein Soc. gold medal, 1983. *Publications:* Cosmology, 1952 (2nd edn, 1960); The Universe at Large, 1961; Relativity and Commonsense, 1964; Assumption and Myth in Physical Theory, 1968; (with Dame Kathleen Ollerenshaw) Magic Squares of Order Four, 1982; papers on astrophysics, etc, in Proc. Royal Society, Monthly Notices, Royal Astronomical Society, Proc. Cam. Phil. Society, etc. *Recreations:* walking, skiing, travelling. *Address:* The Master's Lodge, Churchill College, Cambridge.

BONE, Charles, PRI, ARCA, FRSA; President, Royal Institute of Painters in Water Colours, since 1979; Governor, Federation of British Artists, 1976–81 and since 1983 (Member, Executive Council, 1983–84); *b* 15 Sept. 1926; *s* of William Stanley and Elizabeth Bone; *m* Sheila Mitchell, FRBS, ARCA, sculptor; two *s. Educ:* Farnham Coll. of Art; Royal Coll. of Art (ARCA). FBI Award for Design. Consultant, COSIRA, 1952–70; Craft Adviser, Malta Inds Assoc., Malta, 1952–78; Lecturer, Brighton Coll. of Art, 1950–; Director, RI Galleries, Piccadilly, 1965–70. Many mural paintings completed, including those in Eaton Square and Meretea, Italy; oils and water colours in exhibns of RA, London Group, NEAC and RBA, 1950–; 23 one-man exhibns, 1950–; works in private collections in France, Italy, Malta, America, Canada, Japan, Australia, Norway, Sweden, Germany. Designer of Stourhead Ball, 1959–69; produced Ceramic Mural on the History of Aerial Photography. Critic for Arts Review. Mem. Council, RI, 1964– (Vice-Pres. 1974). Hon. FCA (Can.). Hunting Gp Prize for a British Watercolour, 1984. *Address:* Winters Farm, Puttenham, Guildford, Surrey. *T:* Guildford 810226.

BONE, Ven. John Frank Ewan; Archdeacon of Buckingham, since 1978; *b* 28 Aug. 1930; *s* of Jack and Herberta Blanche Bone; *m* 1954, Ruth Margaret Crudgington; two *s* two *d* and one adopted *s. Educ:* Monkton Combe School, Bath; St Peter's Coll., Oxford (MA); Ely Theological Coll.; Whitelands Coll. of Education (Grad. Cert. in Education). Ordained, 1956; Assistant Curate: St Gabriel's, Warwick Square, 1956–60; St Mary's, Henley on Thames, 1960–63; Vicar of Datchet, 1963–76; Rector of Slough, 1976–78; Rural Dean of Burnham, 1974–77. Mem. of General Synod, 1980–85. *Recreations:* collecting antique maps and prints, classical music, do-it-yourself, gardening. *Address:* 60 Wendover Road, Aylesbury, Bucks HP21 9LW. *T:* Aylesbury 23269.

BONE, Quentin, JP; MA, DPhil; FRS 1984; Zoologist, Marine Biological Assocation UK (Senior Principal Scientific Officer), since 1959; *b* 17 Aug. 1931; *s* of late Stephen Bone and of Mary Adshead, *qv*; *m* 1958, Susan Elizabeth Smith; four *s. Educ:* Warwick Sch.; St John's Coll., Oxon. Naples Scholarship, 1954; Fellow by examination, Magdalen Coll., Oxford, 1956. Zoologist at Plymouth Laboratory, 1959. *Publications:* Biology of Fishes (with N. B. Marshall), 1983; papers on fish and invertebrates, mainly in Jl of Mar. Biol Assoc. UK. *Address:* Marchant House, 98 Church Road, Plymstock, Plymouth, Devon.

BONE, Roger Bridgland; HM Diplomatic Service; Counsellor, Washington, since 1985; *b* 29 July 1944; *s* of late Horace Bridgland Bone and of Dora R. Bone (*née* Tring); *m* 1970, Lena M. Bergman; one *s* one *d. Educ:* William Palmer's Sch., Grays; St Peter's Coll., Oxford (MA). Entered HM Diplomatic Service, 1966; UK Mission to UN, 1966; FCO, 1967; 3rd Sec., Stockholm, 1968–70; 2nd Sec., FCO, 1970–73; 1st Secretary: Moscow, 1973–75; FCO, 1975–78; UK Perm. Rep. to European Communities, Brussels, 1978–82; Asst Private Sec. to Sec. of State for Foreign and Commonwealth Affairs, 1982–84; Vis. Fellow, Harvard Univ. Center for Internat. Affairs, 1984–85. *Recreations:* music, wine. *Address:* c/o Foreign and Commonwealth Office, SW1A 2AH.

BONE, Mrs Stephen; *see* Adshead, Mary.

BONE, Dr Thomas Renfrew; Principal, Jordanhill College of Education, since 1972; *b* 1935; *s* of James Renfrew Bone and Mary Williams; *m* 1959, Elizabeth Stewart; one *s* one *d. Educ:* Greenock High Sch.; Glasgow Univ. MA 1st cl. English 1956, MEd 1st cl. 1962, PhD 1967. Teacher, Paisley Grammar Sch., 1957–62; Lecturer: Jordanhill Coll., 1962–63; Glasgow Univ., 1963–67; Hd of Educn Dept, Jordanhill Coll., 1967–71. Chairman: Scottish Council for Educnl Technology, 1981–; CNAA Educn Organisation and Management Bd, 1984–; Vice-Chm., Scottish Tertiary Educn Adv. Council, 1984–; Member: Gen. Teaching Council for Scotland, 1974–; IBA Educn Adv. Council, 1977–. FCCEA 1984. *Publications:* Studies in History of Scottish Education, 1967; School Inspection in Scotland, 1968; *chapters in:* Whither Scotland, 1971; Education Administration in Australia and Abroad, 1975; Administering Education: international challenge, 1975; European Perspectives in Teacher Education, 1976; Education for Development, 1977; Practice of Teaching, 1978; World Yearbook of Education, 1980; The Management of Educational Institutions, 1982; The Effective Teacher, 1983; Strathclyde: changing horizons, 1985. *Recreation:* golf. *Address:* Jordanhill College of Education, Southbrae Drive, Glasgow G13 1PP. *T:* 041–959 1232. *Clubs:* Royal Commonwealth Society; Western Gailes Golf; Paisley Burns, Paisley Bohemians.

BONFIELD, Peter Leahy; Chairman and Managing Director, STC International Computers Ltd, since 1984; Director, STC plc, since 1985; *b* 3 June 1944; *s* of George and Patricia Bonfield; *m* 1968, Josephine Houghton. *Educ:* Hitchin Boys Grammar School, Loughborough Univ. (BTech Hons). Texas Instruments Inc., Dallas, USA, 1966–81; Group Exec. Dir, ICL, 1981–84. *Recreations:* music, sailing, jogging. *Address:* Truchas House, Towpath, Shepperton, Middx. *T:* Walton-on-Thames 247420; (office) 01–788 7272. *Club:* Royal Automobile.

BONHAM, Major Sir Antony Lionel Thomas, 4th Bt, *cr* 1852; DL; late Royal Scots Greys; *b* 21 Oct. 1916; *o s* of Maj. Sir Eric H. Bonham, 3rd Bt, and Ethel (*d* 1962), *y d* of Col Leopold Seymour; *S* father 1937; *m* 1944, Felicity, *o d* of late Col. Frank L. Pardoe, DSO, Bartonbury, Cirencester; three *s. Educ:* Eton; RMC. Served Royal Scots Greys, 1937–49; retired with rank of Major, 1949. DL Glos 1983. *Heir: s* (George) Martin (Antony) Bonham [*b* 18 Feb. 1945; *m* 1979, Nenon Baillieu, *e d* of R. R. Wilson and Hon. Mrs Wilson, Durford Knoll, Upper Durford Wood, Petersfield, Hants; one *s* two *d*]. *Address:* Ash House, Ampney Crucis, Cirencester, Glos. *T:* Poulton 391.

BONHAM CARTER, family name of **Baron Bonham-Carter.**

BONHAM-CARTER, Baron *cr* 1986 (Life Peer), of Yarnbury in the county of Wiltshire; **Mark Raymond Bonham Carter;** Editorial Consultant, William Collins Publishers, since 1981; Chairman: National Video Corporation Ltd, since 1986; Covent Garden Video Productions Ltd, since 1981; Chairman, Governors of The Royal Ballet, since 1985 (Governor, since 1960); *b* 11 Feb. 1922; *e s* of late Sir Maurice Bonham Carter, KCB, KCVO, and Violet, *d* of 1st Earl of Oxford and Asquith, KG, PC (Baroness Asquith of Yarnbury, DBE); *m* 1955, Leslie, *d* of Condé Nast, NY; three *d* and one step-*d. Educ:* Winchester; Balliol Coll., Oxford (Scholar); University of Chicago (Commonwealth Fund Fellowship). Served Grenadier Guards, 1941–45; 8th Army (Africa) and 21st Army Group (NW Europe); captured, 1943; escaped; (despatches). Contested (L) Barnstaple, 1945; MP (L), Torrington Div. of Devonshire, March 1958–59; Mem., UK Delegn to the Council of Europe, 1958–59; contested (L) Torrington, 1964. Director, Wm Collins & Co. Ltd, 1955–58. First Chm., Race Relations Bd, 1966–70; Chm., Community Relations Commn, 1971–77; Vice-President: Consumers' Assoc., 1972– (Mem. Council, 1966–71); Anglo-Polish Round Table Conf., 1971–; Mem. Council, Inst. of Race Relations, 1966–72. Chm., Writers and Scholars Educnl Trust, 1977–. A Dir, Royal Opera House, Covent Garden, 1958–82; Vice Chm. and a Governor, BBC, 1975–81. Chm., Outer Circle Policy Unit, 1976–80. Mem. Court of Governors, LSE, 1970–81. Hon. Fellow, Manchester Polytechnic. Hon. LLD Dundee, 1978. *Publications:* (ed) The Autobiography of Margot Asquith, 1962; contributor to: Radical Alternative (essays), 1962; articles, reviews in various jls. *Address:* 13 Clarendon Road, W11. *T:* 01–229 5200. *Clubs:* Brooks's, MCC.

See also Hon. R. H. Bonham Carter.

BONHAM-CARTER, John Arkwright, CVO 1975; DSO 1942; OBE 1967; ERD 1952; Chairman and General Manager, British Railways London Midland Region, 1971–75; *b* 27 March 1915; *s* of late Capt. Guy Bonham-Carter, 19th Hussars, and Kathleen Rebecca (*née* Arkwright); *m* 1939, Anne Louisa Charteris; two *s. Educ:* Winchester Coll.; King's Coll., Cambridge (Exhibitioner). 1st class hons Mech. Scis, Cantab, 1936; MA 1970. Joined LNER Co. as Traffic Apprentice, 1936; served in Royal Tank Regt, 1939–46 (despatches, 1940 and 1942); subsequently rejoined LNER; held various appointments; Asst General Manager, BR London Midland Region, 1963–65; Chief Operating Officer, BR Board, 1966–68; Chm. and Gen. Manager, BR Western Region, 1968–71. Lieut-Col, Engr and Transport (formerly Engr and Rly) Staff Corps RE (TA), 1966–71, Col 1971–. FCIT. KStJ 1984; Comdr, St John Ambulance, Dorset, 1984–. *Recreations:* theatre, foreign travel, cabinet making and carpentry. *Address:* Redbridge House, Crossways, Dorchester, Dorset DT2 8DY. *T:* Warmwell 852669. *Club:* Army and Navy.

BONHAM CARTER, Hon. Raymond Henry; Executive Director, S. G. Warburg & Co. Ltd, 1967–77; retired in 1979 following disability; *b* 19 June 1929; *s* of Sir Maurice Bonham Carter, KCB, KCVO, and Lady Violet Bonham Carter, DBE (later Baroness Asquith of Yarnbury); *m* 1958, Elena Propper de Callejon; two *s* one *d. Educ:* Winchester Coll.; Magdalen Coll., Oxford (BA 1952); Harvard Business Sch. (MBA 1954). Irish Guards, 1947–49. With J. Henry Schröder & Co., 1954–58; acting Advr, Bank of England, 1958–63; Alternate Exec. Dir for UK, IMF, and Mem., UK Treasury and Supply Delegn, Washington, 1961–63; S. G. Warburg & Co. Ltd, 1964; Director: Transport Development Group Ltd, 1969–77; Banque de Paris et des Pays Bas NV, 1973–77; Mercury Securities Ltd, 1974–77; seconded as Dir, Industrial Develt Unit, DoI, 1977–79. Mem. Council, Internat. Inst. for Strategic Studies (Hon. Treasurer, 1974–84). *Address:* 7 West Heath Avenue, NW11 7QS. *T:* 01–455 8434.

See also Baron Bonham-Carter.

BONHAM CARTER, Richard Erskine; Physician to the Hospital for Sick Children, Great Ormond Street, 1947–75, to University College Hospital, 1948–66; *b* 27 Aug. 1910; *s* of late Capt. A. E. Bonham-Carter and late M. E. Bonham-Carter (*née* Malcolm); *m* 1946, Margaret (*née* Stace); three *d. Educ:* Clifton Coll.; Peterhouse, Cambridge; St Thomas' Hospital. Resident Asst Physician, Hospital for Sick Children, Great Ormond Street, 1938. Served War of 1939–45 in RAMC; DADMS 1 Airborne Div., 1942–45; despatches, 1944. *Publications:* contributions to Text-Books of Pædiatrics and to medical journals. *Recreations:* gardening, fishing. *Address:* 18 Doughty Mews, WC1N 2PF. *T:* 01–405 3062; Castle Sweyn Cottage, Achnamara, Argyll.

BONHAM-CARTER, Victor; Joint Secretary, Society of Authors, 1971–78, Consultant, 1978–82; Secretary, Royal Literary Fund, 1966–82; *b* 13 Dec. 1913; *s* of Gen. Sir Charles Bonham-Carter, GCB, CMG, DSO, and Gabrielle Madge Jeanette (*née* Fisher); *m* 1st, 1938, Audrey Edith Stogdon (marr. diss. 1979); two *s*; 2nd, 1979, Cynthia Claire Sanford. *Educ:* Winchester Coll.; Magdalene Coll., Cambridge (MA); Hamburg and Paris. Worked on The Countryman, 1936–37; Dir, School Prints Ltd, 1937–39, 1945–60; Army, R Berks Regt and Intell. Corps, 1939–45; farmed in W Somerset, 1947–59; historian of Dartington Hall Estate, Devon, 1951–66; on staff of Soc. of Authors, 1963–82. Active in Exmoor National Park affairs, 1955–; Pres., Exmoor Soc., 1975–; Partner, Exmoor Press, 1969–. *Publications:* The English Village, 1952; (with W. B. Curry) Dartington Hall, 1958; Exploring Parish Churches, 1959; Farming the Land, 1959; In a Liberal Tradition, 1960; Soldier True, 1965; Surgeon in the Crimea, 1969; The Survival of the English Countryside, 1971; Authors by Profession, vol. 1 1978, vol. 2 1984; many contribs to jls, radio, etc on country life and work; also on authorship matters, esp. Public Lending Right. *Recreations:* music, conversation. *Address:* The Mount, Milverton, Taunton TA4 1QZ. *Club:* Authors'.

BONINGTON, Christian John Storey, CBE 1976; mountaineer, writer and photographer; *b* 6 Aug. 1934; *s* of Charles Bonington, journalist, and Helen Anne Bonington (*née* Storey); *m* 1962, Muriel Wendy Marchant; two *s* (and one *s* decd). *Educ:* University Coll. Sch., London. RMA Sandhurst, 1955–56; commnd Royal Tank Regt, 1956–61. Unilever Management Trainee, 1961–62; writer and photographer, 1962–. Climbs: Annapurna II, 26,041 ft (1st ascent) 1960; Central Pillar Freney, Mont Blanc (1st ascent), 1961; Nuptse, 25,850 ft (1st ascent), 1961; North Wall of Eiger (1st British ascent), 1962; Central Tower of Paine, Patagonia (1st ascent), 1963; Mem. of team, first descent of Blue Nile, 1968; Leader: successful Annapurna South Face Expedition, 1970; British Everest Expedition, 1972; Brammah, Himalayas (1st ascent), 1973; co-leader, Changabang, Himalayas (1st ascent), 1974; British Everest Expedition (1st ascent SW face), 1975; Ogre (1st ascent), 1977; jt leader, Kongur, NW China (1st ascent), 1981; Shivling West (1st ascent), 1983; Mt Vinson, highest point of Antarctica (1st British ascent), 1983; reached Everest summit, 1985. Vice-President: British Mountaineering

Council, 1976–79, 1985–; Army Mountaineering Assoc., 1980–; Pres., British Orienteering Fedn, 1985. Pres., LEPRA, 1983. FRGS (Founders' Medal, 1974). Hon. Fellow, UMIST, 1976; Hon. MA Salford, 1973; Hon. DSc: Sheffield, 1976; Lancaster, 1983. Lawrence of Arabia Medal, RSAA, 1986. *Publications:* I Chose to Climb (autobiog.), 1966; Annapurna South Face, 1971; The Next Horizon (autobiog.), 1973; Everest, South West Face, 1973; Everest the Hard Way, 1976; Quest for Adventure, 1981; Kongur: China's elusive summit, 1982; (jtly) Everest: the unclimbed ridge, 1983. *Recreations:* mountaineering, squash, orienteering. *Address:* Badger Hill, Nether Row, Hesket Newmarket, Wigton, Cumbria. *T:* Caldbeck 286. *Clubs:* Alpine, Alpine Ski, Army and Navy, Climbers, Fell and Rock Climbing, Border Liners.

BONNER, Frederick Ernest, CBE 1974; Deputy Chairman, Central Electricity Generating Board, 1975–86; Member (part-time), UKAEA, 1977–86; Chairman, Uranium Institute, 1985–87; *b* 16 Sept. 1923; *s* of late George Frederick Bonner and Mrs Bonner, Hammersmith; *m* 1st, 1957, Phyllis (*d* 1976), *d* of late Mr and Mrs H. Holder; 2nd, 1977, Mary, *widow* of Ellis Walter Aries, AFC, ARICS. *Educ:* St Clement Danes Holborn Estate Grammar Sch. BSc(Econ) London; DPA, JDipMA. Local Govt (Fulham and Ealing Borough Councils), 1940–49. Central Electricity Authority: Sen. Accountant, 1949–50; Asst Finance Officer, 1950–58; Central Electricity Generating Board: Asst Chief Financial Officer, 1958–61; Dep. Chief Financial Officer, 1961–65; Chief Financial Officer, 1965–69; Member, 1969–75; Chm., British Airways Helicopters, 1983–85. FCA, IPFA, CBIM. *Recreations:* music, gardening, reading. *Address:* Joya, Craigweil Manor, The Drive, Bognor Regis, W Sussex PO21 4DJ.

BONNER, Paul Max; Executive Director and Programme Controller, Channel Four Television Co. Ltd, since 1983; *b* 30 Nov. 1934; *s* of Jill and late Frank Bonner; *m* 1956, Jenifer Hubbard; two *s* one *d*. *Educ:* Felsted Sch., Essex. National Service commission, 1953–55. Local journalism, 1955; Radio production, BBC Bristol, 1955–57; Television production, BBC Bristol, 1957–59, BBC Lime Grove, 1959–62; Television Documentary prodn and direction, BBC Lime Grove and Kensington House, 1962–74; Editor, Community Programmes for BBC, 1974–77; Head of Science and Features Programmes for BBC, 1977–80; Channel Controller, Channel Four TV, 1980–83. A Manager, Royal Instn, 1982–85; Governor, Nat. Film and TV School, 1983–; Dir, Broadcasting Support Services, 1982–; Mem., BAFTA, 1971–. *Publications: documentaries include:* Strange Excellency, 1964; Climb up to Hell, 1967; Lost: Four H Bombs, 1967; Search for the Real Che Guevara, 1971; Who Sank the Lusitania?, 1972. *Recreations:* photography, the theatre, sailing, walking, listening to good conversation. *Address:* North View, Wimbledon Common, SW19 4UJ. *Club:* Reform.

BONNET, C. M.; *see* Melchior-Bonnet.

BONNET, Maj.-Gen. Peter Robert Frank, MBE 1975; Director Royal Artillery, since 1986; *b* 12 Dec. 1936; *s* of James Robert and Phyllis Elsie Bonnet; *m* 1961, Sylvia Mary Coy; two *s*. *Educ:* Royal Military Coll. of Science, Shrivenham. BSc (Engrg). Commnd from RMA Sandhurst, 1958; RMCS Shrivenham, 1959–62; apptd to RHA, 1962; Staff trng, RMCS and Staff Coll., Camberley, 1969–70; Comd (Lt-Col), 26 Field Regt, RA, 1978–81; Comd RA (Brig.) 2nd Div., 1982–84; attendance at Indian Nat. Defence Coll., New Delhi, 1985. *Recreations:* tennis, sculpture, painting. *Address:* The Director's House, Royal Military Academy, Woolwich, SE18 4JJ. *T:* 01–856 6691; (office) Headquarters, Director Royal Artillery, Woolwich, SE18 4BH. *T:* 01–856 5533; The Old Rectory, East Street, South Molton, Devon EX36 3DF. *T:* South Molton 2344.

BONNETT, Prof. Raymond, CChem, FRSC; Professor of Organic Chemistry since 1976, and Head of Department of Chemistry since 1982, Queen Mary College, London; *b* 13 July 1931; *s* of Harry and Maud Bonnett; *m* 1956, Shirley Rowe; two *s* one *d*. *Educ:* County Grammar Sch., Bury St Edmunds; Imperial Coll. (BSc, ARCS); Cambridge Univ. (PhD); DSc London 1972. Salters' Fellow, Cambridge, 1957–58; Res. Fellow, Harvard, 1958–59; Asst Prof., Dept of Chemistry, Univ. of British Columbia, 1959–61; Lectr in Organic Chem., 1961–66, Reader in Organic Chem., 1966–74, Prof. 1974–76, QMC, London Univ. *Publications:* sci. papers, esp. in Jls of Royal Soc. of Chemistry and Biochemical Soc. *Recreations:* theatre, private press books, gardening. *Address:* Elmbank, 19 Station Road, Epping, Essex CM16 4HG. *T:* Epping 73203.

BONNEY, George Louis William, MS, FRCS; Consulting Orthopædic Surgeon, St Mary's Hospital, London, since 1984; *b* 10 Jan. 1920; *s* of late Dr Ernest Bonney and Gertrude Mary Williams; *m* 1950, Margaret Morgan; two *d*. *Educ:* Eton (Scholar); St Mary's Hospital Medical Sch. MB, BS, MRCS, LRCP 1943; FRCS 1945; MS (London) 1947. Formerly: Surg.-Lieut RNVR; Research Assistant and Senior Registrar, Royal National Orthopædic Hospital; Consultant Orthopædic Surgeon: Southend Group of Hospitals; St Mary's Hosp., London, 1954–84 (Sen. Consultant, 1979–84). Travelling Fellowship of British Postgraduate Med. Fedn, Univ. of London, 1950. Watson-Jones Lectr, RCS, 1976. Mem. Council, Medical Defence Union; Mem., SICOT. *Publications:* Chapters in Operative Surgery, 1957; papers in medical journals on visceral pain, circulatory mechanisms, nerve injuries and on various aspects of orthopædic surgery. *Recreations:* fishing, shooting, photography, music. *Address:* 71 Porchester Terrace, W2 3TT. *T:* 01–262 4236; Wyeside Cottages, Much Fawley, Hereford HR1 4SP. *Club:* Leander.

BONNICI, Carmelo M.; *see* Mifsud Bonnici.

BONSALL, Sir Arthur (Wilfred), KCMG 1977; CBE 1957; *b* 25 June 1917; *s* of late Wilfred Bonsall and Sarah Bonsall; *m* 1941, Joan Isabel Wingfield; four *s* three *d*. *Educ:* Bishop's Stortford Coll.; St Catharine's Coll., Cambridge. 2nd Cl. Hons Mod. Langs. Joined Air Ministry, 1940; transf. to FO 1942; IDC, 1962; Dir, Govt Communications HQ, 1973–78. *Recreation:* coarse gardening. *Address:* 176 Slad Road, Stroud, Glos GL5 1RJ.

See also F. F. Bonsall.

BONSALL, Prof. Frank Featherstone, FRS 1970; Professor of Mathematics, University of Edinburgh, 1965–84, now Emeritus; *b* 1920; *s* of late Wilfred Bonsall and Sarah Bonsall; *m* 1947, Gillian Patrick. *Educ:* Bishop's Stortford Coll.; Merton Coll., Oxford. *Publications* (all with J. Duncan): Numerical Ranges of Operators on Normed Spaces and of Elements of Normed Algebras, 1971, Numerical Ranges II, 1973; Complete Normed Algebras, 1973. *Recreation:* walking. *Address:* 18 Rossett Park Road, Harrogate HG2 9NP.

See also Sir A. W. Bonsall.

BONSER, Ven. David; Archdeacon of Rochdale, since 1982; Team Rector of the Rochdale team ministry, since 1982 (Vicar of St Chad's, 1982–86); *b* 1 Feb. 1934; *s* of George Frederick and Alice Bonser; *m* 1960, Shirley Wilkinson; one *s* two *d*. *Educ:* Hillhouse Secondary Sch., Huddersfield; King's Coll., London Univ. (AKC); Manchester Univ. (MA). Curate: St James's, Heckmondwike, 1962–65; St George's, Sheffield, 1965–68; Rector of St Clement's, Chorlton-cum-Hardy, 1968–82; Hon. Canon of Manchester Cathedral, 1980–82; Area Dean of Hulme, 1981–82. *Recreations:* theatre, reading, walking, skiing, music. *Address:* The Vicarage, 21 Belmont Way, Rochdale, Lancs OL12 6HR. *T:* Rochdale 48640. *Club:* Royal Commonwealth Society.

BONSER, Air Vice-Marshal Stanley Haslam, CB 1969; MBE 1942; CEng, FRAeS; Director, Easams Ltd, 1972–81; *b* 17 May 1916; *s* of late Sam Bonser and late Phoebe Ellen Bonser; *m* 1941, Margaret Betty Howard; two *s*. *Educ:* Sheffield University. BSc 1938; DipEd 1939. Armament Officer, Appts, 1939–44; British Air Commn, Washington, DC, 1944–46; Coll. of Aeronautics, 1946–47; RAE, Guided Weapons, 1947–51; Chief Instr (Armament Wing) RAF Techn. Coll., 1951–52; Staff Coll., Bracknell, 1953, psa 1953; Project Officer, Blue Streak, Min. of Technology, 1954–57; Asst Dir, GW Engineering, 1957–60; Senior RAF Officer, Skybolt Development Team, USA, 1960–62; Dir, Aircraft Mechanical Engineering, 1963–64; Dir, RAF Aircraft Development (mainly Nimrod), 1964–69; Dep. Controller: of Equipment, Min. of Technology and MoD, 1969–71; Aircraft C, MoD, 1971–72. *Recreations:* scout movement, gardening. *Address:* Chalfont, Waverley Avenue, Fleet, Hants GU13 8NW. *T:* Fleet 615835. *Club:* Royal Air Force.

BONSEY, Mary, (Mrs Lionel Bonsey); *see* Norton, M.

BONSOR, Sir Nicholas (Cosmo), 4th Bt *cr* 1925; MP (C) Upminster, since 1983 (Nantwich, 1979–83); *b* 9 Dec. 1942; *s* of Sir Bryan Cosmo Bonsor, 3rd Bt, MC, TD, and of Elizabeth, *d* of late Captain Angus Valdimar Hambro; *S* father, 1977; *m* 1969, Hon. Nadine Marisa Lampson, *d* of 2nd Baron Killearn, *qv*; two *s* one *d*. *Educ:* Eton; Keble College, Oxford (MA). Barrister-at-law, Inner Temple. Served Royal Buckinghamshire Yeomanry, 1964–69. Practised at the Bar, 1967–75. CLA Legal and Parly Sub-Cttee, 1978–; Sec., Cons. Africa Sub-Cttee, 1979–80; Vice-Chm., Cons. Foreign Affairs Cttee, 1981–83. Chm., Cyclotron Trust for Cancer Treatment, 1984–; Trustee: Baronets' Trust, 1986–; Verdin Trust for Mentally Handicapped, 1983–. FRSA 1970. *Publications:* political pamphlets on law and trades unions and defence. *Recreations:* sailing, shooting, military history. *Heir: s* Alexander Cosmo Walrond Bonsor, *b* 8 Sept. 1976. *Address:* Liscombe Park, Leighton Buzzard, Beds. *Clubs:* White's, Pratt's; Royal Yacht Squadron.

BONY, Prof. Jean V., MA; Professor of the History of Art, University of California at Berkeley, 1962–80, now Emeritus; *b* Le Mans, France, 1 Nov. 1908; *s* of Henri Bony and Marie Normand; *m* 1st, 1936, Clotilde Roure (*d* 1942); one *d*; 2nd, 1953, Mary England. *Educ:* Lycée Louis-le-Grand, Paris; Sorbonne. Agrégé d'Histoire Paris; MA Cantab; Hon. FSA; Corres. Fellow, British Academy. Bulteau-Lavisse Research Scholarship, 1935–37; Asst Master, Eton Coll., 1937–39 and 1945–46. Served War of 1939–45; 1st Lieut, French Infantry, 1939–44; POW, Germany, June 1940–Dec. 1943. Research Scholar, Centre Nat. de la Recherche Scientifique, 1944–45; Lecturer in History of Art at the French Inst. in London, 1946–61. Focillon Fellow and Vis. Lectr, Yale Univ., 1949; Slade Prof. of Fine Art, University of Cambridge, and Fellow of St John's Coll., Cambridge, 1958–61; Vis. Prof. and Mathews Lectr, Columbia Univ., 1961; Lecturer in History of Art at the University of Lille, France, 1961–62; Wrightsman Lectr, New York Univ., 1969; Vis. Fellow, Humanities Res. Centre, ANU, 1978; John Simon Guggenheim Meml Fellow, 1981; Kress Prof., Nat. Gall. of Art, Washington, 1982; Vis. Andrew W. Mellon Prof. of Fine Arts, Univ. of Pittsburgh, 1983; Algur H. Meadows Prof. of Art Hist., Southern Methodist Univ., Dallas, 1984–86. *Publications:* Notre-Dame de Mantes, 1946; French Cathedrals (with M. Hürlimann and P. Meyer), 1951 (revised edn, 1967); (ed) H. Focillon: The Art of the West in the Middle Ages, English edn 1963, new edn 1969; The English Decorated Style, 1979; French Gothic Architecture of the 12th and 13th Centuries, 1983; articles in Bulletin Monumental, Congrès Archéologiques de France, Journal of Warburg and Courtauld Institutes, Journal of British Archæological Assoc., etc. *Address:* Department of History of Art, University of California, Berkeley, California 94720, USA.

BONYNGE, Dame Joan; *see* Sutherland, Dame Joan.

BONYNGE, Richard, AO 1983; CBE 1977; opera conductor; *b* Sydney, 29 Sept. 1930; *s* of C. A. Bonynge, Epping, NSW; *m* 1954, Dame Joan Sutherland, *qv*; one *s*. *Educ:* Sydney Conservatorium (pianist). Official debut, as Conductor, with Santa Cecilia Orch. in Rome, 1962; conducted first opera, Faust, Vancouver, 1963. Has conducted in most leading opera houses in world, and in Edinburgh, Vienna and Florence Fests. Has been Princ. Conductor and Artistic/Musical Dir of cos, incl. Sutherland/Williamson Internat. Grand Opera Co., Aust., 1965; Vancouver Opera, 1974–78; Australian Opera, 1975–85. Many opera and ballet recordings; also recital discs with Sutherland, Tebaldi, Tourangeau and Pavarotti, and many orchestral and ballet anthologies. *Address:* c/o Ingpen and Williams, 14 Kensington Court, W8.

BOOKER, Christopher John Penrice; journalist and author; *b* 7 Oct. 1937; *s* of late John Booker and of Margaret Booker, Shillingstone, Dorset; *m* 1979, Valerie, *d* of late Dr M. S. Patrick, OBE; two *s*. *Educ:* Dragon Sch., Oxford; Shrewsbury Sch.; Corpus Christi Coll., Cambridge (History). Liberal News, 1960; jazz critic, Sunday Telegraph, 1961; Editor, Private Eye, 1961–63, and regular contributor, 1965–; resident scriptwriter, That Was The Week That Was, 1962–63, and Not So Much A Programme, 1963–64; contributor to Spectator, 1962–, Daily Telegraph, 1972–, and to many other newspapers and jls; book reviewer, Sunday Telegraph, 1979–. Wrote extensively on property devlt, planning and housing, 1972–77 (with Bennie Gray, Campaigning Journalist of the Year, 1973); City of Towers—the Rise and Fall of a Twentieth Century Dream (TV prog.), 1979. *Publications:* The Neophiliacs: a study of the revolution in English life in the 50s and 60s, 1969; (with Candida Lycett-Green) Goodbye London, 1973; The Booker Quiz, 1976; The Seventies, 1980; The Games War: a Moscow journal, 1981; contrib. Private Eye anthologies. *Recreations:* Jungian psychology, music, following Somerset cricket team. *Address:* The Old Shop, Lamyatt, near Shepton Mallet, Somerset BA4 6NP. *T:* Bruton 812401.

BOOKER-MILBURN, Donald; Sheriff of Grampian, Highland and Islands, since 1983; *b* Dornoch, 20 May 1940; *s* of late Captain Booker Milburn, DSO, MC, Coldstream Guards, and late Betty Calthrop Calthrop; *m* 1963, Marjorie Lilian Elizabeth Burns; one *s* one *d*. *Educ:* Trinity College, Glenalmond; Grenoble Univ.; Jesus Coll., Cambridge (BA); Edinburgh Univ. (LLB). Admitted to Faculty of Advocates, 1968; Standing Junior Counsel to RAF, 1977–80; Sheriff of Lothian and Borders, 1980–83. *Recreations:* golf, skiing. *Address:* Clashmore House, Clashmore, Dornoch, Sutherland. *Clubs:* New (Edinburgh), Royal Dornoch Golf.

BOOLELL, Sir Satcam, Kt 1977; Minister of Economic Planning, Mauritius, since 1983; *b* New Grove, Mauritius, 11 Sept. 1920; *m* 1948, Inderjeet Kissoodaye; two *s* one *d*. *Educ:* primary and secondary schs in New Grove, Mare d'Albert, Rose Belle, and Port-Louis; LSE (LLB Hons 1951). Called to the Bar, Lincoln's Inn, 1952. Civil servant, Mauritius, 1944–48. Minister of Agric. and Natural Resources, 1959–82. Mem. Central Exec., Mauritius Labour Party, 1955–. Rep. Mauritius, internat. confs. Founder, French daily newspaper, The Nation. *Recreations:* reading travel books, gardening, walking in the countryside. *Address:* 4bis Bancilhon Street, Port-Louis. *T:* 2–0079.

BOON, George Counsell, FSA; FRHistS; FRNS; Senior Keeper of Archaeology and Numismatics, National Museum of Wales, since 1986 (Keeper, since 1976); *b* 20 Sept.

1927; *s* of Ronald Hudson Boon and Eveline Counsell; *m* 1956, Diana Margaret Martyn; two *s* one *d*. *Educ:* Bristol Univ. BA Hons (Latin). FRNS 1954; FSA 1955; FRHistS 1978. Archaeological Assistant, Reading Museum and Art Gallery, 1950–56; Asst Keeper, Dept of Archaeology, 1957–76. Member: Ancient Monuments Bd for Wales, 1979–; Royal Commn on Ancient and Historical Monuments (Wales), 1979–. Pres., Cambrian Archaeol Assoc., 1986–87. Vice-President: Soc. for Promotion of Roman Studies, 1977–; Soc. of Antiquaries, 1979–83. Corresp. Mem., German Archaeological Inst., 1968. *Publications:* Roman Silchester, 1957, 2nd edn 1974; Isca, the Roman Legionary Fortress at Caerleon, Mon., 1972; Welsh Tokens of the Seventeenth Century, 1973; Cardiganshire Silver and the Aberystwyth Mint in Peace and War, 1981; Welsh Hoards 1979–1981; contribs to learned journals. *Recreations:* none worth mention. *Address:* 43 Westbourne Road, Penarth, South Glam CF6 2HA. *T:* Penarth 709588. *Clubs:* unclubbable.

BOON, John Trevor, CBE 1968; Chairman, Mills & Boon Ltd, since 1972; *b* 21 Dec. 1916; 3rd *s* of Charles Boon and Mary Boon (*née* Cowpe); *m* 1943, Felicity Ann, *d* of Stewart and Clemence Logan; four *s*. *Educ:* Felsted Sch.; Trinity Hall, Cambridge (scholar). 1st Cl. Pts I and II History Tripos. Served War, 1939–45: with Royal Norfolk Regt and S Wales Borderers (despatches). Historical Section of War Cabinet, 1945–46. Joined Mills & Boon Ltd, 1938, Man. Dir, 1963, Chm., 1972–. Dir, Wood Bros Glass Works Ltd, 1968, Chm., 1973–75, Dep. Chm., 1975–78. Vice Chm., Harlequin Enterprises Ltd, Toronto, 1972–83. Chairman: Harlequin Overseas, 1978–; Marshall Editions, 1977–; Director: Harmex, 1978–82; Harlequin France, 1980–82 (Chm., 1978–80); Torstar Corp., Toronto, 1981–; Open University Educational Enterprises, 1977–79. President: Soc. of Bookmen, 1981; Internat. Publishers Assoc., 1972–76 (Hon. Mem., 1982); Chairman: Publishers Adv. Panel of British Council, 1977–81; Book Trade Res. Cttee, 1978–82; Director: Book Tokens Ltd, 1964–84; Book Trade Improvements Ltd, 1966–84; Publishers Association: Mem. Council, 1953, Treas., 1959–61, Pres., 1961–63, Vice-Pres., 1963–65. Over-seas missions: for British Council, to SE Asia, USSR (twice), Czechoslovakia; for Book Development Council, to Malaysia, Singapore, and New Zealand. Mem. Management Cttee, Wine Soc., 1971–77. Hon. MA, Open Univ., 1983. *Recreations:* walking, swimming, wine, books, friends. *Address:* c/o Royal Bank of Scotland (Holt's Branch), Kirkland House, Whitehall, SW1. *Clubs:* Beefsteak, Garrick, Royal Automobile, Savile; Hawks (Cambridge).

BOON, Sir Peter Coleman, Kt 1979; Director, Hoover Ltd; Goodyear Professor of Business Administration, Kent State University, USA, since 1983; *b* 2 Sept. 1916; *s* of Frank Boon and Evelyn Boon; *m* 1940, Pamela; one *s* one *d*. *Educ:* Felsted. Stock Exchange, 1933–34; Lloyds & National Provincial Foreign Bank, 1934–35; Dennison Mfg Co., USA, 1936–39; Armed Services, War of 1939–45, 1939–46; Dennison Mfg, 1946; graduate trainee, Hoover Ltd, 1946, Managing Dir (Australia), 1955–65; Managing Dir, Hoover Ltd, 1965–75, Chm., 1975–78. Chm., Highclere Investment Trust, 1979–; Dir, Belden & Blake UK Inc. FBIM; FRSA 1980. Hon. LLD Strathclyde, 1978. Chevalier de l'Ordre de la Couronne, Belgium. *Recreations:* horses, swimming, golf, theatre, economics, National Trust for Scotland, boys clubs, education. *Clubs:* Hurlingham, Royal Wimbledon Golf; Burkes, Western Racing, Australian, Imperial Services, Killara Golf, American National, Royal Sydney Yacht Squadron, Australian Jockey, Sydney Turf (Australia); St Anne, Cercle des Nations (Belgium).

BOON, Dr William Robert, FRS 1974; retired; *b* 20 March 1911; *s* of Walter and Ellen Boon; *m* 1938, Marjorie Betty Oury; one *s* two *d*. *Educ:* St Dunstan's Coll., Catford; King's Coll., London. BSc, PhD, FRSC, FKC 1976. Research, Chemotherapy and Crop Protection, ICI, 1936–69; Dir, Jealott's Hill Res. Station, 1964–69; Man. Dir, Plant Protection Ltd, 1969–73. Vis. Prof., Reading Univ., 1968. Member: Adv. Bd for the Research Councils, 1972–76; NERC, 1976–79. Hon. DSc Cranfield, 1981. Mullard Medal of Royal Society, 1972. *Publications:* papers in Jl Chem. Soc., Jl Soc. Chem. Ind., etc. *Recreations:* gardening, photography, woodwork. *Address:* The Gables, Sid Road, Sidmouth, Devon EX10 9AQ. *T:* Sidmouth 4069. *Club:* Farmers'.

BOORD, Sir Nicolas (John Charles), 4th Bt *cr* 1896; scientific translator; English training specialist; *b* 10 June 1936; *s* of Sir Richard William Boord, 3rd Bt, and of Yvonne, Lady Boord, *d* of late J. A. Hubert Bird; *S* father, 1975; *m* 1965, Françoise Renée Louise Mouret. *Educ:* Eton (Harmsworth Lit. Prize, 1952); Sorbonne, France; Societa Dante Alighieri, Italy; Univ. of Santander, Spain. *Publications:* (trans. jtly) The History of Physics and the Philosophy of Science—Selected Essays (Armin Teske), 1972; numerous translations of scientific papers for English and American scientific and technical jls. *Recreations:* English and French literature and linguistics. *Heir:* *b* Antony Andrew Boord [*b* 21 May 1938; *m* 1960, Anna Christina von Krogh; one *s* one *d*]. *Address:* 61 Traverse Le Mée, 13009 Marseille, France. *T:* 73.13.95.

BOORMAN, Lt.-Gen. Sir Derek, KCB 1986 (CB 1982); Chief of Defence Intelligence, since 1985; *b* 13 Sept. 1930; *s* of late N. R. Boorman, MBE, and of Mrs A. L. Boorman (*née* Patman); *m* 1956, Jennifer Jane Skinner; one *s* two *d*. *Educ:* Wolstanton; RMA Sandhurst. Commnd N Staffords, 1950; Adjt 1 Staffords, 1958–59; Staff Coll., 1961; HQ 48 Gurkha Inf. Bde, 1962–64; Jt Services Staff Coll., 1968; CO 1 Staffords, 1969–71; Instr, Staff Coll., 1972–73; Comdr 51 Inf. Bde, 1975–76; RCDS, 1977; Dir, Public Relations (Army), 1978–79; Director of Military Operations, 1980–82; Comdr, British Forces Hong Kong, and Maj.-Gen. Bde of Gurkhas, 1982–85. Colonel: 6th Queen Elizabeth's Own Gurkha Rifles, 1983–; Staffordshire Regt (Prince of Wales's), 1985–. *Recreations:* shooting, gardening, music. *Address:* c/o Lloyds Bank (Cox's & King's Branch), Pall Mall, SW1. *Club:* Naval and Military.

BOORMAN, Edwin Roy Pratt; Managing Director, Kent Messenger Group, since 1965; Managing Director, Messenger Print Ltd; *b* 7 Nov. 1935; *s* of H. R. P. Boorman, *qv*; *m* 1st, Merrilyn Ruth Pettit (marr. diss. 1982); four *d*; 2nd, 1983, Janine Craske; one *s*. *Educ:* Rydal; Queen's Coll., Cambridge (MA Econ. History). National Service, 1954–56. Cambridge Univ., 1956–59; Kent Messenger, 1959; Editor: South Eastern Gazette, 1960–62; Kent Messenger, 1962–65. Summer sch., S Illinois Univ., Carbondale, St Louis, 1962; Kentucky Colonel 1962. Councillor: Newspaper Soc.; London Chamber of Commerce (Mem., F and GP and Econ. Affairs Cttees). Member: Freedom Assoc. (W Kent Chm.); Kent Co. Show Exec. Cttee; Kent Co. Playing Fields Exec. Cttee; Livery Cttee, Worshipful Co. of Stationers and Newspapermakers; President: Dickens Area Newsagents' Benevolent Assoc.; Maidstone Surgical Aid; Vice-Pres., Kent Br. Royal British Legion; Finance Dir, Royal British Legion Industries; Chairman: Publicity Cttee, Medway Regatta; St John Ambulance Appeals Cttee; Governor: Sutton Valence Sch.; Cornwallis Sch. Trustee, Playhouse Theatre Project, Ashford. Vice-Pres., Age Concern, Kent. Tax Comr, Maidstone District 1. *Recreation:* sailing. *Address:* Redhill Farm, 339 Redhill, Wateringbury, Kent ME18 5LB. *Clubs:* Press, Veteran Car, Locomotive of GB; Kent CCC; Royal Yachting Association, Medway Yacht, Ocean Cruising.

BOORMAN, Henry Roy Pratt, CBE 1966 (MBE 1945); President, Kent Messenger Group, since 1982 (Chairman, 1970–82); *b* 21 Sept. 1900; *s* of Barham Pratt Boorman and Elizabeth Rogers Boorman; *m* 1st, 1933, Enid Starke; one *s*; 2nd, 1947, Evelyn Clinch; one *d*. *Educ:* Leys Sch., Cambridge; Queens' Coll., Cambridge (MA). FJI 1936. Entered journalism, 1922; Proprietor and Editor, Kent Messenger, 1928; Chairman, South Eastern Gazette, 1929. Chairman, Kent Newspaper Proprietors' Assoc., 1931, 1932 and 1951; Mem. Council, Newspaper Soc., 1958, President, 1960. War Service: Regional Information Officer, SE Region, Tunbridge Wells, 1939; Dep. Welfare Officer for Kent, 1941; Major 1944; War Correspondent in Europe, 1939–40 and 1944, Berlin, 1949. Association of Men of Kent and Kentish Men: Editor, Journal Kent, 1931–62 (Chm. Council, 1949–51); Association's Sir Edward Hardy Gold Medal, 1964; in 1981, tenor bell in renewed peal in Canterbury Cathedral presented in his name by Kent Messenger staff. Maidstone Town Council: Councillor, 1934–46 and 1961–70; Mayor of Maidstone, 1962, Alderman, 1964. Liveryman, Worshipful Co. of Stationers and Newspaper Makers, 1933 (Mem. Ct of Assts, 1966–72). JP Maidstone Div. of Kent 1962; DL Kent, 1968–82. SBStJ 1946 (Mem. Council, StJ, 1960–66). *Publications:* Merry America (Royal Tour of Canada and United States), 1939; Hell's Corner, 1940; Kent—Our Glorious Heritage, 1951; Kentish Pride, 1952; Kent and the Cinque Ports, 1958; Kent Messenger Centenary, 1959; Kent—a Royal County, 1966; Spirit of Kent—Lord Cornwallis, 1968; Kent Our County, 1979. *Recreation:* world travel. *Address:* St Augustine's Priory, Bilsington, Ashford, Kent TN25 7AU. *T:* Aldington 252. *Clubs:* City Livery, Royal Commonwealth Society, Press, United Wards.

BOORSTIN, Dr Daniel J.; FRHistS; (12th) Librarian of Congress, since Nov. 1975; *b* 1 Oct. 1914; *s* of Samuel Boorstin and Dora (*née* Olsan); *m* 1941, Ruth Carolyn Frankel; three *s*. *Educ:* schs in Tulsa, Okla; Harvard Univ. (AB, summa cum Laude); Balliol Coll., Oxford (Rhodes Schol., BA Juris. 1st Cl. Hons, BCL 1st Cl. Hons); Yale Univ. Law Sch. (Sterling Fellow, JSD). Called to Bar, Inner Temple, 1937; admitted Mass Bar, 1942. Instr, tutor in history and lit., Harvard Univ. and Radcliffe Coll., 1938–42; Lectr, legal history, Law Sch., Harvard, 1939–42; Sen. Attorney, Office of Lend Lease Admin, Washington, DC, 1942–43; Office of Asst SG, USA, 1942–43; Asst Prof. of History, Swarthmore Coll., 1942–44; Univ. of Chicago, 1944–69: Asst Prof., 1944–49; Associate Prof., Preston and Sterling Morton Distinguished Prof. of Amer. History, 1956–69. During his 25 years tenure at Chicago, Visiting Lectr at Rome and Kyoto Univs, Sorbonne and Cambridge (Fellow, Trinity Coll., and Pitt Prof. of Amer. History and Instns; LittD 1968). Smithsonian Institution: Dir, Nat. Museum History and Techn., 1969–73; Sen. Historian, 1973–75. Many public service membership assignments, trusteeships, and active concern with a number of Amer. Assocs, esp. those relating to Amer. history, educn and cultural affairs. Past Pres., American Studies Assoc. Hon. LittD Sheffield, 1979; Hon. DLitt: Cambridge, 1968; East Anglia, 1980; Sussex, 1983; numerous other hon. degrees. Officier de L'Ordre de la Couronne, Belgium, 1980; Chevalier, Légion d'Honneur, France, 1984; Grand Officer, Order of Prince Henry the Navigator, Portugal, 1985; First Class Order of the Sacred Treasure, Japan, 1986. *Publications: include:* The Mysterious Science of the Law, 1941; The Lost World of Thomas Jefferson, 1948; The Genius of American Politics, 1953; The Americans: The Colonial Experience, 1958 (Bancroft Prize); America and the Image of Europe, 1960; The Image, 1962; The Americans: The National Experience, 1965 (Parkman Prize); The Decline of Radicalism, 1969; The Sociology of the Absurd, 1970; The Americans: The Democratic Experience, 1973 (Pulitzer Prize for History and Dexter Prize, 1974); Democracy and Its Discontents, 1974; The Exploring Spirit (BBC 1975 Reith Lectures), 1976; The Republic of Technology, 1978; (with Brooks M. Kelley) A History of the United States, 1980; The Discoverers, 1984; (for young readers) Landmark History of the American People, vol. I, From Plymouth to Appomattox, 1968; vol. II, From Appomattox to the Moon, 1970; (ed) Delaware Cases 1792–1830, 1943; (ed) An American Primer, 1966; (ed) American Civilization, 1971; (ed) The Chicago History of American Civilization (30 vols). *Address:* (home) 3541 Ordway Street, NW, Washington, DC 20016, USA; (office) Library of Congress, Washington, DC 20540. *T:* Library of Congress 287–5000. *Clubs:* Cosmos, National Press (Washington); Elizabethan (Yale); International House (Japan).

BOOTE, Col Charles Geoffrey Michael, MBE 1945; TD 1943; DL; Vice Lord-Lieutenant of Staffordshire, 1969–76; *b* 29 Sept. 1909; *s* of Lt-Col Charles Edmund Boote, TD, The North Staffordshire Regt (killed in action, 1916); *m* 1937, Elizabeth Gertrude (*d* 1980), *er d* of Evan Richard Davies, Market Drayton, Salop; three *s*. *Educ:* Bedford Sch. 2nd Lt 5th Bn North Staffordshire Regt, 1927. Served 1939–45, UK and NW Europe; despatches, 1945; Lt-Col, 1947. Director, H. Clarkson (Midlands) Ltd, 1969–75. Dir, Brit. Pottery Manufacturers' Fedn (Trustee) Ltd, 1955, retd Dec. 1969; Pres., Brit. Pottery Manufacturers' Fedn, 1957–58; Vice-Chm., Glazed and Floor Tile Manufacturers' Assoc., 1953–57. Hon. Col 5/6 Bn North Staffordshire Regt, 1963–67; Mem. Staffs TAVR Cttee, retd 1976. JP, Stoke-on-Trent, 1955–65; DL, 1958, JP 1959, High Sheriff, 1967–68, Staffordshire. Chm., Eccleshall PSD, 1971–76; Mem. Court of Governors, Keele Univ., 1957. *Recreations:* salmon fishing; British Racing Drivers' Club (Life Mem.); North Staffordshire Hunt (Hon. Sec. 1948–59). *Address:* Morile Mhor, Tomatin, Inverness-shire IV13 7YN. *T:* Tomatin 319. *Club:* Army and Navy.

BOOTE, Robert Edward, CVO 1971; first Director General, Nature Conservancy Council, 1973–80; *b* 6 Feb. 1920; *s* of Ernest Haydn Boote and Helen Rose Boote; *m* 1948, Vera (*née* Badian); one *s* one *d*. *Educ:* London Univ. (BSc Econ). DPA; FCIS 1960–81. War service, 1939–46, Actg Lt-Col, Hon. Major. Admin. Officer, City of Stoke-on-Trent, 1946–48; Chief Admin. Officer, Staffs County Planning and Develt Dept, 1948–54; Principal, 1954–64, Dep. Dir, 1964–73, Nature Conservancy. Sec. 1965–71, formerly Dep. Sec., Countryside in 1970 Confs, 1963, 1965, 1970 and numerous study groups; UK Deleg. to Council of Europe Cttee for Conservation of Nature and Natural Resources, 1963–71; a Chief Marshal to the Queen, 1970; various posts in meetings of UN, UNESCO, EEC and OECD, 1968–81; Chm. Preparatory Gp for Conservation Year 1970; Chm. Organising Cttee for European Conservation Conf. 1970 (Conf. Vice-Pres.); Chm. European Cttee, 1969–71; Consultant for European Architectural Heritage Year 1975; Advr, H of L Select Cttee on Europ. Communities, 1980–81. Founder and Chm., 1974–80, Mem., 1980–85, UK Cttee, IUCN; Mem., Governing Council and Bureau, IUCN, 1975–81, a Vice-Pres., 1978–81 (Treasurer, 1975–78; Election Officer, 1984). FRSA 1971; Council Member: FFPS, 1979–83; RGS, 1983–86; BTCV (Vice-Pres.) 1980–85; RSNC (Vice-Pres.) 1980–; RSNC Wildlife Appeal, 1983–; WWF, 1980–; Ecological Parks Trust, 1980–85; YPTES (Chm.), 1982–; Friends of ENO, 1980–; Common Ground Internat., 1981–85; Cttees for UK Conservation for Develt Prog., 1980–83; HGTAC, Forestry Commn, 1981–; Conservator, Wimbledon and Putney Commons, 1981–; Patron, CSV, 1978–85; Chairman: Instn of Environmental Sciences, 1981–84; Seychelles Appeal Cttee, Royal Soc., 1980–. Hon. Associate, Landscape Inst., 1971; Hon. MRTPI, 1978. Greek Distinguished Service Medal, 1946; van Tienhoven Prize, 1980; Merit Award, IUCN, 1984. Adviser: Macmillan Guide to Britain's Nature Reserves, 1980–; Shell Better Britain Campaign, 1980–. Member Editorial Boards: Internat. Jl of Environmental Studies, 1975–; Town Planning Review, 1979–85; Internat. Jl Environmental Educn and Information, 1981–83. Helped to prepare, and appeared in film, Pacemaker, 1970. *Publications:* (as Robert Arvill) Man and Environment, 1967 (5th edn 1984); numerous papers, articles, addresses, TV and radio broadcasts, over 2 decades in UK and internat. professional confs in 30 countries. *Recreations:* travel, theatre, music. *Address:* 3 Leeward Gardens, SW19 7QR. *T:* 01–946 1551.

BOOTH; *see* Gore-Booth.

BOOTH; *see* Sclater-Booth, family name of Baron Basing.

BOOTH, Alan Shore, QC 1975; **His Honour Judge Alan Booth;** a Circuit Judge, since 1976; *b* Aug. 1922; 4th *s* of Parkin Stanley Booth and Ethel Mary Shore; *m* 1954, Mary Gwendoline Hilton; one *s* one *d*. *Educ:* Shrewsbury Sch.; Liverpool Univ. (LLB). Served War of 1939–45, RNVR, Fleet Air Arm (despatches 1944): Sub-Lt 1942; HMS Illustrious, 1943–45; Lieut 1944. Called to Bar, Gray's Inn, 1949. A Recorder of the Crown Court, 1972–76. Governor, Shrewsbury Sch., 1969. *Recreation:* golf. *Address:* 18 Abbey Road, West Kirby, Wirral L48 7EW. *T:* 051–625 5796. *Clubs:* Royal Liverpool Golf; Royal and Ancient (St Andrews).

BOOTH, Rt. Hon. Albert Edward, PC 1976; CIMechE; a Director, South Yorkshire Passenger Transport Executive, since 1983; *b* 28 May 1928; *e s* of Albert Henry Booth and Janet Mathieson; *m* 1957, Joan Amis; three *s*. *Educ:* St Thomas's Sch., Winchester; S Shields Marine Sch.; Rutherford Coll. of Technology. Engineering Draughtsman. Election Agent, 1951 and 1955. County Borough Councillor, 1962–65. MP (Lab) Barrow-in-Furness, 1966–83; Minister of State, Dept of Employment, 1974–76; Sec. of State for Employment, 1976–79; Opposition spokesman on transport, 1979–83. Chm., Select Cttee on Statutory Instruments, 1970–74. Treasurer, Labour Party, 1984. Contested (Lab): Tynemouth, 1964; Barrow and Furness, 1983. *Address:* South Yorkshire Passenger Transport Executive, Exchange Street, Sheffield S2 5SZ.

BOOTH, Anthony John, CEng, FIEE; Corporate Director, British Telecommunications PLC, since 1984; Managing Director, BT International, since 1983; *b* 18 March 1939; *s* of Benjamin and Una Lavinia Booth; *m* 1965, Elspeth Marjorie, *er d* of Margaret and late Rev. F. S. Gordon Fraser; one *s* one *d*. *Educ:* Bungay Grammar Sch.; London Univ. (BScEng, DMS). Joined Post Office Res. Dept as Scientific Asst, 1957; Exec. Engr and Sen. Exec. Engr, Telecom HQ, 1965–71; Asst Staff Engr, Central HQ Appointments, 1971–74; Head of Section and Div., External Telecom Exec., 1974–78; Head of Div., THQ, 1978–79; Dir, Internat. Networks, 1979–80; Regional Dir, London Region, 1980–83. Member, Guild of Freemen of City of London, 1982–. MInstD 1985; FBIM 1985. *Recreations:* philately, golf, silversmithing, synchronised swimming official. *Address:* 63 Hillsborough Park, Camberley, Surrey GU15 1HG. *T:* Camberley 22476.

BOOTH, Catherine B.; *see* Bramwell-Booth.

BOOTH, Charles Leonard, CMG 1979; LVO 1961; HM Diplomatic Service, retired; re-employed in Foreign and Commonwealth Office, since 1985; *b* 7 March 1925; *s* of Charles Leonard and Marion Booth; *m* 1958, Mary Gillian Emms, two *s* two *d*. *Educ:* Pembroke Coll., Oxford Univ., 1942–43 and 1947–50. Served RA (Capt.), 1943–47. Joined HM Foreign Service, 1950; Foreign Office, 1950–51; Third and Second Secretary, Rangoon, 1951–55; FO, 1955–60 (Private Sec. to Parly Under-Sec. of State, 1958–60); First Sec., Rome, 1960–63; Head of Chancery, Rangoon, 1963–64, and Bangkok, 1964–67; FO, 1967–69. Counsellor, 1968; Deputy High Comr, Kampala, 1969–71; Consul-General and Counsellor (Administration), Washington, 1971–73; Counsellor, Belgrade, 1973–77; Ambassador to Burma, 1978–82; High Comr, Malta, 1982–85. Officer of Order of Merit of Italian Republic, 1961. *Recreations:* opera, gardening, walking. *Address:* 55 Kempshott Road, SW16 5LJ. *Club:* Travellers'.

BOOTH, Sir Christopher (Charles), Kt 1983; Director, Clinical Research Centre, Medical Research Council, since 1978; *b* 22 June 1924; *s* of Lionel Barton Booth and Phyllis Petley Duncan; *m* 1st, 1959, Lavinia Loughridge, Belfast; one *s* one *d*; 2nd, 1970, Soad Tabaqchali; one *d*. *Educ:* Sedbergh Sch., Yorks; University of St Andrews; MB 1951, MD 1958 (Rutherford Gold Medal). Junior appointments at Dundee Royal Infirmary, Hammersmith Hosp. and Addenbrooke's Hosp., Cambridge; successively Medical Tutor, Lecturer in Medicine and Senior Lecturer, Postgraduate Medical School of London; Prof. and Dir of Dept of Medicine, RPMS, London Univ., 1966–77. Member: Adv. Bd to Res. Councils, 1976–78; MRC, 1981–84; Chm., Medical Adv. Cttee, British Council, 1979–85. FRCP 1964; FRCPEd 1967; Hon. FACP 1973. For. Mem., Amer. Philosophical Soc., 1981. Docteur (*hc*): Paris, 1975; Poitiers, 1981; Hon. LLD Dundee, 1982. Dicke Gold Medal, Dutch Soc. of Gastroenterology, 1973; Ludwig Heilmeyer Gold Medal, German Soc. for Advances in Internal Medicine, 1982. Chevalier de l'Ordre National du Mérite (France), 1977. *Publications:* (with Betsy C. Corner) Chain of Friendship: Letters of Dr John Fothergill of London, 1735–1780, 1971; (with G. Neale) Disorders of the Small Intestine, 1985; papers in med. jls on relationship of nutritional disorders to disease of the alimentary tract, and on medical history. *Recreations:* fishing, history. *Address:* 33 Dukes Avenue, W4. *T:* 01–994 4914.

BOOTH, Dr Clive; Director, Oxford Polytechnic, since 1986; *b* 18 April 1943; *m* 1969, Margaret Sardeson. *Educ:* King's Sch., Macclesfield; Trinity Coll., Cambridge (MA 1969); Univ. of California, Berkeley (Harkness Fellow, 1973; MA 1974; PhD 1976). Joined DES, 1965; Prin. Pvte Sec. to Sec. of State for Educn and Science, 1975–77; Asst Sec., 1977–81; Dep. Dir, Plymouth Polytechnic, 1981–84; Mem., HM Inspectorate, DES, 1984–86. Leverhulme Res. Fellow, 1983. Jt Ed., Higher Educn Qly, 1986–. *Recreations:* circuit training, walking, bridge, opera. *Address:* Oxford Polytechnic, Gipsy Lane, Headington, Oxford OX3 0BP. *T:* Oxford 819002.

BOOTH, Rev. Canon David Herbert, MBE 1944; Provost, Shoreham College (formerly Shoreham Grammar School), Sussex, since 1977 (Headmaster, 1972–77); Chaplain to the Queen, 1957–77; *b* 26 Jan. 1907; *s* of Robert and Clara Booth; *m* 1942, Diana Mary Chard; two *s* one *d*. *Educ:* Bedford Sch.; Pembroke Coll., Cambridge; Ely Theological Coll. BA (3rd cl. Hist. Trip. part II), 1931; MA 1936; deacon, 1932; priest, 1933; Curate, All Saints', Hampton, 1932–34; Chaplain, Tonbridge Sch., 1935–40; Chaplain, RNVR, 1940–45; Rector of Stepney, 1945–53; Vicar of Brighton, 1953–59; Prebendary of Waltham in Chichester Cathedral, 1953–59; Archdeacon of Lewes, 1959–71; Prebendary of Bury in Chichester Cathedral, 1972–76; Canon Emeritus of Chichester, 1976. Select Preacher, University of Cambridge, 1947. Mem. of Archbishop's Commission on South East, 1965. Pres., Nat. Schs Jumping Championship, 1963–. *Recreations:* horses, gardening and family life. *Address:* Courtyard Cottage, School Road, Charing, near Ashford, Kent TN27 0HX. *T:* Charing 3349.

BOOTH, Sir Douglas Allen, 3rd Bt, *cr* 1916; writer; *b* 2 Dec. 1949; *s* of Sir Philip Booth, 2nd Bt, and Ethel, *d* of Joseph Greenfield, NY, USA; *S* father 1960. *Educ:* Beverly Hills High Sch.; Harvard Univ. (Harvard Nat. Scholarship, Nat. Merit Scholarship, 1967); BA (*magna cum laude*) 1975. *Recreations:* music, back-packing. *Heir:* *b* Derek Blake Booth, *b* 7 April 1953. *Address:* 438 South Cochran, Apt 108, Los Angeles, Calif 90036, USA.

BOOTH, Eric Stuart, CBE 1971; FRS 1967; FEng 1976; Chairman, Yorkshire Electricity Board, 1972–79; Member Central Electricity Generating Board, 1959–71; *b* 14 Oct. 1914; *s* of Henry and Annie Booth; *m* 1945, Mary Elizabeth Melton; two *d*. *Educ:* Batley Grammar Sch.; Liverpool Univ. Apprentice, Metropolitan Vickers Electrical Co. Ltd, 1936–38; Technical Engineer, Yorks Electric Power Co., 1938–46; Dep., later City Electrical Engineer and Manager, Salford Corporation, 1946–48; various posts associated with construction of Power Stations with British, later Central, Electricity Authority, 1948–57, Dep. Chief Engineer (Generation Design and Construction), 1957; Chief Design and Construction Engineer, Central Electricity Generating Bd, 1958–59. Part-time Mem., UKAEA, 1965–72; Pres., IEE, 1976–77. Consultant to Electricity Council, 1979–84; Dir, British Electricity International, 1979–84. Hon. FIEE 1986. Hon. DTech Bradford, 1980. *Address:* Pinecroft, Upper Dunsforth, York YO5 9RU. *T:* Boroughbridge 2821.

BOOTH, Sir Gordon, KCMG 1980 (CMG 1969); CVO 1976; HM Diplomatic Service, retired; adviser on international trade and investment; Director, Hanson Trust PLC, since 1981; Chairman, Simplification of International Trade Procedures Board, since 1980; Adviser to Bechtel Group, since 1983; Vice Chairman, Bechtel Ltd, since 1986; *b* 22 Nov. 1921; *s* of Walter and Grace Booth, Bolton, Lancs; *m* 1944, Jeanne Mary Kirkham; one *s* one *d*. *Educ:* Canon Slade Sch.; London Univ. (BCom). Served War of 1939–45: Capt. RAC and 13/18th Royal Hussars, 1941–46. Min. of Labour and Bd of Trade, 1946–55; Trade Comr, Canada and West Indies, 1955–65; Mem. HM Diplomatic Service, 1965–80; Counsellor (Commercial), British Embassy in Copenhagen, 1966–69; Dir, Coordination of Export Services, DTI, 1969–71; Consul-General, Sydney, 1971–74; HBM Consul-Gen., NY, and Dir-Gen. of Trade Develt in USA, 1975–80. *Recreations:* golf, bridge. *Address:* Pilgrims Corner, Ebbisham Lane, Walton on the Hill, Surrey KT20 5BT. *T:* Tadworth 3788. *Clubs:* Brooks's; Walton Heath Golf.

BOOTH, His Honour James; a Circuit Judge (formerly a County Court Judge), 1969–84; *b* 3 May 1914; *s* of James and Agnes Booth; *m* 1954, Joyce Doreen Mather; two *s* one *d*. *Educ:* Bolton Sch.; Manchester Univ. Called to Bar, Gray's Inn, 1936 (Arden Scholar, Gray's Inn). Town Clerk, Ossett, Yorks, 1939–41. RAFVR, 1941–46 (Flt-Lieut). Contested (L): West Leeds, 1945; Darwen, 1950. Recorder of Barrow-in-Furness, 1967–69. *Recreation:* fell walking. *Address:* Spinney End, Worsley, Lancs M28 4QN. *T:* 061–790 2003.

BOOTH, John Antony W.; *see* Ward-Booth.

BOOTH, John Dick L.; *see* Livingston Booth.

BOOTH, John Wells; *b* 19 May 1903; *s* of late Charles and Grace Wells Booth, Liverpool; *m* 1929, Margaret, *d* of late Mr and Mrs S. J. Lawry; two *s* one *d*. *Educ:* Royal Naval Colls Osborne and Dartmouth. Royal Navy, 1917–25 (Lieut Comdr). Booth Steamship Co. Ltd., 1926–45 (Chm., 1939–45); Dir, Alfred Booth & Co. Ltd, 1935–79 (Chm., 1952–74). Civil Aviation, 1945–50. Chm., British South American Airways Corporation, 1946–49; Dep. Chm., BOAC, 1949–50; Bd Mem., BOAC, 1950–65; Dir, Phoenix Assurance Co. Ltd, 1945–73. Former Chairman: Liverpool Seamens' Welfare Cttee (Mem. Seamens' Welfare Bd); Liverpool Steamship Owners' Assoc.; former JP for Co. of Cheshire. *Address:* Hilary Lodge, Somerton Road, Hartest, Bury St Edmunds IP29 4NA. *T:* Bury St Edmunds 830426. *Club:* Flyfishers'.

BOOTH, Hon. Dame Margaret (Myfanwy Wood), DBE 1979; **Hon. Mrs Justice Booth;** a Judge of the High Court, Family Division, since 1979; *b* 1933; *d* of late Alec Wood Booth and of Lilian May Booth; *m* 1982, Joseph Jackson, *qv*. *Educ:* Northwood Coll.; University Coll., London (LLM; Fellow, 1982). Called to the Bar, Middle Temple, 1956; Bencher, 1979. QC 1976. Chairman: Family Law Bar Assoc., 1976–78; Matrimonial Causes Procedure Cttee, 1982–85. Governor, Northwood Coll., 1975–; Mem. Council, Univ. Coll. London, 1980–84. *Publications:* (co-ed) Rayden on Divorce, 10th-13th edns; (co-ed) Clarke Hall and Morrison on Children, 9th edn 1977, (cons. ed.) 10th edn 1985. *Address:* c/o Royal Courts of Justice, Strand, WC2A 2LL.

BOOTH, Michael Addison John W.; *see* Wheeler-Booth.

BOOTH, Sir Michael Savile G.; *see* Gore-Booth.

BOOTH, Richard George William Pitt; Chairman, Richard Booth (Hay Castle) Ltd, Bookseller, since 1961; *b* 12 Sept. 1938; *m* (marr. diss.). *Educ:* Rugby; Univ. of Oxford. Established Richard Booth (Booksellers) Ltd, 1961. *Publications:* Country Life Book of Book Collecting, 1976; Independence for Hay, 1977; Bureaucracy in Brecon and Radnor, 1982. *Recreations:* creating a monarchy in Hay (began home rule movement, 1 April 1977); gardening. *Address:* Hay Castle, Hay-on-Wye, via Hereford.

BOOTH, Sir Robert (Camm), Kt 1977; CBE 1967; TD; Chairman, National Exhibition Centre Ltd, 1975–82 (Founder Director, 1970–82; Chief Executive, 1977–78); *b* 9 May 1916; *s* of late Robert Wainhouse Booth; *m* 1939, Veronica Courtenay, *d* of late F. C. Lamb; one *s* three *d*. *Educ:* Altrincham Grammar Sch.; Manchester Univ. (LLB). Called to Bar, Gray's Inn. War Service 8th (A) Bn Manchester Regt, France, Malta, Middle East, Italy, 1939–46. Manchester Chamber of Commerce, 1946–58; Sec., Birmingham Chamber of Industry and Commerce, 1958–65, Dir, 1965–78, Pres., 1978–79. Local non-exec. dir, Barclays Bank, 1977–84; Member: W Midlands Econ. Planning Council, 1974–77; BOTB Adv. Council, 1975–82; Midlands Adv. Bd, Legal and General Assurance Soc., 1979–; Midlands and NW Bd, BR, 1979–85; Bd, Inst. of Occupational Health, 1980–. Trustee, Nuffield Trust for the Forces of the Crown, 1977–. Life Mem., Court of Governors, 1969, Birmingham Univ. (Mem. Council, 1973–78); Governor, Sixth Form Coll., Solihull, 1974–77; Hon. Mem., British Exhbns Promotions Council, 1982. Overseas travel with 20 trade missions and author of marketing and economic publications. Hon. DSc Aston, 1975; Hon. FInstM; FRSA 1975. Midland Man of the Year Press Radio and TV Award, 1970. Officier de la Légion d'Honneur, 1982. *Address:* White House, 7 Sandal Rise, Solihull B9 3ET. *T:* 021–705 5311.

BOOTH, Rev. William James; Chaplain, Westminster School, London, since 1974; *b* 3 Feb. 1939; *s* of William James Booth and Elizabeth Ethel Booth. *Educ:* Ballymena Acad., Co. Antrim; TCD (MA). Curate, St Luke's Parish, Belfast, 1962–64; Chaplain, Cranleigh Sch., Surrey, 1965–74. Priest-in-Ordinary to The Queen, 1976–. Organiser, PHAB annual residential courses at Westminster (and formerly at Cranleigh). *Recreations:* music, hi-fi, cooking. *Address:* 14 Barton Street, SW1P 3NE. *T:* 01–222 3707.

BOOTH-CLIBBORN, Rt. Rev. Stanley Eric Francis; *see* Manchester, Bishop of.

BOOTHBY, Basil; *see* Boothby, E. B.

BOOTHBY, Sir Brooke (Charles), 16th Bt *cr* 1660, of Broadlow Ash, Derbyshire; *b* 6 April 1949; *s* of Sir Hugo Robert Brooke Boothby, 15th Bt and of (Evelyn) Ann, *d* of Late H. C. R. Homfray; *S* father, 1986; *m* 1976, Georgiana Alexandra, *o d* of late Sir John Wriothesley Russell, GCVO, CMG; two *d*. *Educ:* Eton; Trinity Coll., Cambridge (BA Econs). Man. Dir, Fontygary Leisure, 1979–; Chairman: Historic Houses Assoc. Inheritance Cttee, 1984–86; Nat. Caravan Council Parks Div., 1987–. High Sheriff, South Glamorgan, 1986–87. *Recreation:* shooting. *Heir:* *kinsman* George William Boothby [*b* 18 June 1948; *m* 1977, Sally Louisa Thomas; three *d*]. *Address:* Fonman Castle, Barry, South Glamorgan CF6 9ZN. *T:* Rhoose (0446) 710206.

BOOTHBY, (Evelyn) Basil, CMG 1958; HM Diplomatic Service, retired; Tutor, London University Extra-Mural Studies, since 1970; *b* 9 Sept. 1910; *s* of Basil T. B. Boothby and Katherine Knox; *m* 1946, Susan Asquith; two *s* one *d* (and one *s* decd). *Educ:* Winchester; CCC, Cambridge. Student Interpreter, China Consular Service, 1933; appointed a Vice-Consul in China, 1936; served at Shanghai and Hankow (periods Acting

Consul); Vice-Consul, Boston, 1940; employed at New York, Dec. 1941–June 1942, when reappointed a Vice-Consul in China and transf. to Chungking; seconded to Govt of India for service in Chinese Relations Office, Calcutta, Oct. 1943–July 1944; Actg Consul Kweilin and Kunming, also Athens, successively, 1944–45; promoted Consul, Sept. 1945; apptd Foreign Service Officer, Grade 7, in Foreign Office, Nov. 1946; promoted Counsellor, Foreign Service Officer, Grade 6, and became Head of UN (Economic and Social) Dept, Sept. 1949; seconded to Commonwealth Relations Office for service in Ontario and attached to Canadian National Defence Coll., Sept. 1950; apptd Counsellor, Rangoon, Nov. 1951 (Chargé d'Affaires, 1952); Counsellor, British Embassy, Brussels, 1954; Head of African Dept, Foreign Office, 1959; British Ambassador to Iceland, 1962–65; Permanent British Rep. to Council of Europe, 1965–69. Lectr, Morley Coll., 1969–70. *Address:* 23 Holland Park Avenue, W11.

See also P. P. Read.

BOOTHE, Clare; *see* Luce, Mrs Henry R.

BOOTHMAN, Campbell Lester; a Recorder of the Crown Court, since 1985; *b* 3 Sept. 1942; *s* of Gerald and Ann Boothman; *m* 1966, Penelope Evelyn Pepe; three *s*. *Educ:* Oundle; King's College, London. Called to the Bar, Inner Temple, 1965. *Recreations:* skiing, squash. *Address:* The Glen, Tower House Lane, Wraxall, Bristol. *T:* Bristol 852310.

BOOTHMAN, Derek Arnold, FCA; Partner, Binder Hamlyn, Chartered Accountants, since 1974; President, Institute of Chartered Accountants in England and Wales, June 1986–87 (Vice-President, 1983–85; Deputy President, 1985–86); *b* 5 June 1932; *s* of Eric Randolph Boothman and Doris Mary Boothman; *m* 1958, Brenda Margaret; one *s* one *d*. *Educ:* William Hulme's Grammar Sch., Manchester. Articled to J. Needham & Co., 1948; Mem., ICA, 1954; National Service, RAF, 1954–56; Partner, J. Needham & Co. (now part of Binder Hamlyn), 1957; Dir Piccadilly Radio Plc, 1985–. President: Manchester Chartered Accountants Students Soc., 1967–68; Manchester Soc. of Chartered Accountants, 1968–69; ICA: Council Member, 1969–; Chairman of Committees: Internal Services, 1972–75; Grants, 1976–78; Technical, 1978–79; Technical Services, 1979–81; Treasurer, 1981–83. Member, Accounting Standards Cttee, 1974–82. Liveryman, Worshipful Company of Chartered Accountants, 1976–. *Publications:* contribs to professional press and lectures on professional topics, internationally. *Recreations:* cricket, skiing, gardening, travel. *Address:* Ashworth Dene, Wilmslow Road, Mottram St Andrew, Cheshire SK10 4QH. *T:* Prestbury 829101. *Clubs:* St James's (Manchester); Withington Golf (Manchester) (past Captain).

BOOTHROYD, Basil; *see* Boothroyd, J. B.

BOOTHROYD, Betty; MP (Lab) West Bromwich West, since 1974 (West Bromwich, May 1973–1974); *b* Yorkshire, 8 Oct. 1929; *d* of Archibald and Mary Boothroyd. *Educ:* Dewsbury Coll. of Commerce and Art. Personal/Political Asst to Labour Ministers. Accompanied Parly delegns to: European Confs, 1955–60; Soviet Union, China and Vietnam, 1957; delegate to N Atlantic Assembly, 1974. An Asst Govt Whip, Oct. 1974–Nov. 1975; Member: Select Cttee on Foreign Affairs, 1979–81; Speaker's Panel of Chairmen, 1979–; House of Commons Commn, 1983–. Mem., European Parlt, 1975–77. Mem., Labour Party NEC, 1981–. Councillor, Hammersmith Borough Council, 1965–68. Contested (Lab): SE Leicester (by-elec.), 1957; Peterborough (gen. elec.), 1959; Nelson and Colne (by-elec.), 1968; Rossendale (gen. elec.), 1970. Mem. Ct, Birmingham Univ., 1982–. *Recreations:* dominoes, scrabble. *Address:* House of Commons, SW1A 0AA.

BOOTHROYD, (John) Basil; writer and broadcaster; *b* 4 March 1910; *m* 1st, 1939, Phyllis Barbara Youngman (*d* 1980); one *s*; 2nd, 1981, June Elizabeth Leonhardt Mortimer. *Educ:* Lincoln Cathedral Choir Sch.; Lincoln Sch. Bank Clerk, 1927. Served with RAF Police, 1941–45; Personal Asst to Provost-Marshal from 1943. Punch contributor continuously from 1938, an Asst Editor, 1952–70, Mem. Punch Table, 1955. Much broadcasting and miscellaneous frivolous journalism; some lecturing and public speaking. Imperial Tobacco Radio Award, best comedy script, 1976. *Television includes:* adaptation of: The Diary of a Nobody, BBC series, 1979; A. J. Wentworth, BA, ITV series, 1982. *Publications:* Home Guard Goings-On, 1941; Adastral Bodies, 1942; Are Sergeants Human? 1945; Are Officers Necessary?, 1946; Lost, A Double-Fronted Shop, 1947; The House About a Man, 1959; Motor If You Must, 1960; To My Embarrassment, 1961; The Whole Thing's Laughable, 1964; You Can't be Serious, 1966; Let's Stay Married, 1967 (and US, 1967); Stay Married Abroad, 1968; Boothroyd at Bay (radio talks), 1970; Philip (an approved biography of HRH the Duke of Edinburgh), 1971 (and US, 1971); Accustomed As I Am, 1975; Let's Move House, 1977; In My State of Health, 1981; (autobiog.) A Shoulder to Laugh On, 1986. *Recreations:* playing the piano, working. *Address:* Peelers, Church Street, Cuckfield, Sussex. *T:* Haywards Heath 454340/412173. *Club:* Savage.

BOOTLE-WILBRAHAM, family name of **Baron Skelmersdale.**

BOR, Walter George, CBE 1975; FRIBA, DistTP; FRTPI; FRSA; Director, Walter Bor Consultancy Ltd; Consultant, Llewelyn-Davies Weeks, since 1976; Partner, Llewelyn-Davies Weeks Forestier-Walker & Bor, London, 1966–76; *b* 1916, Czech parentage; father chemical engineer; *m* Dr Muriel Blackburn; two *s* one *d*. *Educ:* Prague Univ. (degree of Arch.); Bartlett Sch. of Architecture and Sch. of Planning and Regional Research, London (Dip.). Private architectural practice, London, 1946–47; London County Council, 1947–62 (in charge of planning of London's East End, 1958; Dep. Planning Officer with special responsibility for civic design, 1960–62); Liverpool City Planning Officer, 1962–66. Mem. Minister's Planning Advisory Gp, 1964–65. In private practice as architect and planning consultant, 1966–. Pres., Town Planning Inst., 1970–71; Vice-Pres., Housing Centre Trust, 1971–. Visiting Professor: Princeton Univ., 1977–79; Rice Univ., Houston, 1980–81. Mem., Severn Barrage Cttee, 1978–81; Consultant, UNDP, Cyprus, 1982–83; Advr, Shenzhen City Planning Commn, China. *Publications:* Liverpool Interim Planning Policy, 1965; Liverpool City Centre Plan (jt), 1966; Two New Cities in Venezuela (jt), 1967–69; The Milton Keynes Plan (jt), 1970; Airport City (Third London Airport urbanisation studies) (jt), 1970; The Making of Cities, 1972; SE London and the Fleet Line for LTE (jt), 1973; Bogota Urban Development for UNDP (jt), 1974; Concept Plan for Tehran new city centre, 1974; Shetland Draft Structure Plan, 1975; (jtly) Unequal City: Birmingham Inner Area Study, 1977; articles for jls of RTPI, RIBA, TCPA, ICE, RICS, Amer. Inst. of Planners, Princeton Univ.; L'Architecture d'aujourd'hui, Urbanistica, Habitat Internat.; Ekistics. *Recreations:* music, theatre, skiing, swimming, sketching, sculpting. *Address:* 99 Swains Lane, Highgate, N6 6PJ. *T:* 01–340 6540. *Club:* Reform.

BORDEN, Henry, OC 1969; CMG 1943; QC 1938; Canadian Lawyer; Hon. Director, Canada Trustco Mortgage Co.; *b* Halifax, NS, 25 Sept. 1901; *s* of Henry Clifford and Mabel (Ashmere) Barnstead Borden, both of Halifax, NS; *m* 1929, Jean Creelman, *d* of late Dr D. A. MacRae, Toronto, Ont; three *s* two *d*. *Educ:* King's Coll. Sch., Windsor, NS; McGill Univ.; Dalhousie Law Sch; Exeter Coll., Oxford (Rhodes Schol.). BA Political Science and Economics, McGill, 1921; BA Oxon, 1926. With Royal Bank of Canada, 1921–22. Called to Bar, Lincoln's Inn, 1927; to Bar of Nova Scotia, 1927; to Bar of Ont, 1927. Senior Mem., Borden, Elliot, Kelley, Palmer, 1936–46; Gen. Counsel, Dept of Munitions and Supply, Ottawa, 1939–42; Chairman: Wartime Industries Control Bd, Ottawa, and Co-ordinator of Controls, Dept of Munitions and Supply, Sept. 1942–43; Royal Commission on Energy, 1957–59. Pres., Brazilian Traction Light & Power Co., 1946–63, Chm., 1963–65; Chm. and Pres., Brinco Ltd (formerly British Newfoundland Corporation Ltd), 1965–69; Dir Emeritus, Canadian Imperial Bank of Commerce; Dir, Mem. Exec. Cttee and Past Pres., Royal Agric. Winter Fair. Formerly Lectr, Corp. Law, Osgoode Hall Law Sch; Past President: Canadian Club of Toronto; Lawyers' Club of Toronto. Past Chm., Bd of Governors, Univ. of Toronto. Hon. LLD: St Francis Xavier, 1960; Dalhousie, 1968; Toronto, 1972; Hon. DCL Acadia, 1960. Is an Anglican. Grand Officer, Nat. Order of the Southern Cross (Brazil), 1962; Canada Centennial Medal, 1967. *Publications:* (jtly) Fraser & Borden, Hand Book of Canadian Companies, 1931; ed, Robert Laird Borden: His Memoirs, 1938; ed, Letters to Limbo, by Rt Hon. Sir Robert L. Borden, 1971. *Recreations:* farming, fishing. *Address:* Apt 609, 484 Avenue Road, Toronto M4V 2J4, Canada. *Club:* York (Toronto).

BOREEL, Sir Francis (David), 13th Bt, *cr* 1645; Counsellor, Netherlands Foreign Service, since 1966 (Attaché, 1956); *b* 14 June 1926; *s* of Sir Alfred Boreel, 12th Bt and Countess Reiniera Adriana (*d* 1957), *d* of Count Francis David Schimmelpenninck; *S* father 1964; *m* 1964, Suzanne Campagne; three *d*. *Educ:* Utrecht Univ. *Recreations:* tennis, sailing. *Heir: kinsman* Stephen Gerard Boreel [*b* 9 Feb. 1945; *m* Francien P. Kooyman; one *s*]. *Address:* Netherlands Embassy, Strässchensweg 10, 5300 Bonn 1, Germany.

BOREHAM, Sir (Arthur) John, KCB 1980 (CB 1974); Director, Central Statistical Office, and Head of the Government Statistical Service, 1978–85, retired; *b* 30 July 1925; 3rd *s* of late Ven. Frederick Boreham, Archdeacon of Cornwall and Chaplain to the Queen, and late Caroline Mildred Boreham; *m* 1948, Heather, *o d* of Harold Edwin Horth, FRIBA, and Muriel Horth; three *s* one *d*. *Educ:* Marlborough; Trinity Coll., Oxford. Agricultural Economics Research Inst., Oxford, 1950; Min. of Food, 1951; Min. of Agric., 1952; Gen. Register Office, 1955; Central Statistical Office, 1958; Chief Statistician, Gen. Register Office, 1963; Dir of Economics and Statistics, Min. of Technology, 1967–71; Central Statistical Office: Asst Dir, 1971–72; Dep. Dir, 1972–78. Vis. Fellow, Nuffield Coll., Oxford, 1981–. *Recreations:* music, golf. *Address:* Piperscroft, Brittain's Lane, Sevenoaks, Kent TN13 2NG. *T:* Sevenoaks 454678.

BOREHAM, Hon. Sir Leslie Kenneth Edward, Kt 1972; **Hon. Mr Justice Boreham;** a Judge of the High Court, Queen's Bench Division, since 1972; Presiding Judge, North Eastern Circuit, 1974–79; Deputy Chairman, Agricultural Lands Tribunal; *m*; one *s* one *d*. Served War of 1939–45, RAF. Called to the Bar at Lincoln's Inn, Nov. 1947; Bencher 1972. QC 1965. Recorder of Margate, 1968–71. Joined South-Eastern Circuit. Dep. Chm. 1962–65, Chm. 1965–71, East Suffolk QS. *Recreations:* gardening, golf. *Address:* 1 Paper Buildings, Temple, EC4.

BORG, Alan Charles Nelson, PhD; FSA; Director, Imperial War Museum, since 1982; *b* 21 Jan. 1942; *s* of Charles John Nelson Borg and late Frances Mary Olive Hughes; *m* 1st, 1964, Anne (marr. diss.), *d* of late Dr William Blackmore; one *s* one *d*; 2nd, 1976, Caroline, *d* of late Captain Lord Francis Hill; two *d*. *Educ:* Westminster Sch.; Brasenose Coll., Oxford (MA); Courtauld Inst. of Art (PhD). Lecteur d'anglais, Université d'Aix-Marseille, 1964–65; Lectr, History of Art, Indiana Univ., 1967–69; Asst Prof. of History of Art, Princeton Univ., 1969–70; Asst Keeper of the Armouries, HM Tower of London, 1970–78; Keeper, Sainsbury Centre for Visual Arts, Univ. of E Anglia, 1978–82. *Publications:* Architectural Sculpture in Romanesque Provence, 1972; European Swords and Daggers in the Tower of London, 1974; Torture and Punishment, 1975; Heads and Horses, 1976; Arms and Armour in Britain, 1979; (ed with A. R. Martindale) The Vanishing Past: studies presented to Christopher Hohler, 1981; articles in learned jls. *Recreations:* music, travel. *Address:* Telegraph House, 36 West Square, SE11 4SP.

BORG, Björn Rune; tennis player; *b* 6 June 1956; *s* of Rune and Margaretha Borg; *m* 1980, Mariana Simionescu (marr. diss. 1984); engaged to Jannike Bjorling; one *s*. *Educ:* Blombacka Sch., Södertälje. Started to play tennis at age of 9; won Wimbledon junior title, 1972; became professional player in 1972. Mem., Swedish Davis Cup team, annually 1972–80 (youngest player ever in a winning Davis Cup team, 1975). Championship titles: Italian, 1974, 1978; French, 1974, 1975, 1978, 1979, 1980, 1981; Wimbledon, record of 5 consecutive singles titles, 1976–80; World Champion, 1978, 1979, 1980; Masters, 1980, 1981. *Publication:* (with Eugene Scott) Björn Borg: my life and game, 1980. *Address:* c/o International Management Group, 58 Queen Anne Street, W1.

BORG COSTANZI, Prof. Edwin J.; Head of Department of Computer Science, Brunel University, since 1985; *b* 8 Sept. 1925; 2nd *s* of late Michael Borg Costanzi and M. Stella (*née* Camilleri); *m* 1948, Lucy Valentino; two *s* one *d*. *Educ:* Lyceum, Malta; Royal University of Malta (BSc, BE&A); Balliol College, Oxford (BA 1946, MA 1952); Malta Rhodes Scholar, 1945. Professor of Mathematics, Royal University of Malta, 1950–64; Rector, Old Univ., Malta (formerly Univ. of Malta), 1964–80; Vis. Fellow, Univ. of Southampton, 1980–82; Professorial Res. Fellow, Brunel Univ., 1982–85. Chm., 1976–77, Mem., 1965–66, 1968–69, 1972–74, 1977–78, Council of ACU. *Recreations:* fishing, photography. *Address:* Department of Computer Science, Brunel University, Uxbridge, Middx UB8 3PH. *Club:* Casino (Valletta Malta).

BORGES, Thomas William Alfred; Managing Director, Thomas Borges & Partners Ltd, since 1949; Deputy Chairman, Phoenix Timber Group PLC, 1986; *b* 1 April 1923; *s* of Arthur Borges, Prague, and Paula Borges; *m* 1st (marr. diss.); 2nd, 1966, Serena Katherine Stewart (*née* Jamieson); two *s*. *Educ:* Dunstable Grammar Sch.; Luton Technical Coll. Served War, 1941–45. Trained in banking, shipping and industry, 1945–49; Dir, Borges Law & Co., Sydney and Melbourne, 1951; Chm., Smith Whitworth Ltd, 1974–80. Governor, Royal National Orth. Hosp., 1968– (Dep. Chm., 1978–80, Chm., 1980–82); Dir, Inst. of Orths, Univ. of London, 1968– (Dep. Chm., 1978–80, Chm., 1980–82); Member: Grants Cttee, King Edward VII Hosp. Fund, 1975–80; Council, Professions Supp. to Medicine, 1980– (Dep. Chm., 1982–); Treasurer, Riding for Disabled Assoc., 1977–. Chm., Australian Art Foundn, 1984–. Exec. Mem., Sir Robert Menzies Meml Trust, 1981–. *Publication:* Two Expeditions of Discovery in North West and Western Australia by George Grey, 1969. *Recreations:* collecting Australiana, riding, swimming. *Address:* 10 Regent's Park Terrace, NW1 7EE. *T:* 01–485 4855. *Clubs:* Athenæum, Garrick.

BORINGDON, Viscount; Mark Lionel Parker; *b* 22 Aug. 1956; *s* and *heir* of 6th Earl of Morley, *qv*; *m* 1983, Carolyn Jill, *d* of Donald McVicar, Meols, Wirral, Cheshire; one *d*. *Educ:* Eton. Commissioned, Royal Green Jackets, 1976. *Address:* Pound House, Yelverton, Devon.

BORLAND, David Morton; former Chairman, Cadbury Ltd; Director, Cadbury Schweppes Ltd; *b* 17 Jan. 1911; *s* of David and Annie J. Borland; *m* 1947, Nessa Claire Helwig; one *s* one *d*. *Educ:* Glasgow Academy; Brasenose Coll., Oxford (BA). Management Trainee, etc., Cadbury Bros Ltd, Bournville, Birmingham, 1933. War service, Royal Marines (Lieut-Col), 1940–46. Sales Manager, J. S. Fry & Sons Ltd, Somerdale, Bristol,

1946; Sales Dir and a Man. Dir, J. S. Fry & Sons Ltd, 1948; a Man. Dir, British Cocoa & Chocolate Co. Ltd, 1959, and of Cadbury Bros Ltd, 1963. Mem. Council of Bristol Univ. and of Univ. Appts Bd, 1962; Mem. Govt Cttee of Inquiry into Fatstock and Meat Marketing and Distribution, 1962. Pro-Chancellor, Bristol Univ., 1983–. Hon. LLD Bristol, 1980. *Recreation:* golf. *Address:* Garden Cottage, 3 Hollymead Lane, Stoke Bishop, Bristol BS9 1LN. *T:* Bristol 683978. *Clubs:* Achilles; Vincent's (Oxford).

BORLAUG, Norman Ernest, PhD; Consultant, International Center for Maize and Wheat Improvement; *b* 25 March 1914; *s* of Henry O. and Clara Vaala Borlaug; *m* 1937, Margaret Gibson; one *s* one *d*. *Educ:* Univ. of Minnesota; BS 1937; MS 1940; PhD 1942. US Forest Service (USDA), 1935–1937–1938; Biologist, Dupont de Nemours & Co, 1942–44; Plant Pathologist and Genetist, Wheat Improvement, employed by Rockefeller Foundn (Associate Dir of Agricultural Sciences) and Dir of Wheat Program, International Center for Maize and Wheat Improvement (CIMMYT), 1944–79. Dir, Population Crisis Cttee, 1971; Asesor Especial, Fundación para Estudios de la Población (Mexico), 1971–; Member: Adv. Council, Renewable Natural Resources Foundn, 1973–; Citizens' Commn on Science, Law and Food Supply, 1973–; Council for Agricl Science and Tech., 1973–; Commn on Critical Choices for Americans 1973–. Outstanding Achievement Award, Univ. of Minnesota, 1959; Mem., Nat. Acad. of Sciences (USA), 1968; Sitara-Imtiaz (Star of Distinction) (Pakistan), 1968, Hilal-I-Imtiaz 1978. Nobel Peace Prize, 1970. Holds numerous hon. doctorates in Science, both from USA and abroad; and more than 30 Service Awards by govts and organizations, including US Medal of Freedom, 1977. *Publications:* more than 70 scientific and semi-popular articles. *Recreations:* hunting, fishing, baseball, wrestling, football, golf. *Address:* c/o International Center for Maize and Wheat Improvement (CIMMYT), Apartado Postal 6–641, Londres 40, 06600 Mexico DF, Mexico. *T:* 585–43–55.

BORLEY, Lester; Director, National Trust for Scotland, since 1983; *b* 7 April 1931; *er s* of Edwin Richard Borley and Mary Dorena Davies; *m* Mary Alison, *e d* of Edward John Pearce and Kathleen Florence Barratt; three *d*. *Educ:* Dover Grammar Sch.; Queen Mary Coll. and Birkbeck Coll., London Univ. Pres. of Union, QMC, 1953; Dep. Pres., Univ. of London Union, 1954; ESU debating team tour of USA, 1955. Joined British Travel Assoc., 1955; Asst to Gen. Manager, USA, 1957–61; Manager: Chicago Office, 1961–64; Australia, 1964–67; West Germany, 1967–69; Chief Executive: Scottish Tourist Bd, 1970–75; English Tourist Bd, 1975–83. Member: Council, Scotland's Garden Scheme, 1970–75, 1983–; Council, Nat. Gardens Scheme, 1975–83; Park and Gardens Cttee, Zool Soc. of London, 1979–83. Founder Fellow, Tourism Soc., 1978. FRSA 1982. Honorable Kentucky Col, 1963. *Recreations:* listening to music, looking at pictures, gardening. *Address:* 4 Belford Place, Edinburgh EH4 3DH. *T:* 031–332 2364. *Club:* New (Edinburgh).

BORN, Gustav Victor Rudolf, FRCP 1976; FRS 1972; Professor of Pharmacology, King's College, University of London, since 1978; *b* 29 July 1921; *s* of late Prof. Max Born, FRS; *m* 1st, 1950, Wilfrida Ann Plowden-Wardlaw (marr. diss., 1961); two *s* one *d*; 2nd, 1962, Dr Faith Elizabeth Maurice-Williams; one *s* one *d*. *Educ:* Oberrealschule, Göttingen; Perse Sch., Cambridge; Edinburgh Academy; University of Edinburgh. Vans Dunlop Scholar; MB, ChB, 1943; DPhil (Oxford), 1951, MA 1956. Med. Officer, RAMC, 1943–47; Mem. Scientific Staff, MRC, 1952–53; Research Officer, Nuffield Inst. for Med. Research, 1953–60 and Deptl Demonstrator in Pharmacology, 1956–60, University of Oxford; Vandervell Prof. of Pharmacology, RCS and Univ. of London, 1960–73; Sheild Prof. of Pharmacology, Univ. of Cambridge, and Fellow, Gonville and Caius Coll., Cambridge, 1973–78. Vis. Prof. in Chem., NW Univ., Illinois, 1970–; William S. Creasy Vis. Prof. in Clin. Pharmacol., Brown Univ., 1977; Prof. of Fondation de France, Paris, 1982–84. Hon. Dir, MRC Thrombosis Res. Gp, 1964–73. Scientific Advr, Vandervell Foundn, 1967–; Pres., Internat. Soc. on Thrombosis and Haemostasis, 1977–79; Trustee, Heineman Med. Res. Center, Charlotte, NC, 1981–. Member: Ed. Board, Heffters' Handbook of Experimental Pharmacology; Cttee of Enquiry into Relationship of Pharmaceut. Industry with Nat. Health Service (Sainsbury Cttee), 1965–67; Sci. Council, Fondation Cardiologique Princesse Liliane; Coronary Sclerosis Commn, Fritz-Thyssen Foundn, Cologne; Kuratorium, Ernst Jung Foundn, Hamburg; Med. Cttee, British Council; Forensic Science Adv. Gp, Home Office. Hon. Life Mem., New York Acad. of Scis. Lectures: Beyer, Wisconsin Univ., 1969; Sharpey-Schäfer, Edinburgh Univ., 1973; Cross, RCS, 1974; Wander, Bern Univ., 1974; Johnson Meml, Paris, 1975; Lo Yuk Tong Foundn, Hong Kong Univ., and Heineman Meml, Charlotte, NC, 1978; Carlo Erba Foundn, Milan, 1979; Sir Henry Dale, RCS, 1981; Rokitansky, Vienna, and Oration to Med. Soc., London, 1983. Chevalier de l'Ordre National de Mérite, France, 1980. Mem., Akad. Leopoldina; Corresp. Member: German Pharmacological Soc.; Royal Belgian Acad. of Medicine; Rheinisch-Westfälische Akad. der Wissenschaften, Düsseldorf. Hon. Fellow, St Peter's Coll., Oxford, 1972; Hon. D de l'Univ. Bordeaux, 1978; Hon. MD: Münster, 1980; Leuven, 1981; Edinburgh, 1982. Albrecht von Haller Medal, Göttingen Univ., 1979; Ratschow Medal, Internat. Kur. of Angiology, 1980; Auenbrugger Medal, Graz Univ., 1984. *Publications:* articles in scientific jls and books. *Recreations:* music, walking. *Address:* King's College, Strand, WC2R 2LS; 10 Woodland Gardens, N10. *T:* 01–444 7911. *Club:* Garrick.

BORODALE, Viscount; Sean David Beatty; *b* 12 June 1973; *s* and *heir* of 3rd Earl Beatty, *qv*.

BORODIN, George; *see* Sava, George.

BORRADAILE, Maj.-Gen. Hugh Alastair, CB 1959; DSO 1946; Vice Adjutant-General, War Office, 1960–63, retired; *b* 22 June 1907; *s* of late Lt-Col B. Borradaile, RE, Walnut Cottage, Wylye, Wilts; *m* 1936, Elizabeth Barbara, *d* of late R. Powell-Williams, Woodcroft, Yelverton, Devon; one *s* one *d*. *Educ:* Wellington Coll.; RMC Sandhurst. Commissioned Devon Regt 1926; King's African Rifles, 1931–37; Staff Coll., Camberley, 1939; GSO1, GHQ West Africa, 1942–43; CO 5, E Lancs Regt, 1944; CO 7 Somrset LI, 1944–45; GSO1, 30 Corps 1945; Asst Chief of Staff (Exec.), CCG, 1945–46; CO 1 Devon, 1946–48; Dep. Chief Intelligence Div., CCG, 1948–50; National Defence Coll., Canada, 1950–51; Brig. A/Q AA Command 1951–53; Comd 24 Inf. Bde, 1953–55; Dept Military Sec. (A), War Office, 1955–57; Gen. Officer Commanding South-West District and 43rd (Wessex) Infantry Div., TA, 1957–60. Col, Devon and Dorset Regt, 1962–67. Master, Worshipful Co. of Drapers', 1971–72 (Liveryman 1956–). *Recreations:* golf, shooting, fishing. *Address:* Almora, 33 Park Avenue, Camberley, Surrey. *T:* Camberley 21827. *Club:* Army and Navy.

BORRETT, Ven. Charles Walter; Archdeacon of Stoke-upon-Trent and Hon. Canon of Lichfield Cathedral, 1971–82, now Archdeacon Emeritus; Priest-in-charge of Sandon, Diocese of Lichfield, 1975–82; a Chaplain to the Queen, 1980–86; *b* 15 Sept. 1916; *s* of Walter George Borrett, farmer, and Alice Frances (*née* Mecrow); *m* 1941, Jean Constable, *d* of Charles Henry and Lilian Constable Pinson, Wolverhampton; one *s* two *d*. *Educ:* Framlingham Coll., Suffolk; Emmanuel Coll., Cambridge (MA); Ridley Hall, Cambridge. Deacon, 1941; Priest, 1943; Curate: of All Saints, Newmarket, 1941–45; of St Paul, Wolverhampton, 1945–48; of Tettenhall Regis, 1948–49; Vicar of Tettenhall Regis, 1949–71; Rural Dean of Trysull, 1958–71; Prebendary of Flixton in Lichfield Cathedral, 1964–71. Chm., C of E Council for Deaf, 1976–86. Fellow, Woodard Schs, 1972–86. *Address:* 34 Queensway, Mildenhall, Bury St Edmunds IP28 7JL. *T:* Mildenhall 712718. *Club:* Hawks (Cambridge).

BORRETT, Louis Albert Frank; a Recorder of the Crown Court, since 1980; *b* 8 Aug. 1924; *e s* of late Albert B. Borrett and Louise Alfreda Eudoxie Forrestier; *m* 1946, Barbara Betty, *er d* of late Frederick Charles Bamsey and of Lily Gertrude Thompson. *Educ:* France and England; Folkestone Teachers' Trng Coll.; King's Coll., Univ. of London (LLB 1954). Called to the Bar, Gray's Inn, 1955. Served War, Army: volunteered, 1940; RASC, London Dist and South Eastern Comd; commnd Royal Sussex Regt, 1944; served India and Burma Border; Intell. Officer, 9th Royal Sussex, during invasion of Malaya, 1945; GSO III (Ops), ALFSEA, 1946 (Burma Star, Defence Medal, Victory Medal); demob., 1946 (Captain). Schoolmaster, 1947–53; barrister, in practice on South-Eastern circuit, 1955–86; Assist Comr, Boundary Commn, 1964–67. *Recreations:* hunting, horse riding, music, the French language. *Address:* Queen Elizabeth Building, Temple, EC4Y 9BS. *T:* 01-353 7181; 54 Farm Close, East Grinstead, West Sussex RH19 3QG. *T:* East Grinstead 312350; Chantry Cottage, Tunstall, Woodbridge, Suffolk IP12 2JW.

BORRIE, Sir Gordon (Johnson), Kt 1982; QC 1986; Director General of Fair Trading, since 1976; *b* 13 March 1931; *s* of Stanley Borrie, Solicitor; *m* 1960, Dorene, *d* of Herbert Toland, Toronto, Canada; no *c*. *Educ:* John Bright Grammar Sch., Llandudno; Univ. of Manchester (LLB, LLM). Barrister-at-Law and Harmsworth Scholar of the Middle Temple; called to Bar, Middle Temple, 1952; Bencher, 1980. Nat. Service: Army Legal Services, HQ Brit. Commonwealth Forces in Korea, 1952–54. Practice as a barrister, London, 1954–57. Lectr and later Sen. Lectr, Coll. of Law, 1957–64; Sen. Lectr in Law, Univ. of Birmingham, 1965–68; Prof. of English Law and Dir, Inst. of Judicial Admin, Birmingham Univ., 1969–76, and Dean of Faculty of Law, 1974–76. Member: Law Commn Adv. Panel on Contract Law, 1966–; Parole Bd for England and Wales, 1971–74; CNAA Legal Studies Bd, 1971–76; Circuit Adv. Cttee, Birmingham Gp of Courts, 1972–74; Council, Consumers' Assoc., 1972–75; Consumer Protection Adv. Cttee, 1973–76; Equal Opportunities Commn, 1975–76. Vice-Pres., Inst. of Trading Standards Admin, 1985–. Sen. Treasurer, Nat. Union of Students, 1955–58. Contested (Lab): Croydon, NE, 1955; Ilford, S, 1959. Gov., Birmingham Coll. of Commerce, 1966–70. FRSA 1982. *Publications:* Commercial Law, 1962, 5th edn 1980; The Consumer, Society and the Law (with Prof. A. L. Diamond), 1963, 4th edn 1981; Law of Contempt (with N. V. Lowe), 1973, 2nd edn 1983; The Development of Consumer Law and Policy (Hamlyn Lectures), 1984. *Recreations:* gardening, gastronomy, piano playing, travel. *Address:* Manor Farm, Abbots Morton, Worcestershire. *T:* Inkberrow 792330; 1 Plowden Buildings, Temple, EC4. *T:* 01–353 4434. *Club:* Reform.

BORTHWICK, Jason; *see* Borthwick, W. J. M.

BORTHWICK OF BORTHWICK, Lt-Col John Henry Stuart, TD 1943; DL, JP; The Borthwick of Borthwick; 23rd Lord Borthwick; Baron of Heriotmuir, Borthwick and Locherwart; Hereditary Royal Falconer for Scotland; Chairman: Heriotmuir Properties Ltd, since 1965; Heriotmuir Exporters Ltd, since 1972; Director, Ronald Morrison & Co. Ltd, since 1972; *b* 13 Sept. 1905; *s* of Henry, 22nd Lord Borthwick (*d* 1937); *m* 1938, Margaret Frances (*d* 1976), *d* of Alexander Campbell Cormack, Edinburgh; twin *s*. *Educ:* Fettes Coll., Edinburgh; King's Coll. Newcastle (DipAgric 1926). Formerly RATA, re-employed 1939; served NW Europe, Allied Mil. Govt Staff (Junior Staff Coll., SO 2), 1944; CCG (CO 1, Lt-Col), 1946. Dept of Agriculture for Scotland, 1948–50; farming own farms, 1950–71; Partner in Crookston Farms, 1971–79. National Farmers Union of Scotland: Mid and West Lothian Area Cttee, 1967–73 (Pres. 1970–72); Mem. Council, 1968–72; Member: Lothians Area Cttee, NFU Mutual Insurance Soc., 1969; Scottish Southern Regional Cttee, Wool Marketing Bd, 1966. Mem., Scottish Landowners' Fedn, 1937– (Mem., Land Use Cttee, 1972–83; Mem., Scottish Livestock Export Gp, 1972–83). Chm., Area Cttee, South of Scotland Electricity Bd Consultative Council, 1972–76. Chm., Monitoring Cttee for Scottish Tartans, 1976; Dir, Castles of Scotland Preservation Trust, 1985–. County Councillor, Midlothian, 1937–48; JP 1938; DL Midlothian (now Lothian Region), 1965; Member: Local Appeal Tribunal (Edinburgh and the Lothians), 1963–75; Midlothian Valuation Appeal Cttee, 1966–78. Member: Standing Council of Scottish Chiefs; The Committee of the Baronage of Scotland (International Delegate); Mem. Corresp., Istituto Italiano di Genealogia e Araldica, Rome and Madrid, 1964; Hon. Mem., Council of Scottish Clans Assoc., USA, 1975. Hon. Mem., Royal Military Inst. of Canada, 1976. KLJ, GCLJ 1975; Comdr, Rose of Lippe, 1971. *Recreations:* shooting, travel, history. *Heir:* *er* twin *s* John Hugh, Master of Borthwick [*b* 14 Nov. 1940; *m* 1974, Adelaide, *d* of A. Birkmyre; two *d*]. *Address:* Crookston, Heriot, Midlothian EH38 5YS. *Clubs:* New, Puffins (Edinburgh).

BORTHWICK, Sir John Thomas, 3rd Bt *cr* 1908; MBE 1945; *b* 5 Dec. 1917; *S* to Btcy of uncle (1st and last Baron Whitburgh), 1967; *m* 1st, 1939; three *s*; 2nd, 1962; two *s*. *Heir:* *s* Antony Thomas Borthwick, *b* 12 Feb. 1941.

BORTHWICK, Kenneth W., CBE 1980; JP; DL; Chairman, XIII Commonwealth Games, Scotland 1986, since 1983; Rt Hon. Lord Provost of the City of Edinburgh, 1977–80; Lord Lieutenant of the City and County of Edinburgh, 1977–80; *b* 4 Nov. 1915; *s* of Andrew Graham Borthwick; *m* 1942, Irene Margaret Wilson, *d* of John Graham Wilson, Aberdeen; two *s* one *d*. *Educ:* George Heriot Sch., Edinburgh. Served War of 1939–45: Flying Officer, RAF. Elected Edinburgh Town Council, 1963; Lothian Regional Council, 1974–77; Edinburgh District Council, 1976. Judge of Police, 1972–75. Member: Lothians River Bd, 1969–73; Organising Cttee, Commonwealth Games, Edinburgh, 1970; Edinburgh and Lothian Theatre Trust, 1975–76; Lothian and Borders Police Bd, 1975–77; British Airports Authorities Consultative Cttee, 1977–80; Convention of Scottish Local Authorities, 1977; Scottish Council Develt and Industry, 1977; Chairman: Edinburgh Dist. Licensing Court, 1975–77; Edinburgh Internat. Festival Soc., 1977–80; Edinburgh Military Tattoo Policy Cttee, 1977–80; Queen's Silver Jubilee Edinburgh Appeal Fund, 1977. Curator of Patronage, Univ. of Edinburgh, 1977–80. Governor, George Heriot Sch., 1965–73. Vice-President (ex officio): RZS of Scotland, 1977–80; Lowland TA&VRA, 1977–80. DL City of Edinburgh, 1980. Hon. Consul for Malaŵi, 1982. OStJ. *Recreations:* golf, gardening. *Address:* 62 Trinity Road, Edinburgh EH5 3HT. *Club:* Caledonian (Hon. Mem.).

BORTHWICK, (William) Jason (Maxwell), DSC 1942; *b* 1 Nov. 1910; *er s* of late Hon. William Borthwick and Ruth (*née* Rigby); *m* 1937, Elizabeth Elworthy (*d* 1978), Timaru, NZ; one *s* three *d*. *Educ:* Winchester; Trinity Coll., Cambridge (BA). Called to Bar, Inner Temple, 1933. Commnd RNVR, 1940, Comdr (QO) 1945. Joined Thomas Borthwick & Sons Ltd, 1934, Dir 1946–76; Dir, International Commodities Clearing House Ltd and subsids, 1954–84; Dir, Commonwealth Develt Corp., 1972–78; Mem., Central Council of Physical Recreation, 1955–; Chm., Nat. Sailing Centre, 1965–79. *Recreations:* yachting, shooting. *Address:* Brancaster Staithe, King's Lynn, Norfolk. *T:* Brancaster 210475. *Clubs:* United Oxford & Cambridge University, Royal Thames Ycht.

BORWICK, family name of **Baron Borwick.**

BORWICK, 4th Baron, *cr* 1922; **James Hugh Myles Borwick;** Bt *cr* 1916; MC 1945; Major HLI retired; *b* 12 Dec. 1917; *s* of 3rd Baron and Irene Phyllis, *d* of late Thomas Main Paterson, Littlebourne, Canterbury; *S* father 1961; *m* 1954, Hyllarie Adalia Mary, *y d* of late Lieut-Col William Hamilton Hall Johnston, DSO, MC, DL, Bryn-y-Groes, Bala, N Wales; four *d*. *Educ:* Eton; RMC, Sandhurst. Commissioned as 2nd Lieut HLI, 1937; Capt. 1939; Major 1941; retired, 1947. *Recreations:* field sports, sailing and ocean racing. *Heir: half b* Hon. George Sandbach Borwick [*b* 18 Oct. 1922; *m* 1981, Esther, Lady Ellerman (*d* 1985)]. *Address:* Knap Farm, Owermoigne, Dorchester, Dorset. *T:* Warmwell 852365. *Club:* Royal Ocean Racing.

BOSCAWEN, family name of **Viscount Falmouth.**

BOSCAWEN, Hon. Robert Thomas, MC 1944; MP (C) Somerton and Frome, since 1983 (Wells, 1970–83); comptroller of HM Household, since 1986 (Vice-Chamberlain, 1983–86); *b* 17 March 1923; 4th *s* of 8th Viscount Falmouth and Dowager Viscountess Falmouth, CBE; *m* 1949, Mary Alice, JP London 1961, *e d* of Col Sir Geoffrey Ronald Codrington, KCVO, CB, CMG, DSO, OBE, TD; one *s* two *d*. *Educ:* Eton; Trinity College, Cambridge. Served Coldstream Guards, 1941–50; NW Europe, 1944–45. Mem., London Exec. Council, Nat. Health Service, 1954–65; Underwriting Mem. of Lloyds, 1952–. Contested Falmouth and Camborne (C), 1964, 1966. Asst Govt Whip, 1979–81; a Lord Comr of HM Treasury, 1981–83. Mem., Select Cttee on Expenditure, 1974; Vice-Chm., Conservative Parly Health and Social Security Cttee, 1974–79. Mem. Parly Delegns, USSR 1977, Nepal 1981. *Recreation:* sailing. *Address:* House of Commons, SW1A 0AA. *Clubs:* Pratt's; Royal Yacht Squadron.

BOSSOM, Hon. Sir Clive, 2nd Bt, *cr* 1953; *b* 4 Feb. 1918; *s* of late Baron Bossom (Life Peer); *S* to father's Baronetcy, 1965; *m* 1951, Lady Barbara North, *sister* of 9th Earl of Guilford, *qv*; three *s* one *d*. *Educ:* Eton. Regular Army, The Buffs, 1939–48; served Europe and Far East. Kent County Council, 1949–52; Chm. Council Order of St John for Kent, 1951–56; Mem. Chapter General, Order of St John (Mem., Jt Cttee, 1961–; Chm., Ex-Services War Disabled Help and Homes Dept, 1973–). Contested (C) Faversham Div., 1951 and 1955. MP (C) Leominster Div., Herefordshire, 1959–Feb. 1974; Parliamentary Private Secretary: to Jt Parly Secs, Min. of Pensions and Nat. Insce, 1960–62; to Sec. of State for Air, 1962–64; to Minister of Defence for RAF, 1964; to Home Secretary, 1970–72. Chm., Europ Assistance Ltd. President: Anglo-Belgian Union, 1970–73, 1983–85 (Chm., 1967–70; Vice-Pres., 1974–82, 1985–); Anglo-Netherlands Soc., 1978–; BARC, 1985–; Vice-President: Industrial Fire Protection Assoc., 1981–; Fédération Internationale de L'Automobile, 1975–81 (Vice-Pres. d'Honneur, 1982–); Chairman: RAC, 1975–78; RAC Motor Sports Council, 1975–81; RAC Motor Sports Assoc. Ltd, 1979–82; Iran Soc. 1973–76 (Vice-Pres., 1977–); Mem. Council, RGS, 1982–; Internat. Pres., Internat. Social Service, 1984–. Liveryman of Worshipful Companies of Grocers (Master, 1979), Needlemakers. FRSA. KStJ 1961. Comdr, Order of Leopold II; Order of Homayoun III (Iran), 1977; Comdr, Order of the Crown (Belgium), 1977; Kt Comdr, Order of Orange Nassau (Netherlands), 1980. *Recreation:* travel. *Heir: s* Bruce Charles Bossom, [*b* 22 Aug. 1952; *m* 1985, Penelope Jane, *d* of late Edward Holland-Martin and of Mrs Holland-Martin, Overbury Court, Glos]. *Address:* 3 Eaton Mansions, Cliveden Place, SW1. *T:* 01–730 1108. *Clubs:* Royal Automobile, Carlton.

BOSSY, Rev. Michael Joseph Frederick, SJ; Headmaster, Stonyhurst College, 1972–85; *b* 22 Nov. 1929; *s* of F. J. Bossy and K. Bossy (*née* White). *Educ:* St Ignatius Coll., Stamford Hill; Heythrop Coll., Oxon (STL); Oxford Univ. (MA). Taught at: St Ignatius Coll., Stamford Hill, 1956–59; St Francis Xavier's Coll., Liverpool, 1963–64; Stonyhurst Coll., 1965–85. *Recreation:* watching games. *Address:* Stonyhurst College, via Blackburn, Lancashire BB6 9PZ. *T:* Stonyhurst 247.

BOSTOCK, James Edward, RE 1961 (ARE 1947); ARCA London; painter and engraver; *b* Hanley, Staffs, 11 June 1917; *s* of William George Bostock, pottery and glass-worker, and Amy (*née* Titley); *m* 1939, Gwladys Irene (*née* Griffiths); three *s*. *Educ:* Borden Grammar Sch., Sittingbourne; Medway Sch. of Art, Rochester; Royal College of Art. War Service as Sgt in Durham LI and Royal Corps of Signals. Full-time Teacher, 1946–78; Vice-Principal, West of England Coll. of Art, 1965–70; Academic Develt Officer, Bristol Polytechnic, 1970–78. Elected Mem. of Soc. of Wood Engravers, 1950. Mem. Council. Soc. of Staffs Artists, 1963. Mem., E Kent Art Soc., 1980. Exhibited water-colours, etchings, wood engravings and drawings at RA, NEAC, RBA, RE, RI and other group exhibitions and in travelling exhibitions to Poland, Czechoslovakia, South Africa, Far East, New Zealand, USA, Sweden, Russia and Baltic States, and the provinces. One-man shows: Mignon Gall., Bath; Univ. of Bristol; Bristol Polytechnic; Margate Library Gall.; Deal Lib. Gall.; Broadstairs Lib. Gall. Works bought by V & A Museum, British Museum, British Council, Hull, Swindon, Stoke-on-Trent and Bristol Education Cttees, Hunt Botanical Library, Pittsburgh, Hereford Mus., and private collectors. Commissioned work for: ICI Ltd, British Museum (Nat. Hist.), Odhams Press, and other firms and public authorities. *Publications:* Roman Lettering for Students, 1959; articles in: Times, Guardian, Staffordshire Sentinel, Studio, Artist; reproductions in Garrett, History of British Wood Engraving, 1978. *Address:* White Lodge, 80 Lindenthorpe Road, Broadstairs, Kent CT10 1DB. *T:* Thanet 69782.

BOSTOCK, Rev. Canon Peter Geoffrey, MA; Clergy Appointments Adviser, 1973–76; Deputy Secretary, Board for Mission and Unity, General Synod of Church of England, 1971–73; Canon Emeritus, Diocese of Mombasa, 1958; *b* 24 Dec. 1911; *s* of Geoffrey Bostock; *m* 1937, Elizabeth Rose; two *s* two *d*. *Educ:* Charterhouse; The Queen's Coll., Oxon; Wycliffe Hall, Oxon. Deacon, 1935; Priest, 1937; CMS Kenya, 1935–58; became Canon of Diocese of Mombasa, 1952; Archdeacon, 1953–58; Vicar-Gen., 1955–58. Examining Chaplain to Bishop of Mombasa, 1950–58; Chm., Christian Council of Kenya, 1957–58; Archdeacon of Doncaster and Vicar, High Melton, 1959–67; Asst Sec., Missionary and Ecumenical Council of Church Assembly, 1967–71. *Recreations:* home and gardening. *Address:* 6 Moreton Road, Oxford OX2 7AX. *T:* Oxford 55460. *Club:* Royal Commonwealth Society.

BOSTON, family name of **Baron Boston of Faversham.**

BOSTON, 10th Baron *cr* 1761; **Timothy George Frank Boteler Irby;** Bt 1704; *b* 27 March 1939; *s* of 9th Baron Boston, MBE, and of Erica N., *d* of T. H. Hill; *S* father, 1978; *m* 1967, Rhonda Anne, *d* of R. A. Bate; two *s* one *d*. *Educ:* Clayesmore School, Dorset; Southampton Univ. (BSc Econ.). *Heir: s* Hon. George William Eustace Boteler Irby, *b* 1 Aug. 1971. *Address:* 135 Bishop's Mansions, Stevenage Road, Fulham, SW6. *T:* 01–731 1936.

BOSTON OF FAVERSHAM, Baron *cr* 1976 (Life Peer), of Faversham, Kent; **Terence George Boston;** QC 1981; barrister; Opposition Front Bench Spokesman on Defence, since 1984; Chairman, Television South plc (TVS), since 1980; *b* 21 March 1930; *yr* surv. *s* of George T. Boston and Kate (*née* Bellati); *m* 1962, Margaret Joyce (Member: SE Metropolitan Regional Hospital Board, 1970–74; Mental Health Review Appeals Tribunal (SE Metropolitan area); market research consultant), *er d* of late R. H. J. Head and of Mrs H. F. Winters, and step *d* of late H. F. Winters, Melbourne, Australia. *Educ:* Woolwich Polytechnic Sch.; King's Coll., University of London. Dep. President, University of London Union, 1955–56. Commnd in RAF during Nat. Service, 1950–52; later trained as pilot with University of London Air Sqdn. Called to the Bar: Inner Temple, 1960; Gray's Inn, 1973; BBC News Sub-Editor, External Services, 1957–60; Senior BBC Producer (Current Affairs), 1960–64; also Producer of Law in Action series (Third Programme), 1962–64. Joined Labour Party, 1946; contested (Lab) Wokingham, 1955 and 1959; MP (Lab) Faversham, Kent, June 1964–70; PPS to: Minister of Public Building and Works, 1964–66; Minister of Power, 1966–68; Minister of Transport, 1968–69; Asst Govt Whip, 1969–70; Minister of State, Home Office, 1979; opp. front bench spokesman on home affairs, 1979–84. UK Deleg. to UN Gen. Assembly, XXXIst, XXXIInd and XXXIIIrd Sessions, 1976–78. Member: Executive Cttee, International Union of Socialist Youth, 1950; Select Cttee on Broadcasting Proceedings of Parliament, 1966; Speaker's Conference on Electoral Law, 1965–68. Trustee, Parly Lab. Party Benevolent Fund, 1967–74. Founder Vice-Chm., Great Britain—East Europe Centre, 1967–69; Chm., The Sheppey Gp, 1967–. *Recreations:* opera (going, not singing), fell-walking. *Address:* House of Lords, SW1A 0PW.

BOSTON, David Merrick, OBE 1976; MA; Director (formerly Curator), Horniman Museum and Library, London, since 1965; *b* 15 May 1931; *s* of late Dr H. M. Boston, Salisbury; *m* 1961, Catharine, *d* of Rev. Prof. E. G. S. Parrinder, *qv*; one *s* two *d*. *Educ:* Rondebosch, Cape Town; Bishop Wordsworth's, Salisbury; Selwyn Coll., Cambridge; Univ. of Cape Town. BA History Cantab 1954; MA 1958. RAF, 1950–51; Adjt, Marine Craft Trng School. Field survey, S African Inst. of Race Relations, 1955; Keeper of Ethnology, Liverpool Museums, 1956–62; Assist Keeper, British Museum, New World archaeology and ethnography, 1962–65. Chm., British Nat. Cttee of Internat. Council of Museums, 1976–80; Mem. Council: Museums Assoc., 1969; Royal Anthropological Inst., 1969 (Vice-Pres., 1972–75, 1977–80, Hon. Sec., 1985–). Visiting Scientist: National Museum of Man, Ottawa, 1970; Japan Foundation, Tokyo, 1986. FMA; FRAS; FRGS. Ordenom Jugoslavenske Zastave sa zlatnom zvezdom na ogrlici (Yugoslavia), 1981. *Publications:* Pre-Columbian Pottery of the Americas, 1980; contribs to learned jls and encyclopaedias and on Pre-European America, in World Ceramics (ed R. J. Charleston). *Address:* 10 Oakleigh Park Avenue, Chislehurst, Kent. *T:* 01-467 1049.

BOSTON, Lucy M.; writer; *b* 10 Dec. 1892; *d* of James Wood and Mary Garrett. Has restored, and lives in, the oldest inhabited Norman house in England, which is the source of all her books. Carnegie medal, 1960. *Publications: for children* (many translated into seven languages): The Children of Green Knowe, 1954; The Chimneys of Green Knowe, 1958; The River at Green Knowe, 1959; A Stranger at Green Knowe, 1961; An Enemy at Green Knowe, 1964; The Castle of Yew, 1965; The Sea Egg, 1967; Nothing Said, 1971; The Guardians of the House, 1974; The Fossil Snake, 1975; The Stones of Green Knowe, 1976; *novels:* Yew Hall, 1954; Persephone, 1969; *autobiography:* Memory in a House, 1973; Perverse and Foolish, 1979; *poetry:* Time is Undone; *drama:* The Horned Man, 1970. *Address:* The Manor, Hemingford Grey, Huntingdon PE18 9BN.

BOSTON, Richard; writer; *b* 29 Dec. 1938. *Educ:* Stowe; Regent Street Polytechnic School of Art; King's Coll., Cambridge (MA). Taught English in Sicily, Sweden and Paris; acted in Jacques Tati's Playtime. Editorial staff of Peace News, TLS, New Society; columnist and feature writer, The Guardian, at intervals, 1972–. Editor: The Vole, 1977–80; Quarto, 1979–82. *Publications:* The Press We Deserve (ed), 1969; An Anatomy of Laughter, 1974; The Admirable Urquhart, 1975; Beer and Skittles, 1976; Baldness Be My Friend, 1977; The Little Green Book, 1979; C. O. Jones's Compendium of Practical Jokes, 1982. *Recreations:* shelling peas, going to France. *Address:* The Old School, Aldworth, Reading, Berks. *T:* Compton 587.

BOSVILLE MACDONALD OF SLEAT, Sir Ian Godfrey, 17th Bt, *cr* 1625; ARICS, MRSH; 25th Chief of Sleat; *b* 18 July 1947; *er s* of Sir (Alexander) Somerled Angus Bosville Macdonald of Sleat, 16th Bt, MC, 24th Chief of Sleat and of Mary, Lady Bosville Macdonald of Sleat; *S* father 1958; *m* 1970, Juliet Fleury, *o d* of late Maj.-Gen. J. M. D. Ward-Harrison, OBE, MC; one *s* two *d*. *Educ:* Pinewood Sch.; Eton Coll.; Royal Agricultural Coll. ARICS 1972. Member (for Bridlington South), Humberside CC, 1981–84. MRSH 1972; Mem., Econ. Res. Council, 1979–. *Heir: s* Somerled Alexander Bosville Macdonald, younger of Sleat, *b* 30 Jan. 1976. *Recreation:* ornithology. *Address:* Thorpe Hall, Rudston, Driffield, North Humberside. *T:* Kilham 239; Upper Duntulm, By Portree, Isle of Skye. *T:* Duntulm 206. *Clubs:* Lansdowne, Brooks's; Puffin's (Edinburgh).

BOSWALL, Sir (Thomas) Alford H.; *see* Houstoun-Boswall.

BOSWELL, Lt-Gen. Sir Alexander (Crawford Simpson), KCB 1982; CBE 1974 (OBE 1971; MBE 1962); Lieutenant-Governor and Commander-in-Chief, Guernsey, since 1985; *b* 3 Aug. 1928; *s* of Alexander Boswell Simpson Boswell and Elizabeth Burns Simpson Boswell (*née* Park); *m* 1956, Jocelyn Leslie Blundstone Pomfret, *d* of Surg. Rear-Adm. A. A. Pomfret, CB, OBE; five *s*. *Educ:* Merchiston Castle Sch.; RMA, Sandhurst. Enlisted in Army, 1947; Commnd, Argyll and Sutherland Highlanders, Dec. 1948; regimental appts, Hong Kong, Korea, UK, Suez, Guyana, 1949–58; sc Camberley, 1959; Mil. Asst (GSO2) to GOC Berlin, 1960–62; Co. Comdr, then Second in Comd, 1 A and SH, Malaya and Borneo, 1963–65 (despatches 1965); Directing Staff, Staff Coll., Camberley, 1965–68; CO, 1 A and SH, 1968–71; Col GS Trng Army Strategic Comd, 1971; Brig. Comdg 39 Inf. Bde, 1972–74; COS, 1st British Corps, 1974–76; NDC (Canada), 1976–77; GOC 2nd Armd Div., 1978–80; Dir, TA and Cadets, 1980–82; GOC Scotland and Governor of Edinburgh Castle, 1982–85. Col, Argyll and Sutherland Highlanders, 1972–82; Hon. Col, Tayforth Univs OTC, 1982–86; Col Comdt, Scottish Div., 1982–86. Captain of Tarbet, 1974–82. KStJ 1985. *Address:* Government House, Guernsey, Channel Islands; c/o Bank of Scotland, Palmerston Place Branch, 32 West Maitland Street, Edinburgh EH12 5DZ. *Clubs:* Army and Navy; New (Edinburgh).

BOSWOOD, Anthony Richard; QC 1986; *b* 1 Oct. 1947; *s* of Noel Gordon Paul Boswood and Cicily Ann Watson; *m* 1973, Sarah Bridget Alexander; three *d*. *Educ:* St Paul's Sch.; New Coll., Oxford (BCL, MA). Called to Bar, Middle Temple, 1970. *Recreations:* opera, riding, tennis. *Address:* Fountain Court, Temple, EC4 9DH. *T:* 01–353 7356; Casanuova, Pieveasciata, Castelnuovo Berardenga, Italy. *Club:* Grafton Tennis (Streatham).

BOSWORTH, (John) Michael (Worthington), CBE 1972; FCA; Deputy Chairman, British Railways Board, 1972–83 (Vice-Chairman, 1968–72); *b* 22 June 1921; *s* of Humphrey Worthington Bosworth and Vera Hope Bosworth; *m* 1955, Patricia Mary Edith Wheelock; one *s* one *d*. *Educ:* Bishop's Stortford Coll. Served Royal Artillery, 1939–46. Peat, Marwick, Mitchell & Co., 1949–68, Partner, 1960. Chairman: British Rail Engineering Ltd, 1969–71; British Rail Property Bd, 1971–72; British Rail Shipping and International Services Ltd, now Sealink UK Ltd, 1976–84; BR Hovercraft Ltd, 1976–81; British Transport Hotels, 1978–83; British Rail Investments Ltd, 1981–84; British Rail Trustee Co., 1984–; Director: Hoverspeed (UK) Ltd, 1981–; British Ferries, 1984–. Vice Pres., Société Belgo-Anglaise des Ferry-Boats, 1979–. *Recreations:* ski-ing, vintage cars. *Address:* Old Mill House, Mill Lane, Yetminster, Sherborne, Dorset DT9 6ND. *Club:* Royal Automobile.

BOSWORTH, Neville Bruce Alfred, CBE 1982; Senior Partner, Bosworth, Bailey Cox & Co., Solicitors, Birmingham; *b* 18 April 1918; *s* of W. C. N. Bosworth; *m* 1945, Charlotte Marian Davis; one *s* two *d.* *Educ:* King Edward's Sch., Birmingham; Birmingham Univ. LLB. Admitted Solicitor, 1941. Birmingham City Council, 1950–; County Bor. Councillor (Erdington Ward), 1950–61; Alderman, 1961–74; Dist Councillor (Edgbaston Ward), 1973–; Lord Mayor of Birmingham, 1969–70; Dep. Mayor, 1970–71; Leader of Birmingham City Council, 1976–80, 1982–84; Leader of Opposition, 1972–76, 1980–82 and 1984–; Cons. Gp Leader, 1972– (Dep. Gp Leader, 1971–72); Chairman: Gen. Purposes Cttee, 1966–69; Finance and Priorities Cttee, 1976–80; National Exhibn Centre Cttee, 1976–80. Chm., W Midlands Police Bd, 1985–. County Councillor (Edgbaston Ward), W Midlands CC, 1973–; Chm., Legal and Property Cttee, 1977–79; Vice-Chm., Finance Cttee, 1980–81. Chm., Sutton Coldfield Cons. Assoc., 1963–66; Vice-Chm., Birmingham Cons. Assoc., 1972–; Mem., Local Govt Adv. Cttee, National Union of Cons. and Unionist Assocs, 1973–. Vice Chm., Assoc. of Metropolitan Authorities, 1978–80, and Mem. Policy Cttee, 1976–80; Vice-Pres., Birmingham and Dist Property Owners Assoc.; Dir, Nat. Exhibn Centre Ltd, 1970–72, 1974–; Mem., W Midlands Econ. Council, 1978–79. Trustee, several charitable trusts; Mem. Council, Birmingham Univ.; Governor, King Edward VI Schs, Birmingham (Dep. Bailiff, 1979–80). Hon. Freeman, City of Birmingham, 1982. *Recreations:* politics, football (Dir, Birmingham City Football Club plc). *Address:* Hollington, Luttrell Road, Four Oaks, Sutton Coldfield, Birmingham B74 2SR. *T:* 021–308 0647; 54 Newhall Street, Birmingham B3 3QG. *T:* 021–236 8091. *Club:* Birmingham (Birmingham).

BOTHA, Matthys (Izak); South African Diplomat, retired; *b* 31 Oct. 1913; *s* of Johan Hendrik Jacobus Botha and Anna Botha (*née* Joubert); *m* 1940, Hester le Roux (*née* Bosman); two *s* *Educ:* Selborne Coll.; Pretoria Univ. BA, LLB. Called to the Transvaal Bar, Dept of Finance, Pretoria, 1931–44; S African Embassy, Washington, 1944–51; S African Permanent Mission to UN, NY, 1951–54; Head, Political Div., Dept Foreign Affairs, Pretoria, 1955–59; Envoy Extraordinary and Minister Plenipotentiary, Switzerland, 1959–60; Minister, London, 1960–62; Ambassador and Permanent Rep., UN, NY, 1962–70; Ambassador to: Canada, 1970–73; Italy, 1973–77; Court of St James's, 1977–78; Ciskei, 1983–85. Member: Simon Vanderstel Foundn; South African Foundn. Knight of Grand Cross, Order of Merit (Italy), 1977. *Recreations:* swimming, skiing, cycling. *Address:* 7 de Jongh Street, The Strand, Cape Province, 7140, South Africa.

BOTHA, Pieter Willem, DMS 1976; Star of South Africa, 1979; State President, Republic of South Africa, since 1984 (Prime Minister, and Minister of National Intelligence Service, 1978–84); *b* 12 Jan. 1916; *s* of Pieter Willem and Hendriena Christina Botha; *m* 1943, Anna Elizabeth Rossouw; two *s* three *d.* *Educ:* Paul Roux; Bethlehem, Orange Free State; Univ. of Orange Free State, Bloemfontein. MP for George, 1948–84; Deputy Minister of the Interior, 1958; Minister of Community Development and of Coloured Affairs, 1961; Minister of Public Works, 1964; Minister of Defence, 1966–80. Leader of the National Party in the Cape Province, 1966–. Hon. Doctorate in: Military Science, Stellenbosch Univ., 1976; Philosophy, Orange Free State Univ., 1981; DAdmin *hc* Pretoria Univ., 1985. Grand Cross of Military Order of Christ, Portugal, 1967; Order of Propitious Clouds with Special Grand Cordon, Taiwan, 1980; Grand Collar, Order of Good Hope, 1985. *Recreations:* horseriding, walking, reading, small game hunting. *Address:* Office of the State President, Tuynhuys, Cape Town 8001, South Africa.

BOTHA, Roelof Frederik, (Pik Botha), DMS 1981; Minister of Foreign Affairs, South Africa, since 1977; Minister of Information, since 1978; MP (National Party) for Westdene, since 1977; *b* 27 April 1932; *m* 1953, Helena Susanna Bosman; two *s* two *d.* *Educ:* Volkskool, Potchefstroom; Univ. of Pretoria. Dept of Foreign Affairs, 1953; diplomatic missions, Europe, 1956–62; Mem. team from S Africa, in SW Africa case, Internat. Court of Justice, The Hague, 1963–66, 1970–71; Agent for S African Govt, Internat. Court of Justice, 1965–66; Legal Adviser, Dept of Foreign Affairs, 1966–68; Under-Sec. and Head of SW Africa and UN Sections, 1968–70. National Party, MP for Wonderboom, 1970–74. Mem., SA Delegn to UN Gen. Assembly, 1967–69, 1971, 1973–74. Served on select Parly Cttees, 1970–74. South African Permanent Representative to the UN, NY, 1974–77; South African Ambassador to the USA, 1975–77. Grand Cross, Order of Good Hope, 1980; Order of the Brilliant Star with Grand Cordon, 1980. *Address:* House of Assembly, Cape Town, South Africa; c/o Department of Foreign Affairs, Pretoria, South Africa.

BOTHWELL, Most Rev. John Charles; *see* Niagara, Archbishop of.

BOTT, Ian Bernard, FEng 1985; Director, Admiralty Research Establishment, Ministry of Defence, since 1984; *b* 1 April 1932; *s* of late Edwin Bernard and of Agnes Bott; *m* 1955, Kathleen Mary (*née* Broadbent); one *s* one *d.* *Educ:* Nottingham High Sch.; Southwell Minster Grammar Sch.; Stafford Technical Coll.; Manchester Univ. BSc Hon. Physics; FIEE, FInstP. Nottingham Lace Industry, 1949–53. Royal Air Force, 1953–55. English Electric, Stafford, 1955–57; Royal Radar Estabt, 1960–75 (Head of Electronics Group, 1973–75); Counsellor, Defence Research and Development, British Embassy, Washington DC, 1975–77; Ministry of Defence: Dep. Dir Underwater Weapons Projects (S/M), 1977–79; Asst Chief Scientific Advr (Projects), 1979–81; Dir Gen., Guided Weapons and Electronics, 1981–82; Principal Dep. Dir, AWRE, MoD, 1982–84. *Publications:* papers on physics and electronics subjects in jls of learned socs. *Recreations:* building, horology, music. *Club:* Royal Automobile.

BOTT, Prof. Martin Harold Phillips, FRS 1977; Professor of Geophysics, University of Durham, since 1966; *b* 12 July 1926; *s* of Harold Bott and Dorothy (*née* Phillips); *m* 1961, Joyce Cynthia Hughes; two *s* one *d.* *Educ:* Clayesmore Sch. Dorset; Magdalene Coll., Cambridge (Scholar). MA, PhD. Nat. Service, 1945–48 (Lieut, Royal Signals). Durham University: Turner and Newall Fellow, 1954–56; Lectr, 1956–63; Reader, 1963–66. Anglican Lay Reader. Mem. Council, Royal Soc., 1982–84. Murchison Medallist, Geological Soc. of London, 1977; Clough Medal, Geol Soc. of Edinburgh, 1979; Sorby Medal, Yorkshire Geol Soc., 1981. *Publications:* The Interior of the Earth, 1971, 2nd edn 1982; papers in learned jls. *Recreations:* walking, mountains. *Address:* 11 St Mary's Close, Shincliffe, Durham. *T:* Durham 64021.

BOTTAI, Bruno; Ambassador of Italy to the Court of St James's, since 1985; *b* 10 July 1930; *s* of Giuseppe Bottai and Cornelia Ciocca. *Educ:* Univ. of Rome (law degree). Joined Min. for For. Affairs, 1955; Vice Consul, Tunis, 1956; Second Sec., Perm. Representation to EC, Brussels, 1958; Gen. Secretariat, Co-ord. Service, Min. for For. Affairs, 1961; Counsellor, London, 1966; Dep. Chef de Cabinet, Min. for For. Affairs, 1968; Minister-Counsellor, Holy See, 1969; Diplomatic Advr to Pres., Council of Ministers, 1970; Hd of Press and Inf. Dept 1972, Dir-Gen. of Political Affairs 1976, Min. for For. Affairs; Ambassador to Holy See and Sovereign Mil. Order of Malta, 1979; Dir-Gen. Pol. Affairs, Min. for For. Affairs, 1981. Numerous decorations from Europe, Africa, Latin Amer. countries, Holy See, Malta. *Publications:* political essays and articles. *Recreations:* modern paintings and modern sculpture, theatre, reading, walking. *Address:* Italian Embassy, 4 Grosvenor Square, W1X 9LA. *T:* 01–629 8200. *Club:* Hurlingham.

BOTTINI, Reginald Norman, CBE 1974; General-Secretary, National Union of Agricultural and Allied Workers, 1970–78; Member, General Council of TUC, 1970–78; *b* 14 Oct. 1916; *s* of Reginald and Helena Teresa Bottini; *m* 1946, Doris Mary Balcomb; no *c.* *Educ:* Bec Grammar School. Apptd Asst in Legal Dept of Nat. Union of Agricultural Workers, 1945; Head of Negotiating Dept, 1954; elected Gen.-Sec., Dec. 1969. Member: Agricultural Wages Bd, 1963–78; Agricultural Economic Development Cttee, 1970–78; (part-time) SE Electricity Bd, 1974–83; Food Hygiene Adv. Council, 1973–83; BBC Agric. Adv. Cttee, 1973–78; Econ. and Soc. Cttee, EEC, 1975–78; Clean Air Council, 1975–80; Adv. Cttee on Toxic Substances, 1977–80; Meat and Livestock Commn, 1977–86 (and Chm. of its Consumers Cttee); Panel Mem., Central Arbitration Cttee, 1977–; Commn on Energy and the Environment, 1978–81; Waste Management Adv. Council, 1978–81; Employees' Panel, Industrial Tribunals, 1984–85. Formerly: Secretary: Trade Union Side, Forestry Commn Ind. and Trades Council; Trade Union Side, British Sugar Beet Nat. Negotiating Cttee; Chm., Trade Union Side, Nat. Jt Ind. Council for River Authorities; formerly Member: Central Council for Agric. and Hort. Co-operation; Nat. Jt Ind. Council for County Roadmen. *Recreations:* gardening, driving. *Address:* 43 Knights End Road, Great Bowden, Market Harborough, Leics LE16 7EY. *T:* Market Harborough 64229. *Club:* Farmers'.

BOTTO DE BARROS, Adwaldo Cardoso; Director-General, International Bureau of Universal Postal Union, since 1985; *b* 19 Jan. 1925; *s* of Julio Botto de Barros and Maria Cardoso Botto de Barros; *m* 1951, Neida de Moura; one *s* two *d.* *Educ:* Military Coll., Military Engineering Inst. and Higher Military Engineering Inst., Brazil. Railway construction, 1952–54; Dir, industries in São Paulo and Curitiba; Dir, Handling Sector, São Paulo Prefecture, Financial Adviser to São Paulo Engrg Faculty and Adviser to Suzano Prefecture, 1965–71; Regional Dir, São Paulo, 1972–74, Pres., 1974–84, Brazilian Telegraph and Post Office. Mem. and Head, numerous delegns to UPU and other postal assocs overseas, 1976–84. Numerous Brazilian and foreign hons and decorations. *Recreations:* philately, sports. *Address:* International Bureau of the UPU, Weltpoststrasse 4, 3000 Berne 15, Switzerland. *T:* 031/43 22 11.

BOTTOMLEY, Baron *cr* 1984 (Life Peer), of Middlesbrough in the County of Cleveland, **Arthur George Bottomley,** OBE 1941; PC 1951; *b* 7 Feb. 1907; *s* of late George Howard Bottomley and Alice Bottomley; *m* 1936, Bessie Ellen Wiles (*see* Lady Bottomley); no *c.* *Educ:* Gamuel Road Council Sch.; Extension Classes at Toynbee Hall. London Organiser of National Union of Public Employees, 1935–45, 1959–62. Walthamstow Borough Council, 1929–49; Mayor of Walthamstow, 1945–46; Chairman of Emergency Cttee and ARP Controller, 1939–41. Dep. Regional Commissioner for S-E England, 1941–45. MP (Lab): Chatham Division of Rochester, 1945–50, Rochester and Chatham 1950–59; Middlesbrough East, 1962–74, Teesside, Middlesbrough, 1974–83. Parliamentary Under-Secretary of State for Dominions, 1946–47; Sec. for Overseas Trade, Board of Trade, 1947–51; Sec. of State for Commonwealth Affairs, 1964–66; Minister of Overseas Devel, 1966–67. Land Tax Comr, Becontree Div. of Essex; Special Govt Mission to Burma, 1947; Deleg. to UN, New York, 1946, 1947 and 1949; Leader: UK delegation to World Trade and Employment Conference, Havana, 1947; UK Delegn to Commonwealth Conference, Delhi, 1949; Trade Mission to Pakistan, 1950; Special Mission to West Indies, 1951; Member: Consultative Assembly, Council of Europe, 1952, 1953 and 1954; Leader: Parliamentary Labour Party Mission to Burma, 1962, to Malaysia, 1963; UK Delegation to CPA Conferences, Australia, Canada, Malawi, Malaysia, Mauritius; Member, Parliamentary Missions to: India, 1946; Kenya, 1954; Ghana, 1959; Cyprus, 1963; Hong Kong, 1964; China, 1983. Chairman: Commonwealth Relations and Colonies Group, Parly Labour Party, 1963; Select Parly Cttee on Race Relations and Immigration, 1969; Select Cttee on Cyprus, 1975; Special Parly Cttee on Admin and Orgn of House of Commons Services, 1976; House of Commons Commn, 1980–83; Treasurer, Commonwealth Parly Assoc., 1974 (Vice-Chm., UK Branch, 1968 and 1974–77). Chm., Attlee Foundn, 1978–; President: Britain-India Forum, 1981–; Britain-Burma Soc., 1981–. Hon. Fellow, Hunterian Soc., 1985. Hon. Freeman of Chatham, 1959; Freeman: City of London, 1975; Middlesbrough, 1976. Awarded title of Aung San Tagun, Burma, 1981. *Publications:* Why Britain should Join the Common Market, 1959; Two Roads to Colonialism, 1960; The Use and Abuse of Trade Unions, 1961; Commonwealth Comrades and Friends, 1986. *Recreations:* walking and theatre-going. *Address:* 19 Lichfield Road, Woodford Green, Essex.

BOTTOMLEY, Lady; Bessie Ellen Bottomley, DBE 1970; *b* 28 Nov. 1906; *d* of Edward Charles Wiles and Ellen (*née* Estall); *m* 1936, Baron Bottomley, *qv;* no *c.* *Educ:* Maynard Road Girls' Sch.; North Walthamstow Central Sch. On staff of NUT, 1925–36. Member: Walthamstow Borough Council, 1945–48; Essex CC, 1962–65; Chm., Labour Party Women's Section, E Walthamstow, 1946–71, Chingford, 1973–. Mem., Forest Group Hosp. Man. Cttee, 1949–73; Mem., W Roding Community Health Council, 1973–76. Chm., Walthamstow Nat. Savings Cttee, 1949–65; Vice-Pres., Waltham Forest Nat. Savings Cttee, 1965– (Chm., 1975–). Mayoress of Walthamstow, 1945–46. Mem., WVS Regional Staff (SE England), 1941–45. Past Mem., Home Office Adv. Cttee on Child Care. Chm. of Govs of two Secondary Modern Schools, 1948–68, also group of Primary and Infant Schools; Chm. of Governors of High Schools. Mem., Whitefield Trust. JP 1955–76 and on Juvenile Bench, 1955–71; Dep. Chm., Waltham Forest Bench. *Recreations:* theatre, gardening. *Address:* 19 Lichfield Road, Woodford Green, Essex.

BOTTOMLEY, Sir James (Reginald Alfred), KCMG 1973 (CMG 1965); HM Diplomatic Service, retired; *b* 12 Jan. 1920; *s* of Sir (William) Cecil Bottomley, KCMG, and Alice Thistle Bottomley (*née* Robinson), JP; *m* 1941, Barbara Evelyn (Vardon); two *s* two *d* (and one *s* decd). *Educ:* King's College Sch., Wimbledon; Trinity Coll., Cambridge. Served with Inns of Court Regt, RAC, 1940–46. Dominions Office, 1946; Pretoria, 1948–50; Karachi, 1953–55; Washington, 1955–59; UK Mission to United Nations, 1959; Dep. High Commissioner, Kuala Lumpur 1963–67; Assst Under-Sec. of State, Commonwealth Office (later FCO), 1967–70; Dep. Under-Sec. of State, FCO, 1970–72; Ambassador to South Africa, 1973–76; Perm. UK Rep. to UN and other Internat. Organisations at Geneva, 1976–78; Dir, Johnson, Matthey plc, 1979–85. Mem., British Overseas Trade Bd, 1972. *Recreation:* golf. *Address:* 22 Beaufort Place, Thompson's Lane, Cambridge CB5 8AG. *T:* Cambridge 328760.

BOTTOMLEY, Peter James; MP (C) Eltham, since 1983 (Greenwich, Woolwich West, June 1975–1983); Parliamentary Under Secretary of State, Department of Transport, since 1986; *b* 30 July 1944; *er s* of Sir James Bottomley, *qv;* *m* 1967, Virginia Garnett (*see* V. H. B. M. Bottomley); one *s* two *d.* *Educ:* comprehensive sch.; Westminster Sch.; Trinity Coll., Cambridge (MA). Driving, industrial sales, industrial relations, industrial economics. Contested (C) GLC elect., Vauxhall, 1973; (C) Woolwich West, Gen. Elecs, 1974. PPS to Minister of State, FCO, 1982–83, to Sec. of State for Social Services, 1983–84; Parly Under Sec. of State, Dept of Employment, 1984–86. Secretary: Cons. Parly Social Services Cttee, 1977–79; Cons. Parly For. and Commonwealth Cttee, 1979–81. Mem., Transport House Br., T&GWU, 1971–; Pres., Cons. Trade Unionists,

1978–80; Vice-Pres., Fedn of Cons. Students, 1980–82. Chairman: British Union of Family Orgns, 1973–80; Family Forum, 1980–82. Mem. Council, MIND, 1981–82; Trustee, Christian Aid, 1978–84. Parly Swimming Champion, 1980, 1981 and 1984; Captain, Parly Football Team. *Recreation:* children. *Address:* House of Commons, SW1A 0AA.

BOTTOMLEY, Virginia Hilda Brunette Maxwell, JP; MP (C) Surrey South-West, since May 1984; *b* 12 March 1948; *d* of W. John Garnett, *qv*; *m* Peter Bottomley, *qv*; one *s* two *d*. *Educ:* Putney High Sch.; Univ. of Essex (BA); London Sch. of Econs and Pol Science (MSc). Research for Child Poverty Action Gp, and Lectr in a Further Educn Coll., 1971–73; Psychiatric Social Worker, Maudsley Hosp., Brixton and Camberwell Child Guidance Units, 1973–84. Vice Chm., National Council of Carers and their Elderly Dependants, 1982–. Contested (C) IoW, 1983. JP Inner London, 1975 (Chm., Lambeth Juvenile Court, 1981–84). PPS to Minister of State for Educn and Science, 1985–. *Recreation:* family. *Address:* House of Commons, SW1A 0AA. *T:* 01–219 6499. *Club:* Seaview Yacht.

BOTTOMS, Prof. Anthony Edward; Wolfson Professor of Criminology and Director of the Institute of Criminology, University of Cambridge, since 1984; Fellow of Fitzwilliam College, Cambridge, since 1984; *b* 29 Aug. 1939; *yr s* of James William Bottoms, medical missionary, and Dorothy Ethel Bottoms (*née* Barnes); *m* 1962, Janet Freda Wenger; one *s* two *d*. *Educ:* Eltham Coll.; Corpus Christi Coll., Oxford (MA); Corpus Christi Coll., Cambridge (MA); Univ. of Sheffield (PhD). Probation Officer, 1962–64; Research Officer, Inst. of Criminology, Univ. of Cambridge, 1964–68; Univ. of Sheffield: Lecturer, 1968–72; Sen. Lectr, 1972–76; Prof. of Criminology, 1976–84; Dean of Faculty of Law, 1981–84. Canadian Commonwealth Vis. Fellow, Simon Fraser Univ., BC, 1982. Member: Parole Bd for England and Wales, 1974–76; Social Sciences and Law Cttee, ESRC (formerly SSRC), 1979–85; Govt and Law Cttee, ESRC, 1982–85; Home Office Res. and Adv. Gp on Long-Term Prison System, 1984–. Editor, Howard Journal of Penology and Crime Prevention, 1975–81; Gen. Editor, Cambridge Studies in Criminology, 1984–. *Publications:* (jtly) Criminals Coming of Age, 1973; (jtly) The Urban Criminal, 1976; (jtly) Defendants in the Criminal Process, 1976; The Suspended Sentence after Ten Years (Frank Dawtry Lecture), 1980; (ed jtly) The Coming Penal Crisis, 1980; various articles and reviews. *Address:* Institute of Criminology, 7 West Road, Cambridge CB3 9DT. *T:* Cambridge 337733.

BOTTRALL, (Francis James) Ronald, OBE 1949; MA; FRSL; *b* Camborne, Cornwall, 2 Sept. 1906; *o s* of Francis John and Clara Jane Bottrall; *m* 1st, 1934, Margaret Florence (marr. diss., 1954), *o d* of Rev. H. Saumarez Smith; one *s*; 2nd, 1954, Margot Pamela Samuel. *Educ:* Redruth County Sch.; Pembroke Coll., Cambridge. Foundress' Scholar; First Class English Tripos, Parts I and II (with distinction); Charles Oldham Shakespeare Scholarship, 1927. Lector in English, Univ. of Helsingfors, Finland, 1929–31; Commonwealth Fund Fellowship, Princeton Univ., USA, 1931–33; Johore Prof. of English Language and Literature, Raffles Coll., Singapore, 1933–37; Asst Dir, British Inst., Florence, 1937–38; Sec., SOAS, London Univ., 1939–45; Air Ministry: Temp. Admin. Officer, 1940; Priority Officer, 1941; British Council Representative: in Sweden, 1941; in Italy, 1945; in Brazil, 1954; in Greece, 1957; in Japan (and Cultural Counsellor, HM Embassy, Tokyo), 1959; Controller of Educ. 1950–54. Chief, Fellowships and Training Br., Food and Agriculture Org. of UN, 1963–65. Coronation Medal, 1953; Syracuse Internat. Poetry Prize, 1954. FRSL 1955. Grande Ufficiale dell'Ordine al Merito della Repubblica Italiana, 1973. KStJ 1972; KSJ, Malta, 1977. *Publications: poetry:* The Loosening and other Poems, 1931; Festivals of Fire, 1934; The Turning Path, 1939; Farewell and Welcome, 1945; Selected Poems, 1946; The Palisades of Fear, 1949; Adam Unparadised, 1954; Collected Poems, 1961; Day and Night, 1974; Poems 1955–73, 1974; Reflections on the Nile, 1980; Against a Setting Sun, 1983; *criticism, anthologies:* (with Gunnar Ekelöf) T.S. Eliot: Dikter; Urval, 1942; (with Margaret Bottrall) The Zephyr Book of English Verse, 1945; (with Margaret Bottrall) Collected English Verse, 1946; Rome (Art Centres of the World), 1968. *Recreations:* music, travel. *Address:* Villa Roma, Camino Nuevo de Montemar 6, Albufereta, 03016 Alicante, Spain. *Club:* Athenæum.

BOTVINNIK, Mikhail Moisseyevich; Order of Lenin, 1957; Order of the Badge of Honour, 1936 and 1945; Order of the Red Banner of Labour, 1961; Order of the October Revolution, 1981; Senior Scientist, USSR Research Institute for Elctroenergetics, since 1955; *b* Petersburg, 17 Aug. 1911; *s* of a dental technician; *m* 1935, Gayane Ananova; one *d*. *Educ:* Leningrad Polytechnical Institute (Grad.). Thesis for degree of: Candidate of Technical Sciences, 1937; Doctor of Technical Sciences, 1952; Professor, 1972. Chess master title, 1927; Chess grandmaster title, 1935. Won Soviet chess championship in 1931, 1933, 1939, 1941, 1944, 1945, 1952; World chess title, 1948–57, 1958 and 1961. Honoured Master of Sport of the USSR, 1945. *Publications:* Flohr-Botvinnik Match, 1934; Alekhin-Euwe Return Match, 1938; Selected Games, 1937, 1945, 1960; Tournament Match for the Absolute Champion Title, 1945; Botvinnik-Smyslov Match, 1955; Eleventh Soviet Chess Championship, 1939; Smyslov-Botvinnik Return Match, 1960; Regulation of Excitation and Static Stability of Syndronous Machines, 1950; Asynchronized Synchronous Machines, 1960; Algorithm Play of Chess, 1968; Controlled AC Machines (with Y. Shakarian), 1969; Computers, Chess and Long-Range Planning, 1971; Botvinnik's Best Games 1947–70, 1972; Three matches of Anatoly Karpov, 1975; On Cybernetic Goal of Game, 1975; A Half Century in Chess, 1979; On Solving of Inexact Search, 1979; Fifteen Games and their History, 1981; Selected Games 1967–70, 1981; Achieving the Aim, 1981; Analytical and critical works 1923–41, 1984, 1942–56, 1985, 1957–70, 1986. *Address:* 3 Frunsenskaja 7 (flat 154), Moscow, USSR. *T:* 242.15,86.

BOUCHIER, Prof. Ian Arthur Dennis; Professor of Medicine, University of Edinburgh, since 1986; *b* 7 Sept. 1932; *s* of E. A. and M. Bouchier; *m* 1959, Patricia Norma Henshilwood; two *s*. *Educ:* Rondebosch Boys' High Sch., Cape Town; Univ. of Cape Town. MB, ChB, MD, FRCP, FRCPE, FRSE. Groote Schuur Hospital: House Officer, 1955–58; Registrar, 1958–61; Asst Lectr, Royal Free Hosp., 1962–63; Instructor in Medicine, Boston Univ. Sch. of Medicine, 1964–65; Sen. Lectr 1965–70, Reader in Medicine 1970–73, Univ. of London; Prof. of Medicine, 1973–86, and Dean, Faculty of Medicine and Dentistry, 1982–86, Univ. of Dundee. Sec.-Gen., World Organisation of Gastroenterology, 1982–. Member: Chief Scientist Cttee, Scotland, 1980–; MRC, 1982–. Mem. Council, RCPE, 1984–. *Publications:* (ed) Clinical Investigation of Gastrointestinal Function, 1969, 2nd edn 1981; Gastroenterology, 1973, 3rd edn 1982; (ed) Clinical Skills, 1976, 2nd edn 1981; (ed) Recent Advances in Gastroenterology 5, 1983; (ed) Textbook of Gastroenterology, 1984; 300 scientific papers and communications. *Recreations:* history of whaling, music of Berlioz, cooking. *Address:* Department of Medicine, The Royal Infirmary, Edinburgh EH3 9YW. *T:* 031–229 2477. *Club:* Athenæum.

BOUGH, Francis Joseph; broadcaster; *b* 15 Jan. 1933; *m*; three *s*. *Educ:* Oswestry; Merton College, Oxford (MA). With ICI, 1957–62; joined BBC, 1962; presenter of Sportsview, 1964–67, of Grandstand, 1967–82, of Nationwide, 1972–83, of breakfast television, 1983–. Former Oxford soccer blue, Shropshire sprint champion. *Publication:* Cue Frank! (autobiog.), 1980. *Address:* c/o BBC Television, Lime Grove Studios, Shepherds Bush, W12.

BOUGHEY, John Fenton C.; *see* Coplestone-Boughey.

BOUGHEY, Sir John (George Fletcher), 11th Bt *cr* 1798; *b* 12 Aug. 1959; *s* of Sir Richard James Boughey, 10th Bt, and of Davina Julia (now the Lady Loch), *d* of FitzHerbert Wright; *S* father, 1978. *Heir: b* James Richard Boughey, *b* 29 Aug. 1960. *Address:* Bratton House, Westbury, Wilts.

BOUGHTON, Michael Linnell Gerald; Deputy Chairman and Managing Director (Operations), TI Group PLC (formerly Tube Investments), 1984–85 (Director, since 1964); Chairman, TI Raleigh Industries Ltd, since 1981; *b* 14 May 1925; *s* of Edward Morley Westwood Boughton and Iris Dorothy (*née* Linnell); *m* 1954, Barbara Janette, *d* of Sir Ivan Stedeford, GBE; one *s* two *d*. *Educ:* King Edward's Sch., Birmingham; Rugby Technical Coll. (HNC Product Engrg). Engineering apprentice, B-T-H Co. Ltd, 1942–49; TI Group, 1952–: Man. Dir, Round Oak Steel Works, 1960–61; Jt Man. Dir, Steel Tube Div., 1961–64; Man. Dir, Engrg Div., 1964–74; Man. Dir, Domestic Appliance Div., 1974–83; Director: Condor International, 1969–75; EIS Gp, 1979–84, 1986–. Mem. Bd, PLA, 1986–. *Recreations:* sailing, golf, jobs of construction and destruction. *Address:* Little Heath, Crays Pond, near Pangbourne, Berks RG8 7QG. *T:* Goring-on-Thames 872622.

BOULET, Gilles, OC 1985; President, University of Quebec, since 1978; *b* 5 June 1926; *s* of Georges-A. Boulet and Yvonne Hamel; *m* 1971, Florence Lemire; one *s* one *d*. *Educ:* Coll. St Gabriel de St Tite; Séminaire St Joseph de Trois-Rivières; Laval Univ. (LTh 1951, DèsL 1954); Université Catholique de Paris (LPh, MA 1953). Prof. of Literature and History, Séminaire Ste Marie, Shawinigan, 1953–61; Centre d'Etudes Universitaires de Trois-Rivières: Founder, 1960; Dir, 1960–69; Prof. of Lit. and Hist., 1961–66; Laval University: Prof. of French, Faculty of Lit., 1955–62; Aggregate Prof., Fac. of Arts, 1959; Rector, Univ. du Québec à Trois-Rivières, 1969–78. Dr *hc* Universidade Federal de Rio Grande do Norte, Brazil, 1983; Hon. Master of Administration, Univ. Autonoma de Guerrero, Mexico, 1984. Comdr, Assoc. Belgo-Hispanique, 1980; Comdr, Mérite et Dévouement Français, 1980. Duvernay Award, Soc. St-Jean-Baptiste de Trois-Rivières (literature award), 1978; Gold Medal, Univ. Federal da Bahia, Brazil, 1983. *Publications:* Nationalisme ou Séparatisme, Nationalisme et Séparatisme, 1961; (with Lucien Gagné) Le Français Parlé au Cours Secondaire, vols I and II, 1962, vols III and IV, 1963; Textes et Préceptes Littéraires, vol. I, 2nd edn, 1967, vol. II, 1964; (with others) Le Boréal Express, Album no 1, 1965, Album no 2, 1967. *Recreations:* reading, skiing, skating. *Address:* 3021 de la Promenade, Ste Foy, Quebec G1W 2J5, Canada. *T:* (418) 659–2599. *Club:* Cercle de la Garnison de Québec.

BOULEZ, Pierre; composer; Director, Institut de Recherche et de Coordination Acoustique/Musique, since 1976; *b* Montbrison, Loire, France, 26 March 1925. *Educ:* Saint-Etienne and Lyon (music and higher mathematics); Paris Conservatoire. Studied with Messiaen and René Leibowitz. Theatre conductor, Jean-Louis Barrault Company, Paris, 1948; visited USA with French Ballet Company, 1952. Has conducted major orchestras in his own and standard classical works in Great Britain, Europe and USA, including Edinburgh Festival, 1965; also conducted Wozzeck in Paris and Frankfurt; Parsifal at Bayreuth, 1966; Chief Conductor, BBC Symphony Orchestra, 1971–75; Chief Conductor and Music Dir, NY Philharmonic, 1971–77; Dir, Bayreuth Festival, 1976–80. Hon. DMus Cantab, 1980. Interested in poetry and aesthetics of Baudelaire, Mallarmé and René Char. *Compositions include:* Trois Psalmodies (Piano solo), 1945; Sonata No 1 (piano), 1946; Sonatine for flute and piano, 1946; Sonata No 2 (piano), 1948; Polyphonie X for 18 solo instruments, 1951; Visage nuptial (2nd version), 1951; Structures for 2 pianos, 1952; Le Marteau sans Maître (voice and 6 instruments), 1954; Sonata No 3 (piano), 1956; Deux Improvisations sur Mallarmé for voice and 9 instruments, 1957; Doubles for orchestra, 1958; Poésie pour Pouvoir for voices and orchestra, 1958; Soleil des Eaux (text by René Char) for chorus and orchestra, 1958; Pli selon Pli: Hommage à Mallarmé, for voices and orchestra, 1960; Eclat, 1965; Domaines for solo clarinet, 1968; Cummings ist der Dichter (16 solo voices and instruments), 1970; Eclat/Multiples, 1970; Explosante Fixe (8 solo instruments), 1972; Rituel, for orchestra, 1975; Messagesquisses (7 celli), 1977; Notations, for orch., 1980; Répons, for orch. and live electronics, 1981–86; Dérive, 1985. *Publications:* Penser la musique d'aujourd'hui, 1966 (Boulez on Music Today, 1971); Relevés d'apprenti, 1967; Par volonté et par hasard, 1976; Points de Repère, 1981; Orientations, 1986. *Address:* IRCAM, 31 rue St Merri, 75004 Paris, France. *T:* 277 1233.

BOULIND, Mrs (Olive) Joan, CBE 1975; Fellow, 1973–79, and Tutor, 1974–79, Hughes Hall, Cambridge; *b* 24 Sept. 1912; *e d* of Douglas Siddall and Olive Raby; *m* 1936, Henry F. Boulind, MA, PhD; two *s* one *d*. *Educ:* Wallasey High Sch., Cheshire; Univ. of Liverpool (BA 1st class Hons History, Medieval and Modern; DipEd); MA Cantab 1974. Teacher: Wirral Co. Sch. for Girls, 1934–36; Cambridgeshire High Sch. for Girls, 1963. Mem., Domestic Consumers' Cttee, Min. of Power, 1948–52; Founder Chm., Eastern Regional Cttee, Women's Adv. Council on Solid Fuel, 1962–66; Nat. Pres., Nat. Council of Women, 1966–68 (Sen. Vice-Pres., 1964–66); Co-Chm., Women's Consultative Council, 1966–68; Leader, British delegn to conf. of Internat. Council of Women, Bangkok, 1970; Co-Chm., Women's Nat. Commn, 1973–75; Co-Chm., UK Co-ordinating Cttee for Internat. Women's Year, 1975; Chm., Westminster College Management Cttee, 1980–. Member: Commn on the Church in the Seventies, Congregational Church in England and Wales, 1970–72 (Vice-Chm., 1971–72); Ministerial Trng Cttee, United Reformed Church, 1972–79 and 1982– (Chm., 1982); East Adv. Council, BBC, 1976– (Chm. 1981–). Deacon, Emmanuel Congregational Ch., Cambridge, 1958–66. Trustee, Homerton Coll. of Educn, 1955–. *Recreations:* reading, travel, music. *Address:* 28 Rathmore Road, Cambridge CB1 4AD. *Club:* University Women's.

BOULTER, Prof. Donald, FIBiol; Professor of Botany and Head of Department of Botany, University of Durham, and Director of Durham University Botanic Garden, since 1966; *b* 25 Aug. 1926; *s* of late George Boulter and of Vera Boulter; *m* 1956, Margaret Eileen Kennedy; four *d*. *Educ:* Portsmouth Grammar Sch.; Christ Church, Oxford (BA, MA, DPhil). FIBiol 1970. Served RAF, 1945–48. Sessel Fellow, Yale Univ., 1953–54; Asst Lectr in Botany, King's Coll., London, 1955–57; Lectr 1957–64, Sen. Lectr 1964–66, Liverpool Univ. Vis. Prof., Univ. of Texas, Austin, 1967. Mem., AFRC, 1985–; Pres., Sect. K, BAAS, 1981. FRSA 1972. Tate & Lyle Award for Phytochem., 1975. *Publications:* (ed) Chemotaxonomy of the Leguminosae, 1971; (associate ed) Qualitas Plantarum: Plant Foods for Human Nutrition, 1980; (ed) Encyclopedia of Plant Physiology, vol. 14B: Nucleic Acids and Proteins, 1982; papers in sci. jls on molecular evolution, genetic engrg of crops, biochem. and molecular biol of seed develt. *Recreation:* travel. *Address:* 5 Crossgate, Durham DH1 4PS. *T:* Durham 61199.

BOULTER, Eric Thomas, CBE 1978; Director-General, Royal National Institute for the Blind, 1972–80; *b* 7 July 1917; *s* of Albert and Ethel Boulter; *m* 1946, Martha Mary McClure; one *s* one *d*. *Educ:* St Marylebone Grammar School. World Council for Welfare of Blind: Sec.-General, 1951–59; Vice-Pres., 1959–64; Pres., 1964–69; Hon. Life Mem.,

1969. Chm., Council of World Organisations for Handicapped, 1958–61; Mem. Exec., Internat. Council of Educators of Blind Youth, 1962–70; Assoc. Dir, American Foundn for Overseas Blind, 1956–70; Dep. Dir-Gen., RNIB, 1971–72; Sec., British Council for Prevention of Blindness, 1976–. Hon. Life Mem., World Blind Union, 1984. Order of the Andes (Bolivia), 1960; Silver Medal for service to mankind, City of Paris, 1975; Helen Keller Internat. Award, 1978; Louis Braille Gold Medal, 1978. *Publication:* (with John H. Dobree) Blindness and Visual Handicap—the facts, 1982. *Address:* 40 Snaresbrook Drive, Stanmore, Mddx. *T:* 01–958 8681.

BOULTING, Roy; Producer and Joint Managing Director, Charter Film Productions Ltd, since 1973; *b* 21 Nov. 1913; *s* of Arthur Boulting and Rose Bennett. *Educ:* HMS Worcester; Reading Sch. Formed independent film production company with twin brother John, 1937. Served War of 1939–45, RAC, finishing as Capt.; films for Army included Desert Victory and Burma Victory. Producer: Brighton Rock, 1947; Seven Days to Noon, 1950; Private's Progress, 1955; Lucky Jim (Edinburgh Festival), 1957; I'm All Right Jack, 1959; Heavens Above!, 1962. Director: Pastor Hall, 1939; Thunder Rock, 1942; Fame is the Spur, 1947; The Guinea Pig, 1948; High Treason, 1951; Singlehanded, 1952; Seagulls over Sorrento, Crest of the Wave, 1953; Josephine and Men, 1955; Run for the Sun, 1955; Brothers in Law, 1956; Happy is the Bride, 1958; Carlton-Browne of the FO, 1958–59; I'm All Right Jack, 1959; The Risk, 1960; The French Mistress, 1960; Suspect, 1960; The Family Way, 1966; Twisted Nerve, 1968; There's a Girl in My Soup, 1970; Soft Beds, Hard Battles, 1974; Danny Travis, 1978; The Last Word, 1979; The Moving Finger, 1984. *Play:* (with Leo Marks) Favourites, 1977. Dir, British Lion Films Ltd, 1958–72. *Address:* Charter Film Productions Ltd, Twickenham Film Studios, St Margarets, Twickenham, Middlesex. *Club:* Lord's Taverners.

BOULTING, S. A.; *see* Cotes, Peter.

BOULTON, Sir Christian; *see* Boulton, Sir H. H. C.

BOULTON, Clifford John, CB, CB 1985; Clerk Assistant of the House of Commons, since 1983; *b* 25 July 1930; *s* of Stanley Boulton and Evelyn (*née* Hey), Cocknage, Staffs; *m* 1955, Anne, *d* of Rev. E. E. Raven, Cambridge; one adopted *s* one adopted *d. Educ:* Newcastle-under-Lyme High School; St John's Coll., Oxford (exhibnr). MA (Modern History). National Service, RAC, 1949–50; Lt Staffs Yeomanry (TA). A Clerk in the House of Commons, 1953–: Clerk of Select Cttees on Procedure, 1964–68 and 1976–77; Public Accounts, 1968–70; Parliamentary Questions, 1971–72; Privileges, 1972–77; Clerk of the Overseas Office, 1977–79; Principal Clerk, Table Office, 1979–83. A school Governor and subsequently board mem., Church Schools Company, 1965–79. *Publications:* contribs to Erskine May's Parliamentary Practice, 17th-20th edns, Halsbury's Laws of England, 4th edn, and Parliamentary journals. *Address:* House of Commons, SW1A 0AA. *T:* 01-219 3311; 2 Main Street, Lyddington, Oakham LE15 9LT. *T:* Uppingham 823487.

BOULTON, Prof. Geoffrey Stewart; Regius Professor of Geology, University of Edinburgh, since 1986; *b* 28 Nov. 1940; *s* of George Stewart and Rose Boulton; *m* 1964, Denise Bryers Lawns; two *d. Educ:* Longton High Sch.; Birmingham Univ. BSc, PhD, DSc; FGS. British Geol Survey, 1962–64; Demonstrator, Univ. of Keele, 1964–65; Fellow, Univ. of Birmingham, 1965–68; Hydrogeologist, Kenya, 1968; Lectr, then Reader, Univ. of E Anglia, 1968–86. Prof., Amsterdam Univ., 1982–86. FGS 1961. *Publications:* numerous articles in learned jls on polar, quaternary, glacial and marine geology and glaciology. *Recreations:* violin, mountaineering. *Address:* 19 Lygon Road, Edinburgh EH16 5QD. *Club:* Arctic.

BOULTON, Sir (Harold Hugh) Christian, 4th Bt *cr* 1905; *b* 29 Oct. 1918; *s* of Sir (Denis Duncan) Harold (Owen) Boulton, 3rd Bt, and Louise McGowan (*d* 1978), USA; *S* father, 1968. *Educ:* Ampleforth College, Yorks. Late Captain, Irish Guards (Supplementary Reserve). *Address:* c/o Bank of Montreal, City View Branch, 1491 Merivale Road, Nepean, Ontario K2C 3H3, Canada.

BOULTON, Prof. James Thompson; Professor of English Studies and Head of Department of English Language and Literature, 1975–87, Dean of the Faculty of Arts, 1981–84, Public Orator, 1984–87, University of Birmingham; *b* 17 Feb. 1924; *e s* of Harry and Annie M. P. Boulton; *m* 1949, Margaret Helen Leary; one *s* one *d. Educ:* University College, Univ. of Durham; Lincoln Coll., Oxford. BA Dunelm 1948; BLitt Oxon 1952; PhD Nottingham 1960. FRSL 1968. Served in RAF, 1943–46 (Flt-Lt). Lectr, subseq. Sen. Lectr and Reader in English, Univ. of Nottingham, 1951–64; John Cranford Adams Prof. of English, Hofstra Univ., NY, 1967; Prof. of English Lit., Univ. of Nottingham, 1964–75, Dean, Faculty of Arts, 1970–73. Fellow, Inst. for Advanced Res. in the Humanities, Birmingham Univ., 1985. Editorial Adviser, Studies in Burke and his Time, 1960–77; Mem. Exec. Cttee, Anglo-American Associates (NY), 1968–75. Editor, Renaissance and Modern Studies, 1969–75, 1985. General Editor: The Letters of D. H. Lawrence, 1973–; The Works of D. H. Lawrence, 1975–. *Publications:* (ed) Edmund Burke: A Philosophical Enquiry into . . . the Sublime and Beautiful, 1958; (ed) C. F. G. Masterman: The Condition of England, 1960; The Language of Politics in the Age of Wilkes and Burke, 1963, 2nd edn 1975; (ed) Dryden: Of Dramatick Poesy etc, 1964; (ed) Defoe: Prose and Verse, 1965, 2nd edn 1975; (with James Kinsley) English Satiric Poetry: Dryden to Byron, 1966; (ed) Lawrence in Love: Letters from D. H. Lawrence to Louie Burrows, 1968; (ed) Samuel Johnson: The Critical Heritage, 1971; (with S. T. Bindoff) Research in Progress in English and Historical Studies in the Universities of the British Isles, vol. 1, 1971, vol. 2, 1976; (ed) Defoe: Memoirs of a Cavalier, 1972; (ed) The Letters of D. H. Lawrence, vol. 1, 1979, vol. 2 (jtly), 1982, vol. 3 (jtly), 1984, vol. 4 (jtly), 1987; (contrib.) Renaissance and Modern Essays (ed G. R. Hibbard), 1966; (contrib.) The Familiar Letter in the 18th Century (ed H. Anderson), 1966; papers in Durham Univ. Jl, Essays in Criticism, Renaissance and Modern Studies, Modern Drama, etc. *Recreation:* gardening. *Address:* Department of English Language and Literature, University of Birmingham, PO Box 363, Birmingham B15 2TT.

See also P. H. Boulton.

BOULTON, Rev. Canon Peter Henry; Vicar of Worksop and Surrogate, since 1967; Hon. Canon of Southwell, since 1975; *b* 12 Dec. 1925; *s* of Harry Boulton and Annie Mary Penty Boulton; *m* 1955, Barbara Ethelinda Davies, SRN, SCM; three *s. Educ:* Lady Lumley's Grammar Sch., Pickering, N Yorks; St Chad's Coll., Univ. of Durham (BA Hons Theology); Ely Theol Coll., Cambs. Served War, RNVR, 1943–46. Ordained deacon, 1950, priest, 1951 (Chester). Asst Curate: Coppenhall S Michael, Crewe, 1950–54; S Mark, Mansfield, 1954–55; Vicar: Clipstone Colliery Village, Notts, 1955–60; St John the Baptist, Carlton, Nottingham, 1960–67; Proctor in Convocation, Dio. of Southwell, 1959–; Prolocutor of York Convocation, 1980–; Chaplain-Convenor, Bassetlaw Dist Hosps, 1967–. Chairman: Diocesan Stewardship Cttee, 1978–82; Legal Adv. Commn of Gen. Synod, 1985–. Member: Standing Cttee of Gen. Synod, 1974–; Churches' Council for Covenanting, 1978–82; Howick Commn on Crown Appts, 1962–64; Corp. of Church House, 1980–; Crown Appts Commn, 1982–. C of E Delegate: Anglican Consultative Council, 1972–80; World Council of Churches Assembly, Nairobi, 1975. Pres., Bassetlaw CVS, 1978– (Chm., 1974–78). *Publications:* (co-ed with Bishop of London) Dolphin Papers, 1971–; articles in learned and ecclesiastical jls. *Recreations:* crosswords, local history, pruning, swimming. *Address:* The Vicarage, Cheapside, Worksop, Notts S80 2HX. *T:* Worksop 472180.

See also J. T. Boulton.

BOULTON, Sir William (Whytehead), 3rd Bt *cr* 1944; Kt 1975; CBE 1958; TD 1949; Secretary, Senate of the Inns of Court and the Bar, 1974–75; *b* 21 June 1912; *s* of Sir William Boulton, 1st Bt, and Rosalind Mary (*d* 1969), *d* of Sir John Davison Milburn, 1st Bt, of Guyzance, Northumberland; *S* brother, 1982; *m* 1944, Margaret Elizabeth, *o d* of late Brig. H. N. A. Hunter, DSO; one *s* two *d. Educ:* Eton; Trinity Coll., Cambridge. Called to Bar, Inner Temple, 1936; practised at the Bar, 1937–39. Secretary, General Council of the Bar, 1950–74. Served War of 1939–45: with 104th Regt RHA (Essex Yeo.) and 14th Regt RHA, in the Middle East, 1940–44; Staff Coll., Camberley, 1944. Control Commission for Germany (Legal Div.), 1945–50. Gazetted 2nd Lieut TA (Essex Yeo.), 1934; retired with rank of Hon. Lieut-Col. *Publications:* A Guide to Conduct and Etiquette at the Bar of England and Wales, 1st edn 1953, 6th edn, 1975. *Heir: s* John Gibson Boulton, *b* 18 Dec. 1946. *Address:* The Quarters House, Alresford, near Colchester, Essex. *T:* Wivenhoe 2450; 37 Rutland Gate, SW7. *T:* 01–581 2938.

BOURASSA, Robert; Leader, Quebec Liberal Party, 1970–77 and since 1983; Prime Minister of Québec, 1970–76 and since 1985; Member of Québec National Assembly for St Laurent, since 1986 (for Mercier, 1966–76 and for Bertrand, 1985); *b* 14 July 1933; *s* of Aubert Bourassa and Adrienne Courville; *m* 1958, Andrée Simard; one *s* one *d. Educ:* Jean-de-Brébeuf Coll.; Univs of Montreal, Oxford and Harvard. Gov.-Gen.'s Medal Montreal 1956. MA Oxford 1959. Admitted Quebec Bar 1957. Fiscal Adviser to Dept of Nat. Revenue and Prof. in Econs and Public Finance, Ottawa Univ., 1960–63; Sec. and Dir of Research of Bélanger Commn on Public Finance, 1963–65; Special Adviser to Fed. Dept of Finance on fiscal and econ. matters, 1965–66; financial critic for Quebec Liberal Party, Pres. Polit. Commn and Mem. Liberal Party's Strategy Cttee; Minister of Finance, May-Nov. 1970; Minister of Inter-govtl Affairs, 1971–72. Lectures: Institut d'Etudes Européennes, Brussels, 1977–78; Sch. of Advanced Internat. Studies, Johns Hopkins Univ., 1978; Univ. de Laval, Univ. de Montréal, 1979–81; Yale Univ., 1982. *Address:* 5115 de Gaspé Avenue, Suite 410, Montreal, Québec H2T 3B7, Canada.

BOURDEAUX, Rev. Michael Alan; General Director, Keston College, Keston, Kent, since 1969; *b* 19 March 1934; *s* of Richard Edward and Lillian Myra Bourdeaux; *m* 1st, 1960, Gillian Mary Davies (*d* 1978); one *s* one *d*; 2nd, 1979, Lorna Elizabeth Waterton. *Educ:* Truro Sch.; St Edmund Hall, Oxford (MA Hons Mod. Langs); Wycliffe Hall, Oxford (Hons Theology). Moscow State Univ., 1959–60; Deacon, 1960; Asst Curate, Enfield Parish Church, Mddx, 1960–64; researching at Chislehurst, Kent, on the Church in the Soviet Union, with grant from Centre de Recherches, Geneva, 1965–68; Vis. Prof., St Bernard's Seminary, Rochester, NY, 1969; Vis. Fellow, LSE, 1969–71; Research Fellow, RIIA, Chatham House, 1971–73; Dawson Lectr on Church and State, Baylor Univ., Waco, Texas, 1972; Chavasse Meml Lectr, Oxford Univ., 1976; Kathryn W. Davis Prof. in Slavic Studies, Wellesley Coll., Wellesley, Mass, 1981. Founded Keston College, a research centre on religion in the Communist countries, 1969. Founder of journal, Religion in Communist Lands, 1973–. Templeton Prize for Progress in Religion, 1984. *Publications:* Opium of the People, 1965, 2nd edn 1977; Religious Ferment in Russia, 1968; Patriarch and Prophets, 1970, 2nd edn 1975; Faith on Trial in Russia, 1971; Land of Crosses, 1979; Risen Indeed, 1983. *Recreations:* singing in the Philharmonia Chorus; officiating, as Member British Tennis Umpires Assoc., at Wimbledon and abroad. *Address:* 34 Lubbock Road, Chislehurst, Kent BR7 5JJ. *T:* 01–467 3550. *Club:* Athenæum.

BOURDILLON, Henry Townsend, CMG 1952; Assistant Under-Secretary of State, Department of Education and Science, 1964–73; *b* 19 Aug. 1913; 2nd *s* of late Sir Bernard Henry Bourdillon, GCMG, KBE, and Lady (Violet Grace) Bourdillon; *m* 1942, Margareta d'Almaine (*née* Tham); one *s* two *d. Educ:* Rugby Sch.; Corpus Christi Coll., Oxford. Asst Principal, Colonial Office, 1937; Acting Principal, Colonial Office, 1940; lent to: Foreign Office, 1942; Cabinet Office, 1943; Ministry of Production, 1944; returned to Colonial Office, 1944; Asst Secretary, 1947–54; Asst Under-Secretary of State, Colonial Office, 1954–59; Deputy UK Commissioner for Singapore, 1959–61; returned to Colonial Office, 1961; Under-Secretary, Ministry of Education, 1962–64. *Recreations:* gardening, music. *Address:* Orchard House, Horsenden Lane, Princes Risborough, Bucks. *T:* Princes Risborough 5416.

BOURDILLON, Mervyn Leigh, JP; Lord-Lieutenant of Powys, since 1986; *b* 9 Aug. 1924; *s* of late Prebendary G. L. Bourdillon; *m* 1961, Penelope, *d* of late P. W. Kemp-Welch, OBE; one *s* three *d. Educ:* Haileybury. Served RNVR, 1943–46. Forestry Comr, 1973–76. Mem. Brecon County Council, 1962–73; DL 1962, JP 1970, High Sheriff 1970, Brecon; Vice Lord-Lieutenant, Powys, 1978–86. *Address:* Llwyn Madoc, Beulah, Llanwrtyd Wells, Powys LD5 4TU.

BOURDON, Derek Conway, FIA; Director, 1981–84, and General Manager, 1979–84, Prudential Assurance Co. Ltd; Director, London and Manchester Group PLC, since 1986; *b* 3 Nov. 1932; *s* of Walter Alphonse Bourdon and late Winifred Gladys Vera Bourdon; *m* 1st, Camilla Rose Bourdon (marr. diss.); one *s* one *d*; 2nd, Jean Elizabeth Bourdon. *Educ:* Bancroft's School. FIA 1957. RAF Operations Research (Pilot Officer), 1956–58. Joined Prudential, 1950; South Africa, 1962–65; Dep. General Manager, 1976–79. Chairman, Vanbrugh Life, 1974–79. Member, Policyholders Protection Board, 1980–84; Chm., Industrial Life Offices Assoc., 1982–84 (Vice-Chm., 1980–82). *Recreations:* golf, squash rackets. *Club:* Crowborough Beacon Golf.

BOURKE, family name of **Earl of Mayo.**

BOURKE, Christopher John; Metropolitan Stipendiary Magistrate, since 1974; *b* 31 March 1926; *e s* of late John Francis Bourke of the Oxford Circuit and late Eileen Winifred Bourke (*née* Beddoes); *m* 1956, Maureen, *y d* of late G A. Barron-Boshell; two *s* one *d. Educ:* Stonyhurst; Oriel Coll., Oxford. Called to Bar, Gray's Inn, 1953; Oxford Circuit, 1954–55; Dir of Public Prosecutions Dept, 1955–74. *Recreations:* history of art, music. *Address:* 27 Beverley Road, Barnes, SW13. *T:* 01–876 9939.

BOURKE, Ven. Michael; Archdeacon of Bedford, since 1986; Course Director, St Albans Diocese Ministerial Training Scheme, since 1975; *b* 28 Nov. 1941; *s* of Gordon and Hilda Bourke; *m* 1968, Elizabeth Bieler; one *s* one *d. Educ:* Hamond's Grammar Sch., Swaffham, Norfolk; Corpus Christi Coll., Cambridge (Mod. Langs, MA); Univ. of Tübingen (Theology); Cuddesdon Theological Coll. Curate, St James', Grimsby, 1967–71; Priest-in-charge, Panshanger Conventional Dist (Local Ecumenical Project), Welwyn Garden City, 1971–78; Vicar, All Saints', Southill, Beds, 1978–86. *Recreations:* astronomy, railways, European history. *Address:* 84 Bury Road, Shillington, Hitchin, Herts SG5 3NZ. *T:* Hitchin 711958.

BOURN, James; HM Diplomatic Service, retired; *b* 30 Aug. 1917; *s* of James and Sarah Gertrude Bourn; *m* 1st, 1944, Isobel Mackenzie (*d* 1977); one *s*; 2nd, 1981, Moya Livesey. *Educ:* Queen Elizabeth's Grammar Sch., Darlington; Univ. of Edinburgh (MA Hons 1979). Executive Officer, Ministry of Health, 1936. War of 1939–45; served (Royal Signals), in India, North Africa and Italy; POW; Captain. Higher Exec. Officer, Ministry of National Insurance, 1947; Asst Principal, Colonial Office, 1947; Principal, 1949; Secretary to the Salaries Commission, Bahamas, 1948–49; Private Sec. to Perm. Under-Sec., 1949; seconded to Tanganyika, 1953–55; UK Liaison Officer to Commn for Technical Co-operation in Africa (CCTA), 1955–57; Commonwealth Relations Office, 1961; seconded to Central African Office, 1962; Dar es Salaam, 1963; Deputy High Commissioner in Zanzibar, Tanzania, 1964–65; Counsellor and Dep. High Comr, Malawi, 1966–70; Ambassador to Somalia, 1970–73; Consul-General, Istanbul, 1973–75. *Address:* c/o Lloyds Bank, Butler Place, Victoria Street, SW1. *Club:* Royal Commonwealth Society.

BOURN, John Bryant, CB 1986; Deputy Under-Secretary of State (Defence Procurement), Ministry of Defence, since 1985; *b* 21 Feb. 1934; *s* of Henry Thomas Bryant Bourn and late Beatrice Grace Bourn; *m* 1959, Ardita Ann Fleming; one *s* one *d. Educ:* Southgate County Grammar Sch.; LSE. 1st cl. hons BScEcon 1954, PhD 1958. Air Min. 1956–63; HM Treasury, 1963–64; Private Sec. to Perm. Under-Sec., MoD, 1964–69; Asst Sec. and Dir of Programmes, Civil Service Coll., 1969–72; Asst Sec., MoD, 1972–74; Under-Sec., Northern Ireland Office, 1974–77; Asst Under-Sec. of State, MoD, 1977–82; Dep. Sec., Northern Ireland Office, 1982–84. Vis. Prof., LSE, 1983–. *Publications:* articles and reviews in professional jls. *Recreations:* swimming, squash rackets. *Address:* Main Building, Whitehall, SW1A 2HB.

BOURNE, Lt-Col Geoffrey (H.), FZS; DPhil, DSc; Vice Chancellor, and Professor of Nutrition, St George's University School of Medicine, Grenada, since 1978; *b* West Perth, Western Australia, 17 Nov. 1909; *s* of Walter Howard Bourne and Mary Ann Mellon; *m* 1935, Gwenllian Myfanwy Jones, BA; two *s; m* 1965, Maria Nelly Golarz, PhD. *Educ:* Perth Modern Sch., W Australia; University of Western Australia (BSc 1930, BSc Hons 1931; MSc 1932, DSc 1935); University of Melbourne. DPhil (Oxford), 1943; Hackett Research Student, University of W Australia, 1931–33; Biologist and in charge of Experimental Work, Australian Institute of Anatomy, Canberra, 1933–35; Biochemist Commonwealth of Austr. Advisory Council on Nutrition, 1935–37; Beit Memorial Fellow for Medical Research, Oxford, 1938–41; Mackenzie-Mackinnon Research Fellow of Royal College of Physicians of London and Royal College of Surgeons of England, 1941–44; Demonstrator in Physiology, Oxford, 1941–44, 1946, 1947; in charge of research and development (rations and physiological matters) for Special Forces in South-East Asia, 1944–45; Nutritional Adviser to British Military Administration, Malaya, 1945–46; Reader in Histology, University of London, at the London Hospital Medical Coll., 1947–57; Prof. and Chm. of Anatomy, Emory Univ., Atlanta, Ga, USA, 1957–63; Dir, Yerkes Regional Primate Research Center of Emory Univ., 1962–78. Member: Soc. Experimental Biology; Nutrition Soc. (foundation Mem.); Anatomical Soc. of Gt Brit. and N Ireland, Internat. Soc. for Cell Biology; Aerospace Med. Soc., etc. FRSM. Editor-in-Chief, International Review of Cytology, 1952–. *Publications:* Nutrition and the War, 1940; Wartime Food for Mother and Child, 1942; Cytology and Cell Physiology (ed and part author), 1942, 2nd edn 1951; Starvation in Europe, 1943; How Your Body Works, 1949; The Mammalion Adrenal Gland, 1949; Aids to Histology, 1950; (ed) Biochemistry and Physiology of Nutrition, Vols 1, 2; Introduction to Functional Histology; Biochemistry and Physiology of Bone; (ed) The Biology of Ageing; Structure and Function of Muscle; The Division of Labour in Cells; (ed jtly) Muscular Dystrophy in Man and Animals; World Review of Nutrition and Dietetics, 1962; Atherosclerosis and its origins, 1967; Structure and Function of Nervous Tissue, 1969; The Ape People, 1971; Primate Odyssey, 1974; The Gentle Giants, 1975; (with HSH Prince Rainier III of Monaco) Primate Conservation, 1977; Hearts and Heart-like Organs, 1981; contributor on Famine to Encyclopædia Britannica; contributions to scientific and medical journals. *Recreations:* water ski-ing, tennis, ballet and running (State Mile Championship and Record Holder, Australia). *Address:* St George's University School of Medicine, PO Box 7, St George's, Grenada, West Indies.

BOURNE, Gordon Lionel, FRCS, FRCOG; Consultant, since 1961, and Head of Department, since 1975, Department of Obstetrics and Gynæcology, St Bartholomew's Hospital, London; Consultant Gynæcologist to Royal Masonic Hospital since 1973; *b* 3 June 1921; *s* of Thomas Holland Bourne and Lily Anne (*née* Clewlow); *m* 1948, Barbara Eileen Anderson; three *s* one *d. Educ:* Queen Elizabeth Grammar Sch., Ashbourne; St Bartholomew's Hosp.; Harvard Univ. MRCS, LRCP 1945, FRCS 1954; MRCOG 1956, FRCOG 1962; FRSocMed. Highlands Hosp., 1948; Derbs Royal Infirm., 1949; City of London Mat. Hosp., 1952; Hosp. for Women, Soho, 1954; Gynæcol Registrar, Middlesex Hosp., 1956; Sen. Registrar, Obsts and Gynae., St Bartholomew's Hosp., 1958; Nuffield Trav. Fellow, 1959; Res. Fellow, Harvard, 1959; Cons. Gynæcol., St Luke's Hosp., 1963. Arris and Gale Lectr, RCS, 1964; Mem. Bd of Professions Suppl. to Medicine, 1964; Regional Assessor in Maternal Deaths, 1974; Examr in Obsts and Gynae., Univs of London, Oxford and Riyadh, Jt Conjt Bd and RCOG, Central Midwives Bd; Mem. Ct of Assts, Haberdashers' Co., 1968, Master, 1984; Mem. Bd of Governors, 1971–83, Chm., 1980–83, Haberdashers' Aske's Schs, Hatcham; Mem. Bd of Governors, Haberdashers' Aske's Schs, Elstree, 1983–. *Publications:* The Human Amnion and Chorion, 1962; Shaw's Textbook of Gynæcology, 9th edn, 1970; Recent Advances in Obstetrics and Gynæcology, 11th edn, 1966—13th edn, 1979; Modern Gynæcology with Obstetrics for Nurses, 4th edn, 1969 and 5th edn, 1973; Pregnancy, 1972, 4th edn 1984; numerous articles in sci. and professional jls. *Recreations:* ski-ing, water-ski-ing, shooting, swimming, writing, golf. *Address:* 147 Harley Street, W1N 1DL. *T:* 01–935 4444; Oldways, Bishop's Avenue, N2 0BN. *T:* 01–458 4788. *Club:* Carlton.

BOURNE, James Gerald, MA, MD (Cantab), FFARCS, FDSRCS; Consulting Anæsthetist: St Thomas' Hospital, London; Salisbury Hospital Group; *b* 6 March 1906; *y s* of late W. W. Bourne, Garston Manor, Herts and of late Clara (*née* Hollingsworth); *m* 1957, Jenny Liddell (*d* 1967); one *s; m* 1968, Susan Clarke; two *s. Educ:* Rugby; Corpus Christi Coll., Cambridge; St Thomas' Hospital. 1st class Geographical Tripos Part I, 1925; 1st class Geographical Tripos Part II, 1926; Exhibition and Prizes; MRCS, LRCP 1937; MB, BChir Cantab 1939; DA England 1945; FFARCS 1953; MD (Cantab), 1960; FDSRCS 1986. Major RAMC, 1939–45. *Publications:* Nitrous Oxide in Dentistry: Its Danger and Alternatives, 1960; Studies in Anæsthetics, 1967; contributions to medical literature. *Recreations:* ski-ing, riding, fishing. *Address:* Melstock, Nunton, Salisbury, Wilts. *T:* Salisbury 29734.

BOURNE, Sir (John) Wilfrid, KCB 1979 (CB 1975); QC 1981; Clerk of the Crown in Chancery, and Permanent Secretary, Lord Chancellor's Office, 1977–82; Barrister-at-Law; *b* 27 Jan. 1922; *s* of late Captain Rt Hon. R. C. Bourne, MP, and Lady Hester Bourne; *m* 1958, Elizabeth Juliet, *d* of late G. R. Fox, of Trewardreva, Constantine, Cornwall; two *s. Educ:* Eton; New Coll., Oxford (MA). Served War, Rifle Brigade, 1941–45. Called to Bar, Middle Temple, 1948, Bencher 1977; practised at Bar, 1949–56; Lord Chancellor's Office, 1956–82, Principal Assistant Solicitor, 1970–72, Deputy Sec., 1972–77. *Recreations:* gardening, sailing. *Address:* Povey's Farm, Ramsdell, Basingstoke, Hants. *Club:* Leander (Henley-on-Thames).

BOURNE, Prof. Kenneth, FRHistS; FBA 1984; Professor of International History, London School of Economics and Political Science, University of London, since 1976; *b*

17 March 1930; *s* of Clarence Arthur Bourne and Doris (*née* English); *m* 1955, Eleanor Anne (*née* Wells); one *s* one *d. Educ:* Southend High Sch.; University College of South West; LSE. BA Exeter and London; PhD London. Research Fellow: Inst. of Hist. Research, Univ. of London, 1955–56; Reading Univ., 1956; Asst Lectr, then Lectr, LSE, 1957–69; Reader in Internat. History, Univ. of London, 1969–76. Fulbright Fellow and Sen. Research Fellow, British Assoc. for American Studies, 1961–62; Vis. Lectr, Univ. of California, Davis, 1966–67; Scaife Distinguished Vis. Lectr, Kenyon Coll., 1971; Kratter Prof., Stanford Univ., 1979; Vis. Prof., Univ. of S Mississippi, 1981; Griffin Lectr, Stanford Univ., 1983; Vis. Prof., Univ. of S Alabama, 1983; Albert Biever Meml Lectr, Loyola Univ., 1983; James Pinckney Harrison Prof., Coll. of William and Mary, 1984–85. *Publications:* Britain and the Balance of Power in North America, 1967 (Albert B. Corey Prize); (with D. C. Watt) Studies in International History, 1967; The Foreign Policy of Victorian England, 1970; The Blackmailing of the Chancellor, 1975; Letters of Viscount Palmerston, 1979; Palmerston: the early years, 1982; (ed, with D. C. Watt) British Documents on Foreign Affairs, 1983–. *Recreation:* book-collecting. *Address:* 15 Oakcroft Road, SE13 7ED. *T:* 01–852 6116.

BOURNE, (Rowland) Richard; journalist and author; Deputy Director, The Commonwealth Institute, since 1983; *s* of Arthur Brittan and Edith Mary Bourne; *m* 1966, Juliet Mary, *d* of John Attenborough, CBE; two *s* one *d. Educ:* Uppingham Sch., Rutland; Brasenose Coll., Oxford (BA Mod. Hist.). Journalist, The Guardian, 1962–72 (Education correspondent, 1968–72); Asst Editor, New Society, 1972–77; Evening Standard: Dep. Editor, 1977–78; London Columnist, 1978–79; Founder Editor, Learn Magazine, 1979. Consultant: Internat. Broadcasting Trust, 1980–81; Adv. Council for Adult and Continuing Educn, 1982. Chm., Survival Internat. 1983–. *Publications:* Political Leaders of Latin America, 1969; (with Brian MacArthur) The Struggle for Education, 1970; Getulio Vargas of Brazil, 1974; Assault on the Amazon, 1978; Londoners, 1981; (with Jessica Gould) Self-Sufficiency, 16–25, 1983. *Recreations:* theatre, fishing, supporting Charlton Athletic. *Address:* 65 Lee Road, SE3 9EN. *T:* 01–852 9645. *Club:* Royal Automobile.

BOURNE, Stafford, MA Cantab; Chairman, 1938–72, President, 1972–79, Bourne & Hollingsworth Ltd (relinquished all connection, on retirement after 57 years service); *b* 20 Feb. 1900; *e s* of late Walter William and Clara Louisa Bourne (*née* Hollingsworth), Garston Manor, Herts; *m* 1940, Magdalene Jane, *d* of Frederick and Anne Leeson; one *s* one *d* (and one *s* decd). *Educ:* Rugby; Corpus Christi, Cambridge; and in France. War of 1939–45, Admiralty Ferry Crews. Co-Founder and First Pres., Oxford Street Assoc., 1958–68. Is actively interested in interchange of young people between UK and W Europe for business and cultural purposes. *Recreations:* yachting, painting, chess. *Address:* Drokes Field Cottage, Beaulieu, Brockenhurst, Hants SO4 7XE. *T:* Bucklers Hard 252. *Clubs:* United Oxford & Cambridge University, Royal Cruising.

BOURNE, Sir Wilfrid; *see* Bourne, Sir J. W.

BOURNE-ARTON, Major Anthony Temple, MBE 1944; *b* 1 March 1913; 2nd *s* of W. R. Temple Bourne, Walker Hall, Winston, Co. Durham, and Evelyn Rose, 3rd *d* of Sir Frank Wills, Bristol; assumed surname of Bourne-Arton, 1950; *m* 1938, Margaret Elaine, *er d* of W. Denby Arton, Sleningford Park, Ripon, Yorks; two *s* two *d. Educ:* Clifton. Served Royal Artillery, 1933–48; active service, 1936, Palestine; 1939–45: France, N Africa, Sicily and Italy (despatches, MBE); Malaya, 1947–48. Gen. Commissioner Income Tax, 1952–80; has served on Bedale RDC, and N Riding County Agric. Cttee; County Councillor, N Riding of Yorks, 1949–61; CC, W Riding of Yorks, 1967–70; Chm., Yorkshire Regional Land Drainage Cttee, 1973–80. MP (C) Darlington, 1959–64; PPS to the Home Sec., 1962–64. JP N Riding of Yorks, 1950–80. *Recreations:* fishing and shooting. *Address:* The Old Rectory, West Tanfield, Ripon, N Yorks. *T:* Bedale 70333.

BOURNS, Prof. Arthur Newcombe, OC 1982; FRSC 1964; President and Vice-Chancellor, 1972–80, Professor of Chemistry 1953–81, McMaster University; *b* 8 Dec. 1919; *s* of Evans Clement Bourns and Kathleen Jones; *m* 1943, Marion Harriet Blakney; two *s* two *d. Educ:* schs in Petitcodiac, NB; Acadia Univ. (BSc); McGill Univ. (PhD). Research Chemist, Dominion Rubber Co., 1944–45; Lectr, Acadia Univ., 1945–46; Asst Prof. of Chemistry, Saskatchewan Univ., 1946–47; McMaster Univ.: Asst Prof., 1947–49; Associate Prof., 1949–53; Dean, Faculty of Grad. Studies, 1957–61; Chm., Chemistry Dept, 1965–67; Vice-Pres., Science and Engrg Div., 1967–72; Actg Pres., 1970. Nuffield Trav. Fellow in Science, University Coll., London, 1955–56. Chm., Gordon Res. Conf. on Chem. and Physics of Isotopes (Vice-Chm. 1959–60; Chm., 1961–62); Nat. Res. Council of Canada: Mem. Grant Selection Cttee in Chem., 1966–69 (Chm. 1968–69); Mem. Council, 1969–75; Mem. Exec. Cttee, 1969–75; Mem. or Chm. various other cttees; Natural Scis and Engrg Res. Council: Member: Council, 1978–85; Exec. Cttee, 1978–; Allocations Cttee, 1978–86; Cttee on Strategic Grants, 1978–83; Chm., Grants and Scholarships Cttee, 1978–83; Mem., Adv. Cttee on University/Industry Interface, 1979–83; Vis. Res. Officer, 1983–84. Member: Ancaster Public Sch. Bd, 1963–64; Bd, Royal Botanic Gdns, 1972–80 (Vice-Chm.); Scientific Adv. Council of Canadian Bd, Weizman Inst. of Sci., 1974–; Cttee on Univ. Affairs, Prov. Ontario; Canadian Cttee for Financing Univ. Res., 1978–80; Council of Ontario Univs, 1972–80; Bd of Dirs and Exec. Cttee, Assoc. of Univs and Colleges of Canada, 1974–77; Mohawk Coll. Bd of Dirs, 1975–82; Chm., Internat. Adv. Cttee, Chinese Univ. Develt Project, 1985–; Pres. and Chm. Exec. Cttee, Canadian Bureau for Internat. Educn, 1973–76. McMaster Univ. Med. Centre: Member: Bd of Trustees, 1972–80; Exec. Cttee, 1972–80. Director: Nuclear Activation Services, 1978–80; Slater Steel Industries Ltd, 1975–79. British Council Lectr, 1963. Assoc. Editor, Canadian Jl Chemistry, 1966–69; Mem. Editorial Bd, Science Forum, 1967–73. FCIC 1954 (Chm. Hamilton Section, 1952–53; Mem. Educn Cttee, 1953–59; Mem. Council, 1966–69; Montreal Medal, 1976). Hon. DSc: Acadia, 1968; McGill, 1977; New Brunswick, McMaster, 1981; Hon. LLD Brock, 1980. *Address:* RR No 7, Brantford, Ont N3T 5L9, Canada. *T:* 519–759–0540.

BOURTON, Cyril Leonard, CB 1977; Deputy Secretary (Finance), and Accountant General, Department of Health and Social Security, 1974–76; *b* 28 Dec. 1916; *s* of late Leonard Victor Bourton; *m* 1940, Elizabeth Iris Savage; two *s* one *d. Educ:* St Dunstan's Coll., Catford. Nat. Debt Office, 1933–37; Min. of Health, later DHSS: Dep. Accountant-Gen., 1958; Asst Sec., Exec. Councils Div., 1964; Under-Sec. for Finance and Accountant Gen., 1967. *Recreations:* fishing, photography, genealogy. *Address:* 19 Mytten Close, Cuckfield, Haywards Heath, West Sussex RH17 5LN. *T:* Haywards Heath 456030.

BOUVERIE; *see* Pleydell-Bouverie, family name of Earl of Radnor.

BOVELL, Hon. Sir (William) Stewart, Kt 1976; JP; Agent-General for Western Australia, in London, 1971–74; *b* 19 Dec. 1906; *s* of A. R. Bovell and Ethel (*née* Williams), Busselton, Western Australia. *Educ:* Busselton, WA. Banking, 1923–40. Served War, RAAF, 1941–45, Flt Lt. MLA: for Sussex, WA, 1947–50; for Vasse, WA, 1950–71. Minister: for Labour, WA, 1961–62; for Lands, Forests and Immigration, WA, 1959–71. Govt Whip, WA, 1950–53; Opposition Whip, WA, 1953–57. Rep., Australian States Gen. Council, at British Commonwealth Parly Assoc., in Nairobi, Kenya, and Victoria Falls, S Rhodesia, 1954. Mem. Bd of Governors, Bunbury CofE Cathedral Grammar Sch.,

1974 (Vice-Chm.). Hon. Lay Canon, St Boniface CofE Cathedral, Bunbury, WA, 1975. JP 1949, WA. Patron: Polocrosse Assoc. of WA; Geographe Bay Yacht Club. *Recreations:* swimming, tennis, walking. *Address:* 24 West Street, Busselton, WA 6280, Australia.

BOVENIZER, Vernon Gordon Fitzell, CMG 1948; Assistant Under-Secretary of State, Ministry of Defence, 1964–68, retired; *b* 22 July 1908; *s* of Rev. Michael Fitzell Bovenizer and Mary Gordon; *m* 1937, Lillian Cherry (*d* 1970), *d* of John Henry Rowe, Cork; two *s* two *d*. *Educ:* Liverpool Coll.; Sidney Sussex Coll., Cambridge (Scholar). War Office, 1931–45; Control Commission for Germany, 1945, until return to War Office, 1948; Asst Private Sec. to Secretaries of State for War, 1936, and 1940–42; Resident Clerk, 1934–37; Asst Sec., 1942, civilian liaison with US Armies in the UK; Establishment Officer and Dir of Organisation, CCG, 1945–47; Asst Sec. and Dep. Comptroller of Claims, War Office, 1948–58; Counsellor, UK Delegation to NATO, 1958–60; Asst Under-Sec. of State, War Office, 1960–64. US Medal of Freedom, 1945. *Recreations:* tennis and squash. *Address:* 6 Cambanks, Union Lane, Cambridge; 9 The Square, Annalong, Co. Down. *Club:* Reform.

BOVET, Prof. Daniel; Nobel Prize for Physiology and Medicine, 1957; Hon. Professor, University of Rome, Italy; *b* Neuchatel, Switzerland, 23 March 1907; *s* of Pierre Bovet and Amy Babut; *m* Filomena Nitti; three *s*. Institut Pasteur, Paris, 1929–47 (first as an asst and afterwards Chief of the Laboratory of Therapeutic Chemistry); Chief of the Laboratory of Therapeutic Chemistry, Istituto Superiore di Sanità, Rome, 1947–64; Prof. of Pharmacology, Fac. of Medicine, Univ. of Sassari, Italy, 1964–71; Prof. of Psychobiol., Faculty of Sci., Rome Univ., 1971–77. Mem. of the Accademia Nazionale dei XL, 1949; Mem. of Accademia naz. dei Lincei, 1958; Foreign Mem., Royal Soc., 1962. Grande Ufficiale dell' Ordine della Repubblica Italiana, 1959; Comdr, Légion d'Honneur, 1980. *Publications:* (in collaboration with F. Bovet-Nitti) Structure chimique et activité pharmacodynamique du système nerveux végétatif, 1948 (Bale, Switzerland); (in collaboration with F. Bovet-Nitti and G. B. Marini-Bettolo) Curare and Curare-like Agents, 1957 (Amsterdam, Holland); (in collaboration with R. Blum and others) Controlling Drugs, 1974 (San Francisco). *Recreation:* wandering in Amazonia. *Address:* 33 Piazza S Apollinare, 00186 Rome, Italy. *T:* 6565297.

BOVEY, Dr Leonard; Head of Technological Requirements Branch, Department of Industry, 1977; *b* 9 May 1924; *s* of late Alfred and Gladys Bovey; *m* 1943, Constance Hudson; one *s* one *d*. *Educ:* Heles Sch., Exeter; Emmanuel Coll., Cambridge (BA, PhD). FInstP; CPhys. Dunlop Rubber, 1943–46; Post-doctoral Fellow, Nat. Res. Council, Ottawa, 1950–52; AERE Harwell, 1952–65; Head W Mids Regional Office, Birmingham, Min. of Technology, 1966–70; Regional Dir, Yorks and Humberside, DTI, 1970–73; Counsellor (Scientific and Technological Affairs), High Commn, Ottawa, 1974–77. Editor, Materials & Design. *Publications:* Spectroscopy in the Metallurgical Industry, 1963; papers on spectroscopy in Jl Optical Soc. Amer., Spectrochimica Acta, Jl Phys. Soc. London. *Recreations:* repairing neglected household equipment, work, reading (particularly crime novels), walking, theatre, music. *Address:* 32 Radnor Walk, Chelsea SW3 4BN. *T:* 01–352 4142. *Club:* Civil Service.

BOVEY, Philip Henry; Under Secretary, Department of Trade and Industry, since 1985; *b* 11 July 1948; *s* of Norman Henry Bovey and Dorothy Yvonne Kent Bovey; *m* 1974, Jenet Alison, *d* of late Rev. Canon J. M. McTear and Margaret McTear; one *s* one *d*. Educ: Rugby; Peterhouse, Cambridge (schol.; MA). Solicitor. 3rd Sec., FCO, 1970–71; with Slaughter and May, 1972–75; Legal Assistant, 1976; Sen. Legal Assistant, 1976; Depts of Trade and Industry, 1976–77; Cabinet Office, 1977–78; Depts of Trade, Industry, Prices and Consumer Protection, then DTI, 1978–85; Asst Solicitor, 1982. *Recreation:* photography. *Address:* 102 Cleveland Gardens, Barnes, SW13 0AH. *T:* 01–876 3710.

BOWATER, Sir Euan David Vansittart, 3rd Bt *cr* 1939, of Friston, Suffolk; *b* 9 Sept. 1935; *s* of Sir Noël Vansittart Bowater, 2nd Bt, GBE, MC, and of Constance Heiton, *d* of David Gordon Bett; *S* father, 1984; *m* 1964, Susan Mary Humphrey, *d* of late A. R. O. Slater, FCA; two *s* two *d*. *Educ:* Eton; Trinity Coll., Cambridge. *Heir:* *s* Moray Vansittart Bowater, *b* 24 April 1967. *Address:* Coombe Farmhouse, Chagford, Devon.

BOWATER, Sir J(ohn) Vansittart, 4th Bt *cr* 1914; *b* 6 April 1918; *s* of Captain Victor Spencer Bowater (*d* 1967) (3rd *s* of 1st Bt) and Hilda Mary (*d* 1918), *d* of W. Henry Potter; *S* uncle, Sir Thomas Dudley Blennerhassett Bowater, 3rd Bt, 1972; *m* 1943, Joan Kathleen, (*d* 1982), *d* of late Wilfrid Scullard; one *s* one *d*. *Educ:* Branksome School, Godalming, Surrey. Served Royal Artillery, 1939–46. *Heir:* *s* Michael Patrick Bowater [*b* 18 July 1949; *m* 1968, Alison, *d* of Edward Wall; four *d*]. *Address:* 214 Runnymede Avenue, Bournemouth, Dorset BH11 9SP. *T:* Northbourne 571782.

BOWDELL, Wilfred, CBE 1973; *b* 28 Nov. 1913; *s* of Harry Bowdell and Sarah Alice Bowdell (*née* Roscoe); *m* 1939, Alice Lord. *Educ:* Bury High Sch.; Univ. of London (BScEcon); Inst. of Public Finance and Accountancy (Pres., 1972–73). Finance Asst, Bury County Borough Council, 1930–36; Chief Accountancy Asst, Swinton and Pendlebury Borough Council, 1936–39; Chief Accountant, York City Council, 1939–46; Dep. Treas., Enfield Urban District Council, 1946–48; Dep. Treas. 1948–62, Borough Treas. 1962–65, St Marylebone Borough Council; City Treas., Westminster City Council, 1965–74. Member: Public Works Loan Bd, 1975– (Dep. Chm., 1980–); London Housing Staff Commn, 1979–84. *Recreations:* music, photography, gardening. *Address:* 72 Highfield Way, Rickmansworth, Herts. *T:* Rickmansworth 773459.

BOWDEN, family name of **Baron Aylestone** and **Baron Bowden.**

BOWDEN, Baron, *cr* 1963, of Chesterfield (Life Peer); **Bertram Vivian Bowden,** MA, PhD, FIEE, FIEEE, MScTech; Principal, The University of Manchester Institute of Science and Technology (called Manchester College of Science and Technology until May 1966), 1964–76, retired; *b* 18 Jan. 1910; *s* of B. C. Bowden, Chesterfield; *m* 1939, Marjorie Browne (marr. diss., 1954; she *d* 1957); one *s* two *d*; *m* 1967, Mary Maltby (*d* 1971); *m* 1974, Mrs Phyllis James (*see* P. B. M. Hetzel) (marr. diss. 1983). *Educ:* Chesterfield Grammar Sch.; Emmanuel Coll., Cambridge. Worked with late Lord Rutherford, 1931–34; PhD 1934; University of Amsterdam, 1934–35. Physics Master, Liverpool Collegiate Sch., 1935–37; Chief Physics Master, Oundle Sch., 1937–40; Radar Research in England, 1940–43; Radar Research in USA, 1943–46; Sir Robert Watson Watt and Partners, 1947–50; Ferranti Ltd, Manchester (Digital Computers), 1950–53; Dean of the Faculty of Technology, Manchester Univ., and Principal, Manchester Coll. of Science and Technology, 1953–64. Chm. Electronics Research Council of Ministry of Aviation, 1960–64; Minister of State, Dept of Education and Science, 1964–65 (on leave of absence as Principal of Manchester Coll. of Science and Technology). Pres. The Science Masters Assoc., 1962. Pres., Nat. Television Rental Assoc., 1975–82. Hon. FICE 1975; Hon. DS Rensellaer Polytechnic, USA, 1974; Hon. LLD Manchester, 1976; Hon. DSc Kumasi, Ghana, 1977. Pioneer Award, IEEE Aerospace & Electronic Systems Gp, 1973. *Publications:* Faster Than Thought, 1953; The Development of Manchester College of Science and Technology; numerous papers on education. *Recreations:* listening to music; pottering about at home and in the House of Lords. *Address:* Pine Croft, 5 Stanhope Road, Bowdon, Altrincham, Cheshire WA14 3LB. *T:* 061–928 4005. *Club:* Athenæum.

BOWDEN, Andrew, MBE 1961; MP (C) Kemptown Division of Brighton since 1970; *b* 8 April 1930; *s* of William Victor Bowden, Solicitor, and Francesca Wilson; *m* Benita Napier; one *s* one *d*. *Educ:* Ardingly College. Paint industry, 1955–68; Man. Dir, Personnel Assessments Ltd, 1969–71; Man. Dir, Haymarket Personnel Selection Ltd, 1970–71; Director: Sales Education & Leadership Ltd, 1970–71; Jenkin and Purser (Holdings) Ltd, 1973–77. Mem., Wandsworth Borough Council, 1956–62. Contested (C): N Hammersmith, 1955; N Kensington, 1964; Kemp Town, Brighton, 1966. Jt Chm., All Party Old Age Pensioners Parly Gp, 1972–; Chm., All Party BLESMA Gp; Mem. Select Cttee on Expenditure, 1973–74, on Abortion, 1975, on Employment, 1979–. Nat. Chm., Young Conservatives, 1960–61. Internat. Chm., People to People, 1981–. Nat. Pres., Captive Animals Protection Soc., 1978–. Mem. School Council, Ardingly Coll., 1982–. *Recreations:* fishing, chess, golf. *Address:* House of Commons, SW1. *T:* 01–219 5047. *Club:* Carlton.

BOWDEN, Major Aubrey Henry, DSO 1918; Chairman, Bowden Bros Ltd, 1930–75; *b* 6 June 1895; *e s* of Henry White Bowden, MICE, Great Missenden; *m* 1st, 1918, Helen (*d* 1939), *o d* of late R. G. Modera, Wilbury Lodge, Hove; one *s* one *d*; 2nd, 1941, Andrée Marguerite July; one *s* two *d*. *Educ:* Oundle. Electrical Engineer. Training: Brompton and Kensington Electricity Supply Co.; London Underground Railway; Metropolitan Railway; Oerlikon Co.; from here commissioned: to 11th Service Batt. Royal Warwicks Regt, to Capt. and Brigade Machine Gun Officer, to Machine Gun Corps. *Address:* 28 Berkeley Court, Baker Street, NW1.

BOWDEN, Sir Frank Houston, 3rd Bt *cr* 1915; MA Oxon; retired industrialist and landowner; *b* 10 Aug. 1909; *o s* of Sir Harold Bowden, 2nd Bt, GBE, and of Vera, *d* of Joseph Whitaker, JP, FZS; *S* father 1960; *m* 1st, 1934; one *s*; 2nd, 1937, Lydia Eveline (*d* 1981), *d* of Jean Manolovici, Bucharest; three *s*. *Educ:* Rugby; Merton Coll., Oxford. Served with RNVR, 1939–44. President: University Hall, Buckland, 1967–71; British Kendo Association, 1969. Hon. Vice-Pres., 3rd World Kendo Championships, 1976. *Recreation:* collecting weapons and armour, particularly Japanese (Vice-Chm. Japan Soc. of London, 1970–75, 1979–82, 1984–). *Heir:* *s* Nicholas Richard Bowden, *b* 13 Aug. 1935. *Address:* The Old Vicarage, Winkfield, Windsor, Berks. *Clubs:* White's, Royal Thames Yacht.

BOWDEN, Gerald Francis, TD 1971; MP (C) Dulwich, since 1983; chartered surveyor; *b* 26 Aug. 1935; *s* of Frank Albert Bowden and Elsie Bowden (*née* Burrill); *m* 1967, Heather Elizabeth Hill (*née* Hall) (*d* 1984); two *d*, and one step *s* one step *d*. *Educ:* Battersea Grammar School; Magdalen College, Oxford. MA; FRICS 1984 (ARICS 1971). Called to the Bar, Gray's Inn, 1963. Worked in advertising industry, 1964–68; property marketing and investment, 1968–72; Principal Lecturer in Law, Dept of Estate Management, Polytechnic of the South Bank, 1972–. Mem. GLC for Dulwich, 1977–81; a co-opted Mem., ILEA, 1981–84. Commnd during Nat. Service and continued to serve in TA until 1984 (Lt-Col). *Publication:* An Introduction to the Law of Contract and Tort (with Alan S. Morris), 1977. *Recreations:* reading, gardening, renovating old houses. *Address:* House of Commons, SW1A 0AA. *T:* 01–219 4343. *Club:* United Oxford & Cambridge University.

BOWDEN, Prof. Kenneth Frank, DSc, FInstP; Professor of Oceanography in the University of Liverpool, 1954–82, now Emeritus; *b* 23 Dec. 1916; *s* of Frank and Margaret N. Bowden; *m* 1946, Lilias T. M. Nicol; one *d*. *Educ:* Itchen Secondary Sch.; University Coll., Southampton. Scientific Officer, Anti-Submarine Experimental Establishment (Admiralty), 1939–45; Lecturer in Oceanography, University of Liverpool, 1945–52; Principal Scientific Officer, Nat. Inst. of Oceanography, 1952–54; Dean, Faculty of Science, 1959–62, Pro-Vice-Chancellor, 1968–71, Univ. of Liverpool. *Publications:* Physical Oceanography of Coastal Waters, 1983; papers on physical oceanography in various scientific journals. *Address:* Sailways, 21 Undercliff Road, Wemyss Bay, Renfrewshire PA18 6AJ. *T:* Wemyss Bay 521143.

BOWDEN, Logan S.; *see* Scott Bowden.

BOWDEN, Dr Richard Charles, OBE 1941; PhD, MSc, FRSC, CChem; Consultant, Ministry of Aviation (formerly Ministry of Supply), 1952–60; *b* 31 Aug. 1887; *s* of Richard Charles Bowden, Bristol, and Minnie Clara Thatcher; *m* 1913, Nina Adeline, *er d* of Thomas Fisher, Bristol; no *c*. *Educ:* Merchant Venturers Sch., Bristol; Merchant Venturers Technical Coll., Bristol; Bristol Univ. (Hons, Physical Chemistry). Asst Chemist, Research Dept, Royal Arsenal, Woolwich, 1911; Chemist, Royal Gunpowder Factory, 1912; Chemist 2nd Class, 1915; Chemist in Charge, 1923; Technical Asst (temp.) under Dir of Ordnance Factories, War Office, 1930; Technical Asst, 1932; Chemical Engineer, 1934; Superintendent, Royal Ordnance Factories, 1934–41; Asst Dir of Ordnance Factories (X); Dep Dir of Ordnance Factories (X), 1941; Dir, of Ordnance Factories (X), 1942–52. Patentee or Joint Patentee of various patents relating to chemical processes and chemical plant. Medals: Silver Jubilee, 1935; Coronation, 1937 and 1953. *Publications:* author or joint author of publications in Journal of Chemical Society, 1911, 1912, 1923. *Address:* Villa Maria, 66–68 Croham Road, South Croydon, Surrey CR2 7BB.

BOWDEN, Prof. Ruth Elizabeth Mary, OBE 1980; DSc London, MB, BS, FRCS; Professor of Anatomy: Royal Free Hospital School of Medicine, University of London, 1951–80, now Emeritus; Royal College of Surgeons of England, since 1984; Hon. Research Fellow, Institute of Neurology, since 1980; *b* 21 Feb. 1915; *o c* of late Frank Harold and Louise Ellen Bowden. *Educ:* Westlands Sch.; St Paul's Girls' Sch.; London (Royal Free Hospital) Sch. of Medicine for Women, University of London. House Surg. and later House Physician, Elizabeth Garrett Anderson Hosp. (Oster House branch), 1940–42; House Surg., Royal Cancer Hosp., 1942; Grad. Asst in Nuffield Dept of Orthopædic Surgery, Peripheral Nerve Injury Unit, Oxford, 1942–45; Asst Lecturer in Anatomy, Royal Free Hospital Sch. of Medicine, 1945; later Lecturer, then University Reader in Human Anatomy, 1949; Rockefeller Travelling Fellowship, 1949–50; Hunterian Prof., RCS, 1950; part-time Lectr, Dept of Anatomy, St Thomas's Hosp. Med. Sch., 1980–83. WHO Consultant in anatomy, Khartoum Univ., 1972, 1974, 1977. President: Anat. Soc. of Gt Brit. and Ireland, 1970; Medical Women's Fedn, 1981. Mem., Exec. Cttee, Women's Nat. Commn, 1984–. FRSM; Fellow: Brit. Orthopædic Assoc., Linnean Soc. Vice-President: Chartered Soc. of Physiotherapy (Chm., 1960–70), Inst. of Science Technology (Pres., 1960–65); Riding for the Disabled Assoc. DLJ 1978, CMLJ 1980. Jubilee Medal, 1977. *Publications:* contribs to Peripheral Nerve Injuries Report of Medical Research Council; Peripheral Nerve Injuries; contrib. to Oxford Companion to Medicine; contribs to medical and scientific jls. *Recreations:* reading, music, painting, walking, gardening, carpentry. *Address:* 6 Hartham Close, Hartham Road, N7. *T:* 01–607 3464.

BOWEN, Maj.-Gen. Bryan Morris; Paymaster-in-Chief and Inspector of Army Pay Services, since 1986; *b* 8 March 1932; *s* of Frederick Bowen and Gwendoline Bowen (*née* Morris); *m* 1955, Suzanne Rowena (*née* Howell); two *d*. *Educ:* Newport High Sch.; Exeter Univ. FCCA, FCMA; ndc, psc†, sq, pfc. Joined RE, 1953, served UK and BAOR; transf. RAPC, 1958; Paymaster 1/6 QEO Gurkha Rifles, Malaya and UK, 1960–63;

Army Cost and Management Accounting Services, 1963–68; DAAG, MoD, 1968–70; Exchange Officer, US Army, Washington, DC, 1970–72; Nat. Defence Coll., 1972–73; DS, RMCS Shrivenham, 1973–76; AAG, MOD, 1976–79; Col (Principal), MoD F4(AD), 1979–81; Chief Paymaster, Army Pay Office (Officers Accounts), 1981–82; Dep. Paymaster-in-Chief, 1982–85. *Recreations:* golf, church affairs, gardening. *Clubs:* Lansdowne; Frilford Heath Golf.

BOWEN, Prof. David Aubrey Llewellyn, FRCP, FRCPE, FRCPath; Professor of Forensic Medicine, University of London, since 1977; Head of Department of Forensic Medicine and Toxicology, Charing Cross Hospital Medical School, since 1973 (Charing Cross and Westminster Medical School, since 1985); Hon. Consultant Pathologist, Charing Cross Hospital, since 1973; Lecturer in Forensic Medicine, University of Oxford, since 1974; *b* 31 Jan. 1924; *s* of late Dr Thomas Rufus Bowen and Catherine (*née* Llewellyn); *m* 1st, 1950, Joan Rosemary Davis (*d* 1973); two *s* one *d*; 2nd, 1975, Helen Rosamund Landcastle. *Educ:* Caterham Sch.; Garw Secondary Sch., Pontycymmer; University College of Wales, Cardiff; Corpus Christi Coll., Cambridge (MA); Middlesex Hosp. Med. Sch. (MB BChir 1947); DipPath 1955; DMJ Soc. of Apoth. of London 1962. FRCPE 1971; FRCPath 1975; FRCP 1982. Ho. posts at W Middlesex Hosp. and London Chest Hosp., 1947 and 1950; RAMC, 1947–49; Jun. Resident Pathologist, Bristol Royal Inf., 1950–51; Registrar in Path., London Chest Hosp., 1951–52; Registrar and Sen. Registrar in Clin. Path., National Hosp. for Nervous Diseases, 1952–56; Asst Pathologist and Sen. Registrar, Royal Marsden Hosp., 1956–57; Demonstr 1957–63, Lectr 1963–66, in Forensic Medicine, St George's Hosp. Med. Sch.; Sen. Lectr 1966–73, Reader 1973–77, in Forensic Medicine, Vice-Dean 1974–78, Charing Cross Hosp. Med. Sch. Chairman: Div. of Pathology, Charing Cross Hosp., 1976–78; Apptd and Recog. Teachers in Path., Charing Cross Hosp. Med. Sch., 1980–82; Examiner: Univ. of Riyadh, Saudi Arabia, 1978–81; on Forensic Med., RCPath, 1976–; for Diploma of Med. Jurisprudence, Soc. of Apothecaries of London, 1970–; for MD (Forensic Medicine) and Diploma in Legal Medicine, Univ. of Sri Lanka, 1985. Vice-President: Medico-Legal Soc., 1977–; Medical Defence Union, 1979–; Pres., British Assoc. in Forensic Med., 1977–79; Member: British Academy in Forensic Sci. and Forensic Sci. Soc., 1960– (Mem. Council, 1965–67); British Div. of Internat. Acad. of Path., 1974–; Acad. Internat. de Médicine Légale et de Méd. Sociale, 1976–; RCPath Adv. Cttee on Forensic Path., 1973–76 and 1980–82; W. D. L. Fernando Oration to Medico-Legal Soc. of Sri Lanka, 1985. *Publications:* sci. papers in numerous med., forensic med. and path. jls. *Recreations:* hockey, jogging. *Address:* Department of Forensic Medicine and Toxicology, Charing Cross & Westminster Medical School, Fulham Palace Road, W6 8RF. *T:* 01–748 2040, ext. 2746; 19 Letchmore Road, Radlett, Herts. *T:* Radlett 6936. *Clubs:* West Herts Hockey (Watford); London Welsh Rugby Football (Richmond).

BOWEN, Sheriff Edward Farquharson, TD 1976; Sheriff of Tayside Central and Fife, since 1983; *b* 1 May 1945; *s* of Stanley Bowen, *qv*; *m* 1975, Patricia Margaret Brown, *y d* of Rev. R. Russell Brown, Perth; two *s* one *d*. *Educ:* Melville Coll., Edinburgh; Edinburgh Univ. (LLB 1966). Enrolled as Solicitor in Scotland, 1968; admitted to Faculty of Advocates, 1970. Standing Jun. Counsel: to Scottish Educn Dept, 1977–79; to Home Office in Scotland, 1979; Advocate-Depute, 1979–83. Served RAOC (TA and T&AVR), 1964–80. *Recreation:* golf. *Address:* Westgate, Glamis Drive, Dundee DD2 1QL. *Clubs:* New (Edinburgh); Hon. Company of Edinburgh Golfers; Panmure Golf.

BOWEN, Edward George, CBE 1962; PhD; FRS 1975; FAA; Counsellor (Scientific) at the Australian Embassy in Washington, DC, USA, 1973–76; *b* 14 Jan. 1911; *s* of G. Bowen, Swansea. *Educ:* Univ. of Wales (MSc); London Univ. (PhD); DSc Sydney. FKC 1981. Mem., Radar Develt Team, 1935; Air Ministry Research Station, Bawdsey, 1936–40; British Air Commn Washington, 1940–42; Radiation Lab., MIT, 1943; Chief, Div. of Radiophysics, CSIRO, 1946–71. Chm., Anglo-Australian Telescope Board, 1967–73. Vice-Pres., Aust. Acad. of Science, 1962–63; Foreign Member: Amer. Acad. of Arts and Scis; US Nat. Acad. of Engrg. Thurlow Award, Amer. Inst. of Navigation, 1950. US Medal for Freedom, 1947. *Address:* 1/39 Clarke Street, Narrabeen, NSW 2101, Australia. *Club:* Athenæum.

BOWEN, Maj.-Gen. Esmond John, CB 1982; Director, Army Dental Service, 1978–82; *b* 6 Dec. 1922; *s* of Major Leslie Arthur George Bowen, MC, and Edna Grace Bowen; *m* 1948, Elsie (*née* Midgley); two *s* two *d* (and one *d* decd). *Educ:* Clayesmore Sch.; Univ. of Birmingham. LDS Birmingham 1946. Commd Lieut, RADC, 1947; Captain 1948; Major 1955; Lt-Col 1962; Chief Instructor, Depot and Training Establishment RADC, 1966–69; CO Nos 2 and 3 Dental Groups, 1969–74; Asst Dir, Army Dental Service, 1974–76; Comdt, HQ and Training Centre, RADC, 1976–77; Brig. 1977; Dep. Dir, Dental Service, HQ BAOR, 1977–78. QHDS, 1977–82. Col Comdt, RADC, 1982–. OStJ 1975. *Recreations:* target rifle and muzzle loading shooting. *Address:* 72 Winchester Road, Andover, Hants. *T:* Andover 23252. *Club:* Lansdowne.

BOWEN, (Evan) Roderic, QC 1952; MA, LLD; Master Emeritus of the Middle Temple; Social Security (formerly National Insurance) Commissioner, since 1967; *b* 6 Aug. 1913; 2nd *s* of late Evan Bowen, JP, and late Margaret Ellen Twiss, The Elms, Cardigan. *Educ:* Cardigan Schs; University Coll., Aberystwyth; St John's Coll., Cambridge. Practised at the bar with chambers in Cardiff until 1940; served in HM Forces, 1940–45, in the ranks and subsequently as an officer on staff of Judge Advocate-Gen. MP (L) County of Cardigan, 1945–66; Dep. Chm. of Ways and Means, House of Commons, 1965–66. Recorder of: Carmarthen, 1950; Merthyr Tydfil, 1953–60; Swansea, 1960–64; Cardiff, 1964–67; Chm., Montgomeryshire QS, 1959–71. Chm. Welsh Parliamentary Party, 1955. Pres., St David's UC, Lampeter, 1977–. Hon. LLD Wales, 1972. *Address:* 3 Maynard Court, Fairwater Road, Llandaff, Cardiff. *T:* Cardiff 563207. *Clubs:* National Liberal; County (Cardiff).

BOWEN, Rear-Adm. Frank; Managing Director, Gresham-Cap Ltd; *b* 25 Jan. 1930; *s* of Alfred and Lily Bowen; *m* 1954, Elizabeth Lilian Richards; one *s* two *d*. *Educ:* Cowley Sch., St Helen's; Royal Naval Engineering Coll. CEng; MIMechE; FBIM. RNC Dartmouth, 1948; served various ships and RN establishments incl. HMS Eagle and Excellent, 1956–60, and Scylla, 1971–73; served in Washington, 1968–70 and 1976–78; i/c HMS Collingwood, 1981–82; Special Project Dir, MoD, PE; Captain 1974; Rear-Adm., 1982–84. Chm. and Man. Dir, Naval Systems Exchange Ltd. MInstD. *Recreations:* amateur stage, social golf. *Address:* c/o Midland Bank plc, 102 High Street, Lymington, Hants SO4 9ZP.

BOWEN, Sir Geoffrey Fraser, Kt 1977; Managing Director, Commercial Banking Company of Sydney Ltd, Australia, 1973–76, retired (General Manager, 1970–73); *m* 1st, Ruth (decd), *d* of H. E. Horsburgh; two *s* one *d*; 2nd, Isabel, *d* of H. T. Underwood. *Address:* Cavendish, 16/562 Pacific Highway, Killara, NSW 2071, Australia. *Clubs:* Union (Sydney); Warrawee Bowling; Killara Golf.

BOWEN, Gordon, CB 1962; CMG 1956; Director, Metrication Board, 1969–74; *b* 17 June 1910; *e s* of late Arthur Thomas Bowen and late Dora Drinkwater; *m* 1938, Elsa Catriona, *y d* of late Rev. Dr Alexander Grieve, MA, PhD and late Euphemia Logan Ross Grieve; one *s* (and one *s* decd). *Educ:* Birkenhead Institute Sch.; University of Liverpool.

Asst Lecturer in Geography, University of Glasgow, 1933–36; Commonwealth Fund Fellow, University of Calif., 1936–38; Lecturer in Geography, University of Glasgow, 1938–41; Principal, Board of Trade, 1941–44; Asst Sec., Board of Trade, 1944–53; United Kingdom Senior Trade Commissioner in Canada, 1953–58; Under Secretary: Board of Trade, 1958–66; Min. of Technology, 1966–69. *Address:* 5 Knowehead Gardens, Albert Drive, Pollokshields, Glasgow G41 5RE.

BOWEN, John Griffith; playwright and novelist; freelance drama producer for television; *b* 5 Nov. 1924; *s* of Hugh Griffith Bowen and Ethel May Cook; unmarried. *Educ:* Queen Elizabeth's Grammar Sch., Crediton; Pembroke Coll., Oxford; St Antony's Coll., Oxford. Frere Exhibition for Indian Studies, Oxford, 1951–52 and 1952–53. Asst Editor, The Sketch, 1954–57; Advertising Copywriter and Copy Chief, 1957–60; Consultant on TV Drama, Associated TV, 1960–67; productions for Thames TV, LWT, BBC. *Publications:* The Truth Will Not Help Us, 1956; After the Rain, 1958; The Centre of the Green, 1959; Storyboard, 1960; The Birdcage, 1962; A World Elsewhere, 1965; The Essay Prize, 1965; Squeak, 1983; The McGuffin, 1984 (filmed for TV, 1986); The Girls, 1986; *plays:* I Love You, Mrs Patterson, 1964; After the Rain, 1967; Fall and Redemption, 1967; Little Boxes, 1968; The Disorderly Women, 1968; The Corsican Brothers, 1970; The Waiting Room, 1970; Robin Redbreast, 1972; Heil Caesar, 1973; Florence Nightingale, 1975; Which Way Are You Facing?, 1976; Singles, 1977; Bondage, 1978; The Inconstant Couple (adaptation of Marivaux, L'Heureux Stratagème), 1978; Uncle Jeremy, 1981. *Address:* Old Lodge Farm, Sugarswell Lane, Edgehill, Banbury, Oxon. *T:* Tysoe 401.

BOWEN, Very Rev. Lawrence; Dean of St Davids Cathedral, 1972–84; *b* 9 Sept. 1914; *s* of William and Elizabeth Ann Bowen; *m* 1941, Hilary Myrtle Bowen; two *d*. *Educ:* Llanelli Gram. Sch.; Univ. Coll. of Wales, Aberystwyth (BA 1st Cl.); St Michael's Coll., Llandaff (Crossley Exhibnr and Sen. Student). Ordained in St Davids Cathedral, 1938; Curate of Pembrey, 1938–40; Minor Canon, St Davids Cathedral, 1940–46; Vicar of St Clears with Llanginning, 1946–64; Rector of Tenby, 1964–72; Rector of Rectorial Benefice of Tenby with Gumfreston and Penally, 1970–72; Canon of St Davids Cathedral (Mathry), 1972. Surrogate. *Recreations:* golf, cricket, writing Welsh poetry. *Address:* Saddle Point, Slade Way, Fishguard, Dyfed SA65 9NY.

BOWEN, Hon. Lionel Frost; MP; MHR (Lab) Kingsford-Smith, NSW, since 1969; Deputy Prime Minister of Australia, since 1983; Attorney-General, since 1984; *b* 1922; *m* Claire Clement; eight *c*. *Educ:* Sydney Univ. (LLB). Alderman, 1947, Mayor, 1949–50, Randwick Council; MLA, NSW, 1962–69; Postmaster Gen., 1972–74; Special Minister of State, 1974–75; Minister for Manufg Industry, 1975; Minister for Trade, 1983–84. Dep. Leader, ALP, 1977–. *Recreations:* surfing, reading. *Address:* Parliament House, Canberra, ACT 2600, Australia. *T:* 062–721211.

BOWEN, Most Rev. Michael George; *see* Southwark, Archbishop and Metropolitan of, (RC).

BOWEN, Hon. Sir Nigel (Hubert), KBE 1976; Chief Judge, Federal Court of Australia, since 1976; *b* Summerland, BC, Canada, 26 May 1911; *s* of late O. P. Bowen, Ludlow, England; *m* 1st, 1947, Eileen Cecily (*d* 1983), *d* of F. J. Mullens; three *d*; 2nd, 1984, Ermyn Krippner. *Educ:* King's Sch., Sydney; St Paul's Coll., Sydney Univ. (BA, LLB). Served 2nd AIF, 1942–46 (Captain). Admitted NSW Bar 1936, Victorian Bar 1954; QC (Austr.) 1953; Vice-Pres., Law Council of Australia, 1957–60; Pres., NSW Bar Council, 1959–61. Lectr in Company Law and Taxation, Sydney Univ., 1957–58; Editor, Australian Law Jl 1946–58. MHR (L) Australia for Parramatta, NSW, 1964–73, retired; Attorney-General, Australia, 1966–69 and March-Aug. 1971; Minister for Educn and Science, 1969–71; Minister for Foreign Affairs, Aug. 1971–Dec. 1972. Judge of Court of Appeal of NSW, 1973–76; Chief Judge in Equity, 1974–76. Head of Austr. Delegn and Vice-Pres. of UN Internat. Conf. on Human Rights, 1968; Leader of Austr. Delegations: to Unesco Inter-Govtl Conf. of Ministers on Cultural Policies, 1970; to UN, 1971 and 1972. *Publications* (*Reports*): Conflict between Public Duty and Private Interest, 1979; Legal Education in New South Wales, 1979. *Recreations:* swimming, music. *Address:* 43 Grosvenor Street, Wahroonga, NSW 2076, Australia. *Club:* Union (Sydney).

BOWEN, Roderic; *see* Bowen, (Evan) Roderic.

BOWEN, Stanley, CBE 1972; Hon. Sheriff, Lothian and Borders, since 1975; *b* Carnoustie, Angus, 4 Aug. 1910; *s* of late Edward Bowen and Ellen Esther Bowen (*née* Powles), Birmingham; *m* 1943, Mary Shepherd Greig, *d* of late Alexander Greig and Mary Shand Greig (*née* Shepherd), Carnoustie; two *s* one *d*. *Educ:* Barry Sch., Angus; Grove Academy, Dundee; University Coll., Dundee. Enrolled Solicitor, in Scotland, 1932; entered Procurator Fiscal Service, in Scotland, 1933; Procurator Fiscal Depute at Hamilton, Lanarkshire, 1937; Interim Procurator Fiscal at Airdrie, Lanarkshire, 1938; Crown Office, Edinburgh: Legal Asst, 1941; Principal Asst, 1945; Crown Agent for Scotland, 1967–74. Chm., Sec. of State for Scotland's working party on forensic pathology services, 1975; Member: Sec. of State for the Environment's working party on drinking and driving offences, 1975; Sub-Cttee for legislation on transplantation of human tissues, Council of Europe, 1975–76; Police Adv. Bd for Scotland, 1976–83 (sub-cttee on police discipline, 1976, and working party on Cadet entry, 1979); Sec. of State for Scotland's working group on identification evidence in criminal cases, 1977; Council, Scottish Assoc. for Care and Resettlement of Offenders, 1978–83; Council, Corstorphine Trust, 1978– (Chm., 1982–). *Recreations:* golf, gardening. *Address:* Achray, 20 Dovecot Road, Corstorphine, Edinburgh EH12 7LE. *T:* 031–334 4096. *Clubs:* New, Press (Edinburgh); Carnoustie Golf.

See also E. F. Bowen.

BOWEN, Thomas Edward Ifor L.; *see* Lewis-Bowen.

BOWEN, Sir Thomas Frederic Charles, 4th Bt *cr* 1921; *b* 11 Oct. 1921; *s* of 2nd Bt and May Isobel (*d* 1972), *d* of John Frederick Roberts; *S* brother, 1939; *m* 1947, Jill, *d* of Lloyd Evans, Gold Coast; one *s* two *d*. *Heir:* *s* Mark Edward Mortimer Bowen [*b* 17 Oct. 1958; *m* 1983, Kerry Tessa, *d* of Michael Moriarty, Worthing]. *Address:* 1 Barford Close, Fleet, Hants GU13 9HJ.

BOWEN, Prof. William G(ordon), PhD; President, Princeton University, since 1972; Professor of Economics, Princeton University, since 1958; *b* 6 Oct. 1933; *s* of Albert A. and Bernice C. Bowen; *m* 1956, Mary Ellen Maxwell; one *s* one *d*. *Educ:* Denison Univ. (AB); Princeton Univ. (PhD). Princeton Univ.: Asst Prof. of Economics, Associate Prof. of Economics; Provost, 1967–72. Hon. LLD: Denison, Rutgers, Pennsylvania and Yale, 1972; Harvard, 1973; Jewish Theol Seminary, 1974; Seton Hall Univ., 1975. *Publications:* Economic Aspects of Education, 1964; (with W. J. Baumol) Performing Arts: the Economic Dilemma, 1966; (with T. A. Finegan) Economics of Labor Force Participation, 1969, etc; contribs to Amer. Econ. Review, Economica, Quarterly Jl of Economics, etc. *Address:* 1 Nassau Hall, Princeton University, Princeton, NJ, USA. *T:* 609–452–6100.

BOWER, Air Marshal Sir Leslie William Clement, KCB 1962 (CB 1954); DSO 1945; DFC 1944; *b* 11 July 1909; *s* of William Clarke Bower, Co. Cork, Eire; *m* 1963,

Clare (*d* 1971), *widow* of Commander Jasper Abbott, RN, Uppaton, Yelverton, S Devon, and *d* of H. W. Etkins, OBE, Curlews, Constantine Bay, N Cornwall; *m* 1979, Patricia Fearon, *widow* of Wing Comdr D. N. Fearon. *Educ:* The Harvey Grammar Sch., Folkestone; Cranwell; RAF Staff Coll., 1946; USAF War Coll., 1947–50. Royal Air Force 1929; served War of 1939–45 (despatches twice, DFC, DSO), in Europe and Canada; OC 217 (TB) Sqdn, 1941–42; Dir Op. Trg, HQ, RCAF, Ottawa, 1942–43; OC 138 Wing 2nd TAF, 1943–45; AOC 81 (Fighter) Group, 1952–54; Senior Air Staff Officer, HQ Fighter Command, 1954–57; Senior Air Staff Officer, MEAF, 1957–58; Dep. Commander-in-Chief, Middle East Air Force, 1958–59; Air Officer Commanding No 19 Group, RAF Coastal Command, 1959–61; UK Representative in Ankara on Permanent Military Deputies Group of Central Treaty Organisation (Cento), 1962–65; retired. Air Marshal, 1962. *Address:* c/o Lloyds Bank, Cox's & King's Branch, 6 Pall Mall, SW1. *Club:* Royal Air Force.

BOWER, Michael Douglas; Organiser, Sheffield Co-operative Development Group, since 1981; *b* 25 Aug. 1942; *s* of Stanley Arthur Bower and Rachael Farmer; *m* 1966, Susan Millington; two *d*. *Educ:* Colwyn Bay Grammar Sch.; Royal Coll. of Advanced Technol., Salford. Civil engr, 1961–64; journalist, 1965–77; with The Star, Sheffield, 1968–77; Regional Organiser, NUJ, 1977–81. Mem., Press Council, 1976–77. Mem., Sheffield Metropolitan DC, 1976– (Chm., Educn Cttee, 1983–). Contested (Lab) Hallam Div. of Sheffield, 1979. *Recreations:* walking, golf. *Address:* 155 Steade Road, Sharrow, Sheffield S7 1DT. *T:* Sheffield 580043. *Club:* Carlton Working Men's (Gleadless, Sheffield).

BOWER, Norman; *b* 18 May 1907. *Educ:* Rugby; Wadham Coll., Oxford. Called to Bar, Inner Temple, 1935; contested West Bermondsey, 1931, North Hammersmith, 1935; MP (C) Harrow West, 1941–51; Member Westminster City Council, 1937–45. *Recreations:* golf, cricket, theatre. *Club:* Carlton.

BOWER, Lt-Gen. Sir Roger (Herbert), KCB 1959 (CB 1950); KBE 1957 (CBE 1944); *b* 13 Feb. 1903; *s* of Herbert Morris Bower and Eileen Francis Fitzgerald Bower, Ripon; *m* 1939, Hon. Catherine Muriel Hotham, *d* of late Capt. H. E. Hotham, and *y sister* of 7th Baron Hotham, CBE; (one adopted *s*) one *d* (and one *s* decd). *Educ:* Repton; RMC, Sandhurst. Served in India with KOYLI, 1923–30; Staff Coll., Camberley, 1935–36; Bde Major, Hong Kong, 1937–38. Served War of 1939–45; NW Europe with HQ Airborne Corps, 1944; Comd Air Landing Bdes: 1, Norway, 1945, 6, Palestine, 1945–46 (despatches); Comd Hamburg District, 1948–49, with rank of Maj.-Gen.; Director Land/Air Warfare, War Office, 1950–51; Director of Military Training and Director of Land/Air Warfare, 1951–52; Commander East Anglian District, 1952–55; Chief of Staff, Allied Forces, Northern Europe, 1955–56; GOC and Director of Operations, Malaya, 1956–57; Commander-in-Chief, Middle East Land Forces, 1958–60, retired. Col The KOYLI, 1960–66. Treasurer to HRH Princess Margaret, Nov. 1960–Feb. 1962; Lieut HM Tower of London, 1960–63. US Bronze Star, 1944; King Haakon VII Liberty Cross, 1945. *Recreations:* sailing, shooting, fishing. *Address:* Ash House, St Mary Bourne, Andover, Hants. *T:* St Mary Bourne 263. *Clubs:* Army and Navy, Royal Cruising.

BOWER, Stephen Ernest D.; *see* Dykes Bower.

BOWERING, Christine, MA; Headmistress, Nottingham High School for Girls (GPDST), since 1984; *b* 30 June 1936; *d* of Kenneth Soper and Florence E. W. Soper; *m* 1960, Rev. John Anthony Bowering; one *s* one *d*. *Educ:* St Bernard's Convent, Westcliff-on-Sea; Newnham Coll., Cambridge (MA). Assistant Teacher: St Bernard's Convent; Ursuline Convent, Brentwood; Sheffield High Sch. (GPDST). *Address:* The Vicarage, 2 Sunderland Street, Tickhill DN11 9QJ. *T:* Doncaster 742224. *Club:* University Women's.

BOWERMAN, David Alexander; retired; *b* 19 April 1903; *s* of Frederick and Millicent Bowerman; *m* 1925, Constance Lilian Hosegood (*d* 1959); four *s* one *d*; *m* 1962, June Patricia Ruth Day. *Educ:* Queen's Coll., Taunton. Farmer, 1923–36; Wholesale Fruit and Potato Merchant (Director), 1936–60. Chairman, Horticultural Marketing Council, 1960–63. Director, 1963–75: Jamaica Producers Marketing Co. Ltd; JP Fruit Distributors Ltd; Horticultural Exports (GB) Ltd. *Recreations:* sailing, golf, gardens. *Address:* The Spinney, Brenchley, Kent. *T:* Brenchley 2149. *Clubs:* Lamberhurst Golf; Isle of Purbeck Golf.

BOWERS, Prof. Fredson Thayer; Linden Kent Professor of English, University of Virginia, USA, 1968–75, now Emeritus; *b* 25 April 1905; *s* of Fredson Eugene Bowers and Hattie May Quigley; *m* 1st, 1924, Hyacinth Sutphen; three *s* one *d*; 2nd, 1942, Nancy Hale. *Educ:* Brown Univ. (PhB); Harvard Univ. (PhD). Instructor in English: Harvard Univ., 1926–36; Princeton Univ., 1936–38; Asst Prof., Univ. of Virginia, 1938–46. USNR, Comdr, 1942–46. Associate Prof., Univ. of Virginia, 1946–48, Prof., 1948–75, Alumni Prof., 1959–68 (Dean of the Faculty, 1968–69). Fulbright Fellow for Research in UK, 1953; Guggenheim Fellow, 1959, 1972; Sandars Reader in Bibliography, Cambridge, 1958; Lyell Reader in Bibliography, Oxford, 1959; Vis. Fellow, All Souls Coll., Oxford, 1972, 1974; Fellow Commoner, Churchill Coll., Cambridge, 1975. Exec. Council, Mod. Lang. Assoc. of Amer., 1964–68 (Pres., S Atlantic MLA, 1969); Pres., Soc. for Textual Scholarship, 1985–87. Corresp. FBA, 1968; Fellow: Amer. Acad. Arts and Scis, 1972; Amer. Antiquarian Soc., 1973. Gold Medal, Bibliographical Soc., 1969; Thomas Jefferson Award, 1971. Editor, Studies in Bibliography, 1948–. Hon. DLitt: Brown, 1970; Clark, 1970; Hon. MA Oxon, 1972; Hon. LHD Chicago, 1973. *Publications:* Elizabethan Revenge Tragedy, 1940; Randolph's Fairy Knight (ed), 1942; Principles of Bibliographical Description, 1949; George Sandys: A Bibliographical Catalogue, 1950; Dramatic Works of Thomas Dekker (ed, 4 vols), 1953–61; On Editing Shakespeare and the Elizabethan Dramatists, 1955; Whitman's Manuscripts, 1955; Textual and Literary Criticism, 1959; Works of Nathaniel Hawthorne (text editor, 11 vols), 1962–74; Bibliography and Textual Criticism, 1964; Dramatic Works in the Beaumont and Fletcher Canon (general ed), 1966–; Works of Stephen Crane (ed), 1969–75; Works of Christopher Marlowe (ed, 2 vols), 1973, rev. edn 1981; (ed) Tom Jones, 1975; Works of William James (text editor), 1975–; Essays in Bibliography, Text and Editing, 1975; (ed) Lectures in Literature by V. Nabokov, 1980; (ed) Lectures in Russian Literature by V. Nabokov, 1981; (ed) Lectures on Don Quixote by V. Nabokov, 1983. *Recreation:* music. *Address:* Woodburn, Box 7, Route #14, Charlottesville, Virginia 22901, USA. *T:* 804–973–3629.

BOWERS, Michael John; Managing Director, TW Oil (UK) Ltd, since 1985; *b* 1 Oct. 1933; *s* of Arthur Patrick and Lena Frances Bowers; *m* 1959, Caroline (*née* Clifford); two *d*. *Educ:* Cardinal Vaughan Sch., Kensington. BP Group: various appts in Supply, Distribution Planning and Trading, 1951–73; Vice-Pres. and Dir, BP North America Inc. (NY), 1973–76; Man. Dir and Chief Exec. Officer, BP Gas, 1976–81; Dir, BP Shipping/BP Exploration, 1980–81; Regional Co-ordinator, Western Hemisphere, 1981–83; Chief Exec., International Petroleum Exchange of London Ltd, 1983–85. *Recreations:* gardening, tennis, bridge, chess. *Address:* Wood End, Warren Drive, Kingswood, Surrey KT20 6PZ. *T:* Mogador 832629.

BOWES, Sir Leslie, KCMG 1968; CBE 1943; Chairman, The Pacific Steam Navigation Company, 1960–65, Managing Director, 1952–65 (Deputy Chairman 1959–60); Chairman, Royal Mail Lines Ltd, 1960–65, Managing Director, 1958–65 (Deputy Chairman 1959–60); *b* 18 Nov. 1893; *m* 1st, 1921; two *s* one *d*; 2nd 1950; one *d*. Served European War, RFC and RAF. The Pacific Steam Navigation Company: Manager for Chile, 1921–48; Director and General Manager, 1949–51. Director: Rea Bros Ltd, 1966–84; Ocean Wilsons (Holdings) Ltd, 1966–84. Member: General Purposes Cttee of Shipping Federation, 1958–61; Central Transport Consultative Cttee, 1959–61; Chairman Liverpool Steam Ship Owners' Assoc., 1954; Chairman General Council of British Shipping, 1954; Chairman Liverpool Port Welfare Cttee, 1955–58; Chairman Liverpool Marine Engineers' and Naval Architects Guild, 1955–56; Chairman Govt Cttee of Inquiry into Canals and Inland Waterways, 1956–58; Member General Cttee of Lloyd's Register of Shipping, 1956–65; Director, "Indefatigable" and Nat. Sea Training Sch. for Boys, 1954–58; Chairman Liverpool Chamber of Commerce, 1957–58; Governor, City of Liverpool College of Commerce, 1958–60; President: Institute of Shipping and Forwarding Agents, 1957–58; Vice-President: British Ship Adoption Society, 1968– (Chm. 1958–68); Institute of Transport, 1958–59 (Mem. Council, 1959–; Chairman Shipping Advisory Cttee, 1959–65); Member: Mersey Docks and Harbour Board, 1956–58; Shipping Advisory Council of BTC, 1960–62; Shipping and International Services Cttee of British Railways Board, 1963; Chairman, BNEC Cttee for Exports to Latin America, 1966–67 (Dep. Chm. 1964–66). Member Exec. Cttee: Anglo-Chilean Society, 1960–70 (Vice-Pres., 1970); Anglo-Peruvian Society (Vice-Pres. 1970); Hispanic and Luso-Brazilian Councils, 1960–69 (Vice-Pres. 1969–; Chm. 1963–64 and 1965–66); Anglo-Brazilian Soc.; Member: Cttee of Management, Canning Club; Exec. Cttee, Anglo-Portuguese Society; Vice-Pres., British Mexican Soc., 1974. Liveryman Worshipful Company of Shipwrights (Past Prime Warden). Hon. Citizen of Valparaiso, Chile, 1982. Comdr of Chilean Order of Merit, 1942, Grand Officer, 1952; Comdr, Ecuadorian Order of Merit, 1956; Comdr, Peruvian Order of Merit, 1957, Grand Cross, 1959; Order of Vasco Nuñez de Balboa, 1963; Grand Officer, Orden de Mayo, Argentina, 1964; Grand Cross, Order of San Carlos (Colombia), 1966; Comdr, Cruziero do Sul, Brazil, 1975. *Address:* 7 Chester Row, SW1W 9JF. *T:* 01–730 1523. *Clubs:* Canning, City Livery, Naval and Military.

BOWES LYON, family name of **Earl of Strathmore.**

BOWES LYON, Simon Alexander, FCA; director of insurance and manufacturing companies; Lord-Lieutenant of Hertfordshire, since 1986; *b* 17 June 1932; *s* of Hon. Sir David Bowes Lyon, KCVO, and of Rachel Bowes Lyon (*née* Spender Clay); *m* 1966, Caroline, *d* of Rt Rev. Victor Pike, CB, CBE, and of Dorothea Pike; three *s* one *d*. *Educ:* Eton; Magdalen Coll., Oxford (BA). *Recreations:* botany, gardening, shooting, music. *Address:* St Paul's Walden Bury, Hitchin, Herts. *T:* Whitwell 218. *Clubs:* White's, Brooks's.

BOWETT, Prof. Derek William, CBE 1983; QC 1978; LLD; FBA 1983; Whewell Professor of International Law, Cambridge University, since 1981; a Professorial Fellow of Queens' College, Cambridge; *b* 20 April 1927; *s* of Arnold William Bowett and Marion Wood; *m* 1953, Betty Northall; two *s* one *d*. *Educ:* William Hulme's Sch., Manchester; Downing Coll., Cambridge. MA, LLB, LLD (Cantab), PhD (Manchester). Called to the Bar, Middle Temple, 1953, Hon. Bencher, 1975. Lectr, Law Faculty, Manchester Univ. 1951–59; Legal Officer, United Nations, New York, 1957–59; Lectr, Law Faculty, Cambridge Univ., 1960–76, Reader, 1976–81; Fellow of Queens' Coll., 1960–69, President 1969–82. Gen. Counsel, UNRWA, Beirut, 1966–68. Mem., Royal Commn on Environmental Pollution, 1973–77. *Publications:* Self-defence in International Law, 1958; Law of International Institutions, 1964; United Nations Forces, 1964; Law of the Sea, 1967; Search for Peace, 1972; Legal Régime of Islands in International Law, 1978. *Recreations:* music, cricket, tennis. *Address:* Queens' College, Cambridge. *T:* Cambridge 65511.

BOWEY, Prof. Angela Marilyn, PhD; Professor of Business Administration, Strathclyde Business School, University of Strathclyde, Glasgow, since 1976 (part-time, since 1986); Director, Pay Advice and Research Centre, Glasgow, since 1986; *b* 20 Oct. 1940; *d* of Jack Nicholas Peterson and Kathleen (*née* Griffin); *m* 1st, 1960, Miklos Papp; two *s* one *d*; 2nd, 1965, Gregory Bowey (marr. diss. 1980); one *s* one *d*. *Educ:* Withington Girls Sch., Manchester; Univ. of Manchester (BA Econ, PhD). Technical Asst, Nuclear Power Gp, 1961–62; Asst Lectr, Elizabeth Gaskell Coll. of Educn, 1967–68; Manchester Business School: Res. Associate, 1968–69; Res. Fellow, 1969–72; Lectr, 1972–76. Vis. Professor: Admin. Staff Coll. of India, 1975; Western Australian Inst. of Technology, 1976; Univ. of WA, 1977; Prahran Coll. of Advanced Educn, Australia, 1978; Massey Univ., NZ, 1978. ACAS Arbitrator, 1977–; Dir, Pay and Rewards Res. Centre, 1978–85; Comr, Equal Opportunities Commn, 1980–86; Member: Scottish Econ. Council, 1980–83; Adv. Panel on Police (Scotland), 1983–. Gov., Scottish Police Coll., 1985–. Editor, Management Decision, 1979–82. *Publications:* Job and Pay Comparisons (with Tom Lupton), 1973, 2nd edn 1974; A Guide to Manpower Planning, 1974, 2nd edn 1977; (with Tom Lupton) Wages and Salaries, 1974, 2nd edn 1982; Handbook of Salary and Wage Systems, 1975, 2nd edn 1982; The Sociology of Organisations, 1976; (with Richard Thorpe and Phil Hellier) Payment Systems and Productivity, 1986; articles in Brit. Jl of Indust. Relations, Jl of Management Studies, and Management Decision. *Address:* 9 Grosvenor Crescent, Glasgow G12 9AF. *T:* 041-334 7023.

BOWEY, Olwyn, RA 1975 (ARA 1970); practising artist (painter); *b* 10 Feb. 1936; *o d* of James and Olive Bowey. *Educ:* William Newton Sch., Stockton; West Hartlepool Sch. of Art; Royal Coll. of Art. One-man shows: Zwemmer Gall., 1961; New Grafton Gall., 1969; also exhibited at Leicester Gall., Royal Academy; work purchased through Chantrey Bequest for Tate Gall., Royal Academy, Min. of Works, etc.

BOWICK, David Marshall, CBE 1977; Member, British Railways Board, 1976–80; retired; *b* 30 June 1923; *s* of George Bowick, Corstorphine, Edinburgh; *m* Gladys May (*née* Jeffries); one *d*. *Educ:* Boroughmuir Sch., Edinburgh; Heriot-Watt Coll., Edinburgh. Served with Fleet Air Arm, 1942–46. Movements Supt, Kings Cross, 1962; Planning Officer, British Railways Board Headquarters, 1963; Asst Gen. Man., London Midland Region, BR, 1965; Exec. Dir, Personnel, BRB Headquarters, 1969; Gen. Manager, London Midland Region, BR, 1971; Chief Exec. (Railways), BR, 1971–78; Vice-Chm. (Rail), BRB, 1978–80. Pres., Group of Nine EEC Railways, 1978–80. Mem. Council, Manchester Business Sch. Col RE, T&AVR. FInstM; FREconS; FCIT; FBIM; FRSA. *Recreations:* sailing, swimming, golf, travel, theatre. *Address:* Villa Tuffolina, Shipwreck Promenade, Xemxija, St Paul's Bay, Malta. *Club:* Union (Sliema, Malta).

BOWIE, Rev. (Alexander) Glen, CBE 1984; Principal Chaplain (Church of Scotland and Free Churches), Royal Air Force, 1980–84, retired; *b* 10 May 1928; *s* of Alexander Bowie and Annie (*née* McGhie); *m* 1953, Mary McKillop; two *d*. *Educ:* Stevenston High Sch.; Irvine Royal Acad.; Glasgow Univ. (BSc 1951; Dip Theol 1954); BA Open Univ., 1977. Assistant, Beith High Church, 1952–54; ordained, 1954; entered RAF Chaplains' Br., 1955; served: RAF Padgate, 1955–56; Akrotiri, 1956–59; Stafford, 1959–61; Butzweilerhof, 1961–64; Halton, 1964–67; Akrotiri, 1967–70; RAF Coll., Cranwell, 1970–75; Asst Principal Chaplain, 1975; HQ Germany, 1975–76; HQ Support Comd,

1976–80. QHC 1980–84; Hon. Chaplain, Royal Scottish Corp., 1981–. Editor, Scottish Forces Bulletin, 1985–. *Recreations:* oil painting, travel. *Address:* 16 Weir Road, Hemingford Grey, Huntingdon, Cambs PE18 9EH. *T:* Huntingdon 63269. *Club:* Royal Air Force.

BOWIE, David; international recording artist and performer; film and stage actor; video and film producer; graphic designer; *b* 8 Jan. 1947; *s* of Hayward Stenton Jones and Margaret Mary Burns; *m* (marr. diss.); one *s. Educ:* Stansfield Road Sch., Brixton. Artiste from age of 16; many major recordings, 1970–, and video productions, 1979–; numerous live musical stage performances; guest appearances on television shows. Actor: *films:* The Man who Fell to Earth, 1976; Just a Gigolo, 1978; The Hunger, 1982; Merry Christmas, Mr Lawrence, 1983; Ziggy Stardust and the Spiders from Mars, 1983; Absolute Beginners, 1986; *stage:* The Elephant Man, New York 1980; *television:* Baal, 1982. Recipient of internat. music and entertainment awards. *Recreations:* painting, skiing. *Address:* Suite 2411, 250 West 57th Street, New York, NY 10107, USA.

BOWIE, Rev. Glen; *see* Bowie, Rev. A. G.

BOWIE, Stanley Hay Umphray, DSc; FRS 1975; FEng 1976; FRSE, FIMM; Consultant Geologist; Assistant Director, Chief Geochemist, Institute of Geological Sciences, 1968–77; *b* 24 March 1917; *s* of Dr James Cameron and Mary Bowie; *m* 1948, Helen Elizabeth, *d* of Dr Roy Woodhouse and Florence Elizabeth Pocock; two *s. Educ:* Grammar Sch. and Univ. of Aberdeen (BSc, DSc). Meteorological Office, 1942; commissioned RAF, 1943; HM Geological Survey of Gt Britain: Geologist, Sen. Geologist and Principal Geologist, 1946–55; Chief Geologist, Atomic Energy Div., 1955–67; Chief Consultant Geologist to UKAEA, 1955–77. Visiting Prof. of Applied Geology, Univ. of Strathclyde, 1968–85; Vis. Prof., Imperial Coll., London, 1985–. Chairman: Internat. Mineralogical Assoc., Commn on Ore Microscopy, 1970–78; Royal Soc. Working Party on Envtl Geochem. and Health, 1979–81; DoE Res. Adv. Gp, Radioactive Waste Management, 1984–85; Mem., Radioactive Waste Management Adv. Cttee, 1978–82. Vice-Pres., Geological Soc., 1972–74. FGS 1959; FMSA 1963; FRSE 1970; FIMM 1972 (Pres. 1976–77). Silver Medal, RSA, 1959. *Publications:* (ed jtly) Uranium Prospecting Handbook, 1972; (ed jtly) Mineral Deposits of Europe, Vol. 1: North-West Europe, 1978; (with P. R. Simpson) The Bowie-Simpson System for the Microscopic Determination of Ore Minerals, 1980; (ed jtly) Environmental Geochemistry and Health, 1985; contributions to: Nuclear Geology, 1954; Physical Methods in Determinative Mineralogy, 1967, 2nd edn 1977; Uranium Exploration Geology, 1970; Uranium Exploration Methods, 1973; Recognition and Evaluation of Uraniferous Areas, 1977; Theoretical and Practical Aspects of Uranium Geology, 1979; Nuclear Power Technology, 1983; Applied Environmental Geochemistry, 1983; numerous papers in scientific and technical jls on uranium geology and economics, mineralogy, geophysics and geochemistry. *Recreations:* farming, preservation of rare breeds, gardening, photography. *Address:* Tanyard Farm, Clapton, Crewkerne, Somerset TA18 8PS. *T:* Crewkerne 72093.

BOWKER, Alfred Johnstone, (John), MC 1944; Regional Chairman of Industrial Tribunals, Southampton, since 1978; *b* 9 April 1922; *s* of Alfred Bowker and Isabel Florence (*née* Brett); *m* 1947, Ann, *er d* of late John Christopher Fairweather and Gunhild Fairweather; one *s* one *d. Educ:* Winchester Coll.; Christ Church, Oxford (MA). Served War, Coldstream Guards, 1941–47: Italian Campaign; Captain. Solicitor in private practice, Winchester, 1949–57; Resident Magistrate, Northern Rhodesia, 1957–65; solicitor in private practice, Salisbury, Wilts, 1965–71; Chm. of Indust. Tribunals, Newcastle upon Tyne, 1972–75. Winchester City Councillor, 1954–57. Liveryman, Skinners Co., 1943. Master, Meon Valley Beagles, 1954–56; Jt Master, Hursley Foxhounds, 1968–69 and 1970–71. *Recreations:* hunting, reading history.

BOWKER, Prof. John Westerdale; Fellow and Dean, Trinity College, Cambridge, since 1984; Hon. Canon of Canterbury Cathedral, since 1985; Adjunct Professor of Religion, North Carolina State University, since 1986; *b* 30 July 1935; *s* of Gordon Westerdale Bowker and Marguerite (*née* Burdick); *m* 1963, Margaret Roper; one *s. Educ:* St John's Sch., Leatherhead; Worcester Coll., Oxford (MA); Ripon Hall, Oxford. National Service, RWAFF, N Nigeria, 1953–55. Henry Stephenson Fellow, Sheffield Univ., 1961; Deacon, St Augustine's, Brocco Bank, Sheffield, 1961; Priest and Dean of Chapel, Corpus Christi Coll., Cambridge, 1962; Asst Lectr, 1965, Lectr, 1970, Univ. of Cambridge; Prof. of Religious Studies, Univ. of Lancaster, 1974–85. Lectures: Wilde, Univ. of Oxford, 1972–75; Staley, Rollins Coll., Florida, 1978–79; Public, Univ. of Cardiff, 1984; Riddell, Newcastle Univ., 1985; Boutwood, Univ. of Cambridge, 1985; Harris Meml, Toronto, 1986. Member: Durham Commn on Religious Educn, 1967–70; Root Commn on Marriage and Divorce, 1967–71; Archbps' Commn on Doctrine, 1977–86; Patron, Marriage Research Inst.; Hon. Pres., Stauros; Vice-Pres., Inst. on Religion in an Age of Science, 1980. Editor, Oxford Companion to Religions of the World, 1977–. *Publications:* The Targums and Rabbinic Literature, 1969, 2nd edn 1979; Problems of Suffering in Religions of the World, 1970, 2nd edn 1975; Jesus and the Pharisees, 1973; The Sense of God, 1973; The Religious Imagination and the Sense of God, 1978; Uncle Bolpenny Tries Things Out, 1973; Worlds of Faith, 1983; (ed) Violence and Aggression, 1983. *Recreations:* walking, books, gardening, cooking, painting, poetry. *Address:* 14 Bowers Croft, Cambridge CB1 4RP. *T:* Cambridge 249885. *Club:* Royal Commonwealth Society.

BOWLBY, Sir Anthony Hugh Mostyn, 2nd Bt, *cr* 1923; *b* 13 Jan. 1906; *e s* of Sir Anthony Bowlby, 1st Bt and Maria Bridget (*d* 1957), *d* of Rev. Canon Hon. Hugh W. Mostyn; *S* father, 1929; *m* 1930, Dora Evelyn, *d* of John Charles Allen; two *d. Educ:* Wellington Coll.; New Coll., Oxford. *Heir: b* Edward John Mostyn Bowlby, *qv. Address:* The Old Rectory, Ozleworth, near Wotton-under-Edge, Glos.
See also Sir E. H. P. Brown, J. Dromgoole.

BOWLBY, (Edward) John (Mostyn), CBE 1972; MD; FRCP, FRCPsych, FBPsS; Hon. Consultant Psychiatrist, Tavistock Clinic, London, since 1972; *b* 26 Feb. 1907; 2nd *s* of late Sir Anthony A. Bowlby, 1st Bt (Pres. Roy. Coll. of Surgeons, 1920–23), and late Maria Bridget, *d* of Rev. Canon Hon. Hugh W. Mostyn; *heir-pres.* to *b* Sir Anthony Hugh Mostyn Bowlby, 2nd Bt, *qv*; *m* 1938, Ursula, 3rd *d* of late Dr T. G. Longstaff (Pres. Alpine Club, 1947–49) and Mrs D. H. Longstaff, JP; two *s* two *d. Educ:* RNC Dartmouth; Trinity Coll., Cambridge (MA Nat. Scis); UCH (MD). FRCP 1964; FRCPsych (Foundation Fellow) 1971, Hon. Fellow 1980; FBPsS 1945; Mem., Brit. PsychoAnalyt. Soc. Staff Psych., London Child Guidance Clinic, 1937–40; Consultant Psychiatrist: RAMC, 1940–45 (Temp. Lt-Col, 1944–45); Tavistock Clinic, 1946–72 (Chm., Dept for Children and Parents, 1946–68); pt-time Mem., ext. scientific staff, MRC, 1963–72. Consultant: in mental health, WHO, 1950–; Nat. Inst. of Mental Health, Bethesda, Md, 1958–63. Fellow, Center for Advanced Studies in Behavioral Sciences, Stanford, Calif, 1957–58; Vis. Prof. in Psych., Stanford Univ., Calif, 1968; H. B. Williams Trav. Prof., Aust. and NZ Coll. of Psychiatrists, 1973; Freud Meml Vis. Prof., UCL, 1980. Pres., Internat. Assoc. for Child Psych. and Allied Professions, 1962–66; Foreign Hon. Mem., Amer. Acad. of Arts and Sciences, 1981–. Hon. DLitt Leicester, 1971; Hon. ScD Cambridge, 1977. Sir James Spence Medal, Brit. Paediatric Assoc., 1974; G. Stanley Hall Medal, Amer. Psychol Assoc., 1974; Distinguished Scientific Contrib. Award, Soc. for Res. in Child Develt. 1981; Salmon Medal, NY Acad. of Medicine, 1984. *Publications:* Personal Aggressiveness and War (with E. F. M. Durbin), 1938; Forty-four Juvenile Thieves, 1946; Maternal Care and Mental Health, 1951 (12 trans); Child Care and the Growth of Love, 1953 (2nd edn 1963); Attachment and Loss (6 trans): Vol. 1, Attachment, 1969, 2nd edn 1982; Vol. 2, Separation: anxiety and anger, 1973; Vol. 3, Loss: sadness and depression, 1980; The Making and Breaking of Affectional Bonds, 1979; papers in Brit. and US jls of psych., psychol. and psychoanalysis. *Recreations:* natural history and outdoor activities. *Address:* Wyldes Close Corner, Hampstead Way, NW11 7JB.

BOWLBY, Hon. Mrs Geoffrey, CVO 1937; Extra Woman of the Bedchamber to Queen Elizabeth, the Queen Mother; 4th *d* of 11th Viscount Valentia, Bletchington Park, Oxford; *m* 1911, Capt. Geoffrey Vaux Salvin Bowlby, Royal Horse Guards (killed in action, 1915); one *s* one *d.* Commandant of Auxiliary Hospital, 1916–19 (despatches twice); a Lady-in-Waiting to Duchess of York, 1932; Woman of the Bedchamber to the Queen, 1937–45. *Address:* c/o The Countess of Meath, Kilruddery, Bray, Co. Wicklow.
See also Earl of Meath.

BOWLBY, John; *see* Bowlby, E. J. M.

BOWLBY, Rt. Rev. Ronald Oliver; *see* Southwark, Bishop of.

BOWLER, Geoffrey, FCIS; Chief General Manager, Sun Alliance & London Insurance Group, since 1977; *b* 11 July 1924; *s* of James Henry Bowler and Hilda May Bowler. *Educ:* Sloane Sch., Chelsea. FCIS 1952. Dir, British Aviation Insurance Co., 1976– (Chm., 1977–83). Dep. Chm., British Insurance Assoc., 1977, Chm. 1979–80. *Address:* 13 Green Lane, Purley, Surrey. *T:* 01–660 0756.

BOWLER, Ian John, CBE 1971 (OBE 1957); President, Iranian Management & Engineering Group Ltd, since 1965; Chairman: International Management & Engineering Group Ltd, since 1973 (Managing Director, 1964–68); Wilmeg, Tehran, since 1979; Electron (USA), since 1983; *b* 1920; *s* of Major John Arthur Bowler; *m* 1963, Hamideh, *d* of Prince Yadollah Azodi, GCMG; two *d,* and one step *s* one step *d. Educ:* King's Sch., Worcester; privately; Oxford Univ. Director of Constructors, John Brown, 1961–64. Director: Trading & Processes Ltd, 1967–; IMEG (Offshore) Ltd, 1974–. Mem., RNLI, 1983–. MInstPet. *Publication:* Predator Birds of Iran, 1973. *Recreations:* ornithology, yachting. *Address:* 6 rue Bonaparte, 75006 Paris, France; 28 Mallord Street, SW3. *T:* 01–352 9795. *Clubs:* Royal Thames Yacht, Ocean Cruising; S.R.R. (La Rochelle, France).

BOWLES, Dame Ann P.; *see* Parker Bowles.

BOWLES, Rt. Rev. Cyril William Johnston; *see* Derby, Bishop of.

BOWLES, Peter; actor; *b* 16 Oct. 1936; *s* of Herbert Reginald Bowles and Sarah Jane (*née* Harrison); *m* 1961, Susan Alexandra Bennett; two *s* one *d. Educ:* High Pavement Grammar Sch., Nottingham; RADA (schol.; Kendal Prize 1955). London début in Romeo and Juliet, Old Vic, 1956; *theatre* includes: Happy Haven, Platonov, Royal Court, 1960; Afternoon Men, Arts, 1961; Absent Friends, Garrick, 1975; Dirty Linen, Arts, 1976; Born in the Gardens, Globe, 1980; Some of My Best Friends Are Husbands, nat. tour, 1985; The Entertainer, Shaftesbury, 1986; *films* include: Blow Up, 1966; The Charge of the Light Brigade, 1967; Laughter in the Dark, 1968; A Day in the Death of Joe Egg, 1970; *television series* include: Rumpole of the Bailey, 1976–83; To the Manor Born, 1979–82; Only when I Laugh, 1979–82; The Bounder, 1982–83; The Irish RM, 1983–85; Lytton's Diary, 1984–86 (also co-created series). Comedy Actor of the Year, Pye Awards, 1984; ITV Personality of the Year, Variety Club of GB, 1984. *Recreations:* motoring, physical jerks. *Address:* c/o Michael Whitehall Ltd, 125 Gloucester Road, SW7. *T:* 01–244 8466.

BOWLEY, Martin Richard; QC 1981; a Recorder of the Crown Court, since 1979; *b* 29 Dec. 1936; *s* of late Charles Colin Stuart Bowley and Mary Evelyn Bowley. *Educ:* Magdalen Coll. Sch., Oxford; Queen's Coll., Oxford (Styring Exhibnr, 1955; MA; BCL 1961). National Service, 1955–57: commnd Pilot Officer as a Fighter Controller; served 2nd Tactical Air Force, 1956–57. Called to the Bar, Inner Temple, 1962; Midland and Oxford Circuit; Mem., Senate and Bar Council, 1985–. Chm., Questors Theatre, 1972–84 (Sec., 1963–72); Mem. Standing Cttee, Little Theatre Guild of GB, 1974–84 (Vice-Chm., 1979–81, Chm., 1981–84). *Recreations:* playing at theatre, watching cricket, island hopping. *Address:* Flat E, 23/24 Great James Street, WC1N 3EL. *T:* 01–405 0834; 1 King's Bench Walk, Temple, EC4Y 7DB. *T:* 01–353 8436. *Clubs:* MCC, Questors.

BOWMAN; *see* Kellett-Bowman.

BOWMAN, (Edwin) Geoffrey; Parliamentary Counsel, since 1984; *b* Blackpool, Lancs, 27 Jan. 1946; *er s* of John Edwin Bowman and Lillian Joan Bowman (*née* Nield); *m* 1969, Carol Margaret, *er d* of late Alexander Ogilvie and of Ethel Ogilvie; two *s* one *d. Educ:* Roundhay Sch., Leeds; Trinity Coll., Cambridge (Senior Scholar; MA, LLM). Called to Bar, Lincoln's Inn (Cassel Scholar), 1968; in practice, Chancery Bar, 1969–71; joined Parliamentary Counsel Office, 1971 (with Law Commission, 1977–79); Dep. Parly Counsel, 1981–84. *Publication:* The Elements of Conveyancing (with E. L. G. Tyler), 1972. *Recreations:* music (bassoon), English medieval history. *Address:* 16 Woodberry Avenue, North Harrow, Mddx. *T:* 01–427 4499. *Clubs:* Les Amis du Basson Français (Paris); International Double Reed Society.

BOWMAN, Eric Joseph; Consultant to Property Services Agency, Department of the Environment, since 1986; *b* 1 June 1929; *s* of late Joseph John Bowman and Lilley Bowman; *m* 1951, Esther Kay; one *d. Educ:* Stationers' Company's School; College of Estate Management. FRICS. Private practice, 1945–51; Royal Engineers, 1951–53; private practice, 1953–54; Min. of Works, 1954–63; Min. of Housing and Local Govt, 1963–73; Directorate of Diplomatic and Post Office Services, MPBW, later DoE, 1973–80; Directorate of Quantity Surveying Services, DoE, 1980–83; Dir of Building and Quantity Surveying Services, PSA, DoE, 1983–86. *Recreations:* fly fishing, walking, swimming, gardening, reading. *Address:* Bracken Lodge, Coulsdon Lane, Chipstead, Surrey CR3 3QL. *T:* Downland 51781.

BOWMAN, Geoffrey; *see* Bowman, E. G.

BOWMAN, Sir George, 2nd Bt *cr* 1961, of Killingworth, Northumberland; *b* 2 July 1923; *s* of Sir James Bowman, 1st Bt, KBE, and of Jean, *d* of Henry Brook, Ashington, Northumberland; *S* father, 1978; *m* 1960, Olive (*née* Case); three *d. Heir:* none. *Address:* Parkside, Killingworth Drive, Newcastle upon Tyne NE12 0ES.

BOWMAN, James Thomas; counter-tenor; Teacher of Voice, Guildhall School of Music, since 1983; *b* Oxford, 6 Nov. 1941; *s* of Benjamin and Cecilia Bowman. *Educ:* Ely Cathedral Choir Sch.; King's Sch., Ely; New Coll., Oxford. MA (History) 1967; DipEd 1964. Schoolmaster, 1965–67. Many concert performances with Early Music Consort, 1967–76; operatic performances with: English Opera Gp, 1967; Sadler's Wells Opera, 1970–; Glyndebourne Festival Opera, 1970–; Royal Opera, Covent Gdn, 1972; Sydney Opera, Australia, 1978; Opéra Comique, Paris, 1979; Le Châtelet, Paris, 1982; Geneva, 1983; Scottish Opera, 1985; Badisches Staatsteater, Karlsruhe, 1984; in USA at Santa Fe and Wolf Trap Festivals, Dallas and San Francisco Operas; at Aix-en-Provence Fest., 1979; operatic roles include: Oberon, in A Midsummer Night's Dream; Endymion, in La Calisto; the Priest, in Taverner; Polinesso, in Ariodante; Apollo, in Death in Venice; Astron, in Ice Break; Ruggiero in Alcina; title rôles: Gulio Cesare; Tamerlano; Xerxes; Scipione; Giustino; Orlando. Has made recordings of oratorio and Medieval and Renaissance vocal music. Lay Vicar, Westminster Abbey, 1969. *Recreations:* ecclesiastical architecture; collecting records. *Address:* 19a Wetherby Gardens, SW5 0JP.

BOWMAN, Jeffery Haverstock, FCA; Senior Partner, Price Waterhouse, since 1982; *b* 3 April 1935; *s* of Alfred Haverstock Bowman and Doris Gertrude Bowman; *m* 1963, Susan Claudia Bostock; one *s* two *d. Educ:* Winchester Coll. (schol.); Trinity Hall, Cambridge (major schol.; BA Hons 1st cl. in Law). Served RHG, 1953–55 (commnd. 1954). Price Waterhouse: articled in London, 1958; NY, 1963–64; admitted to partnership, 1966; Mem., Policy Cttee, 1972–; Dir of Tech. Services, 1973–76; Dir, London Office, 1979–81. Auditor, Duchy of Cornwall, 1971–. Vice-Pres., Union of Indep. Cos, 1983–; Member: Accounting Standards Cttee, 1982–; Council, Industrial Soc., 1985–; Governing council, Business in the Community, 1985–; Gov., Brentwood Sch., 1985–. *Recreations:* golf, opera, gardening, sailing. *Address:* The Old Rectory, Boreham, Chelmsford, Essex. *T:* Chelmsford 467233. *Club:* Garrick.

BOWMAN, Dr John Christopher, CBE 1986; PhD; FIBiol; Secretary, Natural Environment Research Council, since 1981; *b* 13 Aug. 1933; *s* of M. C. Bowman and C. V. Simister; *m* 1961, S. J. Lorimer; three *d. Educ:* Manchester Grammar Sch.; Univ. of Reading (BSc); Univ. of Edinburgh (PhD). Geneticist, later Chief Geneticist, Thornbers, Mytholmroyd, Yorks, 1958–66. Post-doctoral Fellow, North Carolina State Univ., Raleigh, NC, USA, 1964–65; University of Reading: Prof. of Animal Production, 1966–81; Head of Dept of Agric., 1967–71; Dir, Univ. Farms, 1967–78; Dir, Centre for Agricl Strategy, 1975–81. *Publications:* An Introduction to Animal Breeding, 1974; Animals for Man, 1977; (with P. Susmel) The Future of Beef Production in the European Community, 1979; (jtly) Hammond's Farm Animals, 1983. *Recreations:* golf, tennis, gardening. *Address:* Farm House, Sonning, Reading, Berks RG4 0TH. *T:* (office) Swindon 40101.

BOWMAN, Maj-Gen. John Francis, CB 1986; Director of Army Legal Services, since 1984; *b* 5 Feb. 1927; *s* of Frank and Gladys Bowman; *m* 1956, Laura Moore; one *s* one *d. Educ:* Queen Elizabeth Grammar Sch., Penrith; Hertford Coll., Oxford (MA). Called to the Bar, Gray's Inn, 1955. Served RN, 1945–48. Journalist and barrister, 1951–56; Directorate of Army Legal Services, 1956–. Chairman: Army Boxing Assoc., 1985–86 (Life Vice-Pres.).; Combined Services Boxing Assoc., 1985. *Recreations:* sailing, skiing, mountain walking. *Address:* c/o Midland Bank, Sloane Square Branch, 145 Sloane Street, SW1X 9BN. *Clubs:* Special Forces, Ski Club of GB; Cruising Association, Army Sailing Association, Army Ski Association.

BOWMAN, Sir John Paget, 4th Bt, *cr* 1884; *b* 12 Feb. 1904; *s* of Rev. Sir Paget Mervyn Bowman, 3rd Bt, and Rachel Katherine (*d* 1936), *d* of late James Hanning, Kilcrone, Co. Cork; *S* father 1955; *m* 1st, 1931, Countess Cajetana Hoyos (*d* 1948), *d* of Count Edgar Hoyos, Schloss Soos, Lower Austria; one *d* (one *s* decd); 2nd, 1948, Frances Edith Marian, *d* of Sir Beethom Whitehead, KCMG (*d* 1928), Efford Park, Lymington. *Educ:* Eton. Formerly 2nd Lieut 98th (Surrey and Sussex Yeomanry) Field Brigade RA. *Heir: cousin* Paul Humphrey Armytage Bowman [*b* 10 Aug. 1921; *m* 1st, 1943, Felicité Anne Araminta MacMichael (marr. diss.); 2nd, 1947, Gabrielle May Currie (marr. diss.); one *d*; 3rd, 1974, Elizabeth Deirdre Churchill]. *Address:* Bishops Green House, Newbury, Berks.

BOWMAN, (Thomas) Patrick; Chairman: PA Management Consultants Ltd, 1966–75; PA International Management Consultants, 1971–75; *b* 25 Sept. 1915; *s* of late Thomas Marshall Bowman and Louisa Hetherington Macfarlane; *m* 1950, Norma Elizabeth Deravin; one *s. Educ:* Oundle Sch.; Hertford Coll., Oxford. Joined Industrial Engineering Div. of Thomas Hedley & Co. (now Proctor & Gamble Ltd), 1937; P A Management Consultants Ltd, 1945 (Dir, 1955; Managing Dir, 1961). Director: London Guardian, 1979–83; Morgan Communications, 1983–85. Member: Monopolies Commn, 1969–72; Council, CBI, 1970–74. Chairman, UK Management Consultants Assoc., 1966, 1974; Founder Member and Fellow of Inst. of Management Consultants; Pres., European Fedn of Management Consultants, 1967–69. Chm., Wimbledon and Putney Conservators Bd, 1976–83; Governor, Sundridge Park Management Centre, 1961–75. FBIM 1959. *Address:* 9 Clement Road, Wimbledon, SW19 7RJ. *T:* 01–946 3828. *Club:* Royal Thames Yacht.

BOWMAN-SHAW, Sir (George) Neville, Kt 1984; Chairman: Lancer Boss Group Ltd, since 1966; Steinbock GmbH, since 1983; Lancer Boss Rentals Ltd, since 1971; Lancer Boss France SA, since 1967; Lancer Boss Fördergeräte Vertriebsgesellschaft, mbH (Austria), since 1966; Lancer Boss Ireland Ltd, since 1966; Lancer Boss Ltd, since 1967; Boss Trucks & Equipment, since 1959; Lancer Boss International SA Lausanne (formerly BS Exports SA Geneva), since 1962; Boss Engineers Ltd, since 1961; Potters Ltd, since 1979; *b* 4 Oct. 1930; *s* of George Bowman-Shaw and Hazel Bowman-Shaw (*née* Smyth); *m* 1962, Georgina Mary Blundell; three *s* one *d. Educ:* Caldicott Preparatory Sch.; then private tutor. Farming Trainee, 1947; Management Trainee in Engineering Co., 1948. Commissioned in 5th Royal Inniskilling Dragoon Guards, 1950. Sales Manager: Matling Ltd, Wolverhampton, 1953; Materials Handling Equipment (GB) Ltd, London, and Matbro Ltd, London, 1955. Member: Development Commn, 1970–77; Design Council, 1979–84; BOTB, 1982–. President: Bedfordshire Rural Community Council; SW Beds and N Luton Conservative Assocs. Governor, Hawtreys School. *Recreations:* shooting, wildfowl collection. *Address:* Toddington Manor, Toddington, Bedfordshire. *T:* Toddington 2576. *Clubs:* Carlton, St Stephen's Constitutional, Cavalry and Guards, Hurlingham.

BOWMAR, Sir (Charles) Erskine, Kt 1984; QSO 1977; JP; *b* 6 May 1913; *s* of Erskine Bowmar and Agnes Julia (*née* Fletcher); *m* 1938, Kathleen Muriel Isobel McLeod; two *s* four *d. Educ:* Gore Public Sch.; Gore High Sch.; Southland Tech Coll. Member: West Gore Sch. Cttee, 1952–; Bd of Governors, Gore High Sch., 1961–; Exec., NZ Counties Assoc. (former Vice-Pres.); PP, Otago and Southland Counties Assoc.); Nat. Roads Board; Chm., Southland County Council (Mem., 1953–); Chm., Southland United Council, 1979–; Mem., Gore Agricl and Pastoral Assoc., 1940, Life Mem., 1964. Mem., Southland Harbour, 1957–65; Vice-Pres., Southland Progress League; former Mem., NZ Territorial Local Govt Council. JP 1964. *Recreations:* mountaineering (Mem., NZ Alpine Club, 1933), trout fishing, golf, gardening. *Address:* Waikaia Plains Station, N6 Rural Delivery, Gore, Southland, New Zealand. *T:* 101M Balfour.

BOWMONT AND CESSFORD, Marquis of; Charles Robert George Innes-Ker; *b* 18 Feb. 1981; *s* and *heir* of Duke of Roxburghe, *qv.*

BOWN, Jane Hope, (Mrs M. G. Moss), MBE 1985; Photographer for The Observer, since 1950; *b* 13 March 1925; *d* of Charles Wentworth Bell and Daisy Bown; *m* 1954, Martin Grenville Moss, *qv;* two *s* one *d. Educ:* William Gibbs Sch., Faversham. Chart corrector, WRNS, 1944–46; student photographer, Guildford School of Art, 1946–50. Hon. DLitt Bradford, 1986. *Publication:* The Gentle Eye: a book of photographs, 1980;

Women of Consequence, 1986. *Recreations:* restoring old houses; chickens. *Address:* Lasham House, near Alton, Hants. *T:* Herriard 216.

BOWN, Prof. Lalage Jean, OBE 1977; Director, Department of Adult and Continuing Education, University of Glasgow, since 1981; *b* 1 April 1927; *d* of Arthur Mervyn Bown, MC and Dorothy Ethel (*née* Watson); two foster *d. Educ:* Wycombe Abbey Sch.; Cheltenham Ladies' Coll.; Somerville Coll., Oxford (MA); Oxford Post-grad. Internship in Adult Education. Resident Tutor: University Coll. of Gold Coast, 1949–55; Makerere University Coll., Uganda, 1955–59; Asst Dir, then Dep. Dir, Extramural Studies, Univ. of Ibadan, Nigeria, 1960–66; Dir, Extramural Studies and Prof. (*ad personam*), Univ., of Zambia, 1966–70; Prof. of Adult Educn, Ahmadu Bello Univ., Nigeria, 1971–76, Univ. of Lagos, Nigeria, 1977–79; Dean of Educn, Univ. of Lagos, 1979–80; Vis. Fellow, Inst. of Development Studies, 1980–81. Member: Bd, British Council, 1981–; Scottish Community Educn Council, 1982–; Exec. Cttee, Scottish Inst. of Adult and Continuing Educn, 1982–. Governor, Inst. of Develt Studies, 1982–; President: Develt Studies Assoc., 1984–86; British Comparative and Internat. Educn Soc., 1985–86. Hon. Vice-Pres., Townswomen's Guilds, 1984–. Hon. Life Member: People's Educnl Assoc., Ghana, 1973; African Adult Educn Assoc., 1976. DUniv Open, 1975. William Pearson Tolley Medal, Syracuse Univ., USA, 1975; Meritorious Service Award, Nigerian Nat. Council for Adult Educn, 1979. *Publications:* (ed with Michael Crowder) Proceedings of First International Congress of Africanists, 1964; Two Centuries of African English, 1973; (ed) Adult Education in Nigeria: the next 10 years, 1975; A Rusty Person is Worse than Rusty Iron, 1976; Lifelong Learning: prescription for progress, 1979; (ed with S. H. O. Tomori) A Handbook of Adult Education for West Africa, 1980; (ed with J. T. Okedara) An Introduction to Adult Education: a multi-disciplinary and cross-cultural approach for developing countries, 1980; numerous articles in learned jls. *Recreations:* travel, reading, entertaining friends. *Address:* 37 Partickhill Road, Glasgow G11 5BP. *T:* (office) 041–339 8855. *Club:* Royal Over-Seas League.

BOWNESS, Alan, CBE 1976; Director of the Tate Gallery, since 1980; *b* 11 Jan. 1928; *er s* of George Bowness and Kathleen (*née* Benton); *m* 1957, Sarah Hepworth-Nicholson, *d* of Ben Nicholson, OM, and Dame Barbara Hepworth, DBE; one *s* one *d. Educ:* University Coll. Sch.; Downing Coll., Cambridge (Hon. Fellow 1980); Courtauld Inst. of Art, Univ. of London. Worked with Friends' Ambulance Unit and Friends' Service Council, 1946–50; Reg. Art Officer, Arts Council of GB, 1955–57; Courtauld Inst., 1957–79, Dep. Dir, 1978–79; Reader, 1967–78, Prof. of Hist. of Art, 1978–79, Univ. of London. Vis. Prof., Humanities Seminar, Johns Hopkins Univ., Baltimore, 1969. Mem. Internat. Juries: Premio Di Tella, Buenos Aires, 1965; São Paulo Bienal, 1967; Lehmbruck Prize, Duisburg, 1970; Rembrandt Prize, 1979–. Arts Council: Mem., 1973–75 and 1978–80; Mem., Art Panel, 1960–80 (Vice-Chm., 1973–75, Chm., 1978–80); Mem., Arts Film Cttee, 1968–77 (Chm., 1972–75). Member: Fine Arts Cttee, Brit. Council, 1960–69 and 1970– (Chm., 1981–); Exec. Cttee, Contemp. Art Soc., 1961–69 and 1970–; Cultural Adv. Cttee, UK National Commn for UNESCO, 1973–82. Governor, Chelsea Sch. of Art, 1965–; Hon. Sec., Assoc. of Art Historians, 1973–76; Dir, Barbara Hepworth Museum, St Ives, Cornwall, 1976–. Mem. Council, RCA, 1978– (Hon. Fellow 1984). Hon. Fellow, Bristol Polytechnic, 1980. Exhibitions arranged and catalogued include: 54:64 Painting and Sculpture of a Decade (with L. Gowing), 1964; Dubuffet, 1966; Sculpture in Battersea Park, 1966; Van Gogh, 1968; Rodin, 1970; William Scott, 1972; French Symbolist Painters (with G. Lacambre), 1972; Ceri Richards, 1975; Courbet (with M. Laclotte), 1977. Chevalier, l'Ordre des Arts et des Lettres, France, 1973. *Publications:* William Scott Paintings, 1964; Impressionists and Post Impressionists, 1965; Henry Moore: complete sculpture 1955–64, 1965; Modern Sculpture, 1965; Barbara Hepworth Drawings, 1966; Alan Davie, 1967; Recent British Painting, 1968; Gauguin, 1971; Barbara Hepworth: complete sculpture 1960–70, 1971; Modern European Art, 1972; Ivon Hitchens, 1973; (contrib.) Picasso 1881–1973, ed R. Penrose, 1973; (contrib.) The Genius of British Painting, ed D. Piper, 1975; Henry Moore: complete sculpture 1964–73, 1977; Henry Moore: complete sculpture 1974–80, 1983; articles in Burlington Magazine, TLS, Observer, and Annual Register. *Recreations:* listening to music; reading, especially poetry and 19th century fiction. *Address:* 91 Castelnau, SW13 9EL. *T:* 01–748 9696; 16 Piazza, St Ives, Cornwall. *T:* St Ives 5444. *Club:* Athenæum.

BOWNESS, Peter Spencer, CBE 1981; DL; Partner, Horsley, Weightman, Richardson and Sadler, Solicitors, Purley, since 1970; Leader of Croydon Council, since 1976; *b* 19 May 1943; *s* of Hubert Spencer Bowness and Doreen (Peggy) Bowness; *m* 1969, Marianne Hall (marr. diss.); one *d*; *m* 1984, Mrs Patricia Jane Cook. *Educ:* Whitgift Sch., Croydon. Admitted Solicitor, 1966. Elected (C) Croydon Council, 1968; Mayor of Croydon, 1979–80; Chm., London Boroughs Assoc., 1978–; Dep. Chm., Assoc. of Metropolitan Authorities, 1978–80. Member: Audit Commn, 1983–; London Residuary Body, 1985–. DL Greater London, 1981. *Recreations:* travel, theatre. *Address:* 1/2 The Exchange, Purley Road, Purley, Surrey CR2 2YY. *T:* 01–660 6455. *Club:* Carlton.

BOWRING, Edgar Rennie Harvey, MC 1945; Director, Marsh & McLennan Cos Inc., New York, since 1980; Chairman, C. T. Bowring & Co. Ltd, 1973–78; *b* 5 Nov. 1915; *y s* of Arthur Bowring; *m* 1940, Margaret Grace (*née* Brook); two *s* one *d. Educ:* Eastbourne Coll.; Clare Coll., Cambridge (MA); Berkeley Coll., Yale, USA (Mellon Fellow). War of 1939–45: commissioned Kent Yeomanry, RA, 1939; served in Iceland, France and Germany (despatches, 1944); demobilised, 1946. Solicitor, 1949; Partner in Cripps Harries Hall & Co., 1950–55. Member of Lloyd's, 1962. Joined C. T. Bowring & Co. (Insurance) Ltd, 1956 (Dir, 1960); Dep. Chm., 1966, Chief Exec., 1970, Chm., 1973–77, C. T. Bowring (Insurance) Holdings Ltd. Chairman: English & American Insurance Co. Ltd, 1965–71; Crusader Insurance Co. Ltd, 1973–77; Bowmaker Ltd, 1973–77. Pres., Insurance Inst. of London, 1971–72 (Dep. Pres., 1970–71); Vice-Pres., Corporation of Insurance Brokers, 1970–77; Mem., Insurance Brokers Registration Council, 1979–81. Chm., City Cttee for Electoral Reform, 1978–82. Comdt, West Kent Special Constab., 1965–71. CBIM. *Recreations:* gardening, golf. *Address:* Leopards Mill, Horam, Sussex. *T:* Horam Road 2687. *Clubs:* City University; Rye Golf; Piltdown Golf.

BOWRING, Maj.-Gen. John Humphrey Stephen, CB 1968; OBE 1958; MC 1941; FICE; *b* 13 Feb. 1913; *s* of late Major Francis Stephen Bowring and late Mrs Maurice Stonor; *m* 1956, Iona Margaret (*née* Murray); two *s* two *d. Educ:* Downside; RMA Woolwich; Trinity Coll., Cambridge. MA 1936. Commissioned, 1933; Palestine, 1936; India, 1937–40; Middle East, 1940–42; India and Burma, 1942–46; British Military Mission to Greece, 1947–50; UK, 1951–55; CRE, 17 Gurkha Div., Malaya, 1955–58; Col GS, War Office, 1958–61; Brig., Chief Engineer, Far East, 1961–64; Brig. GS, Ministry of Defence, 1964–65; Engineer-in-Chief, 1965–68. Col, The Gurkha Engineers, 1966–71; Col Comdt, RE, 1968–73. Dir, Consolidated Gold Fields, 1969–82. High Sheriff, Wiltshire, 1984. Kt SMO Malta, 1986. *Address:* Lower Swillbrook Farm, Minety, Malmesbury, Wilts. *T:* Malmesbury 860439. *Clubs:* Army and Navy, Royal Ocean Racing.

BOWRING, Air Vice-Marshal John Ivan Roy, CB 1977; CBE 1971; CEng, FRAeS; FBIM; Head of Technical Training and Maintenance, British Aerospace (formerly British Aircraft Corporation), Riyadh, Saudi Arabia, since 1978; *b* 28 March 1923; *s* of Hugh

Passmore Bowring and Ethel Grace Bowring; *m* 1945, Irene Mary Rance; two *d*. *Educ:* Great Yarmouth Grammar Sch., Norfolk; Aircraft Apprentice, RAF Halton-Cosford, 1938–40; Leicester Tech. Coll.; commissioned, RAF, 1944; NW Europe, 1944–47; RAF, Horsham St Faith's, Engrg duties, 1947–48; RAF South Cerney, Pilot trng, 1949; Engr Officer: RAF Finningly, 1950–51; RAF Kai-Tak, 1951–53; Staff Officer, AHQ Hong Kong, ADC to Governor, Hong Kong, 1953–54; Sen. Engr Officer, RAF Coltishall, 1954–56; exchange duties with US Air Force, Research and Develt, Wright Patterson Air Force Base, Ohio, 1956–60; RAF Staff Coll., Bracknell, 1960; Air Min. Opl Requirements, 1961–64; OC Engrg Wing, RAF St Mawgan, 1964–67; Head of F111 Procurement Team, USA, 1967–68; OC RAF Aldergrove, NI, 1968–70; RCDS, 1971; Dir of Engrg Policy, MoD, 1972–73; AO Engrg, RAF Germany, 1973–74; SASO, RAF Support Comd, 1974–77; AO Maintenance, 1977. FBIM. *Recreations:* sailing, golf. *Address:* 2 Burdock Close, Goodworth, Clatford, Andover, Hants. *T:* Andover 66229. *Club:* Royal Air Force.

BOWRING, Peter; Chairman, C. T. Bowring & Co. Ltd, 1978–82; Director, Marsh & McLennan Cos Inc., New York, 1980–85 (Vice-Chairman, 1982–84); *b* 22 April 1923; *e s* of Frederick Clive Bowring and Agnes Walker (*née* Cairns); *m* 1946, Barbara Ekaterina Brewis (marr. diss.); one *s* one *d*. *Educ:* Shrewsbury Sch. Served War, 1939–45: commnd Rifle Bde, 1942; served in Egypt, N Africa, Italy, Austria (mentioned in despatches, 1945); demobilised 1946. Joined Bowring Group of Cos, 1947: Dir, C. T. Bowring & Co. Ltd, 1956–84, Dep. Chm. 1973–78; Chairman: C. T. Bowring Trading (Holdings) Ltd, 1967–84; Bowmaker (Plant) Ltd, 1972–83; Bowring Steamship Co. Ltd, 1974–82; Bowmaker Ltd, 1978–82; C. T. Bowring (UK) Ltd, 1980–84. Dir, City Arts Trust Ltd, 1984–. Mem. of Lloyd's, 1968–. Chm., Help the Aged Ltd, 1977–. Dir, Centre for Policy Studies, 1983–. Chm., Aldeburgh Foundn, 1982–. Chm. Bd of Governors, St Dunstan's Educnl Foundn; Mem. Bd of Governors, Shrewsbury Sch. Member: Guild of Freemen of City of London; Worshipful Co. of Insurers; Guild of World Traders. FRSA. *Recreations:* sailing, motoring, listening to music, cooking. *Address:* Flat 79, New Concordia Wharf, Mill Street, SE1 2BA. *T:* 01-237 0818. *Clubs:* Boodle's, Royal Thames Yacht.

BOWRING, Prof. Richard John; Professor of Modern Japanese Studies, and Fellow of Downing College, University of Cambridge, since 1985; *b* 6 Feb. 1947; *s* of Richard Arthur Bowring and Mabel Bowring (*née* Eddy); *m* 1970, Susan (*née* Povey); one *d* *Educ:* Blundell's Sch.; Downing Coll., Cambridge (PhD 1973). Lectr in Japanese, Monash Univ., 1973–75; Asst Prof. of Japanese, Columbia Univ., NY, 1978–79; Associate Prof. of Japanese, Princeton Univ., NJ, 1979–84; Lectr in Japanese, Univ. of Cambridge, 1984. *Publications:* Mori Ogai and the Modernization of Japanese Culture, 1979; Murasaki Shikibu: her diary and poetic memoirs, 1982. *Address:* Downing College, Cambridge CB2 1DQ.

BOWRON, John Lewis, CBE 1986; solicitor; Secretary-General, The Law Society, 1974–87; *b* 1 Feb. 1924; *e s* of John Henry and Lavinia Bowron; *m* 1950, Patricia, *d* of Arthur Cobby; two *d*. *Educ:* Grangefield Grammar Sch., Stockton-on-Tees; King's Coll., London (LLB, FKC 1976). Principal in Malcolm Wilson & Cobby, Solicitors, Worthing, 1952–74. Member of the Council of the Law Society, 1969–74. *Recreations:* golf, music. *Address:* Wellington Cottage, Albourne, Hassocks, W Sussex. *T:* Hurstpierpoint 833345.

BOWSER of Argaty and the King's Lundies, David Stewart, JP; a Forestry Commissioner, 1974–82; landowner since 1947; *b* 11 March 1926; *s* of late David Charles Bowser, CBE and Maysie Murray Bowser (*née* Henderson); *m* 1951, Judith Crabbe; one *s* four *d*. *Educ:* Harrow; Trinity Coll., Cambridge (BA Agric). Captain, Scots Guards, 1944–47. Member: Nat. Bd of Timber Growers Scotland Ltd (formerly Scottish Woodland Owners' Assoc.), 1960–82 (Chm. 1972–74); Regional Adv. Cttee, West Scotland Conservancy, Forestry Commn, 1964–74 (Chm. 1970–74). Mem., Blackface Sheep Breeders' Assoc. (Vice-Pres., 1981–83; Pres., 1983–84); Pres., Highland Cattle Soc., 1970–72. Trustee, Scottish Forestry Trust, 1983–. Mem. Perth CC, 1954–61; JP Co. Perth, 1956. *Recreations:* shooting, fishing, stalking. *Address:* Auchlyne, Killin, Perthshire.

BOWSHER, Peter Charles, QC 1978; a Recorder of the Crown Court, since 1983; *b* 9 Feb. 1935; *s* of Charles and Ellen Bowsher; *m* 1960, Deborah, *d* of Frederick Wilkins and Isobel Wilkins (*née* Copp), Vancouver; two *s*. *Educ:* Ardingly; Oriel Coll., Oxford (MA). Commnd Royal Artillery, 1954; Territorial Army XX Rifle Team, 1957. Called to the Bar, Middle Temple, 1959, Bencher, 1985. Harmsworth Scholar; Blackstone Entrance Scholar; Blackstone Pupillage Prize. A Legal Assessor to GMC and GDC, 1979–. Indep. Review Body, Modified Colliery Review Procedure, 1986–. *Recreations:* photography, music. *Address:* 10 South Square, Gray's Inn, WC1R 5EU. *T:* 01–242–2902. *Clubs:* Brooks's, Royal Automobile.

BOWTELL, Ann Elizabeth; Deputy Secretary, Department of Health and Social Security, since 1986; *b* 25 April 1938; *d* of John Albert and Olive Rose Kewell; *m* 1961, Michael John Bowtell; two *s* two *d*. *Educ:* Kendrick Girls' Sch., Reading; Girton Coll., Cambridge (BA). Asst Principal, Nat. Assistance Board, 1960; Principal: Nat. Assistance Board, 1964; Min. of Social Security, 1966; DHSS, 1968; Asst Sec., 1973, Under Sec., 1980, DHSS. *Recreations:* children, cooking, walking. *Address:* 26 Sidney Road, Walton-on-Thames, Surrey KT12 2NA. *T:* Walton-on-Thames 229260.

BOWYER, family name of **Baron Denham.**

BOWYER, Gordon Arthur, OBE 1970; RIBA; FSIAD; Partner, Gordon Bowyer & Partners, Chartered Architects, since 1948; *b* 21 March 1923; *s* of Arthur Bowyer and Kathleen Mary Bowyer; *m* 1950, Ursula Meyer; one *s* one *d*. *Educ:* Dauntsey's Sch.; Polytechnic of Central London. Architect and designer in private practice, in partnership with Ursula Bowyer, Iain Langlands and Stephen Batchelor, 1948–. Practice started with design of Sports Section, South Bank Exhibn, Fest. of Britain, 1951; schs and hostel for handicapped children in Peckham, Bermondsey and Dulwich, 1966–75; housing for Southwark, GLC, Family Housing Assoc., London & Quadrant Housing Assoc. and Greenwich Housing Soc., 1969–83; numerous office conversions for IBM (UK), 1969–86; Peckham Methodist Church, 1975; new offices and shops for Rank City Wall at Brighton, 1975 and Folkestone, 1976; Treasury at Gloucester Cathedral, 1976; conservation at Vanbrugh Castle, Greenwich, 1973, Charlton Assembly Rooms, 1980, Hill Hall, Essex, 1982; lecture theatre, library and accommodation, Jt Services Defence Coll., RNC, Greenwich, 1983; Cabinet War Rooms Museum, Whitehall (with Alan Irvine), 1984. At present working on refurbishment of galls at Nat. Gall. and Nat. Portrait Gall., and new Japanese Gall. at BM. Hon. Sec., SIAD, 1957–58. Director: NMM Enterprises Ltd, 1985–; Blackheath Concert Halls, 1985–. Mem. Council, Friends of the Nat. Maritime Mus., 1985–. Trustee, Nat. Maritime Museum, 1977–. *Address:* 111 Maze Hill, SE10 8XQ. *T:* (office) 01–836 1452. *Club:* Arts.

BOWYER, William, RA 1981 (ARA 1974); RP, RBA, RWS; Head of Fine Art, Maidstone College of Art, 1971–82; *b* 25 May 1926; *m* 1951, Vera Mary Small; two *s* one *d*. *Educ:* Burslem School of Art; Royal College of Art (ARCA). Hon. Sec., New English Art Club. *Recreations:* cricket (Chiswick and Old Meadonians Cricket Clubs), snooker. *Address:* 12 Cleveland Avenue, Chiswick, W4 1SN. *T:* 01–994 0346. *Club:* Chelsea Arts.

BOWYER-SMYTH, Sir T. W.; *see* Smyth.

BOX, Betty Evelyn, (Mrs P. E. Rogers), OBE 1958; Film Producer; *b* 25 Sept.; *m* 1949, Peter Edward Rogers; no *c*. *Educ:* home. Director: Welbeck Film Distributors Ltd, 1958–; Ulster Television, 1955–85. *Films include:* Dear Murderer; When the Bough Breaks; Miranda; Blind Goddess; Huggett Family series; It's Not Cricket; Marry Me; Don't Ever Leave Me; So Long at the Fair; Appointment with Venus; Venetian Bird; A Day to Remember; The Clouded Yellow; Doctor in the House; Mad About Men; Doctor at Sea; The Iron Petticoat; Checkpoint; Doctor at Large; Campbell's Kingdom; A Tale of Two Cities; The Wind Cannot Read; The 39 Steps; Upstairs and Downstairs; Conspiracy of Hearts; Doctor in Love; No Love for Johnnie; No, My Darling Daughter; A Pair of Briefs; The Wild and the Willing; Doctor in Distress; Hot Enough for June; The High Bright Sun; Doctor in Clover; Deadlier than the Male; Nobody Runs Forever; Some Girls Do; Doctor in Trouble; Percy; The Love Ban; Percy's Progress. *Address:* Pinewood Studios, Iver, Bucks.

BOX, Donald Stewart; Member, The Stock Exchange and Senior Partner, Lyddon & Co., Stockbrokers; *b* 22 Nov. 1917; *s* of late Stanley Carter Box and Elizabeth Mary Stewart Box; *m* 1st, 1940, Margaret Kennington Bates (marr. diss. 1947); 2nd, 1948, Peggy Farr, *née* Gooding (marr. diss. 1973); 3rd, 1973, Margaret Rose Davies; one *d*. *Educ:* Llandaff Cathedral Sch.; St John's Sch., Pinner; County Sch., Harrow. RAF ranks, 1939, commissioned, 1941; overseas service Egypt, Palestine, Transjordan, 1941–44; demobbed with rank of Flt-Lieut, 1945. MP (C) Cardiff North, 1959–66. *Recreations:* indifferent tennis, studying race form, doodling and doggerel. *Address:* Laburnum Cottage, Sully Road, Penarth, S Glam. *T:* Penarth 707966. *Clubs:* City of London; Cardiff and County (Cardiff).

BOX, Prof. George Edward Pelham, BEM 1946; FRS 1985; Professor of Statistics, since 1960, and Vilas Research Professor, Department of Statistics, since 1980, University of Wisconsin-Madison; *b* 18 Oct. 1919; *s* of Harry and Helen (Martin) Box; *m* 1st, 1945, Jessie Ward; 2nd, 1959, Joan G. Fisher; one *s* one *d*; 3rd, 1985, Claire Louise Quist. *Educ:* London University (BSc Maths and Statistics 1947, PhD 1952, DSc 1961). Served War of 1939–45 in Army; res. at Chemical Defence Exptl Station, Porton. Statistician and Head Statn, Statistical Res. Section, ICI, Blackley, 1948–56; Dir, Stats Tech. Res. Group, Princeton Univ., 1956–60. Res. Prof., Univ. of N Carolina, 1952–53; Ford Foundn Vis. Prof., Harvard Business Sch., 1965–66; Vis. Prof., Univ. of Essex, 1970–71. President: Amer. Statistical Assoc., 1978; Inst. of Mathematical Statistics, 1979. Trustee, Biometrika Trust, 1985–. FAAAS, 1975. Hon. DSc Univ. of Rochester, NY, 1975. Numerous medals and awards. *Publications:* Statistical Methods in Research and Production, 1957; Design and Analysis of Industrial Experiments, 1959; Evolutionary Operation: a statistical method for process improvement, 1969; Time Series Analysis Forecasting and Control, 1970; Bayesian Inference in Statistical Analysis, 1973; Statistics for Experimenters, 1977; Empirical Model Building and Response Surfaces, 1986. *Address:* Department of Statistics, University of Wisconsin-Madison, 1210 West Dayton Street, Madison, Wis 53706, USA. *T:* (608) 262–2937, (608) 263–2658.

BOXALL, Bernard, CBE 1963; Deputy Chairman, Lancer Boss Group Ltd; *b* 17 Aug. 1906; *s* of late Arthur Boxall and of Mrs Maud Mary Boxall (*née* Mills); *m* 1931, Marjorie Lilian, *d* of late William George Emery and Mrs Emery; one *s* one *d*. *Educ:* King's Coll. Sch., Wimbledon; Imperial Coll., London Univ. (BSc (Hons), FCGI), Fellow 1971. James Howden & Co. Ltd, 1928–33; J. A. King & Co. Ltd, 1934–42; Production-Engineering Ltd, 1942–59; Management Consultant, 1959–. Chm., British United Trawlers Ltd, 1969–71. Dir, Lindustries Ltd, and Chm. of its engineering cos, 1960–71. Member: Highland Trnspt Bd, 1963–66; IRC, 1966–71; Scottish Economic Planning Council, 1967–71; Monopolies Commn, 1969–74. Mem., Company of Coachmakers and Coach Harness Makers (Master, 1977–78). FIMechE, FIProdE. *Recreation:* golf. *T:* Cranleigh 274340. *Club:* Walton Heath Golf.

BOXALL, Mrs Lewis; *see* Buss, Barbara Ann.

BOXER, Air Vice-Marshal Sir Alan (Hunter Cachemaille), KCVO 1970; CB 1968; DSO 1944; DFC 1943; *b* 1 Dec. 1916; *s* of late Dr E. A. Boxer, CMG, Hastings, Hawkes Bay, NZ; *m* 1941, Pamela Sword; two *s* one *d*. *Educ:* Nelson Coll., New Zealand. Commissioned in RAF, 1939; Trng Comd until 1942; flying and staff appts, Bomber Comd, 1942–45. RAF Staff Coll., 1945; Jt Staff, Cabinet Offices, 1946–47; Staff Coll., Camberley, 1948; Strategic Air Comd, USAF and Korea, 1949–51; Central Fighter Estabt, 1952–53; Mem. Directing Staff, RAF Staff Coll., 1954–56; CO No 7 Sqdn, RAF, 1957; Group Capt. and CO, RAF Wittering, 1958–59; Plans, HQ Bomber Comd, 1960–61; Air Cdre, idc, 1962; SASO: HQ No 1 Gp, RAF, 1963–65; HQ Bomber Comd, 1965–67; Defence Services Sec., MoD, 1967–70. Virtuti Militari (Polish), Bronze Star (US), Air Medal (US).

BOXER, Charles Ian; writer; *b* 11 Feb. 1926; *s* of Rev. William Neville Gordon Boxer and Margaret Boxer; *m* 1968, Hilary Fabienne Boxer. *Educ:* Glasgow High Sch.; Edinburgh Univ. (BL). Church of England ministry, 1950–54; apprentice to solicitors, 1954–58; Mem., Dominican Order (RC), 1958–67; Sen. Community Relations Officer for Wandsworth, 1967–77; Dir, Community Affairs and Liaison Div., Commn for Racial Equality, 1977–81. Communicator of the Year, BAIE Awards, 1976. *Recreation:* music. *Address:* 56 Alder Row, West Woodlands, Frome, Somerset. *T:* Frome 61510.

BOXER, (Charles) Mark (Edward), ('Marc'); cartoonist; Editor, The Tatler, since 1983; *b* 19 May 1931; *s* of Lt-Col Harold Stephen Boxer and Isobel Victoria Hughlings Jackson; *m* 1st, 1956, Lady Arabella Stuart, 3rd *d* of 18th Earl of Moray, MC (marr. diss. 1982); one *s* one *d*; 2nd, 1982, Anna Ford; two *d*. *Educ:* Berkhamsted Sch.; King's Coll., Cambridge. Editor, Granta, 1952–53; Art Director, Queen, 1957–61; 1st Editor, Sunday Times magazine, 1962–65; Dir, Sunday Times, 1964–66; Editorial Dir, London Life, 1965; Asst Editor, Sunday Times, 1966–79; Dir, Weidenfeld and Nicolson, 1980–83; cartoonist: The Times, 1969–83; Guardian, 1983–86; Daily Telegraph, 1986–; caricaturist for New Statesman, 1970–78, London Review of Books, 1981, etc.; Dir, Condé Nast, 1986–. Cartoonist of the Year, 1972. *Publications:* Trendy Ape, 1968; The Times We Live In, 1978; Marc Time, 1984; illus. publications by Clive James: Felicity Fark, 1975, Britannia Bright, 1976, and Charles Charming, 1981. *Recreations:* bridge, chess. *Address:* c/o The Tatler, Vogue House, Hanover Square, W1. *Clubs:* Groucho, Portland.

BOXER, Prof. Charles Ralph, FBA 1957; Emeritus Professor of Portuguese, University of London, since 1968; Fellow, King's Coll., 1967; *b* 8 March 1904; *s* of Col Hugh Boxer and Jane Boxer (*née* Patterson); *m* 1945, Emily Hahn; two *d*. *Educ:* Wellington Coll.; Royal Military Coll., Sandhurst. Commissioned Lincs Regt, 1923. Served War of 1939–45 (wounded, POW in Japanese hands, 1941–45). Retired with rank of Major, 1947. Camoens Prof. of Portuguese, London Univ., 1947–51; Prof. of the History of the Far East, London Univ., 1951–53; resigned latter post and re-apptd Camoens Prof., 1953–67; Prof. of History of Expansion of Europe Overseas, Yale, 1969–72. Visiting Research Prof.,

Indiana Univ., 1967–79; Emeritus Prof. of History, Yale, 1972–. Hon. Fellow, SOAS, 1974. A Trustee of National Maritime Museum, 1961–68. For. Mem., Royal Netherlands Acad. of Scis, 1976. Dr *hc* Universities of Utrecht (1950), Lisbon (1952), Bahia (1959), Liverpool (1966), Hong Kong (1971), Peradeniya (1980); Order of Santiago da Espada (Portugal); Grand Cross of the Order of the Infante Dom Henrique (Portugal); Kt Order of St Gregory the Great, 1969. *Publications*: The Commentaries of Ruy Freyre de Andrade, 1929; The Journal of M. H. Tromp, *Anno* 1639, 1930; Jan Compagnie in Japan, 1600–1817, 1936 (2nd edn 1950); Fidalgos in the Far East, 1550–1770, 1948; The Christian Century in Japan, 1549–1640, 1951, 2nd edn 1967; Salvador de Sá and the Struggle for Brazil and Angola, 1952; South China in the 16th Century, 1953; The Dutch in Brazil, 1624–1654, 1957; The Tragic History of the Sea, 1589–1622, 1959; The Great Ship from Amacon, 1959; Fort Jesus and the Portuguese in Mombasa, 1960; The Golden Age of Brazil, 1695–1750, 1962; Race Relations in the Portuguese Colonial Empire, 1415–1825, 1963; The Dutch Seaborne Empire, 1600–1800, 1965; Portuguese Society in the Tropics, 1966; Further Selections from the Tragic History of the Sea, 1969; The Portuguese Seaborne Empire, 1415–1825, 1969; Anglo-Dutch Wars of the 17th Century, 1974; Mary and Misogyny, 1975; João de Barros: Portuguese humanist and historian of Asia, 1981; From Lisbon to Goa 1500–1750, 1984; Portuguese Conquest and Commerce in Southern Asia 1500–1750, 1985; numerous articles in learned periodicals. *Address*: Ringshall End, Little Gaddesden, Herts HP4 1NF. *Clubs*: Athenæum; Yale (New York).

BOXER, Air Cdre Henry Everard Crichton, CB 1965; OBE 1948; idc, ndc, psc; *b* 28 July 1914; *s* of late Rear-Adm. Henry P. Boxer; *m* 1938, Enid Anne Louise, *d* of late Dr John Moore Collyns; two *s* two *d*. *Educ*: Shrewsbury Sch.; RAF Coll., Cranwell. Commissioned RAF, 1935; No 1 Fighter Squadron, 1935–37; No 1 Flying Training Sch., 1937–39; Specialist Navigator, 1939. Served War of 1939–45, in UK, S Africa and Europe. BJSM, Washington, DC, 1945–48; directing Staff, RAF Staff Coll., 1949–50; Coastal Command, 1951–52; Nat. Defence Coll., Canada, 1952–53; Air Ministry, 1953–56; OC, RAF Thorney Island, 1956–58. ADC to the Queen, 1957–59; IDC, 1959; Sen. Air Liaison Officer and Air Adviser to British High Comr in Canada, 1960–62; AO i/c Admin, HQ Coastal Comd, 1962–65; Dir of Personnel (Air), MoD (RAF), 1965–67; retd, 1967. Counsellor (Defence Equipment), British High Commn, Ottawa, 1967–74; retd, 1975. *Address*: 43 Daniell's Walk, Lymington, Hants SO41 9PP. *T*: Lymington 72584. *Club*: Royal Air Force.

BOXER, Mark; *see* Boxer, Charles M. E.

BOYCE, Air Vice-Marshal Clayton Descou Clement, CB 1946; CBE 1944; Assistant Controller of Aircraft, Ministry of Supply, 1957–59, retired; *b* 19 Sept. 1907; *er s* of Col C. J. Boyce, CBE, late IA; *m* 1928, Winifred (*d* 1981), *d* of late J. E. Mead, Castletown, Isle of Man; one *s*; *m* 1986, Patricia Fielding. *Educ*: Bedford Sch.; Cranwell. Sec.-Gen., Allied Air Forces, Central Europe, 1953; AOC, Cyprus and Levant, 1954–56. *Address*: c/o Lloyds Bank, Cox's and King's Branch, 6 Pall Mall, SW1.

BOYCE, Guy Gilbert L.; *see* Leighton-Boyce.

BOYCE, Joseph Frederick, JP; FRICS; General Manager, Telford Development Corporation, 1980–86; *b* 10 Aug. 1926; *s* of Frederick Arthur and Rosalie Mary Boyce; *m* 1953, Nina Margaret, *o d* of A. F. Tebb, Leeds; two *s*. *Educ*: Roundhay Sch., Leeds; Leeds Coll. of Technology. Pupil and Asst Quantity Surveyor, Rex Procter & Miller, Chartered Quantity Surveyors, 1942–53; Sen. Quantity Surveyor, Bedford Corp., 1953–55; Group Quantity Surveyor, Somerset CC, 1955–60; Principal Asst Quantity Surveyor, Salop CC, 1960–64; Telford Development Corporation: Chief Quantity Surveyor, 1964–71; Technical Dir, 1971–76; Dep. Gen. Manager, 1976–80. JP Shrewsbury, 1975. *Publications*: technical articles and publications on new towns, in learned journals. *Recreations*: reading, travel, hill walking, France. *Address*: The Uplands, 5 Port Hill Gardens, Shrewsbury, Shropshire SY3 8SH.

BOYCE, Sir Robert (Charles) Leslie, 3rd Bt *cr* 1952; *b* 2 May 1962; *s* of Sir Richard (Leslie) Boyce, 2nd Bt, and of Jacqueline Anne (who *m* 2nd, 1974, Christopher Boyce-Dennis), *o d* of Roland A. Hill; *S* father, 1968; *m* 1985, Fiona, second *d* of John Savage, Whitmore Park, Coventry. *Educ*: Cheltenham Coll; Salford Univ. (BSc 1984, 1st cl. hons). Electrical engineer, employed with Plessey Research. *Heir*: *uncle* John Leslie Boyce [*b* 16 Nov. 1934; *m* 1st, 1957, Finola Mary (marr. diss. 1975). *d* of late James Patrick Maxwell; one *s* three *d*; 2nd, 1980, Fusako, *d* of Yoneseku Ishibashi; two *d*]. *Address*: The Barn House, Ascott Earl, Ascott under Wychwood, Oxon OX7 6AG.

BOYCE, Walter Edwin, OBE 1970; Director of Social Services, Essex County Council, 1970–78; *b* 30 July 1918; *s* of Rev. Joseph Edwin Boyce and Alice Elizabeth Boyce; *m* 1942, Edna Lane (*née* Gargett); two *d*. *Educ*: High Sch. for Boys, Trowbridge, Wilts. Admin. Officer, Warwickshire CC, 1938–49. Served war, commnd RA; Gunnery sc, 1943; demob. rank Major, 1946. Dep. County Welfare Officer: Shropshire, 1949–52; Cheshire, 1952–57; Co. Welfare Officer, Essex, 1957–70. Adviser to Assoc. of County Councils, 1965–78; Mem., Sec. of State's Adv. Personal Social Services Council, 1973 until disbanded, 1980 (Chm., People with handicaps Gp); Mem., nat. working parties on: Health Service collaboration, 1972–74; residential accommodation for elderly and mentally handicapped, 1974–78; boarding houses, 1981. Pres., County Welfare Officers Soc., 1967–68. Governor, Queen Elizabeth's Foundn for the Disabled, 1980–. *Recreations*: sailing, golf, in sports, particularly Rugby and athletics, voluntary services, travel. *Address*: Highlanders Barn, Newmans Green, Long Melford, Suffolk CO10 0AD.

BOYCOTT, Prof. Brian Blundell, FRS 1971; Director, Medical Research Council Cell Biophysics Unit, since 1980; Professor of Biology by title, since 1971; *b* 10 Dec. 1924; *s* of Percy Blundell Boycott and Doris Eyton Lewis; *m* 1950, Marjorie Mabel Burchell; one *s* (and one *s* decd). *Educ*: Royal Masonic Sch. Technician, Nat. Inst. Medical Research, and undergraduate (BSc), Birkbeck Coll., London, 1942–46; University Coll., London: Asst Lectr, Zoology, 1946–47; Hon. Res. Asst, Anatomy, 1947–52; Lectr, Zoology, 1952–62; Reader in Zoology, Univ. of London, 1962, Prof. of Zoology, 1968–70. Vis. Lectr, Harvard Univ., 1963. Member: Adv. Council, British Library Board, 1976–80; Council, Open Univ., 1975–; Council, Royal Soc., 1976–78; Univ. of London Cttee on Academic Organization, 1980–82; Comr, 1851 Exhibition, 1974–84. Scientific medal, Zoological Soc. London, 1965. *Publications*: various articles in learned jls on structure and function of nervous systems. *Recreations*: nothing of special notability. *Address*: c/o Department of Biophysics, King's College, 26–29 Drury Lane, WC2. *T*: 01–836 8851.

BOYCOTT, Geoffrey; cricketer; *b* 21 Oct. 1940; *s* of late Thomas William Boycott and Jane Boycott. *Educ*: Kinsley Modern Sch.; Hemsworth Grammar Sch. Played cricket for Yorkshire, 1962–86, received County Cap, 1963, Captain of Yorkshire, 1970–78. Played for England, 1964–74, 1977–82; scored 100th first-class hundred, England v Australia, 1977, 150th hundred, 1986; passed former world record no of runs scored in Test Matches, Delhi, Dec. 1981. Mem., General Cttee, Yorks CCC, 1984–. *Publications*: Geoff Boycott's Book for Young Cricketers, 1976; Put to the Test: England in Australia 1978–79, 1979; Geoff Boycott's Cricket Quiz, 1979; On Batting, 1980; Opening Up, 1980; In the Fast Lane, 1981; Master Class, 1982. *Recreations*: golf, tennis. *Address*: c/o Yorkshire County Cricket Club, Headingley Cricket Ground, Leeds, Yorks LS6 3BY.

BOYD, family name of **Baron Kilmarnock.**

BOYD OF MERTON, 2nd Viscount *cr* 1960, of Merton-in-Penninghame, Co. Wigtown; **Simon Donald Rupert Neville Lennox-Boyd;** Deputy Chairman, Arthur Guinness & Sons plc, 1981–86; *b* 7 Dec. 1939; *e s* of 1st Viscount Boyd of Merton, CH, PC, and of Lady Patricia Guinness, *d* of 2nd Earl of Iveagh, KG, CB, CMG, FRS; *S* father, 1983; *m* 1962, Alice Mary, *d* of late Major M. G. D. Clive and of Lady Mary Clive; two *s* two *d*. *Educ*: Eton; Christ Church, Oxford. Vice-Chm., Save the Children, 1979–82. Chm., Scottish Licensed Trade Assoc., 1983–84, Patron, 1985–; Pres. Council, British Exec. Service Overseas, 1985–. Trustee, Guinness Trust, 1974–. *Heir*: *s* Hon. Benjamin Alan Lennox-Boyd, *b* 21 Oct. 1964. *Address*: Wivelscombe, Saltash, Cornwall PL12 4QY. *T*: Saltash 2672; 9 Warwick Square, SW1V 2AA. *T*: 01–821 1618. *Clubs*: White's; Royal Yacht Squadron.

BOYD, Sir Alexander Walter, 3rd Bt, *cr* 1916; *b* 16 June 1934; *s* of late Cecil Anderson Boyd, MC, MD, and Marjorie Catharine, *e d* of late Francis Kinloch, JP, Shipka Lodge, North Berwick; *S* uncle, 1948; *m* 1958, Molly Madeline, *d* of late Ernest Arthur Rendell; two *s* three *d*. *Heir*: *s* Ian Walter Rendell Boyd, *b* 14 March 1964. *Address*: Box 261, Whistler, BC, Canada.

BOYD, Arthur Merric Bloomfield, AO 1979; OBE 1970; painter; *b* 24 July 1920; *s* of William Merric Boyd and Doris Lucy Eleanor Gough; *m* 1945, Yvonne Hartland Lennie; one *s* two *d*. *Educ*: State Sch., Murrumbeena, Vic, Australia. Was taught painting and sculpture by parents and grandfather, Arthur Merric Boyd; served in Australian Army, 1940–43. Exhibited first in Australia, 1937–59; has lived in Europe and Australia since 1959; first one-man exhibn painting, London, 1960; designed for Ballet at Edinburgh Festival and Sadler's Wells Theatre, 1961, and at Covent Garden Royal Opera House, 1963. *Relevant publications*: Arthur Boyd, by Franz Philipp, 1967; Arthur Boyd Drawings, by Christopher Tadgell, 1973; Artist and River, by Sandra McGrath, 1983; Arthur Boyd—Seven Persistent Images, by Grazia Gunn, 1985; The Art of Arthur Boyd, by Ursula Hoff, 1986. *Address*: c/o Westpac Banking Corporation, Walbrook House, Walbrook, EC4.

BOYD, Atarah, (Mrs Douglas Boyd); *see* Ben-Tovim, A.

BOYD, Christopher; *see* Boyd, T. C.

BOYD, David John; QC 1982; *b* 11 Feb. 1935; *s* of David Boyd and Ellen Jane Boyd (*née* Gruer); *m* 1960, Raija Sinikka Lindholm, Finland; one *s* one *d*. *Educ*: Eastbourne Coll.; St George's Sch., Newport, USA (British-Amer. schoolboy schol.); Gonville and Caius Coll., Cambridge (MA). FCIArb 1979. Various secretarial posts, ICI, 1957–62; Legal Asst, Pfizer, 1962–66; called to the Bar, Gray's Inn, 1963; Sec. and Legal Officer, Henry Wiggin & Co., 1966; Asst Sec. and Sen. Legal Officer (UK), Internat. Nickel, 1968; Dir, Impala Platinum, 1972–78; Sec. and Chief Legal Officer, 1972–86, and Dir, 1984–86, Inco Europe. Gen. Comr of Income Tax, 1978–83. Chm., Bar Assoc. for Commerce, Finance and Industry, 1980–81; Mem., Senate of Inns of Court and Bar, 1978–81. Sec. Gen., Assoc. des Juristes d'Entreprise Européens (European Company Lawyers Assoc.), 1983–84. Legal Advisor to Review Bd for Govt Contracts, 1984–. *Recreations*: theatre-going, holidaying in France. *Address*: 123A Ashley Gardens, Thirleby Road, SW1. *T*: 01–834 1160; Beeches, Upton Bishop, Ross-on-Wye, Herefordshire. *T*: Upton Bishop 214.

BOYD, Dennis Galt; Chief Conciliation Officer, Advisory, Conciliation and Arbitration Service, since 1980; *b* 3 Feb. 1931; *s* of late Thomas Ayre Boyd and Minnie (*née* Galt); *m* 1953, Pamela Mary McLean; one *s* one *d*. *Educ*: South Shields High School for Boys. National Service, 1949–51; Executive Officer, Civil Service: Min. of Supply/Min. of Defence, 1951–66; Board of Trade, 1966–69; Personnel Officer, Forestry Commission, 1969–75; Director of Corporate Services Health and Safety Executive, Dept of Employment, 1975–79; Director of Conciliation (ACAS), 1979–80. Hon. FIPM 1985. *Recreations*: golf, compulsory gardening. *Address*: Dunelm, Silchester Road, Little London, near Basingstoke. *Club*: Civil Service.

BOYD, Sir Francis; *see* Boyd, Sir J. F.

BOYD, Gavin, CBE 1977; Consultant, Boyds, solicitors, since 1978; Chairman, Scottish Opera Theatre Royal Ltd, since 1973; *b* 4 Aug. 1928; *s* of Gavin and Margaret Boyd; *m* 1954, Kathleen Elizabeth Skinner; one *s*. *Educ*: Glasgow Acad.; Univ. of Glasgow. MA (Hons); LLB. Partner, Boyds, solicitors, Glasgow, 1955–77. Director: Stenhouse Holdings Ltd, 1970–79 (Chm., 1971–78); Scottish Opera, 1970–; North Sea Assets plc, 1972– (Dep. Chm., 1981–); Paterson Jenks plc, 1972–81; Scottish Television plc, 1973–; Ferranti plc, 1975–; British Carpets plc, 1977–81; Merchant House of Glasgow, 1982–. Trustee, Scottish Hosps Endowment Res. Trust, 1978. Chm., Court, Univ. of Strathclyde, 1983– (Convener, Finance Cttee, 1979–83); Mem., Law Soc. of Scotland. Hon. LLD Strathclyde, 1982. *Recreations*: music and the performing arts, particularly opera; hill walking. *Address*: 4A Prince Albert Road, Glasgow G12 9JX. *Club*: Glasgow Art.

BOYD, Ian Robertson; HM Stipendiary Magistrate, West Yorkshire, since 1982; a Recorder of the Crown Court, since 1983; *b* 18 Oct. 1922; *s* of Arthur Robertson Boyd, Edinburgh, and Florence May Boyd (*née* Kinghorn), Leeds; *m* 1952, Joyce Mary Boyd (*née* Crabtree); one *s* one *d*. *Educ*: Roundhay Sch.; Leeds Univ. (LLB (Hons)). Served Army, 1942–47: Captain Green Howards; Royal Lincolnshire Regt in India, Burma, Malaya, Dutch East Indies. Leeds Univ., 1947; called to Bar, Middle Temple, 1952; practised North Eastern Circuit, 1952–72; HM Stipendiary Magistrate, sitting at Hull, 1972–82. Sometime Asst/Dep. Recorder of Doncaster, Newcastle, Hull and York. *Recreation*: gardener manqué. *Address*: The Town Hall, Leeds LS1 1UR.

BOYD, James Edward, CA; Director and Financial Adviser, Denholm group of companies, since 1968; *b* 14 Sept. 1928; *s* of Robert Edward Boyd and Elizabeth Reid Sinclair; *m* 1956, Judy Ann Christey Scott; two *s* two *d*. *Educ*: Kelvinside Academy; The Leys Sch., Cambridge. CA Scot. (dist.) 1951. Director: Lithgows (Hldgs), 1962–, Ayrshire Metal Products plc, 1965–; Invergordon Distillers (Holdings) plc, 1966–; GB Papers plc, 1977–; Jebsens Drilling plc, 1978–85; Scottish Widows' Fund & Life Assurance Soc., 1981–; Shanks & McEwan Gp Ltd, 1983–; Scottish Exhibn Centre Ltd, 1983–; British Linen Bank Ltd, 1983– (Gov., 1986–); Bank of Scotland, 1984–; Chairman: London & Gartmore Investment Trust plc, 1978–; English & Caledonian Investment plc, 1981–. Partner, McClelland Ker & Co. CA (subseq. McClelland Moores & Co.), 1953–61; Finance Director: Lithgows Ltd, 1962–69; Scott Lithgow Ltd, 1970–78; Chm., Fairfield Shipbuilding & Engrg Co. Ltd, 1964–65; Man. Dir, Invergordon Distillers (Holdings) Ltd, 1966–67; Chm., Yarrow PLC, 1985–86; Director: Nairn & Williamson (Holdings) Ltd, 1968–75; Carlton Industries plc, 1978–84. Dep. Chm. and part-time Mem., BAA plc (formerly British Airports Authority), 1985–; Member: CAA (part-time), 1984–85; Clyde Port Authority, 1974–80; Working Party on Scope and Aims of Financial Accounts (the Corporate Report), 1974–75; Exec. Cttee, Accountants Jt Disciplinary Scheme,

1979–81; Mem. Council, Inst. of Chartered Accountants of Scotland, 1977–83 (Vice-Pres., 1980–82, Pres., 1982–83). Mem. Council, Glenalmond Coll., 1983–. *Recreations:* tennis, golf, gardening. *Address:* Dunard, Station Road, Rhu, Dunbartonshire, Scotland G84 8LW. *T:* Rhu 820441.

BOYD, James Fleming, CB 1980; Financial Adviser, B. & C. E. Holiday Management Scheme, since 1981; *b* 28 April 1920; *s* of late Walter and late Mary Boyd; *m* 1949, Daphne Steer, Hendon; one *s* one *d. Educ:* Whitehill Sch., Glasgow. Tax Officer, Inland Revenue, 1937; served with HM Forces, RAF, 1940–46; Inspector of Taxes, 1950; Principal Inspector, 1964; Senior Principal Inspector, 1970; Dep. Chief Inspector of Taxes, 1973; Dir of Operations, Inland Revenue, 1975–77, Dir Gen. (Management), 1978–81. *Recreations:* history, gardening. *Address:* 2A The Avenue, Potters Bar, Herts EN6 1EB. *T:* Potters Bar 55905.

BOYD, John Dixon Iklé, CMG 1985; HM Diplomatic Service; Political Adviser, Hong Kong, since 1985; *b* 17 Jan. 1936; *s* of Prof. James Dixon Boyd and Amélie Lowenthal; *m* 1st, 1968, Gunilla Kristina Ingegerd Rönngren; one *s* one *d*; 2nd, 1977, Julia Daphne Raynsford; three *d. Educ:* Westminster Sch.; Clare Coll., Cambridge (BA); Yale Univ. (MA). Joined HM Foreign Service, 1962; Hong Kong, 1962–64; Peking, 1965–67; Foreign Office, 1967–69; Washington, 1969–73; 1st Sec., Peking, 1973–75; secondment to HM Treasury, 1976; Counsellor: (Economic), Bonn, 1977–81; (Economic and Soc. Affairs), UK Mission to UN, 1981–84. *Recreations:* music, fly fishing. *Address:* c/o Foreign and Commonwealth Office, SW1; Low House Farm, Longsleddale, Kendal, Cumbria.

BOYD, Sir (John) Francis, Kt 1976; a Vice-President, Open Spaces Society, since 1982; *b* 11 July 1910; *s* of John Crichton Dick Boyd and Kate Boyd, Ilkley, Yorks; *m* 1946, Margaret, *d* of George Dobson and Agnes Dobson, Scarborough, Yorks; one *s* two *d. Educ:* Ilkley Grammar Sch.; Silcoates Sch., near Wakefield, Yorks. Reporter: Leeds Mercury, 1928–34; Manchester Guardian, 1934–37; Parly Correspondent, Manchester Guardian, 1937–39. Aux. Fire Service, London, 1939; Monitoring Unit, BBC, 1940; Army, 1940–45. Political Correspondent, Manchester Guardian and Guardian, 1945–72; Political Editor, 1972–75. Chm., Lobby Journalists, 1949–50. Hon. LLD Leeds, 1973. *Publications:* Richard Austen Butler, 1956; (ed) The Glory of Parliament, by Harry Boardman, 1960; British Politics in Transition, 1964. *Recreations:* reading, walking, gardening. *Address:* 62 Gainsborough Road, N12 8AH. *T:* 01–445 0607.

BOYD, Sir John (McFarlane), Kt 1979; CBE 1974; General Secretary, Amalgamated Union of Engineering Workers, 1975–82; *b* 8 Oct. 1917; *s* of James and Mary Boyd; *m* 1940, Elizabeth McIntyre; two *d. Educ:* Hamilton St Elem. Sch.; Glencairn Secondary Sch. Engrg apprentice, 1932–37; Engr, 1937–46. AUEW: Asst Div. Organiser, 1946–50; Div. Organiser, 1950–53; Mem. Executive, 1953–75. Pres., Conf. of Shipbuilding and Engineering Unions, 1964; Member: TUC Gen. Council, 1967–75 and 1978–82; Council, ACAS, 1978–82; Director: BSC, 1981–; UKAEA, 1981–85 (Mem., 1980). Director: Industrial Trng Services Ltd, 1980–; ICL (UK) Ltd, 1984–. A Governor, BBC, 1982–. Chm., Labour Party, 1967. Order of the Founder, Salvation Army, 1981. *Recreations:* brass banding, reading. *Address:* 24 Pearl Court, Cornfield Terrace, Eastbourne, Sussex. *Club:* Caledonian.

BOYD, Dr John Morton, FRSE; ecologist; Consultant: Forestry Commission, since 1985; North of Scotland Hydro-Electric Board, since 1985; Director, Scotland, Nature Conservancy Council, 1971–85; *b* Darvel, Ayrshire, 31 Jan. 1925; *s* of Thomas Pollock Boyd and Jeanie Reid Morton; *m* 1954, Winifred Isobel Rome; four *s. Educ:* Kilmarnock Acad.; Glasgow Univ. (BSc, PhD, DSc). FRSE 1968. Served War, 1943–47: Flt Lieut RAF. Nature Conservancy Council: Reg. Officer, 1957–68; Asst Dir, 1969–70. Nuffield Trav. Fellow, ME and E Africa, 1964–65; Leader, British Jordan Expedn, 1966; Mem., Royal Soc. Aldabra Expedn, 1967. Member: Council, Royal Scottish Zool Soc., 1963–69, 1980–85, 1986–; Council, Azraq Internat. Biol Stn, Jordan, 1967–69; Council, National Trust for Scotland, 1971–85; Seals Adv. Cttee, NERC, 1973–79; BBC Scottish Agr. Adv. Cttee, 1973–76; Exec. Bd, Internat. Waterfowl Res. Bureau, 1976–78; Council, Royal Soc. of Edinburgh, 1978–81; Consultative Panel on Conservation of the Line and Phoenix Islands (Central Pacific), 1981–86. Internat. Union for Conservation of Nature and Natural Resources: British Rep., Kinshasa, 1975, Geneva, 1977, Ashkhabad, 1978, Christchurch, 1981, and Madrid, 1985; Mem. Commn on Ecology, 1976–; Confs, Senegal/Gambia and Switzerland, 1980, Holland, 1981, Catalonia and Indonesia, 1982, Malaysia, 1983, Bavaria, 1985. Co-Chm., Area VI Anglo-Soviet Environmental Protection Agreement, 1977–85; Chm., UK Internat. Conservation Cttee, 1980; Council, Scottish Wildlife Trust, 1985–; Vice-Pres., Scottish Conservation Projects Trust, 1985–; Cttee, Centre for Human Ecology, Edinburgh Univ., 1985–. Lectures: Keith Entwistle Meml, Cambridge, 1968; British Council, Amman, Nicosia and Ankara, 1972; Meml in Agr. Zool., W of Scotland Agr. Coll., 1976; Sir William Weipers Meml, Glasgow Univ. Vet. Sch., 1980; Nat. Trust for Scotland Jubilee, 1981; British Council, Jakarta, 1982, Delhi and Kuala Lumpur, 1983. Gen. Editor, Island Biology Series, Edinburgh Univ. Press, 1985–. FRSA 1985; FRZSScot 1985. Neill Prize, Royal Soc. of Edinburgh, 1985. *Publications:* (with K. Williamson) St Kilda Summer, 1960; (with K. Williamson) Mosaic of Islands, 1963; (with F. F. Darling) The Highlands and Islands, 1964; Travels in the Middle East and East Africa, 1966; (with P. A. Jewell and C. Milner) Island Survivors, 1974; (ed) The Natural Environment of the Outer Hebrides, 1979; (ed with D. R. Bowes) The Natural Environment of the Inner Hebrides, 1983; Fraser Darling's Islands, 1986; scientific papers on nature conservation and animal ecology. *Recreations:* hill-walking, painting, photography. *Address:* 57 Hailes Gardens, Edinburgh EH13 0JH. *T:* 031–441 3220; Balephuil, Tiree, Argyll PA77 6UE. *Club:* New (Edinburgh).

BOYD, Leslie Balfour, CBE 1977; Courts Administrator, Central Criminal Court, 1972–77; *b* 25 Nov. 1914; *e s* of late Henry Leslie Boyd, Mem. of Lloyds, of Crowborough, Sussex, and Beatrix Boyd, *d* of Henry Chapman, for many years British Consul at Dieppe; *m* 1936, Wendy Marie, *d* of George and Nancy Blake, Oswestry, Salop; one *s* one *d. Educ:* Evelyn's; Royal Naval College, Dartmouth. Invalided out of Royal Navy, 1931. Called to the Bar, Gray's Inn, 1939; joined staff of Central Criminal Court, 1941; Dep. Clerk of Court, 1948; Clerk of the Court, 1955–71; Dep. Clerk of Peace, 1949–55, Clerk of the Peace, 1955–71, City of London and Town and Borough of Southwark. Master, Worshipful Company of Gold and Silver Wyre Drawers, 1969. *Publications:* contributor to Criminal Law and Juries titles, 3rd edn, Juries title, 4th edn, of Halsbury's Laws of England. *Recreations:* gardening and travel. *Address:* Flat G, Mulberry Court, 2 Highbury Hill, Islington, N5 1BA.

BOYD, Sir Robert (Lewis Fullarton), Kt 1983; CBE 1972; FRS 1969; Professor of Physics in the University of London, 1962–83, now Emeritus; Director, Mullard Space Science Laboratory of Department of Physics and Astronomy of University College, London, 1965–83; *b* 1922; *s* of late William John Boyd, PhD, BSc; *m* 1949, Mary, *d* of late John Higgins; two *s* one *d. Educ:* Whitgift Sch.; Imperial Coll., London (BSc (Eng) 1943); University Coll., London (PhD 1949). FIEE 1967; FInstP 1972. Exp. Officer at Admty Mining Estabt, 1943–46; DSIR Res. Asst, 1946–49; ICI Res. Fellow, 1949–50, Maths Dept, UCL; ICI Res. Fellow, Physics Dept, UCL, 1950–52; Lectr in Physics, UCL, 1952–58, Reader in Physics, UCL, 1959–62. Prof. of Astronomy (part-time), Royal Institution, 1961–67; IEE Appleton Lectr, 1976; Bakerian Lectr, Royal Soc., 1978; Halley Lectr, Univ. of Oxford, 1981. Chairman: Meteorol Res. Cttee, MoD, 1972–75; Astronautics Cttee, MoD, 1972–77; Member: BBC Science Cons. Gp, 1970–79; SRC, 1977–81 (Chm., Astronomy, Space and Radio Bd, 1977–80); Council, Physical Soc., 1958–60; Council, RAS, 1962–66 (Vice-Pres., 1964–66); British Nat. Cttee on Space Res., 1976–. Pres., Victoria Inst., 1965–76. Trustee, Nat. Maritime Museum, 1980–. Governor: St Lawrence Coll., 1965–76; Croydon Coll., 1966–80; Southland Coll., 1976–; Chm., London Bible Coll., 1983–. Hon. DSc Heriot-Watt, 1979. *Publications:* The Upper Atmosphere (with H. S. W. Massey), 1958; Space Research by Rocket and Satellite, 1960; Space Physics, 1975; papers in sci. jls on space sci. and other topics. *Recreation:* elderly Rolls Royce motor cars. *Address:* Roseneath, 41 Church Street, Littlehampton, West Sussex.

BOYD, Robert Stanley, CB 1982; Solicitor of Inland Revenue, 1979–86; *b* 6 March 1927; *s* of Robert Reginald Boyd (formerly Indian Police) and Agnes Maria Dorothea, *d* of Lt-Col Charles H. Harrison; *m* 1965, Ann, *d* of Daniel Hopkin. *Educ:* Wellington; Trinity Coll., Dublin (BA, LLB). Served RN, 1945–48. Called to Bar, Inner Temple, 1954. Joined Inland Revenue, 1959; Prin. Asst Solicitor, 1971–79. *Address:* 28 Canonbury Grove, N1 2HR.

BOYD, Stewart Craufurd, QC 1981; *b* 25 Oct. 1943; *s* of Leslie Balfour Boyd and Wendy Marie Boyd; *m* 1970, Catherine Jay; one *s* two *d. Educ:* Winchester Coll.; Trinity Coll., Cambridge (MA). Called to the Bar, Middle Temple, 1967. *Publications:* (ed) Scrutton, Charterparties, 18th edn 1972; (with Sir Michael Mustill) The Law and Practice of Commercial Arbitration, 1982. *Recreations:* boats, pianos, gardens. *Address:* 1 Gayton Crescent, NW3 1TT. *T:* 01–431 1581.

BOYD, (Thomas) Christopher; farmer; *b* 1916; *m*; one *s* two *d.* Army, 1940–44; civil servant, 1939 and 1944–48; MP (Lab) Bristol NW, 1955–59; Chelsea Borough Councillor, 1953–59. *Address:* Middlegill, Moffat, Dumfriesshire. *T:* Beattock 415.

BOYD, William Andrew Murray, FRSL; author; *b* 7 March 1952; *s* of Dr Alexander Murray Boyd and Evelyn Boyd; *m* 1975, Susan Anne (*née* Wilson). *Educ:* Gordonstoun Sch.; Glasgow Univ. (MA Hons English and Philosophy); Jesus Coll., Oxford. Lecturer in English, St Hilda's Coll., Oxford, 1980–83; Television Critic, New Statesman, 1981–83. FRSL 1983. *Publications:* A Good Man in Africa, 1981 (Whitbread Prize 1981, Somerset Maugham Award 1982); On the Yankee Station, 1981; An Ice-Cream War, 1982 (John Llewellyn Rhys Prize, 1982); Stars and Bars, 1984; School Ties, 1985. *Screenplays:* Good and Bad at Games (TV), 1983; Dutch Girls (TV), 1985. *Recreations:* tennis, strolling. *Address:* c/o Harvey Unna and Stephen Durbridge Ltd, 24 Pottery Lane, Holland Park, W11 4LZ.

BOYD-CARPENTER, family name of **Baron Boyd-Carpenter.**

BOYD-CARPENTER, Baron *cr* 1972 (Life Peer), of Crux Easton in the County of Southampton; **John Archibald Boyd-Carpenter,** PC 1954; Chairman, Rugby Portland Cement, 1976–84 (Director, 1970–76); *b* 2 June 1908; *s* of late Sir Archibald Boyd-Carpenter, MP; *m* 1937, Margaret, *e d* of Lieut-Col G. L. Hall, OBE; one *s* two *d. Educ:* Stowe; Balliol Coll., Oxford. Pres. Oxford Union, 1930; BA (History, 1930); Diploma Economics, 1931; toured USA with Oxford Univ. Debating Team, 1931; Harmsworth Law Scholar, Middle Temple, 1933; Council of Legal Education's Prize for Constitutional Law, 1934; called to Bar, Middle Temple, 1934, and practised in London and SE Circuit. Contested (MR) Limehouse for LCC, 1934. Joined Scots Guards, 1940; held various staff appointments and served with AMG in Italy, retired with rank of Major. MP (C) for Kingston-upon-Thames, 1945–72; Financial Sec., to the Treasury, 1951–54; Minister of Transport and Civil Aviation, 1954–Dec. 1955; Minister of Pensions and National Insurance, Dec. 1955–July 1962; Chief Sec. to the Treasury and Paymaster-Gen., 1962–64; Opposition Front Bench Spokesman on Housing, Local Government and Land, 1964–66; Chm., Public Accounts Cttee, 1964–70. Chairman: Greater London Area Local Govt Cttee, Conservative Party, 1968; London Members Cttee, 1966–72; Pres. Wessex Area, Nat. Union of Conservative and Unionist Assocs, 1977–80. Chm., CAA, 1972–77. Chairman: Orion Insurance Co., 1969–72; CLRP Investment Trust, 1970–72; Dir of other cos; Mem. Council, Trust Houses Forte Ltd, 1977–. Governor, Stowe School; Chairman: Carlton Club, 1979–86; Assoc. of Indep. Unionist Peers, 1979– (Dep. Chm. 1977–79); Mail Users' Assoc., 1986–. High Steward, Royal Borough of Kingston-upon-Thames, 1973–. DL Greater London, 1973–83. *Publications:* Way of Life, 1980; newspaper articles. *Recreations:* tennis and swimming. *Address:* 12 Eaton Terrace, SW1. *T:* 01–730 7765; Crux Easton House, Crux Easton, near Highclere, Hants. *T:* Highclere 253037. *Club:* Carlton.

See also S. E. M. Hogg.

BOYDE, Prof. Patrick, PhD; Serena Professor of Italian, since 1981, and Fellow of St John's College, since 1965, University of Cambridge; *b* 30 Nov. 1934; *s* of Harry Caine Boyde and Florence Colonna Boyde; *m* 1956, Catherine Mavis Taylor; four *s. Educ:* Braintree County High Sch.; Wanstead County High Sch.; St John's Coll., Cambridge. BA 1956, MA 1960, PhD 1963. Nat. service, commnd RA, 1956–58. Research, St John's Coll., Cambridge, 1958–61; Asst Lectr in Italian, Univ. of Leeds, 1961–62; Asst Lectr, later Lectr, Univ. of Cambridge, 1962–81. *Publications:* Dante's Lyric Poetry (with K. Foster), 1967; Dante's Style in his Lyric Poetry, 1971; Dante Philomythes and Philosopher: Man in the Cosmos, 1981. *Recreations:* walking, backpacking, music. *Address:* 23 Hartington Grove, Cambridge CB1 4UA. *T:* Cambridge 247482.

BOYDELL, (The Worshipful Chancellor) Peter Thomas Sherrington, QC 1965; Chairman, Planning and Local Government Committee of the Bar, since 1973; Leader, Parliamentary Bar, since 1975; Chancellor of Dioceses of Truro since 1957, Oxford since 1958 and Worcester since 1959; *b* 20 Sept. 1920; *s* of late Frank Richard Boydell, JP, and late Frances Barton Boydell, Blenheim Lodge, Whitegate Drive, Blackpool; unmarried. *Educ:* Arnold Sch., Blackpool; Manchester Univ. LLB Manchester 1940. Served War of 1939–45; Adjt, 17th Field Regt, RA, 1943; Bde Major, RA, 1st Armoured Div., 1944; Bde Major, RA, 10th Indian Div., 1945. Qualified as Solicitor, 1947. Called to Bar, Middle Temple, 1948, Bencher, 1970. Mem., Legal Board of Church Assembly, 1958–71. Contested (C) Carlisle, 1964. Associate (by invitation and election) RICS, 1982. *Recreations:* mountaineering, music, travel. *Address:* 45 Wilton Crescent, SW1. *T:* 01–235 5505; 2 Harcourt Buildings, Temple, EC4. *T:* 01–353 8415. *Clubs:* Garrick, Royal Automobile; Climbers.

BOYDEN, (Harold) James; *b* 19 Oct. 1910; *s* of late Claude James and late Frances Mary Boyden; *m* 1935, Emily Pemberton. *Educ:* Elementary Sch., Tiffin Boys, Kingston; King's Coll., London. BA (History), 1932; BSc (Econ), London External, 1943; Barrister-at-law, Lincoln's Inn, 1947. Pres., King's Coll. Union Soc., 1931–32. Master: Henry Mellish Grammar Sch., 1933–35; Tiffin Boys Sch., 1935–40; Lectr, Extra-Mural Depts of London, Nottingham and Southampton Univs, 1934–47. RAF, 1940–45; Sqdn-Ldr, 1944–45; Chief Training Officer, Admiralty, 1945–47; Dir Extra-Mural Studies, Durham Univ.,

1947–59. Durham City and County Magistrate, 1951–; CC for Durham City, 1952–59; Chm. Durham County Education Cttee, 1959 (Vice-Chm. 1957–59); Chm., Exec. Cttee Nat. Inst. for Adult Education, 1958–61; Mem. Newcastle Regional Hospital Board, 1958–64; Fabian Soc. Executive, 1961–65. MP (Lab) Bishop Auckland, 1959–79; Jt Parly Under-Sec. of State, Dept of Education and Science, 1964–65; Parliamentary Sec., Ministry of Public Building and Works, 1965–67; Parly Under-Sec. (Army), MoD, 1967–69. Chm., Select Cttee of Expenditure, 1974–79; Sec., Anglo-French Parly Cttee, 1974–79. Overseas Lecture Tours: for Foreign Office, Germany, 1955 and 1957; for British Council, Ghana, Sierra Leone, 1956; Sierra Leone, 1961; for Admiralty, Malta, 1959. Member: WEA; Fabian Soc.; Nat. Union of General and Municipal Workers; National Trust; Council of Europe, 1970–73, WEU, 1970–73. FKC 1969. *Recreations:* walking, gardening, foreign travel, swimming, local government. *Address:* 100 Granary Lane, Budleigh Salterton, Devon EX9 6EP. *T:* Budleigh Salterton 5812. *Clubs:* South Church Workman's, Eldon Lane Workman's (Bishop Auckland); Southerne (Newton Aycliffe).

BOYER, John Leslie, OBE 1982; Chief Executive, Zoological Society of London, since 1984; *b* 13 Nov. 1926; *s* of Albert and Gladys Boyer; *m* 1953, Joyce Enid Thomasson; one *s* two *d*. *Educ:* Nantwich; Acton Grammar Sch. Served Army, 1944–48: commnd into South Lancashire Regt, 1946, and attached to Baluch Regt, then Indian Army. Joined Hongkong and Shanghai Banking Corp., 1948: served Hong Kong, Burma, Japan, India, Malaysia, Singapore; General Manager, Hong Kong, 1973; Director, March 1977; Dep. Chm., Sept. 1977–81; Chm., Antony Gibbs Hldgs Ltd, 1981–83. Chm., Wardley Marine Investment Management Services Ltd, 1981–; Director: Anglo American Securities PLC, 1981–; North Atlantic Securities, 1981–. *Recreations:* walking, swimming, bridge, reading. *Address:* Friars Lawn, Norwood Green Road, Norwood Green, Mddx UB2 4LA. *T:* 01–574 8489. *Clubs:* Oriental; Shek O (Hong Kong); Tanglin (Singapore).

BOYERS, (Raphael) Howard, DFC 1945; Regional Chairman of Industrial Tribunals, Sheffield, since 1984; *b* 20 Oct. 1915; *yr s* of late Bernard Boyers and Jennie Boyers; *m* 1st, 1949, Anna Moyra Cowan (*d* 1984); three *d*; 2nd, 1985, Estell Wolman (*née* Davidson). *Educ:* King Edward VI Grammar School, Retford. Admitted Solicitor, 1939. Served War, RAF, 1940–45; 130 Sqdn, 10 Gp Fighter Comd, 1941; 51 Sqdn, 4 Gp Bomber Comd, 1944–45. Sen. Partner, Boyers Howson & Co., 1946–72. Clerk of the Peace, City of Sheffield, 1964–71; Chairman: VAT Tribunals, 1972–75; Industrial Tribunals, 1975–80; acting Regional Chm., 1980–84. *Recreations:* theatre, music, watching football until it ceased to be fun. *Address:* 49 Cortworth Road, Sheffied S11 9LN. *T:* Sheffield 362041. *Club:* Sheffield (Sheffield).

BOYES, Sir Brian Gerald B.; *see* Barratt-Boyes.

BOYES, James Ashley; Headmaster of City of London School, 1965–84; *b* 27 Aug. 1924; *s* of late Alfred Simeon Boyes and of Edith May Boyes; *m* 1st, 1949, Diana Fay (*née* Rothera), MA Cantab; two *d*; 2nd, 1973, April Tanner (*née* Rothery). *Educ:* Rugby Sch.; Clare Coll., Cambridge. Lieut RNVR; N Russian convoys and Brit. Pacific Fleet, 1942–46. Cambridge Univ., 1942, 1946–48; 1st class Hons Mod. Hist., 1948; Mellon Fellowship, Yale Univ., 1948–50; MA Yale, 1950. Asst Master, Rugby Sch., 1950–55; Headmaster, Kendal Grammar Sch., Westmorland, 1955–60; Dir of Studies, Royal Air Force Coll., Cranwell, 1960–65. *Recreations:* squash racquets, sailing. *Address:* 12 Linver Road, SW6 3RB. *Clubs:* Royal Automobile, Hurlingham; Harlequins RUFC (Hon. Mem.); Hawks (Cambridge); Royal Windermere Yacht.

BOYES, Kate Emily Tyrrell, (Mrs C. W. Sanders); Chairman, Civil Service Selection Boards, since 1978; *b* 22 April 1918; *e d* of S. F. Boyes, Sandiacre, Derbyshire; *m* 1944, Cyril Woods Sanders, *qv*; one *s* three *d*. *Educ:* Long Eaton Grammar Sch.; (Scholar) Newnham Coll., Cambridge. Economics Tripos, 1939; MA (Cantab). Administrative Class, Home Civil Service, 1939; Private Sec. to Parly Sec., 1942–45; Principal, 1945; Sec. to Council on Prices, Productivity and Incomes, 1958–60; Asst Sec., 1961; Speechwriter to President of Bd of Trade, 1963–64; Under-Sec., Europe, Industry and Technology Div., DTI, later Dept of Trade, 1972–78. Member: Council, National Trust, 1967–79; Exec., Keep Britain Tidy Gp, 1980–. *Recreations:* climbing, sailing, ski-ing, archæology. *Address:* 41 Smith Street, SW3 1NQ. *T:* 01–352 8053; Giles Point, Winchelsea, Sussex. *T:* Winchelsea 431; Canower, Cashel, Connemara, Ireland. *Clubs:* Ski Club of Gt Britain; Island Cruising (Salcombe).

BOYES, Roland; MP (Lab) Houghton and Washington, since 1983. Member (Lab) Durham, European Parliament, 1979–84. An opposition frontbench spokesman on the environment, 1985–. Member G&MWU. Chm., Tribune Gp, 1985–. *Address:* (home) 12 Spire Hollin, Peterlee, Co. Durham. *T:* Peterlee 863917; (office) 5A Grangewood Close, Shiney Row, Houghton-le-Spring, Tyne & Wear. *T:* Durham 857825. *Clubs:* Peterlee Labour, Chester le Street Labour; Peterlee Cricket; Houghton Buffs; Easington Lane, North Biddick, Westward, Celtic, Stella Maris, Gardeners, Usworth, and Glendale Working Men's.

BOYLAND, Prof. Eric, PhD London, DSc Manchester; Professor of Biochemistry, University of London, at Chester Beatty Research Institute, Institute of Cancer Research, Royal Marsden Hospital, 1948–70, now Emeritus Professor; Visiting Professor in Environmental Toxicology, London School of Hygiene and Tropical Medicine, 1970–76; *b* Manchester, 24 Feb. 1905; *s* of Alfred E. and Helen Boyland; *m* 1931, Margaret Esther (*d* 1985), *d* of late Maj.-Gen. Sir Frederick Maurice, KCMG, CB; two *s* one *d*. *Educ:* Manchester Central High Sch.; Manchester Univ. BSc Tech. 1926; MSc 1928; DSc 1936. Research Asst in Physiology, Manchester Univ., 1926–28; Grocers' Company Scholar and Beit Memorial Fellow for Med. Research at Lister Institute for Preventive Medicine, 1928–30, and Kaiser Wilhelm Institut für Medizinische Forschung, Heidelberg, 1930–31; Physiological Chemist to Royal Cancer Hosp., London, 1931; Reader in Biochemistry, University of London, 1935–47. Research Officer in Ministry of Supply, 1941–44; Ministry of Agriculture, 1944–45. Consultant to Internat. Agency for Research on Cancer, Lyon, 1970–72, Member WHO Panel on Food Additives. Hon. FFOM, RCP, 1982. Hon. PhD Frankfurt, 1982; Hon. MD Malta, 1985. Judd Award for Cancer Research, New York, 1948. *Publications:* The Biochemistry of Bladder Cancer, 1963; Modern Trends in Toxicology, vol. I, 1962, vol. II, 1974; scientific papers in biochemistry and pharmacology. *Recreations:* walking, looking at paintings. *Address:* London School of Hygiene and Tropical Medicine, WC1; 42 Bramerton Street, SW3. *T:* 01–352 2601. *Clubs:* Athenæum; Rucksack (Manchester).

BOYLE, family name of **Earls of Cork, Glasgow,** and **Shannon.**

BOYLE, Viscount; Richard Henry John Boyle; in catering trade; *b* 19 Jan. 1960; *s* and *heir* of 9th Earl of Shannon, *qv*. *Educ:* Northease Manor School, Lewes. *Recreations:* motocross and trials.

BOYLE, Andrew Philip More; author, journalist, broadcaster; *b* Dundee, 27 May 1919; *er s* of Andrew Boyle and Rose McCann; *m* 1st, 1943, Christina (*d* 1984), *y d* of Jack Galvin; one *s* one *d*; 2nd, 1986, Eleanor Frances Ransome. *Educ:* Blairs, Aberdeen; Paris Univ. Escaped from France as student, June 1940. RAFVR, 1941–43; Military Intelligence, Far East, 1944–45; also Military Corresp., Far East (Major), 1945–46. Joined BBC as scriptwriter/producer, Radio Newsreel, 1947; Asst Editor, 1954; Founding Editor, World At One, 1965, World This Weekend, PM etc, 1967–75; Head of News and Current Affairs (Radio and TV), BBC Scotland, 1976. Successfully resisted Inland Revenue's attempt to tax literary prizes in 1978 Test Case. Work published, 1979, led to exposure of the Blunt affair. *Publications:* No Passing Glory, Biography of Group Captain Cheshire, VC, 1955; Trenchard, Man of Vision, 1962; Montagu Norman: A Biography, 1967; Only the Wind will Listen: Reith of the BBC, 1972; Poor, Dear Brendan: The Quest for Brendan Bracken, 1974 (Whitbread Award for Biography, 1974); The Riddle of Erskine Childers, 1976; The Climate of Treason, 1979, rev. edn 1980; The Fourth Man; A Study of Robert Parsons, 1986; co-author of four other books; occasional contribs to Observer, Sunday Times, Times, Spectator, Listener, Washington Post, and formerly to Catholic Herald, Tablet, etc. *Recreations:* walking, swimming, conversation, music, watching bad football matches from public terraces, especially at Fulham. *Address:* 39 Lansdowne Road, W11 2LQ. *T:* 01–727 5758.

BOYLE, Archibald Cabbourn, MD; FRCP; DPhysMed; Hon. Consultant Physician, King Edward VII, Midhurst, since 1984; Director, Department of Rheumatology, Middlesex Hospital, 1954–83; Honorary Consultant Rheumatologist, King Edward VII Hospital for Officers, 1980–83; Hon. Clinical Adviser, Department of Rheumatological Research, Middlesex Hospital Medical School; *b* 14 March 1918; *s* of late Arthur Hislop Boyle and of Flora Ellen Boyle; *m* 1st, Patricia Evelyn Tallack (*d* 1944); one *d*; 2nd, Dorothy Evelyn (marr. diss. 1982), *widow* of Lieut G. B. Jones; one *s*; 3rd, 1983, June Rosemary Gautrey (*née* Pickett). *Educ:* Dulwich Coll.; St Bartholomew's Hospital. House Physician, St Bartholomew's Hosp., 1941–42. Served War of 1939–45 in Far East, and later as Command Specialist in Physical Medicine. Registrar and Sen. Asst, 1946–49, and Asst Physician, 1949–54, Mddx Hosp.; Consultant in Physical Medicine, Bromley Gp of Hosps, 1950–54; Physician, Arthur Stanley Inst. for Rheumatic Diseases, 1950–65. Member: Bd of Governors, Mddx Hosp.; Bd of Governors, Charterhouse Rheumatism Clinic; Bd of Studies in Medicine, Univ. of London; Council, British Assoc. for Rheumatology and Rehabilitation (Pres., 1973–74); British League against Rheumatism (Vice-Pres., 1972–77; Pres., 1977–81); Council, Section of Physical Medicine, RSM, 1950– (Pres., 1956–58; Vice-Pres., 1970–); Heberden Soc.; Cttee on Rheumatology and Rehabilitation, RCP. Ernest Fletcher Meml Lectr, RSM, 1971. Formerly: Examnr in Physical Medicine, RCP; Examnr to Chartered Soc. of Physiotherapy; Editor, Annals of Physical Medicine, 1956–63; Sec., Internat. Fedn of Physical Medicine, 1960–64; Chm., Physical Medicine Gp, BMA, 1956–58; Pres., London Br., Chartered Soc. of Physiotherapy. Former Member: Council, British Assoc. of Physical Medicine and Rheumatology, 1949–72 (Vice-Pres., 1965–68; Pres., 1970–72); Cttee on Chronic Rheumatic Diseases, RCP; Regional Scientific, and Educn, Sub-Cttees, Arthritis and Rheumatism Council; Physiotherapists Bd, Council for Professions Supplementary to Medicine; Central Consultants and Specialists Cttee, BMA; Med. Adv. Cttee, British Rheumatism and Arthritis Assoc. *Publications:* A Colour Atlas of Rheumatology, 1974; contribs to medical jls, mainly on rheumatic disease. *Recreation:* gardening. *Address:* Iping Barn, Iping, near Midhurst, West Sussex GU29 0PE. *T:* Midhurst 6467.

BOYLE, Marshal of the Royal Air Force Sir Dermot (Alexander), GCB 1957 (CB 1946); KCVO 1953; KBE 1953 (CBE 1945); AFC 1939; Vice-Chairman, British Aircraft Corporation, 1962–71; *b* 2 Oct. 1904; 2nd and *e* surv. *s* of A. F. Boyle, Belmont House, Queen's Co., Ire.; *m* 1931, Una Carey; two *s* one *d* (and one *s* decd). *Educ:* St Columba's Coll., Ireland; RAF (Cadet) Coll., Cranwell. Commissioned RAF 1924; Air ADC to the King, 1943; Air Commodore, 1944; Air Vice-Marshal, 1949; Air Marshal, 1954; Air Chief Marshal, 1956; Marshal of the Royal Air Force, 1958; Dir-Gen. of Personnel, Air Ministry, 1948–49; Dir-Gen. of Manning, Air Ministry, 1949–51; AOC No. 1 Group Bomber Command, 1951–53; AOC-in-C, Fighter Command, 1953–55; Chief of Air Staff, 1956–59. Master, Guild of Air Pilots and Air Navigators, 1965–66. Chairman: Bd of Trustees, RAF Museum, 1965–74; Ct of Governors, Mill Hill Sch., 1969–76; Dep. Chm., RAF Benevolent Fund, 1971–80. J. P. Robertson Meml Trophy, Air Public Relations Assoc., 1973. *Address:* Fair Gallop, Brighton Road, Sway, Hants. *Club:* Royal Air Force.

BOYLE, John Sebastian; Sheriff of South Strathclyde, Dumfries and Galloway at Airdrie, since 1983; *b* 29 March 1933; *s* of Edward Joseph Boyle and Constance Mary Hook or Boyle; *m* 1st, 1955, Catherine Denise Croall; one *s* two *d*; 2nd, 1978, Isobel Margaret Ryan; one *s* one *d*. *Educ:* St Aloysius College, Glasgow; Glasgow University. BL 1955. Solicitor, Glasgow, 1955–83. Pres., Glasgow Bar Assoc., 1962–63; Member: Scottish Arts Council, 1966–72; Council, Law Society of Scotland, 1968–75; Criminal Injuries Compensation Board, 1975–83. *Address:* 5 Great Western Terrace, Glasgow G12 0UP.

BOYLE, Kay, (Baroness Joseph von Franckenstein); writer; Professor in English Department, San Francisco State University, 1963–80, now Emeritus; *b* St Paul, Minn, USA, 19 Feb. 1902; *d* of Howard Peterson Boyle; *m* 1921, 1931 and 1943; one *s* five *d*. Member: National Institute of Arts and Letters, 1958; Amer. Acad. and Inst. of Arts and Letters, 1978. O. Henry Memorial Prize for best short story of the year, 1936, 1941; Guggenheim Fellowship, 1934, 1961; Center for Advanced Studies Wesleyan Univ. Fellowship, 1963; Radcliffe Inst. for Independent Study, 1964, 1965. Writer-in-residence: Hollins Coll., Virginia, 1970–71; Bowling Green State Univ., 1986. Hon. DLitt: Columbia Coll., Chicago, 1971; Southern Illinois, 1982; Bowling Green State Univ., 1986; Hon. DHL Skidmore Coll., 1977. San Francisco Art Commn Award of Honor, 1978; Amer. Book Award, 1983. *Publications: novels:* Plagued by the Nightingale; Year Before Last; Gentlemen, I Address You Privately; My Next Bride; Death of a Man; The Crazy Hunter, 1938; Monday Night; Primer for Combat; Avalanche; A Frenchman Must Die; "1939"; His Human Majesty; The Seagull on the Step, 1955; Three Short Novels, 1958; Generation Without Farewell, 1959; The Underground Woman, 1975; *volumes of short stories:* Wedding Day; The First Lover; The White Horses of Vienna; The Crazy Hunter; Thirty Stories; The Smoking Mountain; Nothing Ever Breaks Except the Heart, 1966; Fifty Stories, 1980; *essays:* Breaking the Silence, 1962; The Long Walk at San Francisco State and other essays, 1970; Words That Must Somehow Be Said, 1985; *memoirs:* The Autobiography of Emanuel Carnevali, 1967; Being Geniuses Together, 1968; *poetry:* A Glad Day; American Citizen; Collected Poems, 1962; Testament for my Students and other poems, 1970; This is Not a Letter, 1985. *For Children:* The Youngest Camel; Pinky, the Cat Who Liked to Sleep, 1966; Pinky in Persia, 1968. *Recreations:* ski-ing, mountain climbing. *Address:* c/o Watkins/Loomis Agency Inc., 150 East 35th Street, New York, NY 10016, USA.

BOYLE, Sir Lawrence, Kt 1979; JP; DL; Director: Short Loan and Mortgage Co. Ltd, since 1980; Scottish Mutual Assurance Society, since 1980; Pension Fund Property Unit Trust, since 1980; Partner, Sir Lawrence Boyle Associates, Financial and Management Consultants, Glasgow, since 1980; *b* 31 Jan. 1920; *s* of Hugh Boyle and Kate (*née* Callaghan); *m* 1952, Mary McWilliam; one *s* three *d*. *Educ:* Holy Cross Acad., Leith, Edinburgh; Edinburgh Univ. BCom, PhD. Depute County Treasurer, Midlothian CC, 1958–62; Depute City Chamberlain, Glasgow, 1962–70; City Chamberlain, Glasgow, 1970–74; Chief Exec., Strathclyde Regional Council, 1974–80. Vis. Prof., Strathclyde

Univ. Business Sch., 1979–85. Mem., Public Works Loan Bd, 1972–74. Vice-Pres., Soc. of Local Authority Chief Execs, 1977–78. Member: Cttee of Inquiry into Functions and Powers of Island Councils of Scotland, 1982–84; Cttee of Inquiry into Conduct of Local Authority Business, 1985–86. Chm., Scottish Nat. Orch. Soc. Ltd, 1980–83. Member: Council, Scottish Business Sch., 1974–79; Strathclyde Univ. Court, 1980–85; Steering Bd, Strathclyde Univ. Business Sch., 1974–82. IPFA (Mem. Council, and Chm. Scottish Br., 1973–74); CBIM (Mem. Adv. Bd for Scotland, 1973–82). JP Glasgow, 1971; DL Renfrewshire, 1985. *Publications:* Equalisation and the Future of Local Government Finance, 1966; articles and papers in economic jls, etc. *Recreation:* music. *Address:* 24 Broomburn Drive, Newton Mearns, Glasgow. *T:* 041–639 3776.

BOYLE, Leonard Butler, CBE 1977; Director and General Manager, Principality Building Society, Cardiff, 1956–78; *b* 13 Jan. 1913; *s* of Harold and Edith Boyle; *m* 1938, Alice Baldwin Yarborough; two *s*. *Educ:* Roundhay Sch., Leeds. FCBSI. Chief of Investment Dept, Leeds Permanent Building Soc., 1937; Asst Man., Isle of Thanet Bldg Soc., 1949; Jt Asst Gen. Man., Hastings and Thanet Bldg Soc., 1951, Sec. 1954. Building Socs Assoc.: Mem. Council, 1956–78 (Chm. Gen. Purposes Cttee, 1958–60; Chm. Develt Cttee, 1967–71); Chm. of Council, 1973–75 (Dep. Chm. 1971–73; Vice-Pres., 1978); Vice-Pres., CBSI, 1982–. Treasurer, Boys' Brigade. Consultant, Manchester Exchange Trust. *Recreations:* gardening, walking, golf. *Address:* Northwick Cottage, Marlpit Lane, Seaton, Devon EX12 2HH. *T:* Seaton 22194.

BOYLE, Sir Stephen Gurney, 5th Bt *cr* 1904; *b* 15 Jan. 1962; *s* of Sir Richard Gurney Boyle, 4th Bt, and of Elizabeth Ann, *yr d* of Norman Dennes; *S* father, 1983. *Heir: b* Michael Desmond Boyle, *b* 16 Sept. 1963.

BOYLES, Edgar William; Under Secretary, Inland Revenue, 1975–81; *b* 24 March 1921; *s* of William John Boyles and Jessie Louisa Boyles; *m* 1950, Heather Iris Hobart, SRN; three *s* one *d*. *Educ:* Bedford Modern Sch. RAF, 1940–46. Tax Officer, Inland Revenue, 1939; Principal Inspector of Taxes, 1962; Sen. Principal Inspector, 1967. *Recreations:* chess, gardening, watching cricket. *Address:* The Keeley, 155 Bedford Road, Wootton, Bedford MK43 9BA. *T:* Bedford 851875.

BOYNE, 10th Viscount *cr* 1717; **Gustavus Michael George Hamilton-Russell,** DL; JP; Baron Hamilton, 1715; Baron Brancepeth, 1866; a Lord in Waiting, since 1981; *b* 10 Dec. 1931; *s* of late Hon. Gustavus Lascelles Hamilton-Russell and *g s* of 9th Viscount; *S* grandfather, 1942; *m* 1956, Rosemary Anne, 2nd *d* of Major Sir Dennis Stucley, 5th Bt; one *s* three *d*. *Educ:* Eton; Sandhurst; Royal Agricl Coll., Cirencester. Commissioned Grenadier Guards, 1952. Dir, Nat. Westminster Bank, 1976– (Chm., W Midlands and Wales Regional Bd). Mem., 1963–83, Dep. Chm., 1975–82, Telford Develt Corp. Governor: Wrekin Coll., Telford; Harper Adams Agricl Coll. CStJ. JP 1961, DL 1965, Salop. *Heir: s* Hon. Gustavus Michael Stucley Hamilton-Russell, *b* 27 May 1965. *Address:* Burwarton House, Bridgnorth, Salop. *T:* Burwarton 203. *Clubs:* Turf, White's.
See also Lord Forbes.

BOYNE, Donald Arthur Colin Aydon, CBE 1977; Consultant, The Architectural Press, since 1984 (Director, 1974–85); *b* 15 Feb. 1921; 2nd *s* of late Lytton Leonard Boyne and Millicent (*née* Nisbet); *m* 1947, Rosemary Pater; two *s* one *d*. *Educ:* Tonbridge Sch.; Architectural Assoc. School of Architecture, 1943–47. Indian Army, 8/13 FF Rifles, 1940–43. Editor, Architects' Jl, 1953–70; Chm., Editorial Bd, Architectural Review and Architects' Jl, 1971–74. Hon. FRIBA 1969. *Address:* Kentlands, Hildenborough, Kent TN11 8NR. *T:* Hildenborough 833539.

BOYNE, Sir Henry Brian, (Sir Harry Boyne), Kt 1976; CBE 1969; Political Correspondent, The Daily Telegraph, London, 1956–76; *b* 29 July 1910; 2nd *s* of late Lockhart Alexander Boyne, Journalist, Inverness, and late Elizabeth Jane Mactavish; *m* 1935, Margaret Little Templeton, Dundee; one *d*. *Educ:* High Sch. and Royal Academy, Inverness. Reporter, Inverness Courier, 1927; Dundee Courier and Advertiser, 1929. On active service, 1939–45, retiring with rank of Major, The Black Watch (RHR). Staff Correspondent, Glasgow Herald, at Dundee, 1945, and Edinburgh, 1949; Political Correspondent, Glasgow Herald, 1950. Dir of Communications, Conservative Central Office, 1980–82. Chairman: Parly Lobby Journalists, 1958–59 (Hon. Sec., 1968–71); Parly Press Gallery, 1961–62. Political Writer of Year, 1972. Mem., Police Complaints Bd, 1977–80; Chm., Bd of Visitors, HM Prison, Pentonville, 1980. Mem. Council, Savers' Union, 1982–. *Publications:* The Houses of Parliament, 1981; Scotland Rediscovered, 1986. *Recreations:* reading, playgoing. *Address:* 122 Harefield Road, Uxbridge UB8 1PN. *T:* Uxbridge 55211. *Clubs:* Press, Victory; Western (Dundee).

BOYNE, Maj.-Gen. John, MBE 1965; CEng, FIMechE; FBIM; Dirctor General of Electrical and Mechanical Engineering, Logistic Executive (Army), since 1985; *b* 7 Nov. 1932; *s* of John Grant Boyne and Agnes Crawford (*née* Forrester); *m* 1956, Norma Beech; two *s*. *Educ:* King's Sch., Chester; Royal Military Coll. of Science, Shrivenham (BScEng 1st Cl. Hons). CEng, FIMechE 1975; FBIM 1975; psc 1963, jssc 1968, rcds 1979. Served in Egypt, Cyprus, Libya and UK, 1951–62; Staff Coll., Camberley, 1963; DAQMG(Ops) HQ MEC, Aden, 1964–66; OC 11 Infantry Workshop, REME, BAOR, 1966–67; Jt Services Staff Coll., 1968; GSO2 MoD, 1968–70; GSO1 (DS), Staff Coll., 1970–72; Comdr REME, 2nd Div., BAOR, 1972–73; AAG MoD, 1973–75; CSO (Personnel) to CPL, MoD, 1975–76; Dep. Dir Elec. and Mech. Engrg, 1st British Corps, 1976–78; RCDS, 1979; Dep. Dir Personal Services (Army), MoD, 1980–82; Vice Adjutant Gen. and Dir of Manning (Army), MoD, 1982–85. *Recreations:* choral singing, football. *Address:* c/o Midland Bank, Runcorn, Cheshire.

BOYNTON, Sir John (Keyworth), Kt 1979; MC 1944; LLB; MRTPI; DL; Chief Executive, Cheshire County Council, 1974–79; Solicitor; *b* 14 Feb. 1918; *s* of late Ernest Boynton, Hull; *m* 1st, 1947, Gabrielle Stanglmaier, Munich (*d* 1978); two *d*; 2nd, 1979, Edith Laane, The Hague. *Educ:* Dulwich Coll. Served War, 15th Scottish Reconnaissance Regt, 1940–46 (despatches, MC). Dep. Clerk, Berks CC, 1951–64; Clerk, Cheshire CC, 1964–74. Member: Planning Law Cttee of Law Soc., 1964–; Economic Planning Council for NW, 1965; Exec. Council of Royal Inst. of Public Admin., 1970; Council of Industrial Soc., 1974–; Council, PSI, 1978–83. Pres., RTPI, 1976. Election Commissioner, Southern Rhodesia, 1979–80. DL Cheshire 1975. *Publications:* Compulsory Purchase and Compensation, 1964 (5th edn 1984); Job at the Top, 1986. *Recreation:* golf. *Address:* Flat 2, 1 Redington Gardens, NW3 7RY. *T:* 01–435 0012. *Club:* Army and Navy.

BOYS-SMITH, Captain Humphry Gilbert, DSO 1940; DSC 1943; RD; RNR, retired; *b* 20 Dec. 1904; *s* of late Rev. Edward Percy Boys Smith, MA, Rural Dean of Lyndhurst, Hants, and Charlotte Cecilia, *d* of late Thomas Backhouse Sandwith, CB, HM Consular Service; *m* 1935, Marjorie Helen (*d* 1981), *d* of Capt. Matthew John Miles Vicars-Miles, JP; no *c*. *Educ:* Pangbourne Nautical Coll. Joined Royal Naval Reserve, 1921; Merchant Navy, 1922–35; Extra Master's Certificate, 1930; HM Colonial Service, 1935–40 (Palestine) and 1946–50 (Western Pacific High Commission as Marine Supt); Addnl Mem. RNR Advisory Cttee, 1949–51; War Course, Royal Naval Coll., Greenwich, 1950–51. Courtaulds Ltd, Central Staff Dept, 1951–68. Placed on Retired List of RNR, 1952; Younger Brother of Trinity House, 1944; Mem. of Hon Company of Master Mariners, 1946; Assoc. Instn Naval Architects, 1948; served War of 1939–45 (DSO and Bar, DSC, despatches and American despatches). *Address:* Dibben's, Semley, Shaftesbury, Dorset SP7 9BW. *T:* East Knoyle 358.

BOYS SMITH, Rev. John Sandwith, MA; Master of St John's College, Cambridge, 1959–69 (Fellow, 1927–59 and since 1969; Senior Bursar, 1944–59); Vice-Chancellor, University of Cambridge, 1963–65; Canon Emeritus of Ely Cathedral since 1948; *b* 8 Jan. 1901; *e s* of late Rev. E. P. Boys Smith, formerly Vicar of Hordle, Hants, and Charlotte Cecilia, *e d* of late T. B. Sandwith, CB; *m* 1942, Gwendolen Sara, *o d* of late W. J. Wynn; two *s*. *Educ:* Sherborne Sch.; St John's Coll., Cambridge. Economics Tripos Part I, Class II, division 2, 1921; BA, Theological Tripos, Part I, Sec. B, Class I, 1922; Scholar and Naden Student in Divinity, St John's Coll., 1922; Theological Tripos Part II, Sec. V, Class 1, 1924; Burney Student, 1924; Marburg University, 1924–25; Deacon, 1926; Curate of Sutton Coldfield, Birmingham, 1926–27; Priest, 1927; Chaplain of St John's Coll., Cambridge, 1927–34, and Director of Theological Studies, 1927–40, and 1944–52; Assistant Tutor, 1931–34; Tutor, 1934–39; Junior Bursar, 1939–40; University Lecturer in Divinity, Cambridge, 1931–40; Stanton Lecturer in the Philosophy of Religion, Cambridge Univ., 1934–37; Ely Professor of Divinity in the University of Cambridge and Canon of Ely Cathedral, 1940–43. Hon. Fellow: Trinity Coll., Dublin, 1968; Darwin Coll., Cambridge, 1969. Hon. LLD, Cambridge, 1970. *Publications:* Religious Thought in the Eighteenth Century (with late J. M. Creed), 1934; Memories of St John's College Cambridge 1919–1969, 1983. *Address:* 12 Abbey Lane, Saffron Walden, Essex CB10 1AG. *T:* Saffron Walden 23692; St John's College, Cambridge.

BOYSE, Prof. Edward Arthur, MD; FRS 1977; Member, Sloan-Kettering Institute for Cancer Research, New York, since 1967; Professor of Biology, Cornell University, since 1969; *b* 11 Aug. 1923; *s* of late Arthur Boyse, FRCO, and Dorothy Vera Boyse (*née* Mellersh); *m* 1951, Jeanette (*née* Grimwood); two *s* one *d*. *Educ:* St Bartholomew's Hosp. Med. Sch., Univ. of London. MB BS 1952; MD 1957. Aircrew, RAF, 1941–46, commnd 1943. Various hospital appts, 1952–57; research at Guy's Hosp., 1957–60; research appts at NY Univ. and Sloan-Kettering Inst., 1960–. Amer. Cancer Soc. Res. Prof., 1977. Member: Amer. Acad. of Arts and Scis, 1977; Nat. Acad. of Scis, USA, 1979. Cancer Research Institute Award in Tumor Immunology, 1975; Isaac Adler Award, Rockefeller and Harvard Univs, 1976. *Publications:* papers relating genetics and immunology to development and cancer. *Address:* Memorial Sloan-Kettering Cancer Center, 1275 York Avenue, New York, NY 10021, USA.

BOYSON, Dr Rhodes; MP (C) Brent North, since Feb. 1974; Minister of State, Department of the Environment, since 1986; *b* 11 May 1925; *s* of Alderman William Boyson, MBE, JP and Mrs Bertha Boyson, Haslingden, Rossendale, Lancs; *m* 1st, 1946, Violet Burletson (marr. diss.); two *d*; 2nd, 1971, Florette MacFarlane. *Educ:* Haslingden Grammar Sch.; UC Cardiff; Manchester Univ.; LSE; Corpus Christi Coll., Cambridge. BA, MA, PhD. Served with Royal Navy. Headmaster: Lea Bank Secondary Modern Sch., Rossendale, 1955–61; Robert Montefiore Secondary Sch., Stepney, 1961–66; Highbury Grammar Sch., 1966–67; Highbury Grove Sch., 1967–74. Chm., Nat. Council for Educnl Standards, 1974–79. Chm., Churchill Press and Constitutional Book Club, 1969–79. Councillor: Haslingden, 1957–61; Waltham Forest, 1968–74 (Chm. Establishment Cttee, 1968–71); Chm., London Boroughs Management Services Unit, 1968–70. Formerly Youth Warden, Lancs Youth Clubs. Contested (C) Eccles, 1970. Vice-Chm., Cons Parly Educn Cttee, 1975–76; Hon. Sec. Cons. Adv. Cttee on Educn, 1975–78; Opposition spokesman on educn, 1976–79; Parly Under-Sec. of State, DES, 1979–83; Minister of State: for Social Security, DHSS, 1983–84; NI Office, 1984–86. Educnl columnist, Spectator, 1969. *Publications:* The North-East Lancashire Poor Law 1838–1871, 1965; The Ashworth Cotton Enterprise, 1970; (ed) Right Turn, 1970; (ed) Down with the Poor, 1971; (ed) Goodbye to Nationalisation, 1972; (ed) Education: Threatened Standards, 1972; (ed) The Accountability of Schools, 1973; Oversubscribed: the story of Highbury Grove, 1974; Crisis in Education, 1975; (jt ed) Black Papers on Education, 1969–77; (ed) 1985: An Escape from Orwell's 1984, 1975; Centre Forward, 1978. *Recreations:* reading, writing, talk, hard work, meeting friends, inciting the millenialistic Left in education and politics. *Address:* Laneham, 71 Paines Lane, Pinner, Harrow, Mddx. *T:* 01–866 2071; House of Commons, SW1. *Clubs:* Carlton, St Stephen's; Churchill (N Wembley).

BOZZOLI, Guerino Renzo, DSc(Eng); Chairman: Council, Mangosuthu Technikon, Kwa Zulu, 1978–85; New Era (non-racial) Schools Trust, 1981–85; Vice-Chancellor and Principal, University of the Witwatersrand, Johannesburg, 1969–77; *b* Pretoria, 24 April 1911; *s* of late B. Bozzoli; *m* 1936, Cora Collins, *d* of late L. N. B. Collins; one *s* three *d*. *Educ:* Sunnyside Sch. and Boys' High Sch., Pretoria; Witwatersrand Univ. BSc(Eng) 1933, DSc(Eng) 1948; PrEng. Major, SA Corps of Signals, 1940–45 (commendation 1944). Asst Engr, African Broadcasting Co., 1934–36; Jun. Lectr, Dept of Electrical Engrg, Witwatersrand Univ., Lectr, 1939, Sen. Lectr, 1942; apptd Prof. and Head of Dept of Electrical Engineering, 1948. Dean, Univ. Residence, Cottesloe, 1948–56; Dean, Faculty of Engrg, 1954–57 and 1962–65; Senate Mem., Council of the Univ., 1957–68; Deputy Vice-Chancellor, 1965–68. Member: Straszacker Commn of Enquiry into Univ. Educn of Engineers, 1957–68; de Vries Commn of Enquiry into SA Univs, 1968–75; Nat. Educn Council, 1975–. President: SAIEE, 1955; AS&TS of SA, 1969–70; SA Assoc. for Advancement of Science, 1972. Hon. FSAIEE; Hon. FRSSAf 1976. Hon. LLD: Univ. of Cape Town, 1977; Univ. of Witwatersrand, 1978. *Publications:* numerous articles and papers on engineering education. *Recreations:* swimming, woodwork, electronics. *Address:* 121 Dundalk Avenue, Parkview, Johannesburg, 2193, South Africa. *T:* Johannesburg 646–1015. *Clubs:* 1926, Scientific and Technical (Johannesburg).

BRAADLAND, Erik; diplomat, retired; *b* 21 Nov. 1910; *m* 1940, Aase Rydtun; one *s* two *d*. *Educ:* Oslo Univ. (Degree in Economics). Served in Hamburg, Marseille, Stockholm, Berlin; various periods Ministry of Foreign Affairs, Oslo; Acting Head of Military Mission in Berlin, 1949; Chargé d'Affaires at Bonn, 1951; Minister in Belgrade, 1952; Ambassador in Moscow, 1954–58, in London, 1959–61, for Norway; Mem. of Storting, 1961–69. Knight Commander, Order of St Olav; Order of the Yugoslav Flag, 1st Class. *Address:* Oer, rute 335, 1750 Halden, Norway. *Clubs:* Norwegian, London; Norske Selskab (Oslo).

BRABAZON, family name of **Earl of Meath.**

BRABAZON OF TARA, 3rd Baron *cr* 1942; **Ivon Anthony Moore-Brabazon;** Parliamentary Under-Secretary of State, Department of Transport, since 1986; *b* 20 Dec. 1946; *s* of 2nd Baron Brabazon of Tara, CBE, and Henriette Mary (*d* 1985), *d* of late Sir Rowland Clegg; *S* father, 1974; *m* 1979, Harriet Frances, *o d* of Mervyn P. de Courcy Hamilton, Salisbury, Zimbabwe; one *s* one *d*. *Educ:* Harrow. Mem., Stock Exchange, 1972–84. A Lord in Waiting (Govt Whip), 1984–86. *Recreations:* sailing, Cresta Run. *Heir: s* Hon. Benjamin Ralph Moore-Brabazon, *b* 15 March 1983. *Address:* 35 Cloncurry Street, SW6 6DR. *T:* 01–736 3705. *Clubs:* White's; Royal Yacht Squadron; Bembridge Sailing, St Moritz Tobogganing.

BRABHAM, Sir John Arthur, (Sir Jack Brabham), Kt 1979; OBE 1966; retired, 1970, as Professional Racing Driver; Managing Director: Jack Brabham (Motors) Ltd; Jack

Brabham (Worcester Park) Ltd; Engine Developments Ltd; *b* Sydney, Australia, 2 April 1926; *m* 1951, Betty Evelyn; three *s*. *Educ:* Hurstville Technical Coll., Sydney. Served in RAAF, 1944–46. Started own engineering business, 1946; Midget Speedway racing, 1946–52; several championships (Australian, NSW, South Australian); numerous wins driving a Cooper-Bristol, Australia, 1953–54; to Europe, 1955; Australian Grand Prix, 1955 and 1963 (debut of Repco Brabham); World Champion Formula II, 1958, also many firsts including Casablanca, Goodwood, Brands Hatch, NZ Grand Prix, Belgian Grand Prix; Formula II Champion of France, 1964. World Champion Driver: (after first full Formula I Season with 2½-litre car), 1959–60, 1960–61, 1966. First in Monaco and British Grandes Epreuves, 1959; won Grand Prix of: Holland, Belgium, France, Britain, Portugal, Denmark, 1960; Belgium, 1961. Elected Driver of the Year by Guild of Motoring Writers, 1959, 1966 and 1970, Sportsman of the Year by Australian Broadcasting Co., 1959; left Cooper to take up building own Grand Prix cars, 1961; debut, 1962; first ever constructor/driver to score world championship points, 1963; cars finished first: French GP; Mexican GP, 1964; Formula II and Formula III cars worldwide success, 1963; awarded Ferodo Trophy, 1964 and again, 1966; won French Grand Prix and British Grand Prix, 1966; won French Grand Prix, 1967. RAC Gold Medal, 1966; BARC Gold Medal, 1959, 1966, 1967; Formula I Manufacturers' Championship, 1966, 1967. *Publications:* Jack Brabham's Book of Motor Racing, 1960; When the Flag Drops, 1971; contribs to British journals. *Recreations:* photography, water ski-ing, underwater swimming, flying. *Address:* c/o 248 Hook Road, Chessington, Surrey. *T:* 01–397 4343. *Clubs:* Royal Automobile, British Racing and Sports Car, British Racing Drivers'; Australian Racing Drivers'.

BRABOURNE, 7th Baron, *cr* 1880; **John Ulick Knatchbull,** 16th Bt, *cr* 1641; film and television producer; *b* 9 Nov. 1924; *s* of 5th Baron and Lady Doreen Geraldine Browne (Order of the Crown of India; DStJ) (*d* 1979), *y d* of 6th Marquess of Sligo; *S* brother, 1943; *m* 1946, Lady Patricia Edwina Victoria Mountbatten (*see* Countess Mountbatten of Burma); four *s* two *d* (and one *s* decd). *Educ:* Eton; Oxford. *Films Produced:* Harry Black, 1958; Sink the Bismarck!, 1959; HMS Defiant, 1961; Othello, 1965; The Mikado, 1966; Romeo and Juliet; Up the Junction, 1967; Dance of Death, 1968; Tales of Beatrix Potter, 1971; Murder on the Orient Express, 1974; Death on the Nile, 1978; Stories from a Flying Trunk, 1979; The Mirror Crack'd, 1980; Evil Under the Sun, 1982; A Passage to India, 1984; Little Dorritt, 1986. TV Series: National Gallery, 1974; A Much-Maligned Monarch, 1976. Director: Thames Television, 1978–; Thorn EMI, 1981–. Governor: BFI, 1979– (Fellow, 1985); National Film Sch., 1980–; Mem., British Screen Adv. Council, 1985–; Trustee: BAFTA, 1975–; Science Museum, 1984–. Pres., Kent Trust for Nature Conservation; Chairman: Council, Caldecott Community; Governors, Norton Knatchbull Sch.; Governor: Wye Coll.; Gordonstoun Sch.; United World Colleges; Dep. Pro-Chancellor, Univ. of Kent. *Heir: s* Lord Romsey, *qv*. *Address:* Newhouse, Mersham, Ashford, Kent TN25 6NQ. *T:* Ashford 23466; Mersham Productions Ltd, 41 Montpelier Walk, SW7 1JH. *T:* 01–589 8829.

BRACEGIRDLE, Dr Brian, FSA, FRPS, FIBiol; Keeper, Wellcome Museum of the History of Medicine, Science Museum, London, since 1977; *b* 31 May 1933; *o c* of Alfred Bracegirdle; *m* 1st, 1958, Margaret Lucy Merrett (marr. diss. 1974); one *d*; 2nd, 1975, Patricia Helen Miles; no *c*. *Educ:* King's Sch., Macclesfield; Univ. of London (BSc, PhD). DipRMS. FRPS 1969; FIBiol 1976; FSA 1981. Technician in industry, 1950–57; Biology Master, Erith Grammar Sch., 1958–61; Sen. Lectr in Biol., S Katharine's Coll., London, 1961–64; Head, Depts of Nat. Science and Learning Resources, Coll. of All Saints, London, 1964–77. Hon. Lectr in History of Medicine, University Coll. London. Hon. Treasurer, ICOM (UK); Pres., Assoc. Européenne de Musées de l'Histoire des Sciences Médicales. Pres., Quekett Microscopical Club. *Publications:* Photography for Books and Reports, 1970; The Archaeology of the Industrial Revolution, 1973; The Evolution of Microtechnique, 1978; (with W. H. Freeman): An Atlas of Embryology, 1963; An Atlas of Histology, 1966; An Atlas of Invertebrate Structure, 1971; An Advanced Atlas of Histology, 1976; (with P. H. Miles): An Atlas of Plant Structure, vol. I, 1971; An Atlas of Plant Structure, Vol. II, 1973; Thomas Telford, 1973; The Darbys and the Ironbridge Gorge, 1974; An Atlas of Chordate Structure, 1977; papers on photography for life sciences, on scientific topics, and on history of science/medicine. *Recreations:* walking, music, travel. *Address:* 67 Limerston Street, Chelsea, SW10 0BL. *T:* 01–351 0548. *Club:* Athenæum.

BRACEWELL, Joyanne Winifred, (Mrs Roy Copeland); QC 1978; **Her Honour Judge Bracewell;** a Circuit Judge, since 1983; *b* 5 July 1934; *d* of Jack and Lilian Bracewell; *m* 1963, Roy Copeland; one *s* one *d*. *Educ:* Manchester Univ. (LLB, LLM). Called to Bar, Gray's Inn, 1955; pupillage at the Bar, 1955–56; in practice, Northern Circuit, 1956–83; a Recorder of the Crown Court, 1975–83. *Recreations:* antiques, cooking, reading, walking, bridge. *Address:* (home) Springfield, Macclesfield Road, Alderley Edge, Cheshire SK9 7BW. *T:* Alderley 582000.

BRACEWELL-SMITH, Sir Charles, 4th Bt *cr* 1947, of Keighley; Director of Park Lane Hotel PLC; *b* 13 Oct. 1955; *s* of Sir George Bracewell Smith, 2nd Bt, MBE, and Helene Marie (*d* 1975), *d* of late John Frederick Hydock, Philadelphia, USA; *S* brother, 1983; *m* 1977, Carol Vivien, *d* of Norman Hough, Cookham, Berks. *Heir:* none. *Address:* Park Lane Hotel, Piccadilly, W1.

BRADBEER, John Derek Richardson, OBE 1973; TD 1965; Partner, Wilkinson Marshall Clayton & Gibson, since 1961; Vice-President of the Law Society, 1986–87; *b* 29 Oct. 1931; *s* of William Bertram Bradbeer and Winifred Bradbeer; *m* 1962, Margaret Elizabeth Chantler; one *s* one *d*. *Educ:* Canford Sch.; Sidney Sussex Coll., Cambridge (MA). Nat. Service, 2nd Lieut RA, 1951–52; TA, 1952–77: Lt-Col Comdg 101 (N) Med. Regt RA(V), 1970–73; Col, Dep. Comdr 21 and 23 Artillery Bdes, 1973–76; Hon. Col, 101 (N) Field Regt, RA(V), 1986–. Admitted Solicitor, 1959. Mem. Council, Law Soc., 1973–. Pres., Newcastle upon Tyne Incorp. Law Soc., 1982–83; Gov., Coll. of Law, 1983–. *Recreations:* reading, gardening. *Address:* Forge Cottage, Shilvington, Ponteland, Newcastle upon Tyne NE20 0AP. *T:* Whalton 214. *Clubs:* Army and Navy; Northern Counties (Newcastle upon Tyne).

BRADBROOK, Prof. Muriel Clara, MA, PhD, 1933; LittD Cantab 1955; *b* 27 April 1909; *d* of Samuel Bradbrook, Supt HM Waterguard at Liverpool and Glasgow. *Educ:* Hutchesons' Sch., Glasgow; Oldershaw Sch., Wallasey; Girton Coll., Cambridge. English Tripos, Class I, 1929, 1930; Harness Prize, 1931, Allen Scholar, 1935–36; in residence, Somerville Coll., Oxford, 1935–36. Cambridge University: Univ. Lecturer, 1945–62; Reader, 1962–65; Professor of English, 1965–76; Mistress of Girton College, 1968–76 (Vice-Mistress, 1962–66; Fellow, 1932–35, 1936–68, and 1976–). Board of Trade, Industries and Manufactures Depts 2 and 3, 1941–45; in residence at Folger Library, Washington, and Huntington Library, California, 1958–59; Fellow, Nat. Humanities Center, N Carolina, 1979. Tour of the Far East for Shakespeare's Fourth Centenary, 1964; Trustee, Shakespeare's Birthplace, 1967–82, 1985–. Freedom of the City of Hiroshima. Visiting Professor: Santa Cruz, California, 1966; Kuwait, 1969; Tokyo, 1975; Kenyon Coll., USA, 1977; Rhodes Univ., SA, 1979; Clark Lecturer, Trinity Coll., Cambridge, 1968. FRSL 1947. Hon. LittD: Liverpool, 1964; Sussex, 1972; London, 1973; Hon. LLD Smith Coll., USA, 1965; Hon. PhD, Gothenburg, 1975; Hon. LHD Kenyon Coll., USA, 1977. Foreign Member Norwegian Acad. of Arts and Sciences, 1966; Hon. Mem., Mod. Lang. Assoc. of America, 1974. *Publications:* Elizabethan Stage Conditions, 1932; Themes and Conventions of Elizabethan Tragedy, 1934; The School of Night, 1936; Andrew Marvell (with M. G. Lloyd Thomas), 1940; Joseph Conrad, 1941; Ibsen the Norwegian, 1947; T. S. Eliot, 1950; Shakespeare and Elizabethan Poetry, 1951; The Queen's Garland, 1953; The Growth and Structure of Elizabethan Comedy, 1955; Sir Thomas Malory, 1957; The Rise of the Common Player, 1962; English Dramatic Form, 1965; That Infidel Place, 1969; Shakespeare the Craftsman, 1969; Literature in Action, 1972; Malcolm Lowry: his art and early life, 1974; The Living Monument, 1976; Shakespeare: the poet in his world, 1978; John Webster, Citizen and Dramatist, 1980; Collected Papers, 3 vols, 1982–83; Muriel Bradbrook on Shakespeare, 1984; numerous articles and reviews. *Recreations:* travel, theatre. *Address:* 91 Chesterton Road, Cambridge CB4 3AP. *T:* Cambridge 352765. *Clubs:* University Women's; ADC (Cambridge).

BRADBURN, John; Chief Registrar of the High Court of Justice in Bankruptcy, since 1984; Clerk of the Restrictive Practices Court, since 1980; *b* 4 April 1915; *s* of Harold and Fanny Louise Bradburn; *m* 1948, Irène Elizabeth Norman, JP, *yr d* of Denham Grindley and Bertha Norman; two *s*. *Educ:* Repton; Trinity Coll., Oxford (MA). Served War, 1939–46; Oxfordshire and Bucks LI; Major. Called to the Bar, Inner Temple, 1939; practised at Chancery Bar, Lincoln's Inn, 1946–79 (Bencher, 1972–); a Conveyancing Counsel of the Supreme Court, 1977–80; Registrar in Bankruptcy and of the Companies Court, High Ct of Justice, 1980–84; Lord Chancellor's Legal Visitor, Ct of Protection, 1980–83. Mem., Gen. Council of the Bar, 1962–66. *Address:* Greenlanes, 7 Green Lane, Burnham, Bucks SL1 8DR. *T:* Burnham 5071. *Club:* MCC.

BRADBURY, family name of **Baron Bradbury.**

BRADBURY, 2nd Baron, *cr* 1925, of Winsford; **John Bradbury;** *b* 7 Jan. 1914; *s* of 1st Baron Bradbury, GCB, and Hilda (*d* 1949), 2nd *d* of W. A. Kirby; *S* father 1950; *m* 1st, 1939, Joan, *o d* of W. D. Knight, Darley, Addlestone, Surrey; one *s* one *d*; 2nd, 1946, Gwerfyl, *d* of late E. S. Roberts, Gellifor, Ruthin; one *d*. *Educ:* Westminster; Brasenose Coll., Oxford. *Heir: s* Hon. John Bradbury [*b* 17 March 1940; *m* 1968, Susan, *d* of late W. Liddiard, East Shefford, Berks; two *s*]. *Address:* Wingham, Summerhays, Leigh Hill Road, Cobham, Surrey. *T:* Cobham 7757.

BRADBURY, Edgar; Managing Director, Skelmersdale Development Corporation, 1976–85; *b* 5 June 1927; *s* of Edgar Furniss Bradbury and Mary Bradbury; *m* 1954, Janet Mary Bouchier Lisle; two *s* one *d*. *Educ:* Grove Park Sch., Wrexham; The High Sch., Newcastle, Staffs; King's Coll., Durham Univ. LLB (Hons). Solicitor. Asst Solicitor: Scarborough BC, 1952–54; St Helens CBC, 1954–57; Dep. Town Clerk, Loughborough, 1957–59; Town Clerk and Clerk of the Peace, Deal, 1960–63; Legal Dir, Skelmersdale Develt Corp., 1963–76. Vice-Chm., W Lancs Health Authority, 1984– (Mem., 1982–). *Recreations:* tennis, bridge. *Address:* Overdale, Granville Park, Aughton, Ormskirk. *T:* Aughton Green 422308.

BRADBURY, (Elizabeth) Joyce, CBE 1970; retired Headmistress; *b* Newcastle upon Tyne, 12 Dec. 1918; *o c* of Thomas Edwin and Anne Bradbury. *Educ:* private sch.; Queen Elizabeth's Grammar Sch., Middleton, near Manchester; Univ. of Leeds. BA (Hons Hist.); Dip. in Educn. Various teaching appts, 1941–57; Dep. Headmistress, Stand Grammar Sch. for Girls, Whitefield, near Manchester, 1957–59; Headmistress: Bede Grammar Sch. for Girls, Sunderland, 1959–67; Pennywell Sch. (co-educnl comprehensive), 1967–72; Thornhill Sch. (co-educnl comprehensive), 1972–78. President, Association of Headmistresses, 1974–76. *Recreations:* travel at home and abroad, walking, pursuing historical interests, music and the theatre, domestic 'arts'. *Address:* 6 Cliffe Court, Roker, Sunderland SR6 9NT. *T:* Sunderland 77135. *Club:* Soroptimist.

BRADBURY, Surgeon Vice-Adm. Sir Eric (Blackburn), KBE 1971; CB 1968; FRCS 1972; Medical Director-General of the Navy, 1969–72; Chairman, Tunbridge Wells District Health Authority, 1981–84; *b* 2 March 1911; *s* of late A. B. Bradbury, Maze, Co. Antrim; *m* 1939, Elizabeth Constance Austin; three *d*. *Educ:* Royal Belfast Academical Instn; Queen's Univ., Belfast; MB, BCh 1934; DMRD (London) 1949; Hon. LLD 1973. Joined RN (Medical Service), 1934; served at sea in HMS Barham, HMS Endeavour, HMS Cumberland, 1935–38 and in HMS Charybdis and HMHS Oxfordshire, 1941–45; served in RN Hospitals: Haslar, Chatham, Plymouth and Malta; Med. Officer-in-Charge, RN Hosp., Haslar, and Comd MO, Portsmouth, 1966–69. QHP 1966–72. *Address:* The Gate House, Nevill Park, Tunbridge Wells, Kent TN4 8NN. *T:* 27661.

BRADBURY, Joyce; *see* Bradbury, E. J.

BRADBURY, Prof. Malcolm Stanley; FRSL; Professor of American Studies, University of East Anglia, since 1970; *b* 7 Sept. 1932; *s* of Arthur Bradbury and Doris Ethel (*née* Marshall); *m* 1959, Elizabeth Salt; two *s*. *Educ:* University Coll. of Leicester (BA); Queen Mary Coll., Univ. of London (MA; Hon. Fellow, 1984); Univ. of Manchester (PhD). Staff Tutor in Literature and Drama, Dept of Adult Education, Univ. of Hull, 1959–61; Lectr in English Language and Literature, Dept of English, Univ. of Birmingham, 1961–65; Lectr (later Sen. Lectr and Reader) in English and American Literature, Sch. of English and American Studies, Univ. of East Anglia, 1965–70. Visiting Professor: Univ. of Zürich, 1972; Washington Univ., St Louis, 1982; Univ. of Queensland, 1983. Chm. of Judges, Booker McConnell Prize for Fiction, 1981. Hon. DLitt Leicester, 1986. Editor: Arnold Stratford-upon-Avon Studies series; Methuen Contemporary Writers series. Adapted for television: Tom Sharpe, Blott on the Landscape, 1985. *Publications: non-fiction:* Evelyn Waugh, 1962; E. M. Forster: a collection of critical essays (ed), 1965; What is a Novel?, 1969; A Passage to India: a casebook, 1970; (ed) Penguin Companion to Literature, vol. 3: American (with E. Mottram), 1971; The Social Context of Modern English Literature, 1972; Possibilities: essays on the state of the novel, 1973; (with J. W. McFarlane) Modernism, 1976; (ed) The Novel Today, 1977; (ed) An Introduction to American Studies (with H. Temperley), 1981; Saul Bellow, 1982; All Dressed Up And Nowhere To Go (humour), 1982; The Modern American Novel, 1983; Why Come to Slaka? (humour), 1986; *fiction:* Eating People is Wrong, 1959; Stepping Westward, 1965; The History Man, 1975; Who Do You Think You Are? (short stories), 1976, The After Dinner Game (television plays), 1982; Rates of Exchange, 1982 (shortlisted, Booker Prize). *Recreations:* none. *Address:* School of English and American Studies, University of East Anglia, Norwich NR4 7TJ. *T:* Norwich 56161. *Club:* Royal Over-Seas League.

BRADBURY, Ray Douglas; author; *b* Waukegan, Ill, USA, 22 Aug. 1920; *s* of Leonard S. Bradbury and Esther Moberg; *m* 1947, Marguerite Susan McClure; four *d*. *Educ:* Los Angeles High Sch. First Science-Fiction stories, 1941–44; stories sold to Harpers', Mademoiselle, The New Yorker, etc., 1945–56. Stories selected for: Best American Short Stories, 1946, 1948, 1952, 1958; O. Henry Prize Stories, 1947, 1948; and for inclusion in numerous anthologies. *Screenplays:* Moby Dick, 1954; Icarus Montgolfier Wright, 1961; The Martian Chronicles, 1964; The Picasso Summer, 1968; The Halloween Tree, 1968; The Dreamers; And The Rock Cried Out. Benjamin Franklin Award for Best Story Published in an Amer. Magazine of General Circulation, 1954; 1000 dollar Grant from

Inst. of Arts and Letters, 1954. *Publications: novels:* Dark Carnival, 1947; Fahrenheit 451, 1953 (filmed); (for children) Switch on the Night, 1955; Dandelion Wine, 1957; Something Wicked This Way Comes, 1962 (filmed 1983; adapted for stage, 1986); The Small Assassin, 1973; Mars and the Minds of Man, 1973; The Mummies of Guanajuato, 1978; The Ghosts of Forever, 1981; Death is a Lonely Business, 1986; *short stories:* The Martian Chronicles, 1950 (English edn, The Silver Locusts, 1957); The Illustrated Man, 1951 (filmed with The Day It Rained Forever); The Golden Apples of the Sun, 1953; The October Country, 1955; A Medicine for Melancholy (English edn, The Day It Rained Forever), 1959; (for children) R Is For Rocket, 1962; (for children) S Is For Space, 1962; The Machineries of Joy, 1964; The Autumn People, 1965; The Vintage Bradbury, 1965; Tomorrow Midnight, 1966; Twice Twenty-Two, 1966; I Sing the Body Electric!, 1969; Long After Midnight, 1976; *general:* Zen and the Art of Writing, 1973; *poems:* When Elephants Last in the Dooryard Bloomed, 1973; Where Robot Mice and Robot Men Run Round in Robot Towns, 1977; This Attic where the Meadow Greens, 1980; The Haunted Computer and the Android Pope, 1981; *plays:* The Meadow, 1947; The Anthem Sprinters (one-act), 1963; The World of Ray Bradbury (one-act), 1964; The Wonderful Ice Cream Suit and Other Plays (one-act), 1965; Any Friend of Nicholas Nickleby's is a Friend of Mine, 1968; Pillar of Fire, 1975. *Recreations:* oil painting, ceramics, collecting native masks. *Address:* 10265 Cheviot Drive, Los Angeles, Calif 90064, USA.

BRADBURY, Rear-Adm. Thomas Henry, CB 1979; Group Personnel Director, Inchcape Group of Cos, since 1979; *b* 4 Dec. 1922; *s* of Thomas Henry Bradbury and Violet Buckingham; *m* 1st, 1945, Beryl Doreen Evans (marr. diss. 1979); one *s* one *d*; 2nd, 1979, Sarah Catherine, *d* of Harley Hillier and Mrs Susan Hillier. *Educ:* Christ's Hosp. CO HMS Jufair, 1960–62; Supply Officer, HMS Hermes, 1965–67; Sec. to Controller of Navy, MoD, 1967–70; CO HMS Terror, 1970–71; RCDS, 1972; Dir, Naval Admin. Planning, MoD, 1974–76; Flag Officer, Admiralty Interview Bd, 1977–79. *Recreations:* sailing, gardening. *Address:* Churches Green, Dallington, Heathfield, Sussex. *T:* Rushlake Green 830657.

BRADBY, Edward Lawrence; Principal, St Paul's College, Cheltenham, 1949–72; *b* 15 March 1907; *y s* of late H. C. Bradby, Ringshall End, near Berkhamsted, Herts; *m* 1939, Bertha Woodall, *y d* of late Henry Woodall, Yotes Court, Mereworth, Maidstone; three *s* one *d*. *Educ:* Rugby Sch.; New College, Oxford (MA). Asst Master, Merchant Taylors' Sch., 1930–34; International Student Service, 1934–39; Secretary to Cttee for England and Wales, 1934–36; Asst General Secretary, Geneva, 1936–37; General Secretary, Geneva, 1937–39; Principal, Royal Coll., Colombo, Ceylon, 1939–46; Principal, Eastbourne Emergency Training Coll., 1946–49. Hon. MEd Bristol, 1972. *Publications:* Editor, The University Outside Europe, a collection of essays on university institutions in 14 countries, 1939; Seend, a Wiltshire Village Past and Present, 1981; The Book of Devizes, 1985; Seend Heritage, 1985. *Address:* Beech House, Seend, Melksham, Wilts. *T:* Seend 456. *Club:* Royal Commonwealth Society.

BRADDON, Russell Reading; author; *b* 25 Jan. 1921; *s* of Henry Russell Braddon and Thelma Doris Braddon (*née* Reading). *Educ:* Sydney Church of England Grammar Sch.; Sydney Univ. (BA). Failed Law finals; began writing, by chance, 1949; been writing ever since. *Publications:* The Piddingtons, 1950; The Naked Island, 1951; Those in Peril, 1954; Cheshire, VC, 1954; Out of the Storm, 1956; Nancy Wake, 1956; End of a Hate, 1958; Gabriel Comes to 24, 1958; Proud American Boy, 1960; Joan Sutherland, 1962; The Year of the Angry Rabbit, 1964; Roy Thomson of Fleet Street, 1965; Committal Chamber, 1966; When the Enemy is Tired, 1968; The Inseparables, 1968; Will You Walk a Little Faster, 1969; The Siege, 1969; Prelude and Fugue for Lovers, 1971; The Progress of Private Lilyworth, 1971; End Play, 1972; Suez: splitting of a nation, 1973; The Hundred Days of Darien, 1974; All the Queen's Men, 1977; The Finalists, 1977; The Shepherd's Bush Case, 1978; The Predator, 1980; The Other Hundred Years War, 1983. *Recreation:* not writing. *Address:* c/o John Farquharson Ltd, 162–168 Regent Street, W1R 5TB.

BRADEN, Bernard; free-lance performer and dabbler; *b* 16 May 1916; *s* of Rev. Dr Edwin Donald Braden and Mary Evelyn Chastey; *m* 1942, Barbara Kelly; one *s* two *d*. *Educ:* Maple Grove Public Sch., Point Grey Junior High Sch., Magee High Sch., Vancouver, Canada. Radio engineer, announcer, singer, actor in Vancouver, Canada, 1937–43; wrote and performed in plays for Canadian Broadcasting Corporation, 1940–43, in Vancouver and Toronto, 1943–49. Moved to England, 1949. London plays include: Street-Car Named Desire; Biggest Thief in Town; The Man; No News From Father; Anniversary Waltz; The Gimmick; Period of Adjustment; Spoon River Anthology; Apple Cart. BBC radio programmes include: Breakfast with Braden; Bedtime with Braden. TV includes: inauguration of BBC School's broadcasts; The Brains Trust; Early to Braden; On the Braden Beat; Braden's Week. Man. Dir, Adanac Productions Ltd; Dir, Prime Performers Ltd. Hon. Chancellor, London School of Economics, 1955. BAFTA Features Personality Award; British Variety Club Light Entertainment Personality; RTS Award for artistry in front of the camera. *Publication:* These English, 1948. *Recreations:* family, tennis, and finding time. *Address:* 2 Ovington Square, SW3 1LN.

BRADEN, Hugh Reginald, CMG 1980; Director, A. B. Jay Ltd, since 1981; *b* 1923; *s* of late Reginald Henry Braden and Mabel Braden (*née* Selby); *m* 1946, Phyllis Grace Barnes; one *d*. *Educ:* Worthing High School for Boys; Brighton College of Technology. Joined War Office, 1939; served War, Royal Navy, 1942–45; Far East Land Forces, 1946–50; British Army of the Rhine, 1953–56; War Office and Min. of Defence, 1956–66; jssc 1967; British Embassy, Washington, 1968–70; Min. of Defence, 1971–80 (Asst Under Sec. of State, 1978–80). Borough Councillor. *Address:* Field House, Honeysuckle Lane, High Salvington, Worthing, West Sussex. *T:* Worthing 60203.

BRADFORD, 7th Earl of, *cr* 1815; **Richard Thomas Orlando Bridgeman;** Bt 1660; Baron Bradford, 1794; Viscount Newport, 1815; *b* 3 Oct. 1947; *s* of 6th Earl of Bradford, TD, and of Mary Willoughby, *er d* of Lt-Col T. H. Montgomery, DSO; *S* father, 1981; *m* 1979, Joanne Elizabeth, *d* of B. Miller; two *s*. *Educ:* Harrow; Trinity College, Cambridge. Owner of Porters Restaurant of Covent Garden. *Publications:* (compiled) My Private Parts and the Stuffed Parrot, 1984; The Eccentric Cookbook, 1985. *Heir:* *s* Viscount Newport, *qv*. *Address:* Woodlands House, Weston-under-Lizard, Shifnal, Salop. *T:* (office) Weston-under-Lizard 201.

BRADFORD, Bishop of, since 1984; **Rt. Rev. Robert Kerr Williamson;** *b* 18 Dec. 1932; *s* of James and Elizabeth Williamson; *m* 1956, Anne Boyd Smith; three *s* two *d*. *Educ:* Elmgrove School, Belfast; Oak Hill College, London. London City Missionary, 1955–61; Oak Hill Coll., 1961–63; Asst Curate, Crowborough Parish Church, 1963–66; Vicar: St Paul, Hyson Green, Nottingham, 1966–71; St Ann w. Emmanuel, Nottingham, 1971–76; St Michael and All Angels, Bramcote, 1976–79; Archdeacon of Nottingham, 1978–84. *Recreations:* walking, bird watching, reading and music. *Address:* Bishopscroft, Ashwell Road, Bradford, W Yorks BD9 4AU.

BRADFORD, Provost of; *see* Jackson, Very Rev. B. D.

BRADFORD, Archdeacon of; *see* Shreeve, Ven. D. H.

BRADFORD, (Sir) Edward Alexander Slade, 5th Bt, *cr* 1902 (but does not use the title); *b* 18 June 1952; *s* of Major Sir Edward Montagu Andrew Bradford, 3rd Bt (*d* 1952) and his 2nd wife, Marjorie Edith (*née* Bere); *S* half-brother, Sir John Ridley Evelyn Bradford, 4th Bt, 1954. *Heir:* *uncle* Donald Clifton Bradford [*b* 22 May 1914; *m* 1949, Constance Mary Morgan; three *d*]. *Address:* Faith Cottage, Pett, near Hastings, E Sussex.

BRADFORD, Prof. Eric Watts, MDS (Sheffield); DDSc (St Andrews); Professor of Dental Surgery, 1959–85, now Emeritus, and Pro-Vice-Chancellor, 1983–85, University of Bristol; *b* 4 Nov. 1919; *e s* of E. J. G. and C. M. Bradford; *m* 1946, Norah Mary Longmuir; two *s* three *d*. *Educ:* King Edward VII Sch., Sheffield; High Storrs Grammar Sch., Sheffield; Univ. of Sheffield (Robert Styring Scholar). LDS, Sheffield, 1943; BDS, Sheffield, 1944; MDS, Sheffield, 1950; DDSc St Andrews, 1954. Lieut, Army Dental Corps, Nov. 1944; Capt. Nov. 1945. Lectr, Univ. of Sheffield, 1947–52; Senior Lectr, Univ. of St Andrews, 1952–59; Dean, Faculty of Medicine, Bristol University, 1975–79. Mem., Gen. Dental Council, 1979–85. *Publications:* many papers on dental anatomy in British and other journals. *Address:* 11 Grove Road, Coombe Dingle, Bristol BS9 2RQ. *T:* 681849.

BRADFORD, Rt. Hon. Roy Hamilton, PC (NI) 1969; Member (U) for East Belfast, Northern Ireland Assembly, 1973–75; Minister for the Environment, Northern Ireland Executive, 1973–74; *b* 7 July 1921; *s* of Joseph Hamilton Bradford, Rockcorry, Co. Monaghan, and Isabel Mary (*née* McNamee), Donemana, Co. Tyrone; *m* 1946, Hazel Elizabeth, *d* of Capt. W. Lindsay, Belfast; two *s*. *Educ:* Royal Belfast Academical Institution; Trinity Coll., Dublin. Foundation Schol. 1940; First Class Hons (BA) German and French (with Gold Medal) 1942 (TCD). Army Intelligence, 1943–47 (France, Belgium, Germany). BBC and ITV Producer and Writer, 1950–. Dir, Geoffrey Sharp Ltd, 1962–. MP (U) for Victoria, Parlt of NI, 1965–73; Asst Whip (Unionist Party), 1966; Parly Sec., Min. of Educn, 1967; Chief Whip, Sept. 1968–April 1969; Minister of Commerce, NI, 1969–71; Minister of Develt, NI, 1971–72. Contested (Off U) North Down, 1974. *Publications:* Excelsior (novel), 1960; The Last Ditch (novel), 1981. *Recreations:* golf, architecture. *Address:* Ardkeen, Carnalea, Bangor, Co. Down, N Ireland. *T:* Bangor 465012. *Club:* Ulster (Belfast).

BRADFORD HILL, Sir Austin; *see* Hill.

BRADING, Keith, CB 1974; MBE 1944; Chief Registrar of Friendly Societies and Industrial Assurance Commissioner, 1972–81; *b* 23 Aug. 1917; *s* of late Frederick C. Brading and late Lilian P. Brading (*née* Courtney); *m* 1949, Mary Blanche Robinson. *Educ:* Portsmouth Grammar Sch. Called to Bar, Gray's Inn, 1950. Entered Inland Revenue (Estate Duty Office), 1936. Served War, Royal Navy, 1941–46 (Lieut RNVR); Solicitor's Office, Inland Revenue, 1950; Asst Solicitor, 1962; Asst Registrar of Friendly Societies and Dep. Industrial Assurance Commissioner, 1969. Vice-President: CBSI, 1981–; Bldg Socs Assoc., 1982–. Pres., Soc. of Co-operative Studies, 1983–. *Publications:* contrib. Halsbury's Laws of England and Atkins Court Forms and Precedents. *Address:* 35 Chiswick Staithe, W4. *T:* 01–995 0517. *Club:* Savile.

BRADING, Brig. Norman Baldwin, CMG 1958; CBE 1945; retired; *b* 25 May 1896; *s* of late Rev. F. C. Brading, Ditton, Kent; *m* Helen Margaret, *d* of G. Gatey, Windermere; one *s* one *d*. *Educ:* Whitgift; Royal Military College, Sandhurst. 2nd Lieut East Surrey Regt, 1915; served European War, 1914–19 (wounded); War of 1939–45; France, Holland, Germany; despatches, 1945; Lieut-Col 1940, Col 1943, Brig. 1944. Lent to UNO as Dep. Dir for Ops in Brit. Zone of Germany; National Health Services, 1949; lent to Nigerian Govt as House Governor, University Coll. Hospital, Ibadan, Nigeria, 1952. FHA. Knight Comdr Order of Orange Nassau, with swords (Netherlands), 1945. *Recreations:* polo, swimming. *Address:* Woodstock House, Woodstock, Oxford OX7 1UG. *Club:* Royal Over-Seas League.

BRADLAW, Prof. Sir Robert (Vivian), Kt 1965; CBE 1950; Hon. Professor of Oral Pathology, Royal College of Surgeons of England, since 1948; Emeritus Professor of Oral Medicine, University of London; Emeritus Consultant, Royal Navy; *b* 14 April 1905; *s* of Philip Archibald Bradlaw, Blackrock, Co. Dublin; unmarried. *Educ:* Cranleigh; Guy's Hosp.; University of London. Hilton Prize, etc, Guy's Hosp.; Hon. Degrees, Univs of Belfast, Birmingham, Boston, Durham, Leeds, Malta, Melbourne, Meshed, Montreal and Newcastle upon Tyne; Fellow, Royal Colleges of Surgeons of England, Edinburgh, Glasgow, Ireland, etc; Hon. Fellow, RSM, 1975. Tomes Prize for Research, RCS 1939–41; Howard Mummery Prize for Research, BDA, 1948–53; Colyer Gold Medal, RCS; Hunterian Prof., RCS 1955; Hon. Gold Medal, RCS, 1972; Chevalier de la Santé Publique (France), 1950; Knight, Order of St Olaf, Norway; Commander, Order of Homayoun, Iran. *Recreations:* fishing, golf, orchids, oriental ceramics. *Address:* The Manse, Stoke Goldington, Newport Pagnell, Bucks. *Club:* Athenæum.

BRADLEY, Prof. Anthony Wilfred; Professor of Constitutional Law, University of Edinburgh, since 1968; Editor, Public Law, since 1986; *b* 6 Feb. 1934; *s* of David and Olive Bradley (*née* Bonsey); *m* 1959, Kathleen Bryce; one *s* three *d*. *Educ:* Dover Grammar Sch.; Emmanuel Coll., Cambridge (BA 1957, LLB 1958, MA 1961). Solicitor of the Supreme Court, England and Wales, 1960 (Clifford's Inn Prize). Asst Lectr, 1960–64, Lectr, 1964–68, Cambridge, and Fellow of Trinity Hall, 1960–68; Dean, Faculty of Law, Univ. of Edinburgh, 1979–82. Vis. Reader in Law, UC, Dar es Salaam, 1966–67; Vis. Prof. of Public Law, Univ. of Florence, 1984. Chairman: Edinburgh Council for Single Homeless, 1984–; Social Security Appeal Tribunal, 1984–; Sub-Cttee on Police Powers, ESRC, 1985–; Member Wolfenden Cttee on Voluntary Orgns, 1974–78; Social Scis and Law Cttee, SSRC, 1975–79; Social Studies Sub-Cttee, UGC, 1985–; Cttee of Inquiry into Local Govt in Scotland, 1980; Cttee to review local govt in Islands of Scotland, 1983–84. *Publications:* (with M. Adler) Justice, Discretion and Poverty, 1976; (with D. J. Christie) The Scotland Act 1978, 1979; (ed) Constitutional and Administrative Law, 10th edn, 1985; Administrative Law (in Stair Meml Encyc. of the Laws of Scotland), 1987; articles in legal jls. *Recreation:* music. *Address:* Old College, South Bridge, Edinburgh EH8 9YL. *T:* 031–667 1011.

BRADLEY, Dr Charles Clive; Counsellor (Science and Technology), British Embassy, Tokyo, since 1982; *b* 11 April 1937; *s* of Charles William Bradley and late Winifred Smith; *m* 1965, Vivien Audrey Godley; one *s* one *d*. *Educ:* Longton High Sch.; Birmingham Univ. (BSc Hons in Physics, 1958); Emmanuel Coll., Cambridge (PhD 1962). Nat. Phys. Lab., 1961–67; MIT, 1967, 1969; Nat. Bureau of Standards, USA, 1968; Nat. Phys. Lab., 1969–75; DoI, 1975–82, SPSO and Head of Energy Unit, 1978–82. Dep. Comr Gen. for Britain, Sci. Expo Tokyo, 1985. A. F. Bulgin Prize, IERE, 1972. *Publications:* High Pressure Methods in Solid State Research, 1969; contribs to jls on lasers, metals and semiconductors. *Recreations:* tennis, gardening. *Address:* British Embassy, Tokyo, Japan; 8 Montrose Gardens, Oxshott, Surrey KT22 0UU.

BRADLEY, Clive; Chief Executive, The Publishers Association (incorporating Book Marketing Council, Book Development Council, Educational Publishers Council and University, College and Professional Publishers Council), since 1976; Director, Confederation of Information Communication Industries, since 1984; *b* 25 July 1934; *s* of Alfred and Kathleen Bradley. *Educ:* Felsted Sch., Essex; Clare Coll., Cambridge (Scholar; MA); Yale Univ. (Mellon Fellow). Called to the Bar, Middle Temple. Current Affairs Producer, BBC, 1961–63; Broadcasting Officer, Labour Party, 1963–64; Political Editor, The Statist, 1965–67; Gp Labour Adviser, IPC, 1967–69; Dep. Gen. Man., Daily and Sunday Mirror, 1969–71; Controller of Admin, IPC Newspapers, 1971–72; i/c IPC local radio applications, 1972–73; Dir i/c new prodn arrangements, The Observer, 1973–75. Dep. Chairman: Central London Valuation Panel; Member: Gen. Assembly, Groupe des Editeurs des Livres des Communautés; WIPO/Unesco Jt Consultative Cttee on Developing Countries; Organising Cttee, World Congress on Books, London, 1982; PA delegns to USSR, China, Australia/NZ, Southern Africa and Canada; IPA Congresses, Stockholm, 1980, Mexico City, 1984. Governor, Felsted Sch. Contested (Lab) S Kensington, bye-election, March 1968. *Publications:* (ed) The Future of the Book, 1982; articles on politics, economics, the press, television, industrial relations. *Recreations:* reading, travel. *Address:* 8 Northumberland Place, Richmond, Surrey TW10 6TS. *T:* 01–940 7172; 19 Bedford Square, WC1B 3HJ. *T:* 01–580 6321. *Clubs:* Reform, Groucho; Elizabethan (Yale).

BRADLEY, Prof. Daniel Joseph, PhD; FRS 1976; FInstP; Professor of Optical Electronics, Trinity College Dublin, since 1980; Emeritus Professor of Optics, London University, 1980; *b* 18 Jan. 1928; *s* of John Columba Bradley and Margaret Mary Bradley; *m* 1958, Winefride Marie Therese O'Connor; four *s* one *d*. *Educ:* St Columb's Coll., Londonderry; St Mary's Trng Coll., Belfast; Birkbeck and Royal Holloway Colls, London (BSc Maths, BSc Physics, PhD). Primary Sch. Teacher, Londonderry, 1947–53; Secondary Sch. Teacher, London area, 1953–57; Asst Lectr, Royal Holloway Coll., 1957–60; Lectr, Imperial Coll. of Science and Technol., 1960–64; Reader, Royal Holloway Coll., 1964–66; Prof. and Head of Dept of Pure and Applied Physics, QUB, 1966–73; Prof. of Optics, 1973–80, and Head of Physics Dept, 1976–80, Imperial Coll., London. Vis. Scientist, MIT, 1965; Consultant, Harvard Observatory, 1966. Lectures: Scott, Cambridge, 1977; Tolansky Meml, RSA, 1977. Chairman: Laser Facility Cttee, SRC, 1976–79; British Nat. Cttee for Physics, 1979–80; Quantum Electronics Commn, IUPAP, 1982–; Member: Rutherford Lab. Estab. Cttee, SRC, 1977–79; Science Bd, SRC, 1977–80; Council, Royal Soc., 1979–80. MRIA 1969; Fellow, Optical Soc. of America, 1975. Hon. DSc NUU, 1983. Thomas Young Medal, Inst. of Physics, 1975; Royal Medal, Royal Soc., 1983. *Publications:* papers on optics, lasers, spectroscopy, chronoscopy and astronomy in Proc. Roy. Soc., Phil. Mag., Phys. Rev., J. Opt. Soc. Amer., Proc. IEEE, Chem. Phys. Letts, Optics Communications. *Recreations:* television, walking, DIY. *Address:* Trinity College, Dublin 2, Ireland. *T:* Dublin 772941.

BRADLEY, Prof. David John, DM; FRCP; FRCPath; FFCM; Professor of Tropical Hygiene, University of London and Director, Ross Institute, since 1974; Chairman, Division of Communicable and Tropical Diseases, London School of Hygiene and Tropical Medicine, since 1982; *b* 12 Jan. 1937; *s* of Harold Robert and Mona Bradley; *m* 1961, Lorne Marie, *d* of late Major L. G. Farquhar and Marie Farquhar; two *s* two *d*. *Educ:* Wyggeston Sch., Leicester; Selwyn Coll., Cambridge (Scholar); University Coll. Hosp. Med. Sch. (Atchison Schol., Magrath Schol., Trotter Medal in Surgery, Liston Gold Medal in Surgery, BA Nat. Scis Tripos, Med. Scis and Zoology, 1st cl. Hons, Frank Smart Prize Zool.; MB, BChir, MA 1960); DM Oxon 1972. FIBiol 1974; FFCM 1979; FRCPath 1981; FRCP 1985. Med. Res. Officer, Ross Inst. Bilharzia Res. Unit, Tanzania, 1961–64; Lectr, 1964–66, Sen. Lectr, 1966–69, Makerere Univ. of East Africa, Uganda; Trop. Res. Fellow of Royal Soc., Sir William Dunn Sch. of Pathology, Oxford, 1969–73; Sen. Res. Fellow, Staines Med. Fellow, Exeter Coll., Oxford, 1971–74; Clinical Reader in Path., Oxford Clinical Med. Sch., 1973–74. Co-Director, Malaria Ref. Lab., PHLS, 1974–; Hon. Specialist Community Physician, NW Thames RHA, 1974–, NE Thames RHA, 1984–; Hon. Consultant in Trop. and Communicable Diseases, Bloomsbury DHA, 1983–; Dir, WHO Collaborating Centre Envtl Control of Vectors, 1983–; Mem., Bd of Trustees, Internat. Centre for Diarrhoeal Disease Res., Bangladesh, 1979–85 (Chm., 1982–83); Consultant Advisor to Dir, Royal Tropical Inst., Amsterdam; Member: WHO Expert Adv. Panel on Parasitic Diseases, 1972–; Tech. Adv. Gp, Diarrhoea Programme, 1979–; Tech. Review Gp on Trop. Diseases Programme, 1976; Panel of Experts on Envtl Management, 1981–. For. Corresp. Mem., Royal Belgian Acad. of Medicine, 1984; Corresp. Mem., German Tropenmediziningesellschaft, 1980; Hon. FIPHE, 1981. Editor, Jl of Trop. Med. and Hygiene, 1981–. Chalmers Medal, RSTM&H, 1980. *Publications:* (with G. F. and A. U. White) Drawers of Water, 1972; (with O. V. Baroyan) Problems and Perspectives in Tropical Diseases (in Russian), 1979; (with E. E. Sabben-Clare and B. Kirkwood) Health in Tropical Africa during the Colonial Period, 1980; (with R. G. Feachem, D. D. Mara and H. Garelick) Sanitation and Disease, 1983; papers in learned jls. *Recreations:* natural history, landscape gardens, travel. *Address:* Ross Institute, London School of Hygiene and Tropical Medicine, Keppel Street, WC1E 7HT. *T:* 01–636 8636; 11 Selwyn House, Lansdowne Terrace, WC1N 1DJ. *T:* 01–278 3918.

BRADLEY, Prof. Donald Charlton, CChem, FRSC; FRS 1980; Professor of Inorganic Chemistry since 1965, and Head of Chemistry Department, 1978–82, Queen Mary College, University of London; *b* 7 Nov. 1924; *m* 1948, Constance Joy Hazeldean (*d* 1985); one *s*. *Educ:* Hove County School for Boys; Birkbeck Coll., Univ. of London (BSc 1st Cl. Hons Chemistry, PhD, DSc). Research Asst, British Electrical and Allied Industries Research Assoc., 1941–47; Asst Lectr in Chemistry, 1949–52, Lectr in Chemistry, 1952–59, Birkbeck Coll.; Prof. of Chemistry, Univ. of Western Ontario, Canada, 1959–64. Univ. of London: Chm., Bd of Studies in Chemistry and Chemical Industries, 1977–79; Mem. Senate, 1981–. Mem., Soc. of Chem. Industry; MRI. Royal Society of Chemistry: Pres. Dalton Div., 1983–85; Ludwig Mond Lectr. Exec. Editor, Polyhedron, 1982–. FRSA 1982. *Publications:* (jtly) Metal Alkoxides, 1978; numerous pubns on synthesis and structure of metallo-organic compounds, co-ordination chemistry and inorganic polymers, mainly in Jl of Chemical Soc. *Recreations:* travelling, gardening, listening to music; amateur interest in archaeology. *Address:* Department of Chemistry, Queen Mary College, Mile End Road, E1 4NS. *T:* 01–980 4811.

BRADLEY, Edgar Leonard, OBE 1979; Metropolitan Stipendiary Magistrate, 1967–83; *b* 17 Nov. 1917; 2nd *s* of Ernest Henry and Letitia Bradley, W Felton, Oswestry; *m* 1942, Elsa, *o d* of Colin and Elizabeth Matheson, Edinburgh; two *s* three *d*. *Educ:* Malvern Coll.; Trinity Hall, Cambridge. BA 1939; MA 1944. Called to Bar, Middle Temple, 1940. Served 1940–46, RA; Capt. and Adjt, 1943–45; Major, GSO2, Mil. Govt of Germany, 1946. Practised at Bar, 1946–51, SE Circuit, Central Criminal Ct, S London and Surrey Sessions. Legal Dept of Home Office, 1951–54. Sec., Departmental Cttee on Magistrates' Courts Bill, 1952; Sec. of Magistrates' Courts Rule Cttee, 1952–54; Clerk to Justices: Wrexham and Bromfield, 1954–57; Poole, 1957–67. Justices' Clerks Society: Mem. Council, 1957–67; Hon. Sec., 1963–67. Mem., Nat. Adv. Council on Trng of Magistrates, 1965–67; Magistrates' Association: Vice Pres., 1984–; Mem. Council, 1968–84; Chm. Legal Cttee, 1973–82. Adv. tour of Magistrates' Courts in Ghana, 1970. *Publications:* (with J. J. Senior) Bail in Magistrates' Courts, 1977; articles in legal jls. *Recreations:* gardening, golf. *Address:* Shallows, Hurst Drive, Walton on the Hill, Tadworth, Surrey KT20 7QX. *T:* Tadworth 3655.

BRADLEY, Maj.-Gen. Peter Edward Moore, CB 1968; CBE 1964 (OBE 1955); DSO 1946; Trustee, Vindolanda Trust, 1982–85 (Secretary, 1975–82); *b* 12 Dec. 1914; *s* of late Col Edward de Winton Herbert Bradley, CBE, DSO, MC, DL; *m* Margaret, *d* of late Norman Wardhaugh of Haydon Bridge, Northumberland; three *s*. *Educ:* Marlborough; Royal Military Academy, Woolwich. 2nd Lieut, Royal Signals, 1934. Served War of 1939–45; India, Middle East, Italy and North West Europe (DSO 6th Airborne Div.). Lieut-Col 1954; Col 1957; Brig. 1962; Maj.-Gen. 1965; Signal Officer in Chief (Army), Ministry of Defence, 1965–67; Chief of Staff to C-in-C Allied Forces Northern Europe, Oslo, 1968–70, retired. Dunlop Ltd, 1970–75. Col Comdt, Royal Signals, 1967–82, Master of Signals, 1970–82; Col. Gurkha Signals, 1967–74. CEng, FIEE, 1966; FBIM, 1970. *Address:* c/o RHQ Royal Signals, Cheltenham Terrace, SW3 4RH.

BRADLEY, Richard Alan; Headmaster, Rivers Country Day School, Massachusetts, USA, since 1981; *b* 6 Oct. 1925; *s* of late Reginald Livingstone Bradley, CBE, MC, and of Phyllis Mary Richardson; *m* 1971, Mary Ann Vicary; one *s* two *d* by previous marriage. *Educ:* Marlborough Coll.; Trinity Coll., Oxford (Scholar). 2nd cl. hons Mod. History. Royal Marines, 1944–46; Oxford, 1946–48; Club Manager, Oxford and Bermondsey Club, 1949. Asst Master: Dulwich Coll., 1949–50; Tonbridge Sch., 1950–66 (Head of History Dept, 1957–66; Housemaster of Ferox Hall, 1961–66); Warden of St Edward's Sch., Oxford, 1966–71; Headmaster, Ridley Coll., Canada, 1971–81. *Recreations:* games, dramatics, mountains. *Address:* Rivers Country Day School, 333 Winter Street, Weston, Mass 02193, USA. *Club:* Vincent's (Oxford).

BRADLEY, Roger Thubron, FICFor; FIWSc; Commissioner, Private Forestry and Development, Forestry Commission, since 1985; *b* 5 July 1936; *s* of Ivor Lewis Bradley and Elizabeth Thubron; *m* 1959, Ailsa Mary Walkden; one *s* one *d*. *Educ:* Lancaster Royal Grammar Sch.; St Peter's Coll., Oxford (MA). FICFor 1980. Asst District Officer, Kendal, 1960; Mensuration Officer, Alice Holt, 1961; Working Plans Officer, 1967; District Officer, North Argyll, 1970; Asst Conservator, South Wales, 1974; Conservator, North Wales, 1977; Forestry Commission: Dir, and Sen. Officer for Wales, 1982–83; Dir, Harvesting and Marketing, Edinburgh, 1983–85. *Publications:* Forest Management Tables, 1966, 2nd edn 1971; Forest Planning, 1967; Thinning Control in British Forestry, 1967, 2nd edn 1971; various articles in Forestry, etc. *Recreation:* sailing. *Address:* Easter Dullater, Callander, Perthshire. *Club:* Royal Commonwealth Society.

BRADLEY, Stanley Walter; Director General, British Printing Industries Federation, since 1983; *b* 9 Sept. 1927; *s* of Walter Bradley; *m* 1955, Jean Brewster; three *s* one *d*. *Educ:* Boys' British Sch., Saffron Walden. Joined Spicers Ltd, 1948: held posts in prodn, marketing and gen. management; Personnel Dir, 1973–83; Dir, Capital Spicers Ltd, Eire, 1971–83. Chm., BPIF Manufg Stationery Industry Gp, 1977–81; Pres., E Anglian Printing Industries Alliance, 1978–79; National Econ. Develt Council: Mem., Printing Industries Sector Working Party, 1979–; Chm., Communications Action Team, 1980–. *Recreations:* painting, tennis, fishing. *Address:* The White Cottage, Henham, Bishop's Stortford, Herts CM22 6AG. *T:* Bishop's Stortford 850264.

BRADLEY, Thomas George; Director, British Section, European League for Economic Co-operation, since 1979; *b* 13 April 1926; *s* of George Henry Bradley, Kettering; *m* 1953, Joy, *d* of George Starmer, Kettering; two *s*. *Educ:* Kettering Central Sch., Northants. Elected to Northants County Council, 1952, County Alderman, 1961; Mem., Kettering Borough Council, 1957–61. Transport Salaried Staffs' Association: Branch Officer, 1946–58; Mem. Exec. Cttee, 1958–77; Treasurer, 1961–64; Pres., 1964–77; Acting Gen. Sec., 1976–77. MP Leicester NE, July 1962–1974, Leicester E, 1974–83 (Lab, 1962–81, SDP, 1981–83); PPS: to Minister of Aviation, 1964–65; to Home Secretary, 1966–67; to Chancellor of the Exchequer, 1967–70; Chm., Select Cttee on Transport, 1979–83. Vice-Chm., Labour Party, 1974–75, Chm., 1975–76; Mem., Labour Party NEC, 1966–81. Contested: (Lab) Rutland and Stamford, 1950, 1951 and 1955; (Lab) Preston S, 1959; (SDP) Leicester E, 1983. *Address:* The Orchard, 111 London Road, Kettering, Northants. *T:* Kettering 3019. *Club:* Savile.

BRADLEY, William Ewart; Special Commissioner of Income Tax, 1950–75; *b* 5 Sept. 1910; *s* of W. E. Bradley, Durham City; *m* 1949, Mary Campbell Tyre; two *s*. *Educ:* Johnston Sch., Durham; LSE, London Univ. Inland Revenue, 1929–50. *Address:* 3 Bourne Lane, Tonbridge, Kent. *T:* Tonbridge 352880.

BRADLEY GOODMAN, Michael; *see* Goodman, M. B.

BRADMAN, Sir Donald (George), AC 1979; Kt 1949; President of South Australian Cricket Association, 1965–73; Chairman, Australian Cricket Board, 1960–63 and 1969–72; *b* Cootamundra, NSW, 27 Aug. 1908; *s* of George and Emily Bradman; *m* 1932, Jessie, *d* of James Menzies, Mittagong, NSW; one *s* one *d*. *Educ:* Bowral Intermediate High Sch. Played for NSW 1927–34; for S Australia, 1935–49; for Australia 1928–48, Capt. 1936–48; records include: highest aggregate and greatest number of centuries in England *v* Australia test matches; highest score for Australia *v* England in test matches (334 at Leeds, 1930). Formerly stock and share broker and Mem. Stock Exchange of Adelaide Ltd. *Publications:* Don Bradman's Book, 1930; How to Play Cricket, 1935; My Cricketing Life, 1938; Farewell to Cricket, 1950; The Art of Cricket, 1958; *relevant publications:* Bradman: The Great, by B. J. Wakley, 1959; Sir Donald Bradman, by Irving Rosenwater, 1978; Bradman—The Illustrated Biography, by Michael Page, 1983. *Recreations:* cricket, golf, tennis, billiards, squash. *Address:* 80 King William Street, Adelaide, South Australia. *Clubs:* MCC (Hon. Life Mem.); Commerce (Adelaide).

BRADNEY, John Robert; HM Diplomatic Service, retired; Oman Government Service, since 1986; *b* 24 July 1931; *s* of Rev. Samuel Bradney, Canon Emeritus of St Alban's Abbey, and Constance Bradney (*née* Partington); *m* 1st, Jean Marion Halls (marr. diss. 1971); one *s* two *d*; 2nd, 1974, Sandra Cherry Smith, *d* of Richard Arthur Amyus Smith, MC. *Educ:* Christ's Hospital. HM Forces, 1949–51, Herts Regt and RWAFF; Colonial Police, Nigeria, 1953–65 (Chief Superintendent); HM Diplomatic Service, 1965; First Sec., Lagos, 1974; FCO, 1977–86 (Counsellor, 1985). *Recreations:* salmon and trout fishing, gardening, ornithology. *Address:* PO Box 5272, Ruwi, Sultanate of Oman. *Club:* Royal Over-Seas League.

BRADSHAW, Prof. Anthony David, PhD; FRS 1982; Holbrook Gaskell Professor of Botany, University of Liverpool, since 1968; *b* 17 Jan. 1926; *m* Betty Margaret Bradshaw; three *d*. *Educ:* St Paul's Sch., Hammersmith; Jesus Coll., Cambridge (BA 1947; MA 1951); PhD Wales 1959. Lectr, 1952–63, Sen. Lectr, 1963–64, Reader in Agricl Botany, 1964–68, UCNW, Bangor. Member: Nature Conservancy Council, 1969–78; Natural Environment Res. Council, 1969–74; Bd of Management, Sports Turf Res. Inst., 1976–. Pres., British Ecological Soc., 1981–83. *Publications:* (ed jtly) Teaching Genetics, 1963; (with M. J. Chadwick) The Restoration of Land, 1980; (with others) Quarry Reclamation, 1982; (with others) Mine Wastes Reclamation, 1982; (with R. A. Dutton) Land Reclamation in Cities, 1982; (with Alison Burt) Transforming our Waste Land: the way forward, 1986; (ed jtly) Ecology and Design in Landscape, 1986; contribs to symposia and learned jls. *Recreations:* dinghy sailing, gardening, appreciating land. *Address:* Botany Department, The University, Liverpool L69 3BX.

BRADSHAW, Sir Kenneth (Anthony), KCB 1986 (CB 1982); Clerk of the House of Commons, since 1983; *b* 1 Sept. 1922; *s* of late Herbert and Gladys Bradshaw. *Educ:*

Ampleforth Coll.; St Catharine's Coll., Cambridge (1st Cl. Hons History); MA 1947. War Service, 1942–45; served with Royal Ulster Rifles (2nd Bn), NW Europe (despatches). Temp. Asst Principal, Min. of Supply, Oct.-Dec. 1946; Asst Clerk, House of Commons, 1947; seconded as Clerk of the Saskatchewan Legislature, 1966 session; Clerk of Overseas Office, 1972–76; Principal Clerk, Table Office, 1976–79; Clerk Asst, 1979–83. Pres., Assoc. of Secs Gen. of Parlts, IPU, 1986– (Jt Sec., 1955–71; Vice-Pres., 1984–86). *Publication:* (with David Pring) Parliament and Congress, 1972, new edn 1982. *Club:* Garrick.

BRADSHAW, Maurice Bernard, OBE 1978; Secretary-General, 1958–79, Governor, 1979–81, a Director, 1981–83, Federation of British Artists; Hon. Member Extraordinary, Royal Society of Portrait Painters, 1983; *b* 7 Feb. 1903; 7th *s* of John Bradshaw; *m* 1927, Gladys (*d* 1983), 2nd *d* of Henry Harvey Frost; one *d. Educ:* Christ's Coll., Finchley. Jun. Clerk, Furness Withy & Co., 1918. Dir, Art Exhibns Bureau, 1926–; Asst Sec., British Artists Exhibns, 1927–35; Organising Sec., Floating Art Gall. aboard Berengaria, 1928; Sec., Empire Art Loan Exhibn Soc., 1932; Sec., Modern Architectural Res. Gp, 1938. Commissioned RAFVR, 1941–45. Sec. following art socs: Royal Inst. Oil Painters, 1966–74, Royal Inst. Painters in Watercolours, 1969–79, Royal Soc. British Artists, 1958–74, Royal Soc. Marine Artists, 1938–72, Royal Soc. Portrait Painters, 1955–83, Royal Soc. Miniature Painters, Sculptors and Gravers, 1959–72, Royal British Colonial Soc. of Artists (temp. known as Commonwealth Soc. of Artists), 1930–83, Artists of Chelsea, 1949–72, National Soc., 1968–74, New English Art Club, 1955–74, Pastel Soc., 1968–77, Soc. Aviation Artists, 1954–83, Soc. Graphic Artists, 1968–75, Soc. Mural Painters, 1968–, Soc. Portrait Sculptors, 1969–83, Soc. Wildlife Artists, 1963–80, Soc. Women Artists, 1968–79, Senefelder Gp, 1968–83. *Recreations:* woodwork, philately. *Address:* Holbrook Park House, Holbrook, near Horsham, W Sussex RH12 4PW.

BRADSHAW, Prof. Peter, FRS 1981; Professor of Experimental Aerodynamics, Aero Department, Imperial College of Science and Technology, University of London, since 1978; *b* 26 Dec. 1935; *s* of Joseph W. N. Bradshaw and Frances W. G. Bradshaw; *m* 1968, Sheila Dorothy (*née* Brown). *Educ:* Torquay Grammar Sch.; St John's Coll., Cambridge (BA). Scientific Officer, Aerodynamics Div., National Physical Lab., 1957–69; Sen. Lectr, Dept of Aeronautics, Imp. Coll. of Science and Technol., 1969–71, Reader, 1971–78. *Publications:* Experimental Fluid Mechanics, 1964, 2nd edn 1971; An Introduction to Turbulence and its Measurement, 1971, 2nd edn 1975; (with T. Cebeci) Momentum Transfer in Boundary Layers, 1977; (ed) Topics in Applied Physics: Turbulence, 1978; (with T. Cebeci and J. H. Whitelaw) Engineering Calculation Methods for Turbulent Flow, 1981; (with T. Cebeci) Convective Heat Transfer, 1984; author or co-author of over 100 papers in Jl of Fluid Mechanics, AIAA Jl, etc. *Recreations:* ancient history, walking. *Address:* 67a Blandford Road, Teddington, Mddx TW11 0LG. *T:* (office) 01–589 5111, ext. 4016.

BRADSHAW, Lt-Gen. Sir Richard (Phillip), KBE 1977; Director General, Army Medical Services, 1977–81; *b* 1 Aug. 1920; *s* of late John Henderson Bradshaw and late May Bradshaw (*née* Phillips); *m* 1946, Estelle, *d* of late Emile Meyer; one *d. Educ:* Newport High Sch.; London Univ.; Westminster Hosp. MRCS, LRCP 1945; FRCPath 1967; FFCM 1977; DTM&H 1953; FRSocMed, FRSTM&H, Mem. BMA. House appts Westminster and Kent and Canterbury Hosps. Commnd RAMC, 1946; appts as Hosp. Pathologist, Mil. Hosps in UK and Ceylon; Staff appts in Path., WO, 1950–52; Comd Cons. Pathologist, E Africa, 1954–57; Exch. Officer, Armed Forces Inst. of Path., Washington, 1959–60; Demonstr in Path., Royal Army Med. Coll., Millbank, 1961–63; Asst Dir of Path., BAOR, 1966–69; Prof. of Path., Royal Army Med. Coll., Millbank, 1969–71; CO, Cambridge Mil. Hosp., Aldershot, 1971–73; Comdt RAMC Trng Centre, 1973–75; DMS, BAOR, 1975–77. QHP 1975–81. Member: Council, Sir Oswald Stoll Foundn, Fulham, 1977– (Chm., Management Cttee, 1983–); Council and Cttee, Phyllis Tuckwell Meml Hospice, Farnham, 1981–; formerly HM Comr, Royal Hosp., Chelsea. CStJ 1977. *Publications:* articles and reports in professional jls. *Recreations:* bird-watching, gardening, working with wood. *Address:* c/o Lloyds Bank, 19 Horseferry Road, SW1P 2AD.

BRADSHAW, Thornton Frederick; Chairman, RCA, New York, since 1981 (Chief Executive Officer, 1981–85); *b* 4 Aug. 1917; *s* of Frederick and Julia Bradshaw; *m* 1st, 1940, Sally Davis (marr. diss. 1974); one *s* two *d;* 2nd, 1974, Patricia Salter West; four step *s. Educ:* Phillips Exeter Acad.; Harvard Coll. (BA); Harvard Grad. Sch. of Business (MBA, Dr of Commercial Science). Associate Prof., Sch. of Bus. Admin, Harvard (with time out for Navy service, seven battle stars), 1942–52; Cresap, McCormick & Paget, 1952–56; Atlantic Richfield Co., 1956–81: Vice Pres. and Gen. Man., Finance and Accounting Dept, Jan. 1958; Mem., Bd of Dirs, Feb. 1958; Exec. Vice Pres., 1962; Pres., and Mem. Exec. Cttee of Bd of Dirs, 1964–81; Chm. Exec. Cttee, Jan.-June 1981. Hon. LLD: Pepperdine Univ., 1974; Southampton Coll., 1983; Hon. DSSc Villanova Univ., 1975. Many awards, including: Freedom and Justice Award, NAACP, 1976; Amer. Jewish Cttee Human Relations Award, 1976; Business Statesman Award, Harvard Bus. Sch., 1977; Earl Warren Award for 1980, Amer. Soc. for Public Admin, 1981. *Publications:* Corporations and their Critics, 1980; articles and pubns. *Recreations:* boating, tennis, swimming; also a prolific reader, fond of history and biography. *Address:* 435 East 52nd Street, Apt 13C, New York, NY 10022, USA; (office) 30 Rockefeller Plaza, New York, NY 10020. *T:* (212) 621–6000. *Clubs:* Mark's; Economic, Harvard, Knickerbocker, River, University (New York); California (LA); Valley Hunt (Pasadena, Calif.).

BRADSHAW, William Peter; Senior Visiting Research Fellow, Centre for Socio-Legal Studies, Wolfson College, Oxford, since 1985; *b* 9 Sept. 1936; *s* of Leonard Charles Bradshaw and Ivy Doris Bradshaw; *m* 1957, Jill Hayward; one *s* one *d. Educ:* Univ. of Reading (BA Pol. Economy, 1957; MA 1960). MCIT 1966. Joined Western Region of British Railways as Management Trainee, 1959; various appts, London and W of England Divs; Divl Manager, Liverpool, 1973; Chief Operating Man., LMR, 1976, Dep. Gen. Man. 1977; Chief Ops Man., BR HQ, 1978; Dir, Policy Unit, 1980; Gen. Man., Western Region, BR, 1983–85. *Recreations:* growing hardy plants; playing member of a brass band. *Address:* Centre for Socio-Legal Studies, Wolfson College, Oxford OX2 6UD. *T:* Oxford 52967. *Club:* National Liberal.

BRADSHAW-ISHERWOOD, Christopher William; see Isherwood, Christopher.

BRADWELL, Area Bishop of; Rt. Rev. (Charles) Derek Bond; appointed Bishop Suffragan of Bradwell, 1976, Area Bishop, 1984; *b* 4 July 1927; *s* of Charles Norman Bond and Doris Bond; *m* 1951, Joan Valerie Meikle; two *s* two *d. Educ:* Bournemouth Sch.; King's Coll., London. AKC (2nd hons). Curate of Friern Barnet, 1952; Midlands Area Sec. of SCM in Schools and Public Preacher, dio. Birmingham, 1956; Vicar: of Harringay, 1958; of Harrow Weald, 1962; Archdeacon of Colchester, 1972–76. Nat. Chm., CEMS, 1983–86. *Recreation:* travel. *Address:* 188 New London Road, Chelmsford CM2 0AR. *T:* Chelmsford 84235.

BRADY, Rev. Canon Ernest William; Dean of Edinburgh, 1976–82 and 1985–86; *b* 10 Nov. 1917; *s* of Ernest and Malinda Elizabeth Brady; *m* 1948, Violet Jeanne Louise Aldworth; one *s* one *d. Educ:* Harris Academy, Dundee (Dux and Classics Medallist,

1936); Univ. of St Andrews; Edinburgh Theological Coll. (Luscombe Schol. 1942). LTh (Dunelm) 1942. Deacon 1942, Priest 1943; Asst Curate, Christ Church, Glasgow, 1942; Asst Curate, St Alphage, Hendon, 1946; Rector, All Saints, Buckie, 1949; Rector, All Saints, Edinburgh, 1957; Chaplain, Royal Infirmary of Edinburgh, 1959–74; Priest-in-Charge, Priory Church of St Mary of Mount Carmel, South Queensferry, 1974–82; Canon of St Mary's Cathedral, Edinburgh, 1967, Hon. Canon, 1983; Synod Clerk, Diocese of Edinburgh, 1969. Sub-dean, Collegiate Church of St Vincent, Edinburgh (Order of St Lazarus of Jerusalem), 1982–. Kt of Holy Sepulchre of Jerusalem (Golden Cross with Crown), 1984. *Recreations:* Holy Land pilgrimage; choral music; ecclesiastical vestments and embroidery. *Address:* 44 Glendevon Place, Edinburgh EH12 5UJ. *T:* 031–337 9528.

BRADY, Prof. (John) Michael; Professor of Information Engineering, Oxford University, since 1985; *b* 30 April 1945; *s* of John and Priscilla Mansfield; *m* 1967, Naomi Friedlander; two *d. Educ:* Manchester Univ. (BSc (1st Cl. Hons Mathematics) 1966; Renold Prize 1967; MSc 1968); Australian National Univ. (PhD 1970). Lectr, Computer Science, 1970, Sen. Lectr 1979, Essex Univ.; Sen. Res. Scientist, MIT, 1980. *Publications:* Theory of Computer Science, 1975; Computer Vision, 1981; Robot Motion, 1982; Computational Theory of Discourse, 1982; Robotics Research, 1984; Artificial Intelligence and Robotics, 1984; contribs to jls on computer vision, robotics, artificial intelligence, computer science. *Recreations:* squash, music, winetasting.

BRADY, Terence Joseph; playwright, novelist and actor, since 1962; *b* 13 March 1939; *s* of late Frederick Arthur Noel and of Elizabeth Mary Brady; *m* Charlotte Mary Thérèse Bingham, *qv;* one *s* one *d. Educ:* Merchant Taylors', Northwood; TCD (BA Moderatorship, History and Polit. Science). Actor: Would Anyone who saw the Accident?, The Dumb Waiter, Room at the Top, 1962; Beyond the Fringe, 1962–64; Present from the Corporation, In the Picture, 1967; Quick One 'Ere, 1968; films include: Baby Love; Foreign Exchange; TV appearances include plays, comedy series and shows, incl. Nanny, 1981, and Pig in the Middle, 1981, 1982, 1983. Writer for *radio:* Lines from my Grandfather's Forehead (BBC Radio Writers' Guild Award, Best Radio Entertainment, 1972); *television:* Broad and Narrow; TWTWTW; with Charlotte Bingham: TV series: Boy Meets Girl; Take Three Girls; Upstairs Downstairs; Away From It All; Play for Today; Plays of Marriage; No—Honestly; Yes—Honestly; Thomas and Sarah; Pig in the Middle; The Complete Lack of Charm of the Bourgeoisie; Nanny; Oh Madeline! (USA TV); Father Matthew's Daughter; A View of Meadows Green; Love with a Perfect Stranger (TV film); *stage:* (contrib.) The Sloane Ranger Revue, 1985. *Publications:* Rehearsal, 1972; The Fight Against Slavery, 1976; with Charlotte Bingham: Victoria, 1972; Rose's Story, 1973; Victoria and Company, 1974; Yes—Honestly, 1977; regular contribs to Daily Mail, Living, Country Homes and Interiors, Punch. *Recreations:* painting, music, horses, avoiding dinner parties. *Address:* c/o A. D. Peters, Literary Agent, 10 Buckingham Street, WC2. *Clubs:* Sloane; Sherborne Golf.

BRAGG, Melvyn; writer; Presenter and Editor, The South Bank Show, for ITV, since 1978; Head of Arts, London Weekend Television, since 1982; Deputy Chairman, Border Television, since 1985; *b* 6 Oct. 1939; *s* of Stanley Bragg and Mary Ethel (*née* Parks); *m* 1st, 1961, Marie-Elisabeth Roche (decd); one *d;* 2nd, 1973, Catherine Mary Haste; one *s* one *d. Educ:* Nelson-Thomlinson Grammar Sch., Wigton; Wadham Coll., Oxford (MA). BBC Radio and TV Producer, 1961–67; writer and broadcaster, 1967–. Novelist, 1964–. FRSL. Mem. ACTT. Presenter, BBC TV series: 2nd House, 1973–77; Read all About It (also editor), 1976–77. Mem. Arts Council, and Chm. Literature Panel of Arts Council, 1977–80. President: Cumbrians for Peace, 1982–; Northern Arts, 1983–; Nat. Campaign for the Arts, 1986–. Hon. DLitt Liverpool, 1986. *Plays:* Mardi Gras, 1976 (musical); Orion (TV), 1977; The Hired Man, 1984 (musical); *screenplays:* Isadora; Jesus Christ Superstar; (with Ken Russell) Clouds of Glory. *Publications:* Speak for England, 1976; Land of the Lakes, 1983 (televised); Laurence Olivier, 1984; *novels:* For Want of a Nail, 1965; The Second Inheritance, 1966; Without a City Wall, 1968; The Hired Man, 1969; A Place in England, 1970; The Nerve, 1971; Josh Lawton, 1972; The Silken Net, 1974; A Christmas Child, 1976; Autumn Manoeuvres, 1978; Kingdom Come, 1980; Love and Glory, 1983; weekly column in Punch; articles for various English jls. *Recreations:* walking, books. *Address:* 12 Hampstead Hill Gardens, NW3. *T:* 01–435 7215. *Clubs:* Garrick, PEN.

BRAGG, Stephen Lawrence, MA, SM; FEng; FIMechE; FRAeS; Director in Industrial Co-operation, University of Cambridge, since 1984; Fellow, Wolfson College, Cambridge, since 1982; *b* 17 Nov. 1923; *e s* of late Sir Lawrence Bragg, CH, OBE, MC, FRS and of Lady Bragg, CBE; *m* 1951, Maureen Ann (*née* Roberts); three *s. Educ:* Rugby Sch.; Cambridge Univ.; Massachusetts Inst. of Technology. BA 1945, MA 1949 (Cambridge); SM 1949 (MIT). FEng 1981. Rolls-Royce Ltd, 1944–48; Commonwealth Fund Fellow, 1948–49; Wm Jessop Ltd, Steelmakers, 1949–51; Rolls-Royce Ltd, 1951–71: Chief Scientist, 1960–63; Chief Research Engineer, 1964–68; Dir, Aero Div., 1969–71. Vice-Chancellor, Brunel Univ., 1971–81. Eastern Region Broker, SERC, 1981–83. Chm., Cambridge DHA, 1982–86. Member: Univ. Grants Cttee, 1966–71; Aeronautical Research Council, 1970–73; Court of ASC, Henley, 1972–81; SRC Engineering Bd, 1976–79; Airworthiness Requirements Bd, 1979–81; Chm., Adv. Cttee on Falsework, 1973–75. Corres. Mem. Venezuelan Acad. Sci., 1975. Hon. DEng Sheffield, 1969; Hon. DTech Brunel, 1982. *Publications:* Rocket Engines, 1962; articles on Jet Engines, Research Management, University/Industry Collaboration, etc. *Recreation:* railway history. *Address:* 22 Brookside, Cambridge CB2 1JQ. *T:* Cambridge 62208. *Club:* Athenæum.
   See also Sir Mark Heath, D. P. Thomson.

BRAGGINS, Maj.-Gen. Derek Henry, CB 1986; Director General, Transport and Movements, Army, 1983–86; *b* 19 April 1931; *s* of Albert Edward Braggins and Hilda Braggins; *m* 1953, Sheila St Clair (*née* Stuart); three *s. Educ:* Rothesay Academy; Hendon Technical College. FBIM 1979, FCIT 1983. Commissioned RASC, 1950; RCT, 1965; regtl and staff appts, Korea, Malaya, Singapore, Ghana, Aden, Germany and UK; student, Staff Coll., Camberley, 1962, JSSC, Latimer, 1970; CO 7 Regt RCT, 1973–75; Col AQ Commando Forces RM, 1977–80; Comd Transport and Movements, BAOR, 1981–83; Col Comdt, RCT, 1986–. Pres., Army Caving Assoc., 1983–. Freeman, City of London, 1983; Hon. Liveryman, Worshipful Co. of Carmen, 1983. *Recreations:* hashing, shooting, fishing, gardening. *Address:* c/o Lloyds Bank, 6 Pall Mall, SW1Y 5NH.

BRAHAM, Allan John Witney, PhD; Keeper and Deputy Director, the National Gallery, since 1978; *b* 19 Aug. 1937; *s* of Dudley Braham and Florence Mears; *m* 1963, Helen Clare Butterworth; two *d. Educ:* Dulwich Coll.; Courtauld Inst. of Art, Univ. of London (BA 1960, PhD 1967). Asst Keeper, National Gall., 1962, Dep. Keeper, 1973. Arts Council Exhibn (with Peter Smith), François Mansart, 1970–71; National Gall. Exhibitions: (co-ordinator and editor) The Working of the National Gallery, 1974; Velázquez, The Rokeby Venus, 1976; Giovanni Battista Moroni, 1978; Italian Renaissance Portraits, 1979; El Greco to Goya, 1981; Wright of Derby "Mr and Mrs Coltman", 1986. *Publications:* Dürer, 1965; Murillo (The Masters), 1966; The National Gallery in London: Italian Painting of the High Renaissance, 1971; (with Peter Smith) François Mansart, 1973; Funeral Decorations in Early Eighteenth Century Rome, 1975; (with Hellmut Hager) Carlo Fontana: The Drawings at Windsor Castle, 1977; The Architecture of the

French Enlightenment, 1980 (Hitchcock Medal, Banister Fletcher Prize); National Gall. catalogues: The Spanish School (revised edn), 1970, and booklets: Velázquez, 1972; Rubens, 1972; Architecture, 1976; Italian Paintings of the Sixteenth Century, 1985; contrib. prof. jls, etc. *Recreation:* history of architecture. *Address:* 15A Acol Road, NW6 3AA.

BRAHAM, Harold, CBE 1960; HM Diplomatic Service, retired; *b* Constantinople, 11 Oct. 1907; *er s* of late D. D. Braham, of The Times; *m* 1941, Cicely Edith Norton Webber; one *s* one *d*. *Educ:* St Peter's Coll., Adelaide; New College, Oxford. Entered HM Consular Service, China, 1931. Retired as HM Consul-Gen., Paris, 1966. *Recreations:* contemporary Spanish history, carpentry. *Address:* Caserio Torret 19, San Luis, Prov. Baleares, Spain.

BRAHIMI, Lakhdar; Assistant Secretary-General, League of Arab States, Tunis, since 1984; *b* 1934; *m* 1964; two *s* one *d*. *Educ:* Faculté de Droit and Institut des Sciences Politiques, Algiers; then Paris. Permanent Rep. of FLN and later of Provisional Govt of Algeria, in SE Asia, 1956–61; Gen. Secretariat, Min. of External Affairs, 1961–63; Ambassador to UAR and Sudan, and Permanent Rep. to Arab League, 1963–70; Ambassador to Court of St James's, 1971–79; Mem., Central Cttee, National Liberation Front, Algeria, 1979–84; Pol Advr to President Chadli, 1982–84. *Address:* The League of Arab States, Tunis, Tunisia.

BRAILSFORD, John William; Keeper, Department of Prehistoric and Romano-British Antiquities, British Museum, 1969–73; *b* 14 July 1918; *o s* of Alfred and Dorothy H. M. Brailsford; *m* 1945, Mary Freeman Boaden; one *s* one *d*. *Educ:* Bedales; Emmanuel College, Cambridge. Sen. Exhibnr and Scholar, BA, MA 1943. Royal Artillery (Survey), 1939–45; Intell. (Air Photo Interpretation), 1945–46. Asst Keeper, Dept of British and Medieval Antiquities, Brit. Mus., 1946; Dep. Keeper, 1963. FMA; FSA 1949; Fellow, German Archaeolog. Inst., 1967. *Publications:* Museum Handbooks to Mildenhall Treasure, 1947; Antiquities of Roman Britain, 1951; Later Prehistoric Antiquities of the British Isles, 1953; Antiquities from Hod Hill in the Durden Collection, 1962; (ed) Hod Hill: Excavations, 1951–58; 1968; Early Celtic Masterpieces from Britain in the British Museum, 1975; papers in learned jls. *Recreations:* various. *Address:* Sunnyside, Brook End, Chadlington, Oxon. *T:* Chadlington 378.

BRAIN, family name of **Baron Brain.**

BRAIN, 2nd Baron *cr* 1962, of Eynsham; **Christopher Langdon Brain;** Bt 1954; *b* 30 Aug. 1926; *s* of 1st Baron Brain, MA, DM, FRS, FRCP and Stella, *er d* of late Reginald L. Langdon-Down; *S* father 1966; *m* 1953, Susan Mary, *d* of George P. and Ethelbertha Morris; three *d*. *Educ:* Leighton Park Sch., Reading; New College, Oxford. MA 1956. Royal Navy, 1946–48. Liveryman, 1955, Upper Warden, 1974–75, Asst, 1980, Renter Bailiff, 1983–84, Upper Bailiff, 1984–85, Worshipful Co. of Weavers. Chm., Rhone-Alps Regional Council, British Chamber of Commerce, France, 1967. ARPS 1970. *Recreations:* bird watching, sailing, fly-fishing. *Heir: b* Hon. Michael Cottrell Brain, MA, DM, FRCP, FRCP Canada, Prof. of Medicine, McMaster Univ. [*b* 6 Aug. 1928; *m* 1960, Dr the Hon. Elizabeth Ann Herbert, *e d* of Baron Tangley, KBE; one *s* two *d*]. *Address:* Laragh, Belmont Road, Combe Down, Bath BA2 5JR. *Club:* Oxford and Cambridge Sailing Society.

BRAIN, Albert Edward Arnold; Regional Director (East Midlands), Department of the Environment, and Chairman of Regional Economic Planning Board, 1972–77; *b* 31 Dec. 1917; *s* of Walter Henry and Henrietta Mabel Brain; *m* 1947, Patricia Grace Gallop; two *s* one *d*. *Educ:* Rendcomb Coll., Cirencester; Loughborough College. BSc (Eng) London, external; DLC hons Loughborough; CEng, MICE, MIMunE. Royal Engineers, 1940–46; Bristol City Corp., 1946–48; Min. of Transport: Asst Engr, London, 1948–54; Civil Engr, Wales, 1954–63; Sen. Engr, HQ, 1963–67; Asst Chief Engr, HQ, 1967–69; Divl Road Engr, W Mids, now Regional Controller (Roads and Transportation), 1969–72. *Recreations:* gardening, campanology. *Address:* Withyholt Lodge, Moorend Road, Charlton Kings, Cheltenham GL53 9BW. *T:* Cheltenham 76264.

BRAIN, Sir (Henry) Norman, KBE 1963 (OBE 1947); CMG 1953; *b* 19 July 1907; *s* of late B. Brain, Rushall, Staffs; *m* 1939, Nuala Mary, *d* of late Capt. A. W. Butterworth; one *s* (and one *s* decd). *Educ:* King Edward's Sch., Birmingham; The Queen's Coll., Oxford (MA). Entered the Consular Service, 1930, and served at Tokyo, Kobe, Osaka, Tamsui, Manila, Mukden, Shanghai and Dairen; interned by Japanese, 1941–42; repatriated and served in Foreign Office, 1943; appointed to Staff of Supreme Allied Comdr, South-East Asia, 1944–46; Political Adviser to Saigon Control Commission, 1945; served with Special Commissioner in South-East Asia, at Singapore, 1946–48; Counsellor in Foreign Office, 1949; Inspector of HM Foreign Service Estabts, 1950–53; Minister, Tokyo, 1953–55; Ambassador to Cambodia, 1956–58; Asst Under-Sec. of State, FO, 1958–61; Ambassador to Uruguay, 1961–66, retired, 1966. Chairman: Royal Central Asian Soc., 1970–74; Japan Soc. of London, 1970–73; Pres., British Uruguayan Soc., 1974–. *Recreations:* music, golf. *Address:* St Andrews, Abney Court, Bourne End, Bucks. *Club:* Canning.

BRAIN, Ronald, CB 1967; Chairman, London and Quadrant Housing Trust, 1977–79; *b* 1 March 1914; *s* of T. T. G. Brain, RN, and E. C. Brain (*née* Fruin); *m* 1943, Lilian Rose (*née* Ravenhill); one *s* one *d*. *Educ:* Trowbridge High Sch. Audit Asst, Min. of Health, 1932; Principal, Min. of Health, 1946; Asst Sec., Min. of Housing and Local Govt, 1952; Under-Sec., 1959; Dep. Sec., Dept of Environment (formerly Min. of Housing and Local Govt), 1966–74. *Recreations:* music, chess. *Address:* Flat 4, Badminton, Galsworthy Road, Kingston-upon-Thames, Surrey.

BRAINE, Rt. Hon. Sir Bernard (Richard), Kt 1972; PC 1985; DL; MP (C) Castle Point, since 1983 (Billericay Division of Essex, 1950–55; South East Essex, 1955–83); *b* Ealing, Middx, 24 June 1914; *s* of Arthur Ernest Braine; *m* 1935, Kathleen Mary Faun (*d* 1982); three *s*. *Educ:* Hendon County Grammar Sch. Served North Staffs Regt in War of 1939–45: West Africa, SE Asia, NW Europe; Staff Coll., Camberley, 1944 (sc); Lt-Col. Chm., British Commonwealth Producers' Organisation, 1958–60; Parly Sec., Min. of Pensions and National Insurance, 1960–61; Parly Under-Sec. of State for Commonwealth Relations, 1961–62; Parly Sec., Min. of Health, 1962–64; Conservative front bench spokesman on Commonwealth Affairs and Overseas Aid, 1967–70; Chm., Select Cttees on Overseas Aid, 1970–71, on Overseas Develt, 1973–74; Treasurer, UK Branch of Commonwealth Parly Assoc., 1974–77 (Dep. Chm., 1964 and 1970–74). Vice-Pres., Commonwealth Youth Exchange Council, 1979–; Chairman: British-German Parly Group, 1970–; British-Greek Parly Group, 1979–; All-party Pro Life Cttee; All-party Misuse of Drugs Cttee; Nat. Council on Alcoholism, 1973–82; UK Chapter, Soc. of Internat. Develt, 1976–83; Vice-Chm., Parly Human Rights Gp, 1979–. President: UK Cttee for Defence of the Unjustly Prosecuted, 1980–; River Thames Soc., 1981–; Greater London Alcohol Adv. Service, 1983–. President, Cons. Clubs of Benfleet, Hadleigh and Canvey Is. Associate Mem., Inst. of Develt Studies, Univ. of Sussex, 1971–; a Governor, Commonwealth Inst., 1968–81, Trustee, 1981–. FRSA 1971. DL Essex, 1978. KStJ 1985. Comdr's Cross, German Order of Merit, 1974, Knight Cmdr's Cross with Star, 1984; Europe Peace Cross, 1979; Comdr's Cross with Star, Order of Polonia Restituta, 1983. *Address:* King's Wood, Rayleigh, Essex. *Club:* Beefsteak.

BRAINE, John (Gerard); author; *b* 13 April 1922; *s* of Fred and Katherine Braine; *m* 1955, Helen Patricia Wood; one *s* three *d*. *Educ:* St Bede's Grammar Sch., Bradford. Furniture-shop asst, bookshop asst, laboratory asst, progress chaser, in rapid succession, 1938–40; Asst, Bingley Public Library, 1940–49; HM Navy, 1942–43; Chief Asst, Bingley Public Library, 1949–51; free-lance writer, London and Yorks, with interval in hospital, 1951–54; Branch Librarian, Northumberland County Library, 1954–56; Branch Librarian, West Riding of Yorks County Library, 1956–57. Writer in Residence, Purdue Univ., 1978. ALA 1950. *Publications:* Room at the Top, 1957 (filmed 1958); The Vodi, 1959; Life at the Top, 1962 (filmed 1965); The Jealous God, 1964; The Crying Game, 1968; Stay with Me till Morning, 1970 (adapted for TV, 1980); The Queen of a Distant Country, 1972 (adapted for TV, 1978); Writing a Novel, 1974; The Pious Agent, 1975; Waiting for Sheila, 1976 (adapted for TV, 1977); Finger of Fire, 1977; J. B. Priestley, 1979; One and Last Love, 1981; The Two of Us, 1984; These Golden Days, 1985. *TV Series:* Man at the Top, 1970, 1972. *Recreations:* walking, talking, Victoriana, and dieting. *Address:* c/o Methuen London Ltd, 11 New Fetter Lane, EC4P 4EE. *Club:* PEN.

BRAINE, Rear-Adm. Richard Allix, CB 1956; Retired; *b* 18 Nov. 1900; *m* 1922; one *s*. *Educ:* Dean Close Memorial Sch., Cheltenham. Joined RN as asst clerk, 1918; Comdr (S), Dec. 1938; Capt. (S), Dec. 1948; Rear-Adm. 1954. Command Supply Officer, Staff of Flag Officer Air (Home), 1954–56, Portsmouth, 1956–57. *Address:* The Old Cottage, Littlewick Green, near Maidenhead, Berks. *T:* Littlewick Green 4484.

BRAININ, Norbert, OBE 1960; Leader of Amadeus String Quartet; Professor of Chamber Music, Hochschule für Musik, Cologne, since 1979; *b* Vienna, 12 March 1923; *s* of Adolph and Sophie Brainin; *m* 1948, Kathe Kottow; one *d*. *Educ:* High Sch., Vienna. Commenced musical training in Vienna at age of seven and continued studies there until 1938; emigrated to London in 1938 and studied with Carl Flesch and Max Rostal; won Carl Flesch prize for solo violinists at the Guildhall Sch. of Music, London, 1946. Formed Amadeus String Quartet, 1947. DUniv York, 1968. Grand Cross of Merit, 1st cl. Fed. Republic of Germany, 1972; Cross of Honour for Arts and Science (Austria), 1972. *Address:* 19 Prowse Avenue, Bushey Heath, Herts. *T:* 01–950 7379.

BRAITHWAITE, Bernard Richard; His Honour Judge Braithwaite; a Circuit Judge (formerly County Court Judge), since 1971; *b* 20 Aug. 1917; *s* of Bernard Leigh Braithwaite and Emily Dora Ballard Braithwaite (*née* Thomas); unmarried. *Educ:* Clifton; Peterhouse, Cambridge. BA (Hons), Law. Served War: 7th Bn Somerset LI, 1939–43; Parachute Regt, 1943–46; Captain, Temp. Major. Called to Bar, Inner Temple, 1946. *Recreations:* hunting, sailing. *Address:* Summerfield House, Uley, Gloucestershire. *Club:* Boodle's.

BRAITHWAITE, Eustace Edward Adolph Ricardo; writer; Ambassador of Guyana to Venezuela, 1968–69; *b* 27 June 1922. *Educ:* New York Univ.; Cambridge Univ. Served War of 1939–45, RAF. Schoolteacher, London, 1950–57; Welfare Officer, LCC, 1958–60; Human Rights Officer, World Veterans Foundation, Paris, 1960–63; Lecturer and Education Consultant, Unesco, Paris, 1963–66; Permanent Rep. of Guyana to UN, 1967–68. Ainsfield-Wolff Literary Award, 1961; Franklin Prize. *Publications:* To Sir With Love, 1959; Paid Servant, 1962; A Kind of Homecoming, 1962; Choice of Straws, 1965; Reluctant Neighbours, 1972; Honorary White, 1976. *Recreations:* dancing and tennis.

BRAITHWAITE, Sir (Joseph) Franklin (Madders), Kt 1980; DL; CBIM; Chairman: Baker Perkins Holdings plc, 1980–84; Peterborough Independent Hospital plc, since 1981; *b* 6 April 1917; *s* of late Sir John Braithwaite and Martha Janette (*née* Baker); *m* 1939, Charlotte Isabel, *d* of late Robert Elmer Baker, New York; one *s* one *d*. *Educ:* Bootham Sch.; King's Coll., Cambridge, 1936–39 (BA 1939, MA 1955). Served Army, 1940–46 (Captain). Joined Baker Perkins Ltd, 1946, Director 1950, Vice-Chm. 1956; Chairman, Baker Perkins Exports Ltd, 1966; Man. Dir, Baker Perkins Holdings Ltd, 1971. Director, Lloyds Bank Ltd, Eastern Counties Regional Board, 1979. Member: Mech. Engrg Industry Economic Development Cttee, 1974–; Management Board, 1978–82, Commercial and Econ. Cttee, 1977–84, Engrg Employers' Fedn; Board of Fellows, 1974–79, Economic and Social Affairs Cttee, 1979–84, BIM. Mem., Peterborough Develt Corp., 1981, Dep. Chm. 1982–. President, Process Plant Assoc., 1977–79, Hon. life Vice-Pres., 1981. DL Cambs, 1983. *Recreations:* music, golf. *Address:* 9 Westhawe, Bretton, Peterborough PE3 8BA. *T:* Peterborough 266161.

BRAITHWAITE, Prof. Richard Bevan, FBA 1957; Emeritus Knightbridge Professor of Moral Philosophy in the University of Cambridge; *b* 15 Jan. 1900; *s* of William Charles Braithwaite, Banbury; *m* 1st, 1925, Dorothea Cotter (*d* 1928), *d* of Sir Theodore Morison; 2nd, 1932, Margaret Mary (*d* 1986), *d* of Rt Hon. C. F. G. Masterman; one *s* one *d*. *Educ:* Sidcot Sch., Somerset; Bootham Sch., York; King's Coll., Cambridge (Scholar, Prizeman, Research Student). MA Camb. 1926; Fellow of King's Coll., Camb. 1924–; University Lectr in Moral Science, 1928–34; Sidgwick Lectr in Moral Science, 1934–53; Knightbridge Prof. of Moral Philosophy, 1953–67; Tarner Lectr at Trinity Coll., Camb., 1945–46; Pres. Mind Assoc., 1946; Pres. Aristotelian Soc., 1946–47; Annual Philosophical Lectr to British Academy, 1950; Pres. Brit. Soc. for the Philosophy of Science, 1961–63; Deems Lectr, New York Univ., 1962; Forwood Lectr, Liverpool Univ., 1968; Visiting Prof. of Philosophy: Johns Hopkins Univ., 1968; Univ. of Western Ontario, 1969; City Univ. of New York, 1970. Syndic Cambridge Univ. Press, 1943–62; Mem. Gen. Bd of Faculties, 1945–48; Mem. Council Senate, 1959–64. Hon. DLitt Bristol, 1963. *Publications:* Moral Principles and Inductive Policies (British Acad. Lecture, 1950); Scientific Explanation, 1953; Theory of Games as a tool for the Moral Philosopher (Inaugural Lecture), 1955; An Empiricist's view of the nature of Religious Belief (Eddington Lecture), 1955; Introd. to trans. of Gödel, 1962. Articles in Mind, Proc. Aristotelian Soc., etc. *Recreation:* reading novels. *Address:* King's College, Cambridge. *T:* Cambridge 350411; 11 Millington Road, Cambridge. *T:* Cambridge 350822.

BRAITHWAITE, Rodric Quentin, CMG 1981; HM Diplomatic Service; Deputy Under-Secretary of State, Foreign and Commonwealth Office, since 1984; *b* 17 May 1932; *s* of Henry Warwick Braithwaite and Lorna Constance Davies; *m* 1961, Gillian Mary Robinson; three *s* one *d* (and one *s* decd). *Educ:* Bedales Sch.; Christ's Coll., Cambridge. 1st cl. Mod. Langs, Pts I and II. Mil. Service, 1950–52. Joined Foreign (subseq. Diplomatic) Service, 1955; 3rd Sec., Djakarta, 1957–58; 2nd Sec., Warsaw, 1959–61; FO, 1961–63; 1st Sec. (Commercial), Moscow, 1963–66; 1st Sec., Rome, 1966–69; FCO, 1969–72; Vis. Fellow, All Souls Coll., Oxford, 1972–73; Head of European Integration Dept (External), FCO, 1973–75; Head of Chancery, Office of Permanent Rep. to EEC, Brussels, 1975–78; Head of Planning Staff, FCO, 1979–80; Asst Under Sec. of State, FCO, 1981; Minister Commercial, Washington, 1982–84. *Recreations:* chamber music (viola); sailing; Russia. *Address:* c/o Foreign and Commonwealth Office, SW1A 2AL.

BRAMALL, Sir Ashley; *see* Bramall, Sir E. A.

BRAMALL, Field Marshal Sir Edwin (Noel Westby), GCB 1979 (KCB 1974); OBE 1965; MC 1945; JP; HM Lord-Lieutenant of Greater London, since 1986; Chief of the Defence Staff, 1982–85; *b* 18 Dec. 1923; *s* of late Major Edmund Haselden Bramall and Mrs Katherine Bridget Bramall (*née* Westby); *m* 1949, Dorothy Avril Wentworth Vernon; one *s* one *d*. *Educ:* Eton College. Commnd into KRRC, 1943; served in NW Europe, 1944–45; occupation of Japan, 1946–47; Instructor, Sch. of Infantry, 1949–51; psc 1952; Middle East, 1953–58; Instructor, Army Staff Coll., 1958–61; on staff of Lord Mountbatten with special responsibility for reorganisation of MoD, 1963–64; CO, 2 Green Jackets, KRRC, Malaysia during Indonesian confrontation, 1965–66; comd 5th Airportable Bde, 1967–69; idc 1970; GOC 1st Div. BAOR, 1972–73; Lt-Gen., 1973; Comdr, British Forces, Hong Kong, 1973–76; Gen., 1976; C-in-C, UK Land Forces, 1976–78; Vice-Chief of Defence Staff (Personnel and Logistics), 1978–79; Chief of the General Staff, 1979–82. ADC (Gen.), 1979–82. Col Comdt, 3rd Bn Royal Green Jackets, 1973–84; Col, 2nd Goorkhas, 1976–; Col Comdt, SAS Regt, 1985–; Pres., Greater London TAVRA, 1986–. A Trustee, Imperial War Museum, 1983–. JP London 1986. *Recreations:* cricket, painting, tennis, travel. *Address:* c/o National Westminster Bank, 34 Lower Sloane Street, SW3. *Clubs:* Travellers', Army and Navy, Pratt's, MCC, I Zingari, Free Foresters, Butterflies.
See also Sir E. A. Bramall.

BRAMALL, Sir (Ernest) Ashley, Kt 1975; DL; Member (Lab), Greater London Council, Bethnal Green and Bow, 1973–86 (Tower Hamlets, 1964–73); Chairman: GLC, 1982–83; ILEA, 1965–67 and 1984–86 (Leader, 1970–81); *b* 6 Jan. 1916; *er s* of late Major E. H. Bramall and Mrs K. B. Bramall (*née* Westby); *m*; three *s*. *Educ:* Westminster and Canford Schs; Magdalen Coll., Oxford. Served in Army, 1940–46; Major; psc 1945. Contested Fareham Div. of Hants, 1945; MP (Lab) for Bexley, 1946–50; contested Bexley, 1950, 1951, 1959; Watford, 1955. Barrister, Inner Temple. Member: LCC (Lab) Bethnal Green, 1961; Westminster CC, 1959–68; Chm., Council of LEAs, 1975–76, 1977–78, Vice-Chm., 1976–77; Leader, Management Panel, Burnham Cttee (Primary and Secondary), 1973–78; Chm., Nat. Council for Drama Trng, 1981–; Mem. Council, City Univ., 1984–. DL Greater London, 1981. Grand Officer, Order of Orange Nassau, 1982. *Address:* 2 Egerton House, 59–63 Belgrave Road, SW1V 2BE. *T:* 01–828 0973.
See also Field Marshal Sir E. N W. Bramall.

BRAMALL, Margaret Elaine, OBE 1969; MA; JP; Vice-President, National Council for One Parent Families (formerly National Council for the Unmarried Mother and her Child) (Director, 1962–79); Lecturer, Applied Social Studies Course, University of Surrey, since 1979; *b* 1 Oct. 1916; *d* of Raymond Taylor, MA and Nettie Kate Taylor, BA; *m* 1939, Sir Ashley Bramall (marr. diss.); two *s*. *Educ:* St Paul's Girls' Sch., Hammersmith; Somerville Coll., Oxford (BA 1939, MA 1942); LSE (Social Science Hon. Certif. 1950); Inst. of Almoners (Certif. 1951). JP Richmond 1965. Member: Probation Case Cttee; Management Cttee, Humming Bird Housing Assoc. *Publications:* contrib., One Parent Families, ed Dulan Barber, 1975; contrib. social work jls. *Recreations:* gardening, family. *Address:* 74 Fifth Cross Road, Twickenham, Mddx TW2 5LE. *T:* 01–894 3998.

BRAMBLE, Courtenay Parker, CIE 1946; *b* 10 June 1900; *s* of Frank Bramble and Violet, *d* of Col M. G. Totterdell, VD; *m* 1st, 1928, Margaret Louise Lawrence, MBE, 1943, *d* of Sir Henry Lawrence, KCSI; two *s* one *d*: 2nd, 1958, Doreen, *d* of C. E. Cornish, Lytham St Annes, Lancs. *Educ:* St Paul's Cathedral Choir Sch. (Coronation Medal, 1911); Cranleigh Sch.; King's Coll., Cambridge (MA, LLB). Barrister-at-law, Middle Temple; with The Bombay Co. Ltd, India, 1922–33; Senior partner Drennan & Co., Bombay, 1933–52; Silver Jubilee Medal, 1935; Coronation Medal, 1937. Dir, East India Cotton Assoc., Bombay, 1925–33; Mem., Indian Central Cotton Cttee, 1935–50. Mem. of Legislature, Bombay, 1935–50 (Leader, Progress Party); JP and Hon. Magistrate, Bombay; Chm. (appointed by Govt), Children's Aid Soc., Bombay, 1931–39; Pres. Bombay Chamber of Commerce, 1940, 1945–46; Dep. Pres. Associated Chambers of Commerce, India, 1945; Chm. European Assoc., Bombay Branch, 1942–44; Mem., Bombay Presidency War Cttee, 1941–45; Trustee of Port of Bombay, 1949. Music critic, Times of India, 1925–41. Chairman: All India Quadrangular Cricket Cttee, 1935–39; UK Citizens Assoc. (Bombay), 1948–50; National Service Advisory Cttee, 1940–45; Bombay European Hospital Trust, 1943–50; Hon. Lieut, RINVR, 1940–45. Dir (Pres. 1962), Liverpool Cotton Association; Man. Dir, Abercrombie, Bramble & Co. Ltd, 1954–73; Member Council: Cotton Research Corp., 1960–72; Liverpool Sch. of Tropical Medicine, 1974–; a Manager, Royal Liverpool Children's Hospital Sch., 1962–75. *Address:* Cross Trees, Birch Way, Heswall, Merseyside. *T:* 051–342 3873. *Clubs:* United Oxford & Cambridge University; Royal Yacht (Bombay).

BRAMLEY, Prof. Sir Paul (Anthony), Kt 1984; FRCS, FDSRCS; Professor of Dental Surgery, University of Sheffield, since 1969; Consultant Oral Surgeon, Trent Region, since 1969; *b* 24 May 1923; *s* of Charles and Constance Bramley; *m* 1952, Hazel Morag Boyd, MA, MB ChB; one *s* three *d*. *Educ:* Wyggeston Grammar Sch., Leicester; Univ. of Birmingham. MB ChB, BDS. HS, Queen Elizabeth Hosp., Birmingham, 1945; Capt., RADC, 224 Para Fd Amb., 1946–48; MO, Church of Scotland, Kenya, 1952; Registrar, Rooksdown House, 1953–54; Consultant Oral Surgeon, SW Region Hosp. Bd, 1954–69; Dir, Dept of Oral Surgery and Orthodontics, Plymouth Gen. Hosp. and Truro Royal Infirmary, 1954–69; Civilian Consultant, RN, 1959–; Dean, Sch. of Clinical Dentistry, Univ. of Sheffield, 1972–75. Member: General Dental Council, 1973–; Council, Medical Protection Soc., 1970–; Council, RCS, 1975–83 (Tomes Lectr, 1980; Dean of Faculty of Dental Surgery, 1980–83); Royal Commission on NHS; Dental Strategy Review Group; Chm., Standing Dental Adv. Cttee; Consultant Adviser, DHSS; Hon. Sec., British Assoc. of Oral Surgeons, 1968–72, Pres., 1975; President: S Yorks Br., British Dental Assoc., 1975; Oral Surgery Club of GB, 1985–86; Inst. of Maxillofacial Technol.; Pres-elect, BDA. Adviser, Prince of Songkla Univ., Thailand, 1982–; External Examiner to RCS, RCSI, RCSG, Univs of Birmingham, Baghdad, Hong Kong, London, Singapore, Trinity College Dublin, Cardiff, NUI. Hon. FRACDS. Fellow, Internat. Assoc. of Oral and Maxillofacial Surgeons. *Publications:* scientific articles in British and foreign medical and dental jls and text books. *Address:* Charles Clifford Dental Hospital, Wellesley Road, Sheffield S10 2SZ.

BRAMMA, Harry Wakefield, FRCO; Organist, Southwark Cathedral, since 1976; *b* 11 Nov. 1936; *s* of Fred and Christine Bramma. *Educ:* Bradford Grammar Sch.; Pembroke Coll., Oxford (MA). FRCO 1958. Dir of Music, King Edward VI Grammar Sch., Retford, Notts, 1961; Asst Organist, Worcester Cathedral, 1963; Dir of Music, The King's Sch., Worcester, 1965. Conductor, Kidderminster Choral Soc., 1972–79. Examnr, Associated Bd of Royal Schs of Music, 1978. Mem. Council, RCO, 1979. *Recreations:* travel, walking. *Address:* 52 Bankside, Southwark, SE1 9JE. *T:* 01–261 1291.

BRAMMER, Leonard Griffith, RE 1956 (ARE 1932); painter and etcher; Supervisor of Art and Crafts, Stoke-on-Trent Education Authority, 1952–69; retired; *b* 4 July 1906; *s* of Frederick William Brammer and Minnie Griffith; *m* 1934, Florence May, *d* of William and Mary Barnett, Hanley; one *d*. *Educ:* Burslem Sch. of Art; Royal College of Art (Diploma Associate); awarded Travelling Scholarship, School of Engraving, Royal College of Art, 1930; represented in Tate Gallery, Victoria & Albert Museum, Ashmolean, Oxford, City of Stoke-on-Trent Art Gallery, City of Carlisle Art Gallery, Wedgwood Museum, Barlaston, Keele Univ., Gladstone Pottery Museum, Collection of Contemporary Art Soc., The Collections of The British Council, etc; was exhibitor at Royal Academy and all leading English and American exhibitions. *Address:* Ŝŵn-y-Wylan, Beach Road, Morfa Bychan, Porthmadog, Gwynedd.

BRAMWELL-BOOTH, Catherine, CBE 1971; a Commissioner of the Salvation Army; *b* London, 20 July 1883; *e c* of late General Bramwell Booth. Entered Salvation Army as an Officer, 1903; engaged in training Cadets at International Training Coll., 1907–17; International Sec. for Salvation Army in Europe, 1917; command of Women's Social Work in Great Britain and Ireland, 1926; International Sec. for Europe, 1946–48; retired 1948. Best Speaker award, Guild of Professional Toastmasters, 1978. *Publications:* Messages to the Messengers; A Few Lines; Bramwell Booth, 1933; (compiler) Bramwell Booth Speaks, 1947; Verse, 1947; Catherine Booth, the story of her loves, 1970; Fighting for the King (poems), 1983; (with Ted Harrison) Commissioner Catherine, 1983. *Address:* North Court, Finchampstead, Berks.

BRANCH, Prof. Michael Arthur, PhD; Director, School of Slavonic and East European Studies, since 1980, and Professor of Finnish, since 1986, University of London; *b* 24 March 1940; *s* of Arthur Frederick Branch and Mahala Parker; *m* 1963, Ritva-Riitta Hannele, *d* of Erkki Kari, Heinola, Finland; three *d*. *Educ:* Shene Grammar Sch.; Sch. of Slavonic and East European Studies, Univ. of London (BA 1963; PhD 1967). School of Slavonic and East European Studies: Asst Lectr and Lectr in Finno–Ugrian Studies, 1967–72; Lectr, 1972–77, and Reader in Finnish, 1977; Chm., Dept of East European Language and Literature, 1979–80. Corresponding Member: Finno–Ugrian Soc., 1977; Finnish Literature Soc. (Helsinki), 1980. Hon. PhD Oulu (Finland), 1983. Comdr, Lion of Finland, 1980. *Publications:* A. J. Sjögren, 1973; (jtly) Finnish Folk Poetry: Epic, 1977; (jtly) A Student's Glossary of Finnish, 1980; (jtly) The Great Bear, 1986. *Recreations:* gardening, walking. *Address:* 33 St Donatt's Road, SE14 6NU. *T:* 01–637 4934. *Club:* Athenæum.

BRANCH, Sir William Allan Patrick, Kt 1977; Managing Director and Grenada Representative on the Windward Islands Banana Association (Mirabeau, Capitol, Hope Development and Dougaldston Estates); *b* 17 Feb. 1915; *m* Thelma (*née* Rapier); one *s*. *Educ:* Grenada Boys' Secondary Sch. Dep. Manager, Mt Horne Agricl Estate, 1936; Manager Mt Horne, Boulogne, Colombier, Industry and Grand Bras Agricl Estates, 1941. Chairman, Eastern Dist Agricl Rehabilitation Cttee; Dep. Chm. Bd of Dirs, Grenada Banana Co-op Soc.; Director: Grenada Cocoa Industry; Parochial and Island Anglican Church Council; Managing Cttee: Grenada Boy Scouts Assoc.; St Andrew's Anglican Secondary Sch; Member, Central Agricl Rehabilitation Cttee. Knighthood awarded for services to agriculture, Grenada, Windward Islands. *Address:* Dougaldston, Gouyave, St John's, Grenada.

BRANCKER, Sir (John Eustace) Theodore, Kt 1969; President of the Senate, Barbados, 1971–76; *b* 9 Feb. 1909; *s* of Jabel Eustace and Myra Enid Vivienne Brancker; *m* 1967, Esme Gwendolyn Walcott. *Educ:* Harrison Coll., Barbados; Grad., Inst. of Political Secretaries; LSE (Certificate in Colonial Admin, 1933). Called to Bar, Middle Temple, 1933; in private practice; QC (Barbados) 1961. Mem., House of Assembly, Barbados, 1937–71 (Leader of Opposition, 1956–61; Speaker, 1961–71). Mem., Medico-Legal Soc. Mem., CPA. Life Fellow, Royal Commonwealth Soc.; Life Mem., Barbados Mus. and Historical Soc. Chm., 1973, Hon. Awards Liaison Officer, 1978, Duke of Edinburgh Award Scheme. Charter Pres., Rotary Club, Barbados. Mem. Adv. Bd, St Joseph Hosp. of Sisters of the Sorrowful Mother. Hon. LLD, Soochow Univ., 1973. FZS; FRSA (Life Fellow). Queen's Coronation Medal, 1953; Silver Jubilee Medal, 1977. *Recreations:* classical music, chess, drama. *Address:* Valencia, Holetown, St James's, Barbados. *T:* 20775. *Clubs:* Royal Over-Seas League (Life Mem.), Challoner (London); Empire, Bridgetown, Sunset Crest (Barbados); Rotary International.

BRAND, family name of **Viscount Hampden.**

BRAND, Hon. Lord; David William Robert Brand; a Senator of the College of Justice in Scotland, since 1972; *b* 21 Oct. 1923; *s* of late James Gordon Brand, Huntingdon, Dumfries, and Frances (*née* Bull); *m* 1st, 1948, Rose Josephine Devlin (*d* 1968); four *d*; 2nd, Bridget Veronica Lynch (*née* Russell), *widow* of Thomas Patrick Lynch, Beechmount, Mallow, Co. Cork. *Educ:* Stonyhurst Coll.; Edinburgh Univ. Served War of 1939–45; Commissioned Argyll and Sutherland Highlanders, 1942; Capt. 1945. Admitted to Faculty of Advocates, 1948; Standing Junior Counsel to Dept of Education for Scotland, 1951; Advocate-Depute for Sheriff Court, 1953; Extra Advocate-Depute for Glasgow Circuit, 1955; Advocate-Depute, 1957–59; QC Scot. 1959; Senior Advocate-Depute, 1964; Sheriff of Dumfries and Galloway, 1968; Sheriff of Roxburgh, Berwick and Selkirk, 1970; Solicitor-General for Scotland, 1970–72. Kt, SMO Malta. *Publications:* Joint Editor, Scottish Edn of Current Law, 1948–61; Scottish Editor, Encyclopedia of Road Traffic Law and Practice, 1960–64; contributor to Scots Law Times. *Recreation:* golf. *Address:* Gospatric House, Dalmeny, W Lothian EH30 9TT. *T:* 031–331 1224. *Clubs:* New (Edinburgh); Honourable Company of Edinburgh Golfers.

BRAND, Alexander George, MBE 1945; Deputy Traffic Commissioner (Scottish Area), since 1979; *b* 23 March 1918; *s* of David Wilson Brand and Janet Ramsay Brand (*née* Paton); *m* 1947, Helen Constance Campbell; one *s* one *d*. *Educ:* Ayr Academy; Univ. of Glasgow. MA 1940, LLB 1948. Admitted Solicitor, 1948. Served in Royal Air Force, 1940–46 (Flt Lt). Legal Asst: Dumbarton CC, 1948; in Office of Solicitor to the Secretary of State for Scotland, 1949; Sen. Legal Asst, 1955; Asst Solicitor, 1964; Dep. Solicitor, 1972–79. Sec. of Scottish Law Commn, 1965–72. *Recreations:* golf, theatre, music, reading. *Address:* 16 Queen's Avenue, Edinburgh EH4 2DF. *T:* 031–332 4472. *Club:* Bruntsfield Links Golfing Society (Edinburgh).

BRAND, Prof. Charles Peter; Professor of Italian, since 1966, and Vice-Principal, since 1984, University of Edinburgh; *b* 7 Feb. 1923; *er s* of Charles Frank Brand and Dorothy (*née* Tapping); *m* 1948, Gunvor, *yr d* of Col I. Hellgren, Stockholm; one *s* three *d*. *Educ:* Cambridge High Sch.; Trinity Hall, Cambridge. War Service, Intelligence Corps, 1943–46. Open Maj. Scholar, Trinity Hall, 1940; 1st Class Hons. Mod. Languages, Cantab, 1948; PhD Cantab, 1951. Asst Lecturer, Edinburgh Univ., 1952; Cambridge University: Asst Lecturer, subsequently Lecturer, 1952–66; Fellow and Tutor, Trinity Hall, 1958–66. Cavaliere Ufficiale, al Merito della Repubblica Italiana, 1975. General Editor, Modern Language Review, 1971–77; Editor, Italian Studies, 1977–. *Publications:* Italy and the English Romantics, 1957; Torquato Tasso, 1965; Ariosto: a preface to the Orlando Furioso, 1974; contributions to learned journals. *Recreations:* sport, travel, gardening. *Address:* 21 Succoth Park, Edinburgh EH12 6BX. *T:* 031–337 1980.

BRAND, David William Robert; *see* Brand, Hon. Lord.

BRAND, Geoffrey Arthur; Under-Secretary, Department of Employment, 1972–85; *b* 13 June 1930; *s* of late Arthur William Charles Brand and Muriel Ada Brand; *m* 1954, Joy Trotman; two *d*. *Educ:* Andover Grammar Sch.; University Coll., London. Entered

Min. of Labour, 1953; Private Sec. to Parly Sec., 1956–57; Colonial Office, 1957–58; Private Sec. to Minister of Labour, 1965–66; Asst. Sec., Industrial Relations and Research and Planning Divisions, 1966–72. *Address:* Cedarwood, Seer Green, Beaconsfield, Bucks. *T:* Beaconsfield 6637.

BRANDES, Lawrence Henry, CB 1982; Under Secretary and Head of the Office of Arts and Libraries, 1978–82; *b* 16 Dec. 1924; *m* 1950, Dorothea Stanyon; one *s* one *d. Educ:* Beltane Sch.; London Sch. of Economics. Min. of Health, 1950; Principal Private Sec. to Minister, 1959; Nat. Bd for Prices and Incomes, 1966; Dept of Employment and Productivity, 1969; Under-Sec., DHSS, 1970; HM Treasury, 1975. Director: Dance Umbrella; Hanover Band; London Internat. Fest. of Theatre. Consultant, British Architectural Library. Member: Dulwich Picture Gall. Management Cttee; Council, League of Friends, Nat. Maritime Museum; Goldsmith's Coll. Delegacy. Trustee, Science Museum, 1986– (Fellow, and Sec. to Trustees, 1983–86). *Address:* 4 Hogarth Hill, NW11.

BRANDO, Marlon; American actor, stage and screen; *b* Omaha, Nebraska, 3 April 1924; *s* of Marlon Brando; *m* 1957, Anna Kashfi (marr. diss., 1959); one *s. Educ:* Libertyville High Sch., Illinois; Shattuck Military Academy, Minnesota. Entered Dramatic Workshop of New School for Social Research, New York, 1943; has studied with Elia Kazan and Stella Adler. *Plays include:* I Remember Mama, Broadway, 1944; Truckline Café, 1946; Candida, 1946; A Flag is Born, 1946; The Eagle Has Two Heads, 1946; A Streetcar Named Desire, 1947. *Films include:* The Men, 1950; A Streetcar Named Desire, 1951; Viva Zapata!, 1952; Julius Cæsar, 1953; The Wild Ones, 1953; Désirée, 1954; On the Waterfront, 1954; Guys and Dolls, 1955; Tea House of the August Moon, 1956; Sayonara, 1957; The Young Lions, 1958; The Fugitive Kind, 1960; Mutiny on the Bounty, 1962; The Ugly American, 1963; Bedtime Story, 1964; The Satoteur, Code Name-Morituri, 1965; The Chase, 1966; Appaloosa, 1966; Southwest to Sonora, 1966; A Countess from Hong Kong, 1967; Reflections in a Golden Eye, 1967; Candy, 1968; The Night of the Following Day, 1969; Quiemad!, 1970; The Nightcomers, 1971; The Godfather, 1972; Last Tango in Paris, 1972; The Missouri Breaks, 1975; Apocalypse Now, 1977; Superman, 1978; The Formula, 1981. Directed, produced and appeared in One-Eyed Jacks, 1959. Academy Award, best actor of year, 1954, 1972.

BRANDON, family name of **Baron Brandon of Oakbrook.**

BRANDON OF OAKBROOK, Baron *cr* 1981 (Life Peer), of Hammersmith in Greater London; **Henry Vivian Brandon;** Kt 1966; MC 1942; PC 1978; a Lord of Appeal in Ordinary, since 1981; *b* 3 June 1920; *y s* of late Captain V. R. Brandon, CBE, RN, and late Joan Elizabeth Maud Simpson; *m* 1955, Jeanette Rosemary, *e d* of J. V. B. Janvrin; three *s* one *d. Educ:* Winchester Coll. (Scholar); King's Coll., Cambridge (Scholar 1938, Stewart of Rannoch Scholar 1939). Commnd 2nd Lieut RA 1939; Major 1944; served Madagascar, 1942, India and Burma, 1942–45. BA 1946. Barrister, Inner Temple, 1946 (Entrance and Yarborough Anderson Scholar); Member Bar Council, 1951–53; QC 1961; Judge of the High Court of Justice, Probate, Divorce and Admiralty Division, 1966–71, Family Division, 1971–78; Judge of the Admiralty Court, 1971–78; Judge of the Commercial Court, 1977–78; a Lord Justice of Appeal, 1978–81. Member panel of Lloyd's arbitrators in salvage cases, 1961–66; Member panel from which Wreck Commissioners chosen, 1963–66. Hon. LLD Southampton, 1984. *Recreations:* cricket, bridge, travelling. *Address:* 6 Thackeray Close, SW19. *T:* 01–947 6344; House of Lords, SW1. *Club:* MCC.

BRANDON, (Oscar) Henry, CBE 1985; Columnist, New York Times World Syndicate, since 1983; Associate Editor and Chief American correspondent of the Sunday Times, retired 1983; *b* 9 March 1916; *m* 1970, Mabel Hobart Wentworth; one *d. Educ:* Univ. of Prague and Lausanne. Joined Sunday Times, 1939; War Correspondent, N Africa and W Europe, 1943–45; Paris Correspondent, 1945–46; Roving Diplomatic Correspondent, 1947–49; Washington Correspondent, 1950–83; Syndicated Columnist for Washington Star, 1979–81. Guest scholar, The Brookings Instn, Washington, DC, 1983–. Hon. LittD Williams Coll., 1979. Foreign corresp. award, Univ. of California, Los Angeles, 1957; award, Lincoln Univ., Jefferson City, Missouri, 1962; Hannen Swaffer award, 1964. *Publications:* As We Are, 1961; In The Red, 1966; Conversations with Henry Brandon, 1966; The Anatomy of Error, 1970; The Retreat of American Power, 1973. *Recreations:* ski-ing, tennis, swimming, photography. *Address:* 3005 O Street NW, Washington, DC 20007, USA. *T:* 338–8506. *Clubs:* National Press, Overseas Writers (Washington, DC).

BRANDON, Prof. Percy Samuel, (Prof. Peter Brandon); Professor of Electrical Engineering, 1971–84, Head of Electrical Division, 1981–84, University of Cambridge, now Professor Emeritus; *b* 9 Nov. 1916; *s* of P. S. Brandon, OBE; *m* 1942, Joan Edith Marriage, GRSM (London), LRAM; two *s. Educ:* Chigwell Sch.; Jesus Coll., Cambridge (MA). Joined The Marconi Company, 1939; Research Div., 1940–71. Frequency Measurement, 1940–44: Aerial Section, 1944–45. FM Radar, 1945–53; Chief of Guidance Systems, 1953–57; Chief of Mathematics and Systems Analysis Gp, 1957–65; Manager of Theoretical Sciences Laboratory, 1965–68; Asst Dir of Research, 1965–68; Manager of Research Div. of GEC-Marconi Electronics, 1968–71. Part-time lecturing at Mid-Essex Technical Coll., and others, 1945–66. FInstP, FIEE. *Publications:* contribs to Marconi Review, IEE Proc., Agardograph, Electronic Engineering, etc. *Recreation:* colour photography. *Address:* New Courts, 8 Bridge Lane, Little Shelford, Cambridge CB2 5HE. *T:* Cambridge 842541.

BRANDON-BRAVO, Martin Maurice; MP (C) Nottingham South, since 1983; *b* 25 March 1932; *s* of late Issac, (Alfred), and Phoebe Brandon-Bravo; *m* 1964, Sally Anne Wallwin; two *s. Educ:* Latymer Sch. FBIM. Joined Richard Stump Ltd, later Richard Stump (1979), 1952; successively Floor Manager, Factory Manager, Production Dir and Asst Man. Dir; Man. Dir., 1979–83; non-exec. Dir, 1983–; Dir, Hall & Earl Ltd, 1970–. Mem., Nottingham City Council, 1968–70 and 1976–; Chm., 1970–73, Pres., 1975–83, Nottingham West Cons. Party Orgn; Dep. Chm., City of Nottingham Cons. Fedn. Contested (C) Nottingham East, 1979. PPS to Minister of State for Housing and Urban Affairs, 1985–. Mem., Nat. Water Sport Centre Management Cttee, 1972–83; Pres., Nottingham and Union Rowing Club. *Recreation:* rowing (Mem., Internat. Umpires' Commn; holder of Internat. Licence). *Address:* The Old Farmhouse, 27 Rectory Place, Barton-in-Fabis, Nottingham NG11 0AL. *T:* Nottingham 830459. *Clubs:* Carlton; Leander.

BRANDRETH, Gyles Daubeney; author, broadcaster, journalist, theatrical producer; Chairman, Victorama Ltd, since 1974; *b* 8 March 1948; *s* of late Charles Brandreth and of Alice Addison; *m* 1973, Michèle Brown; one *s* two *d. Educ:* Lycée Français de Londres; Betteshanger Sch., Kent; Bedales Sch., Hants; New Coll., Oxford (Scholar). Pres. Oxford Union, Editor of Isis. Chm., Archway Productions Ltd, 1971–74; Dir, Colin Smythe Ltd, 1971–73. Freelance journalist, 1968–: contrib. Observer, Guardian, Daily Mail, Daily Mirror, Evening Standard, Spectator, Punch, Homes & Gardens, She, Woman's Own; Columnist: Honey, 1968–69; Manchester Evening News, 1971–72; Woman, 1972–73, 1986–; Press Assoc. weekly syndicated column in USA, 1981–85. Broadcaster, 1969–: TV series incl.: Child of the Sixties, 1969; Puzzle Party, 1977; Chatterbox, 1977–78; Memories, 1982; Countdown, 1983–; TV-am, 1983–; Railway Carriage Game, 1985; Catchword, 1986; (with Hinge and Bracket) Dear Ladies (TV script); (with Julian Slade) Now We Are Sixty (play); Theatrical producer, 1971–: Through the Looking-Glass, 1972; Oxford Theatre Fest., 1974, 1976; The Dame of Sark, Wyndham's, 1974; The Little Hut, Duke of York's, 1974; Dear Daddy, Ambassador's, 1976; also Son et Lumière. Founder, British Pantomime Assoc., 1971. Dir, Europ. Movement's People for Europe campaign, 1975. Appeals Chm., NPFA, 1983–. Founder, National Scrabble Championships, 1971; Europ. Monopoly Champion, 1974; three times holder, world record for longest-ever after-dinner speech (4 hrs 19 mins, 1976; 11 hrs, 1978; 12 hrs 30 mins, 1982). *Publications: general:* Created in Captivity, 1972; Discovering Pantomime, 1973; Brandreth's Bedroom Book, 1973; I Scream for Ice Cream, 1974; A Royal Scrapbook, 1976; Yarooh!, 1976; The Funniest Man on Earth, 1977; The Magic of Houdini, 1978; The Complete Husband, 1978; Pears Book of Words, 1979; The Last Word, 1979; The Joy of Lex, 1980; More Joy of Lex, 1982; Great Theatrical Disasters, 1982; The Books of Mistaikes, 1982; The Complete Public Speaker, 1983; John Gielgud: a celebration, 1984; Great Sexual Disasters, 1984; (with George Hostler) Wit Knits, 1985; *family entertainment:* Brandreth's Party Games, 1972; Complete Book of Home Entertainment, 1974; Games for Trains, Planes & Wet Days, 1974; Brandreth's Christmas Book, 1975; Brandreth's Book of Waiting Games, 1975; (with Cyril Fletcher) Generation Quiz Book, 1975; Knight Book of Scrabble, 1975; Pears Family Quiz Book, 1976; (with David Farris) Scrambled Exits, 1976; Pears All the Year Round Quiz Book, 1977; Teach Yourself Indoor Games, 1977; Pears Round the World Quiz Book, 1978; The Little Red Darts Book, 1978; Everyman's Indoor Games, 1981; The Puzzle Mountain, 1981; Solo Games, 1983; The Christmas Book, 1984; Everyman's Classic Puzzles, 1984; Everyman's Children's Games, 1984; over fifty books for children of stories, jokes, riddles, games, puzzles, magic and fun. *Address:* Victorama Ltd, 14–16 Regent Street, SW1Y 4PS. *T:* 01–727 4290.

BRANDRICK, David Guy, CBE 1981; Secretary, British Coal (formerly National Coal Board), since 1972; *b* 17 April 1932; *s* of Harry and Minnie Brandrick; *m* 1956, Eunice Fisher; one *s* one *d. Educ:* Newcastle-under-Lyme High Sch.; St John's Coll., Oxford (MA). Joined National Coal Board, 1955; Chairman's Office, 1957; Principal Private Secretary to Chairman, 1961; Departmental Sec., Production Dept, 1963; Dep. Sec. to the Board, 1967. *Recreation:* walking. *Address:* c/o Hobart House, Grosvenor Place, SW1.

BRANDT, Paul Nicholas; barrister-at-law; a Recorder of the Crown Court, since 1983; *b* 21 Nov. 1937; *s* of Paul Francis and Barbara Brandt. *Educ:* St Andrew's Sch., Eastbourne; Marlborough Coll.; New Coll., Oxford (BA 2nd Cl. Hons Sch. of Jurisprudence). Called to the Bar, Gray's Inn, 1963. *Recreations:* sailing, shooting, Rugby football. *Address:* 4 Holly Village, N6. *T:* 01–272 1998. *Clubs:* Royal Automobile; Royal Harwich Yacht (Woolverstone, Suffolk), Bar Yacht.

BRANDT, Peter Augustus; Chairman, Atkins Fulford Ltd, since 1977; *b* 2 July 1931; *s* of late Walter Augustus Brandt and late Dorothy Gray Brandt (*née* Crane); *m* 1962, Elisabeth Margaret (*née* ten Bos); two *s* one *d. Educ:* Eton Coll.; Trinity Coll., Cambridge (MA). Joined Wm Brandt's Sons & Co. Ltd, Merchant Bankers, 1954; Mem. Bd, 1960; Chief Executive, 1966; resigned, 1972. Director: London Life Assoc., 1962; Corp. of Argentine Meat Producers (CAP) Ltd and affiliates, 1970; Edward Bates (Holdings) Ltd, 1972–77; Edward Bates & Sons Ltd, 1972–77 (Chm., 1974–77). *Recreations:* sailing, rowing, steam engines, wild fowl. *Address:* Spout Farm, Boxford, Colchester, Essex. *Clubs:* Carlton; Leander (Henley-on-Thames); Royal Harwich Yacht (Ipswich).

BRANDT, Willy; Chairman, Social Democratic Party (SPD), Federal Republic of Germany, since 1964; Member, German Federal Parliament, 1949–57, and since 1969; *b* 18 Dec. 1913; *m* 1948, Rut Hansen (marr. diss.); three *s* one *d*; *m* 1983, Brigitte Seebacher. *Educ:* Johanneum, Lübeck; University of Oslo. Fled from Lübeck to Norway, 1933. Chief Editor, Berliner Stadtblatt, 1950–51. Mem., Social Democratic Party (SPD), 1931–; Rep. Federal Board of SPD (German Social Democratic Party) in Berlin, 1948–49, Deputy Chairman of SPD, 1962–63. President Berlin House of Representatives, 1955–57; Governing Mayor of W Berlin, 1957–66; President German Conference of Mayors, 1958–63; President German Federal Council, 1957–58; Vice-Chancellor and Foreign Minister, 1966–69, Chancellor 1969–74, Federal Republic of Germany; Mem., European Parlt, 1979–83. Pres., Socialist International, 1976. Chm., Commn on Develt Issues, (which produced Brandt reports, North-South: a programme for survival, 1980, and Common Crisis: North-South: cooperation for world recovery, 1983), 1977–79. Dr (*hc*): Pennsylvania Univ., 1959; Maryland Univ., 1960; Harvard Univ., 1963; Hon. DCL: Oxford Univ., 1969; Leeds, 1982. Nobel Prize for Peace, 1971. Grosskreuz des Verdienstordens der Bundesrepublik Deutschland, 1959. *Publications:* Efter segern, 1944; Forbrytere og andre Tyskere, 1946; (with Richard Löwenthal) Ernst Reuter: Ein Leben für die Freiheit, 1957; Von Bonn nach Berlin, 1957; Mein Weg nach Berlin (recorded by Leo Lania), 1960; Plädoyer für die Zukunft, 1961; The Ordeal of Co-existence, 1963; Begegnungen mit Kennedy, 1964; (with Günter Struve) Draussen, 1966 (UK, as In Exile, 1971); Friedenspolitik in Europa, 1968; Essays, Reflections and Letters 1933–47, 1971; Der Wille zum Frieden, 1971; Über den Tag hinaus, 1974; Begegnungen und Einsichten, 1976 (UK as People and Politics, 1978); Frauen heute, 1978; Links und frei, 1982; World Armament and World Hunger, 1986; many publications on topical questions in Sweden and Norway; articles in home and foreign journals. *Address:* (office) Erich-Ollenhauer-Strasse 1, 5300 Bonn 1, Germany. *T:* 5321.

BRANIGAN, Sir Patrick (Francis), Kt 1954; QC; *b* 30 Aug. 1906; *e s* of late D. Branigan and Teresa, *d* of Thomas Clinton, Annagassan, Co. Louth; *m* 1935, Prudence, *yr d* of late Dr A. Avent, Seaton, Devon; one *s* one *d. Educ:* Newbridge Coll., Co. Kildare; Trinity Coll., Dublin. BA 1st Class Hons in Law and Political Science and gold medallist, 1928; called to Irish Bar, Certificate of Honour, 1928 (1st Victoria Prize, 1927); called to Bar, Gray's Inn, 1935. Practised at Irish Bar, 1928–30; Downing Coll., Cambridge, 1930–31; Colonial Administrative Service, Kenya, 1931; Crown Counsel, Tanganyika, 1934; Solicitor-General, N. Rhodesia, 1938; Chairman NR Man-power Cttee, 1939–41; Chairman Conciliation Board, Copperbelt Strike, 1940; Member NR Nat. Arbitration Tribunal, 1940–46; Member Strauss Arbitration Tribunal, Bulawayo, 1944; Chairman, Road Transport Services Board and Electricity Board of N. Rhodesia, 1939–46; Legal Secretary to Govt of Malta and Chairman Malta War Damage Commission, 1946–48; periodically acting Lieut-Governor of Malta, 1947–48. Minister of Justice and Attorney-General, Gold Coast, 1948–54; QC Gold Coast, 1949; retired, 1955. Chairman of Commission of inquiry into Copperbelt industrial unrest, 1956. Dep. Chm. Devon QS, 1958–71; a Recorder of the Crown Court, 1972–75. Chairman: Pensions Appeal Tribunal, 1955–81; Agricultural Land Tribunal for SW Area of England, 1955–79; Nat. Insurance Med. Appeal Tribunal, SW Reg., 1960–78; Mental Health Review Tribunal, SW England, 1960–78; Mem., Industrial Disputes Tribunal, 1955–59. Knight Commander of Order of St Gregory, 1956. *Address:* C'an San Juan, La Font, Pollensa, Majorca. *T:* 3471 530767.

BRANN, Col William Norman, OBE 1967; ERD; JP; Lord Lieutenant for County Down, since 1980; *b* 16 Aug. 1915; *s* of Rev. William Brann, BA, LLB, and Francesca Brann; *m* 1950, Anne Elizabeth Hughes; one *s* two *d. Educ:* Campbell Coll., Belfast. With

Beck & Scott Ltd, Food Importers, Belfast, 1934–80. Served War of 1939–45, Army; TA, 1947–53. High Sheriff, County Down, 1982. *Recreations:* farming, gardening, hunting. *Address:* Drumavaddy, Craigantlet, Newtownards, Co. Down, N Ireland. *T:* Holywood 2224. *Club:* Ulster Reform (Belfast).

BRANNAN, Charles Franklin; lawyer; *b* 23 Aug. 1903; *s* of John Brannan and Ella Louise Street; *m* 1932, Eda Seltzer; no *c. Educ:* Regis Coll., and University of Denver Law Sch., Denver, Colorado, USA. Private law practice, Denver, Colorado, 1929–35; Asst Regional Attorney: Resettlement Administration, Denver, 1935–37; Regional Attorney, Office of the Solicitor, US Dept of Agriculture, Denver, 1937–41; Regional Director of Farm Security Administration, US Dept of Agriculture, Denver, 1941–44; Asst Administrator, Farm Security Administration, US Dept of Agriculture, Washington, DC, April-June 1944; Asst Secretary of Agriculture, Washington, DC, June 1944–48; Secretary of Agriculture, USA, 1948–Jan. 1953. Pres., Bd of Water Commissioners, Denver, 1976. Hon. Degrees: Doctor of Laws from the University of Denver and Doctor of Science from the Colorado Agricultural and Mechanical Coll. Hon. Phi Beta Kappa. *Address:* (home) 3131 East Alameda, Denver, Colorado 80209, USA; (office) 12025 E 45th Avenue, Denver, Colo 80239. *Club:* Denver Athletic (Denver, Colorado).

BRANSON, Rear Adm. Cecil Robert Peter Charles, CBE 1975; *b* 30 March 1924; *s* of Cecil Branson and Marcelle Branson; *m* 1946, Sonia Moss; one *d. Educ:* RNC, Dartmouth. Served, HMS Dragon, W Africa, S Atlantic, Indian Ocean and Far East (present during time of fall of Singapore and Java), 1941–42; Sub-Lieut's Courses, 1942–43; qual. as submarine specialist, served in HM S/M Sea Rover, Far East, 1944–45; various appts in S/Ms, 1945–53; First Lieut, HMS Defender, 1953–55; jssc; CO, HMS Roebuck, Dartmouth Trng Sqdn, 1957; Staff, Flag Officer Flotillas Mediterranean, 1959–60; Jt Planning Staff, MoD, 1960–62; Exec. Officer, HMS Victorious, Far East, 1962–64; CO, HMS Rooke, Gibraltar, 1965; NATO Def. Coll., 1965; Defence Planning Staff, MoD, 1966–68; CO, HMS Phoebe, and Captain (D) Londonderry Sqdn, 1968–70; Naval Attaché, Paris, 1970–73; CO, HMS Hermes, 1973–74 (Hermes headed RN task force evacuating Brit. and foreign subjects from Cyprus beaches after Turkish invasion, 1973); Asst Chief of Naval Staff (Ops), MoD, 1975–77; retired. *Club:* Army and Navy.

BRANSON, Edward James, MA; a Metropolitan Stipendiary Magistrate, since 1971; barrister-at-law; *b* 10 March 1918; *s* of late Rt Hon. Sir George Branson, PC, sometime Judge of High Court, and late Lady (Mona) Branson; *m* 1949, Evette Huntley, *e d* of late Rupert Huntley Flindt; one *s* two *d. Educ:* Bootham Sch., York; Trinity Coll., Cambridge. Served War, 1939–46, Staffordshire Yeomanry: Palestine, Egypt, and Western Desert 1941–42; GSO 3 (Ops) attd 2 NZ Div. for Alamein, 1942; GS02 (Ops), attd 6 (US) Corps for Salerno and Anzio landings, 1943–44; subseq. GSO2 (Ops) 53 (W) Div. in Germany. Called to the Bar, Inner Temple, 1950; practised London and SE Circuit. *Recreations:* shooting, riding, fishing, archaeology. *Address:* Tanyard Farm, Shamley Green, near Guildford, Surrey. *T:* Guildford 893133.

BRANSON, William Rainforth, CBE 1969; retired; *b* 2 Jan. 1905; *s* of late A. W. Branson, JP; *m* 1932, Dorothy Iris Green (*d* 1982); no *c. Educ:* Rydal Sch.; University of Leeds. BSc, 1st Class Hons (Fuel and Gas Engrg), 1927; MSc 1930. Asst Engineer, Gas Light & Coke Co., London, 1927–37; Asst Engineer, later Dep. Engineer, Cardiff Gas Light & Coke Co., 1937–45; Dep. Controller, later Controller, Public Utilities Br., Control Commn for Germany, 1945–49; Planning Engineer, Wales Gas Board, 1949–51; Technical Officer, E Midlands Gas Board, 1952–54; Dep. Chairman, W. Midlands Gas Board, 1954–65; Chm., Scottish Gas Bd, 1965–68; Dir, Woodall-Duckham Group Ltd, 1969–73. President, Instn of Gas Engineers, 1964–65. *Recreation:* music. *Address:* Sidmouth House West, Cotmaton Road, Sidmouth EX10 8ST.

BRANT, Colin Trevor, CMG 1981; CVO 1979; HM Diplomatic Service; Consul General and Director of Trade Promotion, Johannesburg, since 1982; *b* 2 June 1929; *m* 1954, Jean Faith Walker; one *s* two *d. Educ:* Christ's Hospital, Horsham; Sidney Sussex Coll., Cambridge (MA). Served Army, 4th Hussars (now Queen's Royal Irish Hussars), active service, Malaya, 1948–49; Pilot, Cambridge Univ. Air Squadron, 1951–52. Joined Sen. Br., Foreign Office, 1952; MECAS, Lebanon, 1953–54; Bahrain, 1954; Amman, 1954–56; FO, 1956–59; Stockholm, 1959–61; Cairo, 1961–64; Joint Services Staff Coll., Latimer, Bucks, 1964–65 (jssc); FO, 1965–67; Head of Chancery and Consul, Tunis, 1967–68; Asst Head, Oil Dept, FCO, 1969–71; Counsellor (Commercial), Caracas, 1971–73; Counsellor (Energy), Washington, 1973–78; Ambassador to Qatar, 1978–81; FCO Fellow, St Antony's Coll., Oxford, 1981–82. Donation Governor, Christ's Hosp., 1980. *Recreations:* music, painting, history. *Address:* c/o Foreign and Commonwealth Office, SW1; Wethersfield Manor, Braintree, Essex. *Clubs:* Travellers', Royal Commonwealth Society; Rand, Country, Inanda, Turffontein (Johannesburg).

BRASH, Rev. Alan Anderson, OBE 1962; Moderator, Presbyterian Church of New Zealand, 1978–79; *b* 5 June 1913; *s* of Thomas C. Brash, CBE, New Zealand, and Margaret Brash (*née* Allan); *m* 1938, Eljean Ivory Hill; one *s* one *d. Educ:* Dunedin Univ., NZ (MA); Edinburgh Univ. (BD). Parish Minister in NZ, 1938–46 and 1952–56; Gen. Sec., NZ Nat. Council of Churches, 1947–52 and 1957–64, East Asia Christian Conf., 1958–68; Dir, Christian Aid, London, 1968–70; Dir, Commn on Inter-Church Aid, Refuge and World Service, WCC, 1970–73; Dep. Gen. Sec., WCC, 1974–78. Hon. DD Toronto, 1971. *Address:* 13 Knightsbridge Drive, Forrest Hill, Auckland 10, New Zealand.

BRASH, Robert, CMG 1980; HM Diplomatic Service, retired; Ambassador to Indonesia, 1981–84; *b* 30 May 1924; *s* of Frank and Ida Brash; *m* 1954, Barbara Enid Clarke; three *s* one *d. Educ:* Trinity Coll., Cambridge (Exhbnr). War Service, 1943–46. Entered Foreign Service, 1949; Djakarta, 1951–55; FO, 1955–58; First Sec., 1956; Jerusalem, 1958–61; Bonn, 1961–64; Bucharest, 1964–66; FCO, 1966–70; Counsellor, 1968; Canadian Nat. Defence Coll., 1970–71; Counsellor and Consul-Gen., Saigon, 1971–73; Counsellor, Vienna, 1974–78; Consul-Gen., Düsseldorf, 1978–81. *Recreations:* walking, gardening, stained glass, golf. *Address:* Woodbrow, Woodham Lane, Woking, Surrey G21 5SR.

BRASHER, Christopher William; Columnist and Olympic Correspondent, The Observer, since 1961; Race Director, London Marathon since 1980; Managing Director: Brasher Leisure Ltd, since 1977; Fleetfoot Ltd, since 1979; *b* 21 Aug. 1928; *s* of William Kenneth Brasher and Katie Howe Brasher; *m* 1959, Shirley Bloomer; one *s* two *d. Educ:* Rugby Sch.; St John's Coll., Cambridge. MA. Pres., Mountaineering Club and Athletic Club, Cambridge Univ. Management Trainee and Jun. Executive, Mobil Oil Co., 1951–57; Sports Editor, The Observer, 1957–61; BBC Television: Reporter, Tonight, 1961–65; Editor, Time Out, and Man Alive, 1964–65; Head of Gen. Features, 1969–72; reporter/producer, 1972–81. Co-Founder and Chm., British Orienteering Fedn (formerly English Orienteering Assoc.), 1966–69. Rep. GB, Olympic Games, 1952 and 1956; Gold Medal for 3,000 metres Steeplechase, 1956. National Medal of Honour, Finland, 1975; Sports Writer of the Year (British Press Awards), 1968, 1976. *Publications:* The Red Snows (with Sir John Hunt), 1960; Sportsmen of our Time, 1962; Tokyo 1964: a diary of the XVIIIth Olympiad, 1964; Mexico 1968: a diary of the XIXth Olympics, 1968; Munich 72, 1972. *Recreations:* mountains, fishing, orienteering, social running. *Address:* The Navigator's House, River Lane, Richmond, Surrey. *T:* 01–940 8822. *Clubs:* Alpine, Hurlingham; Ranelagh Harriers (Petersham).

BRASNETT, Rev. Dr Bertrand Rippington, DD Oxon, 1935; *b* 22 Jan. 1893; *e s* of Stanley Brasnett, The Manor House, Marham, Norfolk, *g s* of Edward Rowing Brasnett, West Bilney House, Norfolk; unmarried. *Educ:* Oxford High Sch.; private tutor; Keble Coll., Oxford; Cuddesdon Theological Coll. Squire Scholar of the University of Oxford, 1911–15, 2nd class Classical Moderations, 2nd class Literæ Humaniores, BA, MA, Diploma in Theology with Distinction, BD; Deacon, 1916; Priest, 1918; Chaplain and Asst Master, Bradfield Coll., Berks, 1916–18; Priest-in-charge, Coleshill, Bucks, 1918–22; Chaplain and Lecturer, Bishops' Coll., Cheshunt, 1922–25; Vice-Principal, 1925–29, Principal and Pantonian Prof., 1930–42, of the Theological Coll. of the Scottish Episcopal Church, Edinburgh; Hon. Chaplain of St Mary's Cathedral, Edinburgh, 1926–29; Canon, 1930–42, and Chancellor, 1940–42, of St Mary's Cathedral, Edinburgh; Examining Chaplain to the Bishop of Edinburgh, 1930–42; Select Preacher, University of Oxford, 1941–43. *Publications:* The Suffering of the Impassible God, 1928; The Infinity of God, 1933; God the Worshipful, 1935. *Address:* Pleasant View, 15 Jack Straw's Lane, Headington, Oxford OX3 0DL.

BRASNETT, John; HM Diplomatic Service; Deputy High Commissioner, Bombay, since 1985; *b* 30 Oct. 1929; *s* of late Norman Vincent Brasnett and of Frances May Brasnett (*née* Hewlett); *m* 1956, Jennifer Ann Reid; one *s* one *d. Educ:* Blundells Sch.; Selwyn Coll., Cambridge (BA). Served Royal Artillery, 1948–49. Colonial Administrative Service, Uganda, 1953–65; retired from HM Overseas CS as Dep. Administrator, Karamoja District, 1965; entered HM Diplomatic Service, 1965; 1st Sec., OECD Delegn, 1968; Dep. High Comr, Freetown, 1970; FCO, 1973; Olympic Attaché, Montreal, 1975–76; Dep. High Comr, Accra, 1977–80; Counsellor (Econ. and Commercial), Ottawa, 1980–85). *Recreations:* reading, photography. *Address:* c/o Foreign and Commonwealth Office, SW1A 2AH. *Club:* Royal Commonwealth Society.

BRASS, John, CBE 1968; BSc, FEng, FIMinE, MICE; FRSA; Member, National Coal Board, 1971–73; *b* 22 Oct. 1908; 2nd *s* of late John Brass, Mining Engineer, and late Mary Brass (*née* Swainston); *m* 1934, Jocelyn Constance Cape, Stroud, Glos; three *s* (one *d* decd). Educ: Oundle Sch.; Birmingham Univ. (BSc Hons). Various appointments, all in mining; Chm., W Midlands Division, NCB, 1961–67; Regional Chm., Yorks and NW Areas, NCB, 1967–71. *Address:* 2 Fledborough Road, Wetherby, W Yorks.

BRASS, Prof. William, CBE 1981; FBA 1979; Professor of Medical Demography since 1972, Director of Centre for Population Studies since 1978, London School of Hygiene and Tropical Medicine; *b* 5 Sept. 1921; *s* of John Brass and Margaret Tait (*née* Haigh); *m* 1948, Betty Ellen Agnes Topp; two *d. Educ:* Royal High Sch., Edinburgh; Edinburgh Univ. (MA Hons Maths and Nat. Phil., 1943). Scientific Officer, Royal Naval Scientific Service, 1943–46; E African Statistical Dept, Colonial Service, 1948–55; Lectr in Statistics, 1955–64, Sen. Lectr 1964, Aberdeen Univ.; London Sch. of Hygiene and Trop. Medicine: Reader in Med. Demography, 1965–72; Dir, Centre for Overseas Population Studies, 1974–78; Head, Dept of Med. Stats and Epidemiology, 1977–82. Pres., Internat. Union for the Scientific Study of Population, 1985–. For. Associate, US Nat. Acad. of Scis, 1984. Mindel Sheps Award for distinguished contribn to demography, Population Assoc. of America, 1978. *Publications:* The Demography of Tropical Africa, 1968; Metodos para estimar la fecundidad y la mortalidad en poblaciones con datos Limitados: selección de trabajos, 1974; Methods of Estimating Fertility and Mortality from Limited and Defective Data, 1975; Advances in Methods for Estimating Fertility and Mortality from Limited and Defective Data, 1985; about 100 papers in learned jls. *Recreations:* travel, observing art and archaeology. *Address:* 3 Holt Close, N10 3HW. *T:* 01–883 1195.

BRASSEY, family name of **Baron Brassey of Apethorpe.**

BRASSEY OF APETHORPE, 3rd Baron, *cr* 1938, of Apethorpe; **David Henry Brassey;** Bt 1922; JP; DL; *b* 16 Sept. 1932; *er s* of 2nd Baron Brassey of Apethorpe, MC, TD, and late Lady Brassey of Apethorpe; *S* father, 1967; *m* 1st, 1958, Myrna Elizabeth (*d* 1974), *o d* of Lt-Col John Baskervyle-Glegg; one *s*; 2nd, 1978, Caroline, *y d* of late Lt-Col G. A. Evill; two *d.* Commissioned, Grenadier Guards, 1951; Major, 1966, retired, 1967. JP 1970, DL 1972, Northants. *Heir: s* Hon. Edward Brassey, *b* 9 March 1964. *Address:* The Manor House, Apethorpe, Peterborough. *T:* Kingscliffe 231. *Club:* White's.

BRASSEY, Brevet-Col Sir Hugh (Trefusis), KCVO 1985; OBE 1959; MC 1944; Lord Lieutenant of Wiltshire, since 1981; *b* 5 Oct. 1915; *s* of Lieut-Col Edgar Hugh Brassey, MVO, and Margaret Harriet (*née* Trefusis); *m* 1939, Joyce Patricia, *d* of Captain Maurice Kingscote; two *s* two *d* (and one *d* decd). *Educ:* Eton; Sandhurst. Regular Commission, The Royal Scots Greys, 1935–46; served Palestine, Africa, Italy and NW Europe, Lieut-Col Comdg Royal Wilts Yeomanry, 1955–58. ADC (TA) to the Queen, 1964–69; Exon, Queen's Bodyguard, Yeoman of the Guard, 1964–70, Ensign, 1970–79, Lieutenant, 1979–85; Adjutant and Clerk of the Cheque, 1971. Col, The Royal Scots Dragoon Guards, 1974–79. Regional Dir (Salisbury), Lloyds Bank. Chairman, Chippenham Conservative Assoc., 1951–53, 1966–68 (Pres. 1968). Pres., Wilts Assoc. of Boys Clubs, 1968. JP 1951, DL 1955, High Sheriff 1959, Vice Lord-Lieutenant, 1968–81, Wilts. Croix de Guerre (France), 1944. *Recreation:* country. *Address:* Manor Farm, Little Somerford, Chippenham, Wilts. *T:* Malmesbury 2255. *Club:* Cavalry and Guards.

BRASSEY, Lt-Col Hon. Peter (Esmé); DL; Lord-Lieutenant of Cambridgeshire, 1975–81; *b* 5 Dec. 1907; *o* surv. *s* of 1st Baron Brassey of Apethorpe; *m* 1944, Lady Romayne Cecil (OBE 1986), 2nd *d* of 5th Marquess of Exeter, KG, CMG; two *s* one *d. Educ:* Eton; Magdalene Coll., Cambridge. Barrister-at-Law, Inner Temple, Midland Circuit, 1931. Northamptonshire Yeomanry, Lieut-Col, 1945; served NW Europe (wounded). Dir, The Essex Water Co. Ltd, 1970–85 (Chm., 1981–85). DL 1961, High Sheriff, 1966, and Vice-Lieutenant, 1966–74, County of Huntingdon and Peterborough; DL County of Cambridge, 1974. KStJ 1976. *Recreations:* shooting, fishing. *Address:* Pond House, Barnack, Stamford, Lincs PE9 3DN. *T:* Stamford 740 238. *Club:* Carlton.

BRATBY, Jean Esme Oregon; *see* Cooke, J. E. O.

BRATBY, John Randall, RA 1971 (ARA 1959); ARCA; FIAL; RBA; FRSA; Painter and Writer; Member of London Group; Editorial Adviser for Art Quarterly; *b* 19 July 1928; *s* of George Alfred Bratby and Lily Beryl Randall; *m* 1953, Jean Esme Oregon Cooke, RA (*see* Jean E. Cooke) (marr. diss. 1977); three *s* one *d*; *m* 1977, Patti Prime. *Educ:* Tiffin Boys' Sch.; Kingston School of Art; Royal College of Art. Teacher: Carlisle College of Art, 1956; Royal College of Art, 1957–58. Gained prizes and scholarships, 1954–57. Numerous one-man exhibitions at Beaux Arts Gallery from 1954; Zwemmer Gallery from 1959; Thackeray Gallery; Furneaux Gallery; Nat. Theatre, 1978; also in galleries abroad. Exhibited: Royal Academy (yearly) from 1955; has also shown pictures in various international exhibitions and festivals; Venice Biennale, 1956. Guggenheim Award for Great Britain, 1956 and 1958; won junior section of John Moores Liverpool Exhibn, 1957; Paintings for film The Horse's Mouth, 1958. Works in public collections: Tate Gallery; Arts Council of Great Britain; British Council; Contemporary Arts Society. National Galleries: Canada; New Zealand; NSW and Victoria; galleries in many cities and towns of Great Britain; Victoria and Albert Museum; Ashmolean Museum; Museum of Modern Art, New York; also in many other public and private art collections, in Great Britain, the Commonwealth and USA. Paintings for film, Mistral's Daughter, 1984. Has made television appearances and sound broadcasts. *Publications: fiction:* Breakdown, 1960; Breakfast and Elevenses, 1961; Break-Pedal Down, 1962 (also TV play); Break 50 Kill, 1963; *non-fiction:* studio publication of colour reproductions of own work, 1961; Stanley Spencer, 1969; *illustrator:* Horse's Mouth, 1965; (contrib.) Oxford Illustrated Old Testament, 1968; The Devils, 1984; Apocryphal Letters, by Edward Lowerby, 1985. *Recreations:* philosophy, visiting Venice, individualism. *Address:* The Cupola, Belmont Road, Hastings, Sussex TN35 5NR. *T:* Hastings 434037.

BRATT, Guy Maurice, CMG 1977; MBE 1945; HM Diplomatic Service; Counsellor, Foreign and Commonwealth Office, 1977–80 (retired); *b* 4 April 1920; *s* of late Ernst Lars Gustaf Bratt and late Alice Maud Mary Bratt (*née* Raper); *m* 1945, Françoise Nelly Roberte Girardet; two *s* one *d*. *Educ:* Merchant Taylors' Sch.; London Univ. (BA). Served Army, 1939–46 (MBE): Major, Royal Signals. Solicitor 1947. Asst Sec., Colonial Develt Corp.; joined HM Foreign (subseq. Diplomatic) Service, 1952; served FO, 1952–54; Berlin, 1954–56; Brussels, 1956–58; FO, 1958–62; Vienna, 1962–66; FCO, 1966–70; Geneva, 1970–72; FCO, 1972–74; Washington, 1974–77. *Recreations:* music, railways, mountaineering. *Address:* 2 Orchehill Rise, Gerrards Cross, Bucks SL9 8PR. *T:* Gerrards Cross 883106. *Club:* Travellers'.

BRATTAIN, Dr Walter H(ouser); Research Physicist, Bell Telephone Laboratories, Inc., 1929–67; Overseer Emeritus, Whitman College; engaged with others in research investigating the properties of lipid membranes in salt solutions; *b* Amoy, China, 10 Feb. 1902; *s* of Ross R. Brattain and Ottilie Brattain (*née* Houser); *m* 1st, 1935, Keren Gilmore (*d* 1957); one *s*; 2nd, 1958, Emma Jane Miller (*née* Kirsch). *Educ:* Whitman Coll., Walla Walla, Washington; University of Oregon, Eugene, Oregon; University of Minnesota, Minneapolis, Minn. BS 1924, Whitman Coll.; MA 1926, University of Oregon; PhD 1929, University of Minnesota. Asst Physicist, Bureau of Standards, 1928–29; Technical Staff, Bell Telephone Labs, Inc., 1929–67. Division of War Research, Columbia Univ., 1942–44. Visiting Lecturer, Harvard Univ., 1952–53; Visiting Prof. of Physics (part-time) Whitman Coll., 1963–72. Fellow, Explorers' Club, 1977. Hon. Dr of Science: Portland Univ., 1952; Union Coll., 1955; Whitman Coll., 1955; University of Minnesota, 1957; Gustavus Adolphus Coll., 1963; Hon. LHD Hartwick Coll., 1964. Stuart Ballantine Medal, Franklin Institute, 1952; John Scott Medal, City of Philadelphia, 1955; Nobel Prize for Physics (with J. Bardeen and W. Shockley), 1956. Fellow: American Academy of Arts and Sciences, 1956; National Academy of Sciences, 1959; Hon. MIEEE 1981. *Publications:* many scientific papers on Thermionics and Semiconductors in various physics journals. *Recreation:* golf. *Address:* 1869 Rustic Place, Walla Walla, Washington 99362, USA.

BRAVO, Martin Maurice B.; *see* Brandon-Bravo.

BRAY, Denis Campbell, CMG 1977; CVO 1975; Chairman, Denis Bray Consultants Ltd, Hong Kong, since 1985; *b* 24 Jan. 1926; *s* of Rev. Arthur Henry Bray and Edith Muriel Bray; *m* 1952, Marjorie Elizabeth Bottomley; four *d* (one *s* decd). *Educ:* Kingswood Sch.; Jesus Coll., Cambridge (MA). BScEcon London. RN, 1947–49. Colonial Service Devonshire Course, 1949–50; Admin. Officer, Hong Kong, 1950; Dist Comr, New Territories, 1971; Hong Kong Comr in London, 1977–80; Sec. for Home Affairs, Hong Kong, 1973–77 and 1980–84, retd. *Recreations:* ocean racing and cruising. *Address:* D/G Conway Mansion, 29 Conduit Road, Hong Kong. *T:* 5–471621. *Clubs:* Travellers', London Rowing, Royal Ocean Racing; Leander (Henley-on-Thames); Hong Kong, Royal Hong Kong Jockey, Royal Hong Kong Yacht; Tai Po Boat.

See also J. W. Bray.

BRAY, Jeremy William; MP (Lab) Motherwell South, since 1983 (Motherwell and Wishaw, Oct. 1974–1983); Opposition spokesman on science and technology, since 1983; *b* 29 June 1930; *s* of Rev. Arthur Henry Bray and Mrs Edith Muriel Bray; *m* 1953, Elizabeth (*née* Trowell); four *d*. *Educ:* Aberystwyth Grammar Sch.; Kingswood Sch.; Jesus Coll., Cambridge. Researched in pure mathematics at Cambridge, 1953–55; Choate Fellow, Harvard Univ., USA, 1955–56; Technical Officer, Wilton Works of ICI, 1956–62. Contested (Lab) Thirsk and Malton, General Election, 1959; MP (Lab) Middlesbrough West, 1962–70; Member: Select Cttee on Nationalised Industries, 1962–64; Estimates Cttee, 1964–66; Expenditure Cttee, 1978–79; Select Cttee on Treasury and Civil Service, 1979–83 (Chm., Sub-cttee, 1981–82); Chairman: Labour, Science and Technol Group, 1964–66; Economic Affairs Estimates Sub-Cttee, 1964–66; Parly Sec., Min. of Power, 1966–67; Jt Parly Sec., Min. of Technology, 1967–69. Dir, Mullard Ltd, 1970–73; Consultant, Battelle Res. Centre, Geneva, 1973; Sen. Res. Fellow, 1974, Vis. Prof., 1975–79, Univ. of Strathclyde. Dep. Chm., Christian Aid, 1972–84; Co-Dir, Programme of Res. into Econometric Methods, Imperial Coll., 1971–74. Chm., Fabian Soc., 1971–72. *Publications:* Decision in Government, 1970; Production Purpose and Structure, 1982; Fabian pamphlets and articles in jls. *Recreation:* sailing. *Address:* House of Commons, SW1A 0AA.

See also D. C. Bray.

BRAY, Hon. Dr John Jefferson, AC 1979; Chancellor of the University of Adelaide, 1968–83; *b* 16 Sept. 1912; *s* of Harry Midwinter Bray and Gertrude Eleonore Bray (*née* Stow). *Educ:* St Peter's Coll., Adelaide; Univ. of Adelaide. LLB 1932, LLB Hons 1933, LLD 1937. Admitted to South Australian Bar, 1933; QC 1957. Univ. of Adelaide: Actg Lectr in Jurisprudence, 1941, 1943, 1945, 1951; Actg Lectr in Legal History, 1957–58; Lectr in Roman Law, 1959–66; Chief Justice of Supreme Court of SA, 1967–78. DUniv Adelaide, 1983. *Publications:* Poems, 1962; Poems 1961–1971, 1972; Poems 1972–1979, 1979; (ed jtly) No 7 Friendly Street Poetry Reader, 1983; The Bay of Salamis and Other Poems, 1986; contribs to: Well and Truly Tried, 1982 (Festschrift for Sir Richard Eggleston); Adelaide Law School Centenary Essays, 1983; Australian Law Jl. *Address:* 39 Hurtle Square, Adelaide, South Australia 5000. *Club:* University of Adelaide.

BRAY, Prof. Kenneth Noel Corbett, PhD; CEng; Hopkinson and Imperial Chemical Industries Professor of Applied Thermodynamics, Cambridge University, since 1985; *b* 19 Nov. 1929; *s* of Harold H. Bray and Effie E. Bray; *m* 1958, Shirley Maureen Culver; two *s* one *d*. *Educ:* Univ. of Cambridge (BA); Univ. of Southampton (PhD); MSE Princeton; CEng; MRAeS; MAIAA. Engr in Research Dept, Handley Page Aircraft, 1955–56; University of Southampton, 1956–85: Dean, Faculty of Engrg and Applied Science, 1975–78; Head, Dept of Aeronautics and Astronautics, 1982–85. Vis. appt, Avco–Everett Res. Lab., Mass, USA, 1961–62; Vis. Prof., MIT, 1966–67; Vis. Res. Engr, Univ. of California, San Diego, 1975, 1983. *Publications:* on topics in gas dynamics, chemically reacting flows, molecular energy transfer processes and combustion. *Recreations:* walking, wood carving, gardening. *Address:* 23 De Freville Avenue, Cambridge CB4 1HW.

BRAY, Sir Theodor (Charles), Kt 1975; CBE 1964; Chancellor, Griffith University, Brisbane, 1975–85; *b* 11 Feb. 1905; *s* of Horace and Maude Bray; *m* 1931, Rosalie, *d* of Rev. A. M. Trengove; three *s* two *d* (and one *s* one *d* decd). *Educ:* state schs; Adelaide Univ. Apprentice Printer, Reporter, Register, Adelaide; Sub-editor, Chief Sub-editor, The Argus, Melbourne; Editor (26 yrs), Editor-in-Chief, Jt Man. Dir, Queensland Newspapers Pty Ltd, 1936–70, Dir, 1956–80; Chm., Australian Associated Press, 1968–70; Mem., Austr. Council for the Arts, 1969–73; Austr. Chm., Internat. Press Inst., 1962–70; Chm., Griffith Univ. Council, 1970–75. *Recreations:* bowls, travel. *Address:* 10/64 Macquarie Street, St Lucia, Qld 4067, Australia. *T:* 3707442. *Clubs:* Queensland, Johnsonian (Brisbane).

BRAY, William John, CBE 1975; FEng 1978; Director of Research, Post Office, 1966–75 (Dep. Director, 1965); *b* 10 Sept. 1911; British; *m* 1936, Margaret Earp; one *d* (and one *d* decd). *Educ:* Imperial Coll., London Univ. Electrical engineering apprenticeship, Portsmouth Naval Dockyard, 1928–32; Royal and Kitchener Scholarships, Imperial Coll., 1932–34; entered PO Engineering Dept as Asst Engineer, 1934; Commonwealth Fund Fellowship (Harkness Foundation) for study in USA, 1956–57; Staff Engineer, Inland Radio Br., PO Engineering Dept, 1958. Vis. Prof., UCL, 1974–78. External Examr, MSc (Communications), Imperial Coll., London, 1976–80. Participation in work of International Radio Consultative Cttee of International Telecommunication Union and European Postal and Telecommunication Conferences; Consultant to UK Council for Educnl Technology, 1976–78. MSc(Eng), FCGI, DIC, FIEE; DUniv Essex, 1976. J. J. Thomson Medal, IEE, 1978. *Publications:* papers in Proc. IEE (IEE Ambrose Fleming Radio Sect. and Electronics Div. Premium Awards). *Recreations:* sailing, travel. *Address:* The Pump House, Bredfield, Woodbridge, Suffolk IP13 6AH. *T:* Woodbridge 5838.

BRAY, Winston, CBE 1970; Deputy Chairman and Deputy Chief Executive, BOAC, 1972–74; Member Board, BOAC, 1971–74; Member Board, BAAC Ltd (formerly BOAC (AC Ltd), 1969–74; *b* 29 April 1910; *s* of late Edward Bray and Alice Walker; *m* 1937, Betty Atterton Miller; one *s* two *d*. *Educ:* Highgate Sch.; London Univ. (BCom). Missouri Pacific Railroad, USA, 1932; Asst to Traffic Manager, British Airways, 1938; Traffic Dept, BOAC, 1940; Sales Promotion Supt, 1946; Sales Manager, 1950; Sales Planning Manager, 1954; Dir of Planning, 1964; Planning Dir, 1969; Dep. Managing Dir, 1972. FCIT. *Recreations:* sailing, gardening. *Address:* Greenacres, Frith Hill, Great Missenden, Bucks. *Club:* Royal Automobile.

BRAYBROOK, Edward John, CB 1972; *b* 25 Oct. 1911; *s* of late Prior Wormsley Braybrook and Kate Braybrook; *m* 1937, Eva Rosalin Thomas; one *s* two *d*. *Educ:* Edmonton Latymer Secondary Sch. Asst Naval Store Officer, Admty, Chatham, Malta and Devonport, 1930–37; Deputy Naval Store Officer, Admty, 1938–39; Naval Store Officer, Admty and Haslemere, 1940–43; Suptg Naval Store Officer, Levant, 1943; Comdr/Captain (SP) RNVR Suptg Naval Store Officer, Ceylon and Southern India, 1944–46; Supt, Perth, Scotland, 1946–47; Asst Director of Stores, Admty, 1947–53; Suptg Naval Store Officer, Chatham, 1953–55; Deputy Director of Stores, Admty, 1955–64; Director of Stores (Naval), MoD, 1964–70; Dir-Gen. Supplies and Transport (Naval), MoD, 1970–73. *Recreations:* gardening, photography, painting, handicrafts. *Address:* 22 Church Drive, North Harrow, Middlesex. *T:* 01–427 0838.

BRAYBROOKE, 9th Baron *cr* 1788; **Henry Seymour Neville;** JP; DL; Hon. MA Camb. 1948; Hereditary Visitor of Magdalene College, Cambridge; Patron of two livings; *b* 5 Feb. 1897; *er s* of late Rev. Hon. Grey Neville (2nd *s* of 6th Baron) and late Mary Peele, *e d* of late Canon Francis Slater; *S* cousin, 1943; *m* 1st, 1930, Muriel Evelyn (*d* 1962), *d* of late William C. Manning and *widow* of E. C. Cartwright; one *s*; 2nd, 1963, Angela Mary (*d* 1985), *d* of late William H. Hollis and *widow* of John Ree. *Educ:* Shrewsbury Sch. (Scholar); Magdalene Coll., Cambridge. Served European War, 1914–18, in RNA Service and RAF; later held various appointments with Anglo-Iranian and Shell Groups of oil companies. Chm., Diocesan Bd of Finance, Chelmsford, 1950–68. JP Saffron Walden, 1953; DL, 1950–. *Heir: s* Hon. Robin Henry Charles Neville [*b* 29 Jan. 1932; *m* 1st, 1955, Robin Helen (marr. diss. 1974), *d* of late T. A. Brockhoff, Sydney, Australia; four *d* (and one *d* decd); 2nd, 1974, Linda Norman; three *d*]. *Address:* Bruncketts, Wendens Ambo, Saffron Walden, Essex CB11 4JL. *T:* Saffron Walden 40200.

BRAYBROOKE, Rev. Marcus Christopher Rossi; Executive Director, Council of Christians and Jews, since 1984; Hon. Priest-in-charge, Christ Church, Bath, since 1984; *b* 16 Nov. 1938; *s* of Lt-Col Arthur Rossi Braybrooke and Marcia Nona Braybrooke; *m* 1964, Mary Elizabeth Walker, JP, BSc, CQSW; one *s* one *d*. *Educ:* Cranleigh School; Magdalene College, Cambridge (BA, MA); Madras Christian College; Wells Theological College; King's College, London (MPhil). Curate, St Michael's, Highgate, 1964–67; Team Vicar, Strood Clergy Team, 1967–73; Rector, Swainswick, Langridge, Woolley, 1973–79; Dir of Training, Dio. of Bath and Wells, 1979–84; Chm., World Congress of Faiths, 1978–83; Examng Chaplain to Bishop of Bath and Wells, 1984–. Editor, World Faiths Insight, 1976–. *Publications:* Together to the Truth, 1971; The Undiscovered Christ of Hinduism, 1973; Interfaith Worship, 1974; Interfaith Organizations: a historical directory, 1980; contribs to Theology, World Faiths Insight, The Modern Churchman. *Recreations:* gardening, home decorating, tennis, swimming, travel. *Address:* 2 The Bassetts, Box, Wilts SN14 9ER. *T:* Bath 742827.

BRAYBROOKE, Neville Patrick Bellairs; writer; *b* 30 May 1925; *s* of Patrick Philip William Braybrooke and Lettice Marjorie Bellairs; *m* 1953, June Guesdon Jolliffe; one step *d*. *Educ:* Ampleforth. *Publications:* This is London, 1953; London Green: The Story of Kensington Gardens, Hyde Park, Green Park and St James's Park, 1959; London, 1961; The Idler: novel, 1961; The Delicate Investigation (play for BBC), 1969; Four Poems for Christmas, 1986; *edited:* The Wind and the Rain: quarterly, 1941–1951; T. S. Eliot: a symposium for his 70th birthday, 1958, 5th edn 1983; A Partridge in a Pear Tree: a celebration for Christmas, 1960; Pilgrim of the Future: a Teilhard de Chardin symposium, 1966, 2nd edn, 1968; The Letters of J. R. Ackerley, 1975, 2nd edn 1977; contrib. Guardian, New Statesman, New Yorker, Saturday Review, Times, Times Lit. Suppl., Sunday Telegraph, Spectator, Tablet. *Recreations:* cats, walking, reading little reviews. *Address:* Grove House, Castle Road, Cowes, IoW PO31 7QZ. *T:* Cowes 293950; 10 Gardnor Road, NW3 1HA. *T:* 01–435 1851. *Clubs:* Island Sailing; PEN.

BRAYE, Baroness (8th in line) *cr* 1529, of Eaton Braye, Co. Bedford; **Penelope Mary Aubrey-Fletcher;** *b* 28 Sept. 1941; *d* of 7th Baron Braye and of Dorothea, *yr d* of late Daniel C. Donoghue, Philadelphia; *S* father, 1985; *m* 1981, Lt-Col Edward Henry Lancelot Aubrey-Fletcher, Grenadier Guards. *Educ:* Assumption Convent, Hengrave Hall; Univ. of Warwick. High Sheriff of Northants, 1983. *Heir: uncle* Hon. Ambrose Jordan Verney-Cave, *b* 23 Oct. 1906. *Address:* Stanford Hall, Lutterworth, Leics LE17 6DH.

BRAYNE, Richard Bolding, MBE 1957; Clerk of the Worshipful Company of Ironmongers, since 1973; *b* 28 Oct. 1924; 3rd *s* of late Brig. Frank Lugard Brayne, MC, CSI, CIE, ICS, and late Iris Goodeve Brayne, K-i-H; *m* 1947, Anne Stoddart Forrest; one *s* two *d*. *Educ:* Sherborne Sch.; Pembroke Coll., Cambridge. Indian Army, 3rd (Peshawar) Indian Mountain Battery, India, Burma and Far East, 1942–46. Entered Colonial Service as DO, Tanganyika, 1948; Staff Officer to HRH The Princess Margaret's tour of Tanganyika, 1956; Dist Comr, 1957; Principal, Admin. Trng Centre and Local Govt Trng Centre, 1960. Prin. Asst Sec., Min. of Educn, 1963; Mem., E African UGC and Makerere Univ. College Council, 1963; retd from Colonial Service, 1964. Sec., Brit.

Paper and Board Makers' Assoc., 1964; Trng Adviser and Develt Manager, Construction Industry Trng Bd, 1966. Asst Clerk of Worshipful Co. of Ironmongers, 1971. Member: Exec. Cttee, Nat. Assoc. of Almshouses, 1972– (Chm., 1981–); Council, Royal Surgical Aid Soc., 1972– (Chm., 1982–). *Recreations:* shooting, golf, D-I-Y. *Address:* Ironmongers' Hall, Barbican, EC2Y 8AA. *T:* 01–606 2725.

BRAYNE-BAKER, John, CMG 1957; Colonial Administrative Service, Nigeria (retired); *b* 13 Aug. 1905; *s* of Francis Brayne-Baker and Dorothea Mary Brayne-Baker (*née* Porcher); *m* 1947, Ruth Hancock; no *c*. *Educ:* Marlborough Coll.; Worcester Coll., Oxford. Nigeria: Asst District Officer, 1928; District Officer, 1938; Senior District Officer, 1948; Resident, 1953. Senior Resident and Deputy Commissioner of the Cameroons, 1954–56; retired 1956. Member, Tiverton RDC, 1959–74, Tiverton DC, 1973–76. *Recreations:* gardening and golf. *Address:* East Grantlands, Uffculme, Cullompton, Devon. *T:* Craddock 40236. *Club:* Tiverton Golf (Tiverton).

BRAYNE-NICHOLLS, Rear-Adm. (Francis) Brian (Price), CB 1965; DSC 1942; General Secretary, Officers Pensions Society, 1966–79; *b* 1 Dec. 1914; *s* of late Dr G. E. E. Brayne-Nicholls and *g s* of Sir Francis W. T. Brain; *m* 1939, Wendy (*née* Donnelly) (*d* 1983); one *d*. *Educ:* RNC, Dartmouth. Sub-Lieut and Lieut, HMS Bee on Yangtse River, 1936–39; specialised in Navigation, 1939; Navigating Officer of: HM Ships Nelson, Rodney, Cardiff, 1939–41, Manxman (during many mining ops, Malta convoys and Madagascar op.), 1941–42; Combined Ops, taking part in Sicily (despatches), Salerno, and Normandy landings. Navigating Officer: HMS Glory, 1944–46; HMS Vanguard, 1948; Comdr 1948; Comdg Officer: HMS Gravelines, 1952–53; HMS St Kitts, 1953–54; Capt 1954; Naval Asst to First Sea Lord, 1954–55; Comdg Officer, HMS Apollo, 1955–57; NATO Standing Group, Washington, 1957–59; Captain of Navigation Direction Sch., HMS Dryad, 1959–61; Admiralty, 1961–63; Rear-Adm. 1963; Chief of Staff to Commander, Far East Fleet, 1963–65. Younger Brother, Trinity House. Mem., Nautical Inst. *Recreation:* golf. *Address:* 3 Tedworth Square, SW3 4DU. *T:* 01–352 1681. *Club:* Naval and Military.

BRAYNEN, Sir Alvin (Rudolph), Kt 1975; JP; Consultant to Shell, Bahamas, 1969–82; High Commissioner for the Commonwealth of the Bahamas in London, 1973–77; *b* 6 Dec. 1904; *s* of William Rudolph Braynen and Lulu Isabelle Braynen (*née* Griffin); *m* 1969, Ena Estelle (*née* Elden); (one *s* one *d* by a previous marriage). *Educ:* Public Sch., The Current, Eleuthera, Bahamas; Boys' Central Sch., Nassau, Bahamas (teacher trng). Public Sch. Headmaster, 1923–25. Entered commercial world, 1925, as clerk; founded his own petroleum commn firm, 1930, disposing of it in 1965. MP for Cat Island, 1935–42 and constituency for what is now known as St John, 1942–72; Dep. Speaker of House of Assembly, 1949–53, and 1963–66; MEC, 1953–58; Speaker of House of Assembly, 1967–72. During years 1952–58 he was Chairman of several Boards, incl. those responsible for Educn, Public Works, Prisons and Traffic; past Member: Bds of Agriculture, Health, Tourism, Out Island Develt and Educn; Mem., both Constitutional Confs from the Bahamas to London in 1963 and 1968; Chm., Exec. Cttee of Conf. of Commonwealth Caribbean Parliamentary Heads and Clerks; also served as either Chm. or Dep. Chm. of important Nat. Festivities for many years, such as Coronation of the Queen, visit of Princess Margaret, First Constitutional Day, 1964, and supervised arrangements for Conf. of Delegates of Commonwealth Parliamentary Conf. held at Nassau, 1968. Organised Bahamas Chamber of Commerce (first Exec. Sec.); Founder and first Pres., Nassau Mutual Aid Assoc.; first Pres., Kiwanis Club (Montague Branch). JP Bahamas 1952. *Recreations:* swimming; collects books on the Bahamas; collects coins and stamps. *Address:* PO Box N42, Nassau, Bahamas.

BRAYSHAW, (Alfred) Joseph, CBE 1975 (OBE 1964); JP; DL; Secretary, The Magistrates' Association, 1965–77; *b* Manchester, 20 Dec. 1912; *er s* of late Shipley Neave Brayshaw and late Ruth Cotterell (*née* Holmes), JP; *m* 1st, Joan Hawkes (*d* 1940); 2nd, 1943, Marion Spencer, *y d* of late Spencer Johnson, Bury St Edmunds; three *s*. *Educ:* Sidcot Sch., Somerset; engineering factories; Dalton Hall, Univ. of Manchester. Brayshaw Furnaces & Tools Ltd, 1934–40; CBCO, 1941–46; Asst Sec., then Gen. Sec., Friends' Relief Service, 1946–48; Gen. Sec., Nat. Marriage Guidance Council, 1949–64 (a Vice-Pres., 1964–); Pres., Guildford and District Marriage Guidance Council, 1983– (Vice-Pres., 1974–83). JP Surrey, 1958; DL Surrey, 1983; Chm., Farnham Bench, 1979–82; a Vice-Pres., Surrey Magistrates' Soc., 1985– (Chm., 1979–83). *Publication:* Public Policy and Family Life, 1980. *Recreations:* gardening, walking. *Address:* Apple Trees, Beech Road, Haslemere, Surrey GU27 2BX. *T:* Haslemere 2677.

BRAZENDALE, George William, CMG 1958; FCA; *b* 1909; *s* of late Percy Ridout Brazendale, and late Edith Mary Brazendale (*née* Maystre); *m* 1938, Madeleine, *o d* of Thomas and Betty Wroe; two *d*. *Educ:* Arnold Sch., Blackpool, Lancs. Chief Accountant, Colclough China Ltd, Stoke-on-Trent, 1936–41; Asst Area Officer, MAP, 1941–42; Chief Progress Officer, ROF Swynnerton, 1942–43; Secretary, Midland Regional Board, 1943–45; Regional Controller Board of Trade; Northern Region, 1945–46; North-Western Region, 1946–50; Asst Secretary, Board of Trade, 1946; Trade Commissioner for the UK in charge Calcutta, 1950–60. Principal British Trade Commissioner: in the Federation of Rhodesia and Nyasaland, 1961–63; also Economic Adviser to British High Commissioner in Rhodesia, 1964–65; Economic Adviser to Special British Representative in East and Central Africa, 1966–67; retired from HM Diplomatic Service, 1967. ACA 1931. *Recreations:* fishing, gardening. *Address:* 111 Hatherley Court, Hatherley Grove, W2 5RG; 8 Ascot Avenue, Sandy Bay, Hobart, Tas 7005, Australia. *Club:* Oriental.

BRAZIER, Rt. Rev. Percy James; *b* 3 Aug. 1903; *m* 1933, Joan Cooper, MB, BS; one *s* four *d*. *Educ:* Weymouth Coll., Dorset; Emmanuel Coll., Cambridge. 2nd class Hist. Trip., Part I, 1924, 2nd class, Part II, and BA, 1925; MA 1939. Ridley Hall, Cambridge, 1925–27, Deacon, 1927; Priest, 1928; Curate of St John the Evangelist, Blackheath, 1927–29; CMS (Ruanda Mission), 1930; Kabale, 1930–34; Kigeme, Diocese of Uganda, 1934–50; Archdeacon of Ruanda-Urundi, 1946–51; Asst Bishop of Uganda for Ruanda-Urundi, 1951–60; Bishop of Rwanda and Burundi, 1960–64 (name of diocese changed when Ruanda-Urundi was granted independence, 1962); retired 1964. Rector of Padworth and Vicar of Mortimer West End, Diocese of Oxford, 1964–70. Chevalier de l'Ordre Royal du Lion (Belgium), 1955. *Recreations:* photography, gardening, ornithology. *Address:* Lark Rise, Peasemore, Newbury, Berks RG16 0JF. *T:* Chieveley 248548.

See also D. C. Clarke.

BRAZIER-CREAGH, Maj.-Gen. Sir (Kilner) Rupert, KBE 1962 (CBE 1947); CB 1954; DSO 1944; Secretary of the Horse Race Betting Levy Board, 1961–65; Director of Staff Duties, War Office, 1959–61, retired; *b* 12 Dec. 1909; 2nd *s* of late Lt-Col K. C. Brazier-Creagh; *m* 1st, 1938, Elizabeth Mary (*d* 1967), *d* of late E. M. Magor; one *s* two *d*; 2nd, 1968, Mrs Marie Nelson. *Educ:* Rugby; RMA, Woolwich. 2nd Lieut, 1929; served War of 1939–45 (despatches, DSO); Bde Major, 9th Armoured Div., 1941; GSO1 12th Corps, 1943; Commanded 25th Field Regt, 1944; BGS 21st Army Group and BAOR, 1945–48 (CBE); idc 1949; DDRA, War Office, 1950; CRA 11th Armoured Div., 1951–52; Chief of Staff Malaya Command, 1952–55 (despatches, CB); Asst Comdt, Staff Coll., 1955–57; Chief of Staff, Eastern Command, 1957–59. Officer, American Legion of Merit, 1945. *Recreation:* racing. *Address:* Travis Corners Road, Garrison, New York, USA.

BREADALBANE AND HOLLAND, 10th Earl of, *cr* 1677; **John Romer Boreland Campbell;** Mac Chailein Mhic Dhonnachaidh (celtic designation); Viscount of Tay and Paintland; Lord Glenorchy, Benederaloch, Ormelie and Weik, 1677; Bt of Glenorchy; Bt of Nova Scotia, 1625; *b* 28 April 1919; *o s* of 9th Earl of Breadalbane and Holland, MC; *S* father, 1959; *m* 1949, Coralie (marr. diss.), *o d* of Charles Archer. *Educ:* Eton; RMC, Sandhurst; Basil Patterson Tutors; Edinburgh Univ. Entered Black Watch (Royal Highlanders), 1939; served France, 1939–41 (despatches); invalided, 1942. *Recreations:* piobaireachd, Scottish highland culture. *Heir:* none. *Address:* House of Lords, SW1; 29 Mackeson Road, Hampstead, NW3.

BREADEN, Very Rev. Robert William; Dean of Brechin since 1984; Rector of St Mary's, Broughty Ferry, since 1972; *b* 7 Nov. 1937; *s* of Moses and Martha Breaden; *m* 1970, Glenice Sutton Martin; one *s* three *d*. *Educ:* The King's Hospital, Dublin; Edinburgh Theological Coll. Deacon 1961, priest 1962; Asst Curate, St Mary's, Broughty Ferry, 1961–65; Rector, Church of the Holy Rood, Carnoustie, 1965–72; Canon of St Paul's Cathedral, Dundee, 1977. *Recreations:* gardening, horse riding; Rugby enthusiast. *Address:* St Mary's Rectory, 46 Seafield Road, Broughty Ferry, Dundee DD5 3AN. *T:* Dundee 77477.

BREALEY, Prof. Richard Arthur; Deputy Principal, since 1984, and Midland Bank Professor of Corporate Finance, since 1974, London Business School; *b* 9 June 1936; *s* of late Albert Brealey and of Irene Brealey; *m* 1967, Diana Cecily Brown Kelly; two *s*. *Educ:* Queen Elizabeth's, Barnet; Exeter Coll., Oxford (MA, 1st Cl. Hons PPE). Sun Life Assce Co. of Canada, 1959–66; Keystone Custodian Funds of Boston, 1966–68; London Business Sch., 1968–, Governor, 1984–. Pres., European Finance Assoc., 1975; Dir, Amer. Finance Assoc., 1979–81. *Publications:* include: An Introduction to Risk and Return from Common Stocks, 1969, 2nd edn 1983; (with S. C. Myers) Principles of Corporate Finance, 1981, 3rd edn 1987; articles in professional jls. *Recreations:* ski-ing, rock climbing, pottery. *Address:* Haydens Cottage, The Pound, Cookham, Berks SL6 9QE. *T:* Bourne End 20143.

BREAM, Julian, CBE 1985 (OBE 1964); guitarist and lutenist; *b* 15 July 1933; *e s* of Henry G. Bream; *m* 1st, Margaret Williamson; one adopted *s*; 2nd, 1980, Isobel Sanchez. *Educ:* Royal College of Music (Junior Exhibition Award, 1945 and Scholarship, 1948). Began professional career at Cheltenham, 1947; London début, Wigmore Hall, 1950; subsequently has appeared in leading world festivals in Europe, USA, Australia and Far East. A leader in revival of interest in Elizabethan Lute music, on which he has done much research; has encouraged contemporary English compositions for the guitar. Formed Julian Bream Consort, 1960; inaugurated Semley Festival of Music and Poetry, 1971. DUniv Surrey, 1968. *Recreations:* playing the guitar; cricket, table tennis, gardening, backgammon. *Address:* c/o Harold Holt Ltd, 31 Sinclair Road, W14 0NS.

BREARE, William Robert Ackrill; Chairman and Managing Director: R. Ackrill Ltd, 1955–82; Lawrence & Hall Ltd, 1963–81; *b* 5 July 1916; *s* of late Robert Ackrill Breare and late Emily Breare (*née* Waddington); *m* 1942, Sybella Jessie Macduff Roddick, *d* of late John Roddick, Annan; one *s* two *d*. *Educ:* Old College, Windermere; Charterhouse; Wadham Coll., Oxford (MA). BCL Oxon 1938. Sub-Lt RNVSR, 1935–39; Comdr RNVR, 1942–44. Dir, R. Ackrill Ltd, newspaper publishers, 1938. Pres., Yorks Newspaper Soc., 1953 and 1972; Mem. Council, Newspaper Soc., 1967–81; Mem. Press Council, 1972–81. Contested (C) Rother Valley, 1950. *Recreations:* music, sailing. *Address:* Harrison Hill House, Starbeck, Harrogate, N Yorks. *T:* Harrogate 883302.

BREARLEY, Christopher John Scott; Under Secretary, Local Government Finance, Department of the Environment, since 1985; *b* 25 May 1943; *s* of Geoffrey Brearley and Winifred (*née* Scott); *m* 1971, Rosemary Stockbridge; two *s*. *Educ:* King Edward VII Sch., Sheffield; Trinity Coll., Oxford. MA 1964, BPhil 1966. Entered Ministry of Transport, 1966; Private Sec. to Perm. Sec., 1969–70; Principal, DoE, 1970; Sec. to Review of Develt Control Procedures (Dobry), DoE, 1973–74; Private Sec. to the Secretary of the Cabinet, Cabinet Office, 1974–76; Asst Sec., 1977; Under Sec., 1981; Dir of Scottish Services, PSA, 1981–83; Cabinet Office, 1983–85. *Recreations:* crosswords, walking. *Address:* Middlemount, South Road, Chorleywood, Herts WD3 5AS. *T:* Chorleywood 3848. *Club:* New (Edinburgh).

BREARLEY, (John) Michael, OBE 1978; psycho-analyst; Psychotherapist, Camden Psychotherapy Unit; Captain, Middlesex County Cricket Club, 1971–82; *b* 28 April 1942; *s* of Horace and late Midge Brearley; *m* Mana Sarabhai; one *d* and one step *s*; *Educ:* City of London Sch.; St John's Coll., Cambridge (MA). Lectr in Philosophy, Univ. of Newcastle-upon-Tyne, 1968–71. Middlesex County Cricketer, intermittently, 1961–82; capped, 1964; played first Test Match, 1976; Captain of England XI, 1977–80, 1981. *Publications:* (with Dudley Doust) The Return of the Ashes, 1978; (with Dudley Doust) The Ashes Retained, 1979; Phoenix: the series that rose from the ashes, 1982; The Art of Captaincy, 1985; articles for the Sunday Times. *Club:* MCC (Hon. Life Mem.).

BREARLEY, Sir Norman, Kt 1971; CBE 1965; DSO 1916; MC; AFC; FRAeS; Company Director, Western Australia, retired 1977; *b* Geelong, Vic., 22 Dec. 1890; *s* of late Robert Hillard Brearley, Perth, WA; *m* 1917, Violet, *d* of late Hon. Sydney Stubbs, CMG, MLA, Perth; one *s* one *d*. *Educ:* state and private schs, Geelong; Technical Coll., Perth, WA. Enlisted, after engineering training. Served War, RFC and RAF, also Major in Liverpool Regt, France and England, 1914–1919 (wounded, despatches, AFC, MC, DSO); War of 1939–45; Gp Capt., RAAF. Founder (1921) of West Australian Airways; was the first airmail contractor to Australian Govt. Pioneer of Australian Air Services. *Publication:* Australian Aviator, 1971. *Recreations:* tennis, golf. *Address:* 6 Esplanade, Peppermint Grove, Cottesloe, WA 6011, Australia. *T:* 312293. *Club:* Weld (Perth, WA).

BRECHIN, Bishop of, since 1975; **Most Rev. Lawrence Edward Luscombe;** Primus of the Episcopal Church in Scotland, since 1985; *b* 10 Nov. 1924; *s* of Reginald John and Winifred Luscombe; *m* 1946, Doris Carswell Morgan, BSc, MB, ChB; one *d*. *Educ:* Torquay Grammar Sch.; Kelham Theological Coll.; King's Coll., London. CA 1952, ASAA 1957. FSAScot 1980. Served Indian Army, 1942–47. Partner, Galbraith, Dunlop & Co, Chartered Accountants, Glasgow, 1952–63. Ordained deacon, 1963; priest, 1964; Curate, St Margaret's, Glasgow, 1963–66; Rector, St Barnabas', Paisley, 1966–71; Provost of St Paul's Cathedral, Dundee, 1971–75. Hon. Canon, Trinity Cathedral, Davenport, Iowa, 1983. Hon. DLitt Geneva Theological Coll., 1972. OStJ 1986. *Address:* 7 Shaftesbury Road, Dundee DD2 1HF.

BRECHIN, Dean of; *see* Breaden, Very Rev. R. W.

BRECKENRIDGE, Prof. Alasdair Muir, MD; FRCP; Professor of Clinical Pharmacology, University of Liverpool, since 1974; *b* 7 May 1937; *s* of Thomas and Jane Breckenridge; *m* 1967, Jean Margaret Boyle; two *s*. *Educ:* Bell Baxter Sch., Cupar, Fife; Univ. of St Andrews (MB, ChB Hons 1961); Univ. of London (MSc 1968); Univ. of Dundee (MD Hons 1974). FRCP 1974. House Phys. and Surg., Dundee Royal Infirm., 1961–62; Asst, Dept of Medicine, Univ. of St Andrews, 1962–63; successively House

Phys., Registrar, Sen. Registrar, Tutor, Lectr and Sen. Lectr, Hammersmith Hosp. and RPMS, 1964–74. Member: Cttee on Safety of Medicines, 1982–; Council, RCP, 1983–; Exec. Cttee, Internat. Union of Pharmacology, 1983–; Med. Res. Soc., 1966–; British Pharmacol Soc., 1972– (Foreign Sec., 1984–); Assoc of Physicians, 1975–. Goulstonian Lectr, RCP, 1975. Chm., Editorial Bd, British Jl of Clinical Pharmacology, 1983–. *Publications:* papers on clinical pharmacology in various jls. *Recreations:* hill-walking, golf, music. *Address:* Cree Cottage, Feather Lane, Heswall, Wirral L60 4RL. *T:* 051–342 1096.

BRECKNOCK, Earl of; James William John Pratt; *b* 11 Dec. 1965; *s* and *heir* of Marquess Camden, *qv. Educ:* Eton.

BRECKNOCK, Marjorie Countess of, DBE 1967; Superintendent-in-Chief, St John Ambulance Brigade, 1960–70, retired, Chief President, 1972–83; *b* 28 Mar. 1900; *o c* of late Col A. E. Jenkins and of late Mrs Anna Jenkins, Wherwell Priory, Andover, Hants; *m* 1920, Earl of Brecknock (later 5th Marquess Camden; from whom she obtained a divorce, 1941); one *s* (*see* Marquess Camden); one *d. Educ:* at home and Heathfield, Ascot. A Lady-in-waiting to Princess Marina, Duchess of Kent, 1937–39. War of 1939–45: Company Asst, ATS, 1940; Junior Commander, 1941; Senior Commander, 1942 (Senior ATS Officer SHAEF, 1944–45); despatches 1945; Bronze Star (USA), 1945. Commanded 310 (Southern Command) Bn WRAC (TA), 1948–54. Joined St John Ambulance Brigade HQ, 1947; appointed Controller Overseas Dept, 1950. GCStJ 1971 (DStJ 1958). Mem. Order of Mercy. *Publication:* Edwina Mountbatten—her life in pictures, 1961. *Recreations:* gardening, shooting, travelling, fishing. *Address:* Wherwell Priory, Andover, Hampshire. *T:* Chilbolton 388.

BREDIN, Maj.-Gen. Humphrey Edgar Nicholson, CB 1969; DSO 1944 (and bars, 1945 and 1957); MC 1938 (and bar, 1939); DL; Appeals Secretary, Cancer Research Campaign, Essex and Suffolk, 1971–83; *b* 28 March 1916; *s* of Lieut-Colonel A. Bredin, late Indian Army, and Ethel Bredin (*née* Homan); *m* 1st, 1947, Jacqueline Geare (marr. diss., 1961); one *d*; 2nd, 1965, Anne Hardie; two *d. Educ:* King's School, Canterbury; RMC, Sandhurst. Commissioned Royal Ulster Rifles, 1936; Commanded: 6th Royal Inniskilling Fusiliers, 1944; 2nd London Irish Rifles, 1945; Eastern Arab Corps, Sudan Defence Force, 1949–53; 2nd Parachute Regt, 1956–57; 99th Gurkha Infty Bde Group, 1959–62. Campaigns: Dunkirk, 1940; N Africa, 1943; Italy, 1943–45; Palestine, 1937–39 and 1946–47; Suez, 1956; Cyprus, 1956–57; Singapore-Malaya Internal Security, 1959–62; Chief of British Commander-in-Chief's Mission to Soviet Forces in Germany, 1963–65; Commanded 42nd Div. (TA), 1965–68. Brig. 1964; Maj.-Gen. 1965; Dir, Volunteers, Territorials and Cadets, 1968–71; retired 1971. Col Comdt, The King's Division, 1968–71; Col of the Regt, Royal Irish Rangers, 1979–85; Hon. Col D (London Irish Rifles) Co., 4th (V) Bn, The Royal Irish Rangers, 1980–86. Chm. Essex Co. Cttee, Army Benevolent Fund, 1983–. DL Essex, 1984. *Recreations:* shooting, fishing, gardening. *Address:* Bovills Hall, Ardleigh, Essex. *T:* Colchester 230217. *Club:* Army and Navy.

BREDIN, James John; Specialist in television archives; *b* 18 Feb. 1924; *s* of late John Francis and Margaret Bredin; *m* 1958, Virginia Meddowes, *d* of John Meddowes and Mrs K. Thomas; one *s* two *d. Educ:* Finchley Catholic Grammar Sch.; London University. Served Fleet Air Arm, RNVR, S/Lieut, 1943–46. Scriptwriter, This Modern Age Film Unit, 1946–50; Producer, current affairs programmes, BBC TV, 1950–55; Sen. Producer, Independent Television News, 1955–59; Smith-Mundt Fellowship, USA, 1957; Producer of Documentaries, Associated Television, 1959–64; Man. Dir, Border TV Ltd, 1964–82. Chm., Guild of Television Producers and Directors, 1961–64. Director: Independent Television News Ltd, 1970–72; Independent Television Publications Ltd, 1965–82. FRTS 1983. *Address:* 25 Stack House, Cundy Street, SW1W 9JS. *T:* 01–730 2689. *Club:* Beefsteak.

BREEN, Geoffrey Brian; Metropolitan Stipendiary Magistrate, since 1986; *b* 3 June 1944; *s* of Ivor James Breen and Doreen Odessa Breen; *m* 1976, Lucy Bolaños; one *s* one *d. Educ:* Harrow High School. Articled to Stiles Wood & Co., Harrow, 1962–67; admitted Solicitor, 1967; Partner, Stiles, Wood, Head & Co, 1970–75; Sen. Partner, Stiles, Breen & Partners, 1976–86; Partner, Blaser Mills & Newman, Bucks and Herts, 1976–86. *Recreations:* classical guitar, reading, swimming, do-it-yourself. *Address:* Highbury Corner Magistrates' Court, 51 Holloway Road, N7 8JA. *T:* 01–607 6757.

BREEN, Dame Marie (Freda), DBE 1979 (OBE 1958); *b* 3 Nov. 1902; *d* of Frederick and Jeanne Chamberlin; *m* 1928, Robert Tweeddale Breen (*d* 1968); three *d. Educ:* St Michael's C of E Girls' Grammar Sch. Senator for Victoria, 1962–68, retired. Hon. Internat. Sec., Nat. Council of Women of Victoria, 1948–52, Pres., 1954–58, now Hon. Member; Vice-Pres., Australian/Asian Assoc. of Victoria, 1956–74; Chm., UNICEF Victorian Cttee, 1969–73; President: Victorian Family Council, 1958–78; Victorian Assoc. of Citizens' Advice Bureaux, 1970–78; Australian Assoc. of Citizens' Advice Bureaux, 1973–75, 1977–79; Victorian Family Planning Assoc., 1970–71; Patron, FPA of Victoria, 1985; Executive Mem. and Vice-Pres., Queen Elizabeth Hosp. for Mothers and Babies, 1943–78; Chm., Victorian Consultative Cttee on Social Develt, 1980–82. Mayoress of Brighton, Vic., 1941–42; JP 1948. *Recreations:* music, reading. *Address:* 51 Carpenter Street, Brighton, Victoria 3186, Australia. *T:* 592 2314. *Club:* Lyceum (Melbourne).

BREEZE, Alastair Jon; HM Diplomatic Service; Counsellor, UK Mission to the United Nations, New York, since 1983; *b* 1 June 1934; *s* of Samuel Wilfred Breeze and Gladys Elizabeth Breeze; *m* 1960, Helen Burns Shaw; two *s* one *d. Educ:* Mill Hill School; Christ's College, Cambridge (Scholar; MA 1959). Foreign Office, 1958; 3rd Sec., Jakarta, 1960–62; FO, 1962–64; 2nd Sec., seconded to Colonial Office for service in Georgetown, 1964–66; 1st Sec., Tehran, 1967–71; FCO, 1971–72; 1st Sec., Islamabad, 1972–75, Lagos, 1976–79; FCO, 1979–83. *Recreations:* sailing, ornithology. *Address:* c/o Foreign and Commonwealth Office, SW1A 2AH.

BREHONY, Dr John Albert Noel; HM Diplomatic Service; Counsellor, Foreign and Commonwealth Office, since 1984; *b* 11 Dec. 1936; *s* of Patrick Paul Brehony and Agnes Maher; *m* 1961, Jennifer Ann (*née* Cox); one *s* one *d. Educ:* London Oratory Sch.; Univ. of Durham (BA, PhD). Tutor, Durham Univ., 1960; Economist Intell. Unit, 1961; Res. Fellow, Jerusalem (Jordan), 1962; Lectr, Univ. of Libya, 1965–66; FO, 1966; Kuwait, 1967–69; Aden, 1970–71; Amman, 1973–77; Cairo, 1981–84. *Recreations:* Middle Eastern history, tennis, golf, opera. *Address:* c/o Foreign and Commonwealth Office, King Charles Street, SW1A 2AH. *Clubs:* Athenæum; Gezira (Cairo).

BREMRIDGE, Sir John (Henry), KBE 1983 (OBE 1976); Financial Secretary, Hong Kong, 1981–86; *b* 12 July 1925; *m* 1956, Jacqueline Everard; two *s* two *d. Educ:* Dragon Sch.; Cheltenham Coll.; St John's Coll., Oxford (MA). Army service: The Rifle Brigade, 1943–47. Joined John Swire & Sons, 1949; retired as Chm., John Swire & Sons (HK) Ltd, Swire Pacific Ltd, and Cathay Pacific Airways Ltd, 1980. Hon. DSocSc Chinese Univ., 1980; Hon. DCL Hong Kong Univ., 1982. *Recreation:* bad golf. *Address:* 40 Redburn Street, SW3. *T:* 01–351 1657. *Clubs:* Oriental; Hong Kong.

BRENAN, (Edward Fitz-) Gerald, CBE 1982; MC 1918; Author; *b* 7 April 1894; English; *m* 1931, Elisabeth Gamel Woolsey (*d* 1968); one *d. Educ:* self-educated. Served War: Croix de Guerre, 1918. *Publications:* The Spanish Labyrinth, 1943; The Face of Spain, 1950; The Literature of the Spanish People, 1953; South from Granada, 1957; A Holiday by the Sea, 1961; A Life of One's Own (autobiog.), 1962; The Lighthouse Always Says Yes, 1966; St John of the Cross: his life and poetry, 1971; Personal Record (autobiog.), 1974; Thoughts in a Dry Season, 1978. *Recreations:* walking and talking. *Address:* c/o Jonathan Cape, 32 Bedford Square, WC1B 3EL.

BRENAN, Gerald; *see* Brenan, Edward Fitz-Gerald.

BRENCHLEY, Thomas Frank, CMG 1964; MA Oxon; HM Diplomatic Service, retired; *b* 9 April 1918; *m* 1946, Edith Helen Helfand (*d* 1980); three *d. Educ:* Open Univ. (BA). Served with Royal Corps of Signals, 1939–46; Major on Staff of Military Attaché, Ankara, 1943–45; Director, Telecommunications Liaison Directorate, Syria and Lebanon, 1945–46. Civil Servant, GCHQ, 1947; transferred to Foreign Office, 1949; First Secretary: Singapore, 1950–53; Cairo, 1953–56; FO, 1956–58; MECAS, 1958–60; Counsellor, Khartoum, 1960–63; Chargé d'Affaires, Jedda, 1963; Head of Arabian Department, Foreign Office, 1963–67; Assistant Under-Secretary of State, Foreign Office, 1967–68; Ambassador to: Norway, 1968–72; Poland, 1972–74; Dep. Sec., Cabinet Office, 1975–76. Dep. Sec. Gen. and Chief Exec., Arab-British Chamber of Commerce, 1976–83; Chairman: Institute for Study of Conflict, 1983–; Centre for Security Studies, 1984–. *Publications:* New Dimensions of European Security (ed), 1975; Norway and her Soviet Neighbour: NATO's Arctic Frontier, 1982; Diplomatic Immunities and State-sponsored Terrorism, 1984; Living With Terrorism: the problem of air piracy, 1986. *Recreations:* collecting (and sometimes reading) books, studying at the Open University. *Address:* 19 Ennismore Gardens, SW7. *Club:* Travellers'.

BRENDEL, Alfred; concert pianist since 1948; *b* 5 Jan. 1931; *s* of Albert Brendel and Ida Brendel (*née* Wieltschnig); *m* 1960, Iris Heymann-Gonzala (marr. diss. 1972); one *d*; *m* 1975, Irene Semler; one *s* two *d.* Studied piano with: S. Deželić, 1937–43; L. V. Kaan, 1943–47; also under Edwin Fischer, P. Baumgartner and E. Steuermann; composition with Artur Michl. Vienna State Diploma, 1947; Premio Bolzano Concorso Busoni, 1949. Hon. RAM; Hon. Mem., Amer. Acad. of Arts and Sciences, 1984; Hon. DMus: London, 1978; Sussex, 1980; Oxford, 1983. Commandeur des Arts et des Lettres, 1985. Concerts: most European countries, North and Latin America, Australia and New Zealand, also N and S Africa and Near and Far East. Many appearances Vienna and Salzburg Festivals, 1960–. Other Festivals: Athens, Granada, Bregenz, Würzburg, Aldeburgh, York, Cheltenham, Edinburgh, Bath, Puerto Rico, Barcelona, Prague, Lucerne, Dubrovnik, etc. Many long playing records (Bach to Schoenberg) incl. first complete recording of Beethoven's piano works (Grand Prix du Disque, 1965). Cycle of Beethoven Sonatas: London, 1962, 1977, 1982–83; Copenhagen, 1964; Vienna, 1965, 1982–83; Puerto Rico, 1968; BBC and Rome, 1970; Munich and Stuttgart, 1977; Amsterdam, Paris and Berlin, 1982–83; New York, 1983. *Television (series):* Schubert Piano Music (13 films), Bremen, 1978; Alfred Brendel Masterclass, BBC, 1983; Liszt Années de Pèlerinage, BBC, 1986. *Publications:* Musical Thoughts and Afterthoughts (Essays), 1976; essays on music, in: HiFi Stereophonie, Music and Musicians, Phono, Fono Forum, Osterreichische Musikzeitschrift, Gramophone, Die Zeit, New York Rev. of Books, etc. *Recreations:* literature, art galleries, architecture, unintentional humour, "kitsch". *Address:* Ingpen & Williams, 14 Kensington Court, W8.

BRENIKOV, Prof. Paul, FRTPI; Professor and Head of Department of Town and Country Planning, University of Newcastle upon Tyne, 1964–86; *b* 13 July 1921; *o s* of Pavel Brenikov and Joyce Mildred Jackson, Liverpool; *m* 1943, Margaret, *e d* of Albert McLevy, Burnley, Lancs; two *s* one *d. Educ:* St Peter's Sch., York; Liverpool Coll.; Univ. of Liverpool (BA (Hons Geog.), MA), DipCD). War service with RNAS, 1941–46. Sen. Planning Officer, Lancs CC, 1950–55; Lectr, Dept of Civic Design, Univ. of Liverpool, 1955–64; Planning Corresp., Architect's Jl, 1957–63; Environmental Planning Consultant: in UK, for former Bootle CB, 1957–64; Govt of Ireland, 1963–67; overseas, for UN: Chile, 1960–61; E Africa, 1964; OECD; Turkey, 1968. Royal Town Planning Institute: Mem. Council, 1967–78; Chm., Northern Br., 1973–74. Member: Subject Cttee of UGC, 1975–86; DoE Local Plans Inspector's Panel, 1985–. *Publications:* contrib. Social Aspects of a Town Development Plan, 1951; contrib. Land Use in an Urban Environment, 1961; (jtly) The Dublin Region: preliminary and final reports, 1965 and 1967; other technical pubns in architectural, geographical, planning and sociological jls. *Recreations:* drawing, painting, listening to music, walking, reading. *Address:* 46 Mitchell Avenue, Jesmond, Newcastle upon Tyne NE2 3LA. *T:* Tyneside 2812773.

BRENNAN, Anthony John Edward, CB 1981; Deputy Secretary, Northern Ireland Office, 1982–87; *b* 24 Jan. 1927; 2nd *s* of late Edward Joseph Brennan and Mabel Brennan (*née* West); *m* 1958, Pauline Margery, *d* of late Percy Clegg Lees; two *s* one *d. Educ:* St Joseph's; London Sch. of Economics (Leverhulme Schol.). BSc Econ 1946. Served Army, RA, RAEC, 1946–49; Asst Principal, Home Office, 1949; Private Sec. to Parly Under-Sec. of State, 1953–54; Principal, 1954; Principal Private Sec. to Home Sec., 1963; Asst Sec., 1963; Asst Under Sec. of State, Criminal Dept, 1971–75, Immigration Dept, 1975–77; Dep. Under-Sec. of State, Home Office, 1977–82. Sec., Royal Commn on Penal System, 1964–66; Mem., UN Cttee on Crime Prevention and Control, 1979–84. *Recreations:* bridge, theatre, athletics. *Club:* Athenæum.

BRENNAN, Archibald Orr, (Archie Brennan), OBE 1981; Director, Edinburgh Tapestry Co., since 1962; Visiting Artist, Papua New Guinea, since 1978; *s* of James and Jessie Brennan; *m* 1956, Elizabeth Hewitt Carmichael; three *d. Educ:* Boroughmuir Sch., Edinburgh; Edinburgh College of Art (DA). Training as tapestry weaver/student, 1947–62; Lectr, Edinburgh College of Art, 1962–78. Pres., Society of Scottish Artists, 1977–78; Chm., British Craft Centre, 1977–78; travelling lectr, UK, USA, Canada, Australia, Papua New Guinea, 1962–78. Fellow, ANU, 1974–75. *Publications:* articles in various jls. *Address:* 8 Bridge Place, Edinburgh EH3 5JJ. *T:* 031–332 2897.

BRENNAN, Brian John, MC 1944; Deputy Chairman of Lloyd's, 1981–83 (Underwriting Member, since 1950); Non-Executive Director, Sedgwick Group Ltd, since 1981; *b* 17 May 1918; *s* of Alfred Eric Brennan and Jean (*née* Wallace); *m* 1950, Mary Patricia Newbould; one *s* two *d. Educ:* Dulwich College. Joined E. W. Payne, Lloyd's Brokers, 1936. Member, HAC, 1938; commnd Cameronians (Scottish Rifles), 1939; India, 1/Cameronians, 1940–45; Burma, 1942; Burma, 1944; commanded 26 Column 1/Cameronians 111 Bde Special Force; Lt-Col 1/Cameronians, 1944–45. Director, E. W. Payne, 1947, Chm., 1966–74; Director, Montagu Trust, 1967–74; Dep. Chm., Bland Payne Holdings, 1974–78; Chm., Bland Payne Reinsurance Brokers, 1974–78; Dir, Sedgwick Forbes Bland Payne Holdings, 1979; Chm., Sedgwick Payne, 1979; Dir, Sedgwick Gp Ltd, 1980. Mem., Cttee of Lloyd's, 1975–80, 1981–84. *Recreations:* Rugby (played for Old Alleynians, Kent, London, Barbarians); sailing, tennis, gardening. *Address:* Weybank House, Meadrow, Godalming, Surrey GU7 3BZ. *Clubs:* MCC, City of London, Royal London Yacht, Lloyd's Yacht, British Sportsman's.

BRENNAN, Daniel Joseph; QC 1985; a Recorder of the Crown Court, since 1982; *b* 19 March 1942; *s* of late Daniel Brennan and Mary Brennan; *m* 1968, Pilar, *d* of late Luis Sanchez Hernandez; four *s. Educ:* St Bede's Grammar Sch., Bradford; Victoria University of Manchester (LLB Hons). President, University Union, 1964–65. Called to the Bar, Gray's Inn, 1967. *Address:* Brook House, Brook Lane, Alderley Edge SK9 7RU. *T:* Alderley Edge 585552; (chambers) 18 St John Street, Manchester. *T:* 061–834 9843.

BRENNAN, Edward A.; Chairman and Chief Executive Officer, Sears, Roebuck & Co., since 1986; *b* 16 Jan. 1934; *s* of Edward Brennan and Margaret (*née* Bourget); *m* 1955, Lois Lyon; three *s* three *d. Educ:* Marquette Univ., Wisconsin (BA). Joined Sears as salesman in Madison, Wisconsin, 1956; asst store manager, asst buyer, store manager, other positions in diff. locations, to 1969; Asst Manager, NY group, 1969–72; Gen. Manager, Sears Western NY group, 1972–75; Admin. Asst to Vice-Pres., Sears Eastern Territory, 1975; Gen. Manager, Boston group, 1976; Exec. Vice Pres., Southern Territory, 1978; Pres., Sears, Roebuck, 1980; Chm. and Chief Exec., Sears Merchandise Group, 1981; Pres. and chief operating officer, Sears, Roebuck & Co., 1984; dir of other cos. Member: President's Export Council; Business Round-table and business adv. council, Chicago Urban League; Board of Governors, United Way of America; Boards of Trustees of Univs. of Atlanta, DePaul, Marquette, and Chicago Museum of Science and Industry. *Address:* Sears, Roebuck and Co., Sears Tower, Chicago, Ill 60684, USA. *T:* (312) 875–1902.

BRENNAN, Hon. Sir (Francis) Gerard, KBE 1981; **Hon. Mr Justice Brennan;** Justice of the High Court of Australia, since 1981; *b* 22 May 1928; *s* of Hon. Mr Justice (Frank Tenison) Brennan and Mrs Gertrude Brennan; *m* 1953, Patricia (*née* O'Hara); three *s* four *d. Educ:* Christian Brothers Coll., Rockhampton, Qld; Downlands Coll., Toowoomba, Qld; Univ. of Qld (BA, LLB). Called to the Queensland Bar, 1951; QC (Australia) 1965. Judge, Aust. Indust. Court, and Additional Judge of Supreme Court of ACT, 1976–81; Judge, Fed. Court of Australia, 1977–81. President: Admin. Appeals Tribunal, 1976–79; Admin. Review Council, 1976–79; Bar Assoc. of Qld, 1974–76; Aust. Bar Assoc., 1975–76; National Union of Aust. Univ. Students, 1949. Member: Exec. Law Council of Australia, 1974–76; Aust. Law Reform Commn, 1975–77. *Recreation:* gardening. *Address:* 10 Kurundi Place, Hawker, ACT 2614, Australia. *T:* (062) 546794. *Club:* Commonwealth (Canberra).

BRENNAN, Lt-Gen. Michael; retired as Chief Superintendent of Divisions, Office of Public Works, Dublin. Chief of Staff, Irish Army, 1931–40. *Address:* South Hill, Killiney, Co. Dublin.

BRENNAN, William Joseph, Jr; Legion of Merit, 1945; Associate Justice, Supreme Court of the US, since 1956; *b* 25 April 1906; *s* of William J. Brennan and Agnes McDermott; *m* 1st, 1928, Marjorie Leonard (*d* 1982); two *s* one *d;* 2nd, 1983, Mary Fowler. *Educ:* University of Pennsylvania; Harvard. BS Univ. of Pennsylvania, 1928; LLB Harvard, 1931. Admitted to New Jersey Bar, 1931; practised in Newark, New Jersey, 1931–49, Member Pitney, Hardin, Ward & Brennan; Superior Court Judge, 1949–50; Appellate Division Judge, 1950–52; Supreme Court of New Jersey Justice, 1952–56; served War of 1939–45 as Colonel, General Staff Corps, United States Army. Hon. LLD: Pennsylvania, 1957; Wesleyan, 1957; St John's, 1957; Rutgers, 1958; Notre Dame, 1968; Harvard, 1968; Hon. DCL: New York Univ., 1957; Colgate, 1957; Hon. SJD Suffolk Univ., 1956. Hon. Bencher, Lincoln's Inn, 1985.

BRENNER, Sydney, DPhil, FRCP, FRS 1965; Director, Laboratory of Molecular Biology, Cambridge, since 1979 (Member of Scientific Staff, since 1957); Fellow of King's College, Cambridge, since 1959; *b* Germiston, South Africa, 13 Jan. 1927; *s* of Morris Brenner and Lena (*née* Blacher); *m* 1952, May Woolf Balkind; one *s* two *d* (and one step *s*). *Educ:* Germiston High School; University of the Witwatersrand, S Africa; Oxford University (Hon. Fellow, Exeter Coll., 1985). MSc 1947, MB, BCh 1951, Univ. of the Witwatersrand; DPhil Oxon, 1954; FRCP 1979. Mem., MRC, 1978–82, 1986–. Carter-Wallace Lectr, Princeton, 1966, 1971; Gifford Lectr, Glasgow, 1978–79; Dunham Lectr, Harvard, 1984; Croonian Lectr, Royal Soc., 1986. Foreign Hon. Member, American Academy of Arts and Sciences, 1965; Foreign Associate, Nat. Acad. of Sciences, USA, 1977; Mem., Deutsche Akademie der Naturforscher, Leopoldina, 1976 (Gregor Mendel Medal, 1970); For. Mem., Amer. Philosophical Soc., 1979. Hon. FRSE, 1979; Foreign Associate, Royal Soc. of S Africa, 1983. Hon. DSc: Dublin, 1967; Witwatersrand, 1972; Chicago, 1976; London, 1982; Leicester, 1983; Oxford, 1985; Hon. LLD Glasgow, 1981. Warren Triennial Prize, 1968; William Bate Hardy Prize, Cambridge Philosophical Soc., 1969; (jtly) Lasker Award for Basic Medical Research, 1971; Royal Medal, Royal Soc., 1974; (jtly) Prix Charles Leopold Mayer, French Acad. of Science, 1975; Gairdner Foundn Annual Award, 1978; Krebs Medal, FEBS, 1980; CIBA Medal, Biochem. Soc., 1981; Feldberg Foundn Prize, 1983; Rosenstill Award, Brandeis Univ., 1986. *Publications:* papers in scientific journals. *Recreation:* rumination. *Address:* MRC Laboratory of Molecular Biology, Hills Road, Cambridge CB2 2QH. *T:* Cambridge 248011.

BRENT, Prof. Leslie, FIBiol; Professor of Immunology, St Mary's Hospital Medical School, London, since 1969; *b* 5 July 1925; *s* of Charlotte and Arthur Baruch; *m* 1954, Joanne Elisabeth Manley; one *s* two *d. Educ:* Bunce Court Sch., Kent; Birmingham Central Technical Coll.; Univ. of Birmingham; UCL. BSc Birmingham, PhD London; FIBiol 1964. Laboratory technician, 1941–43; Army service, 1943–47; Lectr, Dept of Zoology, UCL, 1954–62; Rockefeller Res. Fellow, Calif Inst. of Technology, 1956–57; Res. scientist, Nat. Inst. for Med. Res., 1962–65; Prof. of Zoology, Univ. of Southampton, 1965–69. European Editor, Transplantation, 1963–68; Gen. Sec., British Transplantation Soc., 1971–75, Pres., The Transplantation Society, 1976–78; Chairman: Organising Cttee, 9th Internat. Congress of The Transplantation Soc., 1978–82; Fellowships Ctte, Inst. of Biol., 1982–85. Pres., Guild of Undergrads, Birmingham Univ., 1950–51. Chairman: Haringey Community Relations Council, 1979–80; Haringey SDP, 1981–83. Vice-Chancellor's Prize, Birmingham Univ., 1951; Scientific Medal, Zool Soc., 1963. Played hockey for UAU and Staffs, 1949–51. Co-editor, Immunology Letters, 1983–. *Publications:* articles in scientific and med. jls on transplantation immunology. *Recreations:* music, fell-walking, chess, squash, cricket. *Address:* 8 Wood Vale, N10.

BRENT, Michael Leon; QC 1983; *b* 8 June 1936; *m* 1965, Rosalind Keller; two *d. Educ:* Manchester Grammar Sch.; Manchester Univ. (LLB Hons). Called to the Bar, Gray's Inn, 1961; practised on: Northern Circuit, 1961–67 (Circuit Junior, 1964); Midland and Oxford Circuit, 1967–. *Address:* 2 Dr Johnson's Buildings, Temple, EC4Y 7AY. *T:* 01–353 5371.

BRENTFORD, 4th Viscount *cr* 1929, of Newick; **Crispin William Joynson-Hicks;** Bt of Holmbury, 1919; Bt of Newick, 1956; Partner, Joynson-Hicks, since 1961; *b* 7 April 1933; *s* of 3rd Viscount Brentford and Phyllis (*d* 1979), *o d* of late Major Herbert Allfrey, Tetbury, Glos; *S* father, 1983; *m* 1964, Gillian Evelyn, *er d* of Gerald Edward Schluter, OBE; one *s* three *d. Educ:* Eton; New College, Oxford. Admitted solicitor, 1960. Master, Girdlers' Co., 1983–84. *Heir: s* Hon. Paul William Joynson-Hicks, *b* 18 April 1971. *Address:* Newick Park, East Sussex BN8 4SB. *T:* Newick 2215.

BRENTON, Howard; playwright; *b* 13 Dec. 1942; *s* of Donald Henry Brenton and Rose Lilian (*née* Lewis); *m* 1970, Jane Fry; two *s. Educ:* Chichester High Sch. for Boys; St Catharine's Coll., Cambridge (BA Hons English). *Full-length stage plays:* Revenge, 1969; Hitler Dances, and Measure for Measure (after Shakespeare), 1972; Magnificence, 1973; The Churchill Play, 1974; Government Property, 1975; Weapons of Happiness, 1976 (Evening Standard Award); Epsom Downs, 1977; Sore Throats, 1979; The Romans in Britain, 1980; Thirteenth Night, 1981; The Genius, 1983; Bloody Poetry, 1984; *one-act stage plays:* Gum and Goo, Heads, The Education of Skinny Spew, and Christie in Love, 1969; Wesley, 1970; Scott of the Antartic, and A Sky-blue Life, 1971; How Beautiful with Badges, 1972; Mug, 1973; The Thing (for children), 1982; *collaborations:* (with six others) Lay-By, 1970; (with six others) England's Ireland, 1971; (with David Hare) Brassneck, 1973; (with Trevor Griffiths, David Hare and Ken Campbell), Deeds, 1978; (with Tony Howard) A Short Sharp Shock, 1980; (with Tunde Ikoli) Sleeping Policemen, 1983; (with David Hare) Pravda, 1985 (London Standard Award); *television plays:* Lushly, 1971; Brassneck (adaptation of stage play), 1974; The Saliva Milkshake, 1975 (also perf. theatre); The Paradise Run, 1976; Desert of Lies, 1984; *television series:* Dead Head, 1986; *translations:* Bertolt Brecht, The Life of Galileo, 1980; Georg Buchner, Danton's Death, 1982; Bertolt Brecht, Conversations in Exile, 1982. *Publications:* many plays published. *Recreation:* painting. *Address:* c/o Margaret Ramsay Ltd, 14A Goodwin's Court, St Martin's Lane, WC2N 4LL. *T:* 01–240 0691.

BRENTWOOD, Bishop of, (RC), since 1980; **Rt. Rev. Thomas McMahon;** *b* 17 June 1936. *Address:* Bishop's House, Stock, Ingatestone, Essex CM4 9BU. *T:* Stock 840268.

BRESSON, Robert; film producer since 1934; *b* 25 Sept. 1907; *s* of Léon Bresson and Marie-Elisabeth Clausels; *m* 1926, Leidia Van der Zee. *Educ:* Lycée Lakanal, Sceaux. Started as painter; then producer of short films, Affaires Publiques. Full-length films produced include: Les Anges du Péché, 1943; Les Dames du Bois de Boulogne, 1948; Journal d'un Curé de Campagne, 1951 (Internat. Grand Prix, Venice); Un Condamné à Mort s'est Echappé, 1956; Pickpocket, 1960; Le Procès de Jeanne d'Arc, 1962 (Jury's special prize, Cannes); Au Hasard Balthazar, 1966; Mouchette, 1967; Une Femme Douce, 1969; Quatre nuits d'un rêveur, 1971; Lancelot du Lac, 1974; Le diable, probablement, 1977; L'Argent, 1983. *Publication:* Notes sur le cinématographe, 1976. *Address:* 49 quai de Bourbon, 75004 Paris, France.

BRETHERTON, Russell Frederick, CB 1951; Under-Secretary, the Treasury, 1961–68; *b* 3 Feb. 1906; *s* of F. H. Bretherton, Solicitor, Gloucester; *m* 1930, Jocelyn Nina Mathews; three *s* one *d. Educ:* Clifton College; Wadham College, Oxford. Fellow of Wadham College, 1928–45, Lecturer and Tutor in Economics and Modern History; University Research Lecturer, 1936–39. Temporary Civil Servant, Ministry of Supply and Board of Trade, 1939–45; Under-Secretary, Raw Materials Dept, Board of Trade, 1946–48; Cabinet Office (Economic Section), 1949–51; Under-Secretary: Min. of Materials, 1951–54; Board of Trade, 1954–61; Treasury, 1961–68. *Publications:* (with R. V. Lennard and others) Englishmen at Rest and Play (17th Century Studies), 1932; (with Burchardt and Rutherford) Public Investment and the Trade Cycle, 1941; (contrib.) Moths and Butterflies of Great Britain and Ireland, vol. 9 1979, vol. 10 1983, vol. 7 1986; articles in Social Survey of Oxford, Economic Journal, Econometrica, and in various entomological journals, etc. *Recreations:* walking, mountaineering, entomology. *Address:* Folly Hill, Birtley Green, Bramley, Guildford, Surrey GU5 0LE. *T:* Guildford 893377.

BRETSCHER, Mark Steven, PhD; FRS 1985; Joint Head, Division of Cell Biology, Medical Research Council Laboratory of Molecular Biology, Cambridge, since 1984; *b* 8 Jan. 1940; *s* of late Egon Bretscher, CBE and of Hanni (*née* Greminger); *m* 1978, Barbara Mary Frances Pearse; one *s* one *d. Educ:* Abingdon Sch., Berks; Gonville and Caius Coll., Cambridge (MA, PhD). Res. Fellow, Gonville and Caius Coll., Cambridge, 1964–70; Mem., Scientific Staff, MRC Lab. of Molecular Biology, Cambridge, 1965–. Vis. Professor: Harvard Univ., 1975; Stanford Univ., 1984. Friedrich Miescher Prize, Swiss Biochemical Soc., 1979. *Publications:* papers in scientific jls on protein biosynthesis, membrane structure and cell locomotion. *Recreation:* gardening. *Address:* Ram Cottage, Commercial End, Swaffham Bulbeck, Cambridge CB5 0ND. *T:* Cambridge 811276.

BRETT, family name of **Viscount Esher.**

BRETT, Charles Edward Bainbridge, CBE 1981; Partner, L'Estrange & Brett, Solicitors, Belfast, since 1954; *b* 30 Oct. 1928; *s* of Charles Anthony Brett and Elizabeth Joyce (*née* Carter); *m* 1953, Joyce Patricia Worley; three *s. Educ:* Rugby Sch.; New Coll., Oxford (Schol.; MA History). Solicitor, 1953. Journalist, Radiodiffusion Française and Continental Daily Mail, 1949–50. Member: Child Welfare Council of Northern Ireland, 1958–61; Northern Ireland Cttee, National Trust, 1956–83 and 1985– (Mem. Council, 1975–); Arts Council of N Ireland, 1970–76; Chairman: N Ireland Labour Party, 1962; Ulster Architectural Heritage Soc., 1968–78 (Pres., 1979–); HEARTH Housing Assoc., 1978 and 1985–; NI Housing Exec., 1979–84 (Mem. Bd, 1971–77, Vice-Chm., 1977–78); Mem. Bd, Irish Architectural Archive, Dublin, 1985–. Hon. Mem., Royal Society of Ulster Architects, 1973. *Publications:* Buildings of Belfast 1700–1914, 1967, rev. edn 1985; Court Houses and Market Houses of Ulster, 1973; Long Shadows Cast Before, 1978; Housing a Divided Community, 1986; lists and surveys for Ulster Architectural Heritage Soc., National Trusts of Guernsey and Jersey, and Alderney Soc. *Address:* 9 Chichester Street, Belfast. *Club:* United Oxford & Cambridge University.

BRETT, Jeremy, (Peter Jeremy William Huggins); actor; *b* 3 Nov. 1935; *s* of Lt-Col H. W. Huggins, DSO, MC, DL, and late Elizabeth Huggins; *m* 1958 (marr. diss.); one *s*; *m* 1978; one *s. Educ:* Eton; Central Sch. of Drama. National Theatre, 1967–71: Orlando, in As You Like It; Berowne, in Love's Labour's Lost; Tesman, in Hedda Gabler; Bassanio, in The Merchant of Venice; Che Guevara, in Macrune's Guevara; The Son, in Voyage round my Father, Haymarket, 1972; Otto, in Design for Living, Phoenix, 1973–74; The Way of the World, Stratford, Ont, 1976; Prospero, in The Tempest, Toronto, 1982; narrator, Martha Graham ballet, Song, New York, 1985; Willie, in Aren't We All, Broadway, 1985. Films include: Nicholas, in War and Peace, 1955; Freddie, in My Fair Lady, 1965; also TV appearances, including: Max de Winter in Rebecca, 1978; George, Duke of Bristol, in On Approval, 1980; Edward Ashburnham in The Good Soldier, 1981; title rôle in Macbeth The Last Visitor, 1982; Robert Browning in The Barretts of Wimpole Street, 1982; title rôle in William Pitt the Younger, 1983; title rôle in The Adventures of Sherlock Holmes, 1984; The Return of Sherlock Holmes, 1986; Mr Nightingale, in Florence Nightingale; Brian Foxworth, in Deceptions, 1986. *Recreation:* archery. *Address:* 9538 Brighton Way, Suite 322, Beverly Hills, Calif 90210, USA. *Club:* Woodmen of Arden (Meriden).

BRETT, John Alfred, MA; Headmaster, Durham School, Durham, 1958–67; retired; *b* 26 Oct. 1915; *s* of Alfred Brett, Harrogate, Yorks; *m* 1939, Margaret Coode; one *s* three *d. Educ:* Durham School; St Edmund Hall, Oxford. MA (Hons Modern History). Temp. teacher, Stowe School, 1938; Teacher, Diocesan College, Rondebosch, South Africa, 1939; restarted Silver Tree Youth Club for non-Europeans, Cape Town. Army: Gunner to Major, RA, 1940–44; Instructor 123 OCTU Catterick; invasion of Normandy, 1944 (lost right eye); Military testing officer, WOSBs, finally Senior Military Testing Officer, War Office Selection Centre. Returned to post at Diocesan College, Rondebosch, 1946; Housemaster, 1948; Temp. teacher, Canford School, Wimborne, Dorset, 1954; Headmaster, Shaftesbury Grammar School, 1954. Diocesan Lay Reader. Member Council:

Brathay Hall Centre; McAlpine Educnl Endowments Ltd. Governor, Bernard Gilpin Society. *Recreations:* sport (Captain Oxford University Rugby Football Club, 1937, and Member British Touring XV to Argentina, 1936); travel; reading. *Address:* The Old School House, Comer Road, Worcester WR2 5HU.

BRETT, Lionel; *see* Esher, 4th Viscount.

BRETT, Sir Lionel, Kt 1961; *b* 19 Aug. 1911; 3rd *s* of late Very Rev. H. R. Brett, Dean of Belfast, and Constance Brett (*née* White). *Educ:* Marlborough; Magdalen College, Oxford. BA 1934; MA 1946. Called to Bar, Inner Temple, 1937. War service, 1939–46, released as Major. Joined Colonial Legal Service as Crown Counsel, Nigeria, 1946; Justice, Supreme Court of Nigeria, 1958–68. *Recreations:* reading, walking. *Address:* The Cottage, Puckington, near Ilminster, Somerset. *Club:* United Oxford & Cambridge University.

BRETT, Michael John Lee; Editor, Investors Chronicle, 1977–82; *b* 23 May 1939; *s* of John Brett and Margaret Brett (*née* Lee). *Educ:* King's Coll. Sch., Wimbledon; Wadham Coll., Oxford (BA Modern Langs). Investors Review, 1962–64; Fire Protection Assoc., 1964–68; Investors Chronicle, 1968–82, Dep. Editor, 1973–77. Past Director: Throgmorton Publications; Financial Times Business Publishing Divn. *Recreations:* travelling, reading. *Address:* 134 Offord Road, N1. *T:* 01–609 2362.

BRETT, Prof. Raymond Laurence; G. F. Grant Professor of English, University of Hull, 1952–82; *b* 10 January 1917; *s* of late Leonard and Ellen Brett; *m* 1947, Kathleen Tegwen, *d* of late Rev. C. D. Cranmer; two *s*. *Educ:* Bristol Cathedral School; University of Bristol; University College, Oxford (Plumptre Exhibitioner). 1st Class Hons BA, English and Philosophy, Bristol, 1937; Taylor Prizeman, Hannam-Clark Prizeman, Haldane of Cloan Post-Grad. Studentship; BLitt, Oxf., 1940. Service in Admiralty, 1940–46; on Staff of First Lord; Lectr in English, Univ. of Bristol, 1946–52; Dean, Faculty of Arts, Hull Univ., 1960–62. Visiting Professor: Univ. of Rochester, USA, 1958–59; Kiel Univ., Osnabrück Univ., 1977; Baroda Univ., Jadavpur Univ., 1978; Univ. of Ottawa, 1981. Hon. DLitt Hull, 1983. *Publications:* The Third Earl of Shaftesbury: A Study in 18th Century Literary Theory, 1951; Coleridge's Theory of Imagination (English Essays), 1949; George Crabbe, 1956; Reason and Imagination, 1961; (with A. R. Jones) a critical edition of Lyrical Ballads by Wordsworth and Coleridge, 1963; Thomas Hobbes (The English Mind), 1964; (ed) Poems of Faith and Doubt, 1965; An Introduction to English Studies, 1965; Fancy and Imagination, 1969; (ed) S. T. Coleridge, 1971, 2nd edn 1978; William Hazlitt, 1978; (ed) Barclay Fox's Journal, 1979; (ed) Andrew Marvell, 1979; articles in: The Times, Time and Tide, Essays and Studies, Review of English Studies, Modern Language Review, Philosophy, English, South Atlantic Qly, Critical Qly, etc. *Address:* 19 Mill Walk, Cottingham, North Humberside HU16 4RP. *T:* Hull 847115.

BRETTEN, George Rex, QC 1980; barrister-at-law; *b* 21 Feb. 1942; *s* of Horace Victor Bretten and Kathleen Edna Betty Bretten; *m* 1965, Maureen Gillian Crowhurst; one *d*. *Educ:* King Edward VII Sch., King's Lynn; Sidney Sussex Coll., Cambridge (MA, LLB). Lectr, Nottingham Univ., 1964–68; Asst Director, Inst. of Law Research and Reform, Alberta, Canada, 1968–70; called to the Bar, Lincoln's Inn; in practice, 1971–. *Publication:* Special Reasons, 1977. *Recreations:* hobby farming, tennis, riding. *Address:* Church Farm, Great Eversden, Cambridgeshire CB3 7HN. *T:* Comberton 3538.

BREW, Richard Maddock, CBE 1982; Chairman, Budget Boilers Ltd, since 1984; *b* 13 Dec. 1930; *s* of late Leslie Maddock Brew and Phyllis Evelyn Huntsman; *m* 1953, Judith Anne Thompson Hancock; two *s* two *d*. *Educ:* Rugby Sch.; Magdalene Coll., Cambridge (BA). Called to the Bar, Inner Temple, 1955. After practising for short time at the Bar, joined family business, Brew Brothers Ltd, SW7, 1955, and remained until takeover, 1972. Chairman: Monks Dormitory Ltd, 1979–; Vice-Chm., NE Thames RHA, 1982–. Farms in Essex. Member: Royal Borough of Kensington Council, 1959–65; Royal Borough of Kensington and Chelsea Council, 1964–70; Greater London Council: Mem., 1968–86; Alderman, 1968–73; Vice-Chm., Strategic Planning Cttee, 1969–71; Chm., Covent Garden Jt Development Cttee, 1970–71 and Environmental Planning Cttee, 1971–73; Mem. for Chingford, 1973–86; Dep. Leader of Council and Leader, Policy and Resources Cttee, 1977–81; Dep. Leader, Cons. Party and Opposition Spokesman on Finance, 1981–82; Leader of the Opposition, 1982–83. Mem., Nat. Theatre Bd, 1982–86. *Recreations:* Pony Club, hunting, tennis. *Address:* The Abbey, Coggeshall, Essex. *T:* Coggeshall 61246. *Clubs:* Carlton, Farmers'.

BREWER, Prof. Derek Stanley, LittD; FSA; Master of Emmanuel College, Cambridge, since 1977; Professor of English, University of Cambridge, since 1983; *b* 13 July 1923; *s* of Stanley Leonard Brewer and Winifred Helen Forbes; *m* 1951, Lucie Elisabeth Hoole; three *s* two *d*. *Educ:* elementary school; The Crypt Grammar Sch.; Magdalen Coll., Oxford (Matthew Arnold Essay Prize, 1948; BA, MA 1948); Birmingham Univ. (PhD 1956). LittD Cantab 1980. Commnd 2nd Lieut, Worcestershire Regt, 1942; Captain and Adjt, 1st Bn Royal Fusiliers, 1944–45. Asst Lectr and Lectr in English, Univ. of Birmingham, 1949–56; Prof. of English, Internat. Christian Univ., Tokyo, 1956–58; Lectr and Sen. Lectr, Univ. of Birmingham, 1958–64; Lectr in English, Univ. of Cambridge, 1965–76, Reader in Medieval English, 1976–83; Fellow of Emmanuel Coll., Cambridge, 1965–77 (Seatonian Prize, 1969, 1972 and 1983, and jtly, 1979 and 1980). Founder, D. S. Brewer Ltd, for the publication of academic books, 1972; now part of Boydell and Brewer Ltd (Dir, 1979–). Mem., Council of the Senate, Cambridge, 1978–83; Chairman: Fitzwilliam Museum Enterprises Ltd, 1978–; Univ. Library Synd., 1980–; English Faculty Bd, Cambridge, 1984–86. Sir Israel Gollancz Meml Lectr, British Academy, 1974; first William Matthews Lectr, Univ. of London, 1982; first Geoffrey Shepherd Meml Lectr, Univ. of Birmingham, 1983. President: The English Assoc., 1982–83; Internat. Chaucer Soc., 1982–84. FSA 1977. Hon. Mem., Japan Acad., 1981. Hon. LLD: Keio Univ., Tokyo, 1982; Harvard Univ., 1984; Hon. DLitt Birmingham, 1985; DUniv York, 1985. Editor, The Cambridge Review, 1981–86. *Publications:* Chaucer, 1953, 3rd edn 1973; Proteus, 1958 (Tokyo); (ed) The Parlement of Foulys, 1960; Chaucer in his Time, 1963; (ed and contrib.) Chaucer and Chaucerians, 1966; (ed) Malory's Morte Darthur: Parts Seven and Eight, 1968; (ed and contrib.) Writers and their Backgrounds: Chaucer, 1974; (ed) Chaucer: the Critical Heritage, 1978; Chaucer and his World, 1978; Symbolic Stories, 1980; (ed jtly) Aspects of Malory, 1981; English Gothic Literature, 1983; Tradition and Innovation in Chaucer, 1983; Chaucer: the Poet as Storyteller, 1984; Chaucer: an introduction, 1984; (ed) Beardsley's Le Morte Darthur, 1985; (with E. Frankl) Arthur's Britain: the land and the legend, 1985; numerous articles in learned jls, reviews, etc. *Recreations:* reading, book-collecting, walking, opera, looking at paintings and antiquities, travelling, publishing other people's books. *Address:* The Master's Lodge, Emmanuel College, Cambridge CB2 3AP. *T:* Cambridge 350484. *Clubs:* Athenæum, United Oxford & Cambridge University.

BREWER, Frank, CMG 1960; OBE 1953; Foreign and Commonwealth Office (formerly Foreign Office), 1960–76; *b* 1915; *s* of late Lewis Arthur Brewer; *m* 1950, Eileen Marian, *d* of A. J. Shepherd. *Educ:* Swindon Commonweal School; Pembroke College, Oxford (MA). Malayan Civil Service, 1937–59; War Service, 1941–45, Special Forces (POW Sumatra) Chinese Secretariat, Labour Dept; Secretary for Chinese Affairs and Dep. Chief Sec., Fed. of Malaya, 1955–57; Sec. for Defence, 1957–59. *Address:* 18 Forest Way, Tunbridge Wells, Kent. *T:* Tunbridge Wells 24850. *Clubs:* Royal Commonwealth Society, Special Forces.

BREWER, Rear-Adm. George Maxted Kenneth, CB 1982; Flag Officer Medway and Port Admiral Chatham, 1980–82; *b* Dover, 4 March 1930; *s* of Captain George Maxted Brewer and Cecilia Victoria (*née* Clark). *Educ:* Pangbourne College. In Command: HMS Carysfort, Far East and Mediterranean, 1964–65; HMS Agincourt, Home, 1967; HMS Grenville, Far East and Mediterranean, 1968–69; HMS Juno, and Captain Fourth Frigate Sqdn, Home and Mediterranean, 1974; rcds 1975; In Command: HMS Tiger, and Flag Captain to Flag Officer Second Flotilla, Far East, 1978; HMS Bulwark, NATO area, 1979–80. *Recreation:* watercolour painting. *Address:* c/o National Westminster Bank, 2 West Street, Portchester, Fareham, Hants. *Clubs:* Royal Navy Club of 1765 and 1785, Royal United Services Institute for Defence Studies.

BREWER, Rt. Rev. John; *see* Lancaster, Bishop of, (RC).

BREWIS, Henry John; Lord-Lieutenant of Wigtown, since 1981; Director, Border Television Ltd, since 1977; Managing Director, Ardwell Estates, Stranraer; farming; *b* 8 April 1920; *s* of Lt-Col F. B. Brewis, Norton Grove, Malton, Yorks; *m* 1949, Faith A. D. MacTaggart Stewart, Ardwell, Wigtownshire; three *s* one *d*. *Educ:* Eton; New College, Oxford. Served Royal Artillery, 1940–46 (despatches twice); on active service, North Africa and Italy; demobilized with rank of Major. Barrister-at-law, 1946. Wigtownshire County Council, 1955; Convener, Finance Cttee, 1958. MP (C) Galloway, April 1959–Sept. 1974; PPS to The Lord Advocate, 1960–61; Speaker's Panel of Chairmen, 1965; Chm., Select Cttee on Scottish Affairs, 1970; Member British Delegn: to Council of Europe, 1966–69; to European Parlt, Strasbourg, 1973–75; Vice-Chm., Cons. Agric. Cttee, 1971; Chm., Scottish Cons. Gp for Europe, 1973–76. Dist Chm., Queen's Jubilee Appeal, 1976–78. Reg. Chm., Scottish Landowners' Fedn, 1977–80; Chm., Timber Growers Scotland Ltd, 1980–83; Vice-Chm., Forestry Cttee for GB; Mem., Comité Central Propriété Forestière, Brussels, 1979, and other forestry cttees. *Recreations:* golf, tennis, shooting. *Address:* Ardwell House, Stranraer. *T:* Ardwell 227; Norton Grove, Malton, N Yorks. *Clubs:* Caledonian; New (Edinburgh).

BREWSTER, George, CVO 1969; MD; practitioner of medicine, retired 1977; formerly Surgeon Apothecary to HM Household at Holyrood Palace, Edinburgh, resigned 1970; formerly Medical Officer to French Consulate-General in Scotland; *b* 27 Sept. 1899; *m* 1930; two *s*. *Educ:* High School, Stirling; Edinburgh Univ. MB, ChB, Edin., 1921; DPH Edin., 1924; MD (with distinction) Edin., 1926. House Surgeon, Edin. Royal Infirmary. Chevalier de la Légion d'Honneur (France), 1957. *Address:* 17 The Limes, Napier Road, Edinburgh EH10 5DL. *T:* 031–447 6183.

BREWSTER, Kingman; Lawyer; Master of University College, Oxford, since 1986; Counsel in London to Winthrop, Stimson, Putnam and Roberts, NYC, since 1981; *b* Longmeadow, Massachusetts, 17 June 1919; *s* of Kingman Brewster and Florence Besse; *m* 1942, Mary Louise Phillips; three *s* two *d*. *Educ:* Yale University; Harvard University. AB Yale, 1941; LLB Harvard, 1948. Military Service: Lieut (Aviation) USNR, 1942–46. Special Asst Coordinator Inter-American Affairs, 1941; Research Assoc., Dept Economics, Massachusetts Inst. of Technology, 1949–50; Asst. General Counsel, Office US Special Representative in Europe, 1948–49; Cons., Pres. Materials Policy Commn, 1951, Mutual Security Agency, 1952; Asst Prof. of Law, Harvard, 1950–58; Prof. of Law, Harvard, 1953–60; Provost, Yale, 1961–63; Pres., Yale Univ., 1963–77; Ambassador to Court of St James's, 1977–81. Member: President's Commn on Law Enforcement and Administration of Justice, 1965–67; President's Commn on Selective Service, 1966–68; Fulbright Commn, 1986–; Bd of Dirs, Carnegie Endowment Fund for Internat. Peace, 1975–; Internat. Bd, United World Colleges (Chm., 1986–); American Trust, British Library; Council of Management, Amer. Ditchley Foundn. Trustee, Reuters, 1984–. Member: Council on Foreign Relations; American Philosophical Soc. Lectures: Stevens, Royal Coll. of Med., 1977; St George's House, 1977; Tanner, Clare Hall, 1984; MacDermott, QUB, 1986; Goodman, 1986. Holds many Hon. Degrees; Hon. Fellow, Clare Coll., Cambridge, 1977. Officer, Legion of Honour, 1977. *Publications:* Antitrust and American Business Abroad, 1959, rev. edn (with J. Atwood), 1981; (with M. Katz) Law of International Transactions and Relations, 1960. *Recreation:* sailing. *Address:* Master's Lodgings, University College, Oxford OX1 4BH; (office) 1–4 College Hill, EC4 2RA. *Clubs:* Athenæum, Buck's; Metropolitan (Washington); Yale, Century Association (New York); Tavern (Boston, Mass).

BRIANCE, John Albert, CMG 1960; HM Diplomatic Service, retired; *b* 19 Oct. 1915; *s* of late Albert Perceval and Louise Florence Briance; *m* 1950, Prunella Mary, *d* of Col. E. Haldane Chapman; one *s* one *d*. *Educ:* King Edward VII School. Colonial Police, Palestine, 1936–48; Foreign Office, 1949; British Embassy, Tehran, 1950–52; British Middle East Office, 1953; Foreign Office, 1954–57; Counsellor, British Embassy, Washington, 1958–60; Counsellor, Office of UK Commissioner for SE Asia Singapore, 1961–63; FCO (formerly FO), 1964–70; retired 1970. *Address:* 14 Pitt Street, W8. *Clubs:* Naval & Military, Hurlingham.

BRIANT, Bernard Christian, CVO 1977 (MVO 1974); MBE 1945; FRICS; Consultant, Messrs Daniel Smith, Chartered Surveyors, since 1982; Church Commissioner, since 1981; *b* 11 April 1917; *s* of Bernard Briant and Cecily (*née* Christian); *m* 1942, Margaret Emslie, *d* of A. S. Rawle; one *s* two *d*. *Educ:* Stowe Sch.; Trinity Coll., Oxford (MA). FRICS 1948. Served War, 1939–45: Tunisia, Italy and Austria; Major, Intell. Corps. Joined Briant & Son, Chartered Surveyors, 1938, Partner 1948; Partner, Daniel Smith, 1970, Sen. Partner, 1976–82. Mem. various cttees, RICS, 1948–70 (Mem. Council, 1962–70); Clerk, Co. of Chartered Surveyors, 1980–85. Director: C of E Bldg Soc., 1953–67; S of England Building Soc., 1967–80; London and S of England Bldg Soc., 1980–83; Anglia Bldg Soc., 1983–; Mem., Cttee of Management, Lambeth and Southwark Housing Soc., 1971– (Vice-Chm., 1983–86). Land Steward, Manor of Kennington of Duchy of Cornwall, 1963–76; Agent, All Souls Coll., Oxford, 1966–79. Governor, Polytechnic of South Bank, 1980–. *Recreations:* golf, walking, reading. *Address:* 32 St James's Street, SW1A 1HT. *Clubs:* United Oxford & Cambridge University; Aldeburgh Golf, Rye Golf.

BRIAULT, Dr Eric William Henry, CBE 1976; Education Officer, Inner London Education Authority, 1971–76; Visiting Professor of Education, University of Sussex, 1977–81 and 1984–85; *b* 24 Dec. 1911; *s* of H. G. Briault; *m* 1935, Marie Alice (*née* Knight); two *s* one *d*. *Educ:* Brighton, Hove and Sussex Grammar Sch.; Peterhouse, Cambridge (Robert Slade Schol.). 1st cl. hons Geography, 1933; MA Cantab 1937; PhD London 1939. School teaching, 1933–47; Inspector of Schools, LCC, 1948–56; Dep. Educn Officer, ILEA, 1956–71. Dir, res. project on falling rolls in secondary schs, 1978–80. Hon. Sec., RGS, 1953–63. Hon. DLitt Sussex, 1975. *Publications:* Sussex, East and West (Land Utilisation Survey report), 1942; (jtly) Introduction to Advanced Geography, 1957; (jtly) Geography In and Out of School, 1960; (jtly) Falling Rolls in Secondary Schools, Parts I and II, 1980. *Recreations:* travel, gardening, music, theatre and ballet; formerly athletics (Cambridge blue) and cross-country running (Cambridge half-blue).

Address: Woodedge, Hampers Lane, Storrington, W Sussex. *T:* Storrington 3919. *Club:* Athenæum.

BRICE, Air Cdre Eric John, CBE 1971 (OBE 1957); CEng; AFRAeS; MBIM; RAF retd; stockbroker; *b* 12 Feb. 1917; *s* of Courtenay Percy Please Brice and Lilie Alice Louise Brice (*née* Grey); *m* 1942, Janet Parks, Roundhay, Leeds, Yorks; two *s* one *d. Educ:* Loughborough Coll. (DLC). Joined RAF, 1939; served War, MEAF, 1943–46 (Sqdn Ldr). Air Ministry, 1946–50; Parachute Trg Sch., 1950–52; Wing Comdr, 1952; RAE, Farnborough, 1952–58; Comd, Parachute Trg Sch., 1958–60; RAF Coll., Cranwell, 1960–61; Gp Capt., 1961; RAF Halton, 1961–64; Comd, RAF Innsworth, Glos, 1964–66; Dir, Physical Educn, RAF, MoD, 1966–68; Air Cdre, 1968; Dep. AOA, RAF Headqrs, Maintenance Comd, 1968–71; April 1971, retd prematurely. *Recreations:* athletics (Combined Services and RAF athletic blues); Rugby football (RAF trialist and Blackheath Rugby Club); captained Loughborough Coll. in three sports. *Address:* Durns, Boldre, Hampshire. *T:* Lymington 72196. *Clubs:* Royal Air Force; Royal Lymington Yacht.

BRICE, Geoffrey James Barrington Groves, QC 1979; barrister; a Recorder of the Crown Court, since 1980; *b* 21 April 1938; *s* of late Lt-Cdr John Edgar Leonard Brice, MBE and Winifred Ivy Brice; *m* 1963, Ann Nuala Brice, LLM, PhD (*née* Connor); one *s. Educ:* Magdalen Coll. Sch., Brackley; University Coll., London (LLB). Called to the Bar, Middle Temple, 1960, Bencher, 1986; Harmsworth Scholar and Robert Garraway Rice Prize, 1960; Bencher, 1986. Lloyd's Arbitrator, 1978–; Wreck Commissioner, 1979–. Mem., UK Govt Delegn to IMO Legal Cttee, 1984–. *Publication:* Maritime Law of Salvage, 1983. *Recreations:* music, opera. *Address:* Yew Tree House, Spring Coppice, Newmer Common, Lane End, Bucks. *T:* High Wycombe 881810; 15 Gayfere Street, Smith Square, SW1. *T:* 01–799 3807; Queen Elizabeth Building, Temple, EC4Y 9BS. *T:* 01–353 9153. *Club:* Athenæum.

BRICKELL, Christopher David, VMH 1976; Director General, Royal Horticultural Society, since 1985; *b* 29 June 1932; *s* of Bertram Tom Brickell and Kathleen Alice Brickell; *m* 1963, Jeanette Scargill Flecknoe; two *d. Educ:* Queen's College, Taunton; Reading Univ. (BSc Horticulture). Joined Royal Horticultural Society Garden, Wisley, 1958: Asst Botanist, 1958; Botanist, 1960; Sen. Scientific Officer, 1964; Dep.Dir, 1968; Dir, 1969–85. *Publications:* Daphne: the genus in cultivation, 1976; Pruning, 1979; The Vanishing Garden, 1986; botanical papers in Flora Europaea and Flora of Turkey; horticultural papers in RHS Jl and Alpine Garden Soc. Bulletin. *Recreations:* gardening, sailing, squash, tennis. *Address:* Royal Horticultural Society, Vincent Square, SW1P 2PE.

BRICKHILL, Paul Chester Jerome; author; *b* 20 Dec. 1916; 3rd *s* of G. R. Brickhill, Sydney, Aust.; *m* 1950, Margaret Olive Slater, Sydney (marr. diss., 1964); one *s* one *d. Educ:* North Sydney High School; Sydney University. Journalist in Sydney, 1935–40; joined RAAF 1940; service in United Kingdom and Middle East as fighter pilot; three times wounded; shot down in Tunisia, 1943; POW Germany; Flight Lieut; Foreign Correspondent in Europe and USA, 1945–47; left journalism to concentrate on books, 1949. *Publications:* Escape to Danger (with Conrad Norton), 1946; The Great Escape, 1951; The Dam Busters, 1951; Escape or Die, 1952; Reach for the Sky, 1954; The Deadline, 1962. *Recreations:* reading, swimming. *Address:* c/o David Higham Associates Ltd, 5–8 Lower John Street, Golden Square, W1R 4HA.

BRICKWOOD, Sir Basil (Greame), 3rd Bt *cr* 1927; *b* 21 May 1923; *s* of Sir John Brickwood, 1st Bt and Isabella Janet Gibson (*d* 1967), *d* of James Gordon; *S* half-brother, 1974; *m* 1956, Shirley Anne Brown; two *d. Educ:* King Edward's Grammar Sch., Stratford-upon-Avon; Clifton College. *Club:* Royal Air Force.

BRIDGE, family name of **Baron Bridge of Harwich.**

BRIDGE OF HARWICH, Baron *cr* 1980 (Life Peer), of Harwich in the County of Essex; **Nigel Cyprian Bridge;** Kt 1968; PC 1975; a Lord of Appeal in Ordinary, since 1980; *b* 26 Feb. 1917; *s* of late Comdr C. D. C. Bridge, RN; *m* 1944, Margaret Swinbank; one *s* two *d. Educ:* Marlborough College. Army Service, 1940–46; commnd into KRRC, 1941. Called to the Bar, Inner Temple, 1947; Bencher, 1964, Reader, 1985, Treasurer, 1986; Junior Counsel to Treasury (Common Law), 1964–68; a Judge of High Court, Queen's Bench Div., 1968–75; Presiding Judge, Western Circuit, 1972–74; a Lord Justice of Appeal, 1975–80. Mem., Security Commn, 1977–85 (Chm. 1982–85). *Address:* House of Lords, SW1.

See also Very Rev. A. C. Bridge.

BRIDGE, Very Rev. Antony Cyprian; Dean of Guildford, 1968–86; *b* 5 Sept. 1914; *s* of late Comdr C. D. C. Bridge, RN; *m* 1937, Brenda Lois Streatfeild; one *s* two *d. Educ:* Marlborough College. Scholarship to Royal Academy School of Art, 1932. Professional painter thereafter. War of 1939–45: joined Army, Sept. 1939; commissioned Buffs, 1940; demobilised as Major, 1945. Ordained, 1955; Curate, Hythe Parish Church till 1958; Vicar of Christ Church, Lancaster Gate, London, 1958–68. Mem., Adv. Council V&A Museum, 1976–79. *Publications:* Images of God, 1960; Theodora: portrait in a Byzantine landscape, 1978; The Crusades, 1980; Suleiman The Magnificent, 1983; One Man's Advent, 1985. *Recreations:* bird-watching, reading. *Address:* 34 London Road, Deal, Kent CT14 9TE.

See also Baron Bridge of Harwich.

BRIDGE, John, GC 1944; GM 1940 and Bar 1941; Director of Education for Sunderland Borough Council (formerly Sunderland County Borough Council), 1963–76, retired; *b* 5 Feb. 1915; *s* of late Joseph Edward Bridge, Culcheth, Warrington; *m* 1945, F. J. Patterson; three *d. Educ:* London Univ. BSc Gen. Hons, 1936 and BSc Special Hons (Physics), 1937; Teacher's Dip., 1938. Schoolmaster: Lancs CC, Sept.-Dec. 1938; Leighton Park, Reading, Jan.-Aug. 1939; Firth Park Grammar Sch., Sheffield, Sept. 1939–Aug. 1946 (interrupted by war service). Served War: RNVR June 1940–Feb. 1946, engaged on bomb and mine disposal; demobilised as Lt Comdr RNVR. *Recreations:* gardening, travel, fell walking, photography, fishing. *Address:* 37 Park Avenue, Roker, Sunderland SR6 9NJ. *T:* Sunderland 486356.

BRIDGE, Keith James; consultant; *b* 21 Aug. 1929; *s* of late James Henry Bridge and Lilian Elizabeth (*née* Nichols); *m* 1960, Thelma Ruby (*née* Hubble); three *d* (and one *s* decd). *Educ:* Sir George Monoux Grammar Sch., Walthamstow; Corpus Christi Coll., Oxford (MA). CIPFA 1959; CBIM 1978. Local govt service, 1953; Dep. City Treasurer, York, 1965; Borough Treas., Bolton, 1967; City Treas., Manchester, 1971; County Treasurer, Greater Manchester Council, 1973; Chief Exec., Humberside CC, 1978–83. Mem., W Yorks Residuary Body, 1985–. Financial Adviser to Assoc. of Metrop. Authorities, 1971–78; Mem. Council, 1972–84, Pres., 1982–83, Chartered Inst. of Public Finance and Accountancy; Pres., Soc. of Metropolitan Treasurers, 1977–78. Member: Audit Commn for Local Authorities in Eng. and Wales, 1983–86; Exec. Council, Business in the Community, 1982–84; Bd, Public Finance Foundn, 1984–. *Publications:* papers in professional jls. *Recreations:* gardening, literature, music. *Address:* Conifers, 11 Eastgate, Lund, Driffield, N Humberside YO25 9TQ. *T:* Driffield 81627.

BRIDGE, Ronald George Blacker, OBE 1985; Secretary for Education and Manpower, Hong Kong, since 1986; *b* 7 Sept. 1932; *s* of Blacker Frank Bridge and Aileen Georgina Edith (*née* Shaw); *m* 1956, Olive Tyrrell Brown; two *s* two *d. Educ:* Charterhouse; Lincoln Coll., Oxford (MA). National Service, 1954–56. Colonial Office Devonshire Course, 1956–57; Hong Kong Admin. Service, 1957–: Dep. Sec. for Civil Service, 1973; Dep. Sec. for Security, 1976; Sec. for CS, 1977; Dir of Immigration, Hong Kong, 1978; Comr for Labour, 1983. *Recreations:* hockey, walking, reading. *Address:* 68 Mount Nicholson, Hong Kong. *T:* Hong Kong 5–734377. *Club:* Football (Hong Kong).

BRIDGEMAN, family name of **Earl of Bradford** and **Viscount Bridgeman.**

BRIDGEMAN, 3rd Viscount *cr* 1929, of Leigh; **Robin John Orlando Bridgeman,** CA; *b* 5 Dec. 1930; *s* of Hon. Geoffrey John Orlando Bridgeman, MC, FRCS (*d* 1974) (2nd *s* of 1st Viscount) and Mary Meriel Gertrude Bridgeman (*d* 1974), *d* of Rt Hon. Sir George John Talbot; *S* uncle, 1982; *m* 1966, (Victoria) Harriet Lucy, *d* of Ralph Meredyth Turton; four *s. Educ:* Eton. CA 1958. Partner: Fenn & Crosthwaite, 1973; Henderson Crosthwaite & Co., 1975–. *Recreations:* shooting, gardening, music. *Heir: s* Hon. William Orlando Caspar Bridgeman, *b* 15 Aug. 1968. *Address:* 19 Chepstow Road, W2 5BP. *T:* 01–229 7420; Watley House, Sparsholt, Winchester SO21 2LU. *T:* Sparsholt 297. *Clubs:* Beefsteak, MCC; Pitt.

BRIDGEMAN, John Michael; Chief Registrar of Friendly Societies and Industrial Assurance Commissioner, since 1982; *b* 26 April 1931; *s* of John Wilfred Bridgeman, *qv*, and Mary Bridgeman; *m* 1958, June Bridgeman, *qv*; one *s* four *d. Educ:* Marlborough Coll.; Trinity Coll., Cambridge. Asst Principal, BoT, 1954; HM Treasury, 1956–81, Under Sec., 1975–81. *Club:* Reform.

BRIDGEMAN, John Wilfred, CBE 1960; BSc London, AKC; retired as Principal, Loughborough Training College, 1950–63; Principal, Loughborough Summer School, 1931–63; *b* 25 Jan. 1895; *s* of late John Edward Bridgeman and Alice Bridgeman, Bournemouth; *m* 1st, 1928, Mary Jane Wallace (*d* 1961); one *s*; 2nd, 1963, Helen Ida Mary Wallace. *Educ:* King's College, University of London; London Day Training College. Industry, 1910–15; taught at technical colleges, Bournemouth, Bath and Weymouth, 1915–20; Asst Master, Lyme Regis Grammar School, 1923; Senior Maths Master, Wolverhampton Secondary Gram. Sch., 1926; Head of Dept for Training of Teachers, Loughborough Coll., 1930. Chm., Assoc. of Teachers in Colls and Depts of Education, 1952; Leader of Staff Panel, Pelham Cttee, 1955–63. Hon. MA Nottingham, 1961; Hon. DLitt Loughborough, 1978. *Recreations:* chess, reading. *Address:* Flat 3, Laleham Court, Woking, Surrey GU21 4AX. *T:* Woking 21523.

See also J. M. Bridgeman.

BRIDGEMAN, Mrs June; Under-Secretary, Department of Transport, since 1979; *b* 26 June 1932; *d* of Gordon and Elsie Forbes; *m* 1958, John Michael Bridgeman, *qv*; one *s* four *d. Educ:* variously, England and Scotland; Westfield Coll., London Univ. (BA). Asst Principal, BoT, 1954; subseq. served in DEA, NBPI, Min. of Housing and Local Govt, DoE; Under Secretary: DoE 1974–76; Central Policy Review Staff, Cabinet Office, 1976–79.

BRIDGER, Rev. Gordon Frederick; Principal, Oak Hill Theological College, since 1987; *b* 5 Feb. 1932; *s* of late Dr John Dell Bridger and Hilda Bridger; *m* 1962, Elizabeth Doris Bewes; three *d. Educ:* Christ's Hospital, Horsham; Selwyn Coll., Cambridge (MA Hons Theology); Ridley Hall, Cambridge. Curate, Islington Parish Church, 1956–59; Curate, Holy Sepulchre Church, Cambridge, 1959–62; Vicar, St Mary, North End, Fulham, 1962–69; Chaplain, St Thomas's Episcopal Church, Edinburgh, 1969–76; Rector, Holy Trinity Church, Heigham, Norwich, 1976–87; RD Norwich (South), 1981–86; Exam. Chaplain to Bishop of Norwich, 1981–86; Hon. Canon, Norwich Cathedral, 1984–87. *Publications:* The Man from Outside, 1969, rev. edn 1978; A Day that Changed the World, 1975; A Bible Study Commentary (I Corinthians—Galatians), 1985; reviews in The Churchman and other Christian papers and magazines. *Recreations:* music, sport, reading. *Address:* The Principal's House, Oak Hill College, Southgate, N14 4PS. *T:* 01–449 0467.

BRIDGER, Pearl, MBE 1947; Director, Central Personnel, Post Office, 1968–72, retired; *b* 9 Dec. 1912; *d* of Samuel and Lottie Bridger. *Educ:* Godolphin and Latymer Girls' Sch., London, W6. BA (Hons) Open Univ., 1978. Entered Post Office as Executive Officer, 1931; Asst Telecommunications Controller, 1938; Principal, 1947; Asst Sec., 1954; Director, 1968. *Address:* 95 Deanhill Court, SW14. *T:* 01–876 8877. *Clubs:* Civil Service, Soroptimist.

BRIDGES, family name of **Baron Bridges.**

BRIDGES, 2nd Baron *cr* 1957; **Thomas Edward Bridges,** KCMG 1983 (CMG 1975); HM Diplomatic Service; Ambassador to Italy, since 1983; *b* 27 Nov. 1927; *s* of 1st Baron Bridges, KG, PC, GCB, GCVO, MC, FRS, and late Hon. Katharine Dianthe, *d* of 2nd Baron Farrer; *S* father, 1969; *m* 1953, Rachel Mary, *y d* of late Sir Henry Bunbury, KCB; two *s* one *d. Educ:* Eton; New Coll., Oxford. Entered Foreign Service, 1951; served in Bonn, Berlin, Rio de Janeiro and at FO (Asst Private Sec. to Foreign Secretary, 1963–66); Head of Chancery, Athens, 1966–68; Counsellor, Moscow, 1969–71; Private Sec. (Overseas Affairs) to Prime Minister, 1972–74; RCDS 1975; Minister (Commercial), Washington, 1976–79; Dep. Under Sec. of State, FCO, 1979–82. *Heir: s* Hon. Mark Thomas Bridges [*b* 25 July 1954; *m* 1978, Angela Margaret, *er d* of J. L. Collinson, Mansfield, Notts; two *d*]. *Address:* c/o Foreign and Commonwealth Office, SW1.

BRIDGES, Brian; Director of Establishments and Personnel, Department of Health and social Security, since 1985; *b* 30 June 1937; *s* of late William Ernest Bridges; *m* 1970, Jennifer Mary Rogers. *Educ:* Harrow Weald County Grammar Sch.; Univ. of Keele (BA 1961). Joined Civil Service, 1961; Principal, 1967; Asst Sec. 1975; Under Sec., 1985. *Recreations:* antiquarian. *Address:* 36 Chiltern Road, Wendover, Bucks.

BRIDGES, Prof. James Wilfrid; Director, Robens Institute of Industrial and Environmental Health and Safety, since 1978 and Professor of Toxicology, since 1979, University of Surrey; *b* 9 Aug. 1938; *s* of Wilfrid Edward Seymour Bridges and Mary Winifred Cameron; *m* 1963, Daphne (*née* Hammond); one *s* one *d. Educ:* Bromley Grammar Sch.; Queen Elizabeth Coll., London Univ.; St Mary's Hosp. Med. Sch., London Univ. BSc, PhD; MRCPath; FRSC, CChem; FIBiol; MInstEnvSci. Lectr, St Mary's Hosp. Med. Sch., 1962–68; Senior Lectr then Reader, Dept of Biochemistry, Univ. of Surrey, 1968–78. Visiting Professor: Univ. of Texas at Dallas, 1973, 1979; Univ. of Rochester, NY, 1974; Sen. Scientist, Nat. Inst. of Envtl Health Scis, N Carolina, 1976. Chm., British Toxicology Soc., 1980–81; First Pres., Fedn of European Toxicology Socs, 1985–. *Publications:* (ed jtly) Progress in Drug Metabolism, 9 vols, 1976–; over 250 research papers and reviews in scientific jls. *Recreations:* theatre going, various sports. *Address:* 3 Chatsworth Close, Caversham Park Village, Reading, Berks RG4 0RS.

BRIDGES, Dame Mary (Patricia), DBE 1981; *b* 6 June 1930; *d* of Austin Edward and Lena Mabel Fawkes; *m* 1951, Bertram Marsdin Bridges; one step *s*. Chm., Honiton Div.

Cons. Assoc., 1968–71; Chm., Western Area, covering 29 constituencies from Cornwall to Glos, 1976–79; past Chm., Cons. Western Area Women's Adv. Cttee and CPC Cttee; Mem. Cttee, Littleham Urban Ward, Exmouth (Pres., 1981). Women's Section of Royal British Legion: Pres., Exmouth Br., 1965–; Chm., Devon County Women's Section, 1979–; Vice Chm., SW Area, 1984, Chm. 1985; SW Area Rep. to Central Cttee, 1985–. Former Mem., Exe Vale HMC; Founder Chm., Exmouth Council of Voluntary Service. Member: Exec., Resthaven, Exmouth, 1970– (Chm., League of Friends, 1971–); Devon FPC, 1985–; President: Exmouth and Budleigh Salterton Br., CRUSE, 1980–; Exmouth Campaign Cttee, Cancer Research, 1981– (Chm., 1975–81); Founder Pres., Exmouth Br., British Heart Foundn, 1984. Mem., SW Electricity Consultative Council, 1982; Mem., Exmouth Cttee, LEPRA, 1962– (Hon. Sec., 1964–); Co-optative Trustee, Exmouth Welfare Trust, 1979–; Governor, Rolle Coll., Exmouth, 1982. Hon. Life Mem., Retford Cricket Club, 1951; Hon. Vice-Pres., Exmouth Cricket Club, 1981. *Recreations:* cricket, reading. *Address:* Walton House, Fairfield Close, Exmouth, Devon EX8 2BN. *T:* Exmouth 265317.

BRIDGES, Ven. Peter Sydney Godfrey; Archdeacon of Warwick since 1983; Canon-Theologian of Coventry Cathedral, since 1977; *b* 30 Jan. 1925; *s* of Sidney Clifford Bridges and Winifred (*née* Livette); *m* 1952, Joan Penlerick (*née* Madge); two *s*. *Educ:* Raynes Park Grammar Sch.; Kingston upon Thames Sch. of Architecture; Lincoln Theol College. ARIBA 1950, Dip. Liturgy and Architecture 1967. Gen. and ecclesiastical practice, 1950–54; Lectr, Nottingham Sch. of Architecture, 1954–56. Deacon, 1958; Priest, 1959. Asst Curate, Hemel Hempstead, 1958–64; Res. Fellow, Inst. for Study of Worship and Religious Architecture, Univ. of Birmingham, 1964–67 (Hon. Fellow, 1967–72 and 1978); Warden, Anglican Chaplaincy and Chaplain to Univ. of Birmingham, 1965–68; Lectr, Birmingham Sch. of Arch., 1967–72; eccles. architect and planning consultant, 1968–75; Chm., New Town Ministers Assoc., 1968–72; Co-Dir, Midlands Socio-Religious Res. Gp, 1968–75; Dir, Chelmsford Diocesan R&D Unit, 1972–77; Archdeacon of Southend, 1972–77; Archdeacon of Coventry, 1977–83. Mem., Cathedrals Advisory Commn for England, 1981–. *Publications:* Socio-Religious Institutes, Lay Academies, etc, 1967; contrib. Church Building, res. bulletins (Inst. for Study of Worship and Relig. Arch.), Clergy Review, Prism, Christian Ministry in New Towns, Cathedral and Mission, Church Architecture and Social Responsibility. *Recreations:* architecture, singing. *Address:* c/o Church House, Palmerston Road, Coventry CV5 6FJ. *T:* Coventry 74328. *Club:* Royal Commonwealth Society.

BRIDGES, Sir Phillip (Rodney), Kt 1973; CMG 1967; *b* 9 July 1922; *e s* of late Captain Sir Ernest Bridges and Lady Bridges; *m* 1st, 1951, Rosemary Ann Streeten (marr. diss. 1961); two *s* one *d*; 2nd, 1962, Angela Mary (*née* Dearden), *widow* of James Huyton. *Educ:* Bedford School. Military Service (Capt., RA) with Royal W African Frontier Force in W. Africa, India and Burma, 1941–47. Admitted Solicitor (England), 1951; Colonial Legal Service, 1954; Barrister and Solicitor, Supreme Court of The Gambia, 1954; Solicitor-General of The Gambia, 1963; QC (Gambia) 1964; Attorney-General of The Gambia, 1964–68; Chief Justice of The Gambia, 1968–83. *Address:* Weavers, Coney Weston, Bury St Edmunds, Suffolk. *Clubs:* Travellers', Royal Commonwealth Society.

BRIDGES-ADAMS, John Nicholas William; a Recorder of the Crown Court, since 1972; *b* 16 Sept. 1930; *s* of late William Bridges-Adams, CBE; *m* 1962, Jenifer Celia Emily, *d* of David Sandell, FRCS. *Educ:* Stowe; Oriel Coll., Oxford (Scholar; MA, DipEd). Commnd Royal Artillery, 1949, transf. to RAFVR 1951 and served with Oxford and London Univ. Air Sqdn; Flying Officer, 2623 Sqdn RAuxAF Regt, 1980–82. Called to Bar, Lincoln's Inn, 1958 (Gray's Inn *ad eundem* 1979); Head of Chambers, 1979; Mem., Young Barristers Cttee, Bar Council, 1960–61; Actg Junior, Mddx Sessions Bar Mess, 1965–67. Mem., Exec. Cttee, Soc. of Cons. Lawyers, 1967–69 (Chairman: Rates of Exchange sub-cttee, 1967–70; Criminal Law sub-cttee, 1983–); Mem., House of Lords Reform Cttee, CAER, 1982–. Chm., panel from which Representations Cttees under Dumping at Sea Act 1974 drawn, 1976–85, and under Food and Environment Protection Act 1985, 1985–. Contested (C) West Bromwich West, Oct. 1974. Governor, St Benedict's Upper Sch., 1980–83. Member: RIIA; IISS; FCIArb. *Publication:* contrib. on collisions at sea, 3rd edn of Halsbury's Laws of England, Vol. 35. *Recreation:* putting cats among pigeons. *Address:* 4 Verulam Buildings, Gray's Inn, WC1R 5LW. *T:* 01–405 6114; Fornham Cottage, Fornham St Martin, Bury St Edmunds, Suffolk. *T:* Bury St Edmunds 5307. *Clubs:* Savile, Garrick.

BRIDGEWATER, Bentley Powell Conyers; Secretary of the British Museum, 1948–73; *b* 6 Sept. 1911; *s* of Conyers Bridgewater, OBE, Clerk to Commissioners of Taxes for City of London, and Violet Irene, *d* of Dr I. W. Powell, Victoria, BC. *Educ:* Westminster School (King's Schol.); Christ Church, Oxford (Westminster Schol., BA 1933, MA 1965). Asst Keeper, British Museum, 1937; Asst Sec., 1940. Seconded to Dominions Office, 1941–42, and to Foreign Office, 1942–45; returned to British Museum, 1946; Deputy Keeper, 1950; Keeper, 1961; retired, 1973. *Recreation:* music. *Address:* 4 Doughty Street, WC1N 2PH. *Club:* Athenæum.

BRIDGLAND, Milton Deane, FTS, FRACI, FAIM; Chairman, ICI Australia Ltd, since 1980; *b* 8 July 1922; *s* of late Frederick H. and Muriel E. Bridgland, Adelaide; *m* 1945, Christine L. Cowell; three *d*. *Educ:* St Peter's Coll., Adelaide; Adelaide Univ. (BSc). Joined ICI Australia Ltd, 1945; Technical Manager, Plastics Gp, 1955–62; Ops Dir, 1962–67, Man. Dir, 1967–71, Dulux Australia Ltd; Exec. Dir 1971, Man. Dir, 1978–84, ICI Australia Ltd. Chm., Jennings Properties Ltd, 1985–; Director: ANZ Banking Group Ltd, 1982–; Jennings Industries Ltd, 1984–. President: Aust. Chemical Industry Council, 1977; Aust. Industry Develt Assoc., 1982–83. Vice President: Aust. Business Roundtable, 1983; Business Council of Australia, 1983–84; Dir, Aust. Inst. of Petroleum, 1980–84; Mem., National Energy Adv. Cttee, 1977–80. Mem., Bd. of Management, Univ. of Melbourne Grad. Sch. of Management, 1983–. Mem., Cook Soc. *Recreations:* tennis, golf. *Address:* 178 Barkers Road, Hawthorn, Vic 3122, Australia. *T:* (03) 819 3939. *Clubs:* Athenæum, Australian, Peninsula Country (Melbourne).

BRIDLE, Rear-Adm. Gordon Walter, CB 1977; MBE 1952; *b* 14 May 1923; *s* of Percy Gordon Bridle and Dorothy Agnes Bridle; *m* 1944, Phyllis Audrey Page; three *s*. *Educ:* King Edward's Grammar Sch., Aston, Birmingham; Northern Grammar Sch., Portsmouth; Royal Dockyard Sch., Portsmouth (Whitworth Scholar); Imperial Coll., London (ACGI). CEng, FIEE. jssc. Loan Service, Pakistan, 1950–52; served HM Ships: Implacable, St James, Gambia, Newfoundland, Devonshire; Proj. Manager, Sea Slug and Sea Dart, Mins of Aviation/Technol.; comd HMS Collingwood, 1969–71; Dir, Surface Weapons Projects, ASWE; Asst Controller of the Navy, 1974–77. Mem. Council, C of E Soldiers', Sailors' and Airmen's Clubs, 1982. *Recreations:* sailing, walking. *Address:* 25 Heatherwood, Midhurst, Sussex GU29 9LH. *T:* Midhurst 2838.

BRIDLE, Ronald Jarman, FEng 1979; Director: (Technology and Development), Mitchell Cotts PLC, since 1984; Key Resources International, since 1984; *b* 27 Jan. 1930; *s* of Raymond Bridle and Dorothy (*née* Jarman); *m* Beryl Eunice (*née* Doe); two *d*. *Educ:* West Monmouth Grammar Sch.; Bristol Univ. (BSc). FEng, FICE, FIHE. Graduate Asst, Monmouthshire CC, 1953–55; Exec. Engr, Gold Coast Govt, 1955–57; Sen. Engr, Cwmbran Develt Corp., 1957–60; Principal Designer, Cardiff City, 1960–62; Project Engr, Sheffield-Leeds Motorway, West Riding CC, 1962–65; Dep. County Surveyor II, Cheshire CC, 1965–67; Dir, Midland RCU, DoE, 1967–71; Dep. Chief Highway Engr, 1971–73, Under-Sec., Highways 1, 1973–75, Chief Highway Engr, 1975–76, DoE; Chief Highway Engr, Dept of Transport, 1976–80; Controller of R&D, Dept of Transport, and Dir, Transport and Road Res. Lab., 1980–84. FRSA. Former Member: Council, ICE; EDC for Civil Engrg; Past Pres., IHE; Mem. Bd., BSI, 1979–; Chm., Building and Civil Engineering Council, BSI, 1979–. *Publications:* papers in jls of ICE, IHE and internat. confs. *Recreations:* golf, painting. *Address:* Parsonage Farm, Kemeys Commander, Usk, Gwent NP5 1SU. *T:* Nantyderry 880929. *Club:* Royal Automobile.

BRIDPORT, 4th Viscount, *cr* 1868; **Alexander Nelson Hood;** Baron Bridport, 1794; 7th Duke of Bronte in Sicily (*cr* 1799); Managing Director, Shearson Lehman Amex Finance SA, since 1986; *b* 17 March 1948; *s* of 3rd Viscount Bridport and Sheila Jeanne Agatha, *d* of Johann van Meurs; *S* father, 1969; *m* 1st, 1972, Linda Jacqueline Paravicini (marr. diss.), *d* of Lt-Col and Mrs V. R. Paravicini, Nutley Manor, Basingstoke, Hants; one *s*; 2nd, 1979, Mrs Nina Rindt-Martyn; one *s*. *Educ:* Eton; Sorbonne. *Heir:* *s* Hon. Peregrine Alexander Nelson Hood, *b* 30 Aug. 1974. *Address:* Villa Jonin, 1261 Le Muids, Vaud, Switzerland. *T:* 022–661705. *Club:* Brooks's.

BRIEGEL, Geoffrey Michael Olver; Legacy Officer, The Institute of Cancer Research: Royal Cancer Hospital, since 1983; *b* 13 July 1923; *s* of late Roy C. Briegel, TD, and Veria Lindsey Briegel; *m* 1947, Barbara Mary Richardson; three *s* one *d*. *Educ:* Highgate Sch. Served War, RAF, 1942–46 (514 Sqdn Bomber Command). Called to Bar, Lincoln's Inn, 1950; Public Trustee Office, 1954; Clerk of the Lists, Queen's Bench Div., and Legal Sec. to Lord Chief Justice of England, 1963; Dep. Circuit Administrator, South Eastern Circuit, 1971; Dep. Master of the Court of Protection, 1977–83. *Recreations:* target rifle and pistol shooting, swimming, cricket, theatre. *Club:* Royal Air Force.

BRIEN, Alan; novelist and journalist; *b* 12 March 1925; *s* of late Ernest Brien and Isabella (*née* Patterson); *m* 1st, 1947, Pamela Mary Jones; three *d*; 2nd, 1961, Nancy Newbold Ryan; one *s* one *d*; 3rd, 1973, Jill Sheila Tweedie, *qv*. *Educ:* Bede Grammar Sch., Sunderland; Jesus Coll., Oxford. BA (Eng Lit). Served war RAF (air-gunner), 1943–46. Associate Editor: Mini-Cinema, 1950–52; Courier, 1952–53; Film Critic and Columnist, Truth, 1953–54; TV Critic, Observer, 1954–55; Film Critic, 1954–56, New York Correspondent, 1956–58, Evening Standard; Drama Critic and Features Editor, Spectator, 1958–61; Columnist, Daily Mail, 1958–62; Columnist, Sunday Dispatch, 1962–63; Political Columnist, Sunday Pictorial, 1963–64; Drama Critic, Sunday Telegraph, 1961–67; Columnist: Spectator, 1963–65; New Statesman, 1966–72; Punch, 1972–84; Diarist, 1967–75, Film Critic, 1976–84, Sunday Times; Contributor various American publications: Saturday Evening Post, Holiday, Vogue, Mademoiselle, Theatre Arts. Regular broadcaster on radio, 1952–, and television, 1955–. Hannen Swaffer Critic of Year, 1966, 1967. *Publications:* Domes of Fortune (essays), 1979; Lenin the Novel (novel), 1986; contrib. novel by several hands, I Knew Daisy Smuten, 1970; various collections of Spectator and Punch pieces. *Recreations:* getting out of London, not getting back to London. *Address:* 14 Falkland Road, NW5. *T:* 01–485 9074; Blaen-y-Glyn, Pont Hyndwr, Llandrillo, Clwyd. *T:* Llandrillo 291. *Club:* Garrick.

BRIERLEY, Christopher Wadsworth; Managing Director, Economic Planning since 1982, and Member of the Board since 1985, British Gas Corporation; *b* 1 June 1929; *s* of Eric Brierley and Edna Mary Lister; *m* 1st, Dorothy Scott (marr. diss. 1980); two *d*; 2nd, 1984, Dilwen Marie Srobat (*née* Morgan). *Educ:* Whitgift Middle School, Croydon. ACMA, ACIS. Branch Accountant, Hubert Davies & Co., Rhodesia, 1953–56; private business, N Rhodesia, 1956–59; Accountant, EMI, 1960; Chief Accountant, EMI Records, 1965; Dir of Finance, Long & Hambly, 1968; Chief Accountant, E Midlands Gas Bd, 1970; Director of Finance: Eastern Gas Bd, 1974; British Gas, 1977; Dir of Economic Planning, British Gas, 1980. *Recreations:* golf, music, sailing. *Address:* 19 Lancaster Avenue, Hadley Wood, Barnet, Herts EN4 0EP. *T:* 01–449 6565. *Club:* Royal Automobile.

BRIERLEY, John David, CB 1978; retired Civil Servant; *b* 16 March 1918; *s* of late Walter George Brierley and late Doris Brierley (*née* Paterson); *m* 1956, Frances Elizabeth Davis; one (adopted) *s* one (adopted) *d*. *Educ:* elementary schools, London and Croydon; Whitgift Sch., Croydon; Lincoln Coll., Oxford. *Lit. Hum.*, BA Hons, 1940. Served War: Army, RASC, 1940–46. Ministry of Education: Asst Principal, 1946; Principal, 1949; Dept of Education and Science: Asst Sec., 1960; Under-Sec., 1969; Principal Finance Officer, 1969–75; Under Sec., DES, 1969–77. Dean of Studies, Working Mens' Coll., NW1, 1978–81, Mem. Corp., 1980–; Governor, Croydon High Sch. (GPDST), 1980–. *Recreations:* fell-walking, cycling, photography, music. *Address:* Little Trees, Winterbourne, near Newbury, Berks. *T:* Chieveley 248870.

BRIERLEY, Zachry, CBE 1978 (MBE 1969); Chairman, Z. Brierley Ltd, since 1957 (Chairman and Managing Director, 1957–73); President, Z. Brierley (USA) Inc., since 1972; *b* 16 April 1920; *s* of late Zachry Brierley and of Nellie (*née* Ashworth); *m* 1946, Iris Macara; one *d*. *Educ:* Rydal Sch., Colwyn Bay. Served War: commnd RAF, 1941. Joined family business, Z. Brierley Ltd, 1938: Dir, 1952; Chm. and Man. Dir, 1957. Dir, Develt Corp. for Wales, 1974–83. Mem., CBI Central Council, 1970–82 (also mem. cttees); Chm., Wales Reg. Council, CBI, 1976–77. Chairman: Small and Medium Firms Commn, Union des Industries de la Communauté Européenne, Brussels, 1975–77; Wales Adv. Cttee, Design Council, 1977–86 (Mem. Design Council, 1976–86). Member: Welsh Indust. Develt Bd, Welsh Office, 1972–82; Welsh Develt Agency, 1975–; Bd, Civic Trust for Wales, 1976–; Cttee to Review Functioning of Financial Instns, 1977–80; Council, Machine Tool Trade Assoc., 1977–80; Bd of Governors, Llandrillo Tech. Coll., 1975–82; Bd of Governors, Penrhos Coll., 1980–. Chairman: Conservative Polit. Centre (Wales), 1975–79; Conway Cons. and Unionist Assoc., 1980–82 (also past Chm. and Vice Pres.); Wales Area Cons. Council, 1982–. Vice Chm., North Wales Medical Centre, 1979–. Liveryman, Basketmakers' Co., 1978–; Freeman, City of London, 1977. *Recreations:* philately, travel, reading, sketching. *Address:* West Point, Gloddaeth Avenue, Llandudno, Gwynedd, N Wales LL30 2AN. *T:* Llandudno 76970. *Club:* Carlton.

BRIERS, Richard; actor since 1955; *b* 14 Jan. 1934; *s* of Joseph Briers and Morna Richardson; *m* 1957, Ann Davies; two *d*. *Educ:* Rokeby Prep. Sch., Wimbledon; Ridgeway Sch., Wimbledon. RADA, 1954–56 (silver medal). First appearance in London in Gilt and Gingerbread, Duke of York's, 1959. *Plays:* (major parts in): Arsenic and Old Lace, 1965; Relatively Speaking, 1966; The Real Inspector Hound, 1968; Cat Among the Pigeons, 1969; The Two of Us, 1970; Butley, 1972; Absurd Person Singular, 1973; Absent Friends, 1975; Middle Age Spread, 1979; The Wild Duck, 1980; Arms and the Man, 1981; Run for Your Wife, 1983; Why Me?, 1985; The Relapse, 1986. *Television series:* Brothers-in-Law; Marriage Lines; The Good Life; OneUpManShip; The Other One; Norman Conquests; Ever-Decreasing Circles; All In Good Faith. *Publication:* Natter Natter, 1981. *Recreations:* reading, gardening. *Address:* c/o ICM Ltd, 388–396 Oxford Street, W1N 9HE.

BRIGDEN, Wallace, MA, MD, FRCP; Consulting Physician: London Hospital, and Cardiac Department, London Hospital; National Heart Hospital; Consulting Cardiologist to the Royal Navy, now Emeritus; *b* 8 June 1916; *s* of Wallis Brigden and Louise Brigden (*née* Clarke). *Educ*: Latymer School; University of Cambridge; King's College Hospital; Yale University. Senior Scholar, King's College, Cambridge; First Class Natural Sciences Tripos, Parts I and II, 1936, 1937; Henry Fund Fellowship, Yale University, USA, 1937–38; Burney Yeo Schol., King's College Hospital, 1938. RAMC, 1943–47, Med. Specialist and O/C Medical Division. Lecturer in Medicine, Post-Grad. Med. School of London; Physician, Hammersmith Hospital, 1948–49; Asst Physician, later Consultant Physician, London Hospital and Cardiac Dept of London Hosp., 1949–81; Asst Physician, later Consultant Physician, National Heart Hospital, 1949–81; Cons. Cardiologist, Special Unit for Juvenile Rheumatism, Taplow, 1955–59; Director Inst. of Cardiology, 1962–66. Cons. Physician to Munich Re-Insurance Co., 1974–. St Cyres Lectr, 1956; R. T. Hall Lectr, Australia and New Zealand, 1961; Hugh Morgan Vis. Prof., Vanderbilt Univ., 1963. Late Assistant Editor, British Heart Journal. Mem. British Cardiac Society and Assoc. of Physicians. *Publications*: Section on Cardio-vascular disease in Price's Textbook of Medicine; Myocardial Disease, Cecil-Loeb Textbook of Medicine; contributor to the Lancet, British Heart Jl, British Medical Jl. *Recreation*: painting. *Address*: 45 Wimpole Street, W1. *T*: 01–935 1201; Willow House, 38 Totteridge Common, N20 8NE. *T*: 01–959 6616.

BRIGGS, family name of **Baron Briggs**.

BRIGGS, Baron *cr* 1976 (Life Peer), of Lewes, E Sussex; **Asa Briggs**, MA, BSc (Econ); FBA 1980; Provost, Worcester College, Oxford, since 1976; Chancellor, Open University, since 1978; *b* 7 May 1921; *o s* of William Walker Briggs and Jane Briggs, Keighley, Yorks; *m* 1955, Susan Anne Banwell, *o d* of late Donald I. Banwell, Keevil, Wiltshire; two *s* two *d*. *Educ*: Keighley Grammar School; Sidney Sussex College, Cambridge (1st cl. History Tripos, Pts I and II, 1940, 1941; 1st cl. BSc (Econ.), Lond., 1941). Gerstenberg studentship in Economics, London, 1941. Served in Intelligence Corps, 1942–45. Fellow of Worcester College, Oxford, 1945–55; Reader in Recent Social and Economic History, Oxford, 1950–55; Member, Institute for Advanced Study, Princeton, USA, 1953–54; Faculty Fellow of Nuffield College, Oxford, 1953–55; Professor of Modern History, Leeds Univ., 1955–61; University of Sussex: Professor of History, 1961–76; Dean, School of Social Studies, 1961–65; Pro Vice-Chancellor, 1961–67; Vice-Chancellor, 1967–76. Chm. Bd of Governors, Inst. of Develt Studies, 1967–76, Mem., 1976–. Visiting Professor: ANU, 1960; Chicago Univ., 1966, 1972. Dep. Pres., WEA, 1954–58, Pres., 1958–67. Member: UGC, 1959–67; Hong Kong UPGC, 1977–; Chm., Cttee on Nursing, 1970–72 (Cmnd 5115, 1972). Trustee: Glyndebourne Arts Trust, 1966–; Internat. Broadcasting Inst., 1968–; (Chm.) Heritage Educn Gp, 1976–86; Civic Trust, 1976–; Chairman: Standing Conf. for Study of Local History, 1969–76; Council, European Inst. of Education, 1975–; Adv. Bd for Redundant Churches, 1983–; Vice-Chm. of Council, UN Univ., 1974–80; Governor, British Film Institute, 1970–77; President: Social History Soc., 1976–; The Ephemera Soc., 1984–; British Assoc. for Local History, 1984–86; Assoc. of Research Associations, 1986–; Vice-Pres., Historical Assoc., 1986–. Mem., Ct of Governors, Administrative Staff Coll., 1971–. Mem., Amer. Acad. of Arts and Sciences, 1970. Hon. Fellow: Sidney Sussex Coll., Cambridge, 1968; Worcester Coll., Oxford, 1969; St Catharine's Coll., Cambridge, 1977. Hon. DLitt: East Anglia, 1966; Strathclyde, 1973; Leeds, 1974; Cincinnati, 1977; Liverpool, 1977; Open Univ., 1979; Hon. DSc Florida Presbyterian, 1966; Hon. LLD: York, Canada, 1968; New England, 1972; Sussex, 1976; Bradford, 1978; Rochester, NY, 1980; Ball State, 1985. Marconi Medal for Communications History, 1975; Médaille de Vermeil de la Formation, Fondation de l'Académie d'Architecture, 1979. *Publications*: Patterns of Peace-making (with D. Thomson and E. Meyer), 1945; History of Birmingham (1865–1938), 1952; Victorian People, 1954; Friends of the People, 1956; The Age of Improvement, 1959; (ed) Chartist Studies, 1959; (ed with John Saville) Essays in Labour History, Vol. I, 1960, Vol. II, 1971, Vol. III, 1977; (ed) They Saw it Happen, 1897–1940, 1961; A Study of the Work of Seebohm Rowntree, 1871–1954, 1961; History of Broadcasting in the United Kingdom: vol. I, The Birth of Broadcasting, 1961; vol. II, The Golden Age of Wireless, 1965; vol. III, The War of Words, 1970; Vol. IV, Sound and Vision, 1979; Victorian Cities, 1963; William Cobbett, 1967; How They Lived, 1700–1815, 1969; (ed) The Nineteenth Century, 1970; (ed with Susan Briggs) Cap and Bell: Punch's Chronicle of English History in the Making 1841–1861, 1973; (ed) Essays in the History of Publishing, 1974; Iron Bridge to Crystal Palace: impact and images of the Industrial Revolution, 1979; Governing the BBC, 1979; The Power of Steam, 1982; Marx in London, 1982; A Social History of England, 1983; Toynbee Hall, 1984; Collected Essays, 2 vols, 1985; The BBC: the first fifty years, 1985; (with Joanna Spicer) The Franchise Affair, 1986. *Recreation*: travelling. *Address*: The Provost's Lodgings, Worcester College, Oxford; (private) The Caprons, Keere Street, Lewes, Sussex. *Club*: Beefsteak.

BRIGGS, Sir Geoffrey (Gould), Kt 1974; President: Pensions Appeal Tribunals for England and Wales, since 1980; Brunei Court of Appeal, since 1979; Justice of Appeal, Court of Appeal of Gibraltar, since 1983; *b* 6 May 1914; 2nd *s* of late Reverend C. E. and Mrs Briggs, Amersham, Buckinghamshire; unmarried. *Educ*: Sherborne; Christ Church, Oxford (BA, BCL; MA 1984). Called to Bar (Gray's Inn), 1938; served War of 1939–45, County of London Yeomanry (Major). Attorney-General, E Region, Nigeria, 1954–58; QC (Nigeria), 1955; Puisne Judge, Sarawak, N Borneo and Brunei, 1958–62; Chief Justice of the Western Pacific, 1962–65; a Puisne Judge, Hong Kong, 1965–73; Chief Justice: Hong Kong, 1973–79; Brunei, 1973–79. DSNB 1974. FRSA 1984. *Address*: 1 Farley Court, Melbury Road, Kensington, W14 8LJ. *Club*: Athenæum.

BRIGGS, Rt. Rev. George Cardell, CMG 1980; *b* Latchford, Warrington, Cheshire, 6 Sept. 1910; *s* of George Cecil and Mary Theodora Briggs; unmarried. *Educ*: Worksop Coll., Notts; Sidney Sussex Coll., Cambridge (MA); Cuddesdon Theological Coll. Deacon 1934; priest 1935; Curate of St Alban's, Stockport, 1934–37; Missionary priest, Diocese of Masasi, Tanzania, 1937; Archdeacon of Newala and Canon of Masasi, 1955–64; Rector of St Alban's, Dar-es-Salaam, 1964–69; Warden of St Cyprian's Theological Coll., Masasi, 1969–73; Bishop of Seychelles, 1973–79; Asst Bishop, Diocese of Derby, and Assistant Priest, parish of St Giles, Matlock, 1979–80. *Recreations*: walking, reading, music. *Address*: PO Box 162, Mtwara, Tanzania. *Club*: Royal Commonwealth Society.

BRIGGS, John; see Briggs, Peter J.

BRIGGS, (Peter) John; a Recorder of the Crown Court, since 1978; *b* 15 May 1928; *s* of late Percy Briggs and of Annie M. Folker; *m* 1956, Sheila Phyllis Walton; one *s* three *d*. *Educ*: King's Sch., Peterborough; Balliol Coll., Oxford. MA, BCL. Called to the Bar, Inner Temple, 1953. Legal Member, Mersey Mental Health Review Tribunal, 1969 (Dep. Chm., 1971, Chm., 1981); Pres., Merseyside Medico-Legal Soc., 1982–84. *Recreations*: badminton, music. *Address*: Park Lodge, 107 Tarbock Road, Huyton, Merseyside L36 5TD. *T*: 051–489 2664.

BRIGGS, Raymond Redvers, DFA; FSIAD; freelance illustrator, since 1957; author, since 1961; *b* 18 Jan. 1934; *s* of Ernest Redvers Briggs and Ethel Bowyer; *m* 1963, Jean Taprell Clark (*d* 1973). *Educ*: Rutlish Sch., Merton; Wimbledon School of Art; Slade School of Fine Art. NDD; DFA London. Part-time Lecturer in Illustration, Faculty of Art,

Brighton Polytechnic, 1961–. *Publications*: The Strange House, 1961; Midnight Adventure, 1961; Ring-A-Ring O'Roses, 1962; Sledges to the Rescue, 1963; The White Land, 1963; Fee Fi Fo Fum, 1964; The Mother Goose Treasury, 1966 (Kate Greenaway Medal, 1966); Jim and the Beanstalk, 1970; The Fairy Tale Treasury, 1972; Father Christmas, 1973 (Kate Greenaway Medal, 1973); Father Christmas Goes On Holiday, 1975; Fungus The Bogeyman, 1977; The Snowman, 1978; Gentleman Jim, 1980 (play, Nottingham Playhouse, 1985); When the Wind Blows, 1982 (play, BBC Radio and Whitehall Th., 1983; text publd 1983; cassette 1984); Fungus the Bogeyman Plop-Up Book, 1982; The Tin-Pot Foreign General and the Old Iron Woman, 1984; The Snowman Pop-Up, 1986. *Recreations*: gardening, reading, walking, second-hand bookshops. *Address*: Weston, Underhill Lane, Westmeston, Hassocks, Sussex BN6 8XG. *Club*: Groucho.

BRIGGS, Rear-Admiral Thomas Vallack, CB 1958; OBE (mil.) 1945; a Vice-Patron, Royal Naval Association (President, 1971–76); *b* 6 April 1906; *e s* of late Admiral Sir Charles John Briggs, and Lady Briggs (*née* Wilson); *m* 1947, Estelle Burland Willing, Boston, USA; one step *s*. *Educ*: The Grange, Stevenage, Herts; Imperial Service College, Windsor. Joined Royal Navy 1924; served HMS Thunderer, Hood, Wishart, Antelope, Wolsey, Nelson, Excellent, and Faulkner, 1924–37; Advanced Gunnery Specialist; served War of 1939–45: HMS Ark Royal, 1939–40; AA Comdr HMS Excellent, 1941–42; HMS Newcastle, 1943–44; staff of Flag Officer 2nd in Command, Eastern Fleet, 1944–45 (despatches twice); HMS Comus, 1945–46; US Naval War Coll., Newport, RI, 1946–47; Dep. Dir. of Naval Ordnance (G), 1947–49; commanded 5th Destroyer Flotilla, HMS Solebay, 1949–50, and HMS Cumberland, 1953–54; IDC, 1951; Chief of Staff: Plymouth, 1952–53, Home Fleet and Eastern Atlantic, 1956–57; Rear-Adm. 1956; Asst Controller of the Navy, 1958, retired. Director: Hugh Stevenson & Sons Ltd, 1958–69; Hugh Stevenson & Sons (North East) Ltd, 1964; Bowater-Stevenson Containers Ltd, 1969–71; Free-Stay Holidays Ltd, 1971; Internat. Consumer Incentives Ltd, 1974–83; Meru Group Ltd, 1978–83. Vice-Chm., City of Westminster Soc. for Mentally Handicapped Children, 1969; Mem., Management Cttee, Haileybury and ISC Junior Sch., Windsor, 1959–80 (Chm., 1978–80); Life Governor, Haileybury and Imperial Service Coll., 1959 (Mem. Council, 1959–80); Pres., Haileybury Soc., 1973–74. Fellow, Inst. of Marketing, 1970–83. Chm., Aldeburgh Festival Club, 1979–80. DL Greater London, 1970–82 (Representative DL, Kingston upon Thames, 1970–79). *Address*: 29 Twin Bridge Road, Madison, Conn 06443, USA. *Recreations*: golf, shooting. *Clubs*: White's; RN Golfing Society, Aldeburgh Golf (Captain, 1981–82); RN Sailing Association; RN Ski; Madison Winter.

BRIGHT, Graham Frank James, MP (C) Luton South, since 1983 (Luton East, 1979–83); *b* 2 April 1942; *s* of Robert Frank Bright and Agnes Mary (*née* Graham); *m* 1972, Valerie Woolliams; one *s*. *Educ*: Hassenbrook County Sch.; Thurrock Technical Coll. Marketing Exec., Pauls & White Ltd, 1958–70; Man. Dir, 1970–, and Chm., 1977–, Dietary Foods Ltd. PPS to Ministers of State, Home Office, 1984–. Jt Sec. to Parly Aviation Gp, 1984–; Chm., Cons. Backbench Smaller Businesses Cttee, 1983–84 (Vice-Chm., 1980); Vice-Chm., Cons. Backbench Food and Drink Sub-Cttee, 1983 (Sec., 1982); former Vice-Chm., Backbench Aviation Cttee; former Sec., Space Sub-Cttee; Mem. Select Cttee on House of Commons Services, 1982–84. Introduced Private Member's Bill (Video Recordings Act), 1984. Member: Thurrock Bor. Council, 1965–79; Essex CC, 1967–70. Contested: Thurrock, 1970 and Feb. 1974; Dartford, Oct. 1974; Chm., Eastern Area CPC, 1977–80; Mem., Nat. CPC, 1980–; Vice Chm., YC Org., 1970–72; Pres., Eastern Area YCs, 1981–. Vice Chm., Smaller Businesses Bureau, 1980–. *Recreations*: foreign travel, motoring, conservation, photography. *Address*: House of Commons, SW1A 0AA. *Club*: Carlton.

BRIGHT, Keith, PhD, CChem, FRSC, FCIT; Chairman and Chief Executive, London Regional Transport (formerly London Transport Executive), since 1982; *b* 30 Aug. 1931; *s* of Ernest William Bright and Lilian Mary Bright; *m* 1st, 1959, Patricia Anne (marr. diss.); one *s* one *d*; 2nd, 1985, Margot Joan Norman. *Educ*: University of London (BSc, PhD). Chief of Research, Passfield Research Laboratories; Supervisor and examiner for higher degrees in Univs of Lancaster, Surrey, City and London, 1961–67; Man. Dir, Formica International Ltd, 1967–73; Group Chief Exec., Sime Darby (Holdings) Ltd, 1974–77; Group Chief Exec., Associated Biscuit Manufacturers Ltd, 1977–82. Mem., British Airports Authy, 1982–85; Director: Extel Group, 1979–; London & Continental Advertising, 1979–. *Publications*: numerous papers in technical and scientific jls. *Recreations*: music, golf. *Address*: c/o London Regional Transport, 55 Broadway, SW1H 0BD.

BRIGHTLING, Peter Henry Miller; Assistant Under Secretary of State, Ministry of Defence, 1973–81; *b* 12 Sept. 1921; *o s* of late Henry Miller Brightling and Eva Emily Brightling (*née* Fry); *m* 1951, Pamela Cheeseright; two *s* two *d*. *Educ*: City of London Sch.; BSc(Econ), London. War of 1939–45: Air Ministry, 1939–40; MAP, 1940–41; served in RAF, 1941–46. Ministry of: Supply, 1946–59; Aviation, 1959–67; Technology, 1967–70; Aviation Supply, 1970–71; MoD (Procurement Executive), 1971. *Address*: 5 Selwyn Road, New Malden, Surrey KT3 5AU. *T*: 01–942 8014.

BRIGHTMAN, family name of **Baron Brightman**.

BRIGHTMAN, Baron *cr* 1982 (Life Peer), of Ibthorpe in the County of Hampshire; **John Anson Brightman;** Kt 1970; PC 1979; a Lord of Appeal in Ordinary, 1982–86; *b* 20 June 1911; 2nd *s* of William Henry Brightman, St Albans, Herts; *m* 1945, Roxane Ambatielo; one *s*. *Educ*: Marlborough College; St John's College, Cambridge (Hon. Fellow, 1982). Called to the Bar, Lincoln's Inn, 1932; Bencher 1966. QC 1961. Able Seaman, Merchant Navy, 1939–40; RNVR (Lieut-Commander), 1940–46; Assistant Naval Attaché, Ankara, 1944. Attorney-General of the Duchy of Lancaster, and Attorney and Serjeant within the County Palatine of Lancaster, 1969–70; Judge of the High Court of Justice, Chancery Div., 1970–79; a Lord Justice of Appeal, 1979–82; Judge, Nat. Industrial Relns Court, 1971–74. Chm., House of Lords Select Cttee on Charities, 1983–84. Member, General Council of the Bar, 1956–60, 1966–70. *Recreations*: sailing, ski-ing, topiary. *Address*: House of Lords, SW1.

BRIGHTY, Anthony David, CMG 1984; CVO 1985; HM Diplomatic Service; Counsellor, Lisbon, since 1983; *b* 7 Feb. 1939; *s* of C. P. J. Brighty and W. G. Turner; *m* 1st, 1963, Diana Porteous (marr. diss. 1979); two *s* two *d*; 2nd, 1982, Jane Docherty. *Educ*: Northgate Grammar Sch., Ipswich; Clare Coll., Cambridge (BA). Entered FO, 1961; Brussels, 1962–63; Havana, 1964–66; FO, 1967–69, resigned; joined S. G. Warburg & Co., 1969; reinstated in FCO, 1971; Saigon, 1973–74; UK Mission to UN, NY, 1975–78; RCDS, 1979; Head of Personnel Operations Dept, FCO, 1980–83. *Address*: c/o Foreign and Commonwealth Office, SW1.

BRIGINSHAW, family name of **Baron Briginshaw**.

BRIGINSHAW, Baron *cr* 1974 (Life Peer), of Southwark; **Richard William Briginshaw;** General Secretary, National Society of Operative Printers, Graphical and Media Personnel, 1951–75; Member, Council, Advisory, Conciliation and Arbitration Service, 1974–76; *b* Lambeth; married. *Educ*: Stuart School, London. Later studied economics, trade union and industrial law, and physical anthropology (UCL diploma course). Elected Asst Secretary, London Machine Branch of Union, 1938. Joined Services, 1940; subseq. in Army, saw service overseas in India, Iraq, Persia, Palestine, Egypt, France, etc; left Army, 1946. Returned to printing trade; re-elected to full-time trade union position, 1949. Vice-Pres. 1961–72, Mem. Exec. Council 1951–72, Printing and Kindred Trades Fedn; TUC: Mem. Gen. Council, 1965–75; Member of Finance and General Purposes, Economic, Organisation, and International Cttees; Member: BOTB, 1975–77; British Nat. Oil Corp., 1976–79. Pres. of two London Confs on World Trade Development, 1963. Member: Joint Committee on Manpower, 1965–70; Bd of Govs, Dulwich Coll., 1967–72; Court, Cranfield Inst. of Technology. Hon. LLD New Brunswick, 1968. *Publications:* (four booklets): Britain's World Rating, 1962; Britain and the World Trade Conference, 1963; Britain's World Rating, 1964; Britain's Oil, the Big Sell Out?, 1979. *Recreations:* swimming, painting, music. *Address:* House of Lords, SW1A 0PW.

BRIGSTOCKE, Mrs Heather Renwick; High Mistress of St Paul's Girls' School since 1974; *b* 2 Sept. 1929; *d* of late Sqdn-Ldr J. R. Brown, DFC and Mrs M. J. C. Brown, MA; *m* 1952, Geoffrey Brigstocke (*d* 1974); three *s* one *d*. *Educ:* Abbey Sch., Reading; Girton Coll., Cambridge (MA). Univ. Winchester Reading Prize, 1950. Classics Mistress, Francis Holland Sch., London, SW1, 1951–53; part-time Classics Mistress, Godolphin and Latymer Sch., 1954–60; part-time Latin Teacher, National Cathedral Sch., Washington, DC, 1962–64; Headmistress, Francis Holland Sch., London, NW1, 1965–74. Member: Council, London House for Overseas Graduates, 1965– (Vice-Chm., 1975–80); Council, Middlesex Hosp. Med. Sch., 1971–80; Trustee, Nat. Gall., 1975–82; Mem., Cttee, AA, 1975–; Governor, Wellington Coll., 1975–; Pres., Bishop Creighton House Settlement, Fulham, 1977–; Mem. Council, Royal Holloway Coll., 1977–85; Governor, The Royal Ballet Sch., 1977–; Mem. Council, The City Univ., 1978–83; Pres., Girls' Schools Assoc., 1980–81; Trustee, Kennedy Meml Trust, 1980–85; Governor, United World College of the Atlantic, 1980–85; Non-exec. Dir, LWT, 1982; Mem. Council, RSA, 1983–; Governor, Forest Sch., 1983–; Mem. Council, St George's House, Windsor, 1984–. *Address:* St Paul's Girls' School, Brook Green, W6 7BS.

BRILLIANT, Fredda, (Mrs Herbert Marshall); sculptor; *b* 7 April 1908; *d* of Mordechai and Raeisell Brilliant; *m* 1935, Herbert P. J. Marshall, *qv*. *Educ:* The Gymnasium (High Sch.), Lodz, Poland; Chelsea Art Sch. (drawing). Sculptor, 1932–; actress and singer, USA, 1930–33; actress and script writer in England, 1937–50. Sculptures include: Nehru, Krishna Menon, Indira Gandhi, Paul Robeson, Herbert Marshall, Mahatma Gandhi (Gandhi model now in the Queen's Collection in Reading Room of St George's, Windsor Castle, 1983), Buckminster Fuller, Carl Albert, Sir Maurice Bowra, Lord Elwyn-Jones, Sir Isaac Hayward, Tom Mann, Dr Delyte Morris. Exhibns in London include: Royal Academy, Leicester Galls, Royal Watercolour Soc., Whitechapel Gall., St Paul's Cathedral; other exhibns in Melbourne, Moscow, Bombay and Washington. Work in permanent collections: Nat. Art Gall., New Delhi; Mayakovsky Mus. and Shevchenko Mus., USSR; Southern Illinois Univ. FRSA; FIAL. Mem. Soc. of Portrait Sculptors. *Publications:* Biographies in Bronze (The Sculpture of Fredda Brilliant), 1986; Women in Power, 1986; The Black Virgin, 1986;. *short stories:* Truth in Fiction, 1986. *Recreations:* writing lyrics, composing songs and singing, attending classical concerts. *Address:* 1204 Chautauqua Street, Carbondale, Illinois 62901, USA.

BRIMACOMBE, Prof. John Stuart, FRSE, FRSC; Roscoe Professor of Chemistry, University of Dundee, since 1969; *b* Falmouth, Cornwall, 18 Aug. 1935; *s* of Stanley Poole Brimacombe and Lillian May Kathleen Brimacombe (*née* Candy); *m* 1959, Eileen (*née* Gibson); four *d*. *Educ:* Falmouth Grammar Sch.; Birmingham Univ. (DSc). DSc Dundee Univ. Lectr in Chemistry, Birmingham Univ., 1961–69. Meldola Medallist, 1964. *Publications:* (co-author) Mucopolysaccharides, 1964; numerous papers, reviews, etc, in: Jl Chem. Soc., Carbohydrate Research, etc. *Recreations:* sport, swimming. *Address:* 29 Dalhousie Road, Barnhill, Dundee. *T:* Dundee 79214.

BRIMELOW, family name of **Baron Brimelow.**

BRIMELOW, Baron *cr* 1976 (Life Peer), of Tyldesley, Lancs; **Thomas Brimelow,** GCMG 1975 (KCMG 1968; CMG 1959); OBE 1954; Chairman, Occupational Pensions Board, 1978–82; *b* 25 Oct. 1915; *s* of late William Brimelow and Hannah Smith; *m* 1945, Jean E. Cull; two *d*. *Educ:* New Mills Grammar School; Oriel College, Oxford; Hon. Fellow, 1973. Laming Travelling Fellow of the Queen's College, Oxford, 1937, Hon. Fellow, 1974. Probationer Vice-Consul, Danzig, 1938; served in Consulate, Riga, 1939 and Consulate-Gen., New York, 1940; in charge of Consular Section of Embassy, Moscow, 1942–45; Foreign Office, 1945; Foreign Service Officer, Grade 7, 1946; First Sec. (Commercial), and Consul, Havana, 1948; trans. to Moscow, 1951; Counsellor (Commercial), Ankara, 1954; Head of Northern Department of the Foreign Office, 1956; Counsellor, Washington, 1960–63; Minister, British Embassy, Moscow, 1963–66; Ambassador to Poland, 1966–69; Dep. Under-Sec. of State, FCO, 1969–73; Permanent Under-Sec. of State, FCO, and Head of the Diplomatic Service, 1973–75. Mem., European Parlt, 1977–78. *Address:* 12 West Hill Court, Millfield Lane, N6 6JJ. *Club:* Athenæum.

BRINCKMAN, Sir Theodore (George Roderick), 6th Bt *cr* 1831; publisher and antiquarian bookseller; *b* 20 March 1932; *s* of Sir Roderick Napoleon Brinckman, 5th Bt, DSO, MC, and Margaret Wilson Southam; *S* father, 1985; *m* 1st, 1958, Helen Mary Anne Cook (marr. diss. 1983); two *s* one *d*; 2nd, 1983, Hon. Greta Sheira Bernadette Murray, formerly wife of Christopher Murray, and *d* of Baron Harvington, *qv*. *Educ:* Trinity College School, Port Hope, Ontario; Millfield; Christ Church, Oxford; Trinity Coll., Toronto (BA). *Heir:* *s* Theodore Jonathan Brinckman, *b* 19 Feb. 1960. *Address:* Somerford Keynes House, Cirencester, Glos GL7 6DN. *T:* Cirencester 861526, 860554. *Clubs:* White's, Buck's; University (Toronto).

BRIND, (Arthur) Henry, CMG 1973; HM Diplomatic Service; High Commissioner to Malaŵi, since 1983; *b* 4 July 1927; *o s* of late T. H. Brind and late N. W. B. Brind; *m* 1954, Barbara Harrison; one *s* one *d*. *Educ:* Barry; St John's Coll., Cambridge. HM Forces, 1947–49. Colonial Administrative Service: Gold Coast/Ghana, 1950–60; Regional Sec., Trans-Volta Togoland, 1959. HM Diplomatic Service, 1960–: Acting High Comr, Uganda, 1972–73; High Comr, Mauritius, 1974–77; Ambassador to Somali Democratic Republic, 1977–80; Vis. Research Fellow, RIIA, 1981–82. Grand Comdr, Order of Lion of Malaŵi. *Recreations:* walking, swimming, books. *Address:* c/o Foreign and Commonwealth Office, SW1; 20 Grove Terrace, NW5 1PH. *Club:* Reform.
See also B. E. Capstick.

BRIND, George Walter Richard; Secretary-General, The Stock Exchange, 1971–75; *b* 13 Oct. 1911; *er s* of late Walter Charles and late Mary Josephine Brind; *m* 1942, Joyce, *er d* of late Matthew and Mary Graham; two *d*. *Educ:* Chiswick. Joined staff of Council of Stock Exchange, London, 1928, and has had no other employment than that with the Exchange. President: English Indoor Bowling Assoc., 1979–80; British Isles Indoor Bowling Assoc., 1983–84. *Recreation:* bowls. *Address:* 7 Amberley Close, Send, Woking, Surrey. *T:* Guildford 223762.

BRIND, Henry; *see* Brind, A. H.

BRIND, Maj.-Gen. Peter Holmes Walter; CBE 1962 (OBE 1948); DSO 1945; DL; Vice President, Surrey Branch, British Red Cross Society, since 1984 (Deputy President, 1977–84); *b* 16 Feb. 1912; *yr s* of late General Sir John Brind, KCB, KBE, CMG, DSO; *m* 1942, Patricia Stewart Walker, *er d* of late Comdr S. M. Walker, DSC, RN, Horsalls, Harrietsham, Kent; three *s*. *Educ:* Wellington College; RMC, Sandhurst. Commissioned Dorset Regt, 1932. ADC to Governor of Bengal, 1936–39; Adjt, NW Europe, 1940; GSO 3 War Office, 1940–41; DAAG, HQ 12 Corps and Canadian Corps, 1941–42; Bde Major 1942; GSO 2 (MO) War Office, 1942; Comdt, Battle School, 1944, Comdg 2 Devons, NW Europe, 1944–45, GSO 1 (MT) War Office, 1946; GSO 1 (Ops), Palestine, 1948; GSO 1 (Plans), Egypt, 1949; GSO 1 (SD), War Office, 1950–54; Bt Lt-Col, 1952; Comdg 5th KAR (Kenya), 1954; Lt-Col, 1954; Col, 1955; Comdg 5 Inf. Bde Gp (BAOR), 1956; IDC 1959; Brig., 1960; Brig., AQ Middle East, 1960; BGS Eastern Comd, 1962; ADC to the Queen, 1964; Maj.-Gen., 1965; COS, Northern Comd, 1965–67. Dir, BRCS (Surrey Branch), 1968–77. DL Surrey, 1970. *Recreations:* gardening, music. *Address:* Pine Ridge, Hill Road, Haslemere, Surrey.

BRINDLEY, Prof. Giles Skey, MA, MD; FRS 1965; FRCP; Professor of Physiology in the University of London at the Institute of Psychiatry, since 1968; Hon. Director, Medical Research Council Neurological Prostheses Unit, since 1968; Hon. Consultant Physician, Maudsley Hospital, since 1971; *b* 30 April 1926; *s* of late Arthur James Benet Skey and Dr Margaret Beatrice Marion Skey (*née* Dewhurst), later Brindley; *m* 1st, 1959, Lucy Dunk Bennell (marr. diss.); 2nd, 1964, Dr Hilary Richards; one *s* one *d*. *Educ:* Leyton County High School; Downing College, Cambridge (Hon. Fellow, 1969); London Hospital Medical College. Various jun. clin. and res. posts, 1950–54; Russian lang. abstractor, British Abstracts of Medical Sciences, 1953–56; successively Demonstrator, Lectr and Reader in physiology, Univ. of Cambridge, 1954–68; Fellow: King's Coll., Cambridge, 1959–62; Trinity Coll., Cambridge, 1963–68. Chm. of Editorial Board, Journal of Physiology, 1964–66 (Member 1959–64). Visiting Prof., Univ. of California, Berkeley, 1968. Liebrecht-Franceschetti Prize, German Ophthalmological Soc., 1971; Feldberg Prize, Feldberg Foundn, 1974. *Publications:* Physiology of the Retina and Visual Pathway, 1960, 2nd edn 1970; papers in scientific, musicological and medical journals. *Recreations:* ski-ing, orienteering, cross-country and track running (UK over-55 record holder, 3000m steeplechase), designing, making and playing various musical instruments (inventor of the logical bassoon). *Address:* 102 Ferndene Road, SE24. *T:* 01–274 2598. *Club:* Thames Hare and Hounds.

BRINK, Prof. André Philippus, DLitt; Professor of Afrikaans and Dutch Literature, Rhodes University, since 1980; *b* 29 May 1935; *s* of Daniel Brink and Aletta Wilhelmina Wolmarans; *m* 1970, Sophia Albertina Miller; one *s* one *d*; two *s* by former marr. *Educ:* Potchefstroom Univ. (MA Eng. Lit. 1958, MA Afr. Lit. 1959); Rhodes Univ. (DLitt 1975). Rhodes University: Lectr, 1961; Sen. Lectr, 1975; Associate Prof., 1977. Hon. DLitt Witwatersrand, 1985. Prix Médicis étranger, 1981; Martin Luther King Meml Prize, 1981. Chevalier de la Légion d'honneur, 1982. *Publications:* in Afrikaans: first book, 1958; over 40 titles (novels, plays, travel books, literary criticism, humour); in English: Looking on Darkness, 1974; An Instant in the Wind, 1976; Rumours of Rain, 1978; A Dry White Season, 1979; A Chain of Voices, 1982; Mapmakers (essays), 1983; The Wall of the Plague, 1984; The Ambassador, 1985. *Address:* Rhodes University, Grahamstown 6140, South Africa. *T:* 0461–23969.

BRINK, Prof. Charles Oscar, LittD Cambridge; PhD Berlin; FBA; Kennedy Professor of Latin in the University of Cambridge, 1954–74, now Kennedy Professor Emeritus; Fellow of Gonville and Caius College, since 1955; *b* 13 March 1907; *m* 1942, Daphne Hope Harvey; three *s*. *Educ:* School and University, Berlin; Travelling Scholarship, Oxford. Member of editorial staff, Thesaurus linguæ Latinæ, 1933–38; Member of editorial staff, Oxford Latin Dictionary, 1938–41; Acting Classical Tutor, Magdalen College, Oxford, 1941–45; Member of Faculty of Literæ Humaniores, Oxford, 1941–48; MA Oxford (decree, 1944); Senior Classics Master, Magdalen College School, Oxford, 1943–48; Senior Lecturer in Humanity, University of St Andrews, 1948–51; Professor of Latin, University of Liverpool, 1951–54; MA Cambridge (BIII 6), 1954. Member Inst. for Advanced Study, Princeton, US, 1960–61, 1966. De Carle Lecturer, University of Otago, NZ, 1965; Vis. Prof., Univ. of Bonn, 1970; Professore Ospite Linceo, Scuola Normale Superiore, Pisa, 1977; James C. Loeb Lectr, Harvard Univ., 1978. Hon. Member, Jt Assoc. of Classical Teachers (Pres. 1969–71). Chm., Classics Committee, Schools Council, 1965–69; Trustee, Robinson Coll., Cambridge, 1973–85 (Chm., 1975–85; Hon. Fellow, 1985). Vice-Pres., Internat. Cttee, Thesaurus Linguæ Latinæ, 1979–. Corresp. Mem., Bayerische Akad. der Wissenschaften, Munich, 1972–. Founding Jt Editor, Cambridge Classical Texts and Commentaries, 1963–. *Publications:* Imagination and Imitation (Inaug. Lect., Liverpool, 1952), 1953; Latin Studies and the Humanities (Inaug. Lect., Cambridge, 1956), 1957; On reading a Horatian Satire, 1965; Horace on Poetry: vol. I, Prolegomena, 1963; vol. II, The Ars Poetica, 1971; vol III, Epistles Book II, 1982; Studi classici e critica testuale in Inghilterra (Pisa), 1978; English Classical Scholarship: historical reflections on Bentley, Porson, and Housman, 1986; papers on Latin and Greek subjects. *Address:* Gonville and Caius College, Cambridge.

BRINK, David Maurice, DPhil; FRS 1981; Fellow and Tutor, Balliol College, Oxford, since 1958; University Lecturer, Oxford, since 1958; *b* 20 July 1930; *s* of Maurice Ossian Brink and Victoria May Finlayson; *m* 1958, Verena Wehrli; one *s* two *d*. *Educ:* Friends' Sch., Hobart; Univ. of Tasmania (BSc); Univ. of Oxford (DPhil). Rhodes Scholar, 1951–54; Rutherford Scholar, 1954–58; Lecturer, Balliol Coll., Oxford, 1954–58. Instructor, MIT, 1956–57. Rutherford Medal and Prize, Inst. of Physics, 1982. *Publications:* Angular Momentum, 1962, 2nd edn 1968; Nuclear Forces, 1965; Semi-classical Methods in Nucleus–Nucleus Scattering, 1985. *Recreations:* birdwatching, mountaineering. *Address:* 21 Northmoor Road, Oxford OX2 6UW. *T:* Oxford 513613.

BRINKWORTH, George Harold, CBE 1960; Legal Adviser and Solicitor to Pay Board, 1973–74; *b* 16 Nov. 1906; *yr s* of George Alban Brinkworth and Hana Mary Brinkworth; *m* 1935, Dorothy Betty Suffield; one *s* one *d*. *Educ:* Wimbledon College; University College, London. LLB (Lond.) 1927. Admitted Solicitor, 1931. Entered Solicitor's Dept, Ministry of Labour, 1935; transf. to Ministry of Nat. Insce, 1945; Asst Solicitor, Min. of Pensions and Nat. Insce, 1948; Principal Asst Sol., DHSS (formerly Min. of Social Security), 1965–71. *Address:* 22 Stevens Parade, Black Rock, Victoria 3193, Australia. *T:* Melbourne 598–6556.

BRINTON, Timothy Denis; MP (C) Gravesham, since 1983 (Gravesend, 1979–83); broadcasting consultant; *b* 24 Dec. 1929; *s* of late Dr Denis Hubert Brinton; *m* 1st, 1954, Jane Mari Coningham; one *s* three *d*; 2nd, 1965, Jeanne Frances Wedge; two *d*. *Educ:* Summer Fields, Oxford; Eton Coll., Windsor; Geneva Univ.; Central Sch. of Speech and Drama. BBC staff, 1951–59; ITN, 1959–62; freelance, 1962–. Member: Kent CC, 1974–81; Court, Univ. of London, 1978–; Med. Sch. Council, St Mary's Hosp., Paddington, 1983–. *Address:* c/o House of Commons, SW1A 0AA. *T:* 01–219 5038. *Club:* Carlton.

BRISBANE, Archbishop of, and Metropolitan of the Province of Queensland, since 1980; also **Primate of Australia,** since 1982; **Most Rev. John Basil Rowland**

Grindrod, KBE 1983; *b* 14 Dec. 1919; *s* of Edward Basil and Dorothy Gladys Grindrod; *m* 1949, Ailsa W. (*d* 1981), *d* of G. Newman; two *d*; *m* 1983, Mrs Dell Cornish, *d* of S. J. Caswell. *Educ:* Repton School; Queen's College, Oxford; Lincoln Theological College. BA 1949; MA 1953. Deacon, 1951; Priest, 1952, Manchester. Curate: St Michael's, Hulme, 1951–54; Bundaberg, Qld, 1954–56; Rector: All Souls, Ancoats, Manchester, 1956–60; Emerald, Qld, 1960–61; St Barnabas, N Rockhampton, Qld, 1961–65; Archdeacon of Rockhampton, Qld, 1960–65; Vicar, Christ Church, S Yarra, Vic, 1965–66; Bishop of Riverina, NSW, 1966–71; Bishop of Rockhampton, 1971–80. *Address:* Bishopsbourne, 39 Eldernell Avenue, Hamilton, Qld 4007, Australia.

BRISBANE, Archbishop of, (RC), since 1973; **Most Rev. Francis Roberts Rush,** DD; *b* 11 Sept. 1916; *s* of T. J. Rush. *Educ:* Christian Brothers' Coll., Townsville; Mt Carmel, Charters Towers; St Columba's Coll., Springwood; Coll. de Propaganda Fide, Rome. Assistant Priest, Townsville, Mundingburra and Ingham; Parish Priest, Abergowrie and Ingham; Bishop of Rockhampton, 1960–73. *Address:* Wynberg, 790 Brunswick Street, New Farm, Queensland 4005, Australia.

BRISBANE, Assistant Bishop of; *see* Wicks, Rt Rev. R. E.

BRISCO, Sir Donald Gilfrid, 8th Bt *cr* 1782; JP; *b* 15 Sept. 1920; *s* of Sir Hylton (Musgrave Campbell) Brisco, 7th Bt and Kathleen (*d* 1982), *d* of W. Fenwick McAllum, New Zealand; *S* father, 1968; *m* 1945, Irene, *o d* of Henry John Gage, Ermine Park, Brockworth, Gloucestershire; three *d*. Served War of 1939–45 with Royal New Zealand Air Force and Royal Air Force (prisoner of war in Germany and Italy). Retired Farmer. JP Hawke's Bay, 1967. *Heir: uncle* Oriel Arthur Brisco [*b* 6 June 1892; *m* 1921, Lilian Frederica, *d* of E. E. D. Saunderson, Christchurch, NZ; *m* 1960, Sarah Louise, RRC (*d* 1971), *d* of R. O. Clark, Auckland, NZ]. *Address:* 27a Chambers Street, PO Box 165, Havelock North, Hawke's Bay, New Zealand.

BRISCOE, Sir John (Leigh Charlton), 4th Bt *cr* 1910; DFC 1945; *b* 3 Dec. 1911; *er s* of Sir Charlton Briscoe, 3rd Bt, MD, FRCP, and Grace Maud (*d* 1973) *d* of late Rev. W. S. Stagg; *S* father 1960; *m* 1948, Teresa Mary Violet, OBE 1972, *d* of late Brig.-Gen. Sir Archibald Home, KCVO, CB, CMG, DSO; two *s* one *d*. *Educ:* Harrow; Magdalen College, Oxford, BA 1933; ACA 1937; MA 1949. Served War of 1939–45 (DFC); RAFVR, 1942–46; Director of Aerodromes, Ministry of Aviation, 1961–66; Dir of Operations, British Airports Authy, 1966–72. *Recreations:* old cars, castles, and carpets. *Heir: s* John James Briscoe, [*b* 15 July 1951; *m* 1985, Felicity M., *e d* of D. M. Watkinson]. *Address:* Little Acres, Grays Park Road, Stoke Poges, Bucks. *T:* Farnham Common 2394. *Club:* Royal Air Force.

BRISE; *see* Ruggles-Brise.

BRISON, Ven. William Stanley; Archdeacon of Bolton, since 1985; *b* 20 Nov. 1929; *s* of William P. Brison and Marion A. Wilber; *m* 1951, Marguerite Adelia Nettleton; two *s* two *d*. *Educ:* Alfred Univ., New York (BS Eng); Berkeley Divinity School, New Haven, Conn (STM, MDiv). United States Marine Corps, Captain (Reserve), 1951–53. Engineer, Norton Co., Worcester, Mass, 1953–54. Vicar, then Rector, Christ Church, Bethany, Conn, 1957–69; Archdeacon of New Haven, Conn, 1967–69; Rector, Emmanuel Episcopal Church, Stamford, Conn, 1969–72; Vicar, Christ Church, Davyhulme, Manchester, 1972–81; Rector, All Saints', Newton Heath, Manchester, 1981–85; Area Dean of North Manchester, 1981–85. *Recreations:* squash, jogging, hiking. *Address:* 52 Manchester Road, Swinton, Manchester M27 1ET. *T:* 061-794 8235.

BRISTER, William Arthur Francis, CB 1984; Deputy Director General of Prison Service, 1982–85; *b* 10 Feb. 1925; *s* of Arthur John Brister and Velda Mirandoli; *m* 1949, Mary Speakman; one *s* one *d* (and one *s* decd). *Educ:* Douai Sch.; Brasenose Coll., Oxford (MA 1949). Asst Governor Cl. II, HM Borstal, Lowdham Grange, 1949–52; Asst Principal, Imperial Trng Sch., Wakefield, 1952–55; Asst Governor II, HM Prison, Parkhurst, 1955–57; Dep. Governor, HM Prison: Camp Hill, 1957–60; Manchester, 1960–62; Governor, HM Borstal: Morton Hall, 1962–67; Dover, 1967–69; Governor II, Prison Dept HQ, 1969–71; Governor, HM Remand Centre, Ashford, 1971–73; Governor I, Prison Dept HQ, 1973–75, Asst Controller, 1975–79; Chief Inspector of the Prison Service, 1979–81; HM Dep. Chief Inspector of Prisons, 1981–82. Nuffield Travelling Fellow, Canada and Mexico, 1966–67. *Recreations:* shooting, music, Venetian history. *Clubs:* United Oxford & Cambridge University, English-Speaking Union.

BRISTOL, 7th Marquess of, *cr* 1826; **Frederick William John Augustus Hervey;** Baron Hervey of Ickworth, 1703; Earl of Bristol, 1714; Earl Jermyn, 1826; Hereditary High Steward of the Liberty of St Edmund; Governing Partner, Jermyn Shipping; Director, Estate Associates Ltd; *b* 15 Sept. 1954; *s* of 6th Marquess of Bristol and Pauline Mary, *d* of Herbert Coxon Bolton; *S* father, 1985; *m* 1984, Francesca, *d* of Douglas Fisher. *Educ:* Harrow; Neuchâtel Univ. MInstD. *Heir:* half-*b* Lord Frederick William Charles Nicholas Wentworth Hervey, *b* 26 Nov. 1961. *Address:* Ickworth, Bury St Edmunds, Suffolk. *Clubs:* House of Lords Yacht, Royal Thames Yacht; Travellers' (Paris); Monte Carlo Country.

BRISTOL, Bishop of, since 1985; **Rt. Rev. Barry Rogerson;** *b* 25 July 1936; *s* of Eric and Olive Rogerson; *m* 1961, Olga May Gibson; two *d*. *Educ:* Magnus Grammar School; Leeds Univ. (BA Theology). Midland Bank Ltd, 1952–57; Leeds Univ. and Wells Theol Coll., 1957–62; Curate: St Hilda's, South Shields, 1962–65; St Nicholas', Bishopwearmouth,. Sunderland, 1965–67; Lecturer, Lichfield Theological Coll., 1967–71, Vice-Principal, 1971–72; Lectr, Salisbury and Wells Theol Coll., 1972–75; Vicar, St Thomas', Wednesfield, 1975–79; Team Rector, Wednesfield Team Ministry, 1979; Bishop Suffragon of Wolverhampton, 1979–85. *Recreations:* cinema and stained glass windows. *Address:* Bishop's House, Clifton Hill, Bristol BS8 1BW.

BRISTOL, Dean of; *see* Dammers, Very Rev. A. H.

BRISTOL, Archdeacon of; *see* Balmforth, Ven. A. J.

BRISTOW, Alan Edgar, OBE 1966; Chairman, Bristow Helicopter Group Ltd, 1967–85; *b* 3 Sept. 1923; *m* 1945; one *s* one *d*. *Educ:* Portsmouth Grammar School. Cadet, British India Steam Navigation Co., 1939–43; Pilot, Fleet Air Arm, 1943–46; Test Pilot, Westland Aircraft Ltd, 1946–49; Helicopair, Paris/Indo-China, 1949–51; Man. Dir, Air Whaling Ltd (Antarctic Whaling Expedns), 1951–54; Man. Dir, Bristow Helicopters Ltd, 1954–68; Dir, British United Airways Ltd, 1960–70, Man. Dir 1967–70. Cierva Memorial Lectr, RAeS, 1967. FRAeS 1967. Croix de Guerre (France), 1950. *Publications:* papers to RAeS. *Recreations:* flying, shooting, sailing, farming, four-in-hand driving. *Address:* Baynards Park Estate, Cranleigh, Surrey. *T:* Cranleigh 274674.

BRISTOW, Hon. Sir Peter (Henry Rowley), Kt 1970; a Judge of the High Court, Queen's Bench Division, 1970–85; *b* 1 June 1913; *s* of Walter Rowley Bristow, FRCS and Florence (*née* White); *m* 1st, 1940, Josephine Noel Leney (*d* 1969); one *s* one *d*; 2nd, 1975, Elsa, *widow* of H. B. Leney. *Educ:* Eton; Trinity College, Cambridge. Pilot, RAFVR, 1936–45. Called to the Bar, Middle Temple, 1936, Bencher 1961, Treasurer 1977; QC 1964; Mem., Inns of Court Senate, 1966–70 (Hon. Treas., 1967–70); Judge, Court of Appeal, Guernsey, and Court of Appeal, Jersey, 1965–70; Dep. Chm., Hants QS, 1964–71; Judge of the Commercial Court and Employment Appeals Tribunal, 1976–78; Vice-Chm., Parole Bd, 1977–78 (Mem. 1976); Presiding Judge, Western Circuit, 1979–82. *Recreations:* sailing, fishing, shooting, gardening. *Address:* The Folly, Membury, Axminster, Devon.

BRITISH COLUMBIA, Metropolitan of Ecclesiastical Province of; *see* New Westminster, Archbishop of.

BRITISH COLUMBIA, Bishop of, since 1985; **Rt. Rev. Ronald Francis Shepherd;** *b* 15 July 1926; *s* of Herbert George Shepherd and Muriel Shepherd (*née* Grant); *m* 1952, Ann Alayne Dundas, *d* of Rt Hon. R. S. Dundas; four *s* two *d*. *Educ:* Univ. of British Columbia (BA Hons 1948); King's Coll., London (AKC 1952). Fellow, Coll. of Preachers, Washington, DC, 1972. Curate, St Stephen's, Rochester Row, London SW, 1952–57; Rector: St Paul's, Glanford, Ont, 1957–59; All Saints, Winnipeg, 1959–65; Dean and Rector: All Saints Cathedral, Edmonton, 1965–69; Christ Church Cathedral, Montreal, 1970–83; Rector, St Matthias, Victoria, 1983–84. *Recreations:* reading, gardening, walking. *Address:* 1256 Beach Drive, Victoria, BC V8S 2N3, Canada. *T:* 604-598 7882. *Club:* Union of British Columbia (Victoria).

BRITTAN, Rt. Hon. Leon, PC 1981; QC 1978; MP (C) Richmond, Yorks, since 1983 (Cleveland and Whitby, Feb. 1974–1983); *b* 25 Sept. 1939; *s* of late Dr Joseph Brittan and Mrs Rebecca Brittan; *m* 1980, Diana Peterson. *Educ:* Haberdashers' Aske's Sch.; Trinity Coll., Cambridge (MA); Yale Univ. (Henry Fellow). Chm., Cambridge Univ. Conservative Assoc., 1960; Pres., Cambridge Union, 1960; debating tour of USA for Cambridge Union, 1961. Called to Bar, Inner Temple, 1962; Bencher, 1983. Chm., Bow Group, 1964–65; contested (C) North Kensington, 1966 and 1970. Editor, Crossbow, 1966–68; formerly Mem. Political Cttee, Carlton Club; Vice-Chm. of Governors, Isaac Newton Sch., 1968–71; Mem. European North American Cttee, 1970–78; Vice-Chm., Nat. Assoc. of School Governors and Managers, 1970–78; Vice-Chm., Parly Cons. Party Employment Cttee, 1974–76; opposition front bench spokesman on Devolution, 1976–79, on employment, 1978–79; Minister of State, Home Office, 1979–81; Chief Sec. to the Treasury, 1981–83; Sec. of State for Home Dept, 1983–85; Sec. of State for Trade and Industry, 1985–86. *Publications:* (contrib.) The Conservative Opportunity; (jtly) Millstones for the Sixties, Rough Justice, Infancy and the Law, How to Save Your Schools (pamphlets). *Recreations:* opera, art, cricket, walking. *Address:* House of Commons, SW1A 0AA. *Clubs:* Carlton, MCC.

See also Samuel Brittan.

BRITTAN, Samuel; Principal Economic Commentator, since 1966, and Assistant Editor, since 1978, Financial Times; *b* 29 Dec. 1933; *s* of late Joseph Brittan, MD, and of Rebecca Brittan (*née* Lipetz). *Educ:* Kilburn Grammar Sch.; Jesus Coll., Cambridge. 1st Class in Economics, 1955; MA Cantab. Various posts in Financial Times, 1955–61; Economics Editor, Observer, 1961–64; Adviser, DEA, 1965. Fellow, Nuffield Coll., Oxford, 1973–74, Vis. Fellow, 1974–82; Vis. Prof. of Economics, Chicago Law Sch., 1978. Mem., Peacock Cttee on Financing the BBC, 1985–86. Hon. DLitt Heriot-Watt, 1985. Financial Journalist of the Year Award 1971; George Orwell Prize (for political journalism), 1980. *Publications:* The Treasury under the Tories, 1964, rev. edn, Steering the Economy, 1969, 1971; Left or Right: The Bogus Dilemma, 1968; The Price of Economic Freedom, 1970; Capitalism and the Permissive Society, 1973; Is There an Economic Consensus?, 1973; (with P. Lilley) The Delusion of Incomes Policy, 1977; The Economic Consequences of Democracy, 1977; How to End the Monetarist Controversy, 1981; The Role and Limits of Government, 1983; articles in various jls. *Address:* c/o Financial Times, Bracken House, Cannon Street, EC4P 4BY.

See also Rt Hon. Leon Brittan.

BRITTEN, Brig. George Vallette, CBE 1947 (OBE 1942, MBE 1940); HM Diplomatic Service, retired; *b* 19 March 1909; *s* of John Britten, Bozeat Manor, Northamptonshire, and Elizabeth Franziska Britten (*née* Vallette); *m* 1937, Shirley Jean Stewart Wink; three *s*. *Educ:* Wellingborough; RMC Sandhurst. Regtl duty in UK, 1929–38; Staff Coll., Camberley, 1938–39. Served War: HQ 2 Corps, France and Belgium, 1939–40; Staff appts in UK, 1940–41; with 1st Airborne Div. in UK, N Africa and Sicily, 1942–43; DCS, 5(US) Army, N Africa and Italy, 1943–44; HQ, 21st Army Gp, NW Europe, 1944–45. DCS, Brit. Military Govt, Germany, 1945–47. Regtl Duty, Berlin and Austria, 1947–49; WO, 1949–51; Comdt, Sch. of Infty, Hythe, 1952–54; Instr, US Army Staff Coll., Kansas, 1954–56; Planning Staff, NATO, Fontainebleau, 1956–58; Mil. Attaché, Brit. Embassy, Bonn, 1958–61; retired from Army, 1961; Ghana Desk, Commonwealth Office, 1961–62; with British High Commissions, Enugu, Kaduna, and Bathurst, 1962–66; Head of Chancery, British Embassy, Berne, 1967–71. American Legion of Merit, 1946; W German Grosses Verdienst Kreuz, 1959. *Recreation:* gardening. *Address:* 41 Bosville Drive, Sevenoaks, Kent.

BRITTEN, Rae Gordon, CMG 1972; HM Diplomatic Service, retired; *b* 27 Sept. 1920; *s* of Leonard Arthur Britten and Elizabeth Percival Taylor; *m* 1952, Valentine Alms (marr. diss. 1974); one *s* three *d*; *m* 1977, Mrs Joan Dorothy Bull. *Educ:* Liverpool Institute High School; Magdalen College, Oxford. Served War 1941–45 (artillery and infantry). Research Assistant with Common Ground Ltd, 1947; apptd Commonwealth Relations Office, 1948; 2nd Sec., Brit. High Commn in India (Calcutta, 1948–49, Delhi, 1949–50): 1st Sec. Brit. High Commn., Bombay, 1955–58, Karachi, 1961–62; Deputy High Commissioner: Peshawar, March 1962; Lahore, June 1962–July 1964; Kingston, Jamaica, 1964–68; Head of Trade Policy Dept, FCO, 1968–71; Dep. High Comr, Dacca, 1971–72; Counsellor and Head of Chancery, Oslo, 1973–76; Head of SW Pacific Dept, FCO, 1976–78; Counsellor on Special Duties, FCO, 1978–80. *Address:* 4 Albany Crescent, Claygate, Esher, Surrey. *Club:* Royal Commonwealth Society.

BRITTEN, Maj.-Gen. Robert Wallace Tudor, CB 1977; MC; *b* 28 Feb. 1922; *s* of Lt-Col Wallace Ernest Britten, OBE; *m* 1947, Elizabeth Mary, *d* of Edward H. Davies, Pentre, Rhondda; one *s* one *d*. *Educ:* Wellington Coll.; Trinity Coll., Cambridge. CBIM; CompICE. 2nd Lieut RE, 1941; served War of 1939–45, Madras Sappers and Miners, 19th Indian Div., India and Burma; Comdr 21 Fd Pk Sqn and 5 Fd Sqn RE, 1947–50; on staff WO, 1951–53; British Liaison Officer to US Corps of Engrs, 1953–56; comd 50 Fd Sqn RE, 1956–58; on staff WO, 1958–61; on staff of 1 (BR) Corps BAOR, 1961–64; Lt-Col in comd 1 Trg Regt RE, 1964–65; GSO1 (DS), Jt Services Staff Coll., 1965–67; Comd 30 Engr Bde (V) and Chief Engr Western Comd, 1967; idc 1969; Dir of Equipment Management, MoD (Army), 1970–71; DQMG, 1971–73; GOC West Midland Dist, 1973–76, retired. Brig. 1967; Maj.-Gen. 1971. Col Comdt, RE, 1977–82. Chm., RE Assoc., 1978–83. Hon. Col, Birmingham Univ. OTC, 1978–. Defence Consultant, Taylor Woodrow Ltd; Chm., IR Management Ltd; Dir, R and E Co-ordination Ltd. *Recreations:* bridge building, fishing, dowsing (Vice Pres., Brit. Soc. Dowsers). *T:* Haslemere 2261. *Club:* Army and Navy

BRITTENDEN, (Charles) Arthur; Director of Corporate Relations, News International, since 1981; General Manager (Editorial), Times Newspapers, since 1982; Member, Press Council, since 1982, Joint Vice-Chairman, since 1983; *b* 23 Oct. 1924; *o s* of late Tom

Edwin Brittenden and Caroline (*née* Scrivener); *m* 1st, 1953, Sylvia Penelope Cadman (marr. diss., 1960); 2nd, 1966, Ann Patricia Kenny (marr. diss. 1972); 3rd, 1975, Valerie Arnison. *Educ:* Leeds Grammar School. Served in Reconnaissance Corps, 1943–46. Yorkshire Post, 1940–43, 1946–49; News Chronicle, 1949–55; joined Sunday Express, 1955: Foreign Editor, 1959–62; Northern Editor, Daily Express, 1962–63; Dep. Editor, Sunday Express, 1963–64; Exec. Editor, 1964–66, Editor, 1966–71, Daily Mail; Dep. Editor, The Sun, 1972–81. Dir, Harmsworth Publications Ltd, 1967–71. Man. Dir, Wigmore Cassettes, 1971–72. Dir, Times Newspapers Ltd, 1982–. *Address:* 22 Park Street, Woodstock, Oxon.

BRITTON, Andrew James Christie; Director, National Institute of Economic and Social Research, since 1982; *b* 1 Dec. 1940; *s* of late Prof. Karl William Britton and Sheila Margaret Christie; *m* 1963, Pamela Anne, *d* of His Honour Edward Sutcliffe, *qv*; three *d*. *Educ:* Royal Grammar Sch., Newcastle upon Tyne; Oriel Coll., Oxford (BA); LSE (MSc). Joined HM Treasury as Cadet Economist, 1966; Econ. Asst, 1968; Econ. Adviser, 1970; Sen. Econ. Adviser: DHSS, 1973; HM Treasury, 1975; London Business Sch., 1978–79; Under Sec., HM Treasury, 1980–82. *Publications:* (ed) Employment, Output and Inflation, 1983; The Trade Cycle in Britain, 1986. *Address:* 15 Hawthorn Road, Wallington, Surrey SM6 0SY. *Club:* United Oxford & Cambridge University.

BRITTON, Prof. Denis King, CBE 1978; Professor of Agricultural Economics at Wye College, 1970–83, now Emeritus Professor; Hon. Fellow, Wye College, 1986; *b* 25 March 1920; *s* of Rev. George Charles Britton and Harriet Rosa (*née* Swinstead); *m* 1942, Margaret Alice Smith; one *s* two *d*. *Educ:* Caterham School; London School of Economics, London University (BSc (Econ.)). Asst Statistician, Ministry of Agriculture and Fisheries, 1943–47; Lecturing and Research at University of Oxford, Agricultural Economics Res. Inst., 1947–52; MA Oxon 1948 (by decree); Economist, United Nations Food and Agriculture Organisation, Geneva, 1952–59; Gen. Manager, Marketing and Economic Res., Massey-Ferguson (UK) Ltd, 1959–61; Prof. of Agricultural Economics, Univ. of Nottingham, 1961–70; Dean, Faculty of Agriculture and Horticulture, Univ. of Nottingham, 1967–70. Member: EDC for Agriculture, 1966–83; Home Grown Cereals Authority, 1969–; Adv. Council for Agriculture and Horticulture, 1973–80; MAFF Gp to review Eggs Authority, 1985; Chairman: Council, Centre for European Agricl Studies, Wye Coll., 1974–79; Adv. Cttee, Nuffield Centre for Agric. Strategy, 1975–80; Forestry Commn Rev. Gp on Integration of Farming and Forestry, 1983–84; President: Internat. Assoc. of Agric. Economists, 1976–79; British Agric. Economics Soc., 1977–78; Special Adviser, House of Commons Select Cttee on Agric., 1980–83. Vis. Prof., Uppsala, 1973; Winegarten Lecture, NFU, 1981. Farmers' Club Cup, 1966. FSS 1943; FRAgS 1970; FRASE 1980. Hon. DAgric, Univ. of Bonn, 1975; Hon. DEcon, Univ. of Padua, 1982. *Publications:* Cereals in the United Kingdom, 1969; (with Berkeley Hill) Size and Efficiency in Farming, 1975; articles in Jl of Royal Statistical Society, Jl of Agricultural Economics, Jl of RSA, Farm Economist, etc. *Recreations:* music, golf, micro-computing. *Address:* 29 Chequers Park, Wye, Ashford, Kent.

BRITTON, Sir Edward (Louis), Kt 1975; CBE 1967; General Secretary, National Union of Teachers, 1970–75; retired; *b* 4 Dec. 1909; *s* of George Edwin and Ellen Alice Britton; *m* 1936, Nora Arnald; no *c*. *Educ:* Bromley Grammar School, Kent; Trinity College, Cambridge. Teacher in various Surrey schools until 1951; Headmaster, Warlingham County Secondary School, Surrey, 1951–60; General Secretary, Association of Teachers in Technical Institutions, 1960–68. Pres., National Union of Teachers, 1956–57. Sen. Res. Fellow, Educn Div., Sheffield Univ., 1975–79. Vice-Pres., NFER, 1979; Member: TUC General Council, 1970–74; Beloe Cttee on Secondary Schs Exams, 1960; Schools Council, 1964–75; Adv. Cttee for Supply and Trng of Teachers, 1973–75; Burnham Primary and Secondary Cttee, 1956–75 (Jt Sec. and Leader of Teachers' Panel, 1970–75); Burnham Further Educn Cttee, 1959–69 (Jt Sec. and Leader of Teachers' Panel, 1961–69); Officers' Panel, Soulbury Cttee (and Leader), 1970–75; Staff Panel, Jt Negotiating Cttee Youth Leaders (and Leader), 1970–75; Warnock Cttee on Special Educn, 1974–78; Council and Exec., CGLI, 1974–77; Central Arbitration Cttee, 1977–83. Fellow College of Preceptors, 1967; Hon. FEIS, 1974. Hon. DEd CNAA, 1969. *Publications:* many articles in educational journals. *Address:* 40 Nightingale Road, Guildford, Surrey.

BRITZ, Jack; General Secretary, Clearing Bank Union, 1980–83; *b* 6 Nov. 1930; *s* of Alfred and Hetty Britz; *m* 1955, Thelma Salaver; one *s* two *d*. *Educ:* Luton Grammar School. Entered electrical contracting industry, 1944; various posts in industry; Director, Rolfe Electrical Ltd, 1964–65. National Recruitment Officer, EETPU, 1969–74; short period with Commission on Industrial Relations as sen. industrial relations officer, 1974; Personnel Manager, Courage Eastern Ltd, 1974–77; Gp Personnel Director, Bowthorpe Group Ltd, 1977–80. *Recreations:* walking, history, wargaming, etc. *Address:* West Wing, Longdown Hollow, Hindhead Road, Hindhead, Surrey GU26 6AY.

See also L. Britz.

BRITZ, Lewis; Executive Councillor, Electrical, Electronic, Telecommunication & Plumbing Union, since 1983; Member, Monopolies and Mergers Commission, since 1986; *b* 7 Jan. 1933; *s* of Alfred and Hetty Britz; *m* 1960, Hadassah Rosenberg; four *d*. *Educ:* Hackney Downs Grammar Sch.; Acton Technical Coll. (OND Elec. Engrg); Nottingham Univ. (BSc (Hons) Engrg). Head of Research, 1967–71, Nat. Officer, 1971–83, EETPU. Dir, LEB, 1976–. *Recreation:* philately. *Address:* 30 Braemarg Gardens, West Wickham, Kent BR4 0JW. *T:* 01–777 5986.

See also J. Britz.

BROACKES, Sir Nigel, Kt 1984; Chairman, Trafalgar House PLC; *b* Wakefield, 21 July 1934; *s* of late Donald Broackes and Nan Alford; *m* 1956, Joyce Edith Horne; two *s* one *d*. *Educ:* Stowe. Nat. Service, commnd 3rd Hussars, 1953–54. Stewart & Hughman Ltd, Lloyds Underwriting agents, 1952–55; various property developments, etc, 1955–57; Trafalgar House Investments Ltd: Man. Dir 1958; Dep. Chm. and Jt Man. Dir 1968; Chm. 1969. Chm., Ship and Marine Technology Requirements Bd, 1972–77; Dep. Chm., Offshore Energy Technology Bd, 1975–77; Chm. Designate, then Chm., London Docklands Develt Corp., 1979–84; British Chm., EuroRoute, 1984–; non-exec. Dir, Distillers Co., 1985–. Hon. Treas., Kensington Housing Trust, 1963–69; Vice-Chairman: Mulberry Housing Trust, 1965–69; London Housing Trust, 1967–70; Mem. Council, Nat. Assoc. of Property Owners, 1967–73. Governor, Stowe Sch., 1974–81. Trustee, Royal Opera House Trust; Mem. Advisory Council, Victoria and Albert Museum, 1980–83. Dir, Horserace Totalisator Bd, 1976–81. Freeman, City of London; Liveryman, Worshipful Co. of Goldsmiths. Guardian Young Businessman of the Year, 1978. *Publication:* A Growing Concern, 1979. *Recreation:* silversmith. *Address:* 41 Chelsea Square, SW3; Checkendon Court, Checkendon, Oxon RG8 0SR.

BROADBENT, Donald Eric, CBE 1974; MA, ScD; FRS 1968; on External Staff, Medical Research Council, since 1974; *b* 6 May 1926; *m* 1st, 1949, Margaret Elizabeth Wright; two *d*; 2nd, 1972, Margaret Hope Pattison Gregory. *Educ:* Winchester College; Pembroke College, Cambridge. RAF Engrg short course, 1st cl., 1944; Moral Science Tripos (Psychology), 1st cl., 1949. Scientific Staff, Applied Psychology Res. Unit, 1949–58 (Dir, 1958–74). Fellow, Pembroke College, Cambridge, 1965–74. Pres., British Psychol. Society, 1965; Pres., Sect. J. Brit. Assoc. for Advancement of Science, 1967; Vis. Fellow, All Souls College, Oxford, 1967–68; Fellow, Wolfson Coll., Oxford, 1974. Member: Biol. Res. Bd, MRC, 1966–70; Psychology Cttee, SSRC, 1969–75; SSRC, 1973–75; Biol Sci. Ctte, SERC, 1984–. Fellow, Acoustical Soc. of Amer.; past or present Council Member: Royal Soc.; British Acoustical Soc.; British Psychol Soc.; Ergonomics Res. Soc.; Experimental Psychology Soc.; Fellow, Human Factors Soc.; Governor, Technical Change Centre, 1980–. For. Associate, US Nat. Acad. Sci., 1971; Hon. FRCP (Faculty of Occupational Medicine), 1982; Hon. FRC Psych 1985. Hon. DSc: Southampton, 1974; York, 1979; Loughborough, 1982; City, 1983. APA Dist. Scientist Award, 1975. *Publications:* Perception and Communication, 1958; Behaviour, 1961; Decision and Stress, 1971; In Defence of Empirical Psychology, 1973; many papers in jls of above societies and of Amer. Psychol Assoc. *Recreations:* reading, camping, photography. *Address:* Department of Experimental Psychology, 1 South Parks Road, Oxford OX1 3UD.

BROADBENT, Dr Edward Granville, FRS 1977; FEng, FRAeS, FIMA; Visiting Professor, Imperial College of Science and Technology (Mathematics Department), London University, since 1983; *b* 27 June 1923; *s* of Joseph Charles Fletcher Broadbent and Lucetta (*née* Riley); *m* 1949, Elizabeth Barbara (*née* Puttick). *Educ:* Huddersfield Coll.; St Catharine's Coll., Cambridge (State Scholarship, 1941; Eng Scholar; MA, ScD). FRAeS 1959; FIMA 1965. Joined RAE (Structures Dept), 1943; worked on aero-elasticity (Wakefield Gold Medal, RAeS, 1960); transf. to Aerodynamics Dept, 1960; worked on various aspects of fluid mechanics and acoustics; DCSO (IM), RAE, 1969–83, retired. *Publication:* The Elementary Theory of Aero-elasticity, 1954. *Recreations:* duplicate bridge, chess, music, theatre. *Address:* 11 Three Stiles Road, Farnham, Surrey GU9 7DE. *T:* Farnham 714621.

BROADBENT, Sir Ewen, KCB 1984 (CB 1973); CMG 1965; Second Permanent Under Secretary of State, Ministry of Defence, 1982–84, retired; Director, International Military Services, since 1985; *b* 9 Aug. 1924; *s* of late Rev. W. Broadbent and of Mrs Mary Broadbent; *m* 1951, Squadron Officer Barbara David, *d* of F. A. David, Weston-super-Mare; one *s*. *Educ:* King Edward VI School, Nuneaton; St John's College, Cambridge. Served with Gordon Highlanders, 1943–47 (Captain); Cambridge, 1942–43 and 1947–49; Air Ministry, 1949; Private Sec. to Secretary of State for Air, 1955–59; Asst Secretary, 1959; Dep. Chief Officer, Sovereign Base Areas, Cyprus, 1961, Chief Officer, 1964; MoD 1965–84: Private Sec. to Sec. of State for Defence, 1967–68; Asst Under-Sec. of State, 1969–72; Dep. Under-Sec. of State (Air), 1972–75; Dep. Under-Sec. of State (Civilian Management), 1975–82. Trustee, RAF Mus., 1985–. *Recreation:* golf. *Address:* 18 Park Hill, Ealing, W5. *T:* 01–997 1978. *Clubs:* Royal Commonwealth Society, Army and Navy.

BROADBENT, Sir William Francis, 3rd Bt, *cr* 1898; *b* 29 Nov. 1904; *s* of Sir John Francis Harpin Broadbent, MD, FRCP, Bt and Margaret Elizabeth Field (*d* 1958); *S* father 1946; *m* 1st, 1935, Veronica Pearl Eustace (*d* 1951); 2nd, 1982, Miranda Hamilton. *Educ:* Winchester College; Trinity College, Oxford (MA). Solicitor, 1933–72, retired. *Heir: cousin* George Walter Broadbent [*b* 23 April 1935; *m* 1962, Valerie Anne, *o d* of C. F. Ward; one *s* one *d*]. *Address:* Flat 43, Ritchie Court, 380 Banbury Road, Oxford. *Club:* United Oxford & Cambridge University.

BROADBRIDGE, family name of **Baron Broadbridge.**

BROADBRIDGE, 3rd Baron *cr* 1945, of Brighton; **Peter Hewett Broadbridge;** Bt 1937; Directorships within the Ravendale Group, since 1980; *b* 19 Aug. 1938; *s* of 2nd Baron Broadbridge and Mabel Daisy (*d* 1966), *o d* of Arthur Edward Clarke; *S* father, 1972; *m* 1967, Mary, *o d* of W. O. Busch; two *d*. *Educ:* Hurstpierpoint Coll., Sussex; St Catherine's Coll., Oxford (MA, BSc). Unilever Ltd, 1963–65; Colgate Palmolive Ltd, 1966; Gallaher Ltd, 1967–70; Peat, Marwick Mitchell & Co., EC2, 1970–77; Management Consultant, Coopers and Lybrand and Associates Ltd, 1977–80. Pres., Nat. Assoc. of Leisure Gardeners, 1978–81. Freeman, City of London, 1980; Liveryman, Worshipful Co. of Goldsmiths, 1983. *Recreations:* tennis, squash, antiques, silversmithing. Heir: *cousin* Martin Hugh Broadbridge [*b* 29 Nov 1929; *m* 1st 1954, Norma, *d* of late Major Herbert Sheffield, MC; one *s* one *d*; 2nd, 1968, Elizabeth, *d* of J. E. Trotman]. *Address:* House of Lords, SW1A 0PW.

BROADHURST, Air Chief Marshal (retd) Sir Harry, GCB 1960 (KCB 1955; CB 1944); KBE 1945; DSO and Bar, 1941; DFC 1940, and Bar, 1942; AFC 1937; Managing Director, A. V. Roe & Co. Ltd, 1961–66; Director, 1961–76, Deputy Managing Director 1965–76, Hawker Siddeley Aviation Ltd; Director, Hawker Siddeley Group Ltd, 1968–76; *b* 1905; *m* 1st, 1929, Doris Kathleen French; one *d*; 2nd, 1946, Jean Elizabeth Townley; one *d*. Joined RAF, 1926; served with: No 11 (B) Sqdn, UK, 1926–28, India, 1928–31; 41 (F) Sqdn, 1932–33; 19 (F) Sqdn, 1933–36; Chief Instr, No 4 FTS, Egypt, 1937; RAF Staff Coll., 1938; served War: OC No 111 (F) Sqdn, 1939–40; Wing Comdr Trng No 11 (F) Gp, Jan.–May 1940; OC No 60 (F) Wing, France, May 1940; OC Fighter Sector, Wittering, June–Dec. 1940, Hornchurch, 1940–42; Dep. SASO No 11 (F) Gp, May–Oct. 1942; SASO and AOC Western Desert, 1942–43; 83 Group Commander Allied Expeditionary Air Force, 1944–45; AO i/c Admin. Fighter Command, 1945–46; AOC 61 Group, 1947–48; idc 1949; SASO, BAFO (now 2nd TAF), Germany, 1950–51; ACAS (Ops), 1952–53; C-in-C 2nd Tactical Air Force, Germany, 1954–56; Air Officer Commanding-in-Chief, Bomber Command, Jan. 1956–May 1959; Cmdr Allied Air Forces, Central Europe, 1959–61. Vice-Pres., 1973–74, Pres., 1974–75, Dep. Pres., 1975–76, SBAC. Kt Grand Cross of Order of Orange Nassau, 1948; Legion of Merit (US). *Address:* Lock's End House, Birdham, Chichester, W Sussex PO20 7BB. *T:* Birdham 512717. *Club:* Royal Air Force.

BROADLEY, John Kenneth Elliott; HM Diplomatic Service; Deputy Governor, Gibraltar, since 1984; *b* 10 June 1936; *s* of late Kenneth Broadley and late Rosamund Venn (*née* Elliott); *m* 1961, Jane Alice Rachel (*née* Gee); one *s* two *d*. *Educ:* Winchester Coll.; Balliol Coll., Oxford (Exhibnr, MA). Served Army, 1st RHA, 1954–56. Entered HM Diplomatic Service, 1960; Washington, 1963–65; La Paz, 1965–68; FCO, 1968–73; UK Mission to UN, Geneva, 1973–76; Counsellor, Amman, 1976–79; Head of Personnel Policy Dept, FCO, 1979–81; Head of Security Dept, FCO, 1982–84. *Recreations:* windsurfing, tennis, family. *Address:* c/o Foreign and Commonwealth Office, SW1. *Club:* Royal Automobile.

BROATCH, James, CBE 1961; Deputy Chairman of the Cotton Board, 1963; Deputy Chairman, Textile Council, 1967–68; *b* 13 May 1900; *s* of Alfred and Mary Broatch; *m* 1927, Mary Booth (*d* 1984). *Educ:* Manchester Grammar School; University College, Oxford. Editor, Manchester Guardian Commercial, 1930–39; Assistant Secretary, The Cotton Board, 1939–43; Secretary 1943–53; Director-General, 1953–62. *Address:* 5 Lynton Drive, Hillside, Southport, Merseyside. *T:* Southport 67976.

BROCAS, Viscount; Patrick John Bernard Jellicoe; *b* 29 Aug. 1950; *s* and *heir* of 2nd Earl Jellicoe, *qv*; *m* 1971, separated 1971, marr. diss. 1980; two *s* (*b* 1970, 1977). *Educ:* Eton. Profession, engineer.

BROCK, Arthur Guy C.; *see* Clutton-Brock.

BROCK, Michael George, CBE 1981; Warden of Nuffield College, Oxford, since 1978; Pro-Vice-Chancellor, Oxford University, since 1980; *b* 9 March 1920; *s* of late Sir Laurence George Brock and Ellen Margery Brock (*née* Williams); *m* 1949, Eleanor Hope Morrison; three *s*. *Educ:* Wellington Coll. (Schol.); Corpus Christi Coll., Oxford (Open Schol.; First Cl. Hons Mod. Hist. 1948; MA 1948). FRHistS 1965; FRSL 1983. War service (Middlesex Regt), 1940–45. Corpus Christi Coll., Oxford: Jun. Res. Fellow, 1948–50; Fellow and Tutor in Modern History and Politics, 1950–66, Fellow Emeritus, 1977; Hon. Fellow, 1982; Oxford University: Jun. Proctor, 1956–57; Univ. Lectr, 1951–70; Mem., Hebdomadal Council, 1965–76, 1978–86; Vice Pres. and Bursar, Wolfson Coll., Oxford, 1967–76; Prof. of Educn and Dir, Sch. of Educn, Exeter Univ., 1977–78. Hon. Fellow, Wolfson Coll., Oxford, 1977; Hon. DLitt Exeter, 1982. *Publications:* The Great Reform Act, 1973; (ed with Eleanor Brock) H. H. Asquith: Letters to Venetia Stanley, 1982; many articles on historical topics and on higher education. *Address:* Nuffield College, Oxford; 186 Woodstock Road, Oxford OX2 7NQ. *Clubs:* Athenæum, United Oxford & Cambridge University; Oxford Union.

BROCK, Rear-Admiral Patrick Willet, CB 1956; DSO 1951; RN retd; Chairman, The Naval Review, 1967–78; *b* 30 Dec. 1902; *e s* of R. W. and M. B. Brock, Kingston, Ontario; *m* 1st, 1931, M. D. Collinson (*d* 1974); 2nd, 1976, Mrs Rosemary Harrison Stanton. *Educ:* Royal Royal Naval College of Canada. Transferred from Royal Canadian Navy to RN, 1921; Commander 1938; Exec. Officer, HMS Mauritius, 1942–44 (despatches); Captain 1944; Senior Naval Officer, Schleswig-Holstein, 1946; commanded HMS Kenya, Far East, 1949–51 (despatches, DSO); Director Operations Div., 1951–53; Rear-Admiral, 1954; Flag Officer, Middle East, 1954–56; Admiralty Material Requirements Committee, 1956–58, retired. Chm., Kipling Soc., 1973–76. Trustee, National Maritime Museum, 1960–74; a Vice-Pres., Soc. for Nautical Research, 1970–. Croix de Guerre (France), 1945; Bronze Star Medal (US), 1951. *Publications:* RUSI Eardley-Wilmot Gold Medal Essay, 1935; (with Basil Greenhill) Steam and Sail in Great Britain and North America, 1973. *Recreations:* gardening, naval history. *Address:* Kiln Cottage, Critchmere, Haslemere, Surrey. *T:* Haslemere 2542.

BROCK, Dr Sebastian Paul, FBA 1977; University Lecturer in Aramaic and Syriac, University of Oxford, since 1974; *b* 1938; *m* 1966, Helen M. C. (*née* Hughes). *Educ:* Eton College; Univ. of Cambridge (BA 1962, MA 1965); MA and DPhil Oxon 1966. Asst Lectr, 1964–66, Lectr, 1966–67, Dept of Theology, Univ. of Birmingham; Lectr, Hebrew and Aramaic, Univ. of Cambridge, 1967–74. Fellow of Wolfson Coll., Oxford, 1974–. Corres. Mem., Syriac Section, Iraqi Acad., 1979. *Publications:* Pseudepigrapha Veteris Testamenti Graece II; Testamentum Iobi, 1967; The Syriac Version of the Pseudo-Nonnos Mythological Scholia, 1971; (with C. T. Fritsch and S. Jellicoe) A Classified Bibliography of the Septuagint, 1973; The Harp of the Spirit: Poems of St Ephrem, 1975, 2nd edn 1983; The Holy Spirit in Syrian Baptismal Tradition, 1979; Sughyotho Mgabyotho, 1982; Syriac Perspectives on Late Antiquity, 1984; Turgome d'Mor Ya'qub da-Srug, 1984; The Luminous Eye: the spiritual world vision of St Ephrem, 1986; contrib. JSS, JTS, Le Muséon, Oriens Christianus, Orientalia Christiana Periodica, Parole de l'Orient, Revue des études arméniennes. *Address:* Wolfson College, Oxford; Oriental Institute, Pusey Lane, Oxford.

BROCK, Prof. William Ranulf; Fellow of Selwyn College, Cambridge, since 1947; Professor of Modern History, University of Glasgow, 1967–81, now Emeritus; *b* 16 May 1916; *s* of Stewart Ernst Brock and Katherine Helen (*née* Temple Roberts); *m* 1950, Constance Helen (*née* Brown); one *s* one *d*. *Educ:* Christ's Hosp.; Trinity Coll., Cambridge (MA, PhD). Prize Fellow 1940 (in absentia). Military service (Army), 1939–45; Asst Master, Eton Coll., 1946–47. Commonwealth Fund Fellow, Berkeley, Calif, Yale and Johns Hopkins, 1952–53, 1958; Vis. Professor: Michigan Univ., 1968; Washington Univ., 1970; Maryland Univ., 1980; Charles Warren Fellow, Harvard Univ., 1976; Leverhulme Emeritus Fellow, 1981. *Publications:* Lord Liverpool and Liberal Toryism, 1941; The Character of American History, 1960; An American Crisis, 1963; The Evolution of American Democracy, 1970; Conflict and Transformation 1844–1877, 1973; The Sources of History: the United States 1790–1890, 1975; Parties and Political Conscience, 1979; Scotus Americanus, 1982; Investigation and Responsibility, 1985; contrib. New Cambridge Mod. History, Vols VII and XI; articles and reviews in Eng. Hist. Review, History, Jl Amer. Studies, etc. *Recreation:* antiques. *Address:* 49 Barton Road, Cambridge CB3 9LG. *T:* Cambridge 313606.

BROCKBANK, (James) Tyrrell, DL; solicitor; *b* 14 Dec. 1920; *y s* of late James Lindow Brockbank; *m* 1950, Pamela, *yr d* of late Lt-Col J. Oxley Parker, TD, and Mary Monica (*née* Hills); four *s*. *Educ:* St Peter's Sch., York; St John's Coll., Cambridge (MA). Served War of 1939–45 with Sherwood Foresters and Inns of Court Regt. Asst Solicitor, Wolverhampton, 1949–51; Asst Clerk, Hertfordshire, 1951–54; Dep. Clerk, Nottinghamshire, 1954–61; Clerk of the Peace, Durham, 1961–71; Clerk of Durham CC, 1961–74; Clerk to the Lieutenancy, 1964–; DL Durham 1970. Member, Local Govt Boundary Commn for England, 1976–85. *Recreations:* fishing, shooting, golf. *Address:* The Orange Tree, Shincliffe Village, Durham DH1 2NN. *T:* Durham 65569. *Clubs:* Travellers'; Durham County (Durham).

BROCKBANK, Maj.-Gen. John Myles, (Robin), CBE 1972; MC 1943; DL; *b* 19 Sept. 1921; *s* of Col J. G. Brockbank, CBE, DSO, and Eireine Marguerite Robinson; *m* 1953, Gillian Findlay, *yr d* of Sir Edmund Findlay, 2nd Bt of Aberlour; three *s* one *d*. *Educ:* Eton Coll.; Oxford Univ. Commissioned into 12 Royal Lancers, 1941. Served War, North Africa, Italy, 1941–45. Served Germany: 1955–58, 1964–68 and 1970–72; Cyprus, 1959; USA, 1961–64; Staff Coll., 1950; IDC 1969; CO, 9/12 Royal Lancers; Comdr, RAC, HQ 1 Corps; Chief of Staff, 1 Corps; Dir, RAC, 1972–74; Vice-Adjutant General, MoD, 1974–76. Col, 9/12 Lancers, 1982–85. Dir, British Field Sports Soc., 1976–84, retd. DL Wilts 1982. *Recreations:* field sports, gardening, bird watching. *Address:* Manor House, Steeple Langford, Salisbury, Wilts. *T:* Salisbury 790353. *Club:* Cavalry and Guards.

BROCKBANK, Prof. (John) Philip, PhD; Director of the Shakespeare Institute and Professor of English, University of Birmingham, since 1979; *b* 4 Jan. 1922; *s* of John Brockbank and Sarah Cooper; *m* 1947, Doreen Winterbottom; two *s*. *Educ:* Oldershaw Grammar Sch., Wallasey; Trinity Coll., Cambridge (MA, PhD). Served RAF, Navigator, 1940–46. Professor of English, Saarbrücken, 1953–54; Asst Lectr, Cambridge, and College Lectr, Jesus Coll., 1954–58; Sen. Lectr, Reading, 1958–62; Prof. of English, York, 1962–79. General Editor, New Cambridge Shakespeare, 1978–. *Publications:* Marlowe's Dr Faustus, 1961, repr. 1979; ed, Pope, Selected Poems, 1962, repr. 1974; ed, Ben Jonson, Volpone, 1967, repr. 1980; ed, Shakespeare, Coriolanus, 1976; (ed) Players of Shakespeare, 1985; contribs to books on Shakespeare, Milton, Pope, Marvell, and to Shakespeare Survey, TLS, etc. *Recreations:* theatre, water-colours. *Address:* 14 Scholars Lane, Stratford-upon-Avon CV37 6HE. *T:* Stratford-upon-Avon 295058.

BROCKBANK, Maj.-Gen. Robin; *see* Brockbank, Maj.-Gen. J. M.

BROCKBANK, Tyrrell; *see* Brockbank, J. T.

BROCKET, 3rd Baron, *cr* 1933; **Charles Ronald George Nall-Cain,** Bt 1921; *b* 12 Feb. 1952; *s* of Hon. Ronald Charles Manus Nall-Cain (*d* 1961), and of Elizabeth Mary (who *m* 2nd, 1964, Colin John Richard Trotter), *d* of R. J. Stallard; *S* grandfather, 1967; *m* 1982, Isabell Maria Lorenzo, *o d* of Gustavo Lorenzo, Whaleneck Drive, Merrick, Long Island, NY; one *s*. *Educ:* Eton. 14/20 Hussars, 1970–75 (Lieut). *Heir: s* Hon. Alexander Christopher Charles Nall-Cain, *b* 30 Sept. 1984. *Address:* Brocket Hall, Welwyn, Herts.

BROCKHOFF, Sir Jack (Stuart), Kt 1979; company director; *b* 1908; *s* of Mr and Mrs Frederick Douglas Brockhoff. *Educ:* Wesley Coll., Vic. Chairman and Managing Director: Brockhoff's Biscuits Pty Ltd; Arnott-Brockhoff-Guest Pty Ltd; Dir, Arnotts Ltd; Chm. of Dirs, Jack Brockhoff Foundn. *Recreations:* golf, bowls, fishing. *Address:* 113 Beach Road, Sandringham, Vic 3191, Australia. *T:* 598 9227. *Clubs:* Woodlands Golf, Victoria Golf, Sandringham, Sandringham Yacht, Royal Automobile of Victoria, Victoria Racing, Victoria Amateur Turf.

BROCKHOLES, Michael John F.; *see* Fitzherbert-Brockholes.

BROCKHOUSE, Dr Bertram Neville, OC 1982; FRS 1965; Professor of Physics, McMaster University, Canada, 1962–84, now Emeritus; *b* 15 July 1918; *s* of Israel Bertram Brockhouse and Mable Emily Brockhouse (*née* Neville); *m* 1948, Doris Isobel Mary (*née* Miller); four *s* two *d*. *Educ:* University of British Columbia (BA); University of Toronto (PhD). Served War of 1939–45 with Royal Canadian Navy. Lectr, University of Toronto, 1949–50; Research Officer, Atomic Energy of Canada Ltd, 1950–59; Branch Head, Neutron Physics Br., 1960–62. Hon. DSc: Waterloo, 1969; McMaster, 1984. *Publications:* some 75 papers in learned journals. *Address:* PO Box 7338, Ancaster, Ontario L9G 3N6, Canada.

BROCKINGTON, Prof. Colin Fraser; Professor of Social and Preventive Medicine, Manchester University, 1951–64, Emeritus, 1964; *b* 8 Jan. 1903; *s* of late Sir William Brockington; *m* 1933, Dr Joyce Margaret Furze; three *s* one *d*. *Educ:* Oakham Sch.; Gonville and Caius Coll., Cambridge; Guy's Hosp., London. MD, MA, DPH, BChir Cantab, MSc Manchester, MRCS, MRCP; barrister-at-law, Middle Temple. Medical Superintendent, Brighton Infectious Diseases Hosp. and Sanatorium, 1929; Asst County Medical Officer, Worcs CC, 1930–33; general medical practice, Kingsbridge, Devon, 1933–36; Medical Officer of Health, Horsham and Petworth, 1936–38; Dep. County Medical Officer of Health, Warwickshire CC, 1938–42; County Medical Officer of Health: Warwickshire CC, 1942–46; West Riding CC, 1946–51. Member: Central Adv. Council for Educn (Eng.), 1945–56; Central Training Council in Child Care (Home Office), 1947–53; Adv. Council for Welfare of Handicapped (Min. of Health), 1949–54; Nursing Cttee of Central Health Services Council (Min. of Health), 1949–51; Council of Soc. of Med. Officers of Health, 1944–66; Public Health Cttee of County Councils Assoc., 1945–49. Chairman: WHO Expert Cttee on School Health, 1950; Symposium on "Mental Health-Public Health Partnership," 5th Internat. Congress on Mental Health, Toronto, 1954; WHO Research Study Group on Juvenile Epilepsy, 1955; UK Cttee of WHO, 1958–61. Took part as Expert in Technical Discussions on Rural Health at World Health Assembly, 1954; Far Eastern Lecture Tour for British Council, 1956–57; visited India, 1959, 1962, S America 1960, Jordan 1966–67, Spain 1967, Arabia 1968, Turkey 1955, 1969, 1970, 1972, Greece 1970, for WHO. Lecture Tour: S Africa and Middle East, 1964. *Publications:* Principles of Nutrition, 1952; The People's Health, 1955; A Short History of Public Health, 1956 (2nd edn 1966); World Health, 1958 (3rd edn 1975); The Health of the Community, 1955, 1960, 1965; Public Health in the Nineteenth Century, 1965; The Social Needs of the Over-Eighties, 1966; The Health of the Developing World, 1985; wide range of contribs to learned jls. *Recreations:* bookbinding, travel. *Address:* Werneth, Silverburn, Ballasalla, Isle of Man. *T:* Castletown (Isle of Man) 3465.

BROCKLEBANK, Sir Aubrey (Thomas), 6th Bt *cr* 1885; ACA; Director, Venture Founders Ltd, since 1986; *b* 29 Jan. 1952; *s* of Sir John Montague Brocklebank, 5th Bt, TD, and of Pamela Sue, *d* of late William Harold Pierce, OBE; *S* father, 1974; *m* 1979, Dr Anna-Marie Dunnet; one *s*. *Educ:* Eton; University Coll., Durham (BSc Psychology). *Recreations:* shooting, motor racing. *Heir: s* Aubrey William Thomas Brocklebank, *b* 15 Dec. 1980. *Address:* 37 Kyrle Road, SW11.

BROCKLEBANK-FOWLER, Christopher; Managing Director, Cambridge Corporate Consultants Ltd, since 1985; *b* 13 Jan. 1934; 2nd *s* of Sidney Straton Brocklebank Fowler, MA, LLB; *m* 1st, 1957, Joan Nowland (marr. diss. 1975); two *s*; 2nd, 1975, Mrs Mary Berry (marr. diss. 1986). *Educ:* Perse Sch., Cambridge. Farm pupil on farms in Suffolk, Cambridgeshire and Norfolk, 1950–55. National service (submarines), Sub-Lt, RNVR, 1952–54. Farm Manager, Kenya, 1955–57; Lever Bros Ltd (Unilever Cos Management Trainee), 1957–59; advertising and marketing consultant, 1959–79; Chm., Overseas Trade and Develt Agency Ltd, 1979–83. Mem. Bow Group, 1961–81 (Chm., 1968–69; Dir, Bow Publications, 1968–71). Mem. London Conciliation Cttee, 1966–67; Vice-Chm. Information Panel, Nat. Cttee for Commonwealth Immigrants, 1966–67; Mem. Exec. Cttee, Africa Bureau, 1970–74; Chm., SOS Childrens Villages, 1978–84. MP King's Lynn, 1970–74, Norfolk North West, 1974–83 (C, 1970–81, SDP, 1981–83); Chm., Conservative Party Sub-Cttee on Horticulture, 1972–74; Vice-Chairman: Cons. Parly Cttee on Agriculture, 1974–75; Cons. Parly Foreign and Commonwealth Affairs Cttee, 1979 (Jt Sec., 1974–75, 1976–77); Cons. Parly Trade Cttee, 1979–80; SDP Agriculture Policy Cttee, 1982–83; Chairman: UN Parly Gp, 1979–83 (Jt Sec., 1971–78); Cons. Parly Overseas Develt Sub-Cttee, 1979–81; SDP Third World Policy Cttee, 1981–; Member: Select Cttee for Overseas Develt, 1973–79; Select Cttee on Foreign Affairs, 1979–81; SDP Nat. Steering Cttee, 1981–82; SDP Nat. Cttee, 1982; SDP Parly spokesman on Agriculture, 1981–82, on Overseas Develt, 1981–83, on Foreign Affairs, 1982–83. Contested: (C) West Ham (North), 1964; (SDP) Norfolk North West, 1983. Vice Chm., Centre for World Develt of Educn, 1980–83; Governor, Inst. of Develt Studies, 1978–81. FRGS; MInstM; M CAM; FInstD; Hon. Fellow IDS. *Publications:* pamphlets and articles on race relations, African affairs, overseas development. *Recreations:* painting, fishing, shooting, swimming. *Address:* The Long Cottage, Flitcham, near King's Lynn, Norfolk. *T:* Hillington 600255. *Club:* Royal Commonwealth Society.

BROCKLEHURST, Major-General Arthur Evers, CB 1956; DSO 1945; late RA; *b* 20 July 1905; *m* 1940, Joan Beryl Parry-Crooke; twin *d*. *Educ:* King's School, Canterbury; RMA Woolwich. 2nd Lieut, RA, 1925; CRA 6th Armoured Div., 1951; IDC 1954; DDPS (B) 1955; Chief of Staff, Malaya Comd, 1956–57; GOC, Rhine Dist, BAOR, 1958–59; Dep. Comdr BAOR, 1959–61; retired 1961. Chm., Devizes Constituency Cons. Assoc., 1963–65. *Recreations:* fishing, gardening. *Address:* Woodborough Manor, Pewsey, Wilts. *Club:* Army and Navy.

BROCKLEHURST, Prof. John Charles, FRCP, FRCPE, FRCPGlas; Professor of Geriatric Medicine, University of Manchester, since 1970; *b* 31 May 1924; *s* of late Harold John Brocklehurst and of Dorothy Brocklehurst; *m* 1956, Susan Engle; two *s* one *d*. *Educ:* Glasgow High Sch.; Ayr Academy; Univ. of Glasgow (MB ChB 1947; MD Hons 1950). Christine Hansen Research Fellow, Glasgow Univ., 1948–49; RAMC (to rank of Major), 1949–51; MO, Grenfell Mission, Northern Newfoundland and Labrador, 1955–57; Medical Registrar, Stobhill Hosp., and Asst Lectr, Dept of Materia Medica and

Therapeutics, Glasgow Univ., 1959–60; Cons. Geriatrician, Bromley Hosp. Gp and Cray Valley and Sevenoaks Hosp. Gp, 1961–69; Cons. in Geriatric and Gen. Med., Guy's Hosp., London, 1969–70. Dir, Geigy Unit for Research in Aging, Univ. of Manchester, 1974–; Chm., Age Concern England, 1973–77, Hon. Vice-Pres., 1980–; Governor, British Foundn for Age Research, 1980–; President: Soc. of Chiropodists, 1977–83; British Geriatrics Soc., 1984–. Vis. Professor of Geriatric Med. and Chm., Div. of Geriatric Med., Univ. of Saskatchewan, Canada, 1978–79. Hon. MSc Manchester 1974. Bellahouston Gold Medal, Univ. of Glasgow, 1950; Willard Thomson Gold Medal, Amer. Geriatrics Soc., 1978. *Publications*: Incontinence in Old People, 1951; The Geriatric Day Hospital, 1971; ed and part author, Textbook of Geriatric Medicine and Gerontology, 1973, 3rd edn 1985; Geriatric Care in Advanced Societies, 1975; (jtly) Geriatric Medicine for Students, 1976, 3rd edn, 1986; (jtly) Progress in Geriatric Day Care, 1980; (jtly) Colour Atlas of Geriatric Medicine, 1983; (ed and part author) Urology: the elderly, 1985; Geriatric Pharmacology and Therapeutics, 1985. *Recreation*: water colour painting. *Address*: 59 Stanneylands Road, Wilmslow, Cheshire SK9 4EX. *T*: Wilmslow 526795. *Clubs*: East India and Devonshire, Royal Society of Medicine.

BROCKLEHURST, Mrs Mary D.; *see* Dent-Brocklehurst.

BROCKLEHURST, Robert James, DM; Emeritus Professor of Physiology, University of Bristol, since 1965; *b* Liverpool, 16 Sept. 1899; *e s* of George and Sarah Huger Brocklehurst, Liverpool; *m* 1st, 1928, Sybille (*d* 1968), *y d* of Captain R. H. L. Risk, CBE, RN; two *s* one *d*; 2nd, 1970, Dora Millicent, *y d* of late Alexander Watts. *Educ*: Harrow Sch.; University College, Oxford (Scholar; 1st Class Honours in Physiology); St Bartholomew's Hospital. BA 1921; MA, BM, BCh, 1924; DM, 1928; MRCS, LRCP, 1925; Demonstrator of Physiology, St Bartholomew's Hosp. Medical Coll., 1925–26; Radcliffe Travelling Fellow, 1926–28; Lecturer, 1928–29, and Senior Lecturer, 1929–30, in Dept of Physiology and Biochemistry, Univ. Coll., London; Prof. of Physiology, 1930–65, and Dean of Med. Fac., 1934–47, Univ. of Bristol, and Univ. Rep. on GMC, 1935–65 (Jt Treas., 1962–65); Long Fox Meml Lectr, 1952; Mem. Inter-departmental Cttee on Dentistry, 1943; Mem. Dental Bd of UK, 1945–56; Additional Mem., GDC, 1956–65; Pres., Bath, Bristol and Somerset Branch, BMA 1959; Fellow BMA, 1967; Pres. Bristol Medico-Chirurgical Society, 1960; Member Council, 1958–63, and President Sect. I (Physiology), 1950, British Association; Mem., S-W Regional Hosp. Bd, and Bd of Govs of United Bristol Hosps, 1947–66; Chm, Moorhaven Hosp. Management Cttee, 1966–71; a representative of Diocese of Bristol in the Church Assembly, 1945–65; Member, Central Board of Finance, 1957–65; Chm., Bristol Diocesan Bd of Finance, 1951–65. Mem., Council Westonbirt School, 1955–75 (Chm., 1956–68); Member Council, Christ Church College, Canterbury, 1961–73; Churchwarden, Stoke Bishop, 1939–60; a Vice-President Gloucester and Bristol Diocesan Association of Church Bell Ringers. Chm., Glos, Somerset and N Devon Regional Group, YHA, 1934–45. Served in Tank Corps, 1918–19. *Publications*: Papers on physiological, biochemical and educational subjects in medical and scientific jls. *Recreation*: gardening. *Address*: Cleeve, Court Road, Newton Ferrers, Plymouth, Devon PL8 1DE. *T*: Plymouth 872397. *Clubs*: Alpine, Royal Commonwealth Society, Royal Over-Seas League.

BROCKLESBY, Prof. David William, FRCPath; Professor of Tropical Animal Health and Director of Centre for Tropical Veterinary Medicine, Royal (Dick) School of Veterinary Studies, University of Edinburgh, since 1978; *b* 12 Feb. 1929; *s* of late David Layton Brocklesby, AFC, and Katherine Jessie (*née* Mudd); *m* 1957, Jennifer Mary Hubble, MB, BS; one *s* three *d*. *Educ*: Terrington Hall Sch.; Sedbergh Sch.; Royal Vet. Coll., Univ. of London; London Sch. of Hygiene and Tropical Med. MRCVS 1954; MRCPath 1964; DrMedVet Zürich 1964. Nat. Service, 4th Queen's Own Hussars, 1947–49. Vet. Res. Officer (Protozoologist), E Afr. Vet. Res. Org., Mugaga, Kenya, 1955–66; Hd of Animal Health Res. Dept, Fisons Pest Control, 1966–67; joined ARC Inst. for Res. on Animal Diseases, Compton, as Parasitologist, 1967; Hd of Parasitology Dept, IRAD, 1969–78. Mem. Editorial Board: Research in Veterinary Science, 1970–; Tropical Animal Health and Production, 1978–; British Vet. Jl, 1982. Mem. Governing Body, Animal Virus Res. Inst., Pirbright, 1979–86. FRCVS (by election) 1985. *Publications*: papers in sci. jls and chapters in review books, mainly on tropical and veterinary protozoa. *Recreations*: formerly squash and golf, now TV and The Times. *Address*: 3 Broomieknowe, Lasswade, Midlothian EH18 1LN. *T*: 031–663 7743. *Club*: Royal Commonwealth Society.

BROCKMAN, John St Leger; Solicitor to the Department of Health and Social Security, to the Office of Population Censuses and Surveys, and the General Register Office, since 1985; *b* 24 March 1928; *s* of late Prof. Ralph St Leger Brockman and Estelle Wilson; *m* 1954, Sheila Elizabeth Jordan; one *s* two *d* (and one *d* decd). *Educ*: Ampleforth; Gonville and Caius Coll., Cambridge. BA, LLB. Called to the Bar, Gray's Inn, 1952. Legal Asst, Min. of National Insurance, 1953; Sen. Legal Asst, Min. of Pensions and National Insurance, 1964; Asst Solicitor, DHSS, 1973; Under Sec. and Principal Asst Solicitor, DHSS, 1978. *Publications*: compiled and edited: The Law relating to Family Allowances and National Insurance, 1961; The Law relating to National Insurance (Industrial Injuries), 1961. *Recreations*: St Vincent de Paul Society, church studies, being a grandfather. *Address*: 304 The Greenway, Epsom, Surrey KT18 7JF. *T*: Epsom 20242.

BROCKMAN, Vice-Admiral Sir Ronald, KCB 1965; CSI 1947; CIE 1946; CVO 1979; CBE 1943; Extra Gentleman Usher to the Queen, since 1979 (Gentleman Usher, 1967–79); *b* 8 March 1909; *er s* of late Rear-Adm. H. S. Brockman, CB; *m* 1932, Marjorie Jean Butt; one *s* three *d*. *Educ*: Weymouth Coll., Dorset. Entered Navy, 1927; Assistant Secretary to First Sea Lord, Admiral of the Fleet Sir Roger Backhouse, 1938–39; Lieut-Commander 1939; Admiral's Secretary to First Sea Lord, Admiral of the Fleet Sir Dudley Pound, 1939–43; Commander 1943; Admiral's Secretary to Admiral of the Fleet Lord Mountbatten in all appointments, 1943–59; Private Secretary to Governor-General of India, 1947–48. Principal Staff Officer to the Chief of Defence Staff, Min. of Defence, 1959–65. Captain, 1953; Rear-Admiral, 1959; Vice-Admiral, 1963; retired list, 1965. Mem., Rugby Football Union Cttee, 1956–; County Pres., St John Ambulance, Devon; Vice Chm., Devon and Exeter Steeplechases Exec.; Pres., Devon County Agric. Assoc., 1980; Governor, Royal Western Sch. for Deaf, Exeter. Liveryman, Tin Plate Workers alias Wireworkers' Company. DL Devon. KStJ 1985; Mem. Chapter-Gen., Order of St John. Special Rosette of Cloud and Banner (China), 1946; Chevalier Legion of Honour and Croix de Guerre, 1946; Bronze Star Medal (USA), 1947. *Address*: 3 Court House, Basil Street, SW3 1AJ. *T*: 01–584 1023; 12 Blueberry Downs, Coastguard Road, Budleigh Salterton, Devon EX9 6NU. *T*: Budleigh Salterton 2687. *Clubs*: White's; MCC; Royal Western Yacht Club of England.

BROCKMAN, Hon. Sir Thomas Charles D.; *see* Drake-Brockman.

BROCKWAY, family name of **Baron Brockway.**

BROCKWAY, Baron *cr* 1964 (Life Peer); **(Archibald) Fenner Brockway;** *b* Calcutta, 1888; *s* of Rev. W. G. Brockway and Frances Elizabeth Abbey; *m* 1914, Lilla, *d* of Rev. W. Harvey-Smith; four *d*; *m* 1946, Edith Violet, *d* of Archibald Herbert King; one *s*. *Educ*: Sch. for the Sons of Missionaries (now Eltham Coll.). Joined staff Examiner, 1907;

sub-editor Christian Commonwealth, 1909; Labour Leader, 1911; editor, 1912–17; secretary No Conscription Fellowship, 1917; sentenced to one month's imprisonment under DORA Aug. 1916, and to three months, six months, and two years hard labour under Military Service Act, Dec. 1916, Feb. 1917, and July 1917; Joint Secretary British Committee of Indian National Congress and editor India, 1919; Joint Secretary Prison System Enquiry Cttee, 1920: Organising Secretary ILP 1922; General Secretary ILP, 1928 and 1933–39; Editor of New Leader, 1926–29, and 1931–46; Labour candidate Lancaster, 1922; Chairman No More War Movement and War Resister's International, 1923–28; Labour candidate Westminster 1924; Exec. Labour and Socialist International, 1926–31; Fraternal Delegate Indian Trade Union Congress and Indian National Congress, 1927; MP (Lab) East Leyton, 1929–31; Chairman ILP, 1931–33; took part in last public Socialist campaign against Hitler in Germany, 1932; Political Secretary ILP, 1939–46; Chairman British Centre for Colonial Freedom, 1942–47; ILP candidate, Upton Division of West Ham, 1934, Norwich, 1935, Lancaster, 1941, and Cardiff East, 1942; ILP Fraternal Delegate Hamburg Trade Union May Day Demonstrations and German Social Democratic Party Conference, Hanover, 1946. Resigned from ILP, 1946, and rejoined Labour Party; MP (Lab) Eton and Slough, 1950–64. Member Internat. Cttee of Socialist Movement for United Europe, 1947–52; first Chairman of Congress of Peoples against Imperialism, 1948–; Fraternal Delegate, Tunisian Trade Union Conf., 1951; Mem. unofficial Fact-finding mission, Kenya, 1952; Chairman: Liberation (formerly Movement for Colonial Freedom), 1954–67 (President, 1967–); British Asian and Overseas Socialist Fellowship, 1959–66; Peace in Nigeria Cttee, 1967–70; Peace Mission to Biafra and Nigeria, 1968; Brit. Council for Peace in Vietnam, 1965–69; Pres., British Campaign for Peace in Vietnam, 1970–; Co-Chm. (with Lord Noel-Baker until 1982), World Disarmament Campaign, 1979–. Hon. LLD Univ. of Lancaster, 1983. *Publications*: Labour and Liberalism, 1913; The Devil's Business, 1915 (proscribed during the war); Socialism and Pacifism, 1917; The Recruit, 1919; Non-Co-operation, 1919; The Government of India, 1920; English Prisons To-day (with Stephen Hobhouse), 1921; A Week in India, 1928; A New Way with Crime, 1928; The Indian Crisis, 1930; Hungry England, 1932; The Bloody Traffic, 1933; Will Roosevelt Succeed?, 1934; Purple Plague (a novel), 1935; Workers' Front, 1938; Inside the Left: a Political Autobiography, 1942; Death pays a Dividend (with Frederic Mullally), 1944; German Diary, 1946; Socialism Over Sixty Years; The Life of Jowett of Bradford, 1946; Bermondsey Story: Life of Alfred Salter, 1949; Why Mau Mau?, 1953; African Journeys, 1955; 1960–Africa's Year of Destiny, 1960; Red Liner (novel in dialogue), 1961; Outside the Right, 1963; African Socialism, 1964; Commonwealth Immigrants: What is the Answer? (with Norman Pannell), 1965; Woman Against the Desert (with Miss Campbell-Purdie) 1967; This Shrinking Explosive World, 1968; The Next Step to Peace, 1970; The Colonial Revolution, 1973; Towards Tomorrow (autobiog.), 1977; Britain's First Socialists, 1980; numerous ILP and Movement for Colonial Freedom pamphlets. *Address*: 31 Ashlyn Close, Bushey, Herts. *T*: Watford 43592.

BRÖDER, Ernst-Günther, DEcon; German economist and financial executive; President, and Chairman of the Board of Directors, European Investment Bank, since 1984 (a Director, 1980–84); *b* Cologne, 6 Jan. 1927; *m* Dr Edith Bleeck-Moll. *Educ*: Univs of Cologne, Mayence, Freiburg and Paris. Corporate staff, Bayer AG Leverkusen, 1956–61; Projects Dept, World Bank, 1961–64; Kreditanstalt für Wiederaufbau, 1964–84: Manager, 1969–75; Mem., Bd of Management, 1975–84; Bd of Management Spokesman, 1980–84. Member: Supervisory Bd, DEG Deutsche Finanzierungsges. für Beteiligungen in Entwicklungsländern GmbH, 1980–84; Special Adv. Gp, Asian Develt Bank, 1981–82; Panel of Conciliators, Internat. Centre for Settlement of Investment Disputes, 1976–. *Address*: European Investment Bank, 100 boulevard Konrad Adenauer, L-2950 Luxembourg. *T*: 43 79–1.

BRODIE, Sir Benjamin David Ross, 5th Bt *cr* 1834; *b* 29 May 1925; *s* of Sir Benjamin Collins Brodie, 4th Bt, MC, and Mary Charlotte (*d* 1940), *e d* of R. E. Palmer, Ballyheigue, Co. Kerry; *S* father, 1971; *m*; one *s* one *d*. *Educ*: Eton. Formerly Royal Corps of Signals. *Heir*: *s* Alan Brodie.

BRODIE, Colin Alexander, QC 1980; *b* 19 April 1929; *s* of Sir Benjamin Collins Brodie, 4th Bt, MC, and late Mary Charlotte, *e d* of R. E. Palmer, Ballyheigue, Co. Kerry; *m* 1955, Julia Anne Irene, *yr d* of Norman Edward Wates; two *s*. *Educ*: Eton; Magdalen Coll., Oxford, 2/Lieut 8th KRI Hussars, 1949–50. Called to the Bar, Middle Temple, 1954. *Recreations*: polo, hunting. *Address*: 24 Old Buildings, Lincoln's Inn, WC2. *T*: 01–404 0946.

BRODIE OF BRODIE, (Montagu) Ninian (Alexander), DL; JP; Chief of Clan Brodie; landowner since 1953; *b* 12 June 1912; *s* of I. A. M. Brodie of Brodie (*d* 1943) and C. V. M. Brodie of Brodie (*née* Hope) (*d* 1958); *m* 1939, Helena Penelope Mills Budgen (*d* 1972); one *s* one *d*. *Educ*: Eton. Stage, films, TV, 1933–40 and 1945–49. Served Royal Artillery, 1940–45. JP Morayshire, 1958; Hon. Sheriff-Substitute, 1958; DL Nairn, 1970. *Recreations*: shooting, collecting pictures. *Heir*: *s* Alastair Ian Ninian Brodie, Younger of Brodie [*b* 7 Sept. 1943; *m* 1968, Mary Louise Johnson; two *s* one *d*]. *Address*: Brodie Castle, Forres, Moray IV36 0TE, Scotland. *T*: Brodie 202.

BRODIE, Peter Ewen, OBE 1954; QPM 1963; an Assistant Commissioner, Metropolitan Police, 1966–72; *b* 6 May 1914; 2nd *s* of late Captain E. J. Brodie, Lethen, Nairn; *m* 1st, 1940, Betty Eve Middlebrook Horsfall (*d* 1975); one *s*; 2nd, 1976, Millicent Joyce Mellor. *Educ*: Harrow School. Metropolitan Police, 1934–49 (Seconded to Ceylon Police, 1943–47); Chief Constable, Stirling and Clackmannan Police force, 1949–58; Chief Constable, Warwicks Constabulary, 1958–64; HM Inspector of Constabulary for England and Wales, 1964–66. Member: Adv. Cttee on Drug Dependence, 1967–70; Exec. Cttee, Internat. Criminal Police Organisation-Interpol, 1967–70. Chm. Council, Order of St John for Warwicks, 1977–84. CStJ 1978. *Address*: Avonbrook, Sherbourne, Warwick CV35 8AN. *T*: Barford 624348.

BRODIE, Very Rev. Peter Philip, DD; Minister of St Mungo's, Alloa, 1947–87; Minister emeritus since 1987; Moderator of General Assembly of Church of Scotland, May 1978–1979; *b* 22 Oct. 1916; *s* of Robert Brodie and Margaret Jack; *m* 1949, Constance Lindsay Hope; three *s* one *d*. *Educ*: Airdrie Acad.; Glasgow Univ. (MA, BD, LLB, DD); Trinity Coll., Glasgow. Minister, St Mary's, Kirkintilloch, 1942. Church of Scotland: Chm., Gen. Trustees, 1985–; Convener, Gen. Admin Cttee, 1976. Hon. DD Glasgow, 1975. *Publications*: Four Ways Sunday School Plan, 1964; contrib. jls. *Recreations*: fishing, gardening. *Address*: 13 Victoria Square, Stirling. *Clubs*: New, Caledonian (Edinburgh).

BRODIE, Robert; Deputy Solicitor to the Secretary of State for Scotland, since 1984; *b* 9 April 1938; *s* of Robert Brodie, MBE and Helen Ford Bayne Grieve; *m* 1970, Jean Margaret McDonald; two *s* two *d*. *Educ*: Morgan Acad., Dundee; St Andrews Univ. (MA 1959, LLB 1962). Admitted Solicitor, 1962. Office of Solicitor to the Sec. of State for Scotland: Legal Asst, 1965; Sen. Legal Asst, 1970; Asst Solicitor, 1975; Dep. Dir, Scottish Courts Admin, 1975–82. *Recreations*: music, hill-walking. *Address*: 45 Stirling Road, Edinburgh EH5 3JB. *T*: 031–552 2028.

BRODIE, Stanley Eric, QC 1975; a Recorder of the Crown Court, since 1975; *b* 2 July 1930; *s* of Abraham Brodie, MB, BS and Cissie Rachel Brodie; *m* 1956, Gillian Rosemary Joseph; two *d*; *m* 1973, Elizabeth Gloster; one *s* one *d*. *Educ*: Bradford Grammar Sch.; Balliol Coll., Oxford (MA). Pres., Oxford Univ. Law Soc., 1952. Called to Bar, Inner Temple, 1954; Bencher, 1984; Mem. NE Circuit, 1954; Lectr in Law, Univ. of Southampton, 1954–55. *Recreations*: opera, boating, winter sports, fishing. *Address*: 45 Phillimore Gardens, W8 7QG. *T*: 01–937 6308. *Clubs*: United Oxford & Cambridge University, Flyfishers'.

BRODIE, Maj.-Gen. Thomas, CB 1954; CBE 1949; DSO 1951; late The Cheshire Regt; *b* 20 Oct. 1903; *s* of Thomas Brodie, Bellingham, Northumberland; *m* 1938, Jane Margaret Chapman-Walker; three *s* one *d*. *Educ*: Durham Univ. (BA 1924). Adjutant, The Cheshire Regt, 1935–37; Instructor, RMA Sandhurst, 1938–39; commanded: 2 Manchester Regt, 1942–43; 14th Infantry Brigade in Wingate Expedition, Burma, 1944; 1 Cheshire Regt, 1946–47; Palestine, 1947–48 (CBE and despatches); commanded 29 Inf. Bde, Korea, 1951 (DSO, US Silver Star Medal, US Legion of Merit); GOC 1 Infantry Div., MELF, 1952–55; Colonel, The Cheshire Regiment, 1955–61; retired 1957. Economic League, 1957–84. *Address*: Greenball, Crawley Ridge, Camberley, Surrey. *Club*: Army and Navy.

BRODIE-HALL, Sir Laurence Charles, Kt 1982; CMG 1976; Director, 1962–82, Consultant, 1975–82, Western Mining Corporation; Chairman, Board of Management, Western Australian School of Mines; *b* 10 June 1910; *m* 1st, 1940, Dorothy Jolly (decd); three *s* two *d*; 2nd, 1978, Jean Verschuer. *Educ*: Sch. of Mines, Kalgoorlie (Dip. Metallurgy 1947, DipME 1948). Served War, RAE. Geologist, Central Norseman Gold Corp., 1948–49; Tech. Asst to Man. Dir, Western Mining Corp., 1950–51; Gen. Supt, Gt Western Consolidated, 1951–58; Gen. Supt, 1958–68, Exec. Dir, WA, 1967–75, Western Mining Corp.; Chm., Westintech Innovation Corp. Ltd, 1984–; former Chm., Gold Mines of Kalgoorlie (Aust.) Pty; Dir, Ansett WA (formerly Airlines WA), 1983–; former Chm. or Dir of many subsidiaries, and Dir, Alcoa of Australia Ltd, 1971–83. Pres., WA Chamber of Mines, 1970–75; Past Pres., Australasian Inst. of Mining and Metallurgy (Institute Medal, 1977); Chm., WA State Cttee, CSIRO, 1971–81. Hon. DTech, WA Inst. Technology, 1978. *Address*: (office) 2 Cliff Street, Perth, WA 6000, Australia.

BRODRICK, family name of **Viscount Midleton.**

BRODRICK, His Honour Norman John Lee, QC 1960; JP; MA; a Circuit Judge (formerly a Judge of the Central Criminal Court), 1967–82; *b* 4 Feb. 1912; 4th *s* of late William John Henry Brodrick, OBE; *m* 1940, Ruth Severn, *d* of late Sir Stanley Unwin, KCMG; three *s* one *d*. *Educ*: Charterhouse; Merton College, Oxford. Called to Bar, Lincoln's Inn, 1935, Bencher, 1965; Mem. Senate of Four Inns of Court, 1970–71. Western Circuit, 1935. Temporary civil servant (Ministry of Economic Warfare and Admiralty), 1939–45. Bar Council, 1950–54 and 1962–66. Recorder: of Penzance, 1957–59; of Bridgwater, 1959–62; of Plymouth, 1962–64. Chairman, Mental Health Review Tribunal, Wessex Region, 1960–63; Deputy Chairman, Middlesex Quarter Sessions, 1961–65; Recorder of Portsmouth, 1964–67; Chm., IoW QS, 1964–67, Dep. Chm. 1967–71. Chm., Deptl Cttee on Death Certification and Coroners, 1965–71. JP Hants, 1967. *Recreations*: gardening, model railways. *Address*: Slade Lane Cottage, Rogate, near Petersfield, Hants GU31 5BL. *T*: Rogate 605. *Club*: Hampshire (Winchester).

BROERS, Prof. Alec Nigel, PhD; FRS 1986; FEng 1985; FIEE; Professor of Electrical Engineering and Head of Electrical Division, Cambridge University, since 1984; Fellow of Trinity College, Cambridge, since 1985; *b* 17 Sept. 1938; *s* of Alec William Broers and Constance Amy (*née* Cox); *m* 1964, Mary Therese Phelan; two *s*. *Educ*: Geelong Grammar School; Melbourne Univ. (BSc Physics 1958, Electronics 1959); Caius College, Cambridge Univ. (BA Mech Scis 1962, PhD Mech Scis 1965). IBM Thomas Watson Research Center: Research Staff Mem., 1965–67; Manager, Electron Beam Technology, 1967–72; Manager, Photon and Electron Optics, 1972–80; IBM East Fishkill Laboratory: Manager, Lithography Systems and Technology Tools, 1981–82; Manager, Semiconductor Lithography and Process Develt, 1982–83; Manager, Advanced Develt, 1983–84; Mem., Corporate Tech. Cttee, IBM Corporate HQ, 1984. IBM Fellow, 1977. Prize for Industrial Applications of Physics, Amer. Inst. of Physics, 1982; Cledo Brunetti Award, IEEE, 1985. *Publications*: patents, papers and book chapters on electron microscopy, electron beam lithography, integrated circuit fabrication. *Recreations*: music, small-boat sailing, skiing, lawn tennis. *Address*: The Oak House, Hinxton, Essex CB10 1RF. *T*: Saffron Walden 30245.

BROGAN, Lt-Gen. Sir Mervyn (Francis), KBE 1972 (CBE 1964; OBE 1944); CB 1970; Chief of the General Staff, Australia, 1971–73, retired; *b* 10 Jan. 1915; *s* of Bernard Brogan, Dubbo, NSW; *m* 1941, Sheila, *d* of David S. Jones, Canberra; two *s*. *Educ*: RMC Duntroon; Wesley Coll., Univ. of Sydney. Commnd 1935; BEng Sydney, 1938. Served War of 1939–45: New Guinea, 1942–45 (despatches 1943); trng UK and BAOR, 1946–47; Chief Instructor, Sch. of Mil. Engrg, 1947–49; trng UK and USA, 1950–52; jssc 1952; Chief Engr, Southern Comd, 1953–54; Dir of Mil. Trng, 1954–55; BGS: Army HQ, 1956; FARELF, 1956–58; idc 1959; Comdt Australian Staff Coll., 1960–62; GOC Northern Comd, 1962–64; Dir Jt Service Plans, Dept of Defence, 1965–66; QMG 1966–68; GOC Eastern Comd, 1968–71. Director: Austmark International; Windsor Resources, NL; Consultant, J. B. Meling and Co. (Australasia) Pty Ltd. Hon. FIEAust; FAIM. JP. *Recreations*: surfing, tennis. *Address*: 71/53 Ocean Avenue, Double Bay, NSW 2028, Australia. *T*: 32–9509. *Clubs*: Union, Australian Jockey, Tattersall's, Royal Sydney Golf, Rose Bay Surf (all Sydney).

BROINOWSKI, John Herbert, CMG 1969; FCA; finance and investment consultant; Senior Partner, J. H. Broinowski & Storey, Chartered Accountants, 1944–54; Founder and Managing Director, Consolidated Metal Products Ltd, 1954–70; Chairman: Orient Lloyd Group, Singapore, since 1970; Clive Hall Ltd, since 1974; Hin Kong Ltd, Hong Kong, since 1977; Utilex Ltd, since 1977; Deputy Chairman, Intersuisse Ltd, since 1984 (Director, since 1984); *b* 19 May 1911; *s* of late Dr G. H. Broinowski and late Mrs Ethel Broinowski (*née* Hungerford); *m* 1939, Jean Gaerloch Broinowski, *d* of Sir Norman and Lady Kater; one *s* one step *s*. *Educ*: Sydney Church of England Grammar Sch. Served Australian Imperial Forces (Captain), 1940–44, New Guinea. Chief Exec. and Dep. Chm., Schroder Darling and Co. Ltd, 1963–73; Exec. Chm., Sims Consolidated Ltd, 1970–83; Director: Electrical Equipment Ltd, 1954–77; Readers Digest Aust., 1955–77; Mount Morgan Ltd, 1962–67 (Chm.); Peko-Wallsend Ltd, 1962–83; South British United Insurance Gp, 1965–73; Hoyts Theatres Ltd, 1968–79 (Chm.); Compunet Ltd, 1969–77 (Chm.); Doulton Aust. Ltd, 1972–77; Robe River Ltd, 1972–73; Aquila Steel Co. Ltd, 1973–81 (Chm.), Formfit Ltd, 1974–79 (Chm.); John Sands Ltd, 1974–77; Castlemaine Tooheys Ltd, 1977–83 (Dep. Chm.); Judson Steel Corp., San Francisco, 1979–83 (Chm.). Hon. Life Member: Aust. Council for Rehabilitation of the Disabled (Pres., 1964–68); NSW Soc. for Crippled Children (Pres., 1970–77); Vice-Pres., Internat. Soc. for Rehabilitation of the Disabled, 1966–72. *Recreation*: cattle breeding. *Address*: 1c Wentworth Place, Point Piper, Sydney, NSW 2027, Australia. *T*: 02/3287534. *Clubs*: Union, Australian, Royal Sydney Golf (all in Sydney).

BROKE; *see* Willoughby de Broke.

BROKE, Lt-Col George Robin Straton, LVO 1977; RA; Equerry-in-Waiting to the Queen, 1974–77; *b* 31 March 1946; *s* of Maj.-Gen. R. S. Broke, *qv*; *m* 1978, Patricia Thornhill Shann, *d* of Thomas Thornhill Shann; one *s*. *Educ*: Eton. Commissioned into Royal Artillery, 1965. *Recreation*: country sports. *Address*: Ivy Farm, Holme Hale, Thetford, Norfolk. *T*: Holme Hale 440225. *Club*: Lansdowne.

BROKE, Maj.-Gen. Robert Straton, CB 1967; OBE 1946; MC 1940; Director, Wellman plc (formerly Wellman Engineering Corporation), since 1968, and Chairman of six companies within the Group; *b* 15 March 1913; *s* of Rev. Horatio George Broke and Mary Campbell Broke (*née* Adlington); *m* 1939, Ernine Susan Margaret Bonsey; two *s*. *Educ*: Eton College (KS); Magdalene College, Cambridge (BA). Commissioned Royal Artillery, 1933. Commander Royal Artillery: 5th Division, 1959; 1st Division, 1960; 1st (British) Corps 1961; Northern Army Group, 1964–66, retired. Col Comdt, RA, 1968–78; Representative Col Comdt, 1974–75. Chm., Iron and Steel Plant Contractors Assoc., 1972, 1977. Pres., Metallurgical Plantmakers' Fedn, 1977–79. *Recreations*: country sports. *Address*: Ivy Farm, Holme Hale, Thetford, Norfolk. *T*: Holme Hale 440225. *Clubs*: Army and Navy, MCC.
		See also G. R. S. Broke.

BROME, Vincent; author; *s* of Nathaniel Gregory and Emily Brome. *Educ*: Streatham Grammar School; Elleston School; privately. Formerly: Feature Writer, Daily Chronicle; Editor, Menu Magazines; Min. of Information; Asst Editor, Medical World. Since then author biographies, novels, plays and essays; broadcaster. Mem., British Library Adv. Cttee, 1975–82. *Plays*: The Sleepless One (prod. Edin), 1962; BBC plays. *Publications*: Anthology, 1936; Clement Attlee, 1947; H. G. Wells, 1951; Aneurin Bevan, 1953; The Last Surrender, 1954; The Way Back, 1956; Six Studies in Quarrelling, 1958; Sometimes at Night, 1959; Frank Harris, 1959; Acquaintance With Grief, 1961; We Have Come a Long Way, 1962; The Problem of Progress, 1963; Love in Our Time, 1964; Four Realist Novelists, 1964; The International Brigades, 1965; The World of Luke Jympson, 1966; Freud and His Early Circle, 1967; The Surgeon, 1967; Diary of A Revolution, 1968; The Revolution, 1969; The Imaginary Crime, 1969; Confessions of a Writer, 1970; The Brain Operators, 1970; Private Prosecutions, 1971; Reverse Your Verdict, 1971; London Consequences, 1972; The Embassy, 1972; The Day of Destruction, 1975; The Happy Hostage, 1976; Jung—Man and Myth, 1978; Havelock Ellis—philosopher of sex, 1981; Ernest Jones: Freud's alter ego, 1983; The Day of the Fifth Moon, 1984; contrib. The Times, Sunday Times, Observer, Manchester Guardian, New Statesman, New Society, Encounter, Spectator, TLS etc. *Recreations*: writing plays and talking. *Address*: 45 Great Ormond Street, WC1. *T*: 01–405 0550. *Club*: Savile.

BROMET, Air Comdt Dame Jean (Lena Annette), (Lady Bromet); *see* Conan Doyle, Air Comdt Dame J. L. A.

BROMHEAD, Sir John Desmond Gonville, 6th Bt *cr* 1806; *b* 21 Dec. 1943; *s* of Sir Benjamin Denis Gonville Bromhead, 5th Bt, OBE, and of Nancy Mary, *d* of late T. S. Lough, Buenos Aires; *S* father, 1981. *Educ*: Wellington; privately. *Heir*: *cousin* John Edmund de Gonville Bromhead [*b* 10 Oct. 1939; *m* 1965, Janet Frances, *e d* of Harry Vernon Brotherton, Moreton-in-Marsh, Glos; one *s* one *d*]. *Address*: Thurlby Hall, Thurlby, near Lincoln, Lincoln LN5 9EG.

BROMLEY, Archdeacon of; *see* Francis, Ven. E. R.

BROMLEY, Lance Lee, MA; MChir; FRCS; Director of Medical and Health Services, Gibraltar, 1982–85; Honorary Consultant Cardiothoracic Surgeon, St Mary's Hospital, W2; *b* 16 Feb. 1920; *s* of late Lancelot Bromley, MChir, FRCS, of London and Seaford, Sussex, and Dora Ridgway Bromley, Dewsbury, Yorks; *m* 1952, Rosemary Anne Holbrook; three *d*. *Educ*: St Paul's School; Caius Coll., Cambridge. Late Capt. RAMC. Late Travelling Fell. Amer. Assoc. for Thoracic Surgery. Consultant Thoracic Surgeon, St Mary's Hosp., 1953–80; Consultant Gen. Surgeon, Teddington Hosp., 1953–80. *Publications*: various contributions to medical journals. *Recreations*: sailing, golf. *Address*: 26 Molyneux Street, W1. *T*: 01–262 7175. *Club*: Royal Ocean Racing.
		See also Sir Charles Knowles, Bt.

BROMLEY, Leonard John, QC 1971; **His Honour Judge Bromley;** a Circuit Judge, since 1984; Chief Social Security Commissioner, since 1984; *b* 21 Feb. 1929; 2nd *s* of George Ernest and Winifred Dora Bromley; *m* 1962, Anne (*née* Bacon); three *d*. *Educ*: City of Leicester Boys' Sch.; Selwyn Coll., Cambridge (exhibnr). MA, LLM (Cantab). National Service: 2nd Lt, RA, Hong Kong, 1947–49. Selwyn Coll., Cambridge, 1949–53; called to Bar, Lincoln's Inn, 1954; Bencher, 1978; Greenland Scholar, Lincoln's Inn. In practice, Chancery Bar, 1954–84; a Recorder, 1980–84. Gen. Council of the Bar: Mem., 1970–74; Chm., Law Reform Cttee, 1972–74; Mem., Exec. Cttee, 1972–74. Chm., Performing Right Tribunal, 1980–83. A Legal Assessor to: GMC, 1977–84; GDC, 1977–84; Governor, Latymer Sch., Edmonton, 1978–84. Vice Cdre, Bar Yacht Club, 1971–75. *Recreations*: sailing, walking. *Address*: 6 Grosvenor Gardens, SW1W 0DH. *T*: 01–730 9236. *Club*: Athenæum.

BROMLEY, Prof. Peter Mann; Professor of English Law, University of Manchester, 1985–86 (Professor of Law, 1965–85), now Professor Emeritus; *b* 20 Nov. 1922; *s* of Frank Bromley and Marion Maud (*née* Moy); *m* 1963, Beatrice Mary, *d* of Eric Charles Cassels Hunter and Amy Madeleine (*née* Renold). *Educ*: Ealing Grammar Sch.; The Queen's College, Oxford (MA 1948). Called to the Bar, Middle Temple, 1951. Served War, Royal Artillery, 1942–45. University of Manchester: Asst Lectr 1947–50, Lectr 1950–61, Sen. Lectr 1961–65; Dean, Faculty of Law, 1966–68, 1972–74 and 1981–83; Pro-Vice-Chancellor, 1977–81; Principal, Dalton Hall, 1958–65. Chm., Cttee on Professional Legal Educn in NI, 1983–85; Member: Adv. Cttee on Legal Educn, 1972–75; University Grants Cttee, 1978–85 (Chm., Social Studies Sub-cttee, 1979–85). Editor, Butterworths Family Law Service, 1983–. *Publications*: Family Law, 1957, 6th edn 1981; (contrib.) Parental Custody and Matrimonial Maintenance, 1966; (contrib.) Das Erbrecht von Familienangehörigen, 1971; (contrib.) The Child and the Courts, 1978; (contrib.) Adoption, 1984; articles in various legal jls. *Recreation*: walking. *Address*: Paddock Brow, Faulkners Lane, Mobberley, Cheshire WA16 7AL. *T*: Mobberley 2183. *Club*: United Oxford & Cambridge University.

BROMLEY, Sir Rupert Charles, 10th Bt, *cr* 1757; *b* 2 April 1936; *s* of Major Sir Rupert Howe Bromley, MC, 9th Bt, and Dorothy Vera (*d* 1982), *d* of late Sir Walford Selby, KCMG, CB, CVO; *S* father, 1966; *m* 1962, Priscilla Hazel, *d* of late Maj. Howard Bourne, HAC; three *s*. *Educ*: Michaelhouse, Natal; Rhodes Univ.; Christ Church, Oxford. *Recreations*: equestrian. *Heir*: *s* Charles Howard Bromley, *b* 31 July 1963. *Address*: PO Box 249, Rivonia, Transvaal, 2128, South Africa.

BROMLEY, Sir Thomas Eardley, KCMG 1964 (CMG 1955); HM Diplomatic Service, retired; Secretary, Churches Main Committee, Dec. 1970–72; *b* 14 Dec. 1911; *s* of late Thomas Edward Bromley, ICS; *m* 1944, Diana Marion, *d* of Sir John Pratt, KBE, CMG; *m* 1966, Mrs Alison Toulmin. *Educ*: Rugby; Magdalen College, Oxford. Entered Consular

Service, 1935; Vice-Consul, Japan, 1938; Asst Private Sec. to the Permanent Under-Secretary of State, 1943, and Private Secretary, 1945; Grade 7, 1945; served in Washington, 1946; Bagdad, 1949; Counsellor, 1953; Head of African Department, Foreign Office, March 1954–Jan. 1956; Imperial Defence College, 1956; Foreign Office Inspectorate, 1957; seconded to Cabinet Office, Oct. 1957; Consul-General at Mogadishu, 1960; Ambassador: to Somali Republic, 1960–61; to Syrian Arab Republic, 1962–64; to Algeria, 1964–65; FO, 1966; Ambassador to Ethiopia, 1966–69. *Address:* 11 Belbroughton Road, Oxford OX2 6UZ.

BROMLEY-DAVENPORT, Lt-Col Sir Walter Henry, Kt 1961; TD; DL; *b* 1903; *s* of late Walter A. Bromley-Davenport, Capesthorne, Macclesfield, Cheshire, and late Lilian Emily Isabel Jane, DBE 1954, JP, *d* of Lt-Col J. H. B. Lane; *m* 1933, Lenette F., *d* of Joseph Y. Jeanes, Philadelphia, USA; one *s* one *d. Educ:* Malvern. Joined Grenadier Guards, 1922; raised and comd 5 Bn Cheshire Regt, Lt-Col 1939. MP (C) Knutsford Div. 1945–70; Conservative Whip, 1948–51. DL Cheshire, 1949. British Boxing Board of Control, 1953. *Address:* Capesthorne Hall, Macclesfield, Cheshire. *T:* Chelford 861221; 39 Westminster Gardens, Marsham Street, SW1. *T:* 01–834 2929; Fiva, Aandalsnes, Norway. *Clubs:* White's, Cavalry and Guards, Carlton, Pratt's.

BROMMELLE, Norman Spencer; Secretary-General, International Institute for Conservation of Historic and Artistic Works, 1957–64 and since 1966; *b* 9 June 1915; *s* of James Valentine Brommelle and Ada Louisa Brommelle (*née* Bastin); *m* 1959, Rosa Joyce Plesters. *Educ:* High Pavement School, Nottingham; University College, Oxford. Scientific research in industry on Metallography and Spectroscopy, 1937–48; Picture Conservation, National Gallery, 1949–60; Keeper, Dept of Conservation, V&A Mus., 1960–77; Dir, Hamilton Kerr Inst., Fitzwilliam Mus., Cambridge, 1978–83 (retd), Technical Adviser (pt-time) 1983–. Governor, Central Sch. of Art and Design, 1971–77. *Publications:* contributions to: Journal of the Institute of Metals; Studies in Conservation; Museums Journal. *Recreation:* gardening. *Address:* 5 Lyndhurst Square, SE15 5AR. *T:* 01–701 0607; 32 Bogliera/Morra, Città di Castello, Italy.

BRON, Eleanor; actress and writer; *d* of Sydney and Fagah Bron. *Educ:* North London Collegiate Sch., Canons, Edgware; Newnham Coll., Cambridge (BA Hons Mod. Langs). De La Rue Co., 1961. Appearances include: revue, Establishment Nightclub, Soho, 1962, and New York, 1963; Not so much a Programme, More a Way of Life, BBC TV, 1964; several TV series written with John Fortune, and TV series: Making Faces, written by Michael Frayn, 1976; Pinkerton's Progress, 1983; *TV plays include:* Nina, 1978; My Dear Palestrina, 1980; Moving on the Edge, 1984; A Month in the Country, 1985. *Stage roles include:* Jennifer Dubedat, The Doctor's Dilemma, 1966; Jean Brodie, The Prime of Miss Jean Brodie, 1967, 1984; title role, Hedda Gabler, 1969; Portia, The Merchant of Venice, 1975; Amanda, Private Lives, 1976; Elena, Uncle Vanya, 1977; Charlotte, The Cherry Orchard, 1978; Margaret, A Family, 1978; On Her Own, 1980; Goody Biddy Bean; The Amusing Spectacle of Cinderella and her Naughty, Naughty Sisters, 1980; Betrayal, 1981; Heartbreak House, 1981; Duet for One, 1982; The Duchess of Malfi, 1985; The Real Inspector Hound, and The Critic (double bill), 1985. *Films include:* Help!; Alfie; Two for the Road; Bedazzled; Women in Love; The National Health; The Day that Christ Died, 1980; Turtle Diary, 1985. Author: song-cycle with John Dankworth, 1973; verses for Saint-Saens' Carnival of the Animals, 1975 (recorded). *Publications:* Is Your Marriage Really Necessary (with John Fortune), 1972; (contrib.) My Cambridge, 1976; (contrib.) More Words, 1977; Life and Other Punctures, 1978; The Pillow Book of Eleanor Bron, 1985. *Address:* c/o Jeremy Conway Ltd, 8 Cavendish Place, W1. *Clubs:* Zoological Society, Actor's Centre.

BRONFMAN, Edgar Miles; Chairman and Chief Executive Officer: The Seagram Company Ltd, since 1975; Joseph E. Seagram & Sons Inc.; *b* 20 June 1929; *s* of late Samuel Bronfman and of Saidye Rosner. *Educ:* Trinity College Sch., Port Hope, Ont., Canada; Williams Coll., Williamstown, Mass, US; McGill Univ., Montreal (BA 1951). President: Joseph E. Seagram & Sons, Inc, 1957; The Seagram Company Ltd, 1971; Dir, E. I. duPont de Nemours & Co. Pres., World Jewish Congress, 1980–. Hon. LHD Pace Univ., NY, 1982; Hon. Dr Laws Williams Coll., Williamstown, 1986. *Address:* 375 Park Avenue, New York, NY 10152, USA. *T:* (212) 572–7000.

BROOK, Anthony Donald, FCA; Managing Director (Television), Television South plc, since 1984; *b* 24 Sept. 1936; *s* of Donald Charles Brook and Doris Ellen (*née* Emmett); *m* 1964, Ann Mary Reeves; two *d. Educ:* Eastbourne Coll. FCA 1970 (ACA 1960). Joined Associated Television Ltd, 1966; Financial Controller, ATV Network Ltd, 1969; Dir of External Finance, IBA, 1974; Finance Dir/Gen. Man., ITC Entertainment Ltd, 1978; Dep. Man. Dir, Television South plc, 1981. *Recreations:* sailing, travel. *Address:* 18 Brookvale Road, Highfield, Southampton SO2 1QP. *T:* Southampton 555689. *Clubs:* Tamesis (Teddington, Mddx); Royal Southern Yacht (Hamble, Hants).

BROOK, Air Vice-Marshal David Conway Grant, CBE 1983; Air Officer Scotland and Northern Ireland, since 1986; *b* 23 Dec. 1935; *s* of late Air Vice-Marshal William Arthur Daville Brook, CB, CBE and of Jean Brook (now Jean Hamilton); *m* 1961, Jessica (*née* Lubbock); one *s* one *d. Educ:* Marlborough Coll.; RAF Coll. (psc) fighter combat leader). Pilot, Nos 263, 1 (Flight-er) and 14 Sqdns, 1957–62 (Hunter aircraft); ADC to AOC-in-C Near East Air Force, 1962–64; CO No 1 (Fighter) Sqdn, 1964–66 (Hunter Mk 9); RN Staff Course, 1967; RAF Adviser to Dir Land/Air Warfare (MoD Army), 1968–69; Wing Comdr Offensive Support, Jt Warfare Estab., 1970–72; CO No 20 (Army Cooperation) Sqdn, 1974–76 (Harrier); Station Comdr, RAF Wittering, 1976–78 (Harrier); Principal Staff Officer to Chief of Defence Staff, 1980–82; SASO, HQ RAF Germany, 1982–85. *Publications:* contrib. to Brasseys Annual. *Recreations:* golf, music, canal boating, walking, fishing. *Address:* Bendameer House, Burntisland, Fife KY3 0AG. *T:* Burntisland 873266; c/o Lloyds Bank, Cranbrook, Kent TN17 3DJ.

BROOK, Prof. George Leslie, MA, PhD; Professor of English Language 1945–77, and of Medieval English Literature, 1951–77, University of Manchester, now Professor Emeritus; Dean of the Faculty of Arts, 1956–57; Pro-Vice-Chancellor, 1962–65; Presenter of Honorary Graduands, 1964–65; *b* 6 March 1910; 3rd *s* of late Willie Brook, Shepley, Huddersfield; *m* 1949, Stella, *d* of Thomas Maguire, Salford. *Educ:* University of Leeds; Ripon English Literature Prize, 1931. Visiting Professor, University of California, Los Angeles, 1951. *Publications:* An English Phonetic Reader, 1935; English Sound-Changes, 1935; Glossary to the Works of Sir Thomas Malory, 1947; An Introduction to Old English, 1955; A History of the English Language, 1958; English Dialects, 1963; The Modern University, 1965; The Language of Dickens, 1970; Varieties of English, 1973; The Language of Shakespeare, 1976; Books and Book Collecting, 1980; Words in Everyday Life, 1981; edited: The Harley Lyrics, 1948; The Journal of the Lancashire Dialect Society, 1951–54; (with R. F. Leslie) Layamon's Brut, Vol. I, 1963, Vol. II, 1978; (with C. S. Lewis) Selections from Layamon's Brut, 1963. *Address:* 33 Priory Lane, Kents Bank, Grange-Over-Sands, Cumbria LA11 7BH. *T:* Grange-Over-Sands 3732.

BROOK, (Gerald) Robert, CBE 1981; Chief Executive, 1977–86, and Chairman, 1985–86, National Bus Company (Deputy Chairman, 1978–85); *b* 19 Dec. 1928; *s* of Charles Pollard Brook and Doris Brook (*née* Senior); *m* 1957, Joan Marjorie Oldfield;

two *s* one *d. Educ:* King James Grammar Sch., Knaresborough. FCIS, FCIT, CBIM. Served Duke of Wellington's Regt, 1947–49. Appointments in bus companies, from 1950; Company Secretary: Cumberland Motor Services Ltd, 1960; Thames Valley Traction Co. Ltd, 1963; General Manager: North Western Road Car Co. Ltd, 1968; Midland Red Omnibus Co. Ltd, 1972; Regional Director, National Bus Company, 1974; Director: Scottish Transport Gp; United Transport Internat. Plc. *Publications:* papers for professional instns and learned socs. *Recreation:* reading military history. *Address:* Hallow Cottage, Crimple Lane, Follifoot, near Harrogate, N Yorks HG3 1DF. *Club:* Army and Navy.

BROOK, Helen, (Lady Brook); Founder, 1963, and President, Brook Advisory Centre for Young People (Chairman, 1964–74); *b* 12 Oct. 1907; *d* of John and Helen Knewstub; *m* 1937, Sir Robin Brook, *qv*; two *d* (and one *d* of previous marriage). *Educ:* Convent of Holy Child Jesus, Mark Cross, Sussex. Voluntary Worker: Family Planning Association, 1949–; Family Planning Sales, 1972– (Chm., 1974–81); Vice President: Nat. Assoc. of Family Planning Nurses, 1980–; FPA, 1982. *Recreations:* painting, gardening. *Address:* 31 Acacia Road, NW8 6AS. *T:* 01–722 5844; Claydene Garden Cottage, Cowden, Kent.

BROOK, Leopold, BScEng, FICE, FIMechE; Chairman: Associated Nuclear Services Ltd, since 1977; Brown & Sharpe Group Ltd, since 1979; Director, Renishaw plc, since 1980; *b* 2 Jan. 1912; *s* of Albert and Kate Brook, Hampstead; *m* 1st, 1940, Susan (*d* 1970), *d* of David Rose, Hampstead; two *s*; 2nd, 1974, Mrs Elly Rhodes; two step *s* one step *d. Educ:* Central Foundation School, London; University College, London. L. G. Mouchel & Partners, Cons. Engineers, 1935–44; Simon Engineering Ltd, 1944–77 (Chief Exec., 1967–70; Chm., 1970–77). Fellow, UCL, 1970–. CBIM; FRSA 1973. *Recreations:* music, theatre, walking. *Address:* 55 Kingston House North, Prince's Gate, SW7 1LW. *T:* 01–584 2041. *Clubs:* Athenæum, Hurlingham.

See also R. E. Rhodes.

BROOK, Peter Stephen Paul, CBE 1965; Producer; Co-Director, The Royal Shakespeare Theatre; *b* 21 March 1925; 2nd *s* of Simon Brook; *m* 1951, Natasha Parry, stage and film star; one *s* one *d. Educ:* Westminster, Greshams and Magdalen College, Oxford. Productions include: The Tragedy of Dr Faustus, 1942; The Infernal Machine, 1945; Birmingham Repertory Theatre: Man and Superman, King John, The Lady from the Sea, 1945–46; Stratford: Romeo and Juliet, Love's Labour's Lost, 1947; London: Vicious Circle, Men Without Shadows, Respectable Prostitute, The Brothers Karamazov, 1946; Director of Productions, Royal Opera House, Covent Garden, 1947–50: Boris Godunov, La Bohème, 1948; Marriage of Figaro, The Olympians, Salome, 1949. Dark of the Moon, 1949; Ring Round the Moon, 1950; Measure for Measure, Stratford, 1950, Paris, 1978; The Little Hut, 1950; The Winter's Tale, 1951; Venice Preserved, 1953; The Little Hut, New York, Faust, Metropolitan Opera House, 1953; The Dark is Light Enough; Both Ends Meet, 1954; House of Flowers, New York, 1954; The Lark, 1955; Titus Andronicus, Stratford, 1955; Hamlet, 1955; The Power and the Glory, 1956; Family Reunion, 1956; The Tempest, Stratford, 1957; Cat on a Hot Tin Roof, Paris, 1957; View from the Bridge, Paris, 1958; Irma la Douce, London, 1958; The Fighting Cock, New York, 1959; Le Balcon, Paris, 1960; The Visit, Royalty, 1960; King Lear, Stratford and Aldwych, 1962; The Physicists, Aldwych, 1963; Sergeant Musgrave's Dance, Paris, 1963; The Persecution and Assassination of Marat..., Aldwych, 1964 (New York, 1966); The Investigation, Aldwych, 1965; US, Aldwych, 1966; Oedipus, National Theatre, 1968; A Midsummer Night's Dream, Stratford, 1970, NY, 1971; Timon of Athens, Paris, 1974 (Grand Prix Dominique, 1975; Brigadier Prize, 1975); The Ik, Paris, 1975, London, 1976; Ubu Roi, Paris, 1977; Antony and Cleopatra, Stratford, 1978, Aldwych, 1979; Ubu, Young Vic, 1978; Conference of the Birds, France, Australia, NY, 1980; The Cherry Orchard, Paris, 1981; La tragédie de Carmen, Paris, 1981, NY, 1983 (Emmy Award, and Prix Italia, 1984); The Mahabharata, Avignon and Paris, 1985, London, 1986; work with Internat. Centre of Theatre Research, Paris, Iran, W Africa, and USA, 1971, Sahara, Niger and Nigeria, 1972–73. *Directed films:* The Beggar's Opera, 1952; Moderato Cantabile, 1960; Lord of the Flies, 1962; The Marat/Sade, 1967; Tell Me Lies, 1968; King Lear, 1969; Meetings with Remarkable Men, 1979; The Tragedy of Carmen, 1983. Hon. DLitt Birmingham. SWET award, for outstanding contribn by UK theatre artist to US theatre season, 1983. Officier de l'Ordre des Arts et des Lettres; Freiherr von Stein Foundn Shakespeare Award, 1973. *Publication:* The Empty Space, 1968. *Recreations:* painting, piano playing and travelling by air. *Address:* c/o CIRT, 9 rue du Cirque, Paris 8, France.

BROOK, Sir Ralph Ellis; *see* Brook, Sir Robin.

BROOK, Robert; *see* Brook, G. R.

BROOK, Sir Robin, Kt 1974; CMG 1954; OBE 1945; Director: United City Merchants; C. E. Coates; Member: City and E London Area Health Authority, 1974–82 (Vice Chairman, 1974–79); City and Hackney District Health Authority, 1982–86; *b* 19 June 1908; *s* of Francis Brook, Harley Street, and Mrs E. I. Brook; *m* 1937, Helen (*see* Helen Brook), *e d* of John Knewstub; two *d. Educ:* Eton; King's College, Cambridge. Served 1941–46; Brig., 1945 (OBE, despatches, Legion of Merit (Commander), Legion of Honour, Croix de Guerre and Bars, Order of Leopold (Officer), Belgian Croix de Guerre). Director, Bank of England, 1946–49. Chm., 1966–68, Pres., 1968–72, London Chamber of Commerce and Industry; Pres., Assoc. of British Chambers of Commerce, 1972–74; Pres., Assoc. of Chambers of Commerce of EEC, 1974–76; Leader of Trade Missions: for HM Govt to Libya and Romania; for London or British Chambers of Commerce to France, Iran, China, Greece, Finland and Hungary; HM Govt Dir, BP Co., 1970–73; Deputy Chairman: British Tourist and Holidays Board, 1946–50; Colonial Development Corp., 1949–53. Mem., Foundn for Management Educn, 1975–82. Sports Council: Mem., 1971–78; Vice-Chm., 1974; Chm., 1975–78; Chm., Sports Develt Cttee, 1971–74. Mem., Cttee on Invisible Exports, 1969–74; Mem. Court, Council, Finance and Hon. Degrees Cttees, City Univ.; Hon. Treasurer: Amateur Fencing Assoc., 1946–61; CCPR, 1961–77 (also Mem. Exec.); Family Planning Association, 1966–75. High Sheriff of County of London, 1950; Mem. Council, Festival of Britain. Mem. Council and Exec. Cttee, King Edward's Fund; Pres., London Homes for the Elderly, 1980– (Chm., 1973–80). St Bartholomew's Hospital: Governor, 1962–74; Treasurer and Chm., 1969–74; Chm., Special Trustees, 1974–; Pres., St Bartholomew's Med. Coll., 1969–; Governor, Royal Free Hosp., 1962–74; Mem. Governors and Exec. Cttee, Sports Aid Foundn, 1975–. Past Master, Wine Warden, Haberdashers' Co.; Governor of schools. *Recreation:* British Sabre Champion, 1936; Olympic Games, 1936, 1948; Capt. British Team, 1933 (3rd in European Championship), etc. *Address:* 31 Acacia Road, NW8 6NS.

BROOK, William Edward; British Council Officer, retired; *b* 18 Jan. 1922; *s* of William Stafford Brook and Dorothy Mary (*née* Thompson); *m* 1950, Rene Dorothy Drew; two *s* one *d. Educ:* Highgate Sch.; St Edmund Hall, Oxford (BA Mod. Langs, 1949; MA 1953). Served RAF, 1940–46: Africa, ME and Italy. Apptd to British Council, 1949; Lectr, Salonika, 1949–51; Asst Dir, Northern Provinces, Nigeria, 1951–56; Lecturer: Kuwait, 1956–59; Tripoli, Libya, 1959–62; Regional Director: Moshi, Tanganyika, 1962–67; Frankfurt, W Germany, 1967–72; Rep., Bahrain (with Qatar, UAE and Oman), 1972–76; Dir, Overseas Educnl Appts Dept, 1976; Controller, Appts Div., 1977–79; Representative, Canada, and Counsellor (Cultural), Ottawa, 1979; retd 1982. *Recreations:*

music, gardening, bird-watching. *Address:* Clarke's Cottage, Rimpton, near Yeovil, Somerset BA22 8AD. *T:* Marston Magna 850828.

BROOK-PARTRIDGE, Bernard; Director, Edmund Nuttall Ltd; Partner, Carsons, Brook-Partridge & Co. (Planning Consultants), since 1972; *b* Croydon, 1927; *o s* of late Leslie Brook-Partridge and Gladys Vere Burchell (*née* Brooks), Sanderstead; *m* 1st, 1951, Enid Elizabeth (marr. diss. 1965), 2nd *d* of late Frederick Edmund Hatfield and late Enid Hatfield (*née* Lucas), Sanderstead; two *d;* 2nd, 1967, Carol Devonald, *o d* of Arnold Devonald Francis Lewis and Patricia (*née* Thomas), Gower, S Wales; two *s. Educ:* Selsdon County Grammar Sch.; Cambridgeshire Tech. Coll.; Cambridge Univ.; London Univ.; Gray's Inn. Military Service, 1945–48. Studies, 1948–50. Cashier/Accountant, Dominion Rubber Co. Ltd, 1950–51; Asst Export Manager, British & General Tube Co. Ltd, 1951–52; Asst Sec., Assoc. of Internat. Accountants, 1952–59; Sec.-Gen., Institute of Linguists, 1959–62; various teaching posts, Federal Republic of Germany, 1962–66; Special Asst to Man. Dir, M. G. Scott Ltd, 1966–68. Business consultancy work on own account, incl. various dirships with several client cos, 1968–72; Dir and Sec., Roban Engineering Ltd and predecessor company, 1971–; Chairman: Brompton Troika Ltd, 1985–; Central Property Index Ltd, 1986–; Thermocare Energy Services Ltd, 1986–; Dir, Alan Wooff Associates Ltd, 1985–. Contested (C) St Pancras North, LCC, 1958; Mem. (C) St Pancras Metropolitan Borough Council, 1959–62. Prospective Parly Cand. (C), Shoreditch and Finsbury, 1960–62; contested (C) Nottingham Central, 1970. Greater London Council: Mem. for Havering, 1967–73, for Havering (Romford), 1973–85; Chm., 1980–81; Chairman: Planning and Transportation (NE) Area Bd, 1967–71; Town Develt Cttee, 1971–73; Arts Cttee, 1977–78; Public Services and Safety Cttee, 1978–79; Opposition spokesman: for Arts and Recreation, 1973–77; for Police Matters, 1983–85; Member: Exec. Cttee, Greater London Arts Assoc., 1973–78; Exec. Council, Area Museums Service for SE England, 1977–78; Council and Exec., Greater London and SE Council for Sport and Recreation, 1977–78; GLC Leaders' Cttee with special responsibility for Law and Order and Police Liaison matters, 1977–79; Dep. Leader, Recreation and Community Services Policy Cttee, 1977–79. Member: Exec. Cttee, Exmoor Soc., 1974–79; BBC Radio London Adv. Council, 1974–79; Gen. Council, Poetry Soc., 1977– (Treas., 1982–); Board Member: Peterborough Develt Corp., 1972– (Chm., Queensgate Management Services); London Festival Ballet (and Trustee), 1977–79; Young Vic Theatre Ltd, 1977– (Chm., 1983–); London Orchestral Concert Bd Ltd, 1977–78; ENO, 1977–78; London Contemp. Dance Trust, 1979–84; Governor and Trustee: SPCK, 1976–; Sadler's Wells Foundn, 1977–79; Chm., London Music Hall Trust, 1983–; Vice-Chm., London Music Hall Protection Soc. Ltd (Wilton's Music Hall), 1983– (Mem. Bd, 1978–; Chm., 1981–83); Chairman: London Symphony Chorus Develt Cttee, 1981–; Samuel Lewis Housing Trust, 1985– (Trustee, 1976–); Pres., British Sch. of Osteopathy Appeal Fund, 1980–84. President: Witan (GLC Staff) Rifle Club, 1979–; City of London Rifle League, 1980–; Gtr London Horse Show, 1982–. FCIS (Mem. Council, 1981–, Treas., 1984, Vice-Pres. 1985, Pres., 1986–); MBIM. Hon. FIE. Hon. PhD Columbia Pacific, 1982. Order of Gorkha Dakshina Bahu (2nd cl.), Nepal, 1981. *Publications:* Europe—Power and Responsibility: Direct Elections to the European Parliament (with David Baker), 1972; innumerable contribs to learned jls and periodicals on linguistics and translation, the use of language, political science and contemporary politics. *Recreations:* hunting, conversation, opera, ballet, classical music and being difficult. *Address:* 14 Redcliffe Street, SW10 9DT. *T:* 01–373 1223. *Clubs:* Athenæum, United and Cecil, Nikaean; Surrey County Cricket.

BROOKE, family name of **Viscount Alanbrooke,** of **Baroness Brooke of Ystradfellte** and of **Viscount Brookeborough.**

BROOKE, Lord; Guy David Greville; *b* 30 Jan. 1957; *s* and *heir* of 8th Earl of Warwick, *qv* and of Mrs Harry Thomson Jones; *m* 1981, Susan McKinley Cobbold; one *s. Educ:* Summerfields, Eton and Ecole des Roches. *Recreations:* golf, surfing. *Heir: s* Hon. Charles Fulke Chester Greville, *b* 27 July 1982. *Address:* 4 Walter Street, Claremont, Western Australia 6010. *T:* 384 9940. *Club:* White's.

BROOKE OF YSTRADFELLTE, Baroness *cr* 1964 (Life Peer); **Barbara Brooke,** DBE 1960; *b* 14 Jan. 1908; *y d* of late Canon A. A. Mathews; *m* 1933, Henry Brooke, PC, CH (later Baron Brooke of Cumnor) (*d* 1984); two *s* two *d. Educ:* Queen Anne's School, Caversham. Joint Vice-Chm., Conservative Party Organisation, 1954–64. Member: Hampstead Borough Council, 1948–65; North-West Metropolitan Regional Hospital Board, 1954–66; Management Cttee, King Edward's Hospital Fund for London, 1966–71; Chairman: Exec. Cttee Queen's Institute of District Nursing, 1961–71; Governing Body of Godolphin and Latymer School, Hammersmith, 1960–78. Hon. Fellow, Westfield College. *Address:* Romans Halt, Mildenhall, Marlborough, Wilts SN8 2LX.

See also H. Brooke, Hon. P. L. Brooke, Rev. A. K. Mathews.

BROOKE, Sir Alistair Weston, 4th Bt *cr* 1919, of Almondbury; *b* 12 Sept. 1947; *s* of Major Sir John Weston Brooke, 3rd Bt, TD, and Rosemary (*d* 1979), *d* of late Percy Nevill, Birling House, West Malling, Kent; *S* father, 1983; *m* 1982, Susan Mary, *d* of Barry Charles Roger Griffiths, MRCVS, Church House, Norton, Powys; one *d. Educ:* Repton; Royal Agricultural Coll., Cirencester. *Recreations:* shooting, farming, racehorse training. *Heir: b* Charles Weston Brooke, *b* 27 Jan. 1951. *Address:* Wootton Farm, Pencombe, Hereford. *T:* Pencombe 615.

BROOKE, Arthur Caffin, CB 1972; retired; *b* 11 March 1919; *s* of late Rev. James M. Wilmot Brooke and Constance Brooke; *m* 1942, Margaret Florence Thompson; two *s. Educ:* Abbotsholme Sch.; Peterhouse, Cambridge (MA). Served War, Royal Corps of Signals, 1939–46. Northern Ireland Civil Service, 1946–79; Ministry of Commerce, 1946–73: Asst Sec., Head of Industrial Development Div., 1955; Sen. Asst Sec., Industrial Development, 1963; Second Sec., 1968; Permanent Sec., 1969; Permanent Sec., Dept of Educn, 1973–79. Chm., Arts Council of NI, 1982–86 (Mem., 1979–). *Address:* 53 Osborne Park, Belfast, Northern Ireland. *T:* 669192.

BROOKE, Prof. Bryan Nicholas, MD, MChir, FRCS; writer and freelance journalist, since 1982; Emeritus Professor (Professor of Surgery, University of London, at St George's Hospital 1963–80); lately consultant surgeon, St George's Hospital; *b* 21 Feb. 1915; *s* of George Cyril Brooke, LitD, FSA (numismatist) and Margaret Florence Brooke; *m* 1940, Naomi Winefride Mills; three *d. Educ:* Bradfield College, Berkshire; Corpus Christi College, Cambridge; St Bartholomew's Hospital, London. FRCSEng 1942; MChir (Cantab.) 1944; MD (Birm.) with hons 1954. Lieut-Colonel, RAMC, 1945–46. Lecturer in Surgery, Aberdeen Univ., 1946–47; Reader in Surgery, Birmingham Univ., 1947–63; Hunterian Prof. RCS, 1951. Examiner in Surgery, Universities of: Birmingham, 1951–63; Cambridge, 1958–; Bristol, 1961–; London, 1962–; Glasgow, 1969; Oxford, 1970; Hong Kong, 1972; Nigeria, 1975; RCS, 1973; Chm., Ct of Examnrs, RCS, 1978. Member, Medical Appeals Tribunal, 1948–. Pres., Ileostomy Assoc. of GB, 1957–82. Chm., Malvern Girls' Coll., 1972–82. Copeman Medal for Scientific Research, 1960; Graham Award (Amer. Proctologic Soc.), 1961; Award of NY Soc., Colon and Rectal Surgeons, 1967. Hon. FRACS, 1977; Hon. Mem., British Soc. of Gastroenterology, 1979. Consultant Editor, World Medicine, 1980–82. *Publications:* Ulcerative Colitis and its Surgical Treatment, 1954; You and Your Operation, 1957; United Birmingham Cancer Reports, 1953, 1954, 1957; (co-editor) Recent Advances in Gastroenterology, 1965; (co-author) Metabolic Derangements in Gastrointestinal Surgery, 1966; Understanding Cancer, 1971; Crohn's Disease, 1977; The Troubled Gut, 1986; Editor, Jl Clinics in Gastroenterology; contrib. to various surgical works. Numerous articles on large bowel disorder, medical education, steroid therapy. *Recreations:* painting, pottery. *Address:* 112 Balham Park Road, SW12 8EA. *Club:* Savage.

BROOKE, Prof. Christopher Nugent Lawrence, MA; LittD; FSA; FRHistS; FBA 1970; Dixie Professor of Ecclesiastical History, since 1977, and Fellow, Gonville and Caius College, 1949–56 and since 1977, University of Cambridge; *b* 1927; *y s* of late Professor Zachary Nugent Brooke and Rosa Grace Brooke; *m* 1951, Rosalind Beckford, *d* of Dr and Mrs L. H. S. Clark; three *s. Educ:* Winchester College (Scholar); Gonville and Caius College, Cambridge (Major Scholar). BA 1948; MA 1952; LittD 1973. Army service in RAEC, Temp. Captain 1949. Cambridge University: College Lecturer in History, 1953–56; Praelector Rhetoricus, 1955–56; Asst Lectr in History, 1953–54; Lectr, 1954–56; Prof. of Mediæval History, University of Liverpool, 1956–67; Prof. of History, Westfield Coll., Univ. of London, 1967–77. Member: Royal Commn on Historical Monuments (England), 1977–83; Reviewing Cttee on Export of Works of Art, 1979–82. Vice-Pres., Soc. of Antiquaries, 1975–79, Pres., 1981–84. Corresp. Fellow, Medieval Acad. of America, 1981. DUniv York, 1984. Lord Mayor's Midsummer Prize, City of London, 1981. *Publications:* The Dullness of the Past, 1957; From Alfred to Henry III, 1961; The Saxon and Norman Kings, 1963; Europe in the Central Middle Ages, 1964; Time the Archsatirist, 1968; The Twelfth Century Renaissance, 1970; Structure of Medieval Society, 1971; Medieval Church and Society (sel. papers), 1971; (with W. Swaan) The Monastic World, 1974; (with G. Keir) London, 800–1216, 1975; Marriage in Christian History, 1977; (with R. B. Brooke) Popular Religion in the Middle Ages, 1000–1300, 1984; A History of Gonville and Caius College, 1985; part Editor: The Book of William Morton, 1954; The Letters of John of Salisbury, vol. I, 1955, vol. II, 1979; Carte Nativorum, 1960; (with A. Morey) Gilbert Foliot and his letters, 1965 and (ed jtly) The Letters and Charters of Gilbert Foliot, 1967; (with D. Knowles and V. London) Heads of Religious Houses, England and Wales 940–1216, 1972; (with D. Whitelock and M. Brett) Councils and Synods, vol. I, 1981; (with Sir Roger Mynors) Walter Map, De Nugis Curialium (revision of M. R. James edn), 1983; contributed to A History of St Paul's Cathedral, 1957; Studies in the Early British Church, 1958; Celt and Saxon, 1963; Studies in Church History, Vol. I, 1964, Vol. VI, 1970, Vol. XXII, 1985; A History of York Minster, 1977; general editor: Oxford (formerly Nelson's) Medieval Texts, Nelson's History of England; articles and reviews in English Historical Review, Cambridge Historical Journal, Bulletin of Inst. of Historical Research, Downside Review, Traditio, Bulletin of John Rylands Library, Jl of Soc. of Archivists, etc. *Address:* Faculty of History, West Road, Cambridge CB3 9EF.

BROOKE, Sir Francis (George Windham), 4th Bt *cr* 1903; *b* 15 Oct. 1963; *s* of Sir George Cecil Francis Brooke, 3rd Bt, MBE, and of Lady Melissa Brooke, *er d* of 6th Earl of Dunraven and Mount-Earl, CB, CBE, MC; *S* father, 1982. *Educ:* Eton; Edinburgh University. *Heir: cousin* Lt-Comdr Geoffrey Arthur George Brooke, DSC, RN retd [*b* 25 April 1920; *m* 1956, Venetia Mabel, *o d* of late Captain the Hon. Oswald Wykeham Cornwallis, OBE, RN; three *d*]. *Address:* Glenbevan, Croom, Co. Limerick, Ireland.

BROOKE, Henry; QC 1981; a Recorder of the Crown Court, since 1983; *b* 19 July 1936; *s* of Lord Brooke of Cumnor, PC, CH and of Lady Brooke of Ystradfellte, *qv*; *m* 1966, Bridget Mary Kalaugher; three *s* one *d. Educ:* Marlborough College; Balliol Coll., Oxford. MA (1st Cl. Classical Hon. Mods, 1st Cl. Lit. Hum.). Called to the Bar, Inner Temple, 1963; Junior Counsel to the Crown, Common Law, 1978–81; Counsel to the Inquiry, Sizewell 'B' Nuclear Reactor Inquiry, 1983–85. *Publication:* (contrib.) Halsbury's Laws of England, 4th edn. *Address:* Fountain Court, Temple, EC4Y 9DH. *T:* 01–353 7356.

See also Hon. P. L. Brooke.

BROOKE, Humphrey; *see* Brooke, T. H.

BROOKE, John; Chairman, Brooke Bond Liebig Ltd, retired 1971; *b* 7 March 1912; *m* 1936, Bridget (*née* May); two *s* one *d. Educ:* Bedales, Petersfield, Hants. Joined Brooke Bond & Co. Ltd, Oct. 1930, as Trainee Salesman. *Address:* 10 Parsonage Lane, Market Lavington, near Devizes, Wilts. *T:* Lavington 2204.

BROOKE, Sir (Norman) Richard (Rowley), Kt 1964; CBE 1958; FCA; *b* 23 June 1910; *s* of William Brooke, JP and Eleanor (*née* Wild), Frodingham, Lincs; *m* 1st, 1948, Julia Dean (marr. diss. 1957); one *s* one *d;* 2nd, 1958, Nina Mari Dolan. *Educ:* Charterhouse School. Joined Guest, Keen & Nettlefolds Ltd, 1935; Commnd TA, 1937; demobilised 1940 on return to GKN; Dir, Guest, Keen & Nettlefolds Ltd, 1961–67; Dir and/or Chm. of several GKN subsidiary cos until retirement in 1967; Director: Eagle Star Insurance Co. (Wales Bd), 1955–80; L. Ryan Hldgs Ltd, 1972–78; a Founder Dir, Develt Corp. for Wales, 1958–67, Hon. Vice-Pres., 1967–83. Founder Mem. and Dep. Chm., British Independent Steel Producers Assoc., 1967. Hon. Life Vice-President, Wales Conservative and Unionist Council, 1966; President, Cardiff Chamber of Commerce, 1960–61; Member Exec. Cttee and Council, British Iron and Steel Federation, to 1967 (Joint Vice-Pres., 1966–67); Vice-Pres., University College, Cardiff, 1965–81, Mem. Council, 1982–. JP Glamorgan, 1952–64, 1970–74. OStJ 1953. *Recreations:* bridge, music, reading. *Address:* New Sarum, Pwllmelin Lane, Llandaff, Cardiff. *T:* Cardiff 563692. *Club:* Cardiff and County (Cardiff).

BROOKE, Hon. Peter Leonard; MP (C) City of London and Westminster South, since Feb. 1977; Minister of State, HM Treasury, since 1985; *b* 3 March 1934; *s* of Lord Brooke of Cumnor, PC, CH and of Lady Brooke of Ystradfellte, *qv*; *m* 1964, Joan Margaret Smith (*d* 1985); three *s* (and one *s* decd). *Educ:* Marlborough; Balliol College, Oxford (MA); Harvard Business School (MBA). Vice-Pres., Nat. Union of Students, 1955–56; Chm., Nat. Conf., Student Christian Movement, 1956; Pres., Oxford Union, 1957; Commonwealth Fund Fellow, 1957–59. Research Assistant, IMEDE, Lausanne, 1960–61. Spencer Stuart & Associates, Management Consultants, 1961–79 (Director of parent company, 1965–79, Chairman 1974–79); lived in NY and Brussels, 1969–73. Director, Ecole St Georges, Switzerland, 1964–79. Mem., Camden Borough Council, 1968–69. Chm., St Pancras N Cons. Assoc., 1976–77. Contested (C) Bedwellty, Oct. 1974; an Asst Govt Whip, 1979–81; a Lord Comr of HM Treasury, 1981–83; Parly Under Sec. of State, DES, 1983–85. Pres., London Council on Alcoholism, 1981–83; Member: Adv. Council, Business Graduates Assoc., 1979–83; Foundn for Management Educn, 1979–83; Pres., Incorp. Assoc. of Prep. Schs, 1980–83; Governor, Marlborough Coll., 1977–83; Trustee: Dove Cottage, 1976–; Cusichaca Project, 1978–; Rantavan Foundn, 1969–. Lay Adviser, St Paul's Cathedral, 1980–. *Recreations:* churches, conservation, cricket, pictures, planting things. *Address:* c/o House of Commons, SW1. *T:* 01–219 5041. *Clubs:* Brooks's, City Livery, MCC, I Zingari, St George's (Hanover Square) Conservative.

See also H. Brooke.

BROOKE, Sir Richard; *see* Brooke, Sir N. R. R.

BROOKE, Sir Richard (Neville), 10th Bt *cr* 1662; *b* 1 May 1915; *s* of Sir Richard Christopher Brooke, 9th Bt, and Marian Dorothea (*d* 1965), *d* of late Arthur Charles Innes, MP, of Dromantine, Co. Down; *S* father, 1981; *m* 1st, 1937, Lady Mabel Kathleen Jocelyn (marr. diss. 1959), *d* of 8th Earl of Roden; two *s*; 2nd, 1960, Jean Evison, *d* of late Lt-Col A. C. Corfe, DSO. *Educ:* Eton. Served as Lieutenant, Scots Guards, 1939–46; prisoner of war (escaped). Chartered Accountant (FCA), 1946; Senior Partner, Price Waterhouse & Co., European Firms, 1969–75; retired, 1975. *Recreations:* racing, fishing. *Heir: s* Richard David Christopher Brooke [*b* 23 Oct. 1938; *m* 1st, 1963, Carola Marion (marr. diss. 1978), *d* of Sir Robert Erskine-Hill, 2nd Bt; two *s*; 2nd, 1979, Lucinda Barlow, *o d* of late J. F. Voelcker and of Jean Constance Voelcker, Lidgetton, Natal]. *Address:* 44 Castellaras-le-Vieux, 06370 Mouans-Sartoux, France. *T:* (93) 752460. *Clubs:* Boodle's; Travellers' (Paris).

BROOKE, Rodney George; Chief Executive, Westminster City Council, since 1984; *b* 22 Oct. 1939; *s* of George Sidney Brooke and Amy Brooke; *m* 1967, Dr Clare Margaret Cox; one *s* one *d*. *Educ:* Queen Elizabeth's Grammar Sch., Wakefield. Admitted solicitor, 1962. Asst Solicitor: Rochdale County Bor. Council, 1962–63; Leicester CC, 1963–65; Stockport County Bor. Council: Sen. Asst Solicitor, 1965–67; Asst Town Clerk, 1967–69; Dep. Town Clerk, 1969–71; Dir of Admin, 1971–73; West Yorkshire Metropolitan County Council: Dir of Admin, 1973–81; Chief Exec. and Clerk, 1981–84. National Order of Merit (France), 1984; Nat. Order of Aztec Eagle (Mexico), 1985; Medal of Merit (Qatar), 1985. *Publications:* articles on local govt. *Recreations:* skiing, opera, Byzantium. *Address:* Stubham Lodge, Clifford Road, Middleton, Ilkley, West Yorks LS29 0AX. *T:* Ilkley 601869; 706 Grenville House, Dolphin Square, SW1V 3LX. *T:* 01–828 6828. *Club:* Ski Club of Great Britain.

BROOKE, (Thomas) Humphrey, CVO 1969 (MVO 1958); Secretary, Royal Academy of Arts, Piccadilly, W1, 1952–68; *b* 31 Jan. 1914; *y s* of late Major Thomas Brooke, Grimston Manor, York, and late B. Gundreda, *d* of Sir Hildred Carlile, 1st and last Bt; *m* 1946, Countess Nathalie Benckendorff, *o d* of Count Benckendorff, DSO; one *d* (one *s* one *d* decd). *Educ:* Wellington Coll.; Magdalen Coll., Oxford. 1st Cl. Hons Mod. History Oxon, 1935; BLitt 1937. Asst Keeper, Public Record Office, 1937. Served War of 1939–45; commissioned KRRC, 1943. Dir of Archives, Sub-Commn for Monuments, Fine Arts and Archives, Allied Control Commn, Italy, 1944–45; Controller, Monuments and Fine Arts Branch, Allied Commission for Austria, 1946; Dep. Director, Tate Gallery, 1948; Ministry of Town and Country Planning, 1949; Resigned from Civil Service on appointment to Royal Acad., 1951. Founded first rosarium in GB in Suffolk for the preservation and conservation of roses, 1971. Member Order of Santiago (Portugal), 1955; Commander Ordine al Merito della Republica Italiana, 1956; Officier de l'Ordre de l'Etoile Noire (France), 1958. *Recreations:* shooting, fishing, gardening. *Address:* Flat 3, 11 Onslow Square, SW7. T: 01–589 5690; Lime Kiln, Claydon, Suffolk. *T:* Ipswich 830334. *Club:* Chelsea Arts.

BROOKE-LITTLE, John Philip Brooke, CVO 1984 (MVO 1969); Norroy and Ulster King of Arms, and King of Arms, Registrar and Knight Attendant on the Most Illustrious Order of St Patrick, since 1980; Librarian, since 1974, and Treasurer, since 1978, College of Arms; *b* 6 April 1927; *s* of late Raymond Brooke-Little, Unicorns House, Swalcliffe; *m* 1960, Mary Lee, *o c* of late John Raymond Pierce and Mrs E. G. Pierce, Lower Heyford, Oxon; three *s* one *d*. *Educ:* Clayesmore Sch; New Coll., Oxford (MA). Earl Marshal's staff, 1952–53; Gold Staff Officer, Coronation, 1953; Bluemantle Pursuivant of Arms, 1956–67; Richmond Herald, 1967–80; Registrar, Coll. of Arms, 1974–82. Asst Dir, Heralds' Museum, Tower of London, 1983–; Adviser on heraldry: Nat. Trust, 1983–; Shrievalty Assoc., 1983–. Founder of Heraldry Soc. and Chm., 1947; Hon. Editor, The Coat of Arms, 1950; Fellow, Soc. of Genealogists, 1969; Hon. Fellow, Inst. of Heraldic and Geneal Studies, 1979. Chm., Harleian Soc., 1984–; Pres., English Language Literary Trust, 1985–. Governor, Clayesmore Sch. (Chm., 1971–83). Freeman and Liveryman, Scriveners' Co. of London (Master, 1985–86). FSA 1961. KStJ 1975; Knight of Malta, 1955 (Chancellor, British Assoc., 1973–77); Comdr Cross of Merit of Order of Malta, 1964; Cruz Distinguida (1st cl.) de San Raimundo de Peñafort, 1955. *Publications:* Royal London, 1953; Pictorial History of Oxford, 1954; Boutell's Heraldry, 1970, 1973, 1978 and 1983 (1963 and 1966 edns with C. W. Scott-Giles); Knights of the Middle Ages, 1966; Prince of Wales, 1969; Fox-Davies' Complete Guide to Heraldry, annotated edn, 1969; (with Don Pottinger and Anne Tauté) Kings and Queens of Great Britain, 1970; An Heraldic Alphabet, 1973; (with Marie Angell) Beasts in Heraldry, 1974; The British Monarchy in Colour, 1976; Royal Arms, Beasts and Badges, 1977; Royal Ceremonies of State, 1979; genealogical and heraldic articles. *Recreations:* cooking, painting. *Address:* Heyford House, Lower Heyford, near Oxford. *T:* Steeple Aston 40337; College of Arms, EC4. *T:* 01–248 1310. *Clubs:* City Livery, Chelsea Arts (Hon. Member).

BROOKE-ROSE, Prof. Christine; novelist and critic; Professor of English Language and Literature, University of Paris, since 1975 (Lecturer, 1969–75). *Educ:* Oxford and London Univs. MA Oxon 1953, PhD London 1954. Research and criticism, 1955–. Reviewer for: The Times Literary Supplement, The Times, The Observer, The Sunday Times, The Listener, The Spectator, and The London Magazine, 1956–68; took up post at Univ. of Paris VIII, Vincennes, 1969. Has broadcast in book programmes on BBC, and on 'The Critics', and ABC Television. Travelling Prize of Society of Authors, 1964; James Tait Black Memorial Prize, 1966; Arts Council Translation Prize, 1969. *Publications: novels:* The Languages of Love, 1957; The Sycamore Tree, 1958; The Dear Deceit, 1960; The Middlemen, 1961; Out, 1964; Such, 1965; Between, 1968; Thru, 1975; Amalgamemnon, 1984; Xorandor, 1986; *criticism:* A Grammar of Metaphor, 1958; A ZBC of Ezra Pound, 1971; A Rhetoric of the Unreal, 1981; *short stories:* Go when you see the Green Man Walking, 1969; short stories and essays in various magazines, etc. *Recreations:* people, travel. *Address:* c/o Cambridge University Press, PO Box 110, Cambridge CB2 3RL.

BROOKE TURNER, Alan, CMG 1980; HM Diplomatic Service, retired; *b* 4 Jan. 1926; *s* of late Arthur Brooke Turner, MC; *m* 1954, Hazel Alexandra Rowan Henderson; two *s* two *d*. *Educ:* Marlborough; Balliol Coll., Oxford (Sen. Schol.). 1st cl Hon. Mods 1949; 1st cl. Lit. Hum. 1951. Served in RAF, 1944–48. Entered HM Foreign (subseq. Diplomatic) Service, 1951; FO, 1951; Warsaw, 1953; 3rd, later 2nd Sec. (Commercial), Jedda, 1954; Lisbon, 1957; 1st Sec., FO, 1959 (UK Delegn to Nuclear Tests Conf., Geneva, 1962); Cultural Attaché, Moscow, 1962; FO, 1965; Fellow, Center for Internat. Affairs, Harvard Univ., 1968; Counsellor, Rio de Janeiro, 1969–71; Head of Southern European Dept, FCO, 1972–73; Counsellor and Head of Chancery, British Embassy, Rome, 1973–76; Civil Dep. Comdt and Dir of Studies, NATO Defense Coll., Rome, 1976–78; Internat. Inst. for Strategic Studies, 1978–79; Minister, Moscow, 1979–82; Ambassador to Finland, 1983–85. *Recreations:* sailing, skiing. *Address:* Poultons, Moor Lane, Dormansland, near Lingfield, Surrey RH7 6NX; 11 Marsham Court, Marsham Street, SW1P 4JY. *Clubs:* Travellers'; Nylands Yacht (Helsinki).

BROOKEBOROUGH, 2nd Viscount *cr* 1952, of Colebrooke; **John Warden Brooke,** PC (NI) 1971; DL; Bt 1822; Member (UPNI) for North Down, Northern Ireland Constitutional Convention, 1975–76; *b* 9 Nov. 1922; *s* of 1st Viscount Brookeborough, KG, PC, CBE, MC, and Cynthia Mary, DBE 1959 (*d* 1970), *d* of late Captain Charles Warden Sergison; *S* father, 1973; *m* 1949, Rosemary Hilda Chichester; two *s* three *d*. *Educ:* Eton. Joined Army, 1941; Captain 10th Royal Hussars; wounded, Italy, 1942; subseq. ADC to Field Marshal Alexander in Italy and to Gen. Sir Brian Robertson in Germany; ADC to Viceroy of India, Field Marshal Lord Wavell, 1946; invalided, 1947. Fermanagh County Councillor, 1947–73, Chairman, 1961–73; pioneered streamlining of local govt by voluntary amalgamation of all councils in the county, 1967. MP (U) Lisnaskea Div., Parlt of NI, 1968–73; Mem. (U), N Down, NI Assembly, 1973–75; Parly Sec. to Min. of Commerce with special responsibilities for tourism, Apr. 1969; Parly Sec. to Dept of the Prime Minister (still retaining Commerce office), with responsibility for general oversight of Government's publicity and information services, Jan. 1970; Minister of State, Min. of Finance and Govt Chief Whip, 1971–72. DL Co. Fermanagh, 1967. *Recreations:* shooting, fishing, riding. *Heir: s* Hon. Alan Henry Brooke [*b* 30 June 1952; *m* 1980, Janet, *o d* of John Cooke, Doagh, Co. Antrim. Commissioned 17/21 Lancers, 1972; Captain, UDR, 1977]. *Address:* Ashbrooke, Brookeborough, Enniskillen, Co. Fermanagh. *T:* Brookeborough 242.

BROOKER, Alan Bernard; JP, DL; FCA; Chairman and Chief Executive, Extel Group plc, since 1980; *b* 24 Aug. 1931; *s* of late Bernard John Brooker and of Gwendoline Ada (*née* Launchbury); *m* 1957, Diana (*née* Coles); one *s* two *d*. *Educ:* Chigwell School, Essex. FCA 1954. Served 2nd RHA (2nd Lieut), 1954–56. Articled, Cole, Dickin & Hills, Chartered Accountants, 1949–54, qualified 1954; Manager, Cole, Dickin & Hills, 1956–58; Accountant, Independent Dairies, 1958–59; Asst Accountant, Exchange Telegraph Co., 1959–64; Dir, Extel Group, 1964–. Vice-Chm., Provident Financial Group, 1983–; Non-exec. Dir, Pauls plc, 1984–85. Member: Council, CBI London Region, 1980–83; Companies Cttee, CBI, 1979–83; Council, CPU, 1975–. Appeal Chm., Newspaper Press Fund, 1985–86. Governor: Chigwell School, 1968– (Chm., 1978–); Felixstowe Coll., 1986–. Freeman, City of London; Liveryman, Stationers and Newspapermakers' Co. (Court Asst, 1985–). Churchwarden, St Bride's, Fleet Street, 1986–. JP Essex 1972, DL Essex 1982. FInstD. *Recreations:* cricket, golf. *Address:* Plowlands, Laundry Lane, Little Easton, Dunmow, Essex CM6 2JW. *Clubs:* East India, MCC.

BROOKES, family name of **Baron Brookes.**

BROOKES, Baron *cr* 1975 (Life Peer), of West Bromwich; **Raymond Percival Brookes,** Kt 1971; Life President, Guest, Keen & Nettlefolds Ltd (Group Chairman and Chief Executive, 1965–74); *b* 10 April 1909; *s* of William and Ursula Brookes; *m* 1937, Florence Edna Sharman; one *s*. Part-time Mem., BSC, 1967–68. First Pres., British Mechanical Engrg Confedn, 1968–70; a Vice-Pres., Engrg Employers' Fedn, 1967–75. Member: Council, UK S Africa Trade Assoc. Ltd, 1967–74; Council, CBI, 1968–75; BNEC, 1969–71; Wilberforce Ct of Inquiry into electricity supply industry dispute, Jan. 1971; Industrial Develt Adv. Bd, 1972–75. Member: Exec. Cttee, 1970–, Council, 1969–, Pres., 1974–75, Soc. of Motor Manufacturers & Traders Ltd; Court of Governors, Univ. of Birmingham, 1966–75; Council, Univ. of Birmingham, 1968–75. Pres., Motor Ind. Res. Assoc., 1973–75. Chm., Rea Brothers (Isle of Man) Ltd; Director: Plessey Co. Ltd. *Recreations:* golf, fly-fishing. *Address:* Guest, Keen & Nettlefolds Ltd, Group Head Office, Smethwick, Warley, Worcs; (private) Mallards, Santon, Isle of Man.

BROOKES, Beata; Member (C) North Wales, European Parliament, since 1979; *b* 1931. *Educ:* Lowther College, Abergele; Univ. of Wales, Bangor; studied politics in USA (US State Dept Scholarship). Former social worker, Denbighshire CC; company secretary and farmer. Contested (C) Widnes, 1955, Warrington, 1963, Manchester Exchange, 1964. Member: Clwyd AHA, 1973–80 (Mem., Welsh Hosp. Bd, 1963–74); Clwyd Family Practitioner Cttee; Clwyd CC Social Services Cttee, 1973–81; Flintshire Soc. for Mentally Handicapped; N Wales Council for Mentally Handicapped; Council for Professions Supplementary to Medicine; Exec. Cttee, N Wales Cons. Group; European Parlt Educn Cttee, and Agricultural Cttee. Pres., N Wales Assoc. for the Disabled. *Address:* The Cottage, Wayside Acres, Bodelwyddan, near Rhyl, North Wales.

BROOKES, Air Vice-Marshal Hugh Hamilton, CB 1954; CBE 1951; DFC 1944; RAF retd; *b* 14 Oct. 1904; *s* of late W. H. Brookes and of Evelyn, *d* of J. Forster Hamilton (she married 2nd Sir John Simpson, KBE, CIE); *m* 1932, Elsie Viola Henry; one *d*. *Educ:* Bedford School; Cranwell. Bomber Command, 1924; 84 Sqdn Iraq, 1929; Staff College, 1933; Sqdn Bomber Command, 1937; Iraq, 1938; Western Desert, 1939; Aden, 1941; Station Bomber Command, 1943; Iraq, 1946; Director of Flying Training, 1949; AOC Rhodesia, 1951; AOC Iraq, 1954; AOC No 25 Group, Flying Training Command, 1956–58, retd. *Club:* Royal Air Force.

BROOKES, Peter C.; *see* Cannon-Brookes, P.

BROOKES, Sir Wilfred (Deakin), Kt 1979; CBE 1972; DSO 1944; AEA 1945; Chairman, Deakin University Foundation, since 1982; *b* 17 April 1906; *s* of Herbert Robinson Brookes and Ivy Deakin; *m* 1928, Betty (*d* 1968), *d* of A. H. Heal; one *s*. *Educ:* Melbourne Grammar Sch.; Melbourne Univ. Exec., later Alternate Dir, Aust. Paper Manufacturers Ltd, 1924–38; Exec. Dir, Box and Container Syndicate, 1938–39. War Service, 1939–45: Sqdn Officer, RAAF, 1939–41 (despatches); CO 24 Sqdn, 1942 (despatches); CO 22 Sqdn, 1942; CO 7 Fighter Section HQ; Comdr, 78th Fighter Wing, New Guinea Offensive, 1943–45; Dir of Postings, RAAF HQ, rank of Gp Captain, 1945. Chairman (retired): Associated Pulp and Paper Mills, 1952–78 (Dir, 1945–78); Colonial Mutual Life Soc., 1965–78 (Dir, 1955–78); Electrolytic Refining & Smelting Co. of Australia Ltd, 1956–80; Apsonor Pty Ltd, to 1983 (Dir, 1960–83); Collins Wales Pty Ltd, 1978–82 (Dir, 1974–82); Director: BH South Group, 1956–82; North Broken Hill, 1970–82; Alcoa of Australia, 1961–83. Past Pres., Inst. of Public Affairs; Chm., Edward Wilson Charitable Trust (Trustee, 1960–); Associate Trustee, Deakin Foundn, 1982; Hon. Dr of Letters Deakin, 1982. Dep. Chm., Corps of Commissionaires, 1979– (Governor, 1975–). *Recreations:* swimming, walking. *Address:* 20 Heyington Place, Toorak, Victoria 3142, Australia. *T:* 20 4553. *Clubs:* Melbourne, Australian (Melbourne).

BROOKING, Maj.-Gen. Patrick Guy, MBE 1975; Commandant and General Officer Commanding British Sector Berlin, since 1985; *b* 4 April 1937; *s* of late Captain C. A. H. Brooking, CBE, RN, and G. M. J. White (*née* Coleridge); *m* 1964, Pamela Mary Walford; one *s* one *d*. *Educ:* Charterhouse Sch. Dip. (French Lang.); Alliance Française, Paris, 1955. Commnd 5th Royal Inniskilling Dragoon Guards, 1956; early career served in England, W Germany, NI, Cyprus, with UN; sc 1969; Mil. Asst to Comdr 1st British Corps, 1970–71; Bde Major 39 Bde, Belfast, 1974–75; comd his regt, 1975–77; Instr Army Staff Coll., 1978; RCDS 1981; Comdr 33 Armd Bde, Paderborn Garrison, 1982–83. *Recreations:* ski-ing, tennis, golf, music (esp. choral singing). *Address:* c/o National Westminster Bank, 26 Haymarket, SW1. *Club:* Cavalry and Guards.

BROOKNER, Dr Anita; Reader, Courtauld Institute of Art, since 1977; *o c* of Newson and Maude Brookner. *Educ:* James Allen's Girls' Sch.; King's Coll., Univ. of London; Courtauld Inst.; Paris. Vis. Lectr, Univ. of Reading, 1959–64; Slade Professor, Univ. of Cambridge, 1967–68; Lectr, Courtauld Inst. of Art, 1964. Fellow, New Hall, Cambridge. *Publications:* Watteau, 1968; The Genius of the Future, 1971; Greuze: the rise and fall of an Eighteenth Century Phenomenon, 1972; Jacques-Louis David, 1980; *novels*: A Start in Life, 1981; Providence, 1982; Look at Me, 1983; Hotel du Lac, 1984 (Booker McConnell Prize; filmed for TV, 1986); Family and Friends, 1985; A Misalliance, 1986; articles in Burlington Magazine, etc. *Address*: 68 Elm Park Gardens, SW10. *T*: 01–352 6894.

BROOKS, family name of **Barons Brooks of Tremorfa** and **Crawshaw.**

BROOKS OF TREMORFA, Baron *cr* 1979 (Life Peer), of Tremorfa in the County of South Glamorgan; **John Edward Brooks;** *b* 12 April 1927; *s* of Edward George Brooks and Rachel Brooks (*née* White); *m* 1948 (marr. diss. 1956); one *s* one *d*; *m* 1958, Margaret Pringle; two *s*. *Educ*: elementary schools; Coleg Harlech. Secretary, Cardiff South East Labour Party, 1966–; Member, South Glamorgan CC, 1973– (Leader, 1973–77; Chm., 1981–82). Contested (Lab) Barry, Feb. and Oct. 1974; Parliamentary Agent to Rt Hon. James Callaghan, MP, Gen. Elections, 1970, 1979. Chm., Labour Party, Wales, 1978–79. Opposition defence spokesman, 1980–. *Recreations*: reading, most sports. *Address*: 57 Janet Street, Splott, Cardiff. *T*: Cardiff 40709.

BROOKS, Prof. Cleanth; Gray Professor of Rhetoric, Yale University, USA, 1947–75, now Emeritus Professor; *b* 16 Oct. 1906; *s* of Rev. Cleanth and Bessie Lee Witherspoon Brooks; *m* 1934, Edith Amy Blanchard; no *c*. *Educ*: The McTyeire School; Vanderbilt, Tulane and Oxford Universities. Rhodes Scholar, Louisiana and Exeter, 1929; Lecturer, later Prof., Louisiana State Univ., 1932–47; Prof. of English, later Gray Prof. of Rhetoric, Yale Univ., 1947–75. Visiting Professor: Univ. of Texas; Univ. of Michigan; Univ. of Chicago; Univ. of Southern California; Bread Loaf School of English; Univ. of South Carolina, 1975; Tulane Univ., 1976; Univ. of North Carolina, 1977; Univ. of Tennessee, 1978. Cultural Attaché at the American Embassy, London, 1964–66. Managing Editor and Editor (with Robert Penn Warren), The Southern Review, 1935–42. Fellow, Library of Congress, 1953–63; Guggenheim Fellow, 1953 and 1960; Sen. Fellow, Nat. Endowment for the Humanities, 1975; Mellon Fellow, Nat. Humanities Center, 1980–81. Member: Amer. Acad. of Arts and Scis; Amer. Acad. Inst. of Arts and Letters; Amer. Philos. Soc.; RSL. Lamar Lectr, 1984; Jefferson Lectr, Nat. Endowment for the Humanities, 1985. Hon. DLitt: Upsala Coll., 1963; Kentucky, 1963; Exeter, 1966; Washington and Lee, 1968; Tulane, 1969; Univ. of the South, 1974; Newberry Coll., 1979; Hon. LHD: St Louis, 1968; Centenary Coll., 1972; Oglethorpe Univ., 1976; St Peter's Coll., 1978; Lehigh Univ., 1980; Millsaps Coll., 1983; Univ. of New Haven, 1984; Univ. of S Carolina, 1984. *Publications*: Modern Poetry and the Tradition, 1939; (ed) Thomas Percy and Richard Farmer, 1946; The Well Wrought Urn, 1947; (with R. P. Warren) Understanding Poetry, 1938; (with R. P. Warren) Modern Rhetoric, 1950; (with W. K. Wimsatt, Jr) Literary Criticism: A Short History, 1957; The Hidden God, 1963; William Faulkner: The Yoknapatawpha Country, 1963; A Shaping Joy, 1971; (with R. W. B. Lewis and R. P. Warren) American Literature: the Makers and the Making, 1973; (ed) Thomas Percy and William Shenstone, 1977; William Faulkner: Toward Yoknapatawpha and Beyond, 1978; William Faulkner: First Encounters, 1983; (Gen. Editor, with David N. Smith and A. F. Falconer) The Percy Letters, 1942–; contrib. articles, reviews to literary magazines, journals. *Address*: 70 Ogden Street, New Haven, Conn 06511, USA. *Club*: Athenæum.

BROOKS, Douglas; Director, Walker Brooks and Partners Ltd, since 1980; *b* 3 Sept. 1928; *s* of Oliver Brooks and Olive Brooks; *m* 1952, June Anne (*née* Branch); one *s* one *d*. *Educ*: Newbridge Grammar Sch.; University Coll., Cardiff (Dip. Soc. Sc.). CIPM; APMI. Girling Ltd: factory operative, 1951–53; Employment Officer, 1953–56; Hoover Ltd: Personnel Off., 1956–60; Sen. Personnel Off., 1960–63; Dep. Personnel Man., 1963–66; Indust. Relations Advr, 1966–69; Gp Personnel Man., 1969–73; Personnel Dir, 1973–78; Group Personnel Manager, Tarmac Ltd, 1979–80. Member: Council, SSRC, 1976–82; BBC Consultative Gp on social effects of television, 1978–80; Hon. Soc. Cymmrodorion, 1981–. Vis. Fellow, PSI, 1982–84. Vice-Pres., IPM, 1972–74. Chm., Wooburn Fest. Soc. Ltd, 1978–86. *Publications*: various articles in professional jls. *Recreations*: talking, music, reading, gardening, cooking. *Address*: Bull Farm House, Park Lane, Beaconsfield, Bucks. *T*: Beaconsfield 5253. *Club*: Reform.

BROOKS, Edwin, PhD; FAIM, FIBA; Dean of Commerce, Riverina-Murray Institute of Higher Education (formerly Riverina College of Advanced Education), Wagga Wagga, New South Wales, since 1982 (Dean of Business and Liberal Studies, 1977–82, and Director, Albury-Wodonga Campus, 1982); *b* Barry, Glamorgan, 1 Dec. 1929; *s* of Edwin Brooks and Agnes Elizabeth (*née* Campbell); *m* 1956, Winifred Hazel Soundie; four *s* one *d*. *Educ*: Barry Grammar Sch.; St John's Coll., Cambridge. PhD (Camb) 1958. National Service, Singapore, 1948–49. MP (Lab) Bebington, 1966–70. Univ. of Liverpool: Lectr, Dept of Geography, 1954–66 and 1970–72; Sen. Lectr, 1972–77; Dean, College Studies, 1975–77. Councillor, Birkenhead, 1958–67. Mem., Courses Cttee, Higher Educn Bd of NSW, 1978–82. FAIM 1983; FIBA 1984. *Publications*: This Crowded Kingdom, 1973; (ed) Tribes of the Amazon Basin in Brazil, 1973. *Recreations*: gardening, listening to music. *Address*: Riverina-Murray Institute of Higher Education, PO Box 588, Wagga Wagga, NSW 2650, Australia. *T*: 069–23–24–84.

BROOKS, Eric Arthur Swatton, MA; Head of Claims Department, Foreign Office, 1960 until retirement, 1967; *b* 9 Oct. 1907; *yr s* of late A. E. Brooks, MA, Maidenhead; *m* 1947, Daphne Joyce, *yr d* of late George McMullan, MD, FRCSE, Wallingford; one *s* one *d*. *Educ*: Reading Sch.; New Coll., Oxford (MA). 2nd cl. hons Jurisprudence, 1929. Solicitor, 1932; practised in London, 1932–39. Mem. Law Soc., 1934– (Mem. Overseas Relations Cttee, 1949–). Served War of 1939–45 in Admty and Min. of Aircraft Production, and in Operational Research as Hon. Ft-Lieut RAFVR until 1944; Disposal of Govt Factories of Min. of Aircraft Production, 1944–Dec. 1945. Foreign Office, 1946–. Served on Brit. Delegns in negotiations with: Polish and Hungarian Governments, 1953, 1954; Bulgarian Government, 1955; Rumanian Government, 1955, 1956, 1960; USSR, 1964, 1965, 1966, 1967. British Representative on Anglo-Italian Conciliation Commn, until 1967. Councillor: Borough of Maidenhead, 1972–74; Royal Borough of Windsor and Maidenhead, 1973–. *Publications*: The Foreign Office Claims Manual, 1968; Maidenhead and its Name, 1985; Earlier Days of Maidenhead Golf Club, 1985; articles, on Compensation in International Law, and Distribution of Compensation, in legal jls, and on local history and amenities. *Recreations*: golf (Oxford Univ. team *v* Cambridge Univ., 1929; various later Amateur European Championships); gardening. *Address*: Kitoha, 116b Grenfell Road, Maidenhead, Berks. *T*: Maidenhead 21621.

BROOKS, Most Rev. Francis Gerard; *see* Dromore, Bishop of, (RC).

BROOKS, John Ashton, FIB; Deputy Group Chief Executive, Midland Bank PLC, since 1981; *b* 24 Oct. 1928; *s* of Victor Brooks and Annie (*née* Ashton); *m* 1959, Sheila (*née* Hulse); one *s* one *d*. *Educ*: Merchant Taylors' Sch., Northwood. Joined Midland Bank, 1949; Manager: 22 Victoria Street Br., 1970; Threadneedle Street Br., 1972; Gen. Man., Computer Operations, 1975; Dir and Dep. Gp Chief Exec., 1981–. *Recreations*: reading, walking. *Address*: 15 The Close, Montreal Park, Sevenoaks, Kent TN13 2HE. *T*: Sevenoaks 454263. *Club*: Overseas Bankers'.

BROOKS, Leslie James, CEng, FRINA; RCNC; Deputy Director of Engineering (Constructive), Ship Department, Ministry of Defence (Procurement Executive), 1973–76, retired; *b* 3 Aug. 1916; *yr s* of late C. J. D. Brooks and Lucy A. Brooks, Milton Regis, Sittingbourne, Kent; *m* 1941, Ruth Elizabeth Olver, Saltash, Cornwall; two *s*. *Educ*: Borden Grammar Sch., Sittingbourne, Kent; HM Dockyard Schs, Sheerness and Chatham; Royal Naval Engrg Coll., Keyham; RNC, Greenwich. War of 1939–45: Asst Constructor, Naval Construction Dept, Admty, Bath, 1941–44; Constr Lt-Comdr on Staff of Allied Naval Comdr, Exped. Force, and Flag Officer, Brit. Assault Area, 1944. Constr in charge Welding, Naval Constrn Dept, Admty, Bath, 1945–47; Constr Comdr, Staff of Comdr-in-Chief, Brit. Pacific Fleet, 1947–49; Constr in charge, No 2 Ship Tank, Admty Experiment Works, Haslar, Gosport, 1949–54. Naval Constrn Dept, Admty, Bath: Constr, Merchant Shipping Liaison, 1954–56; Chief Constr in charge of Conversion of First Commando Ships, and of Operating Aircraft Carriers, 1956–62; Dep. Supt, Admty Exper. Works, Haslar, 1962–65; Ship Dept, Bath: Asst Dir of Naval Constrn, Naval Constrn Div., MoD(N), 1965–68; Asst Dir of Engrg (Ships), MoD(PE), 1968–73; Dep. Dir of Engrg/Constr., MoD(PE), 1973. Mem., Royal Corps of Naval Constructors. *Recreations*: walking, photography, natural history. *Address*: Merrymeet, Perrymead, Bath BA2 5AY. *T*: Bath 832856.

BROOKS, Mel; writer, director, actor; *b* Brooklyn, 1926; *m* Florence Baum; two *s* one *d*; *m* 1964, Anne Bancroft; one *s*. TV script writer for series: Your Show of Shows, 1950–54; Caesar's Hour, 1954–57; Get Smart, 1965–70. Films: (cartoon) The Critic (Academy Award), 1963; writer and director: The Producers (Academy Award), 1968; Young Frankenstein, 1974; writer, director and actor: The Twelve Chairs, 1970; Blazing Saddles, 1973; Silent Movie, 1976; writer, director, actor and producer: High Anxiety, 1977; History of the World Part 1, 1981; actor, producer: To Be Or Not To Be, 1984. Film productions include The Elephant Man, 1980. Several album recordings. *Address*: c/o Twentieth Century-Fox Film Corporation, Box 900, Beverly Hills, Calif 90213, USA.

BROOKS, William Donald Wykeham, CBE 1956; MA, DM (Oxon); FRCP; retired; Consulting Physician: St Mary's Hospital; Brompton Hospital; to the Royal Navy; to the King Edward VII Convalescent Home for Officers, Osborne; Chief Medical Officer, Eagle Star Insurance Co.; *b* 3 Aug. 1905; *er s* of A. E. Brooks, MA (Oxon), Maidenhead, Berks; *m* 1934, Phyllis Kathleen, *e d* of late F. A. Juler, CVO; two *s* two *d*. *Educ*: Reading School; St John's College, Oxford (White Scholar); St Mary's Hospital, London (University Scholar); Strong Memorial Hospital, Rochester, New York. First Class Honours, Final Honour School of Physiology, 1928; Cheadle Gold Medallist, 1931; Fereday Fellow St John's College, Oxford, 1931–34; Rockefeller Travelling Fellow, 1932–33; Goulstonian Lecturer, 1940; Marc Daniels Lecturer, RCP, 1957. Asst Registrar, 1946–50, RCP; Censor, RCP, 1961– (Council, 1959–61, Senior Vice-President and Senior Censor, 1965); Member Association of Physicians of Great Britain and Ireland. Served War 1940–45 as Surgeon Captain, RNVR. Editor, Quarterly Jl of Medicine, 1946–67. *Publications*: numerous articles on general medical topics and on chest diseases in various medical journals; Sections on Chest Wounds, Respiratory Diseases and Tuberculosis, Conybeare's Textbook of Medicine; Respiratory Diseases section in the Official Naval Medical History of the War. *Recreations*: golf, shooting, gardening, bridge. *Address*: Two Acres, Fryern Road, Storrington, Sussex. *T*: Storrington 2159.

BROOKS GRUNDY, Rupert Francis; *see* Grundy, R. F. B.

BROOKSBANK, Sir (Edward) Nicholas, 3rd Bt *cr* 1919; with Christie's, since 1974; *b* 4 Oct. 1944; *s* of Sir Edward William Brooksbank, 2nd Bt, TD, and of Ann, 2nd *d* of Col T. Clitherow; *S* father, 1983; *m* 1970, Emma, *d* of Baron Holderness, *qv*; one *s* one *d*. *Educ*: Eton. Royal Dragoons, 1963–69; Blues and Royals, 1969–73; Adjutant, 1971–73. *Heir*: *s* (Florian) Tom (Charles) Brooksbank, *b* 9 Aug. 1982. *Address*: Ryton Grange, Malton, North Yorks.

BROOKSBANK, Kenneth, DSC and Bar, 1944; Chief Education Officer, Birmingham, 1968–77; *b* 27 July 1915; *s* of Ambrose and Ethel Brooksbank; *m* 1939, Violet Anne Woodrow; two *d*. *Educ*: High Storrs Gram. Sch., Sheffield; St Edmund Hall, Oxford; Manchester University. Asst Master, Hulme Gram. Sch., Oldham, 1937–41; Royal Navy, 1941–46; Dep. Educn Off., York, 1946–49; Sen. Admin. Asst, Birmingham, 1949–52; Asst Sec. for Educn, NR Yorks CC, 1952–56; Dep. Educn Off., Birmingham, 1956–68. Leader, Unesco Educn Planning Mission to Bechuanaland, Basutoland and Swaziland, 1964. Chairman: Management Cttee, Adult Literacy Unit, Nat. Inst. of Adult Educn, 1978–80, Adult Literacy and Basic Skills Unit, 1980–; Council for Environmental Educn, 1978–; Community Educn Centre, 1981–; Member: Engineering Ind. Trng Bd, 1970–79; Ind. Trng Service Bd, 1974–77. President: Educnl Equipment Assoc., 1970–71; Soc. of Educn Officers, 1971–72. Mem. Council, Aston Univ., 1968–84; Vice-Chm., West Hill Coll., 1983–. Hon. Fellow, Birmingham Univ., 1981. Hon. DSc Aston, 1985. *Publications*: (ed) Educational Administration, 1980; (with J. Revell) School Governors, 1981; (ed jtly) County and Voluntary Schools, 1982. *Address*: 29 Wycome Road, Hall Green, Birmingham B28 9EN. *T*: 021–777 4407.

BROOKSBANK, Sir Nicholas; *see* Brooksbank, Sir E. N.

BROOKSBY, John Burns, CBE 1973; FRS 1980; Director, Animal Virus Research Institute, Pirbright, 1964–79; *b* 25 Dec. 1914; *s* of George B. Brooksby, Glasgow; *m* 1940, Muriel Weir; one *s* one *d*. *Educ*: Hyndland Sch., Glasgow; Glasgow Veterinary Coll.; London University. MRCVS 1935; FRCVS 1978; BSc (VetSc) 1936; PhD 1947; DSc 1957; FRSE 1968; Hon. DSc Edinburgh, 1981. Research Officer, Pirbright, 1939; Dep. Dir, 1957; Dir, 1964. *Publications*: papers on virus diseases of animals in scientific jls. *Address*: Heatherdale House, Compton Way, Farnham, Surrey. *T*: Runfold 2164.

BROOM, Prof. Donald Maurice, FIBiol; Colleen Macleod Professor of Animal Welfare, University of Cambridge, since 1986; *b* 14 July 1942; *s* of late Donald Edward Broom and of Mavis Edith Rose Broom; *m* 1971, Sally Elizabeth Mary Riordan; three *s*. *Educ*: Whitgift Sch.; St Catharine's Coll., Cambridge (MA, PhD); FIBiol 1986. Lectr, 1967, Sen. Lectr, 1979, Reader, 1982, Dept of Pure and Applied Zoology, Univ. of Reading. Vis. Asst Prof., Univ. of California, Berkeley, 1969; Vis. Lectr, Univ. of W Indies, Trinidad, 1972; Vis. Scientist, CSIRO Div. of Animal Prodn, Perth, WA, 1983. Invited Expert, EEC Farm Animal Welfare Expert Gp, 1981–; Hon. Res. Associate, Animal and Grassland Res. Inst., 1985–. Hon. Treas., Assoc. for Study of Animal Behaviour, 1971–80; Mem., Internat. Ethological Cttee, 1976–79; Mem. Council, Soc. for Vet. Ethology, 1981–84. Trustee, Farm Animal Care Trust, 1986–. *Publications*: Birds and their Behaviour, 1977; Biology of Behaviour, 1981; (ed jtly) The Encyclopaedia of Domestic Animals, 1986; numerous papers in behaviour, psychol, zool, ornithol, agricl and vet. jls. *Recreations*: squash, water-polo, running, ornithology. *Address*: Department of Clinical Veterinary Medicine, Madingley Road, Cambridge CB3 0ES. *T*: Cambridge 337733. *Club*: Hawks (Cambridge).

BROOM, Air Marshal Sir Ivor (Gordon), KCB 1975 (CB 1972); CBE 1969; DSO 1945; DFC 1942 (Bar to DFC 1944, 2nd Bar 1945); AFC 1956; international aerospace consultant, since 1977; Director, Plessey Airports Ltd, since 1982; Chairman, Gatwick

Handling Ltd, since 1982; *b* Cardiff, 2 June 1920; *s* of Alfred Godfrey Broom and Janet Broom; *m* 1942, Jess Irene Broom (*née* Cooper); two *s* one *d*. *Educ:* West Monmouth Grammar Sch.; Pontypridd County Sch., Glam. Joined RAF, 1940; commissioned, 1941; 114 Sqdn, 107 Sqdn, 1941; CFS Course, 1942; Instr on: 1655 Mosquito Trg Unit; 571 Sqdn, 128 Sqdn, and 163 Sqdn, 1943–45; HQ, ACSEA, 1945–46. Commanded 28 (FR) Sqdn, 1946–48; RAF Staff Coll. Course, Bracknell, 1949; Sqdn Comdr, No 1 ITS, 1950–52; No 3 Flying Coll. Course, Manby, 1952–53; commanded 57 Sqdn, 1953–54; Syndicate Leader, Flying Coll., Manby, 1954–56; commanded Bomber Command Development Unit, Wittering, 1956–59; Air Secretary's Dept, 1959–62; commanded RAF Bruggen, 1962–64; IDC, 1965–66; Dir of Organisation (Establishments), 1966–68; Commandant, Central Flying School, 1968–70; AOC No 11 (Fighter) Gp, Strike Comd, 1970–72. Dep. Controller, 1972–74, Controller, 1974–77, Nat. Air Traffic Services; Mem., CAA, 1974–77. *Recreations:* golf, skiing. *Address:* Cherry Lawn, Bridle Lane, Loudwater, Rickmansworth, Herts WD3 4JB. *Club:* Royal Air Force.

BROOME, David, OBE 1970; farmer; British professional show jumper; *b* Cardiff, 1 March 1940; *s* of Fred and Amelia Broome, Chepstow, Gwent; *m* 1976, Elizabeth, *d* of K. W. Fletcher, Thirsk, N Yorkshire; one *s*. *Educ:* Monmouth Grammar Sch. for Boys. European Show Jumping Champion (3 times); World Show Jumping Champion, La Baule, 1970; Olympic Medallist (Bronze) twice, 1960, 1968; King George V Gold Cup 5 times (a record, in 1981). Mounts include: Sunsalve, Aachen, 1961; Mr Softee, Rotterdam, 1967, and Hickstead, 1969; Beethoven, La Baule, France, 1970, as (1st British) World Champion; Sportsman and Philco, Cardiff, 1974; Professional Champion of the World. *Publications:* Jump-Off, 1971; (with S. Hadley) Horsemanship, 1983. *Recreations:* hunting (MFH), shooting, golf. *Address:* Mount Ballan Manor, Crick, Chepstow, Gwent, Wales. *T:* Caldicot 42077.

BROOMFIELD, Nigel Hugh Robert Allen, CMG 1986; HM Diplomatic Service; Deputy High Commissioner and Minister, New Delhi, since 1985; *b* 19 March 1937; *s* of Arthur Allen Broomfield and Ruth Sheilagh Broomfield; *m* 1963, Valerie Fenton; two *s*. *Educ:* Haileybury Coll.; Trinity Coll., Cambridge (BA (Hons) English Lit.). Commnd 17/21 Lancers, 1959, retired as Major, 1968. Joined FCO as First Sec., 1969; First Secretary: British Embassy, Bonn, 1970–72; British Embassy, Moscow, 1972–74; European Communities Dept, London, 1975–77; RCDS, 1978; Political Advr and Head of Chancery, British Mil. Govt, Berlin, 1979–81; Head of Eastern European and Soviet Dept, 1981–83, and Head of Soviet Dept, 1983–85, FCO. Captain, Cambridge Squash Rackets and Real Tennis, 1957–58; British Amateur Squash Champion, 1958–59 (played for England, 1957–60). *Recreations:* tennis, squash, cricket, gardening, reading, music. *Address:* c/o Foreign and Commonwealth Office, SW1A 2AH. *Clubs:* Royal Automobile, MCC; Hawks (Cambridge).

BROOMHALL, Maj.-Gen. William Maurice, CB 1950; DSO 1945; OBE 1932; *b* 16 July 1897; *o s* of late Alfred Edward Broomhall, London. *Educ:* St Paul's School; Royal Military Academy, Woolwich. Commissioned Royal Engineers, 1915; France and Belgium, 1914–21 (wounded twice); Waziristan, 1921–24 (medal and clasp); NW Frontier of India, 1929–31 (despatches, clasp, OBE); Staff College, Camberley, 1932–33. Served North-West Europe, 1939–45 (Despatches, DSO); Chief Engineer, Allied Forces, Italy, 1946; Chief Engineer, British Army of the Rhine, 1947–48; Chief Engineer, Middle East Land Forces, 1948–51; retired, 1951. Chm., Cellulose Develt Corp., 1965–72. *Address:* The Cottage, Park Lane, Beaconsfield, Bucks HP9 2HR. *Club:* Army and Navy.

BROPHY, Brigid (Antonia), (Lady Levey), FRSL; author and playwright; *b* 12 June 1929; *o c* of late John Brophy; *m* 1954, Sir Michael Levey, *qv*; one *d*. *Educ:* St Paul's Girls' Sch.; St Hugh's Coll., Oxford. Awarded Jubilee Scholarship at St Hugh's Coll., Oxford, 1947 and read classics. Co-organiser, Writers Action Gp campaign for Public Lending Right, 1972–82; Exec. Councillor, Writers' Guild of GB, 1975–78; a Vice-Chm., British Copyright Council, 1976–80. A Vice-Pres., Nat. Anti-Vivisection Soc., 1974–. Awarded Cheltenham Literary Festival First Prize for a first novel, 1954; London Magazine Prize for Prose, 1962. *Publications:* Hackenfeller's Ape, 1953; The King of a Rainy Country, 1956; Black Ship to Hell, 1962; Flesh, 1962; The Finishing Touch, 1963; The Snow Ball, 1964; Mozart the Dramatist, 1964; Don't Never Forget, 1966; (in collaboration with Michael Levey and Charles Osborne) Fifty Works of English Literature We Could Do Without, 1967; Black and White: a portrait of Aubrey Beardsley, 1968; In Transit, 1969; Prancing Novelist, 1973; The Adventures of God in his Search for the Black Girl, and other fables, 1973; Pussy Owl, 1976; Beardsley and his World, 1976; Palace Without Chairs, 1978; The Prince and the Wild Geese, 1983; A Guide to Public Lending Right, 1983. *Plays:* The Burglar, Vaudeville, 1967 (published with preface, 1968); The Waste Disposal Unit, Radio (published 1968). *Visual Art:* (with Maureen Duffy, *qv*) Prop Art, exhibn, London, 1969. *Address:* Flat 3, 185 Old Brompton Road, SW5 0AN. *T:* 01–373 9335.

BROPHY, Michael John Mary; Director, Charities Aid Foundation, since 1982; *b* 24 June 1937; *s* of Gerald and Mary Brophy; *m* 1962, Sarah Rowe; three *s* one *d*. *Educ:* Ampleforth Coll.; Royal Naval Coll., Dartmouth. Entered Royal Navy, 1955; retired as Lt-Comdr (X)(P)(G), 1966. Associate Dir, J. Walter Thompson, 1967–74; Appeals Dir, Spastics Soc., 1974–82. FRSA 1986. *Recreations:* travel, walking. *Address:* Pond House, Isfield, East Sussex TN22 5TY. *T:* Isfield 362. *Club:* Athenæum.

BROSAN, Dr George Stephen, CBE 1982; TD 1960; consulting engineer; Director, North East London Polytechnic, 1970–82; *b* 8 Aug. 1921; *o s* of Rudolph and Margaret Brosan; *m* 1952, Maureen Dorothy Foscoe; three *d*. *Educ:* Kilburn Grammar Sch.; Faraday House; The Polytechnic; Birkbeck Coll., London. Faraday Scholar, 1939. PhD 1951; DFH 1957; Hon. FIProdE 1980; FIEE 1964; FIMA 1966; FIMechE 1971; MRIN 1983; CBIM (formerly FBIM) 1975. Teaching staff, Regent Street Polytechnic, 1950–58; Head of Dept, Willesden Coll. of Technology, 1958–60; Further Educn Officer, Middlesex CC, 1960–62; Principal, Enfield Coll. of Technology, 1962–70. Pres., Tensor Club of GB, 1973–82; Pres., IProdE, 1975–77; Mem. Council, BIM, 1975–79; Chairman: CEI Educn Cttee, 1978–79; Accountancy Educn Consultative Bd, 1979–82. Life Mem., ASME, 1977. Hon. MIED 1968; Hon. Mem., Council for Educn in the Commonwealth, 1983; CNI 1983. Chevalier du Tastevin, 1976. *Publications:* (jtly) Advanced Electrical Power and Machines, 1966; (jtly) Patterns and Policies in Higher Education, 1971; numerous articles and papers in academic and professional press. *Recreation:* yachting. *Address:* High Orchard, Mark Way, Godalming, Surrey GU7 2BB; Tartagli Alti, Paciano 06060, Province of Perugia, Italy. *Clubs:* Reform; Velico Catanese (Perugia).

BROTHERHOOD, Air Cdre William Rowland, CBE 1952; retired as Director, Guided Weapons (Trials), Ministry of Aviation (formerly Supply), 1959–61; *b* 22 Jan. 1912; *s* of late James Brotherhood, Tintern, Mon.; *m* 1939, Margaret (*d* 1981), *d* of late Ernest Sutcliffe, Louth, Lincs; one *s* one *d*. *Educ:* Monmouth School; RAF College, Cranwell. Joined RAF, 1930; Group Captain, 1943; Air Commodore, 1955; Director, Operational Requirements, Air Ministry, 1955–58. *Address:* Inglewood, Llandogo, Monmouth, Gwent. *T:* Dean 530333.

BROTHERS, Air Cdre Peter Malam, CBE 1964; DSO 1944; DFC 1940, and Bar, 1943; Managing Director, Peter Brothers Consultants Ltd, since 1973; *b* 30 Sept. 1917; *s* of late John Malam Brothers; *m* 1939, Annette, *d* of late James Wilson; three *d*. *Educ:* N. Manchester Sch. (Br. of Manchester Grammar). Joined RAF, 1936; Flt-Lieut 1939; RAF Biggin Hill, Battle of Britain, 1940; Sqdn-Ldr 1941; Wing Comdr 1942; Tangmere Fighter Wing Ldr, 1942–43; Staff HQ No. 10 Gp, 1943; Exeter Wing Ldr, 1944; US Comd and Gen. Staff Sch., 1944–45; Central Fighter Estab., 1945–46; Colonial Service, Kenya, 1947–49; RAF Bomber Sqdn, 1949–52; HQ No. 3 Gp, 1952–54; RAF Staff Coll., 1954; HQ Fighter Comd, 1955–57; Bomber Stn, 1957–59; Gp Capt., and Staff Officer, SHAPE, 1959–62; Dir of Ops (Overseas), 1962–65; Air Cdre, and AOC Mil. Air Traffic Ops, 1965–68; Dir of Public Relations (RAF), MoD (Air), 1968–73; retired 1973. Freeman, Guild Air Pilots and Air Navigators, 1966 (Liveryman, 1968; Warden, 1971; Master, 1974–75); Freeman, City of London, 1967. Editorial Adviser, Defence and Foreign Affairs publications, 1973–76. Patron, Spitfire Assoc., Australia, 1971–; Vice-President: Spitfire Soc., 1984–; Devon Emergency Volunteers, 1986– (Chm., 1981–86). MBIM; MIPR. *Recreations:* golf, sailing, fishing, swimming, flying. *Address:* c/o National Westminster Bank, Topsham, Devon. *Clubs:* Royal Air Force; RAF Yacht; Honiton Golf.

BROTHERTON, Michael Lewis; Michael Brotherton Associates, Parliamentary and Financial Consultants, 1986; *b* 26 May 1931; *s* of late John Basil Brotherton and Maud Brotherton; *m* 1968, Julia, *d* of Austin Gerald Comyn King and Katherine Elizabeth King, Bath; three *s* one *d*. *Educ:* Prior Park; RNC Dartmouth. Served RN, 1949–64: qual. Observer 1955; Cyprus, 1957 (despatches); Lt-Comdr 1964, retd. Times Newspapers, 1967–74. Chm., Beckenham Conservative Political Cttee, 1967–68; contested (C) Deptford, 1970; MP (C) Louth, Oct. 1974–1983. Pres., Hyde Park Tories, 1975. Mem., Select Cttee on violence in the family, 1975–76. *Recreations:* cricket, cooking. *Address:* The Old Vicarage, Wrangle, Boston, Lincs. *T:* Boston 870688. *Clubs:* Army and Navy, MCC; Conservative Working Men's (Louth); Castaways (Louth); Cleethorpes Conservative; Immingham Conservative.

BROTHWOOD, John, MRCP, FFCM, FRCPsych, MFOM; Chief Medical Officer, Esso Petroleum (UK), and Esso Chemicals, since 1979; *b* 23 Feb. 1931; *s* of Wilfred Cyril Vernon Brothwood and late Emma Bailey; *m* 1957, Dr Margaret Stirling Meyer; one *s* one *d*. *Educ:* Marlborough Coll.; Peterhouse, Cambridge (Schol.); Middlesex Hosp. MB BChir (Cantab) 1955; MRCP 1960, DPM (London) 1964, FFCM 1972, FRCPsych 1976. Various posts in clinical medicine (incl. Registrar, Maudsley Hosp. and military service as Captain RAMC), 1955–64; joined DHSS (then Min. of Health) as MO, 1964; posts held in mental health, regional liaison, chronic disease policy and medical manpower and educn; SPMO and Under Secretary, DHSS, 1975–78. *Publications:* various, on NHS matters, especially mental health policy and related topics. *Recreations:* diverse. *Address:* 81 Calton Avenue, SE21 7DF. *T:* 01–693 8273.

BROUCHER, David Stuart; HM Diplomatic Service; Counsellor Commercial and Aid, Jakarta, since 1985; *b* 5 Oct. 1944; *s* of Clifford Broucher and Betty Broucher (*née* Jordan); *m* 1971, Marion Monika Blackwell; one *s*. *Educ:* Manchester Grammar School; Trinity Hall, Cambridge (MA Modern Languages). Foreign Office, 1966; British Military Govt, Berlin, 1968; Cabinet Office, 1972; Prague, 1975; FCO, 1978; UK Perm. Rep. to EC, 1983. *Recreations:* music, sailing. *Address:* c/o Foreign and Commonwealth Office, SW1. *Club:* Indonesia Petroleum (Jakarta).

BROUGH, Dr Colin, FRCPE; FFCM; Chief Administrative Medical Officer, Lothian Health Board, since 1980; *b* 4 Jan. 1932; *s* of Peter Brough and Elizabeth C. C. Chalmers; *m* 1957, Maureen Jennings; four *s* one *d*. *Educ:* Bell Baxter Sch., Cupar; Univ. of Edinburgh (MB ChB). DPH 1965; DIH 1965; FFCM 1978; MRCPE 1981; FRCPE 1982. House Officer, Leicester General Hosp. and Royal Infirmary of Edinburgh, 1956–57; Surg.-Lieut, Royal Navy, 1957–60; General Practitioner, Leith and Fife, 1960–64; Dep. Medical Supt, Royal Inf. of Edinburgh, 1965–67; ASMO, PASMO, Dep. SAMO, South-Eastern Regional Hosp. Board, Scotland, 1967–74; Community Medicine Specialist, Lothian Health Board, 1974–80. *Recreations:* golf, shooting, fishing, first aid. *Address:* The Saughs, Gullane, East Lothian EH31 2AL. *T:* Gullane 842179.

BROUGH, Edward; Chairman, Volker Stevin (UK) Ltd, 1980–82; *b* 28 May 1918; *s* of late Hugh and Jane Brough; *m* 1941, Peggy Jennings; two *s*. *Educ:* Berwick Grammar School; Edinburgh University (MA). Joined Unilever Ltd, 1938. War service, KOSB, 1939–46 (Captain). Rejoined Unilever, 1946; Commercial Dir, 1951, Man. Dir, 1954, Lever's Cattle Foods Ltd; Chairman, Crosfields (CWG) Ltd, 1957; Lever Bros & Associates Ltd: Development Dir, 1960; Marketing Dir, 1962; Chm., 1965; Hd of Unilever's Marketing Div., 1968–71; Dir of Unilever Ltd and Unilever NV, 1968–74, and Chm. of UK Cttee, 1971–74. Chm., Adriaan Volker (UK) Ltd, 1974–80. Mem., NBPI, 1967–70. FBIM 1967. *Recreations:* flyfishing, golf. *Address:* Far End, The Great Quarry, Guildford, Surrey. *T:* Guildford 504064; St John's, Chagford, Devon. *Club:* Farmers'.

BROUGHAM, family name of **Baron Brougham and Vaux.**

BROUGHAM AND VAUX, 5th Baron *cr* 1860; **Michael John Brougham;** *b* 2 Aug. 1938; *s* of 4th Baron and Jean, *d* of late Brig.-Gen. G. B. S. Follett, DSO, MVO; *S* father, 1967; *m* 1st, 1963, Olivia Susan (marr. diss. 1968), *d* of Rear-Admiral Gordon Thomas Seccombe Gray; one *d*; 2nd, 1969, Catherine Gulliver (marr. diss. 1981), *d* of W. Gulliver; one *s*. *Educ:* Lycée Jaccard, Lausanne; Millfield School. *Heir:* *s* Hon. Charles William Brougham, *b* 9 Nov. 1971. *Address:* 45 Overstrand Mansions, Prince of Wales Drive, SW11.

BROUGHSHANE, 2nd Baron (UK), *cr* 1945; **Patrick Owen Alexander Davison;** *b* 18 June 1903; *er s* of 1st Baron and Beatrice Mary, *d* of Sir Owen Roberts; *S* father 1953; *m* 1929, Bettine, *d* of Sir Arthur Russell, 6th Bt; one *s*. *Educ:* Winchester; Magdalen College, Oxford. Barrister, Inner Temple, 1926. Served War of 1939–45: with Irish Guards, 1939–41; Assistant Secretary (Military), War Cabinet, 1942–45. Has US Legion of Merit. *Heir:* *s* Hon. Alexander Davison, *b* 1936. *Address:* 21 Eaton Square, SW1; 28 Fisher Street, Sandwich, Kent. *Club:* White's.

BROUGHTON, family name of **Baron Fairhaven.**

BROUGHTON, Air Marshal Sir Charles, KBE 1965 (CBE 1952); CB 1961; RAF retired; Air Member for Supply and Organization, Ministry of Defence, 1966–68; *b* 27 April 1911; *s* of Charles and Florence Gertrude Broughton; *m* 1939, Sylvia Dorothy Mary Bunbury; one *d* (and one *d* decd). *Educ:* New Zealand; RAF College, Cranwell. Commissioned, 1932; India, 1933–37; Flying Instructor, 1937–40. Served War of 1939–45 in Coastal Command and Middle East (despatches four times). Flying Training Command, 1947–49; Air Ministry, 1949–51; Imperial Defence College, 1952; NATO, Washington DC, 1953–55; Far East, 1955–58; Transport Command, 1958–61; Dir-General of Organization, Air Min. (subseq. Min. of Defence), 1961–64; UK Representative in Ankara on Permanent Military Deputies Group of Central Treaty Organization (Cento), 1965–66. *Address:* c/o 52 Shrewsbury House, Cheyne Walk, SW3. *Club:* Royal Air Force.

BROUGHTON, Major Sir Evelyn Delves, 12th Bt, *cr* 1660; *b* 2 Oct. 1915; *s* of Major Sir Henry Delves Broughton, 11th Bt, and Vera Edyth Boscawen (*d* 1968); *S* father, 1942; *m* 1st, 1947, Hon. Elizabeth Florence Marion Cholmondeley (marr. diss., 1953), *er d* of 4th Baron Delamere; 2nd, 1955, Helen Mary (marr. diss. 1974), *d* of J. Shore, Wilmslow, Cheshire; three *d* (one *s* decd); 3rd, 1974, Mrs Rona Crammond. *Educ*: Eton; Trinity Coll., Cambridge. Formerly 2nd Lieut Irish Guards and Major RASC. *Heir presumptive: kinsman* David Delves Broughton, *b* 7 May 1942. *Address*: 37 Kensington Square, W8. *T*: 01–937 8883; Doddington, Nantwich, Cheshire. *Clubs*: Brooks's; White's; Tarporley Hunt.

See also Baron Lovat.

BROUGHTON, Leonard, DL; Member, Lancashire County Council, since 1974 (Chairman and Leader, 1974–81); *b* 21 March 1924; *s* of Charles Cecil Broughton and Florence (*née* Sunman); *m* 1949, Kathleen Gibson; one *d*. *Educ*: Kingston-upon-Hull. Served RASC, 1942–47. Estates Manager, Bedford Borough Council, 1957; business man. Member: Blackpool County Borough Council, 1961–74 (Leader, 1968–73); Blackpool Bor. Council, 1974–79; NW Co. Boroughs' Assoc., 1968–74; NW Economic Planning Council, 1970–72; Assoc. of Co. Councils, 1973–77; Board, Central Lancs Develt Corp., 1976–. Mem. Courts, Lancaster and Salford Univs, 1974–81; Lay Mem., Greater Manch. and Lancs Rent Assessment Panel, 1971–; Vice-President: Lancs Youth Clubs Assoc., 1974–81; NW Arts Assoc., 1974–81; Blackpool Social Service Council, 1974–; Chm., Blackpool and Fylde Civilian Disabled Soc. 1964–. Freeman, Co. Borough of Blackpool, 1973. DL Lancs, 1975; High Sheriff of Lancashire, 1983–84. *Recreations*: gardening, overseas travel. *Address*: Kingsmede, 157 Whitegate Drive, Blackpool, Lancs FY3 9ER. *Club*: Royal Over-Seas League.

BROUMAS, Nikolaos; retired General; Hon. Deputy Chief, Hellenic Armed Forces; Ambassador of Greece to the Court of St James's, 1972–74; *b* 22 Aug. 1916; *s* of Taxiarches and Kostia Broumas; *m* 1945, Claire Pendelis; two *d*. *Educ*: Greek Military Academy. US Infantry Coll., 1947–48; Greek Staff Coll., 1952; Greek Nat. Defence Coll., 1954. Co. Comdr, Greece, 1940–41, Western Desert, 1942–43 and Italy, 1944; Co. and Bn Comdr, Greek Guerrilla War, 1946–49; Liaison Officer, Allied Comd Far East, Korean War, 1951; Dep. Nat. Rep. to NATO Mil. Cttee, 1959–61; Dep. Chief of Greek Armed Forces, 1969–72. Kt Comdr, Orders of George I and of the Phoenix. (Greek) Gold Medal for Valour (4 times); Military Cross (twice); Medal for Distinguished Services (twice); Medal of Greek Italian War; Medal of Middle East War; UN Medal of Korean War, 1951; US Bronze Star Medal with oak leaf cluster, 1951. *Recreation*: hunting. *Address*: 5 Argyrokastrou Street, Papagos, Athens, Greece.

BROUN, Sir Lionel John Law, 12th Bt, *cr* 1686; *b* 25 April 1927; *s* of 11th Bt and Georgie, *y d* of late Henry Law, Sydney, NSW; *S* father 1962. *Heir: c* William Windsor Broun [*b* 1917; *m* 1952, D'Hrie King, NSW; two *d*]. *Address*: 23 Clanalpine Street, Mosman, NSW 2088, Australia.

BROWALDH, Tore; Grand Cross, Order of Star of the North, 1974; Kt Comdr's Cross, Order of Vasa, 1963; Vice Chairman, Svenska Handelsbanken, since 1978; Deputy Chairman, Nobel Foundation, since 1966; *b* 23 Aug. 1917; *s* of Knut Ernfrid Browaldh and Ingrid Gezelius; *m* 1942, Gunnel Eva Ericson; three *s* one *d*. *Educ*: Stockholm Univ. (MA Politics, Economics and Law, 1941). Financial Attaché, Washington, 1943; Asst Sec., Royal Cttee of Post-War Econ. Planning, and Admin. Sec., Industrial Inst. for Econ. and Social Res., 1944–45; Sec. to Bd of Management, Svenska Handelsbanken, 1946–49; Dir of Econ., Social, Cultural and Refugee Dept, Secretariat Gen., Council of Europe, Strasbourg, 1949–51; Exec. Vice Pres., Confedn of Swedish Employers, 1951–54; Chief Gen. Man., Svenska Handelsbanken, 1955–66, Chm., 1966–78. Chairman: Svenska Cellulosa AB, 1965–; Sandrew theater and movie AB; Swedish IBM, 1978–; Swedish Unilever AB, 1977–; Industrivärden, 1976–; Deputy Chairman: Beijerinvest AB, 1975–; AB Volvo, 1977–; Director: Volvo Internat. Adv. Bd, 1980–; IBM World Trade Corp., Europe/ME/Africa, New York, 1979–; Unilever Adv. Bd, Rotterdam and London, 1976–. Member: Swedish Govt's Econ. Planning Commn, 1962–73 and Res. Adv. Bd, 1966–70; Consultative Cttee, Internat. Fedn of Insts for Advanced Study, 1972–; UN Gp of Eminent Persons on Multinational Corporations, 1973–74; Royal Swedish Acad. of Sciences; Hudson Inst., USA; Soc. of Scientists and Members of Parlt, Sweden; Royal Swedish Acad. of Engrg Sciences; Royal Acad. of Arts and Sciences, Uppsala. Dr of Technol. *hc* Royal Inst. of Technol., 1967; Dr of Econs *hc* Gothenburg, 1980. St Erik's Medal, Sweden, 1961; Gold Medal for public service, Sweden, 1981. *Publications*: Management and Society, 1961; (autobiography): vol. I, The Pilgrimage of a Journeyman, 1976; vol. II, The Long Road, 1980; vol. III, Against the Wind, 1984. *Recreations*: jazz, piano, golf, chess. *Address*: (office) Svenska Handelsbanken, Kungsträdgårdsgatan 2, 103 28 Stockholm, Sweden. *T*: 46–08–22 92 20; (home) Sturegatan 14, 114 36 Stockholm. *T*: 46–08–61 96 43. *Club*: Sällskapet (Stockholm).

BROWN, Alan James; HM Diplomatic Service, retired; Deputy Commissioner-General, UN Relief and Works Agency for Palestine Refugees, 1977–84; *b* 28 Aug. 1921; *s* of W. Y. Brown and Mrs E. I. Brown; *m* 1966, Joy Aileen Key Stone (*née* McIntyre); one *s*, and two step *d*. *Educ*: Magdalene College, Cambridge (MA). Served with HM Forces, 1941–47; CRO 1948; 2nd Sec., Calcutta, 1948–50; CRO, 1951; Private Sec. to Parly Under-Secretary of State, 1951–52; 1st Secretary, Dacca, Karachi, 1952–55; CRO, 1955–57; Kuala Lumpur, 1957–62; CRO, 1962–63; Head of Information Policy Dept, 1963–64; Dep. High Comr, Nicosia, 1964; Head of Far East and Pacific Dept, CRO, 1964–66; Dep. High Comr, Malta, 1966–70; Dep High Comr, later Consul-Gen., Karachi, 1971–72; Ambassador to Togo and Benin, 1973–75; Head of Nationality and Treaty Dept, FCO, 1975–77. *Recreation*: sailing. *Address*: Inchiquin, 27 Weybridge Park, Weybridge, Surrey. *Club*: United Oxford & Cambridge University.

BROWN, Alan Thomas, CBE 1978; DL; Chief Executive, Oxfordshire County Council, since 1973; *b* 18 April 1928; *s* of Thomas Henry Brown and Lucy Lilian (*née* Betts); *m* 1962, Marie Christine East; two *d*. *Educ*: Wyggeston Grammar Sch., Leicester; Sidney Sussex Coll., Cambridge (Wrangler, Maths Tripos 1950, MA 1953). Fellow CIPFA, 1961. Asst. Bor. Treasurer's Dept, Wolverhampton, 1950–56; Asst Sec., IMTA, 1956–58; Dep. Co. Treas., Berks CC, 1958–61; Co. Treas., Cumberland CC, 1961–66; Town Clerk and Chief Exec., Oxford City Council, 1966–73. Mem., SE Econ. Planning Council, 1975–79. DL Oxon 1978. *Recreations*: chess, horticulture, music, reading. *Address*: 7 Field House Drive, Oxford OX2 7NT. *T*: Oxford 55809.

BROWN, Alan Winthrop; Director, Personnel and Management Services, Department of Employment, since 1985; *b* 14 March 1934; *s* of James Brown and Evelyn V. Brown (*née* Winthrop); *m* 1959, Rut Berit (*née* Ohlson); two *s* one *d*. *Educ*: Bedford Sch.; Pembroke Coll., Cambridge (BA Hons); Cornell Univ., NY (MSc). Joined Min. of Labour, 1959; Private Sec. to Minister, 1961–62; Principal, 1963; Asst Sec., 1969. Dir of Planning, Employment Service Agency, 1973–74; Under-Sec. and Head of Incomes Div., DoE, 1975; Chief Exec., Employment Service Div., 1976–79, Trng Services Div., 1979–82, MSC; Hd Electricity Div., Dept of Energy, 1983–85. *Publications*: papers on occupational psychology and industrial training. *Recreations*: orienteering, reading history and poetry, gardening. *Address*: Groton, Ballfield Road, Godalming, Surrey GU7 2HE.

BROWN, (Albert) Peter (Graeme); Consultant in Press and Public Relations to the Imperial Cancer Research Fund, 1978–83; Press Officer to Royal Commission on National Health Service, 1979; *b* 5 April 1913; *s* of William Edward Graeme Brown, accountant, and Amy Powell Brown; unmarried. *Educ*: Queen Elizabeth's Sch., Darlington. Reporter, Sub-Editor, Dep.-Chief Sub-Editor, Westminster Press, 1932–40. Served War of 1939–45: Royal Navy, Officer, Western Approaches; Normandy; Far East; destroyers and assault ships. Information Divs, Ministries of Health, Local Govt and Planning, also Housing and Local Govt, 1946; Chief Press and Inf. Officer, Min. of Housing and Local Govt, 1958; Dir of Information, DHSS, and Advr to Sec. of State for Social Services, 1968–77. *Recreations*: cricket, opera (Mem. Friends of Covent Garden), classical music, art (Mem., Friends of RA). *Address*: 107 Hamilton Terrace, St John's Wood, NW8. *T*: 01–286 9192. *Club*: MCC.

BROWN, Alexander Cosens Lindsay, CB 1980; Chief Veterinary Officer, Ministry of Agriculture, Fisheries and Food, 1973–80; *b* Glasgow, 30 Jan. 1920; *s* of William Tait Brown and Margaret Rae; *m* 1945, Mary McDougal Hutchison; two *s*. *Educ*: Hutchesons' Grammar Sch., Glasgow; Glasgow Veterinary Coll. Diploma of RCVS; FRCVS 1980. Ministry of Agriculture, Fisheries and Food: appointed Vet. Officer to Dorset, 1943; Divisional Vet. Officer, HQ Tolworth, 1955; Divisional Vet. Officer, Essex, 1958–62; Dep. Regional Vet. Officer, W Midland Region, Wolverhampton, 1962–63; Regional Vet. Officer, Eastern Region, Cambridge, 1963; HQ Tolworth, 1967; Dep. Dir, Veterinary Field Services, 1969–70, Dir, 1970–73. Mem. ARC, 1975–80. *Publications*: contribs to Jl of Royal Soc. of Medicine, Veterinary Record, State Veterinary Jl. *Recreations*: gardening, swimming, reading. *Address*: 8 Keswick Road, Bookham, Leatherhead, Surrey KT22 9HH. *T*: Bookham 57997.

BROWN, Alexander Douglas G.; *see* Gordon-Brown.

BROWN, Sir Allen (Stanley), Kt 1956; CBE 1953; MA; LLM; Australian Commissioner for British Phosphate Commissioners and Christmas Island Phosphate Commission, 1970–76; *b* 3 July 1911; *m* 1936, Hilda May Wilke; one *s* two *d*. Dir-Gen. of Post-War Reconstruction, 1948. Sec., PM's Dept and Sec. to Cabinet, Commonwealth Govt, 1949–58; Deputy Australian High Commissioner to UK, 1959–65; Australian Ambassador to Japan, 1965–70. *Address*: 3 Devorgilla Avenue, Toorak, Victoria 3142, Australia. *Club*: Melbourne (Melbourne).

BROWN, Gen. Arnold, OC 1982; International Leader, and General, Salvation Army, 1977–81; *b* 13 Dec. 1913; *s* of Arnold Rees Brown and Annie Brown; *m* 1939, Jean Catherine Barclay; two *d*. *Educ*: Belleville Collegiate, Canada. Commnd Salvation Army Officer, 1935; Editor, Canadian War Cry, 1937–47; Nat. Publicity Officer, Canada, 1947–62; Nat. Youth Officer, Canada, 1962–64; Head of Internat. Public Relations, Internat. HQ, London, 1964–69; Chief of Staff, 1969–74; Territorial Comdr, Canada and Bermuda, 1974–77. Freeman, City of London, 1978. Hon. LHD Asbury Coll., USA, 1972; Hon. DD Olivet Coll., USA, 1981. *Publications*: What Hath God Wrought?, 1952; The Gate and the Light, 1984. *Recreations*: reading, writing, music. *Address*: 117 Bannatyne Drive, Willowdale, Ontario M2L 2P5, Canada. *Club*: Rotary of London and Toronto.

BROWN, Rt. Rev. Arthur Durrant; a Suffragan Bishop of Toronto, since 1981; *b* 7 March 1926; *s* of Edward S. Brown and Laura A. Durrant; *m* 1949, Norma Inez Rafuse; three *d*. *Educ*: Univ. of Western Ontario (BA); Huron College (LTh). Ordained deacon, 1949; priest, 1950, Huron. Rector: of Paisley with Cargill and Pinkerton, 1949–51; of St Stephen, London, Ont., 1951–55; with Glanworth, 1951–53; of St John, Sandwich, Windsor, Ont., 1955–64; of St Michael and All Angels, Toronto, 1964–81; Canon of Toronto, 1972–74; Archdeacon of York, Toronto, 1974–81. Member: Judicial Council of Ontario, 1978–85; Multi-Cultural Council of Ontario, 1979–; Special Adv. Cttee, Ontario Assoc. of Homes for the Aged. Chm., Canadian Foundn on Compulsive Gambling (Ontario). Columnist, Toronto Sun, 1979–. City of Toronto Citizens Award, 1981. Hon. DD: Huron Coll., 1979; Wycliffe Coll., 1981. *Address*: Bishop's Room, St Paul's L'Amoreaux, 3333 Finch Avenue East, Agincourt, Ontario M1W 2R9, Canada. *T*: (416) 497–7550.

BROWN, Arthur Godfrey Kilner, MA; Headmaster, Worcester Royal Grammar School, 1950–78; *b* 21 Feb. 1915; *s* of Rev. Arthur E. Brown, CIE, MA, BSc, and Mrs E. G. Brown, MA, formerly of Bankura, India; *m* 1939, Mary Denholm Armstrong; one *s* three *d*. *Educ*: Warwick Sch.; Peterhouse, Cambridge. BA Cantab 1938; MA 1950. Assistant Master, Bedford School, 1938–39; King's School, Rochester, 1939–43; Cheltenham College, 1943–50. Elected to Headmasters' Conference, 1950. Chm. Council, Evendine Court, Malvern, 1968–; Chm. of Directors, Swan Theatre, Worcester, 1978–; Pres., Worcester Br., Historical Assoc., 1951–. *Recreations*: athletics (Gold and Silver Medallist, Olympic Games, 1936); music, gardening, house restoration, drama. *Address*: Hopecroft, 34 The Village, Clifton-upon-Teme, Worcester. *Clubs*: Achilles; Hawks (Cambridge); Probus (Worcester West).

See also Hon. Sir R. K. Brown.

BROWN, A(rthur) I(vor) Parry, FFARCS; Anæsthetist: London Hospital, 1936–73; London Chest Hospital, 1946–73; Harefield Hospital, 1940–73; Royal Masonic Hospital, 1950–73; retired; *b* 23 July 1908; *s* of A. T. J. Brown; *m* Joyce Marion Bash. *Educ*: Tollington Sch., London; London Hospital. MRCS, LRCP, 1931; MB, BS London, 1933; DA, 1935; FFARCS, 1951. Member of the Board of the Faculty of Anæsthetists, RCS; Pres., Sect. of Anæsthetics, RSM, 1972–73; Fellow, Assoc. of Anæsthetists; Member, Thoracic Soc. *Publications*: chapter in Diseases of the Chest, 1952; contributions to: Thorax, Anæsthesia. *Address*: Long Thatch, Church Lane, Balsham, Cambridge CB1 6DS. *T*: Cambridge 893012.

BROWN, Sir (Arthur James) Stephen, KBE 1967; CEng, MIMechE; Director, Porvair Ltd, since 1971; Chairman: Stone-Platt Industries Ltd, 1968–73 (Deputy Chairman, 1965–67); Molins Ltd, 1971–78; Deputy Chairman, Chloride Group, 1965–73; *b* 15 Feb. 1906; *s* of Arthur Mogg Brown, and Ada Kelk (*née* Upton); *m* 1935, Margaret Alexandra McArthur; one *s* one *d*. *Educ*: Taunton School; Bristol University (BSc(Eng.)). Apprenticed British Thomson-Houston Co. Ltd, 1928–32; joined J. Stone & Co. Ltd, 1932, Dir, 1945; Man. Dir J. Stone & Co. (Deptford) Ltd (on formation), 1951; Divisional Dir, Stone-Platt Industries Ltd (on formation), 1958; Dir, Fairey Co., 1971–76. Pres., Engineering Employers' Fedn, 1964–65; Pres., Confedn of British Industry, 1966–68; Founder Mem., Export Council for Europe, 1960 (Dep. Chm., 1962–63); Mem., NEDC, 1966–71. Hon. DSc Aston Univ., 1967. *Recreations*: fishing, golf. *Address*: Cut Hedges, Bolney, Sussex. *T*: Bolney 225.

BROWN, Prof. Arthur Joseph, CBE 1974; FBA 1972; Professor of Economics, University of Leeds, 1947–79, now Emeritus; Pro-Vice-Chancellor, Leeds University, 1975–77; *b* 8 Aug. 1914; *s* of J. Brown, Alderley Edge, Cheshire; *m* 1938, Joan H. M., *d* of Rev. Canon B. E. Taylor, Holy Trinity, Walton Breck, Liverpool; two *s* (and one *s* decd). *Educ*: Bradford Grammar School; Queen's College, Oxford (Hon. Fellow, 1985).

First Class Hons in Philosophy, Politics and Economics, 1936, MA, DPhil 1939. Fellow of All Souls College, Oxford, 1937–46; Lectr in Economics, Hertford College, Oxford, 1937–40; on staff of: Foreign Research and Press Service, 1940–43; Foreign Office Research Dept, 1943–45; Economic Section, Offices of the Cabinet, 1945–47. Head of Dept of Economics and Commerce, University of Leeds, 1947–65. Visiting Professor of Economics, Columbia University, City of New York, Jan.-June 1950. President Section F, British Assoc. for the Advancement of Science, 1958; Member: East African Economic and Fiscal Commn, 1960; UN Consultative Group on Economic and Social Consequences of Disarmament, 1961–62; First Secretary of State's Advisory Group on Central Africa, 1962; Hunt Cttee on Intermediate Areas, 1967–69; UGC, 1969–78 (Vice-Chm., 1977–78). Pres., Royal Economic Soc., 1976–78, Vice-Pres., 1978–. Chairman, Adv. Panel on Student Maintenance Grants, 1967–68. Vis. Prof. ANU, 1963; directing Regional Economics project, National Institute of Economic and Social Research, 1966–72. Hon. DLitt: Bradford, 1975; Kent, 1979; Hon. LLD Aberdeen, 1978; Hon. LittD Sheffield, 1979. *Publications:* Industrialisation and Trade, 1943; Applied Economics-Aspects of the World Economy in War and Peace, 1948; The Great Inflation, 1939–51, 1955; Introduction to the World Economy, 1959; The Framework of Regional Economics in the United Kingdom, 1972; (with E. M. Burrows) Regional Economic Problems, 1977; (with J. Darby) World Inflation since 1950: a comparative international study, 1985; articles in various journals. *Recreations:* gardening and walking. *Address:* 24 Moor Drive, Leeds LS6 4BY. *T:* Leeds 755799. *Club:* Athenæum.

See also W. A. Brown.

BROWN, Brig. Athol Earle McDonald, CMG 1964; OBE 1956; *b* 2 Jan. 1905; *s* of W. J. C. G. and Alice Catherine Brown, Armidale, NSW; *m* 1929, Millicent Alice Heesh, Sydney; two *s* one *d*. *Educ:* The Armidale Sch., NSW; Royal Australian Naval Coll.; Sydney Univ. Served War of 1939–45: Royal Australian Artillery, AIF, Middle East and New Guinea; Director, War Graves Services, AIF, 1944–46; Lt-Col, 1944; Brigadier, 1946. Secretary-General: Imperial War Graves Commn, 1946–60; Commonwealth-Japanese Jt Cttee, 1956–69; Dir and Sec.-Gen., Commonwealth War Graves Commn, Pacific Region, 1960–69. *Recreations:* golf, bowls, motoring. *Address:* 351 Belmore Road, North Balwyn, Victoria 3104, Australia. *T:* 857 7544. *Club:* Royal Automobile of Victoria, Masonic (Melbourne).

BROWN, (Austen) Patrick; Under Secretary, Department of Transport, since 1983; *b* 14 April 1940; *s* of late Austen K. and of Dorothy Mary Brown; *m* 1966, Mary (*née* Bulger); one *d*. *Educ:* Royal Grammar School, Newcastle upon Tyne; School of Slavonic and East European Studies, Univ. of London. Carreras Ltd, 1961–69 (Cyprus, 1965–66, Belgium, 1967–68); Management Consultant, Urwick Orr & Partners, UK, France, Portugal, Sweden, 1969–72; Dept of Envt, 1972; Asst. Sec., Property Services Agency, 1976–80, Dept of Transport, 1980–83. *Address:* Great House Cottage, Hambledon, Surrey. *T:* Wormley 4183.

BROWN, Averil; *see* Brown, D.S.

BROWN, Barry; *see* Brown, James B. C.

BROWN, Dame Beryl P.; *see* Paston Brown.

BROWN, Rear-Adm. Brian Thomas, CBE 1983; Director General, Naval Manpower and Training, since 1986; *b* 31 Aug. 1934; *s* of Walter Brown and Gladys (*née* Baddeley); *m* 1959, Veronica, *d* of late Wing Comdr and Mrs J. D. Bird; two *s*. *Educ:* Peter Symonds School. Pilot in 898 and 848 Sqdns, 1959–62; Dep. Supply Officer, HMY Britannia, 1966–68; Supply Officer, HMS Tiger, 1973–75; Secretary to: VCNS, 1975–78; First Sea Lord, 1979–82; rcds 1983; CO HMS Raleigh, 1984–85; DGNPS, 1986. *Recreations:* cricket, gardening. *Address:* c/o Lloyds Bank, High Street, Winchester, Hants SO23 9BU. *Club:* Army and Navy.

BROWN, Bruce Macdonald; Ambassador Extraordinary and Plenipotentiary for New Zealand to Thailand, Vietnam and Laos, since 1985, to Burma, since 1986; *b* 1930; *s* of John Albert Brown and Caroline Dorothea Brown (*née* Jorgenson); *m* 1953, Edith Irene (*née* Raynor); two *s* one *d*. *Educ:* Victoria University of Wellington (MA Hons). Private Secretary to Prime Minister, 1957–59; Second Sec., Kuala Lumpur, 1960–62; First Sec. (later Counsellor), New Zealand Mission to UN, New York, 1963–67; Head of Administration, Min. of Foreign Affairs, Wellington, 1967–68; Director, NZ Inst. of International Affairs, 1969–71; NZ Dep. High Commissioner, Canberra, 1972–75; Ambassador to Iran, 1975–78, and Pakistan, 1976–78; Asst Sec., Min. of Foreign Affairs, 1978–81; Dep. High Comr in London, 1981–85. *Publications:* The Rise of New Zealand Labour, 1962; ed, Asia and the Pacific in the 1970s, 1971. *Recreations:* reading, golf. *Address:* New Zealand Embassy, 93 Wireless Road, Bangkok, Thailand. *Club:* Reform.

BROWN, Carter; *see* Brown, John C.

BROWN, Charles Dargie, FEng 1981; Joint Chairman, Mott, Hay & Anderson, Consulting Engineers, since 1981; *b* 13 April 1927; *s* of William Henry Brown and Jean Dargie; *m* 1952, Sylvia Margaret Vallis; one *s* one *d*. *Educ:* Harris Acad., Dundee; St Andrews Univ. (BScEng, 1st Cl. Hons.). FICE. Joined staff of Mott, Hay & Anderson, 1947; engaged on highways, tunnels and bridge works, incl. Tamar Bridge, Forth Road Bridge, George Street Bridge, Newport, Kingsferry and Queensferry Bridges, 1947–65; Partner and Director, 1965. Principally concerned with planning, design and supervision of major works, incl. Mersey Queensway tunnels and new London Bridge, and projects in Hong Kong, Malaysia, Singapore, Indonesia, Australia and USA, 1965–. Member, Smeatonian Soc. of Civil Engrs, 1984–. Hon. LLD Dundee, 1982. *Publications:* papers to Instn of Civil Engrs, on Kingsferry Bridge, George St Bridge, London Bridge and Mersey tunnels; also various papers to engrg confs. *Recreations:* golf, gardening, bird watching, reading. *Address:* Mallards Mere, Russell Way, Petersfield, Hants GU31 4LD. *T:* Petersfield 67820. *Club:* Royal Automobile.

BROWN, Lt-Col Sir Charles Frederick Richmond, 4th Bt, *cr* 1863; TD; DL; *b* 6 Dec. 1902; *er s* of Frederick Richmond Brown (*d* 1933; 2nd *s* of 2nd Bt); *S* uncle, 1944; *m* 1st, 1933, Audrey (marr. diss., 1948), 2nd *d* of late Col Hon. Everard Baring, CVO, CBE, and late Lady Ulrica Baring; one *s* two *d*; 2nd, 1951, Hon. Gwendolen Carlis Meysey Thomson (marr. diss. 1969), *y d* of 1st (and last) Baron Knaresborough; 3rd, 1969, Pauline, *widow* of Edward Hildyard, Middleton Hall, Pickering, Yorks. *Educ:* Eton. Joined Welsh Guards, 1921; Captain 1932; retired with a gratuity, 1936; joined 5th Bn Green Howards, Territorial Army, as a Major, March 1939; Lieut-Colonel comdg 7th Bn Green Howards, July 1939, and proceeded to France with 7th Bn, April 1940. DL, North Riding of County of York, 1962. *Heir: s* George Francis Richmond Brown [*b* 3 Feb. 1938; *m* 1978, Philippa Jane, *d* of late E. J. Wilcox; two *s*]. *Address:* Stonely Woods, Fadmoor, York. *T:* Kirby Moorside 31293. *Clubs:* Cavalry and Guards, Pratt's; Yorkshire (York).

BROWN, Admiral Charles Randall, Bronze Star 1943; Legion of Merit 1944; Presidential Unit Citation, 1945; DSM 1960; United States Navy, retired, 1962; *b* Tuscaloosa, Alabama, USA, 13 Dec. 1899; *s* of Robison Brown and Stella Seed Brown; *m* 1921, Eleanor Green, Annapolis, Maryland; two *s*. *Educ:* US Naval Academy; US Air University; US Naval War College. Graduated from US Naval Academy, 1921. During War served on original US Joint Chiefs of Staff and US-British Combined Chiefs of Staff organisations; later, Captain of USS Kalinin Bay and USS Hornet and Chief of Staff of a Fast Carrier Task Force. Commander, US Sixth Fleet, Mediterranean, 1956; C-in-C, Allied Forces Southern Europe, 1959–61. Vice-President for European Affairs, McDonnell Aircraft Corp. of St Louis, Mo, 1962–65. *Recreation:* gardening. *Address:* 4000 Massachusetts Avenue NW, Apartment 1428, Washington, DC 20016, USA. *Clubs:* Army and Navy, Army and Navy Country (Washington, DC); The Brook, New York Yacht (NY).

BROWN, Christopher David, MA; Headmaster, Norwich School, since 1984; *b* 8 July 1944; *s* of E. K. Brown; *m* 1972, Caroline Dunkerley; two *d*. *Educ:* Plymouth College; Fitzwilliam College, Cambridge. MA. Assistant Master: The Leys School, Cambridge, 1967–71; Pangbourne College, 1971–73; Radley College, 1973–84 (Head of English, 1975–84). *Address:* 16 The Close, Norwich NR1 4DZ.

BROWN, Rev. Cyril James, OBE 1956; Rector of Warbleton, 1970–77; Chaplain to the Queen, 1956–74; *b* 12 Jan. 1904; *s* of late James Brown, Clifton, Bristol; *m* 1931, Myrtle Aufrère, *d* of late Mark Montague Ford, London; no *c*. *Educ:* Westminster Abbey Choir School; Clifton College; Keble College, Oxford; St Stephen's House, Oxford. Curate of St Gabriel's, Warwick Square, 1927–31; Chaplain, Missions to Seamen, Singapore, 1931–34, Hong Kong, 1934–41; Chaplain, Hong Kong RNVR, 1941–46; Youth Secretary, Missions to Seamen, 1946–47, Superintendent, 1947–51, General Superintendent, 1951–59, General Secretary, 1959–69; Prebendary of St Paul's, 1958–69. *Publications:* contributions to East and West Review, World Dominion, etc. *Recreation:* choral music. *Address:* 16 Merlynn, Devonshire Place, Eastbourne, Sussex. *Club:* Devonshire (Eastbourne).

BROWN, Sir (Cyril) Maxwell Palmer, (Sir Max), KCB 1969 (CB 1965); CMG 1957; Director, RHP Group plc (formerly Ransome Hoffmann Pollard Ltd), since 1975; *b* 30 June 1914; *s* of late Cyril Palmer Brown; *m* 1940, Margaret May Gillhespy; three *s* one *d*. *Educ:* Wanganui College; Victoria University College, NZ; Clare College, Cambridge. Princ. Private Secretary to Pres. Board of Trade, 1946–49; Monopolies Commn, 1951–55; Counsellor (Commercial) Washington, 1955–57; returned to Board of Trade; Second Permanent Sec., 1968–70; Sec. (Trade), DTI, 1970–74; Permanent Sec., Dept of Trade, March-June 1974. Mem., 1975–81, Dep. Chm., 1976–81, Monopolies and Mergers Commn. Director: John Brown & Co., 1975–82; ERA Technology Ltd, 1974–86. *Address:* 20 Cottenham Park Road, Wimbledon, SW20. *T:* 01-946 7237.

BROWN, Dr Daniel McGillivray, BSc, PhD, ScD; FRS 1982; ARSC; Emeritus Reader in Organic Chemistry, Cambridge University, since 1983; Fellow of King's College, Cambridge, since 1953; Attached Fellow, Laboratory of Molecular Biology, Cambridge; *b* 3 Feb. 1923; *s* of David Cunninghame Brown and Catherine Stewart (*née* McGillivray); *m* 1953, Margaret Joyce Herbert; one *s* three *d*. *Educ:* Glasgow Acad.; Glasgow Univ. (BSc); London Univ. (PhD); Cambridge Univ. (PhD, ScD). Res. Chemist, Chester Beatty Res. Inst., 1945–53; Asst Dir of Res., 1953–58, Lectr, 1959–67, Reader in Org. Chem., 1967–83, Cambridge Univ.; Vice-Provost, King's Coll., Cambridge, 1974–81. Vis. Professor: Univ. of Calif, LA, 1959–60; Brandeis Univ., 1966–67. *Publications:* scientific papers, mainly in chemical jls. *Recreations:* modern art, gardening, spasmodic fly-fishing. *Address:* 60 Hartington Grove, Cambridge CB1 4UE. *T:* Cambridge 245304.

BROWN, Sir David, Kt 1968; Chairman, David Brown Holdings Ltd, and Vosper Ltd, until going to live abroad in 1978; *b* 10 May 1904; *s* of Francis Edwin (Frank) and Caroline Brown; *m* 1st, 1926, Daisie Muriel Firth (marr. diss. 1955); one *s* one *d*; 2nd, 1955, Marjorie Deans (marr. diss. 1980); 3rd, 1980, Paula Benton Stone. *Educ:* Rossall School; Private Tutor in Engineering; Huddersfield Technical Coll. FIMechE. Apprentice, David Brown and Sons (Hudd.), Ltd, 1921; Dir, 1929; Man. Dir, 1932. Founded David Brown Tractors Ltd (first company to manufacture an all-British tractor in England), 1935; Chm., Aston Martin Lagonda Ltd, 1946–72; formed, 1951, The David Brown Corp. Ltd (Chm.), embracing gears, machine tools, castings, etc. Pres., Vosper Ltd, and Chm., Vosper Private Ltd, Singapore, 1978–86; Director: David Brown Corp. of Australia Ltd, 1965–; David Brown Gear Industries Pty Ltd (Australia), 1963–; David Brown Gear Industries (Pty) Ltd (South Africa), 1969–. Past Member: Board of Governors of Huddersfield Royal Infirmary; Council of Huddersfield Chamber of Commerce. Life Governor, RASE. First Englishman to open Canadian Farm and Industrial Equipment Trade Show, Toronto, 1959; inaugurated Chief Flying Sun of Iroquois Tribe of Mohawk Nation, Toronto, 1959. Hon. Dato SPMJ (Johore), 1979. *Address:* L'Estoril, 31 Avenue Princesse Grace, Monte Carlo, Monaco. *Clubs:* Guards Polo (Life Mem.); International des Anciens Pilotes de Grand Prix, Monaco Yacht, Monaco Automobile.

BROWN, Prof. David Anthony, PhD; FIBiol; Professor of Pharmacology, Middlesex Hospital Medical School and University College London, since 1987; *b* 10 Feb. 1936; *s* of Alfred William and Florence Brown; two *s* one *d*. *Educ:* Univ. of London (BSc, BSc, PhD). Asst Lectr 1961–65, Lectr 1965–73, Dept of Pharmacology, St Bart's Hosp. Med. Coll.; Dept of Pharmacology, School of Pharmacy, Univ. of London: Sen. Lectr, 1973–74; Reader, 1974–77; Professor, 1977–79; Wellcome Professor, 1979–87. Visiting Professor: Univ. of Chicago, 1970; Univ. of Iowa, 1971, 1973; Univ. of Texas, 1979, 1980, 1981; Vis. Scientist, Armed Forces Radiobiology Res. Inst., Bethesda, Md, 1976; Fogarty Schol.-in-Residence, NIH, Bethesda, 1985–86. Member: Physiological Soc., 1970; British Pharmacological Soc., 1965–; Biochemical Soc., 1969–. *Publications:* contribs to Jl of Physiology, British Jl of Pharmacology. *Recreation:* family life. *Address:* Department of Pharmacology, Middlesex Hospital Medical School, Mortimer Street, W1P 7PN.

BROWN, David John Bowes, CBE 1982; FSIAD; Chairman/Managing Director, Archer Components Ltd, since 1973; Chairman, Artix Ltd (formerly DJB Engineering Ltd), since 1973; *b* 2 Aug. 1925; *s* of Matthew and Helene Brown; *m* 1954, Patricia Robson (marr. diss. 1982); two *s* two *d*; *m* 1986, Eve Watkinson. *Educ:* King James Grammar Sch., Knaresborough; Leeds College of Technology. Logging Contractor, UK and W Africa, 1946–60; joined Hunslet Engine Co. as Designer/Draughtsman, 1960–62; designed and patented transmission and exhaust gas conditioning systems for underground mines tractors; joined Chaseside as Chief Designer, 1962–65; designed and patented 4 wheel drive loading shovels; became Director and Chief Executive of company; joined Muir-Hill Ltd as Man. Dir, 1965–73; designed and patented 4 wheel drive tractors, cranes, steering systems, transmissions, axles; started DJB Engineering Ltd, 1973; designed, manufactured and sold a range of articulated dump trucks in Peterlee, Co. Durham. The company has gained 3 Queen's Awards and 1 Design Council Award. *Address:* Ravensthorpe Manor, Boltby, Thirsk, North Yorks YO7 2DX; Artix Ltd, Peterlee, Co Durham SR8 2HX. *T:* Peterlee 863333.

BROWN, David K.; *see* Kennett Brown.

BROWN, Vice-Adm. Sir David (Worthington), KCB 1984; self-employed consultant; *b* 28 Nov. 1927; *s* of Captain J. R. S. Brown, RN and Mrs D. M. E. Brown; *m* 1958, Etienne Hester Boileau; three *d*. *Educ:* HMS Conway. Joined RN, 1945; commanded HM

Ships MGB 5036, MTB 5020, Dalswinton, Chailey, Cavendish, Falmouth, Hermione, Bristol; Dir, Naval Ops and Trade, 1971–72; Dir of Officers Appointments (Exec.), 1976–78; Asst Chief of Defence Staff (Ops), 1980–82; Flag Officer Plymouth, Port Adm. Devonport, Comdr Central Sub Area Eastern Atlantic, Comdr Plymouth Sub Area Channel, 1982–85. Younger Brother of Trinity House. *Recreations:* sailing, fishing. *Address:* c/o Barclays Bank, 107 Commercial Road, Portsmouth, Hants PO1 1BT. *Club:* Army and Navy.

BROWN, Denise Lebreton, (Mrs Frank Waters), RE 1959 (ARE 1941); RWA 1986 (ARWA 1980); artist; *d* of Jeanne Lebreton and Frederick Peter Brown; *m* 1938, Frank William Eric Waters; one *s*. *Educ:* Lyzeum Nonnenwerth im Rhein; Royal College of Art. British Instn Schol. in Engraving, 1932; ARCA 1935; *prox. acc.* Rome Scholarship in Engraving, 1936; Royal College of Art Travelling Schol., 1936. Has exhibited at: Royal Academy regularly since 1934; Royal Society of Painter-Etchers and Engravers; Royal West of England Acad.; also in Canada, USA and S Africa. Work represented in British, V&A, and Ashmolean Museums. *Publications:* books illustrated include: several on gardening; children's books, etc. *Recreations:* music, gardening. *Address:* Wintertree, Church Westcote, Oxford OX7 6SF. *Club:* RAF.

BROWN, Denys Downing, CMG 1966; MM 1945; HM Diplomatic Service, retired; *b* 16 Dec. 1918; *s* of A. W. Brown, Belfast, and Marjorie Downing; *m* 1954, Patricia Marjorie, *e d* of Sir Charles Bartley; one *s* one *d*. *Educ:* Hereford Cathedral School; Brasenose College, Oxford (Scholar). Oxf. and Bucks LI, 1939–45 (prisoner-of-war, 1940; escaped, 1945). Entered Foreign Service, 1946; served in Poland, Germany, Egypt, Yugoslavia, Sweden, and FO; Minister (Economic), Bonn, retired 1971; Dir, P&O Steam Navigation Co., 1971–80. *Recreations:* reading, travel. *Address:* Beechcroft, Priorsfield Road, Godalming, Surrey. *T:* Godalming 6635.

BROWN, Sir Derrick H.; *see* Holden-Brown.

BROWN, Sir Douglas (Denison), Kt 1983; Chairman, since 1981, and Managing Director, since 1954, James Corson & Co. Ltd; *b* 8 July 1917; *s* of Robert and Alice Mary Brown; *m* 1941, Marion Cruickshanks Emmerson; one *s* one *d*. *Educ:* Bablake Sch., Coventry. Served Army, 1940–46: RE, 1940–41; commnd RA, 1941; India, ME, N Africa, Italy; mentioned in despatches; retd in rank of Major. Mem. Exec. Cttee, Clothing Manufrs of GB, 1967–82; Chm., Leeds and Northern Clothing Assoc., 1975–77. Chairman: NW Leeds Cons. Assoc., 1961–74 (Pres. 1974); Yorks Area Cons. Assoc., 1978–83 (Treasurer, 1971–78); Mem., Nat. Exec. Cttee, Cons. and Unionist Assoc., 1971–; Mem., Cons. Bd of Finance, 1971–78. Mem., Gas Consumer Council, NE Area, 1981–; Bd Mem., Yorkshire Water Authority, 1983–. Vice-Chm., St Edmund's PCC, Roundhay, 1981–. Chm., Bd of Governors, Jacob Kramer Coll. of Further Educn, 1978–. *Recreations:* gardening, Rugby, cricket, golf. *Address:* Bankfield, 6 North Park Road, Leeds LS8 1JD. *T:* Leeds 662151.

BROWN, Douglas Dunlop, QC 1976; **His Honour Judge Brown;** a Circuit Judge, since 1980; *b* 22 Dec. 1931; *s* of late Robert Dunlop Brown, MICE, and Anne Cameron Brown; *m* 1960, June Margaret Elizabeth McNamara; one *s*. *Educ:* Ryleys Sch., Alderley Edge; Manchester Grammar Sch.; Manchester Univ. (LLB). Served in RN, 1953–55; Lieut, RNR. Called to Bar, Gray's Inn, 1953; practised Northern Circuit from 1955; Mem. General Council of Bar, 1967–71; Asst Recorder, Salford City QS, 1971; a Recorder of the Crown Court, 1972–80. Mem., Parole Bd for England and Wales, 1985–87. *Recreations:* cricket, golf, music. *Address:* Sessions House, Lancaster Road, Preston PR1 2PD. *Club:* Wilmslow Golf.

BROWN, Douglas James, MBE 1959; HM Diplomatic Service, retired; Secretary to the Medical College, St Bartholomew's Hospital; *b* 6 May 1925; *s* of James Stephen Brown and Hilda May (*née* Hinch); unmarried. *Educ:* Edinburgh Univ. (MA). HMOCS, Nigeria, 1951–62 (Private Sec. to Governor-General, 1955–58); joined Diplomatic Service, 1962; Private Sec. to Comr-Gen. for SE Asia, 1962–63; FO, 1963–66; Asst to Special Representative in Africa, 1966–67; British High Commn, Nairobi, 1967–68; British Embassy, Djakarta, 1968–71; Inspector, FCO, 1971–73; Counsellor and Consul-Gen., Algiers, 1974–77; Consul-Gen., St Louis, 1977–80, retired. *Address:* 9 Amherst Avenue, Ealing, W13 8NQ. *T:* 01-997 7125; Via Privata Oliveta 41/18, 16035 Rapallo, Italy. *Club:* Royal Over-Seas League.

BROWN, Edmund Gerald, Jr, (Jerry Brown); lawyer, writer and politician; Attorney, Reavis & McGrath, Los Angeles and New York City; Chairman: National Commission on Industrial Innovation; Institute for National Strategy; *b* 7 April 1938; *s* of Edmund Gerald Brown and Bernice (*née* Layne). *Educ:* Univ. of California at Berkeley (BA 1961); Yale Law School (JD 1964). Admitted to California Bar, 1965; Research Attorney, Calif. Supreme Court, 1964–65; with Tuttle & Taylor, LA, 1966–70; Sec. of State, Calif., 1971–74; Governor of California, 1975–83; Democratic Candidate for US Senator from California, 1982. Trustee, Los Angeles Community Colls, 1969–70. *Address:*Reavis & McGrath, Sixth Floor, Broadway Plaza, 700 South Flower Street, Los Angeles, Calif 90017, USA.

BROWN, Sir Edward (Joseph), Kt 1961; MBE 1958; JP; Laboratory Technician (non-ferrous metals); company director; *b* 15 April 1913; *s* of Edward Brown; *m* 1940, Rosa, *d* of Samuel Feldman; one *s* one *d*. *Educ:* Greencoat Elementary; Morley College (Day Continuation). Leading Aircraftsman, RAF, 1942–46. Formerly Mem. Assoc. Supervisory Staffs Executives and Technicians (Chm., Enfield Branch, 1953–63); Dist Councillor for Union. Member Tottenham Borough Council, 1956–64. Chm., National Union of Conservative and Unionist Associations, 1959, 1960; Chm. Conservative Party Conference, 1960; former Vice-Chm., Assoc. of Conservative Clubs. Contested Stalybridge and Hyde (C), 1959; MP (C) Bath, 1964–79. JP (Middlesex) 1963. *Recreation:* campanology. *Clubs:* Tottenham Conservative; Harringay-West Green Constitutional.

BROWN, Edwin Percy, CBE 1981; Director of Social Services, North Yorkshire County Council, 1973–82; Student, Teeside Polytechnic, 1982–86; *b* 20 May 1917; *s* of late James Percy Brown and of Hetty Brown; *m* 1958, Margaret (*née* Askey); one *s* one *d*. *Educ:* Mundella Grammar Sch., Nottingham; Nottingham Univ. (Certif. in Social Studies). Social worker, Nottinghamshire CC, 1951–54; Sen. social worker, Lancashire CC, 1954–59; Children's Officer: Southampton CC, 1959–65; Wiltshire CC, 1965–71; Dir of Social Services, N Riding CC, 1971–74. Mem., Supplementary Benefits Commn, 1976–80. Adviser to Assoc. of County Councils, 1974–81; President: Assoc. of Directors of Social Services, 1977–78; Nat. Assoc. of Nursery and Family Care, 1984–. *Recreations:* gardening, watching cricket, reading. *Address:* 21 The Green, Romanby, Northallerton, N Yorkshire. *Clubs:* National Liberal; Nottinghamshire County Cricket.

BROWN, Prof. Edwin Thomas, PhD, DSc Eng; FIMM; Professor of Rock Mechanics, since 1979, Head of the Department of Mineral Resources Engineering, since 1985, Imperial College of Science and Technology, University of London; *b* 4 Dec. 1938; *s* of George O. and Bessie M. Brown. *Educ:* Castlemaine High Sch.; Univ. of Melbourne (BE 1960, MEngSc 1964); Univ. of Queensland (PhD 1969); Univ. of London (DSc Eng 1985). MICE 1976; MIEAust 1965; MASCE 1965; FIMM 1980; FGS 1976. Engr, State Electricity Commn of Victoria, 1960–64; James Cook Univ. of North Queensland (formerly UC of Townsville): Lectr, 1965–69; Sen. Lectr, 1969–72; Associate Prof. of Civil Engrg, 1972–75; Imperial College, Univ. of London: Reader in Rock Mechanics, 1975–79; Dean, RSM, 1983–86. Res. Associate, Dept of Civil and Mineral Engrg, Univ. of Minnesota, 1970; Sen. Visitor, Dept of Engrg, Univ. of Cambridge, 1974; Vis. Prof., Dept of Mining and Fuels Engrg, Univ. of Utah, 1979. Chm., British Geotechnical Soc., 1982–83; Pres., Internat. Soc. for Rock Mechanics, 1983–87. Instn of Mining and Metallurgy: Consolidated Gold Fields Gold Medal, 1984; Sir Julius Wernher Meml Lecture, 1985. Editor-in-Chief, Internat. Jl of Rock Mechanics and Mining Sciences, 1975–82. *Publications:* (with E. Hoek) Underground Excavations in Rock, 1980; (ed) Rock Characterization, Testing and Monitoring, 1981; (with B. H. G. Brady) Rock Mechanics for Underground Mining, 1985; papers on rock mechanics in civil engrg and mining jls. *Recreations:* cricket, jazz. *Address:* Department of Mineral Resources Engineering, Imperial College of Science and Technology, SW7 2BP. *T:* 01–589 5111.

BROWN, Prof. Eric Herbert, PhD; Professor of Geography, University College London, since 1966; *b* 8 Dec. 1922; *s* of Samuel Brown and Ada Brown, Melton Mowbray, Leics; *m* 1945, Eileen (*née* Reynolds) (*d* 1984), Llanhowell, Dyfed; two *d*. *Educ:* King Edward VII Grammar Sch., Melton Mowbray; King's Coll., London (BSc 1st Cl. Hons). MSc Wales, PhD London. Served War: RAF Pilot, Coastal Comd, 1941–45. Asst Lectr, then Lectr in Geography, University Coll. of Wales, Aberystwyth, 1947–49; Lectr, then Reader in Geog., UCL, 1950–66; Dean of Students, 1972–75; Mem. Senate, Univ. of London, 1981–86. Vis. Lectr, Indiana Univ., USA, 1953–54; Vis. Prof., Monash Univ., Melbourne, 1971. Mem., NERC, 1981–84. Geographical Adviser, Govt of Argentina, 1965–68; Hon. Mem., Geograph. Soc. of Argentina, 1968. Chairman: British Geomorphol Res. Group, 1971–72; British Nat. Cttee for Geog., 1985–. Hon. Sec., RGS, 1977– (Back Grant, 1961); Pres., Inst. of British Geographers, 1978. *Publications:* The Relief and Drainage of Wales, 1961; (with W. R. Mead) The USA and Canada, 1962; (ed) Geography Yesterday and Tomorrow, 1980; contrib. Geog. Jl, Phil. Trans Royal Soc., Proc. Geologists' Assoc., Trans Inst. of British Geographers, and Geography. *Recreations:* watching Rugby football, wine. *Address:* Monterey, Castle Hill, Berkhamsted, Herts HP4 1HE. *T:* Berkhamsted 4077. *Clubs:* Athenæum, Geographical.

BROWN, Captain Eric Melrose, CBE 1970 (OBE 1945; MBE 1944); DSC 1942; AFC 1947; RN; Chief Executive, British Helicopter Advisory Board, since 1970; *b* 21 Jan. 1919; *s* of Robert John Brown and Euphemia (*née* Melrose); *m* 1942, Evelyn Jean Margaret Macrory; one *s*. *Educ:* Royal High Sch., Edinburgh; Edinburgh University. MA 1947. Joined Fleet Air Arm as Pilot, 1939; Chief Naval Test Pilot, 1944–49; Resident British Test Pilot at USN Air Test Center, Patuxent River, 1951–52; CO No 804 Sqdn, 1953–54; Comdr (Air), RN Air Stn, Brawdy, 1954–56; Head of British Naval Air Mission to Germany, 1958–60; Dep. Dir (Air), Gunnery Div., Admty, 1961; Dep. Dir, Naval Air Warfare and Adviser on Aircraft Accidents, Admty, 1962–64; Naval Attaché, Bonn, 1965–67; CO, RN Air Stn, Lossiemouth, 1967–70. Chm., British Aviation Bicentenary Exec. Cttee, 1984. FRAeS 1964 (Pres., 1982–83; Chm., RAeS Rotorcraft Sect., 1973–76). Hon. FEng (Pakistan) 1984; Hon. Fellow, Soc. of Experimental Test Pilots, 1984. Liveryman, GAPAN, 1978. British Silver Medal for Practical Achievement in Aeronautics, 1949; Anglo-French Breguet Trophy, 1983; Bronze Medal, Fédération Aéronautique Internationale, 1986. *Publications:* Wings on My Sleeve, 1961; (jtly) Aircraft Carriers, 1969; Wings of the Luftwaffe, 1977; Wings of the Navy, 1980; The Helicopter in Civil Operations, 1981; Wings of the Weird and the Wonderful, vol. 1, 1982, vol. 2, 1985. *Recreations:* golf, ski-ing, bridge. *Address:* Carousel, New Domewood, Copthorne, Sussex. *T:* Copthorne 712610. *Clubs:* Naval and Military; Explorers' (NY).

BROWN, Sir (Ernest) Henry Phelps, Kt 1976; MBE 1945; FBA 1960; Professor of Economics of Labour, University of London, 1947–68, now Emeritus Professor; *b* 10 Feb. 1906; *s* of E. W. Brown, Calne, Wiltshire; *m* 1932, Dorothy Evelyn Mostyn, *d* of Sir Anthony Bowlby, 1st Bt, KCB; two *s* one *d*. *Educ:* Taunton School; Wadham College, Oxford (Scholar). Secretary of Oxford Union, 1928; 1st Class Hons Modern History, 1927; Philosophy, Politics and Economics, 1929. Fellow of New College, Oxford, 1930–47; Hon. Fellow, Wadham College, Oxford, 1969–; Rockefeller Travelling Fellow in USA, 1930–31. Served War of 1939–45, with Royal Artillery; BEF; ADGB; First Army; Eighth Army (MBE). Member: Council on Prices, Productivity and Incomes, 1959; Nat. Economic Development Council, 1962; Royal Commn on Distribn of Income and Wealth, 1974–78. Chairman, Tavistock Inst. of Human Relations, 1966–68. Pres., Royal Economic Soc., 1970–72. Hon. DLitt Heriot-Watt, 1972; Hon. DCL Durham, 1981. *Publications:* The Framework of the Pricing System, 1936; A Course in Applied Economics, 1951; The Balloon (novel), 1953; The Growth of British Industrial Relations, 1959; The Economics of Labor, 1963; A Century of Pay, 1968; The Inequality of Pay, 1977; The Origins of Trade Union Power, 1983. *Recreations:* walking; represented Oxford *v* Cambridge cross-country running, 1926. *Address:* 16 Bradmore Road, Oxford. *T:* Oxford 56320. *Club:* Athenæum.

See also M. K. Hopkins.

BROWN, Dr Fred, FRS 1981; Head of Virology Division, Wellcome Research Laboratories, Beckenham, Kent, since 1983; *b* 31 Jan. 1925; *m* 1948, Audrey Alice Doherty; two *s*. *Educ:* Burnley Grammar Sch.; Manchester Univ. BSc 1944, MSc 1946, PhD 1948. Asst Lectr, Manchester Univ., 1946–48; Lectr, Bristol Univ. Food Preservation Res. Station, 1948–50; Senior Scientific Officer: Hannah Dairy Res. Inst., Ayr, 1950–53; Christie Hosp. and Holt Radium Inst., Manchester, 1953–55; Head, Biochemistry Dept, 1955–83, and Dep. Dir, 1980–83, Animal Virus Res. Inst., Pirbright, Surrey. *Publications:* papers on viruses causing animal diseases, in scientific journals. *Recreations:* cricket, Association football, listening to classical music, fell walking. *Address:* Syndal, Glaziers Lane, Normandy, Surrey GU3 2DF. *T:* Guildford 811107.

BROWN, Sir (Frederick Herbert) Stanley, Kt 1967; CBE 1959; BSc; FEng, FIMechE, FIEE; retired; Chairman, Central Electricity Generating Board, 1965–72 (Deputy-Chairman, 1959–64); *b* 9 Dec. 1910; *s* of Clement and Annie S. Brown; *m* 1937, Marjorie Nancy Brown; two *d*. *Educ:* King Edward's School, Birmingham; Birmingham University. Corp. of Birmingham Electric Supply Dept, 1932–46; West Midlands Joint Electricity Authority, 1946–47; Liverpool Corporation Electricity Supply Department, 1947–48; Merseyside and N Wales Division of British Electricity Authority; Generation Engineer (Construction), 1948–49; Chief Generation Engineer (Construction), 1949–51; Deputy Generation Design Engineer of British Electricity Authority, 1951–54; Generation Design Engineer, 1954–57, Chief Engineer, 1957, of Central Electricity Authority; Member for Engineering, Central Elec. Generating Board, 1957–59. President: Instn of Electrical Engineers, 1967–68; EEIBA, 1969–70. Member: Council, City and Guilds of London Inst., 1969–; Court of Govs, Univ. of Birmingham, 1969–. Hon. DSc: Aston, 1971; Salford, 1972. *Publications:* various papers to technical institutions. *Recreations:* gardening, motoring. *Address:* Cobbler's Hill, Compton Abdale, Glos. *T:* Withington 233.

BROWN, Hon. Geoffrey E.; *see* Ellman-Brown.

BROWN, Rev. Canon Geoffrey Harold; Vicar of St Martin-in-the-Fields, since 1985; *b* 1 April 1930; *s* of Harry and Ada Brown; *m* 1963, Elizabeth Jane Williams; two *d. Educ:* Monmouth Sch.; Trinity Hall, Cambridge. MA. Asst Curate, St Andrew's, Plaistow, 1954–60; Asst Curate, St Peter's, Birmingham and Sub-Warden of Pre-Ordination Training Scheme, 1960–63; Rector: St George's, Newtown, Birmingham, 1963–73; Grimsby, 1973–85. *Recreations:* the countryside, photography, theatre. *Address:* 5 St Martin's Place, WC2N 4JJ. *T:* 01–930 1862.

BROWN, Hon. George Arthur, CMG; Associate Administrator, United Nations Development Programme, since 1984 (Deputy Administrator, 1978–84); *b* 25 July 1922; *s* of Samuel Austin Brown and Gertrude Brown; *m* 1964, Leila Leonie Gill; two *d* (and one *s* one *d* by previous marriage). *Educ:* St Simon's College, Jamaica; London School of Economics. Jamaica Civil Service: Income Tax Dept, 1941; Colonial Secretary's Office, 1951; Asst Secretary, Min. of Finance, 1954; Director, General Planning Unit, 1957; Financial Secretary, 1962; Governor, Bank of Jamaica, 1967–78. *Publications:* contrib. Social and Economic Studies (University College of the West Indies). *Recreations:* hiking, boating, fishing. *Address:* c/o United Nations Development Programme, United Nations, New York, NY 10017, USA. *Club:* Jamaica (Jamaica).

BROWN, George Frederick William, CMG 1974; Member, Melbourne Underground Railway Loop Authority, since 1971; *b* 12 April 1908; *s* of late G. Brown; *m* 1933, Catherine Mills; one *d* (and one *d* decd). *Educ:* Christian Brothers' Coll., Essendon; Phahran Techn. Coll.; Royal Melbourne Inst. Technology. FIE (Aust.), AMIME (Aust.), FCIT. Victorian Railways, 1923; Asst Engr 1929; Country Roads Bd, 1934; Plant Engr Newport Workshops, 1939–43; Supt Loco. Maintenance, 1943–53; Chief Mech. Engr, 1953–58; Comr, 1958–61; Dep. Chm., 1961–67; Chm., 1967–73; Mem., Victorian Railway Bd, 1973–77. Mem. Council, Royal Melb. Inst. Technology, 1958–74, Pres. 1970. *Publications:* articles in techn. jls on rail transport. *Recreation:* golf. *Address:* Unit 1, 10 Lucas Street, East Brighton, Victoria 3187, Australia. *Clubs:* Kelvin Victoria, Victoria Golf, MCC (Victoria).

BROWN, George Mackay, OBE 1974; FRSL 1977; author; *b* 17 Oct. 1921; *s* of John Brown and Mary Jane Mackay. *Educ:* Stromness Acad.; Newbattle Abbey Coll.; Edinburgh Univ. (MA). Hon. MA Open Univ., 1976; Hon. LLD Dundee, 1977; Hon. DLitt Glasgow, 1985. *Publications: fiction:* A Calendar of Love, 1967; A Time to Keep, 1969; Greenvoe, 1972; Magnus, 1973; Hawkfall, 1974; The Two Fiddlers, 1975; The Sun's Net, 1976; Pictures in the Cave, 1977; Six Lives of Frankle the Cat, 1980; Andrina, 1983; Time in a Red Coat, 1984; Christmas Stories, 1985; *plays:* A Spell for Green Corn, 1970; Three Plays, 1984; *poetry:* Fishermen with Ploughs, 1971; Winterfold, 1976; Selected Poems, 1977; Voyages, 1983; Christmas Poems, 1984; *essays, etc:* An Orkney Tapestry, 1969; Letters from Hamnavoe, 1975; Under Brinkie's Brae, 1979; Portrait of Orkney, 1981. *Recreations:* ale tasting, watching television, reading. *Address:* 3 Mayburn Court, Stromness, Orkney KW16 3DH.

BROWN, Prof. Sir (George) Malcolm, Kt 1985; FRS 1975; FRSE 1967; United Nations Consultant, since 1986; Director: British Geological Survey (formerly Institute of Geological Sciences), 1979–85; Geological Museum, 1979–85; Geological Survey of Northern Ireland, 1979–85; *b* 5 Oct. 1925; *s* of late George Arthur Brown and Anne Brown; *m* 1st, 1963, Valerie Jane Gale (marr. diss. 1977); 2nd, 1985, Sally Jane Marston, *e d* of A. D. Spencer, *qv;* two step *d. Educ:* Coatham Sch., Redcar; Durham Univ. (BSc, DSc); Oxford Univ. (MA, DPhil). RAF, 1944–47. FGS. Commonwealth Fund (Harkness) Fellow, Princeton Univ., 1954–55; Lectr in Petrology, Oxford Univ., 1955–66; Fellow, St Cross Coll., Oxford, 1965–67; Carnegie Instn Res. Fellow, Geophysical Lab., Washington DC, 1966–67; Prof. of Geology, 1967–79 (now Emeritus), Dean of Faculty of Science, 1978–79, and Pro-Vice-Chancellor, 1979, Durham Univ. NASA Principal Investigator, Apollo Moon Programme, 1967–75; Geol Advr to ODM, 1979–85. Member: Natural Environment Res. Council, 1972–75; Council, Royal Soc., 1980–81. Vis. Prof., Univ. of Berne, 1977–78; Adrian Vis. Fellow, Univ. of Leicester, 1983–. UK Editor, Physics and Chemistry of the Earth, 1977–79. Hon. DSc Leicester, 1984. Daniel Pidgeon Fund Award, 1952, Wollaston Fund Award, 1963, Murchison Medal, 1981, Geol Soc. of London. *Publications:* (with L. R. Wager) Layered Igneous Rocks, 1968; (contrib.) Methods in Geochemistry, 1960; (contrib.) Basalts, 1967; (contrib.) Planet Earth, 1977; (contrib.) Origin of the Solar System, 1978; papers in several sci. jls. *Address:* Dove House, Leafield, Oxford OX8 5NP. *T:* Asthall Leigh 673. *Club:* Royal Over-Seas League.

BROWN, Prof. George William, FBA 1986; Member, External Scientific Staff, Medical Research Council, since 1980; Hon. Professor of Sociology, Royal Holloway and Bedford New College, London University, since 1980; *b* 15 Nov. 1930; *s* of late William G. Brown and of Lily Jane (*née* Hillier); *m* 1st, 1954, Gillian M. Hole (marr. diss. 1970); one *s* one *d*; 2nd, 1978, Seija T. Sandberg; one *d. Educ:* Kilburn Grammar Sch.; University Coll. London (BA Anthropol. 1954); LSE (PhD 1961). Scientific Staff, DSIR, 1955–56; MRC Social Psychiatry Res. Unit, Inst. of Psychiatry, 1956–67; joined Social Res. Unit, Bedford Coll., London Univ., 1967; Prof. of Sociology, London Univ. and Jt Dir, Social Res. Unit, Bedford Coll., 1973–80. *Publications:* (jtly) Schizophrenia and Social Care, 1966; (with J. K. Wing) Institutionalism and Schizophrenia, 1970; (with T. O. Harris) Social Origins of Depression, 1978; numerous contribs to jls. *Address:* 101 Camberwell Grove, SE5 8JH. *T:* 01–701 1483.

BROWN, Dame Gillian (Gerda), DCVO 1981; CMG 1971; HM Diplomatic Service, retired; Member, Panel of Chairmen, Civil Service Selection Board, since 1984; *b* 10 Aug. 1923; *er d* of late Walter Brown and late Gerda Brown (*née* Grenside). *Educ:* The Spinney, Gt Bookham; Stoatley Hall, Haslemere; Somerville Coll., Oxford (Hon. Fellow 1981). FO, 1944–52; 2nd Sec., Budapest, 1952–54; FO, 1954–59; 1st Sec., Washington, 1959–62; 1st Sec., UK Delegn to OECD, Paris, 1962–65; FO, 1965–66; Counsellor and Head of Gen. Dept, FO, subseq. Head of Aviation, Marine and Telecommunications Dept, later Marine and Transport Dept, FCO, 1967–70; Counsellor, Berne, 1970–74; Under Sec., Dept of Energy, 1975–78; Asst Under Sec. of State, FCO, 1978–80; Ambassador to Norway, 1981–83. Council Member: Anglo-Norse Soc., 1983–; Greenwich Forum, 1985–. Hon. LLD Bath, 1981. Grand Cross, Order of St Olav, 1981. *Address:* c/o Midland Bank plc, Central Hall, SW1.

BROWN, Prof. Godfrey Norman; Professor of Education, University of Keele, 1967–80, now Emeritus; Director, Betley Court Gallery, since 1980; *b* 13 July 1926; *s* of Percy Charles and Margaret Elizabeth Brown; *m* 1960, Dr Freda Bowyer; three *s. Educ:* Whitgift Sch.; School of Oriental and African Studies, London; Merton Coll., Oxford (MA, DPhil). Army service, RAC and Intelligence Corps, 1944–48. Social Affairs Officer, UN Headquarters, NY, 1953–54; Sen. History Master, Barking Abbey Sch., Essex, 1954–57; Lectr in Educn, University Coll. of Ghana, 1958–61; Sen. Lectr, 1961, Prof., 1963, Univ. of Ibadan, Nigeria; Dir, Univ. of Keele Inst. of Educn, 1967–80. Visiting Prof., Univ. of Rhodesia and Nyasaland, 1963; Chm., Assoc. for Recurrent Educn, 1976–77; Mem., Exec. Cttee and Bd of Dirs, World Council for Curriculum and Instruction, 1974–77. OECD Consultant on teacher education, Portugal, 1980. Vice-Pres.,

Community Council of Staffs, 1984–. Collector of the Year Award, Art and Antiques, 1981. *Publications:* An Active History of Ghana, 2 vols, 1961 and 1964; Living History, 1967; Apartheid, a Teacher's Guide, 1981; Betley Through the Centuries, 1985; ed (with J. C. Anene) Africa in the Nineteenth and Twentieth Centuries, 1966; ed, Towards a Learning Community, 1971; ed (with M. Hiskett) Conflict and Harmony in Education in Tropical Africa, 1975; contrib. educnl and cultural jls. *Recreations:* family life; art history, conservation. *Address:* Betley Court, Betley, near Crewe, Cheshire. *T:* Crewe 820652.

BROWN, Gordon; *see* Brown, James G.

BROWN, Harold, PhD; Chairman, The Johns Hopkins Foreign Policy Institute, School of Advanced International Studies, since 1984 (Visiting Professor, 1981–84); *b* 19 Sept. 1927; *s* of A. H. Brown and Gertrude Cohen Brown; *m* 1953, Colene McDowell; two *d. Educ:* Columbia Univ. (AB 1945, AM 1946, PhD in Physics 1949). Res. Scientist, Columbia Univ., 1945–50, Lectr in Physics, 1947–48; Lectr in Physics, Stevens Inst. of Technol., 1949–50; Res. Scientist, Radiation Lab., Univ. of Calif, Berkeley, 1951–52; Gp Leader, Radiation Lab., Livermore, 1952–61; Dir, Def. Res. and Engrg, Dept of Def., 1961–65; Sec. of Air Force, 1965–69; Pres., Calif Inst. of Technol., Pasadena, 1969–77; Sec. of Defense, USA, 1977–81. Sen. Sci. Adviser, Conf. on Discontinuance of Nuclear Tests, 1958–59; Delegate, Strategic Arms Limitations Talks, Helsinki, Vienna and Geneva, 1969–77. Member: Polaris Steering Cttee, 1956–58; Air Force Sci. Adv. Bd, 1956–61; (also Consultant) President's Sci. Adv. Cttee, 1958–61. Hon. DEng Stevens Inst. of Technol., 1964; Hon. LLD: Long Island Univ., 1966; Gettysburg Coll., 1967; Occidental Coll., 1969; Univ. of Calif, 1969; Hon. ScD: Univ. of Rochester, 1975; Brown Univ., 1977; Univ. of the Pacific, 1978; Univ. of S Carolina, 1979; Franklin and Marshall Coll., 1982; Chung Ang Univ. (Seoul, Korea), 1983. Member: Amer. Phys. Soc., 1946; Nat. Acad. of Engrg, 1967; Amer. Acad. of Arts and Scis, 1969; Nat. Acad. of Scis, 1977. One of Ten Outstanding Young Men of Year, US Jun. Chamber of Commerce, 1961; Columbia Univ. Medal of Excellence, 1963; Air Force Exceptl Civil. Service Award, 1969; Dept of Def. Award for Exceptionally Meritorious Service, 1969; Joseph C. Wilson Award, 1976; Presidential Medal of Freedom, 1981. Grand Cross, First Class, Order of Merit of Federal Republic of Germany, 1980. *Publication:* Thinking About National Security: defense and foreign policy in a dangerous world, 1983. *Address:* School of Advanced International Studies, The Johns Hopkins Foreign Policy Institute, 1740 Massachusetts Avenue, NW, Washington, DC 20036, USA. *Clubs:* Athenæum; Bohemian (San Francisco); California (Los Angeles); City Tavern (Washington, DC).

BROWN, Harold Arthur Neville, CMG 1963; CVO 1961; HM Diplomatic Service, retired; *b* 13 Dec. 1914; *s* of Stanley Raymond and Gladys Maud Brown; *m* 1939, Mary McBeath Urquhart; one *s* one *d. Educ:* Cardiff High School; University College, Cardiff. Entered Ministry of Labour as 3rd Class Officer, 1939; Asst Principal, 1943; Private Sec. to Permanent Sec. of Min. of Labour and Nat. Service, 1944–46; Principal, 1946; Labour Attaché, Mexico City (and other countries in Central America and the Caribbean), 1950–54; transferred to Foreign Office, 1955; Head of Chancery, Rangoon, 1958 and 1959; British Ambassador in Liberia, 1960–63; Corps of Inspectors, Foreign Office, 1963–66; Ambassador to Cambodia, 1966–70; Consul-General, Johannesburg, 1970–73; Minister, Pretoria, Cape Town, 1973–74. Knight Great Band of the Humane Order of African Redemption, 1962. *Address:* 14 Embassy Court, King's Road, Brighton BN1 2PX.

BROWN, Harold James, AM 1979; BSc, ME; Hon. DSc; FIE(Australia); FIREE; retired; management consultant, Adelaide, South Australia, 1976–85; Technical Director, Philips Industries Holdings Ltd, Sydney, 1961–76; *b* 10 July 1911; *s* of Allison James and Hilda Emmy Brown; *m* 1936, Hazel Merlyn Dahl Helm; two *s* two *d. Educ:* Fort Street Boys' High Sch.; Univ. of Sydney, NSW, Australia. BSc 1933; BE (Univ. Medal) 1935; ME (Univ. Medal) 1945; Hon. DSc 1976. Research Engineer, Amalgamated Wireless Australasia Ltd, 1935–37; Electrical Engineer, Hydro-electric Commission of Tasmania, 1937–39; Research Officer and Principal Research Officer, Council for Scientific and Industrial Research, 1939–45; Chief Communications Engineer, Australian Nat. Airways Pty Ltd, 1945–47; Prof. of Electrical Engineering, Dean of Faculty of Engineering and Asst Director, NSW Univ. of Technology, 1947–52; Controller R&D, Dept of Supply, Melbourne, 1952–54; Controller, Weapons Research Establishment, Department of Supply, Commonwealth Government of Australia, 1955–58; Technical Director, Rola Co. Pty Ltd, Melbourne, 1958–61. Awarded Queen's Silver Jubilee Medal, 1977. *Publications:* numerous technical articles in scientific journals. *Recreations:* gardening, bowling. *Address:* 20 Woodbridge, Island Drive, Delfin Island, South Australia 5021.

BROWN, Sir Henry Phelps; *see* Brown, Sir E. H. P.

BROWN, Henry Thomas C.; *see* Cadbury-Brown.

BROWN, Prof. Herbert Charles, PhD; R. B. Wetherill Research Professor Emeritus, Purdue University, 1978 (Professor, 1947–60, R. B. Wetherill Research Professor, 1960–78); *b* 22 May 1912; *s* of Charles Brown and Pearl (*née* Gorinstein); *m* 1937, Sarah Baylen; one *s. Educ:* Wright Jun. Coll., Chicago (Assoc. Sci. 1935); Univ. of Chicago (BS 1936; PhD 1938). Univ. of Chicago: Eli Lilly Postdoctoral Res. Fellow, 1938–39; Instr, 1939–43; Wayne University: Asst Prof., 1943–46; Associate Prof., 1946–47. Member: Nat. Acad. of Sciences, USA, 1957–; Amer. Acad. of Arts and Sciences, 1966–; Hon. Mem., Phi Lambda Upsilon, 1961–; Hon. Fellow, Chem. Soc., London, 1978– (Centenary Lectr, 1955; C. K. Ingold Medal, 1978); Foreign Fellow, Indian Nat. Science Acad., 1978–. Hon. Dr of Science: Univ. of Chicago, 1968; Wayne State Univ., 1980; Hebrew Univ. Jerusalem, 1980; Pontifica Univ. Catolica de Chile, 1980; Wales, 1982; Purdue, 1982, etc. (Jtly) Nobel Prize in Chemistry, 1979. Amer. Chemical Society: Harrison Howe Award, 1953; Nichols Medal, 1959; Linus Pauling Medal, Oregon and Puget Sound Sects, 1968; Roger Adams Medal, Organic Div., 1971; Priestley Medal, 1981. Award for Creative Res. in Org. Chem., Soc. of Organic Chem. Mfg Assoc., 1960; Herbert Newby McCoy Award, Purdue Univ., 1965 (1st co-recipient); Nat. Medal of Science, US Govt, 1969; Madison Marshall Award, 1975; Allied Chemical Award for Grad. Trng and Innovative Chem., 1978 (1st recipient); Perkins Medal, Amer. Sect., Soc. of Chemical Industry, 1982; Gold Medal, Amer. Inst. Chem., 1985. *Publications:* Hydroboration, 1962; Boranes in Organic Chemistry, 1972; Organic Syntheses via Boranes, 1975; The Non-classical Ion Problem, 1977; over 950 scientific articles in Jl Amer. Chem. Soc., Jl Org. Chem., Jl Organometal. Chem., and Synthesis. *Recreations:* travel, photography. *Address:* Department of Chemistry, Purdue University, West Lafayette, Ind 47907, USA. *T:* (317) 494–5316.

BROWN, Herbert Macauley Sandes; a Judge of the High Court of Nigeria, 1945–58, retd; *b* Dublin, Feb. 1897; *o s* of late William Herbert Brown, KC, sometime County Court Judge, of Glenfern, Blackrock, Co. Dublin, and Elizabeth Rose (*née* Sandes); *m* 1928, Catherine Mary (*née* Hutchinson) (*d* 1971); one *d. Educ:* The Abbey, Tipperary; Trinity College, Dublin. Served War of 1914–18 in Royal Marines. Called to the Irish Bar, 1921. Entered Administrative Service, Nigeria, 1924; Magistrate, 1934; Assistant Judge, 1943; Puisne Judge, 1945. *Address:* 6 Abbotsford Crescent, Edinburgh EH10 5DY.

BROWN, Prof. H(oward) Mayer; Ferdinand Schevill Distinguished Service Professor of Music, University of Chicago, since 1976; *b* 13 April 1930; *s* of Alfred R. and Florence Mayer Brown; unmarried. *Educ:* Harvard Univ. AB 1951, AM 1954, PhD 1959. Walter Naumburg Trav. Fellow, Harvard, 1951–53; Instructor in Music, Wellesley Coll., Mass, 1958–60; Univ. of Chicago: Asst Prof., 1960–63; Assoc. Prof., 1963–66; Prof., 1967–72; Chm., 1970–72; Dir of Collegium Musicum, 1960–83; King Edward Prof. of Music, KCL, 1972–74. Guggenheim Fellow, Florence, 1963–64; Villa I Tatti Fellow, Florence, 1969–70; Andrew D. White Prof.-at-large, Cornell Univ., 1972–76; Prof. of Music, Univ. of Chicago, 1974–. Pres., Amer. Musicological Soc., 1978–80; Vice-Pres., Internat. Musicological Soc., 1982–87. Fellow, Amer. Acad. of Arts and Scis, 1983–. *Publications:* Music in the French Secular Theater, 1963; Theatrical Chansons, 1963; Instrumental Music Printed Before 1600, 1965; (with Joan Lascelle) Musical Iconography, 1972; Sixteenth-Century Instrumentation, 1972; Music in the Renaissance, 1976; Embellishing Sixteenth-Century Music, 1976; Chansonnier from the Time of Lorenzo the Magnificent, 2 vols, 1983. contrib. Jl Amer. Musicological Soc., Acta musicologica, Musical Quarterly, etc. *Address:* 1415 E 54th Street, Chicago, Ill 60615, USA. *Club:* Reform.

BROWN, Hugh Dunbar; MP (Lab) Provan Division of Glasgow since 1964; *b* 18 May 1919; *s* of Neil Brown and Grace (*née* Hargrave); *m* 1947, Mary Glen Carmichael; one *d*. *Educ:* Allan Glen's School and Whitehill Secondary School, Glasgow. Formerly Civil Servant, Ministry of Pensions and National Insurance. Member of Glasgow Corporation, 1954; Magistrate, Glasgow, 1961. Parly Under-Sec. of State, Scottish Office, 1974–79. *Recreation:* golf. *Address:* 29 Blackwood Road, Milngavie, Glasgow G62 7LB.

BROWN, Jack, MBE 1985; JP; General Secretary, Amalgamated Textile Workers Union, since 1976; *b* 10 Nov. 1929; *s* of Maurice Brown and Edith (*née* Horrocks); *m* 1952, Alice (*née* Brown); one *s*. *Educ:* Pennington CofE Primary Sch., Leigh, Lancs; Leigh CofE Secondary Sch., Leigh. Commenced employment in cotton industry as operative, Dec. 1943; Royal Artillery, 1949–51; full time Trade Union Official (Organiser), 1954; District Sec., 1961–72; Asst Gen. Sec., 1972–76. Non-exec. Mem., NW Electricity Bd, 1984–. JP Greater Manchester, 1967. *Recreations:* reading, Rugby League football. *Address:* 11 Thomas Street, Atherton, Manchester M29 9DP. *T:* Atherton 870218. *Clubs:* Soldiers and Sailors, Labour (both Atherton).

BROWN, Lt-Col James, CVO 1985; RNZAC (retd); General Secretary to the Duke of Edinburgh's Award Scheme; *b* 15 Aug. 1925; *y s* of late John Brown and Eveline Bertha (*née* Cooper), Russells Flat, North Canterbury, NZ; *m* 1952, Patricia Sutton; two *d*. *Educ:* Christchurch Boys' High Sch., NZ; Royal Military Coll., Duntroon, Australia (grad 1947). NZ Regular Army, 1947–71: active service, Korea, 1951–52; Reg. Comr of Civil Defence, Dept of Internal Affairs, NZ, 1971–77. Official Sec. to Governor-Gen. of NZ, 1977–85. Col Comdt, RNZAC, 1982–86. *Recreations:* fishing, shooting. *Address:* PO Box 11–467, Wellington, New Zealand. *Club:* United Services Officers (Wellington).

BROWN, Maj.-Gen. James, CB 1982; Director of Management Information Services Division, University of London, since 1986; *b* 12 Nov. 1928; *s* of late James Brown; *m* 1952, Lilian May Johnson; two *s*. *Educ:* Methodist Coll., Belfast; RMA Sandhurst; psc, jssc, rcds. Commissioned RAOC 1948; served UK (attached 1 DWR), Egypt, Cyprus, War Office, 1948–58; Staff Coll., Camberley, 1959; BAOR, UK, 1960–64; JSSC, Latimer, 1964–65; HQ Gurkha Inf. Bde Borneo, 1965–66 (despatches); MoD, 1966–67; Comdr RAOC, 4 Div., 1967–70; AA&QMG (Ops/Plans), HQ 1 (BR) Corps, 1970–72; Central Ordnance Depots, Donnington and Bicester, 1972–75; Dep. Dir, Ordnance Services, MoD, 1975; RCDS, 1976; Dep. Dir, Personal Services, MoD, 1977–80; Dir Gen. of Ordnance Services, 1980–83. Col Comdt, RAOC, 1983–85. Sec., Univ. of London Computer Centre, 1983–86. *Address:* c/o Royal Bank of Scotland, Holt's Branch, Kirkland House, Whitehall, SW1.

BROWN, James Alexander, TD 1948; QC 1956; Recorder of Belfast, 1978–82; *b* 13 June 1914; *s* of Rt Hon. Mr Justice (Thomas Watters) Brown and Mary Elizabeth Brown; *m* 1950, Shirley Wallace Sproule; one *s* two *d*. *Educ:* Campbell College, Belfast; Balliol College, Oxford (BA; Pres., Oxford Union Soc., 1936). Served 1/Royal Ulster Rifles, 1939–45 (wounded; Captain). Called Bar of NI, 1946; called English Bar (GI), 1950. County Court Judge, Co. Down, 1967–78.

BROWN, Dr (James) Barry (Conway), OBE 1978; Deputy Controller, Higher Education Division, British Council, since 1985; *b* 3 July 1937; *s* of Frederick Clarence and Alys Brown; *m* 1963, Anne Rosemary Clough; two *s* one *d*. *Educ:* Cambridge Univ. (BA Nat. Sci 1959; MA 1963); Birmingham Univ. (MSc 1960; PhD 1963). Research Officer, CEGB, Berkeley Nuclear Labs, 1963–67; British Council: Sen. Sci. Officer, Sci. Dept, 1967–69; Sci. Officer, Madrid, 1969–72, Paris, 1972–78; Head, Sci. and Technology Group, 1978–81; Rep. and Cultural Counsellor, Mexico, 1981–85. *Recreations:* music, travel in (and study of) countries of posting, singing, reading. *Address:* British Council, 10 Spring Gardens, SW1A 2AH. *T:* 01–930 8466; 42 Hazel Road, Purley-on-Thames, Reading RG8 8BB. *T:* Reading 417581.

BROWN, (James) Gordon; MP (Lab) Dunfermline East, since 1983; *b* 20 Feb. 1951; *s* of Rev. Dr John Brown and J. Elizabeth Brown. *Educ:* Kirkcaldy High Sch.; Edinburgh Univ. MA 1972; PhD 1982. Rector, Edinburgh Univ., 1972–75; Temp. Lectr, Edinburgh Univ., 1976; Lectr, Glasgow Coll. of Technology, 1976–80; Journalist and Current Affairs Editor, Scottish TV, 1980–83. Member: NUJ; TGWU. Chm., Labour Party Scottish Council, 1983–84. Contested (Lab) S Edinburgh, 1979. *Publications:* (ed) The Red Paper on Scotland, 1975; (with H. M. Drucker) The Politics of Nationalism and Devolution, 1980; (ed) Scotland: the real divide, 1983. *Recreations:* reading and writing, football and tennis. *Address:* 48 Marchmont Road, Edinburgh. *T:* 031–447 7726.

BROWN, Jerry; *see* Brown, E. G.

BROWN, Joe, MBE 1975; Freelance Guide and Climber; *b* 26 Sept. 1930; *s* of J. Brown, Longsight, Manchester; *m* 1957, Valerie Gray; two *d*. *Educ:* Stanley Grove, Manchester. Started climbing while working as plumber in Manchester; pioneered new climbs in Wales in early 1950's; gained internat. reputation after climbing West Face of Petit Dru, 1954; climbed Kanchenjunga, 1955; Mustagh Tower, 1956; Mt Communism, USSR, 1962; Climbing Instructor, Whitehall, Derbs, 1961–65; opened climbing equipment shops, Llanberis, 1965, Capel Curig, 1970; Leader of United Newspapers Andean Expedn, 1970; Roraima Expedn, 1973. Hon. Fellow, Manchester Polytechnic, 1970. *Publication:* (autobiog.) The Hard Years, 1967. *Recreations:* mountaineering, ski-ing, fishing, canoeing. *Address:* Menai Hall, Llanberis, Gwynedd. *T:* Llanberis 327. *Club:* Climbers'.

BROWN, John, CBE 1982; FEng 1984; FIEE; Director, University and Schools Liaison, General Electric Co., since 1983; *b* 17 July 1923; *s* of George Brown and Margaret Ditchburn Brown; *m* 1947, Maureen Dorothy Moore; one *d*. *Educ:* Edinburgh University. Radar Research and Development Estab., 1944–51; Lectr, Imperial Coll., 1951–54; University Coll., London: Lectr, 1954–56; Reader, 1956–64; Prof., 1964–67; seconded to Indian Inst. of Technology as Prof. of Electrical Engrg, 1962–65; Prof. of Elect. Engineering, Imperial Coll. of Science and Technology, 1967–81 (Head of Dept, 1967–79); Tech. Dir, Marconi Electrical Devices Ltd, 1981–83. Member: SRC, 1977–81 (Chm., Engrg Bd, 1977–81); Engrg Group, Nat. Advisory Bd, 1983–84; Engrg Cttee, CNAA, 1985–. Pres., IEE, 1979–80 (Vice-Pres., 1975–78; Dep. Pres., 1978–79); Pres., IEEIE, 1981–85. Governor: S Bank Polytechnic, 1985–; Willesden Coll. of Technology, 1985–. *Publications:* Microwave Lenses, 1953; (with H. M. Barlow) Radio Surface Waves, 1962; Telecommunications, 1964; (with R. H. Clarke) Diffraction Theory and Antennas, 1980; papers in Proc. IEE, etc. *Recreation:* gardening. *Address:* GEC, PO Box 79, Wembley, Middlesex.

BROWN, John; HM Diplomatic Service; Counsellor (Commercial) and Director of Trade Promotion, British Trade Development Office, New York, since 1984; *b* 13 July 1931; *s* of John Coultas Scofield Brown and Sarah Ellen Brown (*née* Brown); *m* 1955, Christine Ann Batchelor; one *d*. *Educ:* South Shields High School. Export Credits Guarantee Dept, 1949; Grenadier Guards, 1949–51; Board of Trade, 1967; seconded to HM Diplomatic Service, 1969; Diplomatic Service, 1975; First Secretary and Head of Chancery, Accra, 1977; FCO, 1979–; Counsellor, 1981. *Recreations:* gardening, golf, walking. *Address:* c/o Foreign and Commonwealth Office, SW1A 2AH. *Club:* Royal Over-Seas League.

BROWN, John B.; *see* Blamire-Brown.

BROWN, (John) Carter; Director, National Gallery of Art, Washington, DC, since 1969; Chairman, Commission of Fine Arts, since 1971; *b* 8 Oct. 1934; *s* of John Nicholas Brown and Anne Kinsolving Brown; *m* 1976, Pamela Braga Drexel; one *s* one *d*. *Educ:* Harvard (AB *summa cum laude* 1956; MBA 1958); Inst. of Fine Arts, NY Univ. (Museum Trng Prog., Metropol. Museum of Art; MA 1961). Studied: with Bernard Berenson, Florence, 1958; Ecole du Louvre, Paris, 1958–59; Rijksbureau voor Kunsthistorische Documentatie, The Hague, 1960. National Gallery of Art: Asst to Dir, 1961–63; Asst Dir, 1964–68; Dep. Dir, 1968–69. Member: President's Cttee on Arts and Humanities; Bd of Govs, John Carter Brown Liby, Brown Univ. Trustee: Amer. Acad. in Rome; Amer. Fedn of Arts; Corning Mus. of Glass; Inst. of Fine Arts, NY Univ.; John F. Kennedy Center for Performing Arts; Nat. Geographic Soc.; Nat. Trust for Historic Preservation; Storm King Art Center; Winterthur Mus. Hon. Mem., Amer. Inst. of Architects, 1975. Holds eight hon. degrees. Gold Medal of Honor, National Arts Soc., 1972. Commandeur, l'Ordre des Arts et des Lettres, France, 1975; Chevalier de la Légion d'Honneur, France, 1976; Knight, Order of St Olav, Norway, 1979; Comdr, Order of the Republic, Egypt, 1979; Comdr, Order of Orange-Nassau, Netherlands, 1982; Commendatore, Order of Merit of Italian Republic, 1984; Kt Comdr, Order of Isabel la Católica, Spain, 1985. Phi Beta Kappa, 1956. Author/Dir, (film), The American Vision, 1966. *Publications:* contrib. professional jls and exhibn catalogues. *Recreations:* sailing, riding, photography. *Address:* 3035 Dumbarton Avenue NW, Washington, DC 20007, USA. *T:* (office) (202) 842–6001. *Clubs:* Knickerbocker, Century Association, New York Yacht, Cruising Club of America (New York), 1925 F Street (Washington).

BROWN, Sir John (Douglas Keith), Kt 1960; Chairman, McLeod Russel plc, London, 1972–79 (Director since 1963); Director of other companies; *b* 8 Sept. 1913; *s* of late Ralph Douglas Brown and Rhoda Miller Keith; *m* 1940, Margaret Eleanor, *d* of late William Alexander Burnet; two *s*. *Educ:* Glasgow Acad. CA 1937. Joined Messrs. Lovelock & Lewes, Chartered Accountants, Calcutta, October 1937 (Partnership, 1946; retired 1948); joined Jardine Henderson Ltd as a Managing Director, 1949; Chairman, 1957–63. Pres. Bengal Chamber of Commerce and Industry and Associated Chambers of Commerce of India, 1958–60; Pres. UK Citizens' Assoc. (India), 1961. Mem. Eastern Area Local Bd, Reserve Bank of India, 1959–63; Mem. Advisory Cttee on Capital Issues, 1958–63; Mem. Technical Advisory Cttee on Company Law, 1958–63; Mem. Companies Act Amendment Cttee, 1957; Mem. Central Excise Reorganisation Cttee, 1960. *Recreations:* gardening, walking. *Address:* Windover, Whitmore Vale Road, Hindhead, Surrey. *T:* Hindhead 4173. *Clubs:* Oriental, City of London; Bengal (Calcutta).

BROWN, Rt. Rev. John Edward; *see* Cyprus and the Gulf, Bishop in.

BROWN, John Francis Seccombe, AO 1977; MC 1942; Agent-General for Queensland, since 1983; *b* 2 May 1917; *s* of George Edward Brown and Ruth Seccombe; *m* 1946, Elwyn Phillips; one *s* one *d*. *Educ:* Queensland, Aust. Committee of Direction of Fruit Marketing, 1939–64; Man. Dir and Chief Exec., Golden Circle Cannery, 1964–82; director of six Queensland public companies, 1975–84. Inaugural and Past Pres., Queensland Confedn of Industry; Trustee, Brisbane Grammar Sch., 1974–. Freedom of City of London, 1985. *Recreations:* social golfer, fishing, boating. *Address:* Flat 7/5 Carlton Gardens, SW1Y 5AD. *T:* 01–839 3763. *Clubs:* East India, Royal Automobile; Queensland, United Services, Royal Queensland Golf (Qld).

BROWN, Sir John (Gilbert Newton), Kt 1974; CBE 1966; MA; Director: Basil Blackwell Ltd (formerly Basil Blackwell Publisher Ltd), since 1983 (Chairman, 1983–85); Blackwell Group Ltd, since 1980; Deputy Chairman, B. H. Blackwell Ltd, since 1983 (Chairman 1980–83); *b* 7 July 1916; *s* of John and Molly Brown, Chilham, Kent; *m* 1946, Virginia, *d* of late Darcy Braddell and Dorothy Braddell; one *s* two *d*. *Educ:* Lancing Coll.; Hertford Coll., Oxford (MA Zoology). Bombay Branch Oxford University Press, 1937–40; commissioned Royal Artillery, 1941; served with 5th Field Regiment, 1941–46; captured by the Japanese at Fall of Singapore, 1942; prisoner of war, Malaya, Formosa and Japan, 1942–45; returned Oxford University Press, 1946; Sales Manager, 1949; Publisher, 1956–80; Chm., University Bookshops (Oxford) Ltd; Director: Book Tokens Ltd; Willshaw Booksellers Ltd, Manchester. President, Publishers' Association, 1963–65. Member: Nat. Libraries Cttee; EDC for Newspapers, Printing and Publishing Industry, 1967–70; Adv. Cttee on Scientific and Technical Information, 1969–73; Communication Adv. Cttee for UK Nat. Cttee for UNESCO; Royal Literary Fund (Asst Treasurer); Bd of British Library, 1973–79; Royal Soc. Cttee on Scientific Information; Mem. Bd, British Council, 1968–81; Open Univ. Visiting Cttee. Professorial Fellow, Hertford Coll., Oxford, 1974–80. FRSA 1964. *Address:* Milton Lodge, Great Milton, Oxon. *T:* Great Milton 217. *Club:* Garrick.

BROWN, (John) Michael, CBE 1986; HM Diplomatic Service retired; *b* 16 Nov. 1929; *m* 1955, Elizabeth Fitton; one *s* one *d*. Served at: Cairo, 1954–55; Doha, 1956–57; FO, 1957–60; Havana, 1960–62; FO, 1962–64; Jedda, 1965–66; Maseru, 1966–67; Bogotá, 1967–69; FCO, 1969–71; Ankara, 1971–73; Tripoli, 1973–75; FCO, 1976–79; Ambassador to Costa Rica and Nicaragua, 1979–82; Consul-Gen., Geneva, 1983–85. *Address:* Chevington Lodge, Chevington, Bury St Edmunds, Suffolk IP29 5QL.

BROWN, Prof. John Russell; Honorary Professor of English, Sussex University, since 1982 (Professor 1971–82); Associate Director, The National Theatre, since 1973; Professor of Theatre and Chairman of Department, University of Michigan, Ann Arbor, since 1985; *b* 15 Sept. 1923; *yr s* of Russell Alan and Olive Helen Brown, Coombe Wood, Somerset; *m* 1961, Hilary Sue Baker; one *s* two *d*. *Educ:* Monkton Combe Sch.; Keble Coll., Oxford. Sub-Lieut (AE) RNVR, 1944–46. Fellow, Shakespeare Inst., Stratford-upon-Avon, 1951–55; Lectr and Sen. Lectr, Dept of English, Birmingham Univ., 1955–63; Hd of Dept of Drama and Theatre Arts, Univ. of Birmingham, 1964–71; Prof. of Theatre Arts, State Univ. of NY at Stony Brook, 1982–85. Reynolds Lectr, Colorado Univ., 1957; Vis. Prof. Graduate Sch., New York Univ., 1959; Mellon Prof. of Drama,

Carnegie Inst., Pittsburgh, 1964; Vis. Prof., Zürich Univ., 1969–70; Univ. Lectr in Drama, Univ. of Toronto, 1970. Robb Lectr, Univ. of Auckland, 1976. Dir, Orbit Theatre Co. Member: Adv. Council of Victoria and Albert Museum, 1980–83; Adv. Council of Theatre Museum, 1974–83 (Chm., 1979–83); Arts Council of GB, 1980–83, and Chm. Drama Panel, 1980–83 (formerly Dep. Chm.). *Theatre productions include:* Twelfth Night, Playhouse, Pittsburgh, 1964; Macbeth, Everyman, Liverpool, 1965; The White Devil, Everyman, 1969; Crossing Niagara, Nat. Theatre at the ICA, 1975; They Are Dying Out, Young Vic, 1976; Old Times, British Council tour of Poland, 1976; Judgement, Nat. Theatre, 1977; Hamlet (tour), 1978; Macbeth, Nat. Theatre (co-director), 1978; The Vienna Notes and The Nest, Crucible, Sheffield, 1979; Company, Nat. Theatre, 1980; Faith Healer, Nat. Theatre and Santa Fe, 1982, and, with Candida, British Council tour of India, 1983; The Double Bass, Nat. Theatre, 1984; The Daughter-in-Law, and Antique Pink, Project Theater, Ann Arbor, Mich, USA, 1985. Gen. Editor: Stratford-upon-Avon Studies, 1960–67; Stratford-upon-Avon Library, 1964–; Theatre Production Studies, 1981–. *Publications:* (ed) The Merchant of Venice, 1955; Shakespeare and his Comedies, 1957; (ed) The White Devil, 1960; Shakespeare: The Tragedy of Macbeth, 1963; (ed) The Duchess of Malfi, 1965; (ed) Henry V, 1965; Shakespeare's Plays in Performance, 1966; Effective Theatre, 1969; Shakespeare's The Tempest, 1969; Shakespeare's Dramatic Style, 1970; Theatre Language, 1972; Free Shakespeare, 1974; Discovering Shakespeare, 1981; Shakespeare and his Theatre, 1982; A Short Guide to Modern British Drama, 1983; articles in Shakespeare Survey, Critical Quarterly, Tulane Drama Review, Studies in Bibliography, etc. *Recreations:* gardening, travel. *Address:* c/o The National Theatre, SE1 9PX.

BROWN, Joseph Lawler, CBE 1978; TD 1953; FInstM; CBIM; DL; Chairman and Managing Director, The Birmingham Post & Mail Ltd, 1973–77; *b* 22 March 1921; *s* of late Neil Brown; *m* 1950, Mabel Smith, SRN, SCM; one *s* one *d. Educ:* Peebles; Heriot-Watt Coll., Edinburgh. BA Open Univ. FInstM 1976; CBIM (formerly FBIM) 1978. Served War, The Royal Scots, 1939–46 (Major). The Scotsman Publications Ltd, 1947–60; Coventry Newspapers Ltd: Gen. Man., 1960; Jt Man. Dir, 1961; Man. Dir, 1964–69; The Birmingham Post & Mail Ltd: Dep. Man. Dir, 1970; Man. Dir, 1971. Director: Cambridge Newspapers Ltd, 1965–69; Press Assoc., 1968–75 (Chm. 1972); Reuters Ltd, 1972–75; BPM (Holdings) Ltd, 1973–81. Pres., Birmingham Chamber of Industry and Commerce, 1979–80. Exec. Chm., Birmingham Venture, 1981–85. Mem., Bromsgrove and Redditch DHA, 1982–84; Mem., Hereford and Worcester Family Practitioner Cttee, 1982–83. Mem. Council, Regular Forces Employment Assoc., 1983–. Warden, Neidpath Castle, Peebles, 1983–84. DL County of W Midlands, 1976. Commendatore, Order Al Merito Della Repubblica Italiana, 1973. *Recreations:* gardening, fishing, Japanese woodcuts. *Address:* Westerly, 37 Mearse Lane, Barnt Green, Birmingham B45 8HH. *T:* 021–445 1234.

BROWN, Kenneth Vincent, CMG 1954; Senior Judge, Supreme Court, Trinidad, 1943–52, retired; *b* 1 Nov. 1890; *m* 1942, Vere Alice Edghill (*d* 1944); one *s. Educ:* St George's Coll., Weybridge, Surrey. Barrister, Gray's Inn, 1915; Magistrate, Trinidad, 1925; Puisne Judge, 1936. Coronation Medals, 1937, 1953. *Recreations:* cricket, racing. *Clubs:* Union, Trinidad Turf, Queen's Park Cricket (Port-of-Spain).

BROWN, Rt. Rev. Laurence Ambrose, MA; *b* 1 Nov. 1907; 2nd *s* of Frederick James Brown; *m* 1935, Florence Blanche, *d* of late William Gordon Marshall; three *d. Educ:* Luton Grammar School; Queens' College, Cambridge (MA); Cuddesdon Theological College, Oxford. Asst Curate, St John-the-Divine, Kennington, 1932–35; Curate-in-Charge, St Peter, Luton, Beds, 1935–40; Vicar, Hatfield Hyde, Welwyn Garden City, 1940–46; Sec. Southwark Dio. Reorganisation Cttee, 1946–60; Sec. S London Church Fund and Southwark Dio. Bd of Finance, 1952–60; Canon Residentiary, Southwark, 1950–60; Archdeacon of Lewisham and Vice-Provost of Southwark, 1955–60; Suffragan Bishop of Warrington, 1960–69; Bishop of Birmingham, 1969–77; Priest-in-Charge of Odstock with Nunton and Bodenham, dio. Salisbury, 1977–84. Mem. Church Assembly, later General Synod, and Proctor in Convocation, 1954–77; Chairman: Advisory Council for Church's Ministry, 1966–71; Industrial Christian Fellowship, 1971–77; Mem., Religious Adv. Bd, Scout Assoc., 1953–83. Mem., House of Lords, 1973–77. *Publications:* pamphlets on church building in post-war period. *Address:* 7 St Nicholas Road, Salisbury, Wilts. *T:* Salisbury 333138.

BROWN, Lawrence Michael, PhD; FRS 1982; Reader in Physics, University of Cambridge, since 1983 (Lecturer 1970–83); Director of Studies, Robinson College, Cambridge, since 1977 (Founding Fellow, 1977); *b* 18 March 1936; *s* of Bertson Waterworth Brown and Edith Waghorne; *m* 1965, Susan Drucker; one *s* two *d. Educ:* Univ. of Toronto (BASc); Univ. of Birmingham (PhD). Athlone Fellow, 1957; W. M. Tapp Research Fellowship to Gonville and Caius Coll., 1963; University Demonstrator, Cavendish Laboratory, 1965. *Publications:* many papers on structure and properties of materials and electron microscopy in Acta Metallurgica and Philosophical Magazine. *Address:* 74 Alpha Road, Cambridge CB4 3DG. *T:* Cambridge 62987.

BROWN, Leslie; Deputy Chairman, Prudential Assurance Co. Ltd, 1970–74 (a Director, 1965–77); *b* 29 Oct. 1902; *s* of late W. H. Brown and late Eliza J. Fiveash; *m* 1930, Frances V., *d* of T. B. Lever; two *s* one *d. Educ:* Selhurst Grammar School. Joined Prudential Assurance Co. Ltd, 1919; Secretary and Chief Investment Manager, Prudential Assurance Co. Ltd, 1955–64 (Joint Secretary 1942); Chairman: Prudential Unit Trust Managers Ltd, 1968–75; Prudential Pensions Ltd, 1970–75. Member, Jenkins Committee on Company Law Amendment, 1960. Deputy-Chairman, Insurance Export Finance Co. Ltd, 1962–65. Inst. of Actuaries: FIA 1929; Vice-Pres., 1949–51. *Recreation:* bowls. *Address:* 12 Park View, Christchurch Road, Purley, Surrey CR2 2NL.

BROWN, Leslie F.; *see* Farrer-Brown.

BROWN, Rt. Rev. Leslie Wilfrid, CBE 1965; *b* 10 June 1912; *s* of Harry and Maud Brown; *m* 1939, Annie Winifred, *d* of Hon. R. D. Megaw, Belfast; one *d. Educ:* Enfield Gram. School; London College of Divinity (London Univ.). BD 1936, MTh 1944, DD 1957. MA Cantab. hon. causa, 1953. Deacon, Curate St James' Milton, Portsmouth, 1935; priest, 1936. Missionary, CMS, 1938 to Cambridge Nicholson Instn, Kottayam, Travancore, S India. Fellow Commoner and Chaplain, Downing College, Cambridge, 1943; Kerala United Theological Seminary, Trivandrum: tutor, 1945, Principal, 1946, and from 1951. Chaplain, Jesus Coll., Cambridge and Select Preacher before Univ. of Cambridge, 1950, 1967, 1979, Oxford, 1967. Archbishop of Uganda, Rwanda and Burundi, 1961–65; Bishop of Namirembe, 1960–65 (of Uganda, 1953–60; name of diocese changed); Bishop of St Edmundsbury and Ipswich, 1966–78. Chm., ACCM, 1972–76. Hon. Fellow, Downing Coll., Cambridge, 1966. DD (*hc*) Trinity Coll., Toronto, 1963. Chaplain and Sub-Prelate, Order of St John, 1968. *Publications:* The Indian Christians of St Thomas, 1956, 2nd edn 1982; The Christian Family, 1959; God as Christians see Him, 1961; Relevant Liturgy, 1965; Three Worlds, One Word, 1981. *Address:* 47 New Square, Cambridge CB1 1EZ. *Club:* Royal Commonwealth Society.

BROWN, Prof. Lionel Neville; Professor of Comparative Law, University of Birmingham, since 1966; *b* 29 July 1923; *s* of Reginald P. N. Brown and Fanny Brown (*née* Carver); *m* 1957, Mary Patricia Vowles; three *s* one *d. Educ:* Wolverhampton Grammar Sch.; Pembroke Coll., Cambridge (Scholar; MA, LLB); Lyons Univ. (Dr en Droit). RAF, 1942–45; Cambridge, 1945–48; articled to Wolverhampton solicitor, 1948–50; Rotary Foundn Fellow, Lyons Univ., 1951–52; Lectr in Law, Sheffield Univ., 1953–55; Lectr in Comparative Law, Birmingham Univ., 1956, Sen. Lectr, 1957; Sen. Res. Fellow, Univ. of Michigan, 1960. Chm., Birmingham Nat. Insurance Local Tribunal, 1977; Mem., Council on Tribunals, 1982–. Visiting Professor: Univ. of Tulane, New Orleans, 1968; Univ. of Nairobi, 1974; Laval, 1975, 1979, 1983. Commonwealth Foundn Lectr (Caribbean), 1975–76. *Publications:* (with F. H. Lawson and A. E. Anton) Amos and Walton's Introduction to French Law, 2nd edn 1963 and 3rd edn 1967; (with J. F. Garner) French Administrative Law, 1967, 3rd edn 1983; (with F. G. Jacobs) Court of Justice of the European Communities, 1977, 2nd edn 1983. *Recreations:* landscape gardening, country walking, music. *Address:* Willow Rise, Waterdale, Compton, Wolverhampton, West Midlands. *T:* Wolverhampton 26666. *Club:* United Oxford & Cambridge University.

BROWN, Sir Malcolm; *see* Brown, Sir G. M.

BROWN, (Marion) Patricia; Under-Secretary (Economics), Treasury, 1972–85; *b* 2 Feb. 1927; *d* of late Henry Oswald Brown and Elsie Elizabeth (*née* Thompson). *Educ:* Norwich High Sch. for Girls; Newnham Coll., Cambridge. Central Economic Planning Staff, Cabinet Office, 1947; Treasury, 1948–54; United States Embassy, London, 1956–59; Treasury, 1959–85. Mem. Council, Royal Holloway and Bedford New Coll., London Univ., 1985–. Godmother of Lucy Harland and Benjamin Watts. *Recreations:* bird watching, gardening, walking. *Address:* 28 The Plantation, SE3 0AB. *T:* 01–852 9011.

BROWN, Sir Max; *see* Brown, Sir C. M. P.

BROWN, Sir Mervyn, KCMG 1981 (CMG 1975); OBE 1963; HM Diplomatic Service, retired; Director, Global Analysis Systems, since 1986; *b* 24 Sept. 1923; *m* 1949, Elizabeth Gittings. *Educ:* Ryhope Gram. Sch., Sunderland; St John's Coll., Oxford. Served in RA, 1942–45. Entered HM Foreign Service, 1949; Third Secretary, Buenos Aires, 1950; Second Secretary, UK Mission to UN, New York, 1953; First Secretary, Foreign Office, 1956; Singapore, 1959; Vientiane, 1960; again in Foreign Office, 1963–67; Ambassador to Madagascar, 1967–70; Inspector, FCO, 1970–72; Head of Communications Operations Dept, FCO, 1973–74; Asst Under-Sec. of State (Dir of Communications), 1974; High Comr in Tanzania, 1975–78, and concurrently Ambassador to Madagascar; Minister and Dep. Perm. Representative to UN, 1978; High Comr in Nigeria, 1979–83, and concurrently Ambassador to Benin. Chm., Visiting Arts Unit of GB, 1983–; Vice-Pres., Commonwealth Youth Exchange Council, 1984–. *Publications:* Madagascar Rediscovered, 1978; articles and reviews on the history of Madagascar in Jl of African History, Tanzania Notes and Records, and Bulletin de l'Académie Malgache. *Recreations:* music, tennis, history. *Address:* c/o Lloyds Bank, 6 Pall Mall, SW1Y 5NH. *Clubs:* Royal Commonwealth Society, Hurlingham, All England Lawn Tennis.

BROWN, Michael; *see* Brown, J. M.

BROWN, Air Vice-Marshal Michael John Douglas; Director General of Strategic Electronic Systems, Procurement Executive, Ministry of Defence, since 1986; *b* 9 May 1936; *s* of late N. H. B. Brown, AMIERE; *m* 1961, Audrey, *d* of late L. J. Woodward, Gidea Park, Essex; one *s. Educ:* Drayton Manor, W7; RAF Technical Coll., Henlow; Trinity Hall, Cambridge (MA); CEng; MRAeS; MRIN; AFIMA. Commnd RAF Technical Br., 1954; Cambridge Univ. Air Sqdn, 1954–57; RAF pilot trng, 1958–59; served in Bomber Comd, 1959–61; signals duties in Kenya (also assisted with formation of Kenya Air Force), 1961–64; advanced weapons course, 1965–66; Defence Operational Analysis Estabt, 1966–69; RAF Staff Coll., 1970; MoD Operational Requirements Staff, 1971–73; RAF Boulmer, 1973–75; USAF Air War Coll., 1975–76; HQ RAF Strike Comd, 1976–78; Comdr, RAF N Luffenham, 1978–80; rcds 1981; Dir, Air Guided Weapons, MoD (PE), 1983–86. *Address:* 75 Lees Gardens, Maidenhead, Berks SL6 4NT. *T:* Maidenhead 36064. *Club:* Royal Air Force.

BROWN, Ven. Michael René Warneford; Archdeacon of Nottingham, 1960–77, now Archdeacon Emeritus; *b* 7 June 1915; *s* of late George and Irene Brown; *m* 1978, Marie Joyce Chaloner, *d* of late Walter Dawson, and of Sarah Dawson, Burbage, Leics; three step *s. Educ:* King's School, Rochester; St Peter's College, Oxford; St Stephen's House, Oxford (MA). Deacon 1941; priest, 1942; Asst Master, Christ's Hospital, 1939–43; Curate of West Grinstead, 1941–43. Chap. RNVR, 1943–46; chaplain and Dean of St Peter's College and Curate of St Mary the Virgin, Oxford, 1946; Lecturer, RN College, Greenwich, 1946–47; Librarian, 1948–50 and Fellow, 1948–52, of St Augustine's Coll., Canterbury; Priest-in-charge of Bekesbourne, 1948–50; Asst Secretary, CACTM, 1950–60. Examining Chaplain: to Bishop of Southwell, 1954–77; to Archbishop of Canterbury, 1959–60; Commissary to Bishop of Waikato, 1958–70. Member: Church of England Pensions Board, 1966–84; Church Commissioners' Redundant Churches Cttee, 1978–; Chm., Redundant Churches' Uses Cttee in Canterbury Dio., 1980–; Vice-Chm., Diocesan Adv. Cttee for the Care of Churches, 1980–; Church Commissioner, 1968–78. *Recreations:* antiquarian and aesthetic, especially English paintings and silver. *Address:* Faygate, 72 Liverpool Road, Walmer, Deal, Kent CT14 7LR. *T:* Deal 361326. *Club:* Athenæum.

BROWN, Michael Russell; MP (C) Brigg and Cleethorpes, since 1983 (Brigg and Scunthorpe, 1979–83); *b* 3 July 1951; *s* of Frederick Alfred Brown and Greta Mary Brown (*née* Russell). *Educ:* Andrew Cairns Sch., Sussex; Univ. of York (BA (Hons) Economics and Politics). Graduate Management Trainee, Barclays Bank Ltd, 1972–74; Lecturer and Tutor, Swinton Conservative Coll., 1974–75; part-time Asst to Michael Marshall, MP, 1975–76; Law Student, 1976–77, Member of Middle Temple; Personal Asst to Nicholas Winterton, MP, 1976–79. Sec., Conservative Parly N Ireland Cttee, 1981–. *Recreations:* cricket, walking. *Address:* House of Commons, SW1. *Clubs:* Reform; Scunthorpe Conservative, Immingham Conservative (Pres.), Cleethorpes Conservative.

BROWN, Prof. Morris Jonathan; Professor of Clinical Pharmacology, Cambridge University, since 1985; *b* 18 Jan. 1951; *s* of Arnold and Irene Brown; *m* 1977, Diana Phylactou; two *d. Educ:* Harrow; Trinity College, Cambridge (MA, MD); MSc London. MRCP. Lectr, Royal Postgraduate Medical School, 1979–82; Senior Fellow, MRC, 1982–85. *Publications:* Advanced Medicine 21, 1985; articles on adrenaline and cardiovascular disease. *Recreations:* violin playing, tennis. *Address:* 104 Grange Road, Cambridge CB3 9AA.

BROWN, Nicholas Hugh; MP (Lab) Newcastle upon Tyne East, since 1983; *b* 13 June 1950; *s* of late R. C. Brown and of G. K. Brown (*née* Tester). *Educ:* Swatenden Secondary Modern Sch.; Tunbridge Wells Tech. High Sch.; Manchester Univ. (BA 1971). Trade Union Officer, GMWU Northern Region, 1978–83. Mem., Newcastle upon Tyne City Council, 1980–. *Address:* 43 Cardigan Terrace, Heaton, Newcastle upon Tyne. *T:* 654353. *Clubs:* Shieldfield Workingmen's, West Walker Social, Newcastle Labour (Newcastle).

BROWN, Ormond John; retired Government Servant; *b* 30 Jan. 1922; *s* of Herbert John Brown and Janie Lee; *m* 1949, Margaret Eileen Beard; two *d*. *Educ:* Gourock High Sch.; Greenock High Sch. Served War, 1941–45: Outer Hebrides, N Africa, Italy, Greece, Austria. Sheriff Clerk Service, Scotland, 1939; Trng Organiser, Scottish Ct Service, 1957; Sheriff Clerk of Perthshire, 1970; Principal Clerk of Justiciary, Scotland, 1971; Principal Clerk of Session and Justiciary, Scotland, 1975–82. Hon. Sheriff of Tayside, Central and Fife at Stirling, 1982. *Recreations:* music, golf, gardening. *Address:* Ormar, 29 Atholl Place, Dunblane, Perthshire. *T:* Dunblane 822186. *Club:* Dunblane New Golf (Dunblane).

BROWN, Patricia; *see* Brown, M. P.

BROWN, Patrick; *see* Brown, A. P.

BROWN, Peter; *see* Brown, A. P. G.

BROWN, Prof. Peter Robert Lamont, FBA 1971; FRHistS; Rollins Professor of History, Princeton University; *b* 26 July 1935; *s* of James Lamont and Sheila Brown, Dublin; *m* 1st, 1959, Friedl Esther (*née* Löw-Beer); two *d*; 2nd, 1980, Patricia Ann Fortini. *Educ:* Aravon Sch., Bray, Co. Wicklow, Ireland; Shrewsbury Sch.; New Coll., Oxford (MA). Harmsworth Senior Scholar, Merton Coll., Oxford and Prize Fellow, All Souls Coll., Oxford, 1956; Junior Research Fellow, 1963, Sen. Res. Fellow, 1970–73, All Souls Coll.; Fellow, All Souls Coll., 1956–75; Lectr in Medieval History, Merton Coll. Oxford, 1970–75; Special Lectr in late Roman and early Byzantine History, 1970–73, Reader, 1973–75, Univ. of Oxford; Prof. of History, Royal Holloway Coll., London Univ., 1975–78; Prof. of History and Classics, Univ. of Calif. at Berkeley, 1978–85. Fellow, Amer. Acad. of Arts and Scis, 1978. Hon. DTheol Fribourg, 1975; Hon. DHL Chicago, 1978. *Publications:* Augustine of Hippo: a biography, 1967; The World of Late Antiquity, 1971; Religion and Society in the Age of St Augustine, 1971; The Making of Late Antiquity, 1978; The Cult of the Saints: its rise and function in Latin Christianity, 1980; Society and the Holy in Late Antiquity, 1982. *Address:* Department of History, Princeton University, Princeton, NJ 08544, USA; 130 Philip Drive, Princeton, NJ 08540, USA.

BROWN, Peter Wilfred Henry; Secretary of the British Academy, since 1983; *b* 4 June 1941; *s* of late Rev. Wilfred George Brown and Joan Margaret (*née* Adams); *m* 1968, Kathleen Clarke (marr. diss.); one *d*. *Educ:* Marlborough Coll.; Jesus Coll., Cambridge (Rustat Schol.). Assistant Master in Classics, Birkenhead Sch., 1963–66; Lectr in Classics, Fourah Bay Coll., Univ. of Sierra Leone, 1966–68; Asst Sec., School of Oriental and African Studies, Univ. of London, 1968–75; Dep. Sec., British Academy, 1975–83 (Actg Sec., 1976–77). Member: British Library Adv. Council, 1983–; Governing Body, GB/E Europe Centre, 1983–; Council: GB/USSR Assoc., 1983–; SSEES, Univ. of London, 1984–; Committee of Management: Inst. of Archaeol., Univ. of London, 1984–; Inst. of Classical Studies, Univ. of London, 1984–; CNAA Cttee for Arts and Humanities, 1985–. Fellow, National Humanities Center, N Carolina, 1978. *Recreations:* travel on business, reading, listening to classical music, photography. *Address:* The British Academy, 20–21 Cornwall Terrace, NW1 4QP. *T:* 01–487 5966; 34 Victoria Road, NW6 6PX. *T:* 01–624 2919. *Club:* Reform.

BROWN, Philip Anthony Russell, CB 1977; Head of External Relations, Lloyd's of London, 1983–85; Director, National Provident Institution, since 1985; *b* 18 May 1924; *e s* of late Sir William Brown, KCB, KCMG, CBE, and of Elizabeth Mabel (*née* Scott); *m* 1954, Eileen (*d* 1976), *d* of late J. Brennan; *m* 1976, Sarah, *d* of late Sir Maurice Dean, KCB, KCMG. *Educ:* Malvern; King's Coll., Cambridge. Entered Home Civil Service, Board of Trade, 1947; Private Sec. to Perm. Sec., 1949; Principal, 1952; Private Sec. to Minister of State, 1953; Observer, Civil Service Selection Board, 1957; returned to BoT, 1959; Asst Sec., 1963; Head of Overseas Information Co-ordination Office, 1963; BoT, 1964; Under-Sec., 1969; Head of Establishments Div. 1, BoT, later DTI, 1969; Head of Cos Div., DTI, 1971; Dep. Sec., Dept of Trade, 1974–83. Mem., Disciplinary Cttee, ICA, 1985–. Mem., London Adv. Bd, Salvation Army, 1982–. *Publication:* contrib. to Multinational Approaches: corporate insiders, 1976; articles in various jls. *Recreations:* reading, gardening, music. *Address:* 32 Cumberland Street, SW1. *T:* 01–821 9342. *Club:* United Oxford & Cambridge University.

BROWN, Ralph, RA 1972 (ARA 1968); ARCA 1955; sculptor; *b* 24 April 1928; *m* 1st, 1952, M. E. Taylor (marr. diss. 1963); one *s* one *d*; 2nd, 1964, Caroline Ann Clifton-Trigg; one *s*. *Educ:* Leeds Grammar School. Studied Royal College of Art, 1948–56; in Paris with Zadkine, 1954; travel scholarships to Greece 1955, Italy 1957. Tutor, RCA, 1958–64. Sculpture Prof., Salzburg Festival, Summer 1972. Work exhibited: John Moores, Liverpool (prizewinner 1957), Tate Gallery, Religious Theme 1958, British Sculpture in the Sixties 1965; Arnhem Internat. Open Air Sculpture, 1958; Middelheim Open Air Sculpture, 1959; Battersea Park Open Air Sculpture, 1960, 1963, 1966, 1977; Tokyo Biennale, 1963; British Sculptors '72, RA, 1972; Holland Park Open Air, 1975; Salisbury Festival Exhibn, 1981; British Art, New Directions, New York, 1983; Yorkshire Sculpture Park, 1984. One man Shows: Leicester Galls, 1961, 1963; Archer Gall., 1972; Salzburg 1972; Munich 1973; Montpellier 1974; Marseilles 1975; Oxford 1975; Taranman Gall., 1976; Browse & Darby Gall., 1979; Charles Foley Gall., Columbus, US, 1984; Lloyd Shine Gall., Chicago, 1984. Work in Collections: Tate Gallery, Arts Council, Contemp. Art Society, Kröller-Müller, Gallery of NSW, Stuyvesant Foundation, City of Salzburg, Nat. Gallery of Wales, Sutton Manor, Winchester, and at Leeds, Bristol, Norwich, Aberdeen, etc. Public Sculpture: at Hatfield, Harlow, LCC Tulse Hill, Loughborough Univ., Newnham Coll., etc. *Address:* Seynckley House, Amberley, Stroud, Glos.

BROWN, Rt. Rev. Mgr Ralph; Vicar General, Diocese of Westminster, since 1976; *b* 30 June 1931; *s* of John William and Elizabeth Josephine Brown. *Educ:* Highgate Sch.; St Edmund's Coll., Old Hall Green, Herts; Pontifical Gregorian Univ., Rome. Licence in Canon Law, 1961, Doctorate, 1963. Commnd Middlesex Regt, 1949; Korea, 1950. Ordained priest, Westminster Cathedral, 1959; Vice-Chancellor, Vice Officialis, dio. of Westminster, 1964–69; Officialis, Westminster, 1969–76; Chancellor, Military Vicariate, 1968–. Pres., Canon Law Soc. of GB and Ireland, 1980–. National Co-ordinator for Papal Visit to England and Wales, 1982. *Publications:* Marriage Annulment, 1969, rev. edn 1977; co-translator, The Code of Canon Law in English Translation, 1983; articles in Heythrop Jl, Studia Canonica, Theological Digest, The Jurist. *Address:* 42 Francis Street, SW1P 1QW. *T:* (office) 01–828 3255/5380. *Club:* Anglo-Belgian.

BROWN, Hon. Sir Ralph Kilner, Kt 1970; OBE 1945; TD 1952; DL; a Judge of the High Court, Queen's Bench Division, 1970–84; a Judge of Employment Appeal Tribunal, 1976–84; *b* 28 Aug. 1909; *s* of Rev. A. E. Brown, CIE, MA, BSc; *m* 1943, Cynthia Rosemary Breffit; one *s* two *d*. *Educ:* Kingswood School; Trinity Hall, Cambridge (Squire Law Scholar). Barrister, Middle Temple (Harmsworth Scholar; Bencher, 1964; Master Reader, 1982); Midland Circuit, 1934 and Northern Circuit, 1975. TA 1938; War Service, 1939–46; DAQMG NW Europe Plans; DAAG HQ53 (Welsh) Div.; AQMG (Planning), COSSAC; Col Q (Ops) and Brig. Q Staff HQ 21 Army Group (despatches, OBE); Hon. Col, TARO, 1952. QC 1958; Recorder of Lincoln, 1960–64; Recorder of Birmingham, 1964–65; Chairman, Warwicks QS, 1964–67 (Dep. Chm., 1954–64); a Judge of the Central Criminal Court, 1965–67; Recorder of Liverpool, and Judge of the Crown Court at Liverpool, 1967–69; Presiding Judge, N Circuit, 1970–75. Chairman, Mental Health Review Tribunal, Birmingham RHB Area, 1962–65. Contested (L) Oldbury and Halesowen, 1945 and 1950; South Bucks, 1959 and 1964; Pres., Birmingham Liberal Organisation, 1946–56; Pres., and Chm., W Midland Liberal Fedn, 1950–56; Mem., Liberal Party Exec., 1950–56. Pres., Birmingham Bn, Boys Bde, 1946–56; Mem., Exec., Boys Bde, 1950–55. DL Warwickshire, 1956. Guild of Freemen, City of London. *Publication:* The Office of Reader in the Middle Temple, 1982. *Recreations:* watching athletics (represented Cambridge University and Great Britain; British AAA Champion 440 yds hurdles, 1934); cricket, Rugby football. *Address:* 174 Defoe House, Barbican, EC2Y 8DN. *Clubs:* Naval and Military; Hawks (Cambridge).
See also A. G. K. Brown.

BROWN, Mrs Ray; *see* Vaughan, Elizabeth.

BROWN, Rev. Raymond; Principal, Spurgeon's College, London, since 1973; *b* 3 March 1928; *s* of Frank Stevenson Brown and Florence Mansfield; *m* 1966, Christine Mary Smallman; one *s* one *d*. *Educ:* Spurgeon's Coll., London (BD, MTh); Fitzwilliam Coll., Cambridge (MA, BD, PhD). Minister: Zion Baptist Church, Cambridge, 1956–62; Upton Vale Baptist Church, Torquay, 1964–71; Tutor in Church History, Spurgeon's Coll., 1971–73. Pres., Evangelical Alliance, 1975–76; Trustee, Dr Daniel Williams's Charity, 1980–. *Publications:* Their Problems and Ours, 1969; Let's Read the Old Testament, 1971; Skilful Hands, 1972; Christ Above All: the message of Hebrews, 1982; Bible Study Commentary: 1 Timothy-James, 1983; (contrib.) Dictionary of Christian Spirituality, 1983; The English Baptists of the Eighteenth Century, 1986; (contrib.) My Call to Preach, 1986. *Recreations:* music, fell walking. *Address:* Spurgeon's College, South Norwood Hill, SE25 6DJ. *T:* 01–653 1235.

BROWN, Sir Raymond (Frederick), Kt 1969; OBE; CompIEE; FIERE; Chairman, Muirhead plc, 1972–85 (Chief Executive and Managing Director, 1970–82); Director, Standard Telephones & Cables, since 1985; *b* 19 July 1920; *s* of Frederick and Susan Evelyn Brown; *m* 1942, Evelyn Jennings (marr. diss. 1949); (one *d* decd); *m* 1953, Carol Jacquelin Elizabeth, *d* of H. R. Sprinks, Paris; two *s* one *d*. *Educ:* Morden Terrace LCC School; SE London Technical College; Morley College. DSc. Joined Redifon as engineering apprentice, 1934; Sales Man., Communications Div., Plessey Ltd, 1949–50; formerly Chm., Man. Dir and Pres., Racal Electronics Ltd (Joint Founder, 1950), and subsidiary companies; Head of Defence Sales, MoD, 1966–69; Chm., Racecourse Technical Services, 1970–84; Dir, National Westminster Bank, Outer London Region, 1978–84. Consultant Adviser on commercial policy and exports to DHSS, 1969–72; Mem., BOTB Working Gp on Innovation and Exports, 1972–74; Adviser to NEDO, to promote export of equipment purchased by nationalised industries, 1976–. Mem., Soc. of Pilgrims. Pres., Electronic Engrg Assoc., 1975; Pres., Egham and Thorpe Royal Agric. and Hort. Assoc., 1977–79. Liveryman: Scriveners' Co.; Scientific Instrument Makers' Co. Governor, SE London Coll., 1980–81. Hon. DSc Bath, 1980. *Recreations:* golf, farming, shooting, polo. *Clubs:* City Livery, Travellers', Canada, Australia; Ends of the Earth; Sunningdale Golf; Guards Polo (life mem.); Swinley Forest Golf; Palm Beach Polo.

BROWN, Prof. Robert, DSc London; FRS 1956; Regius Professor of Botany, Edinburgh University, 1958–77, now Emeritus Professor; *b* 29 July 1908; *s* of Thomas William and Ethel Minnie Brown; *m* 1940, Morna Doris Mactaggart. *Educ:* English School, Cairo; University of London. Assistant Lecturer in Botany, Manchester University, 1940–44; Lecturer in Botany, Bedford College, London, 1944–46; Reader in Plant Physiology, Leeds University, 1946–52; Professor of Botany, Cornell University, 1952–53; Director, Agricultural Research Council Unit of Plant Cell Physiology, 1953–58. *Publications:* various papers on plant physiology in the Annals of Botany, Proceedings of Royal Society and Journal of Experimental Botany. *Recreation:* gardening. *Address:* 5 Treble House Terrace, Blewbury, Didcot, Oxfordshire OX11 9NZ. *T:* Blewbury 850415.

BROWN, Robert; a Recorder of the Crown Court, since 1983; *b* 21 June 1943; *s* of Robert and Mary Brown; *m* 1st, 1964, Susan (marr. diss. 1971); one *s* one *d*; 2nd, 1973, Carole; two step *s*. *Educ:* Arnold Sch., Blackpool; Downing Coll., Cambridge (Exhibnr; BA, LLB). Called to Bar, Inner Temple, 1968 (Major Schol.); practising on Northern Circuit, 1968–. Standing Counsel to DHSS, 1982–. *Recreation:* golf. *Address:* The Cottage, Willow Court, Clifton Drive, Lytham St Anne's, Lancs; (chambers) 2 Old Bank Street, Manchester. *T:* 061–832 3781. *Clubs:* Royal Lytham St Annes Golf; Lytham Yacht.

BROWN, Sir Robert C.; *see* Crichton-Brown.

BROWN, Robert Crofton; MP (Lab) Newcastle upon Tyne North, since 1983 (Newcastle upon Tyne West, 1966–83); *b* 16 May 1921; *m* 1945, Marjorie Hogg, Slaithwaite, Yorks; one *s* one *d*. *Educ:* Denton Road Elementary School; Atkinson Road Technical School; Rutherford Coll. Apprenticed plumber and gasfitter, Newcastle & Gateshead Gas Co., 1937. War Service, 1942–46. Plumber from 1946; Inspector, 1949; in service of Northern Gas Board until 1966. Secretary of Constituency Labour Party and Agent to MP for 16 years. Parly Sec., Ministry of Transport, 1968–70; Parly Under-Sec., Social Security, March-Sept. 1974; Parly Under-Sec. of State for Defence for the Army, 1974–79. Vice-Chm., Parly Lab Party Transport Gp, 1970–. Member Newcastle Co. Borough Council (Chief Whip, Lab. Gp), retd 1968. *Recreations:* walking, reading, gardening. *Address:* 1 Newsham Close, The Boltons, North Walbottle, Newcastle upon Tyne NE5 1QD. *T:* Newcastle upon Tyne 2672199.

BROWN, Robert Glencairn; Deputy Chief Officer, Housing Corporation, since 1986; *b* 19 July 1930; *s* of William and Marion Brown (*née* Cockburn); *m* 1957, Florence May Stalker; two *s*. *Educ:* Hillhead High Sch., Glasgow. Commnd, RCS, 1949–51. Forestry Commn, 1947–68; seconded to CS Pay Res. Unit, 1963–64 and to Min. of Land and Natural Resources, 1964–68; Min. of Housing and Local Govt, later DoE, 1968–71; seconded to Nat. Whitley Council, Staff Side, 1969; Asst Dir, Countryside Commn, 1971–77; Department of the Environment: Asst Sec., 1977–83; Under Sec., 1983–86. *Recreations:* gardening, ski-ing, reading. *Address:* 2 The Squirrels, Pinner, Middx HA5 3BD. *T:* 01–866 8713. *Club:* Ski Club of Great Britain.

BROWN, Prof. Robert Hanbury, AC 1986; FRS 1960; Professor of Physics (Astronomy), in the University of Sydney, 1964–81, now Emeritus Professor; *b* 31 Aug. 1916; *s* of Colonel Basil Hanbury Brown and Joyce Blaker; *m* 1952, Hilda Heather Chesterman; two *s* one *d*. *Educ:* Tonbridge School; Brighton Technical College; City and Guilds College, London. Air Ministry, Bawdsey Research Station, working on radar, 1936–42; British Air Commission, Washington, DC, 1942–45; Principal Scientific Officer, Ministry of Supply, 1945–47; ICI Research Fellow of Manchester University, 1949; Professor of Radio-Astronomy in the University of Manchester, 1960–63. Pres., Internat. Astronomical Union, 1982–. ARAS 1986; FAA 1967; Hon. FNA 1975; Hon. FASc 1975. Hon. DSc: Sydney, 1984; Monash, 1984. Holweck Prize, 1959; Eddington Medal, 1968; Lyle Medal, 1971; Britannica Australia Award, 1971; Hughes Medal, 1971; Michelson Medal, Franklin Inst., 1982. *Publications:* The Exploration of Space by Radio, 1957; The Intensity Interferometer, 1974; Man and the Stars, 1978; Wisdom of Science, 1986; publications in

Physical and Astronomical Journals. *Address:* School of Physics, Sydney University, Sydney, NSW 2006, Australia. *Club:* Athenæum.

BROWN, Robert Ross Buchanan, CBE 1968; Chairman, Southern Electricity Board, 1954–74; *b* 15 July 1909; 2nd *s* of Robert and Rhoda Brown, Sydney, Australia; *m* 1940, Ruth Sarah Aird; one *s* two *d. Educ:* The King's School, Sydney; Sydney University; Cambridge University. BA (Cantab.), BSc. Deputy Gen. Manager, Wessex Electricity Co., 1938. Captain 4th County of London Yeomanry, 1940–45. Gen. Manager, Wessex Electricity Co., 1945; Deputy Chairman, Southern Electricity Board, 1948. *Recreations:* gardening, golf. *Address:* Mumbery Lodge, School Hill, Wargrave, Reading, Berks.

BROWN, Ven. Robert Saville; Archdeacon of Bedford, 1974–79, Archdeacon Emeritus since 1979; *b* 12 Sept. 1914; *s* of John Harold Brown and Frances May Brown; *m* 1947, Charlotte, *d* of late Percy John and Edith Furber; one *s. Educ:* Bedford Modern Sch.; Selwyn Coll., Cambridge (MA). Curate: Gt Berkhamsted, 1940–44; St Mary's, Hitchin, 1944–47; Vicar, Wonersh, 1947–53; Rector, Gt Berkhamsted, 1953–69; Canon of St Albans Cath., 1965; Vicar of St Paul's, Bedford, 1969–74; Priest-in-Charge of Old Warden, 1974–79. *Recreations:* reading, travel, chess. *Address:* 9 Treachers Close, Chesham, Bucks HP5 2HD.

See also F. R. Furber.

BROWN, Roland George MacCormack; Legal Adviser, Technical Assistance Group, Commonwealth Secretariat, since 1975; *b* 27 Dec. 1924; 2nd *s* of late Oliver and of Mona Brown; *m* 1964, Irene Constance, *d* of Rev. Claude Coltman; two *s* one *d. Educ:* Ampleforth College; Trinity College, Cambridge. Called to the Bar, Gray's Inn, Nov. 1949. Practised at the Bar, Nov. 1949–May 1961; Attorney-Gen., Tanganyika, later Tanzania, 1961–65; Legal Consultant to Govt of Tanzania, 1965–72; Fellow, Inst. of Develt Studies, Sussex Univ., 1973–75; on secondment as Special Adviser to Sec. of State for Trade, 1974. *Publication:* (with Richard O'Sullivan, QC) The Law of Defamation. *Recreation:* swimming. *Address:* c/o Commonwealth Secretariat, Marlborough House, Pall Mall, SW1.

BROWN, Rt. Rev. Ronald; *see* Birkenhead, Bishop Suffragan of.

BROWN, Ronald, (Ron); MP (Lab) Edinburgh Leith, since 1979; *b* Edinburgh, 1940; *s* of James Brown and Margaret McLaren; *m* 1963, May Smart; two *s. Educ:* Pennywell Primary Sch., Edinburgh; Ainslie Park High Sch., Edinburgh; Bristo Technical Inst., Edinburgh. National Service, Royal Signals. Five yrs engrg apprenticeship with Bruce Peebles and Co. Ltd, East Pilton, Edinburgh. Chm., Pilton Br., AUEW; formerly: Chm. Works Cttee, Edinburgh Dist of SSEB; Convenor of Shop Stewards, Parsons Peebles Ltd, Edinburgh. Formerly Councillor for Central Leith, Edinburgh Town Council; Regional Councillor for Royston/Granton, Lothian Reg. Council, 1974–79. Member: Lothian and Borders Fire Bd, 1974–79; Central Scotland Water Develt Bd, 1974–79. *Address:* c/o House of Commons, SW1A 0AA.

BROWN, Ronald William; JP; *b* 7 Sept. 1921; *s* of George Brown; *m* 1944, Mary Munn; one *s* two *d. Educ:* Elementary School, South London; Borough Polytechnic. Sen. Lectr in Electrical Engineering, Principal of Industrial Training Sch. Leader, Camberwell Borough Council, 1956; Alderman and Leader, London Bor. of Southwark, 1964. MP Shoreditch and Finsbury, 1964–74, Hackney South and Shoreditch, 1974–83 (Lab, 1964–81, SDP, 1981–83); Asst Govt Whip, 1966–67; contested (SDP) Hackney South and Shoreditch, 1983. Member: Council of Europe Assembly and WEU, 1965–76; European Parlt, 1977–79. Chm., Energy Commn, Rapporteur on Science, Technology and Aerospace questions; Parly Advr to Furniture, Timber and Allied Trades Union, 1967–81. Member: Council of Europe, 1979–83; WEU, 1979–83. FBIM. Assoc. Mem., Inst. of Engineering Designers. JP Co. London, 1961. *Address:* 33 John Street, WC1.

BROWN, Ronald William; Deputy Legal Adviser and Solicitor to Ministry of Agriculture, Fisheries and Food, to Forestry Commission and to (EEC) Intervention Board for Agricultural Produce, 1974–82; *b* 21 April 1917; *o s* of late William Nicol Brown and Eleanor Brown (*née* Dobson); *m* 1958, Elsie Joyce (*d* 1983), *er d* of late Sir Norman Guttery, KBE, CB and Lady Guttery (*née* Crankshaw); two *s. Educ:* Dover Coll.; Corpus Christi Coll., Cambridge (MA). War service, 1939–45, King's Own Royal Regt (Lancaster), France, W Desert, Burma (Chindits) (Major). Called to Bar, Gray's Inn, 1946. Entered Legal Dept, Min. of Agric. and Fisheries, 1948; Asst Solicitor, MAFF, 1970. *Address:* 5 Gomshall Road, Cheam, Surrey SM2 7JZ. *T:* 01–393 4061. *Club:* Royal Automobile.

BROWN, Roy Dudley; Director, Association of West European Shipbuilders, 1977–83; *b* 5 Aug. 1916; *y s* of late Alexander and Jessie Brown; *m* 1941, Maria Margaret Barry McGhee; one *s* one *d. Educ:* Robert Gordon's Coll., Aberdeen; Aberdeen Univ. (MA 1935, LLB 1937). In private law practice, Glasgow, 1937–38; joined Shipbldg Conf., London, 1938; War Service, RN; Jt Sec. on amalgamation of Shipbldg Conf., Shipbldg Employers Fedn, and Dry Dock Owners and Repairers Central Council into Shipbuilders and Repairers National Assoc., 1967; Dep. Dir, 1973, until dissolution of Assoc. on nationalization, 1977. Sec., Shipbldg Corp. Ltd, 1943–77. Liveryman, Worshipful Co. of Shipwrights. *Recreations:* golf, wine, gardening. *Address:* 109 Upper Selsdon Road, Sanderstead, Surrey CR2 0DP. *T:* 01–657 7144.

BROWN, Rear-Adm. Roy S. F.; *see* Foster-Brown.

BROWN, Rt. Rev. Russel Featherstone; *b* Newcastle upon Tyne, 7 Jan. 1900; *s* of Henry John George Brown and Lucy Jane Ferguson; *m* 1940, Priscilla Marian Oldacres (*d* 1948); three *s. Educ:* Bishop's Univ., Lennoxville, PQ, Canada. BA (Theo.) 1933. RAF, 1918–19; business, 1919–29; University, 1929–33; Deacon, 1933; Priest, 1934; Curate, Christ Church Cathedral, Montreal, 1933–36; Priest-in-Charge, Fort St John, BC, 1936–40; Rector of Sherbrooke, PQ, 1940–54; Canon, Holy Trinity Cathedral, Quebec, 1948; Rector, St Matthew's, Quebec, PQ, 1954–60; Archdeacon of Quebec, 1954–60; Bishop of Quebec, 1960–71; subsequently teaching in Papua New Guinea. Assistant Bishop of Montreal, 1976–83. Hon. DCL Bishop's Univ., Lennoxville, 1961; Hon. DD, Montreal Diocesan Theological College, 1968. *Address:* Fyfield Manor, Benson, Oxon OX9 6HA. *T:* 0491–35184.

BROWN, Russell; *see* Brown, J. R.

BROWN, Hon. Sir Simon Denis, Kt 1984; **Hon. Mr Justice Simon Brown;** a Judge of the High Court of Justice, Queen's Bench Division, since 1984; *b* 9 April 1937; *s* of late Denis Baer Brown and of Edna Elizabeth (*née* Abrahams); *m* 1963, Jennifer Buddicom; two *s* one *d. Educ:* Stowe Sch.; Worcester Coll., Oxford (law degree). Commnd 2nd Lt RA, 1955–57. Called to the Bar, Middle Temple, 1961 (Harmsworth Schol.); Master of the Bench, Hon. Soc. of Middle Temple, 1980–; a Recorder, 1979–84; First Jun. Treasury Counsel, Common Law, 1979–84. *Recreations:* golf, skiing, theatre. *Address:* Royal Courts of Justice, Strand, WC2. *Club:* Denham Golf.

BROWN, Sir Stanley; *see* Brown, Sir F. H. S.

BROWN, Sir Stephen; *see* Brown, Sir A. J. S.

BROWN, Rt. Hon. Sir Stephen, Kt 1975; PC 1983; **Rt. Hon. Lord Justice Stephen Brown;** a Lord Justice of Appeal, since 1983; *b* 3 Oct. 1924; *s* of Wilfrid Brown and Nora Elizabeth Brown, Longdon Green, Staffordshire; *m* 1951, Patricia Ann, *d* of Richard Good, Tenbury Wells, Worcs; two *s* (twins) three *d. Educ:* Malvern College; Queens' College, Cambridge (Hon. Fellow, 1984). Served RNVR (Lieut), 1943–46. Barrister, Inner Temple, 1949; Bencher, 1974. Dep. Chairman, Staffs QS, 1963–71; Recorder of West Bromwich, 1965–71; QC 1966; a Recorder, and Honorary Recorder of West Bromwich, 1972–75; a Judge of the High Court, Family Div., 1975–77, QBD, 1977–83; Presiding Judge, Midland and Oxford Circuit, 1977–81. Member: Parole Board, England and Wales, 1967–71; Butler Cttee on mentally abnormal offenders, 1972–75; Adv. Council on Penal System, 1977; Chairman: Adv. Cttee on Conscientious Objectors, 1971–75; Council of Malvern Coll., 1976–. Hon. LLD Birmingham, 1985. *Recreation:* sailing. *Address:* Royal Courts of Justice, Strand, WC2A 2LL. *Clubs:* Garrick, Naval; Birmingham (Birmingham).

BROWN, Sir Thomas, Kt 1974; Chairman, Eastern Health and Social Services Board, Northern Ireland (formerly NI Hospitals Authority), 1967–84, retired; *b* 11 Oct. 1915; *s* of Ephraim Hugh and Elizabeth Brown. *Educ:* Royal Belfast Academical Institution. Admitted Solicitor, 1938. Mem., Royal Commn on NHS, 1976–79. *Recreations:* boating, chairmanship. *Address:* Westgate, Portaferry, Co. Down, Northern Ireland. *T:* Portaferry 28309.

BROWN, Prof. Thomas Julian, MA; FSA; FBA 1982; Professor of Palæography, University of London, since 1961; *b* 24 Feb. 1923; *s* of Tom Brown, land agent, Penrith, Cumberland, and Helen Wright Brown, MBE; *m* 1st, 1959, Alison Macmillan Dyson (marr. diss. 1979); two *d*; 2nd, 1980, Sanchia Mary David (*née* Blair-Leighton). *Educ:* Westminster School (KS); Christ Church, Oxford. 2nd class, Class. Hon. Mods, 1942, and Lit.Hum., 1948. The Border Regt, 1942–45, mostly attached Inf. Heavy Weapons School, Netheravon. Asst Keeper Dept of MSS, British Museum, 1950–60. FSA 1956. Member, Inst. for Advanced Study, Princeton, NJ, 1966–67. Lyell Reader in Bibliography, Univ. of Oxford, 1976–77; Vis. Fellow, All Souls Coll., Oxford, 1976–77. Chm. of Cttee and Trustee, Lambeth Palace Library, 1979–; Pres., Bibliographical Soc., 1986–87. FKC, 1975. *Publications:* (with R. L. S. Bruce-Mitford, A. S. C. Ross, E. G. Stanley and others) Codex Lindisfarnensis, vol. ii, 1960; Latin Palæography since Traube (inaugural lecture), Trans. Camb. Bibliographical Society, 1963; The Stonyhurst Gospel (Roxburghe Club), 1969; The Durham Ritual, 1969; Northumbria and the Book of Kells (Jarrow Lect.), 1972; (with C. D. Verey and E. Coatsworth) The Durham Gospels, 1980. *Address:* King's College, Strand, WC2R 2LS. *T:* 01–836 5454; 1 Edenbridge Road, E9 7DR. *T:* 01–986 0692.

BROWN, Thomas Walter Falconer, CBE 1958; Consultant in Marine Engineering; *b* 10 May 1901; *s* of Walter Falconer Brown, MB, ChB, DPH, and Catherine Edith (*née* McGhie); *m* 1947, Lucy Mason (*née* Dickie); one *s* one *d. Educ:* Ayr Academy; Glasgow University; Harvard University. BSc (special dist. in Nat. Philos.), 1921; DSc (Glas.), 1927; SM (Harvard), 1928; Assoc. of Royal Technical College, Glasgow, 1922. Asst General Manager, Alex Stephen & Sons Ltd, Linthouse, 1928–35; Technical Manager, R. & W. Hawthorn Leslie & Co. Ltd, Newcastle upon Tyne, 1935–44; Director of Parsons and Marine Engineering Turbine Research and Development Assoc., Wallsend, 1944–62; Director of Marine Engineering Research (BSRA), Wallsend Research Station, 1962–66. Liveryman, Worshipful Co. of Shipwrights, Freedom City of London, 1946. Eng Lieut, and Eng Lt-Comdr RNVR, Clyde Div., 1924–36. De Laval Gold Medal, Sweden, 1957. *Publications:* various technical papers in: Trans Instn Mech. Engineers, Inst. Marine Engineers, NE Coast Instn of Engineers & Shipbuilders, etc. *Recreations:* model-making and gardening. *Address:* 12 The Dene, Wylam, Northumberland NE41 8JB. *T:* Wylam 2228.

BROWN, Walter Graham S.; *see* Scott-Brown.

BROWN, William, CBE 1971; Deputy Chairman since 1974, and Managing Director, since 1966, Scottish Television plc; *b* 24 June 1929; *s* of Robert C. Brown, Ayr; *m* 1955, Nancy Jennifer, 3rd *d* of Prof. George Hunter, Edmonton, Alta; one *s* three *d. Educ:* Ayr Academy; Edinburgh University. Lieut, RA, 1950–52. Scottish Television Ltd: London Sales Manager, 1958; Sales Dir, 1961; Dep. Man. Dir, 1963. Director: Independent Television Publications Ltd, 1968–; ITN, 1972–77; Radio Clyde Ltd, 1973–; Channel Four Co. Ltd, 1980–84; Scottish Amicable Life Assurance Soc., 1981–. Director: Scottish Opera Theatre Royal Ltd, 1974–. Mem., Royal Commn on Legal Services in Scotland, 1976–80. Chm., Council, Independent Television Cos Assoc., 1978–80. *Recreations:* gardening, golf, films. *Address:* Scottish Television plc, Cowcaddens, Glasgow G2 3PR. *T:* 041–332 9999. *Clubs:* Caledonian; Glasgow Art; Prestwick Golf, Royal and Ancient Golf (St Andrews).

BROWN, Prof. William Arthur; Montague Burton Professor of Industrial Relations, University of Cambridge, since 1985; Fellow, Wolfson College, Cambridge; *b* 22 April 1945; *s* of Prof. Arthur Joseph Brown, *qv. Educ:* Leeds Grammar Sch.; Wadham Coll., Oxford (BA Hons). Economic Asst, NBPI, 1966–68; Res. Associate, Univ. of Warwick, 1968–70; SSRC's Industrial Relations Research Unit, University of Warwick: Res. Fellow, 1970–79; Dep. Dir, 1979–81; Dir, 1981–85. *Publications:* Piecework Bargaining, 1973; The Changing Contours of British Industrial Relations, 1981; articles in industrial relations jls, etc. *Recreations:* walking, gardening. *Address:* Wolfson College, Cambridge.

BROWN, Sir William B. P.; *see* Pigott-Brown.

BROWN, Dr William Christopher, OBE 1966; RDI 1977; FICE, FIStructE, FASCE; Partner, Freeman, Fox & Partners, since 1970; *b* 16 Sept. 1928; *s* of William Edward Brown and Margaret Eliza Brown; *m* 1964, Celia Hermione Emmett. *Educ:* Monmouth Sch.; University Coll., Southampton (BScEng); Imperial Coll. of Science and Technol., London (DIC, PhD). FICE 1970; FIStructE 1978; FASCE 1978. Principal designer for major bridges, incl.: Volta River, 1956; Forth Road, 1964; Severn and Wye, 1966; Auckland Harbour, 1969; Erskine, 1971; Bosporus, 1973; Avonmouth, 1975; Humber. Holds patents on new concepts for long-span bridges. Designer for radio telescopes in Australia and Canada, and for other special structures. Hon. FRIBA 1978. McRobert Award, 1970; UK and European steel design awards, 1968, 1971, 1976. *Publications:* technical papers for engrg instns in UK and abroad. *Recreations:* archaeology, photography, motoring. *Address:* 1 Allen Mansions, Allen Street, W8 6UY. *T:* 01–937 6550. *Clubs:* Royal Automobile, Royal Over-Seas League.

BROWN, William Eden T.; *see* Tatton Brown.

BROWN, W(illiam) Glanville, TD; Barrister-at-Law; *b* 19 July 1907; *s* of late Cecil George Brown, formerly Town Clerk of Cardiff, and late Edith Tyndale Brown; *m* 1st, 1935, Theresa Margaret Mary Harrison (decd); one *s*; 2nd, 1948, Margaret Isabel Dilks, JP, *o d* of late Thomas Bruce Dilks, Bridgwater. *Educ:* Llandaff Cathedral School; Magdalen College School and Magdalen College, Oxford; in France, Germany and Italy.

Called to Bar, Middle Temple, 1932. Contested (L) Cardiff Central, 1935, St Albans, 1964. Served War of 1939–45, in Army (TA), Aug. 1939–Dec. 1945; attached to Intelligence Corps; served overseas 3½ years in E Africa Command, Middle East and North-West Europe. Junior Prosecutor for UK Internat. Military Tribunal for the Far East, Tokyo, 1946–48; Member: the National Arbitration Tribunal, 1949–51; Industrial Disputes Tribunal, 1959; Deputy-Chairman of various Wages Councils, 1950–64; Joint Legal Editor of English Translation of Common Market Documents for Foreign Office, 1962–63; Lectr in Germany on behalf of HM Embassy, Bonn, 1965–73. Mem., Mental Health Review Tribunal for NE Metropolitan RHB Area, 1960–79. Life Mem., RIIA. Fellow, Inst. of Linguists. *Publication:* Translation of Brunschweig's French Colonialism, 1871–1914, Myths and Realities. *Recreations:* walking, reading, watching cricket, travel. *Address:* 55 Laurel Way, Totteridge, N20. *T:* 01–455 5312. *Club:* National Liberal.

BROWN, Rev. William Martyn; Rural Dean of Holt, since 1984; *b* 12 July 1914; *s* of Edward Brown, artist; *m* 1939, Elizabeth Lucy Hill; one adopted *s. Educ:* Bedford School; Pembroke College, Cambridge (Scholar). 1st Class Honours in Modern Languages, 1936, MA 1947. Assistant Master, Wellington College, 1936–47; Housemaster 1943–47; Headmaster: The King's School, Ely, 1947–55; Bedford School, 1955–75. Commissioner of the Peace, 1954. Ordained 1976; Priest-in-Charge, Field Dalling and Saxlingham, 1977. *Recreation:* watercolour painting. *Address:* Lodge Cottage, Field Dalling, Holt, Norfolk. *T:* Binham 403.

BROWNE, family name of **Baron Craigton, Baron Kilmaine, Baron Oranmore, Marquess of Sligo.**

BROWNE, Major Alexander Simon Cadogan; JP; DL; *b* 22 July 1895; *e s* of late Major Alexander Browne of Callaly Castle, Northumberland; *m* 1918, Dorothy Mary (*d* 1979), *d* of late Major F. J. C. Howard, 8th Hussars of Moorefield, Newbridge, Co. Kildare and Baytown, Co. Meath; one *d. Educ:* Eton; RMC Sandhurst. Major 12th Royal Lancers; served European War, 1914–18; retired, 1925; re-employed, 1939–45; served HQ 23rd (Northumbrian) Div., BEF, 1940 (despatches) and with BLA 1945. Secretary to the Duke of Beaufort's Fox Hounds, 1928–38; Joint Master, Percy Fox Hounds, 1938–46. Pres., Berwick-upon-Tweed Conservative Assoc., 1970–73. Chairman, Rothbury RDC, 1950–55; CC, 1950–67, CA, 1967–74, Hon. Alderman, 1974, Northumberland; High Sheriff of Northumberland, 1958–59; JP 1946, DL 1961, Northumberland. *Address:* Callaly Castle, Alnwick, Northumberland NE66 4TA. *T:* Whittingham (Northumberland) 663. *Clubs:* Cavalry and Guards; Northern Counties (Newcastle upon Tyne).

BROWNE, Andrew Harold; full-time Chairman of Industrial Tribunals, Nottingham Region at Leicester, since 1983; *b* 2 Dec. 1923; *s* of late Harold and Ada Caroline Browne; *m* 1951, Jocelyn Mary Vade Ashmead; two *s* one *d. Educ:* Repton; Trinity Hall, Cambridge (BA). ACIArb. Served Royal Navy, 1942–46; Lieut RNVR. Admitted Solicitor, 1950; Partner in firm of Wells & Hind, Nottingham, 1952–83. Dep. Clerk of the Peace, Nottingham City Sessions, 1951–55. Chairman, National Insurance Local Tribunal, Nottingham, 1965–83; Member, E Midland Rent Assessment Panel, 1966–83 (Vice-Pres., 1972–83). Part-time Chm. of Industrial Tribunals, 1975. *Recreations:* rural England, organ music. *Address:* The House in the Garden, Elton, near Nottingham NG13 9LA. *T:* Whatton 50419. *Clubs:* Aula; Leicestershire (Leicester).

BROWNE, Anthony Arthur Duncan M.; *see* Montague Browne.

BROWNE, Bernard Peter Francis K.; *see* Kenworthy-Browne.

BROWNE, Air Cdre Charles Duncan Alfred, CB 1971; DFC 1944; FBIM; RAF, retired; *b* 8 July 1922; *s* of late Alfred Browne and Catherine (*née* MacKinnon); *m* 1946, Una Felicité Leader; one *s. Educ:* City of Oxford School. War of 1939–45: served Western Desert, Italy, Corsica and S France in Hurricane and Spitfire Sqdns; post war service in Home, Flying Training, Bomber and Strike Commands; MoD; CO, RAF Brüggen, Germany, 1966–68; Comdt, Aeroplane and Armament Exp. Estab., 1968–71; Air Officer i/c Central Tactics and Trials Orgn, 1971–72. *Address:* c/o Midland Bank, Summertown, Oxford. *Club:* Royal Air Force.

BROWNE, Coral (Edith), (Mrs Vincent Price); actress; *b* Melbourne, Australia, 23 July 1913; *d* of Leslie Clarence Brown and Victoria Elizabeth (*née* Bennett); *m* 1950, Philip Westrope Pearman (*d* 1964); *m* 1974, Vincent Price. *Educ:* Claremont Ladies' Coll., Melb. Studied painting in Melbourne. First stage appearance, in Loyalties, Comedy Theatre, Melb., 1931; acted in 28 plays in Australia, 1931–34. First London appearance in Lover's Leap, Vaudeville, 1934, and then continued for some years playing in the West End. From 1940, successes include: The Man Who Came to Dinner, 1941; My Sister Eileen, 1943; The Last of Mrs Cheyney, 1944; Lady Frederick, 1946; Canaries Sometimes Sing, 1947; Jonathan, 1948; Castle in the Air, 1949; Othello, 1951; King Lear, 1952; Affairs of State, 1952; Simon and Laura, 1954; Nina, 1955; Macbeth, 1956; Troilus and Cressida, 1956; (Old Vic season) Hamlet, A Midsummer Night's Dream and King Lear, 1957–58; The Pleasure of His Company, 1959; Toys in the Attic, 1960; Bonne Soupe, 1961–62; The Rehearsal, 1963; The Right Honourable Gentleman, 1964–66; Lady Windermere's Fan, 1966; What the Butler Saw, 1969; My Darling Daisy, 1970; Mrs Warren's Profession, 1970; The Sea, 1973; The Waltz of the Toreadors, 1974; Ardèle, 1975; Charley's Aunt, 1976; The Importance of Being Ernest, 1977; Travesties, 1977. Has also appeared in United States and Moscow. *Films:* Auntie Mame; The Roman Spring of Mrs Stone; Dr Crippen; The Night of the Generals; The Legend of Lylah Clare; The Killing of Sister George, 1969; The Ruling Class, 1972; Theatre of Blood, 1973; The Drowning Pool, 1975; Dreamchild, 1985; *TV series:* Time Express, 1979; *TV films:* Elenor, First Lady of the World, 1982; An Englishman Abroad, 1983. *Recreation:* needlepoint.

BROWNE, Rt. Rev. Denis George; *see* Auckland (NZ), Bishop of, (RC).

BROWNE, Sir (Edward) Humphrey, Kt 1964; CBE 1952; FEng; Chairman, British Transport Docks Board, 1971–82; Deputy Chairman, Haden Carrier Ltd, 1973–84; retired; *b* 7 April 1911; *m* 1934, Barbara Stone (*d* 1970); two *s. Educ:* Repton; Magdalene College, Cambridge (BA 1931, MA 1943); Birmingham University (Joint Mining Degree). Manager, Chanters Colliery; Director and Chief Mining Engineer, Manchester Collieries Ltd, 1943–46; Production Director, North-Western Divisional Coal Board, 1947–48; Director-General of Production, National Coal Board, 1947–55; Chm., Midlands Div., NCB, 1955–60; Dep. Chm., NCB, 1960–67; Chairman: John Thompson Group, 1967–70; Woodall Duckham Gp, 1971–73 (Dep. Chm., 1967–71); Bestobell Ltd, 1973–79 (Dir, 1969). Mem., Commonwealth Develt Corp., 1969–72. President: The British Coal Utilisation Research Assoc., 1963–68; Inst. of Freight Forwarders, 1976–77. Director, National Industrial Fuel Efficiency Service, 1960–69; Pres., Institution of Mining Engineers, 1957. Pro-Chancellor, Univ. of Keele, 1971–75. *Address:* Beckbury Hall, near Shifnal, Salop. *T:* Ryton 207. *Club:* Brooks's.

BROWNE, (Edward) Michael (Andrew); QC 1970; *b* 29 Nov. 1910; *yr s* of Edward Granville Browne, Fellow of Pembroke Coll., Cambridge, and Alice Caroline Browne (*née* Blackburne Daniell); *m* 1937, Anna Florence Augusta, *d* of James Little Luddington; two *d. Educ:* Eton; Pembroke Coll., Cambridge (Scholar); 1st class History Tripos, 1932; MA. Barrister, Inner Temple, 1934, *ad eundem* Lincoln's Inn. Bencher, Inner Temple, 1964. Practiced (mainly in Chancery Div.) until retirement in 1984. FCIArb. Served War of 1939–45: RA (anti aircraft) and GS, War Office (finally GSO3, Capt.). *Address:* 19 Wallgrave Road, SW5. *T:* 01–373 3055. *Club:* Athenæum.

BROWNE, Sir Humphrey; *see* Browne, Sir E. H.

BROWNE, John Ernest Douglas Delavalette; MP (C) Winchester, since 1979; Managing Director, Falcon Finance Management Ltd, since 1978; Director, Churchill Private Clinic, since 1980; *b* Hampshire, 17 Oct. 1938; *s* of Col Ernest Coigny Delavalette Browne, OBE, and late Victoria Mary Eugene (*née* Douglas); *m* 1965, Elizabeth Jeannette Marguerite Garthwaite (marr. diss. 1983). *Educ:* Malvern; RMA Sandhurst (Gwynn-Jones Schol.); Cranfield Inst. of Technology (MSc); Harvard Business Sch. (MBA). Served Grenadier Guards, British Guiana (Battalion Pilot), Cyprus, BAOR, 1959–67; Captain 1963; TA, Grenadier Guards (Volunteers), 1981–. Associate, Morgan Stanley & Co., New York, 1969–72; City of London, 1972–: with Pember & Boyle, 1972–74; Director: Middle East Operations, European Banking Co., 1974–78; Worms Investments, 1981–83; Adviser: Barclays Bank Ltd, 1978–84; Trustees Household Div., 1979–83. Mem., H of C Treasury Select Cttee, 1982–; Secretary: Conservative Finance Cttee, 1982–84; Conservative Defence Cttee, 1982–83; Chm., Conservative Smaller Business Cttee, 1983–. Councillor (C), Westminster Council, 1974–78; Member: NFU; United Services Inst. for Defence Studies, 1972–. Patron: Winchester Preservation Trust, 1980–; Winchester Cadets Assoc., 1980–. Trustee, Winnall Community Assoc., 1981. Pres., Winchester Gp for Disabled People, 1982–. Mem. Court, Univ. of Southampton, 1979–; Governor, Malvern Coll., 1981–. Liveryman, Goldsmiths' Co., 1982–; OStJ. Interests include: economics, gold and internat. monetary affairs. *Publications:* various articles on finance, gold (A New European Currency—The Karl, K̶, 1972), defence, Middle East, Soviet leadership. *Recreations:* riding, skiing, sailing, shooting, squash. *Address:* House of Commons, SW1. *Clubs:* Boodle's, Turf.

BROWNE, Mervyn Ernest, CBE 1976; ERD 1954; HM Diplomatic Service, retired 1976; *b* 3 June 1916; *s* of late Ernest Edmond Browne and of Florence Mary Browne; *m* 1942, Constance (*née* Jarvis); three *s. Educ:* Stockport Sec. Sch.; St Luke's Coll., Exeter; University Coll., Exeter. BScEcon London; BA Exeter. RA, 1940–46; TA, 1947–53; AER, RASC, 1953–60. Distribution of industry res., BoT, 1948–56; HM Trade Comr Service: Trade Comr, Wellington, NZ, 1957–61 and Adelaide, 1961–64; Principal Trade Comr, Kingston, Jamaica, 1964–68; HM Diplomatic Service: Counsellor (Commercial), Canberra, 1968–70; Dir, Brit. Trade in S Africa, Johannesburg, 1970–73; Consul-Gen., 1974–76 and Chargé d'Affaires, 1974 and 1976, Brit. Embassy, Manila. *Recreations:* militaria, lepidoptery, squash rackets. *Address:* 21 Dartmouth Hill, Greenwich, SE10 8AJ. *T:* 01–691 2993.

BROWNE, Michael; *see* Browne, E. M. A.

BROWNE, Lady Moyra (Blanche Madeleine), DBE 1977 (OBE 1962); Superintendent-in-Chief, St John Ambulance Brigade, 1970–83; *b* 2 March 1918; *d* of 9th Earl of Bessborough, PC, GCMG; *m* 1945, Sir Denis John Browne, KCVO, FRCS (*d* 1967); one *s* one *d. Educ:* privately. State Enrolled Nurse, 1946. Dep. Supt-in-Chief, St John Ambulance Bde, 1964; Vice-Chm. Central Council, Victoria League, 1961–65; Vice-Pres., Royal Coll. of Nursing, 1970–85. GCStJ 1984. *Recreations:* music, shooting, fishing, travel. *Address:* 16 Wilton Street, SW1. *T:* 01–235 1419.

BROWNE, Rt. Hon. Sir Patrick (Reginald Evelyn), PC 1974; Kt 1965; OBE (mil.) 1945; TD 1945; a Lord Justice of Appeal, 1974–80, retired; *b* 28 May 1907; *er s* of Edward Granville Browne, Sir Thomas Adams's Prof. of Arabic, Fellow of Pembroke Coll., Cambridge, and Alice Caroline (*née* Blackburne-Daniell); *m* 1st, 1931, Evelyn Sophie Alexandra (*d* 1966), *o d* of Sir Charles and Lady Walston; two *d*; 2nd, 1977, Lena, *y d* of late Mr and Mrs James Atkinson. *Educ:* Eton; Pembroke Coll., Cambridge (Hon. Fellow, 1975). Barrister-at-law, Inner Temple, 1931; QC 1960; Bencher, 1962. Deputy Chairman of Quarter Sessions, Essex, Co. Cambridge and Isle of Ely, 1963–65; a Judge of the High Court of Justice, Queen's Bench Div., 1965–74. Pres., Cambs Branch, Magistrates' Assoc., 1972–85. A Controller, Royal Opera House Development Land Trust, 1981–84. Served Army, 1939–45; GSO 1, Lt-Col. *Publication:* Judicial Reflections, in Current Legal Problems 1982. *Address:* Thriplow Bury, Thriplow, Cambs. *T:* Fowlmere 234. *Clubs:* Garrick; Cambridge County.

BROWNE, Percy Basil; DL; Vice-Chairman, West of England Building Society, since 1985 (Director, Western Counties Building Society, since 1965–85); Chairman, North Devon Meat Ltd, since 1982; *b* 2 May 1923; *s* of late Lt-Col W. P. Browne, MC; *m* 1953, Jenefer Mary, *d* of late Major George Gerald Petherick and the late Lady Jeane Petherick (*née* Pleydell-Bouverie). *Educ:* The Downs, Colwall; Eton College. Served War of 1939–45 (commnd in Royal Dragoons), in Italy and NW Europe. Farmer. Rode in Grand National, 1953. MP (C) Torrington Division of Devon, 1959–64. Dir, Appledore Shipbuilders Ltd, 1965–72 (former Chm.). N Devon District Councillor, 1973–79 (Vice-Chm., 1978–79). Mem., SW Reg. Hosp. Bd, 1967–70; Vice-Chm., N Devon HMC, 1967–74. Chm., Minister of Agriculture's SW Regl Panel, 1985–. High Sheriff, Devon, 1978; DL Devon, 1984. *Address:* Wheatley House, Dunsford, Exeter. *T:* Christow 52037.

BROWNE, Peter K.; *see* Kenworthy-Browne.

BROWNE, Sheila Jeanne, CB 1977; Principal, Newnham College, Cambridge, since 1983; *b* 25 Dec. 1924; *d* of Edward Elliott Browne. *Educ:* Lady Margaret Hall, Oxford (MA; Hon. Fellow 1978); Ecole des Chartes, Paris. Asst Lectr, Royal Holloway Coll., Univ. of London, 1947–51; Tutor and Fellow of St Hilda's Coll., Oxford and Univ. Lectr in French, Oxford, 1951–61, Hon. Fellow, St Hilda's Coll., 1978; HM Inspector of Schools, 1961–70; Staff Inspector, Secondary Educn, 1970–72; Chief Inspector, Secondary Educn, 1972; Dep. Sen. Chief Inspector, DES, 1972–74, Senior Chief Inspector, 1974–83. Hon. DLitt Warwick, 1981; Hon. LLD Exeter, 1984. *Recreations:* medieval France, language, mountains. *Address:* Newnham College, Cambridge CB3 9DF. *T:* Cambridge 335700.

BROWNE, Sir Thomas Anthony G.; *see* Gore Browne.

BROWNE-CAVE, Sir Robert C.; *see* Cave-Browne-Cave.

BROWNE-WILKINSON, Rt. Hon. Sir Nicolas Christopher Henry, Kt 1977; PC 1983; **Rt. Hon. Lord Justice Browne-Wilkinson;** Vice-Chancellor of the Supreme Court, since 1985; *b* 30 March 1930; *s* of late Canon A. R. Browne-Wilkinson and Molly Browne-Wilkinson; *m* 1955, Ursula de Lacy Bacon; three *s* two *d. Educ:* Lancing; Magdalen Coll., Oxford (BA). Called to Bar, Lincoln's Inn, 1953 (Bencher, 1977); QC 1972. Junior Counsel: to Registrar of Restrictive Trading Agreements, 1964–66; to Attorney-General in Charity Matters, 1966–72; in bankruptcy, to Dept of Trade and Industry, 1966–72; a Judge of the Courts of Appeal of Jersey and Guernsey, 1976–77; a

Judge of the High Court, Chancery Div., 1977–83; a Lord Justice of Appeal, 1983–85. Pres., Employment Appeal Tribunal, 1981–83. Pres., Senate of the Inns of Court and the Bar, 1984–86. *Recreations:* farming, gardening. *Address:* Royal Courts of Justice, Strand, WC2A 2LL.

BROWNING, Dame Daphne, (Lady Browning); *see* du Maurier, Dame Daphne.

BROWNING, (David) Peter (James); CBE 1984; MA; Chief Education Officer of Bedfordshire, since 1973; *b* 29 May 1927; *s* of late Frank Browning and Lucie A. (*née* Hiscock); *m* 1953, Eleanor Berry, *d* of late J. H. Forshaw, CB, FRIBA; three *s*. *Educ:* Christ's Coll., Cambridge (Engl. and Mod. Langs Tripos); Sorbonne; Univs of Strasbourg and Perugia. Personal Asst to Vice-Chancellor, Liverpool Univ., 1952–56; Teacher, Willenhall Comprehensive Sch., 1956–59; Sen. Admin. Asst, Somerset LEA, 1959–62; Asst Dir of Educn, Cumberland LEA, 1962–66; Dep. Chief Educn Officer, Southampton LEA, 1966–69; Chief Educn Officer of Southampton, 1969–73. Member: Schools Council Governing Council and 5–13 Steering Cttee, 1969–75; Council, Univ. of Southampton, 1970–73; CofE Bd of Educn Schools Cttee, 1970–75; Council, Nat. Youth Orch., 1972–77; Merchant Navy Trng Bd, 1973–77; British Educnl Administration Soc. (Chm., 1974–78; Founder Mem., Council of Management); UGC, 1974–79; Taylor Cttee of Enquiry into Management and Govt of Schs, 1975–77; Governing Body, Centre for Inf. on Language Teaching and Research, 1975–80; European Forum for Educational Admin (Founder Chm., 1977–84); Library Adv. Council (England), 1978–81; Bd of Governors, Camb. Inst. of Educn. (Vice-Chm., 1980–); Univ. of Cambridge Faculty Bd of Educn, 1983–; British Sch. Tech. Council of Management, 1984–; Bd of Governors, Gordonstoun Sch., 1985–. Consultant, Ministry of Education: Sudan, 1976; Cyprus, 1977; Italy, 1981. Sir James Matthews Meml Lecture, Univ. of Southampton, 1983. FRSA 1981. Cavaliere, Order of Merit (Republic of Italy), 1985; Officier, Order of Palmes Académiques (Republic of France), 1985. *Publications:* Editor: Julius Caesar for German Students, 1957; Macbeth for German Students, 1959; contrib. London Educn Rev., Educnl Administration jl, and other educnl jls. *Recreations:* gardening, music, travel. *Address:* 70 Putnoe Lane, Bedford MK41 9AF. *T:* Bedford 62117; Park Fell, Skelwith, near Ambleside, Cumbria.

BROWNING, Most Rev. Edmond Lee; Presiding Bishop of the Episcopal Church in the United States, since 1986; *b* 11 March 1929; *s* of Edmond Lucian Browning and Cora Mae Lee; *m* 1953, Patricia A. Sparks; four *s* one *d*. *Educ:* Univ. of the South (BA 1952); School of Theology, Sewanee, Tenn (BD 1954). Curate, Good Shepherd, Corpus Christi, Texas, 1954–56; Rector, Redeemer, Eagle Pass, Texas, 1956–59; Rector, All Souls, Okinawa, 1959–63; Japanese Lang. School, Kobe, Japan, 1963–65; Rector, St Matthews, Okinawa, 1965–67; Archdeacon of Episcopal Church, Okinawa, 1965–67; first Bishop of Okinawa, 1967–71; Bishop of American Convocation, 1971–73; Executive for National and World Mission, on Presiding Bishop's Staff, United States Episcopal Church, 1974–76; Bishop of Hawaii, 1976–85. Chm., Standing Commn on World Mission, 1979–82. Member: Exec. Council, Episcopal Church, 1982; Anglican Consultative Council, 1982–. Hon. DD, Univ. of the South, Sewanee, Tenn, 1970. *Publication:* Essay on World Mission, 1977. *Address:* c/o Episcopal Church Center, 815 Second Avenue, New York, NY 10017, USA. *T:* 212–867–8400.

BROWNING, Dr Keith Anthony, FRS 1978; Deputy Director (Physical Research), Meteorological Office, Bracknell, since 1985; *b* 31 July 1938; *s* of late Sqdn Ldr James Anthony Browning and Amy Hilda (*née* Greenwood); *m* 1962, Ann Muriel (*née* Baish), BSc, MSc; one *s* two *d*. *Educ:* Commonweal Grammar Sch., Swindon, Wilts; Imperial Coll. of Science and Technology, Univ. of London. BSc, ARCS, PhD, DIC. Research atmospheric physicist, Air Force Cambridge Research Laboratories, Mass, USA, 1962–66; in charge of Meteorological Office Radar Research Lab., RSRE, Malvern, 1966–85; Principal Research Fellow, 1966–69; Principal Scientific Officer, 1969–72; Sen. Principal Scientific Officer, 1972–79; Dep. Chief Scientific Officer, 1979–; Ch. Scientist, Nat. Hail Res. Experiment, USA, 1974–75. Member: Council, Royal Met. Soc., 1971–74 (Vice-Pres., 1979–81); Editing Cttee, Qly Jl RMetS, 1975–78; Inter-Union Commn on Radio Meteorology, 1975–78; Internat. Commn on Cloud Physics, 1976–84; British Nat. Cttee for Physics, 1979–84; British Nat. Cttee for Geodesy and Geophysics, 1983– (Chm., Met. and Atmos. Phys. Sub-Cttee, 1985–, Vice-Chm., 1979–84); NERC, 1984–. L. F. Richardson Prize, 1968, Buchan Prize, 1972, RMetS; L. G. Groves Meml Prize for Meteorology, Met. Office, 1969; Meisinger Award, 1974, Jule Charney Award, 1985, Amer. Met. Soc. (Fellow of the Society, 1975); Charles Chree Medal and Prize, Inst. of Physics, 1981. *Publications:* (ed) Nowcasting, 1982; meteorological papers in learned jls, mainly in Britain and USA. *Recreations:* home and garden.

BROWNING, Peter; *see* Browning, D. P. J.

BROWNING, Rex Alan, CB 1984; Deputy Secretary, Overseas Development Administration, 1981–86, retired; *b* 22 July 1930; *s* of Gilbert H. W. Browning and Gladys (*née* Smith) *m* 1961, Paula McKain; three *d*. *Educ:* Bristol Grammar Sch.; Merton Coll., Oxford (Postmaster) (MA). HM Inspector of Taxes, 1952; Asst Principal, Colonial Office, 1957; Private Sec. to Parly Under-Sec. for the Colonies, 1960; Principal, Dept of Techn. Co-operation, 1961; transf. ODM, 1964; seconded to Diplomatic Service as First Sec. (Aid), British High Commn, Singapore, 1969; Asst Sec., 1971; Counsellor, Overseas Develt, Washington, and Alternate UK Exec. Dir, IBRD, 1973–76; Under-Secretary: ODM, 1976–78; Dept of Trade, 1978–80; ODA, 1980–81. *Address:* 10 Fieldway, Orpington, Kent. *T:* Orpington 23675.

BROWNING, Prof. Robert, MA; FBA 1978; Professor Emeritus, University of London; *b* 15 Jan. 1914; *s* of Alexander M. Browning and Jean M. Browning (*née* Miller); *m* 1st, 1946, Galina Chichekova; two *d*; 2nd, 1972, Ruth Gresh. *Educ:* Kelvinside Academy, Glasgow; Glasgow Univ. (MA); Balliol Coll., Oxford. Served Army, Middle East, Italy, Balkans, 1939–46. Harmsworth Sen. Scholar, Merton Coll., Oxford, 1946; Lectr, University Coll. London, 1947, Reader, 1955; Prof. of Classics and Ancient History, Birkbeck Coll., Univ. of London, 1965–81. Fellow, Dumbarton Oaks, Washington, DC, 1982, Long-Term Fellow 1983. President, Soc. for Promotion of Hellenic Studies, 1974–77; Chm., National Trust for Greece, 1985. Corresponding Mem., Athens Acad., 1981. Hon. DLitt Birmingham, 1980. Comdr of the Order of the Phoenix, Greece, 1984. *Publications:* Medieval and Modern Greek, 1969, rev. edn 1983; Justinian and Theodora, 1971; Byzantium and Bulgaria, 1975; The Emperor Julian, 1976; Studies in Byzantine History, Literature and Education, 1977; The Byzantine Empire, 1980; (ed) The Greek World, Classical, Byzantine and Modern, 1985; articles in learned jls of many countries. *Address:* 17 Belsize Park Gardens, NW3.

BROWNING, Rev. Canon Wilfrid Robert Francis; Canon Residentiary of Christ Church Cathedral, Oxford, since 1965; *b* 29 May 1918; *s* of Charles Robert and Mabel Elizabeth Browning; *m* 1948, Elizabeth Beeston; two *s* two *d*. *Educ:* Westminster School; Christ Church, Oxford; Cuddesdon Coll., Oxford. MA, BD Oxon. Deacon 1941, priest 1942, dio. of Peterborough; on staff of St Deiniol's Library, Hawarden, 1946–48; Vicar of St Richard's, Hove, 1948–51; Rector of Great Haseley, 1951–59; Lectr, Cuddesdon Coll., Oxford, 1951–59 and 1965–70; Canon Residentiary of Blackburn Cath. and Warden of Whalley Abbey, Lancs, 1959–65; Director of Ordinands and Post-Ordination Trng (Oxford dio.), 1965–85; Dir of Trng for Non-Stipendiary Ordinands and Clergy, 1972–; Examining Chaplain: Blackburn, 1960–70; Manchester, 1970–78; Oxford, 1965–. Member of General Synod, 1973–85; Select Preacher, Oxford Univ., 1972, 1981. *Publications:* Commentary on St Luke's Gospel, 1960, 6th edn 1981; Meet the New Testament, 1964; ed, The Anglican Synthesis, 1965; Handbook of the Ministry, 1985. *Address:* 42 Alexandra Road, Oxford OX2 0DB. *T:* Oxford 723464; Christ Church Cathedral, Oxford OX1 1DP.

BROWNLEE, Prof. George; Professor of Pharmacology, King's College, University of London, 1958–78, retired; now Emeritus Professor; *b* 1911; *s* of late George R. Brownlee and of Mary C. C. Gow, Edinburgh; *m* 1940, Margaret P. M. Cochrane (*d* 1970), 2nd *d* of Thomas W. P. Cochrane and Margaret P. M. S. Milne, Bo'ness, Scotland; three *s*; 2nd, 1977, Betty Jean Gaydon (marr. diss. 1981), *o d* of Stanley H. Clutterham and Margaret M. Fox, Sidney, Australia. *Educ:* Tynecastle Sch.; Heriot Watt Coll., Edinburgh, BSc 1936, DSc 1950, Glasgow; PhD 1939, London. Rammell Schol., Biological Standardization Labs of Pharmaceutical Soc., London; subseq. Head of Chemotherapeutic Div., Wellcome Res. Labs, Beckenham; Reader in Pharmacology, King's Coll., Univ. of London, 1949. Editor, Jl of Pharmacy and Pharmacology, 1955–. FKC, 1971. *Publications:* (with Prof. J. P. Quilliam) Experimental Pharmacology, 1952; papers on: chemotherapy of tuberculosis and leprosy; structure and pharmacology of the polymyxins; endocrinology; toxicity of drugs; neurohumoral transmitters in smooth muscle, etc., in: Brit. Jl Pharmacology; Jl Physiology; Biochem. Jl; Nature; Lancet; Annals NY Acad. of Science; Pharmacological Reviews, etc. *Recreations:* collecting books, making things. *Address:* 602 Gilbert House, Barbican, EC2. *T:* 01–638 9543. *Club:* Athenæum.

See also G. G. Brownlee.

BROWNLEE, Prof. George Gow, PhD; E. P. Abraham Professor of Chemical Pathology, Sir William Dunn School of Pathology, University of Oxford, since 1980; Fellow of Lincoln College, Oxford, since 1980; *b* 13 Jan. 1942; *s* of Prof. George Brownlee, *qv*; *m* 1966, Margaret Susan Kemp; one *s* one *d*. *Educ:* Dulwich College; Emmanuel Coll., Cambridge (MA, PhD). Scientific staff of MRC at Laboratory of Molecular Biology, Cambridge, 1966–80. Fellow, Emmanuel Coll., Cambridge, 1967–71. Colworth Medal, Biochemical Soc., 1977. *Publications:* Determination of Sequences in RNA (Vol. 3, Part I of Laboratory Techniques in Biochemistry and Molecular Biology), 1972; scientific papers in Jl of Molecular Biology, Nature, Cell, Nucleic Acids Research, etc. *Recreations:* gardening, cricket. *Address:* Sir William Dunn School of Pathology, South Parks Road, Oxford. *T:* Oxford 57321.

BROWNLIE, Albert Dempster; Vice-Chancellor, University of Canterbury, Christchurch, New Zealand, since 1977; *b* 3 Sept. 1932; *s* of Albert Newman and Netia Brownlie; *m* 1955, Noelene Eunice (*née* Meyer); two *d*. *Educ:* Univ. of Auckland, NZ (MCom). Economist, NZ Treasury, 1954–55. Lecturer, Sen. Lectr, Associate Prof. in Economics, Univ. of Auckland, 1956–64; Prof. and Head of Dept of Economics, Univ. of Canterbury, Christchurch, 1965–77. Chairman: Monetary and Economic Council, 1972–78; Australia-NZ Foundn, 1979–83; UGC Cttee to Review NZ Univ. Educn, 1980–82; NZ Vice-Chancellors' Cttee, 1983–84; Member: Commonwealth Experts Group on New Internat. Economic Order, 1975–77; Commonwealth Experts Gp on Econ. Growth, 1980; Wage Hearing Tribunal, 1976. Silver Jubilee Medal, 1977. *Publications:* articles in learned jls. *Address:* University of Canterbury, Christchurch, New Zealand. *T:* 488–489.

BROWNLIE, Prof. Ian, QC; DCL; FBA; FRGS; Chichele Professor of Public International Law, and Fellow of All Souls College, University of Oxford, since 1980; *b* 19 Sept. 1932; *s* of John Nason Brownlie and Amy Isabella (*née* Atherton); *m* 1st, 1957, Jocelyn Gale; one *s* two *d*; 2nd, 1978, Christine Apperley. *Educ:* Alsop High Sch., Liverpool; Hertford Coll., Oxford (Gibbs Scholar, 1952; BA 1953); King's Coll., Cambridge (Humanitarian Trust Student, 1955). DPhil Oxford, 1961; DCL Oxford, 1976. Called to the Bar, Gray's Inn, 1958; QC 1979. Lectr, Nottingham Univ., 1957–63; Fellow and Tutor in Law, Wadham Coll., Oxford, 1963–76 and Lectr, Oxford Univ., 1964–76; Prof. of Internat. Law, LSE, Univ. of London, 1976–80. Reader in Public Internat. Law, Inns of Ct Sch. of Law, 1973–76. Dir of Studies, Internat. Law Assoc., 1982–. Delegate, OUP, 1984–. Vis. Professor: Univ. of E Africa, 1968–69; Ghana, 1971; Florence, 1977. Lectr, Hague Acad. of Internat. Law, 1979. Editor, British Year Book of International Law, 1974–. Mem., Inst. of Internat. Law, 1985 (Associate Mem., 1977). FBA 1979; FRGS 1981. Japan Foundn Award, 1978. *Publications:* International Law and the Use of Force by States, 1963; Principles of Public International Law, 1966 (3rd edn 1979; Russian edn, ed G. I. Tunkin, 1977; Certif. of Merit, Amer. Soc. of Internat. Law, 1976); Basic Documents in International Law, 1967 (3rd edn 1983); The Law Relating to Public Order, 1968; Basic Documents on Human Rights, 1971 (2nd edn 1981); Basic Documents on African Affairs, 1971; African Boundaries, a legal and diplomatic encyclopaedia, 1979; State Responsibility, part 1, 1983. *Recreation:* travel. *Address:* 2 Hare Court, Temple, EC4Y 7BH. *T:* 01–583 2681; All Souls College, Oxford OX1 4AL. *T:* Oxford 722251; 43 Fairfax Road, Chiswick, W4 1EN. *T:* 01–995 3647.

BROWNLOW, family name of **Baron Lurgan.**

BROWNLOW, 7th Baron *cr* 1776; **Edward John Peregrine Cust;** Bt 1677; Chairman and Managing Director of Harris & Dixon (Underwriting Agencies) Ltd, 1976–82; *b* 25 March 1936; *o s* of 6th Baron Brownlow and Katherine Hariot (*d* 1952), 2nd *d* of Sir David Alexander Kinloch, 11th Bt, CB, MVO; *S* father, 1978; *m* 1964, Shirlie Edith, 2nd *d* of late John Yeomans, The Manor Farm, Hill Croome, Upton-on-Severn, Worcs; one *s*. *Educ:* Eton. Member of Lloyd's, 1961–; Director, Hand-in-Hand Fire and Life Insurance Soc. (branch office of Commercial Union Assurance Co. Ltd), 1962–82. High Sheriff of Lincolnshire, 1978–79. *Heir:* *s* Hon. Peregrine Edward Quintin Cust, *b* 9 July 1974. *Address:* La Maison des Prés, St Peter, Jersey. *Clubs:* White's, Pratt's; Travellers' (Paris); United (Jersey).

BROWNLOW, Air Vice-Marshal Bertrand, CB 1982; OBE 1967; AFC 1962; Associate Director, Carmichael and Sweet (Portsmouth) Ltd, Defence Consultants, since 1986; *b* 13 Jan. 1929; *s* of Robert John Brownlow and Helen Louise Brownlow; *m* 1958, Kathleen Shannon; two *s* one *d*. *Educ:* Beaufort Lodge Sch. Joined RAF, 1947; 12 and 101 Sqdns, ADC to AOC 1 Gp, 103 Sqdn, 213 Sqdn, Empire Test Pilots' Sch., OC Structures and Mech. Eng Flt RAE Farnborough, RAF Staff Coll., Air Min. Op. Requirements, 1949–64; Wing Comdr Ops, RAF Lyneham, 1964–66; Jt Services Staff Coll., 1966–67; DS RAF Staff Coll., 1967–68; Def. and Air Attaché, Stockholm, 1969–71; CO Experimental Flying, RAE Farnborough, 1971–73; Asst Comdt, Office and Flying Trng, RAF Coll., Cranwell, 1973–74; Dir of Flying (R&D), MoD, 1974–77; Comdt, A&AEE, 1977–80; Comdt, RAF Coll., Cranwell, 1980–82; Dir Gen., Trng, RAF, 1982–83, retired 1984. Silver Medal, Royal Aero Club, 1983, for servs to RAF gliding. *Recreations:* squash, tennis, golf, gliding (Gold C with two diamonds). *Address:* Woodside, Abbotsley Road, Croxton, Huntingdon, Cambs PE19 4SZ. *T:* Croxton 663. *Club:* Royal Air Force.

BROWNLOW, James Hilton, CBE 1984; QPM 1978; HM Inspector of Constabulary for North Eastern England, since 1983; *b* 19 Oct. 1925; *s* of late Ernest Cuthbert

Brownlow and of Beatrice Annie Elizabeth Brownlow; *m* 1947, Joyce Key; two *d*. *Educ*: Worksop Central School. Solicitor's Clerk, 1941–43; served war, RAF, Flt/Sgt (Air Gunner), 1943–47. Police Constable, Leicester City Police, 1947; Police Constable to Det. Chief Supt, Kent County Constabulary, 1947–69; Asst Chief Constable, Hertfordshire Constabulary, 1969–75; Asst to HM Chief Inspector of Constabulary, Home Office, 1975–76; Dep. Chief Constable, Greater Manchester Police, 1976–79; Chief Constable, S Yorks Police, 1979–82. Queen's Commendation for Brave Conduct, 1972. Officer Brother OStJ 1981. *Recreations*: golf, gardening. *Club*: Sheffield.

BROWNLOW, Kevin; author; film director; *b* 2 June 1938; *s* of Thomas and Niña Brownlow; *m* 1969, Virginia Keane; one *d*. *Educ*: University College School. Entered documentaries, 1955; became film editor, 1958, and edited many documentaries; with Andrew Mollo dir. feature films: It Happened Here, 1964; Winstanley, 1975; dir. Charm of Dynamite, 1967, about Abel Gance, and restored his classic film Napoleon (first shown London, Nov. 1980, NY, Jan. 1981). With David Gill produced and directed TV series: Hollywood, 1980; Unknown Chaplin, 1983; Thames Silents, 1985 (incl. The Big Parade); Producer, British Cinema—Personal View, 1986; Supervising Editor, No Surrender, 1986. *Publications*: The Parade's Gone By . . ., 1968; How it Happened Here, 1968; The War, the West and the Wilderness, 1978; Hollywood: the pioneers, 1979; Napoleon: Abel Gance's classic film, 1983; many articles on film history. *Recreation*: motion pictures. *Address*: c/o Thames TV, 306 Euston Road, NW1.

BROWNRIGG, Sir Nicholas (Gawen), 5th Bt, *cr* 1816; *b* 22 Dec. 1932; *s* of late Gawen Egremont Brownrigg and Baroness Lucia von Borosini, *o d* of Baron Victor von Borosini, California; *S* grandfather, 1939; *m* 1959, Linda Louise Lovelace (marr. diss. 1965), Beverly Hills, California; one *s* one *d*; *m* 1971, Valerie Ann, *d* of Julian A. Arden, Livonia, Michigan, USA. *Educ*: Midland Sch.; Stanford Univ. *Heir*: *s* Michael Gawen Brownrigg, *b* Oct. 1961. *Address*: PO Box 548, Ukiah, Calif 95482, USA.

BROWNRIGG, Philip Henry Akerman, CMG 1964; DSO 1945; OBE 1953; TD 1945; *b* 3 June 1911; *s* of late Charles E. Brownrigg, Headmaster of Magdalen Coll. Sch., Oxford; *m* 1936, Marguerite Doreen Ottley; three *d*. *Educ*: Eton; Magdalen Coll., Oxford (BA). Journalist, 1934–52; Editor, Sunday Graphic, 1952. Joined Anglo American Corp. of S Africa, 1953: London Agent, 1956; Dir in Rhodesia, 1961–63; Dir in Zambia, 1964–65; retd, 1969. Director (apptd by Govt of Zambia): Nchanga Consolidated Copper Mines Ltd, 1969–80; Roan Consolidated Mines Ltd, 1969–80. Joined TA, 1938; served War of 1939–45 with 6 R Berks, and 61st Reconnaissance Regt (RAC); Lieut-Col 1944; CO 4/6 R Berks (TA) 1949–52. Insignia of Honour, Zambia, 1981. *Recreations*: golf, sport on TV. *Address*: Wheeler's, Checkendon, near Reading, Berks. *T*: Checkendon 680328.

BROWSE, Lillian Gertrude; author; private archivist; *d* of Michael Browse and Gladys Browse (*née* Meredith); *m* 1st, 1934, Ivan H. Joseph; 2nd, 1964, Sidney H. Lines. *Educ*: Barnato Park, Johannesburg. Studied with Margaret Craske at Cecchetti Ballet Sch., London, 1928–30; joined Dolin-Nemtchinova ballet co., 1930; gave up ballet and worked at Leger Galls, London, 1931–39; organised war-time exhibns at Nat. Gall. and travelling exhibns for CEMA, 1940–45, also exhibns for Inst. of Adult Educn; Organising Sec., Red Cross picture sale, Christie's, 1942; founder partner, Roland, Browse & Delbanco, 1945; Founder Dir, Browse & Darby, 1977–81. Ballet Critic, Spectator, 1950–54. Organised: Sickert exhibn, Edinburgh, 1953; Sickert centenary exhibn, Tate Gall., 1960; exhibited own private collection at Courtauld Inst. Galls, 1983. Hon. Fellow, Courtauld Inst., 1986. *Publications*: Augustus John Drawings, 1941; Sickert, 1943; Degas Dancers, 1949; William Nicholson: Catalogue Raisonné, 1955; Sickert, 1960; Forain, the Painter, 1978; (ed) Ariel Books on the Arts, 1946; contribs to Apollo, Sunday Times, Country Life. *Recreation*: gardening. *Address*: Little Wassell, Ebernoe, near Petworth, West Sussex GU28 9LD.

BROWSE, Prof. Norman Leslie, MD, FRCS; Professor of Surgery, St Thomas's Hospital Medical School, since 1981, and Consultant Surgeon, St Thomas' Hospital, since 1965; *b* 1 Dec. 1931; *s* of Reginald and Margaret Browse; *m* 1957, Dr Jeanne Menage; one *s* one *d*. *Educ*: St Bartholomew's Hosp. Med. Coll. (MB BS 1955); Bristol Univ. (MD 1961). FRCS 1959. Lectr in Surgery, Westminster Hosp., 1962–64; Harkness Fellow, Res. Associate, Mayo Clinic, Rochester, Minn, 1964–65. St Thomas's Hospital Medical School: Reader in Surgery, 1965–72; Prof. of Vascular Surgery, 1972–81. Mem. Council, RCS, 1986–. *Publications*: Physiology and Pathology of Bed Rest, 1964; Symptoms and Signs of Surgical Disease, 1978; Reducing Operations for Lymphoedema, 1986; Diseases of the Veins, 1987; papers on all aspects of vascular disease. *Recreations*: marine art, mediaeval history, sailing. *Address*: Blaye House, Home Farm Close, Esher, Surrey KT10 9HA. *T*: Esher 65058.

BROXBOURNE, Baron *cr* 1983 (Life Peer), of Broxbourne in the County of Hertfordshire; **Derek Colclough Walker-Smith;** 1st Bt *cr* 1960; PC 1957; QC 1955; TD; *b* April 1910; *y s* of late Sir Jonah Walker-Smith; *m* 1938, Dorothy, *d* of late L. J. W. Etherton, Rowlands Castle, Hants; one *s* two *d*. *Educ*: Rossall; Christ Church, Oxford. 1st Class Hons Modern History, Oxford Univ., 1931. Called to Bar, Middle Temple, 1934, Bencher 1963. MP (C) Hertford, 1945–55, Herts East, 1955–83; Parly Sec. to the Board of Trade, 1955–Nov. 1956; Economic Secretary to the Treasury, Nov. 1956–Jan. 1957; Minister of State, Board of Trade, 1957; Minister of Health, 1957–60. Chairman: Cons. Adv. Cttee on Local Govt, 1954–55; 1922 Cttee, 1951–55. Mem., European Parlt, 1973–79 (Chm. of Legal Cttee, 1975–79). Chm., Soc. of Conservative Lawyers, 1969–75; Chm., Nat. House Building Council, 1973–78. ARICS; FCIArb; FIQS. *Publication*: Walker-Smith on the Standard Forms of Building Contracts. *Heir* (to baronetcy only): *s* John Jonah Walker-Smith, *qv*. *Address*: 7 Kepplestone, The Meads, Eastbourne; 20 Albany Court, Palmer Street, SW1. *Club*: Garrick.

BRUBECK, David Warren; musician, USA; composer; *b* Concord, Calif, 6 Dec. 1920; *s* of Howard Brubeck and Elizabeth Ivey; *m* 1942, Iola Whitlock; five *s* one *d*. *Educ*: Pacific Univ. (BA); Mills Coll. (postgrad.). Hon. PhD: Univ. of Pacific; Fairfield Univ. Pianist with dance bands and jazz trio, 1946–49; own trio, touring USA, 1950; formed Dave Brubeck Quartet, 1951; tours to festivals and colls, incl. tour of Europe and Middle East (for US State Dept); Europe and Australia, 1960; Europe, Australia, Canada, S America, with 3 sons, as Two Generations of Brubeck; Quartet semi-annual appearances in London. Fellow, Internat. Inst. of Arts and Sciences; Duke Ellington Fellow, Yale Univ. Exponent of progressive Jazz; many awards from trade magazines; numerous recordings. Has composed: over 250 songs; Points on Jazz (ballet); Elementals (orch.); The Light in the Wilderness (oratorio; perf. Cincinnati Symph. Orch. and mixed chorus of 100 voices, 1968); Gates of Justice (Cantata); Truth (Cantata); They All Sang Yankee Doodle, variations for orch., 1975; La Fiesta de la Posada, 1975; Glances (ballet), 1976; Beloved Son (oratorio), 1978; To Hope (mass), 1980; 6 Variations of Pange Lingua (chorus and orch.); The Voice of the Holy Spirit (cantata), 1985. Hon. PhD: Bridgeport, 1982; Mills Coll., 1982. BMI Jazz Pioneer Award. *Address*: c/o Sutton Artists Corporation, 119 West 57th Street, Suite 512, New York, NY 10019, USA.

BRUCE, family name of **Barons Aberdare,** and **Bruce of Donington,** of **Lord Balfour of Burleigh,** and of **Earl of Elgin.**

BRUCE; *see* Cumming-Bruce and Hovell-Thurlow-Cumming-Bruce.

BRUCE, Lord; Charles Edward Bruce; *b* 19 Oct. 1961; *s* and *heir* of 11th Earl of Elgin, *qv*. *Educ*: Eton College; Univ. of St Andrews (MA Hons). A Page of Honour to HM the Queen Mother, 1975–77. *Address*: Broomhall, Dunfermline KY11 3DU. *T*: Dunfermline 872222.

BRUCE OF DONINGTON, Baron *cr* 1974 (Life Peer), of Rickmansworth; **Donald William Trevor Bruce;** economist; Chartered Accountant, Halpern & Woolf; writer; Member of European Parliament, 1975–79; *b* 3 Oct. 1912; *s* of late W. T. Bruce, Norbury, Surrey; *m* 1st, 1939, Joan Letitia Butcher (marr. diss.); one *s* two *d* (and one *d* decd); 2nd, 1981, Cyrena Shaw Heard. *Educ*: Grammar School, Donington, Lincs; FCA 1947. Rejoined Territorial Army, March 1939; commissioned, Nov. 1939; Major, 1942; served at home and in France until May 1945 (despatches). MP (Lab) for North Portsmouth, 1945–50; Parliamentary Private Sec. to Minister of Health, 1945–50; Member Min. of Health delegn to Sweden and Denmark, 1946, and of House of Commons Select Cttee on Public Accounts, 1948–50. Opposition spokesman on Treasury, economic and industrial questions, House of Lords, 1979–83, on trade and industry, 1983–. *Publications*: miscellaneous contributions on political science and economics to newspapers and periodicals. *Address*: 301–305 Euston Road, NW1.

BRUCE, Alastair Henry, CBE 1951; DL; Chairman and Managing Director, The Inveresk Paper Company Ltd, 1964–68; Member, Monopolies Commission, 1964–68; Chairman, Paper and Paper Products Industry Training Board, 1968–71; *b* 14 April 1900; *s* of Patrick Chalmers Bruce and Lucy Walmsley Hodgson. *Educ*: Cargilfield, Midlothian; Uppingham. President British Paper and Board Makers Association, 1938–42 and 1948–51; President British Paper and Board Research Association, 1948–51. DL Midlothian, 1943–.

BRUCE, Alexander Robson, CMG 1961; OBE 1948; Assistant Secretary, Board of Trade, 1963–67, retired; *b* 17 April 1907; *m* 1936, Isobel Mary Goldie; four *d*. *Educ*: Rutherford Coll., Newcastle upon Tyne; Durham Univ. Asst Trade Comr, 1933–42, Trade Commissioner, 1942–43, Montreal; Commercial Sec., British Embassy, Madrid, 1943–46; Trade Comr, Ottawa, 1946–50; Asst Sec., Bd of Trade, 1950–54 and 1963–; Principal British Trade Commissioner in NSW, 1955–63. *Recreation*: golf. *Address*: 37 North Road, Highgate, N6. *Club*: Highgate Golf.

BRUCE, Sir Arthur Atkinson, KBE 1943; MC 1917; Director: Wallace Brothers & Co. Ltd, 1947–65; Chartered Bank of India, 1949–70; *b* 26 March 1895; *s* of late John Davidson Bruce, Jarrow-on-Tyne; *m* 1928, Kathleen Frances (*d* 1952), *d* of John Emeris Houldey, ICS (retd), Penn, Bucks; three *d*. *Educ*: Cambridge. Director Reserve Bank of India, 1935–46; Chairman Burma Chamber of Commerce, 1936, 1942, 1946. Member of Council, London Chamber of Commerce, 1960–65. *Address*: Silverthorne, 5 Grenfell Road, Beaconsfield, Bucks. *Club*: Oriental.

BRUCE, Christopher; dancer, choreographer, opera producer; Associate Choreographer: Ballet Rambert, since 1979 (Associate Director, 1975–79); Festival Ballet, since 1986; *b* Leicester, 3 Oct. 1945; *m* Marian Bruce; two *s* one *d*. *Educ*: Ballet Rambert Sch. Joined Ballet Rambert Company, 1963; leading dancer with co. when re-formed as modern dance co., 1966; leading roles include: Pierrot Lunaire, The Tempest ((Tetley); L'Apres-Midi d'un Faune (Nijinsky); Cruel Garden (also choreographed with Lindsay Kemp); choreographed: for Ballet Rambert: George Frideric (1st work), 1969; Wings, 1970; For Those Who Die as Cattle, 1971; There Was a Time, 1972; Weekend, 1974; Ancient Voices of Children, 1975; Black Angels, 1976; Cruel Garden, 1977; Night with Waning Moon, 1977; Dancing Day, 1981; Ghost Dances, 1981; Berlin Requiem, 1982; Concertino, 1983; Intimate Pages, 1984; Sergeant Early's Dream, 1984; for London Festival Ballet: Land, 1985; for Tanz Forum, Cologne: Cantata, 1981; for Nederlands Dans Theater: Village Songs, 1981; Curses and Blessings, 1983; works for Royal Ballet, Batsheva Dance Co., Munich Opera Ballet, Gulbenkian Ballet Co., Australian Dance Theatre, Royal Danish Ballet, Royal Swedish Ballet. Kent Opera: choreographed and produced Monteverdi's Il Ballo delle Ingrate, and Combattimento di Tancredi e Clorinda, 1980; chor. John Blow's Venus and Adonis, 1980; co-prod Handel's Agrippina, 1982. Choreographed Mutiny (musical), Piccadilly, 1985. TV productions: Ancient Voices of Children, BBC, 1977; Cruel Garden, BBC, 1981–82; Ghost Dances, Channel 4, 1982; Requiem, Danish-German co-prodn, 1982; Silence is the end of our Song, Danish TV, 1984; The Dream is Over (to John Lennon songs), Danish–German co-prodn, 1985. Evening Standard's inaugural Dance Award, 1974. *Address*: c/o Ballet Rambert, 94 Chiswick High Road, W4 1SH.

BRUCE, David, CA; Partner, Deloitte Haskins & Sells, since 1974; *b* 21 Jan. 1927; *s* of David Bruce and Margaret (*née* Gregson); *m* 1955, Joy Robertson McAslan; four *d*. *Educ*: High School of Glasgow. Commissioned, Royal Corps of Signals, 1947–49. Qualified as Chartered Accountant, 1955; Partner, Kerr McLeod & Co., Chartered Accountants, 1961 (merged with Deloitte Haskins & Sells, 1974). Vice-Pres., Inst. of Chartered Accountants of Scotland, 1978–79 and 1979–80, Pres. 1980–81. Mem., Council on Tribunals, 1984– (Mem., Scottish Cttee, 1984–). *Recreations*: angling, curling, cooking. *Address*: 2 Sandy Road, Hampstead, NW3 7BY. *T*: 01–455 3875. *Club*: Caledonian.

BRUCE, Sir (Francis) Michael Ian; *see* Bruce, Sir Michael Ian.

BRUCE, Prof. Frederick Fyvie, MA Aberdeen, Cantab, Manchester, DD Aberdeen; FBA 1973; Rylands Professor of Biblical Criticism and Exegesis, University of Manchester, 1959–78, now Emeritus; *b* 12 Oct. 1910; *e s* of late P. F. Bruce, Elgin, Morayshire; *m* 1936, Betty, *er d* of late A. B. Davidson, Aberdeen; one *s* one *d*. *Educ*: Elgin Acad.; Univs of Aberdeen, Cambridge, Vienna. Gold Medallist in Greek and Latin; Fullerton Schol. in Classics, 1932; Croom Robertson Fellow, 1933; Aberdeen Univ.; Scholar of Gonville and Caius Coll., Camb., 1932; Sandys Student. Camb., 1934; Ferguson Schol. in Classics, 1933, and Crombie Scholar in Biblical Criticism, 1939, Scottish Univs; Diploma in Hebrew, Leeds Univ., 1943. Asst in Greek, Edinburgh Univ., 1935–38; Lectr in Greek, Leeds Univ., 1938–47: Professor of Biblical History and Literature, University of Sheffield, 1955–59 (Head of Dept, 1947–59). Lectures: John A. McElwain, Gordon Divinity School, Beverly Farms, Massachusetts, 1958; Calvin Foundation, Calvin Coll. and Seminary, Grand Rapids, Michigan, 1958; Payton, Fuller Theolog. Seminary, Pasadena, Calif, 1968; Norton, Southern Baptist Theolog. Seminary, Louisville, Kentucky, 1968; Smyth, Columbia Theological Seminary, Decatur, Ga, 1970; Earle, Nazarene Theological Seminary, Kansas City, Mo, 1970; N. W. Lund, N Park Theological Seminary, Chicago, 1970; Thomas F. Staley, Ontario Bible Coll., Toronto, 1973; Moore Coll., Sydney, 1977; Griffith Thomas, Wycliffe Hall, Oxford, 1982; Griffith Thomas, Dallas Theol Seminary, Texas, 1983. Examr in Biblical Studies: Leeds University, 1943–47, 1957–60, 1967–69; Edinburgh University, 1949–52, 1958–60; Bristol University, 1958–60; Aberdeen University, 1959–61; London University, 1959–60; St Andrews University, 1961–64; Cambridge University, 1961–62; University of Wales, 1965–68; Sheffield University, 1968–70; Newcastle University, 1969–71; Keele Univ., 1971–73; Dublin Univ., 1972–75; Dean of Faculty of Theology, University of

Manchester, 1963–64; President: Yorkshire Soc. for Celtic Studies, 1948–50; Sheffield Branch of Classical Association, 1955–58; Victoria Inst., 1958–65; Manchester Egyptian and Oriental Society, 1963–65; Soc. for Old Testament Study, 1965; Soc. for New Testament Studies, 1975. Burkitt Medal, British Acad., 1979. Editor: Yorkshire Celtic Studies, 1945–57; The Evangelical Quarterly, 1949–80; Palestine Exploration Quarterly, 1957–71. *Publications:* The NT Documents, 1943; The Hittites and the OT, 1948; The Books and the Parchments, 1950; The Acts of the Apostles, Greek Text with Commentary, 1951; The Book of the Acts, Commentary on English Text, 1954; Second Thoughts on the Dead Sea Scrolls, 1956; The Teacher of Righteousness in the Qumran Texts, 1957; Biblical Exegesis in the Qumran Texts, 1959; The Spreading Flame, 1958; The Epistle to the Ephesians, 1961; Paul and his Converts, 1962; The Epistle of Paul to the Romans, 1963; Israel and the Nations, 1963; Commentary on the Epistle to the Hebrews, 1964; Expanded Paraphrase of the Epistles of Paul, 1965; New Testament History, 1969; This is That, 1969; Tradition Old and New, 1970; St Matthew, 1970; The Epistles of John, 1970; First and Second Corinthians (Century Bible), 1971; The Message of the New Testament, 1972; Jesus and Christian Origins outside the New Testament, 1974; Paul and Jesus, 1974; First-Century Faith, 1977; Paul: Apostle of the Free Spirit, 1977; The Time is Fulfilled, 1978; History of the Bible in English, 1979; The Work of Jesus, 1979; Men and Movements in the Primitive Church, 1980; In Retrospect, 1980; The Epistle to the Galatians, 1982; First and Second Thessalonians, 1982; Paternoster Bible History Atlas, 1982; Commentary on Philippians, 1983; The Gospel of John, 1983; The Hard Sayings of Jesus, 1983; Commentary on Colossians, Philemon and Ephesians, 1984; The Pauline Circle, 1985; The Real Jesus, 1985; contribs to classical and theological journals. *Recreation:* foreign travel. *Address:* The Crossways, Temple Road, Buxton, Derbyshire. *T:* Buxton 3250.

BRUCE, George John Done, RP 1959; painter of portraits, landscapes, still life, flowers; *b* 28 March 1930; *s* of 11th Lord Balfour of Burleigh, Brucefield, Clackmannan, Scotland and Violet Dorothy, *d* of Richard Henry Done, Tarporley, Cheshire; *b* of 12th Lord Balfour of Burleigh, *qv. Educ:* Westminster Sch.; Byam Shaw Sch. of Drawing and Painting. Hon. Sec., Royal Soc. of Portrait Painters, 1970–84, Vice-Pres., 1984–. *Recreations:* hang-gliding, ski-ing, windsurfing. *Address:* 6 Pembroke Walk, W8 6PQ. *T:* 01–937 1493. *Club:* Athenæum.

BRUCE, Sir Hervey (James Hugh), 7th Bt *cr* 1804; Major, The Grenadier Guards; *b* 3 Sept. 1952; *s* of Sir Hervey John William Bruce, 6th Bt, and Crista, (*d* 1984), *y d* of late Lt-Col Chandos De Paravicini, OBE; *S* father, 1971; *m* 1979, Charlotte, *e d* of Jack Gore, Tite Street, SW3; one *d. Educ:* Eton; Officer Cadet School, Mons. *Heir: uncle* Ronald Cecil Juckes Bruce [*b* 22 Aug. 1921; *m* 1960, Jean, *d* of L. J. W. Murfitt; one *s*]. *Address:* 23 Cranbury Road, SW6 2NS.

BRUCE, Ian Waugh; Director-General, Royal National Institute for the Blind, since 1983; *b* 21 April 1945; *s* of Thomas Waugh Bruce and Una (*née* Eagle); *m* 1971, Anthea Christine, (Tina), *d* of Dr P. R. Rowland, FRSC; one *s* one *d. Educ:* King Edward VI Sch., Southampton; Central High Sch., Arizona; Univ. of Birmingham (BSocSc Hons 1968). FBIM 1981 (MBIM 1975). Apprentice Chem. Engr, Courtaulds, 1964–65; Marketing Trainee, then Manager, Unilever, 1968–70; Appeals and PR Officer, then Asst Dir, Age Concern England, 1970–74; Dir, National Volunteer Centre, 1975–81; Controller of Secretariat, then Asst Chief Exec., Bor. of Hammersmith and Fulham, 1981–83. Consultant, UN Div. of Social Affairs, 1970–72; Sec., Volunteurope, Brussels, 1979–81; Adviser, BBC Community Progs Unit, 1979–81; Member: Educn Adv. Council, IBA, 1981–83; Exec. Cttee, National Council for Voluntary Orgns, 1978–81; National Good Neighbour Campaign, 1977–79; Council, Retired Executives Action Clearing House, 1978–83; Adv. Council, Centre for Policies on Ageing, 1979–83. Mem., Art Panel, Art Film Cttee and New Activities Cttee, Arts Council of GB, 1967–71; Spokesman, Artists Now, 1973–77. Chm., Coventry Internat. Centre, 1964. Sir Raymond Priestley Expeditionary Award, Univ. of Birmingham, 1968. *Publications:* Public Relations and the Social Services, 1972; (jtly) Patronage of the Creative Artist, 1974, 2nd edn 1975; papers on voluntary and community work, old people, contemporary art and marketing. *Recreations:* the arts, the countryside. *Address:* 54 Mall Road, W6. *Club:* ICA.

BRUCE, Malcolm Gray; MP (L) Gordon, since 1983; *b* 17 Nov. 1944; *s* of David Stewart Bruce and Kathleen Elmslie (*née* Delf); *m* 1969, Veronica Jane Wilson; one *s* one *d. Educ:* Wrekin Coll., Shropshire; St Andrews Univ. (MA 1966); Strathclyde Univ. (MSc 1970). Liverpool Daily Post, 1966–67; Buyer, Boots Pure Drug Co., 1967–68; A. Goldberg & Son, 1968–69; Res. Information Officer, NE Scotland Develt Authority, 1971–75; Marketing Dir, Noroil Publishing House (UK), 1975–81; Jt Editor/Publisher/ Dir, Aberdeen Petroleum Publishing, 1981–84. Dep. Chm., Scottish Liberal Party, 1975–84 (Energy Spokesman, 1975–83); Liberal Parly Spokesman on Scottish Affairs, 1983–85, on Energy, 1985–. Rector of Dundee Univ., 1986–. *Publications:* A New Life for the Country: a rural development programme for West Aberdeenshire; Putting Energy to Work, 1981; (with others) A New Deal for Rural Scotland, 1983; (with Paddy Ashdown) Growth from the Grassroots. *Recreations:* yes please, when I can, theatre, music, travel, hill walking. *Address:* East View, Woodside Road, Torphins AB3 4JR. *T:* Torphins 386. *Clubs:* National Liberal; Royal Northern University (Aberdeen).

BRUCE, Sir Michael Ian, 12th Bt, *cr* 1629; partner, Gossard-Bruce Co., from 1953; *b* 3 April 1926; *s* of Sir Michael William Selby Bruce, 11th Bt and Doreen Dalziel, *d* of late W. F. Greenwell; *S* father 1957; holds dual UK and US citizenship; has discontinued first forename, Francis; *m* 1st, 1947, Barbara Stevens (marr. diss., 1957), *d* of Frank J. Lynch; two *s*; 2nd, 1961, Frances Keegan (marr. diss., 1963); 3rd, 1966, Marilyn Ann (marr. diss., 1975), *d* of Carter Mulally. *Educ:* Forman School, Litchfield, Conn; Pomfret, Conn. Served United States Marine Corps, 1943–46 (Letter of Commendation); *S* Pacific area two years, Bismarck Archipelago, Bougainville, Philippines. Owner, Latitude 57° Marine Shipping Co., 1966; Master Mariner's Ticket, 1968; President: Newport Sailing Club, Inc., 1978–; Newport Academy of Sail, Inc., 1979–; Owner, American Maritime Co. *Recreations:* sailing, spear-fishing. *Heir: s* Michael Ian Richard Bruce, *b* 10 Dec. 1950. *Address:* 3432 Via Oporto #204, Newport Beach, Calif 92663, USA. *T:* 714–675–7100. *Clubs:* Rockaway Hunt; Lawrence Beach; Balboa Bay (Newport Beach); Vikings of Scandia (Los Angeles).

BRUCE, Michael Stewart Rae, QC (Scot.) 1975; *b* 26 July 1938; *s* of late Alexander Eric Bruce, Advocate in Aberdeen, and late Mary Gordon Bruce (*née* Walker); *m* 1963, Alison Mary Monfries Stewart; two *d. Educ:* Loretto Sch.; Aberdeen Univ. (MA, LLB). Admitted Faculty of Advocates, 1963; Standing Counsel: to Dept of Agriculture and Fisheries for Scotland, 1973; to Highlands and Islands Develt Bd, 1973. Advocate Depute, 1983–86. Mem., Criminal Injuries Compensation Bd, 1986. *Recreations:* fishing, golf. *Address:* 17 Wester Coates Terrace, Edinburgh EH12 5LR. *T:* 031–337 5883. *Clubs:* New (Edinburgh); Honourable Company of Edinburgh Golfers.

BRUCE, Robert Nigel (Beresford Dalrymple), CBE 1972 (OBE (mil.) 1946); TD; CEng, Hon. FIGasE; *b* 21 May 1907; *s* of Major R. N. D. Bruce, late of Hampstead; *m* 1945, Elizabeth Brogden, *d* of J. G. Moore; twin *s* two *d. Educ:* Harrow School (Entrance

and Leaving Scholar); Magdalen College, Oxford (Exhibitioner). BA (Hons Chem.) and BSc. Joined Territorial Army Rangers (KRRC), 1931; Major, 1939; served Greece, Egypt, Western Desert, 1940–42; Lt-Col Comdg Regt, 1942; GHQ, MEF, Middle East Supply Centre, 1943–45; Col, Dir. of Materials, 1944. Joined Gas, Light and Coke Co., as Research Chemist, 1929; Asst to Gen. Manager, 1937, Controller of Industrial Relations, 1946; Staff Controller, 1949, Dep. Chm., 1956, North Thames Gas Bd; Chm., S Eastern Gas Bd, 1960–72. President: British Road Tar Assoc., 1964 and 1965; Coal Tar Research Assoc., 1966; Institution of Gas Engineers, 1968; Mem. Bd, CEI, 1968–80. Chm. Governing Body, Westminster Technical Coll., 1958–76. Sec., Tennis and Rackets Assoc., 1974–81. *Publications:* Chronicles of the 1st Battalion the Rangers (KRRC), 1939–45; contribs to Proc. Royal Society, Jl Soc. Chemical Industry, Jl Chemical Society. *Recreations:* travel, golf. *Address:* Fairway, 57 Woodland Grove, Weybridge, Surrey KT13 9EQ. *T:* Weybridge 52372. *Club:* Queen's (Hon. Mem.).

BRUCE, Hon. Mrs Victor, (Mildred Mary), FRGS; *b* 1895; *d* of Lawrence Joseph Petre, Coptfold Hall, Essex; *m* 1926, Hon. Victor Bruce (marr. diss. 1941), *y s* of 2nd Baron Aberdare. *Educ:* Convent of Sion. Travelled furthest north into Lapland by motor car; holds record for Double Channel Crossing, Dover to Calais, by motor boat; holder of 17 World Records, motoring, and of 24–hour record; single-handed drive, covered longest distance for man or woman, 2164 miles, in 24 hours; Coupe des Dames, Monte Carlo Rally, 1927. Flying records: first solo flight from England to Japan, 1930; longest solo flight, 1930; record solo flight, India to French Indo-China, 1930; British Air refuelling endurance flight, 1933. Holds 24 hour record by motor boat, covering 674 nautical miles, single handed, 1929; first crossing of Yellow Sea. Show Jumping, 1st Royal Windsor Horse Show, 1939. Order of the Million Elephants and White Umbrella (French Indo-China). Fellow, Ancient Monuments Society. *Publications:* The Peregrinations of Penelope; 9000 Miles in Eight Weeks; The Woman Owner Driver; The Bluebird's Flight; Nine Lives Plus. *Clubs:* Royal Motor Yacht, British Racing Drivers, Rolls Royce Enthusiasts'.

BRUCE-CHWATT, Prof. Leonard Jan, CMG 1976; OBE 1953; FRCP; FIBiol; Professor of Tropical Hygiene and Director of Ross Institute, London School of Hygiene and Tropical Medicine, University of London, 1969–74, now Emeritus Professor; Editor, Tropical Doctor (Royal Society of Medicine), since 1975; *b* 9 June 1907; *s* of Dr Michael Chwatt and Anna Marquitant; *m* 1948, Joan Margaret Bruce; two *s. Educ:* Univ. of Warsaw (MD); Paris (Dipl. Méd. Col.); Univ. of London (DTM&H); Harvard (MPH). Wartime service Polish Army Med. Corps and RAMC, 1939–45; Colonial Medical Service (Senior Malariologist, Nigeria), 1946–58; Chief Research and Technical Intelligence, Div. of Malaria Eradication, WHO, Geneva, 1958–68. Mem. Expert Cttee on Malaria, WHO, Geneva, 1956–. Pres., Laveran Internat. Foundn; Vice-Pres., Royal Soc. Tropical Med. and Hygiene; Associate, Wellcome Tropical Inst., 1975. Duncan Medal, 1942; North Persian Forces Memorial Medal, 1952; Darling Medal and Prize, 1971; Macdonald Meml Medal, 1978; Laveran Medal, 1983; John Hull Grundy Medal, RAMC, 1984. KStJ 1975. *Publications:* Terminology of Malaria, 1963; chapter on malaria in Cecil and Loeb Textbook of Medicine, 1967 and 1970; Dynamics of Tropical Disease, 1973; The Rise and Fall of Malaria in Europe, 1980; Essential Malariology, 1980, 2nd edn 1985; Chemotherapy of Malaria, 1981, French edn 1984; numerous papers in medical jls. *Recreations:* travel, music, walking. *Address:* 21 Marchmont Road, Richmond, Surrey. *T:* 01–940 5540.

BRUCE-GARDNER, Sir Douglas (Bruce), 2nd Bt, *cr* 1945; Director, Guest, Keen & Nettlefolds Ltd, 1960–82; *b* 27 Jan. 1917; *s* of Sir Charles Bruce-Gardner, 1st Bt; *S* father, 1960; *m* 1st, 1940, Monica Flumerfelt (marr. diss. 1964), *d* of late Sir Geoffrey Jefferson, CBE, FRS; one *s* two *d*; 2nd, 1964, Sheila Jane, *d* of Roger and late Barbara Stilliard, Seer Green, Bucks; one *s* one *d. Educ:* Uppingham; Trinity College, Cambridge. Lancashire Steel, 1938–51; Control Commn, Germany, 1945–46; joined GKN, 1951. Dir, GKN Ltd, 1960, Dep. Chm., 1974–77; Dep. Chm., GKN Steel Co. Ltd, 1962, Gen. Man. Dir, 1963–65, Chm., 1965–67; Chairman: GKN Rolled & Bright Steel Ltd, 1968–72; GKN (South Wales) Ltd, 1968–72; Exors of James Mills Ltd, 1968–72; Parson Ltd, 1968–72; Brymbo Steel Works Ltd, 1974–77; Miles Druce & Co. Ltd, 1974–77; Exec. Vice-Chm., UK Ops, Gen. Products, GKN Ltd, 1972–74; Dep. Chm., GKN (UK) Ltd, 1972–75; Director: Henry Gardner & Co. Ltd, 1952–68; Firth Cleveland Ltd, 1972–75; BHP-GKN Holdings Ltd, 1977–78; Dep.-Chm., Iron Trades Employers' Insurance Assoc., 1984– (Dir, 1977–). President: Iron and Steel Inst., 1966–67; British Indep. Steel Producers' Assoc., 1972; Pres., Iron and Steel Employers' Assoc., 1963–64. *Recreations:* fishing, photography. *Heir: s* Robert Henry Bruce-Gardner [*b* 10 June 1943; *m* 1979, Veronica Ann Hand-Oxborrow, *d* of late Rev. W. E. Hand and of Mrs R. G. Oxborrow, Caterham; two *s*]. *Address:* Stocklands, Lewstone, Ganarew, near Monmouth NP5 3SS. *T:* Symonds Yat 890216. *Club:* Flyfishers'.

BRUCE-GARDYNE, family name of **Baron Bruce-Gardyne.**

BRUCE-GARDYNE, Baron *cr* 1983 (Life Peer), of Kirkden in the District of Angus; **John, (Jock), Bruce-Gardyne;** *b* 12 April 1930; 2nd *s* of late Capt. E. Bruce-Gardyne, DSO, RN, Middleton, by Arbroath, Angus and Joan (*née* McLaren); *m* 1959, Sarah Louisa Mary, *o d* of Comdr Sir John Maitland and Bridget Denny; two *s* one *d. Educ:* Winchester; Magdalen College, Oxford. HM Foreign Service, 1953–56; served in London and Sofia; Paris correspondent, Financial Times, 1956–60; Foreign Editor, Statist, 1961–64. MP (C): South Angus, 1964–Oct. 1974; Knutsford, March 1979–1983; PPS to Secretary of State for Scotland, 1970–72; Minister of State, HM Treasury, 1981; Economic Sec. to HM Treasury, 1981–83. Vice-Chm., Cons. Parly Finance Cttee, 1972–74, 1979–80. Columnist, Sunday Telegraph, 1979–81, 1984–; editorial writer, Daily Telegraph, 1977–81, 1984–. Consultant, Northern Engineering Industries, 1979–81, 1985–. Director: Central Trustee Savings Bank, 1983–; Trustee Savings Bank plc, 1985–; London & Northern Gp plc, 1985–. *Publications:* Whatever happened to the Quiet Revolution?, 1974; Scotland in 1980, 1975; (with Nigel Lawson) The Power Game, 1976; Mrs Thatcher's First Administration: the prophets confounded, 1984. *Address:* 13 Kelso Place, W8; Aswardby Old Rectory, Spilsby, Lincolnshire.

BRUCE LOCKHART, John Macgregor, CB 1966; CMG 1951; OBE 1944; *b* 9 May 1914; *e s* of late John Harold Bruce Lockhart and Mona Brougham; *m* 1939, Margaret Evelyn, *d* of late Rt Rev. C. R. Hone; two *s* one *d. Educ:* Rugby School; St Andrews University (Harkness Scholar). MA 2nd Class Hons Modern Languages, 1937. Asst Master, Rugby School, 1937–39; TA Commission, Seaforth Highlanders, 1938; served War of 1939–45, in UK, Middle East, North Africa, Italy (Lt-Col); Asst Military Attaché, British Embassy, Paris, 1945–47; Control Commission Germany, 1948–51; First Secretary, British Embassy, Washington, 1951–53; served Foreign Office, London, until resignation from the Diplomatic Service, 1965; in charge of planning and development, Univ. of Warwick, 1965–67; Head of Central Staff Dept, Courtaulds Ltd, 1967–71. Pres., Rugby Football Club, 1972–76. Advisor on Post Experience Programme, City Univ. Business Sch., 1971–80 (Hon. Fellow, City Univ., 1980); Chm., Business Educn Council, 1974–80; Member: Schools Council, 1975–80; Naval Educn Adv. Cttee, 1973–80; London and Home Counties Regional Management Council, 1973–80 (Founder Mem.). Vis. Scholar, St Andrews Univ., 1981–82; Vis. Lectr, Rand Africaans Univ., 1983.

Publications: articles and lectures on strategic studies at RCDS, RUSI, Kennedy Inst. of Politics, Harvard and Georgetown Univ., Washington, DC. *Recreations:* music, real tennis, golf, pictures. *Address:* 37 Fair Meadow, Rye, Sussex. *Clubs:* Reform; Rye Dormy.

BRUCE LOCKHART, Logie, MA; Headmaster of Gresham's School, Holt, 1955–82; *b* 12 Oct. 1921; *s* of late John Harold Bruce Lockhart; *m* 1944, Josephine Agnew; two *s* two *d* (and one *d* decd). *Educ:* Sedbergh School; St John's College, Cambridge (Schol. and Choral Studentship). RMC Sandhurst, 1941; served War of 1939–45; 9th Sherwood Foresters, 1942; 2nd Household Cavalry (Life Guards), 1944–45. Larmor Award, 1947; Asst Master, Tonbridge School, 1947–55. Sponsor, Nat. Council for Educnl Standards. *Publication:* The Pleasures of Fishing, 1981. *Recreations:* fishing, writing, music, natural history, games; Blue for Rugby football, 1945, 1946, Scottish International, 1948, 1950, 1953; squash for Cambridge, 1946. *Address:* Church Farm House, Holt, Norfolk. *T:* Holt 2137. *Club:* East India, Devonshire, Sports and Public Schools.

BRUCE LOCKHART, Rab Brougham, MA Cantab; Headmaster, Loretto School, Musselburgh, Edinburgh, 1960–76; *b* 1 Dec. 1916; *s* of late J. H. Bruce Lockhart; *m* 1941, Helen Priscilla Lawrence Crump; one *s* one *d* (and one *s* decd). *Educ:* Edinburgh Academy; Corpus Christi College, Cambridge. BA (Mod. Lang.) 1939; MA 1946. Assistant Master, Harrow, 1939. Served War of 1939–45: Commissioned RA, 1940; Middle East, 1942–44; Major RA 1944; Intelligence, Italy and Austria, 1945. Assistant Master, Harrow, 1946–50; Housemaster, Appleby College, Oakville, Ont, Canada, 1950–54; Headmaster, Wanganui Collegiate School, Wanganui, New Zealand, 1954–60. *Recreations:* squash, golf and photography; formerly: a Scotland cricket XI, 1935; Scotland XV, 1937, 1939; Rugby "Blue" 1937, 1938. *Address:* Saul Hill, Burneside, near Kendal, Cumbria. *T:* Selside 646.

BRUCE-MITFORD, Rupert Leo Scott, FBA 1976; Research Keeper in the British Museum, 1975–77 (Keeper of British and Mediæval Antiquities, 1954–69, of Mediæval and Later Antiquities, 1969–75); *b* 14 June 1914; 4th *s* of C. E. Bruce-Mitford, Madras, and Beatrice (Allison), *e d* of John Fall, British Columbia; *m* 1st, 1941, Kathleen Dent (marr. diss. 1972); one *s* two *d*; 2nd, 1975, Marilyn Roberta (marr. diss. 1984), *o d* of Robert J. Luscombe, Walton on the Hill, Staffs. *Educ:* Christ's Hospital; Hertford College, Oxford (Baring Scholar; Hon. Fellow, 1984). Temp. Asst Keeper, Ashmolean Museum, 1937; Asst Keeper, Dept of British and Mediæval Antiquities, British Museum, 1938; Royal Signals, 1939–45; Deputy Keeper, British Museum, 1954. FSA 1947 (Sec., Soc. of Antiquaries, 1950–54, Vice-Pres., 1972–76); FSA Scot. Slade Professor of Fine Art, Univ. of Cambridge, 1978–79. Vis. Fellow, All Souls Coll., Oxford, 1978–79; Professorial Fellow, Emmanuel Coll., Cambridge, 1978–79; Faculty Visitor, Dept of English, ANU, Canberra, 1981. Excavations: Seacourt, Berks, 1938–39; Mawgan Porth, Cornwall, 1949–54; Chapter House graves, Lincoln Cathedral, 1955; Sutton Hoo, Suffolk, 1965–68. Pres., Soc. for Mediæval Archæol., 1957–59. Member: Ancient Monuments Bd, England, 1954–77; Perm. Council, Internat. Congress of Prehistoric and Protohistoric Scis, 1957–79; German Archæological Inst.; Italian Inst. of Prehistory and Protohistory; Corresp. Member, Jutland Archæological Society; Hon. Mem., Suffolk Inst. of Archaeology; For. Corresp. Mem., Acad. du Var. For. Trustee, Instituto de Valencia de Don Juan, Madrid, 1954–75. Lectures: Dalrymple, Glasgow, 1961; Thomas Davis Radio, Dublin, 1964; Jarrow, 1967; O'Donnell, Wales, 1971; Garmonsway, York, 1973; Crake, Mount Allison Univ., NB, 1980. Liveryman, Worshipful Co. of Clockmakers. Hon. LittD Dublin 1966. *Publications:* The Society of Antiquaries of London; Notes on its History and Possessions (with others), 1952; Editor and contributor, Recent Archæological Excavations in Britain, 1956; (with T. J. Brown, A. S. C. Ross and others), Codex Lindisfarnensis (Swiss facsimile edn), 1957–61; (trans. from Danish) The Bog People, by P. V. Glob, 1969; The Sutton Hoo Ship-burial, a handbook, 1972, revd edn 1979; Aspects of Anglo-Saxon Archaeology, 1974; The Sutton Hoo Ship-burial, Vol. I, 1975, Vol. II, 1978, Vol. III, 1983; (ed) Recent Archaeological Excavations in Europe, 1975; papers and reviews in learned journals. *Recreations:* reading, chess, watching sport, travel. *Address:* 12 Cambray Place, Cheltenham, Glos GL50 1JS. *Clubs:* Athenæum, Garrick, MCC.

BRÜCK, Prof. Hermann Alexander, CBE 1966; DPhil (Munich); PhD (Cantab); Astronomer Royal for Scotland and Regius Professor of Astronomy in the University of Edinburgh, 1957–75; now Professor Emeritus; Dean of the Faculty of Science, 1968–70; *b* 15 Aug. 1905; *s* of late H. H. Brück; *m* 1st, 1936, Irma Waitzfelder (*d* 1950); one *s* one *d*; 2nd, 1951, Dr Mary T. Conway; one *s* two *d*. *Educ:* Augusta Gymnasium, Charlottenburg; Universities of Bonn, Kiel, Munich, and Cambridge. Astronomer, Potsdam Astrophysical Observatory, 1928; Lectr, Berlin University, 1935; Research Associate, Vatican Observatory, Castel Gandolfo, 1936; Asst Observer, Solar Physics Observatory, Cambridge, 1937; John Couch Adams Astronomer, Cambridge University, 1943; Asst Director, Cambridge Observatory, 1946; Director, Dunsink Observatory and Professor of Astronomy, Dublin Institute for Advanced Studies, 1947–57. Mem., Bd of Governors, Armagh Observatory, NI, 1971–84. MRIA, 1948; FRSE, 1958; Member Pontif. Academy of Sciences, Rome, 1955, Mem. Council, 1964–86; Corr. Member Academy of Sciences, Mainz, 1955. Hon. DSc: NUI, 1972; St Andrews, 1973. *Publications* (ed jtly) Astrophysical Cosmology, 1982; The Story of Astronomy in Edinburgh, 1983; scientific papers in journals and observatory publications. *Recreation:* music. *Address:* Craigower, Penicuik, Midlothian EH26 9LA. *T:* Penicuik 75918. *Club:* New (Edinburgh).

BRUDENELL-BRUCE, family name of **Marquess of Ailesbury.**

BRUFORD, Walter Horace, MA; FBA 1963; *b* Manchester, 1894; *s* of Francis J. and Annie Bruford; *m* 1925, Gerda (*d* 1976), *d* of late Professor James Hendrick; one *s* two *d*. *Educ:* Manchester Grammar School; St John's College, Cambridge; University of Zürich. BA Cambridge, 1915 (1st Class Hons Med. and Mod. Langs). Bendall Sanskrit Exhibitioner; Master Manchester Grammar School; served Intelligence Division, Admiralty, with rank of Lieut RNVR. On demobilisation, research in University of Zürich; Lecturer in German, University of Aberdeen, 1920, Reader, 1923; Professor of German, University of Edinburgh, 1929–51. Seconded to Foreign Office, 1939–43. Schröder Professor of German, University of Cambridge, 1951–61. Corresponding member Deutsche Akademie für Sprache und Dichtung, 1957; Goethe-Medal in Gold, of Goethe-Institut, Munich, 1958; President: Mod. Lang. Assoc., 1959; Mod. Humanities Research Assoc., 1965; English Goethe Soc., 1965–75; Corresponding Member, Sächsische Akademie der Wissenschaften, Leipzig, 1965. Hon. LLD Aberdeen, 1958; Hon. DLitt: Newcastle, 1969; Edinburgh, 1974. *Publications:* Sound and Symbol (with Professor J. J. Findlay); Germany in the eighteenth century; Die gesellschaftlichen Grundlagen der Goethezeit; Chekhov and His Russia: two chapters in Essays on Goethe (ed. by W. Rose); Theatre, Drama and Audience in Goethe's Germany; Literary Interpretation in Germany; Goethe's Faust (introd., revised and annotated, Everyman's Library); Chekhov (Studies in Modern European Literature and Thought); The Organisation and Rise of Prussia and German Constitutional and Social Development, 1795–1830 (in Cambridge Modern History, New Series, Vols VII and IX); Culture and Society in Classical Weimar; Deutsche Kultur der Goethezeit; Annotated edition and interpretation of Goethe's Faust, Part I; The German Tradition of Self-Cultivation: *Bildung* from Humboldt to Thomas Mann; articles and reviews in modern language periodicals. *Address:* The Old Vicarage, East Horrington,

Wells, Somerset.
See also H. St J. B. Armitage.

BRUINVELS, Peter Nigel Edward; MP (C) Leicester East, since 1983; management consultant; Director, Aalco Nottingham Ltd, since 1983; *b* 30 March 1950; *er s* of Stanley and Ninette Maud Bruinvels; *m* 1980, Alison Margaret, *o d* of Major David Gilmore Bacon, RA retd; one *d*. *Educ:* St John's Sch., Leatherhead; London Univ. (LLB Hons). Bar Exams, Council of Legal Educn. Co. Sec., BPC Publishing, 1978–81; Asst Sec./Lawyer, Amari PLC, 1981–82; Management Consultant, 1982–. Chairman: Law Students Cons. Assoc. of GB, 1974–76; SE Area Young Conservatives, 1977–79; Dorking CPC, 1979–83; Mem., Cons. Nat. Union Exec., 1977–79; President: Leicester Univ. Cons. Assoc., 1982–; Leics YCs, 1984–. Jt Chm., British Parly Lighting Gp; Vice-Chm., Cons. Backbench Cttee on Urban Affairs and New Towns, 1984– (Jt Sec., 1983–84); Jt Sec., Cons. Backbench Cttee on Education, 1984–; Sec., Anglo-Netherlands Parly Gp, 1983–; Chm., British-Malta Parly Gp, 1984– (Treas., 1983); Member: Cons. Backbench Cttee on Home Affairs, 1983–; Cons. Backbench Cttee on NI, 1983–; Life Mem., British-Amer. Parly Gp, 1983. Sponsor, Cons. Family Campaign, 1986; Founder Chm., Law and Order Soc. of GB, 1985. Member of Court: Univ. of Leicester, 1983–; Univ. of Loughborough, 1983–. Member: Guildford Dio. Synod 1979–; Gen. Synod, 1985–; Bishop's Council, 1985–. MBIM 1981; MIPR 1981; FRSA 1986. Fellow, Industry and Parliament Trust. Granted Freedom, City of London, 1980–. *Publications:* (jtly) Zoning in on Enterprise, 1982; (jtly) Light up the Roads, 1984. *Recreations:* politics (holding my seat), Church of England. *Address:* House of Commons, SW1. *T:* 01–219 6251; 10 Eccleshill, North Holmwood, Surrey. *Clubs:* Carlton, Inner Temple; Leicestershire Far and Near (Leicester).

BRULLER, Jean; *see* Vercors.

BRUNA, Dick; graphic designer; writer and illustrator of children's books; *b* 23 Aug. 1927; *s* of A. W. Bruna and J. C. C. Erdbrink; *m* 1953, Irene de Jongh; two *s* one *d*. *Educ:* Primary Sch. and Gymnasium, Utrecht, Holland; autodidact. Designer of book jackets, 1945–, and of posters, 1947– (many prizes); writer and illustrator of children's books, 1953– (1st book, The Apple); also designer of postage stamps, murals, greeting cards and picture postcards. Exhibn based on Miffy (best-known character in children's books), Gemeentemuseum, Arnhem, 1977. Member: Netherlands Graphic Designers; Authors League of America Inc.; PEN Internat.; Alliance Graphique Internat. *Publications:* 50 titles published and 40 million copies printed by 1983; children's books translated into 28 languages. *Address:* (studio) 3 Jeruzalemstraat, Utrecht. *T:* 030–316042. *Club:* Art Directors (Netherlands).

BRUNDIN, Clark Lannerdahl; PhD; Vice Chancellor, University of Warwick, since 1985; *b* 21 March 1931; *s* of late Ernest Walfrid Brundin and of Elinor Brundin (*née* Clark); *m* 1959, Judith Anne (*née* Maloney); two *s* two *d*. *Educ:* Whittier High Sch., California; California Inst. of Technology; Univ. of California, Berkeley (BSc, PhD); MA Oxford. Electronics Petty Officer, US Navy, 1951–55. Associate in Mech. Engrg, UC Berkeley, 1956–57; Demonstr. Dept of Engrg Science, Univ. of Oxford, 1957–58; Res. Engr, Inst. of Engrg Res., UC Berkeley, 1959–63; Univ. Lectr, Dept of Engrg Sci., Univ. of Oxford, 1963–85, Vice-Chm., Gen. Bd of the Faculties, 1984–85; Jesus College, Oxford: Fellow and Tutor in Engrg, 1964–85; Sen. Tutor, 1974–77; Estates Bursar, 1978–84; Hon. Fellow, 1985. Vis. Prof., Univ. of Calif Santa Barbara, 1978. Chm., Anchor Housing Assoc., 1985–. *Publications:* articles on rarefied gas dynamics in sci. lit. *Recreations:* sailing, mending old machinery, music of all sorts. *Address:* University of Warwick, Coventry CV4 7AL. *T:* Coventry 523630. *Clubs:* Royal Fowey Yacht, Fowey Gallants Sailing (Fowey, Cornwall).

BRUNEI, HM Sultan of; *see* Negara Brunei Darussalam.

BRUNER, Jerome Seymour, MA, PhD; Watts Professor of Psychology, University of Oxford, 1972–80; G. H. Mead University Professor, New School for Social Research, New York; Fellow, New York Institute for the Humanities; *b* New York, 1 Oct. 1915; *s* of Herman and Rose Bruner; *m* 1st, 1940, Katherine Frost (marr. diss. 1956); one *s* one *d*; 2nd, 1960, Blanche Marshall McLane (marr. diss. 1984). *Educ:* Duke Univ. (AB 1937): Harvard Univ. (AM 1939, PhD 1941). US Intelligence, 1941; Assoc. Dir, Office Public Opinion Research, Princeton, 1942–44; govt public opinion surveys on war problems, 1942–43; political intelligence, France, 1943; Harvard University: research, 1945–72; Prof. of Psychology, 1952–72; Dir, Centre for Cognitive Studies, 1961–72. Lectr, Salzburg Seminar, 1952; Bacon Prof., Univ. of Aix-en-Provence, 1965. Editor, Public Opinion Quarterly, 1943–44; Syndic, Harvard Univ. Press, 1962–63. Member: Inst. Advanced Study, 1951; White House Panel on Educnl Research and Develt. Guggenheim Fellow, Cambridge Univ., 1955; Fellow: Amer. Psychol. Assoc. (Pres., 1964–65) (Distinguished Scientific Contrib. award, 1962); Amer. Acad. Arts and Sciences; Swiss Psychol Soc. (hon.); Soc. Psychol Study Social Issues (past Pres.); Amer. Assoc. Univ. Profs; Puerto Rican Acad. Arts and Sciences (hon.). Hon. DHL Lesley Coll., 1964; Hon. DSc: Northwestern Univ., 1965; Sheffield, 1970; Bristol, 1975; Hon. MA, Oxford, 1972; Hon. DSocSci, Yale, 1975; Hon. LLD: Temple Univ., 1965; Univ. of Cincinnati, 1966; Univ. of New Brunswick, 1969; Hon. DLitt: North Michigan Univ., 1969; Duke Univ., 1969; Dr *hc*: Sorbonne, 1974; Leuven, 1976; Ghent, 1977. *Publications:* Mandate from the People, 1944; (with Krech) Perception and Personality: A Symposium, 1950; (with Goodnow and Austin) A Study of Thinking, 1956; (with Smith and White) Opinions and Personality, 1956; (with Bresson, Morf and Piaget) Logique et Perception, 1958; The Process of Education, 1960; On Knowing: Essays for the Left Hand, 1962; (ed) Learning about Learning: A conference report, 1966; (with Olver, Greenfield, and others) Studies in Cognitive Growth, 1966; Toward a Theory of Instruction, 1966; Processes of Cognitive Growth: Infancy, Vol III, 1968; The Relevance of Education, 1971; (ed Anglin) Beyond the Information Given: selected papers of Jerome S. Bruner, 1973; (with Connolly) The Growth of Competence, 1974; (with Jolly and Sylva) Play: its role in evolution and development, 1976; Under Five in Britain, 1980; Communication as Language, 1982; In Search of Mind: essays in autobiography, 1983; Child's Talk, 1983; Actual Minds, Possible Worlds, 1986; contribs technical and professional jls. *Recreation:* sailing. *Address:* 200 Mercer Street, New York, NY 10012, USA. *Clubs:* Royal Cruising, Cruising Club of America.

BRUNNER, Dr Guido; Grand Cross, Order of Federal Republic of Germany; German diplomat and politician; Ambassador of the Federal Republic of Germany in Madrid, since 1982; *b* Madrid, 27 May 1930; *m* 1958, Christa (*née* Speidel). *Educ:* Bergzabern, Munich; German Sch., Madrid; Univs of Munich, Heidelberg and Madrid (law and econs). LLD Munich; Licentiate of Law Madrid. Diplomatic service, 1955–74, 1981–; Private Office of the Foreign Minister, 1956; Office, Sec. of State for For. Affairs, 1958–60; German Observer Mission to the UN, New York, 1960–68; Min. for Foreign Affairs: Dept of scientific and technol relns, 1968–70; Spokesman, 1970–72; Head of Planning Staff, Ambassador and Head of Delegn of Fed. Rep. of Germany, Conf. for Security and Coop. in Europe, Helsinki/Geneva, 1972–74; Mem., Commn of the European Communities, (responsible for Energy, Research, Science and Educn), 1974–80; Mem.,

Bundestag, 1980–81; Mayor of Berlin and Minister of Economics and Transport, Jan.-May 1981; Ambassador, Min. of Foreign Affairs, Bonn, 1981–82. Hon. DLitt Heriot-Watt, 1977; Dr *hc*; Technical Faculty, Patras Univ., Greece: City Univ., London, 1980. Melchett Medal, Inst. of Energy, 1978. Grand Cross, Order of Civil Merit, Spain, 1978; Grand Cross, Order of Leopold, Belgium, 1981; Grand Cross, Order of Merit, FRG, 1981; Grand Cross, Order of Isabel la Católica, Spain, 1986. *Publications:* Bipolarität und Sicherheit, 1965; Friedenssicherungsaktionen der Vereinten Nationen, 1968; Stolz wie Don Rodrigo, 1982; contrib. Vierteljahreshefte für Zeitgeschichte, Aussenpolitik, Europa-Archiv. *Address:* Embajada de la República Federal de Alemania, C/Fortuny 8, 28010 Madrid, Spain.

BRUNNER, Sir John Henry Kilian, 4th Bt *cr* 1895; *b* 1 June 1927; *s* of Sir Felix John Morgan Brunner, 3rd Bt, and of Dorothea Elizabeth, OBE, *d* of late Henry Brodribb Irving; *S* father, 1982; *m* 1955, Jasmine Cecily, *d* of late John Wardrop Moore; two *s* one *d*. *Educ:* Eton; Trinity Coll., Oxford (BA 1950). Served as Lieut RA. On staff, PEP, 1950–53; Talks producer, 1953; Economic Adviser, Treasury, 1958–61; Asst Manager, Observer, 1961. *Heir: s* Nicholas Felix Minturn Brunner, *b* 16 Jan. 1960. *Address:* 13 Glyndon Avenue, Brighton, Vic 3186, Australia.

BRUNSKILL, Ronald William, MA, PhD; FSA; architect, lecturer and author; Reader in Architecture, University of Manchester, since 1984 (Lecturer, 1960–73, Senior Lecturer, 1973–84); *b* 3 Jan. 1929; *s* of William Brunskill and Elizabeth Hannah Brunskill; *m* 1960, Miriam Allsopp; two *d*. *Educ:* Bury High Sch.; Univ. of Manchester (BA Hons Arch. 1951, MA 1952, PhD 1963). Registered Architect and ARIBA, 1951; FSA 1975. National Service, 2nd Lieut RE, 1953–55. Studio Asst in Arch., Univ. of Manchester, 1951–53; Architectural Asst, LCC, 1955; Asst in Arch., Univ. of Manchester, 1955–56; Commonwealth Fund Fellow (arch. and town planning), MIT, 1956–57; Architect to Williams Deacon's Bank, 1957–60; Architect in private practice, 1960–66; Partner, Carter, Brunskill & Associates, chartered architects, 1966–69, Consultant, 1969–73. Vis. Prof., Univ. of Florida, Gainesville, 1969–70. Pres., Vernacular Arch. Gp, 1974–77; Vice-President: Cumberland and Westmorland Antiquarian and Archaeol Soc., 1975–; Weald and Downland Museum Trust, 1980–; Member: Historic Bldgs Council for England, 1978–84; Historic Buildings Adv. Cttee and Ancient Monuments Adv. Cttee of Historic Buildings and Monuments Commn, 1984–; Royal Commn on Ancient and Historical Monuments of Wales, 1983–; Council, Ancient Monuments Soc., 1975– (Hon. Architect, 1983–); Cathedrals Adv. Commn for England, 1981–; Manchester Diocesan Adv. Cttee for Care of Churches, 1973–79; Council, Soc. for Folk Life Studies, 1969–72 and 1980–83. Trustee, British Historic Buildings Trust, 1985–. Neale Bursar, RIBA, 1962; President's Award, Manchester Soc. of Architects, 1977. *Publications:* Illustrated Handbook of Vernacular Architecture, 1971, 3rd edn (enlarged) 1985; Vernacular Architecture of the Lake Counties, 1974; (with Alec Clifton-Taylor) English Brickwork, 1977; Traditional Buildings of Britain, 1981; Houses (in series, Collins Archaeology), 1982; Traditional Farm Buildings of Britain, 1982; Timber Building in Britain, 1985; articles and reviews in archaeol and architectural jls. *Recreation:* enjoying the countryside. *Address:* Three Trees, 8 Overhill Road, Wilmslow SK9 2BE. *T:* Wilmslow 522099; 159 Glan Gors, Harlech, Gwynedd LL46 2SA.

BRUNT, Peter Astbury, FBA 1969; Camden Professor of Ancient History, Oxford University, and Fellow of Brasenose College, 1970–82; *b* 23 June 1917; *s* of Rev. Samuel Brunt, Methodist Minister, and Gladys Eileen Brunt. *Educ:* Ipswich Sch.; Oriel Coll., Oxford. Open Schol. in History, Oriel Coll., Oxford, 1935; first classes in Class. Mods, 1937, and Lit. Hum., 1939; Craven Fellowship, 1939. Temp. Asst Principal and (later) Temp. Principal, Min. of Shipping (later War Transport), 1940–45. Sen. Demy, Magdalen Coll., Oxford, 1946; Lectr in Ancient History, St Andrews Univ., 1947–51; Fellow and Tutor of Oriel Coll., Oxford, 1951–67, Dean, 1959–64, Hon. Fellow, 1973; Fellow and Sen. Bursar, Gonville and Caius Coll., Cambridge, 1968–70. Editor of Oxford Magazine, 1963–64; Chm., Cttee on Ashmolean Museum, 1967; Deleg., Clarendon Press, 1971–79; Mem. Council, British Sch. at Rome, 1972–; Pres., Soc. for Promotion of Roman Studies, 1980–83. *Publications:* Thucydides (selections in trans. with introd.), 1963; Res Gestae Divi Augusti (with Dr J. M. Moore), 1967; Social Conflicts in the Roman Republic, 1971; Italian Manpower 225 BC-AD 14, 1971; ed, Arrian's Anabasis (Loeb Classical Library), vol. I, 1976, vol. II, 1983; articles in classical and historical jls. *Address:* 34 Manor Road, South Hinksey, Oxford. *T:* Oxford 739923.

BRUNT, Peter William, MD, FRCP, FRCPE; Physician to the Queen in Scotland, since 1983; Consultant Physician and Gastroenterologist, Grampian Health Board, Aberdeen, since 1970; Clinical Senior Lecturer in Medicine, University of Aberdeen, since 1970; *b* 18 Jan. 1936; *s* of Harry Brunt and Florence J. J. Airey; *m* 1961, Dr Anne Lewis, *d* of Rev. R. H. Lewis; three *d*. *Educ:* Manchester Grammar Sch.; Cheadle Hulme Sch.; King George V Sch.; Univ. of Liverpool. MB, ChB 1959. Gen. Med. training, Liverpool Royal Infirmary and Liverpool Hosps, 1959–64; Research Fellow, Johns Hopkins Univ. Sch. of Medicine, 1965–67; Lectr in Medicine, Edinburgh Univ., 1967–68; Senior Registrar, Gastrointestinal Unit, Western Gen. Hosp., Edinburgh, 1968–69. Hon. Lectr in Medicine, Royal Free Hosp. Sch. of Medicine, Univ. of London, 1969–70. Mem., Assoc. of Physicians of GB and Ireland. *Publications:* (with M. Losowsky and A. E. Read) Diseases of the Liver and Biliary System, 1984; (with P. F. Jones and N. A. G. Mowat) Gastroenterology, 1984. *Recreations:* mountaineering, music, operatics, Crusaders' Union. *Address:* 17 Kingshill Road, Aberdeen AB2 4JY. *T:* Aberdeen 314204.

BRUNTISFIELD, 1st Baron, *cr* 1942, of Boroughmuir; **Victor Alexander George Anthony Warrender,** MC 1918; 8th Bt of Lochend, East Lothian, *cr* 1715; late Grenadier Guards; *b* 23 June 1899; *s* of 7th Bt and Lady Maud Warrender (*d* 1945), *y d* of 8th Earl of Shaftesbury; *S* to father's Baronetcy, 1917; *m* 1920, Dorothy (marr. diss. 1945), *y d* of late Colonel R. H. Rawson, MP, and Lady Beatrice Rawson; three *s*; *m* 1948, Tania, *yr d* of late Dr Kolin, St Jacob, Dubrovnik, Jugoslavia; one *s* one *d*. *Educ:* Eton. Served European War, 1917–18 (MC, Russian Order of St Stanislas, Star of Roumania, St Ann of Russia with sword); MP (U) Grantham Division of Kesteven and Rutland, 1923–42; an assistant Whip, 1928–31; Junior Lord of the Treasury, 1931–32; Vice-Chamberlain of HM Household, 1932–35; Comptroller of HM Household, 1935; Parliamentary and Financial Secretary to Admiralty, 1935; Financial Secretary, War Office, 1935–40; Parliamentary and Financial Secretary, Admiralty, 1940–42; Parliamentary Secretary, Admiralty, 1942–45. *Heir: s* Col Hon. John Robert Warrender, *qv*. *Address:* Chalet les Pommiers, 3780 Gstaad, OB, Switzerland. *T:* 030 42384. *Club:* Turf.

See also Lord Reay, Hon. R. H. Warrender.

BRUNTON, Sir (Edward Francis) Lauder, 3rd Bt, *cr* 1908; Physician; *b* 10 Nov. 1916; *s* of Sir Stopford Brunton, 2nd Bt, and Elizabeth, *o d* of late Professor J. Bonsall Porter; *S* father 1943; *m* 1946, Marjorie, *o d* of David Sclater Lewis, MSc, MD, CM, FRCP (C); one *s* one *d*. *Educ:* Trinity College School, Port Hope; Bryanston School; McGill Univ. BSc 1940; MD, CM 1942; served as Captain, RCAMC. Hon. attending Physician, Royal Victoria Hosp., Montreal. Fellow: American Coll. of Physicians; Internat. Soc. of Hematology; Member American Society of Hematology; Life Mem., Montreal Mus. of Fine Arts. *Heir: s* James Lauder Brunton, MD, FRCP(C) [*b* 24 Sept. 1947; *m* 1967, Susan, *o d* of Charles Hons; one *s* one *d*]. *Address:* PO Box 140, Guysborough, Nova Scotia, Canada. *Club:* Royal Nova Scotia Yacht Squadron.

BRUNTON, Sir Gordon (Charles), Kt 1985; Chairman: Bemrose Corporation plc, since 1978; Martin Currie Pacific Trust plc, since 1985; The Racing Post plc, since 1985; Euram Consulting Ltd, since 1985; John Silver Holdings Ltd, since 1985; Community Industry Ltd, since 1985; Communications and General Consultants Ltd, since 1985; Mercury Communications, since 1986; *b* 27 Dec. 1921; *s* of late Charles Arthur Brunton and late Hylda Pritchard; *m* 1st, 1946, Nadine Lucile Paula Sohr (marr. diss. 1965); one *s* two *d* (and one *s* decd); 2nd, 1966, Gillian Agnes Kirk; one *s* one *d*. *Educ:* Cranleigh Sch.; London Sch. of Economics. Commnd into RA, 1942; served Indian Army, Far East; Mil. Govt, Germany, 1946. Joined Tothill Press, 1947; Exec. Dir, Tothill, 1956; Man. Dir, Tower Press Gp of Cos, 1958; Exec. Dir, Odhams Press, 1961; joined Thomson Organisation, 1961; Man. Dir, Thomson Publications, 1961; Dir, Thomson Organisation, 1963; Chm., Thomson Travel, 1965–68; Man. Dir and Chief Exec., Internat. Thomson Orgn plc (formerly Thomson British Hldgs) and The Thomson Orgn Ltd, 1968–84; Pres., Internat. Thomson Orgn Ltd, 1978–84. Director: Times Newspapers Ltd, 1967–81; Sotheby Parke Bernet Group, 1978–83 (Chm., 1982–83, Chm. Emeritus, Sotheby's Holding Inc., 1983); Cable and Wireless plc, 1981–; Yattendon Investment Trust Ltd, 1985–; Sports Bureau Internat. Ltd, 1985–; Dir of other printing and publishing cos. President: Periodical Publishers Assoc., 1972–74, 1981–83; Nat. Advertising Benevolent Soc., 1973–75 (Trustee, 1980–); History of Advertising Trust, 1981–84 (Vice Pres., 1985–); Chm., EDC for Civil Engrg, 1978–84; Member: Printing and Publishing Ind. Trng Bd, 1974–78; Supervisory Bd, CBI Special Programmes Unit, 1980–84; Business in the Community Council, 1981–84; Chm., Independent Adoption Service, 1986–. Mem., South Bank Bd, Arts Council, 1985–. Governor: LSE (Fellow, 1978); Ashridge Management Coll., 1983–86; Ct of Governors, Henley—The Management Coll., 1983–85; Mem. Council, Templeton College (formerly Oxford Centre for Management Studies), 1976–; Mem., Finance Cttee, OUP, 1985–. *Recreations:* books, breeding horses. *Address:* North Munstead, Godalming, Surrey. *T:* Godalming 6313. *Club:* Garrick.

BRUNTON, Sir Lauder; *see* Brunton, Sir E. F. L.

BRUS, Prof. Wlodzimierz, PhD; Professor of Modern Russian and East European Studies, University of Oxford and Professorial Fellow, Wolfson College, since 1985; *b* 23 Aug. 1921; *s* of Abram Brus and Helena (*née* Askanas); *m* 1st, 1940, Helena Wolińska; 2nd, 1945, Irena Stergień; two *d*; 3rd, 1956, Helena Wolińska; one *s*. *Educ:* Saratov, USSR (MA Economic Planning); Warsaw, Poland (PhD Pol. Econ.). Polish Army, 1944–46. Junior Editor, Nowe Drogi (theoretical journal of Polish Workers' (later United Workers') Party), 1946–49; Asst (later Associate) Prof. of Political Economy, Central Sch. of Planning & Statistics, Warsaw, 1949–54; Hd of Dept of Political Economy, Inst. of Social Sciences attached to Central Cttee, Polish United Workers' Party, 1950–56; Prof. of Political Econ., Univ. of Warsaw, 1954–68; Dir, Research Bureau, Polish Planning Commn, 1956–68; Vice-Chm., Econ. Adv. Council of Poland, 1957–63; research worker, Inst. of Housing, Warsaw, 1968–72; Vis. Sen. Res. Fellow, Univ. of Glasgow, 1972–73; Sen. Res. Fellow, St Antony's Coll., Oxford, 1973–76; Univ. Lectr and Fellow, Wolfson Coll., Oxford, 1976–85. Visiting Professor (or Senior Fellow): Rome, 1971; Catholic Univ. of Louvain, 1973; Columbia, 1982; Johns Hopkins Bologna Centre, 1983. Consultant to World Bank, 1980–82, 1984. Officers' Cross, Order of Polonia Restituta, Poland, 1954; Polish and Soviet war medals, 1944, 1945. *Publications:* The Law of Value and Economic Incentives, 1956 (trans Hungarian, 1957); General Problems of Functioning of the Socialist Economy, 1961 (trans 10 langs); Economics and Politics of Socialism, 1973 (trans 6 langs); Socialist Ownership and Political Systems, 1975, 8th edn 1986; Economic History of Eastern Europe, 1983, 6th edn 1986; contribs to Soviet Studies, Jl of Comparative Economics, Cambridge Jl of Economics. *Recreations:* walking, swimming. *Address:* 21 Bardwell Court, Bardwell Road, Oxford OX2 6SX. *T:* Oxford 53790.

BRUTON, John (Gerard); TD (Fine Gael), Meath, Dáil Eireann (Parliament of Ireland), since 1969 and Minister for Finance, since 1986; *b* 18 May 1947; *s* of Matthew Joseph Bruton and Doris Bruton (*née* Delany); *m* 1981, Finola Gill; one *s* two *d*. *Educ:* St Dominic's Coll., Dublin; Clongowes Wood Coll., Co. Kildare; University Coll., Dublin (BA, BL); King's Inns, Dublin; called to the Bar, 1972. National Secretary, Fine Gael Youth Group, 1966–69. Mem., Dáil Committee of Procedure and Privileges, 1969–73, 1982–; Fine Gael Spokesman on Agriculture, 1972–73; Parliamentary Secretary: to Minister for Education, 1973–77; to Minister for Industry and Commerce, 1975–77; Fine Gael Spokesman: on Agriculture, 1977–81; on Finance, Jan.-June 1981; Minister: for Finance, 1981–82, for Industry and Energy, 1982–83, for Industry, Trade, Commerce and Tourism, 1983–86. Leader of the House, 1982–86. Pres., EEC internal Monetary, Industry, Research and Internal Market Controls, July–Dec. 1984. Hon. Citizen of Sioux City, Iowa, USA, 1970; Ambassador of Good Will, Hon. Dist. Citizen and Washington General, State of Washington, 1983; Calif. Legislature Assembly Rules Cttee and Calif. Senate Rules Cttee Commendations, 1983. *Publications:* Reform of the Dail, 1980; A Better Way to Plan the Nation's Finances, 1981; Industrial Policy—White Paper, 1984; Tourism Policy—White Paper, 1985; contrib. Furrow magazine. *Recreation:* reading history. *Address:* Department of Finance, Government Buildings, Upper Merrion Street, Dublin 2, Ireland. *T:* 767571; Cornelstown, Dunboyne, Co. Meath. *T:* 255573.

BRYAN, Sir Andrew (Meikle), Kt 1950; DSc; Hon. LLD (Glasgow); FEng, FIMinE, FICE, FRSE; Consulting Mining Engineer; Member of National Coal Board, 1951–57; *b* 1 March 1893; 2nd *s* of John Bryan, Burnbank, Hamilton, Lanarkshire; *m* 1st, 1922, Henrietta Paterson (*d* 1977), *y d* of George S. Begg, Allanshaw, Hamilton; one *s*; 2nd, 1980, Mrs Winifred Henderson Rutledge, widow. *Educ:* Greenfield School; Hamilton Acad.; Glasgow University, graduated 1919 with Special Distinction. Served in University OTC and HM Forces, 1915–18. Obtained practical mining experience in the Lanarkshire Coalfield; HM Junior Inspector of Mines in the Northern Division, 1920; Senior rank, 1926; Dixon Professor of Mining, University of Glasgow, Professor of Mining, Royal College of Science and Technology, Glasgow, 1932–40; Gen. Manager, 1940, Dir, 1942, Managing Director, 1944, Shotts Iron Co. Ltd; also Director Associated Lothian Coal Owners Ltd; Deputy Director of Mining Supplies, Mines Department, 1939–40; Chief Inspector of Mines, 1947–51. Mem. Council, IMinE (Hon. Treas.; Hon. Mem., 1957; Pres., 1950 and 1951; Inst. Medal, 1954); Mem., Mining Qualifications Bd, 1947–62, Chm., 1962–72; former Mem. Council, Inst. Mining and Metallurgy, 1951; Hon. Member: Nat. Assoc. of Colliery Managers, 1957 (Futers Gold Medal, 1937; former Mem. Council; Past Pres.); Geol Soc. of Edinburgh; former Mem. Council and Past Pres., Mining Inst. of Scotland; John Buddle Medal, N England Inst. of Mining and Mech. Engrs, 1967. Fellow, Imperial College of Science and Technology. *Publications:* St George's Coalfield, Newfoundland, 1937; The Evolution of Health and Safety in Mines, 1976; contribs to technical journals. *Address:* 3 Hounslow Gardens, Hounslow, Mddx TW3 2DU.

BRYAN, Sir Arthur, Kt 1976; Chairman, Wedgwood plc, Barlaston, Staffs, since 1968 (Managing Director, 1963–85); Lord-Lieutenant of Staffordshire, since 1968; *b* 4 March

1923; *s* of William Woodall Bryan and Isobel Alan (*née* Tweedie); *m* 1947, Betty Ratford; one *s* one *d*. *Educ:* Longton High Sch., Stoke-on-Trent. Served with RAFVR, 1941–45. Josiah Wedgwood & Sons Ltd, 1947–49; London Man., 1953–57; General Sales Man., 1959–60; Director and President, Josiah Wedgwood & Sons Inc. of America, 1960–62; Director: Josiah Wedgwood & Sons Ltd, Barlaston, 1962; Josiah Wedgwood & Sons (Canada) Ltd; Josiah Wedgwood & Sons (Australia) Pty Ltd; Phoenix Assurance Co., 1976–85; Friends' Provident Life Office, 1985–. Mem., BOTB, 1978–82 (Chm., N American Adv. Gp, 1973–82). Pres., British Ceramic Manufacturers' Fedn, 1970–71; Mem., Design Council, 1977–82. Mem. Ct, Univ. of Keele. FRSA 1964 (Mem. Council, 1980–82); Fellow, Inst. of Marketing (grad. 1950); CBIM (FBIM 1968); Comp. Inst. Ceramics. KStJ 1972. Hon. MUniv. Keele, 1978. *Recreations:* walking, tennis, swimming and reading. *Address:* Parkfields Cottage, Tittensor, Stoke-on-Trent, Staffs. *T:* Barlaston 2686.

BRYAN, Denzil Arnold, CMG 1960; OBE 1947; HM Diplomatic Service, retired; *b* 15 Oct. 1909; *s* of James Edward Bryan; *m* 1965, Hope Ross (*née* Meyer) (*d* 1981). *Educ:* in India; Selwyn Coll., Cambridge. Appointed to Indian Civil Service in 1933 and posted to Punjab. Dep. Commissioner, Hissar, 1938; Registrar, Lahore High Court, 1939–41; Dep. Comr, Dera Ghazi Khan, 1941–44; Sec. to Prime Minister, Punjab, 1944–47; and to Governor of Punjab, 1947; retired from ICS, 1947. Appointed to UK Civil Service, Bd of Trade, as Principal, 1947; Asst Sec., 1950; Under Secretary, 1961; served as a Trade Comr in India, 1947–55; UK Senior Trade Comr: in New Zealand, 1955–58; in Pakistan, 1958–61; in South Africa, 1961; Minister (Commercial, later Economic), S Africa, 1962–69. *Address:* 29 Wildcroft Manor, Wildcroft Road, SW15; c/o Lloyds Bank, 6 Pall Mall, SW1.

BRYAN, Dora, (Mrs William Lawton); actress; *b* 7 Feb. 1924; *d* of Albert Broadbent and Georgina (*née* Hill); *m* 1954, William Lawton; one *s* (and one *s* one *d* adopted). *Educ:* Hathershaw Council Sch., Lancs. Pantomimes: London Hippodrome, 1936; Manchester Palace, 1937; Alhambra, Glasgow, 1938; Oldham Repertory, 1939–44; followed by Peterborough, Colchester, Westcliff-on-Sea. ENSA, Italy, during War of 1939–45. Came to London, 1945, and appeared in West End Theatres: Peace in our Time; Travellers' Joy; Accolade; Lyric Revue; Globe Revue; Simon and Laura; The Water Gypsies; Gentlemen Prefer Blondes; Six of One; Too True to be Good; Hello, Dolly!; They Don't Grow on Trees; Rookery Nook, Her Majesty's, 1979; The Merry Wives of Windsor, Regent's Park, 1984. Chichester Festival seasons, 1971–74; London Palladium season, 1971; London Palladium Pantomime season, 1973–74. Has also taken parts in farces televised from Whitehall Theatre. *Films include:* The Fallen Idol, 1949; A Taste of Honey, 1961 (British Acad. Award); Two a Penny, 1968. *TV series:* appearances on A to Z; Sunday Night at the London Palladium; According to Dora, 1968; Both Ends Meet, 1972. Cabaret in Canada, Hong Kong and Britain. Has made recordings. *Recreations:* reading, patchwork quilts, helping husband and family who run hotel. *Address:* Clarges Hotel, Marine Parade, Brighton, East Sussex. *T:* Brighton 606551.

BRYAN, Gerald Jackson, CMG 1964; CVO 1966; OBE 1960; MC 1941; General Manager, Bracknell Development Corporation, 1973–82; *b* 2 April 1921; *yr s* of late George Bryan, OBE, LLD, and Ruby Evelyn (*née* Jackson), Belfast; *m* 1947, Georgiana Wendy Cockburn, OStJ, *d* of late William Barraud and Winnifred Hull; one *s* two *d*. *Educ:* Wrekin Coll.; RMA, Woolwich; New Coll., Oxford. Regular Commn, RE, 1940; served Middle East with No 11 (Scottish) Commando, 1941; retd 1944, Capt. (temp. Maj.). Apptd Colonial Service, 1944; Asst District Comr, Swaziland, 1944; Asst Colonial Sec., Barbados, 1950; Estabt Sec., Mauritius, 1954; Administrator, Brit. Virgin Is, 1959; Administrator of St Lucia, 1962–67, retired; Govt Sec. and Head of Isle of Man Civil Service, 1967–69; Gen. Man., Londonderry Develt Commn, NI, 1969–73. Dir, Lovaux Engrg Co. Ltd, 1982–; Sec. Gen., Assoc. of Contact Lens Manufacturers, 1983–. Mem. (C), Berks CC, 1983–85. Treasurer, Gordon Boys' Sch., Woking, 1979–; Chm., St John Council for Berks., 1981–. KStJ 1985. FBIM. *Recreation:* riding. *Address:* Whitehouse, Murrell Hill, Binfield, Berks; 30 Queen Street, Castletown, Isle of Man.

BRYAN, Margaret; HM Diplomatic Service; Ambassador to Panama, since 1986; *b* 26 Sept. 1929; *d* of late James Grant and Dorothy Rebecca Galloway; *m* 1952, Peter Bernard Bryan (marr. diss. 1981). *Educ:* Cathedral Sch., Shanghai; Croydon High Sch.; Girton Coll., Cambridge (MA Modern Languages). Second, later First, Secretary, FCO, 1962–80; Head of Chancery and Consul, Kinshasa, 1980–83; Counsellor, Havana, 1983–86. *Recreations:* theatre, travel, cookery, embroidery. *Address:* c/o Foreign and Commonwealth Office, SW1. *Club:* Royal Over-Seas League.

BRYAN, Sir Paul (Elmore Oliver), Kt 1972; DSO 1943; MC 1943; MP (C) Boothferry, since 1983 (Howden Division of Yorkshire (East Riding), 1955–83); *b* 3 Aug. 1913; *s* of Reverend Dr J. I. Bryan, PhD; *m* 1st, 1939, Betty Mary (*née* Hoyle) (*d* 1968); three *d*; 2nd, 1971, Cynthia Duncan (*née* Ashley Cooper), *d* of late Sir Patrick Ashley Cooper and of Lady Ashley Cooper, Hexton Manor, Herts. *Educ:* St John's School, Leatherhead (Scholar); Caius College, Cambridge (MA). War of 1939–45; 6th Royal West Kent Regt; enlisted, 1939; commissioned, 1940; Lieut-Col, 1943; served in France, N Africa, Sicily, Italy; Comdt 164th Inf. OCTU (Eaton Hall), 1944. Sowerby Bridge UDC, 1947; contested Sowerby, By-Election, 1948, and General Elections, 1950 and 1951. Member Parliamentary Delegation: to Peru, 1955, to Algeria, 1956, to Germany, 1960, to USA and Canada, 1961, to India, 1966, to Uganda and Kenya, 1967, to Hong Kong, 1969, to Japan and Indonesia, 1969, to China, 1972, to Mexico, 1981. Assistant Government Whip, 1956–58; Parliamentary Private Secretary to Minister of Defence, 1956; a Lord Commissioner of the Treasury, 1958–61; Vice-Chairman, Conservative Party Organisation, 1961–65; Conservative Front Bench Spokesman on Post Office and broadcasting, 1965; Minister of State, Dept of Employment, 1970–72. Chm., All Party Hong Kong Parly Gp, 1974–; Vice-Chm., Conservative 1922 Cttee, 1977–. Chm., Croydon Cable Television, 1985–; Director: Granada TV Rental Ltd, 1966–70; Granada Television, 1972–83; Granada Theatres, 1973–83; Greater Manchester Independent Radio Ltd, 1972–84; Maritime Union Assurance Co. (Bermuda) Ltd, 1980–; Scottish Lion Insurance Co. Ltd, 1981–; Hewetson Holdings Ltd, 1983–; Dep. Chm., Furness Withy and Co. Ltd, 1984– (Dir, 1983–). *Address:* Park Farm, Sawdon, near Scarborough, North Yorks. *T:* Scarborough 85370; 5 Westminster Gardens, Marsham Street, SW1. *T:* 01–834 2050.

BRYAN, Robert Patrick, OBE 1980; security consultant; Police Adviser to Foreign and Commonwealth Office, and Inspector General of Dependent Territories Police, 1980–85, retired; *b* 29 June 1926; *s* of Maurice Bryan and Elizabeth (*née* Waite); *m* 1948, Hazel Audrey (*née* Braine); three *s*. *Educ:* Plaistow Secondary Sch.; Wanstead County High Sch. Indian Army (Mahratta LI), 1944–47. Bank of Nova Scotia, 1948–49; Metropolitan Police: Constable, 1950; Dep. Asst Commissioner, 1977, retired 1980. National Police College: Intermediate Comd Course, 1965; Sen. Comd Course, 1969; occasional lecturer. RCDS 1974. Governor, Hampton Sch., 1978–. *Publications:* contribs to police and related pubns, particularly on community relations and juvenile delinquency. *Address:* c/o National Westminster Bank, High Street, Teddington, Mddx TW11 8EP.

BRYAN, Willoughby Guy, TD 1945; Director: Barclays Bank, 1957–81 (Vice-Chairman, 1964–70, Deputy Chairman, 1970–74); Barclays Bank Trust Company Ltd, 1970–81 (Chairman, 1970–74); Barclays Unicorn Group Ltd, 1977–81; *b* 16 Jan. 1911; *e s* of late C. R. W. Bryan; *m* 1936, Esther Victoria Loveday, *d* of late Major T. L. Ingram, DSO, MC; one *d*. *Educ:* Winchester; Hertford College, Oxford. Barclays Bank Ltd, 1932; various appointments including: Local Director, Oxford, 1946; Local Director, Reading, 1947; Local Director, Birmingham, 1955; Chm. Local Bd, Birmingham, 1957–64. Served War of 1939–45, Queen's Own Oxfordshire Hussars. *Recreation:* golf. *Address:* 28 Crooked Billet, Wimbledon Common, SW19 4RQ. *T:* 01–946 5645. *Clubs:* Army and Navy; Rye Golf, Royal Wimbledon Golf.

BRYANS, Dame Anne (Margaret), DBE 1957 (CBE 1945); DStJ; Chairman, Order of St John of Jerusalem and BRCS Service Hospitals Welfare and VAD Committee, since 1960; Vice-Chairman, Joint Committee, Order of St John and BRCS, 1976–81; *b* 29 Oct. 1909; *e d* of late Col Rt Hon. Sir John Gilmour, 2nd Bt, GCVO, DSO, MP of Montrave and late Mary Louise Lambert; *m* 1932, Lieut-Comdr J. R. Bryans, RN, retired; one *s*. *Educ:* privately. Joined HQ Staff British Red Cross Society, 1938; Deputy Commissioner British Red Cross and St John War Organisation, Middle East Commission, 1943; Commissioner Jan.-June 1945. Dep. Chm., 1953–64, Vice-Chm., 1964–76, Exec. Cttee, BRCS; Lay Mem., Council for Professions Supplementary to Med., to 1979; Member: Ethical practices Sub-Cttee, Royal Free Hosp., 1974–; Royal Free Hosp. Sch. Council, 1968–; Bd of Governors, Eastman Dental Hosp., 1973–79; Camden and Islington AHA, 1974–79; Vice-Pres., Open Sect., RSocMed, 1975, Pres. 1980–82; former Member: ITA, later IBA; Govt Anglo-Egyptian Resettlement Bd; BBC/ITA Appeals Cttee; Med. Sch. St George's Hosp.; Special Trustee and former Chm., Royal Free Hosp. and Friends of Royal Free Hosp.; former Chairman: Bd of Governors, Royal Free Hosp.; Council, Florence Nightingale Hosp.; Trustee, Florence Nightingale Aid in Sickness Trust, 1979–; Vice-Pres., Royal Coll. of Nursing; former Governor, Westminster Hosp. FRSM 1976. *Address:* 57 Elm Park House, Elm Park Gardens, SW10. *Clubs:* New Cavendish; Royal Lymington Yacht.

BRYANS, Tom, OBE 1983 (MBE 1975); Chief General Manager, Trustee Savings Bank Central Board (formerly TSB Association Ltd), 1975–82; *b* 16 Sept. 1920; *s* of Thomas and Martha Bryans; *m* 1947, Peggy Irene Snelling; two *s*. *Educ:* Royal Belfast Academical Instn. AIB 1950; FSBI 1972. Served War, 1939–46. Joined Belfast Savings Bank, 1938; Asst Gen. Man., 1969; Gen. Man., 1971. *Recreations:* sailing, golfing, gardening and music. *Address:* Redwing, Tamarisk Way, East Preston, W Sussex.

BRYANT, Rear-Adm. Benjamin, CB 1956; DSO 1942 (two bars, 1943); DSC 1940; *b* 16 Sept. 1905; *s* of J. F. Bryant, MA, FRGS, ICS (retd); *m* 1929, Marjorie Dagmar Mynors (*née* Symonds) (*d* 1965); one *s* one *d*; *m* 1966, Heather Elizabeth Williams (*née* Hance). *Educ:* Oundle; RN Colls Osborne and Dartmouth. Entered submarine branch of RN, 1927; Commanded: HMS/M Sea Lion, 1939–41; HMS/M Safari, 1941–43; comd 7th and 3rd Submarine Flotillas, 1943–44; comd 4th s/m Flotilla, British Pacific Fleet, 1945–47; comd HMS Dolphin Submarine School, and 5th Submarine Flotilla, 1947–49; Commodore (submarines), 1948; idc 1950; Commodore, RN Barracks, Devonport, 1951–53; Flag Captain to C-in-C Mediterranean, 1953–54; Rear-Admiral, 1954. Deputy Chief of Naval Personnel (Training and Manning), 1954–57; retired, 1957. Staff Personnel Manager, Rolls Royce Scottish Factories, 1957–68. *Recreations:* fishing, golf, shooting. *Address:* Quarry Cottage, Kithurst Lane, Storrington, West Sussex RH20 4LD.

BRYANT, David John, CBE 1980 (MBE 1969); Director, Drakelite Ltd (International Bowls Consultants), since 1978; international bowler; *b* 27 Oct. 1931; *s* of Reginald Samuel Harold Bryant and Evelyn Claire (*née* Weaver); *m* 1960, Ruth Georgina (*née* Roberts); two *d*. *Educ:* Weston Grammar Sch.; St Paul's Coll., Cheltenham; Redland Coll., Bristol (teacher training colls). National Service, RAF, 1950–52; teacher trng, 1953–55; schoolmaster, 1955–71; company director, sports business, 1971–78. World Singles Champion, 1966 and 1980; World Indoor Singles Champion, 1979, 1980 and 1981; World Indoor Pairs Champion, 1986; Kodak Masters International Singles Champion, 1978, 1979 and 1982; Gateway International Masters Singles Champion, 1984, 1985, 1986; World Triples Champion, 1980; Commonwealth Games Gold Medalist: Singles: 1962, 1970, 1974 and 1978; Fours: 1962. Numerous national and British Isles titles, both indoor and outdoor. *Publications:* Bryant on Bowls, 1966; Bowl with Bryant, 1984; Bryant on Bowls, 1985. *Recreations:* angling, gardening, table tennis. *Address:* 47 Esmond Grove, Clevedon, Avon BS21 7HP. *T:* Clevedon 877551. *Clubs:* Clevedon Bowling, Clevedon Conservative.

BRYANT, Rt. Rev. Denis William, DFC 1942; retired; *b* 31 Jan. 1918; *s* of Thomas and Beatrice Maud Bryant; *m* 1940, Dorothy Linda (*née* Lewis); one *d*. *Educ:* Clark's Coll., Ealing; Cardiff Techn. Coll. Joined RAF; Wireless Operator/Air Gunner, 1936; Navigator, 1939; France, 1940 (despatches); Pilot, 1941; commn in Secretarial Br., 1950; Adjt, RAF Hereford, 1950; Sqdn-Ldr i/c Overseas Postings Record Office, Gloucester, 1951; Sqdn-Ldr DP7, Air Min., 1953. Ordinand, Queen's Coll., Birmingham, 1956; Deacon, 1958; Priest, 1959. Bishop of Kalgoorlie, 1967 until 1973 when Kalgoorlie became part of Diocese of Perth; Asst Bishop of Perth, and Archdeacon and Rector of Northam, 1973–75; Rector of Dalkeith, WA, 1975–85. *Recreations:* squash, tennis, oil painting. *Address:* Sundowner Centre, 416 Stirling Highway, Cottesloe, WA 6011, Australia.

BRYANT, Air Vice-Marshal Derek Thomas, OBE 1974; Air Officer Commanding, Headquarters Command and Staff Training and Commandant, Royal Air Force Staff College, since 1987; *b* 1 Nov. 1933; *s* of Thomas Bryant and Mary (*née* Thurley); *m* 1956, Patricia Dodge; one *s* one *d*. *Educ:* Latymer Upper Grammar Sch., Hammersmith. Fighter pilot, 1953; Qualified Flying Instructor, 1957; Sqdn Comdr, 1968–74; OC RAF Coningsby, 1976–78; SASO HQ 38 Gp, 1982–84; Dep. Comdr, RAF Germany, 1984–87; various courses and staff appts. *Recreations:* gardening, golf. *Address:* Brookham House, Broad Lane, Bracknell, Berks. *Club:* Royal Air Force.

BRYANT, Michael; actor; National Theatre player, since 1977; an Associate of the National Theatre, since 1984; *b* 5 April 1928; *s* of William and Ann Bryant; *m* 1958, Josephine Martin (marr. diss. 1980); two *s* two *d*. *Educ:* Battersea Grammar Sch. Merchant Navy, 1945; Army, 1946–49; drama sch., 1949–51; theatre and television, 1957–77; RSC, 1964–65. Best Actor: SWET awards, 1977; British Theatrical Assoc., 1981. Governor, RADA, 1982–. *Recreation:* rambling. *Address:* 38 Killyon Road, SW8.

BRYANT, Prof. Peter Elwood; Watts Professor of Psychology, Oxford University, since 1980; Fellow of Wolfson College, Oxford, since 1980. *Educ:* Clare College, Cambridge (BA 1963, MA 1967). University Lecturer in Human Experimental Psychology, 1967–80. Fellow, St John's Coll., Oxford, 1967–80. Editor, British Jl of Developmental Psychol., 1983–. President's award, BPsS, 1984. *Publications:* Perception and Understanding in Young Children, 1974; Children's Reading Problems, 1985. *Address:* Wolfson College, Oxford.

BRYANT, Peter George Francis; HM Diplomatic Service (on secondment from Department of Trade and Industry); Consul-General, Düsseldorf, since 1985; *b* 10 May 1932; *s* of late George Bryant, CBE and Margaret Bryant; *m* 1961, Jean (*née* Morriss); one *s* one *d*. *Educ:* Sutton Valence Sch.; Birkbeck Coll., London Univ. (BA). Joined Civil Service as Exec. Officer, Min. of Supply, 1953; Higher Exec. Officer, BoT, 1960; Principal, 1967; 1st Sec. (Commercial), Vienna (on secondment), 1970; Dir of British Trade Drive in S Germany, 1973; Department of Trade (later Department of Trade and Industry): Asst Sec., 1974 (Head, Overseas Projs Gp); Civil Aviation Internat. Relations Div., 1978; Under Sec., Chemicals, Textiles and Paper Div., 1981. *Address:* c/o Foreign and Commonwealth Office, SW1.

BRYANT, Richard Charles, CB 1960; Under-Secretary, Board of Trade, 1955–68; *b* 20 Aug. 1908; *s* of Charles James and Constance Byron Bryant, The Bounds, Faversham, Kent; *m* 1938, Elisabeth Ellington, *d* of Dr. A. E. Stansfeld, FRCP; two *s* two *d*. *Educ:* Rugby; Oriel College, Oxford. Entered Board of Trade, 1932; Ministry of Supply, 1939–44. *Address:* Marsh Farm House, Brancaster, Norfolk. *T:* Brancaster 206. *Club:* Travellers'.

BRYANT, Thomas; HM Diplomatic Service; HM Consul-General, Munich, since 1984; *b* 1 Nov. 1938; *s* of George Edward Bryant and Ethel May Bryant (*née* Rogers); *m* 1961, Vivien Mary Theresa Hill; twin *s* one *d*. *Educ:* William Ellis Sch., London; Polytechnic of Central London (DMS). Nat. service, Army, 1957–59. Entered FO, 1957; Hong Kong, 1963; Peking, 1963–65; Vice Consul, Frankfurt, 1966–68; Second Sec., Tel Aviv, 1968–72; First Sec., FCO, 1973–76; Vienna, 1976–80; FCO, 1980–, Counsellor, 1982; Hd of Finance Dept, 1982–84. *Recreations:* cricket, soccer, tennis, classical music, laughter. *Address:* c/o Foreign and Commonwealth Office, SW1.

BRYARS, Donald Leonard; Commissioner of Customs and Excise, 1978–84 and Director, Personnel, 1979–84, retired; *b* 31 March 1929; *s* of late Leonard and Marie Bryars; *m* 1953, Joan (*née* Yealand); one *d*. *Educ:* Goole Grammar Sch.; Leeds Univ. Joined Customs and Excise as Executive Officer, 1953, Principal, 1964, Asst Sec., 1971; on loan to Cabinet Office, 1976–78; Director, General Customs, 1978–79. *Address:* 15 Ellwood Rise, Chalfont St Giles, Bucks HP8 4SU. *T:* Chalfont St Giles 5466. *Club:* Civil Service (Chm., 1981–85).

BRYARS, John Desmond, CB 1982; Deputy Under Secretary of State (Finance and Budget), Ministry of Defence, 1979–84, retired; *b* 31 Oct. 1928; *s* of William Bryars, MD and Sarah (*née* McMeekin); *m* 1964, Faith, *d* of Frederick Momber, ARCM and Anne Momber. *Educ:* St Edward's Sch., Oxford; Trinity Coll., Oxford (schol.; MA). Army, 1946–48. Entered Civil Service, Air Ministry, 1952; HM Treasury, 1960–62; Private Sec. to Sec. of State for Air, 1963–64, to Minister of Defence, RAF, 1964–65; Asst Sec., MoD, 1965–73; RCDS 1973; Asst Under-Sec. of State, MoD, 1973–75 and 1977–79; Under Sec., Cabinet Office, 1975–77. *Address:* 42 Osterley Road, Osterley, Isleworth, Middlesex. *Club:* Royal Commonwealth Society.

BRYCE; *see* Graham Bryce and Graham-Bryce.

BRYCE, Gabe Robb, OBE 1959; Sales Manager (Operations) British Aircraft Corporation, 1965–75; now occupied in breeding dogs and boarding cats; *b* 27 April 1921; *m* 1943, Agnes Lindsay; one *s* one *d*. *Educ:* Glasgow High School. Served in RAF, 1939–46. Vickers-Armstrongs (Aircraft) Ltd, 1946–60 (Chief Test Pilot, 1951–60). Participated as First or Second Pilot, in Maiden Flights of following British Aircraft: Varsity; Nene Viking; Viscount 630, 700 and 800; Tay Viscount; Valiant; Pathfinder; Vanguard; VC-10; BAC 1–11; Chief Test Pilot, British Aircraft Corporation, 1960–64. Fellow Soc. of Experimental Test Pilots (USA), 1967. Sir Barnes Wallis Meml Medal, GAPAN, 1980. *Recreations:* squash, tennis. *Address:* Meadows, Elm Corner, Ockham, Ripley, Surrey. *T:* Guildford 223916.

BRYCE, Sir Gordon; *see* Bryce, Sir W. G.

BRYCE, Rt. Rev. Jabez Leslie; *see* Polynesia, Bishop in.

BRYCE, Sir (William) Gordon, Kt 1971; CBE 1963; Chief Justice of the Bahamas, 1970–73; *b* 2 Feb. 1913; *s* of James Chisholm Bryce and Emily Susan (*née* Lees); *m* 1940, Molly Mary, *d* of Arthur Cranch Drake; two *d*. *Educ:* Bromsgrove Sch.; Hertford Coll., Oxford (MA). Called to Bar, Middle Temple. War Service, 1940–46 (Major). Colonial Service: Crown Counsel, Fiji, 1949; Solicitor General, Fiji, 1953; Attorney General: Gibraltar, 1956; Aden, 1959; Legal Adviser, S Arabian High Commn, 1963; Attorney General, Bahamas, 1966. Comr, revised edn of Laws: of Gilbert and Ellice Islands, 1952; of Fiji, 1955; Comr, Bahamas Law Reform and Revision Commn, 1976. *Recreations:* riding, gardening. *Address:* Broom Croft, Lydeard St Lawrence, Taunton, Somerset.

BRYCE-SMITH, Prof. Derek, PhD, DSc; CChem, FRSC; Professor of Organic Chemistry, University of Reading, since 1965; *b* 29 April 1926; *s* of Charles Philip and Amelia Smith; *m* 1st, 1956, Marjorie Mary Anne Stewart (*d* 1966); two *s* two *d*; 2nd, 1969, Pamela Joyce Morgan; two step *d*. *Educ:* Bancrofts Sch., Woodford Wells; SW Essex Tech. Coll.; West Ham Municipal Coll.; Bedford Coll., London. Research Chemist: Powell Duffryn Res. Ltd, 1945–46; Dufay-Chromex Ltd, 1946–48; Inst. of Petroleum Student, Bedford Coll., 1948–51; ICI Post-doctoral Fellow, KCL, 1951–55; Asst Lectr in Chem., KCL, 1955–56; Lectr in Chem., 1956–63, Reader, 1963–65, Reading Univ. Founding Chm., European Photochem. Assoc., 1970–72; Founding Vice-Chm., UK Br., Internat. Solar Energy Soc., 1973–74; Chm., RSC Photochemistry Gp, 1981–. John Jeyes Endowed Lectureship and Silver Medal, RSC, 1984–85. *Publications:* (with R. Stephens) Lead or Health, 1980, 2nd edn 1981; (with E. Hodgkinson) The Zinc Solution, 1986; (RSC Senior Reporter and contrib.) Photochemistry: a review of chemical literature, vols 1–17, 1970–; contribs to learned jls in the fields of photochem., organometallic chem., environmental chem. and philosophy of sci. *Recreations:* gardening, making music. *Address:* Highland Wood House, Mill Lane, Kidmore End, Reading, Berks RG4 9HB. *T:* Kidmore End 723132.

BRYDEN, William Campbell Rough, (Bill Bryden); Associate Director, The National Theatre, since 1975; Head of Drama, BBC Scotland, since 1985; *b* 12 April 1942; *s* of late George Bryden and of Catherine Bryden; *m* 1971, Hon. Deborah Morris, *d* of Baron Killanin, *qv*; one *s* one *d*. *Educ:* Hillend Public Sch.; Greenock High Sch. Documentary writer, Scottish Television, 1963–64; Assistant Director: Belgrade Theatre, Coventry, 1965–67; Royal Court Th., London, 1967–69; Associate Dir, Royal Lyceum Th., Edinburgh, 1971–74; Dir, Cottesloe Theatre (Nat. Theatre), 1978–80. Member Board, Scottish Television, 1979–85. Dir of the Year, Laurence Olivier Awards, 1985, Best Dir, Brit. Th. Assoc. and Drama Magazine Awards, 1986, and Evening Standard Best Dir Award, 1985 (for The Mysteries, NT, 1985). *Publications: plays:* Willie Rough, 1972; Benny Lynch, 1974; Old Movies, 1977; *screenplay:* The Long Riders, 1980; *films:* (writer and director) Ill Fares The Land, 1982; The Holy City, 1985. *Recreation:* music. *Address:* The National Theatre, South Bank, SE1 9PX. *T:* 01–928 2033.

BRYMER, Jack, OBE 1960; Hon. RAM; Principal Clarinettist, London Symphony Orchestra, since 1972; *b* 27 Jan. 1915; *s* of J. and Mrs M. Brymer, South Shields, Co. Durham; *m* 1939, Joan Richardson, Lancaster; one *s*. *Educ:* Goldsmiths' College, London University. Schoolmaster, Croydon, general subjects, 1935–40. RAF, 1940–45. Principal Clarinettist: Royal Philharmonic Orchestra, 1946–63; BBC Symphony Orchestra, 1963–72; Prof., Royal Acad. of Music, 1950–58; Prof., Royal Military Sch. of Music, Kneller Hall, 1969–73; Prof., Guildhall Sch. of Music and Drama, 1981–; Member of Wigmore, Prometheus and London Baroque ensembles; Director of London Wind Soloists. Has directed recordings of the complete wind chamber music of Mozart, Beethoven, Haydn and J. C. Bach. Presenter of several BBC music series, inc. At Home (nightly). Has taken a life-long interest in mainstream jazz, and in later life has toured and performed as soloist with many of finest British and American players in that field. Hon. RAM 1955; Hon. MA Newcastle upon Tyne, 1973. *Publications:* The Clarinet (Menuhin Guides), 1976; From Where I Sit (autobiog.), 1979. *Recreations:* golf, tennis, swimming, carpentry, gardening, music. *Address:* Underwood, Ballards Farm Road, South Croydon, Surrey. *T:* 01–657 1698. *Club:* Croham Hurst Golf.

BRYSON, Col (James) Graeme, OBE 1954; TD 1949; JP; Vice-Lord-Lieutenant of Merseyside, since 1979; *b* 4 Feb. 1913; 3rd *s* of John Conway Bryson and Oletta Bryson; *m* Jean (*d* 1981), *d* of Walter Glendinning; two *s* four *d* (and one *s* decd). *Educ:* St Edward's Coll.; Liverpool Univ. (LLM). Admitted solicitor, 1935. Commnd 89th Field Bde RA (TA), 1936; served War, RA, 1939–45 (Lt-Col 1944); comd 470 (3W/Lancs) HAA Regt, 1947–52, and 626 HAA Regt, 1952–55; Bt-Col 1955; Hon. Col 33 Signal Regt (V), 1975–81. Sen. Jt Dist Registrar and Liverpool Admiralty Registrar, High Court of Justice, Liverpool, and Registrar of Liverpool County Court, 1947–78; Dep. Circuit Judge, Northern Circuit, 1978–82. President: Assoc. of County Court Registrars, 1969; Liverpool Law Soc., 1969; NW Area, Royal British Legion, 1979. Chm., Med. Appeal Tribunal, 1978–85; Member: Lord Chancellor's Cttee for enforcement of debts (Payne), 1965–69; IOM Commn to reform enforcement laws, 1972–74; Council, Nat. Assoc. for Employment of Regular Sailors, Soldiers and Airmen, 1952–. JP Liverpool, 1956; DL Lancs, 1965, later Merseyside. The Queen's Commendation for Brave Conduct, 1961. KHS 1974. *Publication:* (jtly) Execution, in Halsbury's Laws of England, 3rd edn 1976. *Recreations:* local history, boating. *Address:* Sunwards, Thirlmere Road, Hightown, Liverpool L38 3RQ. *T:* 051–929 2652. *Club:* Athenæum (Liverpool; Pres., 1969).

BRYSON, Adm. Sir Lindsay (Sutherland), KCB 1981; FRSE 1984; FEng; Controller of the Navy, 1981–84; *b* 22 Jan. 1925; *s* of James McAuslan Bryson and Margaret Bryson (*née* Whyte); *m* 1951, Averil Curtis-Willson; one *s* two *d*. *Educ:* Allan Glen's Sch., Glasgow; London Univ. (External) (BSc (Eng)); FIEE, FRAeS. Engrg Cadet, 1942; Electrical Mechanic, RN, 1944; Midshipman 1946; Lieut 1948; Comdr 1960; Captain 1967; comd HMS Daedalus, RNAS Lee-on-Solent, 1970–71; RCDS 1972; Dir, Naval Guided Weapons, 1973; Dir, Surface Weapons Project (Navy), 1974–76; Dir-Gen. Weapons (Naval), 1977–81, and Chief Naval Engr Officer, 1979–81. Non-exec. Dir, ERA Technology, 1985; Chm., Marine Technology Directorate, 1986. Vice-Pres., 1982–84, Dep. Pres., 1984–85, Pres., 1985–86, IEE (Faraday Lectr, 1976–77). Liveryman, Worshipful Co. of Cooks, 1964, Assistant, 1980, Warden, 1985. *Publications:* contrib. Jl RAeS, Trans RINA, Seaford Papers, Control Engineering. *Recreations:* opera, fair weather sailing, gardening, badminton. *Address:* 74 Dyke Road Avenue, Brighton BN1 5LE. *T:* Brighton 553638. *Club:* Army and Navy.

BUCCLEUCH, 9th Duke of, *cr* 1663, **AND QUEENSBERRY,** 11th Duke of, *cr* 1684; **Walter Francis John Montagu Douglas Scott,** KT 1978; VRD; JP; Baron Scott of Buccleuch, 1606; Earl of Buccleuch, Baron Scott of Whitchester and Eskdaill, 1619; Earl of Doncaster and Baron Tynedale (Eng.), 1662; Earl of Dalkeith, 1663; Marquis of Dumfriesshire, Earl of Drumlanrig and Sanquhar, Viscount of Nith, Torthorwold, and Ross, Baron Douglas, 1684; Lieutenant-Commander RNR; Captain, the Queen's Body Guard for Scotland, Royal Company of Archers; Lord-Lieutenant of Roxburgh, since 1974, of Ettrick and Lauderdale, since 1975; *b* 28 Sept. 1923; *o s* of 8th Duke of Buccleuch, KT, PC, GCVO, and of Vreda Esther Mary, *er d* of late Major W. F. Lascelles and Lady Sybil Lascelles, *d* of 10th Duke of St Albans; *S* father, 1973; *m* 1953, Jane, *d* of John McNeill, QC, Appin, Argyll; three *s* one *d*. *Educ:* Eton; Christ Church, Oxford. Served War of 1939–45, RNVR. MP (C) Edinburgh North, 1960–73; PPS to the Lord Advocate, 1961–62 and to the Sec. of State for Scotland, 1962–64; Chm., Cons. Party Forestry Cttee, 1967–73. Chm., Royal Assoc. for Disability and Rehabilitation; President: Royal Highland & Agricultural Soc. of Scotland, 1969; St. Andrew's Ambulance Assoc.; Royal Scottish Agricultural Benevolent Inst.; Scottish Nat. Inst. for War Blinded; Royal Blind Asylum & School; Galloway Cattle Soc.; East of England Agricultural Soc., 1976; Commonwealth Forestry Assoc.; Vice-Pres., RSSPCC; Hon. President: Animal Diseases Research Assoc.; Scottish Agricultural Organisation Soc. DL, Selkirk 1955, Midlothian 1960, Roxburgh 1962, Dumfries 1974; JP Roxburgh 1975. Countryside Award, Countryside Commn and CLA, 1983. *Heir: s* Earl of Dalkeith, *qv*. *Address:* Bowhill, Selkirk. *T:* Selkirk 20732.

BUCHAN, family name of **Baron Tweedsmuir.**

BUCHAN, 17th Earl of, *cr* 1469; **Malcolm Harry Erskine;** JP; Lord Auchterhouse, 1469; Lord Cardross, 1610; Baron Erskine, 1806; *b* 4 July 1930; *s* of 16th Earl of Buchan and of Christina, Dowager Countess of Buchan, *d* of late Hugh Woolner and adopted *d* of late Lloyd Baxendale; *S* father, 1984; *m* 1957, Hilary Diana Cecil, *d* of late Sir Ivan McLannahan Power, 2nd Bt; two *s* two *d*. *Educ:* Eton. JP Westminster. *Heir: s* Lord Cardross, *qv*. *Address:* Newnham House, Newnham, Basingstoke, Hants. *Club:* Carlton.

BUCHAN OF AUCHMACOY, Captain David William Sinclair, JP; Chief of the Name of Buchan; *b* 18 Sept. 1929; *o s* of late Captain S. L. Trevor, late of Lathbury Park, Bucks, and late Lady Olivia Trevor, *e d* of 18th Earl of Caithness; *m* 1961, Susan Blanche Fionodbhar Scott-Ellis, *d* of 9th Baron Howard de Walden, *qv*; four *s* one *d*. *Educ:* Eton; RMA Sandhurst. Commissioned 1949 into Gordon Highlanders; served Berlin, BAOR and Malaya; ADC to GOC, Singapore, 1951–53; retired 1955. Member of London Stock Exchange. Sen. Partner, Messrs Gow and Parsons, 1963–72. Changed name from Trevor through Court of Lord Lyon King of Arms, 1949, succeeding 18th Earl of Caithness as Chief of Buchan Clan. Member: Queen's Body Guard for Scotland; The Pilgrims; Friends of Malta GC; Alexandra Rose Day Council; Worshipful Company of Broderers. JP Aberdeenshire, 1959–; JP London, 1972–. OStJ 1981. *Recreations:* cricket, tennis, squash. *Address:* 28 The Little Boltons, SW10. *T:* 01–373 0654; Auchmacoy House, Ellon, Aberdeenshire. *T:* Ellon 20229. *Clubs:* White's, Royal Automobile, Turf, MCC, City of London, Pratt's, Pitt; Puffin's (Edinburgh).

BUCHAN, Ven. Eric Ancrum; Archdeacon of Coventry, 1965–77, Archdeacon Emeritus, since 1977; *b* 6 Nov. 1907; *s* of late Frederick Samuel and Florence Buchan. *Educ:* Bristol Grammar School; St Chad's College, University of Durham (BA). Curate of Holy Nativity, Knowle, Bristol, 1933–40. Chaplain RAFVR, 1940–45. Vicar of St Mark's with St Barnabas, Coventry, 1945–59; Hon. Canon of Coventry Cathedral, 1953; Chaplain Coventry and Warwickshire Hospital, 1945–59; Sec. Laymen's Appeal, Dio. of Coventry, 1951–53; Rural Dean of Coventry, 1954–63; Rector of Baginton, 1963–70.

Member Central Board of Finance, 1953–80 (Chm., Develt and Stewardship Cttee, 1976–80; Mem., Church Commrs and CBF Joint Liaison Cttee, 1976–80); Mem. Schools Council, 1958–65; Chm. Dio. Board of Finance, 1958–77; Organiser of Bishop's Appeal, 1958–61; Dio. Director of Christian Stewardship, 1959–65; Domestic Chaplain to Bishop of Coventry, 1961–65; Church Commissioner, 1964–78; Member, Governing Body, St Chad's College, Durham University, 1966–83. Awarded Silver Acorn for outstanding services to the Scout Movement, 1974. *Address:* 6B Millers Green, The Cathedral, Gloucester GL1 2BN. *T:* Gloucester 415944.

BUCHAN, Janey, (Jane O'Neil Buchan); Member (Lab) Glasgow, European Parliament, since 1979; Regional Councillor, Strathclyde Regional Council, since 1974; *b* 30 April 1926; *d* of Joseph and Christina Kent; *m* 1945, Norman Findlay Buchan, *qv*; one *s*. *Educ:* secondary sch.; commercial coll. Housewife; Socialist; Councillor; occasional scriptwriting and journalism. Vice-Chm., Educn Cttee, Strathclyde Reg. Council; Chm., local consumer gp; formerly Chm., Scottish Gas Consumers' Council. *Recreations:* books, music, theatre, television. *Address:* 72 Peel Street, Glasgow G11 5LR. *T:* 041–339 2583.

BUCHAN, Sir John, (Sir Thomas Johnston Buchan), Kt 1971; CMG 1961; Chairman, Buchan Laird International Planners, since 1982; Chairman and Chief Executive, Buchan, Laird and Buchan, Architects, 1957–82; *b* 3 June 1912; *s* of Thomas Johnston Buchan; *m* 1948, Virginia, *d* of William Ashley Anderson, Penn., USA; one *s* two *d*. *Educ:* Geelong Grammar School. Served Royal Aust. Engineers (AIF), 1940–44 (Capt.). Member Melbourne City Council, 1954–60. Member Federal Exec., Liberal Party, 1959–62; President, Liberal Party, Victorian Division, Australia, 1959–62, Treasurer, 1963–67; Pres., Australian American Assoc., Victoria, 1964–68, Federal Pres., Australian American Assoc., 1968–70, Vice-Pres., 1971–82. Member: Council, Latrobe University, 1964–72; Cttee of Management, Royal Melbourne Hosp., 1968–78. Founding Mem. and Dep. Chm., Nat. Cttee for Youth Employment, 1983–86; Co-Founder Apex Association of Australia. *Recreations:* golf, reading. *Address:* 11 Fairlie Court, South Yarra, Vic 3141, Australia. *Club:* Melbourne (Melbourne).

BUCHAN, Norman Findlay; MP (Lab) Paisley South, since 1983 (Renfrewshire West, 1964–83); *b* Helmsdale, Sutherlandshire, 27 Oct. 1922; *s* of John Buchan, Fraserburgh, Aberdeenshire; *m* 1945, Janey Kent (*see* Janey Buchan); one *s*. *Educ:* Kirkwall Grammar School; Glasgow University. Royal Tank Regt (N Africa, Sicily and Italy, 1942–45). Teacher (English and History). Parly Under-Sec., Scottish Office, 1967–70. Opposition Spokesman on Agriculture, Fisheries and Food, 1970–74; Minister of State, MAFF, March-Oct. 1974 (resigned); Opposition Spokesman on: social security, 1980–81; food, agriculture and fisheries, 1981–83; the arts, 1983–. Chm. Bd, Tribune, 1985–. *Publications:* (ed) 101 Scottish Songs; The Scottish Folksinger, 1973; The MacDunciad, 1977. *Address:* 72 Peel Street, Glasgow G11 5LR. *T:* 041–339 2583.

BUCHAN, Dr Stevenson, CBE 1971; Chief Scientific Officer, Deputy Director, Institute of Geological Sciences, 1968–71; *b* 4 March 1907; *s* of late James Buchan and Christian Ewen Buchan (*née* Stevenson), Peterhead; *m* 1937, Barbara, *yr d* of late Reginald Hadfield, Droylsden, Lancs; one *s* one *d*. *Educ:* Peterhead Acad.; Aberdeen Univ. BSc 1st cl. hons Geology, James H. Hunter Meml Prize, Senior Kilgour Scholar, PhD; FRSE, FGS, FIWES, Hon. FIPHE. Geological Survey of Great Britain: Geologist, 1931; Head of Water Dept, 1946; Asst Dir responsible for specialist depts in GB and NI, 1960; Chief Geologist, Inst. of Geological Sciences, 1967. Mem. various hydrological cttees; Founder Mem., Internat. Assoc. of Hydrogeologists (Pres., 1972–77; Advr, 1980–; Hon. Mem., 1985–); Pres., Internat. Ground-Water Commn of Internat. Assoc. of Hydrological Sciences, 1963–67; British Deleg. to Internat. Hydrological Decade; Scientific Editor, Hydrogeological Map of Europe; Vis. Internat. Scientist, Amer. Geol Inst.; Pres. Section C (Geology), Brit. Assoc., Dundee, 1968. Awarded Geol Soc.'s Lyell Fund, and J. B. Tyrell Fund for travel in Canada. *Publications:* Water Supply of County of London from Underground Sources; papers on hydrogeology and hydrochemistry. *Recreations:* travel, photography, gardening, philately. *Address:* Far End, 14 Monks Road, Banstead, Surrey SM7 2EP. *T:* Burgh Heath 54227.

BUCHAN, Sir Thomas Johnston; *see* Buchan, Sir John.

BUCHAN-HEPBURN, Sir Ninian (Buchan Archibald John), 6th Bt, *cr* 1815, of Smeaton-Hepburn; is a painter; Member, Queen's Body Guard for Scotland, Royal Company of Archers; *b* 8 Oct. 1922; *s* of Sir John Buchan-Hepburn, 5th Bt; *S* father 1961; *m* 1958, Bridget (*d* 1976), *er d* of late Sir Louis Greig, KBE, CVO. *Educ:* St Aubyn's, Rottingdean, Sussex; Canford School, Wimborne, Dorset. Served QO Cameron Hldrs, India and Burma, 1939–45. Studied painting, Byam Shaw School of Art. Exhibited at: Royal Academy, Royal Scottish Academy, London galleries. Work in many public and private collections. *Recreations:* music, gardening, shooting. *Heir: kinsman* John Alastair Trant Kidd Buchan-Hepburn [*b* 27 June 1931; *m* 1957, Georgina Elizabeth Turner; one *s* three *d*]. *Address:* Logan, Port Logan, Wigtownshire. *T:* Ardwell 239. *Clubs:* New, Puffin's (Edinburgh).

BUCHANAN, Sir Andrew George, 5th Bt *cr* 1878; DL; farmer; chartered surveyor in private practice; *b* 21 July 1937; *s* of Major Sir Charles Buchanan, 4th Bt, and Barbara Helen (*d* 1986), *o d* of late Lt-Col Rt Hon. Sir George Stanley, PC, GCSI, GCIE; *S* father, 1984; *m* 1966, Belinda Jane Virginia (*née* Maclean), JP, *widow* of Gresham Neilus Vaughan; one *s* one *d*, and one step *s* one step *d*. *Educ:* Eton; Trinity Coll., Cambridge; Wye Coll., Univ. of London. Nat. Service, 2nd Lieut, Coldstream Guards, 1956–58. Chartered Surveyor with Smith-Woolley & Co, 1965–70. Chm., Bd of Visitors, HM Prison Ranby, 1983 (Vice-Chm. 1982). Commanded A Squadron (SRY), 3rd Bn Worcs and Sherwood Foresters (TA), 1971–74. High Sheriff, Notts, 1976–77; DL Notts, 1985. Dep. Chm., Notts Boy Scout Assoc. *Recreations:* skiing, shooting. *Heir: s* George Charles Mellish Buchanan, *b* 27 Jan. 1975. *Address:* Hodsock Priory, Blyth, Worksop, Notts S81 0TY. *T:* Blyth (Notts) 204. *Club:* Boodle's.

BUCHANAN, Sir Charles Alexander James L.; *see* Leith-Buchanan.

BUCHANAN, Prof. Sir Colin (Douglas), Kt 1972; CBE 1964; Lieut-Colonel; consultant with Colin Buchanan & Partners, 47 Princes Gate, London; *b* 22 Aug. 1907; *s* of William Ernest and Laura Kate Buchanan; *m* 1933, Elsie Alice Mitchell (*d* 1984); two *s* one *d*. *Educ:* Berkhamsted School; Imperial College, London. Sudan Govt Public Works Dept, 1930–32; Regional planning studies with F. Longstreth Thompson, 1932–35; Ministry of Transport, 1935–39. War Service in Royal Engineers, 1939–46 (despatches). Ministry of Town and Country Planning (later Ministry of Housing and Local Govt), 1946–61; Urban Planning Adviser, Ministry of Transport, 1961–63; Prof. of Transport, Imperial Coll., London, 1963–72; Prof. of Urban Studies and Dir, Sch. for Advanced Urban Studies, Bristol Univ., 1973–75. Vis. Prof., Imperial Coll., London, 1975–78. Member: Commn on Third London Airport, 1968–70; Royal Fine Art Commn, 1972–74. Pres., CPRE, 1980–85. Pres., Friends of the Vale of Aylesbury, 1985–. Hon. DCL Oxon, 1972; Hon. DSc: Leeds, 1972; City, 1972. *Publications:* Mixed Blessing, The Motor in Britain, 1958; Traffic in Towns (Ministry of Transport report), 1963, (paperback edn), 1964; The State of Britain, 1972; No Way to the Airport, 1981; numerous papers on town planning and allied subjects. *Recreations:* photography, carpentry, caravan touring. *Address:* Appletree House, Lincombe Lane, Boars Hill, Oxford OX1 5DU. *T:* Oxford 739458.

BUCHANAN, Rt. Rev. Colin Ogilvie; *see* Aston, Bishop Suffragan of.

BUCHANAN, George (Henry Perrott); poet; *b* 9 Jan. 1904; 2nd *s* of Rev. C. H. L. Buchanan, Kilwaughter, Co. Antrim, and Florence Moore; *m* 1st, 1938, Winifred Mary Corn (marr. diss. 1945; she *d* 1971); 2nd, 1949, Noel Pulleyne Ritter (*d* 1951); 3rd, 1952, Janet Margesson (*d* 1968), *e d* of 1st Viscount Margesson; two *d*; 4th, 1974, Sandra Gail McCloy, Vancouver. *Educ:* Campbell College; Queen's University, Belfast. On editorial staff of The Times, 1930–35; reviewer, TLS, 1928–40; columnist, drama critic, News Chronicle, 1935–38; Operations Officer, RAF Coastal Command, 1940–45; Chm. Town and Country Development Cttee, N Ireland, 1949–53; Member, Exec. Council, European Soc. of Culture, 1954–. *Publications:* Passage through the Present, 1932; A London Story, 1935; Words for To-Night, 1936; Entanglement, 1938; The Soldier and the Girl, 1940; Rose Forbes, 1950; A Place to Live, 1952; Bodily Responses (poetry), 1958; Green Seacoast, 1959; Conversation with Strangers (poetry), 1961; Morning Papers, 1965; Annotations, 1970; Naked Reason, 1971; Minute-book of a City (poetry), 1972; Inside Traffic (poetry), 1976; The Politics of Culture, 1977; Possible Being (poetry), 1980; Adjacent Columns (poetry), 1982; *plays:* A Trip to the Castle, 1960; Tresper Revolution, 1961; War Song, 1965. *Address:* 27 Ashley Gardens, Westminster, SW1. *T:* 01–834 5722. *Club:* Savile.

BUCHANAN, Isobel Wilson, (Mrs Jonathan King); soprano; *b* 15 March 1954; *d* of Stewart and Mary Buchanan; *m* 1980, Jonathan Stephen Geoffrey King (otherwise Jonathan Hyde, actor); one *d*. *Educ:* Cumbernauld High Sch.; Royal Scottish Academy of Music and Drama (DRSAMD 1974). Australian Opera principal singer, 1975–78; freelance singer, 1978–; British debut, Glyndebourne, 1978; Vienna Staatsoper debut, 1978; American debut: Santa Fé, 1979; Chicago, 1979; New York, 1979; German debut, Cologne, 1979; French debut, Aix-en-Provence, 1981; ENO debut, 1985; Paris Opera debut, 1986. Performances also with Scottish Opera, Covent Garden, Munich Radio, Belgium, Norway, etc. Various operatic recordings. *Recreations:* reading, gardening, cooking, dressmaking, knitting, tennis. *Address:* c/o Harrison/Parrott, 12 Penzance Place, W11.

BUCHANAN, John David, MBE 1944; DL; Headmaster of Oakham School, Rutland, 1958–77; *b* 26 Oct. 1916; *e s* of late John Nevile Buchanan and Nancy Isabel (*née* Bevan); *m* 1946, Janet Marjorie, *d* of late Brig. J. A. C. Pennycuick, DSO; three *s* four *d* (and one *s* decd). *Educ:* Stowe; Trinity College, Cambridge. Served with Grenadier Guards, 1939–46; Adjutant, 3rd Bn Grenadier Guards, 1941–43; Brigade Major, 1st Guards Bde, 1944–45; Private Secretary to Sir Alexander Cadogan, Security Council for the UN, 1946. Assistant Master, Westminster Under School, 1948; Assistant Master, Sherborne School, 1948–57. Administrator, Inchcape Educational Scholarship Scheme, 1978–; Educnl Consultant to Jerwood Foundn, 1978–. DL Leics, 1980. *Publications:* Operation Oakham, 1984; Oakham Overture to Poetry, 1985. *Recreation:* gardening. *Address:* Rose Cottage, Owston, Leics.

BUCHANAN, Vice-Adm. Sir Peter (William), KBE 1980; *b* 14 May 1925; *s* of Lt-Col Francis Henry Theodore Buchanan and Gwendolen May Isobel (*née* Hunt); *m* 1953, Audrey Rowena Mary (*née* Edmondson); three *s* one *d*. *Educ:* Malvern Coll. Joined RN, 1943; served in HM Ships King George V, Birmingham, destroyers and frigates; comd HMS Scarborough 1961–63; Far East, 1963–65 (despatches); HMS Victorious, 1965–67; British Antarctic Survey, 1967–68; comd HMS Endurance, 1968–70; MoD, 1970–72; comd HMS Devonshire, 1972–74; MoD, 1974–76; Rear-Adm. 1976; Naval Sec., 1976–78; Vice-Adm., 1979; Chief of Staff, Allied Naval Forces Southern Europe, 1979–82. Ch. Exec., London World Trade Centre Assoc., 1982–83. Younger Brother of Trinity House. Mem. Council, Malvern Coll. FNI; MRIN; FBIM. *Recreations:* sailing, walking. *Address:* River House, Iping, Midhurst, West Sussex. *T:* Midhurst 6448. *Clubs:* Caledonian; Royal Yacht Squadron.

BUCHANAN, Richard, JP; *b* 3 May 1912; *s* of late Richard Buchanan and late Helen Henderson; *m* 1st, 1938, Margaret McManus (*d* 1963); six *s* two *d*; 2nd, 1971, Helen Duggan, MA, DipEd. *Educ:* St Mungo's Boys' School; St Mungo's Academy; Royal Technical Coll. Councillor, City of Glasgow, 1949–64 (Past Chm. Libraries, Schools and Standing Orders Cttees); Hon. City Treasurer, 1960–63. MP (Lab) Springburn, Glasgow, 1964–79; PPS to Treasury Ministers, 1967–70; Mem. Select Cttees: Public Accounts; Services. Chm., West Day School Management, 1958–64; Governor, Notre Dame College of Education, 1959–64, etc. Chm., Belvidere Hospital; Member Board of Managers, Glasgow Royal Infirmary; Hon. Pres., Scottish Library Assoc. (Pres., 1963); Life Mem., Scottish Secondary Teachers' Assoc., 1979; Chairman: Scottish Central Library; Adv. Cttee, Nat. Library of Scotland; Cttee on Burrell Collection; H of C Library Cttee; St Mungo's Old Folks' Day Centre, 1979–; Director, Glasgow Citizens Theatre. JP Glasgow, 1954. Hon. FLA, 1979. *Recreations:* theatre, walking, reading. *Address:* 18 Gargrave Avenue, Garrowhill, Glasgow. *T:* 041–771 7234. *Club:* St Mungo's Centenary (Glasgow).

BUCHANAN, Dr Robert Angus, FRHistS; Founder and Director, Centre for the History of Technology, Science and Society, University of Bath, since 1964; Head of Humanities Group, School of Humanities and Social Sciences, since 1970; Reader in History of Technology, since 1981; Director, Contemporary Scientific Archives Centre, from March 1987; *b* 5 June 1930; *s* of Roy Graham Buchanan and Bertha (*née* Davis); *m* 1955, Brenda June Wade; two *s*. *Educ:* High Storrs Grammar Sch. for Boys, Sheffield; St Catharine's Coll., Cambridge (MA, PhD). FRHistS 1978. Educn Officer to Royal Foundn of St Katharine, Stepney, 1956–60 (Co-opted Mem., LCC Educn Cttee, 1958–60); Asst Lectr, Dept of Gen. Studies, Bristol Coll. of Science and Technol. (now Univ. of Bath), 1960; Lectr, 1961; Sen. Lectr, 1966. Vis. Lectr, Univ. of Delaware, USA, 1969; Vis. Fellow, ANU, Canberra, 1981; Vis. Lectr, Huazhong (Central China) Univ. of Science and Tech., Wuhan, People's Repub. of China, 1983; Jubilee Chair in History of Technol., Chalmers Univ., Göteborg, Sweden, Autumn term, 1984. Royal Comr, Royal Commn on Historical Monuments (England), 1979–; Sec.-Gen., Internat. Cttee for History of Technol., 1981–; Sec., Res. Cttee on Indust. Archaeology, Council for British Archaeology, 1972–79; President: (Founding), Bristol Indust. Archaeology Soc., 1967–70; Assoc. for Indust. Archaeology, 1974–77; Newcomen Soc. for History of Engrg and Technol., 1981–83; Chm., Water Space Amenity Commn's Working Party on Indust. Archaeology, 1982–83; Member: Properties Cttee, National Trust, 1974–; Technol Preservation Awards Cttee, Science Museum, 1973–81. Hon. DSc (Engrg) Chalmers Univ., Göteborg, Sweden, 1986. *Publications:* Technology and Social Progress, 1965; (with Neil Cossons) Industrial Archaeology of the Bristol Region, 1969; Industrial Archaeology in Britain, 1972, 2nd edn 1982; (with George Watkins) Industrial Archaeology of the Stationary Steam Engine, 1976; History and Industrial Civilization, 1979; (with C. A. Buchanan) Industrial Archaeology of Central Southern England, 1980; (with Michael Williams) Brunel's Bristol, 1982. *Recreations:* Cambridge Judo half-blue, 1955; rambling, travelling, exploring. *Address:* Centre for the History of Technology, Science and Society, University of Bath, Claverton Down, Bath BA2 7AY. *T:* Bath 61244, ext. 833.

BUCHANAN-DUNLOP, Richard, QC 1966; *b* 19 April 1919; *s* of late Canon W. R. Buchanan-Dunlop and Mrs R. E. Buchanan-Dunlop (*née* Mead); *m* 1948, Helen Murray Dunlop; three *d. Educ:* Marlborough College; Magdalene College, Cambridge. Served in Royal Corps of Signals, 1939–46 (Hon. Major). BA (Hons) Law, Cambridge, 1949; Harmsworth Scholar, 1950. Called to the Bar, 1951. *Publications:* Skiathos and other Poems, 1984; Old Olive Men, 1986. *Recreations:* painting, writing. *Address:* Skiathos, Greece.

BUCHANAN-JARDINE, Sir A. R. J.; *see* Jardine.

BUCHANAN-SMITH, Rt. Hon. Alick (Laidlaw); PC 1981; MP (C) Kincardine and Deeside, since 1983 (North Angus and Mearns, 1964–83); Minister of State, Department of Energy, since 1983; *b* 8 April 1932; 2nd *s* of late Baron Balerno, CBE, TD, and Mary Kathleen, *d* of Captain George Smith of Pittodrie; *m* 1956, Janet, *d* of late Thomas Lawrie, CBE; one *s* three *d. Educ:* Edinburgh Academy; Trinity College, Glenalmond; Pembroke College, Cambridge; Edinburgh University. Commissioned Gordon Highlanders, National Service, 1951; subseq. Captain, TA (5th/6th Gordon Highlanders). Parly Under-Sec. of State, Scottish Office, 1970–74; Minister of State, MAFF, 1979–83. *Address:* House of Commons, SW1.

BUCHTHAL, Hugo, FBA 1959; PhD; Ailsa Mellon Bruce Professor, 1970–75, Professor of Fine Arts, 1965–70, New York University Institute of Fine Arts; now Emeritus Professor; *b* Berlin, 11 Aug. 1909; *m* 1939, Amalia Serkin; one *d. Educ:* Universities of Berlin, Heidelberg, Paris and Hamburg. PhD, Hamburg, 1933; Resident in London from 1934; Lord Plumer Fellowship, Hebrew University, 1938; Librarian, Warburg Institute, 1941; Lecturer in History of Art, University of London, 1944; Reader in the History of Art, with special reference to the Near East, 1949; Professor of the History of Byzantine Art in the University of London, 1960. Visiting Scholarship, Dumbarton Oaks, Harvard University, 1950–51, 1965, 1974, 1978; Temp. Member Inst. for Advanced Study, Princeton, NJ, 1959–60, 1968, 1975–76; Visiting Professor Columbia University, New York, 1963. Prix Schlumberger, Académie des Inscriptions et Belles Lettres, 1958, 1981; Guggenheim Fellow, 1971–72; Corres. Mem., Oesterreichische Akad. der Wissenschaften, 1975; Hon. Fellow, Warburg Inst., 1975. *Publications:* The Miniatures of the Paris Psalter, 1938; (with Otto Kurz) A Handlist of illuminated Oriental Christian Manuscripts, 1942; The Western Aspects of Gandhara Sculpture, 1944; Miniature Painting in the Latin Kingdom of Jerusalem, 1957; Historia Trojana, studies in the history of mediaeval secular illustration, 1971; (jtly) The Place of Book Illumination in Byzantine Art, 1976; (with Hans Belting) Patronage in Thirteenth Century Constantinople: an atelier of late Byzantine illumination and calligraphy, 1978; The Musterbuch of Wolfenbüttel and its position in the art of the thirteenth century, 1979; Art of the Mediterranean World, AD 100 to AD 1400, 1983 (collected essays); numerous articles in learned journals. *Address:* 22 Priory Gardens, N6. *T:* 01–348 1664.

BUCHWALD, Art, (Arthur); American journalist, author, lecturer and columnist; *b* Mount Vernon, New York, 20 Oct. 1925; *s* of Joseph Buchwald and Helen (*née* Kleinberger); *m* 1952, Ann McGarry, Warren, Pa; one *s* two *d. Educ:* University of Southern California. Sergeant, US Marine Corps, 1942–45. Columnist, New York Herald Tribune: in Paris, 1949–62; in Washington, 1962–. Syndicated columnist whose articles appear in 550 newspapers throughout the world. Mem., AAIL, 1986–. Pulitzer Prize for outstanding commentary, 1982. *Publications:* (mostly published later in England) Paris After Dark, 1950; Art Buchwald's Paris, 1954; The Brave Coward, 1957; I Chose Caviar, 1957; More Caviar, 1958; A Gift from the Boys, 1958; Don't Forget to Write, 1960; Art Buchwald's Secret List to Paris, 1961; How Much is That in Dollars?, 1961; Is it Safe to Drink the Water?, 1962; I Chose Capitol Punishment, 1963; . . . and Then I told the President, 1965; Son of the Great Society, 1966; Have I Ever Lied to You?, 1968; The Establishment is Alive and Well in Washington, 1969; Sheep on the Runway (Play), 1970; Oh, to be a Swinger, 1970; Getting High in Government Circles, 1971; I Never Danced at the White House, 1973; I Am not a Crook, 1974; Bollo Caper, 1974; Irving's Delight, 1975; Washington is Leaking, 1976; Down the Seine and up the Potomac, 1977; The Buchwald Stops Here, 1978; Laid Back in Washington, 1981; While Reagan Slept, 1984; You Can Fool All of the People All the Time, 1985. *Recreations:* tennis, chess, marathon running. *Address:* 2000 Pennsylvania Avenue NW, Washington, DC 20006, USA. *T:* Washington 393–6680. *Club:* Overseas Press (NY).

BUCK, Albert Charles; business consultant; *b* 1 March 1910; *y s* of William and Mary Buck; *m* 1st, 1937, Margaret Court Hartley; one *d*; 2nd, 1951, Joan McIntyre; one *d*; 3rd, 1970, Mrs Aileen Ogilvy. *Educ:* Alderman Newton's Sch., Leicester; Selwyn Coll., Cambridge (MA). Joined J. J. Colman Ltd, as management trainee, 1931; Export Manager, 1939; Director: Reckitt & Sons Ltd, 1941; Joseph Farrow & Co. Ltd, 1947–69; Thomas Green & Son, 1950–60; Reckitt & Colman (Household) Div.; Industrial Adviser to HM Govt, 1969–73. Member: Incorporated Soc. of British Advertisers (Pres., 1961–63); Internat. Union of Advertiser Societies (Pres. 1963–65); Advertising Standards Authority, 1962–71; Internat. Foundation for Research in Advertising (Pres., 1965–71). Mackintosh medal for personal and public services to Advertising, 1965. *Publications:* sundry articles to jls and newspapers. *Recreations:* winter sports, shooting, fishing. *Address:* Mill Farm, Burton Pidsea, East Yorkshire. *T:* Patrington 70328.

BUCK, Sir Antony; *see* Buck, Sir P. A. F.

BUCK, Sir (Philip) Antony (Fyson), Kt 1983; QC 1974; MP (C) Colchester North, since 1983 (Colchester, 1961–83); Barrister-at-Law; *b* 19 Dec. 1928; *yr s* of late A. F. Buck, Ely, Cambs; *m* 1955, Judy Elaine, *o d* of late Dr C. A. Grant, Cottesloe, Perth, W Australia, and late Mrs Grant; one *d. Educ:* King's School, Ely; Trinity Hall, Cambridge. BA History and Law, 1951, MA 1954. Chm. Cambridge Univ. Cons. Assoc. and Chm. Fedn of Univ. Conservative and Unionist Associations, 1951–52. Called to the Bar, Inner Temple, 1954; Legal Adviser, Nat. Association of Parish Councils, 1957–59, Vice-Pres., 1970–74; sponsored and piloted through the Limitation Act, 1963 PPS to Attorney General, 1963–64; Parly Under-Sec. of State for Defence (Navy), MoD, 1972–74. Sec., Conservative Party Home Affairs Cttee, 1964–70, Vice-Chm., 1970–72, Chm. Oct./Nov. 1972; Chm., Cons. Parly Defence Cttee, 1979–; Mem. Exec., 1922 Cttee, Oct./Nov. 1972, 1977–; Chm., Select Cttee on Parly Comr for Administration (Ombudsman), 1977–. *Recreations:* most sports, reading. *Address:* Pete Hall, Langenhoe, Colchester, Essex CO5 7LN. *T:* Peldon 230; 23 Cardigan Street, SE11. *T:* 01–735 8985; House of Commons, SW1A 0AA. *T:* 01–219 4011. *Club:* United Oxford & Cambridge University.

BUCKEE, His Honour Henry Thomas, DSO 1942; a Circuit Judge (formerly Judge of County Courts), 1961–79; *b* 14 June 1913; *s* of Henry Buckee; *m* 1939, Margaret Frances Chapman; two *d. Educ:* King Edward VI School, Chelmsford. Called to Bar, Middle Temple, 1939. Served RNVR, 1940–46; Lieut-Comdr 1944. *Address:* Rough Hill House, East Hanningfield, Chelmsford, Essex. *T:* Chelmsford 400226.

BUCKHURST, Lord; William Herbrand Sackville; stockbroker with Laing and Cruickshank; *b* 10 April 1948; *s* and *heir* of 10th Earl De La Warr, *qv*; *m* 1978, Anne, Countess of Hopetoun, *e d* of Arthur Leveson; two *s. Educ:* Eton. *Heir: s* Hon. William Herbrand Thomas Sackville, *b* 13 June 1979. *Address:* 75 Eaton Terrace, SW1. *T:* 01–730 4283. *Clubs:* White's, Turf.

BUCKINGHAM, Area Bishop of; Rt. Rev. Simon Hedley Burrows; appointed Bishop Suffragan of Buckingham, 1974, Area Bishop, 1985; *b* 8 Nov. 1928; *s* of late Very Rev. H. R. Burrows, and Joan Lumsden, *d* of Rt Rev. E. N. Lovett, CBE; *m* 1960, Janet Woodd; two *s* three *d. Educ:* Eton; King's Coll., Cambridge (MA); Westcott House, Cambridge. Curate of St John's Wood, 1954–57; Chaplain of Jesus Coll., Cambridge, 1957–60; Vicar of Wyken, Coventry, 1960–67; Vicar of Holy Trinity, Fareham, 1967–74, and Rector of Team Ministry, 1971–74. *Address:* Sheridan, Grimms Hill, Great Missenden, Bucks. *T:* Great Missenden 2173.

BUCKINGHAM, Archdeacon of; *see* Bone, Ven. J. F. E.

BUCKINGHAM, Amyand David, FRS 1975; Professor of Chemistry, University of Cambridge, since 1969, Fellow of Pembroke College, since 1970; *b* 28 Jan. 1930; 2nd *s* of late Reginald Joslin Buckingham and late Florence Grace Buckingham (formerly Elliot); *m* 1965, Jillian Bowles; one *s* two *d. Educ:* Barker Coll., Hornsby, NSW; Univ. of Sydney; Corpus Christi Coll., Cambridge (Shell Postgraduate Schol.). Univ. Medal 1952, MSc 1953, Sydney; PhD 1956, ScD 1985, Cantab. 1851 Exhibn Sen. Studentship, Oxford Univ., 1955–57; Lectr and subseq. Student and Tutor, Christ Church, Oxford, 1955–65; Univ. Lectr in Inorganic Chem. Lab., Oxford, 1958–65; Prof. of Theoretical Chem., Univ. of Bristol, 1965–69. Vis. Lectr, Harvard, 1961; Visiting Professor: Princeton, 1965; Univ. of California (Los Angeles), 1975; Univ. of Illinois, 1976; Univ. of Wisconsin, 1978; Vis. Fellow, ANU, 1979 and 1982. FRACI 1961 (Masson Meml Schol. 1952; Rennie Meml Medal, 1958); FRSC (formerly FCS) (Harrison Meml Prize, 1959; Tilden Lectr 1964; Theoretical Chemistry and Spectroscopy Prize, 1970; Member Faraday Div. (Council, 1965–67, 1975–83); FInstP; Fellow, Optical Soc. of America; Member: Amer. Chem. Soc.; Amer. Phys. Soc. Editor: Molecular Physics, 1968–72; Chemical Physics Letters, 1978–. Member: Chemistry Cttee, SRC, 1967–70; Adv. Council, Royal Mil. Coll. of Science, Shrivenham, 1973–. Senior Treasurer: Oxford Univ. Cricket Club, 1959–64; Cambridge Univ. Cricket Club, 1976–. Hon. Dr, Univ. de Nancy I, 1979. *Publications:* The Laws and Applications of Thermodynamics, 1964; Organic Liquids, 1978; papers in scientific jls. *Recreations:* walking, woodwork, cricket, tennis, travel. *Address:* 37 Millington Road, Cambridge CB3 9HW.

BUCKINGHAM, George Somerset; retired; *b* 11 May 1903; *s* of Horace Clifford Buckingham, Norwich; *m* 1927, Marjorie Lanaway Bateson (*d* 1981); one *s* (one *d* decd). *Educ:* Norwich Sch.; Faraday House Electrical Engrg Coll. (Gold Medallist; Dipl.). BSc (Eng); CEng; FIEE; CBIM. Asst Engr, Yorks Electric Power Co., Leeds, 1924–26; District Engr and Br. Man., Birmingham, for Pirelli-General Cable Works Ltd of Southampton, 1928–48; Midlands Electricity Board: Chief Purchasing Officer, 1948–57; Chief Engr, 1957–62; Dep. Chm., 1962–64; Chm., 1964–69. Member: Electricity Council, 1964–69; Electricity Supply Industry Trng Bd, 1965–69; W Midlands Sports Council, 1966–71; Mem. Council, Univ. of Aston in Birmingham; Mem. Council, Electrical Research Assoc., 1967–72; various sci. and profl Instns and Cttees; Pres. Birmingham Branch, Institute of Marketing, 1967–68. Chairman: South Midland Centre, IEE, 1966–67; Midland Centre, Council of Engineering Instns, 1968–70; Past President, Council of Birmingham Electric Club, 1965; Past President, Faraday House Old Students' Assoc., 1962; Vice-President, Outward Bound Schs Assoc. (Birm. and Dist), 1964–72. *Publications:* papers, articles and reviews in scientific and electrical engrg jls and works of professional engrg bodies. *Recreations:* walking, bridge. *Address:* 15 Parklands, Blossomfield Road, Solihull, West Midlands B91 1NG. *T:* 021–705 2066.

BUCKINGHAM, Prof. Richard Arthur; Professor of Computer Education, Birkbeck College, University of London, 1974–78, now Professor Emeritus; *b* 17 July 1911; *s* of George Herbert Buckingham and Alice Mary Watson (*née* King); *m* 1939 Christina O'Brien; one *s* two *d. Educ:* Gresham's Sch., Holt; St John's Coll., Cambridge. Asst Lecturer in Mathematical Physics, Queen's University, Belfast, 1935–38; Senior 1851 Exhibitioner, University College, London and MIT, 1938–40. At Admiralty Research Laboratory, Teddington, and Mine Design Dept, Havant, 1940–45. University Coll., London: Lecturer in Mathematics, 1945–50; Lecturer in Physics, 1950–51; Reader in Physics, 1951–57; Dir, Univ. of London Computer Unit, later Inst. of Computer Science, 1957–73, and Prof. of Computing Science, 1963–74. FBCS; FRSA. *Publications:* Numerical Methods, 1957; papers in Proc. Royal Soc., Proc. Phys. Soc., London, Jl Chem. Physics, Trans. Faraday Soc., Computer Journal, etc. *Recreation:* travel. *Address:* Challens, Heather Way, Sullington, West Sussex RH20 4DD.

BUCKINGHAMSHIRE, 10th Earl of, *cr* 1746; George Miles Hobart-Hampden; Bt 1611; Baron Hobart 1728; company director; *b* 15 Dec. 1944; *s* of Cyril Langel Hobart-Hampden (*d* 1972) (*g g s* of 6th Earl), and Margaret Moncrieff Hilborne Hobart-Hampden (*née* Jolliffe) (*d* 1985); *S* cousin, 1983; *m* 2nd, 1975, Alison Wightman (*née* Forrest); two step *s. Educ:* Clifton College; Exeter Univ. (BA Hons History); Birkbeck Coll. and Inst. of Commonwealth Studies, Univ. of London (MA Area Studies). With Noble Lowndes and Partners Ltd, 1970–81; Dir, Scottish Pension Trustees Ltd, 1979–81, resigned; Director: Antony Gibbs Pension Services Ltd, 1981–; The Angel Trust Co., 1982–; Wardley Investment Services (UK) Ltd, 1986–; WISL Internat. Ltd, Hongkong Bank Gp, 1986–. Mem., H of L Select Cttee on European Affairs, Sub-Cttee C, 1985–. FInstD. Patron, Hobart Town (1804) First Settlers Assoc. *Recreations:* music, squash, fishing, rugby football. *Heir:* Sir Robert Hobart, Bt, *qv. Address:* The Old Rectory, Church Lane, Edgcott, near Aylesbury, Bucks HP18 0TR. *T:* Aylesbury 77357. *Clubs:* Western (Glasgow); West of Scotland Football.

BUCKLAND, Maj.-Gen. Ronald John Denys Eden, CB 1974; MBE 1956; Chief Executive, Adur District Council, 1975–85; *b* 27 July 1920; *s* of late Geoffrey Ronald Aubert Buckland, CB and Lelgarde Edith Eleanor (*née* Eden); *m* 1968, Judith Margaret Coxhead; two *d. Educ:* Winchester; New College, Oxford (MA). Commissioned into Coldstream Gds, Dec. 1940. Served War of 1939–45: NW Europe, with 4th Coldstream Gds, 1944–45 (wounded twice). GSO3, Gds Div., BAOR, 1946; Adjt, 1st Bn Coldstream Gds, Palestine and Libya, 1948; DAA&QMG, 2nd Guards Bde and 18th Inf. Bde, Malaya, 1950–52 (Dispatches); DAAG, 3rd Div., Egypt, 1954; jssc 1956; Bde Major, 1st Gds Bde, Cyprus, 1958; Bt Lt-Col 1959; Bde Major, 51st Inf. Bde, 1960; commanded 1st Bn, Coldstream Gds, 1961, British Guiana, 1962; GSO1, 4th Div., BAOR, 1963; Brig. 1966; Comdr, 133 Inf. Bde (TA), 1966; ACOS, Joint Exercises Div., HQ AFCENT, Holland, 1967; idc 1968; DA&QMG, 1st British Corps, BAOR, 1969; Maj.-Gen. 1969; Chief of Staff, HQ Strategic Command, 1970; Maj.-Gen. i/c Admin, UKLF, 1972–75. *Recreations:* travel, watching cricket, bricklaying. *Clubs:* Pratt's, Leander; Sussex.

BUCKLE, (Christopher) Richard (Sandford), CBE 1979; writer; critic; exhibition designer; Director, Theatre Museum Association, since 1978; *b* 6 Aug. 1916; *s* of late Lieut-Col C. G. Buckle, DSO, MC, Northamptonshire Regt, and of Mrs R. E. Buckle (*née*

Sandford). *Educ:* Marlborough; Balliol. Founded "Ballet", 1939. Served Scots Guards, 1940–46; in action in Italy (despatches, 1944). Started "Ballet" again, 1946; it continued for seven years. Ballet critic of the Observer, 1948–55: ballet critic of the Sunday Times, 1959–75; advised Canada Council on state of ballet in Canada, 1962; advised Sotheby & Co. on their sales of Diaghilev Ballet material, 1967–69. First play, Gossip Column, prod Q Theatre, 1953; Family Tree (comedy), prod Connaught Theatre, Worthing, 1956. *Organised:* Diaghilev Exhibition, Edinburgh Festival, 1954, and Forbes House, London, 1954–55; The Observer Film Exhibition, London, 1956; Telford Bicentenary Exhibition, 1957; Epstein Memorial Exhibition, Edinburgh Festival, 1961; Shakespeare Exhibition, Stratford-upon-Avon, 1964–65; a smaller version of Shakespeare Exhibition, Edinburgh, 1964; Treasures from the Shakespeare Exhibition, National Portrait Gallery, London, 1964–65; The Communities on the March area in the Man in the Community theme pavilion, Universal and Internat. Exhibition of 1967, Montreal; Exhibition of Beaton Portraits, 1928–68, National Portrait Gallery, 1968; Gala of ballet, Coliseum, 1971; exhibn of Ursula Tyrwhitt, Ashmolean Mus., Oxford, 1974; exhibn Omaggio ai Disegnatori di Diaghilev, Palazzo Grassi, Venice, 1975; exhibn of ballet, opera and theatre costumes, Salisbury Fest., 1975; exhibn Happy and Glorious, 130 years of Royal photographs, Nat. Portrait Gallery, 1977; presented Kama Dev in recital of Indian dancing, St Paul's Church, Covent Garden, 1970; *designed:* (temporary) Haldane Library for Imperial College, South Kensington; new Exhibition Rooms, Harewood House, Yorks, 1959; redesigned interior of Dundee Repertory Theatre, 1963 (burnt down 3 months later). *Publications:* John Innocent at Oxford (novel), 1939; The Adventures of a Ballet Critic, 1953; In Search of Diaghilev, 1955; Modern Ballet Design, 1955; The Prettiest Girl in England, 1958; Harewood (a guide-book), 1959 and (re-written and re-designed), 1966; Dancing for Diaghilev (the memoirs of Lydia Sokolova), 1960; Epstein Drawings (introd. only), 1962; Epstein: An Autobiography (introd. to new edn only), 1963; Jacob Epstein: Sculptor, 1963; Monsters at Midnight: the French Romantic Movement as a background to the ballet Giselle (limited edn), 1966; The Message, a Gothick Tale of the A1 (limited edn), 1969; Nijinsky, 1971; Nijinsky on Stage: commentary on drawings of Valentine Gross, 1971; (ed) U and Non-U revisited, 1978; Diaghilev, 1979; (ed) Self Portrait with Friends, selected diaries of Cecil Beaton, 1979; Buckle at the Ballet, 1980; (with Roy Strong and others) Designing for the Dancer, 1981; *autobiography:* 1, The Most Upsetting Woman, 1981; 2, In the Wake of Diaghilev, 1982. *Recreations:* caricature, light verse. *Address:* Roman Road, Gutch Common, Semley, Shaftesbury, Dorset.

BUCKLE, Maj.-Gen. (Retd) Denys Herbert Vintcent, CB 1955; CBE 1948 (OBE 1945); Legion of Merit (USA) 1944; FCIT; Trustee, South Africa Foundation, since 1969; Director, Prince Vintcent & Co. (Pty) Ltd, Mossel Bay; *b* Cape, South Africa, 16 July 1902; *s* of Major H. S. Buckle, RMLI and ASC and of Agnes Buckle (*née* Vintcent), Cape Town; *m* 1928, Frances Margaret Butterworth; one *d*. *Educ:* Boxgrove School, Guildford; Charterhouse, Godalming; RMC Sandhurst. 2nd Lieut, E Surrey Regt, 1923; transf. to RASC, 1926; Shanghai Def. Force, 1927–28; Asst Adjt, RASC Trg Centre, 1929–32; Adjt 44th (Home Counties) Divnl RASC, TA, 1932–36; Student Staff Coll., Camberley, 1936–37; Adjt Ceylon ASC, 1938; Bde Maj., Malaya Inf Bde, 1938–40; GSO 2, Trg Directorate, WO, 1940; AA & QMG, 8th Armd Div., 1940–41; GSO 1, Staff Coll., Camberley, 1941–42; Brig. Admin. Plans, GHQ Home Forces, "Cossac" and SHAEF, 1942–44; Brig. Q Ops, WO, 1944; DDST and Brig. Q, 21 Army Gp and BAOR, 1945–46; DQMG, FARELF, 1946–48; DDST, S Comd, 1948–49; Spec. Appts (Brig.), USA, 1949–50; Dir of Equipment, WO, 1950–51, and special appt, Paris, 1951; Comdt RASC Trg Centre, 1952–53; DST, MELF, 1953–56; Maj.-Gen. i/c Admin, GHQ, MELF, 1956–58; despatches, 1956 (Suez); retd 1958; ADC to King George VI 1951, to the Queen, 1952–54. FCIT 1971. Bursar, Church of England Training Colleges, Cheltenham, 1958–59. Divisional Manager SE Division, British Waterways, 1961–63; Director of Reorganisation, British Waterways, 1963–65. Dir, UK-S Africa Trade Assoc., 1965–68; Administrative Mem., Southern Africa Cttee, BNEC, 1967–68. Col Comdt RASC, 1959–64; Representative Col Comdt, RASC, 1961; Hon. Col 44th (Home Counties), RASC, 1962–65, Regt, RCT, 1965–67. Legion of Merit (USA), 1944. *Publications:* History of 44th Division, RASC, TA, 1932; The Vintcents of Mossel Bay, 1986. *Recreations:* reading, broadcasting, writing, walking, swimming, travel. *Address:* Flat A, 636 St Martini Gardens, Queen Victoria Street, Cape Town, 8001, South Africa. *Clubs:* Army and Navy; Western Province Sports (Cape Town).

BUCKLE, Rt. Rev. Edward Gilbert; Bishop in the Northern Region, Diocese of Auckland, New Zealand, since 1981; *b* 20 July 1926; *s* of Douglas Gordon Buckle and Claire Ettie Wellman; *m* 1949, Mona Ann Cain; one *s* three *d*. *Educ:* Hurstville Central Coll.; Moore Theological Coll., Univ. of Sydney (LTh); St Augustine's College, Canterbury, Eng. (DipCC). Rector of Koorawatha, 1950–51; Chaplain, Snowy Mountains Hydro-Electric Authority, 1952–54; Rector, All Saints, Canberra, 1955–62; Canon, St Saviour's Cathedral, Goulburn, 1959; Dir of Adult Education for Gen. Bd of Religious Education, Melbourne, 1962–65. New Zealand: Vicar, St Matthew's-in-the-City, Auckland, 1966–67; Bishop's Executive Officer, 1967–70; Diocesan and Ecumenical Develt Officer, 1970–81; Archdeacon of Auckland, 1970–81. *Publications:* The Disturber: The Episcopacy of Ernest Henry Burgmann, Bishop of Canberra and Goulburn, 1957; A Station of the Cross, 1959; Cost of Living, study material on MRI; Family Affair, 1966; Urban Development, 1968; Interview 69, 1969; The Churches and East Coast Bays, 1970; The Isthmus and Redevelopment, 1973; Inner City Churches, 1973; Otara and the Churches, 1974; The Churches East of the Tamaki, 1974; Paroikia—the house alongside, 1978. *Recreations:* reading, sailing, squash. *Address:* 20 Tainui Street, Torbay, Auckland 10, New Zealand. *T:* Auckland 404–6372. *Club:* Wellesley (Wellington, NZ).

BUCKLE, Richard; *see* Buckle, C. R. S.

BUCKLEY, family name of **Baron Wrenbury.**

BUCKLEY, Anthony James Henthorne; consultant; *b* 22 May 1934; *s* of late William Buckley, FRCS; *m* 1964, Celia Rosamund Sanderson, *d* of late C. R. Sanderson; one *s* two *d*. *Educ:* Haileybury and ISC; St John's Coll., Cambridge. MA, LLB, FCA. Peat Marwick Mitchell & Co., 1959–62; Rank Organisation Ltd, 1962–66; Slater Walker Securities Ltd, 1966–75, Man. Dir, 1972–75. *Address:* 2 St Mary's Grove, SW13.

BUCKLEY, Rt. Hon. Sir Denys (Burton), PC 1970; Kt 1960; MBE 1945; a Lord Justice of Appeal, 1970–81; *b* 6 Feb. 1906; 4th *s* of 1st Baron Wrenbury; *m* 1932, Gwendolen Jane (*d* 1985), *yr d* of late Sir Robert Armstrong-Jones, CBE, FRCS, FRCP; three *d*. *Educ:* Eton; Trinity College, Oxford. Called to the Bar, Lincoln's Inn, 1928, Bencher, 1949, Pro-Treasurer, 1967, Treasurer, 1969, Pres., Senate of the Inns of Court, 1970–72. Served War of 1939–45, in RAOC, 1940–45; Temporary Major; GSO II (Sigs Directorate), War Office. Treasury Junior Counsel (Chancery), 1949–60; Judge of High Court of Justice, Chancery Div., 1960–70. Member, Restrictive Practices Ct, 1962–70, President, 1968–70; Member: Law Reform Cttee, 1963–73; Cttee on Departmental Records, 1952–54; Advisory Council on Public Records, 1958–79. Hon. Fellow: Trinity Coll., Oxford, 1969; Amer. Coll. of Trial Lawyers, 1970. Master, Merchant Taylors' Co., 1972, First Upper Warden, 1986–87. CStJ 1966. Medal of Freedom (USA), 1945. *Address:* Flat 6, 105 Onslow Square, SW7. *T:* 01–584 4735; Stream Farm, Dallington, Sussex. *T:* Rushlake Green 830223. *Clubs:* Brooks's, Beefsteak.

BUCKLEY, Eric Joseph, MA; FIOP; Printer to the University of Oxford, 1978–83; Emeritus Fellow of Linacre College, Oxford, 1983 (Fellow, 1979–83); *b* 26 June 1920; *s* of Joseph William Buckley and Lillian Elizabeth Major (*née* Drake); *m* 1st, 1945, Joan Alice Kirby (*d* 1973); one *s* one *d*; 2nd, 1978, Harriett, *d* of Judge and Mrs Robert Williams Hawkins, Caruthersville, Mo, USA. *Educ:* St Bartholomew's, Dover. MA Oxon 1979 (by special resolution; Linacre College). Served War, RAOC and REME, ME and UK, 1939–45. Apprentice, Amalgamated Press, London, 1935; Dir, Pergamon Press Ltd, 1956–74; joined Oxford Univ. Press as Dir, UK Publishing Services, 1974. Liveryman, Stationers and Newspaper Makers Co., 1981; Freeman, City of London, 1980. *Recreations:* reading, theatre, cats. *Address:* 43 Sandfield Road, Oxford OX3 7RN. *T:* Oxford 60588.

BUCKLEY, George Eric; Counsellor, Atomic Energy, British Embassy, Tokyo, 1976–81; *b* 4 Feb. 1916; *s* of John and Florence Buckley; *m* 1941, Mary Theresa Terry; one *s* one *d*. *Educ:* Oldham High Sch.; Manchester Univ. BSc (Hons) Physics; MInstP. Lectr in Physics, Rugby Coll. of Technol., 1938. War service, Sqdn Ldr, RAF, 1940–46. Manager, Health Physics and Safety, Windscale Works, 1949; Works Manager, Capenhurst Works, 1952; Chief Ops Physicist, Risley, 1956; Chief Tech. Manager, Windscale and Calder Works, 1959; Superintendent: Calder Hall and Windscale Advanced Gas Cooled Reactors, 1964; Reactors, and Head of Management Services, 1974. *Recreations:* travel, good food, golf. *Address:* 12 West Water Rise, Seascale, Cumbria CA20 1LB. *T:* Seascale 28405.

BUCKLEY, James; Chief Executive, British Veterinary Association, since 1985; *b* 5 April 1944; *s* of late Harold Buckley and of Mabel Buckley; *m* 1972, Valerie Elizabeth Powles; one *d*. *Educ:* Sheffield City Grammar Sch.; Imperial College of Science and Technology (BSc, ARCS). RAF Operational Res., 1965. Principal Scientific Officer, 1971; Asst Sec., CSD; Private Secretary: to Lord Privy Seal, Lord Peart, 1979; to Lord President of Council, Lord Soames, 1979; to Chancellor of Duchy of Lancaster, Baroness Young, 1981; Sec., Civil Service Coll., 1982. *Recreations:* photography, squash, tennis. *Address:* 29 Spenser Avenue, Weybridge, Surrey KT13 0ST. *T:* Weybridge 43893.

BUCKLEY, James Arthur, CBE 1975; Senior Energy Consultant and Director, CIRS Ltd, Newmarket; *b* 3 April 1917; *s* of late James Buckley and of Elizabeth Buckley; *m* 1939, Irene May Hicks; two *s*. *Educ:* Christ's Hosp., Horsham, Sussex; Westminster Technical Coll.; Bradford Technical Coll. RAFVR, 1940–46. Gas Light & Coke Co.; Gas Supply Pupil, 1934; Actg Service Supervisor, 1939; Service Supervisor, 1946; North Thames Gas Board: Divisional Man., 1954; Commercial Man., 1962; Commercial Man. and Bd Mem., 1964; East Midlands Gas Board: Dep. Chm., 1966–67; Chm., 1967–68; Mem., Gas Council, later British Gas Corp., 1968–76.

BUCKLEY, Sir John (William), Kt 1977; FRSA 1978; Hon. FIChemE; FIProdE; chairman and director of companies; Chairman, Davy Corporation (formerly Davy International Ltd), 1973–82, retired; *b* 9 Jan. 1913; *s* of John William and Florence Buckley; *m* 1st, 1935, Bertha Bagnall (marr. diss. 1967); two *s*; 2nd, 1967, Molly Neville-Clarke; one step *s* (and one step *s* decd). *Educ:* techn. coll. (Dipl. Engrg). George Kent Ltd, 1934–50 (Gen. Man. 1945–50); Man. Dir, Emmco Pty Ltd, 1950–55; Man. Dir, British Motor Corp. Pty Ltd, 1956–60; Vice Chm. and Dep. Chm., Winget, Gloucester Ltd, 1961–68; Man. Dir and Dep. Chm., Davy International Ltd, 1968–73; Chm., Alfred Herbert Ltd, 1975–79; Chairman: Oppenheimer International, 1983–; Engelhard Industries, 1979–85; John Buckley Associates Ltd, 1983–; Harman Ltd, 1985–; Director: Engelhard Corp. Inc., USA, 1982–; Fuerst Day Lawson, 1981–. Dir, British Overseas Trade Bd, 1973–76. Mem., BSC, 1978–81. Hon. FIChemE 1975. Order of the Southern Cross (Brazil), 1977. *Recreations:* gardening, music, photography, fishing, painting. *Address:* 21 Mulberry Walk, SW3. *T:* 01–352 1861. *Clubs:* Boodle's; Union (Sydney).

BUCKLEY, Rear-Adm. Sir Kenneth (Robertson), KBE 1961; FIEE, MBritIRE; *b* 24 May 1904; 2nd *s* of late L. E. Buckley, CSI, TD; *m* 1937, Bettie Helen Radclyffe Dugmore; one *s* two *d*. *Educ:* RN Colleges Osborne and Dartmouth. Joined Navy Jan. 1918. Served War of 1939–45 (despatches). Comdr 1942; Capt. 1949; Rear-Adm. 1958. ADC to the Queen, 1956–58. Director of Engineering and Electrical Training of the Navy, and Senior Naval Electrical Officer, 1959–62. *Recreations:* golf, gardening. *Address:* Meadow Cottage, Cherque Lane, Lee-on-Solent, Hants. *T:* Lee 550646.

BUCKLEY, Michael Sydney; Under Secretary, Department of Energy, since 1985; *b* 20 June 1939; *s* of Sydney Dowsett Buckley and Grace Bew Buckley; *m* 1972, Shirley Stordy; one *s* one *d*. *Educ:* Eltham College; Christ Church, Oxford (MA; Cert. of Stats). Asst Principal, Treasury, 1962; Asst Private Sec. to Chancellor of Exchequer, 1965–66; Principal: Treasury, 1966–68 and 1971–74; CSD, 1968–71; Assistant Secretary: Treasury, 1974–77 and 1980–82; DoI, 1977–80; Under Sec., Cabinet Office, 1982–85. *Recreations:* photography, listening to music, reading. *Address:* 53 Bexley Road, SE9 2PE. *T:* 01–850 8148.

BUCKLEY, Rear-Adm. Peter Noel, CB 1964; DSO 1945; retd; Head of Naval Historical Branch, Ministry of Defence, 1968–75; *b* 26 Dec. 1909; *s* of late Frank and Constance Buckley, Hooton, Cheshire; *m* 1945, Norah Elizabeth Astley St Clair-Ford, *widow* of Lt-Comdr Drummond St Clair-Ford; one *d* (and two step *s* one step *d*). *Educ:* Holmwood School, Formby, Lancs; RNC, Dartmouth. Midshipman, HMS Tiger, 1927, HMS Cornwall, 1928–30; Lieut: qual. 1931. Submarine Service, 1931–38, in submarines; Lieut-Comdr, CO of HMS Shark, 1938. War of 1939–45 (despatches): POW Germany, 1940–45. Comdr 1945; HMS: Rajah and Formidable, 1946; Siskin, 1947; Glory, 1949; RN Barracks, Portsmouth, 1951; Capt. 1952; Capt. D, Plymouth, 1953; Capt. of Dockyard, Rosyth, 1954; Chief Staff Officer to Flag Officer Comdg Reserve Fleet, 1957; Capt of Fleet, Med. Fleet, 1959; Rear-Adm. 1962; Dir-Gen., Manpower, 1962–64; retd 1965. *Address:* Forest Cottage, Sway, Lymington, Hants. *T:* Lymington 682442.

BUCKLEY, Lt-Comdr Sir (Peter) Richard, KCVO 1982 (CVO 1973; MVO 1968); Private Secretary to the Duke and Duchess of Kent since 1961; Director, Vickers International Ltd; *b* 31 Jan. 1928; 2nd *s* of late Alfred Buckley and of Mrs E. G. Buckley, Crowthorne, Berks; *m* 1958, Theresa Mary Neve; two *s* one *d*. *Educ:* Wellington Coll. Cadet, RN, 1945. Served in HM Ships: Mauritius, Ulster, Contest, Defender, and BRNC, Dartmouth. Specialised in TA/S. Invalided from RN (Lt-Comdr), 1961. *Recreations:* fishing, sailing, bee keeping. *Address:* Coppins Cottages, Iver, Bucks SL0 0AT. *T:* Iver 653004. *Clubs:* Army and Navy; Royal Dart Yacht.

BUCKLEY, Roger John, QC 1979; a Recorder, since 1986; *b* 26 April 1939; *s* of Harold and Marjorie Buckley; *m* 1965, Margaret Gillian, *d* of Robert and Joan Cowan; one *s* one *d*. *Educ:* Mill Hill Sch.; Manchester Univ. (LLB (Hons)). Called to the Bar, Middle Temple, 1962 (Harmsworth Schol.). *Recreations:* squash, theatre. *Address:* 1 Brick Court, Temple, EC4Y 9BY. *Club:* Old Mill Hillians.

BUCKLEY, Dr Trevor, CEng, FIEE; Deputy Controller Research, Ministry of Defence (Procurement Executive), since 1986; *b* 4 Feb. 1938; *s* of Harold Buckley and Selina (*née*

Follos); *m* 1960, Mary Pauline Stubbs; one *s* one *d*. *Educ:* Barmouth Grammar Sch.; UCNW Bangor (BSc Hons Electronic Engrg, PhD). RRE, 1962–76 (Head of ATC Res. Div., 1972–76); Admiralty Underwater Weapons Estabt, 1976–82 (Head of Sonar Data Processing Res. Div., 1976–80, Dep. Dir Underwater Weapons Projects (SM), 1980–82); RCDS, 1983; Dir Gen., Air Weapons and Electronic Systems, MoD (PE), 1984–86. *Recreations:* photography, musical appreciation, fixing things. *Address:* 46 Moreland Drive, Gerrards Cross, Bucks SL9 8BD. *T:* Gerrards Cross 885920.

BUCKLEY, Major William Kemmis, MBE 1959; DL; President, Buckley's Brewery Ltd, 1983–86 (Director, 1960, Vice-Chairman, 1963–72, Chairman, 1972–83); *b* 18 Oct. 1921; *o s* of late Lt-Col William Howell Buckley, DL, and Karolie Kathleen Kemmis. *Educ:* Radley Coll.; New Coll., Oxford (MA). Commnd into Welsh Guards, 1941; served N Africa, Italy (despatches, 1945); ADC, 1946–47, Mil. Sec., 1948, to Governor of Madras; Staff Coll., Camberley, 1950; GSO2, HQ London Dist, 1952–53; OC Guards Indep. Para. Co., 1954–57; Cyprus, 1956; Suez, 1956; War Office, 1957; Mil. Asst to Vice-Chief of Imp. Gen. Staff, 1958–59; US Armed Forces Staff Coll., Norfolk, Va., 1959–60. Director: Rhymney Breweries Ltd, 1962–69; Whitbread (Wales) Ltd, 1969–81; Felinfoel Brewery Co., 1975–; Guardian Assurance Co. (S Wales), 1966–83 (Dep. Chm., 1967–83). Mem. Council, Brewers' Soc., 1967; Chm., S Wales Brewers' Assoc., 1971–74; Dep. Chm. and Treas., Nat. Trade Develt Assoc., 1966 (Chm., S Wales Panel, 1965); Lay Mem., Press Council, 1967–73. Chm., Council of St John of Jerusalem for Carms, 1966; Pres., Carms Antiquarian Soc., 1971– (Chm., 1968); Mem., Nat. Trust Cttee for Wales, 1962–70; Mem., T&AFA (Carms), 1962–82 and T&AFA (S Wales and Mon.), 1967–83; Jt Master and Hon. Sec., Pembrokeshire and Carms Otter Hounds, 1962. High Sheriff of Carms, 1967–68, DL Dyfed (formerly Carms) 1969. KStJ 1984 (CStJ 1966). *Publications:* contributions in local history journals. *Recreations:* gardening, bee-keeping, tapestry work. *Address:* Briar Cottage, Ferryside, Dyfed, S Wales. *T:* Ferryside 359. *Clubs:* Brooks's; Cardiff and County (Cardiff).

BUCKMASTER, family name of **Viscount Buckmaster.**

BUCKMASTER, 3rd Viscount *cr* 1933, of Cheddington; **Martin Stanley Buckmaster,** OBE 1979; Baron 1915; HM Diplomatic Service, retired; *b* 11 April 1921; *s* of 2nd Viscount Buckmaster and Joan, Viscountess Buckmaster (*d* 1976), *d* of Dr Garry Simpson; *S* father, 1974. *Educ:* Stowe. Joined TA, 1939; served Royal Sussex Regt (Captain) in UK and Middle East, 1940–46. Foreign Office, 1946; Middle East Centre for Arab Studies, Lebanon, 1950–51; qualified in Arabic (Higher Standard); served in Trucial States, Sharjah (1951–53) and Abu Dhabi (Political Officer, 1955–58) and subsequently in Libya, Bahrain, FO, Uganda, Lebanon and Saudi Arabia, 1958–73; First Sec., FCO, 1973–77; Head of Chancery and Chargé d'Affaires, Yemen Arab Republic, 1977–81. FRGS 1954. *Recreations:* walking, music, railways; Arab and African studies. *Heir:* *b* Hon. Colin John Buckmaster [*b* 17 April 1923; *m* 1946, May, *o d* of late Charles Henry Gibbon; three *s* two *d*]. *Address:* 90 Cornwall Gardens, SW7 4AX. *Club:* Travellers'.

BUCKMASTER, Rev. Cuthbert Harold Septimus; *b* 15 July 1903; *s* of Charles John and Evelyn Jean Buckmaster; *m* 1942, Katharine Mary Zoë (*d* 1974), 3rd *d* of Rev. Canon T. N. R. Prentice, Stratford-on-Avon; two *d*. *Educ:* RN Colls, Osborne and Dartmouth. Asst Curate St John's, Middlesbrough, 1927–30; Curate of Wigan, 1930–33; Chaplain of Denstone Coll., 1933–35; Warden of St Michael's Coll., Tenbury, Worcs, 1935–46; Rector of: Ashprington, with Cornworthy, 1957–59; Chagford, 1959–71. Chaplain RNVR, 1940; RN 1947. *Address:* 2 Pickworth Drive, Anglesea, Vic 3230, Australia.

BUCKMASTER, Colonel Maurice James, OBE 1943; Independent Public Relations Consultant, since 1960; *b* 11 Jan. 1902; *s* of Henry James Buckmaster and Eva Matilda (*née* Nason); *m* 1st, 1927, May Dorothy (*née* Steed); one *s* two *d*; 2nd, 1941, Anna Cecilia (*née* Reinstein). *Educ:* Eton College. J. Henry Schroder & Co., Merchant Bankers, 1923–29; Asst to Chairman, Ford Motor Co. Ltd, 1929–32; Manager, Ford Motor Co. (France), 1932–36; Head of European Dept, Ford Motor Co. Ltd, 1936–39 and 1945–50; Dir of Public Relations, 1950–60. Served War of 1939–45: 50th Div., G3I, Intelligence, 1939–40 (despatches); Intelligence Officer (Captain), Dakar expedition; Special Operations Executive, Head of French Section, 1941–45. Chevalier de la Légion d'Honneur, 1945, Officier 1978 (France); Croix de Guerre with Palms, Médaille de la Résistance (France), 1945; Legion of Merit (US), 1945. *Publications:* Specially Employed, 1961; They Fought Alone, 1964. *Recreation:* family life. *Address:* Bourne Cottage, Ashdown Road, Forest Row, East Sussex. *T:* Forest Row 2379. *Clubs:* Special Forces, Institute of Directors.

BUCKNILL, Peter Thomas, QC 1961; *b* 4 Nov. 1910; *o s* of late Rt Hon. Sir Alfred Bucknill, PC, OBE; *m* 1935, Elizabeth Mary Stark; three *s* two *d* (and one *d* decd). *Educ:* Gresham's Sch., Holt; Trinity Coll., Oxford (MA). Called to the Bar, Inner Temple, 1935 (Bencher, 1967). Ordinand, Chichester Theol. Coll., 1939; Deacon, 1941; Priest, 1942; received into RC Church, 1943; resumed Bar practice. Appointed Junior Counsel to the Treasury (Admiralty), 1958; resigned on becoming QC. On rota for Lloyd's Salvage Arbitrators, Wreck Commissioner, 1962–78, retired from practice, 1978. *Publications:* contributed to Halsbury's Laws of England, shipping vol., 2nd and 3rd edns. *Recreation:* gardening. *Address:* High Corner, The Warren, Ashtead, Surrey KT21 2SL.

BUCKSEY, Verity Ann, (Mrs C. M. Bucksey); *see* Lambert, V. A.

BUCKTON, Raymond William; General Secretary, Associated Society of Locomotive Engineers and Firemen, since 1970; *b* 20 Oct. 1922; *s* of W. E. and H. Buckton; *m* 1954, Barbara Langfield; two *s*. *Educ:* Appleton Roebuck School. MCIT, FCIT 1982. Employed in Motive Power Department, British Railways, 1940–60. Elected Irish Officer of ASLEF, 1960 (Dublin); District Organiser, York, Jan. 1963; Assistant General Secretary, July 1963; General Secretary, 1970. Member: Gen. Council, TUC, 1973–86 (Chm., 1983–84); IBA Gen. Adv. Council, 1976–; Occupational Pensions Bd, 1976–82; Health Services Bd, 1977–80; Health and Safety Commn, 1982–. Member: CIT Council, 1970–; Industrial Soc., 1973–; Standing Adv. Cttee, TUC Centenary Inst. of Occupational Health, 1974–; Nat. Adv. Council on Employment of Disabled People, 1975–; Industrial Injuries Adv. Council, 1976–; Dangerous Substances Adv. Cttee, 1976–; Adv. Cttee on Alcoholism, 1977–; Railway Industry Adv. Cttee, 1977–82; TUC Internat. Cttee, 1978–; EEC Economic and Social Cttee, 1978–82; Exec., ETUC, 1982–; Commonwealth TUC, 1982–. Councillor, York City Council, 1952–55, Alderman, 1955–57. *Address:* 9 Arkwright Road, Hampstead, NW3. *T:* 01–431 0275.

BUDAY, George, RE 1953 (ARE 1939); wood engraver; author on graphic arts subjects; *b* Kolozsvar, Transylvania, 7 April 1907; *s* of late Prof. Arpad Buday, Roman archaeologist, and Margaret Buday. *Educ:* Presbyterian Coll., Kolozsvar; Royal Hungarian Francis Joseph Univ., Szeged (Dr). Apptd Lectr in Graphic Arts, Royal Hungarian F. J. Univ., 1935–41; Rome Scholar, 1936–37; won travelling schol. to England (and has stayed permanently) 1937. Broadcaster, BBC European Service, 1940–42; in a Dept of Foreign Office, 1942–45. Dir, Hungarian Cultural Inst., London, 1947–49, resigned. Illustrated numerous folk-tale and folk-ballad collections, vols of classics and modern authors, publ. in many countries. Since 1938 exhib. Royal Acad., Royal Soc. of Painter-Etchers and Engravers, Soc. of Wood Engravers, and in many countries abroad. Works represented in: Depts of Prints and Drawings, Brit. Mus.; Victoria and Albert Mus.; Glasgow Univ.; New York Public Library; Florence Univ.; Museums of Fine Arts, Budapest, Prague, Warsaw; Phillips Memorial Gall., Washington, DC; etc. Grand Prix, Paris World Exhibn, 1937 (for engravings); subsequently other art and bibliophile prizes. Officer's Cross, Order of Merit (Hungary), 1947. *Publications:* Book of Ballads, 1934; The Story of the Christmas Card, 1951; The History of the Christmas Card, 1954 (1964); (wrote and illustr.): The Dances of Hungary, 1950; George Buday's Little Books, I-XII, incl. The Language of Flowers, 1951; The Cries of London, Ancient and Modern, 1954; Proverbial Cats and Kittens, 1956 (1968); The Artist's Recollections, for a volume of his 82 Selected Engravings, 1970; Multiple Portraiture: Illustrating a Poetical Anthology, 1981; contrib. articles to periodicals. *Relevant publication:* George Buday by Curt Visel, in Illustration 63, 1971. *Recreations:* bibliophile hand-printing on his 1857 Albion hand-press and collecting old Christmas cards (probably most representative collection of Victorian cards extant). *Address:* Downs House, Netherne, PO Box 150, Coulsdon, Surrey CR3 1YE.

BUDD, Bernard Wilfred, MA; QC 1969; *b* 18 Dec. 1912; *s* of late Rev. W. R. A. Budd; *m* 1944, Margaret Alison, MBE, *d* of late Rt Hon. E. Leslie Burgin, PC, LLD, MP; two *s*. *Educ:* Cardiff High Sch.; W Leeds High Sch.; Pembroke Coll., Cambridge (schol. in natural sciences). Joined ICS, 1935; various Dist appts incl. Dep. Comr, Upper Sind Frontier, 1942–43; Collector and Dist Magistrate, Karachi, 1945–46; cont. in Pakistan Admin. Service, 1947; Dep. Sec., Min. of Commerce and Works, Govt of Pakistan, 1947; Anti-corruption Officer and Inspector-Gen. of Prisons, Govt of Sind, 1949. Called to Bar, Gray's Inn, 1952; ceased English practice, 1982. Contested (L), Dover, 1964 and 1966, Folkestone and Hythe, Feb. and Oct. 1974 and 1979. Chm., Assoc. of Liberal Lawyers, 1978–82. Vice-Pres., Internat. Assoc. for the Protection of Industrial Property (British Group), 1978–. *Recreations:* tennis, birds, hill walking. *Address* Highlands, Elham, Canterbury, Kent. *T:* Elham 350. *Clubs:* United Oxford & Cambridge University, National Liberal; Sind (Karachi).

BUDD, Rt. Rev. Mgr. Hugh Christopher; *see* Plymouth, Bishop of, (RC).

BUDD, Stanley Alec; Scottish Representative, Commission of the European Communities, since 1975; *b* 22 May 1931; *s* of Henry Stanley Budd and Ann Mitchell; *m* 1955, Wilma McQueen Cuthbert (*d* 1985); three *s* one *d*. *Educ:* George Heriot's Sch., Edinburgh. Newspaper reporter, feature writer and sub-editor, D. C. Thomson & Co, Dundee, 1947–57 (National Service, 1949–51). Research writer, Foreign Office, 1957–60; 2nd Secretary, Beirut, Lebanon, 1960–63; 1st Sec., Kuala Lumpur, Malaysia, 1963–69; FO, 1969–71; Dep. Head of Information, Scottish Office, 1971–72; Press Secretary to Chancellor of Duchy of Lancaster, 1972–74; Chief Information Officer, Cabinet Office, 1974–75. *Publication:* The EEC—a Guide to the Maze, 1986. *Recreations:* music, painting, oriental antiques, bridge. *Address:* 2 Bellevue Crescent, Edinburgh EH3 6ND; 7 Alva Street, Edinburgh EH2 4PH. *T:* 031–225 2058.

BUDDEN, Kenneth George, FRS 1966; MA, PhD; Reader in Physics, University of Cambridge, 1965–82, now Emeritus; Fellow of St John's College, Cambridge, since 1947; *b* 23 June 1915; *s* of late George Easthope Budden and Gertrude Homer Rea; *m* 1947, Nicolette Ann Lydia de Longesdon Longsdon; no *c*. *Educ:* Portsmouth Grammar Sch.; St John's College, Cambridge (MA, PhD). Telecommunications Research Establishment, 1939–41; British Air Commn., Washington, DC, 1941–44; Air Command, SE Asia, 1945. Research at Cambridge, 1936–39 and from 1947. *Publications:* Radio Waves in the Ionosphere, 1961; The Wave-Guide Mode Theory of Wave Propagation, 1961; Lectures on Magnetoionic Theory, 1964; The Propagation of Radio Waves, 1985; numerous papers in scientific jls, on the propagation of radio waves. *Recreation:* gardening. *Address:* 15 Adams Road, Cambridge. *T:* Cambridge 354752.

BUDGEN, Nicholas William; MP (C) Wolverhampton South-West, since Feb. 1974; *b* 3 Nov. 1937; *s* of Captain G. N. Budgen; *m* 1964, Madeleine E. Kittoe; one *s* one *d*. *Educ:* St Edward's Sch., Oxford; Corpus Christi Coll., Cambridge. Called to Bar, Gray's Inn, 1962; practised Midland and Oxford Circuit. An Asst Govt Whip, 1981–82. *Recreations:* hunting, racing. *Address:* Malt House Farm, Colton, near Rugeley, Staffs. *T:* Rugeley 77059.

BUFFET, Bernard; Chevalier de la Légion d'Honneur; artist, painter; *b* Paris, 10 July 1928; *m* 1958, Annabel May Schwob de Lure; one *s* two *d*. Début at Salon des Moins de Trente Ans, 1944. From 1948 has had one-man shows, annually, at Drouant-David and Visconti Galleries, from 1956 at Galerie Maurice Garnier. Grand Prix de la Critique, 1948. Solo retrospective exhibition of his works was held at Charpentier Gallery, Paris, 1958. He has exhibited, oils, water colours and drawings and is a lithographer, mural painter and illustrator of books. Work represented in permanent collections: Musée du Petit Palais and Musée National d'Art Moderne, in Paris; Buffet Museum founded in Japan, 1973; large room of his mystic works in Vatican Museum; work shown at Venice Biennale, 1956; exhibitions: Lefevre Gallery, London, 1961, 1963, 1965. Stage designs: Le Rendez-vous manqué (ballet), 1959; Patron (musical comedy), 1959; ballets at L'Opéra, Paris, 1969. Mem. Salon d'Automne and Salon des Indépendants. Officier des Arts et des Lettres; Membre de l'Institut, 1974. *Address:* c/o Galerie Maurice Garnier, 6 avenue Matignon, 75008 Paris, France.

BUFTON, Air Vice-Marshal Sydney Osborne, CB 1945; DFC 1940; *b* 12 Jan. 1908; 2nd *s* of late J. O. Bufton, JP, Llandrindod Wells, Radnor; *m* 1943, Susan Maureen, *d* of Colonel E. M. Browne, DSO, Chelsea; two *d*. *Educ:* Dean Close School, Cheltenham. Commissioned RAF 1927; psa, 1939; idc, 1946. Served War of 1939–45, Bomber Comd, Nos 10 and 76 Sqdns, RAF Station, Pocklington, 1940–41; Dep. Dir Bomber Ops, 1941–43; Dir of Bomber Ops, Air Min., 1943–45; AOC Egypt, 1945–46; Central Bomber Establishment, RAF, Marham, Norfolk, 1947–48; Dep. Chief of Staff (Ops/Plans), Air Forces Western Europe, 1948–51; Dir of Weapons, Air Min., 1951–52; AOA Bomber Command, 1952–53; AOC Brit. Forces, Aden, 1953–55; Senior Air Staff Officer, Bomber Comd, 1955–58; Assistant Chief of Air Staff (Intelligence), 1958–61; retired Oct. 1961. Temp. Gp Capt. 1941; Temp. Air Cdre 1943; Subst. Gp Capt. 1946; Air Cdre 1948; Actg Air Vice-Marshal, 1952; Air Vice-Marshal, 1953. FRAeS 1970. High Sheriff of Radnorshire, 1967. Comdr Legion of Merit (US); Comdr Order of Orange Nassau (with swords), Netherlands. *Recreations:* hockey (Welsh International 1931–37, Combined Services, RAF), golf, squash. *Address:* 1 Castle Keep, London Road, Reigate. *T:* Reigate 43707. *Club:* Royal Air Force.

BUGOTU, Francis, CBE 1979; Secretary-General, South Pacific Commission, 1982–86; *b* 27 June 1937; *s* of Tione Kalapalua Bugotu and Rachael Samoa; *m* 1962, Ella Vehe; one *s* one *d*. *Educ:* NZ, Australia, Scotland, England and Solomon Is. Teacher and Inspector of Mission Schs for Ch. of Melanesia (Anglican), 1959–60; Mem., 1st Legislative Council, 1960–62; Lectr, Solomon Is Teachers Coll., 1964–68; Chief Educn Officer and Perm. Sec., Min. of Educn, 1968–75; Perm. Sec. to Chief Minister and Council of Ministers, and titular Head of Civil Service, 1976–78; Sec. for For. Affairs and Roving Ambassador/High Comr of Solomon Is, 1978–82. Chairman: Review Cttee on Educn, 1974–75; Solomon Is Tourist Authority, 1970–73; Solomon Is Scholarship Cttee, 1969–75. Consultant, esp. for S Pacific Commn; Founder Mem. and Chief Adviser, Kakamora Youth Club,

1968–75; Chief Comr of Scouts for Solomon Is, 1970–77; Lay Canon of Ch. of Melanesia, 1970–. *Publications*: (with A. V. Hughes) This Man (play), 1970 (also award winning film); papers on: impact of Western culture on Solomon Is; politics, economics and social aspects in Solomons; recolonising and decolonising; Solomon Is Pidgin. *Recreations*: interested in most ball games (soccer, cricket, basketball, Rugby, tennis, table-tennis, softball, snooker), swimming, music, dancing. *Address*: c/o South Pacific Commission, Post Box D 5, Noumea CEDEX, New Caledonia.

BUHLER, Robert, RA 1956 (ARA 1947); painter; Hon. Fellow, Royal College of Art; tutor, RCA, 1948–75; *b* London, 23 Nov. 1916; *s* of Robert Buhler, journalist; *m* Evelyn Rowell (marr. diss. 1951); one *s*; *m* 1962, Prudence Brochocka (*née* Beaumont) (marr. diss. 1972); two *s*. *Educ*: Switzerland; Bolt Court; St Martin's School of Art; Royal College of Art. Trustee, Royal Academy, 1975–. Exhibited at: Royal Academy, New English Art Club, London Group, London galleries. Work in permanent collections: Chantrey Bequest; Stott Fund; provincial art galleries; galleries in USA, Canada, Australia, NZ, France and Switzerland. *Address*: 33 Alderney Street, SW1V 4ES. *T*: 01–828 2825; (studio) 3 Avenue Studios, Sydney Close, SW3.

BUIST, John Latto Farquharson; Under Secretary, International Division, Foreign and Commonwealth Office (Overseas Development Administration); *b* 30 May 1930; *s* of late Lt-Col Thomas Powrie Buist, RAMC, and of Christian Mary (*née* Robertson). *Educ*: Dalhousie Castle Sch.; Winchester Coll.; New Coll., Oxford (MA). Asst Principal, CO, 1952–54; Sec., Kenya Police Commn, 1953; seconded Kenya Govt, 1954–56; Principal, CO, 1956–61; Dept of Tech. Cooperation, 1961–62; Brit. High Commn, Dar-es-Salaam, 1962–64; Consultant on Admin, E African Common Services Org./Community, 1964–69; Sec., Commn on E African Cooperation and related bodies, 1966–69; Asst Sec., Min. of Overseas Develt, 1966–76; Under Sec., FCO (ODA), 1976–. Co-founder and several times Pres., Classical Assoc. of Kenya; Member: John Bate Choir; United Reformed Church. *Recreations*: singing and other music-making, walking. *Address*: 9 Manor Gate, St John's Avenue, SW15. *T*: 01–789 4490.

BUITER, Prof. Willem Hendrik, PhD; Professor of Economics, Yale University, since 1985; *b* 26 Sept. 1949; *s* of Harm Geert Buiter and Hendrien Buiter, *née* van Schooten. *Educ*: Cambridge Univ. (BA 1971); Yale Univ. (PhD 1975). Asst Prof., Princeton Univ., 1975–76; Lectr, LSE, 1976–77; Asst Prof., Princeton Univ., 1977–79; Prof. of Economics, Univ. of Bristol, 1980–82; Cassel Prof. of Economics, LSE, Univ. of London, 1982–85. Consultant: IMF, 1979–80; World Bank, 1986–; Specialist Adviser, House of Commons Select Cttee on the Treasury and CS, 1980–84; Adviser, Netherlands Min. of Educn and Science, 1985–86. Associate Editor, Econ. Jl, 1980–84. *Publications*: Temporary and Long Run Equilibrium, 1979; articles in learned jls. *Recreations*: tennis, poetry, music. *Address*: 42 East Pearl Street, New Haven, Conn, USA.

BÜLBRING, Edith, MA Oxon; MD Bonn; FRS 1958; Professor of Pharmacology, Oxford University, 1967–71, now Emeritus (University Reader, 1960–67) and Honorary Fellow, Lady Margaret Hall, 1971; *b* 27 Dec. 1903; *d* of Karl Daniel Bülbring, Professor of English, Bonn University, and Hortense Leonore Bülbring (*née* Kann). *Educ*: Bonn, Munich and Freiburg Universities. Postgraduate work in Pharmacology Department of Berlin University, 1929–31; Pediatrics, University of Jena, 1932; Virchow Krankenhaus University of Berlin, 1933; Pharmacological Laboratory of Pharmaceutical Society of Great Britain, University of London, 1933–38; Pharmacology Dept, University of Oxford, 1938–71. Research work on: autonomic transmitters, suprarenals, smooth muscle, peristalsis. Schmiedeberg-Plakette der Deutschen Pharmakologischen Gesellschaft, 1974. Honorary Member: Pharmaceutical Soc., Torino, Italy, 1957; British Pharmacological Soc., 1975; Deutsche Physiolgische Gesellschaft, 1976; Physiol Soc., 1981. Hon. Dr med: Univ. of Groningen, Netherlands, 1979; Leuven, Belgium, 1981. Wellcome Gold Medal in Pharmacology, 1985. *Publications*: mainly in Jl of Physiology, Brit. Jl of Pharmacology and Proc. Royal Soc. of London, Series B. *Recreation*: music. *Address*: 15 Northmoor Road, Oxford. *T*: Oxford 57270; Lady Margaret Hall, Oxford.

BULFIELD, Peter William, CA; Director, Yamaichi International (Europe), since 1986; *b* 14 June 1930; *s* of Wilfred Bulfield and Doris (*née* Bedford); *m* 1958, Pamela June Beckett; two *d*. *Educ*: Beaumont Coll., Old Windsor. Peat Marwick Mitchell & Co., 1947–59; J. Henry Schroder Wagg & Co., 1959–86, Dir, 1967–86; Director: Schroder Finance, 1966–73; Schroder Darling Hldgs, Sydney, 1973–80; Vice-Chm., Mitsubishi Trust & Banking Corporation (Europe) SA, 1973–84; Jt Dep. Chm., Schroder Internat., 1977–86; Dep. Chm., Crown Agents for Oversea Govts and Admin, 1982–85. Member: Overseas Projects Board, 1983–; Overseas Promotions Cttee, BIEC, 1984–; Export Guarantees Adv. Council, 1985–. *Recreations*: sailing, music, painting. *Address*: The Mill House, Merrieweathers, Mayfield, Sussex TN20 6RJ. *T*: Mayfield 872177. *Clubs*: Kildare Street and University (Dublin); Royal Thames Yacht.

BULGER, Anthony Clare, BA, BCL; **His Honour Judge Bulger;** a Circuit Judge (formerly County Court Judge), since 1963; *b* 1912; *s* of Daniel Bulger; *m* Una Patricia Banks; one *s* one *d*. *Educ*: Rugby; Oriel Coll., Oxford. Called to the Bar, Inner Temple, 1936. Oxford Circuit; Dep Chm., 1958–70, Chm. 1970–71, Glos QS; Dep. Chm. Worcs QS, 1962–71; Recorder of Abingdon, 1962–63. *Address*: The Dower House, Forthampton, Glos. *T*: Tewkesbury 293257.

BULKELEY, Sir Richard H. D. W.; *see* Williams-Bulkeley.

BULL, Anthony, CBE 1968 (OBE 1944); Transport Consultant: Kennedy and Donkin, 1971–85; Freeman Fox and Partners, since 1971; *b* 18 July 1908; 3rd *s* of Rt Hon. Sir William Bull, 1st Bt, PC, MP, JP, FSA (*d* 1931), and late Lilian, 2nd *d* of G. S. Brandon, Oakbrook, Ravenscourt Park; *m* 1946, Barbara (*d* 1947), *er d* of late Peter Donovan, Yonder, Rye, Sussex; one *d*. *Educ*: Gresham's Sch., Holt; Magdalene Coll., Cambridge (Exhibitioner; MA). Joined Underground Group of Cos, 1929; served in Staff, Publicity and Public Relations Depts and Chairman's Office. Sec. to Vice-Chm. London Passenger Transport Board, 1936–39. Served War, 1939–45; RE; Transportation Br., War Office, 1939–42; GHQ, Middle East, 1943; Staff of Supreme Allied Comdr, SE Asia (end of 1943); Col 1944; Transp. Div., CCG, 1945–46. Returned to London Transport as Chief Staff and Welfare Officer, 1946; Member: LTE, 1955–62; LTB, 1962–65; Vice-Chm., LTE (formerly LTB), 1965–71. Advr to House of Commons Transport Cttee, 1981–82. Inst. of Transport: served on Council, 1956–59; Vice-Pres., 1964–66; Hon. Librarian, 1966–69; Pres., 1969–70. Mem. Regional Advisory Council for Technological Educn, 1958–62 (Transp. Adv. Cttee, 1950–62; Chm. Cttee, 1953–62); Mem., King's Lynn Area Hosps Management Cttee, 1972–74. CStJ 1969. Bronze Star (USA), 1946. *Publications*: contrib. to transport journals. *Recreation*: travel. *Address*: 35 Clareville Grove, SW7 5AU. *T*: 01–373 5647; Trowland Cottage, Burnham Norton, Norfolk. *T*: Fakenham 738297. *Club*: United Oxford & Cambridge University.

See also Sir S. G. Bull, Bt, Sir Robin Chichester-Clark.

BULL, George Anthony, FRSL 1982; writer, translator and consultant; *b* 23 Aug. 1929; *s* of George Thomas Bull and Bridget Philomena (*née* Nugent); *m* 1957, Doreen Marjorie Griffin; two *s* two *d*. *Educ*: Wimbledon Coll.; Brasenose Coll., Oxford (MA). National Service, Royal Fusiliers, 1947–49. Reporter, Financial Times, 1952–56, Foreign News Editor, 1956–59; News Editor, London Bureau, McGraw-Hill World News, 1959–60; The Director, 1960–84: successively Dep. Editor, Editor, Editor-in-Chief. Dir 1971–, and Trustee 1976–, The Tablet; Trustee, The Universe, 1970–86; Consultant Editor, Penguin Business Library, 1985–. Director: Anvil Prodns (Oxford Playhouse) Ltd, 1980–; Westminster & Overseas Trade Services, 1985–; Hugo Publications Ltd, 1986–. Chm., Commn for Internat. Justice and Peace, Episcopal Conf. of England and Wales, 1971–74; Mem. Council, RSL, 1986–; Hon. Treasurer, Soc. for Renaissance Studies, 1967–; a Governor, St Mary's Coll., Strawberry Hill, 1976–; Foundation Governor, St Thomas More Sch., 1980–. *Publications*: (with A. Vice) Bid for Power, 1958, 2nd edn 1960; Vatican Politics, 1966; The Renaissance, 1968, new edn 1973; (ed) The Director's Handbook, 1969, 2nd edn 1978; (with E. D. Foster) The Director, his Money and his Job, 1970; (with Peter Hobday and John Hamway) Industrial Relations: the boardroom viewpoint, 1972; Venice: the most triumphant city, 1982, Folio Society 1980, USA 1982; Inside the Vatican, 1982, USA 1983, Italy 1983 (as Dentro il Vaticano), Germany 1987; (trans.) Life, Letters and Poetry of Michelangelo, 1987; (trans.) Artists of the Renaissance, 1979–; translations for Penguin Classics: Life of Cellini, 1956 (1986); Machiavelli, The Prince, 1961 (1986); Vasari, Lives of the Artists, 1965 (1986); Castiglione, The Book of the Courtier, 1967 (1985); Aretino, Selected Letters, 1976. *Recreations*: book collecting, travelling. *Address*: 19 Hugh Street, SW1. *Clubs*: Garrick, Savile, Beefsteak.

BULL, Sir Graham (MacGregor), Kt 1976; retired; *b* 30 Jan. 1918; *s* of Dr A. B. Bull; *m* 1947, Megan Patricia Jones (*see* M. P. Bull); three *s* one *d*. *Educ*: Diocesan Coll., Cape Town; Univ. of Cape Town (MD). FRCP. Tutor in Medicine and Asst, Dept of Medicine, Univ. of Cape Town, 1940–46; Lecturer in Medicine, Postgraduate Medical Sch. of London, 1947–52; Professor of Medicine, The Queen's Univ., Belfast, 1952–66; Mem., MRC, 1962–66; Dir, MRC Clinical Research Centre, 1966–78. Research Fellow, SA Council for Scientific and Industrial Research, 1947; Chairman: CIBA Foundn Exec. Cttee, 1977–83; Appropriate Health Resources & Technologies Action Gp Ltd, 1978–80; 2nd Vice-Pres., RCP, 1978–79. *Publications*: contrib. to medical journals. *Address*: 29 Heath Drive, NW3 7SB. *T*: 01–435 1624.

BULL, James William Douglas, CBE 1976; MA, MD, FRCP, FRCS, FRCR; retired; Honorary Consultant Radiologist (diagnostic): National Hospital for Nervous Diseases, Queen Square; Maida Vale Hospital for Nervous Diseases; St Andrew's Hospital, Northampton; St George's Hospital; University Hospital, West Indies; Teacher, Institute of Neurology (University of London); Consultant Adviser in Diagnostic Radiology, Department of Health and Social Security, until 1975; Consultant Neuroradiologist to Royal Navy, until 1975; *b* 23 March 1911; *o s* of late D. W. A. Bull, MD, JP, Stony Stratford, Bucks; *m* 1941, Edith (*d* 1978), *e d* of late Charles Burch, Henley-on-Thames; one *s* one *d*. *Educ*: Repton; Gonville and Caius Coll., Cambridge; St George's Hospital. Entrance schol., 1932. Usual house appts; Asst Curator of Museum, Med. registrar, St George's Hospital, Rockefeller Travelling Schol. (Stockholm), 1938–39. Served War, 1940–46, Temp. Major RAMC (POW Singapore). Dean, Inst. of Neurology, Univ. of London, 1962–68. President: 4th Internat. Symposium Neuroradiologicum, London, 1955; British Inst. of Radiology, 1960; Section of Radiology, 1968–69, Section of Neurology, 1974–75, RSM; Pres., Faculty of Radiologists, 1969–72 (Vice-Pres., 1963). Member: Assoc. of British Neurologists; Brit. Soc. of Neuroradiologists; Pres., European Soc. of Neuroradiology, 1972–75. Examiner in Diagnostic Radiology: Conjoint Board, 1957; Univ. of Liverpool, 1959; for Fellowship, Faculty of Radiologists, London, 1965. Watson Smith Lectr, RCP, 1962; Skinner Lectr, Faculty of Radiologists, 1965; Dyke Meml Lectr, Columbia Univ., New York, 1969; Mackenzie Davidson Meml Lectr, Brit. Inst. Radiol., 1972; Langdon Brown Lectr, RCP, 1974. Member: Council, RCP London, 1964–67; Council, RCS, 1968–73. Hon. Fellow: Royal Soc. of Medicine, 1984; American Coll. of Radiologists; Italian Neuroradiological Soc.; Brazilian Radiological Soc.; Royal Australian Coll. of Radiology; Fac. Radiol. RCSI; Radiological Soc. of N America. Hon. Member: Canadian Neurological Soc.; American Neurological Assoc.; French Radiological Soc.; Amer. Soc. of Neuroradiology. *Publications*: Atlas of Positive Contrast Myelography (jointly), 1962. Contrib. to A. Feiling's Modern Trends in Neurology; various papers in medical journals, mostly connected with neuroradiology. *Recreations*: golf, travel. *Address*: 80 King's Road, Henley-on-Thames RG9 2DQ. *T*: Henley-on-Thames 5374. *Club*: United Oxford & Cambridge University.

BULL, John Michael; QC 1983; a Recorder of the Crown Court, since 1980. *Educ*: Corpus Christi Coll., Cambridge (BA 1958; LLB 1959). Called to the Bar, Gray's Inn, 1960; Standing Counsel to the Board of Inland Revenue. *Address*: 2 Crown Office Row, Temple, EC4Y 7HJ.

BULL, Dr John Prince, CBE 1973; Director of MRC Industrial Injuries and Burns Unit, 1952–82; *b* 4 Jan. 1917; *s* of Robert James Bull and Ida Mary Bull; *m* 1939, Irmgard Bross; four *d*. *Educ*: Burton-on-Trent Grammar Sch.; Cambridge Univ.; Guy's Hospital. MA, MD, BCh Cantab; MRCS, FRCP; MFOM. Casualty Res. Officer, Min. of Home Security, 1941; RAMC, 1942–46; Mem. Research Staff 1947, Asst Dir 1948, MRC Unit, Birmingham Accident Hosp.; Hon. Reader in Traumatology, Univ. of Birmingham. Mem., MRC, 1971–75; Chairman: Regional Res. Cttee, West Midlands RHA, 1966–82; Inst. of Accident Surgery, 1980–83. Mem., Med. Res. Soc. FRSocMed. *Publications*: contrib. scientific and med. jls. *Recreations*: bricolage, gardening. *Address*: 73 Reddings Road, Moseley, Birmingham B13 8LP. *T*: 021–449 0474.

BULL, Megan Patricia, (Lady Bull), OBE 1982; Governor, Holloway Prison, 1973–82; *b* Naauppoort, S Africa, 17 March 1922; *d* of Dr Thomas and Letitia Jones; *m* 1947, Sir Graham MacGregor Bull, *qv*; three *s* one *d*. *Educ*: Good Hope Seminary, Cape Town; Univ. of Cape Town. MB, ChB Cape Town 1944, DCH London 1947, MSc QUB 1961, DPM London 1970, MRCP 1974. Lectr in Physiology, Belfast Coll. of Technology, 1954–61; Med. Officer Student Health Dept, QUB, 1961–66; Prison Med. Officer, Holloway Prison, 1967–73. *Publications*: papers in various medical jls. *Address*: 29 Heath Drive, NW3 7SB.

BULL, Oliver Richard Silvester; Headmaster, Rugby School, since 1985; *b* 30 June 1930; *s* of Walter Haverson Bull and Margaret Bridget Bull; *m* 1956, Anne Hay Fife; two *s* four *d*. *Educ*: Rugby Sch.; Brasenose Coll. Oxford (MA). Mil. Service (1st Beds and Herts), 1949–51. Asst Master, Eton Coll., 1955–77 (Housemaster, 1968–77); Headmaster, Oakham Sch., Rutland, 1977–84. *Recreations*: music, walking, reading, ball games. *Address*: School House, Rugby, Warwicks.

BULL, Richard; *see* Bull, O. R. S.

BULL, Sir Simeon George, 4th Bt *cr* 1922, of Hammersmith; Partner in legal firm of Bull & Bull; *b* 1 Aug. 1934; *s* of Sir George Bull, 3rd Bt and of Gabrielle, *d* of late Bramwell Jackson, MC; *S* father, 1986; *m* 1961, Annick Elizabeth Renée Geneviève, *d* of late Louis Bresson and of Mme Bresson, Chandai, France; one *s* two *d*. *Educ*: Eton; Innsbruck; Paris. Admitted solicitor, 1959. *Heir*: *s* Stephen Louis Bull, *b* 5 April 1966. *Address*: Oakwood, 97 Island Road, Sturry, Canterbury, Kent; Kerlan, Pont l'Abbé, Finistère, France.

BULL, Sir Walter (Edward Avenon), KCVO 1977 (CVO 1964); FRICS; Consultant, Vigers, chartered surveyors, since 1974; *b* 17 March 1902; *s* of Walter Bull, FRICS, and Florence Bull; *m* 1933, Moira Christian, *d* of William John Irwin and Margaret Irwin, Dungannon, N Ireland; one *s. Educ:* Gresham's Sch.; Aldenham. Sen. Partner, Vigers, 1942–74. Dir, City of London Building Soc., 1957–74. Mem. Council, Duchy of Lancaster, 1957–74. Pres., RICS, 1956. Dep. Comr, War Damage Commn 1952–75. Liveryman, Merchant Taylors' Co. Silver Jubilee Medal, 1977. *Publications:* papers to RICS on Landlord and Tenant Acts. *Recreations:* music, golf, bowls. *Address:* The Garden House, 1 Park Crescent, Brighton BN2 3HA. *T:* Brighton 681196. *Clubs:* Naval and Military, Gresham.

BULLARD, Denys Gradwell; Member, Anglian Water Authority and Chairman, Broads Committee, 1974–83; *b* 15 Aug. 1912; *s* of John Henry Bullard; *m* 1970, Diana Patricia Cox; one *s* one *d. Educ:* Wisbech Grammar Sch.; Cambridge Univ. Farmer. Broadcaster on agricultural matters both at home and overseas. MP (C) SW Div. of Norfolk, 1951–55; MP (C) King's Lynn, 1959–64. PPS: to Financial Sec., Treasury, 1955; to Min. of Housing and Local Govt, 1959–64. *Address:* Elm House, Elm, Wisbech, Cambs. *T:* Wisbech 583021.

BULLARD, Sir Giles (Lionel), KCVO 1985; CMG 1981; HM Diplomatic Service, retired; *b* 24 Aug. 1926; 2nd *s* of late Sir Reader Bullard and late Miriam (*née* Smith); *m* 1st, 1952, Hilary Chadwick Brooks (*d* 1978); two *s* two *d*; 2nd, 1982, Linda Rannells Lewis. *Educ:* Blundell's Sch.; Balliol Coll., Oxford. Army service, 1944–48; Oxford Univ., 1948–51 (Capt. OURFC); H. Clarkson & Co. Ltd, 1952–55; HM Foreign (later Diplomatic) Service, 1955; 3rd Sec., Bucharest, 1957; 2nd Sec., Brussels, 1958; 1st Sec., Panama City, 1960; FO, 1964; DSAO, 1965; Head of Chancery, Bangkok, 1967; Counsellor and Head of Chancery, Islamabad, 1969; FCO Fellow, Centre of South Asian Studies, Cambridge, 1973; Inspectorate, FCO, 1974; Consul-Gen., Boston, 1977; Ambassador, Sofia, 1980; High Comr, Barbados, 1983–86. *Address:* Manor House, West Hendred, Wantage, Oxon.
See also Sir J. L. Bullard.

BULLARD, Sir Julian (Leonard), KCMG 1982 (CMG 1975); HM Diplomatic Service; Ambassador to the Federal Republic of Germany, since 1984; *b* 8 March 1928; *s* of late Sir Reader Bullard, KCB, KCMG, CIE, and late Miriam, *d* of late A. L. Smith, Master of Balliol Coll., Oxford; *m* 1954, Margaret Stephens; two *s* two *d. Educ:* Rugby; Magdalen Coll., Oxford. Fellow of All Souls Coll., Oxford, 1950–57; Army, 1950–52; HM Diplomatic Service, 1953–: served at: FO, 1953–54; Vienna, 1954–56; Amman, 1956–59; FO, 1960–63; Bonn, 1963–66; Moscow, 1966–68; Dubai, 1968–70; Head of E European and Soviet Dept, FCO, 1971–75; Minister, Bonn, 1975–79; Dep. Under-Sec. of State, 1979–84 and Dep. to Perm. Under Sec. of State and Political Dir, 1982–84, FCO. *Address:* British Embassy, Bonn, BFPO 19.
See also Sir G. L. Bullard.

BULLEN, Air Vice-Marshal Reginald, CB 1975; GM 1945; MA; Senior Bursar and Fellow, Gonville and Caius College, Cambridge, since 1976; *b* 19 Oct. 1920; *s* of Henry Arthur Bullen and Alice May Bullen; *m* 1952, Christiane (*née* Phillips); one *s* one *d. Educ:* Grocers' Company School. 39 Sqdn RAF, 458 Sqdn RAAF, 1942–44; Air Min., 1945–50; RAF Coll. Cranwell, 1952–54; psa 1955; Exchange USAF, Washington, DC, 1956–58; RAF Staff Coll., Bracknell, 1959–61; Admin. Staff Coll., Henley, 1962; PSO to Chief of Air Staff, 1962–64; NATO Defence Coll., 1965; HQ Allied Forces Central Europe, 1965–68; Dir of Personnel, MoD, 1968–69; idc 1970; Dep. AO i/c Admin, HQ Maintenance Comd, 1971; AOA Training Comd, 1972–75. Chm., Huntingdon DHA, 1981–. MA Cantab, 1975. FBIM 1979 (MBIM 1971). *Publications:* various articles. *Address:* Gonville and Caius College, Cambridge; c/o Lloyds Bank, Cox's & King's Branch, 6 Pall Mall, SW1Y 5NH. *Clubs:* Athenæum, Royal Air Force.

BULLEN, Dr William Alexander; *s* of Francis Lisle Bullen and Amelia Morgan; *m* 1st, 1943, Phyllis, *d* of George Leeson; three *d*; 2nd, 1965, Mary (marr. diss. 1983), *d* of Leigh Crutchley; 3rd, 1983, Rosalind, *d* of Lawrence Gates. *Educ:* Merchant Taylors' Sch., Crosby; London Hosp. Med. Coll. MRCS, LRCP, MRCGP. Royal Tank Regt, UK and Middle East, 1939–45 (Hon. Major). Med. Dir, Boehringer Pfizer, 1957, Sales Man. 1958; Pres., Pfizer Canada, 1962; Gen. Man., Pfizer Consumer Opns UK, 1964–66; Chm., Coty (England), 1965; Man. Dir, Scribbans Kemp, 1966; Man. Dir, 1967–77, Dep. Chm. 1974, Chm., 1975–81, Thomas Borthwick & Sons Ltd; Chm., Whitburgh Investments, 1976–80. Président-Directeur Général, Boucheries Bernard, 1977–81. FBIM 1975. Liveryman, Butchers' Co.; Freeman, City of London. *Publication:* paper on acute heart failure in London Hosp. Gazette. *Recreations:* sailing, reading, music. *Club:* Royal Thames Yacht.

BULLER; *see* Manningham-Buller, family name of Viscount Dilhorne.

BULLER; *see* Yarde-Buller, family name of Baron Churston.

BULLER, Prof. Arthur John, ERD 1969; FRCP; Research Development Director, Muscular Dystrophy Group of GB, since 1982; Emeritus Professor of Physiology, University of Bristol; Research Development Director, Muscular Dystrophy Group of Great Britain and Northern Ireland, since 1982; Honorary Consultant in Clinical Physiology, Bristol District Hospital (T); *b* 16 Oct. 1923; *s* of Thomas Alfred Buller, MBE, and Edith May Buller (*née* Wager); *m* 1946, Helena Joan (*née* Pearson); one *s* one *d* (and one *d* decd). *Educ:* Duke of York's Royal Military Sch., Dover; St Thomas's Hosp. Med. Sch. (MB, BS); BSc; FRCP 1976; FIBiol 1978; FRSA 1979. Kitchener Scholar, 1941–45; Lectr in Physiology, St Thomas' Hosp., 1946–49. Major, RAMC (Specialist in Physiology; Jt Sec., Military Personnel Research Cttee), 1949–53. Lectr in Medicine, St Thomas' Hosp., 1953–57. Royal Society Commonwealth Fellow, Canberra, Aust., 1958–59. Reader in Physiology, King's Coll., London, 1961–65; Gresham Prof. of Physic 1963–65; Prof. of Physiology, Univ. of Bristol, 1965–82, Dean, Fac. of Medicine, 1976–78, on secondment as Chief Scientist, DHSS, 1978–81. Visiting Prof., Monash Univ., Aust., 1972; Long Fox Meml Lectr, Bristol, 1978. Member: Bd of Governors, Bristol Royal Infirmary, 1968–74; Avon Health Authority (T), 1974–78; MRC, 1975–81; Chm., Neurosciences and Mental Health Bd, MRC, 1975–77. External Scientific Advisor, Rayne Inst., St Thomas' Hosp., 1979–. Milroy Lectr, RCP, 1983. *Publications:* contribs to books and various jls on normal and abnormal physiology. *Recreations:* clarets and conversation. *Address:* Lockhall, Cow Lane, Steeple Aston, Oxon OX5 3SG. *T:* Steeple Aston 47502. *Club:* Athenæum.

BULLERS, Ronald Alfred, QFSM 1974; FIFireE, FBIM; Chief Executive Officer, London Fire and Civil Defence Authority, since 1986; *b* 17 March 1931; *m* 1954, Mary M. Bullers. *Educ:* Queen Mary's Grammar Sch., Walsall. Deputy Asst Chief Officer, Lancashire Fire Brigade, 1971; Dep. Chief Officer, Greater Manchester Fire Brigade, 1974, Chief Officer, 1977; Chief Officer, London Fire Bde, 1981–86. Adviser: Nat. Jt Council for Local Authority Fire Brigades, 1977–; Assoc. of Metropolitan Authorities, 1977–. OStJ. *Recreations:* gardening, travel. *Address:* London Fire and Civil Defence Authority, 8 Albert Embankment, SE1 7SD. *T:* 01-587 4000.

BULLEY, Rt. Rev. Sydney Cyril; *b* 12 June 1907; 2nd *s* of late Jethro Bulley, Newton Abbot, Devon; unmarried. *Educ:* Newton Abbot Grammar Sch.; Univ. of Durham. BA 1932; MA 1936; DipTh 1933; Van Mildert Scholar, Univ. of Durham, 1932; Hon. DD Dunelm 1972. Deacon, 1933; priest, 1934; Curate of Newark Parish Church, 1933–42; Director of Religious Education, Diocese of Southwell, 1936–42; Vicar of St Anne's, Worksop, 1942–46; Chaplain to High Sheriff of Notts, 1943; Hon. Canon of Southwell Minster, 1945; Vicar and Rural Dean of Mansfield, 1946–51; Proctor in Convocation of York, 1945–51; Vicar of Ambleside with Rydal, 1951 59; Archdeacon of Westmorland and Dir Religious Education, Diocese Carlisle, 1951–58; Archdeacon of Westmorland and Furness, 1959–65; Suffragan Bishop of Penrith, 1959–66; Hon. Canon of Carlisle Cathedral, 1951–66; Examining Chaplain to the Bishop of Carlisle, 1952–66; Bishop of Carlisle, 1966–72; Chaplain and Tutor, All Saints' Coll., Bathurst, NSW, 1973–74; Hon. Asst Bishop, Dio. Oxford, 1974. Chaplain to the Queen, 1955–59. Chairman: Southwell Diocese Education Cttee, 1942–51; Worksop Youth Cttee, 1943–45; Mansfield Youth Cttee, 1947–48; Member: Southwell Diocese Board of Finance, 1942–51; Central Council of the Church for Education, 1951–54; Westmorland Education Cttee, 1951–64. Gov. Derby Training Coll., 1938–51, Ripon Training Coll., 1953–58, Lancaster Coll. of Education, 1963–69; Chairman of Governing Body: Casterton Sch., 1962–72; St Chad's Coll., Durham Univ., 1969–83; St Mary's Sch., Wantage, 1979–84. *Publications:* The Glass of Time (autobiog.), 1981; Faith, Fire and Fun (verse), 1985. *Address:* 3 Upper Cross Lane, East Hagbourne, Didcot, Oxon.

BULLMORE, (John) Jeremy David, CBE 1985; Chairman, J. Walter Thompson Co. Ltd, since 1976; *b* 21 Nov. 1929; *s* of Francis Edward Bullmore and Adeline Gabrielle Bullmore (*née* Roscow); *m* 1958, Pamela Audrey Green; two *s* one *d. Educ:* Harrow; Christ Church, Oxford. Military service, 1949–50. Joined J. Walter Thompson Co. Ltd, 1954: Dir, 1964; Dep. Chm., 1975; Dir, J. Walter Thompson Co. (USA), 1980–. Mem., Nat. Cttee for Electoral Reform, 1978–. Chm., Advertising Assoc., 1981–. Trustee, Develt Trust for the Young Disabled, 1984. *Address:* 20 Embankment Gardens, SW3. *T:* 01–351 2197. *Club:* Arts.

BULLOCK, family name of **Baron Bullock**.

BULLOCK, Baron *cr* 1976 (Life Peer), of Leafield, Oxon; **Alan Louis Charles Bullock**, Kt 1972; FBA 1967; Founding Master of St Catherine's College, Oxford, 1960–80, Fellow, since 1980; Vice-Chancellor, Oxford University, 1969–73; *b* 13 Dec. 1914; *s* of Frank Allen Bullock; *m* 1940, Hilda Yates, *d* of Edwin Handy, Bradford; three *s* one *d* (and one *d* decd). *Educ:* Bradford Grammar Sch.; Wadham Coll., Oxford (Scholar). MA; 1st Class Lit Hum, 1936; 1st Class, Modern Hist., 1938. DLitt Oxon, 1969. Fellow, Dean and Tutor in Modern Hist., New Coll., 1945–52; Censor of St Catherine's Soc., Oxford, 1952–62; Chairman: Research Cttee of RIIA, 1954–78; Nat. Advisory Council on the Training and Supply of Teachers, 1963–65; Schools Council, 1966–69; Cttee on Reading and Other Uses of English Language, 1972–74 (Report, A Language for Life, published 1975); Trustees, Tate Gallery, 1973–80; Friends of Ashmolean Museum; Cttee of Enquiry on Industrial Democracy, 1976 (Report publ. 1977); Member: Arts Council of Great Britain, 1961–64; SSRC, 1966; Adv. Council on Public Records, 1965–77; Organising Cttee for the British Library, 1971–72. Joined Social Democratic Party, 1981. Sen. Fellow, Aspen Inst., USA; Trustee: Aspen Inst., Berlin; The Observer, 1957–69; Dir, The Observer, 1977–81. Raleigh Lectr, British Acad., 1967; Stevenson Meml Lectr, LSE, 1970; Leslie Stephen Lectr, Cambridge, 1976. Hon. Fellow: Merton Coll.; Wadham Coll.; Linacre Coll.; Wolfson Coll. For. Mem., Amer. Acad. Arts and Sciences, 1972. Hon. Dr Univ. Aix-Marseilles; Hon. DLitt: Bradford; Reading; Open; Newfoundland; Leicester; Sussex. Hon. FRIBA. Chevalier Légion d'Honneur, 1970. *Publications:* Hitler, A Study in Tyranny, 1952 (rev. edn 1964); The Liberal Tradition, 1956; The Life and Times of Ernest Bevin, Vol. I, 1960, Vol. II, 1967, Vol III (Ernest Bevin, Foreign Secretary), 1983; (ed) The Twentieth Century, 1971; (ed with Oliver Stallybrass) Dictionary of Modern Thought, 1977; (ed) The Faces of Europe, 1980; (ed with B. R. Woodings) Fontana Dictionary of Modern Thinkers, 1983; The Humanist Tradition in the West, 1985; Gen. Editor (with Sir William Deakin) of The Oxford History of Modern Europe. *Address:* St Catherine's College, Oxford; Gable End, 30 Godstow Road, Oxford OX2 8AJ. *T:* Oxford 513380.

BULLOCK, Edward Anthony Watson; HM Diplomatic Service, retired; *b* 27 Aug. 1926; *yr s* of late Sir Christopher Bullock, KCB, CBE, and late Lady Bullock (*née* Barbara May Lupton); *m* 1953, Jenifer Myrtle, *e d* of late Sir Richmond Palmer, KCMG, and late Lady Palmer (*née* Margaret Isabel Abel Smith); two *s* one *d. Educ:* Rugby Sch. (Scholar); Trinity Coll., Cambridge (Exhibitioner; MA). HM Forces, 1944–47; Joined Foreign Service, 1950; served: FO, 1950–52; Bucharest, 1952–54; Brussels, 1955–58; FO, 1958–61; La Paz, 1961–65; ODM, 1965–67; FCO, 1967–69; Havana, 1969–72; HM Treasury, 1972–74; Head of Pacific Dependent Territories Dept, FCO, 1974–77; Consul-Gen., Marseilles, 1978–83; Counsellor, FCO, 1983–85. *Recreations:* walking, gardening, tree-planting, reading. *Address:* c/o National Westminster Bank, 36 St James's Street, SW1. *Clubs:* United Oxford & Cambridge University; Union (Cambridge).
See also R. H. W. Bullock.

BULLOCK, Hugh, Hon. GBE 1976 (Hon. KBE 1957; Hon. OBE 1946); FRSA 1958; President, Pilgrims of the United States, since 1955; Chairman and Chief Executive Officer, Calvin Bullock Ltd; retired 1985; *b* 2 June 1898; *s* of Calvin Bullock and Alice Katherine (*née* Mallory); *m* 1933, Marie Leontine Graves; two *d. Educ:* Hotchkiss Sch.; Williams Coll. (BA). Investment banker since 1921; President and Director: Calvin Bullock, Ltd, 1944–66; Bullock Fund, Ltd; Canadian Fund, Inc.; Canadian Investment Fund, Ltd; Dividend Shares, Inc.; Chairman and Director: Carriers & General Corp.; Nation-Wide Securities Co.; US Electric Light & Power Shares, Inc.; High Income Shares Inc.; Money Shares Inc.; Pres., Calvin Bullock Forum. Civilian Aide to Sec. of the Army, for First Army Area, United States, 1952–53 (US Army Certificate of Appreciation). Trustee: Roosevelt Hospital; Estate and Property of Diocesan Convention of New York; Williams Coll., 1960–68. Member Exec. Cttee, Marshall Scholarship Regional Cttee, 1955–58. Member: Amer. Legion; Academy of Political Science; Amer. Museum of Nat. History; Acad. of Amer. Poets (Dir.); Assoc. Ex-mems Squadron A (Gov. 1945–50); Council on Foreign Relations; Ends of the Earth; English-Speaking Union; Foreign Policy Assoc.; Investment Bankers Assoc. of Amer. (Gov. 1953–55); New England Soc.; Nat. Inst. of Social Sciences (Pres. 1950–53); Gold Medal, 1985); Newcomen Soc.; St George's Soc.; France America Assoc. Benjamin Franklyn Fellow, RSA. Hon. LLD: Hamilton Coll., 1954; Williams Coll., 1957. 2nd Lieut Infantry, European War, 1914–18; Lieut-Col, War of 1939–45 (US Army Commendation Ribbon). Distinguished Citizens' Award, Denver, 1958; Exceptional Service Award, Dept of Air Force, 1961; US Navy Distinguished Public Service Award, 1972. Assoc. KStJ 1961, and Vice-Pres. Amer. Society. Knight Comdr, Royal Order of George I (Greece), 1964. Is an Episcopalian. *Publication:* The Story of Investment Companies, 1959. *Address:* (office) 40th Floor, 1 Wall Street, New York, NY 10005, USA. *T:* 809 1920; (home) 1030 Fifth Avenue, New York, NY 10028. *T:* Trafalgar 9–5858. *Clubs:* White's (London); Bond, Century, Racquet and Tennis, Down Town Association, City Midday, River, Union, Williams,

Church, New York Yacht (New York); Sleepy Hollow Country (Scarborough, NY); Denver County (Denver, Colo.); Chevy Chase, Metropolitan (Washington); Edgartown Yacht (Cdre), Edgartown Reading Room (Mass); West Side Tennis (Forest Hills, NY); Mount Royal (Montreal).

BULLOCK, John; Senior Partner, Deloitte Haskins & Sells, since 1985; *b* 12 July 1933; *s* of Robert and Doris Bullock; *m* 1960, Ruth Jennifer (*née* Bullock); two *s* (and one *s* decd). *Educ:* Latymer Upper School. FCA; FCMA; FIMC. Smallfield Fitzhugh Tillet & Co., 1949–56 and 1958–61; RAF Commission, 1956–58; Robson Morrow, 1961, Partner, 1965–70; Robson Morrow merged with Deloitte Haskins & Sells; Partner in charge, Deloitte Haskins & Sells Management Consultants, 1971–79; Deloitte Haskins & Sells: Managing Partner, 1979–85; Dep. Senior Partner, 1984–85. Mem., UKAEA, 1981–. *Recreations:* sailing, swimming, opera. *Address:* Deloitte Haskins & Sells, 128 Queen Victoria Street, EC4P 4JX. *Clubs:* Royal Automobile, Gresham.

BULLOCK, Richard Henry Watson, CB 1971; Consultant, Faulkbourn Consultancy Services, and Company Director; Director-General, Electronic Components Industry Federation, since 1984 (Consultant Director, 1981–84); Consultant Director: Berkeley Seventh Round Ltd; Grosvenor Place Amalgamations Ltd; retired Civil Servant; *b* 12 Nov. 1920; *er s* of late Sir Christopher Bullock, KCB, CBE and late Lady Bullock (*née* Barbara May Lupton); *m* 1946, Beryl Haddan, *o d* of late Haddan J. Markes, formerly Malay Civil Service; one *s* one *d*. *Educ:* Rugby Sch. (Scholar); Trinity Coll., Cambridge (Scholar). Joined 102 OCTU (Westminster Dragoons), Nov. 1940; Commnd Westminster Dragoons, (2nd County of London Yeo.), 1941; served in England, NW Europe (D-day), Italy, Germany, 1941–45; Instructor, Armoured Corps Officers' Training Sch., India, 1945–46; demobilized 1947, rank of Major. Established in Home Civil Service by Reconstruction Competition; joined Min. of Supply as Asst Principal, 1947; Principal, 1949; Asst Sec., 1956; on loan to War Office, 1960–61; Ministry of Aviation, 1961–64; Under-Sec., 1963; Min. of Technology, 1964–70, Head of Space Div., 1969–70, Dep. Sec., 1970; DTI, 1970–74; Dept of Industry, 1974–80; retired Nov. 1980. Mem., BOTB, 1975–78. Vice-Pres. (and Chm. 1978–82), Westminster Dragoons Assoc.; Pres., Old Rugbeian Soc., 1984–86; Dir, Rugby Sch. Develt Campaign, 1981–86. *Recreations:* fly-fishing, hockey (playing and administering) (President: Dulwich Hockey Club, 1962–; Rugby Alternatives HC, 1976–; Civil Service Hockey Cttee/Assoc., 1978–84), lawn tennis, watching cricket. *Address:* 12 Peterborough Villas, SW6 2AT. *T:* 01–736 5132. *Clubs:* Army and Navy, MCC, Hurlingham; Union (Cambridge).

See also E. A. W. Bullock.

BULLOUGH, Prof. Donald Auberon, FSA, FRHistS; Professor of Mediaeval History, since 1973, and Dean, Faculty of Arts, since 1984, University of St Andrews; *b* 13 June 1928; *s* of late William Bullough and of Edith Shirley (*née* Norman); *m* 1963, Belinda Jane Turland; two *d*. *Educ:* Newcastle-under-Lyme High Sch.; St John's Coll., Oxford (BA 1950, MA 1952). FRHistS 1958; FSA 1968. National Service, 1946–48: commnd RA (attached RHA). Harmsworth Scholar, Merton Coll., Oxford, 1951; Medieval Scholar, British Sch. at Rome, 1951; Fereday Fellow, St John's Coll., Oxford, 1952–55; Lectr, Univ. of Edinburgh, 1955–66; Prof. of Med. History, Univ. of Nottingham, 1966–73. Vis. Prof., Southern Methodist Univ., Dallas, Tex, 1965–66; British Acad. Overseas Vis. Fellow, Max-Planck-Inst. für Gesch., 1972–73; Lilly Endowment Fellow, Pennsylvania Univ., 1980–81. Lectures: Ford's, in English Hist., Univ. of Oxford, 1979–80; Scott-Hawkins, Southern Methodist Univ., Dallas, 1980; Andrew Mellon, Catholic Univ., Washington, 1980; Raleigh, British Acad., 1985. Corresponding Fellow, Monumenta Germaniae Historica, 1983–. Mem. Council, Exec., Finance Cttee, British School at Rome, 1975– (Chm., Faculty of Hist., Archeol., and Letters, 1975–79, Acting Dir, 1984). Senate Mem., Nottingham Univ. Council, 1970–73; Mem., Nottingham Univ. Hosp. Management Cttee, 1971–74; Senatus Assessor, St Andrews Univ. Ct, 1977–81. Dir, Paul Elek Ltd, 1968–79. Major RA (TA); seconded OTC, 1957–67. *Publications:* The Age of Charlemagne, 1965 (2nd edn 1974; also foreign trans); (ed with R. L. Storey) The Study of Medieval Records, 1971; contrib. XIX, XX, XXI, Settimana di Studi del Centro ital. di St. sull'Alto Medioevo; contrib. TLS, British and continental hist. jls, philatelic jls. *Recreations:* talk, looking at buildings, postal history. *Address:* 23 South Street, St Andrews, Fife. *T:* St Andrews 72932. *Club:* Athenæum.

BULLOUGH, Dr Ronald, FRS 1985; Head, Materials Development Division, Harwell, since 1984; *b* 6 April 1931; *s* of Ronald Bullough and Edna Bullough (*née* Morrow); *m* 1954, Ruth Corbett; four *s*. *Educ:* Univ. of Sheffield. BSc, PhD, DSc. FIM 1964; FInstP 1962. Res. Scientist, AEI Fundamental Res. Lab., Aldermaston Court, Aldermaston, 1956–63; Theoretical Physicist and Group Leader, Harwell Res. Lab., Didcot, Berks, 1963–84. Visiting Professor: Univ. of Illinois, USA, 1964, 1973, 1979; Univ. of Wisconsin, USA, 1978; Rensselaer Polytechnical Inst., USA, 1968; Visiting Scientist: Nat. Bureau of Standards, USA, 1965; Oak Ridge Nat. Lab., USA, 1969, 1979; Comisión Nacional de Energía Atómica, Buenos Aires, Argentina, 1977. Hon. Citizen of Tennessee, 1967. *Publications:* articles in learned jls such as Proc. Roy. Soc., Phil. Mag., Jl of Nucl. Materials etc., on defect properties in crystalline solids, particularly in relation to the irradiation and mechanical response of materials. *Recreations:* walking, reading, music. *Address:* 4 Long Meadow, Manor Road, Goring-on-Thames, Reading, Berkshire RG8 9EQ. *T:* Goring 873266.

BULLOUGH, Prof. William Sydney, PhD, DSc Leeds; Professor of Zoology, Birkbeck College, University of London, 1952–81, now Emeritus; *b* 6 April 1914; *o s* of Rev. Frederick Sydney Bullough and Letitia Anne Cooper, both of Leeds; *m* 1942, Dr Helena F. Gibbs (*d* 1975), Wellington, NZ; one *s* one *d*. *Educ:* William Hulme Grammar Sch., Manchester; Grammar Sch., Leeds; Univ. of Leeds. Lecturer in Zoology, Univ. of Leeds, 1937–44, McGill Univ., Montreal, 1944–46; Sorby Fellow of Royal Society of London, 1946–51; Research Fellow of British Empire Cancer Campaign, 1951–52; Hon. Fellow, Soc. for Investigative Dermatology (US). Vice-Pres., Zoological Soc., 1983–84. *Publications:* Practical Invertebrate Anatomy, 1950; Vertebrate Sexual Cycles, 1951; (for children) Introducing Animals, 1953; Introducing Animals-with-Backbones, 1954; Introducing Man, 1958; The Evolution of Differentiation, 1967; The Dynamic Body Tissues, 1983; scientific papers on vertebrate reproductive cycles, hormones, and chalones published in a variety of journals. *Recreation:* gardening. *Address:* Oktober, 5 Uplands Road, Kenley, Surrey CR2 5EE. *T:* 01–660 9764.

BULLUS, Wing Comdr Sir Eric (Edward), Kt 1964; journalist; *b* 20 Nov. 1906; 2nd *s* of Thomas Bullus, Leeds; *m* 1949, Joan Evelyn, *er d* of H. M. Denny; two *d*. *Educ:* Leeds Modern Sch.; Univ. of Leeds. Commnd RAFVR Aug. 1940; served War of 1939–45; Air Min. War Room, 1940–43; joined Lord Louis Mountbatten's staff in SE Asia, 1943; Wing Comdr, 1944; served India, Burma and Ceylon; demobilized, 1945. Journalist Yorkshire Post, Leeds and London, 1923–46. Mem. Leeds City Council, 1930–40; Sec., London Municipal Soc., 1947–50; Mem., Harrow UDC, 1947–50; Vice-Pres. Assoc. of Municipal Corps, 1953. MP (C) Wembley N, 1950–Feb. 1974; PPS to Secretary for Overseas Trade, and to Minister of State, 1953–56, to Minister of Aviation, 1960–62, to Secretary of State for Defence, 1962–64. FRGS, 1947; Fellow Royal Statistical Society, 1949. Foundation Mem. of Brotherton Collection Cttee of Univ. of Leeds, 1935; Member: Archdeaconry Council of Delhi, 1944; Management Board, Cambridge Mission to Delhi, 1954; House of Laity, Church Assembly, 1960. Ripon Diocesan Reader, 1929; London Diocesan Reader, 1947; St Alban's Diocesan Reader, 1960; Canterbury Diocesan Reader, 1967; Central Readers' Board, 1960; London Readers' Board, 1954; Council Westfield Coll., Univ. of London. Pres., Soc. of Yorkshiremen in London, 1969–70. *Publications:* History of Leeds Modern School, 1931; History of Church in Delhi, 1944; History of Lords and Commons Cricket, 1959. *Recreations:* played Headingley RU Football Club 15 years and Yorkshire Amateurs Assoc. Football Club; cricket and swimming (bronze and silver medallions). *Address:* Westway, Herne Bay, Kent. *Clubs:* St Stephen's Constitutional, MCC.

BULMER, Esmond; *see* Bulmer, J. E.

BULMER, Dr Gerald; Rector of Liverpool Polytechnic, 1970–85 (sabbatical leave, 1984–85), retired; *b* 17 Nov. 1920; *s* of Edward and Alice Bulmer; *m* 1943, Greta Lucy Parkes, MA; two *d*. *Educ:* Nunthorpe Sch., York; Selwyn Coll., Cambridge. BA 1941; PhD 1944; MA 1945; CChem, FRSC. Asst Master, King's Sch., Canterbury, 1945–49; Sen. Lecturer, Woolwich Polytechnic, 1949–53; Head of Dept of Science and Metallurgy, Constantine Technical Coll., Middlesbrough, 1954–57; Vice-Principal, Bolton Technical Coll., 1958–59; Principal, West Ham Coll. of Technology, 1959–64; Dir, Robert Gordon's Inst. of Technology, Aberdeen, 1965–70. Mem. Council CNAA, 1967–78. Freeman City of York, 1952. *Publications:* papers on organic sulphur compounds in Jl Chem. Soc. and Nature. *Address:* 11 Capilano Park, Winifred Lane, Aughton, Ormskirk, Lancs.

BULMER, (James) Esmond; MP (C) Wyre Forest, since 1983 (Kidderminster, Feb. 1974–1983); *b* 19 May 1935; *e s* of late Edward Bulmer and Margaret Rye; *m* 1959, Morella Kearton; three *s* one *d*. *Educ:* Rugby; King's Coll., Cambridge (BA); and abroad. Commissioned Scots Guards, 1954. Director: H. P. Bulmer Holdings Ltd, 1962– (Dep. Chm., 1980, Chm., 1982–); (non-exec.) Wales and W Midlands Regional Bd, National Westminster Bank PLC, 1982–. Mem. Exec. Cttee, Nat. Trust. *Recreations:* gardening, fishing. *Address:* The Old Rectory, Pudleston, Leominster, Herefordshire HR6 0RA. *T:* Steensbridge 234. *Club:* Boodle's.

BULMER-THOMAS, Ivor, CBE 1984; FSA 1970; writer; Chairman, Ancient Monuments Society; Chairman, Faith Press; Hon. Director, Friends of Friendless Churches; Vice-President, Church Union; *b* 30 Nov. 1905; *s* of late A. E. Thomas, Cwmbran, Newport, Mon.; *m* 1st, 1932, Dilys (*d* 1938), *d* of late Dr W. Llewelyn Jones, Merthyr Tydfil; one *s*; 2nd, 1940, Margaret Joan, *d* of late E. F. Bulmer, Adam's Hill, Hereford; one *s* two *d*. Assumed additional surname Bulmer by deed poll, 1952. *Educ:* West Monmouth Sch., Pontypool; Scholar of St John's (Hon. Fellow, 1985) and Senior Demy of Magdalen Coll., Oxford. 1st Class Math. Mods, 1925; 1st Class Lit. Hum., 1928; Liddon Student, 1928; Ellerton Essayist, 1929; Junior Denyer and Johnson Scholar, 1930; MA 1937; represented Oxford against Cambridge at Cross-country Running, 1925–27, and Athletics, 1926–28, winning Three Miles in 1927; Welsh International Cross-country Runner, 1926; Gladstone Research Student at St Deiniol's Library, Hawarden, 1929–30; on editorial staff of Times, 1930–37; chief leader writer to News Chronicle, 1937–39; acting deputy editor, Daily Telegraph, 1953–54. Served War of 1939–45 with Royal Fusiliers (Fusilier), 1939–40, and Royal Norfolk Regt (Captain, 1941), 1940–42, 1945. Contested (Lab) Spen Valley div., 1935; MP Keighley, 1942–50 (Lab 1942–48; C 1949–50); contested Newport, Mon (C), 1950. Parliamentary Secretary, Ministry of Civil Aviation, 1945–46; Parliamentary Under-Sec. of State for the Colonies, 1946–47. Delegate to Gen. Assembly, UN, 1946; first UK Mem., Trusteeship Council, 1947. Mem. of the House of Laity of the Church Assembly, 1950–70, of General Synod, 1970–85. Lately Chm., Executive Cttee, Historic Churches Preservation Trust; Chm., Redundant Churches Fund, 1969–76. Hon. DSc Warwick, 1979. Stella della Solidarietà Italiana, 1948. *Publications:* Coal in the New Era, 1934; Gladstone of Hawarden, 1936; Top Sawyer, a biography of David Davies of Llandinam, 1938; Greek Mathematics (Loeb Library), 1939–42; Warfare by Words, 1942; The Problem of Italy, 1946; The Socialist Tragedy, 1949; (ed) E. J. Webb, The Names of the Stars, 1952; The Party System in Great Britain, 1953; The Growth of the British Party System, 1965; (ed) St Paul, Teacher and Traveller, 1975; East Shefford Church, 1978; contrib. to Dictionary of Scientific Biography, Classical Review. *Address:* 12 Edwardes Square, W8 6HG. *T:* 01–602 6267; Old School House, Farnborough, Berks; Ty'n Mynydd, Rhoscolyn, Anglesey. *Clubs:* Athenæum; Vincent's (Oxford).

BULPITT, Cecil Arthur Charles, (Philip Bulpitt); Director, BIM Foundation Ltd, 1977–84 (Chairman, 1979–82); *b* 6 Feb. 1919; *s* of A. E. Bulpitt; *m* 1943, Joyce Mary Bloomfield; one *s* one *d*. *Educ:* Spring Grove Sch., London; Regent Street Polytechnic. Territorial Army, to rank of Staff Capt., RA, 1937–45. Carreras Ltd: joined firm, 1935; Gen. Manager, 1960; Asst Managing Dir, 1962; Dep. Chm. and Chief Exec., 1968; Chm. 1969–70. Dir, Thomas Tilling, 1973–81; Chairman: Tilling Construction Services Ltd, 1978–81; InterMed Ltd, 1978–81; Graham Building Services Ltd, 1979–81; Newey & Eyre Gp Ltd, 1979–81. Member: London Reg. Council, CBI, 1978–81; BBC Consultative Gp on Industrial and Business Affairs, 1980–84. MIPM 1955; FBIM 1963 (Vice-Chm. Council, and Dir, Bd of Companions, BIM, 1979–83). Freeman, City of London, 1969. *Publication:* The Chief Executive, 1971. *Recreations:* fishing, climbing, reading, travelling. *Address:* 7 Colinswood, Collinswood Road, Farnham Common, Berks SL2 3LN. *T:* Farnham Common 4778. *Clubs:* Lansdowne; Stoke Poges Golf, Las Brisas Golf (Nueva Andalucia, Spain).

BULTEEL, Christopher Harris, MC 1943; Director, GAP Activity Projects (GAP) Ltd, since 1982; *b* 29 July 1921; *er s* of late Major Walter Bulteel and Constance (*née* Gaunt), Charlestown, Cornwall; *m* 1958, Jennifer Anne, *d* of late Col K. E. Previté, OBE and of Frances (*née* Capper), Hindgaston, Marnhull, Dorset; one *s* two *d*. *Educ:* Wellington Coll.; Merton Coll., Oxford. Served War with Coldstream Guards, 1940–46 (MC). Assistant Master at Wellington Coll., 1949–61; Head of history dept, 1959–61; Hon. Sec., Wellington Coll. Mission, 1959–61; Headmaster, Ardingly Coll., 1962–80. *Recreations:* natural history, sailing. *Address:* GAP, 2 South Drive, Leighton Park School, Reading, Berks RG2 7DP. *T:* Reading 872869; The Old Manor House, Hillesley, near Wotton-under-Edge, Glos. *T:* Dursley 842565.

BUMBRY, Grace; opera singer and concert singer; *b* St Louis, Mo, 4 Jan. 1937. *Educ:* Boston Univ.; Northwestern Univ.; Music Academy of the West (under Lotte Lehmann). Debut: Paris Opera, 1960; Vienna State Opera, 1963; Salzburg Festival, 1964; Metropolitan Opera, 1965; La Scala, 1966. Appearances also include: Bayreuth Festival, 1961–; Royal Opera Covent Garden, London, 1963–, and in opera houses in Europe, S America and USA. Film, Carmen, 1968. Richard Wagner Medal, 1963. Hon. Dr of Humanities, St Louis Univ., 1968; Hon. doctorates: Rust Coll., Holly Spring, Miss; Rockhurst Coll., Kansas City; Univ. of Missouri at St Louis. Has made numerous recordings. *Recreations:* tennis, sewing, flying, body building, psychology, entertaining. *Address:* c/o Columbia Artists Management, attention R. Douglas Sheldon, 165 West 57th Street, New York, NY 10019, USA.

BUMSTEAD, Kenneth, CVO 1958; CBE 1952; *b* 28 April 1908; *s* of Ernest and Nellie Bumstead; *m* 1940, Diana, *e d* of Archibald Smollett Campbell; three *s*. *Educ:* Wallasey Grammar Sch.; Emmanuel Coll., Cambridge. Entered China Consular Service, 1931; served Peking, Tsingtao, Canton, Chungking, Shanghai, 1932–42 (Consul 1939); Madagascar, 1943; London, 1944; Chicago, 1945–48; Shanghai, 1949–52 (Consul-General, 1950); Seattle, 1953–56; Consul-General, Rotterdam, 1957–61; FO Res. Dept, 1963–72, retired. Commander, Order of Oranje Nassau. *Address:* 4 Perry Way, Hilland, Headley, Bordon, Hants GU35 8NE.

BUNBURY; *see* McClintock-Bunbury, family name of Baron Rathdonnell.

BUNBURY, Bishop of, since 1984; **Rt. Rev. Hamish Thomas Umphelby Jamieson;** *b* 15 Feb. 1932; *s* of Robert Marshall Jamieson and Constance Marzetti Jamieson (*née* Umphelby); *m* 1962, Ellice Anne McPherson; one *s* two *d*. *Educ:* Sydney C of E Grammar Sch.; St Michael's House, Crafers (ThL); Univ. of New England (BA). Deacon 1955; Priest 1956. Mem. Bush Brotherhood of Good Shepherd, 1955–62. Parish of Gilgandra, 1957; Priest-in-Charge, Katherine, NT, 1957–62; Rector, Darwin, 1962–67; Canon of All Souls Cathedral, Thursday Island, 1963–67; Royal Australian Navy Chaplain, 1967–74; HMAS Sydney, 1967–68; HMAS Albatross, 1969–71; Small Ships Chaplain, 1972; HMAS Cerberus, 1972–74; Bishop of Carpentaria, 1974–84. *Recreations:* reading, music, gardening. *Address:* Bishopscourt, Bunbury, WA 6230, Australia.

BUNBURY, Brig. Francis Ramsay St Pierre, CBE 1958; DSO 1945, Bar 1953; *b* 16 June 1910; *s* of late Lt-Col Gerald Bruce St Pierre Bunbury, Indian Army, and Frances Mary Olivia (*née* Dixon); *m* 1933, Elizabeth Pamela Somers (*née* Liscombe) (*d* 1969); one *s* one *d*. *Educ:* Rugby and Sandhurst. Commissioned into The Duke of Wellington's Regiment, 1930; Staff Coll., 1941; commanded 1st Bn, The King's Own Royal Regt, Italian Campaign, 1944–45 (despatches, DSO); commanded 1st Bn The Duke of Wellington's Regt, 1951–54, Germany, Korea (Bar to DSO), Gibraltar; AAG, War Office, 1954–56; commanded 50 Independent Infantry Brigade, Cyprus, 1956–59 (despatches, CBE). Dep. Adjt-Gen., Rhine Army, 1959–61; retired 1962.

BUNBURY, Sir Michael; *see* Bunbury, Sir R. D. M. R.

BUNBURY, Sir Michael (William), 13th Bt *cr* 1681, of Stanney Hall, Cheshire; farmer and company director; *b* 29 Dec. 1946; *s* of Sir John William Napier Bunbury, 12th Bt, and of Pamela, *er d* of late Thomas Alexander Sutton; *S* father, 1985; *m* 1976, Caroline Anne, *d* of Col A. D. S. Mangnall, OBE; one *s* one *d*. *Educ:* Eton; Trinity College, Cambridge (MA). *Heir: s* Henry Michael Napier Bunbury, *b* 4 March 1980. *Address:* Naunton Hall, Rendlesham, Woodbridge, Suffolk.

BUNBURY, Lt-Comdr Sir (Richard David) Michael (Richardson-), 5th Bt, *cr* 1787; RN; *b* 27 Oct. 1927; *er s* of Richard Richardson-Bunbury (*d* 1951) and Florence Margaret Gordon, *d* of late Col Roger Gordon Thomson, CMG, DSO, late RA; *S* kinsman 1953; *m* 1961, Jane Louise, *d* of late Col Alfred William Pulverman, IA; two *s*. *Educ:* Royal Naval College, Dartmouth. Midshipman (S), 1945; Sub-Lieut (S), 1947; Lieut (S), 1948; Lieut-Comdr, 1956; retd 1967. *Heir: s* Roger Michael Richardson-Bunbury, *b* 2 Nov. 1962. *Address:* Woodlands, Mays Hill, Worplesdon, Guildford, Surrey. *T:* Guildford 232034.

BUNCE, Michael John; Controller, Information Services, BBC, since 1983; *b* 24 April 1935; *s* of Roland Bunce, ARIBA, and Dorrie Bunce (*née* Woods); *m* 1961, Tina Sims; two *s* two *d*. *Educ:* St Paul's Sch. Joined BBC as engineer; subseq. Producer/Director: People and Politics (World Service), Gallery and various Further Educn Programmes; Editor: Money Programme, 1968–70; Nationwide, 1970–75; Chief Asst, Current Affairs, TV, 1975–78; Head: Television Information, 1978–82; Information Div., 1982–83. Marshall Fund Vis. Fellow, USA, 1975. Mem. Council, and Chm. PR Cttee, RTS. Shell Internat. Television Award, 1969. *Recreations:* gardening, collecting opera and jazz records, visiting fine buildings. *Address:* c/o BBC, Broadcasting House, W1A 1AA. *T:* 01–580 4468. *Club:* Reform.

BUNCH, Sir Austin (Wyeth), Kt 1983; CBE 1978 (MBE 1974); National President, British Limbless Ex-Servicemen's Association, since 1983; Chairman, Queen Mary's Roehampton Hospital Trust, since 1983; Member, Richmond, Twickenham and Roehampton District Health Authority, since 1982; *b* 1918; *s* of Horace William and Winifred Ada Bunch; *m* 1944, Joan Mary Peryer; four *d*. *Educ:* Christ's Hospital. FCA. Deloitte, Plender, Griffiths, 1935–48; Southern Electricity Board, 1949–76: Area Man., Newbury, 1962; Area Man., Portsmouth, 1966; Dep. Chm., 1967; Chm., 1974; Dep. Chm., Electricity Council, 1976–81, Chm., 1981–83; Chm., British Electricity Internat. Ltd, 1977–83; retd. *Recreation:* sports for the disabled. *Address:* Sumner, School Lane, Cookham, Berks SL6 9QJ.

BUNDY, McGeorge; Professor of History, New York University, since 1979; *b* 30 March 1919; *s* of Harvey Hollister Bundy and Katharine Lawrence Bundy (*née* Putnam); *m* 1950, Mary Buckminster Lothrop; four *s*. *Educ:* Yale Univ. AB 1940. Political analyst, Council on Foreign Relations, 1948–49. Harvard University: Vis. Lectr, 1949–51; Associate Prof. of Government, 1951–54; Prof., 1954–61; Dean, Faculty of Arts and Sciences, 1953–61. Special Asst to the Pres. for National Security Affairs, 1961–66; President of the Ford Foundation, 1966–79. Mem., American Political Science Assoc. *Publications:* (with H. L. Stimson) On Active Service in Peace and War, 1948; The Strength of Government, 1968; (ed) Pattern of Responsibility, 1952. *Address:* Department of History, New York University, 19 University Place, New York, NY 10003, USA.

BUNFORD, John Farrant, MA, FIA; Hon.FFA; Director, National Provident Institution for Mutual Life Assurance, 1964–85, retired (Manager and Actuary 1946–64); *b* 4 June 1901; *s* of late John Henry Bunford and Ethel Farrant Bunford; *m* 1929, Florence Louise, *d* of late John and Annie Pearson, Mayfield, Cork; two *s* one *d*. *Educ:* Christ's Hosp.; St Catharine's Coll., Cambridge. (MA). Scottish Amicable Life Assurance Soc., 1923–29. Royal Exchange Assurance, 1929–32; National Provident Institution: Dep. Asst Actuary, 1932; Asst Sec., 1933; Asst Manager, 1937. Institute of Actuaries: Fellow, 1930; Hon. Sec., 1944–45; Vice-Pres., 1948–50; Treas., 1952–53; Pres., 1954–56. Hon. Fellow the Faculty of Actuaries, 1956. *Recreation:* gardening. *Address:* 14 Shepherds Way, Liphook, Hants. *T:* Liphook 722594.

BUNKER, Albert Rowland, CB 1966; Deputy Under-Secretary of State, Home Office, 1972–75; *b* 5 Nov. 1913; *er* and *o surv. s* of late Alfred Francis Bunker and late Ethel Trudgian, Lanjeth, St Austell, Cornwall; *m* 1939, Irene Ruth Ella, 2nd *d* of late Walter and late Ella Lacey, Ealing; two *s*. *Educ:* Ealing Gram. Sch. Served in Royal Air Force, 1943–45. Service in Cabinet Office, HM Treasury, Ministry of Home Security and Home Office. *Recreation:* golf. *Address:* 35 Park Avenue, Ruislip. *T:* Ruislip 35331. *Clubs:* Royal Air Force; Denham Golf.

BUNN, Dr Charles William, FRS 1967; Dewar Research Fellow of the Royal Institution of Great Britain, 1963–72; *b* 15 Jan. 1905; *s* of Charles John Bunn and Mary Grace Bunn (*née* Murray); *m* 1931, Elizabeth Mary Mold; one *s* one *d*. *Educ:* Wilson's Grammar Sch., London, SE; Exeter Coll., Oxford. BA, BSc, (Oxon), 1927; DSc (Oxon), 1953; FInstP, 1944. Mem. Research Staff, Imperial Chemical Industries, Winnington, Northwich, Cheshire (now Mond Div.), 1927–46; transf. to ICI Plastics Div., 1946 (Div. Leader of Molecular Structure Div. of Research Dept, and later of Physics Div.); retd 1963. Chm., X-Ray Analysis Group of The Inst. of Physics and The Physical Soc., 1959–62. Amer. Physical Soc. Award in High Polymer Physics (Ford Prize), 1969. *Publications:* Chemical Crystallography, 1945 (2nd edn 1961); Crystals, Their Role in Nature and in Science, 1964; papers in: Proc. Royal Society; Trans. Faraday Soc.; Acta Crystallographica. *Recreations:* music and horticulture. *Address:* 6 Pentley Park, Welwyn Garden City, Herts. *T:* Welwyn Garden 323581.

BUNN, Douglas Henry David; Chairman: All England Jumping Course, Hickstead; White Horse Caravan Co. Ltd; *b* 1 March 1928; *s* of late George Henry Charles Bunn and Alice Ann Bunn; *m* 1st, 1952, Rosemary Pares Wilson; three *d*; 2nd, 1960, Susan Dennis-Smith; two *s* one *d*; 3rd, 1979, Lorna Kirk; two *d*. *Educ:* Chichester High Sch.; Trinity Coll., Cambridge (MA). Called to Bar, Lincoln's Inn; practised at Bar, 1953–59; founded Hickstead, 1960; British Show Jumping Team, 1957–68; Vice-Chm., British Show Jumping Assoc. (Chm. 1969); Mem. British Equestrian Fedn; founded White Horse Caravan Co. Ltd, 1958; Chm., Southern Aero Club, 1968–72. Jt Master, Mid Surrey Drag Hounds, 1976–. *Recreations:* horses, flying, books, wine. *Address:* Hickstead Place, Sussex RH17 5NU. *T:* Hurstpierpoint 834666. *Clubs:* Buck's, Saints and Sinners, Turf.

BUNSTER, Don Alvaro; Fellow, Institute of Development Studies, University of Sussex, 1977; *b* 25 May 1920; *m* 1965, Raquel de Bunster (*née* Parot); three *s*. *Educ:* National Institute, Santiago; School of Law, Univ. of Chile; Faculty of Law, Central Univ. of Brazil, Rio de Janeiro; Faculty of Jurisprudence, Univ. of Rome, Italy. Judge Advocate of the Army, Chile, 1950–57; Prof. of Penal Law, Univ. of Chile, 1953–73; Gen. Sec., Univ. of Chile, 1957–69. Vis. Prof., Univ. of Calif., Berkeley, 1966–67. Vice-Pres., Inst. of Penal Sciences, 1969–70; Dir, Enciclopedia Chilena, 1970; Chilean Ambassador to Court of St James's, 1971–73; lecturing at Univs of Oxford and Liverpool, 1973–74; Senior Vis. Fellow, Centre of Latin-American Studies, Univ. of Cambridge, 1974–77. *Publications:* La malversación de caudales públicos, 1948; La voluntad del acto delictivo, 1950; articles, descriptive commentaries, etc, in various nat. and foreign magazines. *Recreations:* music, theatre.

BUNTING, Prof. Arthur Hugh, CMG 1971; consultant in tropical agricultural research and development; Professor of Agricultural Development Overseas, Reading University, 1974–82, now Emeritus; *b* 7 Sept. 1917; *e s* of S. P. and R. Bunting; *m* 1941, Elsie Muriel Reynard; three *s*. *Educ:* Athlone High Sch., Johannesburg, S Africa; Univ. of the Witwatersrand, Johannesburg; Oriel Coll., University of Oxford. BSc 1937, BSc (Hons Botany), MSc 1938, Witwatersrand; Rhodes Scholar for the Transvaal, 1938; DPhil Oxford, 1941; CBiol, FIBiol. Asst Chemist, Rothamsted Experimental Station, 1941–45; Member Human Nutrition Research Unit, Medical Research Council, 1945–47; Chief Scientific Officer, Overseas Food Corporation, 1947–51; Senior Research Officer, Sudan Min. of Agriculture, 1951–56; Prof. of Agricultural Botany, 1956–73, Dean, Faculty of Agriculture, 1965–71, Univ. of Reading. Pres., Assoc. of Applied Biologists, 1963–64, Hon. Mem., 1979–; Jt Editor, Journal of Applied Ecology, 1964–68. Foundn Mem., 1968–72, and Mem., 1974–80, Vice-Chm. 1975–77, and Chm. 1977–80, Board of Trustees, Internat. Inst. of Tropical Agriculture, Ibadan, Nigeria; Member: UK Council for Scientific Policy, 1970–72; UN Adv. Cttee on the Applications of Science and Technology to Develt (ACAST), 1972–75; Governing Bodies, Grassland Res. Inst., Hurley, 1959–77, Plant Breeding Inst., Cambridge, 1960–76; Consultant and then Mem., Scientific Cttee, Cotton Res. Corp., 1958–76 (Chm., 1972–76); Member: Panel of Scientific Advisers, CDC, 1967–; Meteorological Cttee, MoD(Air), 1973–; Foundn Mem., Internat. Bd for Plant Genetic Resources, 1974–78. LLD *hc* Ahmadu Bello Univ., 1968. *Publications:* (ed) Change in Agriculture, 1970; (ed jtly) Policy and Practice in Rural Development, 1976; (ed jtly) Advances in Legume Science, 1980; numerous papers in scientific and agricultural journals. *Recreation:* music. *Address:* 27 The Mount, Caversham, Reading, Berks. *T:* Reading 472487; 4 Earley Gate, University of Reading, Berks. *T:* Reading 64640.

BUNTING, Sir (Edward) John, AC 1982; KBE 1977 (CBE 1960); Kt 1964; BA; Australian civil servant (retired); Chairman, Official Establishments Trust, since 1983; Deputy Chairman, since 1983, and National Co-ordinator, since 1978, Sir Robert Menzies Memorial Trust; *b* Ballarat, Vic, 13 Aug. 1918; *s* of late G. B. Bunting; *m* 1942, (Pauline) Peggy, *d* of late D. C. MacGruer; three *s*. *Educ:* Trinity Grammar School, Melbourne; Trinity Coll., Univ. of Melbourne (BA Hons; Hon. Fellow 1981). Asst Sec., Prime Minister's Dept, Canberra, 1949–53; Official Sec., Office of the High Commissioner for Australia, London, 1953–55; Deputy Sec., Prime Minister's Dept, Canberra, 1955–58; Secretary: Australian Cabinet, 1959–75; Prime Minister's Dept, 1959–68; Dept of the Cabinet Office, 1968–71; Dept of the Prime Minister and Cabinet, 1971–75; High Comr for Australia in UK, 1975–77. Chm., Roche-Maag Ltd, 1978–83. Mem., Australia Council, 1978–82. *Recreations:* cricket, music, reading. *Address:* 3 Wickham Crescent, Red Hill, ACT 2603, Australia. *Clubs:* Commonwealth (Canberra); Athenæum (Melbourne); Melbourne Cricket.

BUNTING, John Reginald, CBE 1965; author and educational consultant; *b* 12 Nov. 1916; *s* of John Henry and Jane Bunting, Mansfield; *m* 1940, May Hope Sturdy, Malvern, Jamaica; no *c*. *Educ:* Queen Elizabeth's Grammar Sch., Mansfield; Queen's Coll., Oxford (MA, DipEd). Sen. English Master and Housemaster, Munro Coll., Jamaica, 1939–42; Headmaster, Wolmer's Sch., Jamaica, 1943–49; Principal, King's Coll., Lagos, 1949–54; Actg Dir of Broadcasting, Nigeria, June-Oct. 1952; Actg Inspector of Educn, Western Region, Nigeria, April-Oct. 1954; Dep. Chief Federal Adviser on Educn, Nigeria, 1954–58; Chief Federal Adviser on Educn, Nigeria, 1958–61; Educn Adviser, W Africa, Brit. Council, 1961 and Head, Graduate VSO Unit, 1962; Asst Controller, Educn Div., 1964; Evans Bros Ltd: Editorial Consultant, 1965–68; Dir, Overseas Sales and Publications, 1969; Dir-Gen., Centre for Educnl Develt Overseas, 1970–74; Adviser on Educn to British Council, 1974–76. Hon. Jt Editor, W African Jl of Educn, 1956–61. *Publications:* Civics for Self-Government, 1956; New African English Course (Book 5), 1960; (jtly) Caribbean Civics, 1960; (jtly) Civics for East Africa, 1961; Primary English Course (Book 6): for Ghana, 1962, for Sierra Leone, 1969, for West Cameroon, 1971; Civics: a course in citizenship and character training, 1973; To Light a Candle, 1976. *Recreations:* golf, fishing, painting, bowls. *Address:* 8 Springhill Gardens, Lyme Regis, Dorset. *T:* Lyme Regis 3726. *Club:* Lyme Regis Golf.

BUNTING, Martin Brian, FCA; Director, Imperial Brewing & Leisure Ltd (Deputy Chairman, 1980–84); *b* 28 Feb. 1934; *s* of Brian and Renee Bunting; *m* 1959, Veronica Mary Cope; two *s* one *d*. *Educ:* Rugby School. Director, Courage Ltd, 1972, Man. Dir, later Dep. Chm., 1974–84; Director: Imperial Group plc, 1975–84; George Gale & Co. Ltd, 1984–; Longman Cartermill Ltd, 1985–. Member, Monopolies and Mergers Commission, 1982–. *Address:* The Lodge, Basingstoke Road, Riseley, near Reading RG7 1QD. *T:* Reading 883234.

BUNTON, George Louis, MChir (Cantab), FRCS; Consultant Surgeon to University College Hospital, London, 1955–84, to Metropolitan Hospital, 1957–70, and to

Northwood Hospital, 1958–84, retired; Emeritus Consulting Surgeon to University College and Middlesex Hospitals, 1986; *b* 23 April 1920; *s* of late Surg. Capt. C. L. W. Bunton, RN, and Marjorie Denman; *m* 1948, Margaret Betty Edwards; one *d*. *Educ:* Epsom; Selwyn Coll., Cambridge; UCH. MB, BChir Cantab 1951; MRCS, LRCP 1944; FRCS 1951; MChir Cantab 1955. Served in RNVR 1944–47. University of London: Examr in Surgery, 1974–78; Mem., Academic Council, 1975–77; University College Hospital, London: Chm., Med. Cttee, 1977–80; Mem., Academic Bd, Med. Sch., 1970–78; Mem., Sch. Council, Med. Sch., 1976–81; Mem., Bd of Governors, 1972–74; Mem., Bd of Trustees, UC Gp of Hosps, 1978–82. Chairman: Health Gp, Centre for Policy Studies, 1980–84; S Camden Dist Med. Cttee, 1980–83; Member: Exec., University Hosps Assoc. (England and Wales) (Treasurer, 1980–); Court of Examiners, RCS, 1977–84 (Chm., 1984). Fellow, Assoc. of Surgeons; Fellow, British Assoc. of Pædiatric Surgeons. *Publications:* contribs. to journals and books on surgical subjects. *Recreations:* gardening, music. *Address:* Hither Dennets, Hawridge Common, Chesham, Bucks. *T:* Cholesbury 565.

BUNYAN, Dr Peter John; Head of Agricultural Science Service, Agricultural Development and Advisory Service, Ministry of Agriculture, Fisheries and Food, since 1984; *b* London, 13 Jan. 1936; *o s* of Charles and Jenny Bunyan; *m* 1961, June Rose Child; two *s*. *Educ:* Raynes Park County Grammar Sch.; University Coll., Durham Univ. (BSc, DSc); King's Coll., Univ. of London (PhD). FRSC; CChem; FIBiol; FIFST. Research at KCL, 1960–62, at UCL, 1962–63; Ministry of Agriculture, Fisheries and Food: Sen. Scientific Officer, Infestation Control Lab., 1963–69; PSO, Pest Infestation Control Lab., 1969–73, Head of Pest Control Chemistry Dept, 1973–80; Head of Food Science Div., 1980–84. *Publications:* numerous scientific papers in wide variety of scientific jls. *Recreations:* gardening, jogging. *Address:* c/o Ministry of Agriculture, Fisheries and Food, Great Westminster House, Horseferry Road, SW1P 2AE. *T:* 01-216 6155.

BUNYARD, Robert Sidney, CBE 1986; QPM 1980; Chief Constable, Essex Police, since 1978; *b* 20 May 1930; *s* of Albert Percy Bunyard and Nellie Maria Bunyard; *m* 1948, Ruth Martin; two *d*. *Educ:* Queen Elizabeth Grammar Sch., Faversham; Regent Street Polytechnic Management Sch. (Dip. in Man. Studies). BA (Open). MIPM. Metropolitan Police, 1952; Asst Chief Constable, Leics, 1972; Dep. Chief Constable, Essex, 1977. Man. Editor, Police Jl, 1981–. *Publications:* Police: organization and command, 1978; Police Management Handbook, 1979; contrib. police jls. *Recreations:* music, opera, painting. *Address:* Police Headquarters, Springfield, Chelmsford, Essex CM2 6DA. *T:* Chelmsford 267267.

BURBIDGE, (Eleanor) Margaret, (Mrs Geoffrey Burbidge), FRS 1964; Professor of Astronomy, since 1964, Director, Center for Astrophysics and Space Sciences, since 1979, University of California at San Diego; *d* of late Stanley John Peachey, Lectr in Chemistry and Research Chemist, and of Marjorie Peachey; *m* 1948, Geoffrey Burbidge, *qv*; one *d*. *Educ:* Francis Holland Sch., London; University Coll., London (BSc); Univ. of London Observatory (PhD). Asst Director, 1948–50, Actg Director, 1950–51, Univ. of London Observatory; fellowship from Internat. Astron. Union, held at Yerkes Observatory, Univ. of Chicago, 1951–53; Research Fellow, California Inst. of Technology, 1955–57; Shirley Farr Fellow, later Associate Prof., Yerkes Observatory, Univ. of Chicago, 1957–62; Research Astronomer, Univ. of California at San Diego, 1962–64; Dir, Royal Greenwich Observatory, 1972–73. Abby Rockefeller Mauzé Vis. Prof., MIT, 1968. Member: American Acad. of Arts and Scis, 1969; US Nat. Acad. of Scis, 1978; Nat. Acad. of Scis Cttee on Science and Public Policy, 1979–81; Pres., Amer. Astronomical Soc., 1976–78; Chairwoman Bd of Dirs, Amer. Assoc. for Advancement of Science, 1983 (Pres., 1982). Hon. DSc: Smith Coll., Massachusetts, USA, 1963; Sussex, 1970; Bristol, 1972; Leicester, 1972; City, 1974; Michigan, 1978; Massachusetts, 1978; Williams Coll., 1979; Hon. DSc, State Univ. of NY at Stony Brook, 1984. Fellow University Coll., London, 1967; Hon. Fellow, Lucy Cavendish Collegiate Soc., 1971. Catherine Wolfe Bruce Medal, Astr. Soc. of the Pacific, 1982; Nat. Medal of Science (awarded by President of USA), 1984. *Publications:* Quasi-Stellar Objects (with Geoffrey Burbidge), 1967 (also USA, 1967); contribs to learned jls (mostly USA), Handbuch der Physik, etc. *Address:* Center for Astrophysics and Space Sciences, C-011, University of California at San Diego, La Jolla, California 92093, USA. *T:* (714) 452–4477. *Club:* University Women's.

BURBIDGE, Prof. Geoffrey, FRS 1968; Emeritus Professor of Physics, University of California, 1984; *b* 24 Sept. 1925; *s* of Leslie and Eveline Burbidge, Chipping Norton, Oxon; *m* 1948, Margaret Peachey (*see* E. M. Burbidge); one *d*. *Educ:* Chipping Norton Grammar Sch.; Bristol University; Univ. Coll., London. BSc (Special Hons Physics) Bristol, 1946; PhD London, 1951. Asst Lectr, UCL, 1950–51; Agassiz Fellow, Harvard Univ., 1951–52; Research Fellow, Univ. of Chicago, 1952–53; Research Fellow, Cavendish Lab., Cambridge, 1953–55; Carnegie Fellow, Mount Wilson and Palomar Observatories, Caltech, 1955–57; Asst Prof., Dept of Astronomy, Univ. of Chicago, 1957–58; Assoc. Prof., 1958–62; Assoc. Prof., Univ. of California, San Diego, 1962–63, Prof. of Physics, 1963–78; Dir, Kitt Peak Nat. Observatory, Arizona, 1978–84. Phillips Vis. Prof., Harvard Univ., 1968. Elected Fellow, UCL, 1970. Pres., Astronomical Soc. of the Pacific, 1974–76; Trustee, Assoc. Universities Inc., 1973–82; Editor, Annual Review Astronomy and Astrophysics, 1973–. *Publications:* (with Margaret Burbidge) Quasi-Stellar Objects, 1967; scientific papers in Astrophysical Jl, Nature, Rev. Mod. Phys, Handbuch der Physik, etc. *Address:* Center for Astrophysics and Space Sciences, C-011 University of California at San Diego, La Jolla, Calif 92093, USA. *T:* (619) 452–6626.

BURBIDGE, Mrs Geoffrey; *see* Burbidge, E. M.

BURBIDGE, Sir Herbert (Dudley), 5th Bt *cr* 1916; *b* 13 Nov. 1904; *s* of Herbert Edward Burbidge (*d* 1945) 2nd *s* of 1st Bt, and Harriet Georgina (*d* 1952), *d* of Henry Stuart Hamilton, Londonderry; *S* cousin, 1974; *m* 1933, Ruby Bly, *d* of Charles Ethelbert Taylor; one *s*. *Educ:* University Sch., Victoria, BC, Canada. Harrods Ltd, Knightsbridge, 1923–28; R. P. Clarke (Stock Brokers), Vancouver, BC, 1929–31; Merchandising Manager, Silverwood Industries of Vancouver, BC, 1931–70; retired 1970. President: Vancouver Executive Club, 1942; Vancouver Sales Executive Club, 1948. Mem. Bd of Referees, Workmen's Compensation Bd, 1943–61. *Recreation:* landscape gardening. *Heir:* *s* Peter Dudley Burbidge [*b* 20 June 1942; *m* 1967, Peggy Marilyn, *d* of Kenneth Anderson, Ladner, BC; one *s* one *d*]. *Address:* 12549/27th Avenue, Surrey, British Columbia V4A 2M6, Canada. *Club:* Vancouver Executive.

BURBIDGE, Mrs Margaret; *see* Burbidge, E. M.

BURBRIDGE, Very Rev. (John) Paul, MA Oxon and Cantab; Dean of Norwich, since 1983; *b* 21 May 1932; *e s* of late John Henry Gray Burbridge and Dorothy Vera Burbridge; *m* 1956, Olive Denise Grenfell; four *d*. *Educ:* King's Sch., Canterbury; King's Coll., Cambridge; New Coll., Oxford; Wells Theolog. Coll. Nat. Service Commn in RA, 1957. Jun. Curate, 1959, Sen. Curate, 1961, Eastbourne Parish Church; Vicar Choral of York Minster, 1962–66; Chamberlain, 1962–76; Canon Residentiary, 1966–76; Succentor Canonicorum, 1966; Precentor, 1969–76; Archdeacon of Richmond and Canon Residentiary of Ripon Cathedral, 1976–83. *Recreation:* model engineering. *Address:* The Deanery, Norwich, Norfolk NR1 4EG. *T:* Norwich 623846.

See also S. N. Burbridge.

BURBRIDGE, Stephen Nigel, MA; Secretary, Monopolies and Mergers Commission, since 1986; *b* 18 July 1934; *s* of late John Henry Gray Burbridge and late Dorothy Vera (*née* Pratt). *Educ:* King's Sch., Canterbury; Christ Church, Oxford. National Service, 2 Lieut, RA, 1953–55. Asst Principal, Bd of Trade, 1958–62; Trade Commissioner, Karachi, 1963–65; 1st Secretary (Economic), Rawalpindi, 1965–67; Principal, BoT (marine), 1967–71; CS Selection Bd, 1971; Department of Trade and Industry: Asst Sec. (finance, research, marine, industrial policy), 1971–80; Under Sec. (export promotion, consumer affairs), 1980–86. *Recreations:* sports, reading, collecting. *Address:* Monopolies and Mergers Commission, New Court, 48 Carey Street, WC2A 2JT. *Clubs:* Royal Commonwealth Society; Rye Golf; West Sussex Golf.

See also J. P. Burbridge.

BURBURY, Hon. Sir Stanley Charles, KCMG 1981; KCVO 1977; KBE 1958; Governor of Tasmania, 1973–82; *b* 2 Dec. 1909; *s* of Daniel Charles Burbury and Mary Burbury (*née* Cunningham); *m* 1934, Pearl Christine Barren; no *c*. *Educ:* Hutchins Sch., Hobart; The Univ. of Tasmania. LLB 1933; Hon. LLD 1970. Admitted to Bar, 1934; QC 1950; Solicitor-Gen. for Tasmania, 1952; Chief Justice, Supreme Court of Tasmania, 1956–73. Pres., Nat. Heart Foundn of Australia, 1967–73; Nat. Pres., Winston Churchill Memorial Trust, 1980–85. KStJ 1974. Hon. Col, Royal Tasmanian Regt, 1974–82. *Recreations:* music and lawn bowls. *Address:* 3 Mona Street, Kingston, Tasmania 7150, Australia. *Clubs:* Tasmanian, Athenæum, Royal Hobart Bowls (Hobart).

BURCH, Maj.-Gen. Geoffrey, CB 1977; Director of Management Development, Courtaulds Group, since 1977; *b* 29 April 1923; *s* of late Henry James Burch, LDS, RCS (Eng); *m* 1948, Jean Lowrie Fyfe; one *s*. *Educ:* Felsted Sch. Served War: commissioned 2/Lt RA, 1943; served in Italy, 1943–45. India, 1946–47; ptsc 1951; psc 1953; British Defence Liaison Staff, Ottawa, 1962–65; Comd Flintshire and Denbighshire Yeomanry, 1965–66. Programme Director UK/Germany/Italy 155mm project, 1968–71; Dep. Commandant, Royal Military Coll. of Science, 1971–73; Dir-Gen. Weapons (Army), 1973–75; Dep. Master-General of the Ordnance, 1975–77. Col Comdt, RA, 1978–85. FInstD, FBIM, FIPM. *Recreations:* squash, European defence industry co-operation. *Address:* c/o Lloyds Bank, Cox's & King's Branch, 6 Pall Mall, SW1Y 5NH. *Clubs:* Royal Automobile, MCC.

BURCH, Maj.-Gen. Keith, CB 1985; CBE 1977 (MBE 1965); Director Personnel, Defence Staff, Ministry of Defence, 1985, retired; Chapter Clerk, York Minster, since 1985; *b* 31 May 1931; *s* of Christopher Burch and Gwendoline Ada (*née* James); *m* 1957, Sara Vivette Hales; one *s* two *d*. *Educ:* Bedford Modern Sch.; Royal Military Acad., Sandhurst. Commnd Essex Regt, 1951; DS Staff Coll., Camberley, 1968–69; Comd 3rd Bn Royal Anglian Regt, 1969–71; Asst Sec., Chiefs of Staff Cttee, MoD, 1972–75; Col GS HQ 2nd Armoured Div., 1975–78; Dir, Admin. Planning (Army), MoD, 1978–80; Indian National Defence Coll., New Delhi, 1981; Dep. Dir, Army Staff Duties, MoD, 1981–83; ACDS (Personnel and Logistics), 1984. *Recreations:* country pursuits. *Address:* c/o Lloyds Bank, Cox's & King's Branch, 6 Pall Mall, SW1Y 5NH.

BURCH, Rt. Rev. William Gerald, DD; *b* Winnipeg, Manitoba, 5 March 1911; *m* 1942, Carroll Borrowman; four *d*. *Educ:* University of Toronto (BA); Wycliffe Coll., Toronto. Deacon, 1936; Priest, 1938. Curate, Christ Church, Toronto, 1936–40; Incumbent, Scarborough Junction with Sandown Park, 1940–42; Rector: St Luke, Winnipeg, 1942–52; All Saints, Windsor, 1952–56; Exam. Chaplain to Bishop of Huron, 1955–56; Canon of Huron, 1956; Dean and Rector, All Saints Cathedral, Edmonton, 1956–60; Suffragan Bishop of Edmonton, 1960–61; Bishop of Edmonton, 1961–76. *Address:* 901 Richmond Avenue, Victoria, BC V8S 3Z4, Canada. *T:* (604) 598 4369.

BURCHAM, Prof. William Ernest, CBE 1980; FRS 1957; Emeritus Professor of Physics, Birmingham University, since 1981; *b* 1 Aug. 1913; *er s* of Ernest Barnard and Edith Ellen Burcham; *m* 1st, 1942, Isabella Mary (*d* 1981), *d* of George Richard Todd and of Alice Louisa Todd; two *d*; 2nd, 1985, Patricia Newton, *er d* of Frank Harold Newton Marson and Miriam Eliza Marson. *Educ:* City of Norwich Sch.; Trinity Hall, Cambridge. Stokes Student, Pembroke Coll., Cambridge, 1937; Scientific Officer, Ministry of Aircraft Production, 1940, and Directorate of Atomic Energy, 1944; Fellow of Selwyn Coll., Cambridge, 1944; Univ. Demonstrator in Physics, Cambridge, 1945; Univ. Lecturer in Physics, Cambridge, 1946; Oliver Lodge Prof. of Physics, Univ. of Birmingham, 1951–80. Member: SRC, 1974–78; Council, Royal Soc., 1977–79. Hon. Life Fellow, Coventry Polytechnic, 1984. *Publications:* Nuclear Physics: an Introduction, 1963; Elements of Nuclear Physics, 1979; papers in Nuclear Physics A, Phys. Letters B, Phys. Rev. Letters. *Address:* 95 Witherford Way, Birmingham B29 4AN. *T:* 021–472 1226.

BURCHFIELD, Dr Robert William, CBE 1975; Editor, A Supplement to the Oxford English Dictionary, since 1957; Chief Editor, The Oxford English Dictionaries, 1971–84; Senior Research Fellow, St Peter's College, Oxford, since 1979 (Tutorial Fellow, 1963–79); *b* Wanganui, NZ, 27 Jan. 1923; *s* of Frederick Burchfield and Mary Burchfield (*née* Blair); *m* 1949, Ethel May Yates (marr. diss. 1976); one *s* two *d*; *m* 1976, Elizabeth Austen Knight. *Educ:* Wanganui Technical Coll., New Zealand, 1934–39; Victoria University Coll., Wellington, NZ, 1940–41, 1946–48; MA (NZ) 1948; Magdalen Coll., Oxford, 1949–53; BA (Oxon) 1951, MA 1955. Served War, Royal NZ Artillery, NZ and Italy, 1941–46. NZ Rhodes Scholar, 1949. Junior Lectr in English Lang., Magdalen Coll., Oxford, 1952–53; Lectr in English Lang., Christ Church, Oxford, 1953–57; Lectr, St Peter's Coll., Oxford, 1955–63. Hon. Sec., Early English Text Society, 1955–68 (Mem. Council, 1968–80); Editor, Notes and Queries, 1959–62; Pres., English Assoc., 1978–79. Hon. For. Mem., American Acad. of Arts and Scis, 1977–; Hon. Fellow, Inst. of Linguists, 1984–. Hon. DLitt, Liverpool, 1978; Hon. LitD Victoria Univ. of Wellington, NZ, 1983. *Publications:* (with C. T. Onions and G. W. S. Friedrichsen) The Oxford Dictionary of English Etymology, 1966; A Supplement to the Oxford English Dictionary, vol. I (A-G), 1972, vol. II (H-N), 1976, vol. III (O-Scz), 1982, vol. IV (Se–Z), 1986; (with D. Donoghue and A. Timothy) The Quality of Spoken English on BBC Radio, 1979; The Spoken Language as an Art Form, 1981; The Spoken Word, 1981; The English Language, 1985; The New Zealand Pocket Oxford Dictionary, 1986; contribs to: Times Lit. Supp., Trans Philological Soc., Encounter, etc. *Recreations:* investigating English grammar, travelling, gardening. *Address:* The Barn, 14 The Green, Sutton Courtenay, Oxon OX14 4AE. *T:* Abingdon 848645.

BURCHMORE, Air Cdre Eric, CBE 1972 (OBE 1963; MBE 1945); JP; RAF retired; *b* 18 June 1920; *s* of Percy William Burchmore and Olive Eva Ingledew; *m* 1941, Margaret Ovendale; one *d*. *Educ:* Robert Atkinson Sch., Thornaby; RAF Halton; Heriot-Watt Coll., Edinburgh. CEng, MRAeS. Royal Air Force: Aircraft Apprentice, 1936–39; Fitter 2, 1939–41; Engr Officer, 1941: served in Fighter Comd; Air Comd SE Asia, 1943–45; Air Min. and various home postings; Far East, 1952–55; London and Staff Coll.; Near East, 1960–62; comd RAF Sealand, 1963–66; Far East, 1967–68; Dir RAF Project (subseq. Dir Harrier Projects), MoD(PE), 1969–75; retired 1975. Dep. Dir of Housing, London Borough of Camden, 1975–80; Manager, Defence Support Services, Technicare Internat.,

1981–84. JP Godstone, Surrey, 1979. *Address:* 3 Broad Walk, Caterham, Surrey CR3 5EP. *T:* Caterham 44391. *Club:* Royal Air Force.

BURDEN, family name of **Baron Burden.**

BURDEN, 2nd Baron *cr* 1950, of Hazlebarrow, Derby; **Philip William Burden;** *b* 21 June 1916; *s* of 1st Baron Burden, CBE, and of Augusta, *d* of David Sime, Aberdeen; *S* father, 1970; *m* 1951, Audrey Elsworth, *d* of Major W. E. Sykes; three *s* three *d. Educ:* Raines Foundation School. *Heir: s* Hon. Andrew Philip Burden, *b* 20 July 1959. *Address:* c/o Barclays Bank, 26 Regent Street, Weston-super-Mare, Avon BS23 1SH.

BURDEN, Derrick Frank; HM Diplomatic Service, retired; Counsellor and Head of Claims Department, Foreign and Commonwealth Office, 1973–78; *b* 4 June 1918; *s* of late Alfred Burden and Louisa Burden (*née* Dean); *m* 1942, Marjorie Adeline Beckley; two *d. Educ:* Bec Sch., London. Crown Agents, 1936. Served War, King's Royal Rifle Corps, 1939–41. Joined Foreign Office, 1945; Comr-Gen.'s Office, Singapore, 1950–53; 2nd Sec., Moscow, 1954–56; 2nd Sec., Tokyo, 1957–59; HM Consul, Lourenço Marques, 1959–61; FO, 1962–67 (Asst Head of Protocol Dept, 1965); HM Consul, Khorramshahr (Iran), 1967–69; 1st Sec., Nairobi, 1969–71; HM Consul, Luanda (Angola), 1972–73. *Recreations:* golf, gardening. *Address:* 12 Strathmore Drive, Charvil, Reading, Berks RG10 9QT. *T:* Twyford (Berks) 340564. *Clubs:* Travellers'; Nairobi (Nairobi); Phyllis Court (Henley-on-Thames).

BURDEN, Sqn Ldr Sir Frederick Frank Arthur, Kt 1980; *b* 27 Dec. 1905; *s* of A. F. Burden, Bracknell, Berks; *m* Marjorie Greenwood; one *d. Educ:* Sloane Sch., Chelsea. Served War of 1939–45, RAF: first with a Polish unit, later with SE Asia Command, and on the staff of Lord Louis Mountbatten. MP (C) Gillingham, Kent, 1950–83. Pres., Textile Distributors Assoc., 1981–. Freeman of Gillingham, 1971. *Recreation:* fishing. *Address:* The Knapp, Portesham, Dorset. *T:* Abbotsbury 366.

BURDEN, Major Geoffrey Noel, CMG 1952; MBE 1938; *b* 9 Dec. 1898; *s* of late A. G. Burden, Exmouth, Devon; *m* 1927, Yolande Nancy, *d* of late G. H. B. Shaddick, Kenilworth, Cape Town; one *s* one *d. Educ:* Exeter Sch.; Royal Military College, Sandhurst. Served European War, 1914–18, Devon Regt, 1915–18; Indian Army, 1918–23. Joined Colonial Administrative Service, Nyasaland, 1925; Director of Publicity, 1936; Nyasaland Labour Officer to S Rhodesia, 1937–38; Nyasaland/N Rhodesian Labour Officer in the Union of South Africa, 1939; Chief Recruiting Officer, Nyasaland, 1940. War of 1939–45: military service in Somaliland, Abyssinia, and N Rhodesia, King's African Rifles, 1941–43. Asst Chief Sec., Nyasaland, 1945–46; Commissioner of Labour, Gold Coast, 1946–50; Chief Commissioner, Northern Territories, Gold Coast, 1950–53. Nyasaland Govt Representative in S Rhodesia, 1954–63. Voluntary service under SSAFA (Farnham/Frensham area), 1963–79. *Address:* The Croft, Hillside Road, Frensham, Surrey. *T:* Frensham 2584.

BURDER, Sir John Henry, Kt 1944; ED; *b* 30 Nov. 1900; *s* of late H. C. Burder; *m* 1929, Constance Aileen Bailey; two *d. Educ:* Eton College. Joined Jardine Skinner & Co., 1920; Chm., Jardine Henderson Ltd, 1939–47. Chm., Indian Tea Market Expansion Bd, 1939; President: Local Board, Imperial Bank of India, 1943–44; Bengal Chamber of Commerce, 1943–44; Associated Chambers of Commerce of India, 1943–44; Royal Agricultural and Horticultural Soc. of India, 1938–41; Calcutta Soc. for the Prevention of Cruelty to Animals, 1939–41; Lt-Col Commanding Calcutta Light Horse, 1944; Member of Council of State, 1943–44. *Address:* Plovers, Westhall Hill, Fulbrook, Oxon. *T:* Burford 2287. *Club:* Oriental.

BURDETT, Sir Savile (Aylmer), 11th Bt, *cr* 1665; Managing Director: Rapaway Energy Ltd; Rydraulic Compressors Ltd; *b* 24 Sept. 1931; *s* of Sir Aylmer Burdett, 10th Bt; *S* father, 1943; *m* 1962, June E. C. Rutherford; one *s* one *d. Educ:* Wellington Coll.; Imperial Coll., London. *Heir: s* Crispin Peter Burdett, *b* 8 Feb. 1967. *Address:* Farthings, 35 Park Avenue, Solihull, West Midlands B91 3EJ. *T:* 021–705 3360.

BURDUS, (Julia) Ann; Deputy Chairman, Audits of Great Britain, and a director, AGB International, since 1983; *b* 4 Sept. 1933; *d* of Gladstone Beaty and Julia W. C. Booth; *m* 1981, Ian B. Robertson. *Educ:* Durham Univ. (BA Psychology). Clinical psychologist, 1956–60; Res. Exec., Ogilvy, Benson & Mather, 1961–67; Res. Dir, McCann Erickson, 1971–75, Vice Chm., 1975–77; Senior Vice-Pres., McCann Internat., 1977–79; Chm., McCann & Co., 1979–81; Dir, Strategic Planning and Development, Interpublic, 1981–83. Chairman: Advertising Assoc., 1980–81; EDC for Distributive Trades. *Recreation:* home building. *Address:* Audits of Great Britain Ltd, The Research Centre, Westgate, W5 1UA.

BURFORD, Earl of; Murray de Vere Beauclerk; Partner: Burfords, chartered accountants, since 1981; Burford & Co., since 1981; *b* 19 Jan. 1939; *s* and *heir* of 13th Duke of St Albans, *qv* and 1st wife (later Mrs Nathalie C. Eldrid, *d* 1985); *m* 1st, 1963, Rosemary Frances Scoones (marr. diss. 1974); one *s* one *d*; 2nd, 1974, Cynthia Theresa Mary (Lady Hooper), *d* of late Lt-Col W. J. H. Howard, DSO. *Educ:* Tonbridge. Chartered Accountant, 1962. *Heir: s* Lord Vere of Hanworth, *qv. Address:* 3 St George's Court, Gloucester Road, SW7. *T:* 01–589 1771. *Club:* Hurlingham.

BURFORD, Eleanor; *see* Hibbert, Eleanor.

BURG, Gisela Elisabeth; Managing Director, Expotus Ltd, since 1968; *b* 12 Oct. 1939; *d* of Friedrich and Gerda Schlüsselburg. *Educ:* Gymnasium Philippinum, Weilburg, Germany; Ladies Coll., Wetzlar, Germany; Polytechnic of Central London. Founded Expotus Ltd, 1968. Vice-Pres., Fedn of British Audio, 1979–85 (Chm., 1976); Member: NEDO, 1979–84 (Mem. Electronic Sector Working Party); BOTB, 1982–. The Times/Veuve Clicquot Business Woman of the Year, 1981. *Recreations:* golf, horseracing. *Address:* 82 Kensington Heights, Campden Hill Road, W8 7BD. *T:* 01–727 8884. *Club:* Woburn Golf and Country (Beds).

BURGE, James, QC 1965; a Recorder, 1972–75; *b* 8 Oct. 1906; *s* of George Burge, Masterton, New Zealand; *m* 1938, Elizabeth, *d* of Comdr Scott Williams, RN, Dorset; two *s* one *d. Educ:* Cheltenham Coll.; Christ's Coll., Cambridge. Barrister, 1932, Master of the Bench, 1971, Inner Temple; Yarborough Anderson Scholar, Profumo Prizeman, Paul Methuen Prizeman. Pilot Officer RAFVR, 1940; Sqdn Ldr; Dep. Judge Advocate, 1941–44. Formerly Prosecuting Counsel, GPO, at CCC; Deputy Chairman, West Sussex Quarter Sessions, 1963–71. *Address:* Monte Puchol 151, Jávea, (Alicante), Spain.

BURGE, Stuart, CBE 1974; freelance director and actor; *b* 15 Jan. 1918; *s* of late H. O. Burge and K. M. Haig; *m* 1949, Josephine Parker; three *s* two *d. Educ:* Eagle House, Sandhurst; Felsted Sch., Essex. Served War of 1939–45, Intell. Corps. Actor; trained Old Vic, 1936–37; Oxford Rep., 1937–38; Old Vic and West End, 1938–39; Bristol Old Vic, Young Vic, Commercial Theatre, 1946–49; 1st Dir, Hornchurch, 1951–53; productions for theatre and TV, 1953–; Dir., Nottingham Playhouse, 1968–74; Artistic Dir., Royal Court Theatre, 1977–80. *Theatre:* Measure for Measure, The Devil is an Ass, Edinburgh Fest. and Nat. Theatre, 1977; Another Country, Greenwich 1981 and Queen's 1982; (actor) The Seagull, Royal Court, 1981; The London Cuckolds, Lyric Hammersmith, 1985. *Opera:* La Colombe, Sadler's Wells, 1983. *Television:* Bill Brand, Sons and Lovers, The Old Men at the Zoo, Much Ado About Nothing (BBC Shakespeare), etc. Vis. Prof., UC Davis, USA; Hon. Prof. of Drama, Nottingham Univ. *Publication:* (ed) King John (Folio Society), 1973. *Address:* c/o Harriet Cruickshank, 35 Churton Street, SW1.

BURGEN, Sir Arnold (Stanley Vincent), Kt 1976; FRCP 1969; FRS 1964; Master of Darwin College, Cambridge, since 1982; *b* 20 March 1922; *s* of late Peter Burgen and Elizabeth Wolfers; *m* 1946, Judith Browne; two *s* one *d. Educ:* Christ's Coll., Finchley. Student, Middlesex Hospital Med. Sch., 1939–45; MRCP 1946. Ho. Phys., Middlesex Hospital, 1945; Demonstrator, 1945–48, Asst Lectr, 1948–49, in Pharmacology, Middlesex Hospital Med. Sch. Prof. of Physiology, McGill Univ., Montreal, 1949–62; Dep. Dir, Univ. Clinic, Montreal Gen. Hospital, 1957–62; Sheild Prof. of Pharmacology, Univ. of Cambridge, 1962–71; Fellow of Downing Coll., Cambridge, 1962–71, Hon. Fellow 1972; Dir, Nat. Inst. for Med. Res., 1971–82. Medical Research Council: Member, 1969–71, 1973–77; Hon. Dir, Molecular Pharmacology Unit, 1967–72; Chm., Tropical Medicine Res. Bd, 1977–81; Assessor, 1985–. Pres., Internat. Union of Pharmacology, 1972–75; Member: Council, Royal Soc., 1972–73, 1980– (Vice Pres., 1980–; Foreign Sec., 1981–86); Nat. Biol. Standards Bd, 1975–; Med. Cttee, British Council, 1973–77; Exec. Cttee, Eur. Science Foundn; Chm., Adv. Cttee on Irradiated and Novel Foods, 1982. Dir, Amersham Internat., 1985–. Academico Correspondiente, Royal Acad. of Spain, 1983; Mem., Deutsche Akad. der Naturforscher Leopoldina, 1984. Hon. DSc: Leeds, 1973; McGill, 1973; Hon. MD: Utrecht, 1983; Zûrich, 1983. DUniv. Surrey, 1983. Hon. FRCP (C); Hon. Mem., Amer. Assoc. of Physicians. *Publications:* Physiology of Salivary Glands, 1961; papers in Journals of Physiology and Pharmacology. *Recreation:* sculpture. *Address:* Darwin College, Cambridge CB3 9EU.

BURGER, Warren Earl; Chief Justice of the United States, 1969–86; *b* St Paul, Minn, 17 Sept. 1907; *s* of Charles Joseph Burger and Katharine Schnittger; *m* 1933, Elvera Stromberg; one *s* one *d. Educ:* Univ. of Minnesota; St Paul Coll. of Law, later Mitchell Coll. of Law (LLB *magna cum laude,* LLD). Admitted to Bar of Minnesota, 1931; Mem. Faculty, Mitchell Coll. of Law, 1931–46. Partner in Faricy, Burger, Moore & Costello until 1953. Asst Attorney-Gen. of US, 1953–56; Judge, US Court of Appeals, Washington, DC, 1956–69. Chm., ABA Proj. Standards for Criminal Justice. Past Lectr, Law Schools in US and Europe. Hon. Master of the Bench of the Middle Temple, 1969. Pres. Bentham Club, UCL, 1972–73. Chancellor and Regent, Smithsonian Instn, Washington, DC; Hon. Chm., Inst. of Judicial Admin; Trustee: Nat. Gall. of Art, Washington, DC; Nat. Geographic Soc.; Trustee Emeritus: Mitchell Coll. of Law, St Paul, Minn; Macalester Coll., St Paul, Minn; Mayo Foundn, Rochester, Minn. *Publications:* articles in legal and professional jls. *Address:* c/o Supreme Court, Washington, DC 20543, USA.

BURGES, Alan; *see* Burges, N. A.

BURGES, Mrs (Margaret) Betty (Pierpoint), MBE 1937; Headmistress, Staines Preparatory School, since 1973; Chairman, Surrey County Council Conservative Group, 1981–84; *d* of Frederick Eales Hanson and Margaret Pierpoint Hanson (*née* Hurst); *m* 1937, Cyril Travers Burges, MA (*d* 1975). *Educ:* Edgbaston High Sch., Birmingham. Civil Service, 1929–37 and 1940–45. Councillor, Surrey County Council, 1967–85; Chairman, General Purposes Cttee, 1974–84. *Recreations:* walking, travel. *Address:* 1 Gresham Road, Staines, Mddx TW18 2BT. *T:* Staines 52916 and 52852.

BURGES, (Norman) Alan, CBE 1980; MSc, PhD; FIBiol; FLS; Vice-Chancellor, New University of Ulster, Coleraine, Northern Ireland, 1966–Sept. 1976; *b* 5 Aug. 1911; *s* of late Lieut J. C. Burges, East Maitland, NSW; *m* 1940, Florence Evelyn (*née* Moulton); three *d. Educ:* Sydney Univ., Australia; Emmanuel Coll., Cambridge. Graduated, Sydney, BSc Hons., 1931; MSc, 1932; PhD Cambridge, 1937. Senior 1851 Scholar, 1937. Research Fellow, Emmanuel Coll., 1938; Prof. of Botany, Sydney Univ., 1947–52; Dean of Faculty of Science and Fellow of Senate, 1949–52; Holbrook Gaskell Prof. of Botany, Univ. of Liverpool, 1952–66, Acting Vice-Chancellor, 1964–65; Pro-Vice-Chancellor, 1965–66. Hon. Gen. Sec., ANZAAS, 1947–52; President: British Ecological Soc., 1958, 1959; British Mycological Soc., 1962; Mem. Cttee, Nature Conservancy, England, 1959–66; Mem., Waste Management Adv. Council; Joint Editor, Flora Europæa Project, 1956–. Chm., NI Adv. Council for Education, 1966–75; Chairman: Ulster American Folk Park, 1975–; NI American Bicentennial Cttee, 1975–77; Chm., Nat. Trust NI Cttee, 1978–81. Served War of 1939–45, RAF Bomber Command (despatches). Hon. LLD QUB, 1973; Hon. DTech Loughborough, 1975; Hon. DSc Ulster, 1977. *Publications:* Micro-organisms in the Soil, 1958; (with F. Raw) Soil Biology, 1967; various in scientific journals on plant diseases and fungi. *Recreation:* sailing. *Address:* Beechcroft, Glenkeen Road, Aghadowey, Coleraine, Co. Londonderry. *T:* Aghadowey 224.

BURGES, Maj.-Gen. Rodney Lyon Travers, CBE 1963; DSO 1946; *b* 19 March 1914; *s* of Richard Burges and Hilda Christine Burges (*née* Lyon); *m* 1946, Sheila Marion Lyster Goldby, *d* of H. L. Goldby; one *s* one *d. Educ:* Wellington; RMA, Woolwich. 2nd Lieut RA, 1934; war service in Burma, 1942 and 1944–45; CO The Berkshire Yeomanry (145 Fd Regt, RA), 1945; Comdr, E Battery, RHA, 1949–51; Bt Lt-Col 1953; 2nd in comd, 1 RHA, 1954–55; CO 3 RHA, 1955–57; CRA 3 Div., 1958–59; IDC, 1960; Brig. Q (Ops) WO, 1961–63; CCRA, 1 Corps, BAOR, 1963–64; Maj.-Gen. 1964; GOC, Cyprus District, 1964–66; VQMG, MoD, 1966–67. Joined Grieveson, Grant & Co., 1968, Partner 1971, retd 1978; Consultant to Pat Simon Wines Ltd, 1978–85; Dir, Caroline Fine Wines Ltd, 1982–85. Freeman and Liveryman, Fishmongers' Co., 1974. *Recreations:* racing, drinking wine in the sun. *Address:* Freemantle, Over Wallop, Hants. *Club:* Buck's.

BURGES WATSON, Richard Eagleson Gordon; *see* Watson, R. E. G. B.

BURGESS, Anthony, BA; Hon. DLitt; novelist and critic; *b* 25 Feb. 1917; *s* of Joseph Wilson and Elizabeth Burgess; *m* 1942, Llewela Isherwood Jones, BA (*d* 1968); *m* 1968, Liliana Macellari, *d* of Contessa Maria Lucrezia Pasi della Pergola; one *s. Educ:* Xaverian Coll., Manchester; Manchester Univ. Served Army, 1940–46. Lecturer: Birmingham Univ. Extra-Mural Dept., 1946–48; Ministry of Education, 1948–50; English Master, Banbury Grammar Sch., 1950–54; Education Officer, Malaya and Brunei, 1954–59. Vis. Fellow, Princeton Univ., 1970–71; Distinguished Prof., City Coll., NY, 1972–73. Hon. DLitt Manchester, 1982. Commandeur: de Mérite Culturel, Monaco; des Arts et des Lettres, France. TV scripts: Moses the Lawgiver and Jesus of Nazareth (series), 1977; Blooms of Dublin, 1982 (a musical for radio). *Publications:* Time for a Tiger, 1956; The Enemy in the Blanket, 1958; Beds in the East, 1959 (these three, as The Malayan Trilogy, 1972, and as The Long Day Wanes, 1982); The Right to an Answer, 1960; The Doctor is Sick, 1960; The Worm and the Ring, 1961; Devil of a State, 1961; A Clockwork Orange, 1962 (filmed, 1971); The Wanting Seed, 1962; Honey for the Bears, 1963; The Novel Today, 1963; Language Made Plain, 1964; Nothing like the Sun, 1964; The Eve of Saint Venus, 1964; A Vision of Battlements, 1965; Here Comes Everybody—an introduction to James Joyce, 1965; Tremor of Intent, 1966; A Shorter Finnegans Wake, 1966; The Novel Now, 1967; Enderby Outside, 1968; Urgent Copy, 1968; Shakespeare, 1970; MF, 1971; Joysprick, 1973; Napoleon Symphony, 1974; The Clockwork Testament, 1974; Moses, 1976; A Long Trip to Teatime, 1976; Beard's Roman Women, 1976; ABBA ABBA, 1977; New York, 1977; L'Homme de Nazareth, 1977 (Man of Nazareth, 1979);

Ernest Hemingway and His World, 1978; 1985, 1978; They Wrote in English (Italy), 1979; The Land Where the Ice Cream Grows, 1979; Earthly Powers, 1980; On Going to Bed, 1982; This Man and Music, 1982; The End of the World News, 1982; Enderby's Dark Lady, 1984; Ninety-Nine Novels, 1984; The Kingdom of the Wicked, 1985; Flame into Being, 1985; The Pianoplayers, 1986; (trans. Rostand) Cyrano de Bergerac, 1971; (trans. Sophocles) Oedipus the King, 1973; *translations of stage plays*: Homage to Qwert Yuiop, 1986; as *Joseph Kell*: One Hand Clapping, 1961; Inside Mr Enderby, 1963; as *John Burgess Wilson*: English Literature: A Survey for Students, 1958; contributor to Observer, Spectator, Listener, Encounter, Queen, Times Literary Supplement, Hudson Review, Holiday, Playboy, American Scholar, Corriere della Sera, Le Monde, etc. *Recreations*: music composition, piano-playing, cooking, language-learning, travel. *Address*: 44 rue Grimaldi, Monaco; 1 and 2 Piazza Padella, Bracciano, Italy; 168 Triq Il-Kbira, Lija, Malta.

BURGESS, Anthony Reginald Frank, (Tony), CVO 1983; HM Diplomatic Service; Counsellor and Head of Chancery, Havana, since 1986; *b* 27 Jan. 1932; *s* of Beatrice Burgess; *m* 1960, Carlyn Shawyer; one *s*. *Educ*: Ealing Grammar Sch.; University College London (BScEcon). National Service, 1953–55; TA, 16 Airborne Div., 1955–57. Journalism, 1955–62; European Community Civil Service, 1962–65; HM Diplomatic Service, 1966–: 1st Sec., European Economic Organisations Dept, FCO, 1966–67; 1st Sec. (Political), Dhaka, 1967–69; 1st Sec., SE Asia Dept, FCO, 1970–72; 1st Sec. (Economic), Ottawa, 1972–76; Head of Chancery and HM Consul, Bogota, 1976–79; 1st Sec., Rhodesia Dept, FCO, 1979–80; Asst Head of Information Dept, FCO, 1980–82; Dep. High Comr, Dhaka, 1982–86. *Publication*: (jtly) The Common Market and the Treaty of Rome Explained, 1967. *Recreations*: travel, photography, shooting, riding. *Address*: c/o Foreign and Commonwealth Office, SW1. *Clubs*: Brooks's; British Sporting Rifle (Bisley).

BURGESS, Averil; Headmistress, South Hampstead High School, GPDST, since 1975; *b* 8 July 1938; *d* of David and Dorothy Evans (*née* Owen); *m* 1959, Clifford Burgess (marr. diss. 1973). *Educ*: Ashby-de-la-Zouch Girls' Grammar Sch.; Queen Mary Coll., Univ. of London. BA Hons History. Assistant Mistress: Langleybury Secondary Modern Sch., 1959–60; Ensham Sch., 1960–62; Hatfield Sch., 1963–65; Fulham County Sch., 1965–69; Wimbledon High Sch., GPDST, 1969–74 (Head of History and Second Mistress). Mem., Bursaries Management Cttee, GPDST, 1979–; Mem. Exec Cttee, 1984–, and Chm. Educn Cttee, GSA; Governor, Central Sch. of Speech and Drama, 1981–. *Recreations*: visiting France, listening to music (especially opera), mountain walking in Wales and other forms of non-competitive exercise. *Address*: South Hampstead High School, 3 Maresfield Gardens, NW3. *T*: 01–435 2899.

BURGESS, Claude Bramall, CMG 1958; OBE 1954; Minister for Hong Kong Commercial Relations with the European Communities and the Member States, 1974–82; *b* 25 Feb. 1910; *s* of late George Herbert Burgess, Weaverham, Cheshire, and Martha Elizabeth Burgess; *m* 1952, Margaret Joan Webb (marr. diss. 1965); one *s*; *m* 1969, Linda Nettleton, *e d* of William Grothier Beilby, New York. *Educ*: Epworth Coll.; Christ Church, Oxford. Eastern Cadetship in HM Colonial Administrative Service, 1932. Commissioned in RA, 1940; POW, 1941–45; demobilized with rank of Lieut-Col, RA, 1946. Colonial Office, 1946–48. Attended Imperial Defence Coll., London, 1951. Various Government posts in Hong Kong; Colonial Secretary (and Actg Governor on various occasions), Hong Kong, 1958–63, retd; Head of Co-ordination and Develt Dept, EFTA, 1964–73. *Address*: 75 Chester Row, SW1. *T*: 01–730 8758.

BURGESS, Rev. Canon David John; Canon of St George's Chapel, Windsor, since 1978; *b* 4 Aug. 1939; *e s* of Albert Burgess and Mary Burgess (*née* Kelsey); *m* 1976, Dr Kathleen Louise, *d* of Philip Lindsay Costeloe; one *s* one *d*. *Educ*: King's School, Peterborough; Trinity Hall, Cambridge; Cuddesdon Theological Coll. Orthodox Studentship, Halki, Istanbul, 1963–64. Curate, All Saints, Maidstone, 1965; Assistant Chaplain, University Coll., Oxford, 1966; Fellow, 1969; Chaplain, 1970; Domestic Bursar, 1971. Hon. Fellow, Inst. of Clerks of Works, 1978. *Publications*: articles and reviews. *Recreations*: alpine walking, opera, art, cooking. *Address*: 6 The Cloisters, Windsor Castle, Berks. *T*: Windsor 66313.

BURGESS, Dilys Averil; *see* Burgess, A.

BURGESS, Gen. Sir Edward (Arthur), KCB 1982; OBE 1972; Deputy Supreme Allied Commander, Europe, since 1984; Aide-de-Camp General to the Queen, since 1985; *b* 30 Sept. 1927; *s* of Edward Burgess and Alice Burgess; *m* 1954, Jean Angelique Leslie Henderson; one *s* one *d*. *Educ*: All Saints Sch., Bloxham; Lincoln Coll., Oxford; RMA, Sandhurst. Commnd RA 1948; served Germany and ME, 1949–59; psc 1960; GSO 2 WO, 1961–63; served Germany and Far East, 1963–65; jssc 1966; Mil. Asst to C-in-C BAOR, 1966–67; GSO I (DS) Staff Coll., 1968–70; CO 25 Light Regt, RA, 1970–72; CRA 4th Div., 1972–74; Dir of Army Recruiting, 1975–77; Dir, Combat Development (Army), 1977–79; GOC Artillery Div., 1979–82; Comdr, UK Field Army, and Inspector Gen. TA, 1982–84. Col Comdt, RA, 1982–. *Publications*: articles in military jls. *Recreations*: sailing, fishing, music, reading, gardening. *Address*: c/o Lloyds Bank, Winton, Bournemouth, Dorset. *Club*: Army and Navy.

BURGESS, Geoffrey Harold Orchard; Chief Scientist (Agriculture and Horticulture), Ministry of Agriculture, Fisheries and Food, 1982–86; *b* 28 March 1926; *s* of late Harold Frank and of Eva M. F. Burgess, Reading; *m* 1952, Barbara Vernon, *y d* of late Rev. Gilbert Vernon Yonge; two *s*. *Educ*: Reading Grammar Sch.; Univ. of Reading; UC Hull. BSc Reading, 1951 (Colin Morley Prizewinner 1950); PhD London, 1955. FRSE 1971. Special research appt, Univ. of Hull, 1951; Sen. Scientific Officer, DSIR, Humber Lab., Hull, 1954; PSO, Torry Res. Stn, Aberdeen, 1960; Officer i/c, Humber Lab., Hull, 1962; Director, Torry Res. Station, 1969–79; Head of Biology Div., Agrictl Science Service, and Officer i/c Slough Lab., MAFF, 1979–82. Hon. Res. Lectr in Fish Technology, Univ. of Aberdeen, 1969–79; Buckland Lectr, 1964; Hon. Lectr in Fish Technology, Univ. of Leeds, 1966–69; Mem. Adv. Cttee on Food Science, Univ. of Leeds, 1970–86; Mem., Panel of Fish Technology Experts, FAO, 1962–79. *Publications*: Developments in the Handling and Processing of Fish, 1965; (with Lovern, Waterman and Cutting) Fish Handling and Processing, 1965; The Curious World of Frank Buckland, 1967; scientific and technical papers, reviews, reports etc concerning handling, processing, transport and preservation for food, of fish, from catching to consumption. *Recreations*: music, book collecting, walking. *Address*: 14 Main Road, Naphill, High Wycombe, Bucks.

BURGESS, Rear-Adm. John, MVO 1975; Managing Director, HM Dockyard, Rosyth, since 1984; *b* 13 July 1929; *s* of Albert Burgess and Winifred (*née* Evans); *m* 1952, Avis (*née* Morgan); two *d*. *Educ*: RN Engineering College; Advanced Engineering RN College, Greenwich; nuclear courses, RN College. HM Ships Aisne, Maidstone, Theseus, Implacable, Cumberland, Caprice; Lectr in Thermodynamics, RNEC, 1962–65; HMS Victorious; nuclear reactor design and manufacture at Rolls Royce, 1968–70; Naval Staff, Washington, DC, 1970–72; Royal Yacht Britannia, 1972–75; Head, Forward Design Group, Ship Dept, 1975–77; Naval Asst to Controller of the Navy, 1977–79; in Command, HMS Defiance, 1979–81; in Command, HMS Sultan, 1981–83. *Publications*: papers to professional bodies. *Recreations*: golf, sailing, supporting an old house in the west country. *Address*: c/o Naval Secretary, Ministry of Defence, Whitehall, SW1.

BURGESS, Ven. John Edward; Archdeacon of Bath, since 1975; *b* 9 Dec. 1930; *s* of Herbert and Dorothy May Burgess; *m* 1958, Jonquil Marion Bailey; one *s* one *d*. *Educ*: Surbiton County Gram. Sch.; London Univ. (St John's Hall). BD (2nd Cl.), ALCD (1st Cl.). Shell Chemicals Ltd, 1947–53. Asst Curate, St Mary Magdalen, Bermondsey, 1957–60; Asst Curate, St Mary, Southampton, 1960–62; Vicar of Dunston with Coppenhall, Staffs, 1962–67; Chaplain, Staffordshire Coll. of Technology, 1963–67; Vicar of Keynsham with Queen Charlton and Burnett, Somerset, 1967–75; Rural Dean of Keynsham, 1971–74. *Recreation*: history of railways. *Address*: Birnfels, 56 Grange Road, Saltford, Bristol BS18 3AG. *T*: Saltford 3609.

BURGESS, Sir John (Lawie), Kt 1972; OBE 1944; TD 1945; DL; Chairman, Cumbrian Newspapers Group Ltd, since 1945; *b* 17 Nov. 1912; *s* of late R. N. Burgess, Carlisle and Jean Hope Lawie, Carlisle; *m* 1948, Alice Elizabeth, *d* of late F. E. Gillieron, Elgin; two *s* one *d*. *Educ*: Trinity Coll., Glenalmond. Served War of 1939–45, Border Regt, France, Middle East, Tobruk, Syria, India and Burma; comd 4th Bn, Chindit Campaign, Burma, 1944 (despatches, OBE); Hon. Col 4th Bn The Border Regt, 1955–68. Chm., Reuters Ltd, 1959–68; Dir, Press Assoc. Ltd, 1950–57 (Chm. 1955); Mem. Council, Newspaper Soc., 1947–82; Chm., Border Television Ltd, 1960–81, Vice-Chm. 1981–82. Mem. Council, Commonwealth Press Union. DL Cumberland, 1955; High Sheriff of Cumberland, 1969; JP City of Carlisle, 1952–82. *Recreations*: dowsing; anything to do with Cumbria. *Address*: The Limes, Cavendish Terrace, Carlisle, Cumbria. *T*: Carlisle 37450. *Clubs*: Garrick, Army and Navy.

BURGESS, (Joseph) Stuart, CBE 1984; PhD; FRSC; Chief Executive, Amersham International plc, since 1979; *b* 20 March 1929; *s* of late Joseph and Emma Burgess (*née* Wollerton); *m* 1955, Valerie Ann Street; one *s* one *d*. *Educ*: Barnsley Holgate Grammar School; University College London (1st Class Hons BSc Chem, PhD). Amersham International plc (formerly The Radiochemical Centre), 1953–, Director, 1973–; Pres., Amersham Corp. USA, 1975–77, Group Marketing Controller, 1977–79. Mem., CBI Research and Technology Cttee, 1984–. *Recreations*: golf, music. *Address*: Barrington, Hearn Close, Penn, Bucks. *T*: Penn 6387.

BURGESS, Stuart; *see* Burgess, J. S.

BURGESS, Tony; *see* Burgess, A. R. F.

BURGH, 7th Baron, *cr* 1529 (title called out of abeyance, 1916; by some reckonings he is 9th Baron (from a *cr* 1487) and his father was 8th and grandfather 7th); **Alexander Peter Willoughby Leith;** *b* 20 March 1935; *s* of 6th (or 8th) Baron Burgh; *S* father 1959; *m* 1957, Anita Lorna Eldridge; two *s* one *d*. *Educ*: Harrow; Magdalene Coll., Cambridge (BA). *Heir*: *s* Hon. Alexander Gregory Disney Leith, [*b* 16 March 1958; *m* 1984, Catherine Mary, *d* of David Parkes].

BURGH, Sir John (Charles), KCMG 1982; CB 1975; Director-General of the British Council, 1980–July 1987; Chairman, Court of Governors, London School of Economics, since 1985 (Governor, since 1980); Chairman, International Students House, since 1986 (Member Council, since 1981); *b* 9 Dec. 1925; *m* 1957, Ann Sturge; two *d*. *Educ*: Friends' Sch., Sibford; London Sch. of Economics (BSc Econ.; Leverhulme post-intermediate Schol.; Pres. of Union, 1949; Hon. Fellow, 1983). Asst Principal, BoT, 1950; Private Sec. to successive Ministers of State, BoT, 1954–57; Colonial Office, 1959–62; Mem., UK Delegation to UN Conf. on Trade and Develt, 1964; Asst Sec., DEA, 1964; Principal Private Sec. to successive First Secretaries of State and Secretaries of State for Econ. Affairs, 1965–68; Under-Sec., Dept of Employment, 1968–71; Dep.-Chm., Community Relations Commn, 1971–72; Deputy Secretary: Cabinet Office (Central Policy Rev. Staff), 1972–74; Dept of Prices and Consumer Protection, 1974–79; Dept of Trade, 1979–80. Member: Executive, PEP, 1972–78; Council, Policy Studies Inst., 1978–85; Council, RSA, 1982–85; Council, VSO, 1980–; Acad. Council, Wilton Park, 1984–; Vice-Pres., RIPA, 1985–. Sec., Nat. Opera Co-ordinating Cttee, 1972–; Sec., Opera Cttee, Royal Opera House, Covent Gdn, 1971–80. FRSA 1981. *Recreations*: friends, music, the arts generally. *Address*: (until July 1987) The British Council, 10 Spring Gardens, SW1A 2BN; c/o The London School of Economics, Houghton Street, WC2A 2AE. *Club*: Arts.

BURGHERSH, Lord; Anthony David Francis Henry Fane; *b* 1 Aug. 1951; *s* and *heir* of 15th Earl of Westmorland, *qv*; *m* 1985, Caroline Eldred, *d* of Keon Hughes. *Educ*: Eton. *Address*: 10 Peterborough Villas, SW6 2AT.

BURGHLEY, Lord; William Michael Anthony Cecil; *b* 1 Sept. 1935; *s* and *heir* of 7th Marquess of Exeter, *qv*; *m* 1967, Nancy Rose, *d* of Lloyd Arthur Meeker; one *s* one *d*. *Educ*: Eton. Rancher and businessman in 100 Mile House, 1954–. *Publications*: (jtly) Spirit of Sunrise, 1979; The Long View, 1985; The Rising Tide of Change, 1986. *Heir*: *s* Hon. Anthony John Cecil, *b* 9 Aug. 1970. *Address*: Box 8, 100 Mile House, BC V0K 2EO, Canada. *T*: 604–395–2767; Kingcombe, Chipping Campden, Glos GL55 6UN. *T*: 840253.

BURGNER, Thomas Ulric; Under Secretary, Head of Industry, Agriculture and Employment Group, HM Treasury, since 1985; *b* 6 March 1932; *s* of John Henry Burgner and Clara Doerte Burgner (*née* Wolff); *m* 1958, Marion (*née* Chasik); two *s*. *Educ*: Haberdashers' Aske's, Hampstead; St Catharine's Coll., Cambridge (BA (Hons), MA); Dip. Personnel Management. Flying Officer, RAF, 1954–55. National Coal Board, 1955–61; Assoc. of Chemical and Allied Employers, 1961–65; Principal, Dept of Economic Affairs, 1965–69; HM Treasury: Principal, 1969–72; Asst Secretary, 1972–76; Head of Exchange Control Div., 1972–74; Head of General Aid Div., 1974–76; Under Secretary, 1976; on secondment as Sec., NEDC, 1976–80; Head of Public Enterprises Gp, 1980–85. Mem., BSC, 1980–83. *Address*: 12 Kingsley Place, Highgate, N6 5EA. *T*: 01–340 9759.

BURGON, Geoffrey; composer; *b* 15 July 1941; *s* of Alan Wybert Burgon and Ada Vera Isom; *m* 1963, Janice Elizabeth Garwood (marr. diss.); one *s* one *d*. *Educ*: Pewley Sch., Guildford; Guildhall School of Music and Drama (GGSM). Composer and freelance trumpeter, 1964–71: engagements included Royal Opera House (stage band), Philomusica, Jacques, London Mozart Players, Northern Sinfonia and Capriol Orchestras, also session work, theatres and jazz bands. Full time composer, 1971–; commissions from many Festivals, incl. Bath, Edinburgh, Three Choirs, and Camden; also many works for Dance, incl. Ballet Rambert and London Contemporary Dance Theatre; work performed internationally. *Major works*: Gending, Requiem, Canciones del Alma, The Fire of Heaven, Joan of Arc, Running Figures, Songs, Lamentations and Praises, Mirandola (opera) and Orpheus (one act opera); Chamber Dances, The World Again, Revelations, Mass for Men's Voices; also very many scores for film, television and radio, incl. Life of Brian (film), Tinker, Tailor, Soldier, Spy, Brideshead Revisited, and Bleak House (TV). Prince Pierre of Monaco Award, 1969; Ivor Novello Award, 1979, 1981; Silver Disc for Brideshead record, 1982. *Publications*: over thirty scores of works in most musical genres. *Recreations*: playing jazz, cricket, wasting money on old cars, particularly Bristols. *Address*: c/o J. & W. Chester Ltd, Eagle Court, EC1M 5QD. *T*: 01–253 6947.

BURGOYNE, Rear-Adm. Robert Michael, CB 1982; Director, Royal Institute of Navigation, since 1983; *b* 20 March 1927; *s* of Robert and Elizabeth Burgoyne; *m* 1951, Margaret (Hilda) McCook; one *s* one *d*. *Educ:* Bradfield College; Magdalene College, Cambridge. Joined RN 1945; CO HMS Cleopatra, 1967–68; Captain 2nd Frigate Sqdn and CO HMS Undaunted, 1972–73; Dir, Maritime Tactical Sch., 1974–75; CO HMS Antrim, 1975–77; Comdr, British Navy Staff, Washington and UK Rep. to SACLANT, 1977–80; Senior Naval Member, Directing Staff, RCDS, 1980–82. FBIM (MBIM 1969); MNI 1973. *Address:* c/o Midland Bank, Gerrards Cross, Bucks.

BURKE, Adm. Arleigh Albert; Navy Cross; DSM (3 Gold Stars); Legion of Merit (with 2 Gold Stars and Army Oak Leaf Cluster). Silver Star Medal, Purple Heart, Presidential Unit Citation Ribbon (with 3 stars), Navy Unit Commendation Ribbon; retired as Chief of Naval Operations, US Navy and Member of Joint Chiefs of Staff (1955–61); Member of Board of Directors, Freedoms Foundation, at Valley Forge; *b* 19 Oct. 1901; *s* of Oscar A. and Claire Burke; *m* 1923, Roberta Gorsuch; no *c*. *Educ:* United States Naval Academy; Univ. of Michigan (MSE). Commnd ensign, USN, 1923, advancing through grades to Admiral, 1955. USS Arizona, 1923–28; Gunnery Dept, US Base Force, 1928; Post-graduate course (explosives), 1929–31; USS Chester, 1932; Battle Force Camera Party, 1933–35; Bureau of Ordnance, 1935–37; USS Craven, 1937–39; USS Mugford, Captain, 1939–40; Naval Gun Factory, 1940–43; Destroyer Divs 43 and 44, Squadron 12 Comdg, 1943; Destroyer Squadron 23 Comdg, 1943–44; Chief of Staff to Commander Task Force 58 (Carriers), 1944–45; Head of Research and Development Bureau of Ordnance, 1945–46; Chief of Staff, Comdr Eighth Fleet and Atlantic Fleet, 1947–48; USS Huntington, Captain, 1949; Asst Chief of Naval Ops, 1949–50; Cruiser Div. 5, Comdr, 1951; Dep. Chief of Staff, Commander Naval Forces, Far East, 1951; Director Strategic Plans Div., Office of the Chief of Naval Operations, 1952–53; Cruiser Division 6, Commanding, 1954; Commander Destroyer Force, Atlantic, 1955. Member: American Legion; American Soc. of Naval Engineers and numerous other naval assocs, etc.; National Geographic Society; also foreign societies, etc. Holds several hon. degrees. Ul Chi Medal (Korea), 1954; Korean Presidential Unit Citation, 1954. *Recreations:* reading, gardening. *Address:* The Virginian, Apt 323, 9229 Arlington Boulevard, Fairfax, Va 22031, USA. *Clubs:* Army-Navy Town, Metropolitan, Chevy Chase, Alfalfa, Circus Saints and Sinners, Ends of the Earth, etc (Washington, DC); Quindecum (Newport, US); The Brook, Lotos, Salmagundi, Inner Wheel, Seawanhaka Corinthian Yacht (New York); Bohemian (San Francisco).

BURKE, Sir Aubrey (Francis), Kt 1959; OBE 1941; Vice-Chairman retired from Executive Duties, 1969; *b* 21 April 1904; *m* 1936, Rosalind Laura, *d* of Rt Hon. Sir Henry Norman, 1st Bt, PC, OBE, and Hon. Lady Norman, CBE, JP; one *s* three *d* (and one *d* decd). Pres., SBAC, 1958–1959–1960. FCIT; FRSA. High Sheriff of Hertfordshire, 1966–67. *Recreations:* shooting, fishing, sailing. *Address:* Rent Street Barns, Bovingdon, Hertfordshire. *Club:* Royal Automobile.

BURKE, Hon. Brian Thomas; JP; MLA (Lab) Balga, since 1973; Premier and Treasurer of Western Australia, since 1983 (re-elected as Premier, 1986); also Minister Co-ordinating Economic and Social Development, and Minister for Women's Interests; *b* 25 Feb. 1947; *s* of late Thomas Burke (Federal ALP Member for Perth, 1942–53), and Madeline Burke; *m* 1965, Susanne May Nevill; four *s* two *d*. *Educ:* Brigidine Convent; Marist Brothers' Coll.; Univ. of Western Australia. Asst proof reader, West Australian Newspapers, 1965; cadet journalist, The West Australian, 1966; Journalist: Radio 6PM, 1969; TVW Channel 7, 1970. Opposition Shadow Minister, 1976–81; Leader of the Opposition, 1981–83. Patron, Soccer Fedn of WA. Jaycees Outstanding Young W Australian Award, 1982. *Recreations:* reading, stamp-collecting, writing poetry, swimming, fishing. *Address:* Department of the Premier and Cabinet, 197 St George's Terrace, Perth, WA 6000, Australia. *T:* (09) 420 9444.

BURKE, Desmond Peter Meredyth, MA Oxon; Headmaster, Clayesmore School, 1945–66; *b* 10 May 1912; *yr s* of late Maj. Arthur Meredyth Burke. *Educ:* Cheltenham Coll.; Queen's Coll., Oxford. Honours, Modern Greats, 1933. Housemaster and Senior Modern Language Master, Clayesmore School, 1936–40; served in Army Intelligence Corps at home, Belgium and Germany, 1940–45. *Recreations:* the theatre, travel, tennis, bridge. *Address:* The Old Lodge, 92 Alumhurst Road, Bournemouth West. *T:* Westbourne 762329.

BURKE, Rt. Rev. Geoffrey; Titular Bishop of Vagrauta and Auxiliary Bishop of Salford (RC), since 1967; *b* 31 July 1913; *s* of Dr Peter Joseph Burke and Margaret Mary (*née* Coman). *Educ:* St Bede's Coll., Manchester; Stonyhurst Coll.; Oscott Coll., Birmingham; Downing Coll., Cambridge (MA). Taught History, St Bede's Coll., 1940–66; Prefect of Studies, 1950; Rector, 1966. Consecrated Bishop 29 June 1967. *Address:* St John's Cathedral, 250 Chapel Street, Salford, Lancashire M3 5LL. *T:* 061–834 0333.

BURKE, Jeffrey Peter, QC 1984; a Recorder of the Crown Court, since 1983; *b* 15 Dec. 1941; *s* of Samuel and Gertrude Burke; *m* 1966, Tessa Rachel Marks; two *s* one *d*. *Educ:* Shrewsbury Sch.; Brasenose Coll., Oxford (BA 1963). Called to the Bar, Inner Temple, 1964. *Recreations:* football, cricket, wine, books, music. *Address:* 12 Reynolds Close, NW11 7EA. *T:* 01–455 7825. *Clubs:* Economicals AFC; Caledon Cricket.

BURKE, John Kenneth; QC 1985; a Recorder of the Crown Court, since 1980; *b* 4 Aug. 1939; *s* of Kenneth Burke and Madeline Burke; *m* 1962, Margaret Anne (*née* Scattergood); three *d*. *Educ:* Stockport Grammar Sch. Served Cheshire Regt, 1958–60; TA Parachute Regt, 1962–67. Called to the Bar, Middle Temple, 1965. *Recreations:* painting and drawing, walking. *Address:* 1 Hawthorn View Cottage, Knutsford Road, Mobberley, Cheshire WA16 7BA. *T:* Mobberley 2627; (chambers) 18 St John Street, Manchester M3 4EA. *T:* 061 834 9843; (chambers) 12 South Square, Gray's Inn, WC1R 5EU. *T:* 01–242 0858.

BURKE, Sir Joseph (Terence Anthony), KBE 1980 (CBE 1973; OBE 1946); MA; Professor of Fine Arts, University of Melbourne, 1946–78, now Emeritus Professor; Fellow, Trinity College Melbourne, since 1973; Consultant in Art; *b* 14 July 1913; *s* of late R. M. J. Burke; *m* 1940, Agnes, *d* of late Rev. James Middleton, New Brunswick, Canada; one *s*. *Educ:* Ealing Priory Sch., King's Coll., Univ. of London; Courtauld Institute of Art; Yale Univ., USA (Henry Fellow, 1936–37). Entered Victoria and Albert Museum, 1938; lent to Home Office and Min. of Home Security, Sept. 1939; private sec. to successive Lord Presidents of the Council (Rt Hon. Sir John Anderson, Rt Hon. C. R. Attlee, Rt Hon. Lord Woolton), 1942–45; and to the Prime Minister (Rt Hon. C. R. Attlee), 1945–46; Trustee of Felton Bequest; Fellow, Australian Acad. of the Humanities, Pres., 1971–73. Hon. DLitt Monash, 1977. *Publications:* Hogarth and Reynolds: A Contrast in English Art Theory, 1943; ed William Hogarth's Analysis of Beauty and Autobiographical Notes, 1955; (with Colin Caldwell) Hogarth: The Complete Engravings, 1968; vol. IX, Oxford History of English Art, 1714–1800, 1976; articles in Burlington Magazine, Warburg Journal and elsewhere. *Recreations:* reading, nature study. *Address:* Dormers, Falls Road, Mount Dandenong, Victoria 3767, Australia. *Clubs:* Athenæum; Melbourne (Melbourne).

BURKE, Prof. Philip George, PhD; FRS 1978; MRIA 1974; Professor of Mathematical Physics, Queen's University of Belfast, since 1967; *b* 18 Oct. 1932; *s* of Henry Burke and Frances Mary Sprague; *m* 1959, Valerie Mona Martin; four *d*. *Educ:* Wanstead County High Sch.; Univ. of Exeter (BSc 1953); University Coll. London (PhD 1956, Fellow 1985). Res. Fellow, UCL, 1956–57; Asst Lectr, Univ. of London Inst. for Computer Science, 1957–59; Res. Fellow, Lawrence Berkeley Lab., Calif, 1959–62; Res. Fellow, then Principal Scientific Officer, later Sen. Prin. Sci. Officer, Atomic Energy Res. Estab., Harwell, 1962–67. Hd, Div. of Theory and Computational Sci., SRC (later SERC) Daresbury Lab., 1977–82. Hon. DSc Exeter, 1981. *Publications:* many papers in learned journals. *Recreations:* walking, reading. *Address:* Brook House, Norley Lane, Crowton, near Northwich, Cheshire CW8 2RR. *T:* Kingsley 88301.

BURKE, Richard; Adviser, European Community Office, Ernst & Whinney, Brussels, since 1985; Director, Sedwick Europe BV (Amsterdam), since 1985; *b* 29 March 1932; *s* of David Burke and Elisabeth Burke; *m* 1961, Mary Freeley; two *s* three *d*. *Educ:* University Coll., Dublin (MA). Called to the Bar, King's Inns. Mem., Dublin Co. Council, 1967–73 (Chm., 1972–73); Mem. Dail Eirann, for South County Dublin, 1969–77, for Dublin West, 1981–82; Fine Gael Chief Whip and spokesman on Posts and Telegraphs, 1969–73; Minister for Education, 1973–76. Commission of the European Communities: Member with special responsibility for Transport, Taxation, Consumer Protection, Relations with European Parlt, Research, Educ. and Sci., 1977–81, for Greenland, Greek Memorandum, Personnel and Admin, Jt Interpretation and Conf. Service, Statistical Office and Office of Publications, 1982–85; Vice Pres., 1984–85. Associate Fellow, Center for Internat. Affairs, Harvard Univ., 1980–81. *Recreations:* music, golf, travel. *Address:* 67 Ailesbury Road, Dublin 4, Ireland. *T:* Dublin 692520.

BURKE, Sir Thomas (Stanley), 8th Bt, *cr* 1797; *b* 20 July 1916; *s* of Sir Gerald Howe Burke, 7th Bt and Elizabeth Mary (*d* 1918), *d* of late Patrick Mathews, Mount Hanover, Drogheda; *S* father 1954; *m* 1955, Susanne Margaretha (*d* 1983), *er d* of Otto Salvisberg, Thun, Switzerland; one *s* one *d*. *Educ:* Harrow; Trinity Coll., Cambridge. *Heir:* *s* James Stanley Gilbert Burke [*b* 1 July 1956; *m* 1980, Laura, *d* of Domingo Branzuela; one *s* one *d*]. *Address:* 18 Elmcroft Avenue, NW11 0RR. *T:* 01–455 9407.

BURKE, Tom; Director, The Green Alliance, since 1982; Press Officer, European Environment Bureau, since 1979; Head of Policy and Research, Earthlife Foundation, since 1986; *b* 5 Jan. 1947; *s* of J. V. Burke, DSM, and Mary (*née* Bradley). *Educ:* St Boniface's, Plymouth; Liverpool Univ. (BA (Hons) Philosophy). Great George's Community Arts Project, 1969–70; Lecturer: West Cheshire Coll., 1970–71; Old Swan Technical Coll., 1971–73; Friends of the Earth: Local Groups Co-ordinator, 1973–75; Executive Director, 1975–79; Dir of Special Projects, 1979–80; Vice-Chm., 1980–81. Member: Bd of Dirs, Earth Resources Research, 1975–; Waste Management Adv. Council, 1976–81; Packaging Council, 1978–82; Exec. Cttee, NCVO, 1984–. Royal Humane Society Testimonials: on Vellum, 1966; on Parchment, 1968. Contested (SDP), Brighton Kemptown, 1983. Hon. Vis. Fellow, Manchester Business Sch., 1984. *Publications:* Europe: environment, 1981; (jtly) Pressure Groups in the Global System, 1982; (jtly) Ecology 2000, 1984. *Recreations:* photography, birdwatching. *Address:* 36 Crewdson Road, SW9. *T:* 01–735 9019. *Club:* Reform.

BURKE-GAFFNEY, John Campion; Director-General, The British Red Cross Society, since 1985; *b* 27 Feb. 1932; *s* of late Dr Henry Joseph O'Donnell Burke-Gaffney, OBE and Constance May (*née* Bishop); *m* 1956, Margaret Mary Jennifer (*née* Stacpoole); two *s* two *d*. *Educ:* Douai School. Called to the Bar, Gray's Inn, 1956. Served: RAC, 1950–52; E Riding of Yorks Imperial Yeomanry (Wenlock's Horse), 1952–56. Shell-Mex and BP Ltd, 1956–75; Shell UK Ltd, 1976–77; Man. Dir, Shell and BP Zambia Ltd, 1977–81; Gp Public Affairs, Shell Internat. Petroleum Co. Ltd, 1981–85. *Address:* (office) 9 Grosvenor Crescent, SW1X 7EJ. *T:* 01–235 5454.

See also M. A. B. Burke-Gaffney.

BURKE-GAFFNEY, Michael Anthony Bowes, QC 1977; a Recorder, since 1986; *b* Dar-es-Salaam, Tanzania, 1 Aug. 1928; *s* of late Henry Joseph O'Donnell Burke-Gaffney, OBE and Constance May (*née* Bishop); *m* 1961, Constance Caroline (*née* Murdoch); two *s* one *d*. *Educ:* Douai Sch.; RMA, Sandhurst. Commissioned Royal Irish Fusiliers, 1948; served with 1st Bn, Suez Canal Zone, Akaba, Gibraltar, BAOR and Berlin; served with Royal Ulster Rifles, Korean War, 1951, and in Hong Kong; qual. as interpreter in Turkish (studied at London Univ. and in Istanbul), 1955; Staff Captain, HQ 44 Div., 1956–58, when resigned commn and read for the Bar; joined Gray's Inn, 1956 (Lord Justice Holker Sen. Scholar); called to the Bar, 1959. Jun. Counsel to HM Treasury in certain planning matters, 1974–77; a Legal Assessor to GMC and GDC, 1985–. Author, Three Lakes Inquiry Report, 1976. *Recreations:* family, cricket, wildlife, viniculture, plant breeding. *Address:* Lamb Building, Temple, EC4. *T:* 01–353 6701. *Club:* Naval and Military.

See also J. C. Burke-Gaffney.

BURKETT, Mary Elizabeth, OBE 1978; FRGS; FMA; Director of Abbot Hall Art Gallery, and Museum of Lakeland Life and Industry, 1967–86, and Borough Museum, Kendal, 1977–86; *d* of Ridley Burkett and Mary Alice Gaussen. *Educ:* Univ. of Durham (BA, Teachers' Cert.). FRGS 1978; FMA 1980. Taught art, craft, maths, etc, at Wroxall Abbey, 1948–54; Art and Craft Lectr, Charlotte Mason Coll., Ambleside, 1954–62; seven months in Turkey and Iran, 1962; Asst Dir, Abbot Hall, 1963–66. Formerly part-time Teacher of Art, Bela River Prison. Member: numerous cttees including National Trust (NW Region), 1978–85; Carlisle Diocesan Adv. Cttee, 1980–. Dir, Border Television, 1982–. FRSA; Fellow, Huguenot Soc. Leverhulme Award (to continue research on Lake District portraits). *Publications:* The Art of the Felt Maker, 1979; Kurt Schwitters (in the Lake District), 1979; (with David Sloss) William Green of Ambleside, 1984; contrib. art and archaeol jls, and gall. and museum catalogues. *Recreations:* travel, bird watching, photography, picking up stones. *Address:* Demavend, Bowness-on-Windermere, Cumbria. *T:* Windermere 3767.

BURKILL, John Charles, ScD; FRS 1953; Honorary Fellow, Peterhouse, Cambridge; Emeritus Reader in Mathematical Analysis; *b* 1 Feb. 1900; *s* of Hugh Roberson Burkill and Bertha Burkill (*nee* Bourne); *m* 1928, Margareta, (*d* 1984), *d* of Dr Braun; one *s* one *d* (and one *d* decd). *Educ:* St Paul's; Trinity Coll., Cambridge (Fellow 1922–28). Smith's Prize, 1923; Professor of Pure Mathematics in the University of Liverpool, 1924–29; Fellow of Peterhouse, 1929–67; Master of Peterhouse, 1968–73. Adams Prize, 1949. *Address:* 2 Archway Court, Barton Road, Cambridge CB3 9LW.

BURKITT, Denis Parsons, CMG 1974; MD, FRCSE; FRS 1972; Medical Research Council External Scientific Staff, 1964–76; Hon. Senior Research Fellow, St Thomas's Hospital Medical School, 1976–84; *b* Enniskillen, NI, 28 Feb. 1911; *s* of James Parsons Burkitt and Gwendoline (*née* Hill); *m* 1943, Olive Mary (*née* Rogers); three *d*. *Educ:* Dean Close Sch., Cheltenham; Dublin Univ. BA 1933; MB, BCh, BAO 1935; FRCSE 1938; MD 1946. Surgeon, RAMC, 1941–46. Joined HM Colonial Service: Govt Surgeon, in Uganda, 1946–64, and Lectr in Surgery, Makerere University Coll. Med. Sch.; final appt: Sen. consultant surgeon to Min. of Health, Uganda, 1961. First described a form of cancer common in children in Africa, now named Burkitt's Lymphoma. Foundn and Hon.

Fellow, E Africa Assoc. of Surgeons; Hon. Fellow, Sudan Assoc. of Surgeons; former Pres., Christian Medical Fellowship; a Vice-Pres., CMS. Hon. FRCSI, 1973; Hon. FRCPI, 1977. Harrison Prize, ENT Section of RSM, 1966; Stuart Prize, 1966, Gold Medal, 1978, BMA. Arnott Gold Medal, Irish Hosps and Med. Schs Assoc., 1968; Katharine Berkan Judd Award, Sloan-Kettering Inst., New York, 1969; Robert de Villiers Award, Amer. Leukaemia Soc., 1970; Walker Prize for 1966–70, RCS, 1971; Paul Ehrlich-Ludwig Darmstaedter Prize, Paul Ehrlich Foundn, Frankfurt, 1972; Soc. of Apothecaries' Medal, 1972; Albert Lasker Clinical Chemotherapy Award, 1972; Gairdner Foundn Award, 1973; (jtly) Bristol-Myers Award for Cancer Research, 1982; Charles S. Mott Prize, Gen. Motors Cancer Res. Foundn, 1982; Diplôme de Médaille d'Or, Académie de Médecine, France, 1982; Beaumont Bonelli Award for Cancer Research, Beaumont Foundn, Italy, 1983. Hon. FTCD; Hon. MD Bristol, 1979; Hon. DSc: E Africa, 1970; Leeds, 1982; Hon. DSc (Med) London, 1984. Co-editor, Fibre-depleted Foods and Disease (dietary film), 1985. *Publications:* Co-editor: Treatment of Burkitt's Lymphoma (UICC Monograph 8), 1967; Burkitt's Lymphoma, 1970; Refined Carbohydrate Foods and Disease, 1975; Don't Forget the Fibre in your Diet, 1979; Western Diseases, their emergence and prevention, 1981; over 300 contribs to scientific jls. *Address:* The Old House, Bussage, near Stroud, Glos GL6 8AX. *T:* Brimscombe 882248.

BURLAND, Prof. John Boscawen, FEng; Professor of Soil Mechanics in the University of London, at Imperial College of Science and Technology, since 1980; *b* 4 March 1936; *s* of John Whitmore Burland and Margaret Irene Burland (*née* Boscawen); *m* 1963, Gillian Margaret, *d* of J. K. Miller; two *s* one *d*. *Educ:* Parktown Boys' High Sch., Johannesburg; Univ. of the Witwatersrand (BSc Eng, MSc Eng, DSc Eng); Univ. of Cambridge (PhD). MSAICE; FICE; MIStructE; FEng 1981. Res. Asst, Univ. of the Witwatersrand, 1960; Engineer, Ove Arup and Partners, London, 1961–63; Res. Student, Cambridge Univ., 1963–66; Building Research Station: SSO and PSO, 1966–72; Head of Geotechnics Div., 1972–79; Asst Dir and Head of Materials and Structures Dept, 1979–80. Visiting Prof., Dept of Civil Engineering, Univ. of Strathclyde, 1973–82. Instn of Structural Engineers: Mem. of Council, 1979–82; Murray Buxton Silver Medal; Oscar Faber Bronze Medal; named in Special Award to DoE for Underground Car Park at Palace of Westminster; Instn of Civil Engineers: Telford Premium; Coopers Hill War Meml Medal; Brit. Geotechnical Soc. Prize on three occasions. *Publications:* numerous papers on soil mechanics and civil engineering. *Recreations:* sailing, golf, painting, classical guitar.

BURLEIGH, George Hall; HM Diplomatic Service; Counsellor, Foreign and Commonwealth Office, since 1981; *b* 24 June 1928; *s* of William Burleigh and Hannah (*née* Hall); *m* 1957, Barbara Patricia Rigby; two *d*. *Educ:* Friends Sch., Lisburn; Trinity Coll., Dublin (MA); Trinity Coll., Cambridge. HM Colonial Service (later HMOCS), 1951–62: Asst Dist Comr, Gambaga, Northern Territories, Gold Coast, 1951; Dist Comr, Navrongo, 1952; Govt Agent, Salaga, 1953–54, Tamale, 1955, Zuarungu, 1955–56, Lawra, 1957 and Gambaga, 1958; Sen. (later Principal) Asst Sec., Min. of Communications and Works, 1959–62; FO, 1962–64; Aden, 1965; FO, 1965–68; First Sec., Dubai, 1968–70 and Bahrain, 1970; FCO, 1971; First Sec., Jakarta, 1972–75 and Stockholm, 1976–81. *Recreations:* books, cricket, travel. *Address:* c/o Foreign and Commonwealth Office, SW1; Lawra, Roedean Road, Tunbridge Wells, Kent TN2 5JX. *T:* Tunbridge Wells 22359. *Club:* Travellers'.

BURLEIGH, Thomas Haydon, CBE 1977; Director, John Brown & Co. Ltd, 1965–77; *b* 23 April 1911; *s* of late J. H. W. Burleigh, Great Chesterford; *m* 1933, Kathleen Mary Lenthall, *d* of late Dr Gurth Eager, Hertford; two *s*. *Educ:* Saffron Walden Sch. RAF, short service commission, No 19 (F) Sqdn, 1930–35; Westland Aircraft Ltd, 1936–45; Thos. Firth & John Brown Ltd, 1945–48; Firth Brown Tools Ltd, 1948–77. Pres., Sheffield Chamber of Commerce, 1963–64; Pres. Nat. Fedn of Engineers' Tool Manufacturers, 1968–70; Master of Company of Cutlers in Hallamshire in the County of York, 1970–71. *Recreations:* golf, gardening. *Address:* Kirkgate, Holme next Sea, Hunstanton, Norfolk. *T:* Holme 387. *Clubs:* Royal Air Force; Royal and Ancient Golf (St Andrews).

BURLEY, Sir Victor (George), Kt 1980; CBE 1969; FIE(Aust); FIMechE, FIProdE; Chairman, Advisory Council of Commonwealth Scientific and Research Organization (CSIRO), 1979–81; Chairman, Allied Industries Pty Ltd, since 1984; *b* 4 Dec. 1914; *s* of G. H. Burley and M. A. Luby; *m* 1941, Alpha Loyal Lord; one *s* three *d*. *Educ:* High Sch., Tasmania; Univ. of Tasmania (BE). MIEE, FIFST; FInstD, FAIM. Cadbury-Fry-Pascall Pty Ltd, Australia, 1938–71: Chief Engr, Director and Vice-Chm.; Director, Cadbury Schweppes Aust Ltd, 1971–78; Cons. Dir, Cadbury Fry Hudson NZ; Technical Cons., Cadbury Schweppes UK, 1978–82. Member, Adv. Council, CSIRO, 1961–78; Chm., State Cttee, Tas. CSIRO, 1964–78; Foundn Mem., Commonwealth Adv. Cttee on Advanced Educn, 1965–71; Foundn Chm., Council of Advanced Educn, Tasmania, 1968–76; Mem., Sci. and Industry Forum, Aust. Acad. of Science, 1967–81. Director: Productivity Promotion Council, Australia, 1983–; University Research Co., 1985–. University of Tasmania: Warden of Convocation, 1964–74; Mem., Faculty of Engrg, 1968–; Mem. Council, 1982–84. *Recreations:* music, reading. *Address:* Montaigne, Sandy Bay Road, Hobart, Tasmania 7005. *T:* Hobart (002) 252–583. *Clubs:* Melbourne (Melbourne); Tasmanian (Hobart).

BURLIN, Prof. Terence Eric; Rector, Polytechnic of Central London, since 1984; *b* 24 Sept. 1931; *s* of Eric Jonas Burlin and Winifred Kate (*née* Thomas); *m* 1957, Plessey Pamela Carpenter; one *s* one *d*. *Educ:* Acton County School; University of Southampton; Univ. of London. DSc, PhD; CEng, FIEE; FInstP. Mount Vernon Hosp. and Radium Inst., 1953–57; Hammersmith Hosp., 1957–62; St John's Hosp. for Diseases of the Skin, 1960–; Polytechnic of Central London: Sen. Lectr, 1962; Reader, 1969; Pro-Director, 1971; Sen. Pro-Rector, 1974; Acting Rector, 1982. British Cttee on Radiation Units and Measurements: Mem., 1966–74 and 1979–; Vice-Chm., 1983–84; Chm., 1984–; Member: Council, Inst. for Study of Drug Dependence, 1974–; various Boards, CNAA; Cttee on Practical Determination of Dose Equivalent, Internat. Commn on Radiation Units and Measurements (Chm.), 1979–; Adv. Council on Adult and Continuing Educn, DES, 1980–83; Cttee on Effects of Ionising Radiation, Physics and Dosimetry Sub-Cttee, MRC, 1983–. Mem. Council, BTEC, 1984–. *Publications:* chapters in Radiation Dosimetry, 1968, 2nd edn 1972; papers on radiation dosimetry, radiological protection, biomechanical properties of skin, radiobiology. *Recreations:* music, tennis. *Address:* Polytechnic of Central London, 309 Regent Street, W1R 8AL. *T:* 01–580 2020. *Club:* Athenæum.

BURLINGTON, Earl of; William Cavendish; *b* 6 June 1969; *s* and *heir* of Marquess of Hartington, *qv*. *Address:* Beamsley Hall, Skipton, North Yorks BD23 6HD.

BURMAN, Sir (John) Charles, Kt 1961; DL; JP; *b* 30 Aug. 1908; *o s* of Sir John Burman, JP; *m* 1936, Ursula Hesketh-Wright, JP; two *s* two *d*. *Educ:* Rugby Sch. City Council, 1934–66 (Lord Mayor of Birmingham, 1947–49); General Commissioner of Income Tax, 1941–73; Indep. Chm., Licensing Planning Cttee, 1949–60; Chm. Birmingham Conservative and Unionist Assoc., 1963–72; County Pres. St John Ambulance Brigade, 1950–63; Member, Govt Cttee on Administrative Tribunals, 1955; Member Royal Commission on the Police, 1960. Director: Tarmac Ltd, 1955–71 (Chm., 1961–71); S Staffs Waterworks Co., 1949–82 (Chm. 1959–79). Life Governor and Chm. Trustees, Barber Institute, at University of Birmingham. JP 1942; High Sheriff, Warwickshire, 1958, DL 1967. KStJ, 1961. *Address:* Little Bickerscourt, Danzey Green, Tanworth-in-Arden, Warwickshire B94 5BL. *T:* Tanworth-in-Arden 2711. *Club:* Birmingham (Birmingham).

BURMAN, Sir Stephen (France), Kt 1973; CBE 1954 (MBE 1943); MA; Chairman, Serck Ltd, Birmingham, 1962–70; Director: Averys, Ltd, 1951–73; Imperial Chemical Industries Ltd, 1953–75; Imperial Metal Industries Ltd, 1962–75; J. Lucas Industries Ltd, 1952–75, and of other industrial companies; *b* 27 Dec. 1904; *s* of Henry Burman; *m* 1931, Joan Margaret Rogers; one *s* (and one *s* decd). *Educ:* Oundle. Pres. Birmingham Chamber of Commerce, 1950–51 (Vice-Pres. 1949); Chm. United Birmingham Hosps., 1948–53; Dep. Chm. 1953–56. Dir, Midland Bank Ltd, 1959–76. Governor Birmingham Children's Hosp., 1944–48; Dep. Chm. Teaching Hosps. Assoc., 1949–53; Member, Midlands Electricity Board, 1948–65; Chm. Birmingham and District Advisory Cttee for Industry, 1947–49; Member Midland Regional Board for Industry, 1949–65, Vice-Chm. 1951–65; Member of Council and Governor, Univ. of Birmingham, 1949–76, Pro-Chancellor, 1955–66; General Commissioner for Income Tax, 1950–68. Member Royal Commission on Civil Service, 1953–56. Hon. LLD Birmingham, 1972. *Recreation:* gardening. *Address:* 12 Cherry Hill Road, Barnt Green, Birmingham B45 8LJ. *T:* 021–445 1529.

BURN, Andrew Robert, DLitt; FSA 1979; historian; *b* 25 Sept. 1902; *s* of Rev. A. E. Burn and Celia Mary, *d* of Edward Richardson; *m* 1938, Mary, *d* of Wynn Thomas, OBE, Ministry of Agriculture. *Educ:* Uppingham Sch.; Christ Church, Oxford. DLitt Oxon, 1982. Sen. Classical Master, Uppingham Sch., 1927–40; British Council Rep. in Greece, 1940–41; Intelligence Corps, Middle East, 1941–44; 2nd Sec., British Embassy, Athens, 1944–46; Sen. Lectr and sole Mem. Dept of Ancient History, Univ. of Glasgow, 1946; Reader, 1965; resigned, 1969; Vis. Prof. at "A College Year in Athens", Athens, Greece, 1969–72. Pres. Glasgow Archæological Soc., 1966–69. Silver Cross of Order of Phoenix (Greece). *Publications:* Minoans, Philistines and Greeks, 1930; The Romans in Britain, 1932; The World of Hesiod, 1936; This Scepter'd Isle: an Anthology, 1940 (Athens); The Modern Greeks, 1942 (Alexandria); Alexander and the Hellenistic World, 1947; Pericles and Athens, 1948; Agricola and Roman Britain, 1953; The Lyric Age of Greece, 1960; Persia and the Greeks, 1962; The Pelican History of Greece, 1966; The Warring States of Greece (illustrated), 1968; Greece and Rome (Hist. of Civilisation Vol. II), 1970 (Chicago); (with Mary W. Burn) The Living Past of Greece, 1980; contributions to encyclopædias and historical journals. *Recreations:* travel, reading, classical music (radio). *Address:* 23 Ritchie Court, 380 Banbury Road, Oxford OX2 7PW. *T:* Oxford 50423.

BURN, Angus Maitland P.; *see* Pelham Burn.

BURN, Duncan (Lyall); economist, historian; *b* 10 Aug. 1902; *s* of Archibald William and Margaret Anne Burn; *m* 1930, Mollie White; two *d*. *Educ:* Holloway County Sch.; Christ's Coll. (Scholar), Cambridge. Hist. Tripos, Pts I and II, Cl. I, Wrenbury Schol. 1924, Bachelor Research Schol. 1924, Christ's Coll., Cambridge. Lecturer in Economic History: Univ. of Liverpool, 1925; Univ. of Cambridge, 1927. Min. of Supply (Iron and Steel Control), 1939; Member US-UK Metallurgical Mission, New York and Washington, 1943; leader writer and Industrial Correspondent of the Times, 1946–62. Director of the Economic Development Office set up by AEI, English Electric, GEC, and Parsons, 1962–65. Visiting Professor of Economics: Manchester Univ., 1967–69; Bombay Univ., 1971. Member: Advisory Cttee on Census of Production, 1955–65; Exec. Cttee, Nat. Inst. of Econ. and Social Research, 1957–69; Econ. Cttee, DSIR, 1963–65; Specialist Adviser, House of Commons Select Cttee on Energy, 1980–. *Publications:* Economic History of Steelmaking, 1867–1939, 1940; The Steel Industry, 1939–59, 1961; The Political Economy of Nuclear Energy, 1967; Chemicals under Free Trade, 1971, repr. in Realities of Free Trade: Two Industry Studies (with B. Epstein), 1972; Nuclear Power and the Energy Crisis: politics and the atomic industry, 1978; ed and contrib. The Structure of British Industry, 2 vols, 1958; also contrib. to Journals, Bank Reviews, etc. *Recreations:* walking, gardening. *Address:* 5 Hampstead Hill Gardens, NW3 2PH. *T:* 01–435 5344. *Club:* United Oxford & Cambridge University.

BURN, Michael Clive, MC 1945; writer; *b* 11 Dec. 1912; *s* of late Sir Clive Burn and Phyllis Stoneham; *m* 1947, Mary Booker (*née* Walter); no *c*. *Educ:* Winchester; New Coll., Oxford (open scholar); Hons Degree in Soc. Scis, Oxford, 1945, with distinction in all subjects (awarded whilst POW at Colditz). Journalist, The Times, 1936–39; Lieut 1st Bn Queens Westminsters, KRRC, 1939–40; Officer in Independent Companies, Norwegian Campaign, 1940, subseq. Captain No. 2 Commando; taken prisoner in raid on St Nazaire, 1942; prisoner in Germany, 1942–45. Foreign Correspondent for the Times in Vienna, Jugoslavia and Hungary, 1946–49. Keats Poetry First Prize, 1973. *Plays:* The Modern Everyman (prod. Birmingham Rep., 1947); Beyond the Storm (Midlands Arts Co., and Vienna, 1947); The Night of the Ball (prod. New Theatre, 1956). *Publications: novels:* Yes, Farewell, 1946, repr. 1975; Childhood at Oriol, 1951; The Midnight Diary, 1952; The Trouble with Jake, 1967; *sociological:* Mr Lyward's Answer, 1956; The Debatable Land, 1970; *poems:* Poems to Mary, 1953; The Flying Castle, 1954; Out On A Limb, 1973; Open Day and Night, 1978; *play:* The Modern Everyman, 1948. *Address:* Beudy Gwyn, Minffordd, Gwynedd, N Wales.

BURNELL, (Susan) Jocelyn (Bell), PhD; FRAS; astronomer; Senior Research Fellow, Royal Observatory, Edinburgh, since 1982; *b* 15 July 1943; *d* of G. Philip and M. Allison Bell; *m* 1968, Martin Burnell; one *s*. *Educ:* The Mount Sch., York; Glasgow Univ. (BSc); New Hall, Cambridge (PhD). FRAS 1969. Res. Fellowships, Univ. of Southampton, 1968–73; Res. Asst, Mullard Space Science Lab., UCL, 1974–82. An Editor, The Observatory, 1973–76. Mem., IAU, 1979–. Michelson Medal, Franklin Inst., Philadelphia (jtly with Prof. A. Hewish), 1973; J. Robert Oppenheimer Meml Prize, Univ. of Miami, 1978; Rennie Taylor Award, Amer. Tentative Soc., NY, 1978; (first) Beatrice M. Tinsley Prize, Amer. Astronomical Soc., 1987. *Publications:* papers in Nature, Astronomy and Astrophysics, Jl of Geophys. Res., Monthly Notices of RAS. *Recreations:* Quaker interests, walking. *Address:* Royal Observatory, Blackford Hill, Edinburgh EH9 3HJ.

BURNET, Sir Alastair; *see* Burnet, Sir J. W. A.

BURNET, Sir James William Alexander, (Sir Alastair Burnet), Kt 1984; broadcaster with Independent Television News, since 1976; Associate Editor, News at Ten, since 1982; *b* 12 July 1928; *s* of late Alexander and Schonaid Burnet, Edinburgh; *m* 1958, Maureen Campbell Sinclair. *Educ:* The Leys Sch., Cambridge; Worcester Coll., Oxford. Sub-editor and leader writer, Glasgow Herald, 1951–58; Commonwealth Fund Fellow, 1956–57; Leader writer, The Economist, 1958–62; Political editor, Independent Television News, 1963–64; Editor, The Economist, 1965–74; Editor, Daily Express, 1974–76. Ind. Dir, Times Newspapers Hldgs Ltd, 1982–; Dir, United Racecourses Hldgs Ltd, 1985–. Has appeared regularly on TV progs, News at Ten, Panorama, This Week, TV Eye. Member: Cttee of Award, Commonwealth Fund, 1969–76; Cttee on Reading and Other Uses of English Language, 1972–75; Monopolies Commn specialist panel on newspaper mergers, 1973–; Council, Banking Ombudsman, 1985–. Richard Dimbleby Award, BAFTA, 1966, 1970, 1979; Judges' Award, RTS, 1981. *Address:* 43 Hornton Court,

Campden Hill Road, W8. *T:* 01–937 7563; 33 Westbourne Gardens, Glasgow. *T:* 041–339 8073. *Club:* Reform.

BURNET, Mrs Pauline Ruth, CBE 1970; JP; President, Cambridgeshire Mental Welfare Association, since 1977 (Chairman, 1964–76); Chairman, Cambridge Society for Mentally Handicapped Children, since 1982; *b* 23 Aug. 1920; *d* of Rev. Edmund Willis and Constance Marjorie Willis (*née* Bostock); *m* 1940, John Forbes Burnet, Fellow of Magdalene Coll., Cambridge; one *s* one *d* (and one *s* decd). *Educ:* St Stephen's Coll., Folkestone (now at Broadstairs), Kent. Chm., Cambridgeshire AHA(T), 1973–82. Member: Windsor and Eton Hosp. Management Cttee, 1948–50; Fulbourn and Ida Darwin HMC, 1951–74 (Chm., 1969–74); E Anglian Regional Hosp. Bd, 1968–74; Bd of Governors of United Cambridge Hosps, 1966–74; Council, Assoc. of Hosp. Management Cttees until 1974 (Chm., 1966–68); Cambs FPC, 1985–. Mem., Farleigh Hosp. Cttee of Inquiry, 1970. JP City of Cambridge, 1957–; Chm., Cambs Magistrates' Courts Cttee, 1978–80. *Recreations:* walking, swimming. *Address:* Grange House, Selwyn Gardens, Cambridge CB3 9AZ. *T:* Cambridge 350726.

BURNETT, of Leys, Baronetcy of (unclaimed); *see under* Ramsay, Sir Alexander William Burnett, 7th Bt.

BURNETT, Most Rev. Bill Bendyshe, MA; LTh; *b* 31 May 1917; *s* of Richard Evelyn Burnett and Louisa Dobinson; *m* 1945, Sheila Fulton Trollip; two *s* one *d*. *Educ:* Bishop's College (Rondebosch); Michaelhouse (Natal); Rhodes University College; St Paul's Theological College, Grahamstown and Queen's College, Birmingham. Schoolmaster, St John's College, Umtata, 1940; Army, 1940–45; Deacon, St Thomas', Durban, 1946; Priest, 1947; Assistant priest, St Thomas', Durban, 1946–50; Chaplain, Michaelhouse, 1950–54; Vicar of Ladysmith, 1954–57; Bishop of Bloemfontein, 1957–67; Gen. Secretary, S African Council of Churches, 1967–69; Asst Bishop of Johannesburg, 1967–69; Bishop of Grahamstown, 1969–74; Archbishop of Cape Town and Metropolitan of S Africa, 1974–81. ChStJ 1975. Hon. DD Rhodes, 1980. *Publications:* Anglicans in Natal, 1953; (contrib.) Bishop's Move, 1978. *Recreation:* painting. *Address:* c/o 6 Allenby Road, Selborne, East London, 5201, South Africa.

BURNETT, Air Chief Marshal Sir Brian (Kenyon), GCB 1970 (KCB 1965; CB 1961); DFC 1942; AFC 1939; RAF, retired; Chairman, All England Lawn Tennis Club, Wimbledon, 1974–83; *b* 10 March 1913; *s* of late Kenneth Burnett and Anita Catherine Burnett (*née* Evans); *m* 1944, Valerie Mary (*née* St Ludger); two *s*. *Educ:* Charterhouse; Wadham Coll., Oxford (Hon. Fellow, 1974); Joined RAFO 1932; RAF 1934; Long Distance Record Flight of 7,158 miles from Egypt to Australia, Nov. 1938. Served War of 1939–45, in Bomber and Flying Training Commands; RAF Staff Coll. Course, 1944; Directing Staff, RAF Staff Coll., 1945–47; UN Military Staff Cttee, New York, 1947–48; Joint Planning Staff, 1949–50; SASO HQ No. 3 (Bomber) Group, 1951–53; CORAF Gaydon, 1954–55; ADC to the Queen, 1953–57; Director of Bomber and Reconnaissance Ops, Air Ministry, 1956–57; Imperial Defence Coll., 1958; Air Officer Administration, HQ Bomber Command, 1959–61; AOC No 3 Gp, Bomber Command, 1961–64; Vice-Chief of the Air Staff, 1964–67; Air Secretary, MoD, 1967–70; C-in-C, Far East Command, Singapore, 1970–71; retired 1972. Air ADC to the Queen, 1969–72. Pres., Squash Rackets Assoc., 1972–75. *Recreations:* tennis, squash rackets, golf, ski-ing. *Address:* Heather Hill, Littleworth Cross, Seale, Farnham, Surrey. *Clubs:* Royal Air Force; Vincent's (Oxford); All England Lawn Tennis; Jesters Squash; International Lawn Tennis Club of Great Britain; Hankley Common Golf.

BURNETT, Sir David Humphery, 3rd Bt, *cr* 1913; MBE 1945; TD; Director, Guardian Royal Exchange Assurance and other companies; one of HM Lieutenants of the City of London; *b* 27 Jan. 1918; *s* of Sir Leslie Trew Burnett, 2nd Bt, CBE, TD, DL, and Joan, *d* of late Sir John Humphery; *S* father 1955; *m* 1948, Geraldine Elizabeth Mortimer, *d* of Sir Godfrey Arthur Fisher, KCMG; two *s* (and one *s* decd). *Educ:* Harrow; St John's Coll., Cambridge, MA. Served War of 1939–45 (despatches, MBE), in France, N Africa, Sicily and Italy; Temp. Lt-Col GSO1, 1945. Partner, David Burnett & Son, Chartered Surveyors, 1947–50; Dir, Proprietors of Hay's Wharf Ltd, 1950–80 (Chm., 1965–80). Chairman: South London Botanical Institute, 1976–81 (Pres., 1985–); London Assoc. of Public Wharfingers, 1964–71. Mem. PLA, 1962–75. Mem. Council, Brighton Coll. Master: Company of Watermen and Lightermen of the River Thames, 1964; Girdlers Company, 1970. FRICS 1970 (ARICS 1948); FBIM 1968; FLS 1979. *Heir:* *s* Charles David Burnett, *b* 18 May 1951. *Address:* Tandridge Hall, near Oxted, Surrey RH8 9NJ; Tillmouth Park, Cornhill-on-Tweed, Northumberland TD12 4UT. *Club:* Turf.

BURNETT, Dr John Harrison; Principal and Vice-Chancellor, University of Edinburgh, 1979–Sept. 1987; *b* 21 Jan. 1922; *s* of Rev. T. Harrison Burnett, Paisley; *m* 1945, E. Margaret, *er d* of Rev. Dr E. W. Bishop; two *s*. *Educ:* Kingswood Sch., Bath; Merton Coll., Oxford. BA, MA 1947; DPhil 1953; Christopher Welch Scholar, 1947. FRSE 1957; FIBiol 1969. Lecturer, Lincoln Coll., 1948–49; Fellow (by Exam.) Magdalen Coll., 1949–53; Univ. Lecturer and Demonstrator, Oxford, 1949–53; Lecturer, Liverpool Univ., 1954–55; Prof. of Botany: Univ. of St Andrews, 1955–60; King's Coll., Newcastle, Univ. of Durham, 1961–63, Univ. of Newcastle, 1963–68; Dean of Faculty of Science, St Andrews, 1958–60, Newcastle, 1966–68; Public Orator, Newcastle, 1966–68; Regius Prof. of Botany, Univ. of Glasgow, 1968–70; Oxford University: Sibthorpian Prof. of Rural Economy and Fellow, St John's Coll., 1970–79; Member: Gen. Bd of Faculties, 1972–77 (Vice-Chm, 1974–76); Hebdomodal Council, 1974–79. Lectures: Delgarno, Univ. of Manitoba, 1979–80; Bewley Meml, 1982; Peacock Meml, Dundee Univ., 1982. Chm. Scottish Horticultural Research Inst., 1959–74; Member: Nature Conservancy Scottish Cttee, 1961–66, English Cttee, 1966–69; Nature Conservancy Council, 1987– (Scottish Cttee, 1980–); Nuffield Foundn Biol. Project, 1962–68 (Chm., 1965–68); British Mycol Soc. (Pres., 1982–83); Trustee, The New Phytologist, 1962–85, Advr, 1983–; Mem. Academic Adv. Council, Univs of St Andrews and Dundee, 1964–66. Mem., Newcastle Reg. Hosp. Bd, 1964–68. Served 1942–46 as Lieut RNVR (despatches). Hon. Fellow, RCSE, 1983. Hon. DSc: Buckingham, 1981; Pennsylvania, 1983; Hon. LLD: Dundee, 1982; Strathclyde, 1983. *Publications:* Vegetation of Scotland, ed and contrib., 1964; Fundamentals of Mycology, 1968, 2nd edn 1976; Mycogenetics, 1975; Fungal Walls and Hyphal Growth, ed and contrib., 1979; Speciation and Evolution in Fungi, 1987; papers in various books and scientific journals. *Recreations:* walking, writing, gardens. *Address:* c/o Commonwealth Forestry Institute, South Parks Road, Oxford. *Clubs:* Athenæum; Caledonian, New (Edinburgh).

BURNETT, Lt-Col Maurice John Brownless, DSO 1944; JP; DL; *b* 24 Sept. 1904; *o s* of late Ernest Joseph Burnett, MBE, JP, The Red House, Saltburn-by-the-Sea, Yorks, and late Emily Maud Margaret, 2nd *d* of John Brownless, Whorlton Grange, Barnard Castle and Dunsa Manor, Dalton; *m* 1930, Crystal, *d* of late Col H. D. Chamier, The Connaught Rangers; one *s*. *Educ:* Aysgarth Sch.; Rugby Sch.; RMA, Woolwich; Staff Coll., Camberley. 2nd Lieut RA 1924; psc 1937; Lt-Col 1942; served 1939–45; comd 127th (Highland) Field Regt in 51st Highland Division, Normandy to the Rhine; retd 1948. JP, 1957, DL, 1958, N Yorks. Member: N Riding Yorks Education Cttee, 1956–69; NR Yorks Standing Joint Cttee, and York and NE Yorks Police Cttee, 1958–74; Richmond, Yorks, RDC 1958–74 (Chm., 1967–69); N Riding CC, 1962–74 (Chm., Civil Protection Cttee, 1969–74); N Yorks CC, 1974–85 (Vice Chm., 1981–84; Chm., 1984–85; Hon. County Alderman, 1986); Church Assembly, 1955–70, General Synod, 1970–80; Ripon Diocesan Bd of Finance, 1953–85 (Vice-Chm. 1956–79); Exec. Cttee, N Riding Yorks Assoc. of Youth Clubs, 1950–71 (Chm. 1952 and 1965, Pres. 1971–84, Patron 1984–). Governor, Barnard Castle Sch., 1959–63, 1973–85; Chm. of Governors, Richmond Sch., 1970–; District Comr, Scouts Assoc., (formerly Boy Scouts Assoc.), NR Yorks, 1950, County Comr, 1961–69. Sec., N Riding Yorks Territorial and Auxiliary Forces Assoc., 1950–68. *Recreations:* country sports and pursuits, interest in local government and youth work. *Address:* Dunsa Manor, Dalton, Richmond, N Yorks DL11 7HE. *T:* Darlington 718251. *Club:* Army and Navy.

BURNETT, Rev. Canon Philip Stephen; Church of England Board of Education, 1970–80; *b* 8 Jan. 1914; *s* of late Philip Burnett and Mrs Burnett, Salton, York; *m* 1954, Joan Hardy, *e d* of C. F. Hardy, Sheffield; one *s* one *d*. *Educ:* Scarborough Coll.; Balliol Coll., Oxford; Westcott House, Cambridge. Admitted Solicitor, 1936; Lay Missionary, Dio. Saskatchewan, Canada, 1939–41. Intelligence Corps, 1942–44; Staff Capt., GHQ, New Delhi, 1944–45, Deacon, 1947, Priest, 1948; Curate of St Andrew's, Chesterton, Cambridge, and Staff Sec., Student Christian Movement, 1947–49; Asst Gen. Sec., SCM, 1949–52; Vicar of St Mary, Bramall Lane, Sheffield, 1952–61; Rural Dean of Ecclesall, 1959–65; Canon Residentiary of Sheffield Cathedral, and Educn Secretary, Diocese of Sheffield, 1961–70, Canon Emeritus 1970–. Hon. Sec., Fellowship of the Maple Leaf, 1965–. *Address:* 91 Chelverton Road, Putney, SW15 1RW. *T:* 01–789 9934.

BURNETT, Rear-Adm. Philip Whitworth, CB 1957; DSO 1945; DSC 1943, and Bar, 1944; *b* 10 Sept. 1908; *s* of Henry Ridley Burnett; *m* 1947, Molly, *widow* of Brig. H. C. Partridge, DSO, and *d* of H. M. Trouncer; one *s* two *d*. *Educ:* Preparatory Sch., Seascale; Royal Naval Coll., Dartmouth. Served War of 1939–45; HMS Kelly, 1939–41; HMS Osprey, 1941–43; Western Approaches Escort Groups, 1943–45. Chief of Staff to Comdr-in-Chief, Portsmouth, 1955–57; retd list 1958. Lieut 1930; Comdr 1940; Capt. 1945; Rear-Adm. 1955. Sec. of the Royal Institution of Chartered Surveyors, 1959–65.

BURNETT-STUART, Joseph; Chairman, Robert Fleming Holdings Ltd, since 1981 (Director since 1963); *b* 11 April 1930; *s* of late George Eustace Burnett-Stuart, CBE and Etheldreda Cecily (*née* Edge); *m* 1954, Mary Hermione, *d* of late John A. M. Stewart of Ardvorlich, TD; three *s* one *d*. *Educ:* Eton Coll.; Trinity Coll., Cambridge (BA). Bankers Trust Co., 1953–62. A Church Commissioner, 1984–. *Recreations:* gardening, shooting, fishing. *Address:* Micheldever House, near Winchester, Hants SO21 3DF. *T:* Micheldever 254. *Clubs:* Boodle's; New (Edinburgh).

BURNEY, Sir Anthony (George Bernard), Kt 1971; OBE 1945; MA, FCA; *b* 3 June 1909; *o s* of Theodore and Gertrude Burney; *m* 1947, Dorothy Mary Vere, *d* of Col Clements Parr; no *c*. *Educ:* Rugby; Corpus Christi Coll., Cambridge (Hon. Fellow 1975). MA; FCA. Served War of 1939–45, Army: RE and RASC, Europe (Lt-Col). Partner, Binder, Hamlyn & Co., Chartered Accountants, 1938–71. Chm., Debenhams Ltd, 1971–80 (Dir, 1970–80). Dir, Commercial Union, to 1980; Dir of Reorganisation, The Cotton Bd, 1959–60; Mem. Shipbuilding Inquiry Cttee, 1965–66; Chm., Freight Integration Council, 1968–75; Mem. National Ports Council, 1971; Pres., Charities Aid Foundn. *Publication:* Illustrations of Management Accounting in Practice, 1959. *Recreations:* gardening, photography. *Address:* 6 Greville Place, NW6. *T:* 01–624 4439. *Clubs:* Buck's, Garrick.

BURNEY, Sir Cecil (Denniston), 3rd Bt *cr* 1921; Chairman, Hampton Trust PLC, Since 1975; *b* 8 Jan. 1923; *s* of Sir Charles Dennistoun Burney, 2nd Bt, CMG, and Gladys (*d* 1982), *d* of George Henry High; *S* father, 1968; *m* 1957, Hazel Marguerite de Hamel, *yr d* of late Thurman Coleman; two *s*. *Educ:* Eton; Trinity Coll., Cambridge. Man. Dir, 1951–68, Chm., 1968–78, Northern Motors Ltd; Dir, Security Building Soc., 1959–71. Member of Legislative Council, N Rhodesia, 1959–64; MP Zambia, 1964–68; Chairman, Public Accounts Cttee, Zambia, 1963–67. *Recreations:* tennis, skiing. *Heir:* *s* Nigel Dennistoun Burney, *b* 6 Sept. 1959. *Address:* PO Box 32037, Lusaka, Zambia; 5 Lyall Street, SW1. *T:* 01–235 4014. *Clubs:* White's, Carlton, Turf, Buck's; Leander; Harare, Bulawayo (Zimbabwe); Ndola (Zambia).

BURNHAM, 5th Baron, *cr* 1903; **William Edward Harry Lawson,** Bt 1892; JP; DL; Lieutenant-Colonel; Scots Guards, retired 1968; *b* 22 Oct. 1920; *er s* of 4th Baron Burnham, CB, DSO, MC, TD, and (Marie) Enid, Lady Burnham, CBE (*d* 1979), *d* of Hugh Scott Robson, Buenos Aires; *S* father, 1963; *m* 1942, Anne, *yr d* of late Major Gerald Petherick, The Mill House, St Cross, Winchester; three *d* (one *s* decd). *Educ:* Eton. Royal Bucks Yeomanry, 1939–41; Scots Guards, 1941–68; commanded 1st Bn, 1959–62. Chairman: Sail Training Assoc.; Masonic Housing Assoc., 1980–. JP Bucks 1970, DL Bucks 1977. *Recreations:* sailing, shooting, ski-ing. *Heir:* *b* Hon. Hugh John Frederick Lawson [*b* 15 Aug. 1931; *m* 1955, Hilary Mary, *d* of Alan Hunter; one *s* two *d*]. *Address:* Hall Barn, Beaconsfield, Bucks. *T:* Beaconsfield 3315. *Clubs:* Garrick, Turf; Royal Yacht Squadron.

BURNHAM, James; Writer; an Editor, National Review, since 1955; *b* 22 Nov. 1905; *s* of Claude George Burnham and Mary May Gillis; *m* 1934, Marcia Lightner; two *s* one *d*. *Educ:* Princeton Univ.; Balliol Coll., Oxford Univ. Prof. of Philosophy, New York Univ., 1932–54. *Publications:* (jtly) A Critical Introduction to Philosophy, 1932; The Managerial Revolution, 1941, rev. edn 1972; The Machiavellians, 1943; The Struggle for the World, 1947; (jtly) The Case for De Gaulle, 1948; The Coming Defeat of Communism, 1950; Containment or Liberation, 1953; The Web of Subversion, 1954; Congress and the American Tradition, 1959; Suicide of the West, 1964; The War We Are In, 1967. *Address:* Fuller Mountain Road, Kent, Conn 06757, USA. *T:* Kent, Conn, 203–927–3117.

BURNINGHAM, John Mackintosh; free-lance author-designer; *b* 27 April 1936; *s* of Charles Burningham and Jessie Mackintosh; *m* 1964, Helen Gillian Oxenbury; one *s* two *d*. *Educ:* Summerhill School, Leiston, Suffolk; Central School of Art, Holborn, 1956–59 (Diploma). Now free-lance: illustration, poster design, exhibition, animated film puppets, and writing for children. *Publications:* Borka, 1963 (Kate Greenaway Medal, 1963); Trubloff, 1964; Humbert, 1965; Cannonball Simp, 1966; Harquin, 1967; Seasons, 1969; Mr Gumpy's Outing, 1970 (Kate Greenaway Award, 1971); Around the World in Eighty Days, 1972; Mr Gumpy's Motor Car, 1973; "Little Books" series: The Baby, The Rabbit, The School, The Snow, 1974; The Blanket, The Cupboard, The Dog, The Friend, 1975; The Adventures of Humbert, Simp and Harquin, 1976; Come Away jfrom the Water, Shirley, 1977; Time to Get Out of the Bath, Shirley, 1978; Would You Rather, 1978; The Shopping Basket, 1980; Play and Learn Books: abc, 123, Opposites, Colours, 1985. *Address:* c/o Jonathan Cape Ltd, 32 Bedford Square, WC1.

BURNISTON, George Garrett, CMG 1972; OBE 1968; Consultant Physician, Rehabilitation Medicine; Chairman and Director, Division of Rehabilitation Medicine, Department of Medicine, Prince Henry, Prince of Wales and Eastern Suburbs Hospitals, NSW, 1963–79; *b* Sydney, NSW, 23 Nov. 1914; *s* of George Benjamin Burniston, Melbourne, Vic.; unmarried. *Educ:* Sydney High Sch.; Sydney Univ. (MB, BS). Served in RAAF Medical Service, 1940–47 (RAF Orthopaedic Service, UK, 1941–43); Gp Captain, RAAF Med. Reserve (retired). Dep. Co-ordinator of Rehabilitation, Min. of Post-War Reconstruction (Aust.), 1946–48. SMO, Dept of Social Services, 1948–53; Fulbright Fellow, USA and UK, 1953–54; PMO, Dept of Social Services, 1954–62; Sen. Lectr, 1963–77, Associate Prof., 1977–79, Sch. of Medicine, Univ. of NSW. Member: WHO Expert Advisory Panel on Medical Rehabilitation, 1958–84; Council, Cumberland Coll. of Health Sciences, NSW, 1970–85 (Chm., 1980–85); Bd of Trustees, Cumberland Coll. Foundn, 1979–; Nat. Adv. Council for the Handicapped, Aust., 1977–83; Advanced Educn Council, Tertiary Educn Commn, 1979–; Vice-Pres., Internat. Rehabilitation Med. Assoc., 1978–82; Pres., Aust. Coll. of Rehabilitation Med., 1980–82. Foundation Fellow, Aust. Coll. of Med. Administrators, 1968; Foundn Diplomate, Physical and Rehabilitation Medicine, 1971; FRSH 1973; FRACP 1976. *Recreations:* golf, swimming, painting, reading. *Address:* 701 Tradewinds, Boorima Place, Cronulla, NSW 2230, Australia. *T:* (02) 523–8383; Suite 703, 135 Macquarie Street, Sydney, NSW 2000, Australia. *T:* (02) 27 1951. *Club:* University (Sydney).

BURNLEY, Suffragan Bishop of, since 1970; **Rt. Rev. Richard Charles Challinor Watson;** Hon. Canon of Blackburn Cathedral since 1970; *b* 16 Feb. 1923; *o s* of Col Francis W. Watson, CB, MC, DL, The Glebe House, Dinton, Aylesbury, Bucks; *m* 1955, Anna, *er d* of Rt Rev. C. M. Chavasse, OBE, MC, MA, DD, then Bishop of Rochester; one *s* one *d. Educ:* Rugby; New Coll., Oxford; Westcott House, Cambridge. Served Indian Artillery, Lt and Capt. RA, 1942–45. Oxford Hon. Sch. Eng. Lang. and Lit., 1948, Theology 1949; Westcott House, Cambridge, 1950–51. Curate of Stratford, London E, 1952–53; Tutor and Chaplain, Wycliffe Hall, Oxford, 1954–57; Chaplain of Wadham Coll. and Chaplain of Oxford Pastorate, 1957–61; Vicar of Hornchurch, 1962–70; Examining Chaplain to Bishop of Rochester, 1956–61, to Bishop of Chelmsford, 1962–70; Asst Rural Dean of Havering, 1967–70; Rector of Burnley, 1970–77. *Recreations:* reading, gardening. *Address:* Palace House, 458 Padiham Road, Burnley, Lancashire BB12 6TD. *T:* Burnley 23564. *Club:* Lansdowne.

BURNLEY, Christopher John; Financial Director, British Airports Authority, since 1975; *b* 1 May 1936; *s* of John Fox Burnley and Helena Burnley; *m* 1960, Carol Joan Quirk; two *d. Educ:* King William's College, Isle of Man. Chartered Accountant. Articled Clerk, 1953–59; Military service, 1959–62; Computer Systems Analyst, IBM, 1962–66; Management Consultant, Peat Marwick, 1966–67; Systems Planning Manager, Castrol, 1967–68; Sen. Planner, IBM, 1969–72; Financial Dir, Foseco FS, 1972–74; Group Treasurer, Foseco Minsep, 1974–75. *Recreation:* railway enthusiast. *Address:* Thirlmere, 173 Worcester Road, West Hagley, West Midlands DY9 0PB. *T:* Hagley 3592. *Club:* Royal Automobile.

BURNS, Mrs Anne, (Mrs D. O. Burns); British Gliding Champion, 1966; Principal Scientific Officer, Royal Aircraft Establishment, Farnborough, Hants, 1953–77; *b* 23 Nov. 1915; *d* of late Major Fleetwood Hugo Pellew, W Yorks Regt, and of late Violet Pellew (*née* Du Pré); *m* 1947, Denis Owen Burns; no *c. Educ:* The Abbey Sch., Reading; St Hugh's Coll., Oxford (BA). Joined Min. of Supply, 1940. Engaged in aircraft research at RAE, Farnborough, Hants, under various ministries, 1940–. Feminine International Records: 4 gliding records in S Africa, 1961; records, S Africa, 1963, 1965; Colorado USA, 1967. Queen's Commendation for Valuable Services in the Air, 1955 and 1963. Lilienthal Medal, Fédération Aéronautique Internationale, 1966. *Publications:* contrib. scientific jls. *Recreations:* snooker, fishing. *Address:* Clumps End, Lower Bourne, Farnham, Surrey. *T:* Frensham 3343.

BURNS, Arthur F.; economist; Distinguished Scholar in Residence, American Enterprise Institute, since 1985; *b* Stanislau, Austria, 27 April 1904; *s* of Nathan Burns and Sarah Juran; *m* 1930, Helen Bernstein; two *s. Educ:* Columbia Univ. AB and AM 1925, PhD 1934. Rutgers Univ.: Instructor in Economics, 1927–30; Asst Prof., 1930–33; Associate Prof., 1933–43; Prof., 1943–44; Columbia Univ.: Vis. Prof., 1941–44; Prof., 1944–59; John Bates Clark Prof., 1959–69, now Prof. Emeritus. Nat. Bureau of Econ. Research: Res. Associate, 1930–31; Mem. Res. Staff, 1933; Dir of Res., 1945–53; Pres., 1957–67; Chm. of Bureau, 1967–69; Counsellor to the President of the US, 1969–70; Chm., Bd of Governors of Fed. Reserve System in the US, 1970–78; Alternate Governor, IMF, 1973–78; Distinguished Professorial Lectr, Georgetown Univ., 1978–81; Distinguished Scholar in Residence, Amer. Enterprise Inst., 1978–81; Consultant, Lazard Frères, 1978–81; Mem., Trilateral Commn, 1978–81; Ambassador of USA to FRG, 1981–85. Dir and Trustee of various orgs; Member (or Past Mem. or Consultant) of govt and other advisory bds. Chm., President's Coun. of Economic Advisors, 1953–56; Mem., President's Adv. Cttee on Labor-Management Policy, 1961–66, etc. Fellow: Amer. Statistical Assoc.; Econometric Soc.; Philos. Soc.; Amer. Acad. of Arts and Sciences; Amer. Econ. Assoc. (Pres. 1959); Acad. of Polit. Sci. (Pres., 1962–68); Phi Beta Kappa. Many hon. doctorates, 1952–. Alexander Hamilton Medal, Columbia Univ.; Dist. Public Service Award, Tax Foundn. Mugungwha Decoration, S Korea. Commander, French Legion of Honour; Decoration (1st class), Order of the Rising Sun, Japan. *Publications:* Production Trends in the United States since 1870, 1934; Economic Research and the Keynesian Thinking of our Times, 1946; (jtly) Measuring Business Cycles, 1946; Frontiers of Economic Knowledge, 1954; Prosperity Without Inflation, 1957; The Management of Prosperity, 1966; The Business Cycle in a Changing World, 1969; Reflections of an Economic Policy Maker, 1978. *Address:* 1150 17th Street NW, Washington, DC 20036, USA. *Clubs:* Century Association (New York); Cosmos, City Tavern (Washington).

BURNS, Dr B(enedict) Delisle, FRS 1968; Visitor, Department of Anatomy, University of Newcastle upon Tyne; *b* 22 Feb. 1915; *s* of C. Delisle Burns and Margaret Hannay; *m* 1st, 1938, Angela Ricardo; four *s*; 2nd, 1954, Monika Kasputis; one *d. Educ:* University Coll. Sch.; Tübingen Univ.; King's Coll., Cambridge; University Coll. Hospital. MRCS, LRCP 1939. Univ. extension lecturing for WEA, 1936–38; operational research, 1939–45; Research Asst, Nat. Inst. for Med. Research, 1945–49; Assoc. Prof of Physiology, McGill Univ., Canada, 1950–58; Scientific Advisor to Dept of Veterans' Affairs, 1950–67; Prof. of Physiology, 1958–67, Chm., Dept of Physiology, 1965–67, McGill Univ., Canada; Head, Div. of Physiology and Pharmacology, Nat. Inst. of Medical Research, 1967–76; MRC External Staff, Anatomy Dept, 1976–80, Hon. Prof. of Neurobiology, 1977–80, Univ. of Bristol. *Publications:* The Mammalian Cerebral Cortex, 1958; The Uncertain Nervous System, 1968; about 80 articles on neurophysiology in scientific jls. *Recreations:* tennis, ski-ing, painting, interior decoration. *Address:* Department of Anatomy, University of Newcastle upon Tyne, NE2 4HH. *T:* Newcastle upon Tyne 328511 ext. 2948.

BURNS, Sir Charles (Ritchie), KBE 1958 (OBE 1947); MD, FRCP; FRACP; retired; Consulting Physician and Consulting Cardiologist, Wellington Hospital, since 1958; Director, Clinical Services, National Society on Alcoholism (Inc.), NZ, 1970; Consulting Physician, National Society on Alcoholism and Drug Dependence, 1970–81; *b* Blenheim, Marlborough, NZ, 27 May 1898; *s* of Archibald Douglas Burns, Lands and Survey Dept, NZ; *m* 1st, 1935, Margaret Muriel (decd 1949), *d* of John Laffey, Dunedin, NZ; one *s* one *d*; 2nd, 1963, Doris Ogilvy, *d* of Keith Ramsay (sen.), Dunedin, New Zealand. *Educ:* St Mary's Sch., Blenheim, NZ; Marlborough and Nelson Colls, NZ. MB, ChB (NZ) 1922 (with distinction and Med. Travelling Scholarship; Batchelor Memorial Medal); MRCP 1925; MD (NZ) 1925; Foundation Fellow RACP 1937; FRCP (Lond.) 1943; FMANZ 1979. Med. Registrar Dunedin Hospital, and Medical Tutor Otago Univ., 1925–27; Asst Phys., Dunedin Hospital, 1927–37; Senior Phys. and Cardiologist, Wellington Hospital, NZ, 1940–58; Phys., Home of Compassion, Island Bay, NZ, 1940–68; Mem. Med. Council, NZ, 1943–55; Examr in Medicine, Univ., of NZ, 1947–53, 1959, 1963. Mem. NZ Bd of Censors for RACP, 1954–61; Corresp. Mem. Brit. Cardiac Soc., 1952–71; Life Mem. Cardiac Soc. of Australia and NZ, 1972 (Mem., 1952–72; Mem. Council, 1956–58; Chm. 1964–65); Member: Council and NZ Vice-Pres., RACP, 1956–58; NZ Lepers' Trust Bd, 1958–; Advisory Cttee, The Nat. Soc. on Alcoholism (NZ); Council, Wellington Med. Research Foundn; President: NZ Nutrition Soc., 1967–70; NZ Med. Soc. on Alcohol and Alcoholism, 1978–80; Chm., Industry Cttee, Alcohol Liquor Adv. Council, 1977–80; Patron: NZ Asthma Soc.; NZ Diabetic Soc. (Wellington Br.); Deaf Children's Parents Soc. (Wellington Br.); Soc. for Promotion of Community Standards. Sixth Leonard Ball Oration, Melbourne, 1973. Mem., Guild of Sts Luke Cosmas and Damian, 1954– (Pres., 1966–69). Served War, 1944–47, Military Hospitals, 2nd NZEF, Italy and Japan (OBE). Hon. DSc Otago, 1975. KSG 1977. *Publications:* contrib. medical journals and jls of anciliary medical services. *Recreations:* walking and medical writing. *Address:* 42 Northcote Road, Takapuna, Auckland 9, New Zealand. *T:* Wellington 849–249.

BURNS, David Allan; HM Diplomatic Service; Consul General, Boston, since 1983; *b* 20 Sept. 1937; *s* of Allan Robert Desmond Burns, GM, and Gladys Frances Dine; *m* 1971, Inger Ellen Kristiansson; one *s* one *d. Educ:* Sir Anthony Browne's Sch., Brentwood, Essex. Served HM Forces, 1956–58. Language student and Third Secretary, British Embassy, Belgrade, 1962–65; Second Secretary, Bangkok, 1966–68; First Secretary, Washington, 1969–72; Head of Chancery, Belgrade, 1973–76; Asst Head of Arms Control Dept, FCO, 1976–79; Counsellor, Bangkok, 1979–83. Mem., Marshall Scholarships Selection Cttee for New England, 1983–. *Recreation:* walking. *Address:* c/o Foreign and Commonwealth Office, SW1. *Clubs:* Somerset, St Botolph, Tavern (Boston); Royal Bangkok Sports.

BURNS, Mrs Denis Owen; *see* Burns, Mrs Anne.

BURNS, Maj.-Gen. Sir George; *see* Burns, Maj.-Gen. Sir W. A. G.

BURNS, Ian Morgan; Under Secretary, Department of Health and Social Security, since 1985; *b* 3 June 1939; *s* of Donald George Burns and late Margaret Brenda Burns; *m* 1965, Susan Rebecca (*née* Wheeler); two *d. Educ:* Bootham, York. LLB, LLM London. Examiner, Estate Duty Office, 1960; Asst Principal, 1965, Principal, 1969, Home Office; Principal, 1972, Asst Sec., 1974, NI Office; Asst Sec., Home Office, 1977; Under Sec., NI Office, 1979–84. *Recreations:* listening to music, DIY, gardening.

BURNS, James, CBE 1967; GM 1941; Chairman, Southern Gas Board, 1967–69, retired; *b* 27 Feb. 1902; *s* of William Wilson Burns and Isobella MacDonald; *m* 1934, Kathleen Ida Holt (*d* 1976); one *d* (one *s* decd). *Educ:* Inverness Royal Academy; Aberdeen Univ.; Cambridge Univ. BSc 1st cl. Hons 1925, PhD 1928, Aberdeen. Entered Research Dept, Gas Light & Coke Co., 1929; worked as Chem. Engr with Chemical Reactions Ltd, in Germany, 1930–32; Production Engr, Gas Light & Coke Co., 1941, dep. Chief Engr, 1945; Chief Engr, North Thames Gas Board, 1949, Dep-Chm. 1960–62; Chm, Northern Gas Board, 1962–67. President: Instn Gas Engrs, 1957–58; Inst. Fuel, 1961–62, etc. *Publications:* contrib. Jls Instn Gas Engrs, Inst. Fuel, etc. *Recreations:* golf, shooting, country pursuits. *Address:* 4 Corfu, Chaddesley Glen, Canford Cliffs, Dorset. *T:* Canford Cliffs 707370.

BURNS, James; JP; Convener, Strathclyde Regional Council, 1982–86; *b* 8 Feb. 1931; *s* of late James Burns and of Mary Burns (*née* Magee); *m* 1959, Jean Ward; two *s. Educ:* St Patrick's Sch., Shotts; Coatbridge Tech. Coll. Engineer with NCB, 1966–71. Member: Lanark CC, 1967–75; Lanarks Health Bd, 1973–77; Strathclyde Regional Council, 1974–; Chm., Gen. Purposes Cttee, 1975–82; Vice-Convener, 1978–82. Chm. Vis. Cttee, HM Prison, Shotts, 1980–; Member: Commonwealth Games Council for Scotland, 1982–86; Main Organising Cttee, Commonwealth Games 1986, 1982–86. Vice President: Glasgow Western St Andrew's Youth Club, 1982–86; St Andrew's Ambulance Assoc., 1984–86. Hon. President: Strathclyde CRC, 1982–86; Princess Louise Scottish Hosp. (Erskine Hosp.), 1982–86; Strathclyde Charities Band Assoc., 1982–86; Scottish Retirement Council, 1984–86; Hon. Vice Pres., SNO Chorus, 1982–86; Patron: Strathclyde Youth Club Assoc., 1982–86; YMCA Sports Centre, 1982–86; Scottish Pakistani Assoc., 1984–86. Trustee, The Pearce Institute, 1983–86. JP Motherwell, 1972. *Recreations:* fishing, golf. *Address:* 57 Springhill Road, Shotts ML7 5JA. *T:* Shotts 20187. *Club:* Royal Scottish Automobile (Glasgow).

BURNS, Prof. James Henderson; Professor of the History of Political Thought, University College London, 1966–86, now Emeritus; *b* 10 Nov. 1921; *yr s* of late William Burns and Helen Craig Tait Henderson; *m* 1947, Yvonne Mary Zéla Birnie, *er d* of late Arthur Birnie, MA, and of Yvonne Marie Aline Louis; two *s* (and one *d* decd). *Educ:* George Watson's Boys' Coll., Edinburgh; Univ. of Edinburgh; Balliol Coll., Oxford. MA (Edinburgh and Oxon), PhD (Aberdeen). Sub-Editor, Home News Dept, BBC, 1944–45; Lectr in Polit. Theory, Univ. of Aberdeen, 1947–60; Head of Dept of Politics, 1952–60; Reader in the History of Political Thought, University Coll. London, 1961–66; Head of History Dept, UCL, 1970–75. John Hinkley Vis. Prof., Dept of History, John Hopkins Univ., Baltimore, 1987. Gen. Editor, The Collected Works of Jeremy Bentham, 1961–79; Vice-Chm., Bentham Cttee, 1983– (Sec., 1966–78); Pres., Internat. Bentham Soc., 1986–. FRHistS 1962; Hon. Vice-Pres., RHistS, 1986– (Hon. Sec., 1965–70; Vice-Pres., 1978–82). *Publications:* Scottish University (with D. Sutherland Graeme), 1944; Scottish Churchmen and the Council of Basle, 1962; contributor to: (with S. Rose) The British General Election of 1951, by D. E. Butler, 1952; Essays on the Scottish Reformation, ed D. McRoberts, 1962; Mill: a collection of critical essays, ed J. B. Schneewind, 1968; Bentham on Legal Theory, ed M. H. James, 1973; Jeremy Bentham: ten critical essays, ed B. Parekh, 1974; edited (with H. L. A. Hart): Jeremy Bentham, An Introduction in the Principles of Morals and Legislation, 1970; Jeremy Bentham, A Comment on the Commentaries and A Fragment on Government, 1977; (with F. Rosen) Jeremy Bentham, Constitutional Code, vol. I, 1983; articles and reviews in: English Historical Review, Scottish Historical Review, Innes Review, Political Studies, History, Trans of RHistSoc, Historical Jl, Jl of Eccles. History, etc. *Address:* 6 Chiltern House, Hillcrest Road, Ealing, W5 1HL. *T:* 01–997 7538.

BURNS, Sir John (Crawford), Kt 1957; Director, James Finlay & Co. Ltd, 1957–74; *b* 29 Aug. 1903; *s* of William Barr Burns and Elizabeth Crawford; *m* 1941, Eleanor Margaret Haughton James; one *s* three *d. Educ:* Glasgow High Sch. Commissioned 2/16th Punjab Regt (Indian Army), 1940–46 (despatches). *Recreations:* golf, fishing. *Address:* Blairalan, Dargai Terrace, Dunblane, Perthshire FK15 0AU. *Club:* Oriental.

BURNS, Kevin Francis Xavier, CMG 1984; HM Diplomatic Service; High Commissioner in Barbados, since 1986; *b* 18 Dec. 1930; *m* 1963, Nan Pinto (*d* 1984); one *s* two *d. Educ:* Finchley Grammar Sch.; Trinity Coll., Cambridge (BA 1953). CRO,

1956–58; Asst Private Sec. to Sec. of State, 1958; 2nd Sec., 1959, 1st Sec., 1960–63, Colombo; CRO/FO, 1963–67; 1st Sec., Head of Chancery and Consul, Montevideo, 1967–70; FCO, 1970–73; Counsellor, UK Mission, Geneva, 1973–79; RCDS, 1979–80; Head of SE Asian Dept, FCO, 1980–83; High Comr to Ghana, 1983–86. *Address:* c/o Foreign and Commonwealth Office, SW1.

BURNS, Sir Malcolm (McRae), KBE 1972 (CBE 1959); Principal, Lincoln Agricultural College, New Zealand, 1952–74; *b* 19 March 1910; *s* of J. E. Burns and Emily (*née* Jeffrey); *m* 1936, Ruth, *d* of J. D. Waugh, St Louis, USA; one *s* two *d. Educ:* Rangiora High Sch.; Univs of Canterbury (NZ), Aberdeen and Cornell. Plant Physiologist, DSIR, NZ, 1936; Sen. Lectr, Lincoln Agric. Coll., 1937–48; Dir, NZ Fert. Manuf. Res. Assoc., 1948–52. Chairman: Physical Environment Commn, 1968–70; Fact-finding Gp on Nuclear Power, 1976–77; Member: Nat. Develt Council, 1969–74; Nat. Museum Council, 1974–; Beech Forests Council, 1972–78; Trustee, Norman Kirk Meml, etc. FNZIC; FNZIAS; FRSNZ; FAAAS. Chm., DSIR Research Council, 1959–62. NZ Representative, Harkness Fellowships, 1961–76. Hon. DSc Canterbury, 1974. *Publications:* articles in scientific jls. *Recreations:* bowls, fishing, gardening. *Address:* 7 Royds Street, Christchurch 1, New Zealand.

BURNS, Michael; Chairman: Hatfield and Dunscroft Labour Party, since 1965; South Yorkshire County Association, since 1986; *b* 21 Dec. 1917; *s* of Hugh Burns and Jane Ellin Burns; *m* 1939, Vera Williams (*d* 1984); two *d. Educ:* Thorne Grammar Sch. Served War, 1940–46: 1939–45 Star, France and Germany Star, War Medal, Defence Medal. Miner, Hatfield Main Colliery, 1934–40 and 1946–66; Thorpe Marsh Power Stn, 1966–70; Sch. Caretaker, Hatfield Travis Sch., 1970–81 (due to wife's illness); retd 1981. Mem., Nat. Cttee, NUPE, 1979–81; Chm., Health and Safety Local Govt Nat. Cttee, NUPE, 1979–81. Chairman: Doncaster CVS, 1984– (Mem., 1977–; Mem., Nat. Exec., 1985–); Doncaster Victim Support Scheme, 1985–; Member: S Yorks CC, 1973–86 (Chm., 1982–83); S Yorks Valuation Panel, 1974–; S Yorks Charity Information Service, 1983–; Doncaster FPC, 1985–86; Doncaster Jt Consultative Cttee, 1985–; Goole Constituency Labour Party, 1977–83. Pres., Hatfield Br., Arthritic Care, 1980–. Chairman: Hatfield Ash Hill Sch. Bd of Governors, 1974–; Hatfield High Sch. Bd of Governors, 1974–. Church Warden, Christ Church, Dunscroft, 1964–79. *Recreations:* DIY, oil painting, politics. *Address:* 4A Ash Hill Road, Hatfield, Doncaster, South Yorks DN7 6JG. *T:* Doncaster 841088.

BURNS, Robert Andrew; HM Diplomatic Service; Head of South Asian Department, Foreign and Commonwealth Office, since 1986; *b* 21 July 1943; *e s* of late Robert Burns, CB, CMG and Mary Burns (*née* Goodland); *m* 1973, Sarah Cadogan; two *s* one *d. Educ:* Highgate Sch.; Trinity Coll., Cambridge. BA (Classics), MA. Entered Diplomatic Service, 1965; UK Mission to UN, NY, 1965; FO 1966; Sch. of Oriental and African Studies, 1966–67; Univ. of Delhi, 1967; served New Delhi, FCO, and UK Delegation to CSCE, 1967–76; First Secretary and Head of Chancery, Bucharest, 1976–78; Private Sec. to Perm. Under Sec. and Head of Diplomatic Service, FCO, 1979–82; Fellow, Center for Internat. Affairs, Harvard Univ., 1982–83; Counsellor (Information), Washington, and Head of British Information Services, NY, 1983–86. *Publication:* Diplomacy, War and Parliamentary Democracy, 1985. *Recreations:* music, theatre, country pursuits. *Address:* c/o Foreign and Commonwealth Office, SW1A 2AH. *Clubs:* Royal Automobile; Harvard (New York).

BURNS, Sir Terence, Kt 1983; Chief Economic Adviser to the Treasury and Head of the Government Economic Service, since 1980; *b* 13 March 1944; *s* of Patrick Owen and Doris Burns; *m* 1969, Anne Elizabeth Powell; one *s* two *d. Educ:* Houghton-Le-Spring Grammar Sch.; Univ. of Manchester (BAEcon Hons). London Business School: Research posts, 1965–70; Lecturer in Economics, 1970–74; Sen. Lectr in Economics, 1974–79; Prof. of Economics, 1979; Director, LBS Centre for Economic Forecasting, 1976–79. Member, HM Treasury Academic Panel, 1976–79. *Publications:* various articles in economic jls. *Recreations:* soccer spectator, music, golf. *Address:* c/o HM Treasury, Parliament Street, SW1P 3AG. *T:* 01–233 4508. *Club:* Reform.

BURNS, Thomas Ferrier, OBE 1983; Editor of The Tablet, 1967–82; Chairman of Burns & Oates Ltd, 1948–67; Director, The Tablet Publishing Company, since 1936; *b* 21 April 1906; *s* of late David Burns and late Clara (*née* Swinburne); *m* 1944, Mabel Marañon; three *s* one *d. Educ:* Stonyhurst. Press Attaché, British Embassy, Madrid, 1940–45. *Recreations:* painting and gardening. *Address:* Flat 7, 36 Buckingham Gate, SW1E 6PB. *T:* 01–834 1385. *Club:* Garrick.

BURNS, Prof. Tom, FBA 1982; Professor of Sociology, University of Edinburgh, 1965–81; *b* 16 Jan. 1913; *s* of John and Hannah Burns; *m* 1944, Mary Elizabeth Nora Clark; one *s* four *d. Educ:* Hague Street LCC Elementary Sch.; Parmiters Foundation Sch.; Univ. of Bristol (BA). Teaching in private schools in Tunbridge Wells and Norwich, 1935–39. Friends' Ambulance Unit, 1939–45 (PoW, Germany, 1941–43). Research Asst, W Midland Gp on Post-war Reconstruction and Planning, 1945–49; Lectr, Sen. Lectr and Reader, Univ. of Edinburgh, 1949–65. Vis. Prof., Harvard, 1973–74. Mem., SSRC, 1969–70. *Publications:* Local Government and Central Control, 1954; The Management of Innovation (with G. M. Stalker), 1961; (ed) Industrial Man, 1969; (ed with E. Burns) Sociology of Literature and Drama, 1973; The BBC: Public Institution and Private World, 1977; articles in a number of jls in Britain, USA, France, etc. *Recreations:* music, gardening. *Address:* Inchgarvie Lodge, South Queensferry, West Lothian EH30 9SJ.

BURNS, Maj.-Gen. Sir (Walter Arthur) George, KCVO 1962; CB 1961; DSO 1944; OBE 1953; MC 1940; retired; Lord-Lieutenant of Hertfordshire, 1961–86; *b* 29 Jan. 1911; *s* of late Walter Spencer Morgan and Evelyn Ruth Burns. *Educ:* Eton; Trinity Coll., Cambridge. BA Hons History. Commissioned Coldstream Guards 1932; ADC to Viceroy of India, 1938–40; Adjt 1st Bn, 1940–41 (MC); Brigade Major: 9 Inf. Bde, 1941–42; Sp. Gp Gds Armd Div., 1942; 32 Gds Bde, 1942–43; CO 3rd Bn Coldstream Gds, Italy, 1943–44 (DSO); Staff Coll., Camberley, 1945. Brigade Major, Household Bde, 1945–47; CO 3rd Bn Coldstream Gds, Palestine, 1947–50; AAG, HQ London Dist, 1951, 1952; Regimental Lt-Col Coldstream Gds, 1952–55; Comdg 4th Gds Bde, 1955–59. GOC London District and The Household Brigade, 1959–62; Col, Coldstream Guards, 1966–. Steward, The Jockey Club, 1964–. KStJ 1972. *Recreations:* shooting and racing. *Address:* Home Farm, North Mymms Park, Hatfield, Hertfordshire. *T:* Potters Bar 45117. *Clubs:* Jockey, Pratt's, Buck's.

BURNS, Prof. William, CBE 1966; Emeritus Professor of Physiology, University of London; Professor of Physiology, Charing Cross Hospital Medical School, 1947–77; Hon. Consultant Otologist, Charing Cross Group of Hospitals; *b* 15 Oct. 1909; *e s* of late Charles Burns, MB, ChB, JP and Mary Sillars, lately of Stonehaven, Scotland; *m* 1936, Margaret, *o d* of late W. A. Morgan, Glasgow; one *s* one *d. Educ:* Mackie Acad., Stonehaven; Aberdeen Univ. BSc 1933, MB ChB 1935, DSc 1943 Aberdeen. FRCP 1973. Asst in Physiology, Aberdeen, 1935; Lectr in Physiology, Aberdeen, 1936; War-time duty with Admiralty, 1942; established in RN Scientific Service, 1946; Supt RN Physiological Laboratory, 1947; Chm., Flying Personnel Res. Cttee, RAF, 1978–80; Emeritus Civil Consultant to RN in Audiology; Hon. Consultant to RAF in Acoustic Science; pt-time activity for MRC, 1977–84. Member: Physiological Soc.; Council, British Association for the Advancement of Science, 1956–61; Noise Adv. Council, 1977–81; BMA; formerly Mem., British Inst. of Acoustics; Hon. Life Mem., British Soc. Audiology. *Publications:* Noise and Man, 1968, 2nd edn 1973; (with D. W. Robinson) Hearing and Noise in Industry, 1970; articles on various aspects of hearing, in Journal of the Acoustical Soc. of America, Annals of Occupational Hygiene, Proc. Assoc. of Industrial Med. Officers, etc. *Recreations:* working in wood and metal; interested in engineering in general. *Address:* Cairns Cottage, Blacksmith's Lane, Laleham-on-Thames, Mddx TW18 1UB. *T:* Staines 53066.

BURNSIDE, Dame Edith, DBE 1976 (OBE 1957); *m* W. K. Burnside; one *s* one *d. Educ:* St Michael's C of E Girls' Grammar Sch. President: Prince Henry's Hosp. Central Council of Auxiliary, from 1952 (now retired); Royal Melbourne Hosp. Almoner Ambulance, from 1952. Member of a number of cttees and socs for charities, the arts, and internat. friendship. *Address:* Flat 6–1, 9 Struan Street, Toorak, Victoria 3142, Australia.

BURNSTOCK, Prof. Geoffrey, FRS 1986; FAA 1971; Professor of Anatomy, University of London, and Head of Department of Anatomy and Embryology, University College London, since 1975; Convener, Centre for Neuroscience, University College London, since 1979; *b* 10 May 1929; *s* of James Burnstock and Nancy Green; *m* 1957, Nomi Hirschfeld; three *d. Educ:* King's Coll., London; Melbourne Univ. BSc 1953, PhD 1957 London; DSc Melbourne 1971. National Inst. for Medical Res., Mill Hill, 1956–57; Dept of Pharmacology, Oxford Univ., 1957–59; Rockefeller Travelling Fellowship, Univ. of Ill, 1959; Dept of Zoology, Univ. of Melbourne: Sen. Lectr, 1959–62; Reader, 1962–64; Prof. of Zoology and Chm. of Dept, 1964–75; Associate Dean (Biological Sciences), 1969–72. Vis. Prof., Dept of Pharmacology, Univ. of Calif, LA, 1970. Hon. MSc Melbourne 1962. Silver Medal, Royal Soc. of Victoria, 1970. *Publications:* (with M. Costa) Adrenergic Neurons: their Organisation, Function and Development in the Peripheral Nervous System, 1975; (with Y. Uehara and G. R. Campbell) An Atlas of the Fine Structure of Muscle and its Innervation, 1976; (ed) Purinergic Receptors, 1981; (ed with G. Vrbová and R. O'Brien) Somatic and Autonomic Nerve-Muscle Interactions, 1983; papers on smooth muscle and autonomic nervous system, incl. purinergic nerves, in sci. jls. *Recreations:* tennis, wood sculpture. *Address:* Department of Anatomy and Embryology, University College London, Gower Street, WC1E 6BT. *T:* 01–387 7050.

BURNTON, Stanley Jeffrey; QC 1982; *b* 25 Oct. 1942; *s* of Harry and Fay Burnton; *m* 1971, Gwenyth Frances Castle; one *s* two *d. Educ:* Hackney Downs Grammar Sch.; St Edmund Hall, Oxford. MA. Called to the Bar, Middle Temple, 1965. *Recreations:* music, wine, travel, theatre. *Address:* 1 Essex Court, Temple, EC4Y 9AR. *T:* 01–353 5362.

BURNYEAT, Prof. Myles Fredric, FBA 1984; Laurence Professor of Ancient Philosophy, Cambridge, since 1984; *b* 1 Jan. 1939; *s* of Peter James Anthony Burnyeat and Cynthia Cherry Warburg; *m* 1st, 1971, Jane Elizabeth Buckley (marr. diss. 1982); one *s* one *d*; 2nd, 1984, Ruth Sophia Padel; one *d. Educ:* Bryanston Sch.; King's Coll., Cambridge (BA). Assistant Lecturer in Philosophy 1964, Lecturer in Philosophy 1965, University Coll. London; Lectr in Classics, Cambridge Univ., 1978; Fellow and Lectr in Philosophy, Robinson Coll., Cambridge, 1978. *Publications:* co-editor: Philosophy As It Is, 1979; Doubt and Dogmatism, 1980; Science and Speculation, 1982; (ed) The Skeptical Tradition, 1983; contribs to classical and philosophical jls. *Recreation:* travel. *Address:* Robinson College, Cambridge.

BURRELL, Derek William; Headmaster, Truro School, 1959–86; *b* 4 Nov. 1925; *s* of late Thomas Richard Burrell and of Flora Frances Burrell (*née* Nash). *Educ:* Tottenham Grammar Sch.; Queens' Coll., Cambridge. Assistant Master at Solihull Sch. (English, History, Religious Instruction, Music Appreciation), 1948–52. Senior English Master, Dollar Academy, 1952–59. *Recreations:* music of any kind, theatre, wandering about London. *Address:* Flat 5, 2 Strangways Terrace, Truro, Cornwall TR1 2NY. *T:* Truro 77733; 93 Mountfield Road, Stamford Hill, N16 6TD. *Club:* East India, Devonshire, Sports and Public Schools.

BURRELL, Vice-Adm. Sir Henry Mackay, KBE 1960 (CBE 1955); CB 1959; RAN retired; now a retired grazier; *b* 13 Aug. 1904; British (father *b* Dorset; mother *b* Australia, of Scottish parents); *m* 1944, Ada Theresa Weller (*d* 1981); one *s* two *d. Educ:* Royal Australian Naval Coll., Jervis Bay, Australia. Cadet-Midshipman, 1918; specialist in navigation, psc Greenwich, 1938; Commands: HMAS Norman, 1941–42 (despatches); Bataan, 1945; Dep. Chief of Naval Staff, Navy Office, Melbourne, 1947–48; HMAS Australia, 1949; idc 1950; HMAS Vengeance, 1953–54; Second Naval Mem., Australian Commonwealth Naval Board, 1956–57; Flag Officer Commanding HM Australian Fleet, 1955 and 1958; Chief of the Australian Naval Staff, 1959–62. *Publication:* Mermaids Do Exist (autobiog.), 1986. *Address:* 49 National Circuit, Forrest, Canberra, ACT 2603, Australia. *Club:* Commonwealth (Canberra, ACT).

BURRELL, Sir (John) Raymond, 9th Bt *cr* 1774; *b* 20 Feb. 1934; *s* of Sir Walter Raymond Burrell, 8th Bt, CBE, TD, and of Hon. Anne Judith (OBE), *o d* of 3rd Baron Denman, PC, GCMG, KCVO; *S* father, 1985; *m* 1st, 1959, Rowena Frances (marr. diss. 1971), *d* of late M. H. Pearce; one *s*; 2nd, 1971, Margot Lucy, *d* of F. E. Thatcher, Sydney, NSW; one *s* one *d. Educ:* Eton; Royal Agricultural Coll., Cirencester. *Heir:* *s* Charles Raymond Burrell, *b* 27 Aug. 1962. *Address:* Rosemont, 14 Rosemont Avenue, Woollahra, NSW 2025, Australia. *Club:* Boodle's.

BURRELL, Peter, CBE 1957; Director, The National Stud, 1937–71; *b* 9 May 1905; *s* of Sir Merrik R. Burrell, 7th Bt; *m* 1st, 1929, Pamela Pollen (marr. diss., 1940); two *s*; 2nd, 1971, Mrs Constance P. Mellon (*d* 1980). *Educ:* Eton; Royal Agricultural Coll., Cirencester. *Recreations:* shooting, stalking, hunting. *Address:* Pineland Plantation, PO Box 4, Newton, Ga 31770, USA.

BURRELL, Sir Raymond; *see* Burrell, Sir J. R.

BURRENCHOBAY, Sir Dayendranath, KBE 1978; CMG 1977; CVO 1972; Governor-General of Mauritius, 1978–84; *b* 24 March 1919; *s* of Mohabeer Burrenchobay, MBE, and Anant Kumari Burrenchobay; *m* 1957, Oomawatee Ramphul; one *s* two *d. Educ:* Royal Coll., Curepipe, Mauritius; Imperial Coll., London (BScEng Hons); Inst. of Education, London (Postgrad. CertEd). Education Officer, Govt of Mauritius, 1951–60, Sen. Educn Officer, 1960–64, Chief Educn Officer, 1964; Permanent Secretary: Min. of Education and Cultural Affairs, 1964–68; Min. of External Affairs, Tourism and Emigration, also Prime Minister's Office, 1968–76; Secretary to Cabinet and Head of Civil Service, 1976–78. Attended various confs and seminars as Govt rep.; Chm., Central Electricity Bd, 1968–78. Hon. DCL, Univ. of Mauritius, 1978. Chevalier, Légion d'Honneur, 1975; Grand Cross, 1st Cl., Order of Merit, Fed. Republic of Germany, 1978. *Recreations:* swimming, walking. *Address:* S. Ramphul Street, Curepipe Road, Mauritius.

BURRETT, (Frederick) Gordon, CB 1974; Deputy Secretary, Civil Service Department, 1972–81; Chairman: Redundant Churches Fund, since 1982; Wagner Society, since 1984; Member, Executive Committee, First Division Pensioners Group, since 1984; *b* 31 Oct. 1921; *s* of Frederick Burrett and Marion Knowles; *m* 1943, Margaret Joan Giddins;

one *s* two *d. Educ:* Emanuel Sch.; St Catharine's Coll., Cambridge. Served in Royal Engrs, N Africa, Italy, Yugoslavia, Greece, 1942–45 (despatches). HM Foreign, subseq. Diplomatic, Service, 1946; 3rd Sec., Budapest, 1946–49; FO, 1949–51; Vice-Consul, New York, 1951–54; FO, 1954–57; 1st Sec., Rome, 1957–60; transf. to HM Treasury, 1960; Private Sec. to Chief Sec., Treasury, 1963–64; Asst Secretary: HM Treasury, 1964; Cabinet Office, 1967–68; Secretary: Kindersley Review Body on Doctors' and Dentists' Remuneration; Plowden Cttee on Pay of Higher Civil Service, 1967–68; Civil Service Dept, 1968, Under-Sec. 1969. Mem., Civil Service Pay Res. Unit Bd, 1978–81; conducted govt scrutiny of V&A and Sci. Museums, 1982; Adviser to Govt of Oman on CS reorganisation, 1984; led govt review of policies and operations of Commonwealth Inst., 1986. FSA 1985. *Publication:* article on the watercolours of John Massey Wright (1777–1866) in vol. 54 of the Old Water-Colour Society's Club Annual. *Recreations:* music, books, walking, reading. *Address:* Trinity Cottage, Church Road, Claygate, Surrey. *T:* Esher 62783. *Club:* Athenæum.

BURRIDGE, Alan; Certification Officer for Trade Unions and Employers' Associations, 1981–85; *b* 15 Feb. 1921; *m* 1961, Joan Edith Neale; one *s. Educ:* William Ellis Sch.; Bristol Univ. (BA 1st Cl. Hons 1950). Served War, Army, 1939–46. Northern Assurance Co., 1936–39; Bristol Univ., 1947–50; Swinton Coll., 1950–53; London Municipal Soc., 1953–56; General Electric Co., 1956–67; Dept of Employment, 1967–81. *Address:* 1 Castle Hill Avenue, Berkhamsted, Herts HP4 1HJ. *T:* Berkhamsted 5276.

BURRILL, Timothy; Managing Director, Burrill Productions, since 1966; *b* 8 June 1931; *yr s* of L. Peckover Burrill, OBE and Marjorie S. Burrill; *m* 1st, 1959, Philippa (marr. diss. 1966), *o d* of Maurice and Margot Hare; one *d*; 2nd, 1968, Santa, *e d* of John and Betty Raymond; one *s* two *d. Educ:* Eton Coll.; Sorbonne Univ. Served Grenadier Guards, 1949–52: commnd 1950; served 2nd Bn, 1950–52. Jun. management, Cayzer Irvine & Co., 1952–56; entered film industry, 1956; joined Brookfield Prodns, 1965; Dir, World Film Services, 1967–69; first Prodn Administrator, National Film Sch., 1972; Man. Dir, Allied Stars (resp. for Chariots of Fire), 1979–80; Dir, Dovemead Ltd, 1977–, and Artistry Ltd, 1982– (resp. for Superman and Supergirl films); Consultant, National Film Develt Fund, 1980–81. Chm., BAFTA, 1981–83 (Vice-Chm., 1979–81); Producer Mem., Cinematograph Films Council, 1980–85; Member: Gen. Council, ACTT, 1975–76; Exec. Council, British Film and Television Producers Assoc., 1981–85; Dir, Fourth Protocol Films Ltd, 1985–. Governor: National Film and Television Sch., 1981–; National Theatre, 1982–. *Recreations:* theatre, skiing. *Address:* 51 Lansdowne Road, W11 2LG. *T:* 01–727 1442.

BURRINGTON, Ernest; Editor, The People, since 1985; *b* 13 Dec. 1926; *s* of late Harold Burrington and of Laura Burrington; *m* 1950, Nancy Crossley; one *s* one *d*. Self-educated. Reporter, Oldham Chronicle, 1941–43; Army service, 1943–47; reporter and sub-editor, Oldham Chronicle, 1947–49; sub-editor, Bristol Evening World, 1950; Daily Herald: sub-editor, Manchester, 1950, night editor, 1955; London night editor, 1957; IPC Sun: night editor, 1964; Asst Editor, 1965; Asst Editor and night editor, News International Sun, 1969; dep. night editor, Daily Mirror, 1970; Dep. Editor, Sunday People, 1971. *Recreations:* travel, tennis, bridge. *Address:* c/o The People, Orbit House, New Fetter Lane, EC4A 1AR. *T:* 01–822 3400.

BURROUGH, Alan, CBE 1970; Director, since 1946, President, since 1983, James Burrough plc (Chairman, 1968–82); *b* 22 Feb. 1917; *s* of Ernest James Burrough and Sophie (*née* Burston); *m* 1939, Rosemary June Bruce; two *s* one *d. Educ:* St Paul's Sch., London; Jesus Coll., Cambridge Univ. (MA). Joined James Burrough Ltd, 1935. War of 1939–45: 91st Field Regt, RA, and 5th RHA (Captain). Rejoined James Burrough Ltd, 1945: Director, 1946; Deputy Chairman, 1967; Chairman, 1968; Dir, Corby Distilleries Ltd, Montreal, 1980–82. Dep. Pres., Oxon Br., British Red Cross, 1982–. *Clubs:* Naval and Military; Leander (Henley-on-Thames); Royal Channel Islands Yacht.

BURROUGH, John Outhit Harold, CB 1975; CBE 1963; *b* 31 Jan. 1916; *s* of Adm. Sir Harold M. Burrough, GCB, KBE, DSO, and late Nellie Wills Outhit; *m* 1944, Suzanne Cecile Jourdan; one *s* one *d. Educ:* Manor House, Horsham; RNC Dartmouth. Midshipman, 1934; Sub-Lt 1936; Lieut 1938; Lt-Comdr 1944; retd 1947. Foreign Office (GCHQ), 1946–65; IDC 1964; British Embassy, Washington, 1965–67; Under-Sec., Cabinet Office, 1967–69; an Under Sec., FCO (Govt Communications HQ), 1969–76. Director: Racal Communications Systems Ltd, 1976–79; Racal Communications Ltd, 1979–82. *Address:* The Old Vicarage, Guiting Power, Glos. *T:* Guiting Power 596. *Club:* Naval and Military (Chm., 1969–72).

BURROUGH, Rt. Rev. John Paul, MBE 1946; MA Oxon; *b* 5 May 1916; *s* of Canon E. G. Burrough; *m* 1962, Elizabeth (Bess), *widow* of Stephen John White; one step-*d. Educ:* St Edward's Sch.; St Edmund Hall, Oxford; Ely Theol. College. Coach, Tigre Boat Club, Buenos Aires, 1938–39. Captain, Royal Signals, Malaya Campaign (POW), 1940–45. Asst, Aldershot Parish Church, 1946–51; Mission Priest, Dio. of Korea, 1951–59; Anglican Chaplain to Overseas Peoples in Birmingham, 1959–68; Canon Residentiary of Birmingham, 1967–68; Bishop of Mashonaland, 1968–81; Rector of Empingham and Hon. Asst Bishop, Diocese of Peterborough, 1981–85. Chaplain and Sub-Prelate, Order of St John of Jerusalem, 1969–. *Publications:* Lodeleigh, 1946; God and Human Chance, 1984. *Recreation:* rowing (Oxford crews, 1937 and 1938). *Address:* 6 Mill Green Close, Bampton, Oxon OX8 2HF. *T:* Bampton Castle 850952. *Clubs:* Leander (Henley); Vincent's (Oxford).

BURROW, Prof. Harold, MRCVS, DVSM; Professor of Veterinary Medicine, Royal Veterinary College, University of London, 1944–63; Professor Emeritus since 1963; *b* 24 Aug. 1903; *s* of Henry Wilson and Elizabeth Jane Burrow, Hest Bank Lodge, near Lancaster; *m* 1933, Frances Olivia, *d* of Orlando Atkinson Ducksbury, MRCVS, and Mrs Frances Mary Ducksbury, Lancaster; one *d. Educ:* Lancaster Royal Grammar Sch.; Royal (Dick) Veterinary Coll., Edinburgh. Asst Veterinary Officer, City of Birmingham, 1927–30; Chief Veterinary Officer: Birkenhead, 1930–35; Derbyshire CC, 1935–38; Divisional Veterinary Officer, Min. of Agriculture, 1938–42; Private Veterinary Practice, 1942–44. Examiner: to Royal Coll. of Veterinary Surgeons, 1937–44; to Univs. of Liverpool, London, Reading, Edinburgh, Bristol and Ceylon (various dates). Pres. Old Lancastrian Club, 1953; Member of Council, Royal Society Health, 1950–64 (Chairman, 1956–57, Vice-Pres. 1958–65, Life Vice-Pres., 1965). *Publications:* numerous contributions to veterinary scientific press. *Recreation:* gardening. *Address:* Forge Cottage, Combrook, Warwick. *T:* 641424.

BURROW, Prof. John Anthony, FBA 1986; Winterstoke Professor of English, University of Bristol, since 1976; *b* 3 Aug. 1932; *s* of William and Ada Burrow; *m* 1956, Diana Wynne Jones; three *s. Educ:* Buckhurst Hill County High Sch., Essex; Christ Church, Oxford (BA, MA). Asst Lectr, King's Coll., London, 1955–57; Lectr in English, Christ Church, 1957–61, and Brasenose Coll., 1957–59, Oxford; Fellow in English, Jesus Coll., Oxford, 1961–75. Vis. Prof., Yale Univ., 1968–69. Hon. Dir, EETS, 1983–. *Publications:* A Reading of Sir Gawain and the Green Knight, 1965; Geoffrey Chaucer (critical anthology), 1969; Ricardian Poetry, 1971; (ed) English Verse 1300–1500, 1977; Medieval Writers and their Work, 1982; Essays on Medieval Literature, 1984; The Ages of Man, 1986; reviews in learned jls. *Recreations:* music, cricket. *Address:* 9 The Polygon, Clifton, Bristol BS8 4PW. *T:* Bristol 277845.

BURROW, Prof. John Wyon, FBA 1986; FRHistS 1971; Professor of Intellectual History, University of Sussex, since 1982; *b* 4 June 1935; *s* of Charles and Alice Burrow; *m* 1958, Diane Dunnington; one *s* one *d. Educ:* Exeter School; Christ's College, Cambridge (MA, PhD). Research Fellow, Christ's College, Cambridge, 1959–62; Fellow, Downing Coll., Cambridge, 1962–65; Lectr, Sch. of European Studies, Univ. of East Anglia, 1965–69; Reader in History, Univ. of Sussex, 1969–82. Vis. Prof., Univ. of California, Berkeley, 1981; Vis. Fellow, History of Ideas Unit, ANU, 1983; Carlyle Lectr, Oxford, 1985. *Publications:* Evolution and Society, 1966; A Liberal Descent, 1981 (Wolfson Prize); (with S. Collini and D. Winch) That Noble Science of Politics, 1983; Gibbon, 1985. *Recreation:* cooking. *Address:* 7 Ranelagh Villas, Hove, East Sussex BN3 6HE. *T:* Brighton 731296.

BURROWES, Edmund Stanley Spencer, CMG 1959; Financial Secretary, Barbados, 1951–66; *b* 16 Dec. 1906; *m* 1st, 1934, Mildred B. Jackson (decd); one *s* three *d*; 2nd, 1965, Gwen Searson. *Educ:* Queen's Coll., British Guiana. British Guiana Colonial Secretariat, 1924; Inspector of Labour, 1940; Deputy Commissioner, 1945; Labour Commissioner, Barbados, 1947. *Publication:* Occupational Terms on Sugar Estates in British Guiana, 1945. *Recreations:* diving, gardening. *Address:* 66 Meadow Mount, Churchtown, Dublin.

BURROWES, Norma Elizabeth; opera and concert singer; *d* of Henry and Caroline Burrowes; *m* 1969, Steuart Bedford, *qv* (marr. diss.). *Educ:* Sullivan Upper Sch., Holywood, Co. Down; Queen's Univ., Belfast (BA); Royal Academy of Music (ARAM). Operas include: Zerlina in Don Giovanni, Glyndebourne Touring Opera (début); Blöndchen in Die Entführung aus dem Serail, Salzburg Festival, and again Blöndchen, Paris Opera, 1976 (début); Fiakermili, Royal Opera House (début), also Oscar, Despina, Nanetta, Woodbird; Entführung aus dem Serail, Ballo in Maschera, Der Rosenkavalier, Metropolitan, NY; Daughter of the Regiment, Midsummer Night's Dream, Elisir d'Amore, Canada; Cosi Fan Tutte, Romeo and Juliet, France; Marriage of Figaro, Germany; Gianni Schicchi, Switzerland; Marriage of Figaro, La Scala. Television operas include: Nanetta in Falstaff; Susanna in Marriage of Figaro and Lauretta in Gianni Schicchi. Sings regularly with major opera companies, gives concerts and recitals, GB and abroad; many recordings. Hon. DMus Queen's Univ. Belfast, 1979. *Recreations:* swimming, gardening, needlework. *Address:* 56 Rochester Road, NW1 9JG. *T:* 01–485 7322.

BURROWS, Sir Bernard (Alexander Brocas), GCMG 1970 (KCMG 1955; CMG 1950); Consultant, Federal Trust for Education and Research (Director-General, 1973–76); *b* 3 July 1910; *s* of Edward Henry Burrows and Ione, *d* of Alexander Macdonald; *m* 1944, Ines, *d* of late John Walter; one *s* one *d. Educ:* Eton; Trinity Coll., Oxford. Entered HM Foreign Service (later Diplomatic Service), 1934; served at HM Embassy, Cairo, 1938–45; Foreign Office, 1945–50; Counsellor HM Embassy, Washington, 1950–53; Political Resident in the Persian Gulf, 1953–58; Ambassador to Turkey, 1958–62; Dep. Under-Secretary of State, FO, 1963–66; Permanent British Representative to N Atlantic Council, 1966–70, retired 1970. *Publications:* (with C. Irwin) Security of Western Europe, 1972; Devolution or Federalism, 1980; (with G. Edwards) The Defence of Western Europe, 1982; contributed to: A Nation Writ Large, 1973; Federal Solutions to European Issues, 1978; The Third World War 1985, 1978; The Third World War: the untold story, 1982; articles and reviews in New Europe, etc. *Address:* Rubens West, Droke, East Dean, Chichester, West Sussex. *Club:* Travellers'.

BURROWS, General Eva, AO 1986; General of the Salvation Army, since 1986; *b* 15 Sept. 1929; *d* of Robert John Burrows and Ella Maria Burrows (*née* Watson). *Educ:* Brisbane State High School; Queensland Univ. (BA); London Univ. (PGCE); Sydney Univ. (MEd). Salvation Army: Missionary Educator, Howard Inst., Zimbabwe, 1952–67; Principal, Usher Inst., Zimbabwe, 1967–69; Vice-Principal 1970–73, Principal 1974–75, Internat. Coll. for Officers, London; Leader, Women's Social Services in GB and Ireland, 1975–77; Territorial Commander: Sri Lanka, 1977–79; Scotland, 1979–82; Australia, 1982–86. *Recreations:* classical music, reading, travel. *Address:* Salvation Army International Headquarters, 101 Queen Victoria Street, EC4P 4EP. *T:* 01–236 5222.

BURROWS, Fred, CMG 1981; Law Officer (Special Duties), Hong Kong, since 1985; *b* 10 Aug. 1925; *s* of late Charles Burrows; *m* 1955, Jennifer Winsome Munt; two *s. Educ:* Altrincham Grammar Sch.; Trinity Hall, Cambridge (MA). Served in RAF, 1944–47. Called to Bar, Gray's Inn, 1950; Asst Legal Adviser, Foreign Office, 1956–65; Legal Adviser, British Embassy, Bonn, 1965–67; returned to FO, 1967; Legal Counsellor, FCO, 1968–77; Counsellor (Legal Adviser), Office of UK Perm. Rep. to European Communities, 1977–80; Legal Counsellor, FCO, 1980–85. *Recreations:* sailing, carpentry. *Address:* Attorney General's Chambers, Hong Kong.

BURROWS, Sir John; *see* Burrows, Sir R. J. F.

BURROWS, Lionel John, CBE 1974; Chief Inspector of Schools, Department of Education and Science, 1966–73; Educational Adviser, Methodist Residential Schools, since 1974; *b* 9 March 1912; *s* of H. L. Burrows, HM Inspector of Schools, and Mrs C. J. Burrows; *m* 1939, Enid Patricia Carter; one *s* one *d. Educ:* King Edward VI Sch., Southampton; Gonville and Caius Coll., Cambridge. BA Cantab (1st cl. hons Mod. Langs Tripos) 1933. West Buckland Sch., Devon, Tiffin Sch., Kingston-upon-Thames and primary schools in London and Surrey, 1934–41; HM Forces (RASC and Intell. Corps), 1941–46; Commendation from US Army Chief of Staff, 1945; HM Inspector of Schools, 1946; Divisional Inspector, Metropolitan Div., 1960. Vice-Pres., Nat. Assoc. for Gifted Children, 1975–. *Publication:* The Middle School: high road or dead end?, 1978. *Recreations:* natural history, fell-walking. *Address:* 34 Groby Road, Ratby, Leicester LE6 0LJ. *Club:* English-Speaking Union.

BURROWS, Prof. Malcolm, FRS 1985; Professor of Neuroscience, University of Cambridge, since 1986; *b* 28 May 1943; *s* of William Roy Burrows and Jean Jones Burrows; *m* 1966, Christine Joan Ellis; one *s* one *d. Educ:* Cambridge Univ. (MA; ScD 1983); St Andrews Univ. (PhD 1967). Reader in Neurobiology, Univ. of Cambridge, 1983–86. *Address:* 6 Cherry Bounds Road, Girton, Cambridge CB3 0JT. *T:* Cambridge 276873.

BURROWS, Reginald Arthur, CMG 1964; HM Diplomatic Service, retired; *b* 31 Aug. 1918; *s* of late Arthur Richard Burrows; *m* 1952, Jenny Louisa Henriette Campiche (*d* 1985); one *s* one *d. Educ:* Mill Hill Sch.; St Catharine's Coll., Cambridge. Served with Royal Air Force during War; comd No. 13 (bomber) Sqdn, 1945. Entered the Foreign Service (now the Diplomatic Service), 1947; served in: Paris; Karachi; Tehran; Saigon; The Hague; Istanbul; Foreign Office; Minister, Islamabad, 1970–72; Univ. of Leeds, 1972–73; on secondment as Under-Sec., Civil Service Selection Bd, 1974–75; Asst Under-Sec. of State, 1975–78. *Recreations:* ski-ing, tennis. *Address:* Chemin de Longeraie 9, 1006 Lausanne, Switzerland. *T:* Lausanne 208067.

BURROWS, Sir (Robert) John (Formby), Kt 1965; MA, LLB; Solicitor; *b* 29 May 1901; *s* of Rev. Canon Francis Henry and Margaret Nelson Burrows; *m* 1926, Mary Hewlett (*d* 1986), *y d* of Rev. R. C. Salmon; one *s* one *d*. *Educ:* Eton Coll. (Scholar); Trinity Coll., Cambridge (Scholar); Harvard Law Sch. Pres. of The Law Soc., 1964–65. *Recreation:* small-scale forestry. *Address:* Ridlands Cottage, Limpsfield Chart, Surrey. *T:* Limpsfield Chart 3288.

See also W. Hamilton.

BURROWS, Rt. Rev. Simon Hedley; *see* Buckingham, Area Bishop of.

BURSELL, Rev. Rupert David Hingston; QC 1986; a Recorder of the Crown Court, since 1985; *b* 10 Nov. 1942; *s* of Henry and Cicely Mary Bursell; *m* 1967, Joanna Ruth Gibb; two *s* one *d*. *Educ:* St John's School, Leatherhead; Univ. of Exeter (LLB); St Edmund Hall, Oxford (MA, DPhil). Called to the Bar, Lincoln's Inn, 1968. Deacon, 1968; Priest, 1969; Hon. Curate: St Marylebone, 1968–69; St Mary the Virgin, Almondsbury, 1969–71; St Francis, Bedminster, 1971–83; Christ Church, and St Stephen, Bristol, 1983–. *Publications:* (contrib.) Atkin's Court Forms, 1972, 2nd edn 1985; (contrib.) Halsbury's Laws of England, 1975; (jtly) Crown Court Practice, 1978; (contrib.) Principles of Dermatitis Litigation, 1985. *Recreations:* Church music, military history, archaeology of Greece and Holy Land. *Address:* Brookside, 74 Church Road, Winscombe, Avon BS25 1BP. *T:* Winscombe 3542.

BURSTALL, Dr Clare, FBPsS; Director, National Foundation for Educational Research in England and Wales, since 1983 (Deputy Director, 1972–83); *b* 3 Sept. 1931; *d* of Alfred and Lily Wells; *m* 1955, Michael Lyle Burstall (marr. diss. 1977); one *s* one *d*. *Educ:* King's Coll. and Birkbeck Coll., Univ. of London (BA Hons French, BA Hons Psychology, PhD Psychology); La Sorbonne, Paris. FBPsS 1975. Project Leader of team evaluating teaching of French in British primary schs, NFER, 1964–72. *Publications:* French from Eight: a national experiment, 1968; French in the Primary School: attitudes and achievement, 1970; Primary French in the Balance, 1974; French from Age Eight or Eleven?, 1975; jl articles on various aspects of educnl research (eg, second language learning, large-scale assessment of achievement, class size, and management of educnl res.). *Recreations:* sailing, art collection, music, needlework. *Address:* Flat 2, 26 Lennox Gardens, SW1X 0DQ. *T:* 01–584 3127. *Club:* Royal Over-Seas League.

BURSTEIN, Hon. Dame Rose; *see* Heilbron, Hon. Dame R.

BURSTON, Sir Samuel (Gerald Wood), Kt 1977; OBE 1966; Grazier at Noss Estate, Casterton, Victoria, since 1945; President, Australian Woolgrowers and Graziers Council, 1976–79; *b* 24 April 1915; *s* of Maj.-Gen. Sir Samuel Burston, KBE, CB, DSO, VD, late RAAMC, and late Lady Burston; *m* 1940, Verna Helen Peebles (*d* 1980); one *s* one *d*. *Educ:* St Peter's Coll., Adelaide. Major, AIF, 1939–45 (despatches). Chm., Country Fire Authority, Vic, 1964–65; Pres., Graziers Assoc. of Vic, 1973–76; Councillor, Nat. Farmers Fedn, 1979–82; Vice-Pres., Confedn of Aust. Industry, 1978–82; Member: Nat. Employers Policy Cttee, 1970–78; Australian Wool Industry Policy Cttee, 1976–78; Aust. Sci. and Technol. Council, 1976–85; Aust. Stats Adv. Council, 1976–80; Aust. Govt Econ. Consultative Gp, 1976–82; Nat. Labour Consultative Council, 1976–82; Reserve Bank Bd, 1977–; Aust. Trade Develt Council, 1979–85; Trade Practices Cons. Council, 1979–82; Aust. Manufacturing Council, 1979–84; Chm., Perpetual Executors & Trustee Co. of Australia, 1981–. Mem., Victorian Selection Cttee, Winston Churchill Meml Trust, 1967–81. *Recreations:* golf, swimming. *Address:* 52 Brougham Place, North Adelaide, SA 5006, Australia. *T:* 08 267 3783. *Clubs:* Melbourne (Melbourne); Adelaide, Naval, Military and Air Force of South Australia (Adelaide); Royal Adelaide Golf.

BURT, Alistair James Hendrie; MP (C) Bury North, since 1983; Solicitor, Watts, Vallance & Vallance, London, since 1980; *b* 25 May 1955; *s* of James Hendrie Burt, med. practitioner and Mina Christie Robertson; *m* 1983, Eve Alexandra Twite; one *d*. *Educ:* Bury Grammar Sch.; St John's Coll., Oxford (BA Hons Jurisprudence, 1977). Pres., OU Law Soc., Michaelmas term, 1976. Articled Slater Heelis & Co., Manchester, 1978–80. Councillor, Archway Ward, London Bor. of Haringey, 1982–84. PPS to Sec. of State for the Environment, 1985–86, to Sec. of State for Educn and Science, 1986–. Secretary: NW Cons. MPs Group, 1984–; Parly Christian Fellowship, 1984–. *Recreations:* reading left-wing publications, sport, modern art. *Address:* House of Commons, SW1A 0AA. *T:* 01–219 3000.

BURT, Hon. Sir Francis (Theodore Page), KCMG 1977; Lieutenant-Governor of Western Australia, since 1977; Chief Justice of Western Australia, since 1977 (a Judge of the Supreme Court since 1969); *b* Perth, WA, 14 June 1918; *s* of A. F. G. Burt; *m* 1943, Margaret, *d* of Brig. J. E. Lloyd; two *s* two *d*. *Educ:* Guildford Grammar Sch.; Univ. of Western Australia (LLB, LLM); Hackett Schol., 1941; admitted to Bar of WA, 1941. Served War, RAN and RAAF, 1940–45. QC 1960; Pres., Law Soc. of WA, 1960–62. Visiting Lectr in Law, Univ. of WA, 1945–65. Chairman: Inst. of Radiotherapy, WA, 1960–62; Bd of Management, Sir Charles Gairdner Hosp., Hollywood, WA, 1962–72; Queen Elizabeth II Medical Centre Trust, 1966–85; Mem., Senate of Univ. of WA, 1968–76. *Recreations:* tennis, fishing. *Address:* c/o Supreme Court, Barrack Street, Perth, WA 6000, Australia. *Club:* Weld (Perth).

BURT, Gerald Raymond, OBE 1984; BEM 1947; FCIT; Chief Secretary, British Railways Board, 1976–84; *b* 15 Feb. 1926; *s* of Reginald George Burt and Lilian May Burt; *m* 1948, Edna Ivy Elizabeth Sizeland; two *s*. *Educ:* Latymer Upper Sch. FCIT 1971. Joined GWR as Booking Clerk, 1942; RE (Movement Control), 1944–47; BR Management Trainee, 1951–54; Gen. Staff, British Transport Commn, 1956–59; Divl Planning Officer, Bristol, 1959–62; Planning Officer, LMR, 1962–64; Divl Man., St Pancras, 1965; Traffic Man., Freightliners, 1967–70; Principal Corporate Planning Officer, British Railways Bd, 1970–76. Member: Council, Chartered Inst. of Transport, 1967–70, 1981–84; British Transport Police Cttee, 1984–. Governor, British Transport Staff Coll., 1976–82. FRSA 1983. Scouting Medal of Merit, 1978. *Recreations:* gardening, the countryside. *Address:* Sizelands, Mill Lane, Wingrave, Aylesbury, Bucks HP22 4PL. *T:* Aylesbury 681458.

BURT, Maurice Edward, FRAeS; Deputy Director, Building Research Establishment, 1975–81, retired; *b* 17 Nov. 1921; *s* of Reginald Edward Burt and Bertha Winifred Burt; *m* 1947, Monica Evelyn Amy; one *s* three *d*. *Educ:* Victoria Coll., Jersey; Taunton's Sch., Southampton; BA Hons London, 1948. CEng, MICE; FRAeS 1965. Aircraft industry, 1938–48; RAE, 1948–66 (Supt, Airworthiness, 1961–66); Head of Structures Dept, Transport and Road Res. Lab., 1966–73; Head of Res. Management, Dept of Environment, 1973–75. *Publications:* technical reports and articles. *Recreations:* golf, walking, gardening. *Address:* Roselle, Rue de Haut, St Lawrence, Jersey, CI. *T:* Jersey 35933.

BURT-ANDREWS, Air Commodore Charles Beresford Eaton, CB 1962; CBE 1959; RAF retired; *b* 21 March 1913; *s* of late Major C. Burt-Andrews, RE; *m* 1st, 1941, Elizabeth Alsina Helen, *d* of late Sir Maurice Linford Gwyer, GCIE, KCB, KCSI; one *s* one *d*; 2nd, 1977, Joan Trésor (*née* Cayzer-Evans). *Educ:* Lindisfarne Coll.; Collège des Frères Chrétiens Sophia. Commnd RAF, 1935; served NWF India, 1937–42; S Waziristan ops, 1937; Burma, 1942; comd Army Co-op. Sqdn RAF, 1943; special ops, 1943–44; Air Attaché, British Embassy, Warsaw, 1945–47; Staff Coll., 1948; Sec. Gen. Allied Air Forces Central Europe, Fontainebleau, 1950–52; directing Staff RAF Staff Coll., 1953–55; Head of Far East Defence Secretariat, Singapore, 1955–58; First Comdt, Pakistan Air Force Staff Coll., 1959–61; UK Nat. Mil. Rep., SHAPE, Paris, 1962–65; Asst Comdt, RAF Staff Coll., Bracknell, 1965–68; retd, 1968. *Recreations:* painting, glass engraving. *Address:* 9 Erimi Close, Erimi Village, Limassol District, Cyprus. *Club:* Royal Air Force.

See also S. G. Burt-Andrews.

BURT-ANDREWS, Stanley George, CMG 1968; MBE 1948; retired; *b* 1 Feb. 1908; *s* of Major Charles and Menie Celina Burt-Andrews; *m* 1937, Vera Boyadjieva; one *d*. *Educ:* Lindisfarne Coll., Westcliff-on-Sea; St Andrew's Coll., Bloemfontein, S Africa. Vice-Consul, 1946–47, Consul, 2nd Secretary, Sofia, 1948; Consul, Barranquilla, 1949–52; Commercial Secretary, British Embassy, Buenos Aires, 1952–53; Consul: Baltimore, 1953–59; Bilbao, 1959–62; Venice, 1962–64; Consul-General, St Louis, Mo., 1965–67. *Recreation:* fishing. *Address:* Villa Verial, 1 Aldwick Place, Fish Lane, Aldwick, Bognor Regis, W Sussex. *Club:* Bognor Regis Golf.

See also Air Cdre C. B. E. Burt-Andrews.

BURTON, family name of **Baroness Burton of Coventry.**

BURTON, 3rd Baron, *cr* 1897; **Michael Evan Victor Baillie;** *b* 27 June 1924; *er s* of Brig. Hon. George Evan Michael Baillie, MC, TD (*d* 1941) and *g s* of Baroness Burton (2nd in line); *S* grandmother, 1962; *m* 1st, 1948, Elizabeth Ursula Forster (marr. diss. 1977), *er d* of late Capt. A. F. Wise; two *s* four *d*; 2nd, 1978, Coralie Denise, 2nd *d* of late Claud R. Cliffe. *Educ:* Eton. Lieut, Scots Guards, 1944. Mem. Exec., Scottish Landowners Fedn. Mem., CC, 1948–75, JP 1961–75, DL 1963–65, Inverness-shire; Mem., Dist Council, 1984–. *Heir:* *s* Hon. Evan Michael Ronald Baillie [*b* 19 March 1949; *m* 1970, Lucinda, *e d* of Robert Law, Newmarket; two *s* one *d*]. *Address:* Dochfour, Inverness. *T:* Dochgarroch 252. *Clubs:* Cavalry and Guards, Brooks's; New (Edinburgh).

BURTON OF COVENTRY, Baroness, *cr* 1962, of Coventry (Life Peer); **Elaine Frances Burton;** Chairman, Mail Order Publishers' Authority, and President, Association of Mail Order Publishers, 1970–84; President, Institute of Travel Managers in Industry and Commerce, 1977–86; *b* Scarborough, 2 March 1904; *d* of Leslie and Frances Burton. *Educ:* Leeds Girls' Modern Sch.; City of Leeds Training Coll. Leeds elementary schools and evening institutes, 1924–35; South Wales Council of Social Service and educational settlements, 1935–37; National Fitness Council, 1938–39; John Lewis Partnership, 1940–45. Writer, lecturer, broadcaster, public relations consultant, 1945–50. MP (Lab) Coventry South, 1950–59. Member of parliamentary delegation to Netherlands, 1952 and to Soviet Union, 1954; Siam, 1956; South America, 1958; deleg. to Council of Europe; first woman Chm., Select Cttee on Estimates (sub-Cttee); Mem., Select Cttee on Practice and Procedure (House of Lords). Chairman: Domestic Coal Consumers' Council, 1962–65; Council on Tribunals, 1967–73; Member: Council Industrial Design, 1963–68; ITA, 1964–69; Sports Council, 1965–71; Air Transport Users Cttee, 1973–79. Founder Mem., Social Democratic Party, 1981–. Consultant to: John Waddington Ltd, 1959–61; The Reader's Digest, 1969–70; Courtaulds Ltd, 1960–73; Hon. Consultant, Air Transport Users Cttee, 1979– (Mem., 1973–79); Director: Consultancy Ltd, 1949–73; Imperial Domestic Appliances Ltd, 1963–66. *Publications:* What of the Women, 1941; And Your Verdict?, 1943; articles for press, magazines and political journals. *Recreations:* reading, ballet, opera; World's Sprint Champion, 1920; Yorkshire 1st XI (hockey), 1924–32. *Address:* 47 Molyneux Street, W1. *T:* 01–262 0864.

BURTON, Sir Carlisle (Archibald), Kt 1979; OBE 1968; Chairman: Public Service Commission, Barbados, since 1981; Cave Hill Campus Council, University of the West Indies, Barbados, since 1984; *b* 29 July 1921; *m* 1946, Hyacinth Marjorie Adelle Barker. *Educ:* Harrison Coll., Barbados, WI; Univ. of London (BA); School of Librarianship, Leeds (ALA); Univ. of Pittsburgh (MS). Assistant Master, Harrison Coll., Barbados, 1943–50; Sen. Asst Master, Bishop's High Sch., Tobago, 1950–51; Public Librarian, Barbados, 1953–58; Permanent Secretary: Min. of Educn, 1958–63; Min. of Health, 1963–71; Perm. Sec., Prime Minister's Office, and Head of Civil Service, 1972–81. Director: Barbados National Bank, 1978– (Dep. Chm., 1982–); Insurance Corp. of Barbados, 1978– (Chm., 1981–). FRSA 1953. *Recreations:* (active) table tennis, swimming, bridge, reading; (spectator) cricket (Life Member, Barbados Cricket Assoc.), athletics (Life Member, Barbados Amateur Athletic Assoc.), soccer. *Address:* Caradelle, Mountjoy Avenue, Pine Gardens, St Michael, Barbados, West Indies. *T:* 429 3724.

BURTON, Sir George (Vernon Kennedy), Kt 1977; CBE 1972 (MBE (mil.) 1945); DL; Chairman, Fisons plc, 1973–84 (Chief Executive, 1966–76, Senior Vice-Chairman, 1966–71, Deputy Chairman, 1971–72); *b* 21 April 1916; *s* of late George Ethelbert Earnshaw Burton and Francesca (*née* Holden-White); *g s* of Sir Bunnell Burton, Ipswich; *m* 1st, 1945, Sarah Katherine Tcherniavsky (marr. diss.); two *s*; 2nd, 1975, Priscilla Margaret Gore, *d* of Cecil H. King, *qv*. *Educ:* Charterhouse; Germany. Served RA, 1939–45, N Africa, Sicily, Italy, Austria. Director: Barclays Bank Internat. plc, 1976–82; Thomas Tilling, 1976–83; Rolls-Royce Ltd, 1976–84. Member: Export Council for Europe, 1965–71 (Dep. Chm., 1967–71); Council, CBI, 1970–84 (Chm., CBI Overseas Cttee, 1975–81); BOTB, 1972–73 (BOTB European Trade Cttee, 1972–81; British Overseas Trade Adv. Council, 1975–79); Investment Insce Adv. Cttee, ECGD, 1971–76; Council on Internat. Develt of ODM, 1977–79; Council, BIM, 1968–70 (FBIM); NEDC, 1975–79; Whitford Cttee to Consider Law on Copyright and Designs, 1974–77; Ipswich County Borough Council, 1947–51; Ipswich Gp HMC; Assoc. for Business Sponsorship of the Arts, 1978–84; Governing Body, British National Cttee of Internat. Chamber of Commerce, 1979–; Governor, Sutton's Hosp. in Charterhouse, 1979–; Chm., Ipswich Conservative Assoc., 1982–84. FRSA 1978. DL Suffolk, 1980. Commander: Order of Ouissam Alaouite, Morocco, 1968; Order of Léopold II, Belgium, 1974. *Recreation:* music. *Address:* Aldham Mill, Hadleigh, Suffolk.

BURTON, Graham Stuart; HM Diplomatic Service; Counsellor, Foreign and Commonwealth Office, since 1984; *b* 8 April 1941; *s* of late Cyril Stanley Richard Burton and of Jessie Blythe Burton; *m* 1965, Julia Margaret Lappin; one *s* one *d*. *Educ:* Sir William Borlase's Sch., Marlow. Foreign Office, 1961; Abu Dhabi, 1964; Middle East Centre for Arabic Studies, 1967; Kuwait, 1969; FCO, 1972; Tunis, 1975; UK Mission to United Nations, 1978; Counsellor, Tripoli, 1981. *Recreations:* golf, watching all sport, opera. *Address:* c/o Foreign and Commonwealth Office, SW1.

BURTON, Air Marshal Sir Harry, KCB 1971 (CB 1970); CBE 1963 (MBE 1943); DSO 1941; Air Officer Commanding-in-Chief, Air Support Command, 1970–73, retired; *b* 2 May 1919; *s* of Robert Reid Burton, Rutherglen; *m* 1945, Jean, *d* of Tom Dobie; one *s* one *d*. *Educ:* Glasgow High Sch. Joined RAF 1937; served War of 1939–45, Europe, India, and Pacific (POW, 1940, escaped 1941); CO, RAF Scampton, 1960–62; SASO 3 (Bomber) Group, RAF, 1963–65; Air Executive to Deputy for Nuclear Affairs, SHAPE, 1965–67; AOC 23 Group, RAF, 1967–70. Group Captain 1958; Air Cdre 1963; Air Vice-Marshal 1965; Air Marshal 1971. *Address:* Mayfield, West Drive, Middleton-on-Sea, Sussex. *Club:* Royal Air Force.

BURTON, Humphrey McGuire; Executive Producer, Performing Arts, BBC Television, since 1981; *b* 25 March 1931; *s* of Harry (Philip) and Kathleen Burton; *m* 1st, 1957, Gretel (*née* Davis); one *s* one *d*; 2nd, 1970, Christina (*née* Hellstedt); one *s* one *d*. *Educ:* Long Dene Sch., Chiddingstone; Judd Sch., Tonbridge; Fitzwilliam House, Cambridge (BA). BBC Radio, 1955–58; BBC TV, 1958–67: Editor, Monitor, 1962; Exec. Producer Music Programmes, 1963; Head of Music and Arts Programmes, 1965, productions inc. Workshop, Master Class, In Rehearsal, Britten at 50, Conversations with Glenn Gould. Head of Music and Arts, BBC TV, 1975–81; since 1975, Exec. Producer opera relays from Covent Garden and Glyndebourne (Capriccio, Cosi fan Tutte); Producer, Omnibus at Santa Fe Opera; Producer/Director: TV Proms with Giulini and Solti, 1981; Walton 80th Birthday Concert (Previn), Verdi Requiem (Abbado), and Call me Kiri (Te Kanawa), 1982; Covent Garden opera relays, Manon Lescaut, Die Fledermaus, 1983; Andrea Chénier, 1985; West Side Story (producer), 1985. *Host of BBC series:* Omnibus, 1976–78, 1984–85; Young Musician of the Year, biennially 1978–; Wagner's Ring, 1982; In Performance, 1978–82; Opera Month, 1979; other arts and music programmes; *London Weekend TV:* Head of Drama, Arts and Music, 1967–69; Editor/Introducer, Aquarius, 1970–75, programmes incl. Mahler Festival, Verdi Requiem, Trouble in Tahiti, The Great Gondola Race, Anatomy of a Record, etc; *other ITV companies:* 5 Glyndebourne operas, adapted and produced, Southern, 1972–74; The Beach at Falesa, World Premiere, Harlech, 1974; UN Day Concert with Pablo Casals, 1971; *French TV:* Berlioz' Requiem at Les Invalides, 1975; many free-lance prodns in Austria, Germany, Israel and USA, inc. Mahler, Brahms, Schumann and Beethoven Cycles with Bernstein and Vienna Philharmonic, concerts with von Karajan and Berlin Philharmonic, Giulini with LA Philharmonic, Mehta and NY Philharmonic, and Solti and Chicago SO. Guest Dir, Hollywood Bowl 1983 Summer Music Fest. Chairman: EBU Music Experts Gp, 1976–82; EBU TV Music Working Party, 1982–86; Mem., New Music Sub-Cttee, Arts Council, 1981–83. Hon. Professorial Fellow, University Coll., Cardiff, 1983. Chevalier de l'Ordre des Arts et des Lettres, 1975. Desmond Davis Award, SFTA, 1966; Royal TV Soc. Silver Medal, 1971; Emmy, 1971 for 'Beethoven's Birthday' (CBS TV); Peabody Award, 1972; SFTA Best Specialised Series, 1974; Christopher Award, 1979; RAI Prize, Prix Italia and Robert Flaherty best documentary award, BAFTA (all for West Side Story), 1985. *Publications:* contrib. RSA Jl and Listener. *Recreations:* music-making, tennis, swimming, travel. *Address:* c/o BBC Television, Kensington House, Richmond Way, W14. *Club:* Garrick.

BURTON, Iris Grace; Editor in Chief, G+J of the UK publications, including Prima, since 1986; *d* of Arthur Burton and late Alice Burton; *m*; one *s* one *d*. *Educ:* Roan Girls' Grammar Sch., Greenwich; City of London Coll. Local newspaper, SE London Mercury, until 1966; Writer, then Features Editor, Woman's Own, 1966–78; Asst Editor, TV Times, 1978–80. *Address:* G+J of the UK, Portland House, Stag Place, SW1E 5BJ; (home) Anerley, SE20.

BURTON, Rev. John Harold Stanley, MA Oxon; General Secretary, Church Lads' Brigade, 1954–64 and 1973–Jan. 1977; Member, Church of England Youth Council, 1954–64; *b* 6 Feb. 1913; *o s* of late John Stanley Burton, Grenadier Guards (killed in action 1916), and Lilian Bostock; *m* 1st, 1943, Susan Lella (*d* 1960), *o d* of Sir John Crisp, 3rd Bt; two *d*; 2nd, 1960, Jacqueline Mary Margaret, *o d* of P. L. Forte, Clifton, Bristol; one *d*. *Educ:* Marlborough; University Coll., Oxford; Westcott House, Cambridge. BA 2nd Class Hons. in Theology, Oxford, 1935; MA 1937; Deacon, 1936; Priest, 1938; Curate of Christ Church, Woburn Square, WC1, 1936–39; Cranleigh, Surrey, 1939–40; Head of Cambridge Univ. Settlement, Camberwell, 1940–43; Chaplain RAFVR, 1943; Fighter Command, 1943–44; 2nd Tactical Air Force, 1944; Bomber Command, 1945; Ordination Secretary, Air Command, SE Asia, and Chaplain 9 RAF General Hospital, Calcutta, 1945–46; demobilised Aug. 1946. Chaplain of Middlesex Hospital, W1, 1946–50; Chaplain of the Royal Free Hospital, 1950–54; Chairman of Hospital Chaplains Fellowship, 1953–54. *Publications:* (contrib.) A Priest's Work in Hospital, 1955; (contrib.) Trends in Youth Work, 1967. *Recreations:* Beagling, fishing, shooting, most games. *Address:* 45 Westbourne Terrace, W2. *T:* 01-262 5780. *Club:* Royal Air Force.

BURTON, Prof. Kenneth, FRS 1974; Professor of Biochemistry since 1966, and Dean of Faculty of Science, 1983–86, University of Newcastle upon Tyne; *b* 26 June 1926; *s* of Arthur and Gladys Burton; *m* 1955, Hilda Marsden; one *s* one *d*. *Educ:* High Pavement Sch., Nottingham; Wath-upon-Dearne Grammar Sch.; King's Coll., Cambridge (MA, PhD). Asst Lectr in Biochem., Univ. of Sheffield, 1949, Lectr 1952; Res. Associate, Univ. of Chicago, 1952–54; MRC Unit for Research in Cell Metabolism, Oxford, 1954–66. Vis. Lectr in Medicine, Harvard, 1964; William Evans Vis. Prof., Univ. of Otago, 1977–78. *Publications:* scientific articles, especially on nucleic acids. *Recreations:* music, hill-walking. *Address:* 42 Cade Hill Road, Stocksfield, Northumberland NE43 7PU.

BURTON, Maurice, DSc; retired 1958; now free-lance author and journalist; *b* 28 March 1898; *s* of William Francis and Jane Burton; *m* 1929, Margaret Rosalie Maclean; two *s* one *d*. *Educ:* Holloway County Sch.; London Univ. Biology Master, Latymer Foundation, Hammersmith, 1924–27; Zoology Dept, British Museum (Natural History), SW7, 1927–58. Science Editor, Illustrated London News, 1946–64; Nature Correspondent, Daily Telegraph, 1949–. FZS. Kt of Mark Twain, 1980. *Publications:* The Story of Animal Life, 1949; Animal Courtship, 1953; Living Fossils, 1954; Phœnix Re-born, 1959; Systematic Dictionary of Mammals, 1962; (jtly) Purnell's Encyclopedia of Animal Life, 1968–70; Encyclopaedia of Animals, 1972; Introduction to Nature (for children), 1972; Prehistoric Animals, 1974; Deserts, 1974; How Mammals Live, 1975; Just Like an Animal, 1978; A Zoo at Home, 1979; numerous publications on Sponges in a variety of scientific journals. *Recreation:* gardening. *Address:* Weston House, Albury, Guildford, Surrey GU5 9AE. *T:* Shere 2369.

BURTON, Michael John; QC 1984; *b* 12 Nov. 1946; *s* of late Henry Burton, QC, and Hilda Burton; *m* 1972, Corinne Ruth, *d* of Dr Jack Cowan, MC, and late Dorothy Cowan; four *d*. *Educ:* Eton Coll.; Balliol Coll., Oxford (MA). President, Balliol JCR, 1967; First President, Oxford Univ. SRC, 1968. Called to Bar, Gray's Inn, 1970; Law Lectr, Balliol Coll., Oxford, 1972–74. Contested: (Lab) RBK&C (local elections), 1971; (Lab) Stratford upon Avon, Feb. 1974; (SDP) Putney, GLC, 1981. *Recreations:* amateur theatricals, lyric writing, singing, bridge. *Address:* 2 Crown Office Row, Temple, EC4. *T:* 01-583 2681; 125 Howards Lane, Putney, SW15.

BURTON, Michael St Edmund, CVO 1979; HM Diplomatic Service; Minister and Deputy Commandant, Berlin, since 1985; *b* 18 Oct. 1937; *s* of late Brig. G. W. S. Burton, DSO, and of Barbara Burton (*née* Kemmis Betty); *m* 1967, Henrietta Jindra Hones; one *s* one *d* (and one *d* decd). *Educ:* Bedford Sch.; Magdalen Coll., Oxford. MA. 2nd Lt, Rifle Brigade, 1955–57. Foreign Office, 1960; Asst Political Agent, Dubai, Trucial States, 1962–64; Private Sec. to Minister of State, FO, 1964–67; Second (later First) Sec. (Information), Khartoum, 1967–69; First Sec. (Inf.), Paris, 1969–72; Asst, Science and Technology Dept, FCO, 1972–75; First Sec. and Head of Chancery, Amman, 1975–77; Counsellor, Kuwait, 1977–79; Head of Maritime, Aviation and Environment Dept, FCO, 1979–81; Head of S Asian Dept, FCO, 1981–84; on secondment to BP as Head of Policy Rev. Unit, 1984–85. *Recreations:* tennis, golf, travel. *Address:* c/o Foreign and Commonwealth Office, SW1. *Clubs:* United Oxford & Cambridge University, Hurlingham.

BURTON, Neil Edward David; Secretary, Monopolies and Mergers Commission, 1981–86; *b* 12 May 1930; *s* of late Edward William Burton and Doris Burton; *m* 1954, Jane-Anne Crossley Perry; three *s*. *Educ:* Welwyn Garden City Grammar Sch.; City of London Sch.; Trinity Coll., Oxford (MA). Asst Principal, Min. of Supply; Asst Sec., MAFF, 1966, subseq. CSD and Price Commn; Asst Dir, Office of Fair Trading, 1976; Dir, Restrictive Trade Practices, 1976; Dir of Competition Policy, 1977–81. *Address:* 29 Brittains Lane, Sevenoaks, Kent TN13 2JW. *T:* Sevenoaks 455608.

BURTON, Richard Hilary; Chairman, Cable Authority, since 1984; *b* 28 Dec. 1923; *s* of Robert Claud and Theodora Constance Helen Burton; *m* 1962, Priscilla Jane Coode-Adams; one *s* one *d*. *Educ:* Lancing; Brasenose Coll., Oxford (MA 2nd Cl. Hons Jurisprudence). Served War, 1942–46, 60th Rifles, Captain (mentioned in despatches); Mem., Military Courts, Palestine, 1946. Called to the Bar, Inner Temple, 1951; practised at Bar, 1951–54. Gillette Industries Ltd: Manager, Legal Dept, 1954–65; Legal Dir, 1965–78; Chm., 1978–84; Dep. to the Chm., The Gillette Company (USA), 1984–. Chm., W Mddx Arts Develt Trust, 1978–. Freeman, City of London, 1974. FRSA. *Recreations:* cricket, real tennis, shooting, ornithology, lepidoptery. *Address:* Danmoor House, Heckfield, near Basingstoke, Hants. *T:* Heckfield 233. *Club:* Boodle's.

BURTON, Sydney Harold, JP; FCBSI; Director, Gateway Building Society, since 1981 (Managing Director, 1975–81); *b* 6 April 1916; *s* of Sydney Collard Burton and Maud Burton; *m* 1st, 1941, Jean Cowling (*d* 1985); one *d*; 2nd, 1986, Irene Robertson. *Educ:* Belle Vue High Sch., Bradford. Various appts with Bradford Equitable Building Soc. (excl. war years), 1932–63; joined Temperance Permanent Building Soc., 1963; Jt Gen. Manager, 1965; Gen. Man. and Sec., 1972; following merger of Temperance Permanent and Bedfordshire Bldg Socs became Chief Gen. Man. and Sec. of Gateway Bldg Soc., 1974. Pres., Building Societies Inst., 1976–77; Mem. Council, Building Societies Assoc., 1971–81. JP Worthing, 1974. *Recreations:* music and theatre, social and religious work. *Address:* Cherry Trees, 52 Beehive Lane, Ferring, Sussex BN12 5NR. *T:* Worthing 44704.

BURTON-CHADWICK, Sir Joshua (Kenneth), 3rd Bt *cr* 1935; Sales Manager/Trainer, Joshua Chadwick Marketing Developers; *b* 1 Feb. 1954; *s* of Sir Robert Burton-Chadwick, (Sir Peter), 2nd Bt, and of Beryl Joan, *d* of Stanley Frederick J. Brailsford; *S* father, 1983. *Heir:* none.

BURTON-TAYLOR, Sir Alvin, Kt 1972; FCA (Aust.); FAIM; Director: Email Ltd; NSW Division, National Heart Foundation of Australia; O'Connell Street Associates Pty Ltd; *b* 17 Aug. 1912; *s* of A. A. W. Taylor, Adelaide, and Ruby Ella Burton, Adelaide; *m* 1949, Joan L. Toole; two *s* two *d*. *Educ:* Sydney Church of England Grammar Sch. Cooper Bros Way & Hardie, 1930–37; Asst Gen. Manager, then Gen. Manager, Rheem Aust. Ltd, 1937–57; Man. Dir, Email Ltd (Group), 1957–74. *Recreations:* fishing, bowls, gardening. *Address:* Unit 6 Gainsborough, 50–58 Upper Pitt Street, Kirribilli, NSW 2061, Australia. *Clubs:* Union, Royal Sydney Yacht Squadron, Elanora Country (all in NSW).

BURY, John, OBE 1979; Associate Designer, National Theatre; free-lance designer for theatre, opera and film; *b* 27 Jan. 1925; *s* of C. R. Bury; *m* 1st, 1947, Margaret Leila Greenwood (marr. diss.); one *s*; 2nd, 1966, Elizabeth Rebecca Blackborrow Duffield; two *s* one *d*. *Educ:* Cathedral Sch., Hereford; University Coll., London. Served with Fleet Air Arm (RN), 1942–46. Theatre Workshop, Stratford, E15, 1946–63; Assoc. Designer, Royal Shakespeare Theatre, 1963–73; Head of Design: RSC, 1965–68; NT, 1973–85. Arts Council: Designers' Working Gp, 1962–78; Mem., Drama Panel, 1960–68 and 1975–77; Chm., Soc. of British Theatre Designers, 1975–85. FRSA 1970. Co-winner, Gold Medal for Scene Design, Prague Quadrienale, 1975 and 1979; Antoinette Perry Awards (Best Set Design and Best Lighting), for Broadway prodn of Amadeus, 1981. *Address:* 14 Woodlands Road, Barnes, SW13.

BURY, Michael Oswell, OBE 1968; Director, Education, Training and Technology, Confederation of British Industry, 1985–86; *b* 20 Dec. 1922; *o s* of Lt-Col Thomas Oswell Bury, TD, and Constance Evelyn Bury; *m* 1954, Jean Threlkeld Wood, *d* of late William Threlkeld Wood; two *s* one *d*. *Educ:* Charterhouse; London Sch. of Economics. Served War of 1939–45: The Rifle Brigade (ranks of Rifleman to Captain), 1941–47. Steel Company of Wales, 1947–49; British Iron and Steel Fedn, 1949–64 (Dep. Dir, Labour and Trng, 1962–64); Dir, Iron and Steel Industry Trng Bd, 1964–70; Director, Educn, Trng and Technol., 1970–81, Corporate Affairs, 1981–84, CBI. Mem., Manpower Services Commn, 1974–81, 1985–. *Recreations:* gardening, fishing, travel. *Address:* Hull Bush, Mountnessing, Brentwood, Essex CM13 1UH. *T:* Ingatestone 353958. *Club:* Reform.

BURY, Shirley Joan, FSA; Keeper of Metalwork, Victoria and Albert Museum, 1982–85; *b* 1925; *d* of Ernest Leslie Saxton Watkin and Florence Keen; *m* 1947, John Morley Bury; one *s*. *Educ:* University of Reading. BA Fine Arts 1946, MA 1960; FSA 1972. Joined V & A 1948: Research Asst, 1948, Senior Research Asst, 1961, Circulation Dept; Asst Keeper, Library, 1962–68, Metalwork Dept, 1968–72; Dep. Keeper, Dept of Metalwork, 1972–82. Mem., British Hallmarking Council, 1974–85. Liveryman, Goldsmiths' Co., 1982–. *Publications:* Victorian Electroplate, 1972; V & A Jewellery Gallery Summary Catalogue, 1982; An Introduction to Rings, 1984; Sentimental Jewellery, 1985; (compiled and ed) Catalogue, Copy or Creation, Goldsmiths' Hall, 1967; (ed) Catalogue, Liberty's 1875–1975, V & A 1975; introd. to C. R. Ashbee, Modern English Silver, new edn 1974; contribs to Burlington Magazine, Connoisseur, Apollo, V & A Bulletin, Yearbook and Album. *Recreations:* theatre, walking, gardening. *Address:* 5 Tasker Road, NW3.

BURY, Air Cdre Thomas Malcolm Grahame, CB 1972; OBE 1962; retired as Head of Technical Training and Maintenance, British Aircraft Corporation, Saudi Arabia; *b* 11 Sept. 1918; *s* of late Ernest Bury, OBE; *m* 1951, Dillys Elaine Jenkins, MBE, *d* of Dr Aneurin Jenkins, Swansea; two *s* one *d*. *Educ:* Forest Sch., E17. Served War, 1939–45, NW Europe, Arabia. Joined RAF, 1935; STSO, HQ, 1 Gp, 1961–64; DDME, MoD, 1965–66; Senior Engr Officer, Air Forces Gulf, 1967–68; Command Mech. Engr, HQ Strike Command, 1968–73; retired 1973. *Address:* Las Bayas, 2 Benimeit, Buzón 124, Moraira, Alicante 03724, Spain.

BUSBY, Sir Matthew, Kt 1968; CBE 1958; President, Manchester United Football Club, since 1980; *b* 26 May 1909; *m* 1931, Jean Busby; one *s* one *d* (and four *s* decd). *Educ:* St Brides, Bothwell. Footballer: Manchester City, 1929–36; Liverpool, 1936–39. Served Army, 1939–45. Manchester United Football Club: Manager, 1945–69; Gen. Manager, 1969–71; Dir, 1971–82. Mem., Football League Management Cttee, 1981–82. Freeman of Manchester, 1967. KCSG. *Publication:* My Story, 1957. *Recreations:* golf, theatre. *Address:* 10 Cedar Court, Wilbraham Road, Fallowfield, Manchester M14 6FB.

BUSCH, Rolf Trygve; Comdr, Order of St Olav; Norwegian Ambassador to the Court of St James's and to Ireland, since 1982; *b* 15 Nov. 1920; *s* of Aksel Busch and Alette (*née* Tunby); *m* 1950, Solveig Helle; one *s*. *Educ:* Oslo Univ. (degree in Law); National

Defence Coll. Dep. Judge, 1946–47; entered Norwegian Foreign Service, 1947; Min. of For. Affairs, 1947–50; Sec., Cairo, 1950–52; Vice-Consul, New York, 1952–54; Min. of For. Affairs, 1954–56; National Def. Coll., 1956–57; First Sec., Norwegian Delegn to NATO, Paris, 1957–60; Min. of For. Affairs, 1960–65; Counsellor and Dep. Perm. Rep., Norwegian Delegn to NATO, Paris and Brussels, 1965–70; Dir-Gen., Min. of For. Affairs, 1970–71; Perm. Rep. to N Atlantic Council, 1971–77; Ambassador to Fed. Republic of Germany, 1977–82. Officer, Order of the Nile, Egypt; Comdr with Star, Order of the Falcon, Iceland; Grand Cross, Order of Merit, Fed. Republic of Germany. *Address:* 10 Palace Green, W8. *T:* 01–937 6449.

BUSH, Alan, Composer; Conductor; Pianist; Professor of Composition, Royal Academy of Music, 1925–78; *b* 22 Dec. 1900; *s* of Alfred Walter Bush and Alice Maud (*née* Brinsley); *m* 1931, Nancy Rachel Head; two *d* (and one *d* decd). *Educ:* Highgate Sch.; Royal Academy of Music; Univ. of Berlin. ARAM 1922; Carnegie Award 1924; FRAM 1938; BMus London, 1940; DMus London, 1968. Arts Council Opera Award, 1951; Händel Prize, City Council of Halle (Saale), 1962; Corresp. Member, Deutsche Akademie der Künste, 1955. FRSA 1966. Hon. DMus Dunelm, 1970. Appeared as piano-recitalist, London, Berlin, etc., 1927–33; played solo part in own Piano Concerto, BBC, 1938, with Sir Adrian Boult conducting. Toured Ceylon, India, Australia as Examiner for Assoc. Board of Royal Schools of Music, London, 1932–33; concert tours as orchestral conductor, introducing British Music and own compositions, to USSR, 1938, 1939, 1963, 1967, 1969, 1973, Czechoslovakia, Yugoslavia, Poland, Bulgaria, 1947, Czechoslovakia and Bulgaria again, 1949, Holland, 1950, Vienna, 1951, Berlin (German Democratic Republic) and Hungary, 1952, and Berlin again, 1958; Première of opera "Wat Tyler" at the Leipzig Opera House, 1953 (British première, 1974); Première of opera "Men of Blackmoor" at the German National Theatre, Weimar, 1956; Première of opera "The Sugar Reapers" at the Leipzig Opera House, 1966; Première of opera "Joe Hill (The Man Who Never Died)", German State Opera, Berlin, 1970. Musical Adviser, London Labour Choral Union, 1929–40; Chairman Workers' Music Assoc., 1936–41 (President 1941–). Chairman Composers' Guild of Great Britain, 1947–48. *Publications:* In My Eighth Decade and Other Essays, 1980; *operas:* Wat Tyler; Men of Blackmoor; The Sugar Reapers; Joe Hill (The Man Who Never Died); and children's operettas; *choral works:* The Winter Journey, Op. 29; Song of Friendship, Op. 34; The Ballad of Freedom's Soldier, Op. 44 (mixed voices); The Dream of Llewelyn ap Gruffydd, Op. 35 (male voices); The Alps and Andes of the Living World, Op. 66 (mixed chorus); Song for Angela Davis; Africa is my Name, Op. 85; Turkish Workers' Marching Song (chorus and piano), Op. 101; The Earth in Shadow (mixed chorus and orch.), Op. 102; Mandela Speaking (baritone, mixed chorus and orch.), Op. 110; Folksong arrangements; *song cycles:* Voices of the Prophets, for tenor and piano, Op. 41; Seafarers' Songs for baritone and piano, Op. 57; The Freight of Harvest, for tenor and piano, Op. 69; Life's Span, for mezzo-soprano and piano, Op. 77; Three Songs for baritone and piano, Op. 86; Woman's Life, for soprano and piano, Op. 87; Two Shakespeare Sonnets, Op. 91; *orchestral works:* Dance Overture, Op. 12; Piano Concerto, Op. 18; Symphony No 1 in C, Op. 21; Overture "Resolution", Op. 25; English Suite for strings, Op. 28; Piers Plowman's Day Suite, Op. 30; Violin Concerto, Op. 32; Symphony No 2 "The Nottingham", op. 33; Concert Suite for 'cello and orchestra, Op. 37; Dorian Passacaglia and Fugue, Op. 52; Symphony No 3 "The Byron Symphony", op. 53; Variations, Nocturne and Finale on an English Sea Song for piano and orchestra, Op. 60; Partita Concertante, Op. 63; Time Remembered for Chamber Orchestra, Op. 67; Scherzo for Wind Orchestra with Percussion, Op. 68; Africa: Symphonic Movement for piano and orchestra, Op. 73; Concert Overture for an Occasion, Op. 74; The Liverpool Overture, Op. 76; Lascaux Symphony, Op. 98; Meditation in Memory of Anna Ambrose, Op. 107; *chamber music:* String Quartet, Op. 4; Piano Quartet, Op. 5; Five Pieces for Violin, Viola, Cello, Clarinet and Horn, Op. 6; Dialectic for string quartet, Op. 15; Three Concert Studies for piano trio, Op. 31; Suite for Two Pianos, Op. 65; Serenade for String Quartet, Op. 70; Suite of six for String Quartet, Op. 81; Compass Points, Suite for Pipes, Op. 83; Trio for clarinet, cello and piano, Op. 91; Concertino for two violins and piano, Op. 94; Piano Quintet, Op. 104; Octet for flute, clarinet, horn, string quartet and piano, Op. 105; Canzona for flute, clarinet, violin, cello and piano, Op. 106; *instrumental solos and duos:* Prelude and Fugue for piano, Op. 9; Relinquishment for piano, Op. 11; Concert Piece for 'cello and piano, Op. 17; Meditation on a German song of 1848 for violin and String Orchestra or piano, Op. 22; Lyric Interlude for violin and piano, Op. 26; Le Quatorze Juillet for piano, Op. 38; Trent's Broad Reaches for horn and piano, Op. 36; Three English Song Preludes for organ, Op. 40; Northumbrian Impressions for oboe and piano, Op. 42a; Autumn Poem for horn and piano, Op. 45; Two Ballads of the Sea for piano, Op. 50; Two Melodies for viola with piano accompaniment, Op. 47; Suite for harpsichord or piano, Op. 54; Three African Sketches for flute with piano accompaniment, Op. 55; Two Occasional Pieces for organ, Op. 56; For a Festal Occasion for organ, Op. 58A; Prelude, Air and Dance for violin with accompaniment for string quartet and percussion, Op. 61; Two Dances for Cimbalom, Op. 64; Pianoforte Sonata in A flat, Op. 71; Corentyne Kwe-Kwe for piano, Op. 75; Sonatina for recorders and piano, Op. 82; Twenty-four Preludes for Piano, Op. 84; Sonatina for viola and piano, Op. 88; Rhapsody for cello and piano, Op. 89; Meditation and Scherzo for double-bass and piano, Op. 93; Scots Jigganspiel for piano, Op. 95; Six Short Pieces for piano, Op. 99; Summer Fields and Hedgerows, Two Impressions for clarinet and piano, Op.100; Distant Fields, Op. 109; *Textbook:* Strict Counterpoint in Palestrina Style; *essays:* In My Eighth Decade and other essays, 1980. *Recreations:* walking, foreign travel. *Address:* 25 Christchurch Crescent, Radlett, Herts. *T:* Radlett 6422.

BUSH, Hon. Sir Brian Drex, Kt 1976; **Hon. Mr Justice Bush;** a Judge of the High Court, Family Division, since 1976; *b* 5 Sept. 1925; *s* of William Harry Bush; *m* 1954, Beatrice Marian Lukeman; one *s* one *d. Educ:* King Edward's Sch., Birmingham; Birmingham Univ. (LLB). Served, RNVR, 1943–46. Called to the Bar, Gray's Inn, 1947, Bencher, 1976. Dep. Chm., Derbyshire Quarter Sessions, 1966–71; a Circuit Judge, 1969–76; Presiding Judge, Midland and Oxford Circuit, 1982–85. Chm., Industrial Tribunal, 1967–69; Member: Parole Bd, 1971–74; W Midlands Probation and After Care Cttee, 1975–77. *Recreations:* sailing, golf. *Address:* Royal Courts of Justice, Strand, WC2. *Clubs:* Royal Naval Sailing Association, Bar Yacht.

BUSH, Bryan; His Honour Judge Bush; a Circuit Judge, since 1983; *b* 28 Nov. 1936; *s* of Maurice and Hetty Bush; *m* 1963, Jacqueline (*née* Rayman); two *s* one *d. Educ:* Leeds Grammar Sch.; Keble Coll., Oxford (MA). Called to the Bar, Gray's Inn, 1961; practising on NE Circuit, 1961–83; a Recorder of the Crown Court, 1978–83. *Recreations:* theatre, lawn tennis. *Address:* c/o Leeds Crown Court, Leeds LS1 3BE.

BUSH, George Herbert Walker; Vice-President of the United States of America, since 1981; *b* Milton, Mass, 12 June 1924; *s* of late Prescott Sheldon Bush and of Dorothy (*née* Walker); *m* 1945, Barbara, *d* of Marvin Pierce, NY; four *s* one *d. Educ:* Phillips Acad., Andover, Mass; Yale Univ. (BA Econs 1948). Served War, USNR, Lieut, pilot (DFC, three Air Medals). Co-founder and Dir, Zapata Petroleum Corp., 1953–59; Founder, Zapata Offshore Co., Houston, 1954, Pres., 1956–64, Chm. Bd, 1964–66. Chm., Republican Party, Harris Co., Texas, 1963–64; Delegate, Republican Nat. Convention,

1964, 1968; Republican cand. US Senator from Texas, 1964, 1970; Mem., 90th and 91st Congresses, 7th District of Texas, 1967–70; US Perm. Rep. to UN, 1971–73; Chm., Republican Party Nat. Cttee, 1973–74; Chief, US Liaison Office, Peking, 1974–75; Dir, US Central Intelligence Agency, 1976–77. Cand. for Republican Presidential nomination, 1980. State Chm., Heart Fund. Hon. degrees from many colleges and univs incl. Beaver Coll., Adelphi Univ., Austin Coll., N Michigan Univ. *Recreation:* tennis. *Address:* The Vice-President's House, Washington, DC 20501, USA.

BUSH, Prof. Ian (Elcock), MA; PhD; MB, BChir; Research Professor of Psychiatry and Physiology, Dartmouth Medical School, USA, since 1977 (Senior Research Associate, 1974–77); Associate Chief of Staff, Research and Development, Veterans' Administration Hospital, White River Junction, Vermont, since 1977; *b* 25 May 1928; *s* of late Dr Gilbert B. Bush and of Jean Margaret Bush; *m* 1st, 1951, Alison Mary Pickard (marr. diss., 1966); one *s* two *d*; 2nd, 1967, Joan Morthland (marr. diss. 1972); one *s* one *d*; 3rd, 1982, Mary Calder Johnson. *Educ:* Bryanston Sch.; Pembroke Coll., Cambridge BA 1949. Natural Sciences Tripos, 1st class I and II; MA, PhD 1953; MB, BChir. 1957. Medical Research Council Scholar (Physiology Lab. Cambridge); National Institute for Medical Research), 1949–52; Commonwealth Fellow 1952 (University of Utah; Mass. General Hospital); Part-time Research Asst, Med. Unit, St Mary's Hosp. London and med. student, 1953–56; Grad. Asst, Dept Regius Prof. of Med., Oxford, 1956–59; Mem. ext. Scientific Staff, Med. Research Council (Oxford), 1959–61. Hon. Dir Med. Research Council Unit for research in chem. pathology of mental disorders, 1960; Bowman Prof. of Physiology and Dir of Dept of Physiology, Univ. of Birmingham, 1960–64; Senior Scientist, The Worcester Foundation for Experimental Biology, 1964–67; Chm. of Dept and Prof. of Physiology, Medical Coll. of Virginia, 1967–70; Pres. and Dir of Laboratories, Cybertek Inc., New York, 1970–72, and Prof. of Physiology, New York Univ. Med. Sch., 1970–77. Fellow, Amer. Acad. of Arts and Sciences, 1966. *Publications:* Chromatography of Steroids, 1961; The Siberian Reservoir, 1983; contribs to: Jl Physiol.; Biochem. Jl; Jl Endocrinol.; Nature; The Analyst; Jl Biolog. Chem.; Brit. Med. Bulletin; Acta Endocrinologica; Experientia; Biochem. Soc. Symposia, etc. *Recreations:* music, chess, sailing, fishing, philosophy. *Address:* c/o Dartmouth Medical School, Hanover, NH 03755, USA.

BUSH, Adm. Sir John (Fitzroy Duyland), GCB 1970 (KCB 1965; CB 1963); DSC 1941, and Bars, 1941, 1944; Vice-Admiral of the United Kingdom and Lieutenant of the Admiralty, 1979–84; *b* 1 Nov. 1914; *s* of late Fitzroy Bush, Beach, Glos; *m* 1938, Ruth Kennedy Horsey; three *s* two *d. Educ:* Clifton Coll. Entered Navy, 1933; served in Destroyers throughout War. Commanded HM Ships: Belvoir, 1942–44; Zephyr, 1944; Chevron, 1945–46. Comdr Dec. 1946; Plans Div., Admiralty, 1946–48; graduated Armed Forces Staff Coll., USA, 1949; Comd, HMS Cadiz, 1950–51; Capt. June 1952; Dep. Sec. Chiefs of Staff Cttee, 1953–55; Capt. (F) Sixth Frigate Sqdn, 1955–56; Cdre, RN Barracks, Chatham, 1957–59; Dir. of Plans, Admiralty, 1959–60; Rear-Adm. 1961; Flag Officer Flotillas (Mediterranean), 1961–62; Vice-Adm. 1963; Comdr, British Naval Staff and Naval Attaché, Washington, 1963–65; Vice-Chief of the Naval Staff, Ministry of Defence, 1965–67; C-in-C Western Fleet, C-in-C Eastern Atlantic, and C-in-C Channel (NATO), 1967–70; Admiral 1968; retd, 1970. Rear-Admiral of the UK, 1976–79. Dir, Gordon A. Friesen International Inc., Washington, DC, 1970–73. Adm., Texas (USA) Navy. Governor, Clifton Coll., 1973– (Chm. Council, 1978–81; Pres., 1982–). Pres., Old Cliftonians Soc., 1967–69. Mem., E Hants District Council, 1974–76. *Recreations:* fishing, gardening. *Address:* Becksteddle House, Colemore, near Alton, Hants. *T:* Tisted 367.

BUSH, Maj.-Gen. Peter John, OBE 1968; Controller, Army Benevolent Fund, since 1980; *b* 31 May 1924; *s* of Clement Charles Victor Bush and Kathleen Mabel Peirce; *m* 1948, Jean Mary Hamilton; two *s* one *d. Educ:* Maidenhead County Sch. Commnd Somerset LI, 1944; comd LI Volunteers, 1966; GSO 1 HQ 14 Div./Malaya Dist, 1968; Comdr 3 Inf. Bde, 1971 (mentioned in despatches, 1973); Asst Comdt RMA Sandhurst, 1974; Chief of Staff and Head of UK Delegn to Live Oak, SHAPE, 1977–79, retd. Col, The Light Infantry, 1977–82. *Recreations:* natural history, walking, reading. *Address:* c/o Barclays Bank, High Street, Maidenhead, Berks.

BUSHBY, Frederick Henry; Director of Services, Meteorological Office, 1978–84; *b* 10 Jan. 1924; *s* of Mr and Mrs Frederick George Bushby; *m* 1945, Joan Janet (*née* Gates); one *s. Educ:* Portsmouth Southern Secondary Sch.; Imperial Coll. of Science and Technol. (BSc 1st Cl. Hons Special Maths). ARCS. Meteorol Br., RAF, 1944–48; Meteorol Office, 1948–84; Asst Dir (Forecasting Res.), 1965–74; Dep. Dir (Dynamical Res.), 1974–77, (Forecasting), 1977–78. *Recreations:* bridge, bowls. *Address:* 25 Holmes Crescent, Wokingham, Berks RG11 2SE. *T:* Wokingham 784930.

BUSHELL, John Christopher Wyndowe, CMG 1971; HM Diplomatic Service, retired; Ambassador to Pakistan, 1976–79; *b* 27 Sept. 1919; *s* of late Colonel C. W. Bushell, RE, and Mrs Bushell, Netherbury, Dorset; *m* 1964, Mrs Theodora Todd, *d* of late Mr and Mrs Senior; one *s* (and one step *s* one step *d). Educ:* Winchester; Clare Coll., Cambridge. Served War of 1939–45, RAF. Entered FO, 1945; served in Moscow, Rome, FO; 1st Sec., 1950; NATO Defence Coll., Paris, 1953–54; Deputy Sec.-Gen., CENTO, 1957–59; Counsellor, 1961; Political Adviser to the Commander-in-Chief, Middle East, 1961–64; UK Delegn to NATO, Brussels, 1964–68; seconded to Cabinet Office, 1968–70; Minister and Deputy Commandant, British Mil. Govt, Berlin, 1970–74; Ambassador to Saigon, 1974–75; FCO 1975–76. *Recreations:* varied. *Address:* 19 Bradbourne Street, SW6. *Club:* Travellers'.

BUSHNELL, Alexander Lynn, CBE 1962; County Clerk and Treasurer, Perth County Council, 1946–75, retired; *b* 13 Aug. 1911; *s* of William and Margaret Bushnell; *m* 1939, Janet Braithwaite Porteous; two *d. Educ:* Dalziel High Sch., Motherwell; Glasgow University. *Recreation:* golf. *Address:* 18 Fairies Road, Perth, Scotland. *T:* Perth 22675. *Club:* Royal Perth Golfing Society.

BUSK, Sir Douglas Laird, KCMG 1959 (CMG 1948); *b* 15 July 1906; *s* of late John Laird Busk, Westerham, Kent, and late Eleanor Joy; *m* 1937, Bridget Anne Moyra, *d* of late Brig.-Gen. W. G. Hemsley Thompson, CMG, DSO, Warminster, Wilts; two *d. Educ:* Eton; New Coll., Oxford; Princeton Univ., USA (Davison Scholar). Joined Diplomatic Service, 1929; served in Foreign Office and Tehran, Budapest, Union of S Africa (seconded to United Kingdom High Commission), Tokyo, Ankara, Baghdad; Ambassador to Ethiopia, 1952–56; to Finland, 1958–60; to Venezuela, 1961–64. *Publications:* The Delectable Mountains, 1946; The Fountain of the Sun, 1957; The Curse of Tongues, 1965; The Craft of Diplomacy, 1967; Portrait d'un guide, 1975. *Recreations:* mountaineering and ski-ing. *Address:* Broxton House, Chilbolton, near Stockbridge, Hants. *T:* Chilbolton 272. *Clubs:* Alpine, Lansdowne.

BUSS, Barbara Ann, (Mrs Lewis Boxall); freelance journalist, since 1976; Editor-in-Chief, Woman magazine, 1974–75; Consultant, IPC Magazines Ltd, 1975–76; *b* 14 Aug. 1932; *d* of late Cecil Edward Buss and Victoria Lilian (*née* Vickers); *m* 1966, Lewis Albert Boxall (*d* 1983); no *c. Educ:* Lady Margaret Sch., London. Sec., Conservative Central Office, 1949–52; Sec./journalist, Good Taste magazine, 1952–56; Journalist: Woman and Beauty, 1956–57; Woman, 1957–59; Asst Editor, Woman's Illustrated, 1959–60; Editor, Woman's Illustrated, 1960–61; Journalist, Daily Herald, 1961; Associate Editor, Woman's

Realm, 1961–62; Editor: Woman's Realm, 1962–64; Woman, 1964–74. *Recreations:* reading, theatre, cinema. *Address:* 1 Arlington Avenue, N1. *T:* 01–226 3265.

BUSVINE, Prof. James Ronald; Professor of Entomology as applied to Hygiene in the University of London, 1964–76, Emeritus Professor 1977; *b* 15 April 1912; *s* of William Robert and Pleasance Dorothy Busvine; *m* 1960, Joan Arnfield; one *s* one *d. Educ:* Eastbourne Coll.; Imperial Coll. of Science and Technology, London Univ. BSc Special (1st Class Hons) 1933; PhD 1938; DSc 1948, London. Imperial Chemical Industries, 1936–39; MRC Grants, 1940–42; Entomological Adviser, Min. of Health, 1943–45; London Sch. of Hygiene and Tropical Medicine: Lecturer 1946; Reader 1954; Professor 1964. Member: WHO Panel of Experts on Insecticides, 1956– (Cttee Chm. 1959 and 1968); FAO Panel of Experts on Pest Resistance, 1967– (Cttee Rapporteur). Has travelled professionally in Malaya, Ceylon, Africa, USA, India, etc. *Publications:* Insects and Hygiene, 1951 (3rd edn 1980); A Critical Review of the Techniques for Testing Insecticides, 1957, 2nd edn 1971; Anthropod Vectors of Disease, 1975; Insects, Hygiene and History, 1976; numerous scientific articles. *Recreations:* painting, golf. *Address:* Musca, 26 Braywick Road, Maidenhead, Berks. *T:* Maidenhead 22888.

BUTCHER, Anthony John; QC 1977; a Recorder, since 1985; *b* 6 April 1934; *s* of F. W. Butcher and O. M. Butcher (*née* Ansell); *m* 1959, Maureen Workman (*d* 1982); one *s* two *d. Educ:* Cranleigh Sch.; Sidney Sussex Coll., Cambridge (MA, LLB). Called to the Bar, Gray's Inn, 1957; in practice at English Bar, 1957–. Chm., Official Referees Bar Assoc. *Recreations:* enjoying the Arts and acquiring useless information. *Address:* Anthony Cottage, Polecat Valley, Hindhead, Surrey. *T:* Hindhead 4155; 22 Old Buildings, Lincoln's Inn, WC2A 3UJ. *T:* 01–405 2072. *Club:* Garrick.

BUTCHER, John Patrick; MP (C) Coventry South West, since 1979; Parliamentary Under Secretary of State, Department of Trade and Industry, since 1983 (Department of Industry, 1982–83). *Educ:* Huntingdon Grammar Sch.; Birmingham Univ. (BSocSc). Marketing exec. and Product Manager, computer industry, 1968–79. Mem., Birmingham City Council, 1972–78 (Vice-Chm., Educn Cttee). *Address:* c/o House of Commons, SW1A 0AA.

BUTCHER, Richard James; Under Secretary (Legal), Department of Health and Social Security, 1983–86, retired; *b* 5 Dec. 1926; *s* of late James Butcher, MBE and Kathleen Butcher; *m* 1954, Sheila Joan Windridge; one *s* two *d. Educ:* City of London Sch.; Peterhouse, Cambridge (BA 1948, MA 1961). Called to the Bar, Lincoln's Inn, 1950. Served Educn Br., RAF, 1948–50 (Flying Officer). Entered Legal Civil Service as Legal Asst, 1951; Sen. Legal Asst, 1960; Asst Solicitor, 1971. *Recreation:* gardening. *Address:* The Knoll, Park View Road, Woldingham, Surrey CR3 7DN. *T:*Woldingham 2275.

BUTCHER, Willard Carlisle; Chairman and Chief Executive, Chase Manhattan Bank (formerly Chase National Bank), New York City, since 1981; *b* Bronxville, NY, 25 Oct. 1926; *s* of Willard F. Butcher and Helen Calhoun; *m* 1st, 1949, Sarah C. Payne (*d* 1955); two *d*; 2nd, 1956, Elizabeth Allen (*d* 1978); one *s* one *d*; 3rd, 1979, Carole E. McMahon; one *s. Educ:* Scarsdale High School, New York; Middlebury Coll., Vermont; Brown Univ., Rhode Island (BA). Served with USNR, 1944–45. Joined Chase National Bank, 1947; Asst Vice-Pres., 1956; Vice-Pres., 1958; Sen. Vice-Pres., 1961; assigned Internat. Dept, 1968; Exec. Vice-Pres. in charge of Dept, 1969; Vice-Chm. 1972; Pres. 1972–81; Chief Exec. Officer, 1979. *Address:* 1 Chase Manhattan Plaza, New York City, NY 10081, USA.

BUTE, 6th Marquess of, *cr* 1796; **John Crichton-Stuart,** JP; Viscount Ayr, 1622; Bt 1627; Earl of Dumfries, Lord Crichton of Sanquhar and Cumnock, 1633; Earl of Bute, Viscount Kingarth, Lord Mountstuart, Cumrae, and Inchmarnock, 1703; Baron Mountstuart, 1761; Baron Cardiff, 1776; Earl of Windsor; Viscount Mountjoy, 1796; Hereditary Sheriff of Bute; Hereditary Keeper of Rothesay Castle; Lieutenant (RARO) Scots Guards, 1953; *b* 27 Feb. 1933; *er s* (twin) of 5th Marquess of Bute and of Eileen, Marchioness of Bute, *yr d* of 8th Earl of Granard; *S* father, 1956; *m* 1st, 1955, Nicola (marr. diss. 1977), *o d* of late Lt-Comdr W. B. C. Weld-Forester, CBE; two *s* one *d* (and one *d* decd); 2nd, 1978, Mrs Jennifer Percy. *Educ:* Ampleforth Coll.; Trinity Coll., Cambridge. Pres., Scottish Standing Cttee for Voluntary Internat. Aid, 1968–75 (Chm., 1964–68); Chairman: Council and Exec. Cttee, National Trust for Scotland, 1969–84 (Vice-Pres., 1984–); Scottish Cttee, National Fund for Res. into Crippling Diseases, 1966–; Historic Bldgs Council for Scotland, 1983–; Museums Adv. Bd (Scotland), 1984–85; Member: Countryside Commission for Scotland, 1970–78; Design Council, Scottish Cttee, 1972–76; Development Commission, 1973–78; Oil Develt Council for Scotland, 1973–78. Trustee, Nat. Galleries of Scotland, 1980–87; Chm. Trustees, Nat. Museums of Scotland, 1985–86. Hon. Sheriff-Substitute, County of Bute, 1976. Fellow, Inst. of Marketing, 1967; Hon. FIStructE, 1976; Hon. FRIAS, 1985. Pres., Scottish Veterans' Garden City Assoc. (Inc.), 1971–. Buteshire CC, 1956–75; Convener, 1967–70; DL Bute, 1961, Lord Lieutenant, 1967–75; JP Bute 1967. Hon. LLD Glasgow, 1970. *Heir: s* Earl of Dumfries, *qv. Address:* Mount Stuart, Rothesay, Isle of Bute PA20 9LR. *T:* Rothesay 2730. *Clubs:* Turf, White's; New, Puffin's (Edinburgh); Cardiff and County (Cardiff).

BUTEMENT, William Alan Stewart, CBE 1959 (OBE 1945); DSc (Adel.); retired as Chief Scientist, Department of Supply, Australia, 1967; *b* Masterton, NZ, 18 Aug. 1904; *s* of William Butement, Physician and Surgeon, Otago, and Amy Louise Stewart; *m* 1933, Ursula Florence Alberta Parish; two *d. Educ:* Scots Coll., Sydney; University Coll. Sch., Hampstead, London; University Coll., London Univ. (BSc). Scientific Officer at Signals Exptl Estabt, War Office Outstation, Woolwich (now SRDE, Christchurch, Hants), 1928–38; Senior Scientific Officer Bawdsey Research Stn, War Office Outstation; later, under Min. of Supply, Radar Research, 1938–39 (Station moved to Christchurch, Hants, 1939; now RRE, Malvern); Prin. Scientific Officer, Sen. Prin. Scientific Officer, Asst Dir of Scientific Research, Min. of Supply, HQ London, 1940–46; Dep. Chief Scientific Officer of party to Australia under Lt-Gen. Sir John Evetts to set up Rocket Range, 1947; First Chief Supt of Long Range Weapons Estabt (now Weapons Research Establishment), of which Woomera Range is a part, 1947–49; Chief Scientist, Dept of Supply, in exec. charge Australian Defence Scientific R&D, incl. Rocket Range at Woomera, 1949–67. Dir, Plessey Pacific, 1967–81. FIEE, CEng, FInstP, FAIP, FIREE (Aust.), FTS. *Publications:* Precision Radar, Journal IEE, and other papers in scientific journals. *Address:* 5a Barry Street, Kew, Victoria 3101, Australia. *T:* 861 8375.

BUTENANDT, Prof. Adolf; Dr phil.; Dr med. hc; Dr med. vet. hc; Dr rer. nat. hc; Dr phil. hc; Dr sci. hc; Dr ing. eh; President, Max Planck Society, 1960–72, Hon. President since 1972; Director, Max Planck Institute for Biochemistry, München (formerly Kaiser Wilhelm Institute for Biochemistry, Berlin-Dahlem), 1936–72; Professor Ord. of Physiological Chemistry, München, 1956–71; Nobel Prize for Chemistry, 1939; *b* Bremerhaven-Lehe, 24 March 1903; *m* 1931, Erika von Ziegner; two *s* five *d. Educ:* Universities of Marburg and Göttingen. Privatdozent, Univ. of Göttingen, 1931; Prof. Ord. of Organic Chemistry, Technische Hochschule, Danzig, 1933; Honorarprofessor, Univ. Berlin, 1938; Prof. Ord. of Physiological Chemistry, Tübingen, 1945. Foreign Member: Royal Society, 1968; Académie des Sciences, Paris, 1974. *Publications:* numerous contribs to Hoppe-Seyler, Liebigs Annalen, Berichte der deutschen chemischen Gesellschaft, Zeitschrift für Naturforschung, etc. *Address:* München 60, Marsop Str. 5, Germany. *T:* (089) 885490.

BUTLER, family name of **Earl of Carrick,** of **Baron Dunboyne,** of **Earl of Lanesborough,** of **Viscount Mountgarret,** and of **Marquess of Ormonde.**

BUTLER, Rt. Hon. Sir Adam (Courtauld), Kt 1986; PC 1984; MP (C) Bosworth since 1970; *b* 11 Oct. 1931; *s* of late Baron Butler of Saffron Walden, KG, CH, PC and late Sydney, *o c* of late Samuel Courtauld; *m* 1955, Felicity Molesworth-St Aubyn; two *s* one *d. Educ:* Eton; Pembroke College, Cambridge. National Service, 2nd Lieut KRRC, 1949–51. Cambridge (BA History/Economics), 1951–54. ADC to Governor-General of Canada, 1954–55; Courtaulds Ltd, 1955–73; Director: Aristoc Ltd, 1966–73; Kayser Bondor Ltd, 1971–73; Capital and Counties Property Co., 1973–79. PPS to: Minister of State for Foreign Affairs, 1971–72; Minister of Agriculture, Fisheries and Food, 1972–74; PPS to Leader of the Opposition, 1975–79; an Asst Govt Whip, 1974; an Opposition Whip, 1974–75; Minister of State: DoI, 1979–81; NI Office, 1981–84; Defence Procurement, 1984–85. Mem. NFU. Liveryman of Goldsmiths' Co. FRSA. *Recreations:* field sports, music, pictures. *Address:* The Old Rectory, Lighthorne, near Warwick. *T:* Leamington Spa 651214.

See also Hon. Sir R. C. Butler.

BUTLER, Allan Geoffrey Roy; HM Diplomatic Service; Ambassador to Mongolian People's Republic, since 1984; *b* 25 Aug. 1933; *s* of Frederick William Butler and Florence May Butler; *m* 1965, Pauline Rosalind Birch, SRN; three *d. Educ:* Chatham House School, Ramsgate. RAF, 1952–54. Colonial Office, 1954–66; served in Aden and Washington; Asst Private Sec. to Colonial Sec., 1965–66; transf. to HM Diplomatic Service, 1966; Birmingham University language training, 1966; Consul, Athens, 1967; First Sec., Athens, 1969, Georgetown, 1972, FCO, 1975; Head of Chancery, Dakar, 1977; Nat. Defence Coll., Latimer, 1981; Head of Parly Unit, FCO, 1981. *Recreations:* walking, listening to music. *Address:* c/o Foreign and Commonwealth Office, SW1A 2AH.

BUTLER, Rt. Rev. Arthur Hamilton, MBE 1944; DD; MA; *b* 8 March 1912; *s* of George Booker and Anne Maude Butler; *m* 1938, Betty (*d* 1976), *d* of Seton Pringle, FRCSI; one *s*; *m* 1979, Dr Elizabeth Mayne. *Educ:* Friars School, Bangor; Trinity Coll., Dublin. Curate: Monkstown, Dublin, 1935–37; Christ Church, Crouch End, N8, 1937; Holy Trinity, Brompton, SW3, 1938–39. Army, 1939–45: Chaplain, 2nd DCLI, 1939–43; Senior Chaplain, 1st Div., 1943–45. Incumbent of Monkstown, 1945–58; Bishop of Tuam, Killala and Achonry, 1958–69; Bishop of Connor, 1969–81. *Recreation:* golf. *Address:* 1 Spa Grange, Ballynahinch, Co. Down BT24 8PD. *T:* Ballynahinch 562966. *Club:* Ulster (Belfast).

BUTLER, Mrs Audrey Maude Beman, MA; Headmistress, Queenswood (GSA), Hatfield, Herts, since 1981; *b* 31 May 1936; *d* of Robert Beman Minchin and Vivien Florence Fraser Scott; *m* 1959, Anthony Michael Butler (marr. diss. 1981); two *d. Educ:* Queenswood, Hatfield; St Andrews Univ., Scotland (1st Cl. MA Hons, Geography and Polit. Economy; Scottish Univs Medal, RSGS, 1957–58). Asst Geography Teacher, Queenswood, 1958–59; part-time teacher, Raines Foundn Sch. for Girls, Stepney, 1959–61; Head of Geography, S Michael's, Burton Park, 1970–73, VI Form Tutor/Geography asst, 1974–78; first House Mistress of Manor House, Lancing Coll., 1978–81. Hon. Vice-Pres., Sussex County Ladies Golf Assoc., 1981–83. FRGS; Mem. Geographical Assoc.; MInstD 1986. *Recreations:* tennis and hockey (Blues, St Andrews Univ., 1956–57); golf (Sussex County Colours, 1970). *Address:* Queenswood, Shepherd's Way, Brookmans Park, Hatfield, Herts AL9 6NS. *T:* Potters Bar 52262.

BUTLER, Basil Richard Ryland, OBE 1976; FEng; FIMM; Managing Director, British Petroleum Co. PLC, since 1986; *b* 1 March 1930; *s* of Hugh Montagu Butler and Annie Isabelle (*née* Wiltshire); *m* 1954, Lilian Joyce Haswell; one *s* two *d. Educ:* Denstone Coll., Staffs; St John's Coll., Cambridge (MA). Reservoir Engr, Trinidad Leaseholds Ltd, 1954; Petroleum Engr to Chief Petroleum Engr and Supt Prodn Planning Div., Kuwait Oil Co., 1958–68; transf. to BP, Operations Man., Colombia, 1968; Ops Man., BP Alaska Inc., Anchorage, 1970; seconded to Kuwait Oil Co. as Gen. Man. Ops, 1972; Manager: Ninian Develts, BP Petroleum Development Co. Ltd, London, 1975; Sullom Voe Terminal, Shetland Is, 1976; BP Petroleum Development Ltd: Gen. Man., Exploration and Prodn, Aberdeen, 1978; Chief Exec., London, 1980; Dir, BP Internat. Ltd, and Man. Dir and Chief Exec., BP Exploration Co. Ltd, 1981. *Recreations:* sailing, music. *Address:* British Petroleum Co., Britannic House, Moor Lane, EC2Y 9BU. *T:* 01–920 6165.

BUTLER, (Christopher) David; Under Secretary, HM Treasury, since 1985; *b* 27 May 1942; *s* of Major B. D. Butler, MC (killed in action, 1944) and H. W. Butler (*née* Briggs); *m* 1967, Helen Christine, *d* of J. J. Cornwell and G. Cornwell (*née* Veysey); two *d. Educ:* Christ's Hospital; Jesus College, Oxford (MA). Joined HM Treasury, 1964; Asst Private Sec. to Chancellor of Exchequer, 1967–69; Sec., Cttee to Review Nat. Savings (Page Cttee), 1970–72; Head of public expenditure divs, HM Treasury, 1978–82; Head of corporate planning div., CCTA, 1982–85; HM Treasury: Head of running costs, manpower and superannuation group, 1985–; Principal Estabt and Finance Officer, 1986–. *Recreations:* ballet, opera, running, reading. *Address:* c/o HM Treasury, Parliament Street, SW1.

BUTLER, Sir Clifford (Charles), Kt 1983; FRS 1961; BSc, PhD; Vice-Chancellor of Loughborough University of Technology, 1975–85; *b* 20 May 1922; *s* of C. H. J. and O. Butler, Earley, Reading; *m* 1947, Kathleen Betty Collins; two *d. Educ:* Reading Sch.; Reading Univ. BSc 1942, PhD 1946, Reading. Demonstrator in Physics, Reading Univ., 1942–45; Asst Lecturer in Physics, Manchester Univ., 1945–47, Lecturer in Physics, 1947–53; Imperial College of Science and Technology, London: Reader in Physics, 1953–57; Professor of Physics, 1957–63; Asst Dir, Physics Dept, 1955–62; Prof. of Physics and Head of Physics Dept, 1963–70; Dean, Royal Coll. of Science, 1966–69; Dir, Nuffield Foundn, 1970–75. Charles Vernon Boys Prizeman, London Physical Soc., 1956. Member: Academic Planning Board, Univ. of Kent, 1963–71; Schools Council, 1965–84; Nuclear Physics Board of SRC, 1965–68; University Grants Cttee, 1966–71; Council, Charing Cross Hosp. Med. Sch., 1970–73; Council, Open Univ., 1971–85; Science Adv. Cttee, British Council, 1980–85; Chairman: Standing Education Cttee, Royal Society, 1970–80; Council for the Educn and Training of Health Visitors, 1977–83; Adv. Council for Supply and Educn of Teachers, 1980–85; Steering Cttee, DES Educnl Counselling and Credit Transfer Information Service Project, 1983–; ABRC/NERC Study Gp into Geol Surveying, 1985–. Pres., Internat. Union of Pure and Applied Physics, 1975–78 (Sec.-Gen., 1963–72; first Vice-Pres., 1972–75). Hon. DSc Reading, 1976; DUniv Open, 1986. *Publications:* scientific papers on electron diffraction, cosmic rays and elementary particle physics in Proc. Royal Society and Physical Society, Philosophical Magazine, Nature, and Journal of Scientific Instruments, etc. *Address:* Low Woods Farm House, Belton, near Loughborough, Leics LE12 9TR. *T:* Coalville 223125. *Club:* Athenæum.

BUTLER, Dr Colin Gasking, OBE 1970; FRS 1970; retired as Head of Entomology Department, Rothamsted Experimental Station, Harpenden, 1972–76 (Head of Bee Department, 1943–72); *b* 26 Oct. 1913; *s* of Rev. Walter Gasking Butler and Phyllis

Pearce; *m* 1937, Jean March Innes; one *s* one *d*. *Educ:* Monkton Combe Sch., Bath; Queens Coll., Cambridge. MA 1937, PhD 1938, Cantab. Min. of Agric. and Fisheries Research Schol., Cambridge, 1935–37; Supt Cambridge Univ. Entomological Field Stn, 1937–39; Asst Entomologist, Rothamsted Exper. Stn, 1939–43. Hon. Treas., Royal Entomological Soc., 1961–69, Pres., 1971–72, Hon. FRES, 1984; Pres., Internat. Union for Study of Social Insects, 1969–73; Mem., NT Regional Cttee for Devon and Cornwall, 1982–. FRPS 1957; FIBiol. Hon. Fellow, British Beekeepers' Assoc., 1983. Silver Medal, RSA, 1945. *Publications:* The Honeybee: an introduction to her sense physiology and behaviour, 1949; The World of the Honeybee, 1954; (with J. B. Free) Bumblebees, 1959; scientific papers. *Recreations:* nature photography, fishing, sailing. *Address:* Silver Birches, Porthpean, St Austell, Cornwall PL26 6AU. *T:* St Austell 72480.

BUTLER, David; *see* Butler, C. D.

BUTLER, David Edgeworth; Fellow of Nuffield College, Oxford, since 1954; *b* 1924; *yr s* of late Professor Harold Edgeworth Butler and Margaret, *d* of Prof. A. F. Pollard; *m* 1962, Marilyn Speers Evans (*see* M. S. Butler); three *s*. *Educ:* St Paul's; New Coll., Oxford (MA, DPhil). J. E. Procter Visiting Fellow, Princeton Univ., 1947–48; Student, Nuffield Coll., 1949–51; Research Fellow, 1951–54; Dean and Senior Tutor, 1956–64. Served as Personal Assistant to HM Ambassador in Washington, 1955–56. Hon. DUniv Paris, 1978; Hon. DSSc QUB, 1985. Co-editor, Electoral Studies, 1982–. *Publications:* The British General Election of 1951, 1952; The Electoral System in Britain 1918–51, 1953; The British General Election of 1955, 1955; The Study of Political Behaviour, 1958; (ed) Elections Abroad, 1959; (with R. Rose) The British General Election of 1959, 1960; (with J. Freeman) British Political Facts, 1900–1960, 1963; (with A. King) The British General Election of 1964, 1965; The British General Election of 1966, 1966; (with D. Stokes) Political Change in Britain, 1969; (with M. Pinto-Duschinsky) The British General Election of 1970, 1971; The Canberra Model, 1973; (with D. Kavanagh) The British General Election of February 1974, 1974; (with D. Kavanagh) The British General Election of October 1974, 1975; (with U. Kitzinger) The 1975 Referendum, 1976; (ed) Coalitions in British Politics, 1978; (ed with A. H. Halsey) Policy and Politics, 1978; (with A. Ranney), Referendums, 1978; (with A. Sloman) British Political Facts 1900–79, 1980; (with D. Kavanagh) The British General Election of 1979, 1980; (with D. Marquand) European Elections and British Politics, 1981; (with A. Ranney) Democracy at the Polls, 1981; (with V. Bogdanor) Democracy and Elections, 1983; Governing without a Majority, 1983; (with D. Kavanagh) The British General Election of 1983, 1984; A Compendium of Indian Elections, 1984; (with P. Jowett) Party Strategies in Britain, 1985; (with G. Butler) British Political Facts 1900–85, 1986. *Address:* Nuffield College, Oxford. *T:* Oxford 248014. *Club:* United Oxford & Cambridge University.

BUTLER, Denis William Langford; Comptroller and City Solicitor to the City of London, since 1981; *b* 26 Oct. 1926; *s* of late William H. Butler, Shrewsbury and Kitty Butler; *m* 1953, Marna (*née* Taylor); three *d*. *Educ:* Repton. Admitted Solicitor, 1951. Assistant Solicitor: Norfolk CC, 1953–54; Shropshire CC, 1954–57; Sen. Asst Solicitor, Lindsey (Lincs) CC, 1957–60; Dep. Clerk, 1960–74, County Solicitor and Clerk, 1974–81, Wilts CC. Chm., County Secs Soc., 1974–76. *Recreations:* travel, cinephotography, gardening. *Address:* 5 Stone House, 9 Weymouth Street, W1. *T:* 01–580 2707.

BUTLER, Edward Clive Barber, FRCS; Surgeon: The London Hospital, E1, 1937–69; Haroldwood Hospital, Essex, 1946–69; retired; *b* 8 April 1904; *s* of Dr Butler, Hereford; *m* 1939, Nancy Hamilton Harrison, Minneapolis, USA; two *s* one *d*. *Educ:* Shrewsbury Sch.; London Hospital. MRCS, LRCP 1928; MB, BS London, 1929; FRCS 1931. Resident posts London Hosp., 1928–32; Surgical Registrar, London Hosp., 1933–36; Surgeon, RMS Queen Mary, Cunard White Star Line, 1936. Hunterian Prof., RCS, 1939; examinerships at various times to London Univ. and Coll. of Surgeons. Pres. section of Proctology, Royal Soc. of Medicine, 1951–52; Member: Medical Soc. London; Royal Soc. Medicine. *Publications:* chapter on bacteraemia, in British Surgical Practice, 1948; on hand infections, in Penicillin (by Fleming), 1950; (jointly) on combined excision of rectum, in Treatment of Cancer and Allied Diseases (New York), 1952; articles on various surgical subjects in Lancet, BMJ, Proc. Royal Soc. Med., British Journal Surgery. *Recreations:* golf, gardening and yachting. *Address:* Flat 304, Enterprise House, Chingford, E4. *Club:* United Hospitals Sailing.

BUTLER, Air Vice-Marshal Eric Scott, CB 1957; OBE 1941; RAF; AOA HQ Fighter Command, 1957–61; *b* 4 Nov. 1907; *s* of Archibald Butler, Maze Hill, St Leonards-on-Sea, Sussex; *m* 1936, Alice Evelyn Tempest Meates (*d* 1985); three *s* one *d*. *Educ:* Belfast Academy. Commissioned RAF 1933; Bomber Command European War, 1939–45; idc 1952; Director of Organisation, Air Ministry, 1953–56. *Address:* Camden Cottage, High Street, Pevensey, Sussex BN24 5JP. *T:* Westham 353. *Club:* Royal Air Force.

BUTLER, Esmond Unwin, CVO 1972; Canadian Ambassador to Morocco, since 1985; Secretary-General, Order of Canada, since 1967 and Order of Military Merit, since 1972; *b* 13 July 1922; *s* of Rev. T. B. Butler and Alice Lorna Thompson; *m* 1960, Georgiana Mary North; one *s* one *d*. *Educ:* Weston Collegiate; Univs of Toronto and Geneva; Inst. Internat. Studies, Geneva. BA, Licence ès Sciences politiques. Journalist, United Press, Geneva, 1950–51; Asst Sec.-Gen., Internat. Union of Official Travel Organizations, Geneva, 1951–52; Information Officer, Dept of Trade and Commerce, Dept of Nat. Health and Welfare, 1953–54; Asst Sec. to Governor-Gen., 1955–58; Asst Press Sec. to Queen, London, 1958–59 and Royal Tour of Canada, 1959; Sec. to Governor-Gen., 1959–85. CStJ 1967. *Recreations:* fishing, shooting, collecting Canadiana, ski-ing. *Address:* Canadian Embassy, 13 bis rue Jaâfar-as-Sadik, Rabat-Agdal, Morocco. *T:* (office) 713–75, (residence) 521–02. *Clubs:* Zeta Psi Fraternity (Toronto); White Pine Fishing.

BUTLER, (Frederick Edward) Robin, CVO 1986; Second Permanent Secretary, Public Expenditure, HM Treasury, since 1985; *b* 3 Jan. 1938; *s* of Bernard Butler and Nora Butler; *m* 1962, Gillian Lois Galley; one *s* two *d*. *Educ:* Harrow Sch.; University Coll., Oxford (BA Lit. Hum., 1961). Joined HM Treasury, 1961; Private Sec. to Financial Sec. to Treasury, 1964–65; Sec., Budget Cttee, 1965–69; seconded to Cabinet Office as Mem., Central Policy Rev. Staff, 1971–72; Private Secretary: to Rt Hon. Edward Heath, 1972–74; to Rt Hon. Harold Wilson, 1974–75; returned to HM Treasury as Asst Sec. i/c Gen. Expenditure Intell. Div., 1975; Under Sec., Gen. Expenditure Policy Gp, 1977–80; Prin. Establishments Officer, 1980–82; Principal Private Sec. to Prime Minister, 1982–85. Governor, Harrow Sch., 1975–. *Recreation:* competitive games. *Address:* HM Treasury, Parliament Street, SW1. *Club:* Anglo-Belgian.

BUTLER, George, RWS 1958; RBA; NEAC; painter, principally in water-colour, in England and Provence; *b* 17 Oct. 1904; *s* of John George Butler; *m* 1933, Kcenia Kotliarevskaya; one *s* one *d*. *Educ:* King Edward VII School, Sheffield; Central School of Art. Director and Head of Art Dept, J. Walter Thompson Co. Ltd, 1933–60. Hon. Treas., Artists General Benevolent Institution, 1957–77. Mem., Société des Artistes Indépendants Aixois. *Address:* Riversdale, Castle Street, Bakewell, Derbyshire. *T:* Bakewell 3133. *Club:* Arts.

BUTLER, George William P.; *see* Payne-Butler.

BUTLER, Gerald Norman, QC 1975; **His Honour Judge Butler;** a Circuit Judge, since 1982; Senior Judge at Southwark Crown Court, since 1984; *b* 15 Sept. 1930; *s* of Joshua Butler and Esther Butler (*née* Lampel); *m* 1959, Stella, *d* of Harris and Leah Isaacs; one *s* two *d*. *Educ:* Ilford County High Sch.; London Sch. of Economics; Magdalen Coll., Oxford. LLB London 1952, BCL Oxon 1954. 2nd Lieut, RASC, 1956–57. Called to Bar, Middle Temple, 1955. A Recorder of the Crown Court, 1977–82. *Recreations:* Rugby, bridge, Japanese pottery, Victorian paintings. *Address:* Southwark Crown Court, SE1 2HU. *Club:* MCC.

BUTLER, Maj.-Gen. Hew Dacres George, CB 1975; DL; Secretary, Beit Trust, since 1978; *b* 12 March 1922; *s* of late Maj.-Gen. S. S. Butler, CB, CMG, DSO; *m* 1954, Joanna, *d* of late G. M. Puckridge, CMG, ED; two *s* one *d*. *Educ:* Winchester. Commnd Rifle Bde, 1941; Western Desert, 1942–43; POW, 1943–45; psc 1951; BM 7th Armd Bde, 1951–53; Kenya, 1954–55; Instructor, Staff Coll., 1957–60; CO 1 RB, 1962–64; Cyprus (despatches, 1965); comd 24 Inf. Bde, Aden, 1966–67; idc 1969; ACOS G3 Northag, 1970–72; GOC Near East Land Forces, 1972–74. Chief of Staff (Contingencies Planning), SHAPE, 1975–76; retired 1977. Underwriting Mem. of Lloyds. DL 1980, High Sheriff 1983, Hants. *Recreations:* shooting, racing, horticulture. *Address:* Bury Lodge, Hambledon, Hants. *Clubs:* Boodle's, MCC.

BUTLER, James; *see* Butler, P. J.

BUTLER, James Walter, RA 1972 (ARA 1964); RWA; FRBS; *b* 25 July 1931; *m* (marr. diss.); one *d*; *m* 1975, Angela, *d* of Col Roger Berry, Johannesburg, South Africa; four *d*. *Educ:* Maidstone Grammar Sch.; Maidstone Coll. of Art; St Martin's Art Sch.; Royal Coll. of Art. National Diploma in Sculpture, 1950. Worked as Architectural Carver, 1950–53, 1955–60. Tutor, Sculpture and Drawing, City and Guilds of London Art School, 1960–75, now Visitor. Major commissions include: Portrait statue of Pres. Kenyatta, Nairobi, 1973; Monument to Freedom Fighters of Zambia, Lusaka, 1974; Statue, The Burton Cooper, Burton-on-Trent, 1977; Memorial Statue, Richard III, Leicester, 1980; Memorial Statue, Field Marshal Earl Alexander of Tunis, Wellington Barracks, London, 1985. Mem., British Astronomical Soc. *Recreations:* interested in astronomy, golf. *Address:* Old School House, Greenfield, Beds. *T:* Flitwick 712028.

BUTLER, John Manton, MSc; *b* 9 Oct. 1909; *m* 1940, Marjorie Smith, Melbourne; one *s* one *d*. *Educ:* Southland, NZ; Univ. of Otago (Sen. Schol., NZ, Physics; BSc 1929; Smeaton Schol. Chemistry, 1930, John Edmond Fellow, 1930; MSc 1st class Hons). Pres., Students' Union; Graduate Rep. Univ. Council. Joined Shell, NZ, 1934; served various Shell cos in UK, Australia and S Africa until 1957; Man. Dir, Lewis Berger (GB) Ltd, 1957; Dir, Berger, Jenson & Nicholson Ltd, 1969–74. Chm., BNEC Cttee for Exports to NZ, 1967 (Dep. Chm., 1965). Pres., NZ Soc., 1971. Member: Cttee, Spastics Soc.; St David's Cttee, Conservative Assoc., 1979–80; Aust. Inst. of Internat. Affairs, 1981–. Consultant. *Recreations:* travel, golf, photography. *Address:* Osborne, 28 Ranfurlie Crescent, Glen Iris, Victoria 3146, Australia. *T:* 259 9458. *Club:* Royal Melbourne Golf.

BUTLER, (John) Nicholas, (Nick), RDI 1981; FSIAD; industrial designer; Senior Partner, BIB Design Consultants, since 1967; *b* 21 March 1942; *s* of William and Mabel Butler; *m* 1967, Kari Ann Morrison; two *s*. *Educ:* Leeds Coll. of Art (NDD); Royal Coll. of Art (DesRCA, 1st Cl. Hons). FSIAD 1975. Founded BIB Design Consultants, 1967. Chm., British Design Export Gp, 1980–81. Hon. Sec., SIAD, 1978–81, Treasurer 1981–84. FRSA 1983. *Recreations:* reading, music, country pursuits, watching Rugby, drawing. *Address:* Burnham House, 45 Paradise Road, Richmond, Surrey TW9 1SA. *T:* 01–940 1849.

BUTLER, Mrs Joyce Shore; Chairman, Hornsey Housing Trust, since 1980; *m*; one *s* one *d*. *Educ:* King Edward's High Sch., Birmingham. Member: Wood Green Council, 1947–64 (Leader, 1954–55; Deputy Mayor, 1962–63); First Chm., London Borough of Haringey, 1964–65; First Mayoress, 1965–66. MP (Lab & Co-op) Wood Green, 1955–74, Haringey, Wood Green, 1974–79; Vice-Chm., Labour Parly Housing and Local Govt Gp, 1959–64; Member: Estimates Cttee, 1959–60; Chairman's Panel, House of Commons, 1964–79; Jt Chm., Parly Cttee on Pollution, 1970–79; PPS to Minister for Land and Natural Resources, 1965. A Vice-Chm., Parly Labour Party, 1968–70. Exec. Mem., Housing and Town Planning Council; Founder and First Pres., Women's Nat. Cancer Control Campaign; Pres., London Passenger Action Confedn. *Address:* 8 Blenheim Close, N21. *Club:* University Women's.

BUTLER, Keith Stephenson, CMG 1977; HM Diplomatic Service, retired; Appeal Director for various charities, since 1978; *b* 3 Sept. 1917; *s* of late Raymond R. Butler and Gertrude Stephenson; *m* 1st, 1952, Geraldine Marjorie Clark (*d* 1979); 2nd, 1979, Mrs Priscilla Wittels; no *c*. *Educ:* King Edward's Sch., Birmingham; Liverpool Coll.; St Peter's Coll., Oxford (MA). HM Forces, 1939–47 (despatches): served, RA, in Egypt, Greece and Crete; POW, Germany, 1941–45. Foreign Correspondent for Sunday Times and Kemsley Newspapers, 1947–50. Joined HM Foreign Service, 1950; served: First Sec., Ankara and Caracas; Canadian Nat. Defence Coll.; Paris; Montreal. HM Consul-General: Seville, 1968; Bordeaux, 1969; Naples, 1974–77. *Publications:* contrib. historical and political reviews. *Recreation:* historical research. *Address:* Easter Cottage, Westbrook, Boxford, near Newbury, Berks. *T:* Boxford 557.

BUTLER, Prof. Marilyn Speers, DPhil; King Edward VII Professor of English Literature, University of Cambridge, since 1986; *b* 11 Feb. 1937; *d* of Sir Trevor Evans, CBE and Margaret (*née* Gribbin); *m* 1962, David Edgeworth Butler, *qv*; three *s*. *Educ:* Wimbledon High Sch.; St Hilda's Coll., Oxford (MA; DPhil). Trainee and talks producer, BBC, 1960–62; Oxford University: full-time res. and teaching, 1962–70, Jun. Res. Fellow, 1970–73, St Hilda's Coll.; Fellow and Tutor, St Hugh's Coll., 1973–85; Lectr, 1985–86. Pt-time Lectr, ANU, 1967; British Academy Reader, 1982–85. *Publications:* Maria Edgeworth: a literary biography, 1972; Jane Austen and the War of Ideas, 1975; Peacock Displayed, 1979; Romantics, Rebels and Reactionaries, 1981, 2nd edn 1985; (ed) Burke, Paine, Godwin and the Revolution Controversy, 1984. *Address:* English Faculty, 9 West Road, Cambridge.

BUTLER, Sir Michael; *see* Butler, Sir R. M. T.

BUTLER, Sir Michael (Dacres), GCMG 1984 (KCMG 1980; CMG 1975); HM Diplomatic Service, retired; Director: Hambros PLC, since 1986; Hambros Bank Ltd, since 1986; Wellcome Foundation, since 1986; Consultant, ICL, since 1986; *b* 27 Feb. 1927; *s* of T. D. Butler, Almer, Blandford, and Beryl May (*née* Lambert); *m* 1951, Ann, *d* of Rt Hon. Lord Clyde; two *s* two *d*. *Educ:* Winchester; Trinity Coll., Oxford. Joined HM Foreign Service, 1950; served in: UK Mission to UN, New York, 1952–56; Baghdad, 1956–58; FO, 1958–61 and 1965–68; Paris, 1961–65; Counsellor, UK Mission in Geneva, 1968–70; Fellow, Center for Internat. Affairs, Harvard, 1970–71; Counsellor, Washington, 1971–72; Head of European Integration Dept, FCO, 1972–74; Asst Under-Sec. in charge of European Community Affairs, FCO, 1974–76; Dep. Under-Sec. of State, FCO, 1976–79; Ambassador and Perm. UK Rep. to EC, Brussels, 1979–85. Mem. Council, Oriental Ceramic Soc., 1977–80 and 1985–; Dep. Chm., Bd of Trustees, V&A Museum. *Publications:* Inside the European Community, 1986; Chinese Porcelain, The

Transitional Period 1620–82: a selection from the Michael Butler Collection, 1986; Europe: More than a Continent, 1986; contribs to Trans Oriental Ceramic Soc. *Recreations:* collecting Chinese porcelain, ski-ing, tennis. *Address:* 36A Elm Park Road, SW3. *Club:* Brooks's.

BUTLER, Michael Howard, FCA; Finance Director, British Coal (formerly National Coal Board), since 1985, Member of the Board, since 1986; *b* 13 Feb. 1936; *s* of Howard Butler and Constance Gertrude Butler; *m* 1961, Christine Elizabeth Killer; two *s* one *d*. *Educ:* Nottingham High School. Articled pupil, H. G. Ellis Kennewell & Co., Nottingham, 1952–58; Stewarts & Lloyds Gp, 1960–62; National Coal Board: various posts, NCB HQ, W Midlands Div. and NE Area, 1962–68; Chief Accountant, Coal Products Div., 1968; Dep. Treas., NCB HQ, 1970; Treas. and Dep. Dir Gen. of Finance, 1978; Dir Gen. of Finance, 1981. *Recreations:* gardening, listening to music, playing tennis. *Address:* Banstead Down, Chorleywood Road, Rickmansworth, Herts WD3 4EH. *T:* Rickmansworth 778001; (office) 01-235 2020.

BUTLER, Prof. Neville Roy, MD; FRCP; Director, International Centre for Child Studies, since 1983; Professor of Child Health, Bristol University, 1965–85, Emeritus Professor, since 1985; Hon. Consultant Paediatrician, Bristol & Weston Teaching District and Southmead District, 1965–85; *b* Harrow, 6 July 1920; *o s* of late Dr C. J. Butler, MRCS, LRCP and Ida Margaret Butler; *m* 1954, Jean Ogilvie (marr. diss.), *d* of late John McCormack; two *d*. *Educ:* Epsom Coll.; Charing Cross Hosp. Med. Sch. MB BS 1942, MD 1949; MRCP 1946, FRCP 1965; DCH 1949; FRCOG 1979. Served RAMC, 1942–44, temp. Captain. First Assistant to Paediatric Unit, UCH, 1950; Med. Registrar and Pathologist, Hosp. for Sick Children, Gt Ormond St, 1953; Consultant Paediatrician, Oxford and Wessex RHB, 1957–63; Dir, Perinatal Mortality Survey, Birthday Trust Fund, 1958; Consultant Physician, Hosp. for Sick Children, Gt Ormond St and Sen. Lectr, Inst. of Child Health, London Univ., 1963–65. Co-Dir, Nat. Child Develt Study (1958 cohort), 1965–69; Dir, Child Health and Educn Study (1970 cohort), and Youthscan UK, 1986–87. Harding Meml Lect., RIBA, 1983. Member: BPA, 1958–; Neonatal Soc., 1961–; Cuban Paediatric Soc., 1973–; Hungarian Paediatric Soc., 1979–. *Publications:* jointly: Perinatal Mortality, 1963; 11,000 Seven Year Olds, 1966; Perinatal Problems, 1969; From Birth to Seven, 1972; The Social Life of Britain's Five Year Olds, 1984; Ethnic Minority Children, 1985; The Health of Britain's Five Year Olds, 1986; papers in scientific and med. jls. *Address:* PO Box 328, Bristol BS99 7XQ. *T:* Bristol 739783; 57 Lower Belgrave Street, SW1W 0LR. *T:* 01–730 5607. *Club:* Savage.

BUTLER, Nick; *see* Butler, J. N.

BUTLER, (Percy) James, CBE 1981; FCA; Senior Partner, Peat, Marwick, Mitchell & Co, since 1986; farmer, since 1974; *b* 15 March 1929; *s* of Percy Ernest Butler and Phyllis Mary Butler (*née* Bartholomew); *m* 1954, Margaret Prudence Copland; one *s* two *d*. *Educ:* Marlborough Coll.; Clare Coll., Cambridge (MA). Joined Peat, Marwick, Mitchell & Co., 1952; qualified, 1955; Partner, 1965; Gen. Partner, 1971; Dep. Sen. Partner, 1985–86. Mem. of Lloyd's. Dir, Mersey Docks and Harbour Co., 1972–; Business Advr to Treasury and CS Cttee, 1980–82; Mem., Cttee on review of Railway Finance, 1982. Treasurer, Pilgrims Soc., 1982–. Mem., Marlborough Coll. Council, 1975–. Liveryman: Worshipful Co. of Cutlers, 1965– (Mem. Court, 1985–); Worshipful Co. of Chartered Accountants in England and Wales, 1977–. *Recreations:* bridge, tennis. *Address:* Littleton House, Crawley, near Winchester SO21 2QF. *T:* Winchester 200806; Flat 8, Lennox Gardens, SW1 0DA. *T:* 01–581 8759. *Clubs:* Carlton, Pilgrims.

BUTLER, Sir (Reginald) Michael (Thomas), 3rd Bt *cr* 1922; QC (Canada); Barrister and Solicitor; Partner of Butler, Angus, Victoria, BC; Director: Quinterra Resources Ltd; Teck Corporation; Elco Mining Ltd; *b* 22 April 1928; *s* of Sir Reginald Thomas, 2nd Bt, and Marjorie Brown Butler; *S* father, 1959; *m* Marja McLean (marr. diss.); three *s*; one *s* adopted. *Educ:* Brentwood Coll., Victoria, BC; Univ. of British Columbia (BA). Called to Bar (Hons) from Osgoode Hall Sch. of Law, Toronto, Canada, 1954. Chm., Brentwood Coll. Assoc. *Heir:* *s* (Reginald) Richard Michael Butler, *b* 3 Oct. 1953. *Address:* 634 Avalon Street, Victoria, BC, Canada; 21 Chelsea Towers, Chelsea Manor Street, SW3. *Clubs:* Vancouver (Vancouver); Union (Victoria).

BUTLER, Hon. Sir Richard (Clive), Kt 1981; DL; Director: National Westminster Bank, since 1986; National Farmers' Union Mutual Insurance Society Ltd, since 1985; Life Member, National Farmers' Union (President, 1979–86); farmer since 1953; *b* 12 Jan. 1929; *e s* of late Baron Butler of Saffron Walden, KG, CH, PC and late Sydney, *o c* of late Samuel Courtauld; *m* 1952, Susan Anne Maud Walker; twin *s* one *d*. *Educ:* Eton Coll.; Pembroke Coll., Cambridge (MA). 2nd Lieut, Royal Horse Guards, 1947–49. Mem. Council, NFU, 1962–, Vice-Pres. 1970–71, Dep. Pres., 1971–79. Member: Agricultural Adv. Council, 1968–72; Central Council for Agricultural and Horticultural Co-operation, 1970–79. DL Essex, 1972. *Recreations:* hunting, shooting, tennis. *Address:* Penny Pot, Halstead, Essex. *T:* Halstead 472828. *Club:* Farmers'.

See also Rt Hon Sir . A. C. Butler.

BUTLER, Robin; *see* Butler, F. E. R.

BUTLER, Dr Rohan D'Olier, CMG; MA; DLitt; FRHistS; Laureate, Institute of France; Fellow Emeritus of All Souls, Oxford, since 1984 (Fellow, 1938–84; Sub-Warden, 1961–63; representative at 12th International Historical Congress at Vienna, 1965, at 11th Anglo-American Conference of Historians, 1982); Member, Court, University of Essex, since 1971; *b* St John's Wood, 21 Jan. 1917; *surv. s* of late Sir Harold Butler, KCMG, CB, MA, and Olive, (Lady Butler), *y c* of late Asst Inspector-General S. A. W. Waters, RIC, JP; *m* Lucy Rosemary, FRHS (Lady of the Manor of White Notley, Essex), *y c* of late Eric Byron, Lord of the Manor. *Educ:* Eton; abroad and privately; Balliol Coll., Oxford (Hall Prizeman, 1938). BA (1st Class Hons in History), 1938; on International Propaganda and Broadcasting Enquiry, 1939; on staff of MOI, 1939–41 and 1942–44, of Special Operations Executive, 1941; served with RAPC, 1941–42, with HG, 1942–44 (Defence Medal, War Medal); on staff of FO, 1944–45; Editor of Documents on British Foreign Policy (1919–39), 1945–65 (with late Sir Llewellyn Woodward, FBA, 1945–54; Senior Editor, 1955–65); Sen. Editor, Documents on British Policy Overseas, 1973–82; Leverhulme Res. Fellow, 1955–57, Emeritus Fellow, 1984–86. Mem., Lord Chancellor's Adv. Council on Public Records, 1982–86. Governor, Felsted Sch., 1959–77, representative on GBA, 1964–77; Trustee, Felsted Almshouses, 1961–77; Noel Buxton Trustee, 1961–67. Historical Adviser to Sec. of State for Foreign Affairs, 1963–68, for Foreign and Commonwealth Affairs, 1968–82 (from 14th Earl of Home to 6th Baron Carrington). On management of Inst. of Hist. Research, Univ. of London, 1967–77. *Publications:* The Roots of National Socialism; Documents on British Foreign Policy, 1st series, vols i-ix, 2nd series, vol. ix; The Peace Settlement of Versailles (in New Cambridge Modern History); Paradiplomacy (in Studies in Diplomatic History in honour of Dr G. P. Gooch, OM, CH, FBA); Introduction to Anglo-Soviet historical exhibition of 1967; Choiseul (special award, Prix Jean Debrousse, Acad. des Sciences Morales et Politiques, 1982); Documents on British Policy Overseas, series I, vol. i. *Recreation:* idling. *Address:* White Notley Hall, near Witham, Essex. *Clubs:* Beefsteak, The Lunch.

BUTLER, Rt. Rev. Thomas Frederick; *see* Willesden, Area Bishop of.

BUTLER, Col Sir Thomas Pierce, 12th Bt *cr* 1628; CVO 1970; DSO 1944; OBE 1954; Resident Governor and Major, HM Tower of London, 1961–71, Keeper of the Jewel House, 1968–71; *b* 18 Sept. 1910; *o s* of Sir Richard Pierce Butler, 11th Bt, OBE, DL, and Alice Dudley (*d* 1965), *d* of Very Rev. Hon. James Wentworth Leigh, DD; *S* father, 1955; *m* 1937, Rosemary Liège Woodgate Davidson-Houston, *d* of late Major J. H. Davidson-Houston, Pembury Hall, Kent; one *s* two *d*. *Educ:* Harrow; Trinity Coll., Cambridge. BA (Hons) Cantab, 1933. Grenadier Guards, 1933; served War of 1939–45 (wounded, POW, escaped); BEF France; 6th Bn, Egypt, Syria, Tripoli, N Africa; Staff Coll., 1944 (psc); Comd Guards Composite Bn, Norway, 1945–46; Comd 2nd Bn Grenadier Guards, BAOR, 1949–52; AQMG, London District, 1952–55; Col, Lt-Col Comdg the Grenadier Guards, 1955–58; Military Adviser to UK High Comr in New Zealand, 1959–61. Pres., London (Prince of Wales's) District, St John Ambulance Brigade. JP Co. of London 1961–71. CStJ. *Recreations:* fishing, travelling. *Heir:* *s* Richard Pierce Butler [*b* 22 July 1940; *m* 1965, Diana, *yr d* of Col S. J. Borg; three *s* one *d*]. *Address:* 6 Thurloe Square, SW7. *T:* 01–584 6361; Ballin Temple, Co. Carlow. *Club:* Cavalry and Guards.

See also Maj.-Gen. R. C. Keightley.

BUTLER, Vincent, RSA 1977; sculptor; *b* 1933. *Educ:* Edinburgh Coll. of Art (DA 1955); Accademia di Belle Arti, Milan. One man exhibitions: London, 1969; Manchester, 1973, 1977; Bradford, 1974; Bury, 1977; Torquay, 1976; Haddington, 1978; Wolfsburg, 1979; Edinburgh, 1980. *Address:* 17 Deanpark Crescent, Edinburgh EH4 1PH. *T:* 031–332 5884.

BUTLER, Prof. William Elliott; Professor of Comparative Law in the University of London, since 1976; Director, Centre for the Study of Socialist Legal Systems, University College London, since 1982; *b* 20 Oct. 1939; *s* of William Elliott Butler and Maxine Swan Elmberg; *m* 1961, Darlene Mae Johnson; two *s*. *Educ:* The American Univ. (BA); Harvard Law School (JD); The Johns Hopkins Univ. (MA, PhD); London Univ. (LLD). Res. Asst, Washington Centre of Foreign Policy Res., Sch. of Advanced Internat. Studies, The Johns Hopkins Univ., 1966–68; Res. Associate in Law, and Associate, Russian Res. Centre, Harvard Univ., 1968–70; University of London: Reader in Comparative Law, 1970–76; Mem., 1973–, Vice-Chm., 1983–, SSEES; Dean of Faculty of Laws, UCL, 1977–79; Mem., Cttee of Management, Inst. of Advanced Legal Studies, 1985–. Visiting Scholar: Faculty of Law, Moscow State Univ., 1972, 1980; Inst. of State and Law, USSR Acad. of Scis, 1976, 1981, 1983, 1984; Mongolian State Univ., 1979; Harvard Law Sch., 1982; Visiting Professor: NY Univ. Law Sch., 1978; Harvard Law Sch., 1987; Lectr, Hague Acad. of Internat. Law, 1985. Associé, Internat. Acad. of Comparative Law, 1982–; Member, Bar: Dist of Columbia (Dist Court and Court of Appeals); US Supreme Court. Chm., Civil Rights in Russia Adv. Panel, Univ. of London, 1983–; Co-ordinator, UCL-USSR Acad. of Sciences Protocol on Co-operation, 1981–. Mem., Court of Governors, City of London Polytechnic, 1985–. Sec., The Bookplate Soc., 1978–; Vice Pres., Féd. Internat. des Sociétés d'Amateurs d'Ex-Libris, 1984–. Editor: The Bookplate Jl, 1983–; Year Book on Socialist Legal Systems, 1985–; Mem., editorial bds of learned jls; editor of looseleaf services and microfiche projects. *Publications:* more than 450 books, articles, translations, and reviews, including: The Soviet Union and the Law of the Sea, 1971; Russian Law, 1977; (with others) The Soviet Legal System, 3rd and 4th edns, 1977–84; A Source Book on Socialist International Organizations, 1978; Northeast Arctic Passage, 1978; International Law in Comparative Perspective, 1980; Basic Documents on Soviet Legal System, 1983; Chinese Soviet Republic 1931–1934, 1983; Soviet Law, 1983; Comparative Law and Legal System, 1985; The Law of the Sea and International Shipping, 1985; The Golden Era of American Bookplate Design, 1986; *translations of:* G. I. Tunkin, Theory of International Law, 1974; A. Kuznetsov, The Journey, 1984. *Recreations:* book collecting, bookplate collecting. *Address:* 9 Lyndale Avenue, NW2 2QD. *T:* 01-435 1059. *Club:* Cosmos (Washington, DC).

BUTLER-SLOSS, Hon. Dame (Ann) Elizabeth (Oldfield), DBE 1979; **Hon. Mrs Justice Butler-Sloss;** a Judge of the High Court of Justice, Family Division, since 1979; *b* 10 Aug. 1933; *d* of late Sir Cecil Havers, QC, and late Enid Snelling; *m* 1958, Joseph William Alexander Butler-Sloss, *qv*; two *s* one *d*. *Educ:* Wycombe Abbey Sch. Called to Bar, Inner Temple, Feb. 1955, Bencher, 1979; practice at Bar, 1955–70; Registrar, Principal Registry of Probate, later Family, Division, 1970–79. Contested (C), Lambeth, Vauxhall, 1959. A Vice Pres., Medico-Legal Soc. Pres., Honiton Agricultural Show, 1985–86. *Publications:* Joint Editor: Phipson on Evidence (10th edn); Corpe on Road Haulage (2nd edn); a former Editor, Supreme Court Practice, 1976 and 1979. *Address:* c/o Royal Courts of Justice, Strand, WC2.

See also Rt Hon. Sir R. M. O. Havers.

BUTLER-SLOSS, Joseph William Alexander; Hon. Mr Justice Butler-Sloss; a Judge of the High Court of Kenya, since 1984; *b* 16 Nov. 1926; 2nd and *o* surv. *s* of late Francis Alexander Sloss and Alice Mary Frances Violet Sloss (*née* Patchell); *m* 1958, Ann Elizabeth Oldfield Havers (*see* Hon. Dame (Ann) Elizabeth (Oldfield) Butler-Sloss); two *s* one *d*. *Educ:* Bangor Grammar Sch., Co. Down; Hertford Coll., Oxford. Ordinary Seaman, RN, 1944; Midshipman 1945, Sub-Lieut 1946, RNVR. MA (Jurisprudence) Hertford Coll., Oxford, 1951. Called to Bar, Gray's Inn, 1952; joined Western Circuit, 1954; joined Inner Temple; a Recorder, 1972–84. Joint Master, East Devon Foxhounds, 1970–76. *Recreations:* racing, the violin. *Address:* High Court of Kenya, PO Box 126, Kisumu, Kenya. *T:* Kisumu 2654; Higher Marsh Farm, Marsh Green, Rockbeare, Exeter, Devon. *T:* Whimple 822663. *Clubs:* Carlton; Muthaiga; Nairobi.

BUTLIN, Martin Richard Fletcher; FBA 1984; Keeper of Historic British Collection, Tate Gallery, since 1967; *b* 7 June 1929; *s* of Kenneth Rupert Butlin and Helen Mary (*née* Fletcher); *m* 1969, Frances Caroline Chodzko. *Educ:* Rendcomb Coll.; Trinity Coll., Cambridge (MA); Courtauld Inst. of Art, London Univ. (BA). DLit London 1984. Asst Keeper, Tate Gall., 1955–67. *Publications:* A Catalogue of the Works of William Blake in the Tate Gallery, 1957, 2nd edn 1971; Samuel Palmer's Sketchbook of 1824, 1962; Turner Watercolours, 1962; (with Sir John Rothenstein) Turner, 1964; (with Mary Chamot and Dennis Farr) Tate Gallery Catalogues: The Modern British Paintings, Drawings and Sculpture, 1964; The Later Works of J. M. W. Turner, 1965; William Blake, 1966; The Blake-Varley Sketchbook of 1819, 1969; (with E. Joll) The Paintings of J. M. W. Turner, 1977, 2nd edn 1984 (jtly, Mitchell Prize for the History of Art, 1978); The Paintings and Drawings of William Blake, 1981; selected paintings and prepared catalogues for following exhibitions: (with Andrew Wilton and John Gage) Turner 1775–1851, 1974; William Blake, 1978; articles and reviews in Burlington Mag., Connoisseur, Master Drawings, Blake Newsletter, Blake Studies, Turner Studies. *Recreations:* music, travel. *Address:* Tate Gallery, Millbank, SW1P 4RG. *T:* 01–821 1313.

BUTT, Sir (Alfred) Kenneth (Dudley), 2nd Bt *cr* 1929; Underwriting Member of Lloyd's, 1931–74; farmer and bloodstock breeder; *b* 7 July 1908; *o s* of Sir Alfred Butt, 1st Bt and Lady Georgina Mary Butt (*née* Say); *S* father, 1962; *m* 1st, 1938, Kathleen Farmar (marr. diss., 1948); 2nd, 1948, Mrs Ivor Birts (*née* Bain), *widow* of Lt-Col Ivor Birts, RA (killed on active service). *Educ:* Rugby; Brasenose Coll., Oxford. Lloyd's,

1929–39. Royal Artillery, 1939–45, Major RA. Chairman, Parker Wakeling & Co. Ltd, 1946–54; Managing Director, Brook Stud Co., 1962–81. Pres., Aberdeen-Angus Cattle Soc., 1968–69; Chm., Thoroughbred Breeders Assoc., 1973. *Recreations:* shooting, horse-racing, travelling, paintings. *Address:* Wheat Hill, Sandon, Buntingford, Herts. *T:* Kelshall 203; Flat 29, 1 Hyde Park Square, W2. *T:* 01-262 3988. *Clubs:* Carlton, etc.

BUTT, Geoffrey Frank; Principal Assistant Solicitor, HM Customs and Excise, since 1986; *b* 5 May 1943; *s* of late Frank Thomas Woodman Butt and Dorothy Rosamond Butt; *m* 1972, Lee Anne Davey; two *s* one *d*. *Educ:* Royal Masonic Sch., Bushey; Univ. of Reading (BA). Solicitor 1970. Joined Solicitor's Office, HM Customs and Excise as Legal Asst, 1971; Sen. Legal Asst, 1974; Asst Solicitor, 1982. *Recreations:* family life, classical music, literature and art, gardening, walking, swimming. *Address:* 15 Warwick Park, Tunbridge Wells, Kent TN2 5TA. *T:* Tunbridge Wells 31834.

BUTT, Sir Kenneth; *see* Butt, Sir A. K. D.

BUTT, Richard Bevan; Head of Conservation, English Heritage, since 1986; *b* 27 Feb. 1943; *s* of Roger William Bevan and Jean Mary (*née* Carter); *m* 1975, Amanda Jane Finlay; two *s*. *Educ:* Magdalen Coll., Oxford (BA Hist.); Lancaster Univ. (MA Regional Econs). Asst Principal, Min. of Housing, 1965–68; Res. Associate, Birmingham Univ., 1969–72; Consultant, 1972; HM Treasury: Principal, 1973–78; Asst Sec., 1978–86; seconded as Financial Counsellor, UK Perm. Repn to EC, 1981–84. *Recreations:* pottery, architecture, travel, gardening. *Address:* 35 Gloucester Circus, SE10.

BUTTER, Major David Henry, MC 1941; JP; landowner and farmer; company director; HM Lord-Lieutenant of Perth and Kinross, since 1975; *b* 18 March 1920; *s* of late Col Charles Butter, OBE, DL, JP, Pitlochry, and Agnes Marguerite (Madge), *d* of late William Clark, Newark, NJ, USA; *m* 1946, Myra Alice, *d* of Hon. Maj.-Gen. Sir Harold Wernher, 3rd Bt, GCVO, TD; one *s* four *d*. *Educ:* Eton; Oxford. Served War of 1939–45: 2nd Lieut Scots Guards, 1940, Western Desert and North Africa, Sicily (Staff), 1941–43; Italy (ADC to GOC 8th Army, Gen. Sir Oliver Leese, 1944); Temp. Major, 1946; retd Army, 1948. Brig., Queen's Body Guard for Scotland (Royal Company of Archers); Pres., Highland T&AVR, 1979–84. County Councillor, Perth, 1955–74; DL Perthshire, 1956, Vice-Lieutenant of Perth, 1960–71; HM Lieutenant of County of Perth, 1971–75, and County of Kinross, 1974–75. *Recreations:* shooting, golf, ski-ing, travel. *Address:* Cluniemore, Pitlochry, Scotland. *T:* Pitlochry 2006; 64 Rutland Gate, SW7. *T:* 01-589 6731. *Clubs:* Turf; Royal and Ancient (St Andrews).

See also Lord Ramsay.

BUTTER, John Henry, CMG 1962; MBE 1946; Financial Director to Government of Abu Dhabi, 1970–83; *b* 20 April 1916; *s* of late Captain A. E. Butter, CMG, and late Mrs Baird; *m* 1950, Joyce Platt; three *s*. *Educ:* Charterhouse; Christ Church, Oxford. Indian Civil Service, 1939–47; Pakistan Admin. Service, 1947–50 (served in Punjab, except for period 1942–46 when was Asst to Political Agent, Imphal, Manipur State). HM Overseas Civil Service, Kenya, 1950–65 (Perm. Sec. to the Treasury, 1959–65); Financial Adviser, Kenya Treasury, 1965–69. *Recreations:* golf, bridge. *Address:* PO Box 30181, Nairobi, Kenya; Whitehill, Gordon, Berwickshire. *Club:* East India, Devonshire, Sports, and Public Schools.

See also Prof. P. H. Butter.

BUTTER, Neil (McLaren), QC 1976; **His Honour Judge Butter;** a Circuit Judge, since 1982; a Judge of Bow County Court, since 1986; *b* 10 May 1933; *y s* of late Andrew Butter, MA, MD and late Ena Butter, MB, ChB; *m* 1974, Claire Marianne Miskin. *Educ:* The Leys Sch.; Queens' Coll., Cambridge (MA). Called to Bar, Inner Temple, 1955. An Asst and Dep. Recorder of Bournemouth, 1971; Recorder of the Crown Court, 1972–82. Mem., Senate of the Inns of Court and the Bar, 1976–79. Inspector, for Dept of Trade, Ozalid Gp Hldgs Ltd, 1977–79. A Legal Assessor to GMC and GDC, 1979–82; Mem., Mental Health Review Tribunal, 1983–. Trustee, Kingdon-Ward Speech Therapy Trust, 1980–. *Recreations:* motoring, holidays, browsing through Who's Who. *Address:* c/o 3 Serjeant's Inn, EC4Y 1BQ. *Clubs:* United Oxford & Cambridge University; Hampshire (Winchester).

BUTTER, Prof. Peter Herbert; Regius Professor of English, Glasgow University, 1965–86; *b* 7 April 1921; *s* of Archibald Butter, CMG, and Helen Cicely (*née* Kerr); *m* 1958, Bridget Younger; one *s* two *d*. *Educ:* Charterhouse; Balliol Coll., Oxford. Served in RA, 1941–46. Assistant, 1948, Lecturer, 1951, in English, Univ. of Edinburgh; Professor of English, Queen's Univ., Belfast, 1958–65. *Publications:* Shelley's Idols of the Cave, 1954; Francis Thompson, 1961; Edwin Muir, 1962; Edwin Muir: Man and Poet, 1966; (ed) Shelley's Alastor and Other Poems, 1971; (ed) Selected Letters of Edwin Muir, 1974; (ed) Selected Poems of William Blake, 1982; articles in periodicals. *Address:* Ashfield, Bridge of Weir, Renfrewshire. *T:* Bridge of Weir 613139. *Club:* New (Edinburgh).

See also J. H. Butter.

BUTTERFIELD, Charles Harris, QC (Singapore) 1952; HMOCS, retired; *b* 28 June 1911; 2nd *s* of William Arthur Butterfield, OBE, and Rebecca Butterfield; *m* 1st, 1938, Monica, *d* of Austin Harrison, London; one *d*; 2nd, by special permission of the Holy See, Ellen, *d* of Ernest John Bennett, Singapore and *widow* of J. E. King, Kuala Lumpur, Singapore and Hooe. *Educ:* Downside; Trinity Coll., Cambridge. Barrister-at-law, Middle Temple, 1934. Entered Colonial Legal Service, 1938; Crown Counsel, Straits Settlements, 1938. Served Singapore RA (Volunteer) and RA, 1941–46; POW, 1942–45. Solicitor-General, Singapore, 1948–55, Attorney-General, 1955–57; Legal Adviser's Dept CRO and FCO, 1959–69; DoE and Sec. of State's Panel of Inspectors (Planning), 1969–74. *Address:* 18 Kewhurst Avenue, Cooden, Bexhill on Sea, E Sussex. *Club:* Pevensey Marsh Beagles.

BUTTERFIELD, John Michael; Chief Executive, National Association of Youth Clubs, 1975–86; *b* 2 July 1926; *s* of late John Leslie Butterfield and Hilda Mary Butterfield (*née* Judson); *m* 1955, Mary Maureen, *d* of John Martin; one *s* twin *d* (and one *s* decd). *Educ:* Leeds Modern Sch.; Leeds Univ. John Butterfield & Son, Leeds, 1949–60; John Atkinson & Sons (Sowerby Bridge) Ltd, 1960–61. Youth Officer, Coventry Cathedral, 1961–68; Liverpool Council of Social Service: Head of Youth and Community Dept, 1968–72; Operations Dir, 1972–75. Member: British Council of Churches, 1954–73; British Council of Churches Youth Dept, 1952–68 (Chm. Exec. Cttee, 1962–67); Vice Chm., Nat. Council for Voluntary Youth Services, 1977–83. *Recreations:* music, reading, walking, railways. *Address:* 4 Church Farm Court, Aston Flamville, near Hinckley, Leics LE10 3AW. *T:* Hinckley 611027.

BUTTERFIELD, Prof. Sir (William) John (Hughes), Kt 1978; OBE 1953; DM; FRCP; Regius Professor of Physic, University of Cambridge, since 1976; Master of Downing College, Cambridge, since 1978; *b* 28 March 1920; *s* of late William Hughes Butterfield and of Mrs Doris North; *m* 1st, 1946, Ann Sanders (decd); one *s*; 2nd, 1950, Isabel-Ann Foster Kennedy; two *s* one *d*. *Educ:* Solihull Sch.; Exeter Coll., Oxford (Hon. Fellow, 1978); Johns Hopkins Univ (MD 1951); MA, MD Cantab 1975. Repr. Oxford Univ.: Rugby football, *v* Cambridge, 1940–41; hockey, 1940–42 (Captain); cricket, 1942 (Captain). Member, Scientific Staff, Medical Research Council, 1946–58: Major RAMC, Army Operational Research Group, 1947–50; Research Fellow, Medical Coll. of Virginia, Richmond, Va, USA, 1950–52; seconded to Min. of Supply, 1952; seconded to AEA, 1956; Prof. of Experimental Medicine, Guy's Hospital, 1958–63; Prof. of Medicine, Guy's Hosp. Med. Sch., and Additional Physician, Guy's Hosp., 1963–71; Vice-Chancellor, Nottingham Univ., 1971–75; Professorial Fellow, Downing Coll., Cambridge, 1975–78; Vice-Chancellor, Cambridge Univ., 1983–85. Chairman: Bedford Diabetic Survey, 1962; Woolwich/Erith New Town Medical Liaison Cttee, 1965–71; SE Met. Reg. Hospital Board's Clinical Research Cttee, 1960–71; Scientific Advisory Panel, Army Personnel Research Cttee, 1970–; Council for the Education and Training of Health Visitors, 1971–76; East Midlands Economic Planning Council, 1974–75; Medicines Commn, 1976–81; Member: UGC Medical Sub-Cttee, 1966–71; Council, British Diabetic Assoc., 1963–74 (Chm. 1967–74, Vice-Pres. 1974–); DHSS Cttee on Medical Aspects of Food Policy, 1964–; DHSS Panel on Medical Research, 1974–76; MRC Cttee on General Epidemiology, 1965–74; MRC Clinical Res. Grants Bd, 1969–71; MRC, 1976–80; Anglo-Soviet Consultative Cttee; Minister of Health's Long Term Study Group; Health Educn Council, DHSS, 1973–77; Trent RHA, 1973–75; IUC Council and Exec. Cttee, 1973–; British Council Med. Adv. Cttee, 1971–80; Northwick Park Adv. Cttee, 1971–76; Council, European Assoc. for Study of Diabetes, 1968–71 (Vice-Pres.); Hong Kong Univ. and Polytechnic Grants Cttee, 1975–83. Chairman: Jardine Educnl Trust, 1982–; Health Promotion Res. Trust, 1983–; Trustee: Croucher Foundn, Hong Kong, 1979–; GB-Sasakawa Foundn, 1985–. Consultant, WHO Expert Cttee on Diabetes, 1964–80; Visitor, King Edward's Hospital Fund, 1964–71; Examiner in Medicine: Oxford Univ., 1960–66; Univ. of E Africa, 1966; Cambridge Univ., 1967–75; Pfizer Vis. Professor, NZ and Australia, 1965; Visiting Professor: Yale, 1966; Harvard, 1978. Rock Carling Fellow, RCP, 1968; Lectures: Oliver-Sharpey, RCP, 1967; Banting, BDA, 1970; Linacre, Cambridge 1979; Roberts, Med. Soc. of London, 1981; Clayesmore, Blandford Forum, 1983; Northcott, Exeter, 1984; Cohen, Hebrew Univ. of Jerusalem, 1985. Dir, Prudential Assurance Co., 1981–. Member: Editorial Board, Diabetaloga, 1964–69; Jl Chronic Diseases, 1968–. Hon. Fellow, NY Acad. Science, 1962; Corres. FACP, 1973. Patron, Richmond Soc., 1968–71. FRSA 1971. Hon. LLD Nottingham, 1977; Hon. DMedSci Keio Univ., Tokyo, 1983. Hon. DSc, Florida Internat. Univ., Miami, 1985. *Publications:* (jointly) On Burns, 1953; Tolbutamide after 10 years, 1967; Priorities in Medicine, 1968; Health and Sickness: the choice of treatment, 1971; (ed) International Dictionary of Medicine and Biology, 1986; over 100 contribs to med. and allied literature incl. books, chapters, official reports and articles on diabetes, health care and educnl topics. *Recreations:* tennis (not lawn), cricket (village) and talking (too much). *Address:* The Master's Lodge, Downing College, Cambridge. *T:* Cambridge 334800. *Clubs:* Athenæum, MCC, Queen's; CURUFC (Pres., 1984–); CUCC (Pres., 1979–).

BUTTERFILL, John Valentine; MP (C) Bournemouth West, since 1983; *b* 14 Feb. 1941; *s* of George Thomas Butterfill and Elsie Amelia (*née* Watts); *m* 1965, Pamela Ross Ross-Symons; one *s* three *d*. *Educ:* Caterham Sch.; Coll. of Estate Management. FRICS 1974. Valuer, Jones, Lang, Wootton, 1961–64; Sen. Exec., Hammerson Gp, 1964–69; Dir, Audley Properties Ltd (Bovis Gp), 1969–71; Man. Dir, St Paul's Securities Gp, 1971–76; Sen. Partner, Curchod & Co., chartered surveyors, 1977–. Vice-Chm., Backbench Tourism Cttee, 1986– (Jt Sec., 1984–85). *Publications:* contribs to Estates Gazette. *Recreations:* riding, tennis, bridge, music. *Address:* Perry, Worplesdon, Surrey GU3 3RG. *T:* Worplesdon 232596. *Club:* Sloane.

BUTTERWORTH, family name of **Baron Butterworth.**

BUTTERWORTH, Baron *cr* 1985 (Life Peer), of Warwick in the County of Warwickshire; **John Blackstock Butterworth,** CBE 1982; JP; DL; Vice-Chancellor, University of Warwick, 1963–85; *b* 13 March 1918; *o s* of John William and Florence Butterworth; *m* 1948, Doris Crawford Elder; one *s* two *d*. *Educ:* Queen Elizabeth's Grammar Sch., Mansfield; The Queen's Coll., Oxford. Royal Artillery, 1939–46. MA 1946. Called to Bar, Lincoln's Inn, 1947. New Coll., Oxford: Fellow, 1946–63; Dean, 1952–56; Bursar, 1956–63; Sub Warden, 1957–58. Junior Proctor, 1950–51; Faculty Fellow of Nuffield Coll., 1953–58; Member of Hebdomadal Council, Oxford Univ., 1953–63. Managing Trustee 1964–85, Trustee, 1985–, Nuffield Foundation; Chairman: Inter-Univ. Council for Higher Educn Overseas, 1968–77; Universities Cttee for Non-teaching Staffs, 1970–85; Inquiry into work of Probation Officers and Social Workers in Local Authorities and Nat. Service, 1971–73; Midland Community Radio Ltd (Mercia Sound), 1978–; Standing Cttee on Internat. Co-operation in Higher Educn, British Council, 1981–85; Inter-Univ. and Polytechnic Council, 1981–85. Member: Royal Commn on the Working of the Tribunals of Inquiry (Act), 1921, 1966; Intergovernmental Cttee on Law of Contempt in relation to Tribunals of Inquiry, 1968; Noise Advisory Council, 1974–81; Bd, British Council 1981–85; British delegn to Commonwealth Educn Conferences in Lagos, 1968, Canberra, 1971, Kingston, 1974, Accra, 1977, Colombo, 1980. Governor, Royal Shakespeare Theatre, 1964–. DL Warwickshire, 1967–74, DL West Midlands 1974–; JP City of Oxford, 1962, Coventry, 1963–. Hon. DCL, Univ. of Sierra Leone, 1976; Hon. DSc Univ. of Aston, 1985. *Address:* The Barn, Barton, Guiting Power, Glos GL54 5US. *T:* Guiting Power 297. *Club:* Athenæum.

BUTTERWORTH, Sir (George) Neville, Kt 1973; DL; Chairman, Tootal Ltd (formerly English Calico Ltd), 1968–74; *b* 27 Dec. 1911; *s* of Richard Butterworth and Hannah (*née* Wright); *m* 1947, Barbara Mary Briggs; two *s*. *Educ:* Malvern; St John's Coll., Cambridge. Served with Royal Artillery, at home and overseas, 1939–45. Dir, National Westminster Bank (North Regional Board), 1969–82; Mem., Royal Commn on Distribution of Income and Wealth, 1974–79. Chm., NW Regional Council of CBI, 1968–70; Former Mem., Grand Council of CBI; Trustee, Civic Trust for the North-West, 1967; Mem., Textile Council, 1970; CompTI 1973. Member: Court of Governors, Manchester Univ., 1973–; Council, UMIST, 1973–79. FBIM 1968. High Sheriff 1974, DL 1974, Greater Manchester. *Address:* Oak Farm, Ollerton, Knutsford, Cheshire. *T:* 061-567 3150.

BUTTERWORTH, Henry, CEng, MIMechE; Managing Director, Ammunition (formerly Director General (Ammunition)), Royal Ordnance Factories, since 1979; *b* 21 Jan. 1926; *s* of late Henry and Wilhemena Butterworth; *m* 1948, Ann Smith; two *s*. *Educ:* St Mary's, Leyland, Lancs. DipProd Birmingham. Apprenticeship, 1940–47; Draughtsman, 1947–52; Technical Asst, 1952–53; progressively, Shop Manager, Asst Manager, Manager, 1953–71; Director ROF: Cardiff, Burghfield, Glascoed, 1971–79. *Recreation:* coarse fishing. *Address:* 5 Vicarsfield Road, Worden Park, Leyland, Lancs.

BUTTERWORTH, Prof. Ian, CBE 1984; FRS 1981; Professor of Physics, since 1971, Principal of Queen Mary College, since 1986, University of London; *b* 3 Dec. 1930; *s* of Harry and Beatrice Butterworth; *m* 1964, Mary Therese (*née* Gough); one *d*. *Educ:* Bolton County Grammar Sch.; Univ. of Manchester. BSc 1951; PhD 1954. Sen. Scientific Officer, UK Atomic Energy Authority, 1954–58; Lectr, Imperial Coll., 1958–64; Vis. Physicist, Lawrence Radiation Laboratory, Univ. of California, 1964–65; Sen. Lectr, Imperial Coll., 1965–68; Group Leader, Bubble Chamber Research Gp, Rutherford High Energy Laboratory, 1968–71; Professor, 1971–86, Head of Dept, 1980–83, Dept of Physics, Imperial Coll.; on leave of absence as Res. Dir, CERN, 1983–86. Science and Engineering

Research Council (formerly Science Research Council): Mem., 1979–83 (Mem., Nuclear Physics Bd, 1972–75 and 1978–83, Chm., 1979–83; Mem., Particle Physics Cttee, 1978–79; Chm., Film Analysis Grants Cttee, 1972–75); UK deleg. on Council, CERN, 1979–82 (Mem., Research Bd, 1976–82; Chm., Super Proton Synchroton Cttee, 1976–79). Member: Physics Res. Cttee, Deutsches Elektronen Synchroton, Hamburg, 1981–85; Sci. Policy Cttee, Stanford Linear Accelerator Center, Calif, 1984–86. *Publications:* numerous papers in learned jls (on Hadron Spectroscopy and Application of Bubble Chamber to Strong and Weak Interaction Physics): Annual Review of Nuclear Science; Physical Review; Nuovo Cimento; Nuclear Physics; Physical Review Letters; Physics Letters, etc. *Recreation:* history of art. *Address:* Queen Mary College, Mile End Road, E1 4NS; 1 The Pierhead, Wapping High Street, E1 9PN.

BUTTERWORTH, Sir Neville; *see* Butterworth, Sir G. N.

BUTTFIELD, Dame Nancy (Eileen), DBE 1972; formerly Senator for South Australia; *b* 12 Nov. 1912; *d* of Sir Edward Wheewall Holden and Hilda May Lavis; *m* 1936, Frank Charles Buttfield; two *s. Educ:* Woodlands Church of England Girls' Grammar Sch., Adelaide; Composenea; Paris; Univ. of Adelaide, SA. Senator for South Australia, Oct. 1955–June 1965, re-elected July 1968–74. Exec. Mem., Commonwealth Immigration Adv. Council, 1955–; Vice-President: Good Neighbour Council of SA, 1956–62; Phoenix Soc. for the Physically Handicapped, 1959–. Dir, Co-operative Building Soc. of SA, 1959–. Mem. Council, Bedford Industries, 1965–. Mem., Nat. Council of Women of SA. *Recreations:* farming, dress-making, gourmet cooking, music. *Address:* 52 Strangeways Terrace, North Adelaide, SA 5006, Australia. *Clubs:* Queen Adelaide, Lyceum, Royal Adelaide Golf (all SA).

BUTTON, Air Vice-Marshal Arthur Daniel, CB 1976; OBE 1959; CEng; Director of RAF Education Branch, 1972–76; *b* 26 May 1916; *o s* of late Leonard Daniel Button and of Agnes Ann (*née* Derbyshire); *m* 1944, Eira Guelph Waterhouse, *o d* of late Reginald Waterhouse Jones; one *s* decd. *Educ:* County High Sch., Ilford; University Coll., Southampton (BSc(Hons), (Lond)). Joined RAF Educnl Service, 1938; Gen. Duties Br., RAF, 1941–46; (Queen's Commendation for Valuable Service in the Air, 1946); returned to RAF Educn Br., 1946. Dir, ARELS Examinations Trust, 1976–86. Member Council: RAF Benevolent Fund, 1980–; RAF Assoc., 1980–; Lord Kitchener Nat. Meml Fund, 1983–. Governor, Duke of Kent School, 1981–. *Recreations:* music, do-it-myself. *Address:* Dragons, 23 Upper Icknield Way, Aston Clinton, Aylesbury, Bucks HP22 5NF. *Club:* Royal Air Force.

BUTTON, Henry George; author; *b* 11 Aug. 1913; *e s* of late Rev. Frank S. and Bertha B. Button; *m* 1938, Edith Margaret Heslop (*d* 1972); two *d. Educ:* Manchester Grammar Sch.; Christ's Coll., Cambridge (Scholar). Mod. and Medieval Langs Tripos, Part II, 1st Class (with dist.) 1934; MLitt 1977; Tiarks German Scholar (research at Univ. of Bonn), 1934–35; Sen. Studentship of Goldsmiths' Company, 1935–36. Entered Civil Service, 1937; Board of Trade, 1937–57 (served in Min. of Production, 1942; Counsellor, UK Delegn to OEEC, Paris, 1952–55; on staff of Monopolies Commn, 1955–56); transf. Min. of Agriculture, Fisheries and Food, 1957; Under-Sec., Min. of Agriculture, Fisheries and Food, 1960–73 (Principal Finance Officer, 1965–73). Res. Student, 1974–76, Fellow-Commoner, 1982, Christ's Coll., Cambridge. Mem. Agricultural Research Council, 1960–62. Leader of various UK Delegns to FAO in Rome. BBC Brain of Britain for 1962; rep. Great Britain in radio quiz in Johannesburg, 1966; Bob Dyer's TV show, Sydney, 1967. *Publications:* The Guinness Book of the Business World (with A. Lampert), 1976; contribs to various jls both learned and unlearned, and to newspapers. *Recreations:* reading, writing, studying old businesses (hon. review ed., Business Archives Council, 1966–75; Hon. Sec., Tercentenarians' Club, 1969–), showing visitors round the colleges. *Address:* 7 Amhurst Court, Grange Road, Cambridge CB3 9BH. *T:* 355698. *Club:* Civil Service.

BUTTROSE, Murray; a Deputy Circuit Judge, 1975–77; *b* 31 July 1903; *s* of William Robert and Frances Buttrose, both British; *m* 1935, Jean Marie Bowering; one *s. Educ:* St Peter's Coll. and Adelaide Univ., South Australia. Admitted and enrolled as a barrister and solicitor of the Supreme Court of S Australia, 1927; apptd to HM Colonial Legal Service, 1946; Crown Counsel, Singapore, 1946, Senior Crown Counsel, 1949, and Solicitor-General, Singapore, 1955; Puisne Judge, Singapore, 1956–68, retired. Admitted and enrolled as a solicitor of the Supreme Court of Judicature in England, 1955; a Recorder of the Crown Court, 1972–74. Formerly Temp. Dep. Chm. (part time), London QS. Served with Royal Air Force (RAFVR), 1940–45. *Recreations:* reading, tennis, and golf. *Address:* 2B Metropole Court, Metropole Hotel, Kings Road, Brighton, E Sussex BN1 2FU. *T:* Brighton 204363.

BUXTON, family name of **Barons Buxton of Alsa** and **Noel-Buxton.**

BUXTON OF ALSA, Baron *cr* 1978 (Life Peer), of Stiffkey in the County of Norfolk; **Aubrey Leland Oakes Buxton,** MC 1943; DL; Chairman, Anglia Television, since 1986 (Director, since 1958); Dir, Survival Anglia Ltd; *b* 15 July 1918; *s* of Leland Wilberforce Buxton and Mary, *d* of Rev. Thomas Henry Oakes; *m* 1946, Pamela Mary (*d* 1983), *d* of Sir Henry Birkin, 3rd Bt; two *s* four *d. Educ:* Ampleforth; Trinity Coll., Cambridge. Served 1939–45, RA; combined ops in Arakan, 1942–45 (despatches, 1944). Extra Equerry to Duke of Edinburgh, 1964. A Trustee of the British Museum (Natural History), 1971–73. Member: Countryside Commn, 1968–72; Royal Commission on Environmental Pollution, 1970–74; British Vice Pres., World Wildlife Fund; Trustee, Wildfowl Trust; Treasurer, London Zoological Soc., 1978–83; Former Pres., Royal Television Soc.; Chairman: Independent Television Cos Assoc., 1972–75; UPITN Inc., USA, 1981–83; ITN, 1981–86. Wildlife Film Producer, Anglia TV. Golden Awards, Internat. TV Festival, 1963 and 1968; Silver Medal, Zoological Society of London, 1967; Silver Medal, Royal TV Society, 1968; Queen's Award to Industry, 1974; Gold Medal, Royal TV Soc., 1977. High Sheriff of Essex 1972; DL Essex, 1975–85. *Publications:* (with Sir Philip Christison) The Birds of Arakan, 1946; The King in his Country, 1955. *Recreations:* travel, natural history, painting, sport. *Address:* Old Hall Farm, Stiffkey, Norfolk. *Club:* White's.

BUXTON, Adrian Clarence, CMG 1978; HM Diplomatic Service, retired; Ambassador to Ecuador, 1981–85; *b* 12 June 1925; *s* of Clarence Buxton and Dorothy (*née* Lintott); *m* 1st, 1958, Leonora Mary Cherkas (*d* 1984); three *s*; 2nd, 1985, June Samson. *Educ:* Christ's Hosp., Horsham; Trinity Coll., Cambridge. RNVR, 1944–46; FO, 1947; 3rd Sec., Bangkok, 1948–52; FO, 1952–53; 2nd Sec., Khartoum, 1953–55; 2nd later 1st Sec., Bonn, 1955–58; 1st Sec. (Commercial) and Consul, Bogota, 1958–62; FO, 1962–64; 1st Sec., Saigon, 1964–67; 1st Sec. (Commercial), Havana, 1967–69; UK Dep. Permanent Rep. to UN and other internat. organisations at Geneva, 1969–73; Univ. of Surrey, 1973–74; Head of Training Dept and Dir Language Centre, FCO, 1974–75; Head of Maritime and Gen. Dept, FCO, 1975–77; Ambassador to Bolivia, 1977–81. *Recreations:* golf, choral singing. *Address:* 7 Grove Road, Merrow, Guildford, Surrey.

BUXTON, Andrew Robert Fowell; Vice-Chairman of Barclays Bank PLC, since 1984; Chairman, Barclays Merchant Bank, since 1986; *b* 5 April 1939; *m* 1965, Jane Margery Grant; two *d. Educ:* Winchester Coll.; Pembroke Coll., Oxford. Joined Barclays Bank Ltd, 1963; Dir, Barclays Bank UK Ltd, 1978; Gen. Man., Barclays Bank PLC, 1980. *Club:* Royal Automobile.

BUXTON, Major Desmond Gurney, DL; 60th Rifles, retired; retired as Local Director (Norwich) Barclays Bank, 1958; Member Norfolk County Council, 1958–74; *b* 4 Jan. 1898; *e s* of late Edward G. Buxton, Catton Hall, Norwich, and late Mrs Buxton, The Beeches, Old Catton, Norwich; *m* 1930, Rachel Mary, *yr d* of late Colonel A. F. Morse, Coltishall Mead, Norwich; two *s* three *d* (and one *d* decd). *Educ:* Eton; RMC Sandhurst. 60th Rifles, 1917–29; France and Belgium, 1917–18; NW Europe, 1945. Sheriff of Norwich, 1936–37; Lieut-Colonel Royal Norfolk Regt (TA), 1939–40. High Sheriff, Norfolk, 1960; DL Norfolk, 1961. CStJ 1972. *Recreations:* forestry, chess, bridge. *Address:* Hoveton Hall, Wroxham, Norwich NR12 8RJ.

BUXTON, Prof. John Noel, FBCS; Professor of Information Technology, King's College, London, since 1984; *b* 25 Dec. 1933; *s* of John William Buxton and Laura Frances Buxton; *m* 1958, Moira Jean O'Brien; two *s* two *d. Educ:* Bradford Grammar Sch.; Trinity Coll., Cambridge (BA 1955, MA 1959). FBCS 1968. Flight Trials Engr, De Havilland Propellers, 1955–59; Ops Res. Scientist, British Iron and Steel Res. Assoc., 1959–60; Applied Science Rep., IBM UK, 1960–62; Lectr, Inst. of Computer Science, Univ. of London, 1962–66; Chief Software Consultant, CEIR (now Scicon Ltd) 1966–68; Prof. of Computer Science, Univ. of Warwick, 1968–84. UNDP Proj. Manager, Internat. Computing Educn Centre, Budapest, 1975–77; Vis. Scholar, Harvard Univ., 1979–80. *Publications:* (ed) Simulation Programming Languages, 1968; (ed jtly) Software Engineering Concepts and Techniques (Procs of NATO Confs 1968 and 1969), 1976; three computer programming languages; papers in professional jls. *Recreations:* mountaineering, music, ancient houses. *Address:* Bull's Hall, Yaxley, near Eye, Suffolk IP23 8BZ.

BUXTON, Paul William Jex; Under Secretary, Northern Ireland Office, 1981–85; *b* 20 Sept. 1925; *s* of late Denis Buxton and Emily Buxton (*née* Hollins); *m* 1st, 1950, Katharine Hull (marr. diss. 1971, she *d* 1977); two *s* one *d*; 2nd, 1971, Hon. Margaret Aston (*née* Bridges), PhD; two *d. Educ:* Rugby Sch.; Balliol Coll., Oxford. Coldstream Guards, 1944–47. HM Foreign, later Diplomatic, Service, 1950–71; served Delhi, UN, Guatemala and Washington, latterly as Counsellor. Investment banking, 1972–74. NI Office, 1974–85. *Address:* Castle House, Chipping Ongar, Essex. *T:* Ongar 362642. *Club:* Brooks's.

BUXTON, Raymond Naylor, OBE 1975; BEM 1957; QPM 1971; *b* 16 Sept. 1915; *s* of late Tom Bird Buxton and Ethel Buxton, Rushall, Walsall; *m* 1939, Agatha, *d* of late Enoch and Elizabeth Price, Essington, Wolverhampton; three *s. Educ:* King Edward VI Grammar Sch., Stafford. Constable to Chief Supt in Staffordshire Co. Police. Served War, RAF, Navigator, 1943–45 (FO). Police Coll. Staff, 1958–61; Asst Chief Constable, then Dep. Chief Constable of Herts, 1963–69, Chief Constable, 1969–77; HM Inspector of Constabulary, 1977–79. *Address:* Mannicotts, Radford Rise, Weeping Cross, Stafford.

BUXTON, Richard Joseph, QC 1983; *b* 13 July 1938; *o s* of Bernard Buxton, DSO, chartered mechanical engineer, and Sybil (*née* Hurley), formerly of Burton-upon-Trent. *Educ:* Brighton Coll. (Schol.); Exeter Coll., Oxford (Schol.; First Cl. Final Hon. Sch. of Jurisprudence 1961, First Cl. BCL 1962; Vinerian Schol. 1962; MA). Lectr, Christ Church, 1962–63; Lectr 1963–64, Fellow and Tutor 1964–73, also Sub-Rector 1966–71, Exeter Coll., Oxford. Called to the Bar, Inner Temple, 1969; in practice, 1972–. Second Lieut RAOC, 1957–58. Councillor (Lab) Oxford CC, 1966–69. *Publications:* Local Government, 1970, 2nd edn 1973; articles in legal periodicals. *Recreations:* walking, squash, criminal law. *Address:* Gray's Inn Chambers, WC1. *Clubs:* United Oxford & Cambridge University; Hornsey Squash.

BUXTON, Ronald Carlile; MA Cantab; *b* 20 Aug. 1923; *s* of Murray Barclay Buxton and Janet Mary Muriel Carlile; *m* 1959, Phyllida Dorothy Roden Buxton; two *s* two *d. Educ:* Eton; Trinity Coll., Cambridge. Chartered Structural Engineer (FIStructE). Director of H. Young & Co., London and associated companies. MP (C) Leyton, 1965–66. *Recreations:* travel, music, riding. *Address:* Kimberley Hall, Wymondham, Norfolk; 67 Ashley Gardens, SW1. *Club:* Carlton.

BUXTON, Sir Thomas Fowell Victor, 6th Bt *cr* 1840; *b* 18 Aug. 1925; *s* of Sir Thomas Fowell Buxton, 5th Bt, and Hon. Dorothy Cochrane (*d* 1927), *yr d* of 1st Baron Cochrane of Cults; *S* father, 1945; *m* 1955, Mrs D. M. Chisenhale-Marsh (*d* 1965). *Educ:* Eton; Trinity Coll., Cambridge. *Heir: cousin* Jocelyn Charles Roden Buxton [*b* 8 Aug. 1924; *m* 1960, Ann Frances, *d* of Frank Smitherman, *qv*; three *d*].

BUZZARD, Sir Anthony (Farquhar), 3rd Bt *cr* 1929; Lecturer in Theology, Oregon Bible College, Illinois, since 1982; *b* 28 June 1935; *s* of Rear-Admiral Sir Anthony Wass Buzzard, 2nd Bt, CB, DSO, OBE, and of Margaret Elfreda, *d* of Sir Arthur Knapp, KCIE, CSI, CBE; *S* father, 1972; *m* 1970, Barbara Jean Arnold, Mendon, Michigan, USA; two *d. Educ:* Charterhouse; Christ Church, Oxford (MA); Ambassador Coll., Pasadena, USA (BA). ARCM. Lecturer in French, Ambassador Coll., Pasadena, 1962–65; Peripatetic Music Teacher for Surrey County Council, 1966–68; Lectr in French and Hebrew, Ambassador Coll., Bricket Wood, Herts, 1969–74; teacher of mod. langs, American Sch. in London, 1974–81. Founded Restoration Fellowship, 1981. *Publications:* articles on eschatology and Christology in various jls. *Recreations:* tennis, squash, music. *Heir: b* Timothy Macdonnell Buzzard [*b* 28 Jan. 1939; *m* 1970, Jennifer Mary, *d* of late Peter Patching; one *s* one *d*]. *Address:* Box 100, Oregon, Ill 61061, USA. *T:* (815) 734 4344.

BYAM SHAW, (John) James, CBE 1972; *b* 12 Jan. 1903; *er* surv. *s* of John Byam Shaw and Evelyn Pyke-Nott; *m* 1st, 1929, Eveline (marr. diss., 1938), *d* of Capt. Arthur Dodgson, RN; 2nd, 1945, Margaret (*d* 1965), *d* of Arthur Saunders, MRCVS; one *s*; 3rd, 1967, Christina, *d* of Francis Ogilvy and *widow* of W. P. Gibson. *Educ:* Westminster; Christ Church, Oxford. Scholar of Westminster and Christ Church; MA 1925; Hon. DLitt Oxford 1977. Worked independently in principal museums of Europe, 1925–33; Lecturer and Assistant to the Director, Courtauld Institute of Art, Univ. of London, 1933–34; joined P. & D. Colnaghi & Co., 1934; Director, 1937–68. Served in Royal Scots, UK, India and Burma, 1940–46 (wounded); Major, 1944. Lectr, Christ Church, Oxford, 1964–73; Associate Curator of pictures, Christ Church, Oxford, 1973–74; Hon. Student of Christ Church, 1976. Member: Council of the Byam Shaw Sch. of Art, 1957–77; Exec. Cttee, Nat. Art Collections Fund, 1968–85; Council, British Museum Soc., 1969–74; Gulbenkian Cttee on conservation of paintings and drawings, 1970–72; Conservation Cttee, Council for Places of Worship, 1970–77; Adv. Cttee, London Diocesan Council for Care of Churches, 1974–76. Mem., Cons. Cttee, Burlington Magazine, 1984–; Chm., Adv. Cttee, Master Drawings (NY), 1981–. Trustee, Watts Gall. FSA; FRSA. Hon. Fellow: Pierpont Morgan Library, NY; Ateneo Veneto. Grande Ufficiale, Ordine al Merito, Republic of Italy, 1982. *Publications:* The Drawings of Francesco Guardi, 1951; The Drawings of Domenico Tiepolo, 1962; Catalogue of Paintings by Old Masters at Christ Church Oxford, 1967; Catalogue of Drawings by Old Masters at Christ Church, Oxford, 1976; Catalogue of exhibition, Disegni Veneti della

Collezione Lugt, Venice, 1981; Catalogue of Italian Drawings at the Fondation Custodia (Lugt Collection), Institut Néerlandais, Paris, 1983 (Premio Salimbeni, 1984); (with George Knox) The Robert Lehman Collection, vol. 6: Italian 18th Century Drawings, New York, 1986; publications in Old Master Drawings (1926–39), Print Collectors' Quarterly, Burlington Magazine, Apollo, Master Drawings (New York), Art Quarterly (Detroit), Arte Veneta, etc. *Address:* 4 Abingdon Villas, Kensington, W8. *T:* 01–937 6128. *Club:* Athenæum.

BYAM SHAW, Nicholas Glencairn; Managing Director, Macmillan Publishers Ltd (formerly Macmillan and Co.), since 1969; *b* 28 March 1934; *s* of Lieut. Comdr David Byam Shaw, RN, OBE (killed in action, 19 Dec. 1941) and Clarita Pamela Clarke; *m* 1st, 1956, Joan Elliott; two *s* one *d*; 2nd, 1974, Suzanne Filer (*née* Rastello). *Educ:* Royal Naval Coll., Dartmouth. Commnd RN, 1955 (Lieut). Joined William Collins Sons & Co. Ltd, Glasgow, as salesman, 1956; Sales Manager, 1960; Macmillan and Co.: Sales Manager, 1964; Sales Dir, 1965; Dep. Man. Dir, 1967. Director: St Martins Press, 1980–; Pan Books, 1983–. *Recreations:* gardening, travel. *Address:* 9 Kensington Park Gardens, W11 3HB. *T:* 01–221 4547.

BYATT, Antonia Susan, (Mrs P. J. Duffy), FRSL 1983; writer; *b* 24 Aug. 1936; *d* of His Honour John Frederick Drabble, QC and late Kathleen Marie Bloor; *m* 1st, 1959, Ian Charles Rayner Byatt, *qv* (marr. diss. 1969); one *d* (one *s* decd); 2nd, 1969, Peter John Duffy; two *d*. *Educ:* Sheffield High Sch.; The Mount Sch., York; Newnham Coll., Cambridge (BA Hons); Bryn Mawr Coll., Pa, USA; Somerville Coll., Oxford. Extra-Mural Lectr, Univ. of London, 1962–71; Lectr in Literature, Central Sch. of Art and Design, 1965–69; Lectr in English, 1972–81, Sen. Lectr, 1981–83, UCL. Associate of Newnham Coll., Cambridge, 1977–. Member: Social Effects of Television Adv. Gp, BBC, 1974–77; Bd of Communications and Cultural Studies, CNAA, 1978–84; Bd of Creative and Performing Arts, CNAA, 1985–; PEN (Macmillan Silver Pen of Fiction, 1986); Management Cttee, Soc. of Authors, 1984– (Dep. Chm., 1986). Broadcaster, reviewer; judge of literary prizes (Hawthornden, Booker, David Higham, Betty Trask). FRSL. *Publications:* Shadow of a Sun, 1964; Degrees of Freedom, 1965; The Game, 1967; Wordsworth and Coleridge in their Time, 1970; Iris Murdoch, 1976; The Virgin in the Garden, 1978; (ed) George Eliot, The Mill on the Floss, 1979; Still Life, 1985. *Address:* 37 Rusholme Road, SW15. *T:* 01–789 3109.

BYATT, Sir Hugh Campbell, KCVO 1985; CMG 1979; HM Diplomatic Service, retired; Ambassador to Portugal, 1981–86; *b* 27 Aug. 1927; *e s* of late Sir Horace Byatt, GCMG, and Lady Byatt (*née* Olga Margaret Campbell), MBE; *m* 1954, Fiona, *d* of Ian P. Coats; two *s* one *d*. *Educ:* Gordonstoun; New College, Oxford (MA 1951). Served in Royal Navy, 1945–48; HMOCS Nigeria, 1952–57; Commonwealth Relations Office, 1958; Bombay, 1961–63; CRO, 1964–65; seconded to Cabinet Office, 1965–67; Head of Chancery, Lisbon, 1967–70; Asst Head, South Asian Dept, FCO, 1970–71; Consul-General, Lourenço Marques, 1971–73; Inspector, HM Diplomatic Service, 1973–75; RCDS, 1976; Dep. High Comr, Nairobi, 1977–78; Ambassador to Angola, 1978–81, to São Tomé, 1980–81. Knight Grand Cross, Mil. Order of Christ (Portugal), 1985. *Recreations:* sailing, fishing, gardening. *Address:* Leargnahension, By Tarbert, Loch Fyne, Argyll. *T:* Tarbert 644. *Clubs:* Royal Ocean Racing; New (Edinburgh); Leander.
See also R. A. C. Byatt.

BYATT, Ian Charles Rayner; Deputy Chief Economic Adviser, HM Treasury, since 1978; *b* 11 March 1932; *s* of Charles Rayner Byatt and Enid Marjorie Annie Byatt (*née* Howat); *m* 1959, A. S. Byatt, *qv* (marr. diss. 1969); one *d* (one *s* decd). *Educ:* Kirkham Grammar Sch.; Oxford University. Commonwealth Fund Fellow, Harvard, 1957–58; Lectr in Economics, Durham Univ., 1958–62; Economic Consultant, HM Treasury, 1962–64; Lectr in Economics, LSE, 1964–67; Sen. Economic Adviser, Dept of Educn and Science, 1967–69; Dir of Econs and Stats, Min. of Housing and Local Govt, 1969–70; Dir Economics, DoE, 1970–72; Under Sec., HM Treasury, 1972–78. Chm., Economic Policy Cttee of the European Communities, 1982–85 (Mem., 1978–); Member: Central Council of Educn (England), 1965–66; Economics Cttee, CNAA, 1968–70; ESRC, 1983–; Urban Motorways Cttee, 1970; Cttee on Water Services: Econ. and Financial Objectives, 1970–73; Council, Royal Econ. Soc., 1983. *Publications:* The British Electrical Industry 1875–1914, 1979; articles on economics in books and learned jls; official reports. *Recreation:* painting. *Address:* 17 Thanet Street, WC1. *T:* 01–388 3888.

BYATT, Ronald Archer Campbell, CMG 1980; HM Diplomatic Service; Ambassador to Morocco, since 1985; *b* 14 Nov. 1930; *s* of late Sir Horace Byatt, GCMG and late Olga Margaret Campbell, MBE; *m* 1954, Ann Brereton Sharpe, *d* of C. B. Sharpe; one *s* one *d*. *Educ:* Gordonstoun; New Coll., Oxford; King's Coll., Cambridge. Served in RNVR, 1949–50. Colonial Admin. Service, Nyasaland, 1955–58; joined HM Foreign (now Diplomatic) Service, 1959; FO, 1959; Havana, 1961; FO, 1963; UK Mission to UN, NY, 1966; Kampala, 1970; Head of Rhodesia Dept, FCO, 1972–75; Vis. Fellow, Glasgow Univ., 1975–76; Counsellor and Head of Chancery, UK Mission to UN, NY, 1977–79; Asst Under Sec. of State, FCO, 1979–80; High Comr in Harare, 1980–83; Mem, Directing Staff, RCDS, 1983–84. *Recreations:* sailing, boating (OUBC 1953), bird-watching, gardening. *Address:* c/o Foreign and Commonwealth Office, SW1; Drim-na-Vullin, Lochgilphead, Argyll. *T:* Lochgilphead 2615. *Clubs:* United Oxford & Cambridge University; Leander (Henley-on-Thames).
See also Sir H. C. Byatt.

BYERS, Sir Maurice (Hearne), Kt 1982; CBE 1978; QC 1960; barrister; Solicitor-General of Australia, 1973–83; Chairman: Police Board of New South Wales, since 1984; Australian Constitutional Commission, since 1986; *b* 10 Nov. 1917; *s* of Arthur Tolhurst Byers and Mabel Florence Byers (*née* Hearne); *m* 1949, Patricia Therese Davis; two *s* one *d*. *Educ:* St Aloysius Coll., Milson's Point, Sydney; Sydney Univ. LLB. Called to the Bar, 1944. Mem., Exec. Council, Law Council of Australia, 1966–68; Vice-Pres., NSW Bar Assoc., 1964–65, Pres., 1965–67. Leader, Australian delegations to: UN Commn on Internat. Trade Law, 1974, 1976–82; Diplomatic Conf. on Sea Carriage of Goods, Hamburg, 1979. Member: Council, ANU, 1975–78; Australian Law Reform Commn, 1984–85. *Address:* 14 Morella Road, Clifton Gardens, NSW 2088, Australia. *T:* 969 8257. *Clubs:* Commonwealth (Canberra); Union (Sydney).

BYERS, Dr Paul Duncan; Head of Department of Morbid Anatomy, Institute of Orthopaedics, University of London, since 1980 (Dean of Institute, 1971–79); *b* Montreal, 1922; *s* of A. F. Byers and Marion Taber; *m* 1959, Valery Garden. *Educ:* Bishops College Sch., PQ, Canada; McGill Univ. (BSc, MD, CM); Univ. of London (DCP, PhD). FRCPath. Alan Blair Memorial Fellow, Canadian Cancer Soc., 1955–57. Asst Morbid Anatomist, Inst. of Orthopaedics, 1960; Reader in Morbid Anatomy, Univ. of London, 1974. Hon. Consultant, Royal National Orthopaedic Hosp., 1965; Hon. Senior Lectr, Royal Postgrad. Med. Sch., 1969. Chm., Osteosarcoma Histopathol. Panel, MRC/EORTC, 1983–; Member: Osteosarcoma Wkg Party, MRC, 1982–; Soft Tissue Sarconia Wkg Party, MRC, 1983–84. Mem., Management Cttee, Courtauld Inst. of Art, Univ. of London, 1979–82. *Publications:* articles in medical press on arthritis, metabolic bone disease, bone tumours, medical education. *Recreation:* arts. *Address:* 18 Wimpole Street, W1M 7AD. *T:* 01–580 5206.

BYFORD, Sir Lawrence, Kt 1984; CBE 1979; QPM 1973; HM Chief Inspector of Constabulary, since 1983; *b* 10 Aug. 1925; *s* of George Byford and Monica Irene Byford; *m* 1950, Muriel Campbell Massey; two *s* one *d*. *Educ:* Univ. of Leeds (LLB Hons). Barrister-at-Law. Joined W Riding Police, 1947; served on Directing Staff of Wakefield Detective Sch., 1959–62, and Police Staff Coll., Bramshill, 1964–66; Divl Comdr, Huddersfield, 1966–68; Asst Chief Constable of Lincs, 1968, Dep. Chief Constable 1970, Chief Constable, 1973–77; HM Inspector of Constabulary for: SE Region, 1977–78; NE Region, 1978–82. Lecture tour of univs, USA and Canada, 1976; Headed: British Police Mission to Turkey, 1978–79; official review into Yorkshire Ripper case, 1981. *Publications:* articles in Forensic Science Jl, police magazines and newspapers. *Recreations:* gardening, walking. *Address:* Home Office, Queen Anne's Gate, SW1H 9AT. *Clubs:* Royal Over-Seas League, MCC.

BYGRAVES, Max Walter, OBE 1983; entertainer; *b* 16 Oct. 1922; *s* of Henry and Lilian Bygraves, Rotherhithe, SE16; *m* 1942, Gladys Blossom Murray; one *s* two *d*. *Educ:* St Joseph's, Rotherhithe. Began in advertising agency, carrying copy to Fleet Street, 1936. Volunteered for RAF, 1940; served 5 years as fitter. Performed many shows for troops; became professional, 1946; has appeared in venues all over English-speaking world, incl. 18 Royal Command Performances; best selling record artist. Host, Family Fortunes, TV, 1983–85. *Publications:* I Wanna Tell You a Story (autobiog.), 1976; The Milkman's on his Way (novel), 1977. *Recreations:* golf, painting, reading, writing. *Address:* Roebuck House, Victoria, SW1E 5BE. *T:* 01–828 4595. *Clubs:* St James's, East India.

BYNG, family name of **Earl of Strafford,** and of **Viscount Torrington.**

BYNOE, Dame Hilda Louisa, DBE 1969; in General Medical Practice, Port of Spain, Trinidad, since 1974; *b* Grenada, 18 Nov. 1921; *d* of late Thomas Joseph Gibbs, CBE, JP, Estate Proprietor, and Louisa Gibbs (*née* La Touche); *m* 1947, Peter Cecil Alexander Bynoe, ARIBA, Dip. Arch., former RAF Flying Officer; two *s*. *Educ:* St Joseph's Convent, St George's, Grenada; Royal Free Hospital Medical Sch., Univ. of London. MB, BS (London), 1951, MRCS, LRCP, 1951. Teacher, St Joseph's Convents, Trinidad and Grenada, 1939–44; hospital and private practice, London, 1951–53; public service with Govt of Trinidad and Tobago, 1954–55, with Govt of Guyana (then British Guiana), 1955–58, with Govt of Trinidad and Tobago, 1958–65; private practice, Trinidad, 1961–68; Governor of Associated State of Grenada, WI, 1968–74. Chm. Designate, Nat. Foundn for Arts and Culture, Trinidad and Tobago, 1980–. Patron, Caribbean Women's Assoc., 1970–. *Recreations:* swimming, music, reading, poetry-writing. *Address:* 5A Barcant Avenue, Maraval, Trinidad.

BYRNE, Sir Clarence (Askew), Kt 1969; OBE 1964; DSC 1945; Company Director, Mining, Insurance and Construction, Queensland; *b* 17 Jan. 1903; *s* of George Patrick Byrne, Brisbane, Qld, and Elizabeth Emma Askew, Dalby, Qld; *m* 1928, Nellie Ann Millicent Jones; one *s* one *d*. *Educ:* Brisbane Technical Coll. Mining Develt and Exploration, 1925–30; Oil Exploration, Roma, Qld, 1930–40. Served War, 1940–46 (DSC, Amer. Bronze Star Medal): Lt-Comdr; CO, HMAS Warrego, 1944–45. Pres., Qld Chamber of Mines, 1961–70; Exec. Dir, Conzinc Riotinto of Australia Ltd (Resident, Qld, 1957–68); Formerly: Chm., Qld Alumina Ltd; Director: Thiess Holdings Ltd; Walkers Ltd. Former Mem. Aust. Mining Industries Council, Canberra. *Recreations:* fishing, ocean cruising. *Address:* Culverston, Dingle Avenue, Caloundra, Qld 4551, Australia. *T:* Caloundra 91–1228. *Clubs:* United Service, Queensland (Brisbane).

BYRNE, Douglas Norman; Head of Marine Division, Department of Transport (formerly of Trade), 1980–84; *b* 30 Jan. 1924; *s* of Leonard William Byrne and Clarice Evelyn Byrne; *m* 1949, Noreen Thurlby Giles; one *s* one *d*. *Educ:* Portsmouth Grammar Sch.; St John's Coll., Cambridge (MA). RAF, 1942–46. Asst Principal, Min. of Supply, 1949; BoT, 1956; Cabinet Office, 1961–64; Asst Sec., 1964; on staff of Monopolies Commn, 1966–68; Under-Sec., Dept of Industry, 1974–77; Hd of Fair Trading Div., Dept of Prices and Consumer Protection, 1977–79; Under-Sec., Dept of Trade, 1979–83, Dept of Transport, 1983–84. *Recreations:* hill walking, natural history. *Club:* Royal Air Force.

BYRNE, John Keyes; *see* Leonard, Hugh.

BYRNE, Rev. Father Paul Laurence, OMI; OBE 1976; Secretary General, Conference of Major Religious Superiors of Ireland, since 1980; *b* 8 Aug. 1932; *s* of late John Byrne and Lavinia Byrne. *Educ:* Synge Street Christian Brothers' Sch. and Belcamp Coll., Dublin; University Coll., Dublin (BA, Hons Phil.); Oblate Coll., Piltown. Teacher, Belcamp Coll., 1959–65; Dean of Belcamp Coll., 1961–65; Dir, Irish Centre, Birmingham, 1965–68; Dir, Catholic Housing Aid Soc. (Birmingham) and Family Housing Assoc., Birmingham, 1965–69; Nat. Dir, Catholic Housing Aid Soc., and Dir, Family Housing Assoc., London, 1969–70; Dir SHAC (a housing aid centre), 1969–76. Board Member: Threshold Centre; Servite Houses; SHAC; Housing Corp., 1974–77; Irish Sch. of Ecumenics. Associate, Inst. of Housing, 1972. *Recreations:* golf, theatre-going. *Address:* 170 Merrion Road, Ballsbridge Road, Dublin 4. *T:* 0001–693658. *Club:* Foxrock Golf.

BYRON, 12th Baron *cr* 1643; **Richard Geoffrey Gordon Byron,** DSO 1944; retired; *b* 3 Nov. 1899; *s* of Col Richard Byron, DSO (*d* 1939), and Mabel Mackenzie (*d* 1962), *d* of Charles Albert Winter; *S* kinsman, 1983; *m* 1st, 1926, Margaret Mary Steuart (marr. diss. 1945); 2nd, 1946, Dorigen Margaret (*d* 1985), *o d* of Percival Kennedy Esdaile; one *s* (and one *s* decd). *Educ:* Eton; Sandhurst. Joined 4th Royal Dragoon Guards, 1918; ADC to Governor of Bombay, 1921; Mil. Sec. to Gov.-Gen. of NZ, 1937; comd 4/7th Dragoon Guards, Normandy, 1944; retired, 1948. *Heir:* *s* Hon. Robert James Byron [*b* 5 April 1950; *m* 1979, Robyn Margaret, *d* of John McLean, Hamilton, NZ; three *d*]. *Address:* 62 Burton Court, SW3. *T:* 01–730 2921.

BYRT, (Henry) John, QC 1976; **His Honour Judge Byrt;** a Circuit Judge, since 1983; *b* 5 March 1929; *s* of Dorothy Muriel Byrt and Albert Henry Byrt, CBE; *m* 1957, Eve Hermione Bartlett; one *s* two *d*. *Educ:* Charterhouse; Merton Coll., Oxford (BA, MA). Called to the Bar, Middle Temple, 1953; called within the Bar, 1976; a Recorder of the Crown Court, 1976–83. President: Social Security Appeal Tribunals, 1983–; Medical Appeal Tribunals, 1983–. Vice-Principal, Working Mens' Coll., London, 1978–82, Principal, 1982–; Mem. Council, Queen's Coll., London, 1982–. *Recreations:* building, gardening, sailing, music. *Address:* 65 Gloucester Crescent, NW1. *T:* 01–485 0341. *Club:* Leander.

BYWATERS, Eric George Lapthorne, CBE 1975; MB (London); FRCP; Professor of Rheumatology, Royal Postgraduate Medical School, University of London, 1958–75, now Emeritus; Hon. Consultant Physician, Hammersmith Hospital and Canadian Red Cross Memorial Hospital, Taplow, Bucks; Hon. Librarian, Heberden Library, Royal College of Physicians, since 1970; *b* 1 June 1910; *s* of George Ernest Bywaters and Ethel Penney; *m* 1935, Betty Euan-Thomas; three *d*. *Educ:* Sutton Valence Sch., Kent; Middx Hosp. (Sen. Broderip Schol., Lyell Gold Medallist). McKenzie McKinnon Fellow, RCP,

1935; Asst Clin. Pathologist, Bland Sutton Inst., 1936; Rockefeller Travelling Fellow and Harvard Univ. Research Fellow in Med., 1937–39; Beit Memorial Fellow, 1939; Actg Dir, MRC Clin. Res. Unit (Shock), 1943; Lectr in Med., Postgrad. Med. Sch., 1945; Dir, MRC Rheumatism Res. Unit, Taplow, 1958–75, Sen. MRC Res. Fellow, Bone and Joint Unit, London Hosp., 1977–. Pres., European League against Rheumatism, 1977 (Hon. Mem. 1981); Councillor, Internat. League against Rheumatism. Hon. Mem., Heberden Soc., 1977; Hon. FACP, 1973; Hon. FRCP&S (Canada), 1977; Hon. FRSM, 1983. Hon.

MD Liège, 1973. Gairdner Foundation Medical Award, 1963; Heberden Orator and Medallist, 1966; Croonian Lectr, RCP, 1968; Bunim Lectr and Medallist, 1973; Ewart Angus Lectr, Toronto, 1974; Samuel Hyde Lectr, RSocMed, 1986. Hon. Mem. Dutch, French, Amer., German, Czech, Spanish, Portuguese, Aust., Indian, Canadian, Chilean, Peruvian, Jugoslav and Argentine Rheumatism Assocs. *Publications:* papers on rheumatism, Crush Syndrome, etc. *Recreations:* painting, gardening, tennis. *Address:* Long Acre, 53 Burkes Road, Beaconsfield, Bucks.

C

CABALLÉ, Montserrat; Cross of Lazo de Dama of Order of Isabel the Catholic, Spain; opera and concert singer; *b* Barcelona, 12 April 1933; *d* of Carlos and Ana Caballé; *m* 1964, Bernabé Marti, tenor; one *s* one *d*. *Educ:* Conservatorio del Liceo, Barcelona. Continued to study singing under Mme Eugenia Kemeny. Carnegie Hall début as Lucrezia Borgia, 1965. London début in this role, with the London Opera Society, at the Royal Festival Hall, 1968. Has sung at Covent Garden, Glyndebourne, La Scala, Vienna, Metropolitan Opera, San Francisco and most major opera venues. Major roles include Maria Stuarda, Luisa Miller, Queen Elizabeth in Roberto Devereux, Imogene in Il Pirata, Violetta in La Traviata, Marguerite in Faust, Desdemona in Otello, Norma, Tosca, Turandot, Leonora in La Forza del Destino, Semiramide and also those of contemporary opera. Over 120 roles sung and recorded. Numerous hon. degrees, awards and medals. *Address:* c/o Columbia Artists Management Inc., 165 W 57th Street, New York, NY 10019, USA.

CABLE, Sir James (Eric), KCVO 1976; CMG 1967; HM Diplomatic Service, retired; writer; *b* 15 Nov. 1920; *s* of late Eric Grant Cable, CMG; *m* 1954, Viveca Hollmerus; one *s*. *Educ:* Stowe; CCC, Cambridge. PhD 1973. Served Royal Signals, 1941–46, Major. Entered Foreign (now Diplomatic) Service, 1947; 2nd Sec., 1948; Vice-Consul, Batavia, 1949; 2nd Sec., Djakarta, 1949; acted as Chargé d'Affaires, 1951 and 1952; Helsinki, 1952; FO, 1953; 1st Sec., 1953; Mem. of British Delegn to Geneva Conf. on Indo-China, 1954; 1st Sec. (Commercial), Budapest, 1956; Head of Chancery and Consul, Quito, 1959; acted as Chargé d'Affaires, 1959 and 1960; FO, 1961 and Head of SE Asia Dept, Dec. 1963; Counsellor, Beirut, 1966; acted as Chargé d'Affaires at Beirut, 1967, 1968 and 1969; Research Associate, Institute for Strategic Studies, 1969–70; Head of Western Organisations Dept, FCO, 1970–71; Counsellor, Contingency Studies, FCO, 1971; Head of Planning Staff, 1971–75, and Asst Under-Sec. of State, 1972–75, FCO; Ambassador to Finland, 1975–80; Leverhulme Res. Fellow, 1981–82. *Publications:* Britain in Tomorrow's World, 1969 (as Grant Hugo); Appearance and Reality in International Relations, 1970 (as Grant Hugo); Gunboat Diplomacy, 1971, 3rd edn 1986; The Royal Navy and the Siege of Bilbao, 1979; Britain's Naval Future, 1983; Diplomacy at Sea, 1985; The Geneva Conference of 1954 on Indochina, 1986; articles in various jls. *Address:* c/o Lloyds Bank, 16 St James's Street, SW1A 1EY.

CABLE-ALEXANDER, Sir Desmond William Lionel, 7th Bt (1809); *b* 1910; *S* 1956; *m* 1st, Mary Jane (who obtained a divorce), *d* of James O'Brien, JP, Enniskillen; one *s*; 2nd, Margaret Wood, *d* of late John Burnett, Dublin; two *d*. *Educ:* Harrow; Oxford. Assumed addtl name of Cable before that of Alexander, by deed poll, 1931. *Heir: s* Patrick Desmond William Cable-Alexander, Lt-Col Royal Scots Dragoon Guards [*b* 19 April 1936; *m* 1961, Diana Frances Rogers (marr. diss. 1976); two *d*; *m* 1976, Jane Mary, *d* of Dr Anthony Arthur Gough Lewis, MD, FRCP, of York; one *s*]. *Address:* c/o Barclays Bank, 16 Whitehall, SW1.

CABORN, Richard George; MP (Lab) Sheffield, Central, since 1983; *b* 6 Oct. 1943; *s* of George and Mary Caborn; *m* 1966, Margaret Caborn; one *s* one *d*. *Educ:* Hurlfield Comprehensive Sch.; Granville Coll. of Further Educn; Sheffield Polytechnic. Engrg apprentice, 1959–64; Convenor of Shop Stewards, Firth Brown Ltd, 1967–79. Mem. (Lab) Sheffield, European Parlt, 1979–84. *Recreation:* amateur football. *Address:* 29 Quarry Vale Road, Sheffield S12 3EB. *T:* Sheffield 393802. *Club:* Carlton Working Men's (Sheffield).

CACCIA, family name of **Baron Caccia.**

CACCIA, Baron *cr* 1965 (Life Peer), of Abernant; **Harold Anthony Caccia,** GCMG 1959 (KCMG 1950; CMG 1945); GCVO 1961 (KCVO 1957); *b* 21 Dec. 1905; *s* of late Anthony Caccia, CB, MVO; *m* 1932, Anne Catherine, *d* of late Sir George Barstow, KCB; two *d* (and one *s* decd). *Educ:* Eton; Trinity Coll., Oxford. Laming Travelling Fellowship, Queen's Coll., Oxford, 1928, Hon. Fellow, 1974. Entered HM Foreign Service as 3rd Sec., FO, 1929; transferred to HM Legation, Peking, 1932; 2nd Sec., 1934; FO 1935; Asst Private Sec. to Sec. of State, 1936; HM Legation, Athens, 1939; 1st Sec. 1940; FO 1941; seconded for service with Resident Minister, North Africa, 1943, and appointed Vice-Pres., Political Section, Allied Control Commission, Italy; Political Adviser, GOC-in-C Land Forces, Greece, 1944; Minister local rank, HM Embassy, Athens, 1945; Asst Under-Sec. of State, 1946, Dep. Under-Sec. of State, 1949, Foreign Office; British Ambassador in Austria, 1951–54, and also British High Comr in Austria, 1950–54; Dep. Under-Sec. of State, FO, 1954–56; British Ambassador at Washington, 1956–61; Permanent Under-Sec. of State, FO, 1962–65; Head of HM Diplomatic Service, 1964–65, retired. Provost, Eton Coll., 1965–77. Chairman: Standard Telephones & Cables, 1968–79; ITT (UK) Ltd, 1979–81; Director: Orion Bank (Chm., 1973–74); Westminster, later Nat. Westminster Bank, 1965–75; Prudential Assurance Co., 1965–80; F & C Investment Trust, 1965–78; F & C Eurotrust Ltd, 1972–84. Mem. Adv. Council, Foseco Minsep plc, 1972–. Chm., Gabbitas-Thring Educational Trust, 1967–73. Mem., Advisory Council on Public Records, 1968–73. Pres., MCC, 1973–74. Hon. Fellow, Trinity Coll., Oxford, 1963. Lord Prior of the Order of St John of Jerusalem, 1969–80; GCStJ. *Address:* Abernant, Builth-Wells, Powys LD2 3YR. *T:* Erwood 233.

CACHELIN, Commissioner Francy; British Commissioner, The Salvation Army, since 1984; *b* 4 Aug. 1923; *s* of Maurice Cachelin and France Hauswirth; *m* 1951, Geneviève Irène Catherine Booth; two *s* two *d*. *Educ:* Lausanne School of Arts. Commissioned Salvation Army Officer, 1944; served in Switzerland as Corps Officer; Editor, The War Cry, in Belgium, 1951; responsible for youth work, France, 1957; Field Secretary,

Switzerland, 1966; Chief Secretary, France, 1975, British Territory, 1977; Territorial Commander, Germany, 1979. *Recreation:* reading. *Address:* The Salvation Army, 101 Queen Victoria Street, EC4P 4EP.

CACOYANNIS, Michael; director, stage and screen, since 1954; *b* 11 June 1922; *s* of late Sir Panayotis Cacoyannis and Angeliki, *d* of George M. Efthyvoulos and Zoe Constantinides, Limassol, Cyprus. *Educ:* Greek Gymnasium; Gray's Inn and Old Vic Sch., London. Radio Producer, BBC, Greek Service, 1941–50. Actor on English stage, 1946–51; parts included: Herod, in Salome, 1946; Caligula, in Caligula, 1949, etc. Directed films: Windfall in Athens, 1953; Stella, 1954; Girl in Black, 1956; A Matter of Dignity, 1958; Our Last Spring, 1960; The Wastrel, 1961; Electra, 1962; Zorba the Greek, 1964; The Day the Fish Came Out, 1967; The Trojan Women, 1971; Attila '74, 1975; Iphigenia, 1977; Sweet Country, 1985. Directed plays: produced several of these in Athens for Ellie Lambetti's Company, 1955–61; The Trojan Women, New York, 1963–65, Paris, 1965; Things That Go Bump in the Night, and The Devils, New York, 1965; Mourning Becomes Electra, Metropolitan Opera, NY, 1967; Iphigenia in Aulis, New York, 1968; La Bohème, Juillard, NY, 1972; King Oedipus, Abbey Theatre, Dublin, 1973; Miss Margarita, Athens, 1975; The Bacchae, Comédie Française, 1977, New York, 1980; The Glass Menagerie, Nat. Theatre, Athens, 1978; Antony and Cleopatra, Athens, 1979; La Traviata, Athens, 1983; Zorba (musical), USA, 1983. Hon. DH Columbia Coll., Chicago, 1981. Order of the Phœnix (Greece), 1965; Officier des Arts et des Lettres, 1979. *Recreations:* walking, swimming. *Address:* 15 Mouson Street, Athens 117–41, Greece.

CADBURY, Sir Adrian; *see* Cadbury, Sir G. A. H.

CADBURY, Dominic; *see* Cadbury, N. D.

CADBURY, Sir (George) Adrian (Hayhurst), Kt 1977; Chairman, Cadbury Schweppes plc, since 1975; a Director of the Bank of England, since 1970; *b* 15 April 1929; *s* of late Laurence John Cadbury, OBE and of Joyce, *d* of Lewis O. Mathews, Birmingham; *m* 1956, Gillian Mary, *d* of late E. D. Skepper, Neuilly-sur-Seine; two *s* one *d*. *Educ:* Eton Coll.; King's Coll., Cambridge (MA Economics). Coldstream Guards, 1948–49; Cambridge, 1949–52. Man. Dir, Cadbury Schweppes Ltd, 1969–73; Director: Cadbury Group Ltd, 1962; Cadbury Bros Ltd, 1958; J. S. Fry & Sons, 1964; James Pascall, 1964; IBM UK Ltd, 1975–. Chancellor, Univ. of Aston in Birmingham, 1979–. Chairman: West Midlands Economic Planning Council, 1967–70; Food & Drink Industries Council, 1981–83; Mem., Covent Garden Market Authority, 1974–. Mem. Council: CBI; Industry for Management Educn; Industrial Soc. Chm., Promotion of Non-Exec. Dirs, 1984–. Freeman, City of Birmingham, 1982. Hon. DSc Aston, 1973. *Address:* Cadbury Schweppes plc, Bournville, Birmingham B30 2LU. *T:* 021–458 2000. *Clubs:* Boodle's; Hawks (Cambridge); Leander (Henley).
    See also N. D. Cadbury.

CADBURY, George Woodall; Chairman Emeritus, Governing Body of International Planned Parenthood Federation, since 1975 (Chairman, 1969–75; Vice-Chairman, and Chairman of the Executive, 1963–69, and Special Representative, since 1960); *b* 19 Jan. 1907; *s* of George Cadbury and Edith Caroline Cadbury (*née* Woodall); *m* 1935, Mary Barbara Pearce; two *d*. *Educ:* Leighton Park Sch., Reading; King's Coll., Cambridge; MA (Economics Tripos); Wharton Sch. of Finance and Commerce, Univ. of Pennsylvania. Man. Dir, British Canners Ltd, 1929–35; Marketing Controller and Man. Dir, Alfred Bird & Sons Ltd, 1935–45; Auxiliary, later Nat., Fire Service, 1939–41; Dep. Dir Material Production, Min. of Aircraft Production and British Air Commn (USA), 1941–45; Chm. Economic Advisory and Planning Bd, and Chief Industrial Executive, Prov. of Saskatchewan, 1945–51; Dir, Technical Assistance Administration, UN, 1951–60 (Dir of Ops, 1951–54; Adviser to Govts of Ceylon, Burma, Indonesia, Jamaica and Barbados, 1954–60). New Democratic Party of Canada: Pres., Ont, 1961–66; Fed. Treasurer, 1965–69; Mem., Fed. Council, 1961–71; Life Mem., 1980. Chm., 1972–74 and 1976–78, Pres., 1978–82, Conservation Council of Ontario (now Hon. Pres.). Trustee: Bournville Village Trust, 1928–; Youth Hostels Trust, 1931–; Sponsor and Council Mem., Minority Rights Group, 1967–; Hon. Director, 1961–: Planned Parenthood Fedn of Canada; Planned Parenthood, Toronto; Planned Parenthood Soc., Hamilton, Ont. Member: TGWU (Life Mem., 1973); League for Industrial Democracy, NY, 1928, Bd Mem., 1951–. Mem. Meetings Cttee, RIIA, 1931–35; Sec., W Midland Group for Post-War Reconstruction and Planning, 1939–41; Resident, Toynbee Hall, 1929–35, 1941–43. *Publications:* (jointly) When We Build Again, 1940; English County, 1942; Conurbation, 1942; Essays on the Left, 1971; A Population Policy for Canada, 1973. *Recreation:* railway practice and history. *Address:* 35 Brentwood Road, Oakville, Ont L6J 4B7, Canada. *T:* 416–845 3171.

CADBURY, Kenneth Hotham, CBE 1974; MC 1944; *b* 25 Feb. 1919; *s* of J. Hotham Cadbury, manufacturer, Birmingham; *m* 1st, Margaret R. King (marr. diss.); one *s* one *d*; 2nd, Marjorie I. Lilley; three *d*. *Educ:* Bootham Sch., York; Univ. of Birmingham. Served in Royal Artillery in Middle East and Italy, 1939–46 (despatches, MC; Major). Joined Foreign Service, 1946. Transferred to GPO, 1947; served in Personnel Dept and Inland Telecommunications Dept; Cabinet Office, 1952–55; PPS to PMG, 1956–57; Dep. Director, 1960, Director, 1962, Wales and Border Counties GPO; Director: Clerical Mechanisation and Buildings, GPO, 1964–65; Inland Telecommunications, GPO, 1965–67; Purchasing and Supply, GPO, 1967–69; Sen. Dir, Planning and Purchasing, PO, 1969–75; Asst Man. Dir,Telecommunications, PO, 1975–77; Dep. Man. Dir, Telecommns, PO, 1978–79. Trustee, PO Staff Superannuation Fund, 1969–75. *Recreation:* gardening. *Address:* Lower Graddon Farm, Highampton, Beaworthy, Devon EX21 5JX.

CADBURY, (Nicholas) Dominic; Chief Executive, Cadbury Schweppes plc, since 1984; *b* 12 May 1940; *s* of late Laurence John Cadbury, OBE and of Joyce Cadbury; *m* 1972,

Cecilia Sarah Symes; three *d*. *Educ:* Eton Coll.; Trinity Coll., Cambridge; Stanford Univ. (MBA). Graduate trainee, Cadbury, 1964; Sales Rep., 1965; Sales and Distribution Director: Cadbury Pty Ltd South Africa, 1966–70; Cadbury Ltd, 1970–72; Marketing Dir, Cadbury Ltd, 1972–74; Chm., Cadbury Typhoo, 1975; Dir, 1975, Internat. Marketing Dir, 1977, Chief Operating Officer, N American Reg., 1978–80, Cadbury Schweppes; Man. Dir, Cadbury Ltd, 1980–83. Mem., Royal Mint Adv. Cttee, 1986–. Chm., Edgbaston High Sch. for Girls, Birmingham, 1976–78, 1981–. CBIM 1984. *Recreations:* tennis, golf, shooting. *Address:* Shutford Manor, Shutford, near Banbury, Oxon OX15 6PF.

See also Sir G. A. H. Cadbury.

CADBURY, Peter (Egbert); Chairman: Preston Estates, since 1973; Preston Publications Ltd, since 1985; *b* Great Yarmouth, Norfolk, 6 Feb. 1918; *s* of late Sir Egbert Cadbury, DSC, DFC; *m* 1st, 1947, Eugenie Benedicta (marr. diss. 1968), *d* of late Major Ewen Bruce, DSO, MC and of Mrs Bruce; one *s* one *d*; 2nd, 1970, Mrs Jennifer Morgan-Jones (marr. diss. 1976), *d* of Major Michael Hammond Maude, Ramsden, Oxon; one *s*; 3rd, 1976, Mrs Jane Mead; two *s*. *Educ:* Leighton Park Sch.; Trinity Coll., Cambridge (BA, MA 1939). Called to Bar, Inner Temple, 1946; practised at Bar, 1946–54. Served Fleet Air Arm, 1940, until released to Ministry of Aircraft Production, 1942, as Prodn, Research and Experimental Test Pilot. Contested (L) Stroud (Glos), 1945. Member, London Travel Cttee, 1958–60; Chm. and Man. Dir, Keith Prowse Group, 1954–71; Chairman: Alfred Hays Ltd, 1955–71; Ashton & Mitchell Ltd and Ashton & Mitchell Travel Co. Ltd, 1959–71; Air Westward Ltd, 1977–79; Air West Ltd, 1977–79; Educational Video Index Ltd, 1981–83; Westward Travel Ltd, 1982–84; Exec. Chm., Westward Television Ltd, 1960–80; Director: Independent Television News Ltd, 1972–79; Willett Investments Ltd, 1955–. Chm., George Cadbury Trust, 1979–; Trustee: Help the Aged; Mus. of Army Flying; Winchester Cathedral Trust. Freeman of City of London, 1948. *Recreations:* theatre, racing, flying, golf, tennis, sailing. *Address:* Armsworth Hill, Alresford, Hants SO24 9RJ. *T:* Alresford 4656; Flat 4, 42 Cadogan Square, SW1. *T:* 01–589 8755. *Clubs:* Buck's, Saints & Sinners, XL (Forty), MCC; Hawks (Cambridge); Island Sailing, Royal Motor Yacht, RAF Yacht.

CADBURY-BROWN, Henry Thomas, OBE 1967; TD; RA 1975 (ARA 1971); FRIBA; Professor of Architecture, Royal Academy, since 1975; Hon. Fellow RCA; architect, in partnership with John F. Metcalfe, FRIBA, since 1962; *b* 20 May 1913; *s* of Henry William Cadbury-Brown and Marion Ethel Sewell; *m* 1953, Elizabeth Romeyn, *d* of Prof. A. Elwyn, Croton on Hudson, NY. *Educ:* Westminster Sch.; AA Sch. of Architecture (Hons Diploma). Architect in private practice since winning competition for British Railways Branch Offices, 1937. Work includes pavilions for "The Origins of the People", main concourse and fountain display at Festival of Britain; schools, housing, display and interiors. Architect for new civic centre at Gravesend and halls for residence for Birmingham Univ. and, with Sir Hugh Casson and Prof. Robert Goodden, for new premises for Royal College of Art; awarded London Architecture Bronze Medal, 1963; lecture halls for Univ. of Essex; for RBK & C: Tavistock Cres. housing; World's End redevelt (in gp partnership Eric Lyons, Cadbury-Brown, Metcalfe & Cunningham). Taught at Architectural Association Sch., 1946–49; Tutor at Royal Coll. of Art, 1952–61. Invited as Visiting Critic to Sch. of Architecture, Harvard Univ., 1956. Member: RIBA Council, 1951–53; British Cttee Internat. Union of Architects, 1951–54; MARS (Modern Architectural Research) group. Pres. Architectural Assoc., 1959–60. TA and military service, 1931–45; Major RA (TD). *Recreations:* numerous, including work. *Address:* 10 Macklin Street, WC2. *T:* 01–405 0626; Church Walk, Aldeburgh, Suffolk. *T:* Aldeburgh 2591.

CADELL, Colin Simson, CBE 1944; Air Cdre RAF, retired; Vice Lieutenant for West Lothian since 1972; *b* 7 Aug. 1905; *s* of late Lt-Col J. M. Cadell, DL, Foxhall, Kirkliston, W Lothian; *m* 1939, Rosemary Elizabeth, *d* of Thomas Edward Pooley; two *s* one *d*. *Educ:* Merchiston; Edinburgh Univ.; Ecole Supérieur d'électricité, Paris. MA; AMIEE; Ingénieur ESE. Commnd RAF, 1926; Dir of Signals, Air Min., 1944; retd 1947. Man. Dir, International Aeradio, 1947–58; Director: Carron Company, 1958–71; Royal Bank of Scotland, 1963–69. Mem., Edinburgh Airport Consultative Cttee, 1972– (Chm., 1972–82). Mem. Queen's Body Guard for Scotland (Royal Company of Archers). DL: Linlithgowshire, 1963–72. Officer, US Legion of Merit, 1945. *Address:* 2 Upper Coltbridge Terrace, Edinburgh EH12 6AD. *Club:* New (Edinburgh).

CADELL, Vice-Adm. Sir John (Frederick), KBE 1983; District General Manager, Canterbury and Thanet Health Authority, since 1986; *b* 6 Dec. 1929; *s* of Henry Dunlop Mallock Cadell and Violet Elizabeth (*née* Van Dyke); *m* 1958, Jaquetta Bridget Nolan; one *s* two *d*. *Educ:* Britannia Royal Naval Coll., Dartmouth. Served in HMS Frobisher, 1946, then Mediterranean, Persian Gulf, North and Baltic Seas; 2 years with RNZN, to 1960; served in HMS Ashton, Dartmouth, HMS Leopard, 9th Minesweeping Sqdn, SACLANT, HMS Bulwark, 1960–70; Naval Asst to First Sea Lord, 1970–72; HMS Diomede, 1972–74; RCDS 1974–75; RN Presentation Team, 1975–76; Comd, Sch. of Maritime Ops, 1976–79; Dir Gen. Naval Personal Services, 1979–81; COS to Comdr, Allied Forces Southern Europe, 1982–85. *Recreations:* tennis, skiing, wind surfing.

CADIEUX, Hon. Léo, PC 1965; OC 1975; Ambassador of Canada to France, 1970–75; *b* 28 May 1908; *s* of Joseph E. Cadieux and Rosa Paquette, both French Canadian; *m* 1962, Monique, *d* of Placide Plante; one *s*. *Educ:* Commercial Coll. of St Jerome and Seminary of Ste Thérèse de Blainville, Quebec. Editorial staff of La Presse, Montreal, Quebec, 1930–41; Associate Dir of Public Relations, Can. Army, 1941–44; War Corresp. for La Presse, Montreal, 1944; Mayor of St Antoine des Laurentides, Que., 1948. First elected to House of Commons, gen. elec., 1962; re-elected gen. elec., 1963, 1965, 1968; apptd Associate Minister of Nat. Defence, 1965; Minister of National Defence, Canada, 1967–70. *Address:* 20 Driveway, Appt 1106, Ottawa, Canada.

CADMAN, family name of **Baron Cadman.**

CADMAN, 3rd Baron *cr* 1937, of Silverdale; **John Anthony Cadman**; farmer, 1964–85; *b* 3 July 1938; *s* of 2nd Baron Cadman and Marjorie Elizabeth Bunnis; *S* father, 1966; *m* 1975, Janet Hayes; two *s*. *Educ:* Harrow; Selwyn Coll., Cambridge; Royal Agricultural Coll., Cirencester. *Heir:* *s* Hon. Nicholas Anthony James Cadman, *b* 18 Nov. 1977. *Address:* Heathcourt House, Ironmould Lane, Brislington, Bristol BS4 5RS. *T:* Bristol 775706.

CADMAN, Surg. Rear-Adm. (D) (Albert) Edward; CB 1977; Director of Naval Dental Services, 1974–77; *b* 14 Oct. 1918; *m* 1st, 1946, Margaret Henrietta Tomkins-Russell (*d* 1974); one *s* one *d*; 2nd, 1975, Mary Croil Macdonald, Superintendent, WRNS. *Educ:* Dover Grammar Sch.; Guy's Hosp. Dental Sch. LDS RCS 1941. Surg. Lieut (D) RNVR, 1942; transf. to RN, 1947; served as Asst to Dir, Naval Dental Services, 1967–70; Comd Dental Surgeon on staff of Flag Officer, Naval Air Comd, 1970–74. QHDS 1974–77. *Recreations:* music, gardening, golf. *Address:* Solent House, 2 Solent Way, Alverstoke, Hants. *T:* Gosport 586648.

CADOGAN, family name of **Earl Cadogan.**

CADOGAN, 7th Earl, *cr* 1800; **William Gerald Charles Cadogan,** MC 1943; DL; Baron Cadogan, 1718; Viscount Chelsea, 1800; Baron Oakley, 1831; Lieut-Colonel Royal Wiltshire Yeomanry, RAC; Captain Coldstream Guards R of O until 1964 (retaining hon. rank of Lieut-Colonel); *b* 13 Feb. 1914; *s* of 6th Earl and Lilian Eleanora Marie (who *m* 2nd, 1941, Lt-Col H. E. Hambro, CBE; she *d* 1973), *d* of George Coxon, Craigleith, Cheltenham; *S* father, 1933; *m* 1st, 1936, Hon. Primrose Lillian Yarde-Buller (from whom he obtained a divorce, 1959), *y d* of 3rd Baron Churston; one *s* three *d*; 2nd, 1961, Cecilia, *y d* of Lt-Col H. K. Hamilton-Wedderburn, OBE. *Educ:* Eton; RMC Sandhurst. Served war of 1939–45 (MC); Hereditary Trustee of the British Museum, 1935–63; Mem. Chelsea Borough Council, 1953–59; Mayor of Chelsea, 1964. DL County of London, 1958. *Heir:* *s* Viscount Chelsea, *qv*. *Address:* 28 Cadogan Square, SW1. *T:* 01–584 2335; Snaigow, Dunkeld, Perthshire. *T:* Caputh 223. *Club:* White's.

See also Baron Rockley.

CADOGAN, Prof. John Ivan George, CBE 1985; PhD, DSc London; FRS 1976; FRSE, CChem, FRSC; Director of Research, British Petroleum, since 1981; Director: BP Ventures, since 1981; BPGas International, since 1983; BP Chemicals International, since 1983; BP Venezuela, since 1984; Visiting Professor of Chemistry, Imperial College of Science and Technology, since 1979; Professorial Fellow, University College of Swansea, University of Wales, since 1979; *b* Pembrey, Carmarthenshire, 1930; *er s* of Alfred and Dilys Cadogan; *m* 1955, Margaret Jeanne, *d* of late William Evans, iron founder, Swansea; one *s* one *d*. *Educ:* Grammar Sch., Swansea; King's Coll., London (1st cl. Hons Chem. 1951). Research at KCL, 1951–54. Civil Service Research Fellow, 1954–56; Lectr in Chemistry, King's Coll., London, 1956–63; Purdie Prof. of Chemistry and Head of Dept, St Salvator's Coll., Univ. of St Andrews, 1963–69; Forbes Prof. of Organic Chemistry, Edinburgh Univ., 1969–79; Chief Scientist, BP Res. Centre, 1979–81. Member: Chemistry Cttee, SRC, 1967–71 (Chm. 1972–75); Council, SERC, 1981–85 (Chm., Science Bd, 1981–85; Mem., Science Bd, SRC, 1972–75); Chm., Defence Scientific Adv. Council, 1985–; Member: Council, Chem. Soc., 1966–69, 1973–76; Council, RIC, 1979–80; Chem. Soc.-RIC Unification Cttee, 1975–80; First Council, RSC, 1980–85 (Pres. RSC, 1982–84); Council of Management, Macaulay Inst. for Soil Res., Aberdeen, 1969–79; Council, St George's Sch. for Girls, 1974–79; Council, RSE, 1975–80 (Vice-Pres., 1978–80); Vice-Pres., Royal Instn, 1986– (Mem. Council, 1984–). Mem. Bd of Trustees, Royal Observatory Trust, Edinburgh, 1979–86. Pres., Chem. Sect., BAAS, 1981. Fellow, KCL, 1976 (Mem. Council, 1980–). Tilden Lectr, Chem. Soc., 1971; first RSE Schs Christmas Lectures, 1980; David Martin Royal Soc. BAYS Lectr, 1981; Humphry Davy Lectr, Royal Instn, 1982; Holroyd Meml Lectr, Soc. Chem. Ind., 1984; Salters' Co. Lectr, Royal Instn, 1984; Philips Lectr, Royal Soc., 1985; Pedler Lectr, RSC, 1986. Hon. DSc: St Andrews, 1983; Wales, 1984; Edinburgh, 1986; DUniv Stirling, 1984; Hon. Dr l'Univ Aix-Marseille, 1984. Samuel Smiles Prize, KCL, 1950; Millar Thomson Medallist, KCL, 1951; Meldola Medallist, Soc. of Maccabaeans and Royal Inst. of Chemistry, 1959; Corday-Morgan Medallist, Chem. Soc., 1965. *Publications:* Organophosphorus Reagents in Organic Synthesis; about 220 scientific papers, mainly in Jl Chem. Soc. *Recreations:* gardening, supporting Rugby football (Vice-Pres., Crawshay's Welsh RFC, London Welsh RFC; Patron, Swansea RFCC). *Address:* British Petroleum Company plc, Britannic House, Moor Lane, EC2Y 9BU. *T:* 01–920 6457; *Telex* 888811. *Club:* Athenæum.

CADOGAN, Peter William; lecturer and writer; Secretary, East-West Peace People, since 1978; Editor, ANNE (Active Neutrality Now—Europe) Newsletter, since 1984; *b* 26 Jan. 1921; *s* of Archibald Douglas Cadogan and Audrey Cadogan (*née* Wannop); *m* 1949, Joyce, *d* of William Stones, MP (marr. diss. 1969); one *d*. *Educ:* Tynemouth Sch., Tynemouth; Univ. of Newcastle, 1946–51 (BA (Hons) History, DipEd; Joseph Cowen Meml Prize, 1951). Served War, Air Sea Rescue Service, RAF, 1941–46. Teaching, Kettering and Cambridge, 1951–65. Committed politically to the Far Left, 1945–60; broke with Marxism, 1960. Founding Secretary, East Anglian Committee of 100: exploring theory and practice of non-violent direct action, 1961; Sec., Internat. Sub-Cttee of Cttee of 100: rediscovering internationalism, 1962; Sec. (full-time), National Cttee of 100, 1965–68. Mem., Nat. Council of CND, mix-sixties; Founding Sec., Save Biafra Campaign, 1968–70; Gen. Sec., South Place Ethical Soc., 1970–81; Co-Founder: Turning Point, 1975; Peace Anonymous, Action '84 and Summit '84, 1983–84. *Publications:* Extra-Parliamentary Democracy, 1968; Direct Democracy, 1974, rev. 1975; Early Radical Newcastle, 1975; Six Ballads for the Seventies, 1976; many articles in learned jls, periodicals and elsewhere. *Recreations:* scholarship, conviviality, walking. *Address:* 3 Hinchinbrook House, Greville Road, NW6. *T:* 01–328 3709.

CADWALLADER, Air Vice-Marshal Howard George, CB 1974; RAF retd; Director of Purchasing, Post Office, 1978–79; *b* 16 March 1919; British; *m* 1950, Betty Ethel Samuels; no *c*. *Educ:* Hampton Sch., Mddx. Sen. Equipment Staff Officer: HQ Transport Comd, 1963–65; HQ FEAF Singapore, 1965–68; Dep. Dir of Equipment 14 MoD (Air), 1968–69; Comdt of RAF Supply Control Centre, Hendon, 1969–72; Dir of Movts (RAF), MoD (Air), 1972–73; SASO HQ Support Comd, RAF, 1973–74. Controller of Contracts, PO, 1974–78. *Recreations:* golf, sailing. *Address:* Spain.

CADWALLADER, Sir John, Kt 1967; Chairman and Managing Director of Allied Mills Ltd and subsidiaries, 1949–78; President, Bank of New South Wales, 1959–78, retired; *b* 25 Aug. 1902; *m* 1935, Helen Sheila Moxham; two *s* one *d*. *Educ:* Sydney Church of England Grammar Sch., NSW. *Recreations:* reading, golf. *Address:* 27 Marian Street, Killara, NSW 2071, Australia. *T:* 498 1974. *Clubs:* Commonwealth (Canberra, ACT); Australian, Union, Royal Sydney Golf (all Sydney, NSW); Elanora Country (NSW).

CÆSAR, Rev. Canon Anthony Douglass; Sub-Dean of Her Majesty's Chapels Royal, Deputy Clerk of the Closet, Sub-Almoner and Domestic Chaplain to the Queen, since 1979; *b* 3 April 1924; *s* of Harold Douglass and Winifred Kathleen Cæsar. *Educ:* Cranleigh School; Magdalene Coll., Cambridge; St Stephen's House, Oxford. MA, MusB, FRCO. Served War with RAF, 1943–46. Assistant Music Master, Eton Coll., 1948–51; Precentor, Radley Coll., 1952–59; Asst Curate, St Mary Abbots, Kensington, 1961–65; Asst Sec., ACCM, 1965–70; Chaplain, Royal School of Church Music, 1965–70; Deputy Priest-in-Ordinary to the Queen, 1967–68, Priest-in-Ordinary, 1968–70; Resident Priest, St Stephen's Church, Bournemouth, 1970–73; Precentor and Sacrist, Winchester Cathedral, 1974–79; Hon. Canon of Winchester Cathedral, 1975–76 and 1979–, Residentiary Canon, 1976–79. *Publications:* 2 Part Songs, 1948, 1949. *Recreation:* other people. *Address:* Marlborough Gate, St James's Palace, SW1. *T:* 01–930 6609.

CÆSAR, Irving; author-lyrist; Past President of Songwriters' Protective Association; Member Board of Directors, American Society of Composers, Authors and Publishers; *b* New York, 4 July 1895; *s* of Rumanian Jews. *Educ:* public school; Chappaqua Quaker Inst.; City Coll. of New York. Protégé of Ella Wheeler Wilcox, who, when he was a boy of nine, became interested in bits of verse he wrote and published at the time; at twenty became attached to the Henry Ford Peace Expedition, and spent nine months travelling through neutral Europe (during the War) as one of the secretaries of the Ford Peace Conference; returned to America, and became interested in writing for the musical comedy stage. *Publications:* most important work up to present time, No, No, Nanette; has written hundreds of songs and collaborated in many other musical comedies; writer and publisher of Sing a Song of Safety, a vol. of children's songs in use throughout the public and parochial schools of USA; also Sing a Song of Friendship, a series of songs based on human rights; in England: The Bamboula, Swanee, Tea for Two (successive awards for being among the most performed ASCAP standards), I Want to be Happy, I Was So Young; author of "Peace by Wireless" proposal for freedom of international exchange of radio privilege between governments. *Recreations:* reading, theatre, swimming. *Address:* 850 Seventh Avenue, New York, NY 10019, USA. *Clubs:* Friars, Green Room, City (New York).

CAFFERTY, Michael Angelo; HM Diplomatic Service; Consul-General, Melbourne, Australia, since 1983; *b* 3 March 1927; *m* 1950, Eileen E. Geer; two *s* three *d*. *Educ:* Univ. of London. BoT, 1951; Asst Trade Comr, Johannesburg, 1955, Pretoria, 1957; seconded to FO, Buenos Aires, 1958; Trade Comr, Singapore, 1964; FCO, 1968; Consul (Commercial), Milan, 1974; First Sec. and Head of Chancery, Rome (Holy See), 1977; Ambassador and Consul-Gen., Santo Domingo, 1979–83. *Address:* c/o Foreign and Commonwealth Office, SW1.

CAFFIN, Albert Edward, CIE 1947; OBE 1946; Indian Police (retired); *b* 16 June 1902; *s* of Claud Carter and Lilian Edith Caffin, Southsea; *m* 1929, Hilda Elizabeth Wheeler, Bournemouth; no *c*. *Educ:* Portsmouth. Joined Indian Police as Asst Supt, Bombay Province, 1922; Asst Inspector General, Poona, 1939; Dep. Comr, Bombay, 1944, Comr of Police, Bombay, 1947. *Recreation:* bowls. *Address:* C22 San Remo Towers, Sea Road, Boscombe, Bournemouth, Dorset. *Club:* Royal Bombay Yacht.

CAFFIN, A(rthur) Crawford; a Recorder of the Crown Court, 1972–82; solicitor since 1932; *b* 10 June 1910; *s* of Charles Crawford Caffin and Annie Rosila Caffin; *m* 1933, Mala Pocock; one *d*. *Educ:* King's Sch., Rochester. Asst Solicitor: to Norfolk CC, 1933–37; to Bristol Corporation, 1937–46. Partner in firm of R. L. Frank & Caffin, Solicitors, Truro, 1946–72; Consultant with that firm, 1972–84. Pres., Cornwall Law Soc., 1960; Mem. Council, the Law Society, 1966–76; Dep. Chm., Traffic Commissioners for Western Traffic Area, 1964–84. *Recreation:* swimming. *Address:* Cove Cottage, Portloe, Truro, Cornwall. *Club:* Farmers' (Truro).

CAFFYN, Brig. Sir Edward (Roy), KBE 1963 (CBE 1945; OBE 1942); CB 1955; TD 1950; DL; Chairman, County of Sussex Territorial and Auxiliary Forces Association, 1947–67; Vice-Chairman, Council of Territorial and Auxiliary Forces Associations, 1961–66; *b* 27 May 1904; *s* of Percy Thomas Caffyn, Eastbourne; *m* 1st, 1929, Elsa Muriel, *d* of William Henry Nurse, Eastbourne; two *s*; 2nd, 1946, Delphine Angelique, *d* of Major William Chilton-Riggs. *Educ:* Eastbourne and Loughborough Colleges. Commissioned RE (TA), 1930. Raised and commanded an Army Field Workshop, 1939; served with 51st Highland Division in France, 1940; Brigadier, 1941; a Deputy Director, War Office, on formation of REME, 1942; served on Field Marshal Montgomery's staff as Director of Mechanical Engineering (despatches twice), 1943–45. JP Eastbourne, 1948, transferred East Sussex, 1960; Chairman, Hailsham Bench, 1962–74; DL Sussex, 1956; Chairman, Sussex Agricultural Wages Board, 1951–74. CC for East Sussex, 1958–69, Alderman, 1964, Vice-Chairman 1967; Chm., Sussex Police Authy, 1971–74. *Recreations:* shooting, fishing. *Address:* Norman Norris, Vines Cross, Heathfield, East Sussex. *T:* Horam Road 2674.

CAGIATI, Dr Andrea; Grand Cross, Italian Order of Merit; Hon. GCVO; Italian Ambassador to the Vatican in Rome, since 1985; *b* Rome, 11 July 1922; *m* 1968, Sigrid von Morgen; one *s* one *d*. *Educ:* University of Siena (Dr of Law). Entered Foreign Service, 1948. Served: Secretary, Paris, 1950; Principal Private Sec. to Minister of State, 1951; Vice-Consul-General, New York, 1953; Prin. Private Sec. to Minister of State and subsequently Dept of Political Affairs, 1955; Counsellor, Athens, 1957; Counsellor, Mexico City, 1960; Delegate, Disarmament Cttee, Geneva, March-Dec. 1962; Italian Delegation, UN, June 1962; Head, NATO Dept, Dec. 1962; Minister-Counsellor, Madrid, 1966; Ambassador, Bogotá, 1968; Inst for Diplomatic Studies, 1971; Diplomatic Adviser to Prime Minister, 1972; Ambassador, Vienna, 1973; Ambassador, Court of St James's, 1980. Hon. GCVO during State Visit to Italy of HM The Queen, Oct. 1980. *Recreations:* sculpture, golf. *Address:* Italian Embassy, 2 viale Belle Arti, 00196 Rome, Italy. *Clubs:* White's; Swinley Forest Golf.

CAHILL, Michael Leo; Head of Central and Southern Africa Department, Overseas Development Administration, since 1983; *b* 4 April 1928; *s* of John and Josephine Cahill; *m* 1961, Harriette Emma Clemency, *e d* of late Christopher Gilbert Eastwood, CMG and of Catherine Eastwood; two *d*. *Educ:* Beaumont Coll.; Magdalen Coll., Oxford (Demy). National Service, Intelligence Corps, Trieste, 1950–52, Lieut. FO, 1953; CO, 1955; Asst Private Sec. to Sec. of State, 1956–57; Private Sec. to Parly Under-Sec., 1957–58; Dept of Technical Co-operation, 1961; Asst Sec., ODM, 1969; UK Perm. Deleg. to Unesco, 1972–74. Chm., Woldingham Sch. Parents Assoc., 1981–83. *Recreations:* history of the arts, pianism. *Address:* 9 Murray Road, SW19 4PD. *T:* 01-947 0568.
See also B. S. T. Eastwood.

CAHILL, Patrick Richard, CBE 1970 (OBE 1944); *b* 21 Feb. 1912; *er s* of late Patrick Francis and Nora Christina Cahill; *m* 1st, 1949, Gladys Lilian May Kemp (*d* 1969); one *s*; 2nd, 1969, Mary Frances Pottinger. *Educ:* Hitchin Grammar Sch. Joined Legal & General Assurance Soc. Ltd, 1929; Pensions Manager, 1948; Agency Manager, 1952; Asst Manager, 1954; Asst General Manager, 1957; Gen. Manager, 1958; Chief Exec., 1969–71; Mem. Board, 1969–77. Served War with RASC, 1940–45 (despatches, OBE); N Africa, Italy, and N Europe, 1st, 7th and 11th Armd Divs; rank of Lt-Col. Managing Dir, Gresham Life Assurance Soc. Ltd and Dir, Gresham Fire and Accident Insurance Soc. Ltd, 1958–72. A Vice-Pres., Chartered Insurance Inst., 1961–63, Pres., 1969; Pres., Insurance Charities, 1965–66; Chm., London Salvage Corps, 1964–65; Chm., British Insurance Assoc., 1967–69. *Address:* Flat G, 47 Beaumont Street, W1. *T:* 01-935 2608; Thorndene, Pluckley, Kent. *T:* Pluckley 306.

CAHILL, Teresa Mary; opera and concert singer; *b* 30 July 1944; *d* of Florence and Henry Cahill; *m* 1971, John Anthony Kiernander (marr. diss. 1978). *Educ:* Notre Dame High Sch., Southwark; Guildhall School of Music and Drama; London Opera Centre (LRAM Singing, AGSM Piano). Glyndebourne début, 1969; Covent Garden début, 1970; La Scala Milan, 1976, Philadelphia Opera, 1981, specialising in Mozart and Strauss; concerts: all London orchestras, Boston Symphony Orch., Chicago Symphony Orch., Rotterdam Philharmonic Orch., West Deutscher Rundfunk, Berlin Festival, Vienna Fest., 1983, Promenade concerts; BBC radio and TV; recordings, incl. Strauss and Elgar, for all major companies; master classes, Dartington Fest., 1984, 1986; recitals and concerts throughout Europe, USA, Far East. Silver Medal, Worshipful Co. of Musicians, 1966; John Christie Award 1970. *Recreations:* cinema, theatre, travel, reading, collecting antique furniture. *Address:* 65 Leyland Road, SE12 8DW. *Club:* Royal Over-Seas League (Hon. Mem.).

CAHN, Sir Albert Jonas, 2nd Bt, *cr* 1934; company director; marital, sexual and family therapist; Director, Elm Therapy Centre, New Malden, since 1983; *b* 27 June 1924; *s* of Sir Julien Cahn, 1st Bt, and Phyllis Muriel, *d* of A. Wolfe, Bournemouth; *S* father, 1944; *m* 1948, Malka, *d* of late R. Bluestone; two *s* two *d*. *Educ:* Headmaster's House, Harrow. *Recreations:* cricket, horse riding, photography. *Heir:* *s* Julien Michael Cahn, *b* 15 Jan. 1951. *Address:* 10 Edgecoombe Close, Warren Road, Kingston upon Thames, Surrey. *T:* 01-942 6956; Elm Therapy Centre, 70 Elm Road, New Malden, Surrey.

CAILLARD, Air Vice-Marshal (Hugh) Anthony, CB 1981; retired 1982; Director General, Britain-Australia Society, and Hon. Secretary, Cook Society, since 1982; Specialist Air Adviser, House of Commons Defence Committee, since 1985; *b* 16 April 1927; *s* of late Col F. Caillard, MC, and of Mrs M. Y. Caillard; *m* 1957, Margaret-Ann Crawford, Holbrook, NSW, Australia; four *s*. *Educ:* Downside; Oriel Coll., Oxford. Cranwell, 1947–49; served, 1949–65: 13 Sqdn, Egypt; ADC to C-in-C MEAF, and to AOC-in-C Tech. Trng Comd; 101 Sqdn, Binbrook; RAAF No 2 Sqdn; 49 Sqdn (Sqdn Ldr) and 90 Sqdn; RN Staff Coll.; HQ Bomber Comd (Wg Cdr); OC 39 Sqdn, Malta, 1965–67; Jt Services Staff Coll., 1967; Planning Staffs, MoD, 1967–70; Asst Air Attaché, Washington (Gp Captain), 1970–73; OC Marham, 1974–75; Def. Intell. Staff (Air Cdre), 1975–79; Dep. Chief of Staff, Ops and Intelligence, HQ Allied Air Forces, Central Europe, 1979–82. Member: Britain-Australia Bicentennial Cttee, 1984; Council, Royal Over-Seas League, 1983–. *Address:* 114 Ashley Road, Walton-on-Thames, Surrey KT12 1HW. *Clubs:* Royal Commonwealth Society, Royal Over-Seas League, Royal Air Force.

CAILLAT, Claude; Swiss Ambassador to the Court of St James's, 1980–83; retired; *b* 24 Sept. 1918; *s* of Aymon Caillat and Isabelle Caillat (*née* Bordier); *m* 1948, Béatrice de Blonay; two *s* one *d*. *Educ:* Univ. of Geneva (law degree). Div. of Foreign Interests, Swiss Federal Political Dept, Berne, then served successively in London, Berne, Athens and (as Counsellor) Washington, 1942–60; Federal Office of Foreign Trade, Berne, 1960; Ambassador's Deputy, Swiss Embassy, Paris, 1962; Swiss Federal Council's Rep. at OECD, Paris, with rank of Ambassador, 1967; Swiss Ambassador to the Netherlands, 1969; Head of Swiss Mission to European Communities, Brussels, 1974. *Recreation:* golf. *Address:* 240 route de Lausanne, Chambésy, Geneva. *Clubs:* White's, Travellers'.

CAIN; *see* Nall-Cain.

CAIN, Sir Edney; *see* Cain, Sir H. E. C.

CAIN, Sir Edward (Thomas), Kt 1972; CBE 1966; Commissioner of Taxation, Australia, 1964–76; retired; *b* Maryborough, Qld, Australia, 7 Dec. 1916; *s* of Edward Victor and Kathleen Teresa Cain; *m* 1942, Marcia Yvonne Cain (*née* Parbery); one *s* one *d*. *Educ:* Nudgee Coll., Queensland; Univ. of Queensland (BA, LLB). Commonwealth Taxation Office: in Brisbane, Sydney, Perth and Canberra, 1936–. Served War, 2/9th Bn, AIF, 1939–43. *Recreations:* golf, fishing. *Address:* 99 Buxton Street, Deakin, Canberra, Australia. *T:* 811462. *Clubs:* Commonwealth, Royal Canberra Golf (Canberra); Royal Automobile (Melbourne).

CAIN, Maj.-Gen. George Robert T.; *see* Turner Cain.

CAIN, Sir (Henry) Edney (Conrad), Kt 1986; OBE 1976 (MBE 1965); FCCA; CA (Belize); Financial Secretary, Ministry of Finance, Belize, since 1985; *b* 2 Dec. 1924; *s* of Henry Edney Conrad I and Rhoda (*née* Stamp); *m* 1951, Leonie (*née* Locke). *Educ:* St George's Coll., Belize; St Michael's Coll., Belize; Balham and Tooting Coll. of Commerce, London. FCCA 1977 (ACCA 1961); CA Belize 1984. Belize Government Service, 1940–: Examr of Accts, Audit Dept, 1954; Auditor, Audit Dept, 1959; Asst Accountant Gen., 1961; Accountant Gen., 1963; Man. Dir, Monetary Authority of Belize, 1976; Governor, Central Bank of Belize, 1982; Ambassador of Belize to USA, 1983; High Comr to Canada (resident in Washington, DC), 1984. *Publication:* When the Angel says 'Write' (verse), 1948. *Recreations:* music, reading, current affairs. *Address:* 6 Roseapple Street, Belmopan, Belize. *T:* 082492; 18 Albert Street West, Belize City, Belize. *T:* 022325.

CAIN, Hon. John; MLA (Lab) for Bundoora, since 1976; Premier of Victoria, since 1982; *b* 26 April 1931; *s* of late Hon. John Cain; *m* 1955, Nancye Williams; two *s* one *d*. *Educ:* Melbourne Univ. (LLB). Practised as barrister and solicitor. Mem., Law Reform Commn, 1975–77. Pres., Law Inst. of Victoria, 1972–73 (Treasurer, 1969–70; Chm. of Council, 1971–72); Mem. Exec., Law Council of Australia, 1973–76. Vice-Chm., Vic. Br., Australian Labor Party, 1973–75; Mem., Parly Labor Exec., 1977–; Leader, State Labor Party, 1981–; Leader of Opposition, 1981–82; Minister for Fed. Affairs, 1982; Attorney-General of Vic, 1982–83. *Address:* 9 Magnolia Road, Ivanhoe, Vic 3079, Australia.

CAIN, John Clifford; research historian; Controller, Public Affairs, BBC, 1981–84; Director, Broadcasting Support Services, since 1985 (Chairman, 1980–85); *b* 2 April 1924; *s* of William John Cain and Florence Jessie (*née* Wood); *m* 1954, Shirley Jean Roberts; two *d*. *Educ:* Emanuel Sch.; Imperial Coll., Borough Road Coll., London Univ. (BSc); University Coll., London Univ. (MSc). Served RAF (aircrew), 1944–47. Maths and science teacher in grammar, secondary modern and comprehensive schs and in polytechnic, 1950–59; Lectr, Science Museum, 1959–61; Asst Head of Sch. Broadcasting, Associated-Rediffusion, 1961–63; BBC Television: Producer, subseq. Sen. Producer, 1963–71; Asst Head of Further Educn Dept, 1971–72, Head, 1972–77; Asst Controller, Educn Br., BBC, 1977–80. Dir, Broadcasters' Audience Res. Bd, 1982–84. Mem., Health Educn Council, 1978–83. Member: RTS; BAFTA. *Publications:* Talking Machines, 1961; (jtly) Mathematics Miscellany, 1966; articles in EBU Review, Adult Educn, etc. *Recreations:* reading, gardening, music, theatre. *Address:* 63 Park Road, Chiswick, W4 3EY. *T:* 01-994 2712.

CAIN, Thomas William; HM Attorney General for Isle of Man, since 1980; *b* 1 June 1935; *s* of late James Arthur Cain and Mary Edith Cunningham (*née* Lamb); *m* 1961, Felicity Jane, *d* of Rev. Arthur Stephen Gregory; two *s* one *d*. *Educ:* King's College Choir Sch., Cambridge; Marlborough Coll.; Worcester Coll., Oxford (BA 1958, MA 1961). National Service, 2nd Lieut RAC, 1953–55. Called to the Bar, Gray's Inn, 1959; Advocate, Manx Bar, 1961. *Recreations:* sailing; Chairman, Manx Nature Conservation Trust. *Address:* Ivie Cottage, Kirk Michael, Isle of Man. *T:* Kirk Michael 266.

CAINE, Michael; actor; *b* Old Kent Road, London, 14 March 1933 (Maurice Joseph Micklewhite); *s* of late Maurice and of Ellen Frances Marie Micklewhite; *m* 1st, 1955, Patricia Haines (marr. diss.); one *d*; 2nd, 1973, Shakira Baksh; one *d*. *Educ:* Wilson's Grammar Sch., Peckham. Began acting in youth club drama gp. Served in Army, Berlin and Korea, 1951–53. Asst Stage Manager, Westminster Rep., Horsham, Sx, 1953; actor, Lowestoft Rep., 1953–55; Theatre Workshop, London, 1955; numerous TV appearances (over 100 plays), 1957–63; *play:* Next Time I'll Sing for You, Arts, 1963; *films:* A Hill in Korea, 1956; How to Murder a Rich Uncle, 1958; Zulu, 1964; The Ipcress File, 1965; Alfie, 1966; The Wrong Box, 1966; Gambit, 1966; Hurry Sundown, 1967; Woman Times Seven, 1967; Deadfall, 1967; The Magus, 1968; Battle of Britain, 1968; Play Dirty, 1968; The Italian Job, 1969; Too Late the Hero, 1970; The Last Valley, 1971; Get Carter, 1971; Zee & Co., 1972; Kidnapped, 1972; Pulp, 1972; Sleuth, 1973; The Black Windmill, Marseilles Contract, The Wilby Conspiracy, 1974; Fat Chance, The Romantic Englishwoman, The Man who would be King, Harry and Walter Go to New York, 1975; The Eagle has Landed, A Bridge too Far, Silver Bears, 1976; The Swarm, 1977;

California Suite, 1978; Ashanti, 1979; Beyond the Poseidon Adventure, 1979; The Island, 1979; Dressed to Kill, 1979; Escape to Victory, 1980; Death Trap, 1981; Jigsaw Man, 1982; Educating Rita, 1982; The Honorary Consul, 1982; Blame it on Rio, 1984; Water, 1985; The Holcroft Covenant, 1985; Hannah and Her Sisters, 1986; Half Moon Street, 1986; Mona Lisa, 1986. *Recreations:* cinema, theatre, travel, gardening. *Address:* c/o Jerry Pam, 120 El Camino Drive, Beverly Hills, Calif 90212, USA.

CAINE, Michael Harris; Chairman, since 1979, Vice-Chairman, 1973–79, Chief Executive, 1975–84, Director, since 1964, Booker McConnell plc; *b* 17 June 1927; *s* of Sir Sydney Caine, *qv*; *m* 1952, Janice Denise (*née* Mercer); one *s* one *d*. *Educ:* Bedales; Lincoln Coll., Oxford; George Washington Univ., USA. Joined Booker McConnell Ltd, 1952; Chm., Bookers Shopkeeping Holdings Ltd, 1963; Director, Arbor Acres Farm Inc., 1980–. Chm., Council for Technical Educn and Training for Overseas Countries, 1973–75. Member: Council, Inst. of Race Relations, 1969–72; Council, Bedford Coll., London, 1966–85; IBA, 1984–; Commonwealth Develt Corp., 1985–; Governing Body: Inst. of Develt Studies, Sussex Univ., 1975–; NIESR, 1979–; Queen Elizabeth House, Oxford, 1983–; Chairman: UK Council for Overseas Student Affairs, 1980–; Council, Royal African Soc., 1984–. *Address:* 23 Upper Wimpole Street, W1M 7TA. *T:* 01–935 4044. *Club:* Reform.

CAINE, Sir Sydney, KCMG 1947 (CMG 1945); Director of the London School of Economics and Political Science, 1957–67; *b* 27 June 1902; *s* of Harry Edward Caine; *m* 1st, 1925, Muriel Anne (*d* 1962), *d* of A. H. Harris, MA; one *s*; 2nd, 1965, Doris Winifred Folkard (*d* 1973); 3rd, 1975, Elizabeth, *d* of late J. Crane Nicholls and *widow* of Sir Eric Bowyer, KCB, KBE. *Educ:* Harrow County Sch.; London Sch. of Economics. BSc (Econ.) 1st Class Hons 1922. Asst Inspector of Taxes, 1923–26; entered Colonial Office, 1926; Sec., West Indian Sugar Commn, 1929; Sec., UK Sugar Industry Inquiry Cttee, 1934; Fin. Sec., Hong Kong, 1937; Asst Sec., Colonial Office, 1940; Member Anglo-American Caribbean Commission, 1942; Financial Adviser to Sec. of State for the Colonies, 1942; Assistant Under-Secretary of State, Colonial Office, 1944; Deputy Under-Secretary of State, Colonial Office, 1947–48; Third Secretary, Treasury, 1948; Head of UK Treasury and Supply Delegn, Washington, 1949–51; Chief, World Bank Mission to Ceylon, 1951; Vice-Chancellor, Univ. of Malaya, 1952–56. Chairman: British Caribbean Federation Fiscal Commission, 1955; Grassland Utilisation Cttee, 1957–58; Internat. Inst. of Educational Planning, 1963–70; Governor (new bd), Reserve Bank of Rhodesia, 1965–67; Planning Bd of Independent Univ., 1969–73; Council, University Coll. of Buckingham, 1973–. Mem., ITA, 1960–67 (Dep. Chm., 1964–67). Coordinator, Indonesian Sugar Study, 1971–72. Hon. LLD Univ. of Malaya, 1956. Grand Officer, Orange Nassau (Netherlands), 1947; Comdr, Order of Dannebrog (Denmark), 1965. *Publications:* The Foundation of the London School of Economics, 1963; British Universities: Purpose and Prospects, 1969; The Price of Stability . . . ?, 1983. *Recreations:* reading, walking. *Address:* Buckland House, Tarn Road, Hindhead, Surrey. *Club:* Reform.

See also M. H. Caine.

CAINES, Eric; Director, Personnel and Finance, Prison Department, Home Office, since 1984; *b* 27 Feb. 1936; *s* of Ernest and Doris Caines; *m* 1st, 1958 (marr. diss. 1984); three *s*; 2nd, 1984, Karen Higgs; one *s*. *Educ:* Rothwell Grammar School, Wakefield; Leeds Univ. (LLB Hons). Dip. Hist. Art, London Univ., 1984. Short Service Commission, RAEC, 1958–61. NCB, 1961–65; BBC, 1965–66; as Principal, Min. of Health, Management Side Sec., General Whitley Council, 1966–70; Sec., NHS Reorganisation Management Arrangements Study, 1970–73; Assistant Sec., DHSS, 1973–77; IMF/World Bank, Washington, 1977–79; Under Sec., DHSS, 1979–, Dir, Regl Organisation, 1981–84. *Recreation:* travelling on foot with a book. *Address:* c/o Home Office, Cleland House, SW1.

CAINES, John, CB 1983; Deputy Secretary, Department of Trade and Industry, since 1983; *b* 13 Jan. 1933; *s* of John Swinburne Caines and Ethel May Stenlake; *m* 1963, Mary Large; one *s* two *d*. *Educ:* Westminster Sch.; Christ Church, Oxford (MA). Asst Principal, Min. of Supply, 1957; Asst Private Sec., Min. of Aviation, 1960–61; Principal, Min. of Aviation, 1961–64; Civil Air Attaché in Middle East, 1964–66; Manchester Business Sch., 1967; Asst Sec., BoT, 1968; Sec., Commn on Third London Airport, 1968–71; Asst Sec., DTI, 1971–72; Principal Private Sec. to Sec. of State for Trade and Industry, 1972–74; Under-Sec., Dept of Trade, 1974–77; Sec., 1977–80, Mem. and Dep. Chief Exec., 1979–80, NEB; Dep. Sec., Dept of Trade, and Chief Exec., BOTB, 1980–82; Dep. Sec., Central Policy Review Staff, Cabinet Office, 1983. *Recreations:* travel, music, gardening, theatre. *Address:* 19 College Road, Dulwich, SE21 7BG. *T:* 01–693 5537.

CAIRD, Most Rev. Donald Arthur Richard; *see* Dublin, Archbishop of, and Primate of Ireland.

CAIRD, John Newport; Associate Director, Royal Shakespeare Company, since 1983; *b* 22 Sept. 1948; *s* of late Rev. George Bradford Caird, DPhil, DD, FBA and of Viola Mary Newport, MA; *m* 1982, Ann Dorszynski; one *s* one *d*. *Educ:* Selwyn House Sch., Montreal; Magdalen Coll. Sch., Oxford; Bristol Old Vic Theatre Sch. Resident Dir, RSC, 1977–82; directed, RSC: Dance of Death, 1977; Savage Amusement, 1978; Nicholas Nickleby, London, New York and Los Angeles, 1980–86; Naked Robots, Twin Rivals, 1981; Our Friends in the North, 1982; Peter Pan, 1982–84; Twelfth Night, Romeo and Juliet, 1983; The Merchant of Venice, Red Star, 1984; Philistines, Les Misérables, London, Washington and NY, 1985–86; Every Man in his Humour, 1986. Directed: Song and Dance, London, 1982; As You Like It, Stockholm, 1984 (also for TV, 1985). *Recreation:* music.

CAIRD, William Douglas Sime; Registrar, Family Division of High Court (formerly Probate, Divorce and Admiralty Division), 1964–82; *b* 21 Aug. 1917; *er s* of William Sime Caird and Elsie Amy Caird; *m* 1946, Josephine Mary, *d* of Peter and Elizabeth Seeney, Stratford on Avon; no *c*. *Educ:* Rutlish Sch., Merton. Entered Principal Probate Registry, 1937; Estabt Officer, 1954; Sec., 1959; Mem., Matrimonial Causes Rule Cttee, 1968–79. *Publications:* Consulting Editor, Rayden on Divorce, 10th edn 1967, 11th edn 1971, 12th edn 1974, 13th edn 1979. *Address:* 17 Pine Walk, Bookham, Surrey. *T:* Bookham 56732.

CAIRNCROSS, Sir Alexander Kirkland, (Sir Alec Cairncross), KCMG 1967 (CMG 1950); FBA 1961; Chancellor, University of Glasgow, since 1972; Supernumerary Fellow, St Antony's College, Oxford, since 1978; *b* 11 Feb. 1911; 3rd *s* of Alexander Kirkland and Elizabeth Andrew Cairncross, Lesmahagow, Scotland; *m* 1943, Mary Frances Glynn, *d* of Maj. E. F. Glynn, TD, Ilkley; three *s* two *d*. *Educ:* Hamilton Academy; Glasgow and Cambridge Univs. Univ. Lectr, 1935–39; Civil Servant, 1940–45; Dir of Programmes, Min. of Aircraft Production, 1945; Economic Advisory Panel, Berlin, 1945–46; Mem. of Staff of The Economist, 1946. Mem. of Wool Working Party, 1946; Economic Adviser to: BoT, 1946–49; Organisation for European Economic Co-operation, 1949–50; Prof. of Applied Economics, Univ. of Glasgow, 1951–61; Dir, Economic Development Inst., Washington DC, 1955–56; Economic Adviser to HM Govt, 1961–64; Head of Govt Economic Service, 1964–69. Master of St Peter's Coll., Oxford, 1969–78, Hon. Fellow, 1978. Vis. Prof., Brookings Instn, Washington, DC, 1972; Leverhulme Vis. Prof., Inst. of Economic and Social Change, Bangalore, 1981; Leverhulme Emeritus Fellow, 1983–86. Chairman: independent advrs on reassessment of Channel Tunnel Project, 1974–75 (Adviser to Minister of Transport on Channel Tunnel Project, 1979–81); Commonwealth Secretariat Gp of Experts on Protectionism, 1982; Local Development Cttee, 1951–52; Member: Crofting Commn, 1951–54; Phillips Cttee, 1953–54; Anthrax Cttee, 1957–59; Radcliffe Cttee, 1957–59; Cttee on N Ireland, 1971; Cttee on Police Pay, 1978; Council of Management, Nat. Inst. of Economic and Social Research; Court of Governors, LSE (Hon. Fellow, 1980); Council, Royal Economic Soc. (Pres., 1968–70). President: Scottish Economic Soc., 1969–71; British Assoc. for Advancement of Science, 1970–71 (Pres. Section F, 1969); GPDST, 1972–. Houblon-Norman Trustee, 1982–. Editor, Scottish Journal of Political Economy, 1954–61. For. Hon. Mem., Amer. Acad. of Arts and Scis, 1973. Hon. LLD: Mount Allison, 1962; Glasgow, 1966; Exeter, 1969; Hon. DLitt: Reading, 1968: Heriot-Watt, 1969; Hon. DSc(Econ.): Univ. of Wales, 1971; QUB, 1972; DUniv Stirling, 1973. *Publications:* Introduction to Economics, 1944, 6th edn 1982; Home and Foreign Investment, 1870–1913, 1953; Monetary Policy in a Mixed Economy, 1960; Economic Development and the Atlantic Provinces, 1961; Factors in Economic Development, 1962; Essays in Economic Management, 1971; Control of Long-term International Capital Movements, 1973; Inflation, Growth and International Finance, 1975; Science Studies (Nuffield Foundn report), 1980; Snatches (poems), 1981; (with Barry Eichengreen) Sterling in Decline, 1983; Years of Recovery, 1985; The Price of War, 1986; Economics and Economic Policy, 1986. *Recreations:* colour photography, travel. *Address:* 14 Staverton Road, Oxford OX2 6XJ. *T:* Oxford 52358. *Club:* United Oxford & Cambridge University (Trustee).

See also F. A. Cairncross.

CAIRNCROSS, Frances Anne, (Mrs Hamish McRae); Britain Editor, The Economist, since 1984; *b* 30 Aug. 1944; *d* of Sir Alexander Kirkland Cairncross, *qv*; *m* 1971, Hamish McRae, *qv*; two *d*. *Educ:* Laurel Bank Sch., Glasgow; St Anne's Coll., Oxford (MA History); Brown Univ., Rhode Island (MAEcon). On Staff of: The Times, 1967–69; The Banker, 1969; The Observer, 1970–73; Economics Correspondent 1973–81, Women's Page Editor 1981–84, The Guardian. Member: SSRC Economics Cttee, 1972–76; Newspaper Panel, Monopolies Commn, 1973–80; Council, Royal Economic Soc., 1980–85; Cttee of Inquiry into Proposals to Amend the Shops Act, 1983–84; Inquiry into British Housing, 1984–85. Hon. Treas., Nat. Council for One Parent Families, 1980–83; Trustee, Kennedy Memorial Trust, 1974–. *Publications:* Capital City (with Hamish McRae), 1971; The Second Great Crash (with Hamish McRae), 1973; The Guardian Guide to the Economy, 1981; Changing Perceptions of Economic Policy, 1981; The Second Guardian Guide to the Economy, 1983. *Recreation:* child care. *Address:* 6 Canonbury Lane, N1 2AP. *T:* 01–359 4612.

CAIRNCROSS, Neil Francis, CB 1971; Deputy Under-Secretary of State, Home Office, 1972–80; *b* 29 July 1920; *s* of late James and Olive Hunter Cairncross; *m* 1947, Eleanor Elizabeth Leisten; two *s* one *d*. *Educ:* Charterhouse; Oriel Coll., Oxford. Royal Sussex Regt, 1940–45. Called to the Bar, 1948. Home Office, 1948; a Private Sec. to the Prime Minister, 1955–58; Sec., Royal Commn on the Press, 1961–62; Dep. Sec., Cabinet Office, 1970–72; Dep. Sec., NI Office, March-Nov. 1972. Member: Parole Bd, 1982–85; Home Grown Timber Adv. Cttee, 1981–; (co-opted) Avon Probation Cttee, 1983–. *Recreation:* painting. *Address:* Little Grange, The Green, Olveston, Bristol BS12 3EJ. *T:* Almondsbury 613060. *Club:* United Oxford & Cambridge University.

CAIRNS, family name of **Earl Cairns.**

CAIRNS, 5th Earl, *cr* 1878; **David Charles Cairns,** GCVO 1972 (KCVO 1969); CB 1960; Rear-Admiral; DL; Baron Cairns, 1867; Viscount Garmoyle, 1878; Her Majesty's Marshal of the Diplomatic Corps, 1962–71; Extra Equerry to the Queen, since 1972; *b* 3 July 1909; *s* of 4th Earl and Olive (*d* 1952), *d* of late J. P. Cobbold, MP; *S* father, 1946; *m* 1936, Barbara Jeanne Harrisson, *y d* of Sydney H. Burgess, Heathfield, Altrincham, Cheshire; two *s* one *d*. *Educ:* RNC Dartmouth. Served War of 1939–45 (despatches); Dep. Dir, Signal Dept, Admiralty, 1950, comd 7th Frigate Sqdn, 1952; HMS Ganges, 1953–54; Student Imperial Defence Coll., 1955; comd HMS Superb, 1956–57; Baghdad Pact Plans and Training Div., Admiralty, 1958; Pres., RNC Greenwich, 1958–61; retired. Pres., Navy League, 1966–77. Formerly: Dir, Brixton Estate Ltd; Governor, Nuffield Nursing Home Trust. Prime Warden, Fishmongers' Co., 1972. DL Suffolk, 1973. *Heir:* *s* Viscount Garmoyle, *qv*. *Address:* The Red House, Clopton, near Woodbridge, Suffolk. *T:* Grundisburgh 262. *Club:* Turf.

CAIRNS, Rt. Hon. Sir David (Arnold Scott), PC 1970; Kt 1955; a Lord Justice of Appeal, 1970–77; *b* 5 March 1902; *s* of late David Cairns, JP, Freeman of Sunderland, and late Sarah Scott Cairns; *m* 1932, Irene Cathery Phillips; one *s* two *d*. *Educ:* Bede Sch., Sunderland; Pembroke Coll., Cambridge (Scholar) (Hon. Fellow, 1973); Senior Optime. MA, LLB (Cantab); BSc (London); Certificate of Honour, Bar Final, 1925. Called to Bar, Middle Temple, 1926; Bencher 1958. KC 1947. Liberal Candidate at By-election, Epsom Div., 1947. Mem. of Leatherhead UDC, 1948–54; Chm., Liberal Party Commn on Trade Unions, 1948–49; Mem. of Liberal Party Cttee, 1951–53; Chm., Monopolies and Restrictive Practices Commn, 1954–56; Recorder of Sunderland, 1957–60; Comr of Assize, 1957 (Midland Circuit), May 1959 (Western Circuit), Nov. 1959 (Wales and Chester Circuit); Judge of the High Court, Probate, Divorce and Admiralty Div., 1960–70. Chairman: Statutory Cttee of Pharmaceutical Soc. of Great Britain, 1952–60; Executive of Justice (British Section of International Commn of Jurists), 1959–60; Minister of Aviation's Cttee on Accident Investigation and Licence Control, 1959–60; Govt Adv. Cttee on Rhodesian Travel Restrictions, 1968–70. *Recreations:* swimming, gardening. *Address:* Applecroft, Ashtead, Surrey. *T:* Ashtead 74132.

CAIRNS, Air Vice-Marshal Geoffrey Crerar, CBE 1970; AFC 1960; FRAeS 1979; FBIM; Chief Executive, Trago Mills, since 1981; *b* 1926; *s* of late Dr J. W. Cairns, MD, MCh, DPH and Marion Cairns; *m* 1948, Carol (*d* 1985), *d* of H. I. F. Evernden, MBE; four *d*. *Educ:* Loretto School, Musselburgh; Cambridge Univ. Joined RAF, 1944; served: Sqdns 43 and 93, Italy; Sqdn 73, Malta, 1946–49; Sqdn 72, UK, 1949–51; Adjutant, Hong Kong Auxiliary Air Force; test pilot A&AEE, Boscombe Down, 1957–60; Jt Planning Staff, MoD, 1961; Chief Instructor, Helicopters, CFS, RAF Ternhill, 1963; JSSC 1966; Supt Flying A&AEE 1968; Dir, Defence Operational Requirements Staffs, MoD, 1970; Commandant, Boscombe Down, 1972–74; ACAS (Op. Requirements), MoD, 1974–76; Comdr, Southern Maritime Air Region, 1976–78; Chief of Staff No 18 Group, Strike Command, 1978–80. Consultant, Marconi Avionics, 1980–81. *Recreations:* golf, railways. *Address:* c/o Lloyds Bank, Cox's and King's Branch, 6 Pall Mall, SW1. *Club:* Royal Air Force.

CAIRNS, Hugh John Forster; DM; FRS 1974; Professor of Microbiology, Harvard School of Public Health, since 1980; *b* 21 Nov. 1922. *Educ:* Oxford Univ. BA 1943; BM, BCh 1946; DM 1952. Surg. Registrar, Radcliffe Infirmary, Oxford, 1945; Med. Intern, Postgrad. Med. Sch., London, 1946; Paediatric Intern, Royal Victoria Infirmary, Newcastle, 1947; Chem. Pathologist, Radcliffe Infirmary, 1947–49; Virologist, Hall Inst., Melbourne, Aust., 1950–51; Virus Research Inst., Entebbe, Uganda, 1952–54; Research Fellow, then Reader, Aust. Nat. Univ., Canberra, 1955–63; Rockefeller Research Fellow,

California Inst. of Technology, 1957; Nat. Insts of Health Fellow, Cold Spring Harbor, NY, 1960–61; Dir, Cold Spring Harbor Lab. of Quantitative Biology, 1963–68 (Staff Mem., 1968–); Prof of Biology (Hon.), State Univ. of New York, Stony Brook, 1968–73, Amer. Cancer Soc. Prof. 1968–73; Head of Imperial Cancer Research Fund Mill Hill Laboratories, 1973–80. *Address:* Department of Microbiology, Harvard School of Public Health, 677 Huntington Avenue, Boston, Massachusetts 02115, USA. *T:* (617) 732 1240.

CAIRNS, Dr James Ford; MHR (ALP) for Lalor, 1969–78 (for Yarra, 1955–69); *b* 4 Oct. 1914; *s* of James John Cairns and Letitia Cairns (*née* Ford); *m* 1939, Gwendolyn Olga Robb; two *s*. *Educ:* Melton/Sunbury State Sch.; Northcote High Sch.; Melbourne Univ. MComm and PhD (Melb.). Australian Estates Co. Ltd, 1932; Victoria Police Force, 1935. Served War, AIF, 1945. Melbourne University: Sen. Tutor, Lectr, Sen. Lectr (Economic Hist.), 1946–55; Nuffield Dominion Fellow, Oxford Univ., 1951–52. Minister for Overseas Trade, 1972–74; Treasurer of Australia, 1974–75; Dep. Prime Minister, 1974–75; Minister for the Environment, Australia, 1975. *Publications:* Australia, 1951 (UK); Living with Asia, 1965; The Eagle and the Lotus, 1969; Tariffs or Planning, 1970; Silence Kills, 1970; The Quiet Revolution, 1972; Oil in Troubled Waters, 1976; Vietnam: Scorched Earth Reborn, 1976; Growth to Freedom, 1979; Survival Now, the Human Transformation, 1983; numerous articles in jls and press, incl. title Australia: History in Enc. Brit. *Recreations:* sleeping, reading.

CAIRNS, James George Hamilton Dickson; Chief Architect and Director of Works, Home Office, 1976–80; *b* 17 Sept. 1920; *s* of Percival Cairns and Christina Elliot Cairns; *m* 1944, G. Elizabeth Goodman; one *d*. *Educ:* Hillhead High Sch., Glasgow; London Polytechnic. ARIBA. Served War, Royal Corps of Signals (Intell.), 1941–46. Architects' Dept, GLC, 1946–75. Divisional Architect, Thamesmead New Town, awarded Sir Patrick Abercrombie Prize by Internat. Union of Architects, 1969. *Recreations:* golf, sailing. *Address:* Elmsleigh, 12 Elmstead Park Road, West Wittering, W Sussex. *T:* Birdham 513316. *Clubs:* Roman Way; Goodwood Golf, West Wittering Sailing, Birdham Yacht.

CAIRNS, Julia, (Mrs Paul Davidson); writer and lecturer; Vice-President: London and Overseas Flower Arrangement Society; Society of Women Writers and Journalists; *o c* of late H. W. Akers, Oxford; *m* 1st, 1915, Frank H. James, The Royal Scots; 2nd, 1925, Capt. Paul Davidson, late 12th Royal Lancers (*d* 1942). *Educ:* Oxford. Entered journalism as a free-lance; Woman Editor of The Ideal Home, 1924; House and Home Director of Woman's Journal, 1927; Editor-in-Chief Weldons Publications, 1929–55; Home Editor, The Queen, 1956–58. President Women's Press Club of London Ltd, 1947 and 1948. *Publications:* Home-Making, 1950; How I Became a Journalist, 1960. *Recreation:* gardening. *Club:* University Women's.

CAITHNESS, 20th Earl of, *cr* 1455; **Malcolm Ian Sinclair,** FRICS; Lord Berriedale, 1455; Bt 1631; Minister of State, Home Office, since 1986; *b* 3 Nov. 1948; *s* of 19th Earl of Caithness, CVO, CBE, DSO, DL, JP; *S* father, 1965; *m* 1975, Diana Caroline, *d* of Major Richard Coke, MC; one *s* one *d*. A Lord in Waiting (Govt Whip), 1984–85; parly spokesman on health and social security, 1984–85, on Scotland, 1984–; Parly Under-Sec. of State, Dept of Transport, 1985–86. *Educ:* Marlborough; Royal Agric. Coll., Cirencester. *Heir:* *s* Lord Berriedale, *qv*. *Address:* Finstock Manor, Finstock, Oxford.

CAITHNESS, Archdeacon of; *see* Hadfield, Ven. J. C.

CAKOBAU, Ratu Sir George (Kadavulevu), GCMG 1973; GCVO 1977; OBE 1953; Royal Victorian Chain, 1982; Governor-General of Fiji, 1973–83; *b* 1911; *s* of Ratu Popi Epeli Seniloli Cakobau; *m* Lealea S. Balekiwai, *d* of Vilikesa Balekiwai. *Educ:* Queen Victoria Sch.; Newington Coll., Australia; Wanganui Technical Coll., NZ. Served War, 1939–45; Captain, Fiji Military Forces. Member: Council of Chiefs, Fiji, 1938–72; Legislative Council, Fiji, 1951–70; Minister for Fijian Affairs and Local Government, 1970–71; Minister without Portfolio, 1971–72. KStJ 1973. *Address:* Bau Island, Tailevu, Fiji.

CALCUTT, David Charles; QC 1972; Master of Magdalene College, Cambridge, since 1986 (Fellow Commoner, 1980–85); Chairman: Civil Service Arbitration Tribunal, since 1979; Institute of Actuaries' Appeal Board, since 1985; Deputy President, Lloyd's of London Appeal Tribunal, since 1983; a Judge of the Courts of Appeal of Jersey and Guernsey, since 1978; Chancellor of the Dioceses of Exeter and Bristol, since 1971 and in Europe, since 1983; a Recorder, since 1972; *b* 2 Nov. 1930; *s* of late Henry Calcutt; *m* 1969, Barbara, JP City of London, *d* of late Vivian Walker. *Educ:* Christ Church, Oxford (chorister); Cranleigh Sch. (music schol.); King's Coll., Cambridge (choral schol.; Stewart of Rannoch Schol., 1952; prizeman; MA, LLB, MusB). Called to the Bar, Middle Temple, 1955 (Bencher, 1981); Harmsworth Law Schol., 1956. Staff of The Times, 1957–66; Dep. Chm., Somerset QS, 1970–71. Dept of Trade Inspector, Cornhill Consolidated Gp Ltd, 1974–77; Member: Criminal Injuries Compensation Bd, 1977–; Council on Tribunals, 1980–86; Chairman: Provincial Tribunal of Enquiry, 1979; Falkland Is Commn of Enquiry, 1984; conducted Cyprus Service Police Inquiry, 1985–86; Member: Colliery Indep. Rev. Body, 1985–; Mem., Interception of Communications Tribunal, 1986–; Conciliator, Internat. Centre for the Settlement of Investment Disputes, Washington, 1986–; Indep. Mem., Diplomatic Service Appeal Bd, 1986–. Member: Gen. Council of the Bar, 1968–72; Crown Court Rules Cttee, 1971–77; Senate of the Inns of Court and the Bar, 1979–85 (Chm. of the Senate, 1984–85; Chm. of the Bar, 1984–85); UK Deleg., Consultative Cttee, Bars and Law Socs, EEC, 1979–83. Fellow, Internat. Acad. of Trial Lawyers (NY), 1978–; Hon. Member: American Bar Assoc., 1985–; Canadian Bar Assoc., 1985–. Dir, Edington Music Fest., 1956–64. Member Council: RSCM, 1967–; RCM, 1980–; Vice-Chm. Council, Cranleigh and Bramley Schs, 1983– (Governor, 1963–83); Governor: SPCK, 1980–; Blundell's Sch., 1981–; British Inst. of Human Rights, 1983–. *Recreation:* living on Exmoor. *Address:* Magdalene College, Cambridge; Lamb Building, Temple, EC4. *Clubs:* Athenæum, United Oxford & Cambridge University; New (Edinburgh).

CALCUTTA, Archbishop of, (RC), since 1969; **His Eminence Lawrence Trevor Cardinal Picachy,** SJ; *b* 7 Aug. 1916; Indian. *Educ:* St Joseph's College, Darjeeling and various Indian Seminaries. 1952–60: Headmaster of St Xavier's School, Principal of St Xavier's College, Rector of St Xavier's, Calcutta. Parish Priest of Basanti, large village of West Bengal, 1960–62; (first) Bishop of Jamshedpur, 1962–69, Apostolic Administrator of Jamshedpur, 1969–70. Cardinal, 1976. Pres., Catholic Bishops' Conf. of India, 1976–81 (Vice-Pres., 1972–75). *Address:* Archbishop's House, 32 Park Street, Calcutta 700016, India. *T:* Calcutta 44–4666.

CALCUTTA, Bishop of, since 1982; **Rt. Rev. Dinesh Chandra Gorai;** *b* 15 Jan. 1934. *Educ:* Calcutta Univ. (BA 1956); Serampore Theological Coll. (BD 1959). Ordained, 1962; Methodist Minister in Calcutta/Barrackpore, 1968–70; first Bishop, Church of N India Diocese of Barrackpore, 1970–82; Dep. Moderator, 1980, Moderator, 1983–86, Church of N India. *Publication:* (ed) Transfer of Vision: a leadership development programme for the Church of North India 1983–1986, 1984. *Address:* Bishop's House, 51 Chowringhee Road, Calcutta 700 071, India. *T:* 44–5259.

CALDECOTE, 2nd Viscount *cr* 1939, of Bristol; **Robert Andrew Inskip,** DSC 1941; FEng 1977; Chairman: Delta Group plc (formerly Delta Metal Co.), 1972–82; Investors in Industry (formerly Finance for Industry), 1980–July 1987; *b* 8 Oct. 1917; *o s* of Thomas Walker Hobart Inskip, 1st Viscount Caldecote, PC, CBE, and Lady Augusta Orr Ewing (*d* 1967), *widow* of Charles Orr Ewing, MP for Ayr Burghs and *e d* of 7th Earl of Glasgow; *S* father, 1947; *m* 1942, Jean Hamilla, *d* of late Rear-Adm. H. D. Hamilton; one *s* two *d*. *Educ:* Eton Coll.; King's Coll., Cambridge. BA Cantab 1939; MA 1944; Hon. LLD 1983. RNVR, 1939–45; RNC Greenwich, 1946–47; an Asst Manager, Vickers-Armstrong Naval Yard, Walker-on-Tyne, 1947–48; Mem., Church Assembly, 1950–55; Fellow, King's Coll., and Lectr, Engineering Dept, Cambridge Univ., 1948–55; Man. Dir, English Electric Aviation, 1960–63; Dep. Man. Dir, British Aircraft Corp., 1961–67 (Dir, 1960–69); Dir, English Electric Co., 1953–69; Chm., Legal and General Gp, 1977–80. Chairman: EDC Movement of Exports, 1965–72; Export Council for Europe, 1970–71. President: Soc. of British Aerospace Cos, 1965–66; Internat. Assoc. of Aeronautical and Space Equipment Manufacturers, 1966–68; Parliamentary and Scientific Cttee, 1966–69; Fellowship of Engineering, 1981–86. Director: Consolidated Gold Fields, 1969–78; Lloyds Bank, 1975–; Lloyds Bank International, 1979–85; Equity Capital for Industry, 1980–85. Member: Review Bd for Govt Contracts, 1969–76; Inflation Accounting Cttee, 1974–75; Engineering Industries Council, 1975–82; British Railways Bd, 1979–85; Adv. Council for Applied R & D, 1981–84; Engrg Council, 1981–85. Chairman: Design Council, 1972–80; BBC Gen. Adv. Council, 1982–85; Mary Rose Trust, 1983–. Pro-Chancellor, Cranfield Inst. of Technology, 1976–84. Mem. UK Delegn to UN, 1952; Fellow, Eton Coll., 1953–72; Pres., Dean Close Sch. Hon. FIEE; MRINA; Hon. FIMechE, Hon. FICE, 1982; Hon. FSIAD 1976. Hon. DSc: Cranfield, 1976; Aston, 1979; City; Bristol; Hon. LLD: London, 1981; Cambridge. *Recreations:* sailing, shooting, golf. *Heir:* *s* Hon. Piers James Hampden Inskip [*b* 20 May 1947; *m* 1st, 1970, Susan Bridget, *d* of late W. P. Mellen; 2nd, 1984, Kristine Elizabeth, *d* of Harvey Holbrooke-Jackson; one *s*]. *Address:* Orchard Cottage, South Harting, Petersfield, Hants GU31 5NR. *T:* Harting 264. *Clubs:* Pratt's, Athenæum, Royal Ocean Racing; Royal Yacht Squadron.

CALDECOTT, John Andrew; Chairman, M & G Group PLC, since 1979 (Director, since 1966); Vice Chairman, Kleinwort Benson Ltd, 1974–83; *b* 25 Feb. 1924; *s* of Sir Andrew Caldecott, GCMG, CBE and Lady Caldecott; *m* 1951, Zita Ursula Mary Belloc; three *s* one *d*. *Educ:* Eton; Trinity Coll., Oxford (2nd Cl. BA Hons Jurisprudence). Qualified Solicitor, 1951. Served War, KRRC, 1942–46. Druces & Attlee, Solicitors, 1951–69 (Partner, 1954–69). Director: Kleinwort Benson Ltd, 1970–83; Kleinwort, Benson, Lonsdale Ltd, 1974–; Chloride Group PLC, 1981–; Whitbread and Company PLC, 1983–; Electronic Rentals Group plc, 1983–, Blue Circle Industries PLC, 1983–. Mem., Bd of Banking Supervision, 1986–. *Recreations:* fishing, music. *Address:* 42 Tregunter Road, SW10 9LQ. *T:* 01–370 5616. *Club:* Boodle's.

CALDER, John Mackenzie; Managing Director, John Calder (Publishers) Ltd and Calder & Boyars Ltd, since 1950; President, Riverrun Press Inc., New York, since 1978; Chairman, North American Book Clubs, since 1982; *b* 25 Jan. 1927; *e s* of James Calder, Ardargie, Forgandenny, Perthshire, and Lucianne Wilson, Montreal, Canada; *m* 1st, 1949, Mary Ann Simmonds; one *d*; 2nd, 1960, Bettina Jonic (marr. diss. 1975); one *d*. *Educ:* Gilling Castle, Yorks; Bishops College Sch., Canada; McGill Univ.; Sir George Williams Coll.; Zürich Univ. Studied political economy; subseq. worked in Calders Ltd (timber co.), Director; founded John Calder (Publishers) Ltd, 1950. Organiser of literary confs for Edinburgh Festival, 1962 and 1963, and Harrogate Festival, 1969. Founded Ledlanet Nights, 1963, in Kinross-shire (music and opera festival, closed 1974). Acquired book-selling business of Better Books, London, 1969, expanded Edinburgh, 1971. Dir of other cos associated with opera, publishing, etc, inc. Operabout Ltd, Canadian International Library Ltd, Canada. Active in fields related to the arts and on many cttees; Co-founder, Defence of Literature and the Arts Society; Chm., Fedn of Scottish Theatres, 1972–74. Contested (L): Kinross and W Perthshire, 1970; Hamilton, Oct. 1974; (European Parlt) Mid Scotland and Fife, 1979. FRSA 1974. Chevalier des Arts et des Lettres, 1975; Chevalier de l'Ordre nationale de mérite, 1983. *Publications:* (ed) A Samuel Beckett Reader, 1967; (ed) Beckett at 60, 1967; (ed) William Burroughs Reader, 1982; (ed) New Samuel Beckett Reader, 1983; (ed) Henry Miller Reader, 1985; (ed) The Nouveau Roman Reader, 1985; (ed) Gambit International Drama Review, etc; articles in many jls. *Recreations:* writing (several plays, stories; criticism, etc; translations); music, theatre, opera, reading, chess, lecturing, conversation; travelling, promoting good causes, fond of good food and wine. *Address:* c/o John Calder (Publishers) Ltd, 18 Brewer Street, W1R 4AS. *Clubs:* Caledonian; Scottish Arts (Edinburgh).

CALDER, Julian Richard; Director of Statistics, Board of Inland Revenue, since 1985; *b* 6 Dec. 1941; *s* of Donald Alexander and Ivy O'Nora Calder; *m* 1965, Avril Tucker; two *s*. *Educ:* Dulwich College; Brasenose College, Oxford; Birkbeck College, London. Statistician, 1973, Chief Statistician, 1978, Central Statistical Office; Chief Statistician, Board of Inland Revenue, 1981. *Recreations:* cycling, listening to music. *Address:* Statistics Division, Board of Inland Revenue, Somerset House, Strand, WC2R 1LB. *T:* 01–438 6609.

CALDER, Nigel David Ritchie, MA; science writer; *b* 2 Dec. 1931; *e s* of Baron Ritchie-Calder, CBE; *m* 1954, Elisabeth Palmer; two *s* three *d*. *Educ:* Merchant Taylors' Sch.; Sidney Sussex Coll., Cambridge. Physicist, Mullard Research Laboratories, 1954–56; Editorial staff, New Scientist, 1956–66; Science Editor, 1960–62; Editor, 1962–66. Science Correspondent, New Statesman, 1959–62 and 1966–71; Chairman, Assoc. of British Science Writers, 1962–64. TV series, The Whole Universe Show, 1977. (Jtly) UNESCO Kalinga Prize for popularisation of science, 1972. *Publications:* Electricity Grows Up, 1958; Robots, 1958; Radio Astronomy, 1958; (ed) The World in 1984, 1965; The Environment Game, 1967; (ed) Unless Peace Comes, 1968; Technopolis: Social Control of the Uses of Science, 1969; Living Tomorrow, 1970; (ed) Nature in the Round: a Guide to Environmental Science, 1973; Timescale, 1983; 1984 and After, 1983; The English Channel, 1986; The Green Machines, 1986; *books of own TV programmes:* The Violent Universe, 1969; The Mind of Man, 1970; The Restless Earth, 1972; The Life Game, 1973; The Weather Machine, 1974; The Human Conspiracy, 1975–76; The Key to the Universe, 1977; Spaceships of the Mind (TV series), 1978; Einstein's Universe, 1979; Nuclear Nightmares, 1979; The Comet is Coming!, 1980. *Recreation:* sailing. *Address:* 8 The Chase, Furnace Green, Crawley, W Sussex RH10 6HW. *T:* Crawley 26693. *Clubs:* Athenæum; Cruising Association (Vice-Pres., 1981–84).

CALDER-MARSHALL, Arthur; author; *b* 19 Aug. 1908; *s* of late Arthur Grotjan Calder-Marshall and Alice Poole; *m* 1934, Violet Nancy Sales; two *d*. *Educ:* St Paul's Sch.; Hertford Coll., Oxford. *Publications: novels:* Two of a Kind, 1933; About Levy, 1933; At Sea, 1934; Dead Centre, 1935; Pie in the Sky, 1937; The Way to Santiago, 1940; A Man Reprieved, 1949; Occasion of Glory, 1955; The Scarlet Boy, 1961, rev. edn 1962; *short stories:* Crime against Cania, 1934; A Pink Doll, 1935; A Date with a Duchess, 1937; *for children:* The Man from Devil's Island, 1958; Fair to Middling, 1959; Lone Wolf: the story of Jack London, 1961; *travel:* Glory Dead, 1939; The Watershed, 1947; *biography:* No Earthly Command, 1957; Havelock Ellis, 1959; The Enthusiast, 1962; The Innocent

Eye, 1963; Lewd, Blasphemous and Obscene, 1972; The Two Duchesses, 1978; *autobiography*: The Magic of My Youth, 1951; *miscellaneous*: Challenge to Schools: public school education, 1935; The Changing Scene, 1937; The Book Front, ed J. Lindsay, 1947; Wish You Were Here: the art of Donald McGill, 1966; Prepare to Shed Them Now ...: the biography and ballads of George R. Sims, 1968; The Grand Century of the Lady, 1976; *essays*: Sterne, in The English Novelists, ed D. Verschoyle, 1936; Films, in Mind in Chains, ed C. Day Lewis; *edited*: Tobias Smollett, Selected Writings, 1950; J. London, The Bodley Head Jack London, Vols 1–4, 1963–66; Charles Dickens, David Copperfield, 1967, Nicholas Nickleby, 1968, Oliver Twist, 1970; Bleak House, 1976; The Life of Benvenuto Cellini, 1968; Jack London, The Call of the Wild, and other stories, 1969; Jane Austen, Emma, 1970; Thomas Paine, Common Sense and the Rights of Man, 1970. *Address*: c/o Elaine Greene Ltd, 31 Newington Green, N16 9PW.

CALDERBANK, Emeritus Prof. Philip Hugh; Professor of Chemical Engineering, University of Edinburgh, 1960–80; *b* 6 March 1919; *s* of Leonard and Rhoda Elizabeth Calderbank; *m* 1941, Kathleen Mary (*née* Taylor); one *s* one *d*. *Educ*: Palmer's Sch., Gray's, Essex; King's Coll., London Univ. Research and Development Chemist: Ministry of Supply, 1941–44; Bakelite Ltd, 1944–47. Lecturer in Chemical Engineering Dept, University Coll., London University, 1947–53; Professor in Chem. Engineering Dept, University of Toronto, 1953–56; Senior Principal Scientific Officer, Dept of Scientific and Industrial Research, 1956–60. *Publications*: contributor: Chemical Engineering Progress; Transactions Instn of Chemical Engineers; Chemical Engineering Science. *Recreations*: various crafts.

CALDERWOOD, Robert; Chief Executive, Strathclyde Regional Council, since 1980; *b* 1 March 1932; *s* of Robert Calderwood and Jessie Reid (*née* Marshall); *m* 1958, Meryl Anne (*née* Fleming); three *s* one *d*. *Educ*: William Hulme's Sch., Manchester; Manchester Univ. (LLB (Hons)). Admitted solicitor, 1956; Town Clerk: Salford, 1966–69; Bolton, 1969–73; Manchester, 1973–79. Dir, Glasgow Garden Fest. 1988 Ltd, 1985–. Member: Parole Bd for England and Wales, 1971–73; Soc. of Local Authority Chief Execs, 1974–; Scottish Consultative Cttee, Commn for Racial Equality, 1981–. Mem. Council, Industrial Soc., 1983–; CBIM (Mem., Scottish Bd, 1982–); Companion, IWES, 1983. *Recreations*: theatre, watching Rugby. *Address*: Strathclyde Regional Council, Regional Headquarters, 20 India Street, Glasgow G2 4PF; 6 Mosspark Avenue, Milngavie, Glasgow G62 8NL. *Clubs*: Royal Scottish Automobile (Glasgow); University Union (Manchester).

CALDICOTT, Hon. Sir John Moore, KBE 1963; CMG 1955; *b* 1900; *m* 1945, Evelyn Macarthur; one *s* two step *d*. *Educ*: Shrewsbury School. Joined RAF 1918. Came to Southern Rhodesia, 1925; farmed in Umvukwes District until 1970. President: Rhodesia Tobacco Assoc., 1943–45; Rhodesia National Farmers' Union, 1946–48. MP for Mazoe, S Rhodesia Parliament, 1948; Minister of Agriculture and Lands, 1951, of Agriculture, Health and Public Service, 1953, of Economic Affairs, 1958–62, of The Common Market, 1962, and of Finance, until 1963, Federation of Rhodesia and Nyasaland. *Address*: 24 Court Road, Greendale, Harare, Zimbabwe. *Club*: Harare (Harare, Zimbabwe).

CALDOW, William James, CMG 1977; Consultant, ICI plc, 1981–86; *b* 7 Dec. 1919; *s* of William Caldow and Mary Wilson Grier; *m* 1950, Monique Henriette Hervé; one *s* (and one *s* decd). *Educ*: Marr College (Dux Medallist); Glasgow University (Scholar; MA Hons); Sorbonne. Captain, Intelligence Corps, 1940–45. Colonial Administrative Service, Gold Coast, later Ghana, 1947–59; War Office, later Ministry of Defence, 1959–80. *Recreations*: reading, music, bird watching. *Address*: 3 Pilgrims Way, Guildford, Surrey. *T*: Guildford 62183. *Clubs*: Royal Commonwealth Society; County (Guildford).

CALDWELL, Surg. Vice-Adm. Sir Dick; *see* Caldwell, Surg. Vice-Adm. Sir E. D.

CALDWELL, Edward George; Parliamentary Counsel, since 1981; *b* 21 Aug. 1941; *s* of Arthur Francis Caldwell and Olive Caldwell (*née* Riddle); *m* 1965, Bronwen Anne, *d* of John Andrew Crockett and late Bronwen Crockett; two *d*. *Educ*: St Andrew's, Singapore; Clifton College; Worcester College, Oxford. Solicitor. Law Commission, 1967–69, 1975–77; joined Office of Parly Counsel, 1969. *Recreations*: swimming, motorcycling. *Address*: Office of the Parliamentary Counsel, 36 Whitehall, SW1A 2AY. *T*: 01–210 6611.

CALDWELL, Surg. Vice-Adm. Sir (Eric) Dick, KBE 1969; CB 1965; Medical Director-General of the Royal Navy, 1966–69; Executive Director, Medical Council on Alcoholism, 1970–79; *b* 6 July 1909; *s* of late Dr John Colin Caldwell; *m* 1942, Margery Lee Abbott. *Educ*: Edinburgh Acad.; Edinburgh Univ. MB, ChB Edinburgh 1933; LRCP, LRCSE, LRFPS(G) 1933; MD Edinburgh 1950; MRCP 1956; FRCP(Edin) 1962; FRCP(London) 1967. Joined Royal Navy, 1934. Served War of 1939–45 in Atlantic, Mediterranean and Pacific; survivor from torpedoeing of HMS Royal Oak and HMS Prince of Wales. Medical Specialist, RN Hosp., Hong Kong, 1947; Sen. Med. Specialist at RN Hosp., Haslar, 1956–58; Surg. Captain 1957; MO i/c of RN Hosp., Plymouth, 1963–66. RN Consultant in Medicine, 1962; Surg. Rear-Adm. 1963; Surg. Vice-Adm. 1966. QHP 1963–69. Gilbert Blane Gold Medal, 1962; FRSocMed. CStJ. *Recreations*: reading, travelling, trying to write. *Address*: 9A Holland Park Road, Kensington, W14 8NA. *T*: 01–602 3326.

CALDWELL, Erskine; author; Editor of American Folkways, 1940–55; Member: Authors' League; American PEN; (Hon.) American Academy and Institute of Arts and Letters; *b* 17 Dec. 1903; *s* of Ira Sylvester Caldwell and Caroline Preston Bell; *m* 1st, 1925, Helen Lannigan; two *s* one *d*; 2nd, 1939, Margaret Bourke-White; 3rd, 1942, June Johnson; one *s*; 4th, 1957, Virginia Moffett Fletcher. *Educ*: Erskine Coll.; Univ. of Virginia. Newspaper reporter on Atlanta (Ga) Journal; motion picture screen writer in Hollywood; newspaper and radio correspondent in Russia. Order of Cultural Merit (Poland), 1981; Comdr, Order of Arts and Letters (France), 1983. *Publications*: The Bastard, 1929; Poor Fool, 1930; American Earth, 1931; Tobacco Road, 1932; God's Little Acre, 1933; We Are the Living, 1933; Journeyman, 1935; Kneel to the Rising Sun, 1935; Some American People, 1935; You Have Seen Their Faces, 1937; Southways, 1938; North of The Danube, 1939; Trouble in July, 1940; Jackpot, 1940; Say! Is This the USA?, 1941; All-Out on the Road to Smolensk, 1942; Moscow Under Fire, 1942; All Night Long, 1942; Georgia Boy, 1943; Tragic Ground, 1944; Stories, 1945; A House in the Uplands, 1946; The Sure Hand of God, 1947; This Very Earth, 1948; Place Called Estherville, 1949; Episode in Palmetto, 1950; Call It Experience, 1951; The Courting of Susie Brown, 1952; A Lamp for Nightfall, 1952; The Complete Stories of Erskine Caldwell, 1953; Love and Money, 1954; Gretta, 1955; Gulf Coast Stories, 1956; Certain Women, 1957; Molly Cottontail, 1958 (juvenile); Claudelle Inglish, 1959; When You Think of Me, 1959; Jenny By Nature, 1961; Close to Home, 1962; The Last Night of Summer, 1963; Around About America, 1964; In Search of Bisco, 1965; The Deer at Our House (juvenile), 1966; In the Shadow of the Steeple, 1966; Miss Mamma Aimee, 1967; Writing In America, 1967; Deep South, 1968; Summertime Island, 1968; The Weather Shelter, 1969; The Earnshaw Neighborhood, 1971; Annette, 1973; Afternoons in Mid-America, 1976; Stories of Life: North & South, 1983; With All My Might: an autobiography, 1987. *Address*: c/o McIntosh & Otis Inc., 475 Fifth Avenue, New York, NY 10017, USA. *T*: New York: MU 9–1050; (home) PO Box 4550, Hopi Station,

Scottsdale, Arizona 85258, USA. *Clubs*: Phoenix Press (Phoenix, Arizona); San Francisco Press (San Francisco, Calif).

CALDWELL, Maj.-Gen. Frank Griffiths, OBE 1953 (MBE 1945); MC 1941 and Bar 1942; company director; *b* 26 Feb. 1921; *s* of William Charles Francis and Violet Marjorie Kathleen Caldwell; *m* 1945, Betty, *d* of Captain Charles Palmer Buesden; one *s* one *d*. *Educ*: Elizabeth Coll., Guernsey. Commnd Royal Engrs, 1940; served Western Desert RE, 1940–43 (MC and Bar); Special Air Service NW Europe, 1944–45 (MBE); Malaya, 1951–53 (OBE); Comdr RE, 2 Div. BAOR, 1961–63; Corps Comdr RE, 1 (BR) Corps, 1967–68; Dir Defence Operational Plans, MoD, 1970; Engineer in Chief (Army), 1970–72; Asst CGS (Operational Requirements), 1972–74. Col Comdt, RE, 1975–80. Belgian Croix de Guerre, 1940, and Croix Militaire, 1945. *Recreations*: ornithology, golf. *Address*: Le Courtil Tomar, Rue des Pres, St Pierre du Bois, Guernsey. *Clubs*: Army and Navy, MCC.

CALDWELL, Prof. John Bernard, OBE 1979; PhD; FEng 1976; FRINA; Professor of Naval Architecture, since 1966, and Dean of the Faculty of Engineering, 1983–86, University of Newcastle upon Tyne; *b* 26 Sept. 1926; *s* of John Revie Caldwell and Doris (*née* Bolland); *m* 1955, Jean Muriel Frances Duddridge; two *s*. *Educ*: Bootham Sch., York; Liverpool Univ. (BEng); Bristol Univ. (PhD). CEng, MIStructE; FRINA 1963. Res. Fellow, Civil Engrg, Bristol Univ., 1953; Sen. Scientific Officer 1955, Principal Sci. Off. 1958, Royal Naval Scientific Service; Asst Prof. of Applied Mechanics, RNC Greenwich, 1960–66; Hd of Dept of Naval Architecture, Newcastle upon Tyne Univ., 1966–83. Director: Nat. Maritime Inst. Ltd, 1983–85; Marine Design Consultants Ltd (formerly British Shipbuilders Engrg and Tech. Services Ltd), 1985–; Newcastle Technology Centre, 1985–. Vis. Prof. of Naval Arch., MIT, 1962–63. President: N-E Coast Instn of Engrs and Shipbuilders, 1976–78; RINA, 1984– (Vice-Pres., 1977–84). Hon. DSc Gdansk Tech. Univ., 1985. *Publications*: numerous papers on research and educn in naval arch. in Trans RINA. *Address*: The White House, Cadehill Road, Stocksfield, Northumberland NE43 7PT. *T*: Stocksfield 843445. *Club*: National Liberal.

CALDWELL, Philip; Chief Executive Officer since 1979, and Chairman of the Board since 1980, Ford Motor Co.; *b* Bourneville, Ohio, 27 Jan. 1920; *s* of Robert Clyde Caldwell and Wilhelmina (*née* Hemphill); *m* 1945, Betsey Chinn Clark; one *s* two *d*. *Educ*: Muskingum Coll. (BA Econs 1940); Harvard Univ. Graduate Sch. of Business (MBA Indust. Management, 1942). Served to Lieut, USNR, 1942–46. With Navy Dept, 1946–53 (Dep. Dir, Procurement Policy Div., 1948–53); with Ford Motor Co., 1953–: Vice Pres. and Gen. Man. Truck Ops, 1968–70; Pres. and Dir, Philco-Ford Corp. (subsid. of Ford Motor Co.), 1970–71; Vice Pres. Manufg Gp, N Amer. Automotive Ops, 1971–72; Chm. and Chief Exec. Officer, Ford of Europe, Inc., 1972–73; Exec. Vice Pres., Internat. Automotive Ops, 1973–77; Vice Chm. of Bd, 1977–79; Dep. Chief Exec. Officer, 1978–79; Pres., 1978–80; Dir, Ford Motor Co., Ford of Europe, Ford Latin America, Ford Mid-East and Africa, Ford Asia-Pacific, Ford Motor Credit Co., and Ford of Canada. Chm., Motor Vehicle Manufrs Assoc.; Director: Digital Equipment Corp.; The Chase Manhattan Bank, NA; Chase Manhattan Corp.; Detroit Renaissance; Harvard Univ. Associates of Grad. Sch. of Business Admin; Detroit Symphony Orch.; Vice Chm., Bd of Trustees, New Detroit, Inc.; Member: Internat. Adv. Cttee, Chase Manhattan Bank; Business-Higher Education Forum Exec. Cttee; Business Council; Business Roundtable; Conf. Bd; Trilateral Commn. Trustee: Cttee for Econ. Develt; Muskingum Coll. Hon. DH Muskingum, 1974; Hon. DBA Upper Iowa Univ., 1978; Hon. LLD: Boston Univ. and Eastern Mich Univ., 1979; Miami Univ., 1980; Davidson Coll., 1982. 1st William A. Jump Meml Award, 1950; Meritorious Civilian Service Award, US Navy, 1953; Outstanding Citizen of the Year Award, Mich Assoc. of Broadcasters, 1984; Business Statesman Award, Harvard Business Sch. Club of NY, 1984. *Address*: Ford Motor Co., The American Road, Dearborn, Mich 48121–1899, USA; Bloomfield Hills, Mich 48013, USA. *Clubs*: Detroit, Bloomfield Hills Country Detroit Athletic, Renaissance.

CALDWELL-MOORE, Patrick; *see* Moore, P. C.

CALEDON, 7th Earl of, *cr* 1800; **Nicholas James Alexander;** Baron Caledon, 1790; Viscount Caledon, 1797; *b* 6 May 1955; *s* of 6th Earl of Caledon, and Baroness Anne (*d* 1963), *d* of late Baron Nicolai de Graevenitz; *S* father, 1980; *m* 1979, Wendy (marr. diss.), *d* of Spiro Coumantaros and Mrs Suzanne Dayton. *Educ*: Sandroyd School, Gordonstoun School (Round-Square House). *Recreations*: ski-ing, tennis, swimming, photography, travel. *Heir*: *cousin* Earl Alexander of Tunis, *qv*. *Address*: Caledon Castle, Caledon, Co. Tyrone, Northern Ireland. *T*: Caledon 232.

CALEDONIA, Bishop of, since 1981; **Rt. Rev. John Edward Hannen;** *b* 19 Nov. 1937; *s* of Charles Scott Hannen and Mary Bowman Hannen (*née* Lynds); *m* 1977, Alana Susan Long; two *d*. *Educ*: McGill Univ. (BA); College of the Resurrection (GOE). Asst Curate, St Alphege's, Solihull, Warwicks, 1961–64; Priest in Charge, Mission to the Hart Highway, Diocese of Caledonia, BC, 1965–67; Priest, St Andrew's, Greenville, BC, 1967–68; Priest in Charge, Church of Christ the King, Port Edward, BC, 1969–71; Rector, Christ Church, Kincolith, BC, 1971–81; Regional Dean of Metlakatla, 1972–78. *Recreations*: music, Irish wolfhounds. *Address*: Bishop's Lodge, 208 Fourth Avenue West, Prince Rupert, BC V8J 1P3, Canada. *T*: 624–6013.

CALGARY, Bishop of, since 1983; **Rt. Rev. John Barry Curtis;** *b* 19 June 1933; *s* of Harold Boyd Curtis and Eva B. Curtis (*née* Saunders); *m* 1959, Patricia Emily (*née* Simpson); two *s* two *d*. *Educ*: Trinity Coll., Univ. of Toronto (BA 1955, LTh 1958); Theological Coll., Chichester, Sussex. Deacon 1958, priest 1959; Asst Curate, Holy Trinity, Pembroke, Ont, 1958–61; Rector: Parish of March, Kanata, Ont, 1961–65; St Stephen's Church, Buckingham, Que, 1965–69; Church School Consultant, Diocese of Ottawa, 1969; Rector, All Saints (Westboro), Ottawa, 1969–78; Director of Programme, Diocese of Ottawa, 1978–80; Rector, Christ Church, Elbow Park, Calgary, Alta, 1980–83. Hon. DD Trinity Coll., Toronto, 1985. *Recreations*: reading, hiking, skiing, cycling. *Address*: 3015 Glencoe Road SW, Calgary, Alberta T2S 2L9, Canada. *T*: 403–243–3673; (home) 12 Varanger Place NW, Calgary, Alta T3A 0E9. *T*: 403–286–5127. *Club*: Ranchmen's (Calgary, Alta).

CALLADINE, Christopher Reuben, ScD; FRS 1984; Professor of Structural Mechanics, University of Cambridge, since 1986; Fellow of Peterhouse, since 1960; *b* 19 Jan. 1935; *s* of Reuben and Mabel Calladine (*née* Boam); *m* 1964, Mary R. H. Webb; two *s* one *d*. *Educ*: Nottingham High Sch.; Peterhouse, Cambridge (BA); Massachusetts Inst. of Technology (SM). Development engineer, English Electric Co., 1958; Univ. Demonstrator in Engrg, Univ. of Cambridge, 1960, Lectr, 1963; Reader, 1978. Vis. Research Associate, Brown Univ., 1963; Vis. Prof., Stanford Univ., 1969–70. *Publications*: Engineering Plasticity, 1969; Theory of Shell Structures, 1983; papers in engrg and biological jls. *Address*: 25 Almoners Avenue, Cambridge CB1 4NZ. *T*: Cambridge (0223) 246742.

CALLAGHAN, Sir Allan (Robert), Kt 1972; CMG 1945; agricultural consultant, since 1972; *b* 24 Nov. 1903; *s* of late Phillip George Callaghan and late Jane Peacock; *m* 1928, Zillah May Sampson (*d* 1964); two *s* one *d* (and one *s* decd); *m* 1965, Doreen Rhys Draper. *Educ*: Bathurst High Sch., NSW; St Paul's Coll., Univ. of Sydney (BSc Agr. 1924); St

John's Coll., Oxford (Rhodes Scholar, BSc 1926, DPhil 1928). Asst Plant Breeder, NSW, Dept of Agriculture, 1928–32; Principal, Roseworthy Agricultural Coll., South Australia, 1932–49; Asst Dir (Rural Industry) in Commonwealth Dept of War Organisation of Industry, 1943; Chm., Land Development Executive in South Australia, 1945–51; Dir of Agriculture, South Australia, 1949–59; Commercial Counsellor, Australian Embassy, Washington, DC, 1959–65; Chm., Australian Wheat Bd, 1965–71. Farrer Medal (for distinguished service to Australian Agriculture), 1954; FAIAS 1959. *Publications:* (with A. J. Millington) The Wheat Industry in Australia, 1956; numerous articles in scientific and agricultural jls on agricultural and animal husbandry matters. *Recreations:* swimming, riding, gardening. *Address:* Tralee, 22 Murray Street, Clapham, SA 5062, Australia. *T:* 276–6524.

CALLAGHAN, Sir Bede (Bertrand), Kt 1976; CBE 1968; Managing Director, Commonwealth Banking Corporation, 1965–76; Chancellor of the University of Newcastle, NSW, since 1977; *b* 16 March 1912; *s* of S. K. Callaghan and Amy M. Ryan; *m* 1940, Mary T. Brewer; three *d. Educ:* Newcastle High Sch. FAIB; FAIM. Commonwealth Bank, 1927. Mem. Board Executive Directors, IMF and World Bank, 1954–59; Gen. Man., Commonwealth Develt Bank of Australia, 1959–65; Chm., Aust. European Finance Corp. Ltd, 1971–76; Chm., Foreign Investment Review Bd, 1976–. Chm., Lewisham Hospital Adv. Bd, 1975–. Chairman: Aust. Admin. Staff Coll., 1969–76; Inst. of Industrial Economics, 1976–; Mem. Council, Univ. of Newcastle, NSW, 1966–, Dep. Chancellor, 1973–77. Hon. DSc Newcastle, 1973. *Recreation:* lawn bowls. *Address:* 69 Darnley Street, Gordon, NSW 2072, Australia. *T:* (Sydney) 498–7583. *Club:* Union (Sydney).

CALLAGHAN, Rear-Adm. Desmond Noble, CB 1970; FRSA; Director-General, National Supervisory Council for Intruder Alarms, 1971–77; *b* 24 Nov. 1915; *s* of Edmund Ford Callaghan and Kathleen Louise Callaghan (*née* Noble): *m* 1948, Patricia Munro Geddes; one *s* two *d. Educ:* RNC Dartmouth. HMS Frobisher, 1933; RNEC Keyhan, 1934; HM Ships: Royal Oak, 1937; Iron Duke, 1938; Warspite, 1939; Hereward, 1941; Prisoner of War, 1941; HMS Argonaut, 1945; HMS Glory, 1946; RNC Dartmouth, 1947; Admiralty, 1949; C-in-C Med. Staff, 1950; HMS Excellent, 1953; HMS Eagle, 1956; RN Tactical Sch., 1958; Admiralty, 1960; HMS Caledonia, 1962; Admiralty, 1965; Vice-Pres. and Pres., Ordnance Board, 1968–71, retired 1971. *Recreations:* Rugby, tennis, swimming. *Address:* Bridge End, Abbotsbrook, Bourne End, Bucks. *T:* Bourne End 20519.

CALLAGHAN, James; MP (Lab) Heywood and Middleton (Middleton and Prestwich, Feb. 1974–1983); *b* 28 Jan. 1927. Lectr, Manchester Coll., 1959–74. Metropolitan Borough Councillor, 1971–74. *Recreations:* sport and art. *Address:* 17 Towncroft Avenue, Middleton, Manchester.

CALLAGHAN, Rt. Hon. (Leonard) James, PC 1964; MP (Lab) Cardiff South and Penarth, since 1983 (South-East Cardiff, 1950–83; South Cardiff, 1945–50); Father of the House of Commons, since 1983; *b* 27 March 1912; *s* of James Callaghan, Chief Petty Officer, RN; *m* 1938, Audrey Elizabeth Moulton; one *s* two *d. Educ:* Elementary and Portsmouth Northern Secondary Schs. Entered Civil Service as a Tax Officer, 1929; Asst Sec., Inland Revenue Staff Fed., 1936–47 (with an interval during the War of 1939–45, when served in Royal Navy). Joined Labour Party, 1931. Parly Sec., Min. of Transport, 1947–50; Chm. Cttee on Road Safety, 1948–50; Parliamentary and Financial Sec., Admiralty, 1950–51; Opposition Spokesman: Transport, 1951–53; Fuel and Power, 1953–55; Colonial Affairs, 1956–61; Shadow Chancellor, 1961–64; Chancellor of the Exchequer, 1964–67; Home Secretary, 1967–70; Shadow Home Sec., 1970–71; Opposition Spokesman on Employment, 1971–72; Shadow Foreign Sec., 1972–74; Sec. of State for Foreign and Commonwealth Affairs, 1974–76; Minister of Overseas Develt, 1975–76; Prime Minister and First Lord of the Treasury, 1976–79; Leader, Labour Party, 1976–80; Leader of the Opposition, 1979–80. Deleg. to Council of Europe, Strasburg, 1948–50 and 1954. Mem., Labour Party NEC, 1957–80; Treasurer, Labour Party, 1967–76, Vice-Chm. 1973, Chm. 1974. Consultant to Police Fedn of England and Wales and to Scottish Police Fedn, 1955–64. Chm., Adv. Cttee on Oil Pollution of the Sea, 1952–63; Pres., United Kingdom Pilots Assoc., 1963–76; Hon. Pres., Internat. Maritime Pilots Assoc., 1971–76. Pres., UC Swansea, 1986–. Visiting Fellow, Nuffield Coll., Oxford, 1959–67, Hon. Life Fellow, 1967; Hon. Fellow: UC Cardiff, 1978; Portsmouth Polytechnic, 1981; Hon. LLD: Univ. of Wales, 1976; Sardar Patel Univ., India, 1978, Univ. of Birmingham, 1981. Hon. Bencher, Inner Temple, 1976. Hon. Freeman: City of Cardiff, 1974; City of Sheffield, 1979. Hubert H. Humphrey Internat. Award, 1978. Grand Cross, 1st class, Order of Merit of Federal Republic of Germany, 1979. *Publication:* A House Divided: the dilemma of Northern Ireland, 1973. *Address:* House of Commons, SW1; Upper Clayhill Farm, Ringmer, East Sussex.

See also Peter Jay.

CALLAGHAN, Morley (Edward); Canadian novelist; *b* Toronto, 1903; *s* of Thomas Callaghan and Mary (*née* Dewan); *m* 1929, Lorrete Florence, *d* of late Joseph Dee; two *s. Educ:* St Michael's Coll., Univ. of Toronto (BA); Osgoode Hall Law School. Holds Hon. Doctorates. Canadian Council Prize, 1970; '50,000 Royal Bank of Canada Award, 1970. *Publications:* Strange Fugitive, 1928; Native Argosy, 1929; It's Never Over, 1930; No Man's Meat, 1931; Broken Journey, 1932; Such Is My Beloved, 1934; They Shall Inherit the Earth, 1935; My Joy in Heaven, 1936; Now That April's Here, 1937; Just Ask for George (play), 1940; Jake Baldwin's Vow (for children), 1948; The Varsity Story, 1948; The Loved and the Lost, 1951; The Man with the Coat, 1955 (MacLean's Prize, 1955); A Many Coloured Coat, 1960 (UK 1963); A Passion in Rome, 1961 (UK 1964); That Summer in Paris, 1963; Morley Callaghan, vols 1 and 2, 1964; A Fine and Private Place, 1976; Close to the Sun Again, 1977; No Man's Meat and The Enchanted Pimp, 1978; A Time for Judas, 1983. *Recreation:* sports. *Address:* 20 Dale Avenue, Toronto, Ont M4W 1K4, Canada.

CALLAN, Prof. Harold Garnet, FRS 1963; FRSE; MA, DSc; Professor of Natural History, St Salvator's College, St Andrews, 1950–82, now Emeritus; *b* 5 March 1917; *s* of Garnet George Callan and Winifred Edith Brazier; *m* 1944, Amarillis Maria Speranza, *d* of Dr R. Dohrn, Stazione Zoologica, Naples, Italy; one *s* two *d. Educ:* King's Coll. Sch., Wimbledon; St John's Coll., Oxford (Exhibitioner). Casberd Scholar, St John's Coll., 1937; Naples Biological Scholar, 1938, 1939. Served War of 1939–45, Telecommunications Research Establishment, 1940–45, Hon. Commission, RAFVR. Senior Scientific Officer, ARC, Inst. of Animal Genetics, Edinburgh, 1946–50. Member: Advisory Council on Scientific Policy, 1963–64; SRC, 1972–76; Council, Royal Soc., 1974–76. Trustee, British Museum (Natural History), 1963–66. Vis. Prof., Univ. of Indiana, Bloomington, USA, 1964–65; Master of United Coll. of St Salvator and St Leonard's, 1967–68. Hon. DSc St Andrews, 1984. *Publications:* scientific papers, mostly on cytology and cell physiology. *Recreations:* shooting, carpentry. *Address:* 2 St Mary's Street, St Andrews, Fife. *T:* St Andrews 72311.

CALLAN, Ivan Roy; HM Diplomatic Service; Counsellor, Head of Chancery and Consul-General, Baghdad, since 1983; *b* 6 April 1942; *s* of Roy Ivan Callan and (Gladys) May Callan (*née* Coombe); *m* 1965, Hilary Margaret West Flashman; one *d. Educ:* Reading Sch.; University Coll., Oxford. BA, Dip. Soc. Anthrop., BLitt, MA. Entered FCO, 1969; Middle East Centre for Arab Studies, 1970–71; Second, later First Sec., Beirut, 1971–75; FCO, 1975–80; First Sec. and Head of Chancery, Ottawa, 1980–83. *Recreations:* wilderness travel by foot, canoe and armchair, sailing, bricolage, sketching, painting. *Address:* c/o Foreign and Commonwealth Office, King Charles Street, SW1A 2AH. *Club:* Royal Commonwealth Society.

CALLAN, Maj.-Gen. Michael, CB 1979; consultant in defence logistics and administration; *b* 27 Nov. 1925; *s* of Major John Callan and Elsie Dorothy Callan (*née* Fordham); *m* 1948, Marie Evelyn Farthing; two *s. Educ:* Farnborough Grammar Sch., Hants. rcds, jssc, psc. Enlisted Hampshire Regt, 1943; commnd 1st (KGV's Own) Gurkha Rifles (The Malaun Regt), 1944; resigned commn, 1947; re-enlisted, 1948; re-commnd, RAOC, 1949; overseas service: India, Burma, French Indo China, Netherlands East Indies, 1944–47; Kenya, 1950–53; Malaya/Singapore, 1958–61; USA, 1966–68; Hong Kong, 1970–71; Comdr, Rhine Area, BAOR, 1975–76; Dir Gen., Ordnance Services, 1976–80. Col Comdt, RAOC, 1981–; Hon. Col, SW London ACF, 1982–. Registrar, Corporation of the Sons of the Clergy, 1982–83. *Recreations:* sailing, DIY, gardening. *Address:* c/o Royal Bank of Scotland, Kirkland House, Whitehall, SW1A 2EB.

CALLARD, Sir Eric John, (Sir Jack Callard), Kt 1974; FEng; Chairman, British Home Stores Ltd, 1976–82 (Director 1975–82); *b* 15 March 1913; *s* of late F. Callard and Mrs A. Callard; *m* 1938, Pauline M. Pengelly; three *d. Educ:* Queen's Coll., Taunton; St John's Coll., Cambridge. 1st cl. Hons Mech. Sci. Tripos; BA 1935; MA 1973; Harvard Business Sch. (Adv. Management Programme, 1953). Joined ICI Ltd, 1935; seconded to Min. of Aircraft Prodn, 1942; ICI Paints Div., 1947 (Jt Man. Dir, 1955–59; Chm., 1959–64); Chairman: Deleg. Bd, ICI (Hyde) Ltd, 1959; ICI (Europa) Ltd, 1965–67; ICI Ltd, 1971–75 (Dir, 1964–75; Dep. Chm., 1967–71); Director: Pension Funds Securities Ltd, 1963–67; Imp. Metal Industries Ltd, 1964–67; Imp. Chemicals Insurance Ltd, 1966–70; Midland Bank Ltd, 1971–; Ferguson Industrial Holdings, 1975–86; Commercial Union Assurance Co., 1976–83; Equity Capital for Industry, 1976–84. Member Council: BIM, 1964–69; Manchester Univ. Business Sch., 1964–71; Export Council for Europe, 1965–71; Member: CBI Steering Cttee on Europe, 1965–71; Cambridge Univ. Appointments Bd, 1968–71; CBI Overseas Cttee, 1969–71; Council of Industry for Management Educn, 1967–73; Appeal Cttee of British Sch. of Brussels, 1970–73; Royal Instn of GB, 1971–; Vice-President: Combustion Engnrg Assoc., 1968–75; Manchester Business Sch. Assoc., 1971– (Hon. Mem., 1966–; Pres., 1969–71); Pres., Industrial Participation Assoc., 1971–76 (Chm., 1967–71). Member: Hansard Soc. Commn on Electoral Reform, 1975–76; Cttee of Inquiry into Industrial Democracy, 1976–77. Trustee, Civic Trust, 1972–75; Governor, London Business Sch., 1972–75. Mem. Court, British Shippers' Council, 1972–75. FRSA 1970; CBIM (FBIM 1966); Hon. FIMechE. Hon. DSc Cranfield Inst. of Technology, 1974. *Recreations:* games, fishing, fell walking. *Address:* Crookwath Cottage, High Row, Dockray, Penrith, Cumbria CA11 0LG. *Club:* Flyfishers'.

CALLAWAY, Betty; *see* Callaway-Fittall, B. D.

CALLAWAY, Sir Frank (Adams), Kt 1981; CMG 1975; OBE 1970; Professor and Head of Department of Music, University of Western Australia, 1959–84, Professor Emeritus, since 1985; *b* 16 May 1919; *s* of Archibald Charles Callaway and Mabel Callaway (*née* Adams); *m* 1942, Kathleen Jessie, *d* of R. Allan; two *s* two *d. Educ:* West Christchurch High Sch.; Dunedin Teachers' Coll., NZ; Univ. of Otago, NZ (MusB); Royal Academy of Music. FRAM, ARCM, FTCL; FACE. Head, Dept of Music, King Edward Tech. Coll., Dunedin, NZ, 1942–53; Reader in Music, Univ. of WA, 1953–59. Mem., RNZAF Band, 1940–42. Conductor: King Edward Tech. Coll. Symphony Orchestra, 1945–53; Univ. of WA Orchestral Soc., 1953–64; Univ. of WA Choral Soc., 1953–79; Guest Conductor: WA Symphony Orchestra; S Australia Symphony Orchestra; Adelaide Philharmonic Choir; Orpheus Choir, Wellington, NZ. Member: Australian Music Examinations Bd, 1955–84 (Chm., 1964–66 and 1977–79); Adv. Bd, Commonwealth Assistance to Australian Composers, 1966–72; Australian Nat. Commn for UNESCO, 1968–82; Exec. Bd, Internat. Music Council of UNESCO, 1976–82 (Pres., 1980–81; Individual Mem., 1982–85, Life Mem. of Honour, 1986); Music Bd, Australia Council, 1969–74; Chairman: WA Arts Adv. Bd, 1970–73; WA Arts Council, 1973–79; Organizing Cttees, Aust. Nat. Eisteddfod 1979, Indian Ocean Fests, 1979, 1984; Indian Ocean Arts Assoc., 1980–85 (Life Pres., 1985). Founding Pres. and Life Mem., Australian Soc. for Music Educn, 1966–71; Mem., Bd of Dirs, Internat. Soc. for Music Educn, 1958– (Pres., 1968–72, Treasurer, 1972–). Foundn Mem., 1983, Pres., 1984–, WA Br., Lord's Taverners Australia. Founding Editor: Australian Jl of Music Educn, 1967–82; Studies in Music, 1967–84; Internat. Jl of Music Educn, 1983–85; also General Editor, Music Series and Music Monographs. W Australian Citizen of the Year, 1975. Hon. MusD: W Australia, 1975; Melbourne, 1982. Aust. Nat. Critics' Circle Award for Music, 1977. *Publications:* (General Editor) Challenges in Music Education, 1975; (ed with D. E. Tunley) Australian Composition in the Twentieth Century, 1978. *Recreations:* reading, gardening, cricket. *Address:* 16 The Lane, Churchlands, WA 6018, Australia. *T:* 387.3345.

CALLAWAY-FITTALL, Betty Daphne, (Betty Callaway), MBE 1984; trainer of skaters; *b* 22 March 1928; *d* of William A. Roberts and Elizabeth T. Roberts; *m* 1st, 1949, E. Roy Callaway; 2nd, 1980, Captain W. Fittall, British Airways, retd. *Educ:* Greycoat Sch., and St Paul's Convent, Westminster. Started teaching, Richmond Ice Rink, 1952; Nat. Trainer, W Germany, 1969–72; retired from full-time teaching, 1972. Commentator, ITV, 1984–. Pupils include: Angelika and Erich Buck (European Champions and 2nd in World Championship, 1972); Chrisztine Regoczy and Andras Sally (Hungarian and World Champions and Olympic silver medallists, 1980); Jayne Torvill and Christopher Dean (World Champions, 1981, 1982, 1983, 1984, European Champions, 1981, 1982, and Olympic gold medallists, 1984). Hon. Citizen, Ravensburg, Germany, 1972. Gold Medal, Nat. Skating Assoc., 1955; Hungarian Olympic Medal, 1980. *Recreations:* music, water ski-ing, gardening. *Address:* 35 Long Grove, Seer Green, Beaconsfield, Bucks HP9 2YN.

CALLENDER, Dr Maurice Henry; Ministry of Defence, 1977–80; retired, 1980; *b* 18 Dec. 1916; *s* of Harry and Lizbeth Callender; *m* 1941, Anne Kassel; two *s. Educ:* Univ. of Durham (MA, PhD). FSA. Commissioned: Royal Northumberland Fusiliers, 1939–41; RAF, 1941–45. Lectr, Huddersfield Technical Coll., 1945–47; Research, Univ. of Durham, 1947–49; Lectr, Bristol Univ. Extra-Mural Dept, 1949–53; MoD, 1953–62; Joint Services Staff Coll., 1959–60; Cabinet Office, 1962–64; MoD, 1964–70; Cabinet Office, 1970–73; Counsellor, Canberra, 1973–77. *Publications:* Roman Amphorae, 1965; various articles in archaeological jls. *Recreations:* oil painting, golf, bridge. *Address:* 24 Glanleam Road, Stanmore, Mddx. *T:* 01–954 1435. *Club:* Aldenham Golf and Country.

CALLEY, Sir Henry (Algernon), Kt 1964; DSO 1945; DFC 1943; DL; Owner and Manager of a stud, since 1948; *b* 9 Feb. 1914; *s* of Rev. A. C. M. Langton and Mrs Langton (*née* Calley); changed surname to Calley, 1974; unmarried. *Educ:* St John's Sch., Leatherhead. Taught at Corchester. Corbridge-on-Tyne, 1933–35; Bombay Burmah

Trading Corp., 1935–36; teaching, 1936–38; Metropolitan Police Coll., and Police Force, 1938–41; Royal Air Force, 1941–48; Pilot in Bombers, Actg Wing Comdr, 1944. Mem. Wiltshire CC, 1955; Chm. Finance Cttee, 1959–68; Chm. of Council, 1968–73; Chm. Wessex Area Conservative Assoc., 1963–66. DL Wilts, 1968.

CALLIL, Carmen Thérèse; Chairman, Virago Press, since 1972 (Managing Director, 1972–82); Managing Director, Chatto & Windus: The Hogarth Press, since 1983 (Joint Managing Director, 1982–83); b 15 July 1938; d of Frederick Alfred Louis Callil and Lorraine Clare Allen. Educ: Star of the Sea Convent, Gardenvale, Melbourne; Loreto Convent, Mandeville Hall, Melbourne; Melbourne Univ. (BA). Buyer's Asst, Marks & Spencer, 1963–65; Editorial Assistant: Hutchinson Publishing Co., 1965–66; B. T. Batsford, 1966–67; Publicity Manager, Panther Books, later also of Granada Publishing, 1967–70; André Deutsch, 1971–72; publicity for Ink newspaper, 1972; founded Carmen Callil Ltd, book publicity co., 1972; founded Virago Press, 1972, incorp. as co., 1973. Dir, Channel 4, 1985–. Recreations: friends, reading, animals, films, gardening. Address: 40 William IV Street, WC2. Club: Groucho.

CALLINAN, Sir Bernard (James), AC 1986; Kt 1977; CBE 1971; DSO 1945; MC 1943; Consultant, Gutteridge, Haskins & Davey Pty Ltd, 1978–81 (Chairman and Managing Director, 1971–78); b 2 Feb. 1913; s of Michael Joseph Callinan and Mary Callinan (née Prendergast); m 1943, Naomi Marian Callinan (née Cullinan); five s. Educ: Univ. of Melbourne (BCE; Dip. Town and Regional Planning). Hon. FIE Aust (Pres., 1971–72; P. N. Russell Meml Medal, 1973); FICE; FTS. Lieut to Lt-Col, AIF, 1940–46. Asst Engr, A. Gordon Gutteridge, 1934; Associate, 1946, Sen. Partner, 1948–71, Gutteridge, Haskins & Davey. Director: West Gate Bridge Authority, 1965– (Dep. Chm., 1971–81, Chm., 1981–82); British Petroleum Co. of Aust. Ltd, 1969–85; CSR Ltd, 1978–85. Commissioner: State Electricity Commn, 1963–83; Royal Commn of Inquiry, Aust. PO, 1973–74; Aust. Atomic Energy Commn, 1976–82; Australian Broadcasting Commn, 1977–82; Victorian Post Secondary Educn Commn, 1979–82. Chm., New Parlt House Authority (Canberra), 1979–85. Special Advr, Aust. Overseas Project Corpn, 1978–82. Mem., Pontifical Commn on Justice and Peace, Rome, 1977–82. Councillor: La Trobe Univ., 1964–72; Melbourne Univ., 1976–81. Hon. Col, 4/19 Prince of Wales's Light Horse Regt, 1973–78. Hon. DEng Monash, 1984. Kernot Meml Medal, Melbourne Univ., 1982. Publications: Independent Company, 1953, repr. 1954, 1984; John Monash, 1981; contribs to Jl Instn of Engrs, aust., Jl Royal Soc. of Vic. Address: 111 Sackville Street, Kew, Vic 3101, Australia. T: 80.1230. Clubs: Melbourne, Australian, Naval and Military (Melbourne); Melbourne Cricket (Pres., 1979–85).

CALLMAN, Clive Vernon; His Honour Judge Callman; a Circuit Judge, since 1973, assigned to South-Eastern Circuit; b 21 June 1927; o s of Felix Callman, DMD, LDS, RCS and Edith Callman, Walton-on-Thames, Surrey; m 1967, Judith Helen Hines, BA, DipSocStuds (Adelaide), o d of Gus Hines, OBE, JP, and Hilde Hines, St George's, Adelaide, S Aust.; one s one d. Educ: Ottershaw Coll.; St George's Coll., Weybridge; LSE, Univ. of London. BSc(Econ), Commercial Law. Called to the Bar, Middle Temple, 1951; Blackstone Pupillage Prizeman, 1951; practised as Barrister, London and Norwich, 1952–73 (Head of London chambers, 1963), South-Eastern Circuit; Hon. Mem., Central Criminal Court Bar Mess; Dep. Circuit Judge in Civil and Criminal Jurisdiction, 1971–73. Dir, Woburn Press, Publishers, 1971–73; dir of finance cos, 1961–73. University of London: Fac. Mem., Standing Cttee of Convocation, 1954–79; Senator, 1978–; Mem. Careers Adv. Bd, 1979–; Mem., Commerce Degree Bureau Cttee, 1980; Mem., Adv. Cttee for Magistrates' Courses, 1979–; Vice-Pres., Graduates' Soc.; Governor, Birkbeck Coll., 1982–. Mem. Exec. Cttee, Soc. of Labour Lawyers, 1958; Chm., St Marylebone Constituency Labour Party, 1960–62. Mem. Council, Anglo-Jewish Assoc., 1956–. Editor, Clare Market Review, 1947; Member Editorial Board: Media Law and Practice, 1980–; Professional Negligence, 1985–. Recreations: reading, travelling, the arts. Address: 11 Constable Close, NW11 6UA. T: 01–458 3010. Club: Bar Yacht.

CALLOW, Simon Phillip Hugh; actor; b 15 June 1949; s of Neil Callow and Yvonne Mary Callow. Educ: London Oratory Grammar Sch.; Queen's Univ. Belfast; Drama Centre. West End productions include: Schippel, 1975; A Mad World My Masters, 1977; Arturo Ui, Mary Barnes, 1978; The Beastly Beatitudes of Balthazar B, Total Eclipse, Restoration, 1981; The Relapse, 1983; On the Spot, 1984; Kiss of the Spider Woman, 1985; National Theatre: As You Like It, Amadeus, 1979; directed: Loving Reno, Bush, 1984; The Passport, 1985, Nicolson, 1986, Offstage; Amadeus, Theatr Clwd, 1986; The Infernal Machine, 1986. Films: Amadeus, 1983; A Room with a View, 1986; The Good Father, 1986. Television series: Chance in a Million, 1983. Publications: Being an Actor, 1984; A Difficult Actor: Charles Laughton, 1987; trans. Jacques et son Maître, by Kundera, 1986. Recreation: planning the future of the British theatre. Address: c/o Marina Martin, 7 Windmill Street, W1. T: 01–323 1216.

CALMAN, Prof. Kenneth Charles; FRCP; FRCS; FRSE; Dean of Postgraduate Medicine and Professor of Postgraduate Medical Education, University of Glasgow, since 1984; b 25 Dec. 1941; s of Arthur McIntosh Calman and Grace Douglas Don; m 1967, Ann Wilkie; one s two d. Educ: Allan Glen's Sch., Glasgow; Univ. of Glasgow (BSc, MD, PhD). FRCP 1985; FRCS 1971; FRSE 1979. Hall Fellow in Surgery, Western Infirmary, Glasgow, 1968; Lectr in Surgery, Univ. of Glasgow, 1969; MRC Clinical Res. Fellow, Inst. of Cancer Res., London, 1972; Prof. of Clinical Oncology, Univ. of Glasgow, 1974. Publications: Basic Skills for Clinical Housemen, 1971, 2nd edn 1983; Basic Principles of Cancer Chemotherapy, 1982; Invasion, 1984. Recreations: gardening, golf. Address: 585 Anniesland Road, Glasgow G13 1UX. T: 041–954 9423.

CALMAN, Mel; artist, writer; cartoonist for The Times and others; b 19 May 1931; s of Clement and Anna Calman; m 1st, 1957, Pat McNeill (marr. diss.); two d; 2nd, Karen Usborne (marr. diss. 1982). Educ: Perse School, Cambridge; St Martin's School of Art, London (NDD); Goldsmiths' Coll. London (ATD). Cartoonist for Daily Express, 1957–63; BBC Tonight Programme, 1963–64; Sunday Telegraph, 1964–65; Observer, 1965–66; Sunday Times, 1969–84; The Times, 1979–. Free lance cartoonist for various magazines and newspapers, 1957–; also designer of book-jackets, advertising campaigns, and illustrator of books; started The Workshop-gallery, now The Cartoon Gall., devoted to original cartoons, illustrations etc., 1970; produced animated cartoon, The Arrow; syndicated feature, Men & Women, USA, 1976–82. FRSA; FSIA; AGI. Publications: Through The Telephone Directory, 1962; Bed-Sit, 1963; Boxes, 1964; Calman & Women, 1967; The Penguin Calman, 1968; (contrib.) The Evacuees, ed B. S. Johnson, 1968; My God, 1970; Couples, 1972; This Pestered Isle, 1973; (contrib.) All Bull, ed B. S. Johnson, 1973; The New Penguin Calman, 1977; Dictionary of Psychoanalysis, 1979; "But It's My Turn to Leave You", 1980; "How About a Little Quarrel before Bed?", 1981; Help!, 1982; Calman Revisited, 1983; The Big Novel, 1983; It's Only You That's Incompatible, 1984. Recreations: brooding and worrying. Address: 83 Lambs Conduit Street, WC1. T: 01–242 5335. Club: Garrick.

CALNAN, Prof. Charles Dermod, MA, MB, BChir Cantab; FRCP; Director, Department of Occupational Dermatoses, St John's Hospital for Diseases of the Skin, 1974–82; Honorary Consultant Dermatologist: Royal Free Hospital, 1958–80; St John's

Hospital for Diseases of the Skin, London, 1958–82; b 14 Dec. 1917; s of James Calnan, Eastbourne, Sussex; m 1950, Josephine Gerard Keane, d of late Lt-Col Michael Keane, RAMC; three s one d. Educ: Stonyhurst Coll.; Corpus Christi Coll., Cambridge; London Hospital. 1st Cl. Hons Nat. Sci. Trip., Cambridge 1939. RAMC Specialist in Dermatology, Major, 1942–46; Marsden Prof., Royal Free Hosp., 1958; Visiting Research Associate, Univ. of Pennsylvania, 1959; Prof. of Dermatology, Inst. of Dermatology, 1960–74. WHO Cons. Adviser to Nat. Inst. of Dermatology of Thailand, 1971–. Editor: Transactions of the St John's Hosp. Dermatological Soc., 1958–75; Contact Dermatitis, 1975–. Mem. Brit. Assoc. of Dermatology. FRSocMed (Mem. Dermatological Section). Publications: Atlas of Dermatology, 1974; various papers in med. and dermatological jls. Recreations: squash, books, theatre. Address: 109 Harley Street, W1.

CALNAN, Prof. James Stanislaus, FRCP; FRCS; Professor of Plastic and Reconstructive Surgery, University of London, at the Royal Postgraduate Medical School and Hammersmith Hospital, 1970–81, now Emeritus; b 12 March 1916; e s of James and Gertrude Calnan, Eastbourne, Sussex; m 1949, Joan (formerly County Councillor for Great Berkhamsted and Dacorum District Councillor, and Town Councillor, Berkhamsted), e d of George Frederick and Irene Maud Williams, Roath Park, Cardiff; one d. Educ: Stonyhurst Coll.; Univ. of London at London Hosp. Med. Sch. LDS RCS 1941; MRCS, LRCP 1943; DA 1944; DTM&H 1948; MRCP (London and Edinburgh) 1948; FRCS 1949. Served War of 1939–45, F/Lt RAF, UK, France, India. RMO, Hosp. for Tropical Diseases, 1948; Sen. Lectr, Nuffield Dept of Plastic Surgery, Oxford, 1954; Hammersmith Hospital and Royal Postgraduate Med. Sch.: Lectr in Surgery, 1960; Reader, 1965; Professor, 1970. Hunterian Prof. RCS, 1959. Vis. Prof. in Plastic Surgery, Univ. of Pennsylvania, 1959. Member: BMA; British Assoc. of Plastic Surgeons; Sen. Mem., Surgical Research Soc. Fellow, Royal Soc. of Medicine; FCST 1966. Mem., Soc. of Authors. Clemson Award for Bioengineering, 1980. Publications: Speaking at Medical Meetings, 1972, 2nd edn 1981; Writing Medical Papers, 1973; How to Speak and Write: a practical guide for nurses, 1975; One Way to do Research, 1976; Talking with Patients, 1983; Coping with Research: the complete guide for beginners, 1984; The Hammersmith 1935–1985: the first 50 years of the Royal Postgraduate Medical School, 1985; contribs to medical and scientific jls and chapters in books, on cleft palate, wound healing, lymphatic diseases, venous thrombosis, research methods and organisation. Recreations: gardening, carpentry, reading and writing. Address: White Haven, 23 Kings Road, Berkhamsted, Herts HP4 3BH. T: Berkhamsted 2320; Royal Postgraduate Medical School, Ducane Road, W12 0HS. T: 01–743 2030.
See also Prof. C. D. Calnan.

CALNE, Sir Roy Yorke, Kt 1986; MA, MS; FRCS; FRS 1974; Professor of Surgery, University of Cambridge, since 1965; Fellow of Trinity Hall, Cambridge, since 1965; Hon. Consulting Surgeon, Addenbrooke's Hospital, Cambridge, since 1965; b 30 Dec. 1930; s of Joseph Robert and Eileen Calne; m 1956, Patricia Doreen Whelan; two s four d. Educ: Lancing Coll.; Guy's Hosp. Med. Sch. MB, BS London with Hons (Distinction in Medicine), 1953. House Appts, Guy's Hosp., 1953–54; RAMC, 1954–56 (RMO to KEO 2nd Gurkhas); Deptl Anatomy Demonstrator, Oxford Univ., 1957–58; SHO Nuffield Orthopædic Centre, Oxford, 1958; Surg. Registrar, Royal Free Hosp., 1958–60; Harkness Fellow in Surgery, Peter Bent Brigham Hosp., Harvard Med. Sch., 1960–61; Lectr in Surgery, St Mary's Hosp., London, 1961–62; Sen. Lectr and Cons. Surg., Westminster Hosp., 1962–65. Royal Coll. of Surgeons: Hallet Prize, 1957; Jacksonian Prize, 1961; Hunterian Prof., 1962; Cecil Joll Prize, 1966; Mem. Ct of Examiners, 1970–76; Mem. Council, 1981–86. Fellow Assoc. of Surgeons of Gt Brit.; Mem. Surgical Research Soc.; Pres., European Soc. for Organ Transplantation, 1983; Corresp. Fellow, Amer. Surgical Assoc., 1972, Hon. Fellow 1981. Prix de la Société Internationale de Chirurgie, 1969; Faltin Medal, Finnish Surgical Soc., 1977; Lister Medal, 1984. Publications: Renal Transplantations, 1963, 2nd edn 1967; (with H. Ellis) Lecture Notes in Surgery, 1965, 5th edn 1970; A Gift of Life, 1970; (ed and contrib.) Clinical Organ Transplantation, 1971; (ed and contrib.) Immunological Aspects of Transplantation Surgery, 1973; (ed and contrib.) Liver Transplantation, 1983; (ed and contrib.) Transplantation Immunology, 1984; papers on tissue transplantation and general surgery; sections in several surgical text-books. Recreations: tennis, squash. Address: 22 Barrow Road, Cambridge. T: Cambridge 59831.

CALNE AND CALSTONE, Viscount; Simon Henry George Petty-Fitzmaurice; b 24 Nov. 1970; s and heir of Earl of Shelburne, qv.

CALOVSKI, Mitko; Yugoslav Ambassador to the Court of St James's and to the Republic of Ireland, since 1985; b 3 April 1930; m Ilvana; one s one d. Educ: Higher School of Journalism and Diplomacy, Univ. of Belgrade. Posts with Federal Agencies, 1952–63; with Federal Board, later with Federal Conf. of Socialist Alliance of Working People of Yugoslavia, 1963–67; Consul-General in Toronto, Canada, 1967–71; Dir of Analysis and Policy Planning, 1971–74, Dep. Sec.-Gen. of the Presidency, 1974–77, Fed. Secretariat for Foreign Affairs; Ambassador to Canada, 1977–81; Mem., Federal Exec. Council and Federal Sec. for Information, 1982–85. Mem. of Yugoslavian Delegns to UN Gen. Assembly, non-aligned Summit and ministerial confs. Address: Yugoslav Embassy, 5 Lexham Gardens, W8. T: 01–370 6105.

CALTHORPE; see Anstruther-Gough-Calthorpe, and Gough-Calthorpe.

CALTHORPE, 10th Baron cr 1796; **Peter Waldo Somerset Gough-Calthorpe;** Bt 1728; b 13 July 1927; s of late Hon. Frederick Somerset Gough-Calthorpe and Rose Mary Dorothy, d of late Leveson William Vernon-Harcourt; S brother, 1945; m 1st, 1956, Saranne (marr. diss. 1971), o d of James Harold Alexander, Ireland; 2nd, 1979, Elizabeth, d of James and Sibyl Young, Guildford, Surrey. Heir: none. Address: c/o Isle of Man Bank, 2 Athol Street, Douglas, Isle of Man.

CALVERLEY, 3rd Baron cr 1945; **Charles Rodney Muff;** Member of the West Yorkshire Metropolitan Police; b 2 Oct. 1946; s of 2nd Baron Calverley and of Mary, d of Arthur Farrar, Halifax; S father, 1971; m 1972, Barbara Ann, d of Jonathan Brown, Kelbrook, nr Colne; two s. Educ: Fulneck School for Boys. Heir: s Hon. Jonathan Edward Muff, b 16 April 1975. Address: 110 Buttershaw Lane, Wibsey, Bradford, W Yorks BD6 2DA.

CALVERT, Mrs Barbara Adamson, QC 1975; barrister-at-law; a Recorder of the Crown Court, since 1980; b 30 April 1926; d of late Albert Parker, CBE; m 1948, John Thornton Calvert, CBE; one s one d. Educ: St Helen's, Northwood; London Sch. of Economics (BScEcon). Called to Bar, Middle Temple, 1959, Bencher 1982; admitted Sen. Bar of NI, 1978. Admin. Officer, City and Guilds of London Inst., 1961; practice at Bar, 1962–. Full-time Chm., Industrial Tribunals, London, 1986– (part-time Chm., 1974–86). Recreations: gardening, swimming, poetry. Address: (home) 158 Ashley Gardens, SW1P 1HW; (chambers) 4 Brick Court, Temple, EC4Y 7AN. Club: Royal Fowey Yacht.

CALVERT, Florence Irene, (Mrs W. A. Prowse); Principal, St Mary's College, University of Durham, 1975–77; b 1 March 1912; d of Ernest William Calvert and Florence Alice (née Walton); m 1977, William Arthur Prowse (d 1981). Educ: Univ. of

Sheffield (BA, 1st Cl. Hons French and Latin, MA). Asst Language Teacher, Accrington Grammar Sch., 1936–39; Head, Modern Langs Dept, Accrington Girls' High Sch., 1939–48; Univ. of Durham: Lectr in Educn, 1948; Sen. Lectr, 1964–75. *Publications:* French Plays for the Classroom, 1951; L'Homme aux Mains Rouges, 1954; Contes, 1957; French by Modern Methods in Primary and Secondary Schools, 1965. *Address:* 7 St Mary's Close, Shincliffe, Durham DH1 2ND. *T:* Durham 65502.

CALVERT, Henry Reginald, Dr Phil; Keeper of Department of Astronomy and Geophysics in Science Museum, South Kensington, 1949–67; Keeper Emeritus, 1967–69; *b* 25 Jan. 1904; *e s* of late H. T. Calvert, MBE, DSc, of Min. of Health; *m* 1938, Eileen Mary Frow; two *d. Educ:* Bridlington Sch., East Yorks; St John's Coll., Oxford (Scholar, MA); Univ. of Göttingen, Germany (Dr Phil). 1st Cl. Hons BSc (External) London, 1925; Goldsmiths' Company's Exhibitioner, 1925. Research Physicist, ICI, 1928–30; Research Physicist, Callender's Cable & Construction Co., 1932–34. Entered Science Museum, 1934; Dep. Keeper, 1946. Ballistics research for Min. of Supply, 1940–46. Hon. Treas., British Soc. for History of Science, 1952–63. Fellow Royal Astronomical Soc. *Publications:* Astronomy, Globes, Orreries and other Models, 1967; Scientific Trade Cards, 1971; papers in learned journals. *Recreations:* chess, bridge, croquet, gardening. *Address:* 17 Burnham Drive, Reigate, Surrey RH2 9HD. *T:* Reigate 46893.

CALVERT, Louis Victor Denis, CB 1985; Comptroller and Auditor General for Northern Ireland, since 1980; *b* 20 April 1924; *s* of Louis Victor Calvert, Belfast and Gertrude Cherry Hobson, Belfast; *m* 1949, Vivien Millicent Lawson; two *s* one *d. Educ:* Belfast Royal Academy; Queen's Univ., Belfast (BScEcon); Admin. Staff Coll., Henley-on-Thames. Served with RAF, 1943–47, navigator (F/O). Northern Ireland Civil Service, 1947–: Min. of Agriculture, 1947–56; Dep. Principal 1951; Principal, Min. of Finance, 1956–63; Min. of Health and Local Govt, 1963–65; Asst Sec. 1964; Min. of Development, 1965–73; Sen. Asst Sec. 1970; Dep. Sec. 1971; Min. of Housing, Local Govt and Planning, 1973–76; DoE for NI, 1976–80. *Recreations:* gardening, golf, reading. *Address:* Exchequer and Audit Department, Rosepark House, Upper Newtownards Road, Belfast BT4 2NS.

CALVERT, Norman Hilton; retired; Deputy Secretary, Departments of the Environment and of Transport, 1978–80; *b* 27 July 1925; *s* of Clifford and Doris Calvert; *m* 1st, 1949, May Yates (*d* 1968); one *s* one *d*; 2nd, 1971, Vera Baker. *Educ:* Leeds Modern Sch.; Leeds Univ.; King's Coll., Durham Univ. BA Hons 1st cl. Geography, 1950. Served Royal Signals, 1943–47: 81 (W African) Div., India, 1945–47. Min. of Housing and Local Govt: Asst Principal, 1950–55; Principal, 1956–64; Asst Sec., 1964–71; Sec., Water Resources Bd, 1964–68; Principal Regional Officer, Northern Region, 1969–71; Regional Dir, Northern Region, and Chm, Northern Econ. Planning Bd, 1971–73; Under Sec., DoE, 1971–78. *Recreations:* fell walking, listening to music, motoring. *Address:* Treetops, Roundhill Way, Cobham, Surrey KT11 2EX. *T:* Oxshott 2738.

CALVERT, Phyllis; actress; *b* 18 Feb. 1915; *d* of Frederick and Annie Bickle; *m* 1941, Peter Murray Hill (*d* 1957); one *s* one *d. Educ:* Margaret Morris Sch.; Institut Français. Malvern Repertory Company, 1935; Coventry, 1937; York, 1938. First appeared in London in A Woman's Privilege, Kingsway Theatre, 1939; Punch Without Judy, Embassy, 1939; Flare Path, Apollo, 1942; Escapade, St James's, 1953; It's Never Too Late, Strand, 1954; River Breeze, Phoenix, 1956; The Complaisant Lover, Globe, 1959; The Rehearsal, Globe, 1961; Ménage à Trois, Lyric, 1963; Portrait of Murder, Savoy, Vaudeville, 1963; A Scent of Flowers, Duke of York's, 1964; Present Laughter, Queen's, 1965; A Woman of No Importance, Vaudeville, 1967; Blithe Spirit, Globe, 1970; Crown Matrimonial, Haymarket, 1973; Dear Daddy, Ambassadors, 1976; Mrs Warren's Profession, Worcester, 1977; She Stoops to Conquer, Old World, Exeter, 1978; Suite in Two Keys, tour, 1978; Before the Party, Queen's, 1980; Smithereens, Theatre Royal, Windsor, 1985. Started films, 1939. *Films include:* Kipps, The Young Mr Pitt, Man in Grey, Fanny by Gaslight, Madonna of the Seven Moons, They were Sisters, Time out of Mind, Broken Journey, My Own True Love, The Golden Madonna, A Woman with No Name, Mr Denning Drives North, Mandy, The Net, It's Never Too Late, Child in the House, Indiscreet, The Young and The Guilty, Oscar Wilde, Twisted Nerve, Oh! What a Lovely War, The Walking Stick. TV series: Kate, 1970; Cover her Face, 1985; Death of a Heart, 1985. *Recreations:* swimming, gardening, collecting costume books. *Address:* Hill House, Waddesdon, Bucks.

CALVET, Jacques; President, Peugeot SA, since 1984; Consultant, Audit Office, since 1963; *b* 19 Sept. 1931; *s* of Prof. Louis Calvet and Yvonne Calvet (*née* Olmières); *m* 1956, Françoise Rondot; two *s* one *d. Educ:* Lycée Janson-de-Sailly; Law Faculty, Paris (Licencié en droit; Dipl. Inst. d'Etudes Politiques; Dipl. d'Etudes Supérieures d'Economie Politique et des Sciences Economiques). Trainee, l'Ecole Nationale d'Administration, 1955–57; Audit Office, 1957–59; Office of Sec. of State for Finance, 1959–62, of Minister of Finance, 1962–66; Dep. Dir, 1964, Head of Dept, 1967, Central Finance Admin; Head of Finance Dept, Paris Préfecture, 1967–69; Asst Dir, later Dir, Office of Minister of Economy and Finance, 1969–74; Dir in Ministry of Finance, 1973; Asst Dir Gen., 1974, Dir Gen., 1976, Pres., 1979–82, Banque Nationale de Paris; Director: Groupe de la Populaire, 1983; Compagnie Générale des Eaux; Vice-Pres., Bd of Dirs, Automobiles Peugeot, 1984–; Pres., Bd of Dirs, Automobiles Citroën, 1983–. Chevalier de la Légion d'Honneur; Officier de l'ordre Nationale du Mérite et du Mérite Agricole; Chevalier des Palmes académiques. *Address:* Peugeot SA, 75 avenue de la Grande Armée, 75116 Paris, France. *T:* 502 11 33; Automobiles Citroën, 62 boulevard Victor Hugo, 92208 Neuilly-sur-Seine, France. *T:* 759 41 41; 31 avenue Victor Hugo, 75116 Paris, France.

CALVIN, Prof. Melvin; University Professor of Chemistry, University of California, since 1971; Professor of Molecular Biology, 1963–80; *b* 8 April 1911; *s* of Rose and Elias Calvin; *m* 1942, Marie Genevieve Jemtegaard; one *s* two *d. Educ:* Univ. of Minnesota, Minneapolis (PhD). Fellow, Univ. of Manchester, 1935–37. Univ. of California, Berkeley: Instr., 1937; Asst Prof., 1941–45; Assoc. Prof., 1945–47; Prof., 1947–71; Dir, Laboratory of Chemical Biodynamics, 1960–80; Associate Dir, Lawrence Berkeley Lab., 1967–80. Foreign Mem., Royal Society, 1959. Member: Nat. Acad. of Sciences (US); Royal Netherlands Acad. of Sciences and Letters; Amer. Philos. Society. Nobel Prize in Chemistry, 1961; Davy Medal, Royal Society, 1964; Virtanen Medal, 1975; Gibbs Medal, 1977; Priestley Medal, 1978; Amer. Inst. Chemists Gold Medal, 1979. Hon. Degrees: Michigan Coll. of Mining and Technology, 1955; Univ. of Nottingham, 1958; Oxford Univ., 1959; Northwestern Univ., 1961; Univ. of Notre Dame, 1965; Brooklyn Polytechnic Inst., 1969; Rijksuniversiteit-Gent, 1970; Columbia Univ., 1979. *Publications:* very numerous, including (6 books): Theory of Organic Chemistry (with Branch), 1941; Isotopic Carbon (with Heidelberger, Reid, Tolbert and Yankwich), 1949; Chemistry of Metal Chelate Compounds (with Martell), 1952; Path of Carbon in Photosynthesis (with Bassham), 1957; Chemical Evolution, 1961; Photosynthesis of Carbon Compounds (with Bassham), 1962; Chemical Evolution, 1969. *Address:* University of California, Berkeley, Calif 94720, USA; (home) 2683 Buena Vista Way, Berkeley, Calif 94708, USA. *T:* 848–4036.

CALVO, Roberto Q.; *see* Querejazu Calvo.

CALVOCORESSI, Peter (John Ambrose); author; Chairman, Open University Educational Enterprises Ltd, since 1979; *b* 17 Nov. 1912; *s* of Pandia Calvocoressi and Irene (Ralli); *m* 1938, Barbara Dorothy Eden, *d* of 6th Baron Henley; two *s. Educ:* Eton (King's Scholar); Balliol Coll., Oxford. Called to Bar, 1935. RAF Intelligence, 1940–45; Wing Comdr. Trial of Major War Criminals, Nuremberg, 1945–46. Contested (L) Nuneaton, 1945. Staff of Royal Institute of International Affairs, 1949–54; Mem. Council, Royal Inst. of Internat. Affairs, 1955–70; Reader (part time) in International Relations, Univ. of Sussex, 1965–71; Member: Council, Inst. for Strategic Studies, 1961–71; Council, Inst. of Race Relations, 1970–71; UN Sub-Commn on the Prevention of Discrimination and Protection of Minorities, 1962–71; Chm., The Africa Bureau, 1963–71; Mem., Internat. Exec., Amnesty International, 1969–71; Chm., The London Library, 1970–73; Dep. Chm., N Metropolitan Conciliation Cttee, 1967–71. Dir of Chatto & Windus Ltd and The Hogarth Press Ltd, 1954–65; Editorial Dir, 1972–76, Publisher and Chief Exec., 1973–76, Penguin Books. *Publications:* Nuremberg: The Facts, the Law and the Consequences, 1947; Surveys of International Affairs, vol. 1, 1947–48, 1950; vol. 2, 1949–50, 1951; vol. 3, 1951, 1952; vol. 4, 1952, 1953; vol. 5, 1953, 1954; Middle East Crisis (with Guy Wint), 1957; South Africa and World Opinion, 1961; World Order and New States, 1962; World Politics since 1945, 1968; (with Guy Wint) Total War, 1972; The British Experience 1945–75, 1978; Top Secret Ultra, 1980; Independent Africa and the World, 1985. *Recreation:* walking. *Address:* 1 Queen's Parade, Bath. *T:* Bath 333903. *Club:* Garrick.

CAMBELL, Rear-Adm. Dennis Royle Farquharson, CB 1960; DSC 1940; *b* 13 Nov. 1907; *s* of Dr Archibald Cambell and Edith Cambell, Southsea; *m* 1933, Dorothy Elinor Downes; two *d. Educ:* Westminster Sch. Joined RN, 1925, HMS Thunderer Cadet Training; trained as FAA pilot, 1931; 1st Capt. of HMS Ark Royal IV, 1955–56; retired, 1960. *Address:* The Old School House, Colemore, Alton, Hants.

CAMBRIDGE, Alan John; HM Diplomatic Service, retired; part-time Assessor, Foreign and Commonwealth Office, since 1985; *b* 1 July 1925; *s* of Thomas David Cambridge and Winifred Elizabeth (*née* Jarrett); *m* 1947, Thelma Elliot; three *s* one *d. Educ:* Beckenham Grammar Sch. Served War, FAA and RAFVR, 1943–47 (Air Gunner, Bomber Comd). War Pensions Office and MPNI, 1948–55; entered CRO, 1955; Chief Clerk: Madras, 1956–58; Kuala Lumpur, 1959–62; 2nd Sec., Salisbury, Fedn of Rhodesia and Nyasaland, 1962–65; 1st Sec. (Political), Freetown, 1965–66; UN Dept, FCO, 1966–68; 1st Sec., Prague, 1969; 1st Sec. (Consular/Aid), Suva, 1970–72; HM Consul, Milan, 1972–74; Asst Head of Inf. Dept, FCO, 1974–78; 1st Sec., Ankara, 1978–81; Asst Head, 1981–82, Head and Counsellor, 1983–85, Migration and Visa Dept, FCO. *Recreations:* photography, swimming, tennis. *Address:* 9 The Ferns, Carlton Road, Tunbridge Wells TN1 2JS. *T:* Tunbridge Wells 31223. *Club:* Civil Service.

CAMBRIDGE, Sydney John Guy, CMG 1979; CVO 1979; HM Diplomatic Service, retired; *b* 5 Nov. 1928; *o s* of late Jack and Mona Cambridge; unmarried. *Educ:* Marlborough; King's Coll., Cambridge. Entered HM Diplomatic Service, Sept. 1952; Oriental Sec., British Embassy, Jedda, 1953–56; Foreign Office, 1956–60; First Sec., UK Delegn to United Nations, at New York, 1960–64; Head of Chancery, British Embassy, Djakarta, 1964–66; FO, 1966–70; Counsellor, British Embassy, Rome, 1970–73; Head of Financial Relations Dept, FCO, 1973–75; Counsellor, British High Commn, Nicosia, 1975–77; Ambassador: to Kuwait, 1977–82; to Morocco, 1982–84. *Address:* Saint Peter's House, Filkins, Lechlade, Glos.

CAMDEN, 6th Marquess *cr* 1812; **David George Edward Henry Pratt;** Baron Camden, 1765; Earl Camden, Viscount Bayham, 1786; Earl of Brecknock, 1812; *b* 13 Aug. 1930; *o s* of 5th Marquess Camden, and of Marjorie, Countess of Brecknock, *qv*; *S* father, 1983; *m* 1961, Virginia Ann (marr. diss. 1984), *o d* of late F. H. H. Finlaison, Arklow Cottage, Windsor, Berks; one *s* one *d* (and one *s* decd). Late Lieutenant, Scots Guards. *Educ:* Eton. Dir, Clive Discount Co. Ltd, 1958–69. *Heir: s* Earl of Brecknock, *qv. Address:* Cowdown Farm House, Andover, Hants. *T:* Andover 52085.

CAMDEN, John; Chairman, RMC Group plc, since 1974 (Managing Director, 1966–85); *b* 18 Nov. 1925; *s* of late Joseph Reginald Richard John Camden and Lilian Kate McCann; *m* 1972, Diane Mae Friese; two *d* (and one *s* two *d* of former *m*). *Educ:* Worcester Royal Grammar Sch.; Birmingham Univ. (BSc). Royal Tank Corps and Intell. Corps, 1943–47. Joined RMC Group (formerly Ready Mixed Concrete Group), 1952; Dir responsible for Group's ops in Europe, 1962. Grand Decoration of Honour in Silver (Austria), 1978. *Recreations:* golf, gardening. *Address:* RMC Group plc, RMC House, 55 High Street, Feltham, Mddx TW13 4HA.

CAMERON, family name of **Baron Cameron of Lochbroom.**

CAMERON, Hon. Lord; John Cameron, KT 1978; Kt 1954; DSC; LLD Glasgow and Edinburgh; DLitt Heriot-Watt; HRSA; FRSGS; a Senator of The College of Justice in Scotland and Lord of Session 1955–85; *b* 1900; *m* 1st, 1927, Eileen Dorothea (*d* 1943), *d* of late H. M. Burrell; one *s* two *d*; 2nd, 1944, Iris, *widow* of Lambert C. Shepherd. *Educ:* Edinburgh Acad.; Edinburgh Univ. Served European War, 1918, with RNVR; Advocate, 1924; Advocate-Depute, 1929–36; QC (Scotland), 1936. Served with RNVR, Sept. 1939–44 (despatches, DSC); released to reserve, Dec. 1944. Sheriff of Inverness, Elgin and Nairn, 1945; Sheriff of Inverness, Moray, Nairn and Ross and Cromarty, 1946–48; Dean of Faculty of Advocates, 1948–55. Member: Cttee on Law of Contempt of Court, 1972–; Royal Commn on Civil Liability and Compensation for Personal Injury, 1973–78. DL Edinburgh, 1953–84. Hon. FRSE 1983; Hon. FBA 1983. DUniv Edinburgh, 1983; Hon. LLD Aberdeen. *Address:* 28 Moray Place, Edinburgh. *T:* 031–225 7585. *Clubs:* New, Scottish Arts (Edinburgh); Royal Forth Yacht.
See also Baron Cameron of Lochbroom, Hon. Lord Weir.

CAMERON OF LOCHBROOM, Baron *cr* 1984 (Life Peer), of Lochbroom in the District of Ross and Cromarty; **Kenneth John Cameron;** PC 1984; Lord Advocate since 1984; *b* 11 June 1931; *s* of Hon. Lord Cameron, *qv*; *m* 1964, Jean Pamela Murray; two *d. Educ:* The Edinburgh Academy; Corpus Christi Coll., Oxford (MA); Edinburgh Univ. (LLB). Served RN, 1950–52; commissioned RNVR, 1951 (Lt). Admitted Faculty of Advocates, 1958; QC (Scot.) 1972, Standing Junior to Dept of Transport, 1964–71; to DoE, 1971–72; Chairman of Industrial Tribunals in Scotland, 1966–81; Advocate Depute, 1981–84. Chm. of Pensions Appeal Tribunal (Scotland), 1975, Pres. 1976–84. Chm., Cttee for Investigation in Scotland of Agricultural Marketing Schemes, 1980–84. *Recreations:* fishing, sailing, music. *Address:* 10 Belford Terrace, Edinburgh EH4 3DQ. *T:* 031–332 6636. *Clubs:* Scottish Arts, New (Edinburgh).

CAMERON, Prof. Alan Douglas Edward, FBA 1975; Anthon Professor of Latin Language and Literature, Columbia University, New York, since 1977; *b* 13 March 1938; *er s* of A. D. Cameron, Egham; *m* 1962, Averil Sutton (marr. diss. 1980; *see* Averil Cameron); one *s* one *d. Educ:* St Paul's Sch. (Schol.); New Coll., Oxford (Schol.). Craven Scholar 1958; 1st cl. Hon. Mods 1959; De Paravicini Scholar 1960; Chancellor's Prize for Latin Prose 1960; 1st cl. Lit. Hum. 1961; N. H. Baynes Prize 1967; John Conington Prize 1968. Asst Master, Brunswick Sch., Haywards Heath, 1956–57; Asst Lectr, then Lectr, in

Humanity, Glasgow Univ., 1961–64; Lectr in Latin, 1964–71, Reader, 1971–72, Bedford Coll., London; Prof. of Latin, King's Coll., London, 1972–77. Vis. Prof., Columbia Univ., NY, 1967–68. Vis. Fellow, Humanities Research Centre, Australian National Univ., 1985. Fellow, Amer. Acad. of Arts and Sciences, 1979. *Publications:* Claudian: Poetry and Propaganda at the Court of Honorius, 1970; (contrib.) Prosopography of the Later Roman Empire, ed Jones, Morris and Martindale, i, 1971, ii, 1980; Porphyrius the Charioteer, 1973; Bread and Circuses, 1974; Circus Factions, 1976; Literature and Society in the Early Byzantine World, 1985; The Greek Anthology, 1986; articles and reviews in learned jls. *Recreation:* the cinema. *Address:* 454 Riverside Drive, New York, NY 10027, USA. *T:* 662 9319; Columbia University, Morningside Heights, New York, NY 10027, USA.

CAMERON, Lt-Gen. Sir Alexander (Maurice), KBE 1952; CB 1945; MC; retired; *b* 30 May 1898; *s* of late Major Sir Maurice Alexander Cameron, KCMG; *m* 1922, Loveday (*d* 1965), *d* of Col W. D. Thomson, CMG. *Educ:* Wellington Coll. 2nd Lieut Royal Engineers, 1916. Served European War, France and Belgium (wounded, despatches, MC, 2 medals); S Persia (medal and clasp); Iraq and Kurdistan (two clasps); psc 1929. Brevet Lieut-Col, 1939; RAF Staff Coll., 1939; Brig., 1940; Maj.-Gen. 1943; SHAEF, 1944–45; Dep. QMG, 1945–48; Maj.-Gen. i/c Administration, MELF, 1948–51; GOC East African Comd, 1951–53; retired 1954; Director of Civil Defence South-Eastern Region (Tunbridge Wells), 1955–60. *Club:* Army and Navy.

CAMERON, Major Allan John, JP; Vice Lord-Lieutenant, Highland Region (Ross and Cromarty), since 1977; *b* 25 March 1917; *s* of Col Sir Donald Cameron of Lochiel, KT, CMG (*d* 1951), and Lady Hermione Cameron (*d* 1978), *d* of 5th Duke of Montrose; *m* 1945, Mary Elizabeth Vaughan-Lee, Dillington, Somerset; two *s* two *d* (and one *s* decd.). *Educ:* Harrow; RMC Sandhurst. Served QO Cameron Highlanders, 1936–48; Major, Retd (POW Middle East, 1942). County Councillor, Ross-shire, 1955–75 (Chm. Educn Cttee, 1962–75); former Member: Red Deer Commn; Countryside Commn for Scotland; Broadcasting Council for Scotland. *Recreations:* curling (Past Pres. Royal Caledonian Curling Club), gardening, golf. *Address:* Allangrange, Munlochy, Ross-shire. *T:* Munlochy 249. *Club:* Naval and Military.

See also Col Sir Donald Cameron of Lochiel.

CAMERON, Prof. Averil Millicent, MA, PhD; FBA 1981; FSA 1982; Professor of Ancient History, King's College London, since 1978; *b* 8 Feb. 1940; *d* of T. R. Sutton, Leek, Staffs; *m* 1962, Alan Douglas Edward Cameron, *qv* (marr. diss. 1980); one *s* one *d*. *Educ:* Westwood Hall Girls' High Sch., Leek, Staffs; Somerville Coll., Oxford (Passmore Edwards Schol. 1960; Rosa Hovey Schol. 1962; MA); Univ. of Glasgow; University Coll. London (PhD). King's College London: Asst Lectr, 1965; Lectr, 1968; Reader in Ancient History, 1970. Vis. Prof., Columbia Univ., 1967–68; Sather Vis. Prof., Univ. of Calif. at Berkeley, 1985–86; Vis. Member, Inst. of Advanced Study, Princeton, 1977–78; Summer Fellow, Dumbarton Oaks Center for Byzantine Studies, 1981. Chm., British Nat. Byzantine Cttee, 1983–; Vice-President: Roman Soc., 1983–; British Acad. Council, 1983–; Mem., Council of Hellenic Soc., 1983–. Editor, Jl of Roman Studies, 1985–. *Publications:* Procopius, 1967; Agathias, 1970; Corippus: In laudem Iustini minoris, 1976; Change and Continuity in Sixth-Century Byzantium, 1981; (ed jtly) Images of Women in Antiquity, 1983; (ed jtly) Constantinople in the Eighth Century: the Parastaseis Syntomoi Chronikai, 1984; Procopius and the Sixth Century, 1985; articles in Jl Hellenic Studies, Byzantion, Jl Theol Studies, Annali Scuola Normale di Pisa, Past and Present, Dumbarton Oaks Papers, and others.

CAMERON, Dr Clive Bremner; Dean, Institute of Cancer Research, London, 1978–82; *b* 28 Sept. 1921; *s* of Clive Rutherford and Aroha Margaret Cameron; *m* 1958, Rosalind Louise Paget; two *s* one *d*. *Educ:* King's Coll., Auckland, NZ; Otago Univ., NZ (MD). Consultant in Clinical Pathology, Royal Marsden Hospital, 1961–82; Chairman, SW Thames Regional Cancer Council, 1976–81. Chm., Governing Body, St Mary's Sch., Calne, 1981–. Mem. Bd of Governors, Royal Marsden Hosp., 1977–82. *Publications:* papers on steroid biochemistry, biochemical and other aspects of cancer. *Recreation:* country pursuits. *Address:* 1 St Leonard's Terrace, SW3; East Kennett Manor, Marlborough, Wilts. *T:* Lockeridge 239.

CAMERON OF LOCHIEL, Colonel Sir Donald (Hamish), KT 1973; CVO 1970; TD 1944; JP; 26th Chief of the Clan Cameron; Lord-Lieutenant of County of Inverness, 1971–85 (Vice-Lieutenant, 1963–70); Chartered Accountant; *b* 12 Sept. 1910; *s* of Col Sir Donald Walter Cameron of Lochiel, KT, CMG, 25th Chief of the Clan Cameron, and Lady Hermione Emily Graham (*d* 1978), 2nd *d* of 5th Duke of Montrose; *S* father, as 26th Chief, 1951; *m* 1939, Margaret, *o d* of Lieut-Col Hon. Nigel Gathorne-Hardy, DSO; two *s* two *d*. *Educ:* Harrow; Balliol Coll., Oxford. Joined Lovat Scouts, 1929; Major 1940; Lieut-Col 1945; Lieut-Col comdg 4/5th Bn (TA) QO Cameron Highlanders, 1955–57; Col 1957 (TARO). Hon. Colonel: 4/5th Bn QO Cameron Highlanders, 1958–67; 3rd (Territorial) Bn Queen's Own Highlanders (Seaforth and Camerons), 1967–69; 2nd Bn, 51st Highland Volunteers, 1970–75. Member (part-time): British Railways Bd, 1962–64; Scottish Railways Bd, 1964–72 (Chm. Scottish Area Bd, BTC, 1959–64); Transport Holding Co., 1962–65; Director: Royal Bank of Scotland, 1954–80 (Vice-Chm., 1969–80); Save & Prosper Gp, 1968–84; Culter Guard Bridge Holdings Ltd, 1970–77 (Chm., 1970–76); Scottish Widows Life Assurance Soc., 1955–81 (Chm., 1964–67). Crown Estate Comr, 1957–69. President: Scottish Landowners Fedn, 1979–84; Royal Highland and Agricultural Soc. of Scotland, 1971 and 1979. Governor, Harrow Sch., 1967–77. *Heir: s* Donald Angus Cameron, younger of Lochiel [*b* 2 Aug. 1946; *m* 1974, Lady Cecil Kerr, *d* of Marquess of Lothian, *qv*; one *s* three *d*]. *Address:* Achnacarry, Spean Bridge, Inverness-shire. *T:* Gairlochy 208. *Clubs:* Pratt's; New (Edinburgh).

See also A. J. Cameron, J. A. McL. Stewart of Ardvorlich.

CAMERON, Ellen; *see* Malcolm, E.

CAMERON, Sir (Eustace) John, Kt 1977; CBE 1970; MA Cantab; Tasmanian pastoralist, since 1946; *b* 8 Oct. 1913; *s* of Eustace Noel Cameron and Alexina Maria Cameron; *m* 1934, Nancie Ailsa Sutherland (OBE 1983); one *d*. *Educ:* Geelong Grammar Sch.; Trinity Coll., Cambridge. Served RANVR, 1942–46. ICI, 1938–41. State Pres., Liberal Party, 1948–52. Pres., Tasmanian Stockowners Assoc., 1965–68; Vice-Pres., Aust. Graziers, 1968–71. University of Tasmania: Mem. Council, 1956–82; Dep. Chancellor, 1964–72; Chancellor, 1973–81. Member: Selection Cttee, Winston Churchill Fellowship, 1965–74; CSIRO Adv. Cttee, 1959–77; Housing Loan Insurance Corp., 1970–73. Hon. LLD Tasmania, 1982. *Publications:* contrib. Australian Dictionary of Biography. *Recreations:* Australiana, gardening, pottering. *Address:* Lochiel, Ross, Tas 7209, Australia. *T:* Ross 815253. *Clubs:* Tasmanian (Hobart); Launceston (Launceston).

CAMERON, Rt. Rev. Ewen Donald; Assistant Bishop, Diocese of Sydney, since 1975 (Bishop of North Sydney since 1983); Member, Anglican-Roman Catholic International Commission, since 1983; *b* 7 Nov. 1926; *s* of Ewen Cameron, Balranald, NSW, and Dulce M. Cameron, Sydney, NSW; *m* 1952, Joan R., *d* of T. Wilkins, Mosman, NSW; one *s* two *d*. *Educ:* Sydney C of E Grammar Sch., N Sydney; Moore Theological Coll., Sydney. ACA (Aust.); BD (London); ThSchol (Aust. Coll. of Theol.). Public Accountancy, 1945–57. Lectr, Moore Theological Coll., 1960–63; Rector, St Stephen's, Bellevue Hill, 1963–65; Federal Secretary, CMS of Aust., 1965–72; Archdeacon of Cumberland with Sydney, 1972–75. *Address:* 3 Mildura Street, Killara, NSW 2071, Australia. *T:* 02–498–5816. *Club:* Union (Sydney).

CAMERON, Francis (Ernest), MA, DipEth (Oxon); FRCO(CHM), ARAM; Senior Lecturer in Musical Studies, Oxford Polytechnic, since 1982; Organist, Church of St Mary the Virgin, Iffley, since 1980; *b* London, 5 Dec. 1927; *er s* of Ernest and Doris Cameron; *m* 1952, Barbara Minns; three *d*. *Educ:* Mercers' Sch.; Caerphilly Boys' Secondary Sch.; Royal Acad. of Music; University Coll., Oxford. Henry Richards Prizewinner, RAM, 1946. Organist, St Peter's, Fulham, 1943; Pianist, Canadian Legion, 1944; Organist, St Luke's, Holloway, 1945; Sub-organist, St Peter's, Eaton Square, 1945; Organist, St James-the-Less, Westminster, 1946; commissioned RASC, 1948; Organ Scholar, University Coll., Oxford, 1950; Organist: St Anne's, Highgate, 1952; St Barnabas', Pimlico, 1953; St Mark's, Marylebone Road, 1957–58; received into Roman Catholic Church, Holy Week, 1959; Choirmaster, St Aloysius, Somers Town, 1959; Master of Music, Westminster Cathedral, 1959; Visiting Organist, Church of St Thomas of Canterbury, Rainham, Kent, 1961; Organist and Choirmaster, Church of Our Lady of the Assumption and St Gregory, 1962–68. Travel for UNESCO, 1952–55; Dep. Dir of Music, LCC (subsequently GLC), 1954–68; Asst-Dir of Music, Emanuel Sch., 1954; Music Master, Central Foundation Boys' Grammar Sch., 1956; Prof. of Organ and Composition, RAM, 1959–68; *locum tenens* Dir of Music, St Felix Sch., Southwold, 1963 and 1964; Asst Dir, 1968, Chm. of Musicology, 1974–79, NSW State Conservatorium of Music. Inaugural Conductor, Witan Operatic Soc., 1957–58; Conductor: "I Cantici", 1961–65; Francis Cameron Chorale, 1965–68; Singers of David, 1973–76; British Adjudicator, Fedn of Canadian Music Festivals, 1965; Examr Associated Bd of Royal Schools of Music, 1965–68; Dep. Chm., NSW Adv. Bd, Aust. Music Exams Bd, 1969–74. Field Officer, Deep Creek Aboriginal Monuments res. and recording prog., 1973; Mem., Lancefield Archaeol Expedn, 1975. President: "Open Score", 1946–68; Musicol Soc. of Aust., 1971–75 (jt leader, ethnomusicol expedn to New Hebrides, 1971–72); Sydney Univ. Anthropol Soc., 1974–75; Phoenix Photographic Circle, 1977–79; Conservatorium Professional Staff Assoc., 1978–79; Vice-Pres., Aust. Chapter, Internat. Soc. for Contemporary Music, 1970–77. Beethoven Commemorative Medal, Fed. Repub. of Germany, 1970. *Publications:* editor (with John Steele) Musica Britannica vol. xiv (The Keyboard Music of John Bull, part I), 1960; Old Palace Yard, 1963; Eight dances from Benjamin Cosyn's Second Virginal Book, 1964; I Sing of a Maiden, 1966; John Bull, ausgewählte Werke, 1967; I Believe, 1969; incidental music for film The Voyage of the New Endeavour, 1970; songs and incidental music for Congreve's Love for Love, 1972; contributor to: Church Music; Composer; The Conductor; Liturgy; Musical Times; Australian Jl of Music Education; Studies in Music; Music in Tertiary Educn; Con Brio; Musicology IV; Aust. Nat. Hist.; Nation Review; Quanta. *Address:* 12 Norreys Avenue, Oxford OX1 4SS. *T:* Oxford 240058.

CAMERON, George Edmund, CBE 1970; retired; *b* 2 July 1911; *s* of William Cameron and Margaret Cameron (*née* Craig); *m* 1939, Winifred Audrey Brown; two *s*. *Educ:* Ballymena Academy. Chartered Accountant, 1933; Partner, Wright Fitzsimons & Cameron, 1937–79. Pres., Inst. of Chartered Accountants in Ireland, 1960–61. *Recreations:* golf, gardening. *Address:* Ardavon, Glen Road, Craigavad, Co. Down. *T:* Holywood 2232. *Clubs:* Ulster (Belfast); Royal County Down Golf, Royal Belfast Golf.

CAMERON, Prof. Gordon Campbell; Professor and Head of the Department of Land Economy, and Fellow of Wolfson College, Cambridge University, since 1980; *b* 28 Nov. 1937; *s* of Archibald Arthur Cameron and Elizabeth Forsyth; *m* 1962, Brenda; one *s* one *d*. *Educ:* Quarry Bank High Sch., Liverpool; Hatfield Coll., Univ. of Durham (BA Hons). Res. Asst, Univ. of Durham, 1960–62; Univ. of Glasgow: Asst Lectr in Polit. Econ., 1962–63; Lectr in Applied Econs, 1963–68, Sen. Lectr 1968–71, Titular Prof. 1971–74; Prof. of Town and Regional Planning, 1974–79, Dean of Social Sciences, 1979. Res. Fellow, Resources for the Future, Washington, DC, and Vis. Associate Prof., Pittsburgh Univ., 1966–67; Vis. Prof., Univ. of Calif, Berkeley, 1974. Parly Boundary Comr for Scotland, 1976–83. Chm., Inner City Res. Panel, SSRC, 1980–82; Member: Cttee of Enquiry into Local Govt Finance (Layfield Cttee), 1974–76; Bd, Peterborough Develt Corp., 1981–. Consultant on Urban Policy, Scottish Develt Dept, 1975–79; Economic Consultant to Sec. of State for Scotland, 1977–80; Consultant on Urban Finance, OECD, 1977–80, on Land Markets, 1986–. Consultant, Coopers & Lybrand, 1977–. Governor, Centre for Environmental Studies, London, 1975–82. Editor, Urban Studies Jl, 1968–74. FRSA 1978; Hon. RICS 1982. *Publications:* Regional Economic Development—the federal role, 1971; (with L. Wingo) Cities, Regions and Public Policy, 1974; (ed) The Future of the British Conurbations, 1980. *Recreations:* tennis, musical concerts, theatre. *Address:* Department of Land Economy, 19 Silver Street, Cambridge.

CAMERON, Gordon Stewart, RSA 1971 (ARSA 1958); Senior Lecturer, School of Drawing and Painting, Duncan of Jordanstone College of Art, Dundee, 1952–81, retired; *b* Aberdeen, 27 April 1916; *s* of John Roderick Cameron; *m* 1962, Ellen Malcolm, *qv*. *Educ:* Robert Gordon's Coll., Aberdeen; Gray's Sch. of Art, Aberdeen. Part-time teaching, Gray's Sch. of Art, 1945–50; engaged on anatomical illustrations for Lockhart's Anatomy of the Human Body, 1945–48; apptd Lectr in Duncan of Jordanstone Coll. of Art, 1952. Awarded Davidson Gold Medal, 1939; Guthrie Award, 1944; Carnegie Travelling Schol., 1946. Work in Public Galleries: Aberdeen, Dundee, Perth, Edinburgh, Glasgow; also in private collections in Scotland, England, Ireland and America. *Recreation:* gardening. *Address:* 7 Auburn Terrace, Invergowrie, Perthshire. *T:* Invergowrie 318.

CAMERON, Sir James Clark, Kt 1979; CBE 1969; TD 1947; Visitor to Council, British Medical Association (past Chairman of Council, 1976–79); *b* 8 April 1905; *s* of Malcolm Clark Cameron, Rannoch, Perthshire; *m* 1933, Irene (*d* 1986), *d* of Arthur Ferguson, Perth; one *s* two *d*. *Educ:* Perth Academy; St Andrews Univ. (MB, ChB). FRCGP. Served War of 1939–45, as Captain RAMC attached to 1st Bn, The Rifle Bde (despatches), Calais; POW, 1940. Past Chm., Gen. Med. Services Cttee, BMA, 1964–74, and Hon. Life Member; Chm., Adv. Cttee for Gen. Practice Council for Post Grad. Med. Educn (England and Wales), 1971–79; Member: Jt Cttee on Post Grad. Trng for Gen. Practice, 1976–; Adv. Cttee on Med. Trng, Commn of the European Communities, 1976–; Vice Pres., British Supporting Gp, World Medical Assoc., 1982–. Hon. Mem. Council, Cameron Fund Ltd, 1974. Gold Medal for distinguished merit, BMA, 1974. *Recreation:* medico-politics. *Address:* 201 Croydon Road, Wallington, Surrey SM6 7LT. *T:* 01–647 6123.

See also S. M. C. Cameron, G. C. Ryan.

CAMERON, Prof. J(ames) Malcolm, MD, PhD; FRCSGlas, FRCPath, DMJ; Professor of Forensic Medicine, University of London, at The London Hospital Medical College, since 1973, and Director, Department of Forensic Medicine; Ver Heyden De Lancey Readership in Forensic Medicine, Council of Legal Education, since 1978; Hon. Consultant: to The London Hospital, since 1967; to the Army at Home, in Forensic Medicine, since 1971; to the Royal Navy, in Forensic Medicine, since 1972; Hon. Medical Adviser to Amateur Swimming Association; Editor of Medicine, Science and Law, since

1970; *b* 29 April 1930; *s* of late James Cameron and Doris Mary Robertson; *m* 1956, Primrose Agnes Miller McKerrell, MCST; one *d*. *Educ*: The High Sch. of Glasgow; Univ. of Glasgow (MB, ChB, MD, PhD). Sen. Ho. Officer in Pathology, Southern Gen. Hosp., Glasgow, 1955–56; McIntyre Clin. Res. Schol., Depts of Path. and Surgery, Glasgow Roy. Infirm., 1956–57; Registrar in Orthop. Surg., Western Infirm., Glasgow, and The Royal Hosp. for Sick Children, Glasgow, 1957–59; Registrar in Lab. Med., 1959–60, and Sen. Registrar in Path., 1960–62, Southern Gen. Hosp., Glasgow; Lectr in Path., Univ. of Glasgow, 1962. The London Hosp. Med. Coll.: Lectr in Forensic Med., 1963–65; Sen. Lectr in Forensic Med., 1965–70; Reader in Forensic Med., 1970–72. Lectr in Forensic Med. at St Bartholomew's Hosp. Med. Coll. and Univ. Coll. Hosp. Med. Sch.; Lectr to Metropolitan Police Detective Trng Sch., SW Detective Trng Sch., Bristol, and Special Investigation Br. of RMP; former Examiner in Forensic Med. to Univ. of Dublin; former Convenor for Exams of Dip. in Med. Jurisp. of Honourable Soc. of Apothecaries of London; former Mem. Council, Royal Coll. of Pathologists. Member: BMA; Council, Brit. Assoc. in Forensic Med. (Pres. 1985–); British Acad. of Forensic Sciences (Sec. Gen., 1970–85; Pres., 1978–79); Medico-Legal Soc. (past Vice-Pres.); Assoc. of Police Surgeons of Gt Britain (Hon. Fellow); Forensic Science Soc.; Assoc. of Clinical Pathologists; Pathological Soc. of Gt. Britain and Ire.; Research Defence Soc.; Fellow, Amer. Acad. of Forensic Sciences; Mem., Academic Internationalis Medicinae Legalis et Medicinae Socialis. *Publications*: scientific papers in numerous learned jls, both med. and forensic. *Recreations*: sports medicine and legal medicine. *Address*: c/o Department of Forensic Medicine, The London Hospital Medical College, Turner Street, E1 2AD. *T*: 01–247 5454, ext. 360. *Clubs*: Savage, Royal Naval Medical.

CAMERON, Prof. James Munro; University Professor, St Michaels College, University of Toronto, 1971–78, now Emeritus; *b* 14 Nov. 1910; *o s* of Alan and Jane Helen Cameron; *m* 1933, Vera Shaw (*d* 1985); one *d* (one *s* decd). *Educ*: Central Secondary Sch., Sheffield; Keighley Grammar Sch.; Balliol Coll., Oxford (Scholar). Tutor, Workers' Educational Assoc., 1931–32; Staff Tutor, Univ. Coll., Southampton, 1932–35; Staff Tutor, Vaughan Coll., Leicester (Dept of Adult Education, Univ. Coll., Leicester), 1935–43. Univ. of Leeds: Staff Tutor for Tutorial Classes, 1943–47; Lectr in Philosophy, 1947–60 (Sen. Lectr from 1952); Acting Head of Dept of Philosophy, 1954–55 and 1959–60; Prof. of Philosophy, 1960–67; Master of Rutherford Coll., and Prof. of Philosophy, Univ. of Kent at Canterbury, 1967–71. Vis. Prof., Univ. of Notre Dame, Indiana, 1957–58, 1965; Terry Lectr, Yale Univ., 1964–65. Newman Fellow, Univ. of Melbourne, 1968; Christian Culture Award, Univ. of Windsor, Ont, 1972. *Publications*: Scrutiny of Marxism, 1948; (trans. with Marianne Kuschnitzky) Max Picard, The Flight from God, 1951; John Henry Newman, 1956; The Night Battle, 1962; Images of Authority, 1966; (ed) Essay on Development (1845 edn), by J. H. Newman, 1974; On the Idea of a University, 1978; contribs to other books, and articles and papers in many periodicals. *Address*: 360 Bloor Street E, Apt 409, Toronto, Ontario M4W 3M3, Canada.

CAMERON, Sir John; *see* Cameron, Hon. Lord.

CAMERON, Sir John; *see* Cameron, Sir E. J.

CAMERON, John Alastair, QC (Scot.) 1979; *b* 1 Feb. 1938; *s* of William Philip Legerwood Cameron and Kathleen Milthorpe (*née* Parker); *m* 1968, Elspeth Mary Dunlop Miller; three *s*. *Educ*: Trinity Coll., Glenalmond; Pembroke Coll., Oxford (MA). Called to the Bar, Inner Temple, 1963; admitted Mem., Faculty of Advocates, 1966, Vice-Dean, 1983–. Advocate-Depute, 1972–75; Standing Jun. Counsel: to Dept of Energy, 1976–79; to Scottish Develt Dept, 1978–79. Legal Chm., Pensions Appeal Tribunals for Scotland, 1979–85 (Pres., 1985–). *Publication*: Medical Negligence: an introduction, 1983. *Recreations*: travel, sport, Africana. *Address*: 4 Garscube Terrace, Edinburgh EH12 6BQ. *T*: 031–337 3460.

CAMERON, John Bell, CBE 1982; Chairman, World Meats Group, International Federation of Agricultural Producers, since 1984; *b* 14 June 1939; *s* of John and Margaret Cameron; *m* 1964, Margaret (*née* Clapperton). *Educ*: Dollar Academy. AIAgrE; FRAgS. Studied agriculture in various countries, Scandinavia, S America and Europe, 1956–61; farmed in Scotland, 1961–64. National Farmers' Union of Scotland: Mem. National Council, 1964; Vice-Pres., 1976; Pres., 1979–84 (first long-term Pres.). Mem., Agricultural Praesidium of EEC, 1979–; Chm., EEC Adv. Cttee for Sheep Meat, 1982–. Chm. Governors, Dollar Acad., 1984–. Winner, George Headley Award to the UK Sheep Industry, 1986. *Recreations*: flying, shooting, travelling. *Address*: Balbuthie Farm, By Leven, Fife, Scotland. *T*: St Monans 210.

CAMERON, John Charles Finlay; Director-General and Secretary, Chartered Institute of Transport, since 1984; *b* 8 Feb. 1928; *s* of Robert John and Nancy Angela Cameron; *m*; two *s* two *d*. *Educ*: privately; University Coll., Southampton. CEng, MICE, FCIT, FBIM. Royal Marines, 1946–48. British Railways, Southern Region, Civil Engineering, 1948; BR Transport Commn, 1957; BR Rlys Workshops, 1962; Rank Organisation, 1968. Mem., LTE, 1975–84. Management Cttee, Abbotstone, Ag. Prop. Unit Trust. Chm., Westminster Br., BIM. Major, Engr and Transport Staff Corps, RE (TA). Liveryman, Carmen's Co. Editor-in-Chief, Tranport. *Recreations*: building, garden construction. *Address*: Clunemore Farm, Killiecrankie, Pitlochry, Perthshire PH16 5LS. *T*: Pitlochry 3470; 01–254 8651; (office) 80 Portland Place, W1N 4DP.

CAMERON, Prof. John Robinson; Regius Professor of Logic, University of Aberdeen, since 1979; *b* 24 June 1936; *s* of Rev. George Gordon Cameron and Mary Levering (*née* Robinson); *m* 1959, Mary Elizabeth Ranson (*d* 1984); one *s* two *d*. *Educ*: Dundee High Sch.; Univ. of St Andrews (MA 1st Cl. Hons Maths, BPhil Philosophy); Univ. of Calif, Berkeley; Cornell Univ. Harkness Fellow, Berkeley and Cornell, USA, 1959–61; University of Dundee (formerly Queen's College): Asst in Phil., 1962–63; Lectr in Phil., 1963–73; Sen. Lectr in Phil., 1973–78. *Publications*: articles in phil jls. *Recreation*: bricolage. *Address*: 70 Cornhill Road, Aberdeen AB2 5DH. *T*: Aberdeen 486700.

CAMERON, John Taylor, QC (Scot.) 1973; a Judge of the Courts of Appeal of Jersey and Guernsey, since 1986; *b* 24 April 1934; *s* of late John Reid Cameron, MA, formerly Director of Education, Dundee; *m* 1964, Bridget Deirdre Sloan; no *c*. *Educ*: Fettes Coll.; Corpus Christi Coll., Oxford; Edinburgh Univ. BA (Oxon), LLB (Edinburgh). Admitted to Faculty of Advocates, 1960. Lecturer in Public Law, Edinburgh Univ., 1960–64. Keeper of the Advocates' Library, 1977–; an Advocate-Depute, 1977–79. Chm., Medical Appeal Tribunals, 1985–. *Publications*: articles in legal jls. *Address*: 17 Moray Place, Edinburgh EH3 6DT. *T*: 031–225 7695.

CAMERON, Sir John (Watson), Kt 1981; OBE 1960; President, J. W. Cameron & Co., since 1977; *b* 16 Nov. 1901; *s* of Captain Watson Cameron and Isabel Mann; *m* 1930, Lilian Florence Sanderson; one *s* two *d*. *Educ*: Lancing Coll. Commnd Durham RGA, 1920. Joined J. W. Cameron & Co., brewery co., 1922; Man. Dir, 1940; Chm., 1943–75. Mem., Northern Area, Economic League, 1950–80. Chm., 1964–69, Treasurer, 1967–72, Northern Area Cons. Party; Hartlepool Conservative Party: Chm., 1942–45; Pres., 1945–76; Patron, 1976–78; Pres. and Patron, 1978–. Chm., Hartlepools Hosp. Trust, 1973–80. *Recreations*: gardening, shooting, fishing. *Address*: Cowesby Hall, near Thirsk, N Yorks YO7 2JJ.

CAMERON, Prof. Kenneth, FBA 1976; Professor of English Language, since 1963, and Head of Department of English Studies, since 1984, University of Nottingham; *b* Burnley, Lancs, 21 May 1922; *s* of late Angus W. Cameron and of E. Alice Cameron, Habergham, Burnley; *m* 1947, Kathleen (*d* 1977), *d* of late F. E. Heap, Burnley; one *s* one *d*. *Educ*: Burnley Grammar Sch.; Univ. of Leeds (BA Hons, Sch. of English Language and Literature); PhD Sheffield. Served War, 1941–45; Pilot, RAF. Asst Lectr in English Language, Univ. of Sheffield, 1947–50; Nottingham University: Lectr in English Language, 1950–59; Sen. Lectr, 1959–62; Reader, 1962–63. Sir Israel Gollancz Meml Lecture, British Academy, 1976; O'Donnell Lectr, 1979. Pres., Viking Soc., 1972–74; Hon. Dir, 1966–, Hon. Sec., 1972–, English Place-Name Soc. Gen. Editor, English Place-Name Survey, 1966–; Editor, Jl of the English Place-Name Soc., 1972–. FRHistS 1970; FSA 1984. Hon. FilDr, Uppsala, 1977. Sir Israel Gollancz Meml Prize, British Academy, 1969. *Publications*: The Place-Names of Derbyshire, 1959; English Place-Names, 1961; Scandinavian Settlement in the Territory of the Five Boroughs: the place-name evidence, 1965; The Meaning and Significance of OE *walh* in English Place-Names, 1980; The Place-Names of the County of the City of Lincoln, 1985; contribs to: Nottingham Medieval Studies; Medium Ævum; Mediaeval Scandinavia; Festschrifts, etc. *Recreations*: sports (supporting), home, "The Queens". *Address*: 292 Queens Road, Beeston, Nottingham. *T*: Nottingham 254503.

CAMERON, Roy James, CB 1982; PhD; Australian Statistician, 1977–85; *b* 11 March 1923; *s* of Kenneth Cameron and Amy Jean (*née* Davidson); *m* 1951, Dorothy Olive Lober; two *s* one *d*. *Educ*: Univ. of Adelaide (BEc 1st Cl. Hons, MEc); PhD Harvard. Lecturer in Economics, Canberra University College, 1949–51; Economist, World Bank, 1954–56; Australian Treasury official, 1956–73; Australian Ambassador to OECD, Paris, 1973–77. Chm., Cttee of Inquiry into Distribution of Federal Roads Grants. Mem. Council, Canberra Coll. of Advanced Educn. *Recreation*: lawn bowls. *Address*: 10 Rafferty Street, Chapman, ACT 2611, Australia. *T*: 062 888816. *Club*: Commonwealth (Canberra).

CAMERON, Sheila Morag Clark, (Mrs G. C. Ryan); QC 1983; a Recorder, since 1985; Vicar-General of the Province of Canterbury, since 1983; *b* 22 March 1934; *d* of Sir James Clark Cameron, *qv*, and Lady (Irene M.) Cameron; *m* 1960, Gerard Charles Ryan, *qv*; two *s*. *Educ*: Commonweal Lodge Sch., Purley; St Hugh's Coll., Oxford (MA). Called to the Bar, Middle Temple, 1957; Part-time Lectr in Law, Southampton Univ., 1960–64; part-time Tutor, Council of Legal Educn, 1966–71. Mem., Bar Council, 1967–70. Asst Comr, Boundary Commn for England, 1981–. Official Principal, Archdeaconry of Hampstead, 1968–; Chancellor, Dio. of Chelmsford, 1969–; Member: Legal Adv. Commn, Gen. Synod of C of E, 1975–; Gen. Synod Marriage Commn, 1975–78; Council on Tribunals, 1986–. Mem. Council, Wycombe Abbey Sch., 1972–. *Recreation*: cooking. *Address*: 2 Harcourt Buildings, Temple, EC4Y 9DB. *T*: 01–353 8415.

CAMERON, Stuart Gordon, MC 1943; Chairman and Chief Executive, Gallaher Ltd, since 1980; Director, American Brands Inc., since 1980; *b* 8 Jan. 1924; *s* of James Cameron and Dora Sylvia (*née* Godsell); *m* 1946, Joyce Alice, *d* of Roland Ashley Wood; three *s* one *d*. *Educ*: Chigwell School, Essex. Served War, 2nd Gurkha Rifles, 1942–46 (MC). Managing Director, 1976–78, Dep. Chm., 1978–80, Gallaher Ltd. *Address*: 65 Kingsway, WC2B 6TG. *T*: 01–242 1290. *Club*: Royal Thames Yacht.

CAMERON-RAMSAY-FAIRFAX-LUCY; *see* Fairfax-Lucy.

CAMERON WATT, Prof. Donald; Stevenson Professor of International History in the University of London, since 1981; *b* 17 May 1928; *s* of late Robert Cameron Watt and Barbara, *d* of late Rt Rev. E. J. Bidwell, former Bishop of Ontario; *m* 1st, 1951, Marianne Ruth Grau (*d* 1962); one *s*; 2nd, 1962, Felicia Cobb Stanley; one step *d*. *Educ*: Rugby Sch.; Oriel Coll., Oxford. BA 1951, MA 1954; FRHistS. Asst Editor, Documents on German Foreign Policy, 1918–1945, in Foreign Office, 1951–54; Asst Lectr, Lectr, Sen. Lectr in Internat. History, LSE, 1954–66; Reader in Internat. History in Univ. of London, 1966; Titular Prof. of Internat. History, 1972–81. Editor, Survey of Internat. Affairs, Royal Inst. of Internat. Affairs, 1962–71; Rockefeller Research Fellow in Social Sciences, Inst of Advanced Internat. Studies, Washington, 1960–61; Official Historian, Cabinet Office Historical Section, 1978–. Sec., 1967, Chm., 1976–, Assoc. of Contemporary Historians; Chm., Greenwich Forum, 1974–84; Sec.-Treasurer, Internat. Commn for the Hist. of Internat. Relations, 1982–. Member Editorial Board: Political Quarterly, 1969–; Marine Policy, 1978–; International History, 1984–. *Publications*: Britain and the Suez Canal, 1956; (ed) Documents on the Suez Crisis, 1957; Britain looks to Germany, 1965; Personalities and Policies, 1965; (ed) Survey of International Affairs 1961, 1966; (ed) Documents on International Affairs 1961, 1966; (ed, with K. Bourne) Studies in International History, 1967; A History of the World in the Twentieth Century, Pt I, 1967; (ed) Contemporary History of Europe, 1969; (ed) Hitler's Mein Kampf, 1969; (ed) Survey of International Affairs 1962, 1969; (ed, with James Mayall): Current British Foreign Policy 1970, 1971; Current British Foreign Policy 1971, 1972; Current British Foreign Policy 1972, 1973; Too Serious a Business, 1975; (ed) Survey of International Affairs 1963, 1977; Succeeding John Bull: America in Britain's place 1900–1975, 1984. *Recreations*: exploring London, cats. *Address*: c/o London School of Economics and Political Science, Houghton Street, WC2A 2AE. *Club*: Players Theatre.

CAMILLERI, His Honour Sir Luigi A., Kt 1954; LLD; Chief Justice and President of the Court of Appeal, Malta, 1952–57, retired; *b* 7 Dec. 1892; *s* of late Notary Giuseppe amd Matilde (*née* Bonello); *m* 1914, Erminia, *d* of Professor G. Calì; five *s* three *d*. *Educ*: Gozo Seminary; Royal Univ. of Malta (LLD). Called to the Bar, 1913. Consular Agent for France in Gozo, Malta, 1919–24; Malta Legislative Assembly, 1921–24; Magistrate, 1924–30; Visitor of Notarial Acts, Chairman Board of Prison Visitors, Chairman Licensing Board, Magistrate in charge of Electoral Register, 1927–30; Judicial Bench, 1930; Royal Univ. of Malta representative on General Council of the Univ., 1933–36; Chairman Emergency Compensation Board, 1940–41; Court of Appeal, 1940–57; President Medical Council, Malta, 1959–68; Member Judicial Service Commission, 1959–62. Examiner in Criminal, Roman and Civil Law, Royal Univ. of Malta, 1931–70. Silver Jubilee Medal, 1935; Coronation Medals, 1937 and 1953. Knight of Sovereign Military Order of Malta, 1952. *Recreation*: walking. *Address*: Victoria Avenue, Sliema, Malta. *T*: Sliema 513532. *Club*: Casino Maltese (Malta).

CAMM, Prof. Alan John, MD; FRCP, FACC; Prudential Professor of Clinical Cardiology, St George's Hospital Medical School, London University, since 1986; *b* 11 Jan. 1947; *s* of John Donald and Joan Camm; unmarried. *Educ*: Guy's Hosp. Med. Sch., London Univ. (BSc 1968; MB BS 1971; MD 1981). LRCP, MRCS 1971; FACC 1981; FRCP 1984. Guy's Hospital: House Surgeon, 1971; House Physician, 1971–72; Jun. Registrar, 1972; Jun. Lectr in Medicine, 1972–73; Registrar in Cardiology, 1973–74; Clin. Fellow in Cardiology, Univ. of Vermont, USA, 1974–75; St Bartholomew's Hospital: British Heart Foundn Res. Registrar, 1975–76, Sen. Registrar 1977–79; Wellcome Sen. Lectr and Hon. Consultant Cardiologist, 1979–83; Sir Ronald Bodley Scott Prof. of Cardiovascular

Medicine, 1983–86. Freeman, City of London, 1984. OStJ 1982 (SBStJ 1979). *Publications:* First Aid, Step by Step, 1978; Pacing for Tachycardia Control, 1983; Heart Disease in the Elderly, 1984; Clinical Electrophysiology of the Heart, 1987; approx. 200 papers in major jls. *Recreations:* collector of prints, watercolours and other antiques, model railway enthusiast.

CAMMELL, John Ernest; Head of Mechanical Engineering and Manufacturing Technology Division, Department of Trade and Industry, since 1986; *b* 14 Nov. 1932; *s* of Ernest Alfred Cammell and Gladys Clara (*née* Burroughes); *m* 1976, Janis Linda Moody. *Educ:* Highfield Coll., Leigh-on-Sea, Essex. Mil. Service, Royal Signals. Joined Victualling Dept, Admiralty, 1952; DSIR, 1963; Min. of Technology, 1964; DTI, 1967; Dept of Industry, 1973; Dir, National Maritime Inst., 1981–84. *Recreations:* amateur theatre, golf, cricket, eating. *Address:* 13 Vale Court, Acton, W3 7XW. *T:* 01–749 4747. *Club:* Players Theatre.

CAMOYS, 7th Baron *cr* 1264 (called out of abeyance, 1839); **Ralph Thomas Campion George Sherman Stonor;** Executive Vice-Chairman, Barclays Merchant Bank Ltd, since 1984 (Managing Director, 1978–84); Chief Executive, Barclays de Zoete Wedd (BZW), 1986; Chairman, Jacksons of Piccadilly Ltd, 1968–85; *b* 16 April 1940; *s* of 6th Baron Camoys and of Mary Jeanne, *d* of late Captain Herbert Marmaduke Joseph Stourton, OBE; *S* father, 1976; *m* 1966, Elisabeth Mary Hyde, *d* of Sir William Stephen Hyde Parker, 11th Bt; one *s* three *d*. *Educ:* Eton Coll.; Balliol Coll., Oxford (BA). Gen. Manager and Director, National Provincial and Rothschild (London) Ltd, 1968; Man. Director, Rothschild Intercontinental Bank Ltd, 1969; Chief Exec. Officer and Man. Dir, 1975–77, Chm., 1977–78, Amex Bank Ltd; Director: Barclays Bank Internat. Ltd, 1980–84; Barclays Bank PLC, 1984–; Mercantile Credit Co. Ltd, 1980–84; National Provident Instn, 1982–. Pres., Mail Users' Assoc., 1977–84; Member: House of Lords EEC Select Cttee, 1979–81; Court of Assistants, Fishmongers' Co., 1980–. Order of Gorkha Dakshina Bahu, 1st class (Nepal), 1981. *Recreations:* the arts, shooting. *Heir:* *s* Hon. (Ralph) William (Robert Thomas) Stonor, *b* 10 Sept. 1974. *Address:* Stonor Park, Henley-on-Thames, Oxon RG9 6HF. *Clubs:* Boodle's, Pratt's; Leander (Henley-on-Thames).

CAMP, Jeffery Bruce, RA 1984 (ARA 1974); artist; Lecturer, Slade School of Fine Art. *Educ:* Edinburgh Coll. of Art. DA (Edin.). One-man exhibitions include: Galerie de Seine, 1958; Beaux Arts Gallery, 1959, 1961, 1963; New Art Centre, 1968; Serpentine Gall., 1973; S London Art Gall., 1973 (retrospective); Bradford City Art Gallery, 1979; Browse and Darby, 1984; other exhibitions include: Hayward Annual, 1974, 1982, 1985; British Council touring exhibns to China and Edinburgh, 1982, to India, 1985; Chantrey Bicentenary, Tate Gall., 1981; Narrative Painting, ICA and Arts Council tour; The Hardwon Image, Tate Gall., 1984; group exhibn, Twinning Gall., NY, 1985; Peter Moores exhibn, Liverpool, 1986. *Publication:* Draw, 1981. *Address:* 78 Forthbridge Road, SW11 5NY. *T:* 01–223 5686.

CAMP, William Newton Alexander; writer and political and corporate adviser; *b* 12 May 1926; *s* of I. N. Camp, OBE, Colonial Administrative Service, Palestine, and Freda Camp; *m* 1st, 1950, Patricia Cowan (marr. diss. 1973); two *s* one *d*; 2nd, 1975, Juliet Schubart, *d* of late Hans Schubart, CBE. *Educ:* Bradfield Coll.; Oriel Coll., Oxford (Classical Scholar, MA). Served in Army, 1944–47. Asst Res. Officer, British Travel and Holidays Assoc., 1950–54; Asst Sec., Consumer Adv. Council, 1954–59; Asst Sec., Gas Council, 1960–63; Public Relations Adviser, Gas Council (British Gas Corp.), 1963–67; Dir of Information Services, British Steel Corp., 1967–71; Mem., British Nat. Oil Corp., 1976–78. Special Adviser: milling and baking industries, 1972–; British Leyland Motor Corp., 1975; railway trades unions, 1975–76; C. A. Parsons & Co. Ltd, 1976–77; Prudential Corp., 1978–; Northern Engineering Industries plc, 1978–84; pt-time advr, British Railways Bd, 1977–. Dir, Quartet Books, 1973–76; Chm., Camden Consultants Ltd, 1975–. Chm., Oxford Univ. Labour Club, 1949; contested (Lab) Solihull, 1950; Mem., Southwark Borough Council, 1953–56; Press Adviser (unpaid) to Prime Minister, Gen. Election, 1970. Founder Mem., Public Enterprise Group. *Publications:* *novels:* Prospects of Love, 1957; Idle on Parade, 1958; The Ruling Passion, 1959; A Man's World, 1962; Two Schools of Thought, 1964; Flavour of Decay, 1967; The Father Figures, 1970; Stroke Counterstroke, 1986; *biography:* The Glittering Prizes (F. E. Smith), 1960. *Address:* 61 Gloucester Crescent, NW1. *T:* 01–485 5110; Keeper's Cottage, Marshfield, near Chippenham, Wilts. *Club:* Garrick.

CAMPBELL, family name of **Duke of Argyll,** of **Earl of Breadalbane,** of **Earl Cawdor,** and of **Barons Campbell of Alloway, Campbell of Croy, Campbell of Eskan, Colgrain** and **Stratheden.**

CAMPBELL OF ALLOWAY, Baron *cr* 1981 (Life Peer), of Ayr in the District of Kyle and Carrick; **Alan Robertson Campbell,** QC 1965; a Recorder of the Crown Court, since 1976; *b* 24 May 1917; *s* of late J. K. Campbell; *m* 1957, Vivien, *y d* of late Comdr A. H. de Kantzow, DSO, RN. *Educ:* Aldenham; Ecole des Sciences Politiques, Paris; Trinity Hall, Cambridge. Called to Bar, Inner Temple, 1939, Bencher, 1972; Western Circuit. Commissioned RA (Suppl. Res.), 1939; served France and Belgium, 1939–40; POW, 1940–45. Consultant to sub-cttee of Legal Cttee of Council of Europe on Industrial Espionage, 1965–74; Chm., Legal Res. Cttee, Soc. of Conservative Lawyers, 1968–80. Member: Law Adv. Cttee, British Council, 1974–82; Management Cttee, UK Assoc. for European Law, 1975–. *Publications:* (with Lord Wilberforce) Restrictive Trade Practices and Monopolies, 1956, 2nd edn, 1966, Supplements 1 and 2, 1973; Restrictive Trading Agreements in the Common Market, 1964, Supplement, 1965; Common Market Law, vols 1 and 2, 1969, vol. 3, 1973 and Supplement, 1975; Industrial Relations Act, 1971; EC Competition Law, 1980; Trade Unions and the Individual, 1980. *Address:* 1 Harcourt Buildings, Temple, EC4. *T:* 01–353 2214. *Clubs:* Carlton (Mem., Political Cttee, 1967–79), Pratt's, Beefsteak.

CAMPBELL OF CROY, Baron *cr* 1974 (Life Peer), of Croy in the County of Nairn; **Gordon Thomas Calthrop Campbell,** PC 1970; MC 1944, and Bar, 1945; DL; *b* 8 June 1921; *s* of late Maj.-Gen. J. A. Campbell, DSO; *m* 1949, Nicola Elizabeth Gina Madan; two *s* one *d*. *Educ:* Wellington and Hospital. War of 1939–45: commissioned in Regular Army, 1939; RA, Major, 1942; commanded 320 Field Battery in 15 Scottish Div.; wounded and disabled, 1945. Entered HM Foreign Service, 1946; served, until 1957, in FO, UK Delegn to the UN (New York), Cabinet Office and Vienna. MP (C) Moray and Nairn, 1959–Feb. 1974; Asst Govt Whip, 1961–62; a Lord Comr of the Treasury and Scottish Whip, 1962–63; Joint Parly Under-Sec. of State, Scottish Office, 1963–64; Opposition Spokesman on Defence and Scottish Affairs, 1966–70; Sec. of State for Scotland, 1970–74. Oil industry consultant, 1975–; Partner in Holme Rose Farms and Estate, 1969–; Chm., Scottish Bd, 1976–, Dir, 1983–, Alliance and Leicester (formerly Alliance) Building Soc.; Chm., Stoic Insurance Services, 1979–. Chm., Scottish Cttee, Internat. Year of Disabled, 1981; Trustee, Thomson Foundn, 1980–; First Fellow, Nuffield Provincial Hospitals Trust Queen Elizabeth The Queen Mother Fellowship, 1980. DL Nairn, 1985. *Publication:* Disablement: Problems and Prospects in the UK, 1981. *Recreations:* music, birds. *Address:* Holme Rose, Cawdor, Nairnshire, Scotland. *T:* Croy 223.

CAMPBELL OF ESKAN, Baron *cr* 1966 (Life Peer), of Camis Eskan; **John (Jock) Middleton Campbell;** Kt 1957; Chairman, Commonwealth Sugar Exporters' Association, 1950–84; President, Town & Country Planning Association, since 1980; Trustee: Runnymede Trust; Chequers Trust; *b* 8 Aug. 1912; *e s* of late Colin Algernon Campbell, Colgrain, Dunbartonshire and Underriver House, Sevenoaks, Kent and of Mary Charlotte Gladys (Barrington); *m* 1st, 1938, Barbara Noel (marr. diss. 1948), *d* of late Leslie Arden Roffey; two *s* two *d*; 2nd, 1949, Phyllis Jacqueline Gilmour Taylor (*d* 1983), *d* of late Henry Boyd, CBE. *Educ:* Eton; Exeter Coll., Oxford (Hon. Fellow, 1973). Chairman: Booker McConnell Ltd, 1952–66 (Pres., 1967–79); Statesman and Nation Publishing Co. Ltd, 1964–77; Statesman Publishing Co. Ltd, 1964–81; Milton Keynes Develt Corp., 1967–83; New Towns Assoc., 1975–77; Director: London Weekend TV Ltd, 1967–74 (Dep. Chm., 1969–73); Commonwealth Develt Corp., 1968–81; Pres., West India Cttee, 1957–77. Mem., Community Relations Commn, 1968–77 (a Dep. Chm., 1968–71). Chm., Governing Body, Imperial Coll. of Tropical Agriculture, 1950–60. First Freeman of Milton Keynes, 1982. DUniv Open, 1973. *Recreations:* reading, hitting balls, painting. *Address:* Lawers, Crocker End, Nettlebed, Oxfordshire. *T:* Nettlebed 641202. *Clubs:* Beefsteak, All England Lawn Tennis; Huntercombe Golf.

CAMPBELL, Sir Alan (Hugh), GCMG 1979 (KCMG 1976; CMG 1964); HM Diplomatic Service, retired; Chairman, Society of Pension Consultants, since 1982; Director: National Westminster Bank; Mercantile and General Reinsurance Co.; H. Clarkson (Holdings) plc; *b* 1 July 1919; *y s* of late Hugh Campbell and Ethel Campbell (*née* Warren); *m* 1947, Margaret Taylor; three *d*. *Educ:* Sherborne Sch.; Caius Coll., Cambridge. Served in Devonshire Regt, 1940–46. 3rd Sec., HM Foreign (now Diplomatic) Service, 1946; appointed to Lord Killearn's Special Mission to Singapore, 1946; served in Rome, 1952, Peking, 1955; UK Mission to UN, New York, 1961; Head of Western Dept, Foreign Office, 1965; Counsellor, Paris, 1967; Ambassador to Ethiopia, 1969–72; Asst Under-Sec. of State, FCO, 1972–74; Dep. Under-Sec. of State, FCO, 1974–76; Ambassador to Italy, 1976–79; Foreign Affairs adviser to Rolls Royce Ltd, 1979–81. Chm., British-Italian Soc., 1983–; Member Council: British Sch. at Rome, 1982–; London Philharmonic Orchestra, 1982–. Governor, Sherborne Sch., 1973– (Chm. of Governors, 1982–). *Publications:* articles in Internat. Affairs. *Recreations:* lawn tennis, painting in watercolour. *Address:* 45 Carlisle Mansions, Carlisle Place, SW1. *Clubs:* Brooks's, Beefsteak.

CAMPBELL, Hon. Alexander Bradshaw, PC (Canada) 1967; Judge, Supreme Court of Prince Edward Island, since 1978; *b* 1 Dec. 1933; *s* of Dr Thane A. Campbell and late Cecilia B. Campbell; *m* 1961, Marilyn Gilmour; two *s* one *d*. *Educ:* Dalhousie Univ. (BA, LLB). Called to Bar of Prince Edward Island, 1959; practised law with Campbell & Campbell, Summerside, PEI, 1959–66; QC (Canada) 1966. MLA, Prince Edward Island, 1965–78; Leader of Liberal Party, Dec. 1966–78; Premier, 1966–78; served (while Premier) as Attorney-Gen., 1966–69, Minister of Development, 1969–72, Minister of Agriculture, 1972–74, and Minister of Justice, 1974–78. Dir, Inst. of Man and Resources, 1976–80. Pres., Summerside YMCA, 1981–; Founder Pres., Summerside Area Historical Soc., 1983–; Founder Chm., PEI Council, Duke of Edinburgh Awards (Canada), 1984. Elder of Trinity United Church, Summerside. Hon. LLD: McGill 1967; PEI, 1978. *Recreations:* curling, skiing, golf, boating, gardening. *Address:* 330 Beaver Street, Summerside, PEI C1N 2A3, Canada. *T:* 436–2714. *Club:* Y's Men's (Summerside).

CAMPBELL, Alexander Buchanan, ARSA; FRIBA; architect in private practice, since 1949; Senior Partner, A. Buchanan Campbell and Partners, Glasgow, since 1949; *b* 14 June 1914; *s* of Hugh Campbell and Elizabeth Flett; *m* 1939, Sheila Neville Smith; one *s* one *d*. *Educ:* Royal Technical Coll., Glasgow; Glasgow School of Art; Univ. of Strathclyde (BArch). ARSA 1973; PPRIAS. Assistant: Prof. T. Harold Hughes, 1937; G. Grey Wornum, 1938; City Architect, Glasgow, 1939; served War, Royal Engineers, 1940–46; Inspector, Inspectorate of Elect. and Mech. Equipment, 1947; Chief Technical Officer, Scottish Building Centre, 1948, Dep. Dir, 1949. Principal works include: Dollan Swimming Baths and Key Youth Centre, East Kilbride; Flats, Great Western Road, Glasgow; St Christopher's Church, Glasgow; Priesthill Church, Glasgow; St James Primary Sch., Renfrew; Callendar Park Coll. and Craigie College of Education at Falkirk and Ayr (Civic Trust Awards); High Rise Flats, Drumchapel. President: Glasgow Inst. of Architects, 1974–76; Royal Incorporation of Architects in Scotland, 1977–79. *Recreations:* music, art, golf, exhibiting show dogs. *Address:* 1 Royal Crescent, Glasgow G3 7SL. *T:* 041–332 3553. *Club:* Glasgow Art (President, 1972–74).

CAMPBELL, Prof. (Alexander) Colin (Patton), FRCPath, FRCPE; Procter Professor of Pathology and Pathological Anatomy, University of Manchester, 1950–73, now Professor Emeritus (formerly Dean, Faculty of Medicine and Pro-Vice Chancellor); formerly Director of Studies, Royal College of Pathologists; *b* 21 Feb. 1908; *s* of late A. C. Campbell, Londonderry; *m* 1943, Hon. Elisabeth Joan Adderley, 2nd *d* of 6th Baron Norton; two *s* one *d*. *Educ:* Foyle Coll., Londonderry; Edinburgh Univ. MB, ChB (Hons) Edinburgh 1930; FRCPE 1939. Rockefeller Fellow and Research Fellow in Neuropathology, Harvard Univ., 1935–36; Lectr in Neuropathology, Edinburgh Univ., 1937–39; Lectr in Pathology, Edinburgh Univ., and Pathologist, Royal Infirmary, Edinburgh, 1939–50. War service, 1940–46, RAFVR (Wing-Comdr). Hon. MSc Manchester, 1954. *Publications:* papers on pathological subjects in various medical and scientific jls. *Recreations:* carpentry and cabinet-making. *Address:* The Priory House, Ascott-under-Wychwood, Oxford OX7 6AW.

CAMPBELL, Prof. Alexander Elmslie, PhD; FRHistS; Professor of American History since 1972 (part-time since 1984) and Director of American Studies, 1972–84, University of Birmingham; *b* 12 May 1929; *s* of Rev. John Young Campbell and Emma (*née* Wickert); *m* 1st, 1956, Sophia Anne Sonne (*d* 1972); one *s* one *d*; 2nd, 1983, Juliet Jeanne d'Auvergne Collings (*see* J. J. d'A. Campbell). *Educ:* Paisley Grammar Sch.; Perse Sch., Cambridge; St John's Coll., Cambridge (MA; PhD 1956). MA Oxon 1959. FRHistS 1970. Smith-Mundt Student, Harvard Univ., 1953–54; Fellow, King's Coll., Cambridge, 1955–59; Second Sec., HM Foreign Service, 1958–60; Fellow and Tutor in Mod. Hist., Keble Coll., Oxford, 1960–72, Emeritus Fellow 1981–. Vis. Professor: Hobart and William Smith Colls, NY, 1970; Columbia Univ., 1975; Univ. of Kansas, 1976; Stanford Univ., 1977. Mem., Inst. for Advanced Study, Princeton, 1975. *Publications:* Great Britain and the United States, 1895–1903, 1960; (ed) Expansion and Imperialism, 1970; America Comes of Age: the era of Theodore Roosevelt, 1971; (ed) The USA in World Affairs, 1974; articles and reviews in collections and jls. *Address:* 3 Belbroughton Road, Oxford OX2 6UZ. *T:* Oxford 58685. *Clubs:* Athenæum; Cosmos (Washington, DC).

CAMPBELL, Archibald, CMG 1966; Assistant Under-Secretary of State, Ministry of Defence, 1969–74 (Assistant Secretary, 1967–69); *b* 10 Dec. 1914; *s* of Archibald Campbell and Jessie Sanders Campbell (*née* Halsall); *m* 1939, Peggie Phyllis Hussey; two *s* one *d*. *Educ:* Berkhamsted Sch.; Hertford Coll., Oxford. BA Oxford 1935. Barrister at Law, Middle Temple. Administrative Service, Gold Coast, 1936–46; Colonial Office, 1946;

Colonial Attaché, British Embassy, Washington, 1953–56; Asst Secretary, Colonial Office, 1956–59 and 1962–67; Chief Secretary, Malta, 1959–62. Mem., British observer team, Rhodesian Elections, 1980. *Recreations:* cricket (capped for Bucks in Minor County Competition, 1951); fishing, climbing, gardening. *Address:* Bransbury, Long Park, Chesham Bois, Bucks. *T:* Amersham 7727. *Club:* MCC.

CAMPBELL, Archibald Hunter, LLM, BCL, MA, of Lincoln's Inn, Barrister-at-Law; Regius Professor of Public Law, University of Edinburgh, 1945–72, and Dean of the Faculty of Law, 1958–64; *b* Edinburgh, 1902; *o c* of late Donald Campbell, MA. *Educ:* George Watson's Coll., Edinburgh (Dux); Univ. of Edinburgh (MA, Mackenzie Class. Schol., Ferguson Class. Schol.); University Coll., Oxford (Class. Exhibitioner). 1st Class in Hon. Mods, Lit. Hum., Jurisprudence and BCL; Sen. Demy of Magdalen Coll., 1927–28; Sen. Student of Oxford Univ., 1928; Fellow of All Souls, 1928–30 and 1936–; Stowell Civil Law Fellow, University Coll., Oxford, 1930–35; Barber Professor of Jurisprudence, Univ. of Birmingham, 1935–45. Vice-President Society of Public Teachers of Law, 1961–62, President 1962–63. President Classical Assoc. of Scotland, 1963–. Hon. LLD Aberdeen, 1963. *Address:* Portree Nursing Home, 13–15 Blantyre Terrace, Edinburgh. *Club:* New (Edinburgh).

CAMPBELL, Arthur McLure; Principal Clerk of Session and Justiciary, Scotland, since 1982; *b* 15 Aug. 1932; *s* of late Hector Brownlie Campbell, MBE, AIPA and Catherine Smylie (*née* Renwick). *Educ:* Queen's Park Sch., Glasgow. Deptl Legal Qual., Scottish Court Service, 1956. National Service, FAA, 1950–52. Admiralty Supplies Directorate, 1953–54; entered Scottish Court Service (Sheriff Clerk Br.), 1954; Sheriff Clerk Depute, Kilmarnock, 1957–60; Sheriff Clerk of Orkney, 1961–65; seconded HM Treasury (O & M), 1965–69; Principal Sheriff Clerk Depute, Glasgow, 1969; Sheriff Clerk, Airdrie, 1969–72; Principal, Scottish Court Service Staff Trng Centre, 1973–74; Asst Sheriff Clerk of Glasgow, 1974–81. Secretary: Lord Chancellor's Cttee on Re-sealing of Probates and Confirmations, 1967–68; Scottish Office Cttee on Money Transfer Services, 1968–69; Mem., Review Body on Use of Judicial Time in Superior Courts in Scotland, 1985–86. Chm., Sheriff Clerks' Assoc., 1971–72. *Address:* Parliament House, Edinburgh EH1 1RQ. *T:* 031–225 2595. *Club:* Civil Service.

CAMPBELL, Maj.-Gen. Charles Peter, CBE 1977; Director, H. & J. Quick Group Plc, since 1982; *b* 25 Aug. 1926; *s* of late Charles Alfred Campbell and Blanche Campbell; *m* 1949, Lucy Kitching (*d* 1986); two *s*. *Educ:* Gillingham Grammar Sch.; Emmanuel Coll., Cambridge. FBIM. Commnd RE, 1945; psc 1957; DAA&QMG Trng Bde, RE, 1958–60; OC 11 Indep. Field Sqdn, RE, 1960–62; Jt Services Staff Coll., 1963; DAAG WO, 1963–65; Co. Comd, RMA Sandhurst, 1965–67; CO 21 Engr Regt, 1967–70; GSOI MoD, 1970–71; CRE 3 Div., 1971; Comd 12 Engr Bde, 1972–73; RCDS, 1974; COS HQ NI, 1975–77; Engineer-in-Chief (Army), 1977–80. Col Comdt, RE, 1981–, Rep. Col Comdt, 1982; Hon. Col, RE (Vol.) (Explosive Ordnance Disposal), 1986–. Chm., RE Assoc., 1983–. *Recreations:* painting and collecting militaria. *Address:* c/o Lloyds Bank, Cox's and King's Branch, 6 Pall Mall, SW1Y 5NH. *Club:* Naval and Military.

CAMPBELL, Cheryl (Anne); actress; *b* 22 May 1949. *Educ:* Francis Bacon Grammar Sch., St Albans; London Acad. of Music and Dramatic Art (Rodney Millington Award). Formerly: student and acting Asst Stage Manager, Watford Palace Theatre; acted at Glasgow Citizens Theatre, Watford Rep., Birmingham Rep., King's Head and National Theatre; Nora in A Doll's House (SWET Award, 1983, for best actress of 1982 in a revival), and Diana in All's Well That Ends Well, RSC; title role in Miss Julie, Lyric, Hammersmith, and Duke of York's, 1983; Asta in Little Eyolf, Lyric, Hammersmith, 1985; title rôle in Daughter-in-Law, Hampstead, 1985. BBC Television serials: Pennies from Heaven; Testament of Youth (Best Actress Award, BAFTA, and British Broadcasting Press Guild Award, 1979); Malice Aforethought; A Winter Harvest. Films include Chariots of Fire, 1981; Greystoke, 1983; The Shooting Party, 1985. *Address:* c/o Hope & Lyne, 5 Milner Place, N1 1TN. *T:* 01–359 5407.

CAMPBELL, Christopher James; Executive Member, National Bus Co., since 1986; *b* 2 Jan. 1936; *s* of David Heggie Campbell and Nettie Phyllis Campbell. *Educ:* Epsom College. FCA. Debenhams and subsidiaries, 1966–86, incl. Man. Dir, Hardy Amies, 1978–79; former Director; Harvey Nichols; Lotus; Debenhams Finance; London (M & S). *Recreations:* gardening, reading, listening to music, entertaining. *Address:* 19 Morpeth Mansions, Morpeth Terrace, SW1P 1ER. *T:* 01–630 7527.

CAMPBELL, Sir Clifford (Clarence), GCMG 1962; GCVO 1966; Governor-General of Jamaica, 1962–73; *b* 28 June 1892; *s* of late James Campbell, civil servant, and Blanche, *d* of John Ruddock, agriculturist; *m* 1920, Alice Esthephene, *d* of late William Jolly, planter; two *s* two *d*. *Educ:* Petersfield Sch.; Mico Training Coll., Jamaica. Headmaster: Fullersfield Govt Sch., 1916–18; Friendship Elementary Sch., 1918–28; Grange Hill Govt Sch., 1928–44. Member Jamaica House of Representatives (Jamaica Labour Party) for Westmoreland Western, 1944–49; Chm., House Cttee on Education, 1945–49; 1st Vice-President, Elected Members Assoc., 1945; re-elected 1949; Speaker of the House of Representatives, 1950; Senator and President of the Senate, 1962. KStJ. *Recreations:* agricultural pursuits, reading. *Address:* 8 Cherry Gardens Avenue, Kingston 8, Jamaica. *Clubs:* (Hon. Member) Caymanas Golf and Country, Ex-Services, Kingston Cricket, Liguanea, Rotary, St Andrew's, Trelawny (all in Jamaica).

CAMPBELL, Colin; *see* Campbell, A. C. P.

CAMPBELL, Sir Colin Moffat, 8th Bt *cr* 1667, of Aberuchill and Kilbryde, Dunblane, Perthshire; MC 1945; Chairman: James Finlay plc, since 1975, and associated companies; *b* 4 Aug. 1925; *e s* of Sir John Campbell, 7th Bt and Janet Moffat (*d* 1975); *S* father, 1960; *m* 1952, Mary Anne Chichester Bain, *er d* of Brigadier G. A. Bain, Sandy Lodge, Chagford, Devon; two *s* (one *d* decd). *Educ:* Stowe. Scots Guards, 1943–47, Captain. Employed with James Finlay & Co. Ltd, Calcutta, 1948–58, Nairobi, 1958–71, Dir, 1971–, Dep. Chm., 1973–75. President Federation of Kenya Employers, 1962–70; Chairman: Tea Board of Kenya, 1961–71; E African Tea Trade Assoc., 1960–61, 1962–63, 1966–67. Member: Scottish Council, CBI, 1979–85; Council, CBI, 1981–; Commonwealth Develt Corp., 1981– (Dep. Chm., 1983–). CBIM 1980; FRSA 1982. *Recreations:* gardening, racing, cards. *Heir: s* James Alexander Moffat Bain Campbell, *b* 23 Sept. 1956. *Address:* Kilbryde Castle, Dunblane, Perthshire. *T:* Dunblane 823104. *Clubs:* Boodle's; Western (Glasgow); Royal Calcutta Turf, Tollygunge (Calcutta); Nairobi, Muthaiga (E Africa).

CAMPBELL, David John G.; *see* Graham-Campbell.

CAMPBELL, Prof. Donald, FFARCS; FRCS; FFARCSI; FRCPGlas; Professor of Anaesthesia, University of Glasgow, since 1976; *b* 8 March 1930; *s* of Archibald Peter and Mary Campbell; *m* 1st, 1954, Nancy Rebecca McKintosh (decd); one *s* one *d*; 2nd, 1975, Catherine Conway Bradburn; two *d*. *Educ:* Hutchesons' Boys' Grammar Sch.; Univ. of Glasgow (MB, ChB). Lectr in Anaesthesia, 1959–60, Cons. Anaesthetist, 1960–76, Royal Inf., Glasgow. Vice-Dean, 1981–82, Dean, 1982–85, Faculty of Anaesthetists, RCS; Vice-Pres., RCS, 1985–July 1987. Chm., Scottish Council for Postgrad. Med. Educn, 1985–. *Publications:* A Nurse's Guide to Anaesthetics, Resuscitation and Intensive Care, 1964, 7th edn 1983; Anaesthetics, Resuscitation and Intensive Care, 1965, 6th edn 1985; contribs to med. jls, mainly on anaesthesia and intensive therapy. *Recreations:* angling, curling. *Address:* Novar, 27 Tannoch Drive, Milngavie, Glasgow G62 8AR. *T:* 041–956 1736.

CAMPBELL, Donald le Strange, MC; Chairman, Harvest Hydroponics Ltd; Director: Project Services Overseas Ltd; Hovair Systems Ltd; Beechdean Farms; *b* 16 June 1919; *s* of late Donald Fraser Campbell and of Caroline Campbell, Heacham, Norfolk; *m* 1952, Hon. Shona Catherine Greig Macpherson, *y d* of 1st Baron Macpherson of Drumochter; one *s* one *d*. *Educ:* Winchester Coll.; Clare Coll., Cambridge. Served War, 1939–45, Major RA (MC). EFCO Ltd, 1947–55; MEECO Ltd, 1955–61; Davy-Ashmore Ltd, 1961–67. Dep. Chairman, BNEC Latin America, 1967. *Recreations:* farming, sailing, field sports. *Address:* Bagnor Manor, Newbury, Berks RG16 8AJ. *Clubs:* Buck's; Royal Yacht Squadron.

CAMPBELL, Prof. Fergus William, FRS 1978; Professor of Neurosensory Physiology, Physiological Laboratory, University of Cambridge, since 1983; Fellow of St John's College, Cambridge, since 1955; *b* 30 Jan. 1924; *s* of William Campbell and Anne Fleming; *m* 1948, Helen Margaret Cunningham; one *s* two *d* (and one *d* decd). *Educ:* Univ. of Glasgow (MA, MD, PhD, DOMS). Casualty and Eye Resident Surg., Western Infirmary, Glasgow, 1946–47; Asst, Inst. of Physiol., Glasgow, 1947–49, Lectr, 1949–52; Res. Graduate, Nuffield Lab. of Ophthalmology, Oxford, 1952–53; Univ. Lectr, 1953–72, Reader in Neurosensory Physiol., 1973–83, Physiol Lab., Cambridge; Hon. Prof., Dept of Optometry, UWIST, 1984–. Hon. FBOA 1962. Hon. DSc Glasgow, 1986. Tillyer Medal, Optical Soc. of America, 1980. *Publications:* papers on neurophysiology and psychophysics of vision in Jl Physiol., and Vision Res. *Recreations:* music, photography. *Address:* 96 Queen Ediths Way, Cambridge CB1 4PP. *T:* Cambridge 247578.

CAMPBELL, Graham Gordon, CB 1984; Under-Secretary, Department of Energy, 1974–84; *b* 12 Dec. 1924; *s* of late Lt-Col and Mrs P. H. Campbell; *m* 1955, Margaret Rosamond Busby; one *d*. *Educ:* Cheltenham Coll.; Caius Coll., Cambridge (BA Hist.). Served War, Royal Artillery, 1943–46. Asst Principal, Min. of Fuel and Power, 1949; Private Sec. to Parly Sec., Min. of Fuel and Power, 1953–54; Principal, 1954; Asst Sec., Min. of Power, 1965; Under-Sec., DTI, 1973. *Recreations:* watching birds, music, hill-walking. *Address:* 3 Clovelly Avenue, Warlingham, Surrey CR3 9HZ. *T:* Upper Warlingham 4671.

CAMPBELL, Sir Guy (Theophilus Halswell), 5th Bt *cr* 1815; OBE 1954; MC 1941; Colonel, late 60th Rifles, El Kaimakam Bey, Camel Corps, Sudan Defence Force, and Kenya Regiment; *b* 18 Jan. 1910; *s* of Major Sir Guy Colin Campbell, 4th Bt, late 60th Rifles, and Mary Arabella Swinnerton Kemeys-Tynte, *sister* of 8th Lord Wharton; *S* father, 1960; *m* 1956, Lizbeth Webb, Bickenhall Mansions, W1; two *s*. *Educ:* St Aubyn's, Rottingdean; Eton Coll.; St Andrews Univ. War of 1939–45 (wounded); served in KOYLI, 1931–42; seconded to Camel Corps, Sudan Defence Force, 1939–47; Comd 2/7 and 7 Nuba Bns, 1943–47; Shifta Ops, Eritrea, 1946; Acting Brig., 1945, HQ SDF Group (N Africa); Palestine, 1948; Mil. Adviser to Count Folke Bernadotte and Dr Ralph Bunche of United Nations, 1948; attached British Embassy as Civil Affairs Officer, Cairo, 1948; British Mil. Mission to Ethiopia, in Ogaden Province, 1949–51; 2nd i/c 1/60th Rifles, BAOR, 1951; comd Kenya Regt (TF), 1952–56, Mau Mau ops; Head of British Mil. Mission to Libya, 1956–60; retired Aug. 1960. MoD, 1965–72. Col R of O, 60th Rifles. Provided historical research, costume, weapons etc for United Artists film Khartoum, 1964. C-in-C's (MELF) Commendation, 1945; Gold Medal of Emperor Haile Selassie (non-wearable). *Recreations:* painting, writing, watching cricket, Rugby football, golf. *Heir: s* Lachlan Philip Kemeys Campbell, The Royal Green Jackets [*b* 9 Oct. 1958; *m* 1986, Harriet Jane Sarah, *o d* of F. E. J. Girling, Malvern]. *Address:* The Hermitage, Padbury, Buckingham. *Clubs:* Army and Navy, Special Forces; Puffins (Edinburgh); MCC, I Zingari; Royal and Ancient (St Andrews).

CAMPBELL, Maj.-Gen. Sir Hamish Manus, KBE 1963 (CBE 1958); CB 1961; Rev. Brother Hamish, Order of Prémontré (White Canons), since 1984; *b* 6 Jan. 1905; *s* of late Major A. C. J. Campbell, Middlesex Regt and Army Pay Dept, and of Alice, *d* of late Comdr Yelverton O'Keeffe, RN; *m* 1929, Marcelle (*d* 1983), *d* of late Charles Ortlieb, Neuchâtel, Switzerland; one *s*. *Educ:* Downside School; New Coll., Oxford. Commissioned in Argyll and Sutherland Highlanders, 1927; transferred to Royal Army Pay Corps, 1937; Lieut-Colonel and Staff Paymaster (1st Class), temp. 1945, subs. 1951; Colonel and Chief Paymaster, temp. 1954, subs. 1955; Major-General, 1959. Command Paymaster: Sierra Leone, 1940–42; Burma, 1946–48; Malta, 1953. Deputy Chief, Budget and Finance Division, SHAPE, 1954–56; Commandant, RAPC Training Centre, 1956–59; Paymaster-in-Chief, War Office, 1959–63; retired, 1963. Col Comdt, RAPC, 1963–70. *Address:* Our Lady of England Priory, Storrington, Pulborough, West Sussex RH20 4LN. *T:* Storrington 2150.

CAMPBELL, Harold Edward; Director, Greater London Secondary Housing Association, 1978–83; Chairman, Sutton (Hastoe) Housing Association, 1975–85; *b* 28 Feb. 1915; *s* of Edward Inkerman Campbell and Florence Annie Campbell. *Educ:* Southbury Road Elementary Sch.; Enfield Central Sch. Asst Sec., 1946–64, Sec., 1964–67, Cooperative Party; Mem., 1967–73, Dep. Chm., 1969–73, Housing Corp. Gen. Manager, Newlon Housing Trust, 1970–76; Chairman: Cooperative Planning Ltd, 1964–74; Co-Ownership Develt Soc. Ltd, 1966–76; Sutton Housing Trust, 1973–80 (Trustee, 1967–); Dir, Co-op. Housing Centre, and S British Housing Assoc., 1976–78; Dep. Chm., Stevenage Develt Corp., 1968–80; Mem., Cooperative Develt Agency, 1978–81; Pres., Enfield Highway Cooperative Soc. Ltd, 1976–85 (Dir, 1965–); Dir, CWS Ltd, 1968–73. Chairman: DoE Working Party on Cooperative Housing, 1973–75; DoE Working Group on New Forms of Housing Tenure, 1976–77; Housing Assoc. Registration Adv. Cttee, 1974–79; Hearing Aid Council, 1970–71. Borough Councillor, Enfield, 1959–63. *Recreations:* music, theatre, cinema. *Address:* 235B Kennington Lane, SE11 5QU. *Club:* Sloane.

CAMPBELL, Hugh, PhD; Career Consultant in Paris and London, since 1974; *b* 24 Oct. 1916; *s* of Hugh Campbell and Annie C. Campbell (*née* Spence); *m* 1946, Sybil Marian Williams, MB, ChB, *y d* of Benjamin and Sarah Williams; two *s*. *Educ:* University College Sch., London; St John's Coll., Cambridge (MA, PhD). Research, Dept of Colloid Science, Cambridge, 1938–45; Head of Physical Chem., Research Gp, May and Baker Ltd, 1945–61; Lectr, West Ham Techn. Coll., 1949–54; Research Manager, Chloride Electrical Storage Co. Ltd, 1961–65; Managing Dir: Alkaline Batteries Ltd, 1965–67; Electric Power Storage Ltd, 1968–71; Dir, Chloride Electrical Storage Co. Ltd, 1968–71; Industrial Advr, DTI, 1971–74. *Publications:* papers on various subjects in scientific jls. *Recreations:* skiing, theatre, travelling. *Address:* 4 The Courtyard, Barnsbury Terrace, N1 1JZ. *T:* 01–607 3834.

CAMPBELL, Hugh Hall, QC (Scot.) 1983; *b* 18 Feb. 1944; *s* of William Wright Campbell and Marianne Doris Stuart Hutchison or Campbell; *m* 1969, Eleanor Jane Hare; three *s*. *Educ:* Glasgow Acad.; Trinity Coll., Glenalmond (Alexander Cross Scholar); Exeter Coll., Oxford (Open Scholar in Classics; BA Hons, MA); Edinburgh Univ. (LLB Hons). FCIArb 1986. Called to the Scottish Bar, 1969; Standing Jun. Counsel to

Admiralty, 1976. *Recreations:* music, hill-walking, golf. *Address:* 12 Ainslie Place, Edinburgh EH3 6AS. *T:* 031-225 2067. *Club:* Hon. Company of Edinburgh Golfers.

CAMPBELL, Ian, CEng, MIMechE, JP; MP (Lab) Dumbarton, since 1983 (Dunbartonshire (West), 1970–83); *b* 26 April 1926; *s* of William Campbell and Helen Crockett; *m* 1950, Mary Millar; two *s* three *d. Educ:* Dumbarton Academy; Royal Technical Coll., Glasgow (now Strathclyde Univ.). Engineer with South of Scotland Electricity Board for 17 years. Councillor, Dumbarton, 1958–70; Provost of Dumbarton, 1962–70. PPS to Sec. of State for Scotland, 1976–79. *Address:* The Shanacles, Gartocharn, Alexandria, Dunbartonshire. *T:* Alexandria 52286.

CAMPBELL, Ian Burns; His Honour Judge Ian Campbell; a Circuit Judge, since 1984; *b* 7 July 1938; *s* of late James Campbell and of Laura Woolnough Dransfield; *m* 1967, Mary Elisabeth Poole, BArch, MCD Liverpool; two *s* one *d. Educ:* Tiffin Boys' Sch.; Cambridge Univ. (MA, LLM, PhD). Called to the Bar, Middle Temple, 1966. French Govt Scholar, 1961–62; Asst Lectr in Law, Liverpool Univ., 1962–64, Lectr 1964–69; a Recorder, 1981–84. *Recreation:* cycling.

CAMPBELL, Ian Dugald, QHP 1977; FRCPE, FFCM; Treasurer, Royal College of Physicians of Edinburgh, 1981–85; *b* Dornie, Kintail, 22 Feb. 1916; *s* of John Campbell and Margaret Campbell; *m* 1943, Joan Carnegie Osborn; one *s* two *d. Educ:* Dingwall Acad.; Edinburgh Univ. (MB, ChB 1939). FRCPE 1973, FFCM 1974. Served War, 1941–46: UK, BAOR, MEF, RAMC; final appt OC Field Amb. (Lt-Col). Med. Supt, St Luke's Hosp., Bradford, 1946–49; Asst SMO, Leeds Reg. Hosp. Bd, 1949–57; Dep. Sen. Admin. MO, S-Eastern Reg. Hosp. Bd, Scotland, 1957–72, Sen. Admin. MO, 1972–73; Chief Admin. MO, Lothian Health Bd, 1973–80. WHO assignments, SE Asia, 1969, 1971, 1975. *Publications:* various medical. *Recreations:* fishing, shooting, golf. *Address:* 5 Succoth Park, Edinburgh EH12 6BX. *T:* 031–337 5965. *Clubs:* New (Edinburgh); Hon. Company of Edinburgh Golfers (Muirfield); Royal Burgess Golfing Society (Barnton, Edinburgh).

CAMPBELL, Ian George Hallyburton, TD; QC 1957; Lord Chancellor's Legal Visitor, 1963–79; *b* 19 July 1909; *s* of late Hon. Kenneth Campbell and Mrs K. Campbell; *m* 1949, Betty Yolande, *d* of late Somerset Maclean and *widow* of Lt-Col Allan Bruno, MBE; one adopted *s* one adopted *d. Educ:* Charterhouse, Trinity Coll., Cambridge. Barrister, Inner Temple and Lincoln's Inn, 1932. Served Artists Rifles and Rifle Brigade, 1939–45; Col 1945. Appts include: GSO2, HQ 1st Army; Chief Judicial Officer, Allied Commission, Italy; Chief Legal Officer, Military Govt, Austria (British zone). *Address:* Flat 26, The Abbey, Amesbury, Wilts. *T:* Amesbury 22612.

CAMPBELL, Ian James; defence and marine technology consultant; Technical Director, CAP Scientific, since 1983; *b* 9 June 1923; *s* of Allan and Elizabeth Campbell; *m* 1946, Stella Margaret Smith. *Educ:* George Heriot's Sch.; Edinburgh Univ. (MA). Op. Res. Sect., HQ Bomber Comd, 1943–46; Asst Lectr in Astronomy, St Andrews Univ., 1946–48; Royal Naval Scientific Service, 1948; Dept of Aeronaut. and Eng Res., Admiralty, 1948–49; Admiralty Res. Lab., 1949–59; Admiralty Underwater Weapons Estab., 1959–68; Chief Scientist, Naval Construction Res. Estab., 1969–73; Head of Weapons Dept, Admiralty Underwater Weapons Estab., 1973–76; Ministry of Defence: Dir of Res. (Ships), 1976–78; Scientific Advr to Ship Dept, 1976–81; Dir Gen. Res. Maritime, 1978–81. *Publications:* papers on fluid mechanics in scientific jls. *Address:* Claremont, North Street, Charminster, Dorchester, Dorset. *T:* Dorchester 64270.

CAMPBELL, Ian Macdonald, CVO 1977; BSc; FEng; FICE; FCIT; Part-time Member, British Railways Board, since 1983; Chairman, Scottish Board, British Rail, since 1983; *b* 13 July 1922; *s* of late John Isdale Campbell; *m* 1946, Hilda Ann Williams; one *s* three *d. Educ:* University Coll., London (Fellow, 1984). BSc(Eng). British Rail: District Engr, Kings Cross, 1957–63; Chief Civil Engr, Scottish Region, 1968–70; Gen. Manager, E Region, 1970–73; Exec. Dir, BR, 1973–76; Chief Exec. (Railways), BRB, 1978–80, Exec. Mem. for Engrg and Research, 1977–80; Vice-Chm., BRB, 1980–83. Chm., British Rail Engineering, 1977–79. Mem., Economic and Social Cttee, EEC, 1983–. Pres., ICE, 1981–82 (Vice-Pres., 1978–81). *Recreations:* golf, music. *Address:* Lochearnside, St Fillans, Perthshire.

CAMPBELL, Mrs Ian McIvor; *see* Corbet, Mrs Freda K.

CAMPBELL, Air Vice-Marshal Ian Robert, CB 1976; CBE 1964; AFC 1948; *b* 5 Oct. 1920; *s* of late Major and Hon. Mrs D. E. Campbell; *m* 1st, 1953, Beryl Evelyn Newbigging (*d* 1982); one *s*; 2nd, 1984, Elizabeth Owen. *Educ:* Eton; RAF Coll., Cranwell. Anti-Shipping Ops, 1940–42; POW, Italy and Germany, 1942–45; 540 Sqdn, Benson, 1946; psa 1949; PSO to C-in-C Far East, 1950; 124 (F) Wing Oldenburg, 1953; OC, RAF Sandwich, 1956; pfc 1957; OC 213 Sqdn, Bruggen, 1958; ACOS Plans HQ 2ATAF, 1959; OC, RAF Marham, 1961; MoD (Air) DASB, 1964; SASO, HQ No 1 Group, 1965; Air Attaché, Bonn, 1968; Dir of Management and Support Intell., MoD, 1970–73; C of S, No 18 (M) Group, Strike Command, 1973–75, retired. *Recreations:* shooting, travel. *Address:* Poulton House, Cirencester, Glos. *Clubs:* Boodle's, Royal Air Force.

CAMPBELL, Maj.-Gen. Ian Ross, CBE 1954; DSO and Bar, 1941; *b* 23 March 1900; *m* 1927, Patience Allison Russell (*d* 1961); one *d*; *m* 1967, Irene Cardamatis. *Educ:* Wesley Coll., Melbourne; Scots Coll., Sydney; Royal Military College, Duntroon, Canberra (Sword of Honour, 1922). psc Camberley, 1936–37. Served War of 1939–45, Middle East Campaigns, Libya, Greece and Crete (DSO and bar, Cross of Kt Comdr, Greek Order of Phœnix; pow 1941–45); comd Aust. forces in Korean War, 1951–53 (CBE); Comdt, Australian Staff Coll., 1953–54; Comdt, Royal Mil. Coll. Duntroon, 1954–57; retired, 1957, Mem. Federal Exec., RSL, 1955–56. Chm., NSW Div., Aust. Red Cross Soc., 1967–74. Pres., Great Public Schs Athletic Assoc., NSW, 1966–69. Hon. Col, NSW Scottish Regt, 1957–60. *Recreation:* reading. *Address:* 15/17 Wylde Street, Potts Point, Sydney, NSW 2011, Australia. *Clubs:* Australian, Royal Sydney Golf (Sydney).

CAMPBELL, Sir Ilay (Mark), 7th Bt *cr* 1808, of Succoth, Dunbartonshire; *b* 29 May 1927; *o s* of Sir George Ilay Campbell, 6th Bt; *S* father, 1967; *m* 1961, Margaret Minette Rohais, *o d* of J. Alasdair Anderson; two *d. Educ:* Eton; Christ Church, Oxford. BA 1952. Joint Scottish Agent for Messrs Christie, Manson & Woods; Chm., Christie's & Edmistons, Glasgow. Pres., Assoc. for Protection of Rural Scotland. *Recreations:* heraldry, collecting heraldic bookplates, horticulture. *Heir:* none. *Address:* Crarae Lodge, Inveraray, Argyll PA32 8YA. *T:* Minard 86274; Swiss Cottage, Coldstream, Berwickshire TD12 4EX. *T:* Coldstream 2254. *Clubs:* Turf; Arts (Glasgow).

CAMPBELL, James, FBA 1984; FSA 1971; Fellow of Worcester College, since 1957 and Lecturer in Modern History, since 1958, Oxford University; *b* 26 Jan. 1935. *Educ:* Mill Road Mixed Infants, Clowne, Derbyshire and other primary schools; Lowestoft Grammar School; Magdalen College (Exhibitioner; BA 1955, MA). Junior Research Fellow, Merton College, 1956–57; Worcester College: Tutorial Fellow, 1957; Senior Proctor, 1973–74; Fellow Librarian, 1977–. Vis. Prof., Univ. of South Carolina, 1969. *Publications:* Norwich, 1975; (ed) The Anglo-Saxons, 1982; articles in learned jls. *Recreation:* topography. *Address:* Worcester College, Oxford. *T:* Oxford 247251. *Club:* United Oxford & Cambridge University.

CAMPBELL, James Grant, CMG 1970; Consultant to Atlantic Division, Alcan Aluminium Ltd; *b* Springville, NS, Canada, 8 June 1914; *s* of John Kay Campbell and Wilna Archibald Campbell (*née* Grant); *m* 1941, Alice Isobel Dougall; one *d. Educ:* Mount Allison Univ., Canada. BSc, 1st cl. hons (Chem.). Chemical Engineer, Aluminium Co. of Canada, Arvida, Que, 1937–41; Demerara Bauxite Co. Ltd, Guyana, Gen. Supt, 1941–50; Aluminium Laboratories Ltd, London, England, 1950 (Headqrs for team investigating hydro power, bauxite and aluminium smelting in Asia, Africa and Europe); on staff of Dir of Operations, Aluminium Ltd, Montreal (concerned with world supply of raw materials for Aluminium Ltd), 1951–55; Managing Dir and Chm., Demerara Bauxite Co., Guyana, 1955–71; Vice-Pres., Alcan Ore Ltd, 1971–77; Overseas Representative, Alcan International Ltd, Montreal, 1977–79. Mem. Bd of Regents, Mount Allison Univ., 1972. LLD Mount Allison Univ., 1966. *Recreation:* golf. *Address:* 45 Eaton Square, SW1W 9BD. *Clubs:* Brooks's, Travellers', Oriental; University (New York); University (Montreal).

CAMPBELL, John Davies, CVO 1980; CBE 1981 (MBE 1957); MC 1945, and bar 1945; company director; HM Diplomatic Service, retired; Consul-General, Naples, 1977–81; *b* 11 Nov. 1921; *s* of late William Hastings Campbell and of late The Hon. Mrs Campbell (Eugenie Anne Westenra, subsequently Harbord), *d* of 14th Baron Louth; *m* 1959, Shirley Bouch; one *s* two *d. Educ:* Cheltenham Coll.; St Andrews Univ. Served War, HM Forces, Argyll and Sutherland Highlanders and Popski's Private Army, 1940–46. HM Colonial Service (subseq. HMOCS), 1949–61 (despatches, 1957); HM Foreign (subseq. HM Diplomatic) Service, 1961; First Secretary, 1961; Counsellor, 1972; Counsellor (Information) Ottawa, 1972–77. Commendatore dell'ordine al merito della Repubblica Italiana, 1980. *Recreations:* golf, tennis. *Address:* Ridgeway, The Ludlow Road, Leominster, Herefordshire HR6 0DH. *T:* Leominster 2446. *Clubs:* Special Forces; Muthaiga Country (Nairobi) (Life Mem.); Mombasa.

CAMPBELL, John L.; owner of Heiskeir and Humla, of the Small Isles; formerly owner of Isle of Canna, which he presented to National Trust for Scotland, 1981; farmer (retired) and author; *b* 1 Oct. 1906; *e s* of late Col Duncan Campbell of Inverneill and Ethel Harriet, *e d* of late John I. Waterbury, Morristown, NJ; *m* 1935, Margaret Fay, *y d* of Henry Clay Shaw, Glenshaw, Pennsylvania (US), author; no *c. Educ:* Cargilfield; Rugby; St John's Coll., Oxford (Dipl. Rural Economy 1930; MA 1933, DLitt 1965). Sec., Barra Sea League, 1933–38. Curator of Woods on Isle of Canna for Nat. Trust for Scotland. Hon. LLD, St Francis Xavier Univ., Antigonish, NS, 1953; Hon. DLitt, Glasgow Univ., 1965. *Publications include:* Highland Songs of the Forty-Five, 1933, 2nd edn 1984; The Book of Barra (with Compton Mackenzie and Carl Hj. Borgstrom), 1936; Act Now for the Highlands and Islands (with Sir Alexander MacEwen, in which creation of Highland Develt Bd suggested for first time), 1939; Gaelic in Scottish Education and Life, 1945, 2nd edn 1950; Fr. Allan McDonald of Eriskay, Priest, Poet and Folklorist, 1954; Tales from Barra, told by the Coddy, 1960; Stories from South Uist, 1961; The Furrow Behind Me, 1962; Edward Lhuyd in the Scottish Highlands (with Prof. Derick Thomson), 1963; A School in South Uist (memoirs of Frederick Rea), 1964; Gaelic Poems of Fr. Allan McDonald, 1965; Strange Things (story of SPR enquiry into Highland second sight, with Trevor H. Hall), 1968; Hebridean Folksongs (waulking songs from South Uist and Barra) (with F. Collinson), vol. i, 1969, vol. ii, 1977, vol. iii, 1981; Canna, the Story of a Hebridean Island, 1984; other pubns and articles on Highland history and Gaelic oral tradition, also on Hebridean entomology. *Recreations:* entomology, sea fishing, chamber music. *Address:* Canna House, Isle of Canna, Scotland PH44 4RS.

CAMPBELL, (John) Quentin; Metropolitan Stipendiary Magistrate, since 1981; *b* 5 March 1939; *s* of late John McKnight Campbell, OBE, MC, and late Katharine Margaret Campbell; *m* 1st, Penelope Jane Redman (marr. diss. 1976); three *s* one *d*; 2nd, 1977, Ann Rosemary Beeching; one *s* one *d. Educ:* Loretto Sch., Musselburgh, Scotland; Wadham Coll., Oxford (MA). Admitted as Solicitor, 1965; private practice, Linnell & Murphy, Oxford (Partner, 1968–80). Chairman, Bd of Governors, Bessels Leigh Sch., near Oxford, 1979–. *Recreations:* opera, gardening, golf. *Address:* 12 Park Town, Oxford OX2 6SH. *T:* Oxford 56269. *Clubs:* Chelsea Arts; Frewen (Oxford).

CAMPBELL, Juliet Jeanne d'Auvergne; HM Diplomatic Service; Head of Training Department, Foreign and Commonwealth Office, since 1984; *b* 23 May 1935; *d* of Maj.-Gen. Wilfred d'Auvergne Collings, CB, CBE and of Nancy Draper Bishop; *m* 1983, Prof. Alexander Elmslie Campbell, *qv. Educ:* a variety of schools; Lady Margaret Hall, Oxford. BA. Joined Foreign Office 1957; Common Market Delegation, Brussels, 1961–63; FO, 1963–64; Second, later First Secretary, Bangkok, 1964–66; News Dept, FO, 1967–70; Head of Chancery, The Hague, 1970–74; European Integration Dept, FCO, 1974–77; Counsellor (Inf.), Paris, 1977–80; RCDS, 1981; Counsellor, Jakarta, 1982–83. *Address:* c/o Foreign and Commonwealth Office, SW1. *Club:* United Oxford & Cambridge University.

CAMPBELL, Air Vice-Marshal Kenneth Archibald; Air Officer Maintenance, RAF Support Command, since 1987; *b* 3 May 1936; *s* of John McLean and Christina Campbell; *m* 1959, Isobel Love Millar; two *d. Educ:* George Heriot's Sch.; Glasgow Univ. (BSc); College of Aeronautics, Cranfield (MSc). Various engrg appts, RAF, 1959–; Air Officer, Wales, 1977–79; Dir, Engrg Policy (RAF), 1981–83; AO, Engrg and Supply, RAF Germany, 1983–85; DG, Personal Services (RAF), 1985–87. *Recreations:* golf, skiing. *Club:* Royal Air Force.

CAMPBELL, Laurence Jamieson; Headmaster, Kingswood School, Bath, since 1970; *b* 10 June 1927; *er s* of George S. Campbell and Mary P. Paterson; *m* 1954, Sheena E. Macdonald; two *s* one *d. Educ:* Hillhead High Sch., Glasgow; Aberdeen Univ., Edinburgh Univ. (MA). Lieut RA, 1945–48. Housemaster, Alliance High Sch., Kenya, 1952–56; Educn Sec., Christian Council of Kenya, 1957–62; Headmaster, Alliance High Sch., Kenya, 1963–70. Contested North Kenya Constituency, Kenya General Election, 1961. Mem. Council, Univ. of East Africa, 1963–69; Chm., Heads Assoc. of Kenya, 1965–69; Official of Kenya Commonwealth Games Team, 1970. Schoolmaster Fellow, Balliol Coll., Oxford, 1970. Chairman: Christians Abroad, 1977–81; Bloxham Project, 1981–. *Recreations:* golf, athletics, church. *Address:* Kingswood School, Bath, Avon BA1 5RG. *T:* Bath 311627. *Club:* Royal Commonwealth Society.

CAMPBELL, Leila; Chairman, Inner London Education Authority, 1977–78; *b* 10 Aug. 1911; *d* of Myer and Rebecca Jaffe; *m* 1940, Andrew Campbell (*d* 1968); one *d. Educ:* Belvedere Sch., Liverpool. Art Teacher's Dip. Dress designer, 1932–42; catering, 1942–46. Elected (Lab), Hampstead Bor. Council, 1961–65; elected new London Bor. of Camden, 1964–78 (later Alderman): Mem., Social Services Cttee; Chm., Libraries and Arts Cttee; elected LCC for Holborn and S St Pancras, 1958–65; elected GLC for Camden, 1964–67: Chm., Schools Sub-cttee; Rep. Camden on ILEA, 1970–78: Vice-Chm., Schs Cttee; Vice-Chm. of ILEA, 1967–77. *Recreations:* cooking, theatre, opera, jazz. *Address:* 56 Belsize Park, NW3 4EH. *T:* 01-722 7038.

CAMPBELL of Airds, Brig. Lorne Maclaine, VC 1943; DSO 1940; OBE 1968; TD 1941; Argyll and Sutherland Highlanders (TA); *b* 22 July 1902; *s* of late Col Ian Maxwell Campbell, CBE and Hilda Mary Wade; *m* 1935, Amy Muriel Jordan (*d* 1950), *d* of Alastair Magnus Campbell, Auchendarroch, Argyll; two *s*. *Educ:* Dulwich Coll.; Merton Coll., Oxford (Postmaster, MA). 8th Bn Argyll and Sutherland Highlanders, 1921–42, commanded 7th Bn, 1942–43, and 13th Inf. Brigade, 1943–44; BGS, British Army Staff, Washington, 1944–45; War of 1939–45: despatches four times, DSO and Bar, VC. Hon. Col 8th Bn Argyll and Sutherland Highlanders, 1954–67. Past Master of Vintners' Company (Hon. Vintner). Officer US Legion of Merit. *Address:* 95 Trinity Road, Edinburgh EH5 3JX. *T:* 031–552 6851. *Club:* New (Edinburgh).

CAMPBELL, Sir Matthew, KBE 1963; CB 1959; FRSE; Deputy Chairman, White Fish Authority, and Chairman, Authority's Committee for Scotland and Northern Ireland, 1968–78; *b* 23 May 1907; *s* of late Matthew Campbell, High Blantyre; *m* 1939, Isabella, *d* of late John Wilson, Rutherglen; two *s*. *Educ:* Hamilton Academy; Glasgow Univ. Entered CS, 1928, and after service in Inland Revenue Dept and Admiralty joined staff of Dept of Agriculture for Scotland, 1935; Principal, 1938; Assistant Sec., 1943; Under Sec., 1953; Sec., Dept of Agriculture and Fisheries for Scotland, 1958–68. *Address:* 10 Craigleith View, Edinburgh. *T:* 031–337 5168.

CAMPBELL, Sir Niall (Alexander Hamilton), 8th Bt *cr* 1831, of Barcaldine and Glenure; 15th Chieftain, Hereditary Keeper of Barcaldine Castle; Clerk to Justices of N Devon Divisions of Barnstaple, Bideford and Great Torrington and South Molton, since 1976; *b* 7 Jan. 1925; *o s* of Sir Ian Vincent Hamilton Campbell, 7th Bt, CB, and Madeline Lowe Reid (*d* 1929), *e d* of late Hugh Anglin Whitelocke, FRCS; *S* father, 1978; *m* 1st, 1949, Patricia Mary (marr. diss. on his petition, 1956), *d* of R. G. Turner; 2nd, 1957, Norma Joyce, *d* of W. N. Wiggin; two *s* two *d* (including twin *s* and *d*). *Educ:* Cheltenham College (Scholar); Corpus Christi Coll., Oxford. Called to the Bar, Inner Temple. Served War, 1943–46, Lieut Royal Marines; in Inf. bn, NW Europe campaign and on staff of Comdr RM training bde. Appts as Hosp. Administrator, 1953–70, inside and outside NHS, including St Mary's, Paddington, London Clinic, and Royal Hosp. and Home for Incurables, Putney (Chief Exec.); Dep. Chief Clerk, Inner London Magistrates' Courts, 1970–76, and Dep. Coroner, Inner London (South), Southwark. Mem. Exec. Cttee, N Devon Community Health Council; Governor, Grenville Coll., Bideford; Mem. Management Cttee, N Devon Cheshire Home. *Publication:* Making the Best Use of Bed Resources—monograph based on lecture sponsored by King Edward's Hospital Fund, 1965. *Recreations:* village life, vegetable gardening, birds. *Heir: er s* Roderick Duncan Hamilton Campbell, of Barcaldine, Younger, *b* 24 Feb. 1961. *Address:* The Old Mill, Milltown, Muddiford, Barnstaple, Devon. *T:* Shirwell 341; The Law Courts, Civic Centre, Barnstaple. *T:* Barnstaple 72511; (seat) Barcaldine Castle, Benderloch via Connel, Argyllshire.

CAMPBELL, Prof. Peter Nelson; Courtauld Professor of Biochemistry, and Director of the Courtauld Institute, Middlesex Hospital Medical School, London University, since 1976; *b* 5 Nov. 1921; *s* of late Alan A. Campbell and Nora Nelson; *m* 1946, Mollie (*née* Manklow); one *s* one *d*. *Educ:* Eastbourne Coll.; Univ. Coll., London (Fellow, 1981). BSc, PhD, DSc, London; FIBiol. Research and Production Chemist with Standard Telephones and Cables, Ltd, 1942–46; PhD Student, UCL; 1946–47; Asst Lectr UCL, 1947–49; staff of Nat. Inst. for Med. Research, Hampstead and Mill Hill, 1949–54; Asst, Courtauld Inst. of Biochem., Middx Hosp. Med. Sch., 1954–57; Sen. Lectr, Middx Hosp. Med. Sch., 1957–64; Reader in Biochem., Univ. of London, 1964–67; Prof. and Head of Dept of Biochem., Leeds Univ., 1967–75. Editor in Chief, Biotechnology and Applied Biochemistry, 1981–. Hon. Lectr, Dept of Biochem., UCL, 1954–67. Fellow UCL, 1981. Diplôme d'Honneur, Fedn of European Biochemical Socs. *Publications:* Structure and Function of Animal Cell Components, 1966; (ed with B. A. Kilby) Basic Biochemistry for Medical Students, 1975; (ed) Biology in Profile, 1981; (with A. D. Smith) Biochemistry Illustrated, 1982, 2nd edn 1987; many scientific papers in Biochem. Jl. *Recreations:* theatre, travelling, conversation. *Address:* Department of Biochemistry, The Middlesex Hospital Medical School, W1P 7PN. *T:* 01–380 9498.

CAMPBELL, Prof. Peter (Walter); Professor of Politics, Reading University, since 1964; *b* 17 June 1926; *o s* of late W. C. H. Campbell and of L. M. Locke. *Educ:* Bournemouth Sch.; New Coll., Oxford. 2nd class PPE, 1947; MA 1951; Research Student, Nuffield Coll., Oxford, 1947–49. Asst Lecturer in Govt, Manchester Univ., 1949–52; Lectr, 1952–60; Vice-Warden Needham Hall, 1959–60; Visiting Lectr in Political Science, Victoria Univ. Coll., NZ, 1954; Prof. of Political Economy, 1960–64, Dean, Faculty of Letters, 1966–69, Chm., Graduate Sch. of Contemporary European Studies, 1971–73, Reading University. Hon. Sec. Political Studies Assoc., 1955–58; Chm., Inst. of Electoral Research, 1959–65; Mem. Council, Hansard Soc. for Parly Govt, 1962–77; Editor of Political Studies, 1963–69; Hon. Treas., Joint Univ. Council for Social and Public Administration, 1965–69; Vice-Chm., Reading and District Council of Social Service, 1966–71; Vice-Pres., Electoral Reform Soc., 1972–. Member: CNAA Bds and Panels, 1971–78; Social Studies Sub-Cttee, UGC, 1973–83. Co-Pres., Reading Univ. Cons. Assoc., 1961–. Mem. Council, Campaign for Homosexual Equality, 1978–79; Convenor, Reading CHE, 1979–80; Chm., Conservative Gp for Homosexual Equality, 1982–. *Publications:* (with W. Theimer) Encyclopædia of World Politics, 1950; French Electoral Systems and Elections, 1789–1957, 1958; (with B. Chapman) The Constitution of the Fifth Republic, 1958. Articles in British, French and New Zealand Jls of Political Science. *Recreations:* ambling, idling, advising, meddling. *Address:* The University, Reading RG6 2AA. *T:* Reading 875123.

CAMPBELL, Quentin; *see* Campbell, J. Q.

CAMPBELL, Sir Ralph Abercromby, Kt 1961; Chief Justice of the Bahamas, 1960–70; *b* 16 March 1906; 2nd *s* of Major W. O. Campbell, MC; *m* 1st, 1936, Joan Childers Blake (marr. diss., 1968); one *s* one *d*; 2nd, 1968, Shelagh Moore. *Educ:* Winchester; University Coll., Oxford. Barrister-at-Law, Lincoln's Inn, 1928; Western Circuit; Avocat à la Cour, Egypt, 1929; Pres. Civil Courts, Baghdad, Iraq, 1931–44; British Military Administration, Eritrea, Pres. British Military Court and Italian Court of Appeal, 1945; Resident Magistrate, Kenya, 1946; Judge of the Supreme Court, Aden, 1952 (redesignated Chief Justice, 1956)-1960. *Publications:* editor: Law Reports of Kenya and East African Court of Appeal, 1950; Aden Law Reports, 1954–55; Bahamas Law Reports, 1968. *Recreations:* golf, fishing. *Address:* Lomans Hill, Hartley Wintney, Hants. *T:* Hartley Wintney 3283.

CAMPBELL, Robert, MSc; FICE; Management Consultant; Chairman, Rem Campbell International, since 1981; *b* 18 May 1929; *s* of Robert Stewart Campbell and Isobella Frances Campbell; *m* 1950, Edna Maud Evans. *Educ:* Emmanuel IGS; Loughborough Univ. (DLC (Hons), MSc). MIWES. Member of Gray's Inn, 1960. Contracts Engineer, Wyatts, Contractors, 1954–56; Chief Asst Engr, Stirlingshire and Falkirk Water Board, 1956–59; Water Engr, Camborne, 1959–60; Chief Asst City Water Engr, Plymouth, 1960–65; Civil Engr, Colne Valley Water Co., 1965–69; Engrg Inspector, Min. of Housing and Local Govt/DoE, 1969–74; Asst Dir, Resources, Planning, Anglian Water Authority, 1974–77; Chief Executive, Epping Forest Dist Council, 1977–79; Sec., ICE, 1979–81, and Man. Dir, Thomas Telford Ltd, Dir, Watt Cttee on Energy, and Hon. Sec., ICE Benevolent Fund, 1979–81. Freeman of City of London, 1977; Liveryman of Horners' Co. 1977–. *Publication:* The Pricing of Water, 1973. *Recreations:* golf, music, caravanning, cricket. *Address:* 8 Tansy Close, Northampton NN4 9XW. *Clubs:* Athenæum, MCC.

CAMPBELL, Sir Robin Auchinbreck, 15th Bt *cr* 1628 (NS); *b* 7 June 1922; *s* of Sir Louis Hamilton Campbell, 14th Bt and Margaret Elizabeth Patricia (*d* 1985), *d* of late Patrick Campbell; *S* father, 1970; *m* 1st, 1948, Rosemary, (Sally) (*d* 1978), *d* of Ashley Dean, Christchurch, NZ; one *s* two *d*; 2nd, 1978, Mrs Elizabeth Gunston, *d* of Sir Arthur Colegate, Bembridge, IoW. Formerly Lieut (A) RNVR. *Heir: s* Louis Auchinbreck Campbell [*b* 17 Jan. 1953; *m* 1976, Fiona Mary St Clair, *d* of Gordon King; one *d*]. *Address:* Glen Dhu, Motunau, Scargill, North Canterbury, New Zealand.

CAMPBELL, Ronald Francis Boyd, MA; *b* 28 Aug. 1912; *o s* of Major Roy Neil Boyd Campbell, DSO, OBE and Effie Muriel, *y d* of Major Charles Pierce, IMS; *m* 1939, Pamela Muriel Désirée, *o d* of H. L. Wright, OBE, late Indian Forest Service; one *s* two *d*. *Educ:* Berkhamsted Sch.; Peterhouse, Cambridge. Asst Master, Berkhamsted Sch., 1934–39. War of 1939–45: Supplementary Reserve, The Duke of Cornwall's Light Infantry, Sept. 1939; served in England and Italy; DAQMG, HQ 3rd Div., 1943; demobilized with hon. rank of Lt-Col, 1945. Housemaster and OC Combined Cadet Force, Berkhamsted Sch., 1945–51; Headmaster, John Lyon Sch., Harrow, 1951–68. Dir, Public Sch. Appointments Bureau, later Independent Schs Careers Orgn, 1968–78. Walter Hines Page Travelling Scholarship to USA, 1960. 1939–45 Star, Italy Star, Defence and Victory Medals; ERD (2 clasps). *Recreations:* sailing, fishing. *Address:* 30 Marine Drive, Torpoint, Cornwall PL11 2EN. *T:* Plymouth 813671. *Clubs:* East India, Devonshire, Sports and Public Schools, Royal Cruising.

CAMPBELL, Ross, DSC 1944; Partner, InterCon Consultants, Ottawa, since 1983; *b* 4 Nov. 1918; *s* of late William Marshall Campbell and of Helen Isabel Harris; *m* 1945, Penelope Grantham-Hill; two *s*. *Educ:* Univ. of Toronto Schs; Trin. Coll., Univ. of Toronto. BA, Faculty of Law, 1940. Served RCN, 1940–45. Joined Dept. of Ext. Affairs, Canada, 1945; Third Sec., Oslo, 1946–47; Second Sec., Copenhagen, 1947–50; European Div., Ottawa, 1950–52; First Sec., Ankara, 1952–56; Head of Middle East Div., Ottawa, 1957–59; Special Asst to Sec. of State for Ext. Aff., 1959–62; Asst Under-Sec. of State for Ext. Aff., 1962–64; Adviser to Canadian Delegns to: UN Gen. Assemblies, 1958–63; North Atlantic Coun., 1959–64; Ambassador to Yugoslavia, 1964–67, concurrently accredited Ambassador to Algeria, 1965–67; Ambassador and Perm. Rep. to NATO, 1967–73 (Paris May 1967, Brussels Oct. 1967); Ambassador to Japan, 1973–75, and concurrently to Republic of Korea, 1973. Chm., Atomic Energy of Canada Ltd, 1976–79; President: Atomic Energy of Canada International, 1979–80; Canus Technical Services Corp., Ottawa, 1981–83. *Recreation:* gardening. *Address:* Rivermead House, 890 Aylmer Road, Aylmer, Que J9H 5T8, Canada; (office) Suite 315, 275 Slater Street, Ottawa K1P 5H9, Canada. *Clubs:* Rideau (Ottawa); Country (Lucerne).

CAMPBELL, Ross; Director, International Military Services Ltd, 1979–83, retired; *b* 4 May 1916; 2nd *s* of George Albert Campbell and Jean Glendinning Campbell (*née* Ross); *m* 1st, 1939, Emmy Zoph (marr. diss. 1948); one *s* one *d*; 2nd, 1952, Dr Diana Stewart (*d* 1977); one *d* (and one *d* decd); 3rd, 1979, Jean Margaret Turner (*née* Ballinger) (marr. diss. 1984). *Educ:* Farnborough Grammar Sch.; Reading Univ. CEng, FICE. Articled to Municipal Engr; Local Authority Engr, 1936–39; Air Min. (UK), 1939–44; Sqdn Ldr, RAF, Middle East, 1944–47; Air Min. (UK), 1947–52; Supt Engr, Gibraltar, 1952–55; Air Min. (UK), 1955–59; Chief Engr, Far East Air Force, 1959–62 and Bomber Comd, 1962–63; Personnel Management, MPBW, 1963–66; Chief Resident Engr, Persian Gulf, 1966–68; Dir Staff Management, MPBW, 1968–69; Dir of Works (Air), 1969–72; Under-Sec., and Dir of Defence Services II PSA, DoE, 1972–75. Dir, 1975–77, Dep. Chief Exec., 1977–79, Internat. Military Services Ltd. *Publications:* papers on professional civil engrg and trng in ICE Jl. *Recreations:* golf, tennis, music. *Address:* 41 Nightingale Road, Rickmansworth, Herts. *T:* Rickmansworth 773744. *Clubs:* Royal Air Force; Denham Golf.

CAMPBELL, Sir Thomas C.; *see* Cockburn-Campbell.

CAMPBELL, Maj.-Gen. Victor David Graham, CB 1956; DSO 1940; OBE 1946; JP; DL; *b* 9 March 1905; *s* of late Gen. Sir David G. M. Campbell, GCB; *m* 1947, Dulce Beatrix, *d* of late G. B. Collier, and *widow* of Lt-Col J. A. Goodwin. *Educ:* Rugby; RMC Sandhurst. 2nd Lieut The Queen's Own Cameron Highlanders, 1924; AQMG and DA&QMG HQ AFNEI, 1945–46; Lt-Col Comdg 1st Bn The Gordon Highlanders, 1949; Brig. Comdg 31 Lorried Infantry Brigade, 1951; Chief of Staff, HQ Scottish Command, 1954–57; psc 1938; idc 1953. DL and JP, 1962, High Sheriff, 1968, County of Devon; Chairman: Totnes RDC, 1971–72; Totnes Petty Sessional Div., 1972–75. *Address:* Beggars Bush, South Brent, South Devon.

CAMPBELL, Hon. Sir Walter (Benjamin), Kt 1979; Governor of Queensland, Australia, since 1985; *b* 4 March 1921; *s* of Archie Eric Gordon Campbell and Leila Mary Campbell; *m* 1942, Georgina Margaret Pearce; one *s* one *d* (and one *s* decd). *Educ:* Univ. of Queensland (MA, LLB; Hon. LLD 1980). Served War, RAAF, 1941–46 (pilot). Called to the Qld Bar, 1948; QC 1960; Judge, Supreme Court, Qld, 1967; Chief Justice, Qld, 1982–85. Chairman: Law Reform Commn of Qld, 1969–73; Remuneration Tribunal (Commonwealth), 1974–82; sole Mem., Academic Salaries Tribunal (Commonwealth), 1974–78. President: Qld Bar Assoc., 1965–67; Australian Bar Assoc., 1966–67; Mem. Exec., Law Council of Aust., 1965–67. Dir, Winston Churchill Meml Trust, 1969–80; Chm., Utah Foundn, 1977–85. Mem. Senate 1963–85, and Chancellor 1977–85, Univ. of Qld. KStJ 1986. *Recreations:* golf, fishing. *Address:* Government House, Brisbane, Qld 4001, Australia. *T:* 07 369 7744. *Clubs:* Queensland, Royal Queensland Golf (Brisbane); Australasian Pioneers (Sydney).

CAMPBELL, Walter Menzies, QC (Scot.) 1982; *b* 22 May 1941; *s* of George Alexander Campbell and Elizabeth Jean Adam Phillips; *m* 1970, Elspeth Mary Urquhart or Grant-Suttie, *d* of Maj.-Gen. R. E. Erquhart, *qv*. *Educ:* Hillhead High School, Glasgow; Glasgow Univ. (MA 1962, LLB 1965; President of the Union, 1964–65); Stanford Univ., Calif. Advocate, Scottish Bar, 1968; Advocate Depute, 1977–80; Standing Jun. Counsel to the Army, 1980–82. Member: Clayson Cttee on licensing reform, 1971; Legal Aid Central Cttee, 1983–; Broadcasting Council for Scotland, 1984–. Part-time Chairman: VAT Tribunal, 1984–; Medical Appeal Tribunal, 1985–. Chm., Scottish Liberal Party, 1975–77; contested (L): Greenock and Port Glasgow, Feb. 1974 and Oct. 1974; E Fife, 1979; NE Fife, 1983. Chm., Royal Lyceum Theatre Co., Edinburgh, 1984–. Member: UK Sports Council, 1965–68; Scottish Sports Council, 1971–81. Governor, Scottish Sports Aid Foundn, 1981–; Trustee, Scottish Internat. Educn Trust, 1984–. AAA 220 Yards Champion, 1964 and 1967; UK 100 Metres Record Holder, 1967–74; competed at Olympic Games, 1964 and Commonwealth Games, 1966; Captain, UK Athletics Team, 1965 and 1966. *Recreations:* all sports, reading, music, theatre. *Address:* Advocates' Library, Parliament House, Edinburgh 1. *T:* 031–226 5071. *Clubs:* Scottish Liberal (Edinburgh); Western (Glasgow).

CAMPBELL, William Anthony; QC (NI) 1974; Senior Crown Counsel in Northern Ireland, since 1984; *b* 30 Oct. 1936; *s* of late H. E. Campbell and of Marion Wheeler; *m* 1960, Gail, *e d* of F. M. McKibbin; three *d*. *Educ:* Campbell Coll., Belfast; Queens' Coll., Cambridge. Called to the Bar, Gray's Inn, 1960; called to the Bar of NI, 1960 (Bencher, 1983; Vice-Chm., 1983–, Chm., 1985–, Exec. Council). Jun. Counsel to Attorney-Gen. for NI, 1971–74. Chm., NI Mountain Rescue Co-ordinating Cttee, 1985. Governor, Campbell Coll., 1976– (Chm., 1984–); Mem. Council, St Leonards Sch., St Andrews, 1985–. *Recreations:* sailing, hill walking. *Address:* Royal Courts of Justice, Belfast BT1 3JY. *Club:* Royal Ulster Yacht.
See also J. E. P. Grigg.

CAMPBELL, Maj.-Gen. William Tait, CBE 1945 (OBE 1944); retired; *b* 8 Oct. 1912; *s* of late R. B. Campbell, MD, FRCPE, Edinburgh; *m* 1942, Rhoda Alice, *y d* of late Adm. Algernon Walker-Heneage-Vivian, CB, MVO, Swansea; two *d*. *Educ:* Cargilfield Sch.; Fettes Coll.; RMC Sandhurst. 2nd Lieut, The Royal Scots (The Royal Regt), 1933; served War of 1939–45: 1st Airborne Div. and 1st Allied Airborne Army (North Africa, Sicily, Italy and Europe). Lieut-Col Commanding 1st Bn The Royal Scots, in Egypt, Cyprus, UK and Suez Operation (despatches), 1954–57; Col, Royal Naval War Coll., Greenwich, 1958; Brig. i/c Admin. Malaya, 1962; Maj.-Gen., 1964; DQMG, MoD (Army Dept), 1964–67; Col, The Royal Scots (The Royal Regt), 1964–74. Dir, The Fairbridge Soc., 1969–78. US Bronze Star, 1945. *Recreations:* gardening, golf, shooting, fishing. *Address:* c/o Lloyds Bank (Cox's & King's Branch), 6 Pall Mall, SW1Y 5NH; Ashwood, Boarhills, St Andrews, Fife KY16 8PR.

CAMPBELL-GRAY, family name of **Lord Gray.**

CAMPBELL-JOHNSON, Alan, CIE 1947; OBE 1946; Officer of US Legion of Merit, 1947; MA Oxon; FRSA, MRI; public relations consultant; *b* 16 July 1913; *o c* of late Lieut-Col James Alexander Campbell-Johnson and late Gladys Susanne Campbell-Johnson; *m* 1938, Imogen Fay de la Tour Dunlap; one *d* (one *s* decd). *Educ:* Westminster; Christ Church, Oxford (scholar). BA 2nd Cl. Hons Mod. Hist., 1935. Political Sec. to Rt Hon. Sir Archibald Sinclair, Leader of Parl. Lib. Party, 1937–40; served War of 1939–45, RAF; COHQ, 1942–43; HQ SACSEA (Wing Comdr i/c Inter-Allied Records Section), 1943–46. Contested (L) Salisbury and South Wilts. Div., Gen. Elections, 1945 and 1950. Press Attaché to Viceroy and Gov.-Gen. of India (Earl Mountbatten of Burma), 1947–48. Chm., Campbell-Johnson Ltd, Public Relations Consultants, 1953–78; Dir, Hill and Knowlton (UK) Ltd, 1976–85. Fellow Inst. of Public Relations, Pres. 1956–57. *Publications:* Growing Opinions, 1935; Peace Offering, 1936; Anthony Eden: a biography, 1938, rev. edn 1955; Viscount Halifax: a biography, 1941; Mission with Mountbatten, 1951, repr. 1972. *Recreations:* watching cricket, listening to music. *Address:* 21 Ashley Gardens, Ambrosden Avenue, SW1P 1QD. *T:* 01–834 1532. *Clubs:* Brooks's, National Liberal, MCC.

CAMPBELL ORDE, Alan Colin, CBE 1943; AFC 1919; FRAeS; *b* Lochgilphead, Argyll, NB, 4 Oct. 1898; *s* of Colin Ridley Campbell Orde; *m* 1951, Mrs Beatrice McClure, *e d* of late Rev. Eliott-Drake Briscoe. *Educ:* Sherborne. Served European War, 1916–18, Flight Sub-Lieut, Royal Navy, and Flying Officer, Royal Air Force; active service in Belgium, 1917; one of original commercial Pilots on London-Paris route with Aircraft Transport & Travel Ltd, 1919–20; Instructor and Adviser to Chinese Govt in Peking, 1921–23; Instructor and latterly Chief Test Pilot to Sir W. G. Armstrong-Whitworth Aircraft, Ltd, Coventry, 1924–36; Operational Manager, British Airways, Ltd, 1936–39; subseq. Operations Manager, Imperial Airways Ltd; was Ops Director BOAC, during first 4 years after its inception in 1939; thereafter responsible for technical development as Development Dir until resignation from BOAC Dec. 1957. *Recreation:* reading in bed. *Address:* Smugglers Mead, Stepleton, Blandford, Dorset. *T:* Child Okeford 860268. *Club:* Boodle's.

CAMPBELL-ORDE, Sir John A.; *see* Orde.

CAMPBELL-PRESTON of Ardchattan, Robert Modan Thorne, OBE 1955; MC 1943; TD; Vice-Lieutenant, Argyll and Bute, since 1976; *b* 7 Jan. 1909; *s* of Colonel R. W. P. Campbell-Preston, DL, JP, of Ardchattan and Valleyfield, Fife, and Mary Augusta Thorne, MBE; *m* 1950, Hon. Angela Murray (*d* 1981), 3rd *d* of 2nd Viscount Cowdray and *widow* of Lt-Col George Anthony Murray, OBE, TD (killed in action, Italy, 1945); one *d*. *Educ:* Eton; Christ Church, Oxford (MA). Lt Scottish Horse, 1927; Lt-Col 1945. Hon. Col, Fife-Forfar Yeo./Scottish Horse, 1962–67. Member Royal Company of Archers, Queen's Body Guard for Scotland. Joint Managing Director, Alginate Industries Ltd, 1949–74. DL 1951, JP 1950, Argyllshire. Silver Star (USA), 1945. *Recreations:* shooting, fishing, gardening. *Address:* Ardchattan Priory, Connel, Argyll. *T:* Bonawe 274; 31 Marlborough Hill, NW8. *T:* 01–586 2291. *Club:* Puffin's (Edinburgh).
See also Duke of Atholl.

CAMPBELL-SAVOURS, Dale Norman; MP (Lab) Workington, Cumbria, since 1979; *b* 23 Aug. 1943; *s* of John Lawrence and Cynthia Lorraine Campbell-Savours; *m* 1970, Gudrun Kristin Runolfsdottir; three *s*. *Educ:* Keswick Sch.; Sorbonne, Paris. Dir, manufacturing co., 1969–77. Member, Ramsbottom UDC, 1972–73. Mem., TGWU, 1970–. Contested (Lab): Darwen Division of Lancashire, gen. elections, Feb. 1974, Oct. 1974; Workington, by-election, 1976. *Address:* House of Commons, SW1.

CAMPDEN, Viscount; Anthony Baptist Noel; *b* 16 Jan. 1950; *s* and *heir* of 5th Earl of Gainsborough, *qv*; *m* 1972, Sarah Rose, *er d* of Col T. F. C. Winnington; one *s*. *Educ:* Ampleforth; Royal Agricultural Coll., Cirencester. *Heir: s* Hon. Henry Robert Anthony Noel, *b* 1 July 1977. *Address:* Top House, Exton, Rutland, Leics LE15 8AX. *T:* Oakham 812587; 105 Earls Court Road, W8. *T:* 01–370 5650. *Club:* Turf.
See also Sir F. S. W. Winnington, Bt.

CAMPION, Sir Harry, Kt 1957; CB 1949; CBE 1945; MA; retired as Director of Central Statistical Office, Cabinet Office, 1967; *b* 20 May 1905; *o s* of John Henry Campion, Worsley, Lancs. *Educ:* Farnworth Grammar Sch.; Univ. of Manchester. Rockefeller Foundation Fellow, United States, 1932; Robert Ottley Reader in Statistics, Univ. of Manchester, 1933–39. Dir. of Statistical Office, UN, 1946–47; Mem. of Statistical Commission, United Nations, 1947–67; Pres.: International Statistical Institute, 1963–67; Royal Statistical Society, 1957–59; Hon. LLD, Manchester, 1967. *Publications:* Distribution of National Capital; Public and Private Property in Great Britain; articles in economic and statistical journals. *Address:* Rima, Priory Close, Stanmore, Mddx. *T:* 01–954 3267. *Club:* Reform.

CAMPION, Peter James, DPhil; FInstP; consultant; Deputy Director, National Physical Laboratory, 1976–86; *b* 7 April 1926; *s* of Frank Wallace Campion and Gertrude Alice (*née* Lambert); *m* 1950, Beryl Grace Stanton, *e d* of John and Grace Stanton; one *s* one *d* (and one *s* decd). *Educ:* Westcliff High Sch., Essex; Exeter Coll., Oxford (MA, DPhil). FInstP 1964. RN, 1943. Nuffield Res. Fellow, Oxford, 1954; Chalk River Proj., Atomic Energy of Canada Ltd, 1955; National Physical Lab., Teddington, 1960–: Supt, Div. of Radiation Science, 1964; Supt, Div. of Mech. and Optical Metrology, 1974. Mem., Comité Consultatif pour les Etalons de Mesure des Rayonnements Ionisante, 1963–79; Chm., Sect. II, reconstituted Comité Consultatif, Mesure des radionucléides, 1970–79; Mem., NACCB, 1984–86. Editor, Internat. Jl of Applied Radiation and Isotopes, 1968–71. *Publications:* A Code of Practice for the Detailed Statement of Accuracy (with A. Williams and J. E. Burns), 1973; technical and rev. papers in learned jls on neutron capture gamma rays, measurement of radioactivity, and on metrology generally. *Recreation:* winemaking and wine drinking.

CAMPLING, Very Rev. Christopher Russell; Dean of Ripon, since 1984; *b* 4 July 1925; *s* of Canon William Charles Campling; *m* 1953, Juliet Marian Hughes; one *s* two *d*. *Educ:* Lancing Coll.; St Edmund Hall, Oxford (MA; Hons Theol. cl. 2); Cuddesdon Theol. Coll. RNVR, 1943–47. Deacon 1951, priest 1952; Curate of Basingstoke, 1951–55; Minor Canon of Ely Cathedral and Chaplain of King's School, Ely, 1955–60; Chaplain of Lancing Coll., 1960–67; Vicar of Pershore with Pinvin and Wick and Birlingham, 1968–76; RD of Pershore, 1970–76; Archdeacon of Dudley and Director of Religious Education, Diocese of Worcester, 1976–84. Mem., General Synod of Church of England, 1970–; Chm., House of Clergy, Diocese of Worcester, 1981–84. *Publications:* The Way, The Truth and The Life: Vol. 1, The Love of God in Action, 1964; Vol. 2, The People of God in Action, 1964; Vol. 3, The Word of God in Action, 1965; Vol. 4, God's Plan in Acion, 1965; also two teachers' volumes; Words of Worship, 1969; The Fourth Lesson, Vol. 1 1973, Vol. 2 1974. *Recreations:* music, drama, golf. *Address:* The Minster House, Ripon, N Yorks HG4 1PE. *Club:* Naval.

CAMPOLI, Alfredo; violinist; *b* 20 Oct. 1906; *s* of Prof. Romeo Campoli, Prof. of Violin at Accademia di Santa Cecilia, Rome, and Elvira Campoli, dramatic soprano; *m* 1942, Joy Burbridge. Came to London, 1911; gave regular public recitals as a child; Gold Medal, London Musical Festival, 1919; toured British Isles with Melba and with Dame Clara Butt, and was engaged for series of International Celebrity Concerts at age of 15. Has played all over the world. First broadcast from Savoy Hill, 1930; has subsequently made frequent broadcasts and television appearances, and made many gramophone records. *Recreations:* bridge, cine-photography, table tennis, billiards, croquet.

CAMPOS, Prof. Christophe Lucien; Director, British Institute in Paris, since 1978; *b* 27 April 1938; *s* of Lucien Antoine Campos and Margaret Lilian (*née* Dunn); *m* 1977, Lucy Elizabeth Mitchell; one *s* four *d*. *Educ:* Lycée Lamoricière, Oran; Lycée Français de Londres; Lycée Henri IV, Paris; Gonville and Caius Coll., Cambridge. LèsL (Paris), PhD (Cantab). Lector in French, Gonville and Caius Coll., 1959; Lecturer in French: Univ. of Maryland, 1963; Univ. of Sussex, 1964; Lectr in English, Univ. i Oslo, 1969; Prof. of French, University Coll., Dublin, 1974. Jt Editor, Franco-British Studies. *Publications:* The View of France, 1964; contribs to Th. Qly, TLS, Univs Qly. *Recreations:* bees, football, gastronomy, navigation. *Address:* 53 Houndean Rise, Lewes, Sussex.

CAMPOS, Roberto de Oliveira, Hon. GCVO 1976; Senator, House of Congress, Brazil, since 1982; *b* Cuiabá, Mato Grosso, 17 April 1917. *Educ:* Catholic Seminaries: Guaxupé and Belo Horizonte, Brazil (grad. Philosophy and Theol.); George Washington Univ., Washington (MA Econs); Columbia Univ., NYC (Hon. Dr). Entered Brazilian Foreign Service, 1939; Economic Counsellor, Brazil-US EDC, 1951–53; Dir 1952, Gen. Man. 1955, Pres. 1959, Nat. Economic Develt Bank; Sec. Gen., Nat. Develt Council, 1956–59; Delegate to internat. confs, incl. ECOSOC and GATT, 1959–61; Roving Ambassador for financial negotiations in W Europe, 1961; Ambassador of Brazil to US, 1961–63; Minister of State for Planning and Co-ord., 1964–67; Ambassador to UK, 1975–82. Prof., Sch. of Econs, Univ. of Brazil, 1956–61. Mem. or past Mem., Cttees and Bds on economic develt (particularly inter-Amer. econ. develt). *Publications:* Ensaios de História Econômica e Sociologia; Economia, Planejamento e Nacionalismo; A Moeda, o Govêrno e o Tempo; A Técnica e o Riso; Reflections on Latin American Development; Do outro lado da cerca; Temas e Sistemas; Ensaios contra a maré; Política Econômica e Mitos Políticos (jtly); Trends in International Trade (GATT report); Partners in Progress (report of Pearson Cttee of World Bank); A Nova Economia Brasileira; Formas Criativas do Desenvolvimento Brasileiro; Omundo que vejo e náo desejo; techn. articles and reports on develt and internat. econs, in jls. *Address:* House of Congress, Praça dos Tres Poderes, 70160 Brasilia DF, Brazil; 140 Francisco Otaviano, Ipanema, Rio de Janiero, Brazil.

CAMPS, William Anthony; Master of Pembroke College, Cambridge, 1970–81; *b* 28 Dec. 1910; *s* of P. W. L. Camps, FRCS, and Alice, *d* of Joseph Redfern, Matlock; *m* 1953, Miriam Camp, Washington, DC, *d* of Prof. Burton Camp, Wesleyan Univ., Connecticut. *Educ:* Marlborough Coll.; Pembroke Coll., Cambridge (Schol.). Fellow, Pembroke Coll., 1933; Univ. Lectr in Classics, 1939; Temp. Civil Servant, 1940–45; Asst Tutor, Pembroke Coll., 1945; Senior Tutor, 1947–62; Tutor for Advanced Students, 1963–70; Pres., 1964–70. Mem., Inst. for Advanced Study, Princeton, 1956–57; Vis. Assoc. Prof., UC Toronto, 1966; Vis. Prof., Univ. of North Carolina at Chapel Hill, 1969. *Publications:* edns of Propertius I, 1961, IV, 1965, III, 1966, II, 1967; An Introduction to Virgil's Aeneid, 1969; An Introduction to Homer, 1980; sundry notes and reviews in classical periodicals. *Recreations:* unremarkable. *Address:* c/o Pembroke College, Cambridge. *T:* Cambridge 338100. *Club:* United Oxford & Cambridge University.

CAMROSE, 2nd Viscount, *cr* 1941, of Hackwood Park; **John Seymour Berry,** TD; Bt 1921; Baron 1929; Deputy Chairman (Past Chairman) of The Daily Telegraph Ltd; *b* 12 July 1909; *e s* of 1st Viscount Camrose and Mary Agnes (*d* 1962), *e d* of late Thomas Corns, 2 Bolton Street, W; *S* father, 1954; *m* 1986, Princess Joan Aly Khan. *Educ:* Eton; Christ Church, Oxford. Major, City of London Yeomanry. Served War of 1939–45, North African and Italian Campaigns, 1942–45 (despatches). MP (C) for Hitchin Division, Herts, 1941–45. Vice-Chm. Amalgamated Press Ltd, 1942–59. Younger Brother, Trinity House. *Heir: b* Baron Hartwell, *qv*. *Address:* 8a Hobart Place, SW1. *T:* 01–235 9900; Hackwood, Basingstoke, Hampshire. *T:* Basingstoke 464630. *Clubs:* Buck's, White's, Beefsteak, Marylebone Cricket (MCC); Royal Yacht Squadron (Trustee).
See also Col. Hon. J. Berry.

CANADA, Primate of All; *see* Peers, Most Rev. M. G.

CANADA, Primate of; *see* Quebec, Archbishop of, (RC).

CANADA, Metropolitan of the Ecclesiastical Province of; *see* Fredericton, Archbishop of.

CANAVAN, Dennis Andrew; MP (Lab) Falkirk West, since 1983 (West Stirlingshire, Oct. 1974–1983); *b* 8 Aug. 1942; *s* of Thomas and Agnes Canavan; *m* 1964, Elnor Stewart; three *s* one *d*. *Educ:* St Columba's High Sch., Cowdenbeath; Edinburgh Univ. (BSc Hons, DipEd). Head of Maths Dept, St Modan's High Sch., Stirling, 1970–74; Asst Headmaster, Holy Rood High Sch., Edinburgh, 1974. Treasurer, Scottish Parly Lab. Gp, 1976–79, Vice-Chm., 1979–80, Chm., 1980–81; Convener, Scottish Parly Lab Gp Devolution Sub-Cttee, 1985–. Parly spokesman for Scottish Cttee on mobility for the disabled, 1977–; Mem., H of C Select Cttee on For. Affairs, 1982–; Vice-Chairman: PLP Foreign Affairs Cttee, 1983–; PLP NI Cttee, 1983–. Mem. Local Exec., Educnl Inst. of Scotland, 1972–74; Sec., W Stirlingshire Constituency Labour Party, 1972–74; Labour Party Agent, Feb. 1974; District Councillor, 1973–74; Leader of Labour Gp, Stirling District Council, 1974; Member: Stirling Dist Educn Sub-cttee, 1973–74; Stirlingshire

Youth Employment Adv. Cttee, 1972–74. *Publications:* contribs to various jls on educn and politics. *Recreations:* walking, marathon running, swimming, reading, football (Scottish Univs football internationalist, 1966–67 and 1967–68; Hon. Pres., Milton Amateurs FC). *Address:* 15 Margaret Road, Bannockburn, Stirlingshire. *T:* Bannockburn 812581; House of Commons, SW1A 0AA. *T:* 01–219 3000. *Clubs:* Bannockburn Miners' Welfare (Bannockburn); Camelon Labour (Falkirk).

CANBERRA AND GOULBURN, Bishop of, since 1983; **Rt. Rev. Owen Douglas Dowling;** *b* 11 Oct. 1934; *s* of Cecil Gair Mackenzie Dowling and Winifred Hunter; *m* 1958, Beverly Anne Johnston; two *s* one *d. Educ:* Melbourne High School; Trinity Coll., Melbourne Univ. (BA, DipEd, ThL). Victorian Education Dept, Secondary Teacher, 1956–60; ordained to ministry of Anglican Church, 1960; Asst Curate, Sunshine/Deer Park, Dio. Melbourne, 1960–62; Vicar of St. Philip's, W Heidelberg, 1962–65; Precentor and Organist, St Saviour's Cathedral, Goulburn, 1965–67; Rector of South Wagga Wagga, 1968–72; Rector of St. John's, Canberra, 1972–81; Archdeacon of Canberra, 1974–81; Asst Bishop, Dio. Canberra and Goulburn, 1981–83. *Recreations:* pipe organ and piano playing; squash. *Address:* (office) Jamieson House, Constitution Avenue, Reid, ACT 2601, Australia. *T:* (062) 48.0811; (home) 51 Rosenthal Street, Campbell, ACT 2601. *T:* (062) 48.0716. *Clubs:* Canberra, Southern Cross (Canberra).

CANDELA OUTERINO, Felix; engineer and architect; Professor, Escuela Nacional de Arquitectura, University of Mexico, since 1953 (on leave of absence); *b* Madrid, 27 Jan. 1910; *s* of Felix and Julia Candela; *m* 1940, Eladia Martin Galan (*d* 1964); four *d*; *m* 1967, Dorothy H. Davies. *Educ:* Univ. of Madrid, Spain. Architect, Escuela Superior de Arquitectura de Madrid, 1935. Captain of Engineers, Republican Army, Spanish Civil War, 1936–39. Emigrated to Mexico, 1939; Mexican Citizen, 1941; USA citizen, 1978. General practice in Mexico as Architect and Contractor. Founded (with brother Antonio) Cubiertas ALA, SA, firm specializing in design and construction of reinforced concrete shell structures. Work includes Sports Palace for Mexico Olympics, 1968. Hon. Member: Sociedad de Arquitectos Colombianos, 1956; Sociedad Venezolana de Arquitectos, 1961; International Assoc. for Shell Structures, 1962. Charles Elliot Norton Prof. of Poetry, Harvard Univ., for academic year, 1961–62; Jefferson Meml Prof., Univ. of Virginia, 1966; Andrew D. White Prof., Cornell Univ., 1969–74; Prof., Dept of Architecture, Univ. of Illinois at Chicago, 1971–78; Prof. Honorario: Escuela Tecnica Superior de Arquitectura de Madrid, 1969; Univ. Nacional Federico Villareal, Peru, 1977; William Hoffman Wood Prof., Leeds Univ., 1974–75. Gold Medal, Instn Structural Engineers, England, 1961; Auguste Perret Prize of International Union of Architects, 1961; Alfred E. Lindau Award, Amer. Concrete Inst., 1965; Silver Medal, Acad. d'Architecture, Paris, 1980; Gold Medal, Consejo Superior de Arquitectos de España, 1981. Hon. Fellow American Inst. of Architects, 1963; Hon. Corr. Mem., RIBA, 1963; Plomada de Oro, Soc. de Arquitectos Mexicanos, 1963; Doctor in Fine Arts (*hc*): Univ. of New Mexico, 1964; Univ. of Illinois, 1979; Dr Ing *hc* Univ. de Santa Maria, Caracas, 1968. Order of Civil Merit, Spain, 1978. *Publications:* several articles in architectural and engineering magazines all around the world; *relevant publication:* Candela, the Shell Builder, by Colin Faber, 1963. *Address:* PO Box 356, Bronxville, NY 10708, USA. *T:* (212) 7998715; Avenida America 14–7, Madrid 2, Spain. *T:* 246 0096.

CANDLIN, Prof. Christopher Noel; Professor of Linguistics and Modern English Language, University of Lancaster, since 1981; *b* 31 March 1940; *s* of Edwin Frank Candlin and Nora Candlin (*née* Letts); *m* 1964, Sally (*née* Carter); one *s* three *d. Educ:* Jesus Coll., Oxford (MA); Univ. of London (PGCE); Yale Univ. (MPhil). Research Associate, Univ. of Leeds, 1967–68; Lectr, 1968, later Sen. Lectr, Univ. of Lancaster. Visiting Professor: Univ. of Giessen, 1975; Ontario Inst. for Studies in Educn, Toronto, 1983; East–West Centre, Honolulu, 1978; Univ. of Hawaii at Manoa, 1984; Univ. of Melbourne, 1985. FRSA. General Editor: Applied Linguistics and Language Study; Language in Social Life; Applied Linguistics; IRAL, ELT Documents. *Publications:* Challenges, 1978; The Communicative Teaching of English, 1981; Computers in English Language Teaching and Research, 1985; Language Learning Tasks, 1986. *Recreations:* sailing, upholstery, cooking. *Address:* Northfield House, 19 Quernmore Road, Lancaster LA1 3AB. *T:* Lancaster 66790.

CANDLISH, Thomas Tait, FEng 1980; Managing Director, George Wimpey PLC, 1978–85 (Director since 1973); *b* 26 Nov. 1926; *s* of John Candlish and Elizabeth (*née* Tait); *m* 1964, Mary Trinkwon; two *s. Educ:* Perth Acad.; Glasgow Univ. (BSc Eng). FICE 1971. Served RE, 1946–49 (commnd). Student Engr, George Wimpey & Co. Ltd, 1944–46; rejoined Wimpey, 1951; served in: Borneo, 1951–54; Papua New Guinea, 1955–57; Arabian Gulf area, 1958–62; W Africa, 1962–65; Director: Wimpey Internat., 1973– (Chm., 1979–85); Wimpey ME & C, 1973–85; Wimpey Marine Ltd, 1975–85 (Chm., 1979–85); Brown & Root-Wimpey Highlands Fabricators, 1974– (Chm., 1981–); British Smelter Constructions Ltd, 1977–83 (Chm., 1977–83); Hill Samuel Developments, 1978–85; A & P Appledore Holdings, 1979–; Brown & Root (UK) Ltd, 1985–. Chm., Export Gp for Constructional Industries, 1983–85; Member: EDC for Civil Engrg, 1979–82; British Overseas Trade Bd, 1984–. *Recreations:* motor sport, ski-ing, golf. *Address:* Tithe Cottage, Dorney Wood Road, Burnham, Bucks SL1 8EQ. *T:* Burnham 61893. *Club:* Royal Automobile.

CANE, Prof. Violet Rosina; Professor of Mathematical Statistics, University of Manchester, 1971–81, now Emeritus; *b* 31 Jan. 1916; *d* of Tubal George Cane and Annie Louisa Lansdell. *Educ:* Newnham Coll., Cambridge (MA, Dipl. in Math. Stats). BoT, 1940; Univ. of Aberdeen, 1941; FO, 1942; Min. of Town and Country Planning, 1946; Statistician to MRC Applied Psychol. Unit, 1948; Queen Mary Coll., London, 1955; Fellow, Newnham Coll., Cambridge, 1957; Lectr, Univ. of Cambridge, 1960. Hon. MSc Manchester, 1974. *Publications:* (contrib.) Current Problems in Animal Behaviour, 1961; (contrib.) Perspectives in Probability and Statistics, 1975; papers in Jl of Royal Stat. Soc., Animal Behaviour, and psychol jls. *Recreation:* supporting old houses. *Address:* 13/14 Little St Mary's Lane, Cambridge CB2 1RR. *T:* Cambridge 357277; Statistical Laboratory, University of Cambridge, 16 Mill Lane, Cambridge CB2 1SB.

CANET, Maj.-Gen. Lawrence George, CB 1964; CBE 1956; BE; Master General of the Ordnance, Australia, 1964–67, retired; *b* 1 Dec. 1910; *s* of late Albert Canet, Melbourne, Victoria; *m* 1940, Mary Elizabeth Clift, *d* of Cecil Clift Jones, Geelong, Victoria; one *s. Educ:* RMC Duntroon; Sydney Univ. (BE). Served War of 1939–45 with 7th Australian Div. (Middle East and Pacific). GOC Southern Command, 1960–64. Brigadier 1953; Maj.-Gen. 1957. *Address:* 37 The Corso, Isle of Capri, Surfers Paradise, Qld 4217, Australia.

CANETTI, Elias; writer; *b* Ruschuk, Bulgaria, 25 July 1905; *e s* of late Jacques Canetti and Mathilde (*née* Arditi); *m* 1st, 1934, Venetia Taubner-Calderón (*d* 1963); 2nd; one *c. Educ:* schs in Manchester, Vienna and Zurich; Univ. of Vienna (DSc 1929). Settled in London, 1939. Prizes include: Prix Internat. de Paris, 1949; Austrian Prize for Literature, 1968; Kafka Prize, Austria, 1981; Nobel Prize for Literature, 1981. *Publications: plays:* Hochzeit, 1932; Komödie der Eitelkeit, 1934; Die Befristeten, 1952 (The Numbered, 1956); *novel:* Bie Blendung, 1935 (Auto da Fé, 1946); *non-fiction:* Fritz Wotruba, 1955; Masse und Macht, 1960 (Crowds and Power, 1962); Die Stimmen von Marrakesch, 1967 (The Voices of Marrakesh, 1978); Der andere Prozess, 1969 (Kafka's Other Trial, 1974); Die Provinz des Menschen: Aufzeichnungen 1942–1972, 1973 (The Human Province, 1979); Der Ohrenzeuge: 50 Charaktere, 1974 (Earwitness, 1979); *autobiography:* Die geretete Zunge, 1977 (The Tongue set Free, 1979); Die Fackel im Ohr, 1980 (The Torch in my Ear, US, 1982). *Address:* c/o C. & J. Wolfers Ltd, 3 Regent Square, WC1.

CANHAM, Brian John; Metropolitan Stipendiary Magistrate, since 1975; *b* 27 Dec. 1930; *s* of late Frederick Ernest and of Nora Ruby Canham; *m* 1955, Rachel, *yr d* of late Joseph and Martha Woolley, Bank House, Longnor, Staffs; three *s* one *d. Educ:* City of Norwich Sch.; Queens' Coll., Cambridge. MA, LLB. Called to Bar, Gray's Inn, 1955. Army Legal Services, BAOR: Staff Captain, 1956, Major, 1958. Private practice as barrister on SE Circuit, 1963–75. *Recreations:* gardening, sailing, swimming.

CANHAM, Bryan Frederick, (Peter), MC 1943; FCIS; Chairman, Eurofi UK Ltd, since 1981; *b* 11 April 1920; *s* of Frederick William Canham and Emma Louisa Martin; *m* 1944, Rita Gwendoline Huggett; one *s. Educ:* Trinity County Sch. FCIS 1968 (ACIS 1950). Served War, 1939–46: N Africa, Italy and NW Europe; Captain 1st Royal Tank Regt. Accounting and financial appts, Shell cos in Kenya, Tanzania and French W Africa, 1947–56; Controller, S Europe and N Africa, Shell Internat. Petroleum Co., 1956–60; Finance Dir, Shell Philippines and Ass. Cos, 1960–63; Finance Dir, Shell Malaysia and Ass. Cos, 1963–68; Personnel Adviser, finance and computer staff, Shell Internat. Pet. Co., 1968–73; Div. Hd, Loans, Directorate Gen. XVIII, Commn of European Communities, 1973–76, Dir, Investment and Loans, 1976–80. *Recreations:* reading, chess, pottering. *Address:* The Old Laundry, Penshurst, Kent TN11 8HY. *T:* Penshurst 870239; The Cottage, Stedham Hall, Stedham, W Sussex; (office) 25 London Road, Newbury, Berks. *T:* Newbury 31900. *Club:* Muthaiga Country (Nairobi).

CANHAM, Peter; *see* Canham, B. F.

CANN, Charles Richard; Under Secretary, Plants, Seeds and Flood Protection Policy, Ministry of Agriculture, Fisheries and Food; *b* 3 Feb. 1937; *s* of Charles Alfred Cann and Grace Elizabeth Cann; *m* 1979, Denise Ann Margaret Love; two *s. Educ:* Merchant Taylors' Sch., Northwood, Mddx; St John's Coll., Cambridge (MA). Asst Principal, MAFF, 1960, Principal 1965; Cabinet Office, 1969–71; Asst Sec., MAFF, 1971; Under Sec., 1981. *Address:* c/o Ministry of Agriculture, Fisheries and Food, Whitehall Place, SW1A 2HH.

CANN, Prof. Johnson Robin, ScD; J. B. Simpson Professor of Geology, University of Newcastle upon Tyne, since 1977; *b* 18 Oct. 1937; *er s* of Johnson Ralph Cann and (Ethel) Mary (*née* Northmore); *m* 1963, Janet, *d* of Prof. Charles John Hamson, *qv*; two *s. Educ:* St Alban's Sch.; St John's Coll., Cambridge (MA, PhD, ScD). Research fellow, St John's Coll., 1962–66; post-doctoral work in Depts of Mineralogy and Petrology, and Geodesy and Geophysics, Cambridge, 1962–66; Dept of Mineralogy, British Museum (Natural History), 1966–68; Lectr, then Reader, School of Environmental Sciences, Univ. of East Anglia, 1968–77; research in rocks of ocean floor, creation of oceanic crust, obsidian in archaeology. Member, then Chm., JOIDES ocean crust panel, 1975–78; UK representative on JOIDES planning cttee, 1978–84; co-chief scientist on Glomar Challenger, 1976 and 1979; Mem., UGC physical sciences sub-cttee, 1982–. *Publications:* papers in jls of earth science and archaeology. *Recreations:* gathering, music, local politics. *Address:* Silverlaw House, 138 Newgate Street, Morpeth, Northumberland NE61 1DD. *T:* Morpeth 512789.

CANNAN, Denis; dramatist and script writer; *b* 14 May 1919; *s* of late Captain H. J. Pullein-Thompson, MC, and late Joanna Pullein-Thompson (*née* Cannan); *m* 1st, 1946, Joan Ross (marr. diss.); two *s* one *d*; 2nd, 1965, Rose Evansky; he changed name to Denis Cannan, by deed poll, 1964. *Educ:* Eton. A Repertory factotum, 1937–39. Served War of 1939–45, Queen's Royal Regt, Captain (despatches). Actor at Citizens' Theatre, Glasgow, 1946–48. *Publications: plays:* Max (prod. Malvern Festival), 1949; Captain Carvallo (Bristol Old Vic and St James's Theatres), 1950; Colombe (trans. from Anouilh), New Theatre, 1951; Misery Me!, Duchess, 1955; You and Your Wife, Bristol Old Vic, 1955; The Power and The Glory (adaptation from Graham Greene), Phoenix Theatre, 1956, and Phœnix Theatre, New York, 1958; Who's Your Father?, Cambridge Theatre, 1958; US (original text), Aldwych, 1966; adapted Ibsen's Ghosts, Aldwych, 1966; One at Night, Royal Court, 1971; The Ik (adaptation and collaboration), 1975 (produced Paris, Berlin, London, Venice, Belgrade; tour of American univs, 1976; orig. prod. rev. for Australia, NY, 1980); Dear Daddy, Oxford Festival and Ambassadors, 1976 (Play of the Year award, 1976); the screenplays of several films; plays for TV and radio, adaptations for TV series; contribs to Times Literary Supplement. *Recreation:* loitering. *Address:* 43 Osmond Road, Hove, Sussex.

See also D. L. A. Farr.

CANNAN, Rt. Rev. Edward Alexander Capparis; *b* 25 Dec. 1920; *s* of Alexander and Mabel Capparis; *m* 1941, Eunice Mary Blandford; three *s. Educ:* St Marylebone Grammar School; King's College, London (BD, AKC). Served RAF, 1937–46 (despatches). Deacon 1950, priest 1951, dio. Salisbury; Curate, Blandford Forum, Dorset, 1950–53. Chaplain, RAF, 1953–74; RAF Cosford, 1953–54; Padgate, 1954–57; HQ 2 Gp, Germany, 1957–58; Lecturer, RAF Chaplains' Sch., 1958–60; RAF Gan, Maldive Islands, 1960–61; RAF Halton, 1961–62; Hereford, 1962–64; Khormaksar, Aden, 1964–66; Vice-Principal, RAF Chaplains' School, 1966–69; Asst Chaplain-in-Chief, 1969–74; Far East Air Force, Singapore, 1969–72; HQ Training Comd, 1972–73; Principal, RAF Chaplains' Sch., 1973–74; Hon. Chaplain to the Queen, 1972–74; Chaplain, St Margaret's Sch., Bushey, 1974–79; Bishop of St Helena, 1979–85. *Publication:* A History of the Diocese of St Helena and its Precursors 1502–1984, 1985. *Recreations:* gardening, house maintenance, photography. *Address:* Church Cottage, Allensmore, Hereford HR2 9AQ. *T:* Hereford 277357.

CANNELL, Prof. Robert Quirk; Director, Welsh Plant Breeding Station, Aberystwyth, since 1984; *b* 20 March 1937; *s* of William Watterson Cannell and Norah Isabel Corjeag; *m* 1962, Edwina Anne Thornborough; two *s. Educ:* King's Coll., Newcastle upon Tyne; Univ. of Durham (BSc, PhD). Shell Chemical Co., London, 1959; School of Agriculture, Univ. of Newcastle upon Tyne, 1961; Dept of Agronomy and Plant Genetics, Univ. of Minnesota, 1968–69; Letcombe Lab., AFRC, Oxon, 1970. *Publications:* papers in agricultural science jls. *Address:* Welsh Plant Breeding Station, Plas Gogerddan, near Aberystwyth, Dyfed SY23 3EB. *T:* Aberystwyth 828255.

CANNING, family name of **Baron Garvagh.**

CANNON, Prof. John Ashton, CBE 1985; PhD; Professor of Modern History, University of Newcastle upon Tyne, since 1976; Pro-Vice Chancellor, since 1983; *b* 8 Oct. 1926; *s* of George and Gladys Cannon; *m* 1st, 1948, Audrey Elizabeth, *d* of G. R. Caple (marr. diss. 1953); one *s* one *d*; 2nd, 1953, Minna, *d* of Frederick Pedersen, Denmark; one *s* two *d. Educ:* Hertford Grammar Sch.; Peterhouse, Cambridge (MA 1955). PhD Bristol, 1958. Served RAF, 1947–49 and 1952–55. History of Parlt Trust, 1960–61; Univ. of Bristol: Lectr, 1961; Sen. Lectr, 1967; Reader, 1970; Dean, Faculty of Arts, Univ. of Newcastle upon Tyne, 1979–82. Mem., UGC, 1983–, Vice-Chm., 1986

(Chm., Arts Sub-Cttee, 1983–). Lectures: Wiles, Queen's Univ. Belfast, 1982; Raleigh, British Acad., 1982; Prothero, RHistS, 1985; Stenton, Reading Univ., 1986. Chm., Radio Bristol, 1970–74. *Publications:* The Fox-North Coalition: crisis of the constitution, 1970; Parliamentary Reform, 1640–1832, 1973; (ed with P. V. McGrath) Essays in Bristol and Gloucestershire History, 1976; (ed) The Letters of Junius, 1978; (ed) The Historian at Work, 1980; (ed) The Whig Ascendancy, 1981; Aristocratic Century, 1984. *Recreations:* music, losing at tennis. *Address:* 17 Haldane Terrace, Jesmond, Newcastle upon Tyne NE2 3AN. *T:* Newcastle upon Tyne 815186.

CANNON, John Francis Michael; Keeper of Botany, British Museum (Natural History), since 1977; *b* 22 April 1930; *s* of Francis Leslie Cannon and Aileen Flora Cannon; *m* 1954, Margaret Joy (*née* Herbert); two *s* one *d*. *Educ:* Whitgift Sch., South Croydon, Surrey; King's Coll., Newcastle upon Tyne, Univ. of Durham (BSc 1st Cl. Hons Botany). Dept of Botany, British Museum (Nat. History), 1952, Dep. Keeper 1972. President: Botanical Soc. of the British Isles, 1983–85; Ray Soc., 1986–. *Publications:* papers in scientific periodicals and similar pubns. *Recreations:* travel, music, gardening. *Address:* 26 Purley Bury Avenue, Purley, Surrey CR2 9JD. *T:* 01–660 3223.

CANNON, Richard Walter, CEng, FIEE, FIERE; Joint Managing Director, Cable and Wireless plc, 1977–83; Director: Batelco (Bahrain), since 1981; Teletswana (Botswana), since 1984; *b* 7 Dec. 1923; *s* of Richard William Cannon and Lily Harriet Cannon (*née* Fewins); *m* 1949, Dorothy (formerly Jarvis); two *d*. *Educ:* Eltham Coll. Joined Cable and Wireless Ltd, 1941; Exec. Dir, 1973. *Publications:* telecommunications papers for IEE and IERE.

CANNON-BROOKES, Peter, PhD; FMA, FIIC; Museum Services Director, STIPPLE Database Systems Ltd, since 1986; *b* 23 Aug. 1938; *s* of Victor Montgomery Cannon Brookes and Nancy Margaret (*née* Markham Carter); *m* 1966, Caroline Aylmer, *d* of John Aylmer Christie-Miller; one *s* one *d*. *Educ:* Bryanston; Trinity Hall, Cambridge (MA); Courtauld Inst. of Art, Univ. of London (PhD). FMA 1975. Gooden and Fox Ltd, London, 1963–64; Keeper, Dept of Art, City Museums and Art Gall., Birmingham, 1965–78; Sessional Teacher in History of Art, Courtauld Inst. of Art, London, 1966–68; Keeper of Dept of Art, Nat. Mus. of Wales, Cardiff, 1978–86. Internat. Council of Museums: Mem. Exec. Bd, UK Cttee, 1973–81; Pres., Internat. Art Exhibns Cttee, 1977–79 (Dir, 1974–80; Sec., 1975–77); Dir, Conservation Cttee, 1975–81 (Vice Pres., 1978–81). Member: Town Twinning Cttee, Birmingham Internat. Council, 1968–78; Birm. Diocesan Synod, 1970–78; Birm. Diocesan Adv. Cttee for Care of Churches, 1972–78; Edgbaston Deanery Synod, 1970–78 (Lay Jt Chm., 1975–78); Art and Design Adv. Panel, Welsh Jt Educn Cttee, 1978–; Welsh Arts Council, 1979–84 (Member: Art Cttee, 1978–84; Craft Cttee, 1983–); Projects and Orgns Cttee, Crafts Council, 1985–. President: Welsh Fedn of Museums and Art Galleries, 1980–82; S Wales Art Soc., 1980–86. Editor, Internat. Jl of Museum Management and Curatorship, 1981–. Freeman 1969, Liveryman 1974, Worshipful Co. of Goldsmiths. FRSA. JP Birmingham, 1973–78, Cardiff, 1978–82. *Publications:* (with H. D. Molesworth) European Sculpture, 1964; (with C. A. Cannon-Brookes) Baroque Churches, 1969; Lombard Paintings, 1974; After Gulbenkian, 1976; The Cornbury Park Bellini, 1977; Michael Ayrton, 1978; Emile Antoine Bourdelle, 1983; Ivor Roberts-Jones, 1983; Czech Sculpture 1800–1938, 1983; contrib. Apollo, Art Bull., Arte Veneta, Burlington Mag., Connoisseur, Internat. Jl of Museum Management and Curatorship, and Museums Jl. *Recreations:* photography, growing vegetables, cooking. *Address:* Thrupp House, Abingdon, Oxon OX14 3NE. *T:* Abingdon 20595. *Clubs:* Athenæum; Birmingham (Birmingham).

CANSDALE, George Soper, BA, BSc, FLS, MIWES; *b* 29 Nov. 1909; *y s* of G. W. Cansdale, Paignton, Devon; *m* 1940, Margaret Sheila, *o d* of R. M. Williamson, Indian Forest Service; two *s*. *Educ:* Brentwood Sch.; St Edmund Hall, Oxford. Colonial Forest Service, Gold Coast, 1934–48. Superintendent to Zoological Society of London, Regent's Park, 1948–53. Inventor, SWS Filtration Unit, 1975. *Publications:* The Black Poplars, 1938; Animals of West Africa, 1946; Animals and Man, 1952; George Cansdale's Zoo Book, 1953; Belinda the Bushbaby, 1953; Reptiles of West Africa, 1955; West African Snakes, 1961; Behind the Scenes at a Zoo, 1965; Animals of Bible Lands, 1970; articles in the Field, Geographical Magazine, Zoo Life, Nigerian Field, Natural History, etc. *Recreations:* natural history, photography, sailing. *Address:* Dove Cottage, Great Chesterford, Essex CB10 1PL. *T:* Saffron Walden 30274. *Club:* Royal Commonwealth Society.

CANT, Rev. Harry William Macphail; Minister of St Magnus Cathedral, Kirkwall, Orkney, since 1968; Chaplain to the Queen in Scotland since 1972; *b* 3 April 1921; *s* of late J. M. Cant and late Margaret Cant; *m* 1951, Margaret Elizabeth Loudon; one *s* two *d*. *Educ:* Edinburgh Acad.; Edinburgh Univ. (MA, BD); Union Theological Seminary, NY (STM). Lieut, KOSB, 1941–43; Captain, King's African Rifles, 1944–46; TA Chaplain, 7th Argyll and Sutherland Highlanders, 1962–70. Asst Minister, Old Parish Church, Aberdeen, 1950–51; Minister of Fallin Parish Church, Stirling, 1951–56; Scottish Sec., Student Christian Movt, 1956–59; Minister of St Thomas' Parish Church, 1960–68. *Publication:* Preaching in a Scottish Parish Church: St Magnus and Other Sermons, 1970. *Recreations:* angling, golf. *Address:* Cathedral Manse, Kirkwall, Orkney. *T:* Kirkwall 3312.

CANT, Rev. Canon Reginald Edward; Canon and Chancellor of York Minster, 1957–81, now Canon Emeritus; *b* 1 May 1914; 2nd *s* of late Samuel Reginald Cant; unmarried. *Educ:* Sir Joseph Williamson's Sch., Rochester; CCC, Cambridge; Cuddesdon Theological Coll. Asst Curate, St Mary's, Portsea, 1938–41; Vice-Principal, Edinburgh Theological Coll., 1941–46; Lecturer, Univ. of Durham, 1946–52 (Vice-Principal, St Chad's Coll. from 1949); Vicar, St Mary the Less, Cambridge, 1952–57. *Publications:* Christian Prayer, 1961; part-author, The Churchman's Companion, 1964; (ed jtly) A History of York Minster, 1977. *Address:* 7 Sykes Close, St Olave's Road, York YO3 6HZ. *T:* York 23328. *Clubs:* Royal Commonwealth Society; Yorkshire (York).

CANT, Robert (Bowen); *b* 24 July 1915; *s* of Robert and Catherine Cant; *m* 1940, Rebecca Harris Watt; one *s* two *d*. *Educ:* Middlesbrough High Sch. for Boys; London Sch. of Economics. BSc (Econ.) 1945. Lecturer in Economics, Univ. of Keele, 1962–66. Member: Stoke-on-Trent City Council, 1953–74; Staffs CC, 1973– (Chm., Educn Cttee, 1981–). Contested (Lab) Shrewsbury, 1950, 1951; MP (Lab) Stoke-on-Trent Central, 1966–83. *Publication:* American Journey. *Recreation:* bookbinding. *Address:* (home) 119 Chell Green Avenue, Stoke-on-Trent, Staffordshire. *Club:* Chell Working Men's.

CANTACUZINO, Sherban, FRIBA; Secretary, Royal Fine Art Commission, since 1979; *b* 6 Sept. 1928; *s* of Georges M. Cantacuzino and Sanda Stirbey; *m* 1954, Anne Mary Trafford; two *d* (one *s* decd). *Educ:* Winchester Coll.; Magdalene Coll., Cambridge (MA). Partner, Steane, Shipman & Cantacuzino, Chartered Architects, 1956–65; private practice, 1965–73; Asst Editor, Architectural Review, 1967–73, Exec. Editor, 1973–79. Sen. Lectr, Dept of Architecture, College of Art, Canterbury, 1967–70. Trustee: Thomas Cubitt Trust, 1978–; Conran Foundn, 1981–; Member: Arts Panel, Arts Council, 1977–80; Steering Cttee, Aga Khan Award for Architecture, 1980– (Mem., Master Jury, 1980); Council, RSA, 1980–85; Design Cttee, London Transport, 1981–82; Adv. Panel, Railway Heritage Trust; Vice-Chm., ICOMOS UK Cttee, 1983–. *Publications:* Modern Houses of the World, 1964, 3rd edn 1966; Great Modern Architecture, 1966, 2nd edn 1968; European Domestic Architecture, 1969; New Uses for Old Buildings, 1975; (ed) Architectural Conservation in Europe, 1975; Wells Coates, a monograph, 1978; (with Susan Brandt) Saving Old Buildings, 1980; The Architecture of Howell, Killick, Partridge and Amis, 1981; Charles Correa, 1984; (ed) Architecture in Continuity: building in the Islamic world today, 1985; articles in Architectural Rev. *Recreations:* music, cooking. *Address:* 11 Pembroke Studios, W8 6HX. *T:* 01–602 1029. *Club:* Garrick.

CANTERBURY, Archbishop of, since 1980; **Most Rev. and Rt. Hon. Robert Alexander Kennedy Runcie,** MC 1945; PC 1980; *b* 2 Oct. 1921; *s* of Robert Dalziel Runcie and Anne Runcie; *m* 1957, Angela Rosalind, *d* of J. W. Cecil Turner; one *s* one *d*. *Educ:* Merchant Taylors', Crosby; Brasenose Coll., Oxford (Squire Minor Schol.), Hon. Fellow, 1979; Westcott House, Cambridge. BA (1st Cl. Hons, Lit. Hum.), MA Oxon, 1948; FKC 1981. Served Scots Guards, War of 1939–45 (MC). Deacon, 1950; Priest, 1951; Curate, All Saints, Gosforth, 1950–52; Chaplain, Westcott House, Cambridge, 1953–54; Vice-Principal, 1954–56; Fellow, Dean and Asst Tutor of Trinity Hall, Cambridge, 1956–60, Hon. Fellow 1975; Vicar of Cuddesdon and Principal of Cuddesdon Coll., 1960–69; Bishop of St Albans, 1970–80. Canon and Prebendary of Lincoln, 1969. Hon. Bencher, Gray's Inn, 1980. Chm., BBC and IBA Central Religious Adv. Cttee, 1973–79. Teape Lectr, St Stephen's Coll., Delhi, 1962. Select Preacher: Cambridge, 1957 and 1975, Oxford, 1959 and 1973. Anglican Chm., Anglican-Orthodox Jt Doctrinal Commn, 1973–80. Freeman: St Albans, 1979; City of London, 1981; Canterbury, 1984. Hon. DD: Oxon, 1980; Cantab, 1981; Univ. of the South, Sewanee, 1981; Trinity Coll., Toronto, 1986; Hon. DLitt Keele, 1981; Hon. LittD Liverpool, 1983; Hon. DCL West Indies, 1984. *Publications:* (ed) Cathedral and City: St Albans Ancient and Modern, 1978; Windows onto God, 1983; Seasons of the Spirit, 1983. *Recreations:* opera, reading history and novels, owning Berkshire pigs. *Address:* Lambeth Palace, SE1 7JU. *T:* 01–928 8282; Old Palace, Canterbury. *Club:* Athenæum.

CANTERBURY, Dean of; *see* Simpson, Very Rev. J. A.

CANTERBURY, Archdeacon of; *see* Till, Ven. M. S.

CANTLAY, George Thomson, CBE 1973; Partner, Murray & Co., 1979–83, now Consultant; Chairman, Parkfield Foundries (Tees-side) Ltd, to 1984, now Director; Director: A. B. Electronic Products Group PLC; Christie-Tyler Ltd, to 1983; Welsh National Opera Ltd (since inception); *b* 2 Aug. 1907; *s* of G. and A. Cantlay; *m* 1934, Sibyl Gwendoline Alsop Stoker; one *s* one *d*. *Educ:* Glasgow High Sch. Member of Stock Exchange. Vice-Pres., Welsh Region, Inst. of Directors. KStJ 1985; FRSA. *Recreations:* music (opera), gardening. *Address:* 9 Park Road, Penarth CF6 2BD. *Clubs:* Carlton; Cardiff and County (Cardiff).

CANTLEY, Sir Joseph (Donaldson), Kt 1965; OBE 1945; Judge of the High Court of Justice, Queen's Bench Division, 1965–85; *b* 8 Aug. 1910; *er s* of Dr Joseph Cantley, Crumpsall, Manchester, and Georgina Cantley (*née* Kean); *m* 1966, Lady (Hilda Goodwin) Gerrard, *widow* of Sir Denis Gerrard. *Educ:* Manchester Grammar Sch.; Manchester Univ. Studentship and Certificate of Honour, Council of Legal Education, 1933; Barrister, Middle Temple, 1933 (Bencher 1963; Treasurer 1981); QC 1954. Served throughout War of 1939–45: Royal Artillery and on Staff; 2nd Lieut Royal Artillery 1940; N Africa and Italy, 1942–45 (despatches twice); Lieut-Colonel and AAG, 1943–45. Recorder of Oldham, 1959–60; Judge of Salford Hundred Court of Record, 1960–65; Judge of Appeal, Isle of Man, 1962–65; Presiding Judge: Northern Circuit, 1970–74; South Eastern Circuit, 1980. Member, General Council of the Bar, 1957–61. Hon. Col, Manchester and Salford Univs OTC, 1971–77. Hon. LLD Manchester, 1968. *Club:* Travellers'.

CAPE, Donald Paul Montagu Stewart, CMG 1977; HM Diplomatic Service, retired; Ambassador and UK Permanent Representative to the Council of Europe, Strasbourg, 1978–83; *b* 6 Jan. 1923; *s* of late John Scarvell and Olivia Millicent Cape; *m* 1948, Cathune Johnston; four *s* one *d*. *Educ:* Ampleforth Coll.; Brasenose Coll., Oxford. Scots Guards, 1942–45. Entered Foreign Service, 1946. Served: Belgrade, 1946–49; FO, 1949–51; Lisbon, 1951–55; Singapore, 1955–57; FO, 1957–60; Bogota, 1960–61; Holy See, 1962–67; Head of Information Administration Dept, FCO, 1968–70; Counsellor, Washington, 1970–73; Counsellor, Brasilia, 1973–75; Ambassador to Laos, 1976–78. Administrator: Anglo-Irish Encounter, 1983–; Community Service Volunteers, 1983–. *Recreations:* riding, tennis, walking, swimming, skiing. *Address:* Hilltop, Wonersh, Guildford, Surrey GU5 0QT.

CAPE, Maj.-Gen. Timothy Frederick, CB 1972; CBE 1966; DSO; idc, jssc, psc; FAIM; *b* Sydney, 5 Aug. 1915; *s* of C. S. Cape, DSO, Edgecliff, NSW; *m* 1961, Elizabeth (*d* 1985), *d* of Brig. R. L. R. Rabett; one *d*. *Educ:* Cranbrook Sch., Sydney; RMC Duntroon. Served with RAA, 1938–40; Bde Major Sparrow Force, Timor, 1942; GS01: (Air) New Guinea Force, 1942–43; (Ops) Melbourne, 1944; (Air) Morotai, 1945; (Ops) Japan, 1946–47; (Plans) Melbourne, 1948–49; Instructor, UK, 1950–52; Comdt, Portsea, 1954–56; Dep. Master-Gen. Ordnance, 1957–59; COS Northern Comd, Brisbane, 1961; Dir of Staff Duties, Army HQ, Canberra, 1962–63; Comdr, Adelaide, 1964; GOC Northern Comd, Brisbane, 1965–68; Master-General of the Ordnance, 1968–72; retd 1972. Nat. Chm., Royal United Services Inst. of Australia, 1980–83; Chm., Nat. Disaster Relief Cttee and Mem., Nat. Council, Australian Red Cross Soc., 1975–85. Bronze Star (US). *Address:* 20 Charlotte Street, Red Hill, ACT 2603, Australia. *Clubs:* Melbourne, Naval and Military (Melbourne); Commonwealth (Canberra); Union (Sydney); Royal Sydney Golf.

CAPE TOWN, Archbishop of, and Metropolitan of Southern Africa, since 1986; **Most Rev. Desmond Mpilo Tutu;** *b* 7 Oct. 1931; *s* of Zachariah and Aletta Tutu; *m* 1955, Leah Nomalizo Shenxane; one *s* three *d*. *Educ:* Western High, Johannesburg; Bantu Normal Coll., Pretoria (Higher Teachers' Dip.); Univ. of S Africa (BA); St Peter's Theol Coll., Johannesburg (LTh); King's Coll. London (BD, MTh; FKC 1978). Schoolmaster: Madibane High Sch., Johannesburg, 1954; Munsieville High Sch., Krugersdorp, 1955–57. Theological coll. student, 1958–60; deacon 1960, priest 1961, St Mary's Cathedral, Johannesburg. Curate: St Alban's Church, Benoni, 1960–61; St Philip's Church, Alberton, 1961–62; St Alban's, Golder's Green, London, 1962–65; St Mary's, Bletchingley, Surrey, 1965–66. Lecturer: Federal Theol Seminary, Alice, CP, 1967–69; Univ. of Botswana, Lesotho and Swaziland, Roma, Lesotho, 1970–72; Associate Dir, Theol Education Fund (WCC) based in Bromley, Kent, and Curate, St Augustine's, Grove Park, 1972–75; Dean of Johannesburg, 1975–76; Bishop of Lesotho, 1976–78; Gen. Sec., South African Council of Churches, 1978–85; Asst Bishop of Johannesburg, 1978–85; Rector, St Augustine's Parish, Soweto, 1981–85; Bishop of Johannesburg, 1985–86. Trustee, Phelps Stoke Fund, New York. Holds many hon. degrees from academic institutions in UK, Europe and USA. Athena Prize, Onassis Foundation, 1980; Nobel Peace Prize, 1984. *Publications:* Crying in the Wilderness, 1982; Hope and Suffering, 1983; articles and reviews. *Recreations:* music, reading, jogging. *Address:* Bishopscourt, Claremont, CP, 7700, South Africa.

CAPE TOWN, Bishops Suffragan of; *see* Albertyn, Rt Rev. C. H.; Matolengwe, Rt Rev. P. M.

CAPE TOWN, Dean of; *see* King, Very Rev. E. L.

CAPEL CURE, (George) Nigel, TD; JP; DL; *b* 28 Sept. 1908; *o s* of late Major George Edward Capel Cure, JP, Blake Hall, Ongar; *m* 1935, Nancy Elizabeth, *d* of late William James Barry, Great Witchingham Hall, Norwich; two *s* one *d*. *Educ:* Eton; Trinity Coll., Cambridge. DL and JP, 1947, High Sheriff, 1951, Essex; Vice-Lieutenant, later Vice Lord-Lieutenant, Essex, 1958–78; late of Blake Hall, Ongar. *Recreations:* shooting, cricket. *Address:* Ashlings, Moreton Road, Ongar, Essex. *T:* Ongar 362634. *Clubs:* MCC, City University.

CAPELL, family name of **Earl of Essex.**

CAPLAN, Daniel; Under-Secretary, Department of the Environment, 1970–71; *b* 29 July 1915; *y s* of Daniel and Miriam Caplan; *m* 1945, Olive Beatrice Porter; no *c*. *Educ:* Elem. and Secondary Schools, Blackpool; St Catharine's Coll., Cambridge. Asst Principal, Import Duties Adv. Cttee, 1938; Private Secretary to three Permanent Secretaries, Ministry of Supply, 1940; Principal, 1942; Ministry of Supply Representative and Economic Secretary to British Political Representative in Finland, 1944–45; Asst Secretary, Board of Trade, 1948; Adviser to Chancellor of Duchy of Lancaster, 1957–60; Under-Secretary, Scottish Development Dept, 1963–65; Under-Secretary, National Economic Development Office, 1966; Asst Under-Sec. of State, DEA, 1966–69; Under-Sec., Min. of Housing and Local Govt, 1969–70; Consultant to Minister for Housing for Leasehold Charges Study, 1972–73. Indep. Review of Royal Commn on Historical Manuscripts, for HM Govt, 1980. *Publications:* People and Homes (indep. report on Landlord and Tenant Relations in England for British Property Fedn), 1975; Border Country Branch Lines, 1981; Report on the Work of the Royal Commission on Historical Manuscripts, 1981; The Waverley Route, 1985; The Royal Scot, 1987; numerous papers on religious and economic history in learned journals. *Recreations:* railways, historical research, gardening. *Address:* Knowle Wood, London Road, Cuckfield, West Sussex. *T:* Haywards Heath 454301.

CAPLAN, Leonard, QC 1954; *b* 28 June 1909; *s* of late Henry Caplan, Liverpool; *m* 1st, 1942, Tania (*d* 1974); two *d*; 2nd, 1977, Mrs Korda Herskovits, NY. Called to the Bar, Gray's Inn, 1935; Master of the Bench, 1964; Vice-Treasurer, 1978; Treasurer, 1979; Master of the Library, 1980–86; joined South Eastern Circuit; Middle Temple, 1949; served War of 1939–45, Royal Artillery (Anti-Tank): Staff Captain, 47th Div.; Staff Captain ("Q" Operations), Southern Command, engaged in D-Day Planning; passed Staff Coll., Camberley; Major, DAAG and Lt-Col, AAG, HQ Allied Land Forces, South East Asia. Conservative candidate: Pontypool, 1935; N Hammersmith, 1945; N Kensington, 1950–51. Chm., Coll. Hall (Univ. of London), 1958–67. Chm., Mental Health Review Tribunal, SE Region, 1960–63; Vice-Chm., NI Detention Appeals Tribunal, 1973–75; Senate of Inns of Court and the Bar, 1975–81. Pres., Medico-Legal Soc., 1979–81. *Publication:* (with late Marcus Samuel, MP) The Great Experiment: a critical study of Soviet Five Year Plans, 1935. *Recreation:* yachting. *Address:* 1 Pump Court, Temple, EC4. *T:* 01–353 9332; Skol, Marbella, S Spain; 40 East 66th Street, New York, NY 10021, USA. *Clubs:* Savage, Authors', Royal Automobile; Hurlingham; Marbella Yacht, Bar Yacht.

CAPLAN, Philip Isaac, QC (Scot.) 1970; Sheriff Principal of North Strathclyde, since 1983; *b* 24 Feb. 1929; *s* of Hyman and Rosalena Caplan; *m* 1st, 1953; two *s* one *d*; 2nd, 1974, Joyce Ethel Stone; one *d*. *Educ:* Eastwood Sch., Renfrewshire; Glasgow Univ. (MA, LLB). Solicitor, 1952–56; called to Bar, 1957; Standing Junior Counsel to Accountant of Court, 1964–70; Sheriff of Lothian and Borders, 1979–83. Mem., Sheriff Court Rules Council, 1984–. Chairman: Plant Varieties and Seeds Tribunal, Scotland, 1977–79; Scottish Assoc. for Study of Delinquency, 1985–. Mem., Scottish Photographic Circle, 1986–. ARPS 1982; AFIAP 1985. *Recreations:* photography, sailing, reading, music. *Address:* Auchenlea, Torwoodhill Road, Rhu, Dunbartonshire G84 8LF. *T:* Rhu 820359. *Clubs:* New (Edinburgh); Royal Northern and Clyde Yacht (Rhu).

CAPLAT, Moran Victor Hingston, CBE 1968; General Administrator, Glyndebourne Festival Opera, retired; *b* 1 Oct. 1916; *s* of Roger Armand Charles Caplat and Norah Hingston; *m* 1943, Diana Murray Downton; one *s* two *d* (and one *s* decd). *Educ:* privately; Royal Acad. of Dramatic Art. Actor, etc., 1934–39. Royal Navy, 1939–45. Glyndebourne: Asst to Gen. Man., 1945; Gen. Man., later known as Gen. Administrator, 1949–81. *Publication:* Dinghies to Divas (autobiog.), 1985. *Recreations:* gardening, sailing, wine. *Address:* The Yew Tree House, Barcombe, near Lewes, East Sussex BN8 5EF. *T:* Barcombe 400202. *Clubs:* Garrick, Royal Ocean Racing.

CAPPER, Rt. Rev. Edmund Michael Hubert, OBE 1961; LTh (Dur.); Auxiliary Bishop in the Diocese of Gibraltar in Europe, since 1973; Assistant Bishop of Southwark, since 1981; *b* 12 March 1908; *e s* of Arthur Charles and Mabel Lavinia Capper; unmarried. *Educ:* St Joseph's Academy, Blackheath; St Augustine's College, Canterbury. Deacon, 1932, Priest, 1933. Royal Army Chaplains' Dept, 1942–46 (EA); Archdeacon of Lindi and Canon of Masasi Cathedral, 1947–54; Archdeacon of Dar es Salaam, 1954–58. Provost of the Collegiate Church of St Alban the Martyr, Dar es Salaam, Tanganyika, 1957–62; Canon of Zanzibar, 1954–62; Member, Universities' Mission to Central Africa, 1936–62; Chairman, Tanganyika British Legion Benevolent Fund, 1956–62; President, Tanganyika British Legion, 1960–62; Chaplain, Palma de Mallorca, 1962–67; Bishop of St Helena, 1967–73; Chaplain of St George's, Malaga, 1973–76. *Recreations:* swimming and walking. *Address:* Morden College, Blackheath, SE3 0PW. *T:* 01–858 9169. *Club:* Travellers'.

CAPRA, Frank, Legion of Merit, 1943; DSM 1945; Hon. OBE (mil.) 1946; Writer, Director and Producer of Motion Pictures; President of own producing company, Liberty Films Inc.; *b* 18 May 1897; Italian parents; *m* 1932, Lucille Rayburn; two *s* one *d*. *Educ:* California Institute of Technology. Col, Signal Corps, US Army; released from Army, spring of 1945. Produced and directed following pictures: Submarine, The Strong Man, Flight, Dirigible, Ladies of Leisure, Platinum Blonde, American Madness, Lady for a Day, It Happened One Night, Mr Deeds Goes to Town, Broadway Bill, Lost Horizon, You Can't Take It With You, Mr Smith Goes to Washington, Meet John Doe, Arsenic and Old Lace, It's a Wonderful Life, State of the Union, Here Comes the Groom, A Hole in the Head, Pocketful of Miracles; created: Why We Fight (film series), 1941–46; science series films widely used in schools, incl. Our Mr Sun, Hemo the Magnificent, The Strange Case of Cosmic Rays, The Unchained Goddess, 1956–58. Member of Motion Picture Academy and of Directors' Guild. Hon. Dr Arts Temple Univ., 1971; Hon. Dr Fine Arts Carthage Coll., 1972. Winner of six Academy Awards. *Publication:* Frank Capra: the name above the title (autobiog.), 1971. *Recreations:* hunting, fishing, music. *Address:* PO Box 980, La Quinta, Calif 92253, USA.

CAPRON, (George) Christopher; Head of Parliamentary Broadcasting, BBC, since 1985; *b* 17 Dec. 1935; *s* of late Lt-Col George Capron and of Hon. Mrs Christian Capron (*née* Hepburn-Scott); *m* 1958, Edna Naomi Goldrei; one *s* one *d*. *Educ:* Wellington Coll.; Trinity Hall, Cambridge (BA Hons Mod. Langs). Served Army, 12th Royal Lancers (Prince of Wales's), 1954–56. British Broadcasting Corporation: radio producer, 1963–67; television producer, 1967–76; Editor, Tonight, 1976–77; Editor, Panorama, 1977–79; Asst Head, 1979–81, Head, 1981–85, TV Current Affairs Programmes. *Recreations:* village cricket, tennis. *Address:* 32 Amerland Road, SW18 1PZ; Southwick Hall, Oundle, Northants.

CAPSTICK, Brian Eric, QC 1973; **His Honour Judge Capstick;** a Circuit Judge, since 1985; *b* 12 Feb. 1927; *o s* of late Eric and Betty Capstick; *m* 1960, Margaret Harrison; one *s* one *d*. *Educ:* Sedbergh; Queen's Coll., Oxford (Scholar) (MA). Served HM Forces, 1945–48: 17/21st Lancers, Palestine, 1947–48. Tancred Scholar, and called to Bar, Lincoln's Inn, 1952; Bencher, 1980; a Recorder, 1980–85. Dep. Chm., Northern Agriculture Tribunal, 1976. Asst Boundary Comr, 1978–85. Appeal Steward, British Board of Boxing Control, 1985. *Recreations:* shooting, reading, cooking. *Address:* (home) 71 South End Road, NW3; Blue Mill, Thropton, Northumberland. *Club:* Garrick.

See also A. H. Brind.

CAPSTICK, Charles William, CMG 1972; Director of Economics and Statistics, Ministry of Agriculture, Fisheries and Food, since 1977; *b* 18 Dec. 1934; *s* of William Capstick and Janet Frankland; *m* 1962, Joyce Alma Dodsworth; two *s*. *Educ:* King's Coll., Univ. of Durham (BSc (Hons)); Univ. of Kentucky, USA (MS). MAFF: Asst Agricl Economist, 1961; Principal Agricl Economist, 1966; Senior Principal Agricl Economist, 1968; Sen. Econ. Advr and Head, Milk and Milk Products Div., 1976; Under Sec., 1977. Pres., Agricultural Economics Soc., 1983. *Recreations:* gardening, golf. *Address:* 7 Dellfield Close, Radlett, Herts. *T:* Radlett 7640.

CARADON, Baron (Life Peer) *cr* 1964; **Hugh Mackintosh Foot,** PC 1968; GCMG 1957 (KCMG 1951; CMG 1946); KCVO 1953; OBE 1939; *b* 8 Oct. 1907; *s* of late Rt Hon. Isaac Foot, PC; *m* 1936, Florence Sylvia Tod (*d* 1985); three *s* one *d*. *Educ:* Leighton Park Sch., Reading; St John's Coll., Cambridge. Pres. Cambridge Union, 1929; Administrative Officer, Palestine Govt, 1929–37; attached to the Colonial Office, 1938–39; Asst British Resident, Trans-Jordan, 1939–42; British Mil. Administration, Cyrenaica, 1943; Colonial Secretary: Cyprus, 1943–45, Jamaica, 1945–47; Chief Sec., Nigeria, 1947–51. Acting Governor: Cyprus, 1944, Jamaica, Aug. 1945–Jan. 1946, Nigeria, 1949 and 1950. Capt.-Gen. and Gov.-in-Chief of Jamaica, 1951–57; Governor and Comdr-in-Chief, Cyprus, Dec. 1957–60; Ambassador and Adviser in the UK Mission to the UN and UK representative on Trusteeship Council, 1961–62, resigned; Minister of State for Foreign and Commonwealth Affairs and Perm. UK Rep. at the UN, 1964–70. Consultant, Special Fund of the United Nations, 1963–64. Mem., UN Expert Group on South Africa, 1964; Consultant to UN Develt Programme, 1971–75. Visiting Fellow: Princeton, Harvard and Georgetown Univs, 1979. KStJ 1952. Hon. Fellow, St John's Coll., Cambridge, 1960. *Publication:* A Start in Freedom, 1964. *Address:* House of Lords, SW1; 203 Drake House, Dolphin Square, SW1.

See also Baron Foot, Rt Hon. Michael Foot.

CARBERRY, Sir John (Edward Doston), Kt 1956; Chief Justice, Jamaica, 1954–58, retired; *b* Grenada, WI, 20 Aug. 1893; *e s* of D. A. and Ruth Carberry; *m* 1920, Georgiana, *y d* of Charles Jackson; one *s* one *d*. *Educ:* Wesley Hall, Grenada; McGill Univ., Montreal (LLB). Served European War in 1st Bn British West Indies Regt, 1915–19. Called to Bar, Middle Temple, 1925; in practice in Jamaica until 1927, when joined Government Service as Clerk of the Courts; Resident Magistrate, 1932; Puisne Judge, Supreme Court, 1946; Senior Puisne Judge, Jamaica, 1949. *Recreation:* philately. *Address:* 8 East King's House Road, Kingston 6, Jamaica.

CARBERY, 11th Baron *cr* 1715; **Peter Ralfe Harrington Evans-Freke;** Bt 1768; *b* 20 March 1920; *o s* of Major the Hon. Ralfe Evans-Freke, MBE (*yr s* of 9th Baron) (*d* 1969), and Vera (*d* 1984), *d* of late C. Harrington Moore; *S* uncle, 1970; *m* 1941, Joyzelle Mary, *o d* of late Herbert Binnie; three *s* two *d*. *Educ:* Downside School. MICE. Served War of 1939–45, Captain RE, India, Burmah. Member of London Stock Exchange, 1955–68. *Recreations:* hunting, tennis, winter sports. *Heir: e s* Hon. Michael Peter Evans-Freke [*b* 11 Oct. 1942; *m* 1967, Claudia Janet Elizabeth, *o d* of Captain P. L. C. Gurney; one *s* three *d*]. *Address:* 2 Hayes Court, Sunnyside, Wimbledon, SW19 4SH. *T:* 01–946 6615. *Clubs:* Kennel, Ski Club of Great Britain.

CARBERY, Prof. Thomas Francis, OBE 1983; Professor and Chairman, Department of Information Science, University of Strathclyde, since 1985; *b* 18 Jan. 1925; *o c* of Thomas Albert Carbery and Jane Morrison; *m* 1954, Ellen Donnelly; one *s* two *d*. *Educ:* St Aloysius Coll., Glasgow; Univ. of Glasgow and Scottish Coll. of Commerce. Cadet Navigator and Meteorologist, RAFVR, 1943–47; Civil Servant, Min. of Labour, 1947–61; Sen. Lectr in Govt and Econs, Scottish College of Commerce, Glasgow, 1961–64; Sen. Lectr in Govt-Business Relations, 1964–75, Head of Dept of Office Organisation, 1975–85, and Prof., 1979–85, Univ. of Strathclyde. Member: IBA (formerly ITA), 1970–79 (Chm., Scottish Cttee, 1970–79); Royal Commn on Gambling, 1976–78; Central Transport Users' Consultative Cttee, 1976–80 (Chm., Scottish Transport Users' Consultative Cttee, 1976–80); European Adv. Council, Salzburg Seminar, 1980–; Broadcasting Complaints Commn, 1981–; Data Protection Tribunal, 1984–; Dep. Chm., Scottish Consumer Council, 1980–84 (Mem. 1977–80); Chm., Scottish Cttee, Information Technology, 1982–85; Special Adviser, H of C Select Cttee on Scottish Affairs, 1982. Mem. Court 1968–71 and 1980–83, Mem. Senate 1964–71 and 1973–, Univ. of Strathclyde. Academic Governor, Richmond Coll., 1983–; Governor, St Aloysius' Coll., Glasgow, 1984–. *Publication:* Consumers in Politics, 1969. *Recreations:* golf, conversation, spectating at Association football, watching television. *Address:* 32 Crompton Avenue, Glasgow G44 5TH. *T:* 041–637 0514. *Clubs:* University of Strathclyde, Glasgow Art, Ross Priory (Glasgow).

CARBONELL, William Leycester Rouse, CMG 1956; Commissioner of Police, Federation of Malaya, 1953–58, retired; *b* 14 Aug. 1912; *m* 1937; two *s*. *Educ:* Shrewsbury Sch.; St Catharine's Coll., Cambridge. Probationary Assistant Commissioner of Police, 1935; (title changed to) Asst Superintendent, 1938; Superintendent, 1949; Asst Commissioner, 1952; Senior, 1952; Commissioner, 1953. King's Police Medal, 1950. Perlawan Mangku Negara (PMN), Malaya, 1958. *Address:* Amery End, Tanhouse Lane, Alton, Hants.

CARDEN, Derrick Charles, CMG 1974; JP; HM Diplomatic Service, retired; HM Ambassador, Sudan, 1977–79; *b* 30 Oct. 1921; *s* of Canon Henry Craven Carden and Olive (*née* Gorton); *heir pres.* to Sir John Craven Carden, 7th Bt, *qv*; *m* 1952, Elizabeth Anne Russell; two *s* two *d*. *Educ:* Marlborough; Christ Church, Oxford. Sudan Political Service, 1942–54. Entered HM Diplomatic Service, 1954; Foreign Office, 1954–55; Political Agent, Doha, 1955–58; 1st Sec., Libya, 1958–62; Foreign Office, 1962–65; Head of Chancery, Cairo, 1965; Consul-General, Muscat, 1965–69; Dir, ME Centre of Arab Studies, 1969–73; Ambassador, Yemen Arab Republic, 1973–76. Governor, IDS, Sussex Univ., 1981–. JP Fareham, 1980. *Recreation:* pleasures of the countryside. *Address:* Wistaria Cottage, 174 Castle Street, Portchester, Hants PO16 9QH. *Club:* Vincent's (Oxford).

CARDEN, Sir Henry (Christopher), 4th Bt *cr* 1887; OBE (mil.) 1945; Regular Army Officer (17th/21st Lancers), retired; *b* 16 Oct. 1908; *o s* of Sir Frederick H. W. Carden, 3rd Bt; *S* father, 1966; *m* 1st, 1943, Jane St C. Daniell (whom he divorced, 1960); one *s* one *d*; 2nd, 1962, Gwyneth S. Emerson (*née* Acland), *widow* of Flt-Lt R. Emerson, Argentina (killed in action, RAF, 1944). *Educ:* Eton; RMC Sandhurst. 2/Lieut, 17/21 Lancers, 1928; served Egypt and India, 1930–39. Staff Coll., 1941; comd, 2 Armoured Delivery Regt, in France, 1944–45. CO 17/21 Lancers, in Greece and Palestine, 1947–48; War Office, 1948–51; Military Attaché in Stockholm, 1951–55; retired 1956. Comdr of the Order of the Sword (Sweden), 1954. *Recreations:* most field sports and games. *Heir: s* Christopher Robert Carden, *b* 24 Nov. 1946. *Address:* Moongrove, East Woodhay, near Newbury, Berks. *T:* Highclere 253661. *Club:* Cavalry and Guards.

CARDEN, Sir John Craven, 7th Bt, *cr* 1787; *b* 11 March 1926; *s* of Capt. Sir John V. Carden, 6th Bt and Dorothy Mary, *d* of Charles Luckrart McKinnon; *S* father, 1935; *m* 1947, Isabel Georgette, *y d* of late Robert de Hart; one *d*. *Educ:* Eton. *Heir: cousin* Derrick Charles Carden, *qv*. *Address:* PO Box N4802, Nassau, Bahamas. *Club:* White's.

CARDIFF, Archbishop of, (RC), since 1983; **Most Rev. John Aloysius Ward,** OFM Cap; *b* 24 Jan. 1929; *s* of Eugene Ward and Hannah Ward (*née* Cheetham). *Educ:* Prior Park College, Bath. Received as Capuchin Franciscan Friar, 1945; solemn profession as Friar, 1950; ordained Priest, 1953; Diocesan Travelling Mission, Menevia, 1954–60; Guardian and Parish Priest, Peckham, London, 1960–66; Provincial Definitor (Councillor), 1963–69; Minister Provincial, 1969–70; General Definitor (Councillor), 1970–80; Bishop Coadjutor of Menevia, 1980–81; Bishop of Menevia, 1981–83. *Address:* Archbishop's House, 41–43 Cathedral Road, Cardiff, S Glamorgan CF1 9HD. *T:* Cardiff 20411.

CARDIFF, Auxiliary Bishop in, (RC); *see* Mullins, Rt Rev. D. J.

CARDIFF, Brig. Ereld Boteler Wingfield, CB 1963; CBE 1958 (OBE 1943); *b* 5 March 1909; *m* 1932, Margaret Evelyn, *d* of late Major M. E. W. Pope, Ashwicke Hall, Marshfield; two *d*. *Educ:* Eton, 2nd Lieut, Scots Guards, 1930. Served War of 1939–45: (despatches thrice); 2nd Bn Scots Guards, 201 Guards Bde; 7th Armoured Div., Western Desert. Served Italy, France, Germany, Far ELF, 1955–58; SHAPE, 1958–63. Brig. 1958; retired, Nov. 1963. Chevalier, Order of Leopold, and Croix de Guerre, 1944. *Recreations:* shooting, fishing. *Address:* Easton Court, Ludlow, Salop. *T:* Tenbury Wells 475. *Clubs:* Cavalry and Guards, White's, Pratt's.
See also R. E. B. Lloyd.

CARDIFF, Jack; film director and cameraman; *b* 18 Sept. 1914; *s* of John Joseph and Florence Cardiff; *m* 1940, Julia Lily (*née* Mickleboro); three *s*. *Educ:* various schools, incl. Medburn Sch., Herts. Started as child actor, 1918; switched to cameras, 1928. World travelogues, 1937–39. Photographed, MOI Crown Film Unit: Western Approaches, 1942; best known films include: A Matter of Life and Death, Black Narcissus, The Red Shoes, Scott of the Antarctic, Under Capricorn, Pandora and the Flying Dutchman, African Queen, War and Peace. Started as Director, 1958. *Films include:* Sons and Lovers, My Geisha, The Lion, The Long Ships, Young Cassidy, The Mercenaries, The Liquidator, Girl on a Motorcycle, The Mutation, Catseyes; *photographed:* Ride a Wild Pony, The Prince and the Pauper, Behind the Iron Mask, Death on the Nile, Avalanche Express, The Awakening, The Dogs of War, Ghost Story, The Wicked Lady, Scandalous, The Far Pavilions, The Last Days of Pompeii, Conan II, First Blood II. Awards: Academy Award (Oscar) Photography, Black Narcissus, 1947; Golden Globe Award, 1947; Coup Ce Soir (France), 1951; Film Achievement Award, Look Magazine; BSC Award, War and Peace; New York Critics Award for best film direction, Golden Globe Award, outstanding directorial award (all for Sons and Lovers); six Academy Award nominations. Hon. Dr of Art, Rome, 1953; Hon. Mem., Assoc. Française de Cameramen, 1971. *Publication:* Autobiography, 1975. *Recreations:* tennis, cricket, painting. *Address:* 75 Woodland Rise, N10. *Club:* MCC.

CARDIGAN, Earl of; David Michael James Brudenell-Bruce; *b* 12 Nov. 1952; *s* and *heir* of 8th Marquess of Ailesbury, *qv*; *m* 1980, Rosamond Jane, *er d* of Captain W. R. M. Winkley, Wyke Champflower Manor, near Bruton, Somerset, and of Mrs Jane Winkley, Kepnal Cottage, Kepnal, Marlborough; one *s* one *d*. *Educ:* Eton; Rannoch; Royal Agricultural Coll., Cirencester. *Heir: s* Viscount Savernake, *qv*. *Address:* Savernake Lodge, Savernake Forest, Marlborough, Wilts.

CARDOSO E CUNHA, António José Baptista; Member of the European Commission, since 1986; Member of Portuguese Parliament, 1979–83 and since 1985; *b* 28 Jan. 1934; *s* of Arnaldo and Maria Beatriz Cardoso E Cunha; *m* 1958, Dea Cardoso E Cunha; four *s*. *Educ:* Instituto Superior Tecnico; Lisbon Univ. MSc Chem. Engrg. Professional engineer, Lisbon, 1957–65; Man. Dir/Chief Exec. Officer of private cos, Sa da Bandeira, Angola, 1965–77; in business, director of private cos, Lisbon, 1977–78 and 1982–85; Mem. Portuguese Government: Sec. of State for Foreign Trade, 1978, for Industry, 1979; Minister for Agriculture/Fisheries, 1980–82. Grand Croix, Leopold II, Belgium, 1980; Gran Cruz, Merito Agricola, Spain, 1981. *Address:* Campo Grande 30–7–F, 1700 Lisbon, Portugal. *T:* 772718.

CARDROSS, Lord; Henry Thomas Alexander Erskine; *b* 31 May 1960; *s* and *heir* of 17th Earl of Buchan, *qv*.

CAREW, 6th Baron (UK) *cr* 1838; **William Francis Conolly-Carew,** CBE 1966; Baron Carew (Ireland), 1834; Bt Major retired, Duke of Cornwall's Light Infantry; *b* 23 April 1905; *e s* of 5th Baron and Catherine (*d* 1947), *o d* of late Thomas Conolly, MP, of Castletown, Co. Kildare; *S* father, 1927; *m* 1937, Lady Sylvia Maitland, CStJ, *o d* of 15th Earl of Lauderdale; two *s* two *d*. *Educ:* Wellington; Sandhurst. Gazetted DCLI 1925; ADC to Governor and Comdr-in-Chief of Bermuda, 1931–36. Chm., British Legion, 1963–66; Pres., Irish Grassland Assn, 1949; Br. Govt Trustee, Irish Sailors' and Soldiers' Land Trust. CStJ. *Heir: s* Hon. Patrick Thomas Conolly-Carew, Captain Royal Horse Guards, retd [*b* 6 March 1938; *m* 1962, Celia, *d* of late Col Hon. (Charles) Guy Cubitt, CBE, DSO, TD; one *s* three *d*]. *Address:* Oakville, Donadea, Naas, Co. Kildare, Ireland. *T:* Naas 68196.

CAREW, Sir Rivers (Verain), 11th Bt *cr* 1661; journalist and farmer; *b* 17 Oct. 1935; *s* of Sir Thomas Palk Carew, 10th Bt, and Phyllis Evelyn (*d* 1976), *o c* of Neville Mayman; *S* father, 1976; *m* 1968, Susan Babington, *yr d* of late H. B. Hill, London; one *s* three *d* (and one *s* decd). *Educ:* St Columba's Coll., Rathfarnham, Co. Dublin; Trinity Coll., Dublin. MA, BAgr (Hort.). Asst Editor, Ireland of the Welcomes (Irish Tourist Bd magazine), 1964–67; Joint Editor, The Dublin Magazine, 1964–69; Irish Television, 1967–. *Publication:* (with Timothy Brownlow) Figures out of Mist (verse). *Recreations:* reading; music; reflection. *Heir: s* Gerald de Redvers Carew, *b* 24 May 1975. *Address:* c/o 17 Brighton Avenue, Rathgar, Dublin 6, Ireland.

CAREW, William James, CBE 1937; Retired as Clerk of the Executive Council and Deputy Minister of Provincial Affairs, Newfoundland; *b* 28 Dec. 1890; *s* of late James and Mary Carew; *m* 1920, Mary Florence Channing (decd); one *s* (Titular Archbishop of Telde; Apostolic Pro-Nuncio to Japan) three *d*. *Educ:* St Patrick's Hall (Christian Brothers), St John's, Newfoundland. Newspaper work, 1908–09; staff of Prime Minister's Office, 1909; Sec., 1914–34; acted as Sec. to Newfoundland Delegate to Peace Conference, 1919; Sec. of Newfoundland Delegation to Imperial Conference, 1923, 1926, 1930; Deputy Min. for External Affairs, 1932; Sec. Newfoundland Delegation to Imperial Economic Conference, Ottawa, 1932; Sec. Cttee for Celebration in Newfoundland of Coronation of King George VI, 1937; Sec. Royal Visit Cttees on occasion of visit of King George VI and Queen Elizabeth to Newfoundland, 1939. Hon LLD Newfoundland, 1985. Commemorative Medals of the Royal Jubilee, 1935, the Coronation, 1937 and the Coronation, 1953. Knight Commander, Order of St Sylvester, 1976. *Address:* 74 Cochrane Street, St John's, Newfoundland A1C 3L6, Canada.

CAREW POLE, Col Sir John (Gawen), 12th Bt *cr* 1628; DSO 1944; TD; JP; Lord-Lieutenant of Cornwall, 1962–77; Member of the Prince of Wales's Council, 1952–68; Member, Jockey Club (incorporating National Hunt Committee), since 1969; Steward, National Hunt Committee, 1953–56; Member, Garden Society; *b* 4 March 1902; *e s* of late Lt-Gen. Sir Reginald Pole-Carew, KCB, of Antony, Cornwall, and Lady Beatrice Pole-Carew, *er d* of 3rd Marquess of Ormonde; *S* kinsman, 1926; *m* 1st, 1928, Cynthia Mary, OBE 1959 (*d* 1977), *o d* of Walter Burns, North Mymms Park, Hatfield; one *s* two *d*; 2nd, 1979, Joan, *widow* of Lt-Col Anthony Fulford, Dunsford, Devon. *Educ:* Eton; RMC, Sandhurst. Coldstream Guards, 1923–39; ADC to Commander-in-Chief in India, 1924–25; Comptroller to Governor-General, Union of S Africa, 1935–36; Palestine, 1936; commanded 5th Bn Duke of Cornwall's LI (TA), 1939–43; commanded 2nd Bn Devonshire Regt, 1944; Colonel, Second Army, 1944–45; Normandy, France, Belgium, Holland, Germany, 1944–45 (despatches, immediate DSO); raised and commanded post-war TA Bn, 4/5 Bn, DCLI, 1946–47; Hon. Col, 4/5 Bn DCLI (TA), 1958–60; Hon. Col DCLI (TA) 1960–67. Director: Lloyd's Bank, 1956–72 (Chm., Devon and Cornwall Cttee, 1956–72); English China Clays Ltd, 1969–73; Keith Prowse, 1969; Vice-Chm., Westward Television Ltd, 1960–72. Member: Central Transport Consultative Cttee for Great Britain, 1948–54; SW Electricity Consultative Council, 1949–52 (Vice-Chairman, 1951–52); Western Area Board, British Transport Commission, 1955–61. JP 1939, DL 1947, CA 1954–66, Cornwall; High Sheriff, Cornwall, 1947–48; Vice-Lt, Cornwall, 1950–62; Chairman Cornwall County Council, 1952–63. A Gentleman of HM Bodyguard of the Honourable Corps of Gentlemen-at-Arms, 1950–72, Standard Bearer, 1968–72. Prime Warden Worshipful Company of Fishmongers, 1969–70. KStJ 1972. Hon. LLD Exeter, 1979. *Recreations:* gardening, shooting, travel. *Heir: s* (John) Richard (Walter Reginald) Carew Pole, *qv*. *Address:* Horson House, Antony, Torpoint, Cornwall PL11 2PE. *T:* Plymouth 812406. *Clubs:* Army and Navy, Pratt's, MCC.
See also D. C. T. Quilter.

CAREW POLE, (John) Richard (Walter Reginald); farmer and chartered surveyor; *b* 2 Dec. 1938; *s* and *heir* of Sir John Gawen Carew Pole, *qv*; *m* 1st, 1966, Hon. Victoria Marion Ann Lever (marr. diss. 1974), *d* of 3rd Viscount Leverhulme, *qv*; 2nd, 1974, Mary (MVO 1983), *d* of Lt-Col Ronald Dawnay; two *s*. *Educ:* Eton Coll.; Royal Agricultural Coll., Cirencester. ARICS 1967. Lieut, Coldstream Guards, 1958–63. Asst Surveyor, Laws & Fiennes, Chartered Surveyors, 1967–72. Dir, South West Venture Capital, 1985–. Chm., Devon and Cornwall Police Authority, 1985– (Mem., 1973–); Member: SW Area Electricity Bd, 1981–; NT Cttee for Devon and Cornwall, 1979–83. Pres., Royal Cornwall Agricultural Show, 1981; Governor: Seale Hayne Agric. Coll., 1979–; Plymouth Coll., 1985–. County Councillor, Cornwall, 1973– (Chairman: Planning Cttee, 1980–84; Finance Cttee, 1985–); High Sheriff of Cornwall, 1979. Liveryman, Fishmongers' Co., 1960. *Recreations:* travelling, walking, gardening. *Address:* Antony House, Torpoint, Cornwall PL11 2QA. *T:* Plymouth 814914. *Clubs:* White's, Pratt's.

CAREY, Group Captain Alban M., CBE 1943; Chairman: Chirit Investment Co. Ltd, since 1970; Maden Park Property Investment Co. Ltd, since 1975; East Coast Plastics Ltd, since 1984; Viking Opticals Ltd, since 1986; owner/farmer Church Farm, Great Witchingham, since 1973; *b* 18 April 1906; *m* 1934, Enid Morten Bond; one *s*. *Educ:* Bloxham. Commissioned RAF 1929; served in night bombers, flying boats and as flying boat and landplane instructor; Pilots Cert. no 5283 for Public Transport; Navigator's Licence no 175, 1936; Sen. Op. Trng Officer, Coastal Command, 1939–42; Station Commander: Pembroke Dock, 1942–43; Gibraltar, 1943–45; Haverfordwest, 1945; St Eval, 1945–46. Chairman: Shaw & Sons Ltd, 1946–79; Jordan & Sons Ltd, 1953–68; Hadden Best Ltd, 1957–72; Shaw & Blake Ltd, 1960–68; H. T. Woodrow & Co., 1961–68; Dep. Chm., Trident Group Printers plc 1972–78. Pres., Nat. Assoc. of Engravers and Die Stampers, 1954; Pres., Central London Br., British Fedn of Printing Industries, 1963; Chm., Nat. Assoc. of Law Stationers, 1963–68; Pres., Egham and Thorpe, Royal Agr. Assoc., 1961, 1962; Chm., Egham and Dist Abbeyfield Assoc., 1970–82. *Recreations:* shooting, fishing, yachting. *Address:* Church Farm, Great Witchingham, Norfolk NR9 5PQ. *T:* Norwich 872511. *Clubs:* Royal Air Force; Royal Air Force Yacht.

CAREY, Charles John; Member, European Communities' Court of Auditors, since 1983; *b* 11 Nov. 1933; *s* of Richard Mein Carey and Celia Herbert Amy (*née* Conway). *Educ:* Rugby; Balliol Coll., Oxford. HM Treasury: Asst Principal, 1957; Principal, 1962; Asst Sec., 1971; seconded to HM Diplomatic Service as Counsellor (Econs and Finance), Office of UK Perm. Rep. to EEC, Brussels, 1974–77; Chm., EEC Council Budget Cttee, during UK Presidency of EEC Council, Jan.-June 1977; Under Sec., HM Treasury, 1978–83. *Recreations:* mountaineering, Bavarian baroque churches, Trollope novels. *Clubs:* United Oxford & Cambridge University; Austrian Alpine (UK Br.).

CAREY, D(avid) M(acbeth) M(oir), CBE 1983; MA, DCL Oxon; Joint Registrar to Faculty Office of Archbishop of Canterbury, since 1982; Legal Secretary to the Archbishop of Canterbury and Principal Registrar to the Province of Canterbury, 1958–82; Legal Secretary to the Bishops of Ely, 1953–82 and Gloucester, 1957–82; Registrar to the Diocese of Canterbury, 1959–82; *b* 21 Jan. 1917; *s* of Godfrey Mohun Carey, Sherborne, Dorset, and Agnes Charlotte Carey (*née* Milligan); *m* 1949, Margaret Ruth (*née* Mills), Highfield Sch., Liphook, Hants; three *s* one *d*. *Educ:* Westminster Sch. (King's Scholar); St Edmund Hall, Oxford. Articled Clerk, Messrs Lee, Bolton & Lee, 1938–40. Lt-Cdr (S) RNVR, 1940–46. Qualified Solicitor, 1947; Partnership with Lee, Bolton & Lee, 1948–82, Consultant, 1982–. *Recreation:* fishing. *Address:* Mulberry House, Ash, Canterbury, Kent. *T:* Ash 812534. *Club:* Army and Navy.

CAREY, Rev. Dr George Leonard; Principal, Trinity College, Stoke Hill, Bristol, since 1982; Hon. Canon of Bristol Cathedral, since 1983; *b* 13 Nov. 1935; *s* of George and Ruby Carey; *m* 1960, Eileen Harmsworth Hood, Dagenham, Essex; two *s* two *d*. *Educ:* Bifrons Secondary Modern Sch., Barking; London College of Divinity; King's College, London. BD Hons, MTh; PhD London. National Service, RAF Wireless Operator, 1954–56. Deacon, 1962; Curate, St Mary's, Islington, 1962–66; Lecturer: Oakhill Coll., Southgate, 1966–70; St John's Coll., Nottingham, 1970–75; Vicar, St Nicholas' Church, Durham, 1975–82. *Publications:* I Believe in Man, 1975; God Incarnate, 1976; (jtly) The Great Acquittal, 1980; The Meeting of the Waters, 1985; The Gate of Glory, 1986; contributor to numerous jls. *Recreation:* jogging. *Address:* 16 Ormerod Road, Bristol BS9 1BB.

CAREY, Hugh Leo; Partner and Member, Management Committee, Finley, Kumble, Wagner, Heine, Underberg, Manley & Casey, law firm; Director: American Blood Pressure, Inc.; Rooney, Pace, Inc.; *b* Brooklyn, NY, 11 April 1919; *s* of Denis Carey and Margaret (*née* Collins); *m* 1st, 1947, Helen Owen Twohy (*d* 1974); seven *s* four *d* one step *d* (and two *s* decd); 2nd, 1981, Evangeline Gouletas; one step *d*. *Educ:* St Augustine's Academy and High School, Brooklyn; St John's Coll.; St John's Law School. JD 1951. Served War of 1939–45 (Bronze Star, Croix de Guerre with Silver Star); with US Army in Europe, 1939–46, rank of Lt-Col. Joined family business (petrochemicals), 1947. Called to Bar, 1951. Member US House of Reps, rep. 12th District of Brooklyn, 1960–75 (Democrat); Deputy Whip; Governor of New York State, 1974–83. Chairman: NY City Sports Commn, 1983–; NY State World Trade Council, 1985–. *Address:* 870 United Nations Plaza, New York, NY 10022, USA; (office) 425 Park Avenue, New York, NY 10022, USA.

CAREY, Prof. John; FRSL 1982; Merton Professor of English Literature, Oxford University, since 1976; *b* 5 April 1934; *s* of Charles William Carey and Winifred Ethel Carey (*née* Cook); *m* 1960, Gillian Mary Florence Booth; two *s*. *Educ:* Richmond and East Sheen County Grammar Sch.; St John's Coll., Oxford (MA, DPhil). 2nd Lieut, East Surrey Regt, 1953–54; Harmsworth Sen. Scholar, Merton Coll., Oxford, 1957–58; Lectr, Christ Church, Oxford, 1958–59; Andrew Bradley Jun. Research Fellow, Balliol, Oxford, 1959–60; Tutorial Fellow: Keble Coll., Oxford, 1960–64; St John's Coll., Oxford, 1964–75. Principal book reviewer, Sunday Times, 1977–. *Publications:* The Poems of John Milton (ed with Alastair Fowler), 1968; Milton, 1969; The Violent Effigy: a study of Dickens' imagination, 1973; Thackeray: Prodigal Genius, 1977; John Donne: Life, Mind and Art, 1981; (ed) The Private Memoirs and Confessions of a Justified Sinner, by James Hogg, 1981; articles in Rev. of English Studies, Mod. Lang. Rev., etc. *Recreations:* swimming, gardening, bee-keeping. *Address:* Brasenose Cottage, Lyneham, Oxon; 57 Stapleton Road, Headington, Oxford. *T:* Oxford 64304.

CAREY, Lionel Mohun, TD, MA; JP; Headmaster of Bromsgrove School, 1953–71; *b* 27 Jan. 1911; 4th *s* of late G. M. Carey; *m* 1943, Mary Elizabeth Auld, MBE; two *s*. *Educ:* Sherborne Sch.; Corpus Christi Coll., Cambridge. Teaching Diploma Institute of Education, London, 1934. Assistant Master, Bolton Sch., Lancs., 1934–37; Christ's Hospital, 1937–53, Housemaster 1940–53. JP Sherborne. *Recreations:* walking, gardening, people, contemplation of eternity. *Address:* Westbury Cottage, Sherborne, Dorset.

CAREY, Sir Peter (Willoughby), GCB 1982 (KCB 1976; CB 1972); Chairman, Dalgety PLC, since 1986 (Director, since 1983); Director: Morgan Grenfell Holdings, since 1983; BPB Industries PLC, since 1983; Cable and Wireless PLC, since 1984; NV Philips Gloeilampenfabrieken, since 1984; *b* 26 July 1923; *s* of Jack Delves Carey and Sophie Carey; *m* 1946, Thelma Young; three *d*. *Educ:* Portsmouth Grammar Sch.; Oriel Coll., Oxford; Sch. of Slavonic Studies. Served War of 1939–45: Capt., Gen. List, 1943–45. Information Officer, British Embassy, Belgrade, 1945–46; FO (German Section), 1948–51; Bd of Trade, 1953; Prin. Private Sec. to successive Presidents, 1960–64; IDC, 1965; Asst Sec., 1963–67, Under-Sec., 1967–69, Bd of Trade; Under-Sec., Min. of Technology, 1969–71; Dep. Sec., Cabinet Office, 1971–72; Dep. Sec., 1972–73, Second Permanent Sec., 1973–74, DTI; Second Permanent Sec., 1974–76, Permanent Sec., 1976–83, DoI. Hon. LLD Birmingham, 1983; Hon. DSc Cranfield Inst. of Tech., 1984. *Recreations:* music, theatre, travel. *Address:* Rose Cottage, 67 Church Road, Wimbledon, SW19. *T:* 01–947 5222. *Club:* United Oxford & Cambridge University.

CAREY EVANS, David Lloyd, OBE 1984; JP; farmer; *b* 14 Aug. 1925; *s* of Sir Thomas Carey Evans, MC, FRCS and Lady Olwen Carey Evans, *qv*; *m* 1959, Annwen Williams; three *s* one *d*. *Educ:* Rottingdean Sch.; Oundle Sch.; Univ. of Wales, Bangor. BSc (Agric) 1950. Sub-Lieut, RNVR, 1943–46; farming 1947–; Chm., Welsh Council, NFU, 1976–79; Welsh Representative and Chm., Welsh Panel, CCAHC, 1974–; Vice-Chm., WAOS, 1980–. JP Portmadoc, Gwynedd, 1969. *Address:* Eisteddfa, Criccieth, Gwynedd LL52 0PT. *T:* Criccieth 2104. *Club:* Sloane.

CAREY EVANS, Lady Olwen (Elizabeth), DBE 1969; *b* 3 April 1892; *d* of 1st Earl Lloyd-George of Dwyfor, PC, OM, and Margaret, GBE, *d* of Richard Owen, Mynydd Ednyfed, Criccieth; *m* 1917, Sir Thomas John Carey Evans, MC, FRCS (*d* 1947); two *s* two *d*. *Address:* Eisteddfa, Criccieth, Gwynedd.

See also D. L. Carey Evans.

CAREY-FOSTER, George Arthur, CMG 1952; DFC 1944; AFC 1941; Counsellor, HM Diplomatic (formerly Foreign) Service, 1946–68; *b* 18 Nov. 1907; *s* of George Muir Foster, FRCS, MRCP, and Marie Thérèse Mutin; *m* 1936, Margaret Aloysius Barry Egan; one *d*. *Educ:* Clifton Coll., Bristol. Royal Air Force, 1929–35; Reserve of Air Force Officers, 1935–39; served War of 1939–45: Royal Air Force, 1939–46 (despatches, AFC, DFC), Group Capt. Served at Foreign Office, as Consul General at Hanover, as Counsellor and Chargé d'Affaires at Rio de Janeiro, Warsaw and The Hague, 1946–68; retired, 1968. *Recreations:* wine, gardening. *Address:* Kilkeran, Castle Freke, Co. Cork. *Clubs:* Royal Air Force; Haagsche (The Hague).

CAREY JONES, Norman Stewart, CMG 1965; Director, Development Administration, Leeds University, 1965–77; *b* 11 Dec. 1911; *s* of Samuel Carey Jones and Jessie Isabella Stewart; *m* 1946, Stella Myles; two *s*. *Educ:* Monmouth Sch.; Merton Coll., Oxford. Colonial Audit Service: Gold Coast, 1935; Northern Rhodesia, 1939; British Honduras, 1946; Kenya, 1950; Asst Financial Sec., Treasury, Kenya, 1954; Dep. Sec., Min. of Agric., Kenya, 1956; Perm. Sec., Min. of Lands and Settlement, Kenya, 1962. *Publications:* The Pattern of a Dependent Economy, 1952; The Anatomy of Uhuru, 1966; Politics, Public Enterprise and The Industrial Development Agency, 1974; articles and reviews for: Journal of Rhodes-Livingstone Inst.; E African Economics Review; Africa Quarterly; Geog. Jl. *Address:* Mawingo, Welsh St Donats, near Cowbridge, S Glam CF7 7SS. *Club:* Royal Commonwealth Society.

CARIBOO, Bishop of, since 1974; **Rt. Rev. John Samuel Philip Snowden.** *Educ:* Anglican Theological Coll., Vancouver (LTh 1951); Univ. of British Columbia (BA 1956). Deacon 1951, priest 1952; Curate: Kaslo-Kokanee, 1951–53; Oak Bay, 1953–57; Nanaimo, 1957–60; Incumbent of St Timothy, Vancouver, 1960–64; Priest Pastoral, Christ Church Cathedral, Vancouver, 1964–66; Rector of St Timothy, Edmonton, 1966–71; Dean and Rector of St Paul's Cathedral, Kamloops, 1971–74. Domestic Chaplain to Bishop of Cariboo, 1971–73. *Address:* Suite 3, 465 Victoria Street, Kamloops, BC V2C 2A9, Canada.

CARINGTON, family name of **Baron Carrington.**

CARLESS, Hugh Michael, CMG 1976; HM Diplomatic Service, retired; Vice-President, Hinduja Foundation; Director, GEECO International Consultants; *b* 22 April 1925; *s* of late Henry Alfred Carless, CIE, and of Gwendolen Pattullo; *m* 1956, Rosa Maria, *e d* of Martino and Ada Frontini, São Paulo; two *s*. *Educ:* Sherborne; Sch. of Oriental Studies, London; Trinity Hall, Cambridge. Served in Paiforce and BAOR, 1943–47; entered Foreign (subseq. Diplomatic) Service, 1950; 3rd Sec., Kabul, 1951; 2nd Sec., Rio de Janeiro, 1953; Tehran, 1956; 1st Sec., 1957; FO, 1958; Private Sec. to Minister of State, 1961; Budapest, 1963; Civil Service Fellow, Dept of Politics, Glasgow Univ., 1966; Counsellor and Consul-Gen., Luanda, 1967–70; Counsellor, Bonn, 1970–73; Head of Latin American Dept, FCO, 1973–77; Minister and Chargé d'Affaires, Buenos Aires, 1977–80; on secondment to Northern Engineering Industries International Ltd, 1980–82; Ambassador to Venezuela, 1982–85. *Recreations:* golf, history. *Address:* 15 Bryanston Square, W1H 7FF.

CARLESS, Prof. John Edward, BPharm, MSc, PhD; FPS; Professor and Head of Department of Pharmaceutics, School of Pharmacy, London University, 1977–83, Emeritus Professor, since 1984; *b* 23 Nov. 1922; *s* of Alfred Edward Carless and Frances Mary (*née* Smith); *m* 1950, Dorothy Litherland; one *d* and two step *d*. *Educ:* Leominster Grammar Sch.; Leicester Coll. of Science and Technol. (BPharm); FPS 1947; Univ. of Manchester (MSc, PhD). Asst Lectr in Pharmacy, Univ. of Manchester, 1947–54; Chelsea College: Sen. Lectr in Pharmaceutics, 1954–61; Reader, 1961–67; Prof. of Pharmaceutics, 1967–77. Member: Cttee on Safety of Medicines, 1976–78; Veterinary Products Cttee, 1978–85; Cttee on Review of Medicine, 1980–; Chm., Pharmacy Bd, CNAA, 1978–85. Chm., Reigate Photographic Soc., 1984–. Harrison Meml Medal, 1980. *Publications:* (ed jtly) Advances in Pharmaceutical Sciences: Vol. 1, 1964–vol. 5, 1982; (contrib.) Bentley's Text Book of Pharmaceutics, 1977. *Recreations:* photography, motoring, bowls. *Address:* Manton, Colley Manor Drive, Reigate, Surrey. *T:* Reigate 43670.

CARLESTON, Hadden Hamilton, CIE 1947; OBE 1944; *b* Pretoria, SA, 25 July 1904; *m* 1946, Eirene Leslie, *d* of Rev. H. L. Stevens, Torquay, S Devon; two *s* one *d*. *Educ:* St Olave's Sch., Southwark; Trinity Hall, Cambridge (MA). Indian Civil Service, 1927–47; Dist Magistrate of Civil and Military Station, Bangalore, 1939–43, and of various districts in Madras Presidency, including Vizagapatam, 1944–46, and The Nilgiris, 1947. Civil Liaison Officer with 19th and 25th Indian Inf. Divs, 1944. Sec. of St Cuthbert's Soc., Univ. of Durham, 1948–52; Admin. Sec., Cambridge Univ. Sch. of Veterinary Medicine, 1952–71. *Address:* Selborne, Cae Mair, Beaumaris, Gwynedd. *T:* Beaumaris 810586.

CARLETON, Mrs John; *see* Adam Smith, J. B.

CARLETON-SMITH, Maj.-Gen. Michael Edward, CBE 1980 (MBE 1966); FBIM; Director-General, Marie Curie Memorial Foundation, since 1985; Defence Adviser and Head of British Defence Liaison Staff, Canberra, Australia, also Military Adviser, Canberra, and Wellington, NZ, and Defence Adviser, Papua New Guinea, 1982–85, retired; *b* 5 May 1931; *s* of late Lt-Col D. L. G. Carleton-Smith; *m* 1963, Helga Katja Stoss; three *s*. *Educ:* Radley Coll.; RMA, Sandhurst. Graduate: Army Staff Coll.; JSSC; NDC; RCDS. Commissioned into The Rifle Brigade, 1951; Rifle Bde, Germany, 1951–53; active service: Kenya, 1954–55; Malaya, 1957; Exchange PPCLI, Canada, 1958–60; GSO2 General Staff, HQ1(BR) Corps, 1962–63; Rifle Brigade: Cyprus, Hong Kong, active service, Borneo, 1965–66; Sch. of Infantry Staff, 1967–68; Comd Rifle Depot, 1970–72; Directing Staff NDC, 1972–74; Col General Staff, HQ BAOR, 1974–77; Commander Gurkha Field Force, Hong Kong, 1977–79; Dep. Director Army Staff Duties, MoD, 1981. Member: Exec. Cttee, World Fedn Cancer Care, 1985–; Britain–Australia Bicentennial Cttee, 1985–. *Recreations:* riding, sailing, travel. *Address:* 28 Belgrave Square, SW1X 8QG.

CARLILE, Alexander Charles, QC 1984; MP (L) Montgomery, since 1983; a Recorder, since 1986; *b* 12 Feb. 1948; *s* of Erwin Falik, MD and Sabina Falik; *m* 1968, Frances, *d* of Michael and Elizabeth Soley; three *d*. *Educ:* Epsom Coll.; King's Coll., London (LLB; AKC). Called to the Bar, Gray's Inn, 1970. Chm., Welsh Liberal Party, 1980–82. Contested (L) Flint East, Feb. 1974, 1979. *Recreations:* reading, theatre. *Address:* Cil y Wennol, Berriew, Powys. *Clubs:* Reform, National Liberal.

CARLILE, Rev. Edward Wilson; Liaison Officer, East Africa Church Army Appeal, 1981–84; *b* 11 June 1915; *s* of Victor Wilson and Elsie Carlile; *m* 1946, Elizabeth (*née* Bryant); two *s* one *d*. *Educ:* Epsom Coll.; King's Coll., London (BD). Chartered Accountant, 1939. Deacon, 1943; priest, 1944; Curate, All Saints, Queensbury, 1943–46; Hon. Asst Sec. of Church Army, 1946–49; Chief Sec. of Church Army, 1949–60; Vicar of St Peter's with St Hilda's, Leicester, 1960–73; Rector of Swithland, Leicester, 1973–76; Priest in Charge of St Michael and All Angels, Belgrave, Leicester, 1976–81. *Recreations:* race relations, evangelism, walking, travel, photography. *Address:* Church Cottage, Chadwell, Melton Mowbray, Leics. *T:* Scalford 347.

CARLILE, Thomas, CBE 1975; FEng; Chairman, Burnett and Hallamshire Holdings, since 1985 (Director, since 1984); *b* 9 Feb. 1924; *s* of late James Love Carlile and Isobel Scott Carlile; *m* 1955, Jessie Davidson Clarkson; three *d*. *Educ:* Minchenden County Sch.; City & Guilds Coll., London. Joined Babcock & Wilcox Ltd, 1944; Man. Dir, 1968–84, Dep. Chm., 1978–84, Babcock Internat. plc. Chm., Shipbuilding Industry Training Board, 1967–70. Mem., Energy Commn, 1977–79. Pres., Engineering Employers' Fedn, 1972–74, a Vice-Pres., 1979–84. Director: Chubb & Son plc, 1976–84; French Kier Hldgs Plc, 1985–86. FCGI 1978; FEng 1979. *Address:* 8 Aldenham Grove, Radlett, Herts. *T:* Radlett 7033.

CARLILL, Rear Adm. John Hildred, OBE 1969; FBIM; Secretary, Engineering Council, since 1983; *b* 24 Oct. 1925; *o s* of late Dr and Mrs H. B. Carlill; *m* 1955, (Elizabeth) Ann, *yr d* of late Lt Col and Mrs W. Southern; three *d*. *Educ:* RNC Dartmouth. psc 1961; jssc 1967. Served War 1939–45. Joined RN as Exec. Cadet 1939, transferred to Accountant Branch 1943; HMS Mauritius 1943–45. Comdr 1963, Captain 1972 (Sec. to FO Naval Air Comd, Dir Naval Manning and Training (S), Sec. to Second Sea Lord, Admty Interview Board, Cdre HMS Drake); Rear Admiral 1980; Adm. President, RNC Greenwich, 1980–82. Freeman: City of London, 1980; Drapers' Co., 1983. *Recreations:* walking, skiing, water colour painting. *Address:* Crownpits Barn, Crownpits Lane, Godalming, Surrey GU7 1NY. *T:* Godalming 5022. *Club:* Army and Navy.

CARLILL, Vice-Admiral Sir Stephen Hope, KBE 1957; CB 1954; DSO 1942; *b* Orpington, Kent, 23 Dec. 1902; *s* of late Harold Flamank Carlill; *m* 1928, Julie Fredrike Elisabeth Hildegard, *o d* of late Rev. W. Rahlenbeck, Westphalia; two *s*. *Educ:* Royal Naval Colleges, Osborne and Dartmouth. Lieut RN, 1925; qualified as Gunnery Officer, 1929; Commander 1937; Commanded HM Destroyers Hambledon, 1940, and Farndale, 1941–42; Captain 1942; Captain (D), 4th Destoyer Flotilla, HMS Quilliam, 1942–44 (despatches); Admiralty, 1944–46; Chief of Staff to C-in-C British Pacific Fleet, 1946–48; Captain, HMS Excellent, 1949–50; Commanded HMS Illustrious, 1950–51; Rear-Admiral, 1952; Senior Naval Member, Imperial Defence Coll., 1952–54; Vice-Admiral, 1954; Flag Officer, Training Squadron, 1954–55; Chief of Naval Staff, Indian Navy, 1955–58, retired. Representative in Ghana of West Africa Cttee 1960–66; Adviser to W Africa Cttee, 1966–67. *Recreations:* walking and gardening. *Address:* 22 Hamilton Court, Milford-on-Sea, Lymington, Hants. *T:* Lymington 42958. *Club:* Naval and Military.

CARLISLE, 12th Earl of, *cr* 1661; **Charles James Ruthven Howard,** MC 1945; DL; Viscount Howard of Morpeth, Baron Dacre of Gillesland, 1661; Lord Ruthven of Freeland, 1651; *b* 21 Feb. 1923; *s* of 11th Earl of Carlisle, and Lady Ruthven of Freeland (*d* 1982) (11th in line); *S* father, 1963; *m* 1945, Hon. Ela Beaumont, OStJ, *o d* of 2nd Viscount Allendale, KG, CB, CBE, MC; two *s* two *d*. *Educ:* Eton. Served War of 1939–45 (wounded twice, MC). Lieut late Rifle Brigade. DL Cumbria, 1984–. FRICS (FLAS 1953). *Heir:* s Viscount Morpeth, *qv*. *Address:* Naworth Castle, Brampton, Cumbria. *T:* Brampton 2621.

CARLISLE, Bishop of, since 1972; **Rt. Rev. Henry David Halsey;** *b* 27 Jan. 1919; *s* of George Halsey, MBE and Gladys W. Halsey, DSc; *m* 1947, Rachel Margaret Neil Smith; four *d*. *Educ:* King's Coll. Sch., Wimbledon; King's Coll., London (BA); Wells Theol College. Curate, Petersfield, 1942–45; Chaplain, RNVR, 1946–47; Curate, St Andrew, Plymouth, 1947–50; Vicar of: Netheravon, 1950–53; St Stephen, Chatham, 1953–62; Bromley, and Chaplain, Bromley Hosp., 1962–68; Rural Dean of Bromley, 1965–66; Archdeacon of Bromley, 1966–68; Bishop Suffragan of Tonbridge, 1968–72. Entered House of Lords, 1976. *Recreations:* cricket, sailing, reading, gardening, walking. *Address:* Rose Castle, Dalston, Carlisle CA5 7BZ. *T:* Raughton Head 274.

CARLISLE, Dean of; *see* Churchill, Very Rev. J. H.

CARLISLE, Archdeacon of; *see* Stannard, Ven. C. P.

CARLISLE, Brian Apcar, CBE 1974; DSC 1945; Chairman, Saxon Oil PLC, 1980–85; *b* 27 Dec. 1919; 2nd *s* of Captain F. M. M. Carlisle, MC; *m* 1953, Elizabeth Hazel Mary Binnie, 2nd *d* of Comdr J. A. Binnie, RN; one *s* three *d*. *Educ:* Harrow Sch.; Corpus Christi Coll., Cambridge. Royal Navy, 1940–46, served in N Atlantic, Channel and Mediterranean in HMS Hood and destroyers; Sudan Political Service, 1946–54, served in Kassala, Blue-Nile and Bahr-el-Ghazal Provinces; Royal Dutch/Shell Group, 1955–74: served in India with Burmah Shell, 1960–64; Regional Co-ordinator, Middle East, and Dir, Shell International Petroleum, 1970–74; participated in pricing negotiations with OPEC states, 1970–73; Dir, Home Oil Co. Ltd, 1977–80; Oil Consultant to Lloyds Bank International, 1975–81. Chm., Bd of Governors, Gordon Boys' Sch., 1985–. *Recreations:* gardening, crosswords, golf. *Address:* Heath Cottage, Hartley Wintney, Hants RG27 8RE. *T:* Hartley Wintney 2224.

CARLISLE, Hugh Bernard Harwood, QC 1978; a Recorder of the Crown Court, since 1983; *b* 14 March 1937; *s* of late W. H. Carlisle, FRCS (Ed), FRCOG, and Joyce Carlisle; *m* 1964, Veronica Marjorie, *d* of G. A. Worth, *qv*; one *s* one *d*. *Educ:* Oundle Sch.; Downing Coll., Cambridge. Nat. Service, 2nd Lt, RA. Called to the Bar, Middle Temple, 1961, Bencher, 1985. Jun. Treasury Counsel for Personal Injuries Cases, 1975–78. Inspector: Bryanston Finance Ltd, 1978–83; Milbury plc, 1985–. Mem., Criminal Injuries Compensation Bd, 1982–. *Recreations:* fishing, croquet. *Address:* 18 Ranelagh Avenue, SW6 3PJ. *T:* 01–736 4238. *Clubs:* Garrick, Hurlingham (Chm., 1982–85).

CARLISLE, Sir (John) Michael, Kt 1985; CEng, FIMechE, FIMarE; Chairman, Diesel Marine International Ltd, since 1981; Director, Torday & Carlisle plc, since 1981; Chairman, Trent Regional Health Authority, since 1982; *b* 16 Dec. 1929; *s* of John Hugh Carlisle and Lilian Amy (*née* Smith); *m* 1957, Mary Scott Young; one *s* one *d*. *Educ:* King Edward VII Sch., Sheffield; Sheffield Univ. (BEng). Served Royal Navy (Lieut), 1952–54. Production Engr, Lockwood & Carlisle Ltd, 1954–57, Man. Dir, 1958–70, Chm. and Man. Dir, 1970–81; Dir of several overseas subsid. cos; Dir, Eric Woodward (Electrical) Ltd, 1965–85. Chairman: Sheffield AHA(T), 1974–82; N Sheffield Univ. HMC, 1971–74; Mem., Bd of Governors, United Sheffield Hosps, 1972–74; Mem. Council: Sheffield Chamber of Commerce, 1967–78; Production Engrg Res. Assoc., 1968–73; Chm., Sheffield Productivity Assoc., 1970; Pres., Sheffield Jun. Chamber of Commerce, 1967–68; Governor: Sheffield City Polytechnic, 1979–82 (Hon. Fellow, 1977); Sheffield High Sch. for Girls, 1977–; Member: Sheffield Univ. Court, 1968–; Sheffield Univ. Careers Adv. Bd, 1974–82; Nottingham Univ. Court, 1982–. Freeman, Co. of Cutlers in Hallamshire. FBIM. *Recreations:* golf, sea sailing (in warm climates), country walking, horse riding. *Address:* 7 Rushley Avenue, Dore, Sheffield S17 3EP. *T:* Sheffield 365988. *Clubs:* Sheffield; Sickleholme Golf.

CARLISLE, John Russell; MP (C) Luton North, since 1983 (Luton West, 1979–83); *b* 28 Aug. 1942; *s* of Andrew and Edith Carlisle; *m* 1964, Anthea Jane Lindsay May; two *d*. *Educ:* Bedford Sch.; St Lawrence Coll. Sidney C. Banks Ltd, Sandy, 1964–78; Dir, Granfin Agriculture Ltd, Stoke Ferry, Norfolk, 1978–; Consultant, Louis Dreyfus plc, 1982–; Mem., London Corn Exchange. Chm., Mid Beds Cons. Assoc., 1974–76. Chm., Cons Parly Cttee on Sport, 1981–82, 1983–84, 1985–; Sec., Cons. Parly Foreign Affairs (Africa), 1981–82; Mem., Commons Select Cttee on Agriculture, 1985–. Mem., Internat. Exec. Cttee, Freedom in Sport; Treas., Anglo-Gibraltar Gp, 1981–82; Sec., British - S Africa Gp, 1983–. Vice-Pres., Fedn Cons. Students, 1986. President: Luton 100 Club; Luton Band. *Recreations:* sport, music. *Address:* House of Commons, SW1. *T:* 01–219 4571. *Clubs:* Farmers', MCC, Rugby.

CARLISLE, Kenneth Melville; MP (C) Lincoln, since 1979; *b* 21 March 1941; *s* of late Kenneth Ralph Malcolm Carlisle, TD and of Hon. Elizabeth Mary McLaren, *d* of 2nd Baron Aberconway; *m* 1986, Carla, *d* of A. W. Heffner, Md, USA. *Educ:* Harrow; Magdalen Coll., Oxford (BA History). Called to Bar, Inner Temple, 1965. Brooke Bond Liebig, 1966–74; farming in Suffolk, 1974–. PPS to: Minister of State for Energy, 1981–83; Minister of State for Home Office, 1983–84; Sec. of State for NI, 1984–85; Home Secretary, 1985–. *Recreations:* botany, gardening, walking, history. *Address:* Wyken Hall Farm, Stanton, Bury St Edmunds, Suffolk. *T:* Stanton 50240.

CARLISLE, Rt. Hon. Mark, PC 1979; QC 1971; DL; MP (C) Warrington South, since 1983 (Runcorn, 1964–83); a Recorder of the Crown Court, 1976–79 and since 1981; *b* 7 July 1929; 2nd *s* of late Philip Edmund and Mary Carlisle; *m* 1959, Sandra Joyce Des Voeux; one *d*. *Educ:* Radley Coll.; Manchester Univ. LLB (Hons) Manchester, 1952. Called to the Bar, Gray's Inn, 1953, Bencher 1980; Northern Circuit. Member Home Office Advisory Council on the Penal System, 1966–70; Joint Hon. Secretary, Conservative Home Affairs Cttee, 1965–69; Conservative Front Bench Spokesman on Home Affairs, 1969–70; Parly Under-Sec. of State, Home Office, 1970–72; Minister of State, Home Office, 1972–74; Sec. of State for Educn and Science, 1979–81. Chm., Cons. Home Affairs Cttee, 1983–. Treas., CPA, 1982–85, Dep. Chm., UK Br., 1985–. Mem., Adv. Council, BBC, 1975–79. DL Cheshire, 1983. *Recreation:* golf. *Address:* Queen Elizabeth Building, Temple, EC4. *T:* 01–583 5766; Newstead, Mobberley, Cheshire. *T:* Mobberley 2275. *Club:* Garrick.

CARLISLE, Sir Michael; *see* Carlisle, Sir J. M.

CARLOW, Viscount; Charles George Yuill Seymour Dawson-Damer; *b* 6 Oct. 1965; *s* and *heir* of 7th Earl of Portarlington, *qv*. *Educ:* Eton College. A Page of Honour to the Queen, 1979–80. *Address:* 19 Coolong Road, Vaucluse, NSW 2030, Australia.

CARLYLE, Joan Hildred; soprano; *b* 6 April 1931; *d* of late Edgar James and Margaret Mary Carlyle; *m*; two *d*. *Educ:* Howell's Sch., Denbigh, N Wales. Became Principal Lyric Soprano, Royal Opera House, Covent Garden, 1955; Oscar in Ballo in Maschera, 1957–58 season; Sophie in Rosenkavalier, 1958–59; Micaela in Carmen, 1958–59; Nedda in Pagliacci (new Zeffirelli production), Dec. 1959; Mimi in La Bohème, Dec. 1960; Titania in Gielgud production of Britten's Midsummer Night's Dream, London première, Dec. 1961; Pamina in Klemperer production of The Magic Flute, 1962; Countess in Figaro, 1963; Zdenko in Hartman production of Arabella, 1964; Sœur Angelica (new production), 1965; Desdemona in Otello, 1965, 1967; Sophie in Rosenkavalier (new production), 1966; Pamina in Magic Flute (new production), 1966; Arabella in Arabella, 1967; Marschallin in Rosenkavalier, 1968; Jenifer, Midsummer Marriage (new prod.), 1969; Donna Anna, 1970; Reiza, Oberon, 1970; Adrianna Lecouvreur, 1970; Russalka, for BBC, 1969; Elizabeth in Don Carlos, 1975. Roles sung abroad include: Oscar, Nedda, Mimi, Pamina, Zdenko, Micaela, Desdemona, Donna Anna, Arabella, Elizabeth. Has sung in Buenos Aires, Belgium, Holland, France, Monaco, Naples, Milan, Berlin, Capetown, Munich. Has made numerous recordings; appeared BBC, TV (in film). *Recreations:* gardening, cooking, interior decorating, countryside preservation. *Address:* The Griffin, Ruthin, Clwyd, N Wales. *T:* Ruthin 2792.

CARMAN, George Alfred, QC 1971; a Recorder of the Crown Court, 1972–84; *b* 6 Oct. 1929; *o s* of Alfred George Carman and late Evelyn Carman; *m* 1st, 1960, Cecilia Sparrow (marr. diss. 1976); one *s*; 2nd, 1976, Frances Elizabeth Venning (marr. diss. 1984). *Educ:* St Joseph's Coll., Blackpool; Balliol Coll., Oxford. First Class, Final Hons Sch. of Jurisprudence, 1952. Captain RAEC, 1948–49. Called to the Bar (King George V Coronation Schol.) Lincoln's Inn, 1953, Bencher 1978; practised on Northern Circuit. *Address:* New Court, Temple, EC4Y 9BE; 12 Old Square, Lincoln's Inn, WC2. *Club:* Garrick.

CARMICHAEL, family name of **Baron Carmichael of Kelvingrove.**

CARMICHAEL OF KELVINGROVE, Baron *cr* 1983 (Life Peer), of Camlachie in the District of the City of Glasgow; **Neil George Carmichael;** *b* Oct. 1921; *m* 1948, Catherine McIntosh Rankin (*see* C. M. Carmichael); one *d*. *Educ:* Estbank Acad.; Royal Coll. of Science and Technology, Glasgow. Employed by Gas Board in Planning Dept. Past Member Glasgow Corporation. MP (Lab) Glasgow, Woodside, 1962–74, Glasgow, Kelvingrove, 1974–83; contested (Lab) Glasgow, Hillhead, 1983. PPS to Minister of Technology, 1966–67; Jt Parly Sec., Min. of Transport, 1967–69; Parly Sec., Min. of Technology, 1969–70; Parliamentary Under-Secretary of State: DoE, 1974–75; DoI, 1975–76; Mem., Select Cttee on Transport, 1980–83; Hon. Sec., Scottish Labour Gp of MPs, 1979–83. *Address:* House of Lords, SW1A 0PW; 53 Partick Hill Road, Glasgow G11 5AB.

CARMICHAEL, Mrs Catherine McIntosh, (Kay); social worker; *b* 22 Nov. 1925; *d* of John D. and Mary Rankin; *m* 1948, Neil George Carmichael (now Baron Carmichael of Kelvingrove, *qv*); one *d*. *Educ:* Glasgow and Edinburgh. Social worker, 1955–57; psychiatric social work, 1957–60; Dep. Dir, Scottish Probation Training Course, 1960–62; Lectr, 1962, Sen. Lectr, 1974–80, Dept of Social Administration and Social Work, Univ. of Glasgow. Mem., 1969–75, Dep. Chm., 1975–80, Supplementary Benefits Commn. *Recreation:* Alexander technique. *Address:* 12 Holyrood Crescent, Glasgow G20 6HJ. *T:* 041–339 0247.

CARMICHAEL, Sir David William G. C.; *see* Gibson-Craig-Carmichael.

CARMICHAEL, Ian (Gillett); *b* 18 June 1920; *s* of Arthur Denholm Carmichael, Cottingham, E Yorks, and Kate Gillett, Hessle, E Yorks; *m* 1943, Jean Pyman Maclean (*d* 1983), Sleights, Yorks; two *d*. *Educ:* Scarborough Coll.; Bromsgrove Sch. Studied at RADA, 1938–39. Served War of 1939–45 (despatches). First professional appearance as a Robot in "RUR", by Karel and Josef Capek, The People's Palace, Stepney, 1939; stage appearances include: The Lyric Revue, Globe, 1951; The Globe Revue, Globe, 1952; High Spirits, Hippodrome, 1953; Going to Town, St Martin's, 1954; Simon and Laura, Apollo, 1954; The Tunnel of Love, Her Majesty's, 1958; The Gazebo, Savoy, 1960; Critic's Choice, Vaudeville, 1961; Devil May Care, Strand, 1963; Boeing-Boeing, Cort Theatre, New York, 1965; Say Who You Are, Her Majesty's, 1965; Getting Married, Strand, 1968; I Do! I Do!, Lyric, 1968; Birds on the Wing, O'Keefe Centre, Toronto, 1969; Darling I'm Home, S African tour, 1972; Out on a Limb, Vaudeville, 1976; Overheard, Haymarket, 1981. Films include: (from 1955) Simon and Laura; Private's Progress; Brothers in Law; Lucky Jim; Happy is the Bride; The Big Money; Left, Right and Centre; I'm All Right Jack; School for Scoundrels; Light Up The Sky; Double Bunk; The Amorous Prawn; Hide and Seek; Heavens Above!; Smashing Time; The Magnificent Seven Deadly Sins; From Beyond the Grave; The Lady Vanishes. TV series include: The World of Wooster; Bachelor Father; Lord Peter Wimsey; All For Love. *Publication:* Will the Real Ian Carmichael . . . (autobiog.), 1979. *Recreations:* cricket, gardening, photography and reading. *Address:* c/o London Management, 235/241 Regent Street, W1A 2JT. *Club:* MCC.

CARMICHAEL, Dr James Armstrong Gordon, CB 1978; Chief Medical Adviser (Social Security), Department of Health and Social Security, 1973–78; *b* 28 July 1913; 2nd *s* of Dr Donald Gordon Carmichael and Eileen Mona Carmichael; *m* 1936, Nina Betty Ashton (*née* Heape) (*d* 1981); two *s*. *Educ:* Epsom Coll.; Guy's Hospital. FRCP, MRCS. Commnd RAMC, 1935; Consultant Physician, MELF, 1953–55; Consultant Physician and Prof. of Tropical Medicine, Royal Army Medical Coll., 1957–58, retd; Hon. Colonel 1958. MO 1958, SMO 1965, Min. of Pensions and Nat. Insce; PMO, Min. of Social Security, 1967; Dep. Chief Medical Advr, DHSS, 1971–73. *Publications:* contrib. to BMJ, Jl of RAMC. *Recreation:* gardening. *Address:* Adcote, Branksomewood Road, Fleet, Hants GU13 8JS. *T:* Fleet 615434.

CARMICHAEL, Sir John, KBE 1955; Director, Adobe Oil and Gas Corp., Texas, since 1973; *b* 22 April 1910; *s* of late Thomas Carmichael and Margaret Doig Coupar; *m* 1940, Cecilia Macdonald Edwards; one *s* three *d*. *Educ:* Madras Coll., St Andrews; Univ. of St Andrews; Univ. of Michigan (Commonwealth Fund Fellow). Guardian Assurance Co., Actuarial Dept, 1935–36; Sudan Govt Civil Service, 1936–59; Member, Sudan Resources Board and War Supply Dept, 1939–45; Secretary, Sudan Development Board, 1944–48; Asst Financial Secretary, 1946–48; Dep. Financial Secretary, 1948–53; Director, Sudan Gezira Board, 1950–54; Chm., Sudan Light and Power Co., 1952–54; Acting Financial Secretary, then Permanent Under Secretary to Ministry of Finance, 1953–55; Financial and Economic Adviser to Sudan Government, 1955–59. Member: UK delegation to General Assembly of UN, 1959; Scottish Gas Board, 1960–70; Scottish Industrial Develt Adv. Bd, 1973–80; Dep. Chm., ITA, 1960–64, Acting Chm., ITA, 1962–63; Chm., Herring Industry Bd, 1962–65; Director: Fisons Ltd, 1961–80 (Chief Executive, 1962–66, Dep. Chm., 1965–71); Grampian Television, 1965–72; Jute Industries Ltd, later Sidlaw Industries Ltd, 1966–80 (Dep. Chm., 1969; Chm., 1970–80); Royal Bank of Scotland, 1966–80; Mem., Social and Economic Cttee, EEC, 1973–74. Chm., St Andrews Links Trust, 1984–; Pres., Senior Golfers' Soc., 1982–85. *Recreations:* golf, gardening. *Address:* Hayston Park, Balmullo, St Andrews, Fife. *T:* Balmullo 870268. *Clubs:* Honourable Company of Edinburgh Golfers; Royal and Ancient Golf (St Andrews) (Captain, 1974–75); Augusta National Golf, Pine Valley Golf.

CARMICHAEL, Kay; *see* Carmichael, C. M.

CARMICHAEL, Keith Stanley, CBE 1981; FCA; Managing Partner, Longcrofts, since 1981; *b* 5 Oct. 1929; *s* of Stanley and Ruby Dorothy Carmichael; *m* 1958, Cynthia Mary (*née* Jones); one *s. Educ:* Charlton House Sch.; Bristol Grammar Sch.; qualified as Chartered Accountant, 1951; FTII 1951, FCA 1961. Partner, Wilson Bigg & Co., 1957–69; Dir, H. Foulks Lynch & Co. Ltd, 1957–69; Dir, Radio Rentals Ltd, 1967–69; sole practitioner, 1969–81. Mem., Monopolies and Mergers Commn, 1983–; Lloyd's Underwriter, 1976–. Freeman, City of London. FInstD. Mem., Editl Bd, Simon's Taxes, 1970–82. *Publications:* Spicer and Pegler's Income Tax (ed), 1965; Corporation Tax, 1966; Capital Gains Tax, 1968; Ranking Spicer and Pegler's Executorship Law and Accounts (ed), 1969; (with P. Wolstenholme) Taxation of Lloyd's Underwriters, 1980; contribs to Accountancy. *Recreations:* gardening, reading, golf, tennis, badminton. *Address:* 117 Newberries Avenue, Radlett, Herts WD7 7EN. *T:* Radlett 5098. *Clubs:* Carlton, City of London, MCC, Lord's Taverners, Eccentric.

CARMICHAEL, Peter, CBE 1981; Director, Small Business and Electronics, Scottish Development Agency, since 1982; *b* 26 March 1933; *s* of Robert and Elizabeth Carmichael; *m* 1st; two *s* four *d*; 2nd, 1980, June Carmichael (*née* Philip). *Educ:* Glasgow Univ. (BSc 1st Cl. Hons Physics). Design Engineer with Ferranti Ltd, Edinburgh, 1958–65; Hewlett-Packard: Project Leader, 1965–67 (Leader of Project Team which won Queen's Award to Industry for Technical Innovation, 1967); Production Engrg Manager, 1967–68; Quality Assurance Manager, 1968–73; Engrg Manager, 1973–75; Manufacturing Manager, 1975–76; Division Gen. Man., 1976–82, and Jt Managing Director, 1980–82. Hon. DSc Heriot-Watt, 1984. *Recreations:* fishing, antique clock restoration. *Address:* 86 Craiglea Drive, Edinburgh EH10 5PH. *T:* (business) 031–337 9313.

CARNAC, Rev. Canon Sir (Thomas) Nicholas R.; *see* Rivett-Carnac.

CARNARVON, 6th Earl of, *cr* 1793; **Henry George Alfred Marius Victor Francis Herbert;** Baron Porchester, 1780; Lieut-Colonel 7th Hussars; *b* 7 Nov. 1898; *o s* of 5th Earl and Almina (who *m* 2nd, 1923, Lieut-Colonel I. O. Dennistoun, MVO; she *d* 1969), *d* of late Frederick C. Wombwell; *S* father, 1923; *m* 1st, 1922, Catherine (who obtained a divorce, 1936, and *m* 2nd, 1938, Geoffrey Grenfell (decd), and *m* 3rd, 1950, D. Momand), *d* of late J. Wendell, New York, and Mrs Wendell, Sandridgebury, Sandridge, Herts; one *s* one *d*; 2nd, 1939, Ottilie (marr. diss.), *d* of Eugene Losch, Vienna. *Educ:* Eton. Owns about 4000 acres. *Publications:* No Regrets (memoirs), 1976; Ermine Tales, 1980. *Heir: s* Lord Porchester, *qv. Recreations:* racing and shooting. *Address:* Highclere Castle, near Newbury, Berks. *TA:* Carnarvon Highclere. *T:* Highclere 253204. *Clubs:* White's, Portland.

CARNE, Dr Stuart John, CBE 1986 (OBE 1977); FRCGP; Senior Partner, Grove Health Centre, since 1967; Senior Tutor in General Practice, Royal Postgraduate Medical School, since 1970; *b* 19 June 1926; *s* of late Bernard Carne and Millicent Carne; *m* 1951, Yolande (*née* Cooper); two *s* two *d. Educ:* Willesden County Grammar Sch.; Middlesex Hosp. Med. Sch. MB BS; MRCS; LRCP; DCH. House Surgeon, Middlesex Hosp., 1950–51; House Physician, House Surgeon and Casualty Officer, Queen Elizabeth Hosp. for Children, 1951–52; Flight Lieut, Med. Branch, RAF, 1952–54; general practice in London, 1954–. DHSS appointments: Chm., Standing Med. Adv. Cttee, 1982–86 (Mem., 1974–86); Member: Central Health Services Council, 1976–79; Children's Cttee, 1978–81; Personal Social Services Council, 1976–80; Chm., Jt Cttee on Contraception, 1983–86 (Mem., 1975–86). Hon. Civil Consultant in Gen. Practice to RAF, 1974–. Mem. Council, RCGP, 1961– (Hon.Treasurer, 1964–81); President: Section of General Practice, 1973–74, United Services Sect., 1985–, RSocMed; Mem.Council, World Orgn of Nat. Colls and Acads of Gen. Practice and Family Medicine,1970–80 (Pres., 1976–78); Mem. Exec. Council, British Diabetic Assoc., 1980–. Examnr in medicine, Soc. of Apothecaries, 1980–86. Chm., St Mary Abbots Court Ltd, 1981–. Hon. MO, Queen's Park Rangers FC, 1959–. Hon. Fellow, BPA, 1982. *Publications:* Paediatric Care, 1976; (jtly) DHSS Handbook on Contraceptive Practice, 3rd edn 1984; numerous articles in Lancet, BMJ and other jls. *Recreations:* music, theatre, photography, philately. *Address:* 5 St Mary Abbots Court, Warwick Gardens, W14 8RA. *T:* 01–602 1970. *Club:* Royal Air Force.

CARNEGIE, family name of **Duke of Fife** and of **Earls of Northesk** and **Southesk.**

CARNEGIE, Lt-Gen. Sir Robin (Macdonald), KCB 1979; OBE 1968; Director General of Army Training, 1981–82, retired; *b* 22 June 1926; *yr s* of late Sir Francis Carnegie, CBE; *m* 1955, Iona, *yr d* of late Maj.-Gen. Sir John Sinclair, KCMG, CB, OBE; one *s* two *d. Educ:* Rugby. Commnd 7th Queen's Own Hussars, 1946; comd The Queen's Own Hussars, 1967–69; Comdr 11th Armd Bde, 1971–72; Student, Royal Coll. of Defence Studies, 1973; GOC 3rd Div., 1974–76; Chief of Staff, BAOR, 1976–78; Military Secretary, 1978–80. Col, The Queen's Own Hussars, 1981–. *Address:* c/o Lloyds Bank, 6 Pall Mall, SW1. *Club:* Cavalry and Guards.

CARNEGIE, Sir Roderick (Howard), Kt 1978; FTS; Director, CRA Ltd (Chairman and Chief Executive, 1974–86; Managing Director, 1971–83); *b* 27 Nov. 1932; *s* of Douglas H. Carnegie and Margaret F. Carnegie; *m* 1959, Carmen, *d* of W. J. T. Clarke; three *s. Educ:* Geelong Church of England Grammar Sch.; Trinity Coll., Univ. of Melbourne; New Coll., Oxford Univ.; Harvard Business Sch., Boston. BSc; Dip. Agricl Economics, MA Oxon; MBA Harvard; FTS 1985. McKinsey & Co., New York, 1954–70: Principal, 1964–68, Director, 1968–70. Director: Comalco Ltd, 1970–; Aust. Mining Industry Council, 1974– (a Sen. Vice-Pres., 1985–); Aust. and NZ Banking Gp Ltd. Member: General Motors Aust. Adv. Council, 1979–; Business Council of Aust., 1983–; Chm., Consultative Cttee on Relations with Japan, 1984–; International Councillor: Morgan Guaranty Trust; The Brookings Institn. Hon. DSc Newcastle, 1985. *Recreations:* surfing, tennis, reading. *Address:* 55 Collins Street, Melbourne, Victoria 3000, Australia. *Clubs:* Melbourne (Victoria, Aust.); Links (New York).

CARNEGY OF LOUR, Baroness *cr* 1982 (Life Peer), of Lour in the District of Angus; **Elizabeth Patricia Carnegy of Lour;** Chairman, Scottish Council for Community Education, since 1981 (Member, since 1978); President for Scotland, Girl Guides Association, since 1979; farmer; *b* 28 April 1925; *e d* of late Lt Col U. E. C. Carnegy, DSO, MC, DL, JP, 12th of Lour, and Violet Carnegy, MBE. *Educ:* Downham Sch., Essex. Served Cavendish Lab., Cambridge, 1943–46. With Girl Guides Assoc., 1947–: County Comr, Angus, 1956–63; Trng Adviser, Scotland, 1958–62; Trng Adviser, Commonwealth HQ, 1963–65; Pres. for Angus, 1971–79. Co-opted to Educn Cttee, Angus CC, 1967–75; Tayside Regional Council: Councillor, 1974–82; Convener: Recreation and Tourism Cttee, 1974–76; Educn Cttee, 1977–81. Chm., Working Party on Prof. Trng for Community Education in Scotland, 1975–77; Member: MSC, 1979–82 (Chm., Cttee for Scotland, 1981–83); Council for Tertiary Educn in Scotland, 1979–84; Scottish Economic Council, 1981–; H of L Select Cttee on European Communities, 1983–; Council, Open Univ., 1984–; Admin. Council, Royal Jubilee Trusts, 1985–. Hon. Sheriff, 1969–84. *Address:* Lour, by Forfar, Angus DD8 2LR. *T:* Inverarity 237; 33 Tufton Court, Tufton Street, SW1P 3QH. *T:* 01–222 4464. *Club:* Lansdowne.

CARNELL, Rev. Canon Geoffrey Gordon; Chaplain to The Queen, since 1981; Non-Residentiary Canon of Peterborough Cathedral, 1965–85, Canon Emeritus since 1985; *b* 5 July 1918; *m* 1945, Mary Elizabeth Boucher Smith; two *s. Educ:* City of Norwich Sch.; St John's Coll., Cambridge (Scholar, 1937; BA 1940; Naden Divinity Student, 1940; Lightfoot Scholar, 1940; MA 1944); Cuddesdon Coll., Oxford. Ordained deacon, Peterborough Cathedral, 1942; priest, 1943. Asst Curate, Abington, Northampton, 1942–49; Chaplain and Lectr in Divinity, St Gabriel's Coll., Camberwell, 1949–53; Rector of Isham with Great and Little Harrowden, Northants, 1953–71; Rector of Boughton, Northampton, 1971–85. Examining Chaplain to Bishop of Peterborough, 1962–; Dir, Post-Ordination Trng and Ordinands, 1962–86. Mem., Ecclesiastical History Soc., 1979–; Vice-Chm., Northamptonshire Record Soc., 1982–. *Recreations:* walking, music, art history, local history. *Address:* 52 Walsingham Avenue, Barton Woods, Kettering, Northamptonshire NN15 5ER. *T:* Kettering 511415.

CARNELLEY, Ven. Desmond; Archdeacon of Doncaster, since 1985; *b* 28 Nov. 1929; *m* 1954, Dorothy Frith; three *s* one *d. Educ:* St John's Coll., York; St Luke's Coll., Exeter; William Temple Coll., Rugby; Ripon Hall, Oxford. BA (Open Univ.); Cert. Ed. (Leeds); Cert. Rel. Ed. (Exon). Curate of Aston, 1960–63; Priest-in-charge, St Paul, Ecclesfield, 1963–67; Vicar of Balby, Doncaster, 1967–72; Priest-in-charge, Mosborough, 1973; Vicar of Mosborough, 1974–85; RD of Attercliffe, 1979–84. *Recreations:* reading, theatre, walking in Derbyshire. *Address:* 2 Durham Road, Dunscroft, Doncaster DN7 4NQ. *T:* Doncaster 841769.

CARNEY, Most Rev. James F.; *see* Vancouver, Archbishop of, (RC).

CARNEY, Admiral Robert Bostwick, Hon. CBE 1946; DSM (US), 1942 (and Gold Stars, 1944, 1946, 1955); and numerous other American and foreign decorations; United States Navy; retired; *b* Vallejo, California, 26 March 1895; *s* of Robert E. and Bertha Carney; *m* 1918, Grace Stone Craycroft, Maryland; one *s* one *d. Educ:* United States Naval Acad., Annapolis, Md (BS). Served European War, 1914–18; Gunnery and Torpedo Officer aboard USS Fanning in capture of Submarine U-58 off coast of Ireland; War of 1939–45; North Atlantic, 1941–42; Commanding Officer, USS Denver, serving in Pacific, 1942–43; Chief of Staff to Admiral William Halsey (Commander, S Pacific Force), 1943–45, participating in nine battle engagements. Deputy Chief of Naval Operations, 1946–50; President of US Naval Inst., 1950–51, 1954–56; Commander Second Fleet, 1950; Commander in Chief, United States Naval Forces, Eastern Atlantic and Mediterranean, 1950–52; Commander-in-Chief, Allied Forces, Southern Europe (North Atlantic Treaty Organisation), 1951–53; Chief of Naval Operations, 1953–55; retired 1955. Chm., Bath Iron Works (Ship Building), 1956–67. Hon. LLD, Loras Coll., 1955. *Publications:* various professional. *Recreations:* field sports, music. *Address:* 2801 New Mexico Avenue (NW), Washington, DC 20007, USA. *Clubs:* Chevy Chase Country, Alibi (Washington, DC); The Brook (NY).

CARNLEY, Most Rev. Peter Frederick; *see* Perth (Australia), Archbishop of.

CARNOCK, 4th Baron *cr* 1916, of Carnock; **David Henry Arthur Nicolson;** Bt (NS) of that Ilk and Lasswade 1629, of Carnock 1637; Chief of Clan Nicolson; solicitor; *b* 10 July 1920; *s* of 3rd Baron Carnock, DSO, and Hon. Katharine (*d* 1968), *e d* of 1st Baron Roborough; *S* father, 1982. *Educ:* Winchester; Balliol Coll., Oxford (MA). Admitted Solicitor, 1949; Partner, Clifford-Turner, 1953–86. Served War of 1939–45, Royal Devon Yeomanry and on staff, Major. *Heir: cousin* Nigel Nicolson, *qv. Address:* 90 Whitehall Court, SW1; Ermewood House, Harford, Ivybridge, S Devon.

CARNWATH, Sir Andrew Hunter, KCVO 1975; DL; a Managing Director, Baring Brothers & Co. Ltd, 1955–74; Chairman, London Multinational Bank, 1971–74; *b* 26 Oct. 1909; *s* of late Dr Thomas Carnwath, DSO, Dep. CMO, Min. of Health, and Margaret Ethel (*née* McKee); *m* 1st, 1939, Kathleen Marianne Armstrong (*d* 1968); five *s* one *d*; 2nd, 1973, Joan Gertrude Wetherell-Pepper (Joan Alexander, author). *Educ:* Eton (King's Scholar; Hon. Fellow 1981). Served RAF (Coastal Comd Intelligence), 1939–45. Joined Baring Bros & Co. Ltd, 1928; rejoined as Head of New Issues Dept, 1945. Chm., Save and Prosper Group Ltd, 1961–80 (Dir, 1960–80); Director: Equity & Law Life Assurance Soc. Ltd, 1955–83; Scottish Agricultural Industries Ltd, 1969–75; Great Portland Estates Ltd, 1977–. Member: London Cttee, Hongkong and Shanghai Banking Corp., 1967–74; Council, Inst. of Bankers, 1955– (Dep. Chm., 1969–70, Pres., 1970–72, Vice-Pres., 1972–); Cttee on Consumer Credit; Central Bd of Finance of Church of England (Chm., Investment Management Cttee), 1960–74; Chm., Chelmsford Diocesan Bd of Finance, 1969–75 (Vice-Chm., 1967–68); Member: Council, King Edward's Hosp. Fund for London, 1962– (Treasurer, 1965–74; Governor, 1976–85); Royal Commn for Exhibn of 1851, 1964–85; Council, Friends of Tate Gall., 1962–84 (Treasurer, 1966–82). Trustee: Imp. War Graves Endowment Fund, 1963–74, Chm., 1964–74; Thalidomide Children's Trust, 1980–85. A Governor, Felsted Sch., 1965–81; Treasurer, Essex Univ., 1973–82 (DU Essex, 1983). Pres., Saffron Walden Conservative Assoc. until 1977. Musicians Company: Mem., Ct of Assts, 1973–; Master, 1981–82. Mem., Essex CC, 1973–77; High Sheriff, 1965, DL Essex, 1972–85. FIB; FRSA. DU Essex, 1983. *Publications:* lectures and reviews for Inst. of Bankers, etc. *Recreations:* music (playing piano, etc), pictures, travel. *Address:* Garden Flat, 39 Palace Gardens Terrace, W8 4SB. *T:* 01–727 9145. *Club:* Athenæum.

See also R. J. A. Carnwath.

CARNWATH, Robert John Anderson; QC 1985; *b* 15 March 1945; *s* of Sir Andrew Carnwath, *qv*; *m* 1974, Bambina D'Adda. *Educ:* Eton; Trinity Coll., Cambridge (MA, LLB). Called to the Bar, Middle Temple, 1968. Junior Counsel to Inland Revenue, 1980–85. *Publications:* Knight's Guide to Homeless Persons Act, 1977; (with Rt Hon. Sir Frederick Corfield) Compulsory Acquisition and Compensation, 1978; contrib. Town and Country Planning, in Halsbury's Laws of England, 4th edn, 1984. *Recreations:* violin, singing, tennis, etc. *Address:* 2 Chepstow Place, W2 4TA. *T:* 01-221 6226. *Club:* Garrick.

CARO, Anthony (Alfred), CBE 1969; Sculptor; *b* 8 March 1924; *s* of Alfred and Mary Caro; *m* 1949, Sheila May Girling; two *s. Educ:* Charterhouse; Christ's Coll., Cambridge (Hon. Fellow); Regent Street Polytechnic; Royal Acad. Schs, London. Asst to Henry Moore, 1951–53; taught part-time, St Martin's Sch. of Art, 1953–79; taught sculpture at Bennington Coll., Vermont, 1963, 1965. Initiated Triangle Workshop, Pine Plains, NY, 1982. Member: Council, RCA, 1981–83; Council, Slade Sch. of Art, 1982–. William Townsend Meml Lectr, 1982; Delia Heron Meml Lectr, 1985. Trustee, Tate Gall., 1982–. One-man Exhibitions: Galleria del Naviglio, Milan, 1956; Gimpel Fils, London, 1957; Whitechapel Art Gallery, London, 1963; Andre Emmerich Gallery, NY, 1964, 1966, 1968, 1970, 1972, 1973, 1974, 1977, 1978, 1979, 1981, 1982, 1984; Washington Gallery of Modern Art, Washington, DC, 1965; Kasmin Ltd, London, 1965, 1967, 1971, 1972; David Mirvish Gallery, Toronto, 1966, 1971, 1974; Galerie Bischofberger, Zurich, 1966; Kroller-Muller Museum, Holland, 1967; British Section, X Bienal de São Paulo, 1969; Norfolk and Norwich Triennial Fest., E Anglia, 1973; Kenwood House, Hampstead, 1974, 1981; Galleria dell'Ariete, Milan, 1974; Galerie Andre Emmerich, Zurich, 1974, 1978; Watson/de Nagy Gall., Houston, 1976, 1978; Lefevre Gall., London, 1976; Galerie Wentzel, Hamburg, 1976, 1978; Galerie Piltzer-Rheims, Paris, 1977; Waddington & Tooth, London, 1977; Tel Aviv Mus., 1977; Harkus Krackow Gall., Boston, 1978, 1981; Knoedler, London, 1978, 1984; Ace Gall., Venice, Calif, 1978; Antwerp Gall., 1978; Kasahara, Japan, 1978; Kunstverein Mannheim, 1979; Kunstverein Braunschweig, 1979;

Stadt. Galerie im Lenbachhaus, Munich, 1979; Ace Gall., Vancouver, 1979; York Pieces, Science Center, Boston, 1980; Acquavella Galls, NY, 1980, 1984; Galerie Andre, Berlin, 1980; Downstairs Gall., Edmonton, Alberta, 1981; Saarland Museums, Saarbrucken, 1982; Stadlische Galerie, Frankfurt, 1982; Gallery One, Toronto, 1982; Waddington and Knoedler, London 1983; Gallerie de France, Paris, 1983. British Council touring exhibn, 1977–79: Tel Aviv, NZ, Australia and Germany. Exhibited: First Paris Biennale, 1959 (sculpture Prize); Battersea Park Open Air Exhibitions, 1960, 1963, 1966; Gulbenkian Exhibition, London, 1964; Documenta III Kassel, 1965; Primary Structures, Jewish Museum, NY, 1966 (David Bright Prize); Venice Biennale, 1958 and 1966; Pittsburgh International, 1967 and 1968; Univ. of Pennsylvania, 1969; Everson Mus., Syracuse, 1976. Retrospective Exhibitions: Hayward Gall., London, 1969; Museum of Modern Art, New York, 1975 (toured to Walker Art Center, Minn, Mus. of Fine Arts, Houston, Mus. of Fine Arts, Boston); Serpentine Gall., London, 1984; Arts Council of GB Tour: Whitworth Art Gall., Manchester, 1984; Leeds City Art Gall., 1984; Britih Council Tour of Europe: Ordrupgaard, Samlingen, Copenhagen, 1984; Kunstmuseum, Düsseldorf, 1985; Foundn Joan Miró, Barcelona, 1985. Sculpture commnd by Nat. Gall. of Art, Washington, 1978. Given key to City of NY, 1976. Hon. Mem., Amer. Acad. and Inst. of Arts and Letters, 1979. Hon. DLitt: East Anglia; York Univ., Toronto; Brandeis; Hon. LittD Cambridge, 1985. *Relevant publications:* Anthony Caro, by R. Whelan *et al*, 1974; Anthony Caro, by W. S. Rubin, 1975; Anthony Caro, by D. Blume (catalogue raisonnée), 1979, rev. edn 1981; Anthony Caro, by D. Waldman, 1982. *Recreation:* listening to music. *Address:* 111 Frognal, Hampstead, NW3.

CARO, Prof. David Edmund, AO 1986; OBE 1977; MSc, PhD; FInstP, FAIP, FACE; Vice-Chancellor, University of Melbourne, since 1982; *b* 29 June 1922; *s* of George Alfred Caro and Alice Lillian Caro; *m* 1954, Fiona Macleod; one *s* one *d*. *Educ:* Geelong Grammar Sch.; Univ. of Melbourne (MSc); Univ. of Birmingham (PhD). FInstP 1960, FAIP 1963, FACE 1982. Served War, RAAF, 1941–45. Demonstrator, Univ. of Melbourne, 1947–49; 1851 Overseas Res. Scholar, Birmingham, 1949–51; University of Melbourne: Lectr, 1952; Sen. Lectr, 1954; Reader, 1958; Foundn Prof. of Exper. Physics, 1961; Dean, Faculty of Science, 1970; Dep. Vice-Chancellor, 1972–77; Vice-Chancellor, Univ. of Tasmania, 1978–82. Chairman: Antarctic Res. Policy Adv. Cttee, 1979–85; Aust. Vice-Chancellors Cttee, 1982–83; Melbourne Theatre Co., 1982–; SSAU Nominees Ltd, 1984–. Member: Management Cttee, Royal Melbourne Hosp., 1982–86; Amalg. Melbourne & Essendon Hosps, 1986–. Hon. LLD: Melbourne, 1978; Tasmania, 1982. *Publication:* (jtly) Modern Physics, 1961 (3rd edn 1978). *Recreations:* skiing, gardening, theatre. *Address:* University of Melbourne, Parkville, Melbourne, Vic 3052, Australia. *Clubs:* Melbourne (Melbourne); Peninsula Golf (Vic); Tasmanian (Hobart).

CARÖE, Sir (Einar) Athelstan (Gordon), Kt 1972; CBE 1958; President, Trustee Savings Banks, since 1976; Hon. President, EEC Savings Bank Group, since 1979 (Vice-Chairman, 1973–76; President and Chairman, 1976–78); Director, London Board, Norwich Union Group, 1968–78; Grain Merchant and Broker, W. S. Williamson and Co., Liverpool, 1935–73; Consul for Denmark, in Liverpool, 1931–73, also for Iceland, 1947–84; *b* 6 Oct. 1903; *s* of Johan Frederik Caröe and Eleanor Jane Alexandra Caröe (*née* Gordon); *m* 1st, 1934, Frances Mary Lyon (*d* 1947); two *s*; 2nd, 1952, Doreen Evelyn Jane Sandland; one *s* one *d*. *Educ:* Eton Coll. (King's Scholar); Trinity Coll., Cambridge (Scholar, BA). Chairman: Liverpool Savings Bank, 1947–48; Trustee Savings Banks Assoc., 1966–76 (Dep. 1951–66); Vice-Pres., National Savings Cttee, 1971–78. President, Liverpool Consular Corps, 1952; Chairman, Liverpool Chamber of Commerce, 1950–51. Pres., Minton Ltd, Stoke-on-Trent, 1970– (Chm. 1956–70); Chairman: Maritime Insurance Co. Ltd, Liverpool, 1951–68; Liverpool Corn Trade Assoc., 1963–67; Richards-Campbell Tiles Ltd, 1967–68. Pro-Chancellor, Liverpool Univ., 1966–75 (Dep. Treas., 1948–57; Treas., 1957–66; Pres., 1966–72); President, Lancashire County Lawn Tennis Assoc., 1953; Member Lawn Tennis Assoc. Council, 1954–66; President: Nat. Federation of Corn Trade Assocs, 1957–60; Internat. Savings Banks Inst., 1960–69 (Hon. Pres., 1969–). Hon. LLD, Liverpool, 1976. Officer, 1st Class, Order of Dannebrog, 1957 (Officer, 1945); Kt Commander, Order of Icelandic Falcon, 1974 (Officer 1958); Comdr, Order of Crown of Belgium, 1966; Comdr, Order of Leopold (Belgium), 1978. King Christian X Liberty Medal, 1946; Spanish Medal, Al Merito del Ahorro, 1973. *Recreations:* lawn tennis (Lancashire doubles champion, 1933); philately (Fellow RPS(L) 1939; Roll of Distinguished Philatelists, 1972). *Address:* Pedder's Wood, Scorton, near Preston, Lancs PR3 1BE. *T:* Garstang 4698. *Clubs:* British Pottery Manufacturers (Stoke-on-Trent) (Hon. Mem.); Liverpool Racquet (Hon. Mem).

CARON, Leslie, (Leslie Claire Margaret, *née* Caron); film and stage actress; *b* 1 July 1931; *d* of Claude Caron and Margaret Caron (*née* Petit); *m* 1st, 1951, George Hormel (marr. diss.); 2nd, 1956, Peter Reginald Frederick Hall (marr. diss. 1965); one *s* one *d*; 3rd, 1969, Michael Laughlin (marr. diss.). *Educ:* Convent of the Assumption, Paris. With Ballet des Champs Elysées, 1947–50, Ballet de Paris, 1954. *Films include:* American in Paris, 1950; subsequently, Lili; The Glass Slipper; Daddy Long Legs; Gaby; Gigi; The Doctor's Dilemma; The Man Who Understood Women; The Subterraneans; Fanny; Guns of Darkness; The L-Shaped Room; Father Goose; A Very Special Favour; Promise Her Anything; Is Paris Burning?; Head of the Family; Madron; QB VII; Valentino; Sérail; L'homme qui aimait les femmes; The Contract; The Unapproachable; Master of the Game. *Plays:* Orvet, Paris, 1955; Gigi, London, 1956; Ondine, London, 1961; The Rehearsal, UK tour, 1983; On Your Toes, US tour, 1984. Tales of the Unexpected, Anglia TV, 1982. *Publication:* Vengeance (short stories), 1982. *Recreation:* collecting antiques. *Address:* c/o James Fraser, Fraser & Dunlop, 91 Regent Street, W1R 8RU. *T:* 01–734 7311/5.

CARPENTARIA, Bishop of, since 1984; **Rt. Rev. Anthony Francis Hall-Matthews;** *b* 14 Nov. 1940; *s* of Rev. Cecil Berners Hall and Barbara (who *m* 1944, Rt Rev. Seering John Matthews); *m* 1966, Valerie Joan Cecil; two *s* three *d*. *Educ:* Sanctuary School, Walsingham, Norfolk; Southport School, Queensland; St Francis Theol Coll., Milton, Brisbane. ThL Aust. Coll. of Theology, 1962. Curate of Darwin, 1963–66; Chaplain, Aerial Mission, and Rector of Normanton with Croydon, 1966–76; Hon. Canon of Carpentaria, 1970–76; Archdeacon of Cape York Peninsula, 1976–84; Priest-in-charge of Cooktown, Dio. Carpentaria, 1976–84. *Recreations:* flying, reading, sailing. *Address:* Bishop's House, Thursday Island, Queensland 4875, Australia. *T:* (070) 691455.

CARPENTER; *see* Boyd-Carpenter.

CARPENTER, Very Rev. Edward Frederick, KCVO 1985; Dean of Westminster, 1974–85; Lector Theologiae of Westminster Abbey, 1958; *b* 27 Nov. 1910; *s* of Frederick James and Jessie Kate Carpenter; *m* Lilian Betsy Wright; three *s* one *d*. *Educ:* Strodes Sch., Egham; King's Coll., University of London. BA 1932, MA 1934, BD 1935, PhD 1943; AKC 1935; FKC 1951; Hon. DD London, 1976. Deacon, 1935; Priest, 1936; Curate, Holy Trinity, St Marylebone, 1935–41; St Mary, Harrow, 1941–45; Rector of Great Stanmore, 1945–51; Canon of Westminster, 1951; Treasurer, 1959–74; Archdeacon, 1963–74. Fellow of King's Coll., London University, 1954 (AKC 1935). Chairman Frances Mary Buss Foundation, 1956–; Chairman Governing Body of: North London Collegiate Sch.; Camden Sch. for Girls, 1956–; Chairman of St Anne's Soc., 1958–; Joint Chm., London Soc. of Jews and Christians, 1960–; Chm., CCJ, 1986–; Member, Central Religious Advisory Cttee serving BBC and ITA, 1962–67; Chairman: Recruitment Cttee, ACCM, 1967; Religious Adv. Cttee of UNA, 1969–; President: London Region of UNA, 1966–67; Modern Churchmen's Union, 1966; World Congress of Faiths, 1966. *Publications:* Thomas Sherlock, 1936; Thomas Tenison, His Life and Times, 1948; That Man Paul, 1953; The Protestant Bishop, 1956; (joint author) of Nineteenth Century Country Parson, 1954, and of History of St Paul's Cathedral, 1957; Common Sense about Christian Ethics, 1961; (jtly) From Uniformity to Unity, 1962; (jtly) The Church's Use of the Bible, 1963; The Service of a Parson, 1965; (jtly) The English Church, 1966; (jtly) A House of Kings, 1966; Cantuar: the Archbishops in their office, 1971; contrib. Man of Christian Action, ed Ian Henderson, 1976. *Recreations:* walking, conversation, Association football. *Address:* 6 Selwyn Avenue, Richmond, Surrey.

CARPENTER, Ven. Frederick Charles; Archdeacon of the Isle of Wight, 1977–86, Archdeacon Emeritus since 1986; Priest-in-charge of the Holy Cross, Binstead, Isle of Wight, 1977–86; *b* 24 Feb. 1920; *s* of Frank and Florence Carpenter; *m* 1952, Rachel Nancy, *widow* of Douglas H. Curtis. *Educ:* Sir George Monoux Grammar Sch., Walthamstow; Sidney Sussex Coll., Cambridge (BA 1947, MA 1949); Wycliffe Hall, Oxford. Served with Royal Signals, 1940–46; Italy, 1944 (despatches). Curate of Woodford, 1949–51; Assistant Master and Chaplain, Sherborne School, Dorset, 1951–62; Vicar of Moseley, Birmingham, 1962–68; Director of Religious Education, Diocese of Portsmouth, 1968–75; Canon Residentiary of Portsmouth, 1968–77. *Recreations:* music, gardening. *Address:* Gilston, Mount Pleasant, Stoford, Salisbury SP2 0PP. *T:* Salisbury 790335.

CARPENTER, George Frederick, ERD 1954; Assistant Under-Secretary of State, Ministry of Defence, 1971–77; *b* 18 May 1917; *s* of late Frederick and Ada Carpenter; *m* 1949, Alison Elizabeth (*d* 1978), *d* of late Colonel Sidney Smith, DSO, MC, TD and Elizabeth Smith, Longridge, Lancs; two step *d*. *Educ:* Bec Sch.; Trinity Coll., Cambridge (MA). Commnd Royal Artillery (Supplementary Reserve), July 1939; War Service, 1939–46, France, 1940 and AA Comd; joined War Office, 1946; Asst Sec., 1958; Comd Sec., Northern Comd, 1961–65; Inspector of Establishments (A), MoD, 1965–71. Silver Jubilee Medal, 1977. *Address:* 10 Park Meadow, Hatfield, Herts. *T:* Hatfield 65581. *Club:* Civil Service.

CARPENTER, Rt. Rev. Harry James, DD; *b* 20 Oct. 1901; *s* of William and Elizabeth Carpenter; *m* 1940, Urith Monica Trevelyan; one *s*. *Educ:* Churcher's Coll., Petersfield; Queen's Coll., Oxford. Tutor of Keble Coll., Oxford, 1927; Fellow, 1930; Warden of Keble Coll., 1939–55, Hon. Fellow, 1955; Hon. Fellow, Queen's Coll., Oxford, 1955; Canon Theologian of Leicester Cathedral, 1941–55; Bishop of Oxford, 1955–70. Hon. DD Oxon, 1955; Hon. DLitt Southampton, 1985. *Publications:* (ed) Bicknell, Thirty Nine Articles, 1955; contrib. to: Oxford Dictionary of the Christian Church, ed Cross, 1957; A Theological Word Book of the Bible, ed Richardson, 1963; The Interpretation of the Bible, ed Dugmore, 1944; Jl of Theological Studies. *Address:* St John's Home, St Mary's Road, Oxford OX4 1QE.

CARPENTER, John; *see* Carpenter, V. H. J.

CARPENTER, John McG. K. K.; *see* Kendall-Carpenter.

CARPENTER, Leslie Arthur; Chairman, since 1985 (Chief Executive, 1982–87); Reed International PLC; *b* 26 June 1927; *s* of William and Rose Carpenter. *Educ:* Hackney Techn. Coll. Director: Country Life, 1965; George Newnes, 1966; Odhams Press Ltd (Managing), 1968; International Publishing Corp., 1972; Reed International Ltd, 1974; IPC (America) Inc., 1975; Chairman: Reed Hldgs Inc. (formerly Reed Publishing Hldgs Inc.), 1977; Reed Publishing Hldgs Ltd, 1981; Chm. and Chief Exec., IPC Ltd, 1974; Chief Exec., Publishing and Printing, Reed International Ltd, 1979. *Recreations:* racing, gardening. *Address:* c/o Reed International PLC, Reed House, Piccadilly, W1A 1EJ. *Club:* Royal Automobile.

CARPENTER, Maj.-Gen. (Victor Harry) John, CB 1975; MBE 1945; FCIT; Traffic Commissioner, Western Traffic Area and Licensing Authority, since 1985; *b* 21 June 1921; *s* of Harry and Amelia Carpenter; *m* 1946, Theresa McCulloch; one *s* one *d*. *Educ:* Army schools; Apprentice Artificer RA; RMC Sandhurst. Joined the Army, Royal Artillery, 1936; commissioned into Royal Army Service Corps as 2nd Lieut, 1939. Served War of 1939–45 (Dunkirk evacuation, Western Desert, D-Day landings). Post-war appts included service in Palestine, Korea, Aden, and Singapore; also commanded a company at Sandhurst. Staff College, 1951; JSSC, 1960; served WO, BAOR, FARELF, 1962–71; Transport Officer-in-Chief (Army), MoD, 1971–73; Dir of Movements (Army), MoD, 1973–75; Chairman: Traffic Comrs, NE Traffic Area (formerly Yorks Traffic Area), 1975–85; Northern Traffic Comrs and Licensing Authority, 1982–85. Col Comdt, 1975–86, Representative Col Comdt, 1985, RCT. Nat. Chm., 1940 Dunkirk Veterans Assoc.; President: Artificers Royal Artillery Assoc.; RASC/RCT Assoc. Chm., Yorkshire Section, CIT, 1980–81. *Recreation:* gardening. *Address:* Traffic Commissioner, Western Traffic Area, The Gaunts House, Denmark Street, Bristol BS1 5DR. *Club:* Royal Over-Seas League.

CARR, family name of **Baron Carr of Hadley.**

CARR OF HADLEY, Baron *cr* 1975 (Life Peer), of Monken Hadley; **(Leonard) Robert Carr,** PC 1963; FIC; *b* 11 Nov. 1916; *s* of late Ralph Edward and of Katie Elizabeth Carr; *m* 1943, Joan Kathleen, *d* of Dr E. W. Twining; two *d* (and one *s* decd). *Educ:* Westminster Sch.; Gonville and Caius Coll., Cambridge, BA Nat. Sci. Hons, 1938; MA 1942. FIM 1957. Joined John Dale Ltd, 1938 (Dir, 1948–55; Chm., 1958–63); Director: Metal Closures Group Ltd, 1964–70 (Dep. Chm., 1960–63 and Jt Man. Dir, 1960–63); Carr, Day & Martin Ltd, 1947–55; Isotope Developments Ltd, 1950–55; Metal Closures Ltd, 1959–63; Scottish Union & National Insurance Co. (London Bd), 1958–63; S. Hoffnung & Co., 1963, 1965–70, 1974–80; Securicor Ltd and Security Services PLC, 1961–63, 1965–70, 1974–85; SGB Gp PLC, 1974–; Prudential Assurance Co., 1976–85 (Dep. Chm., 1979–80, Chm., 1980–85); Prudential Corporation PLC, 1978– (Dep. Chm., 1979–80, Chm., 1980–85); Cadbury Schweppes PLC, 1979–; Member: London Adv. Bd, Norwich Union Insurance Gp, 1965–70, 1974–76; Advisory Bd, PA Strategy Partners, 1985–. Mem. Council, CBI, 1976– (Chm., Educn and Trng Cttee, 1977–82); Chm., Business in the Community, 1984–. MP (C) Mitcham, 1950–74, Sutton, Carshalton, 1974–76; PPS to Sec. of State for Foreign Affairs, Nov. 1951–April 1955, to Prime Minister, April-Dec. 1955; Parly Sec., Min. of Labour and Nat. Service, Dec. 1955–April 1958; Sec. for Technical Co-operation, 1963–64; Sec. of State for Employment, 1970–72; Lord President of the Council and Leader of the House of Commons, April-Nov. 1972; Home Secretary, 1972–74. Governor: St Mary's Hosp., Paddington, 1958–63; Imperial Coll. of Science and Technology, 1959–63 and 1976– (Fellow 1985); St Mary's Medical Sch. Council, 1958–63; Hon. Treas., Wright Fleming Inst. of Microbiology, 1960–63. Pres., Consultative Council of Professional Management Orgns, 1976–. Duke of Edinburgh Lectr, Inst. of Building, 1976. Pres., Surrey CCC, 1985–86. *Publications:* (jt) One Nation, 1950; (jt) Change is our Ally, 1954; (jt) The Responsible Society, 1958; (jt)

One Europe, 1965; articles in technical jls. *Recreations:* lawn tennis, music, gardening. *Address:* 14 North Court, Great Peter Street, SW1. *Club:* Brooks's.

CARR, (Albert) Raymond (Maillard), DLitt (Oxon); FRHistS; FRSL; FBA 1978; Warden of St Antony's College, Oxford, since 1968 (Sub-Warden, 1966–68); Fellow since 1964; *b* 11 April 1919; *s* of Reginald and Marion Maillard Carr; *m* 1950, Sara Strickland; three *s* one *d*. *Educ:* Brockenhurst Sch.; Christ Church, Oxford. Gladstone Research Exhnr, Christ Church, 1941; Fellow of All Souls' Coll., 1946–53; Fellow of New Coll., 1953–64. Director, Latin American Centre, 1964–68. Chm. Soc. for Latin American Studies, 1966–68. Prof. of History of Latin America, Oxford, 1967–68. Distinguished Prof., Boston Univ., 1980. Mem., Nat. Theatre Bd, 1968–77. Corresp. Mem., Royal Acad. of History, Madrid. Grand Cross of the Order of Alfonso el Sabio, Spain, 1983. *Publications:* Spain 1808–1939, 1966; Latin America (St Antony's Papers), 1969; (ed) The Republic and the Civil War in Spain, 1971; English Fox Hunting, 1976; The Spanish Tragedy: the Civil War in Perspective, 1977; (jtly) Spain: Dictatorship to Democracy, 1979; Modern Spain, 1980; (with Sara Carr) Fox-Hunting, 1982; Puerto Rico: a colonial experiment, 1984; articles on Swedish, Spanish and Latin American history. *Recreation:* fox hunting. *Address:* St Antony's College, Oxford; 29 Charlbury Road, Oxford. *T:* 58136. *Club:* United Oxford & Cambridge University.

CARR, Christopher; QC 1983; barrister; *b* 30 Nov. 1944; *s* of Edwin Wilfred Carr and Kathleen Carr; *m* 1986, Valerie Esther Marcus; two *d* one *s* of previous marriage. *Educ:* Skegness Grammar Sch.; London Sch. of Economics; Clare Coll., Cambridge. Called to the Bar, Lincoln's Inn, 1968. Lectr in Law, LSE, 1968–69 and 1972–73; Asst Prof. of Law, Univ. of British Columbia, 1969–72; Associate Prof. of Law, Univ. of Toronto, 1973–75; part-time Lectr, QMC, London, 1975–78; in practice at the Bar, 1975–. *Publications:* articles and notes in English and Canadian law jls. *Recreations:* mixed. *Address:* 33 Whistlers Avenue, Morgan's Walk, SW11; 1 Essex Court, Temple, EC4.

CARR, Prof. Denis John; Professor, Research School of Biological Sciences, Australian National University, Canberra, 1968–80; *b* 15 Dec. 1915; *s* of James E. Carr and Elizabeth (*née* Brindley), Stoke-on-Trent, Staffs; *m* 1955, Stella G. M. Fawcett; no *c*. *Educ:* Hanley High Sch., Staffs; Manchester Univ. RAF, 1940–46. Manchester Univ.: undergraduate, 1946–49; Asst Lectr in Plant Ecology, 1949–53; Guest Research Worker at Max-Planck-Inst. (Melchers), Tübingen, 1952; Sen. Lectr in plant physiology, 1953, Reader, 1959, Melbourne; Prof. of Botany, Queen's Univ., Belfast, 1960–67. Hon. MSc Melbourne, 1958. *Publications:* Plant Growth Substances 1970, 1972; numerous papers in scientific jls. *Recreations:* research, music. *Address:* c/o Research School of Biological Sciences, ANU Canberra, PO Box 475, ACT 2601, Australia.

CARR, Donald Bryce, OBE 1985; Secretary, Cricket Council and Test and County Cricket Board, 1974–86; *b* 28 Dec. 1926; *s* of John Lillingston Carr and Constance Ruth Carr; *m* 1953, Stella Alice Vaughan Simpkinson; one *s* one *d*. *Educ:* Repton Sch.; Worcester Coll., Oxford (MA). Served Army, 1945–48 (Lieut Royal Berks Regt). Asst Sec., 1953–59, Sec., 1959–62, Derbyshire CCC; Asst Sec., MCC, 1962–74. *Recreations:* golf, following most sports. *Address:* 28 Aldenham Avenue, Radlett, Herts WD7 8HX. *T:* Radlett 5602. *Clubs:* MCC, British Sportsman's, Lord's Taverners'; Vincent's, Oxford University Cricket (Oxford).

CARR, Dr Eric Francis, FRCP, FRCPsych; Lord Chancellor's Medical Visitor, since 1979; Member, Mental Health Act Commission, since 1983; *b* 23 Sept. 1919; *s* of Edward Francis Carr and Maude Mary Almond; *m* 1954, Janet Gilfillan (marr. diss. 1980); two *s* one *d*. *Educ:* Mill Hill Sch.; Emmanuel Coll., Cambridge. MA, MB BChir; FRCP, 1971, FRCPsych, 1972; DPM. Captain, RAMC, 1944–46. Consultant Psychiatrist: St Ebba's Hosp., 1954–60; Netherne Hosp., 1960–67; Epsom and West Park Hosps, 1967–76; Hon. Consultant Psychiatrist, KCH, 1960–76; SPMO, DHSS, 1976–79. Fellow, RSocMed. *Recreations:* reading, listening to music, cooking. *Address:* 116 Holly Lane East, Banstead, Surrey. *T:* Burgh Heath 53675.

CARR, Frank George Griffith, CB 1967; CBE 1954; MA, LLB; FSA; FRAS; Associate RINA; FRInstNav; Founder and Chairman, World Ship Trust, since 1978; *b* 23 April 1903; *e s* of Frank Carr, MA, LLD, and Agnes Maud Todd, Cambridge; *m* 1932, Ruth, *d* of Harold Hamilton Burkitt, Ballycastle, Co. Antrim; no *c*. *Educ:* Perse and Trinity Hall, Cambridge. BA 1926; LLB 1928; MA 1939. Studied at LCC Sch. of Navigation and took Yacht Master's (Deep Sea) BoT Certificate, 1927; Cambridge Univ.: Squire Law Scholar, 1922; Capt. of Boats, Trinity Hall, 1926; Pres., Law Soc., 1924; Vice-Pres., Conservative Assoc., 1925; Pres., Nat. Union of Students, 1925; Ed., The Cambridge Gownsman, 1925. Asst Librarian, House of Lords, 1929–47. Served War of 1939–45, RNVR, Lt-Comdr. Dir, Nat. Maritime Museum, Greenwich, 1947–66. Chm., Cutty Sark Ship Management Cttee, 1952–72; Mem., HMS Victory Advisory Technical Cttee, 1948–76; Vice-President: Soc. for Nautical Research; Foudroyant Trust; Internat. Sailing Craft Assoc.; Mariners International, 1978; Internat. Chm., Ship Trust Cttee, NY, 1978–; President: Thames Shiplovers and Ship Model Soc., 1982–; Thames Barge Sailing Club, 1984–. Governor, HMS Unicorn Preservation Soc. James Monroe Award, 1974. *Publications:* Sailing Barges, 1931; Vanishing Craft, 1934; A Yachtsman's Log, 1935; The Yachtsman's England, 1936; The Yacht Master's Guide, 1940; (jtly) The Medley of Mast and Sail, 1976; Leslie A. Wilcox, RI, RSMA, 1977; numerous articles in yachting periodicals, etc. *Recreations:* historic ship preservation, nautical research. *Address:* Lime Tree House, 10 Park Gate, Blackheath, SE3. *T:* 01–852 5181. *Clubs:* Athenæum, Royal Cruising, Cruising Association; Cambridge University Cruising (Cambridge).

CARR, Glyn; *see* Styles, F. S.

CARR, Henry Lambton, CMG 1945; LVO 1957; retired 1961; *b* 28 Nov. 1899; *e s* of Archibald Lambton and Ella Carr, Archangel; *m* 1924, Luba (*d* 1975), *d* of John George Edmund Eveleigh, London; two *s*. *Educ:* Haileybury Coll. Served N Russian Exped. Force (2nd Lieut), 1919. Foreign Office, 1920. HBM Passport Control Officer for Finland, 1927–41; Attaché at British Legation, Stockholm, 1941–45; Foreign Office, 1945; First Sec., HM Embassy, Copenhagen, 1955; Foreign Office, 1958. Chevalier (First Grade) of Order of Dannebrog, Denmark, 1957. *Recreation:* walking. *Address:* Redcot, Three Gates Lane, Haslemere, Surrey. *T:* Haslemere 54620; c/o Barclays Bank, East Grinstead, West Sussex. *Club:* Danish.

CARR, Air Marshal Sir John Darcy B.; *see* Baker-Carr.

CARR, John Roger, JP; Director and General Manager, Moray Estates Development Co., since 1967; Chairman, Countryside Commission for Scotland, since 1986; *b* 18 Jan. 1927; *s* of James Stanley Carr and Edith Carr (*née* Robinson); *m* 1951, Catherine Elise Dickson-Smith; two *s*. *Educ:* Ackworth and Ayton (Quaker Schools). FRICS. Royal Marine Commandos, 1944–47; Factor, Walker Scottish Estates Co., 1950–54, Moray Estates Develt Co., 1954–67. Mem., Countryside Commn for Scotland, 1979–84, Vice-Chm., 1984–85. Mem., Moray DC, 1974–80. JP Moray, 1975. *Recreations:* walking, gardening, fishing, shooting. *Address:* Bradbush, Redstone, Darnaway, Moray IV36 0SU. *T:* Brodie 249. *Club:* New (Edinburgh).

CARR, Rear-Adm. Lawrence George, CB 1971; DSC 1954; Chief of Naval Staff, New Zealand, and Member of the Defence Council, 1969–72; management consultant; *b* 31 Jan. 1920; *s* of late George Henry Carr and late Susan Elizabeth Carr; unmarried. *Educ:* Wellington Technical Coll., NZ; Victoria Coll., Univ. of New Zealand. Served War: entered RNZNVR, 1941; commissioned, 1942; on loan to RN, in HM Destroyers in N Atlantic, Medit., W Af. Coast, Eng. Channel, 1941–44; HMNZS Achilles in Pacific Theatre and NZ, 1945–46; permanent Commn, RNZN, 1946. Qual. as communications specialist, 1947; served in: British Medit. Fleet, 1948; RNZN, 1949–; various appts.; in command HMNZS Kaniere, in Korea, 1953–54 (DSC); Comdr Dec. 1953; Exec. Officer, HMNZS Philomel, 1954–55; jssc, 1956; Deputy Chief of Naval Personnel, 1957–59; Qual. Sen. Officers War Coll., Greenwich, 1959–60; Captain June 1960; in command HMNZS: Philomel, 1960–62, Taranaki, 1962–64; idc 1965; Commodore, Auckland, 1966–68. Chief of Naval Personnel, Second Naval Mem., NZ Naval Bd, 1968–69. Nat. Parly Cand., Nov. 1972; Chm., Nat. Party, Pakuranga Electorate, 1976–82. Exec. Dir, Laura Fergusson Trust for Disabled Persons (Auckland). Mem., Spirit of Adventure Trust Bd; Patron, Coastguard (NZ); Vice-Patron, Co. of Master Mariners, NZ. *Recreations:* golf, fishing, shooting, sailing, tennis, chess. *Address:* 57 Pigeon Mountain Road, Half Moon Bay, Auckland, New Zealand. *T:* Auckland 5349692. *Clubs:* Wellington, Royal New Zealand Yacht Squadron.

CARR, Maurice Chapman; His Honour Judge Carr; a Circuit Judge, since 1986; *b* 14 Aug. 1937; *s* of John and Elizabeth Carr; *m* 1959, Caryl Olson; one *s* one *d*. *Educ:* Hookergate Grammar Sch.; LSE (LLB); Harvard Univ. (LLM). Lectr in Law, 1960–62, Asst Prof. of Law, 1963–64, Univ. of British Columbia; Lecturer in Law: UCW, 1964–65; Univ. of Newcastle upon Tyne, 1965–69. Called to the Bar, Middle Temple, 1966. *Recreations:* walking, music. *Address:* 51 Westgate Road, Newcastle upon Tyne. *T:* Tyneside 2320541.

CARR, Peter Derek; Regional Director, Northern Regional Office, Department of Employment and Manpower Services Commission, since 1983; *b* 12 July 1930; *s* of George William Carr and Marjorie (*née* Tailby); *m* 1958, Geraldine Pamela (*née* Ward); one *s* one *d*. *Educ:* Fircroft Coll., Birmingham; Ruskin Coll., Oxford. National Service, RAF, 1951–53. Carpenter and joiner, construction industry, 1944–51 and 1953–56; college, 1956–60; Lectr, Percival Whitley Coll., Halifax, 1960–65; Sen. Lectr in Indust. Relations, Thurrock Coll., and part-time Adviser, NBPI, 1965–69; Director: Commn on Industrial Relations, 1969–74; ACAS, 1974–78; Labour Counsellor, Washington, 1978–83. *Publications:* directed study for CIR on worker participation and collective bargaining in Europe, and study for ACAS on industrial relations in national newspaper industry. *Recreations:* photography and, under marital pressure, occasional woodwork. *Address:* 3 Slayleigh Avenue, Fulwood, Sheffield S10 3RA.

CARR, Philippa; *see* Hibbert, Eleanor.

CARR, Raymond; *see* Carr, A. R. M.

CARR, Dr Thomas Ernest Ashdown, CB 1977; part-time medical referee, Department of Health and Social Security, since 1979; *b* 21 June 1915; *s* of late Laurence H. A. Carr, MScTech, MIEE, ARPS, Stockport, and late Norah E. V. Carr (*née* Taylor); *m* 1940, Mary Sybil (*née* Dunkey); one *s* two *d*. *Educ:* County High Sch. for Boys, Altrincham; Victoria Univ. of Manchester (BSc). MB, ChB 1939; FRCGP 1968; FFCM 1972; DObstRCOG. Jun. hosp. posts, Manchester and Ipswich, 1939–41; RAMC, UK and NW Europe, 1941–46 (Hon. Major, 1946). GP, Highcliffe, Hants, 1947; Mem. Hants Local Med. Cttee, 1952–55; Min. of Health: Regional Med. Officer, Southampton, 1956; Sen. Med. Officer, 1963; Principal Med. Officer, 1966; SPMO in charge of GP and Regional Med. Service, DHSS, 1967–79. Founder Mem., 1953, Provost of SE England Faculty 1962–64, Mem. Council 1964–66, RCGP; Mem. Exec. Cttee, Lambeth and Southwark Div., BMA, 1975–79. FRSocMed (Mem. Council, Gen. Practice Section, 1977–79). Member: Camping Club of GB and Ireland, 1976–83; Southampton Gramophone Soc., 1956–63 (Chm., 1957–58); Guildford Philharmonic Soc., 1964–; Guildford Soc., 1968–; Consumers' Assoc., 1974–; Nat. Soc. of Non-Smokers, 1981– (Chm., 1982–86); British Humanist Assoc., 1965–. *Publications:* papers on NHS practice organisation in Medical World, Practitioner, Update, Health Trends, faculty jls of RCGP, Proc. of RSM. *Recreations:* playing and listening to music, photography, country walks, foreign travel. *Address:* Tollgate House, 2 Pilgrims Way, Guildford, Surrey GU4 8AB. *T:* Guildford 63012. *Clubs:* Civil Service; Yvonne Arnaud Theatre (Guildford).

CARR, William Compton; *b* 10 July 1918; *m*; two *s* one *d*. *Educ:* The Leys Sch., Cambridge. MP (C) Barons Court, 1959–64; PPS to Min. of State, Board of Trade, 1963; PPS to Financial Sec. to the Treasury, 1963–64. *Recreations:* reading, theatre-going, skin diving, eating, dieting.

CARR-ELLISON, Sir Ralph (Harry), Kt 1973; TD; Chairman, Tyne Tees Television Ltd, since 1974 (Director since 1966); Vice-Chairman, Automobile Association, since 1985; Lord-Lieutenant of Tyne and Wear, since 1984; *b* 8 Dec. 1925; *s* of late Major John Campbell Carr-Ellison; *m* 1951, Mary Clare, *d* of late Major Arthur McMorrough Kavanagh, MC; three *s* one *d*. *Educ:* Eton. Served Royal Glos Hussars and 1st Royal Dragoons, 1944–49; Northumberland Hussars (TA), (Lt-Col Comdg), 1949–69; TAVR Col, Northumbrian Dist, 1969–72; Col, Dep. Comdr (TAVR), NE Dist, 1973; Chm., N of England TA&VRA, 1976–80. ADC (TAVR) to HM the Queen, 1970–75; Hon. Colonel: Northumbrian Univs OTC, 1982–86; Northumberland Hussars Sqn QOY, 1986–. Co. Comr, Northumberland Scouts, 1958–68; Mem. Cttee of Council, 1960–67, Mem. Council, 1982–, Scout Assoc. Chm., Berwick-on-Tweed Constituency Cons. Assoc., 1959–62, Pres., 1973–77; Northern Area Cons. Assocs: Treas., 1961–66, Chm., 1966–69; Pres., 1974–78; Vice Chm., Nat Union of Cons. and Unionist Assocs, 1969–71. Director: Newcastle & Gateshead Water Co., 1964–73; Trident Television, 1972–81 (Dep. Chm., 1976–81); Chm: Northumbrian Water Authority, 1973–82; North Tyne Area, Manpower Bd, MSC, 1983–84. Mem. Council, The Wildfowl Trust, 1981–. Chm., Newcastle Univ. Develt Trust, 1978–81; Mem. Ct, Newcastle Univ., 1979–; Governor, Swinton Conservative College, 1967–81. FRSA 1983. High Sheriff, 1972, JP 1953–75, DL 1981–85, Vice Lord-Lieut., 1984, Northumberland. KStJ 1984. *Recreation:* Jt Master, West Percy Foxhounds, 1950–. *Address:* Hedgeley Hall, Powburn, Alnwick, Northumberland NE66 4HZ. *T:* Powburn 273; (office) Newcastle upon Tyne 610181. *Clubs:* Cavalry and Guards, White's, Pratt's; Northern Counties (Newcastle upon Tyne).

CARR-GOMM, Richard Culling, OBE 1985; Executive Consultant to the Carr-Gomm Society and Morpeth Society (charity societies); *b* 2 Jan. 1922; *s* of Mark Culling Carr-Gomm and Amicia Dorothy (*née* Heming); *m* 1957, Susan, *d* of Ralph and Dorothy Gibbs; two *s* three *d*. *Educ:* Stowe School. Served War: commnd Coldstream Guards, 1941; served 6th Guards Tank Bde, NW Europe (twice wounded, mentioned in despatches); Palestine, 1945; ME; resigned commn, 1955. Founded: Abbeyfield Soc., 1956; Carr Gomm Soc., 1965; Morpeth Soc., 1972. Templeton UK Project Award, 1984. Croix de Guerre (Silver Star), France, 1944. KStJ. *Publication:* Push on the Door (autobiog.), 1979. *Recreations:* golf, backgammon, painting. *Address:* 9 The Batch, Batheaston, Avon BA1 7DR. *T:* Bath 858434.

CARR LINFORD, Alan, RWS 1955 (ARWS 1949); ARE 1946; ARCA 1946; *b* 15 Jan. 1926; *m* 1948, Margaret Dorothea Parish; one *s* one *d*. *Educ:* Royal College of Art, and in Rome. Was awarded the Prix de Rome, 1947. *Recreation:* shooting. *Address:* Midfield, Lower Green, Wimbish, Saffron Walden, Essex CB10 2XH. *T:* Radwinter 287.

CARREL, Philip, CMG 1960; OBE 1954; *b* 23 Sept. 1915; *s* of late Louis Raymond Carrel and Lucy Mabel (*née* Cooper); *m* 1948, Eileen Mary Bullock (*née* Hainworth); one *s* one *d*. *Educ:* Blundell's; Balliol. Colonial Admin. Service, 1938, Zanzibar Protectorate. EA Forces, 1940. Civil Affairs, 1941–47 (OETA); Civilian Employee Civil Affairs, GHQ MELF, 1947–49 (on secondment from Som. Prot.); Colonial Admin. Service (Somaliland Protectorate), 1947; Commissioner of Somali Affairs, 1953; Chief Sec. to the Government, Somaliland Protectorate, 1959–60. Cttee Sec., Overseas Relns, Inst. of Chartered Accountants in England and Wales, 1961–77; retired. *Address:* Lych Gates, Chiltley Lane, Liphook, Hants GU30 7HJ. *T:* 722150.

CARRELL, Prof. Robin Wayne, FRSNZ 1980; FRACP; Professor of Haematology, University of Cambridge, since 1986; *b* 5 April 1936; *s* of Ruane George Carrell and Constance Gwendoline Carrell (*née* Rowe); *m* 1962, Susan Wyatt Rogers; two *s* two *d*. *Educ:* Christchurch Boys' High School, NZ; Univ. of Otago (MB ChB 1959); Univ. of Canterbury (BSc 1965); Univ. of Cambridge (MA, PhD 1968). MRCPath 1976; MRCP 1985. Mem., MRC Abnormal Haemoglobin Unit, Cambridge, 1965–68; Dir, Clinical Biochemistry, Christchurch Hosp., NZ, 1968–75; Lectr and Consultant in Clinical Biochem., Addenbrooke's Hosp. and Univ. of Cambridge, 1976–78; Prof. of Clinical Biochem. and Dir, Molecular Path. Res. Lab., Christchurch Sch. of Clinical Medicine, Univ. of Otago, 1978–86. Commonwealth Fellow, St John's Coll. and Vis. Scientist, MRC Lab. of Molecular Biol., 1985. Pharmacia Prize for biochem. res., NZ, 1984; Hector Medal, Royal Soc., NZ, 1986. *Publications:* articles in sci. jls, esp. on genetic abnormalities of human proteins. *Recreations:* gardening, walking. *Address:* 19 Madingley Road, Cambridge CB3 0EG. *T:* Cambridge 312970.

CARRERAS, Sir James, KCVO 1980; Kt 1970; MBE 1945; *b* 30 Jan. 1909; *s* of Henry and Dolores Carreras; *m* 1927, Vera St John; one *s*. Chm. and Chief Exec., Hammer Film Prodns Ltd, 1946–73. Trustee, Royal Naval Film Corporation. Mem. Council, Cinema and Television Benevolent Fund; Vice-Pres., The London Fedn of Boys' Clubs; Past Pres., Variety International; Consultant, Duke of Edinburgh's Award Scheme. Grand Order of Civil Merit (Spain), 1974. *Recreation:* cooking. *Address:* Queen Anne Cottage, Friday Street, Henley-on-Thames, Oxon.

CARRICK, 9th Earl of, *cr* 1748; **Brian Stuart Theobald Somerset Caher Butler;** Baron Butler (UK), 1912; Viscount Ikerrin, 1629; *b* 17 Aug. 1931; *o s* of 8th Earl of Carrick; *S* father, 1957; *m* 1951, (Mary) Belinda (marr. diss. 1976), *e d* of Major David Constable-Maxwell, TD, Bosworth Hall, near Rugby; one *s* one *d*. *Educ:* Downside. Dir., Bowater Industries plc; Chm. and Man. Dir, Ralli Brothers Ltd; Chairman: Ralli Brothers and Coney Ltd; Cargill Maclaine and Co. Ltd; Director: Bowater Incorporated; Nauman Gepp and Co. Ltd; Ralli Hong Kong Ltd; Cargill UK Ltd; Mercantile House Holdings plc. *Heir: s* Viscount Ikerrin, *qv*. *Address:* 10 Netherton Grove, SW10. *T:* 01–352 6328. *Clubs:* White's, Brooks's, Pratt's.

CARRICK, Edward; *see* Craig, E. A.

CARRICK, Senator Hon. Sir John (Leslie), KCMG 1982; Senator, Commonwealth Parliament of Australia, since 1971; *b* 4 Sept. 1918; *s* of late A. J. Carrick and of E. E. Carrick; *m* 1951, Diana Margaret Hunter; three *d*. *Educ:* Univ. of Sydney (BEc). Res. Officer, Liberal Party of Aust., NSW Div., 1946–48, Gen. Sec., 1948–71; Minister: for Housing and Construction, 1975; for Urban and Regional Develt, 1975; for Educn, 1975–79; Minister Assisting Prime Minister in Fed. Affairs, 1975–78; Minister for Nat. Develt and Energy, 1979–83; Dep. Leader, 1978, Leader, 1978–83, Govt in the Senate. Vice-Pres., Exec. Council, 1978–82. *Recreations:* swimming, reading. *Address:* 8 Montah Avenue, Killara, NSW 2071, Australia. *T:* 02 498 6326. *Clubs:* Australian (Sydney); Commonwealth (Canberra).

CARRICK, Roger John, CMG 1983; LVO 1972; HM Diplomatic Service; Consul-General, Chicago, since 1985; *b* 13 Oct. 1937; *s* of John H. and Florence M. Carrick; *m* 1962, Hilary Elizabeth Blinman; two *s*. *Educ:* Isleworth Grammar Sch.; Sch. of Slavonic and East European Studies, London Univ. Served RN, 1956–58. Joined HM Foreign (subseq. Diplomatic) Service, 1956; SSEES, 1961; Sofia, 1962; FO, 1965; Paris, 1967; Singapore, 1971; FCO, 1973; Counsellor and Dep. Head, Personnel Ops Dept, FCO, 1976; Vis. Fellow, Inst. of Internat. Studies, Univ. of Calif, Berkeley, 1977–78; Counsellor, Washington, 1978; Hd, Overseas Estate Dept, FCO, 1982. *Publication:* East-West Technology Transfer in Perspective, 1978. *Recreations:* sailing, squash, music, reading, avoiding gardening. *Address:* c/o Foreign and Commonwealth Office, SW1A 2AH; 33 N Dearborn Street, Chicago, Ill 60602, USA. *Clubs:* Royal Commonwealth Society, Arts; Tavern, Mid-America, Cliff Dwellers, Economic Club of Chicago.

CARRICK, Maj-Gen. Thomas Welsh, OBE 1959; retired; Specialist in Community Medicine, Camden and Islington Area Health Authority (Teaching), 1975–78; *b* 19 Dec. 1914; *s* of late George Carrick and late Mary Welsh; *m* 1948, Nan Middleton Allison; one *s*. *Educ:* Glasgow Academy; Glasgow Univ.; London Sch. of Hygiene and Tropical Med. MB, ChB 1937, FFCM 1972, DPH 1951, DIH 1961. House appts in medicine, surgery and urological surgery at Glasgow Royal Infirmary, 1937–38; Dep. Supt, Glasgow Royal Infirmary, 1939–40. Commissioned, RAMC, 1940. Later service appts include: Asst Dir, Army Health, 17 Gurkha Div., Malaya, 1961–63; Asst Dir, Army Health, HQ Scotland, 1964–65; Dir Army Personnel Research Estabt, 1965–68; Dep. Dir, Army Health, Strategic Command, 1968–70; Prof. of Army Health, Royal Army Med. Coll., 1970; Dir of Army Health and Research, MoD, 1971–72; Comdt and Postgraduate Dean, Royal Army Medical Coll., Millbank, 1973–75, retd. Col Comdt, RAMC, 1975–79. Blackham Lectr, RIPH, 1977. QHS 1973. Pres., Blackmore Vale and Yeovil Centre, National Trust, 1979–85. OStJ 1946. *Publications:* articles in Jl of RAMC, Army Review, Community Health. *Recreations:* gardening, theatre. *Address:* Little Chantry, Gillingham, Dorset SP8 4NA.

CARRINGTON, 6th Baron (Ireland) *cr* 1796, (Great Britain) *cr* 1797; **Peter Alexander Rupert Carington,** KG 1985; CH 1983; KCMG 1958; MC 1945; PC 1959; Secretary-General of NATO, since 1984; Chancellor, Order of St Michael and St George, since 1984; *b* 6 June 1919; *s* of 5th Baron and Hon. Sibyl Marion (*d* 1946), *d* of 2nd Viscount Colville; *S* father, 1938; *m* 1942, Iona, *yr d* of late Sir Francis McClean; one *s* two *d*. *Educ:* Eton Coll.; RMC Sandhurst. Served NW Europe, Major Grenadier Guards. Parly Sec., Min. of Agriculture and Fisheries, 1951–54; Parly Sec., Min. of Defence, Oct. 1954–Nov. 1956; High Comr for the UK in Australia, Nov. 1956–Oct. 1959; First Lord of the Admiralty, 1959–63; Minister without Portfolio and Leader of the House of Lords, 1963–64; Leader of the Opposition, House of Lords, 1964–70 and 1974–79. Secretary of State: for Defence, 1970–74; for Energy, 1974; for For. and Commonwealth Affairs, 1979–82; Minister of Aviation Supply, 1971–74. Chm., Cons. Party Organisation, 1972–74. Chm., GEC, 1983–84. Sec. for Foreign Correspondence and Hon. Mem., Royal Acad. of Arts, 1982–; Chm., Bd of Trustees, V & A Museum, 1983–. Pres., The Pilgrims, 1983–. Hon. Bencher, Middle Temple, 1983. JP 1948, DL Bucks. Fellow of Eton Coll., 1966–81; Hon. Fellow, St Antony's Coll., Oxford, 1982. Hon. LLD: Cambridge, 1981; Leeds, 1981; Aberdeen, 1985; Hon. Dr Laws: Univ. of Philippines, 1982; Univ. of S Carolina, 1983; DUniv Essex, 1983. *Heir: s* Hon. Rupert Francis John Carington, *b* 2 Dec. 1948. *Address:* 32a Ovington Square, SW3 1LR. *T:* 01–584 1476; The Manor House, Bledlow, near Aylesbury, Bucks. *T:* Princes Risborough 3499. *Clubs:* Pratt's, White's.
See also Baron Ashcombe.

CARRINGTON, Prof. Alan, FRS 1971; Royal Society Research Professor, and Fellow of Jesus College, Oxford University, since 1984; *b* 6 Jan. 1934; *o s* of Albert Carrington and Constance (*née* Nelson); *m* 1959, Noreen Hilary Taylor; one *s* two *d*. *Educ:* Colfe's Grammar Sch.; Univ. of Southampton. BSc, PhD; MA Cantab., MA Oxon. Univ. of Cambridge: Asst in Research, 1960; Fellow of Downing Coll., 1960; Asst Dir of Res., 1963; Prof. of Chemistry, Univ. of Southampton, 1967; Royal Soc. Res. Prof., Southampton, 1979–84. Tilden Lectr, Chem. Soc., 1972; Sen. Fellowship, SRC, 1976. Hon. DSc Southampton, 1985. Harrison Mem. Prize, Chem. Soc., 1962; Meldola Medal, Royal Inst. of Chemistry, 1963; Marlow Medal, Faraday Soc., 1966; Corday Morgan Medal, Chem. Soc., 1967; Chem. Soc. Award in Structural Chemistry, 1970; Faraday Medal, RSC, 1985. *Publications:* (with A. D. McLachlan) Introduction to Magnetic Resonance, 1967; Microwave Spectroscopy of Free Radicals, 1974; numerous papers on topics in chemical physics in various learned jls. *Recreations:* family, music, fishing, golf, sailing. *Address:* 46 Lakewood Road, Chandler's Ford, Hants. *T:* Chandler's Ford 65092.

CARRINGTON, Charles Edmund, MC; writer and lecturer; *b* West Bromwich, 21 April 1897; *s* of late Very Rev. C. W. Carrington; *m* 1st, 1932, Cecil Grace MacGregor (marr. diss., 1954); one *d* decd; 2nd, 1955, Maysie Cuthbert Robertson (*d* 1983). *Educ:* Christ's Coll., New Zealand; Christ Church, Oxford. Enlisted, 1914; first commission, 1915; Capt. 5th Royal Warwickshire Regt, 1917; served in France and Italy (MC); Major TA, 1927. BA Oxford, 1921; MA 1929; MA Cambridge, 1929. Asst Master, Haileybury Coll., 1921–24 and 1926–29; Lectr, Pembroke Coll., Oxford, 1924–25; Educational Sec. to the Cambridge Univ. Press, 1929–54. Military service, 1939, France, 1940; Lt-Col Gen. Staff, 1941–45. Prof. of British Commonwealth Relations at Royal Inst. of Internat. Affairs, 1954–62; organised unofficial Commonwealth conferences, New Zealand, 1959, Nigeria, 1962; Visiting Prof., USA, 1964–65. Has served on: LCC Educn Cttee; Classical Assoc. Council; Publishers Assoc. Educational Group; Royal Commonwealth Soc. Council; Inter-Univ. Council; Overseas Migration Board, Islington Soc., etc; Chm., Shoreditch Housing Assoc., 1961–67. *Publications:* An Exposition of Empire, 1947; The British Overseas, 1950; Godley of Canterbury, 1951; Rudyard Kipling, 1955, rev. edn 1978; The Liquidation of the British Empire, 1961; Soldier from the Wars Returning, 1965; (ed) The Complete Barrack-Room Ballads of Rudyard Kipling, 1973; Kipling's Horace, 1978; A History of England (with J. Hampden Jackson), 1932; (under pen-name of Charles Edmonds) A Subaltern's War, 1929; T. E. Lawrence, 1935; contributor to: Camb. Hist. of the British Empire, 1959; An African Survey, 1957; Surveys of International Affairs, 1957–58 and 1959–60, etc. *Recreations:* historical studies, travel. *Address:* 31 Grange Road, N1 2NP. *T:* 01–354 2832. *Club:* Travellers'.

CARROL, Charles Gordon; Director, Commonwealth Institute, Scotland, since 1971; *b* 21 March 1935; *s* of Charles Muir Carrol and Catherine Gray Napier; *m* 1970, Frances Anne, *o d* of John A. and Flora McL. Sinclair; three *s*. *Educ:* Melville Coll., Edinburgh; Edinburgh Univ. (MA); Moray House Coll. (DipEd). Education Officer: Govt of Nigeria, 1959–65; Commonwealth Inst., Scotland, 1965–71. Lay Member, Press Council, 1978–82. *Recreations:* walking, reading, cooking. *Address:* 11 Dukehaugh, Peebles, Scotland EH45 9DN. *T:* Peebles 21296.

CARROLL, Ven. Charles William Desmond; Archdeacon of Blackburn, 1973–86; Archdeacon Emeritus since 1986; Vicar of Balderstone, 1973–86; *b* 27 Jan. 1919; *s* of Rev. William and Mrs L. Mary Carroll; *m* 1945, Doreen Daisy Ruskell; three *s* one *d*. *Educ:* St Columba Coll.; Trinity Coll., Dublin. BA 1943; Dip. Ed. Hons 1945; MA 1946. Asst Master: Kingstown Grammar Sch., 1943–45; Rickerby House Sch., 1945–50; Vicar of Stanwix, Carlisle, 1950–59; Hon. Canon of Blackburn, 1959; Dir of Religious Education, 1959; Hon. Chaplain to Bishop of Blackburn, 1961; Canon Residentiary of Blackburn Cathedral, 1964. *Publication:* Management for Managers, 1968. *Address:* 11 Assheton Road, Blackburn BB2 6SF. *T:* Blackburn 51915. *Clubs:* Royal Commonwealth Society; Rotary (Blackburn).

CARROLL, Maj.-Gen. Derek Raymond, OBE 1958; retired; *b* 2 Jan. 1919; *er s* of late Raymond and Edith Lisle Carroll; *m* 1946, Bettina Mary, *d* of late Leslie Gould; one *s* two *d*. Enlisted TA, 1939; commnd into Royal Engineers, 1943; served Western Desert, 1941–43, Italy, 1943–44; psc 1945; various appts, 1946–66, in War Office (2), Germany (2), Sudan Defence Force, Libya, Malaya; CRE 4 Div., 1962–64; comd 12 Engr Bde, 1966–67; idc 1968; Dir, MoD, 1969–70; Chief Engr, BAOR, 1970–73; RARO, 1973. Bus driver, East Kent Road Car Co., 1974. *Recreations:* sailing, railways, airways. *Club:* Royal Cinque Ports Yacht.

CARROLL, Prof. John Edward, FEng 1985; Professor of Engineering, since 1983, and Deputy Head of Engineering Department, since 1986, University of Cambridge; Fellow of Queens' College, Cambridge, since 1967; *b* 15 Feb. 1934; *s* of Sydney Wentworth Carroll and May Doris Carroll; *m* 1958, Vera Mary Jordan; three *s*. *Educ:* Oundle Sch.; Queens' Coll., Cambridge (Wrangler; Foundn Schol., 1957). BA 1957; PhD 1961; FIEE; ScD 1982. Microwave Div., Services Electronic Res. Lab., 1961–67; Lectr, 1967–76, Reader, 1976–83, Cambridge Univ. Vis. Prof., Queensland Univ., 1982. Editor, IEE Jl of Solid State and Electron Devices, 1976–82. *Publications:* Hot Electron Microwave Generators, 1970; Physical Models of Semiconductor Devices, 1974; Solid State Devices (Inst. of Phys. vol. 57), 1980; Rate Equations in Semiconductor Electronics, 1986; contribs on microwaves, semiconductor devices and optical systems to learned jls. *Recreations:* swimming, piano, walking, reading thrillers, carpentry.

CARROLL, Madeleine; screen, stage, and radio actress; *d* of John Carroll, Co. Limerick, and Hélène de Rosière Tuaillon, Paris; *m* 1st, 1931, Capt. Philip Astley, MC (from whom she obtd a divorce, 1940); 2nd, 1942, Lieut Sterling Hayden, USMC (from whom she obtd a divorce, 1946); 3rd, 1946, Henri Lavorel (marr. diss.); 4th, 1950, Andrew Heiskell (marr. diss.); one *d*. *Educ:* private sch.; Birmingham Univ. (BA Hons French). Started theatrical career in touring company, playing French maid in The Lash; subsequently toured with Seymour Hicks in Mr What's his Name; became leading lady in British films as result of first screen test for The Guns of Loos; subsequently made Young Woodley, The School for Scandal, I was a Spy, and The Thirty Nine Steps; came to America in 1936 and made: The Case against Mrs Ames; The General Died at Dawn; Lloyds of London; On the Avenue; The Prisoner of Zenda; Blockade; Café Society; North-West Mounted Police; Virginia; One Night in Lisbon; Bahama Passage; My Favourite Blonde; White Cradle Inn; An Innocent Affair; The Fan. Radio appearances include the leading parts in: Cavalcade; Beloved Enemy; Romance; There's always Juliet. From 1941 until end of War, engaged exclusively in war activities.

CARRUTHERS, Alwyn Guy; Director of Statistics, Department of Employment, 1981–83 (Deputy Director, 1972–80); *b* 6 May 1925; *yr s* of late John Sendall and of Lily Eden Carruthers, Grimsby; *m* 1950, Edith Eileen, *o d* of late William and Edith Addison Lumb; no *c. Educ:* Wintringham Grammar Sch., Grimsby; King's Coll., London Univ. BA First Cl. Hons in Mathematics, Drew Gold Medal and Prize, 1945. RAE, Farnborough, 1945–46; Instructor Lieut, RN, 1946–49; Rothamsted Experimental Station, 1949. Postgraduate Diploma in Mathematical Statistics, Christ's Coll., Cambridge, 1951. Bd of Trade and DTI Statistics Divisions, 1951–72. *Publications:* articles in official publications and learned jls. *Recreations:* gardening, music. *Address:* 24 Red House Lane, Bexleyheath, Kent. *T:* 01-303 4898.

CARRUTHERS, Colin Malcolm, CMG 1980; HM Diplomatic Service, retired; UK Commissioner, British Phosphate Commissioners, since 1981; *b* 23 Feb. 1931; *s* of Colin Carruthers and late Dorothy Beatrice Carruthers; *m* 1954, Annette Audrey Buckton; three *s* one *d. Educ:* Monkton Combe School; Selwyn College, Cambridge (MA). Royal Signals, 1950–51; joined HMOCS Kenya, 1955; District Officer, Kenya, 1955–63; Dep. Civil Sec., Rift Valley Region, Kenya, 1963–65 (retired on Africanisation of post); Field Dir, Oxfam, Maseru, Lesotho, 1965–67; joined HM Diplomatic Service, 1968; First Sec. (Economic), Islamabad, 1969–73; First Sec., Ottawa, 1973–77; Counsellor and Hd of Chancery, Addis Ababa, 1977–80 (Chargé d'Affaires, 1978–79); Asst Election Comr, Zimbabwe-Rhodesia elecns, 1980; Head of South Pacific Dept, FCO, 1980–83, retired. *Recreations:* tennis, golf, family. *Address:* Thornbury, Frant, near Tunbridge Wells, Kent. *T:* Frant 238. *Club:* Hawks (Cambridge).

CARRUTHERS, George, OBE 1979; FCIT; Member of Board, 1979–82, Deputy Chief Executive, 1981–82, Consultant, 1983–84, National Bus Company; *b* 15 Nov. 1917; *s* of James and Dinah Carruthers; *m* 1941, Gabriel Joan Heath; one *s* one *d. Educ:* Nelson Sch., Wigton, Cumbria; St Edmund Hall, Oxford (BA). FBIM. Served War, Border Regt and Cameronians (Major), 1939–46 (despatches). Various management posts, Bus Industry (all at subsid. cos or Headquarters NBC): Eastern Counties, Norwich, 1946–59; Wilts and Dorset Omnibus Co., 1959–63; Dep. Gen. Manager, Hants and Dorset Omnibus Co., 1963–66; Gen. Manager, United Welsh-Swansea, 1967–69; Vice-Chm., South Wales (NBC), 1969–72; Regional Exec., Western Region (NBC), 1972–73; Gp Exec., NBC Headquarters, 1973–74; Director of Manpower, NBC HQ, 1974–79; Mem. for Personnel Services, 1979–81. Pres., Bus and Coach Council, 1983–84. *Publications:* papers for Jl and meetings of CIT (Road Passenger award for a paper, 1978). *Recreation:* the countryside. *Address:* 2 Mallard Close, Lower Street, Harnham, Salisbury, Wilts SP2 8JB. *T:* Salisbury 23084.

CARRUTHERS, James Edwin; Assistant Under Secretary of State, Ministry of Defence, since 1984; *b* 19 March 1928; *er s* of James and Dollie Carruthers; *m* 1955, Phyllis Williams; one *s. Educ:* George Heriot's Sch.; Edinburgh Univ. (MA; Medallist in Scottish Hist.). FSAScot. Lieut, The Queen's Own Cameron Highlanders, 1949–51, and TA, 1951–55. Air Ministry: Asst Principal, 1951; Private Sec. to DCAS, 1955; Asst Private Sec. to Sec. of State for Air, 1956; Principal, 1956; Min. of Aviation, 1960–62; Private Secretary: to Minister of Defence for RAF, 1965–67; to Parly Under Sec. of State for RAF, 1967; Asst Sec., 1967; Chief Officer, Sovereign Base Areas Admin, Cyprus, 1968–71; Dep. Chief of Public Relations, MoD, 1971–72; Private Sec. to Chancellor of Duchy of Lancaster, Cabinet Office, 1973–74; Sec., Organising Cttee for British Aerospace, DoI, 1975–77; Under-Sec., 1977; seconded as Asst to Chm., British Aerospace, 1977–79; Dir Gen., Royal Ordnance Factories (Finance and Procurement), 1980–83; Chm., C S Selection Bd, 1983–84. Mem., Chorleywood UDC, 1964–65. *Recreations:* painting, gardening, travel. *Address:* 129 Valley Road, Chorleywood, Herts WD3 4BN. *T:* Rickmansworth 776020. *Club:* Royal Commonwealth Society.

CARSBERG, Prof. Bryan Victor; Director General of Telecommunications, since 1984; Director of Research, Institute of Chartered Accountants in England and Wales, since 1981; *b* 3 Jan. 1939; *s* of Alfred Victor Carsberg and Maryllia (*née* Collins); *m* 1960, Margaret Linda Graham; two *d. Educ:* Berkhamsted Sch.; London Sch. of Econs and Polit. Science (MScEcon). Chartered Accountant, 1960. Sole practice, chartered accountant, 1962–64; Lectr in Accounting, LSE, 1964–68; Vis. Lectr, Grad. Sch. of Business, Univ. of Chicago, 1968–69; Prof. of Accounting, Univ. of Manchester, 1969–81 (Dean, Faculty of Econ. and Social Studies, 1977–78); Arthur Andersen Prof. of Accounting, LSE, 1981– (on leave, 1984–). Vis. Prof. of Business Admin, Univ. of Calif, Berkeley, 1974; Asst Dir of Res. and Technical Activities, Financial Accounting Standards Bd, USA, 1978–81. Mem. Council, ICA, 1975–79. Director: Economists Adv. Gp, 1976–84; Economist Bookshop, 1981–; Philip Allan (Publishers), 1981–. Hon. MAEcon Manchester, 1973. *Publications:* An Introduction to Mathematical Programming for Accountants, 1969; (with H. C. Edey) Modern Financial Management, 1969; Analysis for Investment Decisions, 1974; (with E. V. Morgan and M. Parkin) Indexation and Inflation, 1975; Economics of Business Decisions, 1975; (with A. Hope) Investment Decisions under Inflation, 1976; (with A. Hope) Current Issues in Accountancy, 1977, 2nd edn 1984; (with J. Arnold and R. Scapens) Topics in Management Accounting, 1980; (with S. Lumby) The Evaluation of Financial Performance in the Water Industry, 1983; (with M. Page) Current Cost Accounting, 1984; (with M. Page *et al*) Small Company Financial Reporting, 1985. *Recreations:* road running, theatre, music. *Address:* Woodlands, 14 The Great Quarry, Guildford, Surrey GU1 3XN. *T:* Guildford 572672. *Clubs:* London Road Runners; New York Road Runners.

CARSE, William Mitchell, CBE 1953; *b* 23 Aug. 1899; *o s* of Robert Allison Carse, Hawkhead, Renfrewshire; *m* 1928, Helen Knox (*d* 1976), *yr d* of J. B. Beaton, Milliken Park, Renfrewshire; one *s. Educ:* Glasgow High Sch.; Glasgow Univ.; Wellington Military Coll., Madras; St John's Coll., Cambridge. Passed Examination for RMC Sandhurst, 1917; proceeded to Wellington Military Coll., Madras, 1918; gazetted to Indian Army, 1918; served in South Persia until 1920; resigned Commission; entered HM Consular Service, 1923; served in USA, Guatemala, Germany, Portuguese East Africa, Portugal and Portuguese West Africa; Consul-Gen., Luanda, Angola, 1937–39; Consul at Teneriffe, 1939; Consul-Gen. at Reykjavik, Iceland, 1943; attached to British Political Mission in Hungary, 1945–46; Consul-Gen. at Tabriz, Persia, 1946–47, and at Ahwaz, Persia, 1948; Deputy High Comr for the UK in Peshawar, Pakistan, 1948–51; Consul-Gen., São Paulo, Brazil, 1951–56, retd. Appointed to Distillers Company Ltd (Industrial Group), London, 1957. *Recreations:* yachting, riding, chess. *Address:* Little Dene, 16 St Alban's Road, Reigate, Surrey RH2 9LN.

CARSON, Hon. Edward; Lieutenant Life Guards; *b* 17 Feb. 1920; *yr s* of Baron Carson, a Lord of Appeal in Ordinary; *m* 1943, Heather, *d* of Lt-Col Frank Sclater, OBE, MC; one *s* one *d. Educ:* Eton; Trinity Hall, Cambridge. MP (C) Isle of Thanet Div. of Kent, 1945–53. *Address:* Crossways, Westfield, near Hastings, Sussex. *T:* Hastings 751976. *Clubs:* Wig and Pen, MCC.

CARSON, John, CBE 1981; Draper; Member (OUP) for Belfast North, Northern Ireland Assembly, 1982–86; *b* 1934. Member of the Orange Order; Member, Belfast District Council, (formerly Belfast Corporation), 1971–; Official Unionist Councillor for Duncairn; Lord Mayor of Belfast, 1980–81, 1985–86. MP (UU) Belfast North, Feb. 1974–1979. High Sheriff, Belfast, 1978. *Address:* 20 Cardy Road, Greyabbey, Co. Down, N Ireland.

CARSON, Robert Andrew Glendinning, FBA 1980; Keeper, Department of Coins and Medals, British Museum, 1978–83; *b* 7 April 1918; *s* of Andrew and Mary Dempster Carson; *m* 1949, Meta Fransisca De Vries; one *s* one *d. Educ:* Kirkcudbright Acad.; Univ. of Glasgow (MA (1st Cl. Hons Classics) 1940; Foulis Schol. 1940; Hon. DLitt 1983). Served War, RA, 1940–46, NW Europe; 2nd Lieut 1941, Captain 1945. Asst Keeper, 1947, Dep. Keeper, 1965, Dept of Coins and Medals, British Museum. Pres., Internat. Numismatic Commn, 1979–86. Editor, Numismatic Chronicle, 1966–73; Mem., Adv. Cttee on Historic Wreck Sites, 1973–80; Pres., Royal Numismatic Soc., 1974–79 (Medallist, 1972; Hon. Fellow, 1980); Hon. Mem., British Numismatic Soc., 1979. Medallist: Soc. française de Numismatique, 1970; Luxembourg Museum, 1971; Amer. Numismatic Soc., 1978; Corresponding Member: Amer. Num. Soc., 1967; Austrian Num. Soc., 1971; Hon. Mem., Romanian Num. Soc., 1977. FSA 1965. Queen's Jubilee medal, 1977. *Publications:* (with H. Mattingly and C. H. V. Sutherland) Roman Imperial Coinage, 1951–; ed, Essays in Roman Coinage presented to Harold Mattingly, 1956; (with P. V. Hill and J. P. C. Kent) Late Roman Bronze Coinage, 1960; Coins, ancient, mediæval and modern, 1962, 2nd edn 1972; Catalogue of Roman Imperial Coins in the British Museum, vol. VI, 1962; ed, Mints, Dies and Currency, 1971; Principal Coins of the Romans, vol. I, 1978, vol. II, 1980, vol. III, 1981; ed, Essays presented to Humphrey Sutherland, 1978; History of the Royal Numismatic Society, 1986; articles in Numismatic Chron., Rev. Numismatique, etc. *Address:* 2/2A Queen's Parade, Newport, NSW 2106, Australia.

CARSON, Air Cdre Robert John, CBE 1974; AFC 1964; Queen's Commendation (Air), 1962; Director, Leicestershire Medical Research Foundation, University of Leicester, since 1980; *b* 3 Aug. 1924; *e s* of Robert George and Margaret Etta Helena Carson; *m* 1945, Jane, *yr d* of James and Jane Bailie; three *d. Educ:* Regent House Sch., Newtownards, NI; RAF. MRAeS; MBIM; MIOM. India, Burma, Malaya, 1945–48; Rhodesia, 1949–50; Queens Univ. Air Sqdn, 1951–52; RAF HC Examining Unit, 1952–53; AHQ Iraq, 1953–54; RAF Staff Coll., 1955; Plans, Air Min., 1956–59; 16 Sqdn, Laarbruch, Germany, 1959–62; Wing Comdr Flying, RAF Swinderby, 1962–64; Air Warfare Coll., Manby, 1964; Chief Nuclear Ops, 2ATAF Germany, 1964–67; JSSC Latimer, 1967; Chief Air Planner, UK Delegn, Live Oak, SHAPE, 1968–71; Station Comdr, RAF Leeming, 1971–73; Overseas Coll. Defence Studies, Canada, 1973–74; Air Adviser, British High Commission, Ottawa, 1974–75; Defence Advr to British High Comr in Canada, 1975–78; Manager, Panavia Office, Ottawa, and Grumman Aerospace Corp., NY, 1978–80. *Recreations:* Rugby, tennis, golf, gardening. *Address:* 20 Meadow Drive, Scruton, near Northallerton, North Yorks. *T:* Northallerton 748656; c/o Lloyds Bank, 118 High Street, Northallerton, N Yorks. *Clubs:* Royal Air Force; Royal Ottawa (Ottawa).

CARSON, William Hunter Fisher, OBE 1983; jockey; *b* 16 Nov. 1942; *s* of Thomas Whelan Carson and Mary Hay; *m* 1963, Carole Jane Sutton (marr. diss. 1979); three *s*; *m* 1982, Elaine Williams. *Educ:* Riverside, Stirling, Scotland. Apprenticed to Captain G. Armstrong, 1957; trans. to Fred Armstrong, 1963–66; First Jockey to Lord Derby, 1967; first classic win, High Top, 1972; Champion Jockey, 1972, 1973, 1978, 1980 and 1983; became First Jockey to W. R. Hern, 1977; also appointed Royal Jockey, riding Dunfermline to the Jubilee Oaks and St Leger wins in the colours of HM the Queen; won the 200th Derby on Troy, trained by W. R. Hern, 1979; the same combination won the 1980 Derby, with Henbit, and the 1980 Oaks, with Bireme; also won King George VI and Queen Elizabeth Stakes, on Ela-Mana-Mou, 1980, on Petoski, 1985; 1983 Oaks and St Leger, with Sun Princess; Ascot Gold Cup, on Little Wolf, 1983. *Recreation:* hunting. *Address:* West Ilsley, near Newbury, Berks. *T:* West Ilsley 348.

CARSTAIRS, Charles Young, CB 1968; CMG 1950; *b* 30 Oct. 1910; *s* of late Rev. Dr G. Carstairs, DD and Elizabeth Huntly Carstairs (*née* Young); *m* 1939, Frances Mary (*d* 1981), *o d* of late Dr Claude Lionel Coode, Stroud, Glos; one *s* one *d. Educ:* George Watson's Boys' Coll., Edinburgh; Edinburgh Univ. Entered Home Civil Service, 1934, Dominions Office; transf. Colonial Office, 1935; Asst Private Sec. to Sec. of State for the Colonies, 1936; Private Sec. to Perm. Under-Sec. of State for the Colonies, 1937; Asst Sec., West India Royal Commn, 1938–39; West Indian, Prodn, Res. and Mediterranean Depts, 1939–47; Administrative Sec., Development and Welfare Organisation, British West Indies, 1947–50; Sec., British Caribbean Standing Closer Assoc. Cttee, 1948–49; Dir of Information Services, Colonial Office, 1951–53, Asst Under-Sec., 1953–62; Deputy Sec., Medical Research Council, 1962–65; Under-Secretary, MPBW: Directorate-Gen., R and D, 1965–67, Construction Economics, 1967–70; Special Advr, Expenditure Cttee, House of Commons, 1971–75; Clerk to Select Cttee on Commodity Prices, House of Lords, 1976–77. *Address:* St Kea, 9 Ridgegate Close, Reigate, Surrey RH2 0HT. *T:* Reigate 44896. *Club:* Athenæum.

CARSTAIRS, Dr George Morrison, MD; FRCPE, FRCPsych; Vice-Chancellor, University of York, 1973–78; *b* Mussoorie, India, 18 June 1916; *s* of late Rev. Dr George Carstairs, DD, K-i-H, and Elizabeth H. Carstairs; *m* 1950, Vera Hunt; two *s* one *d. Educ:* George Watson's Coll., Edinburgh; Edinburgh Univ. Asst Phys., Royal Edinburgh Hosp., 1942. MO, RAF, 1942–46. Commonwealth Fellow, USA, 1948–49; Rockefeller Research Fellow, 1950–51; Henderson Res. Schol., 1951–52; Sen. Registrar, Maudsley Hosp., 1953; Scientific Staff, MRC, 1954–60. Prof. of Psychiatry, Univ. of Edinburgh, 1961–73. Dir, MRC Unit for Research on Epidemiological Aspects of Psychiatry, 1960–71. Vis. Prof. of Psychiatry, Post Grad. Insts, Bangalore, Chandigarh and New Delhi, India, 1979–81; Fellow, Woodrow Wilson Center, Smithsonian Instn, Washington, 1981–82. Reith Lectr, 1962. Pres., World Federation for Mental Health, 1967–71. *Publications:* The Twice Born, 1957; This Island Now, 1963; (with R.L. Kapur) The Great Universe of Kota, 1976; Death of a Witch, 1983; chapters and articles in medical publications. *Recreations:* travel, theatre; formerly athletics. *Address:* 23 Lancaster Grove, NW3. *Club:* Royal Air Force.

CARSTEN, Prof. Francis Ludwig, DPhil, DLitt Oxon; FBA 1971; Masaryk Professor of Central European History in the University of London, 1961–78; *b* 25 June 1911; *s* of Prof. Paul Carsten and Frida Carsten (*née* Born); *m* 1945, Ruth Carsten (*née* Moses); two *s* one *d. Educ.* Heidelberg, Berlin and Oxford Univs. Barnett scholar, Wadham Coll., Oxford, 1939; Senior Demy, Magdalen Coll., Oxford, 1942; Lectr in History, Westfield Coll., Univ. of London, 1947; Reader in Modern History, Univ. of London, 1960. Co-Editor, Slavonic and East European Review, 1966–84. *Publications:* The Origins of Prussia, 1954; Princes and Parliaments in Germany from the 15th to the 18th Century, 1959; The Reichswehr and Politics, 1918–1933, 1966; The Rise of Fascism, 1967, rev. edn, 1980; Revolution in Central Europe, 1918–1919, 1972; Fascist Movements in Austria, 1977; War against War: British and German Radical Movements in the First World War, 1982; Britain and the Weimar Republic, The British Documents, 1984; Essays in German History, 1985; The First Austrian Republic, 1986; ed and contributor, The New Cambridge Modern History, vol. V: The Ascendancy of France, 1961; articles in English Historical Review, History, Survey, Historische Zeitschrift, etc. *Recreations:* gardening, climbing, swimming. *Address:* 11 Redington Road, NW3. *T:* 01-435 5522.

CARSTENS, Dr Karl; President of the Federal Republic of Germany, 1979–84; *b* 14 Dec. 1914; *s* of Dr Karl Carstens, teacher, and Gertrud (*née* Clausen); *m* 1944, Dr Veronica Carstens (*née* Prior). *Educ:* Univs of Frankfurt, Dijon, München, Königsberg, Hamburg, Yale. Dr Laws Hamburg 1936, LLM Yale 1949. Served with Army, 1939–45; lawyer, Bremen, 1945–49; rep. of Bremen in Bonn, 1949–54; rep. of Fed. Republic of Germany to Council of Europe, Strasbourg, 1954–55; teaching at Cologne Univ., 1950–73; Prof. of Constitutional and Internat. Law, 1960–73; FO, Bonn, 1955–60 (State Sec., 1960–66); Dep. Defence Minister, 1966–67; Head of Chancellor's Office, Bonn, 1968–69; Dir Research Inst., German Foreign Policy Assoc., 1969–72; Mem. German Bundestag (CDU), 1972–79; Leader of the Opposition, 1973–76; Pres. of Bundestag, 1976–79. Hon. Citizen: Berlin, Bonn. Charlemagne Prize, 1984; Bremische Senatsmedaille in Gold, 1985; Robert Schuman Prize, 1985; Stresemann Medaille, 1985. *Publications:* Grundgedanken der amerikanischen Verfassung und ihre Verwirklichung, 1954; Das Recht des Europarats, 1956; Politische Führung—Erfahrungen im Dienst der Bundesregierung, 1971; Bundestagsreden und Zeitdokumente, 1977; Reden und Interviews, 5 vols, 1980–84. *Address:* 5300 Bonn 1, Bundeshaus, West Germany.

CARSWELL, John Patrick, CB 1977; FRSL; Secretary, British Academy, 1978–83, now emeritus; Honorary Research Fellow, Department of History, University College London, since 1983; *b* 30 May 1918; *s* of Donald Carswell, barrister and author, and Catherine Carswell, author; *m* 1944, Ianthe Elstob; two *d. Educ:* Merchant Taylors' Sch.; St John's Coll., Oxford (MA). Served in Army, 1940–46. Entered Civil Service, 1946. Joint Sec., Cttee on Economic and Financial Problems of Provision for Old Age (Phillips Cttee), 1953–54; Asst Sec., 1955; Principal Private Sec. to Minister of Pensions and Nat. Insurance, 1955–56; Treasury, 1961–64; Under-Sec., Office of Lord Pres. of the Council and Minister for Science, 1964, Under-Sec., DES and Ministry of Health, 1964–74; Sec., UGC, 1974–77. Life Mem., Inst. of Historical Research, Univ. of London, 1984; FRSL 1984. *Publications:* The Prospector, 1950; The Old Cause, 1954; The South Sea Bubble, 1960; The Diary and Political Papers of George Bubb Dodington, 1965; The Civil Servant and his World, 1966; The Descent on England, 1969; From Revolution to Revolution: English Society 1688–1776, 1973; Lives and Letters, 1978; The Exile: a memoir of Ivy Litvinov, 1983; Government and the Universities in Britain, 1986; contribs to Times Literary Supplement and other periodicals. *Address:* 5 Prince Arthur Road, NW3. *T:* 01–794 6527. *Club:* Garrick.

CARSWELL, Hon. Robert Douglas; Hon. Mr Justice Carswell; a Judge of the High Court of Northern Ireland, since 1984; *b* 28 June 1934; *er s* of late Alan E. Carswell and of Nance E. Carswell; *m* 1961, Romayne Winifred, *o d* of late James Ferris, JP, Greyabbey, Co. Down, and of Eileen Ferris, JP; two *d. Educ:* Royal Belfast Academical Instn; Pembroke Coll., Oxford (Schol.; 1st Cl. Honour Mods, 1st Cl. Jurisprudence, MA; Hon. Fellow, 1984); Univ. of Chicago Law Sch. (JD). Called to Bar of N Ireland, 1957, and to English Bar, Gray's Inn, 1972; Counsel to Attorney-General for N Ireland, 1970–71; QC (NI), 1971; Sen. Crown Counsel in NI, 1979–84; Bencher, Inn of Court of N Ireland, 1979. Governor, Royal Belfast Academical Instn, 1967–, Chm. Bd of Governors, 1986–; Pro-Chancellor and Chm. Council, Univ. of Ulster, 1984–. *Publications:* Trustee Acts (Northern Ireland), 1964; articles in legal periodicals. *Recreation:* golf. *Address:* Royal Courts of Justice, Belfast BT1 3JF. *Club:* Ulster Reform (Belfast).

CARTER; *see* Bonham-Carter and Bonham Carter.

CARTER, Andrew; HM Diplomatic Service; Counsellor, UK Delegation to NATO, Brussels, since 1986; *b* 4 Dec. 1943; *s* of Eric and Margaret Carter; *m* 1973, Anne Caroline Morgan (marr. diss. 1986); one *d. Educ:* Latymer Upper Sch., Hammersmith; Royal Coll. of Music; Jesus Coll., Cambridge (Scholar 1962; MA). FRCO; LRAM; ARCM. Asst Master, Marlborough Coll., 1965–70. Joined HM Diplomatic Service, 1971; Warsaw, 1972; Geneva, 1975; Bonn, 1975; FCO, 1978; Counsellor, 1984. *Recreation:* music. *Address:* c/o Foreign and Commonwealth Office, SW1.

CARTER, Angela; author and reviewer; *b* 1940. *Educ:* Bristol Univ. Fellow in Creative Writing, Sheffield Univ., 1976–78. Judge, Booker McConnell Prize, 1983. Screenplay (jtly), The Company of Wolves, 1984. *Publications: fiction: novels:* Shadow Dance, 1966; The Magic Toyshop (John Llewellyn Rhys Prize), 1967 (screenplay, 1986); Several Perceptions (Somerset Maugham Award), 1968; Heroes and Villains, 1969; Miss Z, the Dark Young Lady, 1970; Love, 1971; The Infernal Desire Machines of Doctor Hoffman, 1972; The Passion of New Eve, 1977; Nights at the Circus (jtly, James Tait Black Meml Prize), 1984; *short stories:* Fireworks: 9 profane pieces, 1974; The Bloody Chamber and other stories (Cheltenham Fest. of Lit. Award), 1979; Black Venus, 1985; Come unto these Yellow Sands: four radio plays, 1984; *for children:* (jtly) Martin Leman's Comic and Curious Cats, 1979; (jtly) Moonshadow, 1982; (jtly) Sleeping Beauty and other favourite fairy tales (Kate Greenaway Medal), 1983; *non-fiction:* The Sadeian Woman: an exercise in cultural history, 1979; Nothing Sacred: selected writings, 1982; contrib. New Society, Guardian, etc. *Address:* c/o Virago Press Ltd, 41 William IV Street, WC2N 4DB.

CARTER, Bernard Thomas; Hon. RE 1975; artist (painter and etcher); Keeper, Pictures and Conservation, National Maritime Museum, 1974–77; *b* 6 April 1920; *s* of Cecil Carter and Ethel Carter (*née* Darby); *m* Eugenie Alexander, artist and writer; one *s. Educ:* Haberdashers' Aske's; Goldsmith's College of Art, London Univ. NDD, ATD. RAF, 1939–46. Art lectr, critic and book reviewer, 1952–68; Asst Keeper (prints and drawings), Nat. Maritime Museum, 1968; Dep. Keeper (Head of Picture Dept), Nat. Maritime Museum, 1970. One-man exhibns in London: Arthur Jeffress Gall., 1955; Portal Gall. 1963, 1965, 1967, 1969, 1974, 1978, 1979, 1981, 1984; mixed exhibns: Royal Academy, Arts Council, British Council and galleries in Europe and USA; works in public collections, galleries abroad and British educn authorities, etc. TV and radio include: Thames at Six, Pebble Mill at One, Kaleidoscope, London Radio, etc. *Publication:* Art for Young People (with Eugenie Alexander), 1958. *Recreations:* reading, listening to music, gardening, theatre. *Address:* 56 King George Street, Greenwich, SE10 8QD. *T:* 01–858 4281.

CARTER, Dr Brandon, FRS 1981; Directeur de Recherche (Centre National de la Recherche Scientifique), Observatoire de Paris-Meudon, since 1986; *b* Sydney, Australia, 26 May 1942; *s* of Harold Burnell Carter and Mary (*née* Brandon Jones); *m* 1969, Lucette Defrise; three *d. Educ:* George Watson's Coll., Edinburgh; Univ. of St Andrews; Pembroke Coll., Cambridge (MA, PhD 1968, DSc 1976). Res. Student, Dept of Applied Maths and Theoretical Physics, Cambridge, 1964–67; Res. Fellow, Pembroke Coll., Cambridge, 1967–68; Staff Mem., Inst. of Astronomy, Cambridge, 1968–73; Univ. Asst Lectr, 1973–74, Univ. Lectr, 1974–75, Dept of Applied Maths and Theoretical Physics, Cambridge; Maître de Recherche, co-responsable Groupe d'Astrophysique Relativiste (CNRS), Paris-Meudon, 1975–86. *Recreation:* wilderness. *Address:* 19 rue de la Borne au Diable, 92310 Sèvres, France. *T:* (Paris) 4534—46–77.

CARTER, Bruce; *see* Hough, R. A.

CARTER, Sir Charles (Frederick), Kt 1978; FBA 1970; Chairman, Research Committee, Policy Studies Institute, since 1978; Vice-Chancellor, University of Lancaster, 1963–79; *b*

Rugby, 15 Aug. 1919; *y s* of late Frederick William Carter, FRS; *m* 1944, Janet Shea; one *s* two *d. Educ:* Rugby Sch.; St John's Coll., Cambridge. Friends' Relief Service, 1941–45; Lectr in Statistics, Univ. of Cambridge, 1945–51; Fellow of Emmanuel Coll., 1947–51 (Hon. Fellow, 1965–); Prof. of Applied Economics, The Queen's Univ., Belfast, 1952–59; Stanley Jevons Prof. of Political Economy and Cobden Lectr, Univ. of Manchester, 1959–63. Chairman: Science and Industry Cttee, RSA, British Assoc. and Nuffield Foundn, 1954–59; Schools' Broadcasting Council, 1964–71; Joint Cttee of the Univs and the Accountancy Profession, 1964–70; Adv. Bd of Accountancy Educn, 1970–76; North-West Economic Planning Council, 1965–68; Centre for Studies in Social Policy, 1972–78; PO Rev. Cttee, 1976–77; NI Economic Council, 1977–; NI Management Centre, 1983–86; Sec.-Gen., Royal Econ. Soc., 1971–75; Member: UN Expert Cttee on Commodity Trade, 1953; Capital Investment Advisory Cttee, Republic of Ireland, 1956; British Assoc. Cttee on Metric System, 1958; Council for Scientific and Industrial Research, 1959–63; Commn on Higher Education, Republic of Ireland, 1960–67; Heyworth Cttee on Social Studies, 1963; Advisory Council on Technology, 1964–66; North Western Postal Bd, 1970–73; Anglo-Irish Encounter, 1984–85; Learning from Experience Trust, 1986–. President: Manchester Statistical Soc., 1967–69; BAAS, 1981–82. Joint Editor: Journal of Industrial Economics, 1955–61; Economic Journal, 1961–70; Editor, Policy Studies, 1980–. Fellow, Internat. Acad. of Management; Hon. Member, Royal Irish Academy; Trustee: Joseph Rowntree Meml Trust, 1966– (Vice-Chm., 1981–); Sir Halley Stewart Trust, 1969– (Chm., 1986–); Chm., Rosehill Theatre Trust, 1984–. Hon. DEconSc, NUI, 1968; Hon. DSc: NUU, 1979; Lancaster, 1979; QUB, 1980; Hon. LLD: TCD, 1980; Liverpool, 1982. CBIM. *Publications:* The Science of Wealth, 1960, 3rd edn 1973; (with W. B. Reddaway and J. R. N. Stone) The Measurement of Production Movements, 1948; (with G. L. S. Shackle and others) Uncertainty and Business Decisions, 1954; (with A. D. Roy) British Economic Statistics, 1954; (with B. R. Williams) Industry and Technical Progress, 1957; Investment in Innovation, 1958; Science in Industry, 1959; (with D. P. Barritt) The Northern Ireland Problem, 1962, 2nd edn 1972; Wealth, 1968; (with G. Brosan and others) Patterns and Policies in Higher Education, 1971; On Having a Sense of all Conditions, 1971; (with J. L. Ford and others) Uncertainty and Expectation in Economics, 1972; Higher Education for the Future, 1980; (with J. H. M. Pinder) Policies for a Constrained Economy, 1982; articles in Economic Journal, etc. *Recreation:* gardening. *Address:* 1 Gosforth Road, Seascale, Cumbria CA20 1PU. *T:* Seascale 28359. *Clubs:* National Liberal, United Oxford & Cambridge University.
See also Prof. G. W. Carter.

CARTER, David; *see* Carter, R. D.

CARTER, Sir Derrick (Hunton), Kt 1975; TD 1952; Vice-Chairman, Remploy Ltd, 1976–78 (Chairman, 1972–76; Director, 1967–79); *b* 7 April 1906; *s* of Arthur Hunton Carter, MD and Winifred Carter, Sedbergh; *m* 1st, 1933, Phyllis, *d* of Denis Best, Worcester; one *s* one *d*; 2nd, 1948, Madeline, *d* of Col D. M. O'Callaghan, CMG, DSO; one *d. Educ:* Haileybury Coll.; St John's Coll., Cambridge (MA). 2nd Lieut, 27th (LEE) Bn RE, TA, 1936, mobilised Aug. 1939; in AA until Dec. 1941; 1st War Advanced Class; Major RA, Dept Tank Design; comd Armament Wing of DTD, Lulworth, 1942–45 (Lt-Col). Civil Engr, Dominion Bridge Co., Montreal, 1927–28; Res. Engr, Billingham Div., ICI, 1928–33; Asst Sales Controller, ICI, London, 1933–38; Asst Sales Man., ICI, 1938–39 and 1945–47; Gen. Chemicals Div., ICI: Sales Control Man., 1947; Commercial Dir, 1951; Man. Dir, 1953; Chm., 1961; also Chm. Alkali Div., 1963; Chm. (of merged Divs as) Mond Div., 1964; retd from ICI, 1967. Chm., United Sulphuric Acid Corp. Ltd, 1967–71; Chm., Torrance & Sons Ltd, 1971–79; Director: Avon Rubber Co. Ltd, 1970–81; Stothert & Pitt Ltd, 1971–79; BICERI Ltd, 1967–. Mem. Exec. Cttee, Gloucester Council for Small Industries in Rural Areas, 1970–86. Mem. Council of Management, Nat. Star Centre for Disabled Youth, 1977–82; Vice-Pres., Glos Assoc. of Boys' Clubs. Freeman of City of London, 1973; Liveryman, Worshipful Co. of Coachmakers and Coach Harness Makers, 1973. *Recreations:* shooting, gardening. *Address:* Withington House, Withington, Cheltenham, Glos. *T:* Withington 286. *Club:* Army and Navy.

CARTER, Dorothy Ethel Fleming, (Jane); energy consultant; Director, Hardcastle & Co.; Partner, International Energy Efficiency Consultants; *b* 29 Aug. 1928; *d* of late Charles Edward Starkey and of Doris Alma Starkey (*nee* Fleming), Newcastle-upon-Tyne; *m* 1952, Frank Arthur (Nick) Carter; two *d. Educ:* Dame Allen's Girls' Sch.; Swansea High Sch.; LSE (BSc (Econ) 1951). Joined CS as Exec. Officer, BoT, 1947; Principal, 1966; Min. of Technology, 1969–70; DTI, 1970–73; Asst Sec., Pay Bd, 1973–74; Dept of Energy, 1974–82, Under Sec., 1979–82. Ecole Nat. d'Admin, Paris, 1976. Pres., Internat. Assoc. of Energy Economists, 1986– (Vice Pres., 1979–85); Vice Pres., British Inst. of Energy Economics, 1980–. Trustee, Petroleum Law Educn Trust, 1982–. *Recreations:* travelling, reading. *Address:* 27 Gilkes Crescent, Dulwich Village, SE21. *T:* 01–693 1889. *Club:* Reform.

CARTER, Douglas, CB 1969; Under-Secretary, Department of Trade and Industry, 1970–71; *b* 4 Dec. 1911; 3rd *s* of Albert and Mabel Carter, Bradford, Yorks; *m* 1935, Alice, *d* of Captain C. E. Le Mesurier, CB, RN; three *s* one *d. Educ:* Bradford Grammar Sch.; St John's Coll., Cambridge (Scholar). First Cl. Hons, Historical Tripos Part I and Economics Tripos Part II. Wrenbury Research Scholarship in Economics, Cambridge, 1933. Asst Principal, Board of Trade, 1934; Sec., Imperial Shipping Cttee, 1935–38; Princ. BoT, 1939; Asst Sec., BoT, 1943; Chm., Cttee of Experts in Enemy Property Custodianship, Inter-Allied Reparations Agency, Brussels, 1946; Controller, Import Licensing Dept, 1949; Distribution of Industry Div., BoT, 1954; Industries and Manufactures Div., 1957; Commercial Relations and Exports Div., 1960; Under-Sec., 1963; Tariff Div., 1965. *Publications:* articles in bridge magazines. *Recreations:* reading, golf, bridge, travel. *Address:* 12 Garbrand Walk, Ewell Village, Epsom, Surrey. *T:* 01–394 1316. *Club:* Walton Heath Golf.

CARTER, Hon. Sir Douglas (Julian), KCMG 1977; High Commissioner for New Zealand in the United Kingdom, 1976–79; *b* 5 Aug. 1908; *s* of Walter Stephen Carter and Agnes Isobel; *m* Mavis Rose Miles. *Educ:* Palmerston North High Sch.; Waitaki Boys' High Sch. Formerly, Executive Member: Federated Farmers of NZ; Primary Production Council; Pig Production Council. MP (National Party) Raglan, 1957–75; Chm., Govt Transport Cttee, 1960–70; Under Sec., Agriculture, 1966–69; Minister of Agriculture, 1969–72. Chm., Urban Transport Council, NZ, 1980–84. FRSA 1978. *Address:* 6 Edwin Street, St Andrews, Hamilton, New Zealand.

CARTER, Elliott (Cook), DrMus; composer; *b* New York City, 11 Dec. 1908; *m* 1939, Helen Frost-Jones; one *s. Educ:* Harvard Univ. (MA). Ecole Normale, Paris (DrMus). Professor of Greek and Maths, St John's Coll., Annapolis, 1940–42; Professor of Music: Columbia Univ., 1948–50; Yale Univ., 1960–61. *Compositions include:* First Symphony, 1942–43; Quartet for Four Saxophones, 1943; Holiday Overture, 1944; Ballet, The Minotaur, 1946–47; Woodwind Quintet, 1947; Sonata for Cello and Piano, 1948; First String Quartet, 1950–51; Sonata for Flute, Oboe, Cello and Harpsichord, 1952; Variations for Orchestra, 1953; Second String Quartet, 1960 (New York Critics' Circle Award; Pulitzer Prize; Unesco 1st Prize); Double Concerto for Harpsichord and Piano, 1961

(New York Critics' Circle Award); Piano Concerto, 1967; Concerto for Orchestra, 1970; Third String Quartet, 1971 (Pulitzer Prize); Duo for Violin and Piano, 1973–74; Brass Quintet, 1974; A Mirror on which to Dwell (song cycle), 1976; A Symphony of Three Orchestras, 1977; Syringa, 1979; Night Fantasies (for piano), 1980; In Sleep in Thunder, 1982; Triple Duo, 1983; Penthode, 1985. Member: Nat. Inst. of Arts and Letters, 1956 (Gold Medal for Music, 1971); Amer. Acad. of Arts and Sciences (Boston), 1962; Amer. Acad. of Arts and Letters, 1971; Akad. der Kunste, Berlin, 1971. Hon. degrees incl. MusD Cantab, 1983. Sibelius Medal (Harriet Cohen Foundation), London, 1961; Premio delle Muse, City of Florence, 1969; Handel Medallion, New York City, 1978; Mayor of Los Angeles declared Elliott Carter Day, 27 April 1979; Ernst Von Siemens Prize, Munich, 1981; Gold Medal, MacDowell Colony, 1983; National Medal of Arts, USA, 1985. *Publication:* The Writings of Elliott Carter, 1977; *relevant publication:* The Music of Elliott Carter, by David Schiff, 1983.

CARTER, Eric Bairstow, BSc(Eng); CEng, FIMechE, FRAeS, FIProdE; Consultant Engineer, 1972–78; *b* 26 Aug. 1912; *s* of John Bolton Carter and Edith Carter (*née* Bairstow); *m* 1st, 1934, Lily (*d* 1981), *d* of John Charles and Ethel May Roome; one *d*; 2nd, 1981, Olive Hicks Wright, *d* of William George and Olive Theresa Groombridge. *Educ:* Halifax Technical Coll. Staff appt, Halifax Tech. Coll., 1932; Supt and Lectr, Constantine Technical Coll., Middlesbrough, 1936; apptd to Air Min. (Engine Directorate), Sept. 1939; subseq. Air Min. appts to engine firms and at HQ. Asst Dir (Research and Develt, Ramjets and Liquid Propellant Rockets), Dec. 1955; Dir (Engine Prod.), 1960; Dir (Engine R&D), 1963; Dir-Gen. (Engine R&D), Min. of Technology, later MoD (Aviation Supply), 1969–72; Special Advr, Noel Penny Turbines Ltd, 1972–77. *Address:* 15 Colyford Road, Seaton, Devon EX12 2DP.

CARTER, Eric Stephen, CBE 1986; Adviser, Farming and Wildlife Advisory Group, since 1981; *b* 23 June 1923; *s* of Albert Harry Carter, MBE and Doris Margaret (*née* Mann); *m* 1948, Audrey Windsor; one *s*. *Educ:* Grammar Sch., Lydney; Reading Univ. BSc (Agric) 1945. Techn. Officer, Gloucester AEC, 1945–46; Asst District Officer, Gloucester NAAS, 1946–49, Dist Off. 1949–57; Sen. Dist Off., Lindsey (Lincs) NAAS, 1957–63, County Agric. Off. 1963–69; Yorks and Lancs Region: Dep. Regional Dir, NAAS, 1969–71; Regional Agric. Off., ADAS, 1971–73; Regional Off. (ADAS), 1973–74; Chief Regional Off., MAFF, 1974–75; Dep. Dir-Gen., Agricl Develt and Advisory Service, 1975–81. FIBiol 1974, CBiol 1984; FRAgS 1985. *Publications:* (with M. H. R. Soper) Modern Farming and the Countryside, 1985; contrib. agric. and techn. jls. *Recreations:* gardening, reading, music, countryside. *Address:* 15 Farrs Lane, East Hyde, Luton, Beds LU2 9PY. *T:* Harpenden 60504. *Club:* Farmers'.

CARTER, Francis Jackson, CMG 1954; CVO 1963; CBE 1946; Under-Secretary of State of Tasmania and Clerk of Executive Council, 1953–64; also permanent head of Premier's and Chief Secretary's Department; *b* Fremantle, W Australia, 9 Sept. 1899; *s* of late Francis Henry Carter, formerly of Bendigo, Victoria; *m* 1926, Margaret Flora, *d* of late William Thomas Walker, Launceston; two *s* one *d*. *Educ:* Hobart High Sch.; Univ. of Tasmania. Entered Tasmanian Public Service, 1916; transferred to Hydro-Electric Dept, 1925; Asst Secretary, Hydro-Electric Commn, 1934; Secretary to Premier, 1935–39; Dep. Under-Secretary of State, 1939–53; served War of 1939–45 as State Liaison Officer to Commonwealth Dept of Home Security; Official Secretary for Tasmania in London, 1949–50; State Director for Royal Visits, 1954, 1958, 1963, and Thai Royal Visit, 1962. Executive Member, State Economic Planning Authority, 1944–55; Chairman, Fire Brigades Commn of Tasmania, 1945–70. Grand Master GL of Tasmania, 1956–59. FASA; FCIS. JP 1939. *Recreations:* music, golf and lawn bowls. *Address:* 568 Churchill Avenue, Sandy Bay, Hobart, Tasmania 7005. *T:* Hobart 252 382. *Clubs:* Royal Automobile of Tasmania, Masonic (Hobart).

CARTER, Frank Ernest Lovell, CBE 1956 (OBE 1949); FSA; Director General of the Overseas Audit Service, 1963–71; *b* 6 Oct. 1909; *s* of Ernest and Florence Carter; *m* 1966, Gerda (*née* Gruen). *Educ:* Chigwell Sch.; Hertford Coll., Oxford. Served in Overseas Audit Service in: Nigeria, 1933–42; Sierra Leone, 1943; Palestine, 1944–45; Aden and Somaliland, 1946–49; Tanganyika, 1950–54; Hong Kong, 1955–59; Deputy Director in London, 1960–62. Part-time Adviser: FCO, 1972–76; ODM, 1977–81. FSA 1983. *Address:* 8 The Leys, N2 0HE. *T:* 01–458 4684. *Club:* East India.

CARTER, Frederick Brian; QC 1980; **His Honour Judge Carter;** a Circuit Judge, since 1985; *b* 11 May 1933; *s* of late Arthur and Minnie Carter; *m* 1960, Elizabeth Hughes, JP, *d* of late W. B. Hughes and of Mrs B. M. Hughes; one *s* three *d* (and one *s* decd). *Educ:* Stretford Grammar Sch.; King's Coll., London (LLB). Called to Bar, Gray's Inn, 1955, practised Northern Circuit, 1957–85; Prosecuting Counsel for Inland Revenue, Northern Circuit, 1973–80; a Recorder, 1978–85. *Recreations:* golf, travel. *Address:* 55 Ogden Road, Bramhall, Stockport, Cheshire SK7 1HL. *T:* 061–439 3637. *Clubs:* Big Four (Manchester and Hong Kong); Chorlton-cum-Hardy Golf.

CARTER, Prof. Geoffrey William, MA; FIEE; FIEEE; Professor of Electrical Engineering, University of Leeds, 1946–74, now Emeritus; *b* 21 May 1909; *s* of late Frederick William Carter, FRS; *m* 1938, Freda Rose Lapwood; one *s* one *d*. *Educ:* Rugby Sch.; St John's Coll., Cambridge. MA 1937. Student Apprentice, British Thomson-Houston Co. Ltd, Rugby, 1932–35, Research Engineer, 1935–45; University Demonstrator in Engineering Science, Oxford, 1946. *Publications:* The Simple Calculation of Electrical Transients, 1944; The Electromagnetic Field in its Engineering Aspects, 1954 (rev. edn 1967); (with A. Richardson) Techniques of Circuit Analysis, 1972; papers in Proc. IEE and elsewhere. *Recreations:* study of medals, winemaking. *Address:* 14 Church Farm Garth, Leeds LS17 8HD. *T:* Leeds 737488.

See also Sir C. F. Carter.

CARTER, His Eminence Cardinal G(erald) Emmett; *see* Toronto, Archbishop of, (RC).

CARTER, Godfrey James, CBE 1984; Parliamentary Counsel, 1972–79; *b* 1 June 1919; *s* of Captain James Shuckburgh Carter, Grenadier Guards (killed in action, 1918), and Diana Violet Gladys Carter (*née* Cavendish); *m* 1946, Cynthia, *e d* of Eric Strickland Mason; three *s*. *Educ:* Eton (KS); Magdalene Coll., Cambridge. BA 1945, LLM 1946. War Service (Rifle Bde), Middle East, 1940–43 (twice wounded). Called to Bar, Inner Temple, 1946; Asst Parly Counsel, 1949–56; commercial dept, Bristol Aeroplane Co. Ltd, and Bristol Siddeley Engines Ltd, 1956–64; re-joined Parly Counsel Office, 1964; Dep. Counsel, 1970. *Address:* Old Bournstream House, Wotton-under-Edge, Glos. *T:* Dursley 843246. *Club:* Travellers'.

CARTER, James Earl, Jr, (Jimmy); President of the United States of America, 1977–81; *b* Archery, Georgia, USA, 1 Oct. 1924; *s* of late James Earl Carter and Lillian (*née* Gordy); *m* 1946, Rosalynn Smith; three *s* one *d*. *Educ:* Plains High Sch.; Georgia Southwestern Coll.; Georgia Inst. of Technology; US Naval Acad. (BS); Union Coll., Schenectady, NY (post grad.). Served in US Navy submarines and battleships, 1946–53; Ensign (commissioned, 1947); Lieut 1950; retd from US Navy, 1953. Became farmer and warehouseman, 1953, farming peanuts at Plains, Georgia, until 1977. Member: Sumter Co. (Ga) School Bd, 1955–62 (Chm. 1960–62); Americus and Sumter Co. Hosp. Authority, 1956–70; Sumter Co. (Ga) Library Bd, 1961; President: Plains Develt Corp., 1963; Georgia Planning Assoc., 1968; Chm., W Central Georgia Area Planning and Develt Commn, 1964; Dir, Georgia Crop Improvement Assoc., 1957–63 (Pres., 1961). State Chm., March of Dimes, 1968–70; Dist Governor, Lions Club, 1968–69. State Senator (Democrat), Georgia, 1963–67; Governor of Georgia, 1971–75. Chm., Congressional Campaign Cttee, Democratic Nat. Cttee, 1974; Democratic Candidate for the Presidency of the USA, 1976. Distinguished Prof., Emory Univ., 1982–. Baptist. Hon. degrees from: Morehouse Coll., and Morris Brown Coll., 1972; Notre Dame, 1977; Georgia Inst. Tech., and Emory Univ., 1979; Weizmann Inst. of Science, 1980; Kwansei Gakuim Univ., Japan, and Georgia Southwestern Coll., 1981; Tel Aviv Univ., 1983. *Publications:* Why Not the Best?, 1975; A Government as Good as its People, 1977; Keeping Faith: memoirs of a President, 1982; The Blood of Abraham, 1985. *Address:* (home) 1 Woodland Drive, Plains, Georgia 31780, USA; (office) 75 Spring Street, SW, Atlanta, Ga 30303, USA.

CARTER, Maj.-Gen. James Norman, CB 1958; CBE 1955 (OBE 1946). *Educ:* Charterhouse; RMC Sandhurst. Commissioned The Dorset Regt, 1926; Captain, The Royal Warwickshire Regt, 1936; Lieut-Colonel, 1948; Colonel, 1950; Brigadier, 1954; Maj.-General, 1957. Asst Chief of Staff, Organisation and Training Div., SHAPE, 1955–57; Commander British Army Staff, British Joint Services Mission, Washington, 1958–60; Military Attaché, Washington, Jan.–July 1960; General Secretary, The Officers' Assoc., 1961–63.

CARTER, Jane; *see* Carter, D. E. F.

CARTER, Sir John, Kt 1966; QC (Guyana) 1962; Guyana Diplomatic Service, retired; *b* 27 Jan. 1919; *s* of Kemp R. Carter; *m* 1959, Sara Lou (formerly Harris); two *s*. *Educ:* University of London and Middle Temple, England. Called to English Bar, 1942; admitted to Guyana (late British Guiana) Bar, 1945; Member of Legislature of Guyana, 1948–53 and 1961–64; Pro-Chancellor, Univ. of Guyana, 1962–66; Ambassador of Guyana to US, 1966–70; High Comr for Guyana in UK, 1970–76; Ambassador to China and Korea, 1976–81 and to Japan, 1979–81; High Comr to Jamaica, 1981–83. *Recreations:* cricket, swimming. *Address:* 3603 East West Highway, Chevy Chase, Maryland 20815, USA. *Clubs:* MCC; Georgetown (Guyana).

CARTER, John Somers; *b* 26 Feb. 1901; *s* of R. Carter. *Educ:* Edinburgh Academy; Bedford Sch.; Balliol Coll., Oxford, 1st Class Hon. Mods., 3rd Class Lit. Hum. Asst Master, Cheltenham Coll., 1924–32; Headmaster: St John's Sch., Leatherhead, 1933–47; Blundell's Sch., 1948–59. *Address:* 58 Falmouth Road, Truro, Cornwall TR1 2HR. *T:* Truro 78711.

CARTER, Dr (John) Timothy, FFOM; Director of Medical Services, Health and Safety Executive, since 1983; *b* 12 Feb. 1944; *s* of Reginald John Carter and Linda Mary (*née* Briggs); *m* 1967, Judith Ann Lintott; one *s* two *d*. *Educ:* Dulwich Coll.; Corpus Christi Coll., Cambridge (MB, MA); University Coll. Hosp., London. London Sch. of Hygiene, 1972–74 (MSc). MO, British Petroleum, 1974–78; SMO, BP Chemicals, 1978–83. Member: MRC, 1983–; Bd of Management, British Occupational Hygiene Soc., 1978–81; Bd, Faculty of Occupnl Medicine, 1982–; Hon. Sec., Occupnl Medicine Section, RSM, 1979–83. *Publications:* articles on investigation and control of occupnl health hazards and med. history. *Recreation:* history—natural, medical and local. *Address:* 41 Clarence Road, St Albans, Herts AL1 4NP.

CARTER, Peers Lee, CMG 1965; HM Diplomatic Service, retired; Director, 1981–84, Member, since 1984, Afghanistan Support Committee; free-lance conference interpreter; *b* 5 Dec. 1916; *s* of Peers Owen Carter; *m* 1940, Joan Eleanor Lovegrove; one *s*. *Educ:* Radley; Christ Church, Oxford. Entered HM Foreign Service, 1939. Joined the Army in 1940; served in Africa and Europe. HM Embassy, Baghdad, 1945; First Secretary, Commissioner-General's Office, Singapore, 1951; Counsellor HM Embassy, Washington, 1958; (Temp. duty) UK Delegation to UN, New York, 1961; Head of UK Permanent Mission, Geneva, 1961; Inspector of Foreign Service Establishments, 1963–66; Chief Inspector of HM Diplomatic Service, 1966–68; Ambassador to Afghanistan, 1968–72; Ministerial Interpreter and Asst Under-Sec. of State, FCO, 1973–76. Mem., Internat. Assoc. of Conference Interpreters. Sardar-e A'ala, Afghanistan, 1971. *Recreations:* mountain walking, skiing, photography. *Address:* Dean Land Shaw, by Jobes, Balcombe, Sussex RH17 6HZ. *T:* Balcombe 811205. *Clubs:* Special Forces, Travellers'.

CARTER, Philip David, CBE 1982; Managing Director, Littlewoods Organisation, 1976–83; Chairman: Everton Football Club, since 1978; Merseyside Tourism Board, since 1986; *b* 8 May 1927; *s* of Percival Carter and Isobell (*née* Stirrup); *m* 1946, Harriet Rita (*née* Evans); one *s* two *d*. *Educ:* Waterloo Grammar Sch., Liverpool. Professional career in Littlewoods Organisation. Chm., Mail Order Traders Assoc. of GB, 1979–83; Pres., European Mail Order Traders Assoc., 1983; Chm., Man Made Fibres Sector Wkg Party, 1980–; Member: Jt Textile Cttee, NEDO, 1979–; Distributive Trades EDC, 1980–; Merseyside Develt Corp., 1981–. Vice-Chm., 1980–86, Chm., 1986–, Empire Theatre Trust, Liverpool. Chm., Liverpool Conservative Assoc., 1985–. Pres., Football League, 1986–. *Recreations:* football, squash, music, theatre. *Address:* Oak Cottage, Noctorum Road, Noctorum, Wirral, Merseyside L43 9UQ. *T:* 051–652 4053.

CARTER, Raymond John; Executive, Marathon Oil Co., since 1980; *b* 17 Sept. 1935; *s* of John Carter; *m* 1959, Jeanette Hills; one *s* two *d*. *Educ:* Mortlake Co. Secondary Sch.; Reading Technical Coll.; Staffordshire Coll. of Technology. National Service, Army, 1953–55. Sperry Gyroscope Co.: Technical Asst, Research and Development Computer Studies, 1956–65. Electrical Engineer, Central Electricity Generating Bd, 1965–70, Mem., CEGB Management, 1979–80. Mem., Gen. Adv. Council, BBC, 1974–76. Mem. Easthampstead RDC, 1963–68. Contested: Wokingham, Gen. Elec., 1966; Warwick and Leamington, By-elec., March 1968; MP (Lab) Birmingham, Northfield, 1970–79; Parly Under-Sec. of State, Northern Ireland Office, 1976–79. Member: Public Accounts Cttee, 1973–74; Parly Science and Technology Cttee, 1974–76; author of Congenital Disabilities (Civil Liability) Act, 1976. Delegate: Council of Europe, 1974–76; WEU, 1974–76. Trustee, BM (Nat. Hist.), 1986–. Co-cataloguer and exhibitor, works of Sir John Betjeman, 1983. *Recreations:* running, reading, book collecting. *Address:* 1 Lynwood Chase, Warfield Road, Bracknell, Berkshire. *T:* Bracknell 420237.

CARTER, Air Commodore Robert Alfred Copsey, CB 1956; DSO 1942; DFC 1943; Royal Air Force, retired; *b* 15 Sept. 1910; *s* of S. H. Carter and S. Copsey; *m* 1947, Sally Ann Peters, Va, USA; two *s* one *d*. *Educ:* Portsmouth Grammar Sch.; RAF Coll., Cranwell. Cranwell Cadet, 1930–32; commissioned in RAF, 1932; served in India, 1933–36; grad. RAF School of Aeronautical Engineering, 1938; served in Bomber Command, 1940–45; commanded 103 and 150 Sqdns, RAF, Grimsby; grad. RAF Staff Coll., 1945; attended US Armed Forces Staff Coll., Norfolk, Va, USA, 1947; attached to RNZAF, 1950–53; comd. RAF Station, Upwood, 1953–55; SASO, RAF Transport Command, 1956–58; Director of Personal Services, Air Ministry, 1958–61; AO i/c

Admin, HQ, RAF Germany, 1961–64; retired 1964. MRAeS 1960; CEng, 1966. *Club:* Royal Air Force.

CARTER, Robert William Bernard, CMG 1964; HM Diplomatic Service, retired; *b* 1913; 3rd *s* of late William Joseph Carter and late Lucy (*née* How); *m* 1945, Joan Violet, *o d* of Theodore and Violet Magnus; one *s* two *d* (and one *d* decd). *Educ:* St Bees Sch., Cumberland; Trinity Coll., Oxford (Scholar). Asst Master, Glenalmond, Perthshire, 1936. Served with the Royal Navy, 1940–46; Lieut, RNVR. Administrative Assistant, Newcastle upon Tyne Education Cttee, 1946; Principal, Board of Trade, 1949; Trade Commissioner: Calcutta, 1952; Delhi, 1955; Accra, 1956; Principal Trade Commissioner, Colombo (Assistant Secretary), 1959; Senior British Trade Commissioner in Pakistan, 1961; Minister (Commercial), Pakistan, and Dep. High Comr, Karachi, 1967–68; Dep. High Comr, 1969–73 and Consul-Gen., 1973, Melbourne. *Recreations:* reading, travelling, collecting beer-mugs. *Address:* The Old Parsonage, Heywood, Westbury, Wilts. *T:* Westbury 822194. *Club:* Oriental.

CARTER, Roland; Regional Organiser, North East England, National Society for Cancer Relief, since 1980; *b* 29 Aug. 1924; *s* of Ralph Carter; *m* 1950, Elisabeth Mary Green; one *s* two *d*. *Educ:* Cockburn High Sch., Leeds; Leeds Univ. Served War of 1939–45: Queen's Royal Regt, 1944; 6th Gurkha Rifles, 1945; Frontier Corps (South Waziristan and Gilgit Scouts), 1946. Seconded to Indian Political Service, as Asst Political Agent, Chilas, Gilgit Agency, 1946–47; Lectr, Zurich Univ. and Finnish Sch. of Economics, 1950–53. Joined Foreign Service, 1953: FO, 1953–54; Third Sec., Moscow, 1955; Germany, 1956–58; Second Sec., Helsinki, 1959 (First Sec., 1962); FO, 1962–67; Kuala Lumpur, 1967–69; Ambassador to People's Republic of Mongolia, 1969–71; seconded to Cabinet Office, 1971–74; Counsellor: Pretoria, 1974–77; FCO, 1977–80, retired. *Publication:* Näin Puhutaan Englantia (in Finnish; with Erik Erämetsä), 1952. *Recreations:* music, linguistics, Indian studies. *Address:* Barclays Bank, Malton, N Yorks.

CARTER, (Ronald) David, CBE 1980; RDI 1975; Chairman, DCA Design Consultants Ltd; *b* 30 Dec. 1927; *s* of H. Miles Carter and Margaret Carter; *m* 1953, Theo (Marjorie Elizabeth), *d* of Rev. L. T. Towers; two *s* two *d*. *Educ:* Wyggeston Sch., Leicester; Central Sch. of Art and Design, London. Served RN, 1946–48. Appts in industry, 1951–60; Principal, David Carter Associates, 1960–75. Visiting Lectr, Birmingham Coll. of Industrial Design, 1960–65. Examnr, RCA, 1976–79. Mem., Design Council, 1972–84 (Dep. Chm., 1975–84; Chm., Report on Industrial Design Educn in UK, 1977). Pres., Soc. of Industrial Artists and Designers, 1974–75; Mem., Art and Design Cttee, CNAA, 1975–77; Chm., DATEC, 1977–82; Mem., Nat. Adv. Body, Higher Educn Art and Design Working Party, 1982–84; Royal Fine Arts Comr, 1986–. Trustee, Boilerhouse Conran Foundn, 1981–; Moderator, Hong Kong Polytechnic, 1981–; Mem., Prince of Wales Award for Indust. Innovation, 1981–85. Design Awards, 1961, 1969, 1983; Duke of Edinburgh Prize for Elegant Design, 1967. FSIA 1967; FRSA 1975. *Recreations:* making coarse soup, galloping, County Cork. *Address:* 43 Beauchamp Avenue, Leamington Spa, Warwickshire. *T:* Leamington Spa 24864. *Club:* Reform.

CARTER, Ronald Louis, DesRCA; RDI 1971; FSIAD 1961; private consultancy design practice, since 1974; *b* 3 June 1926; *s* of Harry Victor Carter and Ruth Allensen; *m* (marr. diss.); three *d*; *m* 1985, Ann McNab; two step *s* one step *d*. *Educ:* Birmingham Central College of Art: studied Industrial and Interior Design (NDD; Louisa Anne Ryland Schol. for Silver Design), 1946–49; Royal College of Art: studied Furniture Design (1st Cl. Dip.; Silver Medal for work of special distinction; Travelling Schol. to USA), 1949–52; DesRCA; Fellow, RCA, 1966; Hon. Fellow, 1974. Staff Designer with Corning Glass, 5th Avenue, NY City, 1952–53; freelance design practice, Birmingham and London, 1954; Tutor, School of Furniture, RCA, 1956–74; Partner: Design Partners, 1960–68; Carter Freeman Associates, 1968–74. *Recreation:* fishing. *Address:* 35 Great Queen Street, WC2B 5AA. *T:* 01–242 2291.

CARTER, Timothy; *see* Carter, J. T.

CARTER, Air Vice-Marshal Wilfred, CB 1963; DFC 1943; international disaster consultant; *b* 5 Nov. 1912; *s* of late Samuel Carter; *m* 1950, Margaret Enid Bray; one *d* (one *s* decd). Educ: Witney Grammar Sch. RAF, 1929. Served War of 1939–45 with Bomber Command in UK and Middle East. Graduate, Middle East Centre for Arab Studies, 1945–46. Air Adviser to Lebanon, 1950–53; with Cabinet Secretariat, 1954–55; OC, RAF, Ternhill, 1956–58; Sen. RAF Dir, and later Commandant, Jt Services Staff Coll.; Asst Chief of Staff, Cento, 1960–63; Asst Commandant, RAF Staff Coll., 1963–65; AOA, HQ Bomber Command, 1965–67; Dir, Austr. Counter Disaster Coll., 1969–78. Gordon Shephard Memorial Prize (for Strategic Studies), 1955, 1956, 1957, 1961, 1965, 1967. Officer, Order of Cedar of Lebanon, 1953. *Publication:* Disaster Preparedness and Response, 1985. *Recreations:* walking, swimming. *Address:* Blue Range, Macedon, Vic 3440, Australia.

CARTER, William Nicholas, (Will Carter), OBE 1984; Senior Partner, Rampant Lions Press, since 1967; *b* 24 Sept. 1912; *s* of Thomas Buchanan Carter and Margaret Theresa Stone; *m* 1939, Barbara Ruth Digby; one *s* three *d*. *Educ:* Sunningdale Sch.; Radley. Served War, RN, 1941–46: S Atlantic, Coastal Forces Eastern Med.; commnd 1943. Gen. career in printing, advertising, typography and inscriptional letter-carving; founded Rampant Lions Press, 1949. Artist-in-Residence, Dartmouth Coll., NH, USA, 1969. Member: Royal Mint Adv. Cttee, 1971–; Arch. Adv. Panel, Westminster Abbey, 1979–. Hon. Fellow, Magdalene Coll., Cambridge, 1977. Frederick W. Goudy Award, Rochester Inst. of Technol., New York State, 1975; Silver Jubilee Medal, 1977. *Publication:* (with Wilfrid Blunt) Italic Handwriting, 1954. *Address:* 12 Chesterton Road, Cambridge. *T:* Cambridge 357553. *Club:* Double Crown (Pres., 1961).

CARTER, Sir William (Oscar), Kt 1972; Consultant, Hill and Perks, Solicitors, Norwich; *b* 12 Jan. 1905; *s* of late Oscar Carter and Alice Carter; *m* 1934, Winifred Thompson. *Educ:* Swaffham Grammar Sch.; City of Norwich Sch. Admitted Solicitor of Supreme Court of Judicature, 1931. Served War, 1940–45, RAF (Wing Comdr), UK and Middle East. Mem. Council, The Law Society, 1954–75, Vice-Pres. 1970, Pres. 1971–72; President: East Anglian Law Soc., 1952–80; Norfolk and Norwich Incorporated Law Soc., 1959; Internat. Legal Aid Assoc., 1974–80; Life Mem. Council, Internat. Bar Assoc. (first Vice-Pres., 1976–78). Member: County Court Rules Cttee, 1956–60; Supreme Court Rules Cttee, 1960–75; Criminal Injuries Compensation Board, 1967–82 (Dep. Chm., 1977–82). Former Chm., Mental Health Review Tribunals for E Anglian and NE Thames RHA Areas. Upper Warden, 1984, Master, 1985–86, Worshipful Co. of Glaziers; Hon. Mem., The Fellows of American Bar Foundn. *Recreations:* swimming, walking, foreign travel. *Address:* 83 Newmarket Road, Norwich NR2 2HP. *T:* Norwich 53772. *Clubs:* Army and Navy; Norfolk (Norwich).

CARTER-JONES, Lewis; MP (Lab) Eccles since 1964; *b* Gilfach Goch, S Wales, 17 Nov. 1920; *s* of Tom Jones, Kenfig Hill, Bridgend, Glam.; *m* 1945, Patricia Hylda, *d* of late Alfred Bastiman, Scarborough, Yorks; two *d*. *Educ:* Bridgend County Sch.; University Coll. of Wales, Aberystwyth (BA; Chm. Student Finance Cttee; Capt, Coll., Univ. and County Hockey XI). Served War of 1939–45 (Flight Sergeant Navigator, RAF). Head of Business Studies Dept, Yale Grammar-Technical Sch., Wrexham, Denbighshire. Contested (Lab) Chester, by-election, 1956, and general election, 1959. Chairman: Anglo-Columbian Gp; Cttee for Research for Apparatus for Disabled; Parly Labour Party Disablement Gp; Possum Research Foundation; Vice-Chairman: Disabled Income Gp (DIG); All-Party Aviation Gp; Chm., PLP Aviation Gp; Secretary: Indo-British Parly Gp; All-Party BLESMA Gp. Special interest, application of technology for aged and disabled; Mem., Brit. Assoc. for the Retarded; Chm., British Cttee, Rehabilitation International; Exec. Mem., Action Research for the Crippled Child; Vice-Pres., Wales Council for the Disabled. Hon. Parly Adviser to RNIB; Hon. Adviser: British Assoc. of Occupational Therapists; Soc. of Physiotherapists. *Address:* House of Commons, SW1; Cader Idris, 5 Cefn Road, Rhosnessni, Wrexham, Clwyd.

CARTER-RUCK, Peter Frederick; Senior Partner, Peter Carter-Ruck and Partners, Solicitors, since 1981 (Senior Partner, Oswald Hickson, Collier & Co., 1945–81); *b* 26 Feb. 1914; *s* of Frederick Henry Carter-Ruck and Nell Mabel Carter-Ruck; *m* 1940, Pamela Ann, *o d* of late Gp Capt. Reginald Stuart Maxwell, MC, DFC, AFC, RAF; one *d* (one *s* decd). *Educ:* St Edward's, Oxford; Law Society; Solicitor of the Supreme Court (Hons). Admitted Solicitor, 1937; served RA, 1939–44, Captain Instr in gunnery. Specialist Member, Council of Law Soc., 1971–84; Chm. Law Soc. Law Reform Cttee, 1980–83; past Pres., City of Westminster Law Soc.; Chm., Media Cttee, Internat. Bar Assoc., 1983–85; Pres., Media Soc. Governor, St Edward's Sch., Oxford, 1950–78; past Chm. and Founder Governor, Shiplake Coll., Henley; Mem. Livery, City of London Solicitors' Co., 1949–; Underwriting Mem. of Lloyd's. *Publications:* Libel and Slander, 1953, 3rd edn 1985; (with Ian Mackrill) The Cyclist and the Law, 1953; (with Edmund Skone James) Copyright: modern law and practice, 1965. *Address:* Essex House, Essex Street, WC2R 3AH. *T:* 01–379 3456; Latchmore Cottage, Great Hallingbury, Bishop's Stortford, Herts. *T:* Bishop's Stortford 54357; Eilagadale, N Ardnamurchan, Argyll. *T:* Kilchoan 267. *Clubs:* Carlton, Garrick, Press; Royal Yacht Squadron, Lloyd's Yacht, Law Society Yacht (past Commodore), Royal Ocean Racing, Ocean Cruising (past Commodore).

CARTIER, Rudolph; Drama Producer, Television, since 1953; also Producer Television Operas, since 1956; *b* Vienna, Austria, 17 April 1908; *s* of Joseph Cartier; *m* 1949, Margaret Pepper; two *d*. *Educ:* Vienna Academy of Music and Dramatic Art (Max Reinhardt's Master-class). Film director and Scenario writer in pre-war Berlin; came to Britain, 1935; joined BBC Television. Productions include: Arrow to the Heart, Dybbuk, Portrait of Peter Perowne, 1952; It is Midnight, Doctor Schweitzer, L'Aiglon, The Quatermass Experiment, Wuthering Heights, 1953; Such Men are Dangerous, That Lady, Captain Banner, Nineteen-Eightyfour, 1954; Moment of Truth, The Creature, Vale of Shadows, Quatermass II, The Devil's General, 1955; The White Falcon, The Mayerling Affair, The Public Prosecutor, The Fugitive, The Cold Light, The Saint of Bleecker Street, Dark Victory, Clive of India, The Queen and the Rebels, 1956; Salome, Ordeal by Fire, Counsellor-at-Law, 1957; Captain of Koepenick, The Winslow Boy, A Tale of Two Cities, Midsummer Night's Dream, 1958; Quatermass and the Pit, Philadelphia Story, Mother Courage and her Children, (Verdi's) Othello, 1959; The White Guard, Glorious Morning, Tobias and the Angel (Opera), 1960; Rashomon, Adventure Story, Anna Karenina, Cross of Iron, 1961; Doctor Korczuk and the Children, Sword of Vengeance, Carmen, 1962; Anna Christie, Night Express, Stalingrad, 1963; Lady of the Camelias, The Midnight Men, The July Plot, 1964; Wings of the Dove, Ironhand, The Joel Brand Story, 1965; Gordon of Khartoum, Lee Oswald, Assassin, 1966; Firebrand, The Burning Bush, 1967; The Fanatics, Triumph of Death, The Naked Sun, The Rebel, 1968; Conversation at Night, An Ideal Husband, 1969; Rembrandt, The Bear (Opera), The Year of the Crow, 1970; The Proposal, 1971; Lady Windermere's Fan, 1972; The Deep Blue Sea, 1973; Fall of Eagles (episodes Dress Rehearsal, End Game), 1974; Loyalties, 1976; Gaslight, 1977. Prod. Film, Corridor of Mirrors. Directed Film, Passionate Summer. Guild of Television Producers and Directors "Oscar" as best drama producer of 1957. *Recreations:* motoring, serious music, going to films or watching television, stamp-collecting. *Address:* 26 Lowther Road, Barnes, SW13.

CARTIER-BRESSON, Henri; photographer; *b* France, 22 Aug. 1908. Studied painting with André Lhote, 1927–28. Asst Dir to Jean Renoir, 1936–39; Co-founder, Magnum Photos, 1947. Photographs exhibited: Mexico; Japan; Mus. of Modern Art, NY, 1947, 1968; Villa Medicis, Rome; Louvre, 1955, 1967, Grand Palais, 1970, Paris; V&A, 1969; Manege, Moscow, 1972; Edinburgh Festival, 1978; Hayward Gall., London, 1978; drawings exhibited: Carlton Gall., NY, 1975; Bischofberger Gall., Zürich, 1976; Forcalquier Gall., France, 1976; Mus. of Modern Art, Paris, 1981; Mus. of Modern Art, Mexico, 1982; French Inst., Stockholm, 1983; Pavilion of Contemporary Art, Milan, 1983; Mus. of Modern Art, Oxford, 1984; Palace Liechtenstein, Vienna, Salzburg, 1985. Collection of 390 photographs at DeMenil Foundn, Houston, USA, V&A, Univ. of Fine Arts, Osaka, Japan, Bibliothèque Nationale, Paris. Documentary films: on hosps, Spanish Republic, 1937; (with J. Lemare) Le Retour, 1945; (with J. Boffety) Impressions of California, 1969; (with W. Dombrow) Southern Exposures, 1970. Mem., Amer. Acad. of Arts and Scis, 1974. Hon. DLitt Oxon, 1975. Awards: US Camera, 1948; Overseas Press Club of America, 1949; Amer. Soc. of Magazine Photography, 1953; Photography Soc. of America, 1958; Overseas Press Club, 1954 (for Russia), 1960 (for China), 1964 (for Cuba); German Photographic Soc.; Hasselblad Award, 1983. *Publications:* (ed) Images à la Sauvette (The Decisive Moment), 1952; Verve, 1952; The Europeans; Moscow, 1955; From One China to the Other, 1956; Photographs by Cartier-Bresson; Flagrants Délits (The World of Henri Cartier-Bresson, 1968); (with F. Nourrissier) Vive la France, 1970; Cartier-Bresson's France, 1971; (jtly) L'Homme et la Machine, 1972 (Man and Machine, 1969) for IBM; Faces of Asia, 1972; A Propos de l'URSS, 1973 (About Russia, 1974); Henri Cartier-Bresson Pocket Book, 1985; *relevant publications:* Yves Bonnefoy, Henri Cartier-Bresson, Photographer, 1979; André P. de Mandiargues, Photoportrait, 1985. *Address:* c/o Magnum Photos, 20 rue des Grands Augustins, 75006 Paris, France; c/o Helen Wright, 135 East 74th Street, New York, NY 10021, USA; c/o John Hillelson, 145 Fleet Street, EC4A 2BU.

CARTLAND, Barbara (Hamilton); authoress and playwright; *d* of late Major Bertram Cartland, Worcestershire Regiment; *m* 1st, 1927, Alexander George McCorquodale (whom she divorced, 1933; he *d* 1964), of Cound Hall, Cressage, Salop; one *d*; 2nd, 1936, Hugh (*d* 1963), 2nd *s* of late Harold McCorquodale, Forest Hall, Ongar, Essex; two *s*. Published first novel at the age of twenty-one, which ran into five editions; designed and organised many pageants in aid of charity, including Britain and her Industries at British Legion Ball, Albert Hall, 1930; carried the first aeroplane-towed glider-mail in her glider, the Barbara Cartland, from Manston Aerodrome to Reading, June 1931; 2 lecture tours in Canada, 1940; Hon. Junior Commander, ATS and Lady Welfare Officer and Librarian to all Services in Bedfordshire, 1941–49; Certificate of Merit, Eastern Command, 1946; County Cadet Officer for St John Ambulance Brigade in Beds, 1943–47, County Vice-Pres. Cadets, Beds, 1948–50; organised and produced the St John Ambulance Bde Exhibn, 1945–50; Chm., St John Ambulance Bde Exhibn Cttee, 1944–51; County Vice-Pres.: Nursing Cadets, Herts, 1951; Nursing Div., Herts, 1966; CC Herts (Hatfield Div.), 1955–64; Chm., St John Council, Herts, 1972–; Dep. Pres., St John Amb. Bde, Herts,

1978–; Pres., Herts Br. of Royal Coll. of Midwives, 1957–. Founder, Barbara Cartland-Onslow Romany Gypsy Fund (with Earl of Onslow and Earl of Birkenhead) to provide sites for Romany Gypsies, 1961 (first Romany Gypsy Camp at Hatfield); Dep. Pres., National Association of Health, 1965; Pres., 1966–. DStJ 1972 (Mem. Chapter Gen.). FRSA. Bestselling author in the world (Guinness Book of Records). *Publications: novels:* Jigsaw, 1923; Sawdust; If the Tree is Saved; For What?; Sweet Punishment; A Virgin in Mayfair; Just off Piccadilly; Not Love Alone; A Beggar Wished; Passionate Attainment; First Class, Lady?; Dangerous Experiment; Desperate Defiance; The Forgotten City; Saga at Forty; But Never Free; Bitter Winds; Broken Barriers; The Gods Forget; The Black Panther; Stolen Halo; Now Rough-Now Smooth; Open Wings; The Leaping Flame; Yet She Follows; Escape from Passion; The Dark Stream; After the Night; Armour against Love; Out of Reach; The Hidden Heart; Against the Stream; Again this Rapture; The Dream Within; If We Will; No Heart is Free; Sleeping Swords; Love is Mine; The Passionate Pilgrim; Blue Heather; Wings on My Heart; The Kiss of Paris; Love Forbidden; Lights of Love; The Thief of Love; The Sweet Enchantress; The Kiss of Silk; The Price is Love; The Runaway Heart; A Light to the Heart; Love is Dangerous; Danger by the Nile; Love on the Run; A Hazard of Hearts; A Duel of Hearts; A Knave of Hearts; The Enchanted Moment; The Little Pretender; A Ghost in Monte Carlo; Love is an Eagle; Love is the Enemy; Cupid Rides Pillion; Love Me For Ever; Elizabethan Lover; Desire of the Heart; The Enchanted Waltz; The Kiss of the Devil; The Captive Heart; The Coin of Love; Stars in My Heart; Sweet Adventure; The Golden Gondola; Love in Hiding; The Smuggled Heart; Love under Fire; The Messenger of Love; The Wings of Love; The Hidden Evil; The Fire of Love; The Unpredictable Bride; Love Holds the Cards; A Virgin in Paris; Love to the Rescue; Love is Contraband; The Enchanting Evil; The Unknown Heart; The Secret Fear; The Reluctant Bride; The Pretty Horse-Breakers; The Audacious Adventures; Halo for the Devil; The Irresistible Buck; Lost Enchantment; The Odious Duke; The Wicked Marquis; The Complacent Wife; The Little Adventure; The Daring Deception; No Darkness for Love; Lessons in Love; The Ruthless Rake; Journey to Paradise; The Dangerous Dandy; The Bored Bridegroom; The Penniless Peer; The Cruel Count; The Castle of Fear; The Glittering Lights; Fire on the Snow; The Elusive Earl; Moon over Eden; The Golden Illusion; No Time for Love; The Husband Hunters; The Slaves of Love; Passions in the Sand; An Angel in Hell; The Wild Cry of Love; The Blue-Eyed Witch; The Incredible Honeymoon; A Dream from the Night; Conquered by Love; Never Laugh at Love; The Secret of the Glen; The Dream and the Glory; The Proud Princess; Hungry for Love; The Heart Triumphant; The Disgraceful Duke; The Taming of Lady Lorinda; Vote for Love; The Mysterious Maid-Servant; The Magic of Love; Kiss the Moonlight; Love Locked In; The Marquis who Hated Women; Rhapsody of Love; Look Listen and Love; Duel with Destiny; The Wild Unwilling Wife; Punishment of a Vixen; The Curse of the Clan; The Outrageous Lady; A Touch of Love; The Love Pirate; The Dragon and the Pearl; The Temptation of Torilla; The Passion and the Flower; Love, Lords and Ladybirds; Love and the Loathsome Leopard; The Naked Battle; The Hell-Cat and the King; No Escape From Love; A Sign of Love; The Castle Made for Love; The Saint and the Sinner; A Fugitive from Love; Love Leaves at Midnight; The Problems of Love; The Twists and Turns of Love; Magic or Mirage; The Ghost who Fell in Love; The Chieftain without a Heart; Lord Ravenscar's Revenge; A Runaway Star; A Princess in Distress; The Judgement of Love; Lovers in Paradise; The Race for Love; Flowers for the God of Love; The Irresistible Force; The Duke and the Preacher's Daughter; The Drums of Love; Alone in Paris; The Prince and the Pekinese; A Serpent of Satan, 1978; Love in the Clouds, 1978; The Treasure is Love, 1978; Imperial Splendour, 1978; Light of the Moon, 1978; The Prisoner of Love, 1978; Love in the Dark, 1978; The Duchess Disappeared, 1978; Love Climbs In, 1978; A Nightingale Sang, 1978; Terror in the Sun, 1978; Who can Deny Love, 1978; Bride to the King, 1978; Only Love, 1979; The Dawn of Love, 1979; Love Has His Way, 1979; The Explosion of Love, 1979; Women Have Hearts, 1979; A Gentleman in Love, 1979; A Heart is Stolen, 1979; The Power and the Prince, 1979; Free From Fear, 1979; A Song of Love, 1979; Love for Sale, 1979; Little White Doves of Love, 1979; The Perfection of Love, 1979; Lost Laughter, 1979; Punished with Love, 1979; Lucifer and the Angel, 1979; Ola and the Sea Wolf, 1979; The Prude and the Prodigal, 1979; The Goddess and the Gaiety Girl, 1979; Signpost to Love, 1979; Money, Magic and Marriage, 1979; From Hell to Heaven, 1980; Pride and The Poor Princess, 1980; The Lioness and The Lily, 1980; A Kiss of Life, 1980; Love At The Helm, 1980; The Waltz of Hearts, 1980; Afraid, 1980; The Horizons of Love, 1980; Love in the Moon, 1980; Dollars for the Duke, 1981; Dreams Do Come True, 1981; Night of Gaiety, 1981; Count the Stars, 1981; Winged Magic, 1981; River of Love, 1981; Gift of the Gods, 1981; The Heart of the Clan, 1981; An Innocent in Russia, 1981; A Shaft of Sunlight, 1981; Love Wins, 1981; Enchanted, 1981; Wings of Ecstasy, 1981; Pure and Untouched, 1981; In the Arms of Love, 1981; Touch a Star, 1981; For All Eternity, 1981; Secret Harbour, 1981; Looking for Love, 1981; The Vibration of Love, 1981; Lies for Love, 1981; Love Rules, 1981; Moments of Love, 1981; Lucky in Love, 1981; Poor Governess, 1981; Music from the Heart, 1981; Caught by Love, 1981; A King in Love, 1981; Winged Victory, 1981; The Call of the Highlands, 1981; Love and the Marquis, 1981; Kneel for Mercy, 1981; Riding to the Moon, 1981; Wish for Love, 1981; Mission to Monte Carlo, 1981; A Miracle in Music, 1981; From Hate to Love, 1982; Light of the Gods, 1982; Love on the Wind, 1982; The Duke Comes Home, 1982; Journey to a Star, 1983; Love and Lucia, 1983; The Unwanted Wedding, 1983; Gypsy Magic, 1983; Help from the Heart, 1983; A Duke in Danger, 1983; Tempted to Love, 1983; Lights, Laughter and a Lady, 1983; The Unbreakable Spell, 1983; Diona and a Dalmatian, 1983; Fire in the Blood, 1983; The Scots Never Forget, 1983; A Rebel Princess, 1983; A Witch's Spell, 1983; Secrets, 1983; The Storms of Love, 1983; Moonlight on the Sphinx, 1983; White Lilac, 1983; Revenge of the Heart, 1983; Bride of a Brigand, 1983; Love Comes West, 1983; Theresa and a Tiger, 1983; An Island of Love, 1983; Love is Heaven, 1983; Miracle for a Madonna, 1984; A Very Unusual Wife, 1984; The Peril and the Prince, 1984; Alone and Afraid, 1984; Terror for a Teacher, 1984; Royal Punishment, 1984; The Devilish Deception, 1984; Paradise Found, 1984; Love is a Gamble, 1984; A Victory for Love, 1984; Look with Love, 1984; Never Forget Love, 1984; Helga in Hiding, 1984; Safe at Last, 1984; Haunted, 1984; Crowned with Love, 1984; Escape, 1984; The Devil Defeated, 1985; The Secret of the Mosque, 1985; A Dream in Spain, 1985; The Love Trap, 1985; Listen to Love, 1985; The Golden Cage, 1985; Love Casts Out Fear, 1985; A World of Love, 1985; Dancing on a Rainbow, 1985; Love Joins the Clans, 1985; An Angel Runs Away, 1985; Forced into Marriage, 1985; Bewildered in Berlin, 1985; Wanted—a Wedding Ring, 1985; Starlight, 1985; The Earl Escapes, 1985; True Love, 1985; Love and Kisses, 1985; Sapphires in Siam, 1985; A Caretaker of Love, 1985; Secrets of the Heart, 1985; *philosophy:* Touch the Stars; *sociology:* You in the Home; The Fascinating Forties; Marriage for Moderns; Be Vivid, Be Vital; Love, Life and Sex; Look Lovely, Be Lovely; Vitamins for Vitality; Husbands and Wives; Etiquette; The Many Facets of Love; Sex and the Teenager; Charm; Living Together; Woman the Enigma; The Youth Secret; The Magic of Honey; Health Food Cookery Book; Book of Beauty and Health; Men are Wonderful; The Magic of Honey Cookbook; Food for Love; Recipes for Lovers; The Romance of Food; Getting Older, Growing Younger; The Etiquette of Romance, 1985; *biography:* Ronald Cartland, 1942; Bewitching Women; The Outrageous Queen; Polly, My Wonderful Mother, 1956; The Scandalous Life of King Carol; The Private Life of Charles II; The Private Life of

Elizabeth, Empress of Austria; Josephine, Empress of France; Diane de Poitiers; Metternich; The Passionate Diplomat; *autobiography:* The Isthmus Years, 1943; The Years of Opportunity, 1947; I Search for Rainbows, 1967; We Danced All Night, 1919–1929, 1971; I Seek the Miraculous, 1978; *general:* Useless Information (foreword by Earl Mountbatten of Burma); Light of Love (prayers), 1978; Love and Lovers (pictures), 1978; Barbara Cartland's Book of Celebrities, 1982; Barbara Cartland's Scrapbook, 1980; Romantic Royal Marriages, 1981; Written with Love, 1981; *verse:* Lines on Love and Life; *plays:* Blood Money, French Dressing (with Bruce Woodhouse); *revue:* The Mayfair Revue; *radio play:* The Caged Bird; *television:* Portrait of Successful Woman, 1957; This is Your Life, 1958; Success Story, 1959; Midland Profile, 1961; No Looking Back-a Portrait of Barbara Cartland, 1967; The Frost Programme, 1968; *radio:* The World of Barbara Cartland, 1970, and many other radio and television appearances. Editor of the Common Problem, by Ronald Cartland, 1943. *Address:* Camfield Place, Hatfield, Herts. *T:* Potters Bar 42612, 42657.
See also Countess Spencer.

CARTLAND, Sir George (Barrington), Kt 1963; CMG 1956; BA; Vice-Chancellor of the University of Tasmania, 1968–77; Chairman, Australian National Accreditation Authority for Translators and Interpreters, 1977–83; *b* 22 Sept. 1912; *s* of William Arthur and Margaret Cartland, West Didsbury; *m* 1937, Dorothy Rayton; two *s. Educ:* Manchester Central High Sch.; Manchester Univ.; Hertford Coll., Oxford. Entered Colonial Service, Gold Coast, 1935; served Colonial Office, 1944–49; Head of African Studies Br. and Ed. Jl of Afr. Adminis., 1945–49; Sec. London Afr. Conf., 1948; Admin. Sec., Uganda, 1949; Sec. for Social Services and Local Govt, Uganda, 1952; Min. for Social Services, Uganda, 1955; Min. of Education and Labour, Uganda, 1958; Chief Sec., Uganda, 1960; Deputy Gov. of Uganda, 1961–62 (Acting Gov., various occasions, 1952–62); Registrar of Univ. of Birmingham, 1963–67. Part-time Mem., West Midlands Gas Bd, 1964–67. Member: Exec. Cttee, Inter Univ. Council for Higher Educn Overseas (UK), 1963–67; Commonwealth Scholarship Commn (UK), 1964–67. Dep. Chm., Australian Vice-Chancellors' Cttee, 1975 and 1977. Chairman: Adv. Cttee on National Park in SW Tasmania, 1976–78; Tasmanian Council of Australian Trade Union Trng Authority, 1979. Appointed to review: Library and Archives Legislation of Tasmania, 1978; Tasmanian Govt Admin., 1979. Mem., Australian Nat. Cttee of Hoover Awards for Marketing, 1968–82. Chm., St John Council, Uganda, 1958–59; Pres., St John Council, Tasmania, 1969–78. Member Council: Makerere Coll., 1952–60; Royal Tech. Coll., Nairobi, 1952–60; UC of Rhodesia, 1963–67; Univ. of S Pacific, 1972–76. FACE 1970. Hon. LLD Univ. of Tasmania, 1978. KStJ 1972; awarded Belgian Congo medal, 1960. *Publication:* (jtly) The Irish Cartlands and Cartland Genealogy, 1978. *Recreations:* mountaineering, fishing. *Address:* 5 Aotea Road, Sandy Bay, Hobart, Tasmania 7005. *Clubs:* Athenæum; Tasmanian, Royal Tasmanian Yacht (Hobart).

CARTLEDGE, Sir Bryan (George), KCMG 1985 (CMG 1980); HM Diplomatic Service; Ambassador to the Soviet Union, since 1985; *b* 10 June 1931; *s* of Eric Montague George Cartledge and Phyllis (*née* Shaw); *m* 1960, Ruth Hylton Gass, *d* of John Gass; one *s* one *d. Educ:* Hurstpierpoint; St John's Coll., Cambridge (Hon. Fellow, 1985). Queen's Royal Regt, 1950–51. Commonwealth Fund Fellow, Stanford Univ., 1956–57; Research Fellow, St Antony's Coll., Oxford, 1958–59. Entered HM Foreign (subseq. Diplomatic) Service, 1960; served in FO, 1960–61; Stockholm, 1961–63; Moscow, 1963–66; DSAO, 1966–68; Tehran, 1968–70; Harvard Univ., 1971–72; Counsellor, Moscow, 1972–75; Head of E European and Soviet Dept, FCO, 1975–77; Private Sec. (Overseas Affairs) to Prime Minister, 1977–79; Ambassador to Hungary, 1980–83; Asst Under-Sec. of State, FCO, 1983–84; Dep. Sec. of the Cabinet, 1984–85. *Address:* c/o Foreign and Commonwealth Office, SW1A 2AH.

CARTTISS, Michael Reginald Harry; MP (C) Great Yarmouth, since 1983; *b* Norwich, 11 March 1938; *s* of Reginald Carttiss and Doris Culling. *Educ:* Filby County Primary Sch.; Great Yarmouth Tech. High Sch.; Goldsmiths' Coll., London Univ. (DipEd); LSE (part time, 1961–64). Nat. Service, RAF, 1956–58. Teacher: Orpington, Kent, and Waltham Cross, Herts, 1961–64; Oriel Grammar Sch., 1964–69; Cons. Party Agent, Gt Yarmouth, 1969–82. Member: Norfolk CC, 1966–85 (Vice-Chm., 1972, Chm., 1980–85, Educn Cttee); Gt Yarmouth BC, 1973–82 (Leader, 1980–82). Chm., Norfolk Museums Service, 1981–85; Mem., E Anglian RHA, 1981–85; Comr, Gt Yarmouth Port and Haven Commn, 1982–86. *Recreations:* reading, writing, talking, walking, theatre. *Address:* 48 Spruce Avenue, Ormesby St Margaret, Great Yarmouth, Norfolk NR29 3RY.

CARTWRIGHT, David Edgar, DSc; FRS 1984; Senior Research Officer (formerly Assistant Director), Institute of Oceanographic Sciences; *b* 21 Oct. 1926; *s* of Edgar A. Cartwright and Lucienne Cartwright (*née* Tartanson); *m* 1952, Anne-Marie Guerin; two *s* two *d. Educ:* St John's Coll., Cambridge (BA); King's Coll., London (BSc, DSc). Dept of Naval Construction, Admiralty, Bath, 1951–54; Nat. Inst. of Oceanography (later Inst. of Oceanographic Sciences), Wormley, Surrey: Sci. Officer, rising to Individual Merit SPSO, 1954–73; Research Associate, Univ. of California, La Jolla, 1964–65; Asst Dir, Inst. of Oceanographic Scis, Bidston Observatory, Birkenhead, 1973–85. Mem., Royal Astronomical Soc., 1976–. *Publications:* over 60 papers on marine sci. research; reviews, etc, in various learned jls. *Recreations:* music, walking, travel. *Address:* c/o Institute of Oceanographic Sciences, Brook Road, Wormley, Godalming, Surrey GU8 5UB.

CARTWRIGHT, Rt. Rev. (Edward) David; see Southampton, Bishop Suffragan of.

CARTWRIGHT, Frederick; see Cartwright, W. F.

CARTWRIGHT, Harry, CBE 1979 (MBE 1946); MA, CEng, MIMechE, MIEE; Director, Atomic Energy Establishment, Winfrith, 1973–83; *b* 16 Sept. 1919; *s* of Edwin Harry Cartwright and Agnes Alice Cartwright (*née* Gillibrand); *m* 1950, Catharine Margaret Carson Bradbury; two *s. Educ:* William Hulme's Grammar Sch., Manchester; St John's Coll., Cambridge (Schol.). 1st cl. Mechanical Sciences Tripos, 1940. Served War, RAF, 1940–46: Flt Lt, service on ground radar in Europe, India and Burma. Decca Navigator Co., 1946–47; English Electric Co., 1947–49; joined Dept of Atomic Energy, Risley, as a Design and Project Engr, 1949; Chief Engr, 1955; Dir in charge of UKAEA consultancy services on nuclear reactors, 1960–64; Dir, Water Reactors, 1964–70, and as such responsible for design and construction of Winfrith 100 MW(e) SGHWR prototype power station; Dir, Fast Reactor Systems, 1970–73. Pres., British Nuclear Energy Soc., 1979–82; Pres., European Nuclear Soc., 1983–85 (Vice-Pres., 1980–83). *Publications:* various techn. papers. *Recreations:* walking, gardening, golf. *Address:* Tabbit's Hill House, Corfe Castle, Wareham, Dorset BH20 5HZ. *T:* Corfe Castle 480 582. *Club:* United Oxford & Cambridge University.

CARTWRIGHT, John Cameron; JP; MP (SDP) Woolwich, since 1983 (Greenwich, Woolwich East, Oct. 1974–1983: Lab, 1974–81; SDP, 1981–83); *b* 29 Nov. 1933; *s* of Aubrey John Randolph Cartwright and Ivy Adeline Billie Cartwright; *m* 1959, Iris June Tant; one *s* one *d. Educ:* Woking County Grammar School. Exec. Officer, Home Civil Service, 1952–55; Labour Party Agent, 1955–67; Political Sec., RACS Ltd, 1967–72; Director, RACS Ltd, 1972–74. Leader, Greenwich Borough Council, 1971–74. Mem.,

Labour Party Nat. Exec. Cttee, 1971–75 and 1976–78. PPS to Sec. of State for Education and Science, 1976–77; Chm., Parly Labour Party Defence Group, 1979–81; Mem., Select Cttee on Defence, 1979–82; SDP party spokesman on environment, 1981–, on defence and foreign affairs, 1983–; SDP Parly Whip, 1983–. Jt Chm., Council for Advancement of Arab British Understanding, 1983–; Vice-Chm., GB-USSR Assoc., 1983–. Vice-Pres., Assoc. of Metropolitan Authorities, 1974–. Trustee, Nat. Maritime Museum, 1976–83. JP Inner London, 1970–. *Publication:* (jtly) Cruise, Pershing and SS20, 1985. *Recreations:* do-it-yourself, reading, watching television. *Address:* 17 Commonwealth Way, SE2 0JZ. *T:* 01–311 4394.

CARTWRIGHT, Dame Mary Lucy, DBE 1969; FRS 1947; ScD Cambridge 1949; MA Oxford and Cambridge; DPhil Oxford; Hon. LLD (Edin.) 1953; Hon. DSc: Leeds, 1958; Hull, 1959; Wales, 1962; Oxford, 1966; Brown (Providence, RI), 1969; Fellow of Girton College, Cambridge, 1934–49, and since 1968; *b* 1900; *d* of late W. D. Cartwright, Rector of Aynhoe. *Educ:* Godolphin Sch., Salisbury, and St Hugh's Coll., Oxford. Asst Mistress, Alice Ottley Sch., Worcester, 1923–24, Wycombe Abbey Sch., Bucks, 1924–27; read for DPhil, 1928–30; Yarrow Research Fellow of Girton Coll., 1930–34; Univ. Lectr in Mathematics, Cambridge, 1935–59; Mistress of Girton Coll., Cambridge, 1949–68; Reader in the Theory of Functions, Univ. of Cambridge, 1959–68, Emeritus Reader, 1968–; Visiting Professor: Brown Univ., Providence, RI, 1968–69; Claremont Graduate Sch., California, 1969–70; Case Western Reserve, 1970; Polish Acad. of Sciences, 1970; Univ. of Wales (Swansea and Cardiff), 1971; Case Western Reserve, 1971. Consultant on US Navy Mathematical Research Projects at Stanford and Princeton Universities, Jan.-May 1949. Comdt, British Red Cross Detachment, Cambs 112, 1940–44. Fellow of Cambridge Philosophical Soc.; President: London Math. Soc., 1961–63; Mathematical Assoc., 1951–52 (now Hon. Mem.). Hon. FIMA, 1972; Hon. FRSE. Sylvester Medal, Royal Soc., 1964; De Morgan Medal, London Mathematical Soc., 1968; Medal of Univ. of Jyväskylä, Finland, 1973. Commander, Order of the Dannebrog, 1961. *Publications:* Integral Functions (Cambridge Tracts in Mathematics and Mathematical Physics), 1956; math. papers in various journals. *Address:* 38 Sherlock Close, Cambridge CB3 0HP. *T:* Cambridge 352574.
See also W. F. Cartwright.

CARTWRIGHT, Rt. Rev. Richard Fox; Assistant Bishop, Diocese of Truro, since 1982; *b* 10 Nov. 1913; *s* of late Rev. George Frederick Cartwright, Vicar of Plumstead, and Constance Margaret Cartwright (*née* Clark); *m* 1947, Rosemary Magdalen, *d* of Francis Evelyn Bray, Woodham Grange, Surrey; one *s* three *d. Educ:* The King's School, Canterbury; Pembroke Coll., Cambridge (BA 1935, MA 1939); Cuddesdon Theological Coll. Deacon, 1936; Priest, 1937; Curate, St Anselm, Kennington Cross, 1936–40; Priest-in-Charge, Lower Kingswood, 1940–45; Vicar, St Andrew, Surbiton, 1945–52; Proctor in Convocation, 1950–52; Vicar of St Mary Redcliffe, Bristol (with Temple from 1956 and St John Bedminster from 1965), 1952–72; Hon. Canon of Bristol, 1960–72; Suffragan Bishop of Plymouth, 1972–81. Sub-Chaplain, Order of St John, 1957–; Director: Ecclesiastical Insurance Office Ltd, 1964–85; Allchurches Trust Ltd, 1985–. Hon. DD Univ. of the South, Tennessee, 1969. *Recreations:* fly-fishing, gardening. *Address:* Long Hay, Treligga, Delabole, N Cornwall PL33 9EE. *T:* Camelford 212506; 2a Litfield Place, Clifton, Bristol BS8 3LT. *T:* Bristol 738555. *Club:* Army and Navy.

CARTWRIGHT, (William) Frederick, CBE 1977; DL; MIMechE; Director, BSC (International) Ltd; a Deputy Chairman, British Steel Corporation, 1970–72; Group Managing Director, S Wales Group, British Steel Corporation, 1967–70; Chairman, The Steel Co. of Wales Ltd, 1967 (Managing Director, 1962–67); *b* 13 Nov. 1906; *s* of William Digby Cartwright, Rector of Aynhoe; *m* 1937, Sally Chrystobel Ware; two *s* one *d. Educ:* Rugby Sch. Joined Guest, Keen and Nettlefold, Dowlais, 1929; gained experience at steelworks in Germany and Luxembourg, 1930; Asst Works Manager, 1931, Tech. Asst to Managing Director, 1935, Dir and Chief Engineer, 1940, Dir and General Manager, 1943, Guest, Keen and Baldwin, Port Talbot Works; Dir and General Manager, Steel Co. of Wales, 1947; Asst Man. Dir and General Manager of the Steel Div., The Steel Co. of Wales Ltd, 1954. Pres., Iron and Steel Inst., 1960. Dir, Lloyds Bank, 1968–77 (Chm., S Wales Regional Bd, 1968–77). Dir, Develt Corp for Wales. Freeman of Port Talbot, 1970. DL, County of Glamorgan; High Sheriff, Glamorgan, 1961. OStJ. Hon. LLD Wales, 1968. Bessemer Gold Medal, 1958; Frederico Giolitti Steel Medal, 1960. *Recreations:* riding and yachting. *Address:* Castle-upon-Alun, St Brides Major, near Bridgend, Mid Glam. *T:* Southern-down 298. *Clubs:* Royal Ocean Racing, Royal Cruising; Royal Yacht Squadron.
See also Dame Mary Cartwright.

CARTWRIGHT SHARP, Michael; *see* Sharp, J. M. C.

CARUS, Louis Revell, Hon. RAM, FRSAMD, FRCM; Principal, Birmingham School of Music, since 1975; *b* Kasauli, India, 22 Oct. 1927; *s* of Lt-Col Martin and Enid Carus-Wilson; *m* 1951, Nancy Reade Noell; two *s* one *d. Educ:* Rugby Sch.; Brussels Conservatoire (Premier Prix); Peabody Conservatory, USA. LRAM. Scottish National Orchestra, 1950; solo violinist and chamber music specialist, 1951–; Head of Strings, Royal Scottish Academy of Music, 1956; Scottish Trio and Piano Quartet, New Music Group of Scotland, 1956–75; Northern Sinfonia, Monteverdi Orchestras, 1963–73; Orchestra Da Camera, 1975; Adjudicator, 1960–. Pres., ISM, 1986–87; FRSAMD 1976; Hon. RAM 1977; FRCM 1983. *Publications:* various musical journalism, eg, daily press, Strad Magazine, ISM Jl, Gulbenkian Report. *Recreations:* painting, gardening, travel. *Address:* 24 Barlows Road, Edgbaston, Birmingham B15 2PL. *T:* 021–454 3391. *Clubs:* Royal Society of Musicians, Incorporated Society of Musicians, European String Teachers Association; Rotary (Birmingham).

CARVER, family name of **Baron Carver.**

CARVER, Baron *cr* 1977 (Life Peer); **Field-Marshal (Richard) Michael (Power) Carver,** GCB 1970 (KCB 1966; CB 1957); CBE 1945; DSO 1943 and Bar 1943; MC 1941; designated British Resident Commissioner in Rhodesia, 1977–78; Chief of the Defence Staff, 1973–76; *b* 24 April 1915; 2nd *s* of late Harold Power Carver and late Winifred Anne Gabrielle Carver (*née* Wellesley); *m* 1947, Edith, *d* of Lt-Col Sir Henry Lowry-Corry, MC; two *s* two *d. Educ:* Winchester Coll.; Sandhurst. 2nd Lieut Royal Tank Corps, 1935; War of 1939–45 (despatches twice); GSO1, 7th Armoured Div., 1942; OC 1st Royal Tank Regt, 1943; Comdr 4th Armoured Brigade, 1944; Tech. Staff Officer (1), Min. of Supply, 1947; Joint Services Staff Coll., 1950; AQMG, Allied Land Forces, Central Europe, 1951; Col GS, SHAPE 1952; Dep. Chief of Staff, East Africa, 1954 (despatches); Chief of Staff, East Africa, 1955; idc 1957; Dir of Plans, War Office, 1958–59; Comdr 6th Infty Brigade, 1960–62; Maj.-Gen. 1962; GOC, 3 Div., 1962–64, also Comdr Joint Truce Force, Cyprus, and Dep. Comdr United Nations' Force in Cyprus, 1964; Dir, Army Staff Duties, Min. of Defence, 1964–66; Lt-Gen. 1966; comd FE Land Forces, 1966–67; Gen., 1967; C-in-C, Far East, 1967–69; GOC-in-C, Southern Command, 1969–71; Chief of the General Staff, 1971–73; Field-Marshal 1973. Col Commandant: REME 1966–76; Royal Tank Regt, 1968–72; RAC, 1974–77; ADC (Gen.) 1969–72. *Publications:* Second to None (History of Royal Scots Greys, 1919–45), 1954; El Alamein,

1962; Tobruk, 1964; (ed) The War Lords, 1976; Harding of Petherton, 1978; The Apostles of Mobility, 1979; War Since 1945, 1980; A Policy for Peace, 1982; The Seven Ages of the British Army, 1984. *Address:* Wood End House, Wickham, Fareham, Hants PO17 6JZ. *T:* Wickham 832143. *Club:* Anglo-Belgian.

CARVER, James, CB 1978; CEng, FIMinE; consulting mining engineer; *b* 29 Feb. 1916; *s* of late William and Ellen Carver; *m* 1944, Elsie Sharrock; one *s* two *d* (of whom one *s* one *d* are twins). *Educ:* Wigan Mining and Technical Coll. Certificated Mine Manager. Asst Mine Manager, Nos 5, 6 and 7 mines, Garswood Hall, Lancs, 1941–43; HM Jun. Inspector Mines and Quarries, W Midlands Coalfields, 1943; Dist Inspector, Mines and Quarries, N Staffordshire, 1951; Senior District Inspector: M&Q, London Headquarters, 1957; M&Q, Doncaster Dist (in charge), 1962; Principal Inspector, M&Q, London Headquarters, 1967; Dep. Chief, M&Q, 1973; Chief Inspector, M&Q, 1975–77; Member, Health and Safety Exec., 1976–77. *Publications:* author or co-author, papers in Trans IMinE; several papers to internat. mining confs. *Recreation:* golf. *Address:* 196 Forest Road, Tunbridge Wells, Kent TN2 5JB. *T:* Tunbridge Wells 26748. *Club:* Nevill Golf (Tunbridge Wells).

CARVILL, Patrick; Under-Secretary, Department of Finance and Personnel, Belfast, since 1983; *b* 13 Oct. 1943; *s* of Bernard and Susan Carvill; *m* 1965, Vera Abbott; two *s. Educ:* St Mary's Christian Brothers Grammar School, Belfast; Queen's Univ., Belfast (BA Hons). Min. of Fuel and Power, Westminster, 1965; Min. of Development, Stormont, 1967; Min. of Community Relations, 1969; Asst Sec., Dept. of Educn, 1975–83. *Recreations:* reading, windsurfing, diving. *Address:* c/o Department of Finance and Personnel, Stormont, Belfast BT4 3ST.

CARY, family name of **Viscount Falkland.**

CARY, Sir Roger Hugh, 2nd Bt *cr* 1955; a consultant to BBC's Director-General, since 1986; *b* 8 Jan. 1926; *o s* of Sir Robert (Archibald) Cary, 1st Bt, and Hon. Rosamond Mary Curzon (*d* 1985), *d* of late Col Hon. Alfred Nathaniel Curzon; *S* father, 1979; *m* 1st, 1948, Marilda (marr. diss. 1951), *d* of Major Pearson-Gregory, MC; one *d*; 2nd, 1953, Ann Helen Katharine, *e d* of Hugh Blair Brenan, OBE (formerly Asst Sec., Royal Hosp., Chelsea); two *s* one *d. Educ:* Ludgrove; Eton; New Coll., Oxford (BA Mod. Hist. 1949). Enlisted Grenadier Guards, 1943; Lieut 1945; Staff Captain and Instr, Sch. of Signals, Catterick, 1946; Signals Officer, Guards Trng Bn, 1946–47; R of O 1947. Sub-editor and Leader-writer, The Times, 1949–50; Archivist, St Paul's Cathedral, 1950; joined BBC, 1950: attached Home Talks, 1951; Producer, Overseas Talks, 1951–56; Asst, European Talks, 1956–58; Dep. Editor, The Listener, 1958–61; Man. Trng Organiser, 1961–66; Asst, Secretariat, 1966–72; Sen. Asst, 1972–74; Sec., Central Music Adv. Cttee, 1966–77, 1982–83; Special Asst (Public Affairs), 1974–77; Special Asst to Alasdair Milne, when Man. Dir, BBC TV, 1977–82; Chief Asst to Sec., BBC, 1982–83; Chief Asst to Dir of Progs, BBC TV, 1983–86; Research, Richard Cawston's documentary film, Royal Family, 1969; Secretary: Sims Cttee on portrayal of violence on TV, 1979, report revised 1983; Wenham Cttee on Subscription Television, 1980–81; Cotton Cttee on Sponsorship and BBC TV, 1981; British Deleg., Internat. Art-Historical Conf., Amsterdam, 1952; Salzburg Scholar in Amer. Studies, 1956. Associate, RHistS. *Recreations:* looking at pictures, collecting books. Heir: *s* Nicolas Robert Hugh Cary [*b* 17 April 1955; *m* 1979, Pauline Jean, *d* of Dr Thomas Ian Boyd; two *s*]. *Address:* 23 Bath Road, W4 1LJ. *T:* 01–994 7293. *Club:* Pratt's.

CASALONE, Carlo D.; *see* Dionisotti-Casalone.

CASE, Air Vice-Marshal Albert Avion, CB 1964; CBE 1957 (OBE 1943); General Secretary, Hospital Saving Association, 1969–82; *b* Portsmouth, 5 April 1916; *s* of late Group Captain Albert Edward Case and Florence Stella Hosier Case; *m* 1949, Brenda Margaret, *e d* of late A. G. Andrews, Enfield, Middx; one *s* one *d. Educ:* Imperial Service Coll. Commd RAF, 1934; Sqdn Ldr, 1940; Wing Comdr, Commanding No 202 Squadron, 1942; Group Capt., Maritime Ops HQ, ACSEA, 1945; OC, RAF, Koggala, Ceylon, 1945–46; JSSC, 1950–51; OC, RAF, Chivenor, 1953–55; OC, RAF, Nicosia, 1956–57; IDC, 1959; Air Cdre, 1959; Air Min., Dir, Operational Requirements, 1959–62; Air Vice-Marshal, 1962; AOC No 22 Group RAF, Tech. Trg Comd, 1962–66; SASO HQ Coastal Comd, 1966–68; retd. FBIM. *Recreations:* swimming (RAF blue 1946), sailing. *Address:* High Trees, Dean Lane, Winchester. *Clubs:* Royal Air Force; Royal Air Force Yacht.

CASE, Humphrey John; Keeper, Department of Antiquities, Ashmolean Museum, 1973–82; *b* 26 May 1918; *s* of George Reginald Case and Margaret Helen (*née* Duckett); *m* 1st, 1942, Margaret Adelia (*née* Eaton); 2nd, 1949, Jean Alison (*née* Orr); two *s*; 3rd, 1979, Jocelyn (*née* Herickx). *Educ:* Charterhouse; St John's Coll., Cambridge (MA); Inst. of Archaeology, London Univ. Served War, 1939–46. Ashmolean Museum: Asst Keeper, 1949–57; Sen. Asst Keeper, 1957–69; Dep. Keeper, Dept of Antiquities, 1969–73. Vice-Pres., Prehistoric Soc., 1969–73; has directed excavations in England, Ireland and France. FSA 1954. *Publications:* in learned jls (British and foreign): principally on neolithic in Western Europe, prehistoric metallurgy and regional archaeology. *Recreations:* reading, music, swimming. *Address:* 187 Thame Road, Warborough, Oxon OX9 8DH.

CASE, Captain Richard Vere Essex, DSO 1942; DSC 1940; RD; RNR retired; Royal Naval Reserve ADC to the Queen, 1958; Chief Marine Superintendent, Coast Lines Ltd and Associated Companies, 1953–69; *b* 13 April 1904; *s* of late Prof. R. H. Case; *m* 1940, Olive May, *d* of H. W. Griggs, Preston, near Canterbury, Kent; one *s* one *d. Educ:* Thames Nautical Training Coll., HMS Worcester. Joined RNR 1920; commenced service in Merchant Service, 1920; Master's Certificate of Competency, 1928; Captain RNR, 1953; served War of 1939–45 (DSO, DSC and Bar, RD and Clasp). *Recreation:* bowls. *Address:* 14 Aigburth Hall Road, Liverpool L19 9DQ. *T:* 051–427 1016. *Clubs:* Athenæum (Liverpool); Liverpool Cricket.

CASEY, Most Rev. Eamonn; *see* Galway and Kilmacduagh, Bishop of, (RC).

CASEY, Michael Bernard; Chairman, Michael Casey & Associates Ltd, Management Consultants; Director: Marlar International Ltd; Grosvenor Place Amalgamated Ltd; *b* 1 Sept. 1928; *s* of late Joseph Bernard Casey, OBE, and Dorothy (*née* Love); *m* 1963, Sally Louise, *e d* of James Stuart Smith; two *s* two *d. Educ:* Colwyn Bay Grammar Sch.; LSE (Scholar in Laws, 1952; LLB 1954). RAF, 1947–49. Principal, MAFF, 1961; Office of the Minister for Science, 1963–64; Asst Sec., DEA, 1967; DTI (later Dept of Prices and Consumer Protection), 1970; Under Sec., DoI, 1975–77; a Dep. Chm. and Chief Exec., British Shipbuilders, 1977–80; Chm. and Man. Dir, Mather & Platt, 1980–81. *Recreations:* golf, chess, bridge. *Address:* 10 Stanford Road, W8. *T:* 01–937 8357. *Clubs:* Reform, American.

CASEY, Michael Vince, BSc(Eng), FEng 1985; FIMechE; Director of Mechanical and Electrical Engineering, British Railways Board, since 1982; *b* 25 May 1927; *s* of Charles John Casey and May Louise Casey; *m* 1954, Elinor Jane (*née* Harris); two *s* two *d. Educ:* Glossop Grammar Sch.; The College, Swindon. BSc(Eng) Hons London. Premium Apprentice, GWR Locomotive Works, Swindon, 1944–49; Univ. of London External

Degree Course, 1949–52; British Rail Western Region: Locomotive Testing and Experimental Office, Swindon, 1952–58; Supplies and Contracts Dept, Swindon, 1958–61; Chief Mechanical and Electrical Engr's Dept, Paddington, 1961–63; Area Maintenance Engr, Old Oak Common, 1963–66; Chief Mech. and Elec. Engr's Dept, Paddington, 1966–71; Chief Mech. and Elec. Engineer: Scottish Region, Glasgow, 1971–76; Eastern Region, York, 1976–78; Engrg Dir, British Rail Engrg Ltd, 1978–82. Lt-Col, Engr and Transport Staff Corps, RE(TA). *Recreations:* gardening, philately. *Address:* Hunters Ride, Stoke Row Road, Peppard, Henley-on-Thames RG9 5EJ. *T:* Kidmore End 722653.

CASEY, Rt. Rev. Patrick Joseph; Former Bishop of Brentwood; Parish Priest, Our Most Holy Redeemer and St Thomas More, Chelsea, since 1980; *b* 20 Nov. 1913; *s* of Patrick Casey and Bridget Casey (*née* Norris). *Educ:* St Joseph's Parochial Sch., Kingsland; St Edmund's Coll., Ware. Ordained priest, 1939; Asst, St James's, Spanish Place, 1939–61; Parish Priest of Hendon, 1961–63; Vicar Gen. of Westminster, 1963; Domestic Prelate, and Canon of Westminster Cathedral, 1964; Provost of Westminster Cathedral Chapter, 1967; Auxiliary Bishop of Westminster and Titular Bishop of Sufar, 1966–69; Bishop of Brentwood, 1969–79, then Apostolic Administrator. *Address:* 7 Cheyne Row, SW3 5HS.

CASEY, Dr Raymond, FRS 1970; retired; Senior Principal Scientific Officer (Special Merit), Institute of Geological Sciences, London, 1964–79; *b* 10 Oct. 1917; *s* of Samuel Gardiner Casey and Gladys Violet Helen Casey (*née* Garrett); *m* 1943, Norah Kathleen Pakeman (*d* 1974); two *s*. *Educ:* St Mary's, Folkestone; Univ. of Reading. PhD 1958; DSc 1963. Geological Survey and Museum: Asst 1939; Asst Exper. Officer 1946; Exper. Officer 1949; Sen. Geologist 1957; Principal Geologist 1960. *Publications:* A Monograph of the Ammonoidea of the Lower Greensand, 1960–80; (ed, with P. F. Rawson) The Boreal Lower Cretaceous, 1973; numerous articles on Mesozoic palaeontology and stratigraphy in scientific press. *Recreation:* research into early Russian postal and military history (Past Pres., British Soc. of Russian Philately). *Address:* 38 Reed Avenue, Orpington, Kent. *T:* Farnborough (Kent) 51728.

CASEY, Terence Anthony, CBE 1977; KCHS 1976; FCP 1982; retired; General-Secretary, National Association of Schoolmasters/Union of Women Teachers, 1975–83 (National Association of Schoolmasters, 1963–75), now Honorary Life Member; *b* 6 Sept 1920; *s* of Daniel Casey and Ellen McCarthy; *m* 1945, Catherine Wills; two *s* three *d*. *Educ:* Holy Cross, near Ramsgate; Camden Coll. Teacher's Certificate; Diploma in Mod. Hist. Teaching Service, LCC, 1946–63; Headmaster, St Joseph's Sch., Maida Vale, W9, 1956–63. Pres., Nat. Assoc. of Schoolmasters, 1962–63. Member: Burnham Cttee, 1961–83; Council, Open Univ., 1975–; Catholic Educn Council, 1983–; Vice-Chm., "Catch 'em Young" Project Trust, 1983–; Sec. of State's Voluntary Sector Consultative Council, 1984–; formerly Member: Nat. Advisory Cttee on Supply and Training of Teachers; Teachers' Council Working Party; TUC Local Govt Cttee. Treasurer, European Teachers' Trade Union Cttee, 1978–83; Vice Pres., Internat. Fedn of Free Teachers' Unions, 1978–85. Trustee, Westminster Cathedral, 1983–. *Publications:* The Comprehensive School from Within, 1964; contribs to Times Educnl Supplement. *Recreations:* music, opera, motoring. *Address:* 10 Chelsing Rise, Leverstock Green, Hemel Hempstead, Herts. *Club:* Pathfinders'.

CASH, Sir Gerald (Christopher), GCMG 1980; GCVO 1985 (KCVO 1977); OBE 1964; JP; Governor-General, Commonwealth of the Bahamas, since 1979 (Acting Governor-General, 1976–79); *b* Nassau, Bahamas, 28 May 1917; *s* of late Wilfred Gladstone Cash and of Lillian Cash; *m* Dorothy Eileen (*née* Long); two *s* one *d*. *Educ:* Govt High Sch., Nassau. Called to the Bar, Middle Temple, 1948. Counsel and Attorney, Supreme Court of Bahamas, 1940. Member: House of Assembly, Bahamas, 1949–62; Exec. Council, 1958–62; Senate, 1969–73 (Vice-Pres., 1970–72; Pres., 1972–73). Chm., Labour Bd, 1950–52. Member: Bd of Educn, 1950–62; Police Service Commn, 1964–69; Immigration Cttee, 1958–62; Road Traffic Cttee, 1958–62. Rep. Bahamas, Independence Celebrations of Jamaica, Trinidad and Tobago, 1962. Chairman: Vis. Cttee, Boys Indust. Sch., 1952–62; Bd of Governors, Govt High Sch., 1949–63 and 1965–76; Bahamas National Cttee, United World Colls, 1977–. Formerly: Hon. Vice-Consul for Republic of Haiti; Vice-Chancellor, Anglican Dio.; Admin. Adviser, Rotary Clubs in Bahamas to Pres. of Rotary Internat.; Treasurer and Dir, YMCA; Treas., Bahamas Cricket Assoc.; Chm., Boy Scouts Exec. Council; Mem. Board: Dirs of Central Bank of Bahamas; Dirs of Bahamas Assoc. for Mentally Retarded. Formerly: President: Rotary Club of E Nassau; Gym Tennis Club; Florida Tennis Assoc.; Bahamas Lawn Tennis Assoc.; Bahamas Table Tennis Assoc.; Vice-President: Boy Scouts Assoc.; Olympic Assoc., Amateur Athletic Assoc., Swimming Assoc., Football Assoc., Bahamas. JP Bahamas, 1940. Coronation Medal, 1953; Silver Jubilee Medal, 1977; Silver Medal, Olympic Order, 1983. *Recreations:* golf, tennis, table tennis, swimming. *Address:* Government House, PO Box N 8301, Nassau, Bahamas. *T:* 809–21875. *Clubs:* Royal Commonwealth Society; Kingston Cricket (Jamaica); Lyford Cay, Paradise Island Golf, South Ocean Golf, Ambassador Golf, Gym Tennis (Nassau).

CASH, William Nigel Paul; MP (C) Stafford, since 1984; *b* 10 May 1940; *s* of Paul Trevor Cash, MC (killed in action Normandy, July 13, 1944) and Moyra Roberts (*née* Morrison); *m* 1965, Bridget Mary Lee; two *s* one *d*. *Educ:* Stonyhurst Coll.; Lincoln Coll., Oxford (MA History). Qualified as Solicitor, 1967; Partner, Dyson Bell & Co., 1971–79; William Cash & Co. (constitutional and administrative lawyer), 1979–. Chairman: All Party Parly Cttee for Widows and Single Parent Families, 1985–; Simplification of Law Gp, Centre for Policy Studies, 1983–; Gen. Purposes Cttee, Primrose League, 1985–; Vice-Chairman: Cons. Small Business Bureau, 1985–; Cons. Parly Cttee on Constitution, 1985–; Sec., All Party Parly Cttee on E Africa, 1984–; Mem., Select Cttee on European Legislation, 1985–. Mem., Exec. Council, Royal Commonwealth Soc., 1984–. Dir, Ironbridge Gorge Museum Trust, 1980–. *Recreations:* cricket, the heritage. *Address:* Upton Cressett Hall, near Bridgnorth, Shropshire. *T:* Morville 307. *Clubs:* Carlton; Vincent's (Oxford); Free Foresters CC.

CASHEL AND EMLY, Archbishop of, (RC), since 1960; **Most Rev. Thomas Morris,** DD; *b* Killenaule, Co. Tipperary, 16 Oct. 1914; *s* of James Morris and Johanna (*née* Carrigan). *Educ:* Christian Brothers Schs, Thurles; Maynooth Coll. Ordained priest, Maynooth, 1939; studied, Dunboyne Institute, 1939–41. (DD). Professor of Theology, St Patrick's Coll., Thurles, 1942–Dec. 1959, Vice-Pres., 1957–60; appointed Archbishop, 1959; consecrated, 1960. *Recreation:* reading. *Address:* Archbishop's House, Thurles, Co. Tipperary, Ireland. *T:* Thurles 21512.

CASHEL AND OSSORY, Bishop of, since 1980; **Rt. Rev. Noel Vincent Willoughby;** *b* 15 Dec. 1926; *s* of George and Mary Jane Willoughby; *m* 1959, Valerie Moore, Dungannon, Tyrone; two *s* one *d*. *Educ:* Tate School, Wexford; Trinity Coll., Dublin (Scholar, Moderator and Gold Medallist in Philosophy). Deacon 1950, priest 1951, Armagh Cathedral; Curate: Drumglass Parish, 1950–53; St Catherine's, Dublin, 1953–55; Bray Parish, 1955–59; Rector: Delgany Parish, 1959–69; Glenageary Parish, 1969–80; Hon. Sec., General Synod, 1976–80; Treasurer, St Patrick's Cathedral, Dublin, 1976–80; Archdeacon of Dublin, 1979–80. *Recreations:* gardening, golf, tennis, fishing. *Address:* The Palace, Kilkenny, Ireland. *T:* Kilkenny 21560.

CASHMAN, John Prescott; Under-Secretary, Department of Health and Social Security, since 1973; *b* 19 May 1930; *s* of late John Patrick Cashman and late Mary Cashman (*née* Prescott). *Educ:* Balliol Coll., Oxford. MA (English Lang. and Lit.). Army (Intell. Corps), 1948–49. Entered Min. of Health, 1951; Principal 1957; Private Sec. to Minister, 1962–65; Asst Sec. 1965; Nuffield Foundn Trav. Fellow, 1968–69; Private Sec. to Sec. of State, 1969. *Address:* 3 Paul Gardens, Croydon, Surrey CR0 5QL. *T:* 01–681 6578.

CASS, Edward Geoffrey, CB 1974; OBE 1951; Alternate Governor, Reserve Bank of Rhodesia, 1978–79; *b* 10 Sept. 1916; *s* of Edward Charles and Florence Mary Cass; *m* 1941, Ruth Mary Powley; four *d*. *Educ:* St Olave's; Univ. Coll., London (Scholar); The Queen's Coll., Oxford (Scholar). BSc (Econ.) London (1st Cl.) 1937; George Webb Medley Scholarship, 1938; BA Oxon. (1st Cl. PPE) 1939. Lecturer in Economics, New Coll., Oxford, 1939. From 1940 served in Min. of Supply, Treasury, Air Ministry, MoD; Private Sec. to the Prime Minister, 1949–52; Chief Statistician, Min. of Supply, 1952; Private Sec. to Min. of Supply, 1954; Imperial Defence Coll., 1958; Asst Under-Sec. of State (Programmes and Budget), MoD, 1965–72; Dep. Under-Sec. of State (Finance and Budget), MoD, 1972–76. Mem., Review Bd for Govt Contracts, 1977–84; Chm., Verbatim Reporting Study Gp, 1977–79. *Address:* 60 Rotherwick Road, NW11. *T:* 01–455 1664.

CASS, Geoffrey Arthur, MA; CBIM, FIIM; Chief Executive, Cambridge University Press, since 1972; Fellow of Clare Hall, Cambridge, since 1979; *b* 11 Aug. 1932; *o c* of late Arthur Cass and Jessie Cass (*née* Simpson), Darlington and Oxford; *m* 1957, Olwen Mary, *o c* of late William Leslie Richards and Edith Louisa Richards, Llanelli and Brecon; four *d*. *Educ:* Queen Elizabeth Grammar Sch., Darlington (Captain of Sch.); Jesus Coll., Oxford (State Scholar; BA PPE 1954, MA 1958). MA Cantab, 1972. AMIMC 1964; FInstD 1968; FIWM, FIIM 1979; CBIM 1980 (MBIM 1967, FBIM 1979). Sen. Res. Scholar, Dept of Social and Admin. Studies, Oxford Univ., 1956–57; Res. Student, automation, Nuffield Coll., Oxford, 1957–58. Commnd RAFVR, fighter control, 1954; served RAF, 1958–60: Air Min. Directorate of Work Study; Pilot Officer, 1958; Flying Officer, 1960; Editor, Automation, 1960–61; Consultant, PA Management Consultants Ltd, 1960–65; Private Management Consultant, British Communications Corp., and Controls and Communications Ltd, 1965; Dir, Controls and Communications Ltd, 1966–69; Dir, George Allen and Unwin Ltd, 1965–67, Man. Dir, 1967–71; Man. Dir, CUP (Publishing Div.), 1971–72; Dir, Weidenfeld (Publishers) Ltd, 1972–74; Dir, Chicago Univ. Press (UK), 1971–; Sec., Press Syndicate, Univ. of Cambridge, 1974–; Univ. Printer, 1982–83. Chm. Governors, Perse Sch. for Girls, Cambridge, 1978–; Member: Jesus Coll., Cambridge, 1972–; Univ. of Cambridge Cttee of Management of Fenner's (and Exec. Sub-Cttee), 1976–; Univ. of Cambridge Careers Service Syndicate (formerly Appts Bd), 1977– (Exec. Cttee, 1982–); Governing Syndicate, Fitzwilliam Mus., Cambridge, 1977–78; Dining Member: Gonville and Caius Coll., 1976–; St Catharine's Coll., 1976–; Girton Coll., 1977–; Hon. Mem., Ind. Hosp. Gp, 1979–. Royal Shakespeare Theatre Trust: Founder Mem. Council, 1967–; Vice Chm., 1982; Trustee and Guardian, Shakespeare Birthplace Trust, 1982–; Chairman: Governors, Royal Shakespeare Theatre, 1985– (Ct and Council, 1975–; F&GPC, 1976–); Royal Shakespeare Theatre Trust, 1983–; Director: Newcastle Theatre Royal Trust, 1984–; American Friends of Royal Shakespeare Theatre, 1985; Mem. London Council, Cambridge Arts Theatre Appeal, 1982–. Sen. Treasurer, Cambridge Univ. Lawn Tennis Club, 1976–; Cambs County LTA: Mem. Exec., 1974–; Chm., Finance and Gen. Purposes Cttee, 1982–; Captain 1974–78; Pres., 1980–82; Hon. Life Vice-Pres., 1982–; Vice-Pres., Durham and Cleveland LTA, 1977–; Lawn Tennis Assoc. of GB: Member: Bd of Management, 1985–; Council, 1976–, Rules and Internat. Cttee, and Rules Sub-Cttee, 1980–81, Trng and Internat. Match Cttee, 1982–, British Junior Championships Cttee of Management, 1983–; Prentice Cup Cttee, 1979–; Chm., National Trng and Internat. Matches, 1985–. Durham Co. lawn tennis singles champion, 1951; rep. Oxford Univ. against Cambridge: lawn tennis, 1953, 1954, 1955 (Sec., 1955); badminton, 1951, 1952 (Captain, 1952); rep. Oxford and Cambridge against Harvard and Yale, lawn tennis, 1954; played in Wimbledon Championships, 1954, 1955, 1956, 1959; played in inter-county lawn tennis championships for Durham County, then for Cambridgeshire, 1952–82; rep. RAF in Inter-Service lawn tennis championships, 1958, 1959; Cambs Co. lawn tennis singles champion, 1975; Brit. Veterans (over 45) singles champion, Wimbledon, 1978; Mem., Brit. Veterans' Internat. Dubler Cup Team, Eur. Zone, Barcelona, 1978, Milano Marittima, 1979 (Captain). Awarded Hon. Cambridge Tennis 'Blue', 1980. Chevalier, Ordre des Arts et des Lettres (France), 1982. *Publications:* contrib. scientific and technical jls and periodicals (Britain, France, Italy) on econ. and social effects of automation; articles on publishing. *Recreations:* lawn tennis, theatre. *Address:* Middlefield, Huntingdon Road, Cambridge CB3 0LH. *T:* Cambridge 276234. *Clubs:* Hurlingham, Queen's, Royal Automobile, Institute of Directors, International Lawn Tennis of GB, The 45, Veterans' Lawn Tennis of GB; Cambridge University Lawn Tennis, Cambridge Lawn Tennis.

CASS, John, QPM 1979; National Co-ordinator of Regional Crime Squads, 1981–84; Security Consultant; *b* 24 June 1925; *m* 1948, Dilys Margaret Hughes, SRN; three *d*. *Educ:* Nelson Sch., Wigton, Cumbria. Served no 40 RM Commando, 1944–45. Joined Metropolitan Police, 1946; Comdt, Detective Training Sch., Hendon, 1974; Commander: CID, New Scotland Yard, 1975; Complaints Bureau, 1978; Serious Crime Squads, New Scotland Yard, 1980. UK Rep., Interpol Conf. on crime prediction, Paris, 1976. Adviser, Police Staff Coll., on multi-Force major investigations, 1982–83. Mem., British Acad. of Forensic Scis, 1965. Member: Association of Chief Police Officers; Metropolitan Police Commanders' Assoc.; Internat. Police Assoc. Freeman, City of London, 1979. *Recreations:* Lakeland, walking, wild life; and Janet (BA), Anne (BDS) and Sarah (LLB). *Address:* 22 Stradbroke Grove, Buckhurst Hill, Essex IG9 5PF. *T:* 01–504 0505; PO Box 4ER, W1A 4ER. *Clubs:* Special Forces, Sportsman.

CASS, Sir John (Patrick), Kt 1978; OBE 1960; Director: Farmers and Graziers Co-operative Co., since 1962; The Land Newspaper Ltd, since 1964; Queensland Country Life Newspaper, since 1977; *b* 7 May 1909; *s* of Phillip and Florence Cass; *m* 1932, Velma Mostyn; two *s*. *Educ:* Christian Brothers College, Young, NSW. Gen. Pres., Farmers and Settlers Assoc. of NSW, 1954–59; Senior Vice-Pres., Aust. NFU, 1960–70; Chm., NSW Wheat Research Cttee, 1954–72; Mem., Aust. Wheat Board, 1952–77, Chm., 1972–77. Agricultural Man of the Year in Australia, 1977. *Address:* Stoney Ridge, Crowther, NSW 2692, Australia. *Clubs:* Royal Automobile of Australia, Royal Automobile of Victoria.

CASSAR, Francis Felix Anthony; High Commissioner for Malta in London, since 1985; *b* 10 May 1934; *s* of Carmelo and Filomena Cassar; *m* 1969, Doreen Marjorie; two *s*. *Educ:* Primary Sch., Malta; Lyceum, Malta. Emigrated to UK, 1953. Studied mech. engrg, 1953–58; Man. Dir of own motor engrg co.; Co. Sec., Malta Drydocks (UK) Ltd, 1975. Sec., Maltese Labour Movt (UK), 1960–71; active in the Movt for Colonial Freedom; represented Malta Labour Party in the UK, 1971–81, also at meetings of the Bureau of the Socialist International. Mem., Inst of Management, 1977. JP Brentford and Ealing,

Tottenham, 1972–80. *Recreations:* music, football, DIY. *Address:* c/o Malta High Commission, 16 Kensington Square, W8. *T:* 01–938 1712.

CASSEL, Sir Harold (Felix), 3rd Bt *cr* 1920; TD 1975; QC 1970; **His Honour Judge Sir Harold Cassel, Bt;** a Circuit Judge since 1976; *b* 8 Nov. 1916; 3rd *s* of Rt Hon. Sir Felix Cassel, 1st Bt, PC, QC (*d* 1953), and Lady Helen Cassel (*d* 1947); *S* brother, 1969; *m* 1st, 1940, Ione Jean Barclay (marr. diss. 1963); three *s* one *d*; 2nd, 1963, Mrs Eileen Elfrida Smedley. *Educ:* Stowe; Corpus Christi Coll., Oxford. Served War of 1939–45, Captain, 1941, Royal Artillery. Called to Bar, Lincoln's Inn, 1946. Recorder of Great Yarmouth, 1968–71, Hon. Recorder, 1972–. JP Herts, 1959–62; Dep. Chm., Herts QS, 1959–62. *Recreations:* shooting, swimming, opera going. *Heir: s* Timothy Felix Harold Cassel, *qv.* *Address:* 49 Lennox Gardens, SW1. *T:* 01–584 2721.

CASSEL, Timothy Felix Harold; Senior Prosecuting Counsel at Central Criminal Court, since 1986; *b* 30 April 1942; *s* of Sir Harold Cassel, Bt, *qv*; *m* 1st, 1971, Jenifer Puckle (marr. diss. 1976); one *s* one *d*; 2nd, 1979, Ann Mallalieu, *qv*; two *d. Educ:* Eton College. Called to the Bar, Lincoln's Inn, 1965; Jun. Prosecuting Counsel at Central Criminal Court, 1978; Asst Boundaries Comr, 1979–85. *Address:* Studdridge Farm, Stokenchurch, Bucks. *T:* Radnage 2303. *Clubs:* Garrick, Queen's, Aspinall Curzon.

CASSELS, Field-Marshal Sir (Archibald) James (Halkett), GCB 1961 (CB 1950); KBE 1952 (CBE 1944); DSO 1944; Chief of the General Staff, Ministry of Defence, 1965–68; *b* 28 Feb. 1907; *s* of late General Sir Robert A. Cassels, GCB, GCSI, DSO; *m* 1st, 1935, Joyce (*d* 1978), *d* of late Brig.-Gen. Henry Kirk and Mrs G. A. McL. Sceales; one *s*; 2nd, 1978, Joy (Mrs Kenneth Dickson). *Educ:* Rugby Sch.; RMC, Sandhurst. 2nd Lieut Seaforth Highlanders, 1926; Lieut 1929; Capt. 1938; Major 1943; Col 1946; temp. Maj.-Gen. 1945; Maj.-Gen. 1948; Lieut-Gen. 1954; Gen. 1958. Served War of 1939–45 (despatches twice): BGS 1944; Bde Comd 1944; GOC 51st Highland Div., 1945; GOC 6th Airborne Div., Palestine, 1946 (despatches); idc, 1947; Dir Land/Air Warfare, War Office, 1948–49; Chief Liaison Officer, United Kingdom Services Liaison Staff, Australia, 1950–51; GOC 1st British Commonwealth Div. in Korea (US Legion of Merit), 1951–52; Comdr, 1st Corps, 1953–54; Dir-Gen. of Military Training, War Office, 1954–57; Dir of Emergency Operations Federation of Malaya, 1957–59; PMN (Panglima Mangku Negara), 1958; GOC-in-C, Eastern Command, 1959; C-in-C, British Army of the Rhine and Comdr NATO Northern Army Group, 1960–63; Adjutant-Gen. to the Forces, 1963–64; Field-Marshal, 1968. ADC Gen. to the Queen, 1960–63. Col Seaforth Highlanders, 1957–61; Col Queen's Own Highlanders, 1961–66; Colonel Commandant: Corps of Royal Military Police, 1957–68; Army Physical Training Corps, 1961–65. Pres., Company of Veteran Motorists, 1970–73. *Recreations:* follower of all forms of sport. *Address:* Hamble End, Barrow, Bury St Edmunds, Suffolk. *Club:* Cavalry and Guards (Hon. Mem.).

CASSELS, His Honour Francis Henry, TD 1945; Senior Circuit Judge, Inner London Crown Court, 1972–79 (Chairman, SW London Quarter Sessions, 1965–72); *b* 3 Sept. 1910; 2nd *s* of late Sir James Dale Cassels; *m* 1939, Evelyn Dorothy Richardson (*d* 1979); one *s* one *d. Educ:* Sedbergh; Corpus Christi Coll., Cambridge (MA). Called to the Bar, Middle Temple, 1932. Served Royal Artillery, 1939–45. Dep. Chm., County of London Sessions, 1954–65. *Address:* 14 Buckingham House, Courtlands, Richmond, Surrey. *T:* 01–940 4180. *Club:* Royal Wimbledon Golf.

CASSELS, Field-Marshal Sir James; *see* Cassels, Field-Marshal Sir A. J. H.

CASSELS, Prof. James Macdonald, FRS 1959; Lyon Jones Professor of Physics, University of Liverpool, 1960–82, now Emeritus Professor; *b* 9 Sept. 1924; *s* of Alastair Macdonald Cassels and Ada White Cassels (*née* Scott); *m* 1947, Jane Helen Thera Lawrence (*d* 1977); one *s* one *d. Educ:* Rochester House Sch., Edinburgh; St Lawrence Coll., Ramsgate; Trinity College, Cambridge. BA, MA, PhD (Cantab.). Harwell Fellow and Principal Scientific Officer, Atomic Energy Research Establishment, Harwell, 1949–53. Lecturer, 1953, subseq. Senior Lecturer, University of Liverpool. Prof. of Experimental Physics, University of Liverpool, 1956–59; Visiting Prof., Cornell Univ., 1959–60. Hon. Fellow, Univ. of Liverpool, 1982–83. Mem. Council, Royal Soc., 1968–69. Rutherford Medal, Inst. of Physics, 1973. *Publications:* Basic Quantum Mechanics, 1970; contributions to: scientific journals on atomic, nuclear and elementary particle physics; govt reports on district heating and combined heat and power. *Recreations:* fishing, walking, talking. *Address:* 14 Dudlow Court, Dudlow Nook Road, Liverpool L18 2EU. *T:* 051–722 2594.

CASSELS, John Seton, CB 1978; Director General, National Economic Development Office, since 1983; *b* 10 Oct. 1928; *s* of Alastair Macdonald Cassels and Ada White Cassels (*née* Scott); *m* 1956, Mary Whittington; two *s* two *d. Educ:* Sedbergh Sch., Yorkshire; Trinity Coll., Cambridge. Rome Scholar, Classical Archaeology, 1952–54. Entered Ministry of Labour, 1954; Secretary of the Royal Commission on Trade Unions and Employers' Associations, 1965–68; Under-Sec., NBPI, 1968–71; Managing Directors' Office, Dunlop Holdings Ltd, 1971–72; Chief Exec., Training Services Agency, 1972–75; Dir, Manpower Services Commn, 1975–81; Second Permanent Sec., MPO, 1981–83. Member Council: Inst. of Manpower Studies, 1982–; Policy Studies Inst., 1983–. *Recreations:* reading, music, sailing. *Address:* 10 Beverley Road, Barnes, SW13 0LX. *T:* 01–876 6270. *Club:* Reform.

CASSELS, Prof. John William Scott, FRS 1963; FRSE 1981; MA, PhD; Sadleirian Professor of Pure Mathematics, Cambridge University, 1967–84; Head of Department of Pure Mathematics and Mathematical Statistics, 1969–84; *b* 11 July 1922; *s* of late J. W. Cassels (latterly Dir of Agriculture in Co. Durham) and late Mrs M. S. Cassels (*née* Lobjoit); *m* 1949, Constance Mabel Merritt (*née* Senior); one *s* one *d. Educ:* Neville's Cross Council Sch., Durham; George Heriot's Sch., Edinburgh; Edinburgh and Cambridge Univs. MA Edinburgh, 1943; PhD Cantab, 1949. Fellow, Trinity, 1949–; Lecturer, Manchester Univ., 1949; Lecturer, Cambridge Univ., 1950; Reader in Arithmetic, 1963–67. Mem. Council, Royal Society, 1970, 1971 (Sylvester Medal, 1973); Vice Pres., 1974–78, Mem. Exec., 1978–82, Internat. Mathematical Union; Pres., London Mathematical Soc., 1976–78. Dr (*hc*) Lille Univ., 1965; Hon. ScD Edinburgh, 1977. *Publications:* An Introduction to Diophantine Approximation, 1957; An Introduction to the Geometry of Numbers, 1959; Rational Quadratic Forms, 1978; Economics for Mathematicians, 1981; Local Fields, 1986; papers in diverse mathematical journals on arithmetical topics. *Recreations:* arithmetic (higher only), gardening (especially common vegetables). *Address:* 3 Luard Close, Cambridge CB2 2PL. *T:* 246108.

CASSELS, Adm. Sir Simon (Alastair Cassillis), KCB 1982; CBE 1976; Second Sea Lord, Chief of Naval Personnel and Admiral President, Royal Naval College, Greenwich, 1982–86; *b* 5 March 1928; *o s* of late Comdr A. G. Cassels, RN, and Clarissa Cassels (*née* Motion); *m* 1962, Jillian Francies Kannreuther; one *s* one *d. Educ:* RNC, Dartmouth. Midshipman 1945; Commanding Officer: HM Ships Vigilant, Roebuck, and Tenby, 1962–63; HMS Eskimo, 1966–67; HMS Fearless, 1972–73; Principal Staff Officer to CDS, 1973–76; CO HMS Tiger, 1976–78; Asst Chief of Naval Staff (Op. Requirements), 1978–80; Flag Officer, Plymouth, Port Adm. Devonport, Comdr Central Sub Area Eastern Atlantic and Comdr Plymouth Sub Area Channel, 1981–82. Younger Brother of

Trinity House, 1963. Freeman, City of London, 1983; Liveryman, Shipwrights' Co., 1984. FRGS. *Publication:* Peninsular Portrait 1811–1814, 1963. *Recreations:* family, water colours, historical research. *Address:* c/o Lloyds Bank, Broadway, Worcs. *Club:* Army and Navy.

CASSIDI, Adm. Sir (Arthur) Desmond, GCB 1983 (KCB 1978); Commander-in-Chief, Naval Home Command, 1982–85; Flag Aide-de-Camp to the Queen, 1982–85; *b* 26 Jan. 1925; *s* of late Comdr Robert A. Cassidi, RN and late Clare F. (*née* Alexander); *m* 1st, 1950, Dorothy Sheelagh Marie (*née* Scott) (*d* 1974); one *s* two *d*; 2nd, 1982, Dr Deborah Marion Pollock (*née* Bliss), FRCS. *Educ:* RNC Dartmouth. Qual. Pilot, 1945; CO, 820 Sqdn (Gannet aircraft), 1955; 1st Lieut HMS Protector, 1955–56; psc 1957; CO, HMS Whitby, 1959–61; Fleet Ops Officer Home Fleet, 1962–64; Asst Dir Naval Plans, 1964–67; Captain (D) Portland and CO HMS Undaunted, 1967–68; idc 1969; Dir of Naval Plans, 1970–72; CO, HMS Ark Royal, 1972–73; Flag Officer Carriers and Amphibious Ships, 1974–75; Dir-Gen., Naval Manpower and Training, 1975–77; Flag Officer, Naval Air Command, 1978–79; Chief of Naval Personnel and Second Sea Lord, 1979–82. Mem. Adv. Council, Science Museum, 1979–84, Trustee, 1984–; Pres., FAA Museum, 1985–. FRSA 1986. *Recreation:* country pursuits. *Address:* c/o Barclays Bank, 16 Whitehall, SW1A 2EA.

CASSIDY, Bryan Michael Deece; Member (C) Dorset East and Hampshire West, European Parliament, since 1984; *b* 17 Feb. 1934; *s* of late William Francis Deece Cassidy and of Kathleen Selina Patricia Cassidy (*née* Geraghty); *m* 1960, Gillian Mary Isobel Bohane; one *s* two *d. Educ:* Ratcliffe College; Sidney Sussex College, Cambridge. MA (Law). Commissioned RA, 1955–57 (Malta and Libya); HAC, 1957–62. With Ever Ready, Beecham's and Reed International (Dir, European associates). Mem. Council, CBI, 1981–84. Dir Gen., Cosmetic, Toiletry and Perfumery Assoc., 1981–84. Contested (C) Wandsworth Central, 1966; Mem. GLC (Hendon North), 1977–86 (opposition spokesman on industry and employment, 1983–84). *Recreations:* history, spending time in the country, theatre. *Address:* 11 Esmond Court, Thackeray Street, W8 5HB. *T:* 01–937 3558; The Stables, White Cliff Gardens, Blandford DT11 7BU. *T:* Blandford 52420.

CASSILLIS, Earl of; Archibald Angus Charles Kennedy; *b* 13 Sept. 1956; *s* and *heir* of 7th Marquess of Ailsa, *qv*; *m* 1979, Dawn Leslie Anne Keen; two *d. Recreations:* shooting, ski-ing, cadets and youth-work. *Address:* Cassillis House, Maybole, Ayrshire. *T:* Dalrymple 310. *Club:* New (Edinburgh).

CASSILLY, Richard; operatic tenor; *b* Washington, DC, 14 Dec. 1927; *s* of Robert Rogers Cassilly and Vera F. Swart; *m* 1951, Helen Koliopoulos; four *s* three *d. Educ:* Peabody Conservatory of Music, Baltimore, Md. New York City Opera, 1955–66; Chicago Lyric, 1959–; Deutsche Oper, Berlin, 1965–; Hamburgische Staatsoper, 1966–; San Francisco Opera, 1966–; Covent Garden, 1968–; Staatsoper, Vienna, 1969; La Scala, Milan, 1970; Staatsoper, Munich, 1970; Paris Opera, 1972; Metropolitan Opera, NY, 1973–; *Television:* Otello, Peter Grimes, Fidelio, Wozzeck, Die Meistersinger; numerous recordings. *Address:* c/o Robert Lombardo Associates, 30 West 60th Street, New York, NY 10023, USA.

CASSIRER, Mrs Reinhold; *see* Gordimer, Nadine.

CASSON, (Frederick) Michael, OBE 1983; self-employed potter, since 1945 (first workshop, 1952); *b* 2 April 1925; *s* of William and Dorothy Casson; *m* 1955, Sheila Wilmot; one *s* two *d. Educ:* Tollington Grammar Sch.; Hornsey Coll. of Art (Art Teachers Dip.). First pots made 1945; has continued to make functional pots from opening of first workshop, 1952; at present making stoneware and porcelain pots fired with wood. Teaches part-time, all ages, 1946–; at present teaching history of ceramics and lecturing in USA. Founder member: Craftsmen Potters Assoc., 1958 (Chm., 1963–67); Harrow Studio Pottery Course, 1963. Presenter, The Craft of the Potter, BBC TV series, 1975. Gold Medal, Prague Internat. Acad. of Ceramic Art, 1964. *Publications:* Pottery in Britain Today, 1967; The Craft of the Potter, 1976, 2nd edn, 1980; many articles in Crafts, Ceramic Review, Ceramics Monthly (USA). *Recreation:* history - particularly the history of crafts. *Address:* Wobage Farm, Upton Bishop, near Ross-on-Wye, Herefordshire HR9 7QP. *T:* Upton Bishop 233.

CASSON, Sir Hugh (Maxwell), CH 1985; KCVO 1978; Kt 1952; RA 1970; RDI 1951; MA Cantab; RIBA, FSIA; President of the Royal Academy, 1976–84; Professor of Environmental Design, 1953–75; Provost, 1980–86, Royal College of Art; Member, Royal Mint Advisory Committee, since 1972; *b* 23 May 1910; *s* of late Randal Casson, ICS; *m* 1938, Margaret Macdonald Troup (*see* Margaret MacDonald Casson); three *d. Educ:* Eastbourne Coll.; St John's Coll., Cambridge. Craven Scholar, British Sch. at Athens, 1933; in private practice as architect since 1937 with late Christopher Nicholson; served War of 1939–45, Camouflage Officer in Air Ministry, 1940–44; Technical Officer Ministry of Town and Country Planning, 1944–46; private practice, Sen. Partner, Casson Conder & Partners, 1946–48; Dir. of Architecture, Festival of Britain, 1948–51. Master of Faculty, RDI, 1969–71. Mem., Royal Fine Art Commn, 1960–83; Trustee: British Museum (Nat. Hist.), 1976–86; Nat. Portrait Gall., 1976–; Mem. Bd, British Council, 1977–81. Mem., Royal Danish Acad., 1954; Hon. Associate, Amer. Inst of Architects, 1968; Hon. Mem., Royal Canadian Acad. of Arts, 1980. Hon. Dr: RCA 1975; Southampton, 1977; Hon. LLD, Birmingham, 1977; Hon. DLitt Sheffield, 1986. Hon. Fellow University Coll. London, 1983. Albert Medal, RSA, 1984. Italian Order of Merit, 1980. Regular contributor as author and illustrator to technical and lay Press. *Publications:* New Sights of London (London Transport), 1937; Bombed Churches, 1946; Homes by the Million (Penguin), 1947; (with Anthony Chitty) Houses-Permanence and Prefabrication, 1947; Victorian Architecture, 1948; Inscape: the design of interiors, 1968; (with Joyce Grenfell) Nanny Says, 1972; Diary, 1981; London, 1983. *Recreation:* drawing. *Address:* (home) 60 Elgin Crescent, W11 2JJ; (office) 35 Thurloe Place, SW7. *T:* 01–584 4581.

CASSON, Margaret MacDonald, (Lady Casson); Architect, Designer; Senior Tutor, School of Environmental Design, Royal College of Art, retired 1974; *b* 26 Sept. 1913; 2nd *d* of James MacDonald Troup, MD, and Alberta Davis; *m* 1938, Hugh Maxwell Casson, *qv*, three *d. Educ:* Wychwood Sch., Oxford; Bartlett Sch. of Architecture, University Coll. London; Royal Inst. of British Architecture. Office of late Christopher Nicholson, 1937–38; private practice, S Africa, 1938–39; Designer for Cockade Ltd, 1946–51; Tutor, Royal Coll. of Art, 1952; private practice as Architect and Designer for private and public buildings and interiors; also of china, glass, carpets, furniture, etc; Design consultant to various cos; Member: Design Council Index Cttees; Duke of Edinburgh's panel for Award for Elegant Design, 1962–63; Council for Design Council, 1967–73 (Chm. Panel for Design Council Awards for Consumer Goods, 1972); Three-Dimensional Design Panel of NCDAD, 1962–72 (Ext. Assessor for NCDAD, 1962–); Council of RCA, 1970; Arts Council, 1972–75; Cttee of Enquiry into Drama Training, 1973–75; Adv. Council of V&A Museum, 1975; Craft Adv. Cttee, 1976–82; Council, Royal Soc. of Arts, 1977–82; Stamp Adv. Cttee, PO, 1980–; Design Cttee, London Transport, 1980–; Council, Zoological Soc. of London, 1983– (Mem., Gardens and Parks Cttee, 1975–). Mem. Bd of Governors: Wolverhampton Coll. of Art, 1964–66; West of

England Coll. of Art, 1965–67; BFI, 1973–79 (Chm., Regional Cttee, 1976–79). FSIA, Sen. Fellow RCA; Hon. Fellow, Royal Acad., 1985. *Address:* 60 Elgin Crescent, W11 2JJ. *T:* 01-727 2999.

CASSON, Michael; *see* Casson, F. M.

CASTERET, Norbert; Commandeur de la Légion d'Honneur, 1975 (Officier 1947); Croix de Guerre, 1917; archæologist, geologist, speleologist; *b* 19 Aug. 1897; *m* 1924, Elisabeth Martin (*d* 1940); one *s* four *d*. *Educ:* Lycée de Toulouse, Haute-Garonne. Bachelier; lauréat de l'Académie Française, 1934, 1936, 1938; lauréat de l'Académie des Sciences, 1935; mainteneur de l'Académie des Jeux Floraux, 1937; Grande Médaille d'Or de l'Académie des Sports, 1923; Médaille d'Or de l'Education Physique, 1947; Commandeur du Mérite de la Recherche et de l'Invention, 1956; Commandeur du Mérite sportif, 1958; Commandeur des Palmes académiques, 1964; Commandeur du Mérite National; "Oscar" du Courage Français, 1973; Médaille de Sauvetage, 1975; Médaille d'or de la Société d'Encouragement au Bien, 1977; Grande Médaille d'Or de la Société de Géographie de Paris, 1979. *Publications:* 45 works translated into 17 languages: Dix ans sous terre (English edn: Ten Years Under the Earth); Au fond des gouffres; Mes Cavernes (English edn: My Caves); En Rampant; Exploration (English edn: Cave Men New and Old); Darkness Under the Earth; Trente ans sous terre (English edn: The Descent of Pierre Saint-Martin), etc.; contributions to L'Illustration, Illustrated London News, Geographical Magazine, etc. *Recreations:* exploring caves and study on bats. *Address:* Castel Mourlon, 31800 Saint-Gaudens, France. *T:* St Gaudens 61.89.15.13.

CASTILLO, Rudolph Innocent, MBE 1976; first High Commissioner for Belize in London, 1983–85; first Belize Ambassador to: France, Federal Republic of Germany, Holy See, EEC, Unesco, 1983–85; *b* 28 Dec. 1927; *s* of late Justo S. and Marcelina Castillo; *m* 1947, Gwen Frances Powery; three *s* four *d*. *Educ:* St John's Coll., Belize. Training Assignments with BBC and COI, London. Lectr in Maths, Spanish and Hist., St John's Coll., 1946–52; Radio Belize: Announcer, 1952–53; Sen. Announcer, 1953–55; Asst Prog. Organizer, 1955–59; Govt Information Services: Information Officer, 1959–62; Chief Information Officer, 1962–74; Permanent Secretary: Agriculture, 1974–76; Education, 1976–79; Sec. to Cabinet, 1980–83; Chief of Protocol, 1981–83. *Recreations:* photography, theatre. *Address:* 29 Mahogany Street, Belmopan, Belize.

CASTLE, Rt. Hon. Barbara (Anne), PC 1964; BA; Member (Lab) Greater Manchester West, European Parliament, since 1984 (Greater Manchester North, 1979–84); Leader, British Labour Group, 1979–85, Vice-Chairman of Socialist Group, 1979–86, European Parliament; *b* 6 Oct. 1910; *d* of Frank and Annie Rebecca Betts; *m* 1944, Edward Cyril Castle, (later Baron Castle (*d* 1979); she prefers to remain known as Mrs Castle); no *c*. *Educ:* Bradford Girls' Grammar Sch.; St Hugh's Coll., Oxford. Elected to St Pancras Borough Council, 1937; Member Metropolitan Water Board, 1940–45; Asst Editor, Town and County Councillor, 1936–40; Administrative Officer, Ministry of Food, 1941–44; Housing Correspondent and Forces Adviser, Daily Mirror, 1944–45. MP (Lab) Blackburn, 1945–50, Blackburn East, 1950–55, Blackburn, 1955–79. Member of National Executive Cttee of Labour Party, 1950–85; Chairman Labour Party, 1958–59 (Vice-Chm. 1957–58). Minister of: Overseas Development, 1964–65; Transport, 1965–68; First Secretary of State and Sec. of State for Employment and Productivity, 1968–70; Sec. of State for Social Services, 1974–76. Co-Chm., Women's Nat. Commn, 1975–76. Hon. Fellow, St Hugh's Coll., Oxford, 1966. Hon. DTech: Bradford, 1968; Loughborough, 1969. *Publications:* part author of Social Security, edited by Dr Robson, 1943; The Castle Diaries 1974–76, 1980, vol. II, 1964–70, 1984. *Recreations:* poetry and walking. *Address:* European Information Office, 2 Queen Anne's Gate, SW1.

CASTLE, Enid; Headmistress, The Red Maids' School, Bristol, since 1982; *b* 28 Jan. 1936; *d* of Bertram and Alice Castle. *Educ:* Hulme Grammar Sch. for Girls, Oldham; Royal Holloway Coll., Univ. of London. BA Hons History. Colne Valley High Sch., Yorks, 1958–62; Kenya High Sch., Nairobi, 1962–65; Queen's Coll., Nassau, Bahamas, 1965–68; Dep. Head, Roundhill High Sch., Leicester, 1968–72; Headmistress, High Sch. for Girls, Gloucester, 1973–81. *Recreations:* tennis, squash, bridge, choral music. *Address:* The Red Maids' School, Westbury on Trym, Bristol BS9 3AW. *T:* Bristol 622641. *Club:* Soroptimist International.

CASTLE, Mrs G. L.; *see* Sharp, Margery.

CASTLE, Norman Henry; Chairman: Gee & Watson Ltd, since 1978; Paul Developments Ltd, since 1980; Underwriting Member of Lloyds, since 1976; *b* 1 Sept. 1913; *s* of Hubert William Castle, MBE, and Elizabeth May Castle; *m* 1939, Ivy Olive Watson; one *d* decd. *Educ:* Norfolk House; Ludlow Grammar Sch. Joined Hafnia Konserves, Copenhagen, 1931; London: C. & E. Morton Ltd, 1933; Vacuum Packed Produce Ltd, 1938; Vacuum Foods Ltd, 1939. Served War of 1939–45, RAF. General Manager: A. L. Maizel Ltd, 1945; Times Foods Ltd, 1947; Director, Vacuum Foods Ltd, 1951; Managing Dir, Haigh Castle & Co. Ltd, 1956; Man. Dir, Hafnia Ham Co. Ltd, 1956; Chm. and Man. Dir, S. & W. Berisford Ltd, 1971–78 (Dir, 1967); Chairman: Ashbourne Investments Ltd, 1976–82; Wace Ltd, 1978–85; Director: Incentive Investments Ltd, 1976–82; E. S. Schwab & Co. Ltd, 1976–81; Acatos and Hutcheson Ltd, 1979–. *Recreations:* travel, sailing. *Address:* The Penthouse, 39 Courcels, Black Rock, Brighton, E Sussex. *Clubs:* Lloyd's Yacht, Brighton Marina Yacht (Brighton).

CASTLE-MILLER, Rudolph Valdemar Thor; a Recorder of the Crown Court, 1972–75; *b* Britain, 16 March 1905; *s* of late Rudolph Schleusz-Mühlheimer, Randers, Denmark; changed name by deed poll, 1930; *m* 1939, Colleen Ruth, *d* of late Lt-Col N. R. Whitaker; one *s* one *d*. *Educ:* Harrow; Hertford Coll., Oxford (MA). Called to Bar, Middle Temple, 1929. Mem., Gen. Council of the Bar, 1957–60 and 1964–69. Past Master, Loriners' Company, 1968. Flt Lt, Intell. Br., RAF, 1940–46. *Recreations:* motoring, travel. *Address:* 1 Ellesmere Court, Brackley, Northants NN13 6BT. *T:* Brackley 700230.

CASTLE-SMITH, Roger, MBE (mil.) 1971; CEng, FIEE; Major, retired; Chief Engineer, Communications Engineering Department, Foreign and Commonwealth Office, since 1981; *b* 14 June 1934; *s* of George Musgrave Castle-Smith and Esme Josephine Winch; *m* 1960, Pamela Anne Coombes; two *s*. *Educ:* Marlborough Coll.; Royal Military College of Science, Shrivenham. DScEng. Royal Corps of Signals, 1952–71. Communications Engineering Dept, FCO, 1971–. *Recreations:* sailing, model engineering, amateur radio. *Address:* Field House, The Green, Hanslope, Milton Keynes, Bucks MK19 7LS. *T:* Milton Keynes 510457. *Club:* Royal Signals Yacht.

CASTLE STEWART, 8th Earl, *cr* 1800 (Ireland); **Arthur Patrick Avondale Stuart;** Viscount Stuart, 1793; Baron, 1619; Bt 1628; *b* 18 Aug. 1928; 3rd but *e surv. s* of 7th Earl Castle Stewart, MC, and Eleanor May, *er d* of late S. R. Guggenheim, New York; *S* father, 1961; *m* 1952, Edna Fowler; one *s* one *d*. *Educ:* Brambletye; Eton; Trinity Coll., Cambridge (BA). Lieut Scots Guards, 1949. MBIM. *Heir: s* Viscount Stuart, *qv*. *Address:* Stone House Farm, East Pennard, Shepton Mallet, Somerset. *T:* Ditcheat 240; Stuart Hall, Stewartstown, Co. Tyrone. *T:* Stewartstown 208. *Club:* Carlton.

CASTLEMAINE, 8th Baron *cr* 1812; **Roland Thomas John Handcock,** MBE (mil.) 1981; Major, Army Air Corps; *b* 22 April 1943; *s* of 7th Baron Castlemaine and Rebecca Ellen (*d* 1978), *o d* of William T. Soady, RN; *S* father, 1973; *m* 1969, Pauline Anne (marr. diss.), *e d* of John Taylor Bainbridge. *Educ:* Campbell Coll., Belfast. psc, ph (cfs). *Heir: cousin* Terence Robin Handcock [*b* 3 Dec. 1902; *m* 1933, Eva Mary, *d* of Charles Taylor; one *s*]. *Address:* c/o Lloyds Bank, Aldershot, Hants.

CASTLEMAN, Christopher Norman Anthony; Chief Executive, Hill Samuel Group Plc, since 1980; *b* 23 June 1941; *s* of late S. Phillips and of Mrs Joan S. R. Pyper; *m* 1st, 1965, Sarah Victoria (*née* Stockdale) (*d* 1979); one *s* one *d*; 2nd, 1980, Caroline Clare (*née* Westcott); two *d*. *Educ:* Harrow; Clare Coll., Cambridge (MA Law). Joined M. Samuel & Co. Ltd, 1963; General Manager, Hill Samuel Australia Ltd, 1970–72; Director, Hill Samuel & Co. Ltd, 1972; Man. Dir, Hill Samuel Group (SA) Ltd and Hill Samuel (SA) Ltd, 1978–80. *Recreations:* tennis, squash, cricket, travel. *Address:* 23 Chepstow Villas, W11 2QZ. *T:* 01-229 6586.

CASTLEREAGH, Viscount; Frederick Aubrey Vane-Tempest-Stewart; *b* 6 Sept. 1972; *s* and *heir* of 9th Marquess of Londonderry, *qv*.

CASTON, Geoffrey Kemp; Vice-Chancellor, University of the South Pacific, since 1983; *b* 17 May 1926; *s* of late Reginald and Lilian Caston, West Wickham, Kent; *m*; two *s* one *d*. *Educ:* St Dunstans Coll.; (Major Open Scholar) Peterhouse, Cambridge (MA). First Cl. Pt 1 History; First Cl. Pt II Law (with distinction) and Geo. Long Prize for Jurisprudence, 1950; Harvard Univ. (Master of Public Admin. 1951; Frank Knox Fellow, 1950–51). Sub-Lt, RNVR, 1945–47. Colonial Office, 1951–58; UK Mission to UN, New York, 1958–61; Dept of Techn. Co-op., 1961–64; Asst Sec., Dept of Educn and Sci. (Univs and Sci. Branches), 1964–66; Jt Sec., Schools Council, 1966–70; Under-Secretary, UGC, 1970–72; Registrar of Oxford Univ. and Fellow of Merton Coll., Oxford, 1972–79; Sec.-Gen., Cttee of Vice-Chancellors and Principals, 1979–83. Sec., Assoc. of First Div. Civil Servants, 1956–58; Adv. to UK Delegn to seven sessions of UN Gen. Assembly, 1953–63; UK Rep. on UN Cttee on Non-Self-Governing Territories, 1958–60; UN Techn. Assistance Cttee, 1962–64; Mem., UN Visiting Mission to Trust Territory of Pacific Islands, 1961. Chm., SE Surrey Assoc. for Advancement of State Educn, 1962–64; UK Delegn to Commonwealth Educn Conf., Ottawa, 1964. Ford Foundn travel grants for visits to schools and univs in USA, 1964, 1967, 1970. Vis. Associate, Center for Studies in Higher Educn, Univ. of Calif, Berkeley, 1978–81. Chairman: Planning Cttee, 3rd and 4th Internat. Curriculum Confs, Oxford, 1967, New York, 1968; Ford Foundn Anglo-American Primary Educn Project, 1968–70; Library Adv. Council (England), 1973–78; Nat. Inst. for Careers Educn and Counselling, 1975–83; DES/DHSS Working Gp on Under 5s Res., 1980–82; Member: Steering Gp, OECD Workshops on Educnl Innovation, Cambridge 1969, W Germany, 1970, Illinois 1971; Vice-Chm., Educnl Res. Bd, SSRC, 1973–77; Exec. Cttee, Inter-Univ. Council for Higher Educn Overseas, 1977–83. Governor, Centre for Educnl Development Overseas, 1969–70. Hon. LLD Dundee, 1982. *Publications:* contribs to educnl jls. *Address:* University of the South Pacific, PO Box 1168, Suva, Fiji.

CASTRO, Rev. Emilio Enrique; General Secretary, World Council of Churches, since 1985; *b* Uruguay, 2 May 1927; *s* of Ignacio Castro and Maria Pombo; *m* 1951, Gladys Nieves; one *s* one *d*. *Educ:* Union Theol. Seminary, Buenos Aires (ThL); University of Basel (post graduate work, 1953–54); University of Lausanne (doctoral candidate, 1983–84). Ordained, 1948; Pastor: Durazno and Trinidad (Uruguay), 1951–53; Central Methodist Church, La Paz, 1954–56; Central Methodist Church, Montevideo, 1957–65; concurrently Prof. of Contemp. Theol. Thought, Mennonite Seminary, Montevideo; Coordinator, Commn for Evangelical Unity in Latin America, 1965–72; Exec. Sec., S American Assoc. of Theol. Schools, 1966–69; Pres., Methodist Church in Uruguay, 1970–72; Dir, WCC Commn on World Mission and Evangelism, 1973–83. Chm., Fellowship of Christians and Jews in Uruguay, 1962–66; Moderator, Conf. on future of CCIA, Netherlands, 1967; Chm., WCC's Agency for Christian Literature Develt, 1970–72. Hon. DHL Westmar Coll., USA, 1984. *Publications:* Jesus the Conqueror, 1956; When Conscience Disturbs, 1959; Mission, Presence and Dialogue, 1963; A Pilgrim People, 1965; Reality and Faith, 1966; Amidst Evolution, 1975; Towards a Latin American Pastoral Perspective, 1973; Sent Free: Mission and Unity in the Perspective of the Kingdom, 1985; (ed and contrib.) Christian Century, 1971–75; (ed and contrib.) International Review of Mission, 1973–83; numerous articles in several languages. *Recreation:* basket ball. *Address:* World Council of Churches, PO Box 66, 1211 Geneva 20, Switzerland.

CATCHESIDE, David Guthrie, DSc London; FRS 1951; Hon. Research Associate, Waite Agricultural Research Institute, South Australia, since 1975; *b* 31 May 1907; *s* of late David Guthrie Catcheside and Florence Susanna (*née* Boxwell); *m* 1931, Kathleen Mary Whiteman; one *s* one *d*. *Educ:* Strand Sch.; King's Coll., University of London. Asst to Professor of Botany, Glasgow Univ., 1928–30; Asst Lecturer, 1931–33, and Lecturer in Botany, University of London (King's Coll.), 1933–36; International Fellow of Rockefeller Foundation, 1936–37; Lecturer in Botany, University of Cambridge, 1937–50; Lecturer and Fellow, Trinity Coll., Cambridge, 1944–51; Reader in Plant Cytogenetics, Cambridge Univ., 1950–51; Prof. of Genetics, Adelaide Univ., S. Australia, 1952–55; Prof. of Microbiology, Univ. of Birmingham, 1956–64; Prof. of Genetics, 1964–72, Dir, 1967–72, Vis. Fellow, 1973–75, Res. Sch. of Biol Scis, ANU. Research Associate, Carnegie Instn of Washington, 1958. Visiting Professor, California Inst. of Technology, 1961. Foreign Associate, Nat. Acad. of Sciences of USA, 1974. Foundation FAA, 1954; FKC 1959. *Publications:* Botanical Technique in Bolles Lee's Microtomists' Vade-Mecum, 1937–50; Genetics of Micro-organisms, 1951; Genetics of Recombination, 1977; Mosses of South Australia, 1980; papers on genetics and cytology. *Address:* 16 Rodger Avenue, Leabrook, SA 5068, Australia.

CATCHPOLE, Nancy Mona; a part-time Secretary with special responsibility for the Women's Training Roadshow Programme, Women's National Commission (Co-Chairman, 1983–85; Immediate Past Co-Chairman, 1985–86); *b* 6 Aug. 1929; *d* of George William Page and Mona Dorothy Page (*née* Cowin), New Eltham; *m* 1959, Geoffrey David Arthur Catchpole; one *s* one *d*. *Educ:* Haberdashers' Aske's Hatcham Girls' Sch.; Bedford Coll., Univ. of London. BA Hons (History). Asst mistress, Gravesend Grammar Sch. for Girls, 1952–56; i/c History, Ipswich High Sch. GPDST, 1956–62; part time lectr in History and General Studies, Bath Tech. Coll., 1977–. Sec., Bath Assoc. of University Women, 1970–75; Regional Rep. on Exec., BFUW, 1975–77, Vice-Pres., 1977–80, Pres., 1981–84; Vice-Chm., Women's Working Group for Industry Year 1986, 1985–. Sec., Bath Branch, Historical Assoc., 1975–79; a Governor, Weston Infants' Sch., Bath, 1975–85 (Chm., 1981–83; Vice-Chm., 1983–). Member: Managers, Eagle House Community Sch., Somerset CC, 1979–82; Case Cttee, Western Nat. Adoption Soc., 1975–77. *Recreations:* listening, viewing, talking, writing. *Address:* 66 Leighton Road, Weston, Bath, Avon BA1 4NG. *T:* Bath 23338. *Club:* Crosby Hall.

CATER, Antony John E., *see* Essex-Cater.

CATER, Douglass; writer and educator in USA, since 1968; President, Washington College, Chestertown, Maryland, since 1982; Founding Fellow, and Trustee since 1982, Aspen Institute (Director, Programme on Communications and Society, 1970–76); *b* Montgomery, Ala, 24 Aug. 1923; *s* of Silas D. Cater and Nancy Chesnutt; *m* 1950, Libby Anderson; two *s* two *d*. *Educ:* Philip Exeter Acad. (grad.); Harvard Univ. (AB, MA). Served War, 1943–45, with OSS. Washington Editor, The Reporter (Magazine), 1950–63; Nat. Affairs Editor, 1963–64; Special Assistant: to Sec. of Army, 1951; to the President of the United States, 1964–68. Vice-Chm., The Observer, 1976–81. Consultant to Dir, Mutual Security Agency, 1952. Visiting Professor, 1959–: Princeton Univ.; Weslyan Univ., Middletown, Conn; Stanford Univ., etc. Guggenheim Fellow, 1955; Eisenhower Exchange Fellow, 1957; George Polk Meml Award, 1961; NY Newspaper Guild, Page One Award, 1961. Mem., Delta Sigma Chi. *Publications:* (with Marquis Childs) Ethics in a Business Society, 1953; The Fourth Branch of Government, 1959; Power in Washington, 1963; The Irrelevant Man, 1970. *Address:* Office of the President, Washington College, Chestertown, Md 21620, USA.

CATER, Sir Jack, KBE 1979 (CBE 1973; MBE 1956); First Deputy General Manager, Guangdong Nuclear Power Joint Venture Co. Ltd, China, since 1985; *b* 21 Feb. 1922; *yr s* of Alfred Francis Cater and Pamela Elizabeth Dukes; *m* 1950, Peggy Gwenda Richards; one *s* two *d*. *Educ:* Sir George Monoux Grammar Sch., Walthamstow. Served War of 1939–45, Sqdn Ldr, RAFVR; British Military Administration, Hong Kong, 1945; joined Colonial Administrative Service, 1946, appointed Hong Kong; attended 2nd Devonshire Course, Oxford (The Queen's Coll.), 1949–50; various appts, incl. Registrar of Co-operative Societies and Director of Marketing, Dir of Agriculture and Fisheries, Dep. Economic Sec.; IDC 1966; Defence Sec./Special Asst to Governor/Dep. Colonial Sec. (Special Duties), 1967; Executive Dir, HK Trade Development Council, 1968–70; Director, Commerce and Industry, 1970–72; Secretary for Information, 1972; for Home Affairs and Information, 1973; Commissioner, Independent Commn Against Corruption, 1974–78; Chief Secretary, Hong Kong, 1978–81; actg Governor and Dep. Governor on several occasions; Hong Kong Comr in London, 1982–84. Mem., Internat. Bd of Dirs, United World Colls, UK, 1981. Hon. DSSc Univ. of Hong Kong, 1982. *Recreations:* work, walking, squash, bridge, reading, watching television. *Address:* (office) Guangdong Nuclear Power Joint Venture Co. Ltd, Nuclear Power Building, Shenzen City, China. *T:* Shenzen City 38599; (home) 4 Braga Circuit, Kowloon, Hong Kong. *T:* Hong Kong 3:7154004. *Clubs:* Royal Automobile; Hong Kong, Royal Hong Kong Jockey (Hong Kong).

CATER, Sir John Robert, (Sir Robin), Kt 1984; Chairman, Distillers Co. Ltd, 1976–83; *b* 25 April 1919; *s* of Sir John Cater; *m* 1945, Isobel Calder Ritchie; one *d*. *Educ:* George Watson's Coll., Edinburgh; Cambridge Univ. (MA). Trainee, W. P. Lowrie & Co. Ltd, 1946; James Buchanan & Co. Ltd, 1949: Dir 1950; Prodn Dir 1959; Prodn Asst, Distillers Co. Ltd, Edinburgh: Prodn Asst, 1959; Dir, 1967–83 (Mem., Management Cttee); Dep. Chm., 1975–76; Man. Dir, John Haig & Co. Ltd, 1965–70; Non-Exec. Dir, United Glass, 1969, Chm. 1972. *Recreations:* music, theatre, fishing, golf (Walker Cup team, 1955; played for Scotland, 1952–56). *Address:* Avernish, Elie, Fife, Scotland KY9 1DA. *Clubs:* New (Edinburgh); Royal and Ancient (St Andrews); The Golf House (Elie).

CATFORD, John Robin; Secretary for Appointments to the Prime Minister and Ecclesiastical Secretary to the Lord Chancellor, since 1982; *b* 11 Jan. 1923; *er s* of late Adrian Leslie Catford and Ethel Augusta (*née* Rolfe); *m* 1948, Daphne Georgina, *o d* of late Col J. F. Darby, CBE, TD; three *s* one *d*. *Educ:* Hampton Grammar Sch.; Univ. of St Andrews (BSc); St John's Coll., Cambridge (DipAgric). Joined Sudan Civil Service, 1946; with Dept of Agriculture and Forests: Kordofan Province, 1946–48; Equatoria Province, 1948–52; Blue Nile Province (secondment to White Nile Schemes Bd), 1952–55; various posts in industry and commerce, mainly in UK; joined Home Civil Service, MAFF, as Principal, 1966; sec. to Cttee of Inquiry on Contract Farming, 1971; Assistant Secretary: Food and Drink Industries Div., 1972–77; Horticulture Div., 1977–79; Under-Secretary: Agricultural Resources Policy and Horticulture Group, 1979–82; Plant Health, Seeds and Labour, 1981–82. Member: Economic Development Cttee for Hotels and Catering, 1972–76; EDC for Agriculture, 1979–82. Mem. Chichester Dio. Synod, 1979–. *Recreations:* sailing, theatre, avoiding gardening. *Address:* 27 Blackthorns, Lindfield, Haywards Heath, West Sussex RH16 2AX. *T:* Haywards Heath 451896. *Clubs:* United Oxford & Cambridge University; Birdham Yacht (Chichester).

CATHCART, family name of Earl Cathcart.

CATHCART, 6th Earl *cr* 1814; **Alan Cathcart,** CB 1973; DSO 1945; MC 1944; Viscount Cathcart, 1807; Baron Greenock (United Kingdom) and 15th Baron Cathcart (Scotland), 1447; Major-General; *b* 22 Aug. 1919; *o s* of 5th Earl and Vera, *d* of late John Fraser, of Cape Town; *S* father, 1927; *m* 1st, 1946, Rosemary (*d* 1980), *yr d* of late Air Commodore Sir Percy Smyth-Osbourne, CMG, CBE; one *s* two *d*; 2nd, 1984, Marie Isobel Lady Weldon. *Educ:* Eton; Magdalene Coll., Cambridge. Served War of 1939–45 (despatches, MC, DSO). Adjt RMA Sandhurst, 1946–47; Regimental Adjt Scots Guards, 1951–53; Brigade Major, 4th Guards Brigade, 1954–56; Commanding Officer, 1st Battalion Scots Guards, 1957; Lt-Col comd Scots Guards, 1960; Colonel AQ Scottish Command, 1962–63; Imperial Defence Coll., 1964; Brigade Comdr, 152 Highland Brigade, 1965–66; Chief, SHAPEX and Exercise Branch SHAPE, 1967–68; GOC Yorkshire District, 1969–70; GOC and British Comdt, Berlin, 1970–73; retd. A Dep-Chm. of Cttees and Dep. Speaker, House of Lords. Ensign, Queen's Body Guard for Scotland, Royal Company of Archers. Pres., ACFA, 1975–82; Dep. Grand Pres., British Commonwealth Ex-Services League, 1976–. Pres., RoSPA, 1982–. Cdre, RYS, 1974–80. GCStJ 1986 (KStJ 1985); Lord Prior, Order of St John of Jerusalem, 1986– (Vice Chancellor, 1984–86). *Heir:* *s* Lord Greenock, *qv*. *Address:* 2 Pembroke Gardens Close, W8. *T:* 01-602 4535. *Clubs:* Brooks's; Royal Yacht Squadron (Cowes).

CATHERWOOD, Sir (Henry) Frederick (Ross), Kt 1971; Member (C) Cambridge and Bedfordshire North, European Parliament, since 1984 (Cambridgeshire, 1979–84); Deputy Chairman, European Democratic Group, European Parliament, since 1983; Director: The Goodyear Tyre and Rubber Co. (GB) Ltd; *b* 30 Jan. 1925; *s* of late Stuart and of Jean Catherwood, Co. Londonderry; *m* 1954, Elizabeth, *er d* of late Rev. Dr D. M. Lloyd Jones, Westminster Chapel, London; two *s* one *d*. *Educ:* Shrewsbury; Clare Coll., Cambridge. Articled Price, Waterhouse & Co.; qualified as Chartered Accountant, 1951; Secretary, Laws Stores Ltd, Gateshead, 1952–54; Secretary and Controller, Richard Costain Ltd, 1954–55; Chief Executive, 1955–60; Asst Managing Director, British Aluminium Co. Ltd, 1960–62; Managing Director, 1962–64; Chief Industrial Adviser, DEA, 1964–66; Dir-Gen., NEDC, 1966–71; Managing Dir and Chief Executive, John Laing & Son Ltd, 1972–74. Chm., Cttee for External Economic Relations, European Parlt, 1979–84. British Institute of Management: Mem. Council, 1961–66, 1969–79; Vice-Chm., 1972; Chm., 1974–76; Vice-Pres., 1976–. Member of Council: NI Development Council, 1963–64; RIIA, 1964–77; BNEC, 1965–71; NEDC, 1964–71; Chm., BOTB, 1975–79. Vice-Pres., 1976, Pres., 1977, Fellowship of Independent Evangelical Churches; Chm. of Council, 1971–77, Pres., 1983–84, Univs and Colls Christian Fellowship (formerly Inter-Varsity Fellowship); Mem., Central Religious Adv. Cttee to BBC and IBA, 1975–79. Hon. DSc Aston, 1972; Hon. DSc (Econ.) QUB, 1973; Hon. DUniv Surrey, 1979. *Publications:* The Christian in Industrial Society, 1964, rev. edn 1980 (Nine to Five, USA, 1983); The Christian Citizen, 1969; A Better Way, 1976; First Things First, 1979; God's Time God's Money, 1987. *Recreations:* music, gardening, reading. *Address:* Sutton Hall, Balsham, Cambridgeshire; (office) Shire Hall, Castle Hill, Cambridge CB3 0AW. *T:* Cambridge 317672. *Club:* United Oxford & Cambridge University.

CATHERWOOD, Herbert Sidney Elliott, CBE 1979; Chairman of Ulsterbus and Citybus; *b* 1929. *Educ:* Belfast Royal Academy, N Ireland. Chairman, Ulsterbus Ltd, from inception, 1967; Member, NI Transport Holding Co., 1968; became Director of Merger of Belfast Corporation Transport with Ulsterbus, 1972. Director: RMC Catherwood; Sea Ferry Parcels. Member: NE Area Board, Ulster Bank, 1976. *Address:* Ulsterbus Ltd, Milewater Road, Belfast BT3 9BG; Boulderstone House, 917 Antrim Road, Templepatrick, Co. Antrim.

CATHIE, Ian Aysgarth Bewley, MD, BS, MRCP, FRCPath; DL; *b* London, 3 Jan. 1908; 2nd *s* of George Cathie, Ewell, Surrey, and Lilly Pickford Evans; *m* 1938, Josephine (*d* 1982), *o d* of Joseph Cunning, FRCS, Broome Park, Betchworth, Surrey; one *s* three *d*. *Educ:* Guy's Hospital; Zürich Univ. Asst path. to Ancoats Hospital, Manchester, 1932; demonstrator in path. in Manchester Univ. and registrar in path. to Manchester Royal Inf., 1934; path. and res. Fellow in path., Christie Hospital and Holt Radium Inst., also path. to Duchess of York Hospital for Babies, Manchester, 1936. Clinical Pathologist to The Hospital for Sick Children, Great Ormond Street, London, 1938–58, retired. Pathologist in EMS, 1939; war service in RAMC, 1940–46; captured in Tobruk, POW 1942–43. Hon. Member, British Pædiatric Association. Hon. Fellow, Inst. of Child Health, 1983. Lord of the Manor of Barton-on-the-Heath, Warwickshire; CC Warwicks, 1965–77 (Vice-Chm., 1973–74, Chm., 1974–76). DL Warwicks, 1974. *Publications:* Chapters in Moncrieff's Nursing and Diseases of Sick Children and (in collaboration) Garrod, Batten and Thursfield's Diseases of Children; also papers on pathology and pædiatrics in medical journals. Editor, Archives of Disease in Childhood, 1951–63. *Recreation:* gardening. *Address:* Barton House, Moreton-in-Marsh, Glos. *T:* Barton-on-the-Heath 303. *Clubs:* Chelsea Arts, Saintsbury.

CATLING, Hector William, OBE 1980; MA, DPhil, FSA; Director of the British School at Athens since 1971; *b* 26 June 1924; *s* of late Arthur William Catling and Phyllis Norah Catling (*née* Vyvyan); *m* 1948, Elizabeth Anne (*née* Salter); two *s* one *d*. *Educ:* The Grammar Sch., Bristol; St John's Coll., Oxford. Casberd Exhbr, 1948, BA 1950, MA 1954, DPhil 1957. Served War, RNVR, 1942–46. At Univ.: undergrad. 1946–50, postgrad. 1950–54. Goldsmiths' Travelling Schol., 1951–53. Archaeological Survey Officer, Dept of Antiquities, Cyprus, 1955–59; Asst Keeper, Dept of Antiquities, Ashmolean Museum, Univ. of Oxford, 1959–64, Sen. Asst Keeper, 1964–71. Fellow of Linacre Coll., Oxford, 1967–71. Corresp. Mem., German Archaeological Inst., 1961; Hon. Mem., Greek Archaeological Soc., 1975. *Publications:* Cypriot Bronzework in the Mycenaean World, 1964; contribs to jls concerned with prehistoric and classical antiquity in Greek lands. *Recreation:* ornithology. *Address:* The British School at Athens, Odos Souedias 52, Athens 106 76, Greece; 381 Woodstock Road, Oxford.

CATLING, Sir Richard (Charles), Kt 1964; CMG 1956; OBE 1951; *b* 22 Aug. 1912; *y s* of late William Catling, Leiston, Suffolk; *m* 1951, Mary Joan Feyer (*née* Lewis) (*d* 1974). *Educ:* The Grammar School, Bungay, Suffolk. Palestine Police, 1935–48; Federation of Malaya Police, 1948–54; Commissioner of Police, Kenya, 1954–63; Inspector General of Police, Kenya, 1963–64. Colonial Police Medal, 1942; King's Police Medal, 1945. Officer Brother, OStJ, 1956. *Recreations:* fishing, sailing. *Address:* Hall Fen House, Irstead, Norfolk NR12 8XT. *Club:* East India, Devonshire, Sports and Public Schools.

CATO, Hon. Sir Arnott Samuel, KCMG 1983; Kt 1977; PC (Barbados) 1976; President of the Senate of Barbados, 1976–86; *b* St Vincent, 24 Sept. 1912. *Educ:* St Vincent Grammar Sch. (St Vincent Scholar, 1930); Edinburgh Univ. (MB, ChB). Returned to St Vincent; Asst Resident Surgeon, Colonial Hosp., 1936–37; Ho. Surg., Barbados Gen. Hosp., 1937–41; private practice from 1941; Vis. Surgeon, Barbados Gen. Hosp., later Queen Elizabeth Hosp., and Chm. Med. Staff Cttee 1965–70. Past Pres., Barbados Br. BMA. Chm., Barbados Public Service Commn, 1972–76; (Prime Minister's Nominee) Senate of Barbados, following Gen. Election of Sept. 1976; Actg Governor Gen. for periods in 1976, 1980, 1981, 1983, 1984, 1985 and 1986. Hon. LLD, Univ. of West Indies, 1978. *Address:* Government Hill, St Michael, Barbados.

CATO, Brian Hudson; Full-time Chairman of Industrial Tribunals, since 1975; *b* 6 June 1928; *s* of Thomas and Edith Willis Cato; *m* 1963, Barbara Edith Myles; one *s*. *Educ:* LEA elem. and grammar schs; Trinity Coll., Oxford; RAF Padgate. MA Oxon, LLB London. RAF, 1952–54. Called to Bar, Gray's Inn, 1952; in practice NE Circuit, 1954–75; a Recorder of the Crown Court, 1974–75. Special Lectr (part-time) in Law of Town and Country Planning, King's Coll., now Univ. of Newcastle, 1956–75; Hon. Examnr, Inst. of Landscape Architects, 1960–75. Pres., N of England Medico-legal Soc., 1973–75. Freeman of City of Newcastle upon Tyne by patrimony; Mem. Plumbers', Hostmen's, Goldsmiths' and Colliers' Companies; Founder Mem. Scriveners' Co. Freeman, City of London, 1985. Hon. ALI. *Recreations:* bibliomania, antiquarian studies, family life. *Address:* 46 Bemersyde Drive, Newcastle upon Tyne NE2 2HJ. *T:* Newcastle 2814226; The Cottage, Front Street, Embleton, Alnwick, Northumberland NE66 3UH. *T:* Embleton 334.

CATO, Rt. Hon. (Robert) Milton, PC 1981; Barrister; Leader of the Opposition, St Vincent and the Grenadines, since 1984 (Prime Minister, 1979–84); *b* 3 June 1915; *m* Lucy Claxton. *Educ:* St Vincent Grammar Sch. Called to the Bar, Middle Temple, 1948; in private practice. Served War of 1939–45, Canadian Army. Leader, St Vincent Labour Party; Premier of St Vincent, 1967–72, 1974–79; former Minister of Finance. Mem., Kingstown Town Bd, 1952–59 (Chm., 1952–53); former Mem., Public Service Commn. A Governor, Caribbean Reg. Develt Bank for St Vincent. Former Pres., St Vincent Cricket Assoc. *Address:* PO Box 138, Kingstown, St Vincent and the Grenadines. *Club:* Kingstown.

CATTANACH, Brig. Helen, CB 1976; RRC 1963; Matron-in-Chief (Army) and Director of Army Nursing Services, Queen Alexandra's Royal Army Nursing Corps, 1973–77; *b* 21 June 1920; *d* of late Francis Cattanach and Marjory Cattanach (*née* Grant). *Educ:* Elgin Academy; trained Woodend Hospital, Aberdeen. Joined QAIMNS (R) 1945; service in India, Java, United Kingdom, Singapore, Hong Kong and Germany, 1945–52; MELF, Gibraltar and UK, 1953–57; Staff Officer, MoD, 1958–61; Inspector of Recruiting, QARANC, 1961–62; Hong Kong, 1963–64; Matron: BMH Munster, 1968; Cambridge Military Hosp., Aldershot, 1969–71; Dir of Studies, QARANC, 1971–72. QHNS 1973–77. Col Comdt QARANC, 1978–81. CStJ 1976 (OStJ 1971). *Address:* 22 Southview Court, Hill View Road, Woking, Surrey.

CATTELL, George Harold Bernard; Group Managing Director, FMC, 1978–84; Chief Executive, NFU Holdings Ltd, since 1978; Director, Agricultural Credit Corporation, since 1980; *b* 23 March 1920; *s* of H. W. K. Cattell; *m* 1951, Agnes Jean Hardy; three *s* one *d. Educ:* Royal Grammar Sch., Colchester. Served Regular Army, 1939–58; psc 1954; despatches, Malaya, 1957; retired as Major, RA. Asst Director, London Engineering Employers' Assoc., 1958–60; Group Industrial Relations Officer, H. Stevenson & Sons, 1960–61; Director, Personnel and Manufacturing, Rootes Motors Ltd, 1961–68; Managing Director, Humber Ltd, Chm., Hills Precision Diecasting Ltd, Chm., Thrupp & Maberly Ltd, 1965–68; Dir, Manpower and Productivity Services, Dept of Employment and Productivity, 1968–70; Dir-Gen., NFU, 1970–78. Member Council: Industrial Soc. 1965–84; CBI, 1970–84. FRSA; FBIM. AMN Federation of Malaya, 1958. *Recreations:* tennis, fishing. *Address:* Little Cheveney, Yalding, Kent. *T:* Hunton 365. *Club:* Institute of Directors.

CATTERALL, Dr John Ashley, FIM, FInstP; Secretary, Science and Engineering Research Council, since 1983; *b* 26 May 1928; *s* of John William Catterall and Gladys Violet Catterall; *m* 1960, Jennifer Margaret Bradfield; two *s. Educ:* Imperial Coll. of Science and Technol., London (BSc, PhD, DIC). ARSM; FIM 1964; FInstP 1968; CEng 1978. National Physical Lab., 1952–74; Dept of Industry, 1974–81; Head, Energy Technology Div., and Dep. Chief Scientist, Dept of Energy, 1981–83. Inst. of Metals Rosenhain Medal for Physical Metallurgy, 1970. *Publications:* (with O. Kubaschewski) Thermochemical Data of Alloys, 1956; contrib. Philos. Mag., Jl Inst. of Physics, Jl Inst. of Metals. *Recreation:* sailing. *Address:* 65 Hamilton Avenue, Pyrford, Woking, Surrey. *T:* Byfleet 46707.

CATTERMOLE, Joan Eileen, (Mrs J. Cattermole); *see* Mitchell, Prof. J. E.

CATTERMOLE, Lancelot Harry Mosse, ROI 1938; painter and illustrator; *b* 19 July 1898; *s* of Sidney and Josephine Cattermole; *g s* of George Cattermole (1800–1868), painter in water-colours and oils and illustrator of works by Charles Dickens and Sir Walter Scott; *m* 1937, Lydia Alice Winifred Coles, BA; no *c. Educ:* Holmsdale House Sch., Worthing, Sussex; Odiham Grammar Sch., Hants. Senior Art Scholarship to Slade Faculty of Fine Art, University of London, and Central School of Arts and Crafts, London, 1923–26. Exhibitor RA, ROI, RBA, RP, etc, and Provincial Art Galleries; works acquired by National Army Mus., London, and Royal Naval Mus., Portsmouth. Signs work Lance Cattermole. *Recreations:* reading, bridge. *Address:* Horizon, 17 Palmers Way, High Salvington, Worthing, W Sussex. *T:* Worthing 60436.

CATTO, family name of **Baron Catto.**

CATTO, 2nd Baron, *cr* 1936, of Cairncatto; Bt *cr* 1921; **Stephen Gordon Catto;** Chairman: Morgan Grenfell Holdings Ltd, since 1980; Australian Mutual Provident Society (UK Branch), since 1972; Yule Catto & Co. plc, since 1971; Director: The General Electric Co. plc, since 1959; News International plc, since 1969; The News Corporation, since 1979 (Australia); Times Newspapers Holdings Ltd, since 1981, and other companies; *b* 14 Jan. 1923; *o s* of 1st Baron Catto and Gladys Forbes (*d* 1980), *d* of Stephen Gordon; *S* father 1959; *m* 1st, 1948, Josephine Innes (marr. diss. 1965), *er d* of G. H. Packer, Alexandria, Egypt; two *s* two *d*; 2nd, 1966, Margaret, *d* of J. S. Forrest, Dilston, Tasmania; one *s* one *d. Educ:* Eton; Cambridge Univ. Served with RAFVR, 1943–47. Dir, 1957, Chief Exec., 1973–74, and Chm., 1973–79, Morgan Grenfell & Co. Ltd. Member, Advisory Council, ECGD, 1959–65; part-time Mem., London Transport Bd, 1962–68; Mem., London Adv. Cttee, Hong Kong & Shanghai Banking Corp., 1966–80. Chm. Council, RAF Benevolent Fund, 1978–; Trustee and Chm., Exec. Cttee, Westminster Abbey Trust, 1973–. *Heir: s* Hon. Innes Gordon Catto, *b* 7 Aug. 1950. *Address:* Morgan Grenfell Holdings Ltd, 23 Great Winchester Street, EC2P 2AX; 41 William Mews, Lowndes Square, SW1X 9HQ. *Clubs:* Oriental; Melbourne (Australia).

CAUGHEY, Sir Thomas Harcourt Clarke, KBE 1972 (OBE 1966); JP; Managing Director, since 1962, Chairman, since 1975, Smith & Caughey Ltd; *b* Auckland, 4 July 1911; *s* of James Marsden Caughey; *m* 1939, Patricia Mary, *d* of Hon. Sir George Panton Finlay; one *s* two *d. Educ:* King's Coll., Auckland; Auckland Univ. Major, Fiji Military Forces (Pacific), 1942–44. Director: New Zealand Insurance Corp. (Dep. Chm., 1981–); New Zealand Guardian Trust Co. Member: Caughey Preston Trust Bd, 1950–79 (Chm., 1954–79); Eden Park Trustees; Auckland Hosps Bd, 1953–74 (Chm., 1959–74); Hosps Adv. Council, 1960–74; Vice-Pres., NZ Exec. Hosps Bds Assoc., 1960–74; Chairman: NZ MRC, 1966–71; Social Council of NZ, 1971–73; Pres., Auckland Med. Res. Foundn, 1978–84. CStJ. Mem., All Black Rugby Team, 1932–37. *Recreations:* gardening, swimming. *Address:* 7 Judges Bay Road, Auckland, NZ. *Club:* Northern (Auckland, NZ).

CAULCOTT, Thomas Holt; Chief Executive, Birmingham City Council, since 1982; *b* 7 June 1927; *s* of late L. W. Caulcott and Doris Caulcott; *m* 1954, C. Evelyn Lowden; one *d* (and one *s* decd). *Educ:* Solihull Sch.; Emmanuel Coll., Cambridge. Asst Principal, Central Land Bd and War Damage Commn, 1950–53; transferred to HM Treasury, 1953; Private Sec. to Economic Sec. to the Treasury, 1955; Principal, Treasury supply divs, 1956–60; Private Sec. to successive Chancellors of the Exchequer, Sept. 1961–Oct. 1964; Principal Private Sec. to First Sec. of State (DEA), 1964–65; Asst Sec., HM Treasury, 1965–66; Min. of Housing and Local Govt, 1967–69; Civil Service Dept, 1969–70; Under-Sec., Machinery of Govt Gp, 1970–73; Principal Finance Officer, Local Govt Finance Policy, DoE, 1973–76; Sec., AMA, 1976–82. Harkness Fellowship, Harvard and Brookings Instn, 1960–61; Vis. Fellow, Dept of Land Economy, Univ. of Cambridge, 1984–85; Hon. Fellow, Inst. of Local Govt Studies, Univ. of Birmingham, 1979. *Address:* 43 Lee Crescent, Birmingham B15 2BJ. *T:* 021–235 2000.

CAULFEILD, family name of **Viscount Charlemont.**

CAULFIELD, Hon. Sir Bernard, Kt 1968; **Hon. Mr Justice Caulfield;** Judge of the High Court of Justice, Queen's Bench Division, since 1968; Presiding Judge, Northern Circuit, 1976–80; *b* 24 April 1914; *y s* of late John Caulfield and late Catherine Quinn; *m* 1953, Sheila Mary, *o d* of Dr J. F. J. Herbert; three *s* one *d. Educ:* St Francis Xavier's Coll.; University of Liverpool. LLB 1938, LLM 1940, Hon. LLD 1980. Solicitor, 1940. Army Service, 1940–46; Home and MEF; Commnd, Dec. 1942, RAOC; released with Hon. rank of Major. Barrister-at-Law, Lincoln's Inn, 1947 (Bencher, 1968); joined Midland Circuit, 1949; QC 1961; Recorder of Coventry, 1963–68; Dep. Chairman QS, County of Lincoln (Parts of Lindsey), 1963–71; Leader, Midland Circuit, 1965–68; Member: General Council of Bar, 1965–68; Senate, Inns of Court, 1984–. Hon. Mem., Northern Circuit Bar Mess, 1979. *Address:* Royal Courts of Justice, WC2A 2LL.

CAULFIELD, Patrick; artist; *b* London, 29 Jan. 1936; *s* of Patrick and Annie Caulfield; *m* 1968, Pauline Jacobs; three *s. Educ:* Acton Central Secondary Modern Sch.; Chelsea Sch. of Art; RCA. Served RAF, 1953–56. Taught at Chelsea Sch. of Art, 1963–71. First exhibited, FBA Galls, 1961; group exhibitions include: Whitechapel, Tate, Hayward, Waddington and Tooth Galls, and ICA, in London; Walker Art Gall., Liverpool; and exhibns in Paris, Brussels, Milan, NY, São Paulo, Berlin, Lugano, Dortmund, Bielefeld and Helsinki. One-man exhibitions include: Robert Fraser Gall., London, 1965, 1967; Robert Elkon Gall., NY, 1966, 1968; Waddington Galls, 1969, 1971, 1973, 1975, 1979, 1981, and 1985; Tate Gall. (retrospective), 1981; also in Italy, France, Australia, Belgium, USA and Japan. Design for Party Game (ballet), Covent Garden, 1984. Work in public collections incl. Tate Gall.; V&A; Walker Art Gall., Liverpool; Whitworth Art Gall., and Manchester City Art Gall.; and museums and galls in GB, Australia, USA, W Germany and Japan. *Address:* c/o Waddington Galleries, 2 Cork Street, W1X 1PA; 6 Primrose Hill Studios, Fitzroy Road, NW1.

CAUSEY, Prof. Gilbert, FRCS; retired; Sir William Collins Professor of Anatomy, Royal College of Surgeons, Professor of Anatomy, University of London, and Conservator of Hunterian Museum, 1952–70; *b* 8 Oct. 1907; 2nd *s* of George and Ada Causey; *m* 1935, Elizabeth, *d* of late F. J. L. Hickinbotham, JP, and of Mrs Hickinbotham; two *s* three *d. Educ.* Wigan Grammar Sch.; University of Liverpool. MB, ChB (1st Hons.), 1930; MRCS, LRCP, 1930; FRCS 1933; DSc 1964; FDSRCS 1971. Gold Medallist in Anatomy, Surgery, Medicine, and Obstetrics and Gynæcology; Lyon Jones Scholar and various prizes. Member of Anatomical and Physiological Societies. Asst Surgeon, Walton Hospital, Liverpool, 1935; Lecturer in Anatomy, University College, London, 1948; Rockefeller Foundation Travelling Fellow, 1950. John Hunter Medal, 1964; Keith Medal, 1970. *Publications:* The Cell of Schwann, 1960; Electron Microscopy, 1962; contributions to various scientific texts and journals. *Recreation:* music. *Address:* Orchard Cottage, Bodinnick-by-Fowey, Cornwall. *T:* Polruan 433.

CAUSLEY, Charles Stanley, CBE 1986; poet; broadcaster; *b* Launceston, Cornwall, 24 Aug. 1917; *o s* of Charles Causley and Laura Bartlett. *Educ:* Launceston National Sch.; Horwell Grammar Sch.; Launceston Coll.; Peterborough Training Coll. Served on lower-deck in Royal Navy (Communications Branch), 1940–46. Literary Editor, 1953–56, of BBC's West Region radio magazines Apollo in the West and Signature. Awarded Travelling Scholarships by Society of Authors, 1954 and 1966. Mem., Arts Council Poetry Panel, 1962–66. Hon. Vis. Fellow in Poetry, Univ. of Exeter, 1973. FRSL 1958. Hon. DLitt Exeter, 1977; Hon. MA Open, 1982. Awarded Queen's Gold Medal for Poetry, 1967; Cholmondeley Award, 1971. *Publications:* Hands to Dance, 1951; Farewell, Aggie Weston, 1951; Survivor's Leave, 1953; Union Street, 1957; Peninsula (ed), 1957; Johnny Alleluia, 1961; Dawn and Dusk (ed), 1962; Penguin Modern Poets 3 (with George Barker and Martin Bell), 1962; Rising Early (ed), 1964; Modern Folk Ballads (ed), 1966; Underneath the Water, 1968; Figure of 8, 1969; Figgie Hobbin, 1971; The Tail of the Trinosaur, 1973; (ed) The Puffin Book of Magic Verse, 1974; Collected Poems 1951–1975, 1975; The Hill of the Fairy Calf, 1976; (ed) The Puffin Book of Salt-Sea Verse, 1978; Three Heads made of Gold, 1978; The Gift of a Lamb, 1978; The Animals' Carol, 1978; The Last King of Cornwall, 1978; (ed) Batsford Book of Stories in Verse for Children, 1979; (trans.) 25 Poems by Hamdija Demirovíc, 1980; The Ballad of Aucassin and Nicolette (verse play), 1981; (ed) The Sun, Dancing, 1982; Secret Destinations, 1984; 21 Poems, 1986; (trans.) King's Children, 1986; Early in the Morning, 1986; contrib. to many anthologies of verse in Great Britain and America. *Recreations:* the theatre; European travel; the re-discovery of his native town; playing the piano with expression. *Address:* 2 Cyprus Well, Launceston, Cornwall PL15 8BT. *T:* Launceston 2731.

CAUTE, (John) David, MA, DPhil; writer; *b* 16 Dec. 1936; *m* 1st, 1961, Catherine Shuckburgh (marr. diss. 1970); two *s*; 2nd, 1973, Martha Bates; two *d. Educ:* Edinburgh Academy; Wellington; Wadham Coll., Oxford. Scholar of St Antony's Coll., 1959. Spent a year in the Army in the Gold Coast, 1955–56, and a year at Harvard Univ. on a Henry Fellowship, 1960–61. Fellow of All Souls Coll., Oxford, 1959–65; Visiting Professor, New York Univ. and Columbia Univ., 1966–67; Reader in Social and Political Theory, Brunel Univ., 1967–70. Regents' Lectr, Univ. of Calif., 1974; Vis. Prof., Bristol Univ., 1985. Literary Editor, New Statesman, 1979–80. Co-Chm., Writers' Guild, 1981–82. *Plays:* Songs for an Autumn Rifle, staged by Oxford Theatre Group at Edinburgh, 1961; The Demonstration, Nottingham Playhouse, 1969; Fallout, BBC Radio, 1972; The Fourth World, Royal Court, 1973; Brecht and Company, BBC TV, 1979; The Zimbabwe Tapes, BBC Radio, 1983. *Publications:* At Fever Pitch (novel), 1959 (Authors' Club Award and John Llewelyn Rhys Prize, 1960); Comrade Jacob (novel), 1961; Communism and the French Intellectuals, 1914–1960, 1964; The Left in Europe Since 1789, 1966; The Decline of the West (novel), 1966; Essential Writings of Karl Marx (ed), 1967; Fanon, 1970; The Confrontation: a trilogy, 1971 (consisting of The Demonstration (play), 1970; The Occupation (novel), 1971; The Illusion, 1971); The Fellow-Travellers, 1973; Collisions, 1974; Cuba, Yes?, 1974; The Great Fear: the anti-communist campaign under Truman and Eisenhower, 1978; Under the Skin: the Death of White Rhodesia, 1983; The K-Factor (novel), 1983; The Espionage of the Saints, 1986; News from Nowhere (novel), 1986; *as John Salisbury; novels:* The Baby-Sitters, 1978; Moscow Gold, 1980. *Address:* 41 Westcroft Square, W6 0TA.

CAUTHERY, Harold William, CB 1969; *b* 5 May 1914; *s* of Joseph Cauthery, Manchester; *m* 1938, Dorothy Constance, *d* of George E. Sawyer, Sutton Coldfield; one *s* one *d* (and one *d* decd). *Educ:* Bishop Vesey's Grammar Sch., Sutton Coldfield; Christ's College, Cambridge. Asst Inspector of Taxes, Inland Revenue, 1936; Asst Principal, Ministry of Health, 1937; Instructor-Lieut, RN, 1942–45; Principal, Ministry of Health, 1944; Asst Secretary: Ministry of Health, 1950; Ministry of Housing and Local Government, 1951; Under-Sec., Min. of Transport, 1960–66; Dep. Sec., Min. of Land and Natural Resources, 1966; Dir and Sec. and Mem., Land Commn, 1967–71; Dep. Under-Sec. of State (Air), MoD, 1971–72; Sec., Local Govt Staff Commn, 1972–74. *Publication:* Parish Councillor's Guide, 10th Edition, 1958. *Recreations:* music, gardening. *Address:* Eastcote, Petworth Road, Haslemere, Surrey. *T:* Haslemere 51448. *Club:* United Oxford & Cambridge University.

CAVALIERO, Roderick; Deputy Director General, British Council, since 1981 (Assistant Director General, 1977–81); *b* 21 March 1928; *s* of Eric Cavaliero and Valerie (*née* Logan); *m* 1957, Mary McDonnell; one *s* four *d. Educ:* Tonbridge School; Hertford Coll., Oxford. Teaching in Britain, 1950–52; teaching in Malta, 1952–58; British Council Officer, 1958– (service in India, Brazil, Italy). Chm., Educnl and Trng Export Cttee, 1979–; Dir, Open Univ. Educnl Enterprises, 1980–. Mem., British Section, Franco-British Council, 1981–. *Publications:* Olympia and the Angel, 1958; The Last of the Crusaders, 1960. *Address:* British Council, 10 Spring Gardens, SW1A 2BN.

CAVALLERA, Rt. Rev. Charles; *b* Centallo, Cuneo, Italy, 1909. *Educ:* International Missionary College of the Consolata of Turin; Pontifical Univ. of Propaganda Fide of Rome (degree in Missionology) Sec. to Delegate Apostolic of British Africa, 1936–40; Vice-Rector, then Rector, of Urban Coll. of Propaganda Fide of Rome, 1941–47; formerly Titular Bishop of Sufes; Vicar-Apostolic of Nyeri (Kenya), 1947–53; Bishop of Nyeri, 1953–64; Bishop of Marsabit, 1964–81. *Address:* Missioni Consolata, Viale Mura Aurelie 12, 00165 Rome, Italy.

CAVAN, 12th Earl of, *cr* 1647; **Michael Edward Oliver Lambart,** TD; DL; Baron Cavan, 1618; Baron Lambart, 1618; Viscount Kilcoursie, 1647; Vice Lord-Lieutenant, Salop, since 1975; *b* 29 Oct. 1911; *o s* of 11th Earl of Cavan and Audrey Kathleen (*d* 1942), *o d* of late A. B. Loder; *S* father 1950; *m* 1947, Essex Lucy, *o d* of Henry Arthur Cholmondeley, Shotton Hall, Hadnall, Shropshire; one *d* (and two *d* decd). *Educ:* Radley College. Served War of 1939–45, Shropshire Yeomanry (despatches). Lt-Col comdg Shropshire Yeomanry, 1955–58. DL Salop, 1959. *Heir: kinsman* Roger Cavan, *b* 1 Sept. 1944. *Address:* The Glebe House, Stockton, Shifnal, Shropshire TF11 9EF. *T:* Norton 236.

CAVANAGH, John Bryan; Dress Designer; Chairman and Managing Director, John Cavanagh Ltd, retired 1974; *b* 28 Sept. 1914; *s* of Cyril Cavanagh and Anne (*née* Murphy). *Educ:* St Paul's School. Trained with Captain Edward Molyneux in London and Paris, 1932–40. Joined Intelligence Corps, 1940, Captain (GS, Camouflage), 1944. On demobilisation, 1946, travelled throughout USA studying fashion promotion. Personal Assistant to Pierre Balmain, Paris, 1947–51; opened own business, 1952; opened John Cavanagh Boutique, 1959. Elected to Incorporated Society of London Fashion Designers, 1952 (Vice-Chm., 1956–59). Took own complete Collection to Paris, 1953; designed clothes for late Princess Marina and wedding dresses for the Duchess of Kent and Princess Alexandra. Gold Medal, Munich, 1954. *Recreations:* the theatre, swimming, travelling. *Address:* 10 Birchlands Avenue, SW12.

CAVE, Alexander James Edward, MD, DSc, FRCS, FLS; Emeritus Professor of Anatomy, University of London; *b* Manchester, 13 Sept. 1900; *e s* of late John Cave and Teresa Anne d'Hooghe; *m* 1st, 1926, Dorothy M. Dimbleby (*d* 1961); one *d*; 2nd, 1970, Catherine Elizabeth FitzGerald. *Educ:* Manchester High Sch.; Victoria University of Manchester. MB, ChB (distinction Preventive Medicine) 1923; MD (commendation) 1937; DSc, 1944; FRCS, 1959; DSc London, 1967. Senior Demonstrator (later Lecturer) in Anatomy, University of Leeds, 1924–34; Senior Demonstrator of Anatomy and Curator of Anatomical Museum, University College, London, 1934–35; Asst Conservator of Museum (1935–46), Arnott Demonstrator (1936–46), Arris and Gale Lectr, 1932, 1941, Professor of Human and Comparative Anatomy (1941–46), and Wood Jones Medalist 1978, Royal College of Surgeons of England; Prof. of Anatomy, St Bartholomew's Hospital Medical Coll., University of London, 1946–67, now Member Board Governors. Hunterian Trustee; Stopford Lecturer, 1967; Morrison Watson Research Fellow, 1961–72. Late Examiner in Anatomy, University of London, Royal University of Malta, Universities of Cambridge and Ireland, Primary FRCS and English Conjoint Board; Fellow (formerly Council Mem. and Pres.), Linnean Society; Fellow and Hon. Res. Associate (late Vice-Pres. and Council Mem.) and Silver Medallist Zoological Society; Life-Member (late Council Mem., Hon. Secretary and Recorder, Vice-Pres.) Anatomical Soc.; Hon. Associate BM (Nat. Hist.); Mem., American Assoc. of Physical Anthropologists; *Publications:* various papers on human and comparative anatomy, physical anthropology and medical history. *Address:* 18 Orchard Avenue, Finchley, N3. *T:* 01–346 3340. *Club:* Athenæum.

CAVE, Sir Charles (Edward Coleridge), 4th Bt, *cr* 1896; JP; DL; *b* 28 Feb. 1927; *o s* of Sir Edward Charles Cave, 3rd Bt, and Betty (*d* 1979), *o d* of late Rennell Coleridge, Salston, Ottery St Mary; *S* father 1946; *m* 1957, Mary Elizabeth, *yr d* of late John Francis Gore, CVO, TD; four *s*. *Educ:* Eton. Lieut The Devonshire Regt, 1946–48. CC Devon, 1955–64; High Sheriff of Devonshire, 1969. JP Devon 1972, DL Devon 1977. FRICS. *Heir: s* John Charles Cave [*b* 8 Sept. 1958; *m* 1984, Carey D., *er d* of John Lloyd, Langport, Somerset]. *Address:* Sidbury Manor, Sidmouth, Devon. *T:* Sidbury 207.

CAVE, Sir (Charles) Philip H.; *see* Haddon-Cave.

CAVE, John Arthur, FIB; Chairman: Midland Bank Finance Corporation Ltd, 1975–79; Midland Montagu Leasing Ltd, 1975–79; Forward Trust Ltd, 1975–79; Director, Midland Bank Ltd, 1974–79; *b* 30 Jan. 1915; *s* of Ernest Cave and Eva Mary Cave; *m* 1937, Peggy Pauline, *y d* of Frederick Charles Matthews Browne; two *s* two *d*. *Educ:* Loughborough Grammar Sch. FIB 1962. Served War, Royal Tank Regt, 1940–46. Entered Midland Bank, Eye, Suffolk, 1933; Manager, Threadneedle Street Office, 1962–64; Jt Gen. Man., 1965–72; Asst Chief Gen. Man., 1972–74; Dep. Chief Gen. Man., 1974–75. Dir, Midland Bank Trust Co. Ltd, 1972–76. Mem. Council, Inst. of Bankers, 1967–75 (Dep. Chm., 1973–75). Hon. Captain and Founder, Midland Bank Sailing Club (Cdre, 1967–75). *Recreation:* sailing. *Address:* Dolphin House, Centre Cliff, Southwold, Suffolk. *T:* Southwold 722232. *Club:* Royal Norfolk and Suffolk Yacht (Lowestoft).

CAVE, Sir Richard (Guy), Kt 1976; MC 1944; Chairman, Vickers, since 1984; Director: Tate & Lyle Ltd, since 1976; Equity & Law Life Assurance Society, 1972–79 and since 1983; *b* 16 March 1920; *s* of William Thomas Cave and Gwendoline Mary Nicholls; *m* 1957, Dorothy Gillian Fry; two *s* two *d*. *Educ:* Tonbridge; Gonville and Caius Coll., Cambridge. Joined Smiths Industries Ltd, 1946; Man. Dir, Motor Accessory Div., 1963; Chief Exec. and Man. Dir, 1968–73; Chm., 1973–76; Chm., Thorn Electrical Industries Ltd, 1976–79, THORN EMI plc, 1979–84. Dep. Chm., BRB, 1983–85; Dir, Thames Television Ltd, 1981–84. Chm., Industrial Soc., 1979–83. *Recreation:* sailing. *Address:* Stanny, Priors Hill Road, Aldeburgh, Suffolk IP15 5EP. *T:* Aldeburgh 2774.

CAVE, Sir Richard (Philip), KCVO 1977 (MVO 1969); CB 1975; DL; Fourth Clerk at the Table (Judicial), House of Lords, 1965–77 and Principal Clerk, Judicial Department, House of Lords, 1959–77; Taxing Officer of Judicial Costs, House of Lords, 1957–77; Crown Examiner in Peerage Cases 1953–77; Secretary, Association of Lieutenants of Counties and Custodes Rotulorum, 1946–59, and 1964–77; Founder and President, Multiple Sclerosis Society of Great Britain and Northern Ireland (Chairman, 1953–76); a Vice-President, International Federation of Multiple Sclerosis Societies, 1967, Emeritus since 1981; *b* 26 April 1912; 4th *s* of late Charles John Philip Cave and late Wilhelmina Mary Henrietta (*née* Kerr); *m* 1936, Margaret Mary (*d* 1981), *e d* of Francis Westby Perceval; one *s*. *Educ:* Ampleforth Coll.; Trinity Coll., Cambridge (MA); Herts Institute of Agriculture; College of Estate Management. A Gold Staff Officer, Coronation of HM King George VI, 1937. Agent for 6th Earl of Craven's Hamstead Marshall Estate, 1938–39. Royal Wilts Yeomanry (L. Corp.), 1939–40; The Rifle Bde (Captain; Officer i/c Cols Comdt's Office, KRRC and Rifle Bde), 1940–45. Territorial Efficiency Medal, 1946. Vice-Chm., Society for Relief of Distress, 1972; a Governor, Queen Elizabeth's Foundn for the Disabled, 1970. A Confrater of Ampleforth Abbey, 1971. DL Greater London, 1973. Gold Medal, Royal English Forestry Society, 1939; Silver Medal, RASE, 1939. KSG 1966; KCSG 1972; Kt of Honour and Devotion, SMO Malta, 1972; Kt of Justice, Sacred Military Order of Constantine of St George, 1972. *Publications:* Elementary Map Reading, 1941; articles in Atkin's Encyclopedia of Court Forms in Civil Proceedings, 1968 and 1973; Halsbury's Laws of England, 1974. *Recreations:* hill-walking, photography, collecting map postcards. *Address:* Watergate, 34 Ham Common, Richmond, Surrey TW10 7JG. *T:* 01–940 8014. *Clubs:* Royal Commonwealth Society; University Pitt (Cambridge).

CAVE, Dr Terence Christopher; Fellow and Tutor in French, St John's College, Oxford, since 1972; *b* 1 Dec. 1938; *s* of Alfred Cyril Cave and Sylvia Norah (*née* Norman); *m* 1965, Helen Elizabeth Robb; one *s* one *d*. *Educ:* Winchester Coll.; Gonville and Caius Coll., Cambridge (MA; PhD). University of St Andrews: Assistant, 1962–63; Lectr, 1963–65; University of Warwick: Lectr, 1965–70; Sen. Lectr, 1970–72. Visiting Professor: Cornell Univ., 1967–68; Univ. of California, Santa Barbara, 1976; Univ. of Virginia, Charlottesville, 1979; Visiting Fellow: All Souls Coll., Oxford, 1971; Princeton Univ., 1984. *Publications:* Devotional Poetry in France, 1969; Ronsard the Poet, 1973; The Cornucopian Text: problems of writing in the French Renaissance, 1979; articles and essays in learned jls, collective vols, etc. *Recreation:* music. *Address:* St John's College, Oxford OX1 3JP. *T:* Oxford 247671.

CAVE-BROWNE-CAVE, Sir Robert, 16th Bt, *cr* 1641; President of Seaboard Chemicals Ltd; *b* 8 June 1929; *s* of 15th Bt, and Dorothea Plewman, *d* of Robert Greene Dwen, Chicago, Ill; *S* father 1945; *m* 1st, 1954, Lois Shirley, (marr. diss. 1975), *d* of John Chalmers Huggard, Winnipeg, Manitoba; one *s* one *d*; 2nd, 1977, Joan Shirley, *d* of Dr Kenneth Ashe Peacock, West Vancouver, BC. *Educ:* University of BC (BA 1951). *Heir: s* John Robert Charles Cave-Browne-Cave, *b* 22 June 1957. *Address:* 6562 Laurel, Vancouver, BC, Canada.

CAVELL, Rt. Rev. John Kingsmill; Bishop Suffragan of Southampton, 1972–84; Bishop to HM Prisons and Borstals, 1975–85; *b* 4 Nov. 1916; *o s* of late William H. G. Cavell and Edith May (*née* Warner), Deal, Kent; *m* 1942, Mary Grossett (*née* Penman), Devizes, Wilts; one *d*. *Educ:* Sir Roger Manwood's Sch., Sandwich; Queens' Coll., Cambridge; MA; Wycliffe Hall, Oxford. Ryle Reading Prize. Ordained May 1940; Curate: Christ Church, Folkestone, 1940; Addington Parish Church, Croydon, 1940–44; CMS Area Secretary, dio. Oxford and Peterborough, and CMS Training Officer, 1944–52; Vicar: Christ Church, Cheltenham, 1952–62; St Andrew's, Plymouth, 1962–72; Rural Dean of Plymouth, 1967–72; Prebendary of Exeter Cathedral, 1967–72. Hon. Canon, Winchester Cathedral, 1972–84. Proctor in Convocation; Member of General Synod (Mem., Bd for Social Responsibility, 1982–84); Surrogate. Chm., Home Cttee, CMS London; Chm., Sarum Dio. Readers' Bd, 1984–. Chaplain, Greenbank and Freedom Fields Hosps, Plymouth; Member: Plymouth City Educn Cttee, 1967–72; City Youth Cttee; Plymouth Exec. Council NHS, 1968–72; Chm., Hants Assoc. for the Deaf, 1972–84; Pres., Hants Genealogical Soc., 1979–84. Fellow, Pilgrim Soc., Massachusetts, 1974–84. Patron, Southampton RNLI Bd, 1976–84. Governor: Cheltenham Colls of Educn; King Alfred's College of Educn, 1973–84; Croft House Sch., Shillingstone, 1986–; Chairman: St Mary's Coll. Building Cttee, 1957–62; Talbot Heath Sch., Bournemouth, 1975–84; Queensmount Sch., Bournemouth, 1980–84. *Recreations:* historical research, genealogy, philately, cricket. *Address:* Strathmore, 5 Constable Way, West Harnham, Salisbury, Wilts SP2 8LN. *T:* Salisbury 334782.

CAVENAGH, Prof. Winifred Elizabeth, OBE 1977; JP; PhD, BScEcon; Professor of Social Administration and Criminology, University of Birmingham, 1972–76, now Emeritus; Barrister-at-Law; *d* of Arthur Speakman and Ethel Speakman (*née* Butterworth); *m* 1938, Hugh Cavenagh; one step *s*. *Educ:* London Sch. of Economics, Univ. of London. BSc Econ (London); PhD (Birm.). Called to the Bar, Gray's Inn, 1964. With Lewis's Ltd, 1931–38; Min. of Labour, 1941–45. Univ. of Birmingham, 1946–. Birmingham: City Educn Cttee (co-opted expert), 1946–66; City Magistrate, 1949– (Dep. Chm., 1970–78); Police Authority, 1970–78. Governor, Birmingham United Teaching Hosps (Ministerial appt, 1958–64); W Midlands Economic Planning Council, 1967–71; Indep. Mem. of Wages Councils; Home Office Standing Advisory Cttee on Probation, 1958–67; Lord Chancellor's Standing Adv. Cttee: on Legal Aid, 1960–71; on Training of Magistrates, 1965–73. Nat. Chm., Assoc. of Social Workers, 1955–57; Council, Magistrates Assoc. (co-opted expert), 1965–78; BBC Gen. Adv. Council, 1977–80; Vice-Pres., Internat. Assoc. of Juvenile and Family Courts, 1978–; Chm., Industrial Tribunal, 1974–77. Visiting Prof., Univ of Ghana, 1971; Eleanor Rathbone Meml Lectr, 1976; Moir Cullis Lectr Fellowship, USA, 1977, Canada, 1980. *Publications:* Four Decades of Students in Social Work, 1953; The Child and the Court, 1959; Juvenile Courts, the Child and the Law, 1967; contrib. articles to: Public Administration, Brit. Jl Criminology, Justice of the Peace, Social Work To-day, etc. *Recreations:* theatre, music, films. *Address:* 25 High Point, Richmond Hill Road, Edgbaston, Birmingham B15 3RU. *T:* 021–454 0109. *Club:* University Women's.

CAVENAGH-MAINWARING, Captain Maurice Kildare, DSO 1940; Royal Navy; joined Simpson (Piccadilly) Ltd, 1961; *b* 13 April 1908; *yr s* of Major James Gordon Cavenagh-Mainwaring, Whitmore Hall, Whitmore, Staffordshire; *m* Iris Mary, *d* of late Colonel Charles Denaro, OBE; one *s*. *Educ:* RN College, Dartmouth. Joint Services Staff College, 1951–52; HMS St Angelo and Flag Captain to Flag Officer, Malta, 1952–54; President, Second Admiralty Interview Board, 1955–56; Naval Attaché, Paris, 1957–60. ADC to the Queen, 1960. Retired from RN, 1960. Cross of Merit Sovereign Order, Knights of Malta, 1955; Comdr Légion d'Honneur, 1960. *Address:* 47 Cadogan Gardens, SW3. *T:* 01–584 7870; Apollo Court, St Julian's, Malta. *Club:* Naval and Military.

CAVENDISH, family name of **Baron Chesham,** of **Duke of Devonshire,** and of **Baron Waterpark.**

CAVENDISH, Maj.-Gen. Peter Boucher, CB 1981; OBE 1969; retired; Chairman, Military Agency for Standardisation and Director, Armaments Standardisation and Interoperability Division, International Military Staff, HQ NATO, 1978–81; *b* 26 Aug. 1925; *s* of late Brig. R. V. C. Cavendish, OBE, MC (killed in action, 1943) and Helen Cavendish (*née* Boucher); *m* 1952, Marion Loudon (*née* Constantine); three *s*. *Educ:* Abberley Hall, Worcester; Winchester Coll.; New Coll., Oxford. Enlisted 1943; commnd The Royal Dragoons, 1945; transf. 3rd The King's Own Hussars, 1946; Staff Coll., Camberley, 1955; served Palestine, BAOR, Canada and N Africa to 1966; CO 14th/20th King's Hussars, 1966–69; HQ 1st British Corps, 1969–71; Comdt RAC Centre, 1971–74; Canadian Defence Coll., 1975; Sec. to Mil. Cttee and Internat. Mil. Staff, HQ NATO, 1975–78. Colonel, 14th/20th King's Hussars, 1976–81; Hon. Col, The Queen's Own Mercian Yeomanry, TAVR, 1982–; Col Comdt, Yeomanry RAC TA, 1986–. Mem., Peak Park Jt Planning Bd, 1982–. FBIM 1979. High Sheriff, Derbyshire, 1986–87. *Recreations:* shooting, country pursuits, DIY. *Address:* The Rock Cottage, Middleton-by-Youlgrave, Bakewell, Derbys DE4 1LS. *T:* Youlgrave 225.

CAVENDISH-BENTINCK, family name of **Duke of Portland.**

CAWDOR, 6th Earl *cr* 1827; **Hugh John Vaughan Campbell,** FSA; FRICS; Baron Cawdor, 1796; Viscount Emlyn, 1827; *b* 6 Sept. 1932; *er s* of 5th Earl Cawdor, TD, FSA, and Wilma Mairi (*d* 1982), *e d* of late Vincent C. Vickers; *S* father, 1970; *m* 1st, 1957, Cathryn (marr. diss. 1979), 2nd *d* of Maj.-Gen. Sir Robert Hinde, KBE, CB, DSO; two *s* three *d*; 2nd, 1979, Countess Angelika Ilona Lazansky von Bukowa. *Educ:* Eton; Magdalen Coll., Oxford; Royal Agricultural Coll., Cirencester. High Sheriff of Carmarthenshire, 1964. *Heir: s* Viscount Emlyn, *qv*. *Address:* Cawdor Castle, Nairn. *Clubs:* Pratt's, White's.

CAWLEY, family name of **Baron Cawley.**

CAWLEY, 3rd Baron, *cr* 1918; **Frederick Lee Cawley,** 3rd Bt, *cr* 1906; *b* 27 July 1913; *s* of 2nd Baron and Vivienne (*d* 1978), *d* of Harold Lee, Broughton Park, Manchester; *S* father 1954; *m* 1944, Rosemary Joan, *y d* of late R. E. Marsden; six *s* one *d*. *Educ:* Eton; New Coll., Oxford. BA Nat. Science (Zoology), 1935, MA 1942. Called to the Bar, Lincoln's Inn, 1938; practised 1946–73; farmer. Served War of 1939–45, Capt. RA Leicestershire Yeomanry (wounded). Mem. Woking UDC, 1949–57. Dep.-Chm. of Cttees, House of Lords, 1958–67; Mem., Jt Parly Cttees: Consolidation Bills, 1956–73; Delegated Legislation, 1972–73; Ecclesiastical, 1974. *Recreations:* gardening, shooting. *Heir: s* Hon. John Francis Cawley [*b* 28 Sept. 1946; *m* 1979, Regina Sarabia, *e d* of Marqués de Hazas, Madrid; two *s* one *d*]. *Address:* Bircher Hall, Leominster, Herefordshire HR6 0AX. *T:* Yarpole 218. *Club:* Farmers'.

CAWLEY, Sir Charles (Mills), Kt 1965; CBE; Chief Scientist, Ministry of Power, 1959–67; a Civil Service Commissioner, 1967–69; *b* 17 May 1907; *s* of John and Emily Cawley, Gillingham, Kent; *m* 1934, Florence Mary Ellaline, *d* of James Shepherd, York; one *d*. *Educ:* Sir Joseph Williamson's Mathematical Sch., Rochester; Imperial Coll. of Science and Technology (Royal College of Sci.). ARCS, BSc (First Cl. Hons in Chem.), DIC; MSc; PhD; FRSC; DSc(London); SFInstF; FRSA; Fellow, Imperial Coll. of Science and Technology. Fuel Research Station, DSIR, 1929–53. Imperial Defence Coll., 1949. A Dir, Headquarters, DSIR, 1953–59. Chm., Admiralty Fuels and Lubricants Advisory Cttee, 1957–64. Melchett Medal, Inst. of Fuel, 1968. *Publications:* Papers in various scientific and technical journals. *Address:* 8 Glen Gardens, Ferring-by-Sea, Worthing, West Sussex BN12 5HG.

CAWLEY, Prof. Robert Hugh, PhD; FRCP, FRCPsych; Professor of Psychological Medicine, King's School of Medicine and Dentistry (formerly King's College Hospital Medical School), and Institute of Psychiatry, since 1975; Consultant Psychiatrist: King's College Hospital, since 1975; Bethlem Royal and Maudsley Hospitals, since 1967; *b* 16 Aug. 1924; *yr s* of Robert Ernest Cawley and Alice Maud (*née* Taylor); *m* 1985, Elizabeth Ann, *d* of Eugene Malachy Doris and Mary Doris (*née* Crummie). *Educ:* Solihull Sch.; Univ. of Birmingham (BSc Hons Zool., PhD, MB, ChB); Univ. of London (DPM). FRCP 1975; FRCPsych 1971. Univ. of Birmingham: Res. Scholar, 1947; Res. Fellow, 1949; Halley Stewart Res. Fellow, 1954; House Phys. and Surg., Queen Elizabeth Hosp., Birmingham, 1956–57; Registrar, then Sen. Registrar, Bethlem Royal and Maudsley Hosps, 1957–60; Clin. Lectr, Inst. of Psych., 1960–62; Sen. Lectr and First Asst in Psych., Univ. of Birmingham, and Hon. Consultant, United Birm. Hosps and Birm. RHB, 1962–67; Phys., Bethlem Royal and Maudsley Hosps, 1967–75. Mem., MRC, 1979–83; Chm., Neurosciences Bd, 1979–81. Chief Examr, Royal Coll. of Psychiatrists, 1981–. *Publications:* contribns on biological, medical and psychiatric subjects in scientific books and jls. *Address:* 18 Snowbury Road, SW6 2NR. *Club:* Athenæum.

CAWS, Richard Byron, CBE 1984; Partner, Debenham Tewson & Chinnocks, Chartered Surveyors, London, since 1961; *b* 9 March 1927; *s* of Maxwell and Edith S. Caws; *m* 1948, Fiona Muriel Ruth Elton Darling; one *s* two *d* (and one *s* decd). Partner, Nightingale Page & Bennett, Chartered Surveyors, Kingston upon Thames, 1944–60. Crown Estate Comr, 1971–. Member: Commn for the New Towns, 1976– (Chm., Property Cttee, 1978–); Dobry Cttee on Review of the Dev. Control System, 1973–75; DoE Adv. Gp on Commercial Property Dev., 1973–77; DoE Property Adv. Gp, 1978–. Gov., Royal Agricl Coll., 1985. Master, Worshipful Co. of Chartered Surveyors, 1982–83. FRICS (Chm., Jun. Orgn, RICS, 1959–60). *Recreations:* sailing, travel. *Address:* 36 Mount Park Road, Ealing, W5 2RS. *Clubs:* Royal Thames Yacht, Little Ship.

CAWSON, Prof. Roderick Anthony, MD; FDS, RCS and RCPS Glasgow; FRCPath; Professor (Hon. Consultant) and Head of Department of Oral Medicine and Pathology, Guy's Hospital Medical School, since 1966; *b* 23 April 1921; *s* of Capt. Leopold Donald Cawson and Ivy Clunies-Ross; *m* 1949, Diana Hall, SRN; no *c*. *Educ:* King's College Sch. Wimbledon; King's College Hosp. Med. Sch. MD (London); MB, BS, BDS (Hons) (London); FDS, RCS; FDS, RCPS Glasgow; MRCPath; LMSSA. Served RAF, 1944–48; Nuffield Foundn Fellow, 1953–55; Dept of Pathology, King's Coll. Hosp., Sen. Lectr in Oral Pathology, King's Coll. Hosp. Med. Sch., 1955–62; Sen. Lectr in Oral Pathology, Guy's Hosp. Med. Sch., 1962–66. Examinerships: Pathology (BDS) London, 1965–69; Univ. of Wales, 1969–71; Dental Surgery (BDS), Glasgow, 1966–70; BChD Leeds, 1966–70; Newcastle, 1967–71; FDS, RCPS Glasgow, 1967–; BDS Lagos, 1975–; RCPath, 1984–. Chairman: Dental Formulary Sub-cttee (BMA); Dental and Surgical Materials Cttee, Medicines Division, 1976–80; recently First Chm, Univ. Teachers' Gp (BDA). *Publications:* Essentials of Dental Surgery and Pathology 1962, 4th edn, 1984; Medicine for Dental Students (with R. H. Cutforth), 1960; (with R. G. Spector) Clinical Pharmacology in Dentistry, 1975, 3rd edn, 1982; Aids to Oral Pathology and Diagnosis, 1981; (with C. Scully) Medical Problems in Dentistry, 1982; (with A. W. McCracken and P. B. Marcus) Pathologic Mechanisms and Human Disease, 1982; (with A. W. McCracken) Clinical and Oral Microbiology, 1982; numerous papers, etc, in med. and dental jls. *Recreations:* reading, music, gardening (reluctantly). *Address:* 40 Court Lane, Dulwich, SE21 7DR. *T:* 01–693 5781.

CAWTHRA, Rear-Adm. Arthur James, CB 1966; Admiral Superintendent, HM Dockyard, Devonport, 1964–66; *b* 30 Sept. 1911; *s* of James Herbert Cawthra, MIEE, and Margaret Anne Cawthra; *m* 1959, Adrien Eleanor Lakeman Tivy, *d* of Cecil B. Tivy, MCh, Plymouth; one *s* (and one *s* decd). *Educ:* abroad. Joined Royal Navy, 1930; Imperial Defence Course, 1956; HMS Fisgard, 1958–59; Dir Underwater Weapons, Admiralty, 1960–63. Capt. 1955; Rear-Adm. 1964. *Address:* Lower Island, Blackawton, Totnes, Devon.

CAYFORD, Dame Florence Evelyn, DBE 1965; JP; Mayor, London Borough of Camden, 1969; *b* 14 June 1897; *d* of George William and Mary S. A. Bunch; *m* 1923, John Cayford; two *s*. *Educ:* Carlton Road Sch.; St Pancras County Secondary Sch., Paddington Technical Institute. Alderman, LCC, 1946–52; Member: LCC for Shoreditch and Finsbury, 1952–64; GLC (for Islington) and ILEA, 1964–67. Chairman: Hospital and Medical Services Cttee LCC, 1948; (Health Cttee). Division 7, 1948–49, Division 2 in 1949; Health Cttee, 1953–60; Welfare Cttee, 1965, of LCC; Metropolitan Water Bd, 1966–67 (Vice-Chm., 1965–66). Mem. Hampstead Borough Council, 1937–65 (Leader of Labour Group, 1945–58), Councillor for Kilburn until 1945, Alderman, 1945–65; Chm., LCC, 1960–61; Chairman: (Hampstead), Maternity and Child Welfare Cttee, 1941–45, Juvenile Court Panel, 1950–62; Dep. Mayoress, Camden Borough Council, 1967–68. Probation Cttee, 1959–; Leavesden Hosp. Management Cttee, 1948–63; Harben Secondary Sch., 1946–61. Member: Co-operative Political Party (ex-Chm. and Sec.); Co-operative Soc.; Labour Party; National Institute for Social Work Training, 1962–65; Min. of Health Council for Training of Health Visitors, 1962–65; Min. of Health Council for Training in Social Work, 1962–65. Chm., YWCA Helen Graham Hse, 1972–. JP, Inner London, 1941–. Freeman, London Borough of Camden (formerly Borough of Hampstead), 1961. Noble Order, Crown of Thailand, 3rd Class, 1964. *Address:* 26 Hemstal Road, Hampstead, NW6. *T:* 01–624 6181.

CAYLEY, Sir Digby (William David), 11th Bt *cr* 1661; MA Cantab; dealer in fine period furniture; Partner, Lensfield Antiques, Cambridge, since 1985; *b* 3 June 1944; *s* of Lieut-Comdr W. A. S. Cayley, RN (*d* 1964) (*g g s* of 7th Bt), and of Natalie M. Cayley, BA; *S* kinsman, 1967; *m* 1969, Christine Mary Gaunt, BA, *o d* of late D. F. Gaunt and of Mrs A. T. Gaunt, Clitheroe, Lancs; two *d*. *Educ:* Malvern Coll.; Downing Coll., Cambridge. Asst Classics Master, Portsmouth Grammar Sch., 1968–73; Stonyhurst Coll., 1973–81; Manager, C. P. Stockbridge Ltd, Cambs, 1982–83. *Recreations:* .22 rifle shooting, bridge. *Heir: cousin* George Paul Cayley [*b* 23 May 1940; *m* 1967, Shirley Southwell, *d* of Frank Woodward Petford; two *s*]. *Address:* 12 Lensfield Road, Cambridge.

CAYLEY, Henry Douglas, OBE 1946; *b* 20 Jan. 1904; *s* of late Cyril Henry Cayley, MD; *m* 1940, Nora Innes Paton, *d* of Nigel F. Paton; one *s* two *d*. *Educ:* Epsom Coll. Joined National Bank of India Ltd, London, 1922; Eastern Staff, 1926; Dep. Exchange Controller, Reserve Bank of India, 1939–48; rejoined National Bank of India, 1948; appointed to London Head Office, 1952; Asst Gen. Manager 1957, Dep. Gen. Manager 1960, Chief Gen. Manager 1964–69, Director 1966–72, National & Grindlays Bank Ltd. *Recreations:* gardening, walking. *Address:* Virginia Lodge, Boronia Street, Bowral, NSW 2576, Australia.

CAYZER, family name of **Barons Cayzer** and **Rotherwick.**

CAYZER, Baron *cr* 1982 (Life Peer), of St Mary Axe in the City of London; **William Nicholas Cayzer;** Bt 1921; Chairman of: British & Commonwealth Shipping Co. PLC; Clan Line Steamers Ltd; Cayzer, Irvine & Co. Ltd; Caledonia Investments PLC; Union-Castle Mail Steamship Co. Ltd and associated cos; Air Holdings Ltd; Meldrum Investment Trust; *b* 21 Jan. 1910; *s* of Sir August Cayzer, 1st Bt, and Ina Frances (*d* 1935), 2nd *d* of William Stancombe, Blounts Ct, Wilts; *S* to father's baronetcy, 1943; *m* 1935, Elizabeth Catherine, *d* of late Owain Williams and *g d* of Morgan Stuart Williams, Aberpergwm, Glamorgan; two *d*. *Educ:* Eton; Corpus Christi Coll., Cambridge. Chm. Liverpool Steamship Owners Association, 1944–45; Pres. Chamber of Shipping of the UK, 1959; Pres. Inst. of Marine Engineers, 1963. Chairman: Gen. Council of Brit. Shipping, 1959; Chamber of Shipping's British Liner Cttee, 1960–63; Mem., MoT Shipping Adv. Panel, 1962–64; sometime Mem. Mersey Dock and Harbour Board; sometime Mem. National Dock Labour Board. Prime Warden, Shipwrights Company, 1969. *Heir* (to baronetcy): none. *Address:* The Grove, Walsham-le-Willows, Suffolk. *T:* Walsham-le-Willows 263; 95j Eaton Square, SW1. *T:* 01–235 5551. *Club:* Brooks's.

See also M. K. B. Colvin.

CAYZER, Hon. Anthony; *see* Cayzer, Hon. M. A. R.

CAYZER, Sir James Arthur, 5th Bt, *cr* 1904; *b* 15 Nov. 1931; *s* of Sir Charles William Cayzer, 3rd Bt, MP (*d* 1940), and Beatrice Eileen (*d* 1981), *d* of late James Meakin and Emma Beatrice (later wife of 3rd Earl Sondes); *S* brother, 1943. *Educ:* Eton. *Heir: cousin,* Baron Cayzer, *qv*. *Address:* Kinpurnie Castle, Newtyle, Angus PH12 8TW. *T:* Newtyle 207. *Club:* Carlton.

CAYZER, Hon. (Michael) Anthony (Rathborne); shipowner; *b* 28 May 1920; 2nd *s* of 1st Baron Rotherwick; *m* 1952, Hon. Patricia Browne (*d* 1981), *er d* of 4th Baron Oranmore and Browne, *qv*, and late Hon. Mrs Hew Dalrymple; three *d*; *m* 1982, Baroness Sybille de Selys Longchamps. *Educ:* Eton; Royal Military Coll., Sandhurst. Commissioned Royal Scots Greys: served 1939–44 (despatches). Dep. Chairman: British & Commonwealth Shipping Co. Ltd; Airwork Services Ltd; Air Holdings Ltd; Chairman: Servisair Ltd; Avialift Products Ltd; Director: Cayzer, Irvine & Co. Ltd; Caledonia Investments Ltd; Overseas Containers (Holdings) Ltd; Sterling Industries Ltd. President: Inst. of Shipping and Forwarding Agents, 1963–65; Chamber of Shipping of the United Kingdom, 1967; Herts Agric. Soc., 1974; Past Vice-Pres., British Light Aviation Centre. Past Mem. Mersey Docks and Harbour Bd. Chm. Liverpool Steamship Owners Assoc., 1956–57. Trustee: Nat. Maritime Museum, 1968– (Chm., 1977–); Maritime Trust, 1975–; Dep. Chm., Chatham Historic Dockyard Trust, 1984–. Vice-Pres., Missions to Seamen, 1984– (Treasurer, 1974–84). *Address:* Great Westwood, Kings Langley, Herts. *Clubs:* Boodle's, Royal Yacht Squadron.

CAZALET, Edward Stephen, QC 1980; a Recorder, since 1985; *b* 26 April 1936; *s* of late Peter Victor Ferdinand Cazalet and Leonora Cazalet (*née* Rowley); *m* 1965, Camilla Jane (*née* Gage); two *s* one *d*. *Educ:* Eton Coll.; Christ Church, Oxford (MA Jurisprudence). Called to the Bar, Inner Temple, 1960, Bencher, 1985. Chairman, Horserace Betting Levy Appeal Tribunal, 1977–. *Recreations:* riding, ball games, chess. *Address:* 58 Seymour Walk, SW10. *T:* 01–352 0401. *Clubs:* White's, Garrick, Wig and Pen.

CAZALET, Peter Grenville; a Managing Director, since 1981, and Deputy Chairman, since 1986, British Petroleum Co. plc; *b* 26 Feb. 1929; *e s* of Vice-Adm. Sir Peter (Grenville Lyon) Cazalet, KBE, CB, DSO, DSC, and of Lady (Elise) Cazalet (*née* Winterbotham); *m* 1957, Jane Jennifer, *yr d* of Charles and Nancy Rew, Guernsey, CI; three *s*. *Educ:* Uppingham Sch., Uppingham, Rutland; Magdalene Coll., Cambridge (Schol.; MA Hons). General Manager, BP Tanker Co. Ltd, 1968; Regional Co-ordinator, Australasia and Far East, 1970; Pres., BP North America Inc., 1972–75; Director: Standard Oil Co. of Ohio, 1973–75; BP Trading Ltd, 1975; Peninsular & Oriental Steam Navigation Co., 1980–; Chairman, BP Oil International, 1981–. Dir, De La Rue Co., 1983–. Mem., Gen. Cttee, Lloyd's Register of Shipping, 1981– (Mem. Bd, 1981–86). Trustee, Uppingham Sch., 1976–. Liveryman, Tallow Chandlers' Co. (Mem. Court, 1983–). *Recreations:* theatre, fishing. *Address:* Britannic House, Moor Lane, EC2Y 9BU. *T:* 01–920 8000. *Clubs:* Brooks's, Royal Wimbledon Golf, MCC.

CAZALET-KEIR, Thelma, CBE 1952; *d* of late W. M. Cazalet; *m* 1939, David (*d* 1969), *s* of Rev. Thomas Keir. Member of London County Council for East Islington, 1925–31; Alderman of County of London, 1931; contested by-election, East Islington, 1931; MP (Nat. C) East Islington, 1931–45; Parliamentary Private Secretary to Parliamentary Secretary to Board of Education, 1937–40; Parliamentary Secretary to Ministry of Education, May 1945. Member of Committee of Enquiry into conditions in Women's Services, 1942; of Committee on Equal Compensation (Civil Injuries), 1943; Chairman London Area Women's Advisory Committee, Conservative and Unionist Associations, 1943–46. Chairman Equal Pay Campaign Committee; Member Cost of Living Committee; Member Arts Council of Great Britain, 1940–49; Member Executive Committee of Contemporary Art Society; Member Transport Users Consultative Committee for London, 1950–52. A Governor of the BBC, 1956–61. Member Committee Royal UK Beneficent Association, 1962. President Fawcett Society, 1964. *Publications:* From the Wings, 1967; (ed) Homage to P. G. Wodehouse, 1973. *Recreations:* music, lawn tennis. *Address:* Flat J, 90 Eaton Square, SW1. *T:* 01–235 7378.

CECIL, family name of **Baron Amherst of Hackney, Marquess of Exeter, Baron Rockley,** and **Marquess of Salisbury.**

CECIL, Henry Richard Amherst; Trainer of Racehorses; *b* 11 Jan. 1943; *s* of late Hon. Henry Kerr Auchmuty Cecil and of Elizabeth Rohays Mary (who *m* 2nd, Sir Cecil Boyd-Rochfort, KCVO), *d* of Sir James Burnett, 13th Bt, CB, CMG, DSO; *m* 1966, Julia, *d* of Sir Noel Murless, *qv*; one *s* one *d*. *Educ:* Canford School. Commenced training under flat race rules, 1969; previously Assistant to Sir Cecil Boyd-Rochfort. Leading Trainer, 1976, 1978, 1979, 1982, 1984, 1985. *Publication:* On the Level (autobiog.), 1983. *Recreation:* gardening. *Address:* Warren Place, Newmarket, Suffolk CB8 8QQ. *T:* Newmarket 662387.

CECIL, Rear-Adm. Sir (Oswald) Nigel Amherst, KBE 1979; CB 1978; Chairman, Biltmore Restorations Ltd, since 1986; Director, Biltmore, Campbell, Smith Restorations Inc. (USA), since 1986; *b* 11 Nov. 1925; *s* of Comdr the Hon. Henry M. A. Cecil, OBE, RN, and the Hon. Mrs Henry Cecil; *m* 1961, Annette (CStJ 1980), *d* of Maj. Robert Barclay, TD, Bury Hill, near Dorking, Surrey; one *s*. *Educ:* Royal Naval Coll., Dartmouth. Joined Navy, 1939; served during War, 1939–45. In comd, HM MTB 521, 1946–48; Flag Lieut to Admiral, BJSM, Washington, 1950–52; Comdr, 1959; Chief Staff Officer,

London Div. RNR, 1959–61; in comd: HMS Corunna, 1961–63; HMS Royal Arthur, 1963–66; Captain 1966; Staff of Dep. Chief of Defence Staff (Operational Requirements), 1966–69; Captain (D) Dartmouth Trng Sqdn and in comd HMS Tenby and HMS Scarborough, 1969–71; Senior British Naval Officer, S Africa, and Naval Attaché, Capetown, as Cdre, 1971–73; Dir, Naval Operational Requirements, 1973–75; Naval ADC to the Queen, 1975; Rear-Adm., 1975; NATO Comdr SE Mediterranean, 1975–77; Comdr British Forces Malta, and Flag Officer Malta, 1975–79; Lieut Gov., Isle of Man, 1980–85. FIBM 1980. KStJ 1980 (OStJ 1971). *Recreations:* racing, cricket, tennis. *Address:* c/o C. Hoare & Co., 37 Fleet Street, EC4P 4DQ. *Clubs:* White's, MCC.

CECIL, Robert, CMG 1959; author; HM Diplomatic Service, retired; Chairman, Institute for Cultural Research, since 1968; *b* 25 March 1913; *s* of late Charles Cecil; *m* 1938, Kathleen, *d* of late Col C. C. Marindin, CBE, DSO; one *s* two *d. Educ:* Wellington Coll.; Caius Coll., Cambridge. BA Cantab. 1935, MA 1961. Entered HM Foreign Service, 1936; served in Foreign Office, 1939–45; First Sec., HM Embassy, Washington, 1945–48; assigned to Foreign Office, 1948; Counsellor and Head of American Dept, 1951; Counsellor, HM Embassy, Copenhagen, 1953–55; HM Consul-Gen., Hanover, 1955–57; Counsellor, HM Embassy, Bonn, 1957–59; Dir-Gen., British Information Services, New York, 1959–61; Head of Cultural Relations Dept, FO, 1962–67. Reader in Contemp. German Hist., Reading Univ., 1968–78; Chm., Grad. Sch. of Contemp. European Studies, 1976–78. *Publications:* Levant and other Poems, 1940; Time and other Poems, 1955; Life in Edwardian England, 1969; The Myth of the Master Race: Alfred Rosenberg and Nazi ideology, 1972; Hitler's Decision to Invade Russia, 1941, 1976; (ed) The King's Son (anthology), 1980; (contrib.) The Missing Dimension, 1984. *Recreations:* gardening, chess, etc. *Address:* Hambledon, Hants PO7 6RU. *T:* Hambledon 669. *Club:* Royal Automobile.

CELIBIDACHE, Sergiu; Chief Conductor, Munich Philharmonic Orchestra, since 1979; Composer and Guest Conductor to leading orchestras all over the world; *b* Rumania, 28 June 1912; *s* of Demosthene Celibidache; *m* Maria Celibidache. *Educ:* Jassy; Berlin. Doctorate in mathematics, musicology, philosophy and Buddhist religion. Conductor and Artistic Dir, Berlin Philharmonic Orchestra, 1946–51. Member: Royal Acad. of Music, Sweden; Acad. of Music, Bologna. German Critics' Prize, 1953; Berlin City Art Prize, 1955; Grand Cross of Merit, Federal Republic of Germany, 1954. *Recreations:* skiing, water-skiing. *Address:* Munich Philharmonic Orchestra, 8 Munich 2, Rindermarkt 3–4/III, Federal Republic of Germany.

CENTRAL AFRICA, Archbishop of, since 1980; **Most Rev. Walter Paul Khotso Makhulu;** Bishop of Botswana, since 1979; *b* Johannesburg, 1935; *m* 1966, Rosemary Sansom; one *s* one *d. Educ:* St Peter's Theological Coll., Rosettenville; Selly Oak Colls, Birmingham. Deacon 1957, priest 1958, Johannesburg; Curate: Johannesburg, 1957–60; Botswana, 1961–63; St Carantoc's Mission, Francistown, Botswana, 1961–63; St Andrew's Coll., Selly Oak, Birmingham, 1963–64; Curate: All Saints, Poplar, 1964–66; St Silas, Pentonville, with St Clement's, Barnsbury, 1966–68; Vicar of St Philip's, Battersea, 1968–75; Secretary for E Africa, WCC, 1975–79; a President: WCC, 1983–; All Africa Conf. of Churches, 1981–84. Officier, Ordre des Palmes Académiques (France), 1981. *Address:* PO Box 769, Gaborone, Botswana.

CHABAN-DELMAS, Jacques Pierre Michel; Commander Légion d'Honneur; Compagnon de la Libération; President, French National Assembly, since 1985 (Deputy, Department of Gironde, since 1946); Mayor of Bordeaux, since 1947; *b* Paris, 7 March 1915; *s* of Pierre Delmas and Georgette Delmas (*née* Barrouin); *m* 1947 (2nd marr.), Mme Geoffray (*née* Marie Antoinette Iõn) (*d* 1970); two *s* two *d*; *m* 1971, Mme Micheline Chavelet. *Educ:* Lycée Lakanal, Sceaux; Faculté de Droit, Paris; Ecole Libre des Sciences Politiques (Dip.). Licencié en droit. Journalist with l'Information, 1933. Served War of 1939–45: Army, 1939–40 (an Alpine Regt); joined the Resistance; *nom de guerre* of Chaban added (Compagnon de la Libération, Croix de Guerre); attached to Min. of Industrial Production, 1941; Inspector of Finance, 1943; Brig.-Gen., 1944; Nat. Mil. Deleg. (co-ord. mil. planning) Resistance, 1944; Inspector Gen. of Army, 1944; Sec.-Gen., Min. of Inf., 1945. Deputy for Gironde (Radical), 1946. Leader of Gaullist group (Républicans Sociaux) in Nat. Assembly, 1953–56; also Mem. Consultative Assembly of Council of Europe; Minister of State, 1956–57; Minister of Nat. Defence, 1957–58; Pres., Nat. Assembly, France, 1958–69 and 1978–81; Prime Minister, June 1969–July 1972. Président: Communauté urbain de Bordeaux, 1983–; Conseil régional d'Aquitaine, 1985–. *Publication:* L'ardeur, 1976. *Address:* 36 rue Emile Fourcand, 33000 Bordeaux, France; Mairie de Bordeaux, 33000 Bordeaux, France.

CHACKSFIELD, Air Vice-Marshal Sir Bernard, KBE 1968 (OBE 1945); CB 1961; CEng, FRAeS 1968; *b* 13 April 1913; *s* of Edgar Chacksfield, Ilford, Essex; *m* 1st, 1937, Myrtle, (*d* 1984), *d* of Walter Matthews, Rickmansworth, Herts; two *s* two *d* (and one *s* decd); 2nd, 1985, Mrs Elizabeth Beatrice Ody. *Educ:* Co. High Sch., Ilford; RAF, Halton; RAF Coll., Cranwell. NW Frontier, 1934–37; UK, India, Burma, Singapore, 1939–45 (OBE); Air Min., 1945–48; Western Union (NATO), Fontainebleau, 1949–51; RAF Staff Coll., 1951–53; Fighter Command, 1954–55; Director, Guided Weapons (trials), Min. of Supply, 1956–58; IDC, 1959; SASO, Tech. Trg Comd, RAF, 1960; AOC No. 22 Group RAF Technical Training Command, 1960–62; Comdt-Gen., RAF Regiment and Inspector of Ground Defence, 1963–68; retired 1968. Chm., Burma Star Council, 1977– (Vice-Chm., 1974–76). Chm., Wycombe Co-ordinating Cttee for Disabled, 1982–85. Chairman of Governors: Bedstone College, 1978– (Governor, 1977); Deyncourt Sch., 1980–. Order of Cloud and Banner with special rosette (Chinese), 1941. *Recreations:* scouting (HQ Comr, Air Activities, 1959–72; Chief Comr for England, 1968–77), sailing, fencing (Pres. RAF Fencing Union, 1963–68), gliding, travel, model aircraft (Pres. Soc. Model Aircraft Engrs, GB, 1965–), modern Pentathlon (Pres., RAF Pentathlon Assoc., 1963–68), shooting (Chm. RAF Small Arms Assoc., 1963–68); swimming; youth work, amateur dramatics. *Address:* 8 Rowan House, Bourne End, Bucks. *T:* Bourne End 20829. *Club:* Royal Air Force.

CHADDOCK, Prof. Dennis Hilliar, CBE 1962; Professor of Engineering Design, University of Technology, Loughborough, 1966–73, retired; Professor Emeritus, 1974; Consultant Proprietor, Quorn Engineering, since 1974; *b* 28 July 1908; *m* 1937, Stella Edith Dorrington; one *s* one *d* (and one *s* decd). *Educ:* University Coll. Sch. Engineering Apprentice, Sa Adolph Saurer, Switzerland, 1927–30; Research Engineer, Morris Commercial Cars Ltd, Birmingham, 1930–32; Asst Road Motor Engineer, LMS Railway Co., Euston, 1932–41. BSc (Eng) Hons, London, 1933; MSc (Eng) London, 1938. HM Forces, 1941–46; Inspecting Officer, Chief Inspector of Armaments, 1941–43; Dep. Chief Inspecting Officer, 1943–45; Chief Design Officer, Armament Design Estabt, 1945–46; relinquished commission with rank of Lieut-Col, 1946. Superintendent, Carriage Design Branch of Armament Design Estabt, 1947–50; Imperial Defence Coll., 1951; Dep. Chief Engineer, 1952–55; Principal Superintendent, Weapons and Ammunition Div., Armament Research and Development Estabt, 1955–62; Dir of Artillery Research and Development, Ministry of Defence (Army) 1962–66. *Recreation:* model engineering. *Address:* 29 Paddock Close, Quorndon, Leics. *T:* Quorn 412607.

CHADWICK, Charles McKenzie, OBE 1984; British Council Representative, Canada, since 1981; *b* 31 July 1932; *s* of late Trevor McKenzie Chadwick and of Marjorie Baron; *m* 1965, Evelyn Ingeborg Ihlenfeldt; one *s. Educ:* Charterhouse School; Trinity Coll., Toronto (BA). Army service, 1950–52; HMOCS Provincial Administration, Northern Rhodesia, 1958–64; Lectr, 1964–66, and Head, Administrative Training, 1966–67, Staff Trng Coll., Lusaka; British Council Officer, 1967–; service in Kenya, Nigeria, Brazil, London; British Election Supervisor, Zimbabwe, 1980. *Recreations:* music, gardening, cricket. *Address:* c/o British Council, 10 Spring Gardens, SW1A 2BN.

CHADWICK, Gerald William St John, (John Chadwick), CMG 1961; HM Diplomatic Service, retired; Director, London Science Centre, 1981; *b* 28 May 1915; *s* of late John F. Chadwick, Solicitor; *m* 1938, Madeleine Renée Boucheron; two *s. Educ:* Lancing; St Catharine's Coll., Cambridge (open Exhibitioner). Asst Principal, Colonial Office, 1938; transf. Dominions Office, following demobilisation, 1940; Sec., Parl. Mission to Newfoundland, 1943; further missions to Newfoundland and Bermuda, 1946 and 1947; attended United Nations, 1949; Office of UK High Commission, Ottawa, 1949–52; Counsellor, British Embassy, Dublin, 1952–53; UK Delegn to NATO, Paris, 1954–56; Asst Sec., CRO, 1956; Asst Under-Sec. of State, CRO, 1960–66; first Dir, Commonwealth Foundn, 1966–80. Governor, Commonwealth Inst., 1967–80. *Publications:* The Shining Plain, 1937; Newfoundland: Island into Province, 1967; International Organisations, 1969; (ed jtly) Professional Organisations in the Commonwealth, 1976; The Unofficial Commonwealth, 1982; contrib. to A Decade of the Commonwealth 1955–64, 1966; numerous reviews and articles. *Recreation:* travel.

CHADWICK, Rt. Rev. Graham Charles; Chaplain to St Asaph Cathedral, and Adviser on Spirituality, Diocese of St Asaph, since 1983; *b* 3 Jan. 1923; *s* of William Henry and Sarah Ann Chadwick; *m* 1955, Jeanne Suzanne Tyrell; one *s. Educ:* Swansea Grammar School; Keble Coll., Oxford (MA); St Michael's Coll., Llandaff. RNVR, 1942–46. Deacon 1950, priest 1951; Curate, Oystermouth, Dio. Swansea and Brecon, 1950–53; Diocese of Lesotho, 1953–63; Chaplain, University Coll., Swansea, 1963–68; Senior Bursar, Queen's Coll., Birmingham, 1968–69; Diocesan Missioner, Lesotho, and Warden of Diocesan Training Centre, 1970–76; Bishop of Kimberley and Kuruman, 1976–82. *Address:* 2 Llys Trewithan, Mount Road, St Asaph, Clywd LL17 0DF. *T:* St Asaph 583853.

CHADWICK, Very Rev. Prof. Henry, DD; FBA 1960; MRIA; Fellow of Magdalene College, Cambridge, since 1979; Regius Professor Emeritus of Divinity, University of Cambridge, 1983 (Regius Professor, 1979–83); Hon. Canon Emeritus of Ely; *b* 23 June 1920; 3rd *s* of late John Chadwick, Barrister, Bromley, Kent, and Edith (*née* Horrocks); *m* 1945, Margaret Elizabeth, *d* of late W. Pemell Brownrigg; three *d. Educ:* Eton (King's Scholar); Magdalene Coll., Cambridge (Music Schol.). John Stewart of Rannoch Scholar, 1939. MusB. Asst Master, Wellington Coll., 1945; University of Cambridge: Fellow of Queens' Coll., 1946–58; Hon. Fellow, 1958; Junior Proctor, 1948–49. Regius Professor of Divinity and Canon of Christ Church, Oxford, 1959–69; Dean of Christ Church, Oxford, 1969–79 (Hon. Student, 1979); Pro-Vice-Chancellor, Oxford Univ., 1974–75; Delegate, OUP, 1960–79. Hon. Fellow, Magdalene Coll., Cambridge, 1962; Fellow, Eton, 1976–79; Hon. Fellow, St Anne's Coll., Oxford, 1979. Gifford Lectr, St Andrews Univ., 1962–64; Birkbeck Lectr, Cambridge, 1965; Burns Lectr, Otago, 1971; Sarum Lectr, Oxford, 1982–83. Editor, Journal of Theological Studies, 1954–85. Member, Anglican-Roman Catholic International Commn, 1969–81 and 1983–. Mem., Amer. Philosophical Soc.; For. Hon. Mem., Amer. Acad. Arts and Sciences; Correspondant de l'Académie des Inscriptions et des Belles Lettres, Institut de France; Mem., Société des Bollandistes, Brussels. Hon. DD, Glasgow, Yale, Leeds and Manchester; Hon. Teol Dr, Uppsala; D Humane Letters, Chicago. Humboldt Prize, 1983. *Publications:* Origen, Contra Celsum, 1953, 3rd edn 1980; Alexandrian Christianity (with J. E. L. Oulton), 1954; Lessing's Theological Writings, 1956; The Sentences of Sextus, 1959; Early Christian Thought and the Classical Tradition, 1966; The Early Church (Pelican), 1967; The Treatise on the Apostolic Tradition of St Hippolytus of Rome, ed G. Dix (rev. edn), 1968; Priscillian of Avila, 1976; Boethius, 1981; History and Thought of the Early Church, 1982; Augustine, 1986; (contrib.) Oxford History of the Classical World, 1986. *Recreation:* music. *Address:* Magdalene College, Cambridge; 177 Woodstock Road, Oxford OX2 7NB.

See also Sir John Chadwick, W. O. Chadwick, Vice-Adm. Sir A. W. R. McNicoll.

CHADWICK, John; *see* Chadwick, G. W. St J.

CHADWICK, John, FBA 1967; MA; LittD; Perceval Maitland Laurence Reader in Classics, University of Cambridge, 1969–84; Hon. Fellow, Downing College, Cambridge, since 1984 (Collins Fellow, 1960–84); *b* 21 May 1920; *yr s* of late Fred Chadwick; *m* 1947, Joan Isobel Hill; one *s. Educ:* St Paul's Sch.; Corpus Christi Coll., Cambridge. Editorial Asst, Oxford Latin Dictionary, Clarendon Press, 1946–52; Asst Lectr in Classics, 1952–54, Lectr in Classics, 1954–66, Reader in Greek Language, 1966–69, Univ. of Cambridge. Corresponding Member: Deutsches Archäologisches Inst., 1957; Austrian Acad. of Scis, 1974; Associé étranger, Acad. des Inscriptions et Belles-Lettres, Institut de France, 1985. Hon. Fellow, Athens Archaeol Soc., 1974. Hon. Dr of Philosophical Sch., University of Athens, 1958; Hon. Dr, Université Libre de Bruxelles, 1969; Hon. DLitt, Trinity Coll., Dublin, 1971; Hon Dr. Euskal Herriko Unibertsitatea, Vitoria, Spain, 1985. Medal of J. E. Purkyně Univ., Brno, 1966. Comdr, Order of the Phoenix, Greece, 1984. *Publications:* (jtly) The Medical Works of Hippocrates, 1950; (jtly) Documents in Mycenaean Greek, 1956, rev. edn 1973; The Decipherment of Linear B, 1958, 2nd edn 1967 (trans. into 12 languages); The Pre-history of the Greek Language (in Camb. Ancient History), 1963; The Mycenaean World, 1976 (trans. into 5 languages); edns of Linear B Tablets, articles in learned jls on Mycenaean Greek. *Recreation:* travel. *Address:* 75 Gough Way, Cambridge CB3 9LN. *T:* Cambridge 356864.

CHADWICK, Sir John (Edward), KCMG 1967 (CMG 1957); HM Diplomatic Service, retired; *b* 17 Dec. 1911; *e s* of late John Chadwick; *m* 1945, Audrey Lenfestey; one *s* two *d. Educ:* Rugby; Corpus Christi Coll., Cambridge (MA). Dept of Overseas Trade, 1934; Asst Trade Comr, Calcutta, 1938; Eastern Group Supply Council, Simla, 1941; Commercial Secretary, Washington, 1946–48; First Sec., Tel Aviv, 1950–53; Counsellor (Commercial) Tokyo, 1953–56; Minister (Economic), Buenos Aires, 1960–62, (Commercial), Washington, 1963–67; Ambassador to Romania, 1967–68; UK Representative to OECD, Paris, 1969–71. Consultant, Sterling Industrial Securities, 1973; Special Advr, Asian Develt Bank, 1973–83. *Address:* Larkfields, Woodstock Road, Charlbury, Oxford OX7 3ES. *Club:* Travellers'.

See also Very Rev. Prof. Henry Chadwick, W. O. Chadwick, Vice-Adm. Sir A. W. R. McNicoll.

CHADWICK, John Murray, ED; QC 1980; a Judge of the Courts of Appeal of Jersey and Guernsey, since 1986; *b* 20 Jan. 1941; *s* of Hector George Chadwick and Margaret Corry Laing; *m* 1975, Diana Mary Blunt; two *d. Educ:* Rugby School; Magdalene Coll., Cambridge (MA). Called to the Bar, Inner Temple, 1966, Bencher, 1986. *Recreation:* sailing. *Address:* Queen Elizabeth Building, Temple, EC4Y 9BS. *T:* 01–353 0551. *Club:* Cavalry and Guards.

CHADWICK, Sir Joshua Kenneth B.; *see* Burton-Chadwick.

CHADWICK, Lynn Russell, CBE 1964; sculptor since 1948; *b* 24 Nov. 1914; *s* of late Verner Russell Chadwick and Marjorie Brown Lynn; *m* 1942, Charlotte Ann Secord; one *s*; *m* 1959, Frances Mary Jamieson (*d* 1964); two *d*; *m* 1965, Eva Reiner; one *s*. *Educ:* Merchant Taylors' Sch. Architectural Draughtsman, 1933–39; Pilot, FAA, 1941–44. Exhibitions have been held in London, in various galleries, and by the Arts Council; his works have also been shown in numerous international exhibitions abroad, including Venice Biennale, 1956 (Internat. Sculpture Prize). *Works in public collections:* Great Britain: Tate Gallery, London; British Council, London; Arts Council of Great Britain; Victoria and Albert Museum; Pembroke Coll., Oxford; City Art Gallery, Bristol; Art Gallery, Brighton; Whitworth Art Gallery, University of Manchester; France: Musée National D'Art Moderne, Paris; Holland: Boymans van Beuningen Museum, Rotterdam; Germany: Municipality of Recklinghausen; Staatliche Graphische Sammlung, Munich; Staatische Kunstmuseum, Duisburg; Sweden: Art Gallery, Gothenburg; Belgium: Musées Royaux des Beaux-Arts de Belgique, Brussels; Italy: Galleria D'Arte Moderna, Rome; Museo Civico, Turin; Australia: National Gallery of SA, Adelaide; Canada: National Gallery of Canada, Ottawa; Museum of Fine Arts, Montreal; USA: Museum of Modern Art, New York; Carnegie Institute, Pittsburgh; University of Michigan; Albright Art Gallery, Buffalo; Art Institute, Chicago; Chile: Inst. de Artes Contemporáneas, Lima. Officier des Arts et des Lettres (France), 1986. *Address:* Lypiatt Park, Stroud, Glos.

CHADWICK, Owen; *see* Chadwick, W. O.

CHADWICK, Prof. Peter, PhD, ScD; FRS 1977; Professor of Mathematics, University of East Anglia, since 1965; Dean of School of Mathematics and Physics, 1979–82; *b* 23 March 1931; *s* of Jack Chadwick and late Marjorie Chadwick (*née* Castle); *m* 1956, Sheila Gladys Salter, *d* of late Clarence F. and Gladys I. Salter; two *d*. *Educ:* Huddersfield Coll.; Univ. of Manchester (BSc 1952); Pembroke Coll., Cambridge (PhD 1957, ScD 1973). Scientific Officer, then Sen. Scientific Officer, Atomic Weapons Res. Estabt, Aldermaston, 1955–59; Lectr, then Sen. Lectr, in Applied Maths, Univ. of Sheffield, 1959–65. Vis. Prof., Univ. of Queensland, 1972. Member: Exec. Cttee, Internat. Soc. for Interaction of Mechanics and Maths, 1983–; British Nat. Cttee for Theoretical and Applied Mechanics, 1969–75, 1985–. Jt Exec. Editor, Qly Jl of Mechanics and Applied Maths, 1965–72, Trustee, 1977–. *Publications:* Continuum Mechanics, 1976; numerous papers on theoretical solid mechanics and the mechanics of continua in various learned journals and books. *Address:* School of Mathematics and Physics, University of East Anglia, University Plain, Norwich NR4 7TJ. *T:* Norwich 56161; 8 Stratford Crescent, Cringleford, Norwich NR4 7SF. *T:* Norwich 51655.

CHADWICK, Robert Everard; Director, Leeds Permanent Building Society, 1974–86 (President, 1983–85); *b* 20 Oct. 1916; *s* of Robert Agar Chadwick and Aline Chadwick; *m* 1948, Audrey Monica Procter; two *s* one *d*. *Educ:* Oundle; Leeds Univ. (LLB). Served RA, 1939–46. Solicitor, 1938–82; Director: J. Hepworth & Son, 1946–81 (Chm., 1956–81); John Waddington, 1954–77 (Chm., 1969–77); Magnet Joinery, 1969–77; Robert Glew & Co., 1969–77; W Riding Reg. Bd, Barclays Bank, 1972–82. *Recreations:* hill walking, fishing. *Address:* Baxters Fold, Cracoe, Skipton, N Yorks BD23 6LB. *T:* Cracoe 233. *Club:* Leeds (Leeds).

CHADWICK, Rt. Rev. William Frank Percival; Bishop of Barking, 1959–75. *Educ:* Wadham College, Oxford; Harvard Univ., USA (Davison Scholar). Deacon, 1929, Priest, 1930, Diocese Liverpool; Curate, St Helens, 1929–34; Vicar: Widnes, 1934–38; Christ Church, Crouch End, N8, 1938–47; Barking, 1947–59. Proctor, Diocese of London, 1946, Diocese of Chelmsford, 1951; Examining Chaplain to Bishop of Chelmsford, 1951; Asst RD Barking, 1950–53, RD, Barking, 1953; Hon. Canon of Chelmsford, 1954; Pro-Prolocutor, Lower House of Canterbury, 1956; Exchange Preacher, USA, British Council of Churches, 1958; Chm., Church of England's Commn on Roman Catholic Relations, 1968–75; Mem., Dioceses Commn, 1978–80. *Publication:* The Inner Life. *Recreation:* golf. *Address:* Harvard House, Acton, Long Melford, Suffolk. *T:* Sudbury 77015. *Club:* Royal Commonwealth Society.

CHADWICK, (William) Owen, OM 1983; KBE 1982; FBA 1962; Fellow of Selwyn College, Cambridge, since 1983; Chancellor, University of East Anglia, since 1985; *b* 20 May 1916; 2nd *s* of late John Chadwick, Barrister, Bromley, Kent, and Edith (*née* Horrocks); *m* 1949, Ruth Romaine, *e d* of B. L. Hallward, *qv*; two *s* two *d*. *Educ:* Tonbridge; St John's Coll., Cambridge, and took holy orders. Fellow of Trinity Hall, Cambridge, 1947–56, Hon. Fellow, 1959; Master of Selwyn Coll., Cambridge, 1956–83; Dixie Professor of Ecclesiastical History, 1958–68; Regius Prof. of Modern History, 1968–83; Vice-Chancellor, Cambridge Univ., 1969–71. Chm. Trustees, University Coll., later Wolfson Coll., Cambridge, 1965–77, Hon. Fellow 1977. Pres., British Academy, 1981–85. Chm., Archbishops' Commn on Church and State, 1966–70; Mem., Royal Commn on Historical MSS, 1984–. Trustee, Nat. Portrait Gall., 1978–. Hon. Mem., American Acad. of Arts and Scis, 1977. Hon. Fellow, St John's Coll., Cambridge, 1964; Hon. FRSE. Hon. DD: St Andrews; Oxford; Hon. DLitt: Kent; Bristol; London; Leeds; Hon. LittD UEA; Hon. Dr of Letters, Columbia; Hon. LLD Aberdeen. Wolfson Literary Prize, 1980. *Publications include:* John Cassian, 1950; From Bossuet to Newman, 1957; The Mind of the Oxford Movement, 1960; Victorian Miniature, 1960; The Reformation, 1964; The Victorian Church, part I, 1966, 3rd edn 1971; part II, 1970, 3rd edn 1979; The Secularization of the European Mind in the 19th Century, 1976; Acton and Gladstone, 1976; Catholicism and History, 1978; The Popes and European Revolution, 1981; Britain and the Vatican during the Second World War, 1986; contrib. to Studies in Early British History, 1954. *Recreations:* music; Cambridge XV versus Oxford, 1936–38. *Address:* 67 Grantchester Street, Cambridge CB3 9HZ.

See also Very Rev. Prof. Henry Chadwick, Sir John Chadwick, Vice-Adm. Sir A. W. R. McNicoll.

CHADWICK-JONES, Prof. John Knighton, PhD, DSc(Econ); Professor of Psychology, Saint Mary's University, Halifax, Canada, since 1974; *b* 26 July 1928; *s* of late Thomas Chadwick-Jones and Cecilia Rachel (*née* Thomas); *m* 1965, Araceli Carceller y Bergillos; two *s* one *d*. *Educ:* Bromsgrove Sch.; St Edmund Hall, Oxford (MA). PhD Wales, 1960; DSc(Econ) Wales, 1981. FBPsS. Scientific Staff, Nat. Inst. of Industrial Psychol., London, 1957–60; Lectr, then Sen. Lectr, in Industrial Psychol., UC, Cardiff, 1960–66; Reader in Social Psychol., Flinders Univ., SA, 1967–68; Dir, Occupational Psychol. Res. Unit, UC, Cardiff, 1968–74; Mem., Exec. Cttee, Bd of Governors, Saint Mary's Univ., 1975–78. Canada Soc. Scis and Humanities Res. Council Leave Fellow: Darwin Coll., Cambridge, 1980–81; MRC Unit on Develt and Integration of Behaviour, Cambridge, 1984–85; Visiting Fellow: Clare Hall, Cambridge, 1982; Wolfson Coll., Cambridge, 1984–85. Fellow: Amer. Psychol Assoc.; Canadian Psychol Assoc. *Publications:* Automation and Behavior: a social psychological study, 1969; Social Exchange Theory: its structure and influence in social psychology, 1976; (jtly) Brain, Environment and Social Psychology, 1979; Absenteeism in the Canadian Context, 1979; (jtly) Social Psychology of Absenteeism, 1982; articles in academic jls. *Address:* 1105 Belmont-on-the-Arm, Halifax, Nova Scotia B3H 1J2, Canada.

CHADWYCK-HEALEY, Sir Charles (Edward), 5th Bt *cr* 1919, of Wyphurst, Cranleigh, Co. Surrey and New Place, Luccombe, Somerset; Chairman and Managing Director, Chadwyck-Healey Ltd, since 1973; President: Chadwyck-Healey Inc., since 1981; Chadwyck-Healey France SARL, since 1985; *b* 13 May 1940; *s* of Sir Charles Arthur Chadwyck-Healey, 4th Bt, OBE, TD, and of Viola, *d* of late Cecil Lubbock; *S* father, 1986; *m* 1967, Angela Mary, *e d* of late John Metson; one *s* two *d*. *Educ:* Eton; Trinity Coll., Oxford (MA). *Heir: s* Edward Alexander Chadwyck-Healey, *b* 2 June 1972. *Address:* Manor Farm, Bassingbourn, Cambs. *T:* Royston 42447. *Club:* Brooks's.

CHAIR, Somerset de; *see* de Chair.

CHAKAIPA, Most Rev. Patrick; *see* Harare, Archbishop of, (RC).

CHALDECOTT, John Anthony; Keeper, Science Museum Library, South Kensington, 1961–76; *b* 16 Feb. 1916; *o s* of Wilfrid James and Mary Eleanor Chaldecott; *m* 1940, Kathleen Elizabeth Jones; one *d*. *Educ:* Latymer Upper Sch., Hammersmith; Brentwood Sch.; Borough Road Coll., Isleworth; University College, London. BSc 1938, MSc 1949, PhD 1972. FInstP; CPhys. Meteorological Branch, RAFVR, 1939–45 (despatches). Lecturer, Acton Technical Coll., 1945–48; entered Science Museum as Asst Keeper, Dept of Physics, 1949; Deputy Keeper and Secretary to Advisory Council, 1957. Pres., British Society for the History of Science, 1972–74. *Publications:* Josiah Wedgwood: the arts and sciences united (with J. des Fontaines and J. Tindall), 1978; Science Museum handbooks; papers on the history of science. *Address:* 19 The Grove, Ratton, Eastbourne, E Sussex BN20 9DA.

CHALFONT, Baron, *cr* 1964 (Life Peer); **Alun Arthur Gwynne Jones,** PC 1964; OBE 1961; MC 1957; Chairman, All Party Defence Group, House of Lords, since 1980; Director: IBM UK Ltd, since 1973 (Member, IBM Europe Advisory Council, since 1973); Lazard Bros & Co. Ltd, since 1983; President: Nottingham Building Society, since 1983; Abington Corporation (Consultants) Ltd, since 1981; Shandwick plc, since 1985; *b* 5 Dec. 1919; *s* of Arthur Gwynne Jones and Eliza Alice Hardman; *m* 1948, Dr Mona Mitchell; one *c* decd. *Educ:* West Monmouth Sch. Commissioned into South Wales Borderers (24th Foot), 1940; served in: Burma 1941–44; Malayan campaign 1955–57; Cyprus campaign 1958–59; various staff and intelligence appointments; Staff Coll., Camberley, 1950; Jt Services Staff Coll., 1958; Russian interpreter, 1951; resigned commission, 1961, on appt as Defence Correspondent, The Times; frequent television and sound broadcasts and consultant on foreign affairs to BBC Television, 1961–64; Minister of State, Foreign and Commonwealth Office, 1964–70; UK Permanent Rep. to WEU, 1969–70; Foreign Editor, New Statesman, 1970–71. Dir, W. S. Atkins International, 1979–83; Chairman: Industrial Cleaning Papers, 1979–; Peter Hamilton Security Consultants Ltd, 1984–86. President: Hispanic and Luso Brazilian Council, 1975–80; RNID, 1980–; Llangollen Internat. Music Festival, 1979–; Freedom in Sport, 1982–; Chairman: UK Cttee for Free World, 1981–; Eur. Atlantic Gp, 1983–; Member: IISS; Bd of Governors, Sandle Manor Sch. FRSA. MInstD. Hon. Fellow UCW Aberystwyth, 1974. Liveryman, Worshipful Co. of Paviors. Freeman, City of London. *Publications:* The Sword and The Spirit, 1963; The Great Commanders, 1973; Montgomery of Alamein, 1976; (ed) Waterloo: battle of three armies, 1979; Star Wars: suicide or survival, 1985; contribs to The Times, and other national and professional journals. *Recreations:* formerly Rugby football, cricket, lawn tennis; now music and theatre. *Address:* House of Lords, SW1A 0PW. *Clubs:* Garrick, MCC, Lord's Taverners, City Livery.

CHALK, Hon. Sir Gordon (William Wesley), KBE 1971; Hon. LLD; company director and business consultant; MP (Queensland), 1947–76; Minister for Transport, Govt of Queensland, 1957–65, Deputy Premier and Treasurer, 1965–76; Leader, Liberal Party of Australia (Queensland Div.), 1965–76; voluntarily retired, 1976; *b* 1913; of British parentage; *m* 1937, Ellen Clare Grant; one *s* one *d*. *Educ:* Gatton Senior High Sch., Qld. Formerly: Queensland Sales Manager, Toowoomba Foundry Pty Ltd; Registered Taxation Agent. Mem. Senate, Griffith Univ., 1976–84. Hon. LLD Queensland Univ., 1974. *Address:* 277 Indooroopilly Road, Indooroopilly, Qld. 4068, Australia. *T:* Brisbane 3711598. *Clubs:* Tattersall's (Brisbane, Qld); Rotary International (Gatton, Qld); Southport Yacht.

CHALKER, Mrs Lynda; MP (C) Wallasey since Feb. 1974; Minister of State, Foreign and Commonwealth Office, since 1986; *b* 29 April 1942; *d* of Sidney Henry James Bates and late Marjorie Kathleen Randell; *m* 1st, 1967, Eric Robert Chalker (marr. diss. 1973); no *c*; 2nd, 1981, Clive Landa. *Educ:* Roedean Sch.; Heidelberg Univ.; London Univ.; Central London Polytechnic. Statistician with Research Bureau Ltd (Unilever), 1963–69; Dep. Market Research Man. with Shell Mex & BP Ltd, 1969–72; Chief Exec. of Internat. Div. of Louis Harris International, 1972–74. Mem., BBC Gen. Adv. Cttee, 1975–79. Opposition Spokesman on Social Services, 1976–79; Parly Under-Sec. of State, DHSS, 1979–82, Dept of Transport, 1982–83; Minister of State, Dept of Transport, 1983–86. Jt Sec., Cons. Health and Social Services Cttee, 1975–76; Chm., Greater London Young Conservatives, 1969–70; Nat. Vice-Chm., Young Conservatives, 1970–71. *Publications:* (jtly) Police in Retreat (pamphlet), 1967; (jtly) Unhappy Families (pamphlet), 1971; (jtly) We are Richer than We Think, 1978. *Recreations:* music, the disabled, cooking, theatre, driving. *Address:* House of Commons, SW1A 0AA. *T:* 01–219 5098.

CHALKLEY, David Walter; Chairman, Inner London Education Authority, 1979–80; *b* 11 May 1915; *m* 1941, Hilda Davis; one *s* one *d*. *Educ:* Sellincourt Sch.; Battersea Polytechnic. Parliamentary Labour Candidate: NW Croydon, 1959; Brentford-Chiswick, 1964; Mayor of Mitcham, 1961; Mem., GLC, 1964–67 and 1970–81 (for Deptford). *Publication:* article on Labour organisation and class voting in constituencies. *Recreation:* travel. *Address:* 3 Melrose Avenue, Mitcham, Surrey. *Club:* Progressive (Tooting).

CHALLEN, Rt. Rev. Michael Boyd; Assistant Bishop, Diocese of Perth, W Australia, since 1978; *b* 27 May 1932; *s* of late B. Challen; *m* 1961, Judith, *d* of A. Kelly; two *d*. *Educ:* Mordialloc High School; Frankston High School; Univ. of Melbourne (BSc 1955); Ridley College, Melbourne (ThL 1956). Deacon 1957, priest 1958; Curate of Christ Church, Essendon, 1957–59; Member, Melbourne Dio. Centre 1959–63; Director, 1963–69; Priest-in-charge, St Luke, Fitzroy, 1959–61; St Alban's, N Melbourne, 1961–65; Flemington, 1965–69; Dir, Anglican Inner-City Ministry, 1969; Dir, Home Mission Dept, Perth, 1971–78; Priest-in-charge, Lockridge with Eden Hill, 1973; Archdeacon, Home Missions, Perth, 1975–78; Exec. Dir, Anglican Health and Welfare Service, Perth, 1977–78. *Address:* Box W2067, Perth, W Australia 6001.

CHALLENS, Wallace John, CBE 1967 (OBE 1958); Director, Atomic Weapons Research Establishment, Aldermaston, 1976–78; *b* 14 May 1915; *s* of late Walter Lincoln Challens and Harriet Sybil Challens (*née* Collins); *m* 1st, 1938, Winifred Joan Stephenson (*d* 1971); two *s*; 2nd, 1973, Norma Lane. *Educ:* Deacons Sch., Peterborough; University Coll., Nottingham; BSc (Hons) London. Research Dept, Woolwich, 1936; Projectile Develt Estabt, Aberporth, 1939. British Commonwealth Scientific Office, Washington, 1946; Armament Research Estabt, Fort Halstead, 1947; Atomic Weapons Research Estabt: Fort Halstead, 1954; Aldermaston, 1955–78. Scientific Dir of trials at Christmas Island, 1957. Appointed: Chief of Warhead Develt, 1959; Asst Dir, 1965; Dep. Dir, 1972. FInstP 1944. US Medal of Freedom (Bronze) 1946. *Recreation:* golf. *Address:* Far End, Crossborough Hill, Basingstoke, Hampshire RG21 2AG. *T:* Basingstoke 464986.

CHALLIS, Dr Anthony Arthur Leonard, CBE 1980; Chief Scientist, Department of Energy, 1980–83; *b* 24 Dec. 1921; *s* of Leonard Hough Challis and Dorothy (*née* Busby); *m* 1947, L. Beryl Hedley; two *d*. *Educ:* Newcastle upon Tyne Royal Grammar Sch.; King's Coll., Univ. of Durham. 1st cl. hons BSc Chemistry; PhD. Imperial Chemical Industries: joined Billingham Div., 1946; Research Man., HOC Div., 1962; Research Dir, Mond Div., 1966; Head of Corporate Lab., 1967; Gen. Man. Planning, 1970; Sen. Vice-Pres., ICI Americas Inc., 1975–76; Dir, Polymer Engrg, SRC, 1976–80. Mem., SERC (formerly SRC), 1973–83; Pres., PRI, 1985– (Chm. Council, 1983–85). Mem. Court, Univ. of Stirling, 1968–74. Mem., Horners' Co. *Publications:* contrib. chem, energy and managerial jls. *Recreations:* music, walking, sailing. *Address:* Classeys, Low Ham, Langport, Somerset TA10 9DP.

CHALLIS, Margaret Joan, MA; Headmistress of Queen Anne's School, Caversham, 1958–77; *b* 14 April 1917; *d* of R. S. Challis and L. Challis (*née* Fairbairn). *Educ:* Girton Coll., Cambridge. BA Hons., English Tripos, 1939, MA, 1943, Cambridge. English Mistress: Christ's Hospital, Hertford, 1940–44; Dartford Grammar School for Girls, 1944–45; Cheltenham Ladies' Coll., 1945–57. Housemistress at Cheltenham Ladies' Coll., 1949–57. *Recreations:* local history, music, old churches. *Address:* 16 Glencairn Court, Lansdown Road, Cheltenham, Glos.

CHALMERS, George Buchanan, CMG 1978; HM Diplomatic Service, retired; *b* 14 March 1929; *s* of late George and Anne Buchanan Chalmers; *m* 1954, Jeanette Donald Cant. *Educ:* Hutcheson's Grammar Sch.; Glasgow and Leiden Univs. RAF, 1950–52; FO, 1952–54; 3rd Sec., Bucharest, 1954–57; 2nd Sec., Djakarta, 1957–58; 1st Sec., Bangkok, 1958–61; FO, 1961–64; 1st Sec., Seoul, 1964–66; 1st Sec. and subseq. Commercial Counsellor, Tel Aviv, 1966–70; Dir, California Trade Drive Office, 1971; Head of Oil Dept, FCO, 1971–72; Head of S Asian Dept, FCO, 1973–75; Counsellor, Tehran, 1975–76; Minister, Tehran, 1976–79; Consul-General, Chicago, 1979–82. *Recreations:* ski-ing, bridge. *Address:* East Bank House, Bowden, Melrose, Roxburghshire TD6 0ST.

CHALMERS, Ian Pender, OBE 1980; HM Diplomatic Service; Counsellor, UK Mission to United Nations, Geneva, since 1984; *b* 30 Jan. 1939; *s* of John William Pender Chalmers and Beatrice Miriam Emery; *m* 1962, Lisa Christine Hay; two *s* two *d* (and one *d* decd). *Educ:* Hordle House, Harrow; Trinity College Dublin (BA Hons History and Political Science). Joined HM Diplomatic Service, 1963; Second Sec., Beirut, 1966–68; FCO, 1968–70; First Sec., Warsaw, 1970–72; FCO, 1972–76; First Sec., Paris, 1976–80; FCO, 1980–84. *Recreations:* reading, ski-ing, travel, watching sport. *Address:* c/o Foreign and Commonwealth Office, SW1. *Club:* Naval and Military.

CHALMERS, Patrick Edward Bruce; Controller, BBC Scotland, since 1983; *b* Chapel of Garioch, Aberdeenshire, 26 Oct. 1939; *s* of L. E. F. Chalmers, farmer, Lethenty, Inverurie, and Helen Morris Campbell; *m* 1963, Ailza Catherine Reid, *d* of late William McGibbon, Advocate in Aberdeen; three *d* *Educ:* Fettes Coll., Edinburgh; N of Scotland Coll. of Agriculture (NDA); Univ. of Durham (BScA). Joined BBC as radio talks producer, BBC Scotland, 1963; television producer, 1965; sen. producer, Aberdeen, 1970; Head of Television, Scotland, 1979–82; Gen. Man., Co-Productions, London, 1982. Mem., Grampian Region Children's Panel, 1974–79. *Recreations:* skiing, gardening. *Address:* c/o BBC, Queen Margaret Drive, Glasgow G12 8DG. *Clubs:* New (Edinburgh); Royal Northern (Aberdeen); Kandahar Ski.

CHALMERS, Thomas Wightman, CBE 1957; *b* 29 April 1913; *s* of Thomas Wightman Chalmers and Susan Florence Colman. *Educ:* Bradfield Coll.; King's Coll., London. Organ Scholar, King's Coll., London, 1934–36; BSc (Engineering), 1936. Joined BBC programme staff, 1936; successively announcer, Belfast and London; Overseas Presentation Director; Chief Assistant, Light Programme, 1945, Controller, 1948–50; Director, Nigerian Broadcasting Service, 1950–56, on secondment from BBC; Controller, North Region, BBC, 1956–58; Director of the Tanganyika Broadcasting Corporation, 1958–62; Deputy Regional Representative, UN Technical Assistance Board, East and Central Africa, 1962–64; Special Asst, Overseas and Foreign Relations, BBC, 1964–71; Chief Exec., Radio Services, United Newspapers Ltd, and Dir, Radio Fleet Productions Ltd, 1971–75. *Recreations:* travelling, reading and music. *Address:* 75 Ainsworth Street, Cambridge CB1 2PF.

CHALMERS, William Gordon, CB 1980; MC 1944; Crown Agent for Scotland, 1974–84; *b* 4 June 1922; *s* of Robert Wilson Chalmers and Mary Robertson Chalmers (*née* Clark); *m* 1948, Margaret Helen McLeod; one *s* one *d*. *Educ:* Robert Gordon's Coll., Aberdeen; Aberdeen Univ. (BL). University, 1940–42 and 1947–48; served with Queen's Own Cameron Highlanders, 1942–47; Solicitor in Aberdeen, 1948–50; Procurator Fiscal Depute at Dunfermline, 1950–59; Senior Procurator Fiscal Depute at Edinburgh, 1959–63; Asst in Crown Office, 1963–67; Deputy Crown Agent, 1967–74. *Recreations:* golf, bridge. *Address:* 3/4 Rocheid Park, East Fettes Avenue, Edinburgh EH4 1RP. *T:* 031-332 7937.

CHALONER, family name of Baron Gisborough.

CHALONER, Prof. William Gilbert, FRS 1976; Hildred Carlile Professor of Botany, Royal Holloway and Bedford New College, University of London, since 1985 (at Bedford College, 1979–85); *b* London, 22 Nov. 1928; *s* of late Ernest J. and L. Chaloner; *m* 1955, Judith Carroll; one *s* two *d*. *Educ:* Kingston Grammar Sch.; Reading Univ. (BSc, PhD). 2nd Lt RA, 1955–56. Lectr and Reader, University Coll., London, 1956–72. Visiting Prof., Pennsylvania State Univ., USA, 1961–62; Prof. of Botany, Univ. of Nigeria, 1965–66; Prof. of Botany, Birkbeck Coll., Univ. of London, 1972–79. Vis. Prof., Univ. of Mass, 1981. Member: Senate, Univ. of London, 1983–; Bd of Trustees, Royal Botanic Gardens, Kew, 1983–. Vice Pres., Geol Soc. of London, 1985–. Pres., Internat. Orgn of Palaeobotany, 1981–; Pres., Linnean Soc., 1985–. *Publications:* papers in Palaeontology and other scientific jls, dealing with fossil plants. *Recreations:* swimming, tennis, visiting USA. *Address:* 20 Parke Road, SW13 9NG. *T:* 01–748 3863.

CHAMBERLAIN, Rev. Elsie Dorothea; *see* Chamberlain-Garrington, Rev. E. D.

CHAMBERLAIN, Prof. Geoffrey Victor Price, RD 1974; MD; FRCS, FRCOG; Professor and Chairman, Obstetrics and Gynaecology, St George's Hospital Medical School, since 1983; *b* 21 April 1930; *s* of late Albert Chamberlain and Irene Chamberlain (*née* Price); *m* 1956, Jocelyn Oliver Kerley, *d* of late Sir Peter Kerley, KCVO, CBE; three *s* two *d*. *Educ:* Llandaff Cathedral Sch.; Cowbridge; University Coll. and UCH, London (Goldsmith Schol. 1948; MB 1954); MD 1968; FRCS 1960; FRCOG 1978. Residencies at RPMS, Gt Ormond St, Queen Charlotte's and Chelsea Hosps, KCH, 1955–69; Tutor, George Washington Med. Sch., Washington DC, 1965–66; Consultant Obstetrician and Gynaecologist, Queen Charlotte's and Chelsea Hosps, 1970–82. RNR, 1955–74, Surgeon Comdr. Member: Council, RSocMed, 1977–84 (Council, Obst. Sect., 1970–); Council, RCOG, 1971–77, 1982– (Vice-Pres., 1984–); Chairman: Med. Cttee, Nat. Birthday Trust, 1982–; Blair Bell Res. Soc., 1977–80; Fulbright Fellow, RCOG, 1966; Thomas Eden Fellow, RCOG, 1966; Vis. Professor: Beckman, USA, 1984; Daphne Chung, Hong Kong, 1985; Edwin Tooth, Brisbane, 1987; Foundn Prize, Amer. Assoc. of Obstetricians, 1967. *Publications:* Safety of the Unborn Child, 1969; Lecture Notes in Obstetrics, 1975, 5th edn 1985; British Births, 1970; Placental Transfer, 1979; Clinical Physiology in Obstetrics, 1980; Tubal Infertility, 1982; Pregnant Women at Work, 1984; Prepregnancy Care, 1985; contrib. to: Obstetrics by Ten Teachers, 12th edn 1980, 13th edn 1985; Gynaecology by Ten Teachers, 12th edn 1980, 13th edn 1985; contribs to BMJ, Lancet, UK and overseas Jls of Obst. and Gyn. *Recreations:* travel, labouring in wife's garden. *Address:* 10 Burghley Road, Wimbledon, SW19. *T:* 01–947 7558; Groose Cottage, Cwm Ivy, Llanmadoc, Gower, Glamorgan.

CHAMBERLAIN, George Digby, CMG 1950; Chief Secretary, Western Pacific High Commission, 1947–52; *b* 13 Feb. 1898; *s* of Digby Chamberlain, late Knockfin, Knaresborough; *m* 1931, Kirsteen Miller Holmes; one *d* (one *s* decd). *Educ:* St Catharine's Coll., Cambridge. War Service, 1917–19, with Rifle Brigade, Lieut RARO. Asst District Commissioner, Gold Coast, 1925; Asst Principal, Colonial Office, 1930–32; Asst Colonial Secretary, Gold Coast, 1932; Asst Chief Secretary, Northern Rhodesia, 1939; Colonial Secretary, Gambia, 1943–47; Acting Governor, Gambia, July-Nov. 1943, and June-Aug. 1944; Acting High Commissioner, Western Pacific, Jan.-April, and Sept. 1951–July 1952; retired 1952. *Recreations:* shooting, fishing. *Address:* 18 Douglas Crescent, Edinburgh EH12 5BA. *Club:* New (Edinburgh).

CHAMBERLAIN, Air Vice-Marshal George Philip, CB 1946; OBE 1941; RAF, retired; *b* 18 Aug. 1905; *s* of G. A. R. Chamberlain, MA, FLAS, FRICS, Enville, Staffordshire; *m* 1930, Alfreda Rosamond Kedward; one *s* one *d*. *Educ:* Denstone Coll.; Royal Air Force Coll., Cranwell. Commissioned RAF, 1925. On loan to Min. of Civil Aviation, 1947–48; Imperial Defence Coll., 1949; AOA 205 Group, MEAF, 1950; AOC Transport Wing, MEAF, 1951–52; Commandant, RAF Staff Coll., Andover, 1953–54; AO i/c A, HQ Fighter Command, 1954–57; Dep. Controller of Electronics, Min. of Supply, 1957–59, Min. of Aviation, 1959–60; Managing Director, Collins Radio Co. of England, 1961–66, non-executive director, 1967–75. *Recreations:* gardening, walking. *Address:* Little Orchard, Adelaide Close, Stanmore, Middlesex. *Club:* Royal Air Force.

CHAMBERLAIN, Kevin John; Counsellor (Legal Adviser), Office of the UK Permanent Representative to the European Communities, Brussels, since 1983; *b* 31 Jan. 1942; *s* of Arthur James Chamberlain and Gladys Mary (*née* Harris); *m* 1967, Pia Rosita Frauenlob; one *d*. *Educ:* Wimbledon Coll.; King's Coll., London (LLB). Called to the Bar, Inner Temple, 1965. Asst Legal Adviser, FCO, 1965–74; Legal Adviser: British Mil. Govt, Berlin, 1974–76; British Embassy, Bonn, 1976–77; Asst Legal Adviser, FCO, 1977–79; Legal Counsellor, FCO, 1979–83. *Recreations:* opera, riding, tennis, skiing. *Address:* c/o Foreign and Commonwealth Office, SW1.

CHAMBERLAIN, (Leslie) Neville; Chief Executive, British Nuclear Fuels, since 1986; *b* 3 Oct. 1939; *s* of Leslie Chamberlain and Doris Ann Chamberlain (*née* Thompson); *m* 1971, Joy Rachel Wellings; one *s* three *d*. *Educ:* King James Grammar School, Bishop Auckland; King's College, Univ. of Durham. UKAEA, 1962–71; Urenco Ltd, 1971–77; British Nuclear Fuels: Fuel Production, 1977–81; Enrichment Business Manager, 1981–84; Dir, Enrichment Div., 1984–86. *Recreations:* horse racing, swimming, music. *Address:* British Nuclear Fuels plc, Risley, Warrington, Cheshire WA3 6AS. *T:* Warrington 835006.

CHAMBERLAIN, Prof. Owen, AB, PhD; Professor of Physics, University of California, since 1958; *b* San Francisco, 10 July 1920; *s* of W. Edward Chamberlain and Genevieve Lucinda Owen; *m* 1943, Babette Copper (marr. diss. 1978); one *s* three *d*; *m* 1980, June Greenfield Steingart. *Educ:* Philadelphia; Dartmouth Coll., Hanover, NH (AB). Atomic research for Manhattan District, 1942, transferred to Los Alamos, 1943; worked in Argonne National Laboratory, Chicago, 1947–48, and studied at University of Chicago (PhD); Instructor in Physics, University of California, 1948; Asst Professor, 1950; Associate Professor, 1954. Guggenheim Fellowship, 1957; Loeb Lecturer in Physics, Harvard Univ., 1959. Nobel Prize (joint) for Physics, 1959. Fellow: American Phys. Soc.; Amer. Acad. of Arts and Scis; Mem., Nat. Acad. of Sciences, 1960. *Publications:* papers in Physical Review, Physical Review Letters, Nature, Nuovo Cimento. *Address:* Department of Physics, University of California, Berkeley, California 94720, USA.

CHAMBERLAIN, Hon. Sir (Reginald) Roderic (St Clair), Kt 1970; Judge of the Supreme Court of South Australia, 1959–71; *b* 17 June 1901; *s* of late Henry Chamberlain; *m* 1929, Leila Macdonald Haining; one *d*. *Educ:* St Peter's Coll.; Adelaide Univ. Crown Prosecutor, 1928; KC 1945; Crown Solicitor, 1952–59; Chm., SA Parole Board, 1970–75. Chm., Anti-Cancer Foundn. *Publication:* The Stuart Affair, 1973. *Recreations:* golf, bridge. *Address:* 72 Moseley Street, Glenelg South, SA 5045, Australia. *T:* 95.2036. *Clubs:* Adelaide, Royal Adelaide Golf (Adelaide).

CHAMBERLAIN, Richard, TD 1949; Chief Master of the Supreme Court, Chancery Division, 1985–86 (Master, 1964–84); *b* 29 Jan. 1914; *o s* of late John Chamberlain and Hilda (*née* Poynting); *m* 1938, Joan, *d* of late George and Eileen Kay; two *s* one *d*. *Educ:* Radley Coll.; Trinity Coll., Cambridge (MA). Admitted Solicitor, 1938. Served War, 1939–45: Devon Regt, TJFF, Staff Coll., Haifa. Partner, Kingsford Dorman & Co., 1948–64. Asst, Worshipful Co. of Solicitors of the City of London, 1966, Warden, 1973–74, Master, 1975. *Publication:* Asst Editor, Supreme Court Practice, 1967. *Recreations:* gardening, photography, travel, grandparental duties. *Address:* 23 Drax Avenue, Wimbledon, SW20 0EG. *T:* 01–946 4219. *Club:* Garrick.

CHAMBERLAIN, Hon. Sir Roderick; *see* Chamberlain, Hon Sir (Reginald) R.

CHAMBERLAIN, Ronald; Lecturer and Housing Consultant; *b* 19 April 1901; *m* Joan Smith McNeill (*d* 1950), Edinburgh; one *s* one *d*; *m* 1951, Florence Lilian Illingworth, Cricklewood. *Educ:* Owens Sch., Islington; Gonville and Caius Coll., Cambridge (MA). Formerly Secretary to National Federation of Housing Societies and (later) Chief Exec. Officer to the Miners' Welfare Commission; later engaged on administrative work for the National Service Hostels Corporation. MP (Lab) Norwood Division of Lambeth, 1945–50; Member of Middlesex County Council, 1947–52. Governor, Middlesex Hosp., 1947–74. *Recreation:* tennis. *Address:* 145 Hampstead Way, NW11 7YA. *T:* 01–455 1491.

CHAMBERLAIN-GARRINGTON, Rev. Elsie Dorothea, BD (London); Minister, Congregational Centre Church, Nottingham, since 1983; Chairman, Congregational Federation Council, since 1977 (President, 1973–75); *m* 1947, Rev. J. L. St C. Garrington (*d* 1978). *Educ:* Channing Sch.; King's Coll., London (BD). Asst Minister Berkeley Street, Liverpool, 1939–41; Minister: Christ Church, Friern Barnet, 1941–46; Vineyard Congregational Church, Richmond, 1947–54; BBC Religious Dept, 1950–67; Associate Minister, The City Temple, 1968–70; Minister: Hutton Free Church, Brentwood, 1971–80; Chulmleigh, 1980–83; North Street, Taunton, 1980–86. 1st woman chaplain, HM Forces, 1946–47. Chm., Congregational Union of England and Wales, 1956–57; Nat. Pres., Free Church Women's Council, 1984–85. *Publications:* (ed) Lift Up Your Hearts, 1959; (ed) Calm Delight: devotional anthology, 1959; (ed) 12 Mini-Commentaries on the Jerusalem Bible, 1970. *Recreation:* music. *Address:* 4 Castle Gate, Nottingham NG1 7AS. *T:* Nottingham 413801.

CHAMBERS, Prof. Andrew David; Dean, City University Business School, since 1986; *b* 7 April 1943; *s* of Lewis Harold and Florence Lilian Chambers; *m* 1969, Mary Elizabeth Ann Kilbey (marr. diss. 1984); two *s*. *Educ:* St Albans Sch.; Hatfield Coll., Univ. of Durham (BA Hons). FCA, FBCS, FCCA, FIIA. Arthur Andersen & Co., 1965–69; Barker & Dobson, 1969–70; United Biscuits, 1970–71; City University Business School: Lectr in Computer Applications in Accountancy, 1971–74; Leverhulme Sen. Res. Fellow in Internal Auditing, 1974–78; Sen. Lectr in Audit and Management Control, 1978–83; BP Prof. of Internal Auditing, 1983–; Administrative Sub-Dean, 1983–86; Acting Dean, 1985–86. Vis. Prof. in Computer Auditing, Univ. of Leuven, Belgium, 1980–81. Member Council: BCS, 1979–82 (Mem., Tech. Bd; Chm., Meetings Cttee); IIA, 1985–86 (Chm., Res. Cttee). *Publications:* (with O. J. Hanson) Keeping Computers Under Control, 1975; (ed) Internal Auditing: developments and horizons, 1979; Internal Auditing: theory and practice, 1981, 2nd edn (with G. M. Selim and G. Vinten) 1987; Computer Auditing, 1981, 2nd edn (with J. M. Court) 1986; papers in learned jls. *Recreations:* photography, bird watching, conservation. *Address:* City University Business School, Frobisher Crescent, Barbican Centre, EC2Y 8HB. *T:* 01–920 0111. *Club:* Reform.

CHAMBERS, Dr Douglas Robert; HM Coroner, Inner North London, since 1970; *b* 2 Nov. 1929; *s* of Douglas Henry Chambers and Elizabeth Paterson; *m* 1955, Barbara June Rowe; one *s* two *d*. *Educ:* Shene Grammar Sch.; King's College, London. MB BS; AKC 1953; LLB 1960. Called to the Bar, Lincoln's Inn, 1965. RAF Med. Br., 1955–58; Med. Advr, Parke Davis, 1959–61, Nicholas Laboratories, 1961–63, Pharmacia, 1964–65; Med. Dir, Hoechst Pharmaceuticals, 1965–70; Dep. Coroner, West London, 1969–70. Vis. Lectr, City Univ., 1976–; Hon. Sen. Clin. Lectr in med. law, UCL, 1978–; Hon. Sen. Lectr, medical law, Royal Free Hosp., 1978–. Chairman: Richmond Div., BMA, 1969–70; Animal Research and Welfare Panel, Biological Council, 1986–; Pres., Library (sci. research) section, RSocMed, 1979–80; Pres., British sect., Anglo-German Med. Soc., 1980–84; Pres., Coroners' Soc., 1985–86. Hon. Mem., British Micro-circulation Soc., 1986 (Hon. Treas., 1968–86). Dist Comr, Richmond & Barnes Dist Scouts, 1976–85 (Silver Acorn 1984). Pres., Kensington Rowing Club, 1973–78. *Publications:* (jtly) Coroners' Inquiries, 1985; papers on medico-legal subjects. *Recreation:* local history of coroners and of scouting. *Address:* 4 Ormond Avenue, Richmond, Surrey TW10 6TN. *T:* (home) 01–940 7745, (court) 01–387 4882. *Clubs:* Wig and Pen; Auriol-Kensington Rowing.

CHAMBERS, Hon. George Michael; MP (People's National Movement), St Ann's, since 1966; Prime Minister and Minister of Finance and Planning, Trinidad and Tobago, since 1981; *b* 4 Oct. 1928; *m* 1956, Juliana; one *d*. *Educ:* Nelson Street Boys' RC Sch.; Burke's Coll.; Osmond High Sch.; Wolsey Hall, Oxford. Parly Sec., Min. of Finance, 1966; Minister of Public Utilities and Housing, 1969; Minister of State in Min. of National Security and Minister of State in Min. of Finance, Planning and Develt, 1970; Minister of National Security, Nov. 1970; Minister of Finance, Planning and Development, 1971–73; Minister of Finance, 1973–75; Minister of Educn and Culture, 1975–76; Minister of Industry and Commerce and Minister of Agriculture, Lands and Fisheries, 1976–81. Formerly, Asst Gen. Sec. and Mem. Central Exec., Gen. Council, and Res. and Disciplinary Cttees, People's National Movement. Chm. Bd of Governors, World Bank and IMF, 1973; Governor, Caribbean Develt Bank, 1981–. *Address:* Prime Minister's Residence, Port-of-Spain, Trinidad.

CHAMBERS, Harry Heyworth; Counsellor (Defence Supply), British Embassy, Bonn, since 1984; *b* 7 Nov. 1926; *s* of Francis Charles Chambers and Margaret Chambers; *m* 1st, 1955, Stella Howard (decd); 2nd, 1965, Elizabeth Mary Sansom; one *d*. *Educ:* Liverpool Collegiate Sch.; Liverpool Univ. (BComm). RAF 1945–48. Joined Automotive Products Co. Ltd, 1951, Manager, Service Div., 1956; Principal, 1971, Asst Sec., 1976, MoD. *Recreations:* mountaineering, translating. *Address:* 17 Birch Grove, W3. *T:* 01–992 1502.

CHAMBERS, Nicholas Mordaunt; QC 1985; *b* 25 Feb. 1944; *s* of Marcus Mordaunt Bertrand Chambers and Lona Margit Chambers (*née* Gross); *m* 1966, Sarah Elizabeth, *er d* of Thomas Herbert Fothergill Banks; two *s* one *d*. *Educ:* King's School, Worcester; Hertford College, Oxford (BA 1965). Called to the Bar, Gray's Inn, 1966. *Recreation:* sketching. *Address:* 1 Brick Court, Temple, EC4. *T:* 01–583 0777. *Clubs:* Garrick, Lansdowne.

CHAMBERS, Prof. Robert Guy; Professor of Physics, University of Bristol, since 1964; *b* 8 Sept. 1924; *s* of A. G. P. Chambers; *m* 1950, Joan Brislee (marr. diss. 1981); one *d*. *Educ:* King Edward VI Sch., Southampton; Peterhouse, Cambridge. Work on tank armament (Ministry of Supply), 1944–46; Electrical Research Association, 1946–47; Royal Society Mond Laboratory, Cambridge, 1947–57; Stokes Student, Pembroke Coll., 1950–53; PhD 1952; ICI Fellow, 1953–54; NRC Post-doctoral Fellow, Ottawa, 1954–55; University Demonstrator, Cambridge, 1955–57; Bristol University: Sen. Lectr, 1958–61; Reader in Physics, 1961–64; Dean of Science, 1973–76, 1985–; Pro-Vice-Chancellor, 1978–81. Member: Physics Cttee, 1967–71, Nuclear Physics Bd, 1971–74, Sci. Bd, 1975–78, SRC; Physical Sci. Sub-Cttee, UGC, 1974–81. Institute of Physics: Mem., Publications Cttee, 1969–81 (Chm., 1977–81); Vice-Pres., 1977–81. *Publications:* various papers in learned journals on the behaviour of metals at low temperatures. *Recreation:* hill-walking. *Address:* 9 Apsley Road, Clifton, Bristol BS8 2SH. *T:* Bristol 739833.

CHAMIER, Anthony Edward Deschamps; Head of Further and Higher Education Branch 1, Department of Education and Science, since 1984; *b* 16 Aug. 1935; *s* of Brig. George Chamier, OBE and Marion (*née* Gascoigne), Achandounie, Alness, Ross-shire; *m* 1962, Anne-Carole Tweeddale Dalling, *d* of William and Kathleen Dalling, Transvaal, S Africa; one *s* one *d*. *Educ:* Stowe, Buckingham; Trinity Hall, Cambridge; Yale Univ. (Henry Fellow). Military service, 1st Bn Seaforth Highlanders, 1953–55. HM Foreign (later Diplomatic) Service, 1960; Third Secretary, Foreign Office, 1960–62; Second Sec., Rome, 1962–64; Asst Political Adviser, HQ Middle East Comd, Aden, 1964–66; First Sec., FCO, 1966–71; Head of Chancery, Helsinki, 1971–72; seconded, later transf. to Dept of Educn and Science; Principal, 1972–73; Principal Private Sec. to Sec. of State for Educn and Science, 1973–74; Asst Sec., 1974–79; Under Sec., 1980–; Dir of Estabts and Orgn, 1980–84. *Recreations:* walking, shooting, gardening. *Address:* 230 Hanworth Road, Hampton, Mddx TW12 3EP. *T:* 01–979 8475. *Club:* Army and Navy.

CHAMPERNOWNE, David Gawen, MA; FBA 1970; Professor of Economics and Statistics, Cambridge University, 1970–78, now Emeritus; Fellow of Trinity College, Cambridge, since 1959; *b* Oxford, 9 July 1912; *s* of late F. G. Champernowne, MA, Bursar of Keble Coll., Oxford; *m* 1948, Wilhelmina Dullaert; two *s*. *Educ:* The College, Winchester; King's Coll., Cambridge. 1st Class Maths, Pts 1 and 2; 1st Class Economics Pt 2. Asst Lecturer at London Sch. of Economics, 1936–38; Fellow of King's Coll., Cambridge, 1937–48; University Lecturer in Statistics at Cambridge, 1938–40; Asst in Prime Minister's statistical dept, 1940–41; Asst dir of Programmes, Ministry of Aircraft Production, 1941–45; Dir of Oxford Univ. Institute of Statistics, 1945–48; Fellow of Nuffield Coll., Oxford, 1945–59; Prof. of Statistics, Oxford Univ., 1948–59; Reader in Economics, Cambridge Univ., 1959–70. Editor, Economic Jl, 1971–76. *Publications:* Uncertainty and Estimation in Economics (3 vols), 1969; The Distribution of Income between Persons, 1973. *Address:* 25 Worts Causeway, Cambridge CB1 4RJ. *T:* Cambridge 247829; Trinity College, Cambridge.

CHAMPION, John Stuart, CMG 1977; OBE 1963; HM Diplomatic Service, retired; *b* 17 May 1921; *er s* of Rev. Sir Reginald Champion, KCMG, OBE and of Margaret, *d* of late Very Rev. W. M. Macgregor, DD, LLD; *m* 1944, Olive Lawrencina, *o d* of late Lawrence Durning Holt, Liverpool; five *s* two *d*. *Educ:* Shrewsbury Sch.; Balliol Coll., Oxford (Schol., BA). Commnd 11 Hussars PAO, 1941–46. Colonial Service (later HMOCS), Uganda, 1946–63: District Officer; Secretariat, 1949–52; Private Sec. to Governor, 1952; Asst Financial Sec., 1956; Actg Perm. Sec., Min. of Health, 1959; Perm. Sec., Min. of Internal Affairs, 1960; retd 1963; Principal, CRO, 1963; 1st Sec., FCO, 1965; Head of Chancery, Tehran, 1968; Counsellor, Amman, 1971; FCO 1973; British Resident Comr, Anglo/French Condominium of the New Hebrides, 1975–78. Mem., West Midlands RHA, 1980–81; Chm., Herefordshire HA, 1982–86. Dep. County Comr, St John Ambulance, 1985–. Governor, Royal National Coll. for the Blind, 1980– (Vice-Chm., 1985–); Chm., Hereford Cathedral Appeal Fund, 1986–. *Recreations:* hill walking, golf, music. *Address:* Farmore, Callow, Hereford HR2 8DB. *T:* Hereford 274875. *Club:* Royal Commonwealth Society.

CHAN, Rt. Hon. Sir Julius, KBE 1980 (CBE 1975); PC 1981; MP 1968; Deputy Prime Minister and Minister for Finance and Planning, Papua New Guinea, since 1985; Parliamentary Leader, People's Progress Party, Papua New Guinea, since 1970; *b* 29 Aug. 1939; *s* of Chin Pak and Tingoris Chan; *m* 1966, Stella Ahmat; three *s* one *d*. *Educ:* Marist Brothers Coll., Ashgrove, Qld; Univ. of Queensland, Australia (Agricl Science). Co-operative Officer, Papua New Guinea Admin, 1960–62; private business, coastal shipping and merchandise, 1963–70. Minister for Finance, 1972–77; Dep. Prime Minister and Minister for Primary Industry, 1977–78; Prime Minister of PNG, 1980–82. Governor: World Bank/IMF, 1976; Asian Development Bank, 1977. Fellow, Internat. Bankers Assoc., USA, 1976. Attended meetings and conferences worldwide as rep. of PNG, latterly as leader of PNG delegn, 1970–; made State and official visits to Australia, Rep. of Korea, China, Vanuatu, Indonesia, UK, France, Italy, NZ. Hon. DEc Dankook (Republic of Korea) 1978. *Recreations:* swimming, walking, boating. *Address:* PO Box 717, Rabaul, Papua New Guinea.

CHANCE, Sqdn Ldr Dudley Raymond, FRGS; a Recorder of the Crown Court, since 1980; *b* 9 July 1916; *s* of Captain Arthur Chance, Sherwood Foresters, and Byzie Chance; *m* 1958, Jessie Maidstone, widow, *d* of John and Alice Dewing. *Educ:* Nottingham High Sch.; London Univ. (BA Oriental Religions and Philosophies, LLB 1969); BA Hons Internat. Politics and For. Policy, Open Univ., 1980. Called to Bar, Middle Temple, 1955. Commissioned in Royal Air Force, 1936; served Egypt, Transjordan, 1936–37; Bomber Comd (4 Gp), 1938; served in Bomber Comd Nos 97 and 77 Sqdns; took part in first raids on Norway; crashed off Trondheim; picked up later from sea by HMS Basilisk, later sunk at Dunkirk; Air Ministry, Whitehall, 1941–42, later in 2 Group, Norfolk, 21 Sqdn; also served in SEAC, Bengal/Burma. Sqdn Ldr, RAFO, until March 1961; gazetted to retain rank of Sqdn Ldr from that date. Member: panel of Chairmen of Medical Appeal Tribunals (DHSS), 1978–; panel of Independent Inspectors for motorway and trunk road inquiries for DoE, 1978–83. Parly candidate (C), Norwich North, 1959. FRGS 1979. *Recreations:* violin, painting. *Address:* Lamb Buildings, Temple, EC4; Fenners Chambers, 5 Gresham Road, Cambridge. *Clubs:* Goldfish (RAF aircrew rescued from sea); Norfolk (Norwich).

CHANCE, Major Geoffrey Henry Barrington, CBE 1962; *b* 16 Dec. 1893; *s* of Ernest Chance, Burghfield, Berks; *m* 1st, 1914, Hazel Mary Louise Cadell (decd); two *d*; 2nd, 1933, Daphne Corona Wallace; one *s* one *d*. *Educ:* Eton. Engineering, 1913–14. Army, 1914–19. Qualified Chartered Accountant, 1928, practised, 1930–40; HM Treasury, 1941–45. Company director. CC, Alderman (Wilts), 1955–67; Chairman Chippenham Conservative Assoc., 1955–62; High Sheriff of Wiltshire, 1965. *Recreations:* fishing, shooting. *Address:* Flat 2, Hatton's Lodge, Braydon, Swindon, Wilts.

CHANCE, Sir Roger (James Ferguson), 3rd Bt, *cr* 1900; MC; *b* 26 Jan. 1893; *e s* of George Ferguson Chance (2nd *s* of 1st Bt) and Mary Kathleen, *d* of Rev. Henry Stobart; *S* uncle 1935; *m* 1921, Mary Georgina (*d* 1984), *d* of Col William Rowney, and Kate, *d* of Maj.-Gen. Fendall Currie; one *s* two *d* (and one *s* decd). *Educ:* Eton; Trinity Coll., Cambridge (MA); London University (PhD). Served European War, Aug. 1914–April 1918; Capt. and Adjutant 4th (RI) Dragoon Guards, 1916–17; Capt. 1st Batt. The Rifle Brigade, 1918 (twice wounded, despatches twice, MC); Editor, Review of Reviews, 1932–33; Press Attaché, British Embassy, Berlin, 1938; Sqdn Leader RAFVR, 1940–41. *Publications:* Until Philosophers are Kings (political philosophy), 1928; Conservatism and Wealth (with Oliver Baldwin, politics), 1929; Winged Horses (fiction), 1932; Be Absolute for Death (fiction), 1964; The End of Man (theology), 1973; Apple and Eve (a Cambridge symposium). *Heir: s* (George) Jeremy (ffolliott) Chance [*b* 24 Feb. 1926; *m* 1950, Cecilia Mary Elizabeth, *d* of Sir (William) Hugh (Stobart) Chance, CBE; two *s* two *d*]. *Address:* Royal Bank of Scotland, Whitehall, SW1. *Club:* Athenæum.

See also Sir R. T. Armstrong.

CHANCELLOR, Alexander Surtees; Deputy Editor, Sunday Telegraph, since 1986; *b* 4 Jan. 1940; *s* of Sir Christopher Chancellor, *qv*; *m* 1964, Susanna Elisabeth Debenham; two *d*. *Educ:* Eton College; Trinity Hall, Cambridge. Reuters News Agency, 1964–74; ITN, 1974–75; Editor: The Spectator, 1975–84; Time and Tide, 1984–86. *Address:* 1 Souldern Road, W14. *T:* 01–602 2684. *Club:* Garrick.

CHANCELLOR, Sir Christopher (John), Kt 1951; CMG 1948; MA; *b* 29 March 1904; *s* of late Sir John Robert Chancellor, GCMG, GCVO, GBE, DSO; *m* 1926, Sylvia Mary (OBE 1976), *e d* of Sir Richard Paget, 2nd Bt, and Lady Muriel Finch-Hatton, *d* of 12th Earl of Winchilsea and Nottingham; two *s* two *d*. *Educ:* Eton Coll.; Trinity College., Cambridge (1st class in History). Joined Reuters in 1930; Reuters' Gen. Manager and Chief Corresp in Far East with headquarters in Shanghai, 1931–39; Gen. Manager of Reuters, Ltd, 1944–59, Trustee, 1960–65; Chairman: Daily Herald, 1959–61; Odhams Press Ltd, 1960–61 (Vice-Chm., 1959–60); Chm. and Chief Executive, The Bowater Paper Corporation Ltd and associated cos, 1962–69. Director: Northern and Employers Assurance Co. Ltd, 1946–64; Bristol United Press Ltd, 1958–74; Observer Ltd, 1961–64. Chm., Madame Tussaud's, 1961–72. Mem. Court, London Univ., 1956–62; Chm. Exec. Cttee of The Pilgrims Soc. of Great Britain, 1958–67; Mem. Board of Regents, Memorial Univ. of Newfoundland, 1963–68; Vice-Pres., National Council of Social Service, 1959–71; Dep.-Chm., Council of St Paul's Cathedral Trust, 1954–62; Chm., Appeal and Publicity Cttee, King George VI National Memorial Fund, 1952–54; Dep.-Chm., Exec. Cttee, 1955–56; Chm., Bath Preservation Trust, 1969–76. King Haakon VII Liberty Cross, 1947; Officer Order of Orange Nassau, 1950; Comdr Royal Order of Danebrog, 1951; Officer, Legion of Honour, 1951; Comdr Order of Civil Merit (Spain), 1952; Cross of Comdr Order of Phœnix, 1953; Comdr Order of Vasa, 1953; Comdr Order of Merit (Italy), 1959. *Address:* The Priory, Ditcheat, Shepton Mallet, Somerset. *Club:* Travellers'.

See also A. S. Chancellor.

CHANDLER, Colin Michael; Head of Defence Export Services, Ministry of Defence, since 1985; *b* 7 Oct. 1939; *s* of Henry John Chandler and Mary Martha (*née* Bowles); *m* 1964, Jennifer Mary Crawford; one *s* one *d*. *Educ*: St Joseph's Acad.; Hatfield Polytechnic. ACMA. Commercial Apprentice, De Havilland Aircraft Co., 1956–61; Contracts Officer, Hawker Siddeley Aviation, Hatfield, 1962–66; Hawker Siddeley Aviation, Kingston: Commercial Manager, 1967–72; Exec. Dir, Commercial, 1973–76; Exec. Dir and Gen. Manager, 1977; British Aerospace, Kingston: Divl Man. Dir., 1978–82; Gp Marketing Dir, 1983–85. Commander, Order of the Lion of Finland, 1982. *Recreations*: jogging, playing tennis, reading, listening to music. *Address*: Ministry of Defence, Whitehall, SW1. *T*: 01-218 3042. *Clubs*: Les Ambassadeurs, Belfry.

CHANDLER, Edwin George, CBE 1979; FRIBA, FRTPI; City Architect, City of London, 1961–79; *b* 28 Aug. 1914; *e s* of Edwin and Honor Chandler; *m* 1938, Iris Dorothy, *o d* of Herbert William Grubb; one *d*. *Educ*: Selhurst Grammar Sch., Croydon. Asst Architect, Hants County Council and City of Portsmouth, 1936–39. Served in HMS Vernon, Mine Design Dept, 1940–45. Gained distinction in thesis, ARIBA, 1942, FRIBA 1961. Dep. Architect and Planning Officer, West Ham, 1945–47; City Architect and Planning Officer, City of Oxford, 1947–61. Member: RIBA Council, 1950–52; Univ. Social Survey Cttee, Oxford; City of London Archaeological Trust; Trustee, Silver Jubilee Walkway Trust; Chm., Bd of Alleyn's Estate, Dulwich; Gov., James Allen's Sch., Dulwich. Liveryman, Gardeners' Co.; Mem., Court of Common Council, Corp. of London (Cornhill Ward), 1982–. *Publications*: Housing for Old Age, 1939; City of Oxford Development Plan, 1950; articles contrib. to press and professional jls. *Recreations*: landscaping, travel, swimming. *Address*: 1 Perifield, Dulwich, SE21 8NG. *T*: 01-670 3251. *Clubs*: Guildhall, Dulwich.

CHANDLER, Sir Geoffrey, Kt 1983; CBE 1976; Industry Adviser, Royal Society of Arts, 1987; *b* 15 Nov. 1922; *s* of Frederick George Chandler, MD, FRCP, and Marjorie Chandler; *m* 1955, Lucy Bertha Buxton; four *d*. *Educ*: Sherborne; Trinity Coll., Cambridge (MA History). Military Service, 1942–46: Captain 60th Rifles; Political Warfare Exec., Cairo; Special Ops Exec. (Force 133), Greece; Anglo-Greek Information Service, W Macedonia, 1945; Press Officer, Volos and Salonika, 1946. Cambridge Univ., 1947–49; Captain, Univ. Lawn Tennis, 1949. BBC Foreign News Service, 1949–51; Leader Writer and Features Editor, Financial Times, 1951–56; Commonwealth Fund Fellow, Columbia Univ., New York, 1953–54; Shell Internat. Petroleum Co.: Manager, Econs Div., 1957–61; Area Co-ordinator, W Africa, 1961–64; Chm. and Man. Dir, Shell Trinidad Ltd, 1964–69; Shell Internat. Petroleum Co.: Public Affairs Co-ordinator, 1969–78; Dir, 1971–78; Dir, Shell Petroleum Co.; and Shell Petroleum NV, 1976–78; Dir Gen., NEDO, and Mem., NEDC, 1978–83; Dir, Industry Year 1986, 1984–86. Pres., Inst. of Petroleum, 1972–74. Member: Council and Exec. Cttee, Overseas Develt Inst., 1969–78; British Overseas Trade Adv. Council, 1978–82; Council and Exec. Cttee, VSO. Chm., BBC Consultative Group on Industrial and Business Affairs, and Mem. BBC Gen. Adv. Council, 1983–; Chm., Consultative Council, Soc. of Educn Officers Schools Curriculum Award, 1984–; Mem., Wilton Park Academic Council, 1983–; Associate, Ashridge Management Coll., 1983–; Pres., Assoc. of Management Centres, 1985–; Dir, Blackheath Preservation Trust. FRSA. Hon. Fellow: Sheffield City Polytechnic, 1981; Girton Coll., Cambridge, 1986; Hon. FInstPet 1982. Hon. DBA Internat. Management Centre from Buckingham, 1986. *Publications*: The Divided Land: an Anglo-Greek Tragedy, 1959; The State of the Nation: Trinidad & Tobago in the later 1960s, 1969; articles on oil, energy, trans-national corporations, and development; numerous speeches, urging employee participation, coherent British indust. policy and industrially constructive use of N Sea oil revenues. *Recreations*: working in woodland, gardening, playing the oboe. *Address*: (office) 8 John Adam Street, WC2N 6EZ. *T*: 01-930 5115; (home) 46 Hyde Vale, Greenwich, SE10 8HP. *T*: 01-692 5304. *Clubs*: Athenæum; Hawks (Cambridge).

CHANDLER, George, MA, PhD, FLA, FRHistS; FRSA; International Adviser and Editor in Library and Information Science; *b* England, 2 July 1915; *s* of W. and F. W. Chandler; *m* 1937, Dorothy Lowe; one *s*. *Educ*: Central Grammar Sch., Birmingham; Leeds Coll. of Commerce; University of London. ALAA 1974. Birmingham Public Libraries, 1931–37; Leeds Public Libraries, 1937–46; WEA Tutor Organiser, 1946–47; Borough Librarian, Dudley, 1947–50; Dep. City Librarian, Liverpool, 1950–52, City Librarian, 1952–74; Dir-Gen., Nat. Library of Australia, 1974–80. Sec. Dudley Arts Club, 1948–50; Pres., Internat. Assoc. of Met. City Libraries, 1968–71; Pres. 1962–71 (Hon. Sec. 1957–62), Soc. of Municipal and County Chief Librarians; Dir, 1962–74 (Hon. Sec. 1955–62), Liverpool and District Scientific, Industrial and Research Library Advisory Council; Hon. Librarian, 1957–74 (Hon. Sec. 1950–57), Historic Soc. of Lancs and Ches.; Chm., Exec. Cttee, 1965–70, President, 1971, Library Assoc.; Member: DES Library Adv. Council for England and Wales, 1965–72; British Library Organising Cttee, 1972–73; British Library Bd, 1973–74. Hon. Editor, Internat. Library Review, 1969–. Unesco expert in Tunisia, 1964. *Publications*: Dudley, 1949; William Roscoe, 1953; Liverpool 1207–1957; Liverpool Shipping, 1960; Liverpool under James I, 1960; How to Find Out, 1963 (5th edn 1982); Four Centuries of Banking: Martins Bank, Vol. I, 1964, Vol. II, 1968; Liverpool under Charles I, 1965; Libraries in the Modern World, 1965; How to Find Out About Literature, 1968; Libraries in the East, 1971; Libraries, Bibliography and Documentation in the USSR, 1972; Victorian and Edwardian Liverpool and the North West, 1972; An Illustrated History of Liverpool, 1972; (ed) International Librarianship, 1972; Merchant Venturers, 1973; Victorian and Edwardian Manchester, 1974; Liverpool and Literature, 1974; Recent Developments in International and National Library and Information Services, 1982; (ed) International Series of Monographs on Library and Information Science; (ed) series, Recent Advances in Library and Information Services, 1981–; contributions to educl and library press. *Recreations*: writing, research; walking; foreign travel. *Address*: 43 Saxon Close, Stratford-upon-Avon, Warwickshire CV37 7DX.

CHANDLER, Tony John; *b* 7 Nov. 1928; *s* of Harold William and Florence Ellen Chandler; *m* 1954, Margaret Joyce Weston; one *s* one *d*. *Educ*: King's Coll., London. MSc. PhD, AKC, MA. Lectr, Birkbeck Coll., Univ. of London, 1952–56; University Coll. London: Lectr, 1956–65; Reader in Geography, 1965–69; Prof. of Geography, 1969–73; Prof. of Geography, Manchester Univ., 1973–77; Master of Birkbeck Coll., Univ. of London, 1977–79. Sec., Royal Meteorological Soc., 1969–73. Member: Council, NERC; Health and Safety Commn; Cttee of Experts on Major Hazards; Royal Soc. Study Gp on Pollution in the Atmosphere, 1974–77; Clean Air Council; Royal Commn on Environmental Pollution, 1973–77; Standing Commn on Energy and the Environment 1978. *Publications*: The Climate of London, 1965; Modern Meteorology and Climatology, 1972, 2nd edn 1981; contribs to: Geographical Jl, Geography, Weather, Meteorological Magazine, Bulletin of Amer. Meteorological Soc., etc. *Recreations*: music, reading, travel. *Address*: 44 Knoll Rise, Orpington, Kent BR6 0EL. *T*: Orpington 32880.

CHANDOS, 3rd Viscount *cr* 1954, of Aldershot; **Thomas Orlando Lyttelton**; Banker, since 1974, Director, since 1985, Kleinwort, Benson Ltd; *b* 12 Feb. 1953; *s* of 2nd Viscount Chandos and of Caroline Mary (who *m* 1985, Hon. David Hervey Erskine), *d* of Rt Hon. Sir Alan Lascelles, GCB, GCVO, CMG, MC; *S* father, 1980; *m* 1985, Arabella Sarah, *d* of Adrian Bailey and Lady Mary Russell; one *s*. *Educ*: Eton; Worcester College, Oxford (BA). *Heir*: *s* Hon. Oliver Antony Lyttelton, *b* 21 Feb. 1986. *Address*: 149 Gloucester Avenue, NW1. *T*: 01–722 8329.

CHANDOS-POLE, Lt-Col John, CVO 1979; OBE 1951; JP; Lord-Lieutenant for Northamptonshire, 1967–84; *b* 20 July 1909; *s* of late Brig.-Gen. Harry Anthony Chandos-Pole, CBE, DL, JP and late Ada Ismay, Heverswood, Brasted, Kent; *m* 1952, Josephine Sylvia, *d* of late Brig.-Gen. Cyril Randell Crofton, CBE, Limerick House, Milborne Port, near Sherborne; two step-*d*. *Educ*: Eton; Magdalene Coll., Cambridge (MA). 2nd Lieut Coldstream Guards, 1933; ADC: to Governor of Bombay, May-Nov., 1937; to Governor of Bengal, Nov. 1937–June 1938, Oct. 1938–Feb. 1939, also to Viceroy of India, June-Oct., 1938. Served War of 1939–45: France and Belgium (wounded); Palestine, 1948 (wounded, despatches); commanded 1st Bn, Coldstream Guards, 1947–48; Guards Depot, 1948–50; 2nd Bn, Coldstream Guards, 1950–52. Lieut-Col 1949; retired, 1953. A Member of the Hon. Corps of Gentlemen-at-Arms, 1956–79 (Harbinger, 1966–79). DL 1965, JP 1957, Northants. KStJ 1975. *Recreations*: racing and travel. *Address*: Newnham Hall, Daventry, Northants NN11 6HQ. *T*: Daventry 702711. *Clubs*: Boodle's, Pratt's.

CHANDOS-POLE, Major John Walkelyne, DL, JP; *b* 4 Nov. 1913; *o s* of late Col Reginald Walkelyne Chandos-Pole, TD, JP, Radburne Hall; *m* 1947, Ilsa Jill, *er d* of Emil Ernst Barstz, Zürich; one *d* (one *s* decd). *Educ*: Eton; RMC, Sandhurst. Commissioned Grenadier Guards, 1933; ADC to Viceroy of India, 1938–39; retired, 1947. JP 1951, DL 1961, Derbys; High Sheriff of Derbys, 1959. *Recreation*: shooting. *Address*: Radburne Hall, Kirk Langley, Derby DE6 4LZ. *T*: Kirk Langley 246. *Clubs*: Army and Navy, Lansdowne; MCC; County (Derby).

CHANDRA, Ram; *see* Ram Chandra.

CHANDRACHUD, Hon. Yeshwant Vishnu; Chief Justice of India, since 1978; *b* Poona (Maharashtra), 12 July 1920; *s* of Vishnu Balkrishna Chandrachud and Indira; *m* Prabha; one *s* one *d*. *Educ*: Bombay Univ. (BA, LLB). Advocate of Bombay High Court, 1943, civil and criminal work; part-time Prof. of Law, Government Law Coll., Bombay, 1949–52; Asst Govt Pleader, 1952; Govt Pleader, 1958; Judge, Bombay High Court, 1961–72; one-man Pay Commn for Bombay Municipal Corporation officers, later Arbitrator in dispute between Electricity Supply and Transport Undertaking and its employees' union; one-man Commn to inquire into circumstances leading to death of Deen Dayal Upadhyaya; Judge, Supreme Court of India, 1972–78. President: Internat. Law Assoc. (India Branch), 1978–; Indian Law Inst., 1978–. *Address*: (official) Supreme Court of India, New Delhi, India. *T*: 387165; 5 Krishna Menon Marg, New Delhi 110011. *T*: 374053, 372922; (permanent) 131 Budhwar Peth, Balkrishna Niwas, Poona 411002.

CHANDRASEKHAR, Prof. Sivaramakrishna, FRS 1983; Professor, Raman Research Institute, Bangalore, since 1971; Nehru Visiting Professor of Physics and Fellow, Pembroke College, Cambridge, 1986–87; *b* 6 Aug. 1930; *s* of S. Sivaramakrishnan and Sitalaxmi; *m* 1954, Ila Pinglay; one *s* one *d*. *Educ*: Nagpur Univ. (MSc, DSc); Pembroke Coll., Cambridge (PhD 1958). Res. Schol., Raman Res. Inst., Bangalore, 1950–54; 1851 Exhibn Schol., Cavendish Lab., Cambridge, 1954–57; DSIR Fellow, Dept of Crystallography, UCL, 1957–59; Res. Fellow, Davy Faraday Res. Lab., Royal Instn, 1959–61; Prof. and Hd of Dept of Physics, Univ. of Mysore, 1961–71. *Publications*: Liquid Crystals, 1977; editor of several books; contrib. scientific papers to learned jls. *Recreation*: painting. *Address*: Raman Research Institute, Bangalore 560080, India. *T*: (office) 360124 ext. 305, 365267; (home) 362356.

CHANDRASEKHAR, Subrahmanyan, FRS 1944; Morton D. Hull Distinguished Service Professor of Theoretical Astrophysics, University of Chicago, USA, 1937–85; *b* 19 Oct. 1910; *m* 1936, Lalitha Doraiswamy. *Educ*: Presidency Coll., Madras; Trinity Coll., Cambridge (Government of Madras Research Scholar, PhD 1933, ScD 1942). Fellow of Trinity Coll., Cambridge, 1933–37, Hon. Fellow 1981. Managing Editor Astrophysical Journal, 1952–71. Nehru Memorial Lecture, India, 1968. Member: Nat. Acad. of Sciences (Henry Draper Medal, 1971); Amer. Philosophical Soc.; Amer. Acad. of Arts and Sciences (Rumford Medal, 1957). Hon. DSc Oxon 1972. Bruce Gold Medal, Astr. Soc. Pacific, 1952; Gold Medal, Royal Astronomical Soc. London, 1953; Royal Medal, Royal Society, 1962; Nat. Medal of Science (USA), 1966; Heineman Prize, Amer. Phys. Soc., 1974; (jtly) Nobel Prize for Physics, 1983; Copley Medal, Royal Soc., 1984; Dr Tomalla Prize, Eidgenössische Technische Hochschule, Zürich, 1984. *Publications*: An Introduction to the Study of Stellar Structure, 1939; Principles of Stellar Dynamics, 1942; Radiative Transfer, 1950; Hydrodynamic and Hydromagnetic Stability, 1961; Ellipsoidal Figures of Equilibrium, 1969; The Mathematical Theory of Black Holes, 1983; Eddington: the most distinguished astro-physicist of his time, 1983; various papers in current scientific periodicals. *Address*: Laboratory for Astrophysics and Space Research, University of Chicago, 933 East 56th Street, Chicago, Illinois, USA. *T*: (312) 962–7860. *Club*: Quadrangle (Chicago).

CHANEY, Hon. Sir Frederick (Charles), KBE 1982 (CBE 1969); AFC 1945; Chairman, Home Building Society, since 1974; *b* 12 Oct. 1914; *s* of Frederick Charles Chaney and Rose Templar Chaney; *m* 1938; four *s* three *d*. *Educ*: Aquinas Coll.; Claremont Coll. Served War, RAAF, 1940–45. Teacher, 1936–40 and 1946–55. MHR (L) Perth, 1955–69; Govt Whip, 1961–63; Minister for the Navy, 1963–66; Administrator, Northern Territory, 1970–73. Lord Mayor of Perth, WA, 1978–82. Dep. Pres., King's Park Bd, 1981–84. *Recreation*: golf. *Address*: 9A Melville Street, Claremont, WA 6010, Australia. *T*: 384.0596. *Clubs*: West Australian Cricket Assoc., East Perth Football (Perth); Mount Lawley Golf (WA).

CHANG-HIM, Most Rev. French Kitchener; *see* Indian Ocean, Archbishop of the.

CHANNING WILLIAMS, Maj.-Gen. John William, CB 1963; DSO 1944; OBE 1951; jssc; psc; *b* 14 Aug. 1908; *s* of late W. A. Williams, Inkpen, Berks; *m* 1936, Margaret Blachford, *d* of late A. J. Wood, Maidenhead, Berks; three *s*. *Educ*: Trent Coll.; RMC Sandhurst. Commissioned 2nd Lieut, N. Staffs Regt, 1929. Served War of 1939–45 (despatches, DSO): BEF, France, 1939–40; Instructor, Senior Officers' School, 1942–43; GSO1, Staff Coll., Camberley, 1943–44; CO 4th Bn Welch Regt, 1944; served in France, 1944–45, India and Burma, 1945–46. Asst Instructor, Imperial Defence Coll., 1946–48; AA and QMG, 40th Inf. Div., Hong Kong, 1949–50; Colonel General Staff, HQ Land Forces, Hong Kong, 1951–52; Colonel, 1954; BGS (Operations and Plans), GHQ, MELF, 1955–58; Director of Quartering, War Office, 1960–61; Director of Movements, War Office, 1961–63; retired; Brigadier, 1957; Maj.-Gen., 1960. *Recreations*: shooting, fishing. *Address*: Hayes Well, Inkpen, Newbury, Berks.

CHANNON, Rt. Hon. (Henry) Paul (Guinness); PC 1980; MP (C) for Southend West, since Jan. 1959; Secretary of State for Trade and Industry, since 1986; *b* 9 Oct. 1935; *o s* of late Sir Henry Channon, MP, and of late Lady Honor Svejdar (*née* Guinness), *e d* of 2nd Earl of Iveagh, KG; *m* 1963, Ingrid Olivia Georgia Guinness (*née* Wyndham);

one *s* one *d* (and one *d* decd). *Educ:* Lockers Park, Hemel Hempstead; Eton Coll., Christ Church, Oxford. 2nd Lieut Royal Horse Guards (The Blues), 1955–56. Pres. of Oxford Univ. Conservative Association, 1958. Parly Private Sec. to: Minister of Power, 1959–60; Home Sec., 1960–62; First Sec. of State, 1962–63; PPS to the Foreign Sec., 1963–64; Opposition Spokesman on Arts and Amenities, 1967–70; Parly Sec., Min. of Housing and Local Govt, June-Oct. 1970; Parly Under-Sec. of State, DoE, 1970–72; Minister of State, Northern Ireland Office, March-Nov. 1972; Minister for Housing and Construction, DoE, 1972–74; Opposition Spokesman on: Prices and Consumer Protection, March-Sept. 1974; environmental affairs, Oct. 1974–Feb. 1975; Minister of State, CSD, 1979–81; Minister for the Arts, 1981–83; Minister for Trade, 1983–86. Dep. Leader, Cons. Delegn to WEU and Council of Europe, 1976–79. Mem., Gen. Adv. Council to ITA, 1964–66. *Address:* House of Commons, SW1.

CHANTLER, Philip, CMG 1963; Director of Economic Planning, Cyprus, 1969–70, Swaziland, 1970–71; *b* 16 May 1911; *s* of Tom and Minnie Chantler; *m* 1938, Elizabeth Margaret Pentney; one *d*. *Educ:* Manchester Central High Sch.; Manchester Univ.; Harvard Univ Commonwealth Fund Fellow, 1934–36; Asst Lectr in Public Admin., Manchester Univ., 1936–38; Tariffs Adviser, UK Gas Corp. Ltd, 1938–40. Served War of 1939–45: RA 1940–41; War Cabinet Secretariat, 1941–45; Economic Adviser, Cabinet Office, 1945–47; Economic Adviser, Ministry of Fuel and Power, 1947–60 (seconded as Economic Adviser, Government of Pakistan Planning Board, 1955–57); Under-Sec., Electricity Div., Min. of Power, 1961–65; Chm., North-West Economic Planning Bd, 1965–69. *Publication:* The British Gas Industry: An Economic Study, 1938. *Recreations:* gardening, cine-photography, Victorian architecture, industrial archæology, domestic odd-jobbing. *Address:* 4 Tyburn Court, St George's Place, York; 2 The Mill, Rockcliffe, Galloway.

CHANTRY, Dr George William, CEng, FIEE; CPhys; FInstP; Department of Trade and Industry RTP Division, seconded to Ministry of Defence; *b* 13 April 1933; *s* of George William Chantry and Sophia Veronica (*née* Johnston); *m* 1956, Diana Margaret Rhodes (*née* Martin); two *s* one *d*. *Educ:* Christ Church, Oxford (DPhil 1959, MA 1960). CEng, FIEE 1976; FInstP 1974. Res. Associate, Cornell Univ., 1958; National Physical Lab., Dept of Industry: Sen. Res. Fellow, 1960; Sen. Scientific Officer, 1962; Principal Sci. Officer, 1967; Sen. Principal Sci. Officer, 1973; Dep. Chief Sci. Officer, DoI HQ, 1982, seconded to FCO; Counsellor (Sci. and Tech.), Bonn and Berne, 1982. Past Chm., European Molecular Liquids Gp; Mem., Science Educn and Technol. Bd, IEE, 1980–82. Editor, Proc. IEE, Part A, 1981–. *Publications:* Submillimetre Spectroscopy, 1971; High-Frequency Dielectric Measurement, 1972; Submillimetre Waves and their Applications, 1978; Modern Aspects of Microwave Spectroscopy, 1980; Long-Wave Optics, 1983; papers in learned literature. *Recreations:* philately, bridge, gardening, music. *Address:* RTP Division DTI, Ashdown House, 123 Victoria Street, SW1E 6RB; 42 Cranwell Grove, Shepperton, Mddx TW17 0JR. *T:* Chertsey 60524.

CHAPLAIS, Pierre Théophile Victorien Marie; Médaille de la Résistance, 1946; FBA 1973; Reader in Diplomatic in the University of Oxford, since 1957; Professorial Fellow, Wadham College, Oxford, since 1964; *b* Châteaubriant, Loire-Atlantique, France, 8 July 1920; *s* of late Théophile Chaplais and Victorine Chaplais (*née* Roussel); *m* 1948, Mary Doreen Middlemast; two *s*. *Educ:* Collège St-Sauveur, Redon, Ille-et-Vilaine; Univ. of Rennes, Ille-et-Vilaine (Licence en Droit, Licence ès-Lettres); Univ. of London (PhD). Editor, Public Record Office, London, 1948–55; Lectr in Diplomatic, Univ. of Oxford, 1955–57; Literary Dir, Royal Hist. Soc., 1958–64. Corresp. Fellow, Mediaeval Acad. of America, 1979. *Publications:* Some Documents regarding . . . The Treaty of Brétigny, 1952; The War of St Sardos, 1954; Treaty Rolls, vol. I, 1955; (with T. A. M. Bishop) Facsimiles of English Royal Writs to AD 1100 presented to V. H. Galbraith, 1957; Diplomatic Documents, vol. I, 1964; English Royal Documents, King John-Henry VI, 1971; English Medieval Diplomatic Practice, Part II, 1975, Part I, 1983; Essays in Medieval Diplomacy and Administration, 1981; articles in Bulletin of Inst. of Historical Research, English Hist. Review, Jl of Soc. of Archivists, etc. *Recreations:* gardening, fishing. *Address:* Lew Lodge, Lew, Oxford OX8 2BE. *T:* Bampton Castle 850613.

CHAPLIN, Arthur Hugh, CB 1970; Principal Keeper of Printed Books, British Museum, 1966–70; *b* 17 April 1905; *er s* of late Rev. Herbert F. Chaplin and Florence B. Lusher; *m* 1938, Irene Marcousé. *Educ:* King's Lynn Grammar Sch.; Bedford Modern Sch.; University Coll., London. Asst Librarian: Reading Univ. 1927–28; Queen's Univ., Belfast, 1928–29; Asst Keeper, Dept of Printed Books, British Museum, 1930–52; Dep. Keeper, 1952–59; Keeper, 1959–66. Exec. Sec., Organizing Cttee of Internat. Conf. on Cataloguing Principles, Paris, 1961; Mem. Council, Library Assoc. 1964–70; Pres., Microfilm Assoc. of GB, 1967–71; Mem. Senate, Univ. of London, 1973–. Fellow UCL, 1969. *Publications:* contributions to Jl Documentation, Library Assoc. Record, Library Quarterly, and to Cataloguing Principles and Practice (ed M. Piggott), 1954; Tradition and Principle in Library Cataloguing, 1966. *Recreations:* walking; motoring. *Address:* 44 Russell Square, WC1. *T:* 01–636 7217.

CHAPLIN, John Cyril, CEng, FRAeS; Member, Civil Aviation Authority and Group Director, Safety Services, since 1983; *b* 13 Aug. 1926; *s* of late Ernest Stanley Chaplin and Isobel Chaplin; *m* 1949, Ruth Marianne Livingstone; two *s* two *d*. *Educ:* Keswick School. Miles Aircraft, 1946; Vickers-Supermarine, 1948; Handley Page, 1950; Somers-Kendall Aircraft, 1952; Heston Aircraft, 1956; Air Registration Board, 1958; Civil Aviation Authority, 1972, Dir-Gen. Airworthiness, 1979. *Publications:* papers to RAeS. *Recreations:* sailing, photography. *Address:* Civil Aviation Authority, 45–59 Kingsway, WC2B 6TE. *T:* 01–379 7311. *Club:* Cruising Association.

CHAPMAN, family name of **Baron Northfield.**

CHAPMAN, Angela Mary, (Mrs I. M. Chapman); Headmistress, Central Newcastle High School (GPDST), since 1985; *b* 2 Jan. 1940; *d* of Frank Dyson and Mary Rowe; *m* 1959, Ian Michael Chapman; two *s*. *Educ:* Queen Victoria High Sch., Stockton; Univ. of Bristol (BA Hons French); Sorbonne (Dip. de Civilisatin Française). Teacher of French, Bede Sch., Sunderland, 1970–80; Dep. Headmistress, Newcastle-upon-Tyne Church High Sch., 1980–84. *Recreations:* Western Front 1914–18, walking, writing clerihews. *Address:* 14 Alpine Way, Sunderland, Tyne and Wear.

CHAPMAN, Prof. Christopher Hugh; Professor of Geophysics, Department of Earth Sciences, University of Cambridge, since 1984; Fellow, Christ's College, Cambridge, since 1984; *b* 5 May 1945; *s* of John Harold Chapman and Margaret Joan Weeks; *m* 1974, Lillian Tarapaski; one *s* one *d*. *Educ:* Latymer Upper School; Christ's College, Cambridge (MA); Dept of Geodesy and Geophysics, Cambridge (PhD). Asst Prof., Univ. of Alberta, 1969–72, Associate Prof., 1973–74; Asst Prof., Univ. of California, Berkeley, 1972–73; University of Toronto: Associate Prof., 1974–80; Prof., 1980–84; Killam Research Fellow, 1981–83; Adjunct Prof., 1984–. Green Scholar, Univ. of California, San Diego, 1978–79. *Publications:* research papers in sci. jls. *Recreation:* sailing. *Address:* Bullard Laboratories, Department of Earth Sciences, University of Cambridge, Madingley Rise, Madingley Road, Cambridge CB3 0EZ. *T:* Cambridge 337190.

CHAPMAN, His Honour Cyril Donald, QC 1965; a Circuit Judge, 1972–86; *b* 17 Sept. 1920; *s* of Cyril Henry Chapman and Frances Elizabeth Chapman (*née* Braithwaite); *m* 1st, 1950, Audrey Margaret Fraser (*née* Gough) (marr. diss., 1959); one *s*; 2nd, 1960, Muriel Falconer Bristow; one *s*. *Educ:* Roundhay Sch., Leeds; Brasenose Coll., Oxford (MA). Served RNVR, 1939–45. Called to Bar, 1947; Harmsworth Scholar, 1947; North Eastern Circuit, 1947; Recorder of Huddersfield, 1965–69, of Bradford, 1969–71. Contested (C) East Leeds 1955, Goole 1964, Brighouse and Spenborough, 1966. *Recreation:* yachting. *Address:* Hill Top, Collingham, Wetherby, W Yorks. *T:* Collingham Bridge 72813. *Club:* Leeds (Leeds).

CHAPMAN, Daniel Ahmling; *see* Chapman Nyaho.

CHAPMAN, Prof. Dennis, FRS 1986; Professor of Biophysical Chemistry, Royal Free Hospital School of Medicine, University of London, since 1977; *b* 6 May 1927; *s* of George Henry Chapman and Katherine Magnus; *m* 1949, Elsie Margaret; two *s* one *d*. *Educ:* London Univ. (BSc; DSc); Liverpool Univ. (PhD); Cambridge Univ. Comyns Berkeley Fellow, Gonville and Caius Coll., Cambridge, 1960–63; Head of Gen. Research Div., Unilever Ltd, Welwyn, 1963–69; Professor Associate, Biophysical Chem., Sheffield Univ., 1968–76; Sen. Wellcome Trust Research Fellow, Dept of Chemistry, Chelsea Coll., Univ. of London, 1976–77. Hon. DSc: Utrecht, 1976; Meml, Canada, 1980. *Publications:* Biological Membranes, vol. I–vol. V, 1968–84; 300 scientific publications in biochemical jls. *Recreations:* tennis, golf, walking. *Address:* Department of Biochemistry and Chemistry, Royal Free Hospital School of Medicine, Rowland Hill Street, NW3 2PF. *T:* 01–794 0500.

CHAPMAN, (Francis) Ian; Chairman: William Collins plc, since 1981; William Collins Publishers Ltd, since 1979; Radio Clyde Ltd, since 1972; Harvill Press Ltd, since 1976; Hatchards Ltd, since 1976; The Ancient House Bookshop (Ipswich) Ltd, since 1976; *b* 26 Oct. 1925; *s* of late Rev. Peter Chapman and Frances Burdett; *m* 1953, Marjory Stewart Swinton; one *s* one *d*. *Educ:* Shawlands Academy, Glasgow. Served RAF, 1943–44; worked in coal mines as part of national service, 1945–47. Joined Wm Collins Sons & Co. Ltd, 1947 as gen. trainee; Sales Man., 1955; Sales Dir, 1960; Jt Man. Dir, 1968–76; Dep. Chm., 1976–81. Director: Independent Radio News, 1984–85; Pan Books Ltd, 1962–84; Book Tokens Ltd, 1981–; Stanley Botes Ltd; also numerous overseas companies of Collins. Mem. Council, Publishers' Assoc., 1963–76, 1977– (Vice Pres., 1978–79 and 1981–82; Pres., 1979–81; Vice-Chm., 1981); Member: Bd, Book Develt Council, 1970–73; Governing Council, Scottish Business in the Community, 1983–. Chm. Council, Strathclyde Univ. Business School, 1985. FRSA 1985. *Publications:* various articles on publishing in trade jls. *Recreations:* music, golf, reading, skiing. *Address:* Kenmore, 46 The Avenue, Cheam, Surrey. *T:* 01–642 1820. *Clubs:* Garrick, MCC; Royal Wimbledon Golf; Prestwick Golf.

CHAPMAN, Frederick John; Principal Establishment and Finance Officer (Under Secretary), Export Credits Guarantee Department, since 1985; *b* 24 June 1939; *s* of late Reginald John Chapman and Elizabeth Chapman; *m* 1964, Paula Brenda Waller; one *s* two *d*. *Educ:* Sutton County Grammar Sch. Joined ECGD, 1958; Principal, 1969; Asst Sec., 1977; Under Sec., 1982. *Recreations:* reading, music. *Address:* Clinton House, 2 Ludlow Road, Maidenhead, Berks SL6 2RH. *T:* Maidenhead 31908.

CHAPMAN, Prof. Garth; Professor of Zoology, Queen Elizabeth College, University of London, 1958–82, now Emeritus (Vice Principal, 1974–80; Acting Principal, Sept. 1977–March 1978; Fellow, 1984); *b* 8 Oct. 1917; *o s* of E. J. Chapman and Edith Chapman (*née* Attwood); *m* 1941, Margaret Hilda Wigley; two *s* one *d*. *Educ:* Royal Grammar Sch., Worcester; Trinity Hall, Cambridge (Major Scholar); ScD Cantab 1977. FIBiol 1963; FKC 1985. Telecommunications Research Establishment, Ministry of Aircraft Production, 1941–45; Asst Lectr in Zoology, 1945–46, Lectr in Zoology, 1946–58, QMC, Univ. of London; Dean, Faculty of Science, Univ. of London, 1974–78. Vis. Prof., Univ. of California, Berkeley, 1967, Los Angeles, 1970–71. Member: Cttee for Commonwealth Univ. Interchange, British Council, 1978–80; Inter-Univ. Council for Higher Educn Overseas, 1973–83; Council, Westfield Coll., Univ. of London, 1978–84; Central Research Fund Cttee B, 1978–82; Management Cttee of Univ. Marine Biological Station, Millport, 1975–82. *Publications:* Zoology for Intermediate Students (with W. B. Barker), 1964; Body Fluids and their Functions, 1967; various on structure and physiology of marine invertebrates. *Recreations:* gardening; wood-engraving. *Address:* Nunns, Coxtie Green, Brentwood, Essex CM14 5RP. *Club:* Athenæum.

CHAPMAN, Geoffrey Lloyd; Vice Judge Advocate General, since 1984; *b* 20 Oct. 1928; *o s* of Sydney Leslie Chapman and Dora Chapman (*née* Lloyd); *m* 1958, Jean, *er d* of Valentine Harry Coleman and Marjorie Coleman (*née* Poston); one *s* two *d*. *Educ:* Latymer Upper School; Christ Church, Oxford (MA, BCL). National Service, 1947–49 (commissioned RASC). Called to the Bar, Inner Temple, 1953; practised London and Western Circuit; Legal Asst, Min. of Labour and Nat. Service, 1957; Legal Asst, JAG's Office, 1958; Dep. Judge Advocate, 1961 (Germany, 1963–66, Cyprus, 1969–72); Asst JAG, 1971 (Germany, 1972–76); Dep. JAG, British Forces in Germany, 1979–82. *Recreations:* beagling, reading. *Address:* Thurston Lodge, Doods Road, Reigate, Surrey RH2 0NT. *T:* Reigate 47860.

CHAPMAN, Sir George (Alan), Kt 1982; FCA; FCIS; Senior Partner, Chapman Ross & Co., Chartered Accountants; Chairman: BNZ Finance Ltd, since 1979 (Director, since 1977); Landmark Properties Ltd, since 1982; New Zealand Board, Mitel Telecommunications Ltd, since 1984; Norwich Winterthur (NZ) Ltd, since 1985 (Director, since 1982); Kaurex Corporation Ltd, since 1985; Deputy Chairman, Skellerup Industries Ltd, since 1984 (Director since 1982); *b* 13 April 1927; *s* of late Thomas George Chapman and of Winifred Jordan Chapman; *m* 1950, Jacqueline Sidney (*née* Irvine); two *s* five *d*. *Educ:* Trentham Sch.; Hutt Valley High Sch.; Victoria University. Fellow, Chartered Inst. of Secretaries, 1969 (Mem., 1948–); Fellow, NZ Soc. of Accountants, 1969 (Mem., 1948–). Joined Chapman Ross & Co., 1948. Director: Bank of New Zealand, 1968–86 (Dep. Chm., 1976–86); Maui Developments Ltd, 1979–85; Offshore Mining Co. Ltd, 1979–85; Liquigas Ltd, 1981–85 (Chm., 1982–84); NZ Bd, Norwich Union Life Insurance Soc., 1982–; Pilkington Brothers (NZ), 1982–. NZ National Party: Member, 1948–; Vice-Pres., 1966–73; Pres., 1973–82. Councillor, Upper Hutt Bor. Council, 1952–53, Deputy Mayor, Upper Hutt, 1953–55; Member: Hutt Valley Drainage Bd, 1953–55; Heretaunga Bd of Governors, 1953–55; Pres., Upper Hutt Chamber of Commerce, 1956–57. *Publication:* The Years of Lightning, 1980. *Recreations:* golf, reading, tennis. *Address:* 53 Barton Avenue, Heretaunga, Wellington, New Zealand. *T:* 283–512. *Clubs:* Wellington Golf, Wellington Racing.

CHAPMAN, Ian; *see* Chapman, F. I.

CHAPMAN, John Henry Benjamin, CB 1957; CEng; FRINA; RCNC; *b* 28 Dec. 1899; *s* of Robert Henry Chapman and Edith Yeo Chapman (*née* Lillicrap); *m* 1929, Dorothy Rowlerson; one *s* one *d*. *Educ:* HM Dockyard Sch., Devonport; RNC Greenwich. Dir of Naval Construction, Admiralty, 1958–61. Dir, Fairfield S & E Co. Ltd, 1962–66; Consultant, Upper Clyde Shipbuilders, 1966–68. Mem. of Royal Corps of Naval

Constructors, 1922–61; Hon. Vice-Pres., RINA; Mem., Technical Consultative Cttee, RNLI. *Address:* The Small House, Delling Lane, Old Bosham, Sussex. *T:* Bosham 573331. *Club:* Bosham Sailing.

CHAPMAN, Kathleen Violet, CBE 1956; RRC 1953 (ARRC 1945); QHNS 1953–56; Matron-in-Chief, Queen Alexandra's Royal Naval Nursing Service, 1953–56, retired; *b* 30 May 1903; *d* of late Major H. E. Chapman, CBE, DL Kent, Chief Constable of Kent, and Mrs C. H. J. Chapman. *Educ:* Queen Anne's, Caversham. Trained St Thomas's Hospital, 1928–32.

CHAPMAN, Kenneth Herbert; Managing Director, Thomas Tilling Ltd, 1967–73; Director: British Steam Specialities Ltd; Société Générale (France) Bank Ltd; Ready Mixed Concrete Ltd; Goodliffe Garages Ltd; former Director, Royal Worcester Ltd; *b* 9 Sept. 1908; *s* of Herbert Chapman and Anne Bennett Chapman (*née* Poxon); *m* 1937, Jean Martha Mahring; one *s. Educ:* St Peter's Sch., York. Articled Clerk, 1926; qual. Solicitor, 1931; private practice, 1931–36; joined professional staff, HM Land Registry, 1936; transf. Min. of Aircraft Prodn, 1940, Private Sec. to Perm. Sec.; transf. Min. of Supply, 1946. Joined Thomas Tilling Ltd, as Group Legal Adviser, 1948; at various times Chm. or Dir of more than 20 companies in Tilling Group. High Sheriff of Greater London, 1974. *Recreations:* Rugby football (Past Pres. and Hon. Treas. of RFU, mem. cttee various clubs), cricket (mem. cttee various clubs), golf. *Address:* 2 Wyndham Lea, Common Hill, West Chiltington, Sussex RH20 2NP. *T:* West Chiltington 3808. *Clubs:* East India, Devonshire, Sports and Public Schools; West Sussex Golf; Harlequin Football.

CHAPMAN, Leslie Charles; Founder and Chairman, Campaign to Stop Waste in Public Expenditure, since 1981; *b* 14 Sept. 1919; *e s* of Charles Richard Chapman and Lilian Elizabeth Chapman; *m* 1947, Beryl Edith England; one *s. Educ:* Bishopshalt Sch. Served War, Army, 1939–45. Civil Service, 1939 and 1945–74; Regional Dir, Southern Region, MPBW and PSA, 1967–74. Chm. and mem., various cttees; Mem. (pt-time), LTE, 1979–80. *Publications:* Your Disobedient Servant, 1978, 2nd revised edn 1979; Waste Away, 1982. *Recreations:* reading, music, gardening. *Address:* Cae Caradog, Ffarmers, Llanwrda, Dyfed SA19 8NQ. *T:* Pumpsaint 504.

CHAPMAN, Mark Fenger, CVO 1979; HM Diplomatic Service; Ambassador to Iceland, since 1986; *b* 12 Sept. 1934; *er s* of Geoffrey Walter Chapman and Esther Maria Fenger; *m* 1959, Patricia Mary Long; three *s* (and one *s* decd). *Educ:* Cranbrook Sch.; St Catharine's Coll., Cambridge. Entered HM Foreign Service, 1958; served in: Bangkok, 1959–63; FO, 1963–67; Head of Chancery, Maseru, 1967–71; Asst Head of Dept, FCO, 1971–74; Head of Chancery, Vienna, 1975–76; Dep. High Comr and Counsellor (Econ. and Comm.), Lusaka, 1976–79; Diplomatic Service Inspector, 1979–82; Counsellor, The Hague, 1982–86. *Address:* Half Moon House, Briston, Melton Constable, Norfolk; c/o Foreign and Commonwealth Office, SW1. *Club:* Royal Commonwealth Society.

CHAPMAN, Prof. Norman Bellamy, MA, PhD; CChem, FRSC; G. F. Grant Professor of Chemistry, Hull University, 1956–82, now Emeritus; Pro-Vice-Chancellor, 1973–76; *b* 19 April 1916; *s* of Frederick Taylor Chapman and Bertha Chapman; *m* 1949, Fonda Maureen Bungey; one *s* one *d. Educ:* Barnsley Holgate Grammar Sch.; Magdalene Coll., Cambridge (Entrance Scholar). 1st Cl. Parts I and II Nat. Sciences Tripos, 1937 and 1938; BA 1938, MA 1942, PhD 1941. Bye-Fellow, Magdalene Coll., 1939–42; Univ. Demonstrator in Chemistry, Cambridge, 1945; Southampton Univ.: Lectr, 1947; Senior Lectr, 1949; Reader in Chemistry, 1955. R. T. French Visiting Prof., Univ. of Rochester, NY, 1962–63; R. J. Reynolds Vis. Prof., Duke Univ., N Carolina, 1971; Cooch Behar Prof., Calcutta, 1982. Universities Central Council on Admissions: Dep. Chm., 1979–83; Chm., Technical Sub-Cttee, 1974–79; Chm., Statistics Sub-Cttee, 1983–. Hon. DSc Hull, 1984. *Publications:* (ed with J. Shorter) Advances in Free Energy Relationships, 1972; (ed) Organic Chemistry, Series One, vol. 2: Aliphatic Compounds (MTP Internat. Review of Science), 1973, Series Two, vol 2, 1976; Correlation Analysis in Chemistry: recent advances, 1978; contribs to Jl Chem. Soc., Analyst, Jl Medicinal Chem., Tetrahedron, Jl Organic Chemistry, Chemistry and Industry. *Recreations:* music, gardening, cricket, Rugby football. *Address:* 5 The Lawns, Molescroft, Beverley HU17 7LS. *T:* Hull 860553.

CHAPMAN, Sir Robin, (Robert Macgowan), 2nd Bt *cr* 1958; CBE 1961; TD and Bar, 1947; JP; Partner, Chapman and Partners, Chartered Accountants; Chairman, North Eastern Investment Trust Ltd; *b* Harton, Co. Durham, 12 Feb. 1911; *er s* of 1st Bt and Lady (Hélène Paris) Chapman, JP (*née* Macgowan); *S* father, 1963; *m* 1941, Barbara May, *d* of Hubert Tonks, Ceylon; two *s* one *d. Educ:* Marlborough; Corpus Christi Coll., Cambridge (Exhibitioner). 1st Cl. Hons Maths, BA 1933; MA 1937. Chartered Accountant, ACA 1938; FCA 1945. Jt Sec., Shields Commercial Bldg Soc., 1939–83; Partner: Henry Chapman Son and Co., 1939–69; Chapman, Hilton and Dunford, 1969–80; Consultant, Spicer and Pegler, Chartered Accountants, 1980–85. Chairman: Northern Counties Provincial Area Conservative Associations, 1954–57; Jarrow Conservative Association,1957–60; Pres., Northern Area Conservative Council, 1982–86. Pres., Northern Soc. of Chartered Accountants, 1958–59; Mem. Cttee, 1949–60; Member: Police Authority, Co. Durham, 1955–59, 1961–65; Appeals Cttee, 1955–62; Durham Diocesan Conf., 1953–70; Durham Diocesan Synod, 1971–72; Durham Diocesan Bd of Finance, 1953–71 (Chm. 1966–70); Durham County TA, 1948–68; N England TA, 1968–74; Chm., Durham Co. Scout Council, 1972–82 (Scout Silver Acorn Award, 1973). Governor, United Newcastle Hospitals, 1957–64. TA Army officer, 1933–51; served War of 1939–45: RA Anti-Aircraft Command; GSO 2, 1940; CO 325 LAA regt, RA (TA), 1948–51; Hon. Col 1963; JP 1946, DL, 1952; High Sheriff of County Durham, 1960; Vice Lord-Lieutenant, Tyne and Wear, 1974–84. *Heir: er s* David Robert Macgowan Chapman [*b* 16 Dec. 1941; *m* 1965, Maria Elizabeth de Gosztony-Zsolnay, *o d* of Dr N. de Mattyasovsky-Zsolnay, Montreal, Canada; one *s* one *d*]. *Address:* Pinfold House, 6 West Park Road, Cleadon, Sunderland SR6 7RR. *T:* Boldon 367451. *Clubs:* Carlton; County (Durham); Hawks (Cambridge).

CHAPMAN, Roy de Courcy; Headmaster of Malvern College, since Jan. 1983; *b* 1 Oct. 1936; *s* of Edward Frederic Gilbert Chapman and Aline de Courcy Ireland; *m* 1959, Valerie Rosemary Small; two *s* one *d. Educ:* Dollar Academy; St Andrews Univ. (Harkness Schol.; MA 1959); Moray House Coll. of Educn, Edinburgh. Asst Master, Trinity Coll., Glenalmond, 1960–64; Marlborough College: Asst Master, 1964–68; Head of Mod. Langs, 1968–75; OC CCF, 1969–75; Rector of Glasgow Acad., 1975–82. *Publications:* Le Français Contemporain, 1971; (with D. Whiting) Le Français Contemporain: Passages for translation and comprehension, 1975. *Recreations:* squash, France, brewing, wine-making. *Address:* Headmaster's House, Malvern College, Worcs. *T:* Malvern 4472.

CHAPMAN, Hon. Sir Stephen, Kt 1966; Judge of the High Court of Justice, Queen's Bench Division, 1966–81; *b* 5 June 1907; 2nd *s* of late Sir Sydney J. Chapman, KCB, CBE, and of late Lady Chapman, JP; *m* 1963, Mrs Pauline Frances Niewiarowski, *widow* of Dmitri de Lobel Niewiarowski and *d* of late Lt-Col H. Allcard and late Mrs A. B. M. Allcard. *Educ:* Westminster; Trinity Coll., Cambridge. King's Scholar and Capt. Westminster; Entrance Scholar and Major Scholar, Trinity Coll., Cambridge; Browne Univ. Gold Medallist, 1927 and 1928; John Stuart of Rannoch Univ. Scholar, 1928; 1st Cl. Classical Tripos, Pt I, 1927, and in Pt II, 1929. Entrance Scholar, Inner Temple, 1929;

Jardine student, 1931; 1st Cl. and Certificate of Honour, Bar Final, 1931; called to Bar, Inner Temple, 1931; SE Circuit, Herts-Essex Sessions; Asst Legal Adviser, Min. of Pensions, 1939–46; Prosecuting Counsel for Post Office on SE Circuit, 1947–50 (Leader, Circuit, 1962); QC 1955; Comr of Assize, Winchester, Autumn, 1961. Recorder of Rochester, 1959–61, of Cambridge, 1961–63; Judge of the Crown Court and Recorder of Liverpool, 1963–66. Dep. Chm. Herts QS, 1963. Mem. Bar Council, 1956; Hon. Treas. 1958; Vice-Chm. 1959–60. *Publications:* Auctioneers and Brokers, in Atkin's Encyclopædia of Court Forms, vol. 3, 1938; Insurance (non-marine), in Halsbury's Laws of England, 3rd edn, vol. 22, 1958; Statutes on the Law of Torts, 1962. *Recreation:* gardening. *Address:* 72 Thomas More House, Barbican, EC2Y 8AB. *T:* 01–628 9251. *Club:* United Oxford & Cambridge University.

CHAPMAN, Sydney Brookes, RIBA; FRTPI; MP (C) Chipping Barnet, since 1979; Chartered Architect and Chartered Town and Country Planner; private planning consultant (non-practising); freelance writer; *b* 17 Oct. 1935; *m* 1976, Claire Lesley McNab (*née* Davies); two *s* one *d. Educ:* Rugby Sch.; Manchester University. DipArch 1958; ARIBA 1960; DipTP 1961; AMTPI 1962; FFB 1980. Nat. Chm., Young Conservatives, 1964–66 (has been Chm. and Vice-Chm. at every level of Movt); Sen. Elected Vice-Chm., NW Area of Nat. Union of C and U Assocs, 1966–70. Contested (C) Stalybridge and Hyde, 1964; MP (C) Birmingham, Handsworth, 1970–Feb. 1974; PPS to Sec. of State for Transport, 1979–81, to Sec. of State for Social Services, 1981–83; Chm., Parly Consultants Gp, British Consultants Bureau, 1980–; Member: Select Cttee on Environment, 1983–; House of Commons Services Cttee, 1983–. Lectr in Arch. and Planning at techn. coll., 1964–70; Dir (Information), British Property Fedn, 1976–79; Dir (non-exec.), Capital and Counties plc; consultant on urban renewal to YJ Lovell (Holdings) plc. Originator of nat. tree planting year, 1973; President: Arboricultural Assoc., 1983–; London Green Belt Council, 1985–; Chm., Queen's Silver Jubilee London Tree Group, 1977; Vice-Chm., Wildlife Link, 1985–. RIBA: Vice-Pres., 1974–75; Chm., Public Affairs Bd, 1974–75; Mem. Council, 1972–77. President: Friends of Barnet Hosps; Friends of Peter Pan Homes. Hon. Assoc. Mem., BVA; Hon. ALI; FRSA. *Publications:* Town and Countryside: future planning policies for Britain, 1978; regular contributor to bldg and property jls and to political booklets. *Recreation:* tree spotting. *Address:* House of Commons, SW1A 0AA.

CHAPMAN-MORTIMER, William Charles; author; *b* 15 May 1907; *s* of William George Chapman-Mortimer and Martha Jane McLelland; *m* 1934, Frances Statler; *m* 1956, Ursula Merits; one *d. Educ:* privately. *Publications:* A Stranger on the Stair, 1950; Father Goose, 1951 (awarded James Tait Black Memorial Prize, 1952); Young Men Waiting, 1952; Mediterraneo, 1954; Here in Spain, 1955; Madrigal, 1960; Amparo, 1971. *Address:* Gisebo, 56190 Huskvarna, Sweden. *T:* 036–50409.

CHAPMAN NYAHO, Daniel Ahmling, CBE 1961; Director: Pioneer Tobacco Co. Ltd, Ghana (Member of British-American Tobacco Group), since 1967; Standard Bank Ghana Ltd, 1970–75; *b* 5 July 1909; *s* of William Henry Chapman and Jane Atsiamesi (*née* Atriki); *m* 1941, Jane Abam (*née* Quashie); two *s* four *d* (and one *d* decd). *Educ:* Bremen Mission Schs, Gold Coast and Togoland; Achimota Coll., Ghana; St Peter's Hall, Oxford. Postgraduate courses at Columbia Univ. and New York Univ.; Teacher, Government Senior Boys' School, Accra, 1930; Master, Achimota Coll., 1930–33, 1937–46. Area Specialist, UN Secretariat, Lake Success and New York, 1946–54; Sec. to Prime Minister and Sec. of Cabinet, Gold Coast/Ghana, 1954–57; Ghana's Ambassador to USA and Permanent Representative at UN, 1957–59; Headmaster, Achimota Sch., Ghana, 1959–63; Dir, UN Div. of Narcotic Drugs, 1963–66; Ambassador (Special Duties), Min. of External Affairs, Ghana, 1967. Gen. Sec., All-Ewe Conf., 1944–46; Commonwealth Prime Ministers' Conf., 1957; Mem., Ghana delegn to the conf. of indep. African States, Accra, 1958. First Vice-Chm., Governing Council of UN Special Fund, 1959; Chairman: Mission of Indep. African States to Cuba, Dominican Republic, Haiti, Venezuela, Bolivia, Paraguay, Uruguay, Brazil, Argentina, Chile, 1958; Volta Union, 1968–69. Vice-Chairman: Commn on Univ. Educn in Ghana, 1960–61; Ghana Constituent Assembly, 1978–79. Member: Board of Management, UN Internat. Sch., New York, 1950–54, 1958–59; UN Middle East and N. Africa Technical Assistance Mission on Narcotics Control, 1963; Dir, UN Consultative Gp on Narcotics Control in Asia and Far East, Tokyo, 1964; Member: Political Cttee of Nat. Liberation Council, 1967; Board of Trustees of General Kotoka Trust Fund, 1967–83; Chairman: Arts Council of Ghana, 1968–69; Council of Univ. of Science and Technology, Kumasi, 1972; Bd. of Directors, Ghana Film Industry Corporation, 1979–80; Ghana National Honours and Awards Cttee, 1979–80. Darnforth Vis. Lectr, Assoc. Amer. Colls, 1969, 1970. Hon. LLD Greenboro Agric. and Techn. Coll., USA, 1958. Fellow, Ghana Acad. of Arts and Sciences. *Publications:* Human Geography of Eweland, 1946; Our Homeland—Book I: South-East Gold Coast, 1945; (Ed.) The Ewe News-Letter, 1945–46. *Recreations:* music, gardening, walking. *Address:* (office) Tobacco House, Kwame Nkrumah Avenue, PO Box 5211, Accra, Ghana. *T:* 21111; (home) 7 Ninth Avenue, Tesano, Accra, Ghana. *T:* 27180. *Club:* Accra (Ghana).

CHAPPELL, (Edwin) Philip, CBE 1976; a Vice-Chairman, Morgan Grenfell Holdings, 1975–85; Deputy Chairman, London Board, Bank of New Zealand, since 1983; Director: Fisons; Guest Keen & Nettlefolds; *b* 12 June 1929; *s* of late Rev. C. R. Chappell; *m* 1962, Julia Clavering House, *d* of H. W. House, DSO, MC; one *s* three *d. Educ:* Marlborough Coll.; Christ Church, Oxford (MA). Joined Morgan Grenfell, 1954; Dir, Morgan Grenfell & Co. Ltd, 1964–85; Chm., ICL, 1980–81. Chairman: Nat. Ports Council, 1971–77; EDC for Food and Drink Manufacturing Industry, 1976–80. Member: Council, Institute of Bankers, 1971–85; Business Educn Council, 1974–80; SITPRO Board, 1974–77. Governor of BBC, 1976–81. *Address:* 22 Frognal Lane, NW3 7DT. *T:* 01–435 8627. *Club:* Athenæum.

CHAPPELL, William; dancer, designer, producer; *b* Wolverhampton, 27 Sept. 1908; *s* of Archibald Chappell and Edith Eva Clara Blair-Staples. *Educ:* Chelsea School of Art. Studied dancing under Marie Rambert. First appearance on stage, 1929; toured Europe with Ida Rubinstein's company, working under Massine and Nijinska; danced in many ballets, London, 1929–34; joined Sadler's Wells Co., 1934, and appeared there every season; Army service, 1940–45; designed scenery and costumes at Sadler's Wells, 1934–, and Covent Garden, 1947–, including Les Rendezvous, Les Patineurs, Coppelia, Giselle, Handel's Samson, Frederick Ashton's Walk to the Paradise Garden, and Ashton's Rhapsody (costumes); for many revues and London plays. Produced Lyric Revue, 1951, Globe Revue, 1952, High Spirits, Hippodrome, 1953, At the Lyric, 1953, Going to Town, St Martin's, 1954 (also arranging dances for many of these); An Evening with Beatrice Lillie, Globe, 1954 (asst prod.); Time Remembered, New, 1955; Moby Dick, Duke of York's, 1955 (with Orson Welles); The Buccaneer, Lyric, Hammersmith, 1955; The Rivals, Saville; Beaux' Stratagem, Chichester; Violins of St Jacques (also wrote libretto), Sadler's Wells; English Eccentrics; Love and a Bottle; Passion Flower Hotel; Travelling Light; Espresso Bongo; Living for Pleasure; Where's Charley?; appeared in and assisted Orson Welles with film The Trial; The Chalk Garden, Haymarket, 1971; Offenbach's Robinson Crusoe (1st English perf.), Camden Festival, 1973; Cockie, Vaudeville, 1973; Oh, Kay!,

Westminster, 1974; National Tour, In Praise of Love, 1974; Fallen Angels, Gate Theatre, Dublin, 1975; Marriage of Figaro (designed and directed), Sadler's Wells, 1977; The Master's Voice, Dublin, 1977; Memoir, Ambassadors, 1978; Gianni Schicci, Sadler's Wells, 1978; Nijinsky (film), 1979; Same Time Next Year, Dublin, 1980; A Little Bit on the Side (revue, with Beryl Reid), 1983; for Dublin Theatre Festival, 1980: Speak of the Devil (musical); designs for Giselle, inc. 2 prodns for Anton Dolin; design for Merle Park's costume as Fanny Ellsler, Vienna Opera House, 1985; Choreographed: Travesties, RSC Aldwych, 1974, NY, 1975; Bloomsbury, Phoenix, 1974; Directed, designed costumes and choreographed: Purcell's Fairy Queen, London Opera Centre, 1974; Donizetti's Torquato Tasso, Camden Festival, 1975; Lully's Alceste, London Opera Centre, 1975; A Moon for the Misbegotten, Dublin, 1976; The Rivals, Dublin, 1976; teacher and adviser for: Nureyev season, 1979; Joffrey Ballet, NY, 1979. TV shows. Illustrator of several books. *Publications:* Studies in Ballet; Fonteyn; (ed and jt author) Edward Burra: a painter remembered by his friends, 1982; (ed) Well, Dearie: the letters of Edward Burra, 1985. *Recreations:* reading, cinema, painting. *Address:* 25 Rosenau Road, Battersea, SW11 4QN.

CHAPPLE, family name of **Baron Chapple.**

CHAPPLE, Baron *cr* 1985 (Life Peer), of Hoxton in Greater London; **Francis Joseph Chapple;** General Secretary, Electrical, Electronic, Telecommunication and Plumbing Union, 1966–84; *b* Shoreditch, 1921; *m*; two *s*. *Educ:* elementary school. Started as Apprentice Electrician; Member ETU, 1937–83; Shop Steward and Branch Official; Member Exec. Council, 1958; Asst General Secretary, 1963–66. Mem., Gen. Council of TUC, 1971–83, Chm. 1982–83; Gold Badge of Congress, 1983. Member: National Exec. Cttee of Labour Party, 1965–71; Cttee of Inquiry into Shipping, 1967; Royal Commn on Environmental Pollution, 1973–77; Horserace Totalisator Bd, 1976–; Energy Commn, 1977–79; NEDC, 1979–83; Nat. Nuclear Corp., 1980–; Southern Water Authority, 1983–; Dir, Inner City Enterprises, 1983–. *Publication:* (autobiog.) Sparks Fly, 1984. *Recreation:* racing pigeons. *Address:* c/o Electrical, Electronic, Telecommunication and Plumbing Union, Hayes Court, West Common Road, Bromley BR2 7AU.

CHAPPLE, Lt-Gen. Sir John (Lyon), KCB 1985; CBE 1980; Deputy Chief of Defence Staff (Programmes and Personnel), since 1985; *b* 27 May 1931; *s* of C. H. Chapple; *m* 1959, Annabel Hill; one *s* three *d*. *Educ:* Haileybury; Trinity Coll., Cambridge (MA). Joined 2nd KEO Goorkhas, 1954; served Malaya, Hong Kong, Borneo; Staff Coll., 1962; jssc 1969; Commanded 1st Bn 2nd Goorkhas, 1970–72; Directing Staff, Staff Coll., 1972–73; Commanded 48 Gurkha Infantry Bde, 1976; Gurkha Field Force, 1977; Principal Staff Officer to Chief of Defence Staff, 1978–79; Comdr, British Forces Hong Kong, and Maj.-Gen., Brigade of Gurkhas, 1980–82; Dir of Military Operations, 1982–84. Services Fellow, Fitzwilliam Coll., Cambridge, 1973. Member: Council, Nat. Army Museum; Soc. for Army Historical Res. WWF, UK and Hong Kong. FZS, FRGS (Mem. Council). OStJ. *Club:* Beefsteak.

CHAPPLE, Stanley; Director of Symphony and Opera, University of Washington, now Emeritus; *b* 29 Oct. 1900; *s* of Stanley Clements Chapple and Bessie Norman; *m* 1927, Barbara, *d* of late Edward Hilliard; no *c*. *Educ:* Central Foundation Sch., London. Began his musical education at the London Academy of Music at the age of 8, being successively student, professor, Vice-Principal, Principal until 1936; as a Conductor made début at the Queen's Hall, 1927, and has since conducted Symphony Orchestras in Berlin, Vienna, The Hague, Warsaw and Boston, St Louis, Washington, DC, and other American and Canadian cities. Assistant to Serge Koussevitzky at Berkshire Music Centre, 1940, 1941, 1942 and 1946; former conductor St Louis Philharmonic Orchestra and Chorus and Grand Opera Association. Hon. MusDoc Colby Coll., 1947. *Address:* 18270 47th Place NE, Seattle, Washington 98155, USA.

CHAPUT DE SAINTONGE, Rev. Rolland Alfred Aimé, CMG 1953; Bursar; *b* Montreal, Canada, 7 Jan. 1912; *s* of Alfred Edward and Hélène Jeté Chaput de Saintonge; *m* 1940, Barbara Watts; one *s* two *d*. *Educ:* Canada; USA; Syracuse Univ., NY (BA, MA); Geneva Univ. (D ès Sc. Pol.). Extra-Mural Lecturer in International Affairs: University College of the South-West, Exeter, University of Bristol, University College of Southampton, 1935–40; Staff Speaker, Min. of Information, South-West Region, 1940; served Army, 1940–46; Lieut-Col (DCLI); Asst Secretary, Control Office for Germany and Austria, 1946–48; Head of Government Structure Branch, CCG and Liaison Officer to German Parliamentary Council, 1948–49; Head of German Information Dept, FO, 1949–58; UN High Commission for Refugees: Dep. Chief, Information and Public Relations Sect., 1960–64; Rep. in Senegal, 1964–66; Programme Support Officer, 1966–67; Chief, N and W Europe Section, 1967–68; Special Projects Officer, 1968–73. Ordained, Diocese of Quebec, 1975; admitted Community of Most Holy Sacrament, 1976. *Publications:* Disarmament in British Foreign Policy, 1935; British Foreign Policy Since the War, 1936; The Road to War and the Way Out, 1940; Public Administration in Germany, 1961. *Address:* 8 Minley Court, Somers Road, Reigate, Surrey.

CHARKHAM, Jonathan Philip; Chief Adviser, Bank of England, since 1985; *b* 17 Oct. 1930; *s* of late Louis Charkham and Phoebe Beatrice Barquet (*née* Miller); *m* Moira Elizabeth Frances, *d* of late Barnett A. Salmon and of Molly Salmon; twin *s* one *d*. *Educ:* St Paul's Sch. (scholar); Jesus Coll., Cambridge (Exhibitioner). BA 1952. Called to Bar, Inner Temple, 1953. Morris Charkham Ltd, 1953–63 (Man. Dir, 1957–63); Div. Dir, Rest Assured Ltd, 1963–68. Civil Service Department: Principal, Management Services, later Pay, 1969–73; Asst Sec., 1973–78, Personnel Management, 1973–75; Dir, Public Appts Unit, 1975–82; Under Sec., 1978, Management and Organisation, 1980–82; on secondment from Bank of England as Dir, PRO NED, 1982–85. Mem. Council, Royal Inst. of Public Admin., 1981–82. Chm., CU Labour Club, 1952. Master, Worshipful Co. of Upholders, 1979–80, 1980–81. FRSA; FBIM. *Publication:* Effective Boards, 1986. *Recreations:* music, playing golf, watching cricket, antique furniture, wine. *Address:* 22 Montpelier Place, SW7 1HL. *T:* 01–589 9879. *Clubs:* Athenæum, MCC, Roehampton, City Livery.

CHARLEMONT, 14th Viscount *cr* 1665 (Ire.); **John Day Caulfeild;** Baron Caulfeild of Charlemont 1620 (Ire.); *b* 19 March 1934; *s* of Eric St George Caulfeild (*d* 1975) and of Edith Evelyn, *d* of Frederick William Day, Ottawa; *S* uncle, 1985; *m* 1st, 1964, Judith Ann (*d* 1971), *d* of James E. Dodd; one *s* one *d*; 2nd, 1972, Janet Evelyn, *d* of Orville R. Nancekivell. *Heir:* *s* Hon. John Dodd Caulfeild, *b* 15 May 1966. *Address:* 39 Rossburn Drive, Etobicoke, Ontario M9C 2P9, Canada.

CHARLES, Anthony Harold, ERD; TD; MA Cantab; MB; FRCS; FRCOG; Consulting Obstetric and Gynæcological Surgeon, St George's Hospital; Consulting Surgeon, Samaritan Hospital for Women (St Mary's); Consulting Gynæcologist, Royal National Orthopædic Hospital; formerly, Hon. Gynæcologist, King Edward VII Hospital for Officers; Consulting Gynæcologist, Caterham and District Hospital; Consulting Surgeon, General Lying-in-Hospital; late Hon. Consultant in Obstetrics and Gynaecology Army; 2nd *s* of H. P. Charles; *m* 1962, Rosemary Christine Hubert; three *d*. *Educ:* Dulwich; Gonville and Caius Coll., Cambridge. Examiner in Midwifery and Gynæcology: Univ. of Cambridge; Soc. of Apothecaries; RCOG; Univs of London, Hong Kong and Cairo. Past Mem., Board of Governors, St Mary's Hospital. Past President: Chelsea Clinical Soc.; Sect. of Obstetrics and Gynæcology, RSM. Late Vice-Dean, St George's Hospital Medical Sch.; late Resident Asst Surgeon and Hon. Asst Anæsthetist, St George's Hospital. Colonel AMS; late Hon. Colonel and OC, 308 (Co. of London) General Hospital, T&AVR. Hon. Surgeon to the Queen, 1957–59. Served 1939–45, Aldershot, Malta and Middle-East as Surgical Specialist; Officer-in-Charge, Surgical Division, 15 Scottish General Hospital and Gynæc. Adviser MEF. Past Pres., Alleyn Club. *Publications:* Women in Sport, in Armstrong and Tucker's Injuries in Sport, 1964; contributions since 1940 to Jl Obst. and Gyn., Postgrad. Med. Jl, Proc. Royal Soc. Med., Operative Surgery, BMJ. *Recreations:* golf, boxing (Middle-Weight, Cambridge *v* Oxford, 1930); Past President Rosslyn Park Football Club. *Address:* Consulting Suite, Wellington Hospital, NW8. *T:* 01–586 5959; Gaywood Farm, Gay Street, Pulborough, Sussex. *T:* West Chiltington 2223. *Clubs:* Army and Navy, MCC; Hawks (Cambridge).

CHARLES, Bernard Leopold, QC 1980; a Recorder, since 1985; *b* 16 May 1929; *s* of Chaskiel Charles and Mary Harris; *m* 1958, Margaret Daphne Abel; one *s* two *d*. *Educ:* King's Coll., Taunton. Called to the Bar, Gray's Inn, 1955. Practised in London and on South Eastern Circuit, from 1956. *Recreations:* music, politics. *Address:* Lamb Building, Temple, EC4. *T:* 01–353 6701; 12 East 41st Street, New York, NY 10017, USA.

CHARLES, Hon. Eugenia; *see* Charles, Hon. M. E.

CHARLES, Rt. Rev. Harold John; Bishop of St Asaph, 1971–82; *b* 26 June 1914; *s* of Rev. David Charles and Mary Charles, Carmarthenshire; *m* 1941, Margaret Noeline; one *d*. *Educ:* Welsh Univ. Aberystwyth; Keble Coll., Oxford. BA Wales 1935; BA Oxford 1938, MA 1943. Curate of Abergwili, Carms, 1938–40; Bishop's Messenger, Diocese of Swansea and Brecon, 1940–48; Warden of University Church Hostel, Bangor, and Lecturer at University College, Bangor, 1948–52; Vicar of St James, Bangor, 1952–54; Canon Residentiary of Bangor, 1953–54; Warden of St Michael's Coll., Llandaff, 1954–57; Canon of Llandaff, 1956–57; Dean of St Asaph, 1957–71. ChStJ 1973. *Address:* 53 The Avenue, Woodland Park, Prestatyn, Clwyd.

CHARLES, Jack; Director of Establishments, Greater London Council, 1972–77, retired; *b* 18 Jan. 1923; *o s* of late Frederick Walter Charles and of Alice Mary Charles; *m* 1959, Jean, *d* of late F. H. Braund, London; one *s* one *d*. *Educ:* County High Sch., Ilford. Air Min., 1939–42; RAF, 1942–46; Min. of Supply, 1947–59 (Private Sec. to Minister of Supply, 1952–54); War Office, 1959–60; UKAEA, 1960–68 (Authority Personnel Officer, 1965–68); Dep. Dir of Estabs, GLC, 1968–72. *Recreations:* gardening, walking. *Address:* Kings Warren, Enborne Row, Wash Water, Newbury, Berks RG15 0LY. *T:* Newbury 30161.

CHARLES, James Anthony, ScD; FEng 1983; Reader in Process Metallurgy, University of Cambridge, since 1978; Fellow, St John's College, Cambridge, since 1963; *b* 23 Aug. 1926; *s* of John and Winifred Charles; *m* 1951, Valerie E. King; two *s*. *Educ:* Imperial College of Science and Technology, Royal School of Mines (BScEng, ARSM); MA, ScD Cantab; FIM, MIMM. J. Stone & Co. Ltd, 1947–50; British Oxygen Ltd, 1950–60; Dept of Metallurgy and Materials Science, Univ. of Cambridge, 1960–. Sir George Beilby Medal and Prize, RIC, Soc. Chem. Ind. and Inst. of Metals, 1965; Sir Robert Hadfield Medal, Metals Soc., 1977. *Publications:* Oxygen in Iron and Steel Making, 1956; Selection and Use of Engineering Materials, 1984; numerous papers on the science and technology of metals and archaeometallurgy. *Recreations:* gardening, walking, listening to music, archaeology. *Address:* New Lodge, 22 Mingle Lane, Stapleford, Cambridge CB2 5BG. *T:* Cambridge 843812.

CHARLES, Sir Joseph (Quentin), Kt 1984; Managing Director, J. Q. Charles Ltd; *b* 25 Nov. 1908; *s* of Martineau Charles; *m* 1934, Albertha L. Yorke; three *s* two *d*. *Educ:* St Mary's Coll., St Lucia. Commission Agent's Clerk, 1927–33. Started J. Q. Charles as a small provision wholesale and retail business, 1933, incorporated 1944; business has grown to become classified retailer of cars, foods, building materials and hardware, dry goods and wearing apparel; also started several light manufacturing industries; St Lucia Co-operative Bank, 1937 (Founding Director for 43 years, Pres., 1974–79); Past Chairman: St Lucia Agricl & Industrial Bank; St Lucia Banana Growers Assoc., 1963–67; Dir, Copra Manufacturers Ltd. Mem., Castries City Council. *Address:* c/o J. Q. Charles Ltd, PO Box 279, Castries, St Lucia, West Indies. *T:* (home) 20656.

CHARLES, Leslie Stanley Francis; Director, British Aluminium Co. Ltd, since1979 (Deputy Managing Director, 1968–79, Managing Director, 1979–82); Director, Birmid Qualcast plc, since 1981; *b* 28 July 1917; *s* of Samuel Francis Charles and Lena Gwendolyn (*née* Reed); *m* 1941, Henrietta Elizabeth Calvin Thomas; one *s*. *Educ:* Cardiff High Sch.; University Coll. of S Wales and Mon, Univ. of Wales (BScEng London, 1st Cl. Hons). Grad. Engr, Metropolitan Vickers Ltd, 1936–39; Regular Officer, REME, 1939–54; Consultant, Urwick Orr & Partners Ltd, 1954–60; Chief Engr Ops, UKAEA, 1960–63; Dir of Factories, Raleigh Industries Ltd, 1963–66; Man. Dir, Aluminium Wire & Cable Co. Ltd, 1966–68. Chm., European Aluminium Assoc., 1981–84. *Recreations:* golf, bridge, music. *Address:* Crana, Claydon Lane, Chalfont St Peter, Bucks SL9 8JU. *T:* Gerrards Cross 884290. *Club:* Army and Navy.

CHARLES, Hon. (Mary) Eugenia; Prime Minister and Minister of Finance and Foreign Affairs, Commonwealth of Dominica, since 1980; MP (Dominica Freedom Party) Roseau, since 1970; *b* 15 May 1919; *d* of John Baptiste Charles and Josephine (*née* Delauney). *Educ:* Convent High Sch., Roseau, Dominica; St Joseph's Convent, St George's, Grenada; University Coll., Univ. of Toronto (BA); London Sch. of Econs and Pol. Science. Called to the Bar, Inner Temple, 1947; admitted to practice, Dominica, 1949. Entered Parlt, 1970; Leader of the Opposition, 1975–80. *Recreations:* reading, gardening, travelling. *Address:* Office of the Prime Minister, Roseau, Commonwealth of Dominica. *T:* 2401, ext. 300.

CHARLES, Michael Geoffrey A.; *see* Audley-Charles.

CHARLES, Rev. Canon Sebastian; Residentiary Canon, Westminster Abbey, since 1978; Steward since 1978, also Treasurer since 1982; *b* 31 May 1932; *s* of Gnanamuthu Pakianathan Charles and Kamala David; *m* 1967, Frances Rosemary Challen; two *s* two *d*. *Educ:* Madras Univ. (BCom 1953); Serampore Univ. (BD 1965); Lincoln Theological Coll. Curate, St Mary, Portsea, Dio. Portsmouth, 1956–59; Priest-in-charge, St John the Evangelist, Dio. Rangoon, 1959–65; St Augustine's Coll., Canterbury, 1965–66; St Thomas, Heaton Chapel, Dio. Manchester, attached to Industrial Mission Team, 1966–67; Vicar of St Barnabas', Pendleton, 1967–74; Chaplain, Univ. of Salford, 1967–74; Asst Gen. Secretary and Secretary, Div. of Community Affairs, British Council of Churches, 1974–78. Mem., Parole Bd, 1980–83. *Recreations:* reading, tennis. *Address:* 5 Little Cloister, Westminster Abbey, SW1P 3PL. *T:* 01–222 6939.

CHARLES, William Travers; Fellow, Faculty of Law, Monash University, 1976–82 (Special Lecturer, 1966–75); Judge of the High Court, Zambia, 1963–66; *b* Victoria, Australia, 10 Dec. 1908; *s* of William James Charles and Elizabeth Esther Charles (*née* Payne); *m* 1940, Helen Gibson Vale; one *s* one *d*. *Educ:* St Thomas Grammar Sch.,

Essendon, Victoria; University of Melbourne. Admitted to legal practice, Victoria, 1932; practised at bar, 1932–39. Served Australian Army Legal Service including Middle East, 1940–42 (Lieut-Col), seconded AAG (Discipline), AHQ Melbourne, 1942–46. Chief Magistrate and Legal Adviser, British Solomon Islands Protectorate, 1946–51; Judicial Commn, British Solomon Islands, 1951–53; Magistrate, Hong Kong, 1954–56; District Judge, Hong Kong, 1956–58; Judge of the High Court, Western Nigeria, 1958–63. *Recreations:* cricket, football, music, history. *Address:* 2 Burroughs Road, Balwyn, Vic 3103, Australia.

CHARLESTON, Robert Jesse, FSA; FSGT. Keeper of the Department of Ceramics, Victoria and Albert Museum, 1963–76; *b* 3 April 1916; *s* of late Sidney James Charleston, Lektor, Stockholms Högskola; *m* 1941, Joan Randle; one *s* one *d. Educ:* Berkhamsted Sch., Herts; New College, Oxford. Army (Major, RAPC), 1940–46; Asst, Bristol Museum, 1947; Asst Keeper, Victoria and Albert Museum, 1948; Deputy Keeper, 1959. Mem., Reviewing Cttee on Export of Works of Art, 1979–84. *Publications:* Roman Pottery, 1955; (ed) English Porcelain, 1745–1850, 1965; (ed) World Ceramics, 1968; (with Donald Towner) English Ceramics, 1580–1830, 1977; Islamic Pottery, 1979; Masterpieces of Glass, 1980; The James A. de Rothschild Collection: (with J. G. Ayers) Meissen and Oriental Porcelain, 1971; (with Michael Archer and M. Marcheix) Glass and Enamels, 1977; English Glass, 1984; numerous articles and reviews in The Connoisseur, Jl of Glass Studies, Burlington Magazine, etc. *Recreations:* foreign travel, music. *Address:* Whittington Court, Whittington, near Cheltenham, Glos GL54 4HF.

CHARLESWORTH, Peter James; barrister; a Recorder of the Crown Court, since 1982; *b* 24 Aug. 1944; *s* of late Joseph William Charlesworth and of Florence Mary Charlesworth; *m* 1967, Elizabeth Mary Postill; one *s* one *d. Educ:* Hull Grammar Sch.; Leeds Univ. (LLB 1965, LLM 1966). Called to the Bar, Inner Temple, 1966. In practice on North-Eastern Circuit, 1966–. *Recreations:* squash, Rugby football (spectating), walking. *Address:* Daleswood, Creskeld Gardens, Bramhope, Leeds LS16 9EN. *T:* Leeds 674377. *Clubs:* Hull Rugby League Football (Vice-Pres.); Otley Rugby Union Football.

CHARLESWORTH, Stanley, OBE 1980; National Secretary, National Council of YMCAs, 1975–80; *b* 20 March 1920; *s* of Ernest and Amy Charlesworth; *m* 1942, Vera Bridge; three *d. Educ:* Ashton under Lyne Grammar Sch.; Manchester Coll. of Commerce. YMCA: Area Sec., Community Services, 1943–52, Dep. Sec., 1952–57; Asst Regional Sec., NW Region, 1957–67, Regional Sec., 1967–75. *Recreations:* sailing, golf, walking, gardening. *Clubs:* Rotary (Walthamstow); YMCA (Manchester).

CHARLISH, Dennis Norman; Panel Chairman, Civil Service Selection Board, since 1978 (Resident Chairman, 1975–78); *b* 24 May 1918; *s* of Norman Charlish and Edith (*née* Cherriman); *m* 1941, Margaret Trevor, *o d* of William Trevor and Margaret Ann Williams, Manchester; one *d. Educ:* Brighton Grammar Sch.; London Sch. of Economics. Rosebery Schol., 1947; BSc (Econ) 1st class hons., 1951. Joined Civil Service as Tax Officer, Inland Revenue, 1936; Exec. Officer, Dept of Overseas Trade, 1937; Dep. Armament Supply Officer, Admty, 1941; Principal, BoT, 1949; Asst Secretary, 1959; Imperial Defence Coll., 1963; Under-Sec., BoT, 1967–69; Min. of Technology, 1969–70; Head of Personnel, DTI, 1971–74, Dept of Industry, 1974–75. *Address:* 28 Multon Road, SW18 3LH.

CHARLTON, Bobby; see Charlton, Robert.

CHARLTON, (Frederick) Noel, CB 1961; CBE 1946; *b* 4 Dec. 1906; *s* of late Frederick William Charlton and Marian Charlton; *m* 1932, Maud Helen Rudgard; no *c. Educ:* Rugby School; Hertford Coll., Oxford Univ. (MA). Admitted a Solicitor, 1932; in private practice as Solicitor in London, 1932–39. War Service, 1939–46 (attained rank of Colonel, Gen. List). Joined Treasury Solicitor's Dept, 1946; Principal Asst Solicitor (Litigation), Treasury Solicitor's Dept, 1956–71; Sec., Lord Chancellor's Cttee on Defamation, 1971–74; with Dept of Energy (Treasury Solicitor's Branch), 1975–81, retired. Chairman, Coulsdon and Purley UDC, 1953–54 and 1964–65; Hon. Alderman, London Borough of Croydon. Bronze Star (USA), 1945. *Recreations:* golf, travel. *Address:* 4 Newton Road, Purley, Surrey CR2 3DN. *T:* 01–660 2802. *Club:* Army and Navy.
See also T. A. G. Charlton.

CHARLTON, Graham; see Charlton, T. A. G.

CHARLTON, Prof. Graham, MDS; FDSRCSE; Professor of Conservative Dentistry, University of Edinburgh, since 1978 (Dean of Dental Studies, 1978–83); *b* 15 Oct. 1928; *s* of Simpson R. Charlton and Georgina (*née* Graham); *m* 1956, Stella Dobson; two *s* one *d. Educ:* Bedlington Grammar Sch., Northumberland; St John's Coll., York (Teaching Cert.); King's Coll., Univ. of Durham (BDS); Univ. of Bristol (MDS). Teacher, Northumberland, 1948–52; National Service, 1948–50; Dental School, 1952–58; General Dental Practice, Torquay, 1958–64; University of Bristol: Lecturer, 1964–72; Cons. Sen. Lectr, 1972–78; Dental Clinical Dean, 1975–78. *Address:* Carnethy, Bog Road, Penicuik, Midlothian EH26 9BT. *T:* Penicuik 73639.

CHARLTON, John, (Jack Charlton), OBE 1974; Manager, Republic of Ireland Football Team, since 1986; broadcaster; *b* 8 May 1935; *s* of Robert and Elizabeth Charlton; *m* 1958, Patricia; two *s* one *d. Educ:* Hirst Park Sch., Ashington. Professional footballer, Leeds United, 1952–73; Manager: Middlesbrough, 1973–77; Sheffield Wednesday FC, 1977–83; Newcastle United FC, 1984–85. Mem., Sports Council, 1977–82. *Recreations:* shooting, fishing, gardening. *Address:* c/o Football Association of the Republic of Ireland, 8 Merrion Square, Dublin 2, Ireland.
See also Robert Charlton.

CHARLTON, Prof. Kenneth; Emeritus Professor of History of Education, King's College, University of London, since 1983; *b* 11 July 1925; 2nd *s* of late George and Lottie Charlton; *m* 1953, Maud Tulloch Brown, *d* of late P. R. Brown, MBE and M. B. Brown; one *s* one *d. Educ:* City Grammar Sch., Chester; Univ. of Glasgow. MA 1949, MEd 1953, Glasgow. RNVR, 1943–46. History Master, Dalziel High Sch., Motherwell, and Uddingston Grammar Sch., 1950–54; Lectr in Educn, UC N Staffs, 1954–64; Sen. Lectr in Educn, Keele Univ., 1964–66; Prof. of History and Philosophy of Educn, Birmingham Univ., 1966–72; Prof. of History of Educn and Head of Dept of Educn, King's Coll., Univ. of London, 1972–83. *Publications:* Recent Historical Fiction for Children, 1960, 2nd edn 1969; Education in Renaissance England, 1965; contrib. Educnl Rev., Brit. J1 Educnl Psych., Year Bk of Educn, J1 Hist. of Ideas, Brit. J1 Educnl Studies, Internat. Rev. of Educn, Trans Hist. Soc. Lancs and Cheshire, Irish Hist. Studies, Northern Hist. *Recreations:* gardening, listening to music. *Address:* 128 Ridge Langley, Sanderstead, Croydon CR2 0AS.
See also P. Charlton.

CHARLTON, Philip; FIB; CBIM; Chief General Manager, TSB Group, since 1982; *b* 31 July 1930; *s* of George and Lottie Charlton; *m* 1953, Jessie Boulton; one *s* one *d. Educ:* Chester Grammar School. Entered service of Chester Savings Bank, 1947, Gen. Manager, 1966–75; Gen. Manager, Trustee Savings Bank of Wales & Border Counties, 1975–81; Dep. Chief Gen. Manager, TSB Gp Central Exec., 1981–82; Mem., TSB Central Bd,

1976–77, 1981–; Director: TSB Computer Services (Wythenshawe) Ltd, 1976–81; TSB Trust Co. Ltd, 1979–82; TSB Gp Computer Services Ltd, 1981–; Central Trustee Savings Bank Ltd, 1982–; TSB (Holdings) Ltd, 1982–. Council Mem., 1968–71, Hon. Treasurer, 1975–77, Savings Bank Inst.; Council Mem., Inst. of Bankers, 1982–. Chm., TSB Nat. Sports Council, 1979–82. FIB 1977; CBIM 1983. *Recreations:* music, swimming, sport. *Address:* 62 Quinta Drive, Arkley, near Barnet, Herts EN5 3BE. *T:* 01–440 4477. *Club:* City (Chester).
See also Prof. K. Charlton.

CHARLTON, Robert, (Bobby Charlton), CBE 1974 (OBE 1969); Chairman, North West Council for Sport and Recreation, since 1982; Director, Manchester United Football Club, since 1984; *b* 11 Oct. 1937; *s* of Robert and Elizabeth Charlton; *m* 1961, Norma; two *d. Educ:* Bedlington Grammar Sch., Northumberland. Professional Footballer with Manchester United, 1954–73, for whom he played 751 games and scored 245 goals; FA Cup Winners Medal, 1963; FA Championship Medals, 1956–57, 1964–65 and 1966–67; World Cup Winners Medal (International), 1966; European Cup Winners medal, 1968. 100th England cap, 21 April 1970; 106 appearances for England, 1957–73. Manager, Preston North End, 1973–75. Hon. Fellow, Manchester Polytechnic, 1979. *Publications:* My Soccer Life, 1965; Forward for England, 1967; This Game of Soccer, 1967; Book of European Football, Books 1–4, 1969–72. *Recreation:* golf. *Address:* Garthollerton, Chelford Road, Ollerton, near Knutsford, Cheshire.
See also John Charlton.

CHARLTON, (Thomas Alfred) Graham, CB 1970; Secretary, Trade Marks, Patents and Designs Federation, 1973–84; *b* 29 Aug. 1913; 3rd *s* of late Frederick William and Marian Charlton; *m* 1940, Margaret Ethel, *yr d* of A. E. Furst; three *d. Educ:* Rugby School; Corpus Christi Coll., Cambridge. Asst Principal, War Office, 1936; Asst Private Secretary to Secretary of State for War, 1937–39; Principal, 1939; Cabinet Office, 1947–49; Asst Secretary, 1949; International Staff, NATO, 1950–52; War Office, later MoD, 1952–73; Asst Under-Sec. of State, 1960–73. Coronation Medal, 1953. *Recreations:* golf, gardening. *Address:* Victoria House, Elm Road, Penn, Bucks HP10 8LQ. *T:* Penn 3195.
See also Frederick Noel Charlton.

CHARLTON, Prof. Thomas Malcolm, FRSE 1973; historian of engineering science; Jackson Professor of Engineering, University of Aberdeen, 1970–79, now Emeritus; Visiting Professor of Civil Engineering, University of Newcastle upon Tyne, since 1982; *b* 1 Sept. 1923; *s* of William Charlton and Emily May Charlton (*née* Wallbank); *m* 1950, Valerie, *d* of late Dr C. McCulloch, Hexham; two *s* (and one *s* decd). *Educ:* Doncaster Grammar Sch. BSc (Eng) London, MA Cantab. Junior Scientific Officer, Min. of Aircraft Prodn, TRE, Malvern, 1943–46; Asst Engr, Merz & McLellan, Newcastle upon Tyne, 1946–54; Univ. Lectr in Engrg, Cambridge, 1954–63; Fellow and Tutor, Sidney Sussex Coll., 1959–63; Prof. of Civil Engrg, Queen's Univ., Belfast, 1963–70; Dean, Faculty of Applied Science, QUB, 1967–70. For. Mem., Finnish Acad. of Technical Sciences, 1967. *Publications:* Model Analysis of Structures, 1954, new edn 1966; (contrib.) Hydro-electric Engineering Practice, 1958; Energy Principles in Applied Statics, 1959; Analysis of Statically-indeterminate Frameworks, 1961; Principles of Structural Analysis, 1969, new edn 1977; Energy Principles in Theory of Structures, 1973; (contrib.) The Works of I. K. Brunel, 1976; History of Theory of Structures in the Nineteenth Century, 1982; (contrib.) Encyclopaedia of Building Technology, 1986; papers on energy principles, hist. of structures. *Recreations:* ecclesiastical history, golf. *Address:* 18 Queen's Drive, Great Malvern, Worcestershire WR14 4RE. *T:* Malvern 62688. *Club:* New (Edinburgh).

CHARNLEY, Sir John; see Charnley, Sir W. J.

CHARNLEY, Sir (William) John, Kt 1981; CB 1973; MEng, FEng, FRAeS, FRInstNav; consultant in advanced technology; Director, Fairey Holdings Ltd, since 1983; *b* 4 Sept. 1922; *s* of George and Catherine Charnley; *m* 1945, Mary Paden; one *s* one *d. Educ:* Oulton High Sch., Liverpool; Liverpool Univ. MEng 1945. Aerodynamics Dept, RAE Farnborough, 1943–55; Supt. Blind Landing Experimental Unit, 1955–61; Imperial Defence Coll., 1962; Head of Instruments and Electrical Engineering Dept, 1963–65, Head of Weapons Dept, 1965–68, RAE Farnborough; Head of Research Planning, 1968–69, Dep. Controller, Guided Weapons, Min. of Technology, later MoD, 1969–72; Controller, Guided Weapons and Electronics, MoD (PE), 1972–73; Chief Scientist (RAF), 1973–77, and Dep. Controller, R&D Establishments and Res. C, MoD, 1975–77; Controller, R&D Establishments and Res., MoD, 1977–82. Specialist Advr to House of Lords Select Cttee on Science and Technology, 1986. Chm., Civil Aviation Res. and Develt Programme Bd, 1984–; Mem., Air Traffic Control Bd, 1985–. Vice-Pres., RIN, 1985. Gold Medal, RAeS, 1980. *Publications:* papers on subjects in aerodynamics, aircraft all weather operation, aircraft navigation, defence R&D. *Address:* Kirkstones, 29 Brackendale Close, Camberley, Surrey GU15 1HP. *T:* Camberley 22547. *Club:* Royal Air Force.

CHARNOCK, Henry, FRS 1976; Professor of Physical Oceanography, 1966–71 and since 1978, Deputy Vice-Chancellor, 1982–84, Southampton University; *b* 25 Dec. 1920; *s* of Henry Charnock and Mary Gray McLeod; *m* 1946, Eva Mary Dickinson; one *s* two *d. Educ:* Queen Elizabeth's Grammar Sch., Municipal Techn. Coll., Blackburn; Imperial Coll., London. Staff, Nat. Inst. of Oceanography, 1949–58 and 1959–66; Reader in Physical Oceanography, Imperial Coll., 1958–59; Dir, Inst. of Oceanographic Scis (formerly Nat. Inst. of Oceanography), 1971–78. President: Internat. Union of Geodesy and Geophysics, 1971–75; RMetS, 1982–84; Vice-Pres., Scientific Cttee on Oceanic Res., 1980–82 (Sec., 1978–80); Mem., Royal Commn on Environmental Pollution, 1985–. *Publications:* papers in meteorological and oceanographic jls. *Address:* 5 Links View Way, Southampton SO1 7GR. *T:* Southampton 769629.

CHARTERIS, family name of **Baron Charteris of Amisfield** and of **Earl of Wemyss.**

CHARTERIS OF AMISFIELD, Baron *cr* 1978 (Life Peer), of Amisfield, E Lothian; **Martin Michael Charles Charteris,** GCB 1977 (KCB 1972; CB 1958); GCVO 1976 (KCVO 1962; MVO 1953); QSO 1978; OBE 1946; PC 1972; Hon. RA 1981; Provost of Eton, since 1978; Chairman of Trustees, National Heritage Memorial Fund, since 1980; *b* 7 Sept. 1913; 2nd *s* of Hugo Francis, Lord Elcho (killed in action, 1916); *g s* of 11th Earl of Wemyss; *m* 1944, Hon. Mary Gay Hobart Margesson, *yr d* of 1st Viscount Margesson, PC, MC; two *s* one *d. Educ:* Eton; RMC Sandhurst. Lieut KRRC, 1936; served War of 1939–45; Lieut-Colonel, 1944. Private Secretary to Princess Elizabeth, 1950–52; Asst Private Secretary to the Queen, 1952–72; Private Secretary to the Queen and Keeper of HM's Archives, 1972–77. A Permanent Lord in Waiting to the Queen, 1978–. Director: Claridge's Hotel, 1978–; Connaught Hotel, 1978–; De La Rue Co., 1978–85; Rio Tinto Zinc Corp., 1978–84. Trustee, BM, 1979–. Hon. DCL Oxon, 1978; Hon. LLD London, 1981. *Recreation:* sculpting. *Address:* Provost's Lodge, Eton College, Windsor, Berks. *T:* Windsor 866304; Wood Stanway House, Wood Stanway, Glos GL54 5PE. *T:* Stanton 480. *Club:* White's.

CHARTERIS, Leslie; FRSA; author; *b* 12 May 1907; *m* 1st, Pauline Schishkin (divorced, 1937); one *d*; 2nd, Barbara Meyer (divorced, 1941); 3rd, Elizabeth Bryant Borst (divorced, 1951); 4th, Audrey Long. *Educ:* Rossall; Cambridge Univ. Many years of entertaining, but usually unprofitable, travel and adventure; after one or two false starts created character of "The Saint" (trans. into 15 languages besides those of films, radio, television, and the comic strip). *Publications:* Meet the Tiger, 1928; Enter the Saint; The Last Hero; Knight Templar; Featuring the Saint; Alias the Saint; She was a Lady (filmed 1938 as The Saint Strikes Back); The Holy Terror (filmed 1939 as The Saint in London); Getaway; Once More the Saint; The Brighter Buccaneer; The Misfortunes of Mr Teal; Boodle; The Saint Goes On; The Saint in New York (filmed 1938); Saint Overboard, 1936; The Ace of Knaves, 1937; Thieves Picnic, 1937; (trans., with introd.) Juan Belmonte, Killer of Bulls: The Autobiography of a Matador, 1937; Prelude for War, 1938; Follow the Saint, 1938; The Happy Highwayman, 1939; The First Saint Omnibus, 1939; The Saint in Miami, 1941; The Saint Goes West, 1942; The Saint Steps In, 1944; The Saint on Guard, 1945; The Saint Sees it Through, 1946; Call for the Saint, 1948; Saint Errant, 1948; The Second Saint Omnibus, 1952; The Saint on the Spanish Main, 1955; The Saint around the World, 1957; Thanks to the Saint, 1958; Señor Saint, 1959; The Saint to the Rescue, 1961; Trust the Saint, 1962; The Saint in the Sun, 1964; Vendetta for the Saint, 1965 (filmed 1968); The Saint on TV, 1968; The Saint Returns, 1969; The Saint and the Fiction Makers, 1969; The Saint Abroad, 1970; The Saint in Pursuit, 1971; The Saint and the People Importers, 1971; Paleneo, 1972; Saints Alive, 1974; Catch the Saint, 1975; The Saint and the Hapsburg Necklace, 1976; Send for the Saint, 1977; The Saint in Trouble, 1978; The Saint and the Templar Treasure, 1979; Count on the Saint, 1980; The Fantastic Saint, 1982; Salvage for the Saint, 1983; Supervising Editor of the Saint Magazine, 1953–67; Editorial Consultant of the (new) Saint Magazine, 1984–85; columnist, Gourmet Magazine, 1966–68; concurrently has worked as special correspondent and Hollywood scenarist; contributor to leading English and American magazines and newspapers. *Recreations:* eating, drinking, horseracing, sailing, fishing, and loafing. *Address:* 3/4 Great Marlborough Street, W1V 2AR. *Clubs:* Savage; Mensa, Yacht Club de Cannes.

CHARVET, Richard Christopher Larkins, RD 1972; JP; Director, Vogt and Maguire Group of companies, since 1981; *b* 12 Dec. 1936; *s* of Patrice and late Eleanor Charvet; *m* 1961, Elizabeth Joan Johnson; two *s* one *d*. *Educ:* Rugby. MITT, MCIS, ACIArb; FBIM. FRSA 1985. National Service, Royal Navy, 1955–57; Mem., London Div., RNR, 1955–. Union Castle Line, 1957–58; Killick Martin & Co. Ltd, Shipbrokers, 1958–81; Vogt and Maguire Ltd, Shipbrokers, 1981–. Mem., Court of Common Council for Aldgate Ward, City of London, 1970–76; Alderman, Aldgate Ward, 1976–85; Sheriff, 1983–84. Prime Warden, Worshipful Co. of Shipwrights, 1985–86 (Renter Warden, 1984–85). JP 1976. OStJ 1984; Hon. JSM, Malaysia, 1974. *Publication:* Peter and Tom in the Lord Mayor's Show, 1982. *Recreations:* gardening, travel, sailing. *Clubs:* City Livery, United Wards, Aldgate Ward.

CHASE, Anya Seton; *see* Seton, A.

CHASE, Robert John; HM Diplomatic Service; Counsellor (Commercial), British Embassy, Moscow, since 1985; *b* 13 March 1943; *s* of Herbert Chase and Evelyn Chase; *m* 1966, Gillian Ann Chase (*née* Shelton); one *s* two *d*. *Educ:* Sevenoaks Sch.; St John's Coll., Oxford. MA (Mod. Hist.). Entered HM Diplomatic Service, 1965; Third, later Second Sec., Rangoon, 1966–69; UN Dept, FCO, 1970–72; First Sec. (Press Attaché), Brasilia, 1972–76; Hd Caribbean Section, Mexico and Caribbean Dept, FCO, 1976–80; on secondment as a manager to Imperial Chemical Industries PLC, 1980–82; Asst Hd, S American Dept, FCO, 1982–83; Asst Hd, Maritime, Aviation and Environment Dept, FCO, 1983–84. *Recreations:* military history, visiting historic sites, tennis. *Address:* c/o Foreign and Commonwealth Office, King Charles Street, SW1. *T:* 01–243 1110; Forest House, Bishops Down Park Road, Tunbridge Wells, Kent. *T:* Tunbridge Wells 21623.

CHATAWAY, Rt. Hon. Christopher John, PC 1970; Vice Chairman, Orion Royal Bank (formerly Orion Bank), since 1980 (Managing Director, 1974–80); *b* 31 Jan. 1931; *m* 1st, 1959, Anna Lett (marr. diss. 1975); two *s* one *d*; 2nd, 1976, Carola Walker; two *s*. *Educ:* Sherborne Sch.; Magdalen Coll., Oxford. Hons. Degree, PPE. President OUAC, 1952; rep. Great Britain, Olympic Games, 1952 and 1956; briefly held world 5,000 metres record in 1954. Junior Exec. Arthur Guinness Son & Co., 1953–55; Staff Reporter, Independent Television News, 1955–56; Current Affairs Commentator for BBC Television, 1956–59. Elected for N Lewisham to LCC, 1958–61. MP (C): Lewisham North, 1959–66; Chichester, May 1969–Sept. 1974; PPS to Minister of Power, 1961–62; Joint Parly Under-Secretary of State, Dept of Education and Science, 1962–64; Minister of Posts and Telecommunications, 1970–72; Minister for Industrial Develt, DTI, 1972–74. Director: British Electric Traction Co., 1974–; Internat. General Electric Co. of New York Ltd, 1979–; Petrofina UK Ltd, 1985–; Chairman: British Telecommunications Systems, 1979–83; London Broadcasting Co., 1981–. Treasurer, Nat. Cttee for Electoral Reform, 1976–84; Treasurer, Action Aid (formerly Action in Distress), 1976–; Chm., Groundwork Foundn, 1985–. Alderman, GLC, 1967–70; Leader Educn Cttee, ILEA, 1967–69. Nansen Medal, 1960. *Publication:* (with Philip Goodhart) War Without Weapons, 1968. *Address:* 40 Addison Road, W14.

CHATER, Dr Anthony Philip John; Editor, Morning Star, since 1974; *b* 21 Dec. 1929; parents both shoe factory workers; *m* 1954, Janice (*née* Smith); three *s*. *Educ:* Northampton Grammar Sch. for Boys; Queen Mary Coll., London. BSc (1st cl. hons Chem.) 1951, PhD (Phys.Chem.) 1954. Fellow in Biochem., Ottawa Exper. Farm, 1954–56; studied biochem. at Brussels Univ., 1956–57; Teacher, Northampton Techn. High Sch., 1957–59; Teacher, Blyth Grammar Sch., Norwich, 1959–60; Lectr, subseq. Sen. Lectr in Phys. Chem., Luton Coll. of Technology, 1960–69; Head of Press and Publicity of Communist Party, 1969–74; Nat. Chm. of Communist Party, 1967–69. Contested (Com) Luton, Nov. 1963, 1964, 1966, 1970. Mem. Presidential Cttee, World Peace Council, 1969–. *Publications:* Race Relations in Britain, 1966; numerous articles. *Recreations:* walking, swimming, music, camping. *Address:* 8 Katherine Drive, Dunstable, Beds. *T:* Dunstable 64835.

CHATER, Nancy, CBE 1974; Headmistress, Stanley Park Comprehensive School, Liverpool, 1964–75, retired; *b* 18 July 1915; *d* of William John and Ellen Chater. *Educ:* Northampton Sch. for Girls; Girton Coll., Cambridge (Math. Schol., Bell Exhibr, MA); Cambridge Trng Coll. for Women (CertifEd). Asst Mistress, Huddersfield College Grammar Sch. for Boys, 1940–42; Asst Mistress, Fairfield High Sch. for Girls, Manchester, 1942–45; Sen. Maths Mistress, Thistley Hough High Sch., Stoke-on-Trent, 1945–49; Sen. Lectr, Newland Park Trng Coll. for Teachers, 1949–55; Dep. Head, Whitley Abbey Comprehensive Sch., Coventry, 1955–63. *Publications:* contrib. Math. Gazette. *Address:* c/o Stanley Park Comprehensive School, Priory Road, Liverpool L4 2SL. *T:* 051–263 5665. *Clubs:* Soroptomist International, Business and Professional Women's.

CHATFIELD, family name of **Baron Chatfield.**

CHATFIELD, 2nd Baron *cr* 1937, of Ditchling; **Ernle David Lewis Chatfield;** *b* 2 Jan. 1917; *s* of 1st Baron Chatfield, PC, GCB, OM, KCMG, CVO (Admiral of the Fleet Lord Chatfield), and Lillian Emma St John Matthews (*d* 1977); *S* father, 1967; *m* 1969, (Felicia Mary) Elizabeth, *d* of late Dr John Roderick Bulman, Hereford. *Educ:* RNC Dartmouth; Trinity Coll., Cambridge. ADC to Governor-General of Canada, 1940–44. *Heir:* none. *Address:* RR2, Williamstown, Ontario, Canada.

CHATT, Prof. Joseph, CBE 1978; ScD; FRS 1961; Professor of Chemistry, University of Sussex, 1964–80; now Emeritus; Director, Research Unit of Nitrogen Fixation, ARC, 1963–80 (in Sussex, 1964–80); *b* 6 Nov. 1914; *e s* of Joseph and M. Elsie Chatt; *m* 1947, Ethel, *y d* of Hugh Williams, St Helens, Lancs; one *s* one *d*. *Educ:* Nelson Sch., Wigton, Cumberland; Emmanuel Coll., Cambridge (PhD 1940; ScD 1956; Hon. Fellow, 1978). Research Chemist, Woolwich Arsenal, 1941–42; Dep. Chief Chemist, later Chief Chemist, Peter Spence & Sons Ltd, Widnes, 1942–46; ICI Research Fellow, Imperial Coll., London, 1946–47; Head of Inorganic Chemistry Dept, Butterwick, later Akers, Research Laboratories, ICI Ltd, 1947–60; Group Manager, Research Dept, Heavy Organic Chemicals Div., ICI Ltd, 1961–62; Prof. of Inorganic Chem., QMC, Univ. of London, 1964. Visiting Professor: Pennsylvania State Univ., 1960; Yale Univ., 1963; Royal Society Leverhulme, Univ. of Rajasthan, India, 1966–67; Univ. of S Carolina, 1968. Royal Society of Chemistry (formerly Chemical Society): Mem. Council, 1952–65, 1972–76; Hon. Sec., 1956–62; Vice-Pres., 1962–65, 1972–74; Pres. Dalton Div., 1972–74; Organometallic Chem. Award, 1970; Pres., Section B, BAAS, 1974–75; Member: Chemical Council, 1958–60; Commn on Nomenclature of Inorganic Chemistry, Internat. Union of Pure and Applied Chemistry, 1959–81, Hon-Sec., 1959–63, Chm., 1976–81; ARC Adv. Cttee on Plants and Soils, 1964–67; Comité de Direction du Laboratoire de Chimie de Coordination, Toulouse, 1974–77; Council, Royal Soc., 1975–77; national and internat. cttees concerned with chemistry, incl. Parly and Scientific Cttee. Founder, Internat. Confs on Coordination Chemistry, 1950. Lectures: Tilden, 1961–62; Liversidge, 1971–72; Debye, Cornell, 1975; Nyholm, 1976–77; Arthur D. Little, MIT, 1977; Julius Steiglitz, Chicago, 1978; Columbia, 1978 (and Chandler Medal); Univ. of Western Ontario, 1978; John Stauffer, S California, 1979; Dwyer Meml Lectr and Medallist, Univ. of NSW, 1980; Sunner Meml Lectr, Univ. of Lund, 1982. Gordon Wigan Prize for Res. in Chem., Cambridge, 1939; Amer. Chem. Soc. Award for dist. service to Inorganic Chemistry, 1971; Chugaev Commem. Dipl. and Medal, Kurnakov Inst. of Gen. and Inorganic Chemistry, Soviet Acad. of Sciences, 1976; Davy Medal of Royal Soc., 1979; Wolf Foundn Prize for Chemistry, 1981; G.W. Wheland Award (lecture, medal and prize), Univ. of Chicago, 1983. Hon. DSc: East Anglia, 1974; Sussex, 1982; Hon. Dr Pierre et Marie Curie, Paris, 1981; Filosofie Doctor *hc*, Land, 1986. Sócio corresp., Academia das Ciências de Lisboa, 1978; Hon. Life Mem., NY Acad. of Sciences, 1978; For. Fellow, Indian Nat. Science Acad., 1980; Hon. Fellow, Indian Chem. Soc., 1983; Hon. Mem., Royal Physiographical Soc. of Land, 1984; Hon. For. Mem., Amer. Acad. of Arts and Scis, 1985. *Publications:* scientific papers, mainly in Jl Chem. Soc. *Recreations:* numismatics, art, history, gardening. *Address:* 28 Tongdean Avenue, Hove, East Sussex BN3 6TN. *T:* Brighton 554377. *Club:* Civil Service.

CHATTEN, Harold Raymond Percy, CB 1975; RCNC; Chief Executive, Royal Dockyards, 1975–79, and Head of Royal Corps of Naval Constructors, Apr.-Sept. 1979, Ministry of Defence. Production Manager, HM Dockyard, Chatham, 1967–70; General Manager, HM Dockyard, Rosyth, Fife, 1970–75. MA Cambridge 1946. *Address:* c/o National Westminster Bank, 39 Milsom Street, Bath.

CHATTERJEE, Dr Satya Saran, OBE 1971; JP; FRCP, FRCPE; Consultant Chest Physician and Physician in Charge, Department of Respiratory Physiology, Wythenshawe Hospital, Manchester, since 1959; Chairman, Overseas Doctors Association, 1975–81, President, since 1981; *b* 16 July 1922; *m* 1948, Enid May (*née* Adlington); one *s* two *d*. *Educ:* India, UK, Sweden and USA. MB, BS; FCCP (USA). Asst Lectr, Dept of Medicine, Albany Med. Coll. Hosp., NY, 1953–54; Med. Registrar, Sen. Registrar, Dept of Thoracic Medicine, Wythenshawe Hosp., Manchester, 1954–59. Mem., NW RHA, 1976–. Chm., NW Conciliation Cttee, Race Relations Board, 1972–77; Member: Standing Adv. Council on Race Relations, 1977–; GMC, 1979–; Vice-Pres., Manchester Council for Community Relations, 1974–. President: Rotary Club, Wythenshawe, 1975–76; Indian Assoc., Manchester, 1962–71. *Publications:* research papers in various projects related to cardio/pulmonary disorders. *Address:* March, 20 Macclesfield Road, Wilmslow, Cheshire. *T:* Wilmslow 522559.

CHAU, Hon. Sir Sik-Nin, Kt 1960; CBE 1950; JP 1940; Hon. Chairman, Hong Kong Chinese Bank Ltd; Chairman or Director of numerous other companies; President, Firecrackers and Fireworks Co. Ltd (Taiwan); State Trading Corporation (Far East) Ltd; *b* 13 April 1903; *s* of late Cheuk-Fan Chau, Hong Kong; *m* 1927, Ida Hing-Kwai, *d* of late Lau Siu-Cheuk; two *s*. *Educ:* St Stephen's Coll., Hong Kong; Hong Kong Univ.; London Univ.; Vienna State Univ. MB, BS, Hong Kong, 1923; DLO, Eng., 1925; DOMS 1926. LLD (Hon.), Hong Kong 1961. Member Medical Board, Hong Kong, 1935–41; Mem. Urban Council, 1936–41; Chm. Po Leung Kuk, 1940–41; MLC, Hong Kong, 1946–59; MEC, 1947–62. Dep. Chm., Subsid. British Commonwealth Parliamentary Assoc., Hong Kong, 1953–59. Chief Delegate of Hong Kong to ECAFE Conference in India, 1948, in Australia, 1949; Chairman ECAFE Conference in Hong Kong, 1955; Leader, Hong Kong Govt Trade Mission to Common Market countries, 1963; Asian Fair, Bangkok, 1967; first Trade Mission to USA, 1970. Fellow, Internat. Academy of Management; Pres. Indo-Pacific Cttee, 1964–67; Chairman: Hong Kong Trade Develt Council, 1966–70; Hong Kong Management Assoc., 1961–69; Fedn of Hong Kong Inds, 1959–66; Cttee for Expo '70, 1969–70; United Coll., Chinese Univ. of Hong Kong, 1959–61; Hong Kong Productivity Council, 1970–73. President, Japan Soc. of Hong Kong; Mem., Textiles Adv. Bd, 1962–74; Foreign Corresp. Nat. Ind. Conf. Bd Inc.; Member: Advisory Board to Lingnan Inst. of Business Administration; British Universities Selection Cttee, 1945–64; Council and Court of University of Hong Kong, 1945–64; Senior Member Board of Education Hong Kong, 1946–60; Chairman Hong Kong Model Housing Society; Vice-President, Hong Kong Anti-Tuberculosis Assoc.; Hon. Steward Hong Kong Jockey Club, 1974 (Steward 1946–74). Hon. President or Vice-President of numerous Assocs; Hon. Adviser of Chinese General Chamber of Commerce; Permanent Dir Tung Wah Hospital Advisory Board. Coronation Medal, 1937; Defence Medal, 1945; Coronation Medal, 1953; Silver Jubilee Medal, 1977; Freedom of New Orleans, 1966; San Francisco Port Authority Maritime Medal, 1968; 3rd Class Order of Sacred Treasure, Japan, 1969; granted permanent title of Honourable by the Queen, 1962. *Address:* IL 3547 Hatton Road, Hong Kong.

CHAUDHURI, Nirad Chandra, FRSL; FRAS; author and broadcaster; *b* Bengal, 23 Nov. 1897; *s* of Upendra Narayan Chaudhuri and Sushila, of Banagram, Bengal; *m* 1932, Amiya Dhar; three *s*. *Educ:* Calcutta University. BA (Hons) 1918. Resident in UK, 1970–. University Lectures include: Chicago; Texas Univ. at Austin; Pennsylvania; Potsdam; Boston; Oxford; Canadian Univs. DUniv Stirling 1978. Broadcasting on radio and TV; television appearances include: A Brown Man in Search of Civilization (feature on life), 1972; Everyman, 1983; Springing Tiger, 1984. *Publications:* The Autobiography of an unknown Indian, 1951; A Passage to England, 1959; The Continent of Circe, 1965 (Duff Cooper Meml Prize, 1966); The Intellectual in India, 1967; Woman in Bengali Life, 1967 (in Bengali language); To Live or not to Live, 1970; Scholar Extraordinary: life of F. Max Muller, 1974; Clive of India, 1975; Culture in the Vanity Bag, 1976; Hinduism,

1979, Italian trans. 1980, Japanese trans. 1985; contribs to The Times, TLS, The Daily Telegraph, Guardian, London Magazine, Encounter, The New English Review, Spectator, The Atlantic Monthly (USA), Pacific Affairs (USA), major Indian newspapers and magazines. *Recreations:* music, gardening, walks. *Address:* 20 Lathbury Road, Oxford OX2 7AU. *T:* Oxford 57683.

CHAUVIRÉ, Yvette, Officier de la Légion d'Honneur, 1974; Commandeur des Arts et des Lettres, 1975; Commandeur, Ordre National du Mérite, 1981 (Officier, 1972); ballerina assoluta, since 1950; *b* Paris, 22 April 1917. *Educ:* Ecole de la Danse de l'Opéra, Paris. Paris Opera Ballet, 1930; first major rôles in David Triomphant and Les Créatures de Prométhée; Danseuse étoile 1942; danced Istar, 1941; Monte Carlo Opera Ballet, 1946–47; returned to Paris Opera Ballet, 1947–49. Has appeared at Covent Garden, London; also danced in the USA, and in cities of Rome, Moscow, Leningrad, Berlin, Buenos Aires, Johannesburg, Milan, etc; official tours: USA 1948; USSR 1958, 1966, 1968; Canada 1967; Australia. Leading rôles in following ballets: Les Mirages, Lac des Cygnes, Sleeping Beauty, Giselle, Roméo et Juliette, Suite en Blanc, Le Cygne (St Saens), La Dame aux Camélias, etc; acting rôle, Reine Léda, Amphitryon 38, Paris, 1976–77; La Comtessa de Doris in Raymonda, Paris, 1983. Choreographer: La Péri, Roméo et Juliette, Le Cygne; farewell performances: Paris Opera, Giselle, Nov. 1972, Petrouchka and The Swan, Dec. 1972; Berlin Opera, Giselle, 1973. Artistic and Tech. Adviser, Paris Opera, 1963–72, teacher of dance for style and perfection, 1970–; Artistic Director: Acad. Internat. de la Danse, Paris, 1972–76; Acad. ARIMA, Kyoto, Japan, 1981–. *Films:* La Mort du Cygne, 1937 (Paris); Carrousel Napolitain, 1953 (Rome). *Publication:* Je suis Ballerine. *Recreations:* painting and drawing, collections of swans. *Address:* 21 Place du Commerce, Paris 75015, France.

CHAVASSE, Christopher Patrick Grant, MA; Clerk to the Worshipful Company of Grocers, since 1981; *b* 14 March 1928; *s* of late Grant Chavasse and of Maureen Shingler (*née* Whalley); *m* 1955, Audrey Mary Leonard; two *s* one *d*. *Educ:* Bedford Sch.; Clare Coll., Cambridge (Exhibitioner). Commissioned The Rifle Brigade, 1947; served in Palestine (despatches), 1948; RAFVR 1949. Admitted Solicitor, 1955; Partner: Jacobs & Greenwood, 1960; Woodham Smith, 1970; President, Holborn Law Soc., 1977–78. Trustee, NADFAS, 1983–; Chm., NADFAS Tours Ltd, 1986–. Vice-Pres. Chiltern Decorative and Fine Art Soc., 1986–. Hon. Steward of Westminster Abbey, 1950–; Treasurer, St Mary-le-Bow Church, 1981–. Secretary: Governing Body of Oundle and Laxton Schs, 1981–; The Grocers' Charity, 1981–. Mem. Ct, Corp. of Sons of the Clergy, 1985–. *Publications:* Conveyancing Costs, 1971; Non-Contentious Costs, 1975; The Discretionary Items in Contentious Costs, 1980; various articles in Law Society's Gazette, New Law Jl, Solicitors Jl, and others. *Address:* Old Timbers, Badgers Holt, Storrington, W Sussex RH20 3ET. *T:* Storrington 4260; Kingfishers, Aveton Gifford, near Kingsbridge, Devon TQ7 4JL; Grocers' Hall, Princes Street, EC2R 8AQ. *T:* 01–606 3113. *Clubs:* Royal Air Force; Leander.

CHAYTOR, Sir George Reginald, 8th Bt *cr* 1831; *b* 28 Oct. 1912; *s* of William Richard Carter Chaytor (*d* 1973) (*g s* of 2nd Bt) and Anna Laura (*d* 1947), *d* of George Fawcett; *S* cousin, Sir William Henry Clervaux Chaytor, 7th Bt, 1976. *Heir: cousin* (Herbert) Gordon Chaytor [*b* 1922; *m* 1947, Mary Alice, *d* of Thomas Craven; three *s*]. *Address:* 46044 Bonnie Avenue, Chilliwack, BC, Canada.

CHEADLE, Sir Eric (Wallers), Kt 1978; CBE 1973; DL; Deputy Managing Director, International Thomson Organisation Ltd, 1959–74; retired 1974 after 50 years service with the same company (Hultons/Allied Newspapers/Kemsley Newspapers/The Thomson Organisation); Director, Thomson International Press Consultancy Ltd; *b* 14 May 1908; *s* of Edgar and Nellie Cheadle; *m* 1938, Pamela, *d* of Alfred and Charlotte Hulme; two *s*. *Educ:* Farnworth Grammar Sch. Editorial Staff, Evening Chronicle and Daily Dispatch, Manchester, 1924–30; Publicity Manager, Allied Newspapers Ltd, 1931–37; Publicity Manager-in-Chief, Allied Newspapers Group, 1938; Organiser, War Fund for the Services, 1939. Served War, RAFVR, Sqdn Ldr, 1941–46. Dir and Gen. Manager, Kemsley Newspapers Ltd, 1947–53. Mem. Council: Newspaper Publishers Assoc., 1947–74; Newspaper Soc., 1959–78 (Pres., 1970–71; Chm. Editorial Cttee, 1971–78; Mem., Appeal Cttee, 1979–); NEDC for Printing and Publishing Industry; Mem., Jt Bd for Nat. Newspaper Industry, 1965–67; Pres., Assoc. of Lancastrians in London, 1959 and 1973–74; Pres. (former Hon. Sec.), Manchester Publicity Assoc., 1972–74 (Gold Medal, 1973); Pres., Printers' Charitable Corp., 1973–74 (Life Vice-Pres., 1975–, Chm. of Council, 1975–81, Trustee, 1981–); Chm., Jt Cttee, Newspaper and Periodical Publishers and Distributors, 1979–85; Member: Bd, FIEJ/INCA (Fédération Internationale des Editeurs de Journaux et Publications), 1972–76; London Adv. Bd, Nat. and Provincial Building Soc.; UK Newsprint Users' Cttee (Founder Mem.); Caxton Quincentary Commem. Cttee, 1976; Science Mus. Adv. Cttee (Printing); Council, Imp. Soc. of Knights Bachelor, 1979–; Appeal Council, Coll. of Arms Quincentenary Appeal, 1982; Council, Chest, Heart and Stroke Assoc., 1981– (Chm., Appeal Adv. Cttee); Special Cttee, Herts Isotope Cancer Scanner Appeal, 1982–84; Children's Assessment Clinic Appeal, 1984–86; St Albans City Hosp. Rehabilitation Unit Appeal, 1986–; Chm., Nat. Stroke Campaign, 1986–. Chm. of Trustees and Management Group, St Albans Cathedral Trust; Trustee, Herts Groundwork Trust, 1986–; Dir, Herts Bldg Preservation Trust Ltd, 1981–84; Hon. Chm., the PS Tattershall Castle (Victoria Embankment) Trust; Chm., Soc. of St Michaels; Mem., Ver Valley Soc.; Hon. Life Member: Friends of St Albans City Hosp., 1984; Independent Adoption Soc., 1978. DL Hertford, 1985. Editor, Chivalry newspaper. *Publication:* (ed) The Roll of Knights Bachelor, 1981. *Recreations:* watching cricket, talking newspapers. *Address:* The Old Church House, 172 Fishpool Street, St Albans, Herts AL3 4SB. *T:* St Albans 59639. *Clubs:* Wig and Pen, Press, Variety, MCC, Porters Park Golf (Captain, 1974–75).

CHECKETTS, Sqdn Ldr Sir David (John), KCVO 1979 (CVO 1969; MVO 1966); an Extra Equerry to the Prince of Wales, since 1979; *b* 23 Aug. 1930; 3rd *s* of late Reginald Ernest George Checketts and late Frances Mary Checketts; *m* 1958, Rachel Leila Warren Herrick; one *s* three *d*. Flying Training, Bulawayo, Rhodesia, 1948–50; 14 Sqdn, Germany, 1950–54; Instructor, Fighter Weapons Sch., 1954–57; Air ADC to C-in-C Malta, 1958–59; 3 Sqdn, Germany, 1960–61; Equerry to Duke of Edinburgh, 1961–66, to the Prince of Wales, 1967–70; Private Sec. to the Prince of Wales, 1970–79. Chairman: Express Aviation Services Ltd; South East Air Ltd; Man. Dir, ISC Technologies Ltd, 1984–; Director: Penselworth Ltd; ISC Group PLC; Seeatic Marine Ltd. Chairman: Rainbow Boats Trust; Young Enterprise; Wilderness Foundn. *Recreation:* ornithology. *Address:* Church Cottage, Winkfield, Windsor, Berks. *T:* Winkfield Row 2289. *Club:* Whitefriars.

CHECKETTS, Guy Tresham, CBE 1982; Deputy Chairman and Managing Director, Hawker Siddeley International, since 1975; *b* 11 May 1927; *s* of John Albert and Norah Maude Checketts; *m* 1957, Valerie Cynthia Stanley; four *s*. *Educ:* Warwick Sch.; Birmingham Univ. BScEng Hons; CEng, MIEE. British Thompson Houston Co., Rugby, 1948–51; Brush Group, 1951–57; Hawker Siddeley International, 1957–; Exec. Dir, 1960. Chm., SE Asia Trade Adv. Gp, 1979–83; Mem., BOTB, 1981–84. *Recreation:* sailing. *Address:* (office) 32 Duke Street, St James's, SW1Y 6DG. *T:* 01–930 6177. *Clubs:* Royal Over-Seas League; Karachi Yacht (Karachi).

CHECKLAND, Michael; Deputy Director-General, BBC, since 1985; Chairman, BBC Enterprises, since 1986; *b* 13 March 1936; *s* of Leslie and Ivy Florence Checkland; *m* 1960–83; two *s* one *d*. *Educ:* King Edward's Grammar Sch., Fiveways, Birmingham; Wadham Coll., Oxford (BA Modern History). ACMA. Accountant: Parkinson Cowan Ltd, 1959–62; Thorn Electronics Ltd, 1962–64; BBC: Senior Cost Accountant, 1964; Head of Central Finance Unit, 1967; Chief Accountant, Central Finance Services, 1969, Chief Accountant, Television, 1971; Controller, Finance, 1976; Controller, Planning and Resource Management, Television, 1977; Director of Resources, Television, 1982. *Recreations:* sport, music, travel. *Address:* Orchard Cottage, Park Lane, Maplehurst, near Horsham, West Sussex RH13 6LL.

CHEDLOW, Barry William, QC 1969; a Recorder of the Crown Court, since 1974; Member, Criminal Injuries Compensation Board, since 1976; *b* Macclesfield, 8 Oct. 1921; *m* Anne Sheldon, BA; one *s* one *d*. *Educ:* Burnage High Sch.; Manchester Univ. Served RAF, 1941–46: USAAF, Flying Instructor, 1942; Flt-Lt 1943. Called to Bar, Middle Temple, 1947, Bencher, 1976; Prizeman in Law of Evidence. Practises in London, Midland and Oxford Circuit. *Publications:* author and editor of various legal text-books. *Recreations:* flying (private pilot's licence), languages, sailing. *Address:* 12 King's Bench Walk, Temple, EC4. *T:* 01–583 0811; Little Kimblewick Farm, Finch Lane, Amersham, Bucks. *T:* Little Chalfont 2156.

CHEESEMAN, Eric Arthur, BSc (Econ), PhD (Med) (London); Professor of Medical Statistics, The Queen's University of Belfast, 1961–77, now Emeritus; *b* 22 Sept. 1912; 1st *s* of late Arthur Cheeseman and Frances Cheeseman, London; *m* 1943, Henriette Edwina Woollaston; one *s*. *Educ:* William Ellis Sch.; London Univ. Mem. staff of Statistical Cttee of MRC, 1929–39. Served War of 1939–45, RA (TA); GSO3 21 Army Group, 1945. Research Statistician on staff of Statistical Research Unit of MRC and part-time lectr in Med. Statistics, London Sch. of Hygiene and Tropical Medicine, 1946–48; Lectr, later Reader, and Vice-Pres. (Finance), The Queen's Univ. of Belfast, 1948–77; Prof., 1961; Dep. Dean, Faculty of Medicine, 1971–75. Statistical Adviser to Northern Ireland Hospitals Authority, 1948–73; Mem. of Joint Authority for Higher Technicological Studies, 1965–70. Consulting Statistician to Northern Ireland Tuberculosis Authority, 1950–59; Mem., Statistical Cttee of Medical Research Council, 1950–61. Fellow Royal Statistical Soc.; Mem., Soc. for Social Medicine (Chm. 1976, Hon. Mem., 1979); Hon. Associate Mem., Ulster Med. Soc. Silver Jubilee Medal, 1977. *Publications:* Epidemics in Schools, 1950; (with G. F. Adams) Old People in Northern Ireland, 1951; various papers dealing with medical statistical subjects in scientific journals. *Recreation:* cricket. *Address:* 43 Beverley Gardens, Bangor, Co. Down, N Ireland. *T:* Bangor 472822.

CHEESEMAN, Prof. Ian Clifford, PhD; ARCS; CEng, FRAeS, FCIT; Professor of Helicopter Engineering, University of Southampton, 1970–82, now Emeritus; Director of Research, Stewart Hughes Ltd, Southampton, since 1983; *b* 12 June 1926; *s* of Richard Charles Cheeseman and Emily Ethel Clifford; *m* 1957, Margaret Edith Pither; one *s* two *d*. *Educ:* Andover Grammar Sch.; Imperial Coll. of Science and Technology. Vickers Supermarine Ltd, 1951–53; Aeroplane and Armament Estab., 1953–56; Atomic Weapons Res. Estab., 1956–58; Nat. Gas Turbine Estab., 1958–70. *Publications:* contribs to Jl RAeS, Jl CIT, Jl Sound and Vibration, Procs Phys. Soc. 'A'. *Recreations:* dog breeding, gardening, sailing, camping. *Address:* Hill Cottage, Mansbridge Road, West End, Southampton. *T:* Southampton 473387.

CHEETHAM, Prof. Anthony Kevin, FRSC; Professor of Solid State Chemistry, Royal Institution, since 1986; Lecturer in Chemical Crystallography, Oxford, since 1974; Tutor in Inorganic Chemistry, Christ Church, Oxford, since 1974; *b* 16 Nov. 1946; *s* of Norman James Cheetham and Lilian Cheetham; *m* 1984, Janet Clare (*née* Stockwell); one *s* two *d*. *Educ:* Stockport Grammar Sch.; St Catherine's Coll., Oxford (Hon. Scholar); Wadham Coll., Oxford (Sen. Scholar). BA (Chem.) 1968; DPhil 1971. Cephalosporin Fellow, Lincoln Coll., Oxford, 1971–74; Lectr in Inorganic Chem., St Hilda's Coll., Oxford, 1971–85. Visiting Professor: Arizona State Univ., 1977; Univ. of California, Berkeley, 1979; Vis. Foreign Scientist, Amer. Chem. Soc., 1981. Mem., Internat. Science Adv. Cttee of Spallation Neutron Source, 1986–. Corday-Morgan Medal and Prize, RSC, 1982. *Publications:* Inorganic Solids: techniques (with P. Day), 1986; contribs to sci. jls. *Recreations:* cricket, stock market. *Address:* Compas, 62 Iffley Road, Oxford OX4 1EQ. *T:* Oxford 240016.

CHEETHAM, Francis William, OBE 1979; FMA; Director, Norfolk Museums Service, since 1974; *b* 5 Feb. 1928; *s* of Francis Cheetham and Doris Elizabeth Jones; *m* 1954, Monica Fairhurst; three *s* one *d*. *Educ:* King Edward VII Sch., Sheffield; Univ. of Sheffield (BA). Dep. Art Dir and Curator, Castle Museum, Nottingham, 1960–63; Dir, City of Norwich Museums, 1963–74. Winston Churchill Fellow, 1967. Member: Management Cttee, Norfolk and Norwich Triennial Fest., 1966–; Crafts Council, 1978–81; Exec. Cttee, Eastern Arts Assoc., 1978–79; Bd, Norwich Puppet Theatre, 1981–; Founder Mem., National Heritage, 1970; Chairman: Norfolk and Norwich Film Theatre, 1968–70; Norfolk Contemporary Crafts Soc., 1972–85 (Life Pres., 1985). Museums Association: AMA 1959; FMA 1966; Hon. Treasurer, 1970–73; Vice-Pres., 1977–78, 1979–80; Pres., 1978–79; Chm., Soc. of County Museum Dirs, 1974–77; Museum Advr to ACC, 1976–84. Member: Exec. Bd, ICOM (UK), 1981–84; Bd, Radio Broadland (ILR Station), 1983–. *Publications:* Medieval English Alabaster Carvings in the Castle Museum, Nottingham, 1962, revd edn 1973; English Medieval Alabasters, 1984; contrib. Jl of Museums Assoc. *Recreations:* hill-walking, music. *Address:* 25 St Andrew's Avenue, Thorpe St Andrew, Norwich NR7 0RG. *T:* Norwich 34091. *Club:* Rotary (Norwich).

CHEETHAM, John Frederick Thomas, CB 1978; Secretary, Exchequer and Audit Department, 1975–79; *b* 27 March 1919; *s* of late James Oldham Cheetham, MA, BCom; *m* 1943, Yvonne Marie Smith; one *s* one *d*. *Educ:* Penarth Grammar Sch.; Univ. of Wales. Entered Exchequer and Audit Dept, 1938; War Service, Royal Artillery, 1939–46; Office of Parly Comr for Administration, 1966–69; Dep. Sec., Exchequer and Audit Dept, 1973–74. *Recreations:* tennis, food and wine. *Address:* 70 Chatsworth Road, Croydon, Surrey CR0 1HB. *T:* 01–688 3740. *Club:* MCC.

CHEETHAM, Juliet; Professor and Director, Social Work Research Centre, Stirling University, since 1986; *b* 12 Oct. 1939; *d* of Harold Neville Blair and Isabel (*née* Sanders); *m* 1965, Christopher Paul Cheetham; one *s* two *d*. *Educ:* St Andrews Univ. (MA); Oxford Univ. (Dip. in Social and Admin. Studies). Qual. social worker. Probation Officer, Inner London, 1960–65; Lectr in Applied Social Studies, and Fellow of Green Coll., Oxford Univ., 1965–85. Member: Cttee of Enquiry into Immigration and Youth Service, 1966–68; Cttee of Enquiry into Working of Abortion Act, 1971–74; NI Standing Adv. Commn on Human Rights, 1974–77; Central Council for Educn and Trng in Social Work, 1973–; Commn for Racial Equality, 1977–84; Social Security Adv. Cttee, 1983–. *Publications:* Social Work with Immigrants, 1972; Unwanted Pregnancy and Counselling, 1977; Social Work and Ethnicity, 1982; Social Work with Black Children and their Families, 1986; contrib. collected papers and prof. jls. *Recreation:* canal boats. *Address:* 101

Woodstock Road, Oxford OX2 6HL. *T:* Oxford 55105; Centre for Social Work Research, Department of Sociology, University of Stirling, Stirling FK9 4LA. *T:* Stirling 73171.

CHEETHAM, Sir Nicolas (John Alexander), KCMG 1964 (CMG 1953); *b* 8 Oct. 1910; *s* of late Sir Milne Cheetham, KCMG, and late Mrs Nigel Law, CBE, DStJ; *m* 1st, 1937, Jean Evison Corfe (marr. diss. 1960); two *s*; 2nd, 1960, Lady Mabel Brooke (*née* Jocelyn). *Educ:* Eton College; Christ Church, Oxford. Entered HM Diplomatic Service, 1934; served in Foreign Office and at Athens, Buenos Aires, Mexico City and Vienna; UK Deputy Permanent Representative on North Atlantic Council, 1954–59; HM Minister to Hungary, 1959–61; Assistant Under-Secretary, Foreign Office, 1961–64; Ambassador to Mexico, 1964–68. *Publications:* A History of Mexico, 1970; New Spain, 1974; Mediaeval Greece, 1981; Keepers of the Keys: the Pope in history, 1982. *Address:* 50 Cadogan Square, SW1. *Club:* Travellers'.

CHEEVERS, William Harold; Director, Penwell Ltd, since 1971; *b* 20 June 1918; *m* 1964, Shirley Cheevers; one *s*. *Educ:* Christ's Coll., London. Engineer, BBC Television, 1938–39. War Service, Army, PoW, 1941–45. Sen. Engr, BBC Television, 1946–54; Planning Engr, Radio-Corp. of America, in USA and Canada, 1954–55; Head of Engineering, Associated Rediffusion, 1955–60; Gen. Manager, Westward Television, Jt Man. Dir, 1963–67, Man. Dir, 1967–70; Dir, ITN News, 1967–70, and of IT Publications; Dir of Engrg, Granada Television, 1970–72; also Director: Keith Prowse, 1963–70; Prowest, 1967–70; Direct Line Services, 1964–. Chm., British Regional Television Assoc., 1968–69. Fellow British Kinematograph Soc.; MInstD; MBIM; AssIEE. *Publications:* articles for most TV Jls, and Symposiums, at home and abroad. *Recreations:* boating, golf, reading. *Address:* 52 Preston Down Road, Paignton, Devon. *T:* Paignton 524455. *Club:* Royal Western Yacht Club of England (Plymouth).

CHEKE, Dudley John, CMG 1961; MA Cantab; HM Diplomatic Service, retired; *b* 14 June 1912; *s* of late Thomas William Cheke, FRIC; *m* 1944, Yvonne de Méric, *d* of late Rear-Adm. M. J. C. de Méric, MVO; two *s*. *Educ:* St Christopher's, Letchworth; Emmanuel Coll., Cambridge. Entered HM Consular Service, 1934; served in Japan, Manchuria, Korea, 1935–41; served 1942–44, in East Africa and Ceylon; Foreign Office, 1945–49 and 1958–61; UK delegation to OEEC, Paris, 1949–50; Commissioner-Gen.'s Office, Singapore, 1950–51; idc 1952; HM Consul-Gen., Frankfurt-am-Main, 1953–55, Osaka-Kobe, 1956–58; Mem. of Foreign Service Corps of Inspectors, 1961–63; Minister, Tokyo, 1963–67; Ambassador to the Ivory Coast, Niger and Upper Volta, 1967–70. Chm., Japan Soc., 1979–82. *Recreations:* theatre, birdwatching, gardening. *Address:* Honey Farm, Bramley, Basingstoke, Hants RG26 5DE. *Clubs:* United Oxford & Cambridge University; Union Society (Cambridge).

CHELMER, Baron *cr* 1963 (Life Peer), of Margaretting; **Eric Cyril Boyd Edwards,** Kt 1954; MC 1944; TD; JP; DL; *b* 9 Oct. 1914; *s* of Col C. E. Edwards, DSO, MC, TD, DL, JP, and Mrs J. Edwards; *m* 1939, Enid, *d* of F. W. Harvey; one *s*. *Educ:* Felsted Sch. Solicitor, 1937; LLB (London) 1937. Served Essex Yeomanry, 1940–54 (MC), Lieut-Col Commanding, 1945–46. Chairman and Director: Provident Financial Gp, 1970–83; Greycoat Group, 1977–85; Director: NEM Group, 1970–86; NEL Assurance, 1970–86. Chm., Nat. Union of Conservative Associations, 1956, Pres., 1967; Chm., Nat. Exec. Cttee of Conservative and Unionist Assoc., 1957–65; Jt Treasurer of Conservative Party, 1965–77; Chm., Conservative Party Review Cttee, 1970–73; Mem. Adv. Cttee on Policy, 1956–85. Member: Political Cttee, Carlton Club, 1961; Cttee of Musicians' Benevolent Fund; Ralph Vaughan Williams Trust. JP Essex, 1950; DL Essex 1971. *Recreation:* "improving". *Address:* Peacocks, Margaretting, Essex. *Clubs:* Carlton, Buck's, Royal Ocean Racing.

See also D. Edwards, J. T. Edwards.

CHELMSFORD, 3rd Viscount *cr* 1921, of Chelmsford; **Frederic Jan Thesiger;** Baron Chelmsford, 1858; Lloyd's Insurance Broker; Director, Willis Faber plc; *b* 7 March 1931; *s* of 2nd Viscount Chelmsford and of Gilian (*d* 1978), *d* of late Arthur Nevile Lubbock; *S* father, 1970; *m* 1958, Clare Rendle, *d* of Dr G. R. Rolston, Haslemere; one *s* one *d*. Formerly Lieut, Inns of Court Regt. *Heir:* *s* Hon. Frederic Corin Piers Thesiger, *b* 6 March 1962. *Address:* 26 Ormonde Gate, SW3; Hazelbridge Court, Chiddingfold, Surrey.

CHELMSFORD, Bishop of, since 1986; **Rt. Rev. John Waine;** *b* 20 June 1930; *s* of William and Ellen Waine; *m* 1957, Patricia Zena Haikney; three *s*. *Educ:* Prescot Grammar Sch.; Manchester Univ. (BA); Ridley Hall, Cambridge. Deacon 1955, Priest 1956; Curate of St Mary, West Derby, 1955–58; Curate in Charge of All Saints, Sutton, 1958–60; Vicar of Ditton, 1960–64; Vicar of Holy Trinity, Southport, 1964–69; Rector of Kirkby, 1969–75; Bishop Suffragan of Stafford, 1975–78; Bishop of St Edmundsbury and Ipswich, 1978–86. ChStJ 1983. *Recreations:* caravanning, music, gardening. *Address:* Bishopscourt, Margaretting, Ingatestone, Essex CM4 0HD. *Club:* Royal Air Force.

CHELMSFORD, Provost of; *see* Moses, Very Rev. J. H.

CHELSEA, Viscount; Charles Gerald John Cadogan; *b* 24 March 1937; *o s* of 7th Earl Cadogan, *qv*; *m* 1963, Lady Philippa Wallop (*d* 1984), *d* of 9th Earl of Portsmouth; two *s* one *d*. *Educ:* Eton. Chm., Leukaemia Research Fund, 1985–. Freeman, City of London, 1979; Liveryman, GAPAN. *Heir:* *s* Hon. Edward Charles Cadogan, *b* 10 May 1966. *Address:* 7 Smith Street, SW3. *T:* 01–730 2465; Marndhill, Ardington, near Wantage, Oxon. *T:* Abingdon 833273. *Clubs:* White's, Royal Automobile.

CHELTENHAM, Archdeacon of; *see* Evans, Ven. T. E.

CHELWOOD, Baron *cr* 1974 (Life Peer), of Lewes; **Tufton Victor Hamilton Beamish,** Kt 1961; MC 1940; DL; *b* 27 Jan. 1917; *o surv. s* of late Rear-Admiral T. P. H. Beamish, CB, DL; *m* 1950, Janet Stevenson (marr. diss. 1973); two *d*; *m* 1975, Mrs Pia McHenry (*née* von Roretz). *Educ:* Stowe Sch.; RMC, Sandhurst. 2nd Lieut Royal Northumberland Fusiliers, 1937; Active Service, Palestine, 1938–39; War of 1939–45 (wounded twice, despatches, MC); served in France, Belgium, 1940; Malaya, 1942; India and Burma front, 1942–43; North Africa and Italy, 1943–44; Staff Coll., Camberley, 1945 (psc). Hon. Col 411 (Sussex) Coast Regt RA (TA), 1951–57. Mem. Church of England Council on Inter-Church Relations, 1950–60. MP (C) Lewes Div. of E Sussex, 1945–Feb. 1974. Delegate to Council of Europe and Chm. Assembly Cttee, 1951–54; Vice-Chairman: British Group Inter-Parly Union, 1952–54; Conservative and Unionist Members Cttee, 1958–74; Chm. Cons. For. Affairs Cttee, 1960–64; an Opposition defence spokesman, 1965–67; Chm., Cons. Gp for Europe, 1970–73; Jt Dep. Leader, British Delegn to European Parlt, 1973–74. Pres., Lewes Cons. Assoc., 1977–85; Vice-Pres., ACC. Member: Monnet Action Cttee for United States of Europe, 1971–76; Council, RSPB, 1948–61 (Pres., 1967–70; Vice-Pres., 1976–, Gold Medal, 1984); Vice Pres., Soc. for Promotion of Nature Conservation, 1976–84; Nature Conservancy Council, 1978–84. President: Sussex Trust for Nature Conservation, 1968–78; Soc. of Sussex Downsmen, 1975–81. Governor, Stowe Sch., 1966–79; Pres., Old Stoic Soc., 1983. DL East Sussex, 1970–. Hon. Freeman, Borough of Lewes, 1970. Golden Cross of Merit, 1944; Polonia Restituta, Poland; Comdr, Order of the Phoenix, Greece, 1949; Order of the Cedar, Lebanon, 1969. Mem. of the Soc. of Authors. *Publications:* Must Night Fall?, an account of Soviet seizure of power in Eastern Europe, 1950; Battle Royal, a new account for the 700th Anniversary of Simon de Montfort's struggle against Henry III, 1965; Half Marx: a warning that democracy in Britain is threatened by a Marx-influenced Labour Party, 1971; (with Guy Hadley) The Kremlin's Dilemma: the struggle for human rights in Eastern Europe, 1979; contribs to newspapers and periodicals. *Recreations:* gardening, bird-watching, music. *Address:* Plovers' Meadow, Blackboys, Uckfield, Sussex TN22 5NA. *Club:* Buck's.

CHEN Zhaoyuan; Ambassador Extraordinary and Plenipotentiary of the People's Republic of China to the Court of St James's, 1983–85; *b* 14 Nov. 1918; *m* 1946, Ma Lansen; two *s* one *d*. *Educ:* university. Counsellor, Sweden, 1952–58; Dep. Head, Internat. Orgns and Confs Dept, Foreign Ministry, 1958–61; Counsellor, India, 1961–70; Ambassador to: Burma, 1971–73; Spain, 1973–76; India, 1976–79; Head, Second Dept of Asian Affairs, 1980–82. *Recreations:* reading, football, tennis. *Address:* c/o Foreign Ministry, Peking, China.

CHENEY, Christopher Robert, CBE 1984; FBA 1951; Professor of Medieval History, University of Cambridge, 1955–72; Fellow, Corpus Christi College, Cambridge, 1955; *b* 1906; 4th *s* of George Gardner and Christiana Stapleton Cheney; *m* 1940, Mary Gwendolen Hall; two *s* one *d*. *Educ:* Banbury County Sch.; Wadham Coll., Oxford (Hon. Fellow, 1968). 1st class Modern History Sch., 1928; Asst Lectr in History, University Coll., London, 1931–33; Bishop Fraser Lectr in Ecclesiastical History, University of Manchester, 1933–37; Fellow of Magdalen Coll., Oxford, 1938–45; Univ. Reader in Diplomatic, 1937–45; Joint Literary Dir of Royal Historical Society, 1938–45; Prof. of Medieval History, Univ. of Manchester, 1945–55. Hon. Fellow, Wadham Coll., Oxford. Corresp. Fellow, Mediaeval Acad. of America; Corresp. Mem., Monumenta Germaniae Historica. Hon. DLitt: Glasgow, 1970; Manchester, 1978. *Publications:* Episcopal Visitation of Monasteries in the 13th Century, 1931, revd edn 1983; English Synodalia of the 13th Century, 1941; Handbook of Dates, 1945; English Bishops' Chanceries, 1950; (with W. H. Semple) Selected Letters of Pope Innocent III, 1953; From Becket to Langton, 1956; (with F. M. Powicke) Councils and Synods of the English Church, Vol. II, 1964; Hubert Walter, 1967; (with M. G. Cheney) Letters of Pope Innocent III concerning England and Wales, 1967; Notaries Public in England in the XIII and XIV Centuries, 1972; Medieval Texts and Studies, 1973; Pope Innocent III and England, 1976; (with M. G. Cheney) Studies in the Collections of XII Century Decretals, ed from papers of W. Holtzmann, 1979; The Papacy and England, 12th-14th Centuries (Variorum Reprints), 1982; The English Church and its Laws, 12th-14th Centuries (Variorum Reprints), 1982; (with B. E. A. Jones and Eric John) English Episcopal Acta II and III: Canterbury 1162–1205, 2 vols, 1986; articles and reviews in Eng. Hist. Rev., etc. *Address:* 17 Westberry Court, Grange Road, Cambridge CB3 9BG. *T:* Cambridge 351892.

CHERENKOV, Prof. Pavel Alexeevich; Soviet physicist; Member of the Institute of Physics, Academy of Sciences of the USSR; *b* 27 July 1904. *Educ:* Voronezh State Univ., Voronezh, USSR. Discovered the Cherenkov Effect, 1934. Corresp. Mem., 1964–70, Academician, 1970–, USSR Acad. of Scis. Awarded Stalin Prize, 1946; Nobel Prize for Physics (joint), 1958. *Address:* Institute of Physics, Academy of Sciences of the USSR, B Kaluzhskaya 14, Moscow, USSR.

CHERKASSKY, Shura; pianist; *b* 7 Oct. 1911; *s* of late Isaac and Lydia Cherkassky; *m* 1946, Genia Ganz (marr. diss. 1948). *Educ:* Curtis Institute of Music, Pa, USA (diploma). Plays with the principal orchestras and conductors of the world and in all the major series and festivals in Asia, America, Australia and Europe. Has made numerous recordings. *Address:* c/o Ibbs & Tillett Ltd, 450–452 Edgware Road, W2 1EG.

CHERMAYEFF, Serge, FRIBA, FRSA; architect; author; abstract painter; *b* 8 Oct. 1900; *s* of Ivan Chermayeff and Rosalie Issakovitch; *m* 1928, Barbara Maitland May; two *s*. *Educ:* Harrow Sch. Journalist, 1918–22; studied architecture, 1922–25; principal work in England, studios for BBC; Modern Exhibitions; Gilbey's Offices; ICI Laboratories; in Partnership: Bexhill Pavilion. Professor, Brooklyn Coll., 1942–46; Pres. and Dir, Inst. of Design, Chicago, 1946–51; Prof., Harvard Univ., 1953–62; Prof., Yale Univ., 1962–71, now Emeritus. Hon. Fellow, Assoc. of Columbian Architects. Hon. Dr of Fine Art, Washington Univ., 1964; Hon. Dr of Humanities, Ohio State Univ., 1980. Gold Medal, Royal Architectural Inst., Canada, 1974; AIA and Assoc. of Collegiate Schs 1980 Award for excellence in educn; Misha Black Meml Medal for significant contribn to design educn, SIAD, 1980; Gold Medal, NY State Univ. at Buffalo, 1982. *Publications:* Art and Architectural Criticism; ARP, 1939; Community and Privacy, 1963; Shape of Community, 1970; Design and the Public Good (Collected Works), 1982. *Address:* Box NN, Wellfleet, Mass 02667, USA.

CHERMONT, Jayme Sloan, KCVO (Hon.) 1968; Brazilian Ambassador to the Court of St James's, 1966–68, retired; *b* 5 April 1903; *s* of Ambassador E. L. Chermont and Mrs Helen Mary Chermont; *m* 1928, Zaíde Alvim de Mello Franco Chermont (decd); no *c*. *Educ:* Law Sch., Rio de Janeiro Univ. Entered Brazilian Foreign Office, 1928; served in Washington, 1930–32; Rio de Janeiro, 1932–37; London, 1937; transf. to Brazil, 1938; 1st Sec., 1941; Buenos Aires, 1943–45; transf. to Brazil, 1945; Counsellor, Brussels, 1948–50; Minister Counsellor, London (periodically Chargé d'Affaires), 1950–53; various appts, Brazilian FO, 1953–57; Consul-Gen., New York, 1957–60; Ambassador to Haiti, 1960–61; Head of Political and Cultural Depts, Brazil, 1961; Sec.-Gen., FO, 1962–63; Ambassador to Netherlands, 1963–66. Headed Brazilian Delegn to UN Gen. Assembly, 1962. Holds Orders from many foreign countries. *Recreations:* golf, chess, bridge, stamps, coins, books. *Address:* Rua Siqueira Campos no 7–7, Copacabana, Rio de Janeiro, Brasil. *Clubs:* Jockey, Country, Itanhangá Golf (Rio).

CHERRY, Colin; Director of Operations, Inland Revenue, since 1985; *b* 20 Nov. 1931; *s* of late Reginald Cherry and Dorothy (*née* Brooks); *m* 1958, Marjorie Rose Harman; two *d*. *Educ:* Hymers Coll., Hull. Joined Inland Revenue through open executive competition, 1950; HM Inspector of Taxes, 1960; Under Sec., 1985. *Recreations:* music, chrysanthemums, photography. *Address:* Inland Revenue, Operations Division M4, Bush House, Strand, WC2R 4RD. *T:* 01–438 6067.

CHERRY, Prof. Gordon Emanuel; Professor of Urban and Regional Planning, University of Birmingham, since 1976; *b* 6 Feb. 1931; *s* of Emanuel and Nora Cherry; *m* 1957, Margaret Mary Loudon Cox; one *s* two *d*. *Educ:* Holgate and District Grammar Sch., Barnsley; QMC, Univ. of London (BA(Hons) Geog. 1953). Variously employed in local authority planning depts, 1956–68; Research Officer, Newcastle upon Tyne City Planning Dept, 1963–68; University of Birmingham: Sen. Lectr and Dep. Dir, Centre for Urban and Regional Studies, 1968–76; Dean, Fac. of Commerce and Social Science, 1981–86. Member: Local Govt Boundary Commn for England, 1979–; Adv. Cttee on Landscape Treatment of Trunk Roads, 1984–; Trustee, Bournville Village Trust, 1979–. FRICS; Pres., RTPI, 1978–79. Hon. DSc Heriot-Watt, 1984. *Publications:* Town Planning in its Social Context, 1970, 2nd edn 1973; (with T. L. Burton) Social Research Techniques for Planners, 1970; Urban Change and Planning, 1972; The Evolution of British Town Planning, 1974; Environmental Planning, Vol. II: National Parks and Recreation in the Countryside, 1975; The Politics of Town Planning, 1982; (with J. L. Penny) Holford: a study in planning, architecture and civic design, 1986; Editor: Urban Planning Problems,

1974; Rural Planning Problems, 1976; Shaping an Urban World, 1980; Pioneers in British Planning, 1981; (with A. R. Sutcliffe) Planning Perspectives, vol. 1, 1986. *Recreations:* work, professional activities, ecumenical church involvement, sport, reading, music, enjoyment of family life. *Address:* Quaker Ridge, 66 Meriden Road, Hampton in Arden, West Midlands B92 0BT. *T:* Hampton in Arden 3200.

CHERRYMAN, John Richard, QC 1982; *b* 7 Dec. 1932; *s* of Albert James and Mabel Cherryman; *m* 1963, Anna Greenleaf Collis; three *s* one *d*. *Educ:* Farnham Grammar Sch.; London School of Economics (LLB Hons); Harvard Law Sch. Called to Bar, Gray's Inn, 1955. *Recreation:* splitting hairs. *Address:* 4 Stone Buildings, Lincoln's Inn, WC2.

CHESHAM, 5th Baron *cr* 1858; **John Charles Compton Cavendish,** PC 1964; *b* 18 June 1916; *s* of 4th Baron and Margot, *d* of late J. Layton Mills, Tansor Court, Oundle; *S* father, 1952; *m* 1937, Mary Edmunds, 4th *d* of late David G. Marshall, White Hill, Cambridge; two *s* two *d*. *Educ:* Eton; Zuoz Coll., Switzerland; Trinity Coll., Cambridge. Served War of 1939–45, Lieut Royal Bucks Yeomanry, 1939–42; Capt. RA (Air OP), 1942–45. JP Bucks 1946, retd. Delegate, Council of Europe, 1953–56. A Lord-in-Waiting to the Queen, 1955–59; Parly Sec., Min. of Transport, 1959–64. Chancellor, Primrose League, 1957–59. Executive Vice-Chm. Royal Automobile Club, 1966–70; Chairman: British Road Federation, 1966–72 (Vice-Pres., 1972); Internat. Road Fedn, Geneva, 1973–76; Pres., British Parking Assoc., 1972–75; Fellowship of Motor Industry, 1969–71; Hon. Sec., House of Lords Club, 1966–72; Hon. FInstHE, 1970; Hon FIRTE, 1974 (Pres., 1971–73). *Heir: s* Hon. Nicholas Charles Cavendish [*b* 7 Nov. 1941; *m* 1st, 1965, Susan Donne (marr. diss. 1969), *e d* of Dr Guy Beauchamp; 2nd, 1973, Suzanne, *er d* of late Alan Gray Byrne, Sydney, Australia; two *s*]. *Address:* Manor Farm, Preston Candover, near Basingstoke, Hants. *T:* Preston Candover 230. *Club:* Carlton.

CHESHIRE, Group Captain (Geoffrey) Leonard, VC 1944; OM 1981; DSO 1940 and two Bars 1941, 1943; DFC 1941; RAF retired; *b* 7 Sept. 1917; *s* of late Geoffrey Chevalier Cheshire, FBA, DCL, and late Primrose Barstow; *m* 2nd, 1959, Susan Ryder (*see* Baroness Ryder of Warsaw); one *s* one *d*. *Educ:* Stowe Sch.; Merton Coll., Oxford. 2nd Class Hon. Sch. of Jurisprudence, 1939; OU Air Sqdn, 1936; RAFVR, 1937; Perm. Commn RAF, 1939; trained Hullavington; served Bomber Comd, 1940–45: 102 Sqdn, 1940; 35 Sqdn, 1941; CO 76 Sqdn, 1942; RAF Station, Marston Moor, 1943; CO 617 Sqdn (Dambusters), 1943; attached Eastern Air Command, South-East Asia, 1944; British Joint Staff Mission, Washington, 1945; official British observer at dropping of Atomic Bomb on Nagasaki, 1945; retd Dec. 1945. Founder of Cheshire Foundation Homes (220 Homes for the disabled in 45 countries); Co-founder of Ryder Cheshire Mission for the Relief of Suffering. Member: Pathfinders Assoc.; Air Crew Assoc. Hon. LLD: Liverpool, 1973; Manchester Polytechnic, 1979; Nottingham, 1981; Hon. DCL Oxon, 1984. Variety Club Humanitarian Award (jtly with wife), 1975. *Publications:* Bomber Pilot, 1943; Pilgrimage to the Shroud, 1956; The Face of Victory, 1961; The Hidden World, 1981; The Light of Many Suns, 1985. *Relevant publications:* Cheshire, VC, by Russell Braddon, 1954; No Passing Glory, by Andrew Boyle, 1955; New Lives for Old, by W. W. Russell, 1963. *Recreation:* tennis. *Address:* 26 Maunsel Street, SW1. *T:* 01–828 1822. *Clubs:* Royal Air Force, Queen's (Hon. Life Mem.), All England Lawn Tennis.

CHESSHYRE, David Hubert Boothby, FSA; Chester Herald of Arms, since 1978; *b* 22 June 1940; *e s* of late Col Hubert Layard Chesshyre and of Katharine Anne (*née* Boothby), Canterbury, Kent. *Educ:* King's Sch., Canterbury; Trinity Coll., Cambridge (MA); Christ Church, Oxford (DipEd 1967). FSA 1977. Taught French in England and English in France, at intervals 1962–67; wine merchant (Moët et Chandon and Harvey's of Bristol), 1962–65; Hon. Artillery Co., 1964–65 (fired salute at funeral of Sir Winston Churchill, 1965); Green Staff Officer at Investiture of the Prince of Wales, 1969; Rouge Croix Pursuivant, 1970–78, and on staff of Sir Anthony Wagner, Garter King of Arms, 1971–78. Member: Council, Heraldry Soc., 1973–85; Bach Choir, 1979–; Madrigal Soc., 1980–. Lay Clerk, Southwark Cathedral, 1971–; Freeman, City of London, 1975. *Publications:* (Eng. lang. editor) C. A. von Volborth, Heraldry of the World, 1973; The Identification of Coats of Arms on British Silver, 1978; (with A. J. Robinson) The Green: a history of the heart of Bethnal Green, 1978; (ed jtly) Dictionary of British Arms, Vol. 1, 1986; (with Adrian Ailes) Heralds of Today, 1986; genealogical and heraldic articles in British Heritage and elsewhere. *Recreations:* singing, lecturing, gardening, mountain walking, motorcycling, squash. *Address:* Hawthorn Cottage, 1 Flamborough Walk, E14 7LS. *T:* 01-790 7923; College of Arms, Queen Victoria Street, EC4V 4BT. *T:* 01–248 1137.

CHESTER, Bishop of, since 1982; **Rt. Rev. Michael Alfred Baughen;** *b* 7 June 1930; *s* of Alfred Henry and Clarice Adelaide Baughen; *m* 1956, Myrtle Newcomb Phillips; two *s* one *d*. *Educ:* Bromley County Grammar Sch; Univ. of London; Oak Hill Theol Coll. BD (London). With Martins Bank, 1946–48, 1950–51. Army, Royal Signals, 1948–50. Degree Course and Ordination Trng, 1951–56; Curate: St Paul's, Hyson Green, Nottingham, 1956–59; Reigate Parish Ch., 1959–61; Candidates Sec., Church Pastoral Aid Soc., 1961–64; Rector of Holy Trinity (Platt), Rusholme, Manchester, 1964–70; Vicar of All Souls, Langham Place, W1, 1970–75; Rector, 1975–82; Area Dean of St Marylebone, 1978–82; a Prebendary of St Paul's Cathedral, 1979–82. *Publications:* Moses and the Venture of Faith, 1979; The Prayer Principle, 1981; II Corinthians: a spiritual health-warning to the Church, 1982; Chained to the Gospel, 1986; Editor: Youth Praise, 1966; Youth Praise II, 1969; Psalm Praise, 1973; consultant editor, Hymns for Today's Church, 1982. *Recreations:* music, railways, touring. *Address:* Bishop's House, Chester CH1 2JD. *T:* Chester 20864.

CHESTER, Dean of; *see* Smalley, Very Rev. S. S.

CHESTER, Archdeacon of; *see* Williams, Ven. H. L.

CHESTER, Dr Peter Francis, FInstP; FIEE; Director, Technology Planning and Research Division, Central Electricity Generating Board, since 1982; *b* 8 Feb. 1929; *s* of late Herbert and of Edith Maud Chester (*née* Pullen); *m* 1953, Barbara Ann Collin; one *s* four *d*. *Educ:* Gunnersbury Grammar Sch.; Queen Mary College, London. BSc 1st Physics 1950; PhD London 1953. Post-doctoral Fellow, Nat. Research Council, Ottawa, 1953–54; Adv. Physicist, Westinghouse Res. Labs, Pittsburgh, 1954–60; Head of Solid State Physics Section, CERL, 1960–65; Head of Fundamental Studies Section, CERL, 1965–66; Res. Man., Electricity Council Res. Centre, 1966–70; Controller of Scientific Services, CEGB NW Region, 1970–73; Dir, Central Electricity Res. Labs, 1973–82. Science Research Council: Mem., 1976–80; Mem., Science Bd, 1972–75; Chm., Energy Round Table and Energy Cttee, 1975–80. Vice-Pres., Inst. of Physics, 1972–76. A Dir, Fulmer Res. Inst., 1976–83. Faraday Lectr, IEE, 1984–85. Robens Coal Science Medal, 1985. *Publications:* original papers in solid state and low temperature physics, reports on energy and the environment, and acid rain. *Address:* Central Electricity Research Laboratories, Kelvin Avenue, Leatherhead, Surrey KT22 7SE.

CHESTER, Prof. Theodore Edward, CBE 1967; D.jur, MA (Econ) Manchester; Diploma in Commerce; Director, Management Programme for Clinicians, since 1979; Senior Research Fellow and Emeritus Professor, 1976–78, Professor of Social Administration, 1955–75, University of Manchester; Member, Council and Finance and General Purposes Committee, Manchester Business School, since 1964; *b* 28 June 1908; *m* 1940, Mimi; one *s*. Teaching and research in law and administration, 1931–39. Service with HM Forces, 1940–45. Asst Man. in London city firm, 1946–48; Acton Soc. Trust: Senior Research Worker, 1948–52; Dir, 1952–55; Dean, Faculty of Economic and Social Studies, Univ. of Manchester, 1962–63. Research work into problems of large-scale Administration in private and public undertakings including the hosp. and educn service in Britain and comparative studies abroad as well as into the problems of training managers and administrators. Vis. Prof. at many foreign univs and institutions, notably in the United States, Western Europe, Canada, and Australia, 1959–; Kenneth Pray Vis. Prof., Univ. of Pa, 1968; first Kellogg Vis. Prof., Washington Univ., St Louis, 1969 and 1970. Mem. Summer Fac., Sloan Inst. of Health Service Admin, Cornell Univ., 1972–. Ford Foundn Travelling Fellowships, 1960, 1967. WHO Staff Training Programme, 1963–; UN Res. Inst. for Economic and Social Studies, 1968. Member: National Selection Cttee for the recruitment of Sen. Hospital Administrative Staff, 1956–66; Advisory Cttee on Management Efficiency in the Health Service, 1959–65; Cttee of Inquiry into recruitment, training and promotion of clerical and administrative staffs in the Hospital Service, 1962–63; Programme Cttee of Internat. Hosp. Fedn and Chm. study group into problems of trng in hosp. admin, 1959–65; Trng Council for Social Workers and Health Visitors, 1963–65; Cttee on Technical Coll. Resources, 1964–69; Inter Agency Inst. of Fed. Health Execs, USA, 1980–84; Pres., Corp. of Secs, 1956–66; Adviser: Social Affairs Div., OECD, 1965–66; Turkish State Planning Org. on Health and Welfare Problems, 1964. Broadcasts on social problems in Britain and abroad. Golden Needle of Honour, Austrian Hosp. Dirs Assoc., 1970. The Grand Gold Komturcross for services to the Health Service (Austria), 1980. *Publications:* (for Acton Soc. Trust) Training and Promotion in Nationalised Industry, 1951; Patterns of Organisation, 1952; Management under Nationalization, 1953; Background and Blueprint: A Study of Hospital Organisation under the National Health Service, 1955; The Impact of the Change (co-author), 1956; Groups, Regions and Committees, 1957; The Central Control of the Service, 1958; (with H. A. Clegg): The Future of Nationalization, 1953; Wage Policy and the Health Service, 1957; Post War Growth of Management in Western Europe, 1961; Graduate Education for Hospital Administration in the United States: Trends, 1969; The British National Health Service, 1970; The Swedish National Health Service, 1970; Organisation for Change: preparation for reorganisation, 1974 (OECD); (contrib.) Management for Clinicians, 1982; (contrib.) Management for Health Service Administrators, 1983; Alternative Systems in Organising and Controlling Health Services: public health systems in a democratic society, 1985; regular contribs to scientific and other jls. *Recreations:* travel, music, swimming, detective stories. *Address:* 189 Grove Lane, Hale, Altrincham, Cheshire. *T:* 061–980 2828.

CHESTER JONES, Prof. Ian, DSc; Professor of Zoology, University of Sheffield, 1958–81, now Emeritus Professor; Hon. Professor, Wolfson Institute for Research on Ageing, Hull, since 1981; *b* 3 Jan. 1916; *s* of late H. C. Jones; *m* 1942, Nansi Ellis Williams; two *s* one *d*. *Educ:* Liverpool Institute High Sch. for Boys; Liverpool Univ. BSc 1938; PhD 1941; DSc 1958. Served in Army, 1941–46. Commonwealth Fund Fellow, Harvard Univ., 1947–49. Senior Lecturer in Zoology, Univ. of Liverpool, 1955. Chm., Soc. for Endocrinology, 1966 (Sir Henry Dale medal, 1976). Dr de l'Université de Clermont (*hc*), 1967. *Publications:* The Adrenal Cortex, 1957; Integrated Biology, 1971; General, Comparative and Clinical Endocrinology of the Adrenal Cortex, vol. 1, 1976, vol. 2, 1978, vol. 3, 1980. *Address:* Department of Zoology, University of Sheffield S10 2TN.

CHESTERFIELD, Archdeacon of; *see* Phizackerley, Ven. G. R.

CHESTERFIELD, Arthur Desborough, CBE 1962; Director: Singer & Friedlander Ltd, since 1967 (Chairman, 1967–76); Clifford Property Co. Ltd, since 1973 (Chairman); Percy Bilton Ltd, since 1977 (Chairman, 1983–86; President, since 1986); *b* 21 Aug. 1905; *s* of Arthur William and Ellen Harvey Chesterfield; *m* 1932, Betty (*d* 1980), *d* of John Henry Downey; two *s* three *d*. *Educ:* Hastings Grammar Sch. Entered Westminster Bank Ltd, 1923; Joint Gen. Manager, 1947; Chief Gen. Manager, 1950–65, retired; Director: Nat. Westminster Bank, 1963–69 (Local Dir, Inner London, 1969–74); Woolwich Equitable Bldg Soc., 1966–80 (Vice-Chm., 1976–80); Singer & Friedlander (Holdings) Ltd, 1967–84 (Chm., 1967–76). Member: Export Guarantees Adv. Council, 1952–63; Nat. Savings Cttee, 1954–67; Chm., City of London Savings Cttee, 1962–72. FIB (Mem. Council, 1950–65). *Recreations:* music, gardening. *Address:* Coaters, Shirleys, Ditchling, Sussex. *T:* Hassocks 3514.

CHESTERMAN, Sir Ross, Kt 1970; MSc, PhD; DIC; Warden of Goldsmiths' College (University of London), 1953–74; Hon. Fellow, 1980; Master of the College of Design, Craft and Technology (formerly College of Craft Education), since 1982 (Vice-Master, 1960–82; Dean, 1958–60); *b* 27 April 1909; *s* of late Dudley and Ettie Chesterman; *m* 1st, 1938, Audrey Mary Horlick (*d* 1982); one *s* one *d*; 2nd, 1985, Patricia Burns Bell. *Educ:* Hastings Grammar Sch.; Imperial College of Science, London (scholar). Acland English Essay Prizeman, 1930; 1st class hons BSc (Chem.), 1930; MSc 1932; Lecturer in Chemistry, Woolwich Polytechnic; PhD 1937; Science master in various grammar schools; Headmaster, Meols Cop Secondary Sch., Southport, 1946–48. Chief County Inspector of Schools, Worcestershire, 1948–53. Educnl Consultant to numerous overseas countries, 1966–73. Ford Foundation Travel Award to American Univs, 1966. Chairman: Standing Cttee on Teacher Trng; Nat. Council for Supply and Trng of Teachers Overseas, 1971; Adv. Cttee for Teacher Trng Overseas, FCO (ODA), 1972–74. Fellow *hc* of Coll. of Handicraft, 1958. Liveryman and Freeman of Goldsmiths' Co., 1968. *Publications:* The Birds of Southport, 1947; chapter in The Forge, 1955; chapter in Science in Schools, 1958; Teacher Training in some American Universities, 1967; scientific papers in chemical journals and journals of natural history; articles in educational periodicals. *Recreations:* music, painting, travel. *Address:* The Garden House, 6 High Street, Lancaster LA1 1LA.

CHESTERS, Ven. Alan David; Archdeacon of Halifax since 1985; *b* 26 Aug. 1937; *s* of Herbert and Catherine Rebecca Chesters; *m* 1975, Jennie Garrett; one *s*. *Educ:* Elland Grammar Sch., W Yorks; St Chad's Coll., Univ. of Durham (BA Mod. History); St Catherine's Coll., Oxford (BA Theol., MA); St Stephen's House, Oxford. Curate of St Anne, Wandsworth, 1962–66; Chaplain and Head of Religious Education, Tiffin School, Kingston-upon-Thames, 1966–72; Director of Education and Rector of Brancepeth, Diocese of Durham, 1972–84; Hon. Canon of Durham Cathedral, 1975–84. A Church Comr, 1982– (Mem., Bd of Governors, 1984–). Mem., General Synod, 1975–. *Recreations:* railways, hill walking, reading. *Address:* 9 Healey Wood Gardens, Rastrick, Brighouse, West Yorkshire.

CHESTERS, Prof. Charles Geddes Coull, OBE 1977; BSc, MSc, PhD; FRSE; FLS; FInstBiol; Professor of Botany, University of Nottingham, 1944–69, now Emeritus Professor; *b* 9 March 1904; *s* of Charles and Margaret Geddes Chesters; *m* 1928, Margarita Mercedes Cathie Maclean; one *s* one *d*. *Educ:* Hyndland Sch.; Univ. of Glasgow. Lecturer in Botany, 1930, Reader in Mycology, 1942, Univ. of Birmingham. *Publications:* scientific papers on mycology and microbiology, mainly in Trans. British Myc. Soc., Ann. Ap.

Biol., Jl Gen. Microb. *Recreations:* photography and collecting fungi. *Address:* Grandage Cottages, Quenington, near Cirencester, Glos GL7 5DB.

CHESTERS, Dr John Hugh, OBE 1970; FRS 1969; FEng; Consultant, since 1971; *b* 16 Oct. 1906; 2nd *s* of Rev. George M. Chesters; *m* 1936, Nell Knight, Minnesota, USA; three *s* one *d*. *Educ:* High Pavement Sch., Nottingham; King Edward VII Sch., Sheffield; Univ. of Sheffield. BSc Hons Physics, 1928; PhD 1931; DSc Tech 1945; Hon. DSc 1975. Metropolitan-Vickers Research Schol., Univ. Sheff., 1928–31. Robert Blair Fellowship, Kaiser-Wilhelm Inst. für Silikatforschung, Berlin, 1931–32; Commonwealth Fund Fellowship, Univ. of Illinois, 1932–34; United Steel Cos Ltd: in charge of Refractories Section, 1934–45; Asst Dir of Research, 1945–62; Dep. Dir of Research, United Steel Cos Ltd, 1962–67, Midland Group, British Steel Corporation, 1967–70; Dir, Corporate Labs, BISRA, 1970–71. Chm., Watt Cttee on Energy, 1976–86. President: Brit. Ceramic Soc., 1951–52; Inst. of Ceramics, 1961–63; Iron and Steel Inst., 1968–69; Inst. of Fuel, 1972–73. Foreign Associate, Nat. Acad. of Engineering, USA, 1977. Iron and Steel Inst., Bessemer Gold Medal, 1966; John Wilkinson Gold Medal, Staffs Iron and Steel Inst., 1971; American Inst. Met. Eng: Robert Hunt Award, 1952; Benjamin Fairless Award, 1973. Fellow, Fellowship of Engineering, 1978; SFInstF, FIM, FICeram; Fellow, Amer. Ceramic Soc. *Publications:* Steelplant Refractories, 1945, 2nd edn 1957; Iron and Steel, 1948; Refractories: production and properties, 1973; Refractories for Iron- and Steelmaking, 1974; numerous articles in Jl of Iron and Steel Inst., Trans Brit. Cer. Soc., Jl Amer. Cer. Soc., Jl Inst. of Fuel, etc. *Recreations:* foreign travel, fishing. *Address:* 21 Slayleigh Lane, Sheffield S10 3RF. *T:* Sheffield 301257.

CHESTERTON, Elizabeth Ursula, OBE 1977; architect and town planner; *b* 12 Oct. 1915; *d* of late Maurice Chesterton, architect, and Dorothy (*née* Deck). *Educ:* King Alfred Sch.; Queen's Coll., London; Architectural Assoc. Sch. of Architecture, London. AA Dipl. (Hons) 1939; ARIBA 1940; DistTP 1968; FRTPI 1967 (AMTPI 1943). Asst County Planning Officer, E Suffolk CC, 1940–47; Develt Control Officer, Cambs CC Planning Dept, 1947–51; Mem. Staff: Social Res. Unit, Dept of Town Planning, UCL, 1951–53; Architectural Assoc. Sch. of Architecture, 1954–61. Member: Council, Architectural Assoc., 1964–67; Royal Fine Art Commn, 1970–; Historic Buildings Council, 1973–84, Historic Buildings and Historic Areas Adv. Cttees of Historic Buildings and Monuments Commn, 1984–; BR Environment Panel, 1983–; Council, National Trust, 1985–. FRSA 1982. *Publications:* Report on Local Land Use for the Dartington Hall Trustees, 1957; (jtly) The Historic Core of King's Lynn: study and plan, 1964; Plan for the Beaulieu Estate, 1966; North West Solent Shore Estates Report, 1969; Snowdon Summit Report for Countryside Commission, 1974; Plans for Quarries and Rail Distribution Depots, Foster Yeoman and Yeoman (Morvern), 1974–81; Central Area Study, Chippenham, for North Wiltshire District Council, 1975–80; The Crumbles, Eastbourne, for Chatsworth Settlement, 1976; Aldeburgh, Suffolk, for Aldeburgh Soc., 1976; Old Market Conservation and Redevelopment Study, for City of Bristol and Bristol Municipal Charities, 1978; Uplands Landscape Study, for Countryside Commission, 1980; Review of Beaulieu and Cadland Plans, 1985–. *Recreations:* gardening, travel. *Address:* 12 The Mount, NW3 6SZ. *T:* 01–435 0666 and 01–580 6396.

CHESTERTON, Sir Oliver (Sidney), Kt 1969; MC 1943; Consultant, Chestertons, Chartered Surveyors, London, since 1980 (Partner, 1936, Senior Partner, 1945–80); President, Woolwich Equitable Building Society, since 1986; Director, Estates Property Investment Company, since 1979; *b* 28 Jan. 1913; *s* of Frank and Nora Chesterton; *m* 1944, Violet Ethel Jameson; two *s* one *d*. *Educ:* Rugby Sch. Served War of 1939–45, Irish Guards. Director: Woolwich Equitable Building Soc., 1962–86 (Chm., 1976–83); Property Growth Assurance, 1972–85; London Life Assoc., 1975–84. Vice-Chm., Council of Royal Free Med. Sch., 1964–77; Crown Estate Comr, 1969–82. Past Pres., Royal Instn of Chartered Surveyors, Hon. Sec., 1972–79; Pres., Commonwealth Assoc. Surveying and Land Economy, 1969–77; first Master, Chartered Surveyors' Co., 1977–78. Governor, Rugby Sch., 1972–. *Recreations:* golf, fishing, National Hunt racing. *Address:* Hookfield House, Abinger Common, Dorking, Surrey. *Clubs:* White's; Rye Golf.

CHESWORTH, Donald Piers; Warden, Toynbee Hall, 1977–87; *b* 30 Jan. 1923; *s* of late Frederick Gladstone Chesworth and Daisy Radmore. *Educ:* King Edward VI Sch., Camp Hill, Birmingham; London Sch. of Economics. War of 1939–45: Nat. Fire Service; Royal Air Force. Chm., Nat. Assoc. of Labour Student Organisations, 1947; Student and Overseas Sec., Internat. Union of Socialist Youth, 1947–51. Contested (Lab) elections: Warwick and Leamington, 1945; Bromsgrove, 1950 and 1951; Mem. LCC (Kensington N Div.), 1952–65 (Whip and Mem., Policy Cttee); Labour Adviser: Tanganyika Govt (and Chm., Territorial Minimum Wages Bd), 1961–62; Mauritius Govt (and Chm., Sugar Wages Councils), 1962–65; Mem. Economics Br., ILO, Geneva, 1967; Dir, Notting Hill Social Council, 1967–77; Chm. (part time) Mauritius Salaries Commn, 1973–77; Co-opted Mem., ILEA Educn Cttee, 1970–74 and 1975–77; Alderman, Royal Borough of Kensington and Chelsea, 1971–77. Chm., Assoc. for Neighbourhood Councils, 1972–74. Member: Council, War on Want, 1965–76 (Chm., 1967, 1968, 1970–74); Exec. Bd, Voluntary Cttee on Overseas Aid and Develt, 1969–76; Nat. Cttee, UK Freedom from Hunger Campaigns, 1969–76; S Metropolitan Conciliation Cttee, Race Relations Bd, 1975–77; Exec., Internat. Fedn of Settlements, 1983–; British Assoc. of Settlements and Social Action Centres, 1984–; Exec., Britain-Tanzania Assoc., 1984–. Chm., World Development Political Action Trust, 1971–75; Trustee: UK Bangladesh Fund, 1971–72; Campden Charities, 1971–77; Internat. Extension Coll., 1972–; Attlee Meml Foundn, 1977– (Director, 1979–81; Treasurer, 1984–); Mutual Aid Centre, London, 1977–; Hilden Charitable Fund, 1978–; Aldgate Freedom Foundn, 1980–; Centre for World Develt Educn, 1980–; Mem. Bd of Visitors, Hewell Grange Borstal, 1950–52; Chm. Managers Mayford Home Office Approved Sch., 1952–58. Chairman of Governors: Isaac Newton Sch., N Kensington, 1971–77; Paddington Sch., 1972–76; Mem., Ct of Governors, LSE, 1973–78. *Publications:* (contrib.) Statutory Wage Fixing in Developing Countries (ILO), 1968; contrib. Internat. Labour Review. *Recreation:* travel. *Club:* Reform.

CHESWORTH, Air Vice-Marshal George Arthur, CB 1982; OBE 1972; DFC 1954; Chief Executive, Glasgow Garden Festival (1988) Ltd, since 1985; *b* 4 June 1930; *s* of Alfred Matthew Chesworth and Grace Edith Chesworth; *m* 1951, Betty Joan Hopkins; two *d* (one *s* decd). *Educ:* Carshalton and Wimbledon. Joined RAF, 1948; commissioned, 1950; 205 Flying boat Sqdn, FEAF, 1951–53 (DFC 1954); RAF Germany, RAF Kinloss, RAF St Mawgan, 1956–61; RN Staff Coll., 1963; MoD, 1964–67; OC 201 Nimrod Sqdn, 1968–71 (OBE); OC RAF Kinloss, 1972–75; Air Officer in Charge, Central Tactics & Trials Orgn, 1975–77; Director, RAF Quartering, 1977–80; C of S to Air Comdr CTF 317 during Falkland Campaign, Apr.-June 1982 (CB); C of S, HQ 18 Gp, RAF, 1980–84. *Address:* Pindlers Croft, Lower Califer, Forres, Moray IV36 0RN. *T:* Forres 74136.

CHETWODE, family name of **Baron Chetwode.**

CHETWODE, 2nd Baron *cr* 1945, of Chetwode; **Philip Chetwode;** Bt, 1700; *b* 26 March 1937; *s* of Capt. Roger Charles George Chetwode (*d* 1940; *o s* of Field Marshal Lord Chetwode, GCB, OM, GCSI, KCMG, DSO) and Hon. Molly Patricia Berry, *d* of 1st Viscount Camrose (she *m* 2nd, 1942, 1st Baron Sherwood, from whom she obtained a divorce, 1948, and *m* 3rd, 1958, late Sir Richard Cotterell, 5th Bt, CBE); *S* grandfather, 1950; *m* 1967, Mrs Susan Dudley Smith (marr. diss. 1979); two *s* one *d*. *Educ:* Eton. Commissioned Royal Horse Guards, 1956–66. *Heir: s* Hon. Roger Chetwode, *b* 29 May 1968. *Address:* 31 Moore Street, SW3. *T:* 01–584 6300. *Club:* White's.

CHETWOOD, Clifford Jack, FCIOB, FFB, FRSH; Chairman since 1984, a Group Managing Director since 1979, and Chief Executive since 1982, George Wimpey PLC; *b* 2 Nov. 1928; *s* of Stanley Jack Chetwood and Doris May Palmer; *m* 1953, Pamela Phyllis Sherlock; one *s* three *d*. George Wimpey & Co. Ltd, later George Wimpey PLC: Director, 1969; Chm., Bd of Management, 1975–79; Chairman: Wimpey Construction UK, 1979–83; Wimpey Homes Holdings, 1981–83. Trustee, V & A Museum, 1985–. *Address:* Wineberry House, The Drive, Eaton Park, Cobham, Surrey. *T:* Cobham 2389.

CHETWYN, Robert; *b* 7 Sept. 1933; *s* of Frederick Reuben Suckling and Eleanor Lavinia (*née* Boffee). *Educ:* Rutlish, Merton, SW; Central Sch. of Speech and Drama. First appeared as actor with Dundee Repertory Co., 1952; subseq. in repertory at Hull, Alexandra Theatre, Birmingham, 1954; Birmingham Repertory Theatre, 1954–56; various TV plays, 1956–59; 1st prodn, Five Finger Exercise, Salisbury Playhouse, 1960; Dir of Prodns, Opera Hse, Harrogate, 1961–62; Artistic Dir, Ipswich Arts, 1962–64; Midsummer Night's Dream, transf. Comedy (London), 1964; Resident Dir, Belgrade (Coventry), 1964–66; Assoc. Dir, Mermaid, 1966, The Beaver Coat, three one-act plays by Shaw; There's a Girl in My Soup, Globe, 1966 and Music Box (NY), 1967; A Present for the Past, Edinburgh Fest., 1966; The Flip Side, Apollo, 1967; The Importance of Being Earnest, Haymarket, 1968; The Real Inspector Hound, Criterion, 1968; What the Butler Saw, Queens, 1968; The Country Wife, Chichester Fest., 1968; The Bandwaggon, Mermaid, 1968 and Sydney, 1970; Cannibal Crackers, Hampstead, 1969; When We are Married, Strand, 1970; Hamlet, in Rome, Zurich, Vienna, Antwerp, Cologne, then Cambridge (London), 1971; Parents Day, Globe, 1972; Restez Donc Jusq'au Petit Dejeuner, Belgium, 1973; Who's Who, Fortune, 1973; At the End of the Day, Savoy, 1973; Chez Nous, Globe, 1974; Qui est Qui, Belgium, 1974; The Doctor's Dilemma, Mermaid, 1975; Getting Away with Murder, Comedy, 1976; Private Lives, Melbourne, 1976; It's All Right If I Do It, Mermaid, 1977; A Murder is Announced, Vaudeville, 1977; Arms and The Man, Greenwich, 1978; LUV, Amsterdam, 1978; Brimstone and Treacle, Open Space, 1979; Bent, Royal Court and Criterion, 1979; Pygmalion, National Theatre of Belgium, 1979; Moving, Queen's, 1980; Eastward Ho!, Mermaid, 1981; Beethoven's 10th, Vaudeville, 1983 (also Broadway, New York); Number One, Queen's, 1984; Why Me?, Strand, 1985. Has produced and directed for BBC (incl. series Private Shulz, by Jack Pullman and film, That Uncertain Feeling) and ITV (Irish RM first series). Trustee, Dirs' Guild of GB, 1984–. *Publication:* (jtly) Theatre on Merseyside (Arts Council report), 1973. *Recreations:* tennis, films, gardening. *Address:* 1 Wilton Court, Eccleston Square, SW1V 1PH.

CHETWYND, family name of **Viscount Chetwynd.**

CHETWYND, 10th Viscount *cr* 1717 (Ireland); **Adam Richard John Casson Chetwynd;** Baron Rathdowne, 1717 (Ireland); Life Assurance Agent, Prudential Assurance Co. of South Africa Ltd, Sandton Branch, Johannesburg; *b* 2 Feb. 1935; *o s* of 9th Viscount and Joan Gilbert (*d* 1979), *o c* of late Herbert Alexander Casson, CSI, Ty'n-y-coed, Arthog, Merioneth; *S* father, 1965; *m* 1st, 1966, Celia Grace (marr. diss. 1974), *er d* of Comdr Alexander Robert Ramsay, DSC, RNVR, Fasque, Borrowdale, Salisbury, Rhodesia; twin *s* one *d*; 2nd, 1975, Angela May, *o d* of Jack Payne McCarthy, 21 Llanberis Grove, Nottingham. *Educ:* Eton. Fellow, Inst. of Life and Pension Advrs, 1982. 2nd Lieut Cameron Highlanders, 1954–56. With Colonial Mutual Life Assurance Soc. Ltd, Salisbury, Rhodesia, then Johannesburg, 1968–78. Freeman, Guild of Air Pilots and Air Navigators. Life and Qualifying Mem., Million Dollar Round Table, 1979–84; qualified Top of the Table, 1984; Holder, Internat. Quality Award, 1978–84. *Recreations:* squash, travel. *Heir: s* Hon. Adam Douglas Chetwynd, *b* 26 Feb. 1969. *Address:* c/o J. G. Ouvry Esq., Lee Bolton & Lee, 1 The Sanctuary, Westminster, SW1P 3JT. *Clubs:* Rand (Johannesburg); Rotary (Sandton).

CHETWYND, Sir Arthur (Ralph Talbot), 8th Bt *cr* 1795; President, Brocton Hall Communications Ltd, Toronto, since 1978; Chairman, Board of Directors, Chetwynd Films Ltd, Toronto, since 1977 (Founder, President and General Manager, 1950–76); *b* Walhachin, BC, 28 Oct. 1913; *o s* of Hon. William Ralph Talbot Chetwynd, MC, MLA (*d* 1957) (*b* of 7th Bt), and of Frances Mary, *d* of late James Jupe; *S* uncle, 1972; *m* 1940, Marjory May McDonald, *er d* of late Robert Bruce Lang, Vancouver, BC, and Glasgow, Scotland; two *s*. *Educ:* Vernon Preparatory School, BC; University of British Columbia (Physical Education and Recreation). Prior to 1933, a rancher in interior BC; Games Master, Vernon Prep. School, BC, 1933–36, also Instructor, Provincial Physical Education and Recreation; Chief Instructor, McDonald's Remedial Institute, Vancouver, 1937–41; Director of Remedial Gymnastics, British Columbia Workmen's Compensation Board, 1942; RCAF, 1943–45; Associate in Physical and Health Education, Univ. of Toronto, also Publicity Officer, Univ. of Toronto Athletic Assoc., 1946–52. Dir, NZ Lamb Co. Ltd. Chm., Toronto Branch, Royal Commonwealth Soc.; Member: Monarchist League of Canada; St George's Soc. of Canada; Military and Hospitaller Order of St Lazarus of Jerusalem, Canada. KCLJ. *Recreations:* golf, swimming. *Heir: er s* Robin John Talbot Chetwynd [*b* 21 Aug. 1941; *m* 1967, Heather Helen, *d* of George Bayliss Lothian; one *s* one *d*]. *Address:* 214 Gerrard Street East, Toronto, Ont M5A 2E6, Canada. *Clubs:* Naval and Military, Royal Commonwealth Society; Albany, Empire of Canada (Pres., 1974–75), Toronto Hunt (all in Toronto).

CHETWYND-TALBOT, family name of **Earl of Shrewsbury and Waterford.**

CHETWYND-TALBOT, Richard Michael Arthur; *see* Talbot.

CHEVELEY, Stephen William, OBE 1946; farmer; with Cheveley & Co., Agricultural Consultant, since 1959; *b* 29 March 1900; *s* of George Edward Cheveley and Arabella Cheveley; *m* 1926, Joan Hardy (*d* 1977); two *s* one *d*. *Educ:* Leeds Modern Sch.; Leeds Univ. (BSc 1922; MSc). Served War, HAC, 1917–18. Min. of Agric. Scholarship, Farm Costings Res., 1922–23. British Sulphate of Ammonia Fedn, 1924–26; ICI Ltd, 1927–59; Chm., ICI Central Agricultural Control, 1952–59; Man. Dir, Plant Protection Ltd, 1945–51. Min. of Agric., Technical Develt Cttee, 1941–46; Chm., Foot and Mouth Res. Inst., 1950–58. Governor, Wye Coll., 1963–78, Fellow, 1977; Chm., Appeal Cttee, Centre for European Agric. Studies, 1973–75. Chm., Farmers' Club, 1956. Master, Worshipful Co. of Farmers, 1961. *Publications:* Grass Drying, 1937; Out of a Wilderness, 1939; A Garden Goes to War, 1940; (with O. T. W. Price) Capital in UK Agriculture, 1956. *Recreations:* farming, fishing, painting. *Address:* Dunorlan Farm, Tunbridge Wells, Kent. *T:* Tunbridge Wells 26632. *Club:* Farmers'.

CHEVRIER, Hon. Lionel, CC (Canada) 1967; PC (Can.) 1945; QC (Can.); lawyer for Ontario and Quebec, in private practice in Montreal; *s* of late Joseph Elphège Chevrier and late Malvina DeRepentigny; *m* 1932, Lucienne, *d* of Thomas J. Brulé, Ottawa; three *s* three *d*. *Educ:* Cornwall College Institute; Ottawa Univ.; Osgoode Hall. Called to bar,

Ontario, 1928; KC 1938; called to Bar, Quebec, 1957. MP for Stormont, Canada, 1935–54; MP for Montreal-Laurier, 1957–64. Dep. Chief Government Whip, 1940; Chm., Special Parly Sub-Cttee on War Expenditures, 1942; Parliamentary Asst to Minister of Munitions and Supply, 1943; Minister of Transport, 1945–54; Pres., St Lawrence Seaway Authority, 1954–57; Minister of Justice, 1963–64; High Commissioner in London, 1964–67. Delegate, Bretton Woods Conf., 1945; Chm., Canadian Delegn, UN General Assembly, Paris, 1948; Pres., Privy Council, Canada, 1957. Comr-Gen. for State Visits to Canada, 1967; Chairman: Canadian Economic Mission to Francophone Africa, 1968; Mission to study Canadian Consular Posts in USA, 1968; Seminar to study river navigation for Unitar, Buenos Aires, 1970. Hon. degrees: LLD: Ottawa, 1946; Laval, 1952; Queen's, 1956; Concordia, 1984; DCL, Bishops', 1964. *Publication:* The St Lawrence Seaway, 1959. *Recreations:* walking and reading. *Address:* 615 Belmont Street, Lavalin Building, Montreal, Que H3B 2L8, Canada.

CHEW, Victor Kenneth, TD 1958; Fellow of the Science Museum, London; *b* 19 Jan. 1915; *yr s* of Frederick and Edith Chew. *Educ:* Christ's Hospital; Christ Church, Oxford (Scholar). 1st class, Final Honours School of Natural Science (Physics), 1936; BA (Oxon) 1936, MA 1964. Asst Master, King's Sch., Rochester, 1936–38; Winchester Coll., 1938–40. Served War: Royal Signals, 1940–46. Asst Master, Shrewsbury Sch., 1946–48 and 1949–58; Lecturer in Education, Bristol Univ., 1948–49. Entered Science Museum as Asst Keeper, 1958; Deputy Keeper and Sec. to Advisory Council, 1967; Keeper, Dept of Physics, 1970–78. *Publications:* official publications of Science Museum. *Recreations:* choral singing, mountain walking, photography. *Address:* 701 Gilbert House, Barbican, EC2.

CHEWTON, Viscount; James Sherbrooke Waldegrave; *b* 8 Dec. 1940; *e s* of 12th Earl Waldegrave, *qv*; *m* 1986, Mary Alison Anthea, *d* of late Sir Robert Furness, KBE, CMG, and of Lady Furness, Little Shelford, Cambridge. *Educ:* Eton Coll.; Trinity Coll., Cambridge. *Address:* West End Farm, Chewton Mendip, Bath. *Clubs:* Brooks's, Beefsteak.

CHEYNE, Major Sir Joseph (Lister Watson), 3rd Bt *cr* 1908; OBE 1976; Curator, Keats Shelley Memorial House, Rome, since 1976; *b* 10 Oct. 1914; *e s* of Sir Joseph Lister Cheyne, 2nd Bt, MC, and Nelita Manfield (*d* 1977), *d* of Andrew Pringle, Borgue; *S* father, 1957; *m* 1st, 1938, Mary Mort (marr. diss. 1955; she *d* 1959), *d* of late Vice-Adm. J. D. Allen, CB; one *s* one *d*; 2nd, 1955, Cicely, *d* of late T. Metcalfe, Padiham, Lancs; two *s* one *d*. *Educ:* Stowe Sch.; Corpus Christi Coll., Cambridge. Major, The Queen's Westminsters (KRRC), 1943; Italian Campaign. 2nd Sec. (Inf.), British Embassy, Rome, 1968, 1st Sec., 1971, 1st Sec. (Inf.), 1973–76. *Heir: s* Patrick John Lister Cheyne [*b* 2 July 1941; *m* 1968, Helen Louise Trevor, *yr d* of Louis Smith, Southsea; one *s* three *d*]. *Address:* Leagarth, Fetlar, Shetland; Piazza di Spagna 29, Rome 00187, Italy. *T:* Rome 6782334. *Clubs:* Boodle's; Circolo della Caccia (Rome).

CHEYSSON, Claude, Commander Legion of Honour; Croix de Guerre (5 times); Member, Commission of the European Communities, since 1985; Town Councillor, Bargemon, since 1983; *b* 13 April 1920; *s* of Pierre Cheysson and Sophie Funck-Brentano; *m* 1969, Danièle Schwarz; one *s* two *d* (and two *s* one *d* by former marrs). *Educ:* Coll. Stanislas, Paris; Ecole Polytechnique; Ecole Nationale d'Administration. Escaped from occupied France, 1943; Tank Officer, Free French Forces, France and Germany, 1944–45. Liaison Officer with German authorities, Bonn, 1948–52; Political Adviser to Viet Nam Govt, Saigon, 1952–53; Personal Adviser: to Prime Minister of France, Paris, 1954–55; to French Minister of Moroccan and Tunisian Affairs, 1956; Sec.-Gen., Commn for Techn. Cooperation in Africa, Lagos, Nairobi, 1957–62; Dir-Gen., Sahara Authority, Algiers, 1962–66; French Ambassador in Indonesia, 1966–69; Pres., Entreprise Minière et Chimique, 1970–73; European Comr (relations with Third World), 1973–81; Minister for External Relations, 1981–84. Grand Cross, Nat. Orders of Austria, Cameroon, Denmark, Egypt, Finland, Germany, Guinea, Iceland, Italy, Japan, Jordan, Lebanon, Liberia, Mexico, Morocco, Netherlands, Norway, Portugal, Saudi Arabia, Spain, Sweden, Syria, Tunisia and UK; Grand Officer, Nat. Orders of Belgium, Benin, Cameroon, Chad, Gabon, Ivory Coast, Monaco, Nepal, Niger, Portugal, Senegal, Togo, Tunisia, Upper Volta; Comdr, Nat. Orders of Central African Rep., Indonesia, and Mali; US Presidential Citation. Dr *hc* Univ. of Louvain; Joseph Bech Prize, 1978; Luderite Prize, 1983. *Publications:* Une idée qui s'incarne, 1978; articles on Europe, and develt policies. *Recreation:* ski-ing. *Address:* Commission of the European Communities, 200 rue de la Loi, 1049 Brussels, Belgium.

CHIANG KAI-SHEK, Madame (Mayling Soong Chiang); Chinese sociologist; *y d* of C. J. Soong; *m* 1927, Generalissimo Chiang Kai-Shek (*d* 1975). *Educ:* Wellesley Coll., USA. LHD, John B. Stetson Univ., Deland, Fla, Bryant Coll., Providence, RI, Hobart and William Smith Colls, Geneva, NY; LLD, Rutgers Univ., New Brunswick, NJ, Goucher Coll., Baltimore, MD, Wellesley Coll., Wellesley, Mass, Loyola Univ., Los Angeles, Cal., Russell Sage Coll., Troy, NY, Hahnemann Medical Coll., Philadelphia, Pa, Wesleyan Coll., Macon, Ga, Univ. of Michigan, Univ. of Hawaii; Hon. FRCS. First Chinese woman appointed Mem. Child Labor Commn; Inaugurated Moral Endeavor Assoc.; established schools in Nanking for orphans of Revolutionary Soldiers; former Mem. Legislative Yuan; served as Sec.-General of Chinese Commission on Aeronautical Affairs; Member Chinese Commission on Aeronautical Affairs; Director-General of the New Life Movement and Chairman of its Women's Advisory Council; Founder and Director: National Chinese Women's Assoc. for War Relief; National Assoc. for Refugee Children; Chinese Women's Anti-Aggression League; Huashing Children's Home; Cheng Hsin Medical Rehabilitation Center for Post Polio Crippled Children. Chm., Fu Jen Catholic University. Governor, Nat. Palace Museum. Frequently makes inspection tours to all sections of Free China where personally trained girl workers carry on war area and rural service work; accompanies husband on military campaigns; first Chinese woman to be decorated by National Govt of China. Recipient of highest military and Civil decorations; Hon. Chm., British United Aid to China Fund, China; Hon. Chm., Soc. for the Friends of the Wounded; Hon. President, American Bureau for Medical Aid to China; Patroness, International Red Cross Commn; Hon. President, Chinese Women's Relief Assoc. of New York; Hon. Chairman, Canadian Red Cross China Cttee; Hon. Chairman, Board of Directors, India Famine Relief Cttee; Hon. Mem., New York Zoological Soc.; Hon. Pres., Cttee for the Promotion of the Welfare of the Blind; Life Mem., San Francisco Press Club and Associated Countrywomen of the World; Mem., Phi Beta Kappa, Eta Chapter; first Hon. Member, Bill of Rights Commemorative Society; Hon. Member: Filipino Guerrillas of Bataan Assoc.; Catherine Lorillard Wolf Club. Medal of Honour, New York City Federation of Women's Clubs; YWCA Emblem; Gold Medal, New York Southern Soc.; Chi Omega Nat. Achievement Award for 1943; Gold Medal for distinguished services, National Institute for Social Sciences; Distinguished Service Award, Altrusa Internat. Assoc.; Churchman Fifth Annual Award, 1943; Distinguished Service Citation, All-American Conf. to Combat Communism, 1958; Hon. Lieut-Gen. US Marine Corps. *Publications:* China in Peace and War, 1939; China Shall Rise Again, 1939; This is Our China, 1940; We Chinese Women, 1941; Little Sister Su, 1943; Ten Eventful Years, for Encyclopædia Britannica, 1946; Album of Reproduction of Paintings, vol. I, 1952, vol. II, 1962; The Sure Victory, 1955; Madame Chiang Kai-Shek Selected Speeches, 1958–59; Madame Chiang Kai-shek Selected Speeches, 1965–66; Album of Chinese Orchid Paintings, 1971; Album of Chinese Bamboo Paintings, 1972; Album of Chinese Landscape Paintings, 1973; Album of Chinese Floral Paintings, 1974; Conversations with Mikhail Borodin, 1977; Religious Writings 1934–63, 1964.

CHIASSON, Most Rev. Donat; *see* Moncton, Archbishop of, (RC).

CHIBNALL, Albert Charles, PhD (London); ScD (Cantab); FRS 1937; Fellow of Clare College, Cambridge; Fellow of the Imperial College of Science and Technology, London; *b* 28 Jan. 1894; *s* of G. W. Chibnall; *m* 1st, 1931 (wife *d* 1936); two *d*; 2nd, 1947, Marjorie McCallum Morgan (*see* M. McC. Chibnall); one *s* one *d*. *Educ:* St Paul's Sch.; Clare Coll., Cambridge; Imperial Coll. of Science and Technology; Yale Univ., New Haven, Conn. 2nd Lieut, ASC 1914; Capt., 1915; attached RAF, 1917–19, served Egypt and Salonika. Huxley Medal, 1922; Imperial Coll. Travelling Fellow, 1922–23; Seessel Fellow, Yale Univ., 1923–24; Hon. Asst in Biochemistry, University Coll., London, 1924–30; Asst Prof. 1930–36, Prof. 1936–43, Emeritus Prof. 1943, of Biochemistry, Imperial Coll.; Sir William Dunn Prof. of Biochemistry, Univ. of Cambridge, 1943–49. Silliman Lectr, Yale Univ., 1938; Bakerian Lectr, Royal Society, 1942. Hon. Mem., Biochem. Soc.; Vice-Pres., Bucks Record Soc.; FSA 1977. Hon. DSc St Andrews, 1971. *Publications:* Protein Metabolism in the Plant, 1939; Richard de Badew and the University of Cambridge, 1315–1340, 1963; Sherington, fiefs and fields of a Buckinghamshire village, 1965; Beyond Sherington, 1979; papers in scientific journals on plant biochemistry. *Address:* 6 Millington Road, Cambridge. *T:* Cambridge 353923.

CHIBNALL, Marjorie McCallum, MA, DPhil; FSA; FBA 1978; Fellow of Clare Hall, Cambridge, since 1975; *b* 27 Sept. 1915; *d* of J. C. Morgan, MBE; *m* 1947, Prof. Albert Charles Chibnall, *qv*; one *s* one *d* and two step *d*. *Educ:* Shrewsbury Priory County Girls' Sch.; Lady Margaret Hall, Oxford; Sorbonne, Paris. BLitt, MA, DPhil (Oxon); PhD (Cantab). Amy Mary Preston Read Scholar, Oxford, 1937–38; Goldsmiths' Sen. Student, 1937–39; Nursing Auxiliary, 1939; Susette Taylor Research Fellow, Lady Margaret Hall, Oxford, 1940–41; Asst Lectr, University Coll., Southampton, 1941–43; Asst Lectr, 1943–45, Lectr, 1945–47, in Medieval History, Univ. of Aberdeen; Lectr in History, later Fellow of Girton Coll., Cambridge, 1947–65; Research Fellow, Clare Hall, Cambridge, 1969–75; Leverhulme Emeritus Fellowship, 1982. Corresp. Fellow, Medieval Acad. of America, 1983. Hon. DLitt Birmingham, 1979. *Publications:* The English Lands of the Abbey of Bec, 1946; Select Documents of the English Lands of the Abbey of Bec, 1951; The *Historia Pontificalis* of John of Salisbury, 1956; The Ecclesiastical History of Orderic Vitalis, 6 vols, 1969–80; Charters and Custumals of the Abbey of Holy Trinity Caen, 1982; The World of Orderic Vitalis, 1984; Anglo-Norman England 1066–1166, 1986; numerous articles and reviews, principally in English and French historical jls. *Address:* Clare Hall, Cambridge CB3 9AL. *T:* Cambridge 353923. *Club:* University Women's.

CHICHESTER, family name of **Marquess of Donegall.**

CHICHESTER, 9th Earl of, *cr* 1801; **John Nicholas Pelham;** Bt 1611; Baron Pelham of Stanmer, 1762; *b* (posthumous) 14 April 1944; *s* of 8th Earl of Chichester (killed on active service, 1944) and Ursula (she *m* 2nd, 1957, Ralph Gunning Henderson; marr. diss. 1971), *o d* of late Walter de Pannwitz, de Hartekamp, Bennebroek, Holland; *S* father, 1944; *m* 1975, Mrs June Marijke Hall; one *d*. *Recreations:* music, flying. *Heir: kinsman* Richard Anthony Henry Pelham, *b* 1st Aug. 1952. *Address:* Little Durnford Manor, Salisbury, Wilts.

CHICHESTER, Bishop of, since 1974; **Rt. Rev. Eric Waldram Kemp,** MA Oxon, DD; *b* 27 April 1915; *o c* of Tom Kemp and Florence Lilian Kemp (*née* Waldram), Grove House, Waltham, Grimsby, Lincs; *m* 1953, Leslie Patricia, 3rd *d* of late Rt Rev. K. E. Kirk, sometime Bishop of Oxford; one *s* four *d*. *Educ:* Brigg Grammar Sch., Lincs; Exeter Coll., Oxford; St Stephen's House, Oxford. Deacon 1939; Priest 1940; Curate of St Luke, Southampton, 1939–41; Librarian of Pusey House, Oxford, 1941–46; Chaplain of Christ Church Oxford, 1943–46; Actg Chap., St John's Coll., Oxford, 1943–45; Fellow, Chaplain, Tutor, and Lectr in Theology and Medieval History, Exeter Coll., Oxford, 1946–69; Dean of Worcester, 1969–74. Exam. Chaplain: to Bp of Mon, 1942–45; to Bp of Southwark, 1946–50; to Bp of St Albans, 1946–69; to Bp of Exeter, 1949–69; to Bp of Lincoln, 1950–69. Proctor in Convocation for University of Oxford, 1949–69. Bp of Oxford's Commissary for Religious Communities, 1952–69; Chaplain to the Queen, 1967–69. Canon and Prebendary of Caistor in Lincoln Cathedral, 1952; Hon. Provincial Canon of Cape Town, 1960–; Bampton Lecturer, 1959–60. FRHistS 1951. Hon. DLitt Sussex, 1986. *Publications:* (contributions to) Thy Household the Church, 1943; Canonization and Authority in the Western Church, 1948; Norman Powell Williams, 1954; Twenty-five Papal Decretals relating to the Diocese of Lincoln (with W. Holtzmann), 1954; An Introduction to Canon Law in the Church of England, 1957; Life and Letters of Kenneth Escott Kirk, 1959; Counsel and Consent, 1961; The Anglican-Methodist conversations: A Comment from within, 1964; (ed) Man: Fallen and Free, 1969; Square Words in a Round World, 1980; contrib. to English Historical Review, Jl of Ecclesiastical History. *Recreations:* music, travel. *Address:* The Palace, Chichester, W Sussex PO19 1PY. *T:* Chichester 782161. *Club:* National Liberal.

CHICHESTER, Dean of; *see* Holtby, Very Rev. R. T.

CHICHESTER, Archdeacon of; *see* Hobbs, Ven. Keith.

CHICHESTER, Sir (Edward) John, 11th Bt *cr* 1641; *b* 14 April 1916; *s* of Comdr Sir Edward George Chichester, 10th Bt, RN, and late Phyllis Dorothy, *d* of late Henry F. Compton, Minstead Manor, Hants; *S* father, 1940; *m* 1950, Hon. Mrs Anne Rachel Pearl Moore-Gwyn, *widow* of Capt. Howel Moore-Gwyn, Welsh Guards, and *d* of 2nd Baron Montagu of Beaulieu and of Hon. Mrs Edward Pleydell-Bouverie; two *s* two *d* (and one *d* decd). *Educ:* Radley; RMC Sandhurst. Commissioned RSF, 1936. Patron of one living. Served throughout War of 1939–45. Was employed by ICI Ltd, 1950–60. A King's Foreign Service Messenger, 1947–50. Formerly Capt., Royal Scots Fusiliers and Lieut RNVR. *Heir: s* James Henry Edward Chichester, *b* 15 Oct. 1951. *Address:* Battramsley Lodge, Boldre, Lymington, Hants. *Club:* Naval.

CHICHESTER-CLARK, family name of **Baron Moyola.**

CHICHESTER-CLARK, Sir Robert, (Sir Robin Chichester-Clark), Kt 1974; Director, Welbeck Group Ltd; management consultant; *b* 10 Jan. 1928; *s* of late Capt. J. L. C. Chichester-Clark, DSO and Bar, DL, MP, and Mrs C. E. Brackenbury; *m* 1st, 1953, Jane Helen Goddard (marr. diss. 1972); one *s* two *d*; 2nd, 1974, Caroline, *d* of Anthony Bull, *qv*; two *s*. *Educ:* Royal Naval Coll.; Magdalene Coll., Cambridge (BA Hons Hist. and Law). Journalist, 1950; Public Relations Officer, Glyndebourne Opera, 1952; Asst to Sales Manager, Oxford Univ. Press, 1953–55. MP (UU) Londonderry City and Co., 1955–Feb. 1974; PPS to Financial Secretary to the Treasury, 1958; Asst Government Whip (unpaid), 1958–60; a Lord Comr of the Treasury, 1960–61; Comptroller of HM Household, 1961–64; Chief Opposition Spokesman on N Ireland, 1964–70, on Public Building and Works and the Arts, 1965–70; Minister of State, Dept of Employment, 1972–74. Hon. FIWM 1972. *Recreations:* fishing, reading. *Club:* Brooks's.

See also Baron Moyola.

CHICK, John Stephen; HM Diplomatic Service; Consul-General, Geneva, since 1985; *b* 5 Aug. 1935; *m* 1966, Margarita Alvarez de Sotomayor; one *s* three *d. Educ:* St John's Coll., Cambridge (BA 1959). Entered FO, 1961; Madrid, 1963–66; First Sec., Mexico City, 1966–69; FCO, 1969–73; First Sec. and Head of Chancery, Rangoon, 1973–76; Consul, Luxembourg, 1976–78; Consul-Gen., Buenos Aires, 1978–81; Head of Arms Control Dept, FCO, 1981–83; Head of S Pacific Dept, FCO, 1983–85. *Address:* c/o Foreign and Commonwealth Office, SW1.

CHIEF RABBI; *see* Jakobovits, Rabbi Sir Immanuel.

CHIEPE, Hon. Gaositwe Keagakwa Tibe, PMS 1975; MBE 1962; FRSA; Minister for External Affairs, since 1984; *b* 20 Oct. 1922; *d* of late T. Chiepe. *Educ:* Fort Hare, South Africa (BSc, EdDip); Bristol Univ., UK (MA (Ed)). Asst Educn Officer, 1948–53; Educn Officer and Schools Inspector, 1953–62; Sen. Educn Officer, 1962–65; Dep. Dir of Educn, 1965–67; Dir of Educn, 1968–70; Diplomat, 1970–; High Comr to UK and Nigeria, 1970–74; Ambassador: Denmark, Norway, Sweden, France and Germany, 1970–74; Belgium and EEC, 1973–74; Minister of Commerce and Industry, 1974–77; Minister for Mineral Resources and Water Affairs, 1977–84. Chairman: Africa Region, CPA, 1981–83; Botswana Branch, CPA, 1981–. Member: Botswana Society; Botswana Girl Guide Assoc.; Internat. Fedn of University Women. Hon. LLD Bristol, 1972. FRSA 1973. *Recreations:* gardening, a bit of swimming (in Botswana), reading. *Address:* Department of External Affairs, Private Bag 001, Gabarone, Botswana.

CHILCOT, John Anthony; Assistant Under Secretary of State, Home Office, on secondment to Schroders, since 1986; Director, RTZ Pillar Ltd, since 1986; *b* 22 April 1939; *s* of Henry William Chilcot and Catherine Chilcot (*née* Ashall); *m* 1964, Rosalind Mary Forster. *Educ:* Brighton Coll. (Lyon Scholar); Pembroke Coll., Cambridge (Open Scholar; MA). Joined Home Office, 1963; Asst Private Sec. to Home Secretary (Rt Hon. Roy Jenkins), 1966; Private Sec. to Head of Civil Service (late Baron Armstrong of Sanderstead), 1971–73; Principal Private Secretary to Home Secretary (Rt Hon. Merlyn Rees; Rt Hon. William Whitelaw), 1978–80; Asst Under-Sec. of State, Dir of Personnel and Finance, Prison Dept, 1980–84; Under-Sec., Cabinet Office (MPO), 1984–86. *Recreations:* reading, music and opera, travel. *Address:* c/o Home Office, 50 Queen Anne's Gate, SW1.

CHILD, Christopher Thomas; National President, Bakers' Union, 1968–77; former Consultant to Baking Industry, Industrial Relations Officer and Training Officer, Baking Industry and Health Food Products, 1970–85; *b* 8 Jan. 1920; *s* of late Thomas William and Penelope Child; *m* 1943, Lilian Delaney; two *s* one *d. Educ:* Robert Ferguson Sch., Carlisle; Birmingham Coll. of Food and Domestic Science. Apprenticed baker, 1936; gained London City and Guilds final certificates in Breadmaking, Flour Confectionery and Bakery Science, 1951, and became Examiner in these subjects for CGLI. Full-time trade union official in Birmingham, 1958. Member: Birmingham Trades Council Exec., 1958–68; Adv. Council, Midland Regional TUC, 1959–68; Disablement Adv. Cttee, Birmingham, 1959–68. Former Chairman: Nat. Council Baking Education; Nat. Joint Apprenticeship Council for Baking. Mem., Industrial Training Bd, Food, Drink and Tobacco, 1968–78; former Vice-Pres., EEC Food Group and Mem., EEC Cttees on Food Products, Vocational Training, and Food Legislation; former Sec., Jt Bakers' Unions of England, Scotland and Ireland. Mem., TEC C4 programme Cttee, Hotel, Food, Catering and Institutional Management. *Recreations:* fishing, gardening, climbing in English Lake District. *Address:* 200 Bedford Road, Letchworth, Herts SG6 4EA. *T:* Letchworth 672170.

CHILD, Clifton James, OBE 1949; MA, PhM, FRHistS; Administrative Officer, Cabinet Office Historical Section, 1969–76, retired; *b* Birmingham, 20 June 1912; *s* of late Joseph and Georgina Child; *m* 1938, Hilde Hurwitz; two *s. Educ:* Moseley Grammar Sch.; Universities of Birmingham, Berlin and Wisconsin. Univ. of Birmingham: Entrance Schol., 1929; Kenrick Prizeman, 1930; BA 1st class hons, 1932; Francis Corder Clayton Research Schol., 1932–34; MA 1934. Univ. of Wisconsin: Commonwealth Fund Fellow, 1936–38; PhM 1938. Educn Officer, Lancs Community Council, 1939–40. Joined Foreign Office, 1941; Head of American Section, FO Research Dept, 1946–58; African Section, 1958–62; Dep. Librarian and Departmental Record Officer, 1962; Librarian and Keeper of the Papers, FO, 1965–69; Cabinet Office, 1969–76. FRHistS 1965. *Publications:* The German-Americans in Politics, 1939; (with Arnold Toynbee and others) Hitler's Europe, 1954; contribs to learned periodicals in Britain and US. *Recreations:* gardening, foreign travel. *Address:* Westcroft, Westhall Road, Warlingham, Surrey. *T:* Upper Warlingham 2540.

CHILD, Sir (Coles John) Jeremy, 3rd Bt *cr* 1919; actor; *b* 20 Sept. 1944; *s* of Sir Coles John Child, 2nd Bt, and Sheila (*d* 1964), *e d* of Hugh Mathewson; *S* father, 1971; *m* 1971, Deborah Jane (*née* Snelling) (marr. diss. 1976); one *d*; *m* 1978, Jan (marr. diss. 1986), *y d* of B. Todd, Kingston upon Thames; one *s* one *d. Educ:* Eton; Univ. of Poitiers (Dip. in Fr.). Trained at Bristol Old Vic Theatre Sch., 1963–65; Bristol Old Vic, 1965–66; repertory at Windsor, Canterbury and Colchester; Conduct Unbecoming, Queen's, 1970; appeared at Royal Court, Mermaid and Bankside Globe, 1973; Oh Kay, Westminster, 1974; Donkey's Years, Globe, 1977; Hay Fever, Lyric, Hammersmith, 1980; *films include:* Privilege, 1967; Oh What a Lovely War!, 1967; The Breaking of Bumbo, 1970; Young Winston, 1971; The Stud, 1976; Quadrophenia, 1978; Sir Henry at Rawlinson's End, 1979; Chanel Solitaire, 1980; High Road to China, 1982; Give my Regards to Broad Street, 1983; *TV series:* Father, Dear Father, Glittering Prizes, Wings, Edward and Mrs Simpson, When the Boat Comes In, Bird of Prey, The Jewel in the Crown, Fairly Secret Army, Hart to Hart, First Among Equals. *Recreations:* travel, squash, flying, photography. *Heir: s* Coles John Alexander Child, *b* 10 May 1982. *Clubs:* Garrick, Roehampton.

CHILD, Denis Marsden; Deputy Group Chief Executive, National Westminster Bank, since 1982; *b* 1 Nov. 1926; *s* of late Percival Snowden Child and Alice Child (*née* Jackson); *m* 1973, Patricia; three *c* by previous marr. *Educ:* Woodhouse Grove Sch., Bradford. Joined Westminster Bank, Leeds, 1942; RN, 1944–48; rejoined Westminster Bank; National Westminster Bank: Asst Area Manager, Leeds, 1970; Area Manager, Wembley, 1972; Chief Manager, Planning and Marketing, 1975; Head, Management Inf. and Control, 1977; Gen. Manager, Financial Control Div., 1979; Director, 1982–, NatWest Bank and subsids. Chairman: Exec. Cttee, BBA, 1986–; Council, Assoc. for Payment Clearing Services, 1985–; Financial Markets Cttee, Fedn Bancaire, EC, 1985–; Member: Internat. Commodities Clearing House, 1982–; Accounting Standards Cttee, 1985–; Securities and Investments Bd, 1986–; IBM UK Pensions Trust, 1984–; Channel Tunnel Group. FIB; FCT; FBIM. *Recreations:* golf, gardening. *Address:* Carkins, Berry Hill, Taplow, Maidenhead, Berks SL6 0DA. *T:* Maidenhead 34770. *Club:* Stoke Poges Golf.

CHILD, Sir Jeremy; *see* Child, Sir C. J. J.

CHILD-VILLIERS, family name of **Earl of Jersey.**

CHILDS, Most Rev. Derrick Greenslade; *b* 14 Jan. 1918; *er s* of Alfred John and Florence Theodosia Childs; *m* 1951, Elizabeth Cicely Davies; one *s* one *d. Educ:* Whitland Grammar Sch., Carmarthenshire; University Coll., Cardiff (BA Wales, 1st cl. Hons History; Fellow 1981); Sarum Theol College at Wells. Deacon 1941, priest 1942, Diocese of St David's; Asst Curate: Milford Haven, 1941–46; Laugharne with Llansadwrnen, 1946–51; Warden of Llandaff House, Penarth (Hall of Residence for students of University Coll., Cardiff), 1951–61; Gen. Sec., Provincial Council for Education of the Church in Wales, 1955–65; Director of Church in Wales Publications, 1961–65; Chancellor of Llandaff Cathedral, 1964–69; Principal of Trinity Coll. of Education, Carmarthen, 1965–72; Canon of St David's Cathedral, 1969–72; Bishop of Monmouth, 1972–86; Archbishop of Wales, 1983–86. Member: Court University College, Cardiff; Council, St David's Univ. College, Lampeter; Court, Univ. of Wales; Chm., Church in Wales Provincial Council for Educn, 1972–83; Chm. of Council, Historical Soc. of Church in Wales, 1972; Vice-Chm., National Society, 1973; Chm. Bd, Church in Wales Publications, 1974–83. Sub-Prelate, Order of St John of Jerusalem, 1972. *Publications:* Editor: Cymry'r Groes, 1947–49, Province, 1949–68, and regular contributor to those quarterly magazines; contrib.: E. T. Davies, The Story of the Church in Glamorgan, 1962; Religion in Approved Schools, 1967. *Recreations:* music, walking, and watching cricket and Rugby football. *Address:* 30 Birchwood Road, Penylan, Cardiff CF2 5LJ. *T:* Cardiff 483214.

CHILE, Bishop of, since 1977; **Rt. Rev. Colin Frederick Bazley;** *b* 27 June 1935; *s* of Reginald Samuel Bazley and Isabella Davies; *m* 1960, Barbara Helen Griffiths; three *d. Educ:* Birkenhead School; St Peter's Hall, Oxford (MA); Tyndale Hall, Bristol. Deacon 1959, priest 1960; Assistant Curate, St Leonard's, Bootle, 1959–62; Missionary of S American Missionary Society in Chile, 1962–69; Rural Dean of Chol-Chol, 1962–66; Archdeacon of Temuco, 1966–69; Assistant Bishop for Cautin and Malleco, Dio. Chile, Bolivia and Peru, 1969–75; Assistant Bishop for Santiago, 1975–77; Bishop of Chile, Bolivia and Peru, 1977; diocese divided, Oct. 1977; Bishop of Chile and Bolivia until Oct. 1981; Presiding Bishop of the Anglican Council for South America, 1977–83. *Recreations:* football (Liverpool supporter) and fishing on camping holidays. *Address:* Iglesia Anglicana, Casilla 50675, Correo Central, Santiago, Chile. *T:* 2292158.

CHILSTON, 4th Viscount *cr* 1911, of Boughton Malherbe; **Alastair George Akers-Douglas;** Baron Douglas of Baads, 1911; film producer; *b* 5 Sept. 1946; *s* of Ian Stanley Akers-Douglas (*d* 1952) (*g s* of 1st Viscount) and of Phyllis Rosemary (who *m* 2nd, John Anthony Cobham Shaw, MC), *d* of late Arthur David Clere Parsons; *S* cousin, 1982; *m* 1971, Juliet Anne, *d* of Lt-Col Nigel Lovett, Glos Regt; three *s. Educ:* Eton College; Madrid Univ. *Recreation:* sailing. *Heir: s* Hon. Oliver Ian Akers-Douglas, *b* 13 Oct. 1973. *Address:* The Old Rectory, Twyford, near Winchester, Hants. *T:* Twyford 712300.

CHILTON, Air Marshal Sir (Charles) Edward, KBE 1959 (CBE 1945); CB 1951; RAF (retired); *o s* of J. C. Chilton; *m* 1st, 1929, Betty Ursula (*d* 1963), 2nd *d* of late Bernard Temple Wrinch; one *s*; 2nd, 1964, Joyce Cornforth. Royal Air Force general duties branch; Air Commodore, 1950; Air Vice-Marshal, 1954; Air Marshal, 1959. Dep. Air Officer i/c Administration, Air Command, SE Asia, 1944; AOC Ceylon, 1946; Imperial Defence Coll., 1951; AOC Gibraltar, 1952; Asst Chief of the Air Staff (Policy), 1953–54; SASO, HQ Coastal Command, 1955; AOC Royal Air Force, Malta, and Dep. Comdr-in-Chief (Air), Allied Forces Mediterranean, 1957–59; AOC-in-C, Coastal Command and Maritime Air Commander Eastern Atlantic Area, and Commander Maritime Air, Channel and Southern North Sea, 1959–62. Consultant and Dir, IBM (Rentals) UK, 1963–78. Specialist navigator (Air Master navigator certificate) and Fellow (Vice-Pres. 1949–51, 1959–61, 1963–65), Royal Institute of Navigation. Pres. RAF Rowing Club, 1956; Vice-Adm. and Hon. Life Mem. RAF Sailing Assoc.; Hon. Vice-Pres. RAF Swimming Assoc. Vice Patron, Regular Forces Employment Assoc. FInstD. Freeman, City of London. Grand Cross of Prince Henry the Navigator (Portugal), 1960; Order of Polonia Restituta, Poland, 1980. *Publications:* numerous contributions to Service and other journals, on maritime-air operations and air navigation, and biographical papers on Rear-Adm. Sir Murray Sueter, CB, and Wing Comdr J. C. Porte, CMG. *Recreations:* sailing, sea fishing and country walking. *Address:* 11 Charles House, Phyllis Court Drive, Henley-on-Thames, Oxon. *Clubs:* Royal Air Force; (Vice-Patron) Royal Gibraltar Yacht; Phyllis Court (Henley).

CHILTON, Brig. Sir Frederick Oliver, Kt 1969; CBE 1963 (OBE 1957); DSO 1941 and bar 1944; Chairman, Repatriation Commission, Australia, 1958–70; *b* 23 July 1905. *Educ:* Univ. of Sydney (BA, LLB). Solicitor, NSW, 1929. Late AIF; served War of 1939–45, Libya, Greece, New Guinea and Borneo (despatches, DSO and bar); Controller of Joint Intelligence, 1946–48; Asst Sec., Dept of Defence, Australia, 1948–50; Dep. Sec., 1950–58. *Address:* Clareville Beach, NSW, Australia. *Clubs:* Melbourne, Union, Naval and Military (Melbourne); Imperial Service (Sydney).

CHILVER, Sir (Amos) Henry; *see* Chilver, Sir H.

CHILVER, Elizabeth Millicent, (Mrs R. C. Chilver); Principal of Lady Margaret Hall, Oxford, 1971–79, Honorary Fellow, 1979; *b* 3 Aug. 1914; *o d* of late Philip Perceval Graves and late Millicent Graves (*née* Gilchrist); *m* 1937, Richard Clementson Chilver, CB (*d* 1985). *Educ:* Benenden Sch., Cranbrook; Somerville Coll., Oxford (Hon. Fellow, 1977). Journalist, 1937–39; temp. Civil Servant, 1939–45; Daily News Ltd, 1945–47; temp. Principal and Secretary, Colonial Social Science Research Council and Colonial Economic Research Cttee, Colonial Office, 1948–57; Director, Univ. of Oxford Inst. of Commonwealth Studies, 1957–61; Senior Research Fellow, Univ. of London Inst. of Commonwealth Studies, 1961–64; Principal, Bedford Coll., Univ. of London, 1964–71, Fellow, 1974. Mem. Royal Commn on Medical Education, 1965–68. Trustee, British Museum, 1970–75; Mem. Governing Body, SOAS, Univ. of London, 1975–80. Médaille de la Reconnaissance française, 1945. *Publications:* articles on African historical subjects. *Address:* 47 Kingston Road, Oxford OX2 6RH. *T:* Oxford 53082.

CHILVER, Sir Henry, Kt 1978; FRS 1982; FEng 1977; CBIM; Vice-Chancellor, Cranfield Institute of Technology, since 1970; Chairman, Milton Keynes Development Corporation, since 1983; *b* 30 Oct. 1926; *e s* of A. H. Chilver and A. E. Mack; *m* 1959, Claudia M. B. Grigson, MA, MB, BCh, *o d* of Sir Wilfrid Grigson; three *s* two *d. Educ:* Southend High Sch.; Bristol Univ. (Albert Fry Prize 1947). Structural Engineering Asst, British Railways, 1947; Asst Lecturer, 1950, Lecturer, 1952, in Civil Engineering, Bristol Univ.; Demonstrator, 1954, Lectr, 1956, in Engineering, Cambridge Univ.; Fellow of Corpus Christi Coll., Cambridge, 1958–61 (Hon. Fellow, 1981); Chadwick Prof. of Civil Engineering, UCL, 1961–69; Director: Centre for Environmental Studies, 1967–69; Node Course (for civil service and industry), 1974–75. Chm., BASE Internat. Ltd, 1983–; Director: SKF (UK), 1972–80; De La Rue Co., 1973–81; English China Clays, 1973–; SE Reg., Nat. Westminster Bank, 1975–83; Delta Gp, 1977–84; Powell Duffryn, 1979–; TR Technology Investment Trust, 1982–; Hill Samuel Gp, 1983–; Britoil, 1986–. Chairman: PO, 1980–81; Higher Educn Review Body, NI, 1978–81; Univs' Computer Bd, 1975–78; RAF Trng and Educn Adv. Cttee, 1976–80; Adv. Council, RMCS, Shrivenham, 1978–; Working Gp on Advanced Ground Transport, 1978–81; Electronics EDC, 1980–; ACARD, 1982–85. Member: Ferrybridge Enquiry Cttee, 1965; Management Cttee, Inst. of Child Health, 1965–69; ARC, 1967–70 and 1972–75; SRC, 1970–74; Beds Educn Cttee, 1970–74; Planning and Transport Res. Adv. Council, 1972–79; Cttee for Ind. Technologies, 1972–76; ICE Special Cttee on Educn and Trng, 1973 (Chm.); CNAA, 1973–76; Royal Commn on Environmental Pollution, 1976–81;

Standing Commn on Energy and the Environment, 1978–81; Adv. Bd for Res. Councils, 1982–; Bd, Nat. Adv. Body for Local Authority Higher Educn, 1983–85. Dep. Pres., Standing Conf. on Schools Sci. and Technol.; Assessor, Inquiry on Lorries, People and the Envt, 1979–80. President: Inst. of Management Services, 1982–; Inst. Materials Handling, 1986–; Vice-Pres., ICE, 1981–83; Mem., Smeatonian Soc. of Civil Engrs. Member Council: Birkbeck Coll., 1980–82; Cheltenham Coll., 1980–. Lectures: STC Communications, 1981; O'Sullivan, Imperial Coll., 1984; Lady Margaret Beaufort, Bedford, 1985; Fawley, Southampton Univ., 1985. Telford Gold Medal, ICE, 1962; Coopers Hill War Meml Prize, ICE, 1977. Hon. DSc: Leeds; Bristol; Salford; Strathclyde; Bath. *Publications:* Problems in Engineering Structures (with R. J. Ashby), 1958; Strength of Materials (with J. Case), 1959; Thin-walled Structures (ed), 1967; papers on structural theory in engineering journals. *Address:* Cranfield Institute of Technology, Cranfield, Bedford MK43 0AL. *T:* Bedford 750111. *Clubs:* Athenæum, United Oxford & Cambridge University.

CHING, Henry, CBE 1982; Secretary for Health and Welfare, and Member of Legislative Council, Hong Kong, 1983–85, retired; *b* 2 Nov. 1933; *s* of Henry Ching, OBE and Ruby Irene Ching; *m* 1963, Eileen Frances Peters; two *d. Educ:* Diocesan Boys' School, Hong Kong; Hong Kong Univ. (BA Hons); Wadham Coll., Oxford (MA, DipEd). Schoolmaster, 1958–61; Hong Kong Civil Service: various appts, 1961–73; Principal Asst Financial Sec., 1973–76; Dep. Financial Sec., 1976–83. *Recreations:* cricket, rowing. *Address:* 2 Fitzwilliam Road, Vaucluse, Sydney, NSW 2030, Australia.

CHINN, Trevor Edwin; Chairman, since 1973 and Managing Director, since 1968, Lex Service PLC; *b* 24 July 1935; *s* of Rosser and Susie Chinn; *m* 1965, Susan Speelman; two *s. Educ:* Clifton Coll.; King's Coll., Cambridge. Lex Service: Gen. Sales Manager, 1954; Dir, 1959–. Allied Insurance Brokers Gp, 1984–; Rock plc, 1986–. Member: Council, Centre for Business Strategy, London Business Sch., 1983–; Court of Govs, Royal Shakespeare Theatre, 1982–; Bd of Govs, Jewish Agency. Pres., Joint Israel Appeal. Trustee, Duke of Edinburgh's Award Scheme, 1979–. Chief Barker, Variety Club of GB, 1977, 1978. *Address:* Lex House, 17 Connaught Place, W2 2EL. *T:* 01–723 1212.

CHINNERY, (Charles) Derek; Controller, Radio 1, BBC, 1978–85; *b* 27 April 1925; *s* of Percy Herbert and Frances Dorothy Chinnery; *m* 1953, Doreen Grace Clarke. *Educ:* Gosforth Grammar School. Youth in training, BBC, 1941; RAF Cadet Pilot, 1943. BBC: Technical Asst, 1947; Programme Engineer, 1948; Studio Manager, 1950; Producer, 1952; Executive Producer, 1967; Head of Radio 1, 1972. *Recreations:* DIY, sailing. *Address:* 65 Meadway, NW11 6QJ. *Club:* BBC.

CHIONA, Most Rev. James; *see* Blantyre, Archbishop of, (RC).

CHIPIMO, Elias Marko; Chairman, Standard Bank Zambia Ltd, 1976–80 (Deputy Chairman, 1975); *b* 23 Feb. 1931; *s* of Marko Chipimo, Zambia (then Northern Rhodesia); *m* 1959, Anna Joyce Nkole Konie; four *s* three *d. Educ:* St Canisius, Chikuni, Zambia; Munali; Fort Hare Univ. Coll., SA; University Coll. of Rhodesia and Nyasaland; Univ. of Zambia (LLB 1985). Schoolmaster, 1959–63; Sen. Govt Administrator, 1964–67; High Comr for Zambia in London, and Zambian Ambassador to the Holy See, 1968–69; Perm. Sec., Min. of Foreign Affairs, 1969. Chairman: Zambia Stock Exchange Council, 1970–72; Zambia Nat. Bldg Soc., 1970–71; Dep. Chm., Development Bank of Zambia Ltd, 1973–75; Director: Zambia Airways Corp., 1975–81; Zambia Bata Shoe Co. Ltd, 1977–. Mem., Nat Council for Sci. Res., 1977–. Pres., Lusaka Branch, Zambia Red Cross, 1970–75; Vice-Pres., Zambia Red Cross Soc., 1976–; Mem., Zambia Univ. Council, 1970–76; Dir, Internat. Sch. of Lusaka, 1970–76. Cllr, Lusaka City Council, 1974–80. *Publications:* Our Land and People, 1966; Tied Loans and the Role of Banks (vol. 2 of International Financing of Economic Development); A Case for a Capital Market in Zambia; A Statement of Education Reforms—an Irrational View. *Recreations:* rose gardening, reading, general literature, linguistics, philosophy, politics, economics, discussions, chess, growing roses. *Address:* PO Box 32115, Lusaka, Zambia.

CHIPP, David Allan; Editor in Chief of The Press Association 1969–86; *b* 6 June 1927; *s* of late Thomas Ford Chipp and late Isabel Mary Ballinger; unmarried. *Educ:* Geelong Grammar Sch., Australia; King's Coll., Cambridge (MA). Served with Middlesex Regt, 1944–47; Cambridge, 1947–50. Joined Reuters as Sports Reporter, 1950; Correspondent for Reuters: in SE Asia, 1953–55; in Peking, 1956–58; various managerial positions in Reuters, 1960–68; Editor of Reuters, 1968. An Indep. Dir, The Observer, 1985; Director: TV-am News Co.; Reuters, 1986–. *Recreations:* gardening, opera. *Address:* 2 Wilton Court, 59/60 Eccleston Square, SW1V 1PH. *T:* 01–834 5579. *Clubs:* Garrick; Leander (Henley-on-Thames).

CHIPPERFIELD, Geoffrey Howes; Deputy Secretary, Department of the Environment, since 1982; *b* 20 April 1933; *s* of Nelson Chipperfield and Eleanor Chipperfield; *m* 1959, Gillian James; two *s. Educ:* Cranleigh; New Coll., Oxford. Called to the Bar, Gray's Inn, 1955. Joined Min. of Housing and Local Govt, 1956; Harkness Fellow, Inst. of Govtl Studies, Univ. of Calif, Berkeley, 1962–63; Principal Private Sec., Minister of Housing, 1968–70; Sec., Greater London Develt Plan Inquiry, 1970–73; Under Sec., 1976. *Recreations:* reading, gardening. *Address:* Department of the Environment, 2 Marsham Street, SW1. *Club:* United Oxford & Cambridge University.

CHIRAC, Jacques René; Prime Minister of France, since 1986; President, Rassemblement des Français pour la République, 1976–81 and since 1982; Mayor of Paris, since 1977; *b* Paris, 29 Nov. 1932; *s* of François Chirac, company manager and Marie-Louise (*née* Valette); *m* 1956, Bernadette Chodron de Courcel; two *s. Educ:* Lycée Carnot and Lycee Louis-le-Grand, Paris; Diploma of Inst. of Polit. Studies, Paris, and of Summer Sch., Harvard Univ., USA. Served Army in Algeria. Ecole Nat. d'Admin, 1957–59; Auditor, Cour des Comptes, 1959; Head Dept: Sec.-Gen. of Govt, 1962; Private Office of Georges Pompidou, 1962–67; Counsellor, Cour des Comptes, 1965–; State Secretary: Employment Problems, 1967–68; Economy and Finance, 1968–71; Minister for Parly Relations, 1971–72; Minister for Agriculture and Rural Development, 1972–74; Home Minister, March-May 1974; Prime Minister, 1974–76; Sec.-Gen., UDR, Dec. 1974–June 1975. Deputy from Corrèze, elected 1967, 1968, 1973, 1976 (UDR), 1978 (RFR), and 1981; Member from Meymac, Conseil Général of Corrèze, 1968–, Pres. 1970–. Mem., European Parlt, 1979–80. Treasurer, Claude Pompidou Foundn (charity for elderly and for handicapped children), 1969–. Grand-Croix, Ordre national du Mérite; Croix de la valeur militaire; Chevalier du Mérite agricole, des Arts et des Lettres, de l'Etoile noire, du Mérite sportif, du Mérite touristique; Médaille de l'Aéronautique. *Publications:* a thesis on development of Port of New Orleans, 1954; Discours pour la France à l'heure du choix, la lueur d'espérance: réflexion du soir pour le matin, 1978. *Address:* (office) Hôtel Matignon, 57 rue de Varenne, 75007 Paris, France; 110 rue du Bac, 75007 Paris, France.

CHISHOLM, Prof. Alexander William John; Research Professor in Engineering, University of Salford, since 1982; *b* 18 April 1922; *s* of Thomas Alexander Chisholm and Maude Mary Chisholm (*née* Robinson); *m* 1945, Aline Mary (*née* Eastwood); one *s* one *d. Educ:* Brentwood Sch., Essex; Northampton Polytechnic; Manchester Coll. of Science and Technology; Royal Technical Coll., Salford (BSc(Eng) London). CEng, FIMechE, FIProdE. Section Leader, Res. Dept, Metropolitan Vickers Electrical Co. Ltd, 1944–49; Sen. Scientific Officer, then Principal Scientific Officer, Nat. Engrg Lab., 1949–57; UK Scientific Mission, British Embassy, USA, 1952–54; Head of Dept of Mechanical Engrg, then Prof. of Mechanical Engrg, Royal Coll. of Advanced Technology, Salford, 1957–67; Prof. of Mech. Engineering, Univ. of Salford, 1967–82 (Chm., Industrial Centre, 1962–82). Visitor, Cambridge Univ. Engrg Dept and Vis. Fellow, Wolfson Coll., 1973–74. Chm., Industrial Admin and Engrg Prodn Gp, IMechE, 1960–62. Nat. Council for Technological Awards: Chm., Mechanical/Prodn Engrg Cttee, 1960–63; Vice-Chm., Bd of Studies in Engrg and Governor, 1963–65. Pres., Internat. Inst. of Prodn Engrg Res., 1983–84 (Mem. Council, 1972–75; Chm., UK Bd, 1977–). Member: Technology Cttee, UGC, 1969–74; Engrg Profs Conf. (Chm., 1976–80); Court, Cranfield Inst. of Technology, 1974–. Whitworth Prize, IMechE, 1965. *Publications:* numerous on production process technology, manufacturing systems, organization of industrial research, internat. comparisons of educn and training of engineers. *Recreations:* hill walking, sailing. *Address:* 12 Legh Road, Prestbury, Macclesfield, Cheshire SK10 4HX. *T:* Prestbury 829412. *Club:* Athenæum.

CHISHOLM, Archibald Hugh Tennent, CBE 1946; MA; *b* 17 Aug. 1902; 2nd *s* of late Hugh Chisholm and Mrs Chisholm (*née* Harrison), Rush Park, Co. Antrim; *m* 1939, Josephine (*d* 1983), *e d* of J. E. Goudge, OBE, ICS; one *s* one *d* (and one *d* decd). *Educ:* Westminster; Christ Church, Oxford. Wall Street Journal of NY, 1925–27; The British Petroleum Co. (then Anglo-Persian/Anglo-Iranian Oil Co.), Iran and Kuwait, 1928–36 and London, 1945–72. Editor of The Financial Times, 1937–40; Army, 1940–45 (despatches twice, CBE). FZS; FInstPet. Chevalier, Légion d'Honneur. *Publication:* The First Kuwait Oil Concession Agreement: a Record of the Negotiations, 1911–1934, 1975. *Address:* 107 Hamilton Terrace, NW8. *T:* 01–289 0713. *Clubs:* Athenæum, Naval and Military, Beefsteak, MCC.

CHISHOLM, Prof. Michael Donald Inglis; Professor of Geography, University of Cambridge, since 1976; Professorial Fellow, St Catharine's College, Cambridge, since 1976; *b* 10 June 1931; *s* of M. S. and A. W. Chisholm; *m* 1959, Edith Gretchen Emma (*née* Hoof) (marr. diss. 1981); one *s* two *d. Educ:* St Christopher Sch., Letchworth; St Catharine's Coll., Cambridge (MA). MA Oxon. Nat. Service Commn, RE, 1950–51. Deptl Demonstrator, Inst. for Agric. Econs, Oxford, 1954–59; Asst Lectr, then Lectr in Geog., Bedford Coll., London, 1960–64; Vis. Sen. Lectr in Geog., Univ. of Ibadan, 1964–65; Lectr, then Reader in Geog., Univ. of Bristol, 1965–72; Prof. of Economic and Social Geography, Univ. of Bristol, 1972–76. Associate, Economic Associates Ltd, consultants, 1965–77; Mem. SSRC, and Chm. of Cttees for Human Geography and Planning, 1967–72; Member: Local Govt Boundary Commn for England, 1971–78; Develt Commn, 1981–. Mem. Council, Inst. of British Geographers, 1961 and 1962, Junior Vice-Pres., 1977, Sen. Vice-Pres., 1978, Pres. 1979. Conservator of River Cam, 1979–. Gill Memorial Prize, RGS, 1969. Geography Editor for Hutchinson Univ. Lib., 1973–82. *Publications:* Rural Settlement and Land Use: an essay in location, 1962; Geography and Economics, 1966; (ed jtly) Regional Forecasting, 1971; (ed jtly) Spatial Policy Problems of the British Economy, 1971; Research in Human Geography, 1971; (ed) Resources for Britain's Future, 1972; (jtly) Freight Flows and Spatial Aspects of the British Economy, 1973; (jtly) The Changing Pattern of Employment, 1973; (ed jtly) Studies in Human Geography, 1973; (ed jtly) Processes in Physical and Human Geography: Bristol Essays, 1975; Human Geography: Evolution or Revolution?, 1975; Modern World Development, 1982; papers in Farm Economist, Oxford Econ. Papers, Trans Inst. British Geographers, Geography, Applied Statistics, Area, etc. *Recreations:* gardening, theatre, opera, interior design. *Address:* Department of Geography, Downing Place, Cambridge CB2 3EN.

CHISHOLM, Roderick Æneas, CBE 1946; DSO 1944; DFC and bar; AE; ARCS; BSc; *b* 23 Nov. 1911; *s* of Edward Consitt Chisholm and Edith Maud Mary Cary Elwes; *m* 1945, Phillis Mary Sanchia, *d* of late Geoffrey A. Whitworth, CBE; one *s* two *d. Educ:* Ampleforth Coll.; Imperial Coll. of Science and Technology, London. AAF, 1932–40; Royal Air Force, 1940–46 (Air Cdre). *Publication:* Cover of Darkness, 1953. *Address:* Ladywell House, Alresford, Hants.

CHISLETT, Derek Victor; Under Secretary, Department of Health and Social Security, since 1983; *b* 18 April 1929; *s* of Archibald Lynn Chislett and Eva Jessie Collins; *m* 1954, Joan Robson; two *d. Educ:* Christ's Hospital. Clerical Officer, Admiralty, 1946; HM Forces, 1947–49; Exec. Officer, 1953–62, Higher Exec. Officer, 1962–66, Nat. Assistance Board; Sen. Executive Officer, Min. of Social Security, 1967; Department of Health and Social Security: Principal 1968–76; Asst Sec. 1976–83; Controller, Newcastle Central Office, 1983–86. *Recreations:* opera, walking, gardening. *Address:* Balmain, Borders Lane, Etchingham, E Sussex. *T:* Etchingham 220. *Club:* Royal Commonwealth Society.

CHISWELL, Rt. Rev. Peter; *see* Armidale, Bishop of.

CHISWELL, Maj.-Gen. Peter Irvine, CB 1985; CBE 1976 (OBE 1972; MBE 1965); General Officer Commanding Wales, 1983–85; *b* 19 April 1930; *s* of late Col Henry Thomas Chiswell, OBE (late RAMC) and of Gladys Beatrice Chiswell; *m* 1958, Felicity Philippa, *d* of R. F. Martin; two *s. Educ:* Allhallows School; RMA Sandhurst. Commissioned Devonshire Regt, 1951; transf. Parachute Regt, 1958; DAAG HQ Berlin Inf. Bde, 1963–65; Brigade Major, 16 Para Bde, 1967–68; GSO1 (DS), Staff Coll., 1968–69; CO 3 PARA, 1969–71; Col GS (Army Training), 1971–74; Comd British Contingent DCOS UN Force Cyprus, 1974–76; Comd, 44 Para Bde, 1976–78; ACOS (Operations), HQ Northern Army Gp, 1978–81; Comd, Land Forces NI, 1982–83. *Recreations:* travel and sailing.

CHITNIS, family name of **Baron Chitnis.**

CHITNIS, Baron *cr* 1977 (Life Peer), of Ryedale, N Yorks; **Pratap Chidamber Chitnis;** Chief Executive and Director, Joseph Rowntree Social Service Trust, since 1975 (Secretary, 1969–75); *b* 1 May 1936; *s* of late Chidamber N. Chitnis and Lucia Mallik; *m* 1964, Anne Brand; one *s* decd. *Educ:* Penryn Sch.; Stonyhurst Coll.; Univs of Birmingham (BA) and Kansas (MA). Admin. Asst, Nat. Coal Board, 1958–59; Liberal Party Organisation: Local Govt Officer, 1960–62; Agent, Orpington Liberal Campaign, 1962; Trng Officer, 1962–64; Press Officer, 1964–66; Head of Liberal Party Organisation, 1966–69. Mem., Community Relations Commn, 1970–77; Chm., BBC Immigrants Programme Adv. Cttee, 1979–83 (Mem., 1972–77). Chairman: Refugee Action, 1981–; Latin America Cttee, British Refugee Council, 1985–. Reported on elections in: Zimbabwe, 1979; (jtly) Guyana, 1980; El Salvador, 1982 and 1984; Nicaragua, 1984. *Address:* Beverley House, Shipton Road, York. *T:* York 625744.

CHITTY, Dr Anthony; Regional Industrial Adviser, North East Region, Department of Trade and Industry, since 1984; *b* 29 May 1931; *s* of Ashley George Chitty and Doris Ellen Mary Buck; *m* 1956, Audrey Munro; two *s* one *d. Educ:* Glynn Grammar Sch., Epsom; Imperial Coll., London. BSc, PhD, DIC; CEng. GEC Res. Labs, 1955; Hd, Creep of Steels Lab., ERA, 1959; GEC Power Gp, 1963; Chief Metallurgist (Applications), C. A. Parsons, 1966; Dir, Advanced Technol. Div., Clarke Chapman-John Thompson, 1973;

Internat. Res. and Develt, 1978; Gen. Manager, Engrg Products, N. E. I. Parsons, 1979. Vis. Prof., Univ. of Aston in Birmingham, 1977–84. Dep. Chm., Bd of Newcastle Technol. Centre, 1985–. *Publications*: research publications in the fields of materials and welding for power generation. *Recreations*: hill walking, gardening. *Address*: 1 Willow Way, Darras Hall, Ponteland, Northumberland NE20 9RJ. *T*: Ponteland 23899.

CHITTY, Beryl; *see* Chitty, M. B.

CHITTY, (Margaret) Beryl, CMG 1977; HM Diplomatic Service, retired; Appeal Director, St Peter's College, Oxford, since 1982; *b* 2 Dec. 1917; *d* of Wilfrid and Eleanor Holdgate; *m* 1949, Keith Chitty, FRCS (*d* 1958). *Educ*: Belvedere Sch. (GPDST), Liverpool; St Hugh's Coll., Oxford (BA, MA; Hon. Fellow, 1982). Dominions Office, 1940; Private Sec. to Parly Under-Sec. of State, 1943–45; Principal, 1945; CRO, 1947–52; First Sec., Commonwealth Office, 1958; UK Mission to UN, New York, 1968–70; FCO, 1970–71; Dep. British High Comr in Jamaica, 1971–75; Head of Commonwealth Co-ord. Dept, FCO, 1975–77. Appeal Sec., St Hugh's Coll., Oxford, 1978–81. Non-Press Mem., Press Council, 1978–80. Mem., Governing Body, Queen Elizabeth House, Oxford, 1977–80. *Address*: 79 Bainton Road, Oxford OX2 7AG. *T*: Oxford 53384.

CHITTY, Susan Elspeth, (Lady Chitty); author; *b* 18 Aug. 1929; *d* of Rudolph Glossop and Mrs E. A. Hopkinson; *m* 1951, Sir Thomas Willes Chitty, Bt, *qv*; one *s* three *d. Educ*: Godolphin Sch., Salisbury; Somerville Coll., Oxford. Mem. editorial staff, Vogue, 1952–53; subseq. journalist, reviewer, broadcaster and lecturer. *Publications: novels*: Diary of a Fashion Model, 1958; White Huntress, 1963; My Life and Horses, 1966; *biographies*: The Woman who wrote Black Beauty, 1972; The Beast and the Monk, 1975; Charles Kingsley and North Devon, 1976; Gwen John 1876–1939, 1981; Now to My Mother, 1985; *non-fiction*: (with Thomas Hinde) On Next to Nothing, 1976; (with Thomas Hinde) The Great Donkey Walk, 1977; The Young Rider, 1979; *edited*: The Intelligent Woman's Guide to Good Taste, 1958; The Puffin Book of Horses, 1975; As Once in May, by Antonia White, 1983. *Recreations*: riding, travel. *Address*: Bow Cottage, West Hoathly, Sussex RH19 4QF. *T*: Sharpthorne 810269.

CHITTY, Sir Thomas Willes, 3rd Bt *cr* 1924; author (as Thomas Hinde); *b* 2 March 1926; *e s* of Sir (Thomas) Henry Willes Chitty, 2nd Bt, and Ethel Constance (*d* 1971), *d* of S. H. Gladstone, Darley Ash, Bovingdon, Herts; *S* father, 1955; *m* 1951, Susan Elspeth (*see* S. E. Chitty); one *s* three *d. Educ*: Winchester; University Coll., Oxford. Royal Navy, 1944–47. Shell Petroleum Co., 1953–60. Granada Arts Fellow, Univ. of York, 1964–65; Visiting Lectr, Univ. of Illinois, 1965–67; Vis. Prof., Boston Univ., 1969–70. *Publications: novels*: Mr Nicholas, 1952; Happy as Larry, 1957; For the Good of the Company, 1961; A Place Like Home, 1962; The Cage, 1962; Ninety Double Martinis, 1963; The Day the Call Came, 1964; Games of Chance, 1965; The Village, 1966; High, 1968; Bird, 1970; Generally a Virgin, 1972; Agent, 1974; Our Father, 1975; Daymare, 1980; *non-fiction*: (with wife, as Susan Hinde) On Next to Nothing, 1976; (with Susan Chitty) The Great Donkey Walk, 1977; The Cottage Book, 1979; Stately Gardens of Britain, 1983; Forests of Britain, 1985; (ed) The Domesday Book: England's heritage, then and now, 1986; *autobiography*: Sir Henry and Sons, 1980; *biography*: A Field Guide to the English Country Parson, 1983; Capability Brown, 1986; *anthology*: Spain, 1963. *Heir: s* Andrew Edward Willes Chitty, *b* 20 Nov. 1953. *Address*: Bow Cottage, West Hoathly, Sussex RH19 4QF. *T*: Sharpthorne 810269.

CHOLERTON, Frederick Arthur, CBE 1978; *b* 15 April 1917; *s* of Frederick Arthur Cholerton and Charlotte (*née* Wagstaffe); *m* 1939, Ethel (*née* Jackson); one *s* decd. *Educ*: Penkhull Secondary Sch., Stoke-on-Trent. Locomotive driver, British Rail, 1934–77; Trade Union work with ASLEF, 1934–71. City of Stoke-on-Trent: Councillor, 1951–; Leader of Council, 1976–81; Lord Mayor, 1971–72; Staffordshire County Council: Councillor, 1973–; Vice-Chm., 1973–76; Chm., 1977 and 1981–86; Opposition Leader, 1977–81. Director: North Staffordshire South Cheshire Broadcasting (Signal Radio), Ltd, 1982–; Longton Enterprise Ltd, 1980–; 1986 Nat. Garden Festival, Stoke-on-Trent, Staffordshire Ltd, 1983–; W Midlands Industrial Develt Bd, 1983–. JP Stoke-on-Trent, 1956–74. *Recreations*: sports, gardening, politics, voluntary work for charities, particularly RNIB. *Address*: 12 Werburgh Drive, Trentham, Stoke-on-Trent ST4 8JP. *T*: Stoke-on-Trent 657457.

CHOLMELEY, John Adye, FRCS; Surgeon, Royal National Orthopædic Hospital, 1948–70, Hon. Consulting Surgeon, since 1970; Chairman of Joint Examining Board for Orthopædic Nursing, 1959–83; *b* 31 Oct. 1902; *s* of Montague Adye Cholmeley and Mary Bertha Gordon-Cumming; unmarried. *Educ*: St Paul's Sch.; St Bartholomew's Hosp. MRCS, LRCP 1926; MB, BS London 1927; FRCS 1935; Resident appts St Bart's Hosp., 1928–30; Asst MO: Lord Mayor Treloar Cripples' Hosp., Alton, 1930–32; Alexandra Orth. Hosp., Swanley, 1933–34; Resident Surg. and Med. Supt, Country Br., Royal Nat. Orth. Hosp., Stanmore, 1940–48 (Asst Res. Surg., 1936–39); former Orthopædic Surg., Clare Hall Hosp., Neasden Hosp. Mem. Internat. Soc. of Orthopædic Surgery and Trauma (Société Internationale de Chirurgie Orthopédique et de Traumatologie, SICOT); FRSocMed (Pres. Orthopædic Sect., 1957–58); Fellow Brit. Orth. Assoc. *Publications*: History of the Royal National Orthopaedic Hospital, 1985; articles on orthopædic subjects, particularly tuberculosis and poliomyelitis in med. jls. *Address*: 14 Warren Fields, Valencia Road, Stanmore, Mddx. *T*: 01–954 6920.

CHOLMELEY, Sir Montague (John), 6th Bt *cr* 1806; Captain, Grenadier Guards; *b* 27 March 1935; *s* of 5th Bt and Cecilia, *er d* of W. H. Ellice; *S* father, 1964; *m* 1960, Juliet Auriol Sally Nelson; one *s* two *d. Educ*: Eton. Grenadier Guards, 1954–64. *Heir: s* Hugh John Frederick Sebastian Cholmeley, *b* 3 Jan. 1968. *Address*: Church Farm, Burton le Coggles, Grantham, Lincs. *T*: Corby Glen 329. *Clubs*: White's, Cavalry and Guards.

CHOLMONDELEY, family name of **Marquess of Cholmondeley,** and of **Baron Delamere.**

CHOLMONDELEY, 6th Marquess of, *cr* 1815; **George Hugh Cholmondeley,** GCVO 1977; MC 1943; DL; Bt 1611; Viscount Cholmondeley, 1661; Baron Cholmondeley of Namptwich (Eng.), 1689; Earl of Cholmondeley, Viscount Malpas, 1706; Baron Newborough (Ire.), 1715; Baron Newburgh (Gt Brit.), 1716; Earl of Rocksavage, 1815; late Grenadier Guards; Lord Great Chamberlain of England since 1966; *b* 24 April 1919; *e s* of 5th Marquess of Cholmondeley, GCVO, and Sybil (CBE 1946), *d* of Sir Edward Albert Sassoon, 2nd Bt; *S* father, 1968; *m* 1947, Lavinia Margaret, *d* of late Colonel John Leslie, DSO, MC; one *s* three *d. Educ*: Eton; Cambridge Univ. Served War of 1939–45: 1st Royal Dragoons, in MEF, Italy, France, Germany (MC). Retd hon. rank Major, 1949. DL Chester, 1955. *Heir: s* Earl of Rocksavage, *qv. Address*: Cholmondeley Castle, Malpas, Cheshire. *T*: Cholmondeley 202. *Clubs*: Turf, White's.

CHOLMONDELEY CLARKE, Marshal Butler; Master of the Supreme Court of Judicature (Chancery Division), since 1973; *b* 14 July 1919; *s* of Major Cecil Cholmondeley Clarke and Fanny Ethel Carter; *m* 1947, Joan Roberta Stephens; two *s. Educ*: Aldenham. Admitted a solicitor, 1943; Partner, Burton Yeates & Hart, Solicitors, London, WC2, 1946–72. Pres., City of Westminster Law Soc., 1971–72; Mem. Council, Law Soc., 1966–72; Chm., Family Law Cttee, 1970–72; Chm., Legal Aid Cttee, 1972; Chancery

Procedure Cttee, 1968–72; Ecclesiastical Examiner, Dio. London; Trustee, United Law Clerks' Soc.; Mem. Council, Inc. Soc. The Church Lads' and Girls' Brigade. *Publication*: The Supreme Court Practice (Chancery ed.), 1985. *Recreation*: reading. *Address*: 16 Cheyne Court, SW3 5TP. *Club*: Turf.

CHOMSKY, Prof. (Avram) Noam, PhD; Institute Professor, Massachusetts Institute of Technology, since 1976 (Ferrari P. Ward Professor of Modern Languages and Linguistics, 1966–76); *b* Philadelphia, 7 Dec. 1928; *s* of late William Chomsky and of Elsie Simonofsky; *m* 1949, Carol Doris Schatz; one *s* two *d. Educ*: Central High Sch., Philadelphia; Univ. of Pennsylvania (PhD); Society of Fellows, Harvard, 1951–55. Massachusetts Institute of Technology: Asst Prof., 1955–58; Associate Prof., 1958–61; Prof. of Modern Langs, 1961–66. Res. Fellow, Harvard Cognitive Studies Center, 1964–65. Vis. Prof., Columbia Univ., 1957–58; Nat. Sci. Foundn Fellow, Inst. for Advanced Study, Princeton, 1958–59; Linguistics Soc. of America Prof., Univ. of Calif, LA, 1966; Beckman Prof., Univ. of Calif, Berkeley, 1966–67; Vis. Watson Prof., Syracuse Univ., 1982; Lectures: Shearman, UCL, 1969; John Locke, Oxford, 1969; Bertrand Russell Meml, Cambridge 1971; Nehru Meml, New Delhi, 1972; Whidden, McMaster Univ., 1975; Huizinga Meml, Leiden, 1977; Woodbridge, Columbia, 1978; Kant, Stanford, 1979. Member: Nat. Acad. of Scis; Amer. Acad. of Arts and Scis; Linguistic Soc. of America; Amer. Philosophical Assoc.; Bertrand Russell Peace Foundn; Utrecht Soc. of Arts and Scis; Deutsche Akademie der Naturforscher Leopoldina; Aristotelian Soc., GB; Corresp. Mem., British Acad., 1974. Fellow, Amer. Assoc. for Advancement of Science. Mem., Council, Internat. Confedn for Disarmament and Peace, 1967. Hon. FBPsS; Hon. DLitt: London, 1967; Visva-Bharati, West Bengal, 1980; Hon. DHL: Chicago, 1967; Loyola Univ., Chicago, 1970; Swarthmore Coll., 1970; Bard Coll., 1971; Delhi, 1972; Massachusetts, 1973; Pennsylvania, 1985. Distinguished Scientific Contribution Award, Amer. Psychological Assoc., 1984. *Publications*: Syntactic Structures, 1957; Current Issues in Linguistic Theory, 1964; Aspects of the Theory of Syntax, 1965; Cartesian Linguistics, 1966; Topics in the Theory of Generative Grammar, 1966; Language and Mind, 1968; (with Morris Halle) Sound Pattern of English, 1968; American Power and the New Mandarins, 1969; At War with Asia, 1970; Problems of Knowledge and Freedom, 1971; Studies on Semantics in Generative Grammar, 1972; For Reasons of State, 1973; The Backroom Boys, 1973; Peace in the Middle East?, 1974; (with Edward Herman) Bains de Sang, 1974; Reflections on Language, 1975; The Logical Structure of Linguistic Theory, 1975; Essays on Form and Interpretation, 1977; Human Rights and American Foreign Policy, 1978; Language and Responsibility, 1979; (with Edward Herman) Political Economy of Human Rights, 1979; Rules and Representations, 1980; Radical Priorities, 1981; Lectures on Government and Binding, 1981; Towards a New Cold War, 1982; Some Concepts and Consequences of the Theory of Government and Binding, 1982; Fateful Triangle: the United States, Israel and the Palestinians, 1983; Modular Approaches to the Study of the Mind, 1984; Knowledge of Language: its nature, origin, and use, 1985; Turning the Tide, 1985; Barriers, 1986. *Recreation*: gardening. *Address*: Department of Linguistics and Philosophy, Massachusetts Institute of Technology, 20D-219, 77 Massachusetts Avenue, Cambridge, Mass 02139, USA. *T*: 617–253–7819.

CHOPE, Christopher Robert, OBE 1982; barrister; MP (C) Southampton Itchen, since 1983; Parliamentary Under-Secretary of State Department of the Environment, since 1986; *b* 19 May 1947; *s* of His Honour Robert Charles Chope, *qv. Educ*: St Andrew's Sch., Eastbourne; Marlborough Coll.; St Andrews Univ. (LLB Hons). Called to the Bar, Inner Temple, 1972. Mem., Wandsworth Borough Council, 1974–83; Chm., Housing Cttee, 1978–79; Leader of Council, 1979–83. PPS to Minister of State, HM Treasury, 1986–. Jt Sec., Cons. Backbench Environment Cttee, 1983–86; Mem., Select Cttee on Procedure, 1984–86. Mem. Exec. Cttee, Soc. of Cons. Lawyers, 1983–86. *Address*: 12 King's Bench Walk, Temple, EC4. *T*: 01–353 5892. *Clubs*: Roehampton; Royal Southampton Yacht; Hampshire CC; Bisterne Conservative.

CHOPE, His Honour Robert Charles; a Circuit Judge (formerly Judge of County Courts), 1965–85; *b* 26 June 1913; *s* of Leonard Augustine and Ida Florence Chope; *m* 1946, Pamela Durell; one *s* two *d. Educ*: St Paul's Sch.; University Coll., London (BA Hons 1st Cl.) Called to Bar, Inner Temple, 1938. Served Royal Artillery, 1939–45 (Hon. Captain). Dep. Chm., Cornwall QS, 1966–71. *Address*: Carclew House, Perranarworthal, Truro, Cornwall; 12 King's Bench Walk, Temple, EC4.
See also C. R. Chope.

CHORLEY, family name of **Baron Chorley.**

CHORLEY, 2nd Baron *cr* 1945, of Kendal; **Roger Richard Edward Chorley,** FCA; Partner in Coopers & Lybrand, Chartered Accountants, since 1967; *b* 14 Aug. 1930; *er s* of 1st Baron Chorley, QC, and Katharine Campbell (*d* 1986), *d* of late Edward Hopkinson, DSc; *S* father, 1978; *m* 1964, Ann, *d* of late A. S. Debenham; two *s. Educ*: Stowe Sch.; Gonville and Caius Coll., Cambridge (BA). Pres., CU Mountaineering Club. Expedns to Himalayas, 1954 (Rakaposhi), 1957 (Nepal); joined Cooper Brothers & Co. (later Coopers & Lybrand), 1955; New York office, 1959–60; Pakistan (Indus Basin Project), 1961; Hon. Sec., Climbers Club, 1963–67; seconded to Nat. Bd for Prices and Incomes as accounting adviser, 1965–68; Mem. Management Cttee, Mount Everest Foundn, 1968–70; Visiting Prof., Dept of Management Sciences, Imperial Coll. of Science and Technology, Univ. of London, 1979–82; Member: Finance Cttee, National Trust, 1970–; Royal Commn on the Press, 1974–77; Finance Act 1960 Tribunal, 1974–79; Ordnance Survey Rev. Cttee, 1978–79; British Council Rev. Cttee, 1979–80; Nat. Theatre Bd, 1980–; Top Salaries Review Body, 1981–; Bd, British Council, 1981–; Ordnance Survey Adv. Bd, 1983–85; Council, City and Guilds of London Inst.; Council, RGS, 1984– (Vice-Pres., 1986–). Chm., Cttee into Handling of Geographic Information, 1985–. Pres., Alpine Club, 1983–85. *Recreation*: mountains. *Heir: s* Hon. Nicholas Rupert Debenham Chorley, *b* 15 July 1966. *Address*: House of Lords, SW1. *Clubs*: Reform, Alpine.

CHORLEY, (Charles) Harold, CB 1959; Second Parliamentary Counsel, 1968–69; *b* 10 June 1912; *o s* of late Arthur R. Chorley; *m* 1941, Audrey (*d* 1980), *d* of R. V. C. Ash, MC; two *d. Educ*: Radley; Trinity Coll., Oxford. Called to Bar (Inner Temple), 1934. Joined Office of Parliamentary Counsel, 1938; one of the Parliamentary Counsel, 1950–68. *Address*: Paddock Wood, Tisbury, Salisbury, Wilts. *T*: Tisbury 870325.

CHORLEY, Francis Kenneth, CBE 1982; FEng, FIEE, FIERE; A Deputy Chief Executive, The Plessey Co. plc, since 1983 (Director, since 1978); Executive Chairman, Plessey Telecommunications & Office Systems Ltd, since 1983; *b* 29 July 1926; *s* of late Francis Henry Chorley and Eva Ellen Chorley; *m* 1954, Lorna Stella Brooks; two *s. Educ*: Rutlish Sch., Merton. With Plessey Co., 1951–60; Tech. Dir, Epsylon Industries, 1960–63; GEC Electronics: Divl Manager, Communications Div., 1963–64; Man. Dir, GEC-AEI Electronics Ltd, 1964–65; Dir and Gen. Manager, Transmission Div., GEC-AEI Telecommunications Ltd, 1965–74; Man. Dir, Plessey Avionics and Communications Div., 1974–78; Man. Dir, 1976–83, Dep. Chm., 1978–83, Plessey Electronic Systems Ltd; Chm., Plessey Avionics & Communications Ltd, 1978–83. Mem., Engineering Council, 1986–. Vice-President: TEMA, 1986–; IERE, 1986–. Prince Philip Medal, CGLI, 1983. *Recreations*: photography, music, sailing. *Address*: The Plessey Co. plc, Millbank Tower,

21–24 Millbank, SW1 4QP. *T:* 01–834 3855. *Clubs:* Royal Automobile, East India; Royal Air Force Yacht.

CHORLEY, Harold; *see* Chorley, C. H.

CHORLEY, Prof. Richard John; Professor of Geography, University of Cambridge, since 1974; *b* 4 Sept. 1927; *s* of Walter Joseph Chorley and Ellen Mary Chorley; *m* 1965, Rosemary Joan Macdonald More; one *s* one *d.* *Educ:* Minehead Grammar Sch.; Exeter Coll., Oxford. MA (Oxon), ScD (Cantab). Lieut, RE, 1946–48. Fulbright Schol., Columbia Univ., 1951–52; Instructor: in Geography, Columbia Univ., 1952–54; in Geology, Brown Univ., 1954–57; Cambridge Univ.: Demonstrator in Geography, 1958–62; Lectr in Geography, 1962–70, Reader, 1970–74. British rep. on Commn on Quantitative Techniques of Internat. Geographical Union, 1964–68; Dir, Madingley Geog. Courses, 1963–. First Hon. Life Mem., British Geomorphological Res. Gp, 1974. Gill Meml Medal, RGS, 1967; Hons Award, Assoc. of Amer. Geographers, 1981; David Linton Award, 1984. *Publications:* co-author of: The History of the Study of Landforms, Vols I and II, 1964, 1973; Atmosphere, Weather and Climate, 1968; Network Analysis in Geography, 1969; Physical Geography, 1971; Environmental Systems, 1978; Geomorphology, 1984; co-editor of: Frontiers in Geographical Teaching, 1965; Models in Geography, 1967; editor of: Water, Earth and Man, 1969; Spatial Analysis in Geomorphology, 1972; Directions in Geography, 1973; contribs to: Jl of Geology, Amer. Jl of Science, Bulletin of Geolog. Soc. of Amer., Geog. Jl, Geol. Magazine, Inst. of Brit. Geographers, etc. *Recreations:* gardening, theatre. *Address:* 76 Grantchester Meadows, Newnham, Cambridge CB3 9JL.

CHOUFFOT, Geoffrey Charles, CBE 1983 (MBE 1965); Deputy Chairman, Civil Aviation Authority, 1980–83, retired; *m* 1941, June Catherine, *d* of Rev. W. Peebles Fleming; one *s* two *d.* Group Director, Safety Services, Civil Aviation Authority, 1978–80. *Address:* Blundells, Singleton, W Sussex PO18 0EX. *Club:* Royal Air Force.

CHOWDHURY, Abu Sayeed; President of Bangladesh, 12 Jan. 1972-24 Dec. 1973; unanimously elected President of People's Republic of Bangladesh from April 1973, for five year term, resigned December 1973; Member, United Nations Sub-Commission on Prevention of Discrimination and Protection of Minorities, since 1978, re-elected 1981, 1983 (Chairman, Working Group on Slavery Practices, since 1978); *b* 31 Jan. 1921; *s* of late Abdul Hamid Chowdhury (formerly Speaker, the then East Pakistan Assembly); *m* 1948, Khurshid Chowdhury; two *s* one *d.* *Educ:* Presidency Coll.; Calcutta Univ. (MA, BL). Called to the Bar, Lincoln's Inn, 1947. Gen.-Sec., Presidency Coll. Union, 1941–42; Pres. British Br. of All India Muslim Students' Fedn, 1946. Mem., Pakistan Delegn to Gen. Assembly of the UN, 1959; Advocate-Gen., E Pakistan, 1960; Mem., Constitution Commn, 1960–61; Judge, Dacca High Court, July 1961–72; Chm., Central Bd for Develt of Bengali, 1963–68; Leader, Pakistan Delegn to World Assembly of Judges and 4th World Conf. on World Peace through Law, Sept. 1969; Vice-Chancellor, Dacca Univ., Nov., 1969–72, in addition to duties of Judge of Dacca High Court; Mem., UN Commn on Human Rights, 1971, 1982 and 1986– (Chm., 1985–86); Special Rep. for Govt of Bangladesh, designated by Bangladesh Govt as High Comr for UK and N Ireland, 1971, and Head of the Bangladesh Missions at London and New York, April 1971–11 Jan. 1972; Chancellor, all Bangladesh Univs, 1972–73. Special Rep. of Bangladesh, 1973–75; Leader, Bangladesh Delegns: Conf. on Humanitarian Law, Geneva, 1974, 1975 (Chm., Drafting Cttee); World Health Assemblies, Geneva, 1974, 1975; Internat. Labour Confs, Geneva, 1974, 1975 (Chm., Human Resources Cttee); Confs on Law of the Sea, Caracas, 1974, Geneva, 1975; Gen. Conf. Internat. Atomic Energy Agency, Vienna, 1974; UN Special Session, Sept. 1975, NY; 30th Session of Gen. Assembly, UN, 1975; Conf. of IOC, Jeddah, 1975; led goodwill missions to: Saudi Arabia, Egypt, Syria, Lebanon and Algeria, 1974; Turkey, 1975; Japan, 1984. Vis. Prof., Franklin Pierce Law Center, USA, 1983. Hon. Fellow, Open Univ., 1977. Hon. Deshikottama Viswabharati (Shantiniketan), India, 1972; Hon. LLD Calcutta, 1972. *Recreations:* reading, gardening. *Address:* Rosendale, 103 Mymensingh Road, Dhaka-2, Bangladesh. *T:* 402424. *Clubs:* Athenæum, Royal Over-Seas League, Royal Commonwealth Society; (Hon.) Rotarian, Rotary (Dacca).

CHRÉTIEN, Hon. Jean, PC (Canada); QC; Counsel with Lang, Michener, Cranston, Farquharson and Wright; *b* 11 Jan. 1934; *s* of Wellie Chrétien and Marie Boisvert Chrétien; *m* 1957, Aline Chaine; two *s* one *d.* *Educ:* Trois-Rivières; Joliette; Shawinigan; Laval Univ. (BA, LLL). Called to the Bar, and entered Shawinigan law firm of Chrétien, Landry, Deschênes, Trudel and Normand, 1958; Director: Shawinigan Sen. Chamber of Commerce, 1962; Bar of Trois-Rivières, 1962–63. Govt of Canada: MP (L) St Maurice, 1963–86; Parly Sec. to Prime Minister, 1965, and to Minister of Finance, 1966; Minister of State, 1967; Minister of National Revenue, Jan. 1968; Minister of Indian and Northern Affairs, July 1968; Pres., Treasury Bd, 1974; Minister of Industry, Trade and Commerce, 1976; Minister of Finance, 1977–79; Minister of Justice, responsible for constitutional negotiations, Attorney General, Minister of State for Social Develt, 1980–82; Minister of Energy, 1982–84; Deputy Prime Minister and External Affairs Minister, 1984. *Recreations:* skiing, fishing, golf. *Address:* 50 O'Connor Street, Suite 1600, Ottawa, Ont K1P 6L2, Canada.

CHRIMES, Henry Bertram, DL; Chairman, Liverpool Daily Post and Echo Ltd, 1976–85; *b* 11 March 1915; *s* of Sir Bertram Chrimes, CBE, and Mary (*née* Holder); *m* 1946, Suzanne, *d* of W. S. Corbett-Lowe, Sodylt Hall, Ellesmere; one *s* three *d.* *Educ:* Oundle; Clare Coll., Cambridge. Served War of 1939–45: RA, India and Burma, Bde Major (despatches). Cooper & Co.'s Stores Ltd, 1945–60 (Man. Dir, 1954–60); Ocean Transport & Trading Ltd, 1960–85 (Dep. Chm., 1971–75); Liverpool Daily Post & Echo Ltd, 1963–85; Member, Liverpool Bd, Barclays Bank Ltd, 1972–83. Member: Council, Univ. of Liverpool, 1951– (Pres., 1975–; Pro-Chancellor, 1981–Nov. 1987); Univ. Authorities Panel, 1976–; Dir, Univs Superannuation Scheme Ltd, 1980–85; Vice-Pres., Liverpool Sch. of Tropical Medicine, 1981–; Mem., 1951–, Vice-Pres., 1973–, Liverpool Council of Social Service (Chm., 1964–70); President: Merseyside Pre-Retirement Assoc., 1977–; Royal Liverpool Seamen's Orphan Instn, 1980–. DL 1974, High Sheriff 1978–79, Merseyside. *Recreations:* books, bees, gardening. *Address:* Bracken Bank, Heswall, Merseyside L60 4RP. *T:* 051–342 2397. *Club:* Reform.

CHRIST CHURCH, Dublin, Dean of; *see* Salmon, Very Rev. T. N. D. C.

CHRIST CHURCH, Oxford, Dean of; *see* Heaton, Very Rev. E. W.

CHRISTCHURCH, Bishop of, since 1984; **Rt. Rev. Maurice John Goodall,** MBE 1974; *b* 31 March 1928; *s* of John and Alice Maud Goodall; *m* 1st 1953, Nathalie Ruth Cummack; two *s* four *d*; *m* 2nd 1981, Beverley Doreen Moore. *Educ:* Christchurch Technical Coll.; College House, Univ. of NZ (BA 1950); Univ. of Canterbury LTh 1964; Dip. Social Work (Distinction) 1977; CQSW 1982. Asst Curate, St Albans, Dio. of Christchurch, 1951–54; Vicar of: Waikari, 1954–59; Shirley, 1959–67; Hon. Asst, Christchurch, St John's 1967–69; Chaplain, Kingslea Girls' Training Centre, 1967–69; City Missioner (dio. Christchurch), 1969–76; Nuffield Bursary, 1973; Dir, Community Mental Health Team, 1976–82; Dean of Christchurch Cathedral, 1982–84. *Publications:* (with Colin Clark) Worship for Today, 1967; (contrib.) Christian Responsiblity in Society (ed Yule), 1977; contribs to journals. *Recreations:* walking, reading, NZ history. *Address:* PO Box 800, Bishop's House, 80 Bealey Avenue, Christchurch, New Zealand. *T:* 62–653.

CHRISTENSEN, Eric Herbert, CMG 1968; Chairman, Victrose Holdings (Channel Islands) Ltd, since 1985; Director: Seagull Cold Stores, since 1980; Gambia Oil Company Ltd, since 1985; *b* 29 Oct. 1923; *s* of George Vilhelm Christensen and Rose Fleury; *m* 1951, Diana, *d* of Rev. J. Dixon-Baker; four *s* three *d.* Teacher, St Augustine's Sec. Sch., Bathurst, 1941–43; Military Service, W African Air Corps (RAF), Bathurst, 1944–45; Clerk, The Secretariat, Bathurst, 1946–47; Head of Chancery, then Vice-Consul, French Consulate, Bathurst, 1947–60; acted as Consul on several occasions; Attaché, Senegalese Consulate-Gen., Bathurst, 1961–65, acted as Consul-Gen. on several occasions; Asst Sec. (Ext. Affairs), Gambia Govt, 1965; Principal Asst Sec., Prime Minister's Office, Bathurst, 1966–67; Sec.-Gen., President's Office, Perm. Sec., Min. of External Affairs, and Sec. to the Cabinet, The Gambia, 1967–78; also Hd, Public Service, 1967–78. Foreign decorations include: Grand Officer, Order of the Brilliant Star of China (Taiwan), 1966; Officer, Order of Merit of Islamic Republic of Mauritania, 1967; Knight Commander's Cross, Badge and Star, Order of Merit of Federal Republic of Germany, 1968; Order of Republic of Nigeria, 1970; Grand Officer, National Order of Republic of The Gambia, 1970; Order of Diplomatic Merit, Republic of Korea, 1970, and also those from Egypt, Republic of Guinea and Republic of Liberia; Comdr, Nat. Order of the Lion, Senegal, 1972; Chevalier de la Légion d'Honneur, 1975. *Recreations:* reading, photography, philately, chess. *Address:* Sir Dawda Kairaba Jawara Avenue, Kombo St Mary, The Gambia. *T:* Serekunda 2222.

CHRISTENSEN, Jens; Commander First Class, Order of the Dannebrog; Hon. GCVO; Ambassador of Denmark to Austria, since 1984; *b* 30 July 1921; *s* of Christian Christensen and Sophie Dorthea Christensen; *m* 1st, 1950, Tove (*née* Jessen) (*d* 1982); one *s* two *d*; 2nd, 1983, Vibeke Pagh. *Educ:* Copenhagen Univ. (MPolSc 1945). Joined Danish Foreign Service, 1945; Head of Section, Econ. Secretariat of Govt, 1947; Sec. to OECD Delegn in Paris, 1949 and to NATO Delegn, 1952; Hd of Sect., Min. of Foreign Affairs, 1952, Actg Hd of Div., 1954; Chargé d'Affaires *a.i.* and Counsellor of Legation, Vienna, 1957; Asst Hd of Econ.-Polit. Dept, Min. of For. Affairs, 1960; Dep. Under-Sec., 1961; Under-Sec. and Hd of Econ.-Polit. Dept, 1964–71; Hd of Secretariat for Europ. Integration, 1966; Ambassador Extraord. and Plenipotentiary, 1967; State Sec. for Foreign Econ. Affairs, 1971; Ambassador of Denmark to the Court of St James's, 1977–81; Pres., Danish Oil and Natural Gas Co., 1980–84. Governor for Denmark, The Asian Development Bank, 1967–73. Knight Grand Cross: Order of Icelandic Falcon; Order of Northern Star, Sweden; Order of St Olav, Norway; Royal Victorian Order. *Address:* Danish Embassy, Führichgasse 6, 1010 Vienna, Austria.

CHRISTIAN, Clifford Stuart, CMG 1971; consultant in environmental matters; *b* 19 Dec. 1907; *s* of Thomas William and Lily Elizabeth Christian; *m* 1933, Agnes Robinson; four *d.* *Educ:* Univ. of Queensland (BScAgr); Univ. of Minnesota (MS). Officer-in-charge: Northern Australia Regional Survey Section, 1946–50; Land Research and Regional Survey Section, CSIRO, 1950–57; Chief, Div. of Land Research, CSIRO, 1957–60; Mem. Executive, CSIRO, 1960–72. Adviser, Ranger Uranium Environmental Inquiry, 1975–76. Farrer Memorial Medal, 1969. FAIAS; FWA; Fellow, Aust. Acad. of Technological Sciences. Hon. DScAgr Queensland, 1978. *Publications:* A Review Report, Alligator Rivers Study (with J. Aldrick), 1977; chapter contribs to books; articles in various pubns mainly concerning natural resources. *Recreation:* photography. *Address:* 6 Baudin Street, Forrest, ACT 2603, Australia. *T:* 062 952495. *Club:* Commonwealth (Canberra).

CHRISTIAN, Prof. John Wyrill, FRS 1975; Professor of Physical Metallurgy, Oxford University, since 1967; Fellow of St Edmund Hall, Oxford, since 1963; *b* 9 April 1926; *e s* of John Christian and Louisa Christian (*née* Crawford); *m* 1949, Maureen Lena Smith; two *s* one *d.* *Educ:* Scarborough Boys' High Sch.; The Queen's Coll., Oxford. BA 1946, DPhil 1949, MA 1950. Pressed Steel Co. Ltd Research Fellow, Oxford University, 1951–55; Lectr in Metallurgy, 1955–58; George Kelley Reader in Metallurgy, 1958–67. Visiting Prof.: Univ. of Illinois, 1959; Case Inst. of Technology, USA, 1962–63; MIT and Stanford Univ., 1971–72. Lectures: Williams, MIT, 1971; Hume-Rothery Meml, 1976; Inst. of Metals, AIME, 1981; Campbell Meml, ASM, 1982. Rosenhain medallist of Inst. of Metals, 1969; Mehl Medallist of AIME, 1981; Platinum Medallist of Metals Soc., 1984; Gold Medallist Acta Metallurgica, 1984. Editor: Progress in Materials Science, 1970–; Jl Less Common Metals, 1976–85. *Publications:* Metallurgical Equilibrium Diagrams (with others), 1952; The Theory of Transformations in Metals and Alloys, 1965, 2nd rev. edn, 1975; contribs to scientific jls. *Address:* 11 Charlbury Road, Oxford OX2 6UT. *T:* Oxford 58569.

CHRISTIAN, Prof. Reginald Frank; Professor of Russian, St Andrews University, since 1966; *b* Liverpool, 9 Aug. 1924; *s* of late H. A. Christian and late Jessie Gower (*née* Scott); *m* 1952, Rosalind Iris Napier; one *s* one *d.* *Educ:* Liverpool Inst.; Queen's Coll., Oxford (Open Scholar; MA). Hon. Mods Class. (Oxon), 1943; 1st cl. hons Russian (Oxon), 1949. Commnd RAF, 1944; flying with Atlantic Ferry Unit and 231 Sqdn, 1943–46. FO, British Embassy, Moscow, 1949–50; Lectr and Head of Russian Dept, Liverpool Univ., 1950–55; Sen. Lectr and Head of Russian Dept, Birmingham Univ., 1956–63; Vis. Prof. of Russian, McGill Univ., Canada, 1961–62; Prof. of Russian, Birmingham Univ., 1963–66; Exchange Lectr, Moscow, 1964–65. Mem. Univ. Ct, 1971–73 and 1981–85, Associate Dean, Fac. of Arts, 1972–73, Dean, Fac. of Arts, 1975–78, St Andrews Univ. Pres., British Univs Assoc. of Slavists, 1967–70; Member: Internat. Cttee of Slavists, 1970–75; UGC Atkinson Cttee, 1978–81. *Publications:* Korolenko's Siberia, 1954; (with F. M. Borras) Russian Syntax, 1959, 2nd rev. edn, 1971; Tolstoy's War and Peace: a study, 1962; (with F. M. Borras) Russian Prose Composition, 1964, 2nd rev. edn, 1974; Tolstoy: a critical introduction, 1969; Tolstoy's Letters, 2 vols, 1978; Tolstoy's Diaries, 2 vols, 1985; numerous articles and reviews in Slavonic and E European Review, Slavonic and E European Jl, Mod. Languages Review, Survey, Forum, Birmingham Post, Times Lit. Supp., Oxford Slavonic Papers, etc. *Recreations:* fell-walking, violin. *Address:* The Roundel, St Andrews, Fife. *T:* St Andrews 73322; Scioncroft, Knockard Road, Pitlochry, Perthshire. *T:* Pitlochry 2993.

CHRISTIANSON, Alan, CBE 1971; MC 1945; Deputy Chairman, South of Scotland Electricity Board, 1967–72; retired; *b* 14 March 1909; *s* of Carl Robert Christianson; *m* 1936, Gladys Muriel Lewin, *d* of William Barker; two *d.* *Educ:* Royal Grammar Sch., Newcastle upon Tyne; FCA, CompIEE. Served as Major, RA, 1939–45: comd Field Battery, 1943–45. Central Electricity Bd, 1934–48; Divisional Sec., British Electricity Authority, SW Scotland Div., 1948–55; Dep. Sec., S of Scotland Electricity Bd, 1955–62; Chief Financial Officer, 1962–65; Gen. Man., Finance and Administration, 1965–67. *Recreation:* golf. *Address:* Tynedale, Lennox Drive East, Helensburgh, Dunbartonshire. *T:* Helensburgh 4503.

CHRISTIE, Ann Philippa; *see* Pearce, A. P.

CHRISTIE, Campbell; General Secretary, Scottish Trades Union Congress, since 1986; *b* 23 Aug. 1937; *s* of Thomas Christie and Johnina Rolling; *m* 1962, Elizabeth Brown

Cameron; two *s*. *Educ:* Albert Sen. Secondary Sch., Glasgow. Civil Service, 1954–72: Admiralty, 1954–59; DHSS, 1959–72; Society of Civil and Public Servants, 1972–85: Asst Sec., 1972–73; Asst Gen. Sec., 1973–75; Dep. Gen. Sec., 1975–85. *Address:* 31 Dumyat Drive, Falkirk, Stirlingshire FK1 5PA. *T:* Falkirk 24555.

CHRISTIE, Charles Henry; Visiting Professor, United States Naval Academy, Annapolis, 1986–Aug. 1987; Director of Studies, Britannia Royal Naval College, Dartmouth, 1978–86; *b* 1 Sept. 1924; *s* of late Lieut-Comdr C. P. Christie and Mrs C. S. Christie; *m* 1950, Naida Joan Bentley; one *s* three *d*. *Educ:* Westminster Sch. (King's Scholar); Trinity Coll., Cambridge (Exhibitioner). Served 1943–46, RNVR (despatches, 1945). Trinity Coll., Cambridge, 1946–49; Asst Master, Eton Coll., 1949–57; Under Master and Master of Queen's Scholars, Westminster Sch., 1957–63; Headmaster, Brighton Coll., 1963–71; Warden, St Edward's Sch., Oxford, 1971–78. Prime Warden, Dyers' Co., 1983–84. *Address:* c/o 28 Dorothy Road, SW11 2JP.

CHRISTIE, Sir George (William Langham), Kt 1984; DL; Chairman, Glyndebourne Productions Ltd; *b* 31 Dec. 1934; *o s* of John Christie, CH, MC, and Audrey Mildmay Christie; *m* 1958, Patricia Mary Nicholson; three *s* one *d*. *Educ:* Eton. Asst to Sec. of Calouste Gulbenkian Foundation, 1957–62. Chm. of Glyndebourne Productions, 1956–, and of other family companies. Founder Chm., The London Sinfonietta. DL E Sussex, 1983. *Address:* Glyndebourne, Lewes, E Sussex. *T:* Ringmer 812250.

CHRISTIE, Herbert; Director, Research Department, European Investment Bank, since 1983; *b* 26 Sept. 1933; *s* of Brig.-Gen. H. W. A. Christie, CB, CMG, and Mary Ann Christie; *m* 1982, Gilberte F. M. V. Desbois; one *s*. *Educ:* Methodist Coll., Belfast; Univ. of St Andrews (MA). Asst Lectr, Univ. of Leeds, 1958–60; Econ. Asst, HM Treasury, 1960–63; First Sec., Washington, DC, 1963–66; Econ. Adviser, J. Henry Schroder Wagg and Co. Ltd, 1966–71, with secondment as Econ. Adviser, NBPI, 1967–71; Sen. Econ. Adviser, Min. of Posts and Telecommunications, 1971–74, and Dept of Prices and Consumer Protection, 1974–76; Econ. Adviser, EEC Commn, Brussels, 1976–78; Under Sec., HM Treasury, 1978–83. *Publications:* contrib. to books and learned jls. *Recreations:* languages, foreign travel. *Address:* c/o European Investment Bank, 100 boulevard Konrad Adenauer, L2950 Luxembourg. *T:* Luxembourg 4379.

CHRISTIE, Prof. Ian Ralph, FBA 1977; Astor Professor of British History, University of London at University College, 1979–84, now Professor Emeritus; Hon. Research Fellow, University College London, since 1984; *b* 11 May 1919; *s* of John Reid Christie and Gladys Lilian (*née* Whatley). *Educ:* privately; Worcester Royal Grammar Sch.; Magdalen Coll., Oxford, 1938–40 and 1946–48 (MA). Served War, RAF, 1940–46. University Coll. London: Asst Lectr in Hist., 1948; Lectr, 1951; Reader, 1960; Prof. of Modern British History, 1966; Dean of Arts, 1971–73; Chm. History Dept, 1975–79. Ford Lectr, Oxford Univ., 1983–84. Jt Literary Dir, Royal Hist. Soc., 1964–70, Mem. Council, 1970–74. Mem. Editorial Bd, History of Parliament Trust, 1973–. *Publications:* The End of North's Ministry, 1780–1782, 1958; Wilkes, Wyvill and Reform, 1962; Crisis of Empire: Great Britain and the American Colonies, 1754–1783, 1966; (ed) Essays in Modern History selected from the Transactions of the Royal Historical Society, 1968; Myth and Reality in late Eighteenth-century British Politics, 1970; (ed) The Correspondence of Jeremy Bentham, vol. 3, 1971; (with B. W. Labaree) Empire or Independence, 1760–1776, 1976; (with Lucy M. Brown) Bibliography of British History, 1789–1851, 1977; Wars and Revolutions: Britain, 1760–1815, 1982; Stress and Stability in Late Eighteenth Century Britain: reflections on the British avoidance of revolution, 1984; contrib. to jls. *Recreation:* walking. *Address:* 10 Green Lane, Croxley Green, Herts. *T:* Rickmansworth 773008. *Club:* Royal Commonwealth Society.

CHRISTIE, John Arthur Kingsley; Under-Secretary, Ministry of Agriculture, Fisheries and Food, 1970–75; *b* 8 Feb. 1915; *s* of Harold Douglas Christie and Enid Marian (*née* Hall); *m* 1951, Enid Margaret (*née* Owen); one *s* two *d*. *Educ:* Rugby Sch.; Magdalen Coll., Oxford. BA (1st cl. Hon. Mods, 1st cl. Litt. Hum.). Asst Principal, Min. of Agriculture, 1937–41; Sub-Lt, RNVR, 1941–45; Asst Private Sec. to Lord President of the Council, 1945–47; Min. of Agriculture: Principal, 1947–52; Asst Sec., 1952–70. *Recreations:* music, travel. *Address:* Westfield, 16 Knole Road, Sevenoaks, Kent. *T:* Sevenoaks 451423.

CHRISTIE, John Belford Wilson, CBE 1981; Sheriff of Tayside, Central and Fife (formerly Perth and Angus) at Dundee, 1955–83; *b* 4 May 1914; *o s* of late J. A. Christie, Advocate, Edinburgh; *m* 1939, Christine Isobel Syme, *o d* of late Rev. J. T. Arnott; four *d*. *Educ:* Merchiston Castle Sch.; St John's Coll., Cambridge; Edinburgh Univ. Admitted to Faculty of Advocates, 1939. Served War of 1939–45, in RNVR, 1939–46. Sheriff-Substitute of Western Div. of Dumfries and Galloway, 1948–55. Mem., Parole Bd for Scotland, 1967–73; Mem., Queen's Coll. Council, Univ. of St Andrews, 1960–67; Mem. Univ. Court, 1967–75, and Hon. Lectr, Dept of Private Law, Univ. of Dundee. Hon.LLD Dundee, 1977. *Recreations:* curling, golf. *Address:* Annsmuir Farm, Ladybank, Fife. *T:* Ladybank 30480. *Clubs:* New (Edinburgh); Royal and Ancient (St Andrews).

CHRISTIE, John Rankin, CB 1978; Deputy Master and Comptroller of the Royal Mint, 1974–77; *b* 5 Jan. 1918; *s* of Robert Christie and Georgina (*née* Rankin); *m* 1941, Constance May, *d* of Henry Gracie; one *s* two *d*. *Educ:* Ormskirk Gram. Sch.; London Sch. of Economics. War Office, 1936–39; Min. of Supply, 1939; Royal Artillery, 1943–47; Min. of Supply, 1947; Admin. Staff Coll., 1949; Air Ministry, 1954; Private Sec. to Ministers of Supply, 1955–57; Asst Sec., 1957; British Defence Staffs, Washington, 1962–65; Under-Sec., Min. of Aviation, 1965–67, Min. of Technology, 1967–70, Min. of Aviation Supply, 1970–71; Asst Under-Sec. of State, MoD, 1971–74. *Recreations:* travel, bird-watching. *Address:* Twitten Cottage, East Hill, Oxted, Surrey. *T:* Oxted 3047.

CHRISTIE, Julie (Frances); actress; *b* 14 April 1940; *d* of Frank St John Christie and Rosemary Christie (*née* Ramsden). *Educ:* Convent; Brighton Coll. of Technology; Central Sch. of Speech and Drama. *Films:* Crooks Anonymous, 1962; The Fast Lady, 1962; Billy Liar, 1963; Darling, 1964 (Oscar, NY Film Critics Award, Br. Film Academy Award, etc); Young Cassidy, 1964; Dr Zhivago, 1965 (Donatello Award); Fahrenheit 451, 1966; Far from the Madding Crowd, 1966; Petulia, 1967; In Search of Gregory, 1969; The Go-Between, 1971; McCabe and Mrs Miller, 1972; Don't Look Now, 1973; Shampoo, 1974; Heaven Can Wait, 1978; Memoirs of a Survivor, 1981; The Animals Film, 1982; Return of the Soldier, 1982; Heat and Dust, 1983; The Gold Diggers, 1984. Motion Picture Laurel Award, Best Dramatic Actress, 1967; Motion Picture Herald Award, Best Dramatic Actress, 1967. *Address:* c/o ICM Ltd, 388–396 Oxford Street, W1.

CHRISTIE, Hon. Sir Vernon (Howard Colville), Kt 1972; Speaker of the Legislative Assembly, Victoria, 1967–73; MLA (L) for Ivanhoe, Victoria, 1955–73; *b* Manly, NSW, 17 Dec. 1909; *s* of C. Christie, Sydney; *m* 1936, Joyce, *d* of F. H. Hamlin; one *s* one *d*. Chm. Cttees, Legislative Assembly, 1956–61, 1965–68; Director: Australian Elizabethan Theatre Trust, 1969–78; Australian Ballet Foundn, 1969–84; Qld Ballet. Hon. Life Mem., Victoria Br., CPA. AASA; FCIS; AFAIM. *Recreations:* bowls, sailing, music, ballet and the arts, conservation, fly fishing. *Address:* Rothes, 51 Colburn Avenue, Victoria Point, Qld 4163, Australia. *Club:* Queensland (Brisbane).

CHRISTIE, Sir William, Kt 1975; MBE 1970; JP; Lord Mayor of Belfast, 1972–75; a Company Director; *b* 1 June 1913; *s* of Richard and Ellen Christie, Belfast; *m* 1935, Selina (*née* Pattison); one *s* two *d* (and one *s* decd). *Educ:* Ward Sch., Bangor, Northern Ireland. Belfast City Councillor, 1961; High Sheriff of Belfast, 1964–65; Deputy Lord Mayor, 1969; Alderman, 1973–77. JP Belfast, 1951; DL Belfast, 1977. Salvation Army Order of Distinguished Auxiliary Service, 1973. *Recreations:* travel, walking, boating, gardening.

CHRISTIE, William James; Sheriff of Tayside, Central and Fife at Kirkaldy, since 1979; *b* 1 Nov. 1932; *s* of William David Christie and Mrs Anne Christie; *m* 1957, Maeve Patricia Gallacher; three *s*. *Educ:* Holy Cross Acad., Edinburgh; Edinburgh Univ. LLB. Nat. Service, 1954–56; commnd Royal Scots. Private Practice, 1956–79. Mem. Council, Law Soc. of Scotland, 1975–79; President: Soc. of Procurators of Midlothian, 1977–79; Soc. of Solicitors in the Supreme Court, 1979. *Recreations:* music, reading, shooting. *Address:* Sheriff Court House, Whytescauseway, Kirkcaldy, Fife KY1 1XQ. *Club:* New (Edinburgh).

CHRISTISON, Gen. Sir (Alexander Frank) Philip, 4th Bt *cr* 1871; GBE 1948 (KBE 1944); CB 1943; DSO 1945; MC (and Bar); DL; *b* 17 Nov. 1893; 2nd *s* of Sir Alexander Christison, 2nd Bt, and Florence (*d* 1949), *d* of F. T. Elworthy; *S* half-brother, 1945; *m* 1st, 1916, Betty (*d* 1974), *d* of late Rt Rev. A. Mitchell, Bishop of Aberdeen and Orkney; (one *s* killed in action in Burma, 7 March 1942) two *d* (and one *d* decd); 2nd, 1974, Vida Wallace Smith, MBE. *Educ:* Edinburgh Academy; Oxford Univ. (BA); Hon. Fellow, University Coll., Oxford, 1973. 2nd Lieut Cameron Highlanders, 1914; Capt. 1915; Bt Major, 1930; Bt Lt-Col 1933; Lt-Col Duke of Wellington's Regt, 1937; Col 1938; comd Quetta Bde, 1938–40; Comdt Staff Coll., Quetta, 1940–41; Brig. Gen. Staff, 1941; Maj.-Gen. 1941; Lt-Gen. 1942; Gen. 1947; comd XXIII and XV Indian Corps, 1942–45; Temp. Comdr 14th Army, 1945; C-in-C, ALFSEA, 1945; Allied Comdr Netherland East Indies, 1945–46; GOC-in-C Northern Command, 1946; GOC-in-C Scottish Command and Governor of Edinburgh Castle, 1947–49; ADC Gen. to the King, 1947–49; retired pay, 1949. Col, The Duke of Wellington's Regt, 1947–57; Col, 10th Princess Mary's Own Gurkha Rifles, 1947–57; Hon. Col, 414 Coast Regt Royal Artillery, 1950–57. Dir, Cochran and Co. Ltd, 1951–66; Chm., Alban Timber Ltd, 1953–78. Fruit farmer, 1949–. President: Scottish Unionist Party, 1957–58, Army Cadet Force, Scotland; Earl Haig Fund; Vice-President: Burma Star Assoc.; Officers' Assoc.; Scottish Salmon Angling Fedn, 1969; Chm., Lodge Trust for Ornithology, 1969; Chm. and Pres., Clarsach Soc., 1947–. DL Roxburghshire, 1956. FSA Scot, 1957. Chinese Order of Cloud and Banner with Grand Cordon, 1949. Hon. Fellow, Mark Twain Soc., USA, 1977. *Publications:* Birds of Northern Baluchistan, 1940; Birds of Arakan (with Aubrey Buxton), 1946. *Heir:* none. *Recreations:* ornithology, Celtic languages, field sports. *Address:* The Croft, Melrose, Roxburghshire. *T:* Melrose 2456. *Club:* New (Edinburgh).

CHRISTMAS, Arthur Napier, BSc(Eng), CEng, FIEE, FRAeS; Chief Scientific Officer and Director of Materials Quality Assurance, Ministry of Defence, 1971–74, retired; *b* 16 May 1913; *s* of Ernest Napier and Florence Elizabeth Christmas; *m* 1940, Betty Margaret Christmas (*née* Bradbrook); one *s* one *d*. *Educ:* Holloway Sch.; Northampton Technical Coll., London (BSc (Hons)). BEAIRA, 1934–37; Post Office Research Station, 1937–46; Prin. Scientific Officer, Min. of Supply, 1946–51; Sec., British Washington Guided Missile Cttee, 1951–54; Sen. Prin. Scientific Officer, Armament Research and Develt Estabt, 1954–59; DCSO, 1959; Dir, Guided Weapons Research and Techniques, Min. of Aviation, 1959–62; Dir for Engrg Develt, European Launcher Develt Org., 1962–67; Prin. Supt, Royal Armament Research and Develt Estabt, 1967–71. *Recreations:* sailing, mountain walking, music. *Address:* Old Farm Cottage, Itchenor, Sussex. *T:* Birdham 512224. *Clubs:* Itchenor Sailing, Island Sailing.

CHRISTODOULOU, Anastasios, CBE 1978; Secretary-General, Association of Commonwealth Universities, since 1980; Joint Secretary, UK Commonwealth Scholarship Commission; *b* Cyprus, 1 May 1932; *s* of Christodoulos and Maria Haji Yianni; *m* 1955, Joan P. Edmunds; two *s* two *d*. *Educ:* St Marylebone Grammar Sch.; The Queen's Coll., Oxford (MA). Colonial Administrative Service, Tanganyika (Tanzania), 1956–62; served as District Commissioner and Magistrate. Univ. of Leeds Administration, 1963–68: Asst Registrar, 1963–65; Dep. Sec., 1965–68; Secretary, Open Univ., 1969–80. Vice-Chm., Commonwealth Inst., 1981–; Member: Exec. Cttee, Council for Educn in Commonwealth; Fulbright Commn; UKCOSA. Member, Court: Exeter Univ.; Hull Univ.; RCA. Hon. DUniv: Open, 1981; Athabasca, 1981. *Recreations:* sport, music, bridge; international and Commonwealth relations. *Address:* 22 Kensington Court Gardens, W8. *T:* 01–937 4626. *Clubs:* Athenæum, Royal Commonwealth Society.

CHRISTOFAS, Sir Kenneth (Cavendish), KCMG 1983 (CMG 1969); MBE 1944; HM Diplomatic Service, retired; *b* 18 Aug. 1917; *o s* of late Edward Julius Goodwin and of Lillian Christofas (*step-s* of late Alexander Christofas); *m* 1948, Jessica Laura (*née* Sparshott); two *d*. *Educ:* Merchant Taylors' Sch.; University Coll., London (Fellow, 1976). Served War of 1939–45 (MBE): commissioned in The Queen's Own Royal West Kent Regt, 1939; Adjt 1940; Staff Capt. 1941; DAAG 1942; Staff Coll., Quetta, 1944; AAG 1944; GSO1, War Office, 1946. Resigned from Army with Hon. rank of Lieut-Col and joined Sen. Br. of HM Foreign Service, 1948 (HM Diplomatic Service after 1965); served in Foreign Office, 1948–49 and 1951–55; Rio de Janeiro, 1949–51; Rome, 1955–59 and as Dep. Head of UK Delegn to European Communities, Brussels, 1959–61; seconded to CRO for service as Counsellor in the British High Commn, Lagos, 1961–64 and to Colonial Office as Head of Economic Dept, 1965–66; on sabbatical year at Univ. of London, 1964–65; Counsellor in Commonwealth Office, then in FCO, 1966–69; Minister and Dep. Head of UK Delegn to EEC, 1969–72 (acting Head, March-Oct. 1971); Cabinet Office, on secondment, 1972–73; Director General, Secretariat, Council of Ministers of the European Communities, 1973–82, Hon. Dir Gen. 1982–. Pres., Crabtree Foundn, 1985; Hon. Pres. UK Branch, Assoc. of Former Officials of European Communities, 1986–. Gold Medal, Eur. Parlt, 1982. Order of Polonia Restituta (Poland), 1944. *Recreations:* railways, music. *Address:* 3 The Ridge, Bolsover Road, Eastbourne, Sussex BN20 7JE. *T:* Eastbourne 22384. *Club:* East India, Devonshire, Sports and Public Schools.

CHRISTOFF, Boris; opera singer (bass); *b* Plovdiv, near Sofia, Bulgaria, 18 May 1919; *s* of Kyryl and Rayna Teodorova; *m* Franca, *d* of Raffaello de Rensis. *Educ:* Univ. of Sofia (Doctor of Law). Joined Gussla Choir and Sofia Cathedral Choir as soloist. Obtained scholarship, through King Boris III of Bulgaria, to study singing in Rome under Riccardo Stracciari; made concert début at St Cecilia Academy in Rome, 1946 and operatic début, 1946; Covent Garden début, 1950, as Boris Godunov and Philip II; subsequently has appeared at all leading European and American opera houses; American début, Metropolitan Opera House, 1950; as Boris Godunov, San Francisco, 1956. Principal rôles include: Boris Godunov, King Philip, Galitzky, Konchak, Don Quixote, Dositheus, Ivan the Terrible, Ivan Susanin, Mephistopheles, Moses, Don Basilio, Pizarro, Simon Boccanegra. Has made numerous recordings, including opera and songs, winning many prix du disque; these include particularly the complete lyric works of the five great Russian composers. Now making concert appearances. Hon. Mem. Théâtre de l'Opéra, Paris, Mem. La Scala, Milan. Holds foreign decorations. Commendatore della Repubblica Italiana. *Address:* Villa Leccio, Buggiano (PT), Italy.

CHRISTOPHER, Ann, ARA 1980; sculptor; *b* 4 Dec. 1947; *d* of William and Phyllis Christopher; *m* 1969, Kenneth Cook. *Educ:* Harrow School of Art (pre-Diploma); West of England College of Art (DipAD Sculpture). Prizewinner, Daily Telegraph Young Sculptors Competition, 1971; Arts Council grants, 1973–76. *Exhibitions include:* Oxford Gallery, Oxford, 1973, 1974, 1978; Festival Gall., Bath, 1973; London Group exhibns, 1975, 1977; Park Street Gall., Bristol, 1978, 1980; Royal Academy, Summer Exhibns, 1971–. *Work in Collections:* Bristol City Art Gallery; Contemporary Arts Soc.; Chantrey, London; Glynn Vivian Art Gall., Swansea. *Recreation:* cinema. *Address:* The Stable Block, Hay Street, Marshfield, near Chippenham, Wilts SN14 8PF.

CHRISTOPHER, Anthony Martin Grosvenor, CBE 1984; General Secretary, Inland Revenue Staff Federation, since 1976; *b* 25 April 1925; *s* of George Russell Christopher and Helen Kathleen Milford Christopher (*née* Rowley); *m* 1962, Adela Joy Thompson. *Educ:* Cheltenham Grammar Sch.; Westminster Coll. of Commerce. Articled Pupil, Agric. Valuers, Gloucester, 1941–44; RAF, 1944–48; Inland Revenue, 1948–57; Asst Sec. 1957–60, Asst Gen. Sec. 1960–74, Jt Gen. Sec. 1975, Inland Revenue Staff Fedn; Member: TUC General Council, 1976–; TUC Economic Cttee, 1977–; TUC Education Cttee, 1977–85; TUC Educn and Training Cttee, 1985–; TUC Employment Policy and Orgn Cttees, 1985–; TUC International Cttee, 1982–; TUC Finance and General Purposes Cttee, 1983–; TUC Media Working Group, 1979– (Chm., 1985–); TUC Employment Policy and Orgn Cttee, 1979–85. Member: Tax Reform Cttee, 1974–80; Tax Consultative Cttee, 1980–; Royal Commn on Distribution of Income and Wealth, 1978–79; IBA, 1978–83; Council, Inst. of Manpower Studies, 1984; ESRC, 1985–. Vice-Pres., Building Socs Assoc., 1985–; Director: Civil Service Building Soc., 1958– (Chm., 1978–); Trades Union Unit Trust, 1981– (Chm., 1983–); Policy Studies Inst. Council, 1983–; Member: Bd, Civil Service Housing Assoc., 1958–; Council, Nat. Assoc. for Care and Resettlement of Offenders, 1956– (Chm., 1973–); Home Sec.'s Adv. Council for Probation and After-care, 1967–77; Inner London Probation and After-care Cttee, 1966–79; Council, Save the Children Fund, 1985–; Chm., Alcoholics Recovery Project, 1970–76; Mem., Home Sec.'s Working Party on Treatment of Habitual Drunken Offenders, 1969–71. Trustee, Commonwealth Trades Union Council Charitable Trust, 1985–. Vis. Fellow, Univ. of Bath, 1981–; Mem. Council, Royal Holloway and Bedford New Coll., 1985–. *Publications:* (jtly) Policy for Poverty, 1970; (jtly) The Wealth Report, 1979; (jtly) The Wealth Report 2, 1982. *Recreations:* gardening, reading, music. *Address:* Douglas Houghton House, 231 Vauxhall Bridge Road, SW1V 1EH. *T:* 01–834 8254.

CHRISTOPHER, John Anthony, CB 1983; BSc; FRICS; Chief Valuer, Valuation Office, Inland Revenue, 1981–84, retired; *b* 19 June 1924; *s* of John William and Dorothy Christopher; *m* 1947, Pamela Evelyn Hardy; one *s* one *d* (and one *s* decd). *Educ:* Sir George Monoux Grammar Sch., Walthamstow; BSc Estate Management (London). Chartered Surveyor; LCC Valuation Dept, 1941. Served War, RAF, 1943–47. Joined Valuation Office, 1952; District Valuer and Valuation Officer, Lincoln, 1965; Superintending Valuer, Darlington, 1972; Asst Chief Valuer, 1974; Dep. Chief Valuer, Valuation Office, Inland Revenue, 1978. *Recreation:* golf. *Address:* 39 Digswell Road, Welwyn Garden City, Herts AL8 7PB. *T:* Welwyn Garden 335400.

CHRISTOPHERSEN, Henning; a Vice-President, Commission of the European Communities, since 1985; *b* Copenhagen, 8 Nov. 1939; *m* Jytte Christophersen; three *c.* *Educ:* Copenhagen University (Graduated in economics, 1965). Head, Economic Div., Danish Fedn of Crafts and Smaller Industries, 1965–70; economics reporter for periodical NB, 1970–71, for weekly Weekendavisen, 1971–78. MP (Liberal) for Hillerød, 1971–85; Nat. Auditor, 1976–78; Minister for Foreign Affairs, 1978–79; Pres., Liberal Party Parly Gp, 1979–82; Dep. Prime Minister and Minister for Finance, 1982–84. Mem., parly finance and budget cttee, 1972–76 (Vice-Chm., 1975); Chm., parly foreign affairs cttee, 1979–81; Mem., Nordic Council, 1981–82. Dep. Leader, Danish Liberal Party, Venstre, 1972–77; Political spokesman of Liberal MPs, 1973–78; Acting Leader, Liberal Party, 1977, Party Leader, 1978–84. Vice-Pres., Fedn of European Liberals and Democrats, 1980–84. *Address:* Commission of the European Communities, 200 Rue de la Loi, 1049 Brussels, Belgium.

CHRISTOPHERSON, Sir Derman (Guy), Kt 1969; OBE 1946; FRS 1960; FEng 1976; DPhil (Oxon) 1941; MICE, FIMechE; Master, Magdalene College, Cambridge, 1979–85; *b* 6 Sept. 1915; *s* of late Derman Christopherson, Clerk in Holy Orders, formerly of Blackheath, and Edith Frances Christopherson; *m* 1940, Frances Edith, *d* of late James and Martha Tearle; three *s* one *d.* *Educ:* Sherborne Sch.; University Coll., Oxford (Hon. Fellow, 1977). Henry Fellow at Harvard Univ., 1938; Scientific Officer, Research and Experiments Dept, Ministry of Home Security, 1941–45; Fellow, Magdalene Coll., Cambridge, 1945 (Hon. Fellow 1969), Bursar, 1947; University Demonstrator, Cambridge Univ. Engineering Dept, 1945, Lecturer, 1946; Professor of Mechanical Engineering, Leeds Univ., 1949–55; Prof. of Applied Science, Imperial Coll. of Science and Technology, 1955–60; Vice-Chancellor and Warden, Durham Univ., 1960–78. Mem. Council of Institution of Mechanical Engineers, 1950–53; Clayton Prize, Instn of Mechanical Engineers, 1963. Chairman: Cttee of Vice-Chancellors and Principals, 1967–70; Central Council for Educn and Training in Social Work, 1971–79; CNAA (Chm., Educn Cttee), 1966–74; Board of Washington New Town Develt Corp., 1964–78; Science Research Coun., 1965–70. Mem. Council, Royal Soc., 1975; Chm., Royal Fine Art Commn, 1980–85 (Mem., 1978). Fellow, Imperial Coll. of Science and Technology, 1966. Hon. DCL: Kent, 1966; Newcastle, 1971; Hon DSc: Aston, 1967; Sierra Leone, 1970; Cranfield Inst. of Technology, 1985; Hon. LLD: Leeds, 1969; Royal Univ. of Malta, 1969; DTech Brunel, 1979. *Publications:* The Engineer in The University, 1967; The University at Work, 1973; various papers in Proc. Royal Soc., Proc. IMechE, Jl of Applied Mechanics, etc. *Address:* 43 Lensfield Road, Cambridge CB2 1EN. *Club:* United Oxford & Cambridge University.

CHRISTOPHERSON, Harald Fairbairn, CMG 1978; a Senior Clerk, Committee Office, House of Lords; *b* 12 Jan. 1920; *s* of late Captain H. and Mrs L. G. L. Christopherson; *m* 1947, Joyce Winifred Emmett (*d* 1979); one *s* two *d.* *Educ:* Heaton Grammar Sch., Newcastle upon Tyne; King's Coll., Univ. of Durham (BSc and DipEd). Served in RA, 1941–46, Captain 1945. Teacher and lecturer in mathematics, 1947–48. Entered administrative class, Home CS, Customs and Excise, 1948; seconded to Trade and Tariffs Commn, W Indies, 1956–58; Asst Sec., 1959; seconded to Treasury, 1965–66; Under Sec., 1969; Comr of Customs and Excise, 1970–80; Sen. Clerk, Cttee Office, House of Commons, 1980–85. *Recreations:* music, travel. *Address:* 57a York Road, Sutton, Surrey SM2 6HN. *T:* 01–642 2444. *Club:* Reform.

CHRISTY, Ronald Kington, CB 1965; HM Chief Inspector of Factories, 1963–67; *b* 18 Aug. 1905; *s* of William and Edna Christy; *m* 1931, Ivy, *y d* of W. Hinchcliffe, Whitchurch, Salop; one *s* one *d.* *Educ:* Strand Sch.; King's Coll., Univ. of London. Appointed HM Inspector of Factories, 1930; HM Superintending Inspector of Factories, 1953–59; HM Dep. Chief Inspector of Factories, 1959–63. Mem., Nuclear Safety Advisory Cttee, 1963–67. *Recreations:* gardening, travelling. *Address:* The Garden, Thicket Road, Houghton, Huntingdon, Cambs PE17 2BQ. *T:* St Ives 301384.

CHUBB, family name of **Baron Hayter.**

CHUBB, Prof. Frederick Basil, MA, DPhil, LittD; Professor of Political Science, Dublin University, Trinity College, since 1960; *b* 8 Dec. 1921; *s* of late Frederick John Bailey Chubb and Gertrude May Chubb, Ludgershall, Wilts; *m* 1st, 1946, Margaret Gertrude Rafther (*d* 1984); no *c*; 2nd, 1985, Orla, *d* of Seán and Veronica Sheehan. *Educ:* Bishop Wordsworth's Sch., Salisbury; Merton Coll., Oxford. BA 1946; MA Oxon; MA Dublin; DPhil Oxon 1950; LittD Dublin 1976. Lecturer in Political Science, Trinity Coll., Dublin, 1948; Fellow in Polit. Sci., 1952; Reader in Polit. Sci., 1955; Bursar, 1957–62. Vice-Pres. Inst. of Public Administration, 1958; Chm., Comhairle na n-Ospidéal, 1972–78; Chm., Employer-Labour Conf., 1970; MRIA 1969. *Publications:* The Control of Public Expenditure, 1952; (with D. E. Butler (ed) and others) Elections Abroad, 1959; A Source Book of Irish Government, 1964, 2nd edn 1983; (ed with P. Lynch) Economic Development and Planning, 1969; The Government and Politics of Ireland, 1970, 2nd edn 1982; Cabinet Government in Ireland, 1974; The Constitution and Constitutional Change in Ireland, 1978; articles in learned jls. *Recreation:* fishing. *Address:* 19 Clyde Lane, Ballsbridge, Dublin 4. *T:* 684625.

CHUBB, John Oliver, CMG 1976; HM Diplomatic Service, retired; Counsellor, Foreign and Commonwealth Office, 1973–80; *b* 21 April 1920; *s* of Clifford Chubb and Margaret Chubb (*née* Hunt); *m* 1945, Mary Griselda Robertson (marr. diss. 1980); one *s* two *d.* *Educ:* Rugby; Oxford (MA). Served War, Scots Guards, 1940–46. Joined Diplomatic Service, 1946; Beirut, 1947; Bagdad, 1948–49; Canal Zone, 1950–52; Cyprus, 1953; FO, 1954–56; Tokyo, 1957–61; FO, 1961–63; Hong Kong, 1964–66; FO, 1967. Chm., St John's Wood Soc., 1978–83. *Recreations:* reading, spectator sports, golf, gardening, sailing. *Address:* Clayhill House, Clayhill, Beckley, near Rye, East Sussex TN31 6SQ. *T:* Northiam 2268. *Clubs:* Athenæum, MCC; Royal & Ancient Golf (St Andrews); Berkshire Golf, Rye Golf, Senior Golfers' Society.

CHUNG, Kyung-Wha, Korean Order of Merit; concert violinist; *b* 26 March 1948; *d* of Chun-Chai Chung and Won-Sook (Lee) Chung; *m*; one *s. Educ:* Juilliard Sch. of Music, New York. Moved from Korea to New York, 1960; 7 years' study with Ivan Galamian, 1960–67; New York début with New York Philharmonic Orch., 1967; European début with André Previn and London Symphony Orch., Royal Festival Hall, London, 1970. First prize, Leventritt Internat. Violin Competition, NY, 1967. *Address:* c/o 86 Hatton Garden, EC1.

CHUNG, Hon. Sir Sze-yuen, Kt 1978; CBE 1975 (OBE 1968); LLD; DSc; PhD; FEng, Hon. FIMechE, Hon. FHKIE, FIProdE; CBIM; JP; Senior Unofficial Member, Hong Kong Executive Council, since 1980 (Member, 1972–80); Chairman: Hong Kong Polytechnic, since 1972; City Polytechnic, since 1984; Standing Commission on Civil Service Salaries and Conditions of Service, since 1980; Sonca Industries Ltd, since 1978; *b* 3 Nov. 1917; *m* 1942, Nancy Cheung (*d* 1977); one *s* two *d. Educ:* Hong Kong Univ. (BScEng 1st Cl. Hons, 1941); Sheffield Univ. (PhD 1951). FEng 1983; FIMechE 1957, Hon. FIMechE 1983; Hon. FHKIE 1976; FIProdE 1958. CBIM (FBIM 1978). Consulting engr, 1952–56; Gen. Man., Sonca Industries, 1956–60, Man. Dir 1960–77. Dir of cos. Mem., Hong Kong Legislative Council, 1965–74, Sen. Unofficial Mem., 1974–78. Chairman: Hong Kong Productivity Council, 1974–76; Asian Product. Orgn, 1969–70; Hong Kong Industrial Design Council, 1969–75; Fedn of Hong Kong Industries, 1966–70 (Hon. Life Pres. 1974); Hong Kong Metrication Cttee, 1969–73; Hong Kong–Japan Business Co-operation Cttee, 1983–; Hong Kong–US Econ. Co-operation Cttee, 1984–. Pres., Engrg Soc. of Hong Kong, 1960–61. LLD (*hc*) Chinese Univ. of Hong Kong, 1983; DSc (*hc*) Hong Kong Univ., 1976. JP Hong Kong, 1964. Defence Medal, 1948; Silver Jubilee Medal, 1977; Gold Medal, Asian Productivity Orgn, 1980. Japanese Order of Sacred Treasure (3rd cl.), 1983. *Publications:* contrib. Proc. IMechE, Jl Iron and Steel Inst., and Jl Engrg Soc. of Hong Kong. *Recreations:* swimming, hiking, badminton, windsurfing. *Address:* House 25, Bella Vista, Silver Terrace Road, Clear Water Bay, Kowloon, Hong Kong. *T:* Hong Kong 3–213506, 3–7192857. *Clubs:* Les Ambassadeurs; Hong Kong, Royal Hong Kong Jockey, Kowloon Cricket (Hong Kong).

CHURCH, James Anthony; see Church, Tony.

CHURCH, John Carver, CMG 1986; MBE 1970; HM Diplomatic Service; Consul-General, Barcelona, since 1986; *b* 8 Dec. 1929; *s* of Richard Church, CBE, FRSL, and Catherina Church; *m* 1953, Marie-Geneviève Vallette; two *s* two *d. Educ:* Cranbrook Sch., Kent; Ecole Alsacienne, Paris; Christ's Coll., Cambridge (MA 1953). Reuters News Agency, 1953–59; Central Office of Information, 1959–61; Commonwealth Relations Office: Information Officer, Calcutta, 1961–65; Foreign and Commonwealth Office: Second Secretary (Commercial) Rio de Janeiro, 1966–69; First Sec. (Information) Tel Aviv, 1969–74; First Sec., News Dept, FCO, 1974–77; Consul (Commercial) Milan, 1977–78; Consul-Gen., São Paulo, 1978–81; Consul-Gen., Naples, 1981–86. *Recreations:* reading, swimming, skiing. *Address:* c/o Foreign and Commonwealth Office, SW1; 8 Bramshill Gardens, NW5 1JH. *T:* 01–272 6240.

CHURCH, Prof. Ronald James H.; see Harrison-Church.

CHURCH, Tony, (James Anthony Church); Director of Drama, Guildhall School of Music and Drama, since 1982; Associate Artist, Royal Shakespeare Company, since 1960; *b* 11 May 1930; *s* of Ronald Frederic and Margaret Fanny Church; *m* 1958, Margaret Ann Blakeney; one *s* two *d. Educ:* Hurstpierpoint Coll.; Clare Coll., Cambridge. MA 1954. First perf. as professional, Arts Theatre, London, 1953; frequent television, radio, regional theatre perfs; founder mem., RSC, 1960; roles there include: Henry IV; Polonius (twice); King Lear; John of Gaunt; Friar Laurence; Ulysses; Pandarus; York in Richard II; Trelawney in Maydays; Horsham in Waste. Toured USA extensively, 1974–; recorded 26 Shakespeare roles, 1956–66. Founder dir, Northcott Theatre, Exeter, 1967–71; Drama Advr, Hong Kong Govt, 1982–85; Member: Arts Council 1982–85 (Chm., Drama Panel, 1982–85); British Council Drama Cttee, 1985–. Hon. MA Exeter, 1971. *Recreations:* listening to music, narrowboats, travel. *Address:* Guildhall School of Music and Drama, Barbican, EC2Y 8DT. *T:* 01–628 2571; 38 Rosebery Road, N10 2LJ.

CHURCHER, Maj.-Gen. John Bryan, CB 1952; DSO 1944, Bar 1946; retired; Director and General Secretary, Independent Stores Association, 1959–71; *b* 2 Sept. 1905; *s* of late Lieut-Col B. T. Churcher, Wargrave, Berks, and Beatrice Theresa Churcher; *m* 1937, Rosamond Hildegarde Mary, *y d* of late Frederick Parkin, Truro Vean, Truro, Cornwall; one *s* two *d. Educ:* Wellington Coll., Berks; RMC Sandhurst. Commissioned DCLI, 1925; Lieut, 1927; Capt. KSLI, 1936; Staff Coll., 1939; served War of 1939–45 (despatches, DSO and Bar); commanded: 1 Bn Hereford Regt, 1942–44; 159 Inf. Bde, 1944–46; 43 Div., 1946; Northumbrian Dist., 1946; 2 Div., 1946; 3 Div., 1946–47; 5 Div., 1947–48; Brig., Imperial Defence Coll., 1948; BGS, Western Command, 1949–51; Chief of Staff, Southern Comd, 1951–54; GOC, 3rd Inf. Div., 1954–57; Dir of Military Training at the War Office, 1957–59; retired, 1959. ADC to King George VI, 1949–52; ADC to the Queen to 1952. *Address:* 34 Oaks Drive, Colchester, Essex CO3 3PS. *T:* Colchester 74525. *Club:* Army and Navy.

CHURCHHOUSE, Prof. Robert Francis, CBE 1982; PhD; Professor of Computing Mathematics, University College, Cardiff, since 1971; *b* 30 Dec. 1927; *s* of Robert Francis Churchhouse and Agnes Howard; *m* 1954, Julia McCarthy; three *s*. *Educ:* St Bede's Coll., Manchester; Manchester Univ. (BSc 1949); Trinity Hall, Cambridge (PhD 1952). Royal Naval Scientific Service, 1952–63; Head of Programming Gp, Atlas Computer Lab., SRC, 1963–71. Vis. Fellow, St Cross Coll., Oxford, 1972–. Chm., Computer Bd for Univs and Res. Councils, 1979–82. Pres., IMA, 1986–87. *Publications:* (ed jtly) Computers in Mathematical Research, 1968; (ed jtly) The Computer in Literary and Linguistic Studies, 1976; Numerical Analysis, 1978; papers in math. and other jls. *Recreations:* cricket, astronomy. *Address:* 15 Holly Grove, Lisvane, Cardiff CF4 5UJ. *T:* Cardiff 750250. *Club:* Challenor.

CHURCHILL; *see* Spencer-Churchill.

CHURCHILL, 3rd Viscount *cr* 1902; **Victor George Spencer;** Baron 1815; Investment Manager, Central Board of Finance of the Church of England and Charities Official Investment Fund; Director, Local Authorities' Mutual Investment Trust; *b* 31 July 1934; *s* of 1st Viscount Churchill, GCVO, and late Christine Sinclair (who *m* 3rd, Sir Lancelot Oliphant, KCMG, CB); *S* half-brother, 1973. *Educ:* Eton; New Coll., Oxford (MA). Lieut, Scots Guards, 1953–55. Morgan Grenfell & Co. Ltd, 1958–74. *Heir* (to Barony only): Richard Harry Ramsay Spencer [*b* 11 Oct. 1926; *m* 1958, Antoinette Rose-Marie de Charrière; two *s*]. *Address:* 6 Cumberland Mansions, George Street, W1.

CHURCHILL, Diana (Josephine); actress, stage and screen; *b* Wembley, 21 Aug. 1913; *d* of Joseph H. Churchill, MRCS, LRCP and Ethel Mary Nunn; *m* Barry K. Barnes (*d* 1965); *m* 1976, Mervyn Johns. *Educ:* St Mary's Sch., Wantage; Guildhall Sch. of Music (scholarship). First professional appearance in Champion North, Royalty, 1931; subsequently in West End and in Repertory. Old Vic Season, 1949–50, New Theatre, as Rosaline in Love's Labour's Lost, Miss Kate Hardcastle in She Stoops to Conquer, Lizaveta Bogdanovna in A Month in the Country and Elise in The Miser; High Spirits, London Hippodrome, 1953; The Desperate Hours, London Hippodrome, 1955; Hamlet, Stratford-on-Avon Festival, 1956; Lady Fidget in The Country Wife, Royal Court Theatre, 1956; The Rehearsal, Globe Theatre, 1961; The Winter's Tale, Cambridge, 1966; The Farmer's Wife, Chichester, 1967; Heartbreak House, Chichester, later Lyric, 1967. Has also appeared in several films. *Address:* c/o Stella Richards Management, 42 Hazlebury Road, SW6.

CHURCHILL, Hon. Gordon, PC (Canada); DSO 1945; ED; QC; Canadian barrister, retired; *b* Coldwater, Ont, 8 Nov. 1898; *s* of Rev. J. W. and Mary E. Churchill; *m* 1922, Mona Mary, *d* of C. W. McLachlin, Dauphin, Man.; one *d*. *Educ:* Univ. of Manitoba. MA 1931, LLB 1950. Served European War, 1916–18, France; served War of 1939–45 (DSO), commanded First Canadian Armoured Carrier Regt, NW Europe. Principal of a Manitoba High Sch., 1928–38; Mem. Manitoba Legislature, 1946–49; called to Manitoba Bar, 1950; Member Federal Parlt for Winnipeg South Centre, 1951–68, retired; Federal Minister: for Trade and Commerce, 1957–60; of Veterans' Affairs, 1960–63; of National Defence, Feb.-April 1963. Hon. LLD Winnipeg 1976.

CHURCHILL, John George Spencer; mural and portrait, townscape, landscape painter; sculptor, lecturer and author since 1932; *b* 31 May 1909; *s* of John Strange Spencer Churchill and Lady Gwendoline Bertie; *m* 1st, 1934, Angela Culme Seymour; one *d*; 2nd, 1941, Mary Cookson; 3rd, 1953, Kathlyn Tandy (*d* 1957); 4th, 1958, Lullan Boston (marr. diss. 1972). *Educ:* Harrow School; Pembroke Coll., Oxford; Royal Coll. of Art; Central Sch. of Art; Westminster Sch. of Art; Ruskin Sch. of Art, Oxford; private pupil of Meninsky, Hubbard, Nicholson and Lutyens. Stock Exchange, 1930–32. Served War, Major GSO, RE, 1939–45. Mural and portrait, townscape and landscape paintings in England, France, Spain, Portugal, Italy, Switzerland, Belgium and America, 1932–80. Lectr in America, 1961–69. *Work includes:* incised relief carving on slate and cement cast busts, in Marlborough Pavilion at Chartwell, Westerham, Kent (National Trust), 1949; reportage illustrations and paintings of Spanish Revolution, 1936, and Evacuation of BEF from Dunkirk, 1940 (in Illustrated London News); London from the South Bank, in Simpsons, Piccadilly, 1957; painting of forest destruction for WWF, 1985. Mem., Soc. of Mural Painters. *Publications:* Crowded Canvas, 1960; A Churchill Canvas, 1961 (USA), serialised in Sunday Dispatch and Atlantic Monthly, USA; Varnishing Day, 1986; contrib. illustr.: Country Life, Connoisseur, etc. *Recreations:* music, travel. *Address:* (professional) 68 Elgin Crescent, W11 2JJ. *T:* 01–352 2352; (domicile) Appartement Churchill, 83360 Grimaud, France. *T:* 94.43.21.31. *Clubs:* Press, Chelsea Arts; Cincinatti (Washington, DC, USA).

CHURCHILL, Very Rev. John Howard; Dean of Carlisle, since 1973; *b* 9 June 1920; *s* of John Lancelot and Emily Winifred Churchill; *m* 1948, Patricia May, *d* of late John James and Gertrude May Williams; one *s* two *d*. *Educ:* Sutton Valence Sch.; Trinity Coll., Cambridge (Exhibitioner); Lincoln Theological Coll. BA 1942, MA 1946. Deacon, 1943; priest, 1944; Asst curate: St George, Camberwell, 1943–48; All Hallows', Tottenham, 1948–53; Chaplain and Lectr in Theology, King's Coll., London, 1953–60; Vicar of St George, Sheffield, 1960–67; Lectr in Education, Univ. of Sheffield, 1960–67; Canon Residentiary of St Edmundsbury, 1967–73; Director of Ordinands and Clergy Training, Diocese of St Edmundsbury and Ipswich, 1967–73. Lady Margaret Preacher, Univ. of Cambridge, 1969; Proctor in Convocation, 1970–; Mem., Dioceses Commn, 1978–86. Fellow of King's Coll., London, 1982. *Publications:* Prayer in Progress, 1961; Going Up: a look at University life, 1963; Finding Prayer, 1978. *Recreation:* walking. *Address:* The Deanery, Carlisle CA3 8TZ. *T:* Carlisle 23335.

See also A. E. C. Green.

CHURCHILL, Maj.-Gen. Thomas Bell Lindsay, CB 1957; CBE 1949; MC; *b* 1 Nov. 1907; 2nd *s* of late Alec Fleming Churchill, of PWD, Ceylon and Hong Kong, and late Elinor Elizabeth (*née* Bell); *m* 1934, Gwendolen Janie (*d* 1962), *e d* of late Lewis Williams, MD; one *s* one *d*; *m* 1968, Penelope Jane Ormiston (marr. diss. 1974). *Educ:* Dragon Sch., Oxford; Magdalen Coll. Sch., Oxford; RMC Sandhurst. Gained Prize Cadetship to RMC Sandhurst, 1926; Prize for Mil. Hist., 1927. 2nd Lieut, Manchester Regt, 1927; Burma Rebellion, 1930–31 (despatches, MC); Adjt, 1931–34; instructor in interpretation of air photographs, RAF Sch. of Photography, 1934–39; Company Comdr, France, 1939–40; GSO1 Commandos, Sicily and Salerno Landings, 1943; comd 2nd Commando Bde, Italy, 1943; with Marshal Tito and Yugoslav Partisans, 1944 (Partisan Star with Gold Wreath); Albania, 1944; comd 11th and 138th Inf Bdes, Austria, 1945–46; Zone Comdr, Austria, 1947–49; student, Imperial Def. Coll., 1952; Maj.-Gen. i/c Admin., GHQ, Far ELF, 1955–57; Vice-Quartermaster-Gen. to the Forces, 1957–60; Deputy Chief of Staff, Allied Land Forces, Central Europe, 1960–62, retd. Col The Manchester Regt, 1952–58; Col The King's Regt (Manchester and Liverpool), 1958–62. A Vice-President: Commando Assoc., 1950–; British-Jugoslav Soc., 1975–. *Publications:* Manual of Interpretation of Air Photographs, 1939; The Churchill Chronicles, 1986; Commando Crusade, 1987; articles to Yorks Archæolog. Jl, 1935, to Army Quarterly and to Jl of RUSI. *Recreations:* genealogy, heraldry; fine arts. *Address:* Lower Minchingdown Farm, Black Dog, near Crediton, Devon EX17 4QX. *T:* Tiverton 860474.

CHURCHILL, Winston Spencer; MP (C) Davyhulme, Manchester, since 1983 (Stretford, Lancs, 1970–83); author; journalist; company director; Chairman and Managing Director: Gatwick Executive Aviation Ltd; Europe Charter Centre Ltd; *b* 10 Oct. 1940; *s* of late Randolph Frederick Edward Spencer Churchill, MBE and of Mrs Averell Harriman, *e d* of 11th Baron Digby, KG, DSO, MC, TD; *m* 1964, Mary Caroline, (Minnie), d'Erlanger, *d* of late Sir Gerard d'Erlanger, CBE, Chairman of BOAC; two *s* two *d*. *Educ:* Eton; Christ Church, Oxford (MA). Correspondent in Yemen, Congo and Angola, 1963; Presenter, This Time of Day, BBC Radio, 1964–65; Correspondent: Borneo and Vietnam, 1966; Middle East, 1967; Chicago, Czechoslovakia, 1968; Nigeria, Biafra and Middle East, for The Times, 1969–70; Special Correspondent, China, 1972, Portugal, 1975. Lecture tours of the US and Canada, 1965, 1969, 1971, 1973, 1975, 1978, 1980, 1981, 1984, 1985. Contested Gorton Div. of Manchester in Bye-election, Nov. 1967. PPS to Minister of Housing and Construction, 1970–72, to Minister of State, FCO, 1972–73; Sec., Cons. Foreign and Commonwealth Affairs Cttee, 1973–76; Conservative Party front-bench spokesman on Defence, 1976–78. Member: Select Cttee on Defence, 1983–; Select Cttee on H of C (Services), 1985–. Vice-Chm., Cons. Defence Cttee, 1979–83; Cons. Party Co-ordinator for Defence and Multilateral Disarmament, 1982–84; Mem. Exec., 1922 Cttee, 1979–85. Pres., Univ. of Bristol Cons. Assoc., 1977–. Sponsored Motor Vehicles (Passenger Insce) Act 1972. Pres., Trafford Park Indust. Council, 1971–. Trustee: Winston Churchill Meml Trust, 1968–; Nat. Benevolent Fund for the Aged, 1974–; Governor, English-Speaking Union, 1975–80; Vice-Pres., British Technion Soc., 1976–. Hon. Fellow, Churchill Coll., Cambridge, 1969. Hon. LLD, Westminster Coll., Fulton, Mo, USA, 1972. *Publications:* First Journey, 1964; (with late Randolph Churchill) Six Day War, 1967; Defending the West, 1981. *Recreations:* tennis, sailing, ski-ing. *Address:* House of Commons, SW1A 0AA. *Clubs:* White's, Buck's, Press.

CHURSTON, 4th Baron *cr* 1858; **Richard Francis Roger Yarde-Buller;** Bt 1790; VRD; Lieut-Comdr RNVR, retired; *b* 12 Feb. 1910; *er s* of 3rd Baron and Jessie (who *m* 2nd, 1928, Theodore William Wessel), *o d* of Alfred Smither; *S* father, 1930; *m* 1st, 1933, Elizabeth Mary (from whom he obtained a divorce, 1943, and who *m* 1943, Lieut-Col P. Laycock; she *d* 1951), 2nd *d* of late W. B. du Pre; one *s* one *d*; 2nd, 1949, Mrs Jack Dunfee (*d* 1979); 3rd, Mrs Olga Alice Muriel Blair. *Educ:* Eton Coll. *Heir: s* Hon. John Francis Yarde-Buller [*b* 29 Dec. 1934; *m* 1973, Alexandra, *d* of A. Contomichalos; one *s* two *d*]. *Address:* Pendragon, Fort George, Guernsey, Channel Isles. *Club:* Royal Yacht Squadron.

See also Earl Cadogan, Sir G. A. Lyle, Bt.

CHUTE, Marchette; author; *b* 16 Aug. 1909; *d* of William Young Chute and Edith Mary Pickburn; unmarried. *Educ:* Univ. of Minnesota (BA). Doctor of Letters: Western Coll., 1952; Carleton Coll., 1957; Dickinson Coll., 1964. Mem., American Acad. of Arts and Letters. Outstanding Achievement Award, Univ. of Minnesota, 1958; co-winner of Constance Lindsay Skinner Award, 1959. *Publications:* Rhymes about Ourselves, 1932; The Search for God, 1941; Rhymes about the Country, 1941; The Innocent Wayfaring, 1943; Geoffrey Chaucer of England, 1946; Rhymes about the City, 1946; The End of the Search, 1947; Shakespeare of London, 1950; An Introduction to Shakespeare, 1951 (English title: Shakespeare and his Stage); Ben Jonson of Westminster, 1953; The Wonderful Winter, 1954; Stories from Shakespeare, 1956; Around and About, 1957; Two Gentle Men: the Lives of George Herbert and Robert Herrick, 1959; Jesus of Israel, 1961; The Worlds of Shakespeare (with Ernestine Perrie), 1963; The First Liberty: a history of the right to vote in America, 1619–1850, 1969; The Green Tree of Democracy, 1971; PEN American Center: a history of the first fifty years, 1972; Rhymes About Us, 1974; various articles in Saturday Review, Virginia Quarterly Review, etc. *Recreations:* walking, reading, talking. *Address:* 450 East 63rd Street, New York, NY 10021, USA. *T:* Templeton 8–8920. *Clubs:* Royal Society of Arts; PEN, Renaissance Society of America (New York).

CHWATT, Professor Leonard Jan B.; *see* Bruce-Chwatt.

CHYNOWETH, David Boyd; Director of Finance, Lothian Regional Council, since 1985; *b* 26 Dec. 1940; *s* of Ernest and Blodwen Chynoweth; *m* 1968, Margaret Slater; one *s* two *d*. *Educ:* Simon Langton Sch., Canterbury; Univ. of Nottingham (BA). IPFA. Public Finance posts with Derbs CC, 1962 and London Borough of Ealing, 1965; Asst County Treas., Flints CC, 1968; Dep. County Treas., West Suffolk CC, 1970; County Treasurer, S Yorks CC, 1973. Mem. Council, CIPFA; Mem. Investment Protection Cttee, Nat. Assoc. of Pension Funds; Pres., Assoc. of Public Service Finance Officers, 1981–82. *Recreations:* sailing, photography. *Address:* Regional Headquarters, George IV Bridge, Edinburgh EH1 1UQ. *T:* 031-229 9292. *Club:* Royal Over-Seas League.

CHYNOWETH, Rt. Rev. Neville James; *see* Gippsland, Bishop of.

CITRINE, family name of **Baron Citrine.**

CITRINE, 2nd Baron *cr* 1946, of Wembley; **Norman Arthur Citrine,** LLB; solicitor in general practice, retired 1984; author, editor, lecturer; *b* 27 Sept. 1914; *er s* of 1st Baron Citrine, GBE, PC, and Doris Helen (*d* 1973), *d* of Edgar Slade; *S* father, 1983; *m* 1939, Kathleen Alice Chilvers; one *d*. *Educ:* University Coll. Sch., Hampstead; Law Society's Sch., London. Admitted solicitor of Supreme Court (Hons), 1937; LLB (London), 1938. Served War of 1939–45, Lieut RNVR, 1940–46. Legal Adviser to Trades Union Congress, 1946–51; re-entered general legal practice, 1951. Pres., Devon and Exeter Law Soc., 1971. *Publications:* War Pensions Appeal Cases, 1946; Guide to Industrial Injuries Acts, 1948; Trade Union Law, 1950, 3rd edn, 1967; Editor, ABC of Chairmanship, 1952–82. *Recreations:* hiking, boating, engineering, painting, carpentry. *Heir: b* Dr the Hon. Ronald Eric Citrine [*b* 19 May 1919; *m* 1945, Mary, *d* of Reginald Williams]. *Address:* Casa Katrina, The Mount, Opua, Bay of Islands, New Zealand.

CIVIL, Alan, OBE 1985; Principal Horn, BBC Symphony Orchestra, since 1966; *b* 13 June 1928; *m* Shirley Jean Hopkins; three *s* three *d*. *Educ:* Northampton, various schools. Principal Horn, Royal Philharmonic Orchestra, 1953–55; Philharmonia Orchestra, 1955–66. Guest Principal, Berlin Philharmonic Orchestra; international horn soloist; Prof. of Horn, Royal Coll. of Music, London; composer; founder of Alan Civil Horn Trio. Member: London Wind Soloists; London Wind Quintet; Music Group of London. Pres., British Horn Soc., 1979–. *Recreations:* brewing, swimming, Baroque music. *Address:* Downe Hall, Downe, Kent. *T:* Farnborough (Kent) 52982. *Clubs:* Savage, London Sketch.

CLAGUE, Joan; Director of Nursing Services, Marie Curie Memorial Foundation, since 1986; *b* 17 April 1931; *d* of James Henry Clague and Violet May Clague (*née* Johnson). *Educ:* Malvern Girls' Coll.; Guy's Hosp.; Hampstead Gen. Hosp.; Simpson Meml Maternity Pavilion. Asst Regional Nursing Officer, Oxford Regional Hosp. Bd, 1965–67; Principal, then Chief Nursing Officer, St George's Hosp. Bd of Governors, 1967–73; Area Nursing Officer, Merton, Sutton and Wandsworth AHA, 1973–81; Regl Nursing Officer, NE Thames RHA, 1981–86. Pres., Assoc. of Nurse Administrators, 1983–85. WHO Fellow, 1969; Smith and Nephew EEC Scholar, 1981. *Recreations:* walking, domestic pursuits. *Address:* 7 Tylney Avenue, SE19 1LN. *T:* 01–670 5171.

CLAMAGERAN, Alice Germaine Suzanne; Director, School of Social Workers, Centre Hospitalier Universitaire de Rouen, 1942–73; President, International Council of Nurses, 1961–65; *b* 5 March 1906; *d* of William Clamageran, shipowner at Rouen and of Lucie Harlé. *Educ:* Rouen. Nursing studies: Red Cross School of Nurses, Rouen; Ecole Professionnelle d'Assistance aux Malades, Paris. Tutor, Red Cross Sch. for Nurses, Rouen, 1931–42 (leave, for course in Public Health at Florence Nightingale Internat. Foundn, London, 1934–35). War service (6 months), 1939–40. President: Bd of Dirs, Fondation Edith Seltzer (Sanatorium Chantoiseau, Briançon) for Nurses, Social Workers and Medical Auxiliaries; Assoc. Médico-Sociale Protestante de Langue Française; Hon. Pres. Nat. Assoc. of Trained Nurses in France. Hon. Fellow, Royal Coll. of Nursing of UK, 1977. Médaille de Bronze de l'Enseignement Technique, 1960; Officier dans l'Ordre de la Santé Publique, 1961; Chevalier, Légion d'Honneur, 1962. *Address:* Hautonne, 27310 Bourg-Achard, France.

CLANCARTY, 8th Earl of, *cr* 1803; **William Francis Brinsley Le Poer Trench;** Baron Kilconnel, 1797; Viscount Dunlo, 1801; Baron Trench (UK), 1815; Viscount Clancarty (UK), 1823; Marquess of Heusden (Kingdom of the Netherlands), 1818; author; *b* 18 Sept. 1911; 5th *s* of 5th Earl of Clancarty and of Mary Gwatkin, *d* of late W. F. Rosslewin Ellis; *S* half-brother, 1975; *m* 1st, 1940, Diana Joan (marr. diss. 1947), *yr d* of Sir William Younger, 2nd Bt; 2nd, 1961, Mrs Wilma Dorothy Millen Belknap (marr. diss. 1969), *d* of S. R. Vermilyea, USA; 3rd, 1974, Mrs Mildred Alleyn Spong (*d* 1975); 4th, 1976, May, *widow* of Commander Frank M. Beasley, RN and *o d* of late E. Radonicich. *Educ:* Nautical Coll., Pangbourne. Founder Pres., Contact International; Chm., House of Lords UFO Study Gp. *Publications:* (as Brinsley Le Poer Trench): The Sky People, 1960; Men Among Mankind, 1962; Forgotten Heritage, 1964; The Flying Saucer Story, 1966; Operation Earth, 1969; The Eternal Subject, 1973; Secret of the Ages, 1974. *Recreations:* Ufology, travel, walking. *Heir: nephew* Nicholas Power Richard Le Poer Trench, *b* 1 May 1952. *Address:* 51 Eaton Place, Belgravia, SW1. *Club:* Buck's.

CLANCHY, Joan Lesley, (Mrs Michael Clanchy); Headmistress, North London Collegiate School, since 1986; *b* 26 Aug. 1939; *d* of Leslie and Mary Milne; *m* 1962, Dr Michael Clanchy; one *s* one *d*. *Educ:* St Leonard's Sch., St Andrews; St Hilda's Coll., Oxford. MA; DipEd. Schoolteacher: Woodberry Down Sch., London, 1962–63; The Park Sch., Glasgow, 1967–76; Headmistress, St George's Sch., Edinburgh, 1976–85. *Recreation:* cooking. *Address:* North London Collegiate School, Canons, Edgware, Middlesex HA8 7RJ.

CLANCY, Most Rev. Edward Bede; *see* Sydney, Archbishop of, (RC).

CLANFIELD, Viscount; Ashton Robert Gerard Peel; *b* 16 Sept. 1976; *s* and *heir* of 3rd Earl Peel, *qv*.

CLANMORRIS, 7th Baron (Ireland), *cr* 1800; **John Michael Ward Bingham;** *b* 3 Nov. 1908; *o s* of 6th Baron Clanmorris; *S* father, 1960; *m* 1934, Madeleine Mary, *d* of late Clement Ebel, Copyhold Place, Cuckfield, Sussex; one *s* one *d*. *Educ:* Cheltenham Coll.; France and Germany. *Publications:* as John Bingham: My Name is Michael Sibley, 1952; Five Roundabouts to Heaven, 1953; The Third Skin, 1954; The Paton Street Case, 1955; Marion, 1958; Murder Plan Six, 1958; Night's Black Agent, 1960; A Case of Libel, 1963; A Fragment of Fear, 1965; The Double Agent, 1966; I Love, I Kill, 1968; Vulture in the Sun, 1971; The Hunting Down of Peter Manuel, 1974; God's Defector, 1976; The Marriage Bureau Murders, 1977; Brock, 1981; Brock and the Defector, 1982. *Heir: s* Hon. Simon John Ward Bingham [*b* 25 Oct. 1937; *m* 1971, Gizella Maria, *d* of Sandor Zverkó; one *d*]. *Address:* c/o Coutts & Co., 10 Mount Street, W1.
See also Hon. Charlotte Bingham.

CLANWILLIAM, 6th Earl of, *cr* 1776; **John Charles Edmund Carson Meade;** Bt 1703; Viscount Clanwilliam, Baron Gilford, 1766; Baron Clanwilliam (UK), 1828; Major Coldstream Guards (retired); HM Lord-Lieutenant for Co. Down, 1975–79 (HM Lieutenant, 1962–75); *b* 6 June 1914; *o s* of 5th Earl of Clanwilliam; *S* father, 1953; *m* 1948, Catherine, *y d* of late A. T. Loyd, Lockinge, Wantage, Berks; six *d*. *Educ:* Eton; RMC Sandhurst. Adjt, 1939–42; Staff Coll., Haifa, 1942; Bde Major, 201 Guards Motor Brigade, 1942–43; Bde Major, 6 Guards Tank Brigade, 1944; Command and Gen. Staff Sch., Fort Leavenworth, USA, 1944; served in Middle East and France (despatches twice); retd, 1948. *Heir: cousin* John Herbert Meade [*b* 27 Sept. 1919; *m* 1956, Maxine, *o d* of late J. A. Hayden-Scott; one *s* two *d*]. *Address:* Rainscombe Park, Oare, Marlborough, Wilts. *T:* Marlborough 63491. *Clubs:* Carlton, Pratt's.
See also Earl of Belmore.

CLAPHAM, Prof. Arthur Roy, CBE 1969; FRS 1959; MA, PhD Cantab; FLS; Professor of Botany in Sheffield University, 1944–69, Professor Emeritus 1969; Pro-Vice-Chancellor, 1954–58, Acting Vice-Chancellor, 1965; Member of the Nature Conservancy, 1956–72 (Chairman, Scientific Policy Committee, 1963–70); Chairman, British National Committee for the International Biological Programme, 1964–75; President, Linnean Society, 1967–70; *b* 24 May 1904; *o s* of George Clapham, Norwich; *m* 1933, Brenda North Stoessiger; one *s* two *d* (and one *s* decd). *Educ:* City of Norwich Sch.; Downing Coll., Cambridge (Foundation Scholar). Frank Smart Prize, 1925; Frank Smart Student, 1926–27; Crop Physiologist at Rothamsted Agricultural Experimental Station, 1928–30; Demonstrator in Botany at Oxford Univ., 1930–44. Mem., NERC, 1965–70; Trustee, British Museum (Natural History), 1965–75. Hon. LLD Aberdeen, 1970; Hon. LittD, Sheffield, 1970. Linnean Gold Medal (Botany), 1972. *Publications:* (with W. O. James) The Biology of Flowers, 1935; (with T. G. Tutin and E. F. Warburg) Flora of the British Isles, 1952, 1962; Excursion Flora of the British Isles, 1959, 3rd rev. edn 1981; (with B. E. Nicholson) The Oxford Book of Trees, 1975; various papers in botanical journals. *Address:* The Parrock, Arkholme, Carnforth, Lancs. *T:* Hornby 21206.

CLAPHAM, His Honour Brian Ralph; a Circuit Judge, South East Circuit, 1974–85; *b* 1 July 1913; *s* of Isaac Clapham and Laura Alice Clapham (*née* Meech); *m* 1961, Margaret Warburg; two *s*. *Educ:* Tonbridge Sch.; Wadham Coll., Oxford; University Coll. London (LLB; LLM 1976). Called to Bar, Middle Temple, 1936. Contested (Lab): Tonbridge, 1950; Billericay, 1951, 1955; Chelmsford, 1959. Councillor, Tonbridge and Southborough UDCs, 1947–74; Chm., Tonbridge UDC, 1959–60. Mem. Senate, Open Univ.; Governor, West Kent Coll. Freeman of City of London. BA Open, 1981. *Recreations:* walking and talking.

CLAPHAM, Sir Michael (John Sinclair), KBE 1973; Chairman: IMI Ltd, 1974–81; BPM Holdings Ltd, 1974–81; *b* 17 Jan. 1912; *s* of late Sir John Clapham, CBE and Lady Clapham, Cambridge; *m* 1935, Hon. Elisabeth Russell Rea, *d* of 1st Baron Rea of Eskdale; three *s* one *d*. *Educ:* Marlborough Coll.; King's Coll., Cambridge (MA). Apprenticed as printer with University Press, Cambridge, 1933–35; Overseer and later Works Man., Percy Lund Humphries & Co. Ltd, Bradford, 1935–38; joined ICI Ltd as Man., Kynoch Press, 1938; seconded, in conseq. of developing a diffusion barrier, to Tube Alloys Project (atomic energy), 1941–45; Personnel Dir, ICI Metals Div., 1946; Midland Regional Man., ICI, 1951; Jt Man. Dir, ICI Metals Div., 1952; Chm. 1959; Dir, ICI, 1961–74, Dep. Chm. 1968–74; served as Overseas Dir; Dir, ICI of Austr. & NZ Ltd, 1961–74; Director: Imp. Metal Industries Ltd, 1962–70; Lloyds Bank Ltd, 1971–82 (Dep. Chm., 1974–80); Grindlay's Bank Ltd, 1975–84; Associated Communications Corp., 1982–. Mem., General Motors European Adv. Council, 1975–82. Dep. Pres., 1971–72, Pres., 1972–74, CBI. Member: IRC, 1969–71; Standing Adv. Cttee on Pay of Higher Civil Service, 1968–71; Review Body on Doctors' and Dentists' Remuneration, 1968–70; Birmingham Educn Cttee, 1949–56; W Mids Adv. Coun. for Techn., Commercial and Art Educn, and Regional Academic Bd, 1952; Life Governor, Birmingham Univ., 1955 (Mem. Coun., 1956–61); Member: Court, Univ. of London, 1969–85; Govt Youth Service Cttee (Albemarle Cttee), 1958; CNAA, 1964–77 (Chm., 1971–77); NEDC, 1971–76; Pres., Inst. of Printing, 1980–82. Hon. DSc Aston, 1973; Hon. LLD: CNAA, 1978; London, 1984. *Publications:* Printing, 1500–1730, in The History of Technology, Vol. III, 1957; Multinational Enterprises and Nation States, 1975; various articles on printing, personnel management and education. *Recreations:* sailing, canal boating, cooking. *Address:* 26 Hill Street, W1X 7FU. *T:* 01–499 1240. *Clubs:* Royal Yacht Squadron, Royal Cruising.
See also B. D. Till.

CLAPP, Captain Michael Cecil, CB 1982; FBIM, MNI; RN retired; *b* 22 Feb. 1932; *s* of Brig. Cecil Douglas Clapp, CBE and Mary Elizabeth Emmeline Palmer Clapp; *m* 1975, Sarah Jane Alexander; one *s* two *d*. *Educ:* Chafyn Grove Sch., Salisbury; Marlborough College. Joined Royal Navy, 1950; HMS Norfolk, 1972; Directorate of Naval Plans, MoD, 1974; in Command, HMS Leander, 1977; Jt Maritime Op. Trng Staff, 1979; Commodore, Amphibious Warfare, Staff of Third Flotilla, 1980–83 (South Atlantic Campaign, 1982). Governor: Kelly Coll., 1985; St Michael Sch., Tavistock, 1985. *Recreations:* sailing, shooting, fishing, skiing, genealogy, country life. *Address:* c/o Lloyds Bank, PO Box 22, 38 Blue Boar Row, Salisbury, Wilts.

CLARE; *see* Sabben-Clare.

CLARE, Prof. Anthony Ward, MD; FRCPsych; FRCPI; Professor and Head of the Department of Psychological Medicine, St Bartholomew's Hospital Medical College, since 1983; *b* 24 Dec. 1942; *s* of Bernard Joseph Clare and Mary Agnes (*née* Dunne); *m* 1966, Jane Carmel Hogan; three *s* four *d*. *Educ:* Gonzaga Coll., Dublin; University Coll., Dublin. MB, BCh, BAO 1966, MD 1982; MPhil 1972; FRCPsych 1985 (MRCPsych 1973), FRCPI 1983 (MRCPI 1971). Auditor, Literary and Historical Soc., 1963–64. Internship, St Joseph's Hosp., Syracuse, New York, 1967; psychiatric training, St Patrick's Hosp., Dublin, 1967–69; Psychiatric Registrar, Maudsley Hosp., London, 1970–72, Sen. Registrar, 1973–75; research worker, General Practice Research Unit, Inst. of Psychiatry, 1976–79, Sen. Lectr, 1980–82. Radio series: In the Psychiatrist's Chair, 1982–; TV series: Motives, 1983. *Publications:* Psychiatry in Dissent, 1976, 2nd edn 1980; (ed with P. Williams) Psychosocial Disorders in General Practice, 1979; (with S. Thompson) Let's Talk About Me, 1981; (ed with R. Corney) Social Work and Primary Health Care, 1982; (ed with M. Lader) Psychiatry and General Practice, 1982; In the Psychiatrist's Chair, 1984. *Recreations:* tennis, broadcasting, theatre, family life. *Address:* 87 Coper's Cope Road, Beckenham, Kent BR3 1NR. *T:* 01–650 1784.

CLARE, Herbert Mitchell N.; *see* Newton-Clare.

CLARENDON, 7th Earl of, 2nd *cr* 1776; **George Frederick Laurence Hyde Villiers;** Chairman, Seccombe Marshall and Campion plc, since 1985 (a Managing Director, 1962–85); *b* 2 Feb. 1933; *o s* of Lord Hyde (*d* 1935) and Hon. Marion Féodorovna Louise Glyn, Lady Hyde (*d* 1970), *er d* of 4th Baron Wolverton; *S* grandfather, 1955; *m* 1974, Jane Diana, *d* of late E. W. Dawson; one *s* one *d*. Page of Honour to King George VI, 1948–49; Lieut RHG, 1951–53. *Heir: s* Lord Hyde, *qv*. *Address:* 8 Chelsea Square, SW3 6LF. *T:* 01–352 6338.

CLARFELT, Jack Gerald; Chairman: Linhay Meats Ltd; Linhay Frizzell Insurance Brokers Ltd; *b* 7 Feb. 1914; *s* of Barnett Clarfelt and Rene (*née* Frankel); *m* 1948, Baba Fredman; one *s* one *d*. *Educ:* Grocers' Co. Sch.; Sorbonne. Practised as Solicitor in own name, 1938–40; Man. Dir, Home Killed Meat Assoc., 1940–43 and 1945–54; Queen's Royal Surreys, 1943–45; Man. Dir, Fatstock Marketing Corp., 1954–60; Chm., Smithfield & Zwanenberg Gp Ltd, 1960–75; Exec. Dep. Chm., 1975–79, Dir, 1979–83, FMC Ltd. Dir, S. and W. Berisford Ltd, 1973–75. Farming, Hampshire. Master, Worshipful Co. of Butchers, 1978. *Recreations:* golf, swimming. *Address:* Linhay Meads, Timsbury, Romsey, Hants. *T:* Braishfield 68243. *Clubs:* City Livery, Farmers'.
See also R. E. Rhodes.

CLARINGBULL, Sir (Gordon) Frank, Kt 1975; BSc, PhD; FGS; CPhys, FInstP; FMA; Director, British Museum (Natural History), 1968–76; *b* 21 Aug. 1911; *s* of William Horace Claringbull and Hannah Agnes Cutting; *m* 1st, 1938, Grace Helen Mortimer (*d* 1953); one *s* one *d*; 2nd, 1953, Enid Dorothy Phyllis, *d* of late William Henry Lambert. *Educ:* Finchley Grammar Sch.; Queen Mary Coll., Univ. of London (Fellow 1967). British Museum (Natural Hist.): Asst Keeper, 1935–48; Princ. Scientific Officer, 1948–53; Keeper of Mineralogy, 1953–68. Explosives res., Min. of Supply, 1940–43; special scientific duties, War Office, 1943–45. Mineralogical Soc.: Gen. Sec., 1938–59; Vice-Pres, 1959–63; Pres., 1965–67; For. Sec., 1967–71, Managing Trustee, 1969–77; Gemmological Assoc.: Vice-Pres., 1970–72, Pres., 1972–. Mem., Commn on Museums and Galleries, 1976–83. *Publications:* Crystal Structures of Minerals (with W. L. Bragg); papers in journals of learned societies on mineralogical and related topics. *Recreations:* craftwork, gardening, photography. *Address:* Langley House, Main Street, Ash, Martock, Somerset TA12 6PB. *T:* Martock 822983.

CLARK; *see* Chichester-Clark.

CLARK; *see* Stafford-Clark.

CLARK, Rt. Rev. Alan Charles; *see* East Anglia, Bishop of, (RC).

CLARK, Hon. Alan Kenneth McKenzie; MP (C) Plymouth Sutton, since Feb. 1974; Minister for Trade, since 1986; Chairman, International Market Council of EEC Ministers, since 1986; historian; *b* 13 April 1928; *s* of Baron Clark (Life Peer), OM, CH, KCB, CLit, FBA and late Elizabeth Martin; *m* 1958, Caroline Jane Beuttler; two *s*. *Educ:* Eton; Christ Church, Oxford (MA). Household Cavalry (Training Regt), 1946; RAuxAF, 1952–54. Barrister, Inner Temple, 1955. Mem., Inst. for Strategic Studies, 1963. Parly Under Sec. of State, Dept of Employment, 1983–86. Vice-Chm., Parly Defence Cttee, 1980–. Mem., RUSI. *Publications:* The Donkeys, A History of the BEF in 1915, 1961; The Fall of Crete, 1963; Barbarossa, The Russo-German Conflict, 1941–45, 1965; Aces High: the war in the air over the Western Front 1914–18, 1973; (ed) A Good Innings: the private papers of Viscount Lee of Fareham, 1974. *Address:* Saltwood Castle, Kent. *T:* Hythe 67190. *Clubs:* Brooks's, Pratt's.

CLARK, Albert William; His Honour Judge Clark; a Circuit Judge, since 1981; *b* 23 Sept. 1922; *s* of William Charles Clark and Cissy Dorothy Elizabeth Clark; *m* 1951, Frances Philippa, *d* of Dr Samuel Lavington Hart, Tientsin; one *s* one *d*. *Educ:* Christ's Coll., Finchley. War service, 1941–46, Royal Navy. Called to Bar, Middle Temple, 1949; Clerk of Arraigns, Central Criminal Court, 1951–56; Clerk to the Justices, E Devon,

1956–70; Acting Dep. Chm., Inner London QS, 1971; Dep. Circuit Judge, 1972–80; Metropolitan Magistrate, 1970–80. Mem., Central Council of Probation and After-Care Cttees, 1975–81. *Recreations:* fly-fishing, walking, etc. *Address:* 31 Hill Court, Wimbledon Hill Road, Wimbledon, SW19 7PO. *T:* 01–947 8041.

CLARK of Herriotshall, Arthur Melville, MA (Hons); DPhil; DLitt; FRSE; FRSA; Reader in English Literature, Edinburgh University, 1946–60; *b* 20 Aug. 1895; 4th *s* of late James Clark and Margaret Moyes McLachlan, Edinburgh. *Educ:* Stewart's Coll., Edinburgh; Edinburgh University (Sibbald Bursar and Vans Dunlop Scholar); Oriel Coll., Oxford (Scholar); MA First Class Hons and twice medallist, DLitt Edinburgh; DPhil Oxford. Lectr in English Language and Literature, Reading, 1920; Tutor to Oxford Home Students, 1921; Sec. of Oxford Union Soc., 1923; Pres. of Speculative Soc., 1926–29; Lectr in English Literature, Edinburgh Univ., 1928–46; Dir of Studies, Edinburgh Univ., 1931–47; Editor of Edinburgh University Calendar, 1933–45; External Examiner in English, St Andrews Univ., 1939–43, and Aberdeen Univ., 1944–46. Pres. of Scottish Arts Club, 1948–50. Pres. of Edinburgh Scott Club, 1957–58. Exhibitor RSA, SSA. Knight's Cross, Order of Polonia Restituta, 1968; GCLJ 1977. *Publications:* The Realistic Revolt in Modern Poetry, 1922; A Bibliography of Thomas Heywood (annotated), 1924; Thomas Heywood, Playwright and Miscellanist, 1931; Autobiography, its Genesis and Phases, 1935; Spoken English, 1946; Studies in Literary Modes, 1946; Two Pageants by Thomas Heywood, 1953; Sonnets from the French, and Other Verses, 1966; Sir Walter Scott: The Formative Years, 1969; Murder under Trust, or The Topical Macbeth, 1982; contribs to Encyc. Brit., Collier's Encyc., Encyc. of Poetry and Poetics, Cambridge Bibl. of Eng. Lit., Library, Mod. Lang. Review, Classical Review, etc. *Recreations:* walking, pastel-sketching. *Address:* 3 Woodburn Terrace, Edinburgh EH10 4SH. *T:* 031-447 1240; Herriotshall, Oxton, Berwickshire. *Clubs:* New, Scottish Arts (Edinburgh); Union Society (Oxford).

CLARK, Brian Robert; playwright; *b* 3 June 1932; *s* of Leonard and Selina Clark; *m* 1st, 1961, Margaret Paling; two *s*; 2nd, 1983, Anita Modak; one step *s* one step *d*. *Educ:* Merrywood Grammar Sch., Bristol; Redland Coll. of Educn, Bristol; Central Sch. of Speech and Drama, London; Nottingham Univ. BA Hons English. Teacher, 1955–61, and 1964–68; Staff Tutor in Drama, Univ. of Hull, 1968–72. Since 1971 has written some thirty television plays, incl. Whose Life Is It Anyway? and The Saturday Party; also series: Telford's Change; Late Starter. Stage plays: Whose Life Is It Anyway? (SWET award for Best Play, 1977; filmed, 1982); Can You Hear Me At the Back?, 1978; Campions Interview; Post Mortem; The Petition, NY, 1986. Founded Amber Lane Press, publishing plays and books on the theatre, 1978. *Publications:* Group Theatre, 1971; plays. *Address:* c/o Judy Daish Associates, 83 Eastbourne Mews, W2 6LQ. *T:* 01–262 1101. *Club:* Garrick.

CLARK, Charles Anthony; Under Secretary, Department of Education and Science, since 1982; *b* 13 June 1940; *s* of late Stephen and Winifred Clark; *m* 1968, Penelope Margaret (*née* Brett); one *s* two *d*. *Educ:* King's Coll. Sch., Wimbledon; Pembroke Coll., Oxford (MA Nat. Sci.). Pressed Steel Co., 1961; Hilger & Watts Ltd, 1962–65; DES, 1965–; seconded to UGC, 1971–73; Head of Teachers 2, Ext. Relations and General, DES, 1982–. *Recreation:* running, gardening, sailing. *Address:* The Paddock, Effingham, Surrey KT24 5QA. *T:* Bookham 52337.

CLARK, Charles David Lawson; Legal Adviser, Publishers' Association, since 1984; International Copyright Adviser, Association of American Publishers, since 1985; *b* 12 June 1933; *s* of Alec Fulton Charles Clark, CB, and of Mary Clark; *m* 1960, Fiona McKenzie Mill; one *s* three *d*. *Educ:* Edinburgh Acad.; Jesus Coll., Oxford (Exhibnr; MA). Called to the Bar, Inner Temple, 1960. Second Lieut 4th Regt RHA. Editor: Sweet and Maxwell, 1957–60; Penguin Books, 1960–66; Managing Director: Penguin Educn, 1966–72; Allen Lane the Penguin Press, 1967–69; Dir, LWT (Holdings) Ltd, 1982–84. Chairman: Bookrest, 1975–78; Book Marketing Council, 1979–81; Hutchinson Publishing Group, 1972–80 (Man. Dir, 1972); Chief Exec., Hutchinson Ltd, 1980–84. Publishers Association: Mem. Council, 1976–82; Chm., Copyright Panel, 1976–79; Chm., Publishing Law Panel, 1983–85. Member: Book Trade Working Party, 1970–72; Brit. Copyright Council, 1976–79 and 1984–; Council of Management, MIND, the Nat. Assoc. of Mental Health, 1970–79 (Chm. MIND, 1976–79, Vice-Pres., 1980–). *Publications:* (ed) Publishing Agreements, 1980, 2nd edn 1984; articles on publishing topics. *Recreations:* singing lieder, golf. *Address:* 19 Offley Road, SW9 0LR. *T:* 01–735 1422. *Clubs:* Groucho, Le Beaujolais.

CLARK, Rt. Hon. Charles Joseph, (Joe); PC (Canada); MP (Progressive C) Rocky Mountain, later Yellowhead, Constituency, since 1972; Minister of External Affairs, since 1984; *b* 5 June 1939; *s* of Charles and Grace Clark; *m* 1973, Maureen McTeer (she retained her maiden name); one *d*. *Educ:* High River High Sch.; Univ. of Alta (BA History); Univ. of Alberta (MA Polit. Sci.). Journalist, Canadian Press, Calgary Herald, Edmonton Jl, High River Times, 1964–66; Prof. of Political Science, Univ. of Alberta, Edmonton, 1966–67; Exec. Asst to Hon. Robert L. Stanfield, Leader of HM's Loyal Opposition, 1967–70. Leader of HM's Loyal Opposition, Canada, 1976–79; Prime Minister of Canada, 1979–80; Leader of HM's Loyal Opposition, 1980–83. Hon. LLD New Brunswick, 1976. *Recreations:* riding, reading, walking, film going. *Address:* House of Commons, Ottawa, Ont K1A 0A2, Canada.

CLARK, Col Charles Willoughby, DSO 1918; OBE 1945; MC 1916; DL; *b* 6 April 1888; *m* 1916; (one *s* one *d* decd). *Educ:* Atherstone Grammar Sch. Apprentice, Alfred Herbert Ltd, Coventry, 1904; Dir, 1934 (Chm. 1958–66). Served European War, 1914–18, France, Machine Gun Corps, Royal Tank Corps (MC, DSO, despatches twice). Chm. Coventry Conservative Assoc., 1945–48; Pres. Coventry Chamber of Commerce, 1951–53; Chm. Manufacturers' Section Cttee of Machine Tool Trades Assoc., 1946–55. Mem. Bd of Trade Machine Tool Advisory Council, 1957–66. Freeman of the City of London. Fellow Royal Commonwealth Society; FInstD; Mem. Inst of Export. DL Warwickshire, 1965. *Recreations:* shooting, fishing, travelling. *Address:* Flat 41, Regency House, Newbold Terrace, Leamington Spa, Warwickshire. *T:* Leamington Spa 24004; Brooklands Close, Ablington, near Bibury, Glos. *T:* Bibury 326. *Club:* Royal Automobile.

CLARK, Colin Grant, MA, DLitt (Oxon); Corresponding Fellow, British Academy; Research Consultant, Queensland University; Director of Institute for Research in Agricultural Economics, Oxford, 1953–69; Fellow of the Econometric Society; *b* 2 Nov. 1905; *s* of James Clark, merchant and manufacturer, Townsville and Plymouth; *m* 1935, Marjorie Tattersall; eight *s* one *d*. *Educ:* Dragon Sch.; Winchester; Brasenose Coll., Oxford; MA 1931, DLitt 1971; MA Cantab 1931; took degree in chemistry; Frances Wood Prizeman of the Royal Statistical Soc., 1928; Asst to late Prof. Allyn Young of Harvard; worked on the New Survey of London Life and Labour, 1928–29, and Social Survey of Merseyside, 1929–30; on Staff of Economic Advisory Council, Cabinet Offices, 1930–31; University Lectr in Statistics, Cambridge, 1931–37. Contested (Lab): North Dorset, 1929; Wavertree (Liverpool), 1931; South Norfolk, 1935. Visiting Lectr at Univs of Melbourne, Sydney, and Western Australia, 1937–38. Under-Sec. of State for Labour and Industry, Dir of Bureau of Industry, and Financial Adviser to the Treasury, Qld, 1938–52. Hon. ScD, Milan; Hon. DEcon: Tilburg; Queensland, 1985; Hon. DEc Monash, 1983. *Publications:* The National Income, 1924–31, 1932; (with Prof. A. C. Pigou) Economic Position of Great Britain, 1936; National Income and Outlay, 1937; (with J. G. Crawford) National Income of Australia, 1938; Critique of Russian Statistics, 1939; The Conditions of Economic Progress, 1940 (revised edns 1951 and 1957); The Economics of 1960, 1942; Welfare and Taxation, 1954; Australian Hopes and Fears, 1958; Growthmanship, 1961; Taxmanship, 1964; (with Miss M. R. Haswell) The Economics of Subsistence Agriculture, 1964; Economics of Irrigation, 1967, 2nd rev. edn (with Dr D. I. Carruthers), 1981; Population Growth and Land Use, 1967; Starvation or Plenty?, 1970; The Value of Agricultural Land, 1973; Regional and Urban Location, 1982; other pamphlets and numerous articles in Economic periodicals. *Recreations:* walking, gardening. *Address:* Department of Economics, University of Queensland, St Lucia, Qld 4067, Australia. *Club:* Johnsonian (Brisbane).

CLARK, David (George); MP (Lab) South Shields, since 1979; *b* 19 Oct. 1939; *s* of George and Janet Clark; *m* 1970, Christine Kirkby; one *d*. *Educ:* Manchester Univ. (BA(Econ), MSc); Sheffield Univ. (PhD 1978). Forester, 1956–57; Laboratory Asst in Textile Mill, 1957–59; Student Teacher, 1959–60; Student, 1960–63; Pres., Univ. of Manchester Union, 1963–64; Trainee Manager in USA, 1964; University Lecturer, 1965–70. Contested Manchester (Withington), Gen. Elec. 1966; MP (Lab) Colne Valley, 1970–Feb. 1974; contested Colne Valley, Oct. 1974; Opposition spokesman on Agriculture and Food, 1973–74, on Defence, 1980–81, on the Environment, 1981–. Chm., Open Spaces Soc., 1979–. *Publications:* The Industrial Manager, 1966; Colne Valley: Radicalism to Socialism, 1981; Victor Grayson, Labour's Lost Leader, 1985; various articles on Management and Labour History. *Recreations:* fell-walking, ornithology. *Address:* House of Commons, SW1A 0AA.

CLARK, Denis; a Recorder, since 1984; barrister; *b* 2 Aug. 1943; twin *s* of John and Mary Clark; *m* 1967, Frances Mary (*née* Corcoran); four *d*. *Educ:* St Anne's RC Primary, Rock Ferry, Birkenhead; St Anselm's Coll., Birkenhead; Sheffield Univ. LLB. Called to the Bar, Inner Temple, 1966; practised Northern Circuit, 1966–. *Recreations:* medieval history, cricket, theatre. *Address:* (chambers) 1 Exchange Flags, Liverpool L2 3XN. *T:* 051-236 7747.

CLARK, Derek John, FCIS; Secretary, Institution of Structural Engineers, since 1982; *b* 17 June 1929; *s* of Robert Clark and Florence Mary (*née* Wise); *m* 1949, Edna Doris Coome; one *s* one *d*. *Educ:* Selhurst Grammar Sch., Croydon; SE London Technical Coll. FCIS 1982 (ACIS 1961). National Service, RAF, 1948–49. Corp. of Trinity House, 1949–66; RICS, 1966–71; ICMA, 1971–82. *Recreations:* athletics (until 1961), squash. *Address:* 7 Elvington Green, Hayesford Park, Bromley, Kent BR2 9DE. *T:* 01–460 9055. *Club:* Anglo-Belgian.

CLARK, Desmond; *see* Clark, John Desmond.

CLARK, Douglas Henderson, MD, FRCSEd, FRCSGlas, FRCPEd; Consultant Surgeon, Western Infirmary, Glasgow, since 1950; *b* 20 Jan. 1917; *s* of William and Jean Clark; *m* 1950, Morag Clark (decd); three *s*. *Educ:* Ayr Acad.; Glasgow Univ. (ChM 1950, MD Hons 1956). FRCSEd, FRCSGlas 1947, FRCPEd 1982. Captain RAMC, 1941–47. Miners Welfare Scholar, 1936; Fulbright Scholar, 1952; William Stewart Halsted Fellow, Johns Hopkins Hosp., 1952–53. Vis. Lectr in America, S Africa, Australia and NZ. Pres., RCPGlas, 1980–82; Dir, James IV Assoc. of Surgeons, 1979–. Hon. FRCS 1982, Hon. FRCSI 1982. Hon. DSc Glasgow, 1983. *Publications:* papers on gastro-enterology and thyroid disease; chapters in text-books. *Address:* 36 Southbrae Drive, Glasgow G13 1PZ. *T:* 041–959 3556.

CLARK, Lt-Gen. Findlay; *see* Clark, Lt-Gen. S. F.

CLARK, (Francis) Leo, QC 1972; **His Honour Judge Leo Clark;** a Circuit Judge, since 1976; *b* 15 Dec. 1920; *s* of Sydney John Clark and Florence Lilian Clark; *m* 1st, 1957, Denise Jacqueline Rambaud; one *s*; 2nd, 1967, Dr Daphne Margaret Humphreys. *Educ:* Bablake Sch.; St Peter's Coll., Oxford (MA). Called to Bar, Lincoln's Inn, 1947. Dep. Chm., Oxford County QS, 1970; a Recorder of the Crown Court, 1972–76. *Recreations:* tennis, travel. *Address:* The Ivy House, Charlbury, Oxon. *T:* Charlbury 810242. *Clubs:* Hurlingham; Union (Oxford).

CLARK, Sir George Anthony, 3rd Bt *cr* 1917; DL; Captain Reserve of Officers, Black Watch, 1939–64; Senator, N Ireland Parliament, 1951–69; *b* 24 Jan. 1914; *e s* of Sir George Ernest Clark, 2nd Bt and Norah Anne (*d* 1966), *d* of W. G. Wilson, Glasgow; *S* father 1950; *m* 1949, Nancy Catherine, 2nd *d* of George W. N. Clark, Carnabane, Upperlands, Co. Derry; one *d*. *Educ:* Canford. DL Belfast, 1961. Pres., Ulster Unionist Council, 1980. *Recreations:* golf, tennis. *Heir:* *b* Colin Douglas Clark, MC, MA [*b* 20 July 1918; *m* 1946, Margaret Coleman, *d* of late Maj.-Gen. Sir Charlton Watson Spinks, KBE, DSO, and *widow* of Major G. W. Threlfall, MC; one *s* two *d*]. *Address:* Tullygirvan House, Ballygowan, Newtownards, Co. Down, Northern Ireland BT23 6NR. *T:* Ballygowan 528267. *Clubs:* Naval and Military; Royal Ulster Yacht (Bangor, Co. Down).

CLARK, Gerald; Inspector of Companies, Companies Investigation Branch, Department of Trade and Industry, since 1984; *b* 18 Sept. 1933; *s* of John George and Elizabeth Clark (*née* Shaw); *m* 1958, Elizabeth McDermott; one *s*. *Educ:* St Cuthbert's Grammar School, Newcastle upon Tyne. Chartered Secretary. National Health Service, Northumberland Exec. Council, 1949–55; National Coal Board 1955–60; Board of Trade, Official Receiver's Service, 1960–71; Companies Investigation Branch, 1971–79; Official Receiver, High Court of Justice, 1981–83; Principal Examiner, Companies Investigation Branch, 1983–84. *Recreations:* music, photography. *Address:* 141 Sunnybank Road, Potters Bar, Herts EN6 2NG. *T:* Potters Bar 57404.

CLARK, Gerald Edmondson; HM Diplomatic Service; Foreign and Commonwealth Office, since 1984; *b* 26 Dec. 1935; *s* of Edward John Clark and Irene Elizabeth Ada Clark (*née* Edmondson); *m* 1967, Mary Rose Organ; two *d*. *Educ:* Johnston Grammar School, Durham; New College, Oxford. MA. Foreign Office, 1960; Hong Kong, 1961; Peking, 1962–63; FO, 1964–68; Moscow, 1968–70; FCO, 1970–73; Head of Chancery, Lisbon, 1973–77; Asst Sec., Cabinet Office, 1977–79; seconded to Barclays Bank International, 1979–81; Commercial Counsellor, Peking, 1981–83. *Recreations:* architecture, economics and politics. *Address:* c/o Foreign and Commonwealth Office, SW1. *Club:* Athenæum.

CLARK, Grahame; *see* Clark, J. G. D.

CLARK, Henry Maitland; Head of Information, Council for Small Industries in Rural Areas, since 1977; *b* 11 April 1929; *s* of Major H. F. Clark, Rockwood, Upperlands, Co. Londonderry; *m* 1972, Penelope Winifred Tindal; one *s* two *d*. *Educ:* Shrewsbury Sch.; Trinity Coll., Dublin; Trinity Hall, Cambridge. Entered Colonial Service and appointed District Officer, Tanganyika, 1951; served in various Districts of Tanganyika, 1951–59; resigned from Colonial Service, 1959. MP (UU) Antrim North (UK Parliament), Oct. 1959–1970; Chm. Conservative Trade and Overseas Develt Sub-Cttee; Member: British Delegation to Council of Europe and WEU, 1962–65; Advisory Council Food Law Res.

Centre, Univ. of Brussels; Exec. Cttee, Lepra (British Leprosy Relief Assoc.); Select Cttee on Overseas Aid and Devélt, 1969–70; Grand Jury, Co. Londonderry, 1970. A Commonwealth Observer, Mauritius General Election, 1967. Wine merchant, IDV Ltd and Cock Russell Vintners, 1972–76. Vice-Pres., Dublin Univ. Boat Club. *Recreations:* rowing coach, sailing, shooting, golf, collecting old furniture. *Address:* Rockwood, Upperlands, Co. Derry, Northern Ireland. *T:* Maghera 42237; Staddles, Hindon Lane, Tisbury, Wilts. *T:* Tisbury 870330. *Clubs:* Kildare Street and University (Dublin); Royal Portrush Golf.

See also H. W. S. Clark.

CLARK, (Henry) Wallace (Stuart), MBE 1970; DL; Director, Wm Clark & Sons, Linen Manufacturers, since 1972; Chairman, Everbond Interlinings, London, since 1969; *b* 20 Nov. 1926; *s* of Major H. F. Clark, MBE, JP, RA, Rockwood, Upperlands, and Sybil Emily (*née* Stuart); *m* 1957, June Elisabeth Lester Deane; two *s*. *Educ:* Shrewsbury School. Lieut, RNVR, 1945–47 (bomb and mine disposal); Cattleman, Merchant Navy, 1947–48. District Comdt, Ulster Special Constabulary, 1955–70; Major, Ulster Defence Regt, 1970–81. Foyle's Lectr, USA tour, 1964. Led Church of Ireland St Columba commemorative curragh voyage, Derry to Iona, 1963. DL 1962, High Sheriff 1969, Co. Londonderry. *Publications:* (jtly) North and East Coasts of Ireland, 1957; (jtly) South and West Coasts of Ireland, 1962, 2nd edn 1970; Guns in Ulster, 1967; Rathlin Disputed Island, 1972; Sailing Round Ireland, 1976; Linen on the Green, 1982. *Recreation:* running oldest linen company in the world. *Address:* Gorteade Cottage, Upperlands, Co. Londonderry, N Ireland. *T:* Maghera 42737. *Clubs:* Royal Cruising, Irish Cruising (Cdre 1962).

See also H. M. Clark.

CLARK, Ian Robertson, CBE 1979; Chairman, Sigma Resources plc, since 1986; Chairman and Managing Director, Clark and Associates, since 1986; Deputy Chairman, GOC Ltd, since 1985; *b* 18 Jan. 1939; *s* of Alexander Clark and Annie Dundas Watson; *m* 1961, Jean Scott Waddell Lang; one *s* one *d*. *Educ:* Dalziel High Sch., Motherwell. FCCA, IPFA. Trained with Glasgow Chartered Accountant; served in local govt, 1962–76, this service culminating in the post of Chief Executive, Shetland Islands Council; full-time Mem., BNOC, from 1976 until privatisation in 1982; Jt Man. Dir, Britoil plc, 1982–85. Member: Scottish Economic Council, 1978–; Glasgow Univ. Court, 1980–. Hon. LLD Glasgow, 1979. *Publications:* Reservoir of Power, 1980; contribs to professional and religious periodicals. *Recreations:* theology, general reading, walking. *Address:* 48 Auchingramont Road, Hamilton, Lanarks. *T:* Hamilton 425110.

CLARK, James Leonard; Head of Personnel, Securities and Investments Board, since 1985; Under Secretary, Establishment Personnel Division, Departments of Industry and Trade Common Services, 1980–83 (Under Secretary, Department of Trade, 1978–83); *b* 8 Jan. 1923; *s* of James Alfred and Grace Clark; *m* 1954, Joan Pauline Richards. *Educ:* Mercers' School. Lieut (A), Fleet Air Arm, 1942–46. Clerical Officer, HM Treasury, 1939; Private Sec. to successive First Secs of State, 1964–67; Cabinet Office, 1969–71; Asst Sec., Price Commn, 1973–75; Dept of Industry, 1975–78. *Address:* 4 Westcott Way, Cheam, Surrey SM2 7JY. *T:* 01–393 2622.

CLARK, James McAdam, CVO 1972; MC 1944; HM Diplomatic Service, retired; *b* 13 Sept. 1916; *er s* of late James Heriot Clark of Wester Coltfield, and late Ella Catherine McAdam; *m* 1946, Denise Thérèse, *d* of late Dr Léon Dufournier, Paris; two *d*. *Educ:* Edinburgh Univ. BSc (Hons) Tech. Chemistry, 1938. Asst Lectr, Edinburgh Univ., 1938–39. Served Royal Artillery, 1939–46 (MC), rank of Capt.; Royal Mil. Coll. of Science, 1945–46 (pac). Min. of Fuel and Power, 1947–48. Entered Foreign (now Diplomatic) Service, 1948; FO, 1948–50; Head of Chancery, Quito, 1950–53; FO, 1953–56; Head of Chancery, Lisbon, 1956–60; Counsellor, UK Rep. to and Alternate Gov. of Internat. Atomic Energy Agency, Vienna, 1960–64; Head of Scientific Relations Dept, FO, 1964–66; Counsellor on secondment to Min. of Technology, 1966–70; Consul-Gen., Paris, 1970–77. Officer Order of Christ of Portugal, 1957. *Publications:* a number of poems and articles. *Recreations:* golf, sailing, music, disputation. *Address:* Hill Lodge, Aldeburgh, Suffolk. *Clubs:* Aldeburgh Yacht, Aldeburgh Golf.

CLARK, Rt. Hon. Joe; *see* Clark, Rt Hon. C. J.

CLARK, Sir John (Allen), Kt 1971; Chairman and Chief Executive, The Plessey Company plc, since 1970; *b* 14 Feb. 1926; *e s* of late Sir Allen Clark and Lady (Jocelyn) Clark, *d* of late Percy and Madeline Culverhouse; *m* 1952, Deirdre Kathleen (marr. diss. 1962), *d* of Samuel Herbert Waterhouse and Maeve Murphy Waterhouse; one *s* one *d*; *m* 1970, Olivia, *d* of H. Pratt and of Mrs R. S. H. Shepard; twin *s* one *d*. *Educ:* Harrow; Cambridge. Served War of 1939–45; commnd RNVR. Received early industrial training with Metropolitan Vickers and Ford Motor Co.; spent over a year in USA, studying the electronics industry. Asst to Gen. Manager, Plessey International Ltd, 1949; Dir and Gen. Man., Plessey (Ireland) Ltd, and Wireless Telephone Co. Ltd, 1950; appointed to main board, The Plessey Co. Ltd, 1953; Gen. Man., Plessey Components Group, 1957; Man. Dir, 1962–70, and Dep. Chm., 1967–70, The Plessey Co. Ltd. Director: International Computers Ltd, 1968–79; Banque Nationale de Paris Ltd, 1976–. Pres., Telecommunication Engineering and Manufacturing Assoc., 1964–66, 1971–73; Vice-President: Inst. of Works Managers; Engineering Employers' Fedn. Member: Nat. Defence Industries Council; Engineering Industries Council, 1975–. CompIEE; FIM. Order of Henry the Navigator, Portugal, 1973. *Recreations:* horseriding, shooting. *Address:* The Plessey Co. plc, Millbank, SW1P 4QP. *T:* 01–834 3855. *Clubs:* Boodle's, Carlton, Naval and Military.

See also Michael W. Clark.

CLARK, Prof. J(ohn) Desmond, CBE 1960; PhD, ScD; FBA 1961; FSA 1952; FRSSAf 1959; Professor of Anthropology, University of California, Berkeley, USA, since 1961; *b* London, 10 April 1916; *s* of late Thomas John Chown Clark and Catharine (*née* Wynne); *m* 1938, Betty Cable, *d* of late Henry Lea Baume and late Frances M. S. (*née* Brown); one *s* one *d*. *Educ:* Monkton Combe Sch.; Christ's Coll., Cambridge. PhD in Archaeology (Cambridge), 1950; ScD Cantab 1975. Dir, Rhodes-Livingstone Museum, Livingstone, N Rhodesia, 1938–61. Has conducted excavations in Southern, East and Equatorial Africa, the Sahara, Ethiopia, Syria, 1938–, India, 1980–82. Military Service in East Africa, Abyssinia, The Somalilands and Madagascar, 1941–46. Founder Mem. and Sec., N Rhodesia Nat. Monuments Commn, 1948–61. Corr. Mem. Scientific Coun. for Africa South of the Sahara, 1956–64, etc. Faculty Res. Lectr, Berkeley, 1979; Raymond Dart Lectr, Johannesburg, 1979; Mortimer Wheeler Lectr, British Acad., 1981. Fellow, Amer. Acad. of Arts and Sciences, 1965; Foreign Associate, Nat. Acad. of Science, USA, 1986. Hon. DSc: Univ. of the Witwatersrand, 1985; Univ. of Cape Town, 1985. Huxley Medal, RAI, 1974; Gold Medal, Soc. of Antiquaries of London, 1985. Comdr, Nat. Order of Senegal, 1968. *Publications:* The Prehistoric Cultures of the Horn of Africa, 1954; The Prehistory of Southern Africa, 1959; The Stone Age Cultures of Northern Rhodesia, 1960; Prehistoric Cultures of Northeast Angola and their Significance in Tropical Africa, 1963; (ed) Proc. 3rd Pan-African Congress on Pre-history, 1957; (comp.) Atlas of African Pre-history, 1967; (ed, with W. W. Bishop) Background to Evolution in Africa, 1967; Kalambo Falls Prehistoric Site, vol. I, 1969, vol. II, 1973; The Prehistory of Africa, 1970; (ed) Cambridge History of Africa, vol I, 1982; (ed with G. R. Sharma) Palaeoenvironment and Prehistory in the Middle Son Valley, India, 1983; (ed with Steven A. Brandt) From Hunters to Farmers: the causes and consequences of food production in Africa, 1984; contribs to learned journals on prehistoric archaeology. *Recreations:* gardening, walking, photography. *Address:* 1941 Yosemite Road, Berkeley, Calif 94707, USA. *T:* 525/4519 Area Code 415. *Club:* Royal Commonwealth Society.

CLARK, Sir John (Douglas), 4th Bt *cr* 1886; *b* 9 Jan. 1923; *s* of Sir Thomas Clark, 3rd Bt and of Ellen Mercy, *d* of late Francis Drake; *S* father, 1977; *m* 1969, Anne, *d* of Angus and Christina Gordon, Aberfawn, Beauly, Inverness-shire. *Educ:* Gordonstoun School; Edinburgh University. *Heir:* *b* Francis Drake Clark [*b* 16 July 1924; *m* 1958, Mary, *d* of late John Alban Andrews, MC, FRCS; one s]. *Address:* 52 Ormidale Terrace, Edinburgh EH12 6EF. *T:* 031–337 5610.

CLARK, John Edward; Secretary, National Association of Local Councils, since 1978; *b* 18 Oct. 1932; *s* of Albert Edward Clark and Edith (*née* Brown); *m* 1969, Judith Rosemary Lester; one *s* (one *d* decd). *Educ:* Royal Grammar Sch., Clitheroe; Keble Coll., Oxford (MA, BCL). Called to the Bar, Gray's Inn, 1957; practised at the Bar, 1957–61. Dep. Sec., National Assoc. of Local (formerly Parish) Councils, (part-time) 1959–61, (full-time) 1961–78. *Publications:* chapters on local govt, public health, and theatres, in Encyclopaedia of Court Forms, 2nd edn 1964 to 1975. *Recreations:* gardening, walking; indoor games, collecting detective fiction. *Address:* 113 Turney Road, SE21 7JB. *T:* 01–274 1381.

CLARK, Prof. (John) Grahame (Douglas), CBE 1971; FBA 1951; MA, PhD, ScD (Cantab); Master of Peterhouse, 1973–80 (Fellow, 1950–73, Honorary Fellow, 1980); *b* 28 July 1907; *s* of Lt-Col Charles Douglas Clark and Maude Ethel Grahame Clark (*née* Shaw); *m* 1936, Gwladys Maude (*née* White); two *s* one *d*. *Educ:* Marlborough Coll.; Peterhouse, Cambridge. Served War of 1939–45, RAFVR, in Photographic Interpretation, 1941–43, and Air Historical Br., 1943–45. Research Student, 1930–32, and Bye-Fellow, 1933–35, of Peterhouse; Faculty Asst Lectr in Archæology, Cambridge, 1935–46, and Univ. Lectr, 1946–52; Disney Prof. of Archæology, Cambridge, 1952–74; Head of Dept of Archæology and Anthropology, Cambridge, 1956–61 and 1968–71. Lectures: Munro, in Archæology, Edinburgh Univ., 1949; Reckitt, British Acad. 1954; Dalrymple in Archæology, Glasgow Univ., 1955; G. Grant MacCurdy, Harvard, 1957; Mortimer Wheeler Meml, New Delhi, 1978; William Evans Vis. Prof., Univ. of Otago, NZ, 1964; Commonwealth Vis. Fellow, Australia, 1964; Hitchcock Prof., Univ. of California, Berkeley, 1969; Leverhulme Vis. Prof., Uppsala, 1972. Member: Ancient Monuments Board, 1954–77; Royal Commn on Historical Monuments, 1957–69; a Trustee, BM, 1975–80; Pres., Prehistoric Soc., 1958–62; Vice-Pres., Soc. of Antiquaries, 1959–62. Hon. Editor, Proceedings Prehistoric Soc., 1935–70. Hon. Corr. Mem., Royal Soc. Northern Antiquaries, Copenhagen, 1946, and of Swiss Prehistoric Soc., 1951; Fellow, German Archæological Inst., 1954; Hon. Member: RIA, 1955; Archaeol. Inst. of America, 1977; Foreign Member: Finnish Archæological Soc., 1958; Amer. Acad. of Arts and Sciences (Hon.) 1961; Royal Danish Acad. of Sciences and Letters, 1964; Royal Netherlands Acad. of Sciences, 1964; For. Fellow, Royal Society of Sciences, Uppsala, 1964; For. Associate, Nat. Acad. of Sciences, USA, 1974; Royal Soc. of Humane Letters, Lund, 1976. Hon. DLitt: Sheffield, 1971; National Univ. of Ireland, 1976; Fil dr, Uppsala, 1977. Hodgkins Medal, Smithsonian Institution, 1967; Viking Medal, Wenner-Gren Foundn, 1971; Lucy Wharton Drexel Gold Medal, Museum, Univ. of Pennsylvania, 1974; Gold Medal, Soc. of Antiquaries, 1978; Chanda Medal, Asiatic Soc., Calcutta, 1979. Comdr, Order of the Danebrog, 1961. *Publications:* The Mesolithic Settlement of Northern Europe, 1936; Archæology and Society 1939, 1947 and 1957; Prehistoric England, 1940, 1941, 1945, 1948, 1962; From Savagery to Civilization, 1946; Prehistoric Europe, The Economic Basis, 1952; Excavations at Star Carr, 1954; The Study of Prehistory, 1954; World Prehistory, An Outline, 1961; (with Stuart Piggott) Prehistoric Societies, 1965; The Stone Age Hunters, 1967; World Prehistory, a new outline, 1969; Aspects of Prehistory, 1970; The Earlier Stone Age Settlement of Scandinavia, 1975; World Prehistory in New Perspective, 1977; Sir Mortimer and Indian Archaeology (Wheeler Memorial Lectures, 1978), 1979; Mesolithic Prelude, 1980; The Identity of Man (as seen by an archaeologist), 1982; Symbols of Excellence, 1986; numerous papers in archæological journals. *Recreations:* gardening, travel, contemporary art. *Address:* 36 Millington Road, Cambridge CB3 9HP. *Club:* United Oxford & Cambridge University.

CLARK, Sir John S.; *see* Stewart-Clark.

CLARK, Ven. Kenneth James, DSC 1944; Archdeacon of Swindon, since 1982; *b* 31 May 1922; *er s* of Francis James Clark and Winifred Adelaide Clark (*née* Martin); *m* 1948, Elisabeth Mary Monica Helen Huggett; three *s* three *d*. *Educ:* Watford Grammar School; St Catherine's Coll., Oxford (MA); Cuddesdon Theological Coll. Midshipman RN, 1940; Lieutenant RN, 1942; served in submarines, 1942–46. Baptist Minister, Forest Row, Sussex, 1950–52; Curate of Brinkworth, 1952–53; Curate of Cricklade with Latton, 1953–56; Priest-in-Charge, then Vicar (1959), of Holy Cross, Inns Court, Bristol, 1956–61; Vicar: Westbury-on-Trym, 1961–72; St Mary Redcliffe, Bristol, 1972–82; Hon. Canon of Bristol Cathedral, 1974. Member, Gen. Synod of C of E, 1980–. *Recreations:* music, travel, gardening. *Address:* 70 Bath Road, Swindon, Wilts SN1 4AY. *T:* Swindon 695059.

CLARK, Leo; *see* Clark, F. L.

CLARK, Leslie Joseph, CBE 1977; BEM 1942; FEng; Chairman, Victor Products (Wallsend) Ltd, 1977–79; Special Adviser on the international gas industry to the Chairman of British Gas, since 1975; Chairman, Northern Gas Region (formerly Northern Gas Board), 1967–75; *b* 21 May 1914; *s* of Joseph George Clark and Elizabeth (*née* Winslow); *m* 1940, Mary M. Peacock; one *s* one *d*. *Educ:* Stationers' Company's Sch.; King's Coll., London, BSc(Eng), 1st Cl. Hons, 1934; MSc 1948. Engineer, Gas Light & Coke Co., then North Thames Gas Board. Chief Engineer, North Thames Gas Board, 1962–65 (pioneered work for development of sea transp. of liquefied natural gas, 1954–63), Dep. Chm., 1965–67. Pres., Instn of Gas Engineers, 1965–66; Pres., IGU, 1973–76 (Vice.-Pres., 1970–73). Member: Court, Univ. of Newcastle upon Tyne, 1972–; Council, Univ. of Durham, 1975–78. CEng, FICE, FIMechE, FIGasE, FInstE, MIEE, AMIChemE. Founder Fellow, Fellowship of Engineering, 1976. Elmer Sperry Award, USA, 1979. *Publications:* technical papers to Instns of Gas Engineers and Mech. Engrs, Inst. of Fuel, World Energy Conf., Internat. Gas Union, etc. *Recreations:* model engineering, walking, photography, music. *Address:* Hillway, New Ridley Road, Stocksfield, Northumberland. *T:* Stocksfield 842339.

CLARK, Malcolm; Inspector General, Insolvency Service, Department of Trade and Industry, since 1984; *b* 13 Feb. 1931; *s* of late Percy Clark and Gladys Helena Clark; *m* 1956, Beryl Patricia Dale; two *s*. *Educ:* Wheelwright Grammar Sch., Dewsbury, Yorks. FCCA 1980. Department of Trade and Industry Insolvency Service: Examiner, 1953–62; Sen. Examiner, 1962–66; Asst Official Receiver, Rochester, 1966–70; Official Receiver, Lytham St Annes, 1970–79; Principal Inspector of Official Receivers, 1979–81; Dep.

Inspector Gen., 1981–84. *Recreations:* theatre, gardening, reading. *Address:* Shallows, Kingfield Road, Woking, Surrey.

CLARK, Very Rev. Malcolm Aiken; Dean, Collegiate Church of St Vincent since 1982, Dean of Edinburgh, 1983–85; *b* 3 Oct. 1905; *s* of Hugh Aiken Clark, MB, CM, and Agnes Roberta Douglas Baxter; *m* 1936, Margherita Felicinna Columba Gannaway (*d* 1973); two *s* one *d*. *Educ:* Drax, Yorks; High School of Glasgow; Lichfield Theological College. Deacon 1934, priest 1935, Glasgow; Curate, St John's, Greenock; Rector, All Saints, Lockerbie, 1938–49, with All Saints, Langholm, 1939–42. Chaplain, RAFVR, 1942–46. Priest-in-charge, St Mary's, Dalkeith, 1949–56; Rector, Good Shepherd, Murrayfield, 1956–77; retired; warrant to officiate, dio. Edinburgh. Chaplain of St Vincent, Edinburgh, Order of St Lazarus of Jerusalem, 1977; Canon 1980, Dean 1982; also Canon of Cathedral Church of St Mary, Edinburgh and Dean, 1983. FSA (Scot.) 1979. *Address:* 12 St Vincent Street, Edinburgh EH3 6SH. *T:* 031–557 3662.

CLARK, Marjorie, (pen-name, Georgia Rivers); journalist, writer of fiction; *b* Melbourne; *d* of George A. and Gertrude M. Clark. *Educ:* Milverton Girls' Grammar Sch. *Publications:* Jacqueline, 1927; Tantalego, 1928; The Difficult Art, 1929; She Dresses for Dinner, 1933; 12 full-length serials, numerous short stories and articles. *Recreation:* music. *Address:* Flat 2, 374 Auburn Road, Hawthorn, Victoria 3122, Australia. *Club:* PEN (Melbourne Centre).

CLARK, Dr Michael; MP (C) Rochford, since 1983; *b* 8 Aug. 1935; *s* of late Mervyn Clark and of Sybilla Norma Clark (*née* Winscott); *m* 1958, Valerie Ethel, *d* of C. S. Harbord; one *s* one *d*. *Educ:* King Edward VI Grammar School, East Retford; King's College London (BSc (1st cl. Hons) Chemistry, 1956); Univ. of Minnesota (Fulbright Scholar, 1956–57); St John's College, Cambridge (PhD 1960). Research Scientist, later Factory Manager, ICI, 1960–66; Smith's Industries Ltd, 1966–69; PA International Management Consultants, 1969–73; Marketing Manager, St Regis Paper Co., 1973–78; Dir, Courtenay Stewart International, 1978–81; PA International Management Consultants, 1981–. Treasurer, 1975–78, Chm., 1980–83, Cambs Cons. Assoc.; Cons. Eastern Area Exec., 1980–83; contested (C) Ilkeston, 1979. Member: Parly Select Cttee for Energy, 1983–; Council, Parly IT Cttee, 1984–; Hon. Secretary: Parly and Scientific Cttee, 1985–; All Party Gp for the Chemical Industry, 1985–; Parly Anglo Nepalese Soc., 1985–. Governor, Melbourn Village Coll., 1974–83 (Chm., 1977–80). *Recreations:* squash, bridge, gardening. *Address:* 82 Marsham Court, Marsham Street, SW1. *T:* 01–828 0620; 6 Buckingham Road, Hockley, Essex. *T:* Southend-on-Sea 205297. *Clubs:* Carlton; Rochford Conservative.

CLARK, Michael Lindsey, PPRBS; sculptor; *b* 1918; *s* of late Phillip Lindsey Clark, DSO, FRBS, and Truda Mary Calnan; *m* 1942, Catherine Heron; five *s* three *d*. *Educ:* Blackfriars Sch.; City of London Art School. ARBS 1949; FRBS 1960; Pres., RBS, 1971–76. Otto Beit Medal for Sculpture, 1960 and 1978, and Silver Medal, 1967, RBS. *Address:* Barford Court Farm, Lampard Lane, Churt, Surrey GU10 2HJ.

CLARK, Michael William, CBE 1977; Deputy Chairman and Deputy Chief Executive, Plessey Co. plc; Chairman, Plessey Electronic Systems Ltd, since 1976; *b* 7 May 1927; *yr s* of late Sir Allen Clark and late Jocelyn Anina Maria Louise Clark (*née* Emerson Culverhouse); *m* 1st, 1955, Shirley (*née* MacPhadyen) (*d* 1974); two *s* two *d*; 2nd, 1985, Virginia, Marchioness Camden. *Educ:* Harrow. 1st Foot Guards, Subaltern, 1945–48. Ford Motor Co.; Bendix Aviation (USA); Plessey Co. plc, 1950– (formed Electronics Div., 1951; Main Bd Dir, 1953); Dir, Corporate Planning, 1965, Man. Dir, Telecommunications Gp, 1967; Chm., Plessey Electronic Systems Ltd, 1976. Member: Electronics EDC, 1975–80; Council, Inst. of Dirs; Nat. Electronics Council; Ct of Univ. of Essex. Comp. IEE, 1964; Comp. IERE, 1965. FBIM 1974. *Recreations:* fishing, forestry. *Address:* Braxted Park, Witham, Essex. *Clubs:* Boodle's, Pratt's.

See also Sir J. A. Clark.

CLARK, Oswald William Hugh, CBE 1978; Assistant Director-General, Greater London Council, 1973–79; *b* 26 Nov. 1917; *s* of late Rev. Hugh M. A. Clark and Mabel Bessie Clark (*née* Dance); *m* 1966, Diana Mary (*née* Hine); one *d*. *Educ:* Rutlish Sch., Merton; Univ. of London (BA; BD Hons). Local Govt Official, LCC (later GLC), 1937–79. Served War, HM Forces, 1940–46: Major, 2nd Derbyshire Yeo., Eighth Army, Middle East, NW Europe. Member: Church Assembly (later General Synod), 1948–; Standing and Legislative Cttees, 1950–; Standing Orders Cttee (Chm.), 1950–; Chm., House of Laity, 1979–85 (Vice-Chm., 1970–79); a Church Commissioner, 1958–, Mem. Bd of Governors, 1966–68, 1969–73, 1977–; Vice-Pres., Corp. of Church House, 1981–. Life Fellow, Guild of Guide Lectrs, 1982. *Recreations:* London's history and development, commemorative and Goss china, heraldry. *Address:* 8 Courtlands Avenue, Hampton, Middlesex TW12 3NT. *T:* 01–979 1081. *Club:* Cavalry and Guards.

CLARK, Paul Nicholas Rowntree; His Honour Judge Paul Clark; a Circuit Judge, since 1985; *b* 17 Aug. 1940; *s* of late Henry Rowntree Clark and of Gwendoline Victoria Clark; *m* 1967, Diana Barbara Bishop; two *s* one *d*. *Educ:* Bristol Grammar Sch.; New Coll., Oxford (Open Schol.; MA (Lit. Hum.)). Called to the Bar, Middle Temple, 1966 (Harmsworth Schol.), Bencher 1982; in practice on Midland and Oxford (formerly Oxford) Circuit, 1966–85; a Recorder, 1981–85. *Address:* 2 Harcourt Buildings, Temple, EC4Y 9DB. *T:* 01–353 6961.

CLARK, Petula, (Sally Olwen); singer, actress; *b* 15 Nov. 1934; *d* of Leslie Clark; *m* 1961, Claude Wolff; one *s* two *d*. Own BBC radio series, Pet's Parlour, 1943; early British films include: Medal for the General, 1944; I Know Where I'm Going, 1945; Here Come the Huggetts, 1948; Dance Hall, 1950; White Corridors, 1951; The Card, 1951; Made in Heaven, 1952; The Runaway Bus, 1953; That Woman Opposite, 1957. Began career as singer in France, 1959. Top female vocalist, France, 1962; Bravos du Music Hall award for outstanding woman in show business, France, 1965; Grammy awards for records Downtown and I Know A Place. Numerous concert and television appearances in Europe and USA including her own BBC TV series. *Films:* Finian's Rainbow, 1968; Goodbye Mr Chips, 1969; Second to the Right and Straight on till Morning, 1982; *musical:* The Sound of Music, Apollo Victoria, 1981. *Address:* c/o John Ashby, Hindworth Management Ltd, 235 Regent Street, W1.

CLARK, Ramsey; lawyer, New York City, since 1970; *b* Dallas, Texas, 18 Dec. 1927; *s* of late Thomas Campbell Clark, Associate Justice, US Supreme Court, and of Mary Ramsey; *m* 1949, Georgia Welch, Corpus Christi, Texas; one *s* one *d*. *Educ:* Public Schs, Dallas, Los Angeles, Washington; Univ. of Texas (BA); Univ. of Chicago (MA, JD). US Marine Corps, 1945–46. Engaged private practice of law, Dallas, 1951–61; Asst Attorney Gen., Dept of Justice, 1961–65; Dep. Attorney Gen., 1965–67, Attorney Gen., 1967–69. Adjunct Professor: Howard Univ., 1969–72; Brooklyn Law Sch., 1973–. *Publication:* Crime in America, 1970. *Address:* 37 West 12th Street, New York, NY 10011, USA.

CLARK, Richard David; County Education Officer, Hampshire, since 1983; *b* 2 Sept. 1934; *s* of David and Enid Clark; *m* 1958, Pamela Mary (*née* Burgess); two *d*. *Educ:* Keele Univ. (BA, DipEd); Univ. de Paris, Sorbonne. Teaching, Woodberry Down Comprehensive School, 1957–61; Education Admin., Herts CC, 1961–69; Asst Educn Officer, Lancs CC, 1969–71; Second Dep. County Educn Officer, Hants CC, 1972–76; Chief Educn Officer, Glos CC, 1976–83. Fellow Commoner, Churchill Coll., Cambridge, 1983. *Recreations:* books, gardening. *Address:* Little Mount, Church Street, Ropley, Alresford, Hants SO24 0DP. *T:* Ropley 3420.

CLARK, Sir Robert (Anthony), Kt 1976; DSC 1944; Chairman: Hill Samuel & Co. Ltd, since 1974; Hill Samuel Group plc, since 1980 (Chief Executive, 1976–80); IMI, since 1981; Marley plc, since 1985; a Director, Bank of England, 1976–85; *b* 6 Jan. 1924; *yr s* of John Clark and Gladys Clark (*née* Dyer); *m* 1949, Andolyn Marjorie Lewis; two *s* one *d*. *Educ:* Highgate Sch.; King's Coll., Cambridge. Served War, Royal Navy, 1942–46 (DSC). Partner with Slaughter and May, Solicitors, 1953; became a director of merchant bankers, Philip Hill, Higginson, Erlangers Ltd (now known as Hill Samuel & Co. Ltd), 1961–; Director: Alfred McAlpine plc (formerly Marchwiel plc), 1957–; Rover (formerly BL plc), 1977–; Shell Transport and Trading Co., plc, 1982–; Eagle Star Holdings Ltd, 1976–. Chairman: Industrial Development Adv. Bd, 1973–80; Review Body on Doctors' and Dentists' Remuneration, 1979–86; Council, Charing Cross and Westminster Med. Sch., 1982–; Dir, ENO, 1983–. *Recreations:* reading, music. *Address:* Munstead Wood, Godalming, Surrey. *T:* Godalming 7867; Hill Samuel & Co. Ltd, 100 Wood Street, EC2P 2AJ. *T:* 01–628 8011. *Club:* Pratt's.

CLARK, Prof. Robert Bernard, DSc, PhD; FIBiol, FRSE; Professor of Zoology, University of Newcastle upon Tyne, since 1966; *b* 13 Oct. 1923; *s* of Joseph Lawrence Clark and Dorothy (*née* Halden); *m* 1st, 1956, Mary Eleanor (*née* Laurence) (marr. diss.); 2nd, 1970, Susan Diana (*née* Smith); one *s* one *d*. *Educ:* St Marylebone Grammar Sch.; Chelsea Polytechnic (BSc London 1944); University Coll., Exeter (BSc 1950); Univ. of Glasgow (PhD 1956); DSc London 1965. FIBiol 1966, FLS 1969, FRSE 1970. Asst Experimental Officer, DSIR Road Research Laboratory, 1944; Asst to Prof. of Zoology, Univ. of Glasgow, 1950; Asst Prof., Univ. of California (Berkeley), 1953; Lectr in Zoology, Univ. of Bristol, 1956; Head of Dept of Zoology and Dir of Dove Marine Laboratory, Univ. of Newcastle upon Tyne, 1966–77, Dir of Research Unit on Rehabilitation of Oiled Seabirds, 1967–76; Dir of NERC Research Unit on Rocky Shore Surveillance, 1981–. Member: NERC, 1971–77 and 1983–86; Royal Commn on Environmental Pollution, 1979–83; Mem. Council, Nature Conservancy, 1975. *Publications:* Neurosecretion (ed, jtly), 1962; Dynamics in Metazoan Evolution, 1964, corrected repr. 1967; Practical Course in Experimental Zoology, 1966; (jtly) Invertebrate Panorama, 1971; (jtly) Synopsis of Animal Classification, 1971; (ed, jtly) Essays in Hydrobiology, 1972; Marine Pollution, 1986; Founder, 1968, and ed, Marine Pollution Bulletin; numerous papers in learned jls. *Recreations:* architecture, music, unambitious gardening, reading undemanding novels. *Address:* Department of Zoology, The University, Newcastle upon Tyne NE1 7RU. *T:* Newcastle upon Tyne 328511; Highbury House, Highbury, Newcastle upon Tyne NE2 3LN. *T:* Newcastle upon Tyne 2814672.

CLARK, Rev. Canon Robert James Vodden; *b* 12 April 1907; *s* of Albert Arthur Clark and Bessie Vodden; *m* 1934, Ethel Dolina McGregor Alexander; one *d*. *Educ:* Dalry Normal Practising Episcopal Church Sch., Edinburgh; Church Army Coll.; Coates Hall Theol. Coll. Ordained, 1941. Men's Social Dept, Church Army, 1926; varied work in homes for men; special work in probation trng home under Home Office, 1934–39; St Paul and St George, Edinburgh, 1941–44; Rector, St Andrew's, Fort William, 1944–47; seconded to Scottish Educn Dept as Warden-Leader of Scottish Centre of Outdoor Trng, Glenmore Lodge, 1947–49; Curate i/c St David's, Edinburgh, 1949–54; Rector of Christ Church, Falkirk, 1954–69; Rector of St Leonards, Lasswade, 1969–79; Canon, Edinburgh, 1962; Dean of Edinburgh, 1967–76; Hon. Canon, Edinburgh, 1976; retd 1979. Mem., Royal Highland and Agric. Soc. *Recreations:* mountaineering (Mem., Scottish Mountaineering Club); photography. *Address:* 15 North Street, St Andrews, Fife, Scotland KY16 9PW.

CLARK, Prof. Ronald George, FRCSE, FRCS; Professor of Surgery, since 1972, Dean of the Faculty, 1982–85, University of Sheffield; Consultant Surgeon; Northern General Hospital, since 1966; Royal Hallamshire Hospital, since 1966; *b* 9 Aug. 1928; *s* of late George Clark and of Gladys Clark; *m* 1960, Tamar Welsh Harvie; two *d*. *Educ:* Aberdeen Acad.; Univ. of Aberdeen. MB, ChB; FRCSE 1960; FRCS 1980. House appts, Aberdeen Royal Infirmary, 1956–57; Registrar, Western Infirmary, Glasgow, 1958–60; Surgical Res. Fellow, Harvard, USA, 1960–61; Lectr in Surgery, Univ. of Glasgow, 1961–65; Sen. Lectr in Surgery, Univ of Sheffield, 1966–72. Examiner, Universities of: Aberdeen, Glasgow, Edinburgh, Liverpool, Newcastle, Leicester, London, Southampton, Malta, Ibadan, Jos. Chm., European Soc. for Parenteral and Enteral Nutrition, 1982–; Council Mem., Nutrition Soc., 1982–85; Scientific Governor, British Nutrition Foundn, 1982–; Member: GMC, 1983–; Assoc. of Surgeons of GB and Ireland, 1968–; Surgical Res. Soc., 1969–. Mem., Editorial Bd, Scottish Medical Jl, 1962–65; Editor-in-Chief, Clinical Nutrition, 1980–82. *Publications:* contribs to books and jls on surgical topics and metabolic aspects of acute disease. *Recreation:* golf. *Address:* Brookline, 2 Chesterwood Drive, Sheffield S10 5DU. *T:* Sheffield 663601. *Club:* Royal Commonwealth Society.

CLARK, Lt-Gen. (Samuel) Findlay, CBE 1945; CD 1950; MEIC; MCSEE; PEng; *b* 17 March 1909; *m* 1937, Leona Blanche Seagram. *Educ:* Univ. of Manitoba (BScEE); Univ. of Saskatchewan (BScME). Lieut, Royal Canadian Signals, 1933. Associate Prof. of Elec. and Mechan. Engrg (Capt.) at RMC Kingston, 1938. Overseas to UK, Aug. 1940 (Major); Comd 5th Canadian Armd Div. Sigs Regt (Lt-Col), 1941. GSO1 Can. Mil. HQ, London, 1942; Staff Course, Camberley, England (Col), 1942–43; CSO, HQ 2nd Canadian Corps until end of War (Brig. 1943). Dep. Chief of Gen. Staff, 1945; Imperial Defence Coll., 1948; Canadian Mil. Observer on Western Union Mil. Cttee; Maj.-Gen. 1949; Canadian Mil. Rep. NATO, London, 1949; Chm., Joint Staff, CALE, London, 1951; QMG of Canadian Army, 1951; GOC Central Comd, 1955; CGS, Sept. 1958–61. Chm., Nat. Capital Commission, 1961–67. Past Col Comdt, Royal Canadian Corps of Signals; Hon. Lt-Col, 741 Comm. Sqn. FRCGS. Legion of Merit (USA), 1945; Comdr Order of Orange Nassau (Netherlands), 1945. OStJ 1975. *Address:* 301–1375 Newport Avenue, Victoria, BC V8S 5E8, Canada. *T:* 592 4338. *Club:* Union (Victoria).

CLARK, Ven. Sidney H.; *see* Harvie-Clark.

CLARK, Terence Joseph, CMG 1985; CVO 1978; HM Diplomatic Service; Ambassador to Iraq, since 1985; *b* 19 June 1934; *s* of Joseph Clark and Mary Clark; *m* 1960, Lieselotte Rosa Marie Müller; two *s* one *d*. *Educ:* Thomas Parmiter's, London. RAF (attached to Sch. of Slavonic Studies, Cambridge), 1953–55; Pilot Officer, RAFVR, 1955. HM Foreign Service, 1955; ME Centre for Arab Studies, 1956–57; Bahrain, 1957–58; Amman, 1958–60; Casablanca, 1961–62; FO, 1962–65; Asst Polit. Agent, Dubai, 1965–68; Belgrade, 1969–71; Hd of Chancery, Muscat, 1972–73; Asst Hd of ME Dept, FCO, 1974–76; Counsellor (Press and Information), Bonn, 1976–79; Chargé d'Affaires, Tripoli, Feb.-March 1981; Counsellor, Belgrade, 1979–82. Dep. Leader, UK Delegn, Conf. on Security and Co-operation in Europe, Madrid, 1982–83; Hd of Information Dept, FCO, 1983–85. Commander's Cross, Order of Merit of Fed. Republic of Germany, 1978. *Recreations:* aquatic sports, amateur dramatics. *Address:* c/o Foreign and Commonwealth Office, SW1A 2AH. *Club:* Royal Commonwealth Society.

CLARK, Prof. Timothy John Hayes, FRCP; Professor of Thoracic Medicine and Dean, United Medical and Dental Schools; Dean, Guy's Hospital, since 1984; Consultant Physician: to Guy's Hospital, since 1968; to Brompton Hospital, since 1970; *b* 18 Oct. 1935; *s* of John and Kathleen Clark; *m* 1961, Elizabeth Ann Day; two *s* two *d. Educ:* Christ's Hospital; Guy's Hospital Medical Sch. BSc 1958; MB BS (Hons) 1961, MD 1967 London. FRCP 1973 (LRCP 1960, MRCP 1962); MRCS 1960. Fellow, Johns Hopkins Hosp., Baltimore USA, 1963; Registrar, Hammersmith Hosp., 1964; Lecturer and Sen. Lectr, Guy's Hospital Med. Sch., 1966; Prof. of Thoracic Med., Guy's Hosp. Med. Sch., later UMDS, 1977–; Dean, UMDS, 1986–. Mem., Council of Governors, UMDS, 1982–. Specialist Adviser to Social Services Cttee, 1981 and 1985. Special Trustee, Guy's Hosp., 1982–86. *Publications:* (jtly) Asthma, 1977, 2nd edn, 1983; (ed) Small Airways in Health and Disease, 1979; (jtly) Topical Steroid Treatment of Asthma and Rhinitis, 1980; (ed) Clinical Investigation of Respiratory Disease, 1981; (jtly) Practical Management of Asthma, 1985; articles in British Medical Jl, Lancet, and other specialist scientific jls. *Recreation:* cricket. *Address:* 8 Lawrence Court, NW7 3QP. *T:* 01–959 4411. *Club:* MCC.

CLARK, Wallace; *see* Clark, H. W. S.

CLARK, Sir William (Gibson), Kt 1980; MP (C) Croydon South, since 1974 (E Surrey, 1970–74); *b* 18 Oct. 1917; *m* 1944, Irene Dorothy Dawson Rands; three *s* one *d. Educ:* .London. Mem. Association of Certified Accountants, 1941. Served in Army, 1941–46 (UK and India), Major. Mem. Wandsworth Borough Council, 1949–53 (Vice-Chm. Finance Cttee). Contested (C) Northampton, 1955; MP (C) Nottingham South, 1959–66. Opposition Front Bench Spokesman on Economics, 1964–66; Chairman: Select Cttee on Tax Credits, 1973; Cons. Back Bench Finance Cttee, 1979–. Jt Deputy Chm., Conservative Party Organisation, 1975–77 (Jt Treasurer, 1974–75). Hon. Nat. Dir, Carrington £2 million Appeal, 1967–68. *Recreations:* tennis, gardening. *Address:* The Clock House, Box End, Bedford. *T:* Bedford 852361; 3 Barton Street, SW1. *T:* 01–222 5759. *Clubs:* Carlton, Buck's.

CLARK, William P.; Counsel, Rogers & Wells, lawyers, since 1985; *b* 23 Oct. 1931; *s* of William and Bernice Clark; *m* 1955, Joan Brauner; three *s* two *d. Educ:* Stanford Univ., California; Loyola Law Sch., Los Angeles, California. Admitted to practice of law, California, 1959; Sen. Member, law firm, Clark, Cole & Fairfield, Oxnard, Calif, 1959–67. Served on Cabinet of California, Governor Ronald Reagan, first as Cabinet Secretary, later as Executive Secretary, 1967–69; Judge, Superior Court, State of California, County of San Luis Obispo, 1969–71; Associate Justice: California Court of Appeal, Second District, Los Angeles, 1971–73; California Supreme Court, San Francisco, 1973–81; Dep. Secretary, Dept of State, Washington, DC, 1981–82; Assistant to Pres. of USA for Nat. Security Affairs, 1982–83; Sec. of the Interior, 1983–85. Chm., Presidential Task Force on Nuclear Weapons Program Management, 1985; Mem., Commn on Defense Management, 1985–86. *Publications:* judicial opinions in California Reports, 9 Cal. 3d through 29 Cal. 3d. *Recreations:* ranching, horseback riding, outdoor sports. *Address:* (office) 1737 H Street NW, Washington, DC 20006, USA; 201 North Figueroa Street, Los Angeles, Calif 90012–2638, USA. *Clubs:* Bohemian; California Cattleman's Association; Rancheros Visitadores (California).

CLARK HUTCHISON; *see* Hutchison.

CLARKE, Prof. Alan Douglas Benson, CBE 1974; Professor of Psychology, University of Hull, 1962–84, now Emeritus; *b* 21 March 1922; *s* of late Robert Benson Clarke and late Mary Lizars Clarke; *m* 1950, Prof. Ann Margaret (*née* Gravely); two *s. Educ:* Lancing Coll.; Univs of Reading and London. 1st cl. hons BA Reading 1948; PhD London 1950; FBPsS. Reading Univ., 1940–41 and 1946–48. Sen. Psychol., 1951–57 and Cons. Psychol., 1957–62, Manor Hosp., Epsom. Dean of Faculty of Science, 1966–68, and Pro-Vice-Chancellor 1968–71, Univ. of Hull. Rapporteur, WHO Expert Cttee on Organization of Services for Mentally Retarded, 1967; Mem. WHO Expert Adv. Panel on Mental Health, 1968–85; Chm., Trng Council for Teachers of Mentally Handicapped, 1969–74; Hon. Vice-Pres., Nat. Assoc. for Mental Health, 1970–; President: Internat. Assoc. for Sci. Study of Mental Deficiency, 1973–76 (Hon. Past-Pres., 1976–); BPsS, 1977–78. Member: Personal Social Services Council, 1973–77; DHSS/SSRC Organizing Gp Transmitted Deprivation, 1974–83 (Chm. 1978–83); Cons., OECD/NZ Conf. on Early Childhood Care and Educn, 1978; Chairman: Sec. of State's Adv. Cttee on Top Grade Clinical Psychologist Posts and Appts, NHS, 1981–82; Adv. Cttee, Thomas Coram Res. Unit, Univ. of London Inst. of Educn, 1981–. Lectures: Maudsley, RMPA, 1967; Stolz, Guy's Hosp., 1972; Tizard Meml, Assoc. for Child Psychol. and Psychiatry, 1983. Hon. Life Mem., Amer. Assoc. on Mental Deficiency, 1975 (Research award, 1977, with Ann M. Clarke). Hon. DSc Hull, 1986. Distinguished Achievement Award for Scientific Lit., Internat. Assoc. for Scientific Study of Mental Deficiency, 1982. Editor, Brit. Jl Psychol., 1973–79; Mem., Editorial Bds of other jls. *Publications* (with Ann M. Clarke): Mental Deficiency: the Changing Outlook, 1958, 4th edn 1985; Mental Retardation and Behavioural Research, 1973; Early Experience: myth and evidence, 1976; (with B. Tizard) Child Development and Social Policy: the life and work of Jack Tizard, 1983; numerous in psychol and med. jls. *Address:* 55 Newland Park, Hull HU5 2DR. *T:* Hull 444141.

CLARKE, Allen; *see* Clarke, C. A. A.

CLARKE, Anthony Peter; QC 1979; a Recorder, since 1985; *b* 13 May 1943; *s* of Harry Alston Clarke and Isobel Clarke; *m* 1968, Rosemary (*née* Adam); two *s* one *d. Educ:* Oakham Sch.; King's Coll., Cambridge (Econs Pt I, Law Pt II; MA). Called to the Bar, Middle Temple, 1965. *Recreations:* golf, tennis, holidays. *Address:* 2 Essex Court, Temple, EC4Y 9AP. *T:* 01–583 8381.

CLARKE, Arthur Charles; *b* 16 Dec. 1917; *s* of Charles Wright Clarke and Nora Mary Willis; *m* 1953, Marilyn Mayfield (marr. diss. 1964). *Educ:* Huish's Grammar Sch., Taunton; King's Coll., London (BSc); FKC 1977. HM Exchequer and Audit Dept, 1936–41. Served RAF, 1941–46. Instn of Electrical Engineers, 1949–50. Techn. Officer on first GCA radar, 1943; originated communications satellites, 1945. Chm., British Interplanetary Soc., 1946–47, 1950–53. Asst Ed., Science Abstracts, 1949–50. Since 1954 engaged on underwater exploration on Gt Barrier Reef of Australia and coast of Ceylon. Extensive lecturing, radio and TV in UK and US. Chancellor, Moratuwa Univ., Sri Lanka, 1979–; Vikram Sarabhai Prof., Physical Research Lab., Ahmedabad, 1980; Marconi Fellowship, 1982; FRAS. Unesco, Kalinga Prize, 1961; Acad. of Astronautics, 1961; World Acad. of Art and Science, 1962; Stuart Ballantine Medal, Franklin Inst., 1963; Westinghouse-AAAS Science Writing Award, 1969; Amer. Inst. of Aeronautics and Astronautics: Aerospace Communications Award, 1974; Hon. Fellow, 1976; Nebula Award, Science Fiction Writers of America, 1972, 1974, 1979; John Campbell Award, 1974; Hugo Award, World Science Fiction Convention, 1974, 1980. *Publications: non-fiction:* Interplanetary Flight, 1950; The Exploration of Space, 1951; The Young Traveller in Space, 1954 (publ. in USA as Going into Space); The Coast of Coral, 1956; The Making of a Moon, 1957; The Reefs of Taprobane, 1957; Voice Across the Sea, 1958; The Challenge of the Spaceship, 1960; The Challenge of the Sea, 1960; Profiles of the

Future, 1962; Voices from the Sky, 1965; (with Mike Wilson): Boy Beneath the Sea, 1958; The First Five Fathoms, 1960; Indian Ocean Adventure, 1961; The Treasure of the Great Reef, 1964; Indian Ocean Treasure, 1964; (with R. A. Smith) The Exploration of the Moon, 1954; (with Editors of Life) Man and Space, 1964; (ed) The Coming of the Space Age, 1967; The Promise of Space, 1968; (with the astronauts) First on the Moon, 1970; Report on Planet Three, 1972; (with Chesley Bonestell) Beyond Jupiter, 1973; The View from Serendip, 1977; (with Simon Welfare and John Fairley) Arthur C. Clarke's Mysterious World, 1980 (also TV series); (with Simon Welfare and John Fairley) Arthur C. Clarke's World of Strange Powers, 1984 (also TV series); Ascent to Orbit, 1984; (with Peter Hyams) The Odyssey File, 1985; *fiction:* Prelude to Space, 1951; The Sands of Mars, 1951; Islands in the Sky, 1952; Against the Fall of Night, 1953; Childhood's End, 1953; Expedition to Earth, 1953; Earthlight, 1955; Reach for Tomorrow, 1956; The City and the Stars, 1956; Tales from the White Hart, 1957; The Deep Range, 1957; The Other Side of the Sky, 1958; Across the Sea of Stars, 1959; A Fall of Moondust, 1961; From the Ocean, From the Stars, 1962; Tales of Ten Worlds, 1962; Dolphin Island, 1963; Glide Path, 1963; Prelude to Mars, 1965; The Nine Billion Names of God, 1967; (with Stanley Kubrick) novel and screenplay, 2001: A Space Odyssey, 1968; The Lost Worlds of 2001, 1972; Of Time and Stars, 1972; The Wind from the Sun, 1972; Rendezvous with Rama, 1973; The Best of Arthur C. Clarke, 1973; Imperial Earth, 1975; The Fountains of Paradise, 1979; 2010: Space Odyssey II, 1982 (filmed 1984); The Songs of Distant Earth, 1986; papers in Electronic Engineering, Wireless World, Wireless Engineer, Aeroplane, Jl of British Interplanetary Soc., Astronautics, etc. *Recreations:* diving, photography, table-tennis. *Address:* 25 Barnes Place, Colombo 7, Sri Lanka. *T:* Colombo 94255; c/o David Higham Associates, 5 Lower John Street, Golden Square, W1R 3PE. *Club:* British Sub-Aqua.

CLARKE, Arthur Grenfell, CMG 1953; *b* 17 Aug. 1906; *m* 1st, 1934, Rhoda McLean Arnott (*d* 1980); 2nd, 1980, Violet Louise Riley. *Educ:* Mountjoy Sch., Dublin; Dublin Univ. Appointed Cadet Officer, Hong Kong, 1929; entered service of Hong Kong Government, 1929; interned in Stanley Camp during Japanese occupation; Financial Sec., 1952–62; retired, 1962. *Address:* Foxdene, Brighton Road, Foxrock, Co. Dublin. *T:* 894368.

CLARKE, Dr Arthur S.; Keeper, Department of Natural History, Royal Scottish Museum, 1980–83; *b* 11 Feb. 1923; *yr s* of late Albert Clarke and Doris Clarke (*née* Elliot); *m* 1951, Joan, *er d* of Walter Andrassy; one *s* one *d. Educ:* Leeds Boys' Modern School; Aireborough Grammar School; Leeds Univ. (BSc 1948, PhD 1951). Pilot, RAF, 1943–46. Assistant Lecturer, Glasgow Univ., 1951; Asst Keeper, Royal Scottish Museum, 1954; Deputy Keeper, 1973. *Address:* Rose Cottage, Yarrow, Selkirk TD7 5LB.

CLARKE, Sir Ashley; *see* Clarke, Sir H. A.

CLARKE, Bernard; *see* Clarke, J. B.

CLARKE, Prof. Bryan Campbell, DPhil; FRS 1982; Foundation Professor of Genetics, University of Nottingham, since 1971; *b* 24 June 1932; *s* of Robert Campbell Clarke and Gladys Mary (*née* Carter); *m* 1960, Ann Gillian, *d* of Prof. John Jewkes, *qv*; one *s* one *d. Educ:* Fay Sch., Southborough, Mass, USA; Magdalen Coll. Sch., Oxford; Magdalen Coll., Oxford (MA, DPhil). FLS 1980. National Service, 1950–52 (Pilot Officer, RAF). Nature Conservancy Res. Student, Oxford Univ., 1956; Asst 1959, Lectr 1963, Reader 1969, Dept of Zoology, Univ. of Edinburgh. Carnegie Fellow, USA, 1964; National Science Foundn Fellow, USA, 1964 and 1968; Res. Fellow, Stanford Univ., 1973; SRC Sen. Res. Fellow, 1976–81. Joint Founder, Population Genetics Gp, 1967; Vice-President: Genetical Soc., 1981; Linnean Soc., 1985–87; Chm., Terrestrial Life Sciences Cttee, NERC, 1984–87. Scientific expeditions to: Morocco, 1955; Polynesia, 1962, 1967, 1968, 1980 and 1982. Lectures: Special, London Univ., 1973; Official Visitor, Australian Genetics Soc., 1979; Nelson, Rutgers Univ., 1980. Editor, Heredity, 1978–85. *Publications:* Berber Village, 1959; contrib. scientific jls, mostly on ecological genetics and evolution. *Recreations:* sporadic painting and gardening; archaeology, computing. *Address:* Linden Cottage, School Lane, Colston Bassett, Nottingham NG12 3FD. *T:* Kinoulton 243. *Club:* Royal Air Force.

CLARKE, Sir (Charles Mansfield) Tobias, 6th Bt *cr* 1831; *b* Santa Barbara, California, 8 Sept. 1939; *e s* of Sir Humphrey Orme Clarke, 5th Bt, and Elisabeth (*d* 1967), *d* of Dr William Albert Cook; *S* father, 1973; *m* 1971, Charlotte (marr. diss. 1979), *e d* of Roderick Walter; *m* 1984, Teresa L. A. de Chair, *d* of Somerset de Chair, *qv*; one *d. Educ:* Eton; Christ Church, Oxford (MA); Univ. of Paris; New York Univ. Graduate Business Sch. Vice Pres., Bankers Trust Co., NY, 1974–80. Hon. Treasurer, Standing Council of the Baronetage, 1980–. *Recreations:* fox hunting, gardening, photography and meeting people; Pres., Bibury Cricket Club; Vice-Pres., Bibury Association Football Club. *Heir: half b* Orme Roosevelt Clarke [*b* 30 Nov. 1947; *m* 1971, Joanna Valentine, *d* of John Barkley Schuster, TD; one *s*]. *Address:* 80A Campden Hill Road, W8 7AA. *T:* 01–937 6213; The Church House, Bibury, Glos GL7 5NR. *T:* Bibury 225. *Clubs:* Boodle's, Pratt's; Pilgrims; Jockey (Paris); The Brook, Racquet & Tennis (New York).

CLARKE, Christopher Simon Courtenay Stephenson; QC 1984; *b* 14 March 1947; *s* of late Rev. John Stephenson Clarke and of Enid Courtenay Clarke; *m* 1974, Caroline Anne Fletcher; one *s* two *d. Educ:* Marlborough College; Gonville and Caius College, Cambridge (MA). Called to the Bar, Middle Temple, 1969; Attorney of Supreme Court of Turks and Caicos Islands, 1975–. *Address:* 42 The Chase, SW4. *T:* 01–622 0765; 1 Brick Court, Temple, EC4. *T:* 01–583 0777. *Club:* Hurlingham.

CLARKE, (Cyril Alfred) Allen, MA; Headmaster, Holland Park Secondary School, 1957–71; *b* 21 Aug. 1910; *s* of late Frederick John Clarke; *m* 1934, Edna Gertrude Francis (decd); three *s. Educ:* Langley Sch., Norwich; Culham Coll. of Educn, Oxon; Birkbeck Coll., Univ. of London; King's Coll., Univ. of London. Entered London Teaching Service, 1933; Royal Artillery, 1940–46; Staff Officer (Major) in Educn Br. of Mil. Govt of Germany, 1945–46; Asst Master, Haberdashers' Aske's Hatcham Boys' Sch., 1946–51; Headmaster: Isledon Sec. Sch., 1951–55; Battersea Co. Sec. Sch., 1955–57. *Recreations:* photography, writing, reading, archaeology. *Address:* 1 Youl Grange, Link Road, Eastbourne, E Sussex BN20 7TR. *T:* Eastbourne 20792.

CLARKE, Prof. Sir Cyril (Astley), KBE 1974 (CBE 1969); FRS 1970; MD, ScD, FRCP, FRCOG; FIBiol; Emeritus Professor and Hon. Nuffield Research Fellow, Department of Genetics, University of Liverpool (Professor of Medicine, 1965–72, Director, Nuffield Unit of Medical Genetics, 1963–72, and Nuffield Research Fellow, 1972–76); Consultant Physician, United Liverpool Hospitals (David Lewis Northern, 1946–58, Royal Infirmary since 1958) and to Broadgreen Hospital since 1946; Director, Medical Research Unit, Royal College of Physicians, since 1983; *b* 22 Aug. 1907; *s* of Astley Vavasour Clarke, MD, JP, and Ethel Mary Clarke, *d* of H. Simpson Gee; *m* 1935, Frieda (Féo) Margaret Mary, *d* of Alexander John Campbell Hart and Isabella Margaret Hart; three *s. Educ:* Wyggeston Grammar Sch., Leicester; Oundle Sch.; Gonville and Caius Coll., Cambridge; Guy's Hosp. (Schol.). 2nd Class Hons, Natural Science Tripos Pt I; MD Cantab 1937; ScD Cantab 1963. FRCP 1949; FRCOG 1970; FRACP 1973; FRCPI 1973; FRSA 1973;

FFCM 1974; FACP 1976; Fellow Ceylon Coll. of Physicians 1974; FRCPE 1975; FRCP(C) 1977; Fellow Linnean Soc. 1981. House Phys., Demonstr in Physiology and Clin. Asst in Dermatology, Guy's Hosp., 1932–36. Life Insurance practice, Grocers' Hall, EC2, 1936–39. Served, 1939–46, as Med Specialist, RNVR: HM Hosp. Ship Amarapoora (Scapa Flow and N Africa), RNH Seaforth and RNH Sydney. After War, Med. Registrar, Queen Elizabeth Hosp., Birmingham. Visiting Prof. of Genetics, Seton Hall Sch. of Med., Jersey City, USA, 1963; Lectures: Lumleian, RCP, 1967; Ingleby, Univ. of Birmingham, 1968; Foundn, RCPath, 1971; Inaugural Faculty, Univ. of Leeds, 1972; P. B. Fernando Meml, Colombo, 1974; Marsden, Royal Free Hosp., 1976; Linacre, 1978; New Ireland, UCD, 1979; William Meredith Fletcher Shaw, RCOG, 1979; Harveian Oration, RCP, 1979; Sir Arthur Hall Meml, Sheffield, 1981. Examr in Med., Dundee Univ., 1965–69. Pres., RCP, 1972–77 (Censor, 1967–69, Sen. Censor, 1971–72, Dir, Med. Services Study Group, 1977–83); Pres. Liverpool Med. Instn, 1970–71; Chm., British Heart Foundn Council, 1982–; Member: MRC Working Party, 1966; Sub-Cttee of Dept of Health and Social Security on prevention of Rhesus hæmolytic disease, 1967–82 (Chm., 1973–82); Bd of Governors, United Liverpool Hosps, 1969; Assoc. of Hungarian Medical Socs, 1973; Pres., Harveian Soc.; Governor and Councillor, Bedford Coll., 1974, Chm. of Council, 1975–85. Chm., Cockayne Trust Fund, Natural History Museum, 1974–. Hon. Fellow, Caius Coll., Cambridge, 1974; Leverhulme Emeritus Fellow, 1980. Hon. FRCPE 1981; Hon. FRCPath 1981; Hon. FRSM 1982; Hon. Mem., Liverpool Med. Inst., 1981. Hon. DSc: Edinburgh, 1971; Leicester, 1971; East Anglia, 1973; Birmingham, Liverpool and Sussex, 1974; Hull, 1977; Wales, 1978; London, 1980. Gold Medal in Therapeutics, Worshipful Soc. of Apothecaries, 1970; James Spence Medal, Brit. Paediatric Assoc., 1973; Addingham Medal, Leeds, 1973; John Scott Medal and Award, Philadelphia, 1976; Fothergillian Medal, Med. Soc., 1977; Gairdner Award, 1977; Ballantyne Prize, RCPEd, 1979; (jtly) Albert and Mary Lasker Foundn Award, 1980; Linnean Medal for Zoology, 1981; Artois-Baillet Latour Health Prize, 1981; Gold Medal, RSM, 1986. *Publications:* Genetics for the Clinician, 1962; (ed) Selected Topics in Medical Genetics, 1969; Human Genetics and Medicine, 1970, 3rd edn 1986; (with R. B. McConnell) Prevention of Rhesus Hæmolytic Disease, 1972; (ed) Rhesus Hæmolytic Disease: selected papers and extracts, 1975; many contribs med. and scientific jls, particularly on prevention of Rhesus hæmolytic disease and on evolution of mimicry in swallowtail butterflies. *Recreations:* small boat sailing, breeding swallowtail butterflies. *Address:* Royal College of Physicians Research Unit, 11 St Andrews Place, Regent's Park, NW1 4LE. *T:* 01–935 1174; 43 Caldy Road, West Kirby, Wirral, Merseyside L48 2HF. *T:* 051–625 8811. *Clubs:* Athenæum; Explorers' (New York); Oxford and Cambridge Sailing Society (Pres., 1975–77); West Kirby Sailing, Royal Mersey Yacht; United Hospitals Sailing (Pres.).

CLARKE, David Clive; QC 1983; a Recorder, since 1981; *b* 16 July 1942; *s* of Philip George Clarke and José Margaret Clarke; *m* 1969, Alison Claire, *d* of Rt Rev. Percy James Brazier, *qv*; three *s*. *Educ:* Winchester Coll.; Magdalene Coll., Cambridge. BA 1964, MA 1968. Called to the Bar, Inner Temple, 1965. In practice, Northern Circuit, 1965–. *Recreations:* exploring canals, sailing, swimming. *Address:* 5 Essex Court, Temple, EC4Y 9AH. *T:* 01–353 4363.

CLARKE, Maj.-Gen. Desmond Alexander Bruce, CB 1965; CBE 1961 (OBE 1944); *b* 15 July 1912; *yr s* of late R. T. Clarke, ICS, LLD, Weybridge and late Mrs R. T. Clarke (*née* Whyte), Loughbrickland, Co. Down; *m* Madeleine, 2nd *d* of Rear-Adm. Walter Glynn Petre, DSO, Weybridge; three *s* two *d*. *Educ:* Stonyhurst Coll.; RMA Woolwich. Commissioned RA, 1932. Served War of 1939–45 (OBE; despatches 4 times); Middle East, India, France, Germany; AA and QMG, 59 (Staffs) Div., 1943; AA and QMG, 43 (Wessex) Div., Dec. 1944. Brig. i/c Administration, Southern Command, 1960–62; Dir of Personal Services, War Office, 1962–64; Dir of Personal Services (Army), Min. of Defence, 1964–66; retd Oct. 1966. Chevalier, Order of the Crown (Belgium), 1945; Croix de Guerre (Belgium), 1945. *Address:* Elm Cottage, Caldbeck, near Wigton, Cumbria. *T:* Caldbeck 433.

CLARKE, Donald Roberts, FCA, FCT; General Manager—Finance, Investors in Industry Group plc (formerly Finance for Industry plc), since 1979; Director, Société Générale Merchant Bank Ltd, since 1981; *b* 14 May 1933; *s* of Harold Leslie Clarke and Mary Clarke; *m* 1959, Susan Charlotte Cotton; one *s* three *d*. *Educ:* Ealing Grammar Sch.; The Queen's Coll., Oxford (MA). FCA 1970 (ACA 1960); FCT 1981. Articled Peat Marwick Mitchell & Co., 1957–62; Accountant, The Collingwood Group, 1962–64; Industrial and Commercial Finance Corporation: Investigating Accountant, 1964; Controller, 1964–67; Br. Manager, 1967–68; Co. Sec., 1968–73; Finance for Industry: Sec./Treasurer, 1973–76; Asst Gen. Man., 1976–79. Member: UGC, 1982–85; Industrial, Commercial and Prof. Liaison Gp, National Adv. Body for Local Authority Higher Educn, 1983–85; Continuing Educn Standing Cttee, Nat. Adv. Body for Local Authority Higher Educn and UGC, 1985–. Council, Assoc. of Corporate Treasurers, 1983– (Chm., ACT Working Party on Fixed Interest Finance, 1983–85). *Recreations:* music, gardening, photography. *Address:* 67 Cottenham Park Road, Wimbledon, SW20 0DR. *T:* 01–947 3213.

CLARKE, His Honour Edward, QC 1960; a Circuit Judge (Judge of the Central Criminal Court), 1964–81; *b* 21 May 1908; *s* of William Francis Clarke; *m* 1948, Dorothy May, *d* of Thomas Leask, Richmond, Surrey; three *s* one *d*. *Educ:* Sherborne Sch.; King's Coll., London. Called to Bar, Lincoln's Inn, 1935. Served War, 1943–46 in France, Belgium, Holland and Germany, Lieut-Col, Judge Advocate-General's Staff. Bencher, 1955, Treasurer, 1973, Lincoln's Inn; Dep. Chm., Herts Quarter Sessions, 1956–63; Dep. Chm., London Quarter Sessions, 1963–64. FKC, 1965. President: King's Coll. London Assoc., 1972–73, 1978–79; Old Shirburnian Soc., 1975–76. *Publications:* (with Derek Walker Smith) The Life of Sir Edward Clarke; Halsbury's Laws of England (Criminal Law). *Recreation:* criminology. *Address:* 19 Old Buildings, Lincoln's Inn, WC2. *T:* 01–405 2980. *Clubs:* Garrick, MCC.

CLARKE, Rt. Rev. Edwin Kent; *see* Edmonton (Alberta), Bishop of.

CLARKE, Edwin (Sisterson), MD, FRCP; Director, Wellcome Institute for the History of Medicine, 1973–79, retired; *b* Felling-on-Tyne, 18 June 1919; *s* of Joseph and Nellie Clarke; *m* 1st, 1949, Margaret Elsie Morrison (marr. diss.); two *s*; 2nd, 1958, Beryl Eileen Brock (marr. diss.); one *d*; 3rd, 1982, Gaynor Crawford. *Educ:* Jarrow Central Sch.; Univ. of Durham Med. Sch. (MD); Univ. of Chicago Med. Sch. (MD). Neurological Specialist, RAMC, 1946–48; Nat. Hosp., Queen Square, 1950–51; Postgrad. Med. Sch. of London, 1951–58; Lectr in Neurology and Consultant Neurologist to Hammersmith Hosp., 1955–58; Asst Sec. to Wellcome Trust, 1958–60; Asst Prof., History of Medicine, Johns Hopkins Hosp. Med. Sch., 1960–62; Vis. Assoc. Prof., History of Medicine, Yale Univ. Med. Sch., 1962–63; Med. Historian to Wellcome Historical Med. Library and Museum, 1963–66; Sen. Lectr and Head of Sub-Dept of History of Medicine, University Coll. London, 1966–72, Reader, 1972–73. *Publications:* (jtly) The Human Brain and Spinal Cord, 1968; (ed) Modern Methods in the History of Medicine, 1971; (jtly) An Illustrated History of Brain Function, 1972; (trans.) Die historische Entwicklung der experimentellen Gehirn- und Rückenmarksphysiologie vor Flourens, by M. Neuburger, 1981; articles in jls dealing with neurology and with history of medicine. *Address:* c/o University Laboratory of Physiology, Parks Road, Oxford OX1 3PT.

CLARKE, Elizabeth Bleckly, CVO 1969; MA; JP; Headmistress, Benenden School, Kent, 1954–Dec. 1975; *b* 26 May 1915; *d* of Kenneth Bleckly Clarke, JP, MRCS, LRCP, Cranborne, Dorset, and Dorothy Milborough (*née* Hasluck). *Educ:* Grovely Manor Sch., Boscombe, Hants; St Hilda's Coll., Oxford, 1933–37. BA 1936, BLitt and MA 1940. Asst Mistress, The Grove Sch., Hindhead, 1937–39; Benenden Sch., 1940–47; called to the Bar, Middle Temple, 1949; Vice-Principal, Cheltenham Ladies' Coll., 1950–54. JP, County of Kent, 1956. *Recreations:* walking, gardening, local history. *Address:* Minden, 1 Waterloo Place, Cranbrook, Kent TN17 3JH. *T:* Cranbook 712139. *Club:* English-Speaking Union.

CLARKE, Sir Ellis (Emmanuel Innocent), TC 1969; GCMG 1972 (CMG 1960); Kt 1963 (but does not use the title within Republic of Trinidad and Tobago); President of Trinidad and Tobago, since 1976 (Governor General and C-in-C, 1973–76); *b* 28 Dec. 1917; *o c* of late Cecil Clarke and of Mrs Elma Clarke; *m* 1952, Eyrmyntrude (*née* Hagley); one *s* one *d*. *Educ:* St Mary's Coll., Trinidad (Jerningham Gold Medal, 1936, and other prizes). London Univ. (LLB 1940); called to the Bar, Gray's Inn, 1940. Private practice at Bar of Trinidad and Tobago, 1941–54; Solicitor-Gen., Oct. 1954; Dep. Colonial Sec., Dec. 1956; Attorney-Gen., 1957–62; Actg Governor, 1960; Chief Justice designate, 1961; Trinidad and Tobago Perm. Rep. to UN, 1962–66; Ambassador: to United States, 1962–73; to Mexico, 1966–73; Rep. on Council of OAS, 1967–73. Chm. of Bd, British West Indian Airways, 1968–72. KStJ 1973. *Address:* President's House, Port of Spain, Trinidad. *Clubs:* Queen's Park Cricket (Port of Spain); Trinidad Turf, Arima Race (Trinidad); Tobago Golf (President, 1969–75).

CLARKE, Frederick, BSc; FBCS; Chairman: WASP Software Ltd, since 1985; Cutts Ltd, 1986; Director, Leisure Investments, since 1985; *b* 8 Dec. 1928; *s* of George and Edna Clarke; *m* 1955, Doris Thompson; two *d*. *Educ:* King James I Grammar Sch., Bishop Auckland; King's Coll., Durham Univ. (BSc 1951). FBCS 1972. Served RAF, 1951–54. Schoolmaster, 1954–57; IBM, 1957–82 (final appts, Gen. Man. and Dir); Chm., Royal Ordnance plc (formerly Royal Ordnance Factories), 1982–85. *Recreations:* golf, cricket, racing, reading. *Address:* Arran, Bute Avenue, Petersham, Richmond, Surrey TW10 7AX.

CLARKE, Geoffrey, RA 1976 (ARA 1970); ARCA; artist and sculptor; *b* 28 Nov. 1924; *s* of John Moulding Clarke and Janet Petts; two *s*. *Educ:* Royal College of Art (Hons). Exhibitions: Gimpel Fils Gallery, 1952, 1955; Redfern Gallery, 1965; Tranman Gallery, 1975, 1976, 1982. Works in public collections: Victoria and Albert Museum; Tate Gallery; Arts Council; Museum of Modern Art, NY; etc. Prizes for engraving: Triennial, 1951; London, 1953, Tokyo, 1957. Commissioned work includes: iron sculpture, Time Life Building, New Bond Street; cast aluminium relief sculpture, Castrol House, Marylebone Road; mosaics, Liverpool Univ. Physics Block and Basildon New Town; stained glass windows for Treasury, Lincoln Cathedral; bronze sculpture, Thorn Electric Building, Upper St Martin's Lane; relief sculpture on Canberra and Oriana; 3 stained glass windows, high altar, cross and candlesticks, the flying cross and crown of thorns, all in Coventry Cathedral; sculpture, Nottingham Civic Theatre; UKAEA Culham; Westminster Bank, Bond Street; Univs of Liverpool, Exeter, Cambridge, Oxford, Manchester, Lancaster and Loughborough; screens in Royal Military Chapel, Birdcage Walk. Further work at Chichester, Newcastle, Manchester, Plymouth, Ipswich, Canterbury, Taunton, Winchester, St Paul, Minnesota, Lincoln, Nebraska, Newcastle Civic Centre, Wolverhampton, Leicester, Churchill Coll., Aldershot, Suffolk Police HQ, All Souls, W1, The Majlis, Abu Dhabi, York House, N1. *Address:* Stowe Hill, Hartest, Bury St Edmunds, Suffolk. *T:* Bury St Edmunds 830319.

CLARKE, Guy Hamilton, CMG 1959; HM Ambassador to Nepal, 1962–63, retired; *b* 23 July 1910; 3rd *s* of late Dr and Mrs Charles H. Clarke, Leicester. *Educ:* Wyggeston Grammar Sch., Leicester; Trinity Hall, Cambridge. Probationer Vice-Consul, Levant Consular Service, Beirut, 1933; transf. to Ankara, 1936; Corfu, 1940; Adana, 1941; Baltimore, 1944; has since served at: Washington, Los Angeles (Consul 1945), Bangkok, Jedda, Kirkuk (Consul 1949), Bagdad, Kirkuk (Consul-Gen. 1951); Ambassador to the Republic of Liberia, 1957–60, and to the Republic of Guinea, 1959–60; Mem. United Kingdom Delegation to United Nations Gen. Assembly, New York, 1960; HM Consul-General, Damascus, Feb. 1961, and Chargé d'Affaires there, Oct. 1961–Jan. 1962. *Address:* 10 Fairlawn House, Christchurch Road, Winchester, Hants SO23 9SR.

CLARKE, Sir (Henry) Ashley, GCMG 1962 (KCMG 1952; CMG 1946); GCVO 1961; FSA; President, Venice in Peril Fund, since 1983 (Vice-Chairman, 1970–83); *b* 26 June 1903; *e s* of H. H. R. Clarke, MD; *m* 1st, 1937, Virginia (marr. diss. 1960), *d* of Edward Bell, New York; 2nd, 1962, Frances (OBE 1984), *d* of John Molyneux, Stourbridge, Worcs. *Educ:* Repton; Pembroke Coll., Cambridge. Entered Diplomatic Service, 1925; 3rd Sec., Budapest and Warsaw; 2nd Sec., Constantinople, FO and Gen. Disarmament Conf, Geneva; 1st Sec., Tokyo; Counsellor, FO; Minister, Lisbon and Paris; Deputy Under-Sec., FO; Ambassador to Italy, 1953–62, retd. London Adviser, Banca Commerciale Italiana, 1962–71; Sec.-Gen., Europa Nostra, 1969–70. Governor: BBC, 1962–67; Brit. Inst. of Recorded Sound, 1964–67; Member: Council, British Sch. at Rome, 1962–78; Exec. Cttee, Keats-Shelley Assoc., 1962–71; D'Oyly Carte Trust, 1964–71; Adv. Council, V&A Mus., 1969–73; Nat. Theatre Bd, 1962–66; Chairman: British-Italian Soc., 1962–67; Italian Art and Archives Rescue Fund, 1966–70; Royal Acad. of Dancing, 1964–69; Dir, Royal Acad. of Music, 1973–84 (Mem. Governing Body, 1967–73). Mem. Gen. Bd, Assicurazioni Generali of Trieste, 1964–84. Hon. Dr of Political Science, Genoa, 1956; Hon. Academician, Accademia Filarmonica Romana, 1962; FSA 1985; Hon. Fellow: Pembroke Coll., Cambridge, 1962; Ancient Monuments Soc., 1969– (Vice-Pres., 1982–); Royal Acad. of Music, 1971; Ateneo Veneto, 1973. Freeman, City of Venice, 1985. Pietro Torta Prize, 1974 and Bolla Award, 1976 (for conservation in Venice). Knight Grand Cross of the Order of Merit of the Republic of Italy, 1957; Knight Grand Cross, Order of St Gregory the Great, 1976; Knight of St Mark, 1979. *Publication:* Restoring Venice: The Madonna dell'Orto (with P. Rylands), 1977. *Recreation:* music. *Address:* The Glebe House, Halstock, near Yeovil, Som BA22 9SG; Fondamenta Bonlini 1113, Dorsoduro, 30123 Venice, Italy. *Clubs:* Athenæum, Garrick.

CLARKE, Sir Henry O.; *see* Osmond-Clarke.

CLARKE, Hilton Swift, CBE 1984; Chairman: Atlantic International Bank Ltd, since 1973; Astley & Pearce, since 1981; *b* 1 April 1909; *yr s* of Frederick Job Clarke; *m* 1st, 1934, Sibyl Muriel (*d* 1975), *d* of late C. J. C. Salter; one *s*; 2nd, 1984, Ann Elizabeth, *d* of late Leonard Marchant. *Educ:* Highgate School. FIB. Bank of England, 1927–67; former Director: Charterhouse Group Ltd, 1967–82 (Chm. Charterhouse Japhet Ltd, 1971–73); United Dominions Trust Ltd, 1967–81; Guthrie Corp., 1967–79; Bank of Scotland Ltd (London Bd), 1967–79; Chm., Exco International plc, 1981–84. Freeman, City of London, 1973. Hon. FRCGP 1975. *Recreations:* gardening, golf. *Address:* 4 Coverdale Avenue, Cooden, Bexhill, E Sussex TN39 4TY. *Clubs:* City of London, Overseas Bankers'; Royal Fowey Yacht.

CLARKE, James Samuel, MC 1943 and Bar 1944; Under-Secretary and Principal Assistant Solicitor, Inland Revenue, 1970–81, retired; Managing Director, Bishop and Clarke Ltd, Building Contractors, since 1981; *b* 19 Jan. 1921; *s* of James Henry and

Deborah Florence Clarke; *m* 1949, Ilse Cohen; two *d. Educ:* Reigate Grammar Sch.; St Catharine's Coll., Cambridge (MA). Army Service, 1941–45: Royal Irish Fusiliers; served 1st Bn N Africa and Italy; Major 1943. Called to Bar, Middle Temple, 1946. Entered Legal Service (Inland Rev.), 1953; Sen. Legal Asst, 1958; Asst Solicitor, 1965. *Recreation:* gardening. *Address:* Dormers, The Downs, Givons Grove, Leatherhead, Surrey KT22 8LH. *T:* Leatherhead 378254. *Clubs:* National Liberal, Royal Automobile.

CLARKE, Prof. John, FRS 1986; Professor of Physics, University of California, Berkeley, since 1973; *b* 10 Feb. 1942; *s* of Victor Patrick and Ethel May Clarke; *m* 1979, Grethe F. Pedersen; one *d. Educ:* Christ's Coll., Cambridge (BA, MA 1968); Darwin Coll., Cambridge (PhD 1968). Postdoctoral Scholar, 1968, Asst Prof., 1969, Associate Prof., 1971–73, Univ. of California, Berkeley. Alfred P. Sloan Foundn Fellow, 1970; Adolph C. and Mary Sprague Miller Inst. for Basic Research into Science Prof., 1975; John Simon Guggenheim Fellow, 1977. FAAAS 1982; Fellow, Amer. Phys. Soc., 1985. Charles Vernon Boys Prize, Inst. of Physics, 1977. *Publications:* numerous contribs to learned jls. *Address:* Department of Physics, University of California, Berkeley, Calif 94720, USA. *T:* (415) 642–3069.

CLARKE, (John) Bernard; Leader, Greater Manchester County Council, 1981–86; *b* 10 March 1934; *s* of John Clarke and Alice (*née* Hewitt); *m* 1955, Patricia Powell; four *s* two *d. Educ:* St Mary's RC Sch., Stockport. Employed by National Carriers Ltd. Mem., Stockport Metrop. Bor. Council, 1963–74 (Leader, 1972–74); Mem., Greater Manchester CC, 1973–86 (Leader of Labour Gp, 1978–86). *Recreations:* angling, gardening. *Address:* 22 Fallowfield Road, North Reddish, Stockport SK5 6XT.

CLARKE, Prof. John Innes; Professor of Geography, since 1968, Pro-Vice-Chancellor and Sub-Warden, since 1984, University of Durham; *b* 7 Jan. 1929; *s* of Bernard Griffith Clarke and Edith Louie (*née* Mott); *m* 1955, Dorothy Anne Watkinson; three *d. Educ:* Bournemouth Sch.; Univ. of Aberdeen (MA 1st cl., PhD); Univ. of Paris (French Govt scholar). FRGS 1963. RAF 1952–54 (Sword of Merit, 1953). Asst Lectr in Geog., Univ. of Aberdeen, 1954–55; Prof. of Geog., Univ. Coll. of Sierra Leone, 1963–65; University of Durham: Lectr in Geog., 1955–63; Reader in Geog., 1965–68; Acting Principal, Trevelyan Coll., 1979–80. Visiting Professor: Univ. of Wisconsin, 1967–68; Cameroon, 1965, 1966, 1967; Clermont-Ferrand, 1974; Cairo, 1982. Acting Chm., Human Geog. Cttee, SSRC, 1975; RGS rep. on British Nat. Cttee for Geography, 1976–81; Chm., IGU Commn on Population Geography, 1980–. Vice-Pres., Eugenics Soc., 1981–84. Silver Medal, RSGS, 1947. *Publications:* Iranian City of Shiraz, 1963; (jtly) Africa and the Islands, 1964, 4th edn 1977; Population Geography, 1965, 2nd edn 1972; (with B. D. Clark) Kermanshah: an Iranian Provincial City, 1969; Population Geography and the Developing Countries, 1971; (jtly) People in Britain: a census atlas, 1980; *edited:* Sierra Leone in Maps, 1966, 2nd edn 1969; An Advanced Geography of Africa, 1975; Geography and Population: approaches and applications, 1984; *co-edited:* Field Studies in Libya, 1960; Populations of the Middle East and North Africa: a geographical approach, 1972; Human Geography in France and Britain, 1976; Régions Géographiques et Régions d'Aménagements, 1978; Change and Development in the Middle East, 1981; Redistribution of Population in Africa, 1982; Population and Development Projects in Africa, 1985; author of many learned articles. *Recreations:* travel, sports (now vicariously), countryside, family history. *Address:* Tower Cottage, The Avenue, Durham DH1 4EB. *T:* Durham 64971.

CLARKE, (John) Neil; Deputy Chairman and Chief Executive, Charter Consolidated, since 1982; Chairman, Johnson Matthey, since 1984; *b* 7 Aug. 1934; *s* of late George Philip Clarke and Norah Marie Clarke (*née* Bailey); *m* 1959, Sonia Heather Beckett; three *s. Educ:* Rugby School; King's College London (LLB). FICA 1959. Partner: Rowley, Pemberton, Roberts & Co., 1960–69; Charter Consolidated, 1969–; Dir, Consolidated Gold Fields, 1982–. *Recreations:* music, tennis, golf. *Address:* High Willows, 18 Park Avenue, Farnborough Park, Orpington, Kent BR6 8LL. *T:* Farnborough, Kent 51651; (office) 01–353 1545. *Clubs:* MCC; Royal West Norfolk Golf, Addington Golf.

CLARKE, Sir Jonathan (Dennis), Kt 1981; **His Honour Judge Sir Jonathan Clarke;** a Circuit Judge, since 1982; *b* 19 Jan. 1930; *e s* of late Dennis Robert Clarke, Master of Supreme Court, and of Caroline Alice (*née* Hill); *m* 1956, Susan Margaret Elizabeth (*née* Ashworth); one *s* three *d. Educ:* Kidstones Sch.; University Coll. London. Admitted Solicitor, 1956; partner in Townsends, solicitors, 1959–82; a Recorder of the Crown Court, 1972–82. Mem. Council, Law Soc., 1964–82, Pres., 1980–81; Sec., Nat. Cttee of Young Solicitors, 1962–64; Member: Matrimonial Causes Rule Cttee, 1967–78; Legal Studies Bd, CNAA, 1968–75; Judicial Studies Bd, 1979–82; Governor, College of Law, 1970–, Chm. of Governors, 1982. *Recreations:* sailing, skiing. *Address:* c/o Midland Bank, 1 Wood Street, Swindon, Wilts. *Clubs:* Farmers'; Royal Western Yacht, Royal Dart Yacht, Law Society Yacht.

CLARKE, Rt. Hon. Kenneth (Harry); PC 1984; QC 1980; MP (C) Rushcliffe Division of Nottinghamshire since 1970; Paymaster-General, since 1985; *b* 2 July 1940; *e c* of Kenneth Clarke, Nottingham; *m* 1964, Gillian Mary Edwards; one *s* one *d. Educ:* Nottingham High Sch.; Gonville and Caius Coll., Cambridge (BA, LLB). Chm., Cambridge Univ. Conservative Assoc., 1961; Pres., Cambridge Union, 1963; Chm., Fedn Conservative Students, 1963. Called to Bar, Gray's Inn 1963; practising Mem., Midland Circuit, 1963–. Research Sec., Birmingham Bow Group, 1965–66; contested Mansfield (Notts) in General Elections of 1964 and 1966. PPS to Solicitor General, 1971–72; an Asst Govt Whip, 1972–74 (Govt Whip for Europe, 1973–74); a Lord Comr, HM Treasury, 1974; Parly Sec., DoT, later Parly Under Sec. of State for Transport, 1979–82; Minister of State (Minister for Health), DHSS, 1982–85. Mem., Parly delegn to Council of Europe and WEU, 1973–74; Sec., Cons. Parly Health and Social Security Cttee, 1974; Opposition Spokesman on: Social Services, 1974–76; Industry, 1976–79. *Publications:* New Hope for the Regions, 1979; pamphlets published by Bow Group, 1964–. *Recreations:* modern jazz music; watching Association Football and cricket, bird-watching. *Address:* House of Commons, SW1.

CLARKE, Dr Malcolm Roy, FRS 1981; Senior Principal Scientific Officer, Marine Biological Association of the UK, since 1978; *b* 24 Oct. 1930; *s* of Cecil Dutfield Clarke and Edith Ellen Woodward; *m* 1958, Dorothy Clara Knight; three *s* one *d. Educ:* eleven schools and finally Wallingford County Grammar Sch.; Hull Univ. BSc 1955, PhD 1958, DSc 1978. National Service, Private, RAMC, 1949–50. Teacher, 1951; Hull Univ., 1951–58; Whaling Inspector in Antarctic, 1955–56; Scientific Officer, later PSO, Nat. Inst. of Oceanography, 1958–71; led Oceanographic Expedns on RRS Discovery, RRS Challenger and RV Sarsia; PSO, Marine Biol Assoc. of UK, 1972–78. *Publications:* papers on squids and whales in Jl of Marine Biol Assoc. etc, and a Discovery Report, 1980. *Recreations:* boating, painting. *Address:* Ridge Court, Court Road, Newton Ferrers, S Devon PL8 1DD. *T:* Plymouth 872738. *Club:* Yealm Yacht (Newton Ferrers).

CLARKE, Marshal Butler C.; *see* Cholmondeley Clarke.

CLARKE, Prof. Martin Lowther; *b* 2 Oct. 1909; *s* of late Rev. William Kemp Lowther Clarke; *m* 1942, Emilie de Rontenay Moon, *d* of late Dr R. O. Moon; two *s. Educ:* Haileybury Coll.; King's Coll., Cambridge. Asst, Dept of Humanity, Edinburgh Univ., 1933–34; Fellow of King's Coll., Cambridge, 1934–40; Asst Lecturer in Greek and Latin, University Coll., London, 1935–37. Foreign Office, 1940–45. Lecturer, 1946–47, and Reader, 1947–48, in Greek and Latin, University Coll., London; Prof. of Latin, University Coll. of North Wales, 1948–74, Vice-Principal, 1963–65, 1967–74. *Publications:* Richard Porson, 1937; Greek Studies in England, 1700 to 1830, 1945; Rhetoric at Rome, 1953; The Roman Mind, 1956; Classical Education in Britain, 1500–1900, 1959; George Grote, 1962; Bangor Cathedral, 1969; Higher Education in the Ancient World, 1971; Paley, 1974; The Noblest Roman, 1981. *Address:* Lollingdon House, Cholsey, Wallingford OX10 9LS. *T:* Cholsey 651389.

CLARKE, Mary; Editor, Dancing Times, since 1963; *b* 23 Aug. 1923; *d* of Frederick Clarke and Ethel Kate (*née* Reynolds); unmarried. *Educ:* Mary Datchelor Girls' School. London Corresp., Dance Magazine, NY, 1943–55; London Editor, Dance News, NY, 1955–70; Asst Editor and Contributor, Ballet Annual, 1952–63; joined Dancing Times as Asst Editor, 1954. Dance critic, The Guardian, 1977–. *Publications:* The Sadler's Wells Ballet: a history and an appreciation, 1955; Six Great Dancers, 1957; Dancers of Mercury: the story of Ballet Rambert, 1962; (with Clement Crisp) Ballet, an Illustrated History, 1973; (with Clement Crisp) Making a Ballet, 1974; (with Clement Crisp) Introducing Ballet, 1976; ed (with David Vaughan) Encyclopedia of Dance and Ballet, 1977; (with Clement Crisp) Design for Ballet, 1978; (with Clement Crisp) Ballet in Art, 1978; (with Clement Crisp) The History of Dance, 1981; (with Clement Crisp) Dancer, Men in Dance, 1984; contrib. Encycl. Britannica. *Address:* 11 Danbury Street, Islington, N1 8LD. *T:* 01–226 9209. *Club:* Gautier.

CLARKE, Neil; *see* Clarke, J. N.

CLARKE, Norman, OBE 1982; Secretary and Registrar, Institute of Mathematics and its Applications, since 1965; *b* 21 Oct. 1916; *o s* of late Joseph Clarke and of Ellen Clarke, Oldham; *m* 1940, Hilda May Watts; two *d. Educ:* Hulme Grammar Sch., Oldham; Univ. of Manchester (BSc). FInstP, FIMA. Pres., Manchester Univ. Union, 1938–39. External Ballistics Dept, Ordnance Bd, 1939–42; Armament Res. Estabt, Br. for Theoretical Res., 1942–45; Dep. Sec., Inst. Physics, 1945–65; Hon. Sec., Internat. Commn on Physics Educn, 1960–66. Southend-on-Sea County Borough Council: Mem., 1961–74; Alderman, 1964–74; Chm. of Watch Cttee, 1962–69 and of Public Protection Cttee, 1969–78; Vice-Chm., Essex Police Authority, 1969–85; Member: Essex CC, 1973–85; Southend-on-Sea Borough Council, 1974– (Mayor, 1975–76; Chm., Highways Cttee, 1980–84; Leader, 1984–). *Publications:* papers on educn; editor and contributor: A Physics Anthology: (with S. C. Brown) International Education in Physics; Why Teach Physics; The Education of a Physicist; contributor: A Survey of the Teaching of Physics in Universities (Unesco); Metrication. *Recreations:* cricket, gastronomy, photography. *Address:* 106 Olive Avenue, Leigh-on-Sea, Essex SS9 3QE. *T:* Southend-on-Sea 558056; Institute of Mathematics and its Applications, Maitland House, Warrior Square, Southend-on-Sea, Essex SS1 2JY. *T:* Southend-on-Sea 612177.

CLARKE, Norman Eley, CB 1985; Deputy Secretary, Department of Health and Social Security, since 1982; *b* 11 Feb. 1930; *s* of Thomas John Laurence Clarke and May (*née* Eley); *m* 1953, Pamela Muriel Colwill; three *s* one *d. Educ:* Hampton Grammar Sch. Grade 5 Officer, Min. of Labour and National Service, 1948–56; Asst Principal, Principal, Asst Sec., Under Sec., 1956–82, with Nat. Assistance Bd, Cabinet Office, Min. of Social Security and DHSS. *Recreations:* reading, tennis, watching Queens Park Rangers, talking. *Address:* Winton, Guildford Lane, Woking, Surrey. *T:* Woking 64453.

CLARKE, Prof. Patricia Hannah, DSc; FRS 1976; Emeritus Professor, University of London, since 1984; Hon. Research Fellow, Chemical and Biochemical Engineering Department, University College London, since 1984; Leverhulme Emeritus Fellow, since 1984; Hon. Professorial Fellow, UWIST, University of Wales, since 1984; *b* 29 July 1919; *d* of David Samuel Green and Daisy Lilian Amy Willoughby; *m* 1940, Michael Clarke; two *s. Educ:* Howells Sch., Llandaff; Girton Coll., Cambridge (BA). DSc London. Armament Res. Dept, 1940–44; Wellcome Res. Labs, 1944–47; National Collection of Type Cultures, 1951–53; Lectr, Dept of Biochemistry, UCL, 1953; Reader in Microbial Biochemistry, 1966, Prof. of Microbial Biochemistry 1974–84. Kan Tong-Po Prof., Chinese Univ. of Hong Kong, 1986. Hon. Gen. Sec., Soc. for General Microbiology, 1965–70; Mem., CNAA, 1973–79. Lectures: Royal Soc. Leeuwenhoek, 1979; Marjory Stephenson, Soc. for Gen. Microbiology, 1981; A. J. Kluyver, Netherlands Soc. for Microbiology, 1981. A Vice-Pres., Royal Soc., 1981–82. Hon. DSc Kent. *Publications:* Genetics and Biochemistry of Pseudomonas (ed with M. H. Richmond), 1975; papers on genetics, biochemistry and enzyme evolution in Jl of Gen. Microbiol. and other jls. *Recreations:* walking, gardening, dress-making. *Address:* Glebe House, School Hill, Stratton, Cirencester, Glos GL7 2LS.

CLARKE, Paul (Henry Francis); His Honour Judge Paul Clarke; a Circuit Judge since 1974; *b* 14 Oct. 1921; *s* of late Dr Richard Clarke, FRCP, Clifton, Bristol; *m* 1955, Eileen Sheila, *d* of late Lt-Col J. K. B. Crawford, Clifton Coll.; two *s* one *d. Educ:* Clifton Coll.; Exeter Coll., Oxford (MA). Served War, Gloucester Regt and Royal Engineers, 1940–46. Called to Bar, Inner Temple, 1949, practising as Barrister from Guildhall Chambers, Bristol, 1949–74. *Address:* Saffron House, Chudleigh, Devon TQ13 0EE.

CLARKE, Peter, CBE 1983; PhD, CChem, FRSC, FInstPet; Principal, Robert Gordon's Institute of Technology, Aberdeen, 1970–85, retired; Chairman, Scottish Vocational Education Council, since 1985; *b* 18 March 1922; *er s* of Frederick John and Gladys May Clarke; *m* 1947, Ethel Jones; two *s. Educ:* Queen Elizabeth's Grammar Sch., Mansfield; University Coll., Nottingham (BSc). Industrial Chemist, 1942; Sen. Chemistry Master, Buxton Coll., 1947; Lectr, Huddersfield Technl Coll., 1949; British Enka Ltd, Liverpool, 1956; Sen. Lectr, Royal Coll. of Advanced Tech., Salford, 1962; Head of Dept of Chemistry and Biology, Nottingham Regional Coll. of Technology, 1963; Vice-Principal, Huddersfield Coll. of Technology, 1965–70. Dir, Aberdeen Shipbuilders Ltd, 1985–. Member: SERC (formerly SRC), 1978–82; Council for Professions Supplementary to Medicine, 1977–85; Scottish Technical Educn Council, 1982–85; CNAA, 1982– (Chm., Cttee for Scotland, 1983). Chm., Assoc. of Principals of Colleges (Scotland), 1976–78; Pres., Assoc. of Principals of Colleges, 1980–81 (Vice-Pres., 1979–80); Chm., Cttee of Principals and Directors of Central Instns, 1974–75, 1980–81. Chm., Aberdeen Enterprise Trust, 1984–; Pres., Aberdeen Business and Professional Club, 1976–77. FRSA 1986. Burgess of Guild, City of Aberdeen, 1973. LLD Aberdeen, 1985. *Publications:* contribs to Jl of Chem. Soc., Chemistry and Industry. *Recreations:* gardening, swimming. *Address:* Dunaber, 12 Woodburn Place, Aberdeen AB1 8JR.

CLARKE, Major Peter Cecil, CVO 1969 (MVO 1964); Chief Clerk, Duchy of Lancaster, and Extra Equerry to HRH Princess Alexandra, the Hon. Mrs Angus Ogilvy; *b* 9 Aug. 1927; *s* of late Captain E. D. Clarke, CBE, MC, Binstead, Isle of Wight; *m* 1950, Rosemary Virginia Margaret Harmsworth, *d* of late T. C. Durham, Appomattox, Virginia, USA; one *s* two *d. Educ:* Eton; RMA, Sandhurst. 3rd The King's Own Hussars and 14th/20th King's Hussars, 1945–64. Seconded as Asst Private Secretary to HRH Princess Marina, Duchess of Kent, 1961–64; Comptroller, 1964–68; Comptroller to HRH Princess

Alexandra, 1964–69. JP Hants, 1971–81. *Recreations:* golf, fishing. *Address:* 6 Gordon Place, W8. *T:* 01–937 0356. *Club:* Cavalry and Guards.

CLARKE, Peter James; Secretary of the Forestry Commission, since 1976; *b* 16 Jan. 1934; *s* of Stanley Ernest Clarke and Elsie May (*née* Scales); *m* 1966, Roberta Anne, *y d* of Robert and Ada Browne; one *s* one *d. Educ:* Enfield Grammar Sch.; St John's Coll., Cambridge (MA). Exec. Officer, WO, 1952–62 (univ., 1957–60), Higher Exec. Officer, 1962; Sen. Exec. Officer, Forestry Commn, 1967, Principal 1972; Principal, Dept of Energy, 1975. *Recreations:* gardening, hill walking, sailing *Address:* 5 Murrayfield Gardens, Edinburgh EH12 6DG. *T:* 031–337 3145.

CLARKE, Reginald Arnold, CMG 1962; OBE 1960; DFC 1945; Director of Compensation, International Bank for Reconstruction and Development (World Bank), Washington, DC, since 1979; *b* 6 May 1921; *s* of late John Leonard Clarke; *m* 1st, 1949, Dorithea Nanette Oswald; three *s* one *d*; 2nd, 1979, Serena Kwang Ok Han. *Educ:* Doncaster Grammar Sch. Royal Air Force, 1939–46; Provincial Administration, Nigeria, 1947–52; Financial Secretary's Office, Nigeria, 1952–57; Federal Ministry of Finance, Nigeria, 1957, Permanent Sec., 1958–63, retd. Asst Dir of Administration, IBRD, 1964–70, Dir of Personnel, 1970–79. *Recreations:* travel, tennis, bridge. *Address:* c/o Midland Bank, Gosforth, Cumbria; 8104 Hamilton Spring Road, Bethesda, Maryland 20817, USA.

CLARKE, Robert Cyril; Group Chief Executive, United Biscuits (Holdings) plc, since 1986; *b* 28 March 1929; *s* of Robert Henry Clarke and Rose Clarke (*née* Bratton); *m* 1952, Evelyn (Lynne) Mary, *d* of Cyrus Harper and Ann Ellen Harper (*née* Jones); three *s* one *d. Educ:* Dulwich Coll.; Pembroke Coll., Oxford (MA Hist.). Served Royal West Kent Regt, 1947–49. Joined Cadbury Bros, as trainee, 1952; Gen. Manager, John Forrest, 1954; Marketing Dir, Cadbury Confectionery, 1957; Man. Dir, 1962, Chm., 1969, Cadbury Cakes; Dir, Cadbury Schweppes Foods, 1969; Man. Dir, McVitie & Cadbury Cakes, 1971; Dir, 1974, Chm. and Man. Dir, 1984, United Biscuits UK; Man. Dir, UB Biscuits, 1977; Dir, United Biscuits (Holdings), 1984. Member: Council, Cake and Biscuit Alliance, 1965–83; Council, ISBA, 1977–84; Resources Cttee, Food and Drink Fedn, 1984–; EDC, Food and Drink Industry, 1984–. FIGD, CBIM. *Recreations:* reading, walking, renovating old buildings, planting trees. *Address:* Easington Farmhouse, Chilton, Aylesbury, Bucks HP8 9EX. *T:* Long Crendon 208272.

CLARKE, Robin Mitchell, MC 1944; JP; DL; Chairman, Gatwick Airport Consultative Committee, since 1982; *b* 8 Jan. 1917; *e s* of Joseph and Mary Clarke; *m* 1946, Betty Mumford; twin *s* and *d. Educ:* Ruckholt Central Sch., Leyton. Middleton and St Bride's Wharf, Wapping, 1932–34; Town Clerk's Office, City of Westminster, 1935–40. War of 1939–45: 12th Regt, RHA (HAC) and 142 (Royal Devon Yeomanry) Fd Regt, RA; Major, 1944; served Sicily and Italy (wounded, despatches, MC). Town Clerk's Office, Westminster, 1946–48; Crawley Development Corporation, 1948–62; Manager, Crawley, Commn for the New Towns, 1962–78; Chief Exec., New Towns Commn, 1978–82. Chm., St Catherine's Hospice, Crawley, 1983–. Master, Worshipful Co. of Chartered Secs and Administrators, 1984–85. ACIS 1949; FCIS 1959 (Mem. Nat. Council, 1968–; Pres., 1978). JP Crawley, 1971; DL West Sussex, 1982. FRSA 1980. *Address:* Mayford Cottage, 89 Golden Avenue, East Preston, W Sussex BN16 1QT. *T:* Rustington 771739. *Club:* Army and Navy.

CLARKE, Roger Eric; Under Secretary, Civil Aviation Policy Directorate, Department of Transport, since 1985; *b* 13 June 1939; *s* of Frederick Cuérel Clarke and late Hilda Josephine Clarke; *m* 1983, Elizabeth Jane, *d* of Gordon W. Pingstone and Anne Ellen Pingstone. *Educ:* UCS, Hampstead; Corpus Christi Coll., Cambridge (MA). Various posts in civil aviation divs of Min. of Aviation, BoT and Depts of Trade and Transport, 1961–72 and 1980–85; Air Traffic Rights Advr to Govt of Fiji, 1972–74; Asst Sec., Insce and Overseas Trade Divs, Dept of Trade, 1975–80. *Recreations:* family, friends, church, garden, walking, theatre, music, languages, travel. *Address:* CAP Directorate, Department of Transport, 2 Marsham Street, SW1P 3EB. *T:* 01–212 4989. *Club:* Reform.

CLARKE, Roger Simon Woodchurch, JP; Chairman, The Imperial Tobacco Co. Ltd, 1959–64; *b* 29 June 1903; *s* of late Charles S. Clarke, Tracy Park, Wick, Bristol; *m* 1936, Nancy Lingard (*d* 1980), *d* of late William Martin, formerly of St Petersburg; no *c. Educ:* RN Colleges, Osborne and Dartmouth. Joined The Imperial Tobacco Co., 1922; Dir, 1944–68. Pro-Chancellor, Bristol Univ., 1975–83. JP Bristol, 1964. Hon. LLD Bristol, 1975. *Address:* The Little Priory, Bathwick Hill, Bath. *T:* Bath 63103.

CLARKE, Major Sir Rupert William John, 3rd Bt *cr* 1882; MBE 1943; late Irish Guards; Director: Conzinc Riotinto of Australia Ltd, since 1962; Custom Credit Corporation; First National Ltd; Morganite Australia Pty Ltd (Chairman, 1976–84); Vice-Chairman, National Australia Bank Ltd (formerly National Bank of Australasia), since 1978 (Director, since 1955); Chairman: United Distillers Co. since 1960; Cadbury Schweppes Australia Ltd (formerly Schweppes (Australia)); Victory Reinsurance Co. of Australia; International Ranch Management Services Pty Ltd; P & O Australia Ltd, since 1983 (Director, since 1980); *b* 5 Nov. 1919; *s* of 2nd Bt and Elsie Florence (who *m* 2nd, 1928, 5th Marquess of Headfort), *d* of James Partridge Tucker, Devonshire; *S* father, 1926; *m* 1947, Kathleen, *d* of P. Grant Hay, Toorak, Victoria, Australia; two *s* one *d* (and one *s* decd). *Educ:* Eton; Magdalen Coll., Oxford (MA). Hon. Fellow, Trinity Coll., Melbourne, 1981. Served War of 1939–45 (despatches, MBE). Dir, Cadbury Schweppes, 1977–85. Dir, Royal Humane Soc. of Australasia. Chm., Vict. Amateur Turf Club. Hon. Consul General for Monaco, 1975– (Hon. Consul, 1961). Chevalier de la Légion d'Honneur, 1979. *Heir: s* Rupert Grant Alexander Clarke, LLB (Hons) [*b* 12 Dec. 1947; *m* 1978, Susannah, *d* of Sir Robert Law-Smith, *qv*; one *s* two *d*]. *Address:* Bolinda Vale, Clarkefield, Vic 3430, Australia; Richmond House, 56 Avoca Street, South Yarra, Vic 3141. *Clubs:* Cavalry and Guards, Lansdowne; Melbourne, Athenæum, Australian (Melbourne); Union (Sydney); Queensland (Brisbane).

CLARKE, Samuel Harrison, CBE 1956; MSc; Hon. MIFireE; *b* 5 Sept. 1903; *s* of Samuel Clarke and Mary Clarke (*née* Clarke); *m* 1st, 1928, Frances Mary Blowers (*d* 1972); one *s* two *d*; 2nd, 1977, Mrs Beryl N. Wood; two step *d. Educ:* The Brunts Sch., Mansfield; University Coll., Nottingham (MSc London). Forest Products Res. Laboratory of DSIR, 1927; Fire Research Div., Research and Experiments Dept, Ministry of Home Security, 1940; Dir of Fire Research, DSIR, and Fire Offices Cttee, 1946–58; Dir of Fuel Research Station, DSIR, 1958; Dir, Warren Spring Laboratory, DSIR, 1958–63; Careers Officer, Min. of Technology, 1963–67 (DSIR, 1964–65). Mem. Stevenage Development Corporation, 1962–71; Vice-Pres., Herts Assoc. for Care and Resettlement of Offenders. *Publications:* papers in scientific and technical jls. *Recreations:* exchanging ideas, painting. *Address:* 35 Lonsdale Court, Lonsdale Road, Stevenage, Herts SG1 5EL.

See also S. L. H. Clarke.

CLARKE, Samuel Laurence Harrison, CEng, FIEE; Assistant Technical Director, GEC plc (Computing & Automation), since 1981; *b* 16 Dec. 1929; *s* of Samuel Harrison Clarke, *qv; m* 1952, Ruth Joan Godwin, *yr d* of Oscar and Muriel Godwin; one *s* three *d. Educ:* Westminster Sch.; Trinity Coll., Cambridge (BA). Director, Elliott Process Automation

Ltd, 1965–69; Technical Dir, GEC-Elliott Automation Ltd, 1970–74; Technical Dir (Automation), GEC-Marconi Electronics Ltd, 1974–81; Director, GEC Computers Ltd, 1971–83. Chairman, Information Engineering Cttee, SERC, 1981–83; Member, Engineering Board, SERC, 1981–83. Dep. Dir, Alvey Programme, DTI, 1983–. *Publications:* various papers in learned and technical jls. *Recreations:* skiing, Scottish dancing, sailing. *Address:* Furzehill, 7 Williams Way, Radlett, Herts WD7 7EZ. *T:* Radlett 2418.

CLARKE, Stanley George, CBE 1975; Chief Inspector of the Prison Service, 1971–74; Member: Prisons Board, 1971–74; Parole Board, 1975–78; *b* Dunfermline, 5 May 1914; *s* of Stanley and Catherine Clarke; *m* 1940, Mary Preston Lewin; one *s* one *d. Educ:* Sutton High Sch., Plymouth (school colours: cricket, Rugby, soccer). Civil Service Clerk: Dartmoor Prison, 1931; Lowdham Grange Borstal, 1933; North Sea Camp, 1935; Borstal Housemaster: Portland, 1937; North Sea Camp, 1939. Served War, 1941–45 (despatches): Sqdn Ldr, RAF. Borstal Housemaster: Hollesley Bay Colony, 1945; Gaynes Hall, 1946. Dep. Governor, Manchester Prison, 1947; Governor: Norwich Prison, 1949; Nottingham Prison, 1952; Eastchurch Prison, 1955; Liverpool Prison, 1959. Asst Dir of Prisons, in charge of North Region, 1964; Asst Controller, Prison Dept, 1970. *Address:* 17 Grundy's Lane, Malvern Wells, Worcs.

CLARKE, Mrs Stella Rosemary, JP; DL; Chairman, new initiatives in training and housing of the young and unemployed; *b* 16 Feb. 1932; *d* of John Herbert and Molly Isabel Bruce King; *m* 1952, Charles Nigel Clarke; four *s* one *d. Educ:* Cheltenham Ladies' Coll.; Trinity Coll. Dublin. Long Ashton RDC: Councillor, Chm. Council, Housing and Public Health Cttees, 1955–73; Mem., Woodspring Dist Council, 1973–76; co-opted Mem., Somerset CC, Social Services and Children's Cttee, 1957–73. A Governor, BBC, 1974–81. Purchased and restored Theatre Royal, Bath, with husband, 1974–76. Mem. Council, Bristol Univ., 1982–. JP Bristol, 1968 (Chm. Juvenile Bench, 1985–); DL Avon, 1986. *Recreations:* family and the variety of life. *Address:* Gatcombe Court, Flax Bourton, near Bristol BS19 1PX. *T:* Bristol 393141.

CLARKE, Brig. Terence Hugh, CBE 1943; *b* 17 Feb. 1904; *e s* of late Col Hugh Clarke, AM, Royal Artillery, and of Mrs Hugh Clarke, Bunces, Kennel Ride, Ascot; *m* 1928, Eileen Armistead (*d* 1982), Hopelands, Woodville, NZ; two *d. Educ:* Temple Grove; Haileybury Coll.; RMA Sandhurst. 2nd Lieut Glos Regt, 1924; served India, 1924–27; China, 1928; India, 1928–31, in IA Ordnance Corps; England, 1931–33, Glos Regt; transferred to RAOC, 1933; Norway, 1940 (despatches); DDOS 1st Army, 1942, as Brig. (despatches, CBE); DDOS 2nd Army, 1944; Normandy to Luneberg, Germany (despatches); comd RAOC Training Centre, 1946; DDOS Southern Command, 1948–50; retired from Army, 1950, to enter industry as a Dir of public and private companies, retired. MP (C) Portsmouth West, 1950–66; Parly Cand. (C) Portsmouth West, 1966, 1970. *Recreations:* capped six times for the Army at Rugby and boxed heavyweight for Army; sailing, ski-ing and horse racing. *Address:* 46 Hollybank Lane, Emsworth, Hants PO10 7UE. *T:* Emsworth 2256.

CLARKE, Thomas, CBE 1980; JP; MP (Lab) Monklands West, since 1983 (Coatbridge and Airdrie, June 1982–1983); *b* 10 Jan. 1941; *s* of James Clarke and Mary (*née* Gordon). *Educ:* All Saints Primary Sch., Airdrie; Columba High Sch., Coatbridge; Scottish College of Commerce. Started working life as office boy with Glasgow Accountants' firm; Asst Director, Scottish Council for Educational Technology, before going to Parliament. Councillor: (former) Coatbridge Council, 1964; (reorganised) Monklands District Council, 1974; Provost of Monklands, 1975–77, 1977–80, 1980–82. Vice-President, Convention of Scottish Local Authorities, 1976–78, President, 1978–80. Chm., PLP Foreign Affairs Cttee, 1983–. Director, award winning amateur film, Give Us a Goal, 1972; former President, British Amateur Cinematographers' Central Council. JP County of Lanark, 1972. *Recreations:* films, reading, walking. *Address:* 12 Lugar Street, Coatbridge, Lanarkshire. *T:* Coatbridge 22550. *Clubs:* Coatbridge Municipal Golf, Easter Moffat Golf.

CLARKE, Thomas Ernest Bennett, OBE 1952; screenwriter; *b* 7 June 1907; 2nd *s* of late Sir Ernest Michael Clarke; *m* 1932, Joyce Caroline Steele (*d* 1983); one *d* (one *s* decd). *Educ:* Charterhouse; Clare Coll., Cambridge. Staff writer on Answers, 1927–35; editorial staff Daily Sketch, 1936; subsequently free-lance journalist. Wrote screen-plays of films: Johnny Frenchman, Hue and Cry, Against the Wind, Passport to Pimlico, The Blue Lamp, The Magnet, The Lavender Hill Mob (Academy and Venice Awards), The Titfield Thunderbolt, The Rainbow Jacket, Who Done It?, Barnacle Bill, A Tale of Two Cities, Gideon's Day, The Horse Without a Head. Other screen credits include For Those in Peril, Halfway House, Champagne Charlie (lyrics), Dead of Night, Train of Events, Encore, Law and Disorder, Sons and Lovers, A Man Could Get Killed. *Play:* This Undesirable Residence. *Publications:* Go South-Go West, 1932; Jeremy's England, 1934; Cartwright Was a Cad, 1936; Two and Two Make Five, 1938; What's Yours?, 1938; Mr Spirket Reforms, 1939; The World Was Mine, 1964; The Wide Open Door, 1966; The Trail of the Serpent, 1968; The Wrong Turning, 1971; Intimate Relations, 1971; This is Where I Came In (autobiog.), 1974; The Man Who Seduced a Bank, 1977; Murder at Buckingham Palace, 1981; Grim Discovery, 1983. *Recreations:* racing, travel. *Address:* 13 Oakleigh Court, Oxted, Surrey.

CLARKE, Sir Tobias; see Clarke, Sir C. M. T.

CLARKE, Tom; freelance screenwriter, playwright; *b* 7 Nov. 1918; *s* of Herman C. Clarke and May Dora Carter; *m* 1st, 1945, B. D. Gordon; one *s* three *d*; 2nd, 1953, J. I. Hampton; two *s*; 3rd, 1960, Ann Wiltshire; one *d. Educ:* Tonbridge School. Served War, Royal Artillery, 1939–46 (Captain). Called to Bar, Gray's Inn, 1951. Freelance writer, 1958–. TV plays and films include: Mad Jack, 1971; Stocker's Copper, 1972; Billion Dollar Bubble, 1975; Muck and Brass, 1982; Past Caring, 1985; stage play, Come Again, 1983. Grand Prize, Monte Carlo TV Festival, 1972; UNRRA Silver Dove, 1972; Mention d'Honneur, Prague TV Festival, 1973; Writer's Guild Award, 1973; BAFTA Award, 1973; Mention d'Honneur, Venice Film Festival, 1985. *Recreations:* nursing hypochondria and awaiting fulfilment of optimistic astrological predictions. *Address:* c/o Judy Daish Associates, 83 Eastbourne Mews, W2 6LQ. *T:* 01–262 1101.

CLARKE, William Malpas, CBE 1976; Director General and Deputy Chairman, British Invisible Exports Council (formerly Committee on Invisible Exports), since 1976 (Director, 1966–76); *b* 5 June 1922; *o s* of late Ernest and Florence Clarke; *m* 1st, 1946, Margaret Braithwaite; two *d*; 2nd, 1973, Faith Elizabeth Dawson. *Educ:* Audenshaw Grammar Sch.; Univ. of Manchester. Served Royal Air Force, 1941–46; Flying Instructor, 1942–44; Flight-Lieut, 1945. Editorial Staff, Manchester Guardian, 1948–55; The Times, 1955–66: City Editor, 1957–62; Financial and Industrial Editor, 1962–66; Editor, The Banker, March-Sept. 1966, Consultant 1966–76. Chm., Grindlays Bank, Jersey, 1981–; Deputy Chairman: City Communications Centre, 1976–; Trade Indemnity Co. Ltd, 1980–; Director: UK Provident Instn, 1967–; Romney Trust plc, 1976–; Swiss Reinsurance Co (UK) plc, 1977–; Raeburn Investment Trust plc, 1980–; ANZ Holdings, 1985–; ANZ Merchant Bank, 1985–. Chm., Harold Wincott Financial Journalist Press Award Panel. Governor: The Hospitals for Sick Children (Chm., Appeal Trust);

Greenwich Theatre. *Publications:* The City's Invisible Earnings, 1958; The City in the World Economy, 1965; Private Enterprise in Developing Countries, 1966; (ed, as Director of Studies) Britain's Invisible Earnings, 1967; (with George Pulay) The World's Money, 1970; Inside the City, 1979, rev. edn 1983; How the City of London Works: an introduction, 1986. *Recreations:* books, theatre. *Address:* 37 Park Vista, Greenwich, SE10. *T:* 01–858 0979. *Club:* Reform.

CLARKE HALL, Denis; architect; President, Architectural Association, 1958–59; Chairman, Architects Registration Council of the UK, 1963–64; *b* 4 July 1910; *m* 1936, Mary Garfitt; one *s* two *d. Educ:* Bedales. Holds AA Dip. *Address:* Moorhouse, Iping, Midhurst, W Sussex.

CLARKSON, Ven. Alan Geoffrey; Archdeacon of Winchester since 1984; Vicar of Burley, Ringwood, since 1984; *b* 14 Feb. 1934; *s* of Instructor Captain Geoffrey Archibald Clarkson, OBE, RN and Essie Isabel Bruce Clarkson; *m* 1959, Monica Ruth (*née* Lightburne); two *s* one *d. Educ:* Sherborne School; Christ's Coll., Cambridge (BA 1957, MA 1961); Wycliffe Hall, Oxford. Nat. Service Commn, RA, 1952–54. Curate: Penn, Wolverhampton, 1959–60; St Oswald's, Oswestry, 1960–63; Wrington with Redhill, 1963–65; Vicar, Chewton Mendip with Emborough, 1965–74; Vicar of St John Baptist, Glastonbury with Godney, 1974–84; Priest in Charge: West Pennard, 1981–84; Meare, 1981–84; St Benedict, Glastonbury, 1982–84. *Recreations:* music, gardening, carpentry. *Address:* The Vicarage, Church Corner, Burley, Ringwood BH24 4AP. *T:* Burley 2303.

CLARKSON, Prof. Brian Leonard, DSc; FEng 1986; Principal, University College of Swansea, since 1982; *b* 28 July 1930; *s* of L. C. Clarkson; *m* 1953, Margaret Elaine Wilby; three *s* one *d. Educ:* Univ. of Leeds (BSc, PhD). Hon. DSc 1984). FRAeS; Fellow, Soc. of Environmental Engineers; FInst Acoustics. George Taylor Gold Medal, RAeS, 1963. Dynamics Engineer, de Havilland Aircraft Co., Hatfield, Herts, 1953–57; Southampton University: Sir Alan Cobham Research Fellow, Dept of Aeronautics, 1957–58; Lectr, Dept of Aeronautics and Astronautics, 1958–66; Prof. of Vibration Studies, 1966–82; Dir, Inst. of Sound and Vibration Res., 1967–78; Dean, Faculty of Engrg and Applied Science, 1978–80; Deputy Vice-Chancellor, 1980–82. Sen. Post Doctoral Research Fellow, Nat. Academy of Sciences, USA, 1970–71 (one year's leave of absence from Southampton). Sec., Internat. Commn on Acoustics, 1975–81. Pres., Fedn of Acoustical Socs of Europe, 1982–84. Mem., SERC, 1984–. *Publications:* author of sections of three books: Technical Acoustics, vol. 3 (ed Richardson) 1959; Noise and Acoustic Fatigue in Aeronautics (ed Mead and Richards), 1967; Noise and Vibration (ed White and Walker), 1982; (ed) Stochastic Problems in Dynamics, 1977; technical papers on Jet Noise and its effect on Aircraft Structures, Jl of Royal Aeronautical Soc., etc. *Recreations:* walking, gardening, travelling, golf. *Address:* University College of Swansea, Singleton Park, Swansea SA2 8PP. *T:* Swansea 295154.

CLARKSON, Derek Joshua; QC 1969; **His Honour Judge Clarkson;** a Circuit Judge, since 1977; *b* 10 Dec. 1929; *o s* of Albert and Winifred Charlotte Clarkson (*née* James); *m* 1960, Peternella Marie-Luise Ilse Canenbley; one *s* one *d. Educ:* Pudsey Grammar Sch.; King's Coll., Univ. of London. LLB (1st cl. Hons) 1950. Called to Bar, Inner Temple, 1951; Nat. Service, RAF, 1952–54 (Flt Lt). In practice as Barrister, 1954–77; Prosecuting Counsel to Post Office on North-Eastern Circuit, 1961–65; Prosecuting Counsel to Inland Revenue on North-Eastern Circuit, 1965–69; Recorder of Rotherham, 1967–71; Recorder of Huddersfield, 1971; a Recorder of the Crown Court, 1972–77. Mem., Gen. Council of the Bar, 1971–73. Inspector of companies for the Department of Trade, 1972–73, 1975–76. *Recreations:* theatre-going, walking, book collecting. *Address:* 24 John Islip Street, Westminster, SW1; 72A Cornwall Road, Harrogate, N Yorks.

CLARKSON, Prof. Geoffrey Peniston Elliott, PhD; Professor of Business Administration, since 1980, and Dean, College of Business Administration, since 1977, Northeastern University, Boston; Visiting Professor, Sloan School of Management, Massachusetts Institute of Technology, since 1975; *b* 30 May 1934; *s* of George Elliott Clarkson and Alice Helene (*née* Manneberg); *m* 1960, Eleanor M. (*née* Micenko); two *d. Educ:* Carnegie-Mellon Univ., Pittsburgh, Pa (BSc, MSc, PhD). Asst Prof., Sloan Sch. of Management, MIT, 1961–65, Associate Prof., 1965–67. Vis. Ford Foundn Fellow, Carnegie-Mellon Univ., 1965–66; Vis. Prof., LSE, 1966–67; Nat. Westminster Bank Prof. of Business Finance, Manchester Business Sch., Univ. of Manchester, 1967–77. Dir of and consultant to public and private manufng and financial services cos, 1969–. *Publications:* Portfolio Selection: a simulation of trust investment, USA 1962 (Ford Dissertation Prize, 1961); The Theory of Consumer Demand: a critical appraisal, USA 1963; Managerial Economics, 1968; (with B. J. Elliott) Managing Money and Finance, 1969 (3rd edn 1982); Jihad, 1981. *Recreations:* fishing, sailing, reading. *Address:* College of Business Administration, Northeastern University, Boston, Mass 02115, USA. *Clubs:* Royal Automobile, Crockfords.

CLARRICOATS, Prof. Peter John Bell, FEng; Professor of Electrical and Electronic Engineering, Queen Mary College, University of London, since 1968, and Head of Department, since 1979; *b* 6 April 1932; *s* of John Clarricoats and Cecilia (*née* Bell); *m* 1st, 1955, Gillian (*née* Hall) (marr. diss. 1962); one *s* one *d*; 2nd, 1968, Phyllis Joan (*née* Lloyd); two *d* one step *s* one step *d. Educ:* Minchenden Grammar Sch.; Imperial College. BSc (Eng), PhD, DSc (Eng) 1968; FInstP 1964, FIEE 1967, FIEEE 1967, FCGI 1980, FEng 1983. Scientific Staff, GEC, 1953–58; Lectr, Queen's Univ. Belfast, 1959–62; Sheffield Univ., 1962–63; Prof. of Electronic Engineering, Univ. of Leeds, 1963–67. Mem., Governing Body, QMC, 1976–79, Dean of Engineering, 1977–80. Chairman: 1st Internat. Conf. on Antennas and Propagation, IEE, 1978; European Microwave Conf., 1979; IEE Electronics Div., 1978–79; British Nat. Cttee for Radio Science, 1985–; Mem., IEE Council, 1964–67, 1977–80; IEE Awards: Premia, Electronics Section, 1960, 1961; Marconi, 1974; Coopers Hill Meml Prize, 1964. Co-Editor, Electronics Letters (IEE Jl), 1964–. *Publications:* Microwave Ferrites, 1960; (with A.D. Olver) Corrugated Horns for Microwave Antennas, 1984; papers on antennas and waveguides. *Recreations:* music, photography, formerly squash and mountaineering. *Address:* 7 Falcon Close, Sawbridgeworth, Herts. *T:* Bishop's Stortford 723561.

CLATWORTHY, Robert, RA 1973 (ARA 1968); sculptor; *b* 31 Jan. 1928; *s* of E. W. and G. Clatworthy; *m* 1954, Pamela Gordon (marr. diss.); two *s* one *d. Educ:* Dr Morgan's Grammar Sch., Bridgwater. Studied West of England Coll. of Art, Chelsea Sch. of Art, The Slade. Teacher, West of England Coll. of Art, 1967–71. Visiting Tutor, RCA, 1960–72; Mem., Fine Art Panel of Nat. Council for Diplomas in Art and Design, 1961–72; Governor, St Martin's Sch. of Art, 1970–71; Head of Dept of Fine Art, Central Sch. of Art and Design, 1971–75. Exhibited: Hanover Gall., 1954, 1956; Waddington Galls, 1965; Holland Park Open Air Sculpture, 1957; Battersea Park Open Air Sculpture, 1960, 1963; Tate Gallery, British Sculpture in the Sixties, 1965; British Sculptors 1972, Burlington House; Basil Jacobs Fine Art Ltd, 1972; Diploma Galls, Burlington Ho., 1977; Photographers Gall., 1980; Quinton Green Fine Art, London, 1986. Work in Collections: Arts Council, Contemporary Art Soc., Tate Gallery, Victoria and Albert Museum, Greater London Council, Nat. Portrait Gall. (portrait of Dame Elisabeth Frink, 1985). Monumental

Horse and Rider, Finsbury Avenue, London, 1984. *Address:* Moelfre, Cynghordy, Llandovery, Dyfed SA20 0UW.

CLAUSEN, Alden Winship, (Tom); President, The World Bank, 1981–86; Director, Wellcome plc, since 1986; *b* 17 Feb. 1923; *s* of Morton and Elsie Clausen; *m* 1950, Mary Margaret Crassweller; two *s. Educ:* Carthage Coll. (BA 1944); Univ. of Minnesota (LLB 1949); Grad. Harvard Advanced Management Program, 1966. Admitted to Minnesota Bar, 1949. Joined Bank of America, 1949: Vice-Pres., 1961–65; Sen. Vice-Pres., 1965–68; Exec. Vice-Pres., 1968–69; Vice-Chm. of Bd, 1969; Pres. and Chief Exec. Officer, 1970–81. President: Fed. Adv. Council, 1972; Internat. Monetary Conf., Amer. Bankers' Assoc., 1977. Former Director: US-USSR Trade and Econ. Council, 1974–81; Nat. Council for US-China Trade, 1974–81; Co-Chm., Japan-California Assoc., 1973–80. Hon. LLD: Carthage, 1970; Lewis and Clark, 1978; Gonzaga Univ., 1978; Univ. of Notre Dame, 1981; Hon. DPS Univ. Santa Clara, 1981. *Address:* c/o Wellcome plc, 183 Euston Road, NW1 2BP.

CLAVELL, James; author, screenwriter, film director and producer; *s* of late Comdr R. C. Clavell, OBE, RN and Eileen Ross Clavell; *m* 1953, April, *d* of late Comdr W. S. Stride, DSO, RN; two *d. Educ:* Portsmouth Grammar Sch. Served World War II, Captain, RA; POW Far East, 1941–45. Emigrated to USA, 1953. Screenwriter: The Fly, 1958; Watussi, 1958; The Great Escape, 1960; Satan Bug, 1962; 633 Squadron, 1963; director, Where's Jack?, 1968; writer/producer/director: Five Gates to Hell, 1959; Walk Like a Dragon, 1960; To Sir with Love, 1966; Last Valley, 1969; Children's Story . . . But Not for Children, 1982; exec. producer, Shōgun (TV series), 1980. Pilot: Multi-engine, Instrument Rating, Helicopter. Hon. PhD Maryland, 1980; Hon. DLitt Bradford, 1986. Awards: Emmy; Peabody; Critics; Golden Globe. Goldener Eiger (Austria), 1972. *Publications:* King Rat, 1962; Tai-Pan, 1966; Shōgun, 1976; Noble House, 1980; The Children's Story but not for Children (novella), 1982; (forward to) Sun Tsu; The Art of War, 1983; Thrump-O-moto (fantasy), 1985; Whirlwind, 1986. *Address:* c/o Foreign Rights, Inc., Suite 1007, 200 West 57 Street, New York, NY 10019, USA. *Clubs:* Caledonian, Royal Over-Seas League.

CLAXTON, Rt. Rev. Charles Robert, MA, DD; Assistant Bishop, Diocese of Exeter since 1971; *b* 16 Nov. 1903; *s* of Herbert Bailey and Frances Ann Claxton; *m* 1930, Agnes Jane Stevenson; two *s* two *d. Educ:* Monkton Combe Sch.; Weymouth Coll.; Queen's Coll., Cambridge. Deacon, 1927; Priest, 1928; Curate, St John's, Stratford, E15, 1927–29; St John, Redhill, 1929–33; St Martin-in-the-Fields, 1944–46; Vicar Holy Trinity, Bristol, 1933–38; Hon. Canon of Bristol Cathedral, 1942–46; Hon. Chaplain to Bishop of Bristol, 1938–46; Hon. Chaplain to Bishop of Rochester, 1943–46; Rector of Halsall, near Ormskirk, Lancs, 1948–59; Suffragan Bishop of Warrington, 1946–60; Bishop of Blackburn, 1960–71. Hon. Officiating Chaplain, RN, 1978. *Recreation:* golf. *Address:* St Martins, 6 The Lawn, Budleigh Salterton, Devon EX9 6LT. *T:* Budleigh Salterton 2193.

CLAXTON, John Francis, CB 1969; Deputy Director of Public Prosecutions 1966–71; *b* 11 Jan. 1911; *s* of late Alfred John Claxton, OBE, and Dorothy Frances O. Claxton (*née* Roberts); *m* 1937, Norma Margaret Rawlinson (*d* 1983); no *c. Educ:* Tonbridge Sch.; Exeter Coll., Oxford (BA). Called to Bar, 1935. Joined Dept of Dir of Public Prosecutions, 1937; Asst Dir, 1956–66. *Recreations:* model making, gardening. *Address:* The White Cottage, 9 Lock Road, Marlow, Bucks SL7 1QN. *T:* Marlow 2744.

CLAXTON, Maj.-Gen. Patrick Fisher, CB 1972; OBE 1946; General Manager, Regular Forces Employment Association, 1971–81; *b* 13 March 1915; *s* of late Rear-Adm. Ernest William Claxton and Kathleen O'Callaghan Claxton, formerly Fisher; *m* 1941, Jóna Gudrún Gunnarsdóttir (*d* 1980); two *d. Educ:* Sutton Valence Sch.; St John's Coll., Cambridge (BA). Served GHQ, India, 1943–45; Singapore, 1945–46; WO, 1946–48; British Element Trieste Force, 1949–51; HQ, BAOR, 1952–54; RASC Officers' Sch., 1955–56; Amphibious Warfare HQ and Persian Gulf, 1957–58; Col, WO, 1959–60; Brig., WO, 1961–62; DST, BAOR, 1963–65; CTO, BAOR, 1965–66; Comdt, Sch. of Transport, and ADC to the Queen, 1966–68; Transport Officer-in-Chief (Army), 1969–71, retired; Col. Comdt, RCT, 1972–80. Governor and Mem. Administrative Bd, Corps of Commissionaires, 1977–. FCIT. *Publication:* The Regular Forces Employment Association 1885–1985, 1985. *Address:* The Lodge, Beacon Hill Park, Hindhead, Surrey GU26 6HU. *T:* Hindhead 4437. *Club:* MCC.

CLAY, Charles John Jervis; *b* 19 March 1910; *s* of late Arthur J. Clay and Bridget Clay (*née* Parker-Jervis); *m* 1935, Patricia Agnes, *d* of late James and Dorothy Chapman; one *s* two *d. Educ:* Eton; New College, Oxford; Pitmans Business College. Served War, 1939–45, Rifle Bde (Officer), and PoW (despatches). Antony Gibbs & Sons Ltd, 1933–70 (Man. Dir, 1952–70); Dir, Internat. Commodities Clearing House Ltd, 1952–84, Man. Dir, 1971–75, Dep. Chm., 1975–77; Dir, R. J. Rouse & Co. Ltd, 1961–74; Dir-Gen., Accepting Houses Cttee, 1971–76. Chairman: Anton Underwriting Agencies Ltd, 1958–76; Wool Testing Services International Ltd, 1961–74; Automated Real-Time Investments Exchange Ltd, 1972–82; London Bd, National Mutual Life Assoc. of Australasia Ltd, 1969–83; Quality Control International Ltd, 1974–84; Mem. London Cttee, Ottoman Bank, 1955–84; Dir, A. P. Bank Ltd, 1977–86. Member: Public Works Loans Bd, 1958–70; ECGD Adv. Council, 1965–70. Mem. Executive Cttee, BBA, 1973–76; Mem. Council, CBI, 1972–76. *Publications:* Modern Merchant Banking, 1976; papers and speeches on Commodity Futures Trading and Clearing. *Recreations:* sailing, archery, gardening. *Address:* Lamberts, Hascombe, Godalming, Surrey. *T:* Hascombe 240. *Clubs:* Brooks's, MCC.

CLAY, John Lionel, TD 1961; **His Honour Judge Clay;** a Circuit Judge, since 1977; *b* 31 Jan. 1918; *s* of Lionel Pilleau Clay and Mary Winifred Muriel Clay; *m* 1952, Elizabeth, *d* of Rev. Canon Maurice and Lady Phyllis Ponsonby; one *s* three *d. Educ:* Harrow Sch.; Corpus Christi Coll., Oxford (MA). Served War of 1939–45 (despatches): in 1st Bn Rifle Bde, N Africa (8th Army), Italy, 1941–44; Instr, Infantry Heavy Weapons Sch., 1944–45; 1st Bn Rifle Bde, Germany, 1945–46. London Rifle Bde Rangers (TA); Major, 2nd i/c Bn and 23 SAS (TA), 1948–60. Called to the Bar, Middle Temple, 1947; a Recorder of the Crown Court, 1975–76. Chm., Horserace Betting Levy Appeal Tribunal for England and Wales, 1974–77. Freeman of City of London, 1980; Liveryman, Gardeners' Co., 1980. *Recreations:* gardening, fishing, shooting. *Address:* Newtimber Place, Hassocks, Sussex BN6 9BU.

CLAY, John Martin; Vice Chairman, Hambros, since 1986 (Director, since 1970); Deputy Chairman, Hambros Bank Ltd, 1972–84 (Director, 1961–84); *b* 20 Aug. 1927; *s* of late Sir Henry Clay and Gladys Priestman Clay; *m* 1952, Susan Jennifer, *d* of Lt-Gen. Sir Euan Miller, KCB, KBE, DSO, MC; four *s. Educ:* Eton; Magdalen Coll., Oxford. Chairman: Johnson & Firth Brown Ltd, 1973–; Hambro Life Assurance Ltd, 1978–84. Dir, Bank of England, 1973–83. Mem., Commonwealth Develt Corp., 1970–. FBIM 1971. *Recreation:* sailing. *Address:* 41 Bishopsgate, EC2. *Club:* Royal Thames Yacht.

CLAY, Sir Richard (Henry), 7th Bt *cr* 1841, of Fulwell Lodge, Middlesex; *b* 2 June 1940; *s* of Sir Henry Felix Clay, 6th Bt, and of Phyllis Mary, *yr d* of late R. H. Paramore, MD, FRCS; *S* father, 1985; *m* 1963, Alison Mary, *d* of Dr James Gordon Fife; three *s* two *d.*

Educ: Eton. FCA 1966. *Recreation:* sailing. *Heir: s* Charles Richard Clay, *b* 18 Dec. 1965. *Address:* 18 De Freville Avenue, Cambridge CB4 1HS. *Club:* Aldeburgh Yacht.

CLAY, Robert Alan; MP (Lab) Sunderland North, since 1983; *b* 2 Oct. 1946; *m* 1980, Uta Christa. *Educ:* Bedford Sch.; Gonville and Caius Coll., Cambridge. Busdriver, Tyne and Wear PTE, 1975–83. Branch Chm., GMBATU, 1977–83. Treasurer, Campaign Gp of Labour MPs. *Recreations:* walking, reading. *Address:* 12 Park Parade, Roker, Sunderland, Tyne and Wear; House of Commons, SW1A 0AA. *T:* 01–219 6230; (constituency office) Sunderland 78878.

CLAY, Trevor, MPhil; SRN, RMN; FRCN; General Secretary to the Royal College of Nursing of the United Kingdom since 1982 (Deputy General Secretary, 1979–82); *b* 10 May 1936; *s* of Joseph Reginald George and Florence Emma Clay. *Educ:* Nuneaton and Bethlem Royal and Maudsley Hosps. (SRN 1957; RMN 1960); MPhil Brunel Univ. 1976. FRCN 1985. Staff Nurse and Charge Nurse, Guy's Hosp., London, 1960–65; Asst Matron in charge of Psychiatric Unit, Queen Elizabeth II Hosp., Welwyn Garden City, 1965–67; Asst Regional Nursing Officer, NW Metropolitan Regional Hosp. Board, 1967–69; Director of Nursing, Whittington Hosp., London, 1969–70; Chief Nursing Officer, N London Group HMC, 1970–74; Area Nursing Officer, Camden and Islington Area Health Authority, 1974–79. Dir. Internat. Council of Nurses, 1985–. *Publications:* thesis on The Workings of the Nursing and Midwifery Advisory Committees in the NHS since 1974; various articles on nursing and health care. *Recreations:* work, good friends, Mozart. *Address:* The Royal College of Nursing, 20 Cavendish Square, W1M 0AB. *Club:* Reform.

CLAYDON, Geoffrey Bernard; Principal Assistant Treasury Solicitor and Legal Adviser, Department of Energy, since 1980; *b* 14 Sept. 1930; *s* of Bernard Claydon and Edith Mary (*née* Lucas); unmarried. *Educ:* Leeds Modern; King Edward's, Birmingham; Birmingham Univ. (LLB). Articled at Pinsent & Co., Birmingham, 1950; admitted Solicitor, 1954. Legal Asst, 1959, Sen. Legal Asst, 1965, Treasury Solicitor's Dept; Asst Solicitor, DTI, 1973; Asst Treasury Solicitor, 1974. Mem., Editorial Bd, Jl of Energy and Natural Resources Law, 1983–. Sec., National Tramway Museum, 1958–84 (Vice-Chm., 1969–); Vice-Pres., Light Rail Transit Assoc. (formerly Light Railway Transport League), 1968– (Chm. of League, 1963–68); Chairman: Tramway and Light Railway Soc., 1967–; Consultative Panel for Preservation of British Transport Relics, 1982–; Mem., Inst. of Traffic Admin, 1972–. *Recreations:* rail transport, travel. *Address:* 23 Baron's Keep, W14 9AT. *T:* 01–603 6400. *Club:* Royal Automobile.

CLAYSON, Christopher William, CBE 1974 (OBE 1966); retired; *b* 11 Sept. 1903; *s* of Christopher Clayson and Agnes Lilias Montgomerie Hunter; *m* Elsie Webster Breingan. *Educ:* George Heriot's Sch.; Edinburgh University. MB, ChB 1926; DPH 1929; MD (Gold Medal) Edinburgh 1936; FRCPE 1951; FRCP 1967. Physician: Southfield Hosp., Edinburgh, 1931–44; Edinburgh City Hosp., 1939–44; Lectr in Tuberculosis Dept, Univ. of Edinburgh, 1939–44; Med. Supt, Lochmaben Hosp., 1944–48; Consultant Phys. in Chest Medicine, Dumfries and Galloway, 1948–68; retd from clinical practice, 1968. Served on numerous Govt and Nat. Health Service cttees, 1948–; Chairman: Scottish Licensing Law Cttee, 1971–73; Scottish Council for Postgrad. Med. Educn, 1970–74. Pres., RCPE, 1966–70; Mem., Scottish Soc. of Physicians; Mem., Thoracic Soc.; Hon. FACP 1968; Hon. FRACP 1969; Hon. FRCPGlas 1970; Hon. FRCGP 1971. William Cullen Prize, RCPE, 1978. *Publications:* various papers on tuberculosis problem and on alcoholism in leading medical jls. *Recreations:* gardening, fishing. *Address:* Cockiesknowe, Lochmaben, Lockerbie, Dumfriesshire. *T:* Lochmaben 231. *Clubs:* Caledonian; New (Edinburgh).

CLAYSON, Sir Eric (Maurice), Kt 1964; DL; *b* 17 Feb. 1908; *yr s* of late Harry and Emily Clayson; *m* 1933, Pauline Audrey Wright; two *s*. *Educ:* Woodbridge Sch. Chartered Accountant, 1931; Birmingham Post & Mail Group Ltd: Dir, 1944–74; Man. Dir, 1947; Jt Man. Dir, 1957; Chm., 1957–74; Director: Associated TV Ltd, 1964–75; ATV Network Ltd, 1966–78; Sun Alliance & London Insurance Group, 1965–75 (Chm., Birmingham Area Bd, 1967–80); Birmingham Reg. Bd, Lloyds Bank Ltd, 1966–78. President: Birmingham Publicity Assoc., 1948–49 (Chm., 1947–48); W Midlands Newspaper Soc., 1949–50; The Newspaper Soc., 1951–52 (Hon. Treasurer, 1956–60); Birmingham Branch, Incorporated Sales Managers' Assoc., 1953–54; Birmingham and Midland Inst., 1967–68. Vice-Pres., Fédération Internationale des Editeurs de Journaux et Publications, 1954–67. Chairman: Exec. Cttee, British Industries Fair, 1956–57; Midlands Regular Forces Resettlement Cttee, 1961–70 (Mem., 1958–70). Director: The Press Assoc. Ltd, 1959–66 (Chm., 1963–64); Reuters Ltd, 1961–66. Member: Council, Birmingham Chamber of Industry and Commerce, 1951– (Vice-Pres., 1953–54, Pres., 1955–56); Gen. Council of the Press, 1953–72; BBC Midland Regional Adv. Council, 1954–57; W Midland Regional Economic Planning Council, 1965–68. Governor, The Royal Shakespeare Theatre, Stratford-upon-Avon, 1963–83 (Mem. Exec. Council, 1963–74); Life Governor, Birmingham Univ., 1956–, Mem. Council, 1959–71. President: Radio Industries Club of the Midlands, 1965–69; Midland Counties Golf Assoc., 1960–62; Vice-Pres., Professional Golfers' Assoc., 1959–83. Guardian, Standard of Wrought Plate in Birmingham, 1969–84. DL West Midlands, 1975–84. *Recreation:* reading newspapers. *Address:* Clare Park, near Farnham, Surrey. *T:* Farnham 850878.

CLAYTON, Prof. Barbara Evelyn, (Mrs W. Klyne), CBE 1983; MD, PhD; FRCP, PRCPath; Professor of Chemical Pathology and Human Metabolism since 1979, and Dean of the Faculty of Medicine since 1983, University of Southampton; *b* 2 Sept. 1922; *m* 1949, William Klyne; one *s* one *d*. *Educ:* Univ. of Edinburgh (MD, PhD). FRCP 1972; FRCPath 1971; FRCPE 1985. Consultant in Chem. Pathology, Hosp. for Sick Children, London, 1959–70; Prof. of Chem. Pathology, Inst. of Child Health, Univ. of London, 1970–78. Hon Consultant, 1979–, Mem., 1983–, Southampton and SW Hants HA. Member: Commonwealth Scholarship Commn, 1977–; Royal Commn on Environmental Pollution, 1981–; Standing Med. Adv. Cttee (DHSS), 1981–; Cttee on Toxicity of Chemicals in Food, Consumer Products and the Environment, DHSS, 1977–; Systems Bd, MRC, 1974–77; Chairman: Adv. Cttee on Borderline Substances, 1971–83; MRC Adv. Gp on Lead and Neuropsychol Effects in Children, 1983–; Cttee on Med. Aspects of Contaminants in Air, Soil and Water, 1984–. Council, RCPath, 1982–(Pres., 1984–); GMC, 1983–. Past-President: Assoc. of Clinical Biochemists, 1977, 1978; Soc. for Study of Inborn Errors of Metabolism, 1981–82. Mem. Bd of Govs, Hosps for Sick Children, London, 1968–78. Hon. Fellow, British Dietetic Assoc, 1976. Hon. DSc Edinburgh, 1985. Jessie MacGregor Prize for Med. Sci., RCPE, 1985. *Publications:* contrib. learned jls, incl. Jl Endocrinol., Arch. Dis. Childhood, and BMJ. *Recreations:* natural history, walking. *Address:* 16 Chetwynd Drive, Bassett, Southampton SO2 3HZ. *T:* Southampton 769937.

CLAYTON, Captain Sir David (Robert), 12th Bt *cr* 1732, of Marden; Shipmaster since 1970; *b* 12 Dec. 1936; *s* of Sir Arthur Harold Clayton, 11th Bt, DSC, and of Alexandra, Lady Clayton, *d* of late Sergei Andreevsky; *S* father, 1985; *m* 1971, Julia Louise, *d* of late Charles Henry Redfearn; two *s*. *Educ:* HMS Conway. Joined Merchant Service, 1953; promoted to first command as Captain, 1970. *Recreations:* shooting, sailing. *Heir: s* Robert Philip Clayton, *b* 8 July 1975. *Address:* Rock House, Kingswear, Dartmouth, Devon TQ6 0BX. *T:* Kingswear 453. *Club:* Royal Dart Yacht (Kingswear).

CLAYTON, Prof. Frederick William; Professor of Classics, 1948–75, and Public Orator, 1965–73, University of Exeter; *b* 13 Dec. 1913; *s* of late William and Gertrude Clayton, Liverpool; *m* 1948, Friederike Luise Büttner-Wobst; two *s* two *d*. *Educ:* Liverpool Collegiate Sch.; King's Coll., Cambridge. Members' Essay Prizes (Latin and English), Porson Prize, Browne Medal, 1933; Craven Scholar in Classics, 1934; Chancellor's Medal for Classics, 1935; Fellow of King's Coll., 1937. Served War, Nov. 1940–Oct. 1946, Signals, Field Security, RAF Intelligence, India. *Publications:* The Cloven Pine, 1942; various articles. *Address:* Halwill, Clydesdale Road, Exeter, Devon. *T:* Exeter 71810.

See also G. Clayton.

CLAYTON, Air Marshal Sir Gareth (Thomas Butler), KCB 1970 (CB 1962); DFC 1940, and Bar, 1944; Air Secretary, Ministry of Defence, 1970–72, retired; *b* 13 Nov. 1914; *s* of Thomas and Katherine Clayton; *m* 1938, Elisabeth Marian Keates; three *d*. *Educ:* Rossall Sch. Entered RAF, 1936; served in various Bomber and Fighter Squadrons, 1936–44; RAF Staff Coll., 1944; Air Attaché, Lisbon, 1946–48; various command and staff appts, 1948–58; idc 1959; Air Ministry, 1960–61; Air Officer Commanding No. 11 Group, RAF, 1962–63; Chief of Staff, Second Allied Tactical Air Force, Germany, 1963–66; Dir-Gen., RAF Personal Services, 1966–69; Chief of Staff, HQ RAF Strike Command, 1969–70. Life Vice-Pres., RAFA (Chm., 1978–80). *Address:* 41 High Street, Hadleigh, Suffolk IP7 5AE. *Club:* Royal Air Force.

CLAYTON, Prof. George; Newton Chambers Professor of Applied Economics, University of Sheffield, 1967–83, Pro-Vice-Chancellor, 1978–82, now Emeritus Professor; *b* 15 July 1922; *s* of late William Clayton and late Gertrude Alison Clarke Clayton; *m* 1948, Rhiannon Jones, JP; two *s* two *d*. *Educ:* Liverpool Collegiate Sch.; King's Coll., Cambridge. Served War of 1939–45: Pilot, RAF, 1941–45; Pilot, Fleet Air Arm, 1945, Acting Sqdn Ldr. Univ. of Liverpool: Asst Lectr, 1947–50; Lectr, 1950–57; Sen. Lectr, 1957–60 and 1961–63; Sen. Simon Res. Fellow, Univ. of Manchester, 1960–61; Prof. and Head of Dept of Econs, UCW Aberystwyth, 1963–67; Luis Olariaga Lectr, Madrid Univ., 1959; Special Univ. Lectr, London, 1970; Page Fund Lectr, UC Cardiff, 1970. Member: Council, Royal Econ. Soc., 1965–68; (part-time) East Midland Gas Bd, 1967–70; Crowther Cttee on Consumer Credit, 1968–70; Scott Cttee on Property Bonds and Equity-linked Insce, 1970–72; Econs Cttee, SSRC, 1978–82 (Vice-Chm., 1979–82). Non-exec. Director: Pioneer Mutual Assurance Co.; Wagon Finance Corp. Ltd; Western Group Ltd. Chm., British, Canadian and Amer. Mission to British Honduras, 1966; Econ. Adviser: Govt of Tanzania, 1965–66; Govt of Gibraltar, 1973–. Chm., Assoc. of Univ. Teachers of Economics, 1973–78. *Publications:* (contrib.) A New Prospect of Economics, ed G. L. S. Shackle, 1956; (contrib.) Banking in Western Europe, ed R. S. Sayers, 1959; Insurance Company Investment, 1965; Problems of Rail Transport in Rural Wales: Two Case Studies, 1967; Monetary Theory and Monetary Policy in the 1970s, 1971; British Insurance, 1971; articles in Econ. Jl, etc. *Recreations:* tennis, sailing, theatre, fell walking. *Address:* 108 Westbourne Road, Sheffield S10 2GT. *T:* Sheffield 681833. *Clubs:* Hawks (Cambridge); Sheffield (Sheffield).

See also Prof. F. W. Clayton.

CLAYTON, Jack; film director; *b* 1921; *m* Christine Norden (marr. diss.); *m* Katherine Kath (marr. diss.). Entered film industry, 1935. Served War of 1939–45, RAF Film Unit. Production Manager: An Ideal Husband; Associate Producer: Queen of Spades; Flesh and Blood; Moulin Rouge; Beat the Devil; The Good Die Young; I am a Camera; Producer and Director: The Bespoke Overcoat, 1955; The Innocents, 1961; Our Mother's House, 1967; Director: Room at the Top, 1958; The Pumpkin Eater, 1964; The Great Gatsby, 1974; Something Wicked This Way Comes, 1983. *Address:* c/o William Morris Agency, 151 El Camino, Beverly Hills, Calif 90212, USA.

CLAYTON, John Pilkington, CVO 1986 (LVO 1975); MA, MB, BChir; Apothecary to HM Household at Windsor, 1965–86; Surgeon Apothecary to HM Queen Elizabeth the Queen Mother's Household at the Royal Lodge, Windsor, 1965–86; Senior Medical Officer, Eton College, 1965–86 (MO, 1962–65); *b* 13 Feb. 1921; *s* of late Brig.-Gen. Sir Gilbert Clayton, KCMG, KBE, CB, and Enid, *d* of late F. N. Thorowgood. *Educ:* Wellington Coll.; Gonville and Caius Coll., Cambridge; King's Coll. Hospital. RAFVR, 1947–49; Sqdn Ldr 1949. Senior Resident, Nottingham Children's Hosp., 1950. MO, Black and Decker Ltd, 1955–70; MO, 1953–62, SMO 1962–81, Royal Holloway Coll. *Address:* Knapp House, Market Lavington, near Devizes, Wilts.

CLAYTON, Prof. Keith Martin, CBE 1984; Professor of Environmental Sciences, University of East Anglia, since 1967; *b* 25 Sept. 1928; *s* of Edgar Francis Clayton and Constance Annie (*née* Clark); *m* 1st, 1950 (marr. diss. 1976); three *s* one *d*; 2nd, 1976. *Educ:* Bedales Sch.; Univ. of Sheffield (MSc). PhD London. Demonstrator, Univ. of Nottingham, 1949–51. Served RE, 1951–53. Lectr, London Sch. of Economics, 1953–63; Reader in Geography, LSE, 1963–67; Univ. of E Anglia: Founding Dean, Sch. of Environmental Scis, 1967–71; Pro-Vice-Chancellor, 1971–73; Dir, Centre of E Anglian Studies, 1974–81; Vis. Professor, State Univ. of New York at Binghamton, 1960–62. Member: Natural Environment Res. Council, 1970–73; UGC, 1973–84; Nat. Radiological Protection Bd, 1980–85; Nat. Adv. Bd for Local Authority Higher Educn, 1982–84. Pres., IBG, 1984. *Publications:* Editor and publisher, Geo Abstracts, 1960–85. *Recreations:* gardening, work. *Address:* Well Close, Pound Lane, Thorpe, Norwich NR7 0UA. *T:* Norwich 33780.

CLAYTON, Lucie; *see* Kark, Evelyn F.

CLAYTON, Margaret Ann; Assistant Under-Secretary of State (Personnel Management), Home Office, since 1983; *b* 7 May 1941; *d* of late Percy Thomas Clayton and of Kathleen Clayton (*née* Payne). *Educ:* Christ's Hospital, Hertford; Birkbeck Coll., London (part-time) (BA English, 1st Cl. Hons). Entered Home Office, 1960; Executive Officer/Asst Principal, 1960–67; Asst Private Secretary to Home Secretary, 1967–68; Principal, 1968–75 (seconded to Cabinet Office, 1972–73); Asst Sec., 1975–82. Resident Chairman, Civil Service Selection Board, 1983. *Recreations:* equitation, gardening, theatre. *Address:* 5 Cokers Lane, SE21 8NF. *T:* 01–670 4800. *Club:* Reform.

CLAYTON, Michael Aylwin; Editor of Horse and Hound, since 1973; *b* 20 Nov. 1934; *s* of Aylwin Goff Clayton and late Norah (*née* Banfield); *m* 1st, 1959, Mary L. B. Watson (marr. diss.); one *s* one *d*; 2nd, 1979, Barbara Jane Ryman (*née* Whitfield). *Educ:* Bournemouth Grammar School. National Service, RAF, 1954–56. Reporter: Lymington Times and New Milton Advertiser, 1951–54; Portsmouth Evening News, 1956–57; London Evening News, 1957–61; reporter/feature writer, New Zealand Herald, 1961; reporter, London Evening Standard, 1961, Dep. News Editor, 1962–64; News Editor, Southern Ind. Television, 1964–65; staff correspondent, BBC TV and radio (incl. Vietnam, Cambodia, India, Pakistan and Middle East), 1965–73; Presenter, Today, BBC Radio 4, 1973–75. Chm., British Soc. of Magazine Editors, 1986. *Publications:* A Hunting We Will Go, 1967; (with Dick Tracey) Hickstead—the First Twelve Years, 1972; (ed) The

Complete Book of Showjumping, 1975; (ed) Cross-Country Riding, 1977; The Hunter, 1980; The Golden Thread, 1984; Prince Charles: horseman, 1987. *Recreations:* foxhunting, music. *Address:* King's Reach Tower, Stamford Street, SE1 9LS.

CLAYTON, Michael Thomas Emilius, CB 1976; OBE 1958; *b* 15 Sept. 1917; *s* of Lt-Col Emilius Clayton, OBE, RA and Irene Dorothy Constance (*née* Strong); *m* 1942, Mary Margery Pate; one *d.* *Educ:* Bradfield College, Berks. Attached War Office, 1939 and Ministry of Defence, 1964–76. *Recreations:* philately, country pursuits generally. *Address:* Hillside Cottage, Marshwood, Bridport, Dorset. *T:* Hawkchurch 452.

CLAYTON, Richard Henry Michael, (William Haggard); writer; *b* 11 Aug. 1907; *o s* of late Rev. Henry James Clayton and late Mabel Sarah Clayton (*née* Haggard); *m* 1936, Barbara, *e d* of late Edward Sant, Downton, Wilts; one *s* one *d.* *Educ:* Lancing; Christ Church, Oxford. Indian Civil Service, 1931–39; Indian Army, 1939–46 (GS01 1943); BoT, 1947–69 (Controller of Enemy Property, 1965–69). *Publications:* Slow Burner, The Telemann Touch, 1958; Venetian Blind, 1959; Closed Circuit, 1960; The Arena, 1961; The Unquiet Sleep, 1962; The High Wire, 1963; The Antagonists, 1964; The Hard Sell, The Powder Barrel, 1965; The Power House, 1966; The Conspirators, The Haggard Omnibus, 1967; A Cool Day For Killing, 1968; The Doubtful Disciple, Haggard For Your Holiday, 1969; The Hardliners, 1970; The Bitter Harvest, 1971; The Protectors, 1972; The Little Rug Book (non-fiction), 1972; The Old Masters, 1973; The Kinsmen, 1974; The Scorpion's Tail, 1975; Yesterday's Enemy, 1976; The Poison People, 1977; Visa to Limbo, 1978; The Median Line, 1979; The Money Men, 1981; The Mischief Makers, 1982; The Heirloom, 1983; The Need to Know, 1984; The Meritocrats, 1985; The Martello Tower, 1986. *Address:* 3 Linkside, Frinton-on-Sea, Essex CO13 9EN. *Club:* Travellers'.

CLAYTON, Sir Robert (James), Kt 1980; CBE 1970 (OBE 1960); FEng, FIEE, FInstP, FRAeS, FIEEE; Technical Director, The General Electric Co. plc, 1968–83; GEC Director, 1978–83; *b* 30 Oct. 1915; *m* 1949, Joy Kathleen King; no *c.* *Educ:* Cambridge Univ. (Scholar, Christ's Coll.; MA; Hon. Fellow, 1983). GEC Research Labs, 1937; Manager, GEC Applied Electronics Labs, 1955; Dep. Dir, Hirst Research Centre, 1960; Man. Dir, GEC (Electronics), 1963; Man. Dir, GEC (Research), 1966. Member: Adv. Council for Applied R&D, 1976–80 (Chm. of Groups producing reports on Applications of Semiconductors, Computer Aided Design and Manufacture, and Inf. Technology); Adv. Council on R&D for Fuel and Power, 1976–83; NEB, 1978–80; Adv. Council, Science Mus., 1980–83, Trustee, 1984–; British Library Bd, 1981–; UGC, 1982–; Monopolies and Mergers Commn, 1983–; Chairman: Computer Systems and Electronics Requirements Bd, DoI, 1978–81; Open Technology Steering Gp, MSC, 1983–84; Policy Cttee, IT Skills Agency, 1985–. Chm., Electronics Engrg Assoc., 1965; President: IEE, 1975–76 (Chm., Electronics Div., 1968–69); Inst. of Physics, 1982–84; Assoc. for Science Educn, 1983; Vice-President: Fellowship of Engineering, 1980–82; IERE, 1983–84. Vis. Prof., Electrical Engrg Dept, Imperial Coll. of Science and Technology, 1971–77; Lectures: IEE Faraday; CEI Graham Clarke; Christopher Hinton, Fellowship of Engineering. Hon. DSc: Aston, 1979; Salford, 1979; City, 1981; Hon. DEng Bradford, 1985; Hon. Fellow IEE, 1982. *Publications:* papers in Proc. IEE (premium awards). *Address:* GEC Hirst Research Centre, East Lane, Wembley, Mddx. *T:* 01–904 1262. *Club:* United Oxford & Cambridge University.

CLAYTON, Prof. Robert Norman, FRS 1981; Professor, Departments of Chemistry and of the Geophysical Sciences, University of Chicago, since 1966; *b* 20 March 1930; *s* of Norman and Gwenda Clayton; *m* 1971, Cathleen Shelburne Clayton; one *d.* *Educ:* Queen's Univ., Canada (BSc, MSc); California Inst. of Technol. (PhD). Res. Fellow, Calif. Inst. of Technol., 1955–56; Asst Prof., Pennsylvania State Univ., 1956–58; University of Chicago: Asst Prof., 1958–62; Associate Prof., 1962–66. *Publications:* over 100 papers in geochemical journals. *Address:* 5201 South Cornell, Chicago, Ill 60615, USA. *T:* 312–643–2450.

CLAYTON, Stanley James; Town Clerk of the City of London 1974–82; *b* 10 Dec. 1919; *s* of late James John Clayton and late Florence Clayton; *m* 1955, Jean Winifred, *d* of Frederick Etheridge; one *s* one *d.* *Educ:* Ensham Sch.; King's Coll., London (LLB). Served War of 1939–45, commnd RAF. Admitted Solicitor 1958. City of Westminster, 1938–52; Camberwell, 1952–60; Asst Solicitor, Holborn, 1960–63; Deputy Town Clerk: Greenwich, 1963–65; Islington, 1964–69; City of London, 1969–74. Comdr, Order of Dannebrog (Denmark); holds other foreign orders. *Address:* Redriff, 215 East Dulwich Grove, SE22 8SY. *T:* 01–693 1019. *Club:* Royal Air Force.

CLEALL, Charles; music specialist, Northern Division of HM Inspectorate of Schools in Scotland, 1972–June 1987; *b* 1 June 1927; *s* of Sydney Cleal and Dorothy Bound; *m* 1953, Mary, *yr d* of G. L. Turner, Archery Lodge, Ashford, Mddx; two *d.* *Educ:* Hampton Sch.; Univ. of London (BMus); Univ of Wales (MA); Jordanhill Coll. of Educn, Glasgow. ADCM, GTCL, FRCO(CHM), LRAM, HonTSC. Command Music Adviser, RN, 1946–48; Prof., TCL, 1949–52; Conductor, Morley Coll. Orch., 1949–51; Organist and Choirmaster, Wesley's Chapel, City Road, EC4, 1950–52; Conductor, Glasgow Choral Union, 1952–54; BBC Music Asst, Midland Region, 1954–55; Music Master, Glyn County Sch., Ewell, 1955–66; Conductor, Aldeburgh Festival Choir, 1957–60; Organist and Choirmaster: St Paul's, Portman Sq., W1, 1957–61; Holy Trinity, Guildford, 1961–65; Lectr in Music, Froebel Inst., 1967–68; Adviser in Music, London Borough of Harrow, 1968–72; Warden, Music in Education Section, ISM, 1971–72; Regd Teacher, Sch. of Sinus Tone, Ernest George White Soc., 1985–. Delivered two papers at study-conf. of teachers of singing, The Maltings, Snape, 1976, and papers at: Nat. Course on Develt of Young Children's Musical Skills, Univ. of Reading Sch. of Educn, 1979; annual conf., Scottish Fedn of Organists, 1980. Editor, Journal of The Ernest George White Soc., 1983–. Internat. Composition Prizeman of Cathedral of St John the Divine, NY; Limpus Fellowship Prizeman of RCO. *Publications:* Voice Production in Choral Technique, 1955 (2nd edn, 1970); The Selection and Training of Mixed Choirs in Churches, 1960; Music and Holiness, 1964; Plainsong for Pleasure, 1969; Authentic Chanting, 1969; Guide to Vanity Fair, 1982. *Recreations:* watching sea-birds, reading, writing, etymology, indexing, post codes. *Address:* 10 Carronhall, Stonehaven, Kincardineshire AB3 2HF.

CLEARY, Denis Mackrow, CMG 1967; HM Diplomatic Service, retired; *b* 20 Dec. 1907; *s* of late Francis Esmonde Cleary and late Emmeline Marie Cleary (*née* Mackrow); *m* 1st, 1941, Barbara Wykeham-George (*d* 1960); 2nd, 1962, Mary Kent (*née* Dunlop), *widow* of Harold Kent; one step-*d.* *Educ:* St Ignatius Coll. and St Olave's Sch.; St John's Coll., Cambridge (Major Schol.). 1st Class Hons Pts I and II, Math. Tripos; BA 1930; MA 1934. Asst Principal, India Office, 1931; Principal, 1937; seconded to Min. of Home Security, 1940–44; Dep. Principal Officer to Regional Commissioner, Cambridge, March 1943–Sept. 1944; seconded to Foreign Office (German Section) as Asst Sec., 1946–49; transferred to CRO and posted to Delhi as Counsellor, 1949–51; Dep. High Commissioner, Wellington, 1955–58; Mem. of British Delegn to Law of the Sea Conf., Geneva, 1960; Dep. High Comr, Nicosia, 1962–64; Head of Atlantic Dept, Commonwealth Office, 1964–68 (Mem., Cttee for Exports to the Caribbean, 1965–67); retd 1968; re-employed in Internat. Div., DHSS, 1968–72; UK Delegate to Public Health Cttees, Council of Europe, 1968–72; Chm., Council of Europe Med. Fellowships Selection Cttee, 1972–74. *Recreations:* gardening, walking. *Address:* High Gate, Burwash, East Sussex TN19 7LA. *T:* Burwash 882712.

CLEARY, Jon Stephen; novelist; *b* 22 Nov. 1917; *s* of Matthew Cleary and Ida (*née* Brown); *m* 1946, Constantine Lucas; two *d.* *Educ:* Marist Brothers' Sch., Randwick, NSW. Variety of jobs, 1932–40; served with AIF, 1940–45; freelance writer, 1945–48; journalist with Australian News and Information Bureau: London, 1948–49; New York, 1949–51; subseq. full-time writer. Jt winner, Nat. Radio Play Contest, ABC, 1945; regional winner, NY Herald Tribune World Short Story Contest, 1950. *Publications:* These Small Glories (short stories), 1946; You Can't See Round Corners, 1947 (2nd Prize, Novel Contest, Sydney Morning Herald); The Long Shadow, 1949; Just Let Me Be, 1950 (Crouch Gold Medal for best Australian novel); The Sundowners, 1952; The Climate of Courage, 1953; Justin Bayard, 1955; The Green Helmet, 1957; Back of Sunset, 1959; North from Thursday, 1960; The Country of Marriage, 1962; Forests of the Night, 1963; A Flight of Chariots, 1964; The Fall of an Eagle, 1964; The Pulse of Danger, 1966; The High Commissioner, 1967; The Long Pursuit, 1967; Season of Doubt, 1968; Remember Jack Hoxie, 1969; Helga's Web, 1970; Mask of the Andes, 1971; Man's Estate, 1972; Ransom, 1973; Peter's Pence, 1974 (Edgar Award for best crime novel); The Safe House, 1975; A Sound of Lightning, 1976; High Road to China, 1977; Vortex, 1977; The Beaufort Sisters, 1979; A Very Private War, 1980; The Golden Sabre, 1981; The Faraway Drums, 1981; Spearfield's Daughter, 1982; The Phoenix Tree, 1984; The City of Fading Light, 1985. *Recreations:* cricket, tennis, reading. *Address:* c/o Wm Collins Sons & Co. Ltd, 8 Grafton Street, W1.

CLEARY, Rt. Rev. Joseph Francis; Auxiliary Bishop of Birmingham, (RC), and Titular Bishop of Cresima, since 1965; *b* 4 Sept. 1912; *s* of William Cleary and Ellen (*née* Rogers). *Educ:* Dublin; Oscott Coll., Sutton Coldfield. Ordained Priest 1939. Asst, St Chad's Cathedral, 1939–41; Archbishop's Sec., 1941–51; Parish Priest, SS Mary and John's, Wolverhampton, 1951–; Diocesan Treasurer, 1963–65; Provost of Diocesan Chapter, 1966–. Pres., RC Internat. Justice and Peace Commn of England and Wales, 1978–80. *Address:* Presbytery, Snow Hill, Wolverhampton WV2 4AD. *T:* Wolverhampton 21676.

CLEARY, Sir Joseph Jackson, Kt 1965; *b* 26 Oct. 1902; *s* of Joseph Cleary, JP; *m* 1945, Ethel McColl. *Educ:* Holy Trinity C of E Sch., Anfield, Liverpool; Skerry's Coll., Liverpool. Alderman, 1941, JP, 1927 for Liverpool; Lord Mayor of Liverpool, 1949–50. Contested East Toxteth Div., Liverpool, March 1929 and May 1929; West Derby, Oct. 1931; MP (Lab) Wavertree Div. of Liverpool, Feb.-Oct. 1935. Lecture tour to Forces in Middle East, 1945. Freeman, City of Liverpool, 1970. *Recreations:* football (Association), tennis. *Address:* 115 Riverview Heights, Liverpool L19 0LQ. *T:* 051–427 2133.

CLEASBY, Very Rev. Thomas Wood Ingram; Dean of Chester, 1978–86; *b* 27 March 1920; *s* of T. W. Cleasby, Oakdene, Sedbergh, Yorks, and Jessie Brown Cleasby; *m* 1st, 1956, Olga Elizabeth Vibert Douglas (*d* 1967); one *s* one *d* (and one *d* decd); 2nd, 1970, Monica, *e d* of Rt Rev. O. S. Tomkins, *qv*; one *d.* *Educ:* Sedbergh Sch., Yorks; Magdalen Coll., Oxford; Cuddesdon Coll., Oxford. BA, MA (Hons Mod. History) 1947. Commissioned, 1st Bn Border Regt, 1940; served 1st Airborne Div., 1941–45, Actg Major. Ordained, Dio. Wakefield, 1949 (Huddersfield Parish Church). Domestic Chaplain to Archbishop of York, 1952–56; Anglican Chaplain to Univ. of Nottingham, 1956–63; Archdeacon of Chesterfield, 1963–78; Vicar of St Mary and All Saints, Chesterfield, 1963–70; Rector of Morton, Derby, 1970–78. *Recreations:* fell-walking, bird-watching, gardening, fishing. *Address:* Low Barth, Dent, Cumbria. *T:* Dent 476.

CLEAVER, Anthony Brian; Chief Executive, IBM United Kingdom Holdings Ltd, since 1986; *b* 10 April 1938; *s* of William Brian Cleaver and Dorothea Early Cleaver (*née* Peeks); *m* 1962, Mary Teresa Cotter; one *s.* *Educ:* Berkhamsted Sch.; Trinity Coll., Oxford (Schol.; MA). Joined IBM United Kingdom, 1962; IBM World Trade Corp., USA, 1973–74; Dir, DP Div., IBM UK, 1977; Vice-Pres. of Marketing, IBM Europe, Paris, 1981–82; Gen. Man., IBM UK, 1984. Dir, Nat. Computing Centre, 1977–80. Mem. Council: Templeton Coll., Oxford, 1982–; Policy Studies Inst., 1985–; Mem. Board: UK Centre for Econ. and Environmental Develt, 1985–; Business in the Community, 1985–; RIPA, 1986–; Assoc. for Business Sponsorship of the Arts, 1986–. *Recreations:* music, especially opera; sport, especially cricket. *Address:* PO Box 41, North Harbour, Portsmouth, Hants PO6 3AU. *T:* Portsmouth 321212. *Clubs:* Reform, MCC.

CLEAVER, Leonard Harry, FCA; JP; *b* 27 Oct. 1909; *s* of late Harry Cleaver, OBE, JP; *m* 1938, Mary Richards Matthews; one *s.* *Educ:* Bilton Grange and Rugby. Chartered Accountant: articled Agar, Bates, Neal & Co., Birmingham; Sec. and Chief Accountant, Chance Bros Ltd, 1935–51; Partner, Heathcote & Coleman, 1951–59. MP (C) Yardley Div. of Birmingham, 1959–64; PPS to Parly Sec. to Min. of Housing and Local Govt, 1963–64; contested Yardley Div. of Birmingham, 1964, 1966. Member: Smethwick Nat. Savings Cttee, 1939–45; Birmingham Probation Cttee, 1955–73; Central Council, Probation and After-Care Cttees for England and Wales, 1966–73. Treasurer: Deritend Unionist Assoc., 1945–48; Yardley Div. Unionist Assoc., 1971–73 (Chm., 1973–74). Governor, Yardley Educnl Foundn, 1966–70. JP Birmingham, 1954; City Councillor, Birmingham, 1966–70. *Recreations:* Rugby football, fishing, philately. *Address:* 19 Cherry Orchard Close, Chipping Campden, Glos GL55 6DH. *T:* Evesham 840870.

CLEAVER, Air Vice-Marshal Peter (Charles), CB 1971; OBE 1945; *b* 6 July 1919; *s* of William Henry Cleaver, Warwick; *m* 1948, Jean, *d* of J. E. B. Fairclough, Ledbury; two *s.* *Educ:* Warwick Sch.; Coll. of Aeronautics (MSc). Staff Coll., Haifa, 1945; idc 1966. HM Asst Air Attaché, Bucharest, 1947–49; Coll. of Aeronautics, Cranfield, 1950–52; Structural Research, RAE Farnborough, 1952–55; Min. of Supply, 1955–57; HQ FEAF, 1957–60; Maintenance Comd, 1960–63; OC, Central Servicing Develt Estabt, 1963–64; Air Officer Engineering: HQ Flying Trg Comd, 1964–66; HQ FEAF, 1967–69; Air Support Command, 1969–72; retired 1972. Sec., Cranfield Inst. of Technology, 1973–78. Governor, Warwick Schs Foundn, 1978–85; Chm. Governors, Warwick Sch., 1980–85. CEng, FRAeS. *Recreation:* gardening. *Address:* Willow House, Watling Street, Little Brickhill, Milton Keynes MK17 9LS. *Club:* Royal Air Force.

CLEAVER, William Benjamin, CEng, FIMinE; JP; Deputy Director, South Wales Area, National Coal Board, 1969–85; *b* 15 Sept. 1921; *s* of David John Cleaver and Blodwen (*née* Miles); *m* 1943, Mary Watkin (*née* James); one *s* two *d.* *Educ:* Pentre (Rhondda) Grammar Sch.; University Coll. Cardiff (BSc Hons). National Coal Board: Manager: N Celynen Collieries, Gwent, 1947; Oakdale Colliery, Gwent, 1950; Production Manager (Group), S Wales, 1953; Area General Manager, No 2 S Wales Area, 1958. Sec., Contemporary Art Soc. for Wales, 1972–; Member: Welsh Arts Council, 1977–83 (Vice-Chm., 1980–83); Arts Council of GB, 1980–83; Council, Nat. Museum of Wales, 1982–; Exec. Cttee, Council of Museums in Wales, 1983–. Founder Pres., Cardiff Jun. Ch. of Commerce, 1953. Rugby Union Football: Cardiff RFC, 1940–50; Welsh Rugby International, 1947–50 (14 caps); British Lion to NZ and Aust., 1950; Barbarian Rugby Club, 1946; Founder Chm., Welsh Youth Rugby Union, 1949–57. JP Cardiff 1973. OStJ 1961. *Recreations:* theatre, fine arts. *Address:* 29 Lon-y-deri, Rhiwbina, Cardiff CF4 6JN. *T:* Cardiff 693242. *Clubs:* Savile; Cardiff and County (Cardiff).

CLEDWYN OF PENRHOS, Baron *cr* 1979 (Life Peer), of Holyhead in the Isle of Anglesey; **Cledwyn Hughes,** CH 1977; PC 1966; Leader of the Opposition, House of Lords, since 1982 (Deputy Leader of the Opposition, 1981–82); *b* 14 Sept. 1916; *er s* of Rev. Henry David and Emily Hughes; *m* 1949, Jean Beatrice Hughes; one *s* one *d*. *Educ:* Holyhead Grammar Sch.; University Coll. of Wales, Aberystwyth (LLB). Solicitor, 1940. Served RAFVR, 1940–45. Mem. Anglesey County Council, 1946–52. Contested (Lab) Anglesey, 1945 and 1950; MP (Lab) Anglesey, 1951–79; Opposition spokesman for Housing and Local Govt, 1959–64; Minister of State for Commonwealth Relations, 1964–66; Sec. of State for Wales, 1966–68; Min. of Agriculture, Fisheries and Food, 1968–70; Opposition spokesman on Agriculture, Fisheries and Food, 1970–72; Commissioner of the House of Commons, 1979; Chm., House of Lords Select Cttee on Agriculture and Food, 1980–83. Chairman: Welsh Parliamentary Party, 1953–54; Welsh Labour Group, 1955–56; Parly Labour Party, Oct. 1974–1979 (Vice-Chm., March-Oct. 1974); Welsh Cttee on Economic and Industrial Affairs, 1982–84. Member: Cttee of Public Accounts, 1957–64; Cttee of Privileges, 1974–79. Jt Chm. TUC/Labour Party Liaison Cttee, 1974–79. Vice-Pres., Britain in Europe, 1975. Mem. Parly Delegn to Lebanon, 1957; represented British Govt at Kenya Republic Celebrations, 1964; led UK Delegn to The Gambia Independence celebrations, 1965; Mission to Rhodesia, July 1965; led UK Mission on Contingency Planning to Zambia, 1966; led Parliamentary Delegn to USSR, 1977; Prime Minister's Envoy to Southern Africa, Nov.-Dec. 1978. Director: Shell UK Ltd, 1980–84; Anglesey Aluminium Ltd, 1980–; Holyhead Towing Ltd, 1980–; a Regional Advr in Midland Bank, with special responsibilities for Wales, 1979–. Member, County Councils' Assoc., 1980–; Chm., Welsh Theatre Co., 1981–85; President: Housing and Town Planning Council, 1980–; Age Concern, Wales, 1980–85; Soc. of Welsh People Overseas, 1979–; UCW, Aberystwyth, 1976–85. Pro-Chancellor, Univ. of Wales, 1985–. Hon. Freedom of Beaumaris, 1972; Freeman, Borough of Anglesey, 1976. Hon. LLD Wales, 1970. Alderman, Anglesey CC, 1973. *Publication:* Report on Conditions in St Helena, 1958. *Address:* Swynol Le, Trearddur, Holyhead, Gwynedd. *T:* Trearddur 544. *Club:* Travellers'.

CLEERE, Henry Forester, FSA; Director, Council for British Archaeology, since 1974; *b* 2 Dec. 1926; *s* of late Christopher Henry John Cleere and Frances Eleanor (*née* King); *m* 1st, 1950, Dorothy Percy (marr. diss.); one *s* one *d*; 2nd, 1975, Pamela Joan Vertue; two *d*. *Educ:* Beckenham County Sch.; University Coll. London (BA Hons 1951); Univ. of London Inst. of Archaeology (PhD 1981). FBIM. Commissioned Royal Artillery, 1944–48. Successively, Production Editor, Asst Sec., Man. Editor, Dep. Sec., Iron and Steel Inst., 1952–71; Industrial Development Officer, UN Industrial Develt Org., Vienna, 1972–73. Mem. Exec. Cttee, ICOMOS. MIFA 1982. Winston Churchill Fellow, 1979. FSA 1967. *Publications:* Approaches to the Archaeological Heritage, 1984; (with D. W. Crossley) The Iron Industry of the Weald, 1985; papers in British and foreign jls on aspects of early ironmaking, Roman fleets, etc. *Recreations:* gardening, beekeeping, cookery. *Address:* Acres Rise, Lower Platts, Ticehurst, Wadhurst, East Sussex TN5 7DD. *T:* Ticehurst 200752. *Club:* Athenæum.

CLEESE, John Marwood; writer and actor; Founder and Director, Video Arts Ltd; *b* 27 Oct. 1939; *s* of Reginald and Muriel Cleese; *m* 1st, 1968, Connie Booth (marr. diss. 1978); one *d*; 2nd, 1981, Barbara Trentham; one *d*. *Educ:* Clifton Sports Acad.; Downing College, Cambridge (MA). Started making jokes professionally, 1963; started on British television, 1966; TV series have included: The Frost Report, At Last the 1948 Show, Monty Python's Flying Circus, Fawlty Towers. Films include: Interlude, The Magic Christian, And Now For Something Completely Different, Monty Python and the Holy Grail, Romance with a Double Bass, Life of Brian, Privates on Parade, The Meaning of Life, Yellowbeard, Silverado, Clockwise. Hon. LLD St Andrews. *Publications:* (with Robin Skynner) Families and How to Survive Them, 1983; The Golden Skits of Wing Commander Muriel Volestrangler FRHS and Bar, 1984. *Recreations:* gluttony, sloth. *Address:* c/o David Wilkinson, 8 Waterloo Place, SW1.

CLEGG, Brian George Herbert; management consultant and company director; *b* 10 Dec. 1921; *s* of Frederic Bradbury Clegg and Gladys Butterworth; *m* 1st, 1949, Iris May Ludlow; one *s* one *d*; 2nd, 1976, Anne Elizabeth Robertson. *Educ:* Manchester Grammar Sch.; Trinity Coll., Cambridge (Open Math. Schol., MA). FIS, FIM, CEng, FIGasE, MBIM. Sci. Officer, Min. of Supply, 1942; Hon. Flt-Lt, RAFVR. Statistician, Liverpool Gas Co., 1946; Market and Operational Res. Man., Southern Gas Bd, 1957; Commercial Man., Southern Gas Bd, 1961; Dep. Dir of Marketing, Gas Council, 1968; Dir of Marketing, British Gas Corp., 1972; Chairman, Northern Region of British Gas Corp., 1975–82, retired. Dir, Pershke Price Service Organisation Ltd, Mitcham, 1984. *Publications:* numerous articles and papers on marketing and fuel matters. *Recreations:* swimming, ice-skating, electronic organ. *Address:* 30 The Pines, 40 The Avenue, Poole, Dorset BH13 6HJ.

CLEGG, Professor Edward John, MD, PhD; FIBiol; Regius Professor of Anatomy, University of Aberdeen, since 1976; *b* 29 Oct. 1925; *s* of Edward Clegg and Emily Armistead; *m* 1958, Sheila Douglas Walls; two *d* (and one *d* decd). *Educ:* High Storrs Grammar Sch., Sheffield; Univ. of Sheffield (MB, ChB Hons 1948, MD 1964). PhD Liverpool, 1957; FIBiol 1974. RAMC, 1948–50 and RAMC (TA), 1950–61; Major, RAMC (RARO). Demonstr, Asst Lectr and Lectr in Anatomy, Univ. of Liverpool, 1952–63; Lectr, Sen. Lectr and Reader in Human Biology and Anatomy, Univ. of Sheffield, 1963–77. MO, British Kangchenjunga Expedn, 1955; Sci. Mem., Chogolungma Glacier Expedn, 1959; Leader, WHO/IBP Expedn, Simien Mountains, Ethiopia, 1967. *Publications:* The Study of Man: an introduction to human biology, 1968 (2nd edn 1978); papers on anatomy, endocrinology and human biology. *Recreations:* mountaineering, fishing, sailing, music. *Address:* c/o Department of Anatomy, Marischal College, Aberdeen AB9 1AS. *T:* Aberdeen 40241, ext. 233M. *Clubs:* Alpine; Wayfarers (Liverpool).

CLEGG, Prof. Hugh Armstrong; Emeritus Professor of Industrial Relations, University of Warwick, since 1983; *b* 22 May 1920; *s* of late Rev. Herbert Hobson Clegg and of Mabel (*née* Duckering); *m* 1941, Mary Matilda (*née* Shaw); two *s* two *d*. *Educ:* Kingswood Sch., Bath; Magdalen Coll., Oxford. Served War, 1940–45; Official Fellow, Nuffield Coll., Oxford, 1949–66, Emeritus Fellow, 1966–; Prof. of Industrial Relns, Univ. of Warwick, 1967–79, Titular Prof. and Leverhulme Res. Fellow, 1979–83. Chm., Civil Service Arbitration Tribunal, 1968–71; Dir, Industrial Relations Res. Unit, SSRC, 1970–74; Member: Royal Commn on Trade Unions and Employers' Assocs, 1965–68; Cttee of Inquiry into Port Transport Industry, 1964–65; Ct of Inquiry into Seamen's Dispute, 1966–67; Nat. Board for Prices and Incomes, 1966–67; Ct of Inquiry into Local Authorities' Manual Workers' Pay Dispute, 1970; Council, ACAS, 1974–79; Chm., Standing Commn on Pay Comparability, 1979–80. *Publications:* Labour Relations in London Transport, 1950; Industrial Democracy and Nationalisation, 1951; The Future of Nationalisation (with T. E. Chester), 1953; General Union, 1954; Wage Policy in the Health Service (with T. E. Chester), 1957; The Employers' Challenge (with R. Adams), 1957; A New Approach to Industrial Democracy, 1960; Trade Union Officers (with A. J. Killick and R. Adams), 1961; General Union in a Changing Society, 1964; A History of British Trade Unions: Vol. I (with A. Fox and A. F. Thompson), 1964, Vol. II, 1985; The System of Industrial Relations in Great Britain, 1970; How to run an Incomes Policy and Why we made such a Mess of the Last One, 1971; Workplace and Union (with I. Boraston and M. Rimmer), 1975; Trade Unionism under Collective Bargaining, 1976; The Changing System of Industrial Relations in Great Britain, 1979. *Recreations:* walking, beer. *Address:* 7 John Nash Square, Regency Drive, Kenilworth, Warwicks. *T:* Kenilworth 50794.

CLEGG, Philip Charles; a Recorder of the Crown Court, since 1983; *b* 17 Oct. 1942; *s* of Charles and Patricia Clegg; *m* 1965, Caroline Frances Peall; one *s* two *d*. *Educ:* Rossall; Bristol Univ. (LLB Hons). Called to the Bar, Middle Temple, 1966; in practice on Northern Circuit; Asst Recorder, 1980–83. *Recreations:* sailing, model engineering. *Address:* Heath House, Gaskell Avenue, Knutsford, Cheshire WA16 6DA. *T:* Knutsford 3550.

CLEGG, Richard Ninian Barwick, QC 1979; a Recorder of the Crown Court, since 1978; *b* 28 June 1938; *o s* of Sir Cuthbert Clegg, TD; *m* 1963, Katherine Veronica, *d* of A. A. H. Douglas; two *s* one *d*. *Educ:* Aysgarth; Charterhouse; Trinity Coll., Oxford (MA). Captain of Oxford Pentathlon Team, 1959. Called to Bar, Inner Temple, 1960, Bencher, 1985. Chm., NW section of Bow Group, 1964–66; Vice-Chm., Bow Group, 1965–66; Chm., Winston Circle, 1965–66; Pres., Heywood and Royton Conservative Assoc., 1965–68. *Publication:* (jtly) Bow Group pamphlet, Towards a New North West, 1964. *Recreations:* sport, music, travel. *Address:* The Old Rectory, Brereton, via Sandbach, Cheshire CW11 9RY. *T:* Holmes Chapel 32358; 5 Essex Court, Temple, EC4. *T:* 01–353 4365. *Club:* Lansdowne.

CLEGG, Sir Walter, Kt 1980; MP (C) Wyre, since 1983 (North Fylde, 1966–83); *b* 18 April 1920; *s* of Edwin Clegg; *m* 1951, Elise Margaret Hargreaves. *Educ:* Bury Grammar Sch.; Arnold Sch., Blackpool; Manchester Univ. Law Sch. Articled to Town Clerk, Barrow-in-Furness, 1937. Served in Royal Artillery, 1939–46 (commnd 1940). Qualified as Solicitor, 1947; subsequently in practice. Lancashire CC, 1955–61. Opposition Whip, 1967–69; a Lord Comr, HM Treasury, 1970–72; Vice-Chamberlain, HM Household, 1972–73, Comptroller, 1973–74; an Opposition Whip, March-Oct. 1974. Hon. Sec., Cons. Housing and Local Govt Cttee, 1968–69; Mem. Exec., 1922 Cttee, 1975–76, Hon. Treasurer 1976–; Chm., Cons. NW Members Group, 1977–; Mem. Exec., IPU, 1980–85, CPA, 1980–85; Chm., Parly All-Party Solicitors Gp, 1979–. Vice-Chm., Assoc. of Conservative Clubs, 1969–71, Pres. 1977–78, Vice-Pres. 1982; Pres., Cons. NW Provincial Area, 1982–. Pres., Central and W Lancs Chamber of Commerce, 1981. *Recreation:* reading. *Address:* Beech House, Raikes Road, Little Thornton, near Blackpool, Lancs. *T:* Cleveleys 826131. *Club:* Garrick.

CLEGG-HILL, family name of **Viscount Hill.**

CLELAND, Dame Rachel, DBE 1980 (CBE 1966; MBE 1959); *b* Peppermint Grove, Jan. 1906; *d* of W. H. Evans, Perth, WA; *m* 1928, Sir Donald Cleland, *s* of E. D. Cleland; two *s*. *Educ:* Methodist Ladies' Coll., Perth, WA; Kindergarten Training Coll. Pres., Girl Guide Assoc., Papua and New Guinea, 1952–66; President: Red Cross, Papua and New Guinea, 1952–66; Branch of Aust. Pre-Sch. Assoc. (TPNG), 1952–66; Patron WA Branch, Soc. of Women Writers (Aust.). *Publication:* Pathways to Independence: official and family life in Papua New Guinea 1951–1976, 1984, 2nd edn 1985. *Recreations:* gardening, bird-watching. *Address:* 155r Forrest Street, Peppermint Grove, WA 6011, Australia. *Club:* Queen's (Sydney).

CLELAND, William Paton, FRCP, FRCS, FACS; Consulting Surgeon, National Heart and Chest Hospital; Consulting Thoracic Surgeon, King's College Hospital; Emeritus Consultant to the RN; late Adviser in Thoracic Surgery to the Department of Health and Social Security; *b* 30 May 1912; *o s* of late Sir John Cleland, CBE; *m* 1940, Norah, *d* of George E. Goodhart; two *s* one *d*. *Educ:* Scotch Coll., Adelaide; Univ. of Adelaide, S Australia. MB, BS (Adelaide). Resident appts, Royal Adelaide and Adelaide Children's Hosps, 1935–36; MRCP 1939; House Physician and Resident Surgical Officer, Brompton Chest Hosp., 1939–41. Served in EMS as Registrar and Surgeon, 1939–45. FRCS 1946. Consultant Thoracic Surg., King's Coll. Hosp., 1948; Surgeon, Brompton Chest Hospital, 1948; Sen. Lectr in Thoracic Surgery, Royal Postgrad. Med. Sch., 1949; Dir, Dept of Surgery, Cardio-Thoracic Inst., Brompton Hosp. Member: Assoc. Thoracic Surgeons of Gt Brit. and Ire.; Thoracic Soc.; British Cardiac Soc.; Amer. Coll. of Surgeons. Editor, Jl of Cardiovascular Surgery, 1978–83. Comdr, Order of Lion of Finland; Comdr, Order of Icelandic Falcon. *Publications:* (jt author) Medical and Surgical Cardiology, 1969; chapters on thoracic surgery in British Surgical Practice, Diseases of the Chest (Marshall and Perry), Short Practice of Surgery (Bailey and Love), and Operative Surgery (Rob and Rodney Smith); articles on pulmonary and cardiac surgery in medical literature. *Recreations:* fishing, photography, gardening. *Address:* Green Meadows, Goodworth Clatford, Andover, Hants SP11 7HH. *T:* Andover 24327.

CLELLAND, David Gordon; MP (Lab) Tyne Bridge, since Dec. 1985; *b* 27 June 1943; *s* of Archibald and Ellen Clelland; *m* 1965, Maureen; two *d*. *Educ:* Kelvin Grove Boys' School, Gateshead; Gateshead and Hebburn Technical Colleges. Apprentice electrical fitter, 1959–64; electrical tester, 1964–81. Gateshead Borough Council: Councillor, 1972–86; Recreation Chm., 1976–84; Leader of Council, 1984–85. Nat. Sec., Assoc. of Councillors, 1981–85. *Recreation:* golf. *Address:* 216A Rawling Road, Gateshead NE8 4QU. *T:* Tyneside 4773982.

CLEMENS, Clive Carruthers, CMG 1983; MC 1946; HM Diplomatic Service, retired; High Commissioner in Lesotho, 1981–84; *b* 22 Jan. 1924; British; *s* of late M. B. Clemens, Imperial Bank of India, and late Margaret Jane (*née* Carruthers); *m* 1947, Philippa Jane Bailey; three *s*. *Educ:* Blundell's Sch.; St Catharine's Coll., Cambridge. War Service 1943–46: commissioned in Duke of Cornwall's Light Infantry; served in India and Burma, 1944–45. Entered HM Foreign Service and apptd to FO, 1947; Third Sec., Rangoon, 1948; Third (later Second) Sec., Lisbon, 1950; FO, 1953; First Sec., Budapest, 1954; Brussels, 1956; Seoul, 1959; FO, 1961; Strasbourg (UK Delegn to Council of Europe), 1964; Counsellor, Paris, 1967; Principal British Trade Comr, Vancouver, 1970–74; Dep. Consul-Gen., Johannesburg, 1974–78; Consul-Gen., Istanbul, 1978–81. *Recreations:* birdwatching, photography. *Address:* 9 Saxonhurst, Downton, Salisbury, Wilts.

CLEMENT, David James; financial consultant, since 1985; *b* 29 Sept. 1930; *s* of James and Constance Clement; *m* 1958, Margaret Stone; two *s* one *d*. *Educ:* Chipping Sodbury Grammar Sch.; Univ. of Bristol (BA). IPFA. Internal Audit Asst, City of Bristol, 1953–56; Accountancy/Audit Asst, 1956–60, Chief Accountancy Asst, 1960–65, City of Worcester; Dep. Chief Finance Officer, Runcorn Develt Corp., 1965–68; Chief Finance Officer, Antrim and Ballymena Develt Commn, 1968–72; Asst Sec., Dept of Finance, NI, 1972–75, Dep. Sec., 1975–80; Under Sec., DoE, NI, 1980–84. *Recreations:* lawn tennis, Association football, contract bridge, philately.

CLEMENT, David Morris, CBE 1971; FCA, IPFA; Hon. FCGI; Chairman, Joint Mission Hospital Equipment Board Ltd, 1978–85; *b* 6 Feb. 1911; 2nd *s* of Charles William and Rosina Wannell Clement, Swansea; *m* 1938, Kathleen Mary, *o d* of Ernest George Davies,

ACA, Swansea; one *d. Educ:* Bishop Gore's Grammar Sch., Swansea. Mem. Inst. Chartered Accountants, 1933. A. Owen John & Co., Swansea, and Sissons Bersey Gain Vincent & Co., London, Chartered Accts, 1928–35; ICI Ltd, Lime Gp, 1935–40; Chloride Electrical Storage Co. Ltd, 1941–46; National Coal Board: Sec., North Western Div., 1946–49; Chief Acct, Northern and Durham Divs, 1950–55; Dep. Dir-Gen. of Finance, 1955–61; Dir-Gen. of Finance, 1961–69; Bd Mem., 1969–76; Chairman: NCB (Ancillaries) Ltd, 1973–79; Redwood-Corex Services Ltd, 1978–82. Chm., Public Corporations Finance Gp, 1975–76. Dep. Chm., Horizon Exploration Ltd, 1978–80. Underwriting Member of Lloyd's, 1978–. Member: Aircraft and Shipbuilding Industries Arbitration Tribunals, 1980–83; Council, CIPFA, 1975–76; Council, CGLI (Hon. Treas.), 1978–82. *Recreations:* golf, photography. *Address:* 19 The Highway, Sutton, Surrey. *T:* 01–642 3626. *Clubs:* Royal Automobile, Directors'.

CLEMENT, John; Chairman, Unigate Group, since 1977; non-executive Chairman, The Littlewoods Organisation, since 1982; Director, Eagle Star Holdings, since 1981; *b* 18 May 1932; *s* of Frederick and Alice Eleanor Clement; *m* 1956, Elisabeth Anne (*née* Emery); two *s* one *d. Educ:* Bishop's Stortford College. Howards Dairies, Westcliff on Sea, 1949–64; United Dairies London Ltd, 1964–69; Asst Managing Director, Rank Leisure Services Ltd, 1969–73; Chairman, Unigate Foods Div., 1973; Chief Executive, Unigate Group, 1976. Trustee, Rank Prize Funds, 1982–. Mem., Securities and Investments Bd, 1986–. CBIM (FBIM 1977). *Recreations:* tennis, shooting, sailing, skiing, bridge, Rugby. *Address:* Tuddenham Hall, Tuddenham, Ipswich, Suffolk IP6 9DD. *T:* Witnesham 217. *Clubs:* Farmers', London Welsh Rugby Football; Royal Harwich Yacht.
See also R. Clement.

CLEMENT, John Handel, CB 1980; Member: Wales Tourist Board, since 1982; Midland Bank plc Advisory Council for Wales, since 1985; Adviser to Gooding Group, since 1985; *b* 24 Nov. 1920; *s* of late William Clement and Mary Hannah Clement; *m* 1946, Anita Jones; one *d* (and one *d* decd). *Educ:* Pontardawe Grammar Sch. RAF, 1940–46, Flt Lt (despatches). Welsh Board of Health: Clerical Officer, 1938; Exec. Officer, 1946; Higher Exec. Officer, 1948; Sen. Exec. Officer, 1956; Principal, Welsh Office, Min. of Housing and Local Govt, 1960, Asst Sec., 1966; Private Sec. to Sec. of State for Wales, 1966; Under-Sec., 1971–81, Dir of Industry Dept, 1976–81, Welsh Office. Sec., Council for Wales, 1955–59; Chm., Welsh Planning Bd, 1971–76. Hon. MA Wales, 1982. *Recreations:* Welsh Rugby, fishing. *Address:* 6 St Brioc Road, Heath, Cardiff. *T:* Cardiff 624192.

CLÉMENT, René; Chevalier de la Légion d'Honneur; Commandeur, Ordre National du Mérite; Commandeur des Arts et des Lettres; film director; *b* Bordeaux, 18 March 1913; *s* of Jean Clément and Marguérite Clément (*née* Bayle); *m* 1940, Bella Gurwich. *Educ:* Lycée de Bordeaux; Ecole nationale supérieure des beauxarts. *Films:* Soigne ton Gauche (short), 1936; *documentaries:* L'Arabie Interdite, 1937; La Grande Chartreuse, 1938; La Bièvre, 1939; Le Tirage, 1940; Ceux du Rail, 1942; La Grande Pastorale, 1943; Chefs de Demain, 1944; *feature films:* La Bataille du Rail, 1946 (Cannes Fest. Prize); Le Père Tranquille, 1946; Les Maudits, 1947 (Cannes Fest. Prize); Au-delà des Grilles, 1948 (US Academy Award, British award); Le Chateau de Verre, 1950; Jeux Interdits, 1952 (US Academy Award, British award, Cannes Fest. Prize and Grand Internat. Prize Venice Biennale); Monsieur Ripois, 1954 (Cannes Fest. Prize); Gervaise, 1955 (Venice Internat. Prize); Barrage contre le Pacifique, 1958; Plein Soleil, 1959; Quelle Joie de Vivre, 1961; Le Jour et l'Heure, 1962; Les Félins, 1964; Paris, Brûle-t-il?, 1966 (Prix Europa); Le Passager de la Pluie, 1969; La Maison sous les Arbres, 1971; La Course du lièvre à travers les champs, 1971; The Baby Sitter, 1975. Founder Mem., Institut des hautes études cinématographiques; Mem., Institut de France. *Publication:* (with C. Audry) Bataille du rail, 1947. *Recreations:* antiques, painting, music. *Address:* 10 Avenue de St Roman, Monte Carlo, Monaco. *T:* 9350–59–35.

CLEMENT, Richard, (Dick); freelance writer and director; *b* 5 Sept. 1937; *s* of Frederick and Alice Eleanor Clement; *m* 1st, Jennifer F. Sheppard (marr. diss. 1981); three *s* one *d*; 2nd, 1982, Nancy S. Campbell. *Educ:* Bishop's Stortford Coll.; Westminster Sch., Conn, USA. Co-writer (with Ian La Frenais): *television:* The Likely Lads, 1964–66; Whatever Happened to the Likely Lads, 1972–73; Porridge, 1974–76; Thick as Thieves, 1974; Going Straight, 1978; Auf Wiedersehen, Pet, 1984; Mog, 1985; *films:* The Jokers, 1967; Otley, 1968; Hannibal Brooks, 1968; Villain, 1971; Porridge, 1979; Water, 1984; Director: *films:* Otley, 1968; A Severed Head, 1969; Porridge, 1979; Bullshot, 1983; Water, 1984; *stage:* Billy, 1974; Anyone for Denis?, 1981. *Recreations:* work, tennis, dinner; supporting Essex at cricket and Los Angeles Dodgers at baseball. *Address:* 9700 Yoakum Drive, Beverly Hills, Calif 90210, USA. *T:* 213–276–4916.
See also John Clement.

CLEMENTS, Alan William; Finance Director, ICI PLC, since 1979; *b* 12 Dec. 1928; *s* of William and Kathleen Clements; *m* 1953, Pearl Dorling; two *s* one *d. Educ:* Culford School, Bury St Edmunds; Magdalen College, Oxford (BA Hons). HM Inspector of Taxes, Inland Revenue, 1952–56; ICI: Asst Treasurer, 1966; Dep. Treasurer, 1971; Treasurer, 1976. Non-Exec. Director: Trafalgar House PLC, 1980–; Cable & Wireless PLC, 1985–. Lay Mem., Stock Exchange Council, 1984–. *Publications:* articles on finance in jls. *Recreations:* golf, jogging, music, reading. *Address:* Imperial Chemical Industries PLC, IC House, Millbank, SW1P 3JF. *T:* 01–834 4444.

CLEMENTS, Sir John (Selby), Kt 1968; CBE 1956; FRSA; Actor, Manager, Producer; *b* 25 April 1910; *s* of late Herbert William Clements, Barrister-at-Law, and Mary Elizabeth (*née* Stephens); *m* 1st, 1936, Inga Maria Lillemor Ahlgren (marr. diss. 1946); 2nd, 1946, Dorothy Katharine (Kay Hammond) (*d* 1980), *d* of late Sir Guy Standing, KBE, and Dorothy Frances Plaskitt. *Educ:* St Paul's Sch.; St John's Coll., Cambridge. British Actors' Equity: Mem. Council, 1948, 1949; Vice-Pres., 1950–59; Trustee, 1958. Member: Arts Council Drama Panel, 1953–58; Council, RADA, 1957–. First stage appearance, Out of the Blue, Lyric, Hammersmith, 1930; subsequently appeared in: She Stoops to Conquer, Lyric; The Beaux' Stratagem, Royalty, 1930; The Venetian, Little, 1931; Salome, Gate Theatre, 1931; many Shakespearian parts under management of late Sir Philip Ben Greet; founded The Intimate Theatre, Palmers Green, London, 1935, and ran it as weekly repertory theatre until 1940, directing most of and appearing in nearly 200 plays; produced Yes and No, Ambassadors, 1937; appeared in: Skylark, Duchess, 1942; They Came to a City, Globe, 1943; (also produced) Private Lives, Apollo, 1944; (with Old Vic Co.) played Coriolanus, Petruchio and Dunois, New, 1947–48; appeared in Edward My Son, Lyric, 1948–49; as Actor-Manager-Producer, has presented and played in: The Kingmaker; Marriage à la Mode, St James's, 1946; The Beaux' Stratagem, Phoenix and Lyric, 1949–50; Man and Superman, New and Princes, 1951; (also author) The Happy Marriage, Duke of York's, 1952–53; Pygmalion, St James's 1953–54; The Little Glass Clock, Aldwych, 1954–55; personal management of Saville Theatre, 1955–57, where presented and played in: The Shadow of Doubt; The Wild Duck, 1955–56; The Rivals, 1956; The Seagull; The Doctor's Dilemma; The Way of the World, 1956–57; Adviser on Drama to Associated Rediffusion Ltd, 1955–56, where produced films including: A Month in the Country; The Wild Duck; played in: (also co-presented and directed) The Rape of the Belt, Piccadilly, 1957–58; (also presented) Gilt and Gingerbread, Duke of York's, 1959; The Marriage-Go-Round, Piccadilly, 1959–60; produced Will You Walk a Little Faster?, Duke of York's, 1960; played in: J. B., Phœnix, 1961; The Affair, Strand, 1961; The Tulip Tree, Haymarket, 1962; Old Vic American tour, 1962; played in: (also co-presented and directed) The Masters, Savoy, 1963; Robert and Elizabeth, Lyric, 1964; dir and played in, The Case in Question, Haymarket, 1975. Director, Chichester Festival Theatre, 1966–73; 1966 season, presented: The Clandestine Marriage; (also played in) The Fighting Cock (subseq. Duke of York's); The Cherry Orchard; (also played) Macbeth; 1967 season, directed: The Farmer's Wife; (also played Shotover) Heartbreak House (subseq. Lyric); presented: The Beaux' Stratagem; An Italian Straw Hat; 1968 season, presented: The Unknown Soldier and His Wife; The Cocktail Party (subseq. Wyndham's); (played Prospero) The Tempest; The Skin of our Teeth; 1969 season, presented: The Caucasian Chalk Circle; (also directed and played in) The Magistrate (subseq. Cambridge); The Country Wife; (also played Antony) Antony and Cleopatra; 1970 season, presented: Peer Gynt; Vivat! Vivat! Regina!; (also directed) The Proposal; Arms and the Man; The Alchemist; 1971 season presented: (also directed and played in) The Rivals; (also played in) Dear Antoine (subseq. Piccadilly); Caesar and Cleopatra; Reunion in Vienna; 1972 Season, presented: The Beggar's Opera; (also directed and played in) The Doctor's Dilemma; 1973 Season, presented: (also directed and played in) The Director of the Opera; (also directed) Dandy Dick; dir, Waters of the Moon, Chichester, 1977; The Devil's Disciple (General Burgoyne), The Importance of Being Earnest (Canon Chasuble), Chichester, 1979; entered films, 1934; films include: Things to Come; Knight Without Armour; South Riding; Rembrandt; The Four Feathers; Convoy; Ships With Wings; Undercover; They Came to a City; Train of Events; The Silent Enemy; The Mind Benders; Oh What a Lovely War!; Admiral Nelson; Gandhi. *Address:* Rufford Court, 109 Marine Parade, Brighton, E Sussex BN2 1AT. *T:* Brighton 603026. *Club:* Garrick.

CLEMENTS, Julia; *see* Seton, Lady, (Julia).

CLEMENTS, Rt. Rev. Kenneth John; *b* 21 Dec. 1905; *s* of John Edwin Clements and Ethel Evelyn Clark; *m* 1935, Rosalind Elizabeth Cakebread; one *s* two *d. Educ:* Highgate Sch., London; St Paul's Coll., University of Sydney. BA (Hons) 1933; ThD 1949. Registrar, Diocese of Riverina, 1933–37; Rector of: Narrandera, NSW, 1937–39; Tumbarumba, NSW, 1939–43; Gunning, NSW, 1943–44; Director of Studies, Canberra Grammar Sch., Canberra, ACT, 1945; Registrar Diocese of Canberra and Goulburn, 1946–56; Archdeacon of Goulburn, 1946–56; Asst Bishop of Canberra and Goulburn, 1949–56; Bishop of Grafton, NSW, 1956–61; Bishop of Canberra and Goulburn, 1961–71; retired, 1971. *Address:* 5 Quorn Close, Buderim, Qld 4556, Australia.

CLEMENTS, Richard Harry; Executive Officer to the Leader of the Opposition, Rt Hon. Neil Kinnock, since 1983; *b* 11 Oct. 1928; *s* of Harry and Sonia Clements; *m* 1952, Bridget Mary MacDonald; two *s. Educ:* King Alfred Sch., Hampstead; Western High Sch., Washington, DC; Regent Street Polytechnic. Middlesex Independent, 1949; Leicester Mercury, 1951; Editor, Socialist Advance (Labour Party Youth paper), 1953; industrial staff, Daily Herald, 1954; joined Tribune, 1956, Editor, 1961–82; Political Adviser to the Leader of the Opposition, Rt Hon. Michael Foot, 1982–83. *Publication:* Glory without Power: a study of trade unions, 1959. *Recreation:* woodwork. *Address:* 53B Hendon Lane, N3.

CLEMENTS, Prof. Ronald Ernest; Samuel Davidson Professor of Old Testament Studies, King's College, University of London, since 1983; *b* 27 May 1929; *m* 1955, Valerie Winifred (*née* Suffield); two *d. Educ:* Buckhurst Hill County High Sch.; Spurgeon's Coll.; Christ's Coll., Cambridge; Univ. of Sheffield. MA, DD Cantab. Asst Lectr 1960–64, Lectr 1960–67, Univ. of Edinburgh; Lectr, Univ. of Cambridge, 1967–83. Hon. For. Sec., SOTS, 1973–83; Hon. Mem., OTWSA, 1979– (Pres., 1985). Hon. DLitt Acadia, Nova Scotia, 1982. *Publications:* God and Temple, 1965; Prophecy and Covenant, 1965; Old Testament Theology, 1978; Isaiah 1–39, 1979; A Century of Old Testament Study, 1976, 2nd edn 1983; Prayers of the Bible, 1986; contrib. Vetus Testamentum, Jl of Semitic Studies. *Recreations:* reading, travel, photography. *Address:* 8 Brookfield Road, Coton, Cambridge CB3 7PT.

CLEMINSON, Sir James (Arnold Stacey), Kt 1982; MC 1945; DL; Chairman, Reckitt & Colman Ltd, 1977–86 (Chief Executive, 1973–80); President of the CBI, 1984–86 (Member Council, since 1978; Deputy President, 1983); Chairman, British Overseas Trade Board, since 1986; *b* 31 Aug. 1921; *s* of Arnold Russel Cleminson and Florence Stacey; *m* 1950, Helen Juliet Measor; one *s* two *d. Educ:* Rugby Sch. Served War, 1940–46, mainly in Parachute Regt. Reckitt & Colman, 1946–: Overseas Co., 1946; Dir, Reckitt & Colman Overseas, 1957; Chm., Food and Wine Div., Norwich, 1970. Vice-Chm., Norwich Union, 1981– (Dir, 1979–); Director: United Biscuits, 1982–; AP Bank, 1985–. Member: London Cttee, Toronto Dominion Bank, 1982–; NEDC, 1984–. Jt Chm., Netherlands British Chamber of Commerce Council, 1978–84; Chm., Food and Drink Industries Council, 1983–84, Dep. Pres., 1984–85; Pres., Endeavour Trng, 1984–; Trustee: Airborne Forces Security Fund; Army Benevolent Fund. Pro-Chancellor, Hull Univ., 1985; Hon. LLD Hull, 1985. DL Norfolk, 1983. *Recreations:* field sports, golf. *Address:* Loddon Hall, Hales, Norfolk. *Club:* Boodle's.

CLEMITS, John Henry, ARIBA; FRSA; Director for Wales, Property Services Agency, Central Office for Wales, Department of the Environment, since 1985; *b* 16 Feb. 1934; *s* of late Cyril Thomas Clemits and Minnie Alberta Clemits; *m* 1958, Elizabeth Angela Moon; one *s* one *d. Educ:* Sutton High Sch.; Plymouth College of Art. ARIBA (Dist. in Thesis). National Service, RAF, 1959–61; Captain, RE (TA), 43 Wessex Div. and Royal Monmouthshire RE (Militia), 1964–69. Plymouth City Architects Dept, 1954–59; Watkins Gray & Partners, Architects, Bristol, 1961–63; SW RHB, 1963–65; Architect, MPBW, Bristol, 1965–69; Sen. Architect, MPBW, Regional HQ, Rheindahlen, Germany, 1969–71; Naval Base Planning Officer, MPBW, Portsmouth, 1971–73; Suptg Architect, PSA, Directorate of Bldg Develt, 1973–75; Suptg Planning Officer, PSA, Rheindahlen, 1975–79; Dir of Works (Army), PSA, Chessington, 1979–85. *Recreations:* golf, music, travel, DIY. *Address:* The Lodge, Hendrescythan, Creigiau, Cardiff CF4 8NN. *T:* Pentyrch 891786. *Club:* Civil Service.

CLEMITSON, Ivor Malcolm; *b* 8 Dec. 1931; *s* of Daniel Malcolm Clemitson and Annie Ellen Clemitson; *m* 1960, Janet Alicia Meeke; one *s* one *d. Educ:* Harlington Primary Sch.; Luton Grammar Sch.; London Sch. of Economics (BScEcon); Bishops Theol College. Deacon 1958, Priest 1959. Curate: St Mary's (Bramall Lane), Sheffield, 1958–61; Christ Church, Luton, 1962–64; Industrial Chaplain, Dio. St Albans, 1964–69; Dir of Industrial Mission, Dio. Singapore, 1969–70; Research Officer, National Graphical Assoc., 1971–74. MP (Lab) Luton East, Feb. 1974–1979; contested (Lab) Luton South, 1983. *Publication:* (with George Rodgers) A Life to Live, 1981. *Recreations:* watching football, theatre, travel. *Address:* 49 Marlborough Road, Luton, Beds. *T:* Luton 419198.

CLEMOES, Prof. Peter Alan Martin, PhD (Cantab); FRHistS; Elrington and Bosworth Professor of Anglo-Saxon, Cambridge University, 1969–82, Emeritus Professor since 1982; Official Fellow of Emmanuel College, Cambridge, 1962–69, Professorial Fellow 1969–82, Life Fellow since 1982; Fellow, Queen Mary College, London University, since

1975; *b* 20 Jan. 1920; *o s* of Victor Clemoes and Mary (*née* Paton); *m* 1956, Jean Elizabeth, *yr d* of Sidney Grew; two *s*. *Educ:* Brentwood Sch.; Queen Mary Coll., London; King's Coll., Cambridge. BA London (1st Cl. Hons English) 1950; Soley Student, King's Coll., Cambridge, 1951–53; Research Fellow, Reading Univ., 1954–55; PhD Cambridge 1956. Lectr in English, Reading Univ., 1955–61; Lectr in Anglo-Saxon, Cambridge Univ., 1961–69; Coll. Lectr in English, 1963–69 and Dir of Studies in English, 1963–65; Tutor, 1966–68; Asst Librarian, 1963–69. Mem., Council of Early English Text Soc., 1971–. Pres., Internat. Soc. of Anglo-Saxonists, 1983–85; Dir, Fontes Anglo-Saxonici (a register of written sources used by authors in Anglo-Saxon England), 1985–. Founder and Chief Editor, Anglo-Saxon England, 1972–. *Publications:* The Anglo-Saxons, Studies . . . presented to Bruce Dickins (ed and contrib.), 1959; General Editor of Early English Manuscripts in Facsimile (Copenhagen), 1963–74, and co-editor of vol. XIII, 1966, vol. XVIII, 1974; Rhythm and Cosmic Order in Old English Christian Literature (inaug. lecture), 1970; England before the Conquest: Studies . . . presented to Dorothy Whitelock (co-ed and contrib.), 1971; textual and critical writings, especially on the works of Ælfric. *Festschrift:* Learning and Literature in Anglo-Saxon England: studies presented to Peter Clemoes on the occasion of his sixty-fifth birthday, ed Michael Lapidge and Helmut Gneuss, 1985. *Address:* 14 Church Street, Chesterton, Cambridge. *T:* Cambridge 358655.

CLEOBURY, Nicholas Randall, MA; FRCO; conductor; *b* 23 June 1950; *s* of John and Brenda Cleobury; *m* 1978, Heather Kay; one *s* one *d*. *Educ:* King's Sch., Worcester; Worcester Coll., Oxford (BA Hons). Assistant Organist: Chichester Cathedral, 1971–72; Christ Church, Oxford, 1972–76; Chorus Master, Glyndebourne Opera, 1977–79; Asst Director, BBC Singers, 1977–79; Conductor: main BBC, provincial and London orchestras and opera houses, also in Holland, Belgium, Sweden, Italy, Austria, Germany, etc; regular BBC, TV appearances. Principal Opera Conductor, Royal Academy of Music, 1981–. Hon. RAM 1985 (Hon. ARAM 1983). *Recreations:* reading, food, wine, theatre, walking, cricket. *Address:* 23 Abbeville Road, SW4 9LA. *T:* 01–675 1332. *Club:* Savage.
See also S. J. Cleobury.

CLEOBURY, Stephen John, FRCO; Fellow, Director of Music and Organist, King's College, Cambridge, since 1982; *b* 31 Dec. 1948; *s* of John Frank Cleobury and Brenda Julie (*née* Randall); *m* 1971, Penelope Jane (*née* Holloway); two *d*. *Educ:* King's Sch., Worcester; St John's Coll., Cambridge (MA, MusB). FRCO 1968. Organist, St Matthew's, Northampton, 1971–74; Sub-Organist, Westminster Abbey, 1974–78; Master of Music, Westminster Cathedral, 1979–82. Hon. Sec., RCO, 1981–; Pres., IAO, 1985–87; Mem. Council, RSCM, 1982–. Conductor, CUMS, 1983–. *Recreations:* playing chess, watching cricket, reading railway timetables. *Address:* 85 Gough Way, Newnham, Cambridge CB3 9LN. *T:* Cambridge 359461, (King's College) Cambridge 350411, ext. 224.
See also N. R. Cleobury.

CLERK of Penicuik, Sir John Dutton, 10th Bt *cr* 1679; CBE 1966; VRD; FRSE 1977; JP; Lord-Lieutenant of Midlothian since 1972 (Vice-Lieutenant, 1965–72); Cdre RNR; retd; *b* 30 Jan. 1917; *s* of Sir George James Robert Clerk of Penicuik, 9th Bt, and Hon. Mabel Honor (*d* 1974), *y d* of late Col Hon. Charles Dutton and *sister* of 6th Baron Sherborne, DSO; *S* father, 1943; *m* 1944, Evelyn Elizabeth Robertson; two *s* two *d*. *Educ:* Stowe. Brig., Queen's Body Guard for Scotland, Royal Company of Archers, 1973. JP 1955, DL 1956, Midlothian. *Heir:* *s* Robert Maxwell Clerk, Younger of Penicuik [*b* 3 April 1945; *m* 1970, Felicity Faye, *yr d* of George Collins, Bampton, Oxford; two *s* one *d*. *Educ:* London Univ. (BSc (Agric)). FRICS]. *Address:* Penicuik House, Penicuik, Midlothian, Scotland. *T:* Penicuik 74318. *Clubs:* Royal Over-Seas League; New (Edinburgh).

CLERKE, Sir John Edward Longueville, 12th Bt *cr* 1660; Captain Royal Wilts Yeomanry, RAC, TA; *b* 29 Oct. 1913; *er s* of Francis William Talbot Clerke (killed in action, 1916), *e s* of 11th Bt, and late Albinia Mary, *er d* of Edward Henry Evans-Lombe (who *m* 3rd, 1923, Air Chief Marshal Sir Edgar Rainey Ludlow-Hewitt, GCB, GBE, CMG, DSO, MC); *S* grandfather, 1930; *m* 1948, Mary, *d* of late Lt-Col I. R. Beviss Bond, OBE, MC; one *s* two *d*. *Heir:* *s* Francis Ludlow Longueville Clerke [*b* 25 Jan. 1953; *m* 1982, Vanessa Anne, *o d* of late Charles Cosman Citron and of Mrs Olga May Citron, Mouille Point, Cape Town]. *Address:* Holly Tree House, Pound Pill, Corsham, Wilts. *T:* Corsham 713760.

CLEVELAND, Archdeacon of; *see* Woodley, Ven. R. J.

CLEVELAND, Harlan; Professor and Dean, Hubert H. Humphrey Institute of Public Affairs, University of Minnesota, since 1980; *b* 19 Jan. 1918; *s* of Stanley Matthews Cleveland and Marian Phelps (*née* Van Buren); *m* 1941, Lois W. Burton; one *s* two *d*. *Educ:* Phillips Acad., Andover, Mass; Princeton Univ.; Oxford Univ. Farm Security Admin., Dept of Agric., 1940–42; Bd of Econ. Warfare (subseq. Foreign Econ. Admin.), 1942–44; Exec. Dir Econ. Sect., 1944–45, Actg Vice-Pres., 1945–46, Allied Control Commn, Rome; Mem. US Delegn, UNRRA Council, London, 1945; Dept Chief of Mission, UNRRA Italian Mission, Rome, 1946–47; Dir, UNRRA China Office, Shanghai, 1947–48; Dir, China Program, Econ. Coop. Admin., Washington, 1948–49; Dept Asst Adminstr, 1949–51; Asst Dir for Europe, Mutual Security Agency, 1952–53; Exec. Editor, The Reporter, NYC, 1953–56, Publisher, 1955–56; Dean, Maxwell Sch. of Citizenship and Pub. Affairs, Syracuse Univ., 1956–61; Asst Sec. for Internat. Orgn Affairs, State Dept, 1961–65; US Ambassador to NATO, 1965–69; Pres., Univ. of Hawaii, 1969–74; Dir, Program in Internat. Affairs, Aspen Inst. for Humanistic Studies, 1974–80. Distinguished Vis. Tom Slick Prof. of World Peace, Univ. of Texas at Austin, 1979. Delegate, Democratic National Convention, 1960. Chm., Weather Modification Adv. Bd, US Dept of Commerce, 1977–78. Holds hon. degrees and foreign orders; US Medal of Freedom, 1946. Woodrow Wilson Award, Princeton Univ., 1968; Prix de Talloires, Groupe de Talloires, 1981. *Publications:* Next Step in Asia (jtly), 1949; (ed jtly) The Art of Overseasmanship, 1957; (jtly) The Overseas Americans, 1960; (ed) The Promise of World Tensions, 1961; (ed jtly) The Ethic of Power, 1962; (ed jtly) Ethics and Bigness, 1962; The Obligations of Power, 1966; NATO: the Transatlantic Bargain, 1970; The Future Executive, 1972; China Diary, 1976; The Third Try at World Order, 1977; (jtly) Humangrowth: an essay on growth, values and the quality of life, 1978; (ed) Energy Futures of Developing Countries, 1980; (ed jtly) Bioresources for Development, 1980; (ed) The Management of Sustainable Growth, 1981; The Knowledge Executive, 1985. *Address:* Hubert H. Humphrey Institute of Public Affairs, 300 HHH Center, 301 19th Avenue South, Minneapolis, Minn 55455, USA. *Clubs:* Century (NY); International (Washington); Edina Country (Minn); Waikiki Yacht (Honolulu).

CLEVERDON, (Thomas) Douglas (James); publisher and radio producer; *b* 17 January 1903; *er s* of Thomas Silcox Cleverdon, Bristol; *m* 1944, Elinor Nest, *d* of Canon J. A. Lewis, Cardiff; two *s* one *d* (and one *s* decd). *Educ:* Bristol Grammar Sch.; Jesus Coll., Oxford. Bookseller, and publisher of fine printing, Bristol, 1926–39. Free-lance acting and writing for BBC West Region, 1935–39; joined BBC (Children's Hour), 1939; W Regional Features Producer, 1939–43; Features Producer, London, 1943, until retirement in 1969; free-lance producer, 1969–80. Devised and co-produced BBC Brains Trust, 1941. BBC War Corresp. in Burma, 1945; from 1947, mainly concerned with productions for Third Programme including radio works by Max Beerbohm, J. Bronowski, Bill Naughton, George Barker, David Gascoyne, Ted Hughes, David Jones, Stevie Smith, Henry Reed, Dylan Thomas (Under Milk Wood), Peter Racine Fricker, Elizabeth Poston, Humphrey Searle and other poets and composers. Directed first stage prods of Under Milk Wood, in Edinburgh and London, 1955, and in New York, 1957. Directed: Poetry Festivals, Stratford-upon-Avon, 1966–70; Cheltenham Festival of Literature, 1971. Compiled exhibition of paintings, engravings and writings of David Jones, NBL, 1972. Publisher, Clover Hill Edns (illustrated by contemporary engravers), 1964–. Pres., Private Libraries Assoc., 1978–80. *Publications:* Engravings of Eric Gill, 1929; Growth of Milk Wood, 1969; (ed) Sixe Idyllia of Theocritus, 1971; (ed) Under Milk Wood (Folio Soc.), 1972; (ed) Verlaine, Femmes/Hombres, 1972; The Engravings of David Jones: a survey, 1981. *Recreations:* book-collecting; visual arts. *Address:* 27 Barnsbury Square, N1. *T:* 01–607 7392. *Clubs:* Savile, Double Crown.

CLEVERLEY FORD, Rev. Preb. Douglas William; Chaplain to The Queen, 1973–84; *b* 4 March 1914; *yr s* of late Arthur James and Mildred Ford; *m* 1939, Olga Mary, *er d* of late Dr Thomas Bewley Gilbart-Smith; no *c*. *Educ:* Great Yarmouth Grammar Sch.; Univ. of London. BD, MTh, ALCD (1st cl.). Deacon 1937, Priest 1938. London Coll. of Divinity: Tutor, 1937–39; Lectr, 1942–43 and 1952–58; Lectr, Church Army Trng Coll., 1953–60. Curate of Bridlington, Yorks, 1939–42; Vicar of Holy Trinity, Hampstead, 1942–55; Vicar of Holy Trinity with All Saints Church, South Kensington, 1955–74; Senior Chaplain to Archbishop of Canterbury, 1975–80; Hon. Dir, Coll. of Preachers, 1960–73; Rural Dean of Westminster, 1965–74; Prebendary of St Paul's Cathedral, 1968, now Prebendary Emeritus; Provincial Canon of York, 1969–; Lectr, Wey Inst. of Religious Studies, 1980–84; Tutor, Southwark Ordination Course, 1980–. Six Preacher, Canterbury Cathedral, 1982–. Chm., Queen Alexandra's House, Kensington Gore, 1966–74; Mem. Governing Body, Westminster City Sch. and United Westminster Schs, 1965–74; Hon. Life Governor: British and Foreign Bible Soc., 1948; Church's Ministry among the Jews. Queen's Jubilee Medal, 1977. *Publications:* An Expository Preacher's Notebook, 1960; The Christian Faith Explained, 1962; A Theological Preacher's Notebook, 1962; A Pastoral Preacher's Notebook, 1965; A Reading of St Luke's Gospel, 1967; Preaching at the Parish Communion, Vol. 1 1967, Vol. 2 1968, Vol. 3 1969; Preaching Today, 1969; Preaching through the Christian Year, 1971; Praying through the Christian Year, 1973; Have You Anything to Declare?, 1973; Preaching on the Special Occasions, 1974, Vol. 2 1981; Preaching at the Parish Communion (Series III), 1975; New Preaching from the Old Testament, 1976; New Preaching from the New Testament, 1977; The Ministry of the Word, 1979; Preaching through the Acts of the Apostles, 1979; More Preaching from the New Testament, 1982; More Preaching from the Old Testament, 1983; Preaching through the Psalms, 1984; Preaching through the Life of Christ, 1985; Preaching on Devotional Occasions, 1986; From Strength to Strength, 1987; contrib. Churchman's Companion 1967, Expository Times. *Recreations:* gardening, music, languages. *Address:* Rostrevor, Lingfield, Surrey RH7 6BZ. *Club:* Athenæum.

CLEWES, Howard Charles Vivian; novelist; *b* York, 27 Oct. 1912; British parentage; *m* 1946, Renata Faccincani; one *d*. *Educ:* Merchant Taylors' Sch. Various advertising agents, 1931–37. Served War of 1939–45, infantry company Comdr Green Howards, then Major G2; Chief Press and Information Officer, Milan, Italy, 1945–47. Professional novelist, resident Florence, Rome, London, 1948–. *Publications:* (in UK, USA, etc) Dead Ground, 1946; The Unforgiven, 1947; The Mask of Wisdom, 1948; Stendhal, 1949; Green Grow the Rushes, 1950; The Long Memory, 1951; An Epitaph for Love, 1952; The Way the Wind Blows, 1954; Man on a Horse, 1964; I, the King, 1978; *plays:* Quay South, 1947; Image in the Sun, 1955; *films:* The Long Memory, Steel Bayonet, The One that Got Away, The Day They Robbed the Bank of England, Mutiny on the Bounty, The Holiday, Up from the Beach, William the Conqueror, The Novice, The 40 Days of Musa Dagh, etc. *Recreations:* writing, fishing. *Address:* Wildwood, North End, NW3. *T:* 01–455 7110.

CLEWS, Michael Arthur; Master of the Supreme Court Taxing Office, since 1970; *b* Caudebec, France, 16 Sept. 1919; *s* of late Roland Trevor Clews and late Marjorie (*née* Baily); *m* 1947, Kathleen Edith, *d* of late Adam Hollingworth, OBE, JP, and Gertrude (*née* Bardsley); three *c*. *Educ:* Epworth Coll., Rhyl; Clare Coll., Cambridge (MA). Served in Indian Army (Major, RA and V Force), 1940–46. Solicitor, 1953; Partner, W. H. House & Son, and Knocker & Foskett, Sevenoaks, 1957–70. Mem., Lord Chancellor's Adv. Cttee on Legal Aid, 1977–84. *Address:* Royal Courts of Justice, Strand, WC2.

CLIBBORN, Donovan Harold, CMG 1966; HM Diplomatic Service, retired; *b* 2 July 1917; *s* of Henry Joseph Fairley Clibborn and Isabel Sarah Jago; *m* 1st, 1940, Margaret Mercedes Edwige Nelson (*d* 1966); one *s* two *d*; 2nd, 1973, Victoria Ondiviela Garvi. *Educ:* Ilford High Sch.; St Edmund Hall, Oxford (MA). Laming Travelling Fellow, Queen's Coll., Oxford, 1938–40. Entered Consular Service, 1939; Vice-Consul, Genoa, 1939–40. Army Service, 1940–45: Intelligence Corps and Royal Signals, Western Desert, Sicily, Italy, NW Europe (despatches); Major, 1944. Foreign Office, 1945–46; Consul, Los Angeles, 1946–48; Foreign Office, 1948–50; 1st Sec. (UK High Commn, India), Madras, 1950–52; 1st Sec. (Information), Rio de Janeiro, 1952–56; 1st Sec. (Commercial), Madrid, 1956–60; Consul (Commercial), Milan, 1960–62; Counsellor (Economic), Tehran, 1962–64; Counsellor, Rio de Janeiro, 1964–66; Consul-General, Barcelona, 1966–70; Ambassador, El Salvador, 1971–75. *Recreations:* reading, music, perpetrating light verse. *Address:* Paseo del Dr Moragas 188, Atico 1A, Barberá del Vallés, Prov. Barcelona, Spain. *T:* Barcelona 7185377.

CLIBBORN, Rt. Rev. Stanley Eric Francis B.; *see* Manchester, Bishop of.

CLIBURN, Van, (Harvey Lavan Cliburn Jr); pianist; *b* Shreveport, La, 12 July 1934; *o c* of Harvey Lavan Cliburn and Rildia Bee (*née* O'Bryan). *Educ:* Kilgore High Sch., Texas; Juilliard Sch. of Music, New York. Made début in Houston, Texas, 1947; subsequently has toured extensively in United States and Europe. Awards include first International Tchaikovsky Piano Competition, Moscow, 1958, and every US prize, for pianistic ability. *Recreation:* swimming. *Address:* 455 Wilder Place, Shreveport, La 71104, USA.

CLIFFORD, family name of **Baron Clifford of Chudleigh.**

CLIFFORD OF CHUDLEIGH, 13th Baron *cr* 1672; **(Lewis) Hugh Clifford,** OBE 1962; DL; Count of The Holy Roman Empire; farmer and landowner; President: Devon Branch, Country Landowners Association, 1973–75; Devon Branch, Royal British Legion, 1969–80; *b* 13 April 1916; *o s* of 12th Baron and Amy (*d* 1926), *er d* of John A. Webster, MD; *S* father, 1964; *m* 1945, Hon. Katharine Vavasseur Fisher, 2nd *d* of 2nd Baron Fisher; two *s* two *d*. *Educ:* Beaumont Coll.; Hertford Coll., Oxford (BA). 2nd Lieut, Devonshire Regt, 1935. Served War of 1939–45: North Africa; Major, 1941 (prisoner of war, escaped). Retd, 1950. Lieut-Col, 1959; Col, 1961. ADC(TA), 1964–69. Hon. Col, The Royal Devon Yeomanry/1st Rifle Volunteers, RAC, T&AVR (formerly the Devonshire Territorials, RAC), 1968–71; Dep. Hon. Col, The Wessex Yeomanry, 1971–72, Hon. Col D Sqdn, 1972–83. Pres., Devon Co. Agricultural Assoc., 1973–74. DL Devon, 1964–84. *Recreations:* shooting, sailing. *Heir:* *s* Hon. Thomas Hugh Clifford [*b* 17

March 1948; *m* 1980, Suzanne Austin, *yr d* of Mrs Campbell Austin, Limerick, Eire; one *s* one *d*. Commnd Coldstream Guards, 1967, retired 1977 (Captain)]. *Address:* La Colline, St Jacques, St Peter Port, Guernsey, Channel Islands; Morella, Montrose, Vic 3765, Australia. *Clubs:* Army and Navy; Royal Yacht Squadron.

CLIFFORD, Clark McAdams; Senior Partner, Clifford & Warnke, since 1969; Special Counsel and Special Envoy of the President of the United States; *b* 25 Dec. 1906; *s* of Frank Andrew Clifford and Georgia (*née* McAdams); *m* 1931, Margery Pepperell Kimball; three *d*. *Educ:* Washington Univ., St Louis (LLB). Served US Naval Reserve, 1944–46 (Naval Commendation Ribbon). Practised law in St Louis, 1928–43; specialised in trial cases, corporation and labour law; Special Counsel to President of US, 1946–50; Senior Partner, Clifford & Miller, 1950–68; Secretary of Defense, USA, 1968–69. Dir, Knight-Ridder Newspapers; Chm. Bd, First American Bankshares, Inc. (formerly Financial General Bankshares). Medal of Freedom with Distinction, USA, 1969. *Recreation:* golf. *Address:* 815 Connecticut Avenue, Washington, DC 20006, USA.

CLIFFORD, Graham Douglas, CMG 1964; FCIS; Director, The Institution of Electronic and Radio Engineers, 1937–78, Hon. Fellow 1978; *b* 8 Feb. 1913; *s* of John William Clifford and Frances Emily Reece; *m* 1937, Marjory Charlotte Willmot; two *d* (one *s* decd). *Educ:* London schs and by industrial training. Molins Machine Co. Ltd, 1929; Columbia Graphophone Co. Ltd, 1931; American Machinery Co. Ltd, 1934; Dir, Taycliff Investments, 1962–82; formerly dir of other cos. Sec., Radio Trades Exam. Bd, 1942–65 (Hon. Mem. 1965); Jt Founder and Hon. Sec., Nat. Electronics Council, 1961–70 (Hon. Treasurer, 1971–78). For 40 years Editor of The Radio and Electronic Engineer and Electronics Rev. Hon. Mem., Assoc. of Engineers and Architects, Israel, 1966; Hon. Treasurer, UK Cttee for the Gandhi Centenary, 1969–78; Hon. Sec. and Governor, Nehru Meml Trust, 1971–78. Comdr, Order of Merit, Research and Invention, France, 1967. *Publications:* A Twentieth Century Professional Institution, 1960; (ed) Nehru Memorial Lectures, annually 1972–78; contribs to various technical journals. *Recreations:* photography, genealogy, music, but mainly work. *Address:* 45 West Park Lane, West Worthing, W Sussex BN12 4EP. *T:* Worthing 41423.

CLIFFORD, Rev. Paul Rowntree, MA; President, Selly Oak Colleges, Birmingham, 1965–79; *b* 21 Feb. 1913; *s* of Robert and Harriet Rowntree Clifford; *m* 1947, Marjory Jean Tait; one *s* one *d*. *Educ:* Mill Hill Sch.; Balliol Coll., Oxford; Mansfield and Regents Park Colls, Oxford. MA (Oxon) 1939. West Ham Central Mission, London: Asst Minister, 1938–43; Supt Minister, 1943–53; McMaster Univ., Hamilton, Canada: Asst Prof. of Homiletics and Pastoral Theology, 1953–59; Dean of Men and Chm. of Dept of Religion, 1959–64; Prof. of Religion, 1964–65. Hon. Treas., Internat. Assoc. for Mission Studies, 1974–; Sec., Foundn for Study of Christianity and Society, 1980–. *Publications:* The Mission of the Local Church, 1953; The Pastoral Calling, 1959; Now is the Time, 1970; Interpreting Human Experience, 1971; The Death of the Dinosaur, 1977; Politics and the Christian Vision, 1984; Government by the People?, 1986; articles in Jl of Religion, Metaphysical Review, Dialogue, Canadian Jl of Theology, Scottish Jl of Theology, Foundations, Religious Studies. *Recreations:* golf, gardening. *Address:* 2 Kings Stile, Middleton Cheney, Oxon. *Club:* Reform.

CLIFFORD, Sir Roger (Joseph), 7th Bt *cr* 1887; *b* 5 June 1936; *s* of Sir Roger Charles Joseph Gerard Clifford, 6th Bt and Henrietta Millicent Kiver (*d* 1971); *S* father 1982; *m* 1968, Joanna Theresa, *d* of C. J. Ward, Christchurch, NZ; two *d*. *Educ:* Beaumont College, England. *Recreations:* golf, Rugby football. *Heir: b* Charles Joseph Clifford [*b* 5 June 1936; *m* 1983, Sally Green]. *Address:* 135 Totara Street, Christchurch, New Zealand. *T:* 485958. *Clubs:* Blenheim (Bleinheim, NZ); Christchurch Golf.

CLIFFORD, Timothy Peter Plint, BA, AMA; Director, National Galleries of Scotland, since 1984; *b* 26 Jan. 1946; *s* of Derek Plint Clifford and late Anne (*née* Pierson); *m* 1968, Jane Olivia, *yr d* of Sir George Paterson, *qv*; one *d*. *Educ:* Sherborne, Dorset; Perugia Univ. (Dip. Italian); Courtauld Inst., Univ. of London (BA Hons, History of Art). Dip. Fine Art, Museums Assoc., 1972. Asst Keeper, Dept of Paintings, Manchester City Art Galleries, 1968–72, Acting Keeper, 1972; Asst Keeper, Dept of Ceramics, Victoria and Albert Mus., London, 1972–76; Asst Keeper, Dept of Prints and Drawings, British Mus., London, 1976–78; Dir, Manchester City Art Galls, 1978–84. Member: Manchester Diocesan Adv. Cttee for Care of Churches, 1978–84; NACF Cttee (Cheshire and Gtr Manchester Br.), 1978–84; North Western Museum and Art Gall. Service Jt Adv. Panel, 1978–84; Cttee, ICOM (UK), 1980–82; Chm., Internat. Cttee for Museums of Fine Art, ICOM, 1980–83; Mem., Museums and Galleries Commn, 1983–; Founder and Committee Member: Friends of Manchester City Art Galls, 1978–84; Patrons and Associates, Manchester City Art Galls, 1979–; Mem. Exec. Cttee, Scottish Museums Council, 1984–. Cttee Mem., Derby Internat. Porcelain Soc., 1983–86; Vice Pres., Turner Soc., 1984–. FRSA. *Publications:* (with Derek Clifford) John Crome, 1968; (with Dr Ivan Hall) Heaton Hall, 1972; (with Dr T. Friedmann) The Man at Hyde Park Corner: sculpture by John Cheere, 1974; Vues Pittoresques de Luxembourg ... par J. M. W. Turner, (Luxembourg) 1977; Ceramics of Derbyshire 1750–1975 (ed, H. G. Bradley), 1978; J. M. W. Turner, Acquerelli e incisioni, (Rome) 1980; Turner at Manchester, 1982; contrib. Burlington Magazine, etc. *Recreations:* shooting, bird watching, entomology. *Address:* National Galleries of Scotland, The Mound, Edinburgh EH2 2EL. *Clubs:* Turf, Beefsteak; New (Edinburgh).

CLIFFORD, William Henry Morton, CB 1972; CBE 1966; Legal Consultant, Civil Service College, 1974–79, retired; *b* 30 July 1909; *s* of Henry Edward Clifford, FRIBA, Glasgow, and Margaret Alice, *d* of Dr William Gibson, Campbeltown, Argyll; *m* 1936, Katharine Winifred, *d* of Rev. H. W. Waterfield, Temple Grove, Eastbourne; one *s* two *d*. *Educ:* Tonbridge Sch.; Corpus Christi Coll., Cambridge. Admitted a solicitor, 1936. Entered Solicitor's Department, GPO, 1937. Served in Army, 1939–45: Major GS, Army Council Secretariat, WO, 1944–45. Transferred to Solicitor's Office, Min. of National Insurance, 1945; Assistant Solicitor, Min. of Pensions and Nat. Insurance (later Min. of Social Security), 1953; Solicitor, DHSS (formerly Min. of Social Security), 1968–74. *Recreations:* reading, listening to music (especially opera), genealogy, walking, sailing. *Address:* Woodbrook, 9 Lake Road, Tunbridge Wells, Kent. *T:* Tunbridge Wells 21612.

CLIFFORD-TURNER, Raymond; Consultant, Clifford-Turner, solicitors (Senior Partner, 1941–81); *b* 7 Feb. 1906; *s* of Harry Clifford-Turner, solicitor; *m* 1933, Zoë Vachell (*d* 1984); one *s* two *d*. *Educ:* Rugby Sch.; Trinity Coll., Cambridge. Solicitor, 1930; Partner, Clifford-Turner & Co., 1931. Dir, Transport Holding Co., 1962–73. Wing Commander, RAFVR. *Recreations:* golf, racing. *Address:* 86 Eaton Place, SW1. *T:* 01–235 2443; Childown, Longcross, near Chertsey, Surrey KT16 0EH. *T:* Ottershaw 2608. *Clubs:* Portland; Berkshire; Swinley.

CLIFT, Richard Dennis, CMG 1984; HM Diplomatic Service; *b* 18 May 1933; *s* of late Dennis Victor Clift and Helen Wilmot Clift (*née* Evans); *m* 1st, 1957, Barbara Mary Travis (marr. diss. 1982); three *d*; 2nd, 1982, Jane Rosamund Barker (*née* Homfray). *Educ:* St Edward's Sch., Oxford; Pembroke Coll., Cambridge. BA 1956. FO, 1956–57; Office of British Chargé d'Affaires, Peking, 1958–60; British Embassy, Berne, 1961–62; UK Delegn to NATO, Paris, 1962–64; FO, 1964–68; Head of Chancery, British High Commn, Kuala Lumpur, 1969–71; FCO, 1971–73; Counsellor (Commercial), Peking, 1974–76; Canadian Nat. Defence Coll., 1976–77; seconded to NI Office, 1977–79; Hd of Hong Kong Dept, FCO, 1979–84; High Court in Freetown, 1984–86. *Recreations:* sailing, walking. *Address:* c/o Foreign and Commonwealth Office, SW1A 2AL. *Club:* Royal Commonwealth Society.

CLIFTON, Lord; Ivo Donald Stuart Bligh; *b* 17 April 1968; *s* and *heir* of 11th Earl of Darnley, *qv*.

CLIFTON, Bishop of (RC), since 1974; **Rt. Rev. Mervyn Alban Newman Alexander,** DD; *b* London, 29 June 1925; *s* of William Paul Alexander and Grace Evelyn Alexander (*née* Newman). *Educ:* Bishop Wordsworth School, Salisbury; Prior Park College, Bath; Gregorian University, Rome (DD 1951). Curate at Pro-Cathedral, Clifton, Bristol, 1951–63; RC Chaplain, Bristol University, 1953–67; Parish Priest, Our Lady of Lourdes, Weston-super-Mare, 1967–72; Auxiliary Bishop of Clifton and Titular Bishop of Pinhel, 1972–74; Vicar Capitular of Clifton, 1974. *Address:* St Ambrose, Leigh Woods, Bristol BS8 3PW. *T:* Bristol 733072.

CLIFTON, Lt-Col Peter Thomas, CVO 1980; DSO 1945; DL; JP; Standard Bearer, HM Body Guard of Honourable Corps of Gentlemen at Arms, 1979–81; *b* 24 Jan. 1911; *s* of Lt-Col Percy Robert Clifton, CMG, DSO, TD, Clifton Hall, Nottingham; *m* 1st, 1934, Ursula (marr. diss. 1936), *d* of Sir Edward Hussey Packe; 2nd, 1948, Patricia Mary Adela (who *m* 1935, Robert Cobbold, killed in action 1944), *d* of Major J. M. Gibson-Watt, Doldowlod, Radnorshire; two *d*. *Educ:* Eton; RMC Sandhurst. 2nd Lieut Grenadier Guards, 1931; served War of 1939–45: France, 1939–40; Italy, 1944–45; Lt-Col 1944; Palestine, 1945–47. Mem. HM Body Guard of Hon. Corps of Gentlemen at Arms, 1960–81 (Clerk of the Cheque and Adjutant, 1973–79). DL Notts 1954; JP Notts 1952–59, Hants 1964. *Address:* Dummer House, Basingstoke, Hants. *T:* Dummer 306. *Clubs:* Cavalry and Guards, White's; Royal Yacht Squadron.

See also Baron Gibson-Watt, Baron Wrottesley.

CLINCH, David John; Secretary, Open University, since 1981; *b* 14 Feb. 1937; *s* of Thomas Charles Clinch and Madge Isabel Clinch (*née* Saker); *m* 1963, Hilary Jacques; one *s* one *d*. *Educ:* Nautical Coll., Pangbourne; Univ. of Durham (BA); Indiana Univ. (MBA). National Service, Royal Navy (Sub-Lieut), Supply and Secretariat, 1955–57. Administrator, Univ. of Sussex, 1963–69; Deputy Secretary and Registrar, Open University, 1969–81; Registrar Counterpart, Allama Iqbal Open Univ., Pakistan, 1976–77. Member: Conf. of Registrars and Secs; Conf. of Univ. Administrators; British Fulbright Scholars Assoc.; Selection Cttee, ACU Admin. Travel Fellowship. Governor, Bridgewater Hall Sch., Stantonbury Campus, 1981–. *Recreations:* gardening, music, reading, walking. *Address:* 39 Tudor Gardens, Stony Stratford, Milton Keynes MK11 1HX. *T:* Milton Keynes 562475.

CLINTON, 22nd Baron *cr* 1299 (title abeyant 1957–65); **Gerard Nevile Mark Fane Trefusis;** DL; landowner; *b* 7 Oct. 1934; *s* of Capt. Charles Fane (killed in action, 1940); assumed by deed poll, 1958, surname of Trefusis in addition to patronymic; *m* 1959, Nicola Harriette Purdon Coote; one *s* two *d*. *Educ:* Gordonstoun. Took seat in House of Lords, 1965. Mem., Prince of Wales's Councils, 1968–79. JP Bideford, 1963–83; DL Devon, 1977. *Recreations:* shooting, fishing, forestry. *Heir: s* Hon. Charles Patrick Rolle Fane Trefusis, *b* 21 March 1962. *Address:* Heanton Satchville, near Okehampton, North Devon. *T:* Dolton 224, *Club:* Boodle's.

CLINTON, Alan; *see* Clinton, R.A.

CLINTON, (Francis) Gordon, FRCM; Hon. RAM; FBSM; ARCM; baritone; *b* 19 June 1912; *s* of Rev. F. G. Clinton, Broadway, Worcs; *m* 1939, Phyllis Jarvis, GRSM, ARCM; two *s* one *d*. *Educ:* Evesham Grammar Sch.; Bromley Sch. for Boys. Open Schol. RCM, 1935; Vicar Choral, St Paul's Cathedral, 1937–49; served War of 1939–45 in RAF; demobilised as Flt-Lieut. Appearances at over 2,000 major concerts and festivals (50 in Royal Albert Hall, 30 in Festival Hall, inc. inaugural concerts), 1946–; soloist, Beecham 70th birthday concert, 1949; Mem. staff, RCM, 1949–82 (Mem. Bd of Professors, 1975–82); Principal, Birmingham Sch. of Music, 1960–74; Chorus Master and Co-founder, City of Birmingham Symph. Orch. Chorus, 1974–80. Examr to Associated Board, 1956–83. Tours of America, Canada, Europe, Africa, Australasia, Scandinavia, Far East (singing, adjudicating, lecturing). *Recreations:* sport, wild-life. *Address:* 42 Pembroke Croft, Hall Green, Birmingham. *T:* 021–744 3513.

CLINTON, (Robert) Alan; Director, Picton House Ltd and Picton Homes Ltd, property Development cos, since 1986; *b* 12 July 1931; *s* of John and Leah Clinton; *m* 1956, Valerie Joy Falconer. *Educ:* George Dixon Grammar Sch., Edgbaston, Birmingham. On leaving school, joined the Post Office, 1948; Member, North Western Postal Board, 1970; Asst Director (Personnel), London, 1975; Asst Director (Operations), London, 1976; Director of Eastern Postal Region, Colchester, 1978; Director of Postal Operations, London, 1979; Member Post Office Board, 1981–85: for Mails Network and Develt, 1981; for Mails Ops and Estates, 1982; for Corporate Services, 1984–85; Man. Dir, Counter Services, 1984–85. FCIT 1982. Mem., Worshipful Company of Carmen, 1981; Freeman of City of London, 1979. *Recreations:* music, walking. *Address:* Binders, Colchester Road, St Osyth, Clacton-on-Sea, Essex CO16 8HA. *T:* St Osyth 820375. *Club:* City Livery.

CLITHEROE, 2nd Baron *cr* 1955, of Downham; **Ralph John Assheton;** Bt 1945; Lord of the Honor of Clitheroe and Hundred of Blackburn; DL; Chairman and Managing Director, RTZ Borax Ltd, since 1979; *b* 3 Nov. 1929; *s* of 1st Baron Clitheroe, KCVO, PC, FSA, and of Sylvia Benita Frances, Lady Clitheroe, FRICS, FLAS, *d* of 6th Baron Hotham; *S* father, 1984; *m* 1961, Juliet, *d* of Lt-Col Christopher Lionel Hanbury, MBE, TD; two *s* one *d*. *Educ:* Eton; Christ Church, Oxford (Scholar, MA). Served as 2nd Lieut Life Guards, 1948–49. Chairman: Borax Holdings Ltd; RTZ Chemicals Ltd, 1973; RTZ Oil & Gas Ltd, 1983; US Borax & Chemicals Corp., 1979; Director: Rio Tinto-Zinc Corp. PLC, 1968; T. R. Natural Resources Investment Trust, 1982; First Interstate Bank of California; American Mining Congress, 1982. Mem. Council, Chemical Industries Assoc., 1984. Liveryman, Skinners' Co. DL Lancs, 1986. *Heir: s* Hon. Ralph Christopher Assheton, *b* 19 March 1962. *Address:* Downham Hall, Clitheroe, Lancs. *Clubs:* Pratt's, Royal Automobile.

CLIVE, Eric McCredie; a Scottish Law Commissioner, since 1981; *b* 24 July 1938; *s* of Robert M. Clive and Mary L. D. Clive; *m* 1962, Kay M. McLeman; one *s* three *d*. *Educ:* Univs of Edinburgh (MA, LLB with dist.); Michigan (LLM); Virginia (SJD). Solicitor. Lecturer 1962–69, Sen. Lectr 1969–75, Reader 1975–77, Professor of Scots Law 1977–81, Univ. of Edinburgh. *Publications:* Law of Husband and Wife in Scotland, 1974, 2nd edn 1982; (jtly) Scots Law for Journalists, 1965, 4th edn 1984; articles and notes in legal jls. *Recreations:* gardening, beekeeping, hill-walking, ski-ing, chess. *Address:* 14 York Road, Edinburgh EH5 3EH. *T:* 031–552 2875.

CLIVE, Nigel David, CMG 1967; OBE 1959; MC 1944; TD; HM Diplomatic Service, retired; *b* 13 July 1917; *s* of late Horace David and Hilda Mary Clive; *m* 1949, Maria Jeanne Tambakopoulou. *Educ:* Stowe; Christ Church, Oxford (Scholar). Commissioned 2nd Mddx Yeomanry, 1939; served in Middle East and Greece. Joined Foreign Office,

1946; served Athens, 1946–48; Jerusalem, 1948; FO, 1948–50; Baghdad, 1950–53; FO, 1953–58; Tunis, 1958–62; Algiers, 1962–63; FO, 1964–65; Head of Information Research Dept, FCO (formerly FO), 1966–69; Adviser to Secretary-General of OECD, 1970–80. *Publication:* A Greek Experience 1943–1948, 1985. *Recreations:* reading, travel. *Address:* Flat 2, 41 Lowndes Square, SW1. *T:* 01–235 1186. *Clubs:* Brooks's, MCC.

CLOAKE, John Cecil, CMG 1977; HM Diplomatic Service, retired; *b* 2 Dec. 1924; *s* of late Dr Cecil Stedman Cloake, Wimbledon, and Maude Osborne Newling; *m* 1956, Margaret Thomure Morris, Washington, DC, USA; one *s. Educ:* King's Coll. Sch., Wimbledon; Peterhouse, Cambridge. Served in Army, 1943–46 (Lieut RE). Foreign Office, 1948; 3rd Sec., Baghdad, 1949, and Saigon, 1951; 2nd Sec., 1952; FO, 1954; Private Sec. to Permanent Under-Sec., 1956, and to Parly Under-Sec., 1957; 1st Sec., 1957; Consul (Commercial), New York, 1958; 1st Sec., Moscow, 1962; FO, 1963; DSAO, 1965; Counsellor, 1966; Head of Accommodation Dept, 1967; Counsellor (Commercial), Tehran, 1968–72; Fellow, Centre for International Studies, LSE, 1972–73; Head of Trade Relations and Exports Dept, FCO, 1973–76; Ambassador to Bulgaria, 1976–80. Member: Council, British Inst. of Persian Studies, 1981– (Hon. Treas. 1982–); Cttee of Honour for Bulgarian 1300th Anniv., 1981. Chairman: Richmond Museum Project, 1983–; Richmond Soc. History Section, 1975–76, 1984–85; Richmond Local Hist. Soc., 1985–. *Publications:* Templer: Tiger of Malaya, 1985; articles on local history. *Recreations:* gardening, painting, architecture, local history, genealogy. *Address:* 4 The Terrace, Richmond Hill, Richmond, Surrey TW10 6RN.

CLODE, Dame (Emma) Frances (Heather), DBE 1974 (CBE 1969; OBE 1955; MBE 1951); Chairman, Women's Royal Voluntary Service, 1971–74; *b* 12 Aug. 1903; *d* of Alexander and Florence Marc; *m* 1927, Colonel Charles Clode (then Captain in Royal Norfolk Regt); one *s. Educ:* privately. Joined WRVS, 1939; served in Cambridge, 1940–45; WRVS Headquarters, 1945; Vice-Chm. 1967. CStJ 1973. *Address:* 19 Rusher's Close, Pershore, Worcs WR10 1HF. *Club:* Lansdowne.

CLOGHER, Bishop of, since 1986; **Rt. Rev. Brian Desmond Anthony Hannon;** *b* 5 Oct. 1936; *s* of late Ven. Arthur Gordon Hannon and of Hilda Catherine Stewart-Moore Hannon (*née* Denny); *m* 1964, Maeve Geraldine Audley (*née* Butler); three *s. Educ:* Mourne Grange Prep. School, Co. Down; St Columba's Coll., Co. Dublin; Trinity Coll., Dublin (BA Hons 1959, 1st Class Divinity Testimonium 1961). Deacon 1961, priest 1962; Diocese of Derry: Curate-Assistant, All Saints, Clooney, Londonderry, 1961–64; Rector of Desertmartin, 1964–69; Rector of Christchurch, Londonderry, 1969–82; RD of Londonderry, 1977–82; Diocese of Clogher: Rector of St Macartin's Cathedral, Enniskillen, 1982–86; Canon of Cathedral Chapter, 1983; Dean of Clogher, 1985. Chm. of Western (NI) Education and Library Bd, 1985–; Mem. WCC Central Cttee, 1983–. Hon. MA TCD, 1962. *Publication:* (editor/author) Christ Church, Londonderry—1830 to 1980—Milestones, Ministers, Memories, 1980. *Recreations:* walking, music, travel, sport. *Address:* The See House, Fivemiletown, Co. Tyrone, Northern Ireland BT75 0QP. *T:* Fivemiletown 21265.

CLOGHER, Bishop of, (RC), since 1979; **Most Rev. Joseph Duffy,** DD; *b* 3 Feb. 1934; *s* of Edward Duffy and Brigid MacEntee. *Educ:* St Macartan's College, Monaghan; Maynooth College. MA, BD, HDipEd. Ordained priest, 1958; Teacher, 1960–72; Curate, 1972–79. *Publications:* Patrick in his own words, 1972; Lough Derg Guide, 1980. *Recreations:* local history, travel. *Address:* Bishop's House, Monaghan, Ireland. *T:* 047–81019.

CLOSE, Roy Edwin, CBE 1973; Chairman, Broad Street Associates, since 1986; Director: Flextech plc, since 1985; Davies and Perfect, since 1985; Kepner Tregoe Ltd, since 1986; *b* 11 March 1920; *s* of Bruce Edwin and Minnie Louise Close; *m* 1947, Olive Joan Forty; two *s. Educ:* Trinity Grammar Sch., N London. Served Army, 1939–46; SAS, 1943–46 (Captain). Editorial Staff, The Times; Asst Editor, The Times Review of Industry, 1949–56; Executive, Booker McConnell GP; Dir, Bookers Sugar Estates, 1957–65; Directing Staff, Admin. Staff Coll., Henley, 1965; Industrial Adviser, NEDO, 1966–69; Industrial Dir, NEDO, 1969–73; MSc Univ. of Aston in Birmingham, 1973; Chm., Univ. of Aston Management Centre; Dean of Faculty of Management, 1973–76; Dir. Gen., BIM, 1976–85. Chm., Open Univ. Management Educn Sector Bd, 1984–. Dir, Conservation Foundn, 1986–. Trustee, British Engineerium, 1984–. CBIM (FBIM 1979); FIIM (FIWM 1979); FRSA 1980. *Publications:* various articles on industrial, economic subjects. *Recreations:* swimming, walking, reading, listening to music. *Address:* Cathedral Cottage, North Elmham, Dereham, Norfolk NR20 5JU; Flat 20, 3 Cornwall Gardens, SW7 4AJ. *Clubs:* Reform, Special Forces.

CLOSE-SMITH, Charles Nugent, TD 1953; Underwriting Member of Lloyd's (Deputy Chairman, 1970); *b* 7 July 1911; 2nd *s* of Thomas Close Smith, Boycott Manor, Buckingham, and Mary Morgan-Grenville, *d* of 11th Baroness Kinloss; *m* 1946, Elizabeth Vivien, *d* of late Major William Kinsman, DSO, Dublin; three *s. Educ:* Eton; Magdalene Coll., Cambridge. Entered Lloyd's, 1932; 2nd Lt, Royal Bucks Yeomanry, 1938. Served War of 1939–45 France and Burma (despatches); retd as Lt-Col, RA. Chairman Lloyd's Non-Marine Underwriters Assoc., 1965; elected to Committee of Lloyd's, 1967–70. *Recreation:* horticulture. *Address:* The Heymersh, Britford, Salisbury, Wilts. *T:* Salisbury 336760. *Clubs:* Boodle's, Gresham.

CLOSS, Prof. August, MA, DPhil; Professor of German and Head of German Department, University of Bristol, 1931–64, now Emeritus; Dean of the Faculty of Arts, 1962 and 1963; *b* 9 Aug. 1898; 4th *s* of late A. Closs; *m* 1931, Hannah Margaret Mary (*d* 1953), novelist and art-critic, *d* of late Robert Priebsch, Prof. and Medievalist at UCL; one *d. Educ:* Berlin, Vienna, Graz, London. Lectured at Sheffield Univ., 1929–30; at University Coll., London, 1930–31. Guest-Prof. at univs of Amsterdam, Ghent, Berlin, Heidelberg, Frankfurt A/M, Bern, Vienna, Rome, Florence, etc, and in the USA at Univs of Columbia, Princeton, Yale, California and at Canadian and Indian Univs. Hon. Fellow Hannover Univ.; Korresp. Mitglied der Deutschen Akademie; Membre Corresp. de l'Institut International des Arts et des Lettres (Zürich); Fellow of PEN. FRSL. Comdr, Cross of Order of Merit, West Germany, Austrian Cross of Merit *Litteris et Artibus. Publications:* Medieval Exempla: (Dame World) Weltlohn, 1934; The Genius of the German Lyric, 1938 (enlarged 2nd edn 1962, paperback edn 1965); German Lyrics of the Seventeenth Century, 1940, 1947; Hölderlin, 1942, 1944; Tristan und Isolt, 1944, 1974; Die Freien Rhythmen in der deutschen Dichtung, 1947; Novalis-Hymns to the Night, 1948; Die neuere deutsche Lyrik vom Barock bis zur Gegenwart, 1952, 1957; Deutsche Philologie im Aufriss; Woge im Westen, 1954; Medusa's Mirror; Reality and Symbol, 1957; The Harrap Anthology of German Poetry, 1957, new edn 1969; Reality and Creative Vision in German Lyrical Poetry (Symposium), 1963; Introductions to German Literature (4 vols), 1967; Twentieth Century German Literature, 1969, 2nd edn 1971; The Sea in the Shell, 1977; (ed) Briefwechsel, 1979; contribs to Times Literary and Educ. Supplements, German Life and Letters, Modern Lang. Rev., Euphorion, Reallexikon, Deutsches Literatur-Lexikon, Aryan Path, Germanistik, Universitas, and American journals. *Recreations:* music, collecting first editions. *Address:* 40 Stoke Hill, Stoke Bishop, Bristol BS9 1EX. *Club:* University of Bristol.

CLOTHIER, Sir Cecil (Montacute), KCB 1982; QC 1965; Chairman, Police Complaints Authority, since 1985; *b* 28 Aug. 1919; *s* of Hugh Montacute Clothier, Liverpool; *m* 1943, Mary Elizabeth (*d* 1984), *o d* of late Ernest Glover Bush; one *s* two *d. Educ:* Stonyhurst Coll.; Lincoln Coll., Oxford (BCL, MA; Hon. Fellow 1984). Served 1939–46, 51 (Highland) Div.; British Army Staff, Washington, DC; Hon. Lt-Col Royal Signals. Called to Bar, Inner Temple, 1950, Bencher, 1973. Recorder of Blackpool, later of the Crown Court, 1965–78; Judge of Appeal, IoM, 1972–78. A Legal Assessor to Gen. Medical and Gen. Dental Councils, 1972–78; Mem., Royal Commn on NHS, 1976–78; Parly Comr for Admin, and Health Service Comr for England, Wales and Scotland, 1979–84. John Snow Meml lectr (Assoc. of Anaesthetists of GB and Ireland/Amer. Assoc. of Anaesthesiologists), 1981. Hon. LLD Hull, 1982. *Address:* c/o Police Complaints Authority, 10 Great George Street, SW1P 3AE.

CLOUDSLEY-THOMPSON, Prof. John Leonard, MA, PhD (Cantab), DSc (London); FRES, FLS, FZS, FIBiol, FWA; Professor of Zoology, Birkbeck College, University of London, 1972–86, now Emeritus (Reader 1971–72); *b* Murree, India, 23 May 1921; *s* of Dr Ashley George Gyton Thompson, MA, MD (Cantab), DPH, and Muriel Elaine (*née* Griffiths); *m* 1944, Jessie Anne Cloudsley, MCSP, DipBS, LCAD; three *s. Educ:* Marlborough Coll.; Pembroke Coll., Univ. of Cambridge. War of 1939–45: commissioned into 4th Queen's Own Hussars, 1941; transf. 4th Co. of Lond. Yeo. (Sharpshooters); N Africa, 1941–42 (severely wounded); Instructor (Capt.), Sandhurst, 1943; rejoined regt for D Day (escaped from Villers Bocage), Caen Offensive, etc, 1944 (Hon. rank of Capt. on resignation). Lectr in Zoology, King's Coll., Univ. of London, 1950–60; Prof. of Zoology, Univ. of Khartoum, and Keeper, Sudan Nat. Hist. Museum, 1960–71. Nat. Science Foundn Sen. Res. Fellow, Univ. of New Mexico, Albuquerque, USA, 1969; Visiting Professor: Univ. of Kuwait, 1978 and 1983; Univ. of Nigeria, Nsukka, 1981; Univ. of Qatar, 1986; Leverhulme Emeritus Fellow, 1987–. Took part in: Cambridge Iceland Expedn, 1947; Expedn to Southern Tunisia, 1954; univ. expedns with his wife to various parts of Africa, 1960–73, incl. Trans-Sahara crossing, 1967. Chairman: British Naturalists' Assoc., 1974–83 (Vice-Pres., 1985–); Biological Council, 1977–82 (Medal, 1985). President: British Arachnological Soc., 1982–85 (Vice-Pres., 1985–86); British Soc. for Chronobiology, 1985–87. Vice-Pres., Linnean Soc., 1975–76 and 1977–78. Hon. Member: British Herpetological Soc., 1983; Royal African Soc., 1969 (Medal, 1969). Liveryman, Worshipful Co. of Skinners, 1952–. Silver Jubilee Gold Medal and Hon. DSc, Khartoum, 1981. Editor, Jl of Arid Environments (assisted by wife), Vol. 1, 1978–. *Publications:* Biology of Deserts (ed), 1954; Spiders, Scorpions, Centipedes and Mites, 1958 (2nd edn 1968); Animal Behaviour, 1960; Rhythmic Activity in Animal Physiology and Behaviour, 1961; Land Invertebrates (with John Sankey), 1961; Life in Deserts (with M. J. Chadwick), 1964; Desert Life, 1965; Animal Conflict and Adaptation, 1965; Animal Twilight: man and game in eastern Africa, 1967; Microecology, 1967; Zoology of Tropical Africa, 1969; The Temperature and Water Relations of Reptiles, 1971; Desert Life, 1974; Terrestrial Environments, 1975; Insects and History, 1976; Evolutionary Trends in the Mating of Arthropoda, 1976; (ed jtly) Environmental Physiology of Animals, 1976; Man and the Biology of Arid Zones, 1977; The Water and Temperature Relations of Woodlice, 1977; The Desert, 1977; Animal Migration, 1978; Why the Dinosaurs Became Extinct, 1978; Wildlife of the Desert, 1979; Biological Clocks: their functions in nature, 1980; Tooth and Claw: defensive strategies in the animal world, 1980; (ed) Sahara Desert, 1984; Guide to Woodlands, 1985; contribs to Encyclopædia Britannica, Encyclopedia Americana; shorter monographs and ten children's books; many scientific articles in learned jls, etc. *Recreations:* music (especially opera), photography, travel. *Address:* Department of Zoology, University College, Gower Street, WC1E 6BT; c/o National Westminster Bank, 62 Victoria Street, SW1E 6QE; (home) Flat 9, 4 Craven Hill, W2 3DS; Little Clarkes, Little Sampford, Saffron Walden, Essex CB10 2SA.

CLOUGH, (John) Alan, CBE 1972; MC 1945; Chairman, British Mohair Holdings plc (formerly British Mohair Spinners Ltd), 1980–84 (Deputy Chairman, 1970–80, Chief Executive, 1977–80, Joint Managing Director, 1980–83); Chairman, Textile Research Council, since 1984; *b* 20 March 1924; *s* of late John Clough and Yvonne (*née* Dollfus); *m* 1st, 1949, Margaret Joy Catton (marr. diss.); one *s* two *d*; 2nd, 1961, Mary Cowan Catherwood; one *s* one *d. Educ:* Marlborough Coll.; Leeds Univ. HM Forces, Queen's Bays, 1942–47, N Africa and Italy (Captain); TA Major, Yorkshire Hussars, 1947–55. Mayor, Co. of Merchants of Staple of England, 1969–70. Chairman: Wool Industries Res. Assoc., 1967–69; Wool Textile Delegn, 1969–72; Member: Wool Textile EDC, 1967–72; Jt Textile Cttee, NEDO, 1972–74; President: Comitextil (Co-ordinating Cttee for Textile Industries in EEC), Brussels, 1975–77; British Textile Confedn, 1974–77; Textile Inst., 1979–81; Confedn of British Wool Textiles, 1982–84. CompTI 1975. *Recreations:* fishing, gardening, travel. *Address:* The Hays, Monks Eleigh, Suffolk. *T:* Bildeston 740364. *Club:* Boodle's.

CLOUGH, Prunella; painter; *b* 1919; *d* of Eric Clough Taylor, poet and civil servant, and Thora Clough Taylor. *Educ:* privately; Chelsea Sch. of Art. Exhibited at Leger Gallery, 1947; Roland Browse & Delbanco, 1949; Leicester Galleries, 1953; Whitechapel Gallery, 1960; Grosvenor Gallery, 1964, 1968; Graves Art Gallery, Sheffield, 1972; New Art Centre, 1975, 1979; Serpentine Gallery, 1976; Warwick Arts Trust, 1982. City of London Midsummer Prize, 1977. *Address:* 19 Sherbrooke Road, SW6 7HX.

CLOUTMAN, Air Vice-Marshal Geoffrey William, CB 1980; FDSRCS; Director of Dental Services, Royal Air Force, 1977–80; *b* 1 April 1920; *s* of Rev. Walter Evans Cloutman and Dora Cloutman; *m* 1949, Sylvia Brown; three *d. Educ:* Cheltenham Grammar Sch.; Queen Mary Coll., and The London Hosp., Univ. of London. LDSRCS 1942, FDSRCS 1954. House Surg., London Hosp., 1942; joined RAFVR, 1942; War Service, UK and India; specialisation in preventive dentistry, 1948–55; dental hygiene trng; oral surgery appts, 1955–73: RAF Hosps, Fayid, Akrotiri, Aden, Wegberg, Wroughton, Uxbridge; Principal Dental Off., Strike Comd, 1973; QHDS, 1976–80. *Publications:* papers in Brit. Dental Jl and Dental Practitioner. *Recreations:* English church music, cricket, Rugby, Wells Cathedral (Sub-Deacon, 1984–), history of Wells Cathedral and Bishop's Palace. *Address:* Willow Bridge, Easton, Wells, Somerset. *T:* Wells 870580.

CLOVER, His Honour Robert Gordon, TD 1951; QC 1958; JP; a Circuit Judge (formerly Judge of County Courts), 1965–82; *b* 14 Nov. 1911; *m* 1947, Elizabeth Suzanne (*née* McCorquodale); two *s. Educ:* Lancing Coll.; Exeter Coll., Oxford. MA, BCL Oxford. Called to Bar, Lincoln's Inn, 1935. Served in RA, 1939–45 (despatches, 1944). Practised on Northern Circuit, 1935–61; Recorder of Blackpool, 1960–61; Dep. Comr for purposes of Nat. Insurance Acts, 1961–65; Dep. Chm., Bucks QS, 1969–71; Chm., Marlow Magistrates Court, 1972–79. JP Bucks, 1969. *Address:* 10 Westcliff, Sheringham, Norfolk NR26 8JT.

CLOWES, A. W.; General Secretary, Ceramic and Allied Trades Union, since 1980; *b* 17 Dec. 1931. Has been in the Industry since leaving school. Asst Gen. Sec., Ceramic and Allied Trades Union, 1975–80. *Address:* Ceramic and Allied Trades Union, Hillcrest House, Garth Street, Hanley, Stoke-on-Trent, Staffordshire ST1 2AB. *T:* Stoke-on-Trent 272755.

CLOWES, Col Sir Henry (Nelson), KCVO 1981 (CVO 1977); DSO 1945; OBE 1953; *b* 21 Oct. 1911; *yr s* of late Major E. W. Clowes, DSO, Bradley Hall, Ashbourne, Derbs; *m* 1941, Diana Katharine, MBE, *er d* of late Major Basil Kerr, DSC; one *s*. *Educ:* Eton; Sandhurst. Served in Scots Guards, 1931–57: Adjt RMA Sandhurst, 1940–41; psc 1941; Bde Major 4th Inf. Bde, 1942–44; comd 2nd Bn Scots Guards, 1944–46; jssc 1947; cmd 1st Bn Scots Guards, 1947–50; War Office (AG4), 1950–52; AAG Scottish Comd, 1952–54; Lt-Col comdg Scots Guards, 1954–57; retired 1957. Mem. Her Majesty's Body Guard, 1961; Clerk of the Cheque and Adjt, 1966; Standard Bearer, 1973–76; Lieut, 1976–81. *Recreations:* shooting, fishing. *Address:* 57 Perrymead Street, SW6 3SN. *T:* 01–736 7901. *Clubs:* Cavalry and Guards, Pratt's, Shikar.

CLOYNE, Bishop of, (RC), since 1957; **Most Rev. John J. Ahern;** *b* 31 Aug. 1911; *s* of James Ahern and Ellen Mulcahy. *Educ:* St Colman's Coll., Fermoy; St Patrick's Coll., Maynooth; Irish Coll., Rome. Ordained, 1936. Prof. at St Colman's Coll., Fermoy, 1940–44; St Patrick's Coll., Maynooth, 1946–57. *Address:* Bishop's House, Cobh, Co. Cork, Ireland.

CLUCAS, Sir Kenneth (Henry), KCB 1976 (CB 1969); Permanent Secretary, Department of Trade, 1979–82; Chairman, Nuffield Foundation Committee of Inquiry into Pharmacy, 1983–86; *b* 18 Nov. 1921; *o s* of late Rev. J. H. Clucas; *m* 1960, Barbara, *e d* of Rear-Adm. R. P. Hunter, USN (Retd), Washington, DC; two *d*. *Educ:* Kingswood Sch.; Emmanuel Coll., Cambridge. Royal Signals, 1941–46 (despatches). Joined Min. of Labour as Asst Principal, 1948; 2nd Sec. (Labour), British Embassy, Cairo, 1950; Principal, HM Treasury, 1952; Min. of Labour, 1954; Private Sec. to Minister, 1960–62; Asst Sec., 1962; Under-Sec., 1966–68; Sec., Nat. Bd for Prices and Incomes, 1968–71; First Civil Service Comr, and Dep. Sec., CSD, 1971–73; Dep. Sec., DTI, 1974; Permanent Sec., Dept of Prices and Consumer Protection, 1974–79. Director: Gestetner Holdings plc, 1982–; Carreras Rothmans Ltd, 1982–84; Rothmans (UK) Ltd, 1984–85. Member: Council on Tribunals, 1983–; Adv. Panel, Freedom of Information Campaign, 1984–; RIPA Wkg Gp on Politics and the Civil Service, 1985–86; Council, FIMBRA, 1986–; Chm., Cttee of Inquiry into Advertising Controls, 1986–; Dep. Chm., CIBA Foundn Media Resource Steering Cttee, 1984–85; Chm., Lloyd's Wkg Pty on Consumer Guarantees, 1985. Chm., Nat. Assoc. of Citizens' Advice Bureaux, 1984– (Vice Chm., 1983–84; Chm. Surrey and W Sussex Area Cttee, 1982–84); Mem. Management Cttee, Godalming CAB, 1982–85. *Address:* Cariad, Knoll Road, Godalming, Surrey. *T:* Godalming 6430.

CLUFF, Algy; Chairman, since 1979, and Chief Executive, since 1971, Cluff Oil; Chairman: The Spectator, since 1985 (Proprietor, 1981–85); Apollo Magazine Ltd, since 1985; *b* 19 April 1940; *s* of Harold Cluff and Freda Cluff, Waldeshare House, Waldeshare, Kent. *Educ:* Stowe Sch. 2/Lieut, Grenadier Guards, 1959; Captain, Guards Independent Parachute Co., 1963; served W Africa, Cyprus, Malaysia, retd 1964. *Address:* 70 Arlington House, Arlington Street, SW1; Clova House, Lumsden, West Aberdeenshire AB5 4YJ. *T:* Lumsden 336. *Clubs:* White's, Boodle's, Beefsteak, Turf; Royal St George's (Sandwich); Travellers' (Paris).

CLUFF, John Gordon; *see* Cluff, Algy.

CLUSKEY, Frank; *b* April 1930; *m* Eileen Gillespie (decd); one *s* two *d*. *Educ:* St Vincent's Sch., Glasnevin; Harvard Univ., USA. A Branch Sec., Workers' Union of Ireland, 1954–68; Member, Dublin City Council, 1960–63; Lord Mayor of Dublin, 1968–69. TD (Lab) Dublin S Central, 1965–81 and 1982–83; Member: Cttee of Public Accounts and Cttee of Procedure, 1965–69 and 1970–73; Parly Sec. to Min. of Social Welfare, 1973–77; former Labour Opposition Front Bench Spokesman on Justice, Social Welfare, and Labour; Leader of the Labour Party, Ireland, 1977–81; Minister for Trade and Commerce, 1982–83. Mem., European Parlt, 1981–82. *Address:* 1 Glasnevin Park, Dublin 11, Ireland.

CLUTTERBUCK, Vice-Adm. Sir David Granville, KBE 1968; CB 1965; *b* Gloucester, 25 Jan. 1913; *m* 1937, Rose Mere Vaile, Auckland, NZ; two *d*. Joined RN, 1929. Served War of 1939–45 (despatches twice): navigating officer of cruisers HMS Ajax, 1940–42, HMS Newfoundland, 1942–46 (present Japanese surrender at Tokyo). Subsequently commanded destroyers Sluys and Cadiz; Naval Attaché at British Embassy, Bonn; Capt. (D) of Third Training Squadron in HMS Zest, Londonderry, 1956–58; commanded cruiser HMS Blake; Chief of Staff to C-in-C Home Fleet and C-in-C Allied Forces Eastern Atlantic, 1963–66; Rear-Adm., 1963; Vice-Adm. 1966; Dep. Supreme Allied Comdr, Atlantic, 1966–68. Administrative Dir, Business Graduates Assoc. Ltd, 1969–83. *Address:* 29 Elvaston Place, SW7 5NL. *Club:* Army and Navy.

CLUTTERBUCK, Edmund Harry Michael, OBE 1957; Director, Scottish & Newcastle Breweries Ltd, 1960–80 (Deputy Chairman, 1973–77); *b* 22 July 1920; *s* of Maj.-Gen. W. E. Clutterbuck, *qv*; *m* 1945, Anne Agatha Woodsend; one *s* three *d*. *Educ:* Winchester Coll.; New Coll., Oxford (MA). HM Forces, 1940–46. Joined William Younger & Co. Ltd, 1947; Dir, Scottish Brewers Ltd, 1955; Scottish & Newcastle Breweries Ltd: Techn. Man. Dir, 1965; Jt Man. Dir, 1970; Director: Scottish American Mortgage Co., 1962; Scottish Eastern Investment Trust, 1965; Scottish Widows' Fund, 1965 (Chm., 1979–81; Dep. Chm., 1981–82); Pres., European Brewery Convention, 1971–; Member: Heriot-Watt Univ. Court, 1959; Herring Industry Bd, 1963–81; White Fish Authority, 1973–81; Dep. Chm., Royal Inst. of Internat. Affairs (Scottish Br.), 1969. *Recreations:* music, fishing, shooting, travel, languages. *Address:* The Tower, Hornby Castle, Bedale, N Yorks. *Club:* New (Edinburgh).

CLUTTERBUCK, Maj.-Gen. Richard Lewis, CB 1971; OBE 1958; writer, lecturer and broadcaster; *b* London, 22 Nov. 1917; *s* of late Col L. St J. R. Clutterbuck, OBE, late RA, and late Mrs I. J. Clutterbuck; *m* 1948, Angela Muriel Barford; three *s*. *Educ:* Radley Coll.; Pembroke Coll., Cambridge. MA Cantab (Mech. Scis); PhD (Econ. and Pol.), London Univ., 1971. Commd in RE, 1937; War Service: France, 1940; Sudan and Ethiopia, 1941; Western Desert, 1941–43; Italy, 1944; subseq. service in: Germany, 1946 and 1951–53; Italy, 1946; Palestine, 1947; Malaya, 1956–58; Christmas Island (Nuclear Trials), 1958; USA, 1961–63; Singapore, 1966–68. Instructor, British Army Staff Coll., 1953–56; Instructor, US Army Staff Coll., 1961–63; idc 1965; Chief Engr, Far East Land Forces, 1966–68; Engr-in-Chief (Army), 1968–70; Chief Army Instructor, Royal Coll. of Defence Studies, 1971–72, retired. Col Comdt, RE, 1972–77. Sen. Lectr and Reader, Dept of Politics, Univ. of Exeter, 1972–83. FICE. *Publications:* Across the River (as Richard Jocelyn), 1957; The Long Long War, 1966; Protest and the Urban Guerrilla, 1973; Riot and Revolution in Singapore and Malaya, 1973; Living with Terrorism, 1975; Guerrillas and Terrorists, 1977; Britain in Agony, 1978, rev. edn 1980; Kidnap and Ransom, 1978; The Media and Political Violence, 1981, rev. edn 1983; Industrial Conflict and Democracy, 1984; Conflict and Violence in Singapore and Malaysia, 1985; The Future of Political Violence, 1986; Kidnap, Hijack and Extortion, 1987; contribs to British and US jls. *Address:* c/o Lloyds Bank, R Section, 6 Pall Mall, SW1. *Clubs:* Royal Commonwealth Society, Army and Navy.

CLUTTERBUCK, Maj.-Gen. Walter Edmond, DSO 1943; MC; *b* 17 Nov. 1894; *s* of E. H. Clutterbuck, JP, Hardenhuish Park, Chippenham, Wilts; *m* 1919, Gwendolin Atterbury (*d* 1975), *o d* of H. G. Younger, JP, Benmore, Argyllshire; one *s* three *d*. *Educ:* Horris Hill; Cheltenham Coll.; RMC Sandhurst. Commissioned Royal Scots Fusiliers, 1913; served European War, 1914–19, France, Gallipoli, Egypt, Palestine, and S Russia (wounded twice, MC and bar, Crown of Italy, 1914 Star and clasp, despatches twice); Bt Lt-Col 1939; War of 1939–45 commanded: 1st Royal Scots Fusiliers, 1939–40; 10th Inf. Bde, 1940–41; 1st Div., 1941–43, N Africa and Pantellaria (DSO, Legion of Honour); an Inf. Div. Home Forces, 1943. Chief of British Military Mission to Egypt, 1945–46; retired pay, 1946. *Recreations:* hunting, fishing, shooting. *Address:* Hornby Castle, Bedale, N Yorks. *T:* Richmond 811579. *Club:* Naval and Military.

See also E. H. M. Clutterbuck.

CLUTTON, Rafe Henry, FRICS; Partner in Cluttons, Chartered Surveyors, London, since 1955; *b* 13 June 1929; *s* of late Robin John Clutton and Rosalie Muriel (*née* Birch); *m* 1954, Jill Olwyn Evans; four *s* one *d*. *Educ:* Tonbridge Sch., Kent. FRICS 1959. Director, Legal & General Assurance Soc. Ltd, 1972–. Member: National Theatre Bd, 1976–; Salvation Army London Adv. Bd, 1971–. Governor, Royal Foundn of Grey Coat Hosp., 1967–. *Recreations:* family, reading, gardening. *Address:* Fairfield, North Chailey, Sussex. *T:* Newick 2431. *Clubs:* Royal Thames Yacht, City of London.

CLUTTON-BROCK, Arthur Guy; independent social worker, 1965–72, retired; *b* 5 April 1906; *s* of late Henry Alan Clutton-Brock and late Rosa Clutton-Brock; *m* 1934, Francys Mary Allen; one *d*. *Educ:* Rugby Sch.; Magdalene Coll., Cambridge (Hon. Fellow, 1973). Cambridge House, 1927; Rugby House, 1929; Borstal Service, 1933; Principal Probation Officer for the Metropolitan Police Court District, 1936; Head of Oxford House, 1940; Christian Reconstruction in Europe, 1946; Agricultural Labourer, 1947; Agriculturalist at St Faith's Mission, 1949; Field Worker of African Development Trust, 1959–65; deported from Rhodesia by rebel regime, 1971. Treasurer, Cold Comfort Farm Soc., 1966. *Publications:* Dawn in Nyasaland, 1959; Cold Comfort Confronted, 1973. *Address:* Gelli Uchaf, Llandyrnog, Clwyd LL16 4HR.

CLUVER, Eustace Henry, ED; MA; DM, ChB Oxon; DPH London; FRSH; Emeritus Professor of Medical Education, University of the Witwatersrand, Johannesburg, SA, since 1963; *b* 28 Aug. 1894; *s* of late Dr F. A. Cluver, Stellenbosch; *m* 1929, Eileen Ledger; three *d*. *Educ:* Victoria Coll., Stellenbosch; Hertford Coll., Oxford (Rhodes scholar). 1st class Final Hon. Sch. of Physiology, 1916. Elected to a Senior Demyship at Magdalen Coll., 1917; King's Coll. (Burney Yeo Scholarship, 1918). Served European War, 1914–18 (Capt. S Af. Med. Corps, BEF, France); War of 1939–45 (Col Dir of Pathology, S Af. Med. Corps). Prof. of Physiology, Univ. of the Witwatersrand, Johannesburg, 1919–26; Sec. for Public Health and Chief Health Officer for the Union of South Africa, 1938–40; Dir of S African Inst. for Med. Research and Prof. of Preventive Medicine, Univ. Witwatersrand, 1940–59. LLD (*hc*) Witwatersrand, 1974. KStJ. *Publications:* Public Health in South Africa, 1934 (Textbook), 6th edn 1959; Social Medicine, 1951; Medical and Health Legislation in the Union of South Africa, 1949, 2nd edn 1960; papers in scientific and medical journals. *Address:* Mornhill Farm, PO Box 226, Walkerville, Transvaal, 1876, South Africa.

CLWYD, 2nd Baron *cr* 1919; **John Trevor Roberts;** Bt, 1908; Assistant Secretary of Commissions, Lord Chancellor's Department of House of Lords, 1948–61; *b* 28 Nov. 1900; *s* of 1st Baron and Hannah (*d* 1951), *d* of W. S. Caine, MP; *S* father, 1955; *m* 1932, Joan de Bois (*d* 1985), *d* of late Charles R. Murray, Woodbank, Partickhill, Glasgow; one *s* one *d*. *Educ:* Gresham's Sch.; Trinity Coll., Cambridge. BA 1922. Barrister, Gray's Inn, 1930. JP County of London, 1950. *Recreation:* fishing. *Heir:* *s* Hon. (John) Anthony Roberts [*b* 2 Jan. 1935; *m* 1969, Geraldine, *yr d* of C. E. Cannons, Sanderstead; three *s*]. *Address:* 15 Aubrey Road, W8. *T:* 01–727 7911; Trimmings, Gracious Street, Selborne, Hants.

CLWYD, Ann, (Ann Clwyd Roberts); journalist and broadcaster; MP (Lab) Cynon Valley, since May 1984; *b* 21 March 1937; *d* of Gwilym Henri Lewis and Elizabeth Ann Lewis; *m* 1963, Owen Dryhurst Roberts, TV director and producer. *Educ:* Halkyn Primary Sch.; Holywell Grammar Sch.; The Queen's Sch., Chester; University Coll., Bangor. Former: Student-teacher, Hope Sch., Flintshire; BBC Studio Manager; freelance reporter, producer; Welsh corresp., The Guardian and The Observer, 1964–79; Vice-Chm., Welsh Arts Council, 1975–79. Member: Welsh Hospital Board, 1970–74; Cardiff Community Health Council, 1975–; Royal Commn on NHS, 1976–79; Working Party, report, Organisation of Out-Patient Care, for Welsh Hosp. Bd; Working Party, Bilingualism in the Hospital Service; Labour Party Study Gp., People and the Media; Arts Council of Gt Britain, 1975–80; Chm., Cardiff Anti-Racialism Cttee, 1978–80; Labour Party NEC, 1983–84. Chm., Labour back-bench cttee on Health and Social Security; Vice-Chm., Labour back-bench cttee on Defence. Member: NUJ; TGWU. Contested (Lab): Denbigh, 1970; Gloucester, Oct. 1974; Mem. (Lab) Mid and West Wales, European Parlt, 1979–84. *Address:* 70 St Michael's Road, Llandaff, Cardiff. *T:* Cardiff 562245.

CLYDE, Hon. Lord; James John Clyde; a Senator of the College of Justice in Scotland, since 1985; *b* 29 Jan. 1932; *s* of Rt Hon. Lord Clyde; *m* 1963, Ann Clunie Hoblyn; two *s*. *Educ:* Edinburgh Academy; Corpus Christi Coll., Oxford (BA); Edinburgh Univ. (LLB). Called to Scottish Bar, 1959; QC (Scot.) 1971; Advocate-Depute, 1973–74. Chancellor to Bishop of Argyll and the Isles, 1972–85; a Judge of the Courts of Appeal of Jersey and Guernsey, 1979–85. Mem., Scottish Valuation Adv. Council, 1972–; Chairman: Med. Appeal Tribunal, 1974–85; Cttee of Investigation for Scotland on Agricl Mktg, 1984–85. Dir., Edinburgh Acad., 1979–; Trustee, St Mary's Music Sch., 1976–. *Publication:* (ed jtly) Armour on Valuation, 3rd edn, 1961, 5th edn, 1985. *Recreations:* music, gardening. *Address:* 9 Heriot Row, Edinburgh EH3 6HU. *T:* 031–556 7114. *Club:* New (Edinburgh).

CLYDESMUIR, 2nd Baron *cr* 1948, of Braidwood; **Ronald John Bilsland Colville,** KT 1972; CB 1965; MBE 1944; TD; Lord High Commissioner to the General Assembly, Church of Scotland, 1971 and 1972; Lord-Lieutenant, Lanarkshire, since 1963; Captain, Royal Company of Archers, Queen's Body Guard for Scotland, since 1985; *b* 21 May 1917; *s* of 1st Baron Clydesmuir, PC, GCIE, TD, and Agnes Anne (*d* 1970), CI 1947, Kaisar-i-Hind Gold Medal; *S* father, 1954; *m* 1946, Joan Marguerita, *d* of Lt-Col E. B. Booth, DSO, Darver Castle, Co. Louth; two *s* two *d*. *Educ:* Charterhouse; Trinity Coll., Cambridge. Served in The Cameronians (Scottish Rifles), 1939–45 (MBE, despatches). Commanded 6/7th Bn The Cameronians, TA, 1953–56. Director: Colvilles Ltd, 1958–70; British Linen Bank (Governor, 1966–71); Bank of Scotland (Dep. Governor, 1971–72, Governor, 1972–81); Scottish Provident Instn, 1954–; Scotbits Securities Ltd, 1960–; The Scottish Western Investment Co., 1965–78; BSC Strip Mills Div., 1970–73; Caledonian Offshore Co. Ltd, 1971–; Barclays Bank, 1972–82; Chm., North Sea Assets Ltd, 1972–. President: Scottish Council (Development and Industry), 1978– (Chm., Exec. Cttee, 1966–78); Scottish Council of Physical Recreation, 1964–72; Scottish Br., National Playing Fields Assoc.; Chm., Council, Territorial, Auxiliary and Volunteer Reserve Assocs, 1969–73, Pres., 1974–81; Chm., Lanarkshire T&AFA, 1957–63, Pres. 1963–68; Pres., Lowland TA&VRA. Hon. Colonel: 6th/7th (Territorial) Bn, The Cameronians (Scottish Rifles), 1967–71; 52 Lowland Volunteers, T&AVR, 1970–75. Chm., Scottish Outward Bound Assoc. Trustee, MacRobert Trusts. DL Lanarkshire, 1955, Vice-Lieut,

1959–63. Hon. LLD Strathclyde, 1968; Hon. DSc Heriot-Watt, 1971. *Recreations:* shooting, fishing. *Heir: s* Hon. David Ronald Colville [*b* 8 April 1949; *m* 1978, Aline Frances, *er d* of Peter Merriam, Holton Lodge, Holton St Mary, Suffolk; one *s* two *d*]. *Address:* Langlees House, Biggar, Lanarkshire. *T:* Biggar 20057. *Clubs:* Caledonian; New (Edinburgh).

See also Captain N. E. F. Dalrymple Hamilton.

COADY, Aubrey William Burleton, CMG 1959; Chairman, Electricity Commission of NSW, 1959–75 (Member since 1950); *b* Singleton, NSW, 15 June 1915; *s* of W. A. Coady, Belmont; *m* 1964, Phyllis K., *d* of late G. W. Mathews. *Educ:* Newcastle High Sch.; Sydney Univ. (BA, BEc). Under-Sec. and Comptroller of Accounts, NSW Treasury, 1955–59. *Address:* 42 Rickard Avenue, Mosman, NSW 2088, Australia.

COALES, Prof. John Flavell, CBE 1974 (OBE 1945); FRS 1970; FEng; Professor of Engineering (Control), Cambridge University, 1965–74, now Emeritus; Fellow of Clare Hall, 1964–74, now Emeritus; *b* 14 Sept. 1907; *s* of John Dennis Coales and Marion Beatrice Coales (*née* Flavell); *m* 1936, Mary Dorothea Violet, *d* of Rev. Guthrie Henry Lewis Alison; two *s* two *d*. *Educ:* Berkhamsted Sch.; Sidney Sussex Coll., Cambridge (MA; ScD 1985). Admty Dept of Scientific Res., 1929–46; Res. Dir, Elliott Bros (London) Ltd, 1946; Engrg Dept, Cambridge Univ.: Asst Dir of Res., 1953; Lectr, 1956; Reader in Engrg, 1958; Prof., 1965. Part-time Mem., E Electricity Bd, 1967–73. Director: Tube Investments Technological Centre, 1955–60; TI R&D Bd, 1960–65; BSA Metal Components, 1967–73; BSA Gp Res. Bd (Dep. Chm.), 1967–73; Delta Materials Research Ltd, 1974–77. Mackay Vis. Prof. of Electrical Engrg, Univ. of Calif., Berkeley, 1963. Internat. Fedn of Automatic Control: MEC, 1957; Vice-Pres., 1961; Pres., 1963. Brit. Conf. on Automation and Computation: Gp B Vice-Chm., 1958; Chm., 1960. UK Automation Council: Chm. Res. and Develt Panel, 1960–63; Chm. For. Relations Panel, 1960–64; Vice-Chm., 1961–63; Chm., 1963–66. Instn of Electrical Engrs: Mem. Council, 1953–55, 1964–77; Chm., Measurement Section, 1953; Chm., Control and Automation Div., 1965, etc; Vice-Pres., 1966–71; Pres., 1971–72. Council of Engineering Institutions: Vice-Chm., 1974; Chm., 1975 (Mem. Council for Envtl Sci. and Engrg, 1973–); Chm., Commonwealth Bd for Engrg Educn and Training, 1976–80; Pres., World Environment and Resources Council, 1973–74. Pres., Soc. of Instrument Technology, 1958. Past Member, Gen. Bd and Exec. Cttee of Nat. Physical Laboratory; Member: Adv. Council, RMCS, 1963–73; Educn Adv. Cttee for RAF, 1967–76; Trng and Educn Adv. Cttee of RAF, 1976–79; Court of Cranfield Inst. of Technology, 1970–; Governing Body, Nat. Inst. of Agric. Engrg, 1970–75; Envtl Design and Engrg Res. Cttee, DoE Bldg Res. Estab., 1973–; British Council Sci. Adv. Cttee, 1973–75; Engrg and Bldgs Bd, ARC, 1973–77; British Library Adv. Council, 1975–81; Chm., IFAC Pubns Managing Bd, 1976–. Governor: Hatfield Coll. of Technology, 1951–68; Hatfield Polytechnic, 1969–70 (Hon. Fellow, 1971–). FICE, FIEE (Pres., IEE, 1971–72; Hon. FIEE 1985), FIEEE, FIAgrE, FInstP; Founder Fellow, Fellowship of Engineering, 1976 (Mem., Exec. Cttee and Chm., Activities Cttee, 1976–80); Hon. Mem., Inst. of Measurement and Control, 1971. For. Mem., Serbian Acad. of Scis, 1981. Hon. DSc City Univ., 1970; Hon. DTech Loughborough, 1977; Hon. DEng Sheffield, 1978. Harold Hartley Medal, 1971; Giorgio Quazza Medal, IFAC, 1981 (first recipient); Honda Prize, 1982. *Publications:* (ed) Automatic and Remote Control (Proc. First Congr. of Internat. Fedn of Automatic Control), 1961; original papers on radio direction finding, radar, information theory, magnetic amplifiers, automatic control, automation and technical education. *Recreations:* mountaineering, farming, gardening. *Address:* 4 Latham Road, Cambridge CB2 2EQ. *Clubs:* Athenæum, Alpine.

COATES, Sir Anthony Robert M.; *see* Milnes Coates.

COATES, Sir Ernest (William), Kt 1973; CMG 1970; State Director of Finance and Permanent Head of Victoria Treasury, Australia, 1959–77; *b* 30 Nov. 1916; *s* of Thomas Atlee Coates; *m* 1st, 1943, Phylis E. Morris (*d* 1971); one *s* three *d*; 2nd, 1974, Patricia Ann, *d* of late C. A. Fisher, Herts. *Educ:* Ballarat High Sch.; Univ. of Melbourne. BCom. Member: Bd of State Savings Bank of Victoria, 1960–77; Nat. Debt Commn, Australia, 1963–78; Australian Universities Commn, 1968–77; Aust. Administrative Appeals Tribunal, 1978–. Dir, Equity Trustees Executors and Agency Co. Ltd. Chairman: Australian Selection Cttee, Harkness Fellowships, 1975–83; Rhodes Scholarship Selection Cttee (Victoria), 1981 (Mem., 1977–81). Hon. LLD Melbourne, 1979. *Recreations:* golf, music. *Address:* 64 Molesworth Street, Kew, Victoria 3101, Australia. *T:* 8618226. *Clubs:* Melbourne (Melbourne); Green Acres Golf, Lorne Golf.

COATES, Brig. Sir Frederick (Gregory Lindsay), 2nd Bt *cr* 1921; *b* 19 May 1916; *o s* of Sir William Frederick Coates, 1st Bt, Belfast, N Ireland; *S* father, 1932; *m* 1940, Joan Nugent, *d* of late Maj.-Gen. Sir Charlton Spinks, KBE, DSO; one *s* two *d*. *Educ:* Eton; Sandhurst. Commissioned Royal Tank Regt, 1936; Served War of 1939–45, North Africa and NW Europe. Min. of Supply, 1947–53; Asst Military Attaché, Stockholm, 1953–56; British Joint Services Mission, Washington, 1956–58; Comdt, RAC School of Tank Technology, 1958–61; Asst Dir of Fighting Vehicles, and Col GS, War Office and MoD, 1961–66; Brig., British Defence Staff, Washington, DC, 1966–69; Mil. Dep. to Head of Defence Sales, 1969–71; retired 1971. *Heir: s* David Charlton Frederick Coates [*b* 16 Feb. 1948; *m* 1973, Christine Helen, *d* of Lewis F. Marshall; two *s*]. *Address:* Launchfield, Briantspuddle, Dorchester, Dorset DT2 7HN. *Clubs:* Royal Yacht Squadron; RMYC; RLymYC; Island Sailing; RAC Yacht.

COATES, Prof. Geoffrey Edward, MA, DSc; Professor of Chemistry, University of Wyoming, 1968–79, now Emeritus; *b* 14 May 1917; *er s* of Prof. Joseph Edward Coates, OBE; *m* 1951, Winifred Jean Hobbs; one *s* one *d*. *Educ:* Clifton Coll.; Queen's Coll., Oxford. Research Chemist, Magnesium Metal Corp., 1940–45; Univ. of Bristol: Lecturer in Chemistry, 1945–53; Sub-Warden of Wills Hall, 1946–51; Prof. of Chemistry, Univ. of Durham, 1953–68. *Publications:* Organo-metallic Compounds (monograph), 1956, 3rd edn (2 vols), 1967–68; Principles of Organometallic Chemistry, 1968; papers in scientific journals. *Address:* 1801 Rainbow Avenue, Laramie, Wyoming 82070, USA. *Club:* Royal Commonwealth Society.

See also J. F. Coates.

COATES, James Richard; Under Secretary, Railways Directorate, Department of Transport, since 1985; *b* 18 Oct. 1935; *s* of William Richard Coates and Doris Coral (*née* Richmond); *m* 1969, Helen Rosamund Rimington; one *s* one *d*. *Educ:* Nottingham High Sch.; Clare Coll., Cambridge (MA). Joined Ministry of Transport, 1959; Private Sec. to Permanent Sec., 1962–63; Principal, 1963; Private Sec. to Secretary of State for Local Govt and Regional Planning, 1969, and to Minister of Transport, 1970–71; Asst Sec., DoE, 1971; Under Secretary, 1977; Dir, London Reg., PSA, 1979–83; Under Sec., Dept of Transport, 1983–. *Recreations:* listening to music, gardening. *Address:* 10 Alwyne Road, Canonbury, N1 2HH. *T:* 01–359 7827.

COATES, John Francis, OBE 1955; FRINA; Deputy Director, Ship Design, Ministry of Defence, 1977–79, retired; *b* 30 March 1922; *s* of Joseph Edward Coates and Ada Maria Coates; *m* 1954, Jane Waymouth; two *s*. *Educ:* Clifton Coll.; Queen's Coll., Oxford (MA 1946). RCNC; FRINA 1969. Entered RCNC, 1943; RCDS, 1971; Supt, Naval Construction Res. Estabt, Dunfermline, 1974. Dir, The Trireme Trust, 1985. *Publications:* (with J. S. Morrison) The Athenian Trireme, 1986; papers on naval architecture of ancient ships. *Recreation:* nautical research. *Address:* Sabinal, Lucklands Road, Bath BA1 4AU. *T:* Bath 23696.

See also Prof. G. E. Coates.

COATES, Prof. John Henry, FRS 1985; Sadleirian Professor of Pure Mathematics, and Professorial Fellow of Emmanuel College, Cambridge University, since 1986; *b* 26 Jan. 1945; *s* of J. R. Coates and Beryl (*née* Lee); *m* 1966, Julie Turner; three *s*. *Educ:* Australian National Univ. (BSc); Trinity Coll., Cambridge (PhD). Assistant Prof., Harvard Univ., 1969–72; Associate Prof., Stanford Univ., 1972–74; Univ. Lectr, Cambridge, and Fellow, Emmanuel Coll., 1974–77; Prof., ANU, 1977–78; Prof. of Maths, Univ. de Paris, Orsay, 1978–86, Ecole Normale Supérieure, Paris, 1985–86. *Address:* Emmanuel College, Cambridge; 104 Mawson Road, Cambridge CB2 3AP. *T:* Cambridge 60884.

COATES, Michael Arthur, FCA; Chairman, Price Waterhouse, World Firm, since 1982; *b* 12 May 1924; *yr s* of late Joseph Michael Smith Coates, OBE, Elmfield, Wylam, Northumberland, and late Lillian Warren Coates (*née* Murray); *m* 1st, 1952, Audrey Hampton Thorne (marr. diss. 1970); one *s* two *d*; 2nd, 1971, Sally Rogers (marr. diss. 1980). *Educ:* Uppingham Sch. Admitted Mem., Inst. of Chartered Accountants, 1951. Served RA, mainly in ME and Italy, 1942–47. Articled with Price Waterhouse & Co., Newcastle, 1942; returned to Price Waterhouse, 1947; transf. to London, 1954; Partner, Price Waterhouse & Co., 1959–82, Dep. Sen. Partner, 1974–75, Sen. Partner, 1975–82; Chm., Price Waterhouse Internat. Manpower Cttee, 1971–74; Mem., Policy Cttee, 1974–. *Recreations:* diverse, including music, modern painting, antiques, gardens, reading, railways, photography. *Address:* 20 Wilton Crescent, SW1. *T:* 01–235 4423; Aultmore House, Nethybridge, Inverness-shire, Scotland PH25 3ED. *T:* Nethybridge 384.

COATES, Patrick Devereux; Editor for British Academy of Chinese records at Public Record Office, since 1978; *b* 30 April 1916; *s* of late H. H. Coates, OBE, and late Mrs F. J. Coates; *m* 1946, Mary Eleanor, *e d* of late Capt. Leveson Campbell, DSO, RN and late Mrs Campbell; one *s* one *d*. *Educ:* Trinity Coll., Cambridge. Entered Consular Service and served at Peking, Canton and Kunming, 1937–41; attached to Chinese 22nd Div. in Burma (despatches) and to Chinese forces in India, 1941–44; Actg Chinese Sec. to HM Embassy in China, 1944–46; 1st Sec., Foreign Office, 1946–50; transf. to Min. of Town and Country Planning, 1950; Asst Sec., Min. of Housing and Local Govt, 1955; Asst Under-Sec. of State, Dept of Economic Affairs, 1965–68, Min. of Housing and Local Govt, 1968–70, Dept of the Environment, 1970–72. Hon. Vis. Fellow, SOAS, Univ. of London, 1973–76. *Recreations:* Chinese studies, getting into the fresh air. *Address:* Lewesland Cottage, Barcombe, near Lewes, Sussex BN8 5TG. *T:* Barcombe 400407.

COATES, Reginald Charles, FEng 1978; Emeritus Professor of Civil Engineering, University of Nottingham, since 1983; *b* 28 June 1920; *s* of Wilfrid and Margaret Anne Coates; *m* 1942, Doris Sheila (*née* Sharrad); two *s* one *d*. *Educ:* New Mills Grammar Sch.; The Herbert Strutt Sch., Belper, Derbyshire; University Coll., Nottingham. Served War of 1939–45, Corps of Royal Engineers. Univ. of Nottingham: Lectr in Civil Engineering, 1946; Sen. Lectr, 1953; Prof. and Head of Dept of Civil Engrg, 1958–82; Dep. Vice-Chancellor, 1966–69; Prof. and Hd, Dept of Civil Engrg, Papua New Guinea Univ. of Technol., 1982–85. Member: Council, Instn of Civil Engineers, 1967–72 (Vice-Pres., 1975–78, Pres., 1978–79); Sheffield Regional Hosp. Bd, 1971–74; Notts AHA, 1974–75; Council, Construction Industry Research and Information Assoc., 1978–82 (Vice-Chm., 1985–); Adv. Cttee, Books for Overseas, British Council, 1974–82; Construction and Housing Res. Adv. Council, DoE, 1976–79. *Publications:* (with M. G. Coutie and F. K. Kong) Structural Analysis, 1972; occasional articles in technical press. *Recreations:* cooking and idling. *Address:* Tan Y Bracty, Nefyn, Gwynedd.

COATS, Sir Alastair Francis Stuart, 4th Bt, *cr* 1905; *b* 18 Nov. 1921; *s* of Lieut-Col Sir James Stuart Coats, MC, 3rd Bt and Lady Amy Coats (*d* 1975), *er d* of 8th Duke of Richmond and Gordon; *S* father, 1966; *m* 1947, Lukyn, *d* of Capt. Charles Gordon; one *s* one *d*. *Educ:* Eton. Served War of 1939–45, Coldstream Guards (Capt.). *Heir: s* Alexander James Coats, *b* 6 July 1951. *Address:* Birchwood House, Durford Wood, Petersfield, Hants. *T:* Liss 2254.

COATS, Sir William David, Kt 1985; DL; Chairman, Coats Patons PLC, 1981–86 (Deputy Chairman, 1979–81); Deputy Chairman, Clydesdale Bank, since 1985 (Director, since 1962); *b* 25 July 1924; *s* of Thomas Heywood Coats and Olivia Violet Pitman; *m* 1950, Hon. Elizabeth Lilian Graham MacAndrew; two *s* one *d*. *Educ:* Eton Coll. Entered service of Coats Patons PLC, 1948: Director: The Central Agency Ltd (subsid. co.), 1953–55; Coats Patons PLC, 1960–86; Murray Caledonian Trust Co. Ltd, 1961–81; Weir Group Ltd, 1970–83; Murray Investment Trusts, 1986–. Mem., S of Scotland Electricity Bd, 1972–81. Hon. LLD Strathclyde, 1977. DL Ayr and Arran, 1986. *Recreations:* shooting and golf. *Address:* The Cottage, Symington, Ayrshire KA1 5QG. *T:* Symington 830287. *Club:* Western (Glasgow).

See also Baron MacAndrew.

COBB, Henry Stephen, FSA; FRHistS; Clerk of the Records, House of Lords, since 1981; *b* 17 Nov. 1926; *y s* of Ernest Cobb and Violet Kate Cobb (*née* Sleath), Wallasey; *m* 1969, Eileen Margaret Downer. *Educ:* Birkenhead Sch.; London School of Economics (BA, MA); Liverpool Univ. (Dip. Archive Admin). Archivist, Church Missionary Soc., 1951–53; Asst Archivist, House of Lords, 1953–59, Asst Clerk of the Records, 1959–73, Dep. Clerk, 1973–81. Mem. Council: British Records Assoc., 1978–81; Society of Archivists, 1970–82 (Chm., 1982–84); Chm., London Record Soc., 1984–. Lecturer in Palaeography, School of Librarianship, North London Polytechnic, 1973–77. FSA 1967; FRHistS 1970. *Publications:* (ed) The Local Port Book of Southampton 1439–40, 1961; contribs to Economic History Rev., Jl of Soc. of Archivists, Archives, etc. *Recreations:* music, historical research. *Address:* 1 Child's Way, Hampstead Garden Suburb, NW11 6XU. *T:* 01–458 3688.

COBB, Richard Charles, CBE 1978; FBA 1967; Professor of Modern History, University of Oxford, 1973–84; Senior Research Fellow of Worcester College, Oxford, since 1984; *b* 20 May 1917; *s* of Francis Hills Cobb, Sudan Civil Service, and Dora Cobb (*née* Swindale); *m* 1963, Margaret Tennant; four *s* one *d*. *Educ:* Shrewsbury Sch.; Merton Coll., Oxford (Hon. Fellow 1980). Postmastership in History, Merton, 1934. HM Forces, 1942–46. Research in Paris, 1946–55; Lectr in History, UCW Aberystwyth, 1955–61; Sen. Simon Res. Fellow, Manchester, 1960; Lectr, University of Leeds, 1962; Fellow and Tutor in Modern History, Balliol Coll., 1962–72, Hon. Fellow, 1977; Reader in French Revolutionary History, Oxford, 1969–72. Vis. Prof. in the History of Paris, Collège de France, 1971. Lectures: Ralegh, British Academy, 1974; Zaharoff, Oxford, 1976; Helmsley, Brandeis, 1981. DUniv Essex, 1981. Chevalier des Palmes Académiques, 1956; Officier de l'Ordre National du Mérite, 1977; Chevalier de la Légion d'Honneur, 1985. *Publications:* L'armée révolutionnaire à Lyon, 1952; Les armées révolutionnaires du Midi, 1955; Les armées révolutionnaires, vol. 1, 1961, vol. 2, 1963; Terreur et Subsistances, 1965; A Second Identity: essays on France and French history, 1969; The Police and the People: French Popular Protest 1789–1820, 1970; Reactions to the French Revolution,

1972; Paris and its Provinces 1792–1802, 1975; A Sense of Place, 1975; Tour de France, 1976; Death in Paris 1795–1801, 1978 (Wolfson Prize, 1979); Streets of Paris, 1980; Promenades, 1980; French and Germans, Germans and French, 1983; Still Life: sketches from a Tunbridge Wells childhood, 1983 (J. R. Ackerley Prize); A Classical Education, 1985; People and Places, 1985. *Address:* Worcester College, Oxford.

COBB, Timothy Humphry, MA; *b* 4 July 1909; *s* of Humphry Henry Cobb and Edith Muriel (*née* Stogdon); *m* 1952, Cecilia Mary Josephine, *d* of W. G. Chapman; two *s* one *d*. *Educ:* Harrow; Magdalene Coll., Cambridge. Asst Master, Middlesex Sch., Concord, Mass, USA, 1931–32; Bryanston Sch., Blandford, Dorset, 1932–47, Housemaster, Head of Classics, Estate Bursar; Headmaster of King's Coll., Budo, Kampala, Uganda, 1947–58; formerly Sec., Uganda Headmasters' Association; Headmaster, Dover College, 1958–73. *Publication:* Certificate English Language Practice, 1958. *Recreations:* music, railway photography, producing vegetables. *Address:* Parkgate Farm, Framlingham, Woodbridge, Suffolk IP13 9JH. *T:* Badingham 672. *Clubs:* MCC, Royal Commonwealth Society.

COBBAN, Sir James (Macdonald), Kt 1982; CBE 1971; TD; MA; DL; JP; Headmaster of Abingdon School, 1947–70; *b* 14 Sept. 1910; *s* of late A. M. Cobban, MIStructE, Scunthorpe, Lincs; *m* 1942, Lorna Mary (*d* 1961), *er d* of late G. S. W. Marlow, BSc, FRIC, barrister-at-law, Sydenham; four *d* (one *s* decd). *Educ:* Pocklington Sch.; Jesus Coll., Cambridge (Scholar); Univ. of Vienna. Classical Tripos, Part I, 1931, Part II, 1932; Sandys Student, 1932: Thirlwall Medallist and Gladstone Prizeman, 1935; MA, Cambridge; MA, Oxford (Pembroke Coll.). Asst Master, King Edward VI Sch., Southampton, 1933–36; Class. Sixth Form Master, Dulwich Coll., 1936–40, 1946–47. Intelligence Corps (TA), 1941; GSO3, Directorate of Mil. Intelligence, 1941; Intermediate War Course, Staff Coll., 1943; DAQMG, Combined Ops HQ, 1943; Staff Officer, CCG, 1944 (Lt-Col 1945). Rep. Diocese of Oxford on Gen. Synod, 1970–85 (Panel of Chairmen 1979–81); Vice-Pres., Dio. Synod, 1975–82; Chm., Abingdon Co. Bench, 1964–74; Member: Cttee GBA, 1972– (Dep. Chm., 1976–82; Hon. Life Mem., 1981); Direct Grant Schs Jt Cttee, 1966–80 (Chm., 1975–80); Cttee, GBGSA, 1976–81; Council, Ind. Schs Careers Orgn, 1972–80; Cttee, United Soc. Christian Lit., 1974–83; Thames Valley Police Authority, 1973–80; Vale of White Horse DC, 1973–76; Governor: Stowe Sch., 1970–83; Wellington Coll., 1970–81; Campion Sch., Athens, 1980–83; Sch. of St Helen and St Katharine, 1954–80, 1983– (Chm., 1958–67); Abingdon Coll. of Further Education, 1974–80; St Stephen's House, Oxford, 1982–85; Gloucester School of Ministry, 1984–86. JP Berks, 1950, Oxon, 1974; DL Berks, 1966, Oxon, 1974. *Publications:* Senate and Provinces, 78–49 BC, 1935; (in collaboration) Civis Romanus, 1936; Pax et Imperium, 1938; Church and School, 1963. *Address:* 14 St Swithin's Close, Sherborne, Dorset DT9 3DW. *T:* Sherborne 812094.

COBBETT, David John, TD 1973; ERD 1962; railway and transportation management consultant; *b* 9 Dec. 1928; *m* 1952, Beatrix Jane Ogilvie Cockburn; three *s*. *Educ:* Royal Masonic Sch. FCIT. Gen. Railway admin. and managerial positions, 1949–67; Divl Movements Manager, Liverpool Street, 1967; Divl Manager, Norwich (British Railways Bd), 1968–70; Asst Managing Dir, Freightliners Ltd, 1970–73; Dep. Gen. Manager, British Railways Bd Scottish Region, 1973; Gen. Manager, British Railways Scottish Region, 1974–76; Chm., British Transport Ship Management, Scotland, 1974–76; Gen. Manager, BR Eastern Region, 1976–77; British Railways Board: Export Dir (Special Projects), 1977–78; Dir, Strategic Studies, 1978–83; Dir, Information Systems and Technology, 1983–85. Dir, Transmark, 1978. Chm., Railway Benevolent Instn, 1984– (Dep. Chm., 1981–84). Bt Col, Royal Corps of Transport (RARO), 1974. *Recreations:* military matters, historical reading, games. *Address:* The Grange, Strensall, York YO3 5XA. *T:* York 490334. *Clubs:* Army and Navy; MCC.

COBBOLD, family name of **Baron Cobbold.**

COBBOLD, 1st Baron *cr* 1960, of Knebworth; **Cameron Fromanteel Cobbold,** KG 1970; PC 1959; GCVO 1963; DL; Lord Chamberlain of HM Household, 1963–71; Chancellor of the Royal Victorian Order, 1963–71; Governor of Bank of England, 1949–61; one of HM Lieutenants for the City of London; *b* 14 Sept. 1904; *s* of late Lt-Col Clement Cobbold; *m* 1930, Lady (Margaret) Hermione (Millicent) Bulwer-Lytton, *er d* of 2nd Earl of Lytton, KG, PC, GCSI, GCIE; two *s* one *d*. *Educ:* Eton; King's Coll., Cambridge. Entered Bank of England as Adviser, 1933; Exec. Dir, 1938; Dep. Governor, 1945. Director: BIS, 1949–61; British Petroleum, 1963–74; Hudson Bay Co., 1964–74; Guardian Royal Exchange, 1963–74. Chairman: Chemical Bank New York Adv. Commn, 1969–74; Italian International Bank, 1971–74. A Permanent Lord in Waiting to the Queen, 1971–. Vice-Pres., British Heart Foundn (Pres. to 1976); Chm., Middlesex Hosp. Board of Governors and Med. Sch. Council, 1963–74. High Sheriff of County of London for 1946–47. Hon. Fellow Inst. of Bankers, 1961; Fellow of Eton, 1951–67; Steward of the Courts, Eton, 1973–. Chm. Malaysia Commission of Enquiry, 1962. Hon. LLD, McGill Univ., 1961. Hon. DSc (Econ.), London Univ., 1963. DL Herts, 1972. *Heir:* *s* Hon. David Antony Fromanteel Lytton-Cobbold [*b* 14 July 1937; assumed by deed poll, 1960, the additional surname of Lytton; *m* 1961, Christine Elizabeth, 3rd *d* of Major Sir Dennis Frederic Bankes Stucley, 5th Bt; three *s* one *d*]. *Address:* Lake House, Knebworth, Herts. *T:* Stevenage 812310.

COBBOLD, (Michael) David (Nevill), CBE 1983; MA; DL; Consultant, Beachcrofts, Solicitors, since 1983; Senior Partner, Stileman Neate & Topping, 1959–83; *b* 21 Oct. 1919; *s* of late Geoffrey Wyndham Nevill Cobbold and Cicely Helen Cobbold; *m* 1949, Ann Rosemary Trevor; two *s* one *d* (and one *s* decd). *Educ:* Charterhouse; New Coll., Oxford (MA); RMA, Sandhurst. War of 1939–45: commissioned and served with 2nd Bn, The Buffs, 1940–45. Admitted Solicitor, 1949. Westminster City Council: Member, 1949–86; Leader, 1964–65, 1976–83; Alderman, 1962–78; Mayor of Westminster, 1958–59; Lord Mayor and Dep. High Steward of Westminster, 1973–74. London Boroughs Association: Hon. Treas., 1977–84; Chm., Gen. Purposes Cttee, 1978–86; Dep. Chm., 1984–86. Chm., London Boroughs Grants Cttee, 1985–86; Member: DoE Housing Act Gp, 1970–76; Adv. Cttee on Local Govt Audit, 1979–82; Royal Parks Constabulary Cttee, 1985–. Pres., Beckenham Conservative Assoc., 1974–. DL Greater London, 1967–. *Recreations:* watching grandchildren and weeds grow: encouraging the former, discouraging the latter. *Address:* 31 Ashley Court, Morpeth Terrace, SW1P 1EN. *T:* 01-834 5020.

COBBOLD, Patrick Mark; *b* 20 June 1934; *s* of late Captain J. M. Cobbold and of Lady Blanche Cobbold. *Educ:* Eton. Served Scots Guards, 1953–57; ADC to the Governor of the Bahamas, 1957–60; Tolly Cobbold Breweries, 1961–. *Recreations:* fishing, shooting, football. *Address:* Glemham Hall, Woodbridge, Suffolk. *T:* Wickham Market 746219. *Clubs:* White's, Pratt's.

COBHAM, 11th Viscount *cr* 1718; **John William Leonard Lyttelton;** Bt 1618; Baron Cobham 1718; Lord Lyttelton, Baron of Frankley 1756 (renewed 1794); Baron Westcote (Ire.) 1776; *b* 5 June 1943; *e s* of 10th Viscount Cobham, KG, PC, GCMG, GCVO, TD, and Elizabeth Alison Viscountess Cobham (*d* 1986), *d* of J. R. Makeig-Jones, CBE; *S* father, 1977; *m* 1974, Penelope Ann, *e d* of late Roy Cooper, Moss Farm, Ollerton, near Knutsford, Cheshire. *Educ:* Eton; Christ's College, New Zealand; Royal Agricultural College, Cirencester. *Recreations:* cricket, shooting. *Heir:* *b* Hon. Christopher Charles Lyttelton [*b* 23 Oct. 1947; *m* 1973, Tessa Mary, *d* of late Col A. G. J. Readman, DSO; one *s* one *d*]. *Address:* Hagley Hall, near Stourbridge, West Midlands DY9 9LG. *T:* Hagley 885823; 20 Kylestrome House, Cundy Street, Ebury Street, SW1. *T:* 01-730 5756. *Clubs:* Buck's, MCC.

COBHAM, Ven. John Oldcastle, MA; Archdeacon of Durham and Canon Residentiary of Durham Cathedral, 1953–69, now Archdeacon Emeritus; Licence to Officiate, Diocese of Exeter, since 1982, Diocese of Oxford, since 1986; *b* 11 April 1899; *s* of late Ven. John Lawrence Cobham; *m* 1934, Joan (*d* 1967), *d* of late Rev. George Henry Cobham; no *c*. *Educ:* St Lawrence Coll., Ramsgate; Tonbridge Sch.; Corpus Christi Coll., Cambridge; Univ. of Marburg; Westcott House, Cambridge; Académie Goetz. Served in Royal Field Artillery, 1917–19; Curate at St Thomas', Winchester, 1926–30; Vice-Principal of Westcott House, Cambridge, 1930–34; Principal of The Queen's Coll., Birmingham, 1934–53; Vicar of St Benet's, Cambridge, 1940–45; Recognised Lectr, Dept of Theology, Birmingham Univ., 1946–53; Hon. Canon, Derby Cathedral, 1950–53. Chaplain to the Forces (EC), 1943–45. Select Preacher: Univ. of Cambridge, 1933 and 1940; Univ. of Birmingham, 1938; Univ. of Oxford, 1952–53; Examining Chaplain to the Bishop of Durham, 1953–66, to the Bishop of Wakefield, 1959–68; licensed to officiate dio. St Edmundsbury and Ipswich, 1969–82. Member: Liturgical Commn, 1955–62; Archbishop of Canterbury's Commn on Roman Catholic Relations, 1964–69. George Craig Stewart Memorial Lecturer, Seabury-Western Theological Seminary, Evanston, Ill., 1963. *Publications:* Concerning Spiritual Gifts, 1933; co-translator of K. Barth in Revelation, a Symposium, 1937; contributor to: The Parish Communion, 1937; No Other Gospel, 1943; The Significance of the Barmen Declaration for the Oecumenical Church, 1943; DNB 1931–40 (E. C. Hoskyns), 1949; Theological Word Book of the Bible, 1950. *Recreation:* sketching. *Address:* The Old Vicarage, Moulsford, near Wallingford, Oxon OX10 9JB.

COBHAM, Michael John, CBE 1981; FRAeS; CBIM; Chairman and Managing Director, FR Group plc (formerly Flight Refuelling (Holdings) Ltd), since 1969; *b* 22 Feb. 1927; *s* of Sir Alan John Cobham, KBE, AFC, and Lady (Gladys) Cobham; *m* 1st, 1954, June Oakes (marr. diss. 1972); 2nd, 1973, Nadine Felicity, *e d* of William Abbott, Wimborne, Dorset; one *d*. *Educ:* Malvern; Trinity Coll., Cambridge (BA 1949, MA 1965). Served RN, 1945–47. Called to the Bar, Inner Temple, 1952; practised, 1954–55. Flight Refuelling Ltd: Dir, 1952; Man. Dir, 1964–77; Chm., 1969–. *Recreations:* ski-ing, sailing. *Address:* FR Group plc, Brook Road, Wimborne, Dorset BH21 2BJ. *Clubs:* Naval and Military; Royal Southern Yacht (Hamble).

COBURN, Prof. Kathleen; OC 1974; Professor of English, Victoria College, University of Toronto, 1953–71, now Emeritus; author; *b* 1905; *d* of Rev. John Coburn and Susannah Coburn. *Educ:* University of Toronto (MA); Oxford University (BLitt). Imperial Order of the Daughters of the Empire (IODE) Travelling Scholarship, 1930–31. Formerly Lectr, Asst Prof., and Assoc. Prof. of English, Victoria College, University of Toronto. University Women's Internat. Senior Fellowship, 1948–49; John Simon Guggenheim Memorial Fellowship, 1953–54, renewed, 1957–58; Commonwealth Visiting Fellowship (Univ. of London), 1962–63. FRSC 1958. Hon. Fellow, St Hugh's Coll., Oxford, 1970; Hon. Fellow, Champlain Coll., Trent Univ., Ont., 1972; Corresp. FBA, 1973. DHL: Haverford, 1972; Princeton, 1983; Hon. LLD, Queen's Univ., Kingston, Ontario, 1964; Hon. DLitt: Trent Univ., 1972; Cambridge, 1975; Toronto, 1978. Rose Mary Crawshay Prize for English Literature (Brit. Acad.), 1958; Chauveau Medal, RSC. *Publications:* The Philosophical Lectures of S. T. Coleridge, 1949; Inquiring Spirit, 1951, revd edn 1979; The Letters of Sara Hutchinson, 1954; The Notebooks of S. T. Coleridge, vol. i, 1957, vol. ii, 1961, vol. iii, 1973; Coleridge: A Collection of Critical Essays, 1967; The Self-Conscious Imagination (Riddell Meml Lectures), 1972; Coleridge, a Bridge Between Science and Poetry: reflections on the bicentenary of his birth, Discourse, Royal Institution, 1972; In Pursuit of Coleridge, 1977; Experience into Thought: perspectives in the Coleridge notebooks, Alexander Lectures, 1979; general editor, The Collected Coleridge, 1968–. *Address:* Victoria College, 73 Queen's Park Crescent, Toronto, Ontario M5S 1K7, Canada.

COCHRAN, William; PhD, MA; FRS 1962; Professor of Natural Philosophy, University of Edinburgh, since 1975; *b* 30 July 1922; *s* of James Cochran and Margaret Watson Cochran (*née* Baird); *m* 1953, Ingegerd Wall; one *s* two *d*. *Educ:* Boroughmuir Sch., Edinburgh; Edinburgh Univ. Asst Lectr, Edinburgh Univ., 1943–46; Demonstrator and Lectr, Univ. of Cambridge, 1948–62; Reader in Physics, Univ. of Cambridge, 1962–64. Fellow of Trinity Hall, Cambridge, 1951–64; University of Edinburgh: Prof. of Physics, 1964–75; Dean, Faculty of Science, 1978–81; Vice-Principal, 1984–. Research fellowships abroad, 1950–51, 1958–59, 1970. Hon. Fellow, Trinity Hall, Cambridge, 1982. Guthrie medallist, Inst. Physics and Phys. Soc., 1966; Hughes medallist, Royal Soc., 1978; Potts medallist, Franklin Inst., 1985. *Publications:* Vol. III of The Crystalline State (with Prof. H. Lipson), 1954, new edn 1966; Dynamics of Atoms in Crystals, 1973. *Recreations:* Scots verse, family history. *Address:* Department of Physics, The University, The King's Buildings, Edinburgh EH9 3JZ; 71 Clermiston Road, Edinburgh.

COCHRANE, family name of **Earl of Dundonald** and **Baron Cochrane of Cults.**

COCHRANE OF CULTS, 3rd Baron *cr* 1919; **Thomas Charles Anthony Cochrane;** *b* 31 Oct. 1922; *s* of 2nd Baron Cochrane of Cults, DSO, and Hon. Elin Douglas-Pennant (*d* 1934), *y d* of 2nd Baron Penrhyn; *S* father, 1968. *Educ:* privately. Founder and Trustee, Gardeners' Memorial Trust, 1980–. *Heir:* *b* Hon. (Ralph Henry) Vere Cochrane [*b* 20 Sept. 1926; *m* 1956, Janet Mary Watson, *d* of late Dr W. H. W. Cheyne; two *s*]. *Address:* Crawford Priory Estate, Cupar, Fife, Scotland; (residence) East Craigard, East Church Street, Buckie, Banffshire..

COCHRANE, (Alexander John) Cameron, MA; Headmaster, Fettes College, Edinburgh, since 1979; *b* 19 July 1933; *s* of Dr Alexander Younger Cochrane and Jenny Johnstone Cochrane; *m* 1958, Rosemary Aline, *d* of late Robert Alexander Ogg and of Aline Mary Ogg; one *s* two *d*. *Educ:* The Edinburgh Academy; University Coll., Oxford (BA English Lang. and Lit. 1957, MA 1961). National Service in RA, 1952–54. Asst Master, St Edward's Sch., Oxford, 1957–66; Warden, Brathay Hall, Ambleside, Cumbria, 1966–70; Asst Dir of Educn, City of Edinburgh, 1970–74; Headmaster, Arnold Sch., Blackpool, 1974–79. Member: Lancashire CC Educn Cttee, 1976–79; Council, Outward Bound Trust, 1979–; RA Council for Scotland, 1981–; Scottish Cttee, Duke of Edinburgh's Award, 1981–86; Chairman: Outward Bound Ullswater, 1979–84; Lothian Fedn of Boys' Clubs, 1981–84; Outward Bound Loch Eil, 1984–. Governor: Aiglon Coll.; Clifton Hall Sch.; Pocklington Sch. Hon. Fellow, Dept of Educnl Studies, Univ. of Edinburgh, 1973–74. *Recreations:* games, mountains, Rotary. *Address:* The Lodge, Fettes College, Edinburgh EH4 1QX. *Clubs:* Public Schools; MCC; Vincent's (Oxford); New (Edinburgh).

COCHRANE, Sir (Henry) Marc (Sursock), 4th Bt *cr* 1903; *b* 23 Oct. 1946; *s* of Sir Desmond Oriel Alastair George Weston Cochrane, 3rd Bt, and of Yvonne Lady Cochrane (*née* Sursock); *S* father, 1979; *m* 1969, Hala (*née* Es-Said); two *s* one *d*. *Educ:* Eton; Trinity

Coll., Dublin (BBS, MA). Director: Hambros Bank Ltd, 1979–85; GT Management Ltd, 1986–. Hon. Consul General of Ireland in Beirut, 1979–84. *Recreations:* skiing, target shooting, electronics. *Heir: s* Alexander Desmond Cochrane, *b* 7 May 1973. *Address:* Woodbrook, Bray, Co. Wicklow, Ireland. *T:* 821421; Palais Sursock, PO Box 154, Beirut, Lebanon. *T:* 331607.

COCKAYNE, Dame Elizabeth, DBE 1955; Chief Nursing Officer, Ministry of Health, 1948–58, retired; *d* of William and Alice Cockayne, Burton-on-Trent. *Educ:* Secondary Sch., Burton-on-Trent, and privately. Gen. Hospital Training, Royal Infirmary, Sheffield; Fever Training, Mount Gold Hospital, Plymouth; Midwifery Training, Maternity Hospital, Birmingham. Former experience includes: Supervisor of Training Sch., LCC; Matron of West London Hosp., St Charles' Hosp., Royal Free Hosp. *Recreation:* gardening. *Address:* Rushett Cottage, Little Heath Lane, Cobham, Surrey.

COCKBURN, Prof. Forrester, MD; FRCPGlas; FRCPE; Samson Gemmell Professor of Child Health, University of Glasgow, since 1977; *b* 13 Oct. 1934; *s* of Forrester Cockburn and Violet E. Bunce; *m* 1960, Alison Fisher Grieve; two *s*. *Educ:* Leith Acad.; Univ. of Edinburgh (MD). DCH Glasgow. FRCPE 1971; FRCPGlas 1978. Med. trng, Royal Infirmary of Edinburgh, Royal Hosp. for Sick Children, and Simpson Memorial Maternity Pavilion, Edinburgh, 1959–63; Huntingdon Hertford Foundn Res. Fellow, Boston Univ., Mass, 1963–65; Nuffield Sen. Res. Fellow, Univ. of Oxford, 1965–66; Wellcome Trust Sen. Med. Res. Fellow, Univ. of Edin. and Simpson Meml Maternity Pavilion, 1966–71; Sen. Lectr, Dept of Child Life and Health, Univ. of Edin., 1971–77. *Publications:* Neonatal Medicine, 1974; The Cultured Cell in Inherited Metabolic Disease, 1977; Inborn Errors of Metabolism in Humans, 1980; (with O. P. Gray) Children—A Handbook for Children's Doctors, 1984; (with J. H. Hutchison) Practical Paediatric Problems, 6th edn 1986; contrib. Fetal and Neonatal Nutrition. *Recreation:* sailing. *Address:* University Department of Child Health, Royal Hospital for Sick Children, Yorkhill, Glasgow G3 8SJ. *T:* 041–339 8888.

COCKBURN, Sir John (Elliot), 12th Bt of that Ilk, *cr* 1671; Managing Director, Cellar Management Ltd; *b* 7 Dec. 1925; *s* of Lieut-Col Sir John Cockburn, 11th Bt of that Ilk, DSO and Isabel Hunter (*d* 1978), *y d* of late James McQueen, Crofts, Kirkcudbrightshire; *S* father, 1949; *m* 1949, Glory Patricia, *er d* of Nigel Tudway Mullings; three *s* two *d*. *Educ:* RNC Dartmouth; Royal Agricultural Coll., Cirencester. Served War of 1939–45, joined RAF, July 1944. *Recreation:* reading. *Heir: s* Charles Christopher Cockburn [*b* 19 Nov. 1950; *m* 1978, Beverley, *d* of B. Stangroom]. *Address:* 48 Frewin Road, SW18. *Club:* Naval and Military.

COCKBURN, Sir Robert, KBE 1960 (OBE 1946); CB 1953; PhD, MSc, MA; FEng 1977; Senior Research Fellow, Churchill College, Cambridge, 1970–77; Chairman, National Computing Centre, 1970–77; *b* 31 March 1909; 2nd *s* of late Rev. R. T. Cockburn, Columba Manse, Belford, Northumberland; *m* 1935, Phyllis Hoyland; two *d*. *Educ:* Southern Secondary Sch. and Municipal Coll., Portsmouth; London Univ. BSc 1928, MSc 1935, PhD 1939, London; MA Cantab 1973. Taught Science at West Ham Municipal Coll., 1930–37; research in communications at RAE Farnborough, 1937–39; in radar at TRE Malvern, Worcs, 1939–45; in atomic energy at AERE Harwell, 1945–48; Scientific Adviser to Air Min., 1948–53; Princ. Dir of Scientific Research (Guided Weapons and Electronics), Ministry of Supply, 1954–55; Deputy Controller of Electronics, Ministry of Supply, 1955–56; Controller of Guided Weapons and Electronics, Ministry of Supply, 1956–59; Chief Scientist of Ministry of Aviation, 1959–64; Dir, RAE, Farnborough, 1964–69. Chairman: Television Adv. Cttee for Posts and Telecommunications, 1971–; BBC Engineering Adv. Cttee, 1973–81. Hon. Fellow, RAeS, 1970. Congressional Medal for Merit, 1947. *Publications:* scientific papers. *Recreation:* sailing. *Address:* 21 Fitzroy Road, Fleet, Hants. *T:* Fleet 615518. *Club:* Athenæum.

COCKBURN, William, TD; Managing Director of Letters, Post Office, since 1986; *b* 28 Feb. 1943. Entered Post Office, 1961; held various junior and middle management positions; Personal Assistant to Chm. of PO, 1971–73; Asst Dir of Finance and Planning, 1973–77; Dir, Central Finance Planning, 1977–78; Dir, Postal Finance, 1978–79; Dir, London Postal Region, 1979–82; apptd Mem., PO Board, 1981, Mem. for Finance, Counter Services and Planning, 1982–84; Mem. for Royal Mail Operations, 1984–86. Non-exec. Dir, V. A. T. Watkins Holdings Ltd, 1985–. Col, RE Portal and Courier Service (V), 1986–. *Address:* Postal Headquarters, 33 Grosvenor Place, SW1X 1PX.

COCKBURN-CAMPBELL, Sir Thomas; 6th Bt, *cr* 1821; *b* 8 Dec. 1918; *e s* of Sir Alexander Thomas Cockburn-Campbell, 5th Bt, and Maude Frances Lorenzo (*d* 1926), *o d* of Alfred Giles, Kent Town, Adelaide, SA; *S* father, 1935; *m* 1st, 1944, Josephine Zoi (marr. diss. 1981), *e d* of Harold Douglas Forward, Curjardine, WA; one *s*; 2nd, 1982, Janice Laraine, *y d* of William John Pascoe, Bundoora, Vic. *Educ:* Melbourne C of E Grammar Sch. *Heir: s* Alexander Thomas Cockburn-Campbell [*b* 16 March 1945; *m* 1969, Kerry Ann, *e d* of Sgt K. Johnson; one *s* one *d*]. *Address:* 14 Lincoln Street, York, WA 6302, Australia.

COCKCROFT, Dr Janet Rosemary, OBE 1975; Chairman, Bottoms Mill Co. Ltd, Todmorden, since 1980 (Director, since 1961, Deputy Chairman, 1974–80); *b* 26 July 1916; *er d* of late Major W. G. Mowat, MC, TD, JP, of Bucholllie, Lybster, Caithness, Scotland, and late Mary Mowat; *m* 1942, Major Peter Worby Cockcroft (*d* 1980); two *s* one *d*. *Educ:* Glasgow Univ. MB, ChB 1938. Ho. Surg. and Ho. Phys., Glasgow Royal Infirmary, 1938–39; GP, 1939–43; Asst MOH, Co. of Caithness, 1943–46; MO, Maternity and Child Welfare, Halifax, 1950–53; Part-time MOH, WRCC, 1953–67; MO, Family Planning Assoc., 1947–75 (Halifax and Sowerby Bridge Clinics); MO, British Red Cross, Halifax, 1960–66; Chairman: N Midlands FPA Doctors' Gp, 1966–68; Halifax FPA Clinic, 1963–75. Mem., Food Additives and Contaminants Cttee, MAFF, 1972–81; Chm., Consumers' Cttees for England and Wales and for GB, MAFF, 1975–82; Vice-Pres., 1969–70, Pres., 1970–72, Nat. Council of Women of GB; Vice-Pres., Internat. Council of Women, 1973–76; UK Rep., UN Status of Women Commn, 1973–79 (Vice Chm., 1976; Chm., 1978–80); Member: BBC Northern Adv. Council, 1975–79; Gen. Adv. Council, BBC, 1980–. Elder, United Reformed Church, 1973–. *Recreations:* travel, reading. *Address:* Dalemore, Savile Park, Halifax, W Yorks HX1 3EA. *T:* Halifax 52621. *Club:* Naval and Military.

COCKCROFT, John Hoyle; electronics economist and consultant, stockbroking, since 1977; Laurence Prust & Co., since 1986; Director: RSJ Aviation International, since 1979; Spalding Securities, since 1982; Communications Educational Services, since 1983; Open Computer Security, 1984–85; British Rail (Eastern Region), since 1984; Innovare, since 1986; various electronics consultancies, since 1982; *b* 6 July 1934; *s* of Lionel Fielden Cockcroft and Jenny Hoyle; *m* 1971, Tessa Fay Shepley; three *d*. *Educ:* Primary, Trearddur House; Oundle; St John's Coll., Cambridge (Sen. Maj. Scholar (History), 1953). MA Hons History and Econs 1958; Pres., Cambridge Union, 1958. Royal Artillery, 2nd Lieut, 1953–55. Feature Writer and Investment Analyst, Financial Times, 1959–61; Economist, GKN, 1962–67 (re-acquisitions, 1962–65); seconded to Treasury, Public Enterprises Div., 1965–66; Econ. Leader-writer, Daily Telegraph, 1967–74. MP (C) Nantwich, Feb. 1974–1979; Mem. Select Cttee on Nationalised Industries, 1975–79; Company Secretaries Bill (Private Member's), 1978. Consultant: and historian, GKN, 1971–76; British Field Sports Soc., 1975–76; Financial Public Relations Internat., 1975–76; Edman Gp, 1976–77; Mail Users' Assoc., 1976–79; Inst. of Chartered Secretaries, 1977–79; Datsun (Nissan) UK, 1980–81; Cray Electronics, 1982–84; Wedgwood, 1983–84; Camden Associates (political PR), 1984–. Advr and consultant, NEI History Archives, 1980–82. Member Council: European Movement, 1973–74, 1983–84; Conservative Gp for Europe, 1980–; Member: Cttee, Assoc. of Youth Clubs, 1970–74; Cons. Foreign Affairs Forum, 1980; Cons. Computer Forum, 1983–; Treasurer, Cambridge Univ. Cons. Assoc., 1958. Belgium Quarterly Economic Review, EIU, 1969–71. Columnist: and contributor, Microscope, 1982–; electronic money transmission, Banking World, 1984–; Westminster Watch, Electronics Times, 1985–. *Publications:* (jtly) Reforming the Constitution, 1968; (jtly) Self-Help Reborn, 1969; Why England Sleeps, 1971; (jtly) An Internal History of Guest Keen and Nettlefolds, 1976; Microtechnology in Banking, 1984. Westminster Commentary, Investment Report, 1978–79; Political Commentary, Commerce, I. White, 1979–80; Microelectronics (booklet), 1979 and 1982; leaders and leader page articles, Daily and Sunday Telegraphs, 1979–. *Recreations:* walking, reading, swimming, entertaining. *Address:* Mitchell's Farmhouse, Stapleford Tawney, Essex RM4 1SS. *T:* Stapleford 254; 7 Moorgate, EC2R 6AH. *T:* 01–606 8811. *Clubs:* Europe House, 1900, Cannon's, Inst. of Dirs, Press; Cambridge Union Soc.

COCKCROFT, Sir Wilfred (Halliday), Kt 1983; Chairman and Chief Executive, Secondary Examinations Council, since 1983; *b* 7 June 1923; *s* of Wilfred Cockcroft and Bessie Halliday; *m* 1st, 1949, Barbara Rhona Huggan; two *s*; 2nd, 1982, Vivien, *o d* of Mr and Mrs David Lloyd. *Educ:* Keighley Boys' Grammar Sch.; Balliol Coll., Oxford (Williams Exhibnr, 1941, Hon. Scholar, 1946). MA, DPhil Oxon; FIMA 1973; FRSA 1983. Technical Signals/Radar Officer, RAF, 1942–46. Asst Lectr, Univ. of Aberdeen, 1949, Lectr 1950; Lectr, Univ. of Southampton, 1957, Reader 1960; G. F. Grant Prof. of Pure Mathematics, Univ. of Hull, 1961; Vice-Chancellor, NUU, 1976–82. Vis. Lectr and Prof., Univs of Chicago, Stanford, State Univ. of NY, 1954, 1959, 1967. University Grants Committee: Mem., 1973–76; Mem., Math. Sciences Subcttee, 1967–72, Chm. 1973–76; Chm., Educn Subcttee, 1973–76; Mem., Management and Business Studies Subcttee, and Educnl Technology Subcttee, 1973–76. Science and Engineering Research Council (formerly Science Research Council): Mem., 1978–82; Mem., Maths Sub-Cttee, 1964–68 (Chm., 1969–73); Mem., Science Bd, 1969–73; Chm., Postgraduate Trng Cttee, 1979–82. Chairman: Nuffield Maths Project Consultative Cttee, 1963–71; Specialist Conf. on Maths in Commonwealth Schs, Trinidad, 1968; Member: Council, London Math. Soc., 1973–76; Council, Inst. of Maths and its Applications, 1974–77, 1982–85; US/UK Educational Commn, 1977–80; Computer Bd for Univs and Res. Councils, 1975–76; Chairman: Cttee to review Rural Planning Policy, DoE, NI, 1977–78; Cttee to consider teaching of maths in schs in England and Wales, 1978–82; Standing Conference on Univ. Entrance, 1979–82. Hon. DSc: Kent, 1983; Southampton, 1986; DUniv Open, 1984. *Publications:* Your Child and Mathematics, 1968; Complex Numbers, 1972. *Recreations:* golf, swimming, sketching, bad piano playing. *Address:* 140 Sinclair Road, W14. *T:* 01-603 2249; (office) Newcombe House, 45 Notting Hill Gate, W11 3JB. *T:* 01–229 1234.

COCKERAM, Eric (Paul); JP; MP (C) Ludlow, since 1979; *b* 4 July 1924; *er s* of Mr and Mrs J. W. Cockeram; *m* 1949, Frances Irving; two *s* two *d*. *Educ:* The Leys Sch., Cambridge. Served War, 1942–46: Captain The Gloucestershire Regt; "D Day" landings (wounded and later discharged). MP (C) Bebington, 1970–Feb. 1974. PPS: to Minister for Industry, 1970–72; to Minister for Posts and Telecommunications, 1972; to Chancellor of Exchequer, 1972–74. Mem., Select Cttee on Corporation Tax, 1971, on Industry and Trade, 1979–; Mem., Public Accounts Cttee, 1983–. Pres., Menswear Assoc. of Britain, 1964–65. Mem., Bd of Governors, United Liverpool Hosps, 1965–74; Chm., Liverpool NHS Exec. Council, 1970. Chm., Watson Prickard Ltd, 1966–; Director: TSB (NW), 1968–83; TSB (Wales & Border Counties), 1983–; Liverpool Building Soc., 1975–82 (Vice-Chm., 1981–82); Midshires Building Soc., 1982–; Muller Group (UK) Ltd, 1983–; Member of Lloyd's. Liveryman, Worshipful Co. of Glovers, 1969–, Mem. Court, 1979–. Freeman: City of London; City of Springfield, Ill. JP, City of Liverpool, 1960. *Recreations:* bridge, golf, shooting, country walking. *Address:* House of Commons, SW1. *Club:* Carlton.

COCKERELL, Sir Christopher (Sydney), Kt 1969; CBE 1966; MA; FRS 1967; Chairman, Wavepower Ltd, 1974–82 (former Joint Managing Director); *b* 4 June 1910; *s* of late Sir Sydney Cockerell; *m* 1937, Margaret Elinor Belsham; two *d*. *Educ:* Gresham's; Peterhouse, Cambridge (Hon. Fellow, 1974). Pupil, W. H. Allen & Sons, Bedford, 1931–33; Radio Research, Cambridge, 1933–35; airborne and navigational equipment research and development, Marconi Wireless Telegraph Co. Ltd, 1935–50; inventor of and engaged on hovercraft since 1953; Consultant (hovercraft), Ministry of Supply, 1957–58. Consultant: Hovercraft Development Ltd, 1958–70 (Dir, 1959–66); British Hovercraft Corp., 1973–79; Chm., Ripplecraft Co. Ltd, 1950–79. Foundn Pres., Internat. Air Cushion Engrg Soc., 1969–71 (Vice-Pres., 1971–); Pres., UK Hovercraft Soc., 1972–; Member, Min. of Technology's Adv. Cttee for Hovercraft, 1968–70. A Trustee of National Portrait Gallery, 1967–79. Hon. Fellow: Swedish Soc. of Aeronautics, 1963; Soc. of Engineers, 1966; Manchester Inst. of Sci. and Tech., 1967; Downing Coll., Cambridge, 1969. Hon. Mem., Southampton Chamber of Commerce, 1967. Hon. DSc: Leicester, 1967; Heriot-Watt, 1971; London, 1975; Hon. Dr RCA, 1968. Hon. Freeman, Borough of Ramsgate, 1971. Viva Shield, Worshipful Co. of Carmen, 1961; RAC Diamond Jubilee Trophy, 1962. Thulin Medal, Swedish Soc. of Aeronautics, 1963; Howard N. Potts Medal, Franklin Inst., 1965; Albert Medal, RSA, 1966; Churchill Medal, Soc. of Engineers, 1966; Royal Medal, Royal Soc., 1966; Mitchell Memorial Medal, Stoke-on-Trent Assoc. of Engineers, 1967; Columbus Prize, Genoa, 1968; John Scott Award, City of Philadelphia, 1968; Elmer A. Sperry Award, 1968; Gold Medal, Calais Chamber of Commerce, 1969; Bluebird Trophy, 1969; James Alfred Ewing Medal, ICE, 1977; James Watt Internat. Gold Medal, IMechE, 1983. *Recreations:* the visual arts, gardening, fishing. *Address:* 16 Prospect Place, Hythe, Hants SO4 6AU.

COCKERELL, Sydney (Morris), OBE 1980; FSA; bookbinder; Senior Partner in Cockerell Bindery (formerly D. Cockerell & Son), since 1946; *b* 6 June 1906; *er s* of late Douglas Cockerell and Florence Arundel; *m* 1932, Elizabeth Lucy Cowlishaw; one *s* two *d*. *Educ:* St Christopher Sch., Letchworth. Partnership with Douglas Cockerell, 1924. Vis. Lectr, Sch. of Library, Archive and Information Studies, UCL, 1945–76. Assisted with repair and binding of Codex Sinaiticus Manuscript at British Museum, 1934; has repaired and bound many early and medieval manuscripts including Codex Bezae Book of Cerne, Book of Deer, Thornton Romances, Fitzwilliam Virginal Book, Handel's Conducting Score of Messiah, and repaired and treated, amongst others, papers of Wordsworth, Milton, Tennyson, Isaac Newton, Captain Cook's First Circumnavigation of the Globe; mounted Hereford Mappa Mundi; designed and made numbers of tooled bindings for collectors. Revived and developed craft of marbling paper; designed and made tools and equipment for binding and marbling. Visited Ceylon, Ethiopia, Italy, Canada, Tunisia, Portugal, USA, Greece and Jordan to advise on book conservation. Hon. Member: Soc.

of Scribes and Illuminators, 1956; Double Crown Club (Pres., 1976–77); Fellow International Institute for Conservation of Historic and Artistic Works, 1959; Master, Art Workers Guild, 1961. Hon. LittD Cantab, 1982. *Publications:* Marbling Paper, 1934, 4th edn 1985; Appendix to Bookbinding and the Care of Books, 1943, revised and repr. 1973; The Repairing of Books, 1958; contributor to: The Calligrapher's Handbook, 1956, 2nd edn 1985; Encyclopædia Britannica, 1963. *Recreation:* keeping the house up and the weeds down. *Address:* Riversdale, Grantchester, Cambridge. *T:* Cambridge 840124.

COCKERILL, Geoffrey Fairfax, CB 1980; Secretary, University Grants Committee, 1978–82; *b* 14 May 1922; *e s* of late Walter B. Cockerill and of Mary W. Cockerill (*née* Buffery); *m* 1959, Janet Agnes Walters, JP, MA, *d* of late Archibald J. Walters, MBE, and of Elsie Walters; two *s*. *Educ:* Humberstone Foundation Sch.; UC Nottingham. BA London 1947. Royal Artillery, 1941–45 (Captain). Min. of Labour, 1947; Min. of Educn, 1952; Private Sec. to last Minister of Educn and Secs of State for Educn and Science, 1963–65; Asst Sec., 1964; Sec., Public Schools Commn, 1966–68; Jt Sec., Schools Council for Curriculum and Examinations, 1970–72; Under-Sec., DES, 1972–77; Dep. Sec., 1978. Chairman: Anglo-Amer. Primary Educ. Project, 1970–72; Working Party on Nutritional Aspects of School Meals, 1973–75; Kingston-upon-Thames CAB, 1985–; Member: Adv. Gp on London Health Services, 1980–81; RCN, Commn on Nursing Educn, 1984–85; UGC, Univ. of S Pacific, 1984–. Reviewed for Government: Central Bureau for Educational Visits and Exchanges, 1982; Youth Exchanges, 1983; Nat. Youth Bureau, 1983; Consultant to Cttee of Vice-Chancellors and Principals, 1984–85. Hon. Senior Research Fellow, KCL, 1982–. *Recreations:* gardening, photography. *Address:* 29 Lovelace Road, Surbiton, Surrey KT6 6NS. *T:* 01–399 0125. *Clubs:* Athenæum, Royal Commonwealth Society.

COCKERTON, Rev. John Clifford Penn; Rector of Wheldrake with Thorganby, since 1985 (Rector of Wheldrake, 1978–85); *b* 27 June 1927; *s* of late William Penn Cockerton and Eleanor Cockerton; *m* 1974, Diana Margaret Smith, *d* of Mr and Mrs W. Smith, Upper Poppleton, York. *Educ:* Wirral Grammar Sch.; Univ. of Liverpool; St Catherine's Society, Oxford; Wycliffe Hall, Oxford. Asst Master, Prenton Secondary Sch., 1949–51; Deacon 1954; Priest 1955; Asst Curate, St Helens Parish Church, 1954–58; Tutor 1958–60, Chaplain 1960–63, Cranmer Hall, Durham; Vice-Principal, St John's Coll., Durham, 1963–70; Principal, St John's College and Cranmer Hall, Durham, 1970–78. Examining Chaplain to Bishop of Durham, 1971–73; Proctor in Convocation, 1980–85. *Recreation:* music. *Address:* The Rectory, 3 Church Lane, Wheldrake, York YO4 6AW. *T:* Wheldrake 230.

COCKETT, Frank Bernard, MS, FRCS; Consulting Surgeon to: St Thomas' Hospital; King Edward VII Hospital for Officers, London; *b* Rockhampton, Australia, 22 April 1916; *s* of late Rev. Charles Bernard Cockett, MA, DD; *m* 1945, Felicity Ann (*d* 1958), *d* of Col James Thackeray Fisher, DSO, Frieston, near Grantham, Lincs; one *s* two *d*; *m* 1960, Dorothea Anne Newman; twin *s*. *Educ:* Bedford Sch.; St Thomas's Hosp. Med. Sch. BSc (1st Cl. Hons), 1936; MRCS, LRCP 1939; MB, BS (London) 1940; FRCS Eng 1947; MS (London) 1953. Sqdn Ldr (Surgical Specialist) RAFVR, 1942–46; Surgical Registrar, St Thomas' Hosp., 1947–48; Resident Asst Surg., St Thomas' Hosp., 1948–50, Consultant, 1954–81; Senior Lecturer in Surgery, St Thomas's Hosp. Med. Sch., 1950–54; Consultant, King Edward VII Hosp. for Officers, 1974–81. Fellow Assoc. of Surgs of Gt Brit.; Mem. European Soc. of Cardiovascular Surgery; Pres., Vascular Surgical Soc. of GB and Ireland, 1980; Chm., Venous Forum, RSM, 1986–87. *Publications:* The Pathology and Surgery of the Veins of the Lower Limb, 1956, 2nd edn 1976; several contribs to Operative Surgery (ed. C. G. Rob and Rodney Smith), 1956; various papers in medical and surgical journals. *Recreations:* sailing, tennis, squash, gardening, collecting marine paintings. *Address:* 38 Devonshire Place, W1. *T:* 01–580 3612; 14 Essex Villas, Campden Hill, Kensington, W8. *T:* 01–937 9883. *Clubs:* Little Ship; Island Sailing.

COCKETT, Geoffrey Howard; Chief Scientific Officer, Ministry of Defence, since 1983; Deputy Director, Royal Armament Research and Development Establishment, since 1983; *b* 18 March 1926; *s* of late William Cockett and Edith (*née* Dinham); *m* 1951, Elizabeth Bagshaw; two *d*. *Educ:* King Edward VI Sch., Southampton; Univ. of Southampton (BSc, Hons Maths, and Hons Physics). FInstP; CPhys. Royal Aircraft Establishment, 1948–52; Armament Research Estabt, Woolwich, 1952–62; RARDE, 1962–68; Supt of Physics Div., Chemical Defence Estabt, 1968–71; RARDE: Supt, Optics and Surveillance Systems Div., 1971–76; Head, Applied Physics Group, 1976–83; Dep. Director (Systems), 1983–. (Jtly) Gold Medal, Congrès des Materiaux Résistant à Chaud, Paris, 1951. *Publications:* official reports; scientific and technical papers in various learned jls. *Recreations:* opera, photography, under gardening. *Address:* Royal Armament Research and Development Establishment, Fort Halstead, Sevenoaks, Kent TN14 7BP. *T:* Knockholt 32222.

COCKFIELD, family name of **Baron Cockfield.**

COCKFIELD, Baron *cr* 1978 (Life Peer), of Dover in the County of Kent; **Francis Arthur Cockfield,** Kt 1973; PC 1982; a Vice-President, Commission of the European Communities, since 1985; *b* 28 Sept. 1916; 2nd *s* of late Lieut C. F. Cockfield (killed on the Somme in Aug. 1916) and Louisa (*née* James); *m* Aileen Monica Mudie, choreographer. *Educ:* Dover Grammar Sch.; London Sch. of Economics (LLB, BSc (Econ.)). Called to Bar, Inner Temple, 1942. Home Civil Service, Inland Revenue, 1938; Asst Sec. to Board of Inland Revenue, 1945; Commissioner of Inland Revenue, 1951–52; Dir of Statistics and Intelligence to Board of Inland Revenue, 1945–52; Boots Pure Drug Co. Ltd: Finance Dir, 1953–61; Man. Dir. and Chm. Exec. Management Cttee, 1961–67. Chm., Price Commn, 1973–77. Minister of State, HM Treasury, 1979–82; Sec. of State for Trade, 1982–83; Chancellor of the Duchy of Lancaster, 1983–84. Mem., NEDC, 1962–64, 1982–; Advr on Taxation Policy to Chancellor of Exchequer, 1970–73. Mem., Court of Governors, Univ. of Nottingham, 1963–67. Pres., Royal Statistical Soc., 1968–69. Hon. Fellow, LSE, 1972. *Address:* House of Lords, SW1.

COCKIN, Rt. Rev. George Eyles Irwin; Assistant Bishop, Diocese of York, since 1969; *b* 15 Aug. 1908; *s* of late Charles Irwin Cockin, Solicitor, and Judith Cockin. *Educ:* Repton; Leeds University (BA); Lincoln Theological College. Tutor, St Paul's College, Awka, Nigeria, 1933–40; Supervisor, Anglican Schools, E Nigeria, 1940–52. Deacon, 1953, Priest, 1954; Curate, Kimberworth, Rotherham, 1953–55; Sen. Supervisor, Anglican Schools, E Nigeria, 1955–58; Canon, All Saints Cathedral, Onitsha, 1957; first Bishop of Owerri, 1959–69. Rector of Bainton, dio. York, 1969–78; Rural Dean of Harthill, 1973–78. *Address:* 42 Carr Lane, Willerby, Hull. *T:* Hull 653086.

COCKING, Prof. Edward Charles Daniel, FRS 1983; Professor of Botany and Head of Department of Botany, University of Nottingham, since 1969; *b* 26 Sept. 1931; *y s* of late Charles Cocking and of Mary (*née* Murray); *m* 1960, Bernadette Keane; one *s* one *d*. *Educ:* Buckhurst Hill County High Sch., Essex; Univ. of Bristol (BSc, PhD, DSc). FIBiol. Civil Service Commission Research Fellow, 1956–59; Lecturer in Plant Physiology, Univ. of Nottingham, 1959–66, Reader, 1966–69. Member: Bd of Trustees, Royal Botanic Gardens, Kew, 1983–; Governing Body, Glasshouse Crops Res. Inst., 1983–. Pres., Sect. K, BAAS, 1983. *Publications:* Introduction to the Principles of Plant Physiology (with W. Stiles, FRS), 3rd edn 1969; numerous scientific papers in botanical/genetics jls on plant genetic manipulations. *Recreations:* walking, travelling, especially by train, occasional chess. *Address:* Department of Botany, University of Nottingham, University Park, Nottingham NG7 2RD. *T:* Nottingham 506101, ext. 2201; 30 Patterdale Road, Woodthorpe, Nottingham NG5 4LQ. *T:* Nottingham 262452.

COCKRAM, Sir John, Kt 1964; Director, 1952–79, General Manager, 1941–73, The Colne Valley Water Company; Director, 1970–86, Chairman, 1971–86, Rickmansworth Water Co. (formerly Rickmansworth and Uxbridge Valley Water Co.); *b* 10 July 1908; *s* of Alfred John and Beatrice Elizabeth Cockram; *m* 1937, Phyllis Eleanor, *d* of Albert Henning; one *s* two *d*. *Educ:* St Aloysius Coll., Highgate. Chartered Accountant. Member: Herts CC, 1949–74 (Chm. 1961–65); Thames Conservancy, 1954–74; Exec. Cttee, British Waterworks Assoc., 1948–74 (Pres., 1957–58); Central Advisory Water Cttee, 1955–73; Thames Water Authy, 1973–76. Life Mem., Water Cos Assoc., 1985 (Mem., 1950–85; Chm., 1950–79; Dep. Pres., 1979–85). Life Governor, Haileybury. *Recreations:* fishing, gardening. *Address:* Rebels' Corner, The Common, Chorleywood, Hertfordshire. *Club:* MCC.

COCKS, family name of **Baron Somers.**

COCKS, Sir Barnett; *see* Cocks, Sir T. G. B.

COCKS, Rt. Rev. Francis William, CB 1959; *b* 5 Nov. 1913; *o s* of late Canon W. Cocks, OBE, St John's Vicarage, Felixstowe; *m* 1940, Irene May (Barbara), 2nd *d* of H. Thompson, Bridlington; one *s* one *d*. *Educ:* Haileybury; St Catharine's Coll., Cambridge; Westcott House. Played Rugby Football for Cambridge Univ., Hampshire and Eastern Counties, 1935–38. Ordained, 1937. Chaplain RAFVR, 1939; Chaplain RAF, 1945; Asst Chaplain-in-Chief, 1950; Chaplain-in-Chief, and Archdeacon, Royal Air Force, 1959–65; Rector and Rural Dean of Wolverhampton, 1965–70; Bishop Suffragan of Shrewsbury, 1970–80. Hon. Chaplain to HM the Queen, 1959–65. Prebendary of S Botolph in Lincoln Cathedral, 1959; Canon Emeritus, 1965–70; Prebendary of Lichfield Cathedral, 1968–70; Select Preacher, Univ. of Cambridge, 1960; Hon. Canon of Lichfield Cathedral, 1970–. Dir, Mercia Television, 1980–81. Mem. of Council, Haileybury and Imperial Service Coll., 1949–; Pres., Haileybury Soc., 1976–77. Fellow, Woodard Schools, 1970–83; Mem. Council: Denstone Sch., 1970–72; Shrewsbury Sch., 1971–80; Ellesmere Coll., 1971–80. Archbishops' Advr to HMC, 1975–80. President: Shropshire Horticultural Soc., 1979; Shropshire and W Midlands Agric. Soc., 1980; Buccaneers CC, 1965–. *Recreations:* playing golf, watching TV, reading. *Address:* 41 Beatrice Avenue, Felixstowe, Suffolk IP11 9HB. *T:* Felixstowe 283574. *Clubs:* MCC, Royal Air Force; Hawks (Cambridge).

COCKS, Freda Mary, OBE 1972; JP; Deputy Leader, Birmingham City Council, since 1982; *b* 30 July 1915; *d* of Frank and Mary Wood; *m* 1942, Donald Francis Melvin, *s* of Melvin J. Cocks; one *d* (and one *d* decd). *Educ:* St Peter's Sch., Harborne; Queen's Coll., Birmingham. Birmingham Council, 1957–78: Alderman, 1965–74; Lord Mayor of Birmingham, 1977–78; Dep. Chm., Housing Cttee, 1968–70, Chm. 1970–72. Founder Sec., Birmingham Sanatoria League of Friends, 1950–68; Founder, Birm. Hosps Broadcasting Assoc., 1952–78; Member: Little Bromwich Hosp. Management Cttee, 1953–68; West Birmingham Health Authority, 1981–. Conservative Women's Central Council: Chm., 1968–71; Chm., Gen. Purposes Cttee, 1978; service on housing, finance, policies, and land cttees; President: Edgbaston Conservative Assoc., 1980–; Mission to Seamen, Birmingham, 1981–. JP Birmingham, 1968. *Recreations:* hospitals and housing. *Address:* 332–4 Hagley Road, Edgbaston, Birmingham B17 8BH. *T:* 021–420 1140.

COCKS, Rt. Hon. Michael Francis Lovell, PC 1976; MP (Lab) Bristol South since 1970; *b* 19 Aug. 1929; *s* of late Dr H. F. Lovell Cocks; *m* 1st, 1954, Janet Macfarlane; two *s* two *d*; 2nd, 1979, Valerie Davis. *Educ:* Bristol University. Various posts in education from 1954; Lectr, Bristol Polytechnic, 1968. Contested (Lab): Bristol West, 1959; South Gloucestershire, 1964, 1966. An Asst Govt Whip, 1974–76; Parly Sec. to the Treasury and Govt Chief Whip, 1976–79; Opposition Chief Whip, 1979–85. *Recreations:* swimming, listening to music, reading. *Address:* House of Commons, SW1.

COCKS, Sir (Thomas George) Barnett, KCB 1963 (CB 1961); OBE 1949; Clerk of the House of Commons, 1962–73, retired; *b* 1907; *m* 1952, Iris Mary Symon (*née* Coltman); one *s* one step *d*. *Educ:* Blundells Sch.; Worcester Coll., Oxford. Clerk in the House of Commons, from 1931; temporarily attached Min. of Home Security, 1939. Hon. Sec. and later a Trustee of the History of Parliament; Mem., Assoc. of Secretaries-General of Parliaments, 1959–73; Pres., Governing Bd, Internat. Centre of Parliamentary Documentation, Geneva, 1972; Vice-Pres., Westminster Pastoral Foundn, 1984–. Hon. Officer, Saskatchewan Parlt, 1977. *Publications:* The Parliament at Westminster, 1949; (with Strathearn Gordon) A People's Conscience, 1952; The European Parliament, 1973; Mid-Victorian Masterpiece, 1977; Editor: Erskine May's Parliamentary Practice, 15th, 16th, 17th and 18th edns; Council of Europe Manual of Procedure, seven edns. *Address:* 13 Langford Green, SE5 8BX. *T:* 01–274 5448.

COCKSHUT, Mrs Gillian; *see* Avery, G. E.

CODRINGTON, John Ernest Fleetwood, CMG 1968; *b* 1919; *s* of late Stewart Codrington; *m* 1951, Margaret, *d* of late Sir Herbert Hall Hall, KCMG; three *d*. *Educ:* Haileybury; Trinity Coll., Cambridge. Served RNVR, 1940–42: HMS Enchantress, HMS Vanity; Royal Marines, 1942–46: 42 (RM) Commando; Colonial Administrative Service, 1946: Gold Coast (later Ghana), 1947–58; Nyasaland, 1958–64; Financial Sec., Bahamas, 1964–70; Bahamas Comr in London, 1970–73, acting High Comr, 1973–74; Financial Sec., Bermuda, 1974–77. *Recreation:* sailing. *Address:* Chequers Close, Lymington, Hants. *Clubs:* Army and Navy; Royal Lymington Yacht.

CODRINGTON, Sir Simon (Francis Bethell), 3rd Bt *cr* 1876; *b* 14 Aug. 1923; *s* of Sir Christopher William Gerald Henry Codrington, 2nd Bt, and Joan Mary Hague-Cook (*d* 1961); *S* father, 1979; *m* 1st, 1947, Joanne (marr. diss. 1959), *d* of J. W. Molineaux and *widow* of William Humphrey Austin Thompson; 2nd, 1959, Pamela Joy Halliday Wise (marr. diss. 1979); three *s*; 3rd, 1980, Sarah Gwynne Gaze (*née* Pennell). *Educ:* Eton. Late Coldstream Guards. *Heir:* *s* Christopher George Wayne Codrington, *b* 20 Feb. 1960. *Address:* Dodington, Chipping Sodbury, Bristol. *T:* Chipping Sodbury 312354.

CODRINGTON, Sir William (Alexander), 8th Bt *cr* 1721; FNI; in command with Worldwide Shipping; Port Captain, Hong Kong, for Worldwide Shipping Agency, since 1979; *b* 5 July 1934; *e s* of Sir William Richard Codrington, 7th Bt, and Joan Kathleen Birellu, *e d* of Percy E. Nicholas, London, NW; *S* father, 1961. *Educ:* St Andrew Coll., S Africa; S African Naval Coll., General Botha. Joined Merchant Navy, 1952; joined Union Castle Mail Steamship Co., 1960; Master Mariner's Certificate of Competency, 1961. Joined Worldwide Shipping 1976. Mem., Hon. Co. of Master Mariners. Pres., Tooting and Balham Sea Cadet Unit. *Recreations:* model engineering, sailing. *Heir:* *b* Giles Peter Codrington, *b* 28 Oct. 1943. *Address:* 99 St James Drive, Wandsworth Common, SW17. *Club:* Royal Southern Yacht.

CODRON, Michael Victor; theatrical producer; *b* 8 June 1930; *s* of I. A. Codron and Lily (*née* Morgenstern). *Educ:* St Paul's Sch.; Worcester Coll., Oxford (BA). Director: Aldwych Theatre; Hampstead Theatre; Theatres Mutual Insurance Co.; Co-owner, Vaudeville Theatre. Productions include: Share My Lettuce, Breath of Spring, 1957; Dock Brief and What Shall We Tell Caroline?, The Birthday Party, Valmouth, 1958; Pieces of Eight, 1959; The Wrong Side of the Park, The Caretaker, 1960; Three, Stop It Whoever You Are, One Over the Eight, The Tenth Man, Big Soft Nellie, 1961; Two Stars for Comfort, Everything in the Garden, Rattle of a Simple Man, 1962; Next Time I'll sing to You, Private Lives (revival), The Lovers and the Dwarfs, Cockade, 1963; Poor Bitos, The Formation Dancers, Entertaining Mr Sloane, 1964; Loot, The Killing of Sister George, Ride a Cock Horse, 1965; Little Malcolm and his Struggle against the Eunuchs, The Anniversary, There's a Girl in my Soup, Big Bad Mouse, 1966; The Judge, The Flip Side, Wise Child, The Boy Friend (revival), 1967; Not Now Darling, The Real Inspector Hound, 1968; The Contractor, Slag, The Two of Us, The Philanthropist, 1970; The Foursome, Butley, A Voyage Round my Father, The Changing Room, 1971; Veterans, Time and Time Again, Crown Matrimonial, My Fat Friend, 1972; Collaborators, Savages, Habeas Corpus, Absurd Person Singular, 1973; Knuckle, Flowers, Golden Pathway Annual, The Norman Conquests, John Paul George Ringo . . . and Bert, 1974; A Family and A Fortune, Alphabetical Order, A Far Better Husband, Ashes, Absent Friends, Otherwise Engaged, Stripwell, 1975; Funny Peculiar, Treats, Donkey's Years, Confusions, Teeth 'n' Smiles, Yahoo, 1976; Dusa, Stas, Fish & Vi, Just Between Ourselves, Oh, Mr Porter, Breezeblock Park, The Bells of Hell, The Old Country, 1977; The Rear Column, Ten Times Table, The Unvarnished Truth, The Homecoming (revival), Alice's Boys, Night and Day, 1978; Joking Apart, Tishoo, Stage Struck, 1979; Dr Faustus, Make and Break, The Dresser, Taking Steps, Enjoy, 1980; Hinge and Bracket at the Globe, Rowan Atkinson in Revue, House Guest, Quartermaine's Terms, 1981; Season's Greetings, Noises Off, Funny Turns, The Real Thing, 1982; The Hard Shoulder, 1983; Benefactors, 1984; Why Me?, Jumpers, Who Plays Wins, Look, No Hans!, 1985; Made in Bangkok, 1986; *film:* Clockwise, 1986. *Recreation:* collecting Caroline memorabilia. *Address:* Aldwych Theatre Offices, Aldwych, WC2B 4DF. *Club:* Garrick.

COE, Denis Walter; Arts Administrator, Cleveland Arts, since 1983; *b* 5 June 1929; *s* of James and Lily Coe, Whitley Bay, Northumberland; *m* 1953, Margaret Rae (marr. diss. 1979), *d* of William and Ida Chambers; three *s* one *d*; *m* 1979, Diana Rosemary, *d* of Maxwell and Flora Barr. *Educ:* Bede Trng Coll., Durham; London Sch. of Economics. Teacher's Certificate, 1952; BSc (Econ.) 1960; MSc (Econ.) 1966. National Service in RAF, 1947–50; Junior and Secondary Schoolmaster, 1952–59; Dep. Headmaster, Secondary Sch., 1959–61; Lectr in Govt, Manchester Coll. of Commerce, 1961–66. Contested (Lab) Macclesfield, 1964; MP (Lab) Middleton, Prestwich and Whitefield, 1966–70; Parly deleg. to Council of Europe and WEU, 1968–70. Dean of Students, NE London Polytechnic, 1970–74; Asst Dir, Middx Polytechnic, 1974–82. Chairman: Nat. Bureau for Handicapped Students, 1975–83 (Vice Pres., 1983–); Cleveland Music Fest. Mem. Governing Council, Nat. Youth Theatre, 1968–. *Recreations:* music, drama, walking.

COE, Peter; Artistic Director, Churchill Theatre, Bromley, since 1983; *b* 18 April 1929; *s* of Leonard and Gladys Coe; *m* 1st, 1952, Maria Caday; 2nd, 1958, Tsai Chin; 3rd, 1962, Suzanne Fuller; two *d*; 4th, 1977, Ingeborg; one *s* two *d*. *Educ:* Latymer Upper Sch., Hammersmith; Coll. of St Mark and St John, Chelsea; LAMDA. Actor, 1952–54; Lectr in Drama, 1954–56; Theatre Dir, 1956–; Artistic Director at: Her Majesty's, Carlisle, 1956; Arts, Ipswich, 1957–58; Queen's, Hornchurch, 1958–59; Mermaid, London, 1959–60; Bubble, London, 1975; Citadel, Canada, 1978–81; Amer. Shakespeare Th., Stratford, Connecticut, 1981–82. Notable musical prductions in West End: Oliver; Lock Up Your Daughters; Pickwick; On the Twentieth Century; Barnum; plays directed in West End: The World of Suzie Wong; The Miracle Worker; Castle in Sweden; Caligula; In White America; The King's Mare; In the Case of J. Robert Oppenheimer; World War 2½; Mister Lincoln; The Sleeping Prince; plays directed at Chichester Festival Theatre: An Italian Straw Hat; The Skin of Our Teeth; The Caucasian Chalk Circle; Peer Gynt; Tonight We Improvise; Feasting with Panthers; Treasure Island; The Sleeping Prince; Jane Eyre; operas directed at English National Opera: Ernani; The Love of Three Oranges; The Angel of Fire. Plays directed in NY: A Life (Tony nomination, Best Dir, 1981); Othello (Tony Award, Best Revival, 1982); Oliver; Pickwick; The Rehearsal; Mister Lincoln; Next Time I'll Sing to You; Six (musical); productions of Shakespeare include: Twelfth Night (India); Julius Caesar (Israel); Macbeth (Stratford, Ontario); Hamlet (London); The Black Macbeth (Roundhouse); Richard III (Denmark); Henry V, Othello, Henry IV, Hamlet (USA). Plays written and performed: Treasure Island, Mermaid, Chichester; Woman of the Dunes, Cleveland, Ohio; Story Theatre, India; Decameron '73, Roundhouse; The Trials of Oscar Wilde, Oxford, Chichester; Cages, The Great Exhibition, The Trial of Marie Stopes, Bubble; Lucy Crown, tour; Great Expectations, Old Vic; Jane Eyre, Chichester. *Recreation:* tennis. *Address:* The Old Barn, East Clandon, Surrey.

COE, Sebastian Newbold, MBE 1982; Vice-Chairman, since 1986 and Member, since 1983, Sports Council; *b* 29 Sept. 1956; *s* of Peter and Angela Coe. *Educ:* Loughborough University (BSc Hons Economics and Social History). Won gold medal for running 1500m and silver medal for 800m at Moscow Olympics, 1980; gold medal for 1500m and silver medal for 800m at Los Angeles Olympics, 1984; set world records at 800m, 1000m and mile, 1981. Research Assistant, Loughborough Univ., 1981–84; Chm., Olympic Review Group, Sports Council, 1984–85. Associate Mem., Académie des Sports, France; Mem., Athletes Commn, Internat. Olympic Cttee, Lausanne. Hon. DTech Loughborough, 1985. *Publications:* (with David Miller) Running Free, 1981; (with Peter Coe) Running for Fitness, 1983; The Olympians, 1984. *Recreations:* listening to recorded or preferably live jazz, theatre, reading, avoiding all strenuous activity away from the track. *Address:* Strand House, The Embankment, Twickenham, Middx. *Clubs:* East India, Sportsman's.

COEN, Massimo (Aldo), Cavaliere al Merito del Lavoro 1982; Grande Ufficiale nell'Ordine al Merito della Repubblica Italiana 1979; Chairman and Managing Director: Granosa Trading Co. Ltd, since 1946; Florence (Arts & Crafts) Ltd, since 1946; Thames Rugs & Tweed Fabrics Ltd, since 1959; President: Italian Chamber of Commerce for Great Britain, since 1978; Etrufin Reserco Ltd, since 1985; *b* Bologna, 29 July 1918; *s* of Cavaliere Ragioniere Terzo Coen and Delia Coen Guetta; *m* 1946, Thelma Doreen Kelley; one *s* three *d*. *Educ:* Liceo Marco Foscarini, Venice (dipl. 1937); Padua University; London School of Economics. Came to London from Venice because of racial laws, 1939; interned in Isle of Man, June-Dec. 1940; Netherland Shipping & Trading Cttee Ltd, Jan.-April 1941; Italian Section, BBC External Services, 1941–46 (Shift Leader and Senior Announcer Translator); Granosa Trading Co. Ltd and subsidiaries (dealing in textiles), 1946–. Councillor, Italian Chamber of Commerce for GB, 1951–72, Vice-Pres., 1972–78. Hon. Life Governor, Italian Hosp. in London, 1979– (Pres., Cttee of Inquiry into Italian Hosp., 1978). Councillor, Economic Council for Israel, 1979–; Chm., Club di Londra, 1985–. Many radio plays, talks and commentaries during the war years. Acted in Snowbound, 1947, Hotel Sahara, 1951. Cavaliere 1956, Ufficiale 1968, Commendatore 1972, nell'Ordine al Merito della Repubblica Italiana. *Recreations:* shooting, fishing, golf; formerly competition skiing and fencing. *Address:* 14 Acacia Road, St John's Wood, NW8 6AN. *T:* 01–722 2459; (office) 01–626 8827/8.

COETZEE, Prof. John M.; writer; Professor of General Literature, University of Cape Town, since 1983; *b* 9 Feb. 1940; one *s* one *d*. *Educ:* Univ. of Cape Town (MA); Univ. of Texas (PhD). Assistant Professor of English, State University of New York at Buffalo, 1968–71; Lectr in English, Univ. of Cape Town, 1972–82; Butler Prof. of English, State Univ. of New York at Buffalo, 1984; Hinkley Prof. of English, Johns Hopkins Univ., 1986. Hon. DLitt Strathclyde, 1985. *Publications:* Dusklands, 1974; In the Heart of the Country, 1977 (CNA Literary Award, 1977; filmed as Dust, 1985); Waiting for the Barbarians, 1980 (CNA Literary Award, 1980; James Tait Black Prize, 1980; Geoffrey Faber Award, 1980); Life and Times of Michael K, 1983 (CNA Literary Award, 1983; Booker-McConnell Prize, 1983; Prix Femina Etranger, 1985); Foe, 1986; essays in Comp. Lit., Jl of Mod. Lit., Linguistics, Mod. Lang. Notes, Pubns of Mod. Lang. Assoc., etc. *Address:* PO Box 92, Rondebosch, Cape Province, 7700, South Africa.

COFFER, David Edwin, CBE 1973 (OBE 1963); General Secretary, The Royal British Legion, 1959–78; *b* 18 Sept. 1913; *s* of David Gilbertson Coffer and Florence Ellen Gard; *m* 1947, Edith Mary Moulton; three *d*. *Educ:* Colfe Grammar Sch. Member: Supplementary Benefits Appeal Tribunals, 1978–85; Central Advisory Cttee on War Pensions, 1976–; Bromley, Croydon and Sutton War Pensions Cttee, 1953–, Chm., 1976–; Patron, SE County, Royal British Legion, 1978–. *Address:* 47 Malvern Road, Orpington, Kent BR6 9HA. *T:* Orpington 29007.

COFFIN, Cyril Edwin, CBE 1984; Director General, Food Manufacturers' Federation, 1977–84; *b* 29 June 1919; *m* 1947, Joyce Mary Tobitt; one *s* one *d* (and one *d* decd). *Educ:* King's Coll. Sch., Wimbledon; King's Coll., Cambridge. War service, 1939–45, Captain RIASC; jssc 1950. Civil servant, 1946–77; Alternate UK Governor, Internat. Atomic Energy Agency, 1964; Under-Secretary: Min. of Technology, 1966, later DTI; Dept of Prices and Consumer Protection, 1974–77. FRSA 1979. *Recreations:* music, learning languages. *Address:* 54 Cambridge Avenue, New Malden, Surrey. *T:* 01–942 0763. *Clubs:* Athenæum; Union (Cambridge).

COGGAN, Baron *cr* 1980 (Life Peer), of Canterbury and of Sissinghurst in the County of Kent; **Rt. Rev. and Rt. Hon. (Frederick) Donald Coggan;** PC 1961; Royal Victorian Chain, 1980; MA; DD; *b* 9 Oct. 1909; *s* of late Cornish Arthur Coggan and late Fannie Sarah Coggan; *m* 1935, Jean Braithwaite Strain; two *d*. *Educ:* Merchant Taylors' School; St John's College, Cambridge; Wycliffe Hall, Oxford. Late Schol. of St John's Coll., Cambridge, 1st cl. Or. Lang. Trip. pt i, 1930; BA (1st cl. Or. Lang. Trip. pt ii) and Jeremie Sep. Prize, 1931, Naden Div. Student, 1931; Tyrwhitt Hebrew Schol. and Mason Prize, 1932; MA 1935. Asst Lectr in Semitic Languages and Literature, University of Manchester, 1931–34; Curate of St Mary Islington, 1934–37; Professor of New Testament, Wycliffe College, Toronto, 1937–44; Principal of the London College of Divinity, 1944–56; Bishop of Bradford, 1956–61; Archbishop of York, 1961–74; Archbishop of Canterbury, 1974–80. Chairman of the Liturgical Commission, 1960–64. President, Society for Old Testament Studies, 1967–68; first Life President, Church Army, 1981. Pro-Chancellor, York Univ., 1962–74, Hull Univ., 1968–74. Prelate, Order of St John of Jerusalem, 1967–. Wycliffe Coll., Toronto: BD 1941, DD (*hc*) 1944; DD (Lambeth) 1957; Hon. DD: Cambridge, 1962; Leeds, 1958; Aberdeen, 1963; Tokyo, 1963; Saskatoon, 1963; Huron, 1963; Hull, 1963; Manchester, 1972; Moravian Theol Seminary, 1976; Virginia Theol Seminary, 1979. Hon. LLD Liverpool, 1972; HHD Westminster Choir Coll., Princeton, 1966; Hon. DLitt Lancaster, 1967; STD (*hc*) Gen. Theol Seminary, NY, 1967; Hon. DCL Kent, 1975; DUniv York, 1975; FKC, 1975. *Publications:* A People's Heritage, 1944; The Ministry of the Word, 1945; The Glory of God, 1950; Stewards of Grace, 1958; Five Makers of the New Testament, 1962; Christian Priorities, 1963; The Prayers of the New Testament, 1967; Sinews of Faith, 1969; Word and World, 1971; Convictions, 1975; On Preaching, 1978; The Heart of the Christian Faith, 1978; The Name above All Names, 1981; Sure Foundation, 1981; Mission to the World, 1982; Paul—Portrait of a Revolutionary, 1984; contributions to Theology, etc. *Recreations:* gardening, motoring, music. *Address:* Kingshead House, Sissinghurst, Kent TN17 2JE. *T:* Cranbrook 714443. *Club:* Athenæum.

COGHILL, Sir Egerton James Nevill Tobias, (Sir Toby Coghill), 8th Bt *cr* 1778; Headmaster of Aberlour House; *b* 26 March 1930; *s* of Sir Joscelyn Ambrose Cramer Coghill, 7th Bt and Elizabeth Gwendoline (*d* 1980), *d* of John B. Atkins; *S* father, 1983; *m* 1958, Gabriel Nancy, *d* of Major Dudley Claud Douglas Ryder; one *s* one *d*. *Educ:* Gordonstoun; Pembroke College, Cambridge. *Heir: s* Patrick Kendal Farley Coghill, *b* 3 Nov. 1960. *Address:* Aberlour House, Aberlour, Banffshire AB3 9LJ.

COGMAN, Rev. Canon Frederick Walter; Dean of Guernsey, 1967–78; Rector of St Peter Port, Guernsey, 1976–78; *b* 4 March 1913; *s* of William Frederick Cogman and Mabel Cozens; *m* 1940, Rose Hélène Mauger; one *s* one *d*. *Educ:* Rutlish Sch., Merton; King's Coll., London. Asst Priest, Upton-cum-Chalvey, Slough, 1938–42; Chaplain and Housemaster, St George's Sch., Harpenden, 1942–48; Rector of St Martin, Guernsey, 1948–76. *Recreations:* music, painting. *Address:* Oriana Lodge, Rue des Fontenelles, Forest, Guernsey, CI.

COHAN, Robert Paul; Artistic Director, Contemporary Dance Trust; *b* 27 March 1925; *s* of Walter and Billie Cohan. *Educ:* Martha Graham Sch., NYC. Joined Martha Graham Sch., 1946; Partner, 1950; Co-Dir, Martha Graham Co., 1966; Artistic Dir, Contemporary Dance Trust Ltd, 1967; Artistic Dir and Principal Choreographer, London Contemporary Dance Theatre, 1969–83; Artistic Advr, Batsheva Co., Israel, 1980; Director: York Univ., Toronto Choreographic Summer Sch., 1977; Gulbenkian Choreographic Summer Sch., Univ. of Surrey, 1978, 1979, 1982; Banff Sch. of Fine Arts Choreographic Seminar, Canada, 1980; New Zealand Choreographic Seminar, 1982; Choreographic Seminar, Simon Frazer Univ., Vancouver, 1985; Internat. Dance Course for Professional Choreographers and Composers, Surrey Univ., 1985. With London Contemporary Dance Theatre has toured Britain, E and W Europe, S America, N Africa and USA; major works created: Cell, 1969 (recorded for BBC TV, 1982); Stages, 1971; People Together, 1973; Waterless Method of Swimming Instruction, 1974 (recorded for BBC TV); Class, 1975; Stabat Mater, 1975 (recorded for BBC TV); Masque of Separation, 1975; Khamsin, 1976; Nympheas, 1976 (recorded for BBC TV, 1983); Forest, 1977 (recorded by BBC TV); Eos, 1978; Songs, Lamentations and Praises, 1979; Field, 1980; Dances of Love and Death, 1981; Agora, 1984; Skyward, 1984; A Mass for Man, 1985 (recorded for BBC TV). Hon. Fellow, York Univ., Toronto. Evening Standard Award for most outstanding achievement in ballet, 1975; Soc. of West End Theatres Award for most outstanding achievement in ballet, 1978. *Publication:* The Dance Workshop, 1986. *Recreation:* dancing. *Address:* The Place, 17 Dukes Road, WC1. *T:* 01–387 0161.

COHEN; *see* Waley-Cohen.

COHEN, His Honour Arthur; *see* Cohen, His Honour N. A. J.

COHEN, Sir Edward, Kt 1970; company director; Solicitor; Consultant, Corrs, Pavey, Whiting & Byrne, Melbourne, Australia; *b* 9 Nov. 1912; *s* of Brig. Hon. H. E. Cohen; *m* 1939, Meryl D., *d* of D. G. Fink; one *s. Educ:* Scotch Coll., Melbourne (Exhibnr in Greek and Roman History); Ormond Coll., Univ. of Melbourne (LLB; Aust. Blue Athletics, Hockey). Served, 1940–45: AIF, 2/12 Fd Regt, 9th Div. Artillery, Captain 1942. Partner, Pavey, Wilson, Cohen & Carter, 1945–76; Director: Carlton and United Breweries, 1947–84 (Chm., 1967–84); Swan Brewery, 1947–57; Associated Pulp & Paper Mills Ltd, 1951–83 (Dep. Chm. 1981–83); Electrolytic Zinc Co., A'asia, 1951–84 (Chm., 1960–84); Glazebrooks Paints and Chemicals Ltd, 1951–61; Standard Mutual Bldg Soc., 1951–64; E. Z. Industries, 1956–84 (Chm., 1960–84, Pres., 1984–); Pelaco Ltd, 1959–68; Commercial Union Assurance, 1960–82 (Chm., 1964–82); Union Assce Soc. of Aust., 1960–75 (Local Advisor, 1951–60); Michaelis Bayley Ltd, 1964–80; Qld Brewery (later CUB Qld), 1968–84; Herald and Weekly Times Ltd, 1974–77 (Vice-Chm., 1976–77); Chairman: Derwent Metals, 1957–84; CUB Fibre Containers, 1963–84; Emu Bay Railway Co., 1967–84; Manufrs Bottle Co., Vic, 1967–84; Northern Aust. Breweries (CUB (N Qld)), 1967–84; Nat. Commercial Union, 1982–84. Past Member: Faculty of Law of Melbourne Univ.; Internat. Hse Council, Melbourne Univ.; Council of Legal Education and Bd of Examiners. Mem. Council Law Inst. of Victoria, 1959–68, Pres. 1965–66. Chairman: Pensions Cttee, Melbourne Legacy, 1961–84 (Mem., 1955–84); Royal Women's Hosp. 1968 Million Dollar Bldg Appeal; Eileen Patricia Goulding Meml Fund Appeal, 1983; Life Governor: Austin, Prince Henry's, Royal Children's, Royal Melbourne, Royal Women's Hosps; Corps of Commissionaires; Adult Deaf and Dumb Soc. of Victoria. Hon. Solicitor, Queens Fund, 1951–. *Address:* 722 Orrong Road, Toorak, Victoria 3142, Australia; (office) 350 William Street, Melbourne, Victoria 3000, Australia. *Clubs:* Naval and Military, Victoria Racing, Royal Automobile (all in Melbourne).

COHEN, George Cormack; Sheriff-Substitute of the Lothians and Peebles at Edinburgh, 1955–66; *b* 16 Dec. 1909; *s* of J. Cohen and Mary J. Cormack, Melfort House, Bearsden, Dunbartonshire; *m* 1939, Elizabeth, *d* of James H. Wallace, Malvern; one *s* one *d. Educ:* Kelvinside Academy, Glasgow; Glasgow Univ. MA 1930, LLB 1934. Admitted to Scottish Bar, 1935; Sheriff-Substitute of Caithness at Wick, 1944–51; of Ayr and Bute at Kilmarnock, 1951–55. *Recreations:* travel, gastronomy, philately, gardening. *Address:* 37B Lauder Road, Edinburgh EH9 1UE. *T:* 031–668 1689.

COHEN, Prof. Gerald Allan, FBA 1985; Chichele Professor of Social and Political Theory and Fellow of All Souls, Oxford, since Jan. 1985; *b* 14 April 1941; *s* of Morrie Cohen and Bella Lipkin; *m* 1965, Margaret Florence Pearce; one *s* two *d. Educ:* Morris Winchevsky Jewish School, Montreal; Strathcona Academy, Montreal; Outremont High School, Montreal; McGill University (BA 1961); New College, Oxford (BPhil 1963). Lectr in Philosophy, University College London, 1963, Reader, 1978–84. Vis. Asst Prof. of Political Science, McGill Univ., 1965; Vis. Associate Prof. of Philosophy, Princeton Univ., 1975. *Publications:* Karl Marx's Theory of History: a defence, 1978; articles in anthologies, philosophical and social-scientific jls. *Recreation:* Guardian crosswords. *Address:* All Souls College, Oxford. *T:* Oxford 722251.

COHEN, Harry; MP (Lab) Leyton, since 1983; accountant; *b* 10 Dec. 1949. Mem., Waltham Forest Borough Council, 1972– (formerly Chm., Planning Cttee and Sec., Labour Group). Member: CIPFA; NALGO. *Address:* House of Commons, SW1.

COHEN, John Michael, FRSL 1957; critic and translator; *b* 5 Feb. 1903; *s* of late Arthur Cohen and Elizabeth (*née* Abrahams); *m* 1928, Audrey Frances Falk; four *s. Educ:* St Paul's Sch.; Queens' Coll., Cambridge. After short spell in publishing, joined family manufacturing business, 1925–40; war-time Schoolmaster, 1940–46; writing and translating from that date. *Publications: translations:* Don Quixote, 1950; Rousseau's Confessions, 1953; Rabelais, 1955; Life of Saint Teresa, 1957; Montaigne's Essays, 1958; Pascal's Pensées, 1961; Bernal Diaz, The Conquest of New Spain, 1963; The Spanish Bawd, 1964; Zarate, The Discovery and Conquest of Peru, 1968; The Four Voyages of Christopher Columbus, 1969; Sent off the Field, 1974; *criticism and biography:* Robert Browning, 1952; History of Western Literature, 1956; Life of Ludwig Mond, 1956; Poetry of This Age, 1959 (2nd, revised edn, 1966); Robert Graves, 1960; English Translators and Translations, 1962; The Baroque Lyric, 1963; En tiempos difíciles (a study of the new Cuban poetry), 1971; J. L. Borges, 1974; Journeys down the Amazon, 1975; (with J.-F. Phipps) The Common Experience, 1979; *anthologies:* Penguin Book of Comic & Curious Verse, 1952; More Comic & Curious Verse, 1956; Penguin Book of Spanish Verse, 1956; Yet More Comic & Curious Verse, 1959; Latin American Writing Today, 1967; Writers in the New Cuba, 1967; A Choice of Comic and Curious Verse, 1975; Rider Book of Mystical Verse, 1983; *dictionaries:* (with M. J. Cohen) Penguin Dictionary of Quotations, 1960; (with M. J. Cohen) Penguin Dictionary of Modern Quotations, 1971, rev. edn 1981; other translations. *Recreations:* meditation; listening to music; gardening. *Address:* 14 The Moors, Pangbourne, Berks. *T:* Pangbourne 2738.

COHEN, Laurence Jonathan, FBA 1973; Fellow and Praelector in Philosophy, since 1957, Senior Tutor, since 1985, Queen's College, Oxford; British Academy Reader in Humanities, Oxford University, 1982–84; *b* 7 May 1923; *s* of Israel and Theresa Cohen; *m* 1953, Gillian Mary Slee; three *s* one *d. Educ:* St Paul's Sch., London; Balliol Coll., Oxford (MA 1947, DLitt 1982). Served War: Naval Intell. in UK and SEAC, 1942–45, and Lieut (Sp.) RNVR. Asst in Logic and Metaphysics, Edinburgh Univ., 1947; Lectr in Philosophy, St Andrews Univ. at Dundee, 1950; Commonwealth Fund Fellow in Logic at Princeton and Harvard Univs, 1952–53. Vis. Lectr, Hebrew Univ. of Jerusalem, 1952; Visiting Professor: Columbia Univ., 1967; Yale Univ., 1972; British Acad. Philosophical Lectr, 1975; Fry Lectr, Bristol Univ., 1976; Vis. Fellow, ANU, 1980; Austin Lectr, UK Assoc. for Legal and Social Philos., 1982. Sec., Internat. Union of History and Philosophy of Science (Div. of Logic Methodology and Philosophy of Science), 1975–83; Pres., British Soc. for Philosophy of Science, 1977–79. General Editor, Clarendon Library of Logic and Philosophy, 1973–. *Publications:* The Principles of World Citizenship, 1954; The Diversity of Meaning, 1962; The Implications of Induction, 1970; The Probable and the Provable, 1977; (ed jtly) Applications of Inductive Logic, 1980; (ed jtly) Logic, Methodology and Philosophy of Science, 1982; The Dialogue of Reason, 1986. *Recreations:* gardening; work for Council for Protection of Rural England. *Address:* Queen's College, Oxford OX1 4AW.

COHEN, Hon. Leonard Harold Lionel; barrister-at-law; *b* 1 Jan. 1922; *s* of Rt Hon. Lord Cohen, PC (Life Peer), and Adelaide, Lady Cohen (*née* Spielmann); *m* 1949, Eleanor Lucy Quixano Henriques; two *s* one *d. Educ:* Eton Coll.; New Coll., Oxford (MA). War Service, Rifle Bde (wounded), Captain, 1941–45. Called to Bar, Lincoln's Inn, 1948; practised at Chancery Bar, 1949–61. Chm., Ariel Exchange Ltd, 1982–; Director: M. Samuel & Co. Ltd (subseq. Hill Samuel & Co. Ltd), 1961–76; Cayzer Ltd, 1982–; Dir-Gen., Accepting Houses Cttee, 1976–82; Chairman: United Services Trustee, 1976–82; Council, Royal Free Hosp. Med. Sch., 1982–; Pres., Jewish Colonization Assoc., 1976–. Master of the Skinners' Co., 1971–72. Hon. Col, 39th (City of London) Signal Regt (V), 1973–78. *Recreations:* shooting, golf, reading, opera. *Address:* Dovecote House, Swallowfield Park, Reading RG7 1TG. *T:* Reading 884775. *Club:* White's.

COHEN, Dr Louis; Executive Secretary, Institute of Physics, since 1966; *b* 14 Oct. 1925; *s* of late Harry Cohen and Fanny Cohen (*née* Abrahams); *m* 1948, Eve G. Marsh; one *s* two *d. Educ:* Manchester Central High Sch.; Manchester Univ.; Imperial Coll., London. BSc, PhD, FInstP. Research Physicist, Simon-Carves Ltd, 1953–63; Research Manager, Pyrotenax Ltd, 1963–66. Hon. Sec., Council of Science and Technology Insts, 1969–; Treasurer, European Physical Soc., 1968–73; Corresp. Mem., Manchester Literary and Philosophical Soc., 1963. FRSA. *Publications:* papers and articles on physics and related subjects. *Recreations:* cooking, books, music, the theatre. *Address:* 9 Limewood Close, W13 8HL. *T:* 01–997 2001.

COHEN, Lt–Col Mordaunt, TD 1954; DL; Regional Chairman of Industrial Tribunals, since 1976 (Chairman, 1974–76); *b* 6 Aug. 1916; *s* of Israel Ellis Cohen and Sophie Cohen; *m* 1953, Her Honour Judge Myrella Cohen, *qv;* one *s* one *d. Educ:* Bede Collegiate Sch. for Boys, Sunderland. Admitted solicitor, 1938. Served War, RA, 1940–46: seconded RWAFF; despatches, Burma campaign; served TA, 1947–55: CO 463(M) HAA Regt, RA(TA), 1954–55. Alderman, Sunderland Co. Bor. Council, 1967–74; Chm., Sunderland Educn Cttee, 1970–72; Chm., NE Council of Educn Cttees, 1971; Councillor, Tyne and Wear CC, 1973–74; Dep. Chm., Northern Traffic Comrs, 1973–74. Chairman: Mental Health Review Tribunal, 1967–76; Governors, Sunderland Polytechnic, 1969–72; Mem. Court, Univ. of Newcastle upon Tyne, 1968–72. Pres., Sunderland Law Soc., 1970; Trustee and past Pres., Sunderland Hebrew Congregation; Mem., Bd of Deputies of British Jews (Chm., Provincial Cttee); former Mem., Chief Rabbinate Council; Trustee: Ajex Charitable Trust; Ashbrooke Foundn. DL Tyne and Wear, 1986. *Recreations:* watching sport but playing bowls; gardening, communal service, promoting inter-faith understanding. *Address:* c/o Regional Office of Industrial Tribunals, Plummer House, Market Street East, Newcastle upon Tyne NE1 6NF. *T:* Newcastle upon Tyne 328865.

COHEN, Myrella, QC 1970; **Her Honour Judge Myrella Cohen;** a Circuit Judge, since 1972; *b* 16 Dec. 1927; *d* of late Samuel and Sarah Cohen, Manchester; *m* 1953, Lt-Col Mordaunt Cohen, *qv;* one *s* one *d. Educ:* Manchester High Sch. for Girls; Colwyn Bay Grammar Sch.; Manchester Univ. (LLB 1948). Called to the Bar, Gray's Inn, 1950. Recorder of Hull, 1971. Mem., Parole Bd, 1983–. *Address:* c/o Crown Court, Kenton Bar, Newcastle upon Tyne. *Club:* Soroptimist Club of Great Britain.

COHEN, Nat; Executive Consultant, THORN EMI Screen Entertainment (formerly EMI Films Ltd), since 1978 (Chairman, 1970–78); *b* 1905. Entered film industry, 1930. Director: EMI Film Productions Ltd, 1970–79; EMI Film & Theatre Corporation Ltd, 1970–79. *Films produced include:* Carry On Sergeant, and 12 other Carry On films; A Kind of Loving; Billy Liar; Darling; Far From the Madding Crowd; Murder on the Orient Express; Death on the Nile; Clockwise. *Address:* THORN EMI Screen Entertainment, 30 Golden Square, W1A 4QX.

COHEN, Lt-Col Nathan Leslie, TD 1949; JP; *b* 13 Jan. 1908; *s* of Reuben and Maud Cohen; unmarried. *Educ:* Stockton-on-Tees Grammar Sch.; Clifton Coll. In private practice as a Solicitor until 1939; called to the Bar, Lincoln's Inn, 1954. War Service, Aug. 1939–May 1945. Senior Legal Officer (Lt-Col), Military Govt, Carinthia, Austria, 1945–49; Pres. of Sessions Courts, Malaya, 1949–57; Justice of the Special Courts, Cyprus, 1958–59; Judge of HM Court of Sovereign Base Areas of Akrotiri and Dhekalia, Cyprus, 1960–61; Adjudicator under Immigration Appeals Act, 1970–71. Mem., Cleveland Co. Social Services Cttee 1978–80. Vice-President: Northern Area, Royal British Legion; Durham and Cleveland Royal British Legion (Patron, 1985–); Cleveland Co. British Red Cross Soc.; Pres., St John Ambulance Assoc., Stockton. Associate SBStJ, 1980. JP Stockton-on-Tees, 1967. Diamond Jubilee Medal (Johore), 1955; Colonial Police Medal, 1956; Royal Brit. Legion Gold Badge, 1979; Badge of Honour, 1981, Voluntary Medical Service Medal, 1982, British Red Cross Soc. *Recreations:* travelling, reading. *Address:* 35 Richmond Road, Stockton-on-Tees, Cleveland TS18 4DS. *Club:* Royal Over-Seas League.

COHEN, His Honour (Nathaniel) Arthur (Jim), JP; County Court Judge, Circuit No 38, 1955–56, Circuit No 43, 1956–60, Circuit No 56, 1960–70, retired; *b* 19 Jan. 1898; 2nd *s* of late Sir Benjamin Arthur Cohen, KC, and Lady Cohen; *m* 1st, 1927, Judith Luard (marr. diss.); two *s;* 2nd, 1936, Joyce Collingridge. *Educ:* Rugby; CCC, Oxford (BA). Served European War, 1916–19, Royal Navy. Called to Bar, Inner Temple, 1923. War of 1939–45: recalled to RN and placed on Emergency List with rank of Commander. Legal Adviser to UNRRA, 1946–49; Dep. Chm., Foreign Compensation Commn, 1950–55. JP Surrey, 1958. *Recreations:* golf, music. *Address:* Bay Tree Cottage, Crockham Hill, Edenbridge, Kent. *Club:* United Oxford & Cambridge University.

COHEN, Percy, CBE 1936; Joint Director, Conservative Research Department, 1948–59; *b* London, 25 Dec. 1891; *e s* of late M. Cohen; *m* 1917, Rosa Abrams (*d* 1973); one *s* one *d. Educ:* Central Foundation Sch., London. Entered service of Conservative Central Office, 1911; Head of Library and Information Dept, 1928–48. Served first European War, France. Worked in 12 General Elections; Editor, Constitutional Year Book, 1929–39; Editor, Notes on Current Politics, 1942–59. Sec. to several post-war problems Cttees, 1944–45. *Publications:* British System of Social Insurance, 1932; Unemployment Insurance and Assistance in Britain, 1938; (ed) Conservative Election Handbook, 1945; (ed) Campaign Guide, 1950, 1951, 1955 and 1959. *Recreation:* walking. *Address:* Sunridge Court, 76 The Ridgeway, NW11. *T:* 01–455 5203. *Club:* St Stephen's Constitutional.

COHEN, Prof. Philip, PhD; FRS 1984; FRSE 1984; Royal Society Research Professor, University of Dundee, since 1984; *b* 22 July 1945; *s* of Jacob Davis Cohen and Fanny (*née* Bragman); *m* 1969, Patricia Townsend Wade; one *s* one *d. Educ:* Hendon County Grammar Sch.; University Coll. London (BSc 1st Cl. Hons (Biochemistry Special), 1966; PhD Biochem., 1969). SRC/NATO Postdoctoral Res. Fellow, Dept of Biochem., Univ. of Washington, Seattle, USA, 1969–71; Univ. of Dundee: Lectr in Biochem., 1971–78; Reader in Biochem., 1978–81; Prof. of Enzymology, 1981–84. Mem., Eur. Molecular Biology Orgn, 1982–. Anniversary Prize, Fedn of Eur. Biochemical Socs, 1977; Colworth Medal, British Biochemical Soc., 1978. *Publications:* Control of Enzyme Activity, 1976, 2nd edn 1983; (ed series) Molecular Aspects of Cellular Regulation: vol. 1, 1980; vol. 2, 1982; vol. 3, 1984; vol. 4, 1985; 185 original papers and revs in scientific jls. *Recreations:* chess, golf, natural history. *Address:* Inverbay, Invergowrie, Dundee DD2 5QG. *T:* Invergowrie 328.

COHEN, Sir Rex (Arthur Louis), KBE 1964 (OBE 1944); *b* 27 Nov. 1906; *s* of Rex David Cohen, Condover Hall, Shrewsbury; *m* 1932, Nina Alice Castello; one *d. Educ:* Rugby Sch.; Trinity Coll., Cambridge (BA). Served KSLI, 1938–45. Past Mem., BoT Cttee for Consumer Protection. Past Chairman: Lewis's Investment Trust Group, 1958–65 (Joint Man. Dir, 1945); NAAFI, 1961–63; Higgs & Hill Ltd, 1966–72; Meat and Livestock Commn, 1967–72. Officer, Order of Orange Nassau (Netherlands), 1944. *Recreations:* racing, horse breeding, shooting. *Address:* Ruckmans Farm, Oakwood Hill, near Dorking, Surrey. *T:* Oakwood Hill 255. *Clubs:* White's; Jockey (Newmarket).

COHEN, Dr Richard Henry Lionel, CB 1969; Chief Scientist, Department of Health and Social Security, 1972–73, retired; *b* 1 Feb. 1907; *y s* of Frank Lionel and Bertha Hendelah Cohen; *m* 1934, Margaret Clarkson Deas; one *s. Educ:* Clifton Coll.; King's

Coll., Cambridge; St Bartholomew's Hospital. Miscellaneous hosp. appts, 1940–46; MRC, 1948–62; Dep. Chief Med. Off., MRC, 1957–62; Dept of Health and Social Security (formerly Min. of Health), 1962–73. *Address:* The End House South, Lady Margaret Road, Cambridge CB3 0BJ. *Club:* Reform.

COHEN, Prof. Robert Donald, MD, FRCP; Professor of Medicine and Director, Academic Medical Unit, London Hospital Medical College, University of London, since 1981 (Professor of Metabolic Medicine, 1974–81); *b* 11 Oct. 1933; *s* of Dr Harry H. and Ruby Cohen; *m* 1961, Dr Barbara Joan Boucher; one *s* one *d. Educ:* Clifton Coll.; Trinity Coll., Cambridge. MA, MD (Cantab). Hon. Cons. Physician, London Hosp., 1967; Chm., Editorial Bd, Clinical Science and Molecular Medicine, 1973–74; Dir, Academic Unit of Metabolism and Endocrinology, London Hosp. Med. Coll., 1974; Chairman: Adv. Cttee on the Application of Computing Science to Medicine and the Nat. Health Service, 1976–77; DHSS Computer R&D Cttee, 1977–80; Special Adv. Cttee on Gen. Internal Medicine, Jt Cttee on Higher Med. Trng, 1983–; DHSS/MRC Co-ordinating Cttee on Clinical Applications of Magnetic Resonance Imaging, 1986–. *Publications:* Clinical and Biochemical Aspects of Lactic Acidosis (with H. F. Woods), 1976; papers in Clin. Sci. and Molecular Med., BMJ, Lancet, Biochemical Journal. *Address:* The London Hospital, Whitechapel Road, E1 1BB. *T:* 01–377 7000.

COHEN, Ruth Louisa, CBE 1969; MA; Principal, Newnham College, Cambridge, 1954–72; University Lecturer in Economics, Cambridge, 1945–74; *b* 10 Nov. 1906; *d* of late Walter Samuel Cohen and late Lucy Margaret Cohen. *Educ:* Hayes Court, Kent; Newnham Coll., Cambridge. Commonwealth Fund Fellow, Stanford and Cornell Univs., USA, 1930–32; Research Officer, Agricultural Economics Research Inst., Oxford, 1933–39; Fellow of Newnham Coll., Cambridge, 1939–54; Min. of Food, 1939–42; Board of Trade, 1942–45. Lay Mem., Gen. Medical Council, 1961–76. City Cllr, Cambridge, 1973–. *Publications:* History of Milk Prices, 1936; Economics of Agriculture, 1939; articles in Economic Journal, etc. *Address:* 2 Croft Lodge, Cambridge. *T:* Cambridge 62699. *Club:* University Women's.

COHEN, Stanley; *b* 31 July 1927; *s* of Thomas and Teresa Cohen; *m* 1954, Brenda P. Rafferty; three *s* one *d. Educ:* St Patrick's and St Charles' Schools, Leeds. Served in Royal Navy, 1947–49. Employed in Clothing Industry, 1943–47 and 1949–51; Clerical Officer with British Railways, 1951–70. Mem. Leeds City Council, 1952–71; elected Alderman, 1968. Parly Candidate (Lab) Barkston Ash County Constituency, 1966; MP (Lab) Leeds South East, 1970–83. PPS to Minister of State, DES, 1976–79. Mem., Duke of Edinburgh's Commonwealth Study Conf. to Australia, 1968. *Recreations:* walking, camping, driving. *Address:* 164 Ring Road, Halton, Leeds LS15 7AE. *T:* Leeds 649568. *Clubs:* Crossgates Recreational; Irish Centre (Leeds).

COHEN, Prof. Stanley, PhD; Professor of Criminology, Hebrew University, Jerusalem, since 1981; *b* 23 Feb. 1942; *s* of Ray and Sie Cohen; *m* 1963, Ruth Kretzmer; two *d. Educ:* Univ. of Witwatersrand, Johannesburg (BA); LSE, Univ. of London (PhD). Psychiatric social worker, 1963–64; Lectr in Sociology: Enfield Coll., 1965–67; Univ. of Durham, 1967–72; Sen. Lectr in Sociol., Univ. of Essex, 1972–74, Prof. of Sociol., 1974–81. Sellin-Glueck Award, Amer. Soc. of Criminology, 1985. *Publications:* Images of Deviance, 1971; Folk Devils and Moral Panics, 1972; Psychological Survival, 1972; The Manufacture of News, 1973; Escape Attempts, 1976; Prison Secrets, 1978; Social Control and the State, 1984; Visions of Social Control: crime, punishment and classification, 1985. *Address:* Institute of Criminology, Hebrew University, Mount Scopus, Jerusalem 91905, Israel.

COHEN, Prof. Sydney, CBE 1978; FRS 1978; Professor of Chemical Pathology, Guy's Hospital Medical School, since 1965; *b* Johannesburg, SA, 18 Sept. 1921; *s* of Morris and Pauline Cohen; *m* 1950, June Bernice Adler, JP, *d* of Dr and Mrs L. D. Adler; one *s* one *d. Educ:* King Edward VIIth Sch., Johannesburg; Witwatersrand and London Univs. MD, PhD. Lectr, Dept of Physiology, Witwatersrand Univ., 1947–53; Scientific Staff, Nat. Inst. for Med. Research, London, 1954–60; Reader, Dept of Immunology, St Mary's Hosp. Med. Sch., 1960–65. Mem., MRC, 1974–76; Chm., Tropical Med. Research Bd, MRC, 1974–76; Chm., WHO Scientific Gp on Immunity to Malaria, 1976–81; Mem., WHO expert adv. panel on malaria, 1977–; Mem. Council, Royal Soc., 1981–83; Royal Soc. Assessor, MRC, 1982–84. Nuffield Dominion Fellow in Medicine, 1954; Founder Fellow, RCPath, 1964. *Publications:* papers on immunology and parasitic diseases in sci. jls. *Recreations:* golf, gardening, forestry. *Address:* 4 Frognal Rise, NW3 6RD. *T:* 01–435 6507; Hafodfraith, Llangurig, Powys SY18 6QG. *Club:* Royal and Ancient (St Andrews).

COHN, Prof. Norman, MA; DLitt; FBA 1978; FRHistS; historian; Astor-Wolfson Professor, University of Sussex, 1973–80, now Professor Emeritus; *b* London, 12 Jan. 1915; *yr s* of late August Cohn, barrister-at-law, Middle Temple, and Daisy (*née* Reimer); *m* 1941, Vera, *d* of late Mark and Eva Broido, St Petersburg; one *s. Educ:* Gresham's Sch., Holt (Scholar); Christ Church, Oxford (Scholar). 1st Class Hons, Sch. of Medieval and Mod. Languages, 1936; DLitt Glasgow, 1957. Served War of 1939–45, Queen's Royal Regt and Intell. Corps. Lectr in French, Glasgow Univ., 1946–51; Professor of French: Magee Univ. Coll. (then associated with TCD), 1951–60; King's Coll., Durham Univ., 1960–63; changed career to become Dir, Columbus Centre, Sussex Univ. and Gen. Editor, Columbus Centre's Studies in the Dynamics of Persecution and Extermination, 1966–80; Professorial Fellow, Sussex Univ., 1966–73; advr on comparative study of genocide, Concordia Univ., Montreal, 1982–85; advr, Montreal Inst. for Genocide Studies, 1985–; Vis. Prof., KCL, 1986–. Hugh Le May Fellow, Rhodes Univ., 1950; Fellow, Center for Advanced Study in the Behavioral Sciences, Stanford, Calif, 1966; Vis. Fellow, Center for Humanities, Wesleyan Univ., Conn, 1971; Fellow, Netherlands Inst. for Advanced Study, 1975–76; Canadian SSHRC Vis. Fellow, 1982, Canadian Commonwealth Vis. Fellow, 1983. Hon. LLD Concordia Univ., 1985. *Publications:* Gold Khan and other Siberian legends, 1946; The Pursuit of the Millennium: revolutionary millenarians and mystical anarchists of the middle ages, 1957, rev. edns 1961, 1970; Warrant for Genocide: the myth of the Jewish world-conspiracy and the Protocols of the Elders of Zion, 1967, rev. edn 1981 (Anisfield-Wolf Award in Race Relations, 1967); Europe's Inner Demons: an enquiry inspired by the great witch-hunt, 1975, rev. edn 1976; contributor to various symposia, learned jls, and reviews. *Recreations:* walking, travel, looking at pictures, butterfly-watching. *Address:* Orchard Cottage, Wood End, Ardeley, Herts SG2 7AZ. *T:* Stevenage 85247. *Club:* Athenæum.

COHN, Prof. Paul Moritz, FRS 1980; Astor Professor of Mathematics in the University of London, at University College, since 1986; *b* Hamburg, 8 Jan. 1924; *o c* of late James Cohn and late Julia Cohn (*née* Cohen); *m* 1958, Deirdre Sonia Sharon; two *d. Educ:* Trinity Coll., Cambridge. BA 1948, MA, PhD 1951. Chargé de Recherches, Univ. de Nancy, 1951–52; Lectr, Manchester Univ., 1952–62; Reader, London Univ., at Queen Mary Coll., 1962–67; Prof. of Maths, London Univ. at Bedford Coll., 1967–84, at UCL, 1984–86. Visiting Professor: Yale Univ., 1961–62; Univ. of California (Berkeley), 1962; Univ. of Chicago, 1964; State Univ. of New York (Stony Brook), 1967; Rutgers Univ., 1967–68; Univ. of Paris, 1969; Tulane Univ., 1971; Indian Inst. of Technology, Delhi, 1971; Univ. of Alberta, 1972, 1986; Carleton Univ., Ottawa, 1973; Technion, Haifa, 1975; Iowa State Univ., 1978; Univ. of Bielefeld, 1979. Mem., Mathematics Cttee, SRC, 1977–80. London Mathematical Society: Sec., 1965–67; Mem. Council, 1968–71, 1972–75, 1979–84; Pres., 1982–84; Editor, London Math. Soc. Monographs, 1968–77, 1980–. Lester R. Ford Award (Mathematical Assoc. of America), 1972; Senior Berwick Prize, London Mathematical Soc., 1974. *Publications:* Lie Groups, 1957; Linear Equations, 1958; Solid Geometry, 1961; Universal Algebra, 1965, 2nd edn 1981 (trans foreign langs); Free Rings and their Relations, 1971, 2nd edn, 1985; Algebra, vol. I, 1974, 2nd edn 1982, vol. II, 1977; Skewfield Constructions, 1977; papers on algebra in various mathematical periodicals. *Recreations:* linguistics, etymology. *Address:* Department of Mathematics, University College London, Gower Street, WC1E 6BT. *T:* 01–387 7050.

COILEY, John Arthur, PhD; Keeper, National Railway Museum, York, since 1974; *b* 29 March 1932; *o s* of Arthur George Coiley and Stella Coiley (*née* Chinnock); *m* 1956, Patricia Anne Coiley, BA, (*née* Dixon); two *s* one *d. Educ:* Beckenham and Penge Grammar Sch.; Selwyn Coll., Cambridge (BA, PhD Metallurgy). Scientific Officer, UKAEA, Harwell, 1957–60; Aeon Laboratories, Egham, 1960–65; Development Manager, Fulmer Research Laboratories, 1965–73; Asst Keeper, Science Museum, 1973–74. Vice-President, Internat. Assoc. of Transport Museums, 1977–. *Publication:* (jtly) Images of Steam, 1968, 2nd edn 1974. *Recreations:* photography, motoring. *Address:* 4 Beech Close, Farnham, Knaresborough, N Yorkshire HG5 9JJ. *T:* Copgrove 497.

COKAYNE, family name of **Baron Cullen of Ashbourne.**

COKE, family name of **Earl of Leicester.**

COKE, Viscount; Edward Douglas Coke; *b* 6 May 1936; *s* and *heir* of 6th Earl of Leicester, *qv*; *m* 1st, 1962, Valeria Phyllis (marr. diss. 1985), *e d* of late L. A. Potter; two *s* one *d*; 2nd, 1986, Mrs Sarah de Chair. *Educ:* St Andrew's, Grahamstown, CP, S Africa. Pres., Centre of Management in Agriculture, BIM, 1983–. *Recreations:* skiing, sailing, shooting. *Heir:* *s* Hon. Thomas Edward Coke, *b* 6 July 1965. *Address:* Holkham, Wells-next-the-Sea, Norfolk. *Clubs:* Brooks's, White's, Farmers'.

COKE, Gerald Edward, CBE 1967; JP; DL; *b* 25 Oct. 1907; *o s* of late Major the Hon. Sir John Coke, KCVO, and late Hon. Mrs Coke; *m* 1939, Patricia, *e d* of late Rt Hon. Sir Alexander Cadogan, PC, OM, GCMG, KCB; two *s* one *d* (and one *s* decd). *Educ:* Eton; New Coll., Oxford (MA). Served War of 1939–45, Lieut-Col. Treas., Bridewell Royal Hosp. (King Edward's Sch., Witley), 1946–72; Chm., Glyndebourne Arts Trust, 1955–75; Dir, Royal Acad. of Music, 1957–74; Dir, Royal Opera House, Covent Garden, 1958–64; a Governor, BBC, 1961–66. Director: Rio Tinto-Zinc Corp., 1947–75 (Dep. Chm. 1962–66; Chm. Rio Tinto Co., 1956–62); S. G. Warburg & Co., 1945–75; United Kingdom Provident Instn, 1952–74. JP 1952, DL 1974, Hants. Hon. FRAM 1968. *Address:* Jenkyn Place, Bentley, Hants. *T:* Bentley 23118. *Club:* Brooks's.

COKER, Dame Elizabeth, DBE 1979; DL; Chairman: Mid-Essex District Health Authority (formerly Essex Area Health Authority), since 1973; Basildon Development Corporation, 1981–86 (Member, 1971–86; Deputy Chairman, 1980); *d* of William Lowe and Ellen Elizabeth (*née* Winnington); *m* 1947, Frank L. Coker, LDS RCS; one *d. Educ:* Grove Park Sch., Wrexham; Queen Mary Coll., Univ. of London (BSc Hons). Member: Essex CC, 1959–81 (Chm., 1971–74); Exec. Cttee, Assoc. of Educn Cttees, 1965–74 (Vice-Pres., 1972–74); County Councils Assoc., 1968–74; Assoc. of County Councils, 1974–81 (Chm., Exec. Council, 1976–79); Council of Local Educn Authorities, 1974–79 (Chm., 1974–75); Eastern Electricity Bd, 1973–77; Chm., Harlow Development Corporation, 1979–80. Mem. Council, Essex Univ., 1965– (Treasurer, 1982–); Governor: Felsted Sch., 1967–; Brentwood Sch., 1968–; Queen Mary Coll., 1977– (Fellow, 1975–); United World Coll. of the Atlantic, St Donats, 1980–. DL Essex, 1974. *Recreation:* travel. *Address:* Winnington House, Danbury, Chelmsford, Essex. *T:* Danbury 2555.

COKER, Peter Godfrey, RA 1972 (ARA 1965); ARCA 1953; *b* 27 July 1926; *m* 1951, Vera Joyce Crook; one *s* decd. *Educ:* St Martin's Sch. of Art; Royal Coll. of Art (Royal Schol.). Brit. Inst. Schol., 1954. Arts Council Award to Artists, 1976. One-man Exhibitions: Zwemmer Gall., 1956, 1957, 1959, 1964, 1967; Magdalene Street Gall., Cambridge, 1968; Stone Gall., Newcastle, 1969; Thackeray Gall., London, 1970, 1972, 1974, 1975, 1976, 1978; Gallery 10, London, 1980, 1982, 1984. Retrospective Exhibitions: Minories, Colchester, 1972; Victoria Gall., Bath, 1972; Morley Gall., London, 1973; Mappin Art Gall., Sheffield, 1973; Chelmsford and Essex Museum, 1978; Royal Acad., 1979. Represented in Group Exhibitions: Tate Gall., 1958; Jordan Gall., Toronto, 1958; John Moores, Liverpool, 1959, 1961; Northampton, 1960; Europaisches Forum, Alpbach, Austria, 1960; Neue Galerie, Linz, 1960; RCA, 1952–62; Painters in E Anglia, Arts Council, 1966; Bicentenary Exhibn, Royal Acad., 1768–1968, 1968; British Painting 1900–1960, Sheffield and Aberdeen, 1975–76; British Painting 1952–77, RA; Recent Chartrey Purchases, Tate Gall., 1981; Acquisitions since 1980, Tate Gall., 1982; The Forgotten Fifties, Sheffield, Norwich, Coventry, and Camden Arts Centre, London, 1984. Works in permanent collections: Tate Gall.; Arts Council; Contemp. Art Soc., GB; Contemp. Art Soc., Wales; Chantrey Bequest; Nat. Portrait Gall.; V&A; Nat. Maritime Museum; Stedelijk Museum Ostend; Eastern Arts Assoc.; Rugby Library and Museum; Chelmsford and Essex Museum; Castle Museum, Norwich; Art Galls and Mus. of Carlisle, Ipswich, Leicester, Rochdale, Doncaster; Art Galls of Bath (Victoria), Batley, Birmingham, Coventry (Herbert), Kettering, Leeds City, Sheffield City, Southport (Atkinson); RCA; RA; Minories, Colchester; Beecroft Art Gall., Southend-on-Sea; Educn Cttees of Nottingham, Essex, Derbyshire, Lancs, ILEA; Liverpool Univ. *Publication:* Etching Techniques, 1976. *Address:* The Red House, Mistley, Manningtree, Essex. *T:* Manningtree 2179.

COLAHAN, Air Vice-Marshal William Edward, CB 1978; CBE 1973; DFC 1945; retired; Member, Lord Chancellor's Panel of Independent Inquiry Inspectors, since 1983; *b* 7 Aug. 1923; *er s* of Dr W. E. and Dr G. C. J. Colahan; *m* 1949, Kathleen Anne Butler; one *s* two *d. Educ:* Templeton High Sch., S Africa; Univ. of Cape Town. S African Air Force, 1941–46; service in Italy, France (Temp. Captain); Royal Air Force, 1947–: Flt-Lt 1947; Sqdn Ldr 1952; psa 1957; Wing Comdr 1959; jssc 1962; Gp Captain 1965; Air Cdr 1970; idc 1970; Air Comdr Malta, 1971–73; Air Vice-Marshal 1973; ACAS (Operations), 1973–75; AOC and Commandant, RAF College Cranwell, 1975–78; Officer Careers Counsellor (RAF), 1978–83. Mem. Council, St Dunstans, 1978–. Vice Chm. (AIR), E Midlands TAVRA, 1983–; Comdr, St John Ambulance, Lincs, 1985–. OStJ 1986. *Club:* Royal Air Force.

COLBECK-WELCH, Air Vice-Marshal Edward Lawrence, CB 1961; OBE 1948; DFC 1941; Royal Air Force, retired; *b* 29 Jan. 1914; *s* of Major G. S. M. Colbeck-Welch, MC, Collingham, Yorks; *m* 1938, Doreen, *d* of T. G. Jenkin, Sliema, Malta; one *s* two *d. Educ:* Leeds Grammar Sch. Commnd RAF, 1933; No. 22 Sqdn, RAF, 1934–37; CFS Instructor Course, 1937; Flying Instr RAuxAF Sqdns, 1937–39; Staff duties, 1940; OC No. 29 Night Fighter Sqdn, 1941–42; Staff Coll., 1942; Staff duties, 1943–44; Staff duties in 2nd TAF and OC No. 139 (Bomber) Wing, 1944–45; Air Min. Dep. Dir Air Defence, 1945–47; Staff duties in USA, 1947–50; OC Fighter Stations (2), 1950–53; Air Min. Personnel Staff duties, 1954–55; student, idc 1956; Comdt Central Fighter Estab., 1957–58; SASO, HQ No 13 (F) Group, 1959; SASO, HQ Fighter Comd RAF, 1960–63.

Recreation: sailing. *Address:* La Cote au Palier, St Martin, Jersey, CI. *Clubs:* Royal Channel Islands Yacht, St Helier Yacht.

COLBERT, Claudette; stage and film actress; *b* Paris, 13 Sept. 1903; *d* of Georges Chauchoin and Jeanne Loew; *m* 1st, Norman Foster (marr. diss.); 2nd, Dr Joel J. Pressman (*d* 1968). Went to America, 1908. First appearances: New York Stage, 1923; London stage, 1928. Returned to Broadway stage, 1958–60. After success on Broadway, entered films, 1929. *Plays include:* Wild Westcotts, The Marionette Man, We've Got to Have Money, The Cat Came Back, Leah Kleschna, High Stakes, A Kiss in the Taxi, The Ghost Train, The Pearl of Great Price, The Barker, The Mulberry Bush, La Gringa, Within the Law, Fast Life, Tin Pan Alley, Dynamo, See Naples and Die, The Marriage-Go-Round, The Kingfisher, Talent for Murder, Aren't We All?. *Films include:* For the Love of Mike, The Lady Lies, Manslaughter, The Smiling Lieutenant, Sign of the Cross, Cleopatra, Private Worlds, Maid of Salem, It Happened One Night (Academy Award, 1934), The Gilded Lily, I Met Him in Paris, Bluebeard's Eighth Wife, Zaza, Midnight, Drums Along the Mohawk, Skylark, Remember the Day, Palm Beach Story, No Time for Love, So Proudly We Hail, Without Reservations, The Secret Heart, The Egg and I, Sleep My Love, Three Came Home, The Secret Fury, The Planter's Wife, Destiny, Versailles, Parrish. *Address:* Bellerive, St Peter, Barbados, West Indies.

COLBURN, Oscar Henry, CBE 1981; JP; DL; farmer; *m* 1950, Helen Joan (*née* Garne); one *s* two *d*. Crown Estates Commissioner, 1976–; Chairman, Grasslands Research Institute, 1976–84; (Hon. Fellow, 1984); Chairman, Consultative Board of Joint Consultative Organization for Research and Development in Agriculture and Food, 1981–84; Former Chm., Regional Panel, MAFF; former Mem., Northfield Cttee (author, Minority Report); past Mem. Council, RASE. Pioneer breeder of Poll Hereford cattle; during 1960s developed Colbred sheep, first new British breed of sheep for over a century. JP Northleach (Chm., 1976–86); High Sheriff of Glos, 1980–81; DL Glos, 1982. Hon. FRAgS, 1982. Summers Trophy, NFU Glos Br., 1956; George Hedley Meml Award, for services to Sheep Industry, 1963; Bledisloe Lecture, 1972; Farmers' Club Trophy, 1982; instituted Colburn Trophy for annual competition by Gloucestershire Constabulary, 1982. *Address:* Crickley Barrow, Northleach, near Cheltenham, Glos GL54 3QA. *Clubs:* MCC, Farmers', Brooks's.

COLCHESTER, Area Bishop of, until 31 May 1987; **Rt. Rev. Roderic Norman Coote,** DD; appointed Bishop Suffragan of Colchester, 1966; *b* 13 April 1915; *s* of late Comdr B. T. Coote and late Grace Harriet (*née* Robinson); *m* 1964, Erica Lynette, *d* of late Rev. E. G. Shrubbs, MBE; one *s* two *d*. *Educ:* Woking County Sch.; Trinity Coll., Dublin. Curate Asst, St Bartholomew's, Dublin, 1938–41; Missionary Priest in the Diocese of Gambia and the Rio Pongas, 1942; Bishop of Gambia and the Rio Pongas, 1951–57; Suffragan Bishop of Fulham, 1957–66; Archdeacon of Colchester, 1969–72. Member, General Synod of Church of England, 1969–72. *Recreations:* tennis, squash; piano (composer and broadcaster); Irish Champion 120 yds Hurdles. *Address:* The Bishop's House, 32 Inglis Road, Colchester, Essex; (after May 1987) 58 Broom Park, Teddington TW11 9RS.

COLCHESTER, Archdeacon of; *see* Stroud, Ven. E. C. F.

COLCHESTER, Rev. Halsey Sparrowe, CMG 1968; OBE 1960; MA Oxon; Priest in Charge at Great Tew, Oxfordshire, since 1981; *b* 5 March 1918; *s* of late Ernest Charles Colchester; *m* 1946, Rozanne Felicity Hastings Medhurst, *d* of late Air Chief Marshal Sir Charles Medhurst, KCB, OBE, MC; four *s* one *d*. *Educ:* Uppingham Sch.; Magdalen Coll., Oxford. Served Oxf. and Bucks Lt Inf., 1940–43; 2nd SAS Regt, 1944–46 (despatches); Captain. Joined Diplomatic Service, 1947; FO 1948–50; 2nd Sec., Istanbul, 1950–54; FO 1954–56; Consul, Zürich, 1956–60; 1st Sec., Athens, 1960–64; FO 1964–68; Counsellor, Paris, 1968–72; retired from Diplomatic Service, 1972; Ordinand at Cuddesdon Theological Coll., 1972–73; Deacon, 1973; Priest, 1974; Curate, Minchinhampton, Glos, 1973–76; Vicar of Bollington, Cheshire, 1976–81. *Recreations:* walking, theatre-going, wild flowers. *Address:* Great Tew Vicarage, Oxfordshire OX7 4AG. *T:* Great Tew 293. *Club:* Travellers'.

COLCHESTER, Trevor Charles, CMG 1958; *b* London, 18 April 1909; *s* of Charles Colchester; *m* 1937, Nancy Joan Russell; one *d*. *Educ:* Corpus Christi Coll., Cambridge (MA). Colonial Service, 1931–64; in Kenya, Zanzibar, and Northern Rhodesia. Sec. to Cabinet, Kenya, 1954–57; Permanent Sec., Kenya, 1957–61. Sec., Commonwealth Assoc. of Architects, 1964–74; Consultant, Commonwealth Legal Education Assoc., 1974–84. Hon. FRIBA 1975. *Recreations:* conservation, gardening, fly-fishing, music. *Address:* Plomesgate, Aldeburgh, Suffolk.

COLDRICK, Albert Percival, OBE 1974; FCIT 1972; Chairman: National Health Service SE Thames Appeals Tribunal, since 1974; Executive Committee, Industrial Participation Association, since 1974; *b* 6 June 1913; *s* of Albert Percival and Florence Coldrick; *m* 1938, Esther Muriel Blades; three *s*. *Educ:* Britannia Bridge Elementary Sch.; Wigan Mining and Technical College. Railway Controller, 1933–47; Transport Salaried Staffs' Assoc.: full-time Officer, 1948–62; Sen. Asst Sec., 1962–66; Asst Gen. Sec., 1967; Gen. Sec., 1968–73. Member: General Council, TUC, 1968–73; Industrial Tribunal, 1975–84. Mem., Midlands and West Region Rlys Bd, 1975–77. Chm., Foundn for Industrial Understanding, 1979–. Jt Editor, International Directory of the Trade Union Movement, 1977–. *Recreations:* reading, walking, photography. *Address:* 10 Murray Avenue, Bromley, Kent. *T:* 01–464 4089. *Club:* Reform.

COLDSTREAM, Sir George (Phillips), KCB 1955 (CB 1949); KCVO 1968; QC 1960; *b* 20 Dec. 1907; *s* of late Francis Menzies Coldstream; *m* 1st, 1934, Mary Morna (marr. diss. 1948), *o d* of Major A. D. Carmichael, Meigle, Perthshire; one *d* (and one *d* decd); 2nd, Sheila Hope, *widow* of Lt-Col J. H. H. Whitty, DSO, MC. *Educ:* Rugby; Oriel Coll., Oxford. Called to the Bar, Lincoln's Inn, 1930. Bencher, 1954; Asst to Parly Counsel to Treasury, 1934–39; Legal Asst, Lord Chancellor's Office, 1939–44; Dep. Clerk of the Crown, 1944–54; Clerk of the Crown in Chancery and Permanent Sec. to the Lord Chancellor, 1954–68. Member: British War Crimes Executive, 1944–46; British team, Anglo-Amer. Legal Exchanges, 1961–69; Royal Commn on Assizes and Quarter Sessions, 1967–70; Top Salaries Review Body, 1971–82. Special Consultant, Amer. Inst. of Judicial Admin, NY, 1968–71. Part-time Chm., Industrial Tribunals, 1975–80. Chm., Council of Legal Educn, 1970–73. Pres., Old Rugbeian Soc., 1978–80. Hon. Mem., American Bar Assoc., 1969; Hon. Fellow, Amer. Coll. of Trial Lawyers, 1969. Hon. LLD Columbia Univ., 1966. *Address:* The Gate House, Seaford, East Sussex. *T:* Seaford 892801. *Clubs:* Athenæum; Royal Cruising.

COLDSTREAM, Prof. John Nicolas, FSA; FBA 1977; Yates Professor of Classical Art and Archaeology, University College London, since 1983; *b* 30 March 1927; *s* of Sir John Coldstream and Phyllis Mary Hambly; *m* 1970, Imogen Nicola Carr. *Educ:* Eton; King's College, Cambridge (Class. Tripos, BA 1951, MA 1956). FSA 1964. Nat. Service, Buffs and HLI (Egypt and Palestine), 1945–48. Asst Master, Shrewsbury Sch., 1952–56; Temp. Asst Keeper, Dept of Greek and Roman Antiquities, BM, 1956–57; Macmillan Student, British Sch. at Athens, 1957–60; Bedford College, London: Lectr, 1960–66; Reader, 1966–75; Prof. of Aegean Archaeology, 1975–83. Geddes-Harrower Vis. Prof. of Classical Archaeology, Univ. of Aberdeen, 1983. Mem., Managing Cttee, British Sch. at Athens, 1966–. Chm., Nat. Organizing Cttee, XI Internat. Congress of Classical Archaeol., London, 1978. Mem., Deutsches Archäologisches Inst., 1978; Corr. Mem., Rheinisch-Westfälische Akademie der Wissenschaften, 1984. Editor, Annual of the British School at Athens, 1968–73. *Publications:* Greek Geometric Pottery, 1968; (with G. L. Huxley) Kythera: Excavations and Studies, 1972; Knossos: The Sanctuary of Demeter, 1973; Geometric Greece, 1977; articles in British and foreign classical and archaeological journals. *Recreations:* music, travel. *Address:* 180 Ebury Street, SW1.

COLDSTREAM, Sir William (Menzies), Kt 1956; CBE 1952; painter; Slade Professor of Fine Art, at University College, University of London, 1949–75; Vice-Chairman, Arts Council of Great Britain, 1962–70 (Member, 1953); Fellow of University College, London; Senior Fellow, Royal College of Art; *b* 28 Feb. 1908; *yr s* of George Probyn Coldstream, MB, CM, and Lilian Mercer Tod; *m* 1st, 1931, Nancy Culliford Sharp (marr. diss. 1942); two *d*; 2nd, 1961, Monica Mary Hoyer, *d* of A. E. Monrad Hoyer; one *s* two *d*. *Educ:* privately; Slade Sch. of Fine Art, University Coll., London. Member: London Artists Assoc., 1931; London Group, 1933; work represented in exhibitions of: World's Fair, NY, 1938; British Art Since Whistler, Nat. Gallery, 1939; UN Internat. Exhibition, Paris, 1946; Painting and Sculpture of a Decade, Tate Gallery, 1964; retrospective exhibition, South London Gall., 1962; exhibited Anthony d'Offay Gall., 1976; one-man exhibns, Anthony d'Offay Gall., 1978, 1984. Pictures in the collections of: Tate Gallery, National Gallery of Canada, National Museum of Wales, Ashmolean Museum, Imperial War Museum, Arts Council, British Council, Bristol Art Gallery, etc. Works purchased by Contemporary Art Soc. and Chantrey Bequest, 1940. In association with Claude Rogers and Victor Pasmore founded the Sch. of Drawing and Painting, Euston Road, 1937. Served War of 1939–45 with RE; official War Office Artist, Middle East and Italy, 1943–45. Trustee of National Gallery, 1948–55, 1956–63; Trustee of Tate Gallery, 1949–55, 1956–63; a Dir of Royal Opera House, Covent Garden, 1957–62; Chairman: Art Panel of Arts Council, 1953–62; Nat. Adv. Council on Art Education, 1958–71; British Film Institute, 1964–71. Hon. DLitt: Nottingham, 1961; Birmingham, 1962; London, 1984; Hon. DEd CNAA, 1975. *Address:* University College London, Gower Street, WC1. *T:* 01–387 7050. *Clubs:* Athenæum, MCC.

See also Sir J. W. D. Margetson.

COLE, family name of **Earl of Enniskillen.**

COLE, Viscount; Andrew John Galbraith Cole; pilot, and company director; Captain Irish Guards, 1965; *b* 28 April 1942; *s* and *heir* of 6th Earl of Enniskillen, *qv*; *m* 1964, Sarah, *o d* of Maj.-Gen. J. Keith-Edwards, CBE, DSO, MC, Nairobi; three *d*. *Educ:* Eton. Man. Dir, Kenya Airways, 1979–81. *Address:* c/o Royal Bank of Scotland, 9 Pall Mall, SW1.

COLE, Sir (Alexander) Colin, KCVO 1983 (CVO 1979; MVO 1977); TD 1972; FSA; Garter Principal King of Arms, since 1978; *b* 16 May 1922; *er s* of Capt. Edward Harold Cole, and Blanche Ruby Lavinia (*née* Wallis) (both decd); *m* 1944, Valerie, *o d* of late Capt. Stanley Walter Card; four *s* three *d*. *Educ:* Dulwich; Pembroke Coll. Cambridge; Brasenose Coll., Oxford. BCL Oxon; MA Oxon. Served War of 1939–45, Capt. Coldstream Guards. Barrister-at-law (Inner Temple), 1949. Fitzalan Pursuivant of Arms Extraordinary, 1953; Portcullis Pursuivant of Arms, 1957; Windsor Herald of Arms, 1966. One of the Court of Assistants of the Hon. Artillery Company; Major, 6th (Volunteer) Bn, Queen's Regt, 1971–73, Lt-Col RARO (Brevet, 1973); Hon. Col, 6/7 Bn, Queen's Regt, 1981–86. Mem. Court of Common Council of City of London (Castle Baynard Ward), 1964–; Sheriff, City of London, 1976–77. Freeman of City of London, Freeman and Liveryman, Scriveners', Basketmakers and Painter Stainers Companies of London. Fellow Heraldry Soc.; Hon. Heraldic Adviser, Monumental Brass Soc.; Registrar and Librarian, College of Arms, 1967–74. Knight Principal, Imperial Soc. of Knights Bachelor, 1983–; Pres., Royal Soc. of St George, 1982–. FRSA 1979. OStJ. *Publications:* articles on heraldry and kindred subjects in their appropriate journals; illus. Visitations of London (1568) and Wiltshire (1623) (Harleian Soc.). *Recreations:* art, archæology, architecture, wine-bibbing. *Address:* College of Arms, Queen Victoria Street, EC4. *T:* 01–248 1188; Holly House, Burstow, Surrey. *Clubs:* Cavalry and Guards, City Livery.

COLE, Prof. Boris Norman, BSc(Eng) (London), PhD (Birmingham), WhSch, CEng, FIMechE; Professor of Mechanical Engineering and Head of Department of Mechanical Engineering, University of Leeds, since 1962; *b* 8 Jan. 1924; *s* of James Edward Cole and Gertrude Cole; *m* 1945, Sibylle Duijts; two *s* one *d*. *Educ:* King Edward's Sch., Birmingham. Apprenticed to Messrs Belliss and Morcom Ltd, Engineers, Birmingham. Dept of Mech. Engrg, Univ. of Birmingham: Lectr, 1949–55; Sen. Lectr, 1955–58; Reader, 1958–62; Chm. of Faculty Bd of Applied Sciences, Birmingham Univ., 1955–57 and 1959–62. Dir, Univ. of Leeds Industrial Services Ltd. Member: Smethwick Co. Borough Educn Cttee, 1957–60; Engrg Materials Res. Requirements Bd, 1974–78, and various other govt cttees; Governor, Engrg Industries Training Bd, Leeds Training Centre, 1967–82. Prizewinner, IMechE, 1953 and 1962. *Publications:* numerous in fields of solid and fluid mechanics and in engineering education. *Recreations:* walking, music, social history of engineering. *Address:* 6 Wedgewood Grove, Leeds LS8 1EG. *T:* Leeds 664756.

COLE, (Claude Neville) David, CBE 1977; JP; Deputy Managing Director, International Thomson Organisation plc, 1985–86 (Joint Deputy Managing Director, 1980–84); Chairman: Thomson Books, since 1980; Janes Publishing Co., since 1981; *b* 4 June 1928; 2nd *s* of late W. J. Cole and of Mrs M. J. Cole; *m* 1951, Alma Gwlithyn Williams; one *s* one *d* (one *s* decd). *Educ:* Royal Masonic School; Harvard Business Sch. Journalist: Merthyr Express; South Wales Echo; Daily Graphic (Manchester); Daily Sketch (London); Daily Recorder; Empire News (Cardiff); Editor, Western Mail, Cardiff, 1956–59; Managing Director: Western Mail and Echo Ltd, 1959–67 (now Chm.); Newcastle Chronicle and Journal Ltd, 1967–69; Thomson Regional Newspapers Ltd: Asst Man. Dir and Editorial Dir, 1969–72; Man. Dir and Chief Exec., 1972–82; Chm., 1980–82; Chm. and Chief Exec., Thomson Information Services, 1982–84. Chairman: Rainbird Publishing Gp, 1980–85; Hamish Hamilton, 1982–85; Director: Thomson Organisation (Exec. Bd), 1973–80; Reuters Ltd, 1976–81; Scotsman Publications Ltd; Press Consultancy Services Ltd; Press Assoc. (Chm. 1976–77, 1977–78); Welsh Nat. Opera Co. Ltd, 1960–71; Chairman: Celtic Press Ltd; Cole Cttee on Recruitment of Nurses in Wales, 1961–63; Working Party on Welsh Tourism, 1963–64; Member: Council, Newspaper Soc., 1974– (Pres., 1982); Press Council, 1976–80; PIRA Council, 1984–; Trustee, Reuters Ltd, 1983–. Member: Court of Governors of Univ. of Wales, 1962–; Council of Univ. of Wales, 1962–; Council of Welsh National Sch. of Medicine, 1964–67; Governing Body of Cardiff Coll. of Music and Drama, 1963–67; Council of Cardiff New Theatre Trust, 1964–67; Welsh Nat. Theatre Cttee; Aberfan Disaster Fund, 1966–67; Welsh Hospitals Bd, 1962–67. Vice-Patron, Coun. for Wales, Brit. Empire and Commonwealth Games. Pres., Tenovus. OStJ. FBIM. *Publications:* This and Other Worlds (poems), 1975; Meeting Places and other poems, 1977; Mount of Angels (poems), 1978. *Recreations:* two of the three R's. *Address*: 71 Ashley Gardens, Westminster, SW1. *T*: 01–828 1792. *Club*: East India, Devonshire, Sports and Public Schools.

COLE, Sir Colin; *see* Cole, Sir A. C.

COLE, David; *see* Cole, C. N. D.

COLE, Sir David (Lee), KCMG 1975 (CMG 1965); MC 1944; HM Diplomatic Service, retired; *b* 31 Aug. 1920; *s* of late Brig. D. H. Cole, CBE, LittD, and Charlotte Cole (*née* Wedgwood); *m* 1945, Dorothy (*née* Patton); one *s*. *Educ*: Cheltenham Coll.; Sidney Sussex Coll., Cambridge. MA (1st Cl. Hons History). Served Royal Inniskilling Fusiliers, 1940–45. Dominions Office, 1947; seconded to Foreign Office for service with UK Delegn to UN, New York, 1948–51; First Sec., Brit. High Commn, New Delhi, 1953–56; Private Sec. to Rt Hon. the Earl of Home (Sec. of State for Commonwealth Relations and Lord President of the Council), 1957–60; Head of Personnel Dept, CRO, 1961–63; British Dep. High Comr in Ghana, 1963–64; British High Comr in Malawi, 1964–67; Minister (Political), New Delhi, 1967–70; Asst Under-Sec. of State, FCO, 1970–73; Ambassador to Thailand, 1973–78. *Publications*: Thailand: Water Colour Impressions, 1977; Rough Road to Rome, 1983. *Recreation*: watercolour painting (exhibited RI, RBA). *Address*: 19 Burghley House, Somerset Road, Wimbledon, SW19.

COLE, Eileen Marie Lucy; Chief Executive, Research International (Unilever Ltd), 1973–85 (in Rotterdam, 1973–77); Director (non-executive), Post Office, since 1980; Director (part-time) London Regional Transport, since 1984; *b* 22 April 1924; *d* of Arthur Walter Cole and Mary Agnes Boyd. *Educ*: grammar schs; Girton Coll., Cambridge (BA Hons Econ.). Joined Unilever as trainee, 1948; with associated cos and market res. div. of Unilever, 1948–60; Market Research Controller, Lever Bros Ltd, 1960–64; Research Bureau Ltd: Dir, 1964–67; Chm. and Man. Dir, 1967–72. Vice-Pres., 1979–, and Full Mem., UK Market Res. Soc. (Chm., 1977–79); Council Mem., Women in Management, 1971–; Mem., Careers Advisory Services: Cambridge Univ., 1968–75, 1979–83; Reading Univ., 1970–76, 1979–. FBIM; Mem., Inst. of Dirs. *Publications*: various in learned jls connected with market research. *Recreations*: gardening, cooking, reading, theatre. *Address*: Nicholas Farm, Lower Wield, Alresford, Hants.

COLE, Maj.-Gen. Eric Stuart, CB 1960; CBE 1945; retired; Consultant Director, Granger Associates Ltd, Weybridge; *b* 1906; *s* of John William Cole; *m* 1941, Doris Cole. Served Palestine, 1936–39; War of 1939–45 in Italy, France, Greece (despatches, CBE); Maj.-Gen., 1958; Dir of Telecommunications, War Office, 1958–61. Col Comdt Royal Corps of Signals, 1962–67. Pres., Radio Soc. of GB, 1961. Pres., Army Golf Soc., 1971–73. *Address*: 28 Royal Avenue, Chelsea, SW3. *Clubs*: Army and Navy, MCC, Roehampton.

COLE, Frank; *see* Cole, (George) Francis.

COLE, George; actor on stage, screen, radio and television; *b* 22 April 1925; *m* 1st, 1954, Eileen Moore (marr. diss. 1966); one *s* one *d*; 2nd, 1967, Penelope Morrell; one *s* one *d*. *Educ*: Surrey County Council Secondary Sch., Morden. Made first stage appearance in White Horse Inn, tour and London Coliseum, 1939; Cottage to Let, Birmingham, 1940; West End and on tour, 1940–41; subseq. West End plays included Goodnight Children, New, 1942; Mr Bolfry, Playhouse, 1943. Served in RAF, 1943–47. Returned to stage in Dr Angelus, Phoenix, 1947; The Anatomist, Westminster, 1948; Mr Gillie, Garrick, 1950; A Phoenix too Frequent and Thor with Angels, Lyric, Hammersmith, 1951; Misery Me, Duchess, 1955; Mr Bolfry, Aldwych, 1956; Brass Butterfly, Strand, 1958; The Bargain, St Martin's, 1961; The Sponge Room and Squat Betty, Royal Court, 1962; Meet Me on the Fence (tour), 1963; Hedda Gabler, St Martin's, 1964; A Public Mischief, St Martin's, 1965; Too True To Be Good, Strand, 1965; The Waiting Game, Arts, 1966; The Three Sisters, Royal Court, 1967; Doubtful Haunts, Hampstead, 1968; The Passionate Husband, 1969; The Philanthropist, Mayfair, 1971; Country Life, Hampstead, 1973; Déjà Revue, New London, 1974; Motive (tour), 1976; Banana Ridge, Savoy, 1976; The Case of the Oily Levantine, Guildford, 1977; Something Afoot, Hong Kong, 1978; Brimstone and Treacle, Open Space, 1979; Liberty Hall, Greenwich, 1980; The Pirates of Penzance, Drury Lane, 1982; A Month of Sundays, Duchess, 1986. *Films include*: Cottage to Let, 1941; Morning Departure, Laughter in Paradise, Scrooge, Top Secret, 1949–51; Will Any Gentleman?, The Intruder, 1952; Happy Ever After, Our Girl Friday, 1953; Belles of St Trinian's, 1954; Quentin Durward, 1955; The Weapon, It's a Wonderful World, The Green Man, 1956; Blue Murder at St Trinian's, Too Many Crooks, Don't Panic Chaps, The Bridal Path, 1957–59; The Pure Hell of St Trinian's, Cleopatra, Dr Syn, 1961–62; One Way Pendulum, Legend of Dick Turpin, 1964; Great St Trinian's Train Robbery, 1965; The Green Shoes, 1969; Vampire Lovers, 1970; Girl in the Dark, 1971; The Blue Bird, 1975; Minder on the Orient Express (TV film), 1985. TV Series include Life of Bliss (also radio), A Man of our Times, Don't Forget to Write, Minder (5 series), The Bounder (2 series), Blott on the Landscape, Comrade Dad. *Address*: Donnelly, Newnham Hill Bottom, Nettlebed, Oxon.

COLE, George Francis, (Frank); Chairman: Aero Needles Group plc, since 1981; F. J. Neve & Co. Ltd, since 1982; William Mitchell (Sinkers) Ltd, since 1982; M. B. Wild & Co. Ltd, since 1986; Director: Armstrong Equipment Ltd; Alexander Stenhouse UK Ltd (formerly Reed Stenhouse UK Ltd); Frank Cole (consultancy) Ltd; *b* 3 Nov. 1918; *m*; Gwendoline Mary Laver (decd); two *s* one *d*; Barbara Mary Booth (*née* Gornall). *Educ*: Manchester Grammar Sch. Dir and Gen. Manager, Clarkson Engineers Ltd, 1944–53; Gen. Man., Ariel Motors Ltd (BSA Group), 1953–55; Dir, then Man. Dir, Vono Ltd, 1955–67. Past Chairman: Grovewood Products Ltd; Portways Ltd; R. & W. H. Symington Holdings Ltd; National Exhibition Centre Ltd; Crane's Screw (Hldgs); Stokes Bomford (Holdings) Ltd; Debenholt Ltd; Stokes Bomford (Foods) Ltd; James Cooke (Birmingham) Ltd; Franklin Medical Ltd; Past Director: Duport Ltd; Shipping Industrial Holdings Ltd; G. Clancey Ltd. Pres., Birmingham Chamber of Commerce and Industry, 1968–69. Leader of Trade Missions to West Germany, Yugoslavia, Romania and Hungary. CBIM; Life Governor, Birmingham Univ.; Liveryman of City of London. Radio and Television appearances. *Publications*: press articles on economics, exports, etc. *Recreations*: tennis, oil painting. *Address*: Northcot, 128 Station Road, Balsall Common, Coventry, West Midlands CV7 7FF. *T*: Berkswell 32105.

COLE, Humphrey John Douglas; Deputy Secretary and Chief Economic Adviser, Department of Transport, and Chief Economic Adviser, Department of the Environment, since 1983; *b* 30 Jan. 1928; *s* of late G. D. H. Cole and Dame Margaret I. Cole, DBE; *m* 1955, Hilda Annette Robinson; two *s* one *d*. *Educ*: Winchester Coll.; Trinity Coll., Cambridge. Research, Oxford Inst. of Statistics, 1950–61; Head, Economic Indicators and Foreign Trade, OECD Statistics Div., 1961–66; Dept of Economic Affairs: Senior Economic Adviser (Regional), 1966–67; Asst Dir of Economics, 1967–69; Dir of Economics, Min. of Technology, 1969–70; Dir of Econs (Urban and Highways), DoE, 1970–72; Dir Gen., Econs and Resources, DoE, 1972–76; Chief Economic Advr, DoE and Dept of Transport, 1976–82. *Publications*: articles in Bulletin of Inst. of Statistics, 1950–61. *Recreation*: walking. *Address*: 3 The Mead, W13. *T*: 01–997 8285.

COLE, James S.; *see* Stuart-Cole.

COLE, John Morrison; Political Editor, BBC, since 1981; *b* 23 Nov. 1927; *s* of George Cole and Alice Jane Cole; *m* 1956, Margaret Isobel, *d* of Mr and Mrs John S. Williamson, Belfast; four *s*. *Educ*: Fortwilliam and Skegoneill Primary Schs, Belfast; Belfast Royal Acad.; London Univ. (BA External). Belfast Telegraph, 1945–56: successively reporter, industrial, municipal and political correspondent; The Guardian: Reporter, 1956–57; Labour Correspondent, 1957–63; News Editor, 1963–69; Dep. Editor, 1969–75; The Observer: Asst Editor, 1975; Dep. Editor, 1976–81. *Publications*: The Poor of the Earth, 1976; contrib. to books on British and Irish politics. *Recreations*: reading, travel, tennis. *Address*: BBC Office, House of Commons, Westminster, SW1A 0AA. *T*: 01–219 4765. *Club*: Athenæum.

COLE, Prof. John Peter; Professor of Regional Geography, University of Nottingham, since 1975; *b* Sydney, Australia, 9 Dec. 1928; *s* of Philip and Marjorie Cecelia Cole; *m* 1952, Isabel Jesús Cole (*née* Urrunaga); two *s*. *Educ*: Bromley Grammar Sch.; Univ. of Nottingham (State Schol., BA, MA PhD); Collegio Borromeo, Pavia Univ., Italy (British Council Schol.). Demonstrator, Univ. of Nottingham, 1951–52; Nat. Service with RN, Jt Services Sch. for Linguists, Russian Language Interpreter, 1952–54 (Lt Comdr RNR, retired); Oficina Nacional de Planeamiento y Urbanismo, Lima, Peru, 1954–55; Lectr in Geography, Univ. of Reading, 1955–56; Lectr in Geography, Univ. of Nottingham, 1956–69. Reader, 1969–75; Vis. Lectr or Prof., Univs of Washington, Columbia, Mexico, Valparaíso, Nanjing, Beijing. *Publications*: Geography of World Affairs, 1959, 6th edn 1983; (with F. C. German) Geography of the USSR, 1961, 2nd edn 1970; Italy, 1964; Latin America, 1965, 2nd edn 1975; (with C. A. M. King) Quantitative Geography, 1968; (with N. J. Beynon) New Ways in Geography, 1968, 2nd edn 1982; Situations in Human Geography, 1975; The Development Gap, 1981; Geography of the Soviet Union, 1984; China 1950–2000 Performance and Prospects, 1985; contribs to learned jls, UK and overseas. *Recreations*: travel, languages (using Spanish, Italian, Russian, French, Portuguese), pen drawing and painting, gardening, cricket. *Address*: 10 Ranmore Close, Beeston, Nottingham NG9 3FR. *T*: Nottingham 250409.

COLE, John Sydney Richard, QC (Somaliland); MA; FIArb; Barrister-at-Law; Senior Lecturer, Law School, University of Dublin, 1966–77; *b* 24 Jan. 1907; *o s* of late Rev. R. Lee Cole, MA, BD, Dublin; *m* 1st, 1931, Doreen Mathews (d 1966); one *s* one *d*; 2nd, 1968, Mrs Deirdre Gallet. *Educ*: Methodist Coll., Belfast; Cork Gram. Sch.; Trinity Coll., Dublin (Scholar and Moderator). Master, Royal Coll. Mauritius, 1930–36; Education Officer, Nigeria, 1936–40; Crown Counsel, Nigeria, 1940–46; Attorney-Gen., Bahamas, 1946–51; Somaliland Protectorate, 1951–56; Attorney-Gen. and Minister for Legal Affairs, Tanganyika, 1956–61; retired, 1961. English Legal Draftsman to Government of Republic of Sudan, 1962–65. Reid Prof. of Penal Legislation, Univ. of Dublin, 1965–66. *Publication*: (with W. N. Denison) Tanganyika—the Development of its Laws and Constitution, 1964; Irish Cases on the Law of Evidence, 1972, 2nd edn 1979; Irish Cases on Criminal Law, 1975. *Recreations*: walking, swimming. *Address*: 2 Rus in Urbe, Glenageary, Dublin. *T*: 801993. *Club*: Kildare Street and University (Dublin).

COLE, Prof. Monica M.; Professor of Geography, since 1964 and Director of Research in Geobotany, Terrain Analysis and related Resource Use, since 1975, Royal Holloway and Bedford New College (formerly at Bedford College), University of London; *b* 5 May 1922; *d* of William Henry Parnall Cole and Dorothy Mary Cole (*née* Thomas). *Educ*: Wimbledon County Grammar Sch.; Bedford Coll., Univ. of London. Research Asst, Min. of Town and Country Planning, Cambridge, 1944–45; Postgrad. study, Univ. of London, 1945–46; Lectr in Geography: Univ. of Capetown, 1947; Univ. of Witwatersrand, 1948–51, Univ. of Keele, 1951–64. Assoc. Prof., Univ. of Idaho summer sch., 1952; Vis. Lectr, Univs of Queensland, Melbourne, and Adelaide, 1960. Mem. British delegn Internat. Geographical Congress in: Washington, 1952; Rio de Janeiro, 1956; London, 1964; New Delhi, 1968; Montreal, 1972; Tokyo, 1980; Paris, 1984; Participant, Internat. Savannas Symposia, Venezuela, 1964, S Africa, Australia, 1984. Research: savannas, vegetation, soils and geomorphology: S Africa, 1948–51; Brazil, 1956, 1965; Central and E Africa, 1959; Australia, 1960, 1962, 1963, 1965, 1966, 1967, 1968, 1971, 1972, 1975, 1976, 1980, 1984; Venezuela, 1964; Southern Africa, 1967, 1968, 1978, 1979, 1980, 1983; plant indicators of mineralization: Australia, Africa, Brazil, UK, Finland, Japan, 1964–73, 1977, 1978, 1980, 1984, 1985; remote sensing for terrain analysis: Australia, UK, 1970–76, 1983–85, China, 1981. *Publications*: The Transvaal Lowveld, 1956; South Africa, 1961, 1966; The Savannas: biogeography and geobotany, 1986; contribs to Geograph. Jl, Geography, Trans Inst. Brit. Geographers, S African Geograph. Jl, Trans Instn Mining and Metallurgy, Proc. Royal Soc., Jl Applied Ecology, ESRO, Procs Symposium Frascati, Jl Biogeography, S Africa Geol. Soc., CIMM and COSPAR Conf. Procs, Advances in Space Res., Ecological Studies, Environmental Pollution, and many papers in conf. procs. *Recreations*: painting, photography, tennis, walking, climbing. *Address*: Royal Holloway and Bedford New College, Egham Hill, Egham, Surrey TW20 0EX.

COLE, Richard Raymond Buxton; His Honour Judge Richard Cole; a Circuit Judge, since 1984; *b* 11 June 1937; *s* of Raymond Buxton Cole, DSO, TD, DL, and Edith Mary Cole; *m* 1962, Sheila Joy Rumbold; one *s* one *d*. *Educ*: Dragon School, St Edward's, Oxford. Admitted as Solicitor 1960; Partner in Cole & Cole Solicitors, Oxford, 1962–84; Recorder, 1976–84. Mem., Parole Bd, 1981–83. Pres., Berks, Bucks and Oxon Law Soc., 1981–82. Mem. Governing Body, Dragon Sch., 1975–. Chm., Burford Parish Council, 1976–79, first Town Mayor, 1979. *Recreations*: sport, gardening. *Address*: The Malthouse, Honiley, Kenilworth, Warwickshire CV8 1NP. *Clubs*: MCC; Frewen (Oxford).

COLE, Robert Templeman, CBE 1981; FEng 1982; Chairman, Conder Group plc, since 1979; *b* 14 Dec. 1918; *s* of Percival P. Cole and Amy Gladys Cole (*née* Templeman); *m* 1947, Elspeth Lawson; one *s* one *d*. *Educ*: Harrow; Cambridge Univ. (MA). FIStructE. Served RAF, 1940–46. Hampshire County Council, 1946–47; Founder Partner, Conder Engineering, 1947; Chairman: Conder Engineering Co. Ltd, 1950; Conder International Ltd, 1964. Hon. DSc Southampton, 1980. *Recreations*: gliding, jogging, travel. *Address*: Dragons, 69 Chilbolton Avenue, Winchester, Hampshire. *T*: Winchester 54565.

COLE, Sir (Robert) William, Kt 1981; Chairman, Public Service Board, Australia, since 1978; *b* 16 Sept. 1926; *s* of James Henry and Rita Sarah Cole; *m* 1956, Margaret Noleen Martin; one *s* one *d*. *Educ*: Univ. of Melbourne (BCom). Joined Australian Public Service, 1952; Res. Officer, Treasury, 1952–57; Technical Asst, IMF, Washington, 1957–59; various positions, Treasury, 1959–70; Dir, Bureau of Transport Econs, Dept of Shipping and Transport, 1970–72; First Asst Sec., Gen. Financial and Economic Policy Div., Treasury, 1972–76; Australian Statistician, 1976; Sec., Dept of Finance, 1977–78. *Recreations*: reading, fishing, wine. *Address*: 8 Scarborough Street, Red Hill, ACT 2603, Australia. *T*: Canberra 957089. *Club*: Commonwealth (Canberra).

COLE, Robin John, PhD; Head of Life Sciences, Technology, Planning and Research Division, Central Electricity Generating Board; *b* 6 Aug. 1935; *s* of John Richard Cole and Amy Cole (*née* Collins); *m* 1956, Jane Legg; three *d*. *Educ*: East Grinstead Grammar School; University College London (BSc); King's College London (PhD). Research at Univ. of Glasgow, 1961–65; Lectr, Sch. of Biological Scis, Univ. of Sussex, 1965, Reader in Developmental Genetics, 1972, Professor, 1976; Dep. Chief Scientist, DHSS, 1982–85. Mem., ESRC, 1984–85. *Publications:* original papers in developmental biology, experimental haematology, genetic toxicology. *Recreations:* fine and decorative arts; contemporary crafts, especially ceramics. *Address:* c/o CERL, Kelvin Avenue, Leatherhead, Surrey KT22 7SE. *T:* Leatherhead 374488.

COLE, Ven. Ronald Berkeley; Archdeacon Emeritus of Leicester; *b* 20 Oct. 1913; *s* of James William and Florence Caroline Cole; *m* 1943, Mabel Grace Chapman; one *s* one *d*. *Educ:* Bishop's Coll., Cheshunt. Registrar, London County Freehold and Leasehold Properties Ltd, 1934–40. Deacon, 1942; Priest, 1943; Curate, Braunstone, Leicester, 1942–48; Succentor, Leicester Cathedral, 1948–50; Vicar of St Philip, Leicester, 1950–73; Archdeacon of Loughborough, 1953–63, of Leicester, 1963–80; Residentiary Canon of Leicester Cathedral, 1977–80. Hon. Chaplain, 1949–53, Examining Chaplain, 1956–80, to Bishop of Leicester. RD of Repps, dio. Norwich, 1983–86. Hon. DLitt Geneva Theol. Coll., 1972. *Recreations:* gardening, motoring. *Address:* Harland Rise, 70 Cromer Road, Sheringham, Norfolk NR26 8RT.

COLE, Sir William; *see* Cole, Sir R. W.

COLE, William Charles, LVO 1966; DMus; FSA, FRAM, FRCM; FRCO; The Master of the Music at the Queen's Chapel of the Savoy since 1954; Member Council, Royal College of Organists, since 1960 (Hon. Treasurer, 1964–85; President, 1970–72); Member, Central Music Library Council (formerly Committee), since 1964, Chairman, since 1973; *b* 9 Oct. 1909; *s* of Frederick George Cole and Maria (*née* Fry), Camberwell, London; *m* 1st, Elizabeth Brown Caw (*d* 1942); three *d*; 2nd, Winifred Grace Mitchell; one *s*. *Educ:* St Olave's Grammar Sch.; RAM. Organist and Choirmaster, Dorking Parish Church, 1930; Music Master, Dorking County Sch., 1931; served War of 1939–45, in Air Ministry; Hon. Musical Dir, Toynbee Hall, 1947–58; Prof. of Harmony and Composition, and Lectr in History of Music, Royal Academy of Music, 1945–62; Royal Academy of Dancing: Lectr, 1948–62; Chm., Music Cttee, 1961–68; Mem., Exec. Council, 1965–68; Mem., Grand Council, 1976–; Conductor: People's Palace Choral Soc., 1947–63; Leith Hill Musical Festival, 1954–77; Sec., Associated Bd of Royal Schools of Music, 1962–74; Hon. Sec., Royal Philharmonic Soc., 1969–80. President: Surrey County Music Assoc., 1958–76; The London Assoc. of Organists, 1963–66. Member: Governing Cttee, Royal Choral Soc., 1972– (Chm., Music Cttee, 1975–78); Exec. Cttee, Musicians' Benevolent Fund, 1972–. Mem. Education Cttee, Surrey CC, 1951–62. *Publications:* Rudiments of Music, 1951; chapter on Development of British Ballet Music, in The Ballet in Britain, 1962; The Form of Music, 1969; articles in various musical jls and in various learned jls on stained glass. *Recreation:* stained glass. *Address:* Barnacre, Wood Road, Hindhead, Surrey. *T:* Hindhead 4917. *Club:* Garrick.

COLE, Maj.-Gen. William Scott, CB 1949; CBE 1946; *b* 29 March 1902; *s* of late William Scott Cole; *m* 1st, 1948, Kathleen Winifred Coleing (marr. diss. 1970); one *d*; 2nd, 1971, Alice Rose Pitts, *widow* of Dr G. T. Pitts. *Educ:* Victoria Coll., Jersey; RMA Woolwich. Commissioned into the Corps of Royal Engineers, 1921. Served War of 1939–45; Temp. Brig., 1943; Substantive Col, 1945; Subs. Brig., 1951; temp. Maj.-Gen., 1955; Subs. Maj.-Gen., 1956; retd 1958. *Club:* Army and Navy.

COLE-HAMILTON, Arthur Richard; Chief General Manager, Clydesdale Bank PLC, since 1982; *b* 8 May 1935; *s* of John Cole-Hamilton, *qv*; *m* 1963, Prudence Ann; one *s* two *d*. *Educ:* Ardrossan Academy; Loretto School; Cambridge Univ. (BA). CA. Commissioned Argyll and Sutherland Highlanders, 1960–62. Brechin Cole-Hamilton & Co. (Chartered Accountants), 1962–67; Clydesdale Bank: Asst Manager, Finance Corp., 1967; Manager, Finance Corp. and Money Market, 1971; Asst Manager, Chief London Office, 1971; Supt of Branches, 1974; Head Office Manager, 1976; Asst Gen. Manager, 1978; Gen. Manager, 1979; Dep. Chief Gen. Manager, Feb. 1982; Chief Gen. Manager, July 1982; Dir, 1984–. *Recreation:* golf. *Address:* Clydesdale Bank, 30 St Vincent Place, Glasgow G1 2HL. *T:* 041–248 7070. *Clubs:* Western, Royal Scottish Automobile (Glasgow); Highland Brigade; Royal and Ancient Golf, Prestwick Golf.

COLE-HAMILTON, John, CBE 1954; DL; *b* 15 Oct. 1899; *s* of late Col A. R. Cole-Hamilton; *m* 1930, Gladys Cowie; one *s* two *d*. *Educ:* Royal Academy, Irvine. Served European War, 1914–19, with RFC and RAF. Major, Home Guard, 1942. DL for County of Ayr, 1951. *Address:* Beltrim House, Kilwinning, Ayrshire.
See also A. R. Cole-Hamilton.

COLEBROOK, Philip Victor Charles, CEng, MIChemE; retired 1984; Managing Director of Pfizer Ltd, 1958–84; Vice-President, Pfizer International, 1967–84; Managing Director, Imperial Continental Gas Association, 1973–84 (Director, 1971; Director, CompAir Ltd, 1980–84); Director: Calor Group Ltd, 1969–84; Century Power & Light Ltd, 1980–84; Contibel SA (Belgium), 1978–84; *b* 8 March 1924; *s* of Frederick Charles Colebrook and Florence Margaret (*née* Cooper); *m* 1946, Dorothy Ursula Kemp; one *s* three *d*. *Educ:* Andover Grammar Sch.; Guildford Technical Coll.; Battersea Polytechnic, London. Served War of 1939–45, RNVR. Joined Pfizer as Works and Production Manager, 1952; appointed Dir, Pfizer Ltd, 1956; Chm. and Man. Dir, Pfizer Gp, 1961–69; Man. Dir, Calor Gas Holding Co., 1969–80. Member: NHS Affairs Cttee, Assoc. of the British Pharmaceutical Industry, 1963–67; CBI Cttee on State Intervention in Private Business, 1975–78. Trustee and Mem. of Steering Cttee, Univ. of Kent at Canterbury, 1964–65. *Publication:* Going International, 1972. *Recreations:* sailing, ski-ing, golf. *Clubs:* Royal Automobile; Royal Cinque Ports Yacht.

COLEBY, Anthony Laurie; Assistant Director, Bank of England, since 1980; *b* 27 April 1935; *s* of Dr Leslie James Moger Coleby and Laurie Coleby (*née* Shuttleworth); *m* 1966, Rosemary Melian Elisabeth, *d* of Sir Peter Garran, *qv*; one *s* two *d*. *Educ:* Winchester; Corpus Christi, Cambridge (BAEcon, MA). Bank of England: joined, 1961; Assistant Chief, Overseas Dept, 1969; Adviser, Overseas Dept, 1972; Dep. Chief Cashier, 1973. Personal Asst to Managing Director, International Monetary Fund, 1964–67. *Recreations:* choral singing, railways and transport. *Address:* Bank of England, EC2R 8AH. *T:* 01–601 4444. *Club:* Overseas Bankers'.

COLECLOUGH, Peter Cecil; Chairman, Howard Machinery Ltd, 1969–82 (Director, 1950–82); Director: National Westminster Bank (Chairman SE Region), until 1986; NCR Ltd; *b* 5 March 1917; *s* of late Thomas James Coleclough and of Hilda Emma (*née* Ingram); *m* 1944, Pamela Beresford (*née* Rhodes); one *s* (and one *s* decd). *Educ:* Bradfield. Served War, Cheshire Yeomanry, 1939; commnd into Roy. Warwickshire Regt, 1940; served until 1946. Mem., FBI/CBI Council, 1962–72; Chm., E Region, CBI, 1971–72; Leader, OECD/BIAC Investment Gp to Ceylon, 1968 and 1969; Chm., Meat and Livestock Commn, 1971–74; Pres., Agricl Engrs Assoc., 1971–72; Pres., Royal Warrant Holders Assoc., 1971–72. Chm., Appeals and Management Cttee, S Essex Medical Educn and Research Trust, 1969–75. CBIM 1976; FRSA 1977. *Recreation:* fishing. *Address:* Longlands Hall, Stonham Aspal, Stowmarket, Suffolk IP14 6AR. *T:* Stowmarket 711242. *Club:* Naval and Military.

COLEGATE, Raymond, CBE 1982; FCIT 1983; FRAeS 1985; Member, Civil Aviation Authority, since 1974; Group Director, Economic Regulation, (formerly Economic Services), since 1977; *b* 31 Aug. 1927; *s* of Ernest William and Violet Colegate; *m* 1961, Sally Healy; one *s* one *d*. *Educ:* County Sch. for Boys, Gravesend; LSE. BA London (Hons History). Joined BoT, 1949; seconded to Central Statistical Office, 1952–53; Asst Private Sec. to President, 1955–56; seconded to Treasury, 1957–59; seconded to EFTA Secretariat, Geneva and Brussels, 1960–64; CRE Dept, BoT, 1964–67; Aviation Dept, BoT/DTI, 1967–72; Head, Economic Policy and Licensing Div., CAA, 1972–75; Head, Economic Dept, CAA, 1975–77. *Publications:* all anonymous. *Recreations:* music, travel, thinking. *Address:* 40 Lebanon Park, Twickenham TW1 3DG.

COLEMAN, Alice Mary; Reader in Geography, King's College, London, since 1965; *b* 8 June 1923; *d* of Bertie Coleman and Elizabeth Mary (*née* White). *Educ:* Clarendon House Sch.; Furzedown Training Coll. (Cert. of Educn); Birkbeck Coll., Univ. of London (BA Hons 1st Cl.); King's Coll., Univ. of London (MA with Mark of Distinction). FKC 1980. Geography Teacher, Northfleet Central Sch. for Girls, 1943–48; Geography Dept, King's Coll., London: Asst Lectr, 1948; Lectr, 1951; Sen. Lectr, 1963. Vis. Prof. for Distinguished Women Social Scientists, Univ. of Western Ontario, 1976; BC/Mombusho Prof. of Geog., Hokkaido Univ. of Educn at Asahikawa, 1985. Initiated and directed Second Land Utilisation Survey of Britain, 1960–. Gill Meml Award, RGS, 1963; The Times-Veuve Clicquot Award, 1974. *Publications:* The Planning Challenge of the Ottawa Area, 1969; Utopia on Trial, 1985; 120 land-use maps in eleven colours at the scale of 1:25,000; 150 academic papers. *Recreation:* reading. *Address:* King's College, Strand, WC2R 2LS. *T:* 01–836 5454, ext. 2610.

COLEMAN, Arthur Percy; Deputy Director and Secretary to the Board of Trustees, British Museum (Natural History), 1976–82 (Museum Secretary, 1965–76); *b* 8 Feb. 1922; *s* of late Percy Coleman and Gladys May Coleman (*née* Fisher); *m* 1948, Peggy (*née* Coombs); two *d*. *Educ:* Wanstead Co. High Sch.; Bristol Univ. War Service in 1st King George V Own Gurkha Rifles, 1943–47; Min. of Public Building and Works, 1948–61; HM Treasury, 1961–64. *Recreations:* wild life, music. *Address:* Candleford, Hurst, Beaminster, Dorset. *T:* Beaminster 862155.

COLEMAN, Bernard, CMG 1986; HM Diplomatic Service, retired; Ambassador to Paraguay, 1984–86; *b* 3 Sept. 1928; *s* of William Coleman and Ettie Coleman; *m* 1950, Sonia Dinah (*née* Walters); two *d*. *Educ:* Alsop High Sch., Liverpool. HM Forces (RAEC), 1946–48. Entered Foreign (later Diplomatic) Service, 1950; FO, 1950–53; Lima, 1953–56; Detroit, 1956–59; Second Secretary (Information): Montevideo, 1959–62; Caracas, 1962–64; First Sec. (Inf.), Caracas, 1964–66; FCO, 1967–69; First Sec. (Inf.), Ottawa, 1969–73; FCO, 1973–74; seconded to DTI, 1974–75; Consul-Gen., Bilbao, 1976–78; First Sec. (Commercial), Dublin, 1979–80; High Commissioner, Tonga, 1980–83. *Recreations:* golf, reading, walking, travel. *Club:* Royal Commonwealth Society.

COLEMAN, Prof. Donald Cuthbert, LittD; FBA 1972; Professor of Economic History, Cambridge University, 1971–81, now Emeritus; Fellow of Pembroke College, Cambridge; *b* 21 Jan. 1920; *s* of Hugh Augustus Coleman and Marian Stella Agnes Cuthbert; *m* 1954, Jessie Ann Matilda Child (*née* Stevens). *Educ:* Haberdashers' Aske's, Hampstead (now Elstree); London Sch. of Economics, Univ. of London. Worked in London, in insurance, 1937–39; admitted LSE, 1939. Served War, in Army, 1940–46: commissioned Royal Warwickshire Regt, 1941; transf. RA, 1942; active service in N Africa, Italy and Greece. Returned to LSE, 1946; BSc(Econ), 1st Cl. Hons. 1949; Leverhulme Research Studentship, 1949–51; PhD 1951. Lectr in Industrial History, LSE, 1951–58; Reader in Economic History, 1958–69; Prof. of Economic History, 1969–71; Hon. Fellow, LSE, 1984. Visiting Associate Prof. of Economics, Yale Univ., 1957–58. English Editor, Scandinavian Economic History Review, 1952–61; Editor, Economic History Review, 1967–72. FRHistS. *Publications:* The British Paper Industry, 1495–1860, 1958; Sir John Banks: Baronet and Businessman, 1963; Courtaulds: an economic and social history, vols 1 & 2, 1969, vol. 3, 1980; What Has Happened to Economic History? (Inaug. Lect.), 1972; Industry in Tudor and Stuart England, 1975; The Economy of England 1450–1750, 1977; (ed with A. H. John) Trade, Government and Economy in Pre-Industrial England, 1977; (ed with P. Mathias) Enterprise and History, 1984; numerous articles in: Economic History Review, Economica, Historical Jl, etc. *Recreations:* music, cricket, coarse gardening. *Address:* Over Hall, Cavendish, Sudbury, Suffolk. *T:* Glemsford 280325.

COLEMAN, Donald Richard, CBE 1979; JP; DL; MP (Lab) Neath since 1964; *b* 19 Sept. 1925; *s* of late Albert Archer Coleman and of Winifred Marguerite Coleman; *m* 1949, Phyllis Eileen (*née* Williams) (*d* 1963); one *s*; *m* 1966, Margaret Elizabeth Morgan; one *d*. *Educ:* Cadoxton Boys' Sch., Barry; Cardiff Technical Coll. Laboratory Technician, Welsh National Sch. of Medicine, Cardiff, 1940–42; Central Tuberculosis Laboratory, Cardiff, 1942–46; Sen. Technician, Swansea Technical Coll., 1946–50; University Coll., Swansea, 1950–54; Metallurgist, Research Dept, Steel Co. of Wales Ltd, Abbey Works, Port Talbot, 1954 until election to Parliament. PPS to Minister of State for Wales (later Secretary of State for Wales), 1967–70; an Opposition Whip, 1970–74; a Lord Comr, HM Treasury, 1974–79, Vice-Chamberlain of the Household, 1978–79; Opposition Spokesman on Welsh Affairs, 1981–83. Delegate to Council of Europe and WEU, 1968–73; Mem., Panel of Chairmen, H of C, 1984–. JP City of Swansea, 1962–. DL West Glamorgan, 1985. *Address:* Penderyn, 18 Penywern Road, Bryncoch, Neath, West Glamorgan. *T:* Neath 4599.

COLEMAN, John Ennis; Legal Adviser, Department of Education and Science, since 1983; *b* 12 Nov. 1930; *o s* of late Donald Stafford Coleman and Dorothy Jean Balieff (*née* Ennis); *m* 1958, Doreen Gwendoline Hellinger; one *s* one *d*. *Educ:* Dean Close Sch., Cheltenham; Dulwich Coll.; Worcester Coll., Oxford (MA). Solicitor (Hons), 1957. Legal Asst, Treasury Solicitor's Dept, 1958; Senior Legal Asst, 1964; Asst Solicitor, 1971; Under Sec. (Legal), Depts of Industry and Trade, 1980–83. *Address:* 2 Penrith Close, Reigate, Surrey RH2 0LP. *T:* Redhill 63347.

COLEMAN, Rt. Rev. Peter Everard; *see* Crediton, Bishop Suffragan of.

COLEMAN, Prof. Robert George Gilbert; Professor of Comparative Philology, University of Cambridge, since 1985; Fellow of Emmanuel College, Cambridge, since 1960; *b* 2 Oct. 1929; *s* of George Gilbert Coleman and Rosina Emily (*née* Warner); *m* 1958, Dorothy Gabe; one *s*. *Educ:* Rongotai and Wellington Colls, NZ; Victoria Univ. of Wellington (MA 1951); Emmanuel Coll., Cambridge (BA 1954; Burney Prize (shared), 1955; MA 1980). Lecturer: Dept of Humanity, Aberdeen Univ., 1955–60; Faculty of Classics, Cambridge Univ., 1960–85; Tutor, 1963–71, Librarian, 1980–85, Emmanuel Coll., Cambridge. *Publications:* (ed, with commentary) Vergil's Eclogues, 1977; essays and papers in classical and philological jls. *Recreations:* music, conversation, exploring strange towns, golf. *Address:* 60 Gilbert Road, Cambridge CB4 3PE. *T:* Cambridge 357348.

COLEMAN, Ronald Frederick, DSc; CChem, FRSC; Government Chemist, since 1981; *b* 10 Nov. 1931; *s* of late Frederick George Coleman and of Dorothy Alice Coleman (*née* Smith); *m* 1954, Maureen Mary Salt; one *s* one *d*. *Educ:* King Edward VI Sch., Birmingham; College of Technology, Birmingham (BSc, DSc). Chance Brothers Glassworks, Smethwick, 1949–54; UKAEA: Aldermaston, 1954–71; Harwell, 1972;

Laboratory of the Government Chemist, 1973–77 and 1981–; National Physical Laboratory, 1977–81. Visiting Professor: Kingston Polytechnic, 1981–; Royal Holloway and Bedford New Coll. Pres., British Acad. of Forensic Sciences, 1982–83. *Publications:* various papers on analytical chemistry, nuclear chemistry and forensic science. *Recreations:* music, squash, gardening. *Address:* 8 Hogarth Way, Hampton, Middx TW12 2EL. *T:* 01–941 4255.

COLEMAN, Terry, (Terence Francis Frank); reporter and author; *b* 13 Feb. 1931; *s* of J. and D. I. B. Coleman; *m* 1st, 1954, Lesley Fox-Strangeways Vane (marr. diss.); two *d*; 2nd, 1981, Vivien Rosemary Lumsdaine Wallace; one *s* one *d*. *Educ:* 14 schs. LLB London. Formerly: Reporter, Poole Herald; Editor, Savoir Faire; Sub-editor, Sunday Mercury, and Birmingham Post; Reporter and then Arts Corresp., The Guardian, 1961–70, Chief Feature Writer, 1970–74; Special Writer with Daily Mail, 1974–76; The Guardian: Chief Feature Writer, 1976–79, writing mainly political interviews, inc. last seven British Prime Ministers; NY Correspondent, 1981; special corresp., 1982–. Feature Writer of the Year, British Press Awards, 1982. *Publications:* The Railway Navvies, 1965 (Yorkshire Post prize for best first book of year); A Girl for the Afternoons, 1965; (with Lois Deacon) Providence and Mr Hardy, 1966; The Only True History: collected journalism, 1969; Passage to America, 1972; (ed) An Indiscretion in the Life of an Heiress (Hardy's first novel), 1976; The Liners, 1976; The Scented Brawl: collected journalism, 1978; Southern Cross, 1979; Thanksgiving, 1981; The Door to the Open Sea, 1986. *Recreations:* cricket, opera, circumnavigation. *Address:* 18 North Side, SW4. *Clubs:* National Liberal; MCC.

COLEMAN, Rev. Prof. William Robert, DD; Professor of Humanities, York University, Toronto; *b* Ulverton, Quebec, 16 Aug. 1917; *s* of Rev. Stanley Harold Coleman and Mary Ann Coleman (*née* Armstrong); *m* 1947, Mary Elizabeth Charmes, *er d* of Thomas Summers and Marion Wilson; one *s* two *d*. *Educ:* St Mary's Collegiate Inst.; Brantford Collegiate Inst.; University Coll. and Wycliffe Coll. (BD); Univ. of Toronto (MA); Union Theological Seminary, New York (STM); Univs of Cambridge and Edinburgh. Deacon, 1942; Priest, 1943; Curate, Church of the Epiphany, Sudbury, Ont., 1942–43; Priest-in-charge, 1943–45; post-graduate study, 1945–47; Prof. of Religious Philosophy and Ethics, Wycliffe Coll., 1947–50; Dean of Divinity and Harold Prof., Bishop's Coll., Lennoxville, Quebec, 1950–52; Principal, Huron Coll., London, Ont., 1952–61; Bishop of Kootenay, 1961–65. FRSA, London. DD Wycliffe Coll., 1951. DD (Hon.) Huron Coll., 1961; DD (Hon.) Trinity Coll., Toronto, 1962. *Publications:* contributed to: In Such an Age (ed W. C. Lockhart), 1951; The Church in the Sixties (ed. P. Jefferson), 1962. *Address:* 6 Kensington Place, Toronto, Ontario M5T 5K4, Canada.

COLERAINE, 2nd Baron *cr* 1954, of Haltemprice; **James Martin Bonar Law;** *b* 8 Aug. 1931; *s* of 1st Baron Coleraine, PC, and Mary Virginia (*d* 1978), *d* of A. F. Nellis, Rochester, NY; *S* father, 1980; *m* 1st, 1958, Emma Elizabeth (marr. diss.), *o d* of late Nigel Richards; two *d*; 2nd, 1966, Patricia, *yr d* of Major-Gen. R. H. Farrant, *qv*; one *s* two *d*. *Educ:* Eton; Trinity College, Oxford. *Heir:* *s* Hon. James Peter Bonar Law, *b* 23 Feb. 1975. *Address:* 5 Kensington Park Gardens, W11.

See also Baron Ironside.

COLERIDGE, family name of **Baron Coleridge.**

COLERIDGE, 5th Baron *cr* 1873, of Ottery St Mary; **William Duke Coleridge;** *b* 18 June 1937; *s* of 4th Baron Coleridge, KBE, and of Cecilia Rosamund, *d* of Adm. Sir William Wordsworth Fisher, GCB, GCVO; *S* father, 1984; *m* 1st, 1962, Everild Tania (marr. diss. 1977), *d* of Lt-Col Beauchamp Hambrough, OBE; one *s* two *d*; 2nd, 1977, Pamela, *d* of G. W. Baker, *qv*; two *d*. *Educ:* Eton; RMA Sandhurst. Commissioned into Coldstream Guards, 1958; served King's African Rifles, 1962–64; commanded Guards Parachute Company, 1970–72. *Heir:* Hon. James Duke Coleridge, *b* 5 June 1967. *Address:* The Chanters House, Ottery St Mary, Devon EX11 1DQ. *T:* Ottery St Mary 2417.

COLERIDGE, David Ean; Chairman, Sturge Holdings PLC, since 1978; Deputy Chairman of Lloyd's, 1985; *b* 7 June 1932; *s* of Guy Cecil Richard Coleridge, MC and Katherine Cicely Stewart Smith; *m* 1955, Susan Senior; three *s*. *Educ:* Eton. Glanvill Enthoven, 1950–57; R. W. Sturge & Co., 1957–: Dir, 1966–; Chm., A. L. Sturge (Holdings) Ltd (now Sturge Holdings PLC), 1978–; Dir. R. A. Edwards (Holdings) Ltd, 1985–. Member: Cttee of Lloyd's Underwriting Agents Assoc., 1974–82 (Chm., 1981–82); Council and Cttee of Lloyd's, 1983–86. *Recreations:* golf, racing, gardening, family. *Address:* Spring Pond, Wispers, near Midhurst, W Sussex. *T:* Midhurst 3277; 21 Margaretta Terrace, SW3. *T:* 01–351 1773. *Clubs:* City of London, Mark's.

COLERIDGE, Lady (Marguerite) Georgina; *b* 19 March 1916; *d* of 11th Marquess of Tweeddale; *m* 1941, Arthur Coleridge, *yr s* of John Duke Coleridge; one *d*. *Educ:* home, abroad as a child. Joined National Magazine Co.: Circulation Dept, 1937; Advertisement Dept., 1938; joined Country Life, 1945; Editor of Homes and Gardens, 1949–63; Chm., Inst. of Journalists (London District), 1954, Fellow 1970; Chm., Women's Press Club, 1959 (Pres., 1965–67). Dir, Country Life Ltd, 1962–74; Dir, George Newnes Ltd, 1963–69; Publisher: Homes and Gardens; Woman's Journal, 1969–71; Ideal Home, 1970–71; Dir, Special Projects, IPC Women's Magazines, 1971–74; Consultant: IPC Women's Magazines, 1974–82; Public Relations Counsel Ltd, 1974–85 (Dir, 1978–85). Mem., Internat. Assoc. of Women and Home Page Journalists, 1968–74; Associate, Women in Public Relations, 1972–; Associate Mem., Ladies Jockeys Assoc. of GB, 1973–; Founder Mem., Media Soc. Ltd (Inst. of Journalists Foundn), 1973–76; Member: Information Cttee, Brit. Nutrition Foundn, 1975–79; Information Cttee, RCP, 1977–81; Vice-Pres., Greater London Fund for the Blind, 1981; Pres., Friends of Moorfields, 1981. Freeman, Worshipful Co. of Stationers and Newspapermakers, 1973. *Publications:* Grand Smashional Pointers (book of cartoons), 1934; I Know What I Like (clichés), 1959; That's Racing, 1978. *Recreations:* racing, writing, cooking; nothing highbrow. *Address:* 33 Peel Street, W8 7PA. *T:* 01–727 7732.

COLES, Arthur John, CMG 1984; HM Diplomatic Service; Ambassador to Jordan, since 1984; *b* 13 Nov. 1937; *s* of Arthur Strixton Coles and Doris Gwendoline Coles; *m* 1965, Anne Mary Sutherland Graham; two *s* one *d*. *Educ:* Magdalen Coll. Sch., Brackley; Magdalen Coll., Oxford (BA 1960). Served HM Forces, 1955–57. Joined HM Diplomatic Service, 1960; Middle Eastern Centre for Arabic Studies, Lebanon, 1960–62; Third Sec., Khartoum, 1962–64; FO (later FCO), 1964–68; Asst Political Agent, Trucial States (Dubai), 1968–71; FCO, 1971–75; Head of Chancery, Cairo, 1975–77; Counsellor (Developing Countries), UK Perm. Mission to EEC, 1977–80; Head of S Asian Dept, FCO, 1980–81; Private Sec. to Prime Minister, 1981–84. *Recreations:* walking, cricket, bird-watching, reading, music. *Address:* c/o Foreign and Commonwealth Office, King Charles Street, SW1. *Club:* United Oxford & Cambridge University.

COLES, Bruce; *see* Coles, N. B. C.

COLES, Prof. Bryan Randell, DPhil; FInstP; Pro-Rector, since 1986 and Professor of Solid State Physics, since 1966, Imperial College, University of London; Dean of the Royal College of Science, 1984–86; *b* 9 June 1926; *s* of Charles Frederick Coles and Olive Irene Coles; *m* 1955, Merivan Robinson; two *s*. *Educ:* Canton High Sch., Cardiff; Univ. of Wales, Cardiff (BSc); Jesus Coll., Univ. of Oxford (DPhil). FInstP 1972. Lectr in Metal Physics, Imperial Coll., London, 1950; Res. Fellow, Carnegie Inst. of Technol., Pittsburgh, 1954–56. Vis. Prof., Univ. of Calif, San Diego, 1962 and 1969; Hill Vis. Prof., Univ. of Minnesota, 1983. Vice-Pres., Inst. of Physics, 1968–72; Mem. Physics Cttee, SRC, 1972–76 (Chm. 1973–76); Chm., Neutron Beam Cttee, 1985–. Chm. Bd of Dirs, Taylor & Francis Ltd (Scientific Publishers), 1976–. *Publications:* Electronic Structures of Solids (with A. D. Caplin), 1976; papers on structure, electrical properties, superconductivity and magnetic properties of metals and alloys in Philosoph. Magazine, Advances in Physics, Jl of Physics. *Recreations:* music, natural history, theatre. *Address:* 61 Courtfield Gardens, SW5. *T:* 01–373 3539.

COLES, Gerald James Kay; QC 1976; **His Honour Judge Gerald Coles;** a Circuit Judge, since 1985; *b* 6 May 1933; *o s* of James William Coles and Jane Elizabeth Coles; *m* 1958, Kathleen Yolande, *e d* of Alfred John Hobson, FRCS, and Kathleen Elizabeth Hobson; three *s*. *Educ:* Coatham Sch., Redcar; Brasenose Coll., Oxford; Harvard Law Sch., Harvard Univ. Meritorious Award, Hastings Schol., Queen's Coll., Oxford, 1949; Akroyd Open Schol. 1950; BA 1954, BCL 1955, Oxon; Westengard Schol., Harvard Law Sch., 1955; LLM 1956. Called to Bar, Middle Temple, 1957; practised at Bar, London and NE Circuit, 1957–85; Prosecuting Counsel to Inland Revenue, 1971–76; a Recorder, 1972–85. *Recreations:* music, theatre, photography. *Address:* Redwood, Dean Lane, Hawkworth, Guiseley, Leeds, Yorks LS20 8NY. *Clubs:* Carlton; Leeds (Leeds).

COLES, Prof. John Morton, ScD, PhD; FBA 1978; Professor of European Prehistory, University of Cambridge, 1980–86; Fellow of Fitzwilliam College, since 1963; *b* 25 March 1930; *s* of Edward John Langdon Coles and Alice Margaret (*née* Brown); *m* 1985, Bryony Jean Orme; two *s* two *d* of previous marr. *Educ:* Woodstock, Ontario; Univ. of Toronto (BA); Univ. of Cambridge (MA, ScD); Univ. of Edinburgh (PhD). Research Fellow, Univ. of Edinburgh, 1959–60; Asst Lectr, 1960–65, Lectr, 1965–76, Reader, 1976–80, Univ. of Cambridge. President, Prehistoric Soc., 1978–82. FSA 1963, Vice-Pres., 1982–86. *Publications:* The Archaeology of Early Man (with E. Higgs), 1969; Field Archaeology in Britain, 1972; Archaeology by Experiment, 1973; The Bronze Age in Europe (with A. Harding), 1979; Experimental Archaeology, 1979; Prehistory of the Somerset Levels (with B. Orme), 1980; The Archaeology of Wetlands, 1984; (with B. J. Coles) Sweet Track to Glastonbury: the Somerset Levels in prehistory, 1986; contrib. Proc. Prehist. Soc., Antiquaries Jl, Antiquity, Somerset Levels Papers, etc. *Recreations:* music, wetlands, woodlands. *Address:* Fursdon Mill Cottage, Thorverton, Devon EX5 5JS. *T:* Exeter 860125.

COLES, Kenneth George, BE; CEng, FIMechE, FAIM; Chairman, Conveyor Co. of Australia Pty Ltd, since 1957; *b* Melbourne, 30 June 1926; *s* of Sir Kenneth Coles; *m* 1950, Thalia Helen (marr. diss. 1980); one *s* two *d*. *Educ:* The King's Sch., Parramatta, NSW; Sydney Univ. (BE 1948). MIE(Aust); FIMechE 1969; FAIM 1959. Gained engrg experience in appliance manufacturing and automotive industries Nuffield Aust. Pty Ltd, Gen. Motors Holdens Pty Ltd and Frigidaire, before commencing own business manufacturing conveyors, 1955; Chm & Man. Dir, K. G. Coles & Co. Pty Ltd, 1955–76, Chm. 1976–; Chm. & Man. Dir, K. G. C. Magnetic Tape Pty Ltd, 1973–80. Director: Australian Oil & Gas Corp. Ltd, 1969– (Dep. Chm., 1984–); A. O. G. Minerals Ltd, 1969– (Dep. Chm., 1984–); G. J. Coles & Coy Ltd, 1976–; Electrical Equipment Ltd, 1976–84; Permanent Trustee Co. Ltd, 1978–; Centre for Industrial Technol. Ltd, 1985–; Chm., Innovation Council of NSW Ltd, 1984 (Dir, 1982–). Gen. Councillor, NSW Br., Metal Trades Industries Assoc. of Australia, 1976–; Member: Internat. Solar Energy Soc., 1957–; Science & Industry Forum, Australian Academy of Science, 1983–. Mem. Council, Nat. Roads and Motorists Assoc., NSW, 1986–. Councillor and Mem. Bd of Governors, Ascham Sch., 1972–82; Employers' Rep., NSW Secondary Schs Bd, 1979–83. Fellow, Senate, Sydney Univ., 1983–. *Address:* 224 Rosemont Avenue, Woollahra, NSW 2025, Australia. *T:* 328.6084. *Clubs:* Union (Sydney), Sydney Rotary; Royal Sydney Golf; RACV (Melbourne).

COLES, Dame Mabel Irene, DBE 1971 (CBE 1965); President: Royal Women's Hospital, Melbourne, 1968–72; Australian Women's Liberal Club, since 1965; Director, Asthma Foundation of Victoria, 1965; *d* of late E. Johnston; *m* 1927, Sir Edgar Coles (*d* 1981); one *s* two *d*. Associated with Royal Women's Hosp. for 30 years; Chairman: Ladies Cttee for (two) $1,000,000 appeals; (two) Door Knock Appeals; Asthma Ladies' Appeal Cttee; Patroness: Family Planning Assoc. of Vic.; Rheumatism and Arthritis Assoc. of Vic.; Frankston Musical Soc. Life Mem., Australian Nat. Meml Theatre Ltd. Trustee, Mayfield Centre. *Recreations:* dogs, horses, walking. *Address:* Hendra, Williams Road, Mount Eliza, Vic. 3930, Australia. *Clubs:* Alexandra, Peninsula Country (Melbourne).

COLES, Norman, CB 1971; *b* 29 Dec. 1914; *s* of Fred and Emily Coles; *m* 1947, Una Valerie Tarrant; five *s*. *Educ:* Hanson High Sch., Bradford; Royal College of Science; City and Guilds Coll. Head, Armament Dept, RAE, 1959; Dir Gen. Equipment Research and Development, Min. of Aviation, 1962; Dep. Controller: of Aircraft (RAF), Min. of Technology, 1966–68; of Guided Weapons, Min. of Technology, 1968–69; Dep. Chief Adviser (Research and Studies), MoD, 1969–71; Dep. Controller, Establishments and Research, MoD, 1971–75. *Recreations:* carpentry, crossword puzzles. *Address:* Castle Gate, 27 Castle Hill, Banwell, Weston-super-Mare, Avon. *T:* Banwell 822019.

COLES, (Norman) Bruce (Cameron); QC 1984; a Recorder, since 1986; *b* 28 Feb. 1937; *s* of Sir Norman Coles, *qv*; *m* 1961, Sally Fenella Freeman; one *s* three *d*. *Educ:* Melbourne Grammar Sch.; Univ. of Melbourne (LLB); Magdalen Coll., Oxford Univ. (BCL). 2nd Lieut, 6th Bn Royal Melbourne Regt, 1956–59. Associate to Sir Owen Dixon, Chief Justice of High Court of Australia, 1959–60; called to English Bar, Middle Temple, 1963; admitted to Bar of Supreme Court of Victoria, 1964. Assistant Recorder, 1982. Mem. Council, Oxfam, 1985–. *Recreations:* hill walking, cycling, theatre, music. *Address:* Fountain Court, Temple, EC4 9DH. *T:* 01–353 7356. *Clubs:* Gentian Mountaineering (Glos); Cyclist Touring (Surrey); Melbourne Cricket (Melbourne).

COLES, Sir Norman (Cameron), Kt 1977; Chairman, G. J. Coles & Co. Ltd, Melbourne, 1968–79; *b* 10 Sept. 1907; *s* of George Coles and Annie Cameron Coles; *m* 1932, Dorothy Verna Deague; one *s* one *d*. *Educ:* Launceston C of E Grammar Sch., Tas; Trinity Grammar Sch., Kew, Vic. FASA, FCIS. Joined G. J. Coles & Co. Ltd, Australia, 1924: Company Secretary, 1933; Director, 1949–79; Finance Dir, 1963–67; Man. Dir, 1967–75. Mem., Victorian Plastic Surgery Unit, 1978–. *Recreations:* golf, gardening. *Address:* (office) G. J. Coles & Co. Ltd, 236 Bourke Street, Melbourne, Vic 3000, Australia. *T:* 667–4603; (home) 28 Somers Avenue, Malvern, Vic 3144, Australia. *Clubs:* Athenæum (Melbourne), Probus (Melbourne) (Foundn Pres. 1983–84); Melbourne Cricket, Victoria Racing, Peninsula Golf (all Victoria).

See also N. B. C. Coles.

COLFOX, Sir (William) John, 2nd Bt *cr* 1939; JP; DL; *b* 25 April 1924; *yr* and *o* surv. *s* of Sir (William) Philip Colfox, 1st Bt, MC, and Mary (Frances) Lady Colfox (*d* 1973); *S* father, 1966; *m* 1962, Frederica Loveday, *d* of Adm. Sir Victor Crutchley, VC, KCB, DSC; two *s* three *d*. *Educ:* Eton. Served in RNVR, 1942–46, leaving as Lieut. Qualified Land Agent, 1950. Chm., Land Settlement Assoc., 1980–81. JP Dorset, 1962, High Sheriff of Dorset, 1969, DL Dorset, 1977. *Heir: s* Philip John Colfox, *b* 27 Dec. 1962. *Address:* Symondsbury House, Bridport, Dorset. *T:* Bridport 22956.

COLGATE, Dennis Harvey, MM 1944; Registrar of Family Division of Supreme Court, 1975–84; *b* 9 Oct. 1922; *s* of Charles William and Marjorie Colgate; *m* 1961, Kathleen (*née* Marquis); one *d. Educ:* Varndean Sch., Brighton; Univ. Coll. of South West, Exeter; King's Coll., London (LLB). HM Forces, 1942–47; Principal Probate Registry, 1947–64 (Estabt Officer 1959–64); District Probate Registrar of High Court, Manchester, 1964–75. Consulting Editor, Tristram and Coote's Probate Practice, 1975–84. *Publications:* (ed jtly) Rayden on Divorce, 7th edn 1958 and 8th edn 1960; (ed jtly) Atkin's Court Forms (Probate), 2nd edn 1974, rev. 1985. *Recreations:* walking, do-it-yourself. *Address:* 10 Frogmore Close, Hughenden Valley, High Wycombe, Bucks HP14 4LN. *T:* Naphill 2659.

COLGRAIN, 3rd Baron *cr* 1946, of Everlands; **David Colin Campbell;** *b* 24 April 1920; *s* of 2nd Baron Colgrain, MC, and of Margaret Emily, *d* of late P. W. Carver; *S* father, 1973; *m* 1st, 1945, Veronica Margaret (marr. diss. 1964), *d* of late Lt-Col William Leckie Webster, RAMC; one *s* one *d*; 2nd, 1973, Mrs Sheila M. Hudson. *Educ:* Eton; Trinity Coll., Cambridge. Served War of 1939–45, 9th Lancers. Manager, Grindlays Bank Ltd, India and Pakistan, 1945–49; joined Antony Gibbs and Sons Ltd, 1949, Director, 1954–83, retired; Chm., Alexander and Berendt Ltd, 1967–. Jt Treasurer, Royal Assoc. for Disability and Rehabilitation. *Heir: s* Hon. Alastair Colin Leckie Campbell [*b* 16 Sept. 1951; *m* 1979, Annabel Rose, *yr d* of Hon. Robin Warrender, *qv;* one *s*]. *Address:* Bushes Farm, Weald, Sevenoaks, Kent.

COLHOUN, Prof. John; Barker Professor of Cryptogamic Botany, University of Manchester, 1960–80, now Emeritus; Dean, Faculty of Science, 1974 and 1975; Pro-Vice-Chancellor, 1977–80; *b* 15 May 1913; *yr s* of late James Colhoun and Rebecca Colhoun, Castlederg, Co. Tyrone; *m* 1949, Margaret, *e d* of late Prof. Gilbert Waterhouse, LittD, and Mary Elizabeth, *e d* of Sir Robert Woods; three *d. Educ:* Edwards Sch., Castlederg, Co. Tyrone; The Queen's Univ. of Belfast; Imperial Coll. of Science, London Univ. BSc, MAgr (Belfast), PhD, DSc (London), MSc (Manchester), DIC. Min. of Agriculture for Northern Ireland: Research Asst, 1939–46; Senior Scientific Officer, 1946–50; Principal Scientific Officer, 1951–60. The Queen's Univ., Belfast: Asst Lecturer in Agricultural Botany, 1940–42; Asst Lectr 1942–45, Jun. Lectr 1945–46, Lectr 1946–54, Reader 1954–60, in Mycology and Plant Pathology. Warden of Queen's Chambers, 1942–49. FLS 1955. FIBiol 1963. President: British Mycological Soc., 1963; The Queen's Univ. Assoc., 1960–61; The Queen's Univ. Club, London, 1983–85. Chm., Fedn of British Plant Pathologists, 1968. Jt Editor, Phytopathologische Zeitschrift, 1973–. *Publications:* Diseases of the Flax Plant, 1947; Club Root Disease of Crucifers caused by *Plasmodiophora brassicae* Woron, 1958; numerous papers in Annals of Applied Biology, Annals of Botany, Trans Brit. Mycological Soc., Nature, Phytopath. Z. *Address:* 12 Southdown Crescent, Cheadle Hulme, Cheshire SK8 6EQ. *T:* 061–485 2084. *Club:* Athenæum.

COLIN, Rt. Rev. Gerald Fitzmaurice, MA; an Assistant Bishop, Diocese of Lincoln, since 1979; *b* 19 July 1913; *s* of Frederick Constant Colin and Jemima Fitzmaurice; *m* 1941, Iris Susan Stuart Weir; three *s* two *d. Educ:* Mountjoy Sch.; Trinity Coll., Dublin. MA (TCD) 1946. Deacon, 1936; Priest, 1937. St George's, Dublin, 1938; Chancellor's Vicar, St Patrick's Cathedral, Dublin, 1938; RAFVR, 1939–47; Vicar of Frodingham, Dio. of Lincoln, 1947–66; Bishop Suffragan of Grimsby, 1966–78. Canon of Lincoln Cathedral, 1960; Rural Dean of Manlake, 1960; Proctor in Convocation, 1960–65, 1966–70. *Recreation:* fishing. *Address:* Orchard Close, St Mary's Lane, Louth, Lincs. *T:* Louth 602600.

COLL BLASINI, Néstor; Grand Cross, Libertador Simón Bolivar; Venezuelan Ambassador to Israel, since 1984; *b* 10 June 1931; *s* of Guillermo Coll Nuñez and María de Lourdes Blasini de Coll; *m* 1952, Maritza Barrios de Coll; five *s* one *d. Educ:* Colegio La Salle, Caracas; Univ. Católica Andres Bello, Caracas. Entered Foreign Service, 1958, as Third Secretary, later Second Sec.; Head of Office that revised Reciprocal Commercial Treaty between Venezuela and USA; Economic Counsellor, Colombia; Minister Counsellor, Head of Cabinet of Min. of Foreign Affairs; Director of Frontiers, 1969; Ambassador of Venezuela in Panama, 1969–71; Asst Director General, Min. of For. Affairs, actg as Dir Gen. on several occasions, 1971–74; Ambassador of Venezuela: in Sweden and Finland, 1974–76; in Turkey, 1976–78; in Finland, 1978–79; in Italy, 1979–82; in UK, 1982–84. Member: Sociedades Bolivarianas, Venezuela, Italy and Honduras; Academia Tiberina, Rome; Sociedad de Estudios Históricos Mirandinos, Venezuela. Grand Cross: Cavalieri di Gran Croce (Italy), Condor de los Andres (Bolivia), Libertador San Martin (Argentina), Yugoslav Flag (Yugoslavia), Polar Star (Sweden), and other decorations. *Publications:* La Opinion Publica en America Latina (Colombia), 1963; various articles in Latin American newspapers. *Recreations:* reading, music, golf. *Address:* Textile Centre, Kaufman 2, 16th Floor, Tel Aviv 68012, Israel. *Club:* Lagunita Country (Caracas).

COLLARD, Douglas Reginald, OBE 1976; HM Diplomatic Service, retired; Director, Anglo-Arab Association, since 1976; Director, Arab British Centre; *b* 7 April 1916; *s* of late Hebert Carthew Collard and late Mary Ann (*née* Pugh); *m* 1947, Eleni Alkmini Kiortsi (marr. diss. 1969), Greece; two *s* three *d. Educ:* Wallasey Grammar Sch.; privately. Army Service, 1940–46 (despatches); UNRRA, Greece, 1946–47; Asst Commercial Adviser, British Econ. Mission to Greece, 1947; Consul, Patras, Greece, 1947–52; Develt Div., Beirut, 1952–54; 2nd Sec. (Commercial); Khartoum, 1954–56; Copenhagen, 1958–61; FCO, 1956–58 and 1967–69; 1st Sec. (Commercial): Tripoli, 1961–65; Lahore, 1965–67; Montevideo, 1969–71; 1st Sec., later Counsellor (Commercial), Algiers, 1971–73; Consul-Gen., Bilbao, 1973–76. *Recreations:* reading, walking. *Address:* 21 Collingham Road, SW5 0NU. *T:* 01–373 8417.

COLLARD, Prof. Patrick John, JP; MD, FRCP; Professor of Bacteriology and Director of Department of Bacteriology and Virology, University of Manchester, 1962–80, now Professor Emeritus; *b* 22 April 1920; *s* of Rupert John Collard; *m* 1st, 1948, Jessie Robertson (marr. diss. 1955); one *s* one *d*; 2nd, 1956, Kathleen Sarginson; one *s* one *d. Educ:* St Bartholomew's Medical Coll., Univ. of London. Qualified MB, BS, 1942; MD 1951. House Appts, 1942–44. RAMC, 1944–48. Registrar, Westminster Hospital, 1948–50; Lectr, Guy's Hosp. Med. Sch., 1950–54; Prof. of Bacteriology, University Coll. Ibadan, Nigeria, 1954–62; Visiting Professor: London Sch. of Hygiene and Tropical Medicine, 1979; Univ. of Jordan, 1982. FRCP 1972. JP Manchester, 1973. *Publications:* The Development of Microbiology, 1976; papers in: BMJ, Lancet, Jl Soc. Gen. Microbiol., Jl of Hygiene, West African Med. Jl, etc. *Recreations:* talking, reading, playing chess, bookbinding. *Address:* Honor Oak Cottage, Kingham, Oxford. *T:* Kingham 335. *Club:* Athenæum.

COLLENS, John Antony; an Assistant Auditor General, National Audit Office, since 1984; *b* 19 Nov. 1930; *s* of John Collens and Emily Charlotte Collens (*née* Gomm); *m* 1957, Josephine Stark; three *s. Educ:* Harrogate Grammar Sch. Mem. CIPFA, 1979. National Service, 1950–52. Exchequer and Audit Department: Asst Auditor, 1949; Sen. Auditor, 1962; Dep. Dir of Audit, 1973; Dir of Audit, 1977; Dep. Sec., Exchequer and Audit Dept, 1979–83. *Recreations:* cricket, tennis, walking. *Address:* 141 Park Avenue, Orpington, Kent BR6 9ED. *T:* Orpington 29133.

COLLETT, Christopher; JP; Partner in Arthur Young, Chartered Accountants, London; *b* 10 June 1931; 2nd *s* of Sir Henry Seymour Collett, 2nd Bt, and Lady (Ruth Mildred) Collett (*née* Hatch); *m* 1959, Christine Anne, *d* of Oswald Hardy Griffiths, Nunthorpe, Yorks; two *s* one *d. Educ:* Harrow; Emmanuel Coll., Cambridge. MA; FCA. Nat. Service, RA and Surrey Yeomanry; Captain TA (RA). Articled with Cassleton Elliott & Co., Chartered Accountants, 1954; qualified, 1958; Partner, Ghana 1960, London 1963; firm merged to become Josolyne Miles and Cassleton Elliott, Josolyne Layton Bennett & Co., and now Arthur Young. Mem., Court of Common Council (Broad Street Ward), City of London, 1973–79; Alderman, 1979–; Sheriff, City of London, 1985–86. Master, Glovers' Co., 1981; Member: Guild of Freemen, 1983–; Worshipful Co. of Chartered Accts in Eng. and Wales, 1984–; City of London TAVR Cttee, 1980–; Council Mem., Action Research for the Crippled Child, 1984–. Governor, Haberdashers' Aske's Schs, Elstree, 1982–; Hon. Treas., Lee House, Wimbledon. Pres., Broad Street Ward Club, 1979–. JP City of London, 1979. *Recreations:* gardening, fishing. *Address:* 121 Home Park Road, Wimbledon, SW19. *Clubs:* City of London, City Livery.

COLLETT, Sir Ian (Seymour), 3rd Bt *cr* 1934; *b* 5 Oct. 1953; *s* of David Seymour Collett (*d* 1962), and of Sheila Joan Collett (who *m* 1980, Sir James William Miskin, *qv*), *o d* of late Harold Scott; *S* grandfather, 1971; *m* 1982, Philippa, *o d* of James R. I. Hawkins, Preston St Mary, Suffolk; one *s* one *d. Educ:* Lancing College, Sussex. *Recreations:* fishing, cricket, shooting. *Heir: s* Anthony Seymour Collett, *b* 27 Feb. 1984. *Address:* Glebe House, Aspall, Debenham, Suffolk. *Club:* MCC.

COLLETT, Sir (Thomas) Kingsley, Kt 1968; CBE 1956; formerly Director, Adams Bros & Shardlow Ltd (Creative Printers), London and Leicester, retired 1971; *b* 7 March 1906; 6th *s* of late Sir Charles Collett, 1st Bt, Bromley, Kent (Lord Mayor of London, 1933–34); *m* 1930, Beatrice Olive (*d* 1986), *d* of late Thomas H. Brown, Bickley, Kent. *Educ:* Bishop's Stortford Coll. HM Lieut for City of London, 1958. Freeman, City of London, 1930; Liveryman, Worshipful Co. of Distillers, 1934 (Master, 1960–61); Mem., Ct of Common Coun., City of London (Ward of Bridge), 1945–83; Chairman: City of London Freemen's Sch. Cttee, 1949–52; Port of London Health Authority, 1953; City Lands Cttee and Chief Commoner, 1955; Special Cttee, 1956–66; Policy and Parly Cttee, 1967–70. Corp. of London Rep. on Bd of Port of London Authority, 1959–67; Mem., Pollution Control Cttee, PLA, 1966–73; Chm., Lord Mayor's Appeal Cttee; Kennedy Mem. Fund, 1964; Churchill Fund, 1965; Vice-Chm., Lord Mayor's Appeal Cttee: cleaning St Paul's Cath, 1963–64; Attlee Meml Fund, 1967. Governor, Royal Hospitals; Chm., Governing Council, Bishop's Stortford Coll., 1964–76; Life Mem., Court of The City Univ., 1970–84, Hon. DLitt 1980. Chm., East India and Sports Club, 1959–66; Past Pres., City Pickwick Club. Dep. Governor, Irish Soc., 1975. Chevalier, Mil. Order of Christ (Portugal), 1956. *Recreation:* shooting. *Address:* 5 Moorlands, Wilderness Road, Chislehurst, Kent. *Club:* East India, Devonshire, Sports and Public Schools.

COLLEY, Maj.-Gen. David Bryan Hall, CBE 1982 (OBE 1977; MBE 1968); Director General of Transport and Movements (Army), since 1986; *b* 5 June 1934; *s* of Lawson and Alice Colley; *m* 1957, Marie Thérèse (*née* Préfontaine); one *s* one *d. Educ:* King Edward's Sch., Birmingham; RMA, Sandhurst. Commissioned: RASC, 1954; RCT, 1965; regimental appts in Germany, Belgium, UK, Hong Kong and Singapore; Student, Staff Coll., Camberley, 1964; JSSC Latimer, 1970; CO Gurkha Transport Regt and 31 Regt, RCT, 1971–74; Staff HQ 1st (British) Corps, 1974–77; Comd Logistic Support Gp, 1977–80; Col AQ (Ops and Plans) and Dir Admin. Planning, MoD (Army), 1980–82; Comd Transport 1st (British) Corps, 1983–86. Freeman, City of London, 1986; Hon. Liveryman and Mem. Court, Worshipful Co. of Carmen, 1986. *Recreation:* travel. *Address:* c/o Midland Bank, Redditch, Worcs B97 4EA. *Club:* Army and Navy.

COLLEY, Surg. Rear-Adm. Ian Harris, OBE 1963; Chairman, Medical and Survival Committee, Royal National Lifeboat Institution, since 1984; *b* 14 Oct. 1922; *s* of Aubrey James Colley and Violet Fulford Colley; *m* 1952, Joy Kathleen (*née* Goodacre). *Educ:* Hanley Castle Grammar Sch.; King's Coll., London and King's Coll. Hosp. MB, BS 1948; DPH; MFOM; FFCM. Royal Naval Medical Service, 1948–80: MO HMS Cardigan Bay and HMS Consort, 1949–52; service with Fleet Air Arm, 1955–78: as PMO HMS Centaur; MO i/c Air Med. Sch.; Pres., Central Air Med. Bd; Comd MO to Flag Officer, Naval Air Comd; Surg. Rear Adm. (Ships and Estabs), 1978–80, retired. QHP 1978–80. Consultant in Aviation Medicine; former Examr to Conjoint Bd, Royal College of Surgeons and Royal College of Physicians for DipAvMed. Hon. Consultant in Occup. Medicine to RNLI. CStJ 1980. *Publications:* papers in field of aviation medicine. *Address:* c/o Royal Bank of Scotland, Inveraray, Argyll PA32 8TY.

COLLIE, Alexander Conn, MBE 1979; JP; Chairman: Aberdeen Licensing Board, since 1984; Aberdeen Tourist Board, since 1984; Lord Provost of the City of Aberdeen, 1980–84; Member of Aberdeen District Council, since 1975; *b* 1 July 1913; *s* of late Donald and Jane Collie; *m* 1942, Elizabeth Keith Macleod (*d* 1985); two *s. Educ:* Ferryhill Sch., Aberdeen; Ruthrieston Sch., Aberdeen. Member: Aberdeen Town Council, 1947–75; Aberdeen Harbour Board, 1947–74; North of Scotland Hydro-Electric Consultative Council, until Oct. 1980; Past Member: Scottish Sports Council; Scottish Bakers' Union Exec. Council. JP Aberdeen, 1956. OStJ 1981. *Address:* (home) 43 Brimmond Place, Aberdeen AB1 3EN. *T:* Aberdeen 874972.

COLLIER, family name of **Baron Monkswell.**

COLLIER, Andrew James, CB 1976; Chairman, Tripod Engineering Ltd, since 1985; Deputy Secretary, Department of Health and Social Security, 1973–82; *b* 12 July 1923; *s* of Joseph Veasy Collier and Dorothy Murray; *m* 1950, Bridget, *d* of George and Edith Eberstadt, London; two *d. Educ:* Harrow; Christ Church, Oxford. Served Army, RHA, 1943–46. Entered HM Treasury, 1948; Private Sec. to: Sir Henry Wilson Smith, 1950; Sir Leslie Rowan, 1951; Chancellors of the Exchequer, 1956–59 (Rt Hon. Harold Macmillan, Rt Hon. Peter Thorneycroft, Rt Hon. Heathcoat Amory); Asst Sec., 1961; Under-Sec., 1967; Under-Secretary: Civil Service Dept, 1968–71; DHSS, 1971–73. Consultant, 1983–; Chairman: CSTI Health Care Scientific Adv. Cttee Industrial Liaison Unit; Chelsea Housing Improvement Soc.; Health and Educn Cttee, British Consultants Bureau; Director: SMS Europe Ltd; Medical Adv. and Res. Consultants Ltd. *Address:* 10 Lambourne Avenue, SW19 7DW. *Club:* Athenæum.

COLLIER, Andrew John; Chief Education Officer, Lancashire County Council, since 1980; *b* 29 Oct. 1939; *s* of Francis George Collier and Margaret Nancy (*née* Nockles); *m* 1964, Gillian Ann (*née* Churchill); two *d. Educ:* University College Sch.; St John's Coll., Cambridge (MA). Assistant Master, Winchester Coll., 1962–68; Hampshire County Educn Dept, 1968–71; Buckinghamshire County Educn Dept, 1971–77; Dep. Chief Educn Officer, Lancashire, 1977–80. Member: Open Univ. Vis. Cttee, 1982–; Council for Accreditation of Teacher Educn, 1984–. Liveryman, Worshipful Company of Wheelwrights, 1972. Mem. Council, Univ. of Lancaster, 1981–86. *Recreations:* music, walking, gardening. *Address:* County Hall, Preston, Lancs PR1 8RJ. *T:* Preston 263646. *Clubs:* Athenæum; Leander (Henley-on-Thames).

COLLIER, Kenneth Gerald; Principal, College of the Venerable Bede, Durham, 1959–75; *b* 1910; *m* 1938, Gwendoline Halford; two *s*. *Educ:* Aldenham Sch.; St John's Coll., Cambridge. MA 1935; Diploma in Education (Oxon) 1945. Technical translation, Stockholm, 1931–32; Schoolmaster, 1933–41; Royal Ordnance Factories, 1941–44; Physics Master, Lancing Coll., 1944–49; Lectr, St Luke's Coll., Exeter, 1949–59. Editor, Education for Teaching, 1953–58. Chm., Assoc. Teachers in Colls and Depts of Education, 1964–65. Vis. Prof. of Education, Temple Univ., Philadelphia, 1965, 1968. Consultant to Council for Educational Technology, 1971–80. British Council tours to India, Brazil and Portugal, 1976–79. Hon. Research Fellow, Univ. of East Anglia, 1978–81. *Publications:* The Science of Humanity, 1950; The Social Purposes of Education, 1959; New Dimensions in Higher Education, 1968; (ed) Innovation in Higher Education, 1974; (ed) Values and Moral Development in Higher Education, 1974; (ed) Evaluating the New BEd, 1978; (ed) The Management of Peer-Group Learning, 1983; contribs to: Sixth Form Citizens, 1950; Religious Faith and World Culture (New York), 1951; Internat. Encyclopedia of Educn, 1985; articles in educational and other jls. *Recreations:* local history; music; the film. *Address:* 4 Robson Terrace, Shincliffe, Durham DH1 2NL. *T:* Durham 41647.

COLLIER, Lesley Faye, (Mrs Nicholas Dromgoole); Principal Dancer with the Royal Ballet, since 1972; *b* 13 March 1947; *d* of Roy and Mavis Collier; *m* 1977, Nicholas Arthur Dromgoole. *Educ:* The Royal Ballet School, White Lodge, Richmond. Joined Royal Ballet, 1965; has danced most principal roles in the Royal repertory. *Address:* c/o Royal Ballet Company, 155 Talgarth Road, W14.

COLLIER, Prof. Leslie Harold, MD, DSc; FRCP, FRCPath; Professor of Virology, University of London, 1966–86, now Emeritus; *b* 9 Feb. 1921; *s* of late Maurice Leonard Collier and Ruth (*née* Phillips); *m* 1942, Adeline Barnett; one *s*. *Educ:* Brighton Coll.; UCH Med. Sch. MD London 1953; DSc London 1968; MRCP 1969; FRCPath 1975; FRCP 1980. House Phys., UCH, 1943; served RAMC, 1944–47; Asst Pathologist, St Helier Hosp., Carshalton, 1947; Lister Inst. of Preventive Medicine, 1948–78: Head, Dept of Virology, 1955–74; Dep. Dir, 1968–74; Dir, Vaccines and Sera Laboratories, 1974–78; Prof. of Virology and Sen. Lectr, Jt Dept of Virology, London Hosp. Med. Coll. and St Bartholomew's Hosp. Med. Coll., 1978–86; Hd, Dept of Virology, London Hosp. Med. Coll., 1982–86. Hon. Dir, MRC Trachoma Unit, 1957–73; Hon. Consultant in Virology, Tower Hamlets HA, 1978–86. Chibret Gold Medal, Ligue contre le Trachome, 1959; Luys Prize, Soc. de Médecine de Paris, 1963. *Publications:* papers in med. and scientific jls. *Recreations:* various. *Address:* Brontë Cottage, 89 South End Road, NW3 2RJ. *T:* 01–794 6331.

COLLIER-WRIGHT, John Hurrell, CBE 1966; Member, British Transport Docks Board, 1974–77; *b* 1 April 1915; *s* of John Robert Collier-Wright and Phyllis Hurrell Walters; *m* 1940, Pauline Beatrice Platts; three *s* (and one *s* decd). *Educ:* Bradfield Coll.; Queen's Coll., Oxford (MA). FCIT. Traffic Apprentice, LNER, 1936–39. Served War of 1939–45, RE, France, Iraq and Iran (Lt-Col; US Legion of Merit). East African Railways and Harbours, 1946–64; Chief Commercial Supt; joined British Transport Docks Bd, 1964; Chief Commercial Man., 1964–70; Asst Man. Dir, 1970–72; Dep. Man. Dir, 1972–77; Dir, British Transport Advertising, 1966–81. *Address:* Laurel Cottage, 71 Main Street, Mursley, Bucks MK17 0RT. *Club:* Nairobi (Kenya).

COLLIGAN, John Clifford, CBE 1963 (OBE 1957); Director-General, Royal National Institute for the Blind, 1950–72; Secretary, British Wireless for the Blind Fund, 1950–84; Hon. Treasurer and Life Member, World Council for the Blind, since 1969 (British Representative, 1954–69); *b* 27 Oct. 1906; *s* of John and Florence Colligan, Wallasey, Cheshire; *m* 1st, 1934, Ethel May Allton (*d* 1948); one *s* one *d*; 2nd, 1949, Frances Bird. *Educ:* Liscard High Sch., Wallasey. Dep. Sec., National Institute for the Blind, 1945–49. *Publications:* The Longest Journey, 1969; various articles on blind welfare. *Recreations:* fishing, gardening. *Address:* 3 Jonathans, Dene Road, Northwood, Mddx. *T:* Northwood 21988.

COLLIN, Maj.-Gen. Geoffrey de Egglesfield, CB 1975; MC 1944; DL; *b* 18 July 1921; *s* of late Charles de Egglesfield Collin and Catherine Mary Collin; *m* 1949, Angela Stella (*née* Young); one *s* three *d*. *Educ:* Wellington Coll., Berks. Served War of 1939–45: commissioned as 2nd Lt, RA, 1941; in India and Burma, 1942–45. Qualified as Army Pilot, 1946; attended Staff Coll., Camberley, 1951; Instructor at RMA, Sandhurst, 1954–56; served Kenya, 1956–58; JSSC, 1958; Instructor at Staff Coll., Camberley, 1960–62; comd 50 Missile Regt, RA, 1962–64; GSO 1 Sch. of Artillery, 1965; CRA, 4th Div., 1966–67; attended Imperial Defence College, London, 1968; Comdt, Royal School of Artillery, 1969–71; Maj.-Gen. RA, HQ BAOR, 1971–73; GOC North East District, York, 1973–76; retired 1976. Col Comdt, RA, 1976–83 (Rep. Col Comdt, 1982). Part-time Chm., CS Selection Bd, 1981– (Mem., 1978). Hon. Dir, Great Yorks Show, 1976–87. DL N Yorks, 1977. *Recreations:* fishing, ornithology, music, keeping garden under control. *Address:* Old Vicarage, Roecliffe, York YO5 9LY. *Club:* Army and Navy.

COLLIN, Jack, MA, MD; FRCS; Clinical Reader in Surgery, University of Oxford, and Fellow of Trinity College, Oxford, since 1980; *b* 23 April 1945; *s* of John Collin and Amy Maud Collin; *m* 1971, Christine Frances Proud; three *s* one *d*. *Educ:* Univ. of Newcastle (MB BS, MD); Mayo Clinic, Minn. University of Newcastle: Demonstrator in Anatomy, 1969–70; Sen. Res. Associate, 1973–75; Registrar in Surgery, Royal Victoria Infirmary, Newcastle, 1971–80; Mayo Foundn Fellow, Mayo Clinic, Minn, 1977. Moynihan Fellow, Assoc. of Surgeons of GB and Ire., 1980. Arris and Gale Lectr, RCS, 1976. Jacksonian Prize, RCS, 1977. *Publications:* papers on vascular surgery, intestinal myoelectrical activity and absorption, parenteral nutrition and pancreatic transplantation. *Recreations:* gardening, walking. *Address:* Nuffield Department of Surgery, John Radcliffe Hospital, Oxford. *T:* Oxford 64711.

COLLINGRIDGE, Jean Mary, (Mrs A. R. Collingridge); Chief Executive, Employment Division of the Manpower Services Commission, 1979–82, retired; Chairman, Kent Area Manpower Board, since 1983; Member, Civil Service Appeal Board, since 1984; *b* 9 March 1923; *d* of Edgar and Elsie Bishop; *m* 1951, Albert Robert Collingridge; one *d*. *Educ:* County High School, Loughton, Essex; University College London (BSc Econ); LSE (Social Science Course). Asst Personnel Officer, C. and J. Clark, 1945–49; Personnel Manager, Pet Foods Ltd, 1949–50; Ministry of Labour/Department of Employment: Personnel Management Adviser and Industrial Relations Officer, 1950–65; Regl Industrial Relations Officer/Sen. Manpower Adviser, 1965–71; Assistant Secretary, Office of Manpower Economics 1971–73, Pay Board 1973–74, Dept of Employment HQ 1974–76; Dep. Chief Exec., Employment Service Div. of Manpower Services Commn, 1976–79. *Publication:* (jtly) Personnel Management in the Small Firm, 1953. *Recreations:* home and garden. *Address:* Trelawny, Sandy Lane, Ivy Hatch, Sevenoaks, Kent. *T:* Borough Green 885454.

COLLINGS, Juliet Jeanne d'Auvergne; *see* Campbell, J.J. d'A.

COLLINGWOOD, Adrian Redman, CBE 1975; TD 1953; Chairman of the Eggs Authority, 1971–78; *b* Driffield, Yorks, 26 Feb. 1910; *s* of Bernard Joseph Collingwood and Katherine Mary Collingwood; *m* 1939, Dorothy Strong; two *d*. *Educ:* Hull Technical College. FIB. Served War of 1939–45, E Yorks Regt (50th Div.) (Major; despatches, 1944); wounded in Western Desert; POW for a year, then escaped by means of tunnel. Midland Bank: Asst Man., Whitefriargate Branch, Hull, 1947–51; Branch Supt, 1951–55; Gen. Manager's Asst, 1955–59; Asst Gen. Manager, 1959–66; Gen. Manager (Agriculture), 1966–71; retd from bank, 1971. *Publications:* lectures. *Recreations:* previously rugger, cricket, tennis; now golf, bridge, fishing. *Address:* Flat 6, Burrells, 25 Court Downs Road, Beckenham, Kent. *T:* 01–650 2265. *Clubs:* Farmers'; (Pres.) Langley Park Golf.

COLLINGWOOD, John Gildas, FEng, FIChemE; Director: Unilever Ltd, 1965–77; Unilever NV, 1965–77; Head of Research Division of Unilever Ltd, 1961–77; *b* 15 June 1917; *s* of Stanley Ernest Collingwood and Kathleen Muriel (*née* Smalley); *m* 1942, Pauline Winifred (*née* Jones); one *s* one *d*. *Educ:* Wycliffe Coll., Stonehouse, Glos; University Coll. London (BSc). English Charcoal, 1940–41; British Ropeway Engrg Co, 1941–44; De Havilland Engines, 1944–46; Olympia Oil and Cake Mills Ltd, 1946–49; British Oil and Cake Mills Ltd, 1949–51; Mem., UK Milling Group of Unilever Ltd, 1951–60; Dir, Advita Ltd, 1951–60; Dir, British Oil & Cake Mills Ltd, 1955–60. Instn of Chemical Engrs: Mem. Research Cttee, 1963–68; Mem. Council, 1964–67. Mem. Council of Univ. of Aston, 1971–83 (Chm., Academic Advisory Cttee, 1964–71); Mem., Research Cttee, CBI, 1970–71; Member: Council for Scientific Policy, 1971–72; Exec. Cttee, British Nutrition Foundn, 1978–82 (Council, 1970–85); Food Standards Cttee, 1972–80; Royal Commn on Environmental Pollution, 1973–79; Standing Commn on Energy and the Environment, 1978–81. A Gen. Sec., BAAS, 1978–83. Chm., F and GP Cttee, Nat. Children's Home, 1983–. Chm., Council of Governors, Wycliffe Coll., Stonehouse, Glos, 1985– (Mem. Council, 1967–). Hon. DSc, Aston, 1966; Fellow, University Coll. London, 1970. *Recreations:* sailing, music. *Address:* 54 Downs Road, Coulsdon, Surrey. *T:* Downland 54817. *Club:* Athenæum.

COLLINS, Andrew David; QC 1985; a Recorder, since 1986; *b* 19 July 1942; *s* of Rev. Canon Lewis John Collins, MA, and Diana (*née* Elliot); *m* 1970, Nicolette Anne Sandford-Saville; one *s* one *d*. *Educ:* Eton; King's Coll., Cambridge (BA, MA). Called to the Bar, Middle Temple, 1965. *Address:* Lamb Building, Temple, EC4. *T:* 01–353 6701.

COLLINS, Sir Arthur (James Robert), KCVO 1980; *b* 10 July 1911; *s* of Col William Fellowes Collins, DSO, and Lady Evelyn Collins (*née* Innes Ker), OBE; *m* 1965, Elizabeth, *d* of Rear-Adm. Sir Arthur Bromley, Bt, and *widow* of 6th Baron Sudeley (*died* on war service, 1941). *Educ:* Eton; Christ Church, Oxford (MA). Admitted a Solicitor, 1935; Partner, Withers, 1937, Sen. Partner, 1962–81, now Consultant. Served with Royal Horse Guards, 1938–46; Adjt, 2nd Household Cavalry Regt, 1940–44 (despatches), Major 1943. *Address:* Kirkman Bank, Knaresborough, N Yorks HG5 9BT. *T:* Harrogate 863136; 38 Clarence Terrace, NW1. *T:* 01–723 4198. *Clubs:* Turf, White's.

COLLINS, Arthur John, OBE 1973; HM Diplomatic Service; Counsellor, Foreign and Commonwealth Office, since 1986; *b* 17 May 1931; *s* of Reginald and Margery Collins; *m* 1952, Enid Maureen, *d* of Charles and Sarah Stableford; one *s* one *d*. *Educ:* Purley Grammar Sch. Served RAF, 1949–51. Min. of Health, 1951–68 (Private Sec. to Perm. Sec., 1960–61, and to Parly Sec., 1962–63); transf. to HM Diplomatic Service, 1968; FCO, 1968–69; First Secretary and Head of Chancery: Dhaka, 1970–71; Brasilia, 1972–74; Asst Head of Latin America and Caribbean Depts, FCO, 1974–77; Counsellor, UK Del. to OECD, Paris, 1978–81; High Comr, Papua New Guinea, 1982–85. *Recreation:* dabbling in archaeology. *Address:* c/o Foreign and Commonwealth Office, SW1. *Club:* Royal Commonwealth Society.

COLLINS, Basil Eugene Sinclair, CBE 1983; Chairman, Nabisco Group, since 1984; *b* 21 Dec. 1923; *s* of Albert Collins and Pauline Alicia (*née* Wright); *m* 1942, Doris Slott; two *d*. *Educ:* Great Yarmouth Grammar School. Sales Manager, L. Rose & Co. Ltd, 1945; Export Dir, Schweppes (Overseas) Ltd, 1958; Group Admin Dir, Schweppes Ltd, 1964, Chm. of Overseas Gp 1968; Chm. of Overseas Gp, Cadbury Schweppes Ltd, 1969, Dep. Man. Dir 1972, Man. Dir 1974, Dep. Chm. and Group Chief Exec., Cadbury Schweppes plc, 1980–83; Director: Thomas Cook Gp, 1980–85; British Airways Bd, 1982–; Royal Mint, 1984–. Royal College of Nursing: Chm., Finance and General Purposes Cttee, 1970; Hon. Treasurer, 1970; Vice-Pres., 1972. Fellow Inst. of Dirs, 1974, Council Mem., 1982–. FZS 1975; CBIM (FBIM 1976); FIGD; Fellow, Amer. Chamber of Commerce, 1979, Dir 1984–. FRSA 1984. *Recreations:* music, languages, travel, English countryside. *Address:* Wyddial Parva, Buntingford, Herts SG9 0EL. *Club:* Carlton.

COLLINS, Bernard John, CBE 1960; town planner, retired; Controller (formerly Director) of Planning and Transportation, Greater London Council, 1969–74; *b* 3 July 1909; *s* of late John Philip and Amelia Bounevialle Collins; *m* 1937, Grete Elisabeth, *e d* of H. A. Piehler; one *s* three *d*. *Educ:* Ampleforth. Served Royal Artillery, 1939–45, North Africa (despatches) and Italy. Ryde Memorial Prizeman, RICS, 1937. President: Royal Town Planning Inst., 1957–58; International Fedn of Surveyors, 1967–69; Mem. Bureau, Internat. Fedn for Housing and Planning, 1962–66; Vice-Pres., 1968–73, Sen. Vice-Pres., 1973–74, Pres., 1974–75, RICS; Mem. Board of Governors, Coll. of Estate Management, 1959–69; Vice-Chm. of Executive, Town and Country Planning Assoc., 1951–62; Chm., Assoc. of County Planning Officers, 1954–58; County Planning Officer, Middx, 1947–62; Sec. and Chief Exec. Commn for the New Towns, 1962–64; Dir of Planning, GLC, 1964–69; responsible for preparation of Greater London Develt Plan, 1969. Chairman, Technical Panel: Conf. on London and SE Regional Planning, 1964–74; Greater London and SE Regional Sports Council, 1966–74; advised on reorganisation of planning system, City of Jerusalem, 1971. Described by William Hickey of Daily Express as probably the world's top town planner. Pres. Honoraire, Fédération Internationale des Géomètres, 1970–; Hon. Mem., Deutscher Verein für Vermessungswesen (German Soc. of Surveyors), 1965–; Membre d'honneur, Union Belge des Géomètres-experts Immobiliers, 1976–. *Publications:* Development Plans Explained (HMSO), 1951; Middlesex Survey and Development Plan, 1952; numerous addresses, articles and papers on town planning. *Address:* Foxella, Matfield, Kent TN12 7ET. *Club:* Athenæum.

COLLINS, Sir Geoffrey Abdy, Kt 1952; *b* 5 June 1888; *y s* of Philip George and Susan Kate Collins; *m* 1936, Joan Mary, 2nd *d* of Albert Edward and Margaret Alice Ratcliffe; one *s* four *d*. *Educ:* Rugby; Christ's Coll., Cambridge (BA, LLB). Admitted solicitor, 1913. Served European War, 1914–18, in The Rifle Brigade (Capt.). Member: Royal UK Beneficent Assoc. Cttee, 1926–54 (Chm., 1950–54); Council of The Law Society, 1931–56, Pres., 1951–52. Past Master, Tylers and Bricklayers Co. *Address:* Mullion, 20 Ballard Estate, Swanage, Dorset. *T:* Swanage 422030.

COLLINS, Gerard; *see* Collins, James G.

COLLINS, Henry Edward, CBE 1948; FEng 1976; Consulting Mining Engineer; *b* 4 Oct. 1903; *s* of James Collins; *m* 1934, Cecilia Harris (*d* 1975); no *c*. *Educ:* Rotherham Grammar Sch.; Univ. of Sheffield (MEng). Sen. Lectr in Mining, Univ. of Sheffield, 1935–38; Manager, Rossington Main Colliery, Doncaster, 1939–42; Agent, Markham

Colliery, Doncaster, 1942–44; Chief Mining Agent, Doncaster Amalgamated Collieries Ltd, 1944–45; Dir Coal Production, CCG, 1945–47; British Chm., UK/US Coal Control Gp, Germany (later Combined Coal Control Gp), 1947–50; Production Dir, Durham Div., NCB, 1950–56; Dir-Gen. of Reconstruction, NCB, 1956–57; Board Mem. for Production, NCB, 1957–67; Consultant to NCB, 1967–69. Mem., Govtl Cttee on Coal Derivatives, 1959–60; Chairman: NCB Opencast Executive, 1961–67; NCB Brickworks Executive, 1962–67; Whittlesea Central Brick Co. Ltd, 1966–67; Field Research Steering Cttee, Min. of Power, 1964–67; Past Director: Omnia Concrete Sales Ltd; Bradley's (Concrete) Ltd; Powell Duffryn Technical Services Ltd; Inter-Continental Fuels Ltd. Member: Minister of Power's Adv. Council on Research and Develt, 1963–67; Min. of Power Nat. Jt Pneumoconiosis Cttee, 1964–67; Safety in Mines (Adv.) Bd; Mining Qualifications Bd, 1962–69. Pres., Inst. of Mining Engineers, 1962. *Publications:* Mining Memories and Musings: the autobiography of a mining engineer, 1985; numerous papers on mining engineering subjects. *Address:* Rising Sun, 22a West Side, Wimbledon Common, SW19 4UF. *T:* 01-946 3949. *Club:* Athenæum.

COLLINS, (James) Gerard; TD (FF) Limerick West, since 1967; *b* Abbeyfeale, Co. Limerick, 16 Oct. 1938; *s* of late James J. Collins, TD and Margaret Collins; *m* 1969, Hilary Tattan. *Educ:* University Coll., Dublin (BA). Teacher. Asst Gen. Sec., Fianna Fáil, 1965–67. Parly Sec. to Ministers for Industry and Commerce and for the Gaeltacht, 1969–70; Minister for Posts and Telegraphs, 1970–73; opposition front-bench spokesman on agriculture, 1973–75; spokesman on justice, 1975–77; Minister for Justice, 1977–81; Minister for Foreign Affairs, March-Dec. 1982; opposition front-bench spokesman on foreign affairs, 1983–. Mem., Consultative Assembly, Council of Europe, 1973–77; Chm., Parly Cttee on Secondary Legislation of European Communities, 1983–. Mem., Limerick CC, 1974–77. *Address:* The Hill, Abbeyfeale, Co. Limerick.

COLLINS, Prof. Jeffrey Hamilton, FRSE; FEng 1981; Professor of Electrical Engineering and Head of Department, Edinburgh University, 1977–84, Emeritus Professor, 1984; *b* 22 April 1930; *s* of Ernest Frederick and Dora Gladys Collins; *m* 1956, Sally Collins; two *s*. *Educ:* London Univ. (BSc, MSc). FIEE, FInstP, FIERE, FIEEE. GEC Research Laboratories, London, 1951–56; Ferranti Ltd, Edinburgh, 1956–57; Univ. of Glasgow, 1957–66; Research Engr, Stanford Univ., Calif, 1966–68; Dir of Physical Electronics, Rockwell International, Calif, 1968–70; Research Prof., 1970–73, Prof. of Industrial Electronics, 1973–77, Univ. of Edinburgh. Mem., Computer Bd for Univs and Res. Councils, 1985–. Director: MESL, 1970–79; Racal-MESL, 1979–81; Advent Technology, 1981–; Filtronics Components, 1981–85; Burr-Brown Ltd, 1985. *Publications:* Computer-Aided Design of Surface Acoustic Wave Devices, 1976; over 180 articles in learned soc. electrical engrg jls. *Address:* Nether Craigour, Broadgait, Gullane, East Lothian EH31 2DH.

COLLINS, Vice-Adm. Sir John (Augustine), KBE 1951; CB 1940; RAN retired; *b* Deloraine, Tasmania, 7 Jan. 1899; *s* of Michael John Collins, MD; *m* 1930, Phyllis Laishley, *d* of A. J. McLachlan; one *d*. *Educ:* Royal Australian Naval Coll. Served European War with Grand Fleet and Harwich Force, 1917–18; thereafter in various HM and HMA Ships abroad and in Australian waters; Squadron Gunnery Officer, HMA Squadron; Liaison Officer for visit of Duke and Duchess of York to Australia; in command HMAS Anzac; staff course; Asst Chief of Naval Staff, Australia; Capt. HMAS Sydney (CB), 1939–41; Asst Chief of Staff to C-in-C, China, 1941 (despatches); Cdre comdg China Force, 1942 (Comdr of Order of Orange Nassau); Capt. HMAS Shropshire, 1943–44; Cdre comdg HM Australian Sqdn (wounded), 1944–46; idc 1947; Chief of Naval Staff and First Naval Mem., Australian Commonwealth Naval Bd, Melbourne, 1948–55; Australian High Comr to New Zealand, 1956–62. Officer of Legion of Merit (US); Royal Humane Society's Certificate for Saving Life at Sea. *Publication:* As Luck Would Have It, 1965. *Address:* 13 Dumaresq Road, Rose Bay, Sydney, NSW 2029, Australia. *Club:* Royal Sydney Golf.

COLLINS, John Ernest Harley, MBE 1944; DSC 1945 and Bar 1945; DL; Chairman: Morgan Grenfell Holdings Ltd, 1974–79; Guardian Royal Exchange Assurance since 1974; *b* 24 April 1923; *o s* of late G. W. Collins, Taynton, Glos; *m* 1946, Gillian (*d* 1981), *e d* of 2nd Baron Bicester; one *s* one *d*. *Educ:* King Edward's Sch., Birmingham; Birmingham Univ. Royal Navy, 1941–46. Morgan Grenfell & Co. Ltd, 1946, Dir 1957. Director: Royal Exchange Assce, 1957; Rank Hovis McDougall Ltd; Charter Consolidated Ltd, 1966–83; Hudson's Bay Co., 1957–74. Chm. United Services Trustee, 1968–76. DL Oxon, 1975; High Sheriff, Oxon, 1975. KStJ 1983. *Recreations:* shooting, stalking, fishing. *Address:* Tusmore Park, Bicester, Oxon. *T:* Fritwell 209. *Clubs:* Brooks's, White's, Pratt's.

COLLINS, (John) Martin, QC 1972; a Recorder of the Crown Court, since 1972; a Judge of the Courts of Appeal of Jersey and Guernsey, since 1984; *b* 24 Jan. 1929; *s* of John Lissant Collins and Marjorie Mary Collins; *m* 1957, Daphne Mary, *d* of George Martyn Swindells, Prestbury; two *s* one *d*. *Educ:* Uppingham Sch.; Manchester Univ. (LLB). Called to Bar, Gray's Inn, 1952, Bencher, 1981. Dep. Chm., Cumberland QS, 1969–72. Mem., Senate of Inns of Court and Bar, 1981–84. *Address:* 2 Pump Court, Temple, EC4; 20 Chester Row, SW1. *Clubs:* Athenæum, Carlton.

COLLINS, John Morris; a Recorder of the Crown Court, since 1980; *b* 25 June 1931; *s* of late Emmanuel Cohen, MBE, and of Ruby Cohen; *m* 1968, Sheila Brummer; one *d*. *Educ:* Leeds Grammar Sch.; The Queen's Coll., Oxford (MA LitHum). Called to Bar, Middle Temple, 1956, Member of North Eastern Circuit; a Deputy Circuit Judge, 1970. Pres., Leeds Jewish Representative Council, 1986. *Publications:* Summary Justice, 1963; various articles in legal periodicals, etc. *Recreation:* walking. *Address:* (home) 14 Sandhill Oval, Leeds LS17 8EA. *T:* Leeds 686008; (professional) Pearl Chambers, East Parade, Leeds LS1 5BZ. *T:* Leeds 451986.

COLLINS, Maj.-Gen. Joseph Clinton, CB 1953; CBE 1951 (OBE 1946); *b* 8 Jan. 1895; British; *m* 1925, Eileen Patricia Williams; two *d*. *Educ:* London Hosp. Served European War, 1914–18, France and Belgium, 1914; Surgeon Probationer, RNVR, 1915–16; Lieut, RAMC, 1917; Egyptian Army, 1923–33; DDMS, BAOR, 1946–49; DMS Far ELF, 1949–51; DMS Northern Command, 1951–53; KHS 1951–54; Dir Medical Services, BAOR, 1953–Dec. 1954, retired. CStJ 1948. 3rd Class Order of Nile. *Address:* c/o Royal Bank of Scotland, Whitehall, SW1.

COLLINS, Gen. (retd) J(oseph) Lawton, DSM 1942 (Oak Leaf Cluster, 1943, 1944, 1953); Silver Star, 1943 (Army Oak Leaf Cluster, and Navy Gold Star, 1944); Legion of Merit, 1943 (Oak Leaf Cluster, 1945); Bronze Star Medal, 1944; Director, Chas Pfizer & Co. Inc., 1957–72; Vice-Chairman, Pfizer International Subsidiaries 1957–72; *b* New Orleans, La, 1 May 1896; *s* of Jeremiah Bernard Collins and Catherine Lawton; *m* 1921, Gladys Easterbrook; one *s* two *d*. *Educ:* Louisiana State Univ.; US Military Academy. 2nd Lieut, Infantry, 1917; 22nd Infantry, Fort Hamilton, NY, until Jan. 1918; graduated Inf. Sch. of Arms, Fort Sill, Oklahoma, 1918; went overseas and took command of bn of 18th Inf., Coblenz, 1919; Asst Chief of Staff, Plans and Training Div., American Forces in Germany, until 1921; Instr, US Mil. Acad., 1921–25; graduated: Inf. Sch., Fort Benning, Ga, 1926; Advanced Course, Field Artillery Sch., Fort Sill, Oklahoma, 1927; Instr, Inf. Sch., 1927–31; student, Comd and Gen. Staff Sch., Fort Leavenworth, Kansas, 1931–33; with 23rd Bde (Philippine Scouts), Fort William McKinley, and Asst Chief of Staff, Ops and Mil. Intell., Philippine Div., until 1936; Student: Army Industrial Coll., 1936–37; Army War Coll., 1937–38; Instr there, 1938–40. Served War of 1939–45; Office of Sec., War Dept Gen. Staff, 1940–41; Chief of Staff, VII Army Corps, 1941; Chief of Staff, Hawaiian Dept, 1941; Comdg Gen., 25th Inf. Div. in Guadalcanal ops, New Georgia Campaign, 1942–43; comd VII Army Corps, European Theater, for Invasion of France, 1944; and subseq. campaigns to end of hostilities, 1945; Dep. Comdg Gen. and Chief of Staff, HQ, Army Ground Forces, 1945; Dir of Information, War Dept, 1945; Dep. Chief of Staff, US Army, 1947, and Vice Chief of Staff (upon creation of that post), 1948; Chief of Staff, US Army, 1949–53; US Rep., Standing Group, NATO and US Mem. Mil. Cttee, 1953–56; US Special Rep. in Viet Nam with personal rank Ambassador, Nov. 1954–May 1955. Holds hon. degrees. Army of Occupation Medal, Germany, European War, 1914–18, and War of 1939–45; American Defense Service Medal; Asiatic-Pacific Medal; European-African-Middle Eastern Campaign Ribbon. (In addition to above US decorations) Hon. CB (British) 1945; Order of Suvorov, 2nd Class, twice (Russian); Croix de Guerre with Palm, Legion of Honor, Degree of Grand Officer (French); Order of Leopold II, Grand Officer Croix de Guerre with Palm (Belgian). *Address:* 4000 Massachusetts Avenue, NW, Washington, DC 20016, USA. *T:* 362–0971. *Club:* Chevy Chase (Md).

COLLINS, Kenneth Darlingston; Member (Lab) East Strathclyde, European Parliament, since 1979; *b* 12 Aug. 1939; *s* of Nicholas Collins and Ellen Williamson; *m* 1966, Georgina Frances Pollard; one *s* one *d*. *Educ:* St John's Grammar Sch.; Hamilton Acad.; Glasgow Univ. (BSc Hons); Strathclyde Univ. (MSc). Left school, 1956; steelworks apprentice, 1956–59; univ., 1960–65; planning officer, 1965–66; WEA Tutor-Organiser, 1966–67; Lecturer: Glasgow Coll. of Bldg, 1967–69; Paisley Coll. of Technol., 1969–79. Dep. Leader, Labour Gp, Eur. Parlt, 1979–84. Chairman: Environment Cttee, Eur. Parlt, 1979–84 (Vice-Chm., 1984–); NE Glasgow Children's Panel, 1974–76. Member: East Kilbride Town and Dist Council, 1973–79; Lanark CC, 1973–75; East Kilbride Develt Corp., 1976–79. *Recreations:* Labour Party, music, boxer dogs, cycling, squash. *Address:* 11 Stuarton Park, East Kilbride, Lanarkshire G74 4LA. *T:* East Kilbride 37282.

COLLINS, Lesley Elizabeth; *see* Appleby, L. E.

COLLINS, Margaret Elizabeth, CBE 1983; RRC; Matron-in-Chief, Queen Alexandra's Royal Naval Nursing Service, 1980–83; *b* 13 Feb. 1927; *d* of James Henry Collins and Amy Collins. *Educ:* St Anne's Convent Grammar Sch., Southampton. RRC 1978 (ARRC 1965). Royal Victoria Hosp., Bournemouth, SRN 1949; West Middlesex Hosp., CMB Part 1; entered QARNNS as Nursing Sister, 1953; accepted for permanent service, 1958; Matron, 1972; Principal Matron, 1976. SSStJ 1978. QHNS, 1980–83. *Recreations:* gardening, theatre-going. *Address:* Lancastria, First Marine Avenue, Barton-on-Sea, Hants BH25 6DP. *T:* New Milton 612374.

COLLINS, Martin; *see* Collins, J. M.

COLLINS, Michael; aerospace consultant; Vice President, LTV Aerospace and Defense Company (formerly Vought Corporation), 1980–85; former NASA Astronaut; Command Module Pilot, Apollo 11 rocket flight to the Moon, July 1969; *b* Rome, Italy, 31 Oct. 1930; *s* of Maj.-Gen. and Mrs James L. Collins, Washington, DC, USA; *m* 1957, Patricia M. Finnegan, Boston, Mass; one *s* two *d*. *Educ:* St Albans Sch., Washington, DC (grad.). US Mil. Academy, West Point, NY (BSc); advanced through grades to Colonel; Harvard Business Sch. (AMP), 1974. Served as an experimental flight test officer, Air Force Flight Test Center, Edwards Air Force Base, Calif; he was one of the third group of astronauts named by NASA in Oct. 1963; served as backup pilot for Gemini 7 mission; as pilot with John Young on the 3–day 44–revolution Gemini 10 mission, launched 18 July 1966, he shared record-setting flight (successful rendezvous and docking with a separately launched Agena target vehicle; completed two periods of extravehicular activity); Command Module Pilot for Apollo flight, first lunar landing, in orbit 20 July 1969, when Neil Armstrong and Edwin Aldrin landed on the Moon. Asst Sec. of State for Public Affairs, US, 1970–71; Dir, Nat. Air and Space Museum, Smithsonian Institution, 1971–78; Under Sec., Smithsonian Inst., 1978–80. Maj. Gen. Air Force Reserve, retired. Dir, AF Historical Foundn; Member: Bd of Trustees, Rand Corp.; Bd of Trustees, Nat. Geographic Soc.; Washington Historical Monument Soc.; Soc. of Experimental Test Pilots; Internat. Acad. of Astronautics of Internat. Astronautical Fedn; Washington Inst. of Foreign Affairs. FAIAA; Fellow, Amer. Astronautical Soc. Member, Order of Daedalians. Hon. degrees from: Stonehill Coll.; St Michael's Coll.; Northeastern Univ.; Southeastern Univ. Presidential Medal of Freedom, NASA; FAI Gold Space Medal; DSM (NASA); DSM (AF); Exceptional Service Medal (NASA); Astronaut Wings; DFC. *Publications:* Carrying the Fire (autobiog.), 1974; Flying to the Moon and Other Strange Places (for children), 1976. *Recreations:* fishing, handball. *Address:* LTV Corporation, 1025 Thomas Jefferson Street NW, Washington, DC 20007, USA. *Clubs:* Metropolitan, Alfalfa, Alibi (all Washington, DC).

COLLINS, Michael Brendan, OBE 1983 (MBE 1969); HM Diplomatic Service; Counsellor, Economic and Commercial, Brussels, since 1983; *b* 9 Sept. 1932; *s* of Daniel James Collins, GM and Mary Bridget Collins (*née* Kennedy); *m* 1959, Maria Elena Lozar. *Educ:* St Illtyd's College, Cardiff; University College London. HM Forces, 1953–55. FO 1956; Santiago, Chile, 1959; Consul, Santiago, Cuba, 1962; FO, 1964; Second, later First, Sec. (Admin.) and Consul, Prague, 1967; Dep. High Comr, Bathurst, The Gambia, 1970; Head of Chancery, Algiers, 1972; First Sec., FCO, 1975; Consul Commercial, Montreal, 1978; Consul for Atlantic Provinces of Canada, Halifax, 1981. *Recreations:* fishing, shooting, golf, walking, reading, music. *Address:* c/o Foreign and Commonwealth Office, SW1; Avenue des Perdrix 3, 1950 Kraainem, Brussels, Belgium. *T:* 731 54 41. *Club:* Army and Navy.

COLLINS, Miss Nina; *see* Lowry, Mrs N. M.

COLLINS, Pauline; actress (stage and television); *b* Exmouth, Devon, 3 Sept. 1940; *d* of William Henry Collins and Mary Honora Callanan; *m* John Alderton, *qv*; two *s* one *d*. *Educ:* Convent of the Sacred Heart, Hammersmith, London; Central Sch. of Speech and Drama. *Stage:* 1st appearance in A Gazelle in Park Lane, Theatre Royal, Windsor, 1962; 1st London appearance in Passion Flower Hotel, Prince of Wales, 1965; The Erpingham Camp, Royal Court, 1967; The Happy Apple, Hampstead, 1967, and Apollo, 1970; Importance of Being Earnest, Haymarket, 1968; The Night I chased the Women with an Eel, 1969; Come As You Are (3 parts), New, 1970; Judies, Comedy, 1974; Engaged, National Theatre, Old Vic, 1975; Confusions, Apollo, 1976; Rattle of a Simple Man, Savoy, 1980; Romantic Comedy, Apollo, 1983; *television*, 1962–: series: Upstairs Downstairs; No Honestly; P. G. Wodehouse; Thomas and Sarah; The Black Tower; plays: Long Distance Information, 1979; Knockback, 1984. *Address:* c/o Nems Management Ltd, 29–31 King's Road, SW3.

COLLINS, Peter G., RSA 1974 (ARSA 1966); painter in oil; lecturer, Duncan of Jordanstone College of Art, Dundee; *b* Inverness, 21 June 1935; *s* of E. G. Collins, FRCSE; *m* 1959, Myra Mackintosh (marr. diss. 1978); one *s* one *d*. *Educ:* Fettes Coll., Edinburgh;

Edinburgh Coll. of Art. Studied in Italy, on Andrew Grant Major Travelling Scholarship, 1957–58. Work in permanent collections: Aberdeen Civic; Glasgow Civic; Scottish Arts Council. *Recreations:* music and procrastination. *Address:* Royal Scottish Academy, The Mound, Edinburgh; Jasmine Cottage, Newbigging Road, Tealing, Tayside.

COLLINS, Air Vice-Marshal Peter Spencer, CB 1985; AFC 1961; Director, Business Development (Air), Marconi Radar Systems, since 1986; *b* 19 March 1930; *s* of Frederick Wilbore Collins and Mary (*née* Spencer); *m* 1953, Sheila Mary (*née* Perks); three *s* one *d*. *Educ:* Royal Grammar Sch., High Wycombe, Univ. of Birmingham (BA (Hons) History). FBIM 1979. Joined RAF, 1951; flying tours incl. service on squadron nos: 63, 141, 41, AWDS, AFDS; RAF Handling Sqdn, nos 23 and 11; commanded: 111 Sqdn, 1970–72; RAF Gütersloh, 1974–76; staff tours include: Air Ministry, 1962–64; Strike Comd HQ, 1968–70 and 1972–74; Dir of Forward Policy (RAF), 1978–81; SASO, HQ 11 Gp, 1981–83; DG, Communications, Inf. Systems and Orgn (RAF), 1983–85; psc 1965, rcds 1977; retired 1985. *Publications:* contribs to service jls and to Seaford House Papers, 1978. *Recreations:* golf, music, stock market. *Address:* Babylon, Boreham, Essex CM3 3EJ. *Club:* Royal Air Force.

COLLINS, Prof. Philip Arthur William; Emeritus Professor of English, University of Leicester, since 1982; *b* 28 May 1923; *er s* of Arthur Henry and Winifred Nellie Collins; *m* 1st, 1952, Mildred Lowe (marr. diss. 1963); 2nd, 1965, Joyce Dickins; two *s* one *d*. *Educ:* Brentwood Sch.; Emmanuel Coll., Cambridge (Sen. Schol.). MA 1948. Served War (RAOC and Royal Norfolk Regt), 1942–45. Leicester: Staff Tutor in Adult Educn, 1947; Warden, Vaughan Coll., 1954; Sen. Lectr in English, 1962–64; Prof., 1964–82; Head, English Dept, 1971–76, 1981–82; Public Orator, 1975–78, 1980–82. Visiting Prof.: Univ. of California, Berkeley, 1967; Columbia, 1969; Victoria Univ., NZ, 1974. Sec., Leicester Theatre Trust Ltd, 1963–; Member: Drama Panel, Arts Council of Gt Britain, 1970–75; National Theatre Bd, 1976–82; British American Drama Acad. Bd, 1983–; Pres., Dickens Fellowship, 1983–85; Chm. Trustees, Dickens House Museum, 1984–. Many overseas lecture-tours; performances, talks and scripts for radio and television. *Publications:* James Boswell, 1956; (ed) English Christmas, 1956; Dickens and Crime, 1962; Dickens and Education, 1963; The Canker and the Rose (Shakespeare Quatercentenary celebration) perf. Mermaid Theatre, London, 1964; The Impress of the Moving Age, 1965; Thomas Cooper the Chartist, 1969; A Dickens Bibliography, 1970; Dickens's Bleak House, 1971; (ed) Dickens, the Critical Heritage, 1971; (ed) A Christmas Carol: the public reading version, 1971; Reading Aloud: a Victorian Métier, 1972; (ed) Dickens's Public Readings, 1975; Dickens's David Copperfield, 1977; (ed) Dickens: Interviews and Recollections, 1981; (ed) Thackeray: Interviews and Recollections, 1983; Trollope's London, 1983; (ed) Dickens: Sikes and Nancy and other Readings, 1983; Tennyson, Poet of Lincolnshire, 1984; contrib. to: Encyclopaedia Britannica, Listener, TLS, sundry learned journals. *Recreations:* theatre, music. *Address:* 26 Knighton Drive, Leicester LE2 3HB. *T:* Leicester 706026.

COLLINS, Stuart Verdun, CB 1970; retired; Chief Inspector of Audit, Department of the Environment (formerly Ministry of Housing and Local Government), 1968–76; *b* 24 Feb. 1916; *m* 1st, 1942, Helen Simpson (*d* 1968); two *d*; 2nd, 1970, Joan Mary Walmsley (widow); one *step s* two *step d*. *Educ:* Plymouth Coll. Entered Civil Service as Audit Assistant in the District Audit Service of the Ministry of Health, 1934; appointed District Auditor for the London Audit District, 1958. IPFA, FBCS. *Recreations:* golf, do-it-yourself, sailing. *Address:* Kemendine, Court Wood, Newton Ferrers, Devon.

COLLINS, Terence Bernard; Chairman, 1984–87, Group Managing Director, 1975–86, Berger Jenson Nicholson; *b* 3 March 1927; *s* of George Bernard Collins and Helen Teresa Collins; *m* 1956, Barbara (*née* Lowday); two *s* two *d*. *Educ:* Marist Coll., Hull; Univ. of St Andrews (MA Hons). Trainee, Ideal Standard, 1951–52; Blundell Spence: Area Manager, 1953–55; Regl Manager, 1955–57; Nat. Sales Manager, 1957–59; Berger Jenson Nicholson: Sales Manager, 1959–62; Man. Dir, Caribbean, 1962–69; Overseas Regl Exec., 1969–70; Gp Dir UK, 1971–74. Director: A. G. Stanley Hldgs, 1977–; Hoechst UK, 1979–87; Hoechst Australia Investments, 1980–87. Mem. Ct and Council, Cranfield Inst. of Technology, 1977–. *Recreations:* golf, music. *Address:* Aldehurst, Church Walk, Aldeburgh, Suffolk. *Clubs:* Oriental, Directors; Aldeburgh Golf.

COLLINS, Brig. Thomas Frederick James, CBE 1945 (OBE 1944); JP; DL; *b* 9 April 1905; *s* of Capt. J. A. Collins and Emily (*née* Truscott); *m* 1942, Marjorie Morwenna, *d* of Lt-Col T. Donnelly, DSO; one *d*. *Educ:* Haileybury; RMC, Sandhurst. Gazetted to Green Howards, 1924; Staff College, 1938. Served War of 1939–45 (despatches twice, OBE, CBE): France, 1940, NW Europe, 1944–45. Retired, with rank of Brig., 1948. Essex County Council: CC, 1960; Vice-Chm., 1967; Chm., 1968–71. JP 1968, DL 1969, Essex. Comdr, Order of Leopold II (Belgium), 1945. *Recreation:* shooting. *Address:* Ashdon Hall, Saffron Walden, Essex. *T:* Ashdon 232. *Club:* Army and Navy.

COLLINS, William Janson; Chairman, William Collins Sons & Co. (Holdings) Ltd, 1976–81; *b* 10 June 1929; *s* of late Sir William Alexander Roy Collins, CBE, and Lady Collins (Priscilla Marian, *d* of late S. J. Lloyd); *m* 1951, Lady Sara Elena Hely-Hutchinson, *d* of 7th Earl of Donoughmore; one *s* three *d*. *Educ:* Magdalen Coll., Oxford (BA). Joined William Collins Sons & Co. Ltd, 1952; Dir, then Man. Dir, 1967; Vice-Chm., 1971; Chm., 1976. *Recreations:* Royal tennis, shooting, fishing, tennis, golf. *Address:* House of Craigie, by Kilmarnock, Ayrshire KA1 5NA. *T:* Craigie 246. *Clubs:* Boodle's; All England Lawn Tennis and Croquet.

COLLINSON, Prof. Patrick, PhD; FBA 1982; FRHistS, FAHA; Professor of Modern History, University of Sheffield, since 1984; *b* 10 Aug. 1929; *s* of William Cecil Collinson and Belle Hay (*née* Patrick); *m* 1960, Elizabeth Albinia Susan Selwyn; two *s* two *d*. *Educ:* King's Sch., Ely; Pembroke Coll., Cambridge (Exhibnr 1949, Foundn Scholar 1952; BA 1952, 1st Cl. Hons Hist. Tripos Pt II; Hadley Prize for Hist., 1952). PhD London, 1957; FRHistS 1967 (Mem. Council, 1977–81, Vice-Pres., 1983–); FAHA 1974. University of London: Postgrad. Student, Royal Holloway Coll., 1952–54; Res. Fellow, Inst. of Hist. Res., 1954–55; Res. Asst, UCL, 1955–56; Lectr in Hist., Univ. of Khartoum, 1956–61; Asst Lectr in Eccles. Hist., King's Coll., Univ. of London, 1961–62, Lectr, 1962–69 (Fellow 1976); Professor of History: Univ. of Sydney, 1969–75; Univ. of Kent at Canterbury, 1976–84. Vis. Fellow, All Souls Coll., Oxford, 1981; Andrew W. Mellon Fellow, Huntingdon Library, California, 1984. Lectures: Ford's, in Eng. Hist., Univ. of Oxford, 1978–79; Birkbeck, Univ. of Cambridge, 1981; Stenton Meml, Univ. of Reading, 1985; Neale Meml, Univ. of Manchester, 1986; Anstey Meml, Univ. of Kent, 1986. Pres., Ecclesiastical Hist. Soc., 1985–86. Chm., Adv. Editorial Bd, Jl of Ecclesiastical History, 1982–. *Publications:* The Elizabethan Puritan Movement, 1967 (USA 1967; repr. 1982); Archbishop Grindal 1519–1583: the struggle for a Reformed Church, 1979 (USA 1979); The Religion of Protestants: the Church in English Society 1559–1625 (Ford Lectures, 1979), 1982; Godly People: essays on English Protestantism and Puritanism, 1983; English Puritanism, 1983; articles and revs in Bull. Inst. Hist. Res., Eng. Hist. Rev., Jl of Eccles. Hist., Studies in Church Hist., TLS. *Recreations:* mountains, fishing, music, gardening. *Address:* Department of History, University of Sheffield, Sheffield S10 2TN; 45 Parkers Road, Sheffield S10.

COLLISON, family name of **Baron Collison.**

COLLISON, Baron (Life Peer) *cr* 1964, of Cheshunt; **Harold Francis Collison,** CBE 1961; Chairman, Supplementary Benefits Commission, 1969–75; *b* 10 May 1909; *m* 1946, Ivy Kate Hanks. *Educ:* The Hay Currie LCC Sch.; Crypt Sch., Gloucester. Firstly, worked in a commercial office in London; farm worker in Glos, 1934–53. National Union of Agricultural Workers (later Nat. Union of Agricultural and Allied Workers): District Organiser in Gloucester and Worcs, 1944; Nat. Officer, 1946, General Secretary, 1953–69. Mem., TUC Gen. Coun., 1953–69, Chm., 1964–65; Chm., Social Insce and Industrial Welfare Cttee of TUC, 1957–69. President: Internat. Fedn of Plantation, Agricultural and Allied Workers, 1960–76; Assoc. of Agriculture, 1976–84; Member: Coun. on Tribunals, 1959–69; Nat. Insce Adv. Cttee, 1959–69; Governing Body of ILO, 1960–69; Pilkington Cttee on Broadcasting, 1960–62; Central Transport Consultative Cttee, 1962–70; Agric. Adv. Council, 1962–80; Adv. Cttee on Agricultural Educn, 1963; Royal Commn on Trades Unions and Employers' Assocs, 1965–68; Home-Grown Cereals Authority, 1965–78; former Member: Industrial Health Adv. Cttee; Economic Develt for Agriculture; Industrial Consultative Cttee, Approach to Europe; Overseas Labour Consultative Cttee; Agric. Productivity Cttee, British Productivity Council; Chairman: Land Settlement Assoc., 1977–79 (Vice-Chm., 1964–77); Agric. Apprenticeship Council, 1968–74; Mem., N Thames Gas Board (part-time), 1961–72. Mem., Governing Body, Brooklands Technical Coll., Weybridge, 1970– (Chm., 1977–). *Recreations:* gardening, chess. *Address:* Honeywood, 163 Old Nazeing Road, Broxbourne, Herts EN10 6QT. *T:* Hoddesdon 463597.

COLLISON, Lewis Herbert, TD; MA; Headmaster of Liverpool College, 1952–70; *b* 30 July 1908; *s* of late Mr and Mrs W. H. Collison; *m* 1934, Edna Mollie Ivens; two *d*. *Educ:* Mill Hill Sch.; St John's Coll., Cambridge. Asst Master of Sedbergh Sch., 1931–40; Major in King's Own Royal Regt, 1940–45; Housemaster of Sedbergh Sch., 1946–52. Mem. Council, University of Liverpool, 1963–69. JP Liverpool, 1958–70. *Recreations:* pottery, sailing. *Address:* 22 Riverview, Melton, near Woodbridge, Suffolk IP12 1QU. *Club:* Hawks (Cambridge).

COLLYEAR, Sir John Gowen, Kt 1986; FEng 1979; Chairman, AE plc, since 1981; *b* 19 Feb. 1927; *s* of John Robert Collyear and Amy Elizabeth Collyear (*née* Gowen); *m* 1953, Catherine Barbara Newman; one *s* two *d*. *Educ:* Leeds Univ. (BSc). FIMechE, FIProdE; CBIM. Graduate apprentice and Production Engr, Joseph Lucas Industries, 1951; Glacier Metal Company Ltd: Production Engr, 1953; Production Manager, 1956; Chief Production Engr, 1956; Factory Gen. Manager, 1959; Managing Director, 1969; Bearings Div. Man. Dir, Associated Engineering Ltd, 1972; Group Man. Dir, AE plc, 1975. *Publications:* Management Precepts, 1975; The Practice of First Level Management, 1976. *Recreations:* golf, bridge, piano music. *Address:* Walnut Tree House, Nether Westcote, Oxon OX7 6SD. *T:* Shipton-under-Wychwood 831247. *Clubs:* Athenæum, Reform.

COLMAN, Anthony David, QC 1977; barrister-at-law; a Recorder, since 1986; *b* 27 May 1938; *s* of Solomon Colman and Helen Colman; *m* 1964, Angela Glynn; two *d*. *Educ:* Harrogate Grammar Sch.; Trinity Hall, Cambridge (MA). Called to the Bar, Gray's Inn, 1962. *Publications:* Mathew's Practice of the Commercial Court (1902), 2nd edn, 1967; The Practice and Procedure of the Commercial Court, 1983, 2nd edn, 1986. *Recreations:* tennis, music, gardening, the 17th Century, Sifnos, the River Chess. *Address:* 4 Essex Court, Temple, EC4Y 9AJ. *T:* 01–583 9191.

COLMAN, Anthony John; Director, Burton Group PLC, Chief Executive, Development and Concessions for Burton, Top Man, Top Shop, Dorothy Perkins and Evans; *b* 24 July 1943; *s* of late William Benjamin Colman and Beatrice (*née* Hudson); four *s* two *d*. *Educ:* Paston Grammar Sch.; Magdalene Coll., Cambridge (MA); Univ. of E Africa, 1964–69; LSE, 1966. United Africa Co., 1964–69; Burton Group, 1969– (beginning of Top Shop). Member: Price Commn, 1977–79; Exec., Labour Industry & Finance Gp. Contested (Lab), SW Herts, 1979. FRSA 1983. *Address:* Phoebus, 14 Lambourne Avenue, Wimbledon, SW19 7DW. *T:* 01–879 0045. *Club:* Reform.

COLMAN, David Stacy, MA; retired; *b* Broughty Ferry, Angus, 1 May 1906; *yr s* of Dr H. C. Colman; *m* 1934, Sallie Edwards (*d* 1970). *Educ:* Shrewsbury Sch.; Balliol Coll., Oxford (Scholar). 1st Class Hon. Mods, 1926; 1st Class Lit. Hum., 1928. Asst Master at Shrewsbury Sch., 1928–31 and 1935–36; Fellow of Queen's Coll., Oxford and Praelector in Classics and Ancient History, 1931–34; Headmaster, C of E Grammar Sch., Melbourne, 1937–38; Shrewsbury School: Asst Master, 1938–66; Master of Day Boys, 1949–61; Librarian, 1961–66. Mem Council, Soc. for Promotion of Roman Studies, 1958–61, Classical Assoc., 1961–64. *Publication:* Sabrinae Corolla: The Classics at Shrewsbury School under Dr Butler and Dr Kennedy, 1950. *Address:* 19 Woodfield Road, Shrewsbury SY3 8HZ. *T:* 53749. *Clubs:* National Liberal; Leander; Salop (Shrewsbury).

COLMAN, Elijah Alec, JP; Chairman: E. Alec Colman Group of Companies; Langham Life Assurance Co. Ltd; *b* Tipton, Staffs, 7 Jan. 1903; *s* of Abraham and Leah Colman; *m* 1956, Eileen Amelia Graham; no *c*. *Educ:* Tipton Green Coun. Sch., Staffs. Dir of numerous charitable organisations; concerned with rehabilitation of refugees throughout the world; Pres., British Friends of Bar-Ilan Univ., 1981–; Exec. Mem., Jt Palestine Appeal; Vice Pres., British-Israel (formerly Anglo-Israel) Chamber of Commerce, 1981–. Mem. Ct, Patternmakers Co. JP Inner London, 1962. Hon. PhD, Bar-Ilan Univ., 1974. *Recreations:* reading, philosophy. *Clubs:* East India, Devonshire, Sports and Public Schools, City Livery, Royal Automobile.

COLMAN, Sir Michael (Jeremiah), 3rd Bt *cr* 1907; Chairman, Reckitt and Colman Ltd, since 1986; *b* 7 July 1928; *s* of Sir Jeremiah Colman, 2nd Bt, and Edith Gwendolyn Tritton; *S* father, 1961; *m* 1955, Judith Jean Wallop, *d* of Vice-Adm. Sir Peveril William-Powlett, KCB, KCMG, CBE, DSO; two *s* three *d*. *Educ:* Eton. Dir, Reckitt & Colman Ltd; Member: Council of Royal Warrant Holders, 1977–, Pres., 1984–85; Trinity House Lighthouse Bd, 1985–. Member: Council, Chemical Industries Assoc., 1982–84; Bd, UK Centre for Econ. and Environmental Develt, 1985–. Mem., Council, Scout Assoc., 1985–. Capt., Yorks Yeomanry, RARO, 1967. Mem. Ct, Skinners' Co., 1985–. *Recreations:* farming, shooting. *Heir: s* Jeremiah Michael Powlett Colman [*b* 23 Jan. 1958; *m* 1981, Susan Elizabeth, *yr d* of John Henry Britland, York]. *Address:* Malshanger, Basingstoke, Hants. *T:* Basingstoke 780241; 40 Chester Square, SW1; Tarvie, Bridge of Cally, Blairgowrie, Perthshire. *T:* Strathardle 264. *Club:* Cavalry and Guards.

COLMAN, Timothy James Alan; Lord-Lieutenant of Norfolk, since 1978; *b* 19 Sept. 1929; 2nd but *o* surv. *s* of late Captain Geoffrey Russell Rees Colman and Lettice Elizabeth Evelyn Colman, Norwich; *m* 1951, Lady Mary Cecelia (Extra Lady in Waiting to Princess Alexandra), twin *d* of late Lt-Col Hon. Michael Claude Hamilton Bowes Lyon and Elizabeth Margaret, Glamis; two *s* three *d*. *Educ:* RNC, Dartmouth and Greenwich. Lieut RN, 1950, retd 1953. Chm., Eastern Counties Newspapers Group Ltd; Director: Reckitt & Colman plc; Whitbread & Co. PLC. Chm., Carnegie UK Trust, 1983–; Pro-Chancellor, Univ. of E Anglia, 1973– (Chm. Council, 1973–85); Chairman: Trustees, Norfolk and Norwich Triennial Festival, 1974–; Royal Norfolk Agricl Assoc., 1985–

(Pres., 1982). Member: Countryside Commn, 1971–76; Water Space Amenity Commn, 1973–76; Adv. Cttee for England, Nature Conservancy Council, 1974–80; Eastern Regional Cttee, National Trust, 1967–71; Pres., Norfolk Naturalists Trust, 1962–78. JP 1958, DL 1968, High Sheriff 1970, Norfolk. Hon. DCL E. Anglia, 1973. KStJ 1979. *Address:* Bixley Manor, Norwich, Norfolk NR14 8SJ. *T:* Norwich 625298. *Clubs:* Turf, Pratt's.

COLOMBO, Archbishop of, (RC), since 1977; Most Rev. Nicholas Marcus Fernando, STD; *b* 6 Dec. 1932. *Educ:* St Aloysius Seminary, Colombo; Universitas Propaganda Fide, Rome. BA (London); PhL (Rome); STD (Rome). Chairman, Episcopal Commission for Clergy, Religious, Seminaries, Secular Institutes, Sri Lanka. *Address:* Archbishop's House, Colombo 8, Sri Lanka. *T:* 595471/2/3.

COLOMBO, Emilio; Deputy (Christian Democrat), Italian Parliament, since 1948; Minister of Foreign Affairs, Italy, 1980–83; *b* Potenza, Italy, 11 April 1920. *Educ:* Rome Univ. Deputy, Constituent Assembly, 1946–48; Under-Secretary: of Agriculture, 1948–51; of Public Works, 1953–55; Minister: of Agriculture, 1955–58; of Foreign Trade, 1958–59; of Industry and Commerce, 1959–60, March-April 1960, July 1960–63; of the Treasury, 1963–70, Feb.-May 1972, 1974–76; Prime Minister, 1970–72; Minister of State for UN Affairs, 1972–73; Minister of Finance, 1973–74. European Parliament: Mem., 1976–80; Chm., Political Affairs Cttee, 1976–77; Pres., 1977–79. Formerly Vice-Pres., Italian Catholic Youth Assoc. Charlemagne Prize, 1979. *Address:* Camera dei Deputati, Rome, Italy; Via Aurelia 239, Rome, Italy.

COLQUHOUN, Maj.-Gen. Sir Cyril (Harry), KCVO 1968 (CVO 1965); CB 1955; OBE 1945; late Royal Artillery; Secretary of the Central Chancery of the Orders of Knighthood, 1960–68; Extra Gentleman Usher to the Queen since 1968; *b* 1903; *s* of late Capt. Harry Colquhoun; *m* 1930, Stella Irene, *d* of late W. C. Rose, Kotagiri, India, and Cheam, Surrey; one *s.* Served War of 1939–45 (despatches, OBE); Palestine, 1946–48 (despatches); Comdr, 6th, 76th and 1st Field Regiments; CRA 61st Div., 1945; CRA 6th Airborne Div., 1947–48; CRA 1st Infantry Div., 1949–50; Comdt, Sch. of Artillery, 1951–53; GOC 50th (Northumbrian) Infantry Div. (TA), and Northumbrian District, 1954–56; GOC Troops, Malta, 1956–59; retired 1960. Col Commandant: Royal Artillery, 1962–69; Royal Malta Artillery, 1962–70. *Recreations:* gardening, shooting. *Address:* Longwalls, Shenington, Banbury, Oxon OX15 6NQ. *T:* Edgehill 246. *Club:* Army and Navy.

COLQUHOUN, Prof. David, FRS 1985; Professor of Pharmacology, University College London, since 1983; *b* 19 July 1936; *s* of Gilbert Colquhoun and Kathleen Mary (*née* Chambers); *m* 1976, Margaret Ann Boultwood; one *s. Educ:* Birkenhead Sch.; Liverpool Technical Coll.; Leeds Univ. (BSc); Edinburgh Univ. (PhD). Lectr, Dept of Pharmacol., UCL, 1964–70; Vis. Asst, then Associate Prof., Dept of Pharmacol., Yale Univ. Med. Sch., 1970–72; Sen. Lectr, Dept of Pharmacol., Univ. of Southampton Med. Sch., 1972–75; Sen. Lectr, Dept of Pharmacol., St George's Hosp. Med. Sch., 1975–79; Reader, Dept of Pharmacol., UCL, 1979–83. Mem., Editl Bd, Jl of Physiology, 1974–81. Trustee, Sir Ronald Fisher Meml Cttee, 1975–. *Publications:* Lectures on Biostatistics, 1971; articles in Jl of Physiology, British Jl of Pharmacology, Proc. of Royal Soc., etc. *Recreations:* walking, running, sailing, linear algebra. *Address:* 7 Beech Close, Walton-on-Thames, Surrey KT12 5RG. *T:* Walton-on-Thames 244021.

COLQUHOUN, Rev. Canon Frank, MA; Canon Residentiary of Norwich Cathedral, 1973–78, Canon Emeritus, since 1978; Vice-Dean, 1974–78; *b* 28 Oct. 1909; *s* of Rev. R. W. Colquhoun; *m* 1st, 1934, Dora Gertrude Hearne Slater; one *s* one *d*; 2nd, 1973, Judy Kenney. *Educ:* Warwick Sch.; Durham Univ. LTh 1932, BA 1933, MA 1937, Durham. Deacon, 1933; Priest, 1934; Curate, St Faith, Maidstone, 1933–35; Curate, New Malden, Surrey, 1935–39; Vicar, St Michael and All Angels, Blackheath Park, SE3, 1939–46; Editorial Sec., Nat. Church League, 1946–52; Priest-in-Charge, Christ Church, Woburn Square, WC1, 1952–54; Vicar of Wallington, Surrey, 1954–61; Canon Residentiary of Southwark Cathedral, 1961–73; Principal, Southwark Ordination Course, 1966–72. Editor, The Churchman, 1946–53. *Publications:* The Living Church in the Parish (ed), 1952; Harringay Story, 1954; Your Child's Baptism, 1958; The Gospels, 1961; Total Christianity, 1962; The Catechism, 1963; Lent with Pilgrim's Progress, 1965; Christ's Ambassadors, 1965; (ed) Parish Prayers, 1967; (ed) Hard Questions, 1967; Preaching through the Christian Year, 1972; Strong Son of God, 1973; Preaching at the Parish Communion, 1974; Contemporary Parish Prayers, 1975; (ed) Moral Questions, 1977; Hymns that Live, 1980; Prayers that Live, 1981; New Parish Prayers, 1982; Family Prayers, 1984; Fourfold Portrait of Jesus, 1984; A Hymn Companion, 1985; Preaching on Favourite Hymns, 1986. *Recreations:* writing, listening to music. *Address:* 21 Buckholt Avenue, Bexhill-on-Sea, East Sussex TN40 2RS. *T:* Bexhill 221138.

COLQUHOUN OF LUSS, Captain Sir Ivar (Iain), 8th Bt *cr* 1786; JP; DL; Hon. Sheriff (formerly Hon. Sheriff Substitute); Chief of the Clan; Grenadier Guards; *b* 4 Jan. 1916; *s* of Sir Iain Colquhoun, 7th Bt, and Geraldine Bryde (Dinah) (*d* 1974), *d* of late F. J. Tennant; *s* father, 1948; *m* 1943, Kathleen, 2nd *d* of late W. A. Duncan and of Mrs Duncan, 53 Cadogan Square, SW1; one *s* one *d* (and one *s* decd). *Educ:* Eton. JP 1951, DL 1952, Dunbartonshire. *Heir:* *s* Malcolm Rory Colquhoun, Younger of Luss [*b* 20 Dec. 1947; *m* 1978, Susan Timmerman (marr. diss.); one *s*]. *Address:* Camstraddan, Luss, Dunbartonshire; Eilean da Mheinn, Crinan, Argyllshire; 26A Thorney Crescent, SW11. *Clubs:* White's, Royal Ocean Racing.
See also Duke of Argyll.

COLQUHOUN, Ms Maureen Morfydd; political researcher and writer; Member, Hackney Borough Council (New River Ward), since 1982; Director, Democratic Services Limited, since 1983; *b* 12 Aug. 1928; *m* 1949, Keith Colquhoun (marr. diss. 1980); two *s* one *d*. Partner, 1975–, Ms Barbara Todd; extended family, two *d*. Mem. Labour Party, 1945–; Councillor: Shoreham UDC, 1965–74; Adur District Council, 1973–74; County Councillor, West Sussex, 1971–74. MP (Lab) Northampton North, Feb. 1974–1979; Information Officer, Gingerbread, 1980–82. *Publication:* A Woman In the House, 1980. *Recreations:* walking, jazz, opera, theatre, collecting primitive and naieve paintings. *Address:* 19 Vicars Close, E9 7HT.

COLSTON, Colin Charles; QC 1980; **His Honour Judge Colston;** a Circuit Judge, since 1983; *b* 2 Oct. 1937; *yr s* of late Eric Colston, JP, and Catherine Colston; *m* 1963, Edith Helga, JP, *d* of Med. Rat Dr Wilhelm and Frau Gisela Hille, St Oswald/Freistadt, Austria; two *s* one *d. Educ:* Rugby Sch.; The Gunnery, Washington, Conn, USA; Trinity Hall, Cambridge (MA). National Service, RN, 1956–58; commissioned, RNR, 1958–64. Called to the Bar, Gray's Inn, 1962; Midland and Oxford Circuit (formerly Midland Circuit); Recorder of Midland Circuit, 1968–69; Member, Senate of Inns of Court and Bar, 1977–80; Recorder of the Crown Court, 1978–83. *Address:* The Crown Court, St Albans, Herts.

COLSTON, Michael; Chairman and Managing Director, Charles Colston Group Ltd, since 1969; *b* 24 July 1932; *s* of Sir Charles Blampied Colston, CBE, MC, DCM, FCGI and Lady (Eliza Foster) Colston, MBE; *m* 1st, 1956, Jane Olivia Kilham Roberts (marr.

diss.); three *d*; 2nd, 1977, Judith Angela Briggs. *Educ:* Ridley Coll., Canada; Stowe; Gonville and Caius Coll., Cambridge. Joined 17th/21st Lancers, 1952; later seconded to 1st Royal Tank Regt for service in Korea. Founder Dir Charles Colston Group Ltd (formerly Colston Appliances Ltd) together with late Sir Charles Colston, 1955; Chm. and Man. Dir, Colston Domestic Appliances Ltd, 1969–79. Chairman: Tallent Engineering Ltd, 1969–; ITS Rubber Ltd, 1969–85; Dishwasher Council, 1970–75. Chm., Assoc. Manufrs of Domestic Electrical Appliances, 1976–79. Member Council: Inst. of Directors (Pres., Thames Valley Br.); CBI, 1984– (Chm., S Regl Council, 1986–); British Electrotechnical Approvals Bd, 1976–79. *Recreations:* fishing, shooting, tennis; founder Cambridge Univ. Water Ski Club. *Address:* Ewelme Park, Nettlebed, Oxfordshire RG9 6DZ. *T:* Nettlebed 641279.

COLT, Sir Edward (William Dutton), 10th Bt *cr* 1694; MB, MRCP, FACP; Assistant Attending Physician, St Luke's-Roosevelt Hospital, New York; Assistant Professor of Clinical Medicine (part-time), Columbia University, New York; *b* 22 Sept. 1936; *s* of Major John Rochfort Colt, North Staffs Regt (*d* 1944), and of Angela Miriam Phyllis (*née* Kyan; she *m* 1946, Capt. Robert Leslie Cock); *S* uncle, 1951; *m* 1st, 1966, Jane Caroline (marr. diss. 1972), *d* of James Histed Lewis, Geneva and Washington, DC; 2nd, 1979, Suzanne Nelson (*née* Knickerbocker); one *s* one *d. Educ:* Stoke House, Seaford; Douai Sch.; University Coll., London. Lately: Medical Registrar, UCH; House Physician, Brompton Hosp. *Publications:* contribs, especially on sports medicine, particularly running, to British and American med. jls. *Recreations:* cycling, jogging, skiing, squash. *Heir:* *s* Tristan Charles Edward Colt, *b* 27 June 1983. *Address:* 12 E 88 Street, New York, NY 10028, USA; c/o Cock, 11 Stafford Road, Seaford, East Sussex.

COLTHURST, Sir Richard La Touche, 9th Bt *cr* 1744; *b* 14 Aug. 1928; *er s* of Sir Richard St John Jefferyes Colthurst, 8th Bt, and Denys Maida Hanmer West (*d* 1966), *e d* of Augustus William West; *S* father, 1955; *m* 1953, Janet Georgina, *d* of L. A. Wilson-Wright, Coolcarrigan, Co. Kildare; three *s* one *d. Educ:* Harrow; Peterhouse, Cambridge (MA). Dir, K. C. Webb (Underwriting) Ltd. Liveryman of Worshipful Company of Grocers. Mem., Internat. Dendrology Soc. *Recreations:* forestry, cricket, tennis, swimming. *Heir:* *s* Charles St John Colthurst [*b* 21 May 1955. *Educ:* Eton; Magdalene Coll., Cambridge (MA); University Coll., Dublin]. *Clubs:* City University, MCC.

COLTMAN, (Arthur) Leycester (Scott); HM Diplomatic Service; Counsellor and Head of Chancery, Brussels, since 1983; *b* 24 May 1938; *s* of late Arthur Cranfield Coltman and Vera Vaid; *m* 1969, Maria Piedad Josefina Cantos Aberasturi; two *s* one *d. Educ:* Rugby School; Magdalene Coll., Cambridge. Foreign Office, 1961–62; Third Secretary, British Embassy, Copenhagen, 1963–64; Second Secretary, Cairo 1964–65, Madrid 1966–69; Manchester Business School, 1969–70; Foreign Office, 1970–74; Commercial Secretary, Brasilia, 1974–77; Foreign Office, 1977–79; Counsellor, Mexico City, 1979–83. *Recreations:* tennis, squash, chess, bridge, music. *Address:* c/o Foreign and Commonwealth Office, King Charles Street, SW1A 2AH.

COLTON, Cyril Hadlow, CBE 1970; *b* 15 March 1902; *yr s* of Albert Edward Colton and Kate Louise; *m* 1932, Doree Beatrice Coles; one *s* two *d. Educ:* Reigate Grammar School. Man-made fibres industry from 1921: Fabrique de Soie Artificiel de Tubize, 1921; British Celanese Ltd, 1923: Dir, 1945; Chm., 1964; Pres., 1968; Courtaulds Ltd, 1957: Marketing Dir, 1962–67; Dir, Samuel Courtauld Ltd, 1959–64; Dir, Courtaulds SA, 1962–68; Consultant, Courtaulds Ltd, 1967–78. Chm., Rayon Allocation Cttee, 1940–49; Member: Council, British Rayon Research Assoc., 1946–61; BoT Utility Cloth Cttee, 1950–52; BoT Mission to Middle East, 1954; Pres., Textile Inst., 1954–55. Chairman: British Man-Made Fibres Fedn, 1967–75 (Pres., 1976); British Man-Made Fibres Producers Cttee, 1965–72; Silk and Man-Made Fibres Users Assoc., 1968–70; BSI Textile Div., 1969–72; Pres., Bureau International pour la Standardisation de la Rayonne et des Fibres Synthetiques, 1969–72; Vice-Pres., Cttee Internat. des Fibres Synthetiques, 1969–72; Pres., British Display Soc., 1966–79. Mem. Council, Cotton, Silk and Man-Made Fibres Research Assoc. (Shirley Inst.), 1969–72; Dep. Chm., Textile Council, 1967–72; Mem., Crowther Cttee on Consumer Credit, 1968–71. CompTI; FRSA; FInstM. Liveryman, Worshipful Co. of Weavers. *Address:* Appin House, Cobham, Surrey. *T:* Cobham 4477.

COLVILLE, family name of **Viscount Colville of Culross** and of **Baron Clydesmuir.**

COLVILLE OF CULROSS, 4th Viscount *cr* 1902; **John Mark Alexander Colville;** QC; 14th Baron (Scot.) *cr* 1604; 4th Baron (UK) *cr* 1885; Chairman: Mental Health Act Commission, since 1983; Alcohol Research and Education Council, since 1984; *b* 19 July 1933; *e s* of 3rd Viscount and Kathleen Myrtle, OBE 1961, *e d* of late Brig.-Gen. H. R. Gale, CMG, RE, Bardsey, Saanichton, Vancouver Island; *S* father, 1945; *m* 1st, 1958, Mary Elizabeth Webb-Bowen (marr. diss. 1973); four *s*; 2nd, 1974, Margaret Birgitta, Viscountess Davidson, LLB, JP, Barrister, *o d* of Maj.-Gen. C. H. Norton, CB, CBE, DSO; one *s. Educ:* Rugby (Scholar); New Coll., Oxford (Scholar) (MA). Lieut Grenadier Guards Reserve. Barrister-at-law, Lincoln's Inn, 1960 (Buchanan prizeman), Bencher, 1986; QC 1978. Minister of State, Home Office, 1972–74. Chm., Norwich Information and Technology Centre, 1983–85; Director: Rediffusion Television Ltd, 1961–68; British Electric Traction Co. Ltd, 1968–72, 1974–84 (Dep. Chm., 1980–81); Mem., CBI Council, 1982–84. UK rep., UN Human Rights Commn, 1980–83; Mem., UN Working Gp on Disappeared Persons, 1980–84 (Chm., 1981–84); Special Rapporteur on Human Rights in Guatemala, 1983–86. Mem. Council, Univ. of E Anglia, 1968–72. Mem., Royal Company of Archers (Queen's Body Guard for Scotland). Hon. Mem., Rating and Valuation Assoc. *Heir:* *s* Master of Colville, *qv. Address:* House of Lords, SW1A 0PW.
See also Baron Carrington.

COLVILLE, Master of; Hon. Charles Mark Townshend Colville; *b* 5 Sept. 1959; *s* and *heir* of 4th Viscount Colville of Culross, *qv. Educ:* Rugby; Univ. of Durham. *Address:* Rookyards, Spexhall, near Halesworth, Suffolk. *T:* Ilketshall 318.

COLVILLE, Sir John (Rupert), Kt 1974; CB 1955; CVO 1949; Director, Provident Life Association; Chairman: London Committee, Ottoman Bank; Eucalyptus Pulp Mills Ltd; *b* 28 Jan. 1915; *s* of late Hon. George Colville and Lady Cynthia Colville; *m* 1948, Lady Margaret Egerton (*see* Lady Margaret Colville); two *s* one *d. Educ:* Harrow; Trinity Coll., Cambridge (1st Class Hons, History Tripos, and Sen. Scholar). Page of Honour to King George V, 1927–31. 3rd Sec., Diplomatic Service, 1937; Asst Private Sec. to Mr Neville Chamberlain, 1939–40; to Mr Winston Churchill, 1940–41 and 1943–45, and to Mr Clement Attlee, 1945. Served War of 1939–45, Pilot, RAFVR, 1941–44. Private Sec. to Princess Elizabeth, 1947–49; 1st Sec., British Embassy, Lisbon, 1949–51; Counsellor, Foreign Service, 1951; Joint Principal Private Sec. to the Prime Minister, 1951–55. Exec. Dir, Hill Samuel Ltd, 1955–80. President: New Victoria Hospital, 1978–85; Prayer Book Soc., 1981–84; Vice-Pres., National Assoc. of Boys' Clubs. Hon. Fellow, Churchill Coll., Cambridge, 1971. Officier, Légion d'Honneur. *Publications:* Fools' Pleasure, 1935; contrib. to Action This Day-Working with Churchill, 1968; Man of Valour, 1972; Footprints in Time, 1976; The New Elizabethans, 1977; The Portrait of a General, 1980; The Churchillians, 1981; Strange Inheritance, 1983; The Fringes of Power, 1985. *Address:* The

Close, Broughton, near Stockbridge, Hampshire SO20 8AA. *T:* Romsey 301331. *Clubs:* White's, Pratt's.

COLVILLE, Lady Margaret; *b* 20 July 1918; *d* of 4th Earl of Ellesmere; *m* 1948, Sir John Rupert Colville, *qv*; two *s* one *d*. Served War of 1939–45 in ATS (Junior Subaltern). Lady in Waiting to the Princess Elizabeth, Duchess of Edinburgh, 1946–49. *Address:* The Close, Broughton, near Stockbridge, Hants. *T:* Romsey 301331.
See also Duke of Sutherland.

COLVIN, David; Chief Adviser in Social Work, The Scottish Office, since 1980; *b* 31 Jan. 1931; *s* of James Colvin and Mrs Crawford Colvin; *m* 1957, Elma Findlay; two *s* three *d*. *Educ:* Whitehill Sch., Glasgow; Glasgow and Edinburgh Univs. Probation Officer, Glasgow City, 1955–60; Psychiatric Social Worker, Scottish Prison and Borstal Service, Scottish Home and Health Dept, 1960–61; Sen. Psychiatric Social Worker, Crichton Royal Hosp., Child Psychiatric Unit, 1961–65; Director, Family Casework Unit, Paisley, 1965–66; Welfare Officer, SHHD, 1966–68; Social Work Adviser, Social Work Services Gp, Scottish Educn Dept, 1968, and subseq. At various times held office in Howard League for Penal Reform, Assoc. of Social Workers and Inst. for Study and Treatment of Delinquency. Sen. Associate Research Fellow, Brunel Univ., 1978. Gov., Nat. Inst. for Social Work, 1986–. Hon. Adviser, British Red Cross, 1982–. *Recreations:* collector; swimming, climbing, golf, gardens, social affairs. *Address:* 13 Eton Terrace, Edinburgh.

COLVIN, David Hugh; HM Diplomatic Service; Counsellor and Head of Chancery, British Embassy, Budapest, since 1985; *b* 23 Jan. 1941; 3rd *s* of Major Leslie Hubert Boyd Colvin, MC, and Edna Mary (*née* Parrott); *m* 1971, Diana Caroline Carew, *y d* of Gordon MacPherson Lang Smith and Mildred (*née* Carew-Gibson); one *s*. *Educ:* Lincoln Sch.; Trinity Coll., Oxford (MA). Assistant Principal, Board of Trade, 1966. Joined HM Foreign (later Diplomatic) Service, 1967; Central Dept, FO, 1967; Second Secretary, Bangkok, 1968–71; European Integration Dept, FCO, 1971–75; First Sec., Paris, 1975–77; First Sec. (Press and Inf.), UK Permanent Representation to the European Community, 1977–82; Asst Sec., Cabinet Office, 1982–85. *Recreations:* military history, squash, tennis, shooting. *Address:* c/o Foreign and Commonwealth Office, SW1; 15 Westmoreland Terrace, SW1V 4AG. *T:* 01–834 2900. *Club:* Travellers'.

COLVIN, Howard Montagu, CVO 1983; CBE 1964; MA; FBA 1963; FRHistS, FSA; Fellow of St John's College, Oxford, since 1948 (Tutor in History, 1948–78; Librarian, 1950–84); Reader in Architectural History, Oxford University, 1965–Sept. 1987; Member: Historic Buildings Council for England, 1970–84; Historic Buildings and Monuments Commission, 1984–85; Historic Buildings Advisory Committee, since 1986; Royal Commission on Ancient and Historical Monuments of Scotland, since 1977; Royal Commission on Historical Manuscripts, since 1981; Reviewing Committee on the Export of Works of Art, 1982–83; Royal Fine Art Commission, 1962–72; Royal Commission on Historical Monuments, England, 1963–76; President, Society of Architectural Historians of Great Britain, 1979–81; *b* 15 Oct. 1919; *s* of late Montagu Colvin; *m* 1943, Christina Edgeworth, *d* of late H. E. Butler, Prof. of Latin at University Coll., London; two *s*. *Educ:* Trent Coll.; University Coll., London (Fellow, 1974). FRHistS; FSA 1980. Served in RAF, 1940–46 (despatches). Asst Lecturer, Dept of History, University Coll., London, 1946–48. Hon. FRIBA. DUniv York, 1978. Wolfson Literary Award, 1978. *Publications:* The White Canons in England, 1951; A Biographical Dictionary of English Architects 1660–1840, 1954; (General Editor and part author) The History of the King's Works, 6 Vols, 1963–82; A History of Deddington, 1963; Catalogue of Architectural Drawings in Worcester College Library, 1964; Architectural Drawings in the Library of Elton Hall (with Maurice Craig), 1964; (ed with John Harris) The Country Seat, 1970; Building Accounts of King Henry III, 1971; A Biographical Dictionary of British Architects 1600–1840, 1978; (introduction) The Queen Anne Churches, 1980; (ed with John Newman) Roger North, Of Architecture, 1981; Unbuilt Oxford, 1983; Calke Abbey, Derbyshire, 1985; articles on mediæval and architectural history in Archaeological Journal, Architectural Review, etc. *Recreation:* gardening. *Address:* 50 Plantation Road, Oxford. *T:* Oxford 57460.

COLVIN, John Horace Ragnar, CMG 1968; HM Diplomatic Service, retired; Vice-President and Director for International Relations, Chase Manhattan Bank; Director, Hotung Investment (China); *b* Tokyo, 18 June 1922; *s* of late Adm. Sir Ragnar Colvin, KBE, CB and Lady Colvin; *m* 1st, 1948, Elizabeth Anne Manifold (marr. diss., 1963); one *s* one *d*; 2nd, 1967, Moranna Sibyl de Lerisson Cazenove; one *s* one *d*. *Educ:* RNC Dartmouth; University of London. Royal Navy, 1935–51. Joined HM Diplomatic Service, 1951; HM Embassies, Oslo, 1951–53 and Vienna, 1953–55; British High Commn, Kuala Lumpur, 1958–61; HM Consul-General, Hanoi, 1965–67; Ambassador to People's Republic of Mongolia, 1971–74; HM Embassy, Washington, 1977–80. Member: Research Council, Pacific Forum; Political Council, Asiaweek. *Address:* The Old Parsonage, Pamber Heath, Hants. *T:* Silchester 253; Chase Manhattan Bank, 280 Gloucester Road, Hong Kong. *Clubs:* Brooks's, White's.

COLVIN, Brigadier Dame Mary Katherine Rosamond, DBE 1959 (OBE 1947); TD; Extra Lady in Waiting to the Princess Royal, 1964–65 (Lady in Waiting, 1962–64); *b* 25 Oct. 1907; *d* of Lt-Col F. F. Colvin, CBE. Commissioned 1939; Commanded Central Ordnance Depot, ATS Gp, Weedon, Northants, 1943–44; subsequently held staff appointment in Military Government, Germany; Comdt WRAC Sch. of Instruction, 1948–51; Asst Dir, WRAC, HQ. Scottish Comd, 1951–54; Inspector of Recruiting (Women's Services), War Office, 1954–56; Dep. Dir, WRAC, HQ Eastern Command, 1956–57; Dir of the Woman's Royal Army Corps, 1957–61. Hon. ADC to the Queen, 1957–61, retd. *Address:* Pasture House, North Luffenham, Oakham, Rutland LE15 8JU.

COLVIN, Michael Keith Beale; MP (C) Romsey and Waterside, since 1983 (Bristol North West, 1979–83); *b* 27 Sept. 1932; *s* of late Captain Ivan Beale Colvin, RN, and Mrs Joy Colvin, OBE; *m* Hon. Nichola, *e d* of Baron Cayzer, *qv*; one *s* two *d*. *Educ:* Eton; RMA, Sandhurst; Royal Agricultural Coll., Cirencester. Served Grenadier Guards, 1950–57: Temp. Captain; served BAOR, Berlin, Suez campaign, Cyprus. J. Walter Thompson & Co. Ltd, 1958–63. Landowner and farmer. Councillor: Andover RDC, 1965–72; Test Valley Bor. Council, 1972–74 (first Vice Chm.); Dep. Chm., Winchester Constituency Conservative Assoc., 1973–76; Mem. (part-time), Cons. Res. Dept, 1975–79. Chairman: Conservative Aviation Cttee, 1982–83; Cttee of W Country Cons. MPs, 1982–83; Vice-Chm., Conservative Smaller Businesses Cttee, 1980–83; Mem., Select Cttee on Employment, 1981–83; Sec., Conservative Shipping and Shipbuilding Cttee, 1981–83; Parly Adviser to Nat. Union of Licensed Victuallers and NPFA, 1983–; PPS to Baroness Young, Dep. Foreign Sec., FCO, 1983–85, and to Richard Luce, now Minister for Arts, 1983–. President: Hampshire Young Farmers Clubs, 1973–74; Test Valley Br., CPRE, 1974–; Mem., Southern Sports Council, 1970–74. Governor, Enham Village Centre. *Address:* Tangley House, near Andover, Hants SP11 0SH. *T:* Chute Standen 215. *Clubs:* Turf, Pratt's.

COLWYN, 3rd Baron, *cr* 1917; **Ian Anthony Hamilton-Smith;** Bt 1912; Dental Surgeon since 1966; *b* 1 Jan. 1942; *s* of 2nd Baron Colwyn and Miriam Gwendoline, *d* of Victor Ferguson; *S* father 1966; *m* 1st, 1964, Sonia Jane (marr. diss. 1977), *d* of P. H. G. Morgan, The Eades, Upton-on-Severn; one *s* one *d*; 2nd, 1977, Nicola Jeanne, *d* of Arthur Tyers, The Avenue, Sunbury-on-Thames; two *d*. *Educ:* Cheltenham Coll.; Univ. of London. BDS London 1966; LDS, RCS 1966. *Recreations:* music, dance band and orchestra, golf. *Heir: s* Hon. Craig Peter Hamilton-Smith, *b* 13 Oct. 1968. *Address:* (practice) 53 Wimpole Street, W1.

COLYER, John Stuart, QC 1976; a Recorder, since 1986; *b* 25 April 1935; *s* of late Stanley Herbert Colyer, MBE, and Louisa (*née* Randle); *m* 1961, Emily Warner, *o d* of late Stanley Leland Dutrow and Mrs Dutrow, Blue Ridge Summit, Pa, USA; two *d*. *Educ:* Dudley Grammar Sch.; Shrewsbury; Worcester Coll., Oxford (Open History Scholarship; BA 1955, MA 1961). 2nd Lieut RA, 1954–55. Called to the Bar, Middle Temple, 1959 (Bencher, 1983); Instructor, Univ. of Pennsylvania, Philadelphia, 1959–60, Asst Prof., 1960–61; practised English bar, Midland and Oxford Circuit (formerly Oxford Circuit), 1961–; Lectr (Law of Landlord and Tenant), 1970–, Hon. Reader, 1985– and Mem. Council, 1985–, Council of Legal Educn. Chm., Lawyers' Christian Fellowship, 1981–; Mem., Anglo-American Real Property Inst., 1980– (Treasurer, 1984). Blundell Meml Lectr, 1977, 1982, 1986. *Publications:* (ed jtly) Encyclopaedia of Forms and Precedents (Landlord and Tenant), vol. XI, 1965, vol. XII, 1966; A Modern View of the Law of Torts, 1966; Landlord and Tenant, in Halsbury's Laws of England, 4th edn, 1981; (ed) Megarry's The Rent Acts, 11th edn, 1987; articles in Conveyancer and other professional jls. *Recreations:* entertaining my family; opera; cultivation of cacti and of succulents (esp. Lithops); gardening generally; travel. *Address:* 11 King's Bench Walk, Temple, EC4. *T:* 01–353 2484.

COLYER-FERGUSSON, Sir James Herbert Hamilton, 4th Bt, *cr* 1866; *b* 10 Jan. 1917; *s* of Max Christian Hamilton Colyer-Fergusson (*d* on active service, 1940) and Edith Jane (*d* 1936), singer, *d* of late William White Miller, Portage la Prairie, Manitoba; *S* grandfather, 1951. *Educ:* Harrow; Balliol Coll., Oxford. BA 1939; MA 1945. Formerly Capt., The Buffs; served War of 1939–45 (prisoner-of-war, 1940). Entered service of former Great Western Railway Traffic Dept, 1947, later Operating Dept of the Western Region of British Rlys. Personal Asst to Chm. of British Transport Commission, 1957; Passenger Officer in SE Division of Southern Region, BR, 1961; Party and Public Correspondent, BRB, 1967; Deputy to Curator of Historical Relics, BRB, 1968. Retired. *Heir:* none. *Address:* 61 Onslow Square, SW7. *Club:* Naval and Military.
See also Sir Lingard Goulding, Bt, Viscount Monckton of Brenchley.

COLYTON, 1st Baron, *cr* 1956, of Farway and of Taunton; **Henry Lennox d'Aubigné Hopkinson,** PC 1952; CMG 1944; *b* 3 Jan. 1902; *e s* of late Sir Henry Lennox Hopkinson, KCVO; *m* 1st, 1927, Alice Labouisse (*d* 1953), *d* of Henry Lane Eno, Bar Harbor, Maine, USA; one *s*; 2nd, 1956, Mrs Barbara Addams, *d* of late Stephen Barb, New York. *Educ:* Eton Coll.; Trinity Coll., Cambridge (BA History and Modern Languages Tripos). Entered Diplomatic Service, 1924; 3rd Sec., Washington, 1924; 2nd Sec., Foreign Office, 1929; Stockholm, 1931; Asst Private Sec. to Sec. of State for Foreign Affairs, 1932; Cairo, 1934; 1st Sec., 1936; Athens, 1938; War Cabinet Secretariat, 1939; Private Sec. to Permanent Under-Sec. for Foreign Affairs, 1940; Counsellor and Political Advr to Minister of State in the Middle East, 1941; Minister Plenipotentiary, Lisbon, 1943; Dep. Brit. High Comr in Italy, and Vice-Pres., Allied Control Commn, 1944–46. Resigned from Foreign Service to enter politics, 1946; Head of Conservative Parly Secretariat and Jt Dir, Conservative Research Dept, 1946–50; MP (C) Taunton Div. of Somerset, 1950–56; Sec. for Overseas Trade, 1951–52; Minister of State for Colonial Affairs, 1952–Dec. 1955; Mem., Consultative Assembly, Council of Europe, 1950–52; Delegate, General Assembly, United Nations, 1952–55; Chairman: Anglo-Egyptian Resettlement Board, 1957–60; Joint East and Central African Board, 1960–65; Tanganyika Concessions Ltd, 1965–72. Royal Humane Society's Award for saving life from drowning, 1919. OStJ 1959. Grand Cross, Order of Prince Henry the Navigator (Portugal), 1972; Dato, Order of the Stia Negara (Brunei), 1972; Grand Star, Order Paduka Stia Negara Brunei, 1978; Commander, Order of the Zaire (Congo) 1971. *Heir: s* Hon. Nicholas Henry Eno Hopkinson [*b* 18 Jan. 1932; *m* 1957, Fiona Margaret, *o d* of Sir Torquil Munro, 5th Bt; two *s*]. *Address:* Le Formentor, avenue Princesse Grace, Monte Carlo, Monaco. *T:* (93) 30 92 96. *Clubs:* Buck's, White's, Beefsteak; Monte Carlo.

COMAY, Michael; Research Fellow, Leonard Davis Institute for International Relations, Jerusalem, since 1976; *b* Cape Town, 17 Oct. 1908; *s* of Alexander and Clara Comay; *m* 1935, Joan Solomon; one *s* one *d*. *Educ:* Univ. of Cape Town (BA, LLB). Barrister, 1931–40. Served with S African Army, Western Desert and UK, 1940–45 (Major). Settled Palestine as representative S African Zionist Fedn, 1945; Adviser, Political Dept Jewish Agency, 1946–48; Dir, British Commonwealth Div., Israel Foreign Min., 1948–51; Asst Dir-Gen., Israel For. Min., 1951–53 and 1957–59; Minister, then Ambassador to Canada, 1953–57; Perm. Rep. and Ambassador of Israel to UN, 1960–67; Political Adviser to For. Minister and Ambassador-at-Large, 1967–70; Ambassador of Israel to the Court of St James's, 1970–73. Associate Gen. Chm., Chaim Weizmann Centenary. *Recreations:* walking, painting. *Address:* 47 Harav Berlin Street, Jerusalem 92505, Israel.

COMBER, Ven. Anthony James; Archdeacon of Leeds, since 1982; *b* 20 April 1927; *s* of late Norman Mederson Comber and Nellie Comber. *Educ:* Leeds Grammar School; Leeds Univ. (MSc Mining); St Chad's Coll., Durham (DipTh); Munich Univ. Colliery underground official, 1951–53. Vicar: Oulton, 1960–69; Hunslet, 1969–77; Rector of Farnley, 1977–82. *Publication:* (contrib.) Today's Church and Today's World, 1977. *Recreations:* politics; walking in Bavaria. *Address:* 712 Foundry Lane, Leeds LS14 6BL. *T:* Leeds 602069.

COMBERMERE, 5th Viscount, *cr* 1826; **Michael Wellington Stapleton-Cotton;** Bt 1677; Baron Combermere, 1814; Lecturer in Biblical and Religious Studies, University of London, Department of Extra-Mural Studies, since 1972; *b* 8 Aug. 1929; *s* of 4th Viscount Combermere and Constance Marie Katherine (*d* 1968), *d* of Lt-Col Sir Francis Dudley W. Drummond, KBE; *S* father, 1969; *m* 1961, Pamela Elizabeth, *d* of Rev. R. G. Coulson; one *s* two *d*. *Educ:* Eton; King's Coll., Univ. of London. Palestine Police, 1947–48; Royal Canadian Mounted Police, 1948–50; Short-service commn as gen. duties Pilot, RAF, 1950–58, retd as Flt-Lt; Sales Rep., Teleflex Products Ltd, 1959–62; read Theology, KCL, 1962–67 (BD, MTh). Chm., World Congress of Faiths, 1983–. *Heir: s* Hon. Thomas Robert Wellington Stapleton-Cotton, *b* 30 Aug. 1969. *Address:* 46 Smith Street, SW3. *T:* 01–352 1319. *Club:* Royal Automobile.

COMBS, Sir Willis (Ide), KCVO 1974; CMG 1962; HM Diplomatic Service, retired; *b* Melbourne, 6 May 1916; *s* of Willis Ide Combs, Napier, New Zealand; *m* 1942, Grace Willis; two *d*. *Educ:* Dannevirke High Sch.; Victoria Coll., NZ; St John's Coll., Cambridge. Served in HM Forces, 1940–46. Apptd Mem. Foreign Service, 1947; transf. to Paris as 2nd Sec. (Commercial), Dec. 1947; 1st Sec., Nov. 1948; transf. to Rio de Janeiro, as 1st Sec., 1951; to Peking as 1st Sec. and Consul, 1953 (Chargé d'Affaires, 1954); Foreign Office, 1956; to Baghdad as Counsellor (Commercial), 1959; Diplomatic Service Inspector, 1963; Counsellor, British Embassy, Rangoon, 1965; Asst Under-Sec. of State, FCO, 1968; Ambassador to Indonesia, 1970–75. *Address:* Sunset, Wadhurst Park, Wadhurst, East Sussex. *Club:* United Oxford & Cambridge University.

COMFORT, Alexander, PhD, DSc; physician; poet and novelist; Adjunct Professor, Neuropsychiatric Institute, University of California at Los Angeles, since 1980; Consultant, Ventura County Hospital (Medical Education), since 1981; *b* 10 Feb. 1920; *s* of late Alexander Charles and Daisy Elizabeth Comfort; *m* 1st, 1943, Ruth Muriel Harris (marr. diss. 1973); one *s*; 2nd, 1973, Jane Tristram Henderson. *Educ:* Highgate Sch.; Trinity Coll., Cambridge (Robert Styring Scholar Classics, and Senior Scholar, Nat. Sciences); London Hospital (Scholar). 1st Cl. Nat. Sc. Tripos, Part I, 1940; 2nd Cl. Nat. Sc. Tripos, 1st Div. (Pathology), 1941; MRCS, LRCP 1944; MB, BCh Cantab 1944; MA Cantab 1945; DCH London 1945; PhD London 1949 (Biochemistry); DSc London 1963 (Gerontology). Refused military service in war of 1939–45. Lectr in Physiology, London Hospital Medical Coll., 1948–51; Hon. Research Associate, Dept of Zoology, 1951–73, and Dir of Research, Gerontology, 1966–73, UCL; Clin. Lectr, Dept Psychiatry, Stanford Univ., 1974–83; Prof., Dept of Pathol., Univ. of Calif Sch. of Med., Irvine, 1976–78; Consultant psychiatrist, Brentwood VA Hospital, LA, 1978–81. Pres., Brit. Soc. for Research on Ageing, 1967; Member: RSocMed.; Amer. Psychiatric Assoc. *Publications:* The Silver River, 1937; No Such Liberty (novel), 1941; Into Egypt (play), 1942; France and Other Poems, 1942; A Wreath for the Living (poems), 1943; Cities of the Plain (melodrama), 1943; The Almond Tree (novel), 1943; The Powerhouse (novel), 1944; Elegies, 1944; The Song of Lazarus (poems, USA), 1945; Letters from an Outpost (stories), 1947; Art and Social Responsibility (essays), 1947; The Signal to Engage (poems), 1947; Gengulphus (play), 1948; On this side Nothing (novel), 1948; First Year Physiological Technique (textbook), 1948; The Novel and Our Time (criticism), 1948; Barbarism and Sexual Freedom (essays), 1948; Sexual Behaviour in Society (social psychology), 1950; The Pattern of the Future (broadcast lectures), 1950; Authority and Delinquency in the Modern State (social psychology), 1950; And all but He Departed (poems), 1951; A Giant's Strength (novel), 1952; The Biology of Senescence (textbook), 1956 (2nd edn 1964, 3rd edn 1978); Darwin and the Naked Lady (essays), 1961; Come Out to Play (novel), 1961; Haste to the Wedding (poems), 1961; Are you Sitting Comfortably? (songs), 1962; Sex and Society (social psychology), 1963; Ageing, the Biology of Senescence (textbook), 1964; The Koka Shastra (translation), 1964; The Process of Ageing (science), 1965; Nature and Human Nature (science), 1966; The Anxiety Makers (med. history), 1967; The Joy of Sex (counselling), 1973; More Joy (counselling), 1974; A Good Age, 1976; (ed) Sexual Consequences of Disability, 1978; I and That: notes on the Biology of Religion, 1979; Poems, 1979; (with Jane T. Comfort) The Facts of Love, 1979; A Practise of Geriatric Psychiatry, 1979; Tetrarch (trilogy of novels), 1980; What is a Doctor? (essays), 1980; Reality and Empathy, 1983; (with Jane T. Comfort) What about Alcohol? (textbook), 1983. *Address:* The Windmill House, Cranbrook, Kent TN17 3AH.

COMFORT, Anthony Francis; HM Diplomatic Service, retired; *b* Plymouth, 12 Oct. 1920; *s* of Francis Harold Comfort and Elsie Grace (*née* Martin); *m* 1948, Joy Margaret Midson; two *s* one *d. Educ:* Bristol Grammar Sch.; Oriel Coll., Oxford. Entered Foreign Service, 1947; 2nd Sec. (Commercial), Athens, 1948–51; Consul, Alexandria, 1951–53; 1st Sec. (Commercial), Amman, 1953–54; Foreign Office, 1954–57; seconded to Colonial Office, 1957–59; 1st Sec. (Commercial), Belgrade, 1959–60; 1st Sec. and Consul, Reykjavik, 1961–65; Inspector of Diplomatic Establishments, 1965–68, retired 1969. *Recreations:* walking, gardening, looking at churches. *Address:* Nymet Cottage, Trowbridge Road, Bradford on Avon, Wilts BA15 1EE. *T:* Bradford-on-Avon 6046.

COMFORT, Dr Charles Fraser, OC; CD; RCA; artist and author; Emeritus Director, National Gallery of Canada, 1965; *b* Edinburgh, 22 July 1900; *m* 1924, Louise Chase, Winnipeg; two *d. Educ:* Winnipeg Sch. of Art and Art Students' League, New York. Cadet Officer, Univ. of Toronto Contingent of Canadian OTC, 1939; Commnd Instr in Infantry Weapons, 1940; Sen. Canadian War Artist (Army) Major, 1942–46 (UK, Italy and NW Europe). Head of Dept of Mural Painting, Ontario Coll. of Art, 1935–38; Associate Prof., Dept of Art and Archaeology, Univ. of Toronto, 1946–60 (Mem. staff, 1938); Dir, Nat. Gall. of Canada, 1959. Gold Medal and cash award, Great Lakes Exhibn, Albright Gall., Buffalo, NY, 1938; has travelled widely in Europe; Royal Society Fellowship to continue research into problems of Netherlandish painting, 1955–56; studied under Dr William Heckscher of Kunsthistorisch Inst., Utrecht. *Works include:* landscape painting and portraiture (oils and water colour); mural paintings and stone carvings in many public buildings. Pres., Royal Canadian Academy of Arts, 1957–60; Past Pres., Canadian Soc. of Painters in Water Colour; Past Pres. and Charter Mem., Canadian Group of Painters; Mem., Ontario Soc. of Artists. Dr of Laws *hc:* Mount Allison Univ., 1958; Royal Military Coll., Canada, 1980. Medaglia Benemerito della cultura (Italy), 1963; Univ. of Alberta National Award in painting and related arts, 1963. Centennial Decoration, 1967; OC 1972; Queen's Jubilee Medal, 1978. *Publications:* Artist at War, 1956 (Toronto); contrib. to Royal Commission Studies Report on National Development in the Arts, Letters and Sciences, Vol. II, 1951; contrib. various art and literary publications. *Address:* 1201, 100 Bronson Avenue, Ottawa, Ont. K1R 6G8, Canada.

COMINO, Demetrius, OBE 1963; FRSA, FBIM; President, Dexion-Comino International Ltd, 1973 (Chairman, 1947–73); *b* Australia, 4 Sept. 1902; *s* of John and Anna Comino, Greek origin, naturalized British; *m*, Katerina Georgiadis; one *d. Educ:* University Coll., London. BSc 1st cl. hons Engrg 1923. Student Apprentice with The British Thompson Houston Co. Ltd, Rugby, until 1926; started own business, Krisson Printing Ltd, 1927; started present company, 1947; set up, with daughter Anna Comino-James, the Comino Foundn, 1971, aims to promote in all stages of educn learning and application of skills in getting results and solving problems, and an understanding of fundamental importance of industry to our society, one of outcomes being initiation by RSA of Industry Year 1986. FRSA 1971; Fellow, UCL, 1971. Golden Cross, King George I (Greece), 1967. *Publications:* contribs to official jl of Gk Chamber of Technology and to New Scientist. *Recreation:* thinking. *Address:* Silver Birches, Oxford Road, Gerrards Cross, Bucks. *T:* Gerrards Cross (0753) 883170.

COMMAGER, Henry Steele, MA Oxon; MA Cantab; Professor of American History, 1956–72, Simpson Lecturer, since 1972, Amherst College; Professor of History, Columbia University, 1938–56; Hon. Professor, University of Santiago de Chile; *b* 25 Oct. 1902; *s* of James W. Commager and Anna Elizabeth Dan; *m* 1928; Evan Carroll; one *s* two *d. Educ:* Univ. of Chicago; Univ. of Copenhagen. AB, Univ. of Chicago, 1923; MA, 1924; PhD, 1928; Scholar Amer-Scand. Foundation, 1924–25; taught History, New York Univ., 1926–29; Prof. of History, 1929–38. Lectr on American History, Cambridge Univ., 1942–43; Hon. Fellow, Peterhouse; Pitt Prof. of Amer. Hist., Cambridge Univ., 1947–48; Lectr, Salzburg Seminar in Amer. Studies, 1951; Harold Vyvyan Harmsworth Prof. of American History, Oxford Univ., 1952; Gotesman Lectr, Upsala Univ., 1953; Special State Dept lectr to German Univs, 1954; Zuskind Prof., Brandeis Univ., 1954–55; Prof., Univ. of Copenhagen, 1956; Visiting Prof., Univ. of Aix-Provence, summer 1957; Lectr, Univ. of Jerusalem, summer 1958; Commonwealth Lectr, Univ. of London, 1964; Harris Lectr, Northwestern Univ., 1964; Visiting Prof., Harvard, Chicago, Calif, City Univ. NY, Nebraska, etc. Editor-in-Chief, The Rise of the American Nation; Consultant, Office War Information in Britain and USA; Mem. US Army War Hist. Commn; Mem. Historians Commn on Air Power; special citation US Army; Consultant US Army attached to SHAEF, 1945. Trustee; American Scandinavian Foundation; American Friends

of Cambridge Univ. Mem. of the Amer. Acad. of Arts and Letters, USA (Gold Medal for History, 1972). Hon degrees: EdD Rhode I; LittD: Washington, Ohio Wesleyan, Pittsburgh, Marietta, Hampshire Coll., 1970; Adelphi Coll., 1974; DLitt: Cambridge, Franklin-Marshall, W Virginia, Michigan State; LHD: Brandeis, Puget Sound, Hartford, Alfred; LLD: Merrimack, Carleton, Dickinson Coll., 1967; Franklin Pierce Coll., 1968; Columbia Univ., 1969; Ohio State, 1970; Wilson Coll., 1970; W. C. Post Coll., 1974; Alassa Univ., 1974; DHL: Maryville Coll., 1970; Univ. of Mass, 1972. Knight of Order of Dannebrog (Denmark), 1957 (1st cl.). *Publications:* Theodore Parker, 1936; Growth of the American Republic, 1930, 2 vols 1939; sub-ed (with S. E. Morison) Documents of American History, 1934, 9th edn 1974; Heritage of America (with A. Nevins), 1939; America: Story of a Free People (with A. Nevins), 1943, new edn 1966; Majority Rule and Minority Rights, 1944; Story of the Second World War, 1945; ed Tocqueville, Democracy in America, 1947; ed America in Perspective, 1947; ed The St Nicholas Anthology, 1947; The American Mind, 1950; The Blue and the Gray, 2 vols 1950; Living Ideas in America, 1951; Robert E. Lee, 1951; Freedom, Loyalty, Dissent, 1954 (special award, Hillman Foundation); Europe and America since 1942 (with G. Bruun), 1954; Joseph Story, 1956; The Spirit of Seventy-Six, 2 vols (with R. B. Morris); Crusaders for Freedom; History: Nature and Purpose, 1965; Freedom and Order, 1966; Search for a Usable Past, 1967; Was America a Mistake?, 1968; The Commonwealth of Learning, 1968; The American Character, 1970; The Use and Abuse of History, 1972; Britain Through American Eyes, 1974; The Defeat of America, 1974; Essays on the Enlightenment, 1974; The Empire of Reason, 1978; edited: Atlas of American Civil War; Winston Churchill, History of the English Speaking Peoples; Why the Confederacy Lost the Civil War; Major Documents of the Civil War; Theodore Parker, an Anthology; Immigration in American History; Lester Ward and the Welfare State; The Struggle for Racial Equality; Joseph Story, Selected Writings and Judicial Opinions; Winston Churchill, Marlborough, 1968. *Recreation:* music. *Address:* Amherst College, Mass 01002, USA; (summer) Linton, Cambs, England. *Clubs:* Savile, Lansdowne (London); Century, Lotos (New York); St Botolph (Boston); (former Pres.) PEN (American Centre).

COMPSTON, Christopher Dean, MA; **His Honour Judge Compston;** a Circuit Judge, since 1986; *b* 5 May 1940; *s* of Vice Adm. Sir Peter Maxwell Compston, *qv*; *m* 1st, 1968, Bronwen Henniker Gotley (marr. diss. 1982); one *s* one *d* (and one *s* decd); 2nd, 1983, Caroline Philippa, *d* of Paul Odgers, *qv*; one *d. Educ:* Epsom Coll. (Prae Sum.); Magdalen Coll., Oxford (MA). Called to the Bar, Middle Temple, 1965; a Recorder, 1982–86. Mem. Senate, Inns of Court, 1983–86. *Recreation:* the arts. *Address:* 6 King's Bench Walk, Temple, EC4.

COMPSTON, Nigel Dean, CBE 1981; MA, MD, FRCP; Consulting Physician, retired; Royal Free Hospital, 1954–83; Royal Masonic Hospital, 1960–82; St Mary Abbot's Hospital, 1957–73; King Edward VII Hospital for Officers, 1965–72; *b* 21 April 1918; *s* of George Dean Compston and Elsie Muriel Robinson; *m* 1942, Diana Mary (*née* Standish); two *s* one *d. Educ:* Royal Masonic Sch.; Trinity Hall, Cambridge; Middlesex Hospital. BA Cantab 1939; MRCS, LRCP 1942; MB, BCh Cantab 1942; MRCP 1942; MA, MD Cantab 1947; FRCP 1957. RAMC, 1942–47 (Temp. Lt-Col). Research Fellow, Middlesex Hosp. Medical Sch., 1948–51; E. G. Fearnsides Scholar, Cambridge, 1951; Mackenzie Mackinnon Research Fellow, RCP, 1951; Asst Prof. Medicine, Middlesex Hosp., 1952–54; Treasurer, RCP, 1970–85 (formerly Asst Registrar). Examiner: Pharmacology and Therapeutics, Univ. of London, 1958–63, Medicine, 1968; Medicine, RCP, 1965–; Medicine, Univ. of Cambridge, 1971–81. Vice-Dean, Royal Free Hosp. Sch. of Medicine, 1968–70; Mem. Bd of Governors, The Royal Free Hosp., 1963–74. Hon. FFCM 1986. Hon. Editor Proc. RSM, 1966–70. *Publications:* Multiple Sclerosis (jtly), 1955; Recent Advances in Medicine (jtly), 1964, 1968, 1973, 1977, 1981, 1984; contribs to learned jls. *Address:* High Haven, Walton Hill, Littlehaven, near Haverfordwest, Dyfed.

COMPSTON, Vice-Adm. Sir Peter (Maxwell), KCB 1970 (CB 1967); *b* 12 Sept. 1915; *s* of Dr G. D. Compston; *m* 1st, 1939, Valerie Bocquet (marr. diss.); one *s* one *d*; 2nd, 1953, Angela Brickwood. *Educ:* Epsom Coll. Royal Navy, 1937; specialised in flying duties. Served 1939–45, HMS Ark Royal, Anson, Vengeance; HMCS Warrior, 1946; HMS Theseus, 1948–50 (despatches); Directorate of RN Staff Coll., 1951–53; Capt. 1955; in comd HMS Orwell and Capt. 'D' Plymouth, 1955–57; Imperial Defence Coll., 1958; Naval Attaché, Paris, 1960–62; in comd HMS Victorious, 1962–64; Rear-Adm., Jan. 1965; Chief of British Naval Staff and Naval Attaché, Washington, 1965–67; Flag Officer Flotillas, Western Fleet, 1967–68; Dep. Supreme Allied Comdr, Atlantic, 1968–70, retired. Cttee of Management, RNLI; Mem., Cttee, Royal Humane Soc. *Recreations:* theatre, country life. *Address:* Holmwood, Stroud, near Petersfield, Hants. *Club:* Army and Navy.
See also C. D. Compston.

COMPTON, family name of **Marquess of Northampton.**

COMPTON, Earl; Daniel Bingham Compton; *b* 16 Jan. 1973; *s* and *heir* of Marquess of Northampton, *qv.*

COMPTON, Denis Charles Scott, CBE 1958; professional cricketer, retired 1957; Sunday Express Cricket Correspondent, since 1950; BBC Television Cricket Commentator, since 1958; *b* 23 May 1918; *m* 1st; one *s*; 2nd; two *s*; 3rd, 1975, Christine Franklin Tobias; two *d. Educ:* Bell Lane Sch., Hendon. First played for Middlesex, 1936. First played for England *v* New Zealand, 1937; *v* Australia, 1938; *v* West Indies, 1939; *v* India, 1946; *v* S Africa, 1947. Played in 78 Test matches; made 123 centuries in first-class cricket. Association football: mem. of Arsenal XI; England XI, 1943; Editor, Denis Compton's Annual, 1950–57. *Publications:* Playing for England, 1948; Testing Time for England, 1948; In Sun and Shadow, 1952; End of an Innings, 1958; Denis Compton's Test Diary, 1964; (jtly) Cricket and All That, 1978. *Recreation:* golf. *Address:* Royds House, Mandeville Place, W1M 6AE. *T:* 01–935 7733. *Clubs:* MCC; Wanderers (Johannesburg).

COMPTON, Sir Edmund (Gerald), GCB 1971 (KCB 1965, CB 1948); KBE 1955; MA; Hon. FRAM; FRCM; *b* 30 July 1906; *er s* of late Edmund Spencer Compton, MC, Pailton House, Rugby; *m* 1934, Betty Tresyllian, 2nd *d* of late Hakewill Tresyllian Williams, DL, JP, Churchill Court, Kidderminster; one *s* four *d. Educ:* Rugby (Scholar); New Coll., Oxford (Scholar). 1st Class Lit. Hum., 1929; Hon. Fellow 1972. Entered Home Civil Service, 1929; Colonial Office, 1930; transf. to HM Treasury, 1931; Private Sec. to Financial Sec. to Treasury, 1934–36; seconded to Min. of Aircraft Production as Private Sec. to Minister, 1940; Min. of Supply, 1941; Asst Sec., HM Treasury, 1942, Under-Sec., 1947, Third Sec., 1949–58; Comptroller and Auditor General, Exchequer and Audit Dept, 1958–66; Parly Comr for Administration, 1967–71, and in NI, 1969–71. Chm., English Local Govt Boundary Commn, 1971–78. Chairman: Irish Sailors and Soldiers Land Trust, 1946–; Milibern Trust, 1968–; BBC Programmes Complaints Commn, 1972–81; Governing Body, Royal Acad. of Music, 1975–81. *Recreations:* music, water-colour sketching. *Address:* 1/80 Elm Park Gardens, SW10. *T:* 01–351 3790. *Clubs:* Athenæum, Boodle's.
See also Viscount De L'Isle.

COMPTON, Rt. Hon. John George Melvin, PC 1983; Prime Minister of St Lucia and Minister of Foreign Affairs and Finance, since 1982; *b* 1926; *m*; five *c. Educ*: London School of Economics. Called to the Bar, Gray's Inn; practice in St Lucia, 1951. Indep. Mem., Legislative Council, 1954; joined Labour Party, 1954; Dep. Leader, 1957–61; resigned, and formed Nat. Labour Movement, 1961 (later United Workers' Party); Leader, 1964); Chief Minister of St Lucia, 1964–67, Premier, 1967–79, Prime Minister, Feb.–July 1979, 1982–. *Address*: Office of the Prime Minister, Castries, St Lucia.

COMPTON, Michael Graeme; Keeper of Museum Services, Tate Gallery, since 1970; *b* 29 Sept. 1927; *s* of Joseph Nield Compton, OBE, and Dorothy Margaret Townsend Compton; *m* 1952, Susan Paschal Benn; two *d. Educ*: Courtauld Institute, London (BA Hons History of Art). Asst to Director, Leeds City Art Gallery and Templenewsam, 1954–57; Keeper of Foreign Schools, Walker Art Gallery, Liverpool, 1957–59; Dir, Ferens Art Gall., Hull, 1960–65; Asst Keeper, Modern Collection, Tate Gall., 1965–70. Mem., Fine Arts Adv. Cttee, British Council. *Publications*: Optical and Kinetic Art, 1967; Pop Art, 1970; (jtly) Catalogue of Foreign Schools, Walker Art Gallery, 1963; articles in art jls, exhibn catalogues. *Address*: Michaelmas Lodge, Rockfield Road, Oxted, Surrey RH8 0HB.

COMPTON, Robert Edward John; DL; Chairman, since 1979, Chief Executive Officer, since 1985, Time-Life International Ltd; Chairman, Time SARL, since 1985; *b* 11 July 1922; *yr s* of late Major Edward Robert Francis Compton, JP, DL, and Sylvia Farquharson of Invercauld; *m* 1951, Ursula Jane Kenyon-Slaney; two *s. Educ*: Eton; Magdalen Coll., Oxford, 1940–41. Served War, Coldstream Guards, 1941–46 (4 medals, wounded); Mil. Asst to British Ambassador, Vienna (temp. Major), 1946. Studied fruit growing and horticulture (Diploma), 1946–48; with W. S. Crawford Ltd, Advertising Agency, 1951–54; Sen. Acct Exec., Crawfords Internat., 1954; joined Time International, 1954; advertising sales, 1954–58, UK Advtsg Dir, 1958–62; also Dir, Time-Life Internat. Ltd, 1958–79; New Projects Dir, Time-Life Internat. Europe, 1962–65; Public Affairs Dir, Europe, Time-Life Internat. Ltd, 1965. Chairman: Newby Hall Estate Co., 1964–69; CXL UK Ltd, 1971–73; Pres., Highline Finances Services, SA, 1985–; Bd Dir, Extel Corp., Chicago, 1973–80; Dir, Transtel Communications Ltd, Slough, 1974–. FInstD 1958. Vice-Chm., National Trust, Yorks, 1970–85, also Mem. Properties Cttee and Gardens Panel, London, 1970–85, and Pres., Dales Centre Nat. Trust, 1979–85; President: Ripon Tourist Assoc., 1977–; N of England Horticultural Soc., 1984–86; Life Pres., Northern Horticultural Soc., 1986. High Sheriff, 1978–79, DL 1981, N Yorks. *Recreations*: gardening, shooting, golf, music. *Address*: Newby Hall, Ripon, Yorkshire. *T*: Boroughbridge 2583; Flat 2, 17 Brompton Square, SW3. *Clubs*: White's, Buck's; Swinley Forest (Ascot).
    See also Captain A. A. C. Farquharson of Invercauld.

COMPTON, Robert Herbert K.; *see* Keppel-Compton.

COMPTON, Air Vice-Marshal William Vernon C.; *see* Crawford-Compton.

COMPTON MILLER, Sir John (Francis), Kt 1969; MBE (mil.) 1945; TD; MA Oxon; Barrister-at-Law; Senior Registrar, The Family Division (formerly Probate, Divorce and Admiralty Division), 1964–72 (Registrar, 1946–64), retired 1972; *b* 11 May 1900; 3rd *s* of Frederic Richard Miller, MD and Effie Anne, *d* of Samson Rickard Stuttaford; *m* 1st, 1925, Alice Irene Mary (*d* 1931), *er d* of John Scales Bakewell; one *s*; 2nd, 1936, Mary, *e d* of Rev. Alexander MacEwen Baird-Smith; one *s* one *d. Educ*: Colet Court; St Paul's Sch.; New Coll., Oxford. Called to Bar, Inner Temple, 1923; went the Western Circuit, practised Criminal, Common Law, Probate and Divorce Courts. Major, Inns of Court Regt, TA, 1936; OC No 21 Recep. Unit; Asst Comdt, Army Tech. Sch. (Boys), Chepstow. A Deputy Judge Advocate, United Kingdom and North West Europe, 1969. Examiner, Council of Legal Education, 1951–64. UK Rep., Council of Europe Sub-Cttee on Registration of Wills, 1970. *Publications*: I Tried My Hand at Verse, 1968; Further Verse, 1970; The Miraculous Cornfield, 1978; The Chinese Saucer, 1980; Poems '81, 1981; Selected Poems, 1982; Miscellany, 1983; And So It Went, 1985; An Ambit Small, 1986. *Recreations*: painting (Dip., City of London Art Exhibn, 1979), versing, heraldic art. *Address*: 2 Crown Office Row, Temple, EC4. *T*: 01–583 1352.

COMRIE, Rear-Adm. (Alexander) Peter, CB 1982; defence equipment consultant; Director, A. Comrie & Sons Ltd, since 1983; *b* 27 March 1924; *s* of Robert Duncan Comrie and Phyllis Dorothy Comrie; *m* 1945, Madeleine Irene (*née* Bullock) (*d* 1983); one *s* one *d. Educ*: Sutton Valence Sch., Kent; County Technical Coll., Wednesbury, Staffs, and in the Royal Navy. Joined Royal Navy, 1945; served in cruisers, frigates, minesweepers and RN air stations; RCDS 1973; Captain HMS Daedalus, 1974; Director of Weapons Coordination and Acceptance (Naval), 1975; Deputy Controller Aircraft, MoD, 1978–81; Dir-Gen. Aircraft (Navy), 1981–83, retired. Member: IEE Electronics Divisional Bd, 1976–77; Council, IEE, 1981–84; IEE Qualifications Bd, 1981–; Executive Gp Cttee 3, Engrg Council, 1984–. FIEE 1975; FRAeS 1978. *Recreations*: sailing, swimming, DIY. *Address*: c/o National Westminster Bank, 23 West Street, Havant, Hants PO9 1EU. *Clubs*: Royal Commonwealth Society; Hayling Island Sailing, Birdham Yacht.

COMYN, Hon. Sir James, Kt 1978; Judge of the High Court of Justice, Queen's Bench Division, 1979–85; (Family Division, 1978–79); *b* Co. Dublin, 8 March 1921; *o s* of late James Comyn, QC, Dublin and late Mary Comyn; *m* 1967, Anne, *d* of late Philip Chaundler, MC, Biggleswade, and late Mrs Chaundler; one *s* one *d. Educ*: Oratory Sch.; New Coll., Oxford (MA). Ex-Pres. of Oxford Union. Inner Temple, 1942; called to Irish Bar, 1947; QC 1961. Recorder of Andover, 1964–71; Hon. Recorder of Andover, 1972; a Recorder of the Crown Court, 1972–77. Master of the Bench, Inner Temple, 1968; Mem. and Chm., Bar Council, 1973–74. Chm., Court Line Enquiry, 1972–73. Mem., Parole Bd, 1982–84, Vice-Chm. 1983–84. A Governor of the Oratory Sch., 1964; President: Oratory Sch. Assoc., 1983–; Oratory Sch. Soc. (old boys), 1984–. Owner of the "Clareville" herd of pedigree Aberdeen-Angus and the "Beaufield" herd of pedigree Herefords. *Publications*: Their Friends at Court, 1973; Irish at Law: a selection of famous and unusual cases, 1981; Lost Causes, 1982. *Recreations*: farming, golf, planting trees. *Address*: Belvin, Tara, Co. Meath, Ireland. *Clubs*: Athenæum, Royal Dublin Society.

COMYNS, Jacqueline Roberta; a Metropolitan Stipendiary Magistrate, since 1982; *b* 27 April 1943; *d* of late Jack and of Belle Fisher; *m* 1963, Malcolm John Comyns, medical practitioner; one *s. Educ*: Hendon County Grammar Sch.; London Sch. of Econs and Pol. Science (LLB Hons 1964). Called to the Bar, Inner Temple, 1969. Practised on South Eastern Circuit. *Recreations*: theatre, bridge, travel. *Address*: Tower Bridge Magistrates' Court, Tooley Street, SE1 2JY. *T*: 01–407 4232.

CONAN DOYLE, Air Comdt Dame Jean (Lena Annette), (Lady Bromet), DBE 1963 (OBE 1948); AE; Director of the Women's Royal Air Force, 1963–66, retired; *b* 21 Dec. 1912; *d* of late Sir Arthur Conan Doyle and Lady Conan Doyle (*née* Jean Leckie); *m* 1965, Air Vice-Marshal Sir Geoffrey Bromet, KBE, CB, DSO, DL (*d* 1983). *Educ*: Granville House, Eastbourne. Joined No 46 (Co. of Sussex) ATS, RAF Company, Sept.

1938; commnd in WAAF, 1940; served in UK, 1939–45; commnd in RAF, 1949; Comd WRAF Admin Officer: BAFO, Germany, 1947–50; HQ Tech. Trng Comd, 1950–52 and 1962–63; Dep. Dir, 1952–54 and 1960–62; OC, RAF Hawkinge, 1956–59; Inspector of the WRAF, 1954–56 and 1959–60. Hon. ADC to the Queen, 1963–66. A Governor, Royal Star and Garter Home, 1968–82; Mem. Council, Officers' Pensions Soc., 1970–75, a Vice-Pres. 1981–; Mem. Cttee, Not Forgotten Assoc., 1975–, a Pres. 1981–. Holder of USA copyright on her father's published works. *Recreation*: attempting to paint. *Address*: Flat 6, 72 Cadogan Square, SW1. *Clubs*: Naval and Military, Royal Air Force.

CONANT, Sir John (Ernest Michael), 2nd Bt *cr* 1954; farmer and landowner, since 1949; *b* 24 April 1923; *s* of Sir Roger Conant, 1st Bt, CVO, and Daphne, Lady Conant, *d* of A. E. Learoyd; *S* father, 1973; *m* 1950, Periwinkle Elizabeth (*d* 1985), *d* of late Dudley Thorp, Kimbolton, Hunts; two *s* two *d* (and one *s* decd). *Educ*: Eton; Corpus Christi Coll., Cambridge (BA Agric). Served in Grenadier Guards, 1942–45; at CCC Cambridge, 1946–49. Farming in Rutland, 1950–; High Sheriff of Rutland, 1960. *Recreations*: fishing, shooting, tennis. *Heir*: *s* Simon Edward Christopher Conant, *b* 13 Oct. 1958. *Address*: Lyndon Hall, Oakham, Rutland LE15 8TU. *T*: Manton 275.

CONCANNON, Rt. Hon. John Dennis, (Rt. Hon. Don Concannon), PC 1978; MP (Lab) Mansfield, since 1966; *b* 16 May 1930; *m* 1953, Iris May Wilson; two *s* two *d. Educ*: Rossington Sec. Sch. Coldstream Guards, 1947–53; Mem. Nat. Union of Mineworkers, 1953–66; Branch Official, 1960–65. Mem., Mansfield Town Council, 1962–66. Asst Govt Whip, 1968–70; Opposition Whip, 1970–74; Vice-Chamberlain, HM Household, 1974; Parly Under-Sec. of State, NI Office, 1974–76; Minister of State, NI Office, 1976–79; Opposition Spokesman for Defence, 1979–80, for NI, 1980–83. *Recreations*: cricket, basket-ball. *Address*: 69 Skegby Lane, Mansfield, Notts. *T*: Mansfield 27235.

CONCANNON, Terence Patrick, JP; Member, Rotherham Community Health Council, since 1978; *b* 24 Oct. 1932; *s* of Leo Martin Concannon and late Minnie (*née* Foster); *m* 1965, Pauline Marie (*née* Flynn) (*d* 1976); two *s* one *d. Educ*: De La Salle College, Sheffield; Sheffield University. DPA. Nat. Service, 1951–53. Local Govt Finance, West Riding CC, 1948–54; Rotherham CBC, 1954–73; Rotherham MBC, 1974–82, retired as Principal Officer; Mem., S Yorks CC, 1973–86 (Chm., 1984–85). Life Mem., NALGO, 1948. Trustee, S Yorks Racing Apprentice Sch. JP Rotherham, 1971. *Recreations*: camping, music, reading, crosswords. *Address*: 195 Hague Avenue, Rawmarsh, Rotherham, South Yorks S62 7PZ. *T*: Rotherham 522560. *Clubs*: Caravan, One Parent Caravan, Labour (Rawmarsh); South Yorkshire County.

CONDON, Denis David, OBE 1964; retired; Senior Representative at Lloyd's of London for Neilson McCarthy, Consultants, 1968–75; *b* 23 Oct. 1910; *s* of Capt. D. Condon and Mrs A. E. Condon; *m* 1933, Mary Marson; one *d. Educ*: Paston Grammar Sch., North Walsham, Norfolk. Journalist until 1939. War Service with Royal Artillery, UK and Burma (Major). Joined India Office, 1946; CRO, 1947; served India, Ceylon, Australia, Nigeria; Head of News Dept, CO, 1967–68. *Recreations*: fishing, bird-watching, gardening. *Address*: Rose Cottage, Weir, Dulverton, Somerset. *T*: Dulverton 23309. *Clubs*: Gymkhana (Delhi); Australasian Pioneers (Sydney).

CONGLETON, 8th Baron *cr* 1841; **Christopher Patrick Parnell**; Bt 1766; *b* 11 March 1930; 3rd *s* of 6th Baron Congleton (*d* 1932) and Hon. Edith Mary Palmer Howard (MBE 1941) (she *m* 2nd, 1946, Flight Lieut A. E. R. Aldridge, who died 1950), *d* of late R. J. B. Howard and late Lady Strathcona and Mount Royal; *S* brother, 1967; *m* 1955, Anna Hedvig, *d* of G. A. Sommerfelt, Oslo, Norway; two *s* three *d. Educ*: Eton; New Coll., Oxford (BA 1954). Mem., Salisbury and Wilton RDC, 1964–74; Vice-President: RDCA, 1973–74; Assoc. of District Councils, 1974–79; Chm., Salisbury and S Wilts Museum, 1972–77; Pres., Nat. Ski Federation of GB, 1976–81; Mem., Adv. Bd for Redundant Churches, 1981–. Trustee: Sandroyd Sch. Trust, 1975– (Chm., 1980–84); Wessex Med. Sch. Trust, 1984–. *Heir*: *s* Hon. John Patrick Christian Parnell [*b* 17 March 1959; *m* 1985, Marjorie-Anne, *o d* of John Hobdell, Cobham, Surrey]. *Address*: Ebbesbourne Wake, Salisbury, Wilts SP5 5JW.

CONGO, Sonia, (Mrs C. W. Congo); *see* Lawson, S.

CONGREVE, Ambrose, CBE 1965; responsible for Humphreys & Glasgow Ltd, 1939–83; *b* London, 4 April 1907; *s* of Major John Congreve, DL, JP, and Helena Blanche Irene Ponsonby, *d* of 8th Earl of Bessborough; *m* 1935, Marjorie, *d* of Dr Arthur Graham Glasgow, London, and Richmond, Virginia, and Margaret, *d* of John P. Branch, President of Virginia's Merchants National Bank. *Educ*: Eton; Trinity Coll., Cambridge. Employed by Unilever Ltd, in England and China, 1927–36; joined Humphreys & Glasgow Ltd, as Director, 1936; responsible for the company, 1939–83, in succession to Dr Glasgow who founded the firm in 1892. Served War of 1939–45: Air Intelligence for Plans and Bomber Command, then Min. of Supply. Hon. Fellow IChemE 1967. *Recreation*: collection and large-scale outdoor cultivation in Ireland of plant species and hybrids from all over the world. *Address*: Mount Congreve, Waterford, Ireland. *T*: Waterford 84103; Warwick House, Stable Yard, St James's, SW1. *T*: 01–839 3301. *Club*: Beefsteak.

CONI, Peter Richard Carstairs, QC 1980; a Recorder, since 1985; *b* 20 Nov. 1935; *s* of late Eric Charles Coni and Leslie Sybil Carstairs (*née* Pearson). *Educ*: Uppingham; St Catharine's Coll., Cambridge (MA). Called to the Bar, Inner Temple, 1960, Bencher, 1986. Steward, Henley Royal Regatta, 1974 (Chm. Cttee of Management, 1977–); Vice-Pres., London Rowing Club, 1977–; Chm., 1986 World Rowing Championships Cttee, 1982–86; Member: Exec. Cttee, Amateur Rowing Assoc., 1968– (Chm., 1970–77); Exec. Cttee, Central Council of Physical Recreation, 1978–80; Thames Water Authority, 1978–83; Leander Club Cttee, 1983–. Mem., Ct of Assts, Needlemakers' Co., 1983–. *Recreations*: rowing, sports administration, good food, modern art. *Address*: 3 Churton Place, SW1. *T*: 01–828 2135. *Clubs*: Athenæum, Garrick, London Rowing; Leander (Henley-on-Thames).

CONINGSBY, Thomas Arthur Charles; QC 1986; Chancellor of the Diocese of York, since 1977; Vicar General of the Province of York, since 1980; a Recorder, since 1986; *b* 21 April 1933; *s* of Francis Charles and Eilleen Rowena Coningsby; *m* 1959, Elaine Mary Coningsby; two *s* three *d. Educ*: Epsom; Queens' Coll., Cambridge (MA). Called to the Bar, Gray's Inn, 1957. Member, General Synod, 1970–. *Recreation*: lawn tennis. *Address*: Leyfields, Chipstead, Surrey CR3 3SG. *T*: Downland 53304.

CONLAN, Bernard; MP (Lab) Gateshead East since 1964; Engineer; *b* 24 Oct. 1923; *m*; one *d. Educ*: Manchester Primary and Secondary Schs. Mem., AEU, 1940–, Officer, 1943–. City Councillor, Manchester, 1954–66. Joined Labour Party, 1942; contested (Lab) High Peak, 1959. A Vice-Chm., Parly Lab. Party Trade Union Gp, 1974–. Member: House of Commons Expenditure Cttee (since inception), 1971–79; Trade and Industry Select Cttee, 1974–; Select Cttee on Defence, 1979–83. *Address*: House of Commons, SW1; 33 Beccles Road, Sale, Cheshire.

CONN, Edward, CBE 1979; FRCVS; Technical Consultant, Norbrook Laboratories Ltd, Newry, Northern Ireland; *b* 25 March 1918; *s* of late Edward and Elizabeth Conn; *m* 1st, 1943, Kathleen Victoria Sandford (*d* 1974); three *d*; 2nd, 1975, Lilian Frances Miley.

Educ: Coleraine Academical Instn; Royal (Dick) Veterinary Sch., Edinburgh Univ. Qual. Vet. Surgeon, 1940; Diploma; MRCVS 1940; FRCVS 1984. Gen. practice, Coleraine, 1940–43; Chief Vet. Officer to: Hampshire Cattle Breeders, 1943–47; Dept of Agriculture, NI, 1958–83 (Vet. Officer, 1947). Governor, Coleraine Academical Instn, 1972–. *Recreations:* golf, walking; watching all sports, particularly Rugby and athletics. *Address:* Dunedin, 4 Brooklyn Avenue, Bangor, N Ireland BT20 5RB. *T:* Bangor 2383. *Clubs:* Clandeboye Golf; Bangor Rugby and Athletic.

CONN, Prof. John Farquhar Christie, DSc; CEng; FRINA; John Elder Professor of Naval Architecture, University of Glasgow, 1957–73; *b* 5 July 1903; *s* of Alexander Aberdein Conn and Margaret Rhind Wilson; *m* 1935, Doris Maude Yeatman; one *s* one *d. Educ:* Robert Gordon's Coll., Aberdeen; Glasgow Univ. Apprenticeship at Alexander Hall and Co. Ltd, Aberdeen, 1920–25; employed in several shipyards; Scientific staff, Ship Div., National Physical Laboratory, 1929–44; Chief Naval Architect, British Shipbuilding Research Association, 1945–57. Hon. Vice-Pres., RINA. *Publications:* various papers in Trans. of Royal Instn of Naval Architects and other learned societies. *Recreations:* music, reading. *Address:* 14 Elm Walk, Bearsden, Glasgow G61 3BQ. *T:* 041–942 4640.

CONNALLY, John Bowden; lawyer; *b* 27 Feb. 1917; *s* of John Bowden Connally and Lela (*née* Wright); *m* 1940, Idanell Brill; two *s* one *d. Educ:* Univ. of Texas (LLB). Served US Navy, 1941–46. Pres. and Gen. Manager, KVET radio stn, 1946–49; Admin. Asst to Lyndon Johnson, 1949; employed with Powell, Wirtz & Rauhut, 1950–52; Attorney to Richardson & Bass, oil merchants, 1952–61; Sec. US Navy, 1961; Governor of Texas, 1962–68; Secretary of the Treasury, USA, 1971–72. Member: President's Adv. Cttee on Exec. Organisation, 1969–70; President's Foreign Intelligence Adv. Bd, 1972–74 and 1976–77; US Adv. Cttee on reform of Internat. Monetary System, 1973–74; Partner: Vinson Elkins, 1969–71, 1972–85; Barnes/Connally Partnership, Austin, Texas; Director: First City National Bank of Floresville, Texas, 1975–; The Methodist Hospital, 1977–; Ford Motor Co.; The Signal Cos Inc.; Chapman Energy Inc. (Chm.); Cable Advertising Systems, Inc. (Chm.); American Physicians Service Gp Inc.; Art Magazine Publishers Inc.; Consultant, Mason Best, Houston, Texas. Mem. and Trustee, Andrew W. Mellon Foundn, 1973–. *Address:* 515 Post Oak Boulevard, Suite 500, Houston, Texas 77027, USA.

CONNELL, Charles Percy; Puisne Judge, Kenya Colony, 1951–64, retired; *b* 1 Oct. 1902; *s* of late C. R. Connell, Barrister-at-Law and late K. Adlard; *m* 1946, Mary O'Rourke. *Educ:* Charterhouse; New Coll., Oxford (Hons, Jurisprudence). Called to Bar, Lincoln's Inn, 1927. Joined Kenya Judicial Service, 1938 (Resident Magistrate). Served War of 1939–45 (8th Army Clasp and war medals); commissioned King's African Rifles, 1941; British Military Administration (Legal and Judicial), Eritrea and Tripolitania, 1942–46. Acting Puisne Judge, Kenya, 1950, retired 1964. *Recreations:* tennis, cricket and trout fishing. *Address:* c/o National Westminster Bank, 14 Sloane Square, SW1.

CONNELL, George Edward, PhD; FCIC; FRSC; President, University of Toronto, since 1984; *b* 20 June 1930; *m* 1955, Sheila Horan; two *s* two *d. Educ:* Univ. of Toronto (BA, PhD Biochemistry). FCIC 1971; FRSC 1975. Post-doctoral Fellow, Div. of Applied Biol., National Res. Council, Ottawa, Ont, 1955–56; Fellow, National Science Foundn (US), Dept of Biochem., New York University Coll. of Medicine, 1956–57; University of Toronto: Asst Prof. of Biochem., 1957–62; Associate Prof. of Biochem., 1962–65; Prof. and Chm. Dept of Biochem., 1965–70; Associate Dean, Faculty of Med., 1972–74; Vice-Pres., Res. and Planning, 1974–77; Pres. and Vice-Chancellor, Univ. of Western Ontario, 1977–84. Chm., Exec. Cttee, Internat. Congress of Biochem., 1979–; Member: MRC of Canada, 1966–70; Ont Council of Health, 1978–84; Bd of Dirs and Nat. Exec. Cttee, Canadian Arthritis and Rheumatism Soc., 1965–75; Bd of Dirs, Nat. Inst. of Nutrition, 1984–; Bd of Dirs, Southam Inc., 1985–; Council, Ont Univs, 1977– (Chm., 1981–83); Bd of Governors, Upper Canada Coll., 1982–; Bd of Trustees, Royal Ont Mus., 1984–. Hon. LLD: Trent Univ., 1984; Univ. of Western Ont, 1985. *Publications:* scientific papers in jls incl. Canadian Jl of Biochem., Biochemical Jl (UK), and Jl of Immunol. *Recreations:* skiing, tennis. *Address:* Simcoe Hall, University of Toronto, Toronto, Ontario M5S 1A1, Canada. *Clubs:* London Hunt and Country, University of London (London, Ont); York, University, Queen's (Toronto).

CONNELL, John Jeffrey, CBE 1985; PhD; FRSE; FIFST; Director, Torry Research Station, Aberdeen (Ministry of Agriculture, Fisheries and Food), since 1979 (Assistant Director, 1969–79); Hon. Research Professor, Aberdeen University, since 1983; *b* 2 July 1927; *s* of John Edward Connell and Margaret Connell; *m* 1950, Margaret Parsons; one *s* two *d* (and one *d* decd). *Educ:* Burnage High Sch.; Univ. of Manchester (BSc 1947); Univ. of Edinburgh (PhD 1950). FIFST 1970; FRSE 1984. Torry Research Station: Scientific Officer, 1950; Sen. Sci. Officer, 1955; Principal Sci. Officer, 1961; Dep. Chief Sci. Officer, 1979; Officer i/c Humber Lab., Hull (Sen. Principal Sci. Officer), 1968–69. Res. Associate, 1969–79 and Hon. Res. Lectr, 1979–83, Aberdeen Univ. Mem., Fisheries Res. and Develt Bd, 1979–84. *Publications:* Control of Fish Quality, 1975, 2nd edn 1980 (Spanish edn 1978); Trends in Fish Utilisation, 1982; scientific and technical papers related to use of fish as food. *Recreations:* music, hill walking. *Address:* 61 Burnieboozle Crescent, Aberdeen AB1 8NR. *T:* Aberdeen 315852.

CONNELL, John MacFarlane; President, The Distillers Company plc, since 1986 (Chairman, 1983–86; Chief Executive 1986); *b* 29 Dec. 1924; *s* of late John Maclean Connell and Mollie Isobel MacFarlane; *m* 1949, Jean Matheson Sutherland Mackay, *d* of late Major George Sutherland Mackay and late Christine Bourne; two *s. Educ:* Stowe; Christ Church, Oxford. Joined Tanqueray, Gordon & Co. Ltd, 1946, Export Dir 1954, Man. Dir 1962–70; Dir, Distillers Co. Ltd, 1965, Mem., Management Cttee, 1971–86; Chm., United Glass Holdings plc, 1979–83. Chm., Gin Rectifiers and Distillers Assoc., 1968–71. Pres., Royal Warrant Holders Assoc., 1975. *Recreations:* golf, shooting. *Address:* 20 St James's Square, SW1Y 4JF. *T:* 01–930 1040. *Club:* Royal and Ancient (St Andrews).

CONNELL, Michael Bryan; QC 1981; barrister-at-law; a Recorder of the Crown Court, since 1980; *b* 6 Aug. 1939; *s* of Lorraine Connell and of late Joan Connell; *m* 1965, Anne Joan Connell; three *s* one *d. Educ:* Harrow; Brasenose Coll., Oxford (MA Jurisprudence). Called to the Bar, Inner Temple, 1962. *Recreations:* steeplechasing, cricket, foxhunting. *Address:* Queen Elizabeth Buildings, Temple, EC4. *T:* 01–583 7837. *Clubs:* Buck's, Royal Automobile.

CONNELL, Dame Ninette; see de Valois, Dame Ninette.

CONNELL, Philip Henry, CBE 1986; Emeritus Physician, The Bethlem Royal Hospital and The Maudsley Hospital, 1986 (Physician, 1963–86); *b* 6 July 1921; *s* of George Henry Connell and Evelyn Hilda Sykes; *m* 1st, 1948, Marjorie Helen Gilham; two *s*; 2nd, 1973, Cecily Mary Harper. *Educ:* St Paul's Sch.; St Bartholomew's Hosp., London. MD, BS, MRCS, FRCP, FRCPsych, DPM (academic). St Stephen's Hosp., Fulham Road, 1951–53; Registrar and Sen. Registrar, The Bethlem Royal Hosp. and the Maudsley Hosp., 1953–57; Cons. Psychiatrist, Newcastle Gen. Hosp. and Physician i/c Child Psychiatry Unit, Newcastle Gen. Hosp. in assoc. with King's Coll., Durham Univ., and Assoc. Phys., Royal Victoria Infirm., 1957–63. Extensive nat. and internat. work on drug addiction and dependence (incl. work for WHO, Council of Europe and CENTO), and on maladjusted and psychiatrically ill children and adolescents. Mem. numerous adv. cttees and working parties, including: Standing Mental Health Adv. Cttee, DHSS (formerly Min. of Health), 1966–72 (Vice Chm., 1967–72); Standing Adv. Cttee on Drug Dependence (Wayne Cttee), 1966–71; Wootton Cttees on Cannabis and LSD, Amphetamines and Barbiturates, etc.; Consultant Adviser (Addiction) to DHSS, 1968–71 and 1981–86; Pres., Soc. for Study of Addiction, 1973–78; Vice Pres., Internat. Council on Alcohol and Addictions, 1982– (Chm., Scientific and Prof. Adv. Bd, 1971–79); Chairman: Inst. for Study of Drug Dependence, 1975–; Adv. Council on Misuse of Drugs, 1982–; Member: Council, RMPA, 1962–67; GMC, 1979– (Preliminary Screener for Health, 1982–84); Vice-Pres., RCPsych, 1979–81 (Chm., Child and Adolescent Specialist Section, 1971–74). Dent Meml Lectr, KCL and Soc. for Study of Addiction, 1985. Mem., Bd of Governors, Mowden Hall Sch., 1976–82. Mem., editorial bds, various jls. *Publications:* Amphetamine Psychosis (monograph), 1958; (ed jtly) Cannabis and Man, 1975; numerous chapters in books, papers in sci. jls and proc. sci. confs. *Recreations:* theatre, bridge, tennis. *Address:* 25 Oxford Road, Putney, SW15 2LG. *T:* 01–788 1416; 21 Wimpole Street, W1M 7AD. *T:* 01–636 2220. *Club:* Athenæum.

CONNELL-SMITH, Prof. Gordon Edward, PhD; FRHistS; Professor of Contemporary History, University of Hull, 1973–85; *b* 23 Nov. 1917; 2nd *s* of George Frederick Smith and Margaret Smith (*née* Woolerton); surname changed to Connell-Smith by deed-poll, 1942; *m* 1954, Wendy Ann, *o d* of John Bertram and Kathleen Tomlinson; one *s* one *d. Educ:* Richmond County Sch., Surrey; University Coll. of SW of England, Exeter (BA); Birkbeck Coll., London (PhD). FRHistS 1959. Served War, RA and Staff, 1940–46 (Staff Major). Julian Corbett Prize, Inst. of Historical Res., 1949; University of Hull: Staff Tutor/Lectr in Adult Educn and History Depts, 1952–63; Sen. Lectr, 1963–69; Reader in Contemp. Internat. History, 1969–73. Mem., Cttee of Management, Univ. of London Inst. of Latin Amer. Studies, 1973–85. Chm., Latin American Newsletters, Ltd, London, 1969–72. *Publications:* Forerunners of Drake, 1954; Pattern of the Post-War World, 1957; The Inter-American System, 1966 (Spanish edn 1971); (co-author) The Relevance of History, 1972; The United States and Latin America, 1974 (Spanish edn 1977); The Future of History, 1975; Latin American Relations with the World 1826–1976, 1976; contrib. to Bull. Inst. of Historical Res., Contemp. Rev., Econ. History Rev., Eng. Historical Rev., History, Internat. Affairs, Jl of Latin Amer. Studies, World Today, etc. *Recreations:* travel, sport. *Address:* 7 Braids Walk, Kirk Ella, Hull HU10 7PA. *T:* Hull 652624.

CONNELLY, Thomas John; Director of Services, General and Municipal Workers' Union, 1978–85, retired; *b* 24 Dec. 1925; *s* of William and Jane Connelly; *m* 1952, Naomi Shakow; one *s* one *d. Educ:* Priory St Elementary Sch., Colchester; Ruskin Coll.; Lincoln Coll., Oxford. BA 1955. Research Officer: Amalgamated Soc. of Woodworkers, 1955–63; G&MWU, 1963–66; Adviser, Industrial Relations Prices and Incomes Bd, 1966–68; various posts, finally as Chief Officer, Race Relations Bd, 1968–77; apptd Chief Executive, Commn for Racial Equality, 1977, but withdrew from appt. *Publication:* The Woodworkers 1860–1960, 1960. *Recreations:* reading, music. *Address:* 2 Caroline Court, 25 Lovelace Road, Surbiton, Surrey. *T:* 01–399 9223.

CONNER, Rearden; (pen-name of **Patrick Reardon Connor**), MBE 1967; novelist and short-story writer; *b* 19 Feb. 1907; *s* of John and Bridie Connor; *m* 1942, Malinka Marie Smith; no *c. Educ:* Christian Brothers Schs; Presentation Coll., Cork. Worked in Min. of Aircraft Production, during War, in Research and Development of Equipment. Carried on in this field, after war, in Min. of Supply, and later in Min. of Aviation and Min. of Technology. Critic of fiction, The Fortnightly, 1935–37, also on Books of the Month; Reader of fiction for Cassell, 1948–56. Work has been included in: Best Short Stories Anthology (twice); Pick of To-Day's Short Stories; Whit Burnett anthology (USA), Stories of the Forties. *Publications:* Shake Hands with The Devil, 1933 (Literary Guild Selection in USA; filmed, 1958); Rude Earth, 1934; Salute to Aphrodite, 1935 (USA); I am Death, 1936; Time to Kill, 1936 (USA); Men Must Live, 1937; The Sword of Love, 1938; Wife of Colum, 1939; The Devil Among the Tailors, 1947; My Love to the Gallows, 1949; Hunger of the Heart, 1950; The Singing Stone, 1951; The House of Cain, 1952; (under *pseudonym* Peter Malin): To Kill is My Vocation, 1939; River, Sing Me a Song, 1939; Kobo the Brave, 1950. *Recreations:* listening to music; going to the theatre. *Address:* 79 Balsdean Road, Woodingdean, Brighton, Sussex BN2 6PG. *T:* Brighton 34032.

CONNERY, Sean, (Thomas Connery); actor; *b* 25 Aug. 1930; *s* of Joseph and Euphamia Connery; *m* 1st, 1962, Diane (marr. diss. 1974), *d* of Sir Raphael West Cilento, MD and of Lady Cilento; one *s* (and one step *d*); 2nd, 1975, Micheline Roquebrune. Served Royal Navy. Dir, Tantallon Films Ltd, 1972–. Has appeared in films: No Road Back, 1956; Action of the Tiger, 1957; Another Time, Another Place, 1957; Hell Drivers, 1958; Tarzan's Greatest Adventure, 1959; Darby O'Gill and the Little People, 1959; On the Fiddle, 1961; The Longest Day, 1962; The Frightened City, 1962; Woman of Straw, 1964; The Hill, 1965; A Fine Madness, 1966; Shalako, 1968; The Molly Maguires, 1968; The Red Tent (1st Russian co-production), 1969; The Anderson Tapes, 1970; The Offence, 1973; Zardoz, 1973; Ransom, 1974; Murder on the Orient Express, 1974; The Wind and the Lion, 1975; The Man Who Would Be King, 1975; Robin and Marian, 1976; The First Great Train Robbery, 1978; Cuba, 1978; Meteor, 1979; Outland, 1981; The Man with the Deadly Lens, 1982; Wrong is Right, 1982; Five Days One Summer, 1982; as James Bond: Dr No, 1963; From Russia With Love, 1964; Goldfinger, 1965; Thunderball, 1965; You Only Live Twice, 1967; Diamonds are Forever, 1971; Never Say Never Again, 1983. FRSAMD 1984. Hon. DLitt Heriot-Watt, 1981. *Recreations:* oil painting, golf, reading, cooking.

CONNOR, Jeremy George; Metropolitan Stipendiary Magistrate, since 1979; a Recorder, since 1986; *b* 14 Dec. 1938; *s* of Joseph Connor and Mabel Emmeline (*née* Adams), ARCA. *Educ:* Beaumont; University Coll., London (LLB; DRS). Called to the Bar, Middle Temple, 1961; S Eastern Circuit. Apptd to Treasury List, Central Criminal Court, 1973; a Chm., Inner London Juvenile Cts, 1980–. Chairman: Exec. Council, British Acad. of Forensic Scis, 1983–86 (Mem. Council, 1982–); Liaison Cttee, Inner London Probation Service, 1986–; Mem. Exec. Cttee, Central Council of Probation for England and Wales, 1982–. Underwriting Mem. of Lloyd's. Freeman, City of London, 1980; Liveryman, Fanmakers' Co., 1981. *Publications:* chapter in Archbold, Criminal Pleading, Evidence and Practice, 38th and 39th edns. *Recreations:* travel, theatre, occasional broadcasting. *Address:* Marlborough Street Magistrates' Court, WC2. *Clubs:* Garrick, Royal Society of Medicine.

CONNOR, Patrick Reardon; see Conner, Rearden.

CONNOR, Roger David; Metropolitan Stipendiary Magistrate, since 1983; *b* 8 June 1939; *s* of Thomas Bernard Connor and Susie Violet Connor (*née* Spittlehouse); *m* 1967, Sandra Home Holmes; two *s. Educ:* Merchant Taylors' School; Brunel College of Advanced Science and Technology; The College of Law. Solicitor; articled to J. R. Hodder, 1963–68; Asst Solicitor, 1968–70; Partner, Hodders, 1970–83. *Recreations:* music, golf, gardening, bee keeping. *Address:* Bourn's Meadow, Little Missenden, Amersham, Bucks. *Club:* Beaconsfield Golf.

CONOLLY, Mrs Yvonne Cecile; Inspector of Primary Schools, Inner London Education Authority, since 1981; *b* 12 June 1939; *d* of Hugh Augustus and Blanche Foster; *m* 1965, Michael Patrick Conolly; one *d*. *Educ:* Westwood High Sch., Jamaica; Shortwood Coll., Jamaica (Teachers' CertEd); Polytechnic, N London (BEd Hons Primary Educn). Primary school teacher: Jamaica, 1960–63; London, 1963–68; Head Teacher, London, 1969–78; ILEA Inspector, Multi-ethnic Education, 1978–81. Member: Home Secretary's Adv. Council on Race Relations, 1977–86; IBA, 1982–; Consumer Protection Adv. Cttee, 1974–75. Governor, former Centre for Information and Advice on Educnl Disadvantage, 1975–80; (first) Chm., Caribbean Teachers' Assoc., 1974–76. *Publication:* (contributor) Mango Spice, book of 44 Caribbean songs for schools, 1981. *Recreations:* special interest in the activities of ethnic minority groups; travelling, conversing.

CONOLLY-CAREW, family name of **Baron Carew.**

CONQUEST, (George) Robert (Acworth), OBE 1955; writer; *b* 15 July 1917; *s* of late Robert Folger Westcott Conquest and Rosamund, *d* of H. A. Acworth, CIE; *m* 1st, 1942, Joan Watkins (marr. diss. 1948); two *s*; 2nd, 1948, Tatiana Mihailova (marr. diss. 1962); 3rd, 1964, Caroleen Macfarlane (marr. diss. 1978); 4th, 1979, Elizabeth, *d* of late Col Richard D. Neece, USAF. *Educ:* Winchester; Magdalen Coll., Oxford. MA Oxon 1972; DLitt 1975. Oxf. and Bucks LI, 1939–46; Foreign Service, 1946–56; Fellow, LSE, 1956–58; Fellow, Univ. of Buffalo, 1959–60; Literary Editor, The Spectator, 1962–63; Fellow: Columbia Univ., 1964–65; Woodrow Wilson International Center, 1976–77; Hoover Instn, 1977–79 and 1981–; Distinguished Vis. Scholar, Heritage Foundn, 1980–81; Research Associate, Harvard Univ., 1982–83; Adjunct Fellow, Georgetown Univ., 1983–. FRSL 1972. *Publications:* Poems, 1955; A World of Difference, 1955; (ed) New Lines, 1956; Common Sense About Russia, 1960; Power and Policy in the USSR, 1961; Courage of Genius, 1962; Between Mars and Venus, 1962; (ed) New Lines II, 1963; (with Kingsley Amis) The Egyptologists, 1965; The Great Terror, 1968; Arias from a Love Opera, 1969; The Nation Killers, 1970; Lenin, 1972; Kolyma, 1978; The Abomination of Moab, 1979; Present Danger, 1979; Forays, 1979; We and They, 1980; (with Jon Manchip White) What to do when the Russians Come, 1984; Inside Stalin's Secret Police, 1985; The Harvest of Sorrow, 1986; Collected Poems, 1986. *Address:* c/o Brown Shipley & Co., Founder's Court, Lothbury, EC2; 52 Peter Coutts Circle, Stanford, Calif 94305, USA. *Club:* Travellers'.

CONRAN, Elizabeth Margaret, MA, FMA; Curator, The Bowes Museum, Barnard Castle, since 1979; *b* 5 May 1939; *d* of James Johnston and Elizabeth Russell Wilson; *m* 1970, George Loraine Conran, *qv*; one *d*. *Educ:* Falkirk High Sch.; Glasgow Univ. (MA). FMA 1969. Res. Asst, Dept of History of Fine Art, Glasgow Univ., 1959–60; Asst Curator, The Iveagh Bequest, Kenwood, 1960–63; Keeper of Paintings, City Art Galls, Manchester, 1963–74; Arts Adviser, Greater Manchester Council, 1974–79. *Publications:* exhibn catalogues; articles in art and museum jls. *Recreations:* gardens, ballet. *Address:* 31 Thorngate, Barnard Castle, Co. Durham DL12 8QB. *T:* Teesdale 31055.

CONRAN, (George) Loraine, FMA; Director, Manchester City Art Galleries, 1962–76; *b* 29 March 1912; *o s* of Col George Hay Montgomery Conran; *m* 1st, 1938, Jacqueline Elspeth Norah Thullier O'Neill Roe (marr. diss. 1970); one *s* one *d* (and one *d* decd); 2nd, 1970, Elizabeth Margaret Johnston (*see* E. M. Conran); one *d*. *Educ:* RNC Dartmouth. Museum and Art Gallery, Birmingham, 1935; Walker Art Gallery, Liverpool, 1936; Southampton Art Gallery, 1938; Curator, The Iveagh Bequest, Kenwood, 1950. Pres., Museums Assoc. (Hon. Sec., 1959–64); Hon. Sec., Contemporary Art Soc., 1959–65. Chm., Jt Cttee of Museums Assoc. and Carnegie UK Trust; Member: British Nat. Cttee, Internat. Council of Museums, 1959–71; Ct, RCA. Hon. MA Manchester, 1973. Served War of 1939–45 (despatches). *Address:* 31 Thorngate, Barnard Castle, Co. Durham DL12 8QB.

CONRAN, Shirley Ida; writer; *b* 21 Sept. 1932; *d* of W. Thirlby Pearce and Ida Pearce; *m* 1955, Sir Terence Conran (marr. diss. 1962); two *s*. *Educ:* St Paul's Girls' Sch.; Southern College of Art, Portsmouth. Fabric Designer and Director of Conran Fabrics, 1956–62; Member, Selection Cttee, Design Centre, 1961–69. Journalist; (first) Woman's Editor, Observer Colour Magazine, 1964; Woman's Editor, Daily Mail, 1969; Life and Style Editor, Over 21, 1972–74. *Publications:* Superwoman, 1975; Superwoman Year Book, 1976; Superwoman in Action, 1977; (with E. Sidney) Action Woman, 1979; Lace (novel), 1982; The Magic Garden, 1983. *Recreations:* reading, skiing, swimming, Yoga. *Address:* c/o Coutts Bank, 14 Lombard Street, EC4.

CONRAN, Sir Terence (Orby), Kt 1983; Chairman and Chief Executive, Storehouse plc, since 1986; Chairman: Habitat Mothercare PLC, since 1982; Habitat Group Ltd, since 1971; Conran Design Group (formerly Conran Associates), since 1971; Habitat France SA, since 1973; Conran Stores Inc., since 1977; Jasper Conran Ltd, since 1982; Conran Octopus, since 1983; Richard Shops, since 1983; Butlers Wharf Ltd, since 1984; Director: Conran Ink Ltd, since 1969; The Neal Street Restaurant, since 1972; Conran Roche Ltd, since 1982; Michelin House Development Ltd, since 1985; British Home Stores plc, since 1986; Vice President, FNAC, since 1985; *b* 4 Oct. 1931; *m*; two *s*; *m* 1963, Caroline Herbert; two *s* one *d*. *Educ:* Bryanston, Dorset. Chm., Conran Holdings Ltd, 1965–68; Jt Chm., Ryman Conran Ltd, 1968–71; Chm., J. Hepworth & Son Ltd, 1981–83 (Dir, 1979–). Mem., Royal Commn on Environmental Pollution, 1973–76. Member: Council, RCA, 1978–81, 1986–; Adv. Council, V&A Mus., 1979–83; Trustee, V&A Museum, 1984–. RSA Presidential Medal for Design Management to Conran Group; RSA Presidential Award for Design Management to Habitat Designs Ltd, 1975; SIAD Medal, 1981; Assoc. for Business Sponsorship of the Arts and Daily Telegraph Award to Habitat Mothercare, 1982; RSA Bicentenary Medal, 1982. Hon. FRIBA 1984. *Publications:* The House Book, 1974; The Kitchen Book, 1977; The Bedroom & Bathroom Book, 1978; (with Caroline Conran) The Cook Book, 1980; The New House Book, 1985; Conran Directory of Design, 1985; Plants at Home, 1986; The Soft Furnishings Book, 1986. *Recreations:* gardening, cooking. *Address:* The Heal's Building, 196 Tottenham Court Road, W1P 9LD. *T:* 01–631 0101.

CONS, Hon. Derek; Hon. Mr Justice Cons; Vice President, Court of Appeal, Supreme Court of Hong Kong, since 1986; *b* 15 July 1928; *s* of Alfred Henry Cons and Elsie Margaret (*née* Neville); *m* 1952, Mary Roberta Upton Wilkes. *Educ:* Rutlish; Birmingham Univ. (LLB (Hons)). Called to Bar, Gray's Inn, 1953. RASC (2nd Lieut), 1946–48. Magistrate, Hong Kong, 1955–62, Principal Magistrate, 1962–66; District Judge, 1966–72; Judge of Supreme Court of Hong Kong, 1972–80, Justice of Appeal, 1980–86. *Recreations:* golf, skiing. *Address:* The Supreme Court, Hong Kong; Mulberry Mews, Church Street, Fordingbridge, Hants. *Clubs:* Bramshaw Golf (Hants); Hong Kong, Royal Hong Kong Yacht, Shek O Country (Hong Kong).

CONSTABLE, (Charles) John, DBA; CBIM; Director-General, British Institute of Management, 1985–86; *b* 20 Jan. 1936; *s* of Charles and Gladys Constable; *m* 1960, Elisabeth Mary Light; three *s* one *d*. *Educ:* Durham Sch.; St John's Coll., Cambridge (MA); Royal Sch. of Mines, Imperial Coll. London (BSc); Harvard Grad. Sch. of Bus. Admin. (DBA). NCB, 1959–60; Wallis & Linnel Ltd, 1960–63; Arthur Young & Co., 1963–64; Lectr and Sen. Lectr, Durham Univ. Business Sch., 1964–71; Prof. of Operations Management, Business Policy, 1971–82, Dir 1982–85, Cranfield Sch. of Management. Mem., Heavy Electrical EDC, NEDO, 1977–; Governor, Harpur Trust, 1979–; Non-Exec. Dir, IMS Ltd, 1984–. *Publications:* (jtly) Group Assessment Programmes, 1966; (jtly) Operations Management Text and Cases, 1976; (jtly) Cases in Strategic Management, 1980. *Recreations:* golf, family. *Address:* 20 Kimbolton Road, Bedford MK40 2NR. *T:* Bedford 212576. *Club:* Reform.

CONSTABLE, Sir Robert Frederick S.; *see* Strickland-Constable.

CONSTANT, Antony; Group Archivist, the Delta Group plc (formerly Delta Metal Co. Ltd), retired 1980; *b* 1918; *s* of Frederick Charles and Mary Theresa Constant; *m* 1947, Pamela Mary Pemberton; one *s*. *Educ:* Dover Coll.; King's Coll., Cambridge. Asst master, Oundle Sch., 1939–45; Staff of Dir of Naval Intelligence, Admiralty, 1940–44; Educational Adviser to the Control Commission, Germany, 1945. Asst Master, and Asst House Master of School House, Rugby Sch., 1945–49; Rector of Royal Coll., Mauritius, 1949–53; Dir of Studies, RAF Coll., Cranwell, 1953–59; Educational Adviser to the Ministry of Defence and Chm. of Joint-Services Working Party, 1959–62; joined Delta Group of Companies, 1963, as Head of Training Dept; later Group Management Develt Executive. Mem. Bd for Postgraduate Studies, and Mem. Faculty Bd, Management Centre, Univ. of Aston, 1973–77. *Publications:* various papers on historical geography. *Recreations:* ornithology, sailing. *Address:* Old Bonham's, Wardington, near Banbury, Oxon, OX17 1SA.

CONSTANTINE, family name of **Baron Constantine of Stanmore.**

CONSTANTINE OF STANMORE, Baron *cr* 1981 (Life Peer), of Stanmore in Greater London; **Theodore Constantine;** Kt 1964; CBE 1956; AE 1945; DL; *er s* of Leonard and Fanny Louise Constantine; *m* 1935, Sylvia Mary, *y d* of Wallace Henry Legge-Pointing; one *s* one *d*. *Educ:* Acton Coll. Personal Asst to Chm. of public company, 1926–28; Executive in industry, 1928–38; Managing Dir of public company subsidiary, 1938–39. Served War of 1939–45, AAF (AEA 1945). Resumed pre-war Directorships, Oct. 1945. Dir of Industrial Holding Company, 1956–59; Chm. of Public Companies, 1959–84. Organisational work for Conservative Party as Constituency Chm., Area Chm., Mem. Nat. Exec. Cttee, Policy Cttee, Nat. Advisory Cttee on Publicity. Chm., Nat. Union Cons. and Unionist Assocs, 1967–68, Pres. 1980. Trustee, Sir John Wolstenholme Charity; Master, Worshipful Co. of Coachmakers, 1975; Freeman of City of London. High Sheriff of Greater London, 1967; DL Greater London, 1967–85. *Recreations:* watching motor racing, reading, walking. *Address:* House of Lords, SW1. *Clubs:* Carlton, Buck's.

CONSTANTINE, Air Chief Marshal Sir Hugh (Alex), KBE 1958 (CBE 1944); CB 1946; DSO 1942; Co-ordinator, Anglo-American Community Relations, Ministry of Defence (Air), 1964–77; *b* 23 May 1908; *s* of Fleet Paymaster Henry Constantine, RN, and Alice Louise Squire; *m* 1937, Helen, *d* of J. W. Bourke, Sydney, Australia; one *d*. *Educ:* Christ's Hosp.; Royal Air Force Coll., Cranwell. Pilot Officer in RAF, 1927; 56 (F) Sqdn, 1928–29; Flying Instructor, RAF Coll., 1930–31; CFS Instructor, 1932–33 and 1937; No 1 Armoured Car Co. (Iraq), 1934–36 (Palestine, despatches); Sqdn Ldr, 1936; 214 Bomber Sqdn, 1937–38; Sqdn Ldr Examining Wing, CFS, 1939; graduated Staff Coll., Andover, 1940; served in Bomber Comd, 1940–45 (Gp Capt. 1941; despatches four times); Wing Comdr (Ops) No 3 Gp, 1940, (Flying) No 11 OTU, 1941; comd RAF Elsham Wolds, 1941–42; SASO No 1 (B) Gp, 1943; Dep. SASO Bomber Comd, 1944; Air Vice-Marshal, Jan. 1945, and commanded No 5 (B) Group Bomber Command; Chief Intelligence Officer, BAFO and Control Commission, Germany, 1946; idc, 1947; SASO, 205 Gp (Egypt), 1948–49; Dir of Intelligence, Air Min., 1950–51; AO i/c A, Fighter Comd, 1952–53; AOC No 25 Group, Flying Training Command, 1954–56; Deputy Chief of Staff (Plans and Operations), SHAPE, NATO, 1956–59; AOC-in-C, Flg Trng Comd, 1959–61; Commandant, Imperial Defence Coll., 1962–64; retired 1964. Air Marshal, 1957; Air Chief Marshal, 1961. Patron, Central Flying Sch. Assoc., 1979–84. Governor, Christ's Hospital, 1963– (Almoner, 1969–85). Hon. LLD Warwick, 1978. Order of Polonia Restituta (2nd Class), 1945. *Recreations:* Rugby (English Trial, 1934), Eastern Counties, RAF and Leicester; golf. *Address:* 14 Cadogan Court, Draycott Avenue, SW3 3BX. *T:* 01–581 8821. *Club:* Royal Air Force.

CONTI, Rt. Rev. Mario Joseph; *see* Aberdeen, Bishop of, (RC).

CONTI, Tom; actor, since 1960; director; *b* Scotland, 1942; *m* Kara Wilson; one *d*. London appearances include: Savages, Royal Court and Comedy, 1973; The Devil's Disciple, RSC Aldwych, 1976; Whose Life is it Anyway?, Mermaid and Savoy, 1978, NY 1979 (SWET Award for Best Actor in a new play, Variety Club of GB Award for Best Stage Actor, 1978, Tony Award for Best Actor, 1979); They're Playing Our Song, Shaftesbury, 1980; Romantic Comedy, Apollo, 1983; *directed:* Last Licks, Broadway, 1979; Before the Party, Oxford Playhouse and Queen's, 1980; The Housekeeper, Apollo, 1982; *films include:* Galileo, Flame, 1974; Eclipse, 1975; Full Circle, The Duellists, 1977; The Wall, 1980; Merry Christmas, Mr Lawrence, 1983; Reuben, Reuben, 1983; American Dreamer, 1985; Miracles, 1985; Saving Grace, 1985; Heavenly Pursuits, 1986; *television appearances include:* Madame Bovary, The Norman Conquests, Glittering Prizes. *Address:* c/o Chatto and Linnit, Prince of Wales Theatre, Coventry Street, W1V 7FE.

CONTOGEORGIS, George; Member, Commission of the European Communities, 1981–84; *b* 21 Nov. 1912; *s* of Leonidas and Angeliki Contogeorgis; *m* 1949, Mary Lazopoulou. *Educ:* Athens Sch. (now University) of Economic and Commercial Sciences. Ministry of Trade, Greece: Administrator, 1937; Chief of Section, 1945; Dir, 1952; Dir Gen., 1964–67, resigned. Gen. Sec., Tourism, Govt of Nea Dimokratia, 1974; Dep. Minister of Co-ordination (Econs), 1974–77; Minister for EEC Affairs, 1977–81. MP, 1977–81. Grand Comdr, Order of the Phoenix (Greece), 1966; Grand Croix de l'Ordre de Leopold II (Belgium), 1984. *Address:* Rue Anagnostopouloy 26, Athens 10673, Greece. *T:* 361.68.44.

CONWAY, (David) Martin; President, Selly Oak Colleges, Birmingham, since 1986; *b* 22 Aug. 1935; *s* of Geoffrey S. and Dr Elsie Conway; *m* 1962, Ruth, *d* of Rev. Richard Daniel; one *s* two *d*. *Educ:* Sedbergh Sch.; Gonville and Caius Coll., Cambridge (BA, MA); and by friends and fellow Christians in many different cultures. Internat. Sec., SCM of GB and Ire., 1958–61; Study Sec., World Student Christian Fedn, Geneva, 1961–67; Sec. for Chaplaincies in Higher Educn, Gen. Synod of C of E, 1967–70; Publications Sec., WCC, 1970–74; Asst Gen. Sec. for Ecumenical Affairs, BCC, 1974–83; Dir, Oxford Inst. for Church and Society, and Tutor, Ripon Coll., Cuddesdon, Oxford, 1983–86. Simultaneous interpreter at assemblies and major world confs of WCC, 1961–; Consultant, Faith and Order Commn, WCC, 1971–82; Consultant, 1974–83, and Mem., 1986–, C of E Bd for Mission and Unity. Editor: The Ecumenical Review, 1972–74; Christians Together, 1983–; Oxford Papers on Contemporary Society, 1984–86. *Publications:* The Undivided Vision, 1966; (ed) University Chaplain?, 1969; The Christian Enterprise in Higher Education, 1971; Seeing Education Whole, 1971; Look Listen Care, 1983; contribs to Student World, New Christian, Audenshaw Papers, Internat. Rev. of Mission, etc. *Recreations:* other people—family, friends, colleagues; travel, music. *Address:* President's House, Selly Oak Colleges, Birmingham B29 6LQ. *T:* 021–472 4231.

CONWAY, Derek Leslie; MP (C) Shrewsbury and Atcham, since 1983; *b* 15 Feb. 1953; *s* of Leslie and Florence Conway; *m* 1980, Colette Elizabeth Mary (*née* Lamb); two *s*. *Educ:* Beacon Hill Boys' School. Borough Councillor and Dep. Leader of the Opposition, Gateshead Metropolitan Borough Council, 1974–78; Mem., Tyne and Wear Metropolitan County Council, 1977–83 (Leader, 1979–82); Member Board: Washington Develt Corp., 1979–83; North of England Develt Council, 1979–83; Newcastle Airport, 1980–83; Northern Arts, 1980–83. Principal Organiser, Action Research for the Crippled Child, 1974–83. Member, Conservative Party Committees: Nat. Exec. Cttee, 1971–81; Nat. Gen. Purposes Cttee, 1972–74; Nat. Local Govt Cttee, 1979–83; Nat. Vice-Chm., Young Conservatives, 1972–74. Commnd RMA Sandhurst into Royal Regt of Fusiliers; Major, 5th Bn (TA) Light Infantry, OC Headquarter Co. *Recreations:* squash, gardening. *Address:* Grove House, Roman Road, Shrewsbury, Salop. *T:* Shrewsbury 67006. *Club:* Beaconsfield (Shrewsbury).

CONWAY, Most Rev. Dominic J.; *see* Elphin, Bishop of, (RC).

CONWAY, Prof. Gordon Richard, FIBiol; Director, Centre for Environmental Technology, Imperial College of Science and Technology, since 1977; *b* 6 July 1938; *s* of Cyril Gordon Conway and Thelma (*née* Goodwin); *m* 1965, Susan Mary, *d* of Harold Edward Mumford and Ellen Martha (*née* Bingham); one *s* two *d*. *Educ:* Kingston Grammar Sch.; Kingston Polytechnic; University Coll. of North Wales, Bangor (BSc 1959). DipAgricSci, Cambridge, 1960; DTA University Coll. of West Indies, Trinidad, 1961; PhD Univ. of California, Davis, 1969; FIBiol 1978. Research Officer (Entomology), Agric. Res. Centre, State of Sabah, Malaysia, 1961–66; Statistician, Inst. Ecology, Univ. of California, Davis, 1966–69; Res. Fellow and Lectr, Dept of Zoology and Applied Entomology, Imperial Coll., 1970–76; Reader in Environmental Management, Univ. of London, 1976–80; Prof. of Envtl Technology, Univ. of London, 1980–. Vis. Prof., Univ. Chiang Mai, Thailand, 1981–82. Member: Council, Royal Entomol. Soc., 1974–77; Council, British Ecol. Soc., 1972–75; Royal Commn on Environmental Pollution, 1984–; Jt Cttee, SERC/ESRC, 1984–; Inst. of Biology: Chm., Cttee of Envtl Affairs, 1972–76; Mem., Cttee of Envt Div., 1976–81. *Publications:* Pest and Pathogen Control: strategic, tactical and policy models, 1984; papers and reports on agricl ecology. *Recreations:* travel, music. *Address:* Mavins, 6 Greenhill Road, Farnham, Surrey GU9 8JN. *Club:* Royal Commonwealth Society.

CONWAY, Hugh Graham, CBE 1964; FEng; *b* 25 Jan. 1914; *s* of G. R. G. Conway; *m* 1937, Eva Gordon Simpson (*d* 1980); two *s*. *Educ:* Merchiston Castle Sch., Edinburgh; Cambridge Univ. Joined aircraft industry, 1938; Man. Dir, Bristol Engine Division, Rolls Royce Ltd, 1964–70; Dir, Rolls-Royce Ltd, 1966–70, Rolls-Royce (1971) Ltd, 1971; Gp Managing Dir, Gas Turbines, Rolls-Royce Ltd, 1970–71. Member: Decimal Currency Board, 1967–71; Design Council, 1971–76 (Dep. Chm., 1972–76). *Publications:* Engineering Tolerances, 1948; Fluid Pressure Mechanisms, 1949; Landing Gear Design, 1958; Bugatti, 1963; Grand Prix Bugatti, 1968. *Recreation:* vintage motoring. *Address:* 33 Sussex Square, W2.

CONWAY, Prof. John Horton, FRS 1981; Professor of Mathematics, Cambridge University, since 1983; Fellow of Gonville and Caius College, Cambridge, since 1968. *Educ:* Gonville and Caius Coll., Cambridge. BA 1959; MA 1963; PhD 1964. Univ. Lectr in Pure Maths, Cambridge, to 1973; Reader in Pure Mathematics and Mathematical Statistics, 1973–83; Fellow, Sidney Sussex Coll., Cambridge, to 1968. *Publications:* Regular Algebra and Finite Machines, 1971; On Numbers and Games, 1976. *Address:* Gonville and Caius College, Cambridge.

CONWAY, Martin; *see* Conway, D. M.

CONYNGHAM, family name of **Marquess Conyngham.**

CONYNGHAM, 7th Marquess *cr* 1816; **Frederick William Henry Francis Conyngham;** Baron Conyngham, 1781; Viscount Conyngham, 1789; Earl Conyngham, Viscount Mount Charles, 1797; Earl of Mount Charles, Viscount Slane, 1816; Baron Minster (UK), 1821; late Captain Irish Guards; *b* 13 March 1924; *e s* of 6th Marquess Conyngham and Antoinette Winifred (*d* 1966), *er d* of late J. W. H. Thompson; *S* father, 1974; *m* 1st, 1950, Eileen Wren (marr. diss. 1970), *o d* of Capt. C. W. Newsam, Ashfield, Beauparc, Co. Meath; three *s*; 2nd, 1971, Mrs Elizabeth Anne Rudd; 3rd, 1980, Mrs D. G. A. Walker. *Educ:* Eton. *Heir: s* Earl of Mount Charles, *qv*. *Address:* Bifrons, near Canterbury; Cronk Ghennie House, Ramsey, Isle of Man. *Club:* Royal St George Yacht.

COOGAN, Ven. Robert Arthur William; Archdeacon of Hampstead, since 1985; *b* 11 July 1929; *s* of Ronald Dudley Coogan and Joyce Elizabeth Coogan. *Educ:* Univ. of Tasmania (BA); Univ. of Durham (DipTheol). Asst Curate, St Andrew, Plaistow, 1953–56; Rector of Bothwell, Tasmania, 1956–62; Vicar: North Woolwich, 1962–73; St Stephen, Hampstead, 1973–77; Priest in Charge, All Hallows, Gospel Oak, 1974–77; Vicar of St Stephen with All Hallows, Hampstead, 1977–85; Priest in Charge: Old St Pancras with St Matthew, 1976–80; St Martin with St Andrew, Gospel Oak, 1978–81; Area Dean, South Camden 1975–81, North Camden 1978–83; Prebendary of St Paul's Cathedral, 1982–85. Commissary for Bishop of Tasmania, 1968–; Exam. Chaplain to Bishop of Edmonton, 1985–. *Recreations:* reading, gardening, travel. *Address:* 27 Thurlow Road, Hampstead, NW3 5PP. *T:* 01-435 5890. *Club:* Oriental.

COOK, Prof. Alan Hugh, FRS 1969; Jackson Professor of Natural Philosophy, since 1972, and Master of Selwyn College, since 1983, Cambridge University; *b* 2 Dec. 1922; *s* of late Reginald Thomas Cook, OBE, and of Ethel Cook; *m* 1948, Isabell Weir Adamson; one *s* one *d*. *Educ:* Westcliff High Sch. for Boys; Corpus Christi Coll. Cambridge. MA, PhD, ScD. Admty Signal Estabt, 1943–46; Research Student, then Res. Asst, Dept of Geodesy and Geophysics, Cambridge, 1946–51; Metrology Div., Nat. Physical Laboratory, Teddington, 1952; Vis. Fellow, Jt Inst. for Laboratory Astrophysics, Boulder, Colorado, 1965–66; Supt, Standards (subseq. Quantum Metrology) Div., Nat. Physical Laboratory, 1966–69; Prof. of Geophysics, Univ. of Edinburgh, 1969–72; Cambridge University: Fellow, King's Coll., 1972–83 Head of Dept of Physics, 1979–84. Mem. SERC, 1984–. FInstP; FRSE 1970; Foreign Fellow, Acad. Naz. dei Lincei, 1971. Pres., RAS, 1977–79. Fellow, Explorers' Club, NY, 1980. C. V. Boys Prize, Inst. of Physics, 1967. *Publications:* Gravity and the Earth, 1969; Global Geophysics, 1970; Interference of Electromagnetic Waves, 1971; Physics of the Earth and Planets, 1973; Celestial Masers, 1977; Interiors of the Planets, 1980; many contribs learned jls on gravity, artificial satellites, precise measurement, fundamental constants of physics and astronomy. *Recreations:* amateur theatre, travel, painting. *Address:* Master's Lodge, Selwyn College, Cambridge CB3 9DQ. *T:* Cambridge 335889; Cavendish Laboratory, Madingley Road, Cambridge CB3 0HE. *T:* Cambridge 337200.

COOK, (Alfred) Melville, MusDoc, FRCO; Hon. FRCCO; Organist and Choirmaster of the Metropolitan United, Toronto, 1967–86; *b* 18 June 1912; *s* of Harry Melville and Vera Louis Cook; *m* 1944, Marion Weir Moncrieff (*d* 1985); no *c*. *Educ:* King's Sch., Gloucester. Chorister, 1923–28, Asst Organist, 1932–37, Gloucester Cathedral. Organist and Choirmaster: All Saints, Cheltenham, 1935–37; Leeds Parish Church, 1937–56. MusDoc Durham, 1940. Served War in RA, 1941–46. Organist and Master of the Choristers, Hereford Cathedral, 1956–66. Conductor, Three Choirs Festival, Hereford, 1958, 1961, 1964; Conductor, Hereford Choral Soc., 1957–66. Organist and Choirmaster, All Saints', Winnipeg; Conductor of the Winnipeg Philharmonic Choir, Canada, 1966. *Recreations:* walking, swimming.

COOK, Ann; *see* Christopher, A.

COOK, Arthur Herbert, DSc, PhD; FRS 1951; FRSC; Director, Brewing Industry Research Foundation, Nutfield, Surrey, 1958–71 (Assistant Director, 1949–58), retired 1971; *b* London, 10 July 1911; *s* of Arthur Cook, London. *Educ:* Owen's Sch., Islington, London; Universities of London (Imperial Coll. of Science and Technology) and Heidelberg. Joined staff of Imperial Coll., 1937; Asst Prof. and Reader in the University, 1947–49. Hon. DSc Heriot-Watt. *Publications:* (with late Prof. F. Mayer) Chemistry of the Natural Colouring Matters. Numerous articles, mainly in Journal of Chemical Soc. Editor, The Chemistry and Biology of Yeasts, 1958; Barley and Malt: Biology, Biochemistry, Technology, 1962. *Recreations:* gardening, photography. *Address:* Merrylands, Lympstone, Devon. *T:* Exmouth 271426. *Club:* Athenæum.

COOK, Maj.-Gen. Arthur Thompson, FRCP, FRCPE; Director of Army Medicine, 1977–81; *b* 21 Oct. 1923; *s* of Thomas and Mabel Elizabeth Cook; *m* 1960, Kathleen Lane; two *s* one *d*. *Educ:* China Inland Mission Sch., Chefoo, N China; City of London Sch.; St Thomas' Hosp., London (MB). FRCP 1955, FRCPE 1954. Joined RAMC, 1948. QHP, 1977–81. *Address:* Askham, 18A Firwood Drive, Camberley, Surrey GU15 3QD. *T:* Camberley 63043.

COOK, Mrs Beryl Frances; painter; *b* 10 Sept. 1926; *d* of Adrian Lansley and Ella Farmer-Francis; *m* 1948, John Victor Cook; one *s*. *Educ:* Kendrick Girls' Sch., Reading, Berks. *Exhibitions:* Plymouth Arts Centre, 1975; Whitechapel Art Gallery, London, 1976; The Craft of Art, Walker Art Gallery, 1979; Musée de Cahors, 1981; Chelmsford Museum, 1982; Portal Gall., 1985. *Publications:* The Works, 1978; Private View, 1980; Seven Years and a Day (illustrations), 1980; One Man Show, 1981; Bertie and the Big Red Ball (illustrations), 1982; My Granny (illustrations), 1983; Beryl Cook's New York, 1985. *Recreation:* reading. *Address:* Glanville House, 3 Athenæum Street, The Hoe, Plymouth PL1 2RQ.

COOK, Brian (Caldwell); *see* Batsford, Sir B.C.C.

COOK, Brian Francis, FSA; Keeper of Greek and Roman Antiquities, British Museum, since 1976; *b* 13 Feb. 1933; *yr s* of late Harry Cook and Renia Cook; *m* 1962, Veronica Dewhirst. *Educ:* St Bede's Grammar Sch., Bradford; Univ. of Manchester (BA); Downing Coll. and St Edmund's House, Cambridge (MA); British Sch. at Athens. FSA 1971. NCO 16/5 Lancers, 1956–58. Dept of Greek and Roman Art, Metropolitan Museum of Art, New York: Curatorial Asst, 1960; Asst Curator, 1961; Associate Curator, 1965–69; Asst Keeper, Dept of Greek and Roman Antiquities, BM, 1969–76. Corr. Mem., German Archaeol. Inst., 1977. *Publications:* Inscribed Hadra Vases in the Metropolitan Museum of Art, 1966; Greek and Roman Art in the British Museum, 1976; The Elgin Marbles, 1984; The Townley Marbles, 1985; Greek Inscriptions, 1987; articles and revs on Greek, Etruscan and Roman antiquities in Brit. and foreign periodicals. *Recreations:* reading, gardening. *Address:* 4 Belmont Avenue, Barnet, Herts. *T:* 01–440 6590. *Club:* Challoner.

COOK, Brian Hartley K.; *see* Kemball-Cook.

COOK, Charles Alfred George, MC 1945; GM 1945; FRCS; Consultant Ophthalmic Surgeon: Guy's Hospital, 1954–73; Moorfields Eye Hospital, 1956–73; Teacher of Ophthalmology, University of London (Guy's Hospital and Institute of Ophthalmology), 1955–73; *b* 20 Aug. 1913; *s* of late Charles F. Cook and Beatrice Grist; *m* 1939, Edna Constance Dobson; one *s* one *d*. *Educ:* St Edward's Sch., Oxford; Guy's Hospital. MRCS, LRCP 1939; DOMS (Eng.), 1946; FRCS 1950. Capt. and Major RAMC, 1939–45. Moorfields Eye Hospital: Clinical Asst, 1946–47; Ho. Surg., 1948–49; Sen. Resident Officer, 1950; Chief Clin. Asst, 1951–55. Sen. Registrar, Eye Dept, Guy's Hospital, 1951–55; Moorfields Research Fellow, Inst. of Ophthalmology, 1951–58; Ophthalmic Surg., West Middlesex Hospital, 1954–56. Mem., Court of Examrs, RCS; Examr for DOMS, RCP and RCS; Examr Brit. Orthoptic Board; Sec., Ophthalmological Soc. of UK, 1956–57. Member: Cttee of Management, Inst. of Ophthalmology, 1960–63 (Vice-Dean of Inst., 1959–62); Cttee of Management, London Refraction Hosp., 1983–; Council, Coll. of Opth. Opticians, 1979–83 (Hon. Fellow 1982); Bd of Governors, Faculty of Dispensing Opticians, 1980–84. Governor: Royal Nat. Coll. for Blind, 1967–; Moorfields Eye Hosp., 1962–65. Hon. DSc Aston, 1983. Renter Warden, Upper Warden, then Master, Worshipful Co. of Spectacle Makers, 1975–81. Freeman, City of London. *Publications:* (ed) S. Duke Elder, Embryology, vol. 3, 1963; (contrib.) Payling, Wright and Symers, Systematic Pathology, 1966; (jt) May and Worth, Diseases of the Eye, 1968; articles in Brit. Jl of Ophthalmology, Trans Ophthalmological Soc., Jl of Pathology and other Med. Jls. *Recreations:* swimming, reading; an interest in all outdoor recreations. *Address:* 13 Clarence Terrace, Regent's Park, NW1 4RD. *T:* 01–723 5111. *Clubs:* Athenæum, Garrick.

COOK, Sir Christopher Wymondham Rayner Herbert, 5th Bt *cr* 1886; company director since 1979; Director, Diamond Guarantees Ltd, since 1980; *b* 24 March 1938; *s* of Sir Francis Ferdinand Maurice Cook, 4th Bt and Joan Loraine, *d* of John Aloysius Ashton-Case; *S* father, 1978; *m* 1st, 1958, Mrs Malina Gunasekera (from whom he obtained a divorce, 1975); one *s* one *d*; 2nd, 1975, Mrs Margaret Miller, *d* of late John Murray; two *s* two *d*. *Educ:* King's School, Canterbury. *Recreation:* golf. *Heir: s* Richard Herbert Aster Maurice Cook, *b* 30 June 1959. *Address:* La Fontenelle, Ville au Roi, St Peter Port, Guernsey, CI.

COOK, David Somerville; solicitor; Senior Partner, Messrs Sheldon & Stewart, Solicitors, Belfast; Lord Mayor of Belfast, 1978–79; Member (Alliance) for Belfast South, Northern Ireland Assembly, since 1982; *b* 25 Jan. 1944; *s* of Francis John Granville Cook, *qv*; *m* 1972, Mary Fionnuala Ann Deeny; four *s* one *d*. *Educ:* Campbell Coll., Belfast; Pembroke Coll., Cambridge (MA). Alliance Party of Northern Ireland: Founder Member, 1970; Hon. Treasurer, 1972–75; Central Executive Cttee, 1970–78, 1980–85; Dep. Leader, 1980–84. Chm., NI Voluntary Trust, 1979–. Mem., Belfast City Council, 1973–85; contested (Alliance): Belfast South, by-elections, March 1982 and Jan. 1986; N Ireland, European Parly elecn, 1984. Trustee, Ulster Museum, 1974–85; Vice Pres., NI Council on Alcohol, 1978–83; Mem. NI Council, European Movement, 1980–84. Dir, Ulster Actors' Co. Ltd, 1981–85. *Recreations:* football, hill walking, marmalade making. *Address:* Banford House, Tullylish, Gilford, Co. Down BT63 6DL. *Clubs:* Ulster Reform, Ulster Arts (Belfast).

COOK, Eric William; HM Diplomatic Service, retired; *b* 24 Feb. 1920; *s* of Ernest Gordon Cook and Jessie (*née* Hardy); *m* 1949, Pauline Elizabeth Lee; one *s*. *Educ:* various private estabts. RAF, 1940–46. GPO, 1947–49; FO (later FCO), 1949–; Consul, Belgrade,

1961–64; Vice-Consul, Leopoldville, 1964–65; Consul, Cleveland, Ohio, 1967–69; also served at Rome, Moscow, Peking and Djakarta; Consul Gen., Adelaide, 1974–76; FCO, 1977–80. *Recreations:* music, writing and photography. *Address:* 11 St Ann's Court, Nizells Avenue, Hove, East Sussex BN3 1PR. *T:* Brighton 776100.

COOK, Francis; MP (Lab) Stockton North, since 1983; *b* 3 Nov. 1935; *s* of James Cook and Elizabeth May Cook; *m* 1959, Patricia, *d* of Thomas and Evelyn Lundrigan; one *s* three *d*. *Educ:* Corby School, Sunderland; De La Salle College, Manchester; Institute of Education, Leeds. Schoolmaster, 8½ years; Construction Project Manager with Capper-Neill International. *Recreations:* climbing, fell walking, singing, swimming. *Address:* 37 Windlestone Road, Billingham, Cleveland. *T:* Stockton 563041. *Clubs:* Catholic Men's, Low Grange Working Men's, Synthonia, Trade Union, Constitutional (Billingham).

COOK, Francis John Granville, MA Cantab; Headmaster of Campbell College, Belfast, 1954–71; *b* 28 Jan. 1913; *o s* of late W. G. Cook and Nora Braley; *m* 1942, Jocelyn McKay, *d* of late John Stewart, Westholm, Dunblane, Perthshire; one *s* two *d*. *Educ:* Wyggeston Sch.; Downing Coll., Cambridge. Historical Tripos, Law Tripos; Squire Scholar; Tancred Studentship, Lincoln's Inn. Asst Master, Rossall Sch., 1937; served War, 1940–46, with Royal Navy; Headmaster of Junior Sch., Rossall Sch., 1949–54. *Recreations:* gardening, books, people. *Address:* Ryeview Cottage, Butterwick, Malton, N Yorks. *T:* Hovingham 451.
   See also D. S. Cook.

COOK, Frank Patrick; Member, Commission for Local Administration in England and first Local Ombudsman for the North and North Midlands, 1974–85; *b* 28 March 1920; *o c* of Frank Cook, FRCS, FRCOG and Edith Harriet (*née* Reid); *m* 1st, 1945, Rosemary Eason (marr. diss. 1975); two *s* one *d*; 2nd, 1975, Margaret Rodgers, 2nd *d* of Dr J. W. Rodgers, PhD; one *s*. *Educ:* Rugby; Trinity Hall, Cambridge (Open Schol.); LSE (Personnel Management). Royal Marines, 1939–46; Courtaulds Ltd, 1946–56; Nat. Coal Board, 1956–61; Venesta Ltd, 1961–64; Principal, British Transport Staff Coll., 1964–69; First Chief Exec., English Tourist Board, 1970–74. Chm., Microtest Research Ltd, 1982–; A Vice President: IPM, 1965–67; RCN, 1973–; Member: Nat. Nursing Staff Cttee, 1967–72; Brighton and Lewes HMC, 1972–74; Ombudsman Adv. Bd, Internat. Bar Assoc., 1975–85; Exec. Cttee, Fawcett Soc., 1975–77; Council, Univ. of York, 1979–85; Merchant Taylors' Co. of York, 1981–; N Yorks FPC, 1985–. Governor, Martin House Hospice for Children, 1984–86. Hon. LLD Hull, 1986. *Publications:* Shift Work, 1954; Ombudsman (autobiog.), 1981; articles on personnel management. *Address:* 5 Malton Way, Clifton, York YO3 6SG. *Club:* Naval and Military.

COOK, George David, CEng, FIEE; Consultant, Quantel Ltd, since 1985; *b* 23 Sept. 1925; *s* of late John and Jean C. Cook; *m* 1954, Sylvia Ann Sampson; two *d*. *Educ:* Hendon College of Technology. BBC Planning and Installation Dept, 1947; Asst to Supt Engineer, Television Outside Broadcasts, 1955; Head of Engineering, Wales, 1963; Asst Chief Engr, Television, 1967; Chief Engr Transmitters, 1974; Asst Dir of Engrg, 1978; Dep. Dir of Engrg, 1984–85. *Recreations:* golf, theatre. *Address:* 26 Ridge Lane, Watford, Herts WD1 3TA. *T:* Watford 29638.

COOK, George Steveni L.; *see* Littlejohn Cook.

COOK, Sir Halford; *see* Cook, Sir P. H.

COOK, Harold James; a Metropolitan Stipendiary Magistrate, since 1975; *b* 25 Jan. 1926; *s* of Harold Cook and Gwendoline Lydia (*née* List); *m* 1952, Mary Elizabeth (*née* Edwards); one *s*. *Educ:* The John Lyon Sch., Harrow; Edinburgh Univ. RN, 1943–47. Civil Service, 1947–52. Called to the Bar, Gray's Inn, 1952; Dep. Chief Clerk, Bow Street, and later Thames, Magistrates' Courts, 1952–54; Inner London QS, 1955; Dep. Clerk to Justices, Gore Div., Mddx, 1956–60; Clerk to Justices, Highgate Div., 1961, and also Barnet and South Mymms Divs, 1968. *Publications:* contrib. legal jls. *Address:* West London Magistrates' Court, Southcombe Street, W14.

COOK, Rt. Rev. Henry George; retired; *b* Walthamstow, London, England, 12 Oct. 1906; *s* of Henry G. Cook and Ada Mary Evans; *m* 1935, Opal May Thompson, Sarnia, Ont, *d* of Wesley Thompson and Charity Ellen Britney; two *s* one *d*. *Educ:* Ingersoll Collegiate Inst., Ont; Huron Coll. (LTh); Univ. of Western Ont, London, Canada (BA). Deacon, 1935, Priest, 1936; Missionary at Fort Simpson, 1935–43; Canon of Athabasca, 1940–43; Incumbent S Porcupine, Ont., 1943–44; Archdeacon of James Bay, 1945–48; Principal, Bp Horden Sch., Moose Factory, 1945–48; Mem., Gen Synod Exec., 1943–47; Supt of Indian Sch. Admin., 1948–62; Bishop Suffragan of the Arctic, 1963–66, of Athabasca, 1966–70 (the area of Mackenzie having been part first of one diocese and then of the other, constituted an Episcopal District, 1970); Bishop of Mackenzie, 1970–74. RCN(R) Chaplain, 1949–56. Hon. DD Huron Coll. and Univ. of Western Ont. 1946. *Recreations:* fishing, coin collecting, model carving. *Address:* 15 Plainfield Court, Stittsville, Ont K0A 3G0, Canada.

COOK, Cdre Henry Home; Director, C. Gold Associates Ltd, since 1974; Director of Public Relations, Scientific Exploration Society, since 1984; *b* 24 Jan. 1918; *o s* of George Home Cook, Edinburgh; *m* 1943, Theffania, *yr d* of A. P. Saunders, Gerrards Cross; two *s* two *d*. *Educ:* St Lawrence Coll., Ramsgate; Pangbourne College. Entered RN as Paymaster Cadet, 1936; Comdr 1955; Captain 1963; Cdre 1970. Naval Sec. to Vice-Adm. Sir Guy Sayer, 1953–59; Sqdn Supply Officer, 1st S/m Sqdn, 1959; Comdr, RNC Greenwich, 1961; Naval Attaché, Ankara, 1964; Dir of Public Relations (RN), 1966; Defence Adviser to British High Comr, and Head of British Defence Liaison Staff, Ottawa, 1970–72; retired, 1973. ADC to HM the Queen, 1971–72. A Gen. Comr of Income Tax, 1983–. Dir, Ellerman City Liners Ltd, 1973–80. Pres., Anchorites, 1978; Vice-Pres., Inst. of Admin. Management, 1983–. FInstAM 1973 (Chm., 1982). DipCAM 1975. *Recreations:* fencing, swimming, sailing. *Address:* Ramblers Cottage, Layters Green, Chalfont St Peter, Bucks. *T:* Gerrards Cross 83724. *Club:* Army and Navy.

COOK, Rear-Adm. James William Dunbar, CB 1975; Chairman, Surrey Branch of Soldiers', Sailors', and Airmen's Families Association; *b* 12 Dec. 1921; *s* of James Alexander Cook, Pluscarden, Morayshire; *m* 1949, Edith May Williams; one *s* two *d*. *Educ:* Bedford Sch.; HMS Worcester. CO, HM Ships Venus, Dido and Norfolk; Sen. British Naval Officer, S Africa, 1967–69 (as Cdre); Dir RN War College, 1969–71; Asst Chief of Naval Staff (Ops), 1973–75; retired from RN, 1975. Comdr 1957; Captain 1963; Rear-Adm. 1973; jssc 1958; sowc 1970. Appeals Dir, Royal Star and Garter Home for Disabled Sailors, Soldiers and Airmen, Richmond, 1981; Mem. Council, King George's Fund for Sailors. *Recreations:* golf, gardening. *Address:* Springways Cottage, Farnham Lane, Haslemere, Surrey. *T:* Haslemere 3615. *Club:* Army and Navy.

COOK, John, FRCSEd; FRSE 1970; Consultant Surgeon, Eastern General Hospital, Edinburgh, since 1964; *b* 9 May 1926; *s* of George Cook and Katherine Ferncroft (*née* Gauss); *m* 1953, Patricia Mary Bligh; one *s* four *d*. *Educ:* Fettes Coll., Edinburgh; Edinburgh Univ. (MB 1949, ChM 1963). FRCSEd 1954. Served Med. Br., RAF, 1950–52 (Flt Lieut). House Surgeon, Royal Infirmary, Edinburgh, 1949; Res. Asst, Radcliffe Infirm., Oxford, 1954–55; First Asst, Dept of Surg., Makerere University Coll., Uganda, 1955–64

(Reader in Surg., 1962–64). Royal Coll. of Surgeons of Edinburgh: Hon. Sec., 1969–72; Mem. Council, 1974–84. Representative Mem., GMC, 1982–86; Hon. Sec., Internat. Fedn of Surgical Colls, 1974–84. Hon. Fellow, Polish Assoc. of Surgeons, 1981. *Publications:* contrib. surgical jls. *Recreations:* music, fishing. *Address:* 24 Duddingston Park, Edinburgh EH15 1JX. *T:* 031–669 2123.

COOK, Dr John Barry; Headmaster of Epsom College, since 1982; *b* 9 May 1940; *er s* of Albert Edward and late Beatrice Irene Cook, Gloucester; *m* 1964, Vivien Margaret Roxana Lamb, *o d* of Victor and Marjorie Lamb, St Albans; two *s* one *d*. *Educ:* Sir Thomas Rich's Sch., Gloucester; King's Coll., Univ. of London (BSc 1961, AKC 1961); Guy's Hosp. Med. Sch. (PhD 1965). Guy's Hospital Medical School: Biophysics research, 1961–64; Lectr in Physics, 1964–65; Haileybury College: Asst Master, 1965–72; Senior Science Master and Head of Physics Dept, 1967–72; Headmaster of Christ Coll., Brecon, 1973–82. Church in Wales: Mem. Governing Body, 1976–83; Coll. of Episcopal Electors, 1980–83. Chairman: S Wales ISIS, 1978–82; Academic Policy Cttee, HMC, 1985–. *Publications:* (jtly) Solid State Biophysics, 1969; Multiple Choice Questions in A-level Physics, 1969; Multiple Choice Questions in O-level Physics, 1970; papers in Nature, Molecular Physics, Internat. Jl of Radiation Biology, Jl of Scientific Instruments, Educn in Science, Conference and Trends in Education. *Recreations:* sports, philately. *Address:* Headmaster's House, Epsom College, Epsom, Surrey KT17 4JQ. *T:* Epsom 22118.

COOK, John Edward E.; *see* Evan-Cook.

COOK, Prof. John Manuel, FSA; FBA 1974; Professor of Ancient History and Classical Archæology, Bristol University, 1958–76 (formerly Reader); *b* 11 Dec. 1910; *s* of late Rev. C. R. Cook; *m* 1st, 1939, Enid May (*d* 1976), *d* of Dr W. A. Robertson; two *s*; 2nd, 1977, Nancy Easton Law, MA, *widow* of Ralph Hamilton Law. *Educ:* Marlborough; King's Coll., Cambridge. Sir William Browne's Medal for Greek Ode, 1933; Members' Latin Essay Prize, 1933; Augustus Austen Leigh Student in King's Coll., 1934; Asst in Humanity and Lectr in Classical Archæology, Edinburgh Univ., 1936–46; Dir of British Sch. of Archæology at Athens, 1946–54; Dean, Faculty of Arts, 1966–68, Pro-Vice-Chancellor, 1972–75, Bristol Univ. C. E. Norton Lectr of the Archaeological Inst. of America, 1961–62; Visiting Prof., Yale Univ., 1965; Gray Memorial Lectr, Cambridge, 1969; Geddes-Harrower Prof., Univ. of Aberdeen, 1977. Served in Royal Scots, Force 133 (despatches), and HQ Land Forces, Greece (Lt-Col). *Publications:* The Greeks in Ionia and the East, 1962; (with W. H. Plommer) The Sanctuary of Hemithea at Kastabos, 1966; The Troad, an archaeological and historical study, 1973; The Persian Empire, 1983; chapters in: Cambridge Ancient History; Cambridge History of Iran. *Address:* 8 Dalrymple Crescent, Edinburgh EH9 2NU.

COOK, Joseph, CChem, FRSC; management consultant; *b* 7 April 1917; *y s* of Joseph Cook, MBE, JP, and Jane Cook (*née* Adams), Cumberland; *m* 1950, Betty, *d* of James and Elizabeth Barlow, Standish, Lancs; two *d*. *Educ:* Whitehaven Grammar Sch.; Univ. of Liverpool (BSc, DipEd). RAF, 1939–40. Posts in Ministries of Supply, Aviation, Technology and Defence 1941–59; Dir, ROF Burghfield, 1959–65; Gp Dir, Ammunition Factories, 1966; Dir Gen. (Prodn) ROF, 1966–74; Man. Dir, Millbank Tech. Services Ordnance Ltd, 1974–77 (on secondment from MoD). *Recreations:* gardening, golf. *Address:* Abbots-wood, Bramley Road, Pamber End, near Basingstoke, Hants. *T:* Basingstoke 850304.

COOK, Melville; *see* Cook, Alfred Melville.

COOK, Michael John; His Honour Judge Cook; a Circuit Judge, since 1986; *b* 20 June 1930; *s* of George Henry Cook and Nora Wilson Cook (*née* Mackman); *m* 1st, 1958, Anne Margaret Vaughan; three *s* one *d*; 2nd, 1974, Patricia Anne Sturdy; one *d*. *Educ:* Leeds Grammar Sch.; Worksop Coll.; Univ. of Leeds (LLB 2(1) Cl. Hons). Admitted Solicitor, 1953. National Service, commnd Royal Artillery, 1954. Willey Hargrave & Co., Solicitors, to 1957; Ward Bowie, Solicitors, 1957–86 (Senior Partner, 1965–86); a Recorder, 1980–86. Past Hon. Sec. and Pres., London Solicitors' Litigation Assoc.; Member: Solicitors Disciplinary Tribunal, 1975–86; Law Society sub-cttees and working parties. Speaker at professional seminars, broadcaster on Commercial and BBC radio and BBC TV and ITV. *Publications:* The Courts and You, 1976; (contrib.) The Solicitor's Practice, 1981; The Taxation of Solicitors Costs, 1986. *Recreations:* tennis, gardening, theatre, sitting on moving horses. *Clubs:* Athenæum, Law Society.

COOK, Norman Charles, BA; FSA, FMA; Hon. Curator, Wells Museum, Somerset, 1972–82; *b* 24 Jan. 1906; *s* of George and Emily Cook; *m* 1934, Dorothy Ida Waters; one *s* one *d*. *Educ:* Maidstone Grammar Sch. Maidstone Museum, 1924–37; Morven Institute of Archaeological Research, Avebury, 1937–39; Curator, Southampton Museum, 1947–50; Director: Guildhall Museum, 1950–71; Museum of London, 1970–72. Hon. Sec., 1954–59, Pres., 1964–65, Museums Assoc. Vice-Pres., Soc. of Antiquaries, 1967–72. *Recreation:* archæology. *Address:* 6 St Thomas Terrace, Wells, Somerset BA5 2XG.

COOK, Norman Edgar, CBE 1980; writer; *b* 4 March 1920; *s* of Edgar James and Kate Cook; *m* 1942, Mildred Warburton; three *s*. *Educ:* Cowley Grammar Sch., St Helens. TA (Royal Corps of Signals), 1939; served war, UK, Sierra Leone, Gold Coast. Min. of Information, 1943–45; Editor, Northwich Guardian, 1945–47; Liverpool Daily Post, 1947–49; Information Officer, Air Ministry, 1949–53; Liverpool Daily Post and Echo: Night News Editor, 1953–55; Dep. News Editor, 1955–59; London Editor, 1959–72; Exec. News Editor, 1972–77; Editor, Liverpool Daily Post, 1978–79. *Publications:* numerous articles and reviews. *Recreations:* walking and gardening, interspersed with the study of political biographies. *Address:* 84 Boscundle Avenue, Golden Bank, Falmouth, Cornwall TR11 5BX. *T:* Falmouth 317707. *Club:* Athenæum (Liverpool).

COOK, Peter Edward; writer; entertainer; *b* 17 Nov. 1937; *s* of Alexander and Margaret Cook; *m* 1st, 1964, Wendy Snowden; two *d*; 2nd, 1973, Judy Huxtable. *Educ:* Radley Coll.; Pembroke Coll., Cambridge (BA). Part-author and appeared in: *revues:* Pieces of Eight, 1958; One Over the Eight, 1959; Beyond the Fringe, 1959–64 (London and New York); Behind the Fridge, 1971–72 (Australia and London); Good Evening, 1973–75 (US); *television:* Not Only but Also (four series, BBC), 1965–71; Revolver (ITV series), 1978. *Films:* The Wrong Box, 1965; Bedazzled, 1967; A Dandy in Aspic, 1968; Monte Carlo or Bust, 1969; The Bed-Sitting Room, 1970; The Rise and Rise of Michael Rimmer, 1971; The Hound of the Baskervilles, 1978; Derek and Clive, 1981; Yellowbeard, 1983. *Publication:* Dud and Pete: The Dagenham Dialogues, 1971. *Recreations:* gambling, gossip, golf. *Address:* c/o Wright & Webb, Syrett and Sons, 10 Soho Square, W1. *T:* 01–734 9641.

COOK, Sir (Philip) Halford, Kt 1976; OBE 1965; retired; *b* 10 Oct. 1912; *s* of Rev. R. Osborne Cook and May Cook; *m* 1945, Myra V., *d* of M. A. Dean; one *s* one *d*. *Educ:* Wesley Coll., Melbourne; Queen's Coll., Univ. of Melbourne; University Coll., Univ. of London; Columbia and Kansas Univs, USA. MA Melbourne, 1938; PhD Kansas, 1941. FBPsS 1943; FAPsS 1968, Hon. FAPsS 1972. Lectr, Industrial Relations, Univ. of Melbourne, 1945–46, Lectr, Indust. Admin. 1947–50; Professional Staff, Tavistock Inst. of Human Relations, London, 1950–51; Asst Sec., 1952–63, First Asst Sec., 1963–68, Sec., 1968–72, Aust. Dept of Labour and Nat. Service; Ambassador and Special Labour Advr in Europe, Australian Permanent Mission, Geneva, 1973–77. Chm., Governing Body, ILO, 1975–76. Fellow, Queen's Coll., Univ. of Melbourne, 1972. *Publications:* Theory and Technique of Child Guidance, 1944; Productivity Team Technique, 1951; articles in jls on psychology and on indust. relations. *Recreations:* reading and travel. *Address:* 11 Boisdale Street, Surrey Hills, Victoria 3127, Australia. *T:* Melbourne (03) 898 4793. *Club:* Athenæum (Melbourne).

COOK, Reginald, FCA; Chairman, South Wales Electricity Board, 1977–81; Member, Electricity Council, 1977–81; *b* 29 Dec. 1918; *s* of Harold Cook and Gwendolyn Cook, Birmingham; *m* 1945, Constance Irene Holt, Norden, Lancs; one *s* one *d. Educ:* Rochdale High Sch.; Manchester Univ. (BA); Admin. Staff Coll. Served War, 1939–46; Staff Captain, RA. Local Govt Service with Corporations of Manchester, West Bromwich and York, 1946–52; Midlands Electricity Board: accountancy posts, 1952–59; Chief Accountant, 1959–69; Exec. Mem., 1964–69; Dep. Chm., S Wales Electricity Bd, 1969–77. FBIM; CompIEE. Gold Medal, IMTA, 1949. *Recreations:* countryside activities, gardening, golf, bridge. *Address:* Heppleshaw, Itton, Chepstow, Gwent. *T:* Shirenewton 265.

COOK, Brig. Richard Arthur, CBE 1961; *b* 26 May 1908; *m* 1940, Sheila Mary Ostell Prosser; two *s. Educ:* St Paul's; RMA, Woolwich. Commissioned, Royal Artillery, 1928. Posted to India, 1933. Served War of 1939–45 in India and Burma: Staff Coll., 1941; Regimental Comd, 1943; Joint Services Staff Coll., 1947; Col, 1948; Col Administrative Plans, GHQ, MELF, 1948–51; CRA (Brig.) 16th Airborne Div., 1954–56; NATO Defence Coll., 1957; BGS, Southern Command, 1958–61; retired from Army, 1961. *Address:* 3 Meadow Court, Whiteparish, Wilts. *T:* Whiteparish 409. *Club:* Army and Navy.

COOK, Robert Finlayson, (Robin F. Cook); MP (Lab) Livingston, since 1983 (Edinburgh Central, Feb. 1974–1983); *b* 28 Feb. 1946; *s* of Peter Cook, headmaster and Christina Cook (*née* Lynch); *m* 1969, Margaret K. Whitmore, medical consultant; two *s. Educ:* Aberdeen Grammar Sch.; Univ. of Edinburgh. MA Hons English Lit. Tutor-Organiser with WEA, 1970–74. Chm., Scottish Assoc. of Labour Student Organisations, 1966–67; Sec., Edinburgh City Labour Party, 1970–72; Mem., Edinburgh Corporation, 1971–74, Chm. Housing Cttee, 1973–74. An Opposition Treasury spokesman, 1980–83; opposition front bench spokesman on European and community affairs, 1983–85; Labour's Campaigns Co-ordinator, 1985–. Mem., Tribune Group. *Recreations:* eating, reading, talking. *Address:* c/o House of Commons, SW1A 0AA. *T:* 01–219 5120.

COOK, Prof. Robert Manuel, FBA 1976; Laurence Professor of Classical Archaeology, University of Cambridge, 1962–76; *b* 4 July 1909; *s* of Rev. Charles Robert and Mary Manuel Cook; *m* 1938, Kathleen (*d* 1979), *d* of James Frank and Ellen Hardman Porter. *Educ:* Marlborough Coll.; Cambridge Univ. Walston Student, Cambridge Univ., 1932; Asst Lectr in Classics, Manchester Univ., 1934; Lectr, 1938; Sub-warden, St Anselm's Hall, Manchester, 1936–38; Laurence Reader in Classical Archaeology, Cambridge Univ., 1945, Ord. Mem., German Archaeological Inst., 1953. Chm., Managing Cttee, British School at Athens, 1983–. *Publications:* Corpus Vasorum Antiquorum, British Museum 8, 1954; Greek Painted Pottery, 1960, 2nd edn 1972; The Greeks till Alexander, 1962; (with Kathleen Cook) Southern Greece: an archaeological guide, 1968; Greek Art, 1972; Clazomenian Sarcophagi, 1981. *Address:* 15 Wilberforce Road, Cambridge CB3 0EQ. *T:* Cambridge 352863.

See also Prof. J. M. Cook.

COOK, Robin; *see* Cook, Robert F.

COOK, William Birkett, MA; Master of Magdalen College School, Oxford, since 1972; *b* 30 Aug. 1931; *e s* of late William James and Mildred Elizabeth Cook, Headington, Oxford; *m* 1958, Marianne Ruth, *yr d* of late A. E. Taylor, The Schools, Shrewsbury; one *s* one *d* (and one *d* decd). *Educ:* Dragon Sch.; Eton (King's Schol.); Trinity Coll., Cambridge (Schol.). National Service, 1950–51 (commnd in RA). Porson Prizeman, 1953; 1st cl. Classical Tripos Pt I, 1953, Pt II, 1954; Henry Arthur Thomas Student, 1954; MA Oxon by incorporation, 1972. Asst Master, Shrewsbury Sch., 1955–67, and Head of Classical Faculty, 1960–67; Headmaster of Durham Sch., 1967–72; Governor, Oxford High Sch., 1979–. *Recreations:* music, gardening. *Address:* Magdalen College School, Oxford. *T:* Oxford 242191.

COOK, Sir William (Richard Joseph), KCB 1970 (CB 1951); Kt 1958; FRS 1962; Director, Buck & Hickman Ltd, 1970–83; *b* 10 April 1905; *s* of John Cook; *m* 1929, Grace (*née* Purnell); one *d; m* 1939, Gladys (*née* Allen); one *s* one *d. Educ:* Trowbridge High Sch.; Bristol Univ. Entered CS, 1928; various scientific posts in Research Estabs of WO and Min. of Supply, 1928–47; Dir of Physical Research, Admiralty, 1947–50; Chief of Royal Naval Scientific Service, 1950–54; Deputy Dir, Atomic Weapons Research Establishment, Aldermaston, 1954–58; Mem. for Reactors, Atomic Energy Authority, 1961–64 (Mem. for Development and Engineering, 1959–61, for Engineering and Production, 1958–59); Dep. Chief Scientific Adviser, Ministry of Defence, 1964–67; Chief Adviser (Projects and Research) MoD, 1968–70. Director: Rolls-Royce (1971) Ltd, 1971–76; GEC-Marconi Electronics Ltd, 1972–79; Chm., Marconi International Marine Co., 1971–75. FInstP 1967; FINucE 1984. Hon. DSc: Strathclyde, 1967; Bath, 1975. *Address:* Adbury Springs, Newbury, Berks. *T:* Newbury 40409. *Club:* Athenæum.

COOKE, Alexander Macdougall, DM; FRCP; Hon. Consulting Physician, United Oxford Hospitals, 1966; *b* 17 Oct. 1899; *s* of Arthur Clement Cooke, OBE and Isobel Gilles Macdougall; *m* Vera, *d* of Charles Hermann Lea; one *s* three *d. Educ:* Merchant Taylors' School; Jesus College, Oxford; St Thomas's Hosp. (Mead Medal, 1926). 1st Cl. Hons Nat. Sci. 1920; BM 1923; DM 1933; MRCP 1926, FRCP 1935. War Service, Royal Fusiliers, RFC and RAF, 1917–18. Resident Asst Physician, 1927–28, 1st Asst, Professorial Med. Unit, 1928–30 and Dep. Dir, 1930–32, St Thomas's Hosp.; Physician, Radcliffe Infirmary, 1932–66; May Reader in Medicine, 1933–47; Fellow of Merton Coll., Oxford, 1942–66, Emeritus Fellow, 1966–. Lectures: Lumleian, RCP, 1955; Langdon-Brown, RCP, 1968; Litchfield, Oxford, 1964; Stopford Meml, Manchester, 1973. Royal College of Physicians: Examr, 1943–47 and 1952–62; Councillor, 1953–55; Censor, 1956–58; Sen. Censor, 1959–60; Oxford Univ. Rep., GMC, 1963–73. FRSocMed 1924, Hon. Fellow 1972 (Pres., Section of Medicine, 1960–62); Mem., Assoc. of Physicians, 1936 (Exec. Cttee, 1950–53), Hon. Mem., 1966; Hon. Mem., Royal Coll. of Radiologists. Sec. to Editors and Editor, Quarterly Jl of Medicine, 1937–65. *Publications:* A History of the Royal College of Physicians of London, Vol. III, 1972; articles and papers on medicine and med. hist. *Recreation:* inertia. *Address:* Grove Cottage, St Cross Road, Oxford OX1 3TX. *T:* Oxford 242419. *Club:* Athenæum.

COOKE, (Alfred) Alistair, KBE (Hon.) 1973; journalist and broadcaster; *b* 20 Nov. 1908; *s* of Samuel Cooke and Mary Elizabeth Byrne; *m* 1st, 1934, Ruth Emerson; one *s*; 2nd, 1946, Jane White Hawkes; one *d. Educ:* Blackpool Grammar Sch.; Jesus Coll., Cambridge (Scholar; Hon. Fellow, 1986); Yale Univ.; Harvard. Founded Cambridge University Mummers, 1928; First Class, English Tripos, 1929; Second Class, 1930. Editor, The Granta, 1931; Commonwealth Fund Fellow, 1932–34. BBC Film Critic, 1934–37;

London Correspondent for NBC, 1936–37; Commentator on American Affairs for BBC, 1938–; Special Correspondent on American Affairs, The London Times, 1938–40; American Feature Writer, The Daily Herald, 1941–43; UN Correspondent of the Manchester Guardian (which changed name to Guardian, 1959), 1945–48; Chief Correspondent in US of The Guardian, 1948–72. Master of ceremonies: Ford Foundation's television programme, Omnibus, 1952–61; UN television programme, International Zone, 1961–67; Masterpiece Theatre, 1971–. Wrote and narrated, America: a personal history of the United States, BBC TV, 1972–73 (Peabody Award for meritorious services to broadcasting, 1972; Writers' Guild of GB award for best documentary of 1972; Dimbleby Award, Soc. of Film and TV Arts, 1973; four Emmy awards of (US) Nat. Acad. of TV Arts and Sciences, 1973). Hon. LLD: Edinburgh, 1969; Manchester, 1973; Hon. LittD St Andrews, 1975. Peabody Award for internat. reporting, 1952 and 1983; Benjamin Franklin Medal, RSA, 1973; Howland Medal, Yale Univ., 1977. *Publications:* (ed) Garbo and the Night Watchmen, 1937, repr. 1972; Douglas Fairbanks: The Making of a Screen Character, 1940; A Generation on Trial: USA v Alger Hiss, 1950; Letters from America, 1951; Christmas Eve, 1952; A Commencement Address, 1954; (ed) The Vintage Mencken, 1955; Around the World in Fifty Years, 1966; Talk about America, 1968; Alistair Cooke's America, 1973; Six Men, 1977; The Americans: fifty letters from America on our life and times, 1979; (with Robert Cameron) Above London, 1980; Masterpieces, 1982; The Patient has the Floor, 1986. *Recreations:* golf, photography, music, travel. *Address:* 1150 Fifth Avenue, New York City; Nassau Point, Cutchogue, Long Island, NY, USA. *Clubs:* Athenæum; Royal and Ancient (St Andrews); National Press (Washington); Players (New York); San Francisco Golf.

COOKE, Alistair; *see* Cooke, Alfred A.

COOKE, Rear-Adm. Anthony John, CB 1980; Private Secretary to Lord Mayor of London, since 1981; *b* 21 Sept. 1927; *s* of Rear-Adm. John Ernest Cooke, CB; *m* 1951, Margaret Anne, *d* of Frederick Charles Hynard; two *s* three *d. Educ:* St Edward's Sch., Oxford. Entered RN 1945; specialised in navigation, 1953; Army Staff Coll., 1958; Sqdn Navigating Officer, HMS Daring, Second Destroyer Sqdn, 1959–61; Staff Navigating Officer to Flag Officer, Sea Trng, 1961; Comdr 1961; Directorate of Naval Ops and Trade, 1961–63; i/c HMS Brighton, 1964–66; Directorate of Navigation and Tactical Control, 1966; Captain 1966; Captain of Dockyard and Queen's Harbourmaster, Singapore, 1967–69; Captain 1st Destroyer Sqdn, Far East, later Divnl Comdr 3rd Div. Western Fleet, i/c HMS Galatea, 1969–71; Dir, Royal Naval Staff Coll., 1971–73; Cdre Clyde i/c Clyde Submarine Base, 1973–75; Rear-Adm. 1976; Senior Naval Mem., Directing Staff, RCDS, 1975–78; Adm. Pres., RNC Greenwich, 1978–80, retd. Police Foundn, 1980–81. A Younger Brother, Trinity House. Freeman, City of London, 1979; Liveryman, Shipwrights' Co., 1980. *Recreation:* philately. *Address:* Chalkhurst, Eynsford, Kent. *T:* Farningham 862789. *Club:* City Livery.

COOKE, Dr Arthur Hafford, MBE 1946; Warden of New College, Oxford, 1976–85, Hon. Fellow, 1985; Pro-Vice-Chancellor, University of Oxford, 1982–85; *b* 13 Dec. 1912; *er s* of late Sydney Herbert Cooke and Edith Frances (*née* Jee); *m* 1939, Ilse (*d* 1973), *d* of late Prof. Hans Sachs; two *s. Educ:* Wyggeston Grammar Sch., Leicester; Christ Church, Oxford (MA, DPhil). Research Lectr, Christ Church, 1939. Radar research for Admiralty, 1940–45. Fellow of New Coll., Oxford, 1946–76; University Lectr in Physics, 1944–71; Reader in Physics, 1971–76. Member: Gen. Bd of the Faculties, 1962–72 (Vice-Chm., 1969–71); Hebdomadal Council, 1969–83. Hon. DSc Leicester, 1979. *Publications:* articles in scientific jls on magnetism and low temperature physics. *Address:* New College, Oxford; 9 Benson Place, Oxford OX2 6QH. *T:* Oxford 52528.

COOKE, Brian, JP; Secretary of Commissions, Lord Chancellor's Department, since 1982; *b* 16 Jan. 1935; *s* of Norman and Edith Cooke; *m* 1958, Edith Mary Palmer; two *s* one *d. Educ:* Manchester Grammar Sch.; University Coll. London (LLB). Served Royal Air Force, 1956–59. Called to Bar, Lincoln's Inn, 1959; Dept of Director of Public Prosecutions, 1960–68; Deputy Clerk of the Peace, Inner London Quarter Sessions, 1968–71; Dep. Circuit Administrator, North Eastern Circuit, 1971–81; Circuit Administrator 1981–82. JP Mddx, 1985. *Recreations:* tennis, walking, theatre, music. *Address:* Lord Chancellor's Department, Thames House North, Millbank, SW1P 4QE.

COOKE, Prof. Brian Ernest Dudley; Professor Emeritus, University of Wales, 1983; Professor of Oral Medicine and Oral Pathology, University of Wales, Dean of Welsh National School of Medicine Dental School and Consultant Dental Surgeon to University Hospital of Wales, 1962–82; *b* 12 Jan. 1920; *e s* of Charles Ernest Cooke and Margaret Beatrice Wood; *m* 1948, Marion Neill Orkney Hope; one *s* one *d. Educ:* Merchant Taylors' Sch.; London Univ. LDSRCS 1942; LRCP, MRCS 1949; FDSRCS 1952; MDSU London 1959; MRCPath 1965, FRCPath 1974. Served RNVR (Dental Br.), 1943–46. Nuffield Dental Fellow, 1950–52; Trav. Nuffield Fellow, Australia, 1964. Lectr 1952–57, Reader in Dental Med. 1958–62, Guy's Hosp. Dental School. Rep. Univ. of Wales on Gen. Dental Council, 1964–82; Mem. Bd of Faculty of Dental Surgery, RCS England, 1964–72 (Vice-Dean 1971–72); Chm., Dental Educn Adv. Council, GB, 1975–78 (Mem. 1962–82); Sec.-Gen., Assoc. for Dental Educn in Europe, 1982–84. Adviser in Dental Surgery to Welsh Hosp. Bd, 1962–74; Civilian Consultant in Dental Surgery to RN, 1967–. Hon. Adviser, Editorial Bd, British Jl of Dermatology, 1967–76. Mem., S Glamorgan AHA, 1974–76. Mem. Bd of Governors: United Cardiff Hosps, 1965–71; HMC (Cardiff) Univ. Hosp. of Wales, 1971–74. Vice-Provost, Welsh Nat. Sch. of Medicine, 1974–76. Examr in Dental Surgery and Oral Pathology, Liverpool, Manchester and London Univs; Examr for Primary Fellowship in Dental Surgery, RCS, 1967–73. Hon. Mem., Pierre Fauchard Acad., 1967. Charles Tomes Lectr, RCS, 1963; Guest Lectr, Students' Vis. Lectrs Trust Fund, Witwatersrand Univ., 1967; Vis. Prof., Univ. of Sydney Dental Sch., 1986. Pres., Section of Odontology, RSocMed, 1975; Founder Pres., British Soc. for Oral Medicine, 1981. Cartwright Prize and Medal, RCS, 1955; Chesterfield Prize and Medal, St John's Hosp. for Diseases of Skin, 1955. *Publications:* (jtly) Oral Histopathology, 1959, 2nd edn 1970; scientific contribs to medical and dental jls. *Recreations:* various. *Address:* 33 Shanklin Towers, Prospect Road, Shanklin, Isle of Wight PO37 6AE. *T:* Isle of Wight 863734.

COOKE, Cecil; *see* Cooke, R. C.

COOKE, Sir Charles Fletcher F.; *see* Fletcher-Cooke.

COOKE, Cynthia Felicity Joan, CBE 1975; RRC 1969; Matron-in-Chief, Queen Alexandra's Royal Naval Nursing Service, 1973–76; *b* 11 June 1919; *d* of late Frank Alexander Cooke, MBE, DCM, and of Ethel May (*née* Buckle). *Educ:* Rosa Bassett Sch. for Girls; Victoria Hosp. for Children, Tite Street, Chelsea; RSCN, 1940; University Coll. Hosp., London, SRN, 1942; Univ. of London, Sister Tutor Diploma, 1949. Joined QARNNS, 1943; served in: Australia, 1944–45; Hong Kong, 1956–58; Malta, 1964–66. HMS: Collingwood, Gosling, Goldcrest; RN Hospitals: Chatham, Plymouth, Haslar. Principal Tutor, Royal Naval School of Nursing, 1967–70; Principal Matron, RN Hosp., Haslar, 1970–73. QHNS 1973–76. CStJ 1975. *Address:* The Banquet House, Kings Head Mews, The Pightle, Needham Market, Suffolk IP6 8AQ.

COOKE, Col Sir David (William Perceval), 12th Bt *cr* 1661; Commander, Transport and Movements, North West District, Western District and Wales, since 1984; *b* 28 April 1935; *s* of Sir Charles Arthur John Cooke, 11th Bt, and of Diana, *o d* of late Maj.-Gen. Sir Edward Maxwell Perceval, KCB, DSO; *S* father, 1978; *m* 1959, Margaret Frances, *o d* of Herbert Skinner, Knutsford, Cheshire; three *d. Educ:* Wellington College; RMA Sandhurst; Open Univ. (BA). FCIT, MBIM, AMInstTA. Commissioned 4/7 Royal Dragoon Guards, 1955; served BAOR, 1955–58; transferred to RASC, 1958; served: BAOR, 1958–60; France, 1960–62; Far East, 1962–65; UK. Transferred to RCT on formation, 1965, and served UK, 1965–76, and BAOR, 1976–80; AQMG, MoD, 1980–82; Comdr, Transport and Movements, HQ British Forces, Hong Kong, 1982–84. Operational service: Brunei, 1962; Malay Peninsula, 1964–65; N Ireland, 1971–72. Attended Staff Coll., Camberley, 1968 and Advanced Transport Course, 1973–74. Col 1984. Queen's Jubilee Medal, 1977. *Recreations:* fishing, ornithology, military history. *Heir: cousin* Edmund Harry Cooke-Yarborough [*b* 25 Dec. 1918; *m* 1952, Anthea Katharine, *er d* of J. A. Dixon; one *s* one *d*]. *Address:* c/o Midland Bank, Knutsford, Cheshire. *Clubs:* Royal Aeronautical Society, Royal Over-Seas League.

COOKE, George Venables, CBE 1978; *b* 8 Sept. 1918; *s* of William Geoffrey Cooke and Constance Eva (*née* Venables); *m* 1941, Doreen (*née* Cooke); one *s* two *d. Educ:* Sandbach Sch., Cheshire; Lincoln Coll., Oxford, 1936–39 and 1946. MA, DipEd (Oxon). Served Army, 1939–46 (Major). Teacher, Manchester Grammar Sch., 1947–51; Professional Asst (Educn), W Riding of Yorkshire CC, 1951–53; Asst Dir of Educn, Liverpool, 1953–58; Dep. Dir of Educn, Sheffield, 1958–64; Dir of Educn, Lindsey (Lincs) CC, 1965–74; County Educn Officer, Lincolnshire CC, 1974–78; Gen. Sec., Soc. of Education Officers, 1978–84. Chm., Secretary of State's Adv. Cttee on Handicapped Children, 1973–74; Vice-Chm., Nat. Cttee of Enquiry into Special Educn (Warnock Cttee), 1974–78; Member: Jt Adv. Cttee on Agricultural Educn (Hudson Cttee), 1971–74; Parole Bd, 1984–. Pres., Soc. of Educn Officers, 1975–76; Chm., County Educn Officers' Soc., 1976–77 (Hon. Sec. 1970–73). *Recreations:* golf, gardening. *Address:* White House, Grange Lane, Riseholme, Lincoln LN2 2LQ. *T:* Lincoln 22667. *Club:* Royal Over-Seas League.

COOKE, George William, CBE 1975; FRS 1969; Chief Scientific Officer, Agricultural Research Council, 1975–81, retired; *b* 6 Jan. 1916; *s* of late William Harry Cooke and late Sarah Jane Cooke (*née* Whittaker); *m* 1944, Elizabeth Hannah Hill; one *s* one *d. Educ:* Loughborough Grammar Sch.; University Coll., Nottingham. BSc (Chem.) London Univ., 1937, PhD London, 1940. Awarded Min. of Agric. Research Schol., tenable at Rothamsted Experimental Station, 1938; apptd Scientific Officer there, 1941, and Prin. Sc. Officer, 1951; Head of Chemistry Dept, 1956–75; Deputy Dir, 1962–75 (acting Dir, 1972–73). Chm., Agriculture Group of Soc. of Chem. Industry, 1956–58; President: Fertiliser Soc., London, 1961–62; British Soc. of Soil Science, 1976–78. Lectures: Amos Meml, East Malling Res. Station, 1967; Francis New Meml, Fertiliser Soc., 1971; Clive Behrens, Univ. of Leeds, 1972–73; Scott Robertson Meml, QUB, 1973; Macaulay, Macaulay Inst. for Soil Res., 1979; Blackman, Oxford Univ., 1980; Boyd Orr Meml, Nutrition Soc., 1981. Hon. MRIA, 1980; Hon. FRAgS 1981; For. Mem., Lenin All-Union Acad. of Agric. Scis, USSR, 1972. Research Medal of Royal Agricultural Soc., 1967; Soc. of Chem. Industry Medal, 1983. *Publications:* Fertilizers and Profitable Farming, 1960; The Control of Soil Fertility, 1967; Fertilizing for Maximum Yield, 1972, 3rd edn 1982 (trans. Japanese, 1986); many papers in scientific jls on soil science, crop nutrition and fertilizers. *Recreation:* boats. *Address:* 33 Topstreet Way, Harpenden, Herts. *T:* Harpenden 2899. *Club:* Farmers'.

COOKE, Gilbert Andrew, FCA; Chairman and Chief Executive, C. T. Bowring & Co. Ltd, since 1982; Director, Marsh & McLennan Companies Inc., since 1980; *b* 7 March 1923; *s* of Gilbert N. Cooke and Laurie Cooke; *m* 1949, Katherine Margaret Mary McGovern; one *s* one *d. Educ:* Bournemouth Sch. FCA 1950. Sen. Clerk, chartered accountants, 1950–54; Bowmaker Ltd: Chief Accountant, 1955; Dir, 1968; Man. Dir, 1968; Dep. Chm. and Chief Exec., 1972; C. T. Bowring & Co. Ltd: Dir, 1969; Gp Man. Dir, 1976–82. Chm., Bowring UK, 1984–. Chm., Finance Houses Assoc., 1972–74. *Recreations:* music, reading. *Address:* Kilmarth, Onslow Road, Burwood Park, Walton-on-Thames, Surrey. *T:* Walton-on-Thames 240451.

COOKE, Rev. Canon Greville (Vaughan Turner), MA, MusB Cantab; FRAM; FSA; Canon Emeritus, Peterborough Cathedral, since 1956; Composer, Author, Poet, Broadcaster; Adjudicator at Musical Festivals; *b* 14 July 1894; *s* of William Turner Cooke, Chief Clerk of Central Office of Royal Courts of Justice, London, and Adeline Hannah, *d* of David Johnson, MD. *Educ:* Hamilton House, Ealing; Royal Academy of Music (Schol., Exhibitioner, Prizewinner); Christ's Coll., Cambridge (Stewart of Rannoch Schol., 1913, Organ Schol.); Ridley Hall, Cambridge (Theol. Studentship); ARAM 1913; BA 1916; MusBac 1916; MA 1920. Ordained, 1918; Curate, Tavistock, 1918, Ealing, 1920; Dep. Minor Canon of St Paul's Cathedral, 1920–21; Vicar of Cransley, Northants, 1921–56; Rector of Buxted, 1956–71. Canon Non-residentiary of Peterborough Cathedral, 1955. Prof., Royal Academy of Music, 1925–59, FRAM 1927; FSA 1962. Elected FRSA by Council, 1958; Mem., Athenæum, 1931–53. Dir of Music, London Day Training Coll. Examiner for LRAM Diploma, Associated Board Exams, 1927; Lectr for London Univ., Royal Institution of Great Britain, League of Arts, Music Teachers' Association, Sussex Archæological Soc. (Mem. Council), London Appreciation Soc., RSCM, RSA; Lectr in Good English for Shell-Mex and IBM. *Publications:* The Theory of Music, 1928; Art and Reality, 1929; Tonality and Expression, 1929; Poems, 1933; Cransley Broadcast Sermons, 1933; The Light of the World, 1949 (USA 1950, paperback 1965); A Chronicle of Buxted, 1960 (paperback 1965); The Grand Design, 1964; Thus Saith the Lord: a Biblical anthology, 1967; Jenny Pluck Pears, 1972; Night Fancies and other poems, 1976; The Heresies of Orthodoxy, 1980; Who Wrote the Fourth Gospel?, 1981; An Easter Offering, 1982; musical publications include: *orchestral:* Prelude for Strings; *songs:* Three Songs; Day-dreams; The Shepherdess; Bereft; Eileen Aroon; But Yesterday; Your Gentle Care; My Heaven; Weep you no more; The Bells of Heaven; Shepherd Boy's Song; *choral:* Nobody Knows; Deep River; Jillian of Berry; Oh, to be in England; How can I help England; Claribel; Oh, Hush Thee My Baby; Cobwebs; *anthems:* Drop, Slow Tears; Let us with a gladsome mind; This Joyful Eastertide; Bread of the World; Lo! God is Here; *pianoforte:* High Marley Rest; Time Keepers; Meadowsweet; La Petite; Pets' Corner; Up the Ladder; A Day at the Sea; Bargain Basement; Reef's End; Cormorant Crag: Song Prelude; Whispering Willows; Haldon Hills; In the Cathedral; Gothic Prelude; *violin and piano:* High Marley Rest; *'cello and piano:* Sea Croon. Composer of several Hymns and contributor to Hymns Ancient and Modern, 1950, BBC Hymn Book, Baptist Hymn Book, Methodist Hymn Book, etc. *Address:* Waveney, West Close, Middleton-on-Sea, West Sussex.

COOKE, Jean Esme Oregon, RA 1972 (ARA 1965); (professional name Jean E. Cooke); Lecturer in Painting, Royal College of Art, 1964–74; *b* 18 Feb. 1927; *d* of Arthur Oregon Cooke, Grocer, and of Dorothy Emily Cooke (*née* Cranefield); *m* 1953, John Randall Bratby (marr. diss.), *qv*; three *s* one *d. Educ:* Blackheath High Sch.; Central Sch. of Arts and Crafts, Camberwell; City and Guilds; Goldsmiths' Coll. Sch. of Art; Royal Coll. of Art. NDD in Sculpture, 1949. Pottery Workshop, 1950–53. Member: Council, Royal Acad., 1983–85; Academic Bd, Blackheath Sch. of Art; Governor: Central Sch. of Art and Design, 1984–85; Tertiary Educn Bd, Greenwich, 1984–85. Purchase of self-portrait, 1969, and portrait of John Bratby (called Lilly, Lilly on the Brow), 1972, by Chantry Bequest; portraits of Dr Egon Wellesz and Dr Walter Oakshott for Lincoln Coll., Oxford; portrait of Mrs Bennett, Principal, for St Hilda's Coll., Oxford, 1976; started Homage to Birling Gap (large painting), 1985; portrait of Peter Carlisle, 1985–86. Television film: Portrait of John Bratby, BBC, 1978. One-man shows: Establishment Club, 1963; Leicester Gall., 1964; Bear Lane Gall., Oxford, 1965; Arun Art Centre, Arundel; Ashgate Gall., Farnham; Moyan Gall., Manchester; Bladon Gall., Hampshire, 1966; Lane Gall., Bradford, 1967; Gallery 66, Blackheath, 1967; Motley Gall., Lewisham, 1968; Phoenix, Suffolk, 1970; New Grafton Gall., 1971; Ansdell Gall., 1974; Woodlands Gall., Blackheath, 1976; J. K. Taylor Gall., Cambridge, 1976; Garden Gall., Greenwich, 1983; open studio for: Greenwich Festival, 1977, 1978, 1980, 1981, 1982; Blackheath High Sch. Art Fund, 1979; Bakehouse Gall., Blackheath, 1980; open studio in aid of Royal Acad. Trust, 1982. Works exhibited: annually, RA, 1956–; Furneaux Gall., 1968; Upper Grosvenor Gall., 1968; Ashgate Gall., 1973; Agnews, 1974; Gall. 10, Richmond Hill, 1974; Leonie Jonleigh Gall., 1976; Dulwich Coll. Picture Gall., 1976; British Painting 1952–77, Royal Acad., 1977; Business Art Galleries, 1978; New Ashgate Gall., 1979; Tate Gall., 1979; Grosvenor Street Gall., 1979, 1980; Norwich Gall., 1979, 1980; Imp. Coll. Gall., 1980; Patrick Seale Gall., Belgravia, 1981. *Publications:* Contemporary British Artists; The Artist, 1980. *Recreations:* ungardening, talking, shouting, walking along the beach. *Address:* 7 Hardy Road, Blackheath, SE3. *T:* 01–858 6288.

COOKE, Sir John F.; *see* Fletcher-Cooke.

COOKE, Air Vice-Marshal John Nigel Carlyle, CB 1984; OBE 1954; Consultant Physician; *b* 16 Jan. 1922; *s* of Air Marshal Sir Cyril Bertram Cooke, KCB, CBE and Phyllis Amelia Elizabeth Cooke; *m* 1958, Elizabeth Helena Murray Johnstone; two *s* one *d. Educ:* Felsted Sch.; St Mary's Hosp., Paddington (MD, BS(London)). FRCP, FRCPEd, MRCS, MFOM. House Physician, St Mary's, Paddington, 1945; RAF medical Br., 1945–85; Sen. Registrar, St George's, London, 1956–58; Consultant Physician, RAF, 1958–85; overseas service in Germany, Singapore, Aden; Prof. of Aviation Medicine, 1974–79; Dean of Air Force Medicine, 1979–83; Senior Consultant, RAF, 1983–85. UK Mem., Medical Adv. Bd, European Space Agency, 1978–84; Consultant to CAA, UK, 1972–; Chm., Defence Med. Services Postgrad. Council, 1980–82. QHP 1979–85. *Publications:* articles on metabolic and aviation medicine subjects in numerous medical jls. *Recreations:* gliding, fly fishing. *Address:* 4 Lincoln Close, Stoke Mandeville, Bucks HP22 5YS. *T:* Stoke Mandeville 3852. *Club:* Royal Air Force.

COOKE, Kenneth; *see* Cooke, R. K.

COOKE, Peter; *see* Cooke, W. P.

COOKE, Peter Maurice; Regional Administrator, Oxford Regional Health Authority, 1980–85; *b* Feb. 1927; *s* of late Reginald and Grace Cooke; *m* 1956, Daphne Joyce (*née* Annoot); two *s. Educ:* Bristol Grammar Sch.; Corpus Christi Coll., Oxford (MA). 3rd Royal Tank Regt, 1946–48. FHSM. Admin. Assistant, Central Middlesex and Taunton HMCs, 1951–59; Asst Sec., NW Met Regional Hosp. Bd, 1959–63; Group Secretary: W Suffolk and Ipswich and District HMCs, 1963–73; Area Administrator, Suffolk AHA, 1973–80. *Recreations:* golf, choral singing. *Address:* Haremire House, Buckland, near Faringdon, Oxon SN7 8QS. *T:* Buckland 603.

COOKE, Randle Henry, LVO 1971; Managing Director, Mervyn Hughes International Ltd, Recruitment Consultants, since 1986; *b* 26 April 1930; *o s* of late Col H. R. V. Cooke, Dalicote Hall, Bridgnorth, Salop and Mrs E. F. K. Cooke, Brodawel, Tremeirchion, N Wales; *m* 1961, Clare, *d* of C. J. M. Bennett, *qv*; one *s* one *d. Educ:* Heatherdown, Ascot; Eton College. 2nd Lieut, 8th King's Royal Irish Hussars, 1949; served Korea, 1950–53 with Regt and USAF (POW); ADC to GOC 7th Armoured Div., 1955; Regimental Adjt, 1957; Instructor, RMA Sandhurst, 1960; Sqdn Comdr, Queen's Royal Irish Hussars, Malaya, Borneo and Germany, 1963; GSO3 (SD), HQ 1st Div., 1965. Equerry to the Duke of Edinburgh, 1968–71; Private Sec. to Lord Mayor of London, 1972–74. Dir, Personnel and Administration, Alginate Industries plc, 1974–78. Freeman of City of London, 1971. *Recreations:* most things to do with water. *Address:* Coney Hill House, Great Missenden, Bucks. *T:* Great Missenden 2147. *Clubs:* White's, Cavalry and Guards.

COOKE, (Richard) Kenneth, OBE 1945; **His Honour Judge Cooke;** a Circuit Judge, since 1980; *b* 17 March 1917; *s* of Richard and Beatrice Mary Cooke; *m* 1945, Gwendoline Mary Black (*d* 1985); no *c*; *m* 1986, E. A. Rowlands (*née* Bachman). *Educ:* Sebright Sch., Wolverley; Birmingham Univ. Admitted Solicitor (Hons), 1939; Birmingham Law Soc. Prizeman. Sqdn Leader, RAFVR, 1939–45. Solicitor in private practice specialising in Magistrates' Courts, 1945–52; Clerk: to Prescot and St Helens Justices, 1952–57; to Rotherham County Borough and WR Justices, 1957–64; to Bradford City Justices, 1964–70; Metropolitan Stipendiary Magistrate, 1970–80; a Recorder of the Crown Court, 1972–80. Mem. Council, Magistrates' Assoc., 1973– (Chm. Legal Cttee; Hon. Sec. Inner London Branch; a Dep. Chm., 1981–82); Mem., Lord Chancellor's Adv. Cttee on the Training of Magistrates, 1978–85. Reader, Rochester Dio., 1970–. *Publications:* contribs to Criminal Law Review, Justice of the Peace and Local Govt Review, etc. *Recreations:* fishing, choral singing, sampling bin ends. *Address:* 8 St Paul's Square, Church Road, Bromley, Kent. *T:* 01–464 6761.

COOKE, Sir Robert (Gordon), Kt 1979; MA (Oxon); Special Adviser on the Palace of Westminster to the Secretary of State for the Environment, since 1979; *b* 29 May 1930; *er s* of late Robert V. Cooke, FRCS, and Dr Elizabeth Mary Cowie; *m* 1966, Jenifer Patricia Evelyn, *yr d* of Evelyn Mansfield King, *qv*; one *s* one *d. Educ:* Harrow; Christ Church, Oxford. Pres., Oxford Univ. Conservative Assoc., 1952; Editor, Oxford Tory, 1952–53. Councillor, City and Co. of Bristol, 1954–57; contested Bristol SE at Gen. Election, 1955; MP (C) Bristol West, March 1957–1979; Parliamentary Private Secretary to: Minister of State, Home Office, 1958–59; Minister of Health, 1959–60; Minister of Works, 1960–62; introduced: Fatal Accidents Act, 1959; Historic Buildings Bill, 1963; Motorways Commn Bill, 1968; Owner Occupiers Under-occupied Housing Bill, 1973 and 1974. State Dept Foreign Leader Visitor in USA, 1961. Chairman: Cons. Broadcasting and Communications Cttee, 1962–64, 1973–76; Arts and Heritage Cttee of Cons. Party, 1970–79 (Vice-Chm., 1959–62 and 1964–70); House of Commons Administration Cttee, 1974–79; a Commissioner, 1978; Vice-Chm., Media Cttee, 1976–79; Member: Services Cttee, House of Commons, 1967–79; Select Cttee on Wealth Tax, 1974–75 (Chm. Nat. Heritage Sub-Cttee); Select Cttee, Broadcasting Proceedings of Parlt, 1977–79; Parly delegn to Brazil, 1975; Sudan, 1978; Hungary, 1978; Council of Europe, Athens, 1976; Historic Buildings Council for England, 1970–80; Board, BTA, 1980– (Chm., British Heritage Cttee, 1981–). Pres., Dorset Tourism Assoc., 1983–. Trustee: Nat. Heritage Meml Fund, 1980–; Primrose League; Royal Botanic Gardens, Kew, 1986–. Director, Westward Television, 1970–81. Chm., Parish Meeting of Athelhampton. FRSA. *Publications:* West Country Houses, 1957; Government and the Quality of Life, 1974; Palace of Westminster, Houses of Parliament, 1986. *Recreations:* architecture, building, gardening. *Address:* Athelhampton, Dorchester, Dorset. *T:* Puddletown 363. *Clubs:* Carlton, Pratt's, Farmer's, Garrick, MCC.

COOKE, Rt. Hon. Sir Robin (Brunskill), KBE 1986; Kt 1977; PC 1977; PhD; **Rt. Hon. Mr Justice Cooke**; President, Court of Appeal of New Zealand, since 1986 (Judge, 1976–86); *b* 9 May 1926; *s* of Hon. Philip Brunskill Cooke, MC (Judge of Supreme Court), and Valmai Digby Gore; *m* 1952, Phyllis Annette Miller; three *s. Educ:* Wanganui Collegiate Sch.; Victoria University Coll., Wellington (LLM); Clare Coll., Cambridge; Gonville and Caius Coll., Cambridge (MA, PhD). Trav. Scholarship in Law, NZ, 1950; Fellow, Gonville and Caius Coll., Cambridge, 1952 (Yorke Prize, 1954), Hon. Fellow, 1982. Called to the Bar, Inner Temple, 1954, Hon. Bencher 1985; practised at NZ Bar, 1955–72; QC 1964; Judge of Supreme Court, 1972. Chm., Commn of Inquiry into Housing, 1970–71. *Publications:* (ed) Portrait of a Profession (Centennial Book of NZ Law Society), 1969; articles in law reviews. *Recreations:* running, theatre, the Times crossword. *Address:* 4 Homewood Crescent, Karori, Wellington, New Zealand. *T:* 768–059. *Clubs:* United Oxford & Cambridge University; Wellington, Wellington Golf (NZ).

COOKE, (Roland) Cecil, CMG 1959; CBE 1952; Director of Exhibitions, Central Office of Information, 1946–61, retired; *b* 28 June 1899; *m* 1924, Doris Marjorie Fewings (*d* 1982). Architectural Asst, LCC, 1921; Dir of Publicity, Catesbys, Ltd, 1935; Dir of Exhibitions Div., Ministry of Information, 1945. Dir of Exhibitions, Festival of Britain, 1949–51; Dir, Festival Gardens Co., 1951; Dir of Exhibitions, British Government Pavilion, Brussels, 1958; UK representative, International Jury, Brussels Exhibition, 1958. Comr Gen., British Pavilion, Seattle World's Fair. *Publications:* contrib. to periodicals and press, illustrated stories for children, political and strip cartoons. *Recreation:* painting. *Address:* 6 Wells Close, Eastbourne, East Sussex BN20 7TX. *T:* Eastbourne 30258.

COOKE, Prof. Ronald Urwick, MSc, PhD, DSc; Professor and Head of Department of Geography, University College London, since 1981; *b* 1 Sept. 1941; *y s* of Ernest Cooke and Lillian (*née* Mount), Maidstone, Kent; *m* 1968, Barbara Anne, *d* of A. Baldwin; one *s* one *d. Educ:* Ashford Grammar Sch.; University College London, Univ. of London (BSc 1st Cl. Hons, MSc, PhD). Lectr, UCL, 1961–75; Prof. of Geography, 1975–81, Dean of Science, 1978–80, and Vice-Principal, 1979–80, Bedford Coll., Univ. of London. Amer. Council of Learned Societies Fellow, UCLA, 1964–65 and 1973; Vis. Professor: UCLA, 1968; Univ. of Arizona, Tucson, 1970. Desert research in N and S America, N Africa and ME. Chm., British Geomorphological Res. Group, 1979; Mem. Council: RGS, 1980– (Back Grant, 1977); Inst. of British Geographers, 1973–75. *Publications:* (ed with J. H. Johnson) Trends in Geography, 1969; (with A. Warren) Geomorphology in Deserts, 1973; (with J. C. Doornkamp) Geomorphology in Environmental Management, 1974; (with R. W. Reeves) Arroyos and Environmental Change in the American Southwest, 1976; (contrib.) Geology, Geomorphology and Pedology of Bahrain, 1980; (contrib.) Urban Geomorphology in Drylands, 1982; Geomorphological Hazards in Los Angeles, 1984; contribs mainly on desert and applied geomorphology in prof. jls. *Address:* Department of Geography, University College London, 26 Bedford Way, WC1H 0AP. *T:* 01–387 7050.

COOKE, Roy, MA; JP; Director of Coventry School Foundation, since 1977; *b* Manchester, 6 May 1930; *s* of Reginald Herbert Cooke and Alice Cooke; *m* 1957, Claire Marion Medlicott Woodward, *d* of Lt-Col C. S. Woodward, CBE, JP, DL and Irene Anne Woodward, Glamorgan; three *s. Educ:* Manchester Grammar Sch. (schol.); Trinity Coll., Oxford (schol.; BA 1951; MA 1955; DipEd). Army service, 1951–54; commnd RAEC; Staff Officer in Germany (Captain, actg Major). Assistant Master: Gillingham Grammar Sch., Kent, 1955–56; Woking Grammar Sch., Surrey, 1956–58; Manchester Grammar Sch., 1958–64; Head of For. Langs, Stockport Sch., 1964–68; Headmaster: Gravesend Sch. for Boys, 1968–74; King Henry VIII Sch., Coventry, 1974–77. JP Kent, 1972, W Midlands, 1976. *Recreations:* photography, gardening, fell-walking, music. *Address:* 10 Stivichall Croft, Coventry CV3 6GN. *Club:* East India.

COOKE, Thomas Fitzpatrick, TD 1946; Lord Lieutenant, City of Londonderry, 1975–86; *b* 10 July 1911; *s* of Thomas Fitzpatrick Cooke and Aileen Frances Cooke; *m* 1946, Ruth, *d* of Rt Hon. Sir Anthony Brutus Babington, QC; one *s* one *d. Educ:* Stowe; Trinity Coll., Dublin (Dip. in Commerce). Served War, 1939–46, Captain, RA. Chm., Londonderry Port and Harbour Commissioners, 1967–73. Alderman, Londonderry Corp., 1946–52; High Sheriff, County of Londerry, 1949; DL 1950, High Sheriff, 1971–72, City of Londonderry. *Recreations:* gardening, shooting, fishing. *Address:* The Lodge, 5 Edenreagh Road, Eglinton, Londonderry BT47 3AR. *T:* Eglinton 810256. *Club* Northern Counties (Londonderry).

COOKE, Tom Harry; Group Editorial Director, St Regis Newspapers Ltd (publishers of the Bolton Evening News, and weekly newspapers in Lancashire, South Yorkshire and north-east England), 1979–81, retired; *b* 26 March 1923; *er s* of Tom Cooke and Dorothy Cooke; *m* 1952, Jean Margaret Taylor; four *d. Educ:* Bacup and Rawtenstall Grammar Sch. Served RAF, 1942–47. Journalist on weekly, evening and morning papers in Lancs, 1939–51; Parly and Lobby Corresp. with Kemsley (now Thomson) Newspapers, 1951–59; Asst Editor, Evening Telegraph, Blackburn, 1959–64; Dep. Editor, The Journal, Newcastle upon Tyne, 1964–65; Editor-in-Chief, Bolton Evening News and Lancashire Journal Series, 1965–79. Pres., Guild of Brit. Newspaper Editors, 1975–76; Mem., Press Council, 1976–83. *Recreations:* music, esp. opera; travel, reading. *Address:* MG. CA 268, Javea, Alicante, Spain. *T:* (965) 79–39–48. *Club:* Royal Over-Seas League.

COOKE, Victor Alexander, OBE 1981; DL; CEng, FIMechE; Chairman and Managing Director: Henry R. Ayton Ltd, Belfast, since 1970; Springvale EPS (formerly Polyproducts) Ltd, since 1964; Director, Harland & Wolff Ltd, since 1970; *b* 18 Oct. 1920; *s* of Norman Victor Cooke and Alice Harman Cooke (*née* Peavey); *m* 1951, Alison Sheila Casement; two *s* one *d. Educ:* Marlborough Coll., Wilts; Trinity Coll., Cambridge (MA). Engineer Officer, Royal Navy, 1940–46 (Lieut (E) RN). Henry R. Ayton Ltd, Belfast, 1946–; Chairman: Belfast Savings Bank, 1963; Harland & Wolff Ltd, 1980–May 1981; Dir, NI Airports, 1970–85. Member: Senate, Parliament of N Ireland, 1960–68; N Ireland Economic Council, 1974–78; Commissioner, Belfast Harbour, 1968–79; Commissioner of Irish Lights, 1983–. DL Co. Antrim, 1970. *Recreations:* sailing, shooting. *Club:* Naval.

COOKE, (William) Peter; Associate Director, Bank of England, since 1982; *b* 1 Feb. 1932; *s* of late Douglas Edgar Cooke, MC and Florence May (*née* Mills); *m* 1957, Maureen Elizabeth, *er d* of late Dr E. A. Haslam-Fox; two *s* two *d. Educ:* Royal Grammar Sch., High Wycombe; Kingswood Sch., Bath; Merton Coll., Oxford (MA). Entered Bank of England, 1955; Bank for Internat. Settlements, Basle, 1958–59; Personal Asst to Man. Dir, IMF, Washington, DC, 1961–65; Sec., City Panel on Takeovers and Mergers, 1968–69; First Dep. Chief Cashier, Bank of England, 1970–73; Adviser to Governors, 1973–76; Hd of Banking Supervision, 1976–85. Chairman: City EEC Cttee, 1973–80; Group of Ten Cttee on Banking Regulations and Supervisory Practices at BIS, Basle, 1977–. Mem., Management Cttee, Church Housing Assoc. Ltd, 1977–. Governor, Pangbourne Coll., 1982–. *Recreations:* music, golf, travel. *Address:* Bank of England, Threadneedle Street, EC2R 8AH. *Club:* Overseas Bankers.

COOKSLEY, Clarence Harrington, CBE 1973; QPM 1969; DL; one of HM Inspectors of Constabulary, 1975–77; *b* 16 Dec. 1915; *e s* of late Clarence Harrington Cooksley and Elsie Cooksley, Nottingham; *m* 1940, Eunice May White, Nottingham; two *s. Educ:* Nottingham. Joined Nottinghamshire Constabulary, 1938. Served Duke of Wellington's Regt and Dep. Asst Provost Marshal, Special Investigation Branch, Royal Corps of Military Police, 1942–46. Dir. of Dept of Law, Police Coll., Bramshill, 1961; Dep. Chief Constable of Hertfordshire, 1961–63; Chief Constable: Northumberland County Constabulary, 1963–69; Northumberland Constabulary, 1969–74; Northumbria Police, 1974–75. DL Northumberland 1971. OStJ 1966. *Address:* 8 Sandringham Way, Ponteland, Newcastle upon Tyne NE20 9AE.

COOKSON, Catherine Ann, OBE 1985; author, since 1950; *b* 20 June 1906; *d* of Catherine Fawcett; *m* 1940, Thomas Cookson. Member: Society of Authors; Writers' and Authors' Guild. Paul Harris Fellow, Rotary International, Hexham, 1985. Hon. MA Newcastle upon Tyne, 1983. Freeman of South Shields, 1978. *Publications:* Kate Hannigan, 1950; The Fifteen Streets; Colour Blind, 1953; Maggie Rowan, 1954; A Grand Man, 1954 (filmed as Jacqueline, 1956); The Lord and Mary Ann, 1956; Rooney, 1957 (filmed 1958); The Menagerie, 1958; The Devil and Mary Ann, 1958; Slinky Jane, 1959; Fanny McBride, 1959; Fenwick Houses, 1960; Love and Mary Ann, 1961; The Garment, 1962; Life and Mary Ann, 1962; The Blind Miller, 1963; Hannah Massey, 1964; Marriage and Mary Ann, 1964; The Long Corridor, 1965; Mary Ann's Angels, 1965; Matty Doolin, 1965; The Unbaited Trap, 1966; Katie Mulholland, 1967; Mary Ann and Bill, 1967; The Round Tower, 1968 (RSL Winifred Holtby Award for Best Regional Novel); Joe and the Gladiator, 1968; Our Kate (autobiog.), 1969; The Nice Bloke, 1969; The Glass Virgin, 1970; The Invitation, 1970; The Nipper, 1970; The Dwelling Place, 1971; Feathers in the Fire, 1971; Pure as the Lily, 1972; Blue Baccy, 1972; The Mallen Streak, 1973; The Mallen Girl, 1974; The Mallen Litter, 1974; Our John Willie, 1974; The Invisible Cord, 1975; The Gambling Man, 1975 (staged 1985); The Tide of Life, 1976; Mrs Flannigan's Trumpet, 1976; The Girl, 1977; Go Tell It To Mrs Golightly, 1977; The Cinder Path, 1978; The Man Who Cried, 1979; Tilly Trotter, 1980; Lanky Jones, 1980; Tilly Trotter Wed, 1981; Tilly Trotter Widowed, 1982; The Whip, 1983; Hamilton, 1983; The Black Velvet Gown, 1984; Goodbye Hamilton, 1984; A Dinner of Herbs, 1985; Harold, 1985; The Moth, 1986; Catherine Cookson Country (memoirs), 1986; as *Catherine Marchant:* Heritage of Folly, 1962; Fen Tiger, 1963; House of Men, 1964; Martha Mary Crawford, 1975; The Slow Awakening, 1976; The Iron Façade, 1977. *Recreations:* painting, gardening. *Address:* c/o Anthony Sheil Associates, 43 Doughty Street, WC1N 2LF. *Club:* PEN (English Centre).

COOKSON, Prof. Richard Clive, MA, PhD; FRS 1968, FRSC; Research Professor of Chemistry in the University of Southampton, 1983–85, Emeritus Professor, since 1985 (Professor of Chemistry, 1957–83); *b* 27 Aug. 1922; *s* of late Clive Cookson; *m* 1948, Ellen Fawaz; two *s. Educ:* Harrow Sch.; Trinity Coll., Cambridge. BA 1944; MA, PhD Cantab 1947. Research Fellow, Harvard Univ., 1948; Research Div. of Glaxo Laboratories Ltd, 1949–51; Lectr, Birkbeck Coll., London Univ., 1951–57. *Publications:* papers, mainly in Jl Chem. Soc. *Address:* Manor Farm, Stratford Tony, Salisbury, Wilts SP5 4AT.

COOKSON, Roland Antony, CBE 1974 (OBE 1946); Chairman, Lead Industries Group Ltd (until 1967 known as Goodlass Wall & Lead Industries Ltd), 1962–73 (Director, 1948–80, a Managing Director, 1952–62); Chairman, Consett Iron Co. Ltd, 1966–67 (Director 1955; Acting Chairman 1964); Director of Lloyds Bank Ltd, 1964–79 (Chairman, Northern Regional Board, 1965–79); *b* 12 Dec. 1908; *s* of late Bryan Cookson; *m* 1st, 1931, Rosamond Gwladys (*d* 1973), *er d* of late Sir John S. Barwick, 2nd Bt; one *d*; 2nd, 1974, Dr Anne Aitchison, widow of Sir Stephen Charles de Lancey Aitchison, 3rd Bt. *Educ:* Harrow; Magdalen Coll., Oxford. Vice-Chm., Northern Regional Board for Industry, 1949–65; Mem., Northern Economic Planning Council, 1965–68; Pres., Tyneside Chamber of Commerce, 1955–57; Chm., Northern Regional Council, CBI, 1970–72 (Vice-Chm., 1968–70); Mem., Port of Tyne Authority, 1968–74. Mem., Court and Council, Univ. of Newcastle upon Tyne (Vice-Chm. of Council, 1985–); Chm., Careers Adv. Board, Univs of Newcastle upon Tyne and Durham, 1962–73. Hon. DCL Newcastle, 1974. *Recreations:* music, fishing. *Address:* The Brow, Wylam, Northumberland NE41 8DQ. *T:* Wylam 3888. *Clubs:* Brooks's; Northern Counties (Newcastle upon Tyne).

COOLEY, Sir Alan (Sydenham), Kt 1976; CBE 1972; FIE; Secretary, Department of Productivity, 1977–80, retired 1981; *b* 17 Sept. 1920; *s* of Hector William Cooley and Ruby Ann Cooley; *m* 1949, Nancie Chisholm Young; four *d. Educ:* Geelong Grammar Sch.; Melbourne Univ. (BEngSc). Cadet Engr, Dept of Supply, 1940–43; Engrg Rep., London, 1951–52; Manager, Echuca Ball Bearing Factory, 1953–55; Supply Rep., Washington, 1956–57; Manager, Small Arms Factory, Lithgow, 1958–60; Dept of Supply: First Asst Sec. (Management Services and Planning), 1961–62; Controller-Gen. (Munitions Supply), 1962–66; Sec., 1966–71; Chm., Australian Public Service Bd, 1971–77. *Recreations:* golf, fishing. *Address:* 330 Canadian Bay Road, Mt Eliza, Vic 3930, Australia. *Clubs:* Commonwealth (Canberra); Melbourne Cricket (Vic).

COOLS-LARTIGUE, Sir Louis, Kt 1968; OBE 1955; KStJ 1975; Governor of Dominica, 1967–78; *b* 18 Jan. 1905; *s* of Theodore Cools-Lartigue and Emily (*née* Giraud); *m* 1932, Eugene (*née* Royer); two *s* four *d. Educ:* Convents, St Lucia and Dominica; Dominica Grammar Sch. Clerk, Dominica Civil Service, 1924; Chief Clerk to Administrator and Clerk of Councils, 1932; Colonial Treas., Dominica, 1940, St Vincent, 1945; Asst Administrator, St Lucia, 1949; Chief Sec., Windward Is, 1951, retd 1960 on abolition of office; performed duties of Governor's Dep., Windward Is, over fifty times; Speaker of Legislative Council, Dominica, 1961–67; Speaker of House of Assembly, Dominica, March–Oct. 1967. *Recreations:* tennis, swimming. *Address:* 7 Virgin Lane, Roseau, Commonwealth of Dominica, West Indies.

COOMBE, Gerald Hugh; His Honour Judge Gerald Coombe; a Circuit Judge, since 1986; *b* 16 Dec. 1925; *s* of William Stafford Coombe and Mabel Florence Coombe; *m* 1957, Zoë Margaret Richards; one *s* one *d. Educ:* Alleyne's School, Dulwich; Hele's School, Exeter; Exeter College, Oxford. MA 1950. RAF (Navigator), 1944–48; Solicitor, 1953; Partner, Whitehead Monckton & Co., Maidstone, 1956–86; HM Coroner, Maidstone, 1962–86; a Recorder, 1983–86. *Recreation:* gardening. *Club:* Royal Air Force.

COOMBE, Michael Rew; His Honour Judge Coombe; a Circuit Judge, since 1985; *b* 17 June 1930; *s* of late John Rew Coombe and Phyllis Mary Coombe; *m* 1961, Elizabeth Anne Hull; two *s* one *d* (and one *s* decd). *Educ:* Berkhamsted; New Coll., Oxford. MA (Eng. Lang. and Lit.). Called to Bar, Middle Temple, 1957 (Harmsworth Scholar), Bencher 1984. 2nd Prosecuting Counsel to the Inland Revenue at Central Criminal Court and 5 Courts of London Sessions, 1971; 2nd Counsel to the Crown at Inner London Sessions, Sept. 1971; 1st Counsel to the Crown at Inner London Crown Court, 1974; 4th Junior Treasury Counsel at Central Criminal Court, 1974, 2nd Jun. Treasury Counsel, 1975, 1st Jun. Treasury Counsel, 1977; Recorder of the Crown Court, 1976–85; Sen. Prosecuting Counsel to the Crown, CCC, 1978–85. *Recreations:* theatre, antiquity, art and architecture, printing. *Address:* 112 Lupus Street, SW1V 4AJ. *T:* 01–828 8742.

COOMBES, Keva Christopher; Member (Lab) Liverpool City Council, since 1986; *b* 23 Dec. 1949; *s* of Arthur Edward Coombes and Beatrice Claire Coombes; *m* 1970, Kathy Gannon; two *s. Educ:* Chatham House Grammar Sch.; Univ. of East Anglia (BA). Admitted Solicitor, 1977. Member: Liverpool CC, 1976–80; Merseyside CC, 1981–86 (Leader, 1982–86). *Address:* c/o David Phillips Harris & Whalley, 23 Moorfields, Liverpool L2 2BQ.

COOMBS, Derek Michael; *b* 12 Aug. 1937; *m* Patricia O'Toole; one *s* one *d. Educ:* Rydal Prep. Sch.; Bromsgrove. Chm., Hardanger Properties plc, 1976–; Chm. and Man. Dir, S & U Stores plc, 1976–; Dir, Metalrax Holdings plc, 1975–. Political journalist. MP (C) Yardley, 1970–Feb. 1974. Successfully introduced unsupported Private Member's Bill for relaxation of Earnings Rule, 1972, establishing parly record for a measure of its kind; author of Cons. rate scheme for Oct. 1974 Gen. Election; specialist on economic affairs. Lectured on foreign affairs at Cons. weekend confs. Active pro-European. Governor, Royal Hosp. and Home for Incurables. Sponsor: Save the Children Fund; Riding for the Disabled. *Publications:* numerous articles on home, economic and foreign affairs. *Recreations:* friends, tennis, skiing. *Address:* Cheyne Row, SW3. *T:* 01-352 6709; Squalls Farm Estate, Tisbury, Wilts. *T:* Tisbury 870245.

COOMBS, Douglas Stafford, PhD; Controller, Books Division, British Council, 1980–83, retired; *b* 23 Aug. 1924; *s* of Alexander John Coombs and Rosina May (*née* Stafford); *m* 1950, Valerie Nyman; one *s* three *d. Educ:* Royal Liberty Sch., Romford; University College of Southampton; University College London (BA Hons, PhD). Served Royal Air Force, 1943–47. Lecturer in History, University College of the Gold Coast (subseq. Univ. of Ghana), 1952–60; British Council, 1960–: Nigeria, 1960–62; Overseas Student Centre, London, 1962–67; Bombay, 1967–73; Representative: Zambia, 1973–76; Yugoslavia, 1976–79; Visiting Fellow, Postgrad. School of Librarianship and Information Science, Univ. of Sheffield, 1979–80. Chm. Editorial Cttee and Mem. Exec. Cttee, Byways and Bridleways Trust, 1984–; Chm., Wootton Rivers Village Soc., 1985–. *Publications:* The Conduct of the Dutch, 1958; The Gold Coast, Britain and The Netherlands, 1963; articles in historical jls. *Recreations:* travel, slow jogging, watching cricket. *Address:* The Long House, Primrose Hill, Wootton Rivers, Marlborough, Wilts SN8 4NJ. *T:* Marlborough 810201.

COOMBS, Herbert Cole, MA, PhD; FAA; FAHA; FASSA; Visiting Fellow, Centre for Resource and Environmental Studies, Australian National University, since 1976; *b* 24 Feb. 1906; *s* of Francis Robert Henry and Rebecca Mary Coombs; *m* 1931, Mary Alice Ross; three *s* one *d. Educ:* Univ. of Western Australia, Perth, WA (MA); LSE (PhD). School teacher, Education Dept, WA, 1929; Asst Economist, Commonwealth Bank of Australia, 1935; Economist to Commonwealth Treasury, 1939; Mem., Commonwealth Bank Board, 1942; Dir of Rationing, 1942; Dir-Gen. of Post-War Reconstruction, 1943; Governor, Commonwealth Bank of Australia, 1949–60; Chm., Commonwealth Bank Board, 1951–60; Governor and Chm. of Board, Reserve Bank of Australia, 1960–68; Chancellor, ANU, 1968–76. Chairman: Australian Elizabethan Theatre Trust, 1954–68; Australian Council for Arts, 1968–74; Australian Council for Aboriginal Affairs, 1968–76; Royal Commn on Australian Govt Admin, 1974–76. Hon. LLD: Melbourne; ANU; Sydney; Hon. DLitt WA; Hon. DSc NSW; Hon. Fellow LSE, 1961. *Publications:* The Fragile Pattern, 1970; Other People's Money, 1971; Kulinma: Listening to Aboriginal Australians, 1978; Trial Balance—issues in my working life, 1981; (jtly) A Certain Heritage: programs by and for Aborigines, 1983. *Recreations:* golf, squash, theatre-going. *Address:* 119 Milson Road, Cremorne, NSW 2090, Australia.

COOMBS, Ven. Peter Bertram; Archdeacon and Borough Dean of Wandsworth, since 1975; *b* 30 Nov. 1928; *s* of Bertram Robert and Margaret Ann Coombs; *m* 1953, Catherine Ann (*née* Buckwell); one *s* one *d. Educ:* Reading Sch.; Bristol Univ. (MA 1960); Clifton Theological Coll. Curate, Christ Church, Beckenham, 1960–64; Rector, St Nicholas, Nottingham, 1964–68; Vicar, Christ Church, New Malden, 1968–75; Rural Dean of Kingston upon Thames, 1970–75. *Recreations:* walking, sketching. *Address:* 68 Wandsworth Common North Side, SW18 2QX. *T:* 01-874 5766.

COOMBS, Prof. Robert Royston Amos, ScD; FRS 1965; FRCPath 1969; Quick Professor of Biology, Immunology Division, Department of Pathology, University of Cambridge, since 1966; Fellow of Corpus Christi College, since 1962; *b* 9 Jan. 1921; *s* of Charles Royston Amos and Edris Owen Amos (formerly Coombs); *m* 1952, Anne Marion Blomfield; one *s* one *d. Educ:* Diocesan Coll., Cape Town; Edinburgh and Cambridge Univs. BSc, MRCVS Edinburgh 1943; PhD Cambridge 1947; Stringer Fellow, King's Coll., Cambridge, 1947. Asst Director of Research, Dept of Pathology, University of Cambridge, 1948; Reader in Immunology, University of Cambridge, 1963–66. Foreign Corres., Royal Belgium Acad. of Medicine, 1979. Hon. FRCP 1973; Hon. Fellow, Amer. Coll. of Allergists, 1979. Hon. MD Linköping Univ. 1973; Hon. dr med. vet. Copenhagen, 1979; Hon. DSc: Guelph, 1981; Edinburgh, 1984. Landsteiner Award, Amer. Assoc. of Blood Banks, 1961; Gairdner Foundn Award, 1965; Henry Steele Gold Medal, RCVS, 1966; James Calvert Spence Medal, British Paediatric Assoc., 1967. *Publications:* (with Anne M. Coombs and D. G. Ingram) Serology of Conglutination and its relation to disease, 1960; (ed with P. G. H. Gell) Clinical Aspects of Immunology, 1963, 3rd edn (also with P. J. Lachmann), 1975; numerous scientific papers on immunology. *Recreation:* retreat to the country. *Address:* 6 Selwyn Gardens, Cambridge. *T:* Cambridge 352681.

COOMBS, Simon Christopher; MP (C) Swindon, since 1983; *b* 21 Feb. 1947; *s* of late Ian Peter Coombs and of Rachel Robins Coombs; *m* 1983, Kathryn Lee Coe Royce. *Educ:* Reading University (BA, MPhil); Wycliffe College. Marketing Executive, British Telecom and Post Office, Data and Telex, 1970–82; Marketing Manager, Telex Networks, British Telecom, 1982–83. Mem., Southern Electricity Consultative Council, 1981–84. Reading Borough Council: Mem., 1969–84; Chm., Transportation Cttee, 1976–83; Vice-Chm., Policy Cttee, 1976–83; Dep. Leader, 1976–81; Chief Whip, 1983. PPS to Rt Hon. Kenneth Baker, MP, Minister of State for Industry and IT, 1984–85, to Hon. William Waldegrave, MP, Parly Under-Sec. of State DoE, and Rt Hon. Lord Elton, Minister of State for the Environment, 1985–. Member: British-American Parly Gp, 1983–; CPA, 1983–; Secretary: British Malaŵi Parly Gp, 1985–; Parly Food and Health Forum. Chm., Cons. Party, Wessex Area, 1980–83; Chm., Wessex Area Young Conservatives, 1973–76; Pres., Wilts Young Conservatives, 1984–; Vice Pres., N Wilts Disabled Drivers, 1985–. Member University Court: Univ. of Reading; Univ of Bath. *Recreations:* music, cricket, philately, reading, writing. *Address:* House of Commons, SW1A 0AA. *Clubs:* Swindon Constitutional; Hampshire Cricket.

COONEY, Raymond George Alfred, (Ray Cooney); actor, author, director, theatrical producer; created Theatre of Comedy at Shaftesbury Theatre, and Little Theatre of Comedy at Ambassadors Theatre, 1983; *b* 30 May 1932; *s* of Gerard Cooney and Olive (*née* Clarke); *m* 1962, Linda Dixon; two *s. Educ:* Alleyn's Sch., Dulwich. First appeared in Song of Norway, Palace, 1946; toured in Wales, 1954–56; subseq. played in: Dry Rot and Simple Spymen, Whitehall; Mousetrap, Ambassador; Charlie Girl, Adelphi; Not Now Darling, Savoy (also film); Not Now Comrade (film); Run for your Wife, Guildford; Two into One, Leicester and Guildford. Productions (some jointly) include: Thark (revival); Doctor at Sea; The Queen's Highland Servant; My Giddy Aunt; Move Over Mrs Markham; The Mating Game; Lloyd George Knew My Father; That's No Lady-That's My Husband; Say Goodnight to Grandma; Two and Two Make Sex; At the End of the Day; Why Not Stay for Breakfast?; A Ghost on Tiptoe; My Son's Father; The Sacking of Norman Banks; The Bedwinner; The Little Hut; Springtime for Henry; Saint Joan; The Trials of Oscar Wilde; The Dame of Sark; Jack the Ripper; There Goes the Bride (and played leading role, Ambassadors, 1974); Ipi Tombi; What's a Nice Country Like US Doing In a State Like This?; Some of My Best Friends Are Husbands; Banana Ridge; Fire Angel; Elvis; Whose Life is it Anyway? (London and NY); Clouds; Chicago; Bodies; Beatlemania; Not Now Darling (revival); Hello Dolly (revival); Duet for One (London and NY); They're Playing Our Song; Children of a Lesser God; Run for your Wife; Aladdin; See How They Run; Pygmalion; Two Into One; Passion Play; Loot (revival); Intimate Exchanges; Wife Begins at Forty. *Publications:* (with H. and M. Williams) Charlie Girl, 1965; *plays:* (with Tony Hilton) One for the Pot, 1961; Chase Me Comrade, 1964; (with Tony Hilton) Stand by your Bedouin, 1966; (with John Chapman) Not Now Darling, 1967; (with John Chapman) My Giddy Aunt, 1968; (with John Chapman) Move Over Mrs Markham, 1969; (with Gene Stone) Why Not Stay for Breakfast?, 1970; (with John Chapman) There Goes the Bride, 1973; Two into One, 1981, 1983; Run for Your Wife, 1983; Wife Begins at Forty, 1986. *Recreations:* tennis, swimming, golf. *Address:* 219–229 Shaftesbury Avenue, WC2. *Club:* Dramatists'.

COOP, Sir Maurice (Fletcher); Kt 1973; Solicitor; *b* 11 Sept. 1907; *s* of George Harry and Ada Coop; *m* 1948, Elsie Hilda Brazier. *Educ:* Epworth Coll., Rhyl; Emmanuel Coll., Cambridge (BA). Admitted Solicitor of Supreme Court, 1932. Sec., Dunlop Rubber Co. Ltd, 1948–68; Dir, Dunlop Rubber Co. Ltd, 1966–70. Chm., Standing Adv. Cttee to Govt on Patents, 1972–74. *Recreations:* Association football, cricket. *Address:* 39 Hill Street, Berkeley Square, W1X 7FG. *Tel:* 01-491 4549. *Club:* United Oxford & Cambridge University.

COOPER, family name of **Viscount Norwich** and **Baron Cooper of Stockton Heath.**

COOPER; *see* Ashley-Cooper, family name of Earl of Shaftesbury.

COOPER OF STOCKTON HEATH, Baron *cr* 1966, of Stockton Heath (Life Peer); **John Cooper,** MA; General Secretary and Treasurer, National Union of General and Municipal Workers, 1962–73; National Water Council, 1973–77; *b* 7 June 1908; *s* of late John Ainsworth Cooper and of Annie Lily Cooper (*née* Dukes); *m* 1934, Nellie Spencer (marr. diss. 1969); three *d*; *m* 1969, Mrs Joan Rogers. *Educ:* Stockton Heath Council Sch.; Lymm Grammar Sch., Cheshire. Employed Crosfields Soap Works, Warrington, 1924–28; NUGMW, 1928–73. District Sec., Southern Dist, 1944–61; Chm., 1952–61. Member: Manchester CC, 1936–42; LCC, 1949; Alderman, 1952–53; London Labour Party Executive; MP (Lab) Deptford, 1950–51; PPS to Sec. of State for Commonwealth Relations, 1950–51. Member; NEC Labour Party, 1953–57; TUC Gen. Council, 1959–73 (Pres., TUC, 1970–71). Chm., British Productivity Council, 1965–66; Mem., Thames Conservancy, 1955–74. Governor various instns, etc. MA Oxon. Prix de la Couronne Française, 1970. *Address:* 23 Kelvin Grove, Chessington, Surrey. *T:* 01-397 3908.

COOPER, Very Rev. Alan; *see* Cooper, Very Rev. W. H. A.

COOPER, Rev. Albert Samuel; Moderator, Free Church Federal Council, 1973–74; *b* 6 Nov. 1905; *s* of Samuel and Edith Cooper; *m* 1936, Emily (*d* 1983), *d* of Hugh and Emily Williams; one *s* one *d. Educ:* Birkenhead Inst.; London Univ. (external student; BA Hons Philosophy); Westminster Coll., Cambridge (DipTheol); Fitzwilliam House, Cambridge (BA Theol Tripos, MA). Ordained 1936. Pastoral charges: St Columba's Presbyterian Church, Grimsby, 1936–41; Blundellsands Presbyt. Ch., Liverpool, 1941–44; St Columba's Presbyt. Ch., Cambridge, 1944–60; St Columba's Presbyt. (later United Reformed) Ch., Leeds, 1960–72, retd 1972. Free Church Chaplain. Fulbourn Mental Hosp., Cambridgeshire, 1950–60. Moderator, Presbyt. Ch. of England, 1968–69. *Address:* 6 Dacre Hill House, 596 Old Chester Road, Rock Ferry, Birkenhead, Merseyside L42 4NW. *T:* 051-645 0418.

COOPER, Andrew Ramsden, CBE 1965; FEng 1978; Industrial Consultant, since 1966; Member for Operations and Personnel, Central Electricity Generating Board, 1957–66; *b* 1 Oct. 1902; *s* of Mary and William Cooper, Rotherham, Yorks; *m* 1922, Alice Robinson (marr. diss. 1982); one *s* two *d*; *m* 1982, Helen Louise Gordon. *Educ:* Rotherham Grammar Sch.; Sheffield Univ. Colliery Engineer, Yorks and Kent, 1916–28; Chief Electrical Engineer, Pearson & Dorman Long, 1928; Personal Asst to G. A. Mower, London, 1934; joined Central Electricity Board Operation Dept, NW England and N Wales, 1935; transf. to HQ, 1937; Operation Engineeer, SE and E England, 1942; Chief Operation Engineer to Central Electricity Board, 1944; Controller, Merseyside and N Wales Div. (Central Electricity Authority), 1948–52; NW Div., 1952–54; N West, Merseyside and N Wales Div., 1954–57; Mem. Ops and Personnel, CEGB, 1957–66. Inventor, ARCAID Deaf/Blind Conversation Machine; Pres. Electricity Industries Benevolent Assoc., 1964–65; Mem, GB-USSR Cttee, 1967–. Faraday Lectr, 1952–53. CEng, FIEE; SFInstE; FIEEE. Pres., CIGRE, 1966–72. Bernard Price Meml Lectr, S African Inst. of Electr. Engrg, 1970; Meritorious Service Award, Power Engrg Soc. of America, 1972; Willans Medal, IEE, 1952; Thornton Medal, AMEME, 1961; Donor, Power/Life Award, Power Engrg Soc., 1970. Hon. Mem., Batti-Wallahs Assoc. Hon. MEng Liverpool Univ., 1954. *Publications include:* Load Dispatching, with Special Reference to the British Grid System (a paper receiving John Hopkinson Award, 1948, and Willans Medal, 1952, IEE). *Recreations:* golf, art, music, writing, broadcasting. *Address:* 4 Exeter House, Putney Heath, SW15 3SU. *T:* 01-788 5544. *Clubs:* Savile, Energy Industries, 25, Dynamcables; Royal Wimbledon Golf.

COOPER, Beryl Phyllis, QC 1977; a Recorder of the Crown Court, since 1977; *b* 24 Nov. 1927; *o c* of late Charles Augustus Cooper and of Phyllis Lillie (*née* Burrows). *Educ:* Surbiton High Sch. (Head Girl, 1945–46); Univ. of Birmingham (BCom 1950; Hon. Sec., Guild of Undergrads, 1949–50). Called to the Bar, Gray's Inn, 1960. Hosp. Adminstr, Royal Free Hosp., 1951–57. Formerly: Councillor, St Pancras Metrop. Bor. Council; Mem., Homeopathic Hosp. Cttee; Mem., Bd of Visitors, Wandsworth Prison. Conservative Parly Candidate, Stepney, 1966; Founder Mem., Bow Gp (former Sec. and Council Mem.); Mem. Exec. Cttee, Soc. of Cons. Lawyers, 1981–. Chm., Justice Report on Fraud Trials, 1985–86. Member: Cripps Cttee, Women and the Law; Home Office Cttee on Criminal Statistics (Perks Cttee); Housing Corp., 1976–79; Criminal Injuries Compensation Bd, 1978–; Review Body for Nursing Staff, Midwives, Health Visitors, and Professions Allied to Medicine, 1983–; Lambeth, Southwark and Lewisham AHA (Teaching), 1980–82; Council of Justice, 1986–. *Publications:* pamphlets for CPC, etc.; articles on social, legal, criminal and local govt matters. *Recreations:* travel, swimming, golf, gardening. *Address:* 31 Alleyn Park, Dulwich, SE21 8AT. *T:* 01–670 7012; 2 Dr Johnson's Buildings, Temple, EC4Y 7AY. *T:* 01–353 5371; 8d South Cliff Tower, Eastbourne, Sussex. *Clubs:* English-Speaking Union; Caledonian (Edinburgh); Royal Eastbourne Golf, Dulwich and Sydenham Hill Golf.

COOPER, Derek Macdonald; author, broadcaster and journalist; *b* 25 May 1925; *s* of George Stephen Cooper and Jessie Margaret Macdonald; *m* 1953, Janet Marian Feaster; one *s* one *d*. *Educ:* Raynes Park Grammar Sch.; Portree High Sch.; University Coll., Cardiff; Wadham Coll., Oxford (MA Hons). Served RN, 1943–45. Joined Radio Malaya as producer, 1950, retired as Controller of Progs, 1960; Producer, Roving Report, ITN, 1960–61; has worked widely as presenter, interviewer and writer in both television and radio. *Radio* programmes include: Today; Ten O'clock; Newstime; PM; Town and Country; A La Carte; Home This Afternoon; Frankly Speaking; Two of a Kind; You and Yours; Northbeat; New Worlds; Asian Club; Speaking For Myself; Conversations with Cooper; Friday Call; It's Your Line; Offshore Britons; Person to Person; The Food Programme; Meridien book programme; *television* programmes include: World in Action; Tomorrow's World; Breathing Space; A Taste of Britain; The Caterers; World About Us; I Am An Engineer; Men and Materials; Apart from Oil; Money Wise; One in a Hundred; The Living Body; From the Face of the Earth. Columnist: The Listener; Guardian; Observer magazine; World Medicine; Scottish Field; Sunday Standard (House of Fraser Press Award, 1984); Homes & Gardens; Saga magazine; Women's Journal; regular contributor to: In Britain; Taste; A La Carte; The West Highland Free Press. Founder Mem. and first Chm., Guild of Food Writers, 1985–. Glenfiddich Trophy as Wine and Food Writer, 1973, 1980; Broadcaster of the Year, 1984. *Publications:* The Bad Food Guide, 1967; Skye, 1970, 2nd edn 1977; The Beverage Report, 1970; The Gullibility Gap, 1974; Hebridean Connection, 1977; Guide to the Whiskies of Scotland, 1978; Road to the Isles, 1979 (Scottish Arts Council Award, 1980); (with Dione Pattullo) Enjoying Scotch, 1980; Wine With Food, 1982, 2nd edn 1986; (with Fay Godwin) The Whisky Roads of Scotland, 1982; The Century Companion to Whiskies, 1983; Skye Remembered, 1983; The World Of Cooking, 1983; The Road to Mingulay, 1985; The Gunge File, 1986; A Taste of Scotch, 1987. *Address:* 4 St Helena Terrace, Richmond, Surrey TW9 1NR. *T:* 01-940 7051; Seafield House, Portree, Isle of Skye. *T:* Portree 2380.

COOPER, Sir Francis Ashmole, (Sir Frank), 4th Bt *cr* 1905; Chairman, Ashmole Investment Trust Ltd, 1969–74; *b* 9 Aug. 1905; *s* of Sir Richard Ashmole Cooper, 2nd Bt. and Alice Elizabeth (*d* 1963), *d* of Rev. E. Priestland, Spondon; *S* brother, 1970; *m* 1933, Dorothy F. H., *d* of Emile Deen, Berkhamstead, and Maggie Louise Deen; one *s* two *d* (and one *d* decd). *Educ:* Lancing Coll.; King's Coll., Cambridge (MA); University Coll., London (PhD). Joined Cooper, McDougall and Robertson Ltd, 1926; on leave to University College, 1931–36; Technical Director, 1940–62; retired, 1962. *Recreation:* yachting. *Heir: s* Richard Powell Cooper [*b* 13 April 1934; *m* 1957, Angela Marjorie, *e d* of Eric Wilson, Norton-on-Tees; one *s* two *d*]. *Address:* La Bastide de la Maraouro, 06490 Tourrettes sur Loup, France. *Clubs:* Carlton, Royal Thames Yacht, Royal Motor Yacht (Sandbanks, Poole).

COOPER, Rt Hon. Sir Frank, GCB 1979 (KCB 1974; CB 1970); CMG 1961; PC 1983; Chairman, United Scientific Holdings, since 1985; Deputy Chairman, Babcock International, since 1984 (Director, since 1983); Director: Morgan Crucible, since 1983; N. M. Rothschild & Sons, since 1983; Special Adviser, European Commission, since 1985; *b* 2 Dec. 1922; *s* of late V. H. Cooper, Fairfield, Manchester; *m* 1948, Peggie, *d* of F. J. Claxton; two *s* one *d*. *Educ:* Manchester Grammar Sch.; Pembroke Coll., Oxford (Hon. Fellow, 1976). War of 1939–45: Pilot, Royal Air Force, 1941–46. Asst Principal, Air Ministry, 1948; Private Secretary: to Parly Under-Sec. of State for Air, 1949–51; to Permanent Under-Sec. of State for Air, 1951–53; to Chief of Air Staff, 1953–55; Asst Sec., Head of the Air Staff, Secretariat, 1955–60; Dir of Accounts, Air Ministry, 1961–62; Asst Under-Sec. of State, Air Min., 1962–64, Min. of Defence, 1964–68; Dep. Under-Sec. of State, Min. of Defence, 1968–70; Dep. Sec., CSD, 1970–73; Permanent Under-Secretary of State: NI Office, 1973–76; MoD, 1976–82. Hon. Consultant, RUSI, 1982–. Member Council: KCL, 1981–; Imperial Coll., 1983– (Dep. Chm., 1985–); Chm. Delegacy, King's Coll. Med. and Dental Sch., 1983–; Governor: Technical Change Centre, 1982–; Inst. of Manpower Studies; Cranbrook Sch, 1982– (Chm., 1984–). *Recreation:* walking. *Address:* 34 Camden Park Road, Chislehurst, Kent BR7 5HG. *Clubs:* Athenæum, Royal Air Force.

COOPER, Wing Comdr Geoffrey; free-lance writer; *b* 18 Feb. 1907; *s* of Albert Cooper, Leicester, and Evelyn J. Bradham, Hastings. *Educ:* Wyggeston Gram. Sch., Leicester; Royal Grammar School, Worcester. Accountancy, business management. Auxiliary Air Force, 1933; BOAC, 1939. Royal Air Force 1939–45, Pilot (mentioned in despatches). MP (Lab) for Middlesbrough West Div., 1945–51. Farming in Jersey, CI, 1951–61; founder and one of first directors, Jersey Farmers' Co-operative; Chm. Jersey Branch, RAFA. Architecture and land develt, Bahama Is, 1962–77; Pres., Estate Developers Ltd. Writing and social welfare voluntary work in S London, 1977–84; Captain, 56th London Boys' Brigade. *Publications:* Cæsar's Mistress (exposé of BBC and nationalisation); articles in England, Bahamas and USA on civil aviation, business management and government methods. *Recreations:* portrait and landscape painting, swimming. *Address:* PO Box N7117, Nassau, Bahamas; 91 Connor Court, Battersea Park, SW11 5GH. *Club:* Royal Air Force.

COOPER, George A.; Marketing and Business Consultant; Chairman, Independent Television Publications Ltd, since 1971; *b* 9 Oct. 1915; *s* of late Joseph Cooper; *m* 1944, Irene Burns; one *d*. Exec. with internat. publishing gp; served War of 1939–45, Royal Artillery (Captain); Exec., Hulton Press, 1949–55; Director: ABC Television Ltd, 1955–77; Thames Television Ltd, 1968 (Man. Dir, 1974–77); Independent Television News, 1976–77; Chm., Network Programme Cttee of Independent Television, 1975–77. *Recreations:* golf, walking. *Address:* 43 Rivermill, 151 Grosvenor Road, SW1V 3JN. *T:* 01-821 9305. *Clubs:* Royal Automobile, Thirty.

COOPER, George Edward; Chairman, North Thames Gas Region (formerly North Thames Gas Board), 1970–78; Part-time Member, British Gas Corporation, 1973–78; *b* 25 Jan. 1915; *s* of H. E. Cooper and R. A. Jones, Wolverhampton; *m* 1941, Dorothy Anne Robinson; one *s*. *Educ:* Wolverhampton Municipal Grammar Sch. Wolverhampton and Walsall Corp., 1933–40. Served War, 1940–45, with RA in Middle East (Bimbashi Sudan Defence Force), Captain. Qualified as Accountant, Inst. of Municipal Treasurers and Accountants (now Chartered Inst. of Public Accountants), 1947; Hemel Hempstead Development Corp., 1948–50; W Midlands Gas Bd (finally Dep. Chm.), 1950–70. IPFA (FIMTA 1965); CIGasE 1968. Officer OStJ 1976. *Recreations:* photography, geology, golf. *Club:* City Livery.

COOPER, Gen. Sir George (Leslie Conroy), GCB 1984 (KCB 1979); MC 1953; Member, UK Board of Management, and Director of Management Development, The General Electric Company plc, since 1985; *b* 10 Aug. 1925; *s* of late Lt-Col G. C. Cooper and Mrs Y. V. Cooper, Bulmer Tye House, Sudbury; *m* 1957, Cynthia Mary Hume; one *s* one *d*. *Educ:* Downside Sch.; Trinity Coll., Cambridge. Commnd 1945; served with Bengal Sappers and Miners, 1945–48; Korea, 1952–53; psc 1956; jssc 1959; Instructor, RMA Sandhurst, 1959–62 and Staff Coll., Camberley, 1964; GSO1, 1st Div., 1964–66; CRE, 4th Div., 1966–68; MoD, 1968–69; Comdr, 19th Airportable Bde, 1969–71; Royal Coll. of Defence Studies, 1972; Dep. Dir Army Trng, 1973–74; GOC SW District, 1974–75; Dir, Army Staff Duties, 1976–79; GOC SE District, 1979–81; Adjt-Gen., 1981–84, retd. ADC General to the Queen, 1982–84. Colonel Commandant: RE, 1980–; RPC, 1981–85; Col, Queen's Gurkha Engineers, 1981–. Chm., Infantile Hypercalcæmia Foundn, 1980–; Mem. Council, Nat. Fund for Res. into Crippling Diseases, 1982–. *Recreations:* ski-ing, sailing, tennis, shooting, gardening. *Address:* c/o Barclays Bank, 3–5 King Street, Reading, Berks RG1 2HD. *Club:* Army and Navy.

COOPER, Sir Gilbert (Alexander), Kt 1972; CBE 1964; ED 1943; MLC, Bermuda, 1968–72, retired; *b* 31 July 1903; *s* of Alexander Samuel and Laura Ann Cooper. *Educ:* Saltus Grammar Sch., Bermuda; McGill Univ., Canada (BCom). Mem., Corp. of Hamilton, Bermuda, 1946–72; Mayor of Hamilton, 1963–72. Mem., House of Assembly, 1948–68 (Chm. House Finance Cttee, 1959–68). *Recreations:* music, painting, sailing, swimming. *Address:* Shoreland, Pembroke, Bermuda. *T:* 5-4189. *Clubs:* Royal Bermuda Yacht, Royal Hamilton Amateur Dinghy, Bermuda Police.

COOPER, Sir Henry; *see* Cooper, Sir W. H.

COOPER, Henry, OBE 1969; company director since 1972; *b* 3 May 1934; *s* of Henry William Cooper and late Lily Nutkins; *m* 1960, Albina Genepri; two *s*. *Educ:* Athelney Street Sch., Bellingham. Professional boxer, 1954–71. Presenter, Be Your Own Boss (series), Channel 4, 1983. KSG 1978. *Film:* Royal Flash, 1975. *Publications:* Henry Cooper: an autobiography, 1972; The Great Heavyweights, 1978; Henry Cooper's Book of Boxing, 1982. *Recreation:* golf. *Address:* 36 Brampton Grove, NW4.

COOPER, Imogen; concert pianist; *b* 28 Aug. 1949; *d* of late Martin Du Pré Cooper, CBE; *m* 1982, John Alexander Batten. *Educ:* Paris Conservatoire, with Jacques Février and Yvonne Lefébure, 1961–67 (Premier Prix, 1967); privately in Vienna, with Alfred Brendel. Plays regularly with all major British orchestras, inc. annual appearance at Proms, 1975–; first British pianist, and woman, to have appeared in South Bank Piano Series, 1975; British festivals include Bath, Cheltenham, Harrogate, Brighton and Edinburgh. Overseas engagements in Germany, Austria, Holland, France, Scandinavia, Spain, USA and Japan. Recordings include Mozart's Concerto for Two Pianos, with Alfred Brendel and Acad. of St Martin-in-the-Fields, and Mozart's Concerto for Three Pianos. Mozart Meml Prize, 1969. *Recreations:* Romanesque architecture, reading, walking, cooking, clothes. *Address:* c/o Ibbs and Tillett Ltd, 450/452 Edgware Road, W2. *T:* 01-262 2864.

COOPER, Jilly, (Mrs Leo Cooper); Columnist for The Mail on Sunday, since 1982; *b* 21 Feb. 1937; *d* of Brig. W. B. Sallitt, OBE, and Mary Elaine Whincup; *m* 1961, Leo Cooper; one *s* one *d*. *Educ:* Godolphin Sch., Salisbury. Reporter, Middlesex Independent, Brentford, 1957–59; followed by numerous short-lived jobs as account executive, copy writer, publisher's reader, receptionist, puppy fat model, switchboard wrecker, and very temporary typist. Columnist, Sunday Times, 1969–82. *Publications:* How to Stay Married, 1969; How to Survive from Nine to Five, 1970 (new edn as Work and Wedlock, 1978); Jolly Super, 1971; Men and Super Men, 1972; Jolly Super Too, 1973; Women and Super Women, 1974 (new edn as Super Men and Super Women, 1977); Jolly Superlative, 1975; Super Jilly, 1977; Class, 1979; The British in Love, 1980; (with Tom Hartman) Violets and Vinegar, 1980; Supercooper, 1980; Intelligent and Loyal, 1981; Jolly Marsupial, 1982; (with Imperial War Museum) Animals in War, 1983; The Common Years, 1984; Leo and Jilly Cooper on Cricket, 1985; (with Patrick Lichfield) Hot Foot to Zabrieskie Point, the Unipart Calendar Book, 1985; How to Survive Christmas, 1986; Leo and Jilly Cooper on Horse Mania, 1986; *novels:* Emily, 1975; Bella, 1976; Harriet, 1976; Octavia, 1977; Prudence, 1978; Imogen, 1978; Riders, 1985; *short stories:* Love and Other Heartaches, 1981; *for children:* Little Mabel, 1980; Little Mabel's Great Escape, 1981; Little Mabel Wins, 1982; Little Mabel Saves the Day, 1985. *Recreations:* merry-making, wild flowers, music, mongrels. *Address:* The Mail on Sunday, Carmelite House, Carmelite Street, EC4Y 0JA.

COOPER, Joan Davies, CB 1972; Hon. Research Fellow, University of Sussex, since 1979; *b* 12 Aug. 1914; *d* of late Valentine Holland Cooper and of Wynnefred Louisa Cooper; unmarried. *Educ:* Fairfield High Sch., Manchester; University of Manchester (BA). Asst Dir of Educn, Derbyshire CC, 1941; Children's Officer, E Sussex CC, 1948; Chief Inspector, Children's Dept, Home Office, 1965–71; Dir, Social Work Service, DHSS, 1971–76; Nat. Inst. for Social Work, 1976–77. Mem., SSRC, 1973–76. Vice Pres., Nat. Children's Bureau, 1964–; Chairman: Parents for Children, 1979–; NACRO Adv. Council on Juvenile Crime, 1982–; Central Council for Educn and Trng in Social Work, 1984–86; E Sussex Care for the Carers, 1985–. Trustee, Homestart, 1981–. FRAI 1972. *Publications:* Patterns of Family Placement, 1978; Social Groupwork with Elderly Patients, 1981; Creation of the British Personal Social Services, 1962–74, 1983. *Recreation:* walking. *Address:* 2A Gallows Bank, Abinger Place, Lewes, East Sussex BN7 2QA. *T:* Lewes 472604. *Club:* University Women's.

COOPER, Ven. John Leslie; Archdeacon of Aston and Canon Residentiary of St Philip's Cathedral, Birmingham, since 1982; *b* 16 Dec. 1933; *s* of Iris and Leslie Cooper; *m* 1959, Gillian Mary Dodds; two *s* one *d*. *Educ:* Tiffin School, Kingston, Surrey; Chichester Theological Coll. BD 1965, MPhil 1978, London Univ. (External Student). National Service, RA; commissioned, 1952–54. General Electric Co. management trainee, 1954–59; Chichester Theolog. Coll., 1959–62; Asst Curate, All Saints, Kings Heath, Birmingham, 1962–65; Asst Chaplain, HM Prison, Wandsworth, 1965–66; Chaplain: HM Borstal, Portland, Dorset, 1966–68; HM Prison, Bristol, 1968–72; Research Fellow, Queen's Coll., Birmingham, 1972–73; Priest-in-Charge 1973–81, Vicar 1981–82, St Paul's, Balsall Heath, Birmingham. Examining Chaplain to Bishop of Birmingham, 1981–82. *Recreations:* music, reading, squash, walking, travel, carpentry, gardening, photography. *Address:* 51 Moor Green Lane, Moseley, Birmingham B13 8NE. *T:* 021–449 0766.

COOPER, Prof. John Philip, CBE 1983; DSc; FRS 1977; FIBiol; Emeritus Professor of Agricultural Botany, University of Wales, 1984; Visiting Professor, Department of Agriculture and Horticulture, University of Reading, since 1984; *b* Buxton, Derbyshire, 16 Dec. 1923; *o s* of Frank Edward and Nora Goodwin Cooper; *m* 1951, Christine Mary Palmer; one *s* three *d*. *Educ:* Stockport Grammar Sch.; Univ. of Reading (BSc 1945, PhD 1953, DSc 1964); FitzWilliam House, Cambridge (DipAgrSc 1946). Scientific Officer, Welsh Plant Breeding Station, 1946–50; Lectr, Univ. of Reading, 1950–54; Welsh Plant Breeding Station, University College of Wales, Aberystwyth: Plant Geneticist, 1950–59; Head, Dept of Develtl Genetics, 1959–75; Dir, and Prof. of Agricl Botany, 1975–83. Consultant, FAO Headquarters, Rome, 1956; Nuffield Royal Society Bursary, CSIRO, Canberra, 1962; Visiting Professor: Univ. of Kentucky, 1965; Univ. of Khartoum, 1975. Member: UK Seeds Exec., 1979–; Internat. Bd for Plant Genetics Resources, 1981–. *Publications:* (ed, with P. F. Wareing) Potential Crop Production, 1971; (ed) Photosynthesis and Productivity in Different Environments, 1975; various papers on crop physiology and genetics in sc. jls. *Recreations:* walking, field archaeology. *Address:* 31 West End, Minchinhampton, Glos. *T:* Brimscombe 882533. *Club:* Farmers'.

COOPER, Rear-Adm. John Spencer, OBE 1974; Chief Strategic Systems Executive, since 1985; *b* 5 April 1933; *s* of Harold Spencer Cooper and Barbara (*née* Highet); *m* 1966, Jacqueline Street (*née* Taylor); two *d*. *Educ:* St Edward's Sch., Oxford; Clare Coll., Cambridge (MA 1957). Electrical cadet, 1951; Lieut 1957; joined Submarines for Polaris programme, 1966; Comdr 1969, Captain 1976; Director, Trials (Polaris), 1976–78; Cdre 1981; Dir, Weapons (Stragetic Systems), 1981–83; Dir Gen., Strategic Weapon Systems, 1983–85. *Recreation:* wind surfing. *Address:* Ministry of Defence, Whitehall, SW1A 2HB. *T:* 01-218 2526.

COOPER, Joseph, OBE 1982; Pianist and Broadcaster; *b* 7 Oct. 1912; *s* of Wilfrid Needham and Elsie Goodacre Cooper; *m* 1st, 1947, Jean (*d* 1973), *d* of late Sir Louis Greig, KBE, CVO; no *c*; 2nd, 1975, Carol, *d* of Charles and Olive Borg. *Educ:* Clifton Coll. (music schol.); Keble Coll., Oxford (organ schol.). MA (Oxon), ARCM (solo piano). Studied piano under Egon Petri, 1937–39. Served War, in RA, 1939–46. Solo pianist debut, Wigmore Hall, 1947 (postponed, Oct. 1939, owing to War); concerto debut, Philharmonia Orchestra, 1950; BBC debut Promenade Concerts Royal Albert Hall, 1953. Since then has toured in: British Isles, Europe, Africa, India, Canada. Many solo piano records. Chm., BBC TV prog., Face The Music, 1971–84. Hon. Chm., Barclaycard Composer of the Year Competition, 1983. Liveryman, Worshipful Co. of Musicians, 1963–; Mem., Music Panel of Arts Council (and Chm. piano sub-cttee), 1966–71; Trustee, Countess of Munster Musical Trust, 1975–80. Governor, Clifton College. Ambrose Fleming award, Royal Television Soc., 1961; Music Trades Assoc. Record Award, 1976. *Publications:* Hidden Melodies, 1975; More Hidden Melodies, 1976; Still More Hidden Melodies, 1978; Facing the Music (autobiog.), 1979; Arrangement of Vaughan Williams Piano Concerto for 2 pianos (in collab. with composer). *Recreations:* four-footed people, church architecture. *Address:* Octagon Lodge, Ranmore, near Dorking, Surrey RH5 6SX. *T:* East Horsley 2658. *Club:* Garrick.

See also A. C. N. Borg.

COOPER, Prof. Kenneth Ernest; Emeritus Professor of Bacteriology, Bristol University, 1968; *b* 8 July 1903; *s* of E. Cooper; *m* 1930, Jessie Griffiths; no *c*. *Educ:* Tadcaster Grammar Sch.; Leeds Univ. BSc 1925, PhD 1927 Leeds; LRCP MRCS 1936; FIBiol. Leeds University: Research Asst in Chemotherapy, 1928–31; Research Asst in Bacteriology, 1931–36; Lectr in Bacteriology, 1936–38; Bristol University: Lectr in Bacteriology, 1938–46; Reader in Bacteriology, 1946–50; Prof. of Bacteriology, 1951–68; Dep. Dean of the Faculty of Science, 1955–58. Hon. Gen. Sec. of Soc. for Gen. Microbiology, 1954–60, Hon. Treas., 1961–68, Hon. Mem., 1969. *Publications:* numerous papers in medical, chemical and bacteriological journals. *Recreations:* golf, chess. *Address:* Fairfield, 50 Clevedon Road, Tickenham, Clevedon, Avon BS21 6RB. *T:* Nailsea 852375.

COOPER, Kenneth Reginald; Chief Executive, The British Library, since 1984; *b* 28 June 1931; *s* of Reginald and Louisa May Cooper; *m* 1955, Olga Ruth (*née* Harvey); two *s* two *d*. *Educ:* Queen Elizabeth's Grammar Sch., Barnet; New Coll., Oxford (MA). FIPM; FITD (Pres., 1981–83). Various appointments, Min. of Labour, 1954–62; Principal, HM Treasury, 1962–65; Principal Private Secretary to Minister of Labour, 1966–67; Asst Sec. for Industrial Training, Min. of Labour, 1967–70; Chief Executive: Employment Services Agency, 1971–75; Training Services Agency, 1975–79; Dir Gen., Nat. Fedn of Building Trades Employers, 1979–84. *Recreations:* music, Rugby football. *Address:* 2 Sheraton Street, W1V 4BH.

COOPER, Prof. Leon N., PhD ; Thomas J. Watson, Sr, Professor of Science, Brown University, Providence, RI, since 1974; Co-Director, Center for Neural Science; *b* NYC, 28 Feb. 1930; *s* of Irving Cooper and Anna Cooper (*née* Zola); *m* 1969, Kay Anne Allard; two *d*. *Educ:* Columbia Univ. (AB 1951, AM 1953, PhD 1954). Nat. Sci. Foundn post-doctoral Fellow, and Mem., Inst. for Advanced Study, 1954–55; Res. Associate, Univ. of Illinois, 1955–57; Asst Prof., Ohio State Univ., 1957–58; Associate Prof., Brown Univ., 1958–62, Prof., 1962–66, Henry Ledyard Goddard Prof., 1966–74. Consultant, various governmental agencies, industrial and educational organizations. Lectr, Summer Sch., Varenna, Italy, 1955; Visiting Professor: Brandeis Summer Inst., 1959; Bergen Internat. Sch. Physics, Norway, 1961; Scuola Internazionale di Fisica, Erice, Italy, 1965; Ecole Normale Supérieure, Centre Universitaire Internat., Paris, 1966; Cargèse Summer Sch., 1966; Radiation Lab., Univ. of Calif at Berkeley, 1969; Faculty of Scis, Quai St Bernard, Paris, 1970, 1971; Brookhaven Nat. Lab., 1972; Chair of Math. Models of Nervous System, Fondation de France, 1977–83; Mem., Conseil Supérieur de la Recherche, l'Université René Descartes, Paris, 1981–. Alfred P. Sloan Foundn Res. Fellow, 1959–66; John Simon Guggenheim Meml Foundn Fellow, 1965–66. Co-Chm., Bd of Dirs, Nestor Inc. Fellow: Amer. Physical Soc.; Amer. Acad. of Arts and Sciences. Member: Amer. Philosoph. Soc.; National Acad. of Sciences; Sponsor Fedn of Amer. Scientists, Soc. for Neuroscience, Amer. Assoc. for Advancement of Science. (Jtly) Comstock Prize, Nat. Acad. of Scis, 1968; (jtly) Nobel Prize for Physics, 1972; Award of Excellence, Grad. Fac. Alumni, Columbia Univ., 1974; Déscartes Medal, Acad. de Paris, Univ. René Déscartes, 1977. Yrjö Reenpää Medal, Finnish Cultural Foundn, 1982; John Jay Award, Columbia Univ, 1985. Hon. DSc: Columbia, 1973; Sussex, 1973; Illinois, 1974; Brown, 1974; Gustavus Adolphus Coll., 1975; Ohio State Univ., 1976; Univ. Pierre et Marie Curie, Paris, 1977. Public lectures, internat. confs, symposia. *Publications:* Introduction to the Meaning and Structure of Physics, 1968; (contrib.) The Physicist's Conception of Nature, 1973; contrib. The Many Body Problem, 1963; contrib. to numerous jls incl. Physics Rev., Amer. Jl Physics, Biological Cybernetics. *Recreations:* music, theatre, skiing. *Address:* 49 Intervale Road, Providence, RI 02906, USA. *T:* (401)-421–1181; Physics Department, Brown University, Providence, RI 02912, USA. *T:* (401)-863–2172. *Clubs:* University, Faculty (Providence, RI).

COOPER, Louis Jacques B.; *see* Blom-Cooper.

COOPER, Prof. Malcolm McGregor, CBE 1965; Emeritus Professor, University of Newcastle upon Tyne, since 1972; *b* Havelock North, New Zealand, 17 Aug. 1910; *s* of Laurence T. Cooper, farmer, and Sarah Ann Cooper; *m* 1937, Hilary Mathews, Boars Hill, Oxford; three *d*. *Educ:* Napier Boys High Sch., NZ; Massey Agricultural Coll., Palmerston North, NZ; University Coll., Oxford. BAgrSc (NZ), 1933; Rhodes Scholarship, 1933; Oxford, 1934–37; Diploma Rural Econ., 1935; BLitt in Agric. Economics, 1937. Returned to NZ 1937; Mem. of Staff, Dept of Scientific and Industrial Research, till 1940, when appointed Lecturer in Dairy Husbandry at Massey Agric. Coll. Served War of 1939–45, with NZ Mil. Forces, 1941–46; in Italy with 2 NZ Div. in an Infantry battalion, 1943–45; rank of Major on demobilisation; returned to Massey as Head of Dept of Dairy Husbandry, 1946; Prof. of Agriculture, Univ. of London, 1947–54; Prof. of Agriculture and Rural Economy, and Dean, Fac. of Agriculture, Univ. of Newcastle upon Tyne, 1954–72; Pro-Vice-Chancellor, Univ. of Newcastle upon Tyne, 1971–72. Nat. Res. Coordinator, Instituto Nacional Investigaciones Agrarias, Spain, 1972–75. President: British Grassland Soc., 1958–59; British Soc. of Animal Production, 1972–73; formerly Member: Nature Conservancy Council; Agricultural Advisory Council; Advisory Board, Pig Industry Development Authority; Agricultural Research and Advisory Cttee for Government of Sudan; Scientific Advisory Panel of the Minister of Agriculture; Agricultural Cttee of UGC; Chm., Beef Recording Assoc. (UK) Ltd. Hon. Life Mem., British Soc. of Animal Production, 1979. FRSE 1956, Hon. FRASE 1969. Hon. Fellow, Wye Coll., London Univ., 1979. Massey Ferguson Award for services to agriculture, 1970. Hon DSc Massey Univ., NZ, 1972. *Publications:* (in collaboration) Principles of Animal Production (New Zealand), 1945; Beef Production, 1953; Competitive Farming, 1956; Farm Management, 1960; Grass Farming, 1961; Sheep Farming, 1965; (with M. B. Willis) Profitable Beef Production, 1972; technical articles on agricultural topics. *Recreations:* Rugby football (Rugby Blue, 1934, 1935 and 1936; Capt. OURFC 1936, and Sec. 1935; capped for Scotland, 1936); summer sports, reading, farming. *Address:* Holme Cottage, Longhoughton, Alnwick, Northumberland. *Club:* Farmers'.

COOPER, Margaret Jean Drummond, OBE 1980; Chief Education Officer, General Nursing Council for England and Wales, 1974–82; *b* 24 March 1922; *d* of Canon Bernard R. Cooper and A. Jean Cooper (*née* Drackley). *Educ:* School of St Mary and St Anne, Abbots Bromley; Royal College of Nursing. SRN, SCM, RNT. Nursing trng and early posts, Leicester Royal Infirmary, 1941–47; Midwifery trng, General Lying-in Hosp., SW1 and Coventry and Warwicks Hosp.; Nurse Tutor, Middlesex Hosp., 1953–55; Principal Tutor: General Hosp., Northampton, 1956–63; Addenbrooke's Hosp., Cambridge, 1963–68; Principal, Queen Elizabeth Sch. of Nursing, Birmingham, 1968–74. Chm., General Nursing Council for England and Wales, 1971–74 (Mem., 1965 and 1970). *Recreations:* birds, books, buildings. *Address:* 28 Lambert Cross, Saffron Walden, Essex CB10 2DP.

COOPER, Nigel Cookson; General Secretary, British Amateur Athletic Board, since 1982; *b* 7 May 1929; *s* of Richard and Violet Sarah Cooper; *m* 1972, Elizabeth Gillian Smith; two *s* one *d*. *Educ:* Leeds Training Coll., Leeds Univ. (LLB); State Univ. of Iowa, USA (MA). Teacher, primary and secondary schools, 1950–59; Lecturer: Trent Park Training Coll., 1959–61; Loughborough Training Coll., 1961–64; Provincial Supervisor (Schools and Community) for Nova Scotia, Canada, 1964–65; County Organiser of Schools for Norfolk, 1965–68; Asst Education Officer for Oldham, 1970–72; Asst Director of Educn for British Families Educn Service in Europe, 1972–78; Registrar, Kelvin Grove College of Advanced Education, Brisbane, Australia, 1978–82. *Recreations:* playing the trumpet, squash, jogging. *Address:* c/o British Amateur Athletic Board, Francis House, Francis Street, SW1P 1DL. *T:* 01–828 9326.

COOPER, Sir Patrick Graham Astley, 6th Bt *cr* 1821; Director, Crendon Concrete Co. Ltd, Long Crendon, 1973–83; *b* 4 Aug. 1918; *s* of late Col C. G. A. Cooper, DSO, RA and I. M. M. A. Cooper, Abergeldie, Camberley, Surrey; *S* cousin, Sir Henry Lovick Cooper, 5th Bt, 1959; *m* Audrey Ann Jervoise, *d* of late Major D. P. J. Collas, Military Knight of Windsor; one *s* two *d*. *Educ:* Marlborough Coll. Qualified RICS, 1949; Sen. Asst Land Comr, Min. of Agric., Fisheries and Food, 1950–59. Joined Crendon Concrete Co. Ltd, 1959. Served 1939–40, Gunner, RA, 52 AA Bde TA (invalided out). *Recreations:* golf, tennis. *Heir:* *s* Alexander Paston Astley Cooper [*b* 1 Feb. 1943; *m* 1974, Minnie Margaret, *d* of Charles Harrison]. *Address:* Monkton Cottage, Burton Lane, Monks Risborough, Aylesbury, Bucks. *T:* Princes Risborough 4210. *Club:* Farmers'.

COOPER, Philip John; Comptroller-General of Patents, Designs and Trade Marks, Department of Trade and Industry, since 1986; *b* 15 Sept. 1929; *s* of Charles Cooper and Mildred Annie Marlow; *m* 1953, Dorothy Joan Chapman (*d* 1982); two *d*. *Educ:* Deacon's Sch., Peterborough; University Coll., Leicester. BSc (Chem. 1st Cl. Hons). CChem, FRSC. Joined Dept (later Laboratory) of Govt Chemist, 1952; Nat. Service, 2nd Lt, R Signals, 1953–55; Dept of Scientific and Ind. Res., 1956–67; Principal, Min. of Technology, 1967; Prin. Private Sec. to Minister for Industrial Develt, 1972–73; Asst Sec., 1973–79, Under Sec., 1979–, DoI and DTI; Dir, Warren Spring Lab., DTI, 1984–85. *Publications:* various papers on analytical and chemical matters. *Address:* 8 Edenfield Gardens, Worcester Park, Surrey. *T:* 01–337 1035.

COOPER, Robert George; Chairman, Northern Ireland Fair Employment Agency, since 1976; Member, Northern Ireland Standing Advisory Commission on Human Rights, since 1976; *b* 24 June 1936; *er s* of William Hugh Cooper and Annie (*née* Pollock); *m* 1974, Patricia, *yr d* of Gerald and Sheila Nichol, Belfast; one *s* one *d*. *Educ:* Foyle Coll., Londonderry; Queen's Univ., Belfast (LLB). Industrial Relations, International Computers Ltd, Belfast, 1958–63; Asst Sec., Engineering Employers' Fedn, NI, 1963–67, Sec. 1967–72; Gen. Sec., Alliance Party of Northern Ireland, 1972–73. Member (Alliance): West Belfast, NI Assembly, 1973–75; West Belfast, NI Constitutional Convention, 1975–76; Minister, Manpower Services, NI, 1974. *Address:* Lynwood, 104 Bangor Road, Holywood, Co. Down, N Ireland. *T:* Holywood 2071.

COOPER, Ronald Cecil Macleod, CB 1981; Deputy Secretary, Department of Transport; *b* 8 May 1931; *s* of Cecil Redvers Cooper and Norah Agnes Louise Cooper (*née* Macleod); *m* 1st, 1953, June Bicknell (marr. diss. 1967); 2nd, 1967, Christine Savage; one *s* two *d*. *Educ:* Royal Grammar Sch., Newcastle upon Tyne; St Edmund Hall, Oxford (MA). Asst Principal, Min. of Supply, 1954–59; Principal, Min. of Aviation, 1959–62; on loan to European Launcher Develt Org., Paris, 1962–67; Asst Sec., Min. of Technology, 1968–70, DTI, 1970–73; Under Sec., Dept of Trade, 1973–78; Sec., Price Commn, 1979; Dep. Sec. and Principal Estabt and Finance Officer, DTI, 1979–85. *Recreations:* music, reading. *Address:* Department of Transport, 2 Marsham Street, SW1P 3EB. *Club:* United Oxford & Cambridge University.

COOPER, Sidney G.; *see* Grattan-Cooper.

COOPER, Sidney Pool; Head of Public Services, British Museum, 1973–76; *b* 29 March 1919; *s* of late Sidney Charles Henry Cooper and Emily Lilian Baptie; *m* 1940, Denise Marjorie Peverett; two *s* one *d*. *Educ:* Finchley County Sch.; Northern Polytechnic (BSc); University Coll. London (MSc). Laboratory of the Government Chemist, 1947; Asst Keeper, National Reference Library of Science and Invention, British Museum, 1963; Dep. Keeper, NRLSI, 1969. *Recreations:* gardening, golf. *Address:* 98 Kings Road, Berkhamsted, Herts. *T:* Berkhamsted 4145.

COOPER, Maj.-Gen. Simon Christie; Director, Royal Armoured Corps, since 1984; *b* 5 Feb. 1936; *s* of Maj.-Gen. Kenneth Christie Cooper, CB, DSO, OBE and Barbara Harding-Newman; *m* 1967, Juliet Elizabeth Palmer; one *s* one *d*. *Educ:* Winchester College; rcds, psc. Commissioned Life Guards, 1956; served Aden, London, BAOR, 1957–63; Captain Adjt, Household Cavalry Regt, 1963–65; ADC to CDS Earl Mountbatten of Burma, 1965–66; Borneo, Malaya, 1966–67; Staff Coll., 1968; BAOR, 1969–75; CO Life Guards, 1974–76; GSO1, Staff Coll., 1976–78; OC Household Cavalry and Silver Stick in Waiting, 1978–81; Commander, RAC Centre, 1981–82; RCDS, 1983. *Recreations:* cricket, skiing, sailing, shooting. *Address:* c/o Royal Bank of Scotland, Lawrie House, Farnborough, Hants. *Club:* MCC.

COOPER, Susie, (Mrs Susan Vera Barker), OBE 1979; RDI 1940; FRSA; Senior Designer for Josiah Wedgwood & Sons Ltd, since 1966; *b* 29 Oct. 1902; *d* of John Cooper and Mary-Ann (*née* Adams); *m* 1938, Cecil Barker (*d* 1972); one *s*. *Educ:* Mollart House, Hanley; Burslem School of Art. Resident designer, Gray's Pottery, 1924; founded Susie Cooper Pottery, 1929; designed and produced tableware for Royal Pavilion, Festival of Britain, on South Bank, 1951. *Recreation:* gardening. *Address:* The Orchard Cottage, Dilhorne, Stoke-on-Trent, Staffs. *T:* Blythe Bridge 392221.

COOPER, Hon. Warren Ernest; MP Otago, since 1975; National Party spokesman on overseas trade, since 1986; *b* Dunedin, 21 Feb. 1933; *s* of William Cooper; *m* 1959, Lorraine Margaret, *d* of Angus T. Rees; three *s* two *d*. *Educ*: Musselburgh Sch.; King's High Sch., Dunedin. Formerly Postmaster-Gen., Minister of Tourism, Minister of Broadcasting, Minister of Regional Develt, Associate Minister of Finance; Minister of Foreign Affairs and Overseas Trade, 1981–84; Nat. Party spokesman on econ./resource allocation, 1985–86. Member: Dominion Council, National Party, 1973–; Commerce and Energy Select Cttee, 1985–86; Internal Affairs and Local Govt Select Cttee, 1986–; Chm., Local Govt, Justice and Security Core Cttee, 1986–; Member, Core Cttees: Nat. Develt, Regional Develt, Resource Allocation, Industrial Develt, S Island Develt, Privatisation, Economics, 1985–86; Econ., Industry and Develt, 1986–. Mem. Exec., S Island Publicity Assoc., 1971. Mayor of Queenstown, 1968–71. JP Queenstown. *Address*: Parliament House, Wellington, New Zealand; 12 Cluny Avenue, Kelburn, Wellington, New Zealand.

COOPER, Dame Whina, DBE 1981 (CBE 1974; MBE 1953); JP; New Zealand President, Maori Land Rights, since 1975; *b* 9 Dec. 1895; *d* of Heremia Te Wake, JP (a Chief of Ngati-Manawa hapu of Te Rarawa tribe) and Kare Pouro; *m* 1st, 1916, Richard Gilbert (decd); one *d* (one *s* decd); 2nd, 1935, William Cooper (decd); two *s* two *d*. *Educ*: St Joseph's Coll., Greenmeadows, Napier, NZ. Proficiency Cert.; qualified as school teacher. Teacher, Pawarenga Sch., Northland, 1917; postmistress and storekeeper, Panguru, 1940 (Pres., Panguru Federated Farmers, 1940). Active in Maori land develt schemes, 1930; President: (first), Maori Women's Welfare League, 1952; Te Unga Waka Marae Soc., 1960; Maori Progressive Cultural Org., 1966; Pres. and Maori Land Rights Leader who led the Great Maori Land March to Parliament, 1975. Had the honour of being the first woman to cross the threshold of Waitangi House, 1949. Pres., Hokianga Rugby Union, 1947; Mem., Whangarei Gun Club, 1930–38. JP Auckland, 1952. *Publication*: Notable New Zealanders, 1979. *Recreations*: hockey, netball, table tennis. *Address*: 4 McCulloch Road, Panmure, Auckland, New Zealand. *T*: Auckland 578–534.

COOPER, William, (Harry Summerfield Hoff), FRSL; novelist; Adjunct Professor of English Literature, Syracuse University, London Centre, since 1977; *b* 1910; *m* 1951, Joyce Barbara Harris; two *d*. *Educ*: Christ's Coll., Cambridge. Assistant Commissioner, Civil Service Commission, 1945–58; Personnel Consultant to: UKAEA, 1958–72; CEGB, 1958–72; Commn of European Communities, 1972–73; Asst Dir, Civil Service Selection Bd, 1973–75; Mem. Bd of Crown Agents, 1975–77; Personnel Advr, Millbank Technical Services, 1975–77. *Publications*: (as H. S. Hoff) Trina, 1934; Rhéa, 1935; Lisa, 1937; Three Marriages, 1946; (as William Cooper) Scenes from Provincial Life, 1950; The Struggles of Albert Woods, 1952; The Ever-Interesting Topic, 1953; Disquiet and Peace, 1956; Young People, 1958; C. P. Snow (British Council Bibliographical Series, Writers and Their Work, No 115) 1959; Prince Genji (a play), 1960; Scenes from Married Life, 1961; Memoirs of a New Man, 1966; You Want The Right Frame of Reference, 1971; Shall We Ever Know?, 1971; Love on the Coast, 1973; You're Not Alone, 1976; Scenes from Metropolitan Life, 1982; Scenes from Later Life, 1983. *Address*: 22 Kenilworth Court, Lower Richmond Road, SW15. *Club*: Savile.

COOPER, Sir William (Daniel Charles), 6th Bt *cr* 1863, of Woollahra; *b* 5 March 1955; *s* of Sir Charles Eric Daniel Cooper, 5th Bt, and of Mary Elisabeth, *e d* of Captain J. Graham Clarke; *S* father, 1984. *Educ*: Northease Manor, Lewes, Sussex. *Heir*: *b* George John Cooper, *b* 28 June 1956. *Address*: Baronet Shooting School Ltd, 8 Yew Tree Close, Oakley, near Basingstoke, Hants RG23 7HQ.

COOPER, Maj.-Gen. William Frank, CBE 1971; MC 1945; consultant; Director, Gin Rectifiers and Distillers Association and Vodka Trade Association, since 1976; *b* 30 May 1921; *s* of Allan Cooper, Officer of Indian State Railways, and Margaret Cooper; *m* 1945, Elisabeth Mary Finch; one *s* one *d*. *Educ*: Sherborne Sch.; RMA Woolwich. Commnd in RE, 1940; served N Africa and Italy (MC; despatches 1944); Malaya, 1956–58 (despatches); S Arabia, 1963–65 (OBE); Chief Engr FARELF, 1968–70; Dep. Dir Army Staff Duties, MoD, 1970–72; Dir, Mil. Assistance Office, 1972–73; DQMG, 1973–76, retd. Col Comdt, RE, 1978–83. *Recreations*: fishing, birdwatching, theatre, gardening. *Address*: c/o Lloyds Bank, High Street, Guildford, Surrey. *Club*: Army and Navy.

COOPER, Sir (William) Henry, Kt 1985; CBE 1965; ED 1956; Chancellor, University of Auckland, 1968–74, retired; *b* 2 Oct. 1909; *s* of Walter and Ruth Cooper; *m* 1936, Elizabeth McLaren (*d* 1984); one *d* (and one *s* decd). *Educ*: Auckland Grammar Sch.; Univ. of Auckland (MA); Assistant Master: Dilworth Sch., 1933–34; Auckland Grammar Sch., 1935–54; Headmaster, Auckland Grammar Sch., 1954–72; Pro Chancellor, Univ. of Auckland, 1961–67; Mem. Council, Univ. of Auckland, 1955–82. Hon. LLD Auckland, 1974. *Recreations*: golf, music, gardening. *Address*: 22 Ridings Road, Remuera, Auckland 5, New Zealand. *T*: 500.858. *Clubs*: Northern, Grammar (Auckland).

COOPER, Very Rev. (William Hugh) Alan; Priest-in-charge of Chrishall, since 1981; *b* 2 June 1909; *s* of William and Ethel Cooper; *m* 1st, 1940, Barbara (*née* Bentall); one *s* two *d*; 2nd, 1980, Muriel Barnes. *Educ*: King's Coll. Sch., Wimbledon; Christ's Coll., Cambridge (MA); St John's Hall, London. ALCD. Curate of Lee, 1932–36; Holy Trinity, Cambridge, 1936–38; CMS Missionary and Diocesan Missioner of Dio. Lagos, 1938–41; Curate of Farnham, 1941–42; Rector of Ashtead, 1942–51; Vicar of St Andrew, Plymouth, 1951–62; Preb. of Exeter Cathedral, 1958–62; Provost of Bradford, 1962–77; Hon. Assistant to Bishop of Karachi, 1977–80. Hon. MA Bradford, 1978. *Address*: The Vicarage, 5 Engleric, Crawley End, Chrishall, near Royston, Herts; 1 Barton Wood Road, New Milton, Hants BH25 7NN.

COOPER, Prof. Sir William M.; see Mansfield Cooper.

COORAY, (Bulathsinhalage) Anura (Siri); a Metropolitan Stipendiary Magistrate, since 1982; *b* 20 Jan. 1936; *s* of (Bulathsinhalage) Vincent Cooray, accountant, and Dolly Perera Manchanayake, Etul Kotte, Sri Lanka; *m* 1957, Manel Therese, *d* of late George Perera, planter, and late Myrtle Perera, Kandy, Sri Lanka; two *s* three *d*. *Educ*: Christian Coll., Kotte, Sri Lanka; London Univ. Called to the Bar, Lincoln's Inn, 1968. Served RAF, Cranwell and Locking, 1952–55 (RAF Boxing Assoc. Sigrist Trophy, 1953–54); served Royal Ceylon Air Force, 1955–60. Practised in Common Law Chambers at Middle Temple; later, Dep. Head of Chambers at No 1 Gray's Inn Sq.; Mem., South Eastern Circuit; Prosecuting Counsel for DPP and Met. Police Solicitors, 1969–82. *Recreations*: wine making (not too good at it!), gardening. *Address*: 41 Perryn Road, W3 7LS. *T*: 01–743 6458; Kingsland, Etul Kotte, Kotte, Sri Lanka.

COORAY, His Eminence Thomas Benjamin, Cardinal, OMI; BA, PhD, DD; Archbishop of Colombo (RC), 1947–76, now Archbishop Emeritus; *b* 28 Dec. 1901. *Educ*: St Joseph's Coll., Colombo; University Coll., Colombo; St Bernard's Seminary, Colombo; The Angelicum, Rome. Prof. of Botany and Latin, St Joseph's Coll., Colombo, 1931; Superior of Oblate Seminary, Colombo, and Prof. of Moral Theology, Pastoral Theology and Canon Law, St Bernard's Seminary, Colombo, 1937; Pres., Sri Lanka Bishops' Conference, 1947–76; created Cardinal, 1965; Member, Pontifical Commn for Revision of Canon Law, 1968–82. Founder Mem., Fedn of Asian Bishops' Confs (FABC),

1970–. *Publications*: booklets on religious matters. *Address*: Cardinal's Residence, Tewatta, Ragama, Sri Lanka. *T*: 538.208.

COOTE, Sir Christopher (John), 15th Bt *cr* 1621; Senior Baronetcy of Ireland in use; *b* 22 Sept. 1928; *s* of Rear-Adm. Sir John Ralph Coote, 14th Bt, CB, CBE, DSC, and of Noreen Una, *o d* of late Wilfred Tighe; *S* father, 1978; *m* 1952, Anne Georgiana, *d* of Lt-Col Donald Handford; one *s* one *d*. *Educ*: Winchester; Christ Church, Oxford (MA 1957). Coffee and tea merchant. *Heir*: *s* Nicholas Patrick Coote [*b* 28 July 1953; *m* 1980, Mona, *d* of late Moushegh Bedelian; one *d*]. *Address*: Russets, Blackpond Lane, Farnham Royal, Bucks; Knockanattin, Ardnaboha, Belgooly, Co. Cork.

COOTE, John Oldham; Captain, RN; Consultant, Boeing Marine Systems, since 1980; *b* 13 Aug. 1921; *o s* of F. Stanley Coote, OBE, KStJ and Edith F. Coote; *m* 1944, Sylvia Mary (*née* Syson); three *d*. *Educ*: China Inland Mission Sch., Chefoo; Felsted. Royal Navy, as submarine specialist, 1940–60 (despatches 1944). Joined Beaverbrook Newspapers, 1960 (Vice-Chm. and Man. Dir, 1968–74; Dep. Chm. and Gp Man. Dir, 1974–75). Mem., Newspaper Publishers Assoc., 1968–75; Chm., Newsvendors Benevolent Inst. Festival Appeal, 1974. Dir Gen., British Film Prodn Assoc., 1976–77. Council, King George's Fund for Sailors, 1968– (Chm. Appeal Cttee, 1983–); Trustee: Submarine Meml Museum, 1968–; Devas Boys' Club, 1967–85. *Publications*: Shell Pilot to the English Channel: (ed) Part 1 (South Coast), 1982; (author) Part 2 (N France and Channel Islands), 1985; contrib. defence and yachting pubns. *Recreations*: performing arts, offshore sailing, Real tennis. *Address*: Titty Hill, Iping, Midhurst, W. Sussex GU29 0PL. *Clubs*: Garrick, Royal Ocean Racing; Royal Yacht Squadron; Cruising of America, New York Yacht.

COOTE, Rt. Rev. Roderic Norman; see Colchester, Area Bishop of.

COPAS, Most Rev. Virgil; see Kerema, Archbishop of, (RC).

COPE, David Robert, MA; Master of Marlborough College, since April 1986; *b* 24 Oct. 1944; *yr s* of Dr C. L. Cope; *m* 1966, Gillian Margaret Peck; one *s* two *d*. *Educ*: Winchester Coll. (Scholar); Clare Coll., Cambridge (Scholar). 1st Cl. Hons Hist. Tripos Part II, 1965; BA 1965; MA 1972. Asst Master, Eton Coll., 1965–67; Asst British Council Rep. (Cultural Attaché), Mexico City, 1968–70; Asst Master, Bryanston Sch., 1970–73; Headmaster: Dover College, 1973–81; British Sch. of Paris, 1981–86. FRSA. *Recreations*: music, tennis, travel. *Address*: The Master's Lodge, Marlborough College, Wilts. *T*: Marlborough 52140. *Club*: Athenæum.

COPE, Prof. F(rederick) Wolverson, DSc, CEng, FIMinE, FGS; Consultant Geologist; Professor of Geology and Head of Geology Department, University of Keele, 1950–76, now Professor Emeritus; *b* 30 July 1909; *e s* of late Fred and Ida Mary Cope (*née* Chappells), Macclesfield; *m* 1st, 1935, Ethel May Hitchens, BSc (*d* 1961); one *s* two *d*; 2nd, 1962, Evelyn Mary Swales, BA, AKC, *d* of late John Frederick and Ada Mary Swales, Kingston-upon-Hull; one *d*. *Educ*: The King's Sch., Macclesfield; Univs of Manchester (DSc 1946) and London. Brocklehurst Scholar, 1928; John Dalton Prize, 1930; BSc with First Class Honours in Geology, 1931; MSc, Mark Stirrup Res. Scholar, Manchester, 1932. Demonstrator in Geology, Bedford Coll., Univ. of London, 1933–34; Daniel Pidgeon Fund, Geol. Soc. of London, 1937; Prin. Geologist in Geological Survey of GB, 1934–50; Murchison Award of Geol. Soc. of London, 1948; Vis. Prof. of Geology, Univ. of Pisa, 1964. Sometime Examr, Univs of Bristol, Exeter, London, Manchester, Nottingham, Sheffield and Wales. FGS 1934 (Senior Fellow 1984); FIMinE 1968; CEng 1969. Chm., Essex Gp of Geologists' Assoc., 1980–; Hon. Mem., Geologists' Assoc., 1982. *Publications*: The North Staffordshire Coalfields, in Coalfields of Great Britain (ed by late Sir Arthur Trueman), 1954; Geology Explained in the Peak District, 1976; various research publications mainly in the fields of stratigraphy and palaeontology. *Recreations*: hill walking, landscape sketching, cars, ornithology, Italy, reading and speaking Italian. *Address*: 6 Boley Drive, Clacton-on-Sea, Essex CO15 6LA. *T*: Clacton-on-Sea 421829.

COPE, Hon. James Francis, CMG 1978; Speaker of the Australian House of Representatives, 1973–75; *b* 26 Nov. 1907; *s* of G. E. Cope; *m* 1931, Myrtle Irene, *d* of S. J. Hurst; one *d*. *Educ*: Crown Street Public Sch., NSW. Hon. Treaurer, NSW Br., Aust. Glass Workers' Union; Delegate to Federal Council, 1953–55. MHR (Lab) for divs of: Cook, 1955; Watson, 1955–69; Sydney, 1969–75. *Recreations*: billiards, horse racing, cricket, football. *Address*: 1/38–40 Fontainebleau Street, Sans Souci, NSW 2219, Australia.

COPE, John Ambrose; MP (C) Northavon, since 1983 (South Gloucestershire, Feb. 1974–1983); Treasurer of HM Household and Deputy Chief Whip, since 1983; *b* 13 May 1937; *s* of George Cope, MC, FRIBA, Leicester; *m* 1969, Djemila Lovell Payne, *d* of Col P. V. L. Payne, Martinstown, Dorset and Mrs Tanetta Blackden; two *d*. *Educ*: Oakham Sch., Rutland. Chartered Accountant; Company Director. Commnd RA and RE, Nat Service and TA. Conservative Research Dept, 1965–67; Personal Asst to Chm. of Conservative Party, 1967–70; contested (C) Woolwich East, 1970; Special Asst to Sec. of State for Trade and Industry, 1972–74; a Govt Whip, 1979–, and Lord Comr of HM Treasury, 1981–83. Formerly Secretary: Cons. Parly Finance Cttee; Parly Gp for Concorde; Vice Chm., Cons. Parly Smaller Business Cttee, 1977–1979 (Sec., 1975–77). Hon. Vice-Pres., National Chamber of Trade. Patron, Avon Riding for the Disabled. *Publication*: (with Bernard Weatherill) Acorns to Oaks (Policy for Small Business), 1967. *Recreation*: woodwork. *Address*: House of Commons, SW1; Bluegates, Berkeley, Glos. *Clubs*: Carlton, St Stephen's Constitutional; Tudor House (Chipping Sodbury), Chipping Sodbury Yacht.

COPE, John Wigley, MA, MB, BChir Cantab, FRCS; retired; formerly Surgeon in charge Ear, Nose and Throat Department, St Bartholomew's Hospital; *b* 1 Nov. 1907; *o s* of J. J. Cope, Widney Manor, Warwicks; *m* 1937, Muriel Pearce Brown, Reading; two *s* one *d*. *Educ*: King Edward's Sch., Birmingham; Trinity Coll., Cambridge; St Bartholomew's Hosp., London. Demonstrator in Anatomy, St Bartholomew's Med. Coll., 1935. Served with RAFVR (Med. Branch) as Aural Specialist, 1940–45 (Sqdn-Ldr). Aural Surgeon, Royal Waterloo Hosp., 1946; Surgeon, Royal National Throat, Nose and Ear Hosp., 1946. Dean, St Bartholomew's Hosp. Med. Coll., 1962–68. Royal Society of Medicine: Pres., Section of Otology, 1970–71 (formerly Sec.); Hon. Mem., Section of Laryngology, 1983. *Recreations*: shooting, rock-climbing, gardening, golf. *Address*: Owls Hatch Cottage, Seale, near Farnham, Surrey. *T*: Runfold 2456.

COPE, Maclachlan Alan Carl S.; see Silverwood-Cope.

COPELAND, Mrs Roy; see Bracewell, J. W.

COPEMAN, Harold Arthur; Under-Secretary, HM Treasury, 1972–76; *b* 27 Jan. 1918; *s* of H. W. M. and G. E. Copeman; *m* 1948, Kathleen (Kay) Gadd; one *s*. *Educ*: Manchester Grammar Sch.; The Queen's Coll., Oxford. BA, 1st Cl. Hons in PPE, 1939. Served War, Army: Cheshire Regt, RA (Instructor in gunnery) and Ordnance Board (Applied Ballistics Dept), 1940–45. HM Treasury, 1946–76. Consultant, Fiscal Affairs Dept, IMF, 1982. Vis. Fellow, Warwick Univ., 1976–84. *Publications*: (jtly) Health Care: priorities and management, 1980; The National Accounts: a short guide, 1981. *Recreations*: music, gardening, photography. *Address*: 22 Tawney Street, Oxford. *T*: Oxford 243830.

COPISAROW, Alcon Charles, DSc; FInstP; CEng; FIEE; Chairman, Youth Business Initiative, since 1982; External Member, Council of Lloyd's, since 1982; a Chairman, General Commissioners for Income Tax, since 1975; *b* 25 June 1920; *o s* of late Dr Maurice Copisarow, Manchester; *m* 1953, Diana, *y d* of Ellis James Castello, MC, Bucklebury, Berks; two *s* two *d*. *Educ:* Manchester Central Grammar Sch.; University of Manchester; Imperial Coll. of Science and Technology; Sorbonne, Paris. Council of Europe Research Fellow. Served War, 1942–47; Lieut RN, 1943–47; British Admiralty Delegn, Washington, 1945. Home Civil Service, 1946–66; Office of Minister of Defence, 1947–54. Scientific Counsellor, British Embassy, Paris, 1954–60. Dir, Forest Products Research Laboratory, Dept of Scientific and Industrial Research, 1960–62; Chief Technical Officer, Nat. Economic Development Council, 1962–64; Chief Scientific Officer, Min. of Technology, 1964–66. Dir and Vice-Pres., McKinsey & Co. Inc., 1966–76; non-exec. Dir, British Leyland, 1976–77; Mem., BNOC, 1980–83; Dir, Touche Remnant Holdings, 1985–. Chairman: Commonwealth Forest Products Conf., Nairobi, 1962; CENTO Conf. on Investment in Science, Teheran, 1963; Member: Scientific Manpower Cttee, Advisory Council on Scientific Policy, 1963–64; Econ. Develt Cttees for Electronics Industry and for Heavy Electrical Industry; Trop. Prod. Adv. Cttee, 1965–66; Press Council, 1975–81. Dep. Chm., Bd of Governors, English-Speaking Union, 1976–83; Dir, Windsor Fest., 1983–; Trustee, Duke of Edinburgh's Award, 1978–84; Mem. Council, Royal Jubilee Trusts, 1981–; Governor, Benenden Sch., 1976–. Freeman, City of London, 1981. Hon. FTCL. *Address:* The White House, Denham Village UB9 5BE. *Clubs:* Athenæum, Beefsteak, MCC.

COPLAND, Aaron; American composer; *b* Brooklyn, NY, 14 Nov. 1900; *s* of Harris M. Copland and Sarah Mittenthal; unmarried. *Educ:* Boys' High Sch., Brooklyn, NY; studied music privately; Fontainebleau Sch. of Music, France; Paris (with Nadia Boulanger). Guggenheim Fellow, 1925, 1926. Lecturer on music, New School for Social Research, NY, 1927–37; organised Copland-Sessions Concerts, which presented American music, 1928–31; tour of Latin-American countries, as pianist, conductor and lecturer in concerts of American music, 1941 and 1947; Charles Eliot Norton Prof. of Poetry, Harvard Univ., 1951–52. *Principal works:* Symphony for Organ and Orchestra, 1924; First Symphony (orch.), 1928; Short Symphony (No. 2), 1933; El Salon Mexico (orch.), 1936; Billy the Kid (ballet), 1938; Piano Sonata, 1941: Lincoln Portrait (speaker and orch.), 1942; Rodeo (ballet), 1942; Sonata for Violin and piano, 1943; Appalachian Spring (ballet, Pulitzer Prize), 1944; Third Symphony, 1946; Clarinet Concerto, 1948; Piano Quartet, 1950; Twelve Poems of Emily Dickinson, 1950; The Tender Land (Opera), 1954; Symphonic Ode (1929, rev. 1955); Piano Fantasy, 1957; Orchestral Variations, 1958; Nonet, 1960; Connotations for Orchestra, 1962; Dance Panels, 1962; Music for a Great City, 1964; Emblems for Symphonic Band, 1964; Inscape for Orchestra, 1967; Duo for flute and piano, 1971; Three Latin-American Sketches, 1972; various film scores. Pres., American Acad. Arts and Letters, 1971; Member: National Institute of Arts and Letters; American Academy of Arts and Sciences; President of the Edward MacDowell Assoc., 1962; American Soc. of Composers, Authors and Publishers; Hon. Mem., Accademia Santa Cecilia, Rome; Hon. Mem., RAM, 1959; Hon. Dr of Music, Princeton Univ., 1956, Harvard Univ., 1961; Hon. Dr of Humane Letters, Brandeis Univ., 1957. FRSA 1960. Presidential Medal of Freedom, Washington, 1964; Howland Prize, Yale Univ., 1970; Haendel Medallion, NY, 1970; Chancellor's Medal, Syracuse Univ., 1975; Creative Arts Award, Brandeis Univ., 1975; *Publications:* What to listen for in music, 1939 (revised 1957); Our New Music, 1941; Music and Imagination, 1952; Copland on Music, 1960; The New Music 1900–1960, 1968. *Address:* c/o Boosey and Hawkes, 24 West 57 Street, New York, USA. *Clubs:* Harvard, Century Association (New York).

COPLAND, Rev. Canon Charles McAlester; *b* 5 April 1910; *s* of Canon Alexander Copland and of Violet Williamina Somerville McAlester; *m* 1946, Gwendoline Lorimer Williamson; two *d*. *Educ:* Forfar Academy; Denstone Coll.; Corpus Christi Coll., Cambridge (MA); Cuddesdon College. Reserve of Officers, 1933–38. Curate, Peterborough Parish Church, 1934–38; Mission Priest, Chanda, CP, India, 1938–53 (Head of Mission, 1942–53); Canon of Nagpur, 1952; Rector, St Mary's, Arbroath, 1953–59; Canon of Dundee, 1953; Provost of St John's Cathedral, Oban, 1959–79, also Dean of Diocese of Argyll and The Isles, 1977–79; Hon. Canon of Oban, 1979. *Recreations:* formerly Rugby football, athletics; rifle shooting (shot for Cambridge, for Scotland 1932–84). *Address:* Fir Cottage, South Crieff Road, Comrie, Perthshire. *T:* Comrie 70185.

COPLESTON, Ernest Reginald, CB 1954; Secretary, Committee of Enquiry into the Governance of the University of London, 1970–72; *b* 16 Nov. 1909; *s* of F. S. Copleston, former Chief Judge of Lower Burma; *m* Olivia Green. *Educ:* Marlborough Coll.; Balliol Coll., Oxford. Inland Revenue Dept, 1932; Treasury, 1942; Under-Sec., 1950; Dep. Sec., 1957–63, Sec., 1963–69, UGC; retired. *Address:* Holland Hill, Bulmer, Sudbury, Suffolk. *T:* Twinstead 356.

COPLESTON, Rev. Frederick Charles, SJ; MA Oxon, DPhil Rome, Gregorian Univ.; FBA 1970; Principal of Heythrop College, University of London, 1970–74; Emeritus Professor of University of London, 1974; Dean, Faculty of Theology, 1972–74; *b* 10 April 1907; *s* of F. S. Copleston, former Chief Judge of Lower Burma, and N. M. Little. *Educ:* Marlborough Coll.; St John's Coll., Oxford (Hon. Fellow, 1975). Entered Catholic Church, 1925; Soc. of Jesus, 1930; ordained 1937. Prof. of History of Philosophy: Heythrop Coll., Oxford, 1939–70, and Univ. of London, 1972–74; Gregorian Univ., Rome, 1952–68; Dean of Faculty of Theology, Univ. of London, 1972–74; Visiting Professor: Univ. of Santa Clara, Calif., 1974–75 and 1977–82; Univ. of Hawaii, 1976; Gifford Lectr, Univ. of Aberdeen, 1979–80. Hon. Dr (Theology), Uppsala, Sweden, 1983. *Publications:* Friedrich Nietzsche, Philosopher of Culture, 1942, new edn 1975; St Thomas and Nietzsche, 1944; Arthur Schopenhauer, Philosopher of Pessimism, 1946; A History of Philosophy (vol. 1, Greece and Rome, 1946; revised 1947; vol. 2, Augustine to Scotus, 1950; vol. 3, Ockham to Suárez, 1953; vol. 4, Descartes to Leibniz, 1958; vol. 5, Hobbes to Hume, 1959; vol. 6, Wolff to Kant, 1960; vol. 7, Fichte to Nietzsche, 1963; vol. 8, Bentham to Russell, 1966; vol. 9, Maine de Biran to Sartre, 1975); Medieval Philosophy, 1952; Existentialism and Modern Man, 1948; Aquinas (Pelican), 1955; Contemporary Philosophy, 1956, rev. edn 1972; A History of Medieval Philosophy, 1972; Religion and Philosophy, 1974; Philosophers and Philosophies, 1976; On the History of Philosophy, 1979; Philosophies and Cultures, 1980; Religion and the One, 1982; Philosophy in Russia, 1986; articles in learned journals. *Address:* 114 Mount Street, W1Y 6AH. *T:* 01-493 7811.

COPLESTONE-BOUGHEY, His Honour John Fenton; a Circuit Judge (formerly Judge of the County Courts), 1969–85; *b* 5 Feb. 1912; *o s* of late Comdr A. F. Coplestone-Boughey, RN; *m* 1944, Gilian Beatrice, *e d* of late H. A. Counsell, Appleby; one *s* one *d*. *Educ:* Shrewsbury School; Brasenose Coll., Oxford (Open Exhibitioner, Matthew Arnold Prizeman). Inner Temple, Entrance Scholar 1934, Barrister 1935. Legal Assistant, Min. of Health, 1937–40. Royal Artillery, 1940–46; Advanced Class, Military Coll. of Science, 1945. Chester Chronicle & Associated Newspapers, Ltd: Dir, 1947–56; Dep. Chm., 1956–65. Chairman, Nat. Insurance Tribunals (SW London), 1951–69; Referee, Nat. Service and Family Allowances Acts, 1957–69. Battersea etc Hospital Management Cttee: Member 1960–69, Chairman 1969–74; Mem., Wandsworth etc AHA, 1973–82. Chm., Chelsea Housing Improvement Soc., 1981–84. Governor, St Thomas' Hosp., 1971–74; Special Trustee, St George's Hospital, 1974–, Chm. of Trustees 1980–84. Mem. Council, Queen's Coll., London, 1976–, Vice-Chm. 1979–84, Chm. 1984–. *Publications:* contrib. to Halsbury's Laws of England. *Recreations:* walking, travel. *Address:* 82 Oakley Street, SW3 5NP. *T:* 01–352 6287. *Club:* Athenæum.

COPLEY, John (Michael Harold); Principal Resident Producer, Royal Opera, Covent Garden, since 1975; *b* 12 June, 1933; *s* of Ernest Harold Copley and Lilian Forbes. *Educ:* King Edward's, Five Ways, Birmingham; Sadler's Wells Ballet Sch.; Central Sch. of Arts and Crafts, London (Dip. with Hons in Theatre Design). Appeared as the apprentice in Britten's Peter Grimes for Covent Garden Opera Co, 1950; stage managed: both opera and ballet companies at Sadler's Wells, in Rosebery Avenue, 1953–57; also various musicals, plays, etc, in London's West End, incl. The World of Paul Slickey and My Fair Lady. Joined Covent Garden Opera Co.: Dep. Stage Manager, 1960; Asst Resident Producer, 1963; Associate Resident Producer, 1966; Resident Producer, 1972. *Productions include: at Covent Garden:* Suor Angelica, 1965; Cosi fan Tutte, 1968, 1981; Orpheo ed Euridice, 1969; Le Nozze di Figaro, 1971, 1985; Don Giovanni, 1973; La Bohème, 1974, 1985; Faust, 1974; L'elisir d'amore, 1975, 1981, 1985; Benvenuto Cellini, 1976; Ariadne auf Naxos, 1976; Maria Stuarda; Royal Silver Jubilee Gala, 1977; Werther, 1979; La Traviata, Lucrezia Borgia, 1980; Alceste, 1981; Semele, 1982; *at London Coliseum (for Sadler's Wells, subseq. ENO):* Carmen, Il Seraglio, Il Trovatore, La Traviata, Mary Stuart; Rosenkavalier, La Belle Hélène, 1975; Werther, 1977; Manon, Aida, Julius Caesar, Les Mamelles de Tirésias, 1979; *Athens Festival:* Macbeth; *Netherlands Opera:* Lucia; *Opera National de Belge:* Lucia; *Wexford Festival:* La Clemenza di Tito; L'Infedelta delusa; *Dallas Civic Opera, Texas:* Lucia; *Chicago Lyric Opera:* Lucia; La Bohème, 1983; *Canadian Opera, Toronto:* Lucia; Falstaff; La Bohème, 1984; *Greek Nat. Opera:* Madame Butterfly; Otello; *Australian Opera:* Fidelio, Nozze di Figaro, Rigoletto, Magic Flute, Jenufa, Ariadne auf Naxos, Madame Butterfly, Fra Diavolo, Macbeth, La Traviata, Manon Lescaut, Lucia di Lammermoor, Tosca, Manon; Adriana Lecouvreur, 1984; *Victoria State Opera:* Don Carlos, 1984; La Bohème, 1985; *WNO:* La Traviata, Falstaff, Peter Grimes, Tosca; Peter Grimes, 1983; *Opera North:* Les Mamelles de Tirésias, Madama Butterfly; *Scottish Opera:* Lucia, Ballo in Maschera, Dido and Aeneas; Acis and Galatea for English Opera Group in Stockholm, Paris, Aldeburgh Fest.; *New York City Opera:* Le Nozze di Figaro; Der Freischutz; *Ottawa Festival:* Midsummer Night's Dream; Eugene Onegin, 1983; *Vancouver Opera:* Carmen; *San Francisco Opera:* Julius Caesar; The Midsummer Marriage, 1983; Don Giovanni, 1984; Orlando, 1985; *San Diego Opera:* Eugene Onegin, 1985; La Nozze di Figaro, 1986; *Staatsoper Munich:* Adriana Lecouvreur, 1984. Sang as soloist in Bach's St John Passion, Bremen, Germany, 1965; appeared as Ferdy in John Osborne's play, A Patriot for Me, at Royal Court Theatre, 1965. Co-directed (with Patrick Garland) Fanfare for Europe Gala, Covent Garden, 3 Jan. 1973; directed Fanfare for Elizabeth gala, Covent Garden, 21 April 1986. *Recreation:* cooking. *Address:* 9D Thistle Grove, SW10 9RR.

COPP, Darrell John Barkwell, OBE 1981; General Secretary, Institute of Biology, 1951–82; *b* 25 April 1922; *s* of J. J. H. Copp and L. A. Hoad; *m* 1944, Margaret Henderson; two *s* one *d*. *Educ:* Taunton's Sch., Southampton; Southampton Univ. (BSc). Scientific Officer, Admty Signals Estabt, 1942–45; Asst Sec., British Assoc. for Advancement of Science, 1947–51. Sec., Council for Nature, 1958–63; originator and co-ordinator of first National Nature Week, 1963. Hon. Treas., Parly and Scientific Cttee, 1980–83; Sec., European Community Biologists' Assoc., 1975–85. Trustee, Rye Art Gall., 1985–. Hon. MTech Bradford, 1975; Hon. FIBiol 1984. *Publications:* reports and reviews in scientific jls. *Recreations:* mountain walking, renovating country cottages. *Address:* Underhill Farmhouse, Wittersham, Tenterden, Kent TN30 7EU. *T:* Wittersham 633.

COPP, Prof. (Douglas) Harold, CC 1980 (OC 1971); MD, PhD; FRS 1971; FRSC; FRCP(C); Professor of Physiology, University of British Columbia, Canada, since 1950; *b* 16 Jan. 1915; *s* of Charles J. Copp and Edith M. O'Hara; *m* 1939, Winnifred A. Thompson; three *d*. *Educ:* Univ. of Toronto, Canada (BA, MD); Univ. of California, Berkeley, Calif (PhD); British Columbia College of Physicians and Surgeons (Lic.). Asst Prof. of Physiology, Calif, 1945–50. Co-ordinator, Health Scis, Univ. of British Columbia, 1976–77; Head of Dept of Physiology, Univ. of British Columbia, 1950–80. FRSC 1959 (Mem. Council, 1973–75, 1977–; Vice-Pres., and Pres. Academy of Science, 1978–81); FRCP(C) 1974. Hon. LLD: Queen's Univ., Kingston, Ont, 1970; Univ. of Toronto, 1970; Hon. DSc: Univ. of Ottawa, 1973; Acadia Univ., 1975; Univ. of British Columbia, 1980. Discovered calcitonin (ultimobranchial hormone) and teleocalcin (corpuscles of Stannius). *Recreation:* gardening. *Address:* 4755 Belmont Avenue, Vancouver, British Columbia V6T 1A8, Canada. *T:* 604–224–3793.

COPPEN, Dr Alec James, MD, DSc; FRCP, FRCPsych; Director, Medical Research Council Neuropsychiatry Laboratory, and Consultant Psychiatrist, West Park Hospital, Epsom, Surrey, since 1974; *b* 29 Jan. 1923; *y s* of late Herbert John Wardle Coppen and Marguerite Mary Annie Coppen; *m* 1952, Gunhild Margareta, *y d* of late Albert and Sigrid Andersson, Båstad, Sweden; one *s*. *Educ:* Dulwich Coll.; Univ. of Bristol (MB, ChB 1953; MD 1958; DSc 1978); Maudsley Hosp.; Univ. of London (DPM 1957); MRCP 1975, FRCP 1980, FRCPsych 1971. Registrar, then Sen. Registrar, Maudsley Hosp., 1954–59; MRC Neuropsychiatry Research Unit, 1959–74, MRC External Staff, 1974–; Consultant Psychiatrist: St Ebba's Hosp., 1959–64; West Park Hosp., 1964–; Hon. Cons. Psychiatrist, St George's Hosp., 1965–70. Head of WHO designated Centre for Biological Psychiatry in UK, 1974–; Consultant, WHO, 1977–; Examiner, Royal Coll. of Psychiatry, 1973–77; Andrew Woods Vis. Prof., Univ. of Iowa, 1981; Lectr to learned socs and univs in Europe, N and S America, Asia and Africa. Mem. Council, RMPA (Chm., Research and Clinical Section), 1965–70; Chairman, Biolog. Psychiatry Section, World Psychiatric Assoc., 1972; President, British Assoc. of Psychopharmacology, 1975; Member: Internat. Coll. Neuropsychopharm., 1960– (Mem. Council, 1979); RSM, 1960–; British Pharmacol. Soc., 1977–; Special Health Auth., Bethlem Royal and Maudsley Hosp., 1982–; Hon. Member: Mexican Soc. for Biolog. Psychiatry, 1973–; Mexican Inst. of Culture, 1974–; Swedish Psychiatric Assoc., 1977–; Corresp. Mem., Amer. Coll. of Neuropsychopharm., 1977–; Distinguished Fellow, APA, 1981. Freeman, City of London, 1980; Soc. of Apothecaries: Yeoman, 1980; Liveryman 1985. Anna Monika Prize, 1969. *Publications:* (jtly) Recent Developments in Schizophrenia, 1967; (jtly) Recent Developments in Affective Disorders, 1968; (jtly) Psychopharmacology of Affective Disorders, 1979; contribs to text books; papers in Nature, Lancet, BMJ, etc (Current Contents Citation Classic, 1978, Biochemistry of the Affective Disorders). *Recreations:* golf, music, photography. *Address:* 5 Walnut Close, Epsom, Surrey KT18 5JL. *T:* Epsom 20800. *Club:* Athenæum.

COPPLESTONE, Frank Henry; Managing Director, Southern Television Ltd; *b* 26 Feb. 1925; 2nd *s* of late Rev. Frank T. Copplestone; *m* 1st, 1950, Margaret Mary (*d* 1973), *d* of late Edward Walker; three *s*; 2nd, 1977, Penelope Ann Labovitch, *d* of Ben and Eve Perrick; one step *s* one step *d*. *Educ:* Truro Sch.; Nottingham Univ. (BA). Royal Horse Artillery, 1943–47. Pres., Univ. of Nottingham Union, 1952–53; Pres., Nat. Union of Students, 1954–56; Internat. Research Fellow, 1956–58; Regional Officer, Independent

Television Authority, 1958–62; Head of Regional Services, ITA, 1962–63; Head of Programme Services, ITA, 1963–67; Controller, ITV Network Programme Secretariat, 1967–73; Dir, ITV Programme Planning Secretariat, 1973–75; Man. Dir, Southern Television, 1976–; Director: Independent Television News Ltd, 1977–81; Independent Television Publications Ltd, 1976–81. Mem., Broadcasters' Audience Res. Bd, 1981. *Recreations:* sailing, reading, music. *Address:* 4 West Street, Polruan, Cornwall. *Clubs:* Reform; Royal Fowey Yacht, Fowey Gallants Sailing.

COPPOCK, Prof. John Terence, FBA 1975; FRSE 1976; Secretary and Treasurer, Carnegie Trust for the Universities of Scotland, since 1986; *b* 2 June 1921; *s* of late Arthur Coppock and late Valerie Margaret Coppock (*née* Phillips); *m* 1953, Sheila Mary Burnett; one *s* one *d. Educ:* Penarth County Sch.; Queens' Coll., Cambridge. MA (Cantab), PhD (London). Civil Servant: Lord Chancellor's Dept, Min. of Works, Board of Customs and Excise, 1938–47. Served War, Army (commissioned Welch Regt, 1941), 1939–46. Cambridge Univ., 1947–50. University Coll. London (Dept of Geography): successively, Asst Lecturer, Lecturer, Reader, 1950–65; Ogilvie Prof. of Geography, Univ. of Edinburgh, 1965–86. Member: Scottish Sports Council, 1976–; Ordnance Survey Rev. Cttee, 1978–79. FRSA 1980. *Publications:* The Changing Use of Land in Britain (with R. H. Best), 1962; An Agricultural Atlas of England and Wales, 1964, 2nd edn 1976; Greater London (ed, with H. C. Prince), 1964; An Agricultural Geography of Great Britain, 1971; Recreation in the Countryside: a Spatial Analysis (with B. S. Duffield), 1975; Spatial Dimensions of Public Policy (ed, with W. R. D. Sewell), 1976; An Agricultural Atlas of Scotland, 1976; Second Homes: Curse or Blessing? (ed), 1977; Public Participation in Planning (ed, with W. R. D. Sewell), 1977; Land Use and Town and Country Planning (with L. F. Gebbett), 1978; Land Assessment in Scotland (ed, with M. F. Thomas), 1980; Innovation in Scottish Water Management (with W. R. D. Sewell and A. Pitkethly), 1986; numerous papers: mainly in geographical, but also historical, planning and agricultural periodicals, mainly on theme of rural land use in Great Britain. *Recreations:* listening to music, natural history. *Address:* 57 Braid Avenue, Edinburgh EH10 6EB. *T:* 031–447 3443.

COPPOLA, Francis Ford; Artistic Director, Zoetrope Studios, since 1969; *b* 7 April 1939; *s* of Carmine Coppola and Italia Pennino; *m* 1963, Eleanor Neil; one *s* one *d* (and one *s* decd). *Educ:* Hofstra Univ. (BA); Univ. of Calif, LA (MFA). Films directed: Dementia 13, 1963; You're a Big Boy Now, 1967; Finian's Rainbow, 1968; The Rain People, 1969; The Godfather, 1972; The Conversation, 1974; The Godfather, Part II, 1974; Apocalypse Now, 1979; One From the Heart, 1981; The Outsiders, 1983; Rumble Fish, 1983; The Cotton Club, 1984. Commandeur, Ordre des Arts et des Lettres, 1983. *Recreations:* reading, writing, scientific discovery. *Address:* Zoetrope Studios, 916 Kearny Street, San Francisco, Calif 94133, USA. *T:* (415) 788-7500.

CORBEN, Albert Edward; Assistant Under Secretary of State, Radio Regulatory Department, Home Office (and subsequently with Department of Trade and Industry), 1980–83, retired; *b* 25 Nov. 1923; *s* of Ebenezer Joseph James Corben and Frances Flora (*née* Orchard); *m* 1953, Doris Dodd; two *s. Educ:* Portsmouth Grammar Sch.; Sir John Cass Technical Inst. Served Royal Artillery, 1943–47. Entered Home Office, as Executive Officer, 1947; Higher Executive Officer, 1955–62; Sen. Executive Officer, 1962–66; Principal, 1966–72; Secretary to Advisory Council on Penal System, 1966–68; Sen. Principal, 1972–73; Asst Sec., 1973–80. *Recreations:* swimming, tennis, walking. *Address:* 1a Winchester Road, Bromley, Kent BR2 0PZ. *T:* 01–460 4106.

CORBET, Mrs Freda (Kunzlen), (Mrs Ian McIvor Campbell), BA; JP; *b* 1900; *d* of James Mansell; *m* 1925, William Corbet (*d* 1957); *m* 1962, Ian McIvor Campbell (*d* 1976). *Educ:* Wimbledon County Sch.; University Coll., London. Called to Bar, Inner Temple, 1932. MP (Lab) NW Camberwell, later Peckham Div. of Camberwell, 1945–Feb. 1974. Awarded Freedom of Southwark, 1974. JP, Co. London, 1940. *Address:* 39 Gravel Road, Bromley, Kent.

CORBET, Dr Gordon Barclay; Head, Department of Central Services, British Museum (Natural History), since 1976; *b* 4 March 1933; *s* of George and Mary Corbet; *m* 1959, Elizabeth Urquhart; one *s* one *d. Educ:* Morgan Acad., Dundee; Univ. of St Andrews. BSc, PhD. Asst Lectr in Biology, Sir John Cass Coll., London, 1958–59; Sen., later Principal, Scientific Officer, Dept of Zoology, British Museum (Natural History), 1960–71; Dep. Keeper of Zoology, 1971–76. *Publications:* The Terrestrial Mammals of Western Europe, 1966; Finding and Identifying Mammals in Britain, 1975; The Handbook of British Mammals (with H. N. Southern), 1977; The Mammals of the Palaearctic Region, 1978. *Recreations:* bird-watching, walking. *Address:* 27 Farnaby Road, Bromley, Kent BR1 4BL. *T:* 01–460 2439.

CORBET, Lieut-Col Sir John (Vincent), 7th Bt, *cr* 1808; MBE 1946; DL; JP; RE (retired); *b* 27 Feb. 1911; *s* of Archer Henry Corbet (*d* 1950) and Anne Maria (*d* 1951), *d* of late German Buxton; *S* kinsman, Sir Gerald Vincent Corbet, 6th Bt, 1955; *m* 1st, 1937, Elfrida Isobel Francis; 2nd, 1948, Doreen Elizabeth Stewart (*d* 1964), *d* of Arthur William Gibbon Ritchie; 3rd, 1965, Annie Elizabeth Lorimer, MBE, MSc, Dunedin, NZ. *Educ:* Shrewsbury Sch.; RMA; Magdalene Coll., Cambridge. BA 1933, MA 1972. 2nd Lieut, RE, 1931; served North-West Frontier, India, 1935, and War of 1939–45 in India, Burma and Malaya (despatches, MBE); Lieut-Col, 1953; retd 1955. DL County of Salop, 1961; JP 1957; High Sheriff of Salop, 1966; CC Salop, 1963–81. OStJ; Mem., Church Assembly, later General Synod, 1960–75; former Chm., Board of Visitors, Stoke Heath Borstal. *Address:* Acton Reynald, near Shrewsbury, Salop SY4 4DS. *T:* Clive 259. *Club:* Royal Thames Yacht.

CORBET, Air Vice-Marshal Lancelot Miller, CB 1958; CBE 1944; RAF retired; *b* Brunswick, Vic, Australia, 19 April 1898; *s* of late John Miller and late Ella Beatrice Corbet, Caulfield, Vic, Australia; *m* 1924, Gwenllian Elizabeth, *d* of late Thomas Powell and late May Maria Bennett, Claremont, Western Australia; one *s. Educ:* Melbourne High Sch.; Scotch Coll., Melbourne; Melbourne Univ. (MB, BS 1922). RMO, Perth (WA) Hospital, 1922–23, Perth Children's Hospital 1923; Hon. Asst Anæsthetist, Perth Hospital, 1931; Clinical Asst to Out-Patient Surgeon, Perth Hospital, 1931–32. Was Major AAMC; commanded 6th Field Hygiene Sect., 1930–32; entered RAF 1933; served in UK and India, 1933–37; Principal MO, W Africa, 1941–43; Principal MO, Transport Command, RAF, 1943–45; Principal MO, Malaya, 1945–46; Principal MO, British Commonwealth Air Forces, Japan, 1946–48; OC, RAF Hospital, Nocton Hall, 1949–52; Principal MO, HQBF, Aden, 1952–54; Principal MO, 2nd Tactical Air Force, 1954–56; Dep. Dir-Gen. of Medical Services, Air Ministry, 1956–58, retired. Hon. Life Member: BMA; AMA; Aviation Med. Soc. of Aust. and NZ; RAAF Assoc. KStJ. *Recreations:* lacrosse, tennis, squash, golf, etc. *Address:* Unit 201 Ventura House, Air Force Memorial Estate, Bull Creek Drive, Bull Creek, WA 6155, Australia. *T:* Perth 310 1004.

CORBETT, family name of **Baron Rowallan.**

CORBETT, Rev. Canon Charles Eric. *Educ:* Jesus College, Oxford (BA 1939, MA 1943); Wycliffe Hall, Oxford. Deacon 1940, priest 1941, St Asaph; Curate of Gresford, 1940–44; CF, 1944–47; Curate of Eglwys-Rhos, 1947–49; Rector of Harpurhey,

1949–54; Vicar of St Catherine's, Wigan, 1954–61; Vicar of St Luke, Farnworth, 1961–71; Rural Dean of Farnworth, 1964–71; Archdeacon of Liverpool, 1971–79; Canon-Treasurer of Liverpool Cathedral, 1979–83. *Address:* 80 Latham Avenue, Helsby, Cheshire WA6 0EB.

CORBETT, Captain Hugh Askew, CBE 1968; DSO 1945; DSC 1943; RN; (Retired); *b* 25 June 1916; *s* of late Rev. F. St John Corbett, MA, FRSL, FRHistS and late Elsie L. V. Askew; *m* 1945, Patricia Nancy, *d* of late Thomas Patrick Spens, OBE, MC, LLD; three *s. Educ:* St Edmund's Sch., Canterbury. Joined Royal Navy, 1933; IDC 1960; HMS Cæsar as Capt. (D), 8th Destroyer Sqdn, 1961–63; HMS Fearless, 1965–67 (Capt.); Head of Naval Manpower Future Policy Div., 1967–69; Warden, University Centre, Cambridge Univ., 1969–83, retired. *Address:* Holly Cottage, 3 Clare Road, Cambridge. *T:* Cambridge 357735.

CORBETT, Prof. John Patrick, MA; Professor of Philosophy, University of Bradford, 1972–76; *b* 5 March 1916; *s* of E. S. H. and K. F. Corbett; *m* 1st, 1940, Nina Angeloni; two *s*; 2nd, 1968, Jan Adams; two *d. Educ:* RNC, Dartmouth; Magdalen Coll., Oxford. Lieut, RA, 1940; POW in Germany, 1940–45. Fellow of Balliol, 1945–61; Prof. of Philosophy, Univ. of Sussex, 1961–72; Jowett Lectr in Philosophy. Council of Europe Fellow, 1957; Visiting Lectr, Yale Univ., 1958; NATO Fellow, 1960; Vis. Prof., Univ. of Toronto, 1968. *Publications:* Europe and the Social Order, 1959; Ideologies, 1965. *Address:* Kalokhorio, Limassol, Cyprus.

CORBETT, Prof. Peter Edgar; Yates Professor of Classical Art and Archaeology in the University of London (University College), 1961–82, now Professor Emeritus; *b* 19 June 1920; 2nd *s* of Ernest Oliver Corbett and Margaret Edgar. *Educ:* Bedford Sch.; St John's Coll., Oxford. Royal Artillery, 1940–41, RAFVR, 1942–45. Thomas Whitcombe Greene Scholar, and Macmillan Student of British School at Athens, 1947–49; Asst Keeper in Dept of Greek and Roman Antiquities, British Museum, 1949–61. Lectr in Classics, Univ. of Calif, Los Angeles, 1956. Pres., Soc. for Promotion of Hellenic Studies, 1980–83. *Publications:* The Sculpture of the Parthenon, 1959; (with A. Birchall) Greek Gods and Heroes, 1974; articles in Jl of Hellenic Studies, Hesperia, Annual of Brit. School at Athens, BM Quarterly, Bulletin of the Inst. of Classical Studies. *Address:* 30 The Terrace, Barnes, SW13 0NR.

CORBETT, Robin; MP (Lab) Birmingham, Erdington, since 1983; communication and public affairs consultant; *b* 22 Dec. 1933; *s* of Thomas Corbett and Marguerite Adele Mainwaring; *m* 1970, Val Hudson; one *d. Educ:* Holly Lodge Grammar Sch., Smethwick. Newspaper and magazine journalist, 1950–69; Editoral Staff Develt Exec., IPC Magazines, 1969–72; Sen. Lab. Adviser, IPC Magazines, 1972–74. Mem. Nat. Union of Journalists Nat. Exec. Council, 1965–69. MP (Lab) Hemel Hempstead, Oct. 1974–1979; opposition front bench spokesman on home affairs, 1985–. Chairman: PLP Agric. Gp, 1977–78; PLP Home Affairs Cttee, 1984–86; Sec., PLP Civil Liberties Gp, 1974–79; Member: Expenditure Cttee, 1976–79; Commons Home Affairs Cttee, 1984–86; PLP Campaign Unit, 1985–86; Vice Chm., All Party Animal Welfare Gp, 1976–79; Jt Sec., All Party Anzac Gp, 1985–. Mem. Food and Agriculture Sub-Cttee, Labour Party Nat. Exec. Cttee, 1974–79; Chm., farm animal welfare co-ordinating exec., 1977–. Fellow, Industry and Parlt Trust, 1979. *Recreations:* visiting North Wales; pottering. *Address:* House of Commons, SW1A 0AA. *Clubs:* Castle Vale Residents Association; Forget-Me-Not (Erdington).

CORBETT, Lt-Col Uvedale, CBE 1984; DSO 1944; DL; *b* 12 Sept. 1909; *s* of Major C. U. Corbett, Stableford, Bridgnorth, Shropshire; *m* 1st, 1935, Veronica Marian Whitehead (marr. diss., 1952); two *s* one *d*; 2nd, 1953, Mrs Patricia Jane Walker (*d* 1985). *Educ:* Wellington (Berks); RMA, Woolwich. Commissioned Royal Artillery, 1929; relinquished command 3rd Regt RHA 1945; retired. MP (C) Ludlow Div. of Shropshire, 1945–51. Chm., Sun Valley Poultry Ltd, 1961–83. DL Hereford and Worcester, 1983. *Address:* Shobdon Court, Leominster, Herefordshire HR6 9LZ. *T:* Kingsland 260. *Club:* Army and Navy.

CORBETT-WINDER, Col John Lyon, OBE 1949; MC 1942; JP; Lord-Lieutenant of Powys, 1974–86 (of Montgomeryshire, 1960–74); *b* 15 July 1911; *o s* of Major W. J. Corbett-Winder, Vaynor Park, Berriew, Montgomery (Lord Lieutenant of Montgomeryshire, 1944–50); *m* 1944, Margaret Ailsa, *d* of Lt-Col J. Ramsay Tainsh, CBE, VD; one *s* two *d. Educ:* Eton; RMC Sandhurst. 2nd Lieut, 60th Rifles, 1931; Lt-Col, 1942. Served War of 1939–45, Western Desert and N Africa, 1939–43 (despatches twice); Commanded: 44 Reconnaissance Regt; 1st Bn 60th Rifles; GSO1 Infantry Directorate, WO, 1944–47; commanded 2nd Bn 60th Rifles, Palestine, 1947–48 (despatches); AAG, HQ Southern Command, 1948–51; GSO1, HQ 53 Welsh Inf. Div., 1952–55; Col Gen. Staff, SHAPE Mission to Royal Netherlands Army, 1955–57; Dep. Mil. Sec., HQ, BAOR, 1957–58; retd 1958; RARO, 1958–69. Mem., Parly Boundary Commn for Wales, 1963–79. Pres., TA & VR Assoc. for Wales, 1977–81. Chm., Dyfed-Powys Police Authority, 1978–80 (Vice-Chm., 1976–78). JP Powys (formerly Montgomeryshire), 1959. Commander, Order of Orange Nassau, 1958. KStJ 1970 (CStJ 1966). *Recreations:* gardening, forestry. *Address:* Vaynor Park, Berriew, Welshpool, Powys SY21 8QE. *T:* Berriew 204.

CORBIN, Maurice Haig Alleyne; Justice of Appeal, Supreme Court, Trinidad and Tobago, 1972–81; *b* 26 May 1916; *s* of L. A. Corbin; *m* 1943, Helen Jocelyn Child; one *s* two *d*; *m* 1968, Jean Barcant. *Educ:* Harrison Coll., Barbados; Queen's Royal Coll., Trinidad. Solicitor, 1941; appointed Magistrate, Trinidad, 1945; called to the Bar, Middle Temple, 1949; Crown Counsel, 1953; Registrar, Supreme Court, 1954; Puisne Judge, Supreme Court, 1957–72. *Recreation:* tennis. *Address:* 77 Brook Road, Goodwood Park, Trinidad. *Club:* Queen's Park Cricket (Port of Spain, Trinidad).

CORBY, (Frederick) Brian, FIA; Chief Executive, since 1982, Director since 1983, Prudential Corporation plc; Chairman, since 1985, Director, since 1981, Prudential Assurance Co. Ltd; Chairman, since 1985, and Director, since 1982, Mercantile & General Reinsurance Co. plc; a Director, Bank of England, since 1985; *b* 10 May 1929; *s* of Charles Walter and Millicent Corby; *m* 1952, Elizabeth Mairi McInnes; one *s* two *d. Educ:* Kimbolton Sch.; St John's Coll., Cambridge (MA). Joined Prudential Assce Co. Ltd, 1952; Dep. Gen. Manager, 1974; Gen. Manager, 1976–79; Gp Gen. Manager, Prudential Corp. Ltd, 1979–82; Chief Gen. Manager, Prudential Assce Co. Ltd, 1982–85. Vice-President, Inst. of Actuaries, 1979–82; Chm., Assoc. of British Insurers, 1985–. *Publications:* contribs to Jl of Inst. of Actuaries. *Recreations:* reading, golf.

CORBY, George Arthur; international meteorological consultant; *b* 14 Aug. 1917; *s* of Bertie John Corby and Agnes May (*née* Dale); *m* 1951, Gertrude Anne Nicoll; one *s* one *d. Educ:* St Marylebone Grammar Sch.; Univ. of London (BSc Special Maths 1st Cl.). Architect's Dept. LCC, 1936–42; entered Met. Office, 1942; Flt Lt, RAFVR, 1943; Sqdn Leader, Dep. Chief Met. Officer, ACSEA, 1945–46; Sen. Met. Off., Northolt Airport, 1947–53; research, 1953–73; Dep. Dir for Communications and Computing, 1973–76; Dir of Services and Dep. Dir Gen., 1976–78. Vice-Pres., Royal Meteorol Soc., 1975–77. *Publications:* official scientific pubns and res. papers on mountain airflow, dynamical meteorol., and numerical forecasting. *Recreations:* music, photography, cross-country skiing. *Address:* Kings Barn, High Street, Harwell, Oxon. *T:* Abingdon 832883.

CORBYN, Jeremy Bernard; MP (Lab) Islington North, since 1983; *b* 26 May 1949; *s* of David Benjamin Corbyn. *Educ:* Adams Grammar Sch., Newport, Shropshire. NUPE Official, 1975–83; sponsored NUPE MP. Mem., Haringey Borough Council, 1974– (Chm., Community Develt Cttee 1975–78, Public Works 1978–79, Planning Cttee 1980–81, 1982–83). Sec., PLP Latin America, Central America and Caribbean Group. *Address:* 16 Turle Road, N7; (office) 129 Seven Sisters Road, N7 7QG. *T:* 01–263 9450; House of Commons, SW1A 0AA. *T:* 01–219 3545.

CORCORAN, Hon. James Desmond, AO 1982; MP (Labor) Hartley, South Australia, since 1977; *b* 8 Nov. 1928; *s* of James and Catherine Corcoran; *m* 1957, Carmel Mary Campbell; four *s* four *d. Educ:* Tantanoola Public School. Enlisted Australian Regular Army, 1950; served Korea, Japan, Malaya and New Guinea (despatches twice); discharged, rank of Captain, 1962. Entered politics, contested and won House of Assembly seat of Millicen, S Aust. Parliament, 1962, Member for Coles, 1975; held portfolios of Minister of Lands, Irrigation, Repatriation, Immigration and Tourism, in Labor Govt, 1965–68; Dep. Leader of Opposition, 1968–70; Dep. Premier, Minister of Works and Minister of Marine, 1970–77, additionally Minister of Environment, 1977–79; Premier, Treasurer, and Minister of Ethnic Affairs, of S Australia, Feb.-Sept. 1979. *Address:* 1 Aringa Court, Rostrevor, SA 5073, Australia.

CORDEIRO, His Eminence Cardinal Joseph; *see* Karachi, Archbishop of, (RC).

CORDEROY, Rev. Graham Thomas; QHC 1984; Principal Chaplain, Church of Scotland and Free Churches, Royal Air Force, since 1984; *b* 15 April 1931; *s* of Thomas and Gladys Corderoy; *m* 1957, Edna Marian Barnes; six *d. Educ:* Emanuel Sch., London; Manchester Univ. (BA Theology 1957). Ordained 1957; commissioned RAF Chaplain, 1962. *Recreations:* Rugby referee 1964–; Gilbert and Sullivan buff. *Address:* 16 South Road, Brampton, Huntingdon, Cambs PE18 8PX. *T:* Huntingdon 50654. *Club:* Royal Air Force.

CORDINGLEY, Maj-Gen. John Edward, OBE 1959; Chairman, J. W. Carpenter Ltd, since 1984; *b* 1 Sept. 1916; *s* of Air Vice-Marshal Sir John Cordingley, KCB, KCVO, CBE, and late Elizabeth Ruth Carpenter; *m* 1st, 1940, Ruth Pamela (marr. diss. 1961), *d* of late Major S. A. Boddam-Whetham; two *s*; 2nd, 1961, Audrey Helen Anne, *d* of late Maj-Gen. F. G. Beaumont-Nesbitt, CVO, CBE, MC; two step *d. Educ:* Sherborne; RMA, Woolwich. 2nd Lieut RA, 1936; served War of 1939–45, Europe and India. Brigade Comdr, 1961–62; Imperial Defence Coll., 1963; Dir of Work Study, Min. of Defence (Army), 1964–66; Dep. Dir, RA, 1967–68; Maj-Gen., RA, BAOR, 1968–71, retired. Controller, Royal Artillery Instn, 1975–82; Chm. Bd of Management, RA Charitable Fund, 1977–82. Col Comdt, RA, 1973–82. Bursar, Sherborne Sch., 1971–74. Fellow, Inst. of Work Study Practitioners, 1965; MBIM 1966; FInstD 1985. *Recreations:* golf and gardening. *Address:* Church Farm House, Rotherwick, Basingstoke, Hants RG27 9BG. *T:* Hook 2734. *Clubs:* Army and Navy; Senior Golfers.

CORDLE, John Howard; *b* 11 Oct. 1912; *s* of late Ernest William Cordle; *m* 1st, 1938 (marr. diss., 1956); three *s* (and one *s* one *d* decd); 2nd, 1957 (marr. diss. 1971), *e d* of Col A. Maynard, OBE; one *s* three *d*; 3rd, 1976, Terttu, *y d* of Mikko Heikura, Finland; two *s. Educ:* City of London Sch. Served RAF (commissioned), 1940–45. Man. Dir 1946–68, Chm. 1968–81, E. W. Cordle & Son Ltd. Proprietor, Church of England Newspaper, 1959–60, Dir, 1960–71. Member: Archbishops of Canterbury and York Commission on Evangelism, 1945–46; Church Assembly, 1946–53; Oxford Trust of Churches Patronage Board, 1947– (Chm., 1955–); Hon. Treas., The World's Evangelical Alliance, 1949–53. Mem. of Lloyd's, 1952; Mem. Founders Livery Company and Freeman of City of London, 1956. Dir, Presswork Ltd. Prospective Parly Cand. (C) NE Wolverhampton, 1949; contested (C) Wrekin Div., 1951; MP (C) Bournemouth E and Christchurch, Oct. 1959–1974, Bournemouth E, 1974–77; Chairman: West Africa Cttee, Conservative Commonwealth Council, 1962–77; All Party Anglo-Libyan Gp, H of C, 1964–67; Church in Parliament All-Party Gp, 1975–77. Member UK Delegation to: Council of Europe, Strasbourg, 1974–77 (Vice-Chm., Parly and Public Relations Cttee, 1976–77); WEU, Paris, 1974–77; Rapporteur, 1976–77, to Cttee on Social and Health Questions, on the institution of Internat. Medical Card. Primrose League: Chm., Finance Cttee, 1964–67; Hon. Treas., 1964–67; Chm., Gen. Purposes Cttee, 1967–68. Chm., Wessex Aid to Addicts Gp, 1985. Governor, London Coll. of Divinity, 1947–52; Life Governor: St Mary's and St Paul's Coll., Cheltenham; Epsom Coll.; Mem. Court of University of Southampton, 1960–77. Gold Staff Officer, Coronation, 1953. Grand Band, Order of the Star of Africa (Liberia), 1964. *Recreations:* shooting, golf, gardening. *Address:* Malmesbury House, The Close, Salisbury, Wilts. *Clubs:* Carlton, National (Trustee, 1946–), English-Speaking Union, Royal Commonwealth Society.

COREN, Alan; Editor of Punch, since 1978; *b* 27 June 1938; *s* of Samuel and Martha Coren; *m* 1963, Anne Kasriel; one *s* one *d. Educ:* East Barnet Grammar Sch.; Wadham Coll., Oxford (Open scholar; BA); Yale; Univ. of California, Berkeley. Asst Editor, Punch, 1963–66, Literary Editor 1966–69, Dep. Editor 1969–77. TV Critic, The Times, 1971–78; Columnist: Daily Mail, 1972–76; Mail on Sunday, 1984–; contributor to: Sunday Times, Atlantic Monthly, TLS, Observer, Tatler, London Review of Books. Commonwealth Fellowship, 1961–63. Rector, St Andrews Univ., 1973–76. *Publications:* The Dog It Was That Died, 1965; All Except the Bastard, 1969; The Sanity Inspector, 1974; The Bulletins of Idi Amin, 1974; Golfing For Cats, 1975; The Further Bulletins of Idi Amin, 1975; The Lady From Stalingrad Mansions, 1977; The Peanut Papers, 1977; The Rhinestone as Big as the Ritz, 1979; Tissues for Men, 1980; The Best of Alan Coren, 1980; The Cricklewood Diet, 1982; Present Laughter, 1982; (ed) The Penguin Book of Modern Humour, 1983; Bumf, 1984; Something For The Weekend, 1986; (ed) The Pick of Punch (annual), 1979–; (ed) The Punch Book of Short Stories, Bk 1, 1979, Bk 2, 1980, Bk 3, 1981; The Arthur Books (for children), 1976–83. *TV series:* The Losers, 1978. *Recreations:* bridge, riding, broadcasting. *Address:* 23 Tudor Street, EC4.

CORFIELD, Rt. Hon. Sir Frederick (Vernon), PC 1970; Kt 1972; QC 1972; a Recorder of the Crown Court, since 1979; *b* 1 June 1915; *s* of late Brig. F. A. Corfield, DSO, OBE, IA, and M. G. Corfield (*née* Vernon); *m* 1945, Elizabeth Mary Ruth Taylor; no *c. Educ:* Cheltenham Coll. (Scholar); RMA, Woolwich. Royal Artillery, 1935; 8th Field Regt, RA, India, 1935–39; served War of 1939–45; Actg Captain and Adjutant, 23rd Field Regt, BEF, 3rd Div., 1939; 51st (Highland) Div., 1940 (despatches); prisoner of war, Germany, 1940–45. Called to Bar, Middle Temple, 1945; Bencher, 1980; JAG's Branch, WO, 1945–46; retired, 1946; farming, 1946–56. MP (C) South Gloucester, 1955–Feb. 1974; Jt Parly Sec., Min. of Housing and Local Govt, 1962–64; Minister of State, Board of Trade, June-Oct. 1970; Minister of Aviation Supply, 1970–71; Minister for Aerospace, DTI, 1971–72. Mem., British Waterways Bd, 1974–83 (Vice-Chm., 1980–83); Dir, Mid-Kent Water Co. Chm., London and Provincial Antique Dealers' Assoc., 1975–. Pres., Council, Cheltenham Coll., 1985–. *Publications:* Corfield on Compensation, 1959; A Guide to the Community Land Act, 1976; (with R. J. A. Carnworth) Compulsory Acquisition and Compensation, 1978. *Recreation:* gardening. *Address:* Wordings Orchard, Sheepscombe, near Stroud, Glos; 2 Paper Buildings, Temple, EC4. *Club:* Army and Navy.

CORFIELD, Sir Kenneth (George), Kt 1980; FEng; Chairman, 1979–85, and Managing Director, 1969–85, STC PLC (formerly Standard Telephones & Cables plc); Chairman, Standard Telephones and Cables (Northern Ireland), 1974–85; Vice-President, ITT Europe Inc., 1967–85; *b* 27 Jan. 1924; *s* of Stanley Corfield and Dorothy Elizabeth (*née* Mason); *m* 1960; one *d. Educ:* South Staffs Coll. of Advanced Technology. FEng 1979, FIMechE, CBIM. Management Develt, ICI Metals Div., 1946–50; Man. Dir, K. G. Corfield Ltd, 1950–60; Exec. Dir, Parkinson Cowan, 1960–66; Dep. Chm., STC Ltd, 1969–79; Sen. Officer, ITT Corp. (UK), 1974–84. Director: Midland Bank Ltd, 1979–; Britoil PLC, 1982–. Chairman: EDC for Ferrous Foundries Industry, 1975–78; British Engrg Council, 1981–85; Defence Spectrum Review, 1985; Mem., ACARD, 1981–84. President: TEMA, 1974–80; BAIE, 1975–79; Vice-Pres., Engineering Employers' Fedn, 1979–85; Member Council: CBI, 1971–85; Inst. of Dirs, 1981– (Pres. 1984–85); BIM, 1978– (Vice-Pres. 1978–83). Trustee, Science Museum, 1984– (Mem. Adv. Council, 1975–83). CompIEE 1974, Hon. FIEE 1985. Hon. Fellow, Sheffield Polytechnic, 1983. DUniv: Surrey, 1976; Open, 1985; Hon. DSc: City, 1981; Bath, 1982; Aston in Birmingham, 1985; Hon. DScEng London, 1982; Hon. DSc (Engrg) QUB, 1982; Hon. LLD Strathclyde, 1982; Hon. DTech Loughborough, 1983; Hon. DEngrg Bradford, 1984. Bicentennial Medal for design, RSA, 1985. *Publications:* Product Design, Report for NEDO, 1979; No Man An Island, 1982 (SIAD Award). *Recreations:* shooting, photography, music. *Address:* 14 Elm Walk, Hampstead, NW3 7UP.

CORISH, Brendan; TD Wexford, 1945–82, retired; Member of Council of State, 1964–77; *b* 19 Nov. 1918; *m* 1949; three *s. Educ:* Christian Brothers' Sch., Wexford. Vice-Chm. of Labour Party, Republic of Ireland, 1946–49; Party Chm., 1949–53; Parly Party Whip, 1947–54; Parly Sec. to Minister for Local Govt and Defence, 1948–51; Minister for Social Welfare, 1954–57; Party Leader, 1960–77; Tanaiste (Deputy Prime Minister) and Minister for Health and Social Welfare, 1973–77. Mem., Wexford CC, 1979–; Alderman, Wexford Corp., 1979–. *Address:* Belvedere Road, Wexford, Ireland.

CORK AND ORRERY, 13th Earl of, *cr* 1620; **Patrick Reginald Boyle;** Baron Boyle of Youghall, 1616; Viscount Dungarvan, 1620; Viscount Kinalmeaky, Baron Boyle of Bandon Bridge and Baron Boyle of Broghill (Ireland), 1628; Earl of Orrery, 1660; Baron Boyle of Marston, 1711; writer, artist and broadcaster; *b* 7 Feb. 1910; *s* of Major Hon. Reginald Courtenay Boyle, MBE, MC (*d* 1946), and Violet (*d* 1974), *d* of late Arthur Flower; *S* uncle, 12th Earl of Cork and Orrery, 1967; *m* 1952, Dorothy Kate (*d* 1978), *o d* of late Robert Ramsden, Meltham, Yorks; *m* 1978, Mary Gabrielle Walker, *widow* of Kenneth Macfarlane Walker and *o d* of late Louis Ginnett. *Educ:* Harrow Sch.; Royal Military College, Sandhurst. Royal Ulster Rifles, 1930–33; Capt. London Irish Rifles, Royal Ulster Rifles (TA), 1935–38. Served War of 1939–45 with Royal Ulster Rifles, Burma Rifles, Cameronians (Scottish Rifles) in Special Force (Chindits) (severely wounded) and Parachute Regt. Now Hon. Major, late Army Air Corps. Dep. Speaker and Dep. Chm. of Cttees, House of Lords, 1973–78; Mem., British Delegn to Inter-Parly Conf., Tokyo, 1974, Madrid, 1976. Pres. and Exec. Chm., British Cancer Council; Dir, Cancer Research Campaign; Mem., Council of Management, St Christopher's Hospice, Sydenham. Hereditary Life Governor and Exec. Chm., Christian Faith Soc.; Mem., Diocesan Assembly, Russian Orthodox Church in GB. FRSA 1947. *Publications:* (author and illustrator) Sailing in a Nutshell, 1935; (jointly) Jungle, Jungle, Little Chindit, 1946. Contribs to the Hibbert Jl. *Recreations:* sailing, oil-painting, gardening. *Heir: b* Hon. John William Boyle, DSC [*b* 12 May 1916; *m* 1943, Mary Leslie, *d* of late Gen. Sir Robert Gordon Finlayson, KCB, CMG, DSO; three *s*]. *Address:* Flint House, Heyshott, Midhurst, W Sussex. *Clubs:* Royal Thames Yacht; Cork and County (Cork).

CORK, CLOYNE, AND ROSS, Bishop of, since 1978; **Rt. Rev. Samuel Greenfield Poyntz;** *b* 4 March 1926; *s* of James and Katharine Jane Poyntz; *m* 1952, Noreen Henrietta Armstrong; one *s* two *d. Educ:* Portora Royal School, Enniskillen; Univ. of Dublin. Mod., Mental and Moral Sci. and Oriental Langs, 1948; 1st cl. Div. Test., 1950; MA 1951; BD 1953; PhD 1960. Deacon 1950, priest 1951; Curate Assistant: St George's, Dublin, 1950–52; Bray, 1952–55; St Michan and St Paul, Dublin, 1955–59; Rector of St Stephen's, Dublin, 1959–67; Vicar of St Ann's, Dublin, 1967–78; Archdeacon of Dublin, 1974–78; Exam. Chaplain to Archbishop of Dublin, 1974–78. Chairman: Youth Dept, British Council of Churches, 1965–69; Irish Council of Churches, 1986–. *Publications:* The Exaltation of the Blessed Virgin Mary, 1953; St Stephen's—One Hundred and Fifty Years of Worship and Witness, 1974; Journey towards Unity, 1975; St Ann's—the Church in the heart of the City, 1976; (ed) Church the Way, the Truth, and Your Life, 1955; Our Church—Praying with our Church Family, 1983. *Recreations:* interest in Rugby football, stamp collecting. *Address:* The Palace, Bishop Street, Cork. *T:* Cork 271214.

CORK, Sir Kenneth (Russell), GBE 1978; FCA; Senior Partner, Cork Gully, Chartered Accountants, 1980–83 (Senior Partner, W. H. Cork, Gully & Co., 1946–80); Lord Mayor of London for 1978–79; *b* 21 Aug. 1913; *s* of William Henry Cork and Maud Alice (*née* Nunn); *m* 1937, Nina Lippold; one *s* one *d. Educ:* Berkhamsted. ACA 1937, FCA 1946. Enlisted HAC, 1938; called up, 1939; served in North Africa and Italy, 1939–45 (rank Lt-Col). Common Councilman, City of London, 1951–70; Alderman, City of London (Ward of Tower), 1970; Sheriff, City of London, 1975–76; Liveryman, Worshipful Co. of Horners (Mem. Court, 1970, Renter Warden, 1978, Master, 1980); Master, Worshipful Co. of Chartered Accountants in England and Wales, 1984–85 (Sen. Warden, 1983–84). One of HM Lieutenants, City of London, 1979–. Chairman: EEC Bankruptcy Convention Adv. Cttee to Dept Trade, 1973; Insolvency Law Review Cttee, 1977–82. Chairman: NI Finance Corpn, 1974–76; NI Develt Agency, 1976–77, Hon. Consultant, 1977–. Mem., Cttee to Review the Functioning of Financial Institutions, 1977–. President: Inst. of Credit Management Ltd; City Branch, Inst. of Dirs, 1981–. Vice-Chm., Arts Council of GB, 1986– (Mem., 1985–); Chm., Arts Council Enquiry into Professional Theatre in England, 1986–; Governor, Royal Shakespeare Theatre, 1967– (Chm., 1975–85); Dir, Shakespeare Theatre Trust (Chm. 1967–75). Treas., Royal Concert, 1970. Hon. Appeals Patron, Nat. Assoc. of Youth Clubs. Chm. of Governors, Berkhamsted Sch. FRSA 1970; FICM; CBIM 1979 (Pres., S Bucks Br.); FCIS 1979; FInstD. Hon. DLitt City Univ., 1978. Hon. GSM. KStJ 1979. Commandeur de l'Ordre du Merite (France); Order of Rio Branco, cl. III (Brazil); Grande Oficiàl da Ordem Militaire de Cristo (Portugal); Order of Diplomatic Service Merit Gwanghwa Medal (Korea). *Recreations:* sailing, photography, painting. *Address:* Cherry Trees, Grimms Lane, Great Missenden, Bucks. *T:* Great Missenden 2628. *Clubs:* Athenæum; Royal Thames Yacht, City Livery, Little Ship; Bosham Sailing, Itchenor Sailing.

CORKERY, Michael; QC 1981; *b* 20 May 1926; *o s* of late Charles Timothy Corkery and of Nellie Marie Corkery; *m* 1967, Juliet Shore Foulkes, *o d* of late Harold Glyn Foulkes; one *s* one *d. Educ:* The King's Sch., Canterbury. Commissioned in Welsh Guards, 1945; served until 1948. Called to Bar, Lincoln's Inn, 1949, Bencher 1973; Mem., South Eastern Circuit; 3rd Junior Prosecuting Counsel to the Crown at the Central Criminal Court, 1959; 1st Junior Prosecuting Counsel to the Crown, 1964; 5th Senior Prosecuting

Counsel to the Crown, 1970; 3rd Sen. Prosecuting Counsel, 1971; 2nd Sen. Prosecuting Counsel, 1974; 1st Sen. Prosecuting Counsel, 1977–81. Mem., Hong Kong Bar Assoc. *Recreations:* shooting, sailing, gardening, music. *Address:* 5 Paper Buildings, Temple, EC4.

CORLETT, Clive William; Under Secretary, Board of Inland Revenue, since 1985; *b* 14 June 1938; *s* of F. William and Hanna Corlett; *m* 1964, Margaret Catherine Jones; one *s*. *Educ:* Birkenhead Sch.; Brasenose Coll., Oxford (BA PPE). Merchant Navy, 1957. Joined Inland Revenue, 1960; seconded to: Civil Service Selection Bd, 1970; HM Treasury, 1972–74 (as Private Sec. to Chancellor of Exchequer) and 1979–81. *Address:* 40 Mycenae Road, SE3. *T:* 01-858 2804.

CORLETT, Ewan Christian Brew, OBE 1985; MA, PhD; FEng 1978; Chairman and Managing Director, Burness, Corlett Group (formerly Burness, Corlett & Partners Ltd), since 1954; *b* 11 Feb. 1923; *s* of Malcolm James John and Catherine Ann Corlett; *m* 1946, Edna Lilian Büggs; three *s*. *Educ:* King William's Coll., IOM; Oxford Univ. (MA Engrg Sci.); Durham Univ. (PhD Naval Architecture). Dept of Director of Naval Construction, Admiralty, Bath, 1944–46; Tipton Engrg Co., Tipton, 1946–47; Aluminium Develt Assoc. Research Scholar, Durham Univ., 1947–50; Naval Architect, British Aluminium Co., 1950–53; Design Dir, Burness, Corlett & Partners Ltd, 1953–54. Chm. Council, RINA, 1977–79, Vice-Pres., 1971–82, Hon. Vice-Pres., 1982. Home Office Assessor (Technical Inquiries), 1959–80. Mem. Board, Nat. Maritime Inst., 1978–82; Trustee, Nat. Maritime Museum, 1974–. Mem. Court, Shipwrights' Co., 1976–, 4th Warden 1986. *Publications:* The Iron Ship, 1976; The Revolution in Merchant Shipping 1950–1980, 1980. numerous papers to learned instns. *Recreations:* sailing, painting, astronomy. *Address:* Cottimans, Port-e-Vullen, Isle of Man. *T:* Ramsey, IOM, 814009. *Club:* Manx Sailing and Cruising.

CORLETT, Gerald Lingham; Chairman, Higsons Brewery plc, since 1982; *b* 8 May 1925; *s* of Alfred Lingham Corlett and Nancy Eileen Bremner; *m* 1957, Helen Bromfield Williamson; three *s* one *d*. *Educ:* Rossall School; Aberdeen University (short war-time course). RA, 1943–47 (Lieut, Royal Indian Artillery). Higsons Brewery, 1947–. Director: Boddingtons Breweries; Midshires Building Soc. (Northern Bd); Chm., Radio City (Sound of Merseyside). *Recreation:* family. *Address:* Kirk House, Abbey Road, West Kirby, Merseyside. *T:* 051–625 5425. *Clubs:* Liverpool Racquet; West Kirby Sailing.

CORLEY, Sir Kenneth (Sholl Ferrand), Kt 1972; Chairman and Chief Executive, Joseph Lucas (Industries) Ltd, 1969–73; *b* 3 Nov. 1908; *s* of late S. W. Corley and late Mrs A. L. Corley; *m* 1937, Olwen Mary Yeoman; one *s* one *d*. *Educ:* St Bees, Cumberland. Joined Joseph Lucas Ltd, 1927; Director, 1948. Pres., Birmingham Chamber of Commerce, 1964. Governor, Royal Shakespeare Theatre; Life Governor, Birmingham Univ.; Pres., Soc. of Motor Mfrs and Traders, 1971. Chm. Governors, St Bees Sch., 1978–84. Chevalier, Légion d'Honneur, 1975. *Recreations:* fell-walking, bee-keeping, theatre. *Address:* 34 Dingle Lane, Solihull, West Midlands B91 3NG. *T:* 021–705 1597; Yewtree, Wasdale, Cumbria CA20 1EU. *T:* Wasdale 285. *Club:* Royal Automobile.

CORLEY, His Honour Michael Early Ferrand; a Circuit Judge (formerly County Court Judge), 1967–82; *b* 11 Oct. 1909; *s* of late Ferrand Edward Corley, Christian College, Madras, and Elsie Maria Corley. *Educ:* Marlborough; Oriel Coll., Oxford. Called to Bar, 1934. War Service, RNVR, 1940–46. *Publication:* At The Gates—Tomorrow, 1983. *Address:* The Old Rectory, Rectory Road, Broome, Norfolk NR35 2HU.

CORLEY, Peter Maurice Sinclair; Under Secretary, Department of Trade and Industry, since 1981; *b* 15 June 1933; *s* of Rev. James Maurice Corley, MLitt and Mrs Barbara Shearer Corley; *m* 1961, Dr Marjorie Constance Doddridge; two *d*. *Educ:* Marlborough Coll.; King's Coll., Cambridge (MA). Min. of Power, 1957–61; Min. of Transport, 1961–65; BoT, 1965–69; Commercial Sec., Brussels, 1969–71; Asst Sec., DTI, 1972–75; Dir Gen., Econ. Co-operation Office, Riyadh, 1976–78; Dept of Industry, 1978–81. *Recreations:* bookbinding, astronomy. *Address:* c/o Department of Trade and Industry, 1 Victoria Street, SW1H 0ET.

CORLEY, Roger David; General Manager, Clerical, Medical and General Life Assurance Society, since 1982; *b* 13 April 1933; *s* of Thomas Arthur and Erica Trent Corley; *m* 1964, Brigitte Roeder; three *s*. *Educ:* Hymers College, Hull; Univ. of Manchester (BSc). FIA 1960. Joined Clerical Medical, 1956: Investment Manager, 1961–72; Actuary, 1972–80; Dir, 1975–; Dep. Gen. Manager and Actuary, 1980–82. Member: Council, Inst. of Actuaries, 1976– (Vice-Pres., 1985–); Council, Internat. Actuarial Assoc., 1983–; German Assoc. of Actuaries, 1975–. *Recreations:* theatre, travel, music. *Club:* Army and Navy.

CORLEY SMITH, Gerard Thomas, CMG 1952; HM Diplomatic Service, retired; *b* 30 July 1909; *s* of late Thomas and Nina Smith; *m* 1937, Joan Haggard (*d* 1984); one *s* three *d* *Educ:* Bolton Sch.; Emmanuel Coll., Cambridge. Gen. Consular Service, 1931; has served in Paris, Oran, Detroit, La Paz, Milan, St Louis, New York, Brussels, and at various times in the Foreign Office. Became 1st Sec. and Consul, on appt as Labour Attaché to Embassy in Brussels 1945; Counsellor UK Deleg. to UNO at New York and UK Alternate Rep. on UN Economic and Social Council, 1949–52; Press Counsellor, Brit. Embassy, Paris, 1952–54; Labour Counsellor, Brit. Embassy, Madrid, 1954–59; British Ambassador: to Haiti, 1960–62; to Ecuador, 1962–67. Sec. Gen., Charles Darwin Foundn for the Galapagos Islands, 1972–82. Grand Officer, Order of Merit (Ecuador), 1980. *Recreations:* music, mountains, birds. *Address:* Greensted Hall, Chipping Ongar, Essex. *Club:* Travellers'.

CORMACK, Prof. Allan MacLeod; University Professor, Tufts University, since 1980; *b* 23 Feb. 1924; *s* of George Cormack and Amelia MacLeod; *m* 1950, Barbara Jeanne Seavey; one *s* two *d*. *Educ:* Univ. of Cape Town (BSc, MSc). Research Student, St John's Coll., Cambridge. Lecturer, Univ. of Cape Town, 1950–56; Research Fellow, Harvard Univ., 1956–57; Tufts University: Asst Prof., 1957–60; Associate Prof., 1960–64; Prof. of Physics, 1964–80; Chairman, Physics Dept, 1968–76. Nelson Medical Lectr, Univ. of Calif, Davis, 1985; Watkins Vis. Prof., Wichita State Univ., 1986. Fellow, Amer. Physical Soc., 1964; Fellow, Amer. Acad. of Arts and Sciences, 1980; Mem., Nat. Acad. of Sciences, 1983; Hon. Member: Swedish Neuroradiological Soc., 1979; S African Inst. of Physics, 1985; Foreign Fellow, Royal Soc. of S Africa, 1983. Hon. DSc Tufts Univ., 1980. Ballou Medallist, Tufts Univ., 1978; Medal of Merit, Univ. of Cape Town, 1980; Mike Hogg Medallist, Univ. of Texas, 1981. Nobel Prize for Medicine (jtly), 1979. *Publications:* articles on nuclear and particle physics, and computed tomography. *Address:* 18 Harrison Street, Winchester, Mass 01890, USA. *T:* 617–729–0735.

CORMACK, John, CB 1982; Assistant Director, Parliamentary and Law, Institute of Chartered Accountants of Scotland, since 1984; Fisheries Secretary, Department of Agriculture and Fisheries for Scotland, 1976–82; *b* 27 Aug. 1922; *yr s* of late Donald Cormack and Anne Hunter Cormack (*née* Gair); *m* 1947, Jessie Margaret Bain; one *s* one *d* (and one *d* decd). *Educ:* Royal High Sch., Edinburgh. Served RAPC, 1941–46; Captain and Command Cashier, CMF, 1946. Entered Department of Agriculture for Scotland, 1939: Principal, 1959; Private Sec. to Sec. of State for Scotland, 1967–69; Asst Sec., 1969; Under Sec., 1976. *Recreations:* golf, music. *Address:* 57 Craigmount Avenue North, Edinburgh EH12 8DN. *T:* 031–339 5420. *Club:* Royal Commonwealth Society.

CORMACK, Sir Magnus (Cameron), KBE 1970; *b* Caithness, Scotland, 12 Feb. 1906; *s* of William Petrie Cormack and Violet McDonald Cameron; *m* 1935, Mary Gordon Macmeiken; one *s* three *d*. *Educ:* St Peter's Sch., Adelaide, S Aust. Farmer and Grazier. Served War, 1940–44; Aust. Imperial Forces, SW Pacific Area, Major. Pres., Liberal Party Organisation, 1947–49; Senator for Victoria, 1951–53 and 1962–78; President of the Senate, 1971–74. *Recreation:* deep sea sailing. *Address:* 7 Market Court, Portland, Victoria 3305, Australia. *Club:* Australian (Melbourne).

CORMACK, Patrick Thomas; MP (C) Staffordshire South, since 1983 (Cannock, 1970–74; Staffordshire South West, 1974–83); *b* 18 May 1939; *s* of Thomas Charles and Kathleen Mary Cormack, Grimsby; *m* 1967, Kathleen Mary McDonald; two *s*. *Educ:* St James' Choir School and Havelock School, Grimsby; Univ. of Hull. Second Master, St James' Choir School, Grimsby, 1961–66; Company Education and Training Officer, Ross Group Ltd, Grimsby, 1966–67; Assistant Housemaster, Wrekin College, Shropshire, 1967–69; Head of History, Brewood Grammar School, Stafford, 1969–70. Vis. Lectr, Univ. of Texas, 1984. Dir, Historic House Hotels Ltd; Chairman: Aitken Dott Ltd, 1983–; The Scottish Gallery. Trustee, Historic Churches Preservation Trust, 1972–; Pres., Staffs Historic Buildings Trust, 1983–; Member: Historic Buildings Council, 1979–84; Cons. Party Arts and Heritage Cttee, 1979–84 (Chm.); Select Cttee on Educn, Science and Arts, 1979–84; Faculty Jurisdiction Commn, 1979–84; All Party Heritage Cttee (Chm.); Heritage in Danger (Vice-Chm.); Council for British archaeology; Royal Commn on Historical Manuscripts; Council for Independent Educn (Chm.); Lord Chancellor's Adv. Cttee on Public Records, 1979–84; Council, Georgian Gp, 1985–; Council, Winston Churchill Meml Trust, 1983–. Chm. Editorial Bd, Parliamentary Publications. FSA 1978. Rector's Warden, St Margaret's Church, Westminster, 1978–. Mem., Worshipful Co. of Glaziers; Freeman, City of London, 1979. Hon. Citizen of Texas, 1985. *Publications:* Heritage in Danger, 1976; Right Turn, 1978; Westminster: Palace and Parliament, 1981; Castles of Britain, 1982; Wilberforce—the Nation's Conscience, 1983; Cathedrals of England, 1984. *Recreations:* fighting philistines, walking, visiting old churches, avoiding sitting on fences. *Address:* House of Commons, SW1A 0AA. *Clubs:* Athenæum, Brooks's.

CORMACK, Robert Linklater Burke; HM Diplomatic Service; Head of Information Technology Department, Foreign and Commonwealth Office, since 1985; *b* 29 Aug. 1935; *s* of late Frederick Eunson Cormack, CIE, and Elspeth Mary (*née* Linklater), Dounby, Orkney; *m* 1962, Eivor Dorotea Kumlin; one *s* two *d*. *Educ:* Trinity Coll., Glenalmond; Trinity Hall, Cambridge (BA Agric.). National Service, The Black Watch, 1954–56. Dist Officer, Kenya (HMOCS), 1960–64; entered CRO (subseq. Diplomatic Service), 1964: Private Sec. to Minister of State, 1964–66; 1st Secretary: Saigon, 1966–68; Bombay, 1969–70; Delhi, 1970–72; FCO, 1972–77; Counsellor and Consul-Gen., Kinshasa, 1977–79; RCDS, 1980; Counsellor (Economic and Commercial), Stockholm, 1981–85. *Address:* c/o Foreign and Commonwealth Office, SW1.

CORNBERG, Mrs Sol; *see* Gaskin, Catherine.

CORNELIUS, David Frederick, FInstP; Deputy Director, Transport and Road Research Laboratory, Crowthorne, since 1984; *b* 7 May 1932; *s* of Frederick M. N. and Florence K. Cornelius; *m* 1956, Susan (*née* Austin); two *s* two *d*. *Educ:* Teignmouth Grammar Sch.; Exeter University Coll. (BSc (Hons) Physics). Royal Naval Scientific Service, 1953–58; UKAEA, 1958–64; Research Manager, Road Research Laboratory, 1964–72; Asst Director, Building Research Estabt, 1973–78; Head, Research, Transport and Special Programmes, 1978–80, Transport Science Policy Unit, 1980–82, Dept of Transport; Asst Dir, Transport and Road Res. Lab., 1982–84. *Publications:* scientific papers to nat. and internat. confs and in jls of various professional instns on range of topics in tribology and highway transportation. *Recreations:* swimming, cycling, youth work, antiques. *Address:* Transport and Road Research Laboratory, Old Wokingham Road, Crowthorne, Berkshire. *T:* Crowthorne 773131, ext. 2003. *Club:* Civil Service.

CORNELL, Ward MacLaurin; Deputy Minister, Ministry of Housing, Province of Ontario, since 1980; *b* London, Ont, 4 May 1924; *m* Georgina Saxon; three *s* two *d*. *Educ:* Pickering Coll.; Univ. of Western Ontario. Lectr in English and History, Pickering Coll., Ont, 1949–54; Vis. Lectr, Conestoga Coll.; Gen. Manager, Broadcast Div. (Radio), Free Press Printing Co., 1954–67; Pres., Creative Projects in Communications, 1967–72; Agent-Gen. for Ont. in UK, 1972–78; Gen. Manager, European Ops, Lenroc Internat. Ltd, 1978–80; Dep. Minister, Min. of Citizenship and Culture, Province of Ontario, 1980–82. *Recreations:* reading, tennis, travelling. *Address:* RR1, Uxbridge, Ontario, Canada.

CORNER, Edred John Henry, CBE 1972; FRS 1955; FLS; Professor of Tropical Botany, University of Cambridge, 1966–73, now Emeritus; *b* 12 Jan. 1906; *s* of late Edred Moss Corner and Henrietta Corner (*née* Henderson); *m* 1953, Helga Dinesen Sondergoord; one *s* two *d* (by 1st *m*). *Educ:* Rugby Sch. Asst Dir, Gardens Dept, Straits Settlements, 1929–45; Principal Field Scientific Officer, Latin America, Unesco, 1947–48; Lecturer in Botany, Cambridge, 1949–59; Reader in Plant Taxonomy, 1959–65; Fellow, Sidney Sussex Coll., Cambridge, 1959–73. Member: American Mycological Soc.; Brit. Mycological Soc.; French Mycological Soc.; Fellow, American Assoc. for the Advancement of Science; Corr. Member: Botanical Soc. of America; Royal Netherlands Botanical Soc.; Hon. Mem., Japanese Mycological Soc. Mem., Governing Body of Rugby Sch., 1959–75. Darwin Medal, Royal Soc., 1960; Patron's Medal, RGS, 1966; Gold Medal, Linnean Soc. of London, 1970; Victoria Medal of Honour, RHS, 1974; Allerton Award, Pacific Tropical Botanical Garden, Hawaii, 1981; Internat. Prize for Biology, Japan Acad., 1985. *Publications:* Wayside Trees of Malaya (2 vols), 1940 and 1952; A Monograph of Clavaria and allied genera, 1950; Life of Plants, 1964; Natural History of Palms, 1966; Monograph of Cantharelloid Fungi, 1966; Boletus in Malaysia, 1972; Seeds of Dicotyledons, 2 vols, 1976; The Marquis: a tale of Syonan-to, 1981. *Address:* 91 Hinton Way, Great Shelford, Cambs CB2 5AH. *T:* Shelford 842167.

CORNER, Frank Henry, CMG 1980; retired New Zealand Civil Servant and Diplomat; *b* 17 May 1920; *y s* of Charles William Corner, Napier, NZ, and Sybil Corner (*née* Smith); *m* 1943, Lynette Robinson; two *d*. *Educ:* Napier Boys' High Sch.; Victoria Univ. of Wellington. MA, 1st cl. History; James Macintosh and Post-graduate Scholar. External Affairs Dept, NZ, and War Cabinet Secretariat, 1943; 1st Sec., NZ Embassy, Washington, 1948–51; Sen. Counsellor, NZ High Commn, London, 1952–58; Dep. Sec. NZ Dept of External Affairs, 1958–62; Perm. Rep. (Ambassador) to UN, 1962–67; Ambassador of NZ to USA, 1967–72; Permanent Head of Prime Minister's Dept, 1973–75; Secretary of Foreign Affairs, 1973–80; Administrator of Tokelau, 1976–85. Chm., NZ Defence Cttee of Enquiry, 1985–86. Mem., NZ Delegn to Commonwealth Prime Ministers' Meetings, 1944, 1946, 1951–57, 1973, 1975, 1977, 1979; Deleg. to UN Gen. Assembly, 1949–52, 1955, 1960–68, 1973, 1974; NZ Rep. to UN Trusteeship Council, 1962–66 (Pres., 1965–66; Chm., UN Vis. Mission to Micronesia, 1964); NZ Rep. on UN Security Coun., 1966; Adviser, NZ Delegn: Paris Peace Conf., 1946; Geneva Conf. on Korea, 1954;

numerous other internat. confs as adviser or delegate. Mem., Bd of NZ-US Educnl Foundn, 1980–; Patron, Assoc. of NZ Art Socs, 1973–; Mem. Council, Victoria Univ. of Wellington, 1981–. FRSA. *Recreations:* the arts, gardening, wine. *Address:* 26 Burnell Avenue, Wellington 1, NZ. *T:* 737–022; 29 Kakariki Grove, Waikanae. *T:* 36235.

CORNER, Philip; Director General of Quality Assurance, Ministry of Defence Procurement Executive, 1975–84, retired; Chairman, Institute of Quality Assurance's Management Board (for qualification and registration scheme for lead assessors of quality assurance management system), since 1984; *b* 7 Aug. 1924; *s* of late William Henry Corner and of Dora (*née* Smailes); *m* 1st 1948, Nora Pipes (*d* 1984); no *c*; 2nd, 1985, Paula Mason. *Educ:* Dame Allan's Boys' Sch., Newcastle upon Tyne; Bradford Technical Coll.; RNEC Manadon; Battersea Polytechnic. BScEng (London); CEng, MIMechE, MIEE; Hon. FIQA. Short Bros (Aeronautical Engrs), 1942–43; Air Br., RN, Sub-Lieut RNVR, 1944–46; LNER Co., 1946–47; Min. of Works, 1947–50; Min. of Supply, 1950; Ministry of Defence: Dir of Guided Weapons Prodn, 1968–72; Dir of Quality Assurance (Technical), 1972–75. Member: Metrology and Standards Requirements Bd, DoI, 1974–84; Adv. Council for Calibration and Measurement, DoI, 1975–84; BSI Quality Assurance Council, 1979–84; BSI Bd, 1980–84. *Recreations:* gardening, listening to music, building and flying radio controlled model aircraft. *Address:* 3 The Green, Dyke Road, Hove, E Sussex BN3 6TH.

CORNESS, Sir Colin Ross, Kt 1986; Chairman, Redland PLC, since 1977 (Managing Director, 1967–82); *b* 9 Oct. 1931; *s* of Thomas Corness and Mary Evlyne Corness. *Educ:* Uppingham Sch.; Magdalene Coll., Cambridge (BA 1954, MA 1958); Graduate Sch. of Business Admin, Harvard, USA (Advanced Management Program Dip. 1970). Called to the Bar, Inner Temple, 1956. Dir, Taylor Woodrow Construction Ltd, 1961–64; Man. Dir, Redland Tiles Ltd, 1965–70. Director: Chubb & Son Ltd, 1974–84 (Dep. Chm., 1984); W. H. Smith and Son Ltd, 1980–; Giroflex Ltd, 1985–; Courtaulds PLC, 1986–. Chm., Building Centre, 1974–77; Pres., Nat. Council of Building Material Producers, 1985–; Member: EDC for Building, 1980–84; Industrial Develt Adv. Bd, 1982–84. *Recreations:* squash rackets, travel, music. *Address:* Redland House, Reigate, Surrey RH2 0SJ. *T:* Reigate 42488. *Clubs:* White's; Australian (Sydney).

CORNFORD, Sir (Edward) Clifford, KCB 1977 (CB 1966); FEng 1980; Member, Post Office Board, since 1981; Chairman, Raytheon Europe Ltd, since 1985; *b* 6 Feb. 1918; *s* of John Herbert Cornford; *m* 1945, Catherine Muir; three *s* three *d*. *Educ:* Kimbolton Sch.; Jesus Coll., Cambridge (BA). Joined RAE, 1938. Operational Research with RAF, 1939–45. Guided Weapons Res. at RAE, 1945–60; jssc 1951; Head of Guided Weapons Dept, RAE, 1956–61; Min. of Defence: Chm., Def. Res. Policy Staff, 1961–63; Asst Chief Scientific Adviser, 1963–64; Chief Scientist (Army), Mem. Army Board, Ministry of Defence, 1965–67; Chm. Programme Evaluation Group, MoD, 1967–Jan. 1968 Dep. Chief Adviser (Research and Studies), MoD, 1968–69; Controller of Guided Weapons and Electronics, Min. of Technology, later Min. of Aviation Supply and MoD (Procurement Executive), 1969–72; Ministry of Defence (PE): Controller (Policy), 1972–74; Dep. Chief Exec., 1974–75; Chief Exec. and Permanent Under Sec. of State, 1975–77; Chief of Defence Procurement, MoD, 1977–80. FRAeS. *Publications:* on aeronautical subjects in jls of learned socs and technical publications. *Recreation:* travelling. *Address:* Beechurst, Shaftesbury Road, Woking, Surrey. *T:* 68919. *Club:* Athenæum.

CORNFORD, James Peters; Director, Nuffield Foundation, since 1980; *b* 1935; *s* of John Cornford and Rachel Peters; *m* 1960, Avery Amanda Goodfellow; one *s* three *d*. *Educ:* Winchester Coll.; Trinity Coll., Cambridge (MA). Fellow, Trinity Coll., Cambridge, 1960–64; Harkness Fellow, 1961–62; Univ. of Edinburgh: Lectr in Politics, 1964–68; Prof. of Politics, 1968–76; Dir, Outer Circle Policy Unit, 1976–80. Vis. Fellow, All Souls Coll., Oxford, 1975–76; Vis. Prof., Birkbeck Coll., Univ. of London, 1977–80. Mem., Cttee of Inquiry into Educn of Children from Ethnic Minority Gps (DES), 1981–85. Dir, Job Ownership Ltd, 1979–. Chairman of Council: RIPA, 1984–85; Campaign for Freedom of Information, 1984–. Literary Editor, The Political Quarterly, 1976–. *Publications:* contrib.: Cleavages, Ideologies and Party Systems, ed Allardt and Littunen, 1965; Ideas and Institutions of Victorian Britain, ed Robson, 1967; International Guide to Election Statistics, ed Meyriat and Rokkan, 1969; Government and Nationalism in Scotland, ed Wolfe, 1969; Mass Politics, ed Rokkan and Allardt, 1970; Philosophy, Politics and Society IV, ed Laslett, Runciman and Skinner, 1972; (ed) The Failure of the State, 1975; (ed) William Stubbs, The Constitutional History of England, 1979; contrib. to jls. *Address:* The Brick House, Wicken Bonhunt, Saffron Walden, Essex CB11 3UG. *T:* Saffron Walden 40348.

CORNFORTH, Sir John (Warcup), Kt 1977; CBE 1972; FRS 1953; DPhil; Royal Society Research Professor, University of Sussex, 1975–82, now Emeritus; *b* 7 Sept. 1917; *er s* of J. W. Cornforth, Sydney, Aust.; *m* 1941, Rita, *d* of W. C. Harradence; one *s* two *d*. *Educ:* Sydney High Sch.; Universities of Sydney and Oxford. BSc Sydney 1937; MSc Sydney, 1938; 1851 Exhibition Overseas Scholarship, 1939–42; DPhil Oxford, 1941; scientific staff of Med. Research Coun., 1946–62; Dir, Shell Research, Milstead Lab. of Chem. Enzymology, 1962–75. Assoc. Prof. in Molecular Sciences, Univ. of Warwick, 1965–71; Vis. Prof., Univ. of Sussex, 1971–75; Hon. Prof., Beijing Med. Univ., 1986–. Lectures: Pedler, Chem. Soc., 1968–69; Max Tishler, Harvard Univ., 1970; Robert Robinson, Chem. Soc., 1971–72; Sandin, Univ. of Alberta, 1977. For. Hon. Mem., Amer. Acad., 1973; Corresp. Mem., Aust. Acad., 1977; For. Associate, US Nat. Acad. of Scis, 1978; For. Mem., Royal Netherlands Acad. of Scis, 1978. Hon. Fellow, St Catherine's Coll., Oxford, 1976; Hon. DSc: ETH Zürich, 1975; Oxford, Warwick, Dublin, Liverpool, 1976; Aberdeen, Hull, Sussex, Sydney, 1977. Corday-Morgan Medal and Prize, Chem. Soc., 1953; (with G. J. Popjak) CIBA Medal, Biochem. Soc., 1965; Flintoff Medal, Chem. Soc., 1966; Stouffer Prize, 1967; Ernest Guenther Award, Amer. Chem. Soc., 1969; (with G. J. Popjak) Davy Medal, Royal Soc., 1968; Prix Roussel, 1972; (jtly) Nobel Prize for Chemistry, 1975; Royal Medal, Royal Soc., 1976; Copley Medal, Royal Soc., 1982. Has been deaf since boyhood. *Publications:* numerous papers on organic chemical and biochemical subjects. *Recreations:* lawn tennis, chess, gardening. *Address:* Saxon Down, Cuilfail, Lewes, East Sussex BN7 2BE.

CORNISH, Francis; *see* Cornish, R. F.

CORNISH, Jack Bertram; HM Civil Service; Under-Secretary, Department of Health and Social Security, 1976–78; *b* 26 June 1918; *s* of Bertram George John Cornish and Nora Jarmy; *m* 1946, Mary Milton; three *d*. *Educ:* Price's Grammar Sch., Fareham; Cotham Grammar Sch., Bristol. Admiralty, 1937–61: London, Bath, Plymouth, Singapore; DHSS, 1961–78. Supply Ships in Singapore and Newfoundland, 1941 and 1942. *Recreations:* music, painting, gardening. *Address:* 13 Kingsley Road, Kingsbridge, South Devon. *T:* Kingsbridge 2585.

CORNISH, James Easton; Manager, International Department, Phillips & Drew, since 1982; *b* 5 Aug. 1939; *s* of Eric Easton Cornish and Ivie Hedworth (*née* McCulloch); *m* 1968, Ursula Pink; one *s*. *Educ:* Eton Coll.; Wadham Coll., Oxford (BA); Harvard. Joined FO, 1961; Bonn, 1963; British Mil. Govt, Berlin, 1965; FCO, 1968; Washington, 1973; Dep. Head of Planning Staff, FCO, 1977; Central Policy Rev. Staff, 1980; seconded to Phillips & Drew, 1982; resigned HM Diplomatic Service, 1985. *Address:* c/o Phillips & Drew, 120 Moorgate, EC2.

CORNISH, (Robert) Francis, LVO 1978; HM Diplomatic Service; Counsellor (Information), Washington, and Director, British Information Service, New York, since 1986; *b* 18 May 1942; *s* of Mr and Mrs C. D. Cornish; *m* 1964, Alison Jane Dundas; three *d*. *Educ:* Charterhouse; RMA Sandhurst. Commissioned 14th/20th King's Hussars, 1962–68; HM Diplomatic Service 1968; served Kuala Lumpur, Jakarta and FCO, 1969–76; First Sec., Bonn, 1976–80; Asst Private Sec. to HRH the Prince of Wales, 1980–83; High Comr, Brunei Darussalam, 1983–86. *Address:* c/o Foreign and Commonwealth Office, SW1; 28 Embercourt Road, Thames Ditton, Surrey. *T:* 01–398 6080. *Club:* Cavalry and Guards.

CORNISH, William Herbert, CB 1955; Receiver for the Metropolitan Police District, 1961–67; *b* 2 Jan. 1906; *s* of late Rev. Herbert H. Cornish and Susan Emerson; *m* 1938, Eileen May Elizabeth Cooney; two *d*. *Educ:* Wesley Coll., Dublin; Trinity Coll., Dublin. Scholar, 1st Cl. Moderator with Large Gold Medal in Modern History and Political Science. Entered Home Office, 1930; Asst Sec., 1942; Asst Under-Sec. of State, 1952–60. *Recreations:* gardening and music. *Address:* 2 Tormead, Dene Road, Northwood, Mddx. *T:* Northwood 21933.

CORNISH, Prof. William Rodolph, FBA 1984; Professor of English Law, London School of Economics, University of London, since 1970; *b* 9 Aug. 1937; *s* of Jack R. and Elizabeth E. Cornish, Adelaide, S Australia; *m* 1964, Lovedy E. Moule; one *s* two *d*. *Educ:* Univs of Adelaide (LLB) and Oxford (BCL). Lectr in Law, LSE, 1962–68; Reader in Law, Queen Mary Coll., London, 1969–70. *Publications:* The Jury, 1968; (Jt Editor) Sutton and Shannon on Contracts, 1970; (jtly) Encyclopedia of United Kingdom and European Patent Law, 1977; Intellectual Property, 1982; articles etc in legal periodicals. *Address:* 74 Palace Road, SW2.

CORNOCK, Maj.-Gen. Archibald Rae, CB 1975; OBE 1968; FBIM; Chairman, London Electricity Consultative Council, 1980; *b* 4 May 1920; *s* of Matthew Cornock and Mrs Mary Munro MacRae; *m* 1951, Dorothy Margaret Cecilia; two *d*. *Educ:* Coatbridge. MBIM 1965. NW Frontier, 1940–42; Burma, 1942–43; transf. Royal Indian Navy, 1943; Burma (Arakan), 1944–46; Gordon Highlanders, 1947–50; transf. RAOC, 1950; psc 1954; GSO2 Intelligence, 1955–57; DAQMG Northern Army Gp, 1959–61; comd 16 Bn RAOC, 1961–64; SEATO Planning Staff, Bangkok, 1964; Defence Attaché, Budapest, 1965–67; Comdt 15 Base Ordnance Depot, 1967; DDOS Strategic Comd, 1968–70; Brig. Q (Maint.), MoD, 1970–72; Dir of Clothing Procurement, 1972; Dir of Army Quartering, 1973–75. Col Comdt, RAOC, 1976–80. Chm., Army Athletic Assoc., 1968–75; Mem. Council, Back Pain Assoc., 1979–. *Recreations:* sailing, opera, languages, golf. *Address:* 20 Claremont, St Johns Avenue, Putney Hill, SW15 2AB. *T:* 01–789 5892. *Clubs:* Royal Thames Yacht, Army and Navy; Highland Brigade.

CORNOCK, Maj-Gen. Charles Gordon, MBE 1974; Chief of Staff and Head of UK Delegation, Live Oak, SHAPE, since 1986; *b* 25 April 1935; *s* of Gordon Wallace Cornock and Edith Mary (née Keeley); *m* 1963, Kay Smith; two *s*. *Educ:* King Alfred Sch., Plön, Germany; RMA, Sandhurst. Commnd RA, 1956; served, 1957–71: 33 Para Lt Regt; 1 RHA; RMA, Sandhurst; Staff Coll., Camberley; BMRA; Armed Forces Staff Coll., Norfolk, Va; Second in Comd, 1972–74 and CO 1974–76, 7 Para RHA; GSO1 DS Staff Coll., Camberley, 1977–78; Col GS HQ UKLF, 1979; CRA 3rd Armoured Div., 1980–81; RCDS, 1982; Dep. Comdt, Staff Coll., Camberley, 1983; Dir, RA, 1984–86. Col Comdt RA, 1986–. *Recreations:* hockey, tennis, golf, skiing, water skiing. *Address:* Midland Bank plc, 18 Alexandra Road, Farnborough, Hants. *Club:* La Moye Golf (Jersey).

CORNWALL, Archdeacon of; *see* Wood, Ven. Arnold.

CORNWALL, Ian Wolfran, PhD London; Reader in Human Environment, University of London, 1965–74; *b* 28 Nov. 1909; *s* of Lt-Col J. W. Cornwall, CIE, IMS, and Effie E. C. (*née* Sinclair), *d* of Surg.-Gen. D. Sinclair, IMS; *m* 1st, 1937, Anna Margareta (*née* Callear) (*d* 1967); two *s*; 2nd, 1974, Mary L. Reynolds (*née* Miller). *Educ:* private sch.; Wellington Coll., Berks; St John's Coll., Cambridge (BA). Teaching, clerking, pharmaceutical manufacturing, selling, 1931–39; Postal and Telegraph Censorship, Press Censorship, MOI, 1939–45. London Univ. Inst. of Archaeology: Student, 1945–47 (Diploma, 1947); Secretary, 1948–51. University teacher and researcher, 1951–74, retd. (PhD London, 1952). Life Mem., Geologists' Assoc. Henry Stopes Memorial Medal, Geologists' Assoc., 1970. *Publications:* Bones for the Archaeologist, 1956, rev. edn 1975; Soils for the Archaeologist, 1958; The Making of Man, 1960 (Carnegie Medal of Library Assoc.); The World of Ancient Man, 1964; Hunter's Half Moon (fiction), 1967; Prehistoric Animals and their Hunters, 1968; Ice Ages, 1970. Contribs to specialist jls. *Recreations:* geology, gardening, photography. *Address:* Newlands, Cornworthy, Totnes, Devon TQ9 7ES.

CORNWALL-LEGH, C. L. S.; *see* Legh.

CORNWALLIS, family name of **Baron Cornwallis.**

CORNWALLIS, 3rd Baron *cr* 1927, of Linton, Kent; **Fiennes Neil Wykeham Cornwallis,** OBE 1963; DL; *b* 29 June 1921; *s* of 2nd Baron Cornwallis, KCVO, KBE, MC, and Cecily Etha Mary (*d* 1943), *d* of Sir James Walker, 3rd Bt; *S* father, 1982; *m* 1st, 1942, Judith Lacy Scott (marr. diss. 1948); one *s* (one *d* decd); 2nd, 1951, Agnes Jean Russell Landale; one *s* three *d*. *Educ:* Eton. Served War, Coldstream Guards, 1940–44. Pres., British Agricultural Contractors Assoc., 1952–54; Pres., Nat. Assoc. of Agricultural Contractors, 1957–63 and 1986–; Vice-Pres., Fedn of Agricl Co-operatives, 1984–86; Chm., Smaller Firms Council, CBI, 1978–81. Representative, Horticultural Co-operatives in the EEC, 1974–. Director: Checkers Ltd; Checkers Growers Ltd; Town & Country Building Soc.(formerly Planet, then Magnet & Planet, Bld Soc.) 1967– (Chm., 1973–75; Dep. Chm., 1975–77; Chm., 1978–81). Admin. Trustee, Chevening Estate, 1979–. Fellow, Inst. of Horticulture, 1986. Pro Grand Master, United Grand Lodge of England, 1982–. DL Kent, 1976. *Recreation:* fishing. *Heir:* *s* Hon. (Fiennes Wykeham) Jeremy Cornwallis [*b* 25 May 1946; *m* 1969, Sara Gray de Neufville, *d* of Lt-Col Nigel Stockwell, Benenden, Kent; two *d*]. *Address:* Ruck Farm, Horsmonden, Tonbridge, Kent TN12 8DT. *T:* Brenchley 2267; 25B Queen's Gate Mews, SW7. *T:* 01–589 1167. *Clubs:* Brooks's, Farmers'.

CORNWELL, David John Moore, (John le Carré); writer; *b* 19 Oct. 1931; *s* of Ronald Thomas Archibald Cornwell and Olive (*née* Glassy); *m* 1954, Alison Ann Veronica Sharp (marr. diss. 1971); three *s*; *m* 1972, Valerie Jane Eustace; one *s*. *Educ:* Sherborne; Berne Univ.; Lincoln Coll., Oxford (1st cl. Modern Languages; Hon. Fellow 1984). Taught at Eton, 1956–58. Mem. of HM Foreign Service, 1960–64. *Publications:* Call for the Dead, 1961 (filmed as The Deadly Affair, 1967); A Murder of Quality, 1962; The Spy Who Came in from the Cold, 1963 (Somerset Maugham Award; Crime Writers' Assoc. Gold Dagger) (filmed); The Looking-Glass War, 1965 (filmed); A Small Town in Germany, 1968; The Naïve and Sentimental Lover, 1971; Tinker, Tailor, Soldier, Spy, 1974 (televised 1979); The Honourable Schoolboy, 1977 (James Tait Black Meml Prize; Crime

Writers' Assoc. Gold Dagger); Smiley's People, 1980 (televised 1982); The Little Drummer Girl, 1983 (filmed 1985); A Perfect Spy, 1986. *Address:* John Farquharson Ltd, 162–168 Regent Street, W1R 5TB.

CORNWELL, Roger Eliot, FCA; Chairman, Louis Dreyfus & Co. Ltd, since 1982 (Director since 1978); *b* 5 Feb. 1922; *s* of Harold and Kathleen Cornwell. *Educ:* St Albans Sch.; Jesus Coll., Oxford (MA). FCA 1976. *Address:* 42 Brompton Square, SW3 2AF.

CORREA, Charles Mark; Padma Shri, 1972; architect; *b* 1 Sept. 1930; *s* of Carlos M. Correa and Ana Florinda de Heredia; *m* 1961, Monika Sequeira; one *s* one *d*. *Educ:* Univ. of Michigan (BArch); MIT (MArch). Private practice, Bombay, 1958–; work includes: Mahatma Gandhi Memorial, Sabarmati Ashram; State Assembly for Madhya Pradesh; low cost housing projects in Delhi, Bombay, Ahmedabad and other cities in India; Chief Architect for planning of New Bombay; Founder Mem., Steering Cttee, Aga Khan Award for Architecture, 1977–. Jawaharlal Nehru Vis. Prof. and Fellow of Churchill Coll., Cambridge, 1985–86. Hon. FAIA 1979. Hon. Dr Univ. of Michigan, 1980. Royal Gold Medal for Architecture, RIBA, 1984. *Relevant publication:* S. Cantacuzino, Charles Correa, 1984. *Recreations:* tennis, model trains, chess. *Address:* 9 Mathew Road, Bombay 400004, India. *T:* 384858/384714. *Clubs:* Bombay Gymkhana, United Services (Bombay); Bangalore (Bangalore).

CORRIE, John Alexander; MP (C) Cunninghame North, since 1983 (Bute and North Ayr, Feb. 1974–1983); *b* 29 July 1935; *s* of John Corrie and Helen Brown; *m* 1965, Jean Sandra Hardie; one *s* two *d*. *Educ:* Kirkcudbright Acad.; George Watson's Coll.; Lincoln Agric. Coll., NZ. Farmed in NZ, 1955–59, in Selkirk, 1959–65 and in Kirkcudbright, 1965–. Lectr for British Wool Marketing Bd and Agric. Trng Bd, 1966–74; Mem. Cttee, National Farmers Union, 1964–74 (Vice-Chm. Apprenticeship Council, 1971–74); Nuffield Scholar in Agriculture, 1972. District Officer, Rotary International, 1973–74 (Community service). Nat. Chm., Scottish Young Conservatives, 1964; contested (C) North Lanark, 1964 and Central Ayr, 1966; opposition spokesman on educn in Scotland, Oct. 1974–75; an Opposition Scottish Whip, 1975–76 (resigned over Devolution); PPS to Sec. of State for Scotland, 1979–81; Mem., Council of Europe and WEU, 1982–. Treas., Scottish Cons. Back Bench Cttee, 1980, Chm. 1981–82; Leader, Cons. Gp on Scottish Affairs, 1982–; Sec., Cons. Backbench Fish-farming Cttee, 1982–. Mem. European Parlt, 1975–76 and 1977–79 (Mem. Cttees of Agriculture, Reg. Devel and Transport). Vice-President: EEC-Turkey Cttee, 1975–76; EEC Fisheries Cttee, 1977–79; EEC Mediterranean Agricl Cttee, 1977–79; Rapporteur for EEC Fisheries Policy, 1977–78. *Publications:* (jtly) Towards a European Rural Policy, 1978; Towards a Community Forestry Policy, 1979; Fish Farming in Europe, 1979; The Importance of Forestry in the World Economy, 1980. *Recreations:* shooting, fishing, riding, tennis, golf, curling, water ski-ing, hang gliding, bridge. *Address:* Park of Tongland, Kirkcudbright, Scotland DG6 4NE; 3D Morpeth Terrace, SW1; Carlung Farm, West Kilbride, Ayrshire; House of Commons, SW1A 0AA. *T:* 01–219 3591. *Club:* Annabel's.

CORRIE, W(allace) Rodney, CB 1977; *b* 25 Nov. 1919; *o c* of late Edward and Mary Ellen Corrie; *m* 1952, Helen Margaret (*née* Morice), *widow* of Flt-Lt A. H. E. Kahn; one *s* one *d*. *Educ:* Leigh Grammar School; Christ's Coll., Cambridge (BA 1941, MA 1944). Served Royal Signals, 1940–46 (despatches). Entered Civil Service, Min. of Town and Country Planning, 1947; Min. of Housing and Local Govt, 1951; Asst Secretary, 1961; Assistant Under-Secretary of State, DEA, 1969; Under-Secretary: Min. of Housing and Local Govt, 1969; Dept of the Environment, 1970; Chm., NW Econ. Planning Bd, 1969–80, and Regl Dir (NW), DoE, 1971–80, Dept of Transport, 1976–80. *Recreations:* walking, exploring byways, catching up on things. *Address:* Brambledown, Chapel Lane, Hale Barns, Cheshire WA15 0AJ.

CORRIGAN, Thomas Stephen; Chairman: Havelock Europa plc, since 1983; Witchampton Boardmills Ltd, since 1984; Post Office Users' National Council, since 1984; *b* 2 July 1932; *s* of Thomas Corrigan and Renée Victorine Chaborel; *m* 1963, Sally Margaret Everitt; two *d*. *Educ:* Beulah Hill; Chartered Accountant (Scottish Inst.). Nat. Service, Army, 1955–57. Chief Accountant, Lobitos Oilfields, 1957–62; Exec., Keyser Ullmann, 1962–64; Inveresk Group: Finance Controller, 1964; Finance Dir, 1966; Man. Dir, 1971–74; Chm., 1971–83. Pres., British Paper and Board Industry Fedn, 1975–77; Vice-Pres., European Confedn of Pulp, Paper and Board Industries, 1982–83; Mem., NEDC (Tripartite Sector Working Party on paper industry), 1976–77; Master, Makers of Playing Cards Co., 1978–79; FRSA. *Recreations:* golf, bridge, tennis, travel. *Address:* Woodend, The Chase, Kingswood, Surrey KT20 6HZ. *T:* Mogador 832709. *Clubs:* MCC, Royal Automobile, City Livery.

CORRIGAN-MAGUIRE, Mairead; Co-Founder, Community of the Peace People; *b* 27 Jan. 1944; *d* of Andrew and Margaret Corrigan; *m* 1981, Jackie Maguire; one *s* and three step *c*. *Educ:* St Vincent's Primary Sch., Falls Road, Belfast; Miss Gordon's Commercial Coll., Belfast. Secretarial qualification. Confidential Sec. to Managing Director, A. Guinness Son & Co. (Belfast) Ltd, Brewers, Belfast. Initiator of Peace Movement in Northern Ireland, Aug. 1976; Chm., Peace People Organisation, 1980–81. Hon. Dr of Law, Yale Univ., 1976; Nobel Prize for Peace (jtly), 1976; Carl-Von-Ossietzky Medaille for Courage, Berlin, 1976. *Recreations:* voluntary community and youth work. *Address:* 224 Lisburn Road, Belfast 9, N Ireland. *T:* (business) 663465.

CORRIN, John Bowes, OBE 1983; Director, Anglia Building Society, since 1964 (Chairman, 1981–85); Partner, Grant Thornton (formerly Thornton Baker), since 1949; *b* 26 Oct. 1922; *s* of Harold R. Corrin and Mabel F. Corrin; *m* 1948, José M. Sharman; one *s* one *d*. *Educ:* Berkhampsted. FCA 1945 (Auditing Prize). Pres., Leics and Northants Soc. of Chartered Accountants, 1959; past Pres., Northampton Conservative Assoc. Mayor, Northampton, 1964–65; Hon. Freeman, Borough of Northampton, 1972. *Recreation:* golf. *Address:* Tynwald, Sandy Lane, Church Brampton, Northampton NN6 8AX. *T:* Northampton 845301. *Clubs:* Northampton County; Northamptonshire County Golf.

CORRIN, John William; HM Second Deemster, Isle of Man, since 1980; *b* 6 Jan. 1932; *s* of Evan Cain Corrin and Dorothy Mildred Corrin; *m* 1961, Dorothy Patricia, *d* of late J. S. Lace; one *d*. *Educ:* Murrays Road Primary Sch., Douglas; King William's Coll., IOM. Admitted to Manx Bar, 1954. Attorney Gen., IOM, 1974–80. Chairman (all IOM): Criminal Injuries Compensation Tribunal, 1980–; Licensing Appeal Court, 1980–; Prevention of Fraud (Unit Trust) Tribunal, 1980–; Manx Blind Welfare Soc.; Manx Workshop for the Disabled; Council, Postgrad. Med. Centre; Hon. Mem., IOM Med. Soc.; President: Island Bridge Club; Lon Dhoo Male Voice Choir; Chm., Douglas Buxton Music Trust; Trustee: Manx Foundn for Physically Disabled; Manx Methodist Church. *Recreations:* music, gardening, bridge. *Address:* Carla Beck, 28 Devonshire Road, Douglas, Isle of Man. *T:* Douglas 21806. *Club:* Ellan Vannin (Douglas) (Past Pres.).

CORRY; *see* Lowry-Corry, family name of Earl of Belmore.

CORRY, Viscount; John Armar Galbraith Lowry-Corry; *b* 2 Nov. 1985; *s* and *heir* of Earl of Belmore, *qv*.

CORRY, Sir James Perowne Ivo Myles, 3rd Bt, *cr* 1885; a Vice-President of King George's Fund for Sailors, The Royal Alfred Merchant Seamen's Society, and of Royal Merchant Navy School; *b* 10 June 1892; *s* of 2nd Bt and Charlotte, *d* of late J. Collins; *S* father, 1926; *m* 1st, 1921, Molly Irene (marr. diss., 1936), *y d* of late Major O. J. Bell; one *s* two *d*; 2nd, 1946, Cynthia, *widow* of Capt. David Polson, and *o d* of late Capt. F. H. Mahony and Mrs Francis Bliss; one *d*. *Educ:* Eton; Trinity Coll., Cambridge. *Heir:* *s* Lt-Comdr William James Corry, RN retd [*b* 1924; *m* 1945, Diana (*née* Lapsley); four *s* two *d*]. *Address:* Dunraven, Fauvic, Jersey, CI.

CORTAZZI, Sir (Henry Arthur) Hugh, GCMG 1984 (KCMG 1980; CMG 1969); HM Diplomatic Service, retired; Director: Hill Samuel and Co. Ltd, since 1984; Foreign and Colonial Pacific Trust, since 1984; GT Japan Investment Trust plc, since 1984; Austin Rover Japan Ltd, since 1984; Pacific Investment Trust, since 1986; *b* 2 May 1924; *m* 1956, Elizabeth Esther Montagu; one *s* two *d*. *Educ:* Sedbergh Sch.; St Andrews and London Univs. Served in RAF, 1943–47; joined Foreign Office, 1949; Third Sec., Singapore, 1950–51; Third/Second Sec., Tokyo, 1951–54; FO, 1954–58; First Sec., Bonn, 1958–60; First Sec., later Head of Chancery, Tokyo, 1961–65; FO, 1965–66; Counsellor (Commercial), Tokyo, 1966–70; Royal Coll. of Defence Studies, 1971–72; Minister (Commercial), Washington, 1972–75; Dep. Under-Sec. of State, FCO, 1975–80; Ambassador to Japan, 1980–84. Mem., ESRC, 1984–. Pres., Asiatic Soc. of Japan, 1982–83; Chm., Japan Soc. of London, 1985–. *Publications:* trans. from Japanese, Genji Keita: The Ogre and other stories of the Japanese Salarymen, 1972; The Guardian God of Golf and other humorous stories, 1972, reprinted as The Lucky One, 1980; (ed) Mary Crawford Fraser, A Diplomat's Wife in Japan: sketches at the turn of the century, 1982; Isles of Gold: antique maps of Japan, 1983; Higashi No Shimaguni, Nishi No Shimaguni (collection of articles and speeches in Japanese), 1984; Thoughts from a Sussex Garden (essays for Japanese students of English), 1984; Dr Willis in Japan, 1985; (ed) Mitford's Japan, 1985; Second Thoughts (essays for Japanese students of English), 1986; articles on Japanese themes in English and Japanese pubns. *Recreations:* Japanese studies, the arts including antiques. *Address:* c/o Hill Samuel and Co. Ltd, 100 Wood Street, EC2P 2AJ. *Club:* Royal Air Force.

CORVEDALE, Viscount; Benedict Alexander Stanley Baldwin; *b* 28 Dec. 1973; *s* and *heir* of 4th Earl Baldwin of Bewdley, *qv*.

CORY, (Charles) Raymond, CBE 1982; Chairman: John Cory & Sons Ltd, since 1965 (Director since 1948); Milford Haven Conservancy Board, since 1982; Clarkson Puckle (Wales) Ltd, since 1985; *b* 20 Oct. 1922; *s* of Charles and Ethel Cory; *m* 1946, Vivienne Mary Roberts, Kelowna, BC, Canada; three *d*. *Educ:* Harrow; Christ Church, Oxford. Served RNVR, Ord. Seaman to Lieut, 1942–46; Russian and N Atlantic convoys and Normandy landings (C-in-C's Commendation June 1944). Vice-Chm., A. B. Electronics Products Group PLC, 1979–. Dir and Mem. Executive, Baltic and Internat. Maritime Conf., Copenhagen, 1957–67; Mem., Lloyd's Register of Shipping, 1963–67. Chairman: Barry Pilotage Authority, 1963–74 (Mem. 1953); Port Talbot Pilotage Authority, 1970–74; SE Wales Pilotage Authority, 1974–80; Welsh Council Mission to Seamen, 1984–; Vice-Chm., BTDB, 1969–79 (Mem., 1966–79; Chm., S Wales Local Bd, 1966); Pres., Cardiff Chamber of Commerce, 1959–60. Chm., S Glamorgan HA, 1974–84. Member: Governing Body of the Church in Wales, 1957–60; Rep. Body of Church in Wales, 1960– (Dep. Chm., 1985); Finance Cttee of Church in Wales, 1960– (Vice-Chm. 1971, Chm. 1975–). RNLI: Chm. Cardiff Br., 1950–73; Mem. Cttee of Management, 1954–; Vice-Pres. 1969–; Dep. Chm., 1985–; Welsh Mem., Exec. Cttee, 1970. Mem. Council, Univ. of Wales Coll. of Medicine, 1984–. *Publication:* A Century of Family Shipowning, 1954. *Recreations:* skiing, sailing, gardening. *Address:* The Coach House, Llanblethian, Cowbridge, South Glamorgan. *T:* Cowbridge 2251. *Club:* Cardiff and County.

CORY, Sir Clinton James Donald, 4th Bt, *cr* 1919; *b* 1 March 1909; 2nd *s* of Sir Donald Cory, 2nd Bt, shipowner of Llandaff, Glam, and Gertrude (*d* 1981), *d* of Henry Thomas Box; *S* brother, 1941; *m* 1935, Mary, *o d* of Dr A. Douglas Hunt, Park Grange, Derby; one *s*. *Educ:* Brighton Coll.; abroad. *Recreations:* shooting, fishing, gardening. *Heir:* *s* Clinton Charles Donald Cory, *b* 13 Sept. 1937. *Address:* 18 Cloisters Road, Letchworth, Herts SG6 3JS. *T:* Letchworth 77206.

CORY, Raymond; *see* Cory, C. R.

CORY-WRIGHT, Sir Richard (Michael), 4th Bt *cr* 1903; *b* 17 Jan. 1944; *s* of Capt. A. J. J. Cory-Wright (killed in action, 1944), and of Susan Esterel (who *m* 2nd, 1949, late Lt-Col J. E. Gurney, DSO, MC), *d* of Robert Elwes; *S* grandfather, 1969; *m* 1976, Veronica, *o d* of James Bolton; two *s*. *Educ:* Eton; Birmingham Univ. *Heir:* *s* Roland Anthony Cory-Wright, *b* 11 March 1979. *Address:* Cox's Farm, Winterbrook Lane, Wallingford, Oxon OX10 9RE.

COSGRAVE, Liam, SC; *b* April 1920; *s* of late William T. Cosgrave; *m* 1952, Vera Osborne; two *s* one *d*. *Educ:* Synge Street Christian Brothers; Castlenock College, Dublin; King's Inns. Served in Army during Emergency. Barrister-at-Law, 1943; Senior Counsel, 1958. Member, Dail Eireann, 1943–81; Chairman Public Accounts Committee, 1945; Parliamentary Secretary to Taoiseach and Minister for Industry and Commerce, 1948–51; Minister for External Affairs, 1954–57; Leader, Fine Gael Party, 1965–77; Taoiseach (Head of Govt of Ireland), 1973–77; Minister for Defence, 1976. Leader first delegation from Ireland to the UN Assembly. Hon. LLD: Duquesne Univ., Pittsburg, Pa, and St John's Univ., Brooklyn, 1956; de Paul Univ., Chicago, 1958; NUI, 1974; Dublin Univ., 1974. Knight Grand Cross of Pius IX, 1956. *Address:* Beechpark, Templeogue, Co. Dublin.

COSGRAVE, Patrick John, PhD; writer; *b* 28 Sept. 1941; *s* of Patrick John Cosgrave and Margaret FitzGerald; *m* 1st, 1965, Ruth Dudley Edwards (marr. diss.); 2nd, 1974, Norma Alicia Green (marr. diss.); one *d*; 3rd, 1981, Shirley Ward. *Educ:* St Vincent's Sch., Dublin; University Coll., NUI, Dublin (BA, MA); Univ. of Cambridge (PhD). London Editor, Radio Telefis Eireann, 1968–69; Conservative Research Dept, 1969–71; Political Editor, The Spectator, 1971–75; Features Editor, Telegraph Magazine, 1974–76. Special Adviser to Rt Hon. Mrs Margaret Thatcher, 1975–79. Managing Editor, Quartet Crime (Quartet Books), 1979–81. *Publications:* The Public Poetry of Robert Lowell, 1969; Churchill at War: Alone, 1974; Cheyney's Law (novel), 1976; Margaret Thatcher: a Tory and her party, 1978, 2nd edn as Margaret Thatcher: Prime Minister, 1979; The Three Colonels (novel), 1979; R. A. Butler: an English Life, 1981; Adventure of State (novel), 1984; Thatcher: the First Term, 1985; Carrington: a life and a policy, 1985; contribs to Proc. of Royal Irish Academy, Irish Historical Studies, Encounter, Policy Rev., New Law Jl. *Recreations:* thriller fiction, cooking, roses, cricket. *Address:* 21 Thornton Road, SW12 0JX. *T:* 01–671 0637.

COSGROVE, Hazel Josephine, (Mrs J. A. Cosgrove); *see* Aronson, H. J.

COSLETT, Air Marshal Sir (Thomas) Norman, KCB 1963 (CB 1960); OBE 1942; CEng, FIMechE; idc; psc; *b* 8 Nov. 1909; *s* of Evan Coslett; *m* 1938, Audrey Garrett. *Educ:* Barry Grammar Sch.; Halton; Cranwell. Dep. Dir of Engineering Plans, Air Ministry, 1954; Senior Technical Staff Officer, HQ Coastal Command, 1957;

Commandant, No 1 School of Technical Training, 1958–61; AOC No 24 Group, 1961–63; AOC-in-C, RAF Maintenance Command, 1963–66. Air Cdre, 1957; Air Vice-Marshal, 1962; Air Marshal, 1963; retired, 1966. *Recreation:* farming. *Address:* c/o Barclays Bank, Sandton City, Sandton, Republic of South Africa.

COSSLETT, Dr Vernon Ellis, FRS 1972; Reader in Electron Physics, University of Cambridge, 1965–75, now Emeritus; Fellow of Corpus Christi College, Cambridge, since 1963; *b* 16 June 1908; *s* of Edgar William Cosslett and Anne Cosslett (*née* Williams); *m* 1st, 1936, Rosemary Wilson (marr. diss. 1940); 2nd, 1940, Anna Joanna Wischin (*d* 1969); one *s* one *d*. *Educ:* Cirencester Grammar Sch.; Bristol Univ. BSc Bristol 1929; PhD Bristol 1932; MSc London 1939; ScD Cambridge 1963. Research at: Bristol Univ., 1929–30; Kaiser-Wilhelm Institut, Berlin, 1930–31; University Coll., London, 1931–32; Research Fellow, Bristol Univ., 1932–35; Lectr in Science, Faraday House, London, 1935–39; Research (part-time), Birkbeck Coll., London, 1936–39; Keddey-Fletcher-Warr Research Fellow of London Univ. (at Oxford), 1939–41; Lectr in Physics, Electrical Laboratory, Oxford Univ., 1941–46; ICI Fellow, Cavendish Laboratory, Cambridge, 1946–49; Lectr in Physics, Univ. of Cambridge, 1949–65. Past Pres., Royal Microscopical Soc.; Past Vice-Pres., Inst. of Physics; Past Pres., Assoc. of Univ. Teachers. Hon. DSc Tübingen, 1963; Hon. MD Gothenburg, 1974. Royal Medal, Royal Soc., 1979; Röntgen Medal (Remscheid), 1984. *Publications:* Introduction to Electron Optics, 1946 (1951); Practical Electron Microscopy, 1951; X-ray Microscopy (with W. C. Nixon), 1960; Modern Microscopy, 1966; many scientific papers. *Recreations:* gardening, mountain walking, listening to music. *Address:* 31 Comberton Road, Barton, Cambridge. *T:* Comberton 2428.

COSSONS, Neil, OBE 1982; FSA; FMA; Director, Science Museum, since 1986; *b* 15 Jan. 1939; *s* of late Arthur Cossons and Evelyn Cossons (*née* Bettle); *m* 1965, Veronica Edwards; two *s* one *d*. *Educ:* Henry Mellish Sch., Nottingham; Univ. of Liverpool (MA). FSA 1968; FMA 1970. Leicester Museums, 1961; Swindon Museums, 1963; Curator of Technology, Bristol City Museum, 1964; Dep. Dir, City of Liverpool Museums, 1969; Dir, Ironbridge Gorge Museum Trust, 1971; Dir, Nat. Maritime Museum, 1983–86. Member: Curatorium Internat. Committee for the Conservation of the Industrial Heritage, 1973–78; UK Cttee, ICOMOS, 1982–; Ancient Monuments Adv. Cttee, 1984–. President: Assoc. for Industrial Archaeology, 1977–80; Assoc. of Independent Museums, 1983– (Chm., 1978–83); Museums Assoc., 1981–82. Trustee: Maritime Trust, 1983–; Mary Rose Trust, 1983–; Royal Naval Museum, Portsmouth, 1984–. Midlands Press, Radio and Television Award, 1978. Hon. DSocSc Birmingham, 1979; DUniv Open, 1984. *Publications:* Contractors' Locomotives GCR, 1963; (with R. A. Buchanan) Industrial Archaeology of the Bristol Region, 1968; (with K. Hudson) Industrial Archaeologists' Guide, 1969, 2nd edn 1971; Industrial Archaeology, 1975; (ed) Transactions of the First International Congress on the Conservation of Industrial Monuments, 1975; (ed) Rees's Manufacturing Industry, 1975; (with H. Sowden) Ironbridge—Landscape of Industry, 1977; (with B. S. Trinder) The Iron Bridge—Symbol of the Industrial Revolution, 1979; (ed) Management of Change in Museums, 1985; numerous papers in Museums Jl and elsewhere. *Recreations:* travel, design. *Address:* Science Museum, SW7 2DD; Church Hill, Ironbridge, Telford, Shropshire TF8 7PW. *T:* Ironbridge 2701. *Club:* Athenæum.

COSTAIN, Sir Albert (Percy), Kt 1980; *b* 5 July 1910; *s* of William Percy Costain and Maud May Smith; *m* 1933, Joan Mary, *d* of John William Whiter; one *s* one *d*. *Educ:* King James, Knaresborough; Coll. of Estate Management. Production Dir on formation of Richard Costain Ltd, 1933; Chm., Richard Costain Ltd, 1966–69; Chm., Pre-stressed Concrete Development Group, 1952. MP (C) Folkstone and Hythe, 1959–83; Author of Home Safety Act, 1961; Parliamentary Private Secretary: to Minister of Public Bldg and Works, 1962–64; to Minister of Technology, 1970; to Chancellor of Duchy of Lancaster, 1970–72; to Sec. of State for the Environment, 1972–74. Member: Cttee of Public Accts, 1961–64, 1974–83; Estimates Cttee, 1960–61, 1965–70; Estimates Sub-Cttee on Building and Natural Resources, 1965–83; Chairmen's Panel, House of Commons, 1975–83. Joint Vice-Chm., Conservative Party Transport Cttee, 1964. Jt Sec., Conservative Housing and Local Govt Cttee, 1964–65, Jt Vice-Chm., 1965–66; All Party Tourists and Resorts Cttee: Sec., 1964–66; Vice-Chm., 1966–69; Chm., 1970–71; Vice-Chm., Conservative Party Arts, Public Building and Works Cttee, 1965–70; Chm., Cons. Party Horticulture Cttee, 1976–77. London Treas., Nat. Children's Home, 1950–60. FCIOB. *Recreations:* sailing, golf. *Address:* Inwarren, Kingswood, Surrey. *T:* Mogador 832443; 2 Albion Villas, Folkestone, Kent CT20 1RP. *Clubs:* Carlton; Walton Heath Golf.

See also P. J. Costain.

COSTAIN, Noel Leslie, OBE 1964; Director of Works, University of Sheffield, 1964–78; *b* 11 Jan. 1914; *s* of George Wesley Costain and Minnie Grace Pinson; *m* 1945, Marie José Elizabeth (*née* Bishton); two *d*. *Educ:* King Edward's Sch., Five Ways, Birmingham; Univ. of Birmingham (BSc). CEng, MICE, FINucE. Engineer with Sir R. MacAlpine & Sons, 1937–38; Epsom and Ewell BC, 1939; Air Min., Directorate-Gen. of Works; Section Officer, Orkneys and Shetlands, 1940–43; Prin. Works Officer, Sierra Leone, 1944–46; Superintending Engr, Air Ministry, 1946–51; RAF Airfield Construction Br.: Cmdg 5352 Wing, Germany, and OC, RAF Church Lawford, 1951–54; Superintending Engr, Works Area, Bristol, 1954–58; Chief Engr, MEAF, 1958–60; Chief Resident Engr, BMEWS, Fylingdales, 1960–63. Vice-Chm., Yorkshire Univs Air Squadron Cttee. Mem. Council, Instn of Nuclear Engineers, 1965; Vice-Pres., 1969; President, 1972–76. *Recreations:* travel, gardening. *Address:* Villa Marie José, Avenida 3 no 59, Urbanisation Hacienda Las Chapas, Marbella, Málaga, Spain.

COSTAIN, Peter John, FCA; Group Chief Executive, Costain Group Plc, since 1980; *b* 2 April 1938; *s* of Sir Albert Costain, *qv*; *m* 1963, Victoria M. Pope; three *s*. *Educ:* Charterhouse. Peat Marwick Mitchell & Co., 1956–63; Richard Costain Ltd, 1963–65; Costain Australia Ltd, 1965–: Board Member, 1967; Managing Director, 1971; Chief Executive, 1973. FAIB. *Recreations:* sailing, skiing, golf. *Address:* 21 Caroline Terrace, SW1. *Clubs:* Royal Corinthian Yacht; Royal Thames Yacht; Athenæum, Royal Brighton Yacht (Melbourne).

COSTANZI, Edwin J. B.; *see* Borg-Costanzi.

COSTAR, Sir Norman (Edgar), KCMG 1963 (CMG 1953); *b* 18 May 1909. *Educ:* Battersea Grammar School; Jesus Coll., Cambridge. Asst Principal, Colonial Office, 1932; Private Sec. to Permanent Under Sec., Dominions Office, 1935; served in UK High Commissioner's Offices, Australia, 1937–39, New Zealand, 1945–47. Principal, 1938; Asst Sec., 1946. Dep. High Commissioner, Ceylon, 1953–57; Asst Under-Sec., Commonwealth Relations Office, 1958–60; Dep. High Commissioner in Australia, 1960–62; High Commissioner: Trinidad and Tobago, 1962–66; Cyprus, 1967–69. Adjudicator, Immigration Appeals, 1970–81. *Club:* United Oxford & Cambridge University.

COSTELLO, Gordon John; Chief Accountant of the Bank of England, 1975–78; *b* 29 March 1921; *s* of late Ernest James Costello and Hilda May Costello; *m* 1946, Joan Lilian Moore; two *s* one *d*. *Educ:* Varndean Sch. Served War, 1939–45 (RA). Bank of England, 1946; worked in various Departments; Asst Chief Accountant, 1964; Asst Sec., 1965; Dep. Sec., 1968; Dep. Chief Cashier, 1970. *Recreations:* music, travel, walking, tennis. *Address:* 26 Peacock Lane, Brighton, Sussex BN1 6WA. *T:* Brighton 552344.

COT, Pierre Donatien Alphonse, Commander Legion of Honour; Croix de Guerre; Ingénieur général des ponts et chaussées; *b* 10 Sept. 1911; *s* of late Donatien Cot, Engr-Gen. and Naval Hydrographer, Membre de l'Institut, and Yvonne (*née* Bunout); *m* 1939, Claude Bouguen; two *s* two *d*. *Educ:* Lycée Louis-le-Grand, Paris; Ecole Polytechnique, Paris. Licencié ès Sciences. Govt Civil Engr, Paris, 1936; Chief Engineer of Port of Le Havre, 1945; Techn. Manager, 1951, Dir-Gen., 1955–67, and Administrator, 1967–75, Paris Airport Authority; Pres., Air France, 1967–74; Pres.-Dir-Gen., Soc. Gén. d'Entreprises, 1974–79, now Président d'Honneur. Pres., Institut géographique national, 1967–75. Médaille de l'Aéronautique; Officer du Mérite Touristique. Hon. MVO. Médaille de vermeil de la Ville de Paris, 1972. *Address:* 69 rue de l'Assomption, 75016 Paris, France.

COTES, Peter, (Sydney Arthur Boulting); author, lecturer, play producer, stage, film and television director; *e s* of Arthur Boulting and Rose Bennett; *m* 1st, 1938, Myfanwy Jones (marr. diss.); 2nd, 1948, Joan Miller. *Educ:* Taplow; Italia Conti and privately. Was for some years an actor; made theatrical debut, Portsmouth Hippodrome, in the arms of Vesta Tilley. Formed own independent play-producing co. with Hon. James Smith, 1949, presented Rocket to the Moon, St Martin's Theatre, and subsequently produced, in association with Arts Council of Great Britain, notable seasons in Manchester and at Embassy and Lyric Theatres, Hammersmith. Founded: New Lindsey, 1946; New Boltons, 1951. West-End Productions include: Pick Up Girl, 1946; The Animal Kingdom, 1947; The Master Builder, 1948; Miss Julie, 1949; Come Back, Little Sheba, 1951; The Father, 1951; The Biggest Thief in Town, 1951; The Mousetrap, 1952; The Man, 1952; A Pin to see the Peepshow, Broadway, 1953; Happy Holiday, 1954; Hot Summer Night, 1958; Epitaph for George Dillon (Holland), 1959; The Rope Dancers, 1959; Girl on the Highway, 1960; A Loss of Roses, 1962; The Odd Ones, 1963; Hidden Stranger, Broadway, 1963; What Goes Up. . .!, 1963; So Wise, So Young, 1964; Paint Myself Black, 1965; The Impossible Years, 1966; Staring at the Sun, 1968; Janie Jackson, 1968; The Old Ladies, 1969; Look, No Hands!, 1971. Films: The Right Person; Two Letters; Jane Clegg; Waterfront; The Young and the Guilty; has prod. and adapted numerous plays for BBC Television and ITV; was Sen. Drama Dir, AR-TV, 1955–58; producing stage plays and films, 1959–60; Supervising Producer of Drama Channel 7, Melbourne, 1961; produced and adapted plays for Anglia TV, 1964; produced first TV series of P. G. Wodehouse short stories, on BBC; wrote George Robey centenary TV Tribute, BBC Omnibus series, 1969; wrote and dir. in One Pair of Eyes series, BBC TV, 1970; has written, adapted and narrated many productions for radio incl. Back into the Light, The Prime Minister of Mirth, Mervyn Peake, Portrait of an Actor; collaborated 1980–81 on: The Song is Ended, Who Were You With Last Night, Whose Your Lady Friend, The Black Sheep of the Family (BBC); scripted: This Fabulous Genius (BBC), 1980; Wee Georgie Wood (BBC), 1980. FRSA; Member: Theatrical Managers' Assoc.; Medico-Legal Soc.; Our Society; Guild of Drama Adjudicators. Kt of Mark Twain, 1980. *Publications:* No Star Nonsense, 1949; The Little Fellow, 1951; A Handbook of Amateur Theatre, 1957; George Robey, 1972; The Trial of Elvira Barney, 1976; Circus, 1976; Origin of a Thriller, 1977; JP (The Man Called Mitch), 1978; Misfit Midget, 1979; Portrait of an Actor, 1980; The Barbirollis: a musical marriage, 1983; seventh series, Old Stagers, 1986; contrib. to The Field, Spectator, Queen, Guardian, etc. *Address:* 7 Hill Lawn Court, Chipping Norton, Oxon OX7 5NF. *Recreations:* book collecting, writing letters, criminology. *Clubs:* Savage, Our Society.

COTILL, John Atrill T.; *see* Templeton-Cotill.

COTRUBAS, Ileana, (Mme Manfred Ramin); opera singer; *b* Rumania; *d* of Vasile and Maria Cotrubas; *m* 1972, Manfred Ramin. *Educ:* Conservatorul Ciprian Porumbescu, Bucharest. Opera and concert engagements all over Europe, N America and Japan. Permanent guest at Royal Opera House, Covent Garden; Member, Vienna State Opera; also frequently sings in Scala, Milan, Munich, Berlin, Paris, Chicago, NY Metropolitan Opera. Main operatic roles: Susanna, Pamina, Gilda, Traviata, Manon, Tatyana, Mimi, Melisande, Amina, Elisabetta, Nedda, Marguerite, Magda (Roudine). Has made numerous recordings. Kammersängerin, Austria, 1981. *Address:* c/o Royal Opera House, Covent Garden, WC2.

COTT, Hugh Bamford, ScD Cantab, DSc Glasgow; FRPS, FZS; Fellow of Selwyn College, Cambridge, since 1945; *b* 6 July 1900; *s* of late Rev. A. M. Cott, Ashby Magna; *m* 1928, Joyce Radford; one *s* one *d*. *Educ:* Rugby Sch.; RMC, Sandhurst; Selwyn Coll., Cambridge. Joined 1st Bn the Leics Regt; served in Ireland, 1919–21. 2nd class, Nat. Sciences Tripos, Pt I, 1925. Carried out zoological expeditions to SE Brazil, 1923; Lower Amazon, 1925–26; Zoological Society's Expedition to the Zambesi, 1927, Canary Islands, 1931, Uganda, 1952, Zululand, 1956, Central Africa, 1957; Lecturer in Hygiene, Bristol Univ., 1928–32; Asst and Lecturer in Zoology, Glasgow Univ., 1932–38; Strickland Curator and Lectr in the University of Cambridge, 1938–67; Lectr, 1945–67, and Dean, 1966–67, of Selwyn Coll., Cambridge. Founder Member, Soc. Wildlife Artists. War of 1939–45: Mem. Advisory Cttee on Camouflage, 1939–40; Capt. and Major (RE) MEF; served Western Desert, 1941 (despatches); Chief Instructor, Middle East Camouflage Sch., 1941–43; GSO 2 (Cam) Mountain Warfare Trg Centre, 1943–44. *Publications:* Adaptive Coloration in Animals, 1940; Zoological Photography in Practice, 1956; Uganda in Black and White, 1959; Looking at Animals: a zoologist in Africa, 1975; various scientific papers on adaptive coloration, feeding habits of tree frogs, camouflage, edibility of birds, ecology of crocodiles, etc published in Trans and Proc. of Zool Soc. London, Proc. R. Ent. Soc. London, Photographic Jl, Engineers' Jl etc. *Recreations:* travel, pen drawing, photography. *Address:* 10 Stoke Water House, Beaminster, Dorset. *T:* Beaminster 862798.

COTTENHAM, 8th Earl of, *cr* 1850; **Kenelm Charles Everard Digby Pepys;** Bt 1784 and 1801; Baron Cottenham, 1836; Viscount Crowhurst, 1850; *b* 27 Nov. 1948; *s* of 7th Earl of Cottenham and Lady Angela Isabel Nellie Nevill, *d* of 4th Marquess of Abergavenny; *S* father, 1968; *m* 1975, Sarah, *d* of Captain S. Lombard-Hobson, CVO, OBE, RN; two *s* one *d*. *Educ:* Eton. *Heir:* *s* Viscount Crowhurst, *qv*.

See also Baron McGowan.

COTTER, Lt-Col Sir Delaval James Alfred, 6th Bt, *cr* 1763; DSO 1944; late 13th/18th Royal Hussars; *b* 29 April 1911; *s* of 5th Bt and Ethel Lucy (*d* 1956), *d* of Alfred Wheeler; *S* father, 1924; *m* 1st, 1943, Roma (marr. diss., 1949), *widow* of Sqdn Ldr K. A. K. MacEwen and *o d* of late Adrian Rome, Dalswinton Lodge, Salisbury, SR; two *d*; 2nd, 1952, Mrs Eveline Mary Paterson, *widow* of Lieut-Col J. F. Paterson, OBE, and *d* of late E. J. Mardon, ICS (retired). *Educ:* Malvern Coll; RMC, Sandhurst. Served War of 1939–45 (DSO); retired, 1959. JP Wilts, 1962–63. *Heir:* *n* Patrick Laurence Delaval Cotter [*b* 21 Nov. 1941; *m* 1967, Janet, *d* of George Potter, Barnstaple; one *s* two *d*]. *Address:* Green Lines, Iwerne Courtney, Blandford Forum, Dorset.

COTTERELL, Geoffrey; author; *b* 24 Nov. 1919; *yr s* of late Graham Cotterell and Millicent (*née* Crews). *Educ:* Bishops Stortford College. Served War of 1939–45, Royal

Artillery, 1940–46. *Publications:* Then a Soldier, 1944; This is the Way, 1947; Randle in Springtime, 1949; Strait and Narrow, 1950; Westward the Sun, 1952 (repr. 1973); The Strange Enchantment, 1956 (repr. 1973); Tea at Shadow Creek, 1958; Tiara Tahiti, 1960 (filmed 1962, screenplay with Ivan Foxwell); Go, said the bird, 1966; Bowers of Innocence, 1970; Amsterdam, the life of a city, 1972. *Recreation:* golf. *Address:* 2 Fulbourne House, Blackwater Road, Eastbourne, Sussex. *Clubs:* Royal Automobile; Cooden Beach Golf.

COTTERELL, Sir John (Henry Geers), 6th Bt *cr* 1805; Chairman, Radio Wyvern, since 1981; *b* 8 May 1935; *s* of Sir Richard Charles Geers Cotterell, 5th Bt, CBE, and Lady Lettice Cotterell (*d* 1973), *d* of 7th Earl Beauchamp; *S* father, 1978; *m* 1959, Vanda Alexandra Clare, *d* of Major Philip Alexander Clement Bridgewater; three *s* one *d*. *Educ:* Eton; RMA Sandhurst. Officer, Royal Horse Guards, 1955–61. Vice-Chm. Hereford and Worcs CC, 1973–77, Chm., 1977–81. Pres., Nat. Fedn of Young Farmers Clubs, 1986 (Dep. Pres., 1979–86). *Recreations:* cricket, shooting, stuffing hanging baskets. *Heir:* *s* Henry Richard Geers Cotterell [*b* 22 Aug. 1961; *m* 1986, Carolyn, *er d* of John Beckwith-Smith, Maybanks Manor, Rudgwick, Sussex]. *Address:* Garnons, near Hereford. *T:* Bridge Sollars 232. *Club:* White's.

COTTERILL, Kenneth William, CMG 1976; Chairman, Commercial and Political Risk Consultants Ltd, 1986–87 (Deputy Chairman, 1981–86); Consultant, NEI International, 1986–87 (Director, 1981–86); *b* 5 June 1921; *s* of William and Ada May Cotterill; *m* 1948, Janet Hilda Cox; one *d*. *Educ:* Sutton County Sch.; London School of Economics, BSc (Econ). Served War in Royal Navy, 1941–46. After the war, joined ECGD; Principal, 1956; Asst Sec., 1966; Under Sec., 1970; Dep. Head of Dept, 1976–81. Gp Advr on Export Credits, Barclays Bank Internat., 1981–86; Dir, Tarmac Internat., 1981–86. *Recreations:* reading, walking, gardening. *Address:* 15 Minster Drive, Croydon CR0 5UP. *T:* 01-681 6700.

COTTESLOE, 4th Baron (UK) *cr* 1874; **John Walgrave Halford Fremantle,** GBE 1960; TD; Bt 1821; Baron of Austrian Empire, *cr* 1816; *b* 2 March 1900; *s* of 3rd Baron Cottesloe, CB and Florence (*d* 1956), *d* of Thomas Tapling; *S* father 1956; *m* 1st, 1926, Lady Elizabeth Harris (marr. diss., 1945; she *d* 1983), *o d* of 5th Earl of Malmesbury; one *s* one *d*; 2nd, 1959, Gloria Jean Irene Dunn; one *s* two *d*. *Educ:* Eton; Trinity Coll., Cambridge. BA (Hons) Mechanical Sciences 1921; MA 1924. Served as OC 251 (Bucks) AA Battery RA (TA), 1938–39; GSO 1 att. 2nd Armoured Division, 1940; Senior Military Liaison Officer to Regional Commissioner, NE Region, 1940–41; GSO 1 (Technical) AA Command, 1941–42; Commanding Officer, 20 LAA Regt RA, 1942–44; GSO 1 (Radar) War Office, 1944–45. Mem. LCC, 1945–55. Chm., Thomas Tapling & Co. Ltd; Vice-Chm., PLA, 1956–67. Chairman: Tate Gallery, 1959–60; Arts Council of Gt Britain, 1960–65; South Bank Theatre Bd (from inception), 1962–77 (Cottesloe theatre part of Nat. Theatre complex, opened 1976); Adv. Council and Reviewing Cttee on Export of Works of Art, 1954–72; Heritage in Danger, 1973–; Royal Postgrad. Med. Sch., 1949–58 (Fellow); NW Met. Reg. Hosp. Bd, 1953–60; Hammersmith and St Mark's Hospital, 1968–74; Northwick Park Hosp. Adv. Cttee, 1970–74; a Governor, King Edward's Hosp. Fund for London, 1973–83. Chairman: British Postgraduate Medical Fedn, 1958–72; Nat. Rifle Assoc., 1960–72; Vice-Chm., City Parochial Foundn, 1972–77; Pres., Hospital Saving Assoc., 1973–; Hon. Sec. Amateur Rowing Assoc., 1932–46; a Steward of Henley Royal Regatta; Pres., Leander, 1957–62. Chm., The Dogs' Home, Battersea, 1970–83. Former DL County of London (later Greater London). *Recreations:* rowed in winning crews in Oxford and Cambridge Boat Race, 1921 and 1922 and in Grand Challenge Cup, Henley, 1922; Captain of English VIII at Bisley on 25 occasions and has shot in English VIII on 37 occasions and won Match Rifle Championship six times, with many other first prizes for long-range shooting. *Heir:* *s* Comdr Hon. John Tapling Fremantle, *qv*. *Address:* 89 York Mansions, Prince of Wales Drive, Battersea Park, SW11 4BN. *T:* 01–622 9349. *Clubs:* Travellers'; Leander.

COTTHAM, George William; Director General, West Yorkshire Passenger Transport Executive, since 1983; *b* 11 July 1944; *s* of George William and Elizabeth Cottham; *m* 1967, Joan Thomas; two *d*. *Educ:* Univ. of London; Polytechnic of Liverpool; Liverpool Coll. of Commerce. BSc 1st Cl. Hons, LLB 2nd Cl. Hons. MCIT. Various posts, Liverpool City Transport, 1960–74; District Transport Manager, St Helens, 1974–77; Transport General Manager, Newport, 1977–80; Gen. Manager, Cleveland Transit, 1980–83. *Recreations:* family, home, garden, music. *Address:* Brow Lee, 118 Huddersfield Road, Brighouse, West Yorkshire. *T:* Brighouse 713019.

COTTON; *see* Stapleton-Cotton, family name of Viscount Combermere.

COTTON, Bernard Edward, CBE 1976; Deputy Chairman, Baker Perkins plc, 1983–86; Chairman, John Mountford & Co., since 1984; Chairman, South Yorkshire Residuary Body, since 1985; *b* 8 Oct. 1920; *s* of Hugh Harry Cotton and Alice Cotton; *m* 1944, Stephanie Anne, *d* of Rev. A. E. and Mrs Furnival; three *s*. *Educ:* Sheffield City Grammar Sch.; Sheffield Univ. Served Army, 1939–45, latterly as Lieut, Worcs Yeomanry (53rd Airlanding Light Regt RA). Joined Round Oak Steelworks, Brierley Hill, 1949, Sales Man., 1954–57; Gen. Man., Samuel Osborn (Canada) Ltd, Montreal, 1957–63; Samuel Osborn & Co. Ltd: Sales Dir, 1963–69; Man. Dir, 1969; Chm. and Chief Exec., 1969–78; Pres., 1978–80. Dir, Renold Ltd, 1979–84. Chairman: Yorks and Humberside Reg. Econ. Planning Council, 1970–79; Health Service Supply Council, 1980–85; Mem., BR Eastern Bd, 1977–85; Pres., Yorks and Humberside Develt Assoc., 1973–84. Chm., BIM Working Party on Employee Participation, 1975. Pro Chancellor, Sheffield Univ., 1982–. Master, Cutlers' Co. in Hallamshire, 1979–80. Hon. Fellow, Sheffield City Poly., 1980. CBIM. *Recreations:* gardening and other quiet pursuits. *Address:* Stubbin House, Carsick Hill Road, Sheffield S10 3LU. *T:* Sheffield 303082. *Clubs:* Sheffield (Sheffield); St James's (Manchester).

COTTON, Christopher P.; *see* Powell-Cotton.

COTTON, Diana Rosemary, (Mrs R. B. Allan); QC 1983; *b* 30 Nov. 1941; *d* of Arthur Frank Edward and Muriel Cotton; *m* 1966, Richard Bellerby Allan; two *s* one *d*. *Educ:* Berkhamsted School for Girls; Lady Margaret Hall, Oxford (MA). Joined Middle Temple, 1961; called to Bar, 1964; Member, Midland and Oxford Circuit; a Recorder of the Crown Court, 1982. *Recreation:* her family and other animals. *Address:* Devereux Chambers, Devereux Court, Temple, WC2. *T:* 01–353 7534.

COTTON, Henry; *see* Cotton, T. H.

COTTON, John Anthony; His Honour Judge Cotton; a Circuit Judge, since 1973; *b* 6 March 1926; *s* of Frederick Thomas Hooley Cotton and Catherine Mary Cotton; *m* 1960, Johanna Aritia van Lookeren Campagne; three *s* two *d*. *Educ:* Stonyhurst Coll.; Lincoln Coll., Oxford. Called to the Bar, Middle Temple, 1949; Dep. Chm., W Riding of Yorks QS, 1967–71; Recorder of Halifax, 1971; a Recorder and Hon. Recorder of Halifax, 1972–73. Pres., S Yorks Br., Magistrates' Assoc., 1982–. *Recreation:* golf. *Address:* 81 Lyndhurst Road, Sheffield S11 9BJ. *T:* Sheffield 585569.

COTTON, Sir John Richard, KCMG 1969 (CMG 1959); OBE 1947 (MBE 1944); retired from HM Diplomatic Service, 1969; Adjudicator, Immigration Appeals, 1970–81; *b* 22 Jan. 1909; *s* of late J. J. Cotton, ICS, and late Gigia Ricciardi Arlotta; *m* 1937, Mary Bridget Connors, Stradbally, County Waterford, Ireland; three *s*. *Educ:* Wellington Coll.; RMC, Sandhurst. Commissioned 1929; 8th King George's Own Light Cavalry (IA), 1930–34; transferred to Indian Political Service, 1934; served in: Aden, Abyssinia (Attaché HM Legation, 1935), Persian Gulf, Rajputana, Hyderabad, Kathiawar, Baroda, New Delhi (Dep. Sec. Political Dept). Transferred to HM Foreign Service, 1947; served in Karachi (First Sec.), 1947–48, Foreign Office, 1949–51, Madrid (Commercial Counsellor, HM Embassy), 1951–54; Consul-Gen., Brazzaville, 1954–55, Leopoldville, 1955–57; Counsellor (Commercial), HM Embassy, Brussels, 1957–62. Consul-Gen., São Paulo, Brazil, 1962–65; Ambassador to Kinshasa, Congo Republic (now Zaire), and to Burundi, 1965–69. *Recreation:* golf. *Address:* Lansing House, Hartley Wintney, Hants. *T:* Hartley Wintney 2681. *Club:* Army and Navy.

COTTON, Leonard Thomas, MCh; FRCS; Surgeon, King's College Hospital, since 1957; Surgeon, Queen Victoria Hospital, East Grinstead, and St Luke's Nursing Home for the Clergy; Dean, King's College Hospital Medical School, since 1978 (Vice-Dean, 1976–77); *b* 5 Dec. 1922; *s* of Edward Cotton and Elizabeth (*née* Webb); *m* 1946, Frances Joanna Bryan; one *s* two *d*. *Educ:* King's College Sch., Wimbledon; Oriel Coll., Oxford; King's Coll. Hospital. MRCS, LRCP 1946; BM, BCh Oxon 1946; FRCS 1950; MCh Oxon 1957. House Surgeon, King's College Hospital, 1946; Resident Surgical Officer, Royal Waterloo Hospital, 1947; Resident Surgical Officer, Weymouth and District Hospital, 1948; National Service, Surgical Specialist RAMC, 1949–51; Senior Registrar and Registrar, King's College Hospital, 1951–57; Surgical Tutor, King's Coll. Hospital Medical Sch., 1957–65. FRSM; Member: Surgical Research Soc., Assoc. of Surgeons; Vascular Surgical Soc.; Ct of Examiners, RCS. Hunterian Prof., RCS. FKC 1983. *Publications:* (ed) Hey Groves' Synopsis of Surgery; co-author, short text-book of Surgery; contributions to medical journals. *Recreations:* gardening, reading, squash. *Address:* 3 Dome Hill Park, Sydenham Hill, SE26 6SP. *T:* 01-778 8047; Private Wing, King's College Hospital, Denmark Hill, SE5. *T:* 01–274 8670; 22 Harley Street, W1. *T:* 01–637 0491.

COTTON, Hon. Sir Robert Carrington, KCMG 1978; Australian Ambassador to the United States of America, 1982–85; *b* 29 Nov. 1915; *s* of H. L. Carrington Cotton; *m* 1937, Eve Elizabeth MacDougall; one *s* two *d*. *Educ:* St Peter's Coll., Adelaide, SA. FASA. State President of Liberal Party (NSW), 1956–59; Federal Vice-Pres., 1960–61; elected to Senate, 1965; Minister for Civil Aviation, 1969–72; Shadow Minister for Manufacturing Industry (in Opposition), 1972–75; Minister for Industry and Commerce, 1975–77; Australian Consul-Gen. in NY, 1978–81. *Recreations:* swimming, writing, photography. *Address:* 75 Pacific Road, Palm Beach, NSW 2108, Australia. *T:* 919.5456. *Clubs:* The Brook (NY); Australian (Sydney); Commonwealth (Canberra, ACT).

COTTON, (Thomas) Henry, MBE 1946; late Flight Lieutenant RAFVR (invalided, 1943); golfer; Professional Golf Correspondent of Golf Monthly; Director and Founder Golf Foundation for development of youthful golfers; Golf Course Architect; *b* Holmes Chapel, Cheshire, 26 Jan. 1907; *m* 1939, Mrs Maria Isabel Estanguet Moss (*d* 1982). *Educ:* Alleyn's Sch. Played in first Boys' Golf Championship, 1921; asst at Fulwell, 1924; Rye, 1925; Cannes, 1926; professional Langley Park, 1927; Waterloo, Brussels, 1933; Ashridge, 1936; won Kent Professional Championship, 1926–27–28–29–30; Belgian Open, 1930, 1934, 1938; Mar del Plata, 1930; Dunlop Tournament, 1931, 1932, 1953, runner-up, 1959; News of the World Tournament, 1932 and 1939; British Open, 1934, 1937 and 1948 (1934 was First British win for 11 years); Italian Open, 1936; German Open, 1937–38–39; Silver King Tournament, 1937; Czechoslovak Open, 1937–38; Harry Vardon Trophy, 1938; Daily Mail £2000 Tournament, 1939; Penfold Tournament, 1939 and 1954; News Chronicle Tournament, 1945; Star Tournament, 1946; Prof. Golfers' Assoc. Match Play Champion, 1946; French Open Champion, 1946 and 1947; Vichy Open Champion, 1946; represented Great Britain v America, 1929, 1937, 1947, 1953; Ryder Cup Team Capt., 1939, 1947 and 1953; Spalding Tournament, 1947; visited USA in 1929, 1931, 1947, 1948, 1956 and 1957; led US Open Qualifying, 1956; visited Argentine 1929, 1948, 1949 and 1950. Collected over £70,000 for Red Cross and other war charities in 130 matches organised by himself. Golf Consultant: Penina Golf Hotel, Portugal, 1968–75; Penina and Vale do Lobo Golf Clubs, 1978. Architect of golf courses: Abridge, Felixstowe, Canons Brook, Ampfield; Megéve and Deauville (France); Penina, Val de Lobo, Golf de Monte Gorda, and Monte Velho, Algarve (Portugal); Campo de Lagoa (Madeira); Castle Eden Golf Club, Eaglescliffe, Stirling, Gourock, Windmill Hill, Bletchley, Sene Valley, Folkestone, Ely, etc. Hon. Life Mem., Professional Golf Assoc. Vice-President: National Golf Clubs Advisory Bureau; Golf Writers' Assoc. *Publications:* Golf, 1932; This Game of Golf, 1948; My Swing, 1952; (Henry Cotton's) My Golfing Album, 1960; Henry Cotton Says, 1962; Studying the Golf Game, 1964; The Picture World of Golf, 1965; Golf in the British Isles, 1969; A History of Golf, 1973; Thanks for the Game, 1980. *Recreations:* painting, motoring, photography. *Address:* Penina, Golf Hotel, Portimao, Portugal.

COTTON, William Frederick, (Bill Cotton), OBE 1976; Managing Director, Television, BBC, since 1984; Vice Chairman, BBC Enterprises, since 1986 (Chairman, 1982–86); *b* 23 April 1928; *s* of William Edward (Billy) Cotton and Mabel Hope; *m* 1st, 1950, Bernadine Maud (*née* Sinclair); three *d*; 2nd, 1965, Ann Corfield (*née* Bucknall); one step *d*. *Educ:* Ardingly College. Jt Man. Dir, Michael Reine Music Co., 1952–56; BBC-TV: Producer, Light Entertainment Dept, 1956–62; Asst Head of Light Entertainment, 1962–67; Head of Variety, 1967–70; Head of Light Entertainment Gp, 1970–77; Controller, BBC 1, 1977–81; Dep. Man. Dir, 1981–82; Dir of Programmes, Television, and Dir of Develt, BBC, 1982. FRTS 1983. *Recreation:* golf. *Address:* c/o BBC Television Centre, Wood Lane, W12 7RJ.

COTTRELL, Sir Alan (Howard), Kt 1971; FRS 1955; FEng; Master of Jesus College, Cambridge, 1974–86; Vice-Chancellor, University of Cambridge, 1977–79; *b* 17 July 1919; *s* of Albert and Elizabeth Cottrell; *m* 1944, Jean Elizabeth Harber; one *s*. *Educ:* Moseley Grammar Sch.; University of Birmingham. BSc 1939; PhD 1942; ScD(Cantab) 1976. Lectr in Metallurgy, University of Birmingham, 1943–49; Prof. of Physical Metallurgy, University of Birmingham, 1949–55; retired March 1955. Deputy Head of Metallurgy Division, Atomic Energy Research Establishment, Harwell, Berks, 1955–58; Goldsmiths' Prof. of Metallurgy, Cambridge Univ., 1958–65; Dep. Chief Scientific Adviser (Studies), Min. of Defence, 1965–67, Chief Adviser, 1967; Dep. Chief Scientific Advr to HM Govt, 1968–71, Chief Scientific Advr, 1971–74. Part-time Mem., UKAEA, 1962–65, 1983–; Member: Adv. Council on Scientific Policy, 1963–64; Central Adv. Council for Science and Technology, 1967–; Exec. Cttee, British Council, 1974–; Adv. Council, Science Policy Foundn, 1976–; Security Commn, 1981–. Dir, Fisons plc, 1979–. A Vice-Pres., Royal Society, 1964, 1976, 1977. Fellow Royal Swedish Academy of Sciences; Hon. Fellow, Christ's Coll., Cambridge, 1970 (Fellow, 1958–70). Foreign Hon. Mem., American Academy of Arts and Sciences, 1960; Foreign Associate, Nat. Acad. of Sciences, USA, 1972; Hon. Mem., Amer. Soc. for Metals, 1972 (Fellow 1974); Foreign

Associate, Nat. Acad. of Engrng, USA, 1976; Hon. Member: Metals Soc., 1977; Japan Inst. of Metals, 1981. Hon. Fellow, Internat. Congress on Fracture, 1985–. FEng 1979. Hon. DSc: Columbia Univ., 1965; Newcastle Univ., 1967; Liverpool Univ., 1969; Manchester, 1970; Warwick, 1971; Sussex, 1972; Bath, 1973; Strathclyde, 1975; Cranfield, 1975; Aston, 1975; Oxford, 1979; Birmingham, 1983; DUniv Essex, 1982; Hon. DEng Tech. Univ. of Nova Scotia, 1984. Rosenhain Medallist of the Inst. of Metals; Hughes Medal, 1961, Rumford Medal, 1974, Royal Society; Inst. of Metals (Platinum) Medal, 1965; Réaumur Medal, Société Française de Métallurgie, 1964; James Alfred Ewing Medal, ICE, 1967; Holweck Medal, Société Française de Physique, 1969; Albert Sauveur Achievement Award, Amer. Soc. for Metals, 1969; James Douglas Gold Medal, Amer. Inst. of Mining, Metallurgy and Petroleum Engrs, 1974; Harvey Science Prize, Technion Israel Inst., 1974; Acta Metallurgica Gold Medal, 1976; Guthrie Medal and Prize, Inst. of Physics, 1977; Gold Medal, Amer. Soc. for Metals, 1980; Brinell Medal, Royal Swedish Acad. of Engrg Sciences, 1980. *Publications:* Theoretical Structural Metallurgy, 1948, 2nd edn 1955; Dislocations and Plastic Flow in Crystals, 1953; The Mechanical Properties of Matter, 1964; Theory of Crystal Dislocations, 1964; An Introduction to Metallurgy, 1967; Portrait of Nature, 1975; Environmental Economics, 1978; How Safe is Nuclear Energy?, 1981; scientific papers to various learned journals. *Recreation:* music. *Address:* 40 Maids Causeway, Cambridge CB5 8DD. *T:* Cambridge 63806. *Club:* United Oxford & Cambridge University.

COTTRELL, Richard John; Member (C) Bristol, European Parliament, since 1979; *b* 11 July 1943; *s* of John Cottrell and Winifred (*née* Barter); *m* 1965, Dinah Louise (*née* David) (marr. diss. 1986); two *d*. *Educ:* Court Fields Sch., Wellington, Somerset. Journalist: Wellington Weekly News, 1958; South Devon Jl, 1960; Topic (internat. news weekly), 1962; Evening Argus, Brighton, 1963; Lincolnshire Standard, 1964; Evening Post, Bristol, 1965; TWW, subseq. HTV, 1967–79. European Parliament: Sec., backbench cttee, European Dem. Gp, 1979; Member: Transport Cttee, 1979–83; External Econ. Relns Cttee, 1979–82; Information Cttee, 1981–84; ACP-EEC Convention, 1981–84; Agriculture Cttee, 1982–86; Rules Cttee, 1982–; Environment Cttee, 1983–; Budget Cttee, 1983–86; Energy Cttee, 1986–. European Vice-Pres., Assoc. of District Councils; Vice-Pres., Nat. Council on Inland Transport. *Publications:* Energy, the Burning Question for Europe (jtly), 1981; (ed and contrib.) Transport for Europe, 1982; contribs to Encounter. *Recreations:* travel, reading, transport studies, appreciation of real ale. *Address:* Dean House, Bower Ashton, Bristol. *T:* Bristol 663404, Brussels 234.2497.

COTTS, Sir Crichton Mitchell; *see* Cotts, Sir R. C. M.

COTTS, Sir (Robert) Crichton Mitchell, 3rd Bt, *cr* 1921; *b* 20 Oct. 1903; *yr s* of Sir William Dingwall Mitchell Cotts, 1st Bt, KBE, MP (*d* 1932), and Agnes Nivison (*d* 1966), 2nd *d* of late Robert Sloane; *S* brother, 1964; *m* 1942, Barbara (*d* 1982), *o d* of late Capt. Herbert J. A. Throckmorton, Royal Navy; two *s* three *d*. Late Temp. Major, Irish Guards; USSR, White Sea, 1941–42. *Heir:* *s* Richard Crichton Mitchell Cotts, *b* 26 July 1946. *Address:* 16 High Street, Needham Market, Suffolk.

COUCHMAN, James Randall; MP (C) Gillingham, since 1983; *b* 9 Feb. 1942; *s* of Stanley Randall Couchman and Alison Margaret Couchman; *m* 1967, Barbara Jean (*née* Heilbrun); one *s* one *d*. *Educ:* Cranleigh School; King's College, Newcastle upon Tyne; Univ. of Durham. Oil industry, 1964–70; Public House Manager, family company, 1970–74; Gen. Manager, family licensed trade co., 1974–80, Director, 1980–. Councillor, London Borough of Bexley, 1974–82 (Chm., Social Services, 1975–78, 1980–82). Chm., Bexley HA, 1981–83. Member: Assoc. of Metropolitan Authorities Social Services Cttee, 1975–80; Central Council for Educn and Training of Social Workers, 1976–80; Governor, Nat. Inst. for Social Workers, 1976–80. PPS to Minister of State for Social Security, 1984–. Mem., Social Services Select Cttee, 1983–85. Mem., Vintners' Co. *Recreations:* travel, reading, listening to music, politics. *Address:* 21 Norlands Crescent, Chislehurst, Kent BR7 5RN. *T:* 01–467 4567. *Club:* Carlton.

COULL, Prof. Alexander, PhD; FRSE; FICE, FIStructE; Regius Professor of Civil Engineering, University of Glasgow, since 1977; *b* 20 June 1931; *s* of William Coull and Jane Ritchie (*née* Reid); *m* 1962, Frances Bruce Moir; one *s* two *d*. *Educ:* Peterhead Acad.; Univ. of Aberdeen (BScEng, PhD). FRSE 1971; FICE 1972, FIStructE 1973; FASCE 1972. Res. Asst, MIT, USA, 1955; Struct. Engr, English Electric Co. Ltd, 1955–57; Lectr in Engrg, Univ. of Aberdeen, 1957–62; Lectr in Civil Engrg, Univ. of Southampton, 1962–66; Prof. of Struct. Engrg, Univ. of Strathclyde, 1966–76. Chm., Clyde Estuary Amenity Council, 1981–. *Publications:* Tall Buildings, 1967; Fundamentals of Structural Theory, 1972; author or co-author of 100 res. papers in scientific jls. *Recreations:* golf, hill walking. *Address:* 11 Blackwood Road, Milngavie, Glasgow G62 7LB. *T:* 041–956 1655. *Club:* Buchanan Castle Golf (Drymen).

COULSHAW, Rev. Leonard, CB 1949; MC 1917; FKC; Chaplain of the Fleet and Archdeacon of the Royal Navy, 1948–52; *b* 24 Feb. 1896; *s* of late Percy Dean Coulshaw and late Alice Maud Hatt; *m* 1932, Yvonne Cecilia Joan, *d* of Rev. C. Hanmer-Strudwick, Rector of Slawston, Leics; no *c*. *Educ:* Southend-on-Sea High Sch. for Boys; King's Coll., London; Ely Theological Coll. Served European War, 1914–18, Essex Regiment, 1914–20 (MC, despatches); left Army with rank of Captain. Ordained, 1923; Curate, St Andrew's, Romford, Essex; commissioned as Chaplain, RN, 1927; served in HMS Cyclops, 1927–29; RN Barracks, Portsmouth, 1929; HMS Iron Duke, 1929–30; HMS Effingham (Flagship East Indies Station), 1930–32; Royal Hospital Sch., Holbrook, 1932–34; Senior Chaplain HMS Ganges, 1934–37; HMS Royal Sovereign, 1937 (present at Coronation Review, Spithead); HMS Revenge, 1937. Chaplain Royal Naval Hospital, Malta, 1937–40; RM Depot, Lympstone, 1940–42; Senior Chaplain, RN Base, Lyness, 1942–44; Chaplain HM Dockyard, Sheerness, 1944–46; RM Barracks, Portsmouth, 1946–47; KHC, 1948–52; QHC, 1952; Vicar of: West End, Southampton, 1952–54; Frensham, 1954–65. *Address:* 4 Ashurst Court, Alverstoke, Gosport, Hants PO12 2TZ. *T:* Gosport 582467.

COULSHED, Dame (Mary) Frances, DBE 1953 (CBE 1949); TD 1951; Brigadier, Women's Royal Army Corps, retired; *b* 10 Nov. 1904; *d* of Wilfred and Maud Coulshed. *Educ:* Parkfields Cedars, Derby; Convent of the Sacred Heart, Kensington. Served War of 1939–45 (despatches); North-West Europe, 1944–45, with General Headquarters Anti-Aircraft Troops and at Headquarters Lines of Communications; Deputy Dir, Anti Aircraft Command, 1946–50; Dep. Dir, War Office, July-Dec. 1950; Director, WRAC, 1951–54. ADC to the King, 1951, to the Queen, 1952–54. Order of Leopold I of Belgium with palm, Croix de Guerre with palm, 1946. *Address:* 815 Endsleigh Court, Upper Woburn Place, WC1.

COULSON, Mrs Ann Margaret; Regional Planning Administrator, West Midlands Regional Health Authority, since 1983; *b* 11 March 1935; *d* of Sidney Herbert Wood and Ada (*née* Mills); *m* 1958, Peter James Coulson; two *s* one *d*. *Educ:* The Grammar Sch., Chippenham, Wilts; UCL (BScEcon); Univ. of Manchester (DSA); Wolverhampton Technical Teachers' Coll. (CertEd). Hosp. Admin, 1956–62; Lectr in Econs and Management, Bromsgrove Coll. of Further Educn, 1968–76; Asst Dir, North Worchestershire Coll., 1976–80; Service Planning and Develt Co-ordinator, W Midlands RHA, 1980–83. City of Birmingham Dist Council, 1973–79; special interest in Social Services. Mem., IBA, 1976–81. FBIM. *Recreations:* cooking, music, theatre. *Address:* Rowans, Leamington Hastings, near Rugby, Warwicks CV23 8DY. *T:* Leamington Spa 633264.

COULSON, (James) Michael; His Honour Judge Coulson; a Circuit Judge, Midland and Oxford Circuit, since 1983; *b* 23 Nov. 1927; *s* of William Coulson, Wold Newton Hall, Driffield, E Yorks; *m* 1st, 1955, Dilys Adair Jones (marr. diss.); one *s*; 2nd, 1977, Barbara Elizabeth Islay, *d* of Dr Roland Moncrieff Chambers; one *s* one *d*. *Educ:* Fulneck Sch., Yorks; Merton Coll., Oxford; Royal Agricultural Coll., Cirencester. Served E Riding Yeomanry (Wenlocks Horse); Queen's Own Yorks Yeomanry (Major). Called to Bar, Middle Temple, 1951; Mem. North Eastern Circuit; Asst Recorder of Sheffield, 1965–71; Dep. Chm., NR of Yorks QS, 1968–71; a Chm. of Industrial Tribunals, 1968–83; a Recorder of the Crown Court, 1981–83. Dep. Chm., Northern Agricl Land Tribunal, 1967–73. Former Mem., Tadcaster RDC. MP (C) Kingston-upon-Hull North, 1959–64; PPS to Solicitor Gen., 1962–64; Mem., Executive Cttee, Conservative Commonwealth Council. Sometime Sec., Bramham Moor and York and Ainsty Point to Point Race Meetings. *Recreations:* hunting, reading, travel. *Address:* The Tithe Barn, Wymondham, Melton Mowbray, Leics. *Club:* Cavalry and Guards.

COULSON, Sir John Eltringham, KCMG 1957 (CMG 1946); President, Hampshire Branch, British Red Cross Society, 1972–79; Secretary-General of EFTA, 1965–72, retired; *b* 13 Sept. 1909; *er s* of H. J. Coulson, Bickley, Kent; *m* 1944, Mavis Ninette Beazley; two *s*. *Educ:* Rugby; Corpus Christi Coll., Cambridge (Hon. Fellow 1975). Entered Diplomatic Service in 1932. Served in Bucharest, Min. of Econ. Warfare, War Cabinet Office, Foreign Office and Paris. Sometime Dep. UK representative to UN, New York; Asst Under-Sec., Foreign Office, 1952–55; Minister British Embassy, Washington, 1955–57; Asst to Paymaster-Gen., 1957–60; Ambassador to Sweden, 1960–63; Dep. Under-Sec. of State, Foreign Office, 1963–65; Chief of Administration of HM Diplomatic Service, Jan.-Sept. 1965. Director: Atlas Copco (GB), 1972–80; Sheerness Steel Co., 1972–84. Knight Grand Cross, Order of the North Star, Sweden, 1982. *Recreations:* fishing, golf. *Address:* The Old Mill, Selborne, Hants. *Club:* Brooks's.

COULSON, Emeritus Prof. John Metcalfe; Professor of Chemical Engineering, University of Newcastle upon Tyne (formerly University of Durham), 1954–75 (on leave of absence to Heriot-Watt University, 1968–69), now Emeritus; *b* 13 Dec. 1910; *m* 1943, Clarice Dora Scott (*d* 1961); two *s*; *m* 1965, Christine Gould; one *d*. *Educ:* Clifton Coll.; Christ's Coll., Cambridge; Imperial Coll. Royal Arsenal, Woolwich, 1935–39; Asst Lectr, Imperial Coll., 1939; Ministry of Supply (Royal Ordnance Factories), 1939–45; Lectr in Chem. Engineering, Imperial Coll., 1945–52; Reader, 1952–54. Hon. DSc Heriot-Watt, 1973. Davis Medal, IChemE, 1973. *Publications:* Chemical Engineering Vol. I and Vol. II (with Prof. J. F. Richardson), 1954 and 1955, 3rd edn 1977; contrib. Instn of Chem. Eng, Chem. Eng Science, etc. *Recreations:* chess, photography. *Address:* Flat 2, Wheatlands Court, 42 Wheatlands Road East, Harrogate, N Yorks.

COULSON, Michael; *see* Coulson, J. M.

COULTASS, (George Thomas) Clive; Senior Keeper, Imperial War Museum, London, since 1979; Keeper of Audio-Visual Records, since 1983 (Department of Film, 1970–83); *b* 5 July 1931; *m* 1962, Norma Morris. *Educ:* Tadcaster Grammar Sch.; Univ. of Sheffield (BA Hons). Teacher in various London schools, 1955–62; Lectr/Sen. Lectr in History, James Graham Coll., Leeds, 1962–69; Keeper of Film Programming, Imperial War Museum, 1969–70. Vice-Pres., Internat. Assoc. for Audio-Visual Media in Hist. Res. and Educn, 1978–85. Organiser: various film historical confs, 1973–; exhibn on British film and World War II, 1982. *Publications:* section in The Historian and Film, 1976; articles in various historical jls. *Recreations:* travel, music, including opera, reading. *Address:* 39 Fairfield Grove, SE7 8UA.

COULTER, Robert, MC 1945; Controller BBC Scotland, 1973–75, retired 1976; *b* 15 June 1914; *s* of John and Margaret Coulter, Glasgow; *m* 1940, Flora Macleod Bell; no *c*. *Educ:* Irvine Royal Academy; Glasgow Univ. MA Hons English Lit. and Lang. 1st Bn Royal Scots Fusiliers, India, UK, Madagascar and Burma, 1939–46 (Major). Principal English Master, Ayr Grammar Sch., 1946–48; Educn Administration, Belfast, 1948–53; BBC Northern Ireland, 1953–67: radio and TV producer; TV organiser; Asst Head of Programmes; Dir of Television, Uganda, 1967–69; Head of Programmes, BBC Scotland, 1969–73. IBA Res. Fellow at QUB, 1978 (Signposts report on youth employment and radio/TV special output, 1980). *Recreation:* recollections in tranquillity. *Address:* 20 Knockmore Park, Bangor, Co. Down, N Ireland. *T:* Bangor (Co. Down) 462510.

COULTHARD, Alan George Weall; His Honour Judge Alan Coulthard; a Circuit Judge since 1981; *b* Bournemouth, 20 Jan. 1924; *s* of late George Robert Coulthard and Cicely Eva Coulthard (*née* Minns); *m* 1948, Jacqueline Anna, *d* of late Dr T. H. James, Fishguard; two *s* two *d*. *Educ:* Watford Grammar Sch. Pilot, RAF, 1941–46 (Flt-Lt); 1st Officer, BOAC, 1946–48; Pilot and Staff Officer, RAF, 1948–58. Called to Bar, Inner Temple, 1959; practised at Bar, Swansea, 1959–81; Asst Recorder, 1970; a Recorder of the Crown Court, 1972–81; Hon. Recorder of Borough of Llanelli, 1975–81. Chm., Medical Appeals Tribunal for Wales, 1976–81. Contested (L) Pembrokeshire, 1964. Pres., Swansea Festival Patrons' Assoc., 1974–80. BBC sound and TV broadcasts, 1960–. *Recreations:* music, motor sport, ornithology, country life. *Address:* 3 Bolton Road, St John's Wood, NW8 0RJ. *T:* 01–328 8941. *Club:* Royal Air Force.

See also C. W. Coulthard.

COULTHARD, Air Vice-Marshal Colin Weall, CB 1975; AFC 1953 (Bar 1958); retired; *b* 27 Feb. 1921; *s* of late Wing Comdr George Robert Coulthard and Cicely Eva Coulthard (*née* Minns); *m* 1st, 1941, Norah Ellen Creighton (marr. diss.); one *s* two *d*; 2nd, 1957, Eileen Pamela (*née* Barber); one *s*. *Educ:* Watford Grammar Sch.; De Havilland Aeronautical Tech. Sch. Commissioned RAF, 1941; Fighter Pilot, 1942–45 (despatches, 1945); HQ Fighter Comd, 1948–49; RAF Staff Coll., 1950; OC 266 Sqn, Wunstorf, 1952–54, DFLS, CFE, 1955; OC Flying, 233(F) OCU, 1956–57; OC AFDS, CFE, 1957–59; HQ Fighter Comd, 1959–60; Stn Cdr, Gutersloh, 1961–64; MoD, 1964–66; SOA, AHQ Malta, 1966–67; DOR 1(RAF), MoD, 1967–69; Air Attaché, Washington, DC, 1970–72; Mil. Dep. to Head of Defence Sales, MoD, 1973–75. Governor, Truro Sch., 1981–. FRAeS. *Recreations:* walking, shooting, motor sport. *Address:* Fiddlers, Old Truro Road, Goonhavern, Truro TR4 9NN. *T:* Zelah 312. *Club:* Royal Air Force.

See also A. G. W. Coulthard.

COULTHARD, William Henderson, CBE 1968; MSc, CEng, FIMechE, FRPS; Deputy Director, Royal Armament Research and Development Establishment, 1962–74; *b* 24 Nov. 1913; *s* of William and Louise Coulthard, Flimby, Cumberland; *m* 1942, Peggie Frances Platts Taylor, Chiselhurst; one *d* (one *s* decd). *Educ:* Flimby, Workington Schs; Armstrong Coll., University of Durham. Mather Schol., University of Durham, 1932. Linen Industry Research Assoc., 1934; Instrument Dept, Royal Aircraft Estabt, 1935; Air Ministry HQ, 1939; Sqdn Ldr RAFVR, 1944; Official German Translator, 1945; Air Photography Div., RAE, 1946; Supt, later Dep. Dir, Fighting Vehicles Research and Development Estabt, 1951. *Publications:* Aircraft Instrument Design, 1951; Aircraft

Engineer's Handbook, 1953; (trans.) Mathematical Instruments (Capellen), 1948; (trans.) Gyroscopes (Grammel), 1950; articles in technical journals. *Recreations:* art history (Diploma in History of Art, London Univ., 1964); languages. *Address:* Argyll, Francis Close, Ewell, Surrey. *T:* 01-337 4909.

COUNSELL, Hazel Rosemary; Her Honour Judge Hazel Counsell; a Circuit Judge, since 1978; *b* 7 Jan. 1931; *d* of late Arthur Henry Counsell and Elsie Winifred Counsell; *m* 1980, Peter Fallon, *qv. Educ:* Clifton High Sch.; Switzerland; Univ. of Bristol (LLB). Called to the Bar, Gray's Inn, 1956; Western Circuit, 1956–; a Recorder of the Crown Court, 1976–77. Legal Dept, Min. of Labour, 1959–62. Governor, Colston Girls Sch. *Recreations:* reading, swimming, travel. *Address:* The Crown Court, The Guildhall, Broad Street, Bristol.

COUNSELL, John William, OBE 1975; Managing Director of the Theatre Royal, Windsor, since 1938; *b* 24 April 1905; *s* of Claude Christopher Counsell and Evelyn Counsell (*née* Fleming); *m* 1939, Mary Antoinette Kerridge; twin *d. Educ:* Sedbergh Sch.; Exeter Coll., Oxford. Mem. of the OUDS, 1923–26; formerly engaged as a tutor. First appearance on professional stage, Playhouse, Oxford, 1928; two tours of Canada with Maurice Colbourne in Shavian Repertory, 1928–29; leading juvenile, Northampton and Folkestone Repertory Cos, 1929–30; Stage Manager for Baliol Holloway's production of Richard III, New, 1930; Stage Dir, Scenic Artist and eventually Producer, Oxford Repertory Company, 1930–33; Producer and Joint Man.-Dir, Windsor Repertory Company, 1933–34; Lover's Leap, Vaudeville, 1934; toured as Tubbs in Sweet Aloes, 1936; toured S Africa in The Frog, 1936–37; refounded Windsor Repertory Co., 1938. Called to the Colours as Territorial reservist, 1940; served in N Africa, France and Germany, 1942–45; Mem. planning staff of SHAEF; demobilised, 1945, rank of Lieut-Col. Resumed direction of Theatre Royal, Windsor. Has, in addition, produced: Birthmark, Playhouse, 1947; Little Holiday, 1948; Captain Brassbound's Conversion, Lyric, Hammersmith, 1948; The Man with the Umbrella, Duchess, 1950; Who Goes There!, Vaudeville, 1951; His House in Order, 1951; Waggon Load of Monkeys, Savoy, 1951; For Better for Worse, Comedy, 1952; Anastasia, St James's, 1953; Grab Me a Gondola, Lyric, 1956; Three Way Switch, Aldwych, 1958; How Say You?, Aldwych, 1959. *Publications:* Counsell's Opinion (autobiography), 1963; Play Direction: a practical viewpoint, 1973. *Recreations:* gardening, photography. *Address:* 3 Queen's Terrace, Windsor, Berks. *T:* Windsor 65344.

COUNSELL, Paul Hayward; His Honour Judge Counsell; a Circuit Judge since 1973; *b* 13 Nov. 1926; twin *s* of Frederick Charles Counsell and Edna Counsell; *m* 1959, Joan Agnes Strachan; one *s* two *d. Educ:* Colston Sch., Bristol; Queen's Coll., Oxford (MA). Served RAF, 1944–48. Admitted Solicitor, 1951; called to Bar, Inner Temple, 1962. Northern Rhodesia: Crown Solicitor, 1955–56; Crown Counsel, 1956–61; Resident Magistrate, 1958; Dir of Public Prosecutions, 1962–63; Solicitor General, 1963–64; QC 1963; Acting Attorney General, 1964; Solicitor-General, Zambia, 1964, MLC 1963–64. In chambers of Lord Hailsham, Temple, 1965–73; Dep. Circuit Judge, 1971–73. Chm., Industrial Tribunal, 1970–73. *Recreation:* model engineering. *Address:* c/o Hitchin County Court, Park House, 1–12 Old Park Road, Hitchin, Herts SG5 1LX.

COUPER, Prof. Alastair Dougal, FCIT; FNI; FRGS; Professor of Maritime Studies, University of Wales Institute of Science and Technology, since 1970; *b* 4 June 1931; *s* of Daniel Alexander Couper and Davina Couper (*née* Rilley); *m* 1958, Norma Milton; two *s* two *d. Educ:* Robert Gordon's School of Navigation; Univ. of Aberdeen (MA, DipEd; Master Mariner); Australian National Univ. (PhD). Cadet and Navigating Officer, Merchant Navy, 1947–57; student, Univ. of Aberdeen, 1958–62, postgraduate teaching course, 1962–63; Research Schol., Sch. of Pacific Studies, ANU, Canberra, 1963–66; Lectr, Univ. of Durham, 1967–70. UN Consultant, 1972–; Chm., Maritime Bd of Council for National Academic Awards, 1978–85; Assessor, Chartered Inst. of Transport, 1976–85; Founder Mem., Council, British Maritime League, 1982–85. Editor (and Founder), Journal of Maritime Policy and Management, 1973–84. *Publications:* Geography of Sea Transport, 1971; The Law of the Sea, 1978; (ed) Times Atlas of the Oceans, 1983; contrib. Pacific, in World Atlas of Agriculture, 1969; Pacific in Transition (ed Brookfield), 1973; several UN Reports, UNCTAD, ILO, IMO; articles in jls; conf. papers. *Recreations:* hill walking, sailing, archaeology, Pacific history. *Address:* University of Wales Institute of Science and Technology, Cardiff. *T:* Cardiff 42588.

COUPER, Heather Anita; astronomy broadcaster and author, since 1983; *b* 2 June 1949; *o d* of George Couper Elder Couper and late Anita Couper (*née* Taylor). *Educ:* St Mary's Grammar Sch., Northwood, Mddx; Univ. of Leicester (BSc Hons Astronomy and Physics); Univ. of Oxford. Management trainee, Peter Robinson Ltd, 1967–69; Res. Asst, Cambridge Observatories, 1969–70; Lectr, Greenwich Planetarium, Old Royal Observ., 1977–83. Vice-Pres. 1986– (Pres. 1984–86), Brit. Astron. Assoc.; Pres., Jun. Astron. Soc., 1987–. Presenter on television: Heavens Above, 1981; Spacewatch, 1983; The Planets, 1985; Presenter on radio: Astronomy, 1983; Science Now, 1983; Cosmic Pursuits, 1985; also appearances and interviews on wide variety of television and radio progs. *Publications:* (jtly) Space Frontiers, 1978; Exploring Space, 1980; (jtly) Heavens Above, 1981; (jtly) The Restless Universe, 1982; (jtly) Physics, 1983; (jtly) Astronomy, 1983; Journey into Space, 1984; (jtly) Starfinder, 1984; Space Scientist explores Comets and Meteors, 1985; Space Scientist explores the Planets, 1985; Space Scientist explores the Stars, 1985; (jtly) The Halley's Comet Pop-Up Book, 1985; (jtly) The Universe: a 3-dimensional study, 1985; (jtly) The Planets, 1985; numerous articles in nat. newspapers and magazines. *Recreations:* travel, the English countryside, chamber music; wine, food and winemaking. *Address:* 55 Colomb Street, Greenwich, SE10 9EZ. *T:* 01-853 0574.

COUPER, Sir (Robert) Nicholas (Oliver), 6th Bt *cr* 1841; *b* 9 Oct. 1945; *s* of Sir George Robert Cecil Couper, 5th Bt, and Margaret Grace (*d* 1984), *d* of late Robert George Dashwood Thomas; *S* father, 1975; *m* 1972, Curzon Henrietta, *d* of late Major George Burrell MacKean, DL, JP; one *s* one *d. Educ:* Eton; RMA, Sandhurst. Major, Blues and Royals; retired, 1975. Now working with Aylesfords as an estate agent. *Heir: s* James George Couper, *b* 27 Oct. 1977. *Address:* 39 Cloncurry Street, SW6.

COUPLAND, Prof. Rex Ernest; Professor of Human Morphology, since 1967 and Dean of Medicine, since 1981, University of Nottingham; Hon. Consultant, Regional Hospital Board, since 1970; *b* 30 Jan. 1924; *s* of Ernest Coupland, company dir; *m* 1947, Lucy Eileen Sargent; one *s* one *d. Educ:* Mirfield Grammar Sch.; University of Leeds. MB, ChB with honours, 1947; MD with distinction, 1952; PhD 1954; DSc 1970. House appointments, Leeds General Infirmary, 1947; Demonstrator and Lecturer in Anatomy, University of Leeds, 1948, 1950–58; Asst Prof. of Anatomy, University of Minnesota, USA, 1955–56; Prof. of Anatomy, Queen's Coll., Dundee, University of St Andrews, 1958–67. Medical Officer, RAF, 1948–50. FRSE 1960. Member: Biological Research Board of MRC, 1964–70; Med. Adv. Bd, Crippling Diseases Foundn, 1971–75; CMO's Academic Forum, 1984–; Chm., MRC Non-Ionizing Radiations Cttee, 1970–; Derbyshire AHA, 1978–81; Trent RHA, 1981–; Chm., Nottingham Div., BMA, 1978–79; GMC, 1982–. President: Anat. Soc. GB and Ireland, 1976–78; British Assoc. of Clinical Anat., 1977–82. Wood Jones Medal for contrib. to clinical anatomy, RCS, 1984. *Publications:* The Natural History of the Chromaffin Cell, 1965; (ed jtly) Chromaffin, Enterochromaffin and Related Cells, 1976; (ed jtly) Peripheral Neuroendocrine Interaction, 1978; papers in jls of anatomy, physiology, endocrinology, pathology and pharmacology on endocrine and nervous systems and in jls of radiology on NMR imaging; *chapters on:* Anatomy of the Human Kidney, in Renal Disease (ed Black), 1962, 1968, 1973; The Chromaffin System, in Catecholamines (ed Blaschko and Muscholl), 1973; The Blood Supply of the Adrenal Gland, in Handbook of Physiology, 1974; The Adrenal Medulla, in The Cell in Medical Science (ed Beck and Lloyd), 1976; Endocrine System, in Textbook of Human Anatomy (ed W. J. Hamilton), 1976; *contribs to:* Hormones and Evolution, Vol. I, ed Barrington, 1979; Biogenic Amines in Development, ed Parvez and Parvez, 1980; Hormones in Human Tissues, Vol. I, ed Fotherby and Pal, 1981; Asst Editor, Gray's Anatomy (ed Davies), 1967. *Recreations:* shooting, gardening. *Address:* Foxhollow, Quaker Lane, Farnsfield, Newark, Notts NG22 8EE. *T:* Mansfield 882028.

COURAGE, Richard Hubert, DL; *b* 23 Jan. 1915; *s* of Raymond Courage and Mildred Frances Courage (formerly Fisher); *m* 1st, 1941, Jean Elizabeth Agnes Watson (*d* 1977), *d* of late Sir Charles Cuningham Watson, KCIE, CSI, ICS; two *s* (and one *s* decd); 2nd, 1978, Phyllida Anne, *widow* of J. D. Derouet. *Educ:* Eton. Served War of 1939–45: Northants Yeomanry, 1939–46, Major (despatches). Director: Courage Ltd, 1948–75 (Chm., 1959–75); Imperial Group Ltd, 1972–75; Norwich Union Insce Group, 1975–80; Chm., London Adv. Bd, Norwich Union Insce Gp, 1975–80 (Dir, 1964–80). Chm. Governors, Brentwood Sch., Essex, 1976–. JP Essex, 1955–85; DL Essex, 1977. *Recreations:* yachting and shooting. *Address:* Chainbridge, Mountnessing, near Brentwood, Essex. *T:* Brentwood 222206.

COURATIN, Rev. Canon Arthur Hubert; Sixth Canon and Chapter Librarian, Durham Cathedral, 1962–74, Canon Emeritus since 1974; *b* 1902; *s* of Arthur Louis and Marian Couratin. *Educ:* Dulwich Coll.; Corpus Christi Coll., Oxford (Scholar); S Stephen's House, Oxford. 1st Cl. Classical Moderations; 2nd Cl. Literae Humaniores; 2nd Cl. Hons Sch. of Theology; BA 1925; MA 1927. Deacon, 1926; priest, 1927; Asst Curate, S Saviour's, Roath, 1926–30 (in charge of S Francis', Roath, 1927–30); Vice-Principal, Queen's Coll., Birmingham, 1930; Asst Curate, S Stephen's, Lewisham (in charge of Church of the Transfiguration, Lewisham), 1930–35; Chaplain, S Stephen's House, Oxford, 1935–36, Vice-Principal, 1936, Principal, 1936–62; Junior Chaplain, Merton Coll., Oxford, 1936–39. Hon. Canon of Christ Church, 1961–62. *Address:* 7 Pimlico, Durham DH1 4QW. *T:* Durham 64767.

COURCEL, Baron de; (Geoffroy Chodron de Courcel); Grand' Croix de la Légion d'Honneur, 1980; Compagnon de la Libération, 1943; Croix de Guerre, 1939–45; President, France-GB Association, since 1978; *b* Tours, Indre-et-Loire, 11 Sept. 1912; *s* of Louis Chodron de Courcel, Officer, and Alice Lambert-Champy; *m* 1954, Martine Hallade; two *s. Educ:* Stanislas Coll.; University of Paris. DenDr, LèsL, Dip. Ecole des Sciences Politiques. Attaché, Warsaw, 1937; Sec., Athens, 1938–39; Armée du Levant, 1939; joined Free French Forces, June 1940; Chef de Cabinet, Gén. de Gaulle, London, 1940–41; Captain 1st Spahis marocains Regt, Egypt, Libya and Tunisia, 1941–43; Dep.-Dir of Cabinet, Gén de Gaulle, Algiers, 1943–44; Mem. Conseil de l'Ordre de la Libération, 1944; Regional Comr for Liberated Territories, 1944; in charge of Alsace-Lorraine Dept, Min. of Interior, 1944–45; Counsellor, 1945; in Min. of Foreign Affairs: Dep. Dir Central and N European Sections, 1945–47; First Counsellor, Rome, 1947–50; Minister Plen., 1951; Dir Bilateral Trade Agreements Section, 1951; Dir African and ME Section, 1953; Dir Gen., Polit. and Econ. Affairs, Min. of Moroccan and Tunisian Affairs, 1954; Perm. Sec., Nat. Defence, 1955–58; Ambassador, Perm. Rep. to NATO, 1958; Sec.-Gen. Présidence de la République, 1959–62; Ambassador to London, 1962–72; Sec.-Gen., Min. of For. Affairs, 1973–76. Ambassadeur de France, 1965; Hon. DCL Oxon, 1970; Hon. LLD Birmingham, 1972. MC (Great Britain) 1943; Grand Cross of Royal Victorian Order (Hon. GCVO), 1950, etc. *Publication:* L'influence de la Conférence de Berlin de 1885 sur le droit Colonial International, 1936. *Recreations:* shooting, swimming. *Address:* 7 rue de Médicis, 75006 Paris, France; La Ravinière, Fontaines en Sologne, 41250 Bracieux, France.

COURCY; *see* de Courcy.

COURNAND, André Frédéric, MD; Professor Emeritus of Medicine, Columbia University College of Physicians and Surgeons, New York, since 1964 (Professor of Medicine, 1951–60); *b* Paris, 24 Sept. 1895; *s* of Jules Cournand and Marguérite Weber; *m* 1st, Sibylle Blumer (*d* 1959); three *d* (one *s* killed in action, 1944); 2nd, 1963, Ruth Fabian (*d* 1973); 3rd, 1975, Beatrice Berle. *Educ:* Sorbonne, Paris. BA Faculté des Lettres, 1913; PCB Faculté des Sciences, 1914; MD Faculté de Médecine, 1930. Interne des Hôpitaux de Paris, 1925–30. Came to US in 1930; naturalized American Citizen since 1941. Director, Cardio-Pulmonary Laboratory, Columbia University Division, Bellevue Hospital; Visiting Physician, Chest Service, Bellevue Hospital, 1952. Member: American Physiological Soc.; Assoc. of Amer. Physicians; National Acad. of Sciences (USA), 1958; Amer. Acad. of Arts and Sciences, 1975; Académie des Sciences et Belles Lettres et Arts, Lyon, 1982. Hon. Member: British Cardiac Soc.; Swedish Soc. Internal Medicine; Swedish Cardiac Soc.; Soc. Médicale des Hôpitaux, Paris; Foreign Mem., Académie Royale de Médecine de Belgique, 1970; Foreign Member: Académie des Sciences, Institut de France, 1957; Académie Nationale de Médecine, Paris, 1958. Laureate: Andreas Retzius Silver Medal of Swedish Soc. Internal Medicine, 1946; Award, US Public Health Assoc., 1949. Croix de Guerre (1914–18) France, three stars; Commandeur de la Légion d'Honneur, 1970 (Officier, 1957). Nobel Prize for Medicine and Physiology (jointly), 1956; Jimenez Diaz Fondacion Prize, 1970; Trudeau Medal, 1971. Doctor (*hc*): University of Strasburg, 1957; University of Lyons, 1958; Université libre de Bruxelles 1959; University of Pisa, 1961; University of Birmingham, 1961; Gustaphus Adolphus, Coll., Minnesota, 1963; University of Brazil, 1965; Columbia Univ., 1965; Univ. of Nancy, 1968. *Publications:* Cardiac Catheterization in Congenital Heart Disease, 1949; L'Insuffisance cardiaque chronique, 1950; Shaping the Future, 1974; From Roots—to Late Budding, (autobiog.), 1986; numerous articles on human physiopathology of lungs and heart and on the relation between science and society. *Recreations:* Groupe de la Haute Montagne du Club Alpin Français, 1929, and American Alpine Club. *Address:* 142 East 19th Street, New York, NY 10003, USA. *T:* 473 3660. *Club:* Century Association (New York).

COURT, Hon. Sir Charles (Walter Michael), AK 1982; KCMG 1979; Kt 1972; OBE 1946; MLA (Liberal Party) for Nedlands, 1953–82; Premier of Western Australia, 1974–82; also Treasurer, and Minister co-ordinating Economic and Regional Development, 1974–82; *b* Crawley, Sussex, 29 Sept. 1911; *s* of late W. J. Court, Perth; *m* 1936, Rita M., *d* of L. R. Steffanoni; five *s. Educ:* Leederville and Rosalie State Schs; Perth Boys' Sch. Chartered Accountant, 1933; Partner, Hendry, Rae & Court, 1938–70. Served AIF, 1940–46; Lt-Col. State Registrar, Inst. Chartered Accountants in Aust. (WA Br.), 1946–52, Mem. State Council, 1952–55. Dep. Leader, 1957–59, 1971–72, and Leader, 1972–74, of Opposition, WA; Minister, Western Australia: for Industrial Development and the NW, 1959–71; for Railways, 1959–67; for Transport, 1965–66. Chm., Adv. Cttee under WA Prices Control Act, 1948–52; Pres., WA Band Assoc., 1954–59. Hon.

Colonel: WA Univ. Regt, 1969–75; SAS Regt, 1976–80. Paul Harris Fellow, Rotary, 1982. FCA; FCIS; FASA. Hon. FAIM 1980. Freeman: City of Nedlands, 1982; Shire of West Kimberley, WA, 1983. Hon. LLD Univ. of WA, 1969; Hon. DTech WA Inst. of Technol., 1982. Manufacturers' Export Council Award, 1969; James Kirby Award, Inst. of Production Engrs, 1971; Australian Chartered Accountant of the Year, 1983. Life Member: Musicians Union, 1953; ASA, 1979; Returned Services League, 1981; Inst. of Chartered Accountants in Australia, 1982. *Publications:* many professional papers on accountancy, and papers on economic and resource development. *Recreations:* music, yachting. *Address:* 46 Waratah Avenue, Nedlands, WA 6009, Australia. *Clubs:* Weld, Commercial Travellers Association (Perth); Nedlands and Perth Rotary, Lions.

COURT, Emeritus Prof. Seymour Donald Mayneord, CBE 1969; MD; FRCP; *b* 4 Jan. 1912; *s* of David Henry and Ethel Court; *m* 1939, Dr Frances Edith Radcliffe; two *s* one *d*. *Educ:* Adams Grammar Sch., Wem; Birmingham Univ (MB, ChB, 1936; MD 1947); FRCP 1956. Resident Hosp. appts Birmingham Gen. Hosps, and Hosp. for Sick Children, London, 1936–38; Paediatric Registrar, Wander Scholar, Westminster Hosp., 1938–39; Physician, EMS, 1939–46; Nuffield Fellow in Child Health, 1946–47; Reader in Child Health, University of Durham, 1947–55; James Spence Prof. of Child Health, Univ. of Newcastle upon Tyne, 1955–72, Emeritus Professor, 1972. Chm., Child Health Services Cttee for Eng. and Wales, 1973–76. Pres., British Paediatric Assoc., 1973–76. FRCGP *ad eundem* 1982; Hon. FRSM 1986. James Spence Medal, British Paed. Assoc., 1978; Nils Rosén von Rosenstein Medal, Swedish Paed. Assoc., 1979. *Publications:* (jointly) Growing Up in Newcastle upon Tyne, 1960; (ed) The Medical Care of Children, 1963; (ed jointly) Paediatrics in the Seventies, 1972; (jointly) The School Years in Newcastle upon Tyne, 1974; (ed jtly) Fit for the Future, 1976; contributions to special jls and text books on respiratory infection in childhood. *Recreations:* walking, natural history, poetry. *Address:* 8 Towers Avenue, Jesmond, Newcastle upon Tyne NE2 3QE. *T:* Newcastle upon Tyne 2814884.

COURTAULD, Rev. (Augustine) Christopher (Caradoc); Vicar of St Paul's, Knightsbridge, since 1978; *b* 12 Sept. 1934; *s* of late Augustine Courtauld and of Lady Butler of Saffron Walden; *m* 1978, Dr Elizabeth Ann Molland, MD, FRCPath, *d* of late Rev. Preb. John W. G. Molland; two *d*. *Educ:* Trinity College, Cambridge (BA 1958, MA 1961); Westcott House, Cambridge. Deacon 1960, priest 1961, Manchester; Curate of Oldham, 1960–63; Chaplain: Trinity College, Cambridge, 1963–68; The London Hospital, 1968–78. *Recreation:* sailing. *Address:* St Paul's Vicarage, 32 Wilton Place, SW1.

COURTENAY, family name of **Earl of Devon.**

COURTENAY, Lord; Hugh Rupert Courtenay; Partner with Messrs Stratton & Holborow, Chartered Surveyors, Exeter; *b* 5 May 1942; *o s* of 17th Earl of Devon, *qv*; *m* 1967, Dianna Frances, *er d* of J. G. Watherston, Jedburgh, Roxburghshire; one *s* three *d*. *Educ:* Winchester; Magdalene Coll., Cambridge (BA). ARICS. Captain, Wessex Yeomanry, retd. *Recreations:* riding, hunting, shooting. *Heir:* *s* Hon. Charles Peregrine Courtenay, *b* 14 Aug. 1975. *Address:* The Stables House, Powderham, near Exeter, Devon. *T:* Starcross 890370. *Club:* University Pitt (Cambridge).

COURTENAY, Thomas Daniel, (Tom Courtenay); actor; *b* 25 Feb. 1937; *s* of Thomas Henry Courtenay and late Annie Eliza Quest; *m* 1973, Cheryl Kennedy (marr. diss. 1982). *Educ:* Kingston High Sch., Hull; University Coll., London. RADA, 1958–60; started acting professionally, 1960; Old Vic, 1960–61: Konstantin Treplieff, Poins, Feste and Puck; Billy Liar, Cambridge Theatre, June 1961–Feb. 1962 and on tour; Andorra, National Theatre (guest), 1964; The Cherry Orchard, and Macbeth, Chichester, 1966; joined 69 Theatre Co., Manchester, 1966: Charley's Aunt, 1966; Romeo, Playboy of the Western World, 1967; Hamlet (Edinburgh Festival), 1968; She Stoops to Conquer, (transferred to Garrick), 1969; Peer Gynt, 1970; Charley's Aunt, Apollo, 1971; Time and Time Again, Comedy, 1972 (Variety Club of GB Stage Actor Award, 1972); The Norman Conquests, Globe, 1974; The Fool, Royal Court, 1975; Prince of Homburg, The Rivals, Manchester (opening prods of The Royal Exchange), 1976; Otherwise Engaged, NY, 1977; Clouds, Duke of York's, 1978; Crime and Punishment, Manchester, 1978; The Dresser, Manchester and Queen's, 1980 (Drama Critics Award and New Standard Award for best actor, 1980), NY 1981; The Misanthrope, Manchester and Round House, 1981; Andy Capp, Manchester and Aldwych, 1982; Jumpers, Manchester, 1984. Began acting in films, 1962. *Films:* The Loneliness of the Long Distance Runner; Private Potter; Billy Liar; King and Country (Volpi Cup, 1964); Operation Crossbow; King Rat; Dr Zhivago; The Night of the Generals; The Day the Fish Came Out; A Dandy in Aspic; Otley; One Day in the Life of Ivan Denisovitch; Catch Me a Spy; The Dresser. Has appeared on Television. Best Actor Award, Prague Festival, 1968; TV Drama Award (for Oswald in Ghosts), 1968. *Recreations:* listening to music (mainly classical and romantic); watching sport (and occasionally taking part in it, in a light-hearted manner). *Address:* Putney. *Club:* Garrick.

COURTNEY, Comdr Anthony Tosswill, OBE 1949; RN; author and lecturer; Managing Director, New English Typewriting School Ltd, since 1969; *b* 16 May 1908; *s* of Basil Tosswill Courtney and Frances Elizabeth Courtney (*née* Rankin); *m* 1st, 1938, Elisabeth Mary Cortlandt Stokes (*d* 1961); no *c*; 2nd, 1962, Lady (Elizabeth) Trefgarne (marr. diss. 1966); 3rd, 1971, Mrs Angela Bradford. *Educ:* Royal Naval Coll., Dartmouth. Midshipman, HMS Ramillies, 1925; world cruise in HMS Renown with the Duke and Duchess of York, 1927; Sub-Lieut HMS Cornwall, 1930; Lieut HMS Malaya, 1931–33; qualified as Interpreter in Russian after language study in Bessarabia, 1934; qualified in Signals and W/T at Signal Sch., Portsmouth, 1935; served at Admiralty and on staff of C-in-C, Plymouth, 1936; Flag Lieut to Rear-Adm. comdg Third Cruiser Sqdn, Mediterranean Fleet, 1937–39; Staff of Adm. comdg 3rd Battle Squadron and N Atlantic Escort Force, 1939–41; Naval Mission in Russia, 1941–42; Flag Lieut and Signals Officer to Adm. comdg Aircraft Carriers, 1943; Staff of Adm. comdg S Atlantic Station, 1944; Staff of Rear-Adm., Gibraltar, 1945; Intelligence Div., Naval Staff, Admiralty, 1946–48; Chief Staff Officer (Intelligence) Germany, 1949–51; qualified as Interpreter in German; Intelligence Div., Naval Staff, Admiralty, 1952–53; retd with rank of Comdr, 1953. Entered business as Export Consultant (ETG Consultancy Services), until 1965. Contested (C) Hayes and Harlington, 1955. MP (C) Harrow East, 1959–66. Vice-Chm. Conservative Navy Cttee, 1964. Chm. Parliamentary Flying Club, 1965; Chm., Wilts Monday Club, 1977. Chm. of Governors, Urchfont Sch., 1982–. *Publication:* Sailor in a Russian Frame, 1968. *Recreations:* shooting, music, fishing. *Address:* Mulberry House, Urchfont, Devizes, Wilts. *T:* Chirton 357. *Club:* White's.

COURTNEY, Prof. Edward, MA; Professor of Classics, since 1982, Chairman, Classics Department, since 1984, Leonard Ely Professor of Humanistic Studies, since 1986; Stanford University; *b* 22 March 1932; *s* of George and Kathleen Courtney; *m* 1962, Brenda Virginia Meek; two *s*. *Educ:* Royal Belfast Academical Instn; Trinity Coll., Dublin (BA); BA (by incorporation) 1955, MA 1957, Oxford. University studentship, Dublin, 1954–55; Research Lectr, Christ Church, Oxford, 1955–59; Lectr in Classics, 1959, Reader in Classics, 1970, Prof. of Latin, 1977, King's Coll., London. *Publications:* Valerius Flaccus, Argonautica (Leipzig), 1970; (jtly) Juvenal, Satires 1, 3, 10, 1977; (jtly) Ovid, Fasti (Leipzig), 1978; A Commentary on the Satires of Juvenal, 1980; Juvenal, The Satires, a text, 1984; many articles and reviews. *Recreation:* chess (schoolboy champion of Ireland, 1950). *Address:* 1011 Cathcart Way, Stanford, Calif 94305, USA. *T:* (415) 856–3010.

COURTOWN, 9th Earl of, *cr* 1762; **James Patrick Montagu Burgoyne Winthrop Stopford;** Baron Courtown (Ire.), 1758; Viscount Stopford, 1762; Baron Saltersford (GB), 1796; *b* 19 March 1954; *s* of 8th Earl of Courtown, OBE, TD, DL, and of Patricia, 3rd *d* of Harry S. Winthrop, Auckland, NZ; *S* father, 1975; *m* 1985, Elisabeth, *yr d* of I. R. Dunnett, Lower Slaughter, Glos; one *d*. *Educ:* Eton College; Berkshire Coll. of Agriculture. *Heir:* *b* Hon. Jeremy Neville Stopford, MVO 1984 [*b* 22 June 1958; *m* 1984, Bronwen, *d* of Lt-Col David MacDonald Milner; one *d*. Commissioned, Irish Guards; RARO 1984]. *Address:* Beechshade, Cambridge Road, Beaconsfield, Bucks.

COUSINS, Brian Harry, CBE 1981; Assistant Under Secretary of State (General Finance), Ministry of Defence, since 1986; *b* 18 July 1933; *s* of late William and Ethel Margaret Cousins; *m* 1957, Margaret (*née* Spark); two *s*. *Educ:* Devonport High School. Served RAF, pilot, 1952–54. Joined Ministry of Defence, 1954; Private Sec. to Permanent Secretary, 1962–65; Private Sec. Parliamentary Secretary, 1971–72; ndc 1972; Civil Sec., British Forces Germany, 1973–76; Asst Under Sec. of State, MoD, 1981–85; Chm., CSSB, 1985–86. *Recreations:* tennis, music, gardening.

COUSINS, John Peter; General Secretary, Clearing Bank Union, since 1983; *b* 31 Oct. 1931; *s* of Rt Hon. Frank Cousins, PC; *m* 1976, Pauline Cousins (*née* Hubbard); three *d*. *Educ:* Doncaster Central Sch. Motor engineering apprentice, 1947–52; RAF Engineering, 1952–55; BOAC cabin crew and clerical work, 1955–63; Full Time Official, TGWU, 1963–75, Nat. Sec., 1966–75; Dir of Manpower and Industrial Relations, NEDO, 1975–79; Dir of Personnel, Plessey Telecommunications and Office Systems Ltd, 1979–81; Dir of Personnel and Industrial Relns, John Brown PLC, 1981–83. Mem., Transport and Local Govt Cttees, TUC; UK Deleg., ILO; International Transport Workers Federation: Member: Aviation Sect.; Local Govt Cttee; Chemical Cttee; Civil Aviation Cttee; Mem. Industrial Training Bds. Member: Countryside Commn, 1972–; New Towns Commn, 1975–79; Sandford Cttee to review National Parks in England and Wales, 1972–73; Council, RSPB, 1982; Bd of Trustees, Royal Botanic Gardens, Kew, 1983–. Chm., British Council of Productivity Assocs, 1977–82. Travelling Fellow, Kingston Reg. Management Centre, 1977. *Recreations:* hill walking, trout fishing, 17th and 18th century music. *Address:* 19 Papillons Walk, Blackheath Park, SE3 9SF.

COUSINS, Norman; Adjunct Professor, University of California at Los Angeles Medical School, since 1978; *b* 24 June 1915; *s* of Samuel and Sara Cousins; *m* 1939, Ellen Kopf; four *d*. *Educ:* Teachers Coll., Columbia Univ. Educational Editor, New York Evening Post, 1935–36; Managing Editor, Current History Magazine, 1936–39 (World War II edn, USA); Editor, Saturday Review, 1940–71, 1973–78. Chm., Conn Fact-Finding Commission on Education, 1948–51. Vice-Pres. PEN Club, American Center, 1952–55; National Press and Overseas Press Clubs; co-Chm., National Cttee for a Sane Nuclear Policy, 1957–63. Chm., Nat. Educational Television, 1969–70; Mem. Bd of Directors: The Charles F. Kettering Foundn; The Samuel H. Kress Foundn; US Govt Rep. at dedication Nat. Univ., Addis Ababa, 1962; apptd by Pres. John F. Kennedy to Adv. Cttee on Arts, Nat. Cultural Center, 1962; co-Chm., Citizens' Cttee for a Nuclear Test-Ban Treaty, 1963; Chm., Cttee for Culture and Intellectual Exchange, for International Co-operation Year, 1965; US Presidential Rep. at Inauguration of Pres. of Philippines, 1966; US Govt Rep. at Internat. Writers Conf., Finland, 1966. Chm. Mayor's Task Force on Air Pollution, NYC, 1966–. Holds 53 hon. doctorates of letters, medicine, science and law. Awards include: Benjamin Franklin Award for Public Service in Journalism, 1956; Eleanor Roosevelt Peace Award, 1963; Overseas Press Club Award for best interpretation of foreign affairs in magazine writing, 1965; Family of Man Award, 1968; Carr Van Anda Award for Enduring Contribs to Journalism, Ohio Univ., 1971; Peace Medal of UN, 1971; Nat Arts Club Gold Medal for Literature, 1972; Univ. of Missouri Honor Award for Conspicuous Contribs to Journalism, 1972; Drexel Univ. Distinguished Achievement Award, 1972; Irita Van Doren Book Award, 1972; Magazine Publishers Assoc. Award, 1973; Human Resources Award, Nightingale-Conant Corp., 1973; Delbert Clark Award, West Georgia Coll., 1974; Canadian Govt Environment Award, 1975; Medal of Amer. Coll. of Cardiology, 1978; Author of the Year, Soc. of Authors and Journalists, 1980. *Publications:* The Good Inheritance, 1942; The Democratic Chance, 1942; (ed) A Treasury of Democracy, 1942; Modern Man is Obsolete, 1945; (ed jtly) Poetry of Freedom, 1948; Talks with Nehru, 1951; Who Speaks for Man?, 1953; Saturday Review Treasury (ed. sup.), 1957; (ed) In God We Trust, 1958; (ed) Writing for Love or Money, 1958; March's Thesaurus (ed. sup.), 1958; Dr Schweitzer of Lambaréné, 1960; In Place of Folly, 1961; The Improbable Triumvirate, 1962; Present Tense, 1967; (ed) Great American Essays, 1967; (ed) Profiles of Gandhi, 1969; Celebration of Life, 1974; (ed) Memoirs of a Man: Grenville Clark, 1975; Anatomy of an Illness, 1979; Human Options, 1981; (ed) The Physician in Literature, 1982; The Healing Heart, 1983; (ed) The Words of Albert Schweitzer, 1984; Albert Schweitzer's Mission: healing and peace, 1985. *Recreations:* music (especially organ), sports, reading, chess. *Address:* (office) Dean's Office, School of Medicine, 12–138 CHS, University of California, Los Angeles, Calif 90024, USA; (home) 2644 Eden Place, Beverly Hills, Calif 90210, USA.

COUSINS, Philip, CB 1982; Deputy Comptroller and Auditor General, National Audit Office (formerly Secretary, Exchequer and Audit Department), 1979–84; *b* 28 Feb. 1923; *s* of Herbert and Ella Cousins; *m* 1948, Ruby Laura Morris; two *d*. *Educ:* Royal Liberty School, Romford. Served in Royal Air Force, 1943–47. Joined Treasury, 1949; Under Secretary, 1974–79. *Address:* 102 Philbeach Gardens, SW5. *T:* 01–373 6164.

COUSTEAU, Jacques-Yves; Commandeur, Légion d'Honneur; Croix de Guerre with Palm; Officier du Mérite Maritime; Chevalier du Mérite Agricole; Officier des Arts et des Lettres; marine explorer; *b* 11 June 1910; *s* of Daniel and Elizabeth Cousteau; *m* 1937, Simone Melchior; one *s* (and one *s* decd). *Educ:* Stanislas, Paris; Navy Academy, Brest. Lt de vaisseau, War of 1939–45. Was partly responsible for invention of the Aqualung, 1943, a portable breathing device for divers. Established Undersea Research Group, 1946; Founder and President: Campagnes Océanographiques Françaises, 1950; Centre d'Etudes Marines Avancées, 1952; since 1951 has made annual oceanographic expdns on his ship Calypso, and has made film records of his undersea expdns since 1951; took part in making of the Bathyscaphe; promoted Conshelf saturation dive programme, 1962–65. Dir, Musée Océanographique, Monaco, Feb. 1957–; Gen. Sec., Internat. Commn for Scientific Exploration of the Mediterranean Sea, 1966. For. Assoc. Mem., Nat. Acad. Scis, USA, 1968; Corresp. Mem., Hellenic Inst. of Marine Archaeology, 1975; Hon. Mem., Indian Acad. of Scis, 1978. Hon. DSc: California 1970; Brandeis 1970; Rensselaer Polytechnic Inst., 1979; Harvard, 1979; Ghent, 1983. Gold Medal, RGS, 1963; Pott's Medal, Franklin Inst., 1970; Gold Medal, Nat. Geographic Soc., and Gold Medal Grand Prix d'Océanographie Albert Ier, 1971; Grande Médaille d'Or, Soc. d'encouragement au Progrès, 1973; Award of New England Aquarium, 1973; Prix de la couronne d'or, 1973; Polena della Bravura, 1974; Gold Medal "Sciences" (Arts, Sciences, Lettres), 1974; Fellow, BAFTA, 1975; Manley Bendall Prize, Marine Acad., 1976; Special Cervia prize, 1976; Internat. Pahlavi Environment Prize, 1977; Jean Sainteny Prize, 1980; Kiwanis Internat.

Europe Prize, 1980; Lindbergh Award, 1982; Neptune Award, Amer. Oceanic Orgn, 1982; Bruno H. Schubert Foundn Award, 1983. *Publications:* Par 18 mètres de fond, 1946; La Plongée en Scaphandre, 1950; (with Frederic Dumas) The Silent World, 1953 (New York and London), first published in English, then in 21 other languages; (ed with James Dugan) Captain Cousteau's Underwater Treasury, 1960 (London); The Living Sea, 1963 (London); World Without Sun, 1965 (film awarded Oscar, 1966); (with P. Cousteau) The Shark, 1970; with P. Diolé: Life and Death in a Coral Sea, 1971; Diving for Sunken Treasure, 1971; The Whale: mighty monarch of the sea, 1972; Octopus and Squid, 1973; Galapagos, Titicaca, the Blue Holes: three adventures, 1973; The Ocean World of Jacques Cousteau (20 vol encyclopedia), 1973; Diving Companions, 1974; Dolphins, 1975; (with Mose Richards) Jacques Cousteau's Amazon Journey, 1984; articles in National Geographical Magazine, 1952–66. *Films:* The Silent World (Grand Prix, Gold Palm, Cannes 1956; Oscar, 1957); The Golden Fish (Oscar, best short film, 1959); World without Sun (Oscar, 1965); Voyage to the Edge of the World, 1975; Cries from the Deep, 1982; St Lawrence: stairway to the sea, 1982; Jacques Cousteau: the first seventy-five years, 1985; Riders of the Wind, 1986; Haiti: waters of sorrow, 1986; *TV film series:* The Undersea World of Jacques Cousteau, 1968–76 (numerous Emmy awards); Oasis in Space, 1977; The Cousteau Odyssey, 1977–81; Cousteau/Amazon, 1984; Cousteau/Mississippi, 1985. *Address:* The Cousteau Society Inc., 425 E 52nd Street, New York, NY 10022, USA. *Clubs:* Club des Explorateurs (Paris); Club Alpin Sous Marin; Yacht Club de France.

COUTTS; *see* Money-Coutts.

COUTTS, Gordon; *see* Coutts, T. G.

COUTTS, Herbert, FSAScot; FMA; City Curator, City of Edinburgh Museums and Art Galleries, since 1973; *b* 9 March 1944; *s* of late Herbert and Agnes Coutts, Dundee; *m* 1970, Angela Elizabeth Mason Smith; one *s* three *d*. *Educ:* Morgan Acad., Dundee. FSAScot 1965; AMA 1970, FMA 1976. Asst Keeper of Antiquities and Bygones, Dundee City Museums, 1965–68, Keeper, 1968–71; Supt, Edinburgh City Museums, 1971–73. Vice Pres., Museums Assts Gp, 1967–70; Member: Govt Cttee on Future of Scotland's National Museums and Galleries, 1979–80 (report publd 1981); Council, Museums Assoc., 1977–78; Council, Soc. of Antiquaries of Scotland, 1981–82; Bd, Scottish Museums Council, 1985–; Museums Advr, COSLA Arts and Recreation Cttee, 1985–. Building Projects: City of Edinburgh Art Centre (opened 1980); Museum of Childhood Extension (completed 1986). Contested (Lab) Angus South, 1970. SBStJ 1977. *Publications:* Ancient Monuments of Tayside, 1970; Tayside Before History, 1971; Edinburgh: an illustrated history, 1975; guide books, exhibn catalogues; contrib. Museums Jl and archaeol jls. *Recreations:* relaxing with family, gardening, going to the opera, writing, reading, walking. *Address:* Kirkhill House, Queen's Road, Dunbar, East Lothian EH42 1LN. *T:* Dunbar 63113.

COUTTS, Ian Dewar, CBE 1982; in practice as chartered accountant, since 1950; Member: Eastern Electricity Board, since 1982; Local Government Audit Commission, since 1983; Forestry Commission, since 1984; *b* 15 May 1927; *s* of David Dewar Coutts and Dorothy Helen Coutts; *m* 1st, 1950, Sheila Margaret Cargill (marr. diss. 1983); one *s* two *d*; 2nd 1983, Hilary Ballard. *Educ:* Ipswich Sch.; Culford Sch. Chartered Accountant, 1949. Served 1st Essex Regt, 1946–48. Norfolk County Councillor, 1970–; Leader, Norfolk CC, 1973–79. Chm., ACC Finance Cttee, 1977–83; Mem., Consultative Council on Local Govt Finance, 1977–83. Chm., S Norfolk Conservative Assoc., 1970–73; Parly Cand., Norwich S, 1979. Mem., Council, Univ. of East Anglia, 1974–86. *Recreation:* sailing. *Address:* 2 The Close, Norwich NR1 4DJ. *T:* Norwich 612311. *Club:* Royal Automobile.

COUTTS, Prof. John Archibald; Professor of Jurisprudence in the University of Bristol, 1950–75, now Emeritus; Pro-Vice Chancellor, 1971–74; *b* 29 Dec. 1909; *e s* of Archibald and Katherine Jane Coutts; *m* 1940, Katherine Margaret Alldis; two *s*. *Educ:* Merchant Taylors', Crosby; Downing Coll., Cambridge (MA, LLB). Barrister Gray's Inn, 1933; lectured in Law: University Coll., Hull, 1934–35; King's Coll., London, 1935–36; Queen's Univ., Belfast, 1936–37; Trinity Coll., Dublin, 1937–50; Prof. of Laws, University of Dublin, 1944–50. Fellow, Trinity College, Dublin, 1944–50. Visiting Professor: Osgoode Hall Law Sch., Toronto, 1962–63; Univ. of Toronto, 1970–71, 1975–76. *Publications:* The Accused (ed); contributions to legal journals. *Address:* 22 Hurle Crescent, Clifton, Bristol BS8 2SZ. *T:* Bristol 736984.

COUTTS, (Thomas) Gordon, QC (Scotland) 1973; *b* 5 July 1933; *s* of Thomas Coutts and Evelyn Gordon Coutts; *m* 1959, Winifred Katherine Scott, BSc, MA, MLitt; one *s* one *d*. *Educ:* Aberdeen Grammar Sch.; Aberdeen Univ. (MA, LLB). Admitted Faculty of Advocates, 1959; Standing Junior Counsel to Dept Agric. (Scot.), 1965–73. Part-time Chairman: Industrial Tribunals, 1972–; Medical Appeal Tribunal, 1984–. *Recreations:* golf, stamp collecting. *Address:* 6 Heriot Row, Edinburgh EH3 6HU. *Club:* New (Edinburgh).

COUTTS, Sir Walter (Fleming), GCMG 1962 (KCMG 1961; CMG 1953); Kt 1961; MBE 1949; retired; Director: The Farmington Trust, 1971–78; Inchcape (East Africa) Ltd, 1970–78; Assam Investments, 1964–78; Chairman, Grindlays (Commercial) Holdings, 1974–78; *b* Aberdeen, 30 Nov. 1912; *s* of late Rev. John William Coutts, MA, DD, and Mrs R. Coutts, Crieff; *m* 1942, Janet Elizabeth Jamieson, CStJ, 2nd *d* of late Mr and Mrs A. C. Jamieson; one *s* one *d*. *Educ:* Glasgow Academy; St Andrews Univ.; St John's Coll., Cambridge. MA St Andrews, 1934. District Officer Kenya, 1936; Secretariat Kenya, 1946; District Commissioner, 1947; Administrator, St Vincent, 1949; Minister for Education, Labour and Lands, Kenya, 1956–58, Chief Sec., 1958–61; Special Commissioner for African Elections, Feb. 1955; Governor of Uganda, Nov. 1961–Oct. 1962; Governor-Gen. and C-in-C, Uganda, 1962–63. Sec. to Dulverton Trust, 1966–69; Asst Vice-Chancellor (Administration), Univ. of Warwick, 1969–71. Chm., Pergamon Press, 1972–74. *Recreation:* gardening. *Address:* 19 Malindi Street, Willetton, WA 6155, Australia. *T:* Perth 457 2995.

COUVE DE MURVILLE, Maurice; Commandeur de la Légion d'Honneur; Ambassadeur de France; *b* 24 Jan. 1907; *m* 1932, Jacqueline Schweisguth; three *d*. *Educ:* Paris Univ. Inspecteur des finances, 1930; directeur des finances extérieures, 1940; membre du Comité français de la libération nationale (Alger), 1943; représentant de la France, Conseil consultatif pour l'Italie, 1944; Ambassador in Rome, 1945; directeur général des affaires politiques, Ministère des Affaires Etrangères, 1945–50; Ambassador in Egypt, 1950–54; French Permanent Rep., NATO, Sept. 1954–Jan. 1955; Ambassador in the US, 1955–56; Ambassador of France to the Federal Republic of Germany, 1956–58; Ministre des Affaires Etrangères, 1958–68, de l'Economie et des Finances, June-July 1968; Prime Minister of France, 1968–69; Deputy, French Nat. Assembly, Paris 8ème Arrondissement, 1973–86. *Publication:* Une Politique étrangère 1958–69, 1973. *Address:* 44 rue du Bac, 75007 Paris, France.

COUVE DE MURVILLE, Most Rev. Maurice Noël Léon; *see* Birmingham, Archbishop of, (RC).

COUZENS, Sir Kenneth (Edward), KCB 1979 (CB 1976); Deputy Chairman, National Coal Board, since 1985; *b* 29 May 1925; *s* of Albert Couzens and May Couzens (*née* Biddlecombe); *m* 1947, Muriel Eileen Fey; one *s* one *d*. *Educ:* Portsmouth Grammar Sch.; Caius Coll., Cambridge. Inland Revenue, 1949–51; Treasury, 1951–68, and 1970–82; Civil Service Dept, 1968–70. Private Sec. to Financial Sec., Treasury, 1952–55, and to Chief Sec., 1962–63; Asst Sec., 1963–69; Under-Secretary: CSD, 1969–70; Treasury, 1970–73; Dep. Sec., Incomes Policy and Public Finance, 1973–77; Second Perm. Sec. (Overseas Finance), 1977–82; Perm. Under-Sec. of State, Dept of Energy, 1983–85. Chm., Monetary Cttee, European Community, 1982. *Address:* Coverts Edge, Woodsway, Oxshott, Surrey. *T:* Oxshott 3207. *Club:* Reform.

COVACEVICH, Sir (Anthony) Thomas, Kt 1978; DFC 1943; Senior Partner, MacDonnells, Solicitors and Notaries Public, Cairns, Queensland, Australia, since 1963 (Partner, 1939); *b* 1 March 1915; *s* of Prosper and Ellen Covacevich; *m* 1944, Gladys Rose (*née* Bryant); one *s* one *d*. *Educ:* Townsville and Brisbane Grammar Schools. Admitted Solicitor, Supreme Court of Queensland, 1938. Formerly Director of five publicly listed Australian companies, including Foxwood Ltd, a timber company (Chm.). *Recreation:* fishing. *Address:* 17 Temora Close, Edge Hill, Cairns, Queensland, Australia. *T:* 51 4000; Box 5046, Cairns Mail Centre, Queensland 4870, Australia. *Clubs:* North Queensland (Townsville, Qld); Cairns Game Fishing (Cairns, Qld).

COVEN, Major Edwina Olwyn, JP; HM Lieutenant, City of London, since 1981; *b* 23 Oct. 1921; *d* of Sir Samuel Instone, DL, and Lady (Alice) Instone; *m* 1951, Frank Coven, *qv*. *Educ:* Queen's Coll., London; St Winifred's, Ramsgate; Lycée Victor Duruy, Paris; Marlborough Gate Secretarial Coll., London (1st Cl. Business Diploma). Volunteered for Mil. Service, Private ATS; commnd ATS (subseq. WRAC); Army Interpreter (French); served UK and overseas, incl. staff appts, Plans and Policy Div., Western Union Defence Org. and NATO, Directorate Manpower Planning, WO, 1942–56. 1959–: Children's Writer, Fleetway Publications; Gen. Features Writer, National Magazine Co.; Reporter, BBC Woman's Hour; performer and adviser, children's and teenage progs, ITV. Mem. Adv. Council, Radio London (BBC), 1978–81; Dir, TV-am, 1985–. Chm., Davbro Chemists, 1967–71; stores consultant on promotion and fashion, 1960–77; Mem., Women's Adv. Cttee (Clothing and Footwear Sub-Cttee), BSI, 1971–73. JP Inner London, North Westminster, 1965–72 (Dep. Chm., 1971–72); JP City of London Commn, 1969 (Dep. Chm., 1971–); Mem., Central Council Probation and After-Care Cttee, 1971; Chm., City of London Probation and After-Care Cttee, 1971–77; Chm, City of London Police Cttee, 1984– (Dep. Chm., 1983–84). Mem., Jt Cttee of Management, London Court of Internat. Arbitration 1983–. Dowgate Ward, City of London: Court of Common Council, 1972–; elected Alderman, 1973 and 1974; Deputy, 1975–. Freedom, City of London, 1967; Mem., Guild of Freemen, City of London, 1971; Freeman, Loriners Co., 1967; Liveryman, Spectacle Makers Co., 1972. Member: Council, WRAC Assoc., 1973– (Vice Pres., 1984–; Vice-Chm., 1985–); TAVRA, City of London, 1979–86; Associated Speakers, 1975–; London Home Safety Council, 1980–84; Vice Chm., Cities of London and Westminster Home Safety Council, 1984–; Vice Pres., Nat. Org. for Women's Management Educn, 1983–. Mem., Bd of Governors, City of London Sch., 1972–77; Chm., Bd of Governors, City of London Sch. for Girls, 1978–81; Mem., Royal Soc. of St George, 1972–; Chm., Vintry and Dowgate Wards Club, 1977. Hon. Captain of Police, Salt Lake City. *Publication:* Tales of Oaktree Kitchen, 1959 (2nd edn 1960; adapted for ITV children's educnl series). *Recreations:* looking after much-loved husband and homemaking generally; lawn tennis; watching a variety of spectator sports. *Address:* 22 Cadogan Court, Draycott Avenue, SW3 3BX. *T:* 01–589 8286. *Clubs:* Queen's, Hurlingham; Devonshire (Eastbourne).

COVEN, Frank; London and European Director, The Nine Television Network of Australia, since 1974; *b* 26 April 1910; *s* of Isaac L. Coven and Raie Coven; *m* 1951, Edwina Coven (*née* Instone), *qv*. *Educ:* The Perse, Cambridge; France and Germany. Studied film prodn, UFA and EFA Studios, Berlin. TA (Ranks), 1938; War Service, 1939–45 (commnd 1941). Film admin and prodn, Gaumont British Studios, 1932; Studio Manager, Gainsborough Pictures, 1935; TV prodn, BBC/Daily Mail, 1937–38; Jt Dep. Organiser, Daily Mail Ideal Home Exhibition (radio, television, special features), 1945; Manager, Public Relations, Associated Newspapers, 1949; interviews, Wimbledon tennis commentaries, children's series "Write it Yourself" BBC TV, 1949–54 (subseq. ITV); TV Adviser, Bd of Associated Newspapers, 1953, Associated Rediffusion, 1954; London Rep., Television Corporation Ltd, Sydney, and Herald-Sun Pty, Melbourne, 1954; Dir, Compagnie Belge Transmarine SA and Imperial Stevedoring Co. SA, 1959; Head of Publicity and Promotions, Associated Newspapers, 1961; 1962: Dir, Associated Newspapers Gp; Dir, Bouverie Investments Ltd; Managing Director: Northcliffe Developments Ltd; Frank Coven Enterprises Ltd, presenting (with John Roberts) plays in London, incl. The Professor, How's the World Treating You? and, with London Traverse Theatre Co., works by Saul Bellow and others, 1964–69; Gen. Man., United Racecourses Ltd (Epsom, Sandown Park, Kempton Park), 1970, Man. Dir 1970, Vice-Chm. 1972. Mem., Variety Club of GB. Mem., Royal Soc. of St George, 1972. *Publications:* various Daily Mail Guides to Television Development in UK. *Recreations:* lawn tennis, swimming, study of varied media (current affairs). *Address:* 22 Cadogan Court, Draycott Avenue, SW3 3BX. *T:* 01–589 8286. *Clubs:* Savage, Saints and Sinners; Hurlingham, Queen's; Devonshire (Eastbourne).

COVENEY, Prof. James; Professor of French, University of Bath, 1969–85, now Emeritus; Director, Middle East Centre for Higher Education, London, since 1985; *b* 4 April 1920; *s* of James and Mary Coveney; *m* 1955, Patricia Yvonne Townsend; two *s*. *Educ:* St Ignatius Coll., Stamford Hill, London; Univ. of Reading (BA, 1st Cl. hons French, 1950); Univ. of Strasbourg (Dr Univ. 1953). Clerical Officer, LCC, 1936–40. Served War of 1939–45: private, The Welch Regt, 1940; 2nd Lieut, Queen's Own Royal West Kent Regt, 1941; served subsequently as Pilot in RAF; demobilized as Flt-Lt, 1946. Univ. of Strasbourg: French Govt Research Scholar, 1950–51; Lecteur d'Anglais, 1951–53. Lectr in French, Univ. of Hull, 1953–58; Asst Dir of Exams (Mod. Langs), Civil Service Commn, 1958–59; Translator, UNO, New York, 1959–61; Translator/Interpreter, NATO, 1961–64; Sen. Lectr and Head of Mod. Langs, Univ. of Bath, 1964–68; Jt Dir, Centre for European Ind. Studies, Univ. of Bath, 1969–75. Visiting Professor: Ecole Nat. d'Administration, Paris, 1974–85; Univ. of Buckingham, 1974–86; Bethlehem Univ., 1985. Language Trng Consultant, McKinsey & Co. Inc., 1967–73. Governor, Bell Educnl Trust, 1972–. Member: Nat. Council for Modern Languages, 1972–75 (Sec. 1972–74); Jt Sec., Assoc. of Univ. Profs of French, 1973–79. Member: British-French Mixed Cultural Commn, 1973–79; Cttee of Management, British Inst. in Paris, 1975–79; Council, Fédération Britannique de l'Alliance Française, 1976–81. FRSA 1974. Corresp. Mem., Académie des Sciences, Agriculture, Arts et Belles Lettres, Aix-en-Provence, 1975. Chevalier de l'Ordre des Palmes Académiques, 1978; Officier de l'Ordre National du Mérite (France), 1986. *Publications:* La Légende de l'Empereur Constant, 1955; (jtly) Glossary of French and English Management Terms, 1972; International Organization Documents for Translation from French, 1972; (jtly) Le français pour l'ingénieur, 1974; (jtly) Glossary of German and English Management Terms, 1977; (jtly) Glossary of Spanish and English Management Terms, 1978; (jtly) Guide to French Institutions, 1978;

(jtly) English-Portuguese Business Dictionary, 1982; articles in British, French and American periodicals. *Recreation*: Latin-American dancing. *Address*: 40 Westfield Close, Bath BA2 2EB. *T*: Bath 316670.

COVENTRY, family name of **Earl of Coventry.**

COVENTRY, 11th Earl of, *cr* 1697; **George William Coventry;** Viscount Deerhurst, 1697; *b* 25 Jan. 1934; *o s* of 10th Earl and Hon. Nesta Donne Philipps, *e d* of 1st Baron Kylsant; *S* father, 1940; *m* 1st, 1955, Marie Farquhar-Medart (marr. diss. 1963); one *s*; 2nd, 1969, Ann (marr. diss. 1975), *d* of F. W. J. Cripps, Bickley, Kent; 3rd, 1980, Valerie Anne Birch, Southport. *Educ*: Eton; RMA, Sandhurst. *Heir*: *s* Viscount Deerhurst, *qv*. *Address*: Earls Croome Court, Earls Croome, Worcester.
  See also Earl of Harrowby.

COVENTRY, Bishop of, since 1985; **Rt. Rev. Simon Barrington-Ward;** *b* 27 May 1930; *s* of Robert McGowan Barrington-Ward and Margaret Adele Barrington-Ward; *m* 1963, Jean Caverhill Taylor; two *d*. *Educ*: Eton; Magdalene Coll., Cambridge (MA). Lektor, Free Univ., Berlin, 1953–54; Westcott House, Cambridge, 1954–56; Chaplain, Magdalene Coll., Cambridge, 1956–60; Assist Lectr in Religious Studies, Univ. of Ibadan, 1960–63; Fellow and Dean of Chapel, Magdalene Coll., Cambridge, 1963–69; Principal, Crowther Hall, Selly Oak Colls, Birmingham, 1969–74; Gen. Sec., CMS, 1975–85; Hon. Canon of Derby Cathedral, 1975–85; a Chaplain to the Queen, 1984–85. FRAI. Hon. DD Wycliffe Coll., Toronto, 1984. *Publications*: contributor to: Christianity in Independent Africa (ed Fasholé Luke and others), 1978; Today's Anglican Worship (ed C. Buchanan), 1980; Renewal—An Emerging Pattern, by Graham Pulkingham and others, 1980; A New Dictionary of Christian Theology (ed Alan Richardson and John Bowden), 1983; CMS Newsletter, 1975–85. *Address*: Bishop's House, Davenport Road, Coventry, W Midlands CV5 6PW.

COVENTRY, Archdeacon of; *see* Morgan, Ven. A. W.

COVENTRY, Provost of; *see* Semper, Very Rev. C. D.

COVENTRY, Rev. John Seton, SJ; Master, St Edmund's House, Cambridge, 1976–85; *b* 21 Jan. 1915; *yr s* of late Seton and Annie Coventry, Barton-on-Sea, Hants. *Educ*: Stonyhurst; Campion Hall, Oxford. MA Oxon 1945. Entered Society of Jesus, 1932; ordained, 1947; Prefect of Studies, Beaumont, 1950; Rector, Beaumont, 1956–58; Provincial, English Province of Soc. of Jesus, 1958–64; Lectr in Theology, Heythrop Coll., 1965–76. *Publications*: Morals and Independence, 1946; The Breaking of Bread, 1950; Faith Seeks Understanding, 1951; The Life Story of the Mass, 1959; The Theology of Faith, 1968; Christian Truth, 1975; Faith in Jesus Christ, 1980; Reconciling, 1985. *Address*: Heythrop College, 11 Cavendish Square, W1M 0AN. *T*: 01-580 6941.

COVINGTON, Nicholas; Director, Office of Manpower Economics, since 1986; *b* 9 June 1929; *s* of late Cecil Tim Covington and Margaret Joan (*née* Bray); *m* 1st, 1953, Patricia Sillitoe (marr. diss.); one *s* two *d*; 2nd, 1983, Kathleen Hegarty. *Educ*: Cranleigh Sch.; Oriel Coll., Oxford (BA). RAF, 1947–49. Metal Box Co. Ltd, 1952–57; Garnier & Co. Ltd, 1957–66; entered Min. of Labour, 1966; Asst Sec., 1971; Industrial Relns Div., Dept of Employment, 1976–86. *Recreations*: history, walking. *Address*: c/o Office of Manpower Economics, 22 Kingsway, WC2B 6JY.

COWAN, Brig. Alan; *see* Cowan, Brig. J. A. C.

COWAN, Prof. Charles Donald, MA Cantab, PhD London; FRAS; Professor of Oriental History in the University of London, since 1980; Director, School of Oriental and African Studies, London, since 1976; *b* London, 18 Nov. 1923; *s* of W. C. Cowan and Minnie Ethel (*née* Farrow); *m* 1st, 1945, Mary Evelyn, *d* of Otto Vetter, Perth, WA (marr. diss. 1960); two *d*; 2nd, 1962, Daphne Eleanor, *d* of Walter Rishworth Whittam, Rangoon. *Educ*: Kilburn Grammar Sch.; Peterhouse, Cambridge. Served Royal Navy, 1941–45. Lecturer in History, Raffles Coll., Singapore, 1947–48, and University of Malaya, 1948–50; Lectr in the History of South-East Asia, Sch. of Oriental and African Studies, University of London, 1950–60, Prof., 1961–80. Pro-Vice-Chancellor, Univ. of London, 1985–86. Visiting Prof. of South-East Asian History, Cornell Univ., 1960–61. Governor: James Allen's Girls School, 1977–; Alleyn's Coll. of God's Gift, Dulwich, 1980–. *Publications*: Nineteenth Century Malaya, 1961; (ed) The Economic Development of South-East Asia, 1964; (ed) The Economic Development of China and Japan, 1964; (with P. L. Burns) Sir Frank Swettenham's Malayan Journals, 1975; (with O. L. Wolters) Southeast Asian History and Historiography, 1976. *Address*: School of Oriental and African Studies, University of London, WC1.

COWAN, Brig. Colin Hunter, CBE 1984; DL; Chief Executive, Cumbernauld Development Corporation, 1970–85; *b* 16 Oct. 1920; *s* of late Lt-Col S. Hunter Cowan, DSO and Mrs Jean Hunter Cowan; *m* 1949, Elizabeth Williamson, MD (*d* 1985); two *s* one *d*. *Educ*: Wellington Coll.; RMA Woolwich; Trinity Coll., Cambridge (MA). MICE. Comd Engineer Regt, 1960–63; Defence Adviser, UK Mission to the UN, 1964–66; Brigadier Engineer Plans, MoD (Army), 1968–70. DL Dunbartonshire, 1973. *Recreations*: music, photography. *Address*: Hillcroft, Dullatur, by Glasgow G68 0AW. *T*: Cumbernauld 23242. *Club*: Army and Navy.

COWAN, Prof. Ian Borthwick, PhD; FRHistS; Professor in Scottish History, University of Glasgow, since 1983; *b* 16 April 1932; *s* of late William McAulay Cowan and Annie Borthwick; *m* 1954, Anna Little Telford; three *d*. *Educ*: Dumfries Acad.; Univ. of Edinburgh (MA, PhD). FRHistS 1969. Served RAF, Educn Officer, 1954–56. Asst Lectr in Scottish Hist., Univ. of Edinburgh, 1956–59; Lectr in Hist., Newbattle Abbey Coll., 1959–62; Univ. of Glasgow: Lectr in Scottish Hist., 1962–70; Sen. Lectr, 1970–77; Reader, 1977–83. Hon. Treasurer, Scottish Hist. Soc., 1965–; Vice-Pres., Historical Assoc., 1982–. Editor, Scottish Historical Rev., 1983–. *Publications*: Blast and Counterblast, 1960; Parishes of Medieval Scotland, 1962; (with A.I. Dunlop) Calendar of Scottish Supplications to Rome 1428–32, 1970; The Enigma of Mary Stuart, 1971; (with D.E. Easson) Medieval Religious Houses: Scotland, 1976; The Scottish Covenanters 1660–1688, 1976; Regional Aspects of the Scottish Reformation, 1978; The Scottish Reformation—Church and Society, 1982; (with D. Shaw) Renaissance and Reformation in Scotland, 1983; (with P. H. R. MacKay and A. Macquarrie) The Knights of St John of Jerusalem in Scotland, 1983; articles and papers in learned jls. *Recreation*: travel. *Address*: 119 Balshagray Avenue, Glasgow G11 7EG. *T*: 041–954 8494.

COWAN, Brig. (James) Alan (Comrie), MBE 1956; Secretary, Government Hospitality Fund, since 1980; *b* 20 Sept. 1923; *s* of late Alexander Comrie Cowan and of Helen May Isobel (*née* Finlayson); *m* 1948, Jennifer Evelyn Bland; two *s* one *d*. *Educ*: Rugby Sch., Warwicks. Commnd Rifle Bde, 1942; served War, Italy and Egypt, 1942–46; served Army, 1947–60: OU Trng Corps, BAOR, Army Staff Coll., WO, Kenya and Malaya; DS, Army Staff Coll., 1961–63; CO 1 Royal Leicesters, later 4 Royal Anglian, UK, Aden and Malta, 1964–66; GSO1 17 Div., Malaysia, 1966–67; Col GS MoD, 1967–69; Comd 8 Inf. Bde, NI, 1970–71; DAG HQ UKLF, 1972–75; entered Civil Service and joined NI Office, with responsibility for industrial, economic and social affairs, 1975; Principal,

1975–78; Asst Sec., 1978–80. *Recreations*: current affairs, music, theatre, the countryside. *Address*: 1A Templar Street, Myatts Fields, SE5 9JB. *T*: 01–274 7642. *Clubs*: Army and Navy, MCC.

COWAN, James Robertson, CBE 1983 (OBE 1974); CEng, FIMinE; Chairman, NCB Coal Products, since 1985; *b* 12 Sept. 1919; *s* of John and Jean Cowan; *m* 1945, Harriet Good Forrest; two *d*. *Educ*: Dalziel High Sch., Motherwell; Glasgow Univ. (BSc 1st Cl. Hons). CEng, FIMinE 1971. National Coal Board: Dir, Scottish Area, 1970–80; Bd Mem., 1977–85; Mem. for Industrial Relns, 1980–85; Dep. Chm., 1982–85. Chm., Scottish Brick Corp., 1980– (Dir. 1974–); Dir, British Investment Trust, 1978–. Vis. Prof., Strathclyde Univ., 1978. CBIM. *Recreation*: golf. *Address*: 31 Muirfield Park, Gullane, Scotland EH31 2DY. *T*: Gullane 843398. *Club*: Caledonian.

COWAN, Lionel David, (Nick Cowan); Director and Secretary, Federation of London Clearing Bank Employers, since 1980; *b* 18 Dec. 1929; *m* 1953, Pamela Ida, *e d* of Hubert and Winifred Williams, Totton, Hants; one *s* two *d*. *Educ*: Surbiton County Grammar Sch. FBIM 1972; CIPM 1979 (AMIPM 1965). Served Royal Navy, 1945–61: Fleet Air Arm Aircrew (Lieut), 1953; Sen. Instr, RAN, 1958–60. Training Officer, Shoe and Allied Trades Res. Assoc., 1961–62; Perkins Engines Gp, 1962–72 (Dir of Personnel and Industrial Relns 1970–72); Dir of Personnel, Philips Electronic and Associated Industries, 1972–78; Gp Personnel Dir, Unigate Ltd, 1978–79. Chm., W Lambeth HA, 1982–86; Member: Editorial Panel, Personnel Management, 1967–; BIM Adv. Bd on Industrial Relations, 1970–75; Employment Relns Cttee, IPM, 1971–81; Council, Independent Res. and Assessment Centre, 1975–; Engrg Industry Trng Bd, 1976–79; Employment Appeal Tribunal, 1976–; Editorial Panel, Industrial Relns Law Reports, 1977–; Employment Policy Cttee, CBI, 1978–; Civil Service Arbitration Tribunal, 1979–; CBI Council, 1980–; Central Arbitration Cttee, 1984–; Youth Training Bd, 1984–85; NEDO Enquiry, Industrial Relns Trng for Managers, 1976, Supply and Demand for Skilled Manpower, 1977. Vice-Pres. (Employee Relations), IPM, 1977–79. Director, Oxford Univ. Business Summer Sch., 1980. Lecturer and writer on personnel management and industrial relations. *Publications*: Personnel Management and Banking, 1984; The Clearing Banks and the Trade Unions, 1984; numerous articles, papers and other pubns on various aspects of personnel management and industrial relations. *Recreations*: the National Health Service, music and opera, chess, bridge. *Address*: Woodside, 38 Water Lane, Cobham, Surrey KT11 2PB. *T*: Cobham 66945. *Club*: Naval and Military.

COWAN, Robert; Chairman, Highlands and Islands Development Board, Inverness, since 1982; *b* 27 July 1932; *s* of Dr John McQueen Cowan and May Cowan; *m* 1959, Margaret Morton (*née* Dewar); two *d*. *Educ*: Edinburgh Academy; Edinburgh Univ. (MA). Fisons Ltd, 1958–62; Wolsey Ltd, 1962–64; PA Management Consultants Ltd, 1965–82. Member: Bd, Scottish Develt Agency, 1982–; BBC Broadcasting Council for Scotland, 1984–. *Recreation*: sailing. *Address*: The Old Manse, Farr, Inverness-shire. *Clubs*: New (Edinburgh); Royal Scottish Automobile (Glasgow); Hong Kong (Hong Kong).

COWAN, William Graham, MBE 1943; Chairman, J. H. Carruthers & Co. Ltd, since 1981 (Managing Director, 1981–84); *b* 29 April 1919; *s* of William Cowan, WS, Edinburgh, and Dorothy Isobel Horsbrugh; *m* 1960, Karen Wendell Hansen, Crestwood, NY; two *s* one *d*. *Educ*: Edinburgh Academy; Cambridge Univ. (MA). CEng, FIMechE, FSIAD, FRSA. Served 1940–46, Royal Engrs and Gen. Staff, Africa, Italy (Lt-Col). Asst Man. Dir, North British Locomotive Co. Ltd, 1947–50; Man. Dir, J. H. Carruthers and Co. Ltd, 1950–79. Dir, Glasgow Sch. of Art, 1979–82. Mem. Exec. Cttee, Scottish Council (Develt and Industry), 1972–74; Pres., Scottish Engrg Employers' Assoc., 1972. Member: Design Council, 1974–78 (Chm., Scottish Cttee, 1976–78); Council, Nat. Trust for Scotland, 1984–; Dir, Scottish Transport Group, 1977–80. *Address*: The Old Inn, Fowlis Wester, Perthshire. *T*: Madderty 319. *Clubs*: Caledonian; New (Edinburgh).

COWAN, Prof. William Maxwell, FRS 1982; Vice President and Director, Developmental Neurobiology, The Salk Institute, San Diego, since 1981; *b* 27 Sept. 1931; *s* of Adam Cowan and Jessie Sloan Cowan (*née* Maxwell); *m* 1956, Margaret Sherlock; two *s* one *d*. *Educ*: Univ. of the Witwatersrand, S Africa (BSc Hons); Oxford Univ. (MA, DPhil, BM, BCh). University Lecturer in Anatomy, Oxford, 1958–66; Fellow of Pembroke Coll., Oxford, 1958–66 (Hon. Fellow, 1986); Associate Prof., Univ. of Wisconsin, 1966–68; Professor and Head of Dept of Anatomy, Washington Univ. Sch. of Medicine, 1968–80; Director, Div. of Biological Sciences, Washington Univ., 1975–80; Non-Resident Fellow, Salk Institute for Biological Studies, 1977–80, Professor, 1980–. Foreign Associate, US National Academy of Sciences, 1981. Hon. Fellow, Pembroke Coll., Oxford, 1986. *Publications*: The Use of Axonal Transport for Studies of Neuronal Connectivity, 1975; Aspects of Cellular Neurobiology, 1978; Studies in Developmental Neurobiology, 1981; Annual Reviews of Neuroscience, Vol. 1 1978, Vols 2, 3, 4, 5, 6, 1979–83. *Recreations*: photography, reading, travel. *Address*: The Salk Institute for Biological Studies, PO Box 85800, San Diego, California 92138, USA. *T*: (619) 453–4100.

COWARD, David John, CMG 1965; OBE 1962; Registrar General, Kenya, 1955–82; *b* 21 March 1917; *s* of late Robert J. Coward, Exmouth, Devon; *m* 1954, Joan, *d* of late Reginald Frank, Doncaster; three *d*. *Educ*: Exmouth Grammar Sch. and Law Society's Sch. of Law. FCIS 1961; ACIArb 1984. Admitted a solicitor, 1938. Joined RN as a rating at outbreak of war, 1939; commissioned, 1941; demobilized as Lieut-Comdr (S) RNVR, 1947. ADC to Governor of Trinidad, 1947. Joined Colonial Legal Service, 1948, Asst Registrar Gen., Kenya; Dep. Registrar Gen., 1952; Registrar Gen., Official Receiver and Public Trustee, 1955–82. Acted as Permanent Sec. for Justice and Constitutional Affairs, 1963–64. Served in Kenya Police Reserve, 1949–63, latterly as Senior Superintendent i/c Nairobi Area. Chm., Working Party on future of Company Secretarial Profession in Kenya; Mem. Accountants' Registration Bd, 1978–82; Trustee, Nat. Museums of Kenya, 1979–82. Silver Medal, Internat. Olympic Cttee, 1981. *Recreation*: golf. *Address*: North Perretts, Spinney Lane, West Chiltington, W Sussex. *T*: Storrington 2521. *Clubs*: Naval; Nairobi and Limuru Country (Kenya).

COWARD, John Stephen, QC 1984; barrister-at-law; a Recorder of the Crown Court, since 1980; *b* 15 Nov. 1937; *s* of Frank and Kathleen Coward; *m* 1967, Ann Lesley Pye; four *d*. *Educ*: King James Grammar Sch., Almondbury, Huddersfield; University Coll. London (LLB). Lecturer in Law and Constitutional History, University Coll. London and Police Staff Coll., 1962–64; called to the Bar, Inner Temple, 1964; in practice on Midland and Oxford Circuit, 1964–. *Recreation*: trying to grow calceolarias and a decent row of peas. *Address*: The Grange, Scaldwell, Northampton NN6 9JP. *T*: Northampton 880255. *Clubs*: Northampton and County (Northampton); Scaldwell (Scaldwell, Northants).

COWARD, Richard Edgar; retired; Director for Library Planning, OCLC Inc., 1980–81; *b* 1927; *s* of Edgar Frank Coward and Jean (*née* McIntyre); *m* 1949, Audrey Scott Lintern; one *s* two *d*. *Educ*: Richmond Grammar Sch., Surrey. FLA. Dir Gen., Bibliographic Servs Div., British Library, 1975–79. Member: Adv. Cttee on BBC Archives, 1976–79; Library Adv. Council (England), 1976–. *Address*: Gaios, Paxos, Greece; 12 Marylebone Mews, W1M 7LF. *T*: 01–486 7316.

COWBURN, Norman; Deputy Chairman, Britannia Building Society, since 1986 (Managing Director, 1970–84); *b* 5 Jan. 1920; *s* of Harold and Edith Cowburn; *m* 1945, Edna Margaret Heatley; two *s* one *d*. *Educ:* Queen Elizabeth's Grammar Sch., Blackburn. FCIS, FBS. Burnley Building Soc., 1936. Served War, 1940–46. Burnley Building Soc., 1946; Leek and Westbourne Building Soc., 1954 (re-named Britannia Building Soc., Dec. 1975). *Recreations:* golf, gardening. *Address:* Greywoods, Birchall, Leek, Staffs. *T:* Leek 383214.

COWDEROY, Brenda; General Secretary, Girls' Friendly Society, 1978–85; *b* 27 June 1925; *o c* of late Frederick Cowderoy and of Evelyn Cowderoy (*née* Land). *Educ:* Surbiton High Sch.; St Hugh's Coll., Oxford (MA). Called to Bar, Gray's Inn, 1949. John Lewis Partnership: Asst Legal Adviser, 1954–56; Head of Legal Dept, 1956–70; Nat. Gen. Sec., YWCA, 1971–77. FBIM. *Recreations:* history, golf. *Address:* 26 Rossetti Road, Birchington, Kent CT7 9ER. *Clubs:* Royal Commonwealth Society; Prince's (Sandwich).

COWDRAY, 3rd Viscount, *cr* 1917; **Weetman John Churchill Pearson**, TD; Bt, *cr* 1894; Baron, *cr* 1910; Captain, Sussex Yeomanry; Chairman, S. Pearson & Son Ltd, 1954–77; *b* 27 Feb. 1910 (twin); *s* of 2nd Viscount and Agnes Beryl (*d* 1948), *d* of Lord Edward Spencer Churchill; *S* father, 1933; *m* 1st, 1939, Lady Anne Bridgeman (from whom he obtained a divorce, 1950), *d* of 5th Earl of Bradford; one *s* two *d*; 2nd, 1953, Elizabeth Georgiana Mather, 2nd *d* of Sir Anthony Mather-Jackson, 6th Bt; one *s* two *d*. *Educ:* Eton; Christ Church, Oxford. Parliamentary Private Sec. to Under-Sec. of State for Air, 1941–42. *Recreations:* polo, shooting, fishing. *Heir: s* Hon. Michael Orlando Weetman Pearson [*b* 17 June 1944; *m* 1977, Ellen (marr. diss.), *yr d* of late Hermann Erhardt]. *Address:* Cowdray Park, Midhurst, West Sussex. *T:* Midhurst 2461; Dunecht, Skene, Aberdeenshire. *T:* Lyne of Skene 244. *Clubs:* Cavalry and Guards, White's.
See also Duke of Atholl, Baron Cranworth.

COWDREY, (Michael) Colin, CBE 1972; Representative, Barclays Bank PLC; *b* 24 Dec. 1932; *s* of Ernest Arthur Cowdrey and Kathleen Mary Cowdrey (*née* Taylor), BEM; *m* 1956, Penelope Susan Cowdrey (*née* Chiesman) (marr. diss. 1985); three *s* one *d*; *m* 1985, Lady Herries of Terregles, *qv*. *Educ:* Homefield, Sutton, Surrey; Tonbridge; Brasenose Coll., Oxford. Cricket: 5 years Tonbridge Sch. XI (Capt., 1949–50); Public Schs (Lord's) (Capt. 1950); (3 years) Oxford XI (Capt. 1954); Kent Cap, 1951 (Captain, 1957–71); 117 appearances for England, 1954–75; Capt. 23 times; 11 Overseas Tours; 107 centuries in first class cricket, of which 22 were Test centuries; on retirement in 1975, held record for most runs and most catches in Test Matches. Runner-up Amateur Rackets Title, Queen's Club, 1953 and Doubles, 1965. Chm., County Pitches Cttee, TCCB, 1983–. Member: Council, Britain Australia Soc.; Winston Churchill Memorial Trust. Master, Skinners' Co., 1985; Freeman, City of London, 1962. *Publications:* Cricket Today, 1961; Time for Reflection, 1962; Tackle Cricket This Way, 1969; The Incomparable Game, 1970; MCC: the Autobiography of a Cricketer, 1976. *Recreation:* golf. *Address:* 168 Fenchurch Street, EC3. *T:* 01–283 8989. *Clubs:* MCC (Mem. Cttee; Pres., 1987), Boodle's.

COWE, (Robert George) Collin; Fellow and Senior Bursar, Magdalen College, Oxford, 1970–80; *b* 24 Sept. 1917; *s* of Peter and Annie Cowe, Berwick-upon-Tweed; *m* 1943, Gladys May, *d* of William Greenwood Wright and Jessie Wright, Bingley, Yorks; one *d*. *Educ:* The Duke's Sch., Alnwick; The Grammar Sch., Berwick-upon-Tweed; Edinburgh Univ. MA (Hons Classics) 1939; MA Oxon, 1970. Served Royal Regiment of Artillery, Field Branch, 1939–46; Major, RA, 1944–46; Instructor in Gunnery, Sch. of Artillery, UK, and CMF, 1943–46. National Coal Board, 1947–70; Private Sec. to Chm., 1947–49; Principal Private Sec. to Chm., 1949–52; Sec., East Midlands Div., 1952–55; Staff Dir, North-Eastern Div., 1955–58; Dep.-Sec. to NCB, 1958–59; Sec., 1960–67; Man. Dir, Associated Heat Services Ltd (associate co. of NCB), 1967–69. Mem., Advisory Council, BBC Radio Oxford, 1985–. *Recreations:* riding, swimming. *Address:* Brookside Cottage, Brook End, Chadlington, Oxford OX7 3NF. *T:* Chadlington 373.

COWELL, John Richard; Secretary, Royal Horticultural Society, since 1975; *b* 30 April 1933; *er s* of late Frank Richard Cowell, CMG, PhD, and Lilian Margaret (*née* Palin); *m* 1972, Josephine Suzanne Elizabeth, *d* of I.A.F. Craig, Leppington, Yorks; two *s* one *d*. *Educ:* Westminster Sch.; Trinity Coll., Cambridge (MA). Secretariat: London Chamber of Commerce, 1957–58; Royal Horticultural Soc., 1958–. *Recreations:* gardening, fishing. *Address:* Crowdleham House, Kemsing, Sevenoaks, Kent. *T:* Sevenoaks 61192. *Club:* Athenæum.

COWEN, Alan Biddulph, CMG 1961; OBE 1945; retired as Deputy Chairman of Standards Association of Rhodesia and Nyasaland; *b* 26 Sept. 1896; *m*; two *s*. *Educ:* St John's Coll., Johannesburg, S Africa; Sch. of Mines and Technology. Formerly Chm., Southern Rhodesian Electricity Supply Commission; Mem. of Federal Power Board. CEng; FIEE; F(SA)IEE. *Address:* 68 Forest Glade, Tokai Road, Tokai, 7966, S Africa.

COWEN, Rt. Hon. Sir Zelman, AK 1977; GCMG 1977 (CMG 1968); GCVO 1980; Kt 1976; PC 1981; QC; Provost of Oriel College, Oxford, since 1982; Chairman of the Press Council, since 1983; *b* 7 Oct. 1919; *s* of late Bernard and of Sara Cowen; *m* 1945, Anna Wittner; three *s* one *d*. *Educ:* Scotch Coll., Melbourne; Univ. of Melbourne; New and Oriel Colls, Oxford. BA 1939, LLB 1941, LLM 1942, Melbourne; BCL, MA 1947, DCL 1968, Oxford. Lieut, RANVR, 1941–45. Called to Bar, Gray's Inn, 1947; Hon. Bencher, 1978; called to Vic (Aust.) Bar, 1951, Queensland Bar, 1971; QC 1972. Victorian Rhodes Schol., 1941; Vinerian Schol., Oxford Univ., 1947. Fellow and Tutor, Oriel Coll., Oxford, 1947–50, Hon. Fellow 1977; Prof. of Public Law and Dean of Faculty of Law, Univ. of Melbourne, 1951–66; Dominion Liaison Officer to Colonial Office (UK), 1951–66; Prof. Emer., Univ. of Melbourne, 1967; Vice-Chancellor and Professor, Univ. of New England, Armidale, NSW, 1967–70; Vice-Chancellor, Qld Univ., 1970–77; Governor-General of Australia, 1977–82. Vis. Professor: Univ. of Chicago, 1949; Harvard Law Sch. and Fletcher Sch. of Law and Diplomacy, 1953–54 and 1963–64; Univ. of Utah, 1954; Univ. of Illinois, 1957–58; Washington Univ., St Louis, 1959; Tagore Law Prof., Univ. of Calcutta, 1975; Menzies Schol. in Res., Univ. of Va, 1983. For. Hon. Mem., Amer. Acad. of Arts and Sciences, 1965. Broadcaster on radio and TV on nat. and internat. affairs; Mem. and Chm., Victorian State Adv. Cttee of Australian Broadcasting Commn (at various times during 1950's and 1960's); Mem., Chief Justice's Law Reform Cttee, 1951–66; President: Asthma Foundn of Victoria, 1963–66; Adult Educn Assoc. of Australia, 1968–70; Aust. Inst. of Urban Studies, 1973–77; Mem., Law Reform Commn, Australia, 1976–77; Chairman: Aust. Vice-Chancellors' Cttee, 1977; Aust. Studies Centre Cttee, London, 1982–. Mem., Club of Rome, 1974–77. Academic Governor, Bd of Governors, Hebrew Univ. of Jerusalem, 1969–77, 1982–; Mem., Academic Bd of Govrs, Tel Aviv Univ., 1983–. Trustee, Van Leer Inst. of Jerusalem, 1985–. Hon. LLD: Hong Kong, 1967; Queensland, 1972; Melbourne, 1973; Western Australia, 1981; Turin, 1981; Hon. DLitt: New England, 1979; Sydney, 1980; James Cook Univ. of N Qld, 1982; Oxford, 1983; Hon. DHL: Hebrew Union Coll., Cincinnati, 1980; Redlands Univ., Calif., 1986; DUniv.: Newcastle, 1980; Griffith, 1981; Hon. DPhil: Hebrew Univ. of Jerusalem, 1982; Tel Aviv, 1985. FRSA 1971; Hon. FASSA 1977; Hon. FACE 1978; Hon. FRAIA 1978; Hon. FTS 1979; Hon. FRACP 1979; Hon. FAHA 1980; Hon. FASA 1980; Hon. FRACMA 1981; Hon. FRACOG 1981; Hon. FCA 1981; Hon. FACRM 1982; Hon. Fellow: New Coll. Oxford 1978; University House, ANU, 1978; ANZAAS 1983; TCD, 1985. KStJ (A) 1977. *Publications:* (ed jtly) Dicey's Conflict of Laws, 1949; Australia and the United States: Some Legal Comparisons, 1954; (with P. B. Carter) Essays on the Law of Evidence, 1956; American-Australian Private International Law, 1957; Federal Jurisdiction in Australia, 1959; (with D. M. da Costa) Matrimonial Causes Jurisdiction, 1961; Sir John Latham and other papers, 1965; British Commonwealth of Nations in a Changing World, 1964; Isaac Isaacs, 1967; The Private Man, 1969; Individual Liberty and the Law, 1977; articles and chapters in legal works in UK, US, Canada, Germany, Australia. *Recreations:* swimming, tennis, music, performing and visual arts. *Address:* Oriel College, Oxford. *T:* Oxford 241962. *Clubs:* Athenæum, Garrick; Queensland (Brisbane); Pioneer (Sydney).

COWEY, Prof. Alan, PhD; Professor of Physiological Psychology, and Professorial Fellow of Lincoln College, University of Oxford, since 1981; *b* 28 April 1935; *s* of Harry and Mary Cowey; *m* 1959, Patricia Leckonby; three *d*. *Educ:* Bede Grammar Sch., Sunderland; Emmanuel Coll., Cambridge (MA, PhD). Rockefeller Foundn Fellow, Center for Brain Research, Univ. of Rochester, New York, 1961–62; Univ. Demonstrator in Experimental Psychology, Cambridge, 1962–67; Fellow and Coll. Tutor, Emmanuel Coll., Cambridge, 1964–67; Vis. Sen. Fulbright Fellow, Psychology Dept, Harvard Univ., 1967; Sen. Res. Officer, Inst. of Experimental Psychology, Univ. of Oxford, 1967–68; Nuffield Sen. Res. Fellow, Lincoln Coll., Oxford, 1968–81; Henry Head Res. Fellow of Royal Society, 1968–73; Reader in Physiolog. Psychology, Oxford Univ., 1973–81. Member: MRC Neurosciences Grants Cttee, 1974–77 (Chm., 1979–81); MRC Neurosciences Board, 1979–83 (Chm., 1981–83); Mem. Council, MRC, 1981–85. Spearman Medal, British Psychological Soc., 1967. *Publications:* numerous articles in psychological and physiological jls. *Recreations:* squash, swimming, reading. *Address:* Department of Experimental Psychology, South Parks Road, Oxford OX1 3UD. *T:* Oxford 512251.

COWEY, Brig. Bernard Turing Vionnée, DSO 1945; OBE 1976; DL; *b* 20 Nov. 1911; *s* of late Lt-Col R. V. Cowey, DSO, RAMC and late Mrs B. A. Cowey (*née* Blancke); *m* 1947, Margaret Heath Dean (*née* Godwin). *Educ:* Wellington; RMC Sandhurst. Commnd The Welch Regt, 1931; served War of 1939–45: N Africa, 1939–41 (despatches 1941); psc 1941; India, 1942–43; Burma, 1944–45; CO 2 York and Lancs, 1944; CO 2 Welch, 1945–47; Co. Comdr RMA Sandhurst, 1947–49; Chief Instructor, Staff Coll., Quetta, 1952–53; CO 1 Welch, 1953–56; Comd (Brig.) 9 Indep. Armd Bde Gp TA, 1956 and 148 Inf. Bde Gp TA, 1956–58; Inspector of Intelligence, 1961–63; retd 1963. Sec., Notts T&AFA, 1965–67; TAVR Council (formerly TA Council): Dep. Sec., 1967–72; Sec., 1973–75. Regional Organiser, Army Benevolent Fund, 1975–; Regional Sec., British Field Sports Soc., 1976–83. DL Notts, 1973. *Recreations:* Rugby football (played for Wales, Barbarians and Army, 1934–35; Chm., Army Rugby Union Referees Soc., 1963–73); Arab horses (Hon. Show Dir, Arab Horse Show, 1968–81). *Address:* Trent Hills Farm, Flintham, Newark, Notts NG23 5LL. *T:* 063–68 5274. *Clubs:* Army and Navy, British Sportsman's.

COWGILL, Bryan; Deputy Chairman: Mirror Group Newspapers, since 1986; Chairman, SelecTV, since 1986; *b* 27 May 1927; *m* 1966, Jennifer E. Baker; two *s*. *Educ:* Clitheroe Grammar School. Marine, subseq. Lieut, 3rd Royal Marine Commando Bde, SE Asia, 1943–47. Copy boy, then reporter, then feature writer with Lancashire Evening Post and Preston Guardian Group, 1942–50; edited local newspaper, Clitheroe, 1950–55; joined BBC TV as Outside Broadcasts prodn asst, 1955; produced Sportsview and Grandstand, 1957–63; Head of BBC Sport, 1963; Head of TV Outside Broadcasts Group, 1972; Controller, BBC1, 1974–77; Dir, News and Current Affairs, BBC, 1977; Man. Dir, Thames Television, 1977–85. FRTS 1984. *Recreation:* golf. *Address:* 68 Chiswick Staithe, Hartington Road, W4 3TP.

COWIE, Hon. Lord; William Lorn Kerr Cowie; a Senator of the College of Justice in Scotland, since 1977; *b* 1 June 1926; *s* of late Charles Rennie Cowie, MBE and Norah Slimmon Kerr; *m* 1958, Camilla Henrietta Grizel Hoyle; two *s* two *d*. *Educ:* Fettes Coll.; Clare Coll., Cambridge; Glasgow Univ. Sub-Lieut RNVR, 1944–47; Cambridge, 1947–49; Glasgow Univ., 1949–51; Mem., Faculty of Advocates, 1952; QC (Scotland) 1967. *Address:* 20 Blacket Place, Edinburgh EH9 1RL. *T:* 031–667 8238. *Club:* New (Edinburgh).

COWIE, Mervyn Hugh, CBE 1960; ED 1954; FCA; *b* 13 April 1909; *s* of Capt. Herbert Hugh Cowie, JP; *m* 1st, 1934, Erica Mary Beaty (*d* 1956); two *s* one *d*; 2nd, 1957, Valori Hare Duke; one *s* one *d*. *Educ:* Brighton; Brasenose Coll., Oxford. Hon. Game Warden, 1932–; Mem. Nairobi District Council, 1932–36; KAR, Reserve of Officers, 1932–38 (3rd and 5th Battalions); Kenya Regt, 1939; served War of 1939–45; Abyssinia, Middle East, Madagascar (retd Lieut-Col). MLC Kenya, 1951–60; Dir of Manpower, Mau-Mau Emergency, 1953–56. Founder and Dir, Royal National Parks of Kenya, 1946–66. Vice-Pres. E African Tourist Travel Assoc., 1950–65; Mem. Nat. Parks Commn, Internat. Union for Conservation of Nature, 1959–66; Hon. Trustee, Uganda Nat. Parks, 1950–; Vice-Pres., Fauna Preservation Soc., London; Trustee, East African Wild Life Soc.; Financial Dir, African Med. and Res. Foundn (Flying Doctor Services), 1972–79. TV and Radio (BBC Natural History Section). Editor, Royal Nat. Parks of Kenya Annual Reports, 1946–65. Lectures (tours USA and Britain). Gold Medal, San Diego Zool Soc., 1972. Order of the Golden Ark, Netherlands, 1975. *Publications:* Fly Vulture, 1961; I Walk with Lions (USA), 1964; African Lion, 1965. Contributor to International Journals and Conferences. *Recreations:* flying and wild life conservation. *Address:* PO Box 15549, Mbagathi, Nairobi, Kenya. *T:* Nairobi 891914. *Clubs:* Shikar; Explorer's (New York); Muthaiga Country (Nairobi).

COWIE, William Lorn Kerr; *see* Cowie, Hon. Lord.

COWLEY, 7th Earl *cr* 1857; **Garret Graham Wellesley**; Baron Cowley, 1828; Viscount Dangan, 1857; an independent financial consultant; *b* 30 July 1934; 3rd *s* of 4th Earl Cowley (*d* 1962) and of Mary (Elsie May), Countess Cowley; *S* nephew, 1975; *m* Paige Deming, Reno, Nevada; one *s* five *d*, and one *s* one *d* of former marriage. *Educ:* Univ. of S California (BSc Finance 1957); Harvard Univ. (MBA 1962). Investment Research Analyst: Wells Fargo Bank, San Francisco, 1962–64; Dodge & Cox, San Francisco, 1964–66; Asst Head, Investment Research Dept, Wells Fargo Bank, 1966–67; Vice-Pres., Investment Counsel, Thorndike, Doran, Paine & Lewis, Los Angeles, 1967–69; Sen. Vice-Pres., Exec. Cttee Mem., Securities, Real Estate and Company Acquisition Advisor, Shareholders Capital Corp., Los Angeles, 1969–74; Vice-Pres., and Sen. Investment Manager, Trust Dept, Bank of America, San Francisco, 1974–78; Gp Vice-Pres. and Dir, Internat Investment Management Service, Bank of America NT & SA, 1980–85; Director: Bank of America Internat., London, 1978; BankAmerica Trust Co. (Hong Kong), 1980; Bank of America Banking & Trust Co. (Gibraltar), 1981; Bank of America Trust Co. (Jersey), 1982; Bank of America Banking & Trust Co. (Nassau), 1982; Bank of America Banking & Trust Co. (Cayman), 1982. Served US Army Counter Intelligence Corps, primarily in France, 1957–60. *Heir: s* Viscount Dangan, *qv*. *Address:* 10 South Eaton Place, SW1W 9JA. *Clubs:* Brooks's; Harvard (San Francisco).

COWLEY, Rev. Canon Colin Patrick; Rector of Wonston, Winchester, 1955–71; Canon of Winchester, 1950–55, Hon. Canon, 1955; Canon Emeritus, 1971; *b* 3 Aug. 1902; *er s* of Rev. H. G. B. Cowley; *m* 1930, Dorothea Minna Pott (*d* 1980); three *d*. *Educ*: Winchester; Hertford Coll., Oxford. Curate at St Mary's, Bridport, 1926–28; Curate at St Mary Abbots, Kensington, 1928–35; Rector of Shenfield, Essex, 1935–50. Chaplain to the Forces, 1940–45. *Recreation*: coping with old age. *Address*: Cheriton Lodge, 42 Cheriton Road, Winchester, Hants.

COWLEY, Maj.-Gen. John Cain, CB 1971; Paymaster-in-Chief and Inspector of Army Pay Services, Ministry of Defence, 1967–72, retired; with de Zoete and Bevan, Stockbrokers, 1972–79; *b* 17 July 1918; *er s* of late Philip Richard and Eleanor Cowley, Ballaquane, Peel, Isle of Man; *m* 1948, Eileen Rosemary, CBE 1982, *d* of late George Percival Stewart, Aigburth, Liverpool; three *s*. *Educ*: Douglas School, Isle of Man. War of 1939–45: commissioned, RAPC, 1940; served: Palestine, Western Desert, Italy, France, Belgium, Holland, Germany. Dep. Asst Adj.-Gen., Middle East, 1949–51; GSOI, with Permanent Under Sec., War Office, 1952–54; West African Frontier Force, 1956–59; Dep. Paymaster-in-Chief: War Office, 1960–63; BAOR, 1963–65; Chief Paymaster, Eastern Command, 1965–67. Capt. 1946, Maj. 1953, Lt-Col 1955, Col. 1960, Brig. 1963, Maj.-Gen. 1967; psc 1948; jssc 1955; Administrative Staff Coll., 1960. Col Comdt, RAPC, 1974–79. Chm., W Sussex, Duke of Edinburgh's Award Scheme, 1986–. Vice-Pres., St Catherine's Hospice, 1981–; Governor, St Michaels, Burton Park, 1982– (Chm., 1986–). High Sheriff, W Sussex, 1984–85. *Recreations*: shooting, fishing, ornithology. *Address*: The Old Post Office, Nuthurst, Horsham, West Sussex. *T*: Lower Beeding 266. *Club*: Army and Navy.

COWLEY, Lt-Gen. Sir John Guise, GC (AM 1935); KBE 1958 (CBE 1946; OBE 1943); CB 1954; late RE; Chairman, Polamco Ltd, since 1976; *b* 20 Aug. 1905; *s* of Rev. Henry Guise Beatson Cowley, Fourgates, Dorchester, Dorset; *m* 1941, Irene Sybil, *d* of Percy Dreuille Millen, Berkhamsted, Herts; one *s* three *d*. *Educ*: Wellington Coll.; RMA Woolwich. 2nd Lieut RE 1925; Capt. 1936; Major 1940; Lieut-Col 1941; Brig. 1943; Maj.-Gen. 1953; Lieut-Gen. 1957. Served War of 1939–45, Middle East, Italy, and North-West Europe (despatches four times, OBE). Chief of Staff, HQ, Eastern Command, 1953–56; Vice-QMG, 1956–57; Controller of Munitions, Ministry of Supply, 1957–60; Master-Gen. of the Ordnance, War Office, 1960–62; retd, 1962. Col Commandant: Royal Pioneer Corps, 1961–67; Royal Engineers, 1961–70. Chairman: Bowmaker Ltd, 1962–71; Wilverley Securities Ltd, 1970–73; Keith and Henderson Ltd, 1973–76; Director: British Oxygen Ltd, 1962–76; Alastair Watson Ltd, 1962–70; C. T. Bowring and Co. Ltd, 1969–71. Pres., New Forest Preservation Soc., 1982–. Governor, Wellington Coll., 1960–76, Vice-Pres. and Chm. of Governors, 1969–76, Pres. OW Soc. 1979–; Chairman of Governors: Eagle House Sch., 1968–76; Bigshotte Sch., 1968–76; Brockenhurst Sixth Form Coll., 1977–84. Knight Comdr Order of Orange Nassau (Netherlands). FRSA. *Recreations*: golf, bridge, croquet. *Address*: Whitemoor, Sandy Down, Boldre, Lymington, Hants. *T*: Lymington 23369. *Club*: Army and Navy.

COWLEY, Dr John Maxwell, FRS 1979; FAA; Galvin Professor of Physics, Arizona State University, USA, since 1970; *b* 18 Feb. 1923; *s* of Alfred E. and Doris R. Cowley; *m* 1951, Roberta J. (*née* Beckett); two *d*. *Educ*: Univ. of Adelaide (BSc 1942, MSc 1945, DSc 1957); MIT (PhD 1949). FAA 1961. Res. Officer, CSIRO, Australia, 1945–62; Prof. of Physics, Univ. of Melbourne, 1962–70. Mem. Exec. Cttee. Internat. Union of Crystallography, 1963–69. *Publications*: Diffraction Physics, 1975; approx. 200 articles in learned jls. *Recreations*: painting, music. *Address*: 1718 E Gaylon Drive, Tempe, Ariz 85282, USA. *T*: (602) 966–0071.

COWLEY, Kenneth Martin, CMG 1963; OBE 1956; *b* 15 May 1912; *s* of late Robert Martin Cowley, OBE, and late Mabel Priscilla Cowley (*née* Lee); *m* 1948, Barbara (*née* Tannahill); one *s* (and one step *s*). *Educ*: Merchant Taylors' Sch., Crosby; Exeter Coll., Oxford. District Officer, Kenya, 1935–44; Asst Sec., 1944–46; District Comr, 1946–49; Actg Native Courts Officer, 1949–53; Sec. for African Affairs, 1953–56; Provincial Commissioner, Southern Province, Kenya, 1956–63 (despatches, 1957); Sec., Kenya Regional Boundaries and Constituencies Commns, 1962; Sen. Administrative Manager, Express Transport Co. Ltd, Kenya, 1963–70. Sec., Overseas Service Pensioners' Assoc., 1971–79. *Recreation*: natural history. *Address*: Grasmere, 38 Wellington Avenue, Fleet, Hants GU13 9BL. *T*: Fleet 615990. *Club*: Nairobi (Kenya).

COWLEY, Prof. Roger Arthur, FRS 1978; FRSE 1972; Professor of Physics, University of Edinburgh, since 1970; *b* 24 Feb. 1939; *s* of Cecil A. Cowley and Mildred S. Cowley; *m* 1964, Sheila J. Wells; one *s* one *d*. *Educ*: Brentwood Sch., Essex; Cambridge Univ. (MA, PhD). Fellow, Trinity Hall, Cambridge, 1962–64; Research Officer, Atomic Energy of Canada Ltd, 1964–70. Max Born Medal, 1973. *Publication*: Structural Phase Transitions, 1981. *Address*: 54A St Albans Road, Edinburgh EH9 2LX. *T*: 031–667 7630.

COWLING, Richard John, ARICS; Deputy Chief Valuer, Inland Revenue Valuation Office, 1972–74; *b* 2 Feb. 1911; *s* of Sydney George and Madge Prentice Cowling, late of East Grinstead; *m* 1936, Doris Rosa, *o d* of Albert James Puttock, Guildford; one *s*. *Educ*: Skinners' Company's Sch. Articles and private practice as a surveyor, 1928–35; War Office Lands Branch, 1936; Inland Revenue Valuation Office, 1937. TA Commission, Green Howards, 1942. *Recreations*: golf, bridge, sailing. *Address*: 18 Gateways, Epsom Road, Guildford, Surrey GU1 2LF. *T*: Guildford 573473.

COWLING, Thomas George, FRS 1947; Professor of Applied Mathematics, Leeds University, 1948–70, now Professor Emeritus; *b* 17 June 1906; *s* of George and Edith Eliza Cowling; *m* 1935, Doris Moffatt; one *s* two *d*. *Educ*: Sir George Monoux Sch., Walthamstow; Oxford Univ. Teacher of mathematics, Imperial Coll. of Science, University Coll., Swansea, University Coll., Dundee, Manchester Univ., and at University Coll., Bangor (Prof. of Mathematics, 1945–48). Pres., Royal Astronomical Soc., 1965–67. Hon. Fellow, Brasenose Coll., Oxford, 1966. Halley Lectr, Oxford Univ., 1969. Gold Medallist, Royal Astronomical Soc., 1956; Bruce Gold Medallist, Astronomical Soc. of the Pacific, 1985. *Publications*: (with S. Chapman) The Mathematical Theory of Non-Uniform Gases, 1939, 3rd edn 1970; Molecules in Motion, 1950; Magneto-hydrodynamics, 1957, 2nd edn 1976; also a number of papers, chiefly astronomical and gas-theoretic. *Recreation*: gardening. *Address*: 19 Hollin Gardens, Leeds LS16 5NL. *T*: 785342.

COWPER, Sir Norman (Lethbridge), Kt 1967; CBE 1958; *b* 15 Sept. 1896; *yr s* of Cecil Spencer de Grey Cowper; *m* 1925, Dorothea Huntly, *d* of Hugh McCrae; three *d*. *Educ*: Sydney Grammar Sch.; University of Sydney (BA, LLB). Served War of 1939–45, 2nd AIF, Lt-Col. Solicitor, Supreme Court of NSW, 1923. Partner, Allen, Allen & Hemsley, 1924–70. Dir, Australian Inst. of Polit. Science, 1932–69; Australian Inst. of Internat. Affairs: NSW Br. Pres., 1947–49; Commonwealth Pres., 1949–50; Mem. Council, Australian National Univ., 1955–74; Mem. Board of Trustees, Sydney Grammar Sch., 1935–75 (Chm., 1951–75); Chm., Council on New Guinea Affairs, 1965. *Publications*: occasional articles: Australian Quarterly, Australian Outlook, Australian Dictionary of Biography. *Recreations*: reading, gardening. *Address*: Wivenhoe, Millewa

Avenue, Wahroonga, Sydney, Australia. *T*: 48 2336. *Club*: Australian (Sydney) (Pres., 1968–72).

COWPERTHWAITE, David Jarvis; Under-Secretary, Scottish Home and Health Department, 1974–81, retired; *b* 14 Sept. 1921; *s* of J. J. Cowperthwaite and Mrs J. W. B. Cowperthwaite (*née* Jarvis); *m* 1944, Patricia Stockdale; two *d*. *Educ*: Edinburgh Academy; Exeter Coll., Oxford (MA). Nigerian Admin. Service, 1942–48; joined Home Civil Service (Scottish Home Dept), 1948. *Recreations*: cricket, golf. *Address*: 69 Northumberland Street, Edinburgh EH3 6JG. *T*: 031–557 0215.
    See also Sir J. J. Cowperthwaite.

COWPERTHWAITE, Sir John James, KBE 1968 (OBE 1960); CMG 1964; International Adviser to Jardine Fleming & Co. Ltd, Hong Kong, 1972–81; Financial Secretary, Hong Kong, 1961–71; *b* 25 April 1915; *s* of late John James Cowperthwaite and Jessie Wemyss Barron Jarvis Cowperthwaite; *m* 1941, Sheila Mary, *d* of Alexander Thomson, Aberdeen; one *s*. *Educ*: Merchiston Castle Sch.; St Andrews Univ; Christ's Coll., Cambridge. Entered Colonial Administrative Service, Hong Kong, 1941; seconded to Sierra Leone, 1942–45. *Address*: 25 South Street, St Andrews, Fife. *T*: St Andrews 74759. *Clubs*: Royal Hong Kong Jockey, Royal Hong Kong Golf; Royal and Ancient.

COWTAN, Maj.-Gen. Frank Willoughby John, CBE 1970 (MBE 1947); MC 1942 and Bar, 1945; *b* 10 Feb. 1920; *s* of late Air Vice-Marshal F. C. Cowtan, CB, CBE, KHS and late Mrs N. A. Cowtan (*née* Kennedy); *m* 1949, Rose Isabel Cope; one *s* one *d*. *Educ*: Wellington Coll.; RMA Woolwich. 2nd Lieut Royal Engineers, 1939; served War of 1939–45, BEF, N Africa, Italy, NW Europe (Captain); Palestine, Kenya, Middle East, 1945–50 (Major); psc 1951; Middle East, UK, BAOR, 1952–58; Liaison Officer to US Corps of Engrs, USA, 1958–60 (Bt Lt-Col); CO 131 Parachute Engr Regt, 1960–62; CO Victory Coll., RMA Sandhurst, 1962–65 (Lt-Col); Comd 11 Engr Bde, BAOR, 1965–67 (Brig.); ndc (Canada) 1967–68; Dir of Quartering (Army), 1968–70; Dep. QMG, MoD(AD), 1970–71; Comdt, RMCS, 1971–75, retired. Hon. Col, 131 Indep. Commando Sqn, RE, 1975–80; Col Comdt RE, 1977–82. *Recreations*: golf, shooting, wildfowling, sailing, travel, languages. *Address*: Rectory Cottage, Coleshill, Swindon, Wilts. *Club*: Army and Navy.

COX; *see* Roxbee Cox.

COX, family name of **Baroness Cox.**

COX, Baroness *cr* 1982 (Life Peer), of Queensbury in Greater London; **Caroline Anne Cox;** Deputy Speaker, 1986; Director, Nursing Education Research Unit, Chelsea College, University of London, 1977–84; *b* 6 July 1937; *d* of Robert John McNeill Love, MS, FRCS and Dorothy Ida Borland; *m* 1959, Dr Murray Cox, FRCPsych; two *s* one *d*. *Educ*: Channing School. BSc (Sociology, 1st Cl. Hons) 1967, MSc (Economics) 1969, London Univ.; FRCN 1985. SRN, London Hosp., 1958; Staff Nurse, Edgware Gen. Hosp., 1960; Research Associate, Univ. of Newcastle upon Tyne, 1967–68. Department of Sociology, Polytechnic of North London: Lecturer, Senior Lectr, Principal Lectr, 1969–74; Head of Department, 1974–77. Dir, Centre for Policy Studies, 1983–85. A Baroness in Waiting, April–Aug. 1985. Chairman: Academic Council for Peace and Freedom, 1984–; Jagiellonian Trust. Patron, Medical Aid for Poland Fund. Co-editor, Internat. Jl of Nursing Studies. *Publications*: (ed jtly) A Sociology of Medical Practice, 1975; (jtly) Rape of Reason: The Corruption of the Polytechnic of North London, 1975; (jtly) The Right to Learn, 1982; Sociology: A Guide for Nurses, Midwives and Health Visitors, 1983. *Recreations*: campanology, squash, ski-ing, hill walking. *Address*: The White House, Wyke Hall, Gillingham, Dorset SP8 5NS. *T*: Gillingham 3436; 1 Arnellan House, 144–146 Slough Lane, Kingsbury, NW9. *T*: 01–204 2321. *Club*: Royal Commonwealth Society.

COX, Alan Seaforth; Clerk to the Grocers' Company, 1965–81; Secretary, Grocers' Trust Company Ltd, 1968–81; *b* 15 Oct. 1915; *m* 1st, 1944, Jean Heriot-Maitland (marr. diss. 1952); one *s*; 2nd, 1954, Mary Thornton; three *s* one *d*. Served War: London Scottish and Gold Coast Regt, 1939–45; Staff Officer, WO, 1945–46. Farming and banking, Argentine (Patagonia), 1947–52; joined Grocers' Co., 1954. Sec., Governing Body of Oundle Sch., 1965–81. Hon. Mem. Ct, Grocers' Co., 1981–. *Recreations*: bridge, cribbage, dining and wining. *Address*: The Mount, Winchelsea, East Sussex TN36 4EG. *T*: Rye 226543.

COX, Albert Edward; His Honour Judge Edward Cox; a Circuit Judge, since 1977; *b* 26 Sept. 1916; *s* of Frederick Stringer Cox; *m* 1962, Alwyn Winifred Cox, JP. Admitted Solicitor, 1938; Principal Partner, Claude Hornby & Cox, 1946–76. A Recorder of the Crown Court, 1972–77. President: London Criminal Courts Solicitors' Assoc., 1967–68; British Acad. of Forensic Science, 1977–78; Mem., Parole Board, 1971–75; Chm., London (Metropolis) Licensing Planning Cttee, 1979–84. *Address*: 38 Carlton Hill, NW8 0JY; Longhedge, Monckton Deverill, Wilts.

COX, Alister Stransom, MA; Headmaster, Royal Grammar School, Newcastle upon Tyne, since 1972; *b* 21 May 1934; *s* of Rev. Roland L. Cox and F. Ruth Cox; *m* 1960, Janet (*née* Williams); one *s* two *d*. *Educ*: Kingswood School, Bath; New College, Oxford (Scholar). Hon. Mods (1st Class); Lit. Hum. BA 1957, MA 1961. Sixth Form Master, Clifton Coll., 1957–63; Head of Classics, Wellington Coll., 1963–69; Dep. Head, Arnold Sch., Blackpool, 1969–72. Vis. Lectr in Greek, Bristol Univ., 1968. Founder Mem., Sinfonia Chorus, Northern Sinfonia of England, 1973–. FRSA 1982. *Publications*: Lucretius on Matter and Man, 1967; Didactic Poetry, in Greek and Latin Literature (ed Higginbotham), 1969; articles in Greece and Rome, Times Educnl Supp. and educnl jls. *Recreations*: music, especially singing; Lake District fell walking. *Address*: 39 The Grove, Gosforth, Newcastle upon Tyne NE3 1NH. *T*: Tyneside 285 7735.

COX, Anthony; *see* Cox, J. A.

COX, Anthony Robert, PhD, CEng; Counsellor, Science and Technology, British Embassy, Washington DC, since 1983; *b* 30 Nov. 1938; *s* of Robert George Cox and Gladys Cox; *m* 1963, Constance Jean Hammond; one *s* two *d*. *Educ*: Brockley County School; Imperial College, London. BScEng (Metallurgy). ARSM, MIM. RARDE, 1960–69; Exchange Scientist, US Naval Research Lab., Washington DC, 1969–71; Dep. Materials Supt, RARDE, 1971–75; Asst Dir, Armour and Materials, Military Vehicle Engineering Estab., 1975–80; MoD Central Staffs Defence Science, 1980–83. *Publications*: papers on refractory metals, structure and strengthening mechanism on high strength steel, fractography, explosive effects, archaeological artefacts corrosion. *Recreations*: sailing, squash, skiing, foreign travel. *Address*: British Embassy, 3100 Massachusetts Avenue NW, Washington, DC 20008, USA. *T*: 202 462 1340. *Clubs*: International Lions; Cosmos (Washington).

COX, Sir Anthony (Wakefield), Kt 1983; CBE 1972; FRIBA, AADip; Consultant, Architects' Co-Partnership, since 1980; *b* 18 July 1915; *s* of late William Edward Cox, CBE, and of Elsie Gertrude Wakefield; *m* 1943, Susan Babington Smith, ARIBA, AADip; two *d*. *Educ*: Mill Hill Sch.; Architectural Association Sch. of Architecture, London. RIBA Journal, 1938–39; Jt Editor of Focus, 1938–39; founder partner, Architects' Co-

Partnership, 1939; Sir Alexander Gibb & Partners, ordnance factories and hostels, 1940–42. Served War: Royal Engineers, Western Europe and India, 1943–46; Hertfordshire CC Schools, 1946–47; reabsorbed in Architects' Co-Partnership, 1947; part-time teaching AA Sch. of Architecture, 1948–54; Mem. Council: Architectural Assoc., 1956–64 (Pres. 1962–63); RIBA, 1967–72; Member: Bd of Educn, RIBA, 1967–73; Royal Fine Art Commn, 1970–85; Bd, Property Services Agency, 1979–81, Adv. Bd, 1981–84. *Works include* Depts of: Chemistry at Univ. of Leicester and University Coll., London; Chemistry and Biochemistry at Imperial Coll. of Science and Technology; buildings for: Inst. of Psychiatry, London; the Maudsley Hosp., London. *Publication:* (jtly) Design for Health Care, 1981. *Recreations:* reading, listening, looking, making. *Address:* 5 Bacon's Lane, Highgate, N6. *T:* 01–340 2543.

See also O. J. Cox.

COX, Prof. Archibald; Carl M. Loeb University Professor, Harvard University, 1976–84, now Emeritus; Visiting Profssor of Law, Boston University, since 1984; Chairman, Governing Board, Common Cause, since 1980; *b* 17 May 1912; *s* of Archibald Cox and Frances Bruen (*née* Perkins); *m* 1937, Phyllis Ames; one *s* two *d. Educ:* St Paul's Sch., Concord; Harvard Univ. AB 1934, LLB 1937. Admitted to Mass Bar, 1937. Gen. practice with Ropes, Gray, Best, Coolidge & Rugg, 1938–41; Office of Solicitor-Gen., US Dept of Justice, 1941–43; Assoc. Solicitor, Dept of Labor, 1943–45; Lectr on Law, Harvard, 1945–46, Prof. of Law, 1946–61; Solicitor-Gen., US Dept of Justice, 1961–65; Williston Prof. of Law, Harvard Law Sch., 1965–76. Pitt Prof., Univ. of Cambridge, 1974–75. Co-Chm., Constrn Industry Stablizn Commn, 1951–52; Chm., Wage Stablzn Bd, 1952; Mem. Bd Overseers, Harvard, 1962–65. Special Watergate Prosecutor, 1973. Hon. LLD: Loyola, 1964; Cincinnati, 1967; Rutgers, Amherst, Denver, 1974; Harvard, 1975; Michigan, 1976; Wheaton, 1977; Northeastern, 1978; Clark, 1980; Hon. LHD: Hahnemann Med. Coll., 1980; Univ. of Mass, 1981; Illinois, 1985. *Publications:* Cases on Labor Law, 9th edn 1981; (jtly) Law and National Labor Policy, 1960; Civil Rights, the Constitution and the Courts, 1967; The Warren Court, 1968; The Role of the Supreme Court in American Government, 1976; Freedom of Expression, 1981; miscellaneous articles. *Address:* PO Box 393, Wayland, Mass 01778, USA; (office) Harvard Law School, Cambridge, Mass 02138. *T:* 1–617–495–3133. *Clubs:* Somerset (Boston, Mass); Century Association (New York).

COX, Arthur George Ernest S.; *see* Stewart Cox.

COX, Brian; *see* Cox, Charles B.

COX, Brian Robert Escott, QC 1974; a Recorder of the Crown Court, since 1972; *b* 30 Sept. 1932; *yr s* of late George Robert Escott Cox; *m* 1st, 1956; one *s* two *d*; 2nd, 1969, Noelle Gilormini; one *s* one *d. Educ:* Rugby Sch.; Oriel Coll., Oxford (BA, MA). Called to Bar, Lincoln's Inn, 1954, Bencher, 1985. Midland and Oxford Circuit. *Address:* 1 King's Bench Walk, Temple, EC4. *T:* 01–353 8436.

COX, Prof. (Charles) Brian; John Edward Taylor Professor of English Literature, University of Manchester, since 1976; *b* 5 Sept. 1928; *s* of Hedley E. Cox and late Rose Thompson; *m* 1954, Jean Willmer; one *s* two *d. Educ:* Wintringham Sec. Sch.; Pembroke Coll., Cambridge (MA, MLitt). Lectr, Univ. of Hull, 1954–66; Manchester University: Prof. of English Lit., 1966–76; Dean, Faculty of Arts, 1984–86. Vis. Associate Prof., Univ. of Calif, Berkeley, 1964–65; Brown Fellow, Univ. of the South, Sewanee, Tennessee, 1980. Pres., Nat. Council for Educnl Standards, 1984– (Chm., 1979–84). Co-editor: Critical Qly, 1959–; Black Papers on Education, 1969–77. *Publications:* The Free Spirit, 1963; (ed, with A. E. Dyson) Modern Poetry, 1963; (ed, with A. E. Dyson) Practical Criticism of Poetry, 1965; Joseph Conrad: the modern imagination, 1974; Every Common Sight (poems), 1981; The Two-Headed Monster (poems), 1985. *Recreations:* Manchester United, walking. *Address:* 20 Park Gates Drive, Cheadle Hulme, Stockport SK8 7DF. *T:* 061–485 2162. *Club:* Lansdowne.

COX, Prof. Christopher Barry, PhD, DSc; Head of Department of Biology, King's College London, since 1985; *b* 29 July 1931; *s* of Herbert Ernest Cox and May Cox; *m* 1961, Sheila (*née* Morgan); two *s* one *d. Educ:* St Paul's Sch., Kensington; Balliol Coll., Oxford (MA); St John's Coll., Cambridge (PhD); DSc London. Asst Lectr in Zoology, King's Coll. London, 1956–59; Harkness Fellow of Commonwealth Fund, at Mus. of Comparative Zoology, Harvard, 1959–60; King's College London: Lectr in Zoology, 1959–66; Sen. Lectr, 1966–69; Reader, 1970–76; Prof., 1976–82; Head of Dept of Zoology, 1982–85. Mem. Council, Palaeontological Assoc., 1967–69, 1974; Vice-Pres., 1969–81. Editor, Palaeontology, 1975–79. Palaeontological collecting expedns to Central Africa, 1963; Argentina, 1967; N Brasil, 1972; Qld, Aust., 1978. *Publications:* Prehistoric Animals, 1969; Biogeography—an ecological and evolutionary approach, 1973, 4th edn 1985; Prehistoric World, 1975; research papers on vertebrate palaeontology and historical biogeography, in Phil. Trans. Royal Soc., Proc. Zool. Soc., Nature, Bull. Brit. Mus. (Nat. Hist.), Jl Biogeog., etc. *Recreation:* gardening. *Address:* Conifers, Grange Road, Leatherhead, Surrey KT22 7JS. *T:* Ashtead 73167.

COX, Prof. Sir David (Roxbee), Kt 1985; PhD; FRS 1973; Professor of Statistics, Imperial College of Science and Technology, since 1966; Head of Department of Mathematics, 1970–74; *b* 15 July 1924; *s* of S. R. Cox, Handsworth, Birmingham; *m* 1948, Joyce (*née* Drummond), Keighley, Yorks; three *s* one *d. Educ:* Handsworth Grammar Sch., Birmingham; St John's Coll., Cambridge (MA). PhD Leeds, 1949. Posts at Royal Aircraft Establishment, 1944–46; Wool Industries Research Assoc., 1946–50; Statistical Laboratory, Cambridge, 1950–55; Visiting Prof., University of N Carolina, 1955–56; Reader in Statistics, Birkbeck College, 1956–60, Professor of Statistics, 1961–66. SERC Sen. Res. Fellow, 1983–. President: Bernoulli Soc., 1979–81; Royal Statistical Soc., 1980–82. For. Mem., Royal Danish Acad. of Scis and Letters, 1983; For. Hon. Mem., Amer. Acad. of Arts and Sciences, 1974. Hon. DSc: Reading, 1982; Bradford, 1982; Helsinki, 1986. Weldon Meml Prize, Univ. of Oxford, 1984. Editor of Biometrika, 1966–. *Publications:* Statistical Methods in the Textile Industry, 1949 (jt author); Planning of Experiments, 1958; (jtly) Queues, 1961; Renewal Theory, 1962; (jtly) Theory of Stochastic Processes, 1965; (jtly) Statistical Analysis of Series of Events, 1966; Analysis of Binary Data, 1970; (jtly) Theoretical Statistics, 1974; (jtly) Problems and Solutions in Theoretical Statistics, 1978; (jtly) Point Processes, 1980; (jtly) Applied Statistics, 1981; (jtly) Analysis of Survival Data, 1984; papers in Jl of Royal Statistical Society, Biometrika, etc. *Address:* Imperial College, SW7. *T:* 01–589 5111.

COX, Dennis George; Under-Secretary (Industrial Relations), Department of Employment, 1971–74; a Deputy Chairman, Central Arbitration Committee, 1977–84; *b* 23 Feb. 1914; *s* of George and Amelia Cox; *m* 1938, Victoria Barraclough; two *s. Educ:* University College Sch.; Queens' Coll., Cambridge. Royal Navy, 1942–45; served with Netherlands and Norwegian navies, Lieut RNVR. Entered Min. of Labour, 1936; Asst Sec. 1966; Regional Controller, SW Region. *Recreations:* gardening, fishing. *Address:* 22 Ashley Court, Morpeth Terrace, SW1; Church Cottage, Laughton, Lewes, East Sussex. *T:* Ripe 382. *Club:* Army and Navy.

COX, Edward; *see* Cox, A. E.

COX, Sir (Ernest) Gordon, KBE 1964; TD; FRS 1954; FRSC; FInstP; DSc; Secretary of the Agricultural Research Council, 1960–71; *b* 24 April 1906; *s* of Ernest Henry Cox and Rosina Ring; *m* 1st, 1929, Lucie Grace Baker (*d* 1962); one *s* one *d*; 2nd, 1968, Prof. Mary Rosaleen Truter, DSc, *d* of Dr D. N. Jackman. *Educ:* City of Bath Boys' Sch.; University of Bristol. Research Asst, Davy-Faraday Laboratory, Royal Institution, 1927; Chemistry Dept, Univ. of Birmingham, 1929–41 (Reader in Chemical Crystallography, 1940); Prof. of Inorganic and Structural Chemistry, University of Leeds, 1945–60; commissioned in Territorial Army, 1936; special scientific duties, War Office, 1942–44; attached to HQ staff of 21 Army Group, France and Germany, as Technical Staff Officer, Grade I, 1944–45. Vice-Pres., Institute of Physics, 1950–53; Mem. Agric. Research Council, 1957–60. Hon. DSc: Newcastle, 1964; Birmingham, 1964; Bath, 1973; East Anglia, 1973; Hon. LLD Bristol, 1969; Hon. ARCVS, 1972. *Publications:* numerous scientific papers in jls of various learned societies, chiefly on the crystal structures of chemical compounds. *Recreations:* music, gardening, natural history. *Address:* 117 Hampstead Way, NW11 7JN. *T:* 01–455 2618. *Clubs:* Athenæum, English-Speaking Union, Lansdowne.

See also P. A. Cox.

COX, Sir Geoffrey (Sandford), Kt 1966; CBE 1959 (MBE 1945); Director, The Observer, since 1981; *b* 7 April 1910; *s* of Sandford Cox, Wellington, NZ, and Mary Cox (*née* MacGregor); *m* 1935, Cecily Barbara Talbot Turner; two *s* two *d. Educ:* Southland High Sch., New Zealand; Otago Univ., New Zealand (MA); Rhodes Scholar, 1932–35; Oriel Coll., Oxford (BA). Reporter, Foreign and War Corresp. News Chronicle, 1935–37, Daily Express, 1937–40. Enlisted New Zealand Army, 1940; commissioned, Dec. 1940; served in 2 New Zealand Div., Greece, Crete, Libya, Italy; Major, Chief Intelligence Officer, Gen. Freyberg's staff (despatches twice). First Sec. and Chargé d'Affaires, NZ Legation, Washington, 1943; NZ Rep., first UNRRA Conf., 1943; Political Corresp., News Chronicle, 1945; Asst Editor, News Chronicle 1954. Regular Contributor, BBC radio and TV, 1945–56; Editor and Chief Exec., Independent Television News, 1956–68; founded News at Ten, 1967; Dep. Chm., Yorkshire Television, 1968–71; Chm., Tyne Tees Television, 1971–74; Chm., LBC Radio, 1978–81. TV Producers' Guild Award Winner, 1962; Fellow, Royal TV Soc. (Silver Medal, 1963; Gold Medal, 1978); Fellow, British Kinematograph and TV Soc. *Publications:* Defence of Madrid, 1937; The Red Army Moves, 1941; The Road to Trieste, 1946; The Race for Trieste, 1977; See It Happen, 1983. *Recreations:* fishing, tracing Roman roads. *Club:* Garrick.

COX, Sir (George) Trenchard; *see* Cox, Sir Trenchard.

COX, Sir Gordon; *see* Cox, Sir E. G.

COX, Harry Bernard, CBE 1956; Deputy Chairman, Thos Wyatt Nigeria Ltd, 1967–83; Consultant, Knight, Frank & Rutley, 1967–83; retired; *b* 29 Nov. 1906; *e surv. s* of Rev. Charles Henry Cox, BSc; *m* 1955, Joan, *e d* of P. Munn, Brighton; one *s* one *d. Educ:* Upholland Grammar Sch.; Keble Coll., Oxford. Colonial Administrative Service, Nigeria, 1930; Dir of Commerce and Industries, Nigeria, 1949; Acting Development Sec., Nigeria, 1953–54; Acting Commissioner for Nigeria, 1955; Principal Sec. to the Commissioner for Nigeria in the United Kingdom, 1955. John Holt & Co. (Liverpool) Ltd, 1958; Chm., John Holt (Nigeria) Ltd, 1962. Leader, Westminster Chamber of Commerce Mission to Nigeria, 1974. *Address:* 5 Arundel House, 22 The Drive, Hove BN3 3JD. *T:* Brighton 738798. *Club:* Oriental.

COX, Major Horace B. T.; *see* Trevor Cox.

COX, Ian Herbert, CBE 1952; MA; FRGS; FZS; *b* 20 Feb. 1910; *e s* of late Herbert Stanley Cox and Elizabeth Dalgarno; *m* 1945, Susan Mary (*d* 1983), *d* of late Lieut Comdr N. G. Fowler Snelling and *widow* of Flt Lieut D. S. S. Low; two *s* two *d. Educ:* Oundle; Magdalene Coll., Cambridge (Exhibnr). Geologist, Oxford Univ. Hudson Straits Expedition, 1931; research, Dept of Geology, Cambridge, 1932–36; with BBC 1936–39; served War of 1939–45 (Comdr, RNVR); BBC 1946; Science Corresp., London Press Service, 1947–48; Dir of Sci., Festival of Britain Office, 1948–51; Shell Internat. Pet. Co., 1952–70 (Hd Sc. and Develt TR Div., Convener Shell Grants Cttee). Consultant, OECD, 1971–. Mem. Council: RGS, 1953–57, 1959–62; Overseas Develt Inst., 1966–74; BAAS, 1960–70 (Gen. Treasurer, 1965–70); Chelsea Coll., Univ. of London, 1968–74; Mem. Management Cttee, Scott Polar Research Inst., 1955–57; Vice-Pres., Geol. Soc., 1966–68; Mem., Bd of Governors, and Vice-Pres., Exec. Cttee, European Cultural Foundn (Amsterdam), 1972–82. Pres., Arctic Club, 1961. *Publications:* papers on geology and palæontology of the Arctic; (ed) The Queen's Beasts, 1953; The Scallop, 1957; monographs in World Land Use Survey. *Recreations:* working with wood and stone; gardening. *Address:* The Old Post Office, School Hill, Seale, Farnham, Surrey GU10 1HY. *T:* Runfold 2481. *Club:* Athenæum.

COX, Surgeon Rear-Adm. James, OBE 1964; QHS 1982; FFARCS; Surgeon Rear Admiral, Support Medical Services, 1983–84, retired; *b* 4 Feb. 1928; *s* of James Wolseley Cox and Gladys May Cox (*née* Watkinson); *m* 1952, Elizabeth Jennings; one *s* one *d. Educ:* Durham Sch.; Durham Univ. (MB BS 1951). FFARCS 1960. HMS Birmingham, 1952–54; Consultant Anaesthetist, RN Hospitals: Plymouth, 1955–59; Chatham, 1959–61; Plymouth, 1962–65; Gibraltar, 1965–69; Plymouth, 1969–71; Principal Medical Officer, HMS Bulwark, 1971–72; Consultant Anaesthetist, RN Hospitals: Plymouth, 1972–75; Haslar, 1975–77; Staff Medical Officer to MGRM Commando Forces, 1977–80; Medical Officer in Charge, RN Hospital Stonehouse, 1980–82; Surgeon Rear-Adm. (Naval Medicine and Trng), 1982–83. *Recreations:* fishing, gardening. *Address:* c/o National Westminster Bank PLC, 87 Grey Street, Newcastle upon Tyne NE1 6ER.

COX, (James) Anthony; His Honour Judge Anthony Cox; a Circuit Judge, since 1976; *b* 21 April 1924; *s* of Herbert Sidney Cox and Gwendoline Margaret Cox; *m* 1950, Doris Margaret Fretwell; three *s* one *d. Educ:* Cotham Sch., Bristol; Bristol Univ. LLB Hons 1948. War Service, Royal Marines, 1943–46. Called to Bar, Gray's Inn, 1949; a Recorder of the Crown Court, 1972–76. *Recreations:* cricket, sailing, golf, the arts. *Address:* c/o Courts Administrator, The Castle, Exeter, Devon. *Clubs:* MCC; Royal Western Yacht (Plymouth); Yealm Yacht; Bigbury Golf.

COX, John; Artistic Director, Scottish Opera, since 1985 (General Administrator, 1982–85); *b* 12 March 1935; *s* of Leonard John Cox and Ethel M. (*née* McGill). *Educ:* Queen Elizabeth's Hosp., Bristol; St Edmund Hall, Oxford (BA). Freelance producer of plays, opera, revue and musicals in Britain and abroad, incl. La Scala, Milan, and Metropolitan Opera, New York, Vienna, Stockholm, Brussels, Amsterdam, Sydney, Cologne, Frankfurt, Spoleto, Wexford, Santa Fe, Houston, San Francisco, Washington, 1959–; Dir of Prodn, Glyndebourne Festival Opera, 1971–81. Productions include: *opera:* Glyndebourne: Richard Strauss cycle, Rake's Progress, The Magic Flute, La Cenerentola; ENO: Cosi Fan Tutte, Patience; Scottish Opera: L'Egisto, Manon Lescaut, Capriccio, Marriage of Figaro; *plays:* Never The Twain, Mermaid; Miss Julie, Twelfth Night, Greenwich; British Nat. Day Spectacular, Expo '67, Montreal. *Address:* 7 West Grove, SE10 8QT. *T:* 01–692 2450. *Club:* Garrick.

COX, Vice-Adm. Sir John (Michael Holland), KCB 1982; Director, Spastics Society, since 1983; Flag Officer Naval Air Command, 1982–83; *b* Peking, China, 27 Oct. 1928;

s of late Thomas Cox, MBE, and of Daisy Anne Cox; *m* 1962, Anne Garden Farquharson Seth-Smith; one *s* one *d*. *Educ:* Hilton Coll., Natal, SA. Joined BRNC, 1946; ADC to C-in-C Allied Forces, N Europe, 1952–53; ADC to Governor of Victoria, 1955; commanded HM Ships: Dilston, 1957 (despatches); Stubbington, 1958; sc Camberley, 1960; Cadet Trng Officer, BRNC Dartmouth, 1962; CSO, London Div., RNR, 1963; commanded HMS: Surprise, 1964; Naiad, 1965; Comdr, Sea Trng, Staff of Flag Officer Sea Trng, 1967; Naval Attaché, Bonn, 1969; comd HMS Norfolk, 1972; Dir, Naval Ops and Trade, 1973–75; Comdr, Standing Naval Force Atlantic, 1976–77; COS to C in C, Naval Home Command, 1977–79; Flag Officer Third Flotilla and Comdr Anti-Submarine Group Two, 1979–82. *Recreations:* tennis, skiing. *Address:* The Spastics Society, 12 Park Crescent, W1N 4EQ. *Club:* Lansdowne.

COX, Sir John (William), Kt 1951; CBE 1946; Member, 1930–68, and Speaker of the House of Assembly, Bermuda, 1948–68; *b* 29 April 1900; *s* of Henry James and Ellen Augusta Cox; *m* 1st, 1926, Dorothy Carlyle (*d* 1982), *d* of J. D. C. Darrell; three *s*; 2nd, 1984, Joan Maitland Cooper. *Educ:* Saltus Grammar Sch., Bermuda. Merchant; Pres., Pearman, Watlington & Co. Ltd, Hamilton, Bermuda, General and Commission Merchants. Comdr, Royal Netherlands Order of Orange Nassau, 1956. *Address:* The Grove, Devonshire Parish, Bermuda. *T:* 2–0303. *Clubs:* Royal Automobile; Royal Bermuda Yacht, Royal Hamilton Amateur Dinghy, Mid Ocean (Bermuda).

COX, Sir Mencea Ethereal, Kt 1980; Member of the Senate, Barbados; *b* 28 Nov. 1906; *s* of James William Cox and Charlotte Matilda Cox, Plymouth Brethren. *Educ:* elementary and private (languages: English, Latin, French, Spanish). Formerly worked in carpentry, engineering and hired car driving, and as garage owner; also in wholesale and retail business. Elected to Parliament, 1944; Member of the then Governor's Exec. Council, 1948; following the introduction of ministerial system of Govt in 1954, apptd Minister of Communications, Works and Housing, 1954, then Minister of Trade, Industry, Tourism and Labour, 1956–61; concurrently, 1958–61, Dep. Premier and Leader of House of Assembly. *Recreations:* horse racing, cricket. *Address:* Ambury, Clapham St Michael, Barbados, WI. *T:* 77766.

COX, Norman Ernest, CMG 1973; MA; HM Diplomatic Service, retired; *b* 28 Aug. 1921; *s* of late Ernest William Cox and late Daisy Beatrice (*née* Edmonds); *m* 1945, Maruja Margarita (*née* Cruz); one *s* one *d*. *Educ:* Lycée Français de Madrid; King's Coll., London. Tax Officer, Inland Revenue, 1938–41; Army, Intell. Corps, 1941–45: Gibraltar, 1942–45; Attaché, Madrid, 1945–47; FO, 1947–50; 2nd Sec., Sofia, 1950–52; 2nd Sec., Montevideo, 1952–54; FO, 1954–57; Dep. Regional Information Officer for SE Asia, Singapore, 1957–60; FO, 1960–62: Laos Conf., Geneva, 1961; Sec. to UK Conf. Delegn to ECSC, Luxemburg, 1962–63; 1st Sec. (Commercial), Madrid, 1963–66; Counsellor (Information), Mexico, Regional Information Officer for Central American Republics, PRO to Duke of Edinburgh for 1968 Olympics, 1966–68; Counsellor (Commercial), Moscow, 1969–72; Inst. of Latin American Studies, London Univ., 1972–73; Diplomatic Service Inspector, 1973–74; Ambassador to: Ecuador, 1974–77; Mexico, 1977–81. Vice-Pres., British Mexican Soc., 1985– (Chm., 1982–84). *Publication:* (jtly) Politics in Mexico, 1985. *Recreations:* swimming, walking, travelling, archaeology, history, linguistics, comparative religion. *Address:* 36 Meadow Road, Malvern Link, Worcs WR14 2SD. *Club:* Royal Automobile.

COX, Oliver Jasper, CBE 1982; RIBA; retired 1985; Partner, Shankland/Cox Partnership, 1965–85; *b* 20 April 1920; *s* of William Edward and Elsie Gertrude Cox; *m* 1953, Jean; one *s* two *d*. *Educ:* Mill Hill Sch.; Architectural Association School of Architecture (AADip Hons). DistTP. Architects Dept, Herts CC, New Schools Division, 1948–49; Architects Dept, LCC Housing Division, 1950–59; Dep. Chief Architect, and Leader, Research and Development Gp, Min. of Housing and Local Govt, 1960–64. *Recreations:* painting, drawing and screen printing. *Address:* 22 Grove Terrace, NW5 1PL. *T:* 01–485 6929.

See also Sir A. W. Cox.

COX, Patricia Ann; Under Secretary, Scottish Home and Health Department, since 1985; *b* 25 May 1931; *d* of Sir (Ernest) Gordon Cox, *qv*. *Educ:* Leeds Girls' High Sch.; Newnham Coll., Cambridge (MA). Asst Principal, Dept of Health for Scotland, 1953; Principal: SHHD, 1959–62; HM Treasury, 1962–65; SHHD, 1965–67; Asst Sec., 1967–76, Under Sec., 1976–85, Scottish Educn Dept. *Publication:* Sandal Ash (novel for children), 1950. *Recreations:* opera, archaeology, needlework, walking. *Address:* 2 Gloucester Place, Edinburgh EH3 6EF. *T:* 031–225 6370.

COX, Peter Arthur, BSc Eng; FEng, FICE; FCGI; Chairman, Rendel Palmer & Tritton Ltd, Consulting Engineers, since 1985; *b* 30 Oct. 1922; *m* 1944, Rosemary; one *s* two *d*. *Educ:* Westcliff High Sch., Essex; City and Guilds Coll., Imperial Coll., London. Commissioned, Royal Engineers, 1942 (despatches). Lewis & Duvivier, Cons. Engrs, 1947; Rendel Palmer & Tritton, 1952; Peter Lind & Co. Ltd, 1954; Sir Bruce White Wolfe Barry & Partners, Cons. Engrs, 1955; Rendel Palmer & Tritton, 1956, Partner, 1966, Sen. Partner, 1978. Chm., Ceemaid Ltd, 1984–85. Member: Dover Harbour Bd, 1983–; Nat. Maritime Inst. Ltd, 1983–85; British Maritime Technology Ltd, 1986–. Pres., ICE, 1980–81; Mem., Infrastructure Planning Gp, ICE, 1981– (Chm. 1981–84); Mem., Smeatonian Soc. of Civil Engrs, 1980–. *Publications:* papers to Instn of Civil Engrs on Leith Harbour and Belfast Dry Dock; many papers to conferences. *Recreations:* walking, gardening. *Address:* 18 Ranmore Avenue, Croydon, Surrey CR0 5QA. *T:* (office) 01–928 8999. *Club:* East India.

COX, Peter Denzil John H.; *see* Hippisley-Cox, P. D. J.

COX, Peter Richmond, CB 1971; Deputy Government Actuary, 1963–74; *b* 3 Sept. 1914; *s* of Richard R. Cox, Civil Servant, and Nellie (*née* Richmond); *m* 1971, Faith Blake Schenk. *Educ:* King's Coll. Sch., Wimbledon. Entered Government Actuary's Dept, 1933. Qualified as Fellow, Institute of Actuaries, 1939. Joint Hon. Sec., Institute of Actuaries, 1962–64 (Vice-Pres., 1966–68). Pres., Eugenics Soc., 1970–72. Chm., CS Insurance Soc., 1973–78. Silver Medal, Inst. of Actuaries, 1975. *Publications:* Demography, 1950 (5 edns); (with R. H. Storr-Best) Surplus in British Life Assurance, 1962; (ed jtly) Population and Pollution, 1972; Resources and Population, 1973; Population and the New Biology, 1974; Equalities and Inequalities in Education, 1975; various papers on actuarial and demographic subjects. *Recreations:* music, painting, gardening. *Address:* The Level House, Mayfield, East Sussex TN20 6BW. *T:* Mayfield 872217. *Club:* Actuaries.

COX, Philip (Joseph), DSC 1943; QC 1967; a Recorder, and Honorary Recorder of Northampton, since 1972; *b* 28 Sept. 1922; *s* of Joseph Parriss Cox, Rugby; *m* 1951, Margaret Jocelyn Cox, *d* of R. C. H. Cox, Purley, Surrey; one *s* one *d*. *Educ:* Rugby Sch; Queens' Coll., Cambridge. RNVR, 1942–46 (Lieut). Called to Bar, Gray's Inn, 1949; Bencher, 1972; practised at Bar, Birmingham, 1949–67. Mem. County Court Rules Cttee, 1962–68; Dep. Chm., Northants QS, 1963–71; Dep. Chm., Warwicks QS, 1966–71; Leader, Midland and Oxford Circuit, 1975–79; Mem. Senate, Inns of Court and Bar, 1974–80. Legal Assessor to Disciplinary Cttee, RCVS, 1969–; Chm., Cttee of Enquiry into London Smallpox Outbreak, 1973; Chairman: Code of Practice Cttee, Assoc. of British Pharmaceut. Industry, 1978–; Gen. Optical Council, 1985–. Pres., Edgbaston Liberal Assoc., 1974–. *Recreations:* sailing, golf, gardening, reading. *Address:* (home) 9 Sir Harry's Road, Edgbaston, Birmingham B15 2UY. *T:* 021–440 0278; (chambers) 1 King's Bench Walk, Temple, EC4. *Clubs:* Naval; Birmingham; Royal Cruising, Bar Yacht.

COX, Richard Charles, MBE 1961; HM Diplomatic Service, retired; *b* 27 May 1920; *s* of Charles Victor Cox and Marjorie Eleanor Cox (*née* Fox); *m* 1941, Constance (*née* Goddard); one *s*. *Educ:* Gravesend Grammar Sch. Served War of 1939–45, RAF; released with rank of Sqdn Leader, 1946. Entered Colonial Office, 1937; Dominions Office, 1946; High Commn, Colombo, 1949–52; Second Sec., Calcutta, 1953–54; CRO, 1954–56; First Sec., Bombay, 1956–59; CRO, 1960–63; First Sec., Valletta, 1964–68; FCO, 1968–72; NI Office, 1972–74; Dep. Sec. Gen., Cento, 1975–77. *Recreations:* swimming, gardening, watching Rugby football. *Address:* The Old Forge, Hartley, Kent. *T:* Longfield 2035.

COX, Ronald; Director-General, Greater Glasgow Passenger Transport Executive, 1973–77, retired; *b* St Helens, Lancs, 3 Feb. 1916; *s* of Frederick Nisbet Cox and Annie Cox; *m* 1941, Edna Frances Heaton; one *s* one *d*. *Educ:* Higher Grade Boys' Sch., St Helens, Lancs (Oxford Univ. Cert., 6 credits); Trainee Transport Officer, St Helens Corp. Transport (Endorsed Cert. in Commerce, NC Engrg). Served War, Flt Lt (Tech.), RAF Transport Command, 1940–46. Sen. Traffic Officer, St Helens Corp. Transport, 1946–48; Traffic Supt, Salford City Transport, 1948–53; Dep. Engr and Gen. Manager, Rochdale Corp. Transport, 1953–54, Engr and Gen. Manager, 1954–62; Gen. Manager, Bournemouth Corp. Transport, 1962–64; Transport Manager, Edinburgh Corp. Transport, 1964–73. President: Scottish Road Passenger Transport Assoc., 1973–74; Incorp. Assoc. of Public Passenger Transport, 1974–75. RSA Dip. (prizewinner transport subjects); MIRTE, MInstT, FCIT. *Recreation:* sailing. *Address:* 6 Stonehanger Court, Devon Road, Salcombe, Devon TQ8 8HJ. *T:* Salcombe 3456.

COX, Roy Arthur, JDipMA; FCA, FCMA, FCBSI, CBIM; Director, Alliance and Leicester (formerly Alliance) Building Society, 1976–86, non-executive Director, since 1986 (Chief General Manager, 1970–85); *b* 30 Nov. 1925; *s* of J. W. Arthur Cox; *m* 1951; one *s* one *d*. *Educ:* Isleworth Grammar Sch. FCA 1953; FCMA 1957; FCBSI (FBS 1971); CBIM 1980. War Service, 1944–47. Wells & Partners, Chartered Accountants, 1942–49; Colombo Commercial Co. Ltd, 1950–61; Urwick, Orr & Partners, Management Consultants, 1961–65; Alliance Building Society: Sec., 1965; Gen. Man., 1967. Dir, Southern Bd, Legal & General Assce Soc. Ltd, 1972–. Building Societies Association: Chm., S Eastern Assoc., 1972–74; Mem. Council, 1973–87; Chm., Gen. Purposes and Public Relations Cttee, 1975–77; Dep. Chm., Council, 1983–85; Chm., Council, 1985–May 1987. Member: Royal Commn on Distribution of Income and Wealth, 1974–78; SE Electricity Bd, 1983–. Underwriting Mem., Lloyd's. *Recreations:* golf, bridge. *Address:* The Yett, 281 Dyke Road, Hove, E Sussex BN3 6PD.

COX, Thomas Michael; MP (Lab) Tooting, since 1974 (Wandsworth Central, 1970–74); *b* London, 1930. *Educ:* state schools; London Sch. of Economics. Electrical worker. Former Mem., Fulham Borough Council; contested (Lab) GLC elections, 1967; contested (Lab) Stroud, 1966. An Asst Govt Whip, 1974–77; a Lord Comr of the Treasury, 1977–79. Member: ETU; Co-operative Party. *Address:* House of Commons, SW1.

COX, Sir Trenchard, Kt 1961; CBE 1954; MA; FRSA (Vice-President 1964–68); FMA; FSA; Director and Secretary, Victoria and Albert Museum, 1956–66; *b* 31 July 1905; *s* of late William Pallett Cox and Marion Beverley; *m* 1935, Mary Désirée (*d* 1973), *d* of late Sir Hugh Anderson, Master of Gonville and Caius Coll., Cambridge. *Educ:* Eton; King's Coll., Cambridge. Worked as volunteer at the National Gallery and Brit. Museum (Dept of Prints and Drawings), 1929–32; spent a semester at the University of Berlin in the Dept of Arts, 1930; Asst to the Keeper, Wallace Collection, 1932–39; seconded for war-time duties, to Home Office, 1940–44; Dir of Birmingham Museum and Art Gallery, 1944–55. Member: Ancient Monuments Board for England, 1959–69; Standing Commn on Museums and Galleries, 1967–77. People's Warden, St Martin-in-the Fields, 1968–79. Hon. DLitt Birmingham, 1956. Hon. Fellow, Royal Acad., 1981. Chevalier, Légion d'Honneur, 1967. *Publications:* The National Gallery, a Room-to-Room Guide, 1930; Jehan Foucquet, Native of Tours, 1931; part editor of the Catalogue to the Exhibition of French Art at Burlington House, Jan.–March 1932; The Renaissance in Europe, 1933; A General Guide to the Wallace Collection, 1933; A Short Illustrated History of the Wallace Collection and its Founders, 1936; David Cox, 1947; Peter Bruegel, 1951; Pictures: a Handbook for Curators, 1956. *Recreations:* reading, travelling. *Address:* 33 Queen's Gate Gardens, SW7. *T:* 01–584 0231. *Club:* Athenæum.

COX, Maj.-Gen. William Reginald, CB 1956; DSO 1945; Director Territorial Army, Cadets and Home Guard, 1958–60, retired; *b* 13 June 1905; *e s* of late Major W. S. R. Cox; *m* 1947, Dorothy Irene Cox; no *c*. *Educ:* Wellington Coll. Commissioned KSLI, 1925; Adjutant, 2nd Bn, 1932–35; Staff Coll., Camberley, 1938; served War of 1939–45: Bde Major 114 Inf. Bde, 1940; Instr, Staff Coll., Camberley, 1941; GSO 1 Northern Comd, York, 1942; comd 1 Worcs. Regt, 1942–43; GSO 1, 21 Army Gp, 1943–44; comd 7 Green Howards, 1944; 131 Lorried Inf Bde, 1944; 129, 146 and 31 Inf. Bdes, 1945–47; BGS Western Comd, 1948; idc 1949; DAG, GHQ, MEF, 1950–52; Dep. Dir Infty, War Office, 1952–54; Chief of Staff, Southern Command, 1954–55; GOC 53rd (Welsh) Div., TA, and Mid-West District, 1955–58. Col, KSLI, 1957–63. Order of White Lion of Czechoslovakia (3rd Cl.); Military Cross of Czechoslovakia, 1945. *Recreation:* golf. *Address:* Amesbury Abbey, Amesbury, Wilts. *T:* Amesbury 24401. *Club:* Naval and Military.

COX, William Trevor; *see* Trevor, William.

COXETER, Harold Scott Macdonald, FRS 1950; PhD Cambridge, 1931; Professor of Mathematics, University of Toronto, 1948–80, now Emeritus Professor; *b* 9 Feb. 1907; *s* of Harold Samuel Coxeter and Lucy (*née* Gee); *m* 1936, Hendrina Johanna Brouwer, The Hague; one *s* one *d*. *Educ:* King Alfred Sch., London; St George's Sch., Harpenden; Trinity Coll., Cambridge. Entrance Scholar, Trinity Coll., 1926; Smith's Prize, 1931. Fellow Trinity Coll., Cambridge, 1931–36; Rockefeller Foundation Fellow, Princeton, 1932–33; Procter Fellow, Princeton, 1934–35; Asst Prof., 1936–43, Associate Prof., 1943–48, University of Toronto. Visiting Professor: Notre Dame, 1947; Columbia Univ., 1949; Dartmouth Coll., 1964; Univ. of Amsterdam, 1966; Univ. of Edinburgh, 1967; Univ. of E Anglia, 1968; ANU, 1970; Univ. of Sussex, 1972; Univ. of Warwick and Univ. of Utrecht, 1976; Calif. Inst. of Technology, 1977; Univ. of Bologna, 1978. Editor Canadian Jl of Mathematics, 1948–57. President: Canadian Mathematical Congress, 1965–67; Internat. Mathematical Congress, 1974. Foreign Mem., Koninklijke Nederlandse Akademie van Wetenschappen, 1975; Hon. Member: Mathematische Gesellschaft, Hamburg, 1977; Wiskundig Genootschap, Amsterdam, 1978; London Mathematical Soc., 1978. Hon. LLD: Alberta, 1957; Trent, 1973; Toronto, 1979; Hon. DMath Waterloo, 1969; Hon. DSc: Acadia, 1971; Carleton, 1984; Hon. Dr rer. nat. Giessen, 1984. *Publications:* Non-Euclidean Geometry, 1942 and 1965; Regular Polytopes, 1948, 1963 and 1973; The Real Projective Plane, 1949, 1955 and 1959; (with W. O. J. Moser)

Generators and Relations, 1st edn, 1957, 4th edn, 1980; Introduction to Geometry, 1961 and 1969; Projective Geometry, 1964 and 1974; (with S. L. Greitzer) Geometry Revisited, 1967; Twelve Geometric Essays, 1968; Regular Complex Polytopes, 1974; (with W. W. Rouse Ball) Mathematical Recreations and Essays, 12th edn 1974, 13th edn 1986; (with R. W. Frucht and D. L. Powers) Zero-symmetric Graphs, 1981; various mathematical papers. *Recreations:* music, travel. *Address:* 67 Roxborough Drive, Toronto M4W 1X2, Canada.

COYNE, James Elliott; Canadian banker and financial consultant; *b* Winnipeg, 17 July 1910; *s* of James Bowes Coyne and Edna Margaret Coyne (*née* Elliott); *m* 1957, Meribeth Stobie; one *s* one *d. Educ:* University of Manitoba (BA); University of Oxford (BCL). RCAF (Flying Officer), 1942–44. Admitted to the Bar, Manitoba, 1934; solicitor and barrister in Manitoba, 1934–38; Financial Attaché, Canadian Embassy, Washington, DC, 1941; Mem. War-time Prices and Trade Board, Ottawa, 1942 (Dep.-Chm.). Bank of Canada, Ottawa: Asst to the Governors, 1944–49; Deputy-Governor, 1950–54; Governor, 1955–61. *Address:* 29 Ruskin Row, Winnipeg, Manitoba R3M 2R9, Canada.

COZENS, Brig. Dame (Florence) Barbara, DBE 1963; RRC 1958; *b* 24 Dec. 1906; *d* of late Capt. A. Cozens, S Staffs. *Educ:* Seabury Sch., Worthing. Nurse Training: The Nightingale Sch., St Thomas' Hosp., London, 1928–32. Joined QAIMNS, 1933. Served War of 1939–45, England and Continent. Lieut-Col 1954; Col 1958; Brig. 1960; Matron-in-Chief and Dir of Army Nursing Services, 1960–64, retd; Chief Nursing Officer to St John Ambulance Brigade, 1965–72. Col Commandant, QARANC, 1966–69. DStJ 1972.

COZENS, Air Cdre Henry Iliffe, CB 1946; AFC 1939; RAF retired; *b* 13 March 1904; *m* 1956, Gillian Mary, *o d* of Wing Comdr O. R. Pigott, Wokingham, Berks; one *s* two *d. Educ:* St Dunstan's Coll.; Downing Coll., Cambridge. MA 1934. Commissioned in RAF, 1923; Mem. of British Arctic Air Route Expedition, 1930–31. Served War of 1939–45 (AFC, CB). idc 1947. Vice-Pres., British Schs Exploring Soc., 1969–. *Address:* Horley Manor, Banbury, Oxon. *Club:* Royal Air Force.

COZENS, Robert William, QPM 1981; Director, Police Requirements, for Science and Technology, Home Office, since 1985; *b* 10 Nov. 1927; *s* of Sydney Robert and Rose Elizabeth Cozens; *m* 1952, Jean Dorothy Banfield; one *s* one *d. Educ:* Stoke C of E Sch., Guildford. Constable to Chief Superintendent, Surrey Constabulary, 1954–72; Asst Dir, Command Courses, Police Staff Coll., Bramshill, 1972–74; Asst Chief Constable, S Yorks Police, 1974–78; seconded to Federal Judicial Police in Mexico for advisory duties, 1975; Dep. Chief Constable, Lincs Police, 1978–81; Chief Constable, W Mercia Constabulary (Hereford, Worcester and Shropshire), 1981–85. *Recreations:* tennis, squash, badminton. *Address:* (office) Horseferry House, Dean Ryle Street, SW1P 2AW.

CRABB, Most Rev. Frederick Hugh Wright, BD, DD; Associate Rector, St Cyprian, Calgary, and Director, Anglican School of Lay Ministry, since 1983; *b* Luppitt, Devon, 24 April 1915; *s* of William Samuel and Florence Mary Crabb; *m* 1946, Alice Margery Coombs; two *s* two *d. Educ:* Luppitt Parochial Sch.; Univ. of London (St John's Hall, Highbury, London). BD Lond. (1st Cl. Hons); ALCD (1st Cl. Hons). Asst Curate, St James', West Teignmouth, Devon, 1939–41; Asst Priest, St Andrew's, Plymouth, 1941–42; Missionary at Akot, S Sudan, 1942–44; Principal, Bishop Gwynne Divinity Sch., S Sudan, 1944–51; Vice Principal, London Coll. of Divinity, 1951–57; Principal, Coll. of Emmanuel and St Chad, Saskatoon, Sask., 1957–67; Assoc. Priest, Christ Church, Calgary, Alberta, 1967–69; Rector, St Stephen's Church, Calgary, 1969–75; Bishop of Athabasca, 1975–83; Metropolitan of Rupert's Land, 1977–82. Mem. Governing Council, Athabasca Univ., 1982–. Hon. DD: Wycliffe Coll., Toronto, 1960; St Andrew's Coll., Saskatoon, 1967; Coll. of Emmanuel and St Chad, Saskatoon, 1979. *Recreations:* gardening, mountain hiking. *Address:* 3483 Chippendale Drive NW, Calgary, Alberta T2L 0W7, Canada.

CRABBE, Kenneth Herbert Martineau, TD; *b* 4 Nov. 1916; *m* 1st, 1940, Rowena Leete (*d* 1981); one *s*; 2nd, 1982, Belinda V. Fitzherbert (*née* Batt); three step *s* one step *d. Educ:* Stowe Sch. Commnd TA, 1937; psc. Major. Member, Stock Exchange, London, 1937–; Mem. Council, The Stock Exchange, 1963–78 (Dep. Chm., 1970–73). *Recreations:* golf, fishing, shooting, painting. *Address:* Spandrels, Walliswood, Dorking, Surrey RH5 5RJ. *T:* Oakwood Hill 275. *Clubs:* Boodle's; West Sussex Golf.

CRABBE, Mrs Pauline, (Mrs Joseph Benjamin), OBE 1969; JP; National Vice-Chairman, Brook Advisory Centres, since 1980; *b* 1 April 1914; *y d* of Cyril and Edith Henriques, Kingston, Jamaica; *m* 1st, 1936, Geoffrey Henebery (marr. diss. 1948); one *d*; 2nd, 1949, Neville Crabbe (marr. diss. 1960); one *s*; 3rd, 1969, Joseph Benjamin; three step *s. Educ:* Highgate Convent; London Academy of Music and Drama; London Univ. (extra-mural course in Psychology). Actress and broadcaster, 1945–53; secretarial work with British Actors' Equity and WEA, 1953–56; then with Old People's Welfare and London Council of Social Service, 1956–57; Welfare Sec. and Dep. Gen. Sec. to Nat. Council for Unmarried Mother and her Child, 1957–69; Conciliation Officer for Race Relations Bd, 1969–71; Sec., 1971–76, Sen. Counsellor, 1976–80, London Brook Adv. Centres. Founder Mem., Haverstock Housing Trust for Fatherless Families, 1966; Mem. Bd, Housing Corp., 1968–75; Member: Community Relations Commn, 1972–77; Standing Adv. Council on Race Relations, 1977–; Parole Bd, 1978–82. Hon. Fellow, Manchester Polytechnic, 1979. Radio and TV broadcaster and panellist. JP London, 1967. FRSA 1972. *Publications:* articles and book reviews in social work jls. *Recreations:* entertaining, walking, indoor gardening, the theatre and the arts. *Address:* 88 Osprey House, Sillwood Place, Brighton, Sussex. *Club:* Magistrates' Association.

CRABBE, Reginald James Williams, FIA, FSS; Chairman, 1967–82, and President, 1982–86, Provident Life Association of London Ltd; Chairman: United Standard Insurance Co. Ltd, 1967–79; Vigilant Assurance Co. Ltd, 1970–79; *b* 22 June 1909; *e s* of late Harry James and Annie Martha Crabbe; *m* 1948, Phyllis Maud Smith; two *d. Educ:* Chigwell Sch., Essex. Entered National Mutual Life Assurance Soc., 1926; FIA 1933; joined Provident Life as Asst Actuary, 1935; Man. Dir, 1956–74; Dir, 1956–86; Dep. Chm., 1971–85, Chm., 1975–77, Cope & Timmins Holdings. Chm., Life Offices' Assoc., 1965, 1966. *Publication:* (with C. A. Poyser, MA, FIA) Pension and Widows' and Orphans' Funds, 1953. *Recreations:* reading, gardening, music, art. *Address:* Fairways, 166 Lower Green Road, Esher, Surrey KT10 8HA. *T:* Esher 62219.

CRABBIE, Mrs (Margaret) Veronica, CBE 1977; *b* 26 Nov. 1910; *d* of late Sir Christopher Nicholson Johnston (Lord Sands, Senator of the College of Justice, Scotland), and Lady Sands; *m* 1938, John Patrick Crabbie; two *s* one *d. Educ:* St Denis Sch., Edinburgh; Queen Margaret's Sch., Escrick, York. Chairman: Edinburgh Home for Mothers and Infants, 1951–66; Walpole Housing Assoc., 1969–72; Scottish Council for the Unmarried Mother and her Child, 1966–72; WRVS, Scotland, 1972–77. *Recreation:* curling. *Address:* 17 Ravelston Dykes, Edinburgh EH4 3JE. *T:* 031–332 4489. *Club:* New (Edinburgh).

CRABTREE, Maj-Gen. Derek Thomas, CB 1983; Senior Military Adviser Short Brothers, since 1984; *b* 21 Jan. 1930; *s* of late William Edward Crabtree and of Winifred Hilda Burton; *m* 1960, Daphne Christine Mason; one *s* one *d. Educ:* St Brendan's Coll., Bristol. Commissioned, 1953; Regimental Service: 13th/18th Royal Hussars (QMO), UK

and BAOR, 1953–56; Royal Berkshire Regt, UK, Malta and Cyprus, 1956–59; Technical Staff Course, RMCS, 1960–62; sc Camberley, 1964; BM 11 Inf. Bde, BAOR, 1965–67; CO 1st Bn Duke of Edinburgh's Royal Regt, UK and Berlin, 1970–72; DS RMCS, 1972–74; Col GS, MGO Secretariat, MoD, 1974–76; Dep. Comdr and Chief of Staff Headquarters British Forces Hong Kong, 1976–79; Dep. Comdt RMCS, 1979–80; Dir Gen. of Weapons (Army), MoD, 1980–84. Col, Duke of Edinburgh's Royal Regt, 1982–. FBIM. *Recreations:* most outdoor sports, gardening. *Address:* 53 High Street, Shrivenham, Swindon, Wilts. *Clubs:* Cavalry and Guards, Army and Navy.

CRABTREE, Jonathan; a Recorder of the Crown Court, since 1974; barrister-at-law; *b* 17 April 1934; *s* of Charles H. Crabtree and Elsie M. Crabtree; *m* 1st, 1957, Caroline Ruth Keigwin (*née* Oliver) (marr. diss. 1976); one *s* three *d* (and one *s* decd); 2nd, 1980, Wendy Elizabeth Hudson (*née* Ward). *Educ:* Bootham; St John's Coll., Cambridge (MA, LLM). Called to Bar, Gray's Inn, 1958. *Recreations:* cricket, cooking. *Address:* 204 Mount Vale, York YO2 2DL. *T:* York 646609.

CRABTREE, Prof. Lewis Frederick, PhD, FRAeS; FAIAA; Sir George White Professor of Aeronautical Engineering, University of Bristol, 1973–85, now Emeritus; *b* 16 Nov. 1924; *m* 1955, Averil Joan Escott; one *s* one *d. Educ:* Univ. of Leeds; Imperial Coll. of Science and Technology; Cornell Univ., USA. BSc (Mech. Eng) Leeds, 1945; DIC (Aeronautics), 1947; PhD (Aero Eng) Cornell, 1952. Air Engr Officer, RNVR, 1945–46. Grad. apprentice, Saunders-Roe Ltd, E Cowes, IoW, 1947–50; ECA Fellowship, Grad. Sch. of Aero. Engrg, Cornell Univ., 1950–52; Aerodynamics Dept, RAE, Farnborough, 1953–73; Head of: Hypersonics and High temperature Gasdynamics Div., 1961–66; Low Speed Aerodynamics Div., 1966–70; Propulsion Aerodynamics and Noise Div., 1970–73. Visiting Prof., Cornell Univ., 1957. Pres., RAeS, 1978–79 (Usborne Meml Prize, 1955). *Publications:* Elements of Hypersonic Aerodynamics, 1965; contributor to: Incompressible Aerodynamics, 1960; Laminar Boundary Layers, 1963; articles chiefly in Jl RAeS, Aeron. Quart., Jl Aeron. Sci., Jahrbuch der WGLR and Reports and Memos of ARC. *Address:* Dan-y-Coity, Talybont-on-Usk, Brecon LD3 7YN.

CRABTREE, Simon; see Wharton, Michael B.

CRACKNELL, (William) Martin; Chief Executive, Glenrothes Development Corporation, since 1976; *b* 24 June 1929; *s* of John Sidney Cracknell and Sybil Marian (*née* Wood); *m* 1962, Gillian Goatcher; two *s* two *d. Educ:* St Edward's School, Oxford; RMA Sandhurst. Regular Army Officer, Royal Green Jackets, 1949–69; British Printing Industries Fedn, 1969–76. Mem. Exec., Scottish Council (Develt and Industry). Dir, Glenrothes Enterprise Trust. *Address:* Alburne Knowe, Orchard Drive, Glenrothes, Fife. *T:* Glenrothes 752413. *Club:* Guid (Glenrothes) (Chm.).

CRACROFT, Air Vice-Marshal Peter Dicken, CB 1954; AFC 1932; *b* 29 Nov. 1907; *s* of Lt-Col H. Cracroft, Bath; *m* 1932, Margaret Eliza Sugden Patchett; two *s. Educ:* Monkton Combe Sch., Bath. Commissioned RAF 1927; Fleet Air Arm, 1928–31; Central Flying Sch. Instructors' Course, 1931; Flying Instructor, Leuchars, 1931–35; Adjt HMS Courageous, 1936–37; Chief Flying Instructor, Oxford Univ. Air Sqdn, 1937–39; RAF Stn Mount Batten, 1939–40; Air Staff, Coastal Command, 1940–41; OC RAF Station, Chivenor, 1941–43; SASO 19 Gp (later 17 Gp), 1933–44; OC 111 Op. Trg Unit, Bahamas, 1944–45; SASO HQ Air Comd, SE Asia, Mil. Gov. Penang, 1945; AOC Bombay, 1945–46; SASO, HQ 19 Gp, 1946–48; RAF Dir and CO, Jt Anti-Submarine Sch., Londonderry, 1948–50; Sen. Air Liaison Officer, S Africa, 1950–52; AOC 66 Gp, Edinburgh, 1952–53; Senior Air Staff Officer, Headquarters Coastal Command, 1953–55; AOC Scotland and 18 Group, 1955–58; retired from RAF, Dec. 1958. *Recreations:* tennis, fishing, shooting. *Address:* Alderney House, Burton Bradstock, Bridport, Dorset DT6 4NQ. *Club:* Royal Air Force.

CRADDOCK, (William) Aleck; LVO 1981; Director, Harrods Ltd, since 1970 (Managing Director, 1980–84, Chairman, 1981–86); *b* Nov. 1924; *m* 1947, Olive May Brown; one *s* one *d. Educ:* City of London School. Joined Druce and Craddock, Craddock and Tomkins Ltd (family firm), Meat and Provision Merchants, Marylebone, London, 1946; joined Harrods Ltd as Asst to Food Manager, 1954; Member of the Board, 1964; Director and General Manager, 1970; Asst Managing Director, 1975; a Director of House of Fraser Ltd, 1980. Member: Council, Royal Albert Hall; Bd, Drapers Cottage Homes (Pres., Appeal, 1985–86). Liveryman, Worshipful Company of Cooks, 1972. Cavaliere Ufficiale (Fourth Cl.), Order Al Merito Della Repubblica Italiana, 1980. *Address:* c/o Harrods Ltd, Knightsbridge, SW1X 7XL. *T:* 01–730 1234. *Club:* Guards' Polo (Life Mem.).

CRADOCK, John Anthony, CB 1980; MBE 1952; Deputy Secretary, Ministry of Defence, 1981–82; *b* 19 Oct. 1921; *o s* of John Cradock and Nan Cradock (*née* Kelly); *m* 1948, Eileen (*née* Bell); one *s* one *d. Educ:* St Brendan's College, Bristol; Bristol Univ. (BA 1946). Military service, 1941–46 (Captain Royal Signals); Malayan Civil Service, 1946–57; War Office, 1957–67; MoD, 1967–75; Under Sec., N Ireland Office, 1975–77; MoD, 1977–82. *Recreations:* gardening, walking. *Address:* c/o Lloyds Bank, Morpeth, Northumberland NE61 1AN.

CRADOCK, Sir Percy, GCMG 1983 (KCMG 1980; CMG 1968); Adviser to the Prime Minister on Foreign Affairs, since 1984; *b* 26 Oct. 1923; *m* 1953, Birthe Marie Dyrlund. *Educ:* St John's Coll., Cambridge (Hon. Fellow, 1982). Served Foreign Office, 1954–57; First Sec., Kuala Lumpur, 1957–61; Hong Kong, 1961; Peking, 1962; Foreign Office, 1963–66; Counsellor and Head of Chancery, Peking, 1966–68; Chargé d'Affaires, Peking, 1968–69; Head of Planning Staff, FCO, 1969–71; Under-Sec., Cabinet Office, 1971–75; Ambassador to German Democratic Republic, 1976–78; Leader, UK Delegn to Comprehensive Test Ban Discussions at Geneva, 1977–78; Ambassador to People's Republic of China, 1978–83; Dep. Under Sec. of State, FCO, supervising negotiations on Hong Kong, 1984. *Address:* c/o 10 Downing Street, SW1. *Club:* Reform.

CRADOCK-HARTOPP, Sir J. E.; see Hartopp.

CRAFT, Professor Ian Logan, FRCS; Director of Fertility and Obstetric Studies, Humana Hospital Wellington, since 1985; *b* 11 July 1937; *s* of Reginald Thomas Craft and Lois Mary (*née* Logan); *m* 1959, Jacqueline Rivers Symmons; two *s. Educ:* Owens Sch., London; Westminster Med. Sch., Univ. of London (MB, BS). FRCS 1966; MRCOG 1970. Sen. Registrar, Westminster Hosp. Teaching Gp (Westminster Hosp. and Kingston Hosp.), 1970–72; Sen. Lectr and Consultant, Inst. of Obstetrics and Gynaecology, Queen Charlotte's Hosp., London, 1972–76; Prof. of Obstetrics and Gynaecology, Royal Free Hosp., London, 1976–82; Dir of Gynaecology, Cromwell Hosp., 1982–85. FRSocMed. *Publications:* contrib. BMJ, Lancet and other medical jls. *Recreations:* art, music, ornithology, sports of most types. *Address:* 12 Coval Gardens, East Sheen, SW14 7DG. *T:* 01–876 5461; Humana Hospital Wellington, Wellington Place, NW8.

CRAFT, Prof. Maurice, PhD; Professor of Education, since 1980, Head of Advanced Studies in the School of Education and Pro-Vice-Chancellor, since 1983, University of Nottingham; *b* 4 May 1932; *er s* of Jack and Polly Craft, London; *m* 1957, Alma, *y d* of Elio and Dinah Sampson, Dublin; two *d. Educ:* LCC Elem. Sch. and Colfe's Grammar

Sch., SE13; LSE, Univ. of London (BSc Econ); Sch. of Education, Trinity Coll., Univ. of Dublin (HDipEd); Inst. of Education, Univ. of London (AcadDipEd); Dept of Sociology, Univ. of Liverpool (PhD 1972). 2/Lt RAOC (Nat. Service), 1953–55. Asst Master, Catford Secondary Sch., SE6, 1956–60; Princ. Lectr and Head of Dept of Sociology, Edge Hill Coll. of Education, Ormskirk, Lancs, 1960–67; Sen. Lectr in Education, i/c Advanced Courses, Univ. of Exeter, 1967–73; Sub-Dean, Faculty of Educn, 1969–73; Prof. of Education, and Chairman, Centre for the Study of Urban Education, La Trobe Univ., Melbourne, 1973–75; Goldsmiths' Prof. of Education, Inst. of Educn, Univ. of London, and Head of Dept of Advanced Studies in Education, Goldsmiths' Coll., 1976–80; Univ. of Nottingham: Dean, Faculty of Educn, 1981–83; Chm., Sch. of Educn, 1983–85. Adviser: Devon CC, 1970–72; Aust. Federal Poverty Commn, 1974–75; State Coll., Vict., Aust., 1974–75; SSRC, 1974–; Assoc. of Commonwealth Univs, 1976, 1979; CNAA, 1978–; Centre for Advice and Inf. on Educn Disadvantage (Chm., Teacher Educn Working Gp, 1979–80); Schools Council, 1979; CRE (Chm., Teacher Educn Adv. Gp, 1980–84); H of C Home Affairs Cttee, 1981; Swann Cttee, 1982–84; Council for Educn and Trng in Youth and Community Work (Chm., In-service Wkg Gp, 1983); Unesco, 1985. Mem., UK Delegn to EEC Colloquium on Ethnic Min. Educn, Brussels, 1979, 1982; UK delegate to: Council of Europe Seminars on Intercultural Trng of Teachers, Lisbon, 1981, Rome, 1982, Strasbourg, 1983; UNESCO Colloquium on Educnl Disadvantage, Thessalonika, 1984. Member: Management Cttee, Sociology of Educn Abstracts 1965–; Edtl Bd, Jl of Multilingual and Multicultural Develt, 1979–; Edtl Bd, Multicultural Educn Abstracts, 1981–; Council of Validating Univs, 1982–; E Midlands Reg. Consultative Gp on Teacher Educn (Chm., 1980–84); Exec. Cttee, Univs Council for Educn of Teachers, 1984– (Chm., Standing Cttee on Validation, 1984–). *Publications:* (ed jtly) Linking Home and School, 1967 (3rd edn, 1980); (ed jtly) Guidance and Counselling in British Schools, 1969 (2nd edn, 1974); (ed) Family, Class and Education: a Reader, 1970; Urban Education—a Dublin case study, 1974; School Welfare Provision in Australia, 1977; (ed) Teaching in a Multicultural Society: the Task for Teacher Education, 1981; (jtly) Training Teachers of Ethnic Minority Community Languages, 1983; (ed jtly) Change in Teacher Education, 1984; (ed) Education and Cultural Pluralism, 1984; The Democratisation of Education, 1985; Teacher Education in a Multicultural Society, 1986; contrib. to numerous books and to the following jls: Educnl Research, Internat. Review of Educn, Educnl Review, Social and Econ. Admin., Educn for Teaching, Internat. Social Work, Aust. Jl of Social Work, Aust. Educnl Researcher, THES, Higher Educn Jl, New Society, Education, Administration, New Era, Studies. *Recreations:* music, walking. *Address:* School of Education, University of Nottingham, Nottingham NG7 2RD. *T:* Nottingham 506101.

CRAGG, Rt. Rev. (Albert) Kenneth, DPhil; *b* 8 March 1913; *yr s* of Albert and Emily Cragg; *m* 1940, Theodora Melita, *yr d* of John Wesley Arnold; three *s* (one *d* decd). *Educ:* Blackpool Grammar Sch.; Jesus Coll., Oxford; Tyndale Hall, Bristol. BA Oxon 2nd Cl. Hons Mod. Hist., 1934; MA Oxon 1938; DPhil 1950. Ellerton Theol. Essay Prize, Oxford, 1937; Green Moral Philos. Prize, Oxford, 1947. Deacon, 1936; Priest, 1937; Curate, Higher Tranmere Parish Church, Birkenhead, 1936–39; Chaplain, All Saints', Beirut, Lebanon, 1939–47; Warden, St Justin's House, Beirut, 1942–47; Asst Prof. of Philos., Amer. University of Beirut, 1942–47; Rector of Longworth, Berks, 1947–51; Sheriff's Chap., Berks, 1948; Prof. of Arabic and Islamics, Hartford Seminary, Conn, USA, 1951–56; Rockefeller Travelling Schol., 1954; Res. Canon, St George's Collegiate Church, Jerusalem, 1956–61; Fellow, St Augustine's Coll., Canterbury, 1959–60, Sub-Warden, 1960–61, Warden, 1961–67; Examng Chaplain to Archbishop of Canterbury, 1961–67; Hon. Canon of Canterbury, 1961–80; Asst Bishop to Archbishop in Jerusalem, 1970–74; Reader in Religious Studies, Sussex Univ., and Asst Bishop, dio. of Chichester, 1973–78; Vicar of Helme, W Yorks, and Asst Bishop, dio. Wakefield, 1978–81; Asst Bishop, dio. Oxford, 1982–. Select Preacher: Cambridge, 1961; Dublin, 1962; Oxford, 1974. Proctor in Convocation, Canterbury, 1965–68; Visiting Prof., Union Theological Seminary, New York, 1965–66; Lectr, Faculty of Divinity, Cambridge, 1966; Jordan Lectr, Sch. of Oriental and African Studies, University of London, 1967; Vis. Prof., University of Ibadan, Nigeria, 1968; Bye-Fellow, Gonville and Caius Coll., Cambridge, 1968–74; Vis. Prof., Virginia Theol Seminary, 1984, 1985. Editor, The Muslim World Quarterly, 1952–60. *Publications:* The Call of the Minaret, 1956; Sandals at the Mosque, 1959; The Dome and the Rock, 1964; Counsels in Contemporary Islam, 1965; Christianity in World Perspective, 1968; The Privilege of Man, 1968; The House of Islam, 1969; Alive to God, 1970; The Event of the Qur'ān, 1971; The Mind of the Qur'ān, 1973; The Wisdom of the Sufis, 1976; The Christian and Other Religion, 1977; Islam from Within, 1979; This Year in Jerusalem, 1982; Muhammad and the Christian, 1983; The Pen and the Faith, 1985; Jesus and the Muslim, 1985; translated: City of Wrong, 1959; The Theology of Unity, 1965; A Passage to France, 1976; The Hallowed Valley, 1977; Contributor: Journal of World History, 1957; Religion in the Middle East, 1969. *Address:* Appletree Cottage, Ascott-under-Wychwood, Oxford OX7 6AG.

CRAGG, James Birkett; Emeritus Professor of Environmental Science, University of Calgary, Alberta; *b* 8 Nov. 1910; *s* of late A. W. Cragg, N Shields; *m* 1937, Mary Catherine Macnaughtan (marr. diss. 1968); four *s* (and one *s* one *d* decd); *m* Jean Moore. *Educ:* private sch.; Tynemouth High Sch.; Durham Univ. BSc King's Coll., University of Durham, 1933; DThPT, 1934; MSc, 1937; DSc Newcastle, 1965. Demonstrator, Physiology Dept, Manchester Univ., 1935; Asst Lecturer, and later Lecturer, in Zoology, University Coll. of North Wales, 1937; seconded to Agricultural Research Council, 1942; Scientific Officer, ARC Unit of Insect Physiology, 1944; Reader in Zoology, Durham Colls, in University of Durham, 1946; Prof. of Zoology, University of Durham, 1950–61; Dir, Merlewood Research Station (Nature Conservancy, NERC), Grange-over-Sands, Lancs, 1961–66; Dir, Environmental Sciences Centre, and Prof. of Biology, 1966–72, Killam Meml Prof., 1966–76, Vice-Pres. (Academic), 1970–72, Univ. of Calgary, Alberta. Former Chairman: Commn for Ecology; Internat. Union for Conservation of Nature; Convenor, Internat. Biological Programme PT Cttee; Mem., Internat. Biological Programme Cttees; Consultant, Ford Foundation, 1965. Commonwealth Prestige Fellow (New Zealand), 1964. Jubilee medal, 1977. Hon. FIBiol 1981. *Publications:* papers in scientific periodicals; formerly Editor, Advances in Ecological Research. *Recreation:* books. *Address:* 2112 Uralta Road, Calgary, Alberta T2N 4B4, Canada. *Club:* Athenæum.

CRAGG, Rt. Rev. Kenneth; *see* Cragg, Rt. Rev. A. K.

CRAGGS, Prof. James Wilkinson, BSc, PhD; Professor of Engineering Mathematics, University of Southampton, 1967–81; *b* 3 Feb. 1920; *s* of Thomas Gibson Craggs and Margaret (*née* Wilkinson); *m* 1946, Mary Baker; two *s* one *d*. *Educ:* Bede Collegiate Sch., Sunderland; University of Manchester. BSc 1941, PhD 1948, Manchester; PhD Cambridge, 1953. Junior Lectr, Royal Military Coll. of Science, 1941–45; Asst Lectr, University of Manchester, 1947–49; Lecturer, Queen's Coll., Dundee, 1951–52; King's Coll., Newcastle upon Tyne: Lectr, 1952–56; Senior Lecturer, 1956–60; Reader in Mathematics, 1960–61; Prof. of Mathematics, University of Leeds, 1961–63; Prof. of Applied Mathematics, Melbourne Univ., 1963–67. *Publications:* contrib. learned journals regarding the mechanics of solids and fluids. *Recreation:* Methodist lay preacher. *Address:* 23 Redhill, Bassett, Southampton SO1 7BR.

CRAGGS, Prof. John Drummond, MSc, PhD, FInstP; retired; Professor of Electronic Engineering, University of Liverpool, 1955–82; *b* 17 May 1915; *s* of Thomas Lawson Craggs and Elsie Aidrienne Roberts; *m* 1941, Dorothy Ellen Margaret Garfitt; two *d*. *Educ:* Huddersfield Coll.; University of London. Research Student, King's Coll., London Univ., 1937–38; Metropolitan-Vickers High Voltage Research Laboratory, Manchester, 1938–48; University of California, Radiation Laboratory, 1944–45; apptd Sen. Lectr, 1948, and, later, Reader, Dept of Electrical Engineering, University of Liverpool. A Pro-Vice-Chancellor, Liverpool Univ., 1969–72. Hon. DSc. *Publications:* Counting Tubes, 1950 (with S. C. Curran); Electrical Breakdown of Gases, 1953; High Voltage Laboratory Technique, 1954 (with J. M. Meek); Electrical Breakdown of Gases (with J. M. Meek), 1978; papers in various professional jls. *Address:* Stone Cottage, Newton-cum-Larton, West Kirby, Wirral, Merseyside L48 1PG. *T:* 051–625 5055.

CRAIB, Douglas Duncan Simpson, CBE 1974; DL; FRAgS 1971; farmer and company director, since 1937; Member, Potato Marketing Board of Great Britain, since 1968; *b* 5 April 1914; *s* of Peter Barton Salsbury Simpson and Helen Duncan; changed name by deed poll, 1930; *m* 1939, Moyra Louise Booth; one *s* one *d*. *Educ:* Aberdeen Grammar Sch.; Dundee High School. Commerce, 1934. Captain, 7th Bn Seaforth Highlanders, 1939–42. Chm., Elec. Cons. Council, N Scotland Area, 1971–79; Mem., N of Scotland Hydro-Elec. Bd, 1971–79. Chm. of Directors, Royal Highland and Agric. Soc. of Scotland, 1967–69 (Hon. Sec. and Hon. Treas., 1970–74; Vice-Pres., 1978–79); Chm., Highland Agric. Exec. Cttee, 1970–72; Mem., Scottish Agric. Develt Council, 1972–76; Governor: N of Scotland Coll. of Agriculture, 1970–84; Rowett Res. Inst., Aberdeen, 1973–; Trustee, The MacRobert Trusts, Scotland, 1970–84. DL Moray 1974. *Address:* The Old School, Mosstodloch, Fochabers, Morayshire IV32 7LE. *T:* Fochabers 820733. *Club:* Farmers'.

CRAIG, family name of **Viscount Craigavon.**

CRAIG, Sir (Albert) James (Macqueen), GCMG 1984 (KCMG 1981; CMG 1975); HM Diplomatic Service, retired; Director General, Middle East Association, since 1985; Visiting Professor in Arabic, University of Oxford, since 1985; *b* 13 July 1924; *s* of James Craig and Florence Morris; *m* 1952, Margaret Hutchinson; three *s* one *d*. *Educ:* Liverpool Institute High Sch.; Univ. of Oxford. Queen's Coll., Oxford (Exhibr), 1942; 1st cl. Hon. Mods Classics, 1943 (Hon. Schol.); Army, 1943–44; 1st cl. Oriental Studies (Arabic and Persian), 1947; Sen. Demy, Magdalen Coll., 1947–48; Lectr in Arabic, Durham Univ., 1948–55; seconded to FO, 1955 as Principal Instructor at Middle East Centre for Arab Studies, Lebanon; joined Foreign Service substantively, 1956; served: FO, 1958–61; HM Political Agent, Trucial States, 1961–64; 1st Sec., Beirut, 1964–67; Counsellor and Head of Chancery, Jedda, 1967–70; Supernumerary Fellow, St Antony's Coll., Oxford, 1970–71; Head of Near East and N Africa Dept, FCO, 1971–75; Dep. High Comr, Kuala Lumpur, 1975–76; Ambassador to: Syria, 1976–79; Saudi Arabia, 1979–84. Dir, Saudi-British Bank; Special Adviser, Hong Kong Bank Gp. Mem. Council, Order of St John; OStJ 1985. *Address:* c/o 33 Bury Street, SW1. *T:* 01–839 2137. *Club:* Travellers'.

CRAIG, Mrs Barbara Denise, MA Oxon; Principal of Somerville College, Oxford, 1967–80, Honorary Fellow, 1980; *b* 22 Oct. 1915; *o d* of John Alexander Chapman and Janie Denize (*née* Callaway); *m* 1942, Wilson James Craig; no *c*. *Educ:* Haberdashers' Aske's Girls' Sch., Acton; Somerville Coll., Oxford. Craven Fellow, 1938; Goldsmiths' Sen. Student, 1938; Woolley Fellow in Archæology of Somerville Coll., 1954–56. Temp. Asst Principal, Mins of Supply and Labour, 1939–40; Asst to Prof. of Greek, Aberdeen Univ., 1940–42; Temp. Asst Principal, Min. of Home Security, 1942; Temp. Principal, Min. of Production, 1943–45. Unofficial work as wife of British Council officer in Brazil, Iraq, Spain, Pakistan, 1946–65; from 1956, archæological work on finds from British excavations at Mycenae. *Recreations:* bird-watching (Mem. Brit. Ornithologists' Union); walking. *Address:* The Wynd, Gayle, Hawes, North Yorkshire DL8 3SD. *T:* Hawes 289.

CRAIG, Charles (James); opera singer (tenor); *b* 3 Dec. 1920; *s* of James and Rosina Craig; *m* 1946, Dorothy Wilson; one *s* one *d*. *Educ:* in London. Protégé of Sir Thomas Beecham; Principal Tenor with Carl Rosa Opera Co., 1953–56; joined Sadler's Wells Opera Co., 1956. Appears regularly at Internat. Opera Houses, incl. Covent Garden, Milan, Rome, Vienna, Paris, Berlin, Buenos Aires, etc; repertoire of 48 operas, incl. Otello, Aida, Turandot, Norma, Andrea Chenier, Die Walküre, Götterdämmerung, Lohengrin, etc. Concerts, TV and radio, and records. International Opera Medal Award, 1962. *Recreations:* motoring, cooking. *Address:* Whitfield Cottage, Whitfield, Northants.

CRAIG, Air Chief Marshal Sir David (Brownrigg), GCB 1984 (KCB 1981; CB 1978); OBE 1967; Chief of the Air Staff, since 1985; Air ADC to the Queen, since 1985; *b* 17 Sept. 1929; *s* of Major Francis Brownrigg Craig and Mrs Olive Craig; *m* 1955, Elisabeth June Derenburg; one *s* one *d*. *Educ:* Radley Coll.; Lincoln Coll., Oxford (MA; Hon. Fellow 1984). Commnd in RAF, 1951; OC RAF Cranwell, 1968–70; ADC to the Queen, 1969–71; Dir, Plans and Ops, HQ Far East Comd, 1970–71; OC RAF Akrotiri, 1972–73; ACAS (Ops), MoD, 1975–78; AOC No 1 Group, RAF Strike Command, 1978–80; Vice-Chief of Air Staff, 1980–82; AOC-in-C, RAF Strike Command and C-in-C, UK Air Forces, 1982–85. *Recreations:* fishing, shooting, golf. *Address:* c/o Royal Bank of Scotland, 9 Pall Mall, SW1Y 5LX. *Club:* Royal Air Force.

CRAIG, Prof. David Parker, AO 1985; FRS 1968; FAA 1969; FRSC; Fellow and Emeritus Professor, Australian National University, since 1985; *b* 23 Dec. 1919; *s* of Andrew Hunter Craig, Manchester and Sydney, and Mary Jane (*née* Parker); *m* 1948, Veronica, *d* of Cyril Bryden-Brown, Market Harborough and Sydney; three *s* one *d*. *Educ:* Sydney Church of England Grammar Sch.; University of Sydney; University Coll., London. MSc (Sydney) 1941, PhD (London) 1950, DSc (London) 1956. Commonwealth Science Scholar, 1940. War Service: Capt., Australian Imperial Force, 1941–44. Lectr in Chemistry, University of Sydney, 1944–46; Turner and Newall Research Fellow, 1946–49, and Lectr in Chemistry, University Coll., London, 1949–52; Prof. of Physical Chemistry, Univ. of Sydney, 1952–56; Prof. of Chemistry, University Coll., London, 1956–67; Prof. of Chemistry, 1967–85, Dean, Research Sch. of Chemistry, 1970–73 and 1977–81, ANU. Vis. Prof., UCL, 1968–; Firth Vis. Prof., Univ. of Sheffield, 1973; Vis. Prof. University Coll., Cardiff, 1975–. Part-time Mem., CSIRO Exec., 1980–85. Fellow of University Coll., London, 1964–. Hon. Dr Chem Bologna, 1985; Hon. DSc Sydney, 1985. *Publications:* original papers on chemistry in scientific periodicals. *Address:* 199 Dryandra Street, O'Connor, ACT 2601, Australia. *Club:* Athenæum.

CRAIG, Douglas, OBE 1965; freelance opera producer, adjudicator and lecturer; *b* 26 May 1916; *m* 1955, Dorothy Dixon; two *d*. *Educ:* Latymer Upper Sch.; St Catharine's Coll., Cambridge (MA). FRCM, FRSA. Winchester Prize, Cambridge, 1938. Intell. Corps, 1940–46, Major 1944. Baritone, Sadler's Wells Opera and elsewhere, 1946–; Artistic Dir, Opera for All, 1949–65; Stage Dir, Glyndebourne, 1952–55; Asst Gen. Man., Glyndebourne, 1955–59; Producer, Royal Coll. of Music, 1958–; Freelance Opera Producer, 1959–; Dep. Dir, London Opera Centre, 1965–66; Administrator, Welsh Nat. Opera, 1966–70; Dir, Sadler's Wells Theatre, 1970–78; Dir, Opera and Drama Sch., RCM, 1976–80; Mem. Exec. and Editor, Music Jl of ISM, 1979–84. *Publication:* (ed) Delius: Koanga (opera), 1975. *Recreation:* travel. *Address:* 43 Park Road, Radlett, Herts WD7 8EG. *T:* Radlett 7240. *Club:* Garrick.

CRAIG, Edward Anthony, (works also under name of Edward Carrick), FRSA; writer and lecturer, designer for film and theatre; independent film art director; *b* 3 Jan. 1905; *s* of late Edward Gordon Craig, CH; *m* 1960, Mary, *d* of late Lieut-Col H. A. Timewell, OBE. Studied art, the theatre and photography in Italy, 1917–26; has discovered numerous documents of great value to the history of the theatre; Art Dir to the Welsh Pearson Film Co., 1928–29; Art Dir for Associated Talking Pictures, 1932–36; Supervising Art Dir, Criterion Film, 1937–39; established AAT Film Sch., 1937; Art Dir to the Crown Film Unit (Ministry of Information), 1939–46; Executive Art Dir, Independent Producers (Rank), 1947–49; wood-engravings, oil paintings, and scene designs exhibited at: the St George's Gallery, 1927 and 1928; at the Redfern Gallery, 1929, 1931, 1938; The Grubb Group, 1928–38; also in the principal Galleries of Canada and North America; designer of scenes and costumes for numerous London productions and at Stratford-upon-Avon, 1949. *Official Purchasers:* the British Museum; Victoria and Albert Museum; Metropolitan Museum, New York; Yale Univ., USA; The University, Austin, Texas. *Publications:* Designing for Moving Pictures, 1941; Meet the Common People, 1942; Art and Design in British Films, 1948; Designing for Films, 1949; Gordon Craig, The Story of his Life, 1968, Polish trans., 1977, Amer. edn 1985; (in Italian) Fabrizio Carini Motta, 1972; William Nicolson's An Alphabet, 1978; Robinson Crusoe and Gordon Craig, 1979; William Nicolson's An Almanac, 1980; (ed) Gordon Craig: the last eight years, by Ellen Gordon Craig, 1983; Baroque Theatre Construction, 1982. *Illustrations:* The Georgics of Virgil, 1931, etc; books of verse by John Keats, Edith Sitwell, Edmund Blunden, W. H. Davies, etc. *Recreations:* books and music. *Address:* Southcourt Cottage, Long Crendon, Aylesbury, Bucks HP18 9AQ.

CRAIG, Hamish M.; *see* Millar-Craig.

CRAIG, Sir James; *see* Craig, Sir A. J. M.

CRAIG, John Frazer; Under Secretary (Director), Industry Department, Welsh Office, since 1985; *b* 8 Nov. 1943; *s* of late John Frazer Craig and Margaret Jane Gibson Craig; *m* 1973, Janet Elizabeth. *Educ:* Robert Richardson Grammar Sch., Sunderland. Joined Civil Service, 1961; Customs and Excise, 1961–69; Nat. Bd for Prices and Incomes, 1969–70; Welsh Office, 1970–: Private Sec. to Perm. Sec., 1972–74; Private Sec. to Sec. of State for Wales, 1980–82; Asst Sec., Industry Dept, 1982–85. *Recreations:* reading, gardening, photography. *Address:* c/o Welsh Office, Cathays Park, Cardiff CF1 3NQ. *T:* Cardiff 825111.

CRAIG, Rev. Maxwell Davidson; Minister at Wellington Church, Glasgow, since 1973; Convener of the Church and Nation Committee, Church of Scotland, since 1984; Chaplain to the Queen in Scotland, since 1986; *b* 25 Dec. 1931; *s* of Dr William Craig and Alice M. Craig (*née* Semple); *m* 1957, Janet Margaret Macgregor; one *s* three *d. Educ:* Oriel Coll., Oxford (MA (Hons) Lit.Hum.); Edinburgh Univ. (BD); Princeton Theol Seminary, NJ (ThM). 2nd Lieut, 1st Bn Argyll and Sutherland Highlanders, 1954–56. Ministry of Labour: Asst Principal, 1957–61; Pvte Sec. to Parly Sec., 1959–61. Fulbright Schol., Princeton, 1964; ordained minister, Grahamston Parish Church, Falkirk, 1966. Chairman: Falkirk Children's Panel, 1970; Hillhead Housing Assoc., 1977–. *Recreations:* hill-walking, sailing, reading. *Address:* 27 Kingsborough Gardens, Glasgow G12 9NH. *T:* 041–339 3627.

CRAIG, Norman; Assistant Under-Secretary of State, Ministry of Defence, 1972–79; *b* 15 May 1920; *s* of George Craig, OBE; *m* 1st, 1946, Judith Margaret Newling (marr. diss. 1957); one *s*; 2nd, 1960, Jane Hudson; two *s* one *d. Educ:* Penarth County Sch.; Cardiff Univ. Army Service, Royal Sussex Regt, 1940–47. Board of Trade, 1948; Min. of Supply (later Aviation), 1953; Private Sec. to Minister, 1959–60; Min. of Technology, 1964; Sec. to Cttee of Inquiry into Aircraft Industry, 1964–65; course at IDC, 1968; MoD 1971; Asst Sec., LCD, 1979–85. *Publication:* The Broken Plume, 1982. *Address:* 51 Hayes Lane, Beckenham, Kent. *T:* 01–650 7916.

CRAIG, Rt. Rev. Prof. Robert, CBE 1981; Moderator of the General Assembly of the Church of Scotland, May 1986–May 1987 (designation subseq. Very Rev.); Minister, St Andrew's Scots Memorial Church, Jerusalem, 1980–85; Principal and Vice-Chancellor, 1969–80, Professor of Theology, 1963–80, University of Zimbabwe (formerly University of Rhodesia), now Emeritus; *b* 22 March 1917; *s* of late John Craig, stone-mason, and late Anne Peggie, linen-weaver; *m* 1950, Olga Wanda, *d* of late Michael and of Helena Strzelec; one *s* one *d. Educ:* Fife CC schs; St Andrews Univ.; Union Theol Seminary, NY. MA (Ordinary) 1938, BD with distinction in Systematic Theology 1941, PhD 1950, St Andrews; STM *magna cum laude* Union Theol Seminary 1948. Pres., Students' Rep. Council, Chm. Union Debating Soc., Berry Schol. in Theology, St Andrews Univ., 1941; Asst Minister, St John's Kirk, Perth, 1941–42, ordained 1942; Chaplain (4th class), Army, 1942–47: infantry bns, NW Europe, 1944–45 (despatches, Normandy,1944); Palestine, Egypt, 1945–47; HCF 1947. Hugh Black Fellow and Instructor in Systematic Theology, Union Theol Seminary, 1947–48; Dep. Leader, Iona Community, Scotland, 1948–50; Natal Univ.: Prof. of Divinity, 1950–57; College Dean, Adviser of Students and personal rep. of Principal and Vice-Chancellor, 1953–54; Prof. of Religion, Smith Coll., Mass, 1958–63; UC Rhodesia and Nyasaland: Prof. of Theology, 1963; Dean, Faculty of Arts, 1965; Vice-Principal, 1966; Actg Principal, 1967 and 1969. External Examiner: Boston, Cape Town, London, McGill, Natal, Rhodes, S Africa Univs, various times, 1950–80. Vis. Lectr, Ecumenical Inst., Bossey, Switz., 1955; John Dewey Mem. Lectr, Vermont Univ., 1961; Ainslie Meml Lectr, Rhodes Univ., 1965. Jerusalem appointments: Chm., Ecumenical Theol Res. Fraternity, 1983–85 (Mem. 1980–85); Member: Ecumenical Friends Gp, 1980–85; Council, Interfaith Cttee, 1981–85; Bd of Dirs, Internat. YMCA, 1982–85 (Vice-Chm., 1984, Chm., 1984–); Exec. Cttee, Spafford Community Centre, 1982–85; Chm., Church of Scotland Israel Council, 1981–85; Vice-Chm., Soc. of Friends of St Andrew's Church, Jerusalem, 1985–; Moderator, Presbytery of Jerusalem, 1982–84. Brit. Council Commonwealth Interchange Fellow, Cambridge Univ., 1966. Hon. DD St Andrews, 1967; Hon. LLD: Witwatersrand 1979; Birmingham, 1980; Natal, 1981; Hon. DLitt Zimbabwe, 1981. Hon. Fellow, Zimbabwe Instn of Engineers, 1976. Golden Jubilee Medal, Witwatersrand Univ., 1977; Jerusalem Medal, 1985. *Publications:* The Reasonableness of True Religion, 1954; Social Concern in the Thought of William Temple, 1963; Religion: Its Reality and Its Relevance, 1965; The Church: Unity in Integrity, 1966; Religion and Politics: a Christian view, 1972; On Belonging to a University, 1974. *Recreations:* the cinema, theatre, contemporary and recent history, light classical music, listening and talking to people. *Address:* West Port, Falkland, Fife KY7 7BL. *T:* Falkland 57238. *Clubs:* Kate Kennedy, University Staff, Students' Union (St Andrews); YMCA, Rainbow (Jerusalem).

CRAIG, Thomas Rae, CBE 1969 (OBE 1945); TD; DL; retired; Deputy Governor, The Bank of Scotland, 1972–77; *b* 11 July 1906; *s* of Sir John Craig, CBE, and Jessie Craig (*née* Sommerville); *m* 1931, Christina Gay (*née* Moodie); three *s* one *d. Educ:* Glasgow Academy; Lycée Malherbe, Caen, Normandy. Served War of 1939–45: Lt-Col 6th Cameronians; AA and QMG 52nd (Lowland) Div. Dir of Colvilles Ltd, 1935; Man. Dir, 1958; Dep. Chm., 1961; Chm. and Man. Dir, 1965–68. Mem. Bd, BSC, 1967–72. Formerly Dir of companies. Mem., Convocation of Strathclyde Univ. DL Dunbartonshire,

1973. Hon. LLD: Strathclyde, 1968; Glasgow, 1970. OStJ. *Recreation:* farming. *Address:* Invergare, Rhu, Dunbartonshire. *T:* Rhu 820427. *Club:* Royal Scottish Automobile (Glasgow).

CRAIG, Rt. Hon. William, PC (N Ire.) 1963; solicitor and company director; *b* 2 Dec. 1924; *s* of late John Craig and Mary Kathleen Craig (*née* Lamont); *m* 1960, Doris Hilgendorff; two *s. Educ:* Dungannon Royal Sch.; Larne Grammar Sch.; Queen's Univ., Belfast. Served War of 1939–45, Royal Air Force, 1943–46. Qualified as solicitor, 1952. MP (U) Larne Div. of Antrim, NI Parliament, 1960–73; Mem. (Vanguard Unionist Progressive), N Antrim, NI Assembly, 1973–75; Mem. (UUC), E Belfast, NI Constitutional Convention, 1975–76; MP (UU) Belfast East, Feb. 1974–79. Chief Whip, Parliament of Northern Ireland, 1962–63; Minister of Home Affairs, 1963–64, and 1966–68; Minister of Health and Local Government, 1964; Minister of Development, 1965–66. Founder: Ulster Vanguard, 1972 (Leader, 1972–77); Vanguard Unionist Party, 1973 (Leader, 1973–77). Member: Council of Europe, 1976–79; WEU, 1976–79. *Recreations:* travel, motoring, shooting.

CRAIG-McFEELY, Comdt Elizabeth Sarah Ann, CB 1982; Director, Women's Royal Naval Service, 1979–82; *b* 28 April 1927; *d* of late Lt-Col Cecil Michael Craig McFeely, DSO, OBE, MC, and late Nancy Sarah (*née* Mann, later Roberts). *Educ:* St Rose's Convent, Stroud, Glos; Anstey College of Physical Educn, Birmingham. DipPhysEducn London. Taught PE at St Angela's Ursuline Convent Sch., 1948–52; joined WRNS, 1952; Third Officer, 1953; served in various Royal Naval, Royal Marines and Royal Naval Reserve Estabts, 1952–67; in charge, WRNS, Far Eastern Fleet, 1967–69; various appts, MoD (Navy), 1969–74; HMS Centurion, 1974–76; Supt WRNS, 1977. Naval member, NAAFI Bd of Management, 1977–79; Hon. ADC to the Queen, 1979–82; retired 1982. *Recreations:* gardening and country pursuits. *Address:* Moonrakers, Mockbeggar Lane, Biddenden, Kent TN27 8ES. *T:* Biddenden 291325.

CRAIGAVON, 3rd Viscount *cr* 1927, of Stormont, Co. Down; **Janric Fraser Craig;** Bt 1918; *b* 9 June 1944; *s* of 2nd Viscount Craigavon; *S* father, 1974. *Educ:* Eton; London Univ. (BA, BSc). FCA. *Heir:* none. *Address:* Flat 13, 65 Courtfield Gardens, SW5 0NQ. *T:* 01–373 9834.

CRAIGEN, Desmond Seaward; Chairman, Vanbrugh Life Assurance Co. Ltd, since 1982; Director: Prudential Corporation plc, since 1982; Pioneer Concrete (Holdings) Ltd, since 1982; *b* 31 July 1916; *s* of late John Craigen and Ann Amelia Craigen (*née* Brebner); *m* 1961, Elena Ines (*née* Oldham Florez); one *s* one *d. Educ:* Holloway Sch.; King's Coll., London (BA Hons). Prudential Assurance Co. Ltd, 1934–81; India, 1950–57; attached O&M Div., Treasury, 1957–58; Dep. General Manager, 1968–69; General Manager, 1969–78; Chief General Manager, 1979–81. Served War of 1939–45: 53rd Reconnaisance Regt RAC (Major). *Recreations:* music, reading. *Address:* Corrydon House, Blewbury, Oxon OX11 9PF. *T:* Blewbury 850426.

CRAIGEN, James Mark, JP; MP (Lab and Co-op) Glasgow Maryhill since Feb. 1974; *b* 2 Aug. 1938; *e s* of James Craigen, MA and Isabel Craigen; *m* 1971, Sheena Millar. *Educ:* Shawlands Academy, Glasgow; Strathclyde University. MLitt, Heriot-Watt, 1974. FBIM. Compositor, 1954–61. Industrial Relations Asst, Scottish Gas Bd, 1963–64; Head of Organisation and Social Services at Scottish TUC, 1964–68; Asst Sec., and Industrial Liaison Officer, Scottish Business Educn Council, 1968–74. Glasgow City Councillor, 1965–68, Magistrate, 1966–68. Mem. Scottish Ambulance Service Bd, 1966–71; Mem. Police Adv. Bd for Scotland, 1970–74. Contested Ayr constituency, 1970; PPS to Rt Hon. William Ross, MBE, MP, Sec. of State for Scotland, 1974–76; Opposition Spokesman on Scottish Affairs, 1983–85. Mem., Select Cttee on Employment, 1979–83 (Chm., 1982–83); Chairman: Co-op. Party Parly Group, 1978–79; Scottish Group, Labour MPs, 1978–79; PLP Employment Gp, 1981–83. Mem., UK Delegn to Council of Europe Assembly, 1976–80. Mem., GMBATU. Trustee, Industry and Parliament Trust, 1984– (Fellow, 1978–79.). Mem., Bd of Trustees, Nat. Museums of Scotland, 1985–. Hon. Vice-Pres., Building Societies Assoc., 1985–. Hon. Lectr, Strathclyde Univ., 1980–85. JP: Glasgow, 1966; Edinburgh, 1975. *Publications:* contribs to Co-operative News, The Scotsman, Glasgow Herald. *Address:* House of Commons, SW1A 0AA.

CRAIGIE, Dr Hugh Brechin, CBE 1965; Principal Medical Officer, Mental Health Division, Scottish Home and Health Department, retired; *b* 19 May 1908; *s* of late Hugh Craigie; *m* 1st, 1933, Lillia Campbell (*d* 1958), *d* of Dr George Campbell Murray; two *s* (and one *s* decd); 2nd, 1962, Eileen (MBE 1950), *d* of F. S. Lyons. *Educ:* Manchester Grammar Sch.; Manchester Univ. House Physician, Manchester Royal Infirmary, 1931–32; Asst Medical Officer, Monsall Fever Hosp., Manchester, 1932–33; Senior Medical Officer, County Mental Hosp., Lancaster, 1933–46; Dep. Med. Supt, County Mental Hosp., Whittingham, 1946; HM Senior Medical Commissioner, General Board of Control for Scotland, 1947. Served War of 1939–45 (despatches), RAMC (Hon. Lieut-Col). *Publications:* various papers on psychiatry. *Address:* Saviskaill, Westerdunes Park, North Berwick.

CRAIGIE, John Hubert, OC 1967; FRS 1952; *b* 8 Dec. 1887; *s* of John Yorston Craigie and Elizabeth Mary Pollock; *m* 1926, Miriam Louise, *d* of Allen R. Morash and Clara Louise (*née* Smith). *Educ:* Harvard Univ. (AB); University of Minnesota (MSc); University of Manitoba (PhD). Dalhousie Univ., 1914. Served European War, 1914–18, Canadian Expeditionary Force, 1915–18; Indian Army, 1918–20. Canada Dept of Agriculture: Plant Pathologist, 1925–27; Senior Plant Pathologist, 1927–28; Officer-in-Charge (of Laboratory), Dominion Laboratory of Plant Pathology, Winnipeg, 1928–45; Associate Dir. Science Service, Canada Dept of Agriculture, Ottawa, 1945–52; retired 1952. Hon. DSc: University of British Columbia, 1946; University of Manitoba, 1959; Hon. LLD: University of Saskatchewan, 1948; Dalhousie Univ., 1951. *Publications:* papers in scientific journals. *Address:* 950 Bank Street, Ottawa, Ontario K1S 5G6, Canada.

CRAIGMYLE, 3rd Baron, *cr* 1929, of Craigmyle; **Thomas Donald Mackay Shaw;** Chairman: Craigmyle & Co. Ltd; Claridge Mills Ltd; Walsham Mill Ltd; *b* 17 Nov. 1923; *s* of 2nd Baron and Lady Margaret Cargill Mackay (*d* 1958), *e d* of 1st Earl of Inchcape; *S* father, 1944; *m* 1955, Anthea Esther Christine, *y d* of late E. C. Rich; three *s* three *d. Educ:* Eton; Trinity Coll., Oxford (MA). Served RNVR, 1943–46. FRSA. Kt Grand Cross of Obedience, SMO Malta (Hospitaller to British Assoc., 1962–73; Sec.-Gen., 1979–83; Vice-Pres., 1983–). *Publication:* (ed with J. Gould) Your Death Warrant?, 1971. *Recreation:* home baking. *Heir:* *s* Hon. Thomas Columba Shaw, *b* 19 Oct. 1960. *Address:* 18 The Boltons, SW10 9SY; Scottas, Knoydart, Inverness-shire PH41 4PL. *Clubs:* Caledonian; Royal Thames Yacht; Bengal (Calcutta).
See also W. B. Dean.

CRAIGTON, Baron, *cr* 1959 (Life Peer); **Jack Nixon Browne,** PC 1961; CBE 1944; *b* 3 Sept. 1904; *m* 1950, Eileen Nolan, *d* of late Henry Whitford Nolan, London. *Educ:* Cheltenham Coll. Served War of 1939–45, RAF (Balloon Command), Actg Group Capt. Contested (C) Govan Div., Glasgow, in 1945; MP (C) Govan Div., 1950–55; MP (C) Craigton Div. of Glasgow, 1955–Sept. 1959. Parly Private Sec. to Sec. of State for Scotland, 1952–April 1955; Parly Under-Sec., Scottish Office, April 1955–Oct. 1959;

Minister of State, Scottish Office, Nov. 1959–Oct. 1964. Westminster Chamber of Commerce: Mem., General Purposes Cttee, 1948; Mem., Exec. Cttee, 1950; Chm., 1954; Pres., 1966–83. Chm., United Biscuits (Holdings) Ltd, 1967–72. Pres., Commercial Travellers Benevolent Instn, 1976–. Vice-Pres., World Wildlife Fund (British Nat. Appeal), 1979; Chm., Fauna Preservation Soc., 1981–83 (Vice-Chm., 1970–80); Chairman: Council for Environmental Conservation, 1972–83; All-Party Conservation Cttee of both Houses of Parliament, 1972–; Fedn of Zoological Gardens, 1975–81; Mem., Jersey Wildlife Preservation Trust Council, 1970– (Internat. Trustee, 1972–). RSA: Mem. Council, 1975–81; Mem., Environment Cttee, 1975–83. *Recreation:* gardening. *Address:* Friary House, Friary Island, Wraysbury, near Staines, Mddx. *T:* Wraysbury 2213. *Club:* Buck's.

CRAIK, Duncan Robert Steele, CB 1979; OBE 1971; FASA; part-time Member, Administrative Appeals Tribunal, 1981–85; *b* 17 Feb. 1916; *s* of Henry Steele Craik and Lilian Kate Ellis; *m* 1943, Audrey Mavis Ion; four *d*. *Educ:* Univ. of Sydney (BEc). FASA 1973, FAIM 1975. Commonwealth Bank, 1933–40; Taxation Br., 1940–60; Treasury: Asst Sec., 1960–66; First Asst Sec., 1966–69; Dep. Sec., 1969–73; Auditor-General for Australia, 1973–81. Mem. Council, ANU, 1981–83. *Recreations:* bowls, gardening. *Address:* 15 Meehan Gardens, Griffith, ACT 2603, Australia. *T:* 95 8512.

CRAIK, Roger George, QC (Scot.) 1981; Sheriff of Lothian and Borders, since 1984; *b* 22 Nov. 1940; *s* of George and Frances Craik; *m* 1964, Helen Sinclair Sutherland; one *s* one *d*. *Educ:* Lockerbie Academy; Breadalbane Academy, Aberfeldy; George Watson's Boys' Coll.; Edinburgh Univ. (MA 1960, LLB 1962). Qualified as solicitor, 1962; worked for Orr Dignam & Co., Solicitors, Pakistan, 1963–65; called to Scottish Bar, 1966. Standing junior counsel to Min. of Defence (Army), 1974–80; Advocate Depute, 1980–83. *Recreations:* Scottish antiquities, modern jazz. *Address:* Sheriff Court House, Lawnmarket, Edinburgh.

CRAM, Alastair Lorimer, MC 1945; Appellate Judge, Supreme Court of Appeal, Malawi, 1964–68, retired; in private practice at Scots Bar, Edinburgh; *b* 25 Aug. 1909; *m* 1951, Isobel Nicholson; no *c*. *Educ:* Perth Academy; Edinburgh University (LLB). Solicitor, 1933; private practice, 1935–39; admitted Scots Bar, 1946. Served in HM Army, 1939–48: POW, successful escapes; RA, SAS, Intelligence Corps, Counsel War Crimes Group NW Europe, Major; GSO 2. Resident Magistrate, Kenya, 1948; Actg Puisne Judge, 1953–56; Sen. Resident Magistrate, Kenya, 1956; Temp. Puisne Judge, 1958–60; Puisne Judge, High Court of Nyasaland, 1960; acting Chief Justice and (briefly) Governor-General, Malawi, 1965; Legal Dept, Scottish Office, 1971–74. Athlete, climber, and traveller: in Alps, 1930–60, and Himalayas, 1960 and 1963; in African, Asian and South American deserts, 1940–66; in Amazon basin and Peruvian Andes, 1966; in Atlas Mts, 1971; in Great Dividing Range, Australia, N-S traverse, 1981–84. *Publications:* Editor, Kenya Law Reports, 1952–56; contribs law reports, legal and mountaineering jls. *Recreations:* shooting, sound-recordings, photography (still and cine), orchid-collecting, languages. *Address:* 5 Upper Dean Terrace, Edinburgh. *T:* 031–332 5441. *Clubs:* Alpine; Scottish Mountaineering (Edinburgh).

CRAMER, Hon. Sir John (Oscar), Kt 1964; FREI; QRV; MHR (L) for Bennelong, New South Wales, 1949–74; Senior Partner, Cramer Brothers, real estate auctioneers; Managing Director, Higgins (Buildings) Ltd; *b* Quirindi, NSW, 18 Feb. 1897; *s* of J. N. Cramer, Quirindi; *m* 1921, Mary, (Dame Mary Cramer, DBE, decd), *d* of William M. Earls; two *s* two *d*. *Educ:* state public schs; business coll. Mayor of North Sydney, 1940–41; Member: Sydney County Council, 1935– (Chm., 1946–49); Statutory Cttee on Public Works, 1949–56 (Chm., 1955–56); Executive Building Industry Congress of New South Wales; Executive of Liberal Party of Australia, NSW Division (a founder of Provisional Exec.). Minister for the Army, 1956–63. Patron: Anzac Meml Club, N Sydney; RSL, N Ryde, NSW. *Recreation:* bowls. *Address:* Unit 2, 5 Morton Street, Wollstonecraft, NSW 2065, Australia. *T:* 43 5007. *Club:* Rotary.

CRAMOND, Ronald Duncan; Deputy Chairman, Highlands and Islands Development Board, since 1983; *b* 22 March 1927; *s* of Adam and Margaret Cramond; *m* 1954, Constance MacGregor (*d* 1985); one *s* one *d*. *Educ:* George Heriot's Sch.; Edinburgh Univ. (MA). Sen. Medallist History 1949. FBIM; FSAScot 1978. Commnd Royal Scots, 1950. Entered War Office, 1951; Private Sec. to Parly Under-Sec. of State, Scottish Office, 1956; Principal, Dept of Health for Scotland, 1957; Mactaggart Fellow (Applied Econs), Glasgow Univ., 1962; Haldane Medallist in Public Admin, 1964; Asst Sec., Scottish Develt Dept, 1966, Under Sec., 1973; Under Sec., Dept of Agric. and Fisheries for Scotland, 1977. Member: Scottish Museums Adv. Bd, 1984–85; Scottish Tourist Board, 1985–; Bd of Trustees, Nat. Museums of Scotland, 1985–. *Publication:* Housing Policy in Scotland, 1966. *Recreations:* golf, hill walking, geriatric Rugby refereeing. *Address:* c/o Highlands and Islands Development Board, Bridge House, 27 Bank Street, Inverness IV1 1QR. *Club:* Royal Commonwealth Society.

CRAMOND, Dr William Alexander, OBE 1960; FRSE; Hon. Professor of Clinical Psychiatry, Flinders University, South Australia, since 1983; *b* 2 Oct. 1920; *er s* of William James Cramond, MBE and of May Battisby, Aberdeen; *m* 1949, Bertine J. C. Mackintosh, MB, ChB, Dornoch; one *s* one *d*. *Educ:* Robert Gordon's Coll., Aberdeen; Aberdeen Univ. MB, ChB, MD, FRCPsych, FRANZCP, FRACP, DPM. Physician Supt, Woodilee Mental Hosp., Glasgow, 1955–61; Dir of Mental Health, S Australia, 1961–65; Prof. of Mental Health, Univ. of Adelaide, 1963–71; Principal Medical Officer in Mental Health, Scottish Home and Health Dept, 1971–72; Dean of Faculty of Medicine and Prof. of Mental Health, Univ. of Leicester, 1972–75; Principal and Vice-Chancellor, Stirling Univ., 1975–80; Dir of Mental Health Services, NSW, 1980–83; Clinical Dir, Cleland House, Glenside Hosp., SA, 1983–85. Hon. Prof., Clinical Psychiatry, Sydney, 1980–83. DUniv Stirling, 1984. *Publications:* papers on psychosomatic medicine and on care of dying in Brit. Jl Psychiat., Lancet, BMJ. *Recreations:* walking, reading, theatre. *Address:* 28 Tynte Street, North Adelaide, SA 5006, Australia.

CRAMP, Prof. Rosemary Jean; Professor of Archaeology, University of Durham, since 1971; *b* 6 May 1929; *er d* of Robert Kingston and Vera Cramp, Cranoe Grange, Leics. *Educ:* Market Harborough Grammar Sch.; St Anne's Coll., Oxford (MA, BLitt). Lectr, St Anne's Coll., Oxford, 1950–55; Lectr, Durham Univ., 1955, Sen. Lectr, 1966. Commissioner: Royal Commn on Ancient and Historical Monuments of Scotland, 1975–; Historic Bldgs and Monuments Commn, 1984– (Mem., Adv. Cttee (Archaeology), 1984–). Mem., Redundant Churches Fund. Trustee, British Museum, 1978–. Pres., Cumberland and Westmorland Antiquarian and Archaeol Soc., 1984–. Gen. Editor, Corpus of Anglo-Saxon Stone Sculpture, 1974–. *Publications:* Corpus of Anglo-Saxon Stone Sculpture, vol. I, Durham and Northumberland, 1984, vol. 2, (with R. N. Bailey) Cumberland and Westmorland, 1986; contribs in the field of Early Monasticism, Early Medieval Sculpture and Northern Archaeology. *Address:* Department of Archaeology, University of Durham, 46 Saddler Street, Durham DH1 3NU. *T:* Durham 64466.

CRAMPTON, (Arthur Edward) Seán, MC 1943; GM(mil.) 1944; TD 1946; FRBS 1965 (ARBS 1952); sculptor; *b* 15 March 1918; *e s* of late Joshua Crampton, architect, and Ethel Mary (*née* Dyas); *m* 3rd, 1959, Patricia, *e d* of L. J. Cardew Wood; one *s* one *d*; three *d* by former marriages. *Educ:* St Joseph de Cluny, Stafford; Vittoria Jun. Sch. of Art, Birmingham; Birmingham Central Coll. of Art; London; Paris. Served TA, London Irish Rifles, Western Desert, Sicily, Italy, 1938–46 (Captain). Prof. de Sculpture, Anglo-French Art Centre, 1946–50; served on juries for Thomas More and Winston Churchill meml statues. Member, Art Workers Guild, 1971 (Master, 1978); Pres., RBS, 1966–71. Mem., Accademia Italia, 1981. Governor: Camberwell Sch. of Arts and Crafts, 1970– (Chm., 1983–); London Inst., 1986–. FRSA 1973. TEM 1986. *Exhibitions: general:* RA and RI Galls, 1950–; *one-man:* London Gall., 1948; Ashley Gall., 1952; Minories, Colchester, 1971; Alwin Gall. (Grafton St.), eleven exhibns, 1965–82. *Major heroic size works:* Persephone, Crowmallie, Aberdeen; Horseman (RBS Medal for best work of the year, 1965); Simon de Montfort, County Hall, Leics; Three Judges, Churchill Coll., Cambridge; Three Kings, Knochallachie, Aberdeen; Stability, Burgess Hill; Cascade, Duke of Westminster, Eaton, Chester; Two Geese, Goose Green, Altrincham (Civic Trust Award, 1984); *works in RC churches:* St Mary and Child, Midhurst; Our Lady, St Michael and Crucifix, Wolverhampton; Crucifix, Church of Child Jesus, Birmingham; Risen Christ and sanctuary furniture, St Vincent's Convent, Mill Hill; Our Lady and Child, Convent of Sisters of Mercy, Brentwood; Crucifix, St Cedd's, Goodmayes; Our Lady, St Mary's Coll., Wallasey; Cross Motif, St Thomas More, Manor House; Risen Christ, St Albans, Derby; Stations of the Cross, St Edmunds, Calne, etc. *Publication:* Humans, Beasts, Birds (with Hicks and Anderson), 1981. *Recreations:* gardening, painting, cooking. *Address:* Rookery Farmhouse, Calne, Wilts SN11 0LH. *T:* Calne 814068. *Clubs:* Athenæum, Chelsea Arts.

CRAMPTON SMITH, Alex; *see* Smith, Alexander C.

CRANBORNE, Viscount; Robert Michael James Cecil; MP (C) Dorset South, since 1979; *b* 30 Sept. 1946; *s* and *heir* of 6th Marquess of Salisbury, *qv*; *m* 1970, Hannah Ann, *er d* of Lt-Col William Joseph Stirling of Keir; two *s* three *d*. *Educ:* Eton; Oxford. *Heir: s* Hon. Robert Edward William Cecil, *b* 18 Dec. 1970. *Address:* Cranborne Lodge, Dorset.

CRANBROOK, 5th Earl of, *cr* 1892; **Gathorne Gathorne-Hardy;** Viscount Cranbrook, 1878; Baron Medway, 1892; DL; *b* 20 June 1933; *er s* of 4th Earl of Cranbrook, CBE, and of the Dowager Countess of Cranbrook (Fidelity, OBE 1972, *o d* of late Hugh E. Seebohm); *S* father, 1978; *m* 1967, Caroline, *o d* of Col Ralph G. E. Jarvis, Doddington Hall, Lincoln; two *s* one *d*. *Educ:* Eton; Corpus Christi Coll., Cambridge (MA); University of Birmingham (PhD). Asst, Sarawak Museum, 1956–58; Fellow, Yayasan Siswa Lokantara (Indonesia), 1960–61; Sr Lectr in Zoology, Univ. of Malaya, 1961–70. Editor of Ibis, 1973–80. Member: Royal Commn on Environmental Pollution, 1981–; NERC, 1982–; Sub-cttee G (Environment), H of L Select Cttee on European Communities, 1979–85 (Chm., 1980–83); H of L Select Cttee on Science and Technol. 1980–. Mem., Suffolk Coastal DC, 1974–83; President: Suffolk Trust for Nature Conservation, 1979–; British Herpetological Soc., 1981–; Trustee, BM (Natural History), 1982–. Governor, Thomas Mills High Sch., Framlingham, 1978–85; Skinner and Freeman of the City of London. DL Suffolk, 1984. FLS; FZS; FRGS; FRSA; FIBiol; MBOU. OStJ. *Publications:* Mammals of Borneo, 1965, 2nd edn 1977; Mammals of Malaya, 1969, 2nd edn 1978; (with D. R. Wells) Birds of the Malay Peninsula, 1976. *Heir: s* Lord Medway, *qv*. *Address:* c/o National Westminster Bank, St James's Square, SW1Y 4JX.

CRANE, Prof. Francis Roger; Professor of Law, Queen Mary College, University of London, 1965–78, now Emeritus; *b* 19 Dec. 1910; *m* 1938, Jean Berenice Hadfield (*d* 1986); two *s* one *d*. *Educ:* Highgate Sch.; University Coll., London. LLB 1933; Solicitor, 1934, Clifford's Inn Prize. Lecturer in Law; King's Coll. and private practice, 1935–38; Lecturer in Law, University of Manchester, 1938–46; Prof. of Law, University of Nottingham, 1946–52; Prof. of English Law, King's Coll., London, 1952–65; Dean of the Faculty of Law, QMC, London, 1965–76. University of London: Mem. Senate, 1969–71, 1973–78; Chm. Academic Council, 1975–78; Mem. Court, 1975–78. Visiting Professor: Tulane Univ., 1960; University of Khartoum, 1963; Dean of the Faculty of Law and Visiting Prof., University of Canterbury (New Zealand), 1964; Vis. Professor: Univ. of Melbourne, 1972; Monash Univ., 1972; Univ. of Sydney, 1980. Served War of 1939–45: Royal Corps of Signals, Major, 1944. Pres., Soc. of Public Teachers of Law, 1975–76. FKC 1976; Fellow QMC 1980. *Publications:* (jointly) A Century of Family Law, 1957; articles and notes in legal periodicals. *Address:* 25 Winston Drive, Isham, Kettering, Northants NN14 1HS. *T:* Burton Latimer 723938.

See also P. F. Crane.

CRANE, Geoffrey David; Regional Director, Eastern Region, Departments of the Environment and Transport, since 1985; *b* 13 Oct. 1934; *s* of late Frederick David Crane and Marion Doris Crane; *m* 1962, Gillian Margaret, *d* of late Harry Thomas Austin; one *d*. *Educ:* City of London Sch. (John Carpenter Schol.); Trinity Hall, Cambridge (Schol., MA). Served RAF, 1956–58, Flying Officer. Assistant Principal, Min. of Works, 1958; Asst Private Sec. to Minister of Works, 1961–62; Principal, 1962; Secretary, Historic Buildings Council for Scotland and Ancient Monuments Bd for Scotland, 1962–66; Private Sec. to Minister of Public Building and Works, 1968–69; Asst Sec., Machinery of Govt Div., CSD, 1970–72; Dep. Dir, Central Unit on Environmental Pollution, DoE, 1972–76; Personnel Management and Trng, 1976–78, Under Sec. and Dir of Res. Ops, 1978–80, Dir, Personnel Management and Trng, 1981–85, DoE and Dept of Transport. *Recreations:* music, industrial archaeology, mathematics. *Address:* 6 The Paddock, Datchet, Berks SL3 9DL. *T:* Slough 43644. *Clubs:* Royal Air Force, Civil Service.

CRANE, Sir Harry (Walter Victor), Kt 1966; OBE 1949; JP; Industrial Relations Consultant since 1965; *b* 12 Feb. 1903; *s* of William and Ann Crane; *m*, 1st, 1930, Winefride Mary (*d* 1978), *d* of Thomas and Lucy Wing; one *s*; *m* 2nd, 1982, Catherine Elizabeth, *d* of Corby Garland Bevan, Haywards Heath. *Educ:* Nottingham. Engineer Fitter. NUGMW: District Officer, 1934; Nat. Officer, 1943; District Sec., 1957; retd from Union service, 1965. Member: Catering Commn, 1950–52; Catering Hygiene Cttee, 1949–52; Food Hygiene Adv. Coun., 1952–78; Workers' Travel Assoc. (now Galleon World Travel Assoc.) Management Cttee, 1960–; (pt-time) E Midlands Electricity Bd, 1965–73; Milk Marketing Bd, 1966–72. Director (part-time), Transport Holding Co., Ministry of Transport, 1966–73. Hon. Pres., Galleon World Travel, 1973–81. Chairman: Labour Party Conference Arrangements Cttee, 1954–65; Industrial Injuries Advisory Council, 1967–73; Sec. or Chm. of Joint Industrial Councils during Trade Union career. FREconS 1944. JP 1961. *Recreations:* swimming, gardening, reading. *Address:* Riverain, 22 Cliff Drive, Radcliffe-on-Trent, Nottingham. *T:* Radcliffe-on-Trent 2683. *Clubs:* Royal Commonwealth Society, Civil Service.

CRANE, Sir James (William Donald), Kt 1980; CBE 1977; HM Chief Inspector of Constabulary, 1979–82; *b* 1 Jan. 1921; *s* of late William James Crane and Ivy Winifred Crane; *m* 1942, Patricia Elizabeth Hodge; one *s* one *d*. *Educ:* Hampshire schs. Served RE, RA, Royal Hampshire Regt, 1939–46. Joined Metrop. Police, 1946; Comdr and Dep. Asst Comr, Fraud Squad and Commercial Br., 1970–76; Inspector of Constabulary, 1976–79. Member: Parole Bd, 1983–85; Fraud Trials Cttee, 1984–85. *Recreations:* gardening, walking, reading. *Address:* Home Office, 50 Queen Anne's Gate, SW1H 9AT. *Club:* Royal Commonwealth Society.

CRANE, Peter Francis; barrister; a Recorder of the Crown Court, since 1982; *b* 14 Jan. 1940; *s* of Prof. Francis Roger Crane, *qv*, and late Jean Berenice Crane (*née* Hadfield); *m* 1967, Elizabeth Mary Pittman; four *d*. *Educ:* Nottingham High Sch.; Highgate Sch.; Gonville and Caius Coll., Cambridge (MA, LLM); Tulane Univ., New Orleans (LLM). Called to the Bar, Gray's Inn, 1964 (Barstow Scholar, 1963); in practice on Midland and Oxford Circuit. Mem., Senate of Inns of Court and the Bar, 1983–. Chm., Kettering Constituency Liberal Assoc., 1981–84. *Recreations:* walking, gardening, reading, wine. *Address:* The Glebe House, Pytchley, Northants NN14 1EW. *T:* Kettering 790322; 2 Crown Office Row, Temple, EC4Y 7HJ. *T:* 01–353 1365. *Club:* Northampton and County (Northampton).

CRANFIELD, Rev. Prof. Charles Ernest Burland, FBA 1982; Emeritus Professor of Theology, University of Durham, since 1980; *b* 13 Sept. 1915; *s* of Charles Ernest Cranfield and Beatrice Mary Cranfield (*née* Tubbs); *m* 1953, Ruth Elizabeth Gertrude, *d* of Rev. T. Bole; two *d*. *Educ:* Mill Hill Sch.; Jesus Coll., Cambridge; Wesley House, Cambridge. MA Cantab. Research in Basel, cut short before it properly began by outbreak of war. Probationer in Methodist Church, 1939; ordained 1941; Minister, Shoeburyness; Chaplain to the Forces, 1942–46; from end of hostilities worked with German prisoners-of-war and was first staff chaplain to POW Directorate, War Office; Minister, Cleethorpes, 1946–50; admitted to Presbyterian Church of England (now United Reformed Church) as a minister, 1954. Lecturer in Theology, Durham Univ., 1950–62; Sen. Lectr, 1962–66; Reader, 1966–78; Prof. of Theology (personal), 1978–80. Joint general editor, new series of International Critical Commentary, 1966–. Hon. DD Aberdeen, 1980. *Publications:* The First Epistle of Peter, 1950, 4th imp. 1958; The Gospel according to Saint Mark, 1959, supplemented and somewhat revised over the years, 8th imp. 1983; I and II Peter and Jude, 1960; A Ransom for Many, 1963; The Service of God, 1965; A Commentary on Romans 12–13, 1965; A Critical and Exegetical Commentary on the Epistle to the Romans, vol. 1 1975, 5th (corrected) imp. 1985, vol. 2 1979, 3rd (corrected) imp. 1983; Romans: a shorter commentary, 1985; If God Be For Us: a collection of sermons, 1985; The Bible and Christian Life: a collection of essays, 1985; contribs to composite works and to various theological periodicals. *Address:* 30 Western Hill, Durham City DH1 4RL. *T:* Durham 43096.

CRANLEY, Viscount; Rupert Charles William Bullard Onslow; *b* 16 June 1967; *s* and *heir* of 7th Earl of Onslow, *qv*. *Educ:* Eton. *Recreations:* photography, riding, shooting.

CRANMER, Philip; Secretary, Associated Board of the Royal Schools of Music, 1974–83; *b* 1 April 1918; *s* of Arthur Cranmer and Lilian Phillips; *m* 1939, Ruth Loasby; one *s* three *d*. *Educ:* Wellington; Christ Church, Oxford (BMus, MA). Asst Music Master, Wellington Coll. 1938–40; served RA, 1940–46; Major, Education Officer, Guards Div., 1946; Dir of Music, King Edward's Sch., Birmingham, 1946; Staff Accompanist, Midland Region, BBC, 1948; Lectr in Music, Birmingham Univ., 1950; Hamilton Harty Prof. of Music, Queen's Univ., Belfast, 1954–70; Prof. of Music, Univ. of Manchester, 1970–74. Pres., Incorporated Soc. of Musicians, 1971; Chm., Musicians' Benevolent Fund, 1980–. FRCO 1947; Hon. RAM 1967; FRMCM 1974; FRCM 1976. Hon. DMus QUB, 1985. Chevalier de l'Ordre de Léopold II, 1947; Croix de Guerre Belge, 1947. *Publications:* The Technique of Accompaniment, 1970; Sight-reading for Young Pianists, 1979; How to Follow a Score, 1982; Two Sonatinas for piano duet, 1981 and 1985. *Address:* Quince Cottage, Underhill Lane, Clayton, Hassocks, W Sussex BN6 9PJ.

CRANSTON, Prof. Maurice (William); Professor of Political Science at the London School of Economics, 1969–85 (seconded as Professor of Political Science, European University Institute, 1978–81); *b* 8 May 1920; *o c* of William Cranston and Catherine Harris; *m* 1958, Baroness Maximiliana von und zu Fraunberg; two *s*. *Educ:* London Univ.; St Catherine's, Oxford (MA, BLitt; Hon. Fellow, 1984). London Civil Defence during war, 1939–45. Lecturer (part-time) in Social Philosophy, London Univ., 1950–59; Reader (previously Lecturer) in Political Science at London Sch. of Economics, 1959–69. Visiting Prof. of Government: Harvard Univ., 1965–66; Dartmouth Coll., USA, 1970–71; Univ. of British Columbia, 1973–74; Univ. of California, 1976; Ecole des Hautes Etudes, Paris, 1977; Woodrow Wilson Center, Washington, 1982; Fondation Thiers, Paris, 1983; Univ. of California, 1986–87; Carlyle Lectr, Oxford Univ., 1984. Pres., Institut International de Philosophie Politique, 1976–79; Vice-Pres. de l'Alliance Française en Angleterre, 1964–. Literary Adviser to Methuen Ltd, 1959–69. FRSL. Foreign Hon. Mem., Amer. Acad. of Arts and Sciences, 1970–. *Publications:* Freedom, 1953; Human Rights Today, 1954 (revised edn 1962); John Locke: a biography, 1957 (James Tait Black Memorial Prize); Jean-Paul Sartre, 1962; What Are Human Rights? (New York), 1963, 2nd rev. edn (London), 1973; Western Political Philosophers (ed), 1964; A Glossary of Political Terms, 1966; Rousseau's Social Contract, 1967; Political Dialogues, 1968; La Quintessence de Sartre (Montreal), 1969; Language and Philosophy (Toronto), 1969; The New Left (ed), 1970; (ed with R. S. Peters) Hobbes and Rousseau, 1972; The Mask of Politics, 1973; (ed with P. Mair) Idéologie et Politique, 1980; Langage et Politique, 1981; Culture et Politique, 1982; Jean-Jacques: the early life and work of Jean-Jacques Rousseau 1712–1754, 1983; Rousseau's Discourse on Inequality, 1984; Philosophers and Pamphleteers, 1986. *Recreation:* walking. *Address:* 1A Kent Terrace, Regent's Park, NW1 4RP. *T:* 01–262 2698. *Club:* Garrick.

CRANSTON, Prof. William Ian; Professor of Medicine, St Thomas's Hospital Medical School, since 1964; *b* 11 Sept. 1928; *s* of Thomas and Margaret Cranston; *m* Pamela Isabel Pearson; four *s*. *Educ:* High Sch. for Boys, Glasgow; Aberdeen Grammar Sch.; Boys' High Sch., Oswestry; University of Aberdeen, FRCP London 1965 (MRCP 1952); MB, ChB (Hons), 1949; MD Aberdeen 1957; MA Oxon. 1962. Royal Infirmary, Aberdeen: House Physician, 1949–50; Medical Registrar, 1952–53; Asst in Medical Unit, St Mary's Hospital, Paddington, 1953–56; 1st Asst in Dept of Regius Prof. of Med., Radcliffe Inf., Oxford, 1961–64. Mem., Med. Res. Soc. *Recreations:* reading, gardening, painting. *Address:* St Thomas's Hospital Medical School, Albert Embankment, Westminster Bridge, SE1.

CRANSTONE, Bryan Allan Lefevre; Curator, Pitt Rivers Museum, Oxford, 1976–85; *b* 26 Feb. 1918; *s* of late Edgar Arnold Cranstone and late Clarice Edith Cranstone; *m* 1941, Isabel May, *d* of W. Gough-Thomas; one *s*. *Educ:* Bootham Sch., York; St Catharine's Coll., Cambridge (MA). Hampshire Regt, 1939–46. Asst Keeper, Dept of Ethnography, BM, 1947–69; field work, New Guinea, 1963–64; Dep. Keeper, Dept of Ethnography, BM (later Museum of Mankind), 1969–76. Vis. Lectr, University Coll., London, 1955–71. Fellow, Linacre Coll., Oxford, 1976. Vice-Pres., RAI, 1980–83. *Publications:* Melanesia: a short ethnography, 1961; The Australian Aborigines, 1973; (with D. C. Starzecka) The Solomon Islanders, 1974; Arte de Nueva Guinea y Papua, 1977; articles in learned jls and encyclopaedias. *Address:* 38 Granville Court, Cheney Lane, Headington, Oxford OX3 OHS.

CRANWORTH, 3rd Baron, *cr* 1899; **Philip Bertram Gurdon;** Lieutenant, Royal Wiltshire Yeomanry; *b* 24 May 1940; *s* of Hon. Robin Gurdon (killed in action, 1942) and Hon. Yoskyl Pearson (she *m* 2nd, 1944, as his 2nd wife, Lieut-Col. Alistair Gibb, and 3rd, 1962, as his 2nd wife, 1st Baron McCorquodale of Newton, PC, KCVO; she *d* 1979), *d* of 2nd Viscount Cowdray; *S* grandfather, 1964; *m* 1968, Frances Henrietta Montagu Douglas Scott, *d* of late Lord William Scott and of Lady William Scott, Beechwood, Melrose; two *s* one *d*. *Educ:* Eton; Magdalene Coll., Cambridge. *Heir:* *s* Hon. Sacha William Robin Gurdon, *b* 12 Aug. 1970. *Address:* Grundisburgh Hall, Woodbridge, Suffolk IP13 6TW.

See also Earl of Aboyne, C. M. T. Smith-Ryland.

CRASTON, Rev. Canon Richard Colin; Vicar of St Paul with Emmanuel, Bolton, since 1954; Hon. Canon, Manchester Cathedral, since 1968; Area Dean of Bolton, since 1972; Chaplain to the Queen, since 1985; *b* 31 Dec. 1922; *s* of Albert Edward Craston and Ethel Craston; *m* 1948, Ruth Taggart; one *s* one *d*. *Educ:* Preston Grammar Sch.; Univ. of Bristol (BA Hons); Univ. of London (BD Hons); Tyndale Hall, Bristol. Served War, RN, 1941–46. Ordained 1951; Curate, St Nicholas, Durham, 1951–54. Chm., House of Clergy, Dio. of Manchester, 1982–; Member: Gen. Synod, 1970– (Mem., Standing Cttee, 1975–); Anglican Consultative Council, 1981– (Mem., Standing Cttee, 1981–, Vice-Chm., 1986–); Crown Appts Commn, 1982–. *Publications:* contrib. Anvil, and Modern Churchman. *Recreation:* football and cricket spectating. *Address:* St Paul's Vicarage, 174 Chorley New Road, Bolton BL1 4PF. *T:* Bolton 42303. *Club:* Union Jack.

CRATHORNE, 2nd Baron *cr* 1959; **Charles James Dugdale;** Bt 1945; DL; consultant and lecturer in Fine Art; Marketing Director, Blakeney Hotels Ltd, since 1981; *b* 12 Sept. 1939; *s* of 1st Baron Crathorne, PC, TD, and Nancy, OBE (*d* 1969), *d* of Sir Charles Tennant, 1st Bt; *S* father, 1977; *m* 1970, Sylvia Mary, *yr d* of Brig. Arthur Herbert Montgomery, OBE, TD; one *s* two *d*. *Educ:* Eton College; Trinity Coll., Cambridge. MA Cantab (Fine Arts). Impressionist and Modern Painting Dept, Sotheby & Co., 1963–66; Assistant to the President, Parke-Bernet, New York, 1966–69; James Dugdale & Associates, London, Independent Fine Art Consultancy Service, 1969–; James Crathorne & Associates, 1980–. Director: Radio Tees, 1975–; Queen Margarets Sch. York Ltd, 1986. Member: Productions Cttee, Georgian Theatre Royal, Richmond, Yorks, 1969; Exec. Cttee, Georgian Gp, 1985; Cttee of Honour, Pevsner Meml Trust, 1986; Pres., Cleveland Assoc., NT, 1982. Member: Works of Art Sub-Cttee, H of L, 1983; Editorial Bd, House Magazine, 1983; Hon. Sec., All-Party Parly Arts and Heritage Gp, 1981. Trustee, Captain Cook Trust, 1978. Mem., Standing Council of Baronetage, 1978. Annual lecture tours to America, 1970–; lecture series, Metropolitan Mus., NY, 1981. Member: Council, RSA, 1983–; Ct, Univ. of Leeds, 1985–. FRSA 1972. DL Cleveland, 1983. *Exhibition:* Photographs, Middlesbrough Art Gall., 1980. *Publications:* Edouard Vuillard, 1967; (co-author) Tennant's Stalk, 1973; contribs to Apollo and The Connoisseur. *Recreations:* photography, travel, collecting, shooting, fishing. *Heir:* *s* Hon. Thomas Arthur John Dugdale, *b* 30 Sept. 1977. *Address:* Crathorne House, Yarm, Cleveland TS15 0AT. *T:* Stokesley 700431; 52 Lower Sloane Street, SW1W 8BS. *T:* 01–730 9131.

CRAUFURD, Sir Robert (James), 9th Bt *cr* 1781; Member of the London Stock Exchange; *b* 18 March 1937; *s* of Sir James Gregan Craufurd, 8th Bt and of Ruth Marjorie, *d* of Frederic Corder; *S* father, 1970; *m* 1964, Catherine Penelope, *yr d* of late Captain Horatio Westmacott, Torquay; three *d*. *Educ:* Harrow; University College, Oxford. Elected Member of the London Stock Exchange, 1969. Associated with Capel-Cure Myers. *Address:* 7 Waldemar Avenue, SW6 5LB.

CRAVEN, family name of **Earl of Craven.**

CRAVEN, 8th Earl of, *cr* 1801; **Simon George Craven;** Baron Craven, 1665; Viscount Uffington, 1801; *b* 16 Sept. 1961; *s* of 6th Earl of Craven and of Elizabeth (*née* Johnstone-Douglas); *S* brother, 1983. *Educ:* Douai. *Recreation:* sailing. *Heir:* *cousin* Rupert José Evelyn Craven, Lt-Comdr RN [*b* 22 March 1926; *m* 1955, Margaret Campbell (*d* 1985), *d* of Alexander Smith, MBE]. *Address:* Peelings Manor, near Pevensey, Sussex BN24 5AP. *Club:* Royal Ocean Racing.

CRAVEN, Archdeacon of; *see* Smith, Ven. B. A.

CRAVEN, Air Marshal Sir Robert Edward, KBE 1970 (OBE 1954); CB 1966; DFC 1940; *b* 16 Jan. 1916; *s* of Gerald Craven, Port Elizabeth, S Africa, and Edith Craven, York; *m* 1940, Joan Peters; one *s* one *d*. *Educ:* Scarborough Coll. MN, 1932–37; Pilot Officer, RAF, 1937; 201, 210, 228 Sqdns, 1937–41; RAF Staff Coll., 1942; Staff Appts: Coastal Command, 1942 (despatches thrice); Directing Staff, RAF Staff Coll., 1944; HQ, Mediterranean and Middle East, Cairo, 1945; CO Eastleigh, Kenya, 1946; RN Staff Coll., 1948; Directing Staff, Joint Services Staff Coll., 1949; Standing Group, NATO Washington, 1951; RAF St Eval, 1954; Directing Staff, RAF Staff Coll., 1957; Group Capt. 1957; CO RAF Lyneham, 1959; Director, Personal Services, RAF, 1961; Air Cdre 1961; Air Officer Admin., Transport Comd, 1964; Air Vice-Marshal, 1965; SASO, Flying Training Comd, 1967–68, Training Comd, 1968–69; Commander, Maritime Air Forces, 1969–72, retired. Order of Menelik (Ethiopia), 1955. *Recreations:* water fowl breeding, antique furniture restoration and reproduction. *Address:* Letcombe House, Letcombe Regis, Oxon. *Club:* Royal Air Force.

CRAWFORD, 29th Earl of, *cr* 1398, **AND BALCARRES,** 12th Earl of, *cr* 1651; **Robert Alexander Lindsay,** PC 1972; Lord Lindsay of Crawford, before 1143; Lord Lindsay of Balcarres, 1633; Lord Balniel, 1651; Baron Wigan (UK), 1826; Baron Balniel (Life Peer), 1974; Premier Earl of Scotland; Head of House of Lindsay; DL; First Crown Estate Commissioner, 1980–85; *b* 5 March 1927; *er s* of 28th Earl of Crawford and 11th of Balcarres, KT, GBE, and of Mary, 3rd *d* of late Lord Richard Cavendish, PC, CB, CMG; *S* father, 1975; *m* 1949, Ruth Beatrice, *d* of Leo Meyer-Bechtler, Zürich; two *s* two *d*. *Educ:* Eton; Trinity College, Cambridge. Served with Grenadier Guards, 1945–49. MP (C) Hertford, 1955–74, Welwyn and Hatfield, Feb.-Sept. 1974; Parliamentary Private Secretary: to Financial Secretary of Treasury, 1955–57; to Minister of Housing and Local Government, 1957–60; Opposition front-bench spokesman on health and social security, 1967–70; Minister of State for Defence, 1970–72; Minister of State for Foreign and Commonwealth Affairs, 1972–74. Chm., Lombard North Central Bank, 1976–80; Director: Nat. Westminster Bank, 1975–; Scottish American Investment Co., 1978–; a Vice-Chm., Sun Alliance & London Insurance Gp, 1975–. President, Rural District Councils Assoc., 1959–65; Chairman: National Association for Mental Health, 1963–70; Historic Buildings Council for Scotland, 1976–83; Royal Commn on Ancient and Historical Monuments of Scotland, 1985–. DL Fife. *Heir:* *s* Lord Balniel, *qv*. *Address:* Balcarres, Colinsburgh, Fife KY9 1HL.

CRAWFORD, Douglas; *see* Crawford, G. D.

CRAWFORD, Prof. Sir Frederick (William), Kt 1986; FEng 1985; Vice-Chancellor, Aston University, since 1980; *b* 28 July 1931; *s* of William and Victoria Maud Crawford; *m* 1963, Béatrice Madeleine Jacqueline Hutter, LèsL, MA, PhD, Paris; one *s* one *d*. *Educ:* George Dixon Grammar Sch., Birmingham; Univ. of London (BSc Eng (1st cl. hons), MSc, DSc); Univ. of Liverpool (DipEd, PhD, DEng). Pres., Guild of Undergraduates, 1955–56; Mem. Court, 1955–62 and 1981–; Treas., NUS, 1957–59; Winner, NUS-Observer Fifth Nat. Student Debating Tourn., 1958. ACT Birmingham 1952; FIEE 1965; FIEEE 1972; FInstP 1964; FAPS 1965; FIMA 1978. Research Trainee, J. Lucas Ltd, 1948–52; Scientist, NCB Mining Res. Estabt, 1956–57; Sen. Lectr in Elec. Engrg, CAT Birmingham, 1958–59; Stanford University, California, 1959–82: Res. Associate, W. W.

Hansen Labs of Physics, 1959–64; Institute for Plasma Research: Prof. (Research), 1964–67; Associate Prof., 1967–69; Prof., 1969–82; Consulting Prof., 1983–84; Chm., 1974–80; Dir, Centre for Interdisciplinary Res. and Associate Dean of Graduate Studies, 1973–77. Vis. Scientist, French Atomic Energy Commn, and Cons. to Comp. Française Thomson-Houston, 1961–62; Vis. Professor: Japan, 1969; Univ. of Paris, 1971; Australia, 1972; Mathematical Inst., Oxford Univ., also Vis. Fellow, St Catherine's Coll., Oxford, 1977–78. Union Radio-Scientifique Internationale: Member: US Nat. Cttee, 1975–81; UK Nat. Cttee, 1980–84; Commn H (Waves in Plasmas): US Chm., 1975–78; Internat. Chm., 1978–81; UK Rep., 1982–84; Chm. Internat. Sci. Cttee, Internat. Conf. on Phenomena in Ionised Gases, 1979–81; Dir, Sigma Xi, 1976–78; Mem. Council, Amer. Assoc. of Univ. Profs, 1980–82; Univ. Space Research Association: Member: Council, 1973–81 (Chm. 1977–78); Bd of Trustees, 1975–81 (Chm. 1976–77); Mem. numerous cttees on Space Shuttle, NASA, 1972–80. Director: Aston Technical Management and Planning Services, 1980–; Birmingham Technology Ltd, 1982–; West Midlands Technology Transfer Centre, 1985–. Member: City of Birmingham Educn Cttee, 1980–; US-UK Educnl Commn, 1981–84; Ct, Birmingham Univ., 1980–85; Chm., Birmingham Civic Soc., 1983–. Vice-Pres., Birmingham Br. E-SU, 1980–. Patron, Midlands Centre, Royal TV Soc., 1980–. Mem. Editorial Board: Jl of Applied Phys. and Appl. Phys. Letters, 1976–78; Oxford Univ. Press Engrg Science Series, 1979–. *Publications:* numerous papers on plasma physics in sci. books and jls. *Address:* Vice-Chancellor's Office, Aston University, Birmingham B4 7ET. *T:* 021–359 3611. *Club:* Athenæum.

CRAWFORD, (George) Douglas; Director, Polecon Group of Cos, since 1970; *b* 1 Nov. 1939; *s* of Robert and Helen Crawford; *m* 1964, Joan Burnie; one *s* one *d*. *Educ:* Glasgow Academy; St Catharine's Coll., Cambridge (MA). Features Editor, Business, 1961–63; Industrial Corresp., Glasgow Herald, 1963–66; Editor, Scotland Magazine, 1966–70. MP (SNP) Perth and East Perthshire, Oct. 1974–1979; contested (SNP) Perth and Kinross, 1983. *Recreations:* hill-walking, playing piano and clavichord, watching cricket. *Address:* 44 Park Place, Stirling FK7 9JR. *Clubs:* Savile; Scottish Arts, Press (Edinburgh).

CRAWFORD, Hon. Sir George (Hunter), Kt 1972; Judge of the Supreme Court of Tasmania 1958–81; *b* 12 Dec. 1911; *s* of Frederick Charles Crawford and Ruby Priscilla (*née* Simpson); *m* 1st, 1936, Helen Zoë (*d* 1976), *d* of Dr Bruce Arnold Anderson; two *s* one *d*; 2nd, 1979, Nancy Jean Garrott (*née* Findlay). *Educ:* East Launceston State Sch.; Launceston Church Grammar Sch.; Univ. of Tasmania (LLB). Barrister and Solicitor, 1934–58; Mem. Cttee, Northern Law Society, 1946–58 (Vice-Pres. 1957–58). Served (including War): AMF, 1929–40; AIF, 1940–44, Lt-Col. Councillor, Northern Br., Royal Soc. of Tasmania, 1954–72 (Chm., 1957–58 and 1966–68); Mem. Cttee, Tasmanian Historical Res. Assoc., 1960–62 (Chm., 1961–62); Mem. Bd, Launceston Church Grammar Sch., 1946–71 (Chm., 1958–65); Mem. Bd, Cradle Mountain-Lake St Clair Nat. Park; Mem. Adv. Cttee, Cradle Mountain, 1956–71; Pres., N Tasmania Branch, Roy. Commonwealth Soc., 1974–76. Col Comdt, Royal Regt of Australian Artillery, in Tasmania Command, 1972–78. *Recreations:* music, historical research. *Address:* 10A Wentworth Street, Launceston, Tasmania 7250, Australia. *T:* Launceston 311910. *Club:* Launceston (Launceston).

CRAWFORD, Maj.-Gen. George Oswald, CB 1956; CBE 1944; Director of Ordnance Services, War Office, 1958–61; *b* 12 Nov. 1902; *s* of late Col Arthur Gosset Crawford, Nailsworth, Glos; *m* Sophie Cecilia (*d* 1974), *d* of J. C. Yorke, JP, Langton, Dwrbach, Pembs; two *s* one *d*; *m* 1974, Ella Brown. *Educ:* Bradfield; RMC. 2nd Lieut Glos Regt, 1922; transf. RAOC 1928. Served CMF, 1942–45; Lieut-Col 1942; Brig. 1943; Dep. Dir of Ordnance Services, Western Command, 1947–51; DDOS, Southern Command, 1951–55; ADC to the Queen, 1954–55; Maj.-Gen. 1955; Inspector, Royal Army Ordnance Corps, 1955–57; Commandant Mechanical Transport Organisation, Chilwell, 1957–58; Col Comdt RAOC, 1960–66. *Address:* Gwyers, Dinton, Wilts.

See also Wilson Stephens.

CRAWFORD, John Michael; Chief Education Officer, Birmingham, since 1977; *b* 6 Dec. 1938; *s* of James and Emily Crawford; *m* 1962, Geraldine Kay Weaver; two *d*. *Educ:* Ipswich Sch.; University Coll., London (BA); Fitzwilliam House, Cambridge. Asst Master, Merchant Taylor's, Crosby, 1961–63; Admin. Asst, E Suffolk CC, 1963–66; Sen. Admin. Asst, Lancs CC, 1966–68; Asst Educn Officer, W Riding CC, 1968–73; Dep. Educn Officer, Birmingham, 1973–77. *Address:* July Green, Snuff Mill Walk, Bewdley, Worcs. *T:* Bewdley 400174.

CRAWFORD, Michael; actor since 1955; *b* 19 Jan. 1942. *Educ:* St Michael's Coll., Bexley; Oakfield Sch., Dulwich. In orig. prodn of Britten's Noyes Fludde and of Let's Make an Opera; *stage appearances include:* Come Blow Your Horn, Prince of Wales, 1961; Travelling Light, 1965; The Anniversary, 1966; No Sex Please, We're British, Strand, 1971; Billy, Drury Lane, 1974; Same Time, Next Year, Prince of Wales, 1976; Flowers for Algernon, Queen's, 1979; Barnum, Palladium, 1981, 1983, Victoria Palace, 1985–86. *Films include:* Soap Box Derby; Blow Your Own Trumpet; Two Left Feet; The War Lover; Two Living, One Dead; The Knack, 1964; A Funny Thing Happened on the Way to the Forum, 1965; The Jokers, How I Won the War, 1966; Hello Dolly, 1968; The Games, 1969; Hello and Goodbye, 1970; Alice in Wonderland, 1972; The Condorman, 1980. Numerous radio broadcasts and TV appearances; *TV series include:* Some Mothers Do 'Ave 'Em; Chalk and Cheese. *Address:* c/o Duncan Heath Associates Ltd, Paramount House, 162/170 Wardour Street, W1. *T:* 01–439 1471.

CRAWFORD, Prof. Michael Hewson, FBA 1980; Professor of Ancient History, University College London, since 1986; *b* 7 Dec. 1939; *s* of Brian Hewson Crawford and Margarethe Bettina Crawford. *Educ:* St Paul's School; Oriel College, Oxford (BA, MA). Scholar, British School at Rome, 1962–64; Jane Eliza Procter Visiting Fellow, Princeton Univ., 1964–65; Cambridge University: Research Fellow, Christ's Coll., 1964–69; Lectr, 1969–86. Visiting Professor: Univ. of Pavia, 1983; Ecole Normale Supérieure, Paris, 1984; Univ. of Padua, 1986. Jt Dir, Excavations of Fregellae, 1980–86. Chm., JACT Ancient History Cttee, 1978–84; Vice-Pres., Roman Soc., 1981–. Editor: Papers of the British Sch. at Rome, 1975–79; Jl of Roman Studies, 1980–84. *Publications:* Roman Republican Coin Hoards, 1969; Roman Republican Coinage, 1974; The Roman Republic, 1978; La Moneta in Grecia e a Roma, 1981; (with D. Whitehead) Archaic and Classical Greece, 1982; Sources for Ancient History, 1983; Coinage and Money under the Roman Republic, 1985; (with M. Beard) Rome in the Late Republic, 1985; L'impero romano e la struttura economica e sociale delle province, 1986; contribs to Annales, Economic History Rev., Jl of Roman Studies, etc. *Address:* University College, Gower Street, WC1E 6BT.

CRAWFORD, Peter John, QC 1976; a Recorder of the Crown Court, since 1974; *b* 23 June 1930; *s* of William Gordon Robertson and Doris Victoria Robertson (*née* Mann, subseq. Crawford); *m* 1st, 1955, Jocelyn Lavender; two *s* two *d*; 2nd, 1979, Ann Allen Travis. *Educ:* Berkhamsted Sch.; Brasenose Coll., Oxford (MA). Called to Bar, Lincoln's Inn, 1953; Bencher, 1985. Mem., Paddington Borough Council, 1962–65; Chm., W London Family Service Unit, 1972–79; Mem., Family Service Units Nat. Council, 1975–81. *Recreation:* sailing. *Address:* 13 King's Bench Walk, Temple, EC4Y 7EN. *T:* 01–353 7204.

CRAWFORD, Robert Gammie; Chairman, Silver Navigation Ltd and subsidiary companies, since 1974; *b* 20 March 1924; *s* of William and Janet Beveridge Crawford; *m* 1947, Rita Veiss; one *d*. *Educ:* Robert Gordon's Coll., Aberdeen. Solicitor of the Supreme Court, England. Navigator, RAF, 1942–47. Practised as Solicitor, 1950–73, Partner, Ince and Co. (Internat. Shipping Lawyers), Chairman, 1974–: Shipping Industrial Holdings Ltd; Silver Line Ltd; Chm., Highland and Island Airports Ltd, 1986–; Director: UK Freight Demurrage and Defence Assoc. Ltd, 1976–; Donner Underwriting Agencies Ltd, 1976–; Newman Industries PLC, 1983–; Tozer Kemsley and Millbourn (Holdings), 1984–. Mem., Lloyd's, 1975. Member: Bd, CAA, 1984–; Bd, Lloyd's Register of Shipping, 1982–; Bd, PLA, 1985– (Vice Chm., 1986–). Chairman: UK War Risk Club, 1982– (Dir, 1980–); UK Protection & Indemnity Club, 1983–. Governor, Robert Gordon's Coll., Aberdeen. *Recreations:* shooting, golf, reading, conversation. *Address:* 24 Ferncroft Avenue, NW3 7PH. *T:* 01–435 0938; West Mains of Auchenhove, Lumphanan, Aberdeenshire. *T:* Lumphanan 667. *Clubs:* Carlton, City of London.

CRAWFORD, (Robert) Norman, CBE 1973; Chairman, R. N. Crawford & Co., Business Advisors, since 1968; Director, William Clark & Sons, since 1983 (Chief Executive, 1983–85); *b* 14 June 1923; *s* of Wm Crawford and Annie Catherine (*née* Rexter); *m* 1948, Jean Marie Patricia (*née* Carson); one *s* five *d*. *Educ:* Foyle Coll., Londonderry; Queen's Univ., Belfast (BComSc). FCA. Sec./Accountant, John McNeill Ltd, 1948–60; Dep. Man. Dir, McNeill Group Ltd, 1960–66, Man. Dir 1966–68; Chm., N Ireland Transport Holding Co., 1968–75; Divisional Hd, NI Develt Agency, 1976–82. Pres., N Ireland Chamber of Commerce and Industry, 1966–67; Chairman: N Ireland Regional Bd, BIM, 1966–69; Nature Reserves Cttee, 1967–85; NI Outward Bound Assoc., 1969–76 (Pres., 1983–); Open Door Housing Assoc., 1979–84; Retirement Assoc. of NI, 1982–83. Member Senate, Queen's University, Belfast (Pres., Queen's Univ. Assoc., 1982–83); Pres., Foyle Coll. Old Boys' Assoc., 1981–82. Mem. Council, Ulster Trust for Nature Conservation, 1979–81. FRSA. *Address:* 4 Fort Road, Helens Bay, Bangor, Co. Down BT19 1LD. *T:* Helens Bay 853661. *Clubs:* Ulster Reform (Belfast); Kildare Street and University (Dublin).

CRAWFORD, Sir (Robert) Stewart, GCMG 1973 (KCMG 1966; CMG 1951); CVO 1955; HM Diplomatic Service, retired; *b* 27 Aug. 1913; *s* of late Sir William Crawford, KBE, head of W. S. Crawford Ltd, advertising agents; *m* 1938, Mary Katharine, *d* of late Eric Corbett, Gorse Hill, Witley, Surrey; three *s* one *d* (and one *s* decd). *Educ:* Gresham's Sch., Holt, Oriel Coll., Oxford. Home Civil Service (Air Ministry), 1936; Private Sec. to Chief of Air Staff, 1940–46; Asst Sec., Control Office for Germany and Austria, 1946; Foreign Office, 1947; Counsellor, British Embassy, Oslo, 1954–56; Counsellor, later Minister, British Embassy, Baghdad, 1957–59; Dep. UK Delegate to OEEC Paris, 1959–60; Asst Under Sec., Foreign Office, 1961–65; Political Resident, Persian Gulf, 1966–70; Dep. Under-Sec. of State, FCO, 1970–73. Chm., Cttee on Broadcasting Coverage, 1973–74; Mem., BBC Gen. Adv. Council, 1976–84; Chm., Broadcasters' Audience Res. Bd, 1980–. *Recreations:* opera, bookbinding. *Address:* 19 Adam Court, Bell Street, Henley-on-Thames, Oxon. *T:* Henley 574702. *Club:* United Oxford & Cambridge University.

CRAWFORD, Robert William Kenneth; Deputy Director, Imperial War Museum, since 1982; *b* 3 July 1945; *s* of late Hugh Merrall Crawford, FCA, and Mary Crawford (*née* Percival); *m* 1975, Vivienne Sylvia Polakowski; one *d* *Educ:* Culford Sch.; Pembroke Coll., Oxford (Cleobury Schol.; BA). Joined Imperial War Museum as Research Asst, 1968: Head of Research and Information Office, 1971–; Keeper, Dept of Photographs, 1975–83; Asst Director, 1979–82. *Address:* c/o Imperial War Museum, Lambeth Road, SE1 6HZ. *T:* 01–735 8922.

CRAWFORD, Prof. Sir Theodore, (Sir Theo), Kt 1973; Professor of Pathology in the University of London, 1948–77, Professor Emeritus, 1977; Director of Pathological Services, St George's Hospital and Medical School, 1946–77; *b* 23 Dec. 1911; *s* of late Theodore Crawford and late Sarah Mansfield; *m* 1st, 1938, Margaret Donald Green, MD (*d* 1973); two *s* three *d*; 2nd, 1974, Priscilla Leathley Chater. *Educ:* St Peter's Sch., York; Glasgow Academy; Glasgow Univ. BSc, 1932; MB, ChB, 1935; Hon. LLD, 1979. FRFPS, 1938; MD 1941; Bellahouston Gold Medal (Glasgow Univ.), 1941; MRCP 1960; FRCPGlas 1962; FRCPath 1963, FRCP 1964; FRCPA 1972; Hall Tutorial and Research Fellow, 1936–38. Asst Physician, Glasgow, Royal Hosp. for Sick Children, 1936–38; Lecturer in Pathology (Glasgow Univ.), 1939–46. Served War of 1939–45, Major RAMC, 1941–45. Mem. of the Medical Research Council, 1960–64 (and Mem. Cell Board, 1974–78); Registrar, Coll. of Pathologists, 1963–68; Consultant Adviser in Pathology to Dept of Health and Social Security and Chm. of its Central Pathology Cttee, 1969–78. Royal Society of Medicine (Pres. Section of Pathology, 1961–62). Pres., Royal Coll. of Pathologists, 1969–72 (Vice-Pres., 1968–69); Mem., Pathological Soc. of Great Britain, etc.; Chm., Scientific Cttee, British Empire Cancer Campaign, 1969–78 (Hon. Sec., 1955–67; Hon. Sec. of the Campaign, 1967–70); Vice-Pres., Cancer Res. Campaign, 1979–. Member: Council Epsom Coll., 1949–71; Standing Medical Advisory Cttee, Health Services Council, 1964–69; Cttee on Safety of Medicines, 1969–77 (Vice-Chm., 1976–77); Army Pathology Adv. Cttee, 1970–75; DHSS Cttee on Smoking and Health, 1973–79; Chm., Medical Adv. Gp to The Brewers' Soc., 1982– (Mem., 1972–). *Publications:* (ed) Modern Trends in Pathology, 1967; Pathology of Ischaemic Heart Disease, 1977; scientific papers in Lancet, British Medical Journal, British Journal of Surgery, Archives of Disease in Childhood, British Journal of Opthalmology, Journal of Pathology and Bacteriology, etc. *Recreations:* horticulture, growing trees, walking, music. *Address:* 9 Asher Reeds, Langton Green, Tunbridge Wells, Kent TN3 0AL. *T:* Langton 3341. *Club:* Sloane.

CRAWFORD, Vice-Adm. Sir William (Godfrey), KBE 1961; CB 1958; DSC 1941; *b* 14 Sept. 1907; *s* of late H. E. V. Crawford, Wyld Court, Axminster, and late Mrs M. E. Crawford; *m* 1939, Mary Felicity Rosa, *d* of late Sir Philip Williams, 2nd Bt; three *s* one *d*. *Educ:* RN Coll., Dartmouth. Lieut RN, 1929; specialised in gunnery, 1932; Lieut-Comdr, 1937; Gunnery Officer, HMS Rodney, 1940–42; Comdr Dec. 1941; Exec. Officer, HMS Venerable, 1944–46; Capt. 1947; in comd HMS Pelican and 2nd Frigate Flotilla, Med., 1948–49; Dep.-Dir RN Staff Coll., 1950–52; in comd HMS Devonshire, 1952–53; in comd RN Coll., Dartmouth, 1953–56; Rear-Adm. 1956; Imperial Defence Coll., 1956–58; Flag Officer, Sea Training, 1958–60; Vice-Adm. 1959; Comdr British Navy Staff and Naval Attaché Washington, 1960–62; retired list, 1963. Dir, Overseas Offices, BTA, 1964–72. *Recreations:* sailing, fishing. *Address:* Broadlands, Whitchurch Canonicorum, Bridport, Dorset DT6 6RJ. *T:* Chideock 89591. *Clubs:* Naval and Military; Cruising.

CRAWFORD, William Hamilton Raymund, QC 1980; a Recorder of the Crown Court, since 1979; *b* 10 Nov. 1936; *s* of Col Mervyn Crawford, DSO, DL, JP, and Martha Hamilton Crawford; *m* 1965, Marilyn Jean Colville; one *s* two *d*. *Educ:* West Downs, Winchester; Winchester Coll.; Emmanuel Coll., Cambridge (BA). Called to the Bar,

Inner Temple, 1964; Dep. Chm., Agricultural Land Tribunal, 1978. *Recreations:* hill farming, fishing, shooting (shot for GB in Kolapore Match, and for Scotland in Elcho and Twenty Matches on several occasions; mem., Scottish Rifle Team, Commonwealth Games, Jamaica, 1966). *Address:* Dalgonar, Dunscore, Dumfriesshire. *T:* Dunscore 339; Barmoor, Corbridge, Northumberland. *T:* Corbridge 2569. *Clubs:* Naval and Military; Northern Counties (Newcastle).

CRAWFORD-COMPTON, Air Vice-Marshal William Vernon, CB 1965; CBE 1957; DSO 1943, Bar 1945; DFC 1941, Bar, 1942; RAF retired, 1969; *b* 2 March 1915; *s* of William Gilbert Crawford-Compton; *m* 1st, 1949, Chloe Clifford-Brown (marr. diss. 1978); two *d*; 2nd, 1978, Dolores Perle Goodhew, widow. *Educ:* New Plymouth High Sch., New Zealand. Joined RAF, 1939; served War of 1939–45 (DFC and Bar, DSO and Bar); 11 Group and 2nd TAF Group Capt., 1955; SASO, 11 (Fighter) Group; Student, Imperial Defence Coll., 1961; Air Officer in Charge of Administration, Near East Air Force, 1962–63; SASO 1963–66. Air Vice-Marshal, 1963. Legion of Honour (France); Croix de Guerre (France); Silver Star (USA). *Recreations:* golf, tennis, fishing. *Address:* Mother Friday's House, Newtown, Alderney, CI. *T:* Alderney 2578.

CRAWLEY, Aidan Merivale, MBE; Chairman, London Weekend Television, 1967–71, President 1971–73; *b* 10 April 1908; *s* of late Canon A. S. Crawley; *m* 1945, Virginia Cowles, OBE (*d* 1983); two *s* one *d*. *Educ:* Harrow; Oxford. Journalist, 1930–36; Educational Film Producer, 1936–39. AAF, 601 Sqdn, 1936–40; Asst Air Attaché, Ankara, Belgrade (resident Sofia), May 1940–March 1941; joined 73 (F) Sqdn, Egypt; shot down July 1941; prisoner until May 1945. MP (Lab) Buckingham Div. of Bucks, 1945–51; Parliamentary Private Sec. to successive Secs of State for the Colonies, 1945 and 1946–47; Parliamentary Under-Sec. of State for Air, 1950–51; resigned from the Labour Party, 1957; MP (C) West Derbyshire, 1962–68; Editor-in-Chief, Independent Television News Ltd, 1955–56; making television documentaries for BBC, 1956–60; Mem. Monckton Commission on Federation of Rhodesia and Nyasaland, 1960. Pres., MCC, 1973. *Publications:* Escape from Germany, 1956; De Gaulle: A Biography, 1969; The Rise of Western Germany 1945–72, 1973; Dial 200–200, 1980. *Recreation:* cricket; Co-Founder, Haig Nat. Village Cricket Championship, 1971. *Address:* 19 Chester Square, SW1. *T:* 01–730 3030. *Clubs:* White's, Queen's; MCC.

CRAWLEY, Charles William; Hon. Fellow of Trinity Hall, 1971; University Lecturer in History, 1931–66; Vice-Master of Trinity Hall, Cambridge, 1950–66, Emeritus Fellow, 1966; *b* 1 April 1899; *s* of Charles Crawley, barrister of Lincoln's Inn, and Augusta, *d* of Rt Rev. Samuel Butcher, Bishop of Meath; *m* 1930, Kathleen Elizabeth (*d* 1982), *d* of Lieut-Col H. G. Leahy, OBE, RA; four *s* one *d*. *Educ:* Winchester (Scholar); Trinity Coll., Cambridge (Scholar). Fellow of Trinity Hall, 1924–66. Asst Tutor, 1927, Acting Senior Tutor, 1940, Senior Tutor, 1946–58. *Publications:* The Question of Greek Independence, 1821–1833, 1930, repr. 1973; (ed) New Cambridge Modern History, Vol. IX, 1965; John Capodistrias: unpublished documents, 1970; Trinity Hall: the history of a Cambridge College, 1350–1975, 1976. *Address:* 1 Madingley Road, Cambridge. *T:* 352849.

See also J. M. Crawley.

CRAWLEY, Mrs Christine Mary; Member (Lab) Birmingham East, European Parliament, since 1984; Vice-Chairman, Women's Rights Committee; *b* 1 Jan. 1950; *m*; three *c* (incl. twins). *Educ:* Notre Dame Catholic Secondary Girls' School, Plymouth; Digby Stuart Training College, Roehampton. Formerly teacher; S Oxfordshire District Council; contested (Lab) Staffordshire SE, gen. election, 1983. *Address:* 26 Glascote Road, Tamworth, Staffs B77 2AA. *T:* Tamworth 58855.

CRAWLEY, Desmond John Chetwode, CMG 1964; CVO 1961; HM Diplomatic Service, retired; *b* 2 June 1917; *s* of late Lieutenant-Colonel C. G. C. Crawley, OBE and late Agnes Luke; *m* 1945, Daphne Lesley, *y d* of late Sir Vere Mockett, MBE, and late Ethel Norah Gaddum Tomkinson; two *s* one *d*. *Educ:* King's Sch., Ely; Queen's Coll., Oxford. Entered Indian Civil Service, serving in Madras Presidency, 1939; entered Indian Political Service, serving in Baluchistan, 1946; entered Commonwealth Relations Office, 1947, and served in London, Calcutta, and on loan to the Foreign Office in Washington; Principal Private Secretary to Sec. of State for Commonwealth Relations, 1952–53; British Dep. High Commissioner in Lahore, Pakistan, 1958–61; Imperial Defence Coll., 1962; British High Commissioner in Sierra Leone, 1963–66; Ambassador to Bulgaria, 1966–70; Minister to Holy See, 1970–75. Coronation Medal, 1953. Knight Grand Cross, Order of St Gregory the Great, 1973. *Address:* 35 Chartfield Avenue, SW15. *T:* 01–788 9529. *Club:* United Oxford & Cambridge University.

CRAWLEY, Frederick William, FIB; Deputy Chief Executive, since 1985, Director, since 1984, Lloyds Bank; Chairman, Black Horse Agencies, since 1985; *b* 10 June 1926; *s* of William Clement Crawley and Elsie Florence Crawley; *m* 1951, Ruth Eva Jungman; two *d*. Joined Lloyds Bank, 1942; Chief Accountant, 1969–72; Asst Chief Gen. Man., 1977–78; Dep. Chief Gen. Man., 1978–82; Chief Exec., Lloyds Bank, Calif, 1982–83; Dep. Chief Gen. Man., 1983–84, Chief Gen. Man., 1984–85, Lloyds Bank plc. Mem., F&GP Cttee, RAF Benevolent Fund, 1985–. FIB 1971. *Recreations:* aviation, shooting, photography. *Address:* 4 The Hexagon, Fitzroy Park, N6 6HR. *T:* 01–341 2279. *Club:* Overseas Bankers.

CRAWLEY, John Cecil, CBE 1972 (MBE 1944); Chairman of Trustees of Visnews, 1976–86; *b* 1909; *s* of John and Kathleen Crawley; *m* 1933, Constance Mary Griffiths; two *d*. *Educ:* William Ellis Sch. War Service, Army, 1939–45. Journalism: Reynolds, 1927; Central News Agency, 1928; National Press Agency, 1929; Press Secretaries, 1933; BBC: Sub-Editor, 1945; Foreign Correspondent, New York, 1959–63; Foreign News Editor, 1963–67; Editor of News and Current Affairs, 1967–71; Chief Asst to Dir-Gen., BBC, 1971–75. *Recreations:* walking, bird-watching. *Address:* 157 Clarence Gate Gardens, NW1. *T:* 01–723 6876.

CRAWLEY, John Maurice; Under Secretary (Principal Finance Officer and Director of Manpower), Inland Revenue; *b* 27 Sept. 1933; *s* of Charles William Crawley, *qv*; *m* 1978, Jane Meadows Rendel; three *s*. *Educ:* Rugby Sch.; New Coll., Oxford (MA). Assistant Principal, Inland Revenue, 1959; Principal, 1963; Asst Secretary, 1969; Under Sec., 1979; seconded to Cabinet Office (Central Policy Review Staff), 1973–76 and 1979–81. *Recreations:* music, walking. *Address:* 93 Castelnau, SW13.

CRAWLEY-BOEVEY, Sir Thomas (Michael Blake), 8th Bt *cr* 1784; *b* 29 Sept. 1928; *er s* of Sir Launcelot Valentine Hyde Crawley-Boevey, 7th Bt, and Elizabeth Goodeth (*d* 1976), *d* of Herbert d'Auvergne Innes, late Indian Police; *S* father, 1968; *m* 1957, Laura Coelingh (*d* 1979); two *s*. *Educ:* Wellington Coll.; St John's Coll., Cambridge (BA 1952, MA 1956). 2nd Lieut, Durham Light Infantry, 1948. With Shipping Agents, 1952–61; with Consumers' Association, 1961–; Editor: Money Which?, 1968–76; Which?, 1976–82; Editor-in-Chief, Which? magazines, 1980–82. *Heir: er s* Thomas Hyde Crawley-Boevey, *b* 26 June 1958. *Address:* Trebanau, Cilycwm, Llandovery, Dyfed SA20 0HP. *T:* Llandovery 20496.

CRAWSHAW, 4th Baron, *cr* 1892; **William Michael Clifton Brooks;** Bt *cr* 1891; *b* 25 March 1933; *s* of 3rd Baron and Sheila (*d* 1964), *o d* of late Lieut-Col P. R. Clifton, CMG, DSO; *S* father, 1946. *Educ:* Eton; Christ Church, Oxford. Jt Master, Oxford Univ. Drag Hounds, 1952–53. Treasurer, Loughborough Div. Conservative Assoc., 1954–58; County Commissioner, Leics Boy Scouts, 1958–. Pres., Leics Assoc. of the Disabled; Chm., Quorn Hunt Cttee, 1971–. Lord of the Manor of Long Whatton. Patron of the Living of Shepshed. *Heir: b* Hon. David Gerald Brooks [*b* 14 Sept. 1934; *m* 1970, Belinda Mary, *d* of George Burgess, Melbourne, and of Mrs J. P. Allen, Coleman's Hatch, Sussex; two *d*. *Educ:* Eton; Royal Agricultural College, Cirencester]. *Address:* Whatton, Loughborough, Leics. *TA:* Kegworth. *T:* Hathern 225. *Clubs:* Boodle's, MCC.

CRAWSHAW, Sir (Edward) Daniel (Weston), Kt 1964; QC (Aden) 1949; *b* 10 Sept. 1903; British; *m* 1942, Rosemary Treffry; one *s* two *d* (and one *s* decd). *Educ:* St Bees Sch.; Selwyn Coll., Cambridge. Solicitor, Supreme Court of Judicature, England, 1929; Barrister-at-Law, Gray's Inn, 1946; Solicitor, Northern Rhodesia, 1930–32; Colonial Legal Service, Tanganyika, 1933–39; Zanzibar, 1939–47; Attorney-Gen., Aden, 1947–52; Puisne Judge, Tanganyika, 1952–60; Justice of Appeal, Court of Appeal for Eastern Africa, 1960–65. Commissioner, Foreign Compensation Commission, 1965–75. Brilliant Star of Zanzibar, 1947; Coronation Medal, 1953. *Recreation:* golf. *Address:* 1 Fort Road, Guildford, Surrey. *T:* Guildford 576883. *Clubs:* Royal Over-Seas League; County (Guildford).

CRAWSHAY, Elisabeth Mary Boyd, (Lady Crawshay), CBE 1986; JP, DL; Chairman, Local Government Boundary Commission, Wales, since 1979; Deputy Chief Commissioner, St John's Ambulance Brigade, Wales, 1979–84; *b* 2 July 1927; *d* of Lt-Col Guy Franklin Reynolds, late 9th Lancers, and Katherine Isobel (*née* Macdonell); *m* 1950, Col Sir William (Robert) Crawshay, *qv*. *Educ:* Convent of Sacred Heart, Roehampton; St Anne's Coll., Oxford (MA). Mem., Mental Health Act Commn, 1983–. DL Gwent 1978; JP Abergavenny, 1972, Chm., Juvenile Bench, 1980–, Mem., Borstal Board of Visitors, 1975–84. DJStJ 1970. *Address:* Llanfair Court, Abergavenny, Gwent.

CRAWSHAY, Col Sir William (Robert), Kt 1972; DSO 1945; ERD; TD; Vice Lord-Lieutenant of Gwent, since 1979; *b* 27 May 1920; *o s* of late Captain J. W. L. Crawshay, MC, Caversham Park, Oxon, and late Hon. Mrs. George Egerton, Brussels; *m* 1950, Elisabeth Mary Boyd Reynolds (*see* Lady Crawshay). *Educ:* Eton. Served Royal Welch Fus.(SR), 1939–46; SOE 1944 (DSO, despatches twice); TA, 1947–62, Parachute Regt, Welch Regt, SW Brigade. ADC to HM the Queen, 1966–71. Hon. Colonel: 3rd RRW (V) Bn, 1970–82; Cardiff Univ. OTC, 1977–85. Mem., Arts Council of GB, 1962–74; Chairman: Welsh Arts Council, 1968–74; Council, University Coll. of Cardiff, 1966–; Member: Council and Court, Univ. of Wales, 1967; Welsh Council, 1966–69, 1970–; Council and Court, Nat. Museum of Wales, 1966– (Pres., 1977–82). Pres., Royal British Legion, Wales Area, 1974–. Mem., Crafts Adv. Council, 1974–78. Hon. LLD, Univ. of Wales, 1975. DL Glamorgan, 1964, Monmouthshire, 1970, Gwent, 1974. Chevalier, Légion d'honneur, 1956; Croix de Guerre (France) with Palms twice, 1944, 1945. KStJ (formerly KJStJ) 1969. *Address:* Llanfair Court, Abergavenny, Gwent. *Clubs:* White's; Cardiff and County (Cardiff).

CRAXTON, Antony, CVO 1977 (MVO 1968); freelance television consultant; *b* 23 April 1918; 2nd *s* of late Harold Craxton, OBE, and Essie Craxton; *m* 1944, Anne Sybil Cropper (marr. diss. 1978); one *s* one *d*. *Educ:* St George's Chapel Choir Sch., Windsor; Royal Acad. of Music; Gordonstoun Sch., Scotland. Joined BBC Radio, 1941; Home and Overseas Announcer, 1942–45; joined TV Service as Outside Broadcast Producer, 1951; resp. for coverage of all major Royal occasions, 1953–77, Jubilee Day being 200th broadcast involving the Queen and Royal Family; retd, 1979. Helped pioneer presentation of internat. cricket, rugby and golf in early 50s; covered over 100 orchestral concert relays from many parts of country, 1953–71. Chief Royal Occasions: Queen's 1st Christmas Television Broadcast and Prince Philip's 1st major TV appearance, Round the World in 40 Minutes, 1957; Princess Margaret's Wedding, 1960; Duke of Kent's Wedding, 1961; Princess Alexandra's Wedding, 1963; State Funeral of Sir Winston Churchill, 1965; Investiture of Prince Charles as Prince of Wales, 1969; Lying in State of Duke of Windsor, 1972; Queen's Silver Wedding Celebrations, 1972; Princess Anne's Wedding, 1973; Funeral of Duke of Gloucester, 1974; Funeral of Field-Marshal Montgomery, 1976; Queen's Silver Jubilee Day Celebrations, 1977; 10 State visits abroad and 19 visits by Foreign Heads of State to Britain, 1954–76. News Chronicle Readers' Award for Prince Philip's Round the World Documentary, 1957; Guild of TV Producers' Award for Princess Alexandra's Wedding, 1963; French TV Internat. Award for Investiture of Prince Charles, 1970; BAFTA Award for Jubilee Day (1977), 1978. Silver Jubilee Medal, 1977. *Recreations:* golf, cricket, classical music. *Address:* 14 Kidderpore Avenue, NW3. *Clubs:* MCC, Lord's Taverners, Eccentric.

CREAGH, Maj.-Gen. Sir Kilner Rupert B.; *see* Brazier-Creagh.

CREAMER, Brian; Physician, St Thomas' Hospital, London, since 1959; Senior Lecturer in Medicine, United Medical and Dental Schools (St Thomas's), since 1959; Hon. Consultant in Gastroenterology to the Army, since 1970; *b* 12 April 1926; *s* of late L. G. Creamer and Mrs Creamer, Epsom; *m* 1953, Margaret Holden Rees; two *s* one *d*. *Educ:* Christ's Hosp.; St Thomas' Hosp. MB, BS Hons London, 1948; MD London, 1952; FRCP 1966 (MRCP 1950); Research Asst, Mayo Clinic, Rochester, USA, 1955–56; Dean: St Thomas's Hosp. Med. Sch., 1979–84; UMDS of Guy's and St Thomas's Hosps, 1984–86. Vis. Prof., 1977–78, Hon. Prof. of Medicine, 1978–, Shiraz Univ., Iran. Sir Arthur Hurst Memorial Lectr, 1968; Watson Smith Lectr, RCP, 1971. Mem., SE Thames RHA, 1982–85. Member: British Soc. of Gastroenterology; Assoc. of Physicians of GB and NI; Exec. Subcttee, Univ. Hosps Assoc., 1981–86. Member: Collegiate Council, Univ. of London, 1980–86; Senate, Univ. of London, 1981–86; Council of Almoners, Christ's Hosp., 1986–. *Publications:* (ed) Modern Trends in Gastroenterology, vol. 4, 1970; (ed) The Small Intestine, 1974; contributions to med. jls. *Recreations:* drawing and painting, gardening, and listening to music. *Address:* Vine House, Highfields, East Horsley KT24 5AA. *T:* East Horsley 3320.

CREAN, Hon. Frank; *b* Hamilton, Vic, 28 Feb. 1916; *s* of J. Crean; *m* 1946, Mary, *d* of late A. E. Findlay; three *s*. *Educ:* Hamilton High Sch.; Melbourne High Sch.; Melbourne Univ. BA Hons; BCom. DPA; FASA. Income Tax Assessor, 1934–45. MLA: for Albert Park, Vic, 1945–47; for Prahran, 1949–51; MHR for Melbourne Ports, 1951–77; Mem. Exec., Federal Parly Labour Party, 1956–72, Dep. Leader, 1975–76; Mem., Jt Parly Cttee on Public Accounts, 1952–55; Treasurer, Commonwealth of Australia, 1972–74; Minister for Overseas Trade, 1974–75, also Deputy Prime Minister, 1975. Chm., Council of Adult Educn, 1947–74. Pres., Vict. Br., Aust. Inst. Internat. Affairs, 1983–; Chm., Vict. Br., Freedom from Hunger Campaign, 1979. *Publication:* (with W. J. Byrt) Government and Politics in Australia, 1972, 2nd edn 1982. *Address:* 106 Harold Street, Middle Park, Vic 3206, Australia.

CREASY, Leonard Richard, CB 1972; OBE 1961; CEng, FICE, FIStructE; civil engineer in private practice since 1974; *b* 20 Dec. 1912; *s* of William and Ellen Creasy; *m* 1937, Irene Howard; one *s* one *d*. *Educ:* Wimbledon Technical Coll. BSc(Eng) London. Served War, RE, E Africa, 1944–46. Service in Industry, 1928–34; HM Office of Works, Asst Engr, 1935; Min. of Works, Suptg Engr, 1959; MPBW: Dir, Civil Engrg, 1966; Dir,

Central Services, 1968; Dir of Civil Engrg Develt, Dept of the Environment, 1970–73. Concerned with Inquiries into disasters at Aberfan, Ronan Point and Brent, and with design of Radio Towers, London and Birmingham; Plant House, Royal Botanical Gardens, Edinburgh; Wind Tunnels, Bedford RAE; and other structures. Bronze Medal, Reinforced Concrete Assoc.; Manby and Telford Premiums, Instn Civil Engrs; Pres., Instn Struct. Engrs, 1973 (Bronze Medal and Certif. of Merit of the Instn). *Publications:* Pre-stressed Concrete Cylindrical Tanks, 1961; James Forrest Lecture, 1968; many other papers on civil and structural engrg projects and engrg economics. *Recreations:* music, opera, languages. *Address:* 5 The Oaks, Epsom, Surrey KT18 5HH. *T:* Epsom 22361.

CREDITON, Bishop Suffragan of, since 1984; **Rt. Rev. Peter Everard Coleman;** *b* 28 Aug. 1928; *s* of Geoffrey Everard Coleman and Lilian Coleman; *m* 1960, HSH Princess Elisabeth-Donata Reuss; two *s* two *d. Educ:* Haileybury; King's Coll., London Univ. (LLB, AKC); Bristol Univ. (MLitt). Mil. Service, RHG and RA, 1947–49. Called to the bar, Middle Temple, 1965. Ordained, Bristol, 1955; Chaplain and Lectr, King's Coll., London, 1960–66; Vicar of St Paul's, Clifton, and Chaplain, Bristol Univ., 1966–71; Canon Residentiary and Dir of Training, Bristol, 1971–81; Archdeacon of Worcester, 1981–84. Clerical Member, Court of Arches, 1980–; Mem. General Synod, 1974–81. Fellow, Woodard Corp., 1985–. Jt Editor, Theology, 1982–. *Publications:* Experiments with Prayer, 1961; A Christian Approach to Television, 1968; Christian Attitudes to Homosexuality, 1980. *Recreations:* film making, fishing. *Address:* 10 The Close, Exeter EX1 1EZ. *Club:* Royal Commonwealth Society.

CREE, Brig. Gerald Hilary, CBE 1946; DSO 1945; Colonel, The Prince of Wales's Own Regiment of Yorkshire, 1960–70; *b* 23 June 1905; *s* of late Maj.-Gen. Gerald Cree; *m* 1945, Joan Agnes, *d* of late Lt-Col W. R. Eden, RA; one *d. Educ:* Kelly Coll.; RMC Sandhurst. Commissioned, The West Yorks Regt, 1924; King's African Rifles, 1931–36; comd 2nd Bn West Yorks Regt, 1942–44; 1st Bn 1946–48; Comdr 25 (East African) Infantry Bde, 1944–45 and Brig. 1953. Served Palestine, East Africa, Abyssinia, Western Desert, Iraq, Burma, 1938–45. Commander 127 (East Lancs) Infantry Brigade (TA), 1953–56; Col, The West Yorks Regt, 1956–57, Col, PWO Regt of Yorkshire, 1960–70, retd. *Address:* Laurels, Sharpham Drive, Totnes, Devon. *Club:* Naval and Military.

CREED, Albert Lowry, MA; *b* 16 July 1909; *s* of Rev. Albert H. Creed; *m* 1943, Joyce Marian (*née* Hunter), Leeds; two *s* one *d. Educ:* Kingswood Sch.; Downing Coll., Cambridge. MA Cantab 1931. Asst Master: Stretford Grammar Sch., 1932–35; Bishop's Stortford Coll., 1935–39; Housemaster, Christ's Hospital, 1939–42; Headmaster: Staveley-Netherthorpe Grammar Sch., 1942–46; Truro Sch., Cornwall, 1946–59; Kingswood Sch., 1959–70; Volunteer with Botswana Min. of Educn, 1973–74. Chm., West Cornwall Hospital Management Cttee, 1957–59; Vice-Pres., Methodist Conf., 1962–63; a Dir, The Methodist Recorder, 1961–86. Pres., Kingswood Old Boys' Assoc., 1975–76. Hon. Sec., UK-Botswana Soc., 1981–83. *Address:* Greggs House, 73 Manchester Road, Chapel-en-le-Frith, near Stockport, Cheshire SK12 6TH. *T:* Chapel-en-le-Frith 814121. *Club:* Royal Commonwealth Society.

CREEGGAN, Rt. Rev. Jack Burnett; *b* 10 Nov. 1902; *s* of Alfred Henry Creeggan and Mary Laura (*née* Sheffield); *m* 1931, Dorothy Jarman (*née* Embury); one *s* one *d. Educ:* Deseronto (Ont) Public and High Schs; Queen's Univ. (BA); Bishop's Univ. (LST). Priest, 1928; served in many parishes in Dio. Ontario; Canon, St George's Cathedral, Kingston, Ont, 1952; Archdeacon of: Ontario, 1953; Frontenac, 1962; Kingston, 1969; Bishop of Ontario, 1970–74. Prolocutor, Lower House, Provincial Synod of Ont., 1963. Hon. DCL, Bishop's Univ., Lennoxville, PQ, 1971. *Recreations:* curling, golf. *Address:* Apt 112, 32 Ontario Street, Kingston, Ontario K7L 5G4, Canada. *T:* 542–5319.

CREEK, Malcolm Lars, LVO 1980; OBE 1985; HM Diplomatic Service; High Commissioner to Vanuatu, since 1985; *b* 2 April 1931; *s* of Edgar Creek and Lily Creek (*née* Robertshaw); *m* 1st, 1953, Moira Pattison (marr. diss. 1970); one *s* one *d*; 2nd, 1970, Gillian Bell; one *s* two *d. Educ:* Belle Vue School, Bradford. BA Hons London. National Service, 1950–52. Foreign Office, 1953; served Mogadishu, Harar, Mexico City, Abidjan, Chile; First Sec., San José, 1968; Havana, 1971; FCO, 1974; Head of Chancery, Tunis, 1978; Lima, 1981. *Recreations:* reading, family history, cricket. *Address:* c/o Foreign and Commonwealth Office, SW1; 17 Bertram Drive North, Meols, Wirral. *T:* 051–632 5520. *Club:* Yorkshire County Cricket.

CREESE, Nigel Arthur Holloway; Headmaster, Melbourne Grammar School, since 1970; *b* 4 June 1927; *s* of late H. R. Creese; *m* 1951, Valdai (*née* Walters); two *s* two *d. Educ:* Blundell's Sch.; Brasenose Coll., Oxford. Assistant Master: Bromsgrove Sch., 1952–55; Rugby Sch., 1955–63; Headmaster, Christ's Coll., Christchurch, NZ, 1963–70. Chm., Assoc. of Heads of Independent Schs of Australia. *Address:* Melbourne Church of England Grammar School, Domain Road, South Yarra, Victoria 3141, Australia.

CREIGHTMORE, Peter Beauchamp; Master of Supreme Court, Queen's Bench Division, since 1975; *b* 15 Jan. 1928; *s* of Maximilian Louis Creightmore, MRCS, LRCP and Mary Arnell Beauchamp; *m* 1957, June Patricia, *d* of Harold William Hedley, Captain Suez Canal Co. (Pilote Majeur), and Gwendoline Pugh; one *s* one *d. Educ:* Geelong Grammar Sch. (H. H. Whittingham Student, 1945); Worcester Coll., Oxford (MA). O/Sig, RNVR, 1952, commnd 1955. Called to Bar, Inner Temple, 1954; Oxford, later Oxford and Midland, Circuit. *Recreation:* music. *Address:* Royal Courts of Justice, Strand, WC2.

CREIGHTON, Harold Digby Fitzgerald; Deputy Chairman and Chief Executive, Farmer Stedall plc; *b* 11 Sept. 1927; *s* of late Rev. Digby Robert Creighton and Amy Frances Rohde; *m* 1964, Harriett Mary Falconer Wallace, *d* of late A. L. P. F. Wallace of Candacraig (Mem., Queen's Body Guard for Scotland); four *d. Educ:* Haileybury. National Service, Army (Lieut), India and ME, 1945–48. Consolidated Tin Smelters, Penang, 1950–52; Dir, machine tool companies, London, 1952–63; Chm., Scottish Machine Tool Corp. Ltd, Glasgow, 1963–68. Chm., 1967–75, Editor, 1973–75, The Spectator. *Address:* 5 Upper Brook Street, W1. *Club:* Beefsteak.

CREMIN, Cornelius Christopher; Chairman, Irish delegation to 3rd UN Conference on the Law of the Sea, 1973–79; *b* 6 Dec. 1908; 2nd *s* of D. J. Cremin and Ann (*née* Singleton), Kenmare, Co. Kerry; *m* 1st, 1935, Patricia Josephine (decd), Killarney; one *s* three *d*; 2nd, 1974, Dr Mary Eta Murphy, Beare Island. *Educ:* National Univ. of Ireland. BComm 1930; MA (Classics) 1931. Travelling studentship (Classics), NUI, 1931–34; Brit. Sch. at Athens and Rome, 1932; Dipl. in Class. Archaeol., Oxford, 1934; 3rd Sec., Dept of External Affairs, 1935; 1st Sec., Irish Legation, Paris, 1937–43; Chargé d'Affaires, Berlin, 1943–45; Chargé d'Affaires, Lisbon, 1945–46; Couns., Dept of External Affairs, Dublin, 1946–48; Asst Sec., 1948–50; Minister to France, March-Sept. 1950; Ambassador to France, 1950–54; Head of Irish Delegn, OEEC, 1950–54, and Vice-Chm. of OEEC Council (official), 1952–54; Ambassador to the Holy See, 1954–56; Sec. of the Dept of External Affairs, Dublin, 1958–62; Irish Ambassador to Britain, 1963–64 (and 1956–58); Irish Permanent Representative at UN, 1964–74. LLD *hc* National Univ. of Ireland, 1965. Grand Officer of the Legion of Honour, 1954; Knight Grand Cross of the Order of Pius, 1956; Grand Cross of Merit (Fed. Germany), 1960. *Recreations:* golf, boating. *Address:* Tuosist, Killarney, Ireland.

CREMONA, Hon. John Joseph; Judge, European Court of Human Rights, since 1965; Judge, European Tribunal in matters of State immunity, since 1985; Emeritus Professor, University of Malta, since 1965; Chief Justice of Malta and President of the Constitutional Court, Court of Appeal and Court of Criminal Appeal, 1971–81; *b* 6 Jan. 1918; *s* of late Dr Antonio Cremona, KM, MD and Anne (*née* Camilleri); *m* 1949, Marchioness Beatrice Barbaro of St George; one *s* two *d. Educ:* Malta Univ. (BA 1936, LLD *cum laude* 1942); Rome Univ. (DLitt 1939); London Univ. (BA 1st Cl. Hons 1946, PhD in Laws 1951). DrJur Trieste, 1972. Crown Counsel, 1947; Lectr in Constitutional Law, Malta Univ., 1947–65, Prof. of Criminal Law, 1959–65; Attorney-Gen., 1957–64; Vice-Pres., Constitutional Court and Court of Appeal, 1965–71; sometime Actg Governor General and Actg Pres., Republic of Malta. Chm., UN Cttee on Elimination of Racial Discrimination (CERD), 1986– (Mem, 1984–). Chm., Human Rights Section, World Assoc. of Lawyers; Vice-Pres., Internat. Inst. of Studies, Documentation and Info. for the Protection of Envt, Italy; Member: Cttee of Experts of Human Rights and Cttee on State Immunity, Council of Europe, Strasbourg; Scientific Council, Revue des Droits de l'Homme, Paris; Patronage Cttee, Europäische Grundrechte Zeitschrift, Strasbourg; Scientific Council Centro Internazionale per Protezione dei Diritti dell' Uomo, Pesaro, Italy; Editorial Adv. Board: Checklist of Human Rights Documents, NY; Human Rights Law Jl, Arlington, Va; delegate and rapporteur, internat. confs. FRHistS; Fellow *ex titulo*, Internat. Acad. of Legal Medicine and Social Medicine; Hon. Fellow, LSE; Hon. Mem., Real Acad. de Jurisprudencia y Legislacion, Madrid. Kt Comdr, Order of Merit, Italy, 1968; Kt, Sovereign Military Order of Malta, 1966; KSG, 1972; Kt Comdr, 1971, Grand Cross of Merit, 1981, Constantinian Order of St George; KStJ 1984 (Chm., St John Council, Malta, 1983–). *Publications:* The Treatment of Young Offenders in Malta, 1956; The Malta Constitution of 1835, 1959; The Doctrine of Entrapment in Theft, 1959; The Legal Consequences of a Conviction, 1962; The Constitutional Development of Malta, 1963; From the Declaration of Rights to Independence, 1965; Human Rights Documentation in Malta, 1966; articles in French, German, Italian and American law jls. *Recreation:* gardening. *Address:* Villa Barbaro, Main Street, Attard, Malta. *T:* 440818.

CRESPI, (Caesar) James, QC 1984; a Recorder of the Crown Court, since 1973. *Educ:* Trinity Hall, Cambridge (BA). Called to the Bar, Middle Temple, 1951, South Eastern Circuit. *Address:* 5 Paper Buildings, Temple, EC4Y 7HB. *T:* 01–583 6117. *Club:* Garrick.

CRESPIN, Régine; Officier de la Légion d'Honneur, 1981 (Chevalier, 1969); Officier de l'Ordre National du Mérite, (Chevalier, 1965); Commandeur des Arts et des Lettres, 1974; soprano singer; Professor of Singing, Conservatoire National Supérieur de Musique de Paris, since 1976; *b* Marseille, 23 Feb.; *d* of Henri Crespin and Marguerite (*née* Meirone); *m* 1962, Lou Bruder, French novelist, critic, poet, translator. *Educ:* Nîmes; Conservatoire National, Paris (Baccalauréat). Worked at the Opera, Paris, 1951–, in all the famous opera houses of Europe and all over the world, giving concerts, recitals, etc.; *Operas include:* Otello, Tosca, Il Trovatore, Le Nozze di Figaro, Ballo in Maschera, Der Rosenkavalier, Tannhäuser, Lohengrin, Die Walküre, Parsifal, Les Troyens, Dialogues of the Carmelites, Tales of Hoffmann, Iphigenie auf Tauris, Carmen. *Publication:* La vie et l'amour d'une femme (autobiog.), 1982. *Recreations:* sea, sun, sleep, books, theatre; and my dog! *Address:* 3 Avenue Frochot, 75009 Paris, France.

CRESSON, Edith; Commandeur du Mérite Agricole, 1983; Minister for Industrial Redeployment and Foreign Trade, French Republic, 1984–86; *b* 27 Jan. 1934; *née* Campion; *m* Jacques Cresson; two *d. Educ:* Diplômée de l'Ecole des Hautes Etudes Commerciales; Dr en démographie (doctoral thesis: the life of women in a rural district of Guémené-Penfao, Loire-Atlantique). Mem., Convention des Institutions Républicaines (responsible for agricl problems), 1966; Dir of Studies, Bureau des Etudes Economiques privés (dealing especially with industrial investment, particularly in Canada); National Secretary, Parti Socialiste (in charge of youth organisation), 1974; Mem. Directing Cttee, Parti Socialiste; contested (for Parti Socialiste) Châtellerault, 1975; elected to European Assembly, 1979 (Mem., Cttee on Agriculture); Minister: of Agriculture, France, 1981–83; of For. Trade and Tourism, 1983–84. Mayor of Thure, Vienne, 1977, of Châtellerault, Vienne, 1983–; Member, Conseil Général of Vienne, 1982–. *Publication:* Avec le soleil, 1976. *Address:* 101 Rue de Grenelle, 75001 Paris, France.

CRESSWELL, Rev. Amos Samuel; Chairman, Plymouth and Exeter District of the Methodist Church, since 1976; President of the Methodist Conference, 1983–84; *b* Walsall Woods, 21 April 1926; *s* of Amos and Jane Cresswell; *m* 1956, Evelyn Rosemary Marchbanks; two *s* one *d. Educ:* Queen Mary's Grammar School, Walsall; University College, Durham Univ.; Wesley House, Cambridge; Theological Seminary, Bethel bei Bielefeld, Westphalia. BA (Dunelm), Classics, 1947; BA (Cantab), Theology, 1952, MA (Cantab) 1956. Teacher of English and Latin, High School for Boys, Colchester, 1947–49; Methodist Minister, Clitheroe Circuit, 1949–50; Asst Tutor in New Testament, Richmond Coll., London, 1953–56; Minister in Darlaston (Slater St), 1956–61; Tutor in New Testament, Cliff Coll., Derbyshire, 1961–66; Minister in Bramhall Circuit (Cheadle Hulme), 1966–73; Superintendent Minister, Welwyn Garden City, 1973–76. Pres., Devonshire Assoc., 1985–86. Editor, Advance (religious weekly, formerly Joyful News), 1961–63. *Publications:* The Story of Cliff (a history of Cliff College), 1965, 2nd edn 1983; The Story They Told (a short study of the Passion Narratives in the Gospels), 1966; Life Power and Hope—a study of the Holy Spirit, 1972. *Recreations:* compulsive watching of sport (especially West Bromwich Albion); collecting Roman Imperial coins; reading about American Civil War; listening to music and to Shakespeare. *Address:* 18 Velwell Road, Exeter EX4 4LE. *T:* Exeter 72541.

CRESSWELL, Helen, (Mrs Brian Rowe); freelance author; *b* July 1934; *d* of Annie Edna Clarke and Joseph Edward Cresswell; *m* 1962, Brian Rowe; two *d. Educ:* Nottingham Girls' High Sch.; King's College London (BA English Hons). *Television series:* Lizzie Dripping, 1973–75; Jumbo Spencer, 1976; The Bagthorpe Saga, 1980; numerous TV plays. *Publications:* Sonya-by-the-Shire, 1961; Jumbo Spencer, 1963; The White Sea Horse, 1964; Pietro and the Mule, 1965; Jumbo Back to Nature, 1965; Where the Wind Blows, 1966; Jumbo Afloat, 1966; The Piemakers, 1967; A Tide for the Captain, 1967; The Signposters, 1968; The Sea Piper, 1968; The Barge Children, 1968; The Night-watchman, 1969; A Game of Catch, 1969; A Gift from Winklesea, 1969; The Outlanders, 1970; The Wilkses, 1970; The Bird Fancier, 1971; At the Stroke of Midnight, 1971; The Beachcombers, 1972; Lizzie Dripping, 1972; The Bongleweed, 1972; Lizzie Dripping AGain, 1974; Butterfly Chase, 1975; The Winter of the Birds, 1975; My Aunt Polly, 1979; My Aunt Polly By the Sea, 1980; Dear Shrink, 1982; The Secret World of Polly Flint, 1982; Ellie and the Hagwitch, 1984; The Bagthorpe Saga: Pt 1, Ordinary Jack, 1977; Pt 2, Absolute Zero, 1978; Pt 3, Bagthorpes Unlimited, 1978; Pt 4, Bagthorpes *v* The World, 1979; Pt 5, Bagthorpes Abroad, 1984; Pt 6, Bagthorpes Haunted, 1985. *Recreations:* watercolour painting, collecting books, antiques and coincidences, sundial watching. *Address:* Old Church Farm, Eakring, Newark, Notts NG22 0DA. *T:* Mansfield 870401.

CRESSWELL, Peter John; QC 1983; a Recorder, since 1986; *b* 24 April 1944; *s* of Jack Joseph and Madeleine Cresswell; *m* 1972, Caroline Ward; two *s. Educ:* St John's Sch., Leatherhead; Queens' Coll., Cambridge (MA, LLM). Called to the Bar, Gray's Inn, 1966. Mem., Senate of Inns of Court and Bar, 1981–84, 1985–86; Chm., Common Law Bar Assoc., 1985–86. *Publication:* Encyclopaedia of Banking Law, 1982. *Recreation:* fly-fishing. *Address:* 25 Victoria Square, SW1W 0RB. *T:* 01-834 2684. *Clubs:* Athenæum, Flyfishers'.

CRESWELL, Jack Norman; Deputy Chairman of Lloyd's, 1972, 1974; *b* 20 April 1913; *s* of late Sydney and Dora Creswell; *m* 1938, Jean (Lilian Jane) Maxwell; two *s. Educ:* Highgate School. Served War, 1942–46, 2nd Household Cavalry Regt; Captain and Adjt, The Life Guards, 1945–46. Member of Lloyd's, 1946: Mem. Cttee, 1969–72, 1974; Mem. Cttee Lloyd's Underwriters Non-Marine Assoc., 1968–74, Chm. 1973. Dir, Ellinger Heath Western (Underwriting Agencies) Ltd. *Recreations:* photography, family croquet. *Address:* Lullington Court, near Polegate, E Sussex. *T:* Alfriston 870548. *Club:* Cavalry and Guards.

CRESWICK, Harry Richardson, MA; Librarian Emeritus of Cambridge University; *b* 1902; *m* Agnes Isabel (*d* 1982), *d* of late J. W. Stubbings. *Educ:* Barnet Grammar Sch.; Trinity Coll., Cambridge. On staff of University Library, Cambridge, 1926–38; Deputy Librarian, Bodleian Library, Oxford, 1939–45; Bodley's Librarian and Student of Christ Church, 1945–47; Librarian of Cambridge Univ. and Professorial Fellow of Jesus Coll., 1949–67, Emeritus Fellow, 1976. Hon. LittD, Trinity Coll., Dublin.

CRETNEY, Prof. Stephen Michael, DCL; FBA 1985; Professor of Law and Dean of the Faculty of Law, University of Bristol, since 1984; *b* 25 Feb. 1936; *yr s* of late Fred and Winifred M. V. Cretney; *m* 1973, Antonia Lois Vanrenen, *o d* of Lt-Comdr A. G. G. Vanrenen, RN; two *s. Educ:* Queen's Road Primary Sch., Cheadle Hulme; Cheadle Hulme Sch.; Magdalen Coll., Oxford (Demy in Mod. Hist.; 1st Cl. Hons Jurisprudence, 1959; DCL, 1985). Nat. Service, Intell. Corps, 1954–56. Solicitor. Partner, Macfarlanes, London, 1964; Lecturer: Kenya Sch. of Law, Nairobi, 1966; Southampton Univ., 1968; Fellow and Tutor, Exeter Coll., Oxford, 1969–78; a Law Comr, 1978–83. Member: Social Scis and Law Cttee, SSRC, 1979–83; Departmental Cttee on Prison Disciplinary System, 1984–85; Family and Civil Cttee, Judicial Studies Bd, 1985–. Chorley Lectr, 1980. A Gen. Comr of Income Tax, 1970–78. *Publications:* Theobald on Wills, (ed jtly) 13th edn 1970; Principles of Family Law, 1974, 4th edn 1984; Family Law (Teach Yourself series), 1982; The Enduring Power of Attorney, 1986; Elements of Family Law, 1987; articles and notes in legal jls. *Recreations:* cooking, taking snapshots. *Address:* Faculty of Law, Wills Memorial Building, Queen's Road, Bristol BS8 1RJ. *T:* Bristol 303371; 15 Canynge Square, Clifton, Bristol BS8 3LA. *T:* Bristol 732983. *Club:* United Oxford & Cambridge University.

CREW, Air Vice-Marshal Edward Dixon, CB 1973; DSO 1944 and Bar 1950; DFC 1941 and Bar 1942; FRAeS 1972; Planning Inspectorate, Department of the Environment, since 1973; *b* 24 Dec. 1917; *er s* of F. D. Crew, MB, MRCS, LRCP; *m* 1945, Virginia Martin; one *s. Educ:* Felsted Sch.; Downing Coll., Cambridge (MA). Commissioned RAFVR, 1939; served War of 1939–45: night fighter sqdns; 604 sqdn, 85 Sqdn; Comd 96 Sqdn; permanent commission, 1945. Malayan Emergency, Comd No 45 Sqdn, 1948–50; on exchange, RCAF, 1952–54; CFE, 1954–56; Comd RAF Brüggen, Germany, 1959–62; Comdr, Air Forces Borneo, 1965–66; AOC Central Reconnaissance Estabt, 1968; Dep. Controller, Nat. Air Traffic Services, 1969–72; various Air Staff jobs at Air Min. and MoD; retd 1973. *Recreation:* golf. *Address:* National Westminster Bank, 10 Bene't Street, Cambridge. *Club:* Royal Air Force.

CREWE, Albert V., PhD; Professor, Department of Physics and the Enrico Fermi Institute, since 1963 (Assistant Professor, 1956–59; Associate Professor, 1959–63; William E. Wrather Distinguished Service Professor, 1977), Dean of Physical Sciences Division, 1971–81, University of Chicago; *b* 18 Feb. 1927; *m* 1949, Doreen Patricia Blunsdon; one *s* three *d. Educ:* Univ. of Liverpool (BS, PhD). Asst Lectr, 1950–52, Lectr, 1952–55, Univ. of Liverpool; Div. Dir, Particle Accelerator Division, Argonne National Laboratory, 1958–61; Dir, Argonne National Laboratory, 1961–67. Member: Nat. Acad. of Sciences; Amer. Acad. of Arts and Sciences. Hon. FRMS 1984. Named Outstanding New Citizen by Citizenship Council of Chicago, 1962; received Immigrant's Service League's Annual Award for Outstanding Achievement in the Field of Science, 1962; Illinois Sesquicentennial Award, 1968; Industrial Research Award, 1970; Distinguished Service Award, Electron Microscope Soc. of America, 1976; Albert A. Michelson Award, Franklin Inst., 1977; Ernst Abbe Award, NY Microscope Soc., 1979; Duddell Medal, Inst. of Physics, 1980. *Publications:* Research USA (with J. J. Katz), 1964; contribs to: Proc. Royal Soc.; Proc. Phys. Soc.; Physical Review; Science; Physics Today; Jl of Applied Physics; Reviews of Scientific Instruments; Optik; Ultramicroscopy, etc. *Address:* 63 Old Creek Road, Palos Park, Illinois, USA. *T:* Gibson 8–8738. *Clubs:* Quadrangle, Wayfarers' (Chicago).

CREWE, Prof. Ivor Martin; Professor, since 1982, and Chairman, Department of Government, since 1984, University of Essex; *b* 15 Dec. 1945; *s* of Francis and Lilly Crewe; *m* 1968, Jill Barbara (*née* Gadian); two *s* one *d. Educ:* Manchester Grammar Sch.; Exeter Coll., Oxford (BA); London School of Economics (MScEcon). Assistant Lecturer, Univ. of Lancaster, 1967–69; Junior Research Fellow, Nuffield Coll., Oxford, 1969–71; Lectr, Dept of Govt, Univ. of Essex, 1971–74; Dir SSRC Data Archive, 1974–82. Co-Dir, Feb. 1974, Oct. 1974, 1979 British Election Studies; elections analyst for: BBC TV, 1982–; The Guardian, 1983–. Editor, 1977–82, Co-editor, 1984–, British Journal of Political Science. *Publications:* (with A. H. Halsey) Social Survey of the Civil Service (HMSO), 1969; ed, British Political Sociology Yearbook, vol. 1 1974, vol. 2 1975; co-ed, Party Identification and Beyond, 1976; (with Bo Sarlvik) Decade of Dealignment, 1983; (with Anthony Fox) British Parliamentary Constituencies, 1984; (ed jtly) Electoral Change in Western Democracies, 1985; articles in various academic jls on public opinion and elections in Britain. *Address:* 141 Maldon Road, Colchester, Essex CO3 3BJ. *T:* Colchester 561695.

CREWE, Quentin Hugh; writer and journalist; *b* 14 Nov. 1926; *s* of Major Hugh Crewe and Lady Annabel Crewe; *m* 1st, 1956, Martha Sharp; one *s* one *d*; 2nd, 1961, Angela Huth; one *d* (one *s* decd); 3rd, 1970, Susan Cavendish; one *s* one *d. Educ:* Eton; Trinity Coll., Cambridge. Joined Evening Standard, 1953; subseq. worked for Queen, Vogue, Daily Mail, Sunday Mirror; freelance, 1970–, contrib. to Times, Sunday Times, Sunday Telegraph, and Spectator. *Publications:* A Curse of Blossom, 1960; Frontiers of Privilege, 1961; Great Chefs of France, 1978; Pocket Book of Food, 1980; In Search of the Sahara, 1983; The Last Maharaja, 1985. *Recreation:* travel. *Address:* 52 Beauchamp Place, SW3; Le Grand Banc, 04110, Oppedette, France. *T:* (92) 762554.

CRIBB, Air Cdre Peter Henry, CBE 1957; DSO 1942, and Bar, 1944; DFC 1941; JP; retired 1983; *b* 28 Sept. 1918; *s* of late Charles B. Cribb and Mrs Ethel Cribb; *m* 1949, Vivienne Janet, *yr d* of late Col S. T. J. Perry, MC, TD, DL, Oxton, Birkenhead, Ches; three *s. Educ:* Bradford Grammar Sch.; Prince Henry's Sch., Otley. Flt Cadet, RAF Coll., 1936–38; Flying duties in Bomber Comd, 1938–45 (Comd No. 582 Sqdn, RAF Little Staughton); Comdg RAF Salbani, RAF Peshawar, India and Staff No. 1 Indian Gp, 1945–47; OC 203 Sqdn, 1947, and HQ Staff, 1950, Coastal Comd; RAF Staff Coll.,

Bracknell, 1951; Asst Dir Tech. Intell., Air Min., 1951–53; Gp Capt. Plans and Policy, HQ Bomber Comd, 1953–57; 2nd TAF, Germany (OC Oldenburg, Ahlhorn and Gutersloh), 1957–60; Air Min., Dep. Dir Air Staff Briefing, 1959–61, Dir, 1961–62; SASO, Air Forces, Middle East, 1962–63; IDC, 1964; Deputy to Asst Chief of Defence Staff (Joint Warfare), MoD 1965–66; retired, 1966. Administrative Manager, Goldsworthy Mining Ltd, 1966–68. Associate Fellow, Australian Inst. of Management, 1969; Past State Pres., Ryder-Cheshire Foundn of WA, Inc.; Pres., Pathfinder Assoc. of WA; Mem., West Perth (WA) Rotary. Mem., Australian Faceters Guild. JP Western Australia, 1968. *Recreations:* fishing, facetting gem stones. *Address:* Peniston, 66 Sherington Road, Greenwood, WA 6024, Australia.

CRICHTON, family name of **Earl of Erne.**

CRICHTON, Viscount; John Henry Michael Ninian Crichton; *b* 19 June 1971; *s* and *heir* of Earl of Erne, *qv.*

CRICHTON, Sir Andrew Maitland-Makgill-, Kt 1963; Director, P&OSN Co., 1957–81; Vice-Chairman, Port of London Authority, 1967–76 (Member, 1964–67); *b* 28 Dec. 1910; *s* of late Lt-Col D. M.-M.-Crichton, Queen's Own Cameron Highldrs, and Phyllis (*née* Cuthbert); *m* 1948, Isabel, *d* of Andrew McGill, Sydney, NSW. *Educ:* Wellington Coll. Joined Gray, Dawes & Co., 1929; transf. India to Mackinnon Mackenzie & Co. (Agents of BI Co. and for P & O on Indian Continent and in parts of Far East), 1931. Joined IA, 1940; DDM (Shipping), Col, at GHQ India, 1944. Mackinnon Mackenzie, Calcutta, 1945–48; P&O Co., UK (Gen. Manager, 1951); Chm., Overseas Containers Ltd, 1965–73; former Director: Standard Chartered Group; Inchcape Insurance Hldgs Ltd; London Tin Corp.; Dir, Butler's Warehousing & Distrib. Ltd. Chairman: Nat. Assoc. Port Employers, 1958–65; EDC for GPO, 1965–70; Vice-Chm., British Transport Docks Bd, 1963–68; Member: Baltic Exchange; Nat. Freight Corp., 1969–73; Court of The Chartered Bank; Police Council for GB (Arbitrator), 1969–79; Industrial Arbitration Bd. FRSA; FCIT (a past Vice-Pres.). *Recreations:* golf, music. Freeman, Co. of Watermen and Lightermen. *Address:* 55 Hans Place, Knightsbridge, SW1. *T:* 01–584 1209. *Clubs:* City of London, Caledonian.
See also Maj.-Gen. Edward Maitland-Makgill-Crichton.

CRICHTON, David George, LVO 1968; British Consul-General, Nice, 1970–74; *b* 31 July 1914; *e s* of late Col Hon. Sir George Crichton, GCVO; *m* 1941, Joan Fenella, *d* of late Col D. W. Cleaver, DSO; one *s* one *d. Educ:* Eton. Worked as journalist, Reading and Manchester, and on Daily Telegraph, Paris and London, 1933–39; served War of 1939–45 in Derbyshire Yeomanry (despatches); Major 1944; entered Foreign Service, 1946; served in Belgrade, Singapore, Alexandria, Miami, La Paz and Santiago. *Address:* Church House, Medstead, Alton, Hampshire. *T:* Alton 62632; Résidence Bois Joli, 06320–Cap d'Ail, France. *T:* 78 42 52. *Clubs:* Boodle's; MC (Monte Carlo).
See also R. J. V. Crichton.

CRICHTON, Maj.-Gen. Edward Maitland-Makgill-, OBE 1948 (MBE 1945); GOC 51st Highland Division, 1966–68, retired; *b* 23 Nov. 1916; *s* of late Lt-Col D. E. Maitland-Makgill-Crichton, Queen's Own Cameron Highlanders and Phyllis (*née* Cuthbert); *m* 1951, Sheila Margaret Hibbins, Bexhill-on-Sea; three *s. Educ:* Bedford Sch.; RMC Sandhurst. 2nd Lieut Queen's Own Cameron Highlanders, 1937; Adjt 5th Bn Cameron Highlanders, 1939; served with 5th Cameron Highlanders and 51 (Highland) Div., N Africa, Sicily, Normandy, NW Europe, 1940–45; GSO 1, HQ British Commonwealth Occupation Force, Japan, 1946–47; Mobilisation Br., WO 1948–50; 1st Bn Cameron Highlanders, Tripoli and Canal Zone, 1950–52; Jt Services Staff Coll., 1953; GSO 1, 3rd Inf. Div. (UK Strategic Reserve), Canal Zone, Egypt, UK and Suez, 1953–57; with 1st Bn Cameron Highlanders, Aden, 1957; comd 1st Liverpool Scottish, 1958–61; Comdr 152 (Highland) Inf. Bde, 1962–64; Dep. Dir Army Staff Duties, MoD, 1965–66. *Recreations:* shooting, golf, gardening, fishing. *Address:* Clive House, Letham, Forfar, Angus. *T:* Letham 391.
See also Sir Andrew Maitland-Makgill-Crichton.

CRICHTON, Col Richard John Vesey, CVO 1986; MC 1940; *b* 2 Nov. 1916; *s* of late Col Hon. Sir George Crichton, GCVO, and Lady Mary Crichton; *m* 1948, Yvonne Avril Catherine, *d* of late Dr and Mrs H. E. Worthington; three *s. Educ:* Eton; RMC, Sandhurst. Commissioned 2/Lieut Coldstream Guards, 1936; served World War II: Belgium, 1940, Italy, 1943–44 (twice wounded, MC, despatches); Commanded: 1st Bn Coldstream Guards, 1954–57; Coldstream Guards, 1958–61, retired 1961. Comptroller, Union Jack Services Clubs, 1964–66; Member, HM Body Guard, Hon. Corps of Gentlemen at Arms, 1966–86; Clerk of the Cheque and Adjutant, 1979–81; Lieutenant, 1981–86. Mem., Hants CC and Police Authority, 1964–67. *Publication:* The Coldstream Guards 1946–1970, 1972. *Address:* Eglinton Lodge, Hartley Wintney, Hampshire. *T:* Hartley Wintney 2440. *Club:* Cavalry and Guards.
See also D. G. Crichton.

CRICHTON-BROWN, Sir Robert, KCMG 1980; Kt 1972; CBE 1970; TD; *b* Melbourne, 23 Aug. 1919; *s* of late L. Crichton-Brown, Sydney; *m* 1941, Norah Isabelle, *d* of late A. E. Turnbull; one *s* one *d. Educ:* Sydney Grammar Sch. Served War, 1939–45, BEF; Major, Royal Artillery and Gen. Staff, France, Iceland, India, Burma (despatches twice). Exec. Chairman: Rothmans International plc, 1985–; Edward Lumley Ltd, 1974– (Man. Dir, 1952–82); Security Life Assurances Ltd, 1961–85; Security and General Insurance Co. Ltd (Dir, 1952–); NEI Pacific Ltd, 1961–85; Rothmans of Pall Mall (Australia) Ltd, 1981–85 (Dir, 1971–81); Commercial Banking Co. of Sydney Ltd, 1976–82 (Dir, 1970–82); Commercial & General Acceptance Ltd, 1977–82; Westham Dredging Co. Pty Ltd, 1975–85; Vice Chairman: Nat. Australia Bank Ltd, 1982–85; Custom Credit Corp., 1982–85; Director: Royal Prince Alfred Hosp., 1970–84; Daily Mail and General Trust Ltd (UK), 1979–. Fed. Pres., Inst. of Dirs in Aust., 1967–80 (Chm., NSW Branch, 1965–80; Hon. Life Mem.). Pres., Medical Foundn, Sydney Univ; Australian Nat. Chm., United World Colleges (Australia) Trust, 1984–85; Mem. Federal Exec. and Federal Hon. Treas., Liberal Party of Australia, 1973–85; Hon. Life Governor, Aust. Postgraduate Fedn in Medicine; Member: Adv. Bd, Girl Guides Assoc. of Australia, 1973–85; Adv. Bd, Salvation Army, 1973–85; Internat. Forum and Panel, Duke of Edinburgh's Award (Nat. Co-ordinator, Duke of Edinburgh's Award Scheme in Aust., 1979–84); Cttee, Royal Australian Coll. of Physicians, 1973–85; Council, Imperial Soc. of Knights Bachelor (Vice-Chm., Pacific Reg.); Nat. Councillor, Scout Assoc. of Aust., 1980–85. Underwriting Mem. of Lloyd's, 1946–. Mem., Australia's winning Admiral's Cup Team (Balandra), UK, 1967; winner, Sydney-Hobart Yacht Race (Pacha), 1970. *Address:* 15 Hill Street, W1X 7FB. *Clubs:* White's, Royal Cruising; Royal Yacht Squadron; Australian, Union (Sydney); Cruising Yacht Club of Australia, Royal Sydney Yacht Squadron, Royal Prince Alfred Yacht.

CRICHTON-MILLER, Donald, TD; MA; *b* 1906; *s* of late Hugh Crichton-Miller, MA, MD, FRCP; *m* 1931, Monica, *d* of late B. A. Glanvill, JP, Bromley, Kent; two *s* one *d. Educ:* Fettes Coll., Edinburgh; Pembroke Coll., Cambridge (Exhibitioner). Played Rugby Football for Cambridge and Scotland; Asst Master: Monmouth Sch., 1929–31; Bryanston Sch., 1931–34; Stowe Sch., 1934–36; Head Master: Taunton Sch., Somerset,

1936–45; Fettes Coll., 1945–58; Stowe Sch., 1958–63. Carried out education surveys in Pakistan, 1951, and Malta, 1956. *Recreations:* governing schools and managing properties. *Address:* Westridge House, Compton, Berks RG16 0RE.

CRICHTON-STUART, family name of **Marquess of Bute.**

CRICK, Alan John Pitts, OBE 1956; *b* 14 May 1913; *er s* of Owen John Pitts Crick and Margaret Crick (*née* Daw), late of Minehead, Somerset; *m* 1941, Norah (*née* Atkins) (*d* 1984); two *d. Educ:* Latymer Upper Sch.; King's Coll., London Univ. (MA); Heidelberg Univ. (Dr.phil). Vice-Consul, British Consulate-Gen., Free City of Danzig, 1938–39. Served War, Army, 1939–46: Egypt and Libya, 1941–43, HQ Eighth Army; NW Europe, 1944–46 (despatches); Major, GSO2, Intell., SHAEF; HQ 21 Army Group and HQ BAOR. Min. of Defence Jt Intell. Bureau, 1946–63; jssc, 1948; British Jt Services Mission, Washington, 1953–56; Asst Dir, Jt Intell. Bureau, 1957–63; idc, 1960; Counsellor, British Embassy, Washington, 1963–65; Asst Sec., Cabinet Office, 1965–68; Def. Intell. Staff, MoD, 1968–73; Director of Economic Intelligence, MoD, 1970–73. Adviser to Commercial Union Assurance Co., 1973–78. *Recreations:* travel, antiquarian interests, books. *Address:* 16 Church Square, Rye, East Sussex TN31 7HE. *T:* Rye 222050. *Clubs:* Naval and Military; Dormy House (Rye).
See also R. P. Crick.

CRICK, Prof. Bernard, BSc (Econ.), PhD (London); writer; Emeritus Professor, University of London; *b* 16 Dec. 1929; *s* of Harry Edgar and Florence Clara Crick. *Educ:* Whitgift Sch.; University Coll., London. Research student, LSE, 1950–52; Teaching Fellow, Harvard, 1952–54; Asst Prof., McGill, 1954–55; Vis. Fellow, Berkeley, 1955–56; Asst Lectr, later Lectr, later Sen. Lectr, LSE, 1957–65; Prof. of Political Theory and Institutions, Sheffield Univ., 1965–71; Prof. of Politics, Birkbeck Coll., Univ of London, 1971–84. Jt Editor, Political Quarterly, 1966–80. Joint Sec., Study of Parlt Gp, 1964–68. Hon. Pres., Politics Assoc., 1970–76; Mem., Council of the Hansard Soc., 1962–. Hon. DSc Belfast, 1986. *Publications:* The American Science of Politics, 1958; In Defence of Politics, 1962, 3rd edn 1982 (trans. German, Japanese, Spanish, Italian); The Reform of Parliament, 1964, 2nd edn 1968; (ed) Essays on Reform, 1967; (ed with W. A. Robson) Protest and Discontent, 1970; (ed) Machiavelli: The Discourses, 1971; Political Theory and Practice, 1972; (ed with W. A. Robson) Taxation Policy, 1973; Basic Forms of Government, 1973; Crime, Rape and Gin, 1975; (ed with Alex Porter) Political Education and Political Literacy, 1978; George Orwell: a Life, 1980, 2nd edn 1982; (ed) Unemployment, 1981; (ed) Clarendon edn, Orwell's Nineteen Eighty-Four, 1984; (ed with Audrey Coppard) Orwell Observed, 1984. *Recreations:* polemicising, book- and theatre-reviewing, hill-walking, bee-keeping. *Address:* Nether Liberton House, Old Mill Lane, Gilmerton Road, Edinburgh EH16 9TZ. *T:* 031–664 3911. *Clubs:* Savile; Scottish Arts (Edinburgh).

CRICK, Francis Harry Compton, FRS 1959; BSc London, PhD Cantab; J. W. Kieckhefer Distinguished Professor, The Salk Institute, since 1977; Adjunct Professor of Biology, Chemistry and Psychology, University of California, San Diego; *b* 8 June 1916; *e s* of late Harry Crick and late Annie Elizabeth (*née* Wilkins); *m* 1st, 1940, Ruth Doreen Dodd (divorced, 1947); one *s*; 2nd, 1949, Odile Speed; two *d. Educ:* Mill Hill Sch.; University Coll., London; Caius Coll., Cambridge (Hon. Fellow, 1976). Scientist in Admiralty, 1940–47; Strangeways Laboratory, Cambridge, 1947–49; MRC Lab. of Molecular Biology, Cambridge, 1949–77; Brooklyn Polytechnic, NY, USA, 1953–54. Vis. Lectr Rockefeller Inst., NY, USA, 1959; Vis. Prof., Chemistry Dept, Harvard, 1959; Fellow, Churchill Coll., Cambridge, 1960–61; Vis. Biophysics Prof., Harvard, 1962; Non-resident Fellow, Salk Inst. for Biological Studies, San Diego, 1962–73; Ferkauf Foundn Visiting Prof., Salk Inst., 1976–77; Fellow, UCL, 1962; For. Hon. Mem., Amer. Acad. of Arts and Sciences, 1962; Hon. Mem., Amer. Soc. Biological Chem., 1963; Hon. MRIA, 1964; Hon. Fellow: Churchill Coll., Cambridge, 1965; Caius Coll., Cambridge, 1976; FAAAS 1966; Hon. FRSE, 1966; Fellow, INSA, 1982; Hon. Fellow, Indian Acad. of Scis, 1985; For. Associate, US Nat. Acad. of Sciences, 1969; Mem., German Acad. of Science, Leopoldina, 1969; For. Mem., American Philos. Soc., Philadelphia, 1972; Hon. Mem., Hellenic Biochem. and Biophys. Soc., 1974. Associate For. Mem., French Acad. of Scis, 1978. Lectures: Bloor, Rochester, USA, 1959; Korkes Meml, Duke Univ., 1960; Herter, Johns Hopkins Sch. of Medicine, USA, 1960; Franklin Harris, Mount Zion Hosp., 1962; Holme, London, 1962; Henry Sidgewick Meml, Cambridge, 1963; Harveian, London, 1963; Graham Young, Glasgow, 1963; Robert Boyle, Oxford, 1963; James W. Sherrill, Scripps Clinic, 1964; Elisha Mitchel Meml, N Carolina, 1964; Vanuxem, Princeton, 1964; Charles West, London, 1964; William T. Sedgwick Meml, MIT, 1965; A. J. Carlson Meml, Chicago, 1965; Failing, Univ. of Oregon, 1965; Robbins, Pomona Coll., 1965; Telford Meml, Manchester, 1965; Kinnaird, Regent St Polytechnic, 1965; John Danz, Univ. of Washington, 1966; Sumner, Cornell, 1966; Royal Society Croonian, 1966; Cherwell-Simon Meml, Oxford, 1966; Genetical Soc. Mendel, 1966; Rickman Godlee, UCL, 1968; Shell, Stanford Univ., 1969; Evarts A. Graham Meml, Washington Univ., St Louis Missouri; Gehrmann, Illinois Univ., 1973; Cori, Buffalo, NY, 1973; Jean Weigle Meml, Calif Inst. of Technology, 1976; John Stauffer Distinguished, Univ. of Southern Calif, 1976; Smith Kline and French, Univ. of Calif, SF, 1977; Henry Failing Distinguished, Oregon, 1977; Paul Lund, Northwestern, 1977; Steenbock, Wisconsin, 1977; 8th Sir Hans Krebs, and medal, FEBS, Copenhagen, 1977; Lynen, Miami, 1978; Briody Meml, New Jersey, 1979; Dupont, Harvard, 1979; Ferguson, Mo, 1980; George W. Gardiner Meml, New Mexico, 1981; Jean Weigle Meml, Geneva, 1981; Rand Meml, Los Angeles, 1983; Daniel Coir Gilman, Baltimore, 1983; Beatty Memls, McGill Univ., 1985. Warren Triennial Prize, Boston, USA (with J. D. Watson), 1959; Lasker Award (jointly), 1960; Prix Charles Léopold Mayer, French Académies des Sciences, 1961; Research Corp. Award (with J. D. Watson), 1961; Gairdner Foundation Award, Toronto, 1962; Nobel Prize for Medicine (jointly), 1962; Royal Medal, Royal Soc., 1972; Copley Medal, Royal Soc., 1976; Michelson-Morley Award, Cleveland, 1981; Benjamin P. Cheney Medal, Spokane, Washington, 1986. *Publications:* Of Molecules and Men, 1966; Life Itself, 1981; papers and articles on molecular and cell biology and on neurobiology in scientific journals. *Address:* The Salk Institute for Biological Studies, PO Box 85800, San Diego, Calif 92138, USA; 337 Longden Lane, Solana Beach, Calif 92075, USA.

CRICK, R(onald) Pitts, FRCS, DOMS; Honorary Ophthalmic Surgeon, King's College Hospital, since 1982 (Ophthalmic Surgeon, 1950–82); Recognised Teacher in the Faculty of Medicine, University of London, 1960–82, Emeritus Lecturer, King's College Hospital Medical School, 1982; Visiting Research Fellow, University of Sussex, since 1976; *b* 5 Feb. 1917; *yr s* of Owen J. Pitts Crick and Margaret Daw, Minehead, Som; *m* 1941, Jocelyn Mary Grenfell Robins, *yr d* of Leonard A. C. Robins and Geraldine Grenfell, Hendon; four *s* one *d. Educ:* Latymer Upper Sch., London; King's Coll. and (Science Schol.) King's Coll. Hosp. Med. Sch., Univ. of London. MRCS, LRCP 1939. Surgeon, MN, 1939–40; Surg. Lieut, RNVR, 1940–46. Ophthalmic Registrar, King's Coll. Hosp., 1946–48; DOMS 1946. Surgical First Asst, Royal Eye Hosp., 1947–50; Ophth. Surg., Epsom County Hosp., 1948–49; Ophth. Registrar, Belgrave Hosp. for Children, 1948–50; Ophth. Surg., Sevenoaks Hosp., 1948–50; Sen. Ophthalmic Surg., Royal Eye Hosp., 1950–69; Ophthalmic Surg., Belgrave Hosp. for Children, 1950–66. Chm., Ophthalmic Post-Grad. Trng, SE Thames RHA, 1972–82. Examr to RCS for Diploma in Ophthalmology, 1961–68. FRCS, 1950. Hon. Ophth. Surg., Royal London Soc. for the Blind, 1954–57. FRSocMed, Vice-Pres. Ophthalmological Section, 1964, and Mem. Council Ophthalmolog. Section, 1953–54 and 1956–58. Member: Ophthalmolog. Soc. of the UK; Faculty of Ophthalmologists; Oxford Ophthalmolog. Congress; Southern Ophthalmolog. Soc. (Vice-Pres., 1969; Pres., 1970); Chm., Internat. Glaucoma Assoc., 1975; Charter Member: Internat. Glaucoma Congress, USA, 1977–; Internat. Assoc. of Ocular Surgeons, 1981. Sir Stewart Duke-Elder Glaucoma Award, Internat. Glaucoma Congress, 1985; Lederle Medal for Ophthalmology, 1985. *Publications:* All About Glaucoma, 1981; A Textbook of Clinical Ophthalmology, 1986; Cardiovascular Affections, Arteriosclerosis and Hypertension (Section in Systemic Ophthalmology, ed A. Sorsby), 1950 and 1958; Computerised Monitoring of Glaucoma (Section in Glaucoma, ed J. G. Bellows), 1979; Diagnosis of Primary Open Angle Glaucoma (in Glaucoma, ed J. E. Cairns), 1986; medical and ophthalmic contribs to Brit. Jl Ophthalmology, BMJ, Jl RN Med. Service, Trans Ophthalmolog. Soc. of the UK, etc. *Recreations:* walking, motoring, sailing. *Address:* Ophthalmic Department, King's College Hospital, Denmark Hill, SE5 9RS. *T:* 01–274 6222 ext. 2453; 6 Dartford Road, Sevenoaks, Kent TN13 3TQ. *T:* Sevenoaks 452233; Sandbanks House, 2 Panorama Road, Sandbanks, Poole, Dorset BH13 7RD. *T:* Poole 707560. *Clubs:* Royal Automobile; Royal Motor Yacht.
See also A. J. P. Crick.

CRIGHTON, Prof. David George; Professor of Applied Mathematics, University of Cambridge and Fellow of St John's College, Cambridge, since 1986; *b* 15 Nov. 1942; *s* of George Wolfe Johnston Crighton and Violet Grace Crighton (*née* Garrison); *m* 1969, Mary Christine West (marr. diss. 1985); one *s* one *d. Educ:* St John's College, Cambridge (BA 1964, MA 1980); Imperial College London (PhD 1969). Research Asst, Imperial College London, 1967–74; Prof. of Applied Mathematics, Univ. of Leeds, 1974–85. *Publications:* papers on fluid mechanics and wave theory in jls, conf. procs. *Recreations:* music, opera. *Address:* The Laurels, 58 Girton Road, Girton, Cambridge CB3 0LN. *T:* Cambridge 277100.

CRILL, Peter Leslie, CBE 1980; Bailiff of Jersey, 1986; President of the Court of Appeal of Jersey; Mem., Court of Appeal of Guernsey; *b* 1 Feb. 1925; *s* of S. G. Crill, Connetable of St Clement, 1916–58, and Olive Le Gros; *m* 1953, A. F. R. Dodd, MB, *d* of E. A. Dodd, JP, Dromara, NI; three *d. Educ:* Victoria Coll., Jersey; Exeter Coll., Oxford (King Charles I Scholar; MA). Called to the Bar, Middle Temple, 1949; called to the Jersey Bar, 1949. In private practice in Jersey, 1949–62. States of Jersey Deputy for St Clement, 1951–58; States of Jersey Senator, 1960–62; Solicitor General, Jersey, 1962–69; Attorney General, Jersey, 1969–75. Dep. Bailiff, 1975–86. Mem. Council, University of Buckingham. Pres., La Société Jersiaise, 1982. *Recreations:* music, books, horses, boats, pottering about. *Address:* Beechfield House, Trinity, Jersey, Channel Islands. *T:* Jersey 20270. *Clubs:* United Oxford & Cambridge University; United, Victoria (Jersey); Royal Yacht Squadron, Royal CI Yacht, St Helier Yacht.

CRIPPIN, Harry Trevor, FCIS; Chief Executive and Town Clerk, Cardiff City Council, since 1979; *b* 14 May 1929; *s* of Harry and Mary Elizabeth Crippin; *m* 1959, Hilda Green; one *s* one *d. Educ:* Leigh Grammar Sch., Lancs. DMA; FBIM; FCIS 1975. Asst Town Clerk, Manchester, 1970–74; City Sec., Cardiff CC, 1974–79. OStJ. *Address:* 37 Ely Road, Llandaff, Cardiff CF5 2JF. *T:* Cardiff 564103.

CRIPPS, family name of **Baron Parmoor.**

CRIPPS, Anthony L.; *see* Cripps, M. A. L.

CRIPPS, Cyril Humphrey; DL; MA; CChem, FRSC; Managing Director, Pianoforte Supplies Ltd, Roade, Northampton, since 1960, Chairman since 1979; Founder Member, Cripps Foundation, Chairman since 1979; Chairman: Velcro Industries NV, since 1973; Air BVI, since 1971; *b* 2 Oct. 1915; *o s* of Sir Cyril Thomas Cripps, MBE, and Lady (Amy) Cripps; *m* 1942, Dorothea Casson, *o d* of Reginald Percy Cook, architect; three *s* one *d. Educ:* Northampton Grammar Sch. (schol.); St John's Coll., Cambridge (Nat. Sci. Prelim. Cl. 1, Tripos Pts I and II, Cl. 2; BA, MA). FCS 1935; FRIC 1977; FRSC 1979. Founder of private businesses in UK, Australia, Canada and Brit. Virgin Islands. Member, Northamptonshire CC, 1963–74 (Leader of Independents, to 1974; formerly Vice-Chm., Educn and Planning Cttees); Mem., (new) Northants CC, 1973–81; Board Mem., Northampton Develt Corp., 1968–85. Life Mem., Ct, Univ. of Nottingham, 1953; Governor, Northampton Grammar Sch., 1963–74 (Vice-Chm. to 1974 and Vice-Chm. Foundn Trust, 1970–81); Chm. of Governors: Northampton Sch. for Boys, 1977–81; Northampton High Sch. for Girls, 1972–84; Foundn Governor, Bilton Grange Prep. Sch., 1957–80. Trustee, Postgrad. Med. Centre, Sports and Recreation, Residence and Res., Northampton Gen. Hosp., 1969–; Mem. Trusts: Peterborough Cath., 1975–; All Saints Church, Northampton, 1975–. Hon. Fellow: Cambridge Univ.: St John's, 1966; Magdalene, 1971; Selwyn, 1971; Queens', 1979; Cripps Hall, Nottingham Univ., 1959; Hon. DSc Nottingham, 1975; Hon. LLD Cantab 1976; Pres., Johnian Soc., 1966. Liveryman, Worshipful Co. of Wheelwrights, 1957, Mem. Court 1970, Master 1982; Liveryman, Worshipful Co. of Tallow Chandlers, 1983; Freeman, City of London (by redemption), 1957. High Sheriff, Northants, 1985–86; DL Northants, 1986. *Recreations:* travel, photography, natural history—entomological (espec. Rhopalocera), philately. *Address:* Bull's Head Farm, Stoke Goldington, Newport Pagnell, Bucks. *T:* Stoke Goldington 223; Southwold House, Southwold, Suffolk.

CRIPPS, Sir John Stafford, Kt 1978; CBE 1968; Chairman, Countryside Commission, 1970–77; *b* 10 May 1912; *s* of late Rt Hon. Sir Stafford Cripps, PC, CH, FRS, QC, and Isobel (Dame Isobel Cripps, GBE); *m* 1st, 1936, Ursula (marr. diss. 1971), *d* of late Arthur C. Davy; four *s* two *d*; 2nd, 1971, Ann Elizabeth Farwell. *Educ:* Winchester; Balliol Coll., Oxford. 1st Class Hons Politics, Philosophy and Economics (Modern Greats). Editor, The Countryman, 1947–71. Filkins Parish Councillor; Witney Rural District Councillor, 1946–74; Chairman: Rural District Councils' Association, 1967–70; Rural Cttee of Nat. Council of Social Service; Member: Oxfordshire Planning Cttee, 1948–69; W Oxfordshire Technical Coll. Governors, 1951–70; South East Economic Planning Council, 1966–73; Nature Conservancy, 1970–73; Exec. Cttee, CPRE, 1963–69; Inland Waterways Amenity Advisory Council, 1968–73; Defence Lands Cttee, 1971–73; Water Space Amenities Commn, 1977–80; Development Commn, 1978–82. President: Oxfordshire Rural Community Council, 1982–; Camping and Caravanning Club of GB and Ireland, 1981–. Prepared report on Accommodation for Gypsies, 1976. *Address:* Fox House, Filkins, Lechlade, Glos GL7 3JQ. *TA:* Filkins. *T:* Filkins 209. *Club:* Farmers'.
See also A. T. Ricketts.

CRIPPS, (Matthew) Anthony Leonard, CBE 1971; DSO 1943; TD 1947; QC 1958; a Recorder, since 1972 (Recorder of Nottingham, 1961–71); Deputy Senior Judge, British Sovereign Base Areas, Cyprus, since 1978; *b* 30 Dec. 1913; *s* of late Major Hon. L. H. Cripps; *heir-pres.* to 4th Baron Parmoor, *qv*; *m* 1941, Dorothea Margaret (Surrey CC 1965–67), *d* of G. Johnson Scott, Ashby-de-la-Zouch; three *s. Educ:* Eton; Christ Church, Oxford; Combined Army and RAF Staff Coll., 1944–45. Royal Leicestershire Regt, TA, 1933. Served War of 1939–45: Norway, Sweden, Finland, Iceland, N Africa, Italy, Egypt,

1939–44 (Capt. to Lt-Col); Staff Officer, Palestine and Syria, 1944–46. Barrister-at-law, Middle Temple, 1938 (Bencher 1965; Treasurer, 1983), Inner Temple, 1961, and Hong Kong, 1974. Hon. Judge of Court of Arches, 1969–80. Comr for Local Govt Petitions, 1978–. Chairman: Disciplinary Cttees, Milk Marketing Bd, 1956–, Potato and Egg Marketing Bds, 1956–67; Isle of Man Govt Commn on Agricultural Marketing, 1961–62; Home Sec.'s Adv. Cttee on Service Candidates, 1966– (Dep. Chm., 1965); Nat. Panel, Approved Coal Merchants Scheme, 1972–; Nat. Panel, Approved Solid Fuel Distributors Scheme; Legal Adv. Cttee, RSPCA, 1978–; Univ. of London Appeals Cttee, 1980–. Member: Agricultural Wages Bd, 1964–67; Northumberland Cttee of Inquiry into Foot and Mouth Disease, 1968–69; Cttee of Inquiry, Export of Live Animals for Slaughter, 1973–74. Pres., Coal Trade Benevolent Assoc., 1983 Mem., Ct of Assts, Fuellers' Co., 1985–. *Publications:* Agriculture Act 1947, 1947; Agriculture Holdings Act, 1948, 1948; (ed) 9th edn, Cripps on Compulsory Purchase: Powers, Procedure and Compensation, 1950; legal articles, especially on agricultural matters, for Law Jl and Encyclopaedia Britannica. *Recreations:* family life and gardening. *Address:* Alton House, Felbridge, East Grinstead, Sussex RH19 2PP. *T:* 23238; 1 Harcourt Buildings, Temple EC4Y 9DA. *T:* 01–353 9421. *Clubs:* Brooks's, Lansdowne.

CRISHAM, Air Vice-Marshal William Joseph, CB 1953; CBE 1944; RAF, retired; *b* 19 Nov. 1906; Served War of 1939–45; Nos 13 and 23 Sqdns; Central Fighter Establishment, 1950–53; No 12 Group Fighter Command, 1953–56; RAF Levant MEAF, 1956–58; RAF Germany (2nd TAF), 1958–61; retired 1961. *Club:* Royal Air Force.

CRISP, Prof. Arthur Hamilton, MD, DSc; FRCP, FRCPE, FRCPsych; Professor of Psychiatry, University of London at St George's Hospital Medical School, since 1967, and Dean, Faculty of Medicine, University of London, 1976–80; *b* 17 June 1930; *s* of John and Elizabeth Crisp; *m* 1958, Irene Clare (*née* Reid); three *s*. *Educ:* Watford Grammar Sch.; Univ. of London (MD; DSc). FRCP 1973, FRCPE 1972, FRCPsych 1971. Previously Lectr, then Sen. Lectr in Psych., Middlesex Hosp. Med. Sch., London. Chairman: Educn Cttee, GMC, 1982–; Adv. Cttee on Med. Educn, EEC, 1983–85. *Publications:* (jtly) Sleep, Nutrition and Mood, 1976; Anorexia Nervosa: Let Me Be, 1980; approx. 250 articles in learned jls. *Recreations:* golf, study of the River Wandle. *Address:* 113 Copse Hill, Wimbledon, SW20 0NT. *T:* 01–946 0976. *Clubs:* Athenæum; Royal Wimbledon Golf.

CRISP, Prof. Dennis John, CBE 1978; ScD; FRS 1968; Professor in Department of Marine Biology, University College of North Wales, 1962–83, now Professor Emeritus; Hon. Director, Natural Environment Research Council Unit of Marine Invertebrate Biology, 1965–83; *b* 29 April 1916; *m* 1944, Ella Stewart Allpress; one *s* one *d*. *Educ:* St Catharine's Coll., Cambridge. Research Asst, Dept of Colloid Science, Univ. of Cambridge, 1943–46; ICI (Paints Div.), i/c of Marine Paints Res. Stn, Brixham, Devon, 1946–51; Dir, Marine Science Laboratories, University Coll. of N Wales, 1951–70. Hon. FNA, 1984. *Publications:* (ed) Grazing in Terrestrial and Marine Environments, 1964; (ed) 4th European Marine Biology Symposium Volume (1969), 1971; papers in Proc. Royal Soc., Jl Marine Biol. Assoc., Jl Experimental Biology, Jl Animal Ecology, etc. *Recreations:* travel, photography. *Address:* Craig y Pîn, Llandegfan, Menai Bridge, Gwynedd. *T:* Menai Bridge 712775.

CRISP, Sir (John) Peter, 4th Bt *cr* 1913; *b* 19 May 1925; *o s* of Sir John Wilson Crisp, 3rd Bt, and Marjorie (*d* 1977), *d* of F. R. Shriver; *S* father, 1950; *m* 1954, Judith Mary, *d* of late H. E. Gillett; three *s* one *d*. *Educ:* Westminster. *Heir:* *s* John Charles Crisp, *b* 10 Dec. 1955. *Address:* Crabtree Cottage, Drungewick Lane, Loxwood, West Sussex. *T:* Loxwood 752374.

CRISP, Sir Peter; *see* Crisp, Sir (John) P.

CRITCHETT, Sir Ian (George Lorraine), 3rd Bt *cr* 1908; BA Cantab; HM Diplomatic Service, retired; Counsellor, Foreign and Commonwealth Office, 1977–80; *b* 9 Dec. 1920; *s* of Sir Montague Critchett, 2nd Bt, and Innes (*d* 1982), 3rd *d* of late Col F. G. A. Wiehe, The Durham Light Infantry; *S* father, 1941; *m* 1st, 1948, Paulette Mary Lorraine (*d* 1962), *e d* of late Col H. B. Humfrey; 2nd, 1964, Jocelyn Daphne Margret, *e d* of Comdr C. M. Hall, Higher Boswarva, Penzance, Cornwall; one *s* one *d*. *Educ:* Harrow; Clare Coll., Cambridge. RAFVR, 1942–46. Joined Foreign Office, 1948; 3rd Sec. (Commercial), at Vienna, 1950–51; 2nd Sec. (Commercial) at Bucharest, 1951–53; 2nd Sec. at Cairo, 1956; First Sec., FO, 1962. *Heir:* *s* Charles George Montague Critchett, *b* 2 April 1965. *Address:* Uplands Lodge, Pains Hill, Limpsfield, Surrey. *Clubs:* Travellers', MCC.

CRITCHLEY, Julian Michael Gordon; MP (C) Aldershot, since 1974 (Aldershot and North Hants, 1970–74); writer and journalist; *b* 8 Dec. 1930; *s* of Dr Macdonald Critchley, *qv*; *m* 1955, Paula Joan Baron (divorced 1965); two *d*; *m* 1965, Mrs Heather Goodrick; one *s* one *d*. *Educ:* Shrewsbury; Sorbonne; Pembroke Coll., Oxford (MA). MP (C) Rochester and Chatham, 1959–64; contested Rochester and Chatham, 1966. Chm. of the Bow Group, 1966–67. Vice-Chairman: Cons. Party Broadcasting Cttee; Cons. Party Defence Cttee; Chm., Cons. Party Media Cttee, 1976–81. Delegate to WEU and Council of Europe; Chm., WEU Defence Cttee; Deleg. to N Atlantic Assembly. Pres., Atlantic Assoc. of Young Political Leaders, 1968–70. *Publications:* (with O. Pick) Collective Security, 1974; Warning and Response, 1978; The North Atlantic Alliance and the Soviet Union in the 1980s, 1982; (jtly) Nuclear Weapons in Europe, 1984; Westminster Blues, 1985; (ed) Britain: a view from Westminster, 1986; various Bow Group and CPC pamphlets. *Recreations:* watching boxing, the country, reading military history, looking at churches, collecting Staffordshire. *Address:* The Brewer's House, 18 Bridge Square, Farnham, Surrey. *T:* Farnham 722075. *Club:* Carlton.

CRITCHLEY, Macdonald, CBE 1962; MD, ChB 1st Class Hons (Bristol), FRCP; Consulting Neurologist; *s* of Arthur Frank and Rosina Matilda Critchley; *m* 1st, Edna Auldeth Morris (decd); two *s*; 2nd, Eileen Hargreaves. *Educ:* Christian Brothers Coll.; Univ. of Bristol (Lady Haberfield Scholarship in Medicine, Markham Skerritt Prize for Original Research). Goulstonian Lectr, RCP, 1930; Hunterian Prof., RCS, 1935; Royal Coll. of Physicians: Bradshaw Lectr, 1942; Croonian Lectr, 1945; Harveian Orator, 1966; Pres., World Fedn of Neurology, 1965–73; Hon. Consulting Neurologist, King's Coll. Hosp.; Hon. Consulting Physician, National Hosp., Queen Square; formerly Dean, Inst. of Neurology; Neurological Physician, Royal Masonic Hosp.; formerly Neurologist to Royal Hosp. and Home for Incurables, Putney. Consulting Neurologist to Royal Navy, 1939–77; Long Fox Lectr, Univ. of Bristol, 1935; William Withering Lectr, Univ. of Birmingham, 1946; Tisdall Lectr, Univ. of Manitoba, 1951; Semon Lectr, Univ. of London, 1951; Sherrington Lectr, Univ. of Wisconsin; Orator, Medical Soc. of London, 1955. Pres. Harveian Soc., 1947. Hunterian Orator, 1957; Doyne Memorial Lectr, 1961; Wartenberg Lectr, 1961; Victor Horsley Memorial Lectr, 1963; Honyman Gillespie Lectr, 1963; Schorstein Lectr, 1964; Hughlings Jackson Lectr and Medallist, RSM, 1964; Gowers Lectr and Medallist, 1965; Veraguth Gold Medallist, Bern, 1968; Sam T. Orton Award for work on Dyslexia, 1974; Arthur Hall Memorial Lectr, 1969; Rickman Godlee Lectr, 1970; Cavendish Lectr, 1976; Vis. Prof., Winston-Salem, NC, 1983. Pres. Assoc. of British Neurologists, 1962–64; Second Vice-Pres., RCP, 1964; Mem., GMC, 1957–73; Founder-Pres., Migraine Trust. Hon. FACP; MD Zürich *hc*; DenM (Aix-Marseille) *hc*; MD Madrid *hc*; Hon. Fellow: Faculty of History and Philosophy of Medicine and

Pharmacy; Pan-African Assoc. of Neurological Scis; Hon. Mem., RSM; Hon. Corresp. Mem. Académie de Médecine de France, Norwegian Academy of Science and Letters, Royal Academy of Medicine, Barcelona, and Neurological Socs of France, Switzerland, Holland, Turkey, Uruguay, US, Canada, Australia, Brazil, Argentine, Germany, Chile, Spain, Roumania, Norway, Czechoslovakia, Greece, Italy, Bulgaria, Hungary, Peru, Poland and Sweden. Visiting Prof., Univs of: Istanbul, 1949; California, 1950 and 1964; Hawaii, 1966. Master, Worshipful Soc. of Apothecaries, 1956–57. Served European War, 1917–18; Surgeon Captain RNVR, 1939–46. *Publications:* Mirror Writing; Neurology of Old Age; Observations on Pain; Language of Gesture; Shipwreck-survivors; Sir William Gowers; The Parietal Lobes; The Black Hole; Developmental Dyslexia; Aphasiology; The Dyslexic Child; Silent Language; (ed jtly) Music and the Brain, 1976; (jtly) Dyslexia defined, 1978; various articles on nervous diseases. *Address:* National Hospital, Queen Square, WC1. *T:* 01–837 3611. *Clubs:* Athenæum, Garrick, Pilgrims.
See also J. M. G. Critchley.

CRITCHLEY, Philip; Director of Highway Contracts, Administration and Maintenance, Department of Transport, since 1985; *b* 31 Jan. 1931; *s* of Henry Stephen and Edith Adela Critchley; *m* 1962, Stella Ann Barnes; two *s* one *d*. *Educ:* Manchester Grammar Sch.; Balliol Coll., Oxford (MA, 2nd Classical Mods and Greats). National Service, Intelligence Corps, 1953–55. Joined Min. of Housing and Local Govt (now Dept of Environment), 1955: Principal, 1960; Asst Sec., 1969; Under Sec., 1980; Dir of Waste Disposal, 1983. *Recreations:* cycling, walking, writing poetry. *Address:* Redstone House, Maidstone Road, Ashford, Kent TN25 4NP. *T:* Ashford 21037. *Clubs:* Blackheath Harriers; Oxford Union Society.

CRITCHLEY, Thomas Alan, JP; Assistant Under-Secretary of State, Home Office, 1972–76; *b* 11 March 1919; *y s* of Thomas Critchley and Annie Louisa Darvell; *m* 1942, Margaret Carol Robinson; one *s* two *d*. *Educ:* Queen Elizabeth's Grammar Sch., Barnet. Entered Civil Service, 1936. Served War, 1940–46 (commnd in RAOC); Asst Principal, Home Office, 1947; Principal, 1948; Cabinet Office, 1954–56; Principal Private Sec. to Rt Hon. R. A. Butler, Home Secretary, 1957–60; Asst Sec., 1958; Sec., Royal Commn on Police, 1960–62; Sec. to Lord Denning's Enquiry into the Profumo Affair, 1963; Sec. of the Gaming Board for Great Britain, 1971–72; Director (and Mem.), Uganda Resettlement Board, 1972–74; held enquiry into UK Immigrants Adv. Service, 1976; Vice-Chm., WRVS, 1977–81; Chm., Mddx Area Probation Cttee, 1983–85. JP Middlesex 1977. *Publications:* The Civil Service Today, 1951; A History of Police in England and Wales, 1967, 2nd edn 1978 (Amer. edn, 1972); The Conquest of Violence, 1970; (with P. D. James) The Maul and the Pear Tree, 1971, repubd US and GB, 1986; contributor to: The Police We Deserve, 1973, and various jls. *Recreations:* reading, gardening, walking. *Address:* 26 Temple Fortune Lane, NW11. *T:* 01–455 4894. *Clubs:* Reform, Civil Service.

CROAN, Thomas Malcolm; Sheriff of North Strathclyde, since 1983; *b* 7 Aug. 1932; *s* of John Croan and Amelia Sydney; *m* 1959, Joan Kilpatrick Law; one *s* three *d*. *Educ:* St Joseph's Coll., Dumfries; Edinburgh University. MA 1953; LLB 1955. Admitted to Faculty of Advocates, 1956; Standing Junior Counsel, to Scottish Develt Dept, 1964–65 and (for highways work) 1967–69; Advocate Depute, 1965–66; Sheriff of Grampian, Highland and Islands (formerly Aberdeen, Kincardine and Banff), 1969–83. *Recreations:* sailing, reading. *Address:* Overdale, 113 Bentinck Drive, Troon KA10 6JB.

CROCKATT, Lieut Comdr (Douglas) Allan, OBE 1981 (MBE 1971); RD 1978; JP; RNR retd; Vice Lord-Lieutenant of West Yorkshire, since 1985; *b* 31 Jan. 1923; *s* of late Douglas Crockatt, JP, LLD and Ella Crockatt (*née* Lethem); *m* 1946, Helen Townley Tatton (*d* 1985), *d* of late Capt. T. A. Tatton, MC; one *d*. *Educ:* Bootham School, York; Trinity Hall, Cambridge. RNVR 1941–46, Western Approaches and N Russia; RNVSR 1946–64; RNR active list, 1964–82. Director: Johnson Group Cleaners, 1961–84 (Dep. Chm., 1976–84); Johnson Group Inc. (USA) (formerly Apparelmaster Inc.), 1975–84 (Dep. Chm., 1981–84); local Dir, Martins and Barclays Banks W Yorks Bd, 1964–84. Mem., Multiple Shops' Fedn Council, 1972–77. Life Vice-Pres., W Yorks Branch Magistrates' Assoc., 1980 (Hon. Sec., 1958–72; Chm., 1975–77; Pres., 1977–79); Mem. Council, Magistrates' Assoc., 1959–80 (Chm., Training Cttee, 1974–80); Member: Lord Chancellor's Adv. Cttee for training of Magistrates, 1964–79; Lord Chancellor's Magistrates' Courts Rule Cttee, 1979–81. CC, W Riding of Yorks, 1953–58; JP 1956, DL 1971, West (formerly WR) Yorks. Freeman, City of London, 1958; Liveryman, Dyers' Co., 1958. *Recreations:* cricket, sailing, fishing. *Address:* Paddock House, Sicklinghall, Wetherby, W Yorks LS22 4BJ. *T:* Wetherby 62844. *Clubs:* Army and Navy; RN Sailing Association, Driffield Anglers'.

CROCKER, Antony James Gulliford, CB 1973; retired as Under-Secretary, Family Support Division, Department of Health and Social Security (1974–78); *b* 28 Oct. 1918; *s* of late Cyril James Crocker and Mabel Kate Crocker; *m* 1st, 1943, E. S. B. Dent; 2nd, 1949, Nancy Wynell, *d* of late Judge Gamon and Eleanor Margaret Gamon; two *s* one *d*. *Educ:* Sherborne Sch. (Scholar); Trinity Hall, Cambridge (Major Scholar, MA). Served War, 1939–46, Dorsetshire Regt (Major). Asst Princ. 1947, Princ. 1948, Min. of Nat. Insurance. Sec., Nat. Insce Advisory Cttee, 1955–56; Asst Sec., Min. of Pensions and Nat. Insce, 1956; Under-Secretary; War Pensions Dept, 1964 (Min. of Social Security, 1966–68); Supplementary Benefits Commn, 1968; Tax Credits Div., 1972; New Pensions Scheme, 1974. *Recreations:* horticulture, philately. *Address:* Wealdover, Guildown Avenue, Guildford, Surrey. *T:* 66555.

CROCKER, Peter Vernon; His Honour Judge Crocker; a Circuit Judge, since 1974; *b* 29 June 1926; *s* of Walter Angus Crocker and Fanny Victoria Crocker (*née* Dempster); *m* 1950, Nancy Kathleen Sargent. *Educ:* Oundle; Corpus Christi Coll., Cambridge (BA). Called to Bar, Inner Temple, 1949. *Recreations:* gardening, tennis, swimming.

CROCKER, Sir Walter (Russell), KBE 1978 (CBE 1955); Australian diplomat, retired 1970; Lieutenant-Governor of South Australia, 1973–82; *b* 25 March 1902; *e s* of late Robert Crocker and Alma Bray, Parnaroo, SA; *m* 1951, Claire (marr. diss. 1968), *y d* of F. J. Ward, Headmaster of Prince Alfred Coll., Adelaide, and *widow* of Dr John Gooden, Physicist; two *s*. *Educ:* University of Adelaide; Balliol Coll., Oxford; Stanford University, USA. Entered Colonial Administrative Service (Nigeria), 1930; transf. to League of Nations, 1934, and to ILO (Asst to Dir-Gen). Served War, 1940–45 (Lt-Col, Croix de Guerre avec palme, Ordre royal du Lion, Belgium). Farming at Parnaroo, 1946; UN Secretariat (Chief of Africa Sect.), 1946–49; Prof. of Internat. Relations, Aust. Nat. Univ. 1949–52; Actg Vice-Chancellor, 1951; High Commissioner for Australia to India, 1952–55; Ambassador of Australia to Indonesia, 1955–57; High Comr to Canada, 1957–58; High Comr for Australia to India and Ambassador to Nepal, 1958–62; Amb. of Australia to the Netherlands and Belgium, 1962–65; Ambassador to Ethiopia and High Commissioner to Kenya and Uganda, 1965–67; Ambassador to Italy, 1967–70. Hon. Colonel, Royal South Australia Regt, 1977–. L'Ordre royal du Lion (Belgium), 1945; Cavaliere di Gr. Croce dell'Ordine al Merito (Italy), 1970; Order of Malta (Grand' Uffiziale del Merito Melitense), 1975. *Publications:* The Japanese Population Problem, 1931; Nigeria, 1936; On Governing Colonies, 1946; Self-Government for the Colonies, 1949; Can the United Nations Succeed?, 1951; The Race Question as a factor in

International Relations, 1955; Nehru, 1965; Australian Ambassador, 1971; Memoirs, 1981; Sir Thomas Playford, 1983. *Recreations:* gardening, walking, music; previously ski-ing, tennis. *Address:* 256 East Terrace, Adelaide, SA 5000, Australia. *Club:* Adelaide.

CROCKFORD, Brig. Allen Lepard, CBE 1955 (OBE 1945); DSO 1943; MC 1916; TD 1942; late Hon. Colonel RAMC 54 and 56 Division (TA); *b* 11 Sept. 1897; *s* of late J. A. V. Crockford, West Worthing, Sussex; *m* 1924, Doris Ellen Brookes-Smith; one *s* two *d.* *Educ:* Gresham's Sch.; King's Coll., Cambridge; St Thomas's Hosp. Glos Regt, BEF (Capt.; wounded), 1915–19. BA Cantab, 1920; MA 1926, MB, BCh Cantab, 1922; Gen. Practice, 1924–39; RAMC (TA): served with 43rd, Guards Armoured, 46th and 56th Divs, BNAF and CMF (Col), 1939–45; Gen. Practice, 1945–46; Medical Sec., St Thomas's Hosp. Medical Sch., London, SE1, 1946–64. Col (TA), ADMS, 56 Armoured Div., 1947; Brig. (TA); DDMS AA Comd, 1949; KHS 1952; QHS 1952–57; OStJ 1954. *Recreations:* reading, gardening. *Address:* Holly Cottage, Humshaugh, Hexham, Northumberland NE46 4AG. *T:* Humshaugh 298.

CROFT, family name of **Baron Croft.**

CROFT, 2nd Baron *cr* 1940, of Bournemouth; **Michael Henry Glendower Page Croft;** Bt 1924; *b* 20 Aug. 1916; *s* of 1st Baron Croft, PC, CMG, and Hon. Nancy Beatrice Borwick (*d* 1949), *y d* of 1st Baron Borwick; *S* father, 1947; *m* 1948, Lady Antoinette Fredericka Conyngham (*d* 1959), *o d* of 6th Marquess Conyngham; one *s* one *d.* *Educ:* Eton; Trinity Hall, Cambridge (BA). Served War of 1939–45, Capt. RASC. Called to the Bar, Inner Temple, 1952. Director: Henry Page & Co. Ltd, 1946–57; Ware Properties Ltd, 1958–65; Hereford and Worcester, Building Preservation Trust Ltd, 1986. Underwriting Mem., Lloyd's, 1971–. Member Executive Cttee: Contemporary Arts Soc., 1960–68 and 1970–81 (Hon. Sec., 1971–76, Hon. Treasurer, 1976–80, Vice-Chm., 1980–81); British Museum Soc., 1969–76. Hon. Keeper of Contemporary Art, Fitzwilliam Museum, Cambridge, 1984. FRSA. OStJ. *Heir:* *s* Hon. Bernard William Henry Page Croft [*b* 28 Aug 1949. *Educ:* Stowe; Univ. of Wales, Cardiff. BScEcon]. *Address:* Croft Castle, near Leominster, Herefordshire; 19 Queen's Gate Gardens, SW7 5LZ. *Club:* Athenæum.

CROFT, David Legh, QC 1982; a Recorder, since 1985; *b* 14 Aug. 1937; *s* of late Alan Croft and of Doreen Mary Berry (*née* Mitchell); *m* 1963, Susan Mary (*née* Bagnall); two *s.* *Educ:* Haileybury and ISC; Nottingham Univ. (LLB). Called to the Bar, Middle Temple, 1960; called to the Hong Kong Bar, 1984. *Recreation:* dieting. *Address:* Star Hill House, Rochester, Kent ME1 1XB.

CROFT, (Ivor) John, CBE 1982; painter in oils; Head of Home Office Research and Planning Unit, 1981–83 (Head, Home Office Research Unit, 1972–81); *b* 6 Jan. 1923; *s* of Oswald Croft and Doris (*née* Phillips). *Educ:* Westminster Sch.; Christ Church, Oxford (MA); Inst. of Education, Univ. of London (MA); LSE. Temp. jun. admin. officer, FO, 1942–45; asst teacher, LCC, 1949–51; Inspector, Home Office Children's Dept, 1952–66; Sen. Research Officer, Home Office Research Unit, 1966–72. Member: Criminological Scientific Council, Council of Europe, 1978–83, Chm., 1981–83; Conservative Study Gp on Crime, 1983–; Kensington Crime Prevention Panel, 1984–. Governor, ILEA Secondary Schs, 1959–68. Mem. Exec. Cttee, English Assoc., 1966–77 (Hon. Treas. 1972–75); Chm., Pembridge Assoc., 1985–. Group shows, 1958, 1963, 1967, 1968, 1969, 1973; one-man shows, 1970, 1971. *Publications:* Research in Criminal Justice, 1978; Crime and the Community, 1979; Crime and Comparative Research, 1979; Research and Criminal Policy, 1980; Managing Criminological Research, 1981; Concerning Crime, 1982; Criminological Research in Great Britain (with a Note on the Council of Europe), 1983; Confidence in the Law, 1986; contrib. various learned jls. *Address:* Flat 2, 35 Chepstow Villas, W11 3DP. *Club:* Reform.

CROFT, Major Sir John (Archibald Radcliffe), 5th Bt *cr* 1818; Army Officer, retired 1956; *b* 27 March 1910; *s* of Tom Radcliffe Croft, OBE (*d* 1964) (6th *s* of 2nd Bt) and Louise (*d* 1964), *d* of Francis Sales; *S* cousin, 1979; *m* 1953, Lucy Elizabeth, *d* of late Major William Dallas Loney Jupp, OBE; one *s.* *Educ:* King's School, Canterbury. Commissioned The West Yorkshire Regt (PWO), 1935; served India, Burma, 1936–44; France and Germany, 1945. *Recreations:* shooting, fishing, golf. *Heir:* *s* Thomas Stephen Hutton Croft, *b* 12 June 1959. *Address:* Cornerways, Stodmarsh, Canterbury, Kent. *T:* Canterbury 721256. *Clubs:* Army and Navy; Kent and Canterbury (Canterbury).

CROFT, (John) Michael, OBE 1971; Founder of National Youth Theatre, 1956; *b* 8 March 1922. *Educ:* Plymouth Grove Elem. Sch. and Burnage Gram. Sch., Manchester; Keble Coll., Oxford (BA Hons). War Service in RAF and RN, 1940–45. After short career as actor, took up teaching, 1949; Asst English Master, Alleyn's Sch., 1950–55 (prod. series of Shakespeare plays with large schoolboy cos); founded Youth Theatre with group from Alleyn's Sch., 1956; this grew rapidly into nat. organisation with provincial branches; rep. Gt Brit. at Paris Festival, 1960 and W Berlin Festival, 1961; appeared at Old Vic, 1965. Also Dir Shakespeare for leading cos in Belgium and Holland, 1960–65; founded Dolphin Theatre Co., Shaw Theatre, 1971; productions include: Devil's Disciple, 1971; Romeo and Juliet, 1972; Antony and Cleopatra, 1977; Richard II, 1980; Nat. Youth Theatre Productions include: Zigger Zagger, Strand, 1968, Berlin Festival, 1968, Holland Festival, 1970, Shaw, 1981; Little Malcolm and his Struggle, Holland Festival, 1968; Fuzz, Berlin Festival, 1970; a series of plays by Peter Terson and Barrie Keeffe, during 1970s; Good Lads at Heart, tour of Canada, 1978; Brooklyn, NY, 1979; The Bread and Butter Trade, Shaw, 1982; Hamlet, 1983. *Publications:* (novel) Spare the Rod, 1954; (travel book) Red Carpet to China, 1958. *Recreations:* sport, travel. *Address:* 74 Bartholomew Road, NW5. *Club:* Savile.

CROFT, Michael; *see* Croft, J. M.

CROFT, Col Noel Andrew Cotton, DSO 1945; OBE 1970; MA Oxon; Essex Regiment; retired; *b* 30 Nov. 1906; *s* of late Rev. Canon R. W. Croft, MA; *m* 1952, Rosalind, 2nd *d* of late Comdr A. H. de Kantzow, DSO, RN; three *d.* *Educ:* Lancing Coll.; Stowe Sch.; Christ Church, Oxford; Sch. of Technology, Manchester. Cotton Trade, 1929–32; Mem. British Trans-Greenland Expedition, 1933–34; ADC to Maharajah of Cooch Behar, India, 1934–35; Second-in-Command, Oxford Univ. Arctic Expedition to North-East Land, 1935–36; Ethnological Exped. to Swedish Lapland, 1938; Sec. to Dir of Fitzwilliam Museum, Cambridge, 1937–39. Served War of 1939–45, Capt. 1939; WO Mission to Finno-Russian War, 1939–40; Bde Intelligence Officer Independent Companies, Norwegian Campaign, 1940; Combined Ops, 1940–41; Major, 1941; Asst Mil. Attaché, Stockholm, 1941–42; sea or parachute ops in Tunisia, Corsica, Italy, France, and Denmark, 1943–45; Lieut-Col 1945; Asst Dir Scientific Research, War Office, 1945–49; WO Observer on Canadian Arctic "Exercise Musk-Ox", 1945–46, and on NW Frontier Trials, India, 1946–47; attached Canadian Army, 1947–48; GSO1, War Office, 1949–51; Liaison Officer HQ Continental Army, USA, 1952–54; comd The Infantry Junior Leaders Bn, 1954–57; Col 1957; Comdt Army Apprentices Sch., Harrogate, 1957–60; Comdt, Metropolitan Police Cadet Corps, 1960–71. Chm., Women's Transport Service (FANY). Corresp. Fellow, Arctic Inst. of North America; Mem., Reindeer Council of UK, 1949– (Chm., 1962–82). Polar Medal (clasp Arctic, 1935–36), 1942; Back Award, RGS, 1946 and 1947. *Publications:* (with A. R. Glen) Under the Pole Star, 1937; Polar Exploration, 1939. *Recreations:* mountaineering, ski-ing, sailing, photography. *Address:* River House, Strand-on-the-Green, W4. *T:* 01-994 6359. *Clubs:* Alpine, Special Forces.

CROFT, Sir Owen (Glendower), 14th Bt *cr* 1671; grazier; *b* 26 April 1932; *s* of Sir Bernard Hugh Denman Croft, 13th Bt, and of Helen Margaret (*née* Weaver); *S* father, 1984; *m* 1959, Sally Patricia, *d* of Dr T. M. Mansfield, Brisbane; one *s* two *d.* *Educ:* Armidale School, NSW. Member: Council of Advice to Pastures Protection Bds of NSW; Natural Disasters Adv. Cttee of NSW; Vertebrate Pest Control Adv. Cttee of NSW. *Recreations:* tennis; National Trust activities. *Heir:* *s* Thomas Jasper Croft, *b* 3 Nov. 1962. *Address:* Salisbury Court, Uralla, NSW 2358, Australia. *T:* 067/784624.

CROFT, Roy Henry Francis, CB 1983; Chief Executive, Securities and Investments Board, since 1985; *b* 4 March 1936; *s* of late William Henry Croft and Dorothy Croft; *m* 1961, Patricia Ainley; one *s* two *d.* *Educ:* Isleworth Grammar Sch.; Christ's Coll., Cambridge (MA). BoT, 1959; Treasury, 1961–62; DEA, 1964–67; Private Sec. to Pres. Bd of Trade, 1968–70; Cabinet Office, 1970–72; Civil Aviation Div., Dept of Trade, 1973–76; Finance and Economic Appraisal Div., DoI, 1976–79; Posts and Telecommunications Div., DoI, 1979–80; Dep. Sec. DTI, 1980–85. *Address:* 3 Royal Exchange Buildings, EC3V 3NL.

CROFT, Stanley Edward, TD 1951; Senior Associate, Abbey Life Assurance Company; formerly HM Diplomatic Service; *b* 18 Oct. 1917; *s* of Edward John and Alice Lucy Croft; *m* 1950, Joan Mary Kaye; four *s* two *d.* *Educ:* Portsmouth Grammar School. TA, 1939; served War of 1939–45, RA, Middle East, Aden, Italy, Germany. Min. of Labour, 1935; Admty, 1937–39 and 1946–47; transf. to Diplomatic Service, 1947; Vice-Consul, Barcelona, 1950; 2nd Sec., Lahore, 1951; Washington, 1955; Madrid, 1956; 1st Sec., FO, 1960; Consul, Geneva, 1961; FO and CRO, 1965–70; Consul-Gen., Madrid, 1970; Counsellor and Consul-Gen., Luanda, 1974–77. *Recreations:* swimming, tennis, camping, fishing, carpentry. *Clubs:* Royal Commonwealth Society; Foxhills (Ottershaw).

CROFTON, family name of **Baron Crofton.**

CROFTON, 6th Baron *cr* 1797; **Charles Edward Piers Crofton;** Bt 1758; Master Mariner, since 1978; *b* 27 April 1949; *s* of 5th Baron Crofton and of Ann, *e d* of Group Captain Charles Tighe, The Mill House, Kilbride, Co. Wicklow; *S* father, 1974; *m* 1976, Maureen Jacqueline, *d* of S. J. Bray, Taunton, Somerset; one *d.* Ship Master, with Buries Markes (Ship Management) Ltd, 1979–. Mem., Nautical Institute, 1978. *Heir:* *b* Hon. Guy Patrick Gilbert Crofton [*b* 17 June 1951; *m* 1985, Gillian, *o d* of Harry Godfrey Mitchell Bass, *qv.* Commissioned 9/12 Royal Lancers, 1971]. *Address:* Longford House, Beltra, Co. Sligo, Eire.

CROFTON, Denis Hayes, OBE 1948 (MBE 1943); retired Home and Indian Civil Servant; Member, Panel of Inspectors, Department of the Environment, 1969–79; President, Tunbridge Wells and District Branch, Civil Service Retirement Fellowship, since 1985 (Chairman, 1972–85); *b* 14 Dec. 1908; *s* of late Richard Hayes Crofton, Colonial Civil Service and Mabel Annie Crofton (*née* Smith); *m* 1933, Alison Carr, *d* of late Andrew McClure and Ethel McClure; three *s* one *d.* *Educ:* Tonbridge Sch.; Corpus Christi Coll., Oxford (Class. Mods, Lit. Hum., MA). Indian Civil Service, 1932; served in Bihar; subdivisional Magistrate, Giridih, 1934, Jamshedpur, 1935; Under-Sec. to Govt of Bihar, Polit. and Appt Depts, 1936; Under-Sec. to Govt of India, Dept of Labour, 1939; Private Sec. to Indian Mem., Eastern Gp Supply Council, 1941; Dist Mag. and Collector, Shahabad, Bihar, 1942; Sec. to Gov. of Bihar, 1944; apptd to Home Civil Service, 1947; Principal, Min. of Fuel and Power, Petroleum Div. 1948; Asst Sec., Petroleum Div. and Chm., OEEC Oil Cttee, Paris, 1950–53; Asst Sec., Monopolies and Restrictive Practices Commn, 1953; Asst Sec., Min. of Fuel and Power, Electricity Div., 1956; Petroleum Div., 1961; Accountant General and Under-Secretary for Finance, 1962–68. *Publications:* The Children of Edmonstown Park: memoirs of an Irish family, 1981; edited: The Surgery at Aberffrwd: some encounters of a colliery doctor, 1982; A GP's Progress to the Black Country, 1984 (both by Francis Maylett Smith). *Recreations:* reading, gardening. *Address:* 26 Vauxhall Gardens, Tonbridge, Kent. *T:* Tonbridge 353465. *Club:* Royal Commonwealth Society.

CROFTON, Sir John (Wenman), Kt 1977; retired; Professor of Respiratory Diseases and Tuberculosis, University of Edinburgh, 1952–77; *b* 1912; *s* of Dr W. M. Crofton; *m* 1945, Eileen Chris Mercer, MBE 1984; two *s* three *d.* *Educ:* Tonbridge; Sidney Sussex Coll., Cambridge; St Thomas's Hosp. Medical qualification, 1936; War of 1939–45, RAMC; France, Middle East, Germany. Lecturer in Medicine, Postgraduate Medical Sch. of London, 1947–51, Senior Lecturer, 1951; Part-time Tuberculosis Unit, Medical Research Council, Brompton Hosp., 1947–50; Dean of Faculty of Medicine, 1964–66, and Vice-Principal, 1969–70, Univ. of Edinburgh. Vice-Pres., 1972–73, Pres., 1973–76, RCPE. Weber-Parkes Prize, RCP, 1966. *Publications:* (jt author) Respiratory Diseases, 1969, 3rd edn 1981; contributor to BMJ, Lancet, Thorax, etc. *Recreations:* conversation, family life, mountains. *Address:* 13 Spylaw Bank Road, Edinburgh EH13 0JW. *T:* 031-441 3730. *Club:* University Staff (Edinburgh).

CROFTON, Sir Malby (Sturges), 5th Bt *cr* 1838 (orig. *cr* 1661); Partner, Messrs Fenn & Crosthwaite; Member of the London Stock Exchange, 1957–75; *b* 11 Jan. 1923; *s* of Sir Malby Richard Henry Crofton, 4th Bt, DSO and Bar, and Katharine Beatrix Pollard; *S* father, 1962. *Educ:* Eton (King's Scholar); Trinity Coll., Cambridge (scholar). Served with Life Guards, 1942–46, in Middle East and Italy. Member: Kensington Borough Council, 1962, Leader, 1968–77, Mayor, Kensington and Chelsea, 1978; GLC, 1970–73; ILEA, 1970–73; Ealing N, GLC, 1977–81; Leader, GLC Scrutiny Cttee, 1977–78. Vice-Chm., NW Thames RHA, 1980–. Hon.Treasurer, Marie Curie Meml Foundn; Dir, St Edward's Housing Assoc. Freeman, Royal Bor. of Kensington and Chelsea, 1983. Hon. Fellow, Chelsea Coll. *Recreations:* tennis, swimming, motoring, planting trees, farming. *Heir:* *kinsman* Henry Edward Melville Crofton [*b* 15 Aug. 1931; *m* 1955, Brigid, twin of Gerald K. Riddle; two *s* one *d*]. *Address:* 51 Clareville Street, SW7 5AX; Longford House, Co. Sligo, Eire.

CROFTON, Sir Patrick Simon, 7th Bt *cr* 1801; *b* 2 Dec. 1936; *o s* of Major Morgan G. Crofton (*d* 1947); *S* grandfather, 1958; *m* 1967, Mrs Lene Eddowes, *d* of Kai Augustinus, Copenhagen, and Mrs R. Tonnesen, Port Elizabeth, SA; one *d.* *Educ:* Eton Coll. 2nd Lieut Welsh Guards, 1955–57. Entered Steel Industry, 1957; became Public Relations Consultant, 1961. Joint Managing Dir, Crofton Mohill Holdings Ltd; Dir, Blair Eames Suslak, Sir Patrick Crofton Ltd, Advertising Agents; Managing Dir, Sir Patrick Crofton Developments Ltd. *Recreations:* ski-ing, motoring, music, political argument. *Heir:* *uncle* Hugh Denis Crofton, *b* 10 April 1937. *Clubs:* Cavalry and Guards, East India, Devonshire, Sports and Public Schools.

CROHAM, Baron *cr* 1978 (Life Peer), of the London Borough of Croydon; **Douglas Albert Vivian Allen,** GCB 1973 (KCB 1967; CB 1963); Chairman, Guinness Peat Group, since 1983; Head of the Home Civil Service and Permanent Secretary, Civil Service Department, 1974–77; *b* 15 Dec. 1917; *s* of late Albert Allen; *m* 1941, Sybil Eileen Allegro, *d* of late John Marco Allegro; two *s* one *d.* *Educ:* Wallington County

Grammar Sch.; London School of Economics. BSc (Econ.) First Class Hons, 1938. Entered Board of Trade, 1939; Royal Artillery, 1940–45; Cabinet Office, 1947; Treasury, 1948–58; Under-Secretary, Ministry of Health, 1958–60; Under-Secretary, Treasury, 1960–62, Third Secretary, 1962–64; Dept of Economic Affairs: Dep. Under-Sec. of State, 1964–66; Second Permanent Under-Sec. of State, May-Oct. 1966; Permanent Under-Sec. of State, 1966–68; Permanent Sec., HM Treasury, 1968–74. Dir, Pilkington Bros, 1978–; Dep. Chm., 1978–82, Chm., 1982–85, BNOC. An Industrial Advisor to the Governor, Bank of England, 1978–83. Pres., Inst. for Fiscal Studies, 1979–. A Trustee, Anglo-German Foundn, 1977– (Chm., 1982–). CBIM; FRSA 1975. Hon. Fellow, LSE, 1969; Hon. DSc (Social Sciences) Southampton, 1977. *Recreations:* tennis, woodwork. *Address:* 9 Manor Way, South Croydon, Surrey. *T:* 01–688 0496. *Club:* Reform.

See also J. M. Allegro.

CROKER, Edgar Alfred; Secretary and Chief Executive of the Football Association, since 1973; *b* 13 Feb. 1924; *m* 1952, Kathleen Mullins; one *s* two *d*. *Educ:* Kingston Technical Coll. Served War: Flt Lieut, RAF, 1942–46. Flt Lieut, RAFVR, 1947–55. Professional footballer: Charlton Athletic, 1947–51; Headington United, 1951–56. Sales Dir, Douglas Equipment, 1956–61; Chairman and Managing Dir, Liner-Croker Ltd, 1961–73; Chairman, Liner Concrete Machinery Co. Ltd, 1971–73. King's commendation for brave conduct, 1946. *Recreations:* golf, tennis, bridge. *Address:* South Court, The Park, Cheltenham, Glos. *T:* Cheltenham 527618. *Club:* Sportsman.

CROLL, Hon. David Arnold, QC; BA, LLB; Senator; Chairman, Senate Committees on: Poverty, since 1968; Aging, since 1963; Retirement Age Policies, since 1977; *b* Moscow, 12 March 1900; *s* of Hillel and Minnie Croll; *m* 1925, Sarah Levin; three *d*. *Educ:* public schs and Patterson Collegiate Institute, Windsor; Osgoode Hall, Toronto; University of Toronto. Emigrated to Canada with family, 1906, settling at Windsor, Ont; first and only commercial venture operation of news-stand, which greatly facilitated secondary education; after high school and course articled to solicitor; graduation from Osgoode Hall law sch. followed by practice at Windsor, 1925–30; presently senior partner in Croll and Croll, Windsor, Ont., and Croll and Godfrey, Toronto, Ont. Mayor of Windsor, Ont., 1930–34, 1939–40; Mem. for Windsor-Walkerville, Ont. Legislature, 1934–44; late Minister of Labour, Public Welfare and Municipal Affairs for the Province of Ont.; was youngest and first Jewish Cabinet Minister and first Jewish Senator, in Canada. Mem. of House of Commons for Toronto Spadina, 1945–55 when appointed to Senate. Served War of 1939–45, with Canadian Army overseas, enlisting as Private in Sept. 1939 and discharged in rank of Col in Sept. 1945. *Recreations:* golf and the more strenuous sports. *Address:* 1603 Bathurst Street, Suite 508, Toronto, Ont M5P 3J2, Canada. *Club:* Primrose (Toronto).

CROLY, Brig. Henry Gray, CBE 1958; JP; *b* 7 June 1910; *s* of late Lt-Col W. Croly, DSO, late RAMC, Ardvarna, Tralee; *m* 1939, Marjorie Rosanne, *er d* of late Major J. S. Knyvett, late R Warwickshire Regt, Clifford Manor Road, Guildford; two *s* two *d*. *Educ:* Sherborne Sch.; RMA Woolwich. 2nd Lieut RA, 1930; served in India: Mohmand Ops, 1935; Waziristan, 1936–37 (despatches); served War of 1939–45, mostly India and Burma; GSO1, British Mil. Mission to France, 1946–47; 2nd-in-Comd 26 Medium Regt RA, 1947–48; jssc 1949; GSO1, WO, 1950–51; Col GS, SHAPE, 1952; OC 26 Field Regt Suez Canal Zone, 1953–55; Dep. Sec., Chiefs of Staff Cttee, 1955–58; UK Nat. Mil. Rep. to SHAPE, 1959–61; retd 1962. Sec., Health Visitor Trng Council and Council for Trng in Social Work, 1963–66; Asst Sec. of Commns, Lord Chancellor's Office, 1966–74; Sec., Wolfenden Cttee on Voluntary Orgns, 1974–78. JP Surrey, 1968. *Recreations:* golf, reading. *Address:* 20 Middle Bourne Lane, Farnham, Surrey. *T:* Farnham 714851. *Clubs:* Army and Navy, MCC; Hankley Common Golf.

CROMARTIE, 4th Earl of, *cr* 1861 (re-creation, revival of peerage forfeited 1745/46); **Roderick Grant Francis Mackenzie,** MC 1945; TD 1964; JP; DL; Major Seaforth Highlanders, retired; Viscount Tarbat of Tarbat, Baron Castlehaven and Baron MacLeod of Leod, *cr* 1861; Chief of the Clan Mackenzie; *b* 24 Oct. 1904; *er* surv. *s* of Lt-Col Edward Walter Blunt-Mackenzie, DL (*d* 1949) and Countess of Cromartie, (3rd in line); *S* mother, 1962, having discontinued use of surname of Blunt, for himself and son, and reverted to Mackenzie; *m* 1st, 1933, Mrs Dorothy Downing Porter (marr. diss. 1945), *d* of Mr Downing, Kentucky, USA; two *d*; 2nd, 1947, Olga (Mendoza) (marr. diss. 1962), *d* of late Stuart Laurance, Paris; one *s*; 3rd, 1962, Lilias Richard, MB, ChB, *d* of Prof. (James) Walter MacLeod, OBE, FRS, FRSE. *Educ:* Charterhouse; RMC Sandhurst. Commissioned to 1st Bn Seaforth Highlanders in Ireland, 1924; transferred to 2nd Bn Seaforth Highlanders, in India, 1925; seconded to Nigeria Regt of RWAFF, 1928–29; rejoined 2nd Seaforth Highlanders, 1930; Operations North-West Frontier, India, 1930–31; in France in 1940 with 4th Seaforth Highlanders (MC). Sec., Scottish Peers Assoc., House of Lords. JP Ross and Cromarty, 1937, DL Ross and Cromarty, 1976; CC Ross and Cromarty, 1963–77 (Vice-Convener, 1970–71, Convener, 1971–75); Hon. Sheriff (formerly Hon. Sheriff Substitute); Convener, Ross and Cromarty District Council, 1975–77. FSAScot. Freeman of Ross and Cromarty, 1977. *Publication:* A Highland History, 1980. *Heir:* *s* Viscount Tarbat, *qv*. *Address:* Castle Leod, Strathpeffer, Ross and Cromarty, Scotland. *Clubs:* Army and Navy, Pratt's.

CROMARTIE, (Ronald) Ian (Talbot), CMG 1983; HM Diplomatic Service; Ambassador and Leader, UK Delegation to Conference on Disarmament, Geneva, since 1982; *b* 27 Feb. 1929; *s* of late Ronald Duncan Cromartie and of Mrs Margaret Talbot Cromartie; *m* 1962, Jennifer Frances, *er d* of late Captain Ewen Fairfax-Lucy and Mrs Margaret Fairfax-Lucy; two *s* one *d*. *Educ:* Sherborne; Clare Coll., Cambridge (MA, PhD). Scientific research at Univs of Cambridge and Tübingen, 1950–58; Univ. Demonstrator in Organic Chemistry, Cambridge, 1958–60. Entered Foreign (later Diplomatic) Service, 1961; served in: FO, 1961–62; Saigon, 1962–64; FO, 1964–67; UK Disarmament Delegn, Geneva, 1967–69; FCO, 1969–72; Counsellor, 1972–75, Counsellor (Scientific), 1975–78, Bonn; UK Resident Rep. to IAEA and UN Orgs in Vienna, 1978–82, with personal rank of Ambassador, 1981–82. *Publications:* papers in Jl of Chem. Soc. and other scientific periodicals. *Recreations:* walking, sailing, shooting. *Address:* c/o Foreign and Commonwealth Office, SW1; 61 Ashley Gardens, SW1. *Club:* United Oxford & Cambridge University.

CROMBIE, Alistair Cameron, MA, BSc, PhD; Fellow, 1969–83, garden master, 1971–81, Trinity College, Oxford; Lecturer in History of Science, University of Oxford, 1953–83; *b* 4 Nov. 1915; 2nd *s* of William David Crombie and Janet Wilmina (*née* Macdonald); *m* 1943, Nancy Hey; three *s* one *d* (and one *s* decd). *Educ:* Geelong Grammar Sch.; Trinity Coll., Melbourne Univ.; Jesus Coll., Cambridge. Zoological Lab., Cambridge, 1941–46; Lectr in History and Philosophy of Science, University Coll., London, 1946–53, nominated Reader, resigned; All Soul's Coll., Oxford, 1954–69. Kennedy Prof. in the Renaissance, 1982, Prof. of History of Science and Medicine, 1983–85, Smith Coll., Mass. Visiting Professor: Technische Hochschule, Aachen, 1948; Univ. of Washington, 1953–54; Princeton Univ., 1959–60; Australian Univs (guest of Vice-Chancellors' Cttee), 1963; Tokyo Univ. (guest of Japan Soc. for Promotion of Sci.), 1976; All-India Inst. of Med. Scis, and guest of Indian Nat. Sci. Acad., 1976; Virginia Mil. Inst., 1977; Williams Coll., Mass. (Bernhard Vis. Prof.), 1984; Prof. d'Histoire des Sciences, Sorbonne (Univ. of Paris I), 1982–83. Conseil Scientifique, Dépt d'Hist. et Philosophie de la Médecine, Univ. of Paris XII, 1981–. Mem. Council, Science Museum, London, 1962–66; Mem., British Nat. Cttee for History of Science, 1963–69. Editor: Brit. Jl Philos. Sci., 1949–54; Hist. Sci., 1961–; Dir, Oxford Univ. Symp. Hist. Sci., 1961; Pres., Brit. Soc. Hist. Sci., 1964–66; Pres., Internat. Acad. Hist. Sci., 1968–71; Member: Internat. Acad. Hist. Med.; Academia Leopoldina; FRHistS. Galileo Prize, 1969. Hon. DLitt Durham, 1979. *Publications:* Augustine to Galileo, 1952, 4th edn 1979; Robert Grosseteste and the Origins of Experimental Science, 1953, 3rd edn 1971; Scientific Change, 1963; The Mechanistic Hypothesis and the Scientific Study of Vision, 1967; Science Optics and Music in Medieval and Early Modern Thought, 1986; contrib. Annals of Sci., Brit. Jl Hist. Sci., EHR, Isis, Jl Animal Ecol., Physis, Proc. Royal Soc. Lond., Rev. de Synthèse, TLS, Dict. Sci. Biogr., Encyc. Brit., New Cambridge Modern Hist., etc. *Recreations:* literature, travel, landscape gardening. *Address:* Orchardlea, Boars Hill, Oxford. *T:* Oxford 735692. *Club:* Brooks's.

CROMBIE, Prof. Leslie, FRS 1973; CChem, FRSC; Sir Jesse Boot Professor of Organic Chemistry, University of Nottingham, since 1969 (Dean of Science, 1980–83); *b* 10 June 1923; *s* of Walter Leslie Crombie and Gladys May Crombie (*née* Clarkson); *m* 1953 Winifred Mary Lovell Wood; two *s* two *d*. *Educ:* Portsmouth Municipal Coll.; King's Coll., London. PhD, DSc, FKC 1978. Admiralty Chemical Lab., Portsmouth Naval Dockyard, 1941–46. Lectr, Imperial Coll., London, SW7, 1950–58; Reader in Organic Chemistry, King's Coll., London Univ., 1958–63, Fellow, 1978; Prof. of Organic Chemistry, University Coll. (Univ. of Wales), Cardiff, 1963–69. Pres., British Association, Section B, 1978; Chm., Phytochemical Soc. of Europe, 1986 (Vice-Chm., 1984–86). Member: British Libraries Chemical Inf. Review Panel, 1976–77; UGC Physical Scis Sub-Cttee, 1978–85; Royal Society: Travelling Expenses Cttee, 1974–; Govt Grants Cttee, 1976–77 (Chm., 1978–79); Sect. Cttee 3, 1977–78 (Chm., 1978–80); Chemical Educn Cttee, 1981–82 (Chm., 1983–); Educn Cttee, 1983–85 (Chm., 1986–); Council, 1984–86; Science Research Council: Chem. Cttee, 1970–75; Enzyme Cttee, 1973–75; Chemical Society: Council, 1962–64 and 1972–80; Library Cttee, 1959–63; Primary Jls Cttee, 1964–69; Reports and Reviews Cttee, 1964–69 (Chm., 1969–73); Pub. Services Bd, 1969–77; Perkin Div. Council, 1971–85 (Pres., 1976–79); Presidents' Cttee, 1972–74; Tertiary Pub. Cttee, 1974–76; Exec. Cttee, 1976–79; Div. and Annual Congress Cttee, 1976–79; UKCIS Bd, 1972–77; Royal Inst. of Chemistry: Jt Cttee for HNC and HND quals, 1962–84; Council, 1975–78; Exams and Institns Cttee, 1976–78; Quals and Admissions Cttee, 1976–78; Royal Society of Chemistry: Council, 1980–81; Jls Bd, 1981–85; Quals and Exams Bd, 1983–; Chm., Perkin Jls Editorial Bd, 1981–85. Tilden Lectr, 1970, Simonsen Lectr, 1975, Hugo Müller Lectr, 1977, Chem. Soc.; Natural Products Chemistry award, 1980; Pedler Lectr, 1982, Flintoff Medal, 1984, RSC. Hon. Fellow, Portsmouth Polytechnic, 1983. *Publications:* over 300 original papers in learned chemical jls, especially those of RSC, London. *Recreation:* gardening. *Address:* 153 Hillside Road, Bramcote, Beeston, Nottingham. *T:* 259412. *Club:* Athenæum.

CROMER, 3rd Earl of, *cr* 1901; **George Rowland Stanley Baring,** KG 1977; GCMG 1974 (KCMG 1971); MBE (Mil) 1945; PC 1966; Baron Cromer, 1892; Viscount Cromer, 1899; Viscount Errington, 1901; Chairman, International Advisory Council, Morgan Guaranty Trust Co. of New York, since 1977; Advisor to Baring Brothers & Co. Ltd, since 1974; International Advisor to Marsh & McLennan Cos, NY, since 1978; *b* 28 July 1918 (HM King George V stood sponsor); *o s* of 2nd Earl of Cromer, PC, GCB, GCIE, GCVO, and Lady Ruby Elliot, 2nd *d* of 4th Earl of Minto, KG, PC, GCSI, GCMG; *S* father, 1953; *m* 1942, Hon. Esmé Harmsworth (CVO 1980), 2nd *d* of 2nd Viscount Rothermere and of Margaret Hunam (*née* Redhead); two *s* (one *d* decd). *Educ:* Eton Coll.; Trinity Coll., Cambridge. Page of Honour: to King George V, 1931–35; to Queen Mary at Coronation, 1937; Private Sec. to Marquess of Willingdon representing HMG on missions to Argentina, Uruguay, Brazil, 1938, and to NZ and Aust., 1940. Served War, 1939–45: Grenadier Guards; Staff Col., Camberley; NW Europe (despatches, MBE); demob. 1945, Lt-Col. Joined Baring Brothers & Co. Ltd, 1938, rejoined 1945; seconded to: J. P. Morgan & Co.; Kidder Peabody & Co.; Morgan Stanley & Co.; Chemical Bank (all of NYC); Man. Dir, Baring Brothers & Co. Ltd, 1948–61; Mem., Inter-Parly Mission to Brazil; 1954; Econ. Minister and Head of Treasury and Supply Delegn, Washington, 1959–61; UK Exec. Dir, IMF, IBRD, and IFC, 1959–61; Head, UK Delegn to Internat. Coffee Conf., Washington, 1960; Governor of Bank of England, 1961–66; UK Governor, IBRD, IFC, and IDA, 1961–66; Bank of Internat. Settlements, Basle, 1961–66; Sen. Partner and Man. Dir, Baring Brothers & Co. Ltd, 1967–70; HM Ambassador, Washington, 1971–74. Author of report for Pres. of BoT, 1967, and for Cttee of Lloyd's, 1968. Chairman: IBM (UK) Ltd, 1967–70 and 1974–79; London Multinational Bank Ltd, 1967–70; Security & Prosper Fund SA, Luxembourg, 1967–70; Hon. Chm., Harris & Partners Ltd, Toronto, 1967–70. Director, 1949–59: Anglo-Newfoundland Develt Co. Ltd; Royal Ins. Co. Ltd; Liverpool, London & Globe Ins. Co. Ltd; Lewis Investment Trust Ltd; Director: Daily Mail & Gen. Trust Ltd, 1949–61, 1966–70 and 1974–; Union Carbide Corp. of NY, 1967–70; Associated Financial Services, Geneva, 1967–70; Imperial Group Ltd, 1974–80; P & O Steam Navigation Co. Ltd, 1974–80; Shell Trans. & Trading Co. Ltd, 1974–; Compagnie Financiere de Suez, Paris, 1974–82; Robeco Gp of Investment Trusts, Rotterdam, 1977–; Barfield Trust Co. Ltd, Guernsey, 1979–; Baring Henderson Gilt Fund, 1979–; IBM World Trade (Eur./ME/Africa) Corp., NY, 1977–83 (Mem., IBM Eur. Adv. Council, 1967–70 and 1974–). Chairman: Accepting House Cttee, 1967–70; OECD High Level Cttee on Capital Movements, 1967–70; Churchill Meml Trust, 1979; Member: Inst. Internat. d'Etudes Bancaires, 1967–70; Special Cttee on Trans-national Corps, Internat. Chamber of Commerce, 1967–69; Finance Cttee, UCL, 1954–57; British Inst. in Paris, 1952–57. Eur. Advisor to Govt Res. Corp., Washington, DC, 1974–81. A Governor: Atlantic Inst. for Internat. Affairs; Member: The Pilgrims (Mem. Exec. Cttee); Overseas Bankers Club; Trustee: King George's Jubilee Trust; Brain Res. Trust; Comr, Trilateral Commn. HM Lieut, City of London, 1961–; Dep. Lieut, Kent, 1968–79. FIB; Hon. LLD New York Univ., 1966. *Heir:* *s* Viscount Errington, *qv*. *Address:* Beaufield House, St Saviour, Jersey. *T:* Jersey 61671. *Clubs:* White's, Brooks's, Beefsteak; United (Jersey); Brook (NY); Metropolitan (Washington).

CROMPTON, Dr Gareth, FRCP, FFCM; QHP; Chief Medical Officer, Welsh Office, since 1978; *b* 9 Jan. 1937; *s* of Edward Crompton, Drefach-Felindre, Dyfed; *m* 1965; one *d*. *Educ:* Llandysul Grammar Sch.; Welsh Nat. Sch. of Medicine. MB, BCh Wales, 1960; DObstRCOG 1962; DPH Wales, 1964; FFCM 1976; FRCP (MRCP 1980). County Med. Officer, County Welfare Officer and Principal Sch. Med. Officer, Anglesey CC, 1966–73; Area Med. Officer, Gwynedd Health Authority, 1974–77. Specialty Advr, Health Service Comr for England and Wales, 1974–77; Advr in Wales, Faculty of Community Medicine, 1974–77. Chm., Anglesey Disablement Adv. Cttee, 1969–77; Sec., Fluoridation Study Gp, Soc. of Med. Officers of Health, 1969–73; Mem., Welsh Hosp. Bd, 1970–74. Mem. GMC, 1981–83. Med. Fellow, Council of Europe, 1971. QHP 1984–. *Publications:* papers on the effects of fluoridated water supplies on dental caries, and the epidemiology and management of chronic sickness and disablement. *Recreations:* bowls, golf, watching Rugby, reading contemporary Welsh verse. *Address:* Health and Social Work Department, Welsh Office, Cathays Park, Cardiff CF1 3NQ. *T:* Cardiff 823911.

CROMPTON, Ian William; Stipendiary Magistrate for South Yorkshire, since 1983; *b* 28 June 1936; *s* of Thomas and Hilda Crompton; *m* 1962, Audrey (*née* Hopewell); two *s*. *Educ:* Manchester Grammar School; Victoria University of Manchester. LLB. Asst Solicitor, County Magistrates' Court, Strangeways, Manchester, 1961–62; Asst Solicitor, O'Collier, Littler & Kilbeg, 1962–65, Partner, 1965–72; Clerk to the Justices: County Magistrates' Court, Strangeways, 1972–74; Eccles Magistrates' Court, 1974–83. *Recreations:* ballroom and Latin American dancing, golf. *Club:* Hallamshire Golf (Sheffield).

CROMPTON, Air Cdre Roy Hartley, OBE 1962; Group Director, Civil (formerly Home) Defence College, Easingwold, York, 1976–85, retired; *b* 24 April 1921; *er s* of Frank and Ann Crompton, Bedford; *m* 1961, Rita Mabel Leslie; one *d*. *Educ:* Bedford Sch.; University Coll., London (BA Hons). PSO to C-in-C Fighter Comd, 1956–59; OC Flying No 5 FTS, 1959–61; jssc 1962; Chiefs of Staff Secretariat, 1962–64; Stn Comdr No 1 FTS, 1965–67; sowc 1967; Dep. Dir Defence Policy Staff, 1968–70; Gp Dir RAF Staff Coll., 1970; Project Officer, Nat. Defence Coll., 1970–71; AOC and Comdt, Central Flying Sch., RAF, 1972–74. Directing Staff, Home Defence Coll., York, 1974–76. *Recreations:* golf, music, horticulture. *Address:* Sharnford Lodge, Huby, York YO6 1HT. *Club:* Royal Air Force.

CROMPTON-INGLEFIELD, Col Sir John (Frederick), Kt 1963; TD; DL; *b* 1904; *e s* of Adm. Sir F. S. Inglefield, KCB, DL; *m* 1st, 1926, Rosemary (*d* 1978), *d* of Adm. Sir Percy Scott, 1st Bt, KCB, KCVO, LLD; three *d*; 2nd, 1979, Madeline Rose, *widow* of W. E. Dodds and *d* of Col. Conyers Alston, Seven Rivers, Cape Province, South Africa. *Educ:* RN Colls Osborne and Dartmouth. Retired from Royal Navy, 1926. Derbyshire Yeomanry (Armoured Car Co.), Lieut 1936, Major 1939. Served War of 1939–45, with 1st Derbyshire Yeo. and 79th Armoured Div. (despatches) Africa and Europe. Lt-Col Comdg Derbyshire Yeo, 1950–53; Bt Col 1954; Hon. Col, Leics and Derbyshire Yeo., 1962–70. Chm. W Derbyshire Conservative and Unionist Assoc., 1951–66; Vice-Chm., 1957–64, Chm., TA, Derbyshire, 1964–69. CC 1932–55, JP 1933, DL 1953, and High Sheriff, 1938, Derbyshire. OStJ. *Address:* 73 Oakwood Court, Addison Road, W14. *T:* 01–602 1979.

CROMWELL, 7th Baron *cr* 1375 (called out of abeyance, 1923); **Godfrey John Bewicke-Copley;** *b* 4 March 1960; *s* of 6th Baron Cromwell and of Vivian, *y d* of late Hugh de Lisle Penfold, Isle of Man; *S* father, 1982. *Heir: b* Hon. Thomas David Bewicke-Copley, *b* 6 Aug. 1964. *Address:* The Oranges, Sherborne, Northleach, Cheltenham, Glos.

CRONIN, John Walton; Regional Chairman of Industrial Tribunals, since 1972, part-time, since 1985; *b* 14 Oct. 1915; *s* of John and Alice Cronin; *m* 1947, Eileen Veronica Bale (*née* Rector); one *d*; one step *s*. *Educ:* Xaverian Coll., Manchester; Manchester Univ. Solicitor. Served War, 1940–46, Major, Indian Army, latterly Staff appt, DAQMG. Private practice, 1946–55; Resident Magistrate, High Court Registrar, Acting Sheriff, Registrar-General Patents, Trade Marks and Designs, Sen. Resident Magistrate, Acting High Court Judge, Adv. Comr to Governor on Detained Persons, N Rhodesia/Zambia, 1955–65; Circuit Justice, Stipendiary and Circuit Magistrate, Grand Bahama, 1965–71. SBStJ 1969, OStJ 1977. *Address:* 6 Chelsea Court, South Road, Hythe, Kent CT21 6AH. *T:* Hythe (Kent) 67879. *Club:* Royal Commonwealth Society.

CRONIN, Vincent Archibald Patrick; author; *b* 24 May 1924; *s* of late Archibald Joseph Cronin, MD, MRCP, DPH and of Agnes Mary Gibson, MB, ChB; *m* 1949, Chantal, *d* of Comte Jean de Rolland; two *s* three *d*. *Educ:* Ampleforth; Harvard; Trinity Coll., Oxford. Rifle Bde, 1943–45. *Publications:* The Golden Honeycomb, 1954; The Wise Man from the West, 1955; The Last Migration, 1957; A Pearl to India, 1959; The Letter after Z, 1960; Louis XIV, 1964; Four Women in Pursuit of an Ideal, 1965; The Florentine Renaissance, 1967; The Flowering of the Renaissance, 1970; Napoleon, 1971; Louis and Antoinette, 1974; trans., Giscard d'Estaing, Towards a New Democracy, 1977; Catherine, Empress of all the Russias, 1978; The View from Planet Earth, 1981. *Address:* 44 Hyde Park Square, W2 2JT.

CRONNE, Prof. Henry Alfred; Professor of Medieval History in the University of Birmingham, 1946–70, now Emeritus Professor; Dean of the Faculty of Arts, 1952–55; *b* 17 Oct. 1904; *o c* of late Rev. James Kennedy Cronne, Portaferry. Co. Down, N Ireland; *m* 1936, Lilian Mey, *er d* of E. F. Seckler, Bishops Tawton, Barnstaple; one *d*. *Educ:* Campbell Coll., Belfast; Queen's Univ. of Belfast; Balliol Coll., Oxford; Inst. of Historical Research, MA Belfast; MA Oxon; MA Birmingham, *jure officii*. Asst Lecturer in History, QUB, 1928–31; Lecturer in Medieval History, King's Coll., London, 1931, and subsequently Lecturer in Palaeography and Reader in Medieval History. War of 1939–45, served in LDV, Home Guard and Somerset Special Constabulary. *Publications:* Bristol Charters, 1378–1499, 1946; (ed with Charles Johnson) Regesta Regum Anglo-Normannorum, Vol. II, 1100–1135, 1956, (ed with R. H. C. Davis), Vol. III, 1135–1154, 1968, and Vol. IV, Facsimiles and Diplomatic, 1135–54, 1969; The Reign of Stephen, 1970; contribs to historical jls. *Recreations:* writing, drawing. *Address:* Winswood Cottage, Cheldon, Chulmleigh, Devon EX18 7JB. *T:* Chulmleigh 80567.

CROOK, family name of **Baron Crook.**

CROOK, 1st Baron *cr* 1947, of Carshalton, Surrey; **Reginald Douglas Crook;** *b* 2 March 1901; *s* of Percy Edwin Crook; *m* 1922, Ida G. Haddon (*d* 1985); one *s*. *Educ:* Strand Sch. Local Govt Service; Organising Sec. of Poor Law Officers' Union and Editor, Poor Law Gazette, 1920–24; Gen. Sec., Min. of Labour Staff Assoc., 1925–51, and Editor, Civil Service Argus, 1929–51; Sec., Fedn of Min. of Labour Staff, 1944–51; Mem., National Whitley Council for Civil Service, 1925–51; Mem., Min. of Labour Departmental Whitley Council, 1925–51; Chm., N Islington Lab. Party, 1924–26 (and Chm., N Islington Lab. Party Candidates for 1925 Guardians Election); Hon. Sec., Labour Parliamentary Assoc., 1945–47; a Dep. Chm. of Cttees, House of Lords, 1949–75; Mem., Ecclesiastical Cttee of Parliament, 1949–75; Chm. of Interdeptl Cttee of Enquiry as to Optical Services, appointed by Min. of Health, 1949–52, leading to Opticians Act, 1958; Mem., Parl. Delegn to Denmark, 1949; Deleg. to Finland, 1950; Mem., Police Wages Council, 1951; Chm., National Dock Labour Board, 1951–65, also Chm., National Dock Labour Board (Nominees) Ltd and Chm., National Dock Labour Board Pensions Trustees Ltd; Member: London Electricity Board, 1966–72, General Practice Finance Corp., 1972–76; Chm., London Electricity Consultative Council, 1966–72; Delegate, United Nations General Assembly, 1950; Mem., United Nations Administrative Tribunal, 1951–71, Vice-Pres., 1952–71; Mem., UK Goodwill Mission to 350th Anniversary of Virginia, 1957; President: (also Fellow) Brit. Assoc. of Industrial Editors, 1953–61; Assoc. of Optical Practitioners, 1959–84 (Mem., 1959–); Cystic Fibrosis Research Foundation Trust, 1964; The Pre-Retirement Assoc.; Sutton Talking Newspaper, 1975–; Vice-Pres., Royal Soc. for the Prevention of Accidents; Vice-Pres. and Fellow, Inst. of Municipal Safety Officers. Mem., Inst. of Neurology. Master, Worshipful Co. of Spectacle Makers, 1963–65; an Apothecary, 1951–, and Freeman, 1948–, of City of London. Warden, 1968, Senior Warden, 1971, Master, 1972, Guild of Freemen of City of London. JP Surrey. KStJ 1955. Mem. Chapter-Gen. of St John, 1957–. *Heir: s* Hon. Douglas Edwin Crook [*b* 19 Nov. 1926; *m* 1954, Ellenor Rouse; one *s* one *d*]. *Address:* Breedene, Princes Avenue, Carshalton, Surrey. *T:* 01–643 2620.

CROOK, Arthur Charles William; Consultant to Times Newspapers, since 1974; Editor, The Times Literary Supplement, 1959–74; *b* 16 Feb. 1912; *m* 1948, Sarita Mary Vivien Bushell (marr. diss.); one *s* two *d*. Editorial staff of The Times; Asst Editor, The Times Literary Supplement, 1951–59. Pres. and Chm., Royal Literary Fund, 1984–. *Recreation:* theatre. *Address:* 70 Regent's Park Road, NW1. *T:* 01–722 0446. *Club:* Garrick.

CROOK, Colin, FEng; Senior Vice President, Data General Corp., since 1984; *b* 1 June 1942; *s* of Richard and Ruth Crook; *m* 1965, Dorothy Jean Taylor; two *d*. *Educ:* Harris Coll., Preston; Liverpool Polytechnic (ACT Hons; Dip. Elec. Engrg). FEng 1981 (CEng 1977). MIEE 1976; MIERE 1976; MIEEE 1976; MACM 1977. Electronics Engr, Canadian Marconi, 1962–64; Computer Designer, The Plessey Co., 1964–68; Systems Engr, Eli Lilly Co., 1968–69; sen. appts, Motorola Semiconductor Div., Switzerland and USA, 1969–79; sen. appts, The Rank Organisation, 1979–83, including: Man. Dir, RPI, 1979–81; Man. Dir, Zynar, CEO Nestar Systems, USA, 1981–83; Mem. of Bd, British Telecom, and Man. Dir, BT Enterprises, 1983–84. *Publications:* articles and learned papers on electronics and computers. *Recreations:* photography, walking, reading, wine, sailing. *Address:* The Old School House, Harvest Hill, Hedsor, Bourne End, Bucks SL8 5JJ. *T:* Bourne End 27479.

CROOK, Frances Rachel; Director, Howard League for Penal Reform, since 1986; *b* 18 Dec. 1952; *d* of Sheila Sibson-Turnbull and Maurice Crook. *Educ:* Camden School; Liverpool University (BA Hons History). Historical Researcher, Liverpool, 1977–78; Teacher, 1978–79; Campaign Co-ordinator, Amnesty International, 1980–85. Councillor (Lab) Barnet, 1982–. *Recreations:* reading, music, demonstrations. *Address:* The Howard League, 322 Kennington Park Road, SE11 4PP. *T:* 01–735 3317.

CROOK, Maj.-Gen. James Cooper, MD, FRCPath; late RAMC, retired 1981; Civilian Medical Practitioner, Army Blood Supply Depot, Aldershot, since 1982; *b* 19 March 1923; *s* of late Francis William Crook and late Mary Catherine Perry, *d* of late Sir Edwin Cooper Perry, GCVO, MD, Superintendent of Guy's Hospital and Vice-Chancellor of London Univ.; *m* 1950, Ruth, *d* of late W. A. Bellamy of Santa Cruz, Tenerife; one *s* two *d*. *Educ:* Worksop Coll.; Guy's Hosp. Med. Sch., Univ. of London. MB BS 1946, MD 1953; DTM&H 1952; FRCPath 1968. Guy's and Pembury Hosps, 1946; Commnd RAMC 1946; served Egypt and N Africa, 1946–49; Pathologist, Queen Alexandra's Mil. Hosp., 1950; David Bruce Laboratories, 1953; med. liaison officer to MRC Radiobiology Unit, AERE, 1954; Asst Dir of Pathology, Middle East, 1957; Cons. in Pathology, 1958; RAMC Specialist, Chem. Defence Estab., Porton, 1960; Asst Dir of Pathology, Eastern Comd, 1963; ADGMS, 1966; Comd Cons. in Pathology, BAOR, 1969; Prof. of Pathology, Royal Army Med. Coll., 1974; Dir of Army Pathology and Consulting Pathologist to the Army, 1976–81; Hon. Physician to HM The Queen, 1978–81. Hon. Col, 380 Blood Supply Unit RAMC, TAVR, 1982–86. FRSM; Mem., BMA. *Publications:* articles in Jl of Clinical Path., Nature, Med. Sci. and the Law, Jl of RAMC, British Jl of Radiology. *Recreations:* gardening, travelling, history and art. *Address:* Danebury, 2 Wilmerhatch Lane, Epsom, Surrey KT18 7EQ. *T:* Epsom 20967.

CROOK, Prof. John Anthony, MA; Professor of Ancient History, University of Cambridge, 1979–84; Fellow of St John's College, Cambridge, since 1951; *b* 5 Nov. 1921; *s* of Herbert Crook and Hilda Naomi (*née* Flower). *Educ:* St Mary's C of E Sch., Balham; Dulwich Coll.; St John's Coll., Cambridge 1939–41 and 1945–47 (John Stewart of Rannoch Scholar); BA 1947, Craven Student, 1947; Research Student of Balliol Coll., Oxford, 1947–48; MA (Cantab) 1949. Served War, Private and Corporal, 9th Royal Fusiliers, 1941–43 (PoW Stalag VIIIB, 1943–45); Sgt, RAEC, 1945. Univ. Asst Lectr in Classics, Reading Univ., 1948, Lectr, 1949–51; St John's Coll., Cambridge: Tutor, 1956–64; President, 1971–75; Univ. Asst Lectr in Classics, Cambridge Univ., 1953, Lectr, 1955–71, Reader in Roman History and Law, 1971–79, and Brereton Reader, 1974–79. FBA 1970–80. *Publications:* Consilium Principis, 1955; Law and Life of Rome, 1967. *Address:* St John's College, Cambridge CB2 1TP. *T:* Cambridge 338621.

CROOK, Prof. Joseph Mordaunt; Professor of Architectural History, Royal Holloway and Bedford New College (formerly at Bedford College), University of London, since 1981; *b* 27 Feb. 1937; *e s* of late Austin Mordaunt Crook and late Irene Woolfenden; *m* 1st, 1964, Margaret, *o d* of late James Mulholland; 2nd, 1975, Susan, *o d* of late F. H. Mayor. *Educ:* Wimbledon Coll.; Brasenose Coll., Oxford. BA (1st cl. Mod. Hist.) 1958; DPhil 1961, MA 1962, Oxon; FSA 1972. Research Fellow: Inst. of Historical Res., 1961–62; Bedford Coll., London, 1962–63; Warburg Inst., London, 1970–71; Asst Lectr, Univ. of Leicester, 1963–65; Lectr, Bedford Coll., London, 1965–75, Reader in Architectural Hist., 1975–81. Slade Prof. of Fine Art, Oxford Univ., 1979–80; Vis. Fellow: Brasenose Coll., Oxford, 1979–80; Humanities Res. Centre, ANU, Canberra, 1985; Waynflete Lectr and Vis. Fellow, Magdalen Coll., Oxford, 1984–85; Vis. Fellow, Gonville and Caius Coll., Cambridge, 1986. Member: Exec. Cttee, Soc. Architect. Historians of Gt Britain, 1964–77 (Pres., 1980–84); RIBA Drawings Cttee, 1969–75; Exec. Cttee, Georgian Gp, 1970–77; Exec. Cttee, Victorian Soc., 1970–77, Council, 1978–; Historic Buildings Council, DoE, 1974–80; Council, Soc. of Antiquaries, 1980–82; Adv. Council, Paul Mellon Centre for Studies in British Art, 1985–. Freeman, 1979, Liveryman, 1984, Worshipful Co. of Goldsmiths. Editor, Architectural History, 1967–75; Adv. Editor, British Studies Monitor, 1974–. *Publications:* (contrib.) Concerning Architecture, 1967; The Greek Revival, 1968; (contrib.) The Country Seat, 1970; (ed) Eastlake, A History of the Gothic Revival, 1970, revd edn, 1978; Victorian Architecture: A Visual Anthology, 1971; The British Museum, 1972; (contrib.) The Age of Neo Classicism, 1972; The Greek Revival: Neo-Classical Attitudes in British Architecture 1760–1870, 1972; (ed) Emmet, Six Essays, 1972; (ed) Kerr, The Gentleman's House, 1972; (jtly) The History of the King's Works, Vol. VI, 1782–1851, 1973 (Hitchcock Medallion, 1974), Vol. V, 1660–1782, 1976; The Reform Club, 1973; (contrib.) The Building of Early America, 1976; (contrib.) Seven Victorian Architects, 1976; William Burges and the High Victorian Dream, 1981; (ed) The Strange Genius of William Burges, 1981; (contrib.) The Ruskin Polygon, 1982; (contrib.) In Search of Modern Architecture, 1983; (jtly) Axel Haig and The Victorian Vision of the Middle Ages, 1984; The Dilemma of Style: architectural ideas from the picturesque to the modern movement, 1987; numerous articles in Architect. History, Architect. Review, Country Life, History Today, Jl Royal Soc. Arts, RIBA Jl, Antiquaries Jl, TLS, Architect Design, etc. *Recreation:* strolling. *Address:* 55 Gloucester Avenue, NW1 7BA. *T:* 01–485 8280. *Club:* Athenæum.

CROOK, Kenneth Roy, CMG 1978; HM Diplomatic Service, retired; Ambassador to Afghanistan, 1976–79; *b* 30 July 1920; *s* of Alexander Crook, Prescot, Lancs, and Margaret Kay Crook; *m* 1943, Freda Joan Vidler; two *d*. *Educ:* Prescot Grammar Sch., Lancs; Skerry's Coll., Liverpool. Appointed to: Board of Trade, 1937; Min. of War Transport, 1939. Royal Navy, 1941–46. Board of Trade, 1946–49; Commonwealth Relations Office, 1949; Second Sec., Canberra, 1951–54; First Sec., Madras, 1956–59; Deputy High Commissioner: Peshawar, W Pakistan, 1962–64; Dacca, E Pakistan, 1964–67; Counsellor,

FCO, 1967; Head of Information Research Dept, FCO, 1969–71; Governor, Cayman Is, 1971–74; Canadian Nat. Defence Coll., 1974–75; Head of Science and Technology Dept, FCO, 1975–76. *Recreations:* walking, gardening. *Address:* 16 Burntwood Road, Sevenoaks, Kent. *T:* Sevenoaks 452774.

CROOK, Brig. Paul Edwin, CBE 1965 (OBE 1946); DSO 1957; *b* 19 April 1915; *s* of late Herbert Crook and Christine Crook, Lyme Regis; *m* 1st, 1944, Joan (marr. diss. 1967), *d* of late William Lewis; one *d*; 2nd, 1967, Betty, *d* of late John William Wyles. *Educ:* Uppingham Sch.; Emmanuel Coll., Cambridge. BA 1936, MA 1956. Commnd into QORWK Regt, 1935; served: India and Palestine, 1937–39; War of 1939–45, Africa, NW Europe, Burma; Chief Civil Affairs Officer (Col), Netherlands East Indies, 1946; comd 3rd Bn The Parachute Regt, 1954–57; Suez Ops, 1956; comd Army Airborne Trng and Develt Centre, 1959–62; Comdr and Chief of Staff, Jamaica Defence Force, 1962–65; Security Ops Advisor to High Comr for Aden and S Arabia, 1965–67; Comdr, Rhine Area, 1969–70. Col, 1959; Brig., 1963; retired 1971. ADC to The Queen, 1965. Hon. Col, 16 Lincoln Co. Parachute Regt (VR), 1974–79; Dep. Hon. Col, The Parachute Regt (TAVR): 15th (Scottish) Bn, 1979–83; 4th Bn, 1984–85. Bronze Star (US), 1945. *Recreations:* cricket, golf, jazz. *Address:* Frieston House, Frieston, Grantham, Lincs NG32 3DA. *T:* Loveden 72060. *Clubs:* Naval and Military, MCC; Jamaica (W Indies).

CROOKENDEN, Maj.-Gen. George Wayet Derek; DL; Fellow and Senior Bursar, Peterhouse, Cambridge, since 1975; *b* 11 Dec. 1920; *o s* of late Lt-Col John Crookenden and Iris Margherita Gay; *m* 1948, Elizabeth Mary Angela Bourke; one *s* one *d*. *Educ:* Winchester Coll.; Christ Church, Oxford. Commnd Royal Artillery, 1941. GSO1, SHAPE, 1961–62; CO, 19 Field Regt, RA, 1962–64; Comdr, 7 Artillery Bde, 1964–67; Exercise Controller, CICC (West), 1969–71; Chief, British Commanders-in-Chief Liaison Mission, 1971–72; C of S, Contingencies Planning, SHAPE, 1972–75. Col Comdt, RA, 1977–82. DL Cambs, 1984. *Address:* c/o Lloyds Bank, 95–97 Regent Street, Cambridge CB2 1BQ. *Club:* Army and Navy.

CROOKENDEN, Lt-Gen. Sir Napier, KCB 1970 (CB 1966); DSO 1945; OBE 1954; DL; Lieutenant, HM Tower of London, 1975–81; *b* 31 Aug. 1915; 2nd *s* of late Col Arthur Crookenden, CBE, DSO; *m* 1948, Patricia Nassau, *d* of 2nd Baron Kindersley, CBE, MC, and of Nancy Farnsworth, *d* of Dr Geoffrey Boyd; two *s* two *d*. *Educ:* Wellington Coll.; RMC, Sandhurst. Commissioned, Cheshire Regt, 1935; Bde Major, 6th Airlanding Bde, 1943–44; CO, 9th Bn, The Parachute Regt, 1944–46; GSO1 (Plans) to Dir of Ops, Malaya, 1952–54; Comdr, 16th Parachute Bde, 1960–61; idc 1962; Dir, Land/Air Warfare MoD (Army Dept), 1964–66; Commandant, RMCS, Shrivenham, 1967–69; GOC-in-C, Western Comd, 1969–72. Col, The Cheshire Regt, 1969–71; Col Comdt, The Prince of Wales Div., 1971–74. Director: SE Regional Bd, Lloyds Bank Ltd, 1973–86; Flextech Ltd, 1978–. A Trustee, Imperial War Museum, 1973–83. Chm., SS&AFA, 1974–85; a Vice-Pres., RUSI, 1978–85. DL Kent, 1979. *Publications:* Dropzone Normandy, 1976; Airborne at War, 1978; Battle of the Bulge 1944, 1980. *Address:* Twin Firs, Four Elms, Edenbridge, Kent TN8 6PL. *Club:* Army and Navy.

CROOKS, Air Vice-Marshal David Manson, CB 1985; OBE 1969; Chief of Air Staff, Royal New Zealand Air Force, since 1983; *b* 8 Dec. 1931; *s* of James and Gladys Meta Crooks; *m* 1954, Barbara Naismith McDougall; four *d*. *Educ:* Rangiora, NZ. Joined RNZAF, 1951; Head, NZ Defence Liaison Staff, Singapore, 1967–70; CO RNZAF Base Wigram, 1973–74; RCDS, UK, 1974–75; AOC RNZAF Ops Gp, 1978–80; DCAS, 1980–83. *Recreations:* tramping, gardening, reading. *Address:* 13 Burrows Avenue, Karori, Wellington, New Zealand. *T:* 764-588. *Club:* Wellesley (Wellington, NZ).

CROOKS, Very Rev. John Robert Megaw; Dean of Armagh and Keeper of the Library, since 1979; *b* 9 July 1914; *s* of Canon the Rev. Louis Warden Crooks, OBE, MA, and Maria Kathleen Megaw; *m* 1941, Elizabeth Catherine Vance; two *s*. *Educ:* Campbell College, Belfast; Trinity College Dublin (MA). Deacon, 1938; priest, 1939; Curate Assistant, St Peter's, Dublin, 1938–43; Hon. Vicar Choral, St Patrick's Cathedral, Dublin, 1939–43; Catechist, High School, Dublin, 1939–43; Curate Assistant, Leighlin, 1943–44; Incumbent, Killylea, Dio. Armagh, 1944–56; Vicar Choral, St Patrick's Cathedral, 1956–73; Diocesan Sec., 1963–79; Hon. Clerical Sec., General Synod, 1970–; Prebendary of Ballymore, 1971, of Mullabrack 1972; Archdeacon of Armagh, 1973–79. *Recreation:* golf. *Address:* 44 Abbey Street, Armagh. *T:* 522540. *Club:* University (Dublin).

CROOKS, Air Vice-Marshal Lewis M.; *see* Mackenzie Crooks.

CROOM-JOHNSON, Rt. Hon. Sir David Powell, Kt 1971; DSC 1944; VRD 1953; PC 1984; **Rt. Hon. Lord Justice Croom-Johnson;** a Lord Justice of Appeal, since 1984; *b* 28 Nov. 1914; 3rd *s* of late Hon. Sir Reginald Powell Croom-Johnson, sometime a Judge of the High Court, and late Lady (Ruby) Croom-Johnson; *m* 1940, Barbara Douglas, *y d* of late Erskine Douglas Warren, Toronto; one *d*. *Educ:* The Hall, Hampstead; Stowe Sch.; Trinity Hall, Cambridge (MA; Hon. Fellow, 1985). RNVR (London Div.) 1936–53; served with Royal Navy, 1939–46. Called to Bar, Gray's Inn, 1938, Master of the Bench, 1964, Treasurer, 1981; Western Circuit. QC 1958; Recorder of Winchester, 1962–71; Judge of Courts of Appeal, Jersey and Guernsey, 1966–71; Judge of High Court of Justice, Queen's Bench Div., 1971–84. Member: Gen. Council of the Bar, 1958–62; Senate of Inns of Court, 1966–70. Home Office Inquiry concerning amalg. of Lancs Police Areas, 1967–68; Vice-Chm., Home Office Cttee on Mentally Abnormal Offenders, 1972–75; Chm., Crown Agents Tribunal, 1978–82. Mem., Council, Oakdene Sch., 1956–79; Chm., Knightsbridge Assoc., 1965–71. *Recreations:* books, music. *Address:* Royal Courts of Justice, WC2. *Club:* Garrick.

See also H. P. Croom-Johnson.

CROOM-JOHNSON, Henry Powell, CMG 1964; CBE 1954 (OBE 1944); TD 1948; *b* 15 Dec. 1910; *e s* of late Hon. Sir Reginald Croom-Johnson, sometime Judge of High Court, and of late Lady (Ruby) Croom-Johnson; *m* 1947, Jane, *er d* of late Archibald George Mandry; two *s*. *Educ:* Stowe Sch.; Trinity Hall, Cambridge. Asst Master, Bedford Sch., 1932–34. Joined staff of British Council, 1935. Served with Queen's Westminsters and King's Royal Rifle Corps, 1939–46 (staff Sicily, Italy, Greece; Lt-Col). Rejoined British Council, 1946: Controller Finance Div., 1951; Controller European Div., 1956; Representative in India, 1957–64; Controller, Overseas Div. B, 1964; Asst Dir-Gen., 1966–72, retired 1973. *Recreations:* climbing, books, music. *Address:* 3a Ravenscourt Square, W6. *T:* 01–748 3677. *Club:* Savile.

See also Sir D. P. Croom-Johnson.

CROOME, (John) Lewis, CMG 1957; *b* 10 June 1907; *s* of John and Caroline Croome; *m* 1st, 1931, Honoria Renée Minturn (*née* Scott; as Honor Croome, Editorial Staff of The Economist) (*d* 1960); four *s* one *d* (and one *s* decd); 2nd, 1961, Pamela Siola, *o d* of Lt-Col Tyrrel Hawker, Hurstbourne Priors, Hants; one *s*. *Educ:* Henry Thornton Sch., Clapham; London Sch. of Economics. Imperial Economic Cttee, 1931–39; Ministry of Food, 1939–48; Deputy (later Head), British Food Mission, Ottawa, 1942–46; HM Treasury (Central Economic Planning Staff), 1948–51; Min. of Food, 1951–54; UK Delegation to OEEC, Paris, 1954–57; Ministry of Agriculture, Fisheries and Food, 1957–58; Chief Overseas Relations Officer, UKAEA, 1958–72, retired. *Recreations:* painting, gardening. *Address:* 8 The Holdens, Bosham, West Sussex. *T:* Bosham 572292.

CROPPER, Peter John; Special Adviser to the Chancellor of the Exchequer, since 1984; *b* 18 June 1927; *s* of Walter Cecil Cropper and late Kathleen Cropper; *m* 1965, Rosemary Winning; one *s*. *Educ:* Hitchin Grammar Sch.; Gonville and Caius Coll., Cambridge (MA). Served Royal Artillery, 1945–48. Conservative Research Dept, 1951–53, 1975–79; Investment Analyst, Stockbroker, 1953–75; Special Adviser to Chief Sec. to the Treasury, 1979–82; Dir, Cons. Res. Dept, 1982–84. *Address:* 77 Hadlow Road, Tonbridge, Kent. *Club:* Reform.

CROSBIE, Hon. John Carnell; PC (Canada); MP (PC) St John's West, Newfoundland, since 1976; Minister of Transport, Canada, since 1986; *b* 30 Jan. 1931; *s* of Chesley Arthur Crosbie and Jessie Carnell; *m* 1952, Jane Furneaux; two *s* one *d*. *Educ:* Bishop Field Coll., St John's, Nfld; St Andrew's Coll., Aurora, Ont.; Queen's Univ., Kingston, Ont. (Pol. Sc. and Econs); Dalhousie Univ., Halifax, NS (Law); LSE, London, Eng. Joined Newfoundland Law Soc. and Newfoundland Bar; entered law practice, St John's, 1957; Mem. City Council, St John's, 1965; Dep. Mayor, 1966; Minister of Municipal Affairs and Housing, Province of Newfoundland, (Lib. Admin), July 1966; MHA, Prov. of Newfoundland, Sept. 1966; Minister of Health, 1967; resigned from Govt, 1968; re-elected Member for St John's West (Progressive Conservative), Provincial election, 1971; Minister of Finance, Pres. of Treasury Bd and Minister of Econ. Develt, 1972–74; Minister of Fisheries, Min. for Intergovtl Affairs and Govt House Leader, 1974–75; Minister of Mines and Energy and Minister for Intergovtl Affairs, 1975–76; resigned from Newfoundland Govt, Sept. 1976; elected to House of Commons, Oct. 1976; Chm. of Progressive Conservative Caucus Cttee on Energy, 1977; PC parly critic for Industry, Trade and Commerce, 1977–79; Minister of Finance, 1979–80; Party Finance Critic, 1980; Party External Affairs Critic, 1981–83; Minister of Justice and Attorney General, 1984–86. *Address:* 16 Circular Road, St John's, Newfoundland; House of Commons, Ottawa, Ontario.

CROSBIE, William, BA; RSA 1973; RGI 1977; artist; *b* Hankow, China, 31 Jan. 1915; *s* of Archibald Shearer Crosbie, marine engineer, and Mary Edgar, both Scottish; *m* 1st, 1944, M. G. McPhail (decd); one *d* (and one *d* decd); 2nd, 1975, Margaret Anne Roger. *Educ:* Chinese Tutor; Renfrew primary sch.; Glasgow Academy; Glasgow Sch. of Art, Glasgow Univ. (4 yrs under Forrester Wilson). Haldane Travelling Schol., 1935, for 3 yr period of study in British Schs in Athens, Rome and Paris (Beaux Arts); studied history and theory of techniques, in Beaux Arts and Sorbonne, and finally took a post-grad. qualif. in these (continues to acquire craftsmanship); passed into studio of Fernand Leger, Paris, and remained until war declared. Served War of 1939–45: ambulance service, WVS driving pool, and at sea. Has exhibited, on average, every two yrs, 1946–; principally one-man exhibns: Glasgow, Edinburgh, London, etc; also in USA, Brussels, Hamburg, etc. *Works in:* Kelvingrove Galls, Glasgow; Scottish provincial galls; Edinburgh City Arts Centre (mural), 1980; Scottish Gall. of Modern Art, 1980; Sydney State Gall., Australia; Wellington, NZ; Royal collection, UK, etc; also in many private collections. *Recreation:* sailing. *Address:* Studio, 12 Ruskin Lane, Glasgow G12 8EA. *T:* 041–334 4573; Rushes House, 10 Winchester Road, Petersfield, Hants GU32 3BY. *Clubs:* Glasgow Art; Royal Northern and Clyde Yacht (Rhu).

CROSBY, John Michael, LVO 1976; HM Diplomatic Service; High Commissioner in Belize, since 1984; *b* 2 Aug. 1940; *s* of Rev. B. Crosby and Norah Crosby (*née* Copeland); *m* 1963, Mary Collinge Smethurst; one *s* one *d*. *Educ:* Kingswood Sch., Bath; Magdalene Coll., Cambridge (MA). Social work in North Kensington and for SCM in Schools, 1962–65; entered Diplomatic Service, 1965; Third, later Second, Secretary, Addis Ababa, 1966–70; Second, later First, Secretary, FCO, 1970–73; seconded to Cabinet Office, 1973; First Secretary and Head of Chancery: Luxembourg, 1973–76; Mexico City, 1977–79; First Secretary, FCO, 1979–81; Counsellor and Dep. High Comr, Dar es Salaam, 1981–84. *Recreations:* sport, history, travel. *Address:* c/o Foreign and Commonwealth Office, SW1A 2AH. *Club:* United Oxford & Cambridge University.

CROSBY, Theo, ARA 1982; RIBA, FSIAD; Partner, Pentagram Design, since 1972; *b* 3 April 1925; *s* of N. J. Crosby and N. J. A. Goosen; *m* 1960, Finella Anne Buchanan; one *s* one *d*. *Educ:* Univ. of the Witwatersrand (BArch 1947). RIBA 1948; FSIAD 1964. Technical Editor, Architectural Design, 1953–62; now engaged in private architectural practice in exhibns, interiors and conservation. Mem., Berlin Acad., 1977–. Triennale of Milan Gran Premio, 1964; 2 Architectural Heritage Year Awards, 1973. *Publications:* Architecture: City Sense, 1965; The Necessary Monument, 1970; How to Play the Environment Game, 1973. *Recreation:* art. *Address:* Tower 3, Whitehall Court, SW1A 2EL. *T:* 01–930 0730 and 01–229 3477.

CROSFIELD, Very Rev. (George) Philip (Chorley); Provost of St Mary's Cathedral, Edinburgh, since 1970; *b* 9 Sept. 1924; *s* of James Chorley Crosfield and Marjorie Louise Crosfield; *m* 1956, Susan Mary Jullion (*née* Martin); one *s* two *d*. *Educ:* George Watson's Coll., Edinburgh; Selwyn Coll., Cambridge. Royal Artillery, 1942–46 (Captain). Priest, 1952; Asst Curate: St David's, Pilton, Edinburgh, 1951–53; St Andrew's, St Andrews, 1953–55; Rector, St Cuthbert's, Hawick, 1955–60; Chaplain, Gordonstoun School, 1960–68; subseq. Canon and Vice Provost, St Mary's Cathedral, Edinburgh. *Recreations:* walking, reading, carpentry. *Address:* 8 Lansdowne Crescent, Edinburgh, EH12 5EQ. *T:* 031–225 2978.

CROSS, family name of **Viscount Cross** and **Baron Cross of Chelsea.**

CROSS, 3rd Viscount, *cr* 1886; **Assheton Henry Cross;** late Lieut Scots Guards; *b* 7 May 1920; *e s* of 2nd Viscount and Maud Evelyn (who *m* 2nd, 1944, Guy Hope Coldwell (*d* 1948), Stoke Lodge, Ludlow, Salop; she *d* 1976), *d* of late Maj.-Gen. Inigo Jones, CVO, CB, Kelston Park, Bath; *S* father, 1932; *m* 1952, Patricia Mary (marr. diss., 1957; she *m* 1960, Comdr G. H. H. Culme-Seymour), *e d* of E. P. Hewetson, JP, The Craig, Windermere, Westmorland; two *d*; *m* 1972, Mrs Victoria Webb (marr. diss. 1977); *m* 1983, Mrs Patricia J. Rossiter. *Educ:* Shrewsbury; Magdalene Coll., Cambridge. *Heir:* none. *Club:* Cavalry and Guards.

CROSS OF CHELSEA, Baron *cr* 1971 (Life Peer), of the Royal Borough of Kensington and Chelsea; **(Arthur) Geoffrey (Neale) Cross,** PC 1969; Kt 1960; a Lord of Appeal in Ordinary, 1971–75; Chairman, Appeals Committee, Takeover Panel, 1976–81; *b* 1 Dec. 1904; *e s* of late Arthur George Cross and Mary Elizabeth Dalton; *m* 1952, Joan, *d* of late Major Theodore Eardley Wilmot, DSO, and *widow* of Thomas Walton Davies; one *d*. *Educ:* Westminster; Trinity College, Cambridge. Craven Scholar, 1925. Fellow of Trinity College, 1927–31, Hon. Fellow, 1972; called to the Bar, Middle Temple, 1930, Master of the Bench, 1958, Reader, 1971; QC 1949. Chancellor of the County Palatine of Durham, 1959. A Judge of the High Court of Justice, Chancery Div., 1960–69; a Lord Justice of Appeal, 1969–71. *Publications:* Epirus, 1932; (with G. R. Y. Radcliffe) The English Legal System (6th edn 1977). *Address:* The Bridge House, Leintwardine, Craven Arms, Shropshire. *T:* Leintwardine 205.

CROSS, Alexander Galbraith, MA, MD, FRCS; Ophthalmic Surgeon; lately Dean of the Medical School, St Mary's Hospital; Civilian Consultant in Ophthalmology, RN,

1946–76; Consultant Surgeon, Moorfields Eye Hospital, 1947–73; Consultant Ophthalmic Surgeon, St Mary's Hospital, 1946–73; Consultant Ophthalmic Surgeon, Royal National Throat, Nose, and Ear Hospital, 1954–73; Ophthalmic Surgeon, St Dunstan's, 1946–84; Hon. Consultant Ophthalmologist, Royal National Institute for the Blind, 1968–82; *b* 29 March 1908; *er s* of late Walter Galbraith Cross and Mary Stewart Cross, Wimbledon; *m* 1939, Eileen Longman, twin *d* of late Dr H. B. Corry, Liss, Hants; one *d*. *Educ*: King's Coll. Sch.; Gonville and Caius Coll., Cambridge; St Mary's Hosp., London (University Scholar) Meadows Prize, 1932, Broadbent and Agnes Cope Prizes, 1933, Cheadle Gold Medallist, 1933, St Mary's Hospital. House Phys. and House Surg., St Mary's, 1933–35; House Surg. and Sen. Res. Officer, Moorfields Eye Hosp., 1937–39; Ophthalmic Surgeon: West Middlesex Hosp., 1938–48; Tite Street Children's Hosp., 1939–48; Princess Beatrice Hosp., 1939–47; Royal Masonic Hosp., 1961–71. Wing Comdr, RAFVR, 1941–46 and Adviser in Ophthalmology, South-East Asia Air Forces. Examiner in Fellowship and in Diploma of Ophthalmology for RCS and in Ophthalmology for Univ. of Bristol; Recognised Teacher of Ophthalmology, University of London. Co-opted Mem. Council RCS, 1963–68. Mem. Bd of Governors: St Mary's Hosp., 1951–60; Moorfields Eye Hosp., 1962–65 and 1968–75. Mem. Paddington Group Hosp. Management Cttee, 1952–60. Pres. Ophthalmological Soc. of UK, 1975–77 (Sec. 1949–51; Vice-Pres., 1963–66); Member: RSocMed (Sec., Ophthalmic Section, 1951; Vice-Pres., 1960; Hon. Mem. 1979); BMA (Sec., Ophthalmic Section, 1948; Vice-Pres., 1957). Chm., Ophthalmic Gp Cttee, 1963–75; Mem. Council, Faculty of Ophthalmologists, 1963–72, Vice-Pres. 1964, Pres. 1968–71; Dean, Inst. of Ophthalmology, 1967–75 (Deputy Dean, 1966–67); Mem., Orthoptists Bd, 1970, Vice-Chm. 1971, Chm. 1972–75. *Publications*: 12th Edn, May and Worth's Diseases of the Eye; articles in British Jl of Ophthalmology, the Lancet, and other med. jls, dealing with ophthalmology. *Recreations*: gardening, lawn tennis, golf, squash racquets. *Address*: 4 Cottenham Park Road, Wimbledon, SW20 0RZ. *T*: 01–946 3491.

CROSS, Alexander Urquhart, TD 1959; JP; Lord Provost of Perth, 1972–75; *b* 24 Dec. 1906; *m* 1936; one *s* one *d*. *Educ*: Univ. of Glasgow (MA). Owner of private school, 1931–70 (except war years, 1939–45). JP 1972, DL 1972–75, Hon. Sheriff, 1974–, Perth. CStJ 1981. *Address*: 6 Craigie Road, Perth. *T*: Perth 25013.

CROSS, Prof. Anthony Glenn; Professor of Slavonic Studies, since 1985, and Fellow of Fitzwilliam College, since 1986, Cambridge University; *b* 21 Oct. 1936; *s* of Walter Sidney Cross and Ada Cross; *m* 1960, Margaret (*née* Elson); two *d*. *Educ*: High Pavement Sch., Nottingham; Trinity Hall, Cambridge (BA 1960, MA 1964, PhD 1966); Harvard Univ. (AM 1961); LittD East Anglia 1981. Frank Knox Fellow, Harvard Univ., 1960–61; Univ. of East Anglia: Lectr in Russian, 1964–69; Sen. Lectr in Russian, 1969–72; Reader, 1972–81; Roberts Prof. of Russian, Univ. of Leeds, 1981–85. Vis. Fellow: Univ. of Illinois, 1969–70; All Souls Coll., Oxford, 1977–78. Pres., British Univs Assoc. of Slavists, 1982–84; Chm., British Academic Cttee for Liaison with Soviet Archives, 1983–. Editor, Study Group on Eighteenth-Century Russia Newsletter, 1973–. *Publications*: N. M. Karamzin, 1971; Russia Under Western Eyes 1517–1825, 1971; (ed) Russian Literature in the Age of Catherine the Great, 1976; Anglo-Russian Relations in the Eighteenth Century, 1977; (ed) Great Britain and Russia in the Eighteenth Century, 1979; By the Banks of the Thames, 1980; (ed) Russia and the West in the Eighteenth Century, 1981; The Tale of the Russian Daughter and her Suffocated Lover, 1982; (ed jtly) Eighteenth Century Russian Literature, Culture and Thought: a bibliography, 1984; The Russian Theme in English Literature, 1985. *Recreations*: book collecting, cricket watching. *Address*: Department of Slavonic Studies, University of Cambridge, Sidgwick Avenue, Cambridge CB3 9DA. *T*: Cambridge 335007.

CROSS, Dr Barry Albert, CBE 1981; FRS 1975; Director of Animal Physiology and Genetics Research, Agricultural and Food Research Council, since 1986; *b* 17 March 1925; *s* of Hubert Charles and Elsie May Cross; *m* 1949, Audrey Lilian Crow; one *s* two *d*. *Educ*: Reigate Grammar Sch.; Royal Veterinary Coll. London, MRCVS, BSc (Vet Sci); St John's Coll., Cambridge, BA Hons, MA, PhD, ScD 1964. ICI Research Fellow, Physiological Lab., Cambridge, 1949–51, Gedge Prize 1952; Demonstrator, Zoological Lab., Cambridge, 1951–55; Lectr, 1955–58; Rockefeller Fellow at UCLA, 1957–58; Lectr, Dept. of Anatomy, Cambridge 1958–67; Supervisor in Physiology at St John's Coll., 1955–67; Corpus Christi College, Cambridge: Fellow, 1962–67, 1974–; Tutor for Advanced Students, 1964–67. Warden of Leckhampton, 1975–80; President, 1985–86; WHO Consultant, Geneva 1964; Prof. and Head of Dept of Anatomy, Univ. of Bristol, 1967–74, and Chm., Sch. of Preclinical Studies, 1969–73; Dir, AFRC Inst. of Animal Physiology, Babraham, 1974–86. Lectures: Share Jones, RCVS, 1967; Charnock Bradley, Edinburgh Univ., 1968; Glaxo, 1975; Entwhistle, Cambridge, 1976; McFadyean, London Univ., 1976; Wilmott, 1978, Long Fox, 1980, Bristol Univ. Member: Council, Anatomical Soc., 1968–73 (Vice Pres. 1973–74); Council, Assoc. for Study of Animal Behaviour, 1959–62, 1973–75; Cttee, Soc. for Study of Fertility, 1961–65; Cttee, Physiological Soc., 1971–75 (Chm. 1974–75); Internat. Soc. for Neuroendocrinology (Vice-Pres., 1972–75, Pres., 1976–80); Council, Zoological Soc. of London, 1985–; Adv. Cttee, Inst. of Zoology, 1982–. Mem. Farm Animals Welfare Adv. Cttee, MAFF, 1975–78. FIBiol 1975; FRVC 1979. Bledisloe Veterinary Award, RASE, 1982. Chevalier, Order of Dannebrog, 1968; Comdr d'honneur de l'Ordre du Bontemps de Médoc et des Graves, 1973. *Publications*: sci. papers on neuroendocrine topics in various biol. jls. *Address*: 6 Babraham Road, Cambridge. *Club*: Athenæum.

CROSS, Beverley; playwright; *b* 13 April 1931; *s* of George Cross, theatrical manager, and Eileen Williams, actress; *m* 1975, Maggie Smith, *qv*. *Educ*: Nautical Coll., Pangbourne; Balliol Coll., Oxford. Mem. Shakespeare Memorial Theatre Company, 1954–56; then began writing plays. One More River, Duke of York's, 1959; Strip the Willow, Arts, Cambridge, 1960 (Arts Council Drama Award for both, 1960); The Singing Dolphin, Oxford, 1960; The Three Cavaliers, Birmingham Rep., 1960; Belle, or The Ballad of Dr Crippen, Strand, 1961; Boeing-Boeing, Apollo, 1962; Wanted On Voyage, Marlowe, Canterbury, 1962; Half A Sixpence, Cambridge, London, 1963; Jorrocks, New, London, 1966; The Owl on the Battlements, Nottingham, 1971; Catherine Howard, York, 1972; The Great Society, Mermaid, 1974; Hans Andersen, Palladium, 1974; Happy Birthday, Apollo, 1979; Haworth, Birmingham Rep., 1981; The Scarlet Pimpernel, Chichester, Her Majesty's, 1985. *Libretti*: The Mines of Sulphur, Sadler's Wells, 1965; All the King's Men, 1969; Victory, Covent Garden, 1970; The Rising of the Moon, Glyndebourne, 1970; A Capital Transfer, British Council, London, 1981. *Screen plays of*: Jason and the Argonauts, 1962; The Long Ships, 1963; Genghis Khan, 1965; Half A Sixpence, 1966; (with Carlo Lizzani) Mussolini: Ultimo Atto, 1973; Sinbad and the Eye of the Tiger, 1977; The Clash of the Titans, 1981. *Television plays*: The Nightwalkers, 1960; The Dark Pits of War, 1960; Catherine Howard, 1969; March on, Boys!, 1975; A Bill of Mortality, 1975. *Directed*: Boeing-Boeing, Sydney, 1964; The Platinum Cat, Wyndham's, 1965. *Publications*: Mars in Capricorn, 1955; The Nightwalkers, 1956; Plays For Children, 1960. *Address*: c/o Curtis Brown Ltd, 162 Regent Street, W1R 5TA. *T*: 01–437 9700.

CROSS, Sir Cecil Lancelot Stewart, (Sir Lance Cross), Kt 1984; CBE 1977; *b* 12 Nov. 1912; *s* of Cecil Thomas Cross; *m* 1940, Amy, *d* of Albert Taylor; two *d*. *Educ*: Timaru Boys' High School; Canterbury University. Fellow, Phys. Ed. Soc., NZ. Served RNZAF, war of 1939–45. Dir, Phys. Educn, YMCA, 1933–39; NZ Supt, Phys. Welfare and Recreation, 1939–52; Head of Sports Broadcasts, 1953–75, of Sporting Services, 1976–77, NZ Broadcasting Council. Chairman: NZ Olympic and Commonwealth Games Assoc., 1967–82 (Pres., 1982–); NZ Sports Council, 1977–84; Mem., IOC, 1969–; Pres., Oceania Assoc. of Nat. Olympic Cttees, 1980–; Vice-Pres., Internat. Basketball Fedn, 1972–. *Address*: 1 Otaki Street, Wellington 3, New Zealand. *Club*: Wellesley (Wellington).

CROSS, Clifford Thomas, CB 1977; Commissioner, Customs and Excise, 1970–79; *b* 1 April 1920; *o s* of late Arthur and Helena Cross; *m* 1942, Ida Adelaide Barker; one *s* two *d*. *Educ*: Latymer Upper Sch., Hammersmith; Univ. of London (LLB). Joined Inland Revenue, 1939; Customs and Excise, 1946; Asst Sec. 1959; Comr 1970. *Recreations*: squash rackets, bonsai culture, watching television, etc. *Address*: Longacre, 101 Histon Road, Cottenham, Cambs. *T*: Cottenham 50757.

CROSS, Rt. Rev. David Stewart; see Blackburn, Bishop of.

CROSS, Prof. George Alan Martin, FRS 1984; André and Bella Meyer Professor of Molecular Parasitology, Rockefeller University, New York, since 1982; *b* 27 Sept. 1942; *s* of George Bernard and Beatrice Mary Cross. *Educ*: Cheadle Hulme Sch.; Downing Coll., Univ. of Cambridge (BA, PhD). ICI Postdoctoral Fellow, Biochemistry, Cambridge, 1967–69; Research Fellow, Fitzwilliam Coll., Cambridge, 1967–70; Scientist, MRC Biochemical Parasitology Unit, Molteno Inst., Cambridge, 1969–77; Head, Dept of Immunochemistry, Wellcome Research Laboratories, 1977–82. Fleming Lectr, Soc. for General Microbiology, 1978. Chalmers Medal, Royal Soc. for Tropical Medicine and Hygiene, 1983; (jtly) Paul Ehrlich and Ludwig Darmstaedter Prize, 1984. *Publications*: in journals of parasitology, biochemistry, microbiology and molecular biology. *Recreations*: sailing, tennis, building projects, observing people. *Address*: Rockefeller University, 1230 York Avenue, New York, NY 10021, USA. *T*: 212–570–7571.

CROSS, Hannah Margaret, (Mrs E. G. Wright); barrister-at-law; *b* 25 April 1908; *o d* of late F. J. K. Cross and Eleanor Mary Cross (*née* Phillimore); *m* 1936, Edmund Gordon Wright, Barrister-at-Law (*d* 1971); one *s* one *d*. *Educ*: Downe House Sch.; St Hilda's Coll., Oxford. BA 1929. Called to Bar, Lincoln's Inn, 1931; first woman Mem. of Gen. Council of Bar, 1938–45; Civil Defence, 1939–45. *Address*: The Quay House, Sidlesham, near Chichester, West Sussex. *T*: Sidlesham 258.

CROSS, James Richard, (Jasper), CMG 1971; Under-Secretary, Principal Establishment Officer, Department of Energy, 1978–80; *b* 29 Sept. 1921; *s* of J. P. Cross and Dinah Cross (*née* Hodgins); *m* 1945, Barbara Dagg; one *d*. *Educ*: King's Hosp., Dublin; Trin. Coll., Dublin. Scholar, First Cl. Moderatorship Economics and Polit. Science. RE (Lieut). Asst Principal, Bd of Trade, 1947; Private Sec. to Parly Sec., 1947–49; Principal, 1950; Trade Commissioner: New Delhi, 1953–56; Halifax, 1957–60; Winnipeg, 1960–62; Asst Sec., 1962; Sen. Trade Comr, Kuala Lumpur, 1962–66; Bd of Trade, 1966–67; Under Sec., 1968; Sen. British Trade Comr, Montreal, 1968–70 (kidnapped by terrorists and held for 59 days, Oct.-Dec. 1970); Under-Sec., Export Planning and Develt Div., DTI, 1971–73; Sec., British Overseas Trade Bd, 1972; Coal Div., DTI, later Dept of Energy, 1973–78. *Recreations*: theatre, bridge, the New Forest. *Address*: The Small House, Queen Katherine Road, Lymington, Hants.

CROSS, Joan, CBE 1951; opera singer; *b* Sept. 1900. *Educ*: St Paul's Girls' Sch. Principal soprano, Old Vic and Sadler's Wells, 1924–44; Dir of Opera, Sadler's Wells, 1941–44; subsequently Principal, National Sch. of Opera (Ltd), Morley Coll., London, resigned. *Address*: 4 The Timberyard, Great Glemham, Saxmundham, Suffolk.

CROSS, Air Chief Marshal Sir Kenneth (Brian Boyd), KCB 1959 (CB 1954); CBE 1945; DSO 1943; DFC 1940; *b* 4 Oct. 1911; *s* of Pembroke H. C. Cross and Mrs Jean Cross; *m* 1945, Brenda Megan, *d* of Wing-Comdr F. J. B. Powell; two *s* one *d*. *Educ*: Kingswood Sch., Bath. Pilot Officer, RAF, 1930; Flying Badge, 1931; 25 Fighter Sqdn, 1931; Flying Officer, 1932; Flying Instructor, No 5 FTS Sealand and Cambridge Univ. Air Sqdn, 1934; Flt Lt 1935; Sqdn Ldr 1938; commanded No 46 Fighter Sqdn UK, Norway, 1939–40; Wing Comdr 1940; posted Middle East, 1941; Actg Group Capt. 1941; Actg Air Commodore, 1943; Director Overseas Operations, Air Ministry, 1944; Imperial Defence Coll., 1946; reverted Group Capt., 1946; Group Capt. Operations HQ BAFO Germany, 1947; OC Eastern Sector Fighter Command, 1949; Dir of Weapons, Air Ministry, 1952; subs. Air Cdre, 1953; Dir of Ops, Air Defence, 1954–Dec. 1955; Air Vice-Marshal, 1956; AOC No 3 (Bomber) Group, 1956–59; Air Marshal, 1961; AOC-in-C, Bomber Comd, 1959–63; Air Chief Marshal, 1965; AOC-in-C, Transport Comd, 1963–66, retd, 1967. Director: Suffolk Branch, 1968, London Branch, 1974, British Red Cross Soc. Norwegian War Cross, 1941; USA Legion of Merit, 1944; French Legion of Honour, 1944; French Croix de Guerre, 1944; Dutch Order of Orange Nassau, 1945. *Recreations*: Rugby football and golf (colours RAF). *Address*: 12 Callow Street, Chelsea, SW3. *Club*: Royal Air Force.

CROSS, Prof. Kenneth William, MB, DSc, FRCP; Professor of Physiology, London Hospital Medical College, 1960–81, now Emeritus; Hon. Physiologist to The London Hospital; *b* 26 March 1916; *s* of late George Cross, Ealing; *m* 1942, Joyce M. Wilson (*née* Lack, *d* 1970); one step *d*; *m* 1970, Dr Sheila R. Lewis. *Educ*: St Paul's Sch.; St Mary's Hospital Medical Sch. Qualified, 1940; House appointments in St Mary's Hospital Sector; graded Physician EMS Amersham Emergency Hosp. 1945; Friends' Ambulance Unit, China, 1946–47. Lecturer in Physiology, 1947, Reader, 1952, St Mary's Hosp. *Publications*: contrib. to Journal of Physiology.

CROSS, Sir Lance; see Cross, Sir C. L. S.

CROSS, Mrs Margaret Natalie; see Smith, Maggie.

CROSS, Prof. Robert Craigie, CBE 1972; MA Glasgow, MA Oxford; FRSE; Regius Professor of Logic, 1953–78, Vice-Principal, 1974–77, University of Aberdeen; *b* 24 April 1911; *s* of Matthew Cross and Margaret Dickson; *m* 1943, Peggy Catherine Elizabeth Vernon; two *d*. *Educ*: Glasgow Univ.; Queen's Coll., Oxford. MA 1st Cl. Hons Classics, Glasgow, 1932; 1st Cl. Hons Classical Mods, Oxford, 1934; 1st Cl. Lit. Hum., Oxford, 1936. Fellow and Tutor in Philsophy, Jesus Coll., Oxford, 1938; served War, 1941–45, Navy and Admiralty; Senior Tutor, Jesus Coll., Oxford, 1948–53. Trustee, Scottish Hospital Endowments Research Trust, 1968–80; Mem., University Grants Cttee, 1965–74; Mem., North Eastern Regional Hospital Bd, 1958–65. *Publications*: (with A. D. Woozley) Plato's Republic: A Philosophical Commentary, 1964; contributions to learned jls. *Address*: Heatherlands, Ancrum, Roxburghshire. *T*: Ancrum 282.

CROSSE, Gordon; composer; *b* 1 Dec. 1937; *s* of Percy and Marie Crosse; *m* 1965, Elizabeth Bunch. *Educ*: Cheadle Hulme Sch.; St Edmund Hall, Oxford; Accad. di S Cecilia, Rome. Music Fellow, Essex Univ., 1969–74; Composer in residence, King's Coll., Cambridge, 1974–76; Vis. Lectr, Univ. of Calif at Santa Barbara, 1977–78. Hon. RAM, 1980. *Operas*: Purgatory, 1966; The Grace of Todd, 1967; The Story of Vasco, 1970; Potter Thompson, 1973; *ballets*: Playground, 1979; Wildboy, 1981; *other compositions*:

Concerto da Camera, 1962; Meet My Folks, 1963; "Symphonies", 1964; Second Violin Concerto, 1970; Memories of Morning: Night, 1972; Ariadne, 1973; Symphony 2, 1975; Wildboy (clarinet concerto), Play Ground, 1977; Dreamsongs, 1978; Cello Concerto, 1979; String Quartet, 1980; Dreamcanon (chorus), 1981; much other orchestral, vocal and chamber music. *Address:* Brant's Cottage, Wenhaston, Halesworth, Suffolk.

CROSSETT, Robert Nelson, DPhil; Chief Scientist (Fisheries and Food), Ministry of Agriculture, Fisheries and Food, since 1985; *b* 27 May 1938; *s* of Robert Crossett and Mary Nelson; *m* 1966, Susan Marjorie Legg; two *s*. *Educ:* British School, Hamburg; Campbell College, Belfast; Queen's Univ., Belfast (BSc, BAgr); Lincoln College, Oxford (DPhil); Univ. of East Anglia. Group Leader Environmental Studies, Aust. Atomic Energy Commn, 1966; Sen. Sci. Officer, ARC Letcombe Lab., 1969; Develt Officer (Crops), Scottish Agricl. Develt Council, 1972; PSO, Dept of Agric. and Fisheries for Scotland, 1975; Sci. Liaison Officer (Horticulture and Soils), MAFF, 1978; Head, Food Sci. Div., MAFF, 1984. *Publications:* papers in plant physiology and marine biology. *Recreations:* walking, gardening, orienteering, boats. *Address:* Ministry of Agriculture, Fisheries and Food, Great Westminster House, Horseferry Road, SW1P 2AE. *T:* 01-216 6704.

CROSSLAND, Anthony, FRCO; Organist and Master of the Choristers, Wells Cathedral, since 1971; *b* 4 Aug. 1931; *s* of Ernest Thomas and Frances Elizabeth Crossland; *m* 1960, Barbara Helen Pullar-Strecker; one *s* two *d*. *Educ:* Christ Church, Oxford. MA, BMus (Oxon), FRCO (CHM), ARCM. Asst Organist: Christ Church Cathedral, Oxford, 1957–61; Wells Cathedral, 1961–71. Conductor: Wells Cathedral Oratorio Soc., 1966–; Wells Sinfonietta, 1985–; Organs Advr to dio. of Bath and Wells, 1971–. Pres., Cathedral Organists' Assoc., 1983–85. *Recreations:* reading, photography. *Address:* 15 Vicars' Close, Wells, Somerset. *T:* Wells (Somerset) 73526.

CROSSLAND, Prof. Bernard, CBE 1980; MSc (London); PhD (Bristol); DSc (Nottingham); FRS 1979; FEng 1979; MRIA; FIMechE; FIProdE; FIW; FIEI; Emeritus Professor, The Queen's University, Belfast, since 1984 (Professor and Head of Department of Mechanical and Industrial Engineering, 1959–82, Research Professor, 1982–84; Dean, 1964–67; Pro-Vice-Chancellor, 1978–82); *b* 20 Oct. 1923; *s* of R. F. Crossland and K. M. Rudduck; *m* 1946, Audrey Elliott Birks; two *d*. *Educ:* Simon Langton's, Canterbury. Apprentice, Rolls Royce Ltd, 1940–41; Nottingham Univ., 1941–43; Technical Asst, Rolls Royce, 1943–45; Asst Lectr, Lectr and then Senior Lectr in Mechanical Engineering, Univ. of Bristol, 1946–59. Member: AFRC, 1981–; Engrg Council, 1983–; Chairman: Bd for Engineers' Registration, 1983–; Youth Careers Guidance Cttee, N Ireland, 1975–79, 1979–81; NI Manpower Council, 1981–; Member: NI Training Council, 1964–76, 1977–81; NI Economic Council, 1981–85; NI Industrial Develt Bd, 1982–. Institution of Mechanical Engineers: Chm., Engineering Sciences Div., 1980–84; Vice-Pres., 1983–84; Dep. Pres., 1984–86; Pres., 1986–; George Stephenson and Thomas Hawksley Medals; Mem. Council and a Vice-Pres., Royal Soc., 1984–86; Mem. Council, Fellowship of Engrg, 1985–. Trustee, Mackie Foundn, 1983–. Hon. DSc: NUI, 1984; Dublin, 1985. *Publications:* An Introduction to the Mechanics of Machines, 1964; Explosive Welding and its Application, 1982; various papers on fatigue of metals and effect of very high fluid pressures on properties of materials; strength of thick-walled vessels, explosive welding, friction welding, design and history of engineering. *Recreation:* walking. *Address:* The Queen's University, 2 Fitzwilliam Street, Belfast BT7 1NN. *T:* Belfast 245133 ext. 3126; Crossland Consultants, Belfast BT7 1JR. *T:* Belfast 244503. *Club:* Athenæum.

CROSSLAND, Sir Leonard, Kt 1969; farmer since 1974; Chairman: Eaton Ltd (UK), since 1972; Ford Motor Co. Ltd, 1968–72; Energy Research and Development Ltd (formerly Sedgeminster Technical Developments Ltd), since 1974; *b* 2 March 1914; *s* of Joseph and Frances Crossland; *m* 1st, 1941, Rhona Marjorie Griffin; two *d*; 2nd, 1963, Joan Brewer. *Educ:* Penistone Grammar Sch. Purchase Dept, Ford Motor Co. Ltd, 1937–39. Royal Army Service Corps, 1939–45. Ford Motor Co. Ltd: Purchase Dept. 1945–54; Chief Buyer, Tractor and Implement Dept, 1954–57; Chief Buyer, Car and Truck Dept, 1957–59; Asst Purchase Manager, 1959–60; Purchase Manager, 1960–62; Exec. Dir, Supply and Services, 1962–66; Dir, Manufacturing Staff and Services, 1966; Asst Man. Dir, 1966–67; Man. Dir, 1967; Dep. Chm., 1967; Chm., Autolite Motor Products Ltd; Director: Henry Ford & Son Ltd, Cork; Eaton Corp. (US), 1974–81. Farmer. *Recreations:* shooting, fishing, golf. *Address:* Abbotts Hall, Great Wigborough, Colchester, Essex. *T:* Peldon 456. *Clubs:* City Livery, Royal Automobile, British Racing Drivers'; American.

CROSSLAND, Prof. Ronald Arthur, FSA 1982; Professor of Greek, University of Sheffield, 1958–82, now Emeritus; *b* 31 Aug. 1920; *s* of late Ralph Crossland, BSc, and late Ethel Crossland (*née* Scattergood). *Educ:* Stanley Road Elementary Sch., Nottingham; Nottingham High Sch.; King's Coll., Cambridge. Major Scholar in Classics, King's Coll., Cambridge, 1939–41 and 1945–46. National Service in Royal Artillery, 1941–45. Henry Fellow, Berkeley Coll., Yale Univ., 1946–47; Instructor in Classics, Yale Univ., 1947–48; Senior Student of Treasury Cttee for Studentships in Foreign Languages and Cultures (for research in Hittite Philology and Linguistics), 1948–51; Hon. Lectr in Ancient History, University of Birmingham, 1950–51; Lecturer in Ancient History, King's Coll., University of Durham, Newcastle upon Tyne, 1951–58. Harris Fellow of King's Coll., Cambridge, 1952–56. Vis. Prof., Univ. Texas, 1962; Collitz Vis. Prof., Univ. Michigan, 1967; Vis. Fellow, Victoria Univ. of Wellington, NZ, 1979. Pres., South Shields Archaeological and Historical Soc., 1976–77. *Publications:* Bronze Age Migrations in the Aegean (with A. Birchall), 1973; Teaching Classical Studies, 1976; chapters on: Immigrants from the North, in Cambridge Ancient History, rev. edn, 1967; Linguistic Problems of the Balkan Area, in Cambridge Ancient History, rev. edn, 1982; articles in Trans Philological Soc., Archivum Linguisticum, Studia Balcanica, Past and Present. *Recreations:* music, travel. *Address:* 59 Sherlock Close, Cambridge CB3 0HP. *T:* Cambridge 358085; (*enquiries*) Sheffield 78555 ext. 4603.

CROSSLEY, family name of **Baron Somerleyton.**

CROSSLEY, Sir Christopher John, 3rd Bt *cr* 1909; Lieutenant-Commander Royal Navy, retired; Middle East business consultant; *b* 25 Sept. 1931; *s* of late Lt-Comdr Nigel Crossley, RN (*s* of late Eric Crossley, OBE, 2nd *s* of 1st Bt); *S* great uncle (Sir Kenneth Crossley, 2nd Bt), 1957; *m* 1959, Carolyne Louise (marr. diss. 1969), *d* of late L. Grey Sykes; two *s*; *m* 1977, Lesley, *e d* of late Dr K. A. J. Chamberlain. *Educ:* Canford Sch. Entered Royal Navy, 1950. *Recreations:* royal tennis, squash. *Heir:* *s* Nicholas John Crossley, *b* 10 Dec. 1962. *Address:* PO Box 100, Heliopolis, Egypt.

CROSSLEY, Geoffrey Allan, CMG 1974; HM Diplomatic Service, retired; Director, External Relations, Continuing Education, European Institute of Business Administration, INSEAD, Fontainebleau, 1980–84; *b* 11 Nov. 1920; *s* of Thomas Crossley and Winifred Mary Crossley (*née* Ellis); *m* 1945, Aline Louise Farcy; two *s* one *d*. *Educ:* Penistone; abroad; Gonville and Caius Coll., Cambridge (Scholar). Served War of 1939–45: Min. of Supply, 1941–; Foreign Office, 1942–; in Algeria and France. Foreign Service, 1945–: Second Sec., Paris, 1945–48; FO, 1948–49; Alternate UK Deleg. on UN Balkans Commn, Greece, 1949–52; Dep. Regional Inf. Officer with Commissioner-Gen. for SE Asia, Singapore, 1952–55; FO, 1955–57; Consulate-Gen., Frankfurt, for Saar Transition from France to Germany, 1957–59; Political Office, NE Command, Cyprus (later in charge), 1959–61; Head of Chancery, Berne, 1961–65; on secondment to Min. of Overseas Development, as Head of W and N African Dept, 1965–67; Dep. High Comr, Lusaka, 1967–69; Counsellor, Oslo, 1969–73; Ambassador to Colombia, 1973–77; Envoy to the Holy See, 1978–80. *Recreations:* various. *Address:* 22 Rue Emeriau, 75015 Paris, France.

CROSSLEY, Harry; DL; Chief Executive, Derbyshire County Council, 1974–79, retired; *b* 2 Sept. 1918; *s* of late Percy Crossley and Nellie McMinnies Crossley, Burnley, Lancs; *m* 1949, Pamela, *e d* of late Ald. E. A. C. Woodcock, Kettering, Northants; two *s*. *Educ:* Burnley Grammar Sch. Solicitor. LAM RTPI. War service, RA, attached Indian Army (Major), 1939–46. Private practice and local govt service as solicitor; Derbyshire CC: Dep. Clerk of Peace and of CC, 1960–69; Clerk of Peace and of CC, 1969–74. Clerk to Derbyshire Lieutenancy, 1969–79; Sec., Lord Chancellor's Adv. Cttee for Derbyshire, 1969–79. Clerk, Peak Park Planning Bd, 1969–74. DL Derbyshire, 1978. *Publications:* articles for legal and local govt jls. *Recreations:* golf, tennis, gardening. *Address:* Alpine, Bracken Lane, Holloway, Matlock DE4 5AS. *T:* Dethick 382.

CROSSLEY, Wing-Comdr Michael Nicholson, DSO 1940; OBE 1946; DFC; Fighter Command; farming in South Africa since 1955; *b* 29 May 1912; *s* of late Major E. Crossley, OBE; *m* 1957, Sylvia Heyder (*d* 1975); one *s* two *d*; *m* 1977, Moyra Birkbeck, *widow* of Maj.-Gen. T. H. (John) Birkbeck. *Educ:* Eton Coll.; Munich. Commissioned in RAF, 1935. *Recreation:* golf. *Address:* Loughrigg, White River 1240, E Transvaal, S Africa. *Clubs:* Army and Navy; Rand (Johannesburg).

CROSSLEY, Maj.-Gen. Ralph John, CBE 1981; Director General of Weapons (Army), 1984–86; *b* 11 Oct. 1933; *s* of Edward Crossley and Eva Mary Crossley (*née* Farnworth); *m* 1957, Marion Hilary Crossley (*née* Bacon); one *s* one *d*. *Educ:* Quainton Sch., Harrow; Felsted School. FBIM. Commnd 1952 (Nat. Service); Air Observation Post Pilots course, 1953; Regimental Duty: Canal Zone,1954–56; BAOR, 1956–59; Instructor in Gunnery, Larkhill, 1959–63; Technical Staff Course, 1963–65; Regtl Duty, BAOR, 1965–67, 1969–71; Weapons Staff, UK, 1967–69; Gen. Staff, UK, 1971–72; Instructor, RMCS, 1972–74; CO, 94 Locating Regt, 1974–77; Project Manager, 155 Systems, 1977–81; Dep. Comdt, RMCS, 1981–84. *Recreations:* golf, walking, gardening. *Address:* c/o Midland Bank, Eastcote, Pinner, Middlesex.

CROSSMAN, Sir (Douglas) Peter, Kt 1982; TD 1944; DL; *b* 25 Sept. 1908; *s* of late Percy Crossman, Gt Bromley Hall, Colchester; *m* 1st, 1932, Monica, *d* of late C. F. R. Barnett; two *s* one *d*; 2nd, 1939, Jean Margaret, *d* of late Douglas Crossman, Cokenach, Royston. *Educ:* Uppingham; Pembroke Coll., Cambridge. Commission Warwicks Yeomanry, 1934–45. Chairman: Mann Crossman Paulin Ltd, 1961–65; Watney Mann Ltd, 1965–70. President: Licensed Victuallers' Sch., 1958; Shire Horse Soc., 1958; Beer and Wine Trade Benev., 1960; Licensed Victuallers' Nat. Homes, 1963; Hunts Agricultural Soc., 1965; Chairman: Govs, Dame Alice Owen's Sch., 1951–65; Hunts Conservative Assoc., 1954–61; Eastern Area, Nat. Union of Conservative Party, 1965; Nat. Union of Conservative Party, 1969. Master, Brewers' Co., 1950. Chairman, Brewers' Soc., 1968, 1969. DL Huntingdonshire, 1958. Master: Essex and Suffolk Foxhounds, 1938–40; Cambridgeshire Foxhounds, 1947–49. *Recreations:* hunting, shooting, fishing, gardening. *Address:* Tetworth Hall, Sandy, Beds. *T:* Gamlingay 212. *Club:* Cavalry and Guards.

CROSTHWAIT, Timothy Leland, CMG 1964; MBE 1944; HM Diplomatic Service, retired; *b* 5 Aug. 1915; *s* of Lt-Col L. G. Crosthwait, Survey of India; *m* 1959, Anne Marjorie, *d* of Col T. M. M. Penney. *Educ:* Wellington Coll.; Peterhouse, Cambridge (MA). Appointed to Indian Civil Service, 1937; Asst Private Sec. to Viceroy, 1942–44; Air Min., 1948–55; Commonwealth Relations Office, 1955; British Deputy High Commissioner in Ceylon, 1957–61; Asst Sec., CRO, 1961–63; British High Commissioner, Zanzibar, 1963–64; British Deputy High Commissioner, Malta, 1965–66; British High Commissioner, Guyana, 1966–67; Ambassador, Malagasy Republic, 1970–75. *Address:* 39 Eaton Terrace, SW1. *T:* 01-730 9553. *Club:* United Oxford & Cambridge University.

CROSTHWAITE, Sir (Ponsonby) Moore, KCMG 1960 (CMG 1951); *b* 13 Aug. 1907; *o s* of late P. M. Crosthwaite, MICE, and late Agnes Alice, *y d* of J. H. Aitken, Falkirk, Stirlingshire. *Educ:* Rugby; CCC, Oxford. Laming Fellowship, Queen's Coll., 1931. Entered Diplomatic Service, 1932; has served in Bagdad, Moscow, Madrid, Athens and Foreign Office; Deputy UK Representative to United Nations, New York, 1952–58; Ambassador to the Lebanon, 1958–63; Ambassador to Sweden, 1963–66. *Recreations:* travel, the arts. *Address:* 17 Crescent Grove, SW4. *Club:* Athenæum.

CROUCH, David (Lance); MP (C) Canterbury since 1966; Director: David Crouch & Co. Ltd; Pfizer Ltd; Foster Crouch (Consultants) Ltd; Kingsway Public Relations (Holdings) Ltd; ITM (Offshore) Ltd; *b* 23 June 1919; *s* of late Stanley Crouch and Rosalind Kate Crouch (*née* Croom); *m* 1947, Margaret Maplesden, *d* of Major Sydney Maplesden Noakes, DSO and Norah Parkyns Maplesden Noakes (*née* Buckland), Shorne, Kent; one *s* one *d*. *Educ:* University Coll. Sch. Served in City of London Yeomanry (TA), 1938–39; served War of 1939–45, Royal Artillery: Major 1943; attached RAF Staff (GSO2), 1944–45. Joined British Nylon Spinners Ltd, 1946; ICI Ltd, 1950; Dir of Publicity, Internat. Wool Secretariat, 1962–64. Formed own co., David Crouch & Co. Ltd, as international marketing and public relations consultants (Chairman, 1964–). Contested (C) West Leeds, 1959. Chairman: British-Egyptian Parly Gp; British-Algerian Gp; All-Party Gp for the Chemical Industry, 1970–85; All-Party Gp for Energy Studies, 1980–85; British Gp, Inter-Parly Union, 1985–; Vice-Chm., Cons. Middle East Council; Member: Select Cttee for Nationalized Industries, 1966–74; Public Accounts Cttee, 1974–79; Select Cttee for Social Services, 1983–84. Trustee, Theatres Trust, 1977– (Dep. Chm., 1979–); Chm., Channel Theatre Co., 1984–. Member: SE Thames RHA, 1970–85; MRC, 1984–; Soc. of Chemical Industry; Council, Univ. of Kent; Council, RSA, 1974– (Fellow, 1971). *Recreations:* cricket, tennis, golf. *Address:* 3 Tufton Court, Tufton Street, SW1; The Oast House, Fisher Street, Badlesmere, Faversham, Kent. *Club:* Athenæum.

CROWDEN, James Gee Pascoe, JP; FRICS, FCIArb; Senior Partner, Grounds & Co., since 1974; Vice Lord-Lieutenant of Cambridgeshire, since 1985; *b* 14 Nov. 1927; *yr s* of late Lt-Col R. J. C. Crowden, MC, and late Mrs Crowden; *m* 1955, Kathleen Mary, *widow* of Captain F. A. Grounds and *d* of late Mr and Mrs J. W. Loughlin, Upwell; one *s* decd. *Educ:* Bedford Sch.; Pembroke Coll., Cambridge (MA). Chartered surveyor; FRICS 1959; FCIArb 1977. Commissioned Royal Lincs Regt, 1947. Rowed in Oxford and Cambridge Boat Race, 1951 and 1952 (Pres., 1952); Captain, Great Britain VIII, European Championships, Macon, 1951 (Gold Medallists); also rowed in 1950 European Championships and 1952 Olympics; coached 20 Cambridge crews, 1953–75; Steward and Mem., Cttee of Management, Henley Royal Regatta; Mem. Council, Amateur Rowing Assoc., 1957–77; Mem. of Court and Freeman, Co. of Watermen and Lightermen of River Thames. Chairman: Cambridgeshire Olympic Appeal, 1984; Appeal Exec. Cttee, Peterborough Cathedral, 1979–80; Mem., Ely Diocesan Pastoral Cttee, 1969–. Governor:

King's Sch., Peterborough; St Hugh's Sch., Woodhall Spa. JP Wisbech, 1969; DL Cambridgeshire, 1971; High Sheriff, Cambridgeshire and Isle of Ely, 1970. *Recreations:* rowing, shooting. *Address:* 19 North Brink, Wisbech, Cambridgeshire PE13 1JR. *T:* Wisbech 583320. *Clubs:* East India, Devonshire, Sports and Public Schools; Hawks', University Pitt, Cambridge County (Cambridge); Leander (Henley-on-Thames).

CROWDER, F(rederick) Petre, QC 1964; a Recorder (formerly Recorder of Colchester), since 1967; Barrister-at-Law; *b* 18 July 1919; *s* of late Sir John Ellenborough Crowder; *m* 1948, Hon. Patricia Stourton, *d* of 25th Baron Mowbray, MC (also 26th Baron Segrave and 22nd Baron Stourton); two *s. Educ:* Eton; Christ Church, Oxford. Served War of 1939–45; joined Coldstream Guards, 1939, and served in North Africa, Italy, Burma; attained rank of major. Called to the Bar, Inner Temple, 1948, Master of the Bench, 1971. South Eastern Circuit; North London Sessions. Recorder of Gravesend, 1960–67; Herts QS: Dep. Chm., 1959–63; Chm., 1963–71. Contested (C) North Tottenham, by-elec. 1945; MP (C) Ruislip-Northwood, 1950–74, Hillingdon, Ruislip-Northwood, 1974–79; PPS to Solicitor-Gen., 1952–54; PPS to Attorney General, 1954–62. *Address:* 2 Harcourt Buildings, Temple, EC4. *T:* 01–353 2112; 8 Quarrendon Street, SW6 3SU. *T:* 01–731 6342; Pond House, Charlestown, St Austell, Cornwall PL25 3NN. *T:* St Austell 61515. *Clubs:* Carlton, Pratt's, Turf.

CROWDER, Michael; Visiting Professor, Amherst College, USA, 1987; *b* 9 June 1934; *s* of Henry Cussons Crowder and late Molly Gladys Elizabeth Crowder (*née* Burchell). *Educ:* Mill Hill Sch.; Hertford Coll., Oxford (BA 1st Cl. Hons PPE, MA). 2/Lieut, Middx Regt, seconded to Nigeria Regt, 1953–54. Editor, Nigeria Magazine, Lagos, 1959–62; Secretary, Inst. of African Studies, Univ. of Ibadan, Nigeria, 1962–64; Vis. Lectr in African History, Univ. of Calif, Berkeley, 1964–65; Director, Inst. of African Studies, Fourah Bay Coll., Univ. of Sierra Leone, 1965–67; Research Prof. and Dir, Inst. of African Studies, Univ. of Ife, Nigeria, 1968–71; Prof. of History, Ahmadu Bello Univ., 1971–75 (Head, Dept of History, Kano Campus, 1971–74; Dean, Faculty of Arts and Islamic Studies, 1972–73; Dir, Univ. Centre for Nigerian Cultural Studies, 1972–75); Research Prof. in History, Centre for Cultural Studies, Univ. of Lagos, 1975–78; Editor, 1979–81, Consultant Editor, 1981–, History Today; Prof. of History, Univ. of Botswana, 1982–85; Hon. Sen. Res. Fellow, Inst. of Commonwealth Studies, Univ. of London, 1985–86. Mem. Exec. Council, 1979–, Jt Hon. Dir, 1981–82, Internat. African Inst.; Jt Editor, Journal of African History, 1985–. Visiting Professor: Columbia Univ., 1964, 1965; Ibadan Univ., 1967, Georgetown Univ., 1970; Vis. Fellow, Centre for Internat. Studies, LSE, 1981–82; Vis. Distinguished Prof., Univ. of Calif, Berkeley, 1985; Sen. Associate Mem., St Antony's Coll., Oxford, 1986. Hon. Exec. Sec., Internat. Congress of Africanists, 1962–68 (jtly with Prof. Lalage Bown, 1965–68); Member Council, African Studies Assoc. of UK, 1979–82; Minority Rights Gp, 1980–; Mem. Exec. Council, International African Inst., 1979– (Chm., Publication Cttee, 1979–82). General Editor, Hutchinson University Library for Africa, 1976–. Officer, National Order of Senegal, 1964. FRHistS, 1979. *Publications:* The Story of Nigeria, 1962, 4th edn 1977; Senegal: a study in French assimilation policy, 1962, 2nd edn 1967; West Africa under Colonial Rule, 1968; ed jtly, West African Chiefs, 1970; West African Resistance, 1971, 2nd edn 1981; ed jtly, History of West Africa, vol. I 1971, 3rd edn 1986, vol. II 1974, 2nd edn 1987; Revolt in Bussa: a study in British 'Native' Administration in Nigerian Borgu 1902–1936, 1973; Colonial West Africa: collected essays, 1978; Jt Gen. Editor: Cambridge Encyclopaedia of Africa, 1981; Historical Atlas of Africa, 1986; (ed) Cambridge History of Africa, vol. VIII, 1984. *Recreations:* music, travelling, gardening. *Address:* 13 Addington Square, SE5 7JZ. *T:* 01–703 8938; Dar Demdam, rue Merrouche, Casbah, Tangier, Morocco. *Club:* Travellers'.

CROWDER, Ven. Norman Harry; Archdeacon of Portsmouth, since 1985; *b* 20 Oct. 1926; *s* of Laurence Smethurst Crowder and Frances Annie (*née* Hicks); *m* 1971, Pauleen Florence Alison (*née* Styles); one *s. Educ:* Nottingham High School; St John's Coll., Cambridge (MA); Westcott House, Cambridge. Curate, St Mary's, Radcliffe-on-Trent, 1952–55; Residential Chaplain to Bishop of Portsmouth, 1955–59; Asst Chaplain, Canford School, 1959–64, Chaplain 1964–72; Vicar, St John's, Oakfield, Ryde, IoW, 1972–75; Dir of Religious Educn, Portsmouth Dio., and Res. Canon of Portsmouth Cathedral, 1975–85. *Recreations:* water colour, travel. *Address:* Victoria Lodge, 36 Osborn Road, Fareham, Hampshire PO16 7DS. *T:* Fareham 280101. *Club:* MCC.

CROWDY, Maj.-Gen. Joseph Porter, CB 1984; Commandant and Postgraduate Dean, Royal Army Medical College, 1981–84, retired; Hon. Consultant on nutrition to Army, since 1985; *b* 19 Nov. 1923; *s* of late Lt-Col Charles R. Crowdy and Kate Crowdy (*née* Porter); *m* 1948, Beryl Elisabeth Sapsford; four *d. Educ:* Gresham's Sch.; Edinburgh Univ. MB, ChB 1947, DTM&H 1956, DPH 1957, DIH 1957; FFCM 1974; MFOM 1981; FRIPHH 1982. House Surgeon, Norfolk and Norwich Hosp., 1947–48; joined RAMC, 1949; North Africa, 1952–55; Singapore, 1960–62; Head of Applied Physiology, Army Personnel Res. Estabt, 1963–73; Prof. of Army Health, Royal Army Med. Coll., 1973–76; SMO, Land Forces Cyprus, 1976–78; Dir, Army Preventive Medicine, 1978–81. Col Comdt, RAMC, 1985–. QHP 1981–84. Editor, RAMC Jl, 1978–83. *Publications:* articles in medical jls, on smoking and health, nutrition, physical fitness and obesity. *Recreation:* antique furniture restoration. *Address:* Pepperdon Mine, Lustleigh, Newton Abbot, Devon TQ13 9SN. *T:* Lustleigh 419.

CROWE, Brian Lee, CMG 1985; HM Diplomatic Service; Minister, Commercial, Washington, since 1985; *b* 5 Jan. 1938; *s* of Eric Crowe and Virginia Crowe; *m* 1969, Virginia Willis; two *s. Educ:* Sherborne; Magdalen Coll., Oxford (1st Cl. Hons PPE). Joined FO, 1961; served: Moscow, 1962–64; London, 1965–67; Aden, 1967; Washington, 1968–73; Bonn, 1973–76; Counsellor and Hd of Policy Planning Staff, FCO, 1976–78; Hd of Chancery, UK Perm. Representation to EEC, Brussels, 1979–81; Counsellor and Hd of EEC Dept (External), FCO, 1982–84. *Recreations:* winter sports, tennis, riding, squash, swimming. *Address:* c/o Foreign and Commonwealth Office, SW1.

CROWE, Sir Colin Tradescant, GCMG 1973 (KCMG 1963; CMG 1956); HM Diplomatic Service, retired; *b* 7 Sept. 1913; *s* of late Sir Edward Crowe, KCMG; *m* 1938, Bettina Lum (*d* 1983). *Educ:* Stowe Sch.; Oriel Coll., Oxford. Served at HM Embassy, Peking, 1936–38 and 1950–53; Shanghai, 1938–40; HM Embassy, Washington, 1940–45; Foreign Office, 1945–48, 1953–56; UK Delegn to OEEC, Paris, 1948–49; HM Legation, Tel Aviv, 1949–50; Imperial Defence Coll., 1957; Head, British Property Commn, Cairo, 1959; British Chargé d'Affaires, Cairo, 1959–61; Deputy UK Representative to the UN, New York, 1961–63; Ambassador to Saudi Arabia, 1963–64; Chief of Administration, HM Diplomatic Service, 1965–68; High Comr in Canada, 1968–70; UK Permanent Rep. to UN, 1970–73. Supernumerary Fellow, St Antony's Coll., Oxford, 1964–65. Dir, Grindlay's Bank Ltd, 1976–84. Chm., Marshall Aid Commemoration Commn, 1973–85. Chm. Council, Cheltenham Ladies Coll., 1974–86. *Address:* Pigeon House, Bibury, Glos. *Club:* Travellers'.

CROWE, Gerald Patrick, QC 1973; **His Honour Judge Crowe;** a Circuit Judge, since 1980; *b* 3 April 1930; *y s* of Patrick Crowe and Ethel Maud Crowe (*née* Tooth); *m* 1954, Catherine Mary, *d* of Joseph and Rose Murphy, Newry, N Ireland. *Educ:* St Francis Xavier's Coll.; Liverpool Univ. (LLB). Called to Bar, Gray's Inn, 1952; practised Northern Circuit. A Recorder of the Crown Court, 1976–80. Mem., Lord Chancellor's Adv. Cttee on Legal Aid, 1984–. *Recreations:* golf, fishing. *Address:* The Spinney, Long Hey Road, Caldy, Cheshire. *T:* 051–625 8848; Goldsmith Building, Temple, EC4Y 7BL.

CROWE, Prof. Ralph Vernon, FRIBA; Professor Emeritus, School of Architecture, Newcastle-upon-Tyne University, since 1981 (Professor of Architecture and Head of Department, 1976–81); now in private practice; *b* 30 Sept. 1915; *s* of Sidney John Crowe and Sarah Emma (*née* Sharp); *m* 1943, Nona Heath Eggington; two *s* one *d. Educ:* Westminster City Sch.; Architectural Assoc., London (AA Dipl. Hons); Sch. of Planning and Res. for Reg. Develt. MA Newcastle upon Tyne; ARIBA 1945; MRTPI 1949. War Service, 1941–45: Captain, RE. Govt Architect and Planning Officer, Govt of Barbados, BWI, 1947–50; teaching, Arch. Assoc., 1950–52; Basildon New Town, 1952–53; LCC, 1953–58; County Architect: Shropshire, 1958–66; Essex, 1966–76. *Publications:* contribs to professional and tech. jls. *Recreations:* music (flute), hill walking. *Address:* Holly Hall Barn, Sandhoe, Hexham, Northumberland NE46 4LX. *Club:* Savage.

CROWE, Dame Sylvia, DBE 1973 (CBE 1967); landscape architect in private practice since 1945; *b* 1901; *d* of Eyre Crowe; unmarried. *Educ:* Berkhamsted; Swanley Hort. Coll. Designed gardens, 1927–39. Served FANY and ATS, 1939–45. Since 1945, private practice as landscape architect has included: work as consultant to: Harlow and Basildon New Town Corporations; Wimbleball and Rutland Water reservoirs; Central Electricity Generating Board, for Trawsfynydd and Wylfa Nuclear Power Stations; Forestry Commission; reclamation of land after 1952 floods and design of public gardens at Mablethorpe and Sutton on Sea; gardens for Oxford Univ., various Colls and Commonwealth Inst., London; Sec., Internat. Federation Landscape Architecture, 1948–59; Vice-Pres., 1964; Pres., Inst. Landscape Architects, 1957–59; Corresp. Mem., Amer. Soc. of Landscape Architects, 1960; Hon. Fellow, Aust. Inst. of Landscape Architects, 1978. Chm., Tree Council, 1974–76. Hon. FRIBA, 1969; Hon. FRTPI, 1970. Hon. DLitt: Newcastle, 1975; Heriot-Watt, 1976; Hon. LLD Sussex, 1978. *Publications:* Tomorrow's Landscape, 1956; Garden Design, 1958, 2nd edn 1981; The Landscape of Power, 1958; Landscape of Roads, 1960; Forestry in the Landscape, 1966; The Landscapes of Forests and Woodlands, 1979; Patterns of Landscape, 1986. *Recreations:* walking and gardening. *Address:* 59 Ladbroke Grove, W11 3AT. *T:* 01–727 7794.

CROWFOOT, Maj.-Gen. Anthony Bernard, CBE 1982 (MBE 1974); Director General Army Manning and Recruiting, Ministry of Defence, since 1986; *b* 12 Aug. 1936; *s* of Thomas Bernard Crowfoot and Gladys Dorothy Crowfoot; *m* 1960, Bridget Sarah Bunting; three *s* one *d. Educ:* King Edward VII Sch., Norfolk; Royal Military Academy, Sandhurst, psc. Commissioned 1956; 1 E Yorks 1PWO: BAOR, UK, Aden, Gibraltar, 1956–60; Instructor, School of Infantry, 1960–62; 1PWO: BAOR, UK, Aden, 1962–66; Army Staff Coll. 1967; Brigade Major, HQ 5 Inf. Bde, 1968–69; Coy Comd 1PWO, Cyprus, 1970–71; DAAG, MoD, 1971–73; CO 1PWO: UK, BAOR, N Ireland, 1973–76; Instructor, Army Staff College, 1976–77; Col GS, MoD, 1977–80; Comd 39 Inf. Bde, N Ireland, 1980–82; Student, US Army War Coll., 1982–83; Dep. Comdr/COS, HQ British Forces Hong Kong, 1983–86. Col, PWO Regt of York, 1986–. *Recreations:* sailing, philately, golf. *Address:* c/o National Westminster Bank, 45 Park Street, Camberley, Surrey GU15 3PA. *T:* Camberley 65171. *Club:* Army and Navy.

CROWHURST, Viscount; Mark John Henry Pepys; *b* 11 Oct. 1983; *s* and *heir* of 8th Earl of Cottenham, *qv*.

CROWLEY, Rear-Adm. George Clement, CB 1968; DSC 1942, and Bar 1944; Official Fellow and Domestic Bursar of Corpus Christi College, Oxford University, 1969–75; *b* 9 June 1916; *s* of Charles Edmund Lucas Crowley and Beatrice Cicely Crowley; *m* 1948, Una Margaret Jelf; two *s. Educ:* Pangbourne Coll. Cadet, HMS Frobisher, 1933; served in China and New Zealand, 1934–39; served War of 1939–45, destroyers; comdg HMS Walpole, 1943–45; comdg HMS Tenacious, 1945–46 (despatches); RN Staff Course, 1947; Staff appts, 1948–53; Exec. Off., HMS Newfoundland, 1953–55; Drafting Comdr, Chatham, 1955–57; Asst Dir Plans, 1957–59; Capt. (D) 7th Destroyer Sqdn, 1959–61; CO New Entry, Trng Estab. HMS Raleigh, 1961–63; Capt. of Fleet to Flag Off. C-in-C Far East Fleet, 1963–64; Staff of Jt Exercise Unison, 1964–65; Staff of Defence Operational Analysis Estab., W Byfleet, 1965–66; Director-General, Naval Personal Services, 1966–68. Capt. 1957; Rear-Adm. 1966. *Recreations:* fishing, tennis, gardening. *Address:* Windrush, Shroton, Blandford, Dorset.

CROWLEY, John Desmond, QC 1982; a Recorder of the Crown Court, since 1980; *b* 25 June 1938; *s* of John Joseph Crowley and Anne Marie (*née* Fallon); *m* 1977, Sarah Maria, *er d* of Christopher Gage Jacobs and Joan Zara (*née* Atkinson); two *d. Educ:* St Edmund's College, Ware; Christ's College, Cambridge (BA 1961, LLB 1962). National Service, 2/Lieut 6th Royal Tank Regt, 1957–58. Called to the Bar, Inner Temple, 1962. Mem., Criminal Injuries Compensation Bd, 1985–. *Recreations:* tennis, the turf, wine. *Address:* 2 Crown Office Row, Temple, EC4Y 7UJ. *T:* 01–353 9337.

CROWLEY, Niall, FCA; Chairman, Allied Irish Banks Ltd Group, since 1977; *b* 18 Sept. 1926; *s* of Vincent Crowley and Eileen (*née* Gunning); *m* 1953, Una Hegarty; five *s* one *d. Educ:* Xavier Sch.; Castleknock Coll. FCA 1955. Entered father's accounting firm, Stokes Kennedy Crowley & Co., as articled clerk, 1944: qualified, 1949; Partner, 1950, subseq. Managing Partner; Consultant to the firm, which also represents Peat Marwick Mitchell & Co. in Ireland, 1977–84. Dir, Irish Life Assurance Co. Ltd, 1964–84 (Chm., 1974–83). President: Inst. of Chartered Accountants in Ireland, 1971–72; Dublin Chamber of Commerce, 1983–84; Irish Bankers Fedn, 1985–. Chm., Financial Services Industry Assoc., 1984–. Mem. Exec. Bd, Anglo-Irish Encounter Gp, 1983–. Member, Company of Goldsmiths of Dublin, 1973–. Hon. LLD NUI, 1982. *Recreations:* bridge, golf. *Address:* 18 Herbert Park, Ballsbridge, Dublin 4. *T:* 683637. *Clubs:* Stephens Green; Portmarnock Golf; Milltown Golf; Fitzwilliam Lawn Tennis (Dublin).

CROWLEY, Thomas Michael, CMG 1970; Assistant Secretary, Ministry of Defence, 1971–77; *b* 28 June 1917; *s* of late Thomas Michael Crowley; *m* 1965, Eicke Laura, *d* of late Carl Jensen; one *s* two *d. Educ:* Forres Acad.; Aberdeen Univ. Entered Civil Service in 1940; Assistant Secretary: Min. of Technology, 1953–70; DTI, 1970; Min. of Aviation Supply, 1970–71. *Address:* 116 Barnett Wood Lane, Ashtead, Surrey.

CROWLEY-MILLING, Air Marshal Sir Denis, KCB 1973; CBE 1963; DSO 1943; DFC 1941, Bar 1942; Registrar and Secretary, Order of the Bath, since 1985 (Gentleman Usher of the Scarlet Rod, 1979–85); *b* 22 March 1919; *s* of T. W. and G. M. Crowley-Milling (*née* Chinnery); *m* 1943, Lorna Jean Jeboult (*née* Stuttard); two *d* (one *s* decd). *Educ:* Malvern Coll., Worcs. Rolls Royce apprentice and RAF Volunteer Reserve, 1937–39; Fighters and Fighter Bombers, Nos 615, 242, 610 and 181 Sqdns, 1939–44; Air Ministry Operational Requirements, 1945–47; OC No 6 Sqdn, Middle East, 1947–50; Personal Staff Officer C-in-C Fighter Comd, 1950–52; Wing Comdr Flying, RAF Odiham, 1952–54; Directing Staff, RAF Staff Coll., Bracknell, 1954–57; Flying Coll., RAF Manby, 1957–58; Plans Staff Fighter Comd, 1958–59; Group Capt. Operations Central Fighter Establishment, 1959–62; Station Comdr, RAF Leconfield, 1962–64; AOC RAF Hong Kong, 1964–66; Dir Operational Requirements, MoD (Air), 1966–67;

Comdr, RAF Staff and Principal Air Attaché, Washington, 1967–70; AOC No 38 Gp, RAF Odiham, 1970–72; AOC 46 Gp RAF Upavon, 1973; UK Rep., Perm. Mil. Deputies Gp, Cento, 1974–75. Controller, RAF Benevolent Fund, 1975–81, Mem. Council, 1981–; Mem. Council, Malvern Coll., 1972–. *Recreations:* golf and shooting. *Address:* Church Cottages, North Creake, Fakenham, Norfolk NR21 9JJ. *Club:* Royal Air Force.
See also M. C. Crowley-Milling.

CROWLEY-MILLING, Michael Crowley, CMG 1982; CEng, FIEE; Consultant to Los Alamos National Laboratory, New Mexico, since 1986; *b* 7 May 1917; *s* of Thomas William Crowley-Milling and Gillian May (*née* Chinnery); *m* 1958, Gee Dickson. *Educ:* Radley Coll.; St John's Coll., Cambridge (MA 1943). CEng, FIEE 1956. R&D on radar systems, Metropolitan-Vickers Electrical Co. Ltd, Manchester, 1938–46; design and develt of electron linear accelerators for physics, medical and irradiation purposes, 1946–63; contrib. to construction of electron synchrotron, Daresbury Nuclear Physics Lab., Warrington, 1963–71; CERN, Geneva: resp. for control system for Super Proton Synchrotron (SPS), 1971–75; SPS Div. Leader, 1977–78; Dir, Accelerator Prog., 1979–80; Consultant, 1982–83; Consultant to SLAC, Calif., 1984–85. Crompton Premium, IEE, 1959; Glazebrook Medal, Inst. of Physics, 1980. Captain LMBC, 1938. *Publications:* articles and chapters in books on particle accelerators and computer control systems. *Recreations:* vintage cars, sailing. *Address:* c/o Barclays Bank PLC, Conway Road, Colwyn Bay, Clwyd.
See also Sir Denis Crowley-Milling.

CROWSON, Richard Borman, CMG 1986; HM Diplomatic Service; High Commissioner in Mauritius, since 1985, and concurrently Ambassador (non-resident) to the Comoros, since 1986; *b* 23 July 1929; *s* of late Clarence Borman Crowson and Cecilia May Crowson (*née* Ramsden); *m* 1st, 1960, Sylvia Cavalier (marr. diss. 1974); one *s* one *d*; 2nd, 1983, Judith Elaine Turner. *Educ:* Downing Coll., Cambridge (MA). FCIS. HMOCS, Uganda, 1955–62; Foreign Office, 1962–63; First Sec. (Commercial), Tokyo, 1963–68; Dep. High Commissioner, Barbados, 1968–70; FCO, 1970–75; Counsellor (Commercial and Aid), Jakarta, 1975–77; Counsellor for Hong Kong Affairs, Washington, 1977–82; Counsellor and Head of Chancery, Berne, 1983–85. *Recreations:* music, drama, travel. *Address:* c/o Foreign and Commonwealth Office, SW1; 67 Crofton Road, Orpington, Kent. *T:* Orpington 30781. *Clubs:* Royal Commonwealth Society; Grande Société (Berne).

CROWTHER, Eric (John Ronald), OBE 1977; Metropolitan Magistrate, since 1968; a Recorder of the Crown Court, since 1983; *b* 4 Aug. 1924; *s* of Stephen Charles Crowther, company secretary, and Olive Beatrix Crowther (*née* Selby); *m* 1959, Elké Auguste Ottilie Winkelmann; one *s* one *d*. *Educ:* University College Sch., Hampstead. Royal Navy, 1943–47 (Medit. Area of Ops). Awarded Tancred Studentship in Common Law, 1948; Called to Bar, Lincoln's Inn, 1951; winner of Inns of Court Contest in Advocacy, 1951; Lectr and Student Counsellor, British Council, 1951–81; Lecturer: on Elocution and Advocacy for Council of Legal Educn, 1955– (Dir of Studies, Post-Final Gps, 1975–77); on Evidence to RN, 1968–. Joined Inner Temple *ad eundem*, 1960. Practised at Criminal Bar, 1951–68. Chairman: Inner London Magistrates' Assoc. Trng Sub-Cttee, 1981–; Prisoners' Wives Service, 1982–85. Mem. Council, British Council, 1985–; Mem., Bd of Academic Studies, St Catherine's, Cumberland Lodge, 1977–82; Trustee, Professional and Academic Regional Visits Organisation, 1977–. Mem. Cttee, RADA, 1979–84. Hon. Officer, Internat. Students' Hse, 1981–. Editor, Commonwealth Judicial Jl, 1973–77. *Publication:* Advocacy for the Advocate, 1984. *Recreations:* travel, transport, the theatre, debating, student welfare, Scottish dancing. *Address:* 21 Old Buildings, Lincoln's Inn, WC2.

CROWTHER, (Joseph) Stanley; MP (Lab) Rotherham, since June 1976; *b* 30 May 1925; *s* of Cyril Joseph Crowther and Florence Mildred (*née* Beckett); *m* 1948, Margaret Royston; two *s*. *Educ:* Rotherham Grammar Sch.; Rotherham Coll. of Technology. Royal Signals, 1943–47. Journalist: Rotherham Advertiser, 1941–43 and 1947–50; Yorkshire Evening Post, 1950–51; freelance, 1951–. Mem., Rotherham Borough Council, 1958–59, 1961–76; Mayor of Rotherham, 1971–72, 1975–76; Chm., Yorkshire and Humberside Develt Assoc., 1972–76; Council Mem., Town and Country Planning Assoc. *Recreations:* walking, singing, listening to jazz. *Address:* 15 Clifton Crescent South, Rotherham S65 2AR. *T:* Rotherham 364559. *Clubs:* Central Labour, Eastwood View Working Men's (Rotherham).

CROWTHER, Thomas Rowland; QC 1981; **His Honour Judge Crowther;** a Circuit Judge since 1985; *b* 11 Sept. 1937; *s* of Kenneth Vincent Crowther, MB, BCh, and Winifred Anita Crowther, MPS; *m* 1969, Gillian Jane (*née* Prince); one *s* one *d*. *Educ:* Newport High Sch.: Keble Coll., Oxford (MA). President, Oxford Univ. Liberal Club, 1957; Editor, Oxford Guardian, 1957. Called to the Bar, Inner Temple, 1961; Junior and Wine Steward, Wales and Chester Circuit, 1974. A Recorder, 1980–85. Contested (L) General Elections: Oswestry, 1964 and 1966; Hereford, 1970. Founder Mem., Gwent Area Broadcasting, 1981. *Recreation:* garden. *Address:* Lansor, Llandegfedd, Caerleon, Gwent NP6 1LS. *T:* Tredunnock 224. *Clubs:* Cardiff and County; Newport Golf.

CROWTHER, William Ronald Hilton; QC 1980; a Recorder, since 1985; *b* 7 May 1941; *s* of Ronald Crowther and Ann Bourne Crowther; *m* 1964, Valerie Meredith (*née* Richards); one *s*. *Educ:* Oundle Sch.; Univ. of Oxford (BA Jurisprudence). Called to the Bar, Inner Temple, 1963, Bencher, 1985. *Recreations:* bird-watching and all aspects of natural history, scuba diving. *Address:* 83 South End Road, NW3. *T:* 01–794 4619.

CROWTHER-HUNT, family name of **Baron Crowther-Hunt.**

CROWTHER-HUNT, Baron *cr* 1973 (Life Peer), of Eccleshill in the West Riding of the County of York; **Norman Crowther Crowther-Hunt,** PhD; Rector, Exeter College, Oxford, since 1982; *b* 13 March 1920; *s* of late Ernest Angus Hunt, and of Florence Hunt, Bradford, Yorks; *m* 1944, Joyce, *d* of late Rev. Joseph Stackhouse, Walsall Wood, Staffs; three *d*. *Educ:* Wellington Road Council Sch.; Belle Vue High Sch., Bradford; Sidney Sussex Coll., Cambridge. Exhibitioner, 1939–40, Open Scholar, 1945–47, Sidney Sussex Coll.; MA 1949, PhD 1951; Hon. Fellow, 1982. Served RA, 1940–45; War Office (GSO3), 1944–45. First Cl. Hist. Tripos, 1946 and 1947; Res. Fellow, Sidney Sussex Coll., 1949–51; Commonwealth Fund Fellow, Princeton Univ., USA, 1951–52; Fellow and Lectr in Politics, 1952–82, Domestic Bursar, 1954–70, Exeter Coll., Oxford. Deleg., Oxford Univ. Extra-Mural Delegacy, 1956–70; Vis. Prof., Michigan State Univ., 1961. Constitutional Adviser to the Govt, March-Oct. 1974; Minister of State: DES, 1974–76; Privy Council Office, 1976. Member: Cttee on the Civil Service (Fulton Cttee), 1966–68 (Leader of Management Consultancy Group); Commn on the Constitution, 1969–73 (principal author of the Memorandum of Dissent); Civil Service Coll. Adv. Council, 1970–74. Chm., BBC Gen. Adv. Council, 1986–. Mem. Council, Headington Sch., Oxford, 1966–74. Hon. DLitt Bradford, 1974; Hon. LLD Williams Coll., Mass., 1985. *Publications:* Two Early Political Associations, 1961; (ed) Whitehall and Beyond, 1964; (ed with Graham Tayar) Personality and Power 1970; (with Peter Kellner) The Civil Servants, 1980. *Recreations:* playing tennis, squash and the piano; broadcasting. Cambridge Univ. Assoc. Football XI, 1939–40. *Address:* 14 Apsley Road, Oxford. *T:* Oxford 58342; Exeter College, Oxford. *T:* Oxford 244681 and 247422.

CROXON, Raymond Patrick Austin, QC 1983; *b* 31 July 1928; *s* of late Randolph Croxon and of Rose Harvey; *m* 1952, Monica Howard; two *s* two *d*. *Educ:* Strand College; King's College London. LLB. Served in RAMC, 1946–49. Called to the Bar, Gray's Inn, 1960. *Recreations:* gardening, fishing, golf, travel. *Address:* 1 Paper Buildings, Temple, EC4. *Club:* Orpington Sports.

CROXTON-SMITH, Claude; Chartered Accountant in public practice, Bristol, 1946–83, retired; President, Institute of Chartered Accountants in England and Wales, 1970–71; *b* 24 Aug. 1901; *m* 1928, Joan Norah Bloss Watling; two *d*. *Educ:* Dulwich Coll.; Gonville and Caius Coll., Cambridge. The Sales Staff, Anglo American Oil Co. Ltd, 1924–31; Articled Clerk, Inst. of Chartered Accountants in England and Wales, 1932–36; Chartered Accountant, 1936–39. Served War of 1939–45, RAOC (Major). *Recreations:* walking, reading. *Address:* New Cote Rest Home, Cote House Lane, Westbury-on-Trym, Bristol BS9 3UW. Club: Bristol (Bristol).

CROYDON, Bishop Suffragan of, since 1985; **Rt. Rev. Wilfred Denniston Wood;** *b* Barbados, WI, 15 June 1936; *s* of Wilfred Coward and Elsie Elmira Wood; *m* 1966, Ina Eileen, *d* of L. E. Smith, CBE, Barbadian MP; three *s* two *d*. *Educ:* Combermere Sch. and Codrington Coll., Barbados. Lambeth Dip. in Theol., 1962. Ordained deacon, St Michael's Cath., Barbados, 1961; ordained priest, St Paul's Cath., London, 1962. Curate of St Stephen with St Thomas, Shepherd's Bush, 1962–66, Hon. Curate, 1966–74; Bishop of London's Officer in Race Relations, 1966–74; Vicar of St Laurence, Catford, 1974–82; RD of East Lewisham, 1977–82; Archdeacon of Southwark, 1982–85; Hon. Canon of Southwark Cathedral, 1977–85. Chm., Martin Luther King Meml Trust. Member: Royal Commn on Criminal Procedure, 1978–80; Archbishop of Canterbury's Commn on Urban Priority Areas, 1983–85; Housing Corp., 1986–. JP Inner London, 1971–85. Hon. DD Gen. Theol Seminary, NY, 1986. *Publications:* (contrib.) The Committed Church, 1966; (with John Downing) Vicious Circle, 1968. *Recreations:* reading, cricket; armchair follower of most sports. *Address:* Croydon Episcopal Area Office, St Matthew's House, 100 George Street, Croydon CR0 1PE. *T:* 01–681 5496/7.

CROYDON, Archdeacon of; *see* Hazell, Ven F. R.

CROYDON, Rear-Adm. John Edward Kenneth, JP; CEng, FIEE; consultant engineer; *b* 25 Feb. 1929; *s* of late Kenneth P. Croydon and Elizabeth V. Croydon; *m* 1953, Brenda Joyce Buss, MA; one *s* two *d*. *Educ:* King Edward's Sch., Birmingham; Selwyn Coll., Cambridge (MA). BA London; CEng, FIEE 1975; jssc 1969. RN Special Entry Cadet (L), 1947; HMS Verulam and HMS Undine, 1954–55; Royal Naval Coll., Dartmouth, 1959–61; HMS Devonshire, 1961–64; HMS London, 1970–72; MoD, 1972–74; Captain Weapon Trials, 1974–77; Dir, Underwater Weapon Projects (Naval), 1978–80; Dir Gen. Weapons (Naval), 1981–83; Dep. Controller, Warships Equipment, MoD (Navy), 1983–84, retd. Rear Cdre (Dinghies), Royal Naval Sailing Assoc., 1980. Gov., Milton Abbey Sch., 1985–. JP Weymouth, 1985. *Recreations:* sailing, music, walking. *Clubs:* Royal Naval Sailing Association; Weymouth Sailing.

CROZIER, Brian Rossiter; writer and consultant on international affairs; Columnist: National Review, New York, since 1978; The Free Nation, London, since 1982; Co-founder Institute for the Study of Conflict, 1970, and Director, 1970–79; *b* 4 Aug. 1918; *s* of R. H. Crozier and Elsa (*née* McGillivray); *m* 1940, Mary Lillian Samuel; one *s* three *d*. *Educ:* Lycée, Montpellier; Peterborough Coll., Harrow; Trinity Coll. of Music, London. Music and art critic, London, 1936–39; reporter-sub-editor, Stoke-on-Trent, Stockport, London, 1940–41; aeronautical inspection, 1941–43; sub-editor: Reuters, 1943–44; News Chronicle, 1944–48; and writer, Sydney Morning Herald, 1948–51; corresp., Reuters-AAP, 1951–52; features editor, Straits Times, 1952–53; leader writer and corresp., Economist, 1954–64; commentator, BBC English, French and Spanish overseas services, 1954–66; Chm., Forum World Features, 1965–74; Columnist: Now!, 1979–81; The Times, 1982–83. *Publications:* The Rebels, 1960; The Morning After, 1963; Neo-Colonialism, 1964; South-East Asia in Turmoil, 1965 (3rd edn 1968); The Struggle for the Third World, 1966; Franco, 1967; The Masters of Power, 1969; The Future of Communist Power (in USA: Since Stalin), 1970; De Gaulle, vol. 1 1973, vol. 2 1974; A Theory of Conflict, 1974; The Man Who Lost China (Chiang Kai-shek), 1976; Strategy of Survival, 1978; The Minimum State, 1979; Franco: crepúsculo de un hombre (Spanish orig.), 1980; The Price of Peace, 1980, new edn 1983; (jtly) Socialism Explained, 1984; (jtly) This War Called Peace, 1984; (as John Rossiter) The Andropov Deception (novel), 1984 (pubd under own name, NY, 1986); contrib. to jls in many countries. *Recreations:* piano, taping stereo, Polaroid photography. *Address:* Kulm House, Dollis Avenue, Finchley, N3 1DA. *T:* 01–346 8124. *Clubs:* Royal Automobile, Arts.

CROZIER, Eric John; writer and theatrical producer; *b* 14 Nov. 1914; *s* of John and Ethel Mary Crozier, London; *m* 1st, 1936, Margaret Johns (marriage dissolved, 1949); two *d*; 2nd, 1950, Nancy Evans. *Educ:* University Coll. Sch., London; Royal Academy of Dramatic Art; British Institute, Paris. Play producer for BBC Television Service, 1936–39. Produced plays and operas for Sadler's Wells Opera, Stratford-on-Avon Memorial Theatre, Glyndebourne Opera and other theatres, 1944–46. Closely associated with Benjamin Britten as producer or author of his operas, 1945–51, and was co-founder with him of The English Opera Group, 1947, and The Aldeburgh Festival of Music and the Arts, 1948. *Publications:* Christmas in the Market Place (adapted from French of Henri Ghéon), 1944; The Life and Legends of Saint Nicolas, 1949; Noah Gives Thanks, a play, 1950; (with Benjamin Britten): Albert Herring, a comic opera in three acts, 1947; Saint Nicolas, a cantata, 1948; Let's Make an Opera, an entertainment for children, 1949; (with E. M. Forster and Benjamin Britten) Billy Budd, an opera in four acts, 1951; opera translations include: The Bartered Bride, Otello, Falstaff, La Traviata, Idomeneo, Salome, The Woman without a Shadow. *Recreation:* listening to music. *Address:* 1 White House Farm, Great Glemham, Saxmundham, Suffolk IP17 1LS. *T:* Rendham 683.

CRUDDAS, Rear-Adm. Thomas Rennison, CB 1974; Director, Pressure Vessels Quality Assurance Board, since 1977; *b* 6 Feb. 1921; *s* of late Thomas Hepple Wheatley Cruddas, MBE, and Lily (*née* Rennison); *m* 1943, Angela Elizabeth Astbury; one *s* one *d*. *Educ:* Queen Elizabeth Grammar Sch., Darlington; RN Engineering College, Keyham. Joined RN 1938; RNEC, 1939–42. Served War, 1939–45: in Mediterranean and E Indies, in HM Ships Unicorn and Valiant. HMS Cardigan Bay, 1948–50; specialised Aero. Engrg, 1950; RNAY Donibristle, 1951–53; Comdr, 1953; HMS Ark Royal, 1953–55; RNAY Fleetlands, 1956–58; Admty, 1958–61; Staff of Flag Officer Aircraft Carriers, 1961–63; Captain, 1963; Asst Dir Ship Production, 1964–66; service with USN, Washington, DC, as Programme Manager UK Phantom Aircraft, 1967–69; Command Engr Officer, Staff FONAC, 1970–72; Rear-Adm. Engineering, Naval Air Comd, 1972; Dep. Controller Aircraft B, MoD (PE), 1973–76, retired. FIMechE. *Recreations:* golf, horticulture. *Address:* Beeches Close, Bishop's Waltham, Hants. *T:* Bishop's Waltham 2335.

CRUFT, John Herbert; Hon. Treasurer, Royal Society of Musicians since 1976; *b* 4 Jan. 1914; *er s* of late Eugene and Winifred Cruft; *m* 1938, Mary Margaret Miriam, *e d* of late Rev. Pat and Miriam McCormick; two *s*. *Educ:* Westminster Abbey Choir Sch.; Westminster Sch.; Royal College of Music (K. F. Boult Conducting Scholar). Oboist in BBC Television, London Philharmonic and Suisse Romande Orchestras, 1936–40. Served with Royal Corps of Signals, 1940–46. London Symphony Orchestra: Oboist, 1946–49; Sec., 1949–59. British Council: Dir of Music Dept, 1959–61; Dir of Drama and Music Dept, 1961–65; Music Dir, Arts Council of GB, 1965–79; a Dir, National Jazz Centre, 1982–. Mem. Council, RCM, 1983–. Trustee: Loan Fund for Musical Instruments, 1980–; Electro-Acoustic Music Trust, 1980–; Governor: London Festival Ballet Trust Ltd, 1980–84; Contemporary Dance Trust Ltd, 1982–. FRCM, Hon. RAM. *Publication:* The Royal College of Music: a Centenary Record 1883–1983 (with late H. C. Colles), 1982. *Address:* 11 Broadhinton Road, Clapham, SW4 0LU. *T:* 01–720 2330.

CRUICKSHANK, Andrew John Maxton, MBE 1945; FRSAMD; actor; *b* 25 Dec. 1907; *m* 1939, Curigwen Lewis; one *s* two *d*. *Educ:* Aberdeen Grammar Sch. Hon. DLitt St Andrews, 1977. With Baynton Shakespearean Company, 1929; appeared in Richard of Bordeaux, New York, 1934; Mary Tudor, London Playhouse, 1935; Lysistrata, Gate, 1936; Macbeth, Old Vic, 1937 (Mem. of Old Vic Company, 1937–40). Served Royal Welch Fus., and GS, 1940–45. Spring 1600, Lyric, Hammersmith, 1945–46; The White Devil, Duchess, 1947; The Indifferent Shepherd, Criterion, 1949; Memorial Theatre, Stratford (Parts included Wolsey, Kent and Julius Caesar), 1950; St Joan, Cort Theatre, New York, 1951; Dial M for Murder, Westminster Theatre, 1952; Dead on Nine, Westminster, 1955; The House by the Lake, Duke of York's, 1956; Inherit The Wind, 1960; Look Homeward Angel, 1960; The Lady From the Sea, Queen's, 1961; The Master Builder, Ashcroft Theatre, Croydon, 1963; Alibi for a Judge, Savoy, 1965; Lloyd George Knew my Father, Savoy, 1973; When We Dead Awaken, Haymarket Leicester, 1975; The Thrie Estates, Edinburgh, 1984; *National Theatre:* The Woman, 1978; Strife, 1978; The Fruits of Enlightenment, 1979; The Wild Duck, 1980; Sisterly Feelings, 1980. Has appeared in many films, also in radio and on television; TV series, Dr Finlay's Casebook; author of play, Games, 1975. *Publications:* The Infinite Guarantee, 1971; A Scottish Bedside Book, 1977; After the Wager, the Dice and the Games, 1984. *Address:* 33 Carlisle Mansions, Carlisle Place, SW1. *Club:* Garrick.

CRUICKSHANK, Charles Greig, MA, DPhil; FRHistS; author; *b* 10 June 1914; *s* of late George Leslie Cruickshank, Fyvie; *m* 1943, Maire Kissane; three *s*. *Educ:* Aberdeen Grammar Sch.; Aberdeen Univ.; Hertford Coll., Oxford; Edinburgh University. Min. of Supply, 1940–46; BoT, 1946–51; Trade Comr, Ceylon, 1951–55 (economic mission to Maldive Is, 1953); Canada, 1955–58; Sen. Trade Comr, NZ, 1958–63; Exec. Sec., Commonwealth Econ. Cttee, 1964–66; Dir, Commodities Div., Commonwealth Secretariat, 1967–68; BoT (Regional Export Dir, London and SE), 1969–71; Inspector, FCO, 1971–72; CAA, 1972–73; Asst Sec., DTI, 1973. *Publications: non-fiction:* Elizabeth's Army, 1966; Army Royal, 1969; The English Occupation of Tournai, 1971; (jtly) A Guide to the Sources of British Military History, 1971; The German Occupation of the Channel Islands (official history), 1975; Greece 1940–41, 1976; The Fourth Arm: psychological warfare, 1938–45, 1977; Deception in World War II, 1979; SOE in the Far East (official history), 1983; SOE in Scandinavia (official history), 1986; History of the Royal Wimbledon Golf Club, 1986; *fiction: novels:* The V-Mann Papers, 1976; The Tang Murders, 1976; The Ebony Version, 1978; The Deceivers, 1978; Kew for Murder, 1984; Scotch Murder, 1985; contrib. to English Historical Review, Army Quarterly, History Today, Punch, War Monthly, DNB, History of Parliament, etc. *Recreation:* golf. *Address:* 15 McKay Road, Wimbledon Common, SW20 0HT. *T:* 01–947 1074. *Club:* Royal Wimbledon Golf.

CRUICKSHANK, Prof. Durward William John, PhD, ScD; FRS 1979; CChem, FRSC; Professor of Chemistry (Theoretical Chemistry), 1967–83, now Emeritus, and Hon. Professorial Research Fellow, since 1983, University of Manchester Institute of Science and Technology; *b* 7 March 1924; *s* of William Durward Cruickshank, MB, ChB, and Margaret Ombler Meek, MA, MRCS, LRCP; *m* 1953, Marjorie Alice Travis (*d* 1983), MA, PhD; one *s* one *d*. *Educ:* St Lawrence Coll., Ramsgate; Loughborough Coll. (DLC 1944; BScEng 1st Cl. Hons London, 1944); Cambridge Univ. (Wrangler, Math. Tripos, 1949; Dist. Pt III Math. Tripos, 1950; BA 1949, MA 1954, ScD 1961). PhD Leeds, 1952; CChem, FRIC 1971. Engrg Asst, WO and Admiralty (Naval Opl Res.), 1944–46; Leeds University: Res. Asst, Chemistry Dept, 1946–47; Lectr, 1950–57; Reader in Math. Chemistry, 1957–62; Fellow, St John's Coll., Cambridge, 1953–56; Joseph Black Prof. of Chem. (Theor. Chem.), Glasgow Univ., 1962–67; Dep. Principal, UMIST, 1971–72. Hon. Vis. Prof. of Physics, York Univ., 1985–. Treasurer, 1966–72, and Gen. Sec., 1970–72, Internat. Union of Crystallography. 1977 Chemical Soc. Award for Struct. Chem., 1978. *Publications:* scientific papers on crystallography, molecular structure determination and theoretical chemistry in Acta Cryst., Proc. Royal Soc., and Jl Chem. Soc. *Recreations:* golf, genealogy. *Address:* 105 Moss Lane, Alderley Edge, Cheshire SK9 7HW. *T:* Alderley Edge 582656; Chemistry Department, University of Manchester Institute of Science and Technology, Manchester M60 1QD. *T:* 061–236 3311.

CRUICKSHANK, Prof. Eric Kennedy, OBE 1961; MD; FRCP, FRCPGlas; Dean of Postgraduate Medicine, University of Glasgow, 1972–80, retired; *b* 29 Dec. 1914; *s* of John Cruickshank, CBE, and Jessie (*née* Allan); *m* 1st, 1951, Ann Burch; two *s* two *d*; 2nd, 1969, Josephine Williams. *Educ:* Aberdeen Grammar Sch.; Univ. of Aberdeen (MB, ChB Hons, 1937; MD Hons and gold medal, 1948). Fellow, Harvard and Massachusetts Gen. Hosp., USA, 1938–39; Lectr, then Sen. Lectr, Dept of Medicine, Univ. of Aberdeen, 1939–50; Hon. Consultant in Medicine, NHS, 1948–50; First Dean, Medical Faculty, and Prof. of Medicine, Univ. of West Indies, Kingston, Jamaica, 1950–72. Served War of 1939–45: Captain RAMC, Medical Specialist, Changi Prisoner of War Camp, Singapore (despatches twice). WHO Consultant in Medical Educn, 1959–, Nutrition, 1955–; Member: GMC, 1972–80; Inter-Univ. Council, 1972–84; Greater Glasgow Health Bd, 1972–80. Hon. FACP 1969. *Publications:* on nutrition, neurology, medical educn. *Recreations:* tennis, golf, gardening, ornithology. *Address:* Parsonage House, Oare, Wilts SN8 4JA.

CRUICKSHANK, Herbert James, CBE 1969; CEng, FIMechE; FCIOB; *b* 12 July 1912; *s* of late James William Cruickshank and of Dorothy Adeline Cruickshank; *m* 1st, 1939, Jean Alexandra Payne (*d* 1978); no *c*; 2nd, 1985, Susan Elizabeth Bullen. *Educ:* Charlton Central Sch.; Regent Street Polytechnic (Schol.). Bovis Ltd: Staff Trainee, 1931; Plant and Labour Controller, 1937; Gilbert-Ash Ltd: (formed within Bovis Gp), 1945; Director, 1949; Civil Engineering Works in Nyasaland, 1949–55; Managing Dir, UK, 1960–63; Chm. and Man. Dir, 1964; Dir, Bovis Holdings, 1964–72; Group Man. Dir, 1966, Dep. Chm. 1970–72. Member: Metrication Bd, 1969–73; SE Thames RHA, 1972–78; BSI Quality Assurance Council, 1976–81. FRSA. *Recreations:* amateur theatre, photography, sketching. *Address:* 45 Bidborough Ridge, Tunbridge Wells, Kent. *T:* Tunbridge Wells 27270. *Clubs:* Oriental, MCC.

CRUICKSHANK, Prof. John; Professor of French, University of Sussex, since 1962; *b* Belfast, N Ireland, 18 July 1924; *s* of Arthur Cruickshank, parliamentary reporter, and Eva Cruickshank (*née* Shummacher); *m* 1st, 1949, Kathleen Mary Gutteridge; one *s*; 2nd, 1972, Marguerite Doreen Penny. *Educ:* Royal Belfast Academical Institution; Trinity Coll., Dublin. Awarded Mod. Lang. Sizarship, TCD, 1943; Cryptographer in Mil. Intell., 1943–45; 1st class Moderatorship in Mod. Langs (French and German) and 2nd class Moderatorship (Mental and Moral Science), TCD, 1948; Lecteur d'Anglais, Ecole Normale Supérieure, Paris, 1948–49; Asst Lectr in French and German, Univ. of Southampton, 1951; Sen. Lectr in French, Univ. of Southampton, 1961. Mem., UGC, 1970–77. *Publications:* Albert Camus and the Literature of Revolt, 1959; Critical Readings in the Modern French Novel, 1961; The Novelist as Philosopher, 1962; Montherlant, 1964; (ed) French Literature and Its Background: vols 1–6, 1968–70; Aspects of the Modern European Mind, 1969; Benjamin Constant, 1974; Variations on Catastrophe, 1982; Pascal: Pensées, 1983; articles in: French Studies; Modern Language Review; Times Literary Supplement; Times Higher Education Supplement, etc. *Recreations:* bird-watching, painting in oils, watching cricket. *Address:* Woodpeckers, East Hoathly, Sussex BN8 6QL. *T:* Halland 364.

CRUICKSHANK, Flight-Lieut John Alexander, VC 1944; late RAF; with Grindlay's Bank Ltd, London, 1952–76; retired; Administrator, Northern Division, North West Securities Ltd, 1977–85; *b* 20 May 1920; *s* of James C. Cruickshank, Aberdeen, and Alice Bow, Macduff, Banffshire; *m* 1955, Marion R. Beverley (*d* 1985), Toronto, Canada. *Educ:* Aberdeen Grammar Sch.; Daniel Stewart's Coll., Edinburgh. Entered Commercial Bank of Scotland, 1938; returned to banking, 1946. Mem. of Territorial Army and called for service, Aug. 1939, in RA; transferred to RAF 1941 and commissioned in 1942; all RAF service was with Coastal Command. ADC to Lord High Commissioner to the Gen. Assembly of the Church of Scotland, 1946–48. *Address:* 34 Frogston Road West, Edinburgh EH10 7AJ. *T:* 031–445 1215.

CRUMP, Maurice, CBE 1959; *b* 13 Jan. 1908; *s* of William Hamilton Crump and Jean Morris Alan Crump (*née* Esplen); *m* 1946, Mary Arden, *d* of Austin Stead, Montreal, PQ, Canada. *Educ:* Harrow; Oxford. Called to Bar, Inner Temple, 1931, practised Western Circuit. RAF Reserve, 1929–35; recommissioned RAF Volunteer Reserve, 1940; served War of 1939–45, as pilot, 1940–45; Capt. in Command on North Atlantic Return Ferry, 1944–45. In Dept of Dir of Public Prosecutions, 1945; Asst Dir, 1951–58, Deputy Dir, 1958–66. *Recreations:* flying, travelling. *Address:* No 2, 46 Elm Park Road, SW3 6AX. *T:* 01–351 2126. *Club:* Royal Air Force.

CRUMP, Rt. Rev. William Henry Howes; *b* London, Ontario, Canada, 13 March 1903; *m* 1932, Betty Margaret Dean Thomas; one *s* one *d*. *Educ:* London, Ontario; University of Western Ontario; Huron College; Trinity College, Toronto. Ordained Deacon, 1926; Curate, Wawanesa, Manitoba, 1926; Priest, 1927. Rector: Glenboro, Manitoba, 1927; Holland, Manitoba, 1931; Boissevain, Manitoba, 1933; St Aidan's, Winnipeg, 1933–44; Christ Church, Calgary, 1944–60; Canon of St Paul, Diocese of Calgary, 1949; Bishop of Saskatchewan, 1960–71. *Address:* Apt 815 Lions Place, 610 Portage Avenue, Winnipeg, Manitoba R3C 0G5, Canada.

CRUMP, William Maurice Esplen; *see* Crump, Maurice.

CRUMPTON, Michael Joseph, PhD; FRS 1979; Deputy Director of Research, Imperial Cancer Research Fund Laboratories, London, since 1979; *b* 7 June 1929; *s* of Charles E. and Edith Crumpton; *m* 1960, Janet Elizabeth Dean; one *s* two *d*. *Educ:* Poole Grammar Sch., Poole; University Coll., Southampton; Lister Inst. of Preventive Medicine, London. BSc, PhD, London. Member, scientific staff, Microbiological Research Estabt, Porton, Wilts, 1955–58; Visiting Scientist Fellowship, Nat. Insts of Health, Bethesda, Maryland, USA, 1959–60; Research Fellow, Dept of Immunology, St Mary's Hosp. Med. Sch., London, 1960–66; Mem., scientific staff, Nat. Inst. for Med. Research, Mill Hill, 1966–79, Head of Biochemistry Div., 1977–79. Visiting Fellow, John Curtin Sch. for Med. Research, ANU, Canberra, 1973–74. Member: EMBO; Cell Board, MRC, 1979–83; Scientific Adv. Commn, Lister Inst., 1986–; Member Council: Royal Instn, 1986–; MRC, 1986–; Mem. Sci. Council, Celltech Ltd, 1980–. Biochem. Soc. Vis. Lectr, Australia, 1983. *Publications:* contribs to Biochemical Jl and various other learned scientific jls. *Recreations:* gardening, reading. *Address:* 33 Homefield Road, Radlett, Herts WD7 8PX. *T:* Radlett 4675.

CRUTCHLEY, Brooke, CBE 1954; Printer of the University of Cambridge, 1946–74; Fellow of Trinity Hall, 1951–73, Emeritus Fellow, 1977 (Vice-Master, 1966–70); Honorary Fellow of St Edmund's House, Cambridge, since 1980; *b* 31 July 1907; *yr s* of late Ernest Tristram Crutchley, CB, CMG, CBE, and Anna, *d* of James Dunne; *m* 1936, Diana, *d* of late Lt-Col Arthur Egerton Cotton, DSO, and Beryl Marie (who *m* 2nd, John Lee Booker); two *s* one *d*. *Educ:* Shrewsbury; Trinity Hall, Cambridge. Editorial Staff of Yorkshire Post, 1929–30; Asst Univ. Printer at Cambridge, 1930–45; Secretary's Dept of the Admiralty, 1941–45. Pres., Inst. of Printing, 1972–74. Hon. Col, Commonwealth of Kentucky, 1974. Bicentenary Medal, RSA, 1977. *Publication:* To be a printer, (autobiog.), 1980. *Address:* 2 Courtyards, Little Shelford, Cambridge CB2 5ER. *T:* Cambridge 842389. *Club:* Double Crown.

CRUTHERS, Sir James (Winter), Kt 1980; company director; Chairman, Satellite Television plc, since 1985 (Director, since 1984); Vice-Chairman: News America Publishing Inc., since 1984 (Director, since 1983); News America Holdings, since 1984 (Director, since 1984); *b* 20 Dec. 1924; *s* of James William and Kate Cruthers; *m* 1950, Alwyn Sheila Della; one *s* one *d*. *Educ:* Claremont Central State Sch.; Perth Technical College. Started as junior in Perth Daily News, 1939; war service, AIF and RAAF (Pilot), 1942; Journalist, Perth Daily News, 1946; Editor, Weekly Publications, West Australian Newspapers Ltd, 1953; TVW Enterprises Ltd: General Manager, 1958; Managing Director, 1969; Dep. Chm., 1974; Chm., 1976–81; Chm., Australian Film Commn, 1982–83. Dir, News Corp. Ltd, 1981–. Western Australian Citizen Of The Year, Industry and Commerce, 1980. *Recreations:* golf, jogging. *Address:* c/o News America Publishing Inc., 210 South Street, New York, NY 10002, USA; c/o McLaren and Stewart, GPO Box L892, Perth, WA 6001, Australia. *Clubs:* Weld (Perth); Lake Karrinyup Country; Friars (New York).

CRUTTWELL, Mrs Geraldine; *see* McEwan, Geraldine.

CRUTTWELL, Hugh (Percival); Principal of Royal Academy of Dramatic Art, 1966–84, retired; *b* 31 Oct. 1918; *s* of Clement Chadwick Cruttwell and Grace Fanny (*née* Robin); *m* 1953, Geraldine McEwan, *qv*; one *s* one *d*. *Educ:* King's Sch., Bruton; Hertford Coll., Oxford.

CRYER, (George) Robert; Member (Lab) Sheffield, European Parliament, since 1984; *b* 3 Dec. 1934; *m* 1963, Ann (*née* Place); one *s* one *d*. *Educ:* Salt High Sch., Shipley; Hull Univ. BSc Econ Hons, Certif. Educn. Secondary Sch. Teacher, Hull, 1959, Bradford, 1961 and Keighley, 1962; Asst Personnel Officer, 1960; Dewsbury Techn. Coll., 1963; Blackburn Coll. of Technology, 1964–65; Keighley Techn. Coll., 1965–74. MP (Lab) Keighley, Feb. 1974–1983; Parly Under-Sec. of State, DoI, 1976–78. Chm., Jt and Select Cttees on Statutory Instruments, 1979–83; Vice-Chairman: PLP Defence Group, 1980–83; PLP Industry Gp, 1982–83. Contested (Lab): Darwen Div. of Lancs, 1964;

Keighley, 1983. Labour Councillor, Keighley Borough Council, 1971–74. *Publications:* Steam in the Worth Valley, Vol. 1 1969, Vol. 2 1972. *Recreations:* working on Worth Valley Railway, cinematography, film appreciation. *Address:* Holyoake, Providence Lane, Oakworth, Keighley, W Yorks. *T:* Haworth 42595. *Club:* Workers Union Social (Keighley).

CRYSTAL, Prof. David; author, lecturer, and broadcaster on language and linguistics; Hon. Professorial Fellow, University College of North Wales, since 1985; *b* 6 July 1941; *s* of Samuel Cyril Crystal and Mary Agnes Morris; *m* 1st, 1964, Molly Irene Stack (*d* 1976); one *s* two *d* (and one *s* decd); 2nd, 1976, Hilary Frances Norman; one *s*. *Educ:* St Mary's Coll., Liverpool; University Coll. London (BA 1962); London Univ. (PhD 1966). Res. Asst, UCL, 1962–63; Asst Lectr, UCNW, 1963–65; University of Reading: Lectr, 1965–69; Reader, 1969–75; Prof., 1975–85. Vis. Prof., Bowling Green State Univ., 1969. Sec., Linguistics Assoc. of GB, 1965–70. Mem., Academic Bd, Coll. of Speech Therapists, 1972–79. Editor: Language Res. in Progress, 1966–70; Jl of Child Language, 1973–85; The Language Library, 1978–; Applied Language Studies, 1980–84; Child Language Teaching and Therapy, 1985–; Linguistics Abstracts, 1985–; Blackwells Applied Language Studies, 1986–; Consultant Editor, English Today, 1985–; Adv. Editor, Penguin Linguistics, 1968–75; Associate Editor, Jl of Linguistics, 1970–73; Co-Editor, Studies in language Disability, 1974–. Regular BBC broadcasts on English language and linguistics. FCST 1983; FRSA 1983. *Publications:* Systems of prosodic and paralinguistic features in English (with R. Quirk), 1964; Linguistics, language and religion, 1965; (ed jtly) Proceedings, Modern approaches to language teaching at university level, 1967; What is linguistics?, 1968, 5th edn 1985; Prosodic systems and intonation in English, 1969; (with D. Davy) Investigating English style, 1969; (ed with W. Bolton) The English language, vol. 2, 1969; Linguistics, 1971, 2nd edn 1985; Basic linguistics, 1973; Language acquisition, 1973; The English tone of voice, 1975; (with D. Davy) Advanced conversational English, 1975; (with J. Bevington) Skylarks, 1975; (jtly) The grammatical analysis of language disability, 1976; Child language, learning and linguistics, 1976, 2nd edn 1986; Working with LARSP, 1979; Introduction to language pathology, 1980; A first dictionary of linguistics and phonetics, 1980, 2nd edn 1985; (ed) Eric Partridge: in his own words, 1980; Clinical linguistics, 1981; Directions in applied linguistics, 1981; Profiling linguistic disability, 1982; (ed) Linguistic controversies, 1982; Who cares about English usage?, 1984; Language handicap in children, 1984; Linguistic encounters with language handicap, 1984; Listen to your child, 1986; Cambridge Encyclopaedia of Language, 1986; (with J. L. Foster) Databank series: Heat, Light, Sound, Roads, Railways, Canals, Manors, Castles, Money, Monasteries, Parliament, Newspapers, 1979; The Romans, The Greeks, The Ancient Egyptians, 1981; Air, Food, Volcanoes, 1982; Deserts, Dinosaurs and Electricity, 1983; Motorcycles, Computers, Horses and Ponies, Normans, Vikings, Anglo-Saxons, Celts, 1984; The Stone Age, Fishing, 1985; contributions to: The Library of Modern Knowledge, 1978; A Dictionary of Modern Thought, 1978; Reader's Digest Great Illustrated Dictionary, 1984; Reader's Digest Book of Facts, 1985; A Comprehensive Grammar of the English Language, 1985; and to numerous volumes on language, style, prosody, communication, religion, handicap, teaching and reading; symposia and proceedings of learned socs; articles and reviews in jls on linguistics, English language, speech pathology and education. *Recreations:* cinema, music, bibliophily. *Address:* Akaroa, Gors Avenue, Holyhead, Anglesey, Gwynedd LL65 1PB. *T:* Holyhead 2764.

CRYSTAL, Michael; QC 1984; *b* 5 March 1948; *s* of Dr Samuel Cyril Crystal, OBE, and Rachel Ettel Crystal; *m* 1972, Susan Felicia Sniderman; one *s* one *d*. *Educ:* Leeds Grammar Sch.; Queen Mary Coll., Univ. of London (LLB Hons); Magdalen Coll., Oxford (BCL). Called to the Bar, Middle Temple, 1970; Lecturer in Law, Pembroke Coll., Oxford, 1971–76. *Publications:* various legal text books. *Recreations:* travel, music. *Address:* 27 Rosslyn Hill, NW3 5UJ. *T:* 01–435 7290; The Quadrangle, Naunton, Glos. *T:* Guiting Power 620. *Club:* Royal Automobile.

CUBBON, Sir Brian (Crossland), GCB 1984 (KCB 1977; CB 1974); Permanent Under Secretary of State, Home Office, since 1979; *b* 9 April 1928; *m* 1956, Elizabeth Lorin Richardson; three *s* one *d*. *Educ:* Bury Grammar Sch.; Trinity Coll., Cambridge. Entered Home Office, 1951; Cabinet Office, 1961–63, 1971–75; Private Sec. to Home Sec., 1968–69; Permanent Under-Sec. of State, Northern Ireland Office, 1976–79. *Address:* c/o Home Office, SW1. *Club:* United Oxford & Cambridge University.

CUBBON, Maj.-Gen. John Hamilton, CB 1962; CBE 1958 (OBE 1940); DL; *b* 15 March 1911; *s* of Joseph Cubbon; *m* 1951, Amelia Margaret Yates; two *s* one *d*. *Educ:* St Bees Sch.; RMC Sandhurst. 2nd Lieut Ches Regt, 1931; Commanded: 1st Bn The Parachute Regt, 1946–49; 1st Bn The Ches Regt, 1951–54; 18th Infantry Bde, Malaya, 1956–57. Maj.-Gen. 1960; GOC SW Dist, 1960–63; GOC Land Forces, Middle East Command, 1963–65. DL Devon, 1969. *Recreation:* sailing. *Address:* The Hayes, Harpford, Sidmouth, Devon.

CUBITT, family name of **Baron Ashcombe.**

CUBITT, Sir Hugh (Guy), Kt 1983; CBE 1977; FRICS; JP; DL; Director: National Westminster Bank (Chairman, Outer London Region); Property Security Investment Trust; Chairman: Lombard North Central PLC, since 1980; The Housing Corporation, since 1980; *b* 2 July 1928; *s* of late Col Hon. (Charles) Guy Cubitt, CBE, DSO, TD, and Rosamond Mary Edith, *d* of Sir Montagu Cholmeley, 4th Bt; *m* 1958, Linda Ishbel, *d* of late Hon. Angus Campbell, CBE; one *s* two *d*. *Educ:* RNC Dartmouth and Greenwich. Lieut RN, 1949; served in Korea, 1949–51; Flag Lieut to Adm., BJSM Washington, 1952 and to C-in-C Nore, 1953; retd 1953. Qual. Chartered Auctioneer and Estate Agent, 1958; Chartered Surveyor (FRICS) 1970. Partner: Rogers Chapman & Thomas, 1958–67; Cubitt & West, 1962–79. Mem. Westminster City Council, 1963–78; Chairman: Highways Cttee, 1968–71; Town Planning Cttee, 1971–72; Leader of Council, 1972–76; Alderman, 1974–78; Lord Mayor and dep. High Steward of Westminster, 1977–78. Hon. Treas., London Boroughs Assoc., 1974–77. Mem. Home Office Cttee on London Taxicab Trade (Stamp Cttee), 1967–70. Governor: Cranleigh Sch. (Chm. of Governors, 1981); West Heath Sch. (Chm., 1978); Dir and Mem. Governing Body, RAM. Hon. Steward, Westminster Abbey, 1978. Mem., Bd of Green Cloth Verge of Palaces, 1980–. FRSA; Hon. FRAM 1985. JP Surrey, 1964; Dep. Chm., Dorking PSD, 1974–; High Sheriff of Surrey, 1983–84. DL Greater London, 1978. Liveryman, Needlemakers' Co. *Recreations:* country sports, travel, photography. *Address:* Chapel House, West Humble, Dorking, Surrey. *T:* Dorking 882994. *Club:* Boodle's.

CUCKNEY, Sir John (Graham), Kt 1978; Chairman: Thomas Cook Group, since 1978; John Brown plc, since 1983 (Director, since 1981; Deputy Chairman, 1982–83); Royal Insurance plc, since 1985 (Deputy Chairman, 1983–85; Director, since 1979); Westland plc, since 1985; Investors in Industry, from July 1987; Deputy Chairman, TI Group plc, since 1985; Director: Midland Bank plc, since 1978; Touche Remnant Holdings Ltd, since 1985; Brixton Estate plc, since 1985; *b* 12 July 1925; *s* of late Air Vice-Marshal E. J. Cuckney, CB, CBE, DSC; *m* 2nd, 1960, Muriel, *d* of late Walter Scott Boyd. *Educ:* Shrewsbury; St Andrews Univ. (MA). War Service, Royal Northumberland Fusiliers, King's African Rifles, followed by attachment to War Office (Civil Asst, Gen. Staff), until 1957; subseq. chm. and dir of various industrial and financial cos including Brooke Bond Group plc, 1978–84 and Lazard Brothers (Dir, 1964–70). Public appointments include: Chm., Mersey Docks and Harbour Board, 1970–72; Chief Executive (Second Perm. Sec.), Property Services Agency, DoE, 1972–74; Chm., International Military Services Ltd (an MoD company), 1974–85; Sen. Crown Agent and Chm. of Crown Agents, for Oversea Governments and Administrations, 1974–78. Independent Mem., Railway Policy Review Cttee, 1966–67; special Mem., Hops Marketing Bd, 1971–72; Chairman: EDC for Building, 1976–80; Port of London Authority, 1977–79; Internat. Maritime Bureau, Internat. Chamber of Commerce, 1981–85; Member: Docklands Joint Cttee, 1977–79; Council, British Exec. Service Overseas, 1981–84; Dir, SBAC, 1986–. Governor, Centre for Internat. Briefing, Farnham Castle, 1974–84; Trustee, Venture Trust, 1982– (Chm., 1984). Elder Brother of Trinity House, 1980. *Address:* 45 Berkeley Street, W1. *Club:* Athenæum.

CUDLIPP, family name of **Baron Cudlipp.**

CUDLIPP, Baron *cr* 1974 (Life Peer), of Aldingbourne, W Sussex; **Hugh Cudlipp,** Kt 1973; OBE 1945; Personal consultant to Robert Maxwell, MC, publisher, Mirror Group Newspapers, since 1984; Chairman: International Publishing Corporation Ltd, 1968–73 (Deputy Chairman, 1964–68); International Publishing Corporation Newspaper Division, 1970–73; Deputy Chairman (editorial), Reed International Board, 1970–73; Director, Associated Television Ltd, 1956–73; *b* 28 Aug. 1913; *s* of William Cudlipp, Cardiff; *m* 2nd, 1945, Eileen Ascroft (*d* 1962); 3rd, 1963, Jodi, *d* of late John L. Hyland, Palm Beach, Fla, and Mrs D. W. Jones, Southport. *Educ:* Howard Gardens Sch., Cardiff. Provincial newspapers in Cardiff and Manchester, 1927–32; Features Ed., Sunday Chronicle, London, 1932–35; Features Ed., Daily Mirror, 1935–37; Ed., Sunday Pictorial, 1937–40. Military Service, 1940–46; CO, British Army Newspaper Unit, CMF, 1943–46. Ed., Sunday Pictorial, 1946–49; Managing Ed., Sunday Express, 1950–52; Editorial Dir, Daily Mirror and Sunday Pictorial, 1952–63; Joint Managing Dir, Daily Mirror and Sunday Pictorial, 1959–63; Chm., Odhams Press Ltd, 1961–63; Chm., Daily Mirror Newspapers Ltd, 1963–68. Mem., Royal Commn on Standards of Conduct in Public Life, 1974–76. *Publications:* Publish and be Damned!, 1955; At Your Peril, 1962; Walking on the Water, 1976; The Prerogative of the Harlot, 1980. *Address:* The Dene, Hook Lane, Aldingbourne, Chichester, West Sussex. *Club:* Garrick.

CUDLIPP, Michael John; consultant on internal and external corporate communications; Director, The History of Advertising Trust, since 1987; *b* 24 April 1934; *o s* of late Percy Cudlipp and Mrs Gwendoline May Cudlipp; *m* 1st, 1957, Margaret Susannah Rees (marr. diss. 1975); one *d*; 2nd, 1985, Jane Gale; two *d*. *Educ:* Tonbridge Sch., Kent. Trainee reporter, feature writer, gossip columnist, sub-editor, South Wales Echo, Cardiff, 1953–57; Sub-editor, Evening Chronicle, Manchester (various freelance jobs on daily and Sunday newspapers in Manchester), 1957–58; News Editor and Asst Editor (News), Sunday Times, 1958–67; Asst Editor (Night), Jt Man. Editor and sen. Dep. Editor, The Times, 1967–73; Chief Editor, London Broadcasting Co., 1973–74; Consultant on Public Relations to NI Office (temp. Civil Servant with rank of Under-Sec.), 1974–75; Dir of Information, Nat. Enterprise Bd, 1975–78; Dir, External and Internal Communications, Internat. Thomson Orgn, 1979–85. Gov., History of Advertising Trust, 1984–86. FZS. *Recreations:* Arts, Welsh rugby football. *Address:* c/o The History of Advertising Trust, Unit 202 Butlers Wharf Business Centre, 45 Curlew Street, SE1 2ND. *T:* 01–403 0756.

CUDLIPP, Reginald; Director, Anglo-Japanese Economic Institute, London, since 1961; *b* Cardiff, 11 Dec. 1910; *s* of William Cudlipp, Cardiff; *m* 1945, Rachel Joyce Braham. *Educ:* Cardiff Technical Coll. Began journalistic career on Penarth News, Glamorgan; Sub-Ed., Western Mail, Cardiff; joined News of the World Sub-Editorial Staff, 1938; served War, 1940–46; rejoined News of the World and became Special Correspondent in USA, 1946–47; Features Ed., 1948–50, Dep. Ed., 1950–53, Ed., 1953–59; Dir, News of the World Ltd, 1955–60. Extensive industrial tours and on-the-spot economic study of Japan regularly, 1962–. Member: Japan Soc.; RSAA; RSA; RIIA; Life Mem., NUJ, 1929–. Editor, Japan (quarterly review and monthly survey), and special publications on the Japanese scene. Lecturer and writer on Japan's past, present and future; also first-hand research on developing nations and economic co-operation, especially in Africa and Asia. Order of the Sacred Treasure, Japan, 1982. *Publications:* numerous contribs to newspapers and periodicals, on Japan and Anglo-Japanese affairs. *Recreations:* music, travel, and reading, writing and talking about Japan. *Address:* 342 Grand Buildings, Trafalgar Square, WC2. *T:* 01–930 5567.

CUEVAS-CANCINO, Francisco, GCVO (Hon.) 1985; Mexican Ambassador to Austria and Permanent Mexican Representative to UNIDO and AEIO, since 1986; *b* 7 May 1921; *s* of José Luis Cuevas and Sofia Cancino; *m* 1946, Ana Hilditch; two *s* one *d*; *m* Cristina Flores de Cuevas. *Educ:* Free School of Law, Mexico (lawyer, 1943); McGill Univ., Montreal (MCL 1946). Entered Mexican Foreign Service, as Vice-Consul, 1946, reaching rank of Ambassador by own merit; Permanent Representative to UN, 1965–70; Mexican Rep. to UNESCO, 1971–75, and Mem. Exec. Council during first four years; Perm. Rep. to UN, 1978–79; Ambassador: to Brazil, 1979–80; to Belgium, 1980–83; to UK and to Republic of Ireland, 1983–85. Order of the Liberator, 1970, Order Andrés Bello, 1971, (Venezuela); Medal of Mexican For. Service (25 years), 1972; Order Cruzeiro do Sur (Brazil), 1980; Great Cross of Order of the Crown (Belgium), 1983. *Publications:* La nullité des actes juridiques, 1947; La doctrina de Suárez en el derecho natural (award, Madrid), 1952; Roosevelt y la buena vecindad, 1955; Del Congreso de Panamá a la Conferencia de Caracas, 1955, re-ed 1979; Tratado sobre la organización internacional, 1962; (ed) Porvenir de México by Luis G. Cuevas, 1961; (ed) Pacto de Familia (vol. forms part of Hist. Archives of Mexican Diplomatic Service, 2nd series), 1963; (ed) Foro Internacional, 1961–62; contrib. to book of essays in homage to Hans Morgenthau, 1978; several works and articles on Bolivarian theatre, and on Simón Bolívar (The Liberator), incl.: Visión Surrealista del Libertador, (Bogotá) 1980; Homenaje a Bolívar en el Sesquicentenario de su Muerte, (Bogotá) 1980. *Address:* Mexican Embassy, Mattiellistrasse 2–4, 1040 Vienna, Austria. *T:* 52 99 11. *Clubs:* Travellers', Garrick.

CULHAM, Michael John; Assistant Under Secretary of State (Adjutant-General), Ministry of Defence, since 1982; *b* 24 June 1933; *s* of Cecil and Constance Culham; *m* 1963, Christine Mary Daish; one *s* two *d*. *Educ:* Reading Sch.; Lincoln Coll., Oxford (MA). National Service, Queen's Own Royal West Kent Regt, RAEC, 1952–54. Exec. Officer, WO, 1957–61; Asst Principal, Air Min., 1962; Private Sec. to Under-Sec. of State for Air, 1962–64; Principal, MoD, 1964–72; Jt Services Staff Coll., 1969; 1st Sec. (Defence), UK Delegn to NATO, Brussels, 1972–74; Asst Sec., MoD, 1974–82. Member: Royal Patriotic Fund Corp., 1983–; Adv. Council, RMCS, Shrivenham, 1983–. Commissioner: Duke of York's Royal Mil. Sch., 1982–; Queen Victoria Sch., 1982–; Welbeck Coll., 1985–; Royal Hosp. Chelsea, 1985–. Chm., Farnham Town Boys' FC, 1983–85. Trustee, Nat. Army Mus., 1985–. *Recreations:* music, sailing, watching cricket. *Address:* 39 Waverley Lane, Farnham, Surrey GU9 8BH. *T:* Farnham 726707. *Clubs:* Civil Service; Surrey County Cricket.

CULHANE, Prof. John Leonard, FRS 1985; Professor of Physics, University College London, since 1981, and Director, Mullard Space Science Laboratory, since 1983; *b* 14

Oct. 1937; *s* of late John Thomas Culhane and Mary Agnes Culhane; *m* 1961, Mary Brigid, *d* of James Smith; two *s*. *Educ:* Clongowes Wood College, Co. Kildare; University College Dublin (BSc Phys 1959; MSc Phys 1960); UCL (PhD Phys 1966). Physics Department, University College London: Res. Asst, 1963; Lectr, 1967; Reader, 1976; Prof., 1981. Sen. Scientist, Lockheed Palo Alto Res. Lab., 1969–70. Member: Council, RAS, 1975–78; SERC Astronomy, Space and Radio Board, 1981–85, Engineering Board, 1984–85; Space Sci. Adv. Cttee, ESA, 1985– (Chm., Astrophysics Working Group, 1985–); Council, Surrey Univ., 1985–; IAU; Amer. Astronomical Soc.; IEEE Professional Group on Nuclear Sci. Governor, Oxted County Sch., 1983–85. *Publications:* X-ray Astronomy (with P. W. Sanford), 1981; papers on X-ray instrumentation, plasma spectroscopy, solar and cosmic X-ray astronomy. *Recreations:* music, racing cars. *Address:* Ariel House, Holmbury St Mary, Dorking, Surrey.

CULHANE, Rosalind, (Lady Padmore), LVO 1938; OBE 1949; Treasury Welfare Adviser, 1943–64; *y d* of late F. W. S. Culhane, MRCS, LRCP, Hastings, Sussex; *m* 1964, Sir Thomas Padmore, *qv*. Joined Treasury in 1923 and attached to office of Chancellor of Exchequer; Asst Private Sec. to Mr Chamberlain, 1934, Sir John Simon, 1937, Sir Kingsley Wood, 1940. *Address:* 39 Cholmeley Crescent, N6. *T:* 01–340 6587.

CULLEN, Hon. Lord; (William) Douglas Cullen; a Senator of the College of Justice in Scotland, since 1986; *b* 18 Nov. 1935; *s* of late Sheriff K. D. Cullen and Mrs G. M. Cullen; *m* 1961, Rosamond Mary Downer; two *s* two *d*. *Educ:* Dundee High Sch.; St Andrews Univ. (MA); Edinburgh Univ. (LLB). Called to the Scottish Bar, 1960. Standing Jun. Counsel to HM Customs and Excise, 1970–73; QC (Scot.) 1973; Advocate-depute, 1978–81. Chm., Medical Appeal Tribunal, 1977–86; Mem., Scottish Valuation Adv. Council, 1980–. Chm. Council, Cockburn Assoc. (Edinburgh Civic Trust), 1984–86. *Publication:* The Faculty Digest Supplement 1951–60, 1965. *Recreations:* gardening, natural history. *Address:* 62 Fountainhall Road, Edinburgh EH9 2LP. *T:* 031–667 6949. *Club:* New (Edinburgh).

CULLEN OF ASHBOURNE, 2nd Baron *cr* 1920; **Charles Borlase Marsham Cokayne,** MBE 1945; a Lord in Waiting (Government Whip), 1979–82; Major, Royal Signals; *b* 6 Oct. 1912; *e s* of 1st Baron and Grace Margaret (*d* 1971), *d* of Rev. Hon. John Marsham; *S* father, 1932; *m* 1942, Valerie Catherine Mary (marr. diss. 1947), *o d* of late W. H. Collbran; one *d*; *m* 1948, Patricia Mary, *er d* of late Col S. Clulow-Gray and late Mrs Clulow-Gray, formerly of Clare Priory, Suffolk. *Educ:* Eton. Served War of 1939–45 (MBE). Amateur Tennis Champion, 1947, 1952. One of HM Lieutenants, City of London, 1976–. Chairman: National Listening Library; Osteopathic Educnl Foundn; Pres., Fedn of Ophthalmic & Dispensing Opticians (formerly Fedn of Optical Corporate Bodies), 1983–. *Heir: b* Hon. Edmund Willoughby Marsham Cokayne [*b* 18 May 1916; *m* 1943, Janet Manson, *d* of late William Douglas Watson and of Mrs Lauritson, Calgary]. *Address:* 75 Cadogan Gardens, SW3 2RB. *T:* 01–589 1981. *Club:* MCC.

CULLEN, Prof. Alexander Lamb, OBE 1960; DSc(Eng); FRS 1977; FEng 1977, FIEE, FIEEE, FInstP, FCGI; Emeritus Professor, University of London; Hon. Research Fellow, Department of Electronic and Electrical Engineering, University College London, since 1984 (SERC Senior Research Fellow, 1980–84); *b* 30 April 1920; *s* of Richard and Jessie Cullen, Lincoln; *m* 1940, Margaret, *er d* of late Alexander Lamb, OBE; two *s* one *d*. *Educ:* Lincoln Sch.; City and Guilds Coll., London. Staff of Radio Dept, RAE Farnborough, working on development of radar, 1940–46; Lectr in Electrical Engineering, University Coll., London, 1946–55 (title of Reader conferred 1955); Prof. of Electrical Engineering, University of Sheffield, 1955–67; Pender Prof. of Electrical Engineering, University College London, 1967–80. Hon. Prof., Northwestern Polytechnical Univ., Xian, China, 1981. Mem., IBA, 1982–. Instn of Electrical Engineers: Kelvin premium, 1952; Extra premium, 1953 (with Prof. H. M. Barlow and Dr A. E. Karbowiak); Radio Sect. premium, 1954; Ambrose Fleming premium, 1956 (with J. C. Parr), 1975 (with Dr J. R. Forrest); Duddell premium, 1957 (with Dr H. A. French); Electronics and Communications Sect. premium, 1959; Faraday Medal, 1984. Chm., Brit. Nat. Cttee, URSI, 1981–85; Vice-Pres., Internat. URSI, 1981–. Clifford Paterson Lecture, Royal Soc., 1984; Clerk Maxwell Lecture, IERE, 1986. Hon. DSc: Chinese Univ. of Hong Kong, 1981; Kent, 1986. Hon. DEng Sheffield, 1985. Royal Medal, Royal Soc., 1984. *Publications:* Microwave Measurements (jointly with Prof. H. M. Barlow), 1950; a number of papers on electromagnetic waves and microwave measurement techniques in IEE proceedings and elsewhere. *Recreations:* music and reading. *Address:* Department of Electronic and Electrical Engineering, University College London, Torrington Place, WC1E 7JE.

CULLEN, Douglas; *see* Cullen, Hon. Lord.

CULLEN, Dr (Edward) John; Chairman, Health and Safety Commission, since 1983; *b* 19 Oct. 1926; *s* of William Henry Pearson Cullen and Ellen Emma Cullen; *m* 1954, Betty Davall Hopkins; two *s* two *d*. *Educ:* Cambridge Univ. (MA 1952, PhD 1956); Univ. of Texas (MS 1953). UKAEA, 1956–58; ICI, 1958–67; Rohm and Haas Co., 1967–83: Eur. Dir for Engrg and Regulatory Affairs, 1981–83; Dep. Chm., Rohm and Haas (UK) Ltd, 1981–83. MInstD 1978. *Publications:* articles on gas absorption, in Trans Faraday Soc., Trans IChemE, Chem. Engrg Science. *Recreations:* reading (detective stories), photography, swimming, gardening. *Address:* 14 Gloucester Walk, W8 5JH. *T:* 01–937 0709. *Club:* Institute of Directors.

CULLEN, Gordon; *see* Cullen, T. G.

CULLEN, James Reynolds; *b* 13 June 1900; *s* of Rev. James Harris Cullen, London Missionary Society; *m* 1931, Inez (*d* 1980), *e d* of M. G. Zarifi, MBE; one *s* two *d*. *Educ:* Weimar Gymnasium; Tonbridge Sch.; Balliol Coll., Oxford (Scholar). Hertford Schol., 1919; Craven Schol., 1920; 1st class Hon. Mods, 1920; 2nd class Lit. Hum. 1922; MA 1925. Asst Master, Winchester Coll., 1922–30; archæological expeditions to Asia Minor, 1925, and Mytilene, 1930; Dir of Education, Cyprus, 1930–45; Dir of Education, Uganda, 1945–52; Asst Master, Oundle Sch., 1953–60, Cranbrook and Benenden Schs, 1960–68. *Address:* Weathercock House, Hawkhurst, Kent TN18 4QA. *Club:* Royal Commonwealth Society.

CULLEN, John; *see* Cullen, E. J.

CULLEN, Raymond; Chairman, The Calico Printers' Association Ltd and subsidiaries, 1964–68; *b* 27 May 1913; *s* of late John Norman Cullen and Bertha (*née* Dearden); *m* 1940, Doris (*d* 1984), *d* of A. W. Paskin; two *d*. *Educ:* King's Sch., Macclesfield; St Catharine's Coll., Cambridge (Scholar, MA). Joined The Calico Printers' Assoc. Ltd Commn Printing, 1934; transf. overseas, 1938; service in India and China. Dir, W. A. Beardsell & Co. (Private) Ltd, Madras, 1946 (Chm. and Man. Dir, 1949–55); Chm. and Man. Dir, Mettur Industries Ltd, 1949–55; Chm. and Man. Dir, Marshall Fabrics Ltd, 1955–62; Director: Calico Printers' Assoc. Ltd, 1962–68; Barclays Bank Ltd Manchester Local Bd, 1965–69. Member: Textile Coun., 1967–69; Coun., Inst. of Directors, 1967–69; NW Economic Planning Coun., 1968–69; Governor, Manchester Grammar Sch., 1968–83. *Recreations:* fishing, golf (Pres., Cheshire Union of Golf Clubs, 1977–78). *Address:* Cranford, Ladybrook Road, Bramhall, Cheshire SK7 3NB. *T:* 061–485 3204.

CULLEN, Terence Lindsay Graham, QC 1978; *b* 29 Oct. 1930; *s* of Eric Graham Cullen and Jean Morrison Hunter (*née* Bennett); *m* 1958, Muriel Elisabeth Rolfe; three *s*. *Educ:* RNC, Dartmouth. RN, 1948–55; Prestige Group Ltd, 1955–61. Called to the Bar: Lincoln's Inn, 1961 (Bencher, 1986); Singapore, 1978; Malaysia, 1980. *Recreation:* the Turf. *Address:* 13 Old Square, Lincoln's Inn, WC2A 3UA. *T:* 01–404 4800; Calico House, Newnham, Kent ME9 0LN.

CULLEN, (Thomas) Gordon, CBE 1978; RDI 1976; planning consultant, artist and writer; *b* 9 Aug. 1914; *s* of Rev. T. H. Cullen and Mary Anne (*née* Moffatt); *m* 1955, Comtesse Jacqueline de Chabameix du Chambon; three *d*. *Educ:* Prince Henry's Grammar Sch., Otley, Yorks; Regent Street Polytechnic Sch. of Architecture, London. Fraternal Delegate, Runcorn Trades Council, 1942; Mem. Planning Div., Develt and Welfare, Barbados, 1944–46; Asst Editor, Architectural Rev., 1946–56. Townscape Consultant: with Ford Foundn, New Delhi, 1960, and Calcutta, 1962; Liverpool, Llantrisant, Tenterden, Peterborough and Ware, 1962–76. Exhib. drawings, Paris Salon, Royal Acad.; One-Man Exhibn, Sweden and Holland, 1976. Member: Eton RDC, 1963–73; Wraysbury Parish Council, 1960–. Hon. FRIBA 1972. Hon. LittD Sheffield, 1975; Dr-IngEh Munich, 1973. Amer. Inst. of Architects Gold Medal, 1976. *Publications:* Townscape, 1964; planning reports. *Recreations:* observation, writing poetry, sleep. *Address:* 29 The Drive, Wraysbury, Staines, Mddx TW19 5ES. *T:* Wraysbury 2147. *Club:* Wraysbury Village Club and Institute (Wraysbury).

CULLIMORE, Charles Augustine Kaye; HM Diplomatic Service; Foreign and Commonwealth Office, since 1986; *b* 2 Oct. 1933; *s* of Charles Cullimore and Constance Alicia Kaye Cullimore (*née* Grimshaw); *m* 1956, Val Elizabeth Margot (*née* Willemsen); one *s* one *d*. *Educ:* Portora Royal Sch., Enniskillen; Trinity Coll., Oxford (MA). N Ireland Short Service Commn, 1955–57. HMOCS, Tanganyika, 1958–61; ICI Ltd, 1961–71; joined HM Diplomatic Service, 1971; FCO, 1971–73; Bonn, 1973–77; FCO, 1977–79; Counsellor, New Delhi, 1979–82; Dep. High Comr, Canberra, 1982–86. *Recreations:* theatre, walking, tennis. *Address:* c/o Foreign and Commonwealth Office, SW1A 2AH. *Clubs:* Royal Commonwealth Society; Commonwealth (Canberra).

CULLIMORE, Colin Stuart, CBE 1978; Director: several Union International plc Cos; Albion Insurance; *b* 13 July 1931; *s* of Reginald Victor Cullimore and May Maria Cullimore; *m* 1952, Kathleen Anyta Lamming; one *s*. *Educ:* Westminster Sch.; National Coll. of Food Technol. Commnd Royal Scots Fusiliers, 1951; seconded Parachute Regt; transf. when perm. officer cadre formed; Major 1956; 10th Bn Parachute Regt TA, 1960. Gen. Man., Payne & Son (Butchers) Ltd, 1960; Asst Gen. Man., J. H. Dewhurst Ltd, 1965, Gen. Man. 1969, Man. Dir, 1976. Non-Exec. Dir, NAAFI, 1984–. Chairman: Retail Consortium Food Cttee, 1973–74; Multiple Shops Fedn, 1977–78. Vice-Chairman: Multiple Food Retailers Assoc., 1972–74; Governors, Coll. for Distributive Trades, 1976–79, 1984– (Gov., 1980–84); Retail Consortium, 1985–; Pres., British Retailers Assoc., 1984– (Vice Pres., 1978–84); Dep. Chm., Meat Promotion Exec., 1975–78. Member: Distribn and Consumer Cttees, 1969–72, Finance Cttee, 1980–, Diet and Health Cttee, 1986–, Meat and Livestock Commn; EDC for Distrib. Trades, 1972–80; Council, Inst. of Meat (Vice-Chm., 1981–83); Bd of Admin, European Retailers, 1981–85; Cttee of Commerce and Distribn, EEC, 1984–. Gov., Court of London Inst.; Exec. Trustee, Airborne Assault Normandy Trust, 1983–. FInstD, 1979; CBIM, 1984. Gold Medal: Inst. of Meat, 1956; Butchers' Co., 1956. *Address:* 29 Eaton Mews North, SW1. *T:* 01–235 1420. *Clubs:* Naval and Military, Institute of Directors.

CULLINAN, Edward Horder; Senior Partner, Edward Cullinan Architects, since 1965; *b* 17 July 1931; *s* of Dr Edward Cullinan and Joy (*née* Horder); *m* 1961, Rosalind Yeates; one *s* two *d*. *Educ:* Ampleforth Coll.; Cambridge Univ. (Anderson and Webb Schol., 1951; BA); Univ. of California at Berkeley (George VI Meml Fellow, 1956). AADip; RIBA. With Denys Lasdun, 1958–65. Bannister Fletcher Prof., UCL, 1978–79; Graham Willis Prof., Univ. of Sheffield, 1985–. Vis. Prof., MIT, 1985. FRSA. *Publications:* contribs to many architectural jls. *Recreations:* horticulture, cycling, surfing, ski-ing, Sahara travel, building. *Address:* 62 Camden Mews, NW1 9BX. *T:* 01–485 7738.

CULLINGFORD, Rev. Cecil Howard Dunstan, MA; FRSA; *b* 13 Sept. 1904; *s* of Francis James and Lilian Mabel Cullingford; *m* 1st, 1933, Olive Eveline (*d* 1971), *d* of Lt-Col P. H. Collingwood, Clifton, Bristol; one *s* one *d*; 2nd, 1972, Penelope Wood-Hill, *e d* of Dr H. Wood-Hill, Beccles. *Educ:* City of London Sch.; Corpus Christi Coll., Cambridge (Foundation Scholar). 1st Class Hons in Classical Tripos, Parts 1 and 2, and Historical Tripos, Part 2. VIth Form Master, Brighton Coll., 1928–32; Vice-Principal, Clifton Theological Coll., 1932–34; Chaplain of Oundle Sch., 1935–46. Army Chaplain, 1939–45; Guards Armoured Div., 1939–43; Staff Chaplain, 21st Army Group, 1943–44; Senior Chaplain, 79th Armoured Div., 1944–45. Headmaster of Monmouth Sch., 1946–56; Lectr in Naval History at Britannia RNC Dartmouth, 1957–60; Chaplain: St John's Sch., Leatherhead, 1960–64; St Michael's Sch., Limpsfield, 1964–67; Vicar of Stiffkey with Morston, 1967–72; Rural Dean of Beccles, 1973–76. Pres., Silleren Ski Club, 1966; Vice-Pres., Wessex Cave Club; Hon. Member: Cave Res. Group of GB; British Speleological Assoc.; British Cave Res. Assoc. *Publications:* Exploring Caves, 1951; (ed) British Caving: an Introduction to Speleology, 1953 (2nd edn 1961); (ed) A Manual of Caving Techniques, 1969; The Thornhill Guide to Caving, 1976; (ed) The Science of Speleology, 1976. *Recreations:* hockey, pot-holing, music, archæology. *Address:* The Staithe, Beccles, Suffolk. *T:* Beccles 712182.

See also E. C. M. Cullingford.

CULLINGFORD, Eric Coome Maynard, CMG 1963; *b* 15 March 1910; *s* of Francis James and Lilian Mabel Cullingford; *m* 1938, Friedel Fuchs; two *s* one *d*. *Educ:* City of London Sch.; St Catharine's Coll., Cambridge (Exhibitioner). Entered Ministry of Labour as Third Class Officer, 1932; Principal, 1942. Served with Manpower Div. of CCG, 1946–50. Asst Sec., Min. of Labour, 1954. Labour Attaché, Bonn, 1961–65, 1968–72. Regional Controller, Eastern and Southern Region, Dept of Employment and Productivity, 1966–68; retired 1973. *Publications:* Trade Unions in West Germany, 1976; Pirates of Shearwater Island, 1983. *Address:* Combermere, Flat 1, 25 Avenue Road, Malvern, Worcs.

See also Rev. C. H. D. Cullingford.

CULLINGWORTH, Prof. (John) Barry; Unidel Professor of Urban Affairs and Public Policy, University of Delaware, since 1983; Visiting Professor, University of Strathclyde; *b* 11 Sept. 1929; *s* of Sidney C. and Winifred E. Cullingworth; *m* 1951, Betty Violet (*née* Turner); one *s* two *d*. *Educ:* High Pavement Sch., Nottingham; Trinity Coll. of Music, London; London Sch. of Economics. Research Asst, Asst Lectr and Lectr, Univ. of Manchester, 1955–60; Lectr, Univ. of Durham, 1960–63; Sen. Lectr and Reader, Univ. of Glasgow, 1963–66; Dir, Centre for Urban and Regional Studies, Univ. of Birmingham, 1966–72. Dir, Planning Exchange, Scotland, 1972–75; Official Historian, Cabinet Office, 1975–77. Chm., Dept of Urban and Regional Planning, 1977–80, Res. Prof., Centre for Urban and Community Studies, 1980–82, Prof. of Planning, 1982–83, Univ. of Toronto. Vice-Chm., Scottish Housing Adv. Cttee; Chairman: Cttee on Community Facilities in Expanding Towns (Report, The Needs of New Communities, 1967); Cttee on Unfit Housing in Scotland (Report, Scotland's Older Houses, 1967); Cttee on Allocation of

Council Houses (Report, Council Housing: Purposes, Procedures and Practices, 1968); Adv. Cttee on Rent Rebates and Rent Allowances, 1973–77. Mem., Ont. Council of Health, 1979–83; Vice-Pres., Housing Centre Trust, 1972–. FRSA 1974; Hon. MRTPI. *Publications:* Housing Needs and Planning Policy, 1960; Housing in Transition, 1963; Town and Country Planning in England and Wales, 1964, 9th edn 1985; English Housing Trends, 1965; Housing and Local Government, 1966; Scottish Housing in 1965, 1967; A Profile of Glasgow Housing, 1968; (with V. Karn) Ownership and Management of Housing in New Towns, 1968; Housing and Labour Mobility, (Paris) 1969; Problems of an Urban Society (3 vols), 1973; Environmental Planning—Reconstruction and Land Use Planning, 1975; Essays on Housing Policy, 1979; New Towns Policy, 1980; Canadian Housing Policy Research, 1980; Land Values, Compensation and Betterment, 1981; Rent Control, 1983; Canadian Planning and Public Participation, 1984; Urban and Regional Planning in Canada, 1985. *Address:* College of Urban Affairs and Public Policy, University of Delaware, Newark, Delaware 19716, USA.

CULLIS, Prof. Charles Fowler; Saddlers' Research Professor, City University, London, since 1984; *b* 31 Aug. 1922; 2nd *s* of late Prof. C. G. Cullis, Prof. of Mining Geology, Univ. of London, and Mrs W. J. Cullis (*née* Fowler); *m* 1958, Marjorie Elizabeth, *er d* of late Sir Austin Anderson and of Lady Anderson; two *s* two *d*. *Educ:* Stowe Sch. (Open Schol.); Trinity Coll., Oxford. BA 1944, BSc 1st Cl. Hons Chem. 1945, DPhil 1948, MA 1948, DSc 1960; FRSC (FRIC 1958); FRSA. ICI Research Fellow in Chem., Oxford, 1947–50; Lectr in Phys. Chem., Imperial Coll., London, 1950–59; Sen. Lectr in Chem. Engrg and Chem. Tech., Imperial Coll., 1959–64; Reader in Combustion Chemistry, Univ. of London, 1964–66; City University: Prof. of Physical Chemistry, 1967–84; Head, Chemistry Dept, 1973–84; a Pro-Vice-Chancellor, 1980–84. Vis. Prof., College of Chem., Univ. of California, Berkeley, 1966; Vis. Scientist, CSIRO, Sydney, 1970. Mem. Council, Chem. Soc., 1969–72, 1975–78; Hon. Sec., Brit. Sect. of Combustion Inst., 1969–74; Mem., Rockets Sub-cttee, 1968–73, and of Combustion Sub-cttee, 1969–72, Aeronautical Research Council; Member: Navy Dept Fuels and Lubricants Adv. Cttee (Fire and Explosion Hazards Working Gp), 1967–; Safety in Mines Research Adv. Bd, 1973– (Chm., 1980–); Chem. Cttee, Defence Sci. Adv. Council, 1979–82; Chem. Bd, CNAA, 1982–; Scientific Editor, Internat. Union of Pure and Applied Chem., 1976–78. Governor, City of London Polytechnic, 1982–84. Freeman, City of London, 1983; Liveryman, Bakers' Co., 1983. Joseph Priestley Award, 1974, Combustion Chem. Medal and Award, 1978, Chem. Soc. *Publications:* The Combustion of Organic Polymers (jtly with M. M. Hirschler), 1981; numerous sci. papers in Proc. Royal Soc., Trans Faraday Soc., Jl Chem. Soc., etc, mainly concerned with chemistry of combustion reactions. *Recreations:* music, travel. *Address:* Chieveley, Black Hill, Lindfield, Sussex RH16 2HF. *T:* Lindfield 2188; Chemistry Department, City University, Northampton Square, EC1V 0HB. *T:* 01-253 4399, ext. 3500. *Club:* Athenæum.
See also M. F. Cullis.

CULLIS, Michael Fowler, CVO 1955; HM Diplomatic Service, retired; Director, UK Committee, European Cultural Foundation, Amsterdam, since 1983; *b* 22 Oct. 1914; *s* of late Prof. Charles Gilbert Cullis, Imperial Coll. of Science and Technology, London Univ., and late Winifred Jefford Cullis (*née* Fowler); *m* Catherine Robertson, Arbroath, Scotland; no *c*. *Educ:* Wellington Coll. (scholar); Brasenose Coll., Oxford (Hulme Open Scholar). MA, classics. Law (Lincoln's Inn), and journalism, 1938–39. Military Intelligence, Gibraltar, 1939–40; served Min. of Economic Warfare (London, Spain and Portugal), 1940–44; joined FO as head of Austrian Section, 1945; Political Adviser on Austrian Treaty negotiations (London, Moscow, Vienna, Paris, New York), 1947–50; Special Asst, Schuman Plan, 1950; First Sec., British Embassy, Oslo, 1951–55; Regional (Information) Counsellor for the five Nordic countries, British Embassy, Copenhagen, 1955–58; Dep. Gov. of Malta, 1959–61; Sen. Research Associate, Atlantic Institute, Paris, 1962–65; writing, lecturing, etc, at various European centres, 1965–66; Dir, Arms Control and Disarmament Res., FO, then FCO, 1967–74; Advr on relations with non-govtl bodies, FCO, 1974–79; consultant for acad. and institutional fund-raising, and European parly affairs, 1980–82. Unsuccessful candidate (C), European Elections, 1979. Vice-President: Inst. of Linguists, 1984–; Internat. Eisteddfod 1984–. FRSA. Chevalier (1st cl.) Order of Dannebrog, 1957. *Publications:* articles and broadcasts on international affairs. *Address:* County End, Bushey Heath, Herts WD2 1NY. *T:* 01–950 1057. *Club:* Athenæum.
See also C. F. Cullis.

CULLITON, Hon. Edward Milton, CC 1981; QC 1947; retired; Chief Justice of Saskatchewan, 1962–81; *b* Grand Forks, Minnesota, USA, 9 April 1906; *s* of John J. Culliton and Katherine Mary Kelly, Canadians; *m* 1939, Katherine Mary Hector. *Educ:* Primary educn in towns in Saskatchewan; Univ. of Saskatchewan. BA 1926, LLB 1928. Practised law in Gravelbourg, Sask., 1930–51. Served War: Canadian Armed Forces (active, overseas, Judges' Advocate Br.), 1941–46. MLA for Gravelbourg, 1935–44, re-elected, 1948; Mem. Opposition until 1951; Provincial Sec., 1938–41; Minister without portfolio, 1941–44. Apptd Judge of Court of Appeal for Sask., 1951. Chm., Sask. Jubilee Cttee, 1952–55. Univ. of Sask.: Mem. Bd of Governors, 1955–61; Chancellor, 1963–69; Mem. Bd, Can. Nat. Inst. for the Blind, 1955– (Pres. Sask. Div., 1962–); Chm., Adv. Bd, Martha House (unmarried mothers), 1955–; Chm., Sask. Revision of Statutes Cttee, 1963–65, and again 1974 until completion 1975–76. Mem., Knights of Columbus, 1930–. Hon. DCL Saskatchewan, 1962. Kt Comdr of St Gregory (Papal) 1963. *Recreations:* golf, curling; interested in football. *Address:* 1303–1830 College Avenue, Regina, Saskatchewan S4P 1C2, Canada. *T:* 569–1758. *Clubs:* Wascana Country, Assiniboia, Royal United Services Institute (all Regina, Sask.).

CULME-SEYMOUR, Comdr Sir Michael; *see* Seymour.

CULSHAW, John Douglas; Assistant Chief Scientific Adviser (Capabilities), Ministry of Defence, since 1985; *b* 22 Oct. 1927; *s* of Alfred Henry Douglas Culshaw and Dorothy Yeats Culshaw (*née* Hogarth); *m* 1951, Hazel Speirs Alexander; one *s* one *d*. *Educ:* Alderman Smith Grammar Sch., Washington, Co. Durham; University Coll., Nottingham. BSc London 1949; MSc Nottingham 1950. Joined Weapons Dept, Royal Aircraft Estabt, Min. of Supply, Farnborough, 1950; OC (Scientific) 6 Joint Services Trials Unit RAF (UK), 1956; OC (Sci.) 16 JSTU RA Weapons Research Estabt, Salisbury, S Australia, 1961; Co-ordinating Research and Development Authority Technical Project Officer, RAE, 1964; Supt Mine Warfare Br., Royal Armament R&D Estabt, MoD, Sevenoaks, 1967; Director, Scientific Adv. Br., Home Office, 1970; Dept of Chief Scientific Adviser (Army), 1972; Head of Mathematics and Assessment Dept, RARDE, MoD, Sevenoaks, 1974; Head of Defence Science II, MoD, 1975; RCDS 1976; Dep. Dir, Scientific and Technical Intelligence, 1977; Dir, Defence Operational Analysis Estabt and Asst Chief Scientific Advr (Studies), MoD, 1979–84. *Recreations:* war games, wine-making, folk-song collecting, bee-keeping. *Club:* Civil Service.

CULYER, Prof. Anthony John; Professor of Economics, University of York, since 1979; *b* 1 July 1942; *s* of late Thomas Reginald Culyer and Betty Ely (*née* Headland); *m* 1966, Sieglinde Birgit; one *s* one *d*. *Educ:* King's Sch., Worcester; Exeter Univ. (BA Hons); Univ. of California at Los Angeles. Tutor and Asst Lectr, Exeter Univ., 1965–69; Lectr, Sen. Lectr and Reader, Univ. of York, 1969–79; Deputy Director, Inst. of Social and Economic Research, Univ. of York, 1971–82. Sen. Research Associate, Ontario Economic Council, 1976, Vis. Professorial Lectr, Queen's Univ., Kingston, 1976; William Evans Vis. Professor, Otago Univ., 1979; Vis. Fellow, Australian National Univ., 1979; Vis. Prof., Trent Univ., 1985–86. *Publications:* The Economics of Social Policy, 1973; (with M. H. Cooper) Health Economics, 1973; Economic Policies and Social Goals, 1974; Need and the National Health Service, 1976; (with J. Wiseman and A. Walker) Annotated Bibliography of Health Economics, 1977; (with V. Halberstadt) Human Resources and Public Finance, 1977; Measuring Health: Lessons for Ontario, 1978; (with K. G. Wright) Economic Aspects of Health Services, 1978; The Political Economy of Social Policy, 1980; (ed) Health Indicators, 1983; (with B. Horisberger) Economic and Medical Evolution of Health Care Technologies, 1983; Economics, 1985; (with G. Terny) Public Finance and Social Policy, 1985; (with B. Jonsson) Public and Private Health Services: complementarities and conflicts, 1986; (jtly) The International Bibliography of Health Economics: a comprehensive annotated guide to English language sources since 1914; articles in Oxford Econ. Papers, Economica, Scottish Jl of Political Economy, Public Finance, Jl of Public Economics, Kyklos, Qly Jl of Economics, Jl Royal Statistical Soc., and others. *Recreation:* church music. *Address:* The Laurels, Barmby Moor, York YO4 5EJ. *T:* Pocklington 2639.

CUMBER, Sir John Alfred, Kt 1985; CMG 1966; MBE 1954; TD; Director-General, Save the Children Fund, 1976–85; *b* 30 Sept. 1920; *s* of A. J. Cumber, FRIBA, AMICE; *m* 1945, Margaret Anne Tripp; two *s*. *Educ:* Richmond County Sch.; LSE. Served War of 1939–46 (Major). HMOCS, Kenya, 1947–63 (Sen. District Comr); Administrator of the Cayman Islands, 1964–68; Comr in Anguilla, 1969; Dep. Election Comr, Southern Rhodesia/Zimbabwe, 1979–80. *Recreations:* art, music. *Address:* 7 Barton Cottages, Throwleigh, Devon EX20 2HS. *Club:* Royal Commonwealth Society.

CUMBERLEGE, Julia Frances, CBE 1985; JP; Chairman, Brighton Health Authority, since 1981; *b* 27 Jan. 1943; *d* of Dr L. U. Camm and late M. G. G. Camm; *m* 1961, Patrick Francis Howard Cumberlege; three *s*. *Educ:* Convent of the Sacred Heart, Tunbridge Wells. Mem., East Sussex AHA, 1977–81; Mem. Council, NAHA, 1982– (Vice-Chm., 1984–). Member: Lewes DC, 1966–79 (Leader, 1977–78); East Sussex CC, 1974–85 (Chm., Social Services Cttee, 1979–82). Mem., Social Security Adv. Cttee, 1980–82; Chm., Review of Community Nursing for England, 1985 (report, Community Nursing—a focus for care, 1986). Lay Mem., 1977–83, Mem. Appts Commn, 1984–, Press Council. Vice Pres., Age Concern, Brighton, 1984–. Governor: Chailey Comprehensive Sch., 1972–; Ringmer Comprehensive Sch., 1979–85; Newick Primary Sch., 1977–85. Founder: Newick Playgp; Newick Youth Club. JP East Sussex, 1973. *Recreations:* cycling, editing the Newick News, other people's gardens. *Address:* Vuggles Farm, Newick, Lewes, Sussex. *T:* Barcombe 400453.

CUMING, Frederick George Rees, RA 1974 (ARA 1969); ARCA 1954; NDD 1948; NEAC 1960; painter; *b* 16 Feb. 1930. *Educ:* University School, Bexley Heath; Sidcup Art School; Royal College of Art; travelling schol., Italy. Exhbns in Redfern, Walker, New Grafton, Thackeray, Fieldborne Galleries; Group shows at NEAC, RA, Schools' Exhbn, John Moores London Group; One Man exhbns at Thackeray Gall., galls in Chichester, Lewes, Eastbourne, Guildford, Durham, Chester, Folkstone, Canterbury, New York; works in collections: Dept. of Envt; Treasury; Chantrey Bequest; RA; Kendal Mus.; Scunthorpe Mus.; Bradford; Carlisle; Nat. Mus. of Wales; Brighton and Hove Mus.; Maidstone Mus.; Towner Gall., Eastbourne; Monte Carlo Mus.; works in galls in Canada, France, Germany, Greece, Holland. *Address:* Drayton Lodge, 23 Swan Street, Wittersham, Kent.

CUMING, Mariannus Adrian, CMG 1962; retired; Chairman, Cuming Smith & Co. Ltd, Melbourne, 1945–78, and formerly associated fertiliser companies; formerly Director: Broken Hill Pty Co. Ltd and subsidiaries; Imperial Chemical Industries of Australia and New Zealand Ltd; *b* 26 Nov. 1901; *s* of J. Cuming, Melbourne; *m* 1926, Wilma Margaret, *d* of W. C. Guthrie; three *s* one *d*. *Educ:* Melbourne Grammar Sch.; Melbourne Univ. (BSc); Imperial Coll., London (Dip.). FTS. Dir, Alfred Hospital, Melbourne, 1945–76. *Recreations:* golf, fishing. *Address:* 29 Stonnington Place, Toorak, Vic 3142, Australia. *T:* Melbourne 20 5319. *Clubs:* Australian, Melbourne, Royal Melbourne Golf (Melbourne); Weld (Perth).

CUMMING; *see* Gordon Cumming and Gordon-Cumming.

CUMMING, (John) Alan, CBE 1983; CA, FCBSI, CBIM; Executive Vice Chairman, since 1986, and Director since 1978, Woolwich Equitable Building Society; *b* 6 March 1932; *s* of John Cumming; *m* 1958, Isobel Beaumont Sked; three *s*. *Educ:* George Watson's Coll., Edinburgh. CA 1956; FCBSI 1971; CBIM (FBIM 1976). Woolwich Equitable Building Society, 1958–: Gen. Manager's Asst, 1965; Asst Gen. Man., 1967; Gen. Man., 1969; Chief Gen. Man., 1976. Pres., Bldg Socs Inst., 1973–74; Chm., Metrop. Assoc. of Bldg Socs., 1977–78; Mem. Council: Bldg Socs Assoc. (Chm., 1981–83); Internat. Union of Bldg Socs and Savings Assocs; European Fedn of Bldg Socs. Pres., Europ. Community Mortgage Fedn, 1984–87. *Recreations:* golf, bridge. *Address:* 8 Prince Consort Drive, Chislehurst, Kent BR7 5SB. *T:* 01–467 8382. *Club:* Caledonian.

CUMMING, Ronald William, ME; FTS; Director, Caulfield Institute of Technology, 1979–82, retired; *b* 9 April 1920; *s* of John Borland Cumming and Muriel Cumming (*née* Hackford); *m* 1945, Betty Lovell Gent; two *s* two *d*. *Educ:* Sydney Univ. (BEAero); Univ. of Michigan (AMPsychol); Univ. of Melbourne (ME). Research Scientist, Aeronautical Research Labs, Melbourne, 1941–55; Head, Human Engineering Gp, Aero Res. Labs, 1956–66 (research on human factors in aviation); set up Human Factors Cttee of Aust. Road Research Bd, 1962 (Chm. to 1969); Reader in Mechanical Engrg, Univ. of Melbourne, 1966–71; Prof. of Psychology, Monash Univ., 1971–78. Vis. Prof., Dept of Mech. Engrg, Univ. of Melbourne, 1982–85. Pt-time Comr, Road Safety & Standards Authority, 1975–76; Member, Adv. Council, CSIRO, 1973–78. Pres., Australian Psychological Soc., 1972–73. Hon. DEng Melbourne, 1983. *Publications:* various research papers in jls. *Recreation:* classical music. *Address:* 46 Westbrook Street, East Kew, Victoria 3102, Australia.

CUMMING-BRUCE, Rt. Hon. Sir (James) Roualeyn Hovell-Thurlow-, PC 1977; Kt 1964; MA; a Lord Justice of Appeal, 1977–85; *b* 9 March 1912; *s* of 6th Baron Thurlow and Grace Catherine, *d* of Rev. Henry Trotter; *m* 1955, Lady (Anne) Sarah Alethea Marjorie Savile, *d* of 6th Earl of Mexborough; two *s* one *d*. *Educ:* Shrewsbury; Magdalene Coll., Cambridge (Hon. Fellow, 1977). Barrister, Middle Temple, 1937 (Harmsworth Scholar); Master of the Bench, 1959; Treasurer, 1975. Served War of 1939–45 (Lt-Col RA). Chancellor of Diocese of Ripon, 1954–57; Recorder of Doncaster, 1957–58; Recorder of York, 1958–61; Junior Counsel to the Treasury (Common Law), 1959–64; Judge of the High Court, Family Div. (formerly Probate, Divorce and Admiralty Div.), 1964–77; Judge of the Restrictive Practices Court, 1968; Presiding Judge, North Eastern Circuit, 1971–74. *Address:* 1 Mulberry Walk, Chelsea, SW3. *T:* 01–352 5754. *Clubs:* Pratt's, United Oxford & Cambridge University.
See also Baron Thurlow.

CUMMINGS, Constance, CBE 1974; actress; *b* Seattle, USA; *d* of Kate Cummings and Dallas Vernon Halverstadt; *m* 1933, Benn Wolfe Levy, MBE (*d* 1973); one *s* one *d*. *Educ:* St Nicholas Girls Sch., Seattle, Washington, USA. Began stage work, 1932; since then has appeared in radio, television, films and theatre; joined National Theatre Co., 1971. Member: Arts Council, 1965–71; Council, English Stage Co., 1978–; Chm., Young People's Theatre Panel, 1966–70. *Plays include:* Goodbye, Mr Chips, 1938; The Taming of the Shrew, 1938; The Good Natured Man, 1939; St Joan, 1939; Romeo and Juliet, 1939; The Petrified Forest, 1942; Return to Tyassi, 1952; Lysistrata, 1957; The Rape of the Belt, 1957; JB, 1961; Who's Afraid of Virginia Woolf?, 1964; Justice is a Woman, 1966; Fallen Angels, 1967; A Delicate Balance, 1969; Hamlet, 1969; Children, 1974; Stripwell, 1975; All Over, 1976; Wings, 1978 (televised, USA, 1982); Hay Fever, 1980; The Chalk Garden, NY, 1982; Mrs Warren's Profession, Vienna, 1982; Eve, 1984; The Glass Menagerie, USA, then London, 1985; *National Theatre:* Coriolanus, Amphitryon 38, 1971; A Long Day's Journey into Night, 1972; The Cherry Orchard, The Bacchae, 1973; The Circle, 1974–75. Fanny Kemble at Home, one woman show, 1986; has appeared Albert Hall, performing with orchestra Peter and the Wolf and Honegger's Jeanne d'Arc au Bûcher. *Recreations:* anthropology and music. *Address:* 68 Old Church Street, SW3. *T:* 01–352 0437.

CUMMINS, Frank; Headmaster, Thomas Telford High School, Sandwell, West Midlands, since 1973; *b* 20 Jan. 1924; *s* of Archibald Ernest and Ruth Elizabeth Cummins; *m* 1st, 1943, Joyce Swale (marr. diss.); three *s*; 2nd, 1973, Brenda Valerie Swift. *Educ:* Whitgift Middle Sch., Croydon; London School of Economics and Institute of Education, London Univ. Served Royal Signals, 1943–46. Assistant Teacher, Shireland Boys' Sch., Smethwick, 1949; Dep. Headmaster, 1956, Headmaster, 1961, Sandwell Boys' Sch., Smethwick. Chm., Exams Cttee, W Midlands Exams Bd, 1983– (Vice-Chm., 1980–83); Mem. Jt Management Cttee, Midland Examining Gp for GCSE, 1985–. Chairman, Community Relations Councils: Warley, 1969, Sandwell, 1974; part-time Commissioner for Racial Equality, 1977–82; Chm., Schools Council Steering Group on Educn in a Multi-Cultural Soc., 1981–83. *Recreations:* cooking, camping, walking, theatre, City of Birmingham Symphony Orchestra. *Address:* 21 Green Street, Smethwick, Warley, West Midlands B67 7EB. *T:* (home) 021–558 8484; (school) 021–553 2615.

CUNARD, Major Sir Guy (Alick), 7th Bt *cr* 1859; *b* 2 Sept. 1911; *s* of Captain Alick May Cunard (*d* 1926) (*s* of William Samuel Cunard, *g s* of 1st Bt) and Cecil Muriel (*d* 1964), *d* of late Guy St Maur Palmes, Lingcroft, York; *S* brother, 1973; unmarried. *Educ:* Eton; RMC, Sandhurst. Gazetted 16/5th Lancers, 1931; transferred to 4/7th Royal Dragoon Guards, 1933; Captain, 1939; Major, 1946; active service France and Belgium, 1940, and Western Desert; retired, 1949. *Recreations:* steeplechasing, point-to-pointing, hunting, cricket. *Heir:* none. *Address:* The Garden House, Wintringham, Malton, N Yorks. *T:* Rillington 286.

CUNEO, Terence Tenison; portrait and figure painter, ceremonial, military and engineering subjects; *b* 1 Nov. 1907; *s* of Cyrus Cuneo and Nell Marion Tenison; *m* 1934, Catherine Mayfield Monro (*d* 1979), *yr d* of Major E. G. Monro, CBE; one *d*. *Educ:* Sutton Valence Sch.; Chelsea and Slade. Served War of 1939–45: RE, and as War Artist; special propaganda paintings for Min. of Information, Political Intelligence Dept of FO, and War Artists Advisory Cttee; representative of Illustrated London News, France, 1940. Royal Glasgow Inst. of Fine Arts; Pres. of Industrial Painters Group; Exhibitor, RA, RP, ROI Paris Salon (Hon. Mention, 1957). Has painted extensively in North Africa, South Africa, Rhodesia, Canada, USA, Ethiopia and Far East; one-man exhibition, Underground Activities in Occupied Europe, 1941; one-man exhibitions: RWS Galleries, London, 1954 and 1958; Sladmore Gall., 1971, 1972, 1974. Best known works include: Meml Paintings of El Alamein and The Royal Engineers, King George VI at The Royal Artillery Mess, Woolwich, King George VI and Queen Elizabeth at The Middle Temple Banquet, 1950; Meml Painting of The Rifle Brigade, 1951; Visit to Lloyd's of Queen Elizabeth II with the Duke of Edinburgh to lay Foundation Stone of Lloyd's New Building, 1952; Queen's Coronation Luncheon, Guildhall, The Duke of Edinburgh at Cambridge, 1953; Portraits of Viscount Allendale, KG, as Canopy Bearer to Her Majesty, 1954; Coronation of Queen Elizabeth II in Westminster Abbey (presented to the Queen by HM's Lieuts of Counties), 1955; Queen's State Visit to Denmark, Engineering Mural in Science Museum, 1957; Queen Elizabeth II at RCOG, 1960; Queen Elizabeth II at Guildhall Banquet after Indian Tour, 1961; Equestrian Portrait of HM the Queen as Col-in-Chief, Grenadier Guards, 1963; Garter Ceremony, 1964; Commonwealth Prime Ministers' Banquet, Guildhall, 1969; first official portraits of Rt Hon. Edward Heath, 1971, of Field Marshal Viscount Montgomery of Alamein, 1972; HM the Queen as Patron of Kennel Club, 1975; King Hussein of Jordan, 1980; Col H. Jones, VC, 1984; 40th Anniversary of D-Day, 1984. Set of stamps commemorating the 150th anniv. of GWR. *Publications:* (autobiog.) The Mouse and his Master, 1977; The Railway Painting of Terence Cuneo, 1984; articles in the The Studio, The Artist. *Recreations:* writing, sketching, travel, riding. *Address:* 201 Ember Lane, East Molesey, Surrey. *T:* 01–398 1986. *Club:* Junior Carlton.

CUNINGHAME, Sir John Christopher Foggo M.; *see* Montgomery Cuninghame, Sir J. C. F.

CUNINGHAME, Sir William Henry F.; *see* Fairlie-Cuninghame.

CUNLIFFE, family name of **Baron Cunliffe.**

CUNLIFFE, 3rd Baron *cr* 1914, of Headley; **Roger Cunliffe,** RIBA; MBIM; consulting architect; *b* 12 Jan. 1932; *s* of 2nd Baron and Joan Catherine Lubbock (*d* 1980); *S* father, 1963; *m* 1957, Clemency Ann Hoare; two *s* one *d*. *Educ:* Eton; Trinity Coll., Cambridge (MA); Architectural Association (AA Dipl.); Open Univ. With various architectural firms in UK and USA, 1957–65; Associate, Robert Matthew, Johnson-Marshall & Partners, 1966–69; Dir, Architectural Assoc., 1969–71; Partner, SCP, 1973–78; own practice as architectural, planning and management consultant, 1977–. Mem., Urban Motorways Cttee, 1969–72. Governor: Lancing Coll., 1967–86; Goldsmiths' Coll., 1972–78. Mem. Ct, Goldsmiths' Co., 1986–. *Publications:* (with Leonard Manasseh) Office Buildings, 1962; contrib. various professional jls. *Recreations:* photography, taxonomy, planting trees. *Heir:* *s* Hon. Henry Cunliffe, *b* 9 March 1962. *Address:* The Broadhurst, Brandeston, Woodbridge, Suffolk IP13 7AG.

CUNLIFFE, Prof. Barrington Windsor, FBA 1979; FSA; Professor of European Archaeology, Oxford University, and Fellow of Keble College, since 1972; *b* 10 Dec. 1939. *Educ:* Portsmouth; St John's Coll., Cambridge (MA, PhD, LittD). Lecturer, Univ. of Bristol, 1963–66; Prof. of Archæology, Univ. of Southampton, 1966–72. O'Donnell Lectr in Celtic Studies, Oxford Univ., 1983–84. Member: Ancient Monuments Bd for England, 1976–84; Ancient Monuments Adv. Cttee of Historic Bldgs and Monuments Commn for England, 1984–; Pres., Council for British Archaeology, 1976–79; Vice-Pres., Soc. of Antiquaries, 1982–. Hon. DLitt Sussex, 1983; Hon. DSc Bath, 1984. *Publications:* Fishbourne, a Roman Palace and its Garden, 1971; Roman Bath Discovered, 1971, rev. edn 1984; The Cradle of England, 1972; The Making of the English, 1973; The Regni, 1973; Iron Age Communities in Britain, 1974; Rome and the Barbarians, 1975; Hengistbury Head, 1978; Rome and her Empire, 1978; The Celtic World, 1979; Danebury: the anatomy of an Iron Age hillfort, 1984; contribs to several major excavation reports and articles to Soc. of Antiquaries, and in other learned jls. *Recreation:* mild self-indulgence. *Address:* Institute of Archaeology, 36 Beaumont Street, Oxford.

CUNLIFFE, His Honour Christopher Joseph; a Circuit Judge (formerly County Court Judge), 1966–82; *b* 28 Feb. 1916; *s* of Lt-Col E. N. Cunliffe, OBE, RAMC, Buckingham Crescent, Manchester, and Harriet Cunliffe (*née* Clegg); *m* 1942, Margaret Hamer Barber; two *d*. *Educ:* Rugby Sch.; Trinity Hall, Cambridge. BA 1937. Called to the Bar, Lincoln's Inn, 1938. Legal Cadet, Br. North Borneo Civil Service. 1939–40. Served RAFVR, 1941–46; Intelligence, Judge Advocate General's Branch. Practised on Northern Circuit, 1946; Dep. Coroner, City of Liverpool, 1953; Chairman: National Insurance Tribunal, Bootle, 1956–; Mental Health Review Tribunal for SW Lancs and W Ches, 1961–. *Recreations:* golf, gardening.

CUNLIFFE, Sir David Ellis, 9th Bt *cr* 1759; salesman; *b* 29 Oct. 1957; *s* of Sir Cyril Henley Cunliffe, 8th Bt and of Eileen Lady Cunliffe, *d* of Frederick William and Nora Anne Parkins; *S* father, 1969; *m* 1983, Linda Carol, *d* of John Sidney and Ella Mary Batchelor; one *d*. *Educ:* St Albans Grammar School. *Heir:* *b* Andrew Mark Cunliffe [*b* 17 April 1959; *m* 1980, Janice Elizabeth, *d* of Ronald William Kyle; one *s*]. *Address:* Sunnyside, Burnthouse Lane, Needham, near Harleston, Norfolk.

CUNLIFFE, Lawrence Francis; MP (Lab) Leigh, since 1979; *b* 25 March 1929; *m* 1950, Winifred (marr. diss.), *d* of William Haslem; three *s* two *d*. *Educ:* St Edmund's RC Sch., Worsley, Manchester. Engr, NCB, 1949–79. Member, Farnworth Borough Council, 1960–74, Bolton MDC, 1974–79; contested (Lab) Rochdale, Oct. 1972 and Feb. 1974. JP 1967–79. *Address:* House of Commons, SW1A 0AA.

CUNLIFFE, Prof. Marcus Falkner; University Professor, George Washington University, Washington DC, since 1980; *b* 5 July 1922; *s* of Keith Harold and Kathleen Eleanor Cunliffe. *Educ:* Oriel Coll., Oxford. Commonwealth Fund Fellow, Yale Univ., 1947–49; Lectr in American Studies, 1949–56, Sen Lectr, 1956–60, Prof. of Amer. Hist. and Instns, 1960–64, Univ. of Manchester; Prof. of Amer. Studies, Univ. of Sussex, 1965–80. Fellow, Center for Advanced Study in the Behavioral Sciences, Stanford, Calif., 1957–58; Vis. Prof. in American History, Harvard Univ., 1959–60; Vis. Prof., Michigan Univ., 1973; Fellow, Woodrow Wilson Internat. Centre, Washington DC, 1977–78. Member: Massachusetts Historical Soc.; Soc. of American Historians. Hon. Dr Humane Letters: Univ. of Pennsylvania, 1976; New England Coll., 1979. *Publications:* The Literature of the United States, 1954, rev. edn 1986; George Washington: Man and Monument, 1958, rev. edn 1982; The Nation Takes Shape, 1789–1837, 1959; (ed) Weems' Life of Washington, 1962; Soldiers and Civilians: The Martial Spirit in America, 1775–1865, 1968; American Presidents and the Presidency, 1969, rev. edn 1986; (ed with R. Winks) Pastmasters: Some Essays on American Historians, 1969; (ed) Sphere History of Literature, Vols 8 and 9 (American Literature), 1974–75, rev. edns 1986, 1987; The Age of Expansion 1848–1917, 1974; (ed) The Divided Loyalist: Crèvecoeur's America, 1978; Chattel Slavery and Wage Slavery, 1979. *Recreation:* the pursuit of happiness. *Address:* 1823 Lamont Street NW, Washington, DC 20010, USA. *T:* 202–387–4459.

CUNLIFFE, Peter Whalley, CBE 1980; Chairman, Pharmaceuticals Division, Imperial Chemical Industries PLC, 1976–March 1987; *b* 29 Oct. 1926; *s* of Fred Cunliffe and Lillie Whalley; *m* 1951, Alice Thérèse Emma Brunel; one *d*. *Educ:* Queen Elizabeth's Grammar Sch., Blackburn; Trinity Hall, Cambridge (Scholar; BA 1st Class Hons, 1948). Joined ICI Ltd, Pharmaceuticals Div., 1950; Services Dir, 1968; Overseas Dir, 1970; Dep. Chm., 1971. Pres., Assoc. of British Pharmaceutical Industry, 1981–83; Member: Council, Internat. Fedn of Pharmaceutical Manufrs Assoc., 1979–87 (Vice Pres., 1982–84, Pres. 1984–86); Exec. Cttee, European Fedn of Pharmaceutical Industries Assocs, 1982–85. FRSA 1981. *Recreations:* reading, walking. *Address:* c/o ICI Pharmaceuticals Division, Alderley Park, Macclesfield, Cheshire SK10 4TF.

CUNLIFFE, Captain Robert Lionel Brooke, CBE 1944; Royal Navy, retired; *b* 15 March 1895; *s* of Col Foster Cunliffe and Mrs Cunliffe (*née* Lyon); *m* 1st, 1926, Barbara Eleanor Cooper (*d* 1970); three *d*; 2nd, 1971, Christina Cooper. *Educ:* RN Colls Osborne and Dartmouth. Comdr 1930; Capt. 1936; commanded HMS Milford, 1938–39; RNC Dartmouth, 1939–42; Commodore, Dover, 1942; commanded HMS Illustrious, 1942–44 (despatches); Cdre, RN Barracks, Devonport, 1944–46; Retd, 1946. Naval Asst to UK High Comr, Canada, 1946–48. Grand Officer Order of Leopold II, Belgium, 1948. *Recreations:* cricket, shooting. *Address:* The Garden House, Pakenham, Bury St Edmunds, Suffolk. *T:* Pakenham 30236. *Club:* Army and Navy.

See also Baron Sackville.

CUNLIFFE, Stella Vivian; consultant statistician; *b* 12 Jan. 1917; *d* of Percy Cunliffe and Edith Blanche Wellwood Cunliffe. *Educ:* privately, then Parsons Mead, Ashtead; London School of Economics (BScEcon). Danish Bacon Co, 1939–44; Voluntary Relief Work in Europe, 1945–47; Arthur Guinness Son and Co. Ltd, 1947–70; Head of Research Unit, Home Office, 1970–72; Dir of Statistics, Home Office, 1972–77. Statistical Adviser to Cttee of Enquiry into Engineering Profession, 1978–80. Pres., Royal Statistical Soc., 1975–77. *Recreations:* work with youth organisations; gardening; prison after-care. *Address:* 69 Harriotts Lane, Ashtead, Surrey. *T:* Ashtead 72343.

CUNLIFFE, His Honour Thomas Alfred; a Circuit Judge (formerly County Court Judge), 1963–75; *b* 9 March 1905; *s* of Thomas and Elizabeth Cunliffe, Preston; *m* 1938, Constance Isabella Carden; one *s* one *d*. *Educ:* Lancaster Royal Grammar Sch.; Sidney Sussex Coll., Cambridge (Classical Scholar). Inner Temple: Profumo Prize, 1926; Paul Methven Prize, 1926. Called to the Bar, Inner Temple, 1927; Yarborough Anderson Scholar, 1927. Practised Northern Circuit, 1927–63; Dep. Chm., Lancs County Quarter Sessions, 1961–63; Recorder, Barrow-in-Furness, 1962–63. RAFVR (Squadron Leader), 1940–45. *Recreations:* music, gardening. *Address:* Wycoller, 3 Downham Road North, Heswall, Wirrall, Merseyside L61 6UR. *T:* 051–342 3949.

CUNLIFFE-JONES, Rev. Prof. Hubert, DD (Hon.); Professor of Theology, University of Manchester, 1968–73, now Professor Emeritus; *b* Strathfield, Sydney, NSW, Australia, 30 March 1905; *s* of Rev. Walter and Maud Cunliffe-Jones; *m* 1933, Maude Edith Clifton, BSc, DipEd Sydney; two *s* two *d*. *Educ:* Newington Coll., Sydney; Sydney and Oxford Univs; Camden Coll., Sydney; Mansfield Coll., Oxford. Congregational Minister, Warrnambool, Vic., Australia, 1928–29; Travelling Sec., Australian SCM 1929–30; Congregational Minister, Witney, Oxon, 1933–37; Tutor in Systematic Theology, Yorks United Independent Coll., Bradford, 1937–47; Principal Yorks United Independent Coll., Bradford, 1947–58; Associate Principal, Northern Congregational Coll., Manchester, 1958–66; Prof., History of Doctrine, Univ. of Manchester, 1966–68 (Lectr, 1958–66). Chm. of the Congregational Union of England and Wales, 1957–58. Hon. DD Edinburgh, 1956. *Publications:* The Holy Spirit, 1943; The Authority of the Biblical Revelation, 1945; Deuteronomy, 1951; Jeremiah, 1960; Technology, Community and Church, 1961; Christian Theology since 1600, 1970; (ed) History of Christian Doctrine, 1979; articles in Theology, Expository Times, etc. *Recreation:* drama. *Address:* 5 Wood Road, Manchester M16 9RB.

CUNLIFFE-LISTER, family name of **Baroness Masham of Ilton** and **Earl of Swinton.**

CUNLIFFE-OWEN, Sir Hugo Dudley, 3rd Bt *cr* 1920, of Bray; *b* 16 May 1966; *s* of Sir Dudley Herbert Cunliffe-Owen, 2nd Bt, and of Jean, *o d* of late Surg.-Comdr A. N. Forsyth, RN; *S* father, 1983. *Heir:* none. *Address:* Eyreton House, Quarterbridge, Douglas, Isle of Man.

CUNNANE, Most Rev. Joseph; *see* Tuam, Archbishop of, (RC).

CUNNINGHAM, Alexander Alan; Executive Vice President, General Motors, since 1984; *b* Bulgaria, 7 Jan. 1926; naturalised citizen, US; *m* 1976, Mary Helen; one *s* three *d* of former marr. *Educ:* General Motors Inst., Michigan. BSc (Industrial Engrg) 1951. Served War of 1939–45, navigation electronics radar specialist, RAF. General Motors: Jun. Process Engr, Frigidaire Div., 1951; Asst to Frigidaire Man., NY, Gen. Motors Overseas Ops, 1952; Prodn Planning Technician for Adam Opel AG, Germany, 1953; Exec. Asst to Man. Dir, GM Ltd, London, 1956; Master Mechanic, Gen. Motors do Brasil, 1957, Works Man. 1958; Works Man., Gen. Motors Argentina SA, 1962; Man. Dir, Gen. Motors do Brasil, 1963; Man., Adam Opel's Bochum plant, 1964; Asst Gen. Manufrg Man., Adam Opel AG, 1966, Gen. Manufrg Man. 1969; Man. Dir, Adam Opel AG, 1970; Gen. Dir, European Organisations, Gen. Motors Overseas Corp., 1974–76; Vice Pres., Group Exec. Overseas, 1978; Group Exec., Body Assembly, 1980. *Address:* General Motors Corporation, 3044 West Grand Boulevard, Detroit, Mich 48202, USA. *T:* (313) 556–3525.

CUNNINGHAM, Sir Charles (Craik), GCB 1974 (KCB 1961; CB 1946); KBE 1952; CVO 1941; *b* Dundee, 7 May 1906; *s* of late Richard Yule Cunningham, Abergeldie, Kirriemuir, and Isabella Craik; *m* 1934, Edith Louisa Webster; two *d*. *Educ:* Harris Acad., Dundee; University of St Andrews. Entered Scottish Office, 1929; Private Sec. to Parliamentary Under Sec. of State for Scotland, 1933–34; Private Sec. to Sec. of State for Scotland, 1935–39; Asst Sec., Scottish Home Dept, 1939–41; Principal Asst Sec., 1941–42; Dep. Sec., 1942–47; Sec., 1948–57; Permanent Under-Sec. of State, Home Office, 1957–66; Dep. Chm., UKAEA, 1966–71; Chm., Radiochemical Centre Ltd, 1971–74. Dir, Securicor Ltd, 1971–81. Chm., Uganda Resettlement Bd, 1972–73. Mem., Nat. Radiological Protection Bd, 1971–74. Hon. LLD St Andrews, 1960. *Address:* Bankside, Peaslake, Surrey GU5 9RL. *T:* Dorking 730402. *Clubs:* Reform; New (Edinburgh).

CUNNINGHAM, David, CB 1983; Solicitor to the Secretary of State for Scotland, 1980–84; *b* 26 Feb. 1924; *s* of Robert Cunningham and Elizabeth (*née* Shields); *m* 1955, Ruth Branwell Crawford; one *s* two *d*. *Educ:* High School of Glasgow; Univ. of Glasgow (MA, LLB). Served war, 1942–47: commnd, Cameronians, 1943; Intelligence Corps (Captain), and Control Commission for Germany, 1945–47. Admitted Solicitor, 1951; entered Office of Solicitor to Secretary of State for Scotland as Legal Asst, 1954; Sen. Legal Asst, 1960; Asst Solicitor, 1966; Cabinet Office Constitution Unit, 1975–77; Dep. Solicitor, 1978–80. *Recreations:* hill walking, reading, theatre, motor-cars. *Address:* The Green Gates, Innerleithen, Peeblesshire, Scotland EH44 6NH. *T:* Innerleithen 830436.

CUNNINGHAM, George, BA, BSc; Chief Executive, Library Association, since 1984; *b* 10 June 1931; *s* of Harry Jackson Cunningham and Christina Cunningham, Dunfermline; *m* 1957, Mavis Walton; one *s* one *d*. *Educ:* Univs of Manchester and London. Nat. Service in Royal Artillery (2nd Lieut), 1954–56; on staff of Commonwealth Relations Office, 1956–63; 2nd Sec., British High Commn, Ottawa, 1958–60; Commonwealth Officer of Labour Party, 1963–66; Min. of Overseas Development, 1966–69. MP South West Islington, 1970–74, Islington South and Finsbury, 1974–83 (Lab, 1970–81, Ind, 1981–82, SDP, 1982–83). Opposition front bench spokesman (Lab) on home affairs, 1979–81. Contested: (Lab) Henley Div. of Oxfordshire, 1966; (SDP) Islington South and Finsbury, 1983. Mem., Parlt of European Community, 1978–79. *Publications:* (Fabian pamphlet) Rhodesia, the Last Chance, 1966; (ed) Britain and the World in the Seventies, 1970; The Management of Aid Agencies, 1974; Careers in Politics, 1984. *Address:* 28 Manor Gardens, Hampton, Middlesex. *T:* 01–979 6221.

CUNNINGHAM, Prof. George John, MBE 1945; Professor and Chairman, Department of Academic Pathology, Virginia Commonwealth University, Richmond, 1974–77, now Emeritus Professor; Conservator of Pathological Collection, Royal College of Surgeons; Consultant Pathologist to South East and South West Regional Health Authorities; *b* 7 Sept. 1906; *s* of George S. Cunningham and Blanche A. Harvey; *m* 1957, Patricia Champion, Brisbane, Australia. *Educ:* Royal Belfast Academical Institution; Dean Close Sch., Cheltenham; St Bartholomew's Hospital Medical Coll. MRCS, LRCP, 1931; MB, BS London, 1933; MD London, 1937; FRCPath 1964. Asst Pathologist, Royal Sussex County Hosp., Brighton, 1934–42. War Service, RAMC, Middle East and Italy (temp. Lt-Col). Senior Lectr in Pathology, St Bartholomew's Hosp., London, 1946–55; Sir William Collins Prof. of Pathology, Univ. of London, at RCS, 1955–68; Prof. of Pathology, Medical Coll. of Virginia, and Chief Laboratory Service, McGuire VA Hosp., Richmond, 1968–74. Dorothy Temple Cross Travelling Fellow in America, 1951–52; Vis. Prof., New York State Univ., 1961; Vis. Prof., Cairo Univ., 1963. Past Pres., Assoc. Clin. Path., Internat. Acad. of Pathology, Quekett Microscopical Club. Freeman, City of London. *Publications:* chap. on Gen. Pathology of Malignant Tumours in Cancer, Vol. 2, 1957; chap. on Microradiography, in Tools of Biological Research, Vol. 2, 1960; and several articles on Pathology, in medical press. *Recreation:* golf. *Address:* 57 Albany Road, St Leonard's-on-Sea, E Sussex TN38 0LJ. *Clubs:* National Liberal; Royal Blackheath Golf.

CUNNINGHAM, Lt-Gen. Sir Hugh (Patrick), KBE 1975 (OBE 1966); Director: Fairey Holdings Ltd, since 1978; Fairey Engineering Ltd, since 1981; MEL, since 1982; TREND Communications Ltd, since 1984; Chairman, LL Consultants Ltd, since 1984; *b* 4 Nov. 1921; *s* of late Sir Charles Banks Cunningham, CSI; *m* 1955, Jill, *d* of J. S. Jeffrey, East Knoyle; two *s* two *d*. *Educ:* Charterhouse. 2nd Lieut, RE, 1942; served War of 1939–45, India, New Guinea, Burma; Greece, 1950–51; Egypt, 1951–53; Instructor, Sch. of Infantry, 1955–57, RMA Sandhurst, 1957–60; Cameroons, 1960–61; CRE 3 Div., Cyprus and Aden, 1963–66; comd 11 Engr Bde, BAOR, 1967–69; comd Mons OCS, 1969–70; Nat. Defence Coll., Canada, 1970–71; GOC SW District, 1971–74; ACGS (OR), 1974–75; DCDS (OR), 1976–78, retired. Lieutenant of Tower of London, 1983–86. Col, Queen's Gurkha Engineers (formerly Gurkha Engrs), 1976–81; Col Comdt, RE, 1976–81; Col, Bristol Univ. OTC, 1977–. Master, Glass Sellers' Co., 1981. Chm. of Governors, Port Regis School, 1982–. *Recreations:* bird-watching, opera, golf. *Address:* Little Leigh, East Knoyle, Salisbury, Wilts. *T:* East Knoyle 281; 406 Howard House, Dolphin Square, SW1. *T:* 01–821 7960. *Clubs:* Athenæum, Army and Navy, MCC.

CUNNINGHAM, Group Captain John, CBE 1963 (OBE 1951); DSO 1941; DFC; Executive Director, British Aerospace, Hatfield, 1978–80; *b* 27 July 1917; *s* of late A. G. Cunningham and of E. M. Cunningham. *Educ:* Whitgift. Apprenticed to De Havilland Aircraft Co., Hatfield, 1935–38; employed, 1938–Aug. 1939, with De Havillands, Light Aircraft Development and Test Flying. Called up Aug. 1939; joined AAF, 1935; commanded 604 Sqdn, 1941–42; Staff job, 1942–43; commanded 85 Sqdn, 1943–44 (DSO and two bars, DFC and bar); Group Capt. Night Operations HQ 11 Group, 1944. Chief Test Pilot, de Havilland Aircraft Co., 1946–77; Exec. Dir, Hawker Siddeley Aviation, 1963–77. International Record Flight, 16 Oct. 1957: London to Khartoum direct; distance 3,064 statute miles in 5 hrs 51 mins, by Comet 3; average speed 523 statute mph. Derry and Richards Memorial Medal of Guild of Air Pilots and Air Navigators for 1965; Segrave Trophy, 1979; Air League Founders' Medal, 1979. *Address:* Canley, Kinsbourne Green, Harpenden, Herts.

CUNNINGHAM, Dr John A., (Jack); MP (Lab) Copeland, since 1983 (Whitehaven, Cumbria, 1970–83); *b* 4 Aug. 1939; *s* of Andrew Cunningham; *m* 1964, Maureen; one *s* two *d*. *Educ:* Jarrow Grammar Sch.; Bede Coll., Durham Univ. Hons Chemistry, 1962; PhD Chemistry, 1966. Formerly: Research Fellow in Chemistry, Durham Univ.; School Teacher; Trades Union Officer. PPS to Rt Hon. James Callaghan, 1972–76; Parly Under-Sec. of State, Dept of Energy, 1976–79; Opposition Spokesman on Industry, 1979–83; elected to Shadow Cabinet, 1983; spokesman on the Environment, 1983–. *Recreations:* fell walking, squash, gardening, classical and folk music, reading, listening to other people's opinions. *Address:* House of Commons, SW1.

CUNNINGHAM, Merce; Artistic Director, Merce Cunningham Dance Company, since 1953; *b* 18 April 1919; *s* of Clifford D. Cunningham. *Educ:* Cornish Inst. of Allied Arts, Seattle, Washington. Martha Graham Dance Co., 1939–45; 1st solo concert, NY, 1944; choreographed: The Seasons, for Ballet Society (later NY City Ballet), 1947; Un Jour ou deux, for Ballet of Paris Opéra, 1973; more than 100 works for own company; other works revived for NY City Ballet, American Ballet Theatre, Ballet Rambert, Théâtre du Silence, France, Ohio Ballet, Boston Ballet. Hon. Mem., Amer. Acad. and Inst. of Arts and Letters, 1984. DLitt Univ. of Illinois, 1972. Samuel H. Scripps American Dance Festival Award for lifetime contribs to dance, 1982; Award of Honor for Arts and Culture, NY, 1983; MacArthur Award, 1985; Kennedy Center Honors, 1985; Laurence Olivier Award, 1985. Comdr, Order of Arts and Letters, France, 1982. *Publications:* Changes: notes on choreography (ed Frances Starr), 1968; Le Danseur et la danse: entretiens avec Jacqueline Lesschaeve, 1980, English edn The Dancer and the Dance, 1985; articles in 7 Arts, trans/formation, TriQuarterly. *Address:* 463 West Street, New York, NY 10014, USA. *T:* 212 255 8240.

CUNNINGHAM, Robert Kerr, CMG 1983; PhD; FIBiol; FRSC; Chief Natural Resources Adviser, Overseas Development Administration, 1976–83, and Head of Natural Resources Department, 1980–83; *b* 7 June 1923; *s* of John Simpson Cunningham and Agnes Stewart Cunningham; *m* 1947, Jean Sinclair (*née* Brown); one *s* one *d*. *Educ:* Bathgate Acad., Scotland; Edinburgh Univ. (BSc); London Univ. (PhD). FRIC 1964. Served War, RAF, 1942–46. Science Teacher, W Lothian County Educn Cttee, 1947–50; Science Lectr and Chemist, Govt of Bahamas, 1950–55; Colonial Res. Fellowship, Rothamsted Experimental Stn, 1955–56; Res. Off., W African Cocoa Res. Inst., Gold Coast and Ghana, 1956–60; Principal Scientific Off., Rothamsted Experimtl Stn, 1960–64; Prof. of Chemistry and Soil Science, Univ. of WI, Trinidad, 1964–67; Adviser on Res. and Nat. Resources, Min. of Overseas Develt, 1967–76. *Publications:* many scientific papers dealing mainly with soil chem. and plant nutrition in jls; several reports on organisation of R&D in developing countries; (co-author) reports on Brit. and internat. aid in natural resources field. *Recreations:* walking, reading, golf. *Address:* 35 Clarence Road, Harpenden, Herts AL5 4AH. *T:* Harpenden 4203. *Club:* Royal Air Force.

CUNYNGHAME, Sir Andrew (David Francis), 12th Bt *cr* 1702; FCA; *b* 25 Dec. 1942; *s* of Sir (Henry) David St Leger Brooke Selwyn Cunynghame, 11th Bt, and of Hon. Pamela Margaret Stanley, *qv*; *S* father, 1978; *m* 1972, Harriet Ann, *d* of C. T. Dupont, Montreal; two *d*. *Educ:* Eton. *Heir:* *b* John Philip Henry Michael Selwyn Cunynghame [*b* 9 Sept. 1944; *m* 1981, Marjatta, *d* of Martti Markus; one *s* one *d*]. *Address:* 69 Hillgate Place, W8; The Old School House, Williamscote, Banbury, Oxon. *Club:* Brooks's.

CUNYNGHAME, Sir James Ogilvy B.; *see* Blair-Cunynghame.

CUOMO, Mario Matthew; Governor of New York State, since 1983; lawyer; Democrat; *b* 15 June 1932; *s* of Andrea and Immaculata Cuomo; *m* 1954, Matilda M. Raffa; two *s* three *d*. *Educ:* St John's Coll., NY (Latin Amer. Studies, English, Philosophy; BA 1953); St John's Univ. (LLB 1956). Admitted to NY Bar, 1956, US Supreme Court, 1960; Asst to Judge A. P. Burke, NY State Court of Appeals, 1956–58; joined Corner, Weisbrod, Froeb & Charles (later Corner, Finn, Cuomo & Charles), 1958, Partner, 1963–75; Prof., St John's Univ. Law Sch., 1963–73; Sec. of State for NY, 1975–78 (Chm., NY Urban & Rural Affairs, Adv. Council on Disabled; 1st NY Ombudsman); Lt-Governor, NY, 1979–82. *Publications:* The Forest Hills Controversy: a report and comment, 1972; Forest Hills Diary: the crisis of low income housing, 1974; Diaries of Mario M. Cuomo: the campaign for Governor, 1984; articles in legal jls. *Address:* State Capitol, Albany, NY 12224, USA.

CUPITT, Rev. Don; Dean of Emmanuel College, since 1965 and University Lecturer in Divinity, Cambridge, since 1973; *b* 22 May 1934; *s* of Robert and Norah Cupitt; *m* 1963, Susan Marianne (*née* Day); one *s* two *d*. *Educ:* Charterhouse; Trinity Hall, Cambridge; Westcott House, Cambridge. Curate, St Philip's Church, Salford, 1959–62; Vice-Principal, Westcott House, Cambridge, 1962–65. Hon. DLitt Bristol, 1985. *Publications:* Christ and the Hiddenness of God, 1971; Crisis of Moral Authority, 1972; The Leap of Reason, 1976; The Worlds of Science and Religion, 1976; (with Peter Armstrong) Who Was Jesus?, 1977; Jesus and the Gospel of God, 1979; The Nature of Man, 1979; The Debate about Christ, 1979; Explorations in Theology, 1979; Taking Leave of God, 1980; The World to Come, 1982; The Sea of Faith, 1984 (TV series, 1984); Only Human, 1985; Life Lines, 1986. *Recreation:* family life. *Address:* Emmanuel College, Cambridge CB2 3AP.

CURE, (George) Nigel C.; *see* Capel Cure.

CURIE, Eve, (Mrs Henry R. Labouisse), writer and journalist; *b* Paris, 6 Dec. 1904; *d* of late Marie and Pierre Curie; *m* 1954, Henry Richardson Labouisse, *qv*. *Educ:* by governesses, generally Polish; Sévigné College; Bachelor of Science and Bachelor of Philosophy. Accompanied her mother in her tour of the US 1921; devoted several years to the study of the piano and gave her first concert in 1925 in Paris; later she took up musical criticism and under a pseudonym acted for several years as musical critic of the weekly journal Candide; after the death of her mother in 1934 she collected and classified all the papers, manuscripts, and personal documents left by Mme Curie and went to Poland in 1935 to obtain material as to Mme Curie's youth; wrote Mme Curie's biography; went to America again in 1939 and has gone several times since on lecture tours; was a co-ordinator of the women's war activities at the Ministry of Information in Paris at the beginning of the war, until she went on a lecture tour in the USA; came back to Paris 2 May 1940; after the French capitulation went to live in London for six months, then to America for her third lecture tour; Vichy Govt deprived her of French citizenship in April 1941; in 1942, travelled, as a war correspondent to the battlefronts of Libya, Russia, Burma, China; enlisted in the Fighting French corps, Volontaires Françaises, 1943, as a private; received basic training in England; 2nd Lieut 1943; 1st Lieut 1944. Co-publisher of Paris-Presse, an evening paper in Paris, 1944–49. Special Adviser to the Sec.

Gen. of NATO, Paris, Aug. 1952–Nov. 1954. *Publications:* Madame Curie (in US), 1937 (trans. into 32 langs); Journey Among Warriors, 1943. *Recreation:* swimming. *Address:* 1 Sutton Place South, New York, NY 10022, USA.

CURLE, James Leonard; Member and Managing Director, Civil Aviation Authority, since 1984; *b* 14 Nov. 1925; *s* of Leonard and Mary Curle; *m* 1952, Gloria Madaleine Roch; one *s* one *d*. *Educ:* St Joseph's Academy, Blackheath; SE London Technical College; Borough Polytechnic. CEng, MIEE. Royal Signals, 1944–49; joined Telecommunications Div., MTCA, 1957; Dir Telecommunications, ATS, 1976–79, Dir Gen. Telecommunications, NATS, 1979–84. *Address:* Civil Aviation Authority, CAA House, 45–59 Kingsway, WC2B 6TE.

CURLE, Sir John (Noel Ormiston), KCVO 1975 (CVO 1956); CMG 1966; HM Diplomatic Service, retired; *b* 12 Dec. 1915; *s* of Major W. S. N. Curle, MC, Melrose, Scotland; *m* 1st, 1940, Diana Deane; one *s* one *d*; 2nd, 1948, Pauline, *widow* of Capt. David Roberts; one step *s* two step *d*. *Educ:* Marlborough; New Coll., Oxford. 1st Class Hons, MA, Laming Travelling Fellow of Queen's Coll. Diplomatic Service, 1939; Irish Guards, 1939; War Cabinet Secretariat, 1941–44. Has served in Lisbon, Ottawa, Brussels, Stockholm (Counsellor), Athens (Counsellor); Boston (Consul-Gen., 1962–66); Ambassador to: Liberia, 1967–70 and Guinea, 1968–70; the Philippines, 1970–72; Vice Marshal of Diplomatic Corps, 1972–75; retired 1975; Dir of Protocol, Hong Kong, 1976–85. Liveryman, Masons Company. *Recreations:* skiing (represented Oxford *v* Cambridge, and British Univs *v* Swiss Univs). *Address:* Appletree House, near Aston-le-Walls, Daventry, Northants NN11 6UG. *T:* Chipping Warden 211. *Clubs:* Cavalry and Guards, Beefsteak; Hong Kong.

CURNOW, Elizabeth Ann Marguerite; QC 1985; a Recorder of the Crown Court, since 1980; *b* 5 June 1935; *d* of Cecil Curnow and Doris Curnow (*née* Behr); *m* 1981, William Neil Denison, *qv*. *Educ:* St Hilda's Sch., Whitby, Yorks; King's Coll., London (LLB). Called to the Bar, Gray's Inn, 1957, Bencher, 1985. Treasury Counsel, Mddx Crown Court, 1972–77; Central Criminal Court: Jun. Treasury Counsel, 1977–81; Sen. Prosecuting Counsel to the Crown, 1981–85. *Recreations:* reading, gardening, listening to music, walking and (recently) tapestry. *Address:* 6 King's Bench Walk, Temple, EC4Y 7DR. *T:* 01–583 0410.

CURRALL, Alexander, CB 1970; CMG 1965; Director: National Counties Building Society, since 1977 (Chairman, 1984–86); Applied Photophysics Ltd, since 1980 (Chairman, since 1981); Photophysics Research Ltd, since 1980 (Chairman, since 1981); Grantham House Ltd, since 1980 (Chairman, since 1981); The Pryors Ltd, since 1983; *b* 30 Jan. 1917; *s* of late R. T. Currall, Edinburgh; *m* 1940, Madeleine Crombie Saunders; one *s*. *Educ:* George Watson's Coll., Edinburgh; Edinburgh Univ. Min. of Supply, 1939–40; Royal Artillery and Indian Artillery, 1940–46. Successively in Min. of Supply, Min. of Materials and Board of Trade, concerned mainly with internat. economic negotiations, excepting the period 1950–54, when responsible for public trading in non-ferrous metals, and 1954–55, when holding a Commonwealth Fellowship for travel and study in USA. Seconded to Foreign Office as Dep. Consul-Gen., New York, and Dir of British Industrial Development Office, 1960–62; Minister (Commercial), British High Commn, Ottawa, 1962–66; Under-Secretary: Board of Trade, 1966–67; DEA, 1967–68; Dir, Dept for Nat. Savings, 1968–72; Man. Dir (Posts), Post Office, 1972–77. Dir, Renold Ltd, 1977–84. Manager, Royal Instn, 1972–75, 1977–80, 1981–84. *Address:* Fairlawn, Buckden, Skipton, North Yorkshire BD23 5JA. *Club:* Caledonian.

CURRAN, Harry Gibson, CMG 1953; *b* 1901; *s* of late James P. and Jessie M. Curran; *m* 1962, Betty, *d* of Harold Beazley. *Educ:* Royal Naval College, Dartmouth; University College, Oxford (MA). Served War of 1914–18 in Grand Fleet; served War of 1939–45, Middle East (despatches). Treasury Representative, South Asia, India, 1946–53; Canada, 1953–56; Head of Economic Mission, Ecuador, 1956–58; Representative World Bank, India, 1959–61; Dep. Dir, European Office, World Bank, 1961–66. *Address:* Fairmile, St Mark's Avenue, Salisbury, Wilts. *Club:* Travellers'.

CURRAN, Leo Gabriel Columbanus, CEng, FIMechE, FIMarE; Chairman, Camac Transport Co. Ltd, since 1981; *b* 23 Nov. 1930; *s* of B. L. Curran and R. Fanning; *m* 1957, Margaret Hickey; one *s* two *d*. *Educ:* St Malachy's Coll., Belfast; Dublin Coll. of Higher Technol. CEng 1974, FIMechE 1969; FIMarE 1974; MIProdE 1970. Managing Director: British Silverware Ltd, 1970–71; Delta Electrical (South African Delta Metal Electrical Pty) Ltd, 1971–73; Gen. Man. and Dir, Harland & Wolff Ltd, 1973–76; Man. Dir, Plessey Hydraulics International Ltd, 1976–79; Bd Mem. for Enginebuilding and Gen. Engrg, British Shipbuilders, 1979–80; Chm., Kenny Lithographic Printers, 1982–85. *Recreations:* music, walking. *Address:* Camac Transport Co. Ltd, Camac House, John F. Kennedy Park, Bluebell, Dublin 12, Ireland. *Club:* Institute of Directors.

CURRAN, Prof. Robert Crowe, MD; FRSE 1962; Leith Professor of Pathology, Birmingham University, 1966–86; Hon. Consultant Pathologist, Birmingham Central Health District; *b* 28 July 1921; *s* of John Curran and Sarah Crowe, Netherton, Wishaw, Lanarkshire; *m* 1947, Margaret Marion Park; one *s* one *d*. *Educ:* Glasgow Univ. MB, ChB 1943, MD 1956; FRCPath 1967; FRCP 1969; Hon. FFPath, RCPI, 1983. RAMC, 1945–47. Lectr in Pathology, Glasgow Univ., 1950–55. Sen. Lectr and Cons. Pathologist, Sheffield Univ., 1955–58; Prof. of Pathology, St Thomas's Hospital Medical Sch., 1959–66. Registrar, Royal Coll. of Pathologists, 1968–73, Vice-Pres., 1977–80, Pres., 1981–84; Mem., GMC, 1979–86; Hon. Sec., Conf. of Med. Royal Colls and their Faculties in UK, 1982–86. *Publications:* Colour Atlas of Histopathology, 1966, 3rd edn 1985; The Pathological Basis of Medicine, 1972; Gross Pathology—a Colour Atlas, 1974; scientific papers on lymphoid tissue, disorders of connective tissue, etc. *Recreations:* golf, music. *Address:* 34A Carpenter Road, Edgbaston, Birmingham B15 2JH.

See also Sir S. C. Curran.

CURRAN, Sir Samuel (Crowe), Kt 1970; FRS 1953; FRSE 1947; FEng 1983; Visiting Professor in Energy Studies at the University of Glasgow, since 1980; Principal and Vice-Chancellor, University of Strathclyde, 1964–80; *b* 23 May 1912; *s* of John Curran, Kinghorn, Fife, and Sarah Owen Crowe, Ballymena, Ulster; *m* 1940, Joan Elizabeth, *yr d* of Charles William Strothers and Margaret Beatrice (*née* Millington); three *s* one *d*. *Educ:* Glasgow Univ. (MA, BSc; PhD 1937; DSc 1950); St John's Coll., Cambridge (PhD Cantab, 1941; Hon. Fellow, 1971). Cavendish Laboratory, 1937–39; RAE, 1939–40; Min. of Aircraft Production and Min. of Supply, 1940–44; Manhattan Project (Min. of Supply), Univ. of California, 1944–45 (Invention of Scintillation Counter, 1944). Natural Philosophy, Glasgow Univ. 1945–55; UK Atomic Energy Authority, 1955–58; Chief Scientist, AWRE, Aldermaston, Berks, 1958–59. Principal, Royal Coll. of Science and Technology, Glasgow, 1959–64. Pres., Scottish Soc. for the Mentally Handicapped, 1954–. Member: Council for Scientific and Industrial Research, 1962–65; Science Research Council, 1965–68; Adv. Council on Technology, 1965–70; Chairman: Adv. Cttee on Med. Research, 1962–75; Adv. Bd on Relations with Univs, 1966–70; Electricity Supply Res. Council, 1978–80 (Dep. Chm., 1980–82); Dep. Chm., Electricity Council, 1977–79; Chief Scientific Adviser to the Sec. of State for Scotland, 1967–77; Member: Oil Develt Council for Scotland, 1973–78; Adv. Cttee on Safety of Nuclear Installations, 1977–80; Radioactive Waste Management Adv. Cttee, 1978–81; Adv. Council of A Power for Good (APG), 1978–; UK Nat. Commn for Unesco, and Educn Adv. Cttee, 1978–. Director: Scottish Television, 1964–82; Hall Thermotank Ltd, 1969–76; Cetec Systems Ltd, 1965–77; Internat. Res. & Develt Co. Ltd, 1970–78; Gen. Steels Div., BSC, 1970–73; Nuclear Structures (Protection) Ltd, 1981–. Hon. Pres., Scottish Polish Cultural Assoc., 1972–; Pres., St Andrews' Soc., Glasgow, 1982–. FRCPS (Hon.) 1964; Hon. LLD: Glasgow, 1968; Aberdeen, 1971; Hon. ScD Lodz, 1973; Hon. DSc Strathclyde, 1980; Hon. DEng Nova Scotia, 1982. Freeman, Motherwell and Wishaw, 1966; City of Glasgow, 1980. DL Glasgow, 1969. St Mungo Prize, 1976. Comdr, St Olav (Norway), 1966; Comdr, Order Polish People's Republic, 1976. *Publications:* (with J. D. Craggs) Counting Tubes, 1949; Luminescence and the Scintillation Counter, 1953; Alpha, Beta and Gamma Ray Spectroscopy, 1964; (jt) Energy Resources and the Environment, 1976; (with J. S. Curran) Energy and Human Needs, 1979; papers on nuclear researches and education in Proc. Royal Society. *Recreations:* horology, golf. *Address:* 93 Kelvin Court, Glasgow G12 0AH. *Clubs:* Caledonian; Royal Scottish Automobile (Glasgow).

See also R. C. Curran.

CURREY, Rear-Adm. Edmund Neville Vincent, CB 1960; DSO 1944; DSC 1941; *b* 1 Oct. 1906; *s* of Dr and Mrs E. F. N. Currey, Lismore, Co. Waterford, Ireland; *m* 1941, Rosemary Knight; one *d*. *Educ:* Royal Naval Colls, Osborne and Dartmouth. Joined RNC Osborne 1920; served in submarines and destroyers as junior officer; served War of 1939–45; commanded HM ships Wrestler, Escapade and Musketeer; Comdr, 1942; Capt., 1949; subsequently served with British Naval Mission to Greece; Naval Asst to Adm. Commanding Reserves; in command of HMS Bermuda; Naval Asst to Second Sea Lord; Rear-Adm., 1958; Chief of Staff to C-in-C, Portsmouth, 1958–61, retired. Polish Gold Cross of Merit, with swords, 1943. *Recreation:* golf. *Address:* 75 Great Pulteney Street, Garden Flat, Bath, Avon. *T:* Bath 63743.

CURREY, Prof. Harry Lloyd Fairbridge, FRCP; Arthritis and Rheumatism Council Professor of Rheumatology, University of London, since 1983; Director, Bone and Joint Unit, London Hospital Medical College, since 1976; *b* 5 June 1925; *s* of late Ronald Fairbridge Currey and of Dorothy (*née* White); *m* 1st, 1950, Chrystal Komlosy (decd); one *s* two *d*; 2nd, 1973, Jacqueline Harris. *Educ:* Cordwalles, S Africa; Michaelhouse, Natal; Univ. of Cape Town (MB, ChB 1950, MMed 1960). FRCP 1971 (MRCP 1962). Intern, Groote Schuur Hosp., and House Officer, City Hosp. and Peninsular Maternity Hosps, Cape Town, 1951–53; gen. practice, Port Elizabeth, 1953–58; Med. Registrar, Groote Schuur Hosp., Cape Town, 1959–61; Intern, Hammersmith Hosp., London, 1962; Registrar, Dept of Rheumatology, London Hosp., 1963–65; London Hosp. Med. College: Sen. Lectr, 1965–70; Reader in Rheumatol., 1970–74; Prof of Rheumatol., 1974–83; Res. Fellow, Southwestern Med. Sch., Dallas, Texas, 1966. Philip Ellman Lectr, RCP, 1977. Pres., Heberden Soc., 1980–81; Heberden Round presented 1972. Editor, Annals of the Rheumatic Diseases, 1983–. *Publications:* Mason and Currey's Clinical Rheumatology, 1970, 4th edn 1986; Essentials of Rheumatology, 1983; (with S. A. Hull) Rheumatology for GPs, 1986; articles on rheumatol topics in learned jls. *Recreations:* gardening, music. *Address:* The Heights, Galloway Road, Bishop's Stortford, Herts CM23 2HS. *T:* Bishop's Stortford 54717.

CURRIE, Prof. Sir Alastair (Robert), Kt 1979; Professor of Pathology, Edinburgh University, 1972–86; Pathologist, Royal Infirmary of Edinburgh; Consultant Pathologist, Lothian Health Board; *b* 8 Oct. 1921; *s* of late John Currie and Maggie Mactaggart; *m* 1949, Jeanne Marion Clarke, MB, ChB; three *s* two *d*. *Educ:* High Sch. and Univ. of Glasgow. BSc; MB, ChB Glasgow; FRCPE; FRCP Glasgow; FRCP; FRCPath; FRSE. RAMC 1949–51; Lectr in Pathology, Univ. of Glasgow 1947–54; Sen. Lectr in Pathology, Univ. of Glasgow, and Cons. Pathologist, Royal Infirmary, Glasgow, 1954–59; Head, Div. of Pathology, Imperial Cancer Research Fund, London, 1959–62; Regius Prof. of Pathology, Univ. of Aberdeen, 1962–72. Chairman: Standing Adv. Cttee on Laboratory Services, 1968–72; Biomedical Res. Cttee, 1975–78; Jt MRC and NRPB Cttee on Radiological Protection, 1974–81; MRC/CRC Cttee for Jtly Supported Insts, 1978–80; CRC/MRC Cttee for Inst. of Cancer Research, 1980–83; Co-ordinating Cttee for Cancer Res., 1980–81; Member: MRC, 1964–68 and 1976–80 (Chm., Cell Biology and Disorders Bd, 1976–78); Scottish NE Regional Hosp. Bd, 1966–71; Council, RCPath, 1968–71; Council, RSE, 1980–83; Scottish Health Services Council, 1969–72; Chief Scientist's Cttee, Scottish Home and Health Dept, 1974–78; Court, Edinburgh Univ., 1975–78; Bd of Dirs, Inveresk Research International, 1980–; Sci. Adv. Council, Alberta Heritage Foundn for Med. Res., 1982–; Assembly, Gen. Motors Cancer Research Foundn, 1982–86; UK Co-ordinating Cttee for Cancer Res., 1984–; Cancer Research Campaign: Mem. Exec. Cttee and Council, 1977– (Chm. Exec. Cttee, 1983–); Mem., 1969–83, Chm., 1978–83, Scientific Cttee. Chm., Bd of Govrs, Beatson Inst. of Cancer Res., 1984–. Hon. DSc: Birmingham, 1983; Aberdeen, 1985. *Publications:* papers in scientific and med. jls. *Address:* 42 Murrayfield Avenue, Edinburgh EH12 6AY. *T:* 031–337 3100; Grianan, Strathlachlan, Strachur, Argyll. *T:* Strachur 769. *Club:* New (Edinburgh).

CURRIE, Sir Alick Bradley, 6th Bt *cr* 1847; retired; *b* 8 June 1904; *s* of George Hugh Currie (*d* 1951) (*g s* of 1st Bt) and Grace, *d* of A. F. Miller, Farmington, New Mexico, USA; *S* kinsman, Sir Walter Mordaunt Cyril Currie, 5th Bt, 1978. Formerly in Radio Communications with US Navy and Federal Aviation, 1923–50; US Representative, ICAO, 1945–50, attending numerous world-wide confs. *Heir: nephew* Donald Scott Currie [*b* 1930; *m* 1st, 1948, Charlotte (marr. diss. 1951), *d* of Charles Johnstone; one *s* two *d*; 2nd, 1952, Barbara Lee, *d* of A. P. Garnier; one *s* two *d*]. *Address:* Tenacre Ranch, 13467 County Road 501, Bayfield, Colorado 81122, USA.

CURRIE, Austin; *see* Currie, J. A.

CURRIE, Edwina; MP (C) Derbyshire South, since 1983; Parliamentary Under-Secretary of State for Health and Social Security, since 1986; *b* 13 Oct. 1946; *m* 1972, Raymond F. Currie, BA, FCA; two *d*. *Educ:* Liverpool Inst. for Girls; Oxford Univ. (MA 1972); London Sch. of Econs and Pol Science (MSc 1972). Teaching and lecturing posts in econs, econ. history and business studies, 1972–81. Birmingham City Council: Mem., 1975–86; Chm., Social Services Cttee, 1979–80; Chm., Housing Cttee, 1982–83. Chm., Central Birmingham HA, 1981–83; Member: Birmingham AHA, 1975–82; Birmingham Community Relations Council, 1979–83; Local Review Cttee, HM Prison Winson Green, 1981–83. PPS to Sec. of State for Educn and Science, 1985–86; Mem., Parly Select Cttee on Social Services, 1983–86. Mem., BBC Gen. Adv. Council, 1985–. Vice-Pres., Fedn of Conservative Students, 1983–84; Vice-Pres., various univ. conservative assocs. *Publications:* Financing our Cities (Bow Group pamphlet), 1976; newspaper articles in national and local press. *Recreations:* family, domestic arts, swimming. *Address:* House of Commons, SW1A 0AA. *T:* 01–219 3611. *Club:* Swadlincote Conservative (Derbyshire).

CURRIE, James McGill; Counsellor, UK Permanent Representation to EEC, since 1982; *b* 17 Nov. 1941; *s* of late David Currie and of Mary (*née* Smith); *m* 1968, Evelyn Barbara McIntyre; one *s* one *d*. *Educ:* Blairs Coll., Aberdeen; Royal Scots Coll., Valladolid; Univ. of Glasgow (MA). Asst Principal, Scottish Home and Health Dept, 1968–72; Principal, Scottish Educn Dept, 1972–75; Secretary, Management Gp, Scottish Office, 1975–77;

Scottish Development Dept: Principal, 1977–79; Asst Sec., 1979–81; Asst Sec., Scottish Economic Planning Dept, 1981–82. *Recreations:* sport, music. *Address:* 35 Hermitage Gardens, Edinburgh. *T:* 031–447 2641.

CURRIE, (Joseph) Austin; Adviser to the European Commission, since 1984; *b* 11 Oct. 1939; *s* of John Currie and Mary (*née* O'Donnell); *m* 1968, Anne Ita Lynch; two *s* three *d. Educ:* Edendork Sch.; St Patrick's Academy, Dungannon; Queen's Univ., Belfast (BA). MP (Nat) Tyrone, Parlt of N Ireland, 1964–72; Mem. (SDLP), Fermanagh and S Tyrone, NI Assembly, 1973–75, NI Constitutional Convention, 1975–76, NI Assembly, 1982–86; Minister of Housing, Planning and Local Govt, 1974. Res. Fellow, Faculty of Economic and Social Studies, TCD, 1977–78. *Address:* Tullydraw, Donaghmore, Co. Tyrone.

CURRIE, Sir Neil (Smith), Kt 1982; CBE 1977; Australian Ambassador to Japan, since 1982; *b* 20 Aug. 1926; *s* of Sir George Currie; *m* 1951, Geraldine Evelyn; two *s* two *d. Educ:* Wesley Coll., Perth, W Australia; Univ. of Western Australia (BA). Department of External Affairs, 1948–59; Dept of Trade and Industry, 1959–71; Secretary: Dept of Supply, 1971–74; Dept of Manufacturing Industry, 1974–76; Dept of Industry and Commerce, 1976–82. *Recreations:* golf, tennis. *Address:* Australian Embassy, 1–14 Mita 2–Chome, Minato-Ku, Tokyo. *T:* 453–0251/9. *Clubs:* Commonwealth, Federal Golf (Canberra).

CURRIE, Rev. Piers William Edward, MC 1945; Staff member, Glaven Association of Parishes, since 1986; *b* 26 Feb. 1913; *e c* of late P. A. Currie, OBE and Mrs L. A. Currie; *m* 1956, Ella Rosaleen, *y c* of late Rev. W. and Mrs Bennett-Hughes; no *c. Educ:* Rugby Sch.; Brasenose Coll., Oxford (MA). Solicitor, admitted Dec. 1939. Served War, 1940–45, in 4th Regt RHA. Sen. Legal Asst, Nat. Coal Bd, 1946–53; Asst Sec., 1953–55; Sec., W Midlands Divisional Bd, 1955–60; Sec. and Legal Adviser, 1960–62; Dep. Sec., NCB, 1962–67; Legal Adviser, Land Commission, 1967–71; Deputy Master, Court of Protection, 1971–77. Ordained deacon, 1980; priest, 1981; Hon. Curate of Holt with Edgefield, 1980–82; permanent permission to officiate, dio. Norwich, 1982; Priest in charge of Baconsthorpe and Hempstead by Holt, dio. Norwich, 1983–85. *Recreations:* gardening, natural history. *Address:* Westward House, Woodlands Close, Holt, Norfolk.

CURRIE, Rear-Adm. Robert Alexander, CB 1957; DSC 1944, bar 1945; DL; *b* 29 April 1905; 5th *s* of John Currie, Glasgow, and Rachel Thomson, Dundee; *m* 1944, Lady (Edith Margaret) Beevor (*d* 1985), *widow* of Sir Thomas Beevor, 6th Bt, and *d* of Frank Agnew, Eccles, Norfolk; one step *s* (*see* Sir Thomas Beevor, 7th Bt) three step *d. Educ:* RN Colleges, Osborne and Dartmouth. Specialised in Gunnery, 1930. Served War, 1939–45: HMS Hood; HMS Warspite, 2nd Battle of Narvik; Plans Division, Admiralty; Convoy Escort Comdr; Assault Gp Comdr, Far East; Captain RN, 1945; Captain (D) Fifth Flotilla, 1948–49; idc 1950; Director, Royal Naval Staff Coll., 1951–52; Comdg Officer, HMS Cumberland, 1953; Rear-Adm., 1954; Chief of Staff to Chairman, British Joint Service Mission, Washington, DC, 1954–57; retired, 1957. Member: Cttee of Enquiry into the Fishing Industry, 1958–60; W Suffolk County Council, 1962–74. DL, Suffolk, 1968. King Haakon VII Liberty Cross, Norway, 1945. *Recreation:* painting. *Address:* Saffron Pane, Hall Road, Lavenham, Suffolk CO10 9QU.

CURRIE, Prof. Ronald Ian, CBE 1977; FIBiol; FRSE; Director and Secretary, Scottish Marine Biological Association, since 1966; *b* 10 Oct. 1928; *s* of Ronald Wavell Currie and Elizabeth Currie; *m* 1956, Cecilia, *d* of William and Lilian de Garis; one *s* one *d. Educ:* The Univ., Glasgow (BSc 1st Cl. Hons Zool., 1949); Univ. of Copenhagen. FIBiol 1967; FRSE 1969. Hon. Prof., Heriot-Watt Univ., 1979–. Joined Royal Naval Scientific Service, 1949; seconded to National Inst. of Oceanography; Head of Biol. Dept, 1962–66. William Scoresby Expedn, S Africa, 1950; Discovery Expedn, Antarctica, 1951; res. voyages, N Atlantic, 1955–64; Chm., Biol. Planning Cttee, Internat. Indian Ocean Expedn, 1960; Indian Ocean Expedn, 1963 and 1964. Secretary: Internat. Assoc. for Biol Oceanography, 1964–66 (Pres., 1966–70); Scientific Cttee on Oceanic Res., Internat. Council of Scient. Unions, 1972–78. Chm., NERC Adv. Cttee on Internat. Ocean. Affairs, 1981–; Member: Scottish Adv. Cttee, Nature Conservancy Council; Council, N British Hotels Trust; Royal Nat. Mission to Deep Sea Fishermen; Chm., Kilmore Community Council, 1977–; Hon. Sec., Challenger Soc., 1956–. *Publications:* (with T. J. Hart) The Benguela Current (Discovery Report), 1960; scientific papers on organic prodn in the sea and fertility of the ocean. *Recreations:* cooking, hill walking, shooting, local history. *Address:* Kilmore House, Kilmore, by Oban, Argyll. *T:* Kilmore 248. *Club:* Royal Over-Seas League.

CURRY, Dr Alan Stewart; retired; Controller, Forensic Science Service, Home Office, 1976–82; *b* 31 Oct. 1925; *s* of late Richard C. Curry and of Margaret Curry; *m* 1973, J. Venise Hewitt; one *s* (by previous marriage). *Educ:* Arnold Sch., Blackpool; Trinity Coll., Cambridge (Scholar). MA, PhD, CChem, FRSC, FRCPath. Served War of 1939–45 with RAF. Joined Home Office Forensic Science Service, 1952; served in NE Region, 1952–64; Dir, Nottingham Forensic Sci. Lab., 1964–66; Dir, Home Office Central Research Estabt, Aldermaston, 1966–76. Pres., Internat. Assoc. of Forensic Toxicologists, 1969–75; UN Consultant in Narcotics; Hon. Consultant in Forensic Toxicology to RAF; Consultant in Toxicology to British Airways. Fellow, Indian Acad. of Forensic Scis; Mem., Amer. Acad. of Forensic Scis; Hon. Mem., Belg. Pharmaceutical Soc. Hon. DSc Ghent. Stas Gold Medal, Gesellschaft für Toxicologische und Forensische Chemie, 1983. *Publications:* Poison Detection in Human Organs, 1962 (3rd edn 1976); (ed) Methods in Forensic Science, vols 3 and 4, 1964–65; Advances in Forensic and Clinical Toxicology, 1973; (ed) Analytical Methods in Human Toxicology, Part 1 1985, Part 2 1986; (ed, with wife) The Biochemistry of Women: Clinical Concepts; Methods for Clinical Investigation, 1974; over 100 papers in med. and sci. and police jls. *Recreations:* sailing, amateur radio. *T:* Reading 581481. *Club:* Athenæum.

CURRY, David Maurice; Member (C) Essex North East, European Parliament, since 1979; *b* 13 June 1944; *s* of Thomas Harold Curry and Florence Joan (*née* Tyerman); *m* 1971, Anne Helene Maud Roullet; one *s* two *d. Educ:* Ripon Grammar Sch.; Corpus Christi Coll., Oxford (MA Hons); Kennedy Sch. of Govt, Harvard (Kennedy Scholar, 1966–67). Reporter, Newcastle Jl, 1967–70; Financial Times: Trade Editor, Internat. Cos Editor, Brussels Corresp., Paris Corresp., and European News Editor, 1970–79. Sec., Anglo-American Press Assoc. of Paris, 1978; Founder, Paris Conservative Assoc., 1977. European Parliament: Chm., Agriculture Cttee, 1982–84; Vice-Chm., Budgets Cttee, 1984–85; spokesman on budgetary matters for European Democratic Gp, 1985–; Gen. Rapporteur for EEC's 1987 budget. *Publication:* The Food War: the EEC, the US and the battle for world food markets, 1982. *Recreations:* digging, windsurfing, bee-keeping. *Address:* Newland End, Arkesden, Essex CB11 4HF. *T:* Clavering 368.

CURRY, John Anthony, OBE 1976; professional skater; *b* 9 Sept. 1949; *s* of Joseph Henry Curry and Rita Agnes Pritchard. *Educ:* Solihull Sch. British, European, World, and Olympic Figure Skating Champion, 1976. Founder and Director: John Curry Theatre of Skating, 1977; John Curry Sch. of Skating, 1978; Artistic Dir, John Curry Skating Co. Appeared in: A Midsummer Night's Dream, Nottingham and Open Air Theatre, Regent's Park; As You Like It, Open Air Theatre, Regent's Park; A Symphony On Ice, Royal Albert Hall, Metropolitan Opera House, NY, 1984. *Publication:* (with photographs by Keith Money) John Curry, 1978. *Recreation:* theatre. *Address:* c/o London Management, 235 Regent Street, W1.

CURRY, (Thomas) Peter (Ellison), QC 1966, 1973; *s* of Maj. F. R. P. Curry; *m* 1950, Pamela Joyce, *d* of late Group Capt. A. J. Holmes, AFC, JP; two *s* two *d. Educ:* Tonbridge; Oriel Coll., Oxford. BA 1948; MA 1951. Served War of 1939–45; enlisted 1939; commnd, 1941; 17th Indian Div., India and Burma, 1941–45. War Office, 1946. Called to Bar, Middle Temple, 1953, Bencher, 1979. QC 1966. Solicitor, 1968; partner in Freshfields, Solicitors, 1968–70; returned to Bar; re-appointed QC 1973. Pres., Aircraft and Shipbuilding Industries Arbitration Tribunal, 1978–80. Hon. Treas., Barristers' Benevolent Assoc., 1964–71, 1984–; Chm., Chancery Bar Assoc., 1980–85. Rep. Army, Oxford and Sussex at Squash Racquets (described as fastest mover in squash, 1947; triple blue, Oxford; twice cross country winner); World Student Games (5000 m), 1947; British Steeplechase champion 1948, Olympic Games, 1948. Served on AAA Cttee of Inquiry, 1967. Holder of French certificate as capitaine-mécanicien for mechanically propelled boats. *Publications:* (Joint Editor) Palmer's Company Law, 1959; (Joint Editor) Crew on Meetings, 1966, 1975. *Recreations:* work, gardening, the Turf. *Address:* Hurlands, Dunsfold, Surrey. *T:* Dunsfold 356. *Club:* Army and Navy.

CURSON, Bernard Robert, CMG 1967; HM Diplomatic Service, retired; *b* 14 Nov. 1913; *e s* of late Robert and Mabel Curson; *m* 1949, Miriam Olive Johnson (*d* 1986), Lynchburg, Virginia; one *s. Educ:* University Coll. Sch. Asst Private Sec. to Sec. of State for India, 1943–44, and 1945–46; Mem., UK Delegn to UN Assembly, 1946, 1947, 1948; Private Sec. to Sec. of State for Commonwealth Relations, 1948–50; Office of High Comr, Ceylon, 1950–52; Mem., UK Delegn to UN Wheat Conf., Geneva, 1956; Mem., UK Delegn to Colombo Plan Consultative Cttee, Wellington, 1956, and Saigon, 1957; British Information Services, Canada, 1958–64; Consul-Gen., Atlanta, USA, 1970–73. *Address:* 3804 Peachtree Road, NE, Atlanta, Ga 30319, USA. *Club:* Travellers'.

CURTEIS, Ian Bayley; television playwright; *b* 1 May 1935; *m* 1st, 1964, Mrs Joan Macdonald (marr. diss.); two *s*; 2nd, 1985, Joanna Trollope; two step *d. Educ:* unorthodox. Director and actor in theatres all over Great Britain, and BBC-tv script reader, 1956–63; BBC and ATV staff director (drama), directing plays by John Betjeman, John Hopkins, William Trevor and others, 1963–67. Chm., Cttee on Censorship, Writers' Guild of GB, 1981–85. *Television plays:* Beethoven, Sir Alexander Fleming (BBC's entry at 1973 Prague Fest.), Mr Rolls and Mr Royce, Long Voyage out of War (trilogy), The Folly, The Haunting, Second Time Round, A Distinct Chill, The Portland Millions, Philby, Burgess and Maclean (British entry 1978 Monte Carlo Fest., BAFTA nomination), Hess, The Atom Spies, Churchill and the Generals (BAFTA nomination; Grand Prize, Best Programme of 1980, NY Internat. Film and TV Fest.), Suez 1956 (BAFTA nomination), Miss Morison's Ghosts (British entry 1982 Monte Carlo Fest.), The Mitford Girls, BB and Joe (trilogy), The Falklands Play, Lost Empires (adapted from J. B. Priestley), The Trials of Lady Sackville, Eureka (1st Euroserial to be simultaneously shown in UK, Germany, Austria, Switzerland, Italy and France), George Blake Triple Spy. Also originated and wrote numerous popular television drama series; *film screenplays:* Andre Malraux's La Condition humaine, 1982; Graham Greene's The Man Within, 1983; Tom Paine (for Sir Richard Attenborough), 1983; *play:* A Personal Affair, Globe, 1982. *Publications: plays:* Long Voyage out of War (trilogy), 1971; Churchill and the Generals, 1979; Suez 1956, 1980. *Address:* The Mill House, Coln St Aldwyns, Cirencester, Glos. *Club:* Beefsteak.

CURTIN, Rt. Rev. Mgr. Canon Jeremiah John, DD; Priest-Director and Ecclesiastical Adviser, Universe Enquiry Bureau, since 1953; Canon of Southwark Diocesan Chapter, 1958; Domestic Prelate to HH Pope John XXIII, 1961, Protonotary Apostolic, 1972; Canon Theologian, Metropolitan Chapter, 1981; *b* Sileby, Leics, 19 June 1907; *e s* of late Jeremiah John Curtin and Mary Bridget Curtin (*née* Leahy). *Educ:* Battersea Polytechnic; Wimbledon Coll.; St Joseph's Coll., Mark Cross; St John's Seminary, Wonersh; Gregorian Univ., Rome. BA London 1927; DD Rome 1933 (Gregorian Univ.). Priest, 1931; Prof. of Philosophy and Theology, St John's Seminary, Wonersh, 1933–48; Vice-Rector, 1947–48; Parish Priest, St Paul's, Hayward's Heath, 1948–56; Parish Priest, Our Lady of Ransom, Eastbourne, 1956–61; Rector, Pontificio Collegio Beda, Rome, 1961–72. *Recreations:* archæology, music. *Address:* 48 Castle Street, Farnham, Surrey GU9 7JQ. *T:* Farnham 714659. *Club:* Athenæum.

CURTIS, Colin Hinton Thomson, CVO 1970; ISO 1970; Chairman, Metropolitan Public Abattoir Board, 1971–81; Member, Queensland Meat Industry Authority, 1972–78; *b* 25 June 1920; *s* of A. Curtis, Brisbane; *m* 1943, Anne Catherline Drevesen; one *s. Educ:* Brisbane Grammar School. RANR Overseas Service, 1940–45. Sec. and Investigation Officer to Chm., Sugar Cane Prices Board, 1948–49; Asst Sec. to Central Sugar Cane Prices Board, 1949; Sec. to Premier of Queensland, 1950–64; Mem., Qld Trade Missions to SE Asia, 1963 and 1964; Asst Under-Sec., Premier's Dept, 1961–64; Assoc. Dir and Dir of Industrial Development, 1964–66; Under-Sec., Premier's Dept and Clerk of Exec. Council, 1966–70; State Dir, Royal Visit, 1970; Agent-General for Queensland in London, 1970–71. *Recreations:* squash, yachting, swimming. *Address:* 117 Carlton Terrace, Manly, Qld 4179, Australia. *Clubs:* RSL Memorial, Royal Queensland Yacht, Rugby League (Queensland).

CURTIS, Prof. David Roderick, FRS 1974; FAA 1965; Professor of Pharmacology, John Curtin School of Medical Research, Australian National University, since 1973; *b* 3 June 1927; *s* of E. D. and E. V. Curtis; *m* 1952, Lauris Sewell; one *s* one *d. Educ:* Univ. of Melbourne; Australian National Univ. MB, BS Melbourne 1950, PhD ANU 1957. Dept of Physiology, John Curtin Sch., ANU: Research Scholar, 1954–56; Research Fellow, 1956–57; Fellow, 1957–59; Sen. Fellow, 1959–62; Professorial Fellow, 1962–66; Prof. of Pharmacology, 1966–68; Prof. of Neuropharmacology, 1968–73. Pres., Aust. Acad. of Sci, 1986– (Burnet Medal, 1983). *Publications:* papers in fields of neurophysiology, neuropharmacology in Jl Physiology, Jl Neurophysiol., Brain Research, Exper. Brain Research, etc. *Recreation:* tennis. *Address:* 7 Patey Street, Campbell, Canberra, ACT 2601, Australia. *T:* Canberra (062) 48–5664: John Curtin School of Medical Research, Australian National University, GPO Box 334, ACT 2601. *T:* Canberra (062) 49–2757.

CURTIS, Sir (Edward) Leo, Kt 1965; Lord Mayor of Melbourne, Australia, 1963–64 and 1964–65; *b* London, 13 Jan. 1907; *m* 1938, Elvira Lillian Prahl. Joined Melbourne City Council, Dec. 1955; retired March 1975. Past President of Retail Traders Association of Victoria. *Address:* 168 Kooyong Road, Toorak, Vic 3142, Australia. *Clubs:* Athenæum, Kelvin (Melbourne); various sporting.

CURTIS, Most Rev. Ernest Edwin, CBE 1976; Hon. Assistant Bishop of Portsmouth, since 1976; *b* 24 Dec. 1906, *s* of Ernest John and Zoe Curtis; *m* 1938, Dorothy Anne Hill (*d* 1965); one *s* one *d*; *m* 1970, Evelyn Mary Josling. *Educ:* Sherborne; Foster's Sch.; Royal College of Science, London. BSc (hons Chem.) London, 1927; ARCSc 1927; Dipl. Educn, London, 1928. Asst Master, Lindisfarne Coll., Westcliff, 1928–31; Wells Theol Coll., 1932–33; Asst Curate, Holy Trinity, Waltham Cross, 1933–36; Chaplain i/c parishes Rose Hill and Bambous, and Principal, St Paul's Theol Coll., Mauritius, 1937–44; Missions to Seamen Chaplain, Port Louis, 1944; Priest i/c St Wilfrid, Portsmouth, 1945–47; Vicar, All Saints, Portsmouth, and Chaplain, Royal Portsmouth Hospital, 1947–55; Priest i/c St

Agatha, Portsmouth, 1954–55; Vicar, St John Baptist, Locks Heath, 1955–66; Warden of Readers, Dio. Portsmouth, 1956–66; Rural Dean of Alverstoke, 1964–66; Bishop of Mauritius and Seychelles, 1966–72, of Mauritius, 1973–76; Archbishop of the Indian Ocean, 1973–76; Priest-in-charge of St Mary and St Rhadagunde, Whitwell, 1976–82. *Recreations:* walking, hill-climbing, piano. *Address:* 5 Elizabeth Gardens, Havenstreet, Ryde, Isle of Wight PO33 4DU. *T:* Isle of Wight 883049.

CURTIS, Frank; *see* Curtis, R. F.

CURTIS, Very Rev. Frank; *see* Curtis, Very Rev. W. F.

CURTIS, Rt. Rev. John Barry; *see* Calgary, Bishop of.

CURTIS, John Henry, CB 1981; FAIM, FTS; Chairman, D. Richardson & Sons Ltd, since 1982; Commissioner, Overseas Telecommunications Commission (Australia), since 1974; *b* 20 March 1920; *s* of K. H. and E. M. Curtis; *m* 1943, Patricia Foote; one *s* one *d*. *Educ:* Ipswich Grammar Sch.; Queensland Univ. (BE Hons 1950, BSc 1951, BA 1957). FIEAust 1981; FAIM 1970; FTS 1979. Dir of Posts and Telegraphs, Qld, 1971–73; Dep. Dir Gen., Postmaster-Gen.'s Dept, 1973–75; Man. Dir, Australian Telecommunications Commn, 1975–81. Pres., Victorian Div., Aust. Inst. of Management, 1979–81. Mem., Bd of Management, Defence Aerospace, 1984–. Gov., Internat. Council for Computer Communication, 1982–. Hon. Life Mem., IREE, 1982. *Address:* 36 Boyd Street, Blackburn, Vic 3130, Australia. *T:* 877 4848.

CURTIS, John S.; *see* Sutton Curtis.

CURTIS, Sir Leo; *see* Curtis, Sir E. L.

CURTIS, Michael Howard; Executive Aide to HH The Aga Khan; Director, Nation Printers and Publishers, Nairobi, Kenya, since 1959, Chairman, 1976–77; *b* 28 Feb. 1920; *e s* of Howard and late Doris May Curtis; *m* 1st, 1947, Barbara Winifred Gough; two *s* two *d*; 2nd, 1961, Marian Joan Williams (*d* 1984); two step *s*. *Educ:* St Lawrence Coll.; Sidney Sussex Coll., Cambridge (MA). Eastern Daily Press, Norwich, 1945; News Chronicle: Leader Writer, 1946; Dep. Editor, 1952; Editor, 1954–57; Dir, News Chronicle Ltd, 1954–57; Personal Aide to HH The Aga Khan, 1957–59. *Address:* La Vieille Maison, Villemetrie, 60300 Senlis, France. *Clubs:* Garrick, East India; Muthaiga (Nairobi).

CURTIS, His Honour Philip; a Circuit Judge (formerly a Judge of County Courts), 1969–80; *b* 29 April 1908; *s* of James William and Emma Curtis; *m* 1937, Marjorie Lillian Sharp; two *s* one *d*. *Educ:* St Mary's RC, Denton, Lancs; Manchester Grammar; Brasenose Coll., Oxford. Called to the Bar, Gray's Inn, 1944. *Address:* Mottram Hall Farm, Mottram St Andrew, near Macclesfield, Cheshire. *T:* Prestbury 829509.

CURTIS, Richard Herbert, QC 1977; a Recorder of the Crown Court, since 1974. *Educ:* Oxford Univ. (MA). Called to Bar, Inner Temple, 1958, Master of the Bench, 1985. Hon. Recorder, City of Hereford, 1980. *Address:* 1 King's Bench Walk, Temple, EC4. *T:* 01–353 8436.

CURTIS, Prof. (Robert) Frank, CBE 1985; PhD, DSc; FRSC, FIFST; Director, Agricultural and Food Research Council Institute of Food Research, Reading, since 1985; Professor, University of East Anglia, since 1977; *b* 8 Oct. 1926; *s* of late William John Curtis, Somerset, and Ethel Irene Curtis, Bath; *m* 1954, Sheila Rose, *y d* of Bruce Rose, Huddersfield; two *s* one *d*. *Educ:* City of Bath Sch.; Univ. of Bristol (BSc 1949, PhD 1952, DSc 1972). FRIC 1966, FIFST 1977. Johns Hopkins University: W. H. Grafflin Fellow, 1952; Instr in Chemistry, 1953; Technical Officer, ICI Ltd, Manchester, 1954–56; Res. Fellow, Univ. of WI, 1956–57; Lectr in Chem., University Coll., Swansea, 1957–62, Sen. Lectr, 1962–69; Reader, Univ. of Wales, 1969–70; Head, Chem. Div., 1970–77, Dir, 1977–85, ARC Food Res. Inst. Chm., Food Adv. Cttee, MAFF, 1983– (Chm., Food Standards Cttee, 1979–83). *Publications:* res. papers on chemistry and food science in jls of learned socs. *Address:* Manor Barn, Colton, Norwich NR9 5BZ. *T:* Norwich 880379.

CURTIS, Very Rev. (Wilfred) Frank; Provost of Sheffield, since 1974; *b* 24 Feb. 1923; *s* of W. A. Curtis, MC and Mrs M. Curtis (*née* Burbidge); *m* 1951, Muriel (*née* Dover); two *s* two *d*. *Educ:* Bishop Wordsworth's Sch., Salisbury; King's Coll., London (AKC). Served in RA, 1942–47; Major 1946. London Univ., 1947–52; Curate of High Wycombe, 1952–55; staff of Church Missionary Soc., 1955–74: Area Sec., Devon and Cornwall, 1955–65; Adviser in Rural Work, 1957–65; SW Regional Sec., 1962–65; Home Sec., 1965–74. Vice-Pres., Church Missionary Soc., 1977–; Mem., General Synod, 1977–85. Chm., Community Action Panel (S Yorks Police), 1983–86; Mem., Sheffield Council Voluntary Service, 1978–; Chm., Radio Sheffield Religious Adv. Panel, 1985–. Chaplain to Master Cutler, 1976, 1978, 1982, 1984; Chaplain (ACU) Crucible Th., Sheffield, 1986–. Hon. Fellow, Sheffield City Polytechnic, 1980. Hon. Canon, 1982, and Bishop's Comissary, 1983–, Maseno North Diocese, Kenya. *Recreations:* walking, photography, nature study. *Address:* Provost's Lodge, 22 Hallam Gate Road, Sheffield S10 5BS. *T:* Sheffield 662373 or 753434.

CURTIS, Wilfred Harry, CB 1953; CBE 1950; *b* 23 May 1897; retired as Assistant Under-Secretary of State, War Office, 1958. *Educ:* Summerleaze, Harptree, Somerset. JP County of London, 1950–58. *Address:* Rose Cottage, Hindon, Salisbury, Wilts SP3 6DP.

CURTIS, Sir William (Peter), 7th Bt *cr* 1802; *b* 9 April 1935; *s* of Sir Peter Curtis, 6th Bt, and of Joan Margaret, *d* of late Reginald Nicholson; *S* father, 1976. *Educ:* Winchester College; Trinity College, Oxford (MA); Royal Agricultural College, Cirencester. *Heir:* *cousin* Major Edward Philip Curtis, 16th/5th The Queen's Royal Lancers (retd) [*b* 25 June 1940; *m* 1978, Catherine, *d* of H. J. Armstrong, Christchurch, NZ; one *s* two *d*. *Educ:* Bradfield; RMA Sandhurst]. *Address:* Oak Lodge, Bank Street, Bishop's Waltham, Hants.

CURTISS, Air Marshal Sir John (Bagot), KCB 1981 (CB 1979); KBE 1982; FRAeS; Director and Chief Executive, Society of British Aerospace Companies, since 1984; Secretary, Defence Industries Council, since 1985; *b* 6 Dec. 1924; *s* of Major E. F. B. Curtiss, RFC; *m* 1946, Peggy Drughorn Bowie; three *s* one *d*. *Educ:* Radley Coll.; Wanganui Collegiate Sch., NZ; Worcester Coll., Oxford. Served War: Oxford Univ. Air Sqdn, 1942–43; Bomber Comd, 578 and 158 sqdns, 1944–45; Transport Comd, 51 and 59 sqdn, 1945–49; Training Comd, 1950–53; Fighter Comd, 29 and 5 sqdns, 1953–64; Dir, RAF Staff Coll., 1967–69; Stn Comdr RAF Bruggen, RAFG, 1970–72; Gp Capt Ops, HQ Strike Comd, 1972–74; SASO, HQ 11 Gp, 1974–75; Dir-Gen. Organisation, RAF, 1975–77; Comdt, RAF Staff Coll., 1977–80; Air Comdr, South Atlantic Operations, 1982; AOC No 18 Gp, 1980–83, retd. Member, Executive Committee: Air League, 1982–; Forces Help Soc., 1984–86. CBIM 1981. FRAeS 1984. *Recreations:* squash, sailing, cricket. *Address:* c/o Coutts & Co., 1 Old Park Lane, W1Y 4BS. *Clubs:* MCC, Royal Air Force, Pilgrims; Royal Lymington Yacht; Keyhaven Yacht; Royal Yacht Squadron.

CURWEN, Sir Christopher (Keith), KCMG 1986 (CMG 1982); HM Diplomatic Service; Foreign and Commonwealth Office, since 1980; *b* 9 April 1929; *s* of late Rev. R. M. Curwen and Mrs M. E. Curwen; *m* 1st, 1956, Noom Tai (marr. diss. 1977); one *s* two *d*; 2nd, 1977, Helen Anne Stirling; one *s* one *d*. *Educ:* Sherborne Sch.; Sidney Sussex Coll., Cambridge (BA). Served HM Forces, 4th Queen's Own Hussars, 1948–49 (despatches). Joined FO, 1952; Bangkok, 1954; Vientiane, 1956; FO, 1958; Bangkok, 1961; Kuala Lumpur, 1963; FO, 1965; Washington, 1968; FCO, 1971; Geneva, 1977. *Recreations:* books, gardening, motoring. *Address:* c/o Foreign and Commonwealth Office, SW1. *Club:* Travellers'.

CURZON; *see* Roper-Curzon, family name of Baron Teynham.

CURZON, family name of **Earl Howe** and **Viscount Scarsdale.**

CURZON, Leonard Henry, CB 1956; *b* 4 Jan. 1912; *s* of late Frederick Henry Curzon; *m* 1935, Greta, *e d* of late Willem and Anny van Praag; one *s*. *Educ:* Sir Walter St John's Sch.; Jesus Coll., Cambridge (Scholar, BA, LLB). Civil Servant, 1934–72: Import Duties Adv. Cttee; Air Ministry, Ministries of Aircraft Production, Supply, Aviation and Defence. IDC 1947. *Address:* Southease, Derringstone Hill, Barham, Kent. *T:* Canterbury 831449.

CUSACK, Henry Vernon, CMG 1955; CBE 1947; HM Overseas Civil Service (retired); Deputy Director General of the Overseas Audit Service, 1946–55; *b* 26 June 1895; 2nd *s* of late Edward Cusack, Bray, Co. Wicklow, and of Constance Louisa Vernon, *e d* of late Col Vernon, DL, JP, Clontarf Castle, Dublin; unmarried. *Educ:* Aravon Sch., Ireland. Served European War, 1914–19 (General Service and Victory medals), France, Belgium and North Russia, as Captain, RASC, attached RGA; entered Colonial Audit Service, 1920; Asst Auditor: Sierra Leone, 1920–22, Nigeria, 1922–28; Sen. Asst Auditor, Nyasaland, 1928–33; Asst Director, Central Office, Colonial Audit Dept London, 1933–37; Auditor, Gold Coast, 1937–46; a Governor of the King's Hospital Sch., Dublin (Chm., 1964–69). FRGS. Coronation Medal, 1953. *Address:* Our Lady's Manor, Bulloch Castle, Dalkey, Co. Dublin. *Clubs:* Naval and Military; Royal St George Yacht (Dun Laoghaire, Co. Dublin).

CUSDIN, Sidney Edward Thomas, OBE 1946; DSc (Hong Kong); FRIBA, AADip; Consultant to Firm of Cusdin, Burden and Howitt, Architects; *b* 28 July 1908; *s* of Sidney Herbert Cusdin, London; *m* 1936, Eva Eileen (Peggy), *d* of F. P. Dorizzi, London; no *c*. *Educ:* Municipal School of Arts and Crafts, Southend-on-Sea, Essex; Architectural Assoc., London. AA Holloway Scholarship, 1927; Fifth Year Travelling Studentship, 1929; joined staff of Stanley Hall & Easton and Robertson: British Pavilions at Brussels Internat. Exhibition and Johannesburg Exhibition; elected Member of AA Council, 1937, and worked on RIBA Cttees. Served War of 1939–45, RAF, on staff of HQ, No. 26 Group (despatches twice, OBE). Re-joined firm of Easton & Robertson, 1946 (firm later known as Easton & Robertson, Cusdin, Preston and Smith, until 1965 when this partnership was dissolved). Pres. AA, 1950–51; Mem. Council RIBA, 1950–51. Awarded Henry Saxon Snell Prize and Theakston Bequest, 1950; Principal works: London: Development of the Hosp. for Sick Children, Great Ormond Street, British Postgraduate Medical Fedn, and London Univ., Inst. of Child Health; Medical Coll. of St Bartholomew's Hosp., New Hostel and Labs; Middlesex Hosp. Medical Sch.; New Sch. Buildings and Astor Coll.; National Inst. for Medical Research Develt, Mill Hill; Cambridge: Dept of Engineering, New Workshops and Laboratories; Univ. Chemistry Laboratories; United Cambridge Hosps, Addenbrooke's Hosp., Hills Rd, New Develt; MRC, extension of Lab. of Molecular Biology; Harlow: Princess Alexandra Hosp.; Belfast: Queen's Univ. of Belfast, Inst. of Clin. Science; Royal Victoria Hosp. Develt; Royal Belfast Hosp. for Sick Children, alterations and additions; Malaya: plans for Develt of Univ. of Malaya; Hong Kong; plans for develt of Univ. of Hong Kong; Cons. Architect for: Queen Elizabeth Hosp., Hong Kong (awarded RIBA Bronze Medal); Faculty of Medicine, Univ. of Riyad, Saudi Arabia. Chm., British Consultants Bureau, 1972–74. Dir, Brendoncare Foundn, 1984–. Hon. Freeman, Apothecaries' Soc., 1981. *Publications:* (with James Crooks) Suggestions and Demonstration Plans for Hospitals for Sick Children, 1947. *Recreations:* theatre, travel, fishing; spending time in believing that "WS" was Shakespeare. *Address:* 27 Devonshire Close, W1N 1LG. *T:* 01–637 1891; 34 Ringshall, Little Gaddesden, near Berkhamsted, Herts. *Clubs:* Savile, Royal Air Force, The Sette of Odd Volumes.

CUSENS, Prof. Anthony Ralph, PhD; FRSE; FICE, FIStructE, FAmSCE; Professor and Head of Department of Civil Engineering, University of Leeds, since 1979; *b* 24 Sept. 1927; *s* of James Cusens and May Edith (*née* Thomas); *m* 1953, Pauline Shirin German; three *d*. *Educ:* St John's Coll., Southsea, University Coll. London (BSc Eng; PhD 1955). FICE 1966; FIStructE 1972; FAmSCE 1972; FRSE 1974. Res. Engr, British Cast Concrete Fedn, 1952–54; Sen. Lectr, RMCS, Shrivenham, 1954–56; Sen. Lectr, Univ. of Khartoum, Sudan, 1956–60; Prof. of Structl Engrg, Asian Inst. of Technol., Bangkok, 1960–65; Prof. of Civil Engineering: Univ. of St Andrews, 1965–67; Univ. of Dundee, 1967–78. Dir, Harry Stanger Ltd, 1984–; Consultant, Posford Pavry and Partners, 1977–. Visitor, Transport and Road Res. Lab., 1982–; Pres., Concrete Soc., 1983–84; Vice Chm., British Gp, Internat. Assoc. for Bridge and Structl Engrg, 1977–; Chm., Jt Bd of Moderators of ICE and IStructE, 1986– (Dep. Chm., 1982–86); Mem., Structl Bd, ICE, 1981–85. Chm., Editorial Bd, Magazine of Concrete Research, 1984– (Mem. Bd, 1970–). *Publications:* (jtly) Bridge Deck Analysis, 1975; Finite Strip Method in Bridge Engineering, 1978; res. papers on concrete technol. and structures. *Recreations:* golf, gardening. *Clubs:* East India; Pannal Golf (Harrogate).

CUSHING, David Henry, DPhil; FRS 1977; Deputy Director, Fisheries Research, England and Wales, 1974–80; *b* 14 March 1920; *s* of W. E. W. Cushing and Isobel (*née* Batchelder); *m* 1943, Diana R. C. Antona-Traversi; one *d*. *Educ:* Duke's Sch., Alnwick; Newcastle upon Tyne Royal Grammar Sch.; Balliol Coll., Oxford (MA, DPhil). RA, 1940–45; 1st Bn, Royal Fusiliers, 1945–46. Fisheries Lab., 1946–80. Rosenstiel Gold Medal for Oceanographic Science, Rosenstiel Inst. for Marine and Atmospheric Scis, Miami, 1980; Albert Medal for Oceanography, Institut Océanographique, Paris, 1984. *Publications:* The Arctic Cod, 1966; Fisheries Biology, 1968 (USA); Detection of Fish, 1973; Fisheries Resources and their Management, 1974; Marine Ecology and Fisheries, 1975; Science and the Fisheries, 1977; Climate and Fisheries, 1982. *Address:* 198 Yarmouth Road, Lowestoft, Suffolk. *T:* Lowestoft 65569.

CUST, family name of **Baron Brownlow.**

CUSTANCE, Michael Magnus Vere, CB 1959; *b* 3 Jan. 1916; *e s* of late Mrs Arthur Long (Marjorie Bowen, novelist); *m*; one *s* one *d*. *Educ:* St Paul's (schol.); The Queen's Coll., Oxford (open hist. schol., BA Hons, 1st cl., Mod. Hist., 1937). Asst Principal, Board of Trade, 1938; Ministry of Shipping, 1939; Royal Air Force, 1941–45; Principal, Ministry of War Transport, 1943; Asst Sec., Min. of Transport, 1948; Under-Sec., Min. of Transport and Civil Aviation, 1956; Dep. Sec., Min. of Transport and Civil Aviation, 1958; in Ministry of Aviation, 1959–63; in Ministry of Transport, 1963–66; in Min. of Social Security, later DHSS, 1966–75; Chief Advr to Supplementary Benefits Commn, 1968–75. IDC (1952 Course). *Address:* The Patch, Lodsworth, Petworth, Sussex.

CUSTIS, Patrick James, CBE 1981; FCA, FCMA, FCIS; director of companies; *b* 19 March 1921; *er s* of late Alfred and Amy Custis; *m* 1954, Rita, *yr d* of late Percy and Annie Rayner; one *s*. *Educ:* The High Sch., Dublin. JDipMA. FCA 1951; FCMA 1950; FCIS

1945. Served articles with Josolyne Miles & Co., Chartered Accountants, Cheapside, London, 1945–51; Asst to Gen. Man., Rio Tinto Co. Ltd, London, 1952–54; Gp Chief Accountant and Dir of subsid. cos, Glynwed Ltd, W Midlands, 1955–66; Guest Keen & Nettlefolds Ltd, W Midlands, 1967–81 (Dir of Finance, 1974–81); various sen. appts prior to 1974. Mem., Birmingham and W Midlands Reg. Bd, Lloyds Bank plc, 1979–; Director: New Court Property Fund Managers Ltd, 1978–; Associated Heat Services plc, 1981–; Wolseley plc, 1982–; Birmingham Technology Ltd, 1983–; Wyko Group PLC, 1985–; Dep. Chm., Leigh Interests plc, 1982–; Chm., MCD Group plc, 1983–86. Member: HM Prisons Bd, Home Office, 1980–85; Bi-Centenary Adv. Bd, Birmingham Gen. Hosp. Co-opted Mem. Council, Inst. of Chartered Accountants in England and Wales, 1979–85; Liveryman, Worshipful Co. of Chartered Accountants in England and Wales; Pres., Wolverhampton Soc. of Chartered Accountants, 1985–86. *Recreations:* walking, gardening, reading. *Address:* West Barn, Westmancote, near Tewkesbury, Glos GL20 7ES. *T:* Bredon 72865. *Clubs:* Royal Over-Seas League, Lansdowne.

CUSTIS, Ronald Alfred; Director General, Energy Industries Council, since 1981; *b* 28 Feb. 1931; *m* 1st, 1957, Enid Rowe (*d* 1984); one *s* one *d*; 2nd, 1986, Mrs Valerie Mackett. *Educ:* The High Sch., Dublin. Joined HM Treasury, 1947; DES, 1964; Min. of Technology, 1964–70: Private Sec. to Permanent Under Sec., 1964–66; Principal, 1967; Sec. to Cttee of Inquiry into the Brain Drain, 1967–68; Min. of Aviation Supply, later MoD (Procurement Exec.), 1970–74: Private Sec. to Sec. of State for Defence, 1971–73; Asst Sec., 1973; Dept of Energy, 1974–81: Private Sec. to successive Secs of State for Energy, 1974–75; Under Sec., 1978; Dir Gen., Offshore Supplies Office, 1980–81. *Recreations:* reading, hill walking, listening to music. *Address:* Woodbrook, London Road, Offham, Maidstone, Kent ME19 5AL. *T:* West Malling 848751.

See also P. J. Custis.

CUTHBERT, Prof. Alan William, PhD; FRS 1982; Sheild Professor of Pharmacology, University of Cambridge, since 1979; Fellow of Jesus College, Cambridge, since 1968; *b* 7 May 1932; *s* of Thomas William Cuthbert and late Florence Mary (*née* Griffin); *m* 1957, Harriet Jane Webster; two *s*. *Educ:* Leicester Coll. of Technol.; St Andrews Univ. (BSc); London Univ. (BPharm, PhD). MA Cantab. Res. Fellow, then Asst Lectr, Dept of Pharmacology, Sch. of Pharmacy, Univ. of London, 1959–63; Demonstrator in Pharmacol., 1963–66, Lectr, 1966–73, and Reader, 1973–79, Dept of Pharmacol., Univ. of Cambridge. Chm. Editorial Bd, British Jl of Pharmacology, 1974–82. Pereira Medal in Materia Medica, Pharmaceutical Soc. of GB, 1953; Sir James Irvine Medal in Chemistry, St Andrews Univ., 1955. *Publications:* scientific papers in pharmacol and physiol jls. *Recreations:* screen printing, painting, squash, Duodecimos. *Address:* 7 Longstanton Road, Oakington, Cambridge. *T:* Histon 3676.

CUTHBERT, Lady, (Betty Wake), CBE 1946 (OBE 1943); OStJ 1944; *b* 1904; *d* of Guy Shorrock and Emma Wake; *m* 1928, Vice-Adm. Sir John Cuthbert, *qv*; no *c*. Joined Auxiliary Fire Service, London, as driver, 1938; Fire Staff, Home Office, 1941; Chief Woman Fire Officer, National Fire Service, 1941–46. Nat. Chm., Girls' Venture Corps, 1946–67 (Pres. 1967). Mem., Hampshire CC, 1967–74. *Address:* Ibthorpe Manor Farm, Hurstbourne Tarrant, Andover, Hants.

CUTHBERT, Ian Holm; *see* Holm, Ian.

CUTHBERT, Vice-Adm. Sir John (Wilson), KBE 1957 (CBE 1945); CB 1953; JP; DL; *b* 9 April 1902; *s* of William Cuthbert, Glasgow; *m* 1928, Betty Wake, *d* of Guy Shorrock (*see* Lady Cuthbert); no *c*. *Educ:* Kelvinside Acad.; RN Colleges. Midshipman, 1919; Commander, 1936; Captain, 1941; Rear-Adm., 1951; Vice-Adm., 1954. Commanded: HMS Glasgow, 1942; Ajax, 1944–46; Vengeance, 1949–50; Joint Planning Staff, London, 1942–44; Deputy Controller Admiralty, 1951–53; Flag Officer Flotillas, Home Fleet, 1953–54. Admiral Commanding Reserves, 1955–56; Flag Officer, Scotland, 1956–58. Retired List, 1958. Member Royal Company of Archers (Queen's Body Guard for Scotland); JP Hants 1959; DL Hants 1977. *Address:* Ibthorpe Manor Farm, Hurstbourne Tarrant, near Andover, Hants. *T:* Hurstbourne Tarrant 237.

CUTHBERT, William Moncrieff; DL; Managing Director, Clyde Shipping Company Ltd, since 1971; Chairman, Scottish Amicable Life Assurance Society, since 1985 (Director, since 1976); Chairman of Council and Executive Committee, National Trust for Scotland, since 1984; *b* 22 June 1936; *s* of Alan Dalrymple Cuthbert and Elspeth Moncrieff Cuthbert (*née* Mitchell); *m* 1960, Caroline Jean Balfour Mitchell; two *s* one *d*. *Educ:* Shrewsbury School. Dir, the Murray Johnstone managed Investment Trusts, 1982–. Member: Exec. Bd, Lloyd's Register of Shipping, 1982–; Council, Royal Glasgow Inst. of Fine Arts, 1981–. Mem., Royal Co. of Archers (Queen's Body Guard for Scotland, 1968–). DL Stirling and Falkirk, 1984. *Address:* 78 Carlton Place, Glasgow G5 9TG. *T:* 041–429 2181.

CUTHBERTSON, Sir David (Paton), Kt 1965; CBE 1957; MD, DSc Glasgow; FRSE, FRCPE; Hon. Senior Research Fellow in Pathological Biochemistry, Glasgow University, and Hon. Consultant in the Biochemical Department of the Royal Infirmary, Glasgow; late Director Rowett Research Institute, 1945–65; *b* 9 May 1900; *s* of John Cuthbertson, MBE, Kilmarnock; *m* 1928, Jean Prentice, *d* of late Rev. Alexander P. Telfer, MA, Tarbet, Dunbartonshire; two *s* one *d*. *Educ:* University of Glasgow. BSc 1921; MB, ChB, 1926; DSc, 1931; MD, 1937. Bellahouston Gold Medallist. 2nd Lieut (temp.) Royal Scots Fusiliers, 1919. Lecturer in Pathological Biochemistry and Clinical Biochemist, Royal Infirmary and University of Glasgow, 1926–34; Grieve Lecturer in Physiological Chemistry, University of Glasgow, 1934–45; Arris and Gale Lecturer Royal College of Surgeons, 1942. Lieut-Col and Zone Medical Advisor (No. 1) Glasgow Home Guard, 1941–43; seconded to Administrative Headquarters, Medical Research Council, 1943–45. Consultant Director Commonwealth Bureau of Animal Nutrition, 1945–65; Hon. Consultant in Physiology and Nutrition to the Army, 1946–65. Member: UK Agricultural Mission to Canada, 1950; Tech. Cttee, Scottish Agricultural Improvement Council, 1951–64; Advisory Cttee on Pesticides and other Toxic Chemicals, 1966–71. Chairman: General and Organising Cttees, 9th International Congress of Animal Production, 1966; ARC Tech. Cttee on Nutrient Requirements of Livestock, 1959–65. President: International Union of Nutritional Sciences, 1960–66 (Hon. Pres., 1972–); Sect. I (1953) and Sect. M (1958) of British Assoc.; Nutrition Soc., 1962–65; British Soc. of Animal Production, 1966–67. Scientific Governor, British Nutrition Foundn, 1968–76 (Pres., 1976–79; Hon. Pres., 1979–82). Sir David Cuthbertson Foundn (charitable trust for research), founded by industry, 1985. Baxter Lectr, American Coll. of Surgeons, 1959; 1st W. H. Sebrell Jr Internat. Nutrition Lectr, 1974; Mackdougall-Brisbane Prize Lectr, RSE, 1975; 2nd Jonathan E. Rhoads Lectr, Amer. Soc. Parenteral and Enteral Nutrition, 1979. Hon. Member: European Soc. of Parenteral and Enteral Nutrition, 1981 (Sir David Cuthbertson Lectureship founded 1979); American Institute of Nutrition; Society Biochemistry, Biophysics et Microbiol. Finland; British Soc. of Animal Production; British Nutrition Soc.; Assoc. of Clinical Biochemists. Hon. DSc Rutgers, 1958; Hon. LLD: Glasgow, 1960; Aberdeen, 1972; Dr *hc* Zagreb, 1969. Hon. FRCSE 1967; Hon. FRCPath 1970; Hon. FRCPS Glas; Hon. FIFST 1972. Gold Medal, Czechoslovak Acad. of Agriculture, 1969. *Publications:* Dominions No 4 Report on Nutrition in Newfoundland, with specific recommendations for improvement, 1947; papers on Physiology of Protein Nutrition and Metabolism and on Metabolic Response to Injury, Ruminant Digestion, etc. *Recreations:* water-colour painting and golf. *Address:* Glenavon, 11 Willockston Road, Troon, Ayrshire. *T:* Troon 312028. *Club:* Athenæum.

CUTHBERTSON, Sir Harold (Alexander), Kt 1983; President, Savings Bank of Tasmania; Managing Director, Blundstone Pty Ltd, since 1957; *b* 16 Nov. 1911; *s* of Thomas Alexander Cuthbertson and Vera Rose Cuthbertson; *m* 1937, Jean Westbrook; two *d*. *Educ:* Hutchins Sch., Hobart. Entered family business, Blundstone Pty Ltd, 1932; after tertiary training, became Dir, 1939. Dir of cos, public and private, incl. Phoenix Prudential of Australia, 1970–. Pres., Tas Chamber of Manufrs, 1964–67; Vice Pres., Assoc. of Aust. Chambers of Manufrs, 1966–67; Mem., Commonwealth Immigration Planning Council, 1968–75; Warden, Marine Bd of Hobart, 1963–75. *Recreations:* bowls, fishing. *Address:* 3 David Avenue, Sandy Bay, Tas 7005, Australia. *T:* (002) 251619. *Clubs:* Tasmanian, Athenæum (Pres. 1970), Rotary (Pres., 1959–60) (Hobart).

CUTLER, Sir (Arthur) Roden, VC 1941; AK 1981; KCMG 1965; KCVO 1970; CBE 1957; Governor of New South Wales, 1966–81; company director; Chairman, State Bank of New South Wales, 1981–86; *b* 24 May 1916; *s* of Arthur William Cutler and Ruby Daphne (*née* Pope); *m* 1946, Helen Gray Annetta (*née* Morris), AC 1980; four *s*. *Educ:* Sydney High Sch.; University of Sydney (BEc). Public Trust Office (NSW), 1935–42; War of 1939–45 (VC). State Secretary, RSS & AILA (NSW), 1942–43; Mem., Aliens Classification and Adv. Cttee to advise Commonwealth Govt, 1942–43; Asst Dep. Dir, Security Service, NSW, 1943; Asst Comr Repatriation, 1943–46; High Comr for Australia to New Zealand, 1946–52; High Comr for Australia to Ceylon, 1952–55; HM's Australian Minister to Egypt, 1955–56; Secretary General, SEATO Conference, 1957; Chief of Protocol, Dept of External Affairs, Canberra, 1957–58; State President of RSL, formerly RSSAILA (ACT), 1958; Australian High Comr to Pakistan, 1959–61; Australian Representative to Independence of Somali Republic, 1960; Australian Consul-General, New York, 1961–65; Ambassador to the Netherlands, 1965. Delegate to UN General Assembly, and Australian Rep., Fifth Cttee. 1962–63–64. Hon. Col, Royal New South Wales Regt, 1966–85; Hon. Col, Sydney Univ. Regt, 1966–85; Hon. Air Cdre RAAF. Hon. LLD, Univ. of Sydney; Hon. DSc: Univ. of New South Wales; Univ. of Newcastle; Hon. DLitt: Univ. of New England; Univ. of Wollongong. KStJ 1965. *Recreations:* swimming, shooting, yachting. *Address:* 22 Ginahgulla Road, Bellevue Hill, NSW 2023, Australia. *T:* Sydney 326 1233. *Clubs:* Australian, Union (Sydney); Royal Sydney Yacht Squadron, Royal Prince Alfred Yacht (Sydney), Royal Sydney Golf.

CUTLER, Hon. Sir Charles (Benjamin), KBE 1973; ED 1960; Director, since 1976, Chairman, since 1978, Sun Alliance (Australia); *b* Forbes, NSW, 20 April 1918; *s* of George Hamilton Cutler and Elizabeth Cutler; *m* 1943, Dorothy Pascoe (OBE 1976); three *s* one *d*. *Educ:* rural and high schs, Orange, NSW. MLA for Orange, NSW, 1947; Leader of Country Party (NSW), 1959; Dep. Premier and Minister for Educn, 1965; Dep. Premier, 1972–76, Minister for Local Govt, 1972–76, and Minister for Tourism, 1975–76, NSW. Chm., United World Colls (Aust.) Trust, 1977. Hon. DLitt Newcastle Univ., NSW, 1968. *Recreation:* golf. *Address:* 52 Kite Street, Orange, NSW 2800, Australia. *T:* 62–6418. *Clubs:* Royal Automobile, Imperial Service, Union (Sydney); Orange Golf.

CUTLER, Sir Horace (Walter), Kt 1979; OBE 1963; DL; Member of Greater London Council for Harrow West, 1964–86; Chairman, Branch Retirement Homes PLC, since 1985; *b* London, N16, 28 July 1912; *s* of Albert Benjamin and Mary Ann Cutler; *m* 1957, Christiane, *d* of Dr Klaus Muthesius; one *s* three *d* (and one *s* of previous marriage). *Educ:* Harrow Grammar Sch.; Hereford. Served War of 1939–45: RNVR, 1941–46, Lieut. Harrow Borough Council: elected 1952; Chm. Planning Cttee, 1954; Chm. Housing Cttee, 1955–58; Dep. Mayor, 1958; Alderman, 1959; Mayor, 1959–60; Leader of Council, 1961–65; Chm., Gen. Purposes Cttee, 1962–65; Middlesex CC: elected, 1955; Vice-Chm., Estates and Housing Cttee, 1957; Chm. Planning Cttee, 1961–65; Dep. Leader of CC, 1962; Leader, 1963–65; Greater London Council: Dep. Leader of Opposition, 1964–67 and 1973–74; Dep. Leader, 1967–73; Leader of Opposition, 1974–77 and 1981–82; Leader, 1977–81; Chm. Housing Cttee, 1967–70; Policy and Resources Cttee, 1970–73. Member: Milton Keynes New City Develt Corp. (Chm., Central Milton Keynes Shopping Management Co. Ltd); Central Housing Adv. Cttee, Min. of Housing and Local Govt, 1967–74; Nat. Housing and Town Planning Exec. Cttee, 1967–74 (Vice-Chm., London Region, 1968); Dir, S Bank Theatre Bd; Mem., Nat. Theatre Bd, 1975–82; Trustee, Nat. Theatre, 1976–83. Contested (C) Willesden East, 1970; Pres., Harrow West Conservative Assoc., 1964– (Chm., 1961–64). Freeman of Harrow, and City of London. DL Greater London, 1981. FRSA. OStJ. *Publication:* The Cutler Files, 1982. *Recreations:* golf, ski-ing, classical music, travel. *Address:* Hawkswood, Hawkswood Lane, Gerrards Cross, Bucks. *T:* Fulmer 3182. *Clubs:* Constitutional, United & Cecil.

CUTLER, Ivor; humorist, since 1957; *b* 1923; *s* of Jack and Polly Cutler; two *s*. *Educ:* Shawlands Academy. *Radio and television:* Monday Night at Home, Radio 4, 1959–63; John Peel, Radio 1, 1971–; 11 radio plays, Radio 3, 1979–82; Prince Ivor (opera), Radio 3, 1983; Magical Mystery Tour, TV, 1967; *stage:* Establishment Club (cabaret), 1961–62; An Evening of British Rubbish, Comedy Th., 1963. Contrast, Private Eye and Observer, 1962–63. Pye Radio Award for humour, 1980. *Gramophone records:* Ivor Cutler of Y'hup, 1959; Get Away from the Wall, 1961; Who Tore Your Trousers?, 1961; Ludo, 1967; Dandruff, 1974; Velvet Donkey, 1975; Jammy Smears, 1976; Life in a Scotch Sitting Room, vol. 2, 1978; Privilege, 1983; Women of the World (single), 1983; Prince Ivor, 1986; Gruts, 1986. *Publications: stories:* Gruts, 1961, repr. 1986 (illustr. M. Honeysett); Cockadoodle don't, 1967; (illustr. Martin Honeysett) Life in a Scotch Sitting Room, vol. 2, 1984; *children's books:* (illustr. Helen Oxenbury): Meal One, 1971; Balooky Klujypop, 1974; The Animal House, 1977; (illustr. Alfreda Benge): Herbert the Chicken, 1984; Herbert the Elephant, 1984; *poetry:* Many Flies Have Feathers, 1973; A Flat Man, 1977; Private Habits, 1981; Large et Puffy, 1984; Fresh Carpet, 1986. *Recreations:* fighting noise pollution, nuclear profusion, race hatred; cycling, conversation. *Address:* c/o BBC, Broadcasting House, W1A 1AA.

CUTLER, Sir Roden; *see* Cutler, Sir A. R.

CUTT, Rev. Canon Samuel Robert; Canon Residentiary since 1979 and Treasurer since 1985 of Wells Cathedral (Chancellor, 1979–85); Examining Chaplain to the Bishop of Bath and Wells, since 1980; *b* 28 Nov. 1925; *er s* of Robert Bush Cutt and Lilian Elizabeth Cutt (*née* Saint); *m* 1972, Margaret Eva (*d* 1975), *yr d* of Norman and Eva McIntyre. *Educ:* Skegness Grammar Sch.; Selwyn Coll., Cambridge; Cuddesdon Coll., Oxford. BA Cantab 1950, MA 1954. Deacon 1953, Priest 1954. Asst Curate, St Aidan, West Hartlepool, 1953–56; Tutor for King's Coll. London at St Boniface Coll., Warminster, 1956–59; Sub-Warden for KCL at St Boniface Coll., 1959–65; Lectr and Tutor of Chichester Theol Coll., 1965–71; Priest Vicar of Chichester Cath., 1966–71; Minor Canon, 1971–79, and Succentor, 1974–79, St Paul's Cathedral, and Warden, Coll. of Minor Canons, 1974–79; part-time Lectr, Theological Dept, KCL, 1973–79; Priest in Ordinary to the Queen, 1975–79. Dio. Dir of Ordinands, Bath and Wells, 1979–86. OStJ 1981. *Recreations:*

walking, music, biographical studies, heraldry, cooking. *Address:* 8 The Liberty, Wells, Somerset BA5 2SU. *T:* Wells 78763.

CUTTER, Prof. Elizabeth Graham, PhD, DSc; FRSE; FLS; George Harrison Professor of Botany, University of Manchester, since 1979; *b* 9 Aug. 1929; *d* of Roy Carnegie Cutter and Alexandra (*née* Graham). *Educ:* Rothesay House Sch., Edinburgh; Univ. of St Andrews (BSc, DSc); Univ. of Manchester (PhD). Asst Lecturer in Botany, 1955–57, Lectr in Botany, 1957–64, Univ. of Manchester; Associate Professor of Botany, 1964–68, Professor of Botany, 1968–72, Univ. of California, Davis; Sen. Lectr in Cryptogamic Botany, 1972–74, Reader in Cryptogamic Botany, 1974–79, Univ. of Manchester. *Publications:* Trends in Plant Morphogenesis (principal editor), 1966; Plant Anatomy: Experiment and Interpretation, pt 1, Cells and Tissues, 1969, 2nd edn 1978; pt 2, Organs, 1971. *Recreations:* photography, fishing. *Address:* 8 Huxley Close, Bramhall, Stockport, Cheshire SK7 2PJ. *T:* 061–439 1566. *Club:* Royal Over-Seas League.

CUTTS, Rt. Rev. Richard Stanley; *see* Argentina and Eastern South America, Bishop in.

CYPRUS AND THE GULF, Bishop in, since 1987; **Rt. Rev. John Edward Brown;** *b* 13 July 1930; *s* of Edward and Muriel Brown; *m* 1956, Rosemary (*née* Wood); one *s*. *Educ:* Wintringham Grammar Sch., Grimsby; Kelham Theological Coll., Notts. BD London. Deacon 1955, priest 1956; Master, St George's School, Jerusalem; Curate, St George's Cathedral, Jerusalem; Chaplain of Amman, Jordan, 1954–57; Curate-in-Charge, All Saints, Reading, 1957–60; Missionary and Chaplain, All Saints Cathedral, Khartoum, Sudan, 1960–64; Vicar: Stewkley, Buckingham, 1964–69; St Luke's, Maidenhead, 1969–73; Bracknell, Berkshire, 1973–77; Rural Dean of Sonning, 1974–77; Archdeacon of Berkshire, 1978–86. Representative of Archbishop of the Sudan. *Recreations:* walking; Middle East and African studies. *Address:* 5A John Clerides Street, PO Box 2075, Nicosia, Cyprus.

CZIFFRA; pianist; *b* Budapest, Hungary; *m* 1942, Madame Soleyka Cziffra; one *s*. *Educ:* Academy of Music Franz Liszt, Budapest. Has given recitals and taken part in concerts at the Festival Hall, London, and throughout the world: USA, Canada, France, Israel, Benelux, Germany, Italy, Switzerland, Hungary, Austria, Japan, S America, also BBC and BBC Television, London. Records for HMV: Liszt, Grieg, Tchaikowski, Rackmaninof, Beethoven, Schumann, paraphrases by G. Cziffra, Brahms's Hungarian dances, transcition by Cziffra, etc. Founded, 1968, biennial Concours International de Piano, Versailles, for young pianists; Founder, with son, 1966, Festival of La Chaise Dieu; undertook the creation, in the Chapelle Royale Saint Frambourg, Senlis, of an Auditorium Franz Liszt, 1973; first cultural exchanges between France and Hungary (Foundation Cziffra of Budapest), 1983; Pres., Foundation Cziffra, 1975– (created for young artists). Chevalier de la Légion d'Honneur, 1973. Comdr, Ordre des Arts et des Lettres, 1975. Médaille d'or de l'Académie Française, 1981. *Publication:* Des canons et des fleurs, 1977. *Address:* 4 rue Saint Pierre, 60300 Senlis, France. *T:* (4)-453–39–99.

D

d'ABREU, Francis Arthur, ERD 1954; Surgeon, since 1946, Consultant Surgeon, since 1969, Westminster Hospital; Surgeon, 1950–69, now Emeritus, Hospital of St John and St Elizabeth; Surgeon to Jockey Club and National Hunt Committee, since 1964; *b* 1 Oct. 1904; *s* of Dr John Francis d'Abreu and Teresa d'Abreu; *m* 1945, Margaret Ann Bowes-Lyon; one *s* two *d*. *Educ:* Stonyhurst Coll.; Birmingham Univ. MB, ChB Birmingham 1929; MRCS, LRCP 1929; FRCS, 1932; ChM Birmingham 1935. House Surgeon, Gen. Hosp., Birmingham, 1929; Res. Surgical Officer, Gen. and Queen's Hosps, Birmingham, 1930–34; Surg. Registrar, St Bartholomew's Hosp., London, and Westminster Hosp., 1934–39. Formerly: Examiner to Soc. of Apothecaries; Examiner to Univs of Cambridge and London; Mem., Ct of Examiners, RCS. Mem. Bd of Management, Inst. of Sports Medicine. Lieut RAMC (Supp. Reserve), 1939. Served War of 1939–45: Major, RAMC, 1939, Lt-Col 1942–45. Kt of Magistral Grace, Sov. and Mil. Order of Malta; Kt Comdr, Order of St Gregory (Holy See), 1977. *Publications:* contrib. to various medical jls. *Recreation:* gardening. *Address:* 36 Cumberland Terrace, Regent's Park, NW1.

DACCA; *see* Dhaka.

DACIE, Prof. Sir John (Vivian), Kt 1976; FRS 1967; MD, FRCP; Professor of Haematology, Royal Post-graduate Medical School of London, University of London, 1957–77, now Emeritus; *b* 20 July 1912; British; *s* of John Charles and Lilian Maud Dacie, Putney; *m* 1938, Margaret Kathleen Victoria Thynne; three *s* two *d*. *Educ:* King's Coll. Sch., Wimbledon; King's Coll., London: King's Coll. Hospital, London. MB, BS London 1935; MD 1952; MRCP 1936; FRCP 1956; Hon. FRSM 1984; MD (Hon.): Uppsala, 1961; Marseille, 1977; FRCPath (Pres., 1973–75); Pres., RSM, 1977. Various medical appointments, King's Coll. Hospital, Postgraduate Medical Sch. and Manchester Royal Infirmary, 1936–39. Pathologist, EMS, 1939–42; Major, then Lieut-Col, RAMC, 1943–46. Senior Lecturer in Clinical Pathology, then Reader in Haematology, Postgraduate Medical Sch., 1946–56. Chm., Med. and Scientific Adv. Panel, Leukaemia Research Fund, 1975–85. *Publications:* Practical Haematology, 1950, 2nd edn, 1956, 6th edn (jointly), 1984; Haemolytic Anaemias, 1954: 2nd edn, Part I, 1960, Part II, 1962, Parts III and IV, 1967, 3rd edn, Part I, 1985; various papers on anaemia in medical journals. *Recreations:* music, entomology, gardening. *Address:* 10 Alan Road, Wimbledon, SW19. *T:* 01–946 6086.

da COSTA, Harvey Lloyd, CMG 1962; **Hon. Mr Justice da Costa;** Judge of Appeal, Court of Appeal for Bermuda, since 1982; *b* 8 Dec. 1914; *s* of John Charles and Martha da Costa. *Educ:* Calabar High Sch., Jamaica; St Edmund Hall (Sen. Exhibnr; Rhodes Schol.), Oxford. BA (Hons) London; MA, BLitt Oxon; Practised at Chancery Bar, 1950–52; Crown Counsel, Jamaica, 1952–54; Sen. Crown Counsel, Jamaica, 1954–56; Asst Attorney-Gen., Jamaica, 1956–59; QC Jamaica 1959; Attorney-Gen. of West Indies, 1959–62; practised Private Bar, Jamaica, 1962–77; Puisne Judge 1978–80, Chief Justice, 1980–81, Bahamas Supreme Court; Judge of Appeal, Court of Appeal for Bahamas, 1982–85. Mem., Anguilla, British Virgin Is and Seychelles Commns. *Recreation:* swimming. *Address:* c/o Court of Appeal, Hamilton, Bermuda.

da COSTA, Sergio Corrêa, GCVO; Brazilian Ambassador to the United States of America, since 1983; *b* 19 Feb. 1919; *s* of Dr I. A. da Costa and Lavinia Corrêa da Costa; *m* 1943, Zazi Aranha; one *s* two *d*. *Educ:* Law Sch., Univ. of Brazil; post grad. UCLA; Brazilian War Coll. Career diplomat: Sec. of Embassy, Buenos Ayres, then Washington, 1944–48; Acting Deleg., Council of OAS, Wash., 1946–48; Inter-American Econ. and Social Coun., Washington, 1946–48; Dep. Head, Economic Dept, Min. of Ext. Relations, 1952; Actg Pres., Braz. Nat. Techn. Assistance Commn, 1955–58; Minister-Counsellor, Rome, 1959–62; Permanent Rep. to FAO, Rome, 1960; Mem., Financial Cttee of FAO, 1962–63; Ambassador to Canada, 1962–65; Asst Sec.-Gen. for Internat. Organizations at Min. Ext. Relations, 1966; Sec.-Gen., Min. of Ext. Relations, 1967–68; Acting Minister for External Relations, 1967–68; Ambassador to UK, 1968–75; Permanent Rep. to UN in NY, 1975–83. Mmber: Brazilian Acad. of Letters; Brazilian Hist. and Geographical Inst.; Brazilian Soc. of Internat. Law; American Soc. of Internat. Law. Grand Officer: Military Order of Aeronautical Merit, Brazil, 1967; Order of Naval Merit, Brazil, 1967; Grand Cross of Victorian Order (Hon. GCVO), Gt Britain, 1968; also numerous Grand Crosses, etc, of Orders, from other countries, 1957–. *Publications:* (mostly in Brazil): As 4 Coroas de Pedro I, 1941; Pedro I e Metternich, 1942; Diplomacia Brasileira na Questao de Leticia, 1943; A Diplomacia do Marechal, 1945; Every Inch a King—A biography of Pedro I, Emperor of Brazil, 1950 (NY 1964, London 1972). *Recreations:* reading, writing, boating. *Address:* Brazilian Embassy, 3006 Massachusetts Avenue NW, Washington, DC 20008, USA. *Clubs:* White's, Travellers' (London); Rideau, Country (Ottawa); Circolo della Caccia (Rome).

DACRE, Baroness (27th in line), *cr* 1321; **Rachel Leila Douglas-Home;** *b* 24 Oct. 1929; *er* surv. *d* of 4th Viscount Hampden, CMG (*d* 1965) (whose Barony of Dacre was called out of abeyance in her favour, 1970) and of Leila Emily, *o d* of late Lt-Col Frank Evelyn Seely; *m* 1951, Hon. William Douglas-Home, *qv*; one *s* three *d*. Heir: *s* Hon. James Thomas Archibald Douglas-Home [*b* 16 May 1952; *m* 1979, Christine (*née* Stephenson); one *d*]. *Address:* Drayton House, East Meon, Hants.

DACRE OF GLANTON, Baron *cr* 1979 (Life Peer), of Glanton in the County of Northumberland; **Hugh Redwald Trevor-Roper;** Master of Peterhouse, Cambridge, since 1980; *b* 15 January 1914; *er s* of late Dr B. W. E. Trevor-Roper, Glanton and Alnwick, Northumberland; *m* 1954, Lady Alexandra Howard-Johnston, *e d* of late Field-Marshal Earl Haig, KT, GCB, OM. *Educ:* Charterhouse; Christ Church, Oxford. Research

Fellow Merton Coll., 1937–39 (Hon. Fellow, 1980). Student of Christ Church, Oxford, 1946–57; Censor 1947–52; Hon. Student, 1979; Regius Prof. of Modern Hist., and Fellow of Oriel Coll., Oxford Univ., 1957–80 (Hon. Fellow, 1980). Dir, Times Newspapers Ltd, 1974–. Chevalier, Legion of Honour, 1975. *Publications:* Archbishop Laud, 1940; The Last Days of Hitler, 1947; The Gentry, 1540–1640, 1953; (ed) Hitler's Table Talk, 1953; (ed with J. A. W. Bennett) The Poems of Richard Corbett, 1955; Historical Essays, 1957; (ed) Hitler's War Directives, 1939–45, 1964; (ed) Essays in British History Presented to Sir Keith Feiling, 1964; The Rise of Christian Europe, 1965; Religion, The Reformation and Social Change, 1967; (ed) The Age of Expansion, 1968; The Philby Affair, 1968; The European Witch-Craze of the 16th and 17th Centuries, 1970; The Plunder of the Arts in the Seventeenth Century, 1970; Princes and Artists, 1976; A Hidden Life, 1976; (ed) The Goebbels Diaries, 1978; Renaissance Essays, 1985. *Address:* Master's Lodge, Peterhouse, Cambridge; Chiefswood, Melrose. *Clubs:* Athenæum, Savile, Beefsteak.
See also Earl Haig, P. D. Trevor-Roper.

da CUNHA, John Wilfrid, JP; **His Honour Judge da Cunha;** a Circuit Judge (formerly Judge of County Courts), since 1970; *b* 6 Sept. 1922; 2nd *s* of Frank C. da Cunha, MD, DPH, and Lucy (*née* Finnerty); *m* 1953, Janet, MB, ChB, *d* of Louis Savatard, (Hon.) MSc, LSA, and Judith Savatard, MB, BS; one *s* four *d*. *Educ:* Stonyhurst Coll., Lancs; St John's Coll., Cambridge. MA Cantab 1954. Served 1942–47, 23rd Hussars (RAC) and Judge Advocate Gen. (War Crimes), Hon. Major. Called to Bar, Middle Temple, 1948; Northern Circuit. Chm., Local Appeal Tribunal, Min. of Social Security (Wigan), 1964–69. Asst Recorder, Oldham County Borough QS, 1966–70; Chm., Industrial Tribunals, 1966–70; Dep. Chm., Lancs County QS, 1968–71. Comr, NI (Emergency Provisions) Act, 1973; Member: Appeals Tribunal; Parole Bd, 1976–78. JP Lancs 1968. *Recreations:* gardening, pottering. *Address:* c/o Circuit Administrator, Aldine House, New Bailey Street, Salford M3 5EU. *Club:* Manchester.

D'AETH, Prof. Richard, PhD; President, Hughes Hall, Cambridge, 1978–84; *b* 3 June 1912; *e s* of Walter D'Aeth and Marion Turnbull; *m* 1943, Pamela Straker; two *d*. *Educ:* Bedford Sch.; Emmanuel Coll., Cambridge (Scholar; 1st Cl. Hons Nat. Sci., PhD); Harvard Univ. (Commonwealth Fellow; AM). Served War, RAF, 1941–46 (Wing Comdr). Master, Gresham's Sch., 1938–40; HM Inspector of Schs, 1946–52; Prof. of Education: University Coll. of West Indies, 1952–58; Univ. of Exeter, 1958–77. Mem., Internat. Assoc. for Advancement of Educnl Res. (Pres., Warsaw, 1969); sometime mem. cttees of Schools Council, BBC, Schs Broadcasting Council, RCN and NSPCC. *Publications:* Education and Development in the Third World, 1975; articles in jls. *Address:* 57 Highsett, Cambridge CB2 1NZ.

DAHL, Murdoch Edgcumbe; *b* 11 March 1914; *s* of Oscar Horace and Edith Gladys Dahl; *m* 1940, Joan, *d* of Daniel Charles and Edith Marion Woollaston; three *s*. *Educ:* Royal Grammar Sch., Newcastle upon Tyne; Armstrong Coll. (subsq. King's Coll.), Newcastle upon Tyne; St John's Coll., Durham. BA 1936, MA 1956, Durham. Deacon 1937; Priest 1938. Curate of: St Paul, Astley Bridge, 1937–39; Fallowfield, 1939–43; Harpenden, 1943–49; Vicar of Arlesey and Rector of Astwick, 1949–51; Minister, St Oswald's, Croxley Green, 1951–56; Vicar of Great with Little Hormead and Rector of Wyddial, 1956–65; Examining Chaplain to Bishop of St Albans, 1959; Hon. Canon of St Albans, 1963–65, Canon Residentiary, 1965–68, Canon Theologian, 1968–79; Canon Emeritus, 1979. Resigned all ecclesiastical (C of E) titles, Dec. 1982, when he became a Roman Catholic. *Publications:* Resurrection of the Body, 1962; Sin Streamlined, 1966; The Christian Materialist, 1968; Final Loss—Final Gain, 1980. *Address:* 52 Fleet Street, Beaminster, Dorset DT8 3EH.

DAHL, Roald; writer; *b* 13 Sept. 1916; *s* of Harald Dahl and Sofie Magdalene Hesselberg; *m* 1st, 1953, Patricia Neal (marr. diss. 1983); one *s* three *d* (and one *d* decd); 2nd, 1983, Mrs Felicity Ann Crosland (*née* d'Abreu). *Educ:* Repton. Public Schools Exploring Soc. expedn to Newfoundland, 1934; Eastern Staff of Shell Co., 1934–39, served in Dar-es-Salaam; RAF flying trng, Nairobi and Habbanyah, 1939–40; No 80 Fighter Sqdn, Western Desert, 1940 (wounded); Greece, 1941; Syria, 1941; Asst Air Attaché, Washington, 1942–43; Wing Comdr, 1943; British Security Co-ordination, N America, 1943–45. Edgar Allan Poe Award, Mystery Writers of America, 1954 and 1959. *Publications: short stories:* Over to You, 1945; Someone Like You, 1953; Kiss Kiss, 1960; Switch Bitch, 1974; Tales of the Unexpected, 1979; More Tales of the Unexpected, 1980; The Best of Roald Dahl, 1983; Roald Dahl's Book of Ghost Stories, 1983; *novels:* Sometime Never (A Fable for Supermen), 1948; My Uncle Oswald, 1979; *autobiography:* Going Solo, 1986; *children's books:* (with Walt Disney) The Gremlins, 1943; James and the Giant Peach, 1962; Charlie and the Chocolate Factory, 1964 (staged, Sadler's Wells, 1986); The Magic Finger, 1966; Fantastic Mr Fox, 1970; Charlie and the Great Glass Elevator, 1972; Danny, the Champion of the World, 1975; The Wonderful Story of Henry Sugar and Six More, 1977; The Enormous Crocodile, 1978; The Twits, 1980; George's Marvellous Medicine, 1981; Revolting Rhymes, 1982; The BFG, 1982; Dirty Beasts, 1983; The Witches, 1983 (Whitbread Award); Boy, Tales from Childhood, 1984; The Giraffe and The Pelly and Me, 1985; *play:* The Honeys, 1955; *screenplays:* You Only Live Twice, 1967; Chitty Chitty Bang Bang, 1968; Willy Wonka and the Chocolate Factory, 1971; *television series:* Tales of the Unexpected, 1979; contrib. New Yorker, Harper's Magazine, Atlantic Monthly, Saturday Evening Post, Colliers, etc. *Recreation:* picking wild mushrooms. *Address:* Gipsy House, Great Missenden, Bucks HP16 0PB. *T:* Great Missenden 2757.

DAHL, Robert Henry, TD 1950; MA Oxford; Head Master of Wrekin College, 1952–71; *b* 21 April 1910; *y s* of Murdoch Cameron Dahl, London, and Lilian May Edgcumbe; *m* 1936, Lois Helen Allanby; three *s*. *Educ:* Sedbergh Sch.; Exeter Coll.,

Oxford. Asst Master (Modern Langs) at Merchant Taylors' Sch., 1934–38. Asst Master and Housemaster at Harrow Sch., 1938–52. Served War of 1939–45: Intelligence Corps, Middle East, 1941–43; Major, 1943; Political Intelligence Dept of Foreign Office, 1943–46. FRSA 1969. *Publication*: Joint Editor, Selections from Albert Schweitzer, 1953. *Recreations*: golf, music, painting. *Address*: 72 Eastgate Street, Bury St Edmunds, Suffolk IP33 1YR.

DAHRENDORF, Prof. Ralf, Hon. KBE 1982; PhD, DrPhil; FBA 1977; Professor of Social Science, Universität Konstanz, since 1984; *b* Hamburg, 1 May 1929; *s* of Gustav Dahrendorf and Lina Dahrendorf (*née* Witt); *m* 1980, Ellen Joan (*née* Krug). *Educ*: several schools, including Heinrich-Hertz Oberschule, Hamburg; studies in philosophy and classical philology, Hamburg, 1947–52; DrPhil 1952; postgrad. studies at London Sch. of Economics, 1952–54; Leverhulme Research Schol., 1953–54; PhD 1956. Habilitation, and University Lecturer, Saarbrücken, 1957; Fellow at Center for Advanced Study in the Behavioural Sciences, Palo Alto, USA, 1957–58; Prof. of Sociology, Hamburg, 1958–60; Vis. Prof. Columbia Univ., 1960; Prof. of Sociology, Tübingen, 1960–64; Vice-Chm., Founding Cttee of Univ. of Konstanz, 1964–66; Prof. of Sociology, Konstanz, 1966–69; Parly Sec. of State, Foreign Office, W Germany, 1969–70; Dir, 1974–84, Governor, 1986–, LSE; Member: Commn of European Communities, Brussels, 1970–74; Hansard Soc. Commn on Electoral Reform, 1975–76; Royal Commn on Legal Services, 1976–79; Cttee to Review Functioning of Financial Instns, 1977–80. Trustee, Ford Foundn, 1976–. Chm. Bd, Friedrich Naumann Stiftung, 1982–; Non-Exec. Dir, Glaxo Holdings PLC, 1984–. Vis. Prof. at several Europ. and N American univs. Reith Lecturer, 1974; Jephcott Lectr, RSocMed, 1983. Hon. Fellow: LSE; Imperial Coll. Hon. MRIA 1974; Fellow, St Antony's Coll., Oxford, 1976. Foreign Hon. Member: Amer. Acad. of Arts and Sciences, 1975–; Nat. Acad. of Sciences, USA, 1977; Amer. Philosophical Soc., 1977; FRSA 1977; Hon. FRCS 1982. Hon. DLitt: Reading, 1973; Dublin, 1975; Hon. LLD: Manchester, 1973; Wagner Coll., NY, 1977; York, Ontario, 1979; Hon. DHL: Kalamazoo Coll., 1974; Johns Hopkins, 1982; Hon. DSc: Ulster, 1973; Bath, 1977; Queen's Univ. Belfast, 1984; DUniv: Open, 1974; Maryland, 1978; Surrey, 1978; Hon. Dr Univ. Catholique de Louvain, 1977. Journal Fund Award for Learned Publication, 1966. Grand Croix de l'Ordre du Mérite du Sénégal, 1971; Grosses Bundesverdienstkreuz mit Stern und Schulterband (Federal Republic of Germany), 1974; Grand Croix de l'Ordre du Mérite du Luxembourg, 1974; Grosses goldenes Ehrenzeichen am Bande für Verdienste um die Republik Österreich (Austria), 1975; Grand Croix de l'Ordre de Léopold II (Belgium), 1975. *Publications include*: Marx in Perspective, 1953; Industrie- und Betriebssoziologie, 1956 (trans. Italian, Spanish, Dutch, Japanese, Chinese); Soziale Klassen und Klassenkonflikt, 1957 (Class and Class Conflict, 1959; also trans. French, Italian, Spanish, Finnish, Japanese); Homo Sociologicus, 1959 (trans. English, Italian, Portuguese, Finnish); Die angewandte Aufklärung, 1963; Gesellschaft und Demokratie in Deutschland, 1965 (Society and Democracy in Germany, 1966; also trans. Italian); Pfade aus Utopia, 1967 (Uscire dall'Utopia, 1971); Essays in the Theory of Society, 1968; Konflikt und Freiheit, 1972; Plädoyer für die Europäische Union, 1973; The New Liberty, 1975 (trans. German, Italian, Urdu, Arabic, Japanese, Korean); Life Chances, 1979 (trans. German, Japanese, Italian); On Britain, 1982; Die Chancen der Krise, 1983; Reisen nach innen und aussen, 1984; Law and Order, 1985. *Address*: Universität Konstanz, D 7750 Konstanz, Postfach 5560, W Germany. *Clubs*: PEN, Reform, Political Economy.

DAICHES, David, MA Edinburgh; MA, DPhil Oxon; PhD Cantab; FRSL; FRSE; Director, Institute for Advanced Studies in the Humanities, Edinburgh University, since 1980; Professor of English, University of Sussex, 1961–77, and Dean of the School of English Studies, 1961–68; now Emeritus Professor; *b* 2 Sept. 1912; *s* of late Rabbi Dr Salis Daiches and Flora Daiches (*née* Levin); *m* 1st, 1937, Isobel J. Mackay (*d* 1977); one *s* two *d*; 2nd, 1978, Hazel Neville (*née* Newman) (*d* 1986). *Educ*: George Watson's Coll., Edinburgh; Edinburgh Univ. (Vans Dunlop Schol., Elliot Prize); Balliol Coll., Oxford (Elton Exhibnr). Asst in English, Edinburgh Univ., 1935–36; Andrew Bradley Fellow, Balliol Coll., Oxford, 1936–37; Asst Prof. of English, Univ. of Chicago, 1939–43; Second Sec., British Embassy, Washington, 1944–46; Prof. of English, Cornell Univ., USA, 1946–51; University Lecturer in English at Cambridge, 1951–61; Fellow of Jesus Coll., Cambridge, 1957–62. Visiting Prof. of Criticism, Indiana Univ., USA, 1956–57; Hill Foundation Visiting Prof., Univ. of Minnesota, Spring 1966. Lectures: Elliston, Univ. of Cincinnati, 1960; Whidden, McMaster Univ., Canada, 1964; Ewing, Univ. of Calif, 1967; Carpenter Meml, Ohio Wesleyan Univ., 1969; Alexander, Univ. of Toronto, 1980; Gifford, Univ. of Edinburgh, 1983. Hon. Prof., Stirling Univ., 1980. Fellow, Centre for the Humanities, Wesleyan Univ., Middletown, Conn, 1970. Hon. Fellow, Sunderland Polytechnic, 1977. Hon. LittD, Brown Univ; Docteur *hc* Sorbonne; Hon. DLitt: Edinburgh, 1976; Sussex, 1978; DUniv Stirling, 1980. *Publications*: The Place of Meaning in Poetry, 1935; New Literary Values, 1936; Literature and Society, 1938; The Novel and the Modern World, 1939 (new edn, 1960); Poetry and the Modern World, 1940; The King James Bible: A Study of its Sources and Development, 1941; Virginia Woolf, 1942; Robert Louis Stevenson, 1947; A Study of Literature, 1948; Robert Burns, 1950 (new edn 1966); Willa Cather: A Critical Introduction, 1951; Critical Approaches to Literature, 1956; Two Worlds (autobiog.), 1956; Literary Essays, 1956; John Milton, 1957; The Present Age, 1958; A Critical History of English Literature, 1960; George Eliot's Middlemarch, 1963; The Paradox of Scottish Culture, 1964; (ed) The Idea of a New University, 1964; English Literature (Princeton Studies in Humanistic Scholarship), 1965; More Literary Essays, 1968; Some Late Victorian Attitudes, 1969; Scotch Whisky, 1969; Sir Walter Scott and his World, 1971; A Third World (autobiog.), 1971; (ed) The Penguin Companion to Literature: Britain and the Commonwealth, 1971; Robert Burns and his World, 1971; (ed with A. Thorlby) Literature and Western Civilization, vol. I, 1972, vols II and V, 1973, vols III and IV, 1975; vol. VI, 1976; Charles Edward Stuart: the life and times of Bonnie Prince Charlie, 1973; Robert Louis Stevenson and his World, 1973; Was, 1975; Moses, 1975; James Boswell and his World, 1976; Scotland and the Union, 1977; Glasgow, 1977; Edinburgh, 1978; (with John Flower) Literary Landscapes of the British Isles: a narrative atlas, 1979; (ed) Selected Writings and Speeches of Fletcher of Saltoun, 1979; (ed) Selected Poems of Robert Burns, 1979; (ed) A Companion to Scottish Culture, 1981; Literature and Gentility in Scotland, 1982; Robert Fergusson, 1982; Milton's Paradise Lost, 1983; God and the Poets, 1984; Edinburgh, A Travellers' Companion, 1986; Gen. Editor, Studies in English Literature, 1961–. *Recreations*: talking, music. *Address*: 9 Randolph Crescent, Edinburgh EH3 7TT.
See also L. H. Daiches.

DAICHES, Lionel Henry, QC (Scot) 1956; *b* 8 March 1911; *s* of late Rev. Dr. Salis Daiches, Edinburgh, and Mrs Flora Daiches; *m* 1947, Dorothy Estelle Bernstein (marr. diss. 1973); two *s*. *Educ*: George Watson's Coll., Edinburgh; Edinburgh Univ. (MA, LLB). Pres., Edinburgh Univ. Diagnostic Soc., 1931; Convener of Debates, Edinburgh Univ. Union, 1933; Editor, The Student, 1933. Served 1940–46 in N Stafford Regt and Major, JAG Branch in N Africa and Italy, including Anzio Beach-head. Admitted Scots Bar, 1946. Standing Junior Counsel to Board of Control, Scotland, 1950–56; Sheriff-Substitute of Lanarkshire at Glasgow, 1962–67. Fellow, Internat. Acad. of Trial Lawyers, 1976. Contested (L) Edinburgh South, 1950. *Publication*: Russians at Law, 1960. *Recreations*: walking and talking. *Address*: 10 Heriot Row, Edinburgh. *T*: 031–556 4144. *Clubs*: Puffin's, Scottish Arts (Edinburgh); RNVR (Scotland).
See also D. Daiches.

DAIN, Rt. Rev. Arthur John, OBE 1979; Honorary Consultant to Lausanne Committee for World Evangelization, since 1985 (General Co-Ordinator, 1982–85); *b* 13 Oct. 1912; *s* of Herbert John Dain and Elizabeth Dain; *m* 1939, Edith Jane Stewart, MA, *d* of Dr Alexander Stewart, DD; four *d*. *Educ*: Wolverhampton Gram. Sch.; Ridley Coll., Cambridge. Missionary in India, 1935–40; 10th Gurkha Rifles, 1940–41; Royal Indian Navy, 1941–47; Gen. Sec., Bible and Medical Missionary Fellowship, formerly Zenana Bible and Medical Mission, 1947–59; Overseas Sec., British Evangelical Alliance, 1950–59; Federal Sec., CMS of Australia, 1959–65; Hon. Canon of St Andrew's Cathedral, 1963; Asst Bishop, Diocese of Sydney, 1965–82; Sen. Asst Bishop and Chief Executive Officer, 1980–82. *Publications*: Mission Fields To-day, 1956; Missionary Candidates, 1959. *Recreation*: sport. *Address*: 3 Mitchell Place, 4 Mitchell Road, Darling Point, NSW 2027, Australia. *T*: 328 7940.

DAIN, David John Michael; HM Diplomatic Service; Head of Western European Department, Foreign and Commonwealth Office, since 1985; *b* 30 Oct. 1940; *s* of John Gordon Dain and Gladys Ellen (*née* Connop); *m* 1969, Susan Kathleen Moss; one *s* four *d*. *Educ*: Merchant Taylors' Sch.; St John's Coll., Oxford (MA Lit.Hum.). Entered HM Diplomatic Service, 1963; Third, later Second Sec., Tehran and Kabul, 1964–68; seconded to Cabinet Office, 1969–72; First Sec., Bonn, 1972–75; FCO, 1975–78; First Sec., Athens, 1978–81; Counsellor, Nicosia, 1981–85. *Recreations*: tennis, bridge, walking, natural history. *Address*: c/o Foreign and Commonwealth Office, SW1; Manor Cottage, Frant, Tunbridge Wells, Kent TN3 9DR. *T*: Frant 427.

DAINTON, family name of **Baron Dainton.**

DAINTON, Baron *cr* 1986 (Life Peer), of Hallam Moors in South Yorkshire; **Frederick Sydney Dainton;** Kt 1971; FRS 1957; MA, BSc Oxon, PhD, ScD Cantab; Chancellor, Sheffield University, since 1978; *b* 11 Nov. 1914; *y s* of late George Whalley and Mary Jane Dainton; *m* 1942, Barbara Hazlitt, JP, PhD, *o d* of late Dr W. B. Wright, Manchester; one *s* two *d*. *Educ*: Central Secondary Sch., Sheffield; St John's Coll., Oxford; Sidney Sussex Coll., Cambridge. Open Exhibitioner, 1933; Casberd Prizeman, 1934, Casberd Scholar, 1935, Hon. Fellow 1968, St John's Coll., Oxford; Goldsmiths' Co. Exhibitioner, 1935, 1st class Hons Chemistry, 1937, University of Oxford; Research Student, 1937, Goldsmiths' Co. Senior Student, 1939, University Demonstrator in Chemistry, 1944, H. O. Jones Lecturer in Physical Chemistry, 1946, University of Cambridge. Fellow, 1945, Praelector, 1946, Hon. Fellow 1961, St Catharine's Coll., Cambridge. Prof. of Physical Chemistry, University of Leeds, 1950–65; Vice-Chancellor, Nottingham Univ., 1965–70; Dr Lee's Prof. of Chemistry, Oxford University, 1970–73; Chm., UGC, 1973–78. Vis. Prof., Univ. Toronto, 1949; Tilden Lectr, 1950, Faraday Lectr, 1973, Chem. Soc.; Peter C. Reilly Lectr, Univ. of Notre Dame, Ind., USA, 1952; Arthur D. Little Visiting Prof., MIT, 1959; George Fisher Baker Lectr, Cornell Univ., 1961; Boomer Lectr, Univ. of Alberta, 1962; Rede Lectr, Cambridge, 1981; Crookshank Lectr, RCR, 1981. Chm., Cttee on Swing away from Science (report published as Enquiry into the Flow of Candidates in Science and Technology into Higher Education, Cmnd 3541, 1968). Chairman: Assoc. for Radiation Research, 1964–66; Nat. Libraries Cttee, 1968–69; Adv. Cttee on Sci. and Tech. Information, 1966–70; Adv. Bd for Res. Councils, 1972–73; British Cttee, Harkness Fellowship, 1977–81 (Mem., 1973–); British Library Bd, 1978–85; Nat. Radiological Protection Bd, 1978–85. President: Faraday Soc., 1965–67; Chemical Soc., 1972–73 (Hon. Fellow, 1983–); Assoc. for Science Education, 1967; Library Assoc., 1977; BAAS, 1980; Soc. of Designer Craftsmen, 1985–. Member: Council for Scientific Policy, 1965– (Chm. 1969–72); Central Advisory Council for Science and Technology, 1967–70; Crafts Council, 1984–; Museums and Galleries Commn, 1985–; Trustee: Natural Hist. Museum, 1974–84; Wolfson Foundn, 1978–. Chairman: Edward Boyle Meml Trust, 1982–; Council, Royal Post-grad. Med. Sch., 1980–. Prime Warden, Goldsmiths' Co., 1982–83. Foreign Member: Swedish Acad. of Sci., 1968; Amer. Acad. of Arts and Scis, 1972; Acad. of Scis, Göttingen, 1975. Hon. Fellow: Goldsmiths' Coll., London; Queen Mary Coll., London, 1985; Birkbeck Coll., London, 1986; Hon. FRCP 1979; Hon. FRSC 1983; Hon. FRCR 1984; Hon. FLA 1986. Hon. ScD: Łódź, 1966; Dublin, 1968; Hon. DSc: Bath Univ. of Technology, 1970; Loughborough Univ. of Technology, 1970; Heriot-Watt, 1970; Warwick, 1970; Strathclyde, 1971; Exeter, 1971; QUB, 1971; Manchester, 1972; E Anglia, 1972; Leeds, 1973; McMaster, 1975; Uppsala, 1977; Liverpool, Salford, 1979; Kent, 1981; Hon. LLD: Nottingham, 1970; Aberdeen, 1972; Sheffield, Cambridge, 1979; London, 1984. Sylvanus Thompson Medal, BIR, 1958; Davy Medal, Royal Soc., 1969; Crookshank Medal, RCR, 1981; Curie Medal, Poland, 1983. Kt Comdr, Order of Merit (Poland), 1985. *Publications*: Chain Reactions, 1956; Choosing a British University, 1981; (contrib.) The Parliament of Science, 1981; Universities and the Health Service, 1983; papers on physico-chemical subjects in scientific jls. *Recreations*: walking, colour photography. *Address*: Fieldside, Water Eaton Lane, Oxford OX5 2PR. *T*: Kidlington 5132. *Club*: Athenæum.

DAKERS, Lionel Frederick, CBE 1983; DMus; FRCO; Director, Royal School of Church Music (Special Commissioner, 1958–72), since 1972; Examiner to the Associated Board of the Royal Schools of Music, since 1958; *b* Rochester, Kent, 24 Feb. 1924; *o s* of late Lewis and Ethel Dakers; *m* 1951, Mary Elisabeth, *d* of Rev. Claude Williams; four *d*. *Educ*: Rochester Cathedral Choir Sch. Studied with H. A. Bennett, Organist of Rochester Cathedral, 1933–40, with Sir Edward Bairstow, Organist of York Minster, 1943–45, and at Royal Academy of Music, 1947–51. Organist of All Saints', Frindsbury, Rochester, 1939–42. Served in Royal Army Educational Corps, 1943–47. Cairo Cathedral, 1945–47; Finchley Parish Church, 1948–50; Asst Organist, St George's Chapel, Windsor Castle, 1950–54; Asst Music Master, Eton Coll., 1952–54; Organist of Ripon Cathedral, 1954–57; Conductor Ripon Choral Soc. and Harrogate String Orchestra, 1954–57; Hon. Conductor, Exeter Diocesan Choral Association, 1957; Lectr in Music, St Luke's Coll., Exeter, 1958–70; Organist and Master of the Choristers, Exeter Cathedral, 1957–72; Conductor: Exeter Musical Soc., 1957–72; Exeter Chamber Orchestra, 1959–65. President: Incorporated Assoc. of Organists, 1972–75; London Assoc. of Organists, 1976–78; Mem. Council, Royal Coll. of Organists, 1967– (Pres., 1976–78). Sec., Cathedral Organists' Assoc., 1972–. Chm., Organs Adv. Cttee of Council for Care of Churches of C of E, 1974. Hon. Mem., US Assoc. of Anglican Musicians, 1978. ARCO, 1944; FRCO, 1945; ADCM, 1952; BMus Dunelm, 1951; ARAM 1955; FRAM, 1962; FRSCM 1969; DMus Lambeth, 1979; FRCM 1980. Fellow, St Michael's Coll., Tenbury, 1973. Hon. Fellow, Westminster Choir Coll., USA, 1975. Compositions: church music, etc. *Publications*: Church Music at the Crossroads, 1970; A Handbook of Parish Music, 1976; Making Church Music Work, 1978; (ed) Music and the Alternative Service Book, 1980; (ed) The Choristers Companion, 1980; (ed) The Psalms—their use and performance today, 1980; The Church Musician as Conductor, 1982; Church Music in a Changing World, 1984; Choosing and Using Hymns, 1985. *Recreations*: book collecting, gardening, continental food, travel. *Address*: Addington Palace, Croydon CR9 5AD. *T*: 01–654 7676. *Clubs*: Athenæum; St Wilfrid's (NY) (Hon. mem.).

DAKIN, Dorothy Danvers, OBE 1982; Assistant Chaplain: HM Prison and Remand Centre, Pucklechurch, since 1984; Southmead Hospital, Bristol, since 1985; *b* 22 Oct.

1919; *d* of Edwin Lionel Dakin, chartered civil engr and Mary Danvers Dakin (*née* Walker), artist. *Educ:* Sherborne Sch. for Girls; Newnham Coll., Cambridge. MA Geography. 2nd Officer WRNS (Educn), 1943–50; Housemistress, Wycombe Abbey Sch., 1950–60; Headmistress, The Red Maids' School, Bristol, 1961–81; Chm., ISIS Assoc., 1982–84. President: West of England Br., Assoc. of Headmistresses, 1969–71; Assoc. of Headmistresses of Girls' Boarding Schs, 1971–73; Girls' Schs Assoc. (Independent and Direct Grant), 1973–75; Chm. Council, ISIS, 1977–81. Licensed Reader, C of E, 1982–. Governor: Bath High Sch.; St George's Sch., Ascot; Bristol Cathedral Sch.; Notton Special Sch., Lacock; Collegiate Sch., Winterbourne; Embledon Infants' Sch., Bristol. *Recreations:* fencing, painting, travel, embroidery. *Address:* 41 Park Grove, Henleaze, Bristol BS9 4LF.

DALAL, Maneck Ardeshir Sohrab; Managing Director, Tata Ltd, SW1, since 1977; Director, Tata Industries, Bombay, since 1979; *b* 24 Dec. 1918; *s* of Ardeshir Dalal and Amy Dalal; *m* 1947, Kathleen Gertrude Richardson; three *d*. *Educ:* Trinity Hall, Cambridge (MA). Called to the Bar, Middle Temple, 1945. Manager: Air-India New Delhi, 1946–48; Air-India London, 1948–53; Regional Traffic Manager, 1953–59; Regional Director, 1959–77; Minister for Tourism and Civil Aviation, High Commn for India, 1973–77. President: Indian Chamber of Commerce in Great Britain, 1959–62; Indian Management Assoc. of UK, 1960–63; UK Pres., World Conf. on Religions and Peace, UK and Ireland Gp, 1985–; Vice-Pres., Friends of Vellore, 1979–; Chairman: Foreign Airlines Assoc. of UK, 1965–67; Indian YMCA in London, 1972–; Bharatiya Vidhya Bhavan in London (Indian Cultural Inst. of Gt Britain), 1975–; Vice-Chm., Fest. of India in GB, 1980–81; Member: Sub-Cttee on Transport, Industrial Trng Bd of GB, 1975–77; Assembly, British Council of Churches, 1984–86; Internat. Bd, United World Colls, 1985–; Bd Govs, Nat. Inst. for Social Work, 1986–; Chm., Royal Over-Seas League, 1986– (Dep. Chm., 1982–86; Mem., 1974–, Dep. Chm., 1982–, Central Council). Patron, Internat. Centre for Child Studies, 1984–. FCIT 1975; FBIM. *Recreations:* squash rackets, reading. *Address:* Tall Trees, Marlborough Road, Hampton, Mddx TW12 3RX. *T:* 01–979 2065. *Clubs:* Hurlingham, Royal Over-Seas League.

DALBY, Dr (Terry) David (Pereira); Reader in West African Languages, School of Oriental and African Studies, University of London, 1967–83, now Emeritus; *b* 7 Jan. 1933; *s* of Ernest Edwin Dalby and Rose Cecilia Dalby; *m* 1st, 1957, Winifred Brand (marr. diss.); two *d*; 2nd, 1982, Catherine Jansens; one *s*. *Educ:* Cardiff High Sch.; Queen Mary Coll., London (BA 1954, PhD 1961; Hon. Life Mem., Queen Mary Coll. Union Soc., 1954). Served to Lieut, Intell. Corps, 1954–56. United Africa Co. Ltd, London and W Africa, 1957–60; Lectr in Mod. Languages, University Coll. of Sierra Leone, 1961–62; Lectr in W African Langs, SOAS, Univ. of London, 1962–67. Hanns Wolff Vis. Prof., Indiana Univ., 1969. Chm., Centre for Afr. Studies, Univ. of London, 1971–74; Dir, Internat. African Inst., 1974–80; Chairman: Internat. Conf. on Manding Studies, 1972, and Drought in Africa Conf., 1973; UK Standing Cttee on Univ. Studies of Africa, 1978–82 (Dep. Chm., 1975–78). Vice-Pres., Unesco Meeting on Cultural Specificity in Africa, Accra, 1980. Member: Governing Body, SOAS, 1969–70; Council, African Studies Assoc. of UK, 1970–73; Cttee of Management, British Inst. in Paris, 1975–82; Comité d'Honneur, Société d'Etudes Linguistiques et Anthropologiques de France, 1980–; Conseil Internat. de Recherche et d'Etude en Linguistique Fondamentale et Appliquée, 1980– (Président, 1984); Centre Internat. de Recherche sur le Bilinguisme, Laval Univ., Que, 1981–; Conseil Scientifique, Assoc. d'Etudes Linguistiques Interculturelles Africaines, Paris, 1982–; Comité Scientifique de Linguistique et Sciences Humaines, Zaire, 1984–; Eur. Council on African Studies, 1985–; Hon. Mem., SOAS, 1983. Editor, African Language Review, 1962–72; Co-editor, Africa, 1976–80. *Publications:* Lexicon of the Mediaeval German Hunt, 1965; Black through White: patterns of communication in Africa and the New World, 1970; (ed) Language and History in Africa, 1970; (ed jtly) Drought in Africa, 1st vol. 1973, 2nd vol. 1978; Language Map of Africa and the adjacent islands, 1977; Clavier international de Niamey, 1984; (jtly) Les langues et l'espace du français, 1985; articles in linguistic and other jls. *Recreations:* cartography, local history. *Address:* Cressenville, 27440 Ecouis, France. *T:* 32.49.35.60.

DALDRY, Sir Leonard (Charles), KBE 1963 (CBE 1960); Chairman, St Loye's College for the Disabled, Exeter, 1969–84; *b* 6 Oct. 1908; *s* of Charles Henry Daldry; *m* 1938, Joan Mary (*d* 1976), *d* of John E. Crisp; no *c*; *m* 1976, Monica Mary, *d* of late G. E. Benson and of Helen Benson, Moretonhampstead, Devon; one *s* one *d*. Joined Barclays Bank DCO 1929; Kenya and New York, 1936–52; Local Dir in W Africa at Lagos, 1952–63; Chm., Nigeria Bd, 1961–63. Assoc. Inst. of Bankers, 1936. Mem. Nigerian Railway Corp., 1955–60; Special Mem., Nigerian House of Reps, 1956–59; Senator, Federal Legislature, Nigeria, 1960–61. *Address:* Prospect House, Budleigh Salterton, Devon. *Club:* Athenæum.

DALE, Barry Gordon, FCA; Board Member for Finance, London Regional Transport, since 1985; *b* 31 July 1938; *s* of Francis and Catherine Dale; *m* 1963, Margaret (*née* Fairbrother); one *s* one *d*. *Educ:* Queen Elizabeth Grammar Sch., Blackburn. Coopers Lybrand, Montreal, 1960–62; Pilkington Brothers Glass, St Helens, 1962–65; ICI, 1965–85: Mond Div., Cheshire, 1966–68; Head Office, 1968–72; Dep. Chief Acct, Mond Div., 1972–78; Finance Dir, ICI Latin America (Wilmington, USA), 1978–80; Chief Acct, Organics Div., Manchester, 1980–84; Director: Magadi Soda Co. (Kenya), 1980–82; Ellis & Everard, 1978–81; London Buses Ltd, 1985–; London Underground Ltd, 1985–; LRT Bus Engineering Ltd, 1985–; Chairman: London Transport Trustee Co., 1985–; London Transport Pension Fund Trustees, 1985–. *Recreations:* golf, walking, other sports. *Address:* London Regional Transport, 55 Broadway, SW1H 0BD. *T:* 01-227 3164. *Clubs:* Royal Commonwealth Society; Tatton (Knutsford).

DALE, David Kenneth Hay, CBE 1976; Governor, Montserrat, West Indies, 1980–85; Clerk, Worshipful Company of Shipwrights, since 1986; *b* 27 Jan. 1927; *s* of Kenneth Hay Dale and Francesca Sussana Hoffman; *m* 1956, Hanna Szydlowska; one *s*. *Educ:* Dorchester Grammar Sch. Joined Queen's Royal Regt, 1944; 2/Lieut 8th Punjab Regt, 1945; Lieut 4 Bn (PWO) 8th Punjab Regt, 1946; Lieut Royal Regt of Artillery, 1948, Captain 1955: served Kenya and Malaya (despatches); Dist Officer, Kenya, 1960, Dist Comr, 1962; Admin Officer Cl. B, subseq. Cl. A, Anglo-French Condominium, New Hebrides, W Pacific, 1965–73; Perm. Sec., Min. of Aviation, Communications and Works, Seychelles, 1973–75; Dep. Governor, Seychelles, 1975; Sec. to Cabinet, Republic of Seychelles, 1976; FCO, 1977–80. *Recreations:* birdwatching, walking, colonial and military history. *Address:* Chatley Cottage, Batcombe, near Shepton Mallet, Somerset BA4 6AF. *T:* Upton Noble 449. *Club:* East India.

DALE, Jim; actor, singer, composer, lyricist; *b* 15 Aug. 1935; *m*; three *s* one *d*. *Educ:* Kettering Grammar School. Music Hall comedian, 1951; singing, compèring, directing, 1951–61; films, 1965–, include: Lock Up Your Daughters, The Winter's Tale, The Biggest Dog in the World, National Health, Adolf Hitler—My Part in his Downfall, Joseph Andrews, Pete's Dragon, Bloodshy, The Spaceman and King Arthur, Scandalous. Joined Frank Dunlop's Pop Theatre for Edinburgh Festival, 1967–68; National Theatre, 1969–71: main roles in National Health, Love's Labour's Lost, Merchant of Venice, Good-natured Man, Captain of Kopenick; also appeared at Young Vic in Taming of the Shrew, Scapino (title rôle and wrote music); title rôle in musical The Card, 1973; Compère of Sunday Night at the London Palladium, 1973–74; Scapino (title rôle), Broadway, 1974–75 (Drama Critics' and Outer Circle Awards for best actor; Tony award nomination for best actor); Barnum, Broadway, 1980 (Tony award for best actor in a musical, Drama Desk Award); A Day in the Death of Joe Egg, NY, 1985 (Tony nomination for best actor; Outer Circle Award for best actor). Composed film music for: The Winter's Tale, Shaliko, Twinky, Georgy Girl (nominated for Academy Award), Joseph Andrews. *Address:* c/o Gottlieb, Schiff, Ticktin & Schachter, 555 5th Avenue, New York, NYC 10017, USA. *T:* 212 922 1880.

DALE, Sir William (Leonard), KCMG 1965 (CMG 1951); International legal consultant; Director of Studies, Government Legal Advisers Course, since 1976; *b* 17 June 1906; *e s* of late Rev. William Dale, Rector of Preston, Yorks; *m* 1966, Mrs Gloria Spellman Finn, Washington, DC; one *d*. *Educ:* Hymers Coll., Hull; London (LLB); Barrister, Gray's Inn, 1931. Asst Legal Adviser, Colonial and Dominions Offices, 1935; Min. of Supply, 1940–45; Dep. Legal Adviser, Colonial and Commonwealth Relations Offices, 1945; Legal Adviser, United Kingdom of Libya, 1951–53; Legal Adviser: Min. of Educn, 1954–61; CRO, subseq. CO, 1961–66. Special Asst to the Law Officers, 1967–68; Gen. Counsel, UNRWA, Beirut, 1968–73. Hon. LLD Hull, 1978. *Publications:* Law of the Parish Church, 1932 (5th edn, 1975); Legislative Drafting: a new approach, 1977; The Modern Commonwealth, 1983; contributions to journals. *Recreation:* music (except Wagner). *Address:* 20 Old Buildings, Lincoln's Inn, WC2A 3UP. *T:* 01–242 9365; 12 New Square, Lincoln's Inn, WC2. *Club:* Travellers'.

DALES, Richard Nigel; HM Diplomatic Service; Deputy High Commissioner, Harare, since 1986; *b* 26 Aug. 1942; *s* of Kenneth Richard Frank Dales and Olwen Mary (*née* Preedy); *m* 1966, Elizabeth Margaret Martin; one *s* one *d*. *Educ:* Chigwell Sch.; St Catharine's Coll., Cambridge (BA 1964). Entered FO, 1964; Third Sec., Yaoundé, Cameroon, 1965–67; FCO, 1968–70; Second Sec., later First Sec., Copenhagen, 1970–73; FCO, 1973; Asst Private Sec. to Foreign and Commonwealth Sec., 1974–77; First Sec., Head of Chancery and Consul, Sofia, Bulgaria, 1977–81; FCO, 1981; Counsellor and Head of Chancery, Copenhagen, 1982–86. *Recreations:* music, walking. *Address:* c/o Foreign and Commonwealth Office, King Charles Street, SW1.

DALGARNO, Prof. Alexander, PhD; FRS 1972; Phillips Professor of Astronomy, since 1977, Chairman of Department of Astronomy, 1971–76, Associate Director of Centre for Astrophysics, 1973–80, Harvard University; Member of Smithsonian Astrophysical Observatory, since 1967; *b* 5 Jan. 1928; *s* of William Dalgarno; *m* 1st, 1957, Barbara Kane (marr. diss. 1972); two *s* two *d*; 2nd, 1972, Emily Izsák. *Educ:* Southgate Grammar Sch.; University Coll., London (Fellow 1976). BSc Maths, 1st Cl. Hons London, 1947; PhD Theoretical Physics London, 1951; AM Harvard, 1967. The Queen's University of Belfast: Lectr in Applied Maths, 1952; Reader in Maths, 1956; Dir of Computing Lab, 1960; Prof. of Quantum Mechanics, 1961; Prof. of Mathematical Physics, 1966–67; Prof. of Astronomy, Harvard Univ., 1967–77; Acting Dir, Harvard Coll. Observatory, 1971–73. Chief Scientist, Geophysics Corp. of America, 1962–63. Editor, Astrophysical Journal Letters, 1973–. Fellow: Amer. Acad. of Arts and Sciences, 1968; Amer. Geophysical Union, 1972; Amer. Physical Soc., 1980; Corresp. Mem., Internat. Acad. Astronautics, 1972. Hon. DSc QUB, 1980. Prize of Internat. Acad. of Quantum Molecular Sci., 1969; Hodgkins Medal, Smithsonian Instn, 1977; Davisson-Germer Prize, Amer. Physical Soc., 1980; Gold Medal, Royal Astronomical Soc., 1986. *Publications:* numerous papers in scientific journals. *Recreations:* squash, books. *Address:* c/o Harvard-Smithsonian Center for Astrophysics, 60 Garden Street, Cambridge, Mass 02138, USA.

DALGLISH, Captain James Stephen, CVO 1955; CBE 1963; *b* 1 Oct. 1913; *e s* of late Rear-Adm. Robin Dalglish, CB; *m* 1939, Evelyn Mary, *e d* of late Rev. A. Ll. Meyricke, Vicar of Aislaby, near Whitby; one *s* one *d*. *Educ:* RN Coll., Dartmouth. Commanded HMS Aisne, 1952–53; HM Yacht Britannia, 1954, HMS Woodbridge Haven and Inshore Flotilla, 1958–59; HMS Excellent, 1959–61; HMS Bulwark, 1961–63; jssc 1950; idc 1957; retired from RN, 1963. Welfare Officer, Metropolitan Police, 1963–73. *Recreations:* gardening, painting. *Address:* Park Hall, Aislaby, Whitby, North Yorks. *T:* Whitby 810213.

DALHOUSIE, 16th Earl of, *cr* 1633; **Simon Ramsay,** KT 1971; GCVO 1979; GBE 1957; MC 1944; LLD; Baron Ramsay, 1619; Lord Ramsay, 1633; Baron Ramsay (UK), 1875; Lord Chamberlain to the Queen Mother, 1965; Lord-Lieutenant of Angus, since 1967; Chancellor, Dundee University, since 1977; *b* 17 Oct. 1914; 2nd *s* of 14th Earl (*d* 1928) and Lady Mary Adelaide Heathcote Drummond Willoughby (*d* 1960), *d* of 1st Earl of Ancaster; *S* brother, 1950; *m* 1940, Margaret Elizabeth, *d* of late Brig.-Gen. Archibald and Hon. Mrs Stirling of Keir; three *s* two *d*. *Educ:* Eton; Christ Church, Oxford. Served TA, Black Watch, 1936–39; embodied, 1939. MP (C) for County of Angus, 1945–50; Conservative Whip, 1946–48 (resigned). Governor-General, Fedn of Rhodesia and Nyasaland, 1957–63. Hon. LLD: Dalhousie, 1952; Dundee, 1967. *Heir:* *s* Lord Ramsay, *qv*. *Address:* Brechin Castle, Brechin. *T:* Brechin 2176; 5 Margaretta Terrace, SW3. *T:* 01–352 6477. *Club:* White's.

See also Earl of Scarbrough.

DALI, Salvador (Felipe Jacinto); Marqués de Dali y de Pubol, 1982; Spanish painter; stage-designer; book-illustrator; writer; interested in commercial art and films; *b* Figueras, Upper Catalonia, 11 May 1904; *s* of Salvador Dali, notary and Felipa Dome (Doménech); *m* 1935, Gala (*d* 1982) (*née* Elena Diaranoff); she *m* 1st, Paul Eluard. *Educ:* Academy of Fine Arts, Madrid; Paris. First one-man show, Barcelona, 1925; became prominent Catalan painter by 1927; began surrealist painting in Paris, 1928; first one-man show, Paris, Nov. 1929; first one-man show, New York, Nov. 1933; visited United States, 1934, 1939, 1940; lectured in Museum of Modern Art, New York, 1935; later, came to London; first visited Italy, 1937. Designer of scenery and costumes for ballet, etc., also of film scenarios. Has held exhibitions of paintings in many American and European Cities; Exhibition of jewels, London, 1960; major exhibition, Rotterdam, 1970; retrospective, Paris, and Tate Gallery, 1980, Madrid and Barcelona, 1983. *Publications:* Babaouo (ballet and film scenarios), 1932; Secret Life of Salvador Dali, 1942; Hidden Faces (novel), 1944; Fifty Secrets of Magic Craftsmanship, 1948; Diary of a Genius, 1966; The Unspeakable Confessions of Salvador Dali, 1976. *Address:* Hotel St Regis, 5th Avenue, and 55th Street, New York, NY 10022, USA; Port-Lligat, Cadaqués, Spain.

DALITZ, Prof. Richard Henry, FRS 1960; Royal Society Research Professor at Oxford University, since 1963; *b* 28 Feb. 1925; *s* of Frederick W. and Hazel B. Dalitz, Melbourne, Australia; *m* 1946, Valda (*née* Suiter) of Melbourne, Australia; one *s* three *d*. *Educ:* Scotch Coll., Melbourne; Univ. of Melbourne; Trinity Coll., Univ. of Cambridge, PhD Cantab, 1950. Lecturer in Mathematical Physics, Univ. of Birmingham, 1949–55; Research appointments in various Univs, USA, 1953–55; Reader in Mathematical Physics, Univ. of Birmingham, 1955–56; Prof. of Physics, Univ. of Chicago, 1956–66. Mem. Council, Royal Soc., 1979–81. Corresp. Mem., Australian Acad. of Science, 1978; For. Mem., Polish Acad. of Sci., 1980. Maxwell Medal and Prize, Institute of Physics and the Physical Soc., 1966; Bakerian Lectr and Jaffe Prize, 1969, Hughes Medal, 1975, Royal Medal, 1982, Royal Soc.; J. Robert Oppenheimer Meml Prize, Univ. of Miami, 1980. *Publications:* Strange Particles and Strong Interactions, 1962 (India); Nuclear Interactions of the

Hyperons, 1965 (India); numerous papers on theoretical physics in various British and American scientific jls. *Recreations:* mountain walking, travelling. *Address:* 1 Keble Road, Oxford OX1 3NP; All Souls College, Oxford.

DALKEITH, Earl of; Richard Walter John Montagu Douglas Scott; *b* 14 Feb. 1954; *s* and *heir* of 9th Duke of Buccleuch, *qv*; *m* 1981, Lady Elizabeth Kerr, *d* of Marquess of Lothian, *qv*; one *s* one *d*. *Educ:* Eton; Christ Church, Oxford. *Heir:* *s* Lord Eskdaill, *qv*. *Address:* Dabton, Thornhill, Dumfriesshire. *T:* Thornhill 30467; 24 Lansdowne Road, W11 3LL. *T:* 01–727 6573.

DALLEY, Christopher Mervyn, CMG 1971; MA Cantab; CEng; Director: London and Scottish Marine Oil Co. Ltd, 1979–84; *b* 26 Dec. 1913; *er s* of late Christopher Dalley; *m* 1947, Elizabeth Alice, *yr d* of late Lt-Gen. Sir James Gammell, KCB, DSO, MC; one *s* three *d*. *Educ:* Epsom Coll., Surrey; Queens' Coll., Cambridge. Served in RN, 1939–45. Joined British Petroleum Co., 1946; joined Oil Operating Companies in Iran, 1954: Asst Gen. Managing Dir, 1958; joined Iraq Petroleum Co. and associated companies, 1962, Man. Dir, 1963, Chm., 1970–73; Chm., Oil Exploration Holdings Ltd, 1973–79; Dir, Viking Resources Trust, 1973–84. Pres., Inst. of Petroleum, 1970; Mem. Council, World Petroleum Congress, 1970. Mem., Governing Body, Royal Medical Foundn (Epsom Coll.), 1970. Order of Homoyoun (Iran), 1963. *Address:* Mead House, Woodham Walter, near Maldon, Essex. *T:* Danbury 2404. *Club:* Athenæum.

DALMENY, Lord; Harry Ronald Neil Primrose; *b* 20 Nov. 1967; *s* and *heir* of 7th Earl of Rosebery, *qv*.

DALRYMPLE, family name of **Earl of Stair.**

DALRYMPLE, Viscount; John David James Dalrymple; *b* 4 Sept. 1961; *s* and *heir* of 13th Earl of Stair, *qv*.

DALRYMPLE, Sir Hew (Fleetwood) Hamilton-, 10th Bt, *cr* 1697; KCVO 1985 (CVO 1974); late Major, Grenadier Guards; Vice-Lieutenant of East Lothian, since 1973; Chairman, Scottish American Investment Company, since 1985 (Director, since 1967); *b* 9 April 1926; *er s* of Sir Hew (Clifford) Hamilton-Dalrymple, 9th Bt, JP; *S* father, 1959; *m* 1954, Lady Anne-Louise Mary Keppel, *d* of 9th Earl of Albemarle, MC, and of (Diana Cicely) Countess of Albemarle, *qv*; four *s*. *Educ:* Ampleforth. Commnd, Grenadier Guards, 1944; Staff Coll., Camberley, 1957; DAAG HQ 3rd Div., 1958–60; Regimental Adjt, Grenadier Guards, 1960–62; retd 1962. Adjt, 1964–85, and Lieut, Queen's Body Guard for Scotland (Royal Company of Archers). Vice-Chm., Scottish & Newcastle Breweries, 1983–86 (Dir, 1967–86). President: E Lothian Scout Council; E Lothian Council for Voluntary Services. DL East Lothian, 1964. *Heir:* *e s* Hew Richard Hamilton-Dalrymple [*b* 3 Sept. 1955. *Educ:* Ampleforth; Corpus Christi Coll., Oxford (MA); Clare Hall, Cambridge (MPhil); Birkbeck Coll., London (MSc). ODI Fellow, Swaziland, 1982–84]. *Address:* Leuchie, North Berwick, East Lothian. *T:* North Berwick 2903. *Club:* Cavalry and Guards.

DALRYMPLE, Ian Murray, FRSA; Film Producer, Writer and Director; *b* 26 Aug. 1903; *s* of late Sir William Dalrymple, KBE, LLD; *m* 2nd, Joan Margaret, *d* of late James Douglas Craig, CMG, CBE; one *s* and one *d* of previous marriage and two *s*. *Educ:* Rugby Sch.; Trinity Coll., Cambridge (Editor of The Granta, 1924–25). Executive Producer, Crown Film Unit, Min. of Information, 1940–43; subseq. op. through Wessex Film Productions Ltd and Ian Dalrymple (Advisory) Ltd. Chm. Brit. Film Acad., 1957–58. Film Editor, 1927–35. Screen writer, 1935–39, films including The Citadel, South Riding, Storm in a Teacup, The Lion Has Wings. Produced for Crown Film Unit; Fires Were Started, Western Approaches, Coastal Command, Ferry Pilot, Close Quarters, Wavell's 30,000, Target for To-Night, London Can Take It, etc. Independent productions: The Woman in the Hall, Esther Waters, Once a Jolly Swagman, All Over The Town, Dear Mr Prohack, The Wooden Horse, Family Portrait, The Changing Face of Europe (series), Royal Heritage, Raising a Riot, A Hill in Korea. Commissioned productions include: The Heart of the Matter, The Admirable Crichton, A Cry from the Streets, Bank of England (Educational Films), The Boy and the Pelican. Film Adviser, Decca Ltd, 1967–68. Supervising Film Projects, Argo Record Co. (Div. of Decca Ltd), 1969. Prod Chaucer's Tale, 1970. *Address:* 3 Beaulieu Close, Cambridge Park, Twickenham TW1 2JR.

DALRYMPLE-HAMILTON of Bargany, Captain North Edward Frederick, CVO 1961; MBE 1953; DSC 1943; JP; DL; Royal Navy; *b* 17 Feb. 1922; *s* of Admiral Sir Frederick Dalrymple-Hamilton of Bargany, KCB; *m* 1st, 1949, Hon. Mary Colville (*d* 1981), *d* of 1st Baron Clydesmuir, PC, GCIE, TD; two *s*; 2nd, 1983, Antoinette, *widow* of Major Rowland Beech. *Educ:* Eton. Entered Royal Navy, 1940; Comdr 1954; Captain 1960. Comdg Officer HMS Scarborough, 1958; Executive Officer, HM Yacht Britannia, 1959; Captain (F) 17th Frigate Squadron, 1963; Dir of Naval Signals, 1965; Dir, Weapons Equipment Surface, 1967; retd, 1970. Ensign, Royal Company of Archers, Queen's Body Guard for Scotland. DL 1973, JP 1980, Ayrshire. *Address:* Lovestone House, Bargany, Girvan, Ayrshire KA26 9RF. *T:* Old Dailly 227. *Clubs:* Pratt's, MCC; New (Edinburgh).

DALRYMPLE-HAY, Sir James Brian, 6th Bt, *cr* 1798; estate agent; Principal, Dalrymple-Hay Overseas, since 1985; *b* 19 Jan. 1928; *e s* of Lt-Col Brian George Rowland Dalrymple-Hay (*d* on active service, 1943) and Beatrice (*d* 1935), *d* of A. W. Inglis; *S* cousin, 1952; *m* 1958, Helen Sylvia, *d* of late Stephen Herbert Card and of Molly M. Card; three *d*. *Educ:* Hillsbrow Preparatory Sch., Redhill; Blundell's Sch., Tiverton, Devon. Royal Marine, 1946–47; Lieut Royal Marine Commando, 1947–49; Palestine Star, 1948. Estate Agent and Surveyor's Pupil, 1949; Principal, 1955–67. Partner, Whiteheads PLC, Estate Agents, 1967, Dir, 1983–85. *Heir:* *b* John Hugh Dalrymple-Hay [*b* 16 Dec. 1929; *m* 1962, Jennifer, *d* of late Brig. Robert Johnson, CBE; one *s*]. *Address:* The Red House, Church Street, Warnham, near Horsham, W Sussex.

DALRYMPLE-SMITH, Captain Hugh, RN (retired); *b* 27 Sept. 1901; *s* of late Arthur Alexander Dalrymple-Smith and late Mary Glover; *m* 1939, Eleanor Mary Hoare; two *s* one *d*. *Educ:* Ovingdean; Osborne; Dartmouth. Midshipman, 1917; Ronald Megaw Prize for 1921–22; qualified gunnery 1925, advanced course, 1928. Capt. 1941 (despatches); Admiralty Operations Div., 1942–43; commanding HMS Arethusa, including Normandy landings, 1943–45 (despatches). Naval Attaché, Nanking, 1946–48; commanding HMS King George V, 1948–49. Retired, Dec. 1950, and recalled as Actg Rear-Adm.; Chief of Staff to C-in-C Allied Forces, Northern Europe, 1951–53; retired as Captain. Dir, Television Audience Measurement Ltd, 1958–66. *Recreation:* painting. *Address:* Dale Cottage, Bridge Street, Wickham, Hants PO17 5JE. *T:* Wickham 833103.

DALRYMPLE-WHITE, Sir Henry Arthur Dalrymple, 2nd Bt, *cr* 1926; DFC 1941 and Bar 1942; *b* 5 Nov. 1917; *o s* of Lt-Col Sir Godfrey Dalrymple-White, 1st Bt, and late Hon. Catherine Mary Cary, *d* of 12th Viscount Falkland; *S* father 1954; *m* 1948, Mary (marr. diss. 1956), *o d* of Capt. Robert H. C. Thomas; one *s*. *Educ:* Eton; Magdalene Coll., Cambridge; London Univ. Formerly Wing Commander RAFVR. Served War of 1939–45. *Heir:* *s* Jan Hew Dalrymple-White, *b* 26 Nov. 1950. *Address:* c/o Aero Club of East Africa, PO Box 40813, Nairobi, Kenya.

DALSAGER, Poul; Member, Commission of the European Communities, 1981–84; *b* 5 March 1929; *m* 1951, Betty Jørgensen; two *s*. *Educ:* grammar sch. Bank employee, 1945–64; Mem. (Social Democrat), Danish Parliament, 1964–81; Chm., Market Cttee of Parlt, 1971–73; Chm., Social-Democratic Gp in Parlt, 1978–79; Minister for: Agriculture and Fisheries, 1975–77 and 1979–81; Agriculture, 1977–78. Mem. and Vice Pres., European Parlt, 1973 and 1974. Delegate to UN Gen. Assembly, 1969–71. Dep. Mayor. *Address:* Gram Mikkelsensvej 12, 9800 Hjørring, Denmark.

DALTON, Sir Alan (Nugent Goring), Kt 1977; CBE 1969, DL, Chairman, English China Clays PLC, since 1984 (Deputy Chairman, 1968–84); Managing Director, English Clays, Lovering Pochin & Co. Ltd, 1961–84; *b* 26 Nov. 1923; *s* of Harold Goring Dalton and Phyllis Marguerite (*née* Ash). *Educ:* Shendish Prep. Sch., King's Langley; King Edward VI Sch., Southampton. Chm., British Railways (Western) Bd, 1978–; Member: Sun Alliance & London Assurance Group Bd, 1976–; SW Reg. Bd, Nat. Westminster Bank PLC, 1977–; Director, Westland plc (formerly Westland Aircraft), 1980–85. CBIM; FRSA. DL Cornwall, 1982. *Recreations:* sailing, painting, reading. *Address:* English China Clays PLC, John Keay House, St Austell, Cornwall PL25 4DG.

DALTON, Alfred Hyam, CB 1976; Deputy Chairman, Board of Inland Revenue, 1973–82 (Commissioner of Inland Revenue, 1970–82); *b* 29 March 1922; *m* 1946, Elizabeth Stalker; three *d*. *Educ:* Merchant Taylors' Sch., Northwood; Aberdeen Univ. Served War, REME, 1942–45 (despatches). Entered Inland Revenue, 1947; Asst Sec., 1958; Sec. to Board, 1969. *Address:* 10 Courtmead Close, Burbage Road, SE24 9HW. *T:* 01–733 5395.

DALTON, Maj.-Gen. Sir Charles (James George), Kt 1967; CB 1954; CBE 1949 (OBE 1941); *b* 28 Feb. 1902; *s* of late Maj.-Gen. James Cecil Dalton, Col Comdt, RA, and late Mary Caroline, *d* of late Gen. Sir George Barker, GCB; *m* 1936, Daphne, *d* of Col Llewellyn Evans, and late Mrs F. A. Macartney; one *s* two *d* (and one *s* decd). *Educ:* Aysgarth Sch., Yorks; Cheltenham Coll.; RMA Woolwich. Commissioned, RA, 1921; Staff Coll., Camberley, 1935–36; served in Egypt and India, 1922–39; staff appts in India and Burma, 1939–45 (CRA 26 Ind. Div., BGS 33 Ind. Corps, CRA 14 Ind. Div.); served with CCG, 1946; War Office (Brig. AG Coordination), 1946–49; Comdr 8 AA Bde, 1949–51; Services Relations Adviser to UK High Comr Control Commn for Germany, 1951–54; Dir of Manpower Planning, War Office, 1954–57, retired. Capt. 1934, Major 1939, Lt-Col 1946, Col 1947, Brig. 1951, Maj.-Gen. 1954. Col Comdt RA, 1960–65. Dir-Gen. of Zoological Soc. of London, 1957–67. High Sheriff of Yorks 1972. CStJ. *Recreations:* shooting and fishing. *Address:* The Hutts, Grewelthorpe, Ripon, North Yorks. *T:* Kirkby Malzeard 355.

DALTON, Vice-Adm. Sir Geoffrey (Thomas James Oliver), KCB 1986; Deputy Supreme Allied Commander Atlantic, 1984–April 1987; *b* 14 April 1931; *s* of late Jack Rowland Thomas Dalton and Margaret Kathleen Dalton; *m* 1957, Jane Hamilton (*née* Baynes); four *s*. *Educ:* Parkfield, Sussex; Reigate Grammar Sch.; RNC Dartmouth. Midshipman 1950; served in HM Ships Illustrious, Loch Alvie, Cockade, Virago, Flag Lieut to C-in-C The Nore, and HMS Maryton (in comd), 1950–61; served HMS Murray, RN Staff Course and HMS Dido, 1961–66; served HMS Relentless (in Comd), RN Sch. of PT, HMS Nubian (in Comd), Staff of Flag Officers Second in Comd Far East Fleet and Second Flotilla, 1966–72; Asst Dir of Naval Plans, 1972–74; RCDS, 1975; Captain RN Presentation Team, 1976–77; in Comd HMS Jupiter, 1977–79 and HMS Dryad, 1979–81; Asst Chief of Naval Staff (Policy), 1981–84. Commander, 1966; Captain, 1972; Rear-Adm. 1981. *Recreations:* squash, fishing, gardening, walking. *Address:* c/o Lloyds Bank, Cox's and King's Branch, Pall Mall, SW1.

DALTON, Irwin, CBE 1986; Executive Vice-Chairman, National Bus Company, since 1985; *b* 25 July 1932; *s* of Harry Farr Dalton and Bessie Dalton; *m* 1954, Marie Davies; two *d*. *Educ:* Cockburn High Sch., Leeds. FCA 1973; FCIT 1978. Accountancy profession, 1947–62; Asst Company Sec., 1962–67, Company Sec., 1968–70, West Riding Automobile, Wakefield; Company Sec., Crosville Motor Services, 1971–74; Dir and Gen. Manager, Ribble Motor Services, 1974–76; National Bus Company: Regional Dir, 1977–81; Mem. for Personnel Services, 1981–83; Exec. Bd Mem., 1983–84. A Vice-Pres., Bus and Coach Council, 1983–. *Recreations:* golf, other sporting activities. *Address:* Westview, 1 Birling Park Avenue, Birling Road, Tunbridge Wells, Kent TN2 5LQ. *T:* Tunbridge Wells 33459. *Club:* Tunbridge Wells Golf.

DALTON, Vice-Adm. Sir Norman (Eric), KCB 1959 (CB 1956); OBE 1944; *b* 1 Feb. 1904; *s* of late William John Henry Dalton, Portsmouth; *m* 1927, Teresa Elizabeth (*d* 1982), *d* of late Richard Jenkins, Portsmouth; one *s* one *d*. *Educ:* RN Colls Osborne and Dartmouth. Joined RN, 1917; Capt. 1946; Rear-Adm. 1954; Vice-Adm. 1957. Deputy Engineer-in-Chief of the Fleet, 1955–57; Engineer-in-Chief of the Fleet, 1957–59; Dir-Gen. of Training, 1959–60; retired 1960. *Address:* New Lodge, Peppard Lane, Henley-on-Thames, Oxon. *T:* Henley 575552. *Club:* Army and Navy.

DALTON, Peter Gerald Fox, CMG 1958; *b* 12 Dec. 1914; *s* of late Sir Robert (William) Dalton, CMG; *m* 1944, Josephine Anne Helyar; one *s* one *d*. *Educ:* Uppingham Sch.; Oriel Coll., Oxford. HM Embassy, Peking 1937–39; HM Consulate-Gen., Hankow, 1939–41; HM Embassy, Chungking, 1941–42; Foreign Office, 1942–46; HM Legation, Bangkok, 1946; HM Embassy, Montevideo, 1947–50; Foreign Office, 1950–53; Political Adviser, Hong Kong, 1953–56; Foreign Office, 1957–60; HM Embassy, Warsaw, 1960–63; HM Consul-General: Los Angeles, 1964–65; San Francisco, 1965–67; Minister, HM Embassy, Moscow, 1967–69; retd from HM Diplomatic Service, 1969. *Address:* Rotherdale Cottage, Fir Toll Road, Mayfield, Sussex. *T:* Mayfield 873421.

DALTON, Philip Neale; Vice President, Immigration Appeal Tribunal, 1970–82; *b* 30 June 1909; *o s* of late Sir Llewelyn Dalton, MA; *m* 1947, Pearl, *d* of Mark Foster, Kenya; one *s* two *d*. *Educ:* Downside Sch.; Trinity Coll., Cambridge. Barrister-at-law. Inner Temple, 1933; Resident Magistrate, Ghana, 1937; military service, 1939–45; Crown Counsel, Ghana, 1945–51; Solicitor-Gen., Fiji, 1951–53; Attorney-Gen., British Solomon Islands, and Legal Adviser, Western Pacific High Commission, 1953–56; Attorney-Gen., Zanzibar, 1957–63; Puisne Judge, Kenya, 1963–69. Order of the Brilliant Star (second class) Zanzibar, 1963. *Recreations:* cricket, golf. *Address:* Spring Lane, Aston Tirrold, Oxon. *Clubs:* Royal Commonwealth Society; Nairobi (Nairobi).

DALY, Most Rev. Cahal Brendan; *see* Down and Connor, Bishop of, (RC).

DALY, Hon. Francis Lenton; barrister; Chief Justice: Solomon Islands, 1980–84; Nauru, 1983; *b* 23 June 1938; *s* of Sydney Richard Daly and Lilian May Daly (*née* Lindholm); *m* 1964, Joyce Brenda (*née* Nicholls). *Educ:* Forest School; London School of Economics (LLB). Called to Bar, Gray's Inn, 1961 (Lord Justice Holker Exhibn). English Bar, 1961–66; Legal Secretary, Lord Chancellor's Office, 1966; Bermudian Bar, 1966–72; Asst Judge Advocate General to the Forces, UK, 1972–78; Principal Magistrate, Malaita, Solomon Islands, 1978; Attorney General, Solomon Islands, 1979; admitted, Qld Bar, 1984. *Publications:* contribs to International and Comparative Law Qly, Commonwealth Judicial Jl. *Recreations:* yachting, rowing, reading. *Address:* 18 Abbott Street, Cairns, Qld 4870, Australia. *T:* 070–51–9133. *Clubs:* Royal Commonwealth Society; Cairns Yacht.

DALY, Rt. Rev. John Charles Sydney; Assistant to the Bishop of Coventry, since 1968; *b* 13 Jan. 1903; *s* of S. Owen Daly. *Educ:* Gresham's Sch., Holt; King's Coll., Cambridge; Cuddesdon Coll., Oxford. Curate, St Mary's Church, Tyne Dock, South Shields, 1926–29; Vicar, Airedale with Fryston, Yorks, 1929–35; Bishop of Gambia, 1935–51; Bishop of Accra, 1951–55; Bishop in Korea, 1955–65, of Taejon (Korea), 1965–68; Priest-in-charge of Honington with Idlicote and Whatcote, 1968–70; Vicar of Bishop's Tachbrook, 1970–75. *Address:* Rye Croft, Honington, Shipston-on-Stour, Warwicks CV36 5AA. *T:* Shipston-on-Stour 62140.

DALY, John Daniel; General Secretary, National and Local Government Officers' Association, since 1983 (Deputy General Secretary, 1982–83); *b* 27 Aug. 1930. *Educ:* Ruskin Coll., Oxford (Oxford Univ. Dip. in Econs and Pol. Science). WEA, 1954–57; National Union of Tailors and Garment Workers, 1957–65; TUC, 1965–68; NALGO, 1968–. Member: TUC Internat. Cttee, 1985–; Employment Appeal Tribunal, 1986–. *Recreations:* music, reading, walking. *Address:* National and Local Government Officers' Association, 1 Mabledon Place, WC1H 9AJ. *T:* 01–388 2366.

DALY, Lawrence; General Secretary, National Union of Mineworkers, 1968–84; *b* 20 Oct. 1924; *s* of James Daly and late Janet Taylor; *m* 1948, Renée M. Baxter; four *s* one *d*. *Educ:* primary and secondary schools. Glencraig Colliery (underground), 1939; Workmen's Safety Inspector, there, 1954–64. Part-time NUM lodge official, Glencraig, 1946; Chm., Scottish NUM Youth Committee, 1949; elected to Scottish Area NUM Exec. Cttee, 1962; Gen. Sec., Scottish NUM, 1964; National Exec., NUM, 1965. Mem., TUC General Council, 1978–81. *Publications:* (pamphlets): A Young Miner Sees Russia, 1946; The Miners and the Nation, 1968. *Recreations:* literature, politics, folk-song. *Address:* Glencraig, 45 Hempstead Lane, Potten End, Berkhamsted, Herts. *Club:* Railway (Euston, London).

DALY, Margaret Elizabeth; Member (C) Somerset and Dorset West, European Parliament, since 1984; *b* 26 Jan. 1938; *d* of Robert and Elizabeth Bell; *m* 1964, Kenneth Anthony Edward Daly; one *d*. *Educ:* Methodist Coll., Belfast. Departmental Head, Phoenix Assurance Co., 1956–60; Trade Union Official, Guild of Insurance Officials, later Union of Insurance Staffs, and subseq. merged with ASTMS, 1960–71; Consultant, Cons. Party, 1976–79; Nat. Dir of Cons. Trade Unionists, 1979–84. *Recreations:* swimming, music, travel. *Address:* The Old School House, Aisholt, Spaxton, Bridgwater, Somerset.

DALY, Michael de Burgh, MA, MD, ScD Cambridge; FRCP; Emeritus Professor of Physiology in the University of London, since 1984; Visiting Scientist, Department of Physiology, Royal Free Hospital School of Medicine, London, since 1984; *b* 7 May 1922; *s* of late Dr Ivan de Burgh Daly, CBE, FRS; *m* 1948, Beryl Esmé, *y d* of late Wing Commander A. J. Nightingale; two *s*. *Educ:* Loretto Sch., Edinburgh; Gonville and Caius Coll., Cambridge; St Bartholomew's Hospital. Nat. Science Tripos. Part I, 1943, Part II, 1944, Physiology. House-physician, St Bartholomew's Hospital, 1947; Asst Lecturer, 1948–50, and Lecturer, 1950–54, in Physiology, University Coll., London. Rockefeller Foundation Travelling Fellowship in Medicine, 1952–53; Locke Research Fellow of Royal Soc., 1955–58; St Bartholomew's Hospital Medical College: Prof. of Physiology, 1958–84; Governor, 1975–; Treas., 1983–84. Vis. Prof. of Physiology, Univ. of NSW, 1966; Vis. Lectr, Swedish Univs, 1961; G. L. Brown Lectr, Physiological Soc., 1985–86. Member: Adv. Panel for Underwater Personnel Res., MoD, 1975–; MRC/RN Personnel Res. Cttee, Underwater Physiology Sub-Cttee, 1975–; Res. Funds Cttee, British Heart Foundn, 1982–85. Chm., Editorial Bd of Monographs of Physiological Soc., 1981–; Co-Editor of Journal of Physiology, 1956–63, 1984–. FRSM 1959. Member: Soc. of Experimental Biol., 1965; Physiological Soc., 1951–85 (Hon. Mem., 1986); Osler Med. Club, 1974–; European Underwater Biomed. Soc., 1971–; Undersea Med. Soc. Inc., 1971–. Schafer Prize in Physiology, University Coll., London, 1953; Thruston Medal, Gonville and Caius Coll., 1957; Sir Lionel Whitby Medal, Cambridge Univ., 1963; Gold Medal, BMA, 1972. *Publications:* contributor to: Lippold and Winton, Human Physiology; Starling, Principles of Human Physiology; Bell, Emslie-Smith and Paterson, Textbook of Physiology; papers on the integrative control of respiration and the cardiovascular system in Journal of Physiology; contrib. to film on William Harvey and the Circulation of the Blood. *Recreation:* model engineering. *Address:* 7 Hall Drive, Sydenham, SE26 6XL. *T:* 01–778 8773.

DALY, Michael Francis; HM Diplomatic Service; Ambassador to Costa Rica, and Ambassador (non-resident) to Nicaragua, since 1986; *b* 7 April 1931; *s* of late William Thomas Daly and of Hilda Frances Daly; *m* 1st, 1963, Sally Malcolm Angwin (*d* 1966); one *d*; 2nd, 1971, Juliet Mary Siragusa (*née* Arning); one step-*d*. *Educ:* Downside; Gonville and Caius Coll., Cambridge (BA Hons). Mil. Service, 1952–54: 2nd Lieut, Intell. Corps. E. D. Sassoon Banking Co., London, 1954; Transreef Industrial & Investment Co., Johannesburg, 1955–66; General Electric Co., London, 1966; HM Diplomatic Service: 1st Sec., FCO, 1967; 1st Sec. (Commercial), Rio de Janeiro, 1969; 1st Sec. (Inf.) and Head of Chancery, Dublin, 1973; Asst, Cultural Relations Dept, FCO, 1976; Counsellor, Consul-Gen. and Head of Chancery, Brasilia, 1977–78; Ambassador to Ivory Coast, Upper Volta and Niger, 1978–83; Head of West African Dept, FCO, and Ambassador (non-resident) to Chad, 1983–86. *Recreations:* skiing, sailing, theatre, golf. *Address:* c/o Foreign and Commonwealth Office, SW1.

DALY, Lt-Gen. Sir Thomas (Joseph), KBE 1967 (CBE 1953; OBE 1944); CB 1965; DSO 1945, Chief of the General Staff, Australia, 1966–71; *b* 19 March 1913; *s* of late Lt-Col T. J. Daly, DSO, VD, Melbourne; *m* 1946, Heather, *d* of late James Fitzgerald, Melbourne; three *d*. *Educ:* St Patrick's Coll., Sale; Xavier Coll., Kew, Vic; RMC, Duntroon (Sword of Honour). 3rd LH, 1934; attached for training 16/5 Lancers, India, 1938; Adj, 2/10 Aust. Inf. Bn, 1939; Bde Major, 18 Inf. Bde, 1940; GSO2 6 Aust. Div., 1941; GSO1 5 Aust. Div., 1942; Instructor, Staff Sch. (Aust.), 1944; CO 2/10 Inf. Bn, AIF, 1944; Instr, Staff Coll., Camberley, UK, 1946; Joint Services Staff Coll., Latimer, 1948; Dir of Mil. Art, RMC Duntroon, 1949; Dir of Infantry, AHQ, 1951; Comd 28 Brit. Commonwealth Inf. Bde, Korea, 1952; Dir, Ops and Plans, AHQ, 1953; IDC, London, 1956; GOC Northern Command, Australia, 1957–60; Adjt Gen., 1961–63; GOC, Eastern Command, Australia, 1963–66. Col Comdt, Royal Australian Regt, and Pacific Is Regt, 1971–75. Director: Jennings Industries Ltd, 1974–85; Fruehauf Trailers (Aust.) Ltd, 1974–; Associated Merchant Bank (Singapore), 1975–77. Mem., Nat. Council, Australian Red Cross, 1972–75; Chm., Council, Australian Nat. War Memorial, 1974–82 (Mem., 1966–74); Councillor, Royal Agricl Soc. of NSW, 1972–. Legion of Merit (US), 1953. *Recreations:* golf, tennis, cricket, ski-ing. *Address:* 16 Victoria Road, Bellevue Hill, NSW 2023, Australia. *Clubs:* Australian, Ski Club of Australia (Sydney); Naval and Military (Melbourne); Royal Sydney Golf, Melbourne Cricket.

DALYELL, Tam; MP (Lab) Linlithgow, since 1983 (West Lothian, 1962–83); *b* 9 Aug. 1932; *s* of late Gordon and Eleanor Dalyell; *m* 1963, Kathleen, *o d* of Baron Wheatley, *qv*; one *s* one *d*. *Educ:* Eton; King's Coll., Cambridge; Moray House Teachers' Training Coll., Edinburgh. Trooper, Royal Scots Greys, 1950–52; Teacher, Bo'ness High Sch., 1956–60. Contested (Lab) Roxburgh, Selkirk, and Peebles, 1959. Dep.-Director of Studies on British India ship-school, Dunera, 1961–62. Member Public Accounts Cttee, House of Commons, 1962–66; Secretary, Labour Party Standing Conference on the Sciences, 1962–64; PPS to Rt Hon. Richard Crossman, Minister of Housing, Leader of H of C, Sec. of State for the Social Services, 1964–70; Opposition spokesman on science, 1980–82; Chairman: PLP Education Cttee, 1964–65; PLP Sports Group, 1964–74; PLP Foreign Affairs Gp, 1974–75; Vice-Chairman: PLP Defence and Foreign Affairs Gps, 1972–74; Scottish Labour Group of MPs, 1973–75; Parly Lab. Party, Nov. 1974–; Sub-Cttee on Public Accounts; Member: European Parlt, 1975–79; European Parlt Budget Cttee, 1976–79; European Parlt Energy Cttee, 1979; Member: House of Commons Select Cttee on Science and Technology, 1967–69; Liaison Cttee between Cabinet and Parly Labour Party, 1974–76; Council, National Trust for Scotland. Mem. Scottish Council for Devlt and Industry Trade Delegn to China, Nov. 1971. Political columnist, New Scientist, 1967–. *Publications:* The Case of Ship-Schools, 1960; Ship-School Dunera, 1963; Devolution: the end of Britain?, 1977; One Man's Falklands, 1982; A Science Policy for Britain, 1983; Thatcher's Torpedo, 1983. *Recreations:* tennis, swimming. *Address:* The Binns, Linlithgow, Scotland. *T:* Philipstoun 4255.

DALZELL-PAYNE, Maj.-Gen. Henry Salusbury Legh, CBE 1973; international business consultant, R. H. Sanbar Group, New York, since 1982; *b* 1929; *s* of late Geoffrey Legh Dalzell-Payne; *m* 1963, Serena Helen (marr. diss. 1980), *d* of Col Clifford White Gourlay, MC, TD; two *d*. *Educ:* Cheltenham; RMA Sandhurst. Commissioned, 7th Hussars, 1949; Major, Sultan of Muscat's Armed Forces, 1959–60; Staff Coll., Camberley, 1961; BM 20 Armd Brigade Gp, 1962–64; Queen's Own Hussars, 1964–65; Instructor, Staff Coll., Camberley, 1966; Comd 3rd Dragoon Guards, 1967–69; Gen. Staff, Mil. Ops, MoD, 1970–72; student, RCDS, 1973; Comdr, 6th Armoured Brigade, 1974–75; Chief of Staff, 1 (BR) Corps, 1976–78; GOC 3 Armoured Div., 1978–80. *Clubs:* White's, Cavalry and Guards, Turf, Hurlingham.

DALZIEL, Geoffrey Albert; British Commissioner, Leader of Salvation Army activities in Gt Britain, 1974–80; *b* 10 Dec. 1912; *s* of Alexander William and Olive Mary Dalziel; *m* 1937, Ruth Edith Fairbank; two *s* one *d*. *Educ:* Harrow Elementary Sch. Commissioned Salvation Army Officer, 1934; Corps Officer in Gt Britain, to 1946; on Internat. Trng Coll. Staff, 1946–51; Divisional Youth Sec., 1951–59; Trng Coll. Principal, Melbourne, Aust., 1959–64; Chief Side Officer, Internat. Trng Coll., London, 1964–66; Chief Secretary: Sydney, Aust., 1966–68; Toronto, Canada, 1968–70; Territorial Comdr, Kenya, Uganda and Tanzania, E Africa, 1970–74. *Recreations:* walking, gardening, reading. *Address:* 407 Wickham Road, Shirley, Croydon, Surrey CR0 8DP.

DALZIEL, Ian Martin; Director, Adam & Co. plc, since 1983; *b* 21 June 1947; *s* of late John Calvin Dalziel and of Elizabeth Roy Dalziel, *e d* of Rev. Ian Bain, FRSE and Mrs Christian Stuart Fisher Bain, Gairloch; *m* 1972, Nadia Maria Iacovazzi; four *s*. *Educ:* Daniel Stewart's Coll., Edinburgh; St John's Coll., Cambridge (BA Hons 1968, LLB Hons 1969); Université Libre de Bruxelles (Weiner Anspach Foundation Scholarship, 1970). MA 1972. Mullens & Co., 1970–72; Manufacturers Hanover Ltd, 1972–83. Mem., Richmond upon Thames Council, 1978–79. Mem. (C) Lothian, European Parlt, 1979–84. *Recreations:* golf, shooting. *Address:* 21 Greenhill Gardens, Edinburgh EH10 4BL. *T:* 031–447 3441; (office) 22 Charlotte Square, Edinburgh EH2 4DF. *T:* 031–225 8484. *Club:* New (Edinburgh).

DALZIEL, Dr Keith, FRS 1975; Reader in Biochemistry, University of Oxford, 1978–83; Fellow of Wolfson College, 1970–83, now Emeritus; *b* 24 Aug. 1921; *s* of late Gilbert and Edith Dalziel; *m* 1945, Sallie Farnworth; two *d*. *Educ:* Grecian Street Central Sch., Salford; Royal Techn. Coll., Salford; 1st cl. hons BSc London 1944; PhD London; MA Oxon. Lab. Technician, Manchester Victoria Meml Jewish Hosp., 1935–44, Biochemist 1944–45; Asst Biochemist, Radcliffe Infirmary, Oxford, 1945–47; Res. Asst, Nuffield Haematology Res. Fund, Oxford, 1947–58; Rockefeller Trav. Fellowship in Medicine, Nobel Inst., Stockholm, 1955–57; Sorby Res. Fellow of Royal Soc., Sheffield Univ., 1958–63; Univ. Lectr in Biochem., Oxford, 1963–78. Vis. Prof. of Biochemistry, Univ. of Michigan, 1967. Member: Enzyme Chem. and Tech. Cttee, SRC, 1974; Council, Royal Soc., 1979–80; Editorial Bds, European Jl of Biochemistry and Biochimica Biophysica Acta, 1971–74; Adv. Bd, Jl Theor. Biol., 1976–79; an Associate Editor, Royal Soc., 1983–. *Publications:* sci. papers in Biochem. Jl, European Jl of Biochemistry, etc. *Recreations:* music, golf, walking. *Address:* 25 Hampden Drive, Kidlington, Oxford. *T:* Kidlington 2623.

DALZIEL, Malcolm Stuart, CBE 1984; Controller, Higher Education Division, British Council, since 1983, and Secretary, Inter University and Polytechnic Council; *b* 18 Sept. 1936; *s* of late Robert Henderson Dalziel and Susan Aileen (*née* Robertson); *m* 1961, Anne Elizabeth Harvey; one *s* two *d*. *Educ:* Banbury Grammar Sch.; St Catherine's Coll., Oxford (BA 1960, MA 1965). National Service, 2nd Lieut Northamptonshire Regt, 1955–57. Joined The British Council, 1960; Asst Educn Officer, Lahore, Pakistan, 1961–63; Regional Dir, Penang, Malaya, 1963–67; Regional Rep., Lahore, 1967–70; Rep., Sudan, 1970–74; Dir, Management Services Dept, and Dep. Controller, Estabs Div., 1975–79; Rep., Egypt, and Counsellor (Cultural) British Embassy, Cairo, 1979–83. Sec., CICHE, 1983. Mem., Court, Univ. of Essex, 1986–. *Recreations:* theatre, ballet, walking, Rugby (now only spectating). *Address:* c/o The British Council, 10 Spring Gardens, SW1A 2BN. *T:* 01–930 8466. *Club:* United Oxford & Cambridge University.

DAMER; *see* Dawson-Damer, family name of Earl of Portarlington.

DAMERELL, Derek Vivian; Governor, since 1974, and Deputy Chairman, since 1984, BUPA (Chief Executive, 1974–84); Director, Murrayfield plc, since 1982; *b* 4 Aug. 1921; *s* of William James Damerell (Lt-Col), MBE and Zoe Damerell; *m* 1942, Margaret Isabel Porritt, *d* of Prof. B. D. Porritt; two *s* three *d*. *Educ:* ISC; Edinburgh Univ.; Harvard Business Sch. Parent Bd, BPB Industries, 1953–64; Regional Dir, Internat. Wool Secretariat, 1965–73. Governor, Nuffield Nursing Homes Trust, 1974–80; Founder, Independ. Hosp. Gp (Chm., 1975–80); Internat. Fedn of Voluntary Health Service Funds: Mem. Council, 1976–; Dep. Pres., 1980–81, Pres., 1981–84; Mem. Bd of Governors, Assoc. Internat. de la Mutualité, 1974–83. *Recreations:* sailing (jt founder, BCYC, 1947); travel. *Address:* The Miller's House, Houghton, near Huntingdon, Cambs PE17 2BQ. *T:* St Ives 63285. *Clubs:* various yacht.

DAMMERS, Very Rev. Alfred Hounsell, (Horace), Dean of Bristol, 1973–May 1987; *b* 10 July 1921; *s* of late B. F. H. Dammers, MA, JP; *m* 1947, Brenda Muriel, *d* of late Clifford Stead; two *s* two *d*. *Educ:* Malvern Coll. (Schol.); Pembroke Coll., Cambridge (Schol., MA); Westcott House, Cambridge. Served RA (Surrey and Sussex Yeo.), 1941–44. Asst Curate, Adlington, Lancs, 1948; Asst Curate, S Bartholomew's, Edgbaston, Birmingham, and Lectr at Queen's Coll., Birmingham, 1950; Chaplain and Lectr at S John's Coll., Palayamkottai, S India, 1953; Vicar of Holy Trinity, Millhouses, Sheffield, and Examining Chaplain to Bishop of Sheffield, 1957; Select Preacher at Univ. of Cambridge, 1963; Select Preacher at Univ. of Oxford, 1975; Chairman, Friends of Reunion, 1965; Canon Residentiary and Director of Studies, Coventry Cathedral, 1965. Founder, The Life Style Movement, 1972. Companion, Community of the Cross of Nails, 1975. *Publications:* Great Venture, 1958; Ye Shall Receive Power, 1958; All in Each Place, 1962; God is Light, God is Love, 1963; AD 1980, 1966; Lifestyle: a parable of sharing,

1982; A Christian Life-style, 1986. *Recreations:* travel (home and abroad); walking, candle making, sailing. *Address:* The Deanery, 20 Charlotte Street, Bristol BS1 5PZ. *T:* Bristol 22443.

DANCE, Brian David, MA; Headmaster, St Dunstan's College, Catford, since 1973; *b* 22 Nov. 1929; *s* of late L. H. Dance and late Mrs M. G. Swain (*née* Shrivelle); *m* 1955, Chloe Elizabeth, *o d* of J. F. A. Baker, *qv*; two *s* two *d*. *Educ:* Kingston Grammar Sch.; Wadham Coll., Oxford. BA 1952, MA 1956. Asst Master, Kingston Grammar Sch., 1953–59; Sen. History Master: Faversham Grammar Sch., 1959–62; Westminster City Sch., 1962–65; Headmaster: Cirencester Grammar Sch., 1965–66; Luton Sixth Form Coll., 1966–73. Cambridge Local Examination Syndicate, 1968–73; Headmasters' Assoc. Council, 1968–76 (Exec. Cttee, 1972–76, Hon. Legal Sec. 1975–76); Chm., London Area, SHA, 1984–85. *Publications:* articles in: Times Educnl Supp.; Headmasters' Assoc. 'Review'. *Recreations:* watching most ball games (especially cricket and Rugby football), music, philately. *Address:* Headmaster's House, St Dunstan's College, Catford SE6 4TY. *T:* 01–690 1277. *Club:* East India, Devonshire, Sports and Public Schools.

d'ANCONA, John Edward William; Director General, Offshore Supplies Office of the Department of Energy, since 1981; *b* 28 May 1935; *o s* of late Adolph and late Margaret d'Ancona; *m* 1958, Mary Helen, *o d* of late Sqdn-Ldr R. T. Hunter and late Mrs Hunter; three *s*. *Educ:* St Edward's Coll., Malta; St Cuthbert's Grammar Sch., Newcastle upon Tyne. BA (Hons) Mod. History, DipEd (Durham). Teacher, 1959–61; Civil Service, 1961–: Asst Principal, Dept of Educn and Science, 1961; Private Sec. to Minister of State, DES, 1964–65; Principal: DES, 1965–67; Min. of Technology and DTI, 1967–74; Asst Sec., DoE, 1974; Under Sec., DoE OSO, 1981. *Recreations:* cricket, philately, wine-bibbing. *Address:* c/o Department of Energy, Thames House South, Millbank, SW1.

DANCY, Prof. John Christopher, MA; Professor of Education, University of Exeter, 1978–84, now Emeritus; *b* 13 Nov. 1920; *e s* of late Dr J. H. Dancy and Dr N. Dancy; *m* 1944, Angela Bryant; two *s* one *d*. *Educ:* Winchester (Scholar); New Coll., Oxford (Scholar, MA). 1st Class, Classical Hon. Mods., 1940; Craven Scholar, 1946; Gaisford Greek Prose Prize, 1947; Hertford Scholar, 1947; Arnold Historical Essay Prize, 1949. Served in Rifle Brigade, 1941–46; Capt. GSO(3)I, 30 Corps, 1945; Major, GSO(2)I, 1 Airborne Corps, 1945–46. Lecturer in Classics, Wadham Coll., 1946–48; Asst Master, Winchester Coll., 1948–53; Headmaster of Lancing Coll., 1953–61; Master, Marlborough Coll., 1961–72; Principal, St Luke's Coll. of Educn, Exeter, 1972–78. Dir, St Luke's Coll. Foundn, 1978–86. Member, Public Schools' Commission, 1966–68. Chm., Higher Educn Foundn, 1981–86. *Publications:* Commentary on 1 Maccabees, 1954; The Public Schools and the Future, 1963; Commentary on Shorter Books of Apocrypha, 1972. *Address:* Wharf House, Mousehole, Penzance, Cornwall TR19 6RX. *T:* Penzance 731137.

DANGAN, Viscount; Garret Graham Wellesley, (Jr); student at Franklin College, Switzerland (Economics and Art History); *b* 30 March 1965; *s* and *heir* of 7th Earl Cowley, *qv*.

DANIEL, Gerald Ernest, IPFA, FCA, FRVA; SAT; FRSA; Public Sector Adviser, Pannell Kerr Forster, Chartered Accountants, since 1984; *b* 7 Dec. 1919; *s* of Ernest and Beata May Daniel; *m* 1942, Ecila Roslyn Dillow; one *s* one *d*. *Educ:* Huish's Grammar Sch., Taunton. Served War, 1939–46, Somerset LI. Various appts in Borough Treasurers' Depts at Taunton, Scunthorpe and Bexhill, 1935–50; Cost and machine accountant, subseq. Chief Accountant, City Treasury, Bristol, 1950–60; Dep. Borough Treasurer, Reading, 1960–64; Borough Treasurer, West Bromwich, 1965–68; City Treasurer, Nottingham, 1968–74; County Treasurer, Nottinghamshire CC, 1974–84. Sec., 1971–76, Chm., 1976–81, Officers Side, Jt Negotiating Cttee for Chief Officers in Local Govt. Dir, Horizon Travel, 1975–85. Treasurer: E Midlands Airport, 1968–84; E Midlands Arts Assoc., 1969–84. President: Nottingham Soc. of Chartered Accountants, 1976; Assoc. of Public Service Finance Officers, 1978; Soc. of County Treasurers, 1979; Chartered Inst. of Public Finance and Accountancy, 1983–84 (Mem. Council, 1971–85; Vice-Pres., 1982); Mem. Council, Assoc. of Accounting Technicians, 1981–83. *Recreations:* gardening, music. *Address:* Brookvale, Star Lane, Blackboys, Uckfield, East Sussex TN22 5LD. *T:* Framfield 712. *Club:* Royal Over-Seas League.

DANIEL, Prof. Glyn Edmund, MA, LittD; FBA 1982; Fellow of St John's College, Cambridge, since 1938; Disney Professor of Archæology, University of Cambridge, 1974–81, Emeritus Professor since 1981 (Lecturer, 1948–74); *b* 23 April 1914; *o s* of John Daniel and Mary Jane (*née* Edmunds); *m* 1946, Ruth, *d* of late Rev. R. W. B. Langhorne, Exeter. *Educ:* Barry County Sch.; University College, Cardiff; St John's Coll., Cambridge (Scholar; BA 1st Class Hons with Distinction, Archaeological and Anthropological Tripos). Strathcona Student, 1936; Allen Scholar, 1937; Wallenberg Prizeman, 1937; Research Fellowship, St John's Coll., 1938; PhD 1938; MA 1939; LittD 1962. Intelligence Officer, RAF, 1940–45; in charge Photo Interpretation, India and SE Asia, 1942–45 (despatches); Wing Comdr, 1943. Faculty Asst Lectr in Archaeology, 1945–48; Steward of St John's Coll., 1946–55; Leverhulme Research Fellow, 1948–50; Leverhulme Emeritus Fellow, 1985–87. Lecturer: Munro, Archaeology, Edinburgh Univ., 1954; Rhŷs, British Acad., 1954; O'Donnell, Edinburgh Univ., 1956; Josiah Mason, Birmingham Univ., 1956; Gregynog University College, Wales, 1968; Ballard-Matthews, University Coll. of North Wales, 1968; George Grant MacCurdy, Harvard, 1971. Visiting Prof., Univ. Aarhus, 1968; Ferrens Prof., Univ. Hull, 1969. Pres., South Eastern Union of Scientific Socs, 1955. President: Bristol and Gloucestershire Archaeological Soc., 1962–63; RAI, 1977–79; Somerset Archaeol and Nat. Hist. Soc., 1984–85. Chm., Duchy of Cornwall Adv. Cttee on Archaeology, 1983–. Fellow: UC Cardiff, 1981; Royal Danish Acad. of Science and Letters, 1984. Hon. Mem. Istituto Italiano di Preistoria e Protostoria; Corresponding Fellow, German Archaeological Institute; Corresponding Mem., Jutland Archaeological Soc.; Foreign Hon. Mem., Archaeol Inst. of Amer. Editor, Ancient Peoples and Places, 1955–, and of Antiquity, 1958–86. Director: Anglia Television, Ltd, 1959–81; Antiquity Publications Ltd; Trustee, Cambridge Arts Theatre. FSA 1942. Knight (First Class) of the Dannebrog, 1961. *Publications:* The Three Ages, 1942; A Hundred Years of Archaeology, 1950; The Prehistoric Chamber Tombs of England and Wales, 1950; A Picture Book of Ancient British Art (with S. Piggott), 1951; Lascaux and Carnac, 1955; ed Myth or Legend, 1955; Barclodiad y Gawres (with T. G. E. Powell), 1956; The Megalith Builders of Western Europe, 1958; The Prehistoric Chamber Tombs of France, 1960; The Idea of Prehistory, 1961, rev. edn (with Colin Renfrew), 1986; The Hungry Archaeologist in France, 1963; New Grange and the Bend of the Boyne (with late S. P. O'Riordain), 1964; (ed with I. Ll. Foster), Prehistoric and Early Wales, 1964; Man Discovers his Past, 1966; The Origins and Growth of Archaeology, 1967; The First Civilisations, 1968; Archaeology and the History of Art, 1970; Megaliths in History, 1973; (ed jtly) France before the Romans, 1974; A Hundred and Fifty Years of Archaeology, 1975; Cambridge and the Back-Looking Curiosity: an inaugural lecture, 1976; A Short History of Archaeology, 1981; (ed) Towards a History of Archaeology, 1981; Some Small Harvest (memoirs), 1986; and articles in archaeological journals; *festschrift:* (ed John D. Evans, Barry Cunliffe and Colin Renfrew) Antiquity and Man, 1981. *Recreations:* travel, walking, food, wine, writing detective stories (The Cambridge Murders, 1945; Welcome Death, 1954). *Address:* The Flying Stag, 70 Bridge Street, Cambridge. *T:* 356082; La Marnière, Zouafques-par-Tournehem, 62890 France. *T:* Calais 35.61.40. *Club:* United Oxford & Cambridge University.

DANIEL, Sir Goronwy Hopkin, KCVO 1969; CB 1962; DPhil Oxon; HM Lieutenant for Dyfed, since 1978; *b* Ystradgynlais, 21 March 1914; *s* of David Daniel; *m* 1940, Lady Valerie, *d* of 2nd Earl Lloyd George; one *s* two *d*. *Educ:* Pontardawe Secondary Sch.; Amman Valley County Sch.; University College of Wales, Aberystwyth; Jesus Coll., Oxford (Hon. Fellow, 1979). Fellow of University of Wales; Meyricke Scholar, Jesus Coll.; Oxford Institute of Statistics, 1937–40; Lecturer, Dept of Economics, Bristol Univ., 1940–41; Clerk, House of Commons, 1941–43; Ministry of Town and Country Planning, 1943–47; Ministry of Fuel and Power, Chief Statistician, 1947–55; Under-Sec., Coal Div., 1955–62, Gen. Div., 1962–64; Permanent Under-Sec. of State, Welsh Office, 1964–69; Principal, Aberystwyth UC, 1969–79; Vice-Chancellor, Univ. of Wales, 1977–79; Chm., Welsh Fourth Channel Authority, 1981–86. Chm., British Nat. Conf. on Social Welfare, 1970; Pres., West Wales Assoc. for the Arts, 1971–85; Member: Welsh Language Council, 1974–78; Gen. Adv. Council, BBC, 1974–79; Adv. Council on Energy Conservation, 1977–79; SSRC, 1980–83; Dep. Chm., Prince of Wales Cttee, 1980–. Dir, Commercial Bank of Wales, 1972– (Dep. Chm., 1985–). Chairman: Home-Grown Timber Adv. Cttee, 1974–81; Cttee on Water Charges in Wales, 1974–75. Hon. LLD, Univ. of Wales, 1980. Hon. Freeman, City of London, 1982. *Publications:* papers in statistical, fuel and power, and other journals. *Recreations:* country pursuits, sailing. *Address:* Ridge Farm, Letterston, Dyfed. *T:* Letterston 840586; 4 Deans Close, Llandaf, Cardiff. *T:* Cardiff 553150. *Club:* Travellers'.

DANIEL, Gruffydd Huw Morgan; His Honour Judge Daniel; a Circuit Judge, since 1986; *b* 16 April 1939; *s* of Prof. John Edward Daniel, MA, and Catherine Megan Daniel; *m* 1968, Phyllis Margaret (*née* Bermingham); one *d*. *Educ:* Ampleforth; University College of Wales (LLB); Inns of Court School of Law. Commissioned 2nd Lieut First Bn Royal Welch Fusiliers, 1959; Captain 6/7 Bn Royal Welch Fusiliers (TA), 1965. Called to the Bar, Gray's Inn, 1967; Wales and Chester Circuit (Circuit Junior, 1975); Recorder, 1980–86; Asst Liaison Judge, Gwynedd, 1983–. Asst Parly Boundary Comr for Wales, 1981–82, 1985–86. *Publication:* contributor to Ampleforth Country, 1957. *Recreations:* gardening, shooting, fishing, sailing. *Address:* (residence) Rhiwgoch, Halfway Bridge, Bangor, Gwynedd; 10 Stanley Place, Chester. *Clubs:* Reform; Royal Anglesey Yacht.

DANIEL, Jack; *see* Daniel R. J.

DANIEL, Norman Alexander, CBE 1974 (OBE 1968); PhD; Consultant, Hassan Khalifa, since 1984; historian of the Middle Ages and intercultural relations; *b* 8 May 1919; *s* of George Frederick Daniel and Winifred Evelyn (*née* Jones); *m* 1941, Marion Ruth (*d* 1981), *d* of Harold Wadham Pethybridge; one *s*. *Educ:* Frensham Heights Sch.; Queen's Coll., Oxford (BA); Edinburgh Univ. (PhD). Asst Dir, British Inst., Basra, 1947; British Council Asst Representative: Baghdad, 1948; Beirut, 1952; Edinburgh, 1953; Dir, Brit. Inst., Baghdad, 1957; Dep. Rep., Brit. Council, Scotland, 1960; Brit. Council Rep., Sudan, 1962; Vis. Fellow, University Coll., Cambridge, 1969–70; Dir, Visitors Dept, Brit. Council, London, 1970; Cultural Attaché, Cairo, 1971; British Council Rep. and Cultural Counsellor, British Embassy, Cairo, 1973–79; Planning Advr, Hassan Khalifa, 1979–84; Gen. Sec., Coptic Archaeological Soc., Cairo, 1979–83. Green Vis Prof., Univ. of British Columbia, 1982. Egyptian Order of Merit, 2nd class, 1977. *Publications:* Islam and the West: the making of an image, 1960, 3rd edn 1966, repr. 1980; Islam, Europe and Empire, 1966; The Arabs and Mediaeval Europe, 1975, enlarged and rev. edn 1979, trans. Italian (Premio Lao Silesu Terzo Mondo, 1981); The Cultural Barrier, 1975; Heroes and Saracens, 1984; (contrib.) History of the Crusades, vol. 6 (Wisconsin, in progress); (contrib.) Islam: Past Influence and Future Challenge (ed Cachia), 1979; contrib. to learned jls. *Recreation:* gardening. *Address:* 1 rue Masna al-Tarabich, Abbasiah, Cairo, Egypt. *T:* 825509; Le Grammont, rue Nationale, St Gingolph, 74500 Evian, France. *T:* 50 76 72 62.

DANIEL, Prof. Peter Maxwell, MA, MB, BCh Cambridge; MA, DM Oxon; DSc London; FRCP; FRCS; FRCPath (Founder Fellow); FRCPsych (Founder Fellow); FLS; FInstBiol; Senior Research Fellow, Department of Applied Physiology and Surgical Science, Hunterian Institute, Royal College of Surgeons, since 1976; Visiting Senior Research Fellow, St Thomas's Hospital Medical School, since 1981; Emeritus Professor, lately Professor of Neuropathology, University of London, at the Institute of Psychiatry, Maudsley Hospital, 1957–76; *b* 14 Nov. 1910; *s* of Peter Daniel, FRCS, surgeon to Charing Cross Hospital, and Beatrice Laetitia Daniel; *m* 1st, Sarah Shelford; two *s* three *d*; 2nd, F. Dawn Bosanquet; one *s*; 3rd, Marion F. Bosanquet. *Educ:* Westminster Sch.; St John's Coll., Cambridge; New Coll., Oxford. Hon. Consultant Pathologist, Radcliffe Infirmary, 1948–56; Senior Research Officer, University of Oxford, 1949–56; Hon. Consultant in Neuropathology to the Army at Home, 1952–76; Hon. Consultant Neuropathologist, Bethlem Royal and Maudsley Hosps, 1956–76. Emeritus Fellow, Leverhulme Trust, 1978–80; Hon. Librarian, RCPath, 1981–. John Hunter Medal and Triennial Prize, 1946–48, and Erasmus Wilson Lectr, 1964, RCS. Editorial Board of: Jl of Physiology, 1958–65; Jl of Neurology, Neurosurgery and Psychiatry, 1953–64; Journal of Neuroendocrinology, 1966–77; Brain, 1974–76; Qly Jl Exp. Physiol., 1980–84. President: British Neuropathological Society, 1963–64; Neurological Section, RSM, 1970–71; Harveian Soc. London, 1966 (Trustee, 1971–); Section of Hist. of Med., RSM, 1979–82; Osler Club, 1979–82; Mem. Council: Royal Microscopical Soc., 1968–72; Neonatal Soc., 1959–61; Assoc. of British Neurologists, 1966–69 (Hon. Mem., 1985); Med. Soc. of London, 1981– (Hon. Librarian, 1984; Pres. elect, 1986). Hon. Mem., Physiological Soc., 1981. Member: Bd of Govs, Bethlem Royal and Maudsley Hosps, 1966–75; Council, Charing Cross Hosp. Medical Sch., 1972–85. Chm., Academic Bd, Inst. of Psychiatry, 1966–70; Vice-Chm., Central Academic Council, British Postgrad. Med. Fedn, 1975–76; Mem., Bd of Studies in Physiology, Univ. of London, 1981–. Life Mem., Anatomical Soc. of GB. Liveryman, Soc. of Apothecaries, 1952–. *Publications:* (jointly) Studies of the Renal Circulation, 1947; The Hypothalamus and Pituitary Gland, 1975; papers in various medical and scientific journals. *Recreations:* books, medical history. *Address:* 5 Seaforth Place, Buckingham Gate, SW1E 6AB. *T:* 01–834 3087. *Clubs:* Athenæum, Garrick, Green Room.

DANIEL, (Reginald) Jack, OBE 1958; FEng, FRINA, FIMarE; RCNC, Managing Director, Warship Design Services Ltd, since 1984; *b* 27 Feb. 1920; *o s* of Reginald Daniel and Florence Emily (*née* Woods); *m* 1st, Joyce Earnshaw (marr. diss.); two *s*; 2nd, 1977, Elizabeth, *o d* of George Mitchell, Long Ashton, Som. *Educ:* Royal Naval Engineering Coll., Keyham; Royal Naval Coll., Greenwich. Grad., 1942; subseq. engaged in submarine design. Served War of 1939–45; Staff of C-in-C's Far East Fleet and Pacific Fleet, 1943–45. Atomic Bomb Tests, Bikini, 1946; Admty, Whitehall, 1947–49; Admty, Bath, Aircraft Carrier Design, 1949–52; Guided Missile Cruiser design, 1952–56; Nuclear and Polaris Submarine design, 1956–65; IDC, 1966; Materials, R&D, 1967–68; Head of Forward Design, 1968–70; Director, Submarine Design and Production, 1970–74; Dir-Gen. Ships and Head of RCNC, MoD, 1974–79; British Shipbuilders: Bd Mem., 1979; Man. Dir, for Warshipbuilding, 1980–83; Dir (Training, Educn, Safety), 1981–85; Dir of Technology (Warships), British Shipbuilders, 1983–84; Dir, British Shipbuilders Australia

Pty, 1983–. Dep. Chm., Internationale Schiff Studien GmbH Hamburg, 1984–. Vice Pres., RINA, 1982. Liveryman, Worshipful Co. of Shipwrights, 1980. Hon. Res. Fellow, UCL, 1974; Founder Fellow, Fellowship of Engineering, 1976. *Publications:* Warship Design, New Concepts and New Technology, Parsons Meml Lecture, 1976; papers for RINA, etc. *Recreations:* gardening, motoring, music. *Address:* Meadowland, Cleveland Walk, Bath BA2 6JU.

DANIELL, Brig. Averell John, CBE 1955 (MBE 1939); DSO 1945; *b* 19 June 1903; *s* of late Lt-Col Oswald James Daniell, QO Royal West Kent Regt, and late May Frances Drummond Daniell (*née* Adams); *m* 1934, Phyllis Kathleen Rhona Grove-Annesley; two *s* one *d*. *Educ:* Wellington Coll.; RM Acad., Woolwich. Commissioned, Royal Field Artillery, 1923; Captain, RA, 1936; Major, 1940; Lt-Col, 1943. Served War of 1939–45; Middle East, Iraq, Burma. Col, 1948; Brig., 1952; retired, 1955. Administrative Officer, Staff Coll., Camberley, 1955–61. Colonel Commandant, Royal Artillery, 1956–66. *Address:* Oak Lodge, Hillside Street, Hythe, Kent. *T:* Hythe 66494.

DANIELL, Sir Peter (Averell), Kt 1971; TD 1950; DL; Senior Government Broker, 1963–73; *b* 8 Dec. 1909; *s* of R. H. A. Daniell and Kathleen Daniell (*née* Monsell); *m* 1935, Leonie M. Harrison; two *s* one *d*. *Educ:* Eton Coll.; Trinity Coll., Oxford (MA). Joined Mullens & Co., 1932, Partner, 1945; retd 1973. Served KRRC, 1939–45, Middle East and Italy. Master, Drapers' Co., 1980–81. DL Surrey 1976. *Recreations:* shooting, fishing, golf. *Address:* Glebe House, Buckland, Surrey. *T:* Betchworth 2320. *Clubs:* Brooks's, Alpine.

DANIELL, Ralph Allen, CBE 1965 (OBE 1958); HM Diplomatic Service, retired; *b* 26 Jan. 1915; 2nd *s* of late Reginald Allen Daniell; *m* 1943, Diana Lesley (*née* Tyndale); one *s* three *d*. *Educ:* Lancing Coll.; University Coll., Oxford. Appointed to Board of Trade, 1937. Joined HM Forces, 1942; served with Royal Tank Regt in North Africa and Italian campaigns, 1943–45. Appointed to HM Foreign Service as First Sec., 1946; Mexico City, 1946; Rome, 1949; Foreign Office, 1951; Helsinki, 1953; Counsellor, 1958; Washington, 1958; New York, 1959; Cairo, 1962; Wellington, 1967; Consul-Gen., Chicago, 1972–74. *Address:* 1A Collins Lane, Ringwood, Hants BH24 1LD. *T:* Ringwood 3662.

DANIELL, Roy Lorentz, CBE 1957; Barrister-at-Law; Charity Commissioner, 1953–62; *s* of late Edward Cecil Daniell, Abbotswood, Speen, Bucks; *m* 1936, Sheila Moore-Gwyn, *d* of late Maj. Moore-Gwyn, Clayton Court, Liss, Hants. *Educ:* Gresham's Sch., Holt; New Coll., Oxford. *Address:* Common Side, Russell's Water, Henley on Thames, Oxon. *T:* Nettlebed 641696. *Club:* United Oxford & Cambridge University.

DANIELS, George, MBE 1982; FSA, FBHI; author, watch maker, horological consultant; *b* 19 Aug. 1926; *s* of George Daniels and Beatrice (*née* Cadou); *m* 1964, Juliet Anne (*née* Marryat); one *d*. *Educ:* elementary. 2nd Bn E Yorks Regt, 1944–47. Started professional horology, 1947; restoration of historical watches, 1956–; hand watch making to own designs, 1969–. President: British Horological Inst., 1980 (Fellow, 1951); British Clock and Watchmakers' Benevolent Soc., 1980; Chm., Horological Industries Cttee, 1985–. Worshipful Co. of Clockmakers: Liveryman, 1968; Warden, 1977; Master, 1980; Tompion Gold Medal, 1981; Asst Hon. Surveyor. Freeman, Goldsmiths' Co., 1979; FSA 1976. Arts, Sciences and Learning Award, City Corporation, London, 1974; Victor Kullberg Medal, Stockholm Watch Guild, 1977; Gold Medal, British Horol Inst., 1981; Gold Badge and Hon. Fellow, Amer. Watchmakers Inst., 1985. *Publications:* Watches (jtly), 1965 (3rd edn 1978); English and American Watches, 1967; The Art of Breguet, 1975 (3rd edn 1985); (jtly) Clocks and Watches of the Worshipful Company of Clockmakers, 1975; Sir David Salomons Collection, 1978; Watchmaking, 1981 (2nd edn 1985). *Recreations:* vintage cars, fast motorcycles, opera, Scotch whisky. *Address:* 34 New Bond Street, W1A 2AA.

DANIELS, Harold Albert; *b* 8 June 1915; *s* of Albert Pollikett Daniels and Eleanor Sarah Maud Daniels (*née* Flahey); *m* 1946, Frances Victoria Jerdan; one *s*. *Educ:* Mercers' Sch.; Christ's Coll., Cambridge. BA 1937; Wren Prize 1938; MA 1940. Asst Principal, Post Office, 1938; Admiralty, 1942; Post Office, 1945; Principal, 1946; Asst Sec., 1950; Under-Sec., 1961; Min. of Posts and Telecommunications, 1969. Asst Under Sec. of State, Home Office, 1974–76. *Address:* Lyle Court Cottage, Bradbourne Road, Sevenoaks, Kent. *T:* Sevenoaks 454039.

DANIELS, Prof. Henry Ellis, FRS 1980; Professor of Mathematical Statistics, University of Birmingham, 1957–78, now Emeritus Professor; Senior Research Associate, Statistical Laboratory, University of Cambridge, 1978–81; *b* 2 Oct. 1912; *s* of Morris and Hannah Daniels; *m* 1950, Barbara Edith Pickering; one *s* one *d*. *Educ:* Sciennes Sch., Edinburgh; George Heriot's Sch., Edinburgh; Edinburgh Univ.; Clare Coll., Cambridge. MA Edinburgh 1933, BA Cantab 1935, PhD Edinburgh 1943. Statistician, Wool Industries Research Assoc., 1935–47; Ministry of Aircraft Production, 1942–45; Lecturer in Mathematics, University of Cambridge, 1947–57; Fellow, King's Coll. Cambridge, 1975–76. Pres., Royal Statistical Soc., 1974–75; Fellow Inst. of Mathematical Statistics; elected Mem. Internat. Statistical Inst., 1956. Freeman, Clockmakers' Co., 1981, Liveryman 1984. Guy Medal (Silver) 1957, (Gold) 1984, Royal Statistical Society. *Publications:* papers in Journal of the Royal Statistical Society, Annals of Mathematical Statistics, Biometrika, etc. *Recreations:* playing the English concertina, repairing watches. *Address:* 12 Kimberley Road, Cambridge CB4 1HH. *T:* Cambridge 313402.

DANIELS, Laurence John, CB 1979; OBE 1970; Secretary, Department of Capital Territory, Australia, 1977–81, retired; *b* 11 Aug. 1916; *s* of Leslie Daniels and Margaret (*née* Bradley); *m* 1943, Joyce Carey; two *s* eight *d*. *Educ:* Rostrevor Coll., South Australia; Sydney Univ. (BEc 1943). AASA 1939. Commonwealth (Australian) Taxation Office, 1934–53; Commonwealth Dept of Health, 1953–72; Director-General, Dept of Social Security, 1973–77. *Address:* 5 Nares Crest, Forrest, ACT 2603, Australia. *T:* 062–95 1896.

DANIELS, Robert George Reginald, CBE 1984; JP; DL; Chairman, Dartford Tunnel Joint Committee, since 1974 (Member, since 1968, Vice-Chairman, 1970–74); *b* 17 Nov. 1916; *s* of Robert Henry Daniels and Edith Daniels; *m* 1940, Dora Ellen Hancock; one *d*. *Educ:* private and state. Insurance Representative, Prudential Assurance, 1938–76, retd. Mem., Essex CC, 1965– (Alderman, 1969; Vice-Chm., 1977–80, Chm. 1980–83). Member: Theydon Bois Parish Council, 1952– (Chm., 1969–); Epping RDC, 1952–55 and Epping and Ongar RDC, 1955–74 (Vice-Chm., 1958–59 and 1964–65; Chm., 1959–60 and 1965–66); Epping Forest District Council, 1974–79. Gen. Comr of Income Tax for Epping Div., 1970–. President: Theydon Bois Br., British Legion, 1985– (Chm., 1973–85); Outward Bound Trust, Essex, 1985–; Mem., Chelmsford Engrg Soc., 1980–. JP Essex (Epping and Ongar Bench), 1969; DL Essex, 1980. *Recreation:* reading. *Address:* 42 Dukes Avenue, Theydon Bois, Epping CM16 7HF. *T:* Theydon Bois 3123. *Club:* Essex (Chelmsford).

DANILOVA, Alexandra, lecturer, teacher and choreographer, actress; *b* Pskoff, Russia, 20 Nov. 1906; *d* of Dionis Daniloff and Claudia Gotovzeffa; *m* 1st, 1931, Giuseppe Massera (*d* 1936); 2nd, 1941, Kazimir Kokic (marr. annulled, 1949). *Educ:* Theatrical Sch., Petrograd. Maryinski Theatre, Leningrad, 1923–24; Diaghileff Company, 1925–29; Waltzes from Vienna, 1931; Colonel de Basil Company, 1933–37; Prima Ballerina, Ballet Russe de Monte Carlo, 1938–58. Teacher (on Faculty) of School of American Ballet. Guest artist Royal Festival Hall, London, 1955; Ballerina in Oh Captain (Musical), New York, 1958. With own Company has toured West Indies, Japan, Philippines, USA, Canada and S Africa. Capezio Award (for outstanding services to Art of the Dance), 1958; Guest Choreographer Metropolitan Opera House, Guest Teacher and Choreographer, Germany (Krefeld Festival of Dance) and Amsterdam, 1959–60; Choreographed Coppelia for La Scala di Milano, 1961; Lecture performances throughout US; Guest Choreographer, Washington Ballet, 1962–64. Choreographed Coppelia (with George Balanchine), NY City Ballet, 1975. Screen acting debut in film, The Turning Point, 1977. *Recreations:* needlework, ping-pong, gardening. *Address:* Carnegie House, 100 West 57 Street, New York, NY 10019, USA.

DANINOS, Pierre; French Author; *b* Paris, 26 May 1913; *m* 1st, 1942, Jane Marrain; one *s* two *d*; 2nd, 1968, Marie-Pierre Dourneau. *Educ:* Lycée Janson de Sailly, Paris. Began to write for newspapers, 1931; reporter for French press in England, USA, etc. Liaison agent with British Army, Dunkirk, 1940. Published first book in Rio de Janeiro, 1940; returned to France, 1941, from South America, Chronicler for Le Figaro. *Publications:* Les Carnets du Bon Dieu (Prix Interallié 1947); L'Eternel Second, 1949; Sonia les autres et moi (Prix Courteline, 1952) (English trans., Life with Sonia, 1958); Les Carnets du Major Thompson, 1954 (English trans., Major Thompson Lives in France, 1955); Le Secret du Major Thompson, 1956 (English trans., Major Thompson and I, 1957); Vacances à Tous Prix, 1958; Un certain Monsieur Blot, 1960 (English trans., 1961); Le Jacassin, 1962; Snobissimo, 1964; Le 36ème dessous, 1966; Le Major Tricolore, 1968; Ludovic Morateur, 1970; Le Pyjama, 1972; Les Touristocrates, 1974; Made in France, 1977; La Composition d'Histoire, 1979; Le Veuf Joyeux, 1981; La Galérie des Glaces, 1983; La France dans tous ses états, 1985. *Recreations:* tennis, ski-ing, collecting British hobbies. *Address:* 81 rue de Grenelle, 75007 Paris, France.

DANKERT, Pieter; Member of the European Parliament, since 1977 (President, 1982–84); *b* Jan. 1934; *m* 1962, Paulette Puig; one *s* two *d*. *Educ:* Amsterdam Free Univ. Mem. (Partij van de Arbeid) Tweede Kamer, Netherlands; formerly: Internat. Sec., Partij van de Arbeid; Mem., NATO Assembly, WEU Assembly and Assembly of Council of Europe. *Address:* Secretariat of the European Parliament, Post Box 1601, Centre Européen, Kirchberg, Luxembourg; Hoogstraat 1, 1135 BZ Edam, Netherlands.

DANKS, Sir Alan (John), KBE 1970; Chairman: New Zealand University Grants Committee, 1966–77; Information Authority, since 1982; *b* 9 June 1914; *s* of T. E. Danks; *m* 1943, Loma Beryl Hall (*née* Drabble). *Educ:* West Christchurch High Sch.; Canterbury Coll. (MA). Teaching profession, 1931–43; Economics Dept, Univ. of Canterbury (formerly Canterbury University Coll.), 1943–66; Prof., 1962; Pro-Vice Chancellor, 1964. Hon. LLD Canterbury, 1973. *Address:* 116 Upland Road, Wellington 5, New Zealand.

DANKWORTH, Mrs C. D.; *see* Laine, Cleo.

DANKWORTH, John Philip William, CBE 1974; FRAM 1973; musician; *b* 20 Sept. 1927; British; *m* 1958, Cleo Laine, *qv*; one *s* one *d*. *Educ:* Monoux Grammar Sch. Studied Royal Academy of Music, 1944–46. ARAM 1969. Closely involved with post-war development of British jazz, 1947–60; formed large jazz orchestra, 1953. Composed works for combined jazz and symphonic musicians including: Improvisations (with Matyas Seiber, 1959); Escapade (commissioned by Northern Sinfonia Orch., 1967); Tom Sawyer's Saturday, for narrator and orchestra (commissioned by Farnham Festival), 1967; String Quartet, 1971; Piano Concerto (commissioned by Westminster Festival, 1972); Grace Abounding (for RPO), 1980; The Diamond and the Goose (for City of Birmingham Choir and Orch.), 1981. Many important film scores (1964–) including: Saturday Night and Sunday Morning, Darling, The Servant, Morgan, Accident; other works include: Palabras, 1970; dialogue and lyrics for Colette, Comedy, 1980. Variety Club of GB Show Business Personality Award (with Cleo Laine), 1977. Hon. MA Open Univ., 1975; Hon. DMus Berklee Sch. of Music, 1982. *Recreations:* driving, household maintenance. *Address:* The Old Rectory, Wavendon, Milton Keynes MK17 8LT; World Wide Management, Laurie Mansfield, International Artistes Representation, 235 Regent Street, W1. *T:* 01–439 8401.

DANN, Mrs Jill; *b* 10 Sept. 1929; *d* of Harold Norman Cartwright and Marjorie Alice Thornton; *m* 1952, Anthony John Dann; two *s* two *d* (and one *s* decd). *Educ:* Solihull High Sch. for Girls, Malvern Hall; Birmingham Univ. (LLB); St Hilda's Coll., Oxford (BCL). Called to the Bar, Inner Temple, 1952. Mayoress of Chippenham, 1964–65. Church Commissioner, 1968–; Member: General Synod of Church of England, and of its Standing Cttee, 1971– (Vice-Chm. House of Laity, 1985–); Crown Appointments Commn, 1977–; Chairman: House of Laity, Bristol Diocesan Synod, 1982–; C of E Evangelical Council, 1985–. Dir, Wiltshire Radio, 1981–. Chm., Chippenham Old People's Housing Assoc.; Pres., Inner Wheel, 1978–79. *Recreations:* reading, sport. *Address:* Harnish Mead, 30 Hardenhuish Lane, Chippenham, Wilts SN14 6HN. *T:* Chippenham 653142. *Club:* Royal Commonwealth Society.

DANN, Most Rev. Robert William; *b* 28 Sept. 1914; *s* of James and Ruth Dann; *m* 1949, Yvonne (*née* Newnham); one *s* two *d*. *Educ:* Trinity Coll., Univ. of Melbourne. BA Hons Melbourne 1946. Deacon, 1945; Priest, 1946. Dir of Youth and Religious Education, Dio. Melbourne, 1946; Incumbent: St Matthew's, Cheltenham, 1951; St George's, Malvern, 1956; St John's, Footscray, 1961; Archdeacon of Essendon, 1961; Dir of Evangelism and Extension, Dio. Melbourne, 1963; Bishop Coadjutor, Dio. Melbourne, 1969–77; Archbishop of Melbourne and Metropolitan of Province of Victoria, 1977–83. *Address:* 1 Myrtle Road, Canterbury, Vic 3126, Australia. *Club:* Melbourne (Melbourne).

DANNATT, Prof. (James) Trevor, MA; RA 1983 (ARA 1977); FRIBA; Senior Partner, Trevor Dannatt & Partners, Architects; Professor of Architecture, Manchester University, since 1975; *b* 15 Jan. 1920; *s* of George Herbert and Jane Ellen Dannatt; *m* 1953, Joan Howell Davies; one *s* one *d*. *Educ:* Colfes Sch.; Sch. of Architecture, Regent Street Polytechnic (Dip. Arch.). Professional experience in office of Jane B. Drew and E. Maxwell Fry, 1943–48; Architects Dept, LCC (Royal Festival Hall Gp), 1948–52; commenced private practice, 1952. Vis. Prof., Washington Univ., St Louis, 1976. Assessor for national and international architectural competitions, Civic Trust; Mem., Cathedrals Adv. Commn. Editor, Architects' Year Book, 1945–62. Architectural work includes private houses, housing, school, university and welfare buildings, conservation and restoration, interiors for private, corporate and public clients; Architects for British Embassy and Diplomatic Staff housing, Riyadh, 1980–85. Won internat. competition for conference complex in Riyadh, Saudi Arabia, 1974. *Publications:* Modern Architecture in Britain, 1959; Trevor Dannatt: Buildings and Interiors 1951–72, 1972; (Editorial Adviser, and foreword) Buildings and Ideas 1933–83 from the Studio of Leslie Martin, 1983; contribs to Architectural Rev., Architects' Jl, and various foreign journals. *Recreations:* the arts, including architecture. *Address:* 115 Crawford Street, W1. *T:* 01–486 6844. *Club:* Travellers'.

DANSON, Hon. Barnett Jerome, PC (Canada); consultant, since 1984; *s* of Joseph B. Danson and Saidie W. Danson, Toronto; *m* 1943, Isobel, *d* of Robert John Bull, London, England; four *s*. *Educ:* Toronto public and high schs. Served War: enlisted Queen's Own Rifles as Rifleman, 1939; commnd, 1943; wounded in France, 1944; retd 1945, Lieut. Manager, Jos. B. Danson & Sons Ltd, Toronto, 1945–50; Sales Man., Maple Leaf Plastics Ltd, 1950–53; Principal (Pres.), Danson Corp. Ltd, Scarborough, 1953–74; Chairman: CSPG Consultants, 1980–84; de Havilland Aircraft of Canada Ltd, 1981–84; Canadian Consul General, Boston, Mass, 1984–86. Active in Liberal Party, 1946–: MP (L) for York North, 1968–79; Parly Sec. to Prime Minister Trudeau, 1970–72; Minister of State for Urban Affairs, 1974–76; Minister of Nat. Defence, Canada, 1976–79; former Mem., Standing Cttee on Finance, Trade and Econ. Affairs, and Ext. Affairs and National Defence. Former Pres. and first Chm. Bd, Soc. of Plastics Engineers Inc. Former Member: Bd of Trade of Metrop. Toronto; Canadian Manufacturers Assoc.; Canadian Chamber of Commerce. *Recreations:* fishing, reading, music. *Address:* 500 Avenue Road, Toronto, Ontario, Canada.

DANTZIC, Roy Matthew, CA; Director: Wood Mackenzie & Co. Ltd, since 1985; Hill Samuel & Co. Ltd, since 1986; *b* 4 July 1944; *s* of David and Renee Dantzic; *m* 1969, Diane Clapham; one *s* one *d*. *Educ:* Brighton Coll., Sussex. CA 1968. Coopers & Lybrand, 1962–69; Kleinwort, Benson Ltd, 1970–72; Drayton Corporation Ltd, which merged in 1974 with Samuel Montagu & Co. Ltd, 1972–80 (Exec. Dir, 1975; Mem. for Finance, BNOC, subseq. Finance Dir, Britoil plc, 1980–84; Man. Dir, Dillon, Read Ltd, 1984–85; Chm., Premier Portfolio Ltd, 1985–. Pt-time Mem., CEGB, 1984–. *Recreations:* theatre, playing golf, watching cricket. *Address:* 12 Bedford Road, Moor Park, Northwood, Mddx HA6 2AZ. *Clubs:* MCC; Moor Park Golf.

DAR-ES-SALAAM, Archbishop of, (RC), since 1969; **HE Cardinal Laurean Rugambwa;** *b* Bukongo, 12 July 1912; *s* of Domitian Rushubirwa and Asteria Mukaboshezi. *Educ:* Rutabo, Rubya Seminary; Katigondo Seminary; Univ. of Propaganda, Rome (DCL 1951). Priest 1943; Bishop of Rutabo, 1952–60; Cardinal 1960; Bishop of Bukoba, 1960–69. Member: Knights of Columbus; Knights of St Peter Claver. Hon. Dr of Laws: Notre Dame, 1961; St Joseph's Coll., Philadelphia, 1961; Rosary Hill Coll., Buffalo, 1965; Hon. DHL New Rochelle, 1961; Hon. Dr Civil and Canon Law, Georgetown Univ. (Jesuits), 1961; Giving of the Scroll, Catholic Univ. of America, 1961. *Address:* Archbishop's House, PO Box 167, Dar-es-Salaam, Tanzania, East Africa.

DARBISHIRE, David Harold, JP; Chairman, FMC plc, 1975–83; Director, ACC Ltd, since 1972; *b* 23 Oct. 1914; *s* of H. D. Darbishire and Hester E. Bright (*g d* of Rt Hon. John Bright, MP); *m* 1939, Phebe Irene Lankester, *d* of Captain Felix Lankester, MC; three *d*. *Educ:* Sidcot; Wye Agric. Coll. (Wye DipAgric). Farmer; Vice-Pres., NFU, 1971–74. Mem., Metrication Bd, 1970–77. *Recreations:* hunting, fishing. *Address:* Manor Farm, Wormleighton, Leamington Spa CV33 0XW. *Club:* Farmers'.

DARBOURNE, John William Charles, CBE 1977; RIBA; Partner, Darbourne & Darke, Architects and Landscape Planners, since 1961; *b* 11 Jan. 1935; *s* of late William Leslie Darbourne and Violet Yorke; *m* 1960, Noreen Fifield; one *s* three *d*. *Educ:* Battersea Grammar Sch.; University Coll., London Univ. (BA Hons Arch. 1958); Harvard (MLA). RIBA 1960; AILA. Asst Architect in private practice, 1958–60; Post-grad. study in landscape arch. and planning, Harvard, 1960, completed degree course, 1964; estabd own practice with Geoffrey Darke (following successful entry in national architect. competition), 1961; practice moved to Richmond, 1963, and, 1966–, has grown steadily to undertake several large commns, particularly public housing, laboratories and offices; in recent years practice has expanded into Europe (through internat. competitions) and is currently building in Stuttgart, Hannover and Bolzano. Architectural and Landscape Consultant to City of Bath. Involved in professional and local cttees, and national confs. Fritz Schumacher Award, 1979. *Recreations:* working late, the piano; latterly tennis and squash and now the obsessive folly of golf. *Address:* 6 The Green, Richmond, Surrey. *T:* 01–940 7182; 10 Dynevor Road, Richmond, Surrey. *T:* 01–940 2241. *Club:* Athenæum.

DARBY, Dr Francis John, TD 1964; MRCGP; MFOM; *b* 24 Feb. 1920; *o s* of Col John Francis Darby, CBE, late Royal Signals, and Georgina Alice (*née* Dean); *m* 1969, Pamela Lisbeth, *o d* of Sydney Hill, Sutton Coldfield; one *s* by former *m*. *Educ:* Nottingham High Sch.; Edinburgh Acad.; Edinburgh Univ. (MB ChB 1950). MRCGP 1970; DIH 1963; DMJ 1965; MFOM RCP 1982. Commissioned, Royal Signals, 1938–46: N Africa (despatches), Italy and Egypt, 1942–46. House appts, 1950–51; general practice, Warwickshire, and member medical staff, Tamworth General Hosp. and St Editha's Hosp., Tamworth, 1951–64; joined DHSS, 1964; Dep. Chief Medical Advr, 1978–80; Chief Medical Advr (Social Security), 1980–82; CMO and Consultant Physician, Cayman Is, 1983–85. Mem. BMA, 1950. Mem., Worshipful Soc. of Apothecaries of London, 1978–; Freeman, City of London, 1979. FRSM 1974. QHP, 1980–84. *Publications:* various papers on drug prescribing and medical administration. *Recreations:* sailing, swimming. *Address:* Ruardean, Captains Row, Lymington, Hants SO4 9RP. *T:* Lymington 77119. *Clubs:* Army and Navy; Royal Signals Yacht; Royal Lymington Yacht.

DARBY, Rt. Rev. Harold Richard; *see* Sherwood, Bishop Suffragan of.

DARBY, Henry Clifford, CBE 1978 (OBE 1946); LittD 1960; FBA 1967; Professor of Geography in the University of Cambridge, 1966–76, now Emeritus; Honorary Fellow: St Catharine's College, Cambridge, 1960; King's College, Cambridge, 1983; *b* 7 Feb. 1909; *s* of Evan Darby, Resolven, Glamorgan; *m* 1941, Eva Constance Thomson; two *d*. *Educ:* Neath County Sch.; St Catharine's Coll., Cambridge. 1st Class Geographical Tripos, Parts I, 1926, II, 1928; PhD 1931; MA 1932. Lecturer in Geography, University of Cambridge, 1931–45; Fellow, King's Coll., Cambridge, 1932–45, 1966–81; Intelligence Corps, 1940–41 (Capt.); Admiralty, 1941–45; John Rankin Prof. of Geography, University of Liverpool, 1945–49; Prof. of Geography, University Coll. London, 1949–66; Leverhulme Research Fellow, 1946–48; Visiting Prof. Univ. of Chicago, 1952, Harvard Univ., 1959, 1964–65, and Univ. of Washington, 1963. Member: Royal Commission on Historical Monuments (England), 1953–77; National Parks Commn, 1958–63; Water Resources Board, 1964–68. President: Institute of British Geographers, 1961; Section E British Assoc., 1963; English Place-Name Soc., 1985–86; Chm., British National Cttee for Geography, 1973–78. Carl Sauer Lectr, Univ. of Calif, Berkeley, 1985. Hon. Member: Croatian Geog. Soc., 1957; Royal Netherlands Geog. Soc., 1958; RGS, 1976; Inst. of British Geographers, 1977. Victoria Medal, RGS, 1963. Daly Medal, American Geog. Soc., 1963; Honors Award, Assoc. of Amer. Geographers, 1977. Hon. degrees: Chicago, 1967; Liverpool, 1968; Durham, 1970; Hull, 1975; Ulster, 1977; Wales, 1979. *Publications:* An Historical Geography of England before AD 1800 (ed and contrib.), 1936; (with H. Fullard) The University Atlas, 1937, 22nd edn 1983; (with H. Fullard) The Library Atlas, 1937, 15th edn 1981; The Cambridge Region (ed and contrib.), 1938; The Medieval Fenland, 1940; The Draining of the Fens, 1940, 3rd edn 1968; (with H. Fullard) The New Cambridge Modern History Atlas, 1970; (ed and contrib.) A New Historical Geography of England, 1973, 2 vol. edn 1976; The Changing Fenland, 1983; General Editor and Contributor, The Domesday Geography of England, 7 vols, 1952–77; articles in geographical and historical journals. *Address:* 60 Storey's Way, Cambridge. *T:* Cambridge 354745.

DARBY, Dr Michael Douglas, FRES, FRGS; Deputy Director, Victoria and Albert Museum, since 1983; *b* 2 Sept. 1944; *s* of Arthur Douglas Darby and Ilene Doris Darby (*née* Eatwell); *m* 1977, Elisabeth Susan Done. *Educ:* Rugby School; Reading Univ. (PhD). FRES 1977; FRGS 1984. Asst to Barbara Jones, 1963; Victoria and Albert Museum: Textiles Dept, 1964–72; Prints and Drawings Dept, 1973–76; Exhibitions Officer, 1977–83. Member: Crafts Council, 1984–; IoW Adv. Cttee, English Heritage. *Publications:* Marble Halls, 1973; Early Railway Prints, 1974, 2nd edn 1979; British Art in the Victoria and Albert Museum, 1983; John Pollard Seddon, 1983; The Islamic Perspective, 1983; articles in art, architectural and entomological periodicals. *Recreations:* beetles, books. *Address:* c/o Victoria and Albert Museum, SW7 2RL. *T:* 01-589 6371.

DARBY, Sir Peter (Howard), Kt 1985; CBE 1973; QFSM 1970; HM Chief Inspector of Fire Services, 1981–86; *b* 8 July 1924; *s* of William Cyril Darby and Beatrice Colin; *m* 1948, Ellen Josephine Glynn; one *s* one *d*. *Educ:* City of Birmingham Coll. of Advanced Technology. Fire Brigades: Dep. Ch. Officer, Suffolk and Ipswich FB, 1963; Chief Officer, Nottingham FB, 1966; Chief Officer, Lancashire FB, 1967; County Fire Officer, Greater Manchester FB, 1974; Regional Fire Comdr (No 10) NW Region, 1974–76; Regional Fire Adviser (No 5) Greater London Region, 1977; Chief Officer of the London Fire Brigade, 1977–80. Pres., Chief and Asst Chief Fire Officers' Assoc., 1975–76; Mem. Adv. Council, Central Fire Brigades, 1977; Principal Adviser to Sec. of State on Fire Service matters, 1981–86; Chm., Fire Services Central Examinations Bd, 1985. Foundation Gov., St James's Secondary Modern Sch., Hendon, 1985–. Freeman, City of London; Liveryman, Worshipful Co. of Basketmakers. CStJ 1983. *Recreations:* fell-walking, golf, fishing, sailing. *Address:* 10 Moor Lane, Rickmansworth, Herts WD3 1LG. *Clubs:* City Livery, KSC.

D'ARCY, Surgeon Rear-Adm. Thomas Norman, CB 1953; CBE 1950; retired; *b* 12 Feb. 1896; *s* of Dr S. A. D'Arcy, Rosslea, County Fermanagh, Ireland; *m* 1922, Eleanor Lennox Broadbent (*d* 1982); two *s* two *d*. *Educ:* Royal School, Cavan; RCS Dublin. Qualified, 1919; Surgeon Probationer RNVR, 1915–18; Surgeon Lieut RN, 1919; Surgeon Lieut-Comdr 1925; Surgeon Comdr 1930; Surgeon Capt. 1943; Surgeon Rear-Adm., 1951; Medical Officer in Charge, RN Hospital, Plymouth, and Command Medical Officer, 1951–54. KHS 1951; QHS 1952–54. CStJ 1953. Gilbert Blane medal, 1929. *Publications:* surgical articles to Jl of RN Medical Service (Co-Editor, 1946–47). *Recreation:* hockey (old Irish International). *Address:* South Wind, Witley, Surrey GU8 5RB. *T:* Godalming 5751.

DARCY DE KNAYTH, Baroness (18th in line), *cr* 1332; **Davina Marcia Ingrams** (*née* **Herbert**); *b* 10 July 1938; *d* of late Squadron Leader Viscount Clive (*d* on active service, 1943), and of Vida, *o d* of late Captain James Harold Cuthbert, DSO, Scots Guards (she *m* 2nd, 1945, Brig. Derek Schreiber, MVO (*d* 1972)); *S* to father's Barony, 1943; *m* 1960, Rupert George Ingrams (*d* 1964), *s* of late Leonard Ingrams and of Mrs Ingrams; one *s* two *d*. *Heir:* *s* Hon. Caspar David Ingrams, *b* 5 Jan. 1962. *Address:* Camley Corner, Stubbings, Maidenhead, Berks.

D'ARCY HART, Philip Montagu; *see* Hart, P. M. D'A.

DARELL, Brig. Sir Jeffrey (Lionel), 8th Bt, *cr* 1795; MC 1945; *b* 2 Oct. 1919; *s* of late Lt-Col Guy Marsland Darell, MC (3rd *s* of 5th Bt); *S* cousin, 1959; *m* 1953, Bridget Mary, *e d* of Maj.-Gen. Sir Allan Adair, 6th Bt, *qv*; one *s* two *d*. *Educ:* Eton; RMC, Sandhurst. Commissioned Coldstream Guards, July 1939; served War of 1939–45: ADC to GOC-in-C, Southern Comd, 1942; Bde Major, Guards Bde, 1953–55; Officer Comdg 1st Bn Coldstream Guards, 1957–59; GSO1, PS12, War Office, 1959; College Comdr RMA Sandhurst, 1961–64; Comdg Coldstream Guards, 1964–65; Comdr, 56 Inf. Brigade (TA), 1965–67; Vice-Pres., Regular Commns Bd, 1968–70; Comdt, Mons OCS, 1970–72; MoD, 1972–74; retd 1974. ADC to HM the Queen, 1973–74. Trustee and Mem., London Law Trust, 1981–. High Sheriff, Norfolk, 1985. *Recreations:* normal. *Heir:* *s* Guy Jeffrey Adair Darell, *b* 8 June 1961. *Address:* 55 Green Street, W1. *T:* 01–629 3860; Denton Lodge, Harleston, Norfolk. *T:* Homersfield 206. *Club:* Cavalry and Guards.

DARESBURY, 2nd Baron, *cr* 1927, of Walton, Co. Chester; **Edward Greenall,** Bt, *cr* 1876; late Life Guards; *b* 12 Oct. 1902; *o* surv. *s* of 1st Baron Daresbury, CVO, and late Frances Eliza, OBE 1945, *d* of Capt. Wynne-Griffith, 1st Royal Dragoons; *S* father 1938; *m* 1st 1925, Joan Madeline (*d* 1926), *d* of Capt. Robert Thomas Oliver Sheriffe, of Goadby Hall, Melton Mowbray; 2nd, 1927, Josephine (*d* 1958), *y d* of Brig.-Gen. Sir Joseph Laycock, KCMG, DSO; one *s*; 3rd, 1966, Lady Helena Hilton Green (*née* Wentworth-Fitzwilliam) (*d* 1970), 4th *d* of 7th Earl Fitzwilliam. *Educ:* Wixenford; Eton. *Heir:* *s* Hon. Edward Gilbert Greenall [*b* 27 Nov. 1928; *m* 1952, Margaret Ada, *y d* of late C. J. Crawford and of Mrs Crawford, Wayside, St Andrews; three *s* one *d*]. *Address:* Altavilla, Askeaton, Co. Limerick, Eire. *T:* Limerick 64281.

DARGIE, Sir William Alexander, Kt 1970; CBE 1969 (OBE 1960); FRSA 1951; artist; portrait, figure and landscape painter; Chairman, Commonwealth Art Advisory Board, Prime Minister's Department, 1969–73 (Member, 1953–73); *b* 4 June 1912; *s* of Andrew and Adelaide Dargie; *m* 1937, Kathleen, *d* of late G. H. Howitt; one *s* one *d*. *Educ:* Melbourne, and in studio of A. D. Colquhoun. Official War Artist (Capt.) with AIF in Middle East, Burma, New Guinea, India, 1941–46. Dir, National Gallery of Victoria Art Schs, 1946–53. Member: Interim Council of Nat. Gallery Canberra, 1968–72; Nat. Capital Planning Cttee, Canberra, 1970–73; Aboriginal Arts Adv. Cttee, 1970–72; Trustee: Native Cultural Reserve, Port Moresby, Papua-New Guinea, 1970–73; Museum of Papua-New Guinea, 1970–73; Mem. Council, Nat. Museum, Victoria, 1978–83; Chm., Bd of Trustees, McClelland Gall., 1981–. Archibald Prize for portraiture, 1941, 1942, 1945, 1946, 1947, 1950, 1952, 1956; Woodward Award, 1940; McPhillimy Award, 1940; McKay Prize, 1941. Painted portrait of The Queen for Commonwealth of Aust., 1954; the Duke of Gloucester, 1947; the Duke of Edinburgh for City of Melbourne, 1956. Portraits of Sir Macfarlane Burnet, Sir William Ashton, Sir Lionel Lindsay, acquired for Commonwealth Nat. Collection. Rep. in public and private collections in Aust., NZ, England and USA. One-man exhibition, Leger Galls, London, 1958. Exhibits with RA and Royal Soc. of Portrait Painters. *Publication:* On Painting a Portrait, 1956. *Recreations:* books, chess, tennis. *Address:* 19 Irilbarra Road, Canterbury, Victoria 3126, Australia. *T:* 836 3396 Melbourne. *Clubs:* Melbourne, Naval and Military, Savage (Melbourne).

DARK, Anthony Michael B.; *see* Beaumont-Dark.

DARKE, Geoffrey James, RIBA; Partner, Darbourne and Darke, Architects and Landscape Planners, since 1961; *b* 1 Sept. 1929; *s* of late Harry James Darke and Edith Anne (*née* Rose); *m* 1959, Jean Yvonne Rose, ARCM; one *s* two *d*. *Educ:* Prince Henry's Grammar Sch., Evesham, Worcs; Birmingham School of Architecture (DipArch); ARIBA 1956. National Service, Malaya, commnd RE, 1954–56. Asst architect, Stevenage Development Corp., 1952–58; private practice, 1958–61; established present practice, with John Darbourne, 1961. Work includes several large commissions, particularly public buildings. Success in national and internat. competitions, latterly in Stuttgart, 1977, Hanover, 1979,

W Germany, also in Bolzano, Italy, 1980; numerous medals and awards for architectural work; with John Darbourne, co-recipient of Fritz Schumacher Award, Hamburg, 1978, for services to architecture and townplanning. Mem. Council, RIBA, 1977–83; Chm., RIBA Competitions Cttee, 1979–84; has served on many professional committees. FRSA 1981. Mem., Aldeburgh Festival Snape Maltings Foundn, 1979–. *Recreation:* music. *Address:* 41 The Avenue, St Margarets, Twickenham, Mddx. *Club:* Reform.

DARKE, Marjorie Sheila; writer, since 1962; *b* 25 Jan. 1929; *d* of Christopher Darke and Sarah Ann (*née* Palin); *m* 1952; two *s* one *d*. *Educ:* Worcester Grammar Sch. for Girls; Leicester Coll. of Art and Technol.; Central Sch. of Art, London. Worked in textile studio of John Lewis Partnership, 1950–54. *Publications:* Ride the Iron Horse, 1973; The Star Trap, 1974; A Question of Courage, 1975; The First of Midnight, 1977; A Long Way to Go, 1978; Comeback, 1981; Tom Post's Private Eye, 1982; Messages and Other Shivery Tales, 1984; *for young children:* Mike's Bike, 1974; What Can I Do, 1975; Kipper's Turn, 1976; The Big Brass Band, 1976; My Uncle Charlie, 1977; Carnival Day, 1979; Kipper Skips, 1979; Imp, 1985. *Recreations:* reading, music, sewing, country walks, jogging. *Address:* c/o Penguin Books Ltd, 27 Wright's Lane, W8 5TZ; c/o Patricia White, Deborah Rogers Ltd, 49 Blenheim Crescent, W11 2EF. *Clubs:* Society of Authors; International PEN.

DARKIN, Maj.-Gen. Roy Bertram, CBE 1969; Commander Base Organisation RAOC, 1971–73, retired; *b* 3 Sept. 1916; *s* of late Bertram Duncan and of late Isobel Doris Darkin, Aylsham, Norfolk; *m* 1945, Louise Margaret, *d* of late Francis Charles Sydney Green and Lilian Green, Buckden, Hunts, and *widow* of Sqn Ldr J. C. D. Joslin, RAF (killed in action); no *c*. *Educ:* Felsted School. Commnd Baluch Regt, IA, 1940; war service, NW Frontier, Iraq, Persia (despatches); psc 1943; G2 HQ ALFSEA service, Burma; DAQMG India Office, 1945; transf. RAOC, 1946; Sen. Instructor, RAAOC Sch., Melbourne, 1952–54; DAQMG HQ Aldershot District, 1954–55; jssc 1955; AA&QMG Land Forces, Hong Kong, 1960–62; AAG (Col) MoD, 1962–65; Sen. Provision Officer, COD Bicester, 1965–66; Dir of Ordnance Services, FARELF (Brig.), 1966–69; Dep. Dir Ordnance Services MoD, 1969–71. Hon. Col, RAOC, T&AVR, 1971–73; Col Comdt, RAOC, 1975–79. FBIM. *Recreation:* travel. *Clubs:* MCC; Hankley Common Golf.

DARLING; *see* Stormonth Darling and Stormonth-Darling.

DARLING, family name of **Baron Darling.**

DARLING, 2nd Baron, *cr* 1924, of Langham; **Robert Charles Henry Darling;** DL; Major retired, Somerset Light Infantry; *b* 15 May 1919; *s* of late Major Hon. John Clive Darling, DSO; *S* grandfather, 1936; *m* 1942, Bridget Rosemary Whishaw, *d* of Rev. F. C. Dickson; one *s* two *d*. *Educ:* Wellington Coll.; RMC Sandhurst. Retired, 1955. Sec., later Chief Executive, Royal Bath and West and Southern Counties Soc., 1961–79. DL Somerset 1972, Avon 1974. *Recreations:* fishing, gardening. *Heir:* *s* Hon. Robert Julian Henry Darling, FRICS [*b* 29 April 1944; *m* 1970, Janet, *yr d* of Mrs D. M. E. Mallinson, Richmond, Yorks; two *s* one *d*]. *Address:* Puckpits, Limpley Stoke, Bath, Avon. *T:* Limpley Stoke 2146.

DARLING, Prof. Arthur Ivan, CBE 1971; Emeritus Professor of Dental Medicine, University of Bristol, 1982; *b* 21 Nov. 1916; *s* of John Straughan Darling and Henrietta Jeffcoat; *m* 1948, Kathleen Brenda Pollard; one *s* three *d*. *Educ:* Whitley Bay and Monkseaton Grammar Sch.; King's Coll., Univ. of Durham, LDS Dunelm, 1937, BDS Dunelm, 1938; Parker Brewis Research Fellow, 1938–41; MDS Dunelm, 1942; LRCP, MRCS 1947; FDSRCS 1948; DDSc Dunelm 1957; FFDRCSI 1964; FRCPath 1967. Univ. of Durham: Lectr in Operative Dental Surgery, 1941; Lectr in Oral Anatomy, 1943; Lectr in Dental Materia Medica, 1945; Univ. of Bristol: Prof. of Dental Surgery, 1947–59; Prof. of Dental Medicine, 1959–82; Dir of Dental Studies, 1947–82; Dean of Med. Faculty, 1963–66; Pro-Vice-Chancellor, 1968–72. Mem., Avon AHA (Teaching); Vice-Dean, Bd of Dental Faculty, RCS, 1977–78. Hon. Dir, Dental Unit of MRC, 1961–82. Hon. DSc Wales, 1981; Hon. Dr Univ. of René Déscartes, Paris, 1982. *Publications:* scientific papers on professional subjects in journals. *Recreations:* cabinet making, music. *Address:* 7 Rylestone Grove, Bristol BS9 3UT. *Club:* Athenæum.

DARLING, Hon. Sir Clifford, Kt 1977; MP (Bahamas); Speaker, House of Assembly, Bahamas, since 1977; *b* Acklins Island, 6 Feb. 1922; *s* of Charles and Aremelia Darling; *m* Igrid Smith. *Educ:* Acklins Public Sch.; several public schs in Nassau. Became taxi-driver (Gen. Sec. Bahamas Taxicab Union for 8 yrs, Pres. for 10 yrs). An early Mem., Progressive Liberal Party; MHA for Englerston; Senator, 1964–67; Dep. Speaker, House of Assembly, 1967–69; Minister of State, Oct. 1969; Minister of Labour and Welfare, Dec. 1971; Minister of Labour and Nat. Insurance, 1974–77. Past Chm., Tourist Advisory Bd; instrumental in introd. of a comprehensive Nat. Insce Scheme in the Bahamas, Oct. 1974. Member: Masonic Lodge; Elks Lodge; Acklins, Crooked Is and Long Cays Assoc. *Address:* House of Assembly, Nassau, Bahamas.

DARLING, Rt. Rev. Edward Flewett; *see* Limerick and Killaloe, Bishop of.

DARLING, Gerald Ralph Auchinleck, RD 1967; QC 1967; MA; Lieutenant-Commander, retired; Judge, Admiralty Court of the Cinque Ports, since 1979; *b* 8 Dec. 1921; *er s* of late Lieut-Col R. R. A. Darling and Moira (*née* Moriarty); *m* 1954, Susan Ann, *d* of late Brig. J. M. Hobbs, OBE, MC; one *s* one *d*. *Educ:* Harrow Sch. (Reginald Pole Schol.); Hertford Coll., Oxford (Baring Schol., Kitchener Schol.; MA 1948). Served with RNVR, 1940–46: Fleet Fighter Pilot with 807 Seafire Sqdn in HM Ships Furious, Indomitable, Battler and Hunter; Test Pilot, Eastern Fleet and Chief Test Pilot, British Pacific Fleet in HMS Unicorn; RNR until 1967. Called to Bar, Middle Temple, 1950 (Harmsworth Law Schol.), Bencher, 1972; Barrister, Northern Ireland, 1957; QC Hong Kong 1968. Member: Panel of Lloyd's Arbitrators in Salvage Cases, 1967–78, Appeal Arbitrator, 1978–; Panel of Wreck Commissioners, 1967–. Trustee, Royal Naval Museum, 1985–. Freeman of City of London, 1968. *Publication:* (contrib.) 3rd edn Halsbury's Laws of England (Admiralty and Ship Collisions). *Recreations:* fly fishing, shooting. *Address:* Crevenagh House, Omagh, Northern Ireland BT79 0EH; Queen Elizabeth Building, Temple, EC4Y 9BS. *T:* 01–353 9153. *Clubs:* Naval and Military; Tyrone County (Omagh).

DARLING, Henry Shillington, CBE 1967; Director-General, International Centre for Agricultural Research in Dry Areas, 1977–81, retired; Fellow of Wye College, since 1982; *b* 22 June 1914; *s* of late J. S. Darling, MD, FRCS, and Marjorie Shillington Darling, BA, Lurgan, N Ireland; *m* 1940, Vera Thompson Chapman, LDS, Belfast; one *s* two *d*. *Educ:* Watts' Endowed Sch.; Greenmount Agric. Coll., N Ireland; Queen's Univ., Belfast; Imp. Coll. Tropical Agriculture, Trinidad. BSc (1st Hons), 1938, BAgr (1st Hons) 1939, MAgr 1950, Belfast; AICTA 1942; PhD London, 1959. Middle East Anti-Locust Unit, Iran and Arabia, 1942–44; Research Div., Dept of Agriculture: Uganda, 1944–47; Sudan, 1947–49; Faculty of Agriculture, University Coll., Khartoum, 1949–54; Head of Hop Research Dept, Wye Coll., London Univ., 1954–62; Prof. of Agriculture and Dir of Inst. for Agric. Research, Ahmadu Bello Univ., Zaria, Nigeria, 1962–68; Dep. Vice-Chancellor, Ahmadu Bello Univ., 1967–68; Principal, Wye College, Univ. of London, 1968–77. Technical Adviser, Parly Select Cttee for Overseas Develt, 1970–71. Chairman: Agricultural Panel, Intermediate Technology Develt Gp; British Council Agricl Adv. Panel; Member: Senate and Collegiate Council, London Univ. (Chm., Senate European Studies Cttee), and other univ. cttees; Council, Royal Veterinary Coll.; Council, Ahmadu Bello Univ. Exec. Cttee, and Acad. Policy Cttee, Inter-Univ. Council for Higher Educn Overseas (also Chm., W African Gp and Mem., working parties and gps); Kent Educn Cttee; Exec. Cttee East Malling Res. Station; Council S and E Kent Productivity Assoc. Pres., Agricultural Sect., British Assoc., 1971–72. Technical Adviser: Tear Fund; Methodist Missionary Soc.; Pres., Inter-Collegiate Christian Fellowship, 1971–72. FInstBiol 1968. Hon. DSc: Ahmadu Bello Univ., 1968; Queen's Univ. Belfast, 1984. Order of the Hop, 1959. *Publications:* many papers in jls and reports dealing with applied biology, entomology, agricultural science and rural development in the Third World. *Recreations:* reading, walking, Christian dialogue. *Address:* 9 Jemmett Road, Ashford, Kent TN23 2QA. *Clubs:* Farmers'; Samaru (Nigeria).

DARLING, Sir James Ralph, Kt 1968; CMG 1958; OBE 1953; MA Oxon; Hon. DCL, Hon. LLD; FACE; Headmaster, Geelong Church of England Grammar School, Corio, Victoria, Australia, 1930–61; *b* 18 June 1899; *s* of late Augustine Major Darling and Jane Baird Nimmo; *m* 1935, Margaret Dunlop, *er d* of late John Dewar Campbell; one *s* three *d*. *Educ:* Repton Sch.; Oriel Coll., Oxford. 2nd Lieut Royal Field Artillery, 1918–19, France and Germany; Asst Master Merchant Taylors' Sch., Crosby, Liverpool, 1921–24; Asst Master Charterhouse Sch., Godalming, 1924–29; in charge of Public Schs Empire Tour to NZ, 1929; Hon. Sec. Headmasters' Conference of Australia, 1931–45, Chm., 1946–48; Member: Melbourne Univ. Council, 1933–71 (Hon. MA Melbourne); Commonwealth Univs Commission, 1942–51; Commonwealth Immigration Advisory Council, 1952–68; Australian Broadcasting Control Board, 1955–61. President: Australian Coll. of Educn, 1959–63 (Hon. Fellow 1970); Australian Road Safety Council, 1961–70; Chairman: Australian Expert Gp on Road Safety, 1970–71; Australian Frontier Commission, 1962–71 (President, 1971–73); Australian Broadcasting Commission, 1961–67; Commonwealth Immigration Publicity Council, 1962–71; Pres., Elizabethan Trust, 1970–82. Hon. DCL Oxon, 1948; Hon. LLD Melbourne, 1973. *Publications:* The Education of a Civilized Man, 1962; Timbertop (with E. H. Montgomery), 1967; Richly Rewarding, 1978. *Address:* 3 Myamyn Street, Armadale, Victoria 3143, Australia. *T:* 20.6262. *Clubs:* Australian (Sydney); Melbourne (Melbourne).

DARLING, Gen. Sir Kenneth (Thomas), GBE 1969 (CBE 1957); KCB 1963 (CB 1957); DSO 1945; Commander-in-Chief, Allied Forces, Northern Europe, 1967–69, retired; *b* 17 Sept. 1909; *s* of late G. K. Darling, CIE; *m* 1941, Pamela Beatrice Rose Denison-Pender. *Educ:* Eton; Royal Military College, Sandhurst. Commissioned 7th Royal Fusiliers, 1929; jssc 1946; idc 1953. Served NW Europe, 1944–45: Comd 5th Parachute Bde, 1946; Comd Airborne Forces Depot, 1948; Comd 16th Parachute Bde, 1950; Brig. A/q 1st (Br) Corps, 1954; Chief of Staff 1st (Br) Corps, 1955; Chief of Staff 2nd Corps, 1956. Dep. Dir of Staff Duties (D), WO, 1957–58; GOC Cyprus District and Dir of Ops, 1958–60; Dir of Infantry, 1960–62; GOC 1st (Br) Corps, 1962–63; GOC-in-C, Southern Command, 1964–66. Colonel: The Royal Fusiliers (City of London Regt), 1963–68; The Royal Regt of Fusiliers, 1968–74; Col Comdt, The Parachute Regt, 1965–67. ADC Gen., 1968–69. *Recreation:* riding. *Address:* Vicarage Farmhouse, Chesterton, Bicester, Oxon. *T:* Bicester 252092. *Club:* Army and Navy.

DARLINGTON, Rear-Adm. Sir Charles (Roy), KBE 1965; BSc; Director of the Naval Education Service and Head of Instructor Branch, Royal Navy, Oct. 1960–Oct. 1965, retired; on staff of Haileybury, 1965–75; *b* 2 March 1910; *o s* of C. A. Darlington, Newcastle under Lyme, Staffs; *m* 1935, Nora Dennison Wright, Maulds Meaburn, Westmorland; one *s* one *d*. *Educ:* Orme Sch., Newcastle under Lyme; Manchester Univ. (BSc). Double First in Maths 1931; Sen. Maths Master, William Hulme's Gram. Sch., 1937–40. Entered Royal Navy, 1941 (Instructor Lieut); served in: HM Ships Valiant and Malaya during War, and later in HM Ships Duke of York, Implacable, Vanguard and Tyne. On Staff of C-in-C Home Fleet, 1954–55, as Fleet Meteorological Officer; for various periods in Admty, HMS Excellent and HMS Collingwood. Rear-Adm. 1960. *Recreations:* cricket, hill-walking, mathematics and trying to avoid ignorance of the arts, and particularly of history. *Address:* 11 Freestone Road, Southsea, Hants. *T:* Portsmouth 825974.

DARLINGTON, Joyce, (Mrs Anthony Darlington); *see* Blow, Joyce.

DARLINGTON, Stephen Mark, FRCO; Organist and Official Student in Music, Christ Church, Oxford, since 1985; *b* 21 Sept. 1952; *s* of John Oliver Darlington and Bernice Constance Elizabeth (*née* Murphy); *m* 1975, Moira Ellen (*née* Hill); three *d*. *Educ:* King's Sch., Worcester; Christ Church, Oxford (Organ Schol.; MA). Asst Organist, Canterbury Cathedral, 1974–78; Master of the Music, St Albans Abbey, 1978–85. Artistic Dir, Internat. Organ Fest., 1979–85. *Recreations:* travel, walking, punting, Italian food. *Address:* 110 Staunton Road, Headington, Oxford OX3 7TN. *T:* Oxford 751256.

DARNLEY, 11th Earl of, *cr* 1725; **Adam Ivo Stuart Bligh;** Baron Clifton of Leighton Bromswold, 1608; Baron Clifton of Rathmore, 1721; Viscount Darnley, 1723; *b* 8 Nov. 1941; *s* of 9th Earl of Darnley and of Rosemary, *d* of late Edmund Basil Potter; *S* half-brother, 1980; *m* 1965, Susan Elaine, JP, *y d* of late Sir Donald Anderson; one *s* one *d*. *Educ:* Harrow; Christ Church, Oxford. Governor, Cobham Hall Sch., 1981–. *Heir:* *s* Lord Clifton, *qv*. *Address:* Netherwood Manor, Tenbury Wells, Worcs WR15 8RT. *Clubs:* Brooks's, MCC.

DARNLEY-THOMAS, Mrs John; *see* Hunter, Rita.

DART, Raymond Arthur; United Steelworkers of America Professor of Anthropology, The Institutes for the Achievement of Human Potential, Philadelphia, since 1966; Emeritus Professor since 1959, Professor of Anatomy, 1923–58, and Dean of the Faculty of Medicine, 1925–43, University of the Witwatersrand, Johannesburg; *b* Toowong, Brisbane, Australia, 4 Feb. 1893; *s* of Samuel Dart and Eliza Anne Brimblecombe; *m* 1936, Marjorie Gordon Frew, Boksburg, Transvaal; one *s* one *d*. *Educ:* Ipswich Grammar Sch., Queensland (Scholarship holder); University of Queensland (Scholarship holder and Foundation scholar); graduated BSc (Hons) 1913; MSc 1915; Sydney Univ., 1914–17; graduated MB, ChM (Hons) 1917; MD 1927; Demonstrator of Anatomy and Acting Principal of St Andrew's Coll., Sydney, 1917; House Surgeon at Royal Prince Alfred Hospital, Sydney, 1917–18; Capt., AAMC, Australia, England, France, 1918–19; Senior Demonstrator of Anatomy, University Coll., London, 1919–20; Fellow of Rockefeller Foundation, 1920–21; Senior Demonstrator of Anatomy and Lecturer in Histology, University Coll., London, 1921–22; Capt., SAMC, 1925; Major, 1928; Lieut-Col Reserve Officers, 1940; Pres. of Anthropological Section SAAAS, 1926 (Gold Medal, 1939); Vice-Pres., SAAAS, 1952; Vice-Pres. of Anthropological Section, BAAS, Johannesburg, 1929; Mem. of International Commission on Fossil Man since 1929; FRSSAF 1930, Hon. FRSSAF 1983 (Mem. of Council, 1938, Vice-Pres. 1938–39, 1939–40, 1950–51); Mem. Board, SA Institute for Medical Research, 1934–48; Mem. SA Med. Council, 1935–48, Executive Cttee, 1940–48; Mem. SA Nursing Council from its inception in 1944 until 1951; Mem. Medical Advisory Cttee, SA Council for Scientific and Industrial Research, 1946–48; Pres. Anthropological Section, First Pan-African Congress of Prehistory,

1947–51; guest-lecturer at The Viking Fund Seminar, New York, and public lecturer of The Lowell Inst., Boston, 1949; Inaugural Lecturer, John Irvine Hunter Memorial, Univ. of Sydney, NSW, 1950; Woodward Lecturer, Yale Univ., USA, 1958; Inaugural Van Riebeeck Lecturer; R. J. Terry Meml Lectr, Washington Univ. Sch. of Medicine, St Louis, 1971. SA Broadcasting Corp., 1959. Pres. SA Archaeological Soc., 1951; Pres. SA Assoc. for Advancement of Science, Bulawayo, S Rhodesia, 1953; Vice-Pres., Fourth Pan-African Congress of Prehistory, 1959–62; Pres. SA Museums Assoc., 1961–62; Vice-Pres., Assoc. Scientific and Technical Socs of S Africa, 1961–62, 1962–63, Pres., 1963–64; Pres. SA Soc. of Physiotherapy, 1961–68, Hon. Life Vice-Pres., 1968–; Mem., Internat. Primatological Cttee, 1963–; Mem., Municipal Library Advisory Cttee, Johannesburg, 1964–. Coronation Medal, 1953; Sen. Capt. Scott Memorial Medal, SA Biological Soc., 1955; Viking Medal and Award for Physical Anthropology, Wenner-Gren Foundation of New York, 1957; Simon Biesheuvel Medal (Behavioural Sciences), 1963; Gold Medal, SA Nursing Assoc., 1970; Silver Medal, SA Medical Assoc., 1972. Hon. DSc: Natal, 1956; Witwatersrand, 1964; La Salle, 1968. Fellow Odontological Soc. of SA, 1937; Fellow Institute of Biology, 1964; For. Fellow, Linnaean Soc., 1974; Hon. FSA 1986. Raymond Dart Lectureship in Institute for Study of Man in Africa, estab. 1964; Museums of Man and Science, Johannesburg, initiated 1966, Board of Governors, 1968. Life Mem., S African Soc. for Quaternary Res., 1983; Hon. Life Member: Dental Assoc. of South Africa, 1958, Medical Assoc. of South Africa, 1959, Anatomical Society of Great Britain and Ireland, 1961, Anatomical Soc. of Southern Africa, 1970, S African Nursing Assoc., 1970; Archaeological Soc. of SA, 1973; NY Acad. of Scis, 984; Hon. Fellow, Coll. of Medicine of SA, 1985. *Publications:* Racial Origins, chapter in The Bantu-speaking Tribes of South Africa, 1937; chapters on genealogy and physical characters, in Bushmen of the Southern Kalahari, 1937; (ed) Africa's Place in the Human Story, 1954; The Oriental Horizons of Africa, 1955; Adventures with the Missing Link, 1959; Africa's Place in the Emergence of Civilisation, 1960; Beyond Antiquity, 1965; over 250 articles on anthropological, archaeological, neurological and comparative anatomical subjects in scientific and lay periodicals. *Recreations:* swimming, music. *Address:* 20 Eton Park, Eton Road, Sandhurst, Sandton, Transvaal, 2196, South Africa. *Clubs:* Associated Scientific and Technical, Country (Johannesburg); Explorers' (NY) (Hon. Mem.).

DARTMOUTH, 9th Earl of, *cr* 1711; **Gerald Humphry Legge;** Baron Dartmouth, 1682; Viscount Lewisham, 1711; *b* 26 April 1924; *s* of 8th Earl of Dartmouth, CVO, DSO; *S* father, 1962; *m* 1948, Raine (marr. diss. 1976), *d* of late Alexander McCorquodale; three *s* one *d*; *m* 1980, Mrs G. M. Seguin. *Educ:* Eton. Served War, 1943–45, Coldstream Guards, Italy (despatches). FCA 1951. Dir, Rea Bros PLC, Bankers, 1958. Chairman: Royal Choral Soc.; Anglo-Brazilian Soc. Hon. LLD Dartmouth Coll., USA, 1969. *Heir: s* Viscount Lewisham, *qv*. *Address:* The Manor House, Chipperfield, King's Langley, Herts WD4 9BN. *Club:* Buck's.

See also Baron Herschell.

DARTNALL, Gary; Chairman and Chief Executive, Screen Entertainment Ltd, since 1986; *b* 9 May 1937; *s* of Enid and Gordon Dartnall; *m* 1962, Zena Chidiac; two *d*. *Educ:* King's College, Taunton. Asst Overseas Sales Manager, Associated British Pathé, 1958–60; Far East rep., British Lion Films, 1960–64; Pres., Alliance Inc., 1964–68; Man. Dir, Internat. Dept, Walter Reade Organization (USA) Inc., 1968–71; Pres., EMI Films Inc., 1971–76; Vice-Chm., EMI Television Programs Inc., 1976–80; Pres., VHD Programs Inc. and VHD Disc Manufacturing Inc., 1980–83; Chm. and Chief Exec., THORN EMI Screen Entertainment Ltd, 1983–86; Associate Dir, THORN EMI, 1985–. *Recreation:* sailing. *Address:* Flat 3, Green Park House, 90 Piccadilly, W1. *T:* 01–499 5663.

DARVALL, Sir (Charles) Roger, Kt 1971; CBE 1965; former company director; *b* 11 Aug. 1906; *s* of late C. S. Darvall; *m* 1931, Dorothea M., *d* of late A. C. Vautier; two *d*. *Educ:* Burnie, Tasmania. FASA. Gen. Manager, Australia & New Zealand Bank Ltd, Melbourne, 1961–67; former Director: Broken Hill Pty; Rothmans of Pall Mall Aust.; H. C. Sleigh Ltd; Australia New Guinea Corp.; Electrolux Pty; L. M. Ericsson Pty; Munich Re-Insurance Co. of Aust; Australian Eagle Insurance Co. Comr, State Electricity Commn of Vic, 1969–79. *Recreations:* motoring, gardening, outdoors. *Address:* 2 Martin Court, Toorak, Vic 3142, Australia. *T:* 241–4647. *Clubs:* Athenæum, Melbourne (Melbourne).

DARVALL, Frank Ongley, CBE 1954; retired from HM Diplomatic Service, 1970; a Governor: Sulgrave Manor; Haileybury; Imperial Service College; *b* 16 April 1906; 5th *s* of late R. T. Darvall and Annie E. Johnson, Reading; *m* 1931, Dorothy (*d* 1979), *er d* of Harry Edmonds and late Jane Quay, NY City; one *s* decd. *Educ:* Dover Coll.; Reading (BA); London (BA, PhD); Columbia (MA). President Nat. Union of Students, 1927–29; Commonwealth Fund Fellow, 1929–31; Assoc. Sec. for Internat. Studies, Internat. Students Service, 1931–32; Dir, Geneva Students Internat. Union, 1933. Lecturer in Economics and History, Queen's Coll., Harley Street, 1933–36; Director Research and Discussion, English-Speaking Union, 1936–39; Dep. Director American Div., Ministry of Information, 1939–45; British Consul, Denver, 1945–46; 1st Secretary HM Embassy, Washington, 1946–49; Vice-Chairman Kinsman Trust, 1949–56; Editor, The English-Speaking World, 1950–53; Director-General, English-speaking Union of the Commonwealth, 1949–57; Chairman, Congress of European-American Assoc., 1954–57. European Editor, World Review, 1958–59. Hon. Dir, UK Cttee, Atlantic Congress, 1959; Attached British High Commn, Cyprus, 1960–62; Dir, British Information Services, Eastern Caribbean, 1962–66; attached, British Consulate-Gen., Barcelona, 1966; Consul, Boston, 1966–68; FCO (formerly CO), 1968–70. Dean of Academics, Alvescot Coll., 1970–71, Vice-Pres., 1971–72. Contested (L) Ipswich, 1929, King's Lynn, 1935, Hythe bye-election, 1939. Extension Lecturer and Tutorial Classes Tutor, Cambridge and London Universities, 1933–39. *Publications:* Popular Disturbances and Public Order in Regency England, 1934; The Price of European Peace, 1937; The American Political Scene, 1939. *Address:* c/o Lloyds Bank, 1 Butler Place, SW1.

DARVALL, Sir Roger; *see* Darvall, Sir C. R.

DARWEN, 2nd Baron, *cr* 1946, of Heys-in-Bowland; **Cedric Percival Davies;** Publisher; President, Independent Publishers' Guild, since 1973; *b* 18 Feb. 1915; *e s* of 1st Baron and M. Kathleen Brown; *S* father 1950; *m* 1934, Kathleen Dora, *d* of George Sharples Walker; three *s* one *d*. *Educ:* Sidcot; Manchester Univ. BA Hons English Lit. and Language, Manchester, 1947. Engaged in Cotton Industry, 1932–40. On staff of school for Maladjusted Children, 1942–44. Manchester Univ., 1944–48, Teaching Diploma, 1948. Warden of Letchworth Adult Education Centre, 1948–51; Secretary to Training and Education Dept of National Assoc. for Mental Health, 1951–53; Founded Darwen Finlayson Ltd, Publishers, 1954, Chm., and Man. Dir, 1954–73; Dep. Editor of John O'London's, 1959–62. Chm., Hollybank Engineering Co. Ltd., 1957–70. Is a Quaker. *Publications:* designed and ed, Illustrated County History Series. *Recreations:* sailing, painting, cinéphotography. *Heir: s* Hon. Roger Michael Davies, [*b* 28 June 1938; *m* 1961, Gillian Irene, *d* of Eric G. Hardy, Bristol; two *s* three *d*]. *Address:* White Lodge, Sandelswood End, Beaconsfield, Bucks. *T:* Beaconsfield 3355.

DARWENT, Rt. Rev. Frederick Charles; *see* Aberdeen and Orkney, Bishop of.

DARWIN, Henry Galton, CMG 1977; MA; Second Legal Adviser, Foreign and Commonwealth Office, since 1984; *b* 6 Nov. 1929; *s* of late Sir Charles Darwin, KBE, FRS; *m* 1958, Jane Sophia Christie; three *d*. *Educ:* Marlborough Coll.; Trinity Coll., Cambridge. Called to Bar, Lincoln's Inn, 1953. Asst Legal Adviser, FO, 1954–60 and 1963–67; Legal Adviser, British Embassy, Bonn, 1960–63; Legal Counsellor: UK Mission to UN, 1967–70; FCO, 1970–73; a Dir-Gen., Legal Service, Council Secretariat, European Communities, Brussels, 1973–76. Dep. Legal Adviser, FCO, 1976–84. *Publications:* contribs in Report of a Study Group on the Peaceful Settlement of International Disputes, 1966 and International Regulation of Frontier Disputes, 1970; notes in British Yearbook of International Law and American Jl of International Law. *Address:* 30 Hereford Square, SW7. *T:* 01–373 1140. *Club:* Athenæum.

DARWIN, Kenneth; Editor, Familia: Ulster Genealogical Review, since 1985; *b* 24 Sept. 1921; *s* of late Robert Lawrence and Elizabeth Darwin (*née* Swain), Ripon, Yorks. *Educ:* Elementary Sch.; Ripon Grammar Sch.; University Coll., Durham; Oflag VIIB (1943–45). BA 1947, MA 1948. Served 2nd Bn Lancs Fus., N Africa, (Captain) POW, 1942–46; TA Captain (Intelligence Corps), 1949–54. Asst Keeper, Public Record Office (NI), 1948; Dep. Keeper of Records of N Ireland, 1955–70; Vis. Lectr in Archives, UC Dublin, 1967–71; Fellow Commoner, Churchill Coll., Cambridge, 1970; Asst Sec., Min. of Commerce (NI), 1970–74; Sen. Asst Sec., Dept of Finance (NI) and Dept of Civil Service (NI), 1974–77; Dep. Sec., Dept of Finance (NI), 1977–81. Member: Irish MSS Commn, Dublin, 1955–70; Adv. Bd for New History of Ireland, Royal Irish Acad., 1968–; Trustee: Ulster Historical Foundn, 1956–; Ulster Museum, 1982– (Vice-Chm., 1984–86); Lyric Th., Belfast, 1966–69. Mem., Bangor Br., British Legion. *Publications:* articles on archives, history and genealogy, in jls and Nat. Trust guides. *Recreations:* travel and fine arts; walking, gardening. *Address:* 18 Seymour Road, Bangor, Co. Down BT19 1BL. *T:* 460718. *Club:* Royal Commonwealth Society.

DARYNGTON, 2nd Baron, *cr* 1923, of Witley; **Jocelyn Arthur Pike Pease;** *b* 30 May 1908; *s* of 1st Baron Daryngton, PC and Alice (*d* 1948), 2nd *d* of Very Rev. H. Mortimer Luckock, sometime Dean of Lichfield; *S* father 1949. *Educ:* Eton; privately; Trinity Coll., Cambridge (MA). Member Inner Temple, 1932. *Heir:* none. *Address:* 7 Stocks Mead, Washington, Pulborough, W Sussex RH20 4AU. *T:* Ashington 892246.

DASGUPTA, Prof. Partha Sarathi, PhD; Professor of Economics, Cambridge University, and Fellow of St John's College, Cambridge, since 1985; *b* 17 Nov. 1942; *s* of Prof. Amiya Dasgupta and Shanti Dasgupta, Santiniketan, India; *m* 1968, Carol Margaret, *d* of Prof. James Meade, *qv*; one *s* two *d*. *Educ:* Univ. of Delhi (BSc Hons 1962); Univ. of Cambridge (BA 1965, PhD 1968; Stevenson Prize, 1967). Res. Fellow, Trinity Hall, Cambridge, 1968–71, Supernumerary Fellow, 1971–74; Lectr, 1971–75, Reader, 1975–78, Prof. of Econs, 1978–84, LSE. Vis. Professor: Stanford Univ., 1974–75 and 1983–84; Delhi Univ., 1978. Consultant: on Proj. Planning, UNIDO, 1969–72; on Resource Management, World Bank, 1977; on Environmental Component of Natural Resource Pricing, UNCTAD, 1977–80. Member: Expert Panel on Environmtl Health, WHO, 1975–85; Expert Gp on Management of Environmtl Resources, UNEP, 1979–. Fellow, Econometric Soc., 1975. *Publications:* (with S. Marglin and A. K. Sen) Guidelines for Project Evaluation, 1972; (with G. Heal) Economic Theory and Exhaustible Resources, 1979; The Control of Resources, 1982; articles on develt planning, optimum population, taxation and trade, welfare and justice, nat. resources, game theory, indust. org. and technical progress in Econ. Jl, Econometrica, Rev. of Econ. Stud., etc. *Address:* 1 Dean Drive, Holbrook Road, Cambridge. *T:* Cambridge 212179.

DASHWOOD, Sir Francis (John Vernon Hereward), 11th Bt, *cr* 1707; (Premier Baronet of Great Britain); *b* 7 Aug. 1925; *s* of Sir John Lindsay Dashwood, 10th Bt, CVO, and Helen Moira Eaton; *S* father, 1966; *m* 1st, 1957, Victoria Ann Elizabeth Gwynne de Rutzen (*d* 1976); one *s* three *d*; 2nd, 1977, Marcella (*née* Scarafia), formerly wife of Giuseppe Sportoletti Baduel and *widow* of Jack Frye, CBE; one step *s* (from wife's first *m*). *Educ:* Eton; Christ Church, Oxford (BA 1948, MA 1953); Henry Fellow, Harvard Business Sch., USA. Foreign Office, 1944–45. Aluminium Company of Canada Ltd, 1950–51; EMI Ltd, 1951–53. Member of Buckinghamshire County Council, 1950–51; Member Lloyd's, 1956. Contested (C) West Bromwich, 1955, Gloucester, 1957. High Sheriff Bucks, 1976. SBStJ. *Heir: s* Edward John Francis Dashwood, *b* 25 Sept. 1964. *Address:* West Wycombe Park, Buckinghamshire. *T:* High Wycombe 23720. *Club:* White's.

DASHWOOD, Sir Richard (James), 9th Bt *cr* 1684, of Kirtlington Park; *b* 14 Feb. 1950; *s* of Sir Henry George Massy Dashwood, 8th Bt, and Susan Mary (*d* 1985), *er d* of late Major V. R. Montgomerie-Charrington, Hunsdon House, Herts; *S* father, 1972; *m* 1984, Kathryn Ann, *er d* of Frank Mahon, Eastbury, Berks. *Educ:* Maidwell Hall Preparatory Sch.; Eton College. Commissioned 14/20th King's Hussars, 1969; T&AVR, 1973–. *Heir: kinsman* Alexander Thomas Whitburn Dashwood, *b* 1950. *Address:* Ledwell Cottage, Sandford St Martin, Oxfordshire OX5 4AN. *T:* Great Tew 267. *Club:* Cavalry and Guards.

da SILVA, John Burke, CMG 1969; HM Diplomatic Service, retired; Adviser, Commercial Union Assurance Co., 1973–84; *b* 30 Aug. 1918; *o s* of late John Christian da Silva and Gabrielle Guittard; *m* 1st, 1940, Janice (decd), *d* of Roy Mayor, Shrewsbury, Bermuda; one *d*; 2nd, 1963, Jennifer, *yr d* of late Capt. the Hon. T. T. Parker, DSC, RN, Greatham Moor, Hants; one *s* two *d*. *Educ:* Stowe Sch.; Trinity Coll., Cambridge (MA). Commnd Intell. Corps 1940, served with 1st Airborne Div., N Africa and Italy, GS02 SHAEF, France and Germany (despatches); Control Commn Germany and Austria. Joined Foreign Service, 1948; served Rome, Hamburg, Bahrain, Aden, Washington, FCO; retired 1973. Chm., Governors, Virginia Water Junior Sch., 1973–83; a Vice-Pres., Royal Soc. for Asian Affairs, 1983–86; Mem. Council, Oriental Ceramic Soc., 1977–80, 1984–. *Publications:* contributor: Oriental Art, Trans OCS, Asian Affairs, etc. *Recreation:* Oriental Art. *Address:* Copse Close, Virginia Water, Surrey. *T:* Wentworth 2342. *Club:* Travellers'.

DATE, William Adrian, CBE 1973; Chairman, Grenada Public Service Board of Appeal, since 1967; Member, Judicial and Legal Services Commission, Organisation of Eastern Caribbean States, since 1967; Income Tax Appeal Commissioner, Grenada, since 1985; *b* 1 July 1908; *er s* of James C. Date; *m* 1st, 1933, Dorothy MacGregor Grant (*d* 1979); two *d*; 2nd, 1981, Rhoda Elaine Minors. *Educ:* Queen's Royal Coll., Trinidad; Grenada Boys' Secondary Sch.; Lodge Sch., Barbados; Middle Temple, London. Magistrate and District Govt Officer, St Lucia, 1933–39; Crown Attorney, St Vincent, 1939–44; Legal Draughtsman, Jamaica, 1944–47; Chief Secretary, Windward Islands, 1947–50; Puisne Judge of the Supreme Court of the Windward and Leeward Islands, 1950–56; Puisne Judge, British Guiana, 1956–64, retd. Vice-Pres., Grenada Building and Loan Assoc., 1976–; Grenada Co-operative Bank, 1976–. *Recreations:* golf, tennis, bridge. *Address:* PO Box 133, St George's, Grenada, West Indies.

DATTA, Dr Naomi, FRS 1985; Professor Emeritus, London University; *b* 17 Sept. 1922; *d* of Alexander and Ellen Henrietta Goddard; *m* 1943, S. P. Datta; two *d* one *s*. *Educ:* St Mary's Sch., Wantage; University Coll. London; W London Hosp. Med. Sch. MB BS (external); MD London. Junior medical posts, 1946–47; Bacteriologist in PHLS, 1947–57; Lectr, later Prof. of Microbial Genetics, RPMS, London Univ., 1957–84; retired 1984. *Publications:* papers on the genetics and epidemiology of antibiotic resistance in bacteria. *Recreations:* gardening, cooking, sewing, knitting. *Address:* 9 Duke's Avenue, W4 2AA. *T:* 01-995 7562.

DAUBE, Prof. David, MA, DCL, PhD, Dr jur; FBA 1957; Director of the Robbins Hebraic and Roman Law Collections and Professor-in-Residence at the School of Law, University of California, Berkeley, 1970–81, Emeritus Professor of Law, since 1981; Emeritus Regius Professor, Oxford University, since 1970; Member, Academic Board, Institute of Jewish Studies, London, since 1953; *b* Freiburg, 8 Feb. 1909; 2nd *s* of Jakob Daube; *m* 1936 (marr. diss., 1964); three *s*. *Educ:* Berthold-gymnasium, Freiburg; Universities of Freiburg, Göttingen and Cambridge. Fellow of Caius Coll., 1938–46, Hon. Fellow, 1974; Lecturer in Law, Cambridge, 1946–51; Professor of Jurisprudence at Aberdeen, 1951–55; Regius Prof. of Civil Law, Oxford Univ., and Fellow of All Souls Coll., 1955–70, Emeritus Fellow, 1980. Senior Fellow, Yale Univ., 1962; Delitzsch Lecturer, Münster, 1962; Gifford Lecturer, Edinburgh, for 1962 and 1963 (lectures delivered, 1963–64); Olaus Petri Lecturer, Uppsala, 1963; Ford Prof. of Political Science, Univ. of California, Berkeley, 1964; Riddell Lectr, Newcastle, 1965; Gray Lectr, Cambridge, 1966; Lionel Cohen Lectr, Jerusalem, 1970; inaug. Frosty Gerard Lectr, UC Irvine, 1981. Vis. Prof. of History, 1966–78, Hon. Prof., 1980, Univ. of Constance. President: Société d'Histoire des Droits de l'Antiquité, 1957–58; Classical Assoc. of GB, 1976–77; Jewish Law Assoc., 1983–85; Founder-Pres., B'nai B'rith Oxford, 1961. Corresp. Mem., Akad. Wiss., Göttingen, 1964, Bayer. Akad. Wiss., Munich, 1966; Hon. Mem. Royal Irish Acad., 1970; Fellow: Amer. Acad. of Arts and Sciences, 1971; World Acad. of Art and Sci., 1975; Amer. Acad. for Jewish Research, 1979; Amer. Soc. for Legal History, 1983; Hon. Fellow, Oxford Centre for Postgraduate Hebrew Studies, 1973. Hon. LLD: Edinburgh 1960; Leicester 1964; Cambridge 1981; Dr *hc* Paris 1963; Hon. DHL Hebrew Union Coll., 1971; Dr jur *hc* Munich, 1972. *Publications:* Studies in Biblical Law, 1947; The New Testament and Rabbinic Judaism, 1956; Forms of Roman Legislation, 1956; The Exodus Pattern in the Bible, 1963; The Sudden in the Scriptures, 1964; Collaboration with Tyranny in Rabbinic Law, 1965; He that Cometh, 1966; Roman Law, 1969; Civil Disobedience in Antiquity, 1972; Ancient Hebrew Fables, 1973; Wine in the Bible, 1975; Medical and Genetic Ethics, 1976; Duty of Procreation, 1977; Typologie im Werk des Flavius Josephus, 1977; Ancient Jewish Law, 1981; Geburt der Detektivgeschichte, 1983; Das Alte Testament im Neuen, 1984; Sons and Strangers, 1984; (ed) Studies in memory of F. de Zulueta, 1959; (with W. D. Davies) Studies in honour of C. H. Dodd, 1956, and articles; *Festschriften:* Daube Noster, 1974; Studies in Jewish Legal History in Honour of D.D., 1974; Donum Gentilicium, 1978. *Address:* School of Law, University of California, Berkeley, Calif 94720, USA.

DAULTANA, Mumtaz Mohammad Khan; Ambassador of Pakistan to the Court of St James's, 1972–78; *b* 23 Feb. 1916; *o s* of Nawab Ahmadyar Daultana; *m* 1943, Almas Jehan; one *s* one *d*. *Educ:* St Anthony's Sch., Lahore; Government Coll., Lahore (BA (Hons)); Corpus Christi Coll., Oxford (MA); Called to Bar, Middle Temple, 1940; 1st cl. 1st position in Bar exam. Mem., All India Muslim League, 1942–; unopposed election as Mem. Punjab Legislative Assembly, 1943; Gen. Sec., Punjab Muslim League, 1944; Sec., All India Muslim League Central Cttee of Action, 1945; Elected Member: Punjab Assembly, 1946; Constituent Assembly of India, 1947; Constituent Assembly, Pakistan, 1947; Finance Minister, Punjab, 1947–48; Pres., Punjab Muslim League, 1948–50; Chief Minister of Punjab, 1951–53; Finance Minister, West Pakistan, 1955–56; Defence Minister, Pakistan, 1957; Pres., Pakistan Muslim League, 1967–72. Elected Member: Nat. Assembly of Pakistan, 1970; Constitution Cttee of Nat. Assembly, 1972. *Publications:* Agrarian Report of Pakistan Muslim League, 1950; Thoughts on Pakistan's Foreign Policy, 1956; Kashmir in Present Day Context, 1965. *Recreations:* music, squash. *Address:* 8 Durand Road, Lahore, Pakistan. *T:* 302459 (Lahore), 532387 (Karachi). *Clubs:* United Oxford & Cambridge University; Gymkhana (Lahore).

DAUNCEY, Brig. Michael Donald Keen, DSO 1945; DL; Hon. Colonel, 1st Cadet Battalion, Gloucestershire Regiment (ACF), since 1981; *b* 11 May 1920; *o s* of late Thomas Gough Dauncey and Alice Dauncey (*née* Keen); *m* 1945, Marjorie Kathleen, *d* of H. W. Neep, FCA; one *s* two *d*. *Educ:* King Edward's School, Birmingham; Inter. Exam., Inst. of Chartered Accountants. Commissioned, 22nd (Cheshire) Regt, 1941; seconded to Glider Pilot Regt, 1943; Arnhem, 1944 (wounded three times; taken prisoner, later escaped); MA to GOC-in-C, Greece, 1946–47; seconded to Para. Regt, 1948–49; Staff Coll., 1950; Instructor, RMA, 1957–58; CO, 1st Bn 22nd (Cheshire) Regt, 1963–66, BAOR and UN peace keeping force, Cyprus; DS plans, JSSC, 1966–68; Comdt, Jungle Warfare Sch., 1968–69; Comdt, Support Weapons Wing Sch. of Infantry, 1969–72; Defence and Military Attaché, Madrid, 1973–75; retired 1976. Col, 22nd (Cheshire) Regt, 1978–85. DL Glos 1983. *Recreations:* rough shooting, travelling, tennis; also under-gardener. *Address:* Uley Lodge, Uley, near Dursley, Glos GL11 5SN. *T:* Dursley 860216. *Club:* Army and Navy.

DAUNT, Maj.-Gen. Brian, CB 1956; CBE 1953; DSO 1943; late RA; *b* 16 March 1900; *s* of Dr William Daunt, Parade House, Hastings; *m* 1938, Millicent Margaret, *d* of Capt. A. S. Balfour, Allermuir House, Colinton, Edinburgh; two *d* (one *s* decd). *Educ:* Tonbridge; RMA, Woolwich. Commissioned RA, 1920; served NW Frontier, India, 1929–30; War of 1939–45; France, 1940, as 2 i/c Regt; CO Anti-Tank Regt, 1941; Italy, as CO 142 Field Regt, RA, Royal Devon Yeo., 1943 (DSO); CRA: 1st Armoured Div., 1944; 46 Div., 1944; 10 Indian Div., 1946; Italy, 1945 (despatches). Has had various Brigadier's appts. Commandant Coast Artillery Sch. and Inspector Coast Artillery, 1950–53; General Officer Commanding Troops, Malta, 1953–Nov. 1956; retired, 1957; Controller, Home Dept, British Red Cross Society, 1957–66. Col Comdt RA, 1960–65. CStJ 1966. *Recreations:* gardening, music, drama. *Address:* Blackstone House, Sotwell, near Wallingford, Oxon OX10 0PX. *T:* Wallingford 37060. *Club:* Army and Navy.

DAUNT, Patrick Eldon; Head of Bureau for Action in favour of Disabled People, EEC, since 1982; *b* 19 Feb. 1925; *s* of Dr Francis Eldon Daunt and Winifred Doggett Daunt (*née* Wells); *m* 1958, Jean Patricia, *d* of Lt-Col Percy Wentworth Hargreaves and of Joan (*née* Holford); three *s* one *d*. *Educ:* Rugby Sch.; Wadham Coll., Oxford. BA, 1st Cl. Hons Lit. Hum., 1949, MA 1954, Oxon. Housemaster, Christ's Hosp., 1959; Headmaster, Thomas Bennett Comprehensive Sch., Crawley, 1965. Chm., Campaign for Comprehensive Educn, 1971–73; Principal Administrator, EEC, 1974–82. *Publication:* Comprehensive Values, 1975. *Address:* Avenue des Cactus 29, 1150 Brussels, Belgium. *T:* Brussels 770-64-12; Cambridge 891485.

DAUNT, Timothy Lewis Achilles, CMG 1982; HM Diplomatic Service; Ambassador to Turkey, since 1986; *b* 11 Oct. 1935; *s* of L. H. G. Daunt and Margery (*née* Lewis Jones); *m* 1962, Patricia Susan Knight; one *s* two *d*. *Educ:* Sherborne; St Catharine's Coll., Cambridge. 8th KRI Hussars, 1954–56. Entered Foreign Office, 1959; Ankara, 1960; FO, 1964; Nicosia, 1967; Private Sec. to Permanent Under-Sec. of State, FCO, 1970; Bank of England, 1972; UK Mission, NY, 1973; Counsellor, OECD, Paris, 1975; Head of South European Dept, FCO, 1978–81; Associate at Centre d'études et de recherches internationales, Paris, 1982; Minister and Dep. UK Perm. Rep. to NATO, Brussels, 1982–85; Asst Under-Sec. of State (Defence), FCO, 1985–86. *Address:* c/o Foreign and Commonwealth Office, SW1.

DAUSSET, Prof. Jean Baptiste Gabriel Joachim; Commandeur de la Légion d'Honneur; Professeur de Medécine Expérimentale au Collège de France, since 1977; *b* 19 Oct. 1916; *s* of Henri Dausset and Elizabeth Brullard; *m* 1962, Rose Mayoral; one *s* one *d*. *Educ:* Lycée Michelet, Paris; Faculty of Medicine, University of Paris. Associate Professor, 1958–68, Professor of Immunohaematology, 1968–77, University of Paris. Institut Nationale de la Santé et de la Recherche Médicale: Director of Research Unit on Immunogenetics of Human Transplantation, 1968–84; Centre National de la Recherche Scientifique: Co-Director, Oncology and Immuno-haematology Laboratory, 1968–84. Gairdner Foundn Prize, 1977; Koch Foundn Prize, 1978; Wolf Foundn Prize, 1978; Nobel Prize for Physiology or Medicine, 1980. *Publications:* Immuno-hématologie biologique et clinique, 1956; (with F. T. Rapaport) Human Transplantation, 1968; (with G. Snell and S. Nathanson) Histocompatibility, 1976; (with M. Fougereau) Immunology 1980, 1980; (with M. Pla) HLA, 1985. *Recreation:* plastic art. *Address:* 9 rue de Villersexel, 75007 Paris, France. *T:* 42 22 18 82.

DAVENPORT, (Arthur) Nigel; President, British Actors' Equity Association, since 1986; *b* 23 May 1928; *s* of Arthur Henry Davenport and Katherine Lucy (*née* Meiklejohn); *m* 1st, 1951, Helena White (decd); one *s* one *d*; 2nd, 1972, Maria Aitken (marr. diss.); one *s*. *Educ:* Cheltenham Coll.; Trinity Coll., Oxford (MA). Entered acting profession, 1951; for first ten years worked almost exclusively in theatre; original mem. English Stage Co. at Royal Court Th., 1956; A Taste of Honey, on Broadway, 1960; mainly television and films, 1961–; starred or co-starred in over 30 cinema films, incl. A High Wind in Jamaica, 1964; Man for All Seasons, 1966; *television:* South Riding; George III in The Prince Regent. Mem. Council, British Actors' Equity, 1976; Vice Pres., 1978–82, 1985–86. *Recreations:* gardening, travel. *Club:* Garrick.

DAVENPORT, Brian John, QC 1980; a Law Commissioner, since 1981; *b* 17 March 1936; *s* of R. C. Davenport, FRCS, and Mrs H. E. Davenport; *m* 1969, Erica Tickell, *yr d* of Prof. E. N. Willmer, *qv*; two *s* one *d*. *Educ:* Bryanston Sch.; Worcester Coll., Oxford (MA). 2 Lieut RE, 1955–56. Called to the Bar, Gray's Inn, 1960 (Atkin Scholar); Bencher, 1983. Junior Counsel: to Export Credit Guarantees Dept, 1971–74; to Dept of Employment, 1972–74; (Common Law), to Bd of Inland Revenue, 1974–80; (Common Law), to the Crown, 1978–80. Mem., Gen. Council of the Bar, 1969–73. Mem. Cttee of Management, Barristers Benevolent Assoc., 1963–78, Jt Hon. Sec. 1978–. *Publications:* (ed jtly with F. M. B. Reynolds) 13th and 14th edns of Bowstead on Agency. *Address:* 43 Downshire Hill, NW3 1NU. *T:* 01–435 3332; c/o Law Commission, 37 John Street, WC2. *T:* 01–242 0861.

DAVENPORT, Major (retd) David John Cecil, DL; Chairman, Council for Small Industries in Rural Areas (CoSIRA), since 1982; Development Commissioner, since 1982; *b* 28 Oct. 1934; *s* of Major John Lewes Davenport, DL, JP, and Louise Aline Davenport; *m* 1st, 1959, Jennifer Burness (marr. diss. 1969); two *d*; 2nd, 1971, Lindy Jane Baker; one *s*. *Educ:* Eton College; Royal Military Academy, Sandhurst. Commnd into Grenadier Guards, 1954, retired 1967. Chairman, Leominster District Council, 1975–76. Chm., Regional Adv. Cttee of the Forestry Commn (SW), 1974–; Member, Forestry Commn's National Adv. Cttee for England, 1974–; Mem. Council, Country Landowners' Assoc., 1980–. DL Hereford and Worcester 1974. *Address:* Mansel Lacy House, Hereford HR4 7HQ. *T:* Bridge Sollars 224. *Club:* Boodle's.

DAVENPORT, Rear-Adm. Dudley Leslie, CB 1969; OBE 1954; *b* 17 Aug. 1919; *s* of Vice-Adm. R. C. Davenport, CB, Catherington, Hants; *m* 1950, Joan, *d* of Surg. Comdr H. Burns, OBE; two *s*. *Educ:* RNC, Dartmouth. Served in Destroyers, Mediterranean and Atlantic, 1939–45; commanded HMS Holmes, 1945 and HMS Porlock Bay, 1946; served in HMS Sheffield, 1947–48; at HMS Ganges, 1949–51; Naval Staff Course, 1951; Naval Instructor, Indian Defence Services Staff Coll., 1951–53; comd HMS Virago, 1954–55; NATO Defence Course, 1955–56; Comdr RN Barracks, Chatham, 1956–57; Captain, 1957; Staff of Admiral Comdg Reserves, 1958–60; Captain Inshore Flotilla Far East, 1960–62; Director Naval Officers Appointments (Seaman Officers), 1962–64; comd HMS Victorious, 1964–66; Rear-Admiral, 1967; Flag Officer, Malta, 1967–69; retd, 1969. *Recreation:* gardening. *Address:* Rose Cottage, Halnaker, Chichester, West Sussex. *T:* Chichester 773210. *Club:* Army and Navy.

DAVENPORT, Maurice Hopwood, FIB; Director, First National Finance Corporation plc, since 1985; *b* 19 March 1925; *s* of Richard and Elizabeth Davenport; *m* 1954, Sheila Timms; one *s* two *d*. *Educ:* Rivington and Blackrod Grammar Sch. FIB 1982. Served RN, 1943–46. Joined Williams Deacon's Bank, 1940; Sec., 1960; Asst Gen. Man., 1969; Dir, 1978–85, Man. Dir, 1982–85, Williams & Glyn's Bank; Dir, Royal Bank of Scotland Gp and Royal Bank of Scotland, 1982–85. Mem., Tunbridge Wells HA, 1985–. *Recreations:* walking, gardening, reading. *Address:* Pines, Dormans Park, East Grinstead, West Sussex RH19 2EN. *T:* Dormans Park 439.

DAVENPORT, Nigel; *see* Davenport, A. N.

DAVENPORT, Lt-Col Sir Walter Henry B.; *see* Bromley-Davenport.

DAVENPORT-HANDLEY, Sir David (John), Kt 1980; OBE 1962; JP; DL; Chairman, Clipsham Quarry Co., since 1947; *b* 2 Sept. 1919; *s* of John Davenport-Handley, JP; *m* 1943, Leslie Mary Goldsmith; one *s* one *d*. *Educ:* RNC Dartmouth. RN retd 1947. Chm., Rutland and Stamford Conservative Assoc., 1952–65; Treasurer, East Midlands Area Conservative Assoc., 1965–71, Chm. 1971–77; Vice-Chm., Nat. Union of Conservative & Unionist Assocs, 1977–79, Chm., 1979–80. Member: Consumers' Cttees for GB and for England and Wales, 1956–65; Parole Bd, 1981–84. Governor, Swinton Conservative Coll., 1973–77; Chairman: Board of Visitors, Ashwell Prison, 1955–73; Governors, Casterton Community Coll., 1960–78; Trustee, Oakham Sch., 1970–86. JP 1948, High Sheriff 1954, DL 1962, Vice-Lieutenant 1972, Rutland; Chm., Rutland Petty Sessional Div., 1957–84; DL Leicestershire 1974. *Recreations:* gardening, music, travel. *Address:* Clipsham Hall, Oakham, Rutland, Leics. *T:* Castle Bytham 204. *Club:* English-Speaking Union.

DAVENTRY, 3rd Viscount *cr* 1943; **Francis Humphrey Maurice FitzRoy Newdegate,** DL; *b* 17 Dec. 1921; *s* of Comdr Hon. John Maurice FitzRoy Newdegate, RN (*y s* of 1st Viscountess; he assumed by Royal Licence, 1936, additional surname and arms of Newdegate and *d* 1976) and Lucia Charlotte Susan, OBE (*d* 1982), *d* of Sir Francis Alexander Newdigate Newdegate, GCMG; *S* uncle, 1986; *m* 1959, Hon. Rosemary, *e d* of 1st Baron Norrie, GCMG, GCVO, CB, DSO, MC; two *s* one *d*. *Educ:* Eton. Served War of 1939–45 with Coldstream Guards, N Africa and Italy; Captain 1943. ADC to Viceroy of India, 1946–48. JP 1960, DL 1970, High Sheriff 1970, Warwickshire; Vice-Lieut 1974. *Heir:* *s* Hon. James Edward FitzRoy Newdegate, *b* 27 July 1960. *Address:* Temple House, Arbury, Nuneaton, Warwickshire. *T:* Nuneaton 383514. *Club:* Boodle's.

DAVEY, David Garnet, OBE 1949; MSc, PhD; Research Director of Pharmaceuticals Division, Imperial Chemical Industries Ltd, 1969–75; *b* 8 Aug. 1912; *y s* of I. W. Davey, Caerphilly, Glamorgan; *m* 1938, Elizabeth Gale; one *s* two *d. Educ:* University Coll., Cardiff (1st cl. Hons Zoology; MSc 1935); Gonville and Caius Coll., Cambridge (PhD 1938); Harvard Univ. Med. Sch. (Research Fellow). Inst. of Animal Pathology, Univ. of Cambridge, 1938; Lectr, University Coll., Cardiff, 1939–40; Min. of Supply (Radar), 1941; joined ICI 1942; Biological Research Manager, Pharmaceuticals Div., 1957–69. Pres., European Soc. for Study of Drug Toxicity, 1964–69; Member: MRC, 1971–75; Cttee on Review of Medicines, 1975–81; Sub-cttee on Toxicity, Clinical Trials, and Therapeutic Efficacy, Cttee on Safety of Medicines, 1976–81. Chalmers Gold Medal, Royal Soc. Tropical Medicine and Hygiene, 1947; Therapeutics Gold Medal, Apothecaries Soc., 1947. *Publications:* contribs to Annals Trop. Med.; Trans Royal Soc. Tropical Medicine and Hygiene; British Med. Bulletin; Proc. European Soc. for Study of Drug Toxicity, etc. *Recreation:* gardening. *Address:* Aragon Lodge, Star Lane, Morcombelake, Dorset DT6 6DN. *T:* Chideock 89458.

DAVEY, Francis, MA; Headmaster of Merchant Taylors' School, 1974–82; *b* 23 March 1932; *er s* of Wilfred Henry Davey, BSc and Olive (*née* Geeson); *m* 1960, Margaret Filby Lake, MA Oxon, AMA, *o d* of Harold Lake, DMus Oxon, FRCO; one *s* one *d. Educ:* Plymouth Coll.; New Coll., Oxford (Hon. Exhibr); Corpus Christi Coll., Cambridge (Schoolmaster Fellow Commoner). 1st cl. Class. Hon. Mods 1953, 2nd cl. Lit. Hum. 1955, BA 1955, MA 1958. RAF, 1950–51; Classical Upper Sixth Form Master, Dulwich Coll., 1955–60; Head of Classics Dept, Warwick Sch., 1960–66; Headmaster, Dr Morgan's Grammar Sch., Bridgwater, 1966–73. *Publications:* articles in Enciclopedia dello Spettacolo and Classical Review. *Recreations:* Rugby, swimming, gardening, travel. *Address:* Crossings Cottage, Dousland, Yelverton, S Devon PL20 6LU. *T:* Yelverton 853928. *Clubs:* East India, Devonshire, Sports and Public Schools; Union (Oxford).

DAVEY, Geoffrey Wallace; a Recorder of the Crown Court, since 1974; *b* 16 Oct. 1924; *s* of late Hector F. T. Davey and Alice M. Davey; *m* 1964, Joyce Irving Steel; two *s* one *d. Educ:* Queen Elizabeth Grammar Sch., Faversham; Wadham Coll., Oxford (MA). Called to Bar, Lincoln's Inn, 1954; admitted Ghana Bar, 1957; resumed practice NE Circuit, 1970. Chm., Med. Appeal Tribunal, 1982–; Dep. Chm., Agricl Land Tribunal, 1982–. *Recreations:* golf, cooking, carpentry. *Address:* 22 Mill Hill Lane, Northallerton, N Yorkshire. *T:* Northallerton 5943; 19 Baker Street, Middlesbrough, Cleveland. *T:* Middlesbrough 217037–8; 5 King's Bench Walk, Temple, EC4.

DAVEY, Idris Wyn; Under-Secretary, Welsh Office, 1972–77; Member, Sports Council for Wales, since 1978; Deputy Chairman, Local Government Boundary Commission for Wales, since 1979; *b* 8 July 1917; *m* 1943, Lilian Lloyd-Bowen; two *d.* Admiralty, 1940–47; Welsh Bd of Health: Asst Principal, 1948; Principal, 1951; Sec. Local Govt Commn for Wales, 1959–62; Welsh Office: Asst Sec. (in Min. of Housing and Local Govt), 1962; Establishment Officer, 1966–72; Under-Sec., 1972; seconded as Sec. and Mem., Local Govt Staff Commn for Wales and NHS Staff Commn for Wales, 1972–73. *Recreations:* watching Rugby football, gardening. *Address:* 4 Southgate Road, Pennard, Gower, West Glam. *T:* Bishopston 4320.

DAVEY, Jocelyn; *see* Raphael, Chaim.

DAVEY, Jon Colin; Director General, Cable Authority, since 1985; *b* 16 June 1938; *s* of Frederick John Davey and late Dorothy Mary Davey; *m* 1962, Ann Patricia Streames; two *s* one *d. Educ:* Raynes Park Grammar Sch. Joined Home Office, 1957; served in Civil Defence, Immigration, Criminal Policy, Prison and Criminal Justice Depts; Asst Sec., Broadcasting Dept, 1981–85. Asst Sec., Franks Cttee on Sect. 2 of Official Secrets Act, 1971–72; Secretary: Williams Cttee on Obscenity and Film Censorship, 1977–79; Hunt Inquiry into Cable Expansion and Broadcasting Policy, 1982. Vice-Chm., Media Policy Cttee, Council of Europe, 1983–84 *Recreations:* lawnmaking, Bach, English countryside. *Address:* Cable Authority, 38–44 Gillingham Street, SW1V 1HU. *T:* 01-821 6161.

DAVEY, Keith Alfred Thomas, CB 1973; Solicitor and Legal Adviser, Department of the Environment, 1970–82; *b* 1920; *s* of W. D. F. Davey; *m* 1949, Kathleen Elsie, *d* of Rev. F. J. Brabyn; one *s* one *d. Educ:* Cambridge and County High Sch.; Fitzwilliam House, Cambridge (MA). Served War of 1939–45, Middle East (Captain). Called to the Bar, Middle Temple, 1947. Principal Asst Solicitor, DHSS, 1968–70. *Recreations:* looking at churches, reading history, keeping cats and dogs. *Address:* 165 Shelford Road, Trumpington, Cambridge CB2 2ND. *Clubs:* Athenæum, Sette of Odd Volumes.

DAVEY, Peter Gordon, CBE 1986; Managing Director, Meta Machines Ltd, since 1984; Senior Research Fellow, St Cross College, Oxford, since 1981; *b* 6 Aug. 1935; *s* of late Lt-Col Frank Davey, Royal Signals and H. Jean Davey (*née* Robley); *m* 1961; two *s* two *d. Educ:* Winchester Coll.; Gonville and Caius Coll., Cambridge (Mech. Scis Tripos, pt 2 Electrical; MA 1961). MIEE; MBCS 1967. Engineer: GEC Applied Electronics Labs, Stanmore, 1958–61; Lawrence Radiation Lab, Berkeley, Calif, 1961–64; Guest Researcher, Heidelberg Univ., 1964–65; Oxford University: Project Engr, Nuclear Physics Lab., 1966–79; Co-ordinator, Indust. Robotics Research Prog., SERC, 1979–84; Head of Inter-active Computing Facility, Rutherford Lab, SRC, 1978–80; of Robot Welding Project, Engrg Sci. Lab., 1979–. Tech. Dir, Electro Pneumatic Equipment Ltd, Letchworth, 1968–. *Publications:* (with W. F. Clocksin) A Tutorial Introduction to Industrial Robotics; artificial intelligence skills, 1982; (contrib.) Robot Vision, 1982; contribs to learned jls on robotics and image analysis systems. *Recreations:* buildings restoration, squash, sailing. *Address:* Asham Cottage, Horton-cum-Studley, Oxon OX9 1BB.

DAVEY, Peter John; Editor, Architectural Review, since 1981; *b* 28 Feb. 1940; *s* of John Davey and Mary (*née* Roberts); *m* 1968, Carolyn Pulford; two *s. Educ:* Oundle Sch.; Edinburgh University (BArch). RIBA. News and Features Editor, Architects' Journal, 1974; Managing Editor, Architectural Review, 1980. *Publications:* Architects' Journal Legal Handbook (ed), 1973; Arts and Crafts Architecture, 1980; numerous articles in architectural jls. *Recreations:* pursuit of edible fungi, fishing, cooking. *Address:* 44 Hungerford Road, N7 9LP.

DAVEY, Dr Ronald William; Physician to the Queen, since 1986; *b* 25 Oct. 1943; *s* of Frederick George Davey and Cissy Beatrice Lawday; *m* 1966, Geraldine Evelyn Maureen Croucher; one *s* one *d. Educ:* Trinity School of John Whitgift; King's College London; King's College Hosp. (MB BS; MFHom; AKC). Gen. med. practice, 1970–77; Private homoeopathic medical practice, 1978–; research into electro-stimulation and drug addiction, 1978–79; Med. Res. Dir, Blackie Foundn Trust, 1980–. Trustee, Res. Council for Complementary Medicine, 1985– (Vice-Chm., 1986–); Editor, Internat. Soc. of Biophysical Medicine Jl, 1986–. *Publications:* medical papers. *Recreations:* fishing, riding, golf, music, writing. *Address:* 101 Harley Street, W1N 1DF. *T:* 01–580 5489. *Club:* Royal Society of Medicine.

DAVEY, Roy Charles; Headmaster, King's School, Bruton, 1957–72; *b* 25 June 1915; *s* of William Arthur Davey and Georgina (*née* Allison); *m* 1940, Kathleen Joyce Sumner; two *d. Educ:* Christ's Hospital; Brasenose Coll., Oxford (Open Scholar). Asst Master, Weymouth Coll., 1937–40. War Service, Royal Artillery, 1940–46. Senior Master,

1946–49, Warden, 1949–57, The Village Coll., Impington. FRSA. *Recreations:* poetry, botany, gardening, games. *Address:* Fir Trees, Buckland Newton, Dorchester, Dorset DT2 7BY. *T:* Buckland Newton 262. *Club:* East India, Devonshire, Sports and Public Schools.

DAVEY, Prof. William, CBE 1978; PhD; FRSC; President, Portsmouth Polytechnic, 1969–82; Honorary Professor, Polytechnic of Central London, since 1979; *b* Chesterfield, Derbyshire, 15 June 1917; *m* 1941, Eunice Battye; two *s. Educ:* University Coll., Nottingham; Technical Coll., Huddersfield. BSc, PhD (London, external). Chemist: ICI Scottish Dyes, 1940; Boots, 1941; Shell, 1942–44. Lectr and Sen. Lectr in Organic Chemistry, Acton Techn. Coll., 1944–53; Head of Dept of Chemistry and Biology, The Polytechnic, Regent Street, London, W1, 1953–59; Principal, Coll. of Technology, Portsmouth, 1960–69. FRSA, FRSC, CBIM. *Publications:* Industrial Chemistry, 1961; numerous original papers in: Jl Chem. Soc., Inst. Petroleum, Jl Applied Chem. *Recreations:* motoring, foreign travel. *Address:* 67 Ferndale, Waterlooville, Portsmouth PO7 7PH. *T:* Waterlooville 263014.

DAVID, family name of **Baroness David.**

DAVID, Baroness *cr* 1978 (Life Peer), of Romsey in the City of Cambridge; **Nora Ratcliff David;** JP; Deputy Chief Opposition Whip, since 1982; *b* 23 Sept. 1913; *d* of George Blockley Blakesley, JP, and Annie Edith Blakesley; *m* 1935, Richard William David, *qv*; two *s* two *d. Educ:* Ashby-de-la-Zouch Girls' Grammar School; St Felix, Southwold; Newnham Coll., Cambridge (MA; Hon. Fellow 1986). Mem. Bd, Peterborough Develt Corp., 1976–78. A Baroness-in-Waiting (Government Whip), 1978–79; Opposition Whip, 1979–82. Member: Cambridge City Council, 1964–67, 1968–74; Cambs County Council, 1974–78. JP Cambridge City, 1965–. *Recreations:* swimming, theatre. *Address:* 50 Highsett, Cambridge CB2 1NZ. *T:* Cambridge 350376; Cove, New Polzeath, Cornwall PL27 6UF. *T:* Trebetherick 3310.

DAVID, Brian Gurney, CBE 1986; Deputy Receiver for the Metropolitan Police District, 1976–86; *b* 25 Jan. 1926; *s* of Constantine and Gladys Emma David; *m* 1950, Jean Valerie (*née* Young). *Educ:* Alleyn's School, Dulwich. Joined Metropolitan Police Office, 1946; Private Secretary to Receiver for the Metropolitan Police District, 1958; Asst Secretary (Director of Finance), 1973. *Recreations:* cats, cooking, crossword puzzles. *Address:* 26 Woodwarde Road, Dulwich, SE22 8UJ.

DAVID, Mrs Elizabeth, CBE 1986 (OBE 1976); FRSL 1982; 2nd *d* of Rupert Sackville Gwynne, MP, and Hon. Stella Ridley; *m* 1944, Lt-Col Ivor Anthony David (marr. diss. 1960). DUniv Essex, 1979. Chevalier du Mérite Agricole (France), 1977. *Publications:* A Book of Mediterranean Food, 1950; French Country Cooking, 1951; Italian Food, 1954; Summer Cooking, 1955; French Provincial Cooking, 1960; English Cooking, Ancient and Modern: vol. I, Spices, Salt and Aromatics in the English Kitchen, 1970; English Bread and Yeast Cookery, 1977; An Omelette and a Glass of Wine, 1984. *Address:* c/o Penguin Books Ltd, Harmondsworth, Middlesex.

DAVID, Sir (Jean) Marc, Kt 1986; CBE 1982; QC (Mauritius) 1969; Barrister, in private practice since 1964; *b* 22 Sept. 1925; *s* of late Joseph Claudius David and Marie Lucresia David (*née* Henrisson); *m* 1948, Mary Doreen Mahoney; three *s* three *d. Educ:* Royal Coll., Port Louis; Royal Coll., Curepipe, Mauritius (Laureate (classical side) of English Scholarship, 1945); LSE (LLB Hons). Called to the Bar, Middle Temple, 1949. Barrister in private practice, 1950–54; Dist Magistrate, then Crown Law Officer (Crown Counsel, Sen. Crown Counsel and Actg AAG), 1954–64. Chm., Mauritius Bar Assoc., 1968, 1979. Chairman: various arbitration tribunals, commns of enquiry and cttees apptd by govt, 1958–; Electoral Supervisory and Boundaries Commns, 1973–82 (Mem., 1968–73); Mem., Panel of Conciliators and Arbitrators, Internat. Centre for Settlement of Investment Disputes, 1969–. Visitor, Univ. of Mauritius, 1980–81. *Recreations:* reading, listening to music, horse racing. *Address:* (home) Hillview, Jenner Lane, Quatre Bornes, Mauritius. *T:* 54–3811; (chambers) 11 Jules Koenig Street, Port-Louis, Mauritius. *T:* 2–2177. *Clubs:* Royal Over-Seas League; Lions, City (Port Louis), Turf, Racing (Mauritius).

DAVID, Richard (William), CBE 1967; formerly Publisher to the University, Cambridge University Press; Fellow of Clare Hall, Cambridge; *b* 28 Jan. 1912; *e s* of Rev. F. P. and Mary W. David, Winchester; *m* 1935, Nora (*see* Baroness David); two *s* two *d. Educ:* Winchester Coll. (Scholar); Corpus Christi Coll., Cambridge (Scholar). Joined editorial staff, CUP, 1936. Served RNVR, 1940–46, in Mediterranean and Western Approaches; qualified navigator, 1944; Lt-Comdr, 1945. Transferred to London Office of CUP, 1946; London Manager, 1948–63; Sec. to the Syndics of the Press, 1963–70. Member of Council of Publishers Assoc., 1953–63; Chairman of Export Research Cttee, 1956–59; President, 1959–61. Pres., Botanical Soc. of British Isles, 1979–81. *Publications:* The Janus of Poets, 1935; Love's Labour's Lost (The Arden Edition of Shakespeare), 1951; Shakespeare in the Theatre, 1978; (ed) Hakluyt's Voyages: a selection, 1981; (jtly) Review of the Cornish Flora, 1981; (ed jtly) John Raven: by his friends, 1981; (jtly) Sedges of the British Isles, 1982; journal articles on the production of Shakespeare plays, and on botanical subjects, especially Carex. *Recreations:* music, botanising, fly-fishing. *Address:* 50 Highsett, Cambridge; Cove, New Polzeath, Wadebridge, Cornwall. *Club:* Garrick.

DAVID, Robin (Robert) Daniel George, QC 1968; DL; **His Honour Judge David;** a Circuit Judge (formerly Chairman, Cheshire Quarter Sessions), since 1968; *b* 30 April 1922; *s* of late Alexander Charles Robert David and late Edrica Doris Pole David (*née* Evans); *m* 1944, Edith Mary David (*née* Marsh); two *d. Educ:* Christ Coll., Brecon; Ellesmere Coll., Salop. War Service, 1943–47, Captain, Royal Artillery. Called to Bar, Gray's Inn, 1949; joined Wales and Chester Circuit, 1949. Dep. Chairman, Cheshire QS, 1961; Dep. Chairman, Agricultural Land Tribunal (Wales), 1965–68; Commissioner of Assize, 1970; Mem., Parole Bd for England and Wales, 1971–74. DL Cheshire 1972. *Publication:* The Magistrate in the Crown Court, 1982. *Recreation:* boating. *Address:* (home) Hallowsgate House, Kelsall, Cheshire. *T:* Kelsall 51456; (chambers) 4 Paper Buildings, Temple, EC4. *T:* 01–353 8408, 01–353 0196; (chambers) 40 King Street, Chester. *T:* Chester 23886.

DAVID, Tudor, OBE 1984; journalist; Executive Editor, Journal of Oil and Gas Accountancy, since 1986; *b* 25 April 1921; *s* of Thomas and Blodwen David; *m* 1943, Nancy Ramsay (*d* 1984); one *s* one *d. Educ:* Barry Grammar Sch.; Univ. of Manchester (BA Hons); Univ. of Oxford. Technical Officer, RAF, 1942–47; Extra-mural Lectr, Univ. of Newcastle upon Tyne, 1947–49; Careers Officer, 1950–55; Asst Editor, Education, 1955–65; Editor, The Teacher, 1965–69; Managing Editor, Education, 1969–86. Member: Council, Cymmrodorion, 1968–; Welsh Acad., 1969–; Exec., Assoc. of Isle of Dogs, 1979–. FCP 1980. *Publications:* (ed) Scunthorpe and its Families, 1954; Defence and Disarmament, 1959; Church and School, 1963. *Recreations:* Wales, the Isle of Dogs, opera. *Address:* 83 Saunders Ness Road, Isle of Dogs, E14 9EB. *T:* 01–987 8631. *Club:* London Welsh.

DAVIDSON, family name of **Viscount Davidson.**

DAVIDSON, 2nd Viscount *cr* 1937, of Little Gaddesden; **John Andrew Davidson;** Captain of the Yeomen of the Guard (Deputy Government Chief Whip), since 1986; *b*

22 Dec. 1928; *er s* of 1st Viscount Davidson, PC, GCVO, CH, CB, and Frances Joan, Viscountess Davidson (Baroness Northchurch), DBE (*d* 1985), *y d* of 1st Baron Dickinson, PC, KBE; *S* father, 1970; *m* 1st, 1956, Margaret Birgitta Norton (marr. diss. 1974); four *d* (including twin *d*); 2nd, 1975, Mrs Pamela Dobb (*née* Vergette). *Educ*: Westminster School; Pembroke College, Cambridge (BA). Served in The Black Watch and 5th Bn KAR, 1947–49. A Lord in Waiting (Govt Whip), 1985–86. Director: Strutt & Parker (Farms) Ltd, 1960–75; Lord Rayleigh's Farms Inc., 1960–75; Member of Council: CLA, 1965–75; RASE, 1973; Chm., Management Committee, Royal Eastern Counties Hospital, 1966–72; Mem., East Anglia Economic Planning Council, 1971–75. *Recreation*: music. *Heir*: *b* Hon. Malcolm William Mackenzie Davidson [*b* 28 Aug. 1934; *m* 1970, Mrs Evelyn Ann Carew Perfect, *yr d* of William Blackmore Storey; one *s* one *d*]. *Address*: 25 Cliveden Place, SW1.

DAVIDSON, Hon. Lord; Charles Kemp Davidson, FRSE 1985; a Senator of the College of Justice in Scotland, since 1983; *b* Edinburgh, 13 April 1929; *s* of Rev. Donald Davidson, DD, Edinburgh; *m* 1960, Mary, *d* of Charles Mactaggart, Campbeltown, Argyll; one *s* two *d*. *Educ*: Fettes Coll., Edinburgh; Brasenose Coll., Oxford; Edinburgh Univ. Admitted to Faculty of Advocates, 1956; QC (Scot.) 1969; Vice-Dean, 1977–79; Dean, 1979–83; Keeper, Advocates' Library, 1972–76. Procurator to Gen. Assembly of Church of Scotland, 1972–83. Dep. Chm., Boundary Commn for Scotland, 1985–. *Address*: 22 Dublin Street, Edinburgh EH1 3PP. *T*: 031–556 2168.

DAVIDSON, Alan Eaton, CMG 1975; author; HM Diplomatic Service, retired; Managing Director, Prospect Books Ltd, since 1982; *b* 30 March 1924; *s* of William John Davidson and Constance (*née* Eaton); *m* 1951, Jane Macatee; three *d*. *Educ*: Leeds Grammar Sch.; Queen's Coll., Oxford. 1st class hons Class. Mods. and Greats. Served in RNVR (Ordinary Seaman, later Lieut) in Mediterranean, N Atlantic and Pacific, 1943–46. Member of HM Foreign Service, 1948; served at: Washington, 1950–53; The Hague, 1953–55; FO, 1955–59; First Secretary, British Property Commission, and later Head of Chancery, British Embassy, Cairo, 1959–61; Head of Chancery and Consul, Tunis, 1962–64; FO, 1964; Counsellor, 1965; Head, Central Dept, FO, 1966–68; Head of Chancery, UK Delegn to NATO, Brussels, 1968–71; seconded, as Vis. Fellow, Centre for Contemporary European Studies, Univ. of Sussex, 1971–72; Head of Defence Dept, FCO, 1972–73; Ambassador to Vientiane, 1973–75. *Publications*: Seafish of Tunisia and the Central Mediterranean, 1963; Snakes and Scorpions Found in the Land of Tunisia, 1964; Mediterranean Seafood, 1972; The Role of the Uncommitted European Countries in East-West Relations, 1972; Fish and Fish Dishes of Laos, 1975; Seafood of South East Asia, 1976; (with Jane Davidson) Dumas on Food, 1978; North Atlantic Seafood, 1979; (with Jennifer Davidson) Traditional Recipes of Laos, 1981. *Address*: 45 Lamont Road, World's End, SW10 0HU. *T*: 01–352 4209.

DAVIDSON, Alfred Edward; international lawyer; Vice-President, General Counsel, Technical Studies, 1957–70, and since 1973; *b* New York, 11 Nov. 1911; *s* of Maurice Philip Davidson and Blanche Reinheimer; *m* 1934, Claire H. Dreyfuss (*d* 1981). *Educ*: Harvard Univ. (AB); Columbia Law Sch. (LLB). Advocate, Bar of New York, 1936; of Dist of Columbia, 1972; Asst to Gen. Counsel, US Dept of Labour, Wash., 1938–40; review section, Solicitor's Office, 1940–41; Legis. Counsel, Office of Emergency Management, in Exec. Office of President, 1941–43; Asst Gen. Counsel, Lend-Lease Admin. (later Foreign Economic Admin.), 1943–45; Gen. Counsel, 1945–; Gen. Counsel, UNRRA, Nov. 1945; Counsel, Preparatory Commn for Internat. Refugee Org., 1947; Dir, European Headqrs of UNICEF, 1947–51; Advisor, Office of Sec.-Gen. of UN, 1951–52; Gen. Counsel, UN Korean Reconstr. Agency, 1952–54; Exec. Asst to Chm., Bd of Rio Tinto of Canada, 1955–58; European Representative, Internat. Finance Corp., 1970–72; Counsel to Wilmer, Cutler & Pickering, Attorneys at Law, 1972–75. Dir, Channel Tunnel Study Gp, 1960–70; Dir, Gen. Counsel, Construction Capital Co., 1964–69. Hon. Chm., Democratic Party Cttee, France. Co-Founder, Assoc. for Promotion of Humor in Internat. Affairs; Co-Chm., Bipartisan Cttees on Medicare Overseas and Absentee Voting; Hon. Chm., Common Cause Overseas. *Publications*: contribs. various periodicals and newspapers. *Recreations*: tennis, bridge, chess, reading. *Address*: 5 rue de la Manutention, 75116 Paris, France. *Clubs*: Lansdowne (London); Standard (France).

DAVIDSON, Arthur; QC 1978; *b* 7 Nov. 1928. *Educ*: Liverpool Coll.; King George V Sch., Southport; Trinity Coll., Cambridge. Served in Merchant Navy. Barrister, Middle Temple, 1953. Trinity Coll., Cambridge, 1959–62; Editor of the Granta. MP (Lab) Accrington, 1966–83; PPS to Solicitor-General, 1968–70; Chm., Home Affairs Gp, Parly Labour Party, 1971–74; Parly Sec., Law Officers' Dept, 1974–79; Opposition spokesman on Defence (Army), 1980–81, on legal affairs, 1981–83, frontbench spokesman, 1982–83; Member: Home Affairs Select Cttee, 1980–83; Armed Forces Bill Select Cttee, 1981–83. Contested (Lab): Blackpool S, 1955; Preston N, 1959; Hyndburn, 1983. Member: Council, Consumers' Association, 1970–74; Exec. Cttee, Soc. of Labour Lawyers, 1981–; Nat. Exec., Fabian Soc.; Council, Nat. Youth Jazz Orchestra; Chm., House of Commons Jazz Club, 1973–83. *Recreations*: lawn tennis, ski-ing, theatre, listening to good jazz and playing bad jazz; formerly Member Cambridge Univ. athletics team. *Address*: 11 South Square, Gray's Inn, WC1R 5EU. *Clubs*: James Street Men's Working (Oswaldtwistle); Free Gardeners (Rishton); King Street, Marlborough Working Men's (Accrington).

DAVIDSON, Basil Risbridger, MC 1945; author and historian; *b* 9 Nov. 1914; *s* of Thomas and Jessie Davidson; *m* 1943, Marion Ruth Young; three *s*. Served War of 1939–45 (despatches twice, MC, US Bronze Star, Jugoslav Zasluge za Narod); British Army, 1940–45 (Balkans, N Africa, Italy); Temp. Lt-Col demobilised as Hon. Major. Editorial staff of The Economist, 1938–39; The Star (diplomatic correspondent, 1939); The Times (Paris correspondent, 1945–47; chief foreign leader-writer, 1947–49); New Statesman (special correspondent, 1950–54); Daily Herald (special correspondent, 1954–57); Daily Mirror (leader-writer, 1959–62). Vis. Prof., Univ. of Ghana, 1964; Regents' Lectr, Univ. of California, 1971; Montagu Burton Vis. Prof. of Internat. Relations, Edinburgh Univ., 1972; Sen. Simon Res. Fellow, Univ. of Manchester, 1975–76; Hon. Res. Fellow, Univ. of Birmingham, 1978–. A Vice-Pres., Anti-Apartheid Movement, 1969–. Freeman of City of Genoa, 1945. DLitt *hc*: Ibadan, 1975; Dar es Salaam, 1985; DUniv: Open, 1980; Edinburgh, 1981. Haile Selassie African Research Award, 1970; Medalha Amílcar Cabral, 1976. *Publications*: *novels*: Highway Forty, 1949; Golden Horn, 1952; The Rapids, 1955; Lindy, 1958; The Andrassy Affair, 1966; *non-fiction*: Partisan Picture, 1946; Germany: From Potsdam to Partition, 1950; Report on Southern Africa, 1952; Daybreak in China, 1953; The New West Africa (ed.), 1953; The African Awakening, 1955; Turkestan Alive, 1957; Old Africa Rediscovered, 1959; Black Mother, 1961, rev. edn 1980; The African Past, 1964; Which Way Africa?, 1964; The Growth of African Civilisation: West Africa AD 1000–1800, 1965; Africa: History of a Continent, 1966; A History of East and Central Africa to the late 19th Century, 1967; Africa in History: Themes and Outlines, 1968; The Liberation of Guiné, 1969; The Africans, An Entry to Cultural History, 1969; Discovering our African Heritage, 1971; In the Eye of the Storm: Angola's People, 1972; Black Star, 1974; Can Africa Survive?, 1975; Discovering Africa's Past, 1978 (Children's Rights Workshop Award, 1978); Africa in Modern History, 1978; Crossroads in Africa, 1980; Special Operations Europe, 1980; The People's Cause, 1980; No Fist is Big Enough, 1981; Modern Africa, 1982; The Story of Africa, 1984. *Address*: Old Cider Mill, North Wootton, Somerset BA4 4HA. *Club*: Savile.

DAVIDSON, Brian, CBE 1965; *b* 14 Sept. 1909; *o s* of late Edward Fitzwilliam Davidson and late Esther Davidson (*née* Schofield); *m* 1935, Priscilla Margaret (*d* 1981), *d* of late Arthur Farquhar and Florence Chilver; one *s* one *d* (and one *s* decd). *Educ*: Winchester Coll. (Scholar); New Coll., Oxford (Scholar). Gaisford Prize for Greek Verse; 1st class Honour Mods.; 2nd class LitHum; President, Oxford Union Society; President OU Conservative Assoc.; BA 1932. Cholmeley Student Lincoln's Inn; Barrister-at-Law, 1933; Law Society Sheffield Prize; Solicitor, 1939; Air Ministry and Ministry of Aircraft Production, 1940. With Bristol Aeroplane Co., 1943–68: Business Manager, 1946; Director, 1950–68; Director, Bristol Siddeley Engines Ltd, 1959–68. Solicitor with Gas Council, later British Gas Corp., 1969–75. Member: Monopolies Commission, 1954–68; Gloucestershire CC (and Chairman Rating Valuation Appeals Cttee), 1953–60; Cttee Wine Society, 1966–83. *Recreations*: fox-hunting, sailing (represented Oxford Univ.), Scottish country dancing, bridge. *Address*: Sands Court, Dodington, Avon BS17 6SE. *T*: Chipping Sodbury 313077.

DAVIDSON, Charles Kemp; *see* Davidson, Hon. Lord.

DAVIDSON, Charles Peter Morton; Metropolitan Stipendiary Magistrate, since 1984; a Chairman, Inner London Juvenile Courts, since 1985; *b* 29 July 1938; *s* of late William Philip Morton Davidson, MD, and Muriel Maud Davidson (*née* Alderson); *m* 1966, Pamela Louise Campbell-Rose. *Educ*: Harrow; Trinity Coll., Dublin (MA, LLB). Called to the Bar, Inner Temple, 1963; employed by Legal and General Assurance Soc., 1963–65; in practice at Bar, 1966–84. Chairman, London Rent Assessment Panel, 1973–84; part-time Immigration Appeals Adjudicator, 1976–84. Contested (C) North Battersea, 1966 General Election; Councillor, London Boroughs: of Wandsworth, 1964–68, of Merton, 1968–71. *Recreations*: music, gardening. *Address*: c/o Horseferry Road Magistrates Court, 70 Horseferry Road, SW1P 2AX.

DAVIDSON, Francis, CBE 1961; Finance Officer, Singapore High Commission, London, 1961–71; *b* 23 Nov. 1905; *s* of James Davidson and Margaret Mackenzie; *m* 1937, Marial Mackenzie, MA; one *s* one *d*. *Educ*: Millbank Public Sch., Nairn; Nairn Academy. Commercial Bank of Scotland Ltd, 1923–29; Bank of British West Africa Ltd, 1929–41; Colonial Service (Treasury), 1941–61; retired from Colonial Service, Nov. 1961, as Accountant-General of Federation of Nigeria. *Recreation*: philately. *Address*: Woolton, Nairn, Scotland. *T*: Nairn 52187. *Club*: Royal Over-Seas League.

DAVIDSON, Howard William, CMG 1961; MBE 1942; *b* 30 July 1911; *s* of late Joseph istopher Davidson, Johannesburg, and Helen, *d* of James Forbes; *m* 1st, 1941, Anne Elizabeth, *d* of late Captain R. C. Power; one *d*; 2nd, 1956, Dorothy (marr. diss. 1972), *d* of late Sir Wm Polson, KCMG; one step *s*. *Educ*: King Edward VII Sch., Johannesburg; Witwatersrand Univ.; Oriel Coll., Oxford (1st cl. Greats 1934; MA 1984). Cadet, Colonial Admin. Service, Sierra Leone, 1935; District Commissioner, 1942; Dep. Fin. Secretary, 1949; Fin. Secretary, Fiji, 1952; Fin. Secretary, N Borneo, 1958; State Financial Secretary and Member Cabinet, Sabah, Malaysia, 1963–64; Financial Adviser, 1964–65; Member of Inter-Governmental Cttee which led to establishment of new Federation of Malaysia; retired, 1965. Inspector (part-time) Min. of Housing and Local Government, 1967–70. Consultant with Peat, Marwick Mitchell & Co, to report on finances of Antigua, 1973. Appointed PDK (with title of Datuk) in first Sabah State Honours List, 1963, now SPDK. *Recreations*: cricket, croquet, gardening, learning. *Address*: Glebe Cottage, Tillington, Petworth, West Sussex. *Clubs*: East India; Sussex County Cricket, Sussex County Croquet.

DAVIDSON, Ian Douglas, CBE 1957; *b* 27 Oct. 1901; *s* of Rev. John Davidson, JP, and Elizabeth Helen (*née* Whyte); *m* 1st, 1936, Claire Louise (*d* 1937), *d* of E. S. Gempp, St Louis, Missouri; one *d*; 2nd, 1938, Eugenia, *d* of late Marques de Mohernando and Lorenza, Marquesa de Mohernando; one *d*. *Educ*: King William's Coll. Royal Dutch Shell Group of Companies, 1921–61; President: Mexican Eagle Oil Co., 1936–47; Cia Shell de Venezuela, 1953–57; Canadian Shell Ltd, 1957–61. Order of St Mark (Lebanon), 1957; Orden del Libertador (Venezuela), 1957. *Address*: One Benvenuto Place, Apt 105, Toronto, Ontario M4V 2L1, Canada. *Clubs*: Caledonian (London); York (Toronto); Links (NY).

DAVIDSON, Ian Thomas Rollo, QC 1977; **His Honour Judge Ian Davidson;** a Circuit Judge, since 1984; *b* 3 Aug. 1925; *s* of late Robert Davidson and Margaret Davidson; *m* 1954, Gyöngyi (marr. diss. 1982), *d* of Prof. Cs. Anghi; one *s* one *d*.; *m* 1984, Barbara Ann Watts. *Educ*: Fettes Coll.; Corpus Christi Coll., Oxford (Schol.). MA, Lit. Hum. Royal Armoured Corps, 1943–47, Lieut Derbs Yeomanry. Called to Bar, Gray's Inn, 1955. Asst Lectr, University Coll., London, 1959–60; Deputy Recorder, Nottingham, 1971; a Recorder of the Crown Court, 1974. *Recreations*: music, golf, photography. *Address*: 1 Ludlow Avenue, Luton, Beds LU1 3RW. *T*: Luton 422624.

DAVIDSON, Ivor Macaulay; Chairman, D. O. Sanbiet Ltd, since 1980; *b* 27 Jan. 1924; *s* of late James Macaulay and Violet Alice Davidson; *m* 1948, Winifred Lowes; four *s* one *d*. *Educ*: Bellahouston Sch.; Univ. of Glasgow. Royal Aircraft Establishment, 1943; Power Jets (R&D) Ltd, 1944; attached RAF, 1945; National Gas Turbine Establishment, 1946: Dep. Dir, 1964; Dir, 1970–74; Dir-Gen. Engines, Procurement Exec., MoD, 1974–79. *Publications*: numerous, scientific and technical. *Recreations*: music, gardening.

DAVIDSON, James Alfred, OBE 1971; retired RN and Diplomatic Service; *b* 22 March 1922; *s* of Lt-Comdr A. D. Davidson and Mrs (Elizabeth) Davidson; *m* 1955, Daphne (*née* While); two *d*, and two step *s*. *Educ*: Christ's Hospital; RN Coll., Dartmouth. Royal Navy, 1939–60 (war Service Atlantic, Mediterranean and Far East); commanded HM Ships Calder and Welfare; Comdr 1955; retd 1960. Holds Master Mariner's Cert. of Service. Called to the Bar, Middle Temple, 1960. Joined CRO (later FCO) 1960; served Port of Spain, Phnom Penh (periods as Chargé d'Affaires 1970 and 1971); Dacca (Chargé d'Affaires, later Dep. High Comr, 1972–73); Vis. Scholar, Univ. of Kent, 1973–74; British High Comr, Brunei, 1974–78; participated, Sept. 1978, in finalisation of Brunei Independence Treaty; Governor, British Virgin Islands, 1978–81. Vis. Fellow, LSE Centre for Internat. Studies, 1982–84. Legal Mem., Mental Health Review Tribunal, 1982–; a Chm., Pensions Appeals Tribunals, 1984–. *Publications*: Brunei Coinage, 1977; Indo-China: Signposts in the Storm, 1979. *Address*: Little Frankfield, Seal Chart, near Sevenoaks, Kent. *T*: Sevenoaks 61600. *Club*: Army and Navy.

DAVIDSON, James Duncan Gordon, OBE 1984; MVO 1947; Chief Executive, Royal Highland and Agricultural Society of Scotland, since 1970; *b* 10 Jan. 1927; *s* of Alastair Gordon Davidson and M. Valentine B. Davidson (*née* Osborne); *m* 1st, 1955, Catherine Ann Jamieson; one *s* two *d*; 2nd, 1973, Janet Stafford; one *s*. *Educ*: RN Coll., Dartmouth; Downing Coll., Cambridge. Active List, RN, 1944–55. Subseq. farming, and political work; contested (L) West Aberdeenshire, 1964; MP (L) West Aberdeenshire, 1966–70. FRAgS; FBIM; MIEx. *Recreations*: family, walking, ski-ing, fishing, music. *Address*: Coire Cas, Newtonmore, Inverness-shire. *T*: Newtonmore 322.

DAVIDSON, James Patton, CBE 1980; *b* 23 March 1928; *s* of Richard Davidson and Elizabeth Ferguson Carnichan; *m* 1st, 1953, Jean Stevenson Ferguson Anderson (marr. diss. 1981); two *s*; 2nd, 1981, Esmé Evelyn Ancill. *Educ:* Rutherglen Acad.; Glasgow Univ. (BL). Mil. service, commissioned RASC, 1948–50. Clyde Navigation Trust, 1950; Asst Gen. Manager, 1958. Clyde Port Authority: Gen. Manager, 1966; Managing Dir, 1974; Dep. Chm. and Man. Dir, 1976; Chm., 1980–83. Chairman: Ardrossan Harbour Co. Ltd, 1976–83; Clydeport Stevedoring Services Ltd, 1977–83; Clyde Container Services Ltd, 1968–83; S. & H. McCall Transport (Glasgow) Ltd, 1972–; Rhu Marina Ltd, 1976–80; Scotway Haulage Ltd, 1976–81; R. & J. Strang Ltd, 1976–81; Nat. Assoc. of Port Employers, 1974–79; British Ports Assoc., 1980–83 (Dep. Chm., 1978–80); Port Employers' & Registered Dock Workers' Pension Fund Trustee Ltd, 1978–83; Pilotage Commn, 1983– (Mem., 1979–83); UK Dir, 1976–83 and Mem., Exec. Cttee, 1977–83, Hon. Mem., 1983, Internat. Assoc. of Ports and Harbours. Dir, Iron Trades Insurance Gp, 1981–; Chm., Foods & Feeds (UK), 1982–83. FCIT, CBIM; FRSA. *Recreations:* golf, travel, reading. *Address:* 44 Guthrie Court, Gleneagles Village, Gleneagles, Perthshire. *Clubs:* Oriental; Cambuslang Golf; Royal Troon Golf.

DAVIDSON, Prof. John Frank, FRS 1974; FEng; Shell Professor of Chemical Engineering, University of Cambridge, since 1978 (Professor of Chemical Engineering, 1975–78); *b* 7 Feb. 1926; *s* of John and Katie Davidson; *m* 1948, Susanne Hedwig Ostberg; one *s* one *d.* *Educ:* Heaton Grammar Sch., Newcastle upon Tyne; Trinity Coll., Cambridge. MA, PhD, ScD; FEng, FIChemE, MIMechE. 1st cl. Mech. Scis Tripos, Cantab, 1946, BA 1947. Engrg work at Rolls Royce, Derby, 1947–50; Cambridge Univ.: Research Fellow, Trinity Coll., 1949; research, 1950–52; Univ. Demonstrator, 1952; Univ. Lectr, 1954; Steward of Trinity Coll., 1957–64; Reader in Chem. Engrg, Univ. of Cambridge, 1964–75. Visiting Professor: Univ. of Delaware, 1960; Univ. of Sydney, 1967. Member: Flixborough Ct of Inquiry, 1974–75; Adv. Cttee on Safety of Nuclear Installations, HSC, 1977–. Pres., IChemE, 1970–71. Founder FEng, 1976. For. Associate, Nat. Acad. of Engrg, US, 1976. Dr *hc* Institut Nat. Polytech. de Toulouse, 1979. Leverhulme Medal, Royal Soc., 1984. *Publications:* (with D. Harrison): Fluidised Particles, 1963; Fluidization, 1971; 2nd edn with R. Clift and D. Harrison), 1985; (with D. L. Keairns) Fluidization (Conference Procs), 1978. *Recreations:* hill walking, gardening, mending bicycles and other domestic artefacts. *Address:* 5 Luard Close, Cambridge CB2 2PL. *T:* Cambridge 246104.

DAVIDSON, Keith; *see* Davidson, W. K.

DAVIDSON, Mrs Paul; *see* Cairns, Julia.

DAVIDSON, Rev. Prof. Robert; Professor of Old Testament Language and Literature, University of Glasgow, since 1972; Principal, Trinity College, Glasgow, since 1982; *b* 30 March 1927; *s* of George Braid Davidson and Gertrude May Ward; *m* 1952, Elizabeth May Robertson; four *s* three *d.* *Educ:* Univ. of St Andrews (MA 1st Cl Hons Classics, 1949; BD, Distinction in Old Testament, 1952). Asst Lectr, then Lectr in Biblical Studies, Univ. of Aberdeen, 1953–60; Lectr in Hebrew and Old Testament, Univ. of St Andrews, 1960–66; Lectr in Old Testament Studies, Univ. of Edinburgh, 1966–69, Sen. Lectr, 1969–72. Hon. DD Aberdeen, 1985. *Publications:* The Bible Speaks, 1959; The Old Testament, 1964; (with A. R. C. Leaney) Biblical Criticism (Vol. 3 of Pelican Guide to Modern Theology), 1970; Genesis 1–11 (Cambridge Bible Commentary), 1973; Genesis 12–50 (Cambridge Bible Commentary), 1979; The Bible in Religious Education, 1979; The Courage to Doubt, 1983; Jeremiah 1–20 (Daily Study Bible), 1983; Jeremiah II, Lamentations (Daily Study Bible), 1986; Ecclesiastes and Song of Songs (Daily Study Bible), 1986; articles in Vetus Testamentum, Annual Swedish Theol Inst., Expository Times, and Scottish Jl of Theol. *Recreations:* music, gardening. *Address:* 357 Albert Drive, Glasgow G41 5PH. *T:* 041–427 5793.

DAVIDSON, Air Vice-Marshal Rev. Sinclair Melville, CBE 1968; Priest-in-charge, Holy Trinity, High Hurstwood, since 1982; *b* 1 Nov. 1922; *s* of late James Stewart Davidson and Ann Sinclair Davidson (*née* Cowan); *m* 1944, Jean Irene, *d* of late Edward Albert Flay; one *s* (and one *s* decd). *Educ:* Bousfield Sch., Kensington; RAF Cranwell; RAF Techn. College; Chichester Theolog. College. CEng, FRAeS, FIERE. War service with 209, 220 and 53 Sqdns RAF, 1941–45 (despatches); Staff RAF Coastal and Fighter Comds, 1946–53; Air Staff, Egypt, Iraq and Cyprus, 1954–55; psa 1956; Air Staff, Air Min., 1957–60; jssc 1960; Dirg Staff, RAF Staff Coll., Bracknell, 1961–63; Asst Comdt, RAF Locking, 1963–64; Chm. Jt Signal Bd (Middle East), 1965; Chief Signal Officer and Comd Electrical Engr, Near East Air Force, 1966–67; idc 1968; Dir of Signals (Air), MoD, 1969–71; AO Wales and Stn Comdr, RAF St Athan, 1972–74; Asst Chief of Defence Staff (Signals), 1974–77. Sec., IERE, 1977–82. Deacon 1981, priest 1982. *Address:* Trinity Cottage, High Hurstwood, E Sussex TN22 4AA. *T:* Buxted 2151. *Club:* Royal Air Force.

DAVIDSON, William Bird; a Deputy Chairman, National Westminster Bank Ltd, 1973–76 (Director and Chief Executive, 1970–72); Chairman, Lombard North Central, 1973–76; Director, Allied London Properties Ltd, 1976–84; *b* 18 May 1912; 2nd *s* of late J. N. Davidson; *m* 1941, Christina M. Ireton (*d* 1984); two *s.* *Educ:* Queen Elizabeth Grammar Sch., Penrith. War Service, Royal Artillery, 1939–45. Entered Nat. Provincial Bank, 1929; Jt Gen Manager, 1961; Chief Gen. Manager, 1967–68; Dir, 1968; Dir and Jt Chief Executive, Nat. Westminster Bank, 1968–70. FIB. *Recreation:* golf. *Address:* Rose Cottage, 9 Starrock Road, Coulsdon, Surrey. *T:* Downland 53687.

DAVIDSON, Dr (William) Keith, CBE 1982; FRCGP; JP; Chairman, Scottish Health Service Planning Council, since 1984; *b* 20 Nov. 1926; *s* of James Fisher Keith Davidson and Martha Anderson Davidson (*née* Milloy); *m* 1952, Dr Mary Waddell Aitken Davidson (*née* Jamieson); one *s* one *d.* *Educ:* Coatbridge Secondary Sch.; Glasgow Univ. DPA 1967; FRCGP 1980. MO 1st Bn Royal Scots Fusiliers, 1950; 2nd Command (Major) 14 Field Ambulance, 1950–51; MO i/c Holland, 1952. Gen. Medical Practitioner, 1953–. Chairman: Glasgow Local Medical Cttee, 1971–75; Scottish Gen. Medical Services Cttee, 1972–75; Dep. Chm., Gen. Medical Services Cttee (UK), 1975–79; Member: Scottish Medical Practices Cttee, 1968–80; Scottish Council on Crime, 1972–75; GMC, 1984–; Scottish Health Service Policy Bd, 1985–. British Medical Association: Mem. Council, 1972–81; Fellow, 1975; Chm., Scottish Council, 1978–81; Vice-Pres., 1983–. Hon. Pres., Glasgow Eastern Med. Soc., 1984–85; Pres., Scottish Midland and Western Med. Soc., 1985–86. Mem., Bonnetmaker Craft. Elder, Church of Scotland, 1956–; Session Clerk, 1983–. JP Glasgow, 1962. SBStJ 1976. *Recreations:* gardening, caravanning. *Address:* Dunvegan, Stepps, Glasgow G33 6DE. *T:* 041–779 2103. *Club:* Royal Scottish Automobile (Glasgow).

DAVIDSON-HOUSTON, Major Aubrey Claud; portrait painter since 1952; *b* 2 Feb. 1906; *s* of late Lt-Col Wilfred Bennett Davidson-Houston, CMG, and Annie Henrietta Hunt; *m* 1938, Georgina Louie Ethel (*d* 1961), *d* of late Capt. H. S. Dobson; one *d.* *Educ:* St Edward's Sch., Oxford; RMC, Sandhurst; Slade Sch. of Fine Art. 2nd Lieut, Royal Sussex Regt, 1925; ADC to Governor of Western Australia, 1927–30; Nigeria Regt, RWAFF, 1933–37; PoW (Germany), 1940–45; Sch. of Infty, 1946–47; MS Branch, WO, 1948–49; retd, 1949. Slade Sch. of Fine Art, 1949–52 (diploma). *Portraits include:* The

Queen, for RWF; The Duke of Edinburgh, for 8th King's Royal Irish Hussars, for Duke of Edinburgh's Royal Regt, for the House of Lords, and for United Oxford & Cambridge University Club; Queen Elizabeth, The Queen Mother, for Black Watch of Canada; The Prince of Wales, for Royal Regt of Wales; The Princess Royal, for WRAC; The Duke of Gloucester, for Royal Inniskilling Fusiliers, for Scots Guards and for Trinity House; The Duchess of Kent for ACC; also portraits for Lincoln Coll., Keble Coll., and St Cross Coll., Oxford, and for Selwyn Coll., Cambridge; also for a number of other regts and for City Livery cos, schools, etc. Founder Trustee, Jt Educn Trust, 1971–86. *Address:* Hillview, West End Lane, Esher, Surrey KT10 8LA. *T:* Esher 64769; 4 Chelsea Studios, 412 Fulham Road, SW6 1EB. *T:* 01–385 2569. *Clubs:* Buck's, Naval and Military, MCC.

DAVIE, Alan, CBE 1972; HRSA 1977; painter, poet, musician, silversmith and jeweller; *b* 1920. *Educ:* Edinburgh Coll. of Art. DA. Gregory Fellowship, Leeds Univ., 1956–59. Teaching, Central Sch. of Arts and Crafts, London, 1953–56 and 1959–60, and Emily Carr Coll. of Art, Vancouver, 1982. One-man exhibitions in GB, USA and most European countries and at Gimpel Fils Galleries in London, Zürich and New York, 1946–; Edinburgh Fest., 1972; Brussels, Paris, Athens and London, 1977; London, Florida, Stuttgart, Zürich, Amsterdam, St Andrews and Edinburgh, 1978; Florida, Edinburgh Fest., Belgium, Sydney and Perth, Australia, 1979; New York, Australia, Colchester and Philadelphia, 1980; London, Frankfurt, NY and Toronto, 1981; Toronto, Edinburgh, Basle, Harrogate, Hong Kong, Paris (Foire Internat. d'Art Contemporain) and Vancouver, 1982; Amsterdam, FIAC Paris, Basel, Madrid, Glasgow and London, 1983; New York, Frankfurt, Cologne, Edinburgh, Windsor, Hertford and Bath, 1984; London (Art Fair, Olympia), Edinburgh and Bonn, 1985; London, Arizona and NY, 1986. Work represented in exhibitions: 4th Internat. Art Exhibn, Japan; Pittsburgh Internat.; Documenta II & III, Kassel, Germany; British Painting 1700–1960, Moscow; Salon de Mai, Paris; Peggy Guggenheim Collection; ROSC Dublin; Peter Styvesant Collection; British Painting and Sculpture 1960–1970, Washington; III Bienal de Arte Coltejer, Colombia; Hannover, 1973; British Paintings, 1974; Hayward Gall., 1974; Paris, 1975; Lausanne, 1975; 25 years of British Art, RA, 1977; South America, 1977; Kassell, 1977; Sydney, 1979. Works in Public Collections: Tate Gall., Gulbenkian Foundn London, Belfast, Bristol, Durham, Edinburgh, Hull, Leeds, Manchester, Newcastle, Wakefield; Boston, Buffalo, Dallas, Detroit, Yale New Haven, Phoenix, Pittsburgh, Rhode Island, San Francisco; Ottawa, Adelaide, Sydney, Auckland, São Paulo, Tel Aviv, Venice, Vienna, Baden-Baden, Bochum, Munich, Amsterdam, Eindhoven, The Hague, Rotterdam, Oslo, Basle, Stockholm, Gothenburg, St Paul de Vence and Paris. First public recital of music, Gimpel Fils Gall., 1971; music and lecture tour, Sydney, Melbourne, Canberra, 1979. Prize for Best Foreign Painter, VII Bienal de São Paulo, 1963; Saltire Award, 1977. *Relevant Publication:* Alan Davie (ed Alan Bowness), 1967. *Address:* Gamels Studio, Rush Green, Hertford.

DAVIE, Rev. Sir (Arthur) Patrick; *see* Ferguson Davie.

DAVIE, Prof. Donald Alfred; Andrew W. Mellon Professor of Humanities, Vanderbilt University, since 1978; *b* 17 July 1922; *s* of George Clarke Davie and Alice (*née* Sugden); *m* 1945, Doreen John; two *s* one *d.* *Educ:* Barnsley Holgate Gram. Sch.; St Catharine's Coll., Cambridge (Hon. Fellow, 1973). BA 1947; PhD 1951. Served with Royal Navy, 1941–46 (Sub-Lieut RNVR). Lecturer in Dublin Univ., 1950–57; Fellow of Trinity Coll., Dublin, 1954–57, Hon. Fellow, 1978; Visiting Prof., University of Calif., 1957–58; Lecturer, Cambridge Univ., 1958–64; Fellow of Gonville and Caius Coll., Cambridge, 1959–64; George Elliston Lecturer, University of Cincinnati, 1963; Prof. of Literature, University of Essex, 1964–68, and Pro-Vice-Chancellor, 1965–68; Prof. of English, 1968–74, Olive H. Palmer Prof. in Humanities, 1974–78, Stanford Univ. Clark Lectr, Trinity Coll., Cambridge, 1976. Hon. DLitt Univ. of Southern California, 1978. Fellow, Amer. Acad. of Arts and Scis, 1973. *Publications:* poetry: Brides of Reason, 1955; A Winter Talent, 1957; The Forests of Lithuania, 1959; A Sequence for Francis Parkman, 1961; Events and Wisdoms, 1964; Essex Poems, 1969; Six Epistles to Eva Hesse, 1970; Collected Poems, 1972; The Shires, 1975; In the Stopping Train, 1977; Three for Water-Music, 1981; Collected Poems 1971–1983, 1983; *criticism and literary history:* Purity of Diction in English Verse, 1952; Articulate Energy, 1957, 2nd edn 1976; The Heyday of Sir Walter Scott, 1961; Ezra Pound: Poet as Sculptor, 1965; Introduction to The Necklace by Charles Tomlinson, 1955; Thomas Hardy and British Poetry, 1972; Pound, 1976; The Poet in the Imaginary Museum: essays of two decades, 1978; A Gathered Church: the literature of the English dissenting interest 1700–1930, 1978; Trying to Explain (essays), 1980; Dissentient Voice, 1982; *anthologies:* The Late Augustans, 1958; (with Angela Livingstone) Modern Judgements: Pasternak, 1969; Augustan Lyric, 1974; The New Oxford Book of Christian Verse, 1981. *Recreations:* verse-translation; literary politics; travel. *Address:* 4400 Belmont Park Terrace, Nashville, Tenn 37215, USA. *Clubs:* Savile; Union (Cambridge).

DAVIE, Sir Paul (Christopher), Kt 1967; *b* 30 Sept. 1901; *s* of Charles Christopher Davie and Beatrice Paulina Mabel (*née* Walrond); *m* 1938, Betty Muriel, *d* of late Captain Ronald Henderson, MP for Henley div. of Oxfordshire, 1924–32, of Studley Priory, Oxon; one *s* one *d.* *Educ:* Winchester; New Coll., Oxford. Called to Bar, Lincoln's Inn, 1925; 2nd Asst Legal Advisor, Home Office, 1936; Asst Legal Advisor, 1947. Remembrancer, City of London, 1953–67. Chairman: Nat. Deaf Children's Soc., 1970–74; Council and Gen. Devel't Services Ltd, 1971–82. *Publications:* Silicosis and Asbestosis Compensation Schemes, 1932; Joint Managing Ed., Encyclopædia of Local Government Law and Administration, 1934. *Recreations:* history, gardening. *Address:* The Old Rectory, Bentley, Farnham, Surrey GU10 5HU. *T:* Bentley 23128. *Club:* Travellers'.

DAVIE, Ronald, PhD; FBPsS; Director, National Children's Bureau, since 1982; *b* 25 Nov. 1929; *s* of late Thomas Edgar Davie and Gladys (*née* Powell); *m* 1957, Kathleen, *d* of William Wilkinson, Westhoughton, Lancs; one *s* one *d.* *Educ:* King Edward VI Grammar Sch., Aston, Birmingham; Univ. of Reading (BA 1954); Univ. of Manchester (PGCE and Dip. Deaf Educn 1955); Univ. of Birmingham (Dip. Educnl Psych. 1961); Univ. of London (PhD 1970). FBPsS 1973. Teacher, schs for normal and handicapped children, 1955–60; Co. Educnl Psychologist, IoW, 1961–64; Nat. Children's Bureau, London: Sen. Res. Officer, 1964; Dep. Dir, 1968; Dir of Res., 1972; Prof. of Educnl Psychology, Dept of Educn, UC Cardiff, 1974–81; Vis. Fellow, Inst. of Educn, Univ. of London, 1985–. Co-Dir, Nat. Child Develt Study, 1968–77; Scientific Adviser: Local Authority Social Services Res. Liaison Gp. DHSS, 1975–77; Mental Handicap in Wales Res. Unit, 1977–79; Mental Handicap Res. Liaison Gp, DHSS, 1977–81; Prof. Advr, All Party Parly Gp for Children, 1983–. Pres., Links Assoc., 1977–; Vice-Pres., British Assoc. for Early Childhood Educn, 1984–; Chairman: Trng and Educn. Cttee, Nat. Assoc. Mental Health, 1969–72; Working Gp rep. nat. vol. orgs concerned with handicapped children, 1971–74; Assoc. for Child Psychol. and Psychiatry, 1972–73 (Hon. Sec. 1965–70); Working Gp rep. professional assocs in S Wales concerned with children, 1974–84; Working Party, Children Appearing Before Juvenile Courts, Children's Reg. Planning Cttee for Wales, 1975–77; Develt Psychol. Section, Brit. Psychol. Soc., 1975–77 (Treas. 1973–75); Wales Standing Conf. for Internat. Year of the Child, 1978–79; Steering Cttee, Child Health and Educn Study, 1979–84; Adv. Bd, Whitefield Library, 1983–. Member: Council of Management, Nat. Assoc. Mental Health, 1969–77; Working

Party, Children at Risk, DHSS, 1970–72; Educn and Employment Cttee, Nat. Deaf Children's Soc., 1972–78; Management Cttee, Craig y Parc Sch., 1974–76; Cttee, Welsh Br., Assoc. for Child Psychol. and Psychiatry, 1975–80; Bd of Assessors, Therapeutic Educn, 1975–82; Council, British Psychol. Soc., 1977–80; Experimental Panel on Children in Care, SSRC, 1978–79; NCSE Internat. Conf. Prog. Cttee, 1982–; Council, Child Accident Prevention Trust, 1982–; Evaluation Panel, Royal Jubilee Trusts, 1982–; Steering Cttee on Special Educn Needs Res., DES, 1983–86; Steering Cttee on Special Needs Res. Dissem., DES, 1986–; Bd of Trustees, Stress Syndrome Foundn, 1983–85; Adv. Bd, Ravenswood Village, 1984–; Bd of Governors, Elizabeth Garrett Anderson Sch. 1985–; Council, Caldecott Community, 1985–. Hon. Consultant, Play Board, 1984–. Hon. Mem., BPA, 1985. *Publications:* (co-author) 11,000 Seven-Year Olds, 1966; Directory of Voluntary Organisations concerned with Children, 1969; Living with Handicap, 1970; From Birth to Seven, 1972; chapters in books and papers in sci. and other jls on educn, psychol., child care and health. *Recreations:* photography, antiques, Rugby, athletics. *Address:* 3 Grange Grove, Canonbury, N1 2NP. *T:* 01–226 3761; (office) 8 Wakley Street, EC1. *Club:* Royal Over-Seas League.

DAVIES, family name of **Barons Darwen, Davies** and **Davies of Penrhys.**

DAVIES; *see* Edmund-Davies.

DAVIES; *see* Llewelyn-Davies.

DAVIES; *see* Prys-Davies.

DAVIES, 3rd Baron, *cr* 1932, of Llandinam; **David Davies,** MA; CEng, MICE, MBA; Chairman, Welsh National Opera Company, since 1975; *b* 2 Oct. 1940; *s* of 2nd Baron and Ruth Eldrydd (*d* 1966), 3rd *d* of Major W. M. Dugdale, CB, DSO; *S* father (killed in action), 1944; *m* 1972, Beryl, *d* of W. J. Oliver; two *s* two *d. Educ:* Eton; King's Coll., Cambridge. *Heir: s* Hon. David Daniel Davies, *b* 23 Oct. 1975. *Address:* Plas Dinam, Llandinam, Powys.

DAVIES OF PENRHYS, Baron *cr* 1974 (Life Peer), of Rhondda; **Gwilym Elfed Davies;** *b* 9 Oct. 1913; *s* of David Davies and Miriam Elizabeth (*née* Williams); *m* 1940, Gwyneth Rees, *d* of Daniel and Agnes Janet Rees; two *s* one *d. Educ:* Tylorstown Boys' Sch. Branch Official Tylorstown Lodge, NUM, 1935–59. Member Glamorgan CC, 1954–61. Chairman Local Government Cttee, 1959–61. MP (Lab) Rhondda East, Oct. 1959–Feb. 1974; PPS to Minister of Labour, 1964–68, to Minister of Power, 1968. Part-time Mem., S Wales Electricity Bd, 1974–80. Mem., Nat. Sports Council for Wales, 1978–84. Freeman, Borough of Rhondda, 1975. *Recreations:* Rugby football and cricket. *Address:* Maes-y-Ffrwd, Ferndale Road, Tylorstown, Rhondda, Glam. *T:* Ferndale 730254.

DAVIES, Air Marshal Sir Alan (Cyril), KCB 1979 (CB 1974); CBE 1967; Co-ordinator of Anglo-American Relations, Ministry of Defence, since 1984; *b* 31 March 1924; *s* of Richard Davies, Maidstone; *m* Julia Elizabeth Ghislaine Russell; two *s* (and one *s* decd). Enlisted RAF, 1941; commnd 1943; comd Joint Anti-Submarine School Flight, 1952–54; comd Air Sea Warfare Development Unit, 1958–59; comd No 201 Sqdn, 1959–61; Air Warfare Coll., 1962; Dep. Dir, Operational Requirements, MoD, 1964–66; comd RAF Stradishall, Suffolk, 1967–68; idc 1969; Dir of Air Plans, MoD, 1969–72; ACAS (Policy), MoD, 1972–74; Dep. COS (Ops and Intell.), HQ Allied Air Forces Central Europe, 1974–77; Dep. C-in-C, RAF Strike Command, 1977; Dir, Internat. Mil. Staff, NATO, Brussels, 1978–81; Hd, Support Area Economy Review Team, RAF, 1981–83; *Address:* 10 Crispin Close, Caversham, Reading RG4 7JS. *Club:* Royal Air Force.

DAVIES, Albert John; Chief Agricultural Officer, Agricultural Development and Advisory Service, Ministry of Agriculture, Fisheries and Food, 1971–79; *b* 21 Jan. 1919; *s* of David Daniel Davies and Annie Hilda Davies; *m* 1944, Winnifred Ivy Caroline Emberton; one *s* one *d. Educ:* Amman Valley Grammar Sch.; UCW Aberystwyth. BSc Hons Agric. 1940. FIBiol. Adv. Staff, UCW Aberystwyth, 1940–41; Asst Techn. Adviser, Montgomeryshire War Agricultural Cttee, 1941–44; Farm Supt, Welsh Plant Breeding Stn, 1944–47; Nat. Agricultural Adv. Service: Crop Husbandry Adviser Wales, 1947–51; Grassland Husbandry Adviser Wales, 1951–57 and E Mids, 1957–59; Dep. Dir Wales, 1959–64; Regional Dir SW Region, 1964; Chief Farm Management Adviser, London Headquarters, 1964–67; Sen. Agric. Adviser, 1967–68; Dep. Dir, 1968–71. *Publications:* articles in learned jls and agric. press. *Recreations:* golf, Rugby, gardening. *Address:* Cefncoed, 38A Ewell Downs Road, Ewell, Surrey. *T:* 01–393 0069. *Clubs:* Farmers'; Epsom Golf.

DAVIES, (Albert) Meredith, CBE 1982; Principal, Trinity College of Music, since 1979; Guest Conductor, Royal Opera House, Covent Garden, and Sadler's Wells; also BBC; *b* 30 July 1922; 2nd *s* of Reverend E. A. Davies; *m* 1949, Betty Hazel, *d* of late Dr Kenneth Bates; three *s* one *d. Educ:* Royal College of Music; Stationers' Company's Sch.; Keble Coll., Oxford; Accademia di S. Cecilia, Rome. Junior Exhibitioner, RCM, 1930; Organist to Hurstpierpoint Coll., Sussex, 1939; elected Organ Scholar, Keble Coll., 1940. Served War of 1939–45, RA, 1942–45. Conductor St Albans Bach Choir, 1947; Organist and Master of the Choristers, Cathedral Church of St Alban, 1947–49; Musical Dir, St Albans Sch., 1948–49; Organist and Choirmaster, Hereford Cathedral, and Conductor, Three Choirs' Festival (Hereford), 1949–56; Organist and Supernumerary Fellow of New Coll., Oxford, 1956; Associate Conductor, City of Birmingham Symphony Orchestra, 1957–59; Dep. Musical Dir, 1959–60; Conductor, City of Birmingham Choir, 1957–64; Musical Dir, English Opera Group, 1963–65; Musical Dir, Vancouver Symphony Orchestra, 1964–71; Chief Conductor, BBC Trng Orchestra, 1969–72; Music Dir, Royal Choral Soc., 1972–85; Conductor, Leeds Phil. Soc., 1975–84. Pres., ISM, 1985–86. *Address:* c/o Trinity College of Music, Mandeville Place, W1M 6AQ.

DAVIES, Hon. Sir (Alfred William) Michael, Kt 1973; **Hon. Mr Justice Michael Davies;** a Judge of the High Court of Justice, Queen's Bench Division, since 1973; *b* 29 July 1921; *er s* of Alfred Edward Davies, Stourbridge; *m* 1947, Margaret, *y d* of Robert Ernest Jackson, Sheffield; one *s* three *d. Educ:* King Edward's Sch., Birmingham; University of Birmingham (LLB). Called to Bar, Lincoln's Inn, 1948, Bencher 1972; QC 1964; Dep. Chm. Northants QS, 1962–71; Recorder of: Grantham, 1963–65; Derby, 1965–71; Crown Court, 1972–73. Leader of Midland Circuit, 1968–71, Jt Leader of Midland and Oxford Circuit, 1971–73. Chm. Mental Health Review Tribunal, for Birmingham Area, 1965–71; Comr of Assize (Birmingham), 1970; Chancellor, Dio. of Derby, 1971–73; Mem., Gen. Council of the Bar, 1968–72. Chm., Hospital Complaints Procedure Cttee, 1971–73. *Recreations:* golf and the theatre. *Address:* Royal Courts of Justice, WC2. *Club:* Garrick.

DAVIES, Alun B. O.; *see* Oldfield-Davies.

DAVIES, Very Rev. Alun Radcliffe; Dean of Llandaff, since 1977; *b* 6 May 1923; *s* of Rev. Rhys Davies and Jane Davies; *m* 1952, Winifred Margaret Pullen; two *s* one *d. Educ:* Cowbridge Grammar Sch.; University Coll., Cardiff (BA 1945; Fellow, 1983); Keble Coll., Oxford (BA 1947, MA 1951); St Michael's Coll., Llandaff. Curate of Roath, 1948–49; Lecturer, St Michael's Coll., Llandaff, 1949–53; Domestic Chaplain to Archbishop of Wales, 1952–57, to Bishop of Llandaff, 1957–59; Chaplain RNR, 1953–60; Vicar of Ystrad Mynach, 1959–75; Chancellor of Llandaff Cathedral, 1969–71; Archdeacon of Llandaff, 1971–77; Residentiary Canon of Llandaff Cathedral, 1975–77. *Address:* The Deanery, The Cathedral Green, Llandaff, Cardiff. *T:* Cardiff 561545.

DAVIES, Sir Alun Talfan, Kt 1976; QC 1961; MA; LLB; barrister-at-law; a Recorder, and Honorary Recorder of Cardiff, since 1972; *b* Gorseinon, 22 July 1913; *s* of late Rev. W. Talfan Davies, Presbyterian Minister, Gorseinon; *m* 1942, Eiluned Christopher, *d* of late Humphrey R. Williams, Stanmore, Middx; one *s* three *d. Educ:* Gowerton Gram. Sch.; Aberystwyth Univ. Coll. of Wales (LLB), Hon. Professorial Fellow, 1971; Gonville and Caius Coll., Cambridge (MA, LLB). Called to the Bar, Gray's Inn, 1939; Bencher, 1969–. Practised on Wales and Chester circuit. Contested (Ind.) University of Wales (by-elec.), 1943; contested (L): Carmarthen Div., 1959 and 1964; Denbigh, 1966. Mem. Court of University of Wales and of Courts and Councils of Aberystwyth and Swansea University Colls. Recorder: of Merthyr Tydfil, 1963–68; of Swansea, 1968–69; of Cardiff, 1969–71; Dep. Chm., Cardiganshire QS, 1963–71; Judge of the Courts of Appeal, Jersey and Guernsey, 1969–84. Member: Commn on the Constitution, 1969–73; Criminal Injuries Compensation Bd, 1977–85. President: Court of Nat. Eisteddfod of Wales, 1977–80; Court, Welsh Nat. Opera, 1978–; Welsh Centre of Internat. Affairs. Dep. Chm., Commercial Bank of Wales, 1973– (Dir, 1971–); Dir, HTV Ltd, 1967–83 (Vice-Chm., and Chm. Welsh Bd, 1978–83); Vice-Chm., HTV (Group) Ltd, 1978–83. Chm. Trustees, Aberfan Fund (formerly Aberfan Disaster Fund), 1969–. Hon. LLD Wales: Aberystwyth, 1973. *Address:* 10 Park Road, Penarth, South Glam. *T:* Penarth 701341; 34 Park Place, Cardiff. *T:* Cardiff 382731. *Clubs:* Cardiff and County (Cardiff); Bristol Channel Yacht (Swansea).

DAVIES, (Angie) Michael; Chairman, Tozer Kemsley & Millbourn (Holdings) plc, since 1985; *b* 23 June 1934; *s* of Angelo Henry and Clarice Mildred Davies; *m* 1962, Jane Priscilla, *d* of Oliver Martin and Kathleen White; one *s* one *d. Educ:* Shrewsbury Schools; Queens' College, Cambridge. Director: Ross Group, 1964–82; Fenchurch Insurance Holdings, 1969–76; Brown Brothers Corp., 1976–81; Imperial Group, 1972–82; Chm., Imperial Foods, 1979–82; Director: Littlewoods Organisation, 1982–; Newman Industries, 1983–; British Airways, 1983–; TV-am, 1983–; TI Group, 1984–; Alva Investment Trust, 1984–; CC Conversions, 1984–. *Address:* Little Woolpit, Ewhurst, Cranleigh, Surrey GU6 7NP. *T:* Cranleigh 277344.

DAVIES, Prof. Anna Elbina, (A. Morpurgo Davies), FBA 1985; Professor of Comparative Philology, Oxford University, since 1971; Fellow of Somerville College, Oxford, since 1971; *b* Milan, 21 June 1937; *d* of Augusto Morpurgo and Maria (*née* Castelnuovo); *m* 1962, J. K. Davies, *qv* (marr. diss. 1978). *Educ:* Liceo-Ginnasio Giulio Cesare, Rome; Univ. of Rome. Dott.lett. Rome, 1959; Libera docente, Rome, 1963; MA Oxford, 1964. Asst in Classical Philology, Univ. of Rome, 1959–61; Junior Research Fellow, Center for Hellenic Studies, Harvard Univ., 1961–62; Univ. Lectr in Classical Philology, Oxford, 1964–71; Fellow of St Hilda's Coll., Oxford, 1966–71, Hon. Fellow, 1972–. Visiting Professor: Univ. of Pennsylvania, 1971; Yale Univ., 1977; Collitz Prof. of Ling. Soc. of America, Univ. of South Florida, 1975. Pres., Philological Soc., 1976–80, Hon. Vice-Pres., 1980–. FSA 1974. Hon. DLitt St Andrews, 1981. *Publications:* (as A. Morpurgo) Mycenaeae Graecitatis Lexicon, 1963; articles and reviews on comparative and classical philology in Italian, German, British and American jls. *Address:* Somerville College, Oxford. *T:* Oxford 57595.

DAVIES, Rear-Adm. Anthony, CB 1964; CVO 1972; Royal Navy, retired; *b* 13 June 1912; *s* of late James Arthur and Margaret Davies; *m* 1940, Lilian Hilda Margaret (*d* 1980), *d* of late Admiral Sir Harold Martin Burrough, GCB, KBE, DSO, and Lady (Nellie Wills) Burrough; two *s* two *d. Educ:* Royal Naval College, Dartmouth; Open Univ. (BA 1983). Midshipman, HMS Danae, 1930–32; Sub-Lieut, HMS Despatch, 1934; Lieut, HMS Duncan, 1935–37; Gunnery course, 1938; HMS Repulse, 1939; HMS Cossack 1940–41; Lieut-Comdr, HMS Indefatigable, 1943–45; Comdr, HMS Triumph, 1950; HMS Excellent, 1951–54; Capt., HMS Pelican, 1954–55; Dep. Dir, RN Staff Coll., 1956–57; Far East Fleet Staff, 1957–59; Dep. Dir, Naval Intelligence, 1959–62; Head of British Defence Liaison Staff, Canberra, Australia, 1963–65. Warden, St George's House, Windsor Castle, 1966–72. *Address:* Witts Piece, 11A South Street, Aldbourne, Marlborough, Wilts. *T:* Marlborough 40418.

DAVIES, (Anthony) Roger; Metropolitan Stipendiary Magistrate, since 1985; *b* 1 Sept. 1940; *er s* of late R. George Davies and of Megan Davies, Penarth, Glam; *m* 1967, Clare, *e d* of Comdr W. A. Walters, RN; twin *s* one *d. Educ:* Bridgend; King's Coll., London. LLB (Hons); AKC. Called to the Bar, Gray's Inn, 1965 (Lord Justice Holker Sen. Schol.). Practised at Bar, London and SE Circuit, 1965–85. *Recreations:* reading (history, biography), music (especially opera), travel, family life. *Address:* Chobham House, Chobham, Surrey GU24 8NA. *T:* Chobham 6578.

DAVIES, Prof. Arthur; Reardon-Smith Professor of Geography, University of Exeter, 1948–71; Deputy Vice-Chancellor, University of Exeter, 1969–71; Dean of the Faculty of Social Studies, 1961–64; *b* 13 March 1906; *s* of Richard Davies, Headmaster, and Jessie Starr Davies, Headmistress; *m* 1933, Lilian Margaret Morris; one *d. Educ:* Cyfarthfa Castle Sch.; University Coll. of Wales, Aberystwyth, 1st cl. Hons in Geography and Anthropology, 1927; MSc Wales 1930; Fellow, University of Wales, 1929–30, Asst Lecturer in Geography, Manchester Univ., 1930–33; Lecturer in Geography, Leeds Univ., 1933–40. Served War of 1939–45, RA 1940–45, Normandy (despatches twice, Major); Mem., High Mil. Tribunal of Hamburg, 1945. Hon. FRGS 1982. *Publications:* Yugoslav Studies, Leplay Soc., London, 1932; Polish Studies, Leplay Soc., London, 1933; numerous papers in learned jls on Great Age of Discovery, Columbus, Drake (resolving California/San Francisco problem), John Lloyd's discovery of America in 1477, etc. *Recreations:* gardening and architecture. *Address:* Morlais, Winslade Park, Clyst St Mary, Devon. *T:* Topsham 3296.

DAVIES, Sir Arthur; *see* Davies, Sir D. A.

DAVIES, Dr Arthur Gordon; Coroner to the Greater London Council (formerly London County Council), since 1959; Managing Director, Medical & Electrical Instrumentation Co. Ltd, since 1965; *b* 6 Nov. 1917; *s* of Louis Bernard Davies and Elizabeth Davies; *m* 1945, Joan (*née* Thompson); two *d. Educ:* Westminster Hosp. (MB, BS 1943). LRCP, MRCS 1943. Called to the Bar, Lincoln's Inn, 1955. Served War, RAMC (Captain). Coroner to the Royal Household, 1959–83. *Recreations:* chess, bridge, photography, electronics.

DAVIES, Brian Meredith; *see* Davies, J. B. M.

DAVIES, Bryan; Secretary, Parliamentary Labour Party, since 1979; *b* 9 Nov. 1939; *s* of George William and Beryl Davies; *m* 1963, Monica Rosemary Mildred Shearing; two *s* one *d. Educ:* Redditch High Sch.; University Coll., London; Inst. of Education; London Sch. of Economics. BA Hons History London, Certif. Educn, BScEcons London. Teacher, Latymer Sch., 1962–65; Lectr, Middlesex Polytechnic at Enfield, 1965–74. MP (Lab)

Enfield North, Feb. 1974–1979; an Asst Govt Whip, 1979; Member: Select Cttee on Public Expenditure, 1975–79; Select Cttee on Overseas Develt, 1975–79. Contested (Lab) Newport West, 1983. Mem., MRC, 1977–79. *Recreations:* playing cricket, squash, tennis; going to the theatre. *Address:* 28 Churchfields, Broxbourne, Herts. *T:* Hoddesdon 466427.

DAVIES, Bryn, MBE 1978; Member, General Council, Wales Trades Union Congress, since 1974 (Vice-Chairman, 1983–84, Chairman, 1984–85); *b* 22 Jan. 1932; *s* of Gomer and Ann Davies; *m* 1956, Esme Irene Gould; two *s*. *Educ:* Cwmlai School, Tonyrefail. Served HM Forces (RAMC), 1949–51; Forestry Commn, 1951–56; South Wales and Hereford Organiser, Nat. Union of Agricultural and Allied Workers, 1956–. Chm., Mid Glamorgan AHA, 1978–; Member: Welsh Council, 1965–81; Development Commn, 1975–81; Nat. Cttee (Wales), Forestry Commn, 1978–; Nat. Water Council, 1982–; Council, British Heart Foundn, 1986–. *Recreations:* cricket and Rugby football. *Address:* Derwendeg, 36 Hall Drive, North Cornelly, Bridgend, Mid Glamorgan. *T:* Bridgend 740426. *Clubs:* Tonyrefail Rugby (Pres., 1985–); Glamorgan CC.

DAVIES, Caleb William, CMG 1962; FFCM; MRCS; LRCP; DPH; retired; Regional Specialist in Community Medicine, 1974–82 (Acting Regional Medical Officer, 1977–78, 1979–80), South Western Regional Health Authority; *b* 27 Aug. 1916; *s* of Caleb Davies, KIH, MB, ChB, and Emily (*née* Platt); *m* 1939, Joan Heath; three *s* one *d*. *Educ:* Kingswood Sch., Bath; University Coll. and University Coll. Hosp. Med. Sch., London; Edinburgh Univ.; London Sch. of Hygiene and Tropical Med. Kenya: MO, 1941; MOH, Mombasa, 1946; Tanganyika: Sen. MO, 1950; Asst Dir of Med. Services, 1952; Uganda: Dep. Dir of Medical Services, 1958; Permanent Sec. and Chief Medical Officer, Ministry of Health, 1960; retired 1963; South-Western Regional Hosp. Bd: Asst SMO, 1963–66; Principal Asst SMO, 1966–74. *Recreations:* swimming, photography. *Address:* Dolphins, Homefield Road, Saltford, Bristol BS18 3EG. *T:* Saltford 3522.

DAVIES, Ven. Carlyle W.; *see* Witton-Davies.

DAVIES, Christopher Evelyn K.; *see* Kevill-Davies.

DAVIES, (Claude) Nigel (Byam); *b* 2 Sept. 1920; unmarried. *Educ:* Eton. Studied at Aix en Provence University, 1937, and at Potsdam, 1938. PhD London (archaeology). Entered Sandhurst, 1939, and later commissioned Grenadier Guards. Served Middle East, Italy and Balkans, 1942–46. Formerly Managing Dir of Windolite Ltd from 1947. MP (C) Epping Div. of Essex, 1950–51. *Publications:* Los Señoríos Independientes del Imperio Azteca, 1968; Los Mexicas: Primeras Pasos Hacia el Imperio, 1973; The Aztecs, 1973; The Toltecs, 1977; Voyagers to the New World: fact and fantasy, 1979; The Toltec Heritage, 1980; Human Sacrifice, 1981; The Ancient Kingdoms of Mexico, 1983; The Rampant God, 1984. *Recreation:* travel. *Address:* Sondra 75, Colonia Chapultepec, Tijuana, Baja California, Mexico. *T:* 86–10–36. *Club:* Carlton.

DAVIES, Cyril James; Chief Executive, City of Newcastle upon Tyne, since 1980; *b* 24 Aug. 1923; *s* of James and Frances Davies; *m* 1948, Elizabeth Leggett; two *s* two *d*. *Educ:* Heaton Grammar Sch. CIPFA, ACIS, FRVA. Served RN, Fleet Air Arm, 1942–46. City Treasurer's Dept, Newcastle upon Tyne, 1946–: Dep. City Treas., 1964; City Treas., 1969; Treas., Tyne and Wear Co., 1973–80. Chm., Northern Sinfonia Orch., 1982–; Mem. Council: Northern Arts, 1981–; Univ. of Newcastle upon Tyne, 1982–. *Recreations:* theatre, walking, music. *Address:* 36 Lindisfarne Close, Jesmond, Newcastle upon Tyne NE2 2HT. *T:* Newcastle upon Tyne 815402. *Club:* Naval.

DAVIES, Dr David; Director, Dartington North Devon Trust, since 1980; *b* 11 Aug. 1939; *s* of Trefor Alun and Kathleen Elsie Davies; *m* 1968, Joanna Rachel Peace; one *s* three *d*. *Educ:* Nottingham High Sch.; Peterhouse, Cambridge. MA, PhD. Res. Scientist, Dept of Geophysics, Cambridge, 1961–69; Leader, Seismic Discrimination Gp, MIT Lincoln Laboratory, 1970–73; Editor of Nature, 1973–79. Rapporteur, Seismic Study Gp of Stockholm Internat. Peace Res. Inst. (SIPRI), 1968–73. Mem., Warnock Cttee on artificial human fertilisation, 1982–84. Member Council: Internat. Disaster Inst., 1979; Beaford Arts Centre, 1980–; Trustee, Bristol Exploratory, 1983–. Musical Dir, Blackheath Opera Workshop, 1977–79; Conductor, Exmoor Chamber Orchestra, 1980–. *Publications:* Seismic Methods for Monitoring Underground Explosions, 1968; numerous scientific papers. *Recreations:* orchestral and choral conducting. *Address:* Wester Ground, Chittlehamholt, N Devon.

DAVIES, Sir (David) Arthur, KBE 1980; Secretary-General Emeritus, World Meteorological Organization, Geneva, Switzerland, since 1980 (Secretary-General, 1955–79); Vice-President, since 1983 and Honorary Consultant, since 1982, Welsh Centre for International Affairs; *b* 11 Nov. 1913; *m* 1938, Mary Shapland; one *s* two *d*. *Educ:* University of Wales (MSc) (1st cl. Hons Maths; 1st cl. Hons Physics); Fellow, University Coll., Cardiff, 1985. Technical Officer, Meteorological Office, 1936–39. War Service, RAF, 1939–47 (despatches). Principal Scientific Officer, Met. Office, 1947–49; Dir, E African Met. Dept, Nairobi, 1949–55; Pres. World Meteorological Organization Regional Assoc. for Africa, 1951–55. United Nations Peace Medal, 1979. Hon. Member: Amer. Meteorological Soc., 1970; Hungarian Meteorol Soc., 1975. FInstP, FRMet Soc. Dr *hc* Univ. of Bucharest, 1970; Dr *hc* Univ. of Budapest, 1976; Dr ès Sc *hc* Swiss Fed. Inst. of Technology, 1978; Hon. DSc Wales, 1981. Gold Medal of Merit, Czech. Acad. of Scis, 1978; Silver Medal, Royal Swedish Acad. of Science, 1979; Cleveland Abbe Award, Amer. Meteorol Soc., 1985; Internat. Meteorological Orgn Prize, WMO, 1985. *Publications:* various meteorological papers and articles. *Recreations:* music, Listener crossword. *Address:* 2 Ashley Close, Patcham, Brighton, East Sussex BN1 8YT. *T:* Brighton 509437. *Clubs:* Anglo-Belgian, Royal Commonwealth Society.

DAVIES, David Cyril, BA, LLB; Headmaster, Crown Woods School, 1971–84; *b* 7 Oct. 1925; *s* of D. T. E. Davies and Mrs G. V. Davies, JP; *m* 1952, Joan Rogers, BSc; one *s* one *d*. *Educ:* Lewis Sch., Pengam; UCW Aberystwyth. Asst Master, Ebbw Vale Gram. Sch., 1951–55; Head, Lower Sch., Netteswell Bilateral Sch., 1955–58; Sen. Master and Dep. Headmaster, Peckham Manor Sch., 1958–64; Headmaster: Greenway Comprehensive Sch., 1964–67; Woodberry Down Sch., 1967–71. Pres., Inverliever Lodge Trust, 1971–84. *Recreations:* reading, Rugby and roughing it. *Address:* 9 Plaxtol Close, Bromley, Kent. *T:* 01–464 4187.

DAVIES, Prof. David Evan Naunton, CBE 1986; PhD, DSc; FRS 1984; FEng 1979; Professor of Electrical Engineering, since 1971, and Head of the Department of Electronic and Electrical Engineering, since 1985, University College London; *b* 28 Oct. 1935; *s* of David Evan Davies and Sarah (*née* Samuel); *m* 1962, Enid Patilla; two *s*. *Educ:* Univ. of Birmingham (MSc 1958; PhD 1960; DSc 1968). FIEE 1969; FIERE 1975. Lectr and Sen. Lectr in Elec. Engrg, Univ. of Birmingham, 1961–67 (also Hon. SPSO, RRE, Malvern, 1966–67); Asst Dir of Elec. Res., BR Bd, Derby, 1967–71; Vis. Industrial Prof. of Elec. Engrg, Loughborough Univ. of Technol., 1969–71. Mem., SERC, 1985–. *Publications:* technical papers and articles on radar, antennae and aspects of fibre optics. *Address:* Department of Electronic and Electrical Engineering, University College London, Torrington Place, WC1E 7JE. *T:* 01–387 7050.

DAVIES, (David) Garfield; General Secretary, Union of Shop, Distributive and Allied Workers, since 1986; *b* 24 June 1935; *s* of David John Davies and Lizzie Ann Davies; *m* 1960, Marian (*née* Jones); four *d*. *Educ:* Heolgam Secondary Modern School; Bridgend Tech. Coll. (part time). Junior operative, Electrical Apprentice and Electrician, British Steel Corp., Port Talbot, 1950–69; Area Organiser, USDAW, Ipswich, 1969–73; Dep. Divl Officer, USDAW, London/Ipswich, 1973–78; Nat. Officer, USDAW, Manchester, 1978–85. JP 1972–79. *Recreations:* most sport, badminton, squash, swimming, jogging; formerly soccer, cricket, Rugby. *Address:* USDAW, Oakley, 188 Wilmslow Road, Fallowfield, Manchester M14 6LJ. *T:* 061–224 2804; 64 Dairyground Road, Bramhall, Stockport, Cheshire SK7 2QW. *T:* 061–439 9548.

DAVIES, Sir David (Henry), Kt 1973; first Chairman, Welsh Development Agency, 1976–79; General Secretary, Iron and Steel Trades Confederation, 1967–75; *b* 2 Dec. 1909; British; *m* 1934, Elsie May Battrick; one *s* one *d* (and one *d* decd). *Educ:* Ebbw Vale, Mon. Organiser, 1950, Asst. Gen. Sec., 1953–66, Iron and Steel Trades Confederation. Chm., Jt Adv. Cttee on Safety and Health in the Iron and Steel Industry, 1965–67; Vice-Chm., Nat. Dock Labour Bd, 1966–68; Hon. Treas. WEA, 1962–69 (Mem. Central Coun. and Central Exec. Cttee, 1954–69); Hon. Treas., British Labour Party, 1965–67 (Chm., 1963; Mem. Nat. Exec., 1954–67); Hon. Sec., Brit. Sect., Internat. Metalworkers Federation, 1960–; Member: Ebbw Vale UDC, 1945–50; Royal Institute of International Affairs, 1954–; Iron and Steel Operatives Course Adv. Cttee, City and Guilds of London Institute Dept of Technology, 1954–68; Iron and Steel Industry Trng Bd, 1964–; Constructional Materials Gp, Economic Development Cttee for the Building and Civil Engrg Industries, 1965–68; Iron and Steel Adv. Cttee, 1967–; English Industrial Estates Corporation, 1971–; Vice-Pres., European Coal and Steel Community Consultative Cttee, 1975– (Pres., 1973–74). Governor: Ruskin Coll., Oxford, 1954–68; Iron and Steel Industry Management Trng Coll., Ashorne Hill, Leamington Spa, 1966–. Mem. TUC Gen. Coun., 1967–75. *Address:* 82 New House Park, St Albans, Herts. *T:* St Albans 56513.

DAVIES, Hon. Sir (David Herbert) Mervyn, Kt 1982; MC 1944; TD 1946; **Hon. Mr Justice Mervyn Davies;** a Judge of the High Court of Justice, Chancery Division, since 1982; *b* 17 Jan. 1918; *s* of Herbert Bowen Davies and Esther Davies, Llangunnor, Carms; *m* 1951, Zita Yollanne Angelique Blanche Antoinette, 2nd *d* of Rev. E. A. Phillips, Bale, Norfolk. *Educ:* Swansea Gram. Sch. Solicitor, 1939. 18th Bn Welch Regt and 2nd London Irish Rifles, Africa, Italy and Austria, 1939–45. Called to Bar, Lincoln's Inn, 1947; Bencher, 1974; QC 1967; a Circuit Judge, 1978–82. Mem., Bar Council, 1972; Mem., Senate of Inns of Court, 1975. *Address:* The White House, Great Snoring, Norfolk. *T:* Walsingham 575; 7 Stone Buildings, Lincoln's Inn, WC2. *T:* 01–242 8061.

DAVIES, (David) Hywel, MA, PhD, FIEE; Deputy Director-General for Science, Research and Development, Commission of the European Communities, Brussels, since 1982; *b* 28 March 1929; *s* of John and Maggie Davies; *m* 1961, Valerie Elizabeth Nott; one *s* two *d*. *Educ:* Cardiff High Sch.; Christ's Coll., Cambridge. Radar Research Estabt, 1956; Head of Airborne Radar Group, RRE, 1970; Head of Weapons Dept, Admty Surface Weapons Estabt, 1972; Asst Chief Scientific Advr (Projects), MoD, 1976–79; Dir, RARDE, MoD, 1979–80; Dep. Controller, Res. Programmes, MoD, 1980–82. *Publications:* papers on electronics, radar and remote sensing, in Proc. IEE, etc. *Recreations:* do-it-yourself, photography, knots. *Address:* 52 Brittains Lane, Sevenoaks, Kent TN13 2JP. *T:* Sevenoaks 456359.

DAVIES, David John; Managing Director, The Hongkong Land Group, 1983–86; *b* 1 April 1940; *s* of Stanley Kenneth Davies, *qv*; *m* 1967, Deborah Frances Loeb (marr. diss.); one *s*; *m* 1985, Linda Wong Lin-Tye. *Educ:* Winchester Coll., Winchester; New Coll., Oxford (MA); Harvard Business Sch. (Advanced Management Program). Chase Manhattan Bank, 1963–67; Hill Samuel Group, 1967–73: Dir, Hill Samuel Inc., New York, 1970–73; Dir, Hill Samuel Ltd, London, 1973; Finance Dir, 1973–83, and Vice-Chm., 1977–83, MEPC Ltd. Chm., Wire Ropes Ltd, Wicklow, 1979–; Director: Letheby & Christopher Ltd, 1979–; Jardine, Matheson & Co. Ltd, 1983–. *Recreations:* farming, skiing, tennis, travel. *Address:* Killoughter House, Ashford, Co. Wicklow, Ireland. *T:* Wicklow 4126. *Clubs:* Turf; Cardiff and County (Cardiff); Kildare Street and University (Dublin); Royal Hong Kong Jockey, Hong Kong (Hong Kong).

DAVIES, Rt. Hon. (David John) Denzil; PC 1978; MP (Lab) Llanelli since 1970; *b* 9 Oct. 1938; *s* of G. Davies, Conwil Elfed, Carmarthen; *m* 1963, Mary Ann Finlay, Illinois; one *s* one *d*. *Educ:* Queen Elizabeth Grammar Sch., Carmarthen; Pembroke Coll., Oxford. Bacon Scholar, Gray's Inn, 1961; BA (1st cl. Law) 1962; Martin Wronker Prize (Law), 1962. Teaching Fellow, Univ. of Chicago, 1963; Lectr in Law, Leeds Univ., 1964; called to Bar, Gray's Inn, 1964. Member: Select Cttee on Corporation Tax, 1971; Jt Select Cttee (Commons and Lords) on Delegated Legislation, 1972; Public Accounts Cttee, 1974–; PPS to the Secretary of State for Wales, 1974–76; Minister of State, HM Treasury, 1975–79; Opposition spokesman on Treasury matters, 1979–81, on foreign affairs, 1981–82, on defence, 1982–83; chief opposition spokesman: on Welsh affairs, 1983; on defence and disarmament, 1983–. *Address:* House of Commons, SW1.

DAVIES, Sir David (Joseph), Kt 1969; Chairman, Wales Tourist Board, 1965–70; *b* 30 Aug. 1896; *s* of David and Catherine Davies; *m* 1924, Eleanor Irene Davies (*née* Bowen); one *s*. *Educ:* Maesteg Higher Grade and Bridgend County Schools. Served in Welch Regt, 1915–19, Acting Captain. Mem. Court, University Coll., Cardiff, 1959–76; Mem. Court and Council, National Museum of Wales, 1961–73. *Address:* 28 Queen Anne Square, Cardiff CF1 3ED. *T:* Cardiff 382695. *Club:* Cardiff and County (Cardiff).

DAVIES, David Levric, CB 1982; OBE 1962; Under Secretary (Legal), Treasury Solicitor's Office, 1977–82; *b* 11 May 1925; *s* of Benjamin and Elizabeth Davies; *m* 1955, Beryl Justine Hammond. *Educ:* Llanrwst Grammar Sch.; University Coll. of Wales, Aberystwyth (LLB Hons). Called to the Bar, Middle Temple, 1949. Served War, 1943–46: Sub-Lt RNVR. Crown Counsel, Aden, 1950–55; Tanganyika: Asst to Law Officers, 1956–58; Parly Draftsman, 1958–61; Solicitor-Gen., 1961–64; Home Civil Service, 1964–82: seconded to Jamaica as Sen. Parly Draftsman, 1965–69, and to Seychelles as Attorney-Gen., 1970–72; Sen. Legal Asst, Treasury Solicitor's Office, 1972–73; Asst Treasury Solicitor, 1973–77. *Recreations:* gardening, loafing, reading. *Address:* Greystones, Breach Lane, Shaftesbury, Dorset. *T:* Shaftesbury 51224. *Club:* RNVR.

DAVIES, David Ronald, MB, BS, FRCS; Surgeon, University College Hospital, London, 1946–75, retired; *b* Clydach, Swansea, 11 May 1910; 3rd *s* of late Evan Llewelyn and Agnes Jane Davies; *m* 1940, Alice Christine, 2nd *d* of Rev. John Thomson; three *s*. *Educ:* University Coll. and University Coll. Hosp., London. MRCS, LRCP 1934; MB BS London, 1934; FRCS, 1937. House appts at UCH, Asst, Surgical Unit, UCH, 1937–39; Asst Surg. EMS at UCH and Hampstead Gen. Hosp., 1939–41; served RAMC, Surgical Specialist and Officer-in-Charge Surgical Div., 1941–46; Surgeon: Queen Mary's Hospital, Roehampton, 1947–69; Harrow Hosp., 1946–69. Mem., BMA. Fellow: University Coll. London; Assoc. of Surgeons; RSocMed; British Assoc. of Urological Surgeons; Internat. Assoc. of Urologists. *Publications:* The Operations of Surgery (with A. J. Gardham); various papers on surgical subjects. *Address:* 15 Camden Square, NW1 9UY; Newland Farm, Withypool, Somerset. *T:* Exford 352. *Club:* Oriental.

DAVIES, Prof. David Roy, PhD; Professor of Applied Genetics and Dean of School of Biological Sciences, University of East Anglia; Deputy Director, John Innes Institute; *b* 10 June 1932; *s* of late J. O. Davies and A. E. Davies; *m* 1957, Winifred Frances Davies, JP, BA (*née* Wills); two *s* two *d*. *Educ:* Llandyssul and Grove Park, Wrexham Grammar Schs; Univ. of Wales. BSc, PhD. UK Atomic Energy Authority, 1956–62 and 1963–68; US Atomic Energy Commn, 1962–63. Editor, Heredity, 1975–82. *Publications:* papers on radiobiology and plant genetics in scientific jls. *Address:* 57 Church Lane, Eaton, Norwich. *T:* Norwich 51049.

DAVIES, David Theodore Alban; a Registrar, Family Division of the High Court of Justice, since 1983; *b* 8 June 1940; *s* of late John Rhys Davies, Archdeacon of Merioneth, and Mabel Aeronwy Davies; *m* 1966, Janet Mary, *er d* of Frank and Barbara Welburn, Cheadle Hulme, Cheshire; one *s* one *d*. *Educ:* Rossall School (Scholar); Magdalen College, Oxford (Exhibnr, 2nd cl. Mods 1960, 1st cl. Lit Hum, 1962, BA 1962; Eldon Law Schol., 1963; MA 1967). Called to the Bar, Gray's Inn, 1964 (Entrance Schol., Arden Atkin and Mould Prize, Lord Justice Holker Sen. Schol.). Practised SE Circuit, 1965–83. Sec., Family Law Bar Assoc., 1976–80, Treasurer, 1980–83; Mem., Senate Law Reform Cttee, 1979–83. *Publication:* (ed jtly) Jackson's Matrimonial Finance and Taxation, 2nd edn 1975, 4th edn 1986. *Recreations:* reading, walking, history. *Address:* 134 Court Lane, SE21 7EB. *T:* 01-693 4132.

DAVIES, Rt. Hon. Denzil; *see* Davies, Rt. Hon. David J. D.

DAVIES, Donald, CBE 1978 (OBE 1973); Chairman: NCB (Ancillaries) Ltd, since 1979; National Fuel Distributors Ltd, since 1973; Southern Depot Co. Ltd, since 1973; Horizon Exploration Ltd, since 1981; consultant; *b* 13 Feb. 1924; *s* of late Wilfred Lawson Davies and Alwyne Davies; *m* 1948, Mabel (*née* Hellyar); two *d*. *Educ:* Ebbw Vale Grammar Sch.; UC Cardiff (BSc). CEng, FIMinE. Nationl Coal Board: Colliery Man., 1951–55; Gp Man., 1955–58; Dep. Prodn Man., 1958–60; Prodn Man., 1960–61; Area Gen. Man., 1961–67; Area Dir, 1967–73; Bd Mem., 1973–84. FRSA, FBIM. *Recreations:* golf, walking. *Address:* Wendy Cottage, Dukes Wood Avenue, Gerrards Cross, Bucks SL9 7LA. *T:* Gerrards Cross 85083.

DAVIES, Douglas; *see* Davies, Percy D.

DAVIES, Duncan Sheppey, CB 1982; Consulting Technical Director, Tate & Lyle, Unilever, US National Bureau of Standards, etc; Chairman, BCRA Ltd, since 1984; Governor, Technical Change Centre, since 1982; *b* 20 April 1921; *o s* of Duncan S. Davies and Elsie Dora, Liverpool; *m* 1944, Joan Ann Frimston, MA; one *s* three *d*. *Educ:* Liverpool Coll.; Trinity Coll., Oxford (Minor Scholar). MA, BSc, DPhil. CEng, FIChemE, Hon. FIMechE. Joined ICI Dyestuffs Div., 1945; Research Dir, Gen. Chemicals Div., 1961; first Dir, ICI Petrochemical and Polymer Lab., 1962; Dep. Chm., Mond Div., 1967; Gen. Manager, Research, ICI, 1969–77; Chief Engineer and Scientist, DoI, 1977–82; Consulting Technical Dir, BCRA Ltd, 1982–84. Member: SERC (formerly SRC), 1969–73, 1977–82; SRC/SSRC, 1973–79 (Chm.); Adv. Bd for Res. Councils, 1977–82; Adv. Council on Applied R&D, NERC, 1977–82; Swann Manpower Working Gp, 1964–66; Council, Liverpool Univ., 1967–69; Council, QEC London, 1975–78; President: R & D Soc., 1983–; SCI, 1986–87. Visiting Professor: Imperial Coll., 1968–70; Univ. of York, 1983–; Vis. Fellow, St Cross Coll., Oxford, 1970; Vis. Prof. Fellow, UC Swansea, 1974–79. DUniv Stirling, 1975; DUniv Surrey, 1980; Hon. DSc Bath, 1981. Castner Medal, SCI, 1967. Foreign Associate, Nat. Acad. of Engineering, USA, 1978. Hon. DSc Technion, Haifa, 1982. *Publications:* (with M. C. McCarthy) Introduction to Technological Economics, 1967; The Humane Technologist, 1976; (with D. M. Bathurst) Pictures and Words, 1986; various papers in engineering and economics, pure and applied chemistry jls. *Recreations:* music, writing. *Address:* 3 Broadlands Close, N6 4AF. *T:* 01–341 2421. *Club:* United Oxford & Cambridge University.

DAVIES, Ednyfed Hudson, BA (Wales); MA (Oxon); barrister; *b* 4 Dec. 1929; *s* of Rev. E. Curig Davies and Enid Curig (*née* Hughes); *m* 1972, Amanda Barker-Mill, *d* of Peter Barker-Mill and Elsa Barker-Mill; two *d*. *Educ:* Friars Sch., Bangor; Dynevor Grammar Sch., Swansea; University College of Swansea; Balliol Coll., Oxford. Called to the Bar, Gray's Inn, 1975. Lecturer in Dept of Extra-Mural Studies, University of Wales, Aberystwyth, 1957–61; Lecturer in Political Thought, Welsh Coll. of Advanced Technology, Cardiff, 1961–66. MP: (Lab) Conway, 1966–70; Caerphilly, 1979–83 (Lab, 1979–81, SDP, 1981–83); Mem., H of C Select Cttee on Energy, 1980–83; Sec., H of C All-Party Tourism Cttee, 1979–83. Contested (SDP) Basingstoke, 1983. Part-time TV and Radio Commentator and Interviewer on Current Affairs, 1962–66; on full-time contract to BBC presenting Welsh-language feature programmes on overseas countries, 1970–76; Chm., Wales Tourist Board, 1976–78. Dir, New Forest Butterfly Farm, 1984–. *Address:* 2 King's Bench Walk, Temple, EC4Y 7DE. *Club:* Cardiff and County (Cardiff).

DAVIES, (Edward) Hunter; author and broadcaster; *b* Renfrew, Scotland, 7 Jan. 1936; *s* of late John Hunter Davies and Marion (*née* Brechin); *m* 1960, Margaret Forster, *qv*; one *s* two *d*. *Educ:* Creighton Sch., Carlisle; Carlisle Grammar Sch.; University Coll., Durham. BA 1957, DipEd 1958; Editor of Palatinate. Reporter: Manchester Evening Chronicle, 1958–59; Sunday Graphic, London, 1959–60; Sunday Times, 1960–84: Atticus, 1965–67; Chief Feature Writer, 1967; Editor, Look pages, 1970; Editor, Scene pages, 1975; Editor, Sunday Times Magazine, 1975–77; Columnist: Punch, 1979–; Stamp News, 1981–; Presenter, Bookshelf, Radio 4, 1983–86. *Television:* The Playground (play), 1967; The Living Wall, 1974; George Stephenson, 1975; A Walk in the Lakes, 1979. *Publications:* Here We Go, Round the Mulberry Bush, 1965 (filmed, 1968); The Other Half, 1966; (ed) The New London Spy, 1966; The Beatles, 1968, 2nd edn 1985; The Rise and Fall of Jake Sullivan, 1970; (ed) I Knew Daisy Smuten, 1970; A Very Loving Couple, 1971; Body Charge, 1972; The Glory Game, 1972, 2nd edn 1985; A Walk Along the Wall, 1974, 2nd edn 1984; George Stephenson, 1975; The Creighton Report, 1976; (ed) Sunday Times Book of Jubilee Year, 1977; A Walk Around the Lakes, 1979; William Wordsworth, 1980; The British Book of Lists, 1980; The Grades, 1981; Father's Day, 1981 (television series, 1983); Beaver Book of Lists, 1981; A Walk Along the Tracks, 1982; England!, 1982; (with Frank Herrmann) Great Britain: a celebration, 1982; Flossie Teacake's Fur Coat, 1982; A Walk Round London Parks, 1983; The Joy of Stamps, 1983; Flossie Teacake—Again!, 1983; London at its Best, 1984; (also publisher) The Good Guide to the Lakes, 1984, 2nd edn 1986; Flossie Teacake Strikes Back, 1984; Come on Ossie!, 1985; The Grand Tour, 1986; Ossie Goes Supersonic, 1986. *Recreations:* collecting stamps, postal history, US railway bonds, autographs, Lakeland books, Beatles memorabilia, parking fines. *Address:* 11 Boscastle Road, NW5. *T:* 01–485 3785; John Peel Farm, Caldbeck, Cumbria.

DAVIES, Elidir (Leslie Wish), FRIBA, FRSA; Chartered Architect in private practice; *b* 3 Jan. 1907; *yr s* of late Rev. Thomas John Landy Davies and Hetty Boucher (*née* Wish); *m* 1st, Vera (*née* Goodwin) (*d* 1974); 2nd, 1976, Kathleen Burke-Collis. *Educ:* privately; Colchester Sch.; Bartlett Sch. of Architecture, University of London (under Prof. Albert Richardson). Min. of Supply Air Defence, 1939–44; Min. of Town and Country Planning, London and Wales, 1944–47; University Lectr and Cons. to Argentinian and Uruguay Govts on planning and low cost housing, 1947–49; private practice (Devereux and Davies); rebuilding of Serjeants' Inn, Fleet Street; Royal Vet. Coll., London Univ. (Research and Field Labs); King's Coll. Sch., Wimbledon (Jun. Sch. and Sci. Labs); St James's Hosp., Balham (Out-patients' and other Depts); St Benedict's Hosp. (Hydrotherapy Dept), 1950–61. West Indies: 5-year Hospital progr. for Trinidad (incl. new gen. and maternity hosps, trg schs, specialist depts, and hosp. services). Cons. Arch. Hosps to Govts of Guiana, Barbados and Grenada, 1957–63. Private practice (Elidir L. W. Davies & Partners). Architect to: St David's Coll., Lampeter, restoration and new bldgs; London Borough of Camden; Central Library, Shaw Theatre and arts centre; Mermaid Theatre; Dynevor Castle, Carmarthen, Wales; new arts centre for drama and films; Chigwell Central Public Library; church work: The Temple, White Eagle Lodge, Hants; rebuilding of Wren's church, St Michael Paternoster Royal; Burrswood Nursing Home of Healing, Groombridge, Kent, new garden Hydrotherapy, gen. maintenance and upgrading; Cons. Architect to: St David's Trust, Welsh Nat. Arts Theatre Centre, Cardiff; Govt Offices, Century House, Waterloo; BP Offices, 100 Euston Road; private houses and housing developments in London and the country. Chm., Soc. of Theatre Consultants, 1969–71; Mem. of Exec., Assoc. of British Theatre Technicians, 1965–71. Bronze Medal, RIBA, 1953. *Publications:* lectures and articles; contrib. to pubn relating to hospital architecture. *Recreations:* theatre, travel, sailing, visual arts. *Address:* St David's, Burrswood, Groombridge, Kent TN3 9PY. *T:* Groombridge 810. *Clubs:* Garrick, Art Workers' Guild.

DAVIES, Emlyn Glyndwr, MSc; Chief Scientific Officer, Controller, Forensic Science Service, Home Office, 1974–76; *b* 20 March 1916; *yr s* of late William and Elizabeth Davies; *m* 1940, Edwina, *d* of late Lemuel and Alice Morgan, Blaengarw; two *s*. *Educ:* Bargoed Grammar Sch.; Maesycwmmer Grammar Sch.; University Coll of Wales, Aberystwyth (MSc). Asst Master, Ardwyn Sch., 1939–42; Ministry of Supply, 1942–44; Forensic Science Laboratory, Cardiff, 1944–58; Director, Forensic Science Laboratories: Nottingham, 1958–59; Preston, 1959–63; Forensic Science Adviser, Home Office, 1963–74. Pres., Forensic Science Soc., 1975–77. *Publications:* contribs to scientific jls. *Recreation:* Rugby football. *Address:* 14 Church Hill Close, Llanblethian, Cowbridge, S Glamorgan CF7 7JH. *T:* Cowbridge 2234.

DAVIES, Emrys Thomas; HM Diplomatic Service; Deputy UK Permanent Representative to the OECD, and Counsellor (Economic and Financial) to the UK Delegation, Paris, since 1984; *b* 8 Oct. 1934; *s* of Evan William Davies and Dinah Davies (*née* Jones); *m* 1960, Angela Audrey, *er d* of late Paul Robert Buchan May, ICS and of Esme May; one *s* two *d*. *Educ:* Parmiters Foundation Sch. RAF, 1953–55. Sch. of Slavonic Studies, Cambridge Univ., 1954; Sch. of Oriental and African Studies, London Univ., 1955–56. Served Peking, 1956–59; FO, 1959–60; Bahrain, 1960–62; FO, 1962–63; Asst Political Adviser to Hong Kong Govt, 1963–68; First Sec., British High Commn, Ottawa, 1968–71; FCO, 1972–76; Commercial Counsellor, Peking, 1976–78 (Chargé, 1976 and 1978); Oxford Univ. Business Summer Sch., 1977; NATO Defense Coll., Rome, 1979; Dep. High Comr, Ottawa, 1979–82; Overseas Inspector, FCO, 1982–84. *Address:* c/o Foreign and Commonwealth Office, SW1A 2AH. *Club:* Royal Commonwealth Society.

DAVIES, Ernest Albert John; journalist, author; *b* London, 18 May 1902; *s* of late Alderman Albert Emil Davies; *m* 1st, 1926, Natalie Rossin, New York (marr. diss. 1944; she *d* 1955); two *s* one *d*; 2nd, 1944, Peggy Yeo (*d* 1963); one *d* (*decd*). *Educ:* Wycliffe Coll.; London Univ. (Diploma in Journalism). Managing Editor, Traffic Engineering and Control, 1960–76; Managing Editor, Antique Finder, 1962–72; Editor Clarion, 1929–32; Associate Editor, New Clarion, 1932. Served on Fabian Soc. Exec., 1940; Gov. National Froebel Foundation, 1938–40. With British Broadcasting Corporation, 1940–45, and its North American Service Organiser, 1944–45. Contested (Lab) Peterborough, 1935; MP (Lab) Enfield Division of Middx, 1945–50, East Enfield, 1950–59. Parl. Private Sec. to Min of State, 1946–50; Parliamentary Under-Sec. of State, Foreign Office, 1950–51. Chm. Transport Group Parliamentary Labour Party, 1945–50 and 1951–59; Jt Chm. Parliamentary Roads Study Group, 1957–59; Mem. Select Cttee on Nationalised Industries, 1952–59; Vice-Pres., British Yugoslav Soc., 1980– (Chm., 1957–80); Mem., Exec. Cttee, European-Atlantic Gp, 1958–65 (Vice-Pres., 1966–82). Mem. British Delegation to Gen. Assembly, UN, 1947, 1948–49 and 1950; Dep. Leader British Deleg. to UN Conf. on Freedom of Information, 1948; Mem. British Deleg. to London Conf. 1950; Leader UK Deleg., Economic Commn for Europe, Geneva, 1950; UK Representative at Foreign Ministers' Deputies' Four Power Talks, Paris, 1951. Vice-Chm., British Parking Assoc., 1969–71, 1976–77 (Pres., 1977–80; Hon. Sec. 1971–76; Mem. Council, 1968–80); Hon. FInstHE. Managing Dir, Printerhall Ltd. Orden de la Liberatión de España, Republican Govt, 1960; Ordenom Jugoslovenske Zvezde sa zlatnim vencem (Yugoslavia), 1976. *Publications:* How Much Compensation, 1935; National Capitalism, 1939; The State and the Railways, 1940; American Labour, 1943; British Transport, 1945; National Enterprise, 1946; Problems of Public Ownership, 1952; (ed) Roads and Their Traffic, 1960; Transport in Greater London, 1962; (ed) Traffic Engineering Practice, 1963, new edn 1968; Contrib. Encyclopaedia Britannica. *Address:* 16 Redcliffe Square, SW10 9JZ. *T:* 01–373 3962. *Clubs:* Wig and Pen, National Liberal.

DAVIES, Dr Ernest Arthur, JP; management consultant and lecturer; *b* 25 Oct. 1926; *s* of Daniel Davies and Ada (*née* Smith), Nuneaton; *m* 1st, 1956, Margaret Stephen Tait Gatt (marr. diss. 1967), *d* of H. Gatt, Gamesley, near Glossop; no *c*; 2nd, 1972, Patricia (marr. diss. 1980), *d* of S. Bates, Radford, Coventry; no *c*. *Educ:* Coventry Jun. Techn. Coll.; Westminster Trng Coll., London; St Salvator's Coll., University of St Andrews; St John's Coll., Cambridge. PhD Cantab 1959; MInstP 1959. RAF Aircraft Apprentice, 1942–43 (discharged on med. grounds). Westminster Trng Coll., 1946–48; Teacher, Foxford Sch., Coventry, 1948–50; University of St Andrews, 1950–54 (1st cl. hons Physics, Neil Arnott Prize, Carnegie Schol.); subseq. research in superconductivity, Royal Society Mond Lab., Cambridge; AEI Research Scientist, 1957–63; Lectr in Physics, Faculty of Technology, University of Manchester, 1963–66. Management Selection Consultant, MSL, 1970–81. MP (Lab) Stretford, 1966–70; Parliamentary Private Secretary to: PMG (Mr Edward Short), Nov.-Dec. 1967; Foreign Secretary (Mr George Brown), Jan.-Mar. 1968; Foreign and Commonwealth Sec. (Mr Michael Stewart), 1968–69; Jt Parly Sec., Min. of Technology, 1969–70. Co-Vice-Chm., Parly Labour Party's Defence and Services Group; Mem., Select Cttee on Science and Technology, 1966–67, 1967–68, 1968–69; Parly Deleg. to 24th Gen. Assembly of UN (UK Rep. on 4th Cttee). Councillor: Borough of Stretford, 1961–67; Borough of Southwark, 1974–82. JP Lancs, 1962, Inner London, 1972. *Publications:* contribs to Proc. Royal Society, Jl of Physics and Chem. of Solids. *Recreations:* reading, walking. *Address:* Flat 3, 5 Rye Hill Park, Peckham, SE15.

DAVIES, Prof. Eurfil Rhys, FRCR, FRCPE; Professor of Radiodiagnosis, University of Bristol, since 1981; *b* 18 April 1929; *s* of late Daniel Haydn Davies and Mary Davies; *m* 1962, Zoë Doreen Chamberlain; three *s*. *Educ:* Rhondda Grammar Sch.; Llandovery Coll.; Clare Coll., Cambridge (MB, BChir 1953; MA); St Mary's Hosp., London. FRCR (FFR 1964); FRCPE 1971. Served RAMC, 1954–56. Sen. Registrar, St Mary's Hosp., 1963–66; Consultant Radiologist, United Bristol Hosps, 1966–81; Clinical Lectr, Univ. of Bristol, 1972–81. Vis. Sen. Lectr, Lagos Univ., 1971; Mayne Vis. Prof., Queensland

Univ., 1982. Mem., Bristol and Weston DHA, 1983–86. Mem., Admin of Radio Active Substances Adv. Cttee, DHSS, 1978–83. Royal Coll. of Radiologists: Sen. Examr, 1973–74; Mem., Fellowship Bd, 1974–76; Registrar, 1976–81; Warden of the Fellowship, 1984–86; Pres., 1986–; Chairman: Nuclear Medicine Cttee, 1972–78; Examng Bd, 1982–84. Pres., Nuclear Medicine Soc., 1974–76; Chm., Inter Collegiate Standing Cttee for Nuclear Medicine, 1982–84 (Sec., 1980–82). Hon. Fellow, Faculty of Radiologists, RCSI, 1978. *Publications:* (contrib.) Textbook of Radiology, ed Sutton, 1969, 3rd edn 1980; (contrib.) Textbook of Urology, ed J. P. Blandy, 1974; (jtly) Radioisotopes in Radiodiagnosis, 1976; (contrib.) Radiological Atlas of Biliary and Pancreatic Disease, 1978; Textbook of Radiology by British Authors, 1984; papers in Clin. Radiology, British Jl of Radiology, Lancet. *Recreations:* theatre, walking, wine. *Address:* 19 Hyland Grove, Bristol BS9 3NR.

DAVIES, Gareth; Group Chief Executive since 1984, Chairman since 1987, Glynwed International plc; *b* 13 Feb. 1930; *s* of Lewis and Margaret Ann Davies; *m* 1953, Joan Patricia Prosser; one *s*. *Educ:* King Edward's Grammar School, Aston, Birmingham. FCA. Joined Glynwed Group, 1957; Computer Manager, 1964; Financial Dir, 1969; Man. Dir, 1981. *Recreations:* music, gardening. *Address:* 4 Beechgate, Roman Road, Little Aston Park, West Midlands. *T:* 021–353 4780.

DAVIES, Garfield; *see* Davies, D. G.

DAVIES, George Francis, CMG 1962; Chairman, Davies Brothers Ltd, since 1954; *b* 26 Jan. 1911; *yr s* of late C. B. Davies, CBE, MIEA, and late Ruby A. Davies; *m* 1935, Margaret Ingles; one *s* three *d*. *Educ:* Clemes Coll., Hobart, Tasmania. Director: Commercial Broadcasters Pty Ltd (Chm., 1950–); Australian Newsprint Mills Ltd, 1954–; Tasmanian Fibre Containers Pty Ltd (Chm., 1975–); Packaging Investments Pty Ltd (Chm., 1965–); Perpetual Trustees and National Executors Ltd, 1968–. *Recreations:* golf, fishing, racing. *Address:* 5/46 Marieville Esplanade, Sandy Bay, Tasmania 7005, Australia. *T:* 34.6411. *Clubs:* Tasmanian, Athenæum (Hobart).

DAVIES, George Raymond, (Gerry), OBE 1977; FLA; Director, The Booksellers Association of Great Britain and Ireland, 1964–66 and 1970–81 (Hon. Life Member, 1981); *b* 3 Oct. 1916; *s* of George John Davies and Eva Florence Davies; *m* 1945, Sylvia Newling; one *s* one *d*. *Educ:* East Ham Grammar Sch. FLA 1948. Local govt service, 1934–40; land reclamation, 1940–45; estate under-bailiff, 1945–46; W Suffolk and Cambridge Public Libraries, 1947–54 (Dep. City Librarian, 1953); Gen. Sec., Booksellers Assoc., 1955–64; Man. Dir, Bowker Publishing Co. Ltd, 1966–67; Editor, Publishers Inf. Card Services Ltd, 1968–69; Jt Dep. Editor, The Bookseller, 1969–70. Founder-Mem., Internat. Community of Booksellers Assocs, 1956 (Mem. Council, 1972–78); Mem. Council, Internat. Booksellers Fedn, 1978– (Pres. 1978–81; Editor, Booksellers International, 1982–); Chm., BA Service House Ltd, 1977–82; Pres., Book Trade Benevolent Soc., 1986– (Chm., 1974–86). *Publications:* (ed jtly) Books are Different, 1966; A Mortal Craft, 1980; (contrib.) The Book of Westminster, 1964; (contrib.) Books and Their Prices, 1967; contrib. to Library Rev., Library World, Year's Work in Librarianship, Canadian Bookseller, American Bookseller, Australian Bookseller and Publisher, and The Bookseller. *Recreations:* estate management, writing words and music. *Address:* Crotchets, Rotherfield Lane, Mayfield, East Sussex. *T:* Mayfield 872356. *Club:* Savile.

DAVIES, Prof. Graeme John; Vice-Chancellor, University of Liverpool, since 1986; *b* 7 April 1937; *s* of Harry John Davies and Gladys Edna Davies (*née* Pratt); *m* 1959, Florence Isabelle Martin; one *s* one *d*. *Educ:* Mount Albert Grammar School, Auckland, NZ; Univ. of Auckland (BE, PhD); St Catharine's College, Cambridge (MA, ScD). FIM, MIMechE. Junior Lectr, Univ. of Auckland, 1960–62; University of Cambridge: TI Research Fellow, 1962–64; Univ. Demonstrator in Metallurgy, 1964–66; Lectr, 1966–77; Fellow of St Catharine's Coll., 1967–77; Prof. of Metallurgy, Univ. of Sheffield, 1978–86. Visiting Professor: Brazil, 1976–77; Israel, 1978; Argentina, 1980; China, 1981, 1985. Guardian, Sheffield Assay Office, 1983–86; Member: Council, Inst. Metals, 1981–; Council, Sheffield Metallurgical and Engineering Assoc., 1978–86 (Pres., 1984–85). Rosenhain Medal, Inst. of Metals, 1982. *Publications:* Solidification and Casting, 1973; Texture and Properties of Materials, 1976; Solidificacao e Fundicao das Metais e Suas Ligas, 1978; Hot Working and Forming Processes, 1980; Superplasticity, 1981; Essential Metallurgy for Engineers, 1985; papers to learned jls. *Recreations:* cricket, birdwatching. *Address:* Vice-Chancellor's Lodge, 12 Sefton Park Road, Liverpool L8 3SL. *T:* 051–709 6022. *Club:* Athenæum.

DAVIES, Gwen F.; *see* Ffrangcon-Davies.

DAVIES, (Gwilym) E(dnyfed) Hudson; *see* Davies, Ednyfed H.

DAVIES, Rev. Gwynne Henton; Principal, Regent's Park College, Oxford, 1958–72; *b* 19 Feb. 1906; *m* 1935, Annie Bronwen (*née* Williams), BA Wales; two *d*. *Educ:* Perse Sch., Cambridge; University College of South Wales, Cardiff (BD, MA); St Catherine's and Regent's Park Colls, Oxford Univ. (MLitt, MA); Marburg/Lahn, Germany. Minister West End Baptist Church, London, W6, 1935–38; Tutor Bristol Baptist Coll., 1938–51; special Lecturer in Hebrew, University of Bristol, 1948–51; (First) Prof. of Old Testament Studies, Faculty of Theology, Durham Univ., 1951–58; Select Preacher to the Universities of Cambridge and Oxford. OT Editor, The Teachers' Commentary (revised 7th edn), 1955. Secretary, Society for Old Testament Study, 1946–62 (President, 1966); Vice-Pres., Baptist Union of GB and Ireland, 1970–71, Pres., 1971–72. OT Lecture, Pantyfedwen Foundn, 1975; Distinguished Visiting Professor: Meredith Coll., USA, 1978, 1979; William Jewell Coll., 1982, 1983. Hon. DD: Glasgow, 1958; Stetson, 1965. *Publications:* (with A. B. Davies) The Story in Scripture, 1960; Exodus, 1967; Who's Who in the Bible, 1970; Deuteronomy, in Peake's Commentary on the Bible, rev. edn, 1962; 20 articles in The Interpreter's Bible Dictionary, 1962; The Ark in the Psalms, in Promise and Fulfilment (ed F. F. Bruce), 1963; essay in R. Goldman's Breakthrough, 1968; Genesis, in The Broadman Bible Commentary, 1969; Gerhard von Rad, in O.T. Theology in Contemporary Discussion (ed R. Laurin). *Address:* Headlands, Broad Haven, Haverfordwest, Dyfed SA62 3JP. *T:* Broad Haven 339.

DAVIES, Handel, CB 1962; MSc; FEng; Hon. FRAeS; FAIAA; aeronautical engineering consultant; *m* 1942, Mary Graham Harris. *Educ:* Aberdare Grammar Sch.; University of Wales. FRAeS 1948, Hon. FRAeS 1982. Royal Aircraft Establishment and Ministry of Aircraft Production, 1936–47; Head of Aerodynamics Flight Division, RAE, 1948–52. Chief Superintendent, Aeroplane and Armament Experimental Establishment, Boscombe Down, 1952–55; Scientific Adviser to Air Ministry, 1955–56; Director-General, Scientific Research (Air), Ministry of Supply, 1957–59; Dep. Director, RAE, Farnborough, 1959–63. Dep. Controller of Aircraft, (R&D), Ministry of Aviation, 1963–67, Ministry of Technology, 1967–69. Tech. Dir, British Aircraft Corp., 1969–77. Pres., RAeS, 1977 78. Chm., Standing Conf. on Schools Sci. and Technology, 1978–82. Fellow, University Coll., Cardiff, 1981. Gold Medal, RAeS, 1974. Wilbur and Orville Wright Meml Lectr, 1979. *Publications:* papers in Reports and Memoranda of Aeronautical Research Council and in Journal of Royal Aeronautical Society. *Recreation:* sailing. *Address:* Keel Cottage, Woodham Road, Horsell, Woking, Surrey GU21 4DL. *T:* Woking 4192. *Clubs:* Naval and Military; Royal Air Force Yacht (Hamble).

DAVIES, Harry, JP; Member, Greater Manchester County Council, 1973–86 (Chairman, May 1984–85); *b* 5 March 1915; *s* of Herbert Jacob Davies and Mary Elizabeth Johnson; *m* 1941, Elsie Gore; three *d*. *Educ:* Bedford Methodist Primary School; Leigh Grammar School; Padgate Teacher Training College. 6th Royal Tank Regt, 1941 46. Dep. Head, Westleigh C of E School, 1958; Headmaster, Bedford Methodist School, 1964–77. Mem., Leigh Borough Council, 1959; Mayor, Borough of Leigh, 1971–72. JP Leigh, 1969. Silver Jubilee Medal, 1977. *Recreations:* gardening, bread baking, wine making. *Address:* 45 Edale Road, Leigh WN7 2BD. *T:* Leigh 672583.

DAVIES, Hugh Llewelyn; HM Diplomatic Service; Commercial Counsellor, Peking, since 1984; *b* 8 Nov. 1941; *m* 1968, Virginia Ann Lucius; one *d* one *s*. *Educ:* Rugby School; Churchill College, Cambridge (Hons History degree). Joined Diplomatic Service, 1965; Chinese Language Studies, Hong Kong, 1966–68; Second Sec., Office of British Chargé d'Affaires, Peking, 1969–71; Far Eastern Dept, FCO, 1971–74; First Sec. (Econ.), Bonn, 1974–79; Head of Chancery, Singapore, 1977–79; Asst Head, Far Eastern Dept, FCO, 1979–82; on secondment, Barclays Bank International, 1982–83. *Recreations:* dreaming of Cornwall while away, sketching, tennis, gardens, living. *Address:* c/o Foreign and Commonwealth Office, SW1A 2AH.

DAVIES, Humphrey; *see* Davies, Morgan Wynn Humphrey.

DAVIES, Hunter; *see* Davies, E. H.

DAVIES, Hywel; *see* Davies, D. H.

DAVIES, Ian Hewitt, TD; **His Honour Judge Ian Davies;** a Circuit Judge, since 1986; *b* 13 May 1931; *s* of late Rev. J. R. Davies; *m* 1962, Molly Cecilia Vaughan Vaughan. *Educ:* Kingswood Sch.; St John's Coll., Cambridge (MA). Nat. Service, commnd KOYLI; served with 3rd Bn Parachute Regt, 1950–51; TA, 1952–71 (Lt-Col). Called to the Bar, Inner Temple, 1958. *Address:* c/o Snaresbrook Crown Court, Hollybush Hill, E11. *Clubs:* Boodle's, MCC, Hurlingham.

DAVIES, Ian Leonard, CB 1983; MA; CEng, FIEE; Director, Admiralty Underwater Weapons Establishment, 1975–84; *b* 2 June 1924; *s* of late H. Leonard Davies and of Mrs J. D. Davies; *m* 1951, Hilary Dawson, *d* of late Rear-Adm. Sir Oswald Henry Dawson, KBE; two *s* two *d*. *Educ:* Barry County Sch.; St John's Coll., Cambridge. Mechanical Sciences Tripos, 1944, and Mathematical Tripos Pt 2, 1949. Telecommunications Research Estabt, 1944; Blind Landing Experimental Unit, 1946. TRE (later the Royal Radar Establishment), 1949–69; Imperial Defence Coll., 1970; Asst Chief Scientific Adviser (Projects), MoD, 1971–72; Dep. Controller Electronics, 1973, Dep. Controller Air Systems (D), 1973–75, MoD(PE). Mem. Council, IEE, 1974–77 (Chm., Electronics Div. Bd, 1975–76). *Publications:* papers on information theory, radar, and lasers. *Recreations:* music, walking. *Address:* 37 Bowleaze Coveway, Preston, Weymouth, Dorset. *T:* Weymouth 832206. *Club:* Athenæum.

DAVIES, Ven. Ivor Gordon; Archdeacon Emeritus; *b* 21 July 1917; *m* 1946, Kristine Wiley, SRN; one *s* two *d*. *Educ:* University of Wales (BA); Oxford; London (BD). Deacon 1941, Priest 1942, Llandaff; Curate of St Paul's, Cardiff, 1941–44; CF 1944–47; Curate of St John the Baptist, Felixstowe, 1947–49; Vicar of St Thomas', Ipswich, 1950–57; Residentiary Canon of Southwark Cathedral and Diocesan Missioner, 1957–72; Dean of Lewisham, 1970–72; Archdeacon of Lewisham, 1972–85; Proctor-in-Convocation, 1965–85. *Address:* 10 Garfield Road, Felixstowe, Suffolk. *T:* Felixstowe 271546.

DAVIES, Jack Gale Wilmot, OBE 1946; Executive Director of the Bank of England, 1969–76; *b* 10 Sept. 1911; *s* of Langford George Davies, MD, BCh, MRCS, LRCP, and Lily Barnes Davies; *m* 1949, Georgette O'Dell (*née* Vanson); one *s*. *Educ:* Tonbridge Sch.; St John's Coll., Cambridge. Nat. Institute of Industrial Psychol., 1935–39. Regimental service, The Middlesex Regt, 1940–42; Chief Psychologist, Directorate for Selection of Personnel, War Office, 1942–46. Bureau of Personnel, UN Secretariat, 1946–48; Secretariat, Human Factors Panel, Cttee on Industrial Productivity, 1948–49; Staff Training Section, UN Secretariat, 1950–52; Secretary, Cambridge Univ. Appointments Board, 1952–68; Asst to the Governor, Bank of England, 1968. Director: Portals Holdings Ltd, 1976–83; Portals Water Treatment Ltd, 1983–. FBPsS 1946. Fellow St John's Coll., Cambridge, 1959–68; Dep. Pro-Chancellor, City Univ., 1984–. Hon. DLitt City, 1976. *Publications:* articles in Occupational Psychology and similar journals. *Recreations:* cricket, golf, music. *Address:* 31 Wingate Way, Cambridge. *Clubs:* Royal Automobile, MCC (Pres., 1985–86).

DAVIES, Rev. Jacob Arthur Christian; Assistant Director-General, Regional Representative for Africa, FAO, since 1982; *b* 24 May 1925; *s* of Jacob S. Davies and Christiana; *m* Sylvia Onikeh Cole; two *s* two *d*. *Educ:* Univ. of Reading (BSc 1950); Selwyn Coll., Cambridge; Imperial Coll. of Tropical Agriculture. Permanent Secretary, Min. of Agriculture and Natural Resources, Sierra Leone, 1961–63; Chief Agriculturist, 1962–67; Project Co-manager, UNDP, FAO, 1967–69; Chm., Public Service Commn, 1969–71; Ambassador to USA, 1971–72; High Comr for Sierra Leone in London, 1972–74; Non-resident Ambassador to Denmark, Sweden and Norway, 1972–74; Dep. Dir, Agricl Ops Div., 1974–76, Dir, Personnel Div., 1976–82, FAO. *Recreations:* philately, sports. *Address:* FAO Regional Office for Africa, PO Box 1628, Accra, Ghana.

DAVIES, (James) Brian Meredith, MD, DPH, FFCM; Director of Social Services, City of Liverpool, 1971–81; Hon. Lecturer in (Preventive) Paediatrics, University of Liverpool, 1964–84; *b* 27 Jan. 1920; *s* of late Dr G. Meredith Davies and Caroline Meredith Davies; *m* 1944, Charlotte (*née* Pillar); three *s*. *Educ:* Bedford Sch.; Medical Sch., St Mary's Hosp., London Univ. MB, BS (London) 1943 MD (London) 1948, DPH 1948, MFCM 1972, FFCM 1974. Various hosp. appts. Served War, RAMC, Captain, 1944–47. Asst MOH, Lancashire CC, 1948–50; Dep. MOH, City of Oxford, 1950–53; Clin. Asst (infectious Diseases), United Oxford Hosps, 1950–53; Dep. MOH, 1953–69, Dir of Personal Health and Social Services, 1969–71, City of Liverpool; pt-time Lectr in Public Health, Liverpool Univ., 1953–71. Chm., Liverpool div., BMA, 1958–59; Council of Europe Fellowship, to study Elderly: in Finland, Sweden, Norway and Denmark, 1964 (report awarded special prize); Mem. Public Health Laboratory Service Bd, 1966–71. Teaching Gp of Soc. of Community Med. (Sec. of Gp, 1958–72, Pres. Gp, 1972–73). Member: Personal Social Services Council, 1978–80; Mental Health Review Tribunal, Mersey Area, 1982–. Governor, Occupational Therapy Coll., Huyton, Liverpool, 1969–85; Dir of MERIT (Merseyside Industrial Therapy Services Ltd), 1970–75; Mem. Council, Queen's Inst. of District Nursing, 1971–78; Assoc. of Dirs of Social Services: Chm., NW Br., 1971–73; Mem. Exec. Council, 1973–78; Pres. 1976–77; Mem. Exec. Cttee of Central Council for the Disabled, 1972–76; Adviser to Social Services Cttee of Assoc. of Metropolitan Authorities, 1974–81; Member: RCP Cttee on Rheumatism and Rehabilitation, 1974–83; DES Cttee of Enquiry into Special Educn for Disabled Children, 1975–78; Exec. Cttee, Liverpool Personal Services Soc., 1973–81; Adv. Panel Inf. Service, Disabled Living

Foundn, 1979–81; UK Steering Cttee, Internat. Year for the Disabled, 1979–80; Jt Cttee on Mobility of Blind and Partially Sighted People, 1980–81; Exec. Cttee, N Regional Assoc. for the Blind, 1980–81. Vice Pres., MIND Appeal, 1978–79. Christopher Kershaw Meml Lectr, London, 1984. Pres., Merseyside Ski Club, 1970–77. Mem. Council, Prospect Hall Coll., 1973–77; Chm., Bd of Governors, William Rathbone Staff Coll., Liverpool, 1961–75. *Publications:* Community Health and Social Services, 1965, 4th edn 1984; Community Health, Preventive Medicine and Social Services, 1966, 5th edn 1983; (contrib.) Going Home, 1981; The Disabled Child and Adult, 1982; (contrib.) Rehabilitation: a practical guide to the management of physical disability in adults, 1987; numerous papers on Public Health, Physically and Mentally Handicapped and various social services, in scientific and other jls. *Recreations:* skiing, golf, fishing, gardening, music. *Address:* Tree Tops, Church Road, Thornton Hough, Wirral, Merseyside. *T:* 051–336 3435. *Clubs:* Royal Over-Seas League; Bromborough Golf; Holyhead Golf.

DAVIES, Janet Mary H.; *see* Hewlett-Davies.

DAVIES, Dame Jean; *see* Lancaster, Dame J.

DAVIES, John; *see* Davies, L. J.

DAVIES, John Alun Emlyn; retired 1977; *b* 4 May 1909; *s* of Robert Emlyn and Mary Davies; *m* 1941, Elizabeth Boshier; three *s*. *Educ:* Ruabon Grammar Sch.; Trinity Coll., Cambridge (Scholar). BA 1st cl. Pts I and II, History Tripos, MA 1984. Called to Bar, Lincoln's Inn, 1936. Served War of 1939–45: DAA&QMG 2nd Parachute Bde, 1943; DAAG 1st Airborne Div., 1944. Joined BoT, 1946; Asst Solicitor, 1963; Principal Asst Solicitor, DTI, 1968–72; Asst Solicitor, Law Commn, 1972–74; part-time Asst, Law Commn, 1974–77. Asst Sec. to Jenkins Cttee on Company Law, 1959–62. *Recreations:* gardening, walking. *Address:* 29 Crescent Road, Sidcup, Kent DA15 7HN. *T:* 01–300 1421. *Club:* Reform.

DAVIES, John Duncan, OBE 1984; DSc, PhD; Director, Polytechnic of Wales, since 1978; *b* 19 March 1929; *s* of Ioan and Gertrude Davies; *m* 1949, Barbara, *d* of Ivor and Alice Morgan; three *d*. *Educ:* Pontardawe School; Treforest School of Mines. BSc, MSc, PhD, DSc, Univ. of London. Junior Engineer, Consulting Engineers, 1949; Site Engineer, Cleveland Bridge Co., 1950–54; Royal Engineers, 1952–53; Design Engineer, Local Authority, 1955–56; Asst Lectr, Manchester Univ., 1957–58; University College, Swansea: Lecturer, 1959; Senior Lecturer, 1965; Reader, 1968; Professor of Civil Engineering, 1971–76; Dean, 1974–76; Principal, West Glamorgan Inst. of Higher Education, 1976–77. Mem., Open University Delegacy, 1978–83. Member: Manpower Services Cttee (Wales), 1980–83; Wales Adv. Bd for Public Sector Higher Educn, 1982–83, 1986–; Council, CNAA, 1985–. *Publications:* contribs to Structural Mechanics. *Address:* Polytechnic of Wales, Treforest, Pontypridd, Mid Glamorgan CF37 1DL. *T:* Pontypridd 405133.

DAVIES, Rev. John Gordon, MA, DD; Edward Cadbury Professor of Theology and Head of Department of Theology, University of Birmingham, 1960–86, now Emeritus; Director of Institute for Study of Worship and Religious Architecture, University of Birmingham, 1962–86; *b* 20 April 1919; *s* of late A. G. Davies and of Mrs Davies, Chester; *m* 1945, Emily Mary Tordoff; one *s* two *d*. *Educ:* King's Sch., Chester; Christ Church, Oxford; Westcott House, Cambridge. Curate of Rotherhithe, Dec. 1943–Sept. 1948; Univ. of Birmingham: Asst Lecturer in Theology, 1948–50; Lecturer, 1950–57; Senior Lecturer, 1957–59; Reader, 1959–60; Dean of Faculty of Arts, 1967–70. BA Oxon., 1942; MA 1945; BD 1946; DD 1956; MA (Official) Birmingham, 1952; Hon. DD St Andrews, 1968. Hereditary Freeman, City of Chester; Brother of Ancient and Worshipful Company of Skinners and Felt Makers. Bampton Lecturer, 1958. Hon. Canon, Birmingham, 1965–86; Canon Emeritus, Birmingham, 1986. Hon. Mem., Guild for Religious Architecture, USA. Conover Memorial Award, New York, 1967. *Publications:* The Theology of William Blake, 1948 (USA 1966); The Origin and Development of Early Christian Church Architecture, 1952 (USA 1953); Daily Life in the Early Church: Studies in the Church Social History of the First Five Centuries, 1952 (repr. 1955); Daily Life of Early Christians, 1953 (trans. as La Vie quotidienne des premiers chrétiens, 1956); Social Life of Early Christians, 1954; The Spirit, the Church, and the Sacraments, 1954 (trans. as Der Heilige Geist, die Kirche, und die Sakramente, 1958); Members One of Another: Aspects of Koinonia, 1958; He Ascended into Heaven: a Study in the History of Doctrine (Bampton Lectures, 1958), 1958 (USA 1958); The Making of the Church, 1960, repr. 1983; Intercommunion, 1961; The Architectural Setting of Baptism, 1962; Holy Week, a Short History, 1963 (USA 1963); The Early Christian Church, 1965 (USA 1965; trans. as La Chiesa delle Origini, 1966; as Origens do Cristianismo, 1967); A Select Liturgical Lexicon, 1965 (USA 1965; trans. as Liturgiskt Handlexikon, 1968); Worship and Mission, 1966 (USA 1967; Japan, 1968); Dialogue with the World, 1967 (trans. as Dialogo con el Mundo, 1967); The Secular Use of Church Buildings, 1968 (USA 1968); Every Day God: encountering the Holy in World and Worship, 1973; Christians, Politics and Violent Revolution, 1976 (USA 1976; trans. as Los Christianos, la Politica y la Revolucion violenta, 1977; Kristendom, Politikk, Vold og Revolusjon, 1979); New Perspectives on Worship Today, 1978 (trans. as Nya perspektiv på gudštjänsten, 1984); Temples, Churches and Mosques: a guide to the appreciation of religious architecture, 1982 (USA 1982); Liturgical Dance: an historical, theological and practical handbook, 1984; *translated editions include:* French, German, Italian, Spanish, Finnish, Japanese, Norwegian, Portuguese, Swedish; *co-author:* An Experimental Liturgy, 1958; translator: Essays on the Lord's Supper, 1958; The Eucharistic Memorial Vol. I, 1960, Vol. II, 1961; Mission in a Dynamic Society, 1968; *editor:* A Dictionary of Liturgy and Worship, 1972; Worship and Dance, 1975; The Recreational Use of Churches, 1978; A New Dictionary of Liturgy and Worship, 1986; *contributor to:* Becoming a Christian, 1954; The Teachers' Commentary, 1955; The Concise Encyclopædia of Living Faiths, 1959; Making the Building Serve the Liturgy, 1962; The Modern Architectural Setting of the Liturgy, 1964; A Manual for Holy Week, 1967; Preface to Christian Studies, 1971; Journal of Theological Studies; Journal of Hellenic Studies; Vigiliae Christianae; Harvard Theological Review; Encyclopædia Britannica; Theologische Realenzyklopädie, etc. *Recreation:* cooking. *Address:* 28 George Road, Edgbaston, Birmingham B15 1PJ. *T:* 021–454 6254.

DAVIES, John Henry Vaughan, CB 1981; Deputy Secretary, Ministry of Agriculture, Fisheries and Food, 1979–81; *b* 15 Sept. 1921; *s* of late Rev. James Henry Davies and Ethel Sarah Davies; *m* 1st, 1950, Dorothy Rosa Mary Levy (marr. diss.); 2nd, 1959, Claire Daphne Bates (marr. diss.); one *d*; 3rd, 1971, Barbara Ann, *o d* of late David L. Davies, Portland, Oregon. *Educ:* Monkton Combe Sch.; Worcester Coll., Oxford (MA). Served Royal Air Force, FO, 1942–46. Entered Ministry of Agriculture and Fisheries as Asst Principal, 1947; Principal, 1951; Asst Sec., 1964; Under Sec., 1970. Chairman, Joint FAO/WHO Codex Alimentarius Commn, 1968–70. *Publications:* contributor to The Country Seat, 1970; articles on architecture. *Recreations:* reading, architecture. *Address:* 17 Cherrywood Drive, SW15 6DS. *T:* 01–789 1529.

DAVIES, Rev. Canon John Howard; Director of Theological and Religious Studies, University of Southampton, since 1981; Canon Theologian of Winchester, since 1981; *b* 19 Feb. 1929; *s* of Jabez Howard and Sarah Violet Davies; *m* 1956, Ina Mary (*d* 1985), *d* of Stanley William and Olive Mary Bubb; three *s* (and one *s* decd). *Educ:* Southall Grammar Sch.; St John's Coll., Cambridge (MA); Westcott House, Cambridge; Univ. of Nottingham (BD); FRCO 1952. Ordained deacon, 1955, priest 1956. Succentor of Derby Cathedral, 1955; Chaplain of Westcott House, 1958; Lectr in Theology, Univ. of Southampton, 1963, Sen. Lectr 1974. *Publication:* A Letter to Hebrews, 1967. *Recreations:* music, architecture, the countryside. *Address:* 13 Glen Eyre Road, Southampton SO2 3GA. *T:* Southampton 769359.

DAVIES, John Howard Gay; Editorial Director, Thomson Regional Newspapers Ltd, 1972–82; *b* 17 Jan. 1923; *er s* of late E. E. Davies, Nicholaston Hall, Gower, Glamorgan; *m* 1st, 1948, Eira Morgan (marr. dissolved, 1953); 2nd, 1955, Betty Walmsley; one *s*. *Educ:* Bromsgrove Sch.; Wadham Coll., Oxford. Welsh Guards, 1942–46 (despatches). Western Mail, 1950–52; Daily Telegraph, 1952–55; Deputy Editor, Western Mail, 1955–58; an Assistant Editor, Sunday Times, 1958–62; Exec. Assistant to Editorial Director, Thomson Newspapers Ltd, 1962–64; Editor, Western Mail, 1964, 1965. *Address:* 41 Chartfield Avenue, SW15. *T:* 01–788 8685.

DAVIES, John Irfon; MBE (mil.) 1963; Under Secretary, Welsh Office, since 1985; *b* 8 June 1930; *s* of Thomas M. Davies and Mary M. Davies (*née* Harris); *m* 1950, Jean Marion Anderson; one *d*. *Educ:* Stanley School; Croydon Polytechnic. psc, awc; Specialist Navigator course. Joined RAF, 1948, commissioned 1950; No 13 Swn, MEAF, 1951; HQ 205 Gp, 1952; No 24 Sqn, 1953–54; staff and flying appts, 1954–66; Chief Navigation Instructor, Cranwell, 1967; OC Flying, Muharraq, 1967–69; MoD, 1970–72; Cabinet Office, 1972–74; Principal, Welsh Office, 1974, Asst Sec., 1978. *Recreations:* golf, piano, fishing, books. *Address:* Friston, 15 Windsor Road, Radyr, Cardiff. *T:* Cardiff 842617. *Clubs:* Royal Air Force; Radyr Golf.

DAVIES, Prof. John Kenyon, MA , DPhil; FBA 1985; Rathbone Professor of Ancient History and Classical Archaeology, since 1977, and Pro-Vice-Chancellor, since 1986, University of Liverpool; *b* 19 Sept. 1937; *s* of Harold Edward Davies and Clarice Theresa (*née* Woodburn); *m* 1st, 1962, Anna Elbina Morpurgo (*see* Anna Elbina Davies) (marr. diss. 1978); 2nd, 1978, Nicola Jane, *d* of Dr and Mrs R. M. S. Perrin; one *s* one *d*. *Educ:* Manchester Grammar Sch.; Wadham Coll., Oxford (BA 1959; MA 1962; DPhil 1966). Harmsworth Sen. Scholar, Merton Coll., Oxford, 1960–61 and 1962–63; Jun. Fellow, Center for Hellenic Studies, Washington, DC, 1961–62; Dyson Jun. Res. Fellow, Balliol Coll., Oxford, 1963–65; Lectr in Ancient History, Univ. of St Andrews, 1965–68; Fellow and Tutor in Ancient History, Oriel Coll., Oxford, 1968–77. Vis. Lectr, Univ. of Pennsylvania, 1971. Chairman: St Patrick's Isle (IOM) Archaeological Trust Ltd, 1982–; NW Archaeol Trust, 1982–. Editor: Jl of Hellenic Studies, 1972–77; Archaeol Reports, 1972–74. *Publications:* Athenian Propertied Families 600–300 BC, 1971; Democracy and Classical Greece, 1978 (Spanish trans. 1981, German and Italian trans. 1983); Wealth and the Power of Wealth in Classical Athens, 1981; (ed with L. Foxhall) The Trojan War: its historicity and context, 1984; articles and reviews in learned jls. *Recreation:* choral singing. *Address:* 39 Holmefield Road, Aigburth, Liverpool L19 3PE. *T:* 051–427 2126.

DAVIES, John Michael; Principal Clerk, Private Bill and Overseas Offices, and Examiner of Petitions for Private Bills, House of Lords, since 1985; *b* 2 Aug. 1940; *s* of Vincent Ellis Davies and Rose Trench (*née* Temple); *m* 1971, Amanda Mary Atkinson; two *s* one *d*. *Educ:* The King's Sch., Canterbury; Peterhouse, Cambridge. Joined Parliament Office, House of Lords, 1964; seconded to Civil Service Dept as Private Sec. to Leader of House of Lords and Govt Chief Whip, 1971–74; Establishment Officer and Sec. to Chm. of Cttees, 1974–83; Principal Clerk, Overseas and European Office, H o L, 1983–85. Secretary: Soc. of Clerks-at-the-Table in Commonwealth Parlts, and Jt Editor, The Table, 1967–83; Statute Law Cttee, 1974–83. *Address:* 26 Northchurch Terrace, N1 4EG.

DAVIES, J(ohn) R(obert) Lloyd, CMG 1953; *b* 24 March 1913; *o s* of late J. R. and Mrs Davies, Muswell Hill; *m* 1st, 1943, Margery (*née* McClelland), Nottingham (*d* 1978); one *s* one *d*; 2nd, 1982, Grace, *widow* of Frederick Reynolds, Bethesda, Md, USA. *Educ:* Highgate Sch.; Oriel Coll., Oxford. Served War of 1939–45: Royal Navy; Lieut RNVR; Asst Sec., Dept of Employment; Labour Counsellor, Paris and Washington, FCO. Part-time Teacher, Working Men's Coll., London, 1970–. *Recreations:* key-board music, reading. *Address:* 59 Elm Park Court, Pinner, Middlesex. *Club:* United Oxford & Cambridge University.

DAVIES, Prof. John Tasman, PhD, DSc London; MA, ScD Cantab; Professor of Chemical Engineering and Head of Department, University of Birmingham, 1960–83, Research Professor since 1983; *b* 1 May 1924; *m* 1948, Ruth Batt; two *s*. *Educ:* Boys' High Sch., Christchurch, NZ; Canterbury University Coll.; London Univ. MA Cantab. 1955; PhD London 1949; DSc London 1955; ScD Cantab 1967. Worked with Sir Eric Rideal, FRS, Royal Institution London, 1946–48; Research Associate and Bristol-Myers Fellow, Stanford Univ., Calif. (USA) (worked with late Prof. J. W. McBain, FRS), 1948–49; Beit Mem. Fellow for Medical Research, Royal Instn and KCL, 1949–52; Lectr in: Chemistry, KCL, 1952–55; Chemical Engineering, Cambridge Univ., 1955–60. Overseas guest lecturer at Gordon Conference, USA, 1956, 1980. Visiting Professor: Univ. of Minnesota, 1963; Univ. of Auckland, NZ, 1976, 1980. Member: UN Consultative Commn to Indian Inst. of Petroleum, 1967–71; UNESCO Advisory Group on Petroleum Technology, Arab States, 1967; (part-time) West Midlands Gas Board, 1968–72. Member Sigma-Xi, 1949 (USA), FIChemE. *Publications:* (with Sir Eric Rideal, FRS) Interfacial Phenomena, 1961; The Scientific Approach, 1965, 2nd edn 1973; Turbulence Phenomena, 1972; many on Surface Phenomena and Chemical Engineering. *Address:* Department of Chemical Engineering, The University, Birmingham B15 2TT. *T:* 021–472 1301.

DAVIES, Joseph Marie, QC 1962; **His Honour Judge J. M. Davies;** a Circuit Judge (formerly Judge of County Courts), since 1971; *b* 13 Jan. 1916; *s* of Joseph and Mary Davies, St Helen's; *m* 1948, Eileen Mary (*née* Dromgoole); two *s* two *d*. *Educ:* Stonyhurst Coll.; Liverpool Univ. Called to Bar, Gray's Inn, Nov. 1938; practice in Liverpool. Recorder of Birmingham, 1970–71; Cumberland Co. QS: Dep. Chm., 1956–63, 1970–71; Chm., 1963–70. Served War of 1939–45; The King's Regt, Nov. 1939–Dec. 1941; RIASC and Staff Allied Land Forces, SE Asia, 1942–46. *Address:* 4 Elm Grove, Eccleston Park, Prescot, Lancs. *T:* 051–426 5415. *Clubs:* Athenæum (Liverpool); Cumberland County.

DAVIES, Keith Laurence M.; *see* Maitland Davies.

DAVIES, Kenneth; *see* Davies, S. K.

DAVIES, Kenneth Arthur, CMG 1952; OBE 1946; *b* 28 Jan. 1897; *s* of William and Alice Davies; *m* 1932, Edna Myfanwy, *d* of Rev. T. Rowlands; one *s*. *Educ:* Pontypridd Grammar Sch.; University Coll., Wales, Aberystwyth; Trinity Coll., Cambridge. Served European War, 1914–18, with RFA in France and Belgium, 1916–19; 1st Class Hons Geology BSc, University Coll., Aberystwyth. Research Scholar, 1923–26; Fellow of University of Wales, 1926; MSc 1925; PhD (Cantab.), 1928. Field Geologist, Govt of Uganda, 1929; Senior Geologist, 1936; Director, Geological Survey, 1939, retired 1951. Adviser on Mineral Development to Uganda Govt, 1952–54 and 1965; Commonwealth

Geological Liaison Officer, 1954. Dep.-Dir Overseas Geological Surveys, 1957–65. Adviser to United Nations, 1966. Fellow, Geological Society, 1928; FIMM 1950. Murchison Medallist, Geological Society, 1954. *Publications:* various on Stratigraphy of Central Wales and graptolites in British Geological journals, and on African Geology in British and American journals. *Recreation:* gardening. *Address:* Park Cottage, 36 Somerset Road, SW19.

DAVIES, Sir Lancelot Richard B.; *see* Bell Davies.

DAVIES, (Lewis) John, QC 1967; **His Honour Judge John Davies;** a Circuit Judge (Official Referee), since 1984; *b* 15 April 1921; *s* of William Davies, JP, and Esther Davies; *m* 1956, Janet Mary Morris; one *s* two *d. Educ:* Pontardawe Grammar Sch.; University College of Wales, Aberystwyth; Trinity Hall (Common Law Prizeman, 1943; Scholar, 1943–44), Cambridge. LLB Wales 1942 (1st cl.); BA Cantab (1st cl.); LLB Cantab (1st cl.). Asst Principal, HM Treasury, 1945–46; Senior Law Lecturer, Leeds Univ., 1946–48; Administrative Asst, British Petroleum, 1949–52. Called to the Bar, Middle Temple, 1948, Bencher, 1973; a Recorder, 1974–84. Mem., Bar Council, 1969–71; Mem., Senate, 1976–78. Mem., Council of Legal Educn, 1976–79. Inspector, DoT, 1977. *Recreations:* gardening, golf. *Address:* Old Manor Cottage, 24 Park Road, Teddington, Mddx. *T:* 01–977 3975. *Club:* Travellers'.

DAVIES, Lewis Mervyn, CMG 1966; CBE 1984 (OBE 1962); HM Overseas Civil Service, retired; *b* 5 Dec. 1922; *s* of late Rev. Canon L. C. Davies; *m* 1st, 1950, Ione Podger (*d* 1973); one *s*; 2nd, 1975, Mona A. Birley; two step *s. Educ:* St Edward's Sch., Oxford. Served with Fleet Air Arm, 1941–46: Lieut A, RNVR. District Commissioner, Gold Coast, 1948; Western Pacific: Senior Asst Secretary, 1956–62; Financial Secretary, 1962–65; Chief Secretary, 1965–70; Deputy Governor, Bahamas, 1970–73; Secretary for Security, Hong Kong, 1973–82; Secretary (Gen. Duties), Hong Kong, 1983–85. Lay Canon, Cathedral Church of St Barnabas, Honiara, 1965–70. Commandeur de l'Ordre National du Mérite, 1966. *Recreations:* sailing, tennis. *Address:* Apartado 123, Felanitx, Mallorca, Spain. *Clubs:* Oriental, Royal Commonwealth Society; Vall D'or Golf; Bosham Sailing, Royal Hong Kong Yacht.

DAVIES, Lloyd; *see* Davies, J. R. L.

DAVIES, Col Lucy Myfanwy, CBE 1968 (OBE 1962); Deputy Controller Commandant, WRAC, 1967–77; *b* 8 April 1913; *d* of late Col A. M. O. Anwyl-Passingham, CBE, DL, JP, and late Margaret Anwyl-Passingham; *m* 1955, Major D. W. Davies, TD, RAMC (*d* 1959); no *c. Educ:* Francis Holland Graham Street Sch. Driver FANY, 1939; commnd ATS, 1941; served in Egypt, 1945–48; Asst Director, WRAC Middle East (Cyprus), 1957–59; Comdt WRAC Depot, 1961–64; Dep. Director WRAC, 1964–68; retired, 1968. An underwriting Member of Lloyd's, 1971–. OStJ 1938. *Recreations:* travel, racing, reading. *Address:* 6 Elm Place, SW7. *T:* 01–373 5731. *Clubs:* Aspinall Curzon House; Lingfield Park.

DAVIES, Marcus John A.; *see* Anwyl-Davies.

DAVIES, Meredith; *see* Davies, Albert Meredith.

DAVIES, Hon. Sir Mervyn; *see* Davies, Hon. Sir D. H. M.

DAVIES, Hon. Sir Michael; *see* Davies, Hon. Sir A. W. M.

DAVIES, Michael; *see* Davies, A. M.

DAVIES, Prof. (Morgan Wynn) Humphrey, LLM, MSc; CEng, FIEE; FCGI; Professor of Electrical Engineering, Queen Mary College, University of London, 1956–79, now Emeritus (Fellow of the College, 1984); *b* 26 Dec. 1911; *s* of late Richard Humphrey Davies, CB; *m* 1944, Gwendolen Enid, *d* of late Canon Douglas Edward Morton, Camborne, Cornwall; one *s. Educ:* Westminster Sch.; University College of N Wales, Bangor; Charlottenburg Technische Hochschule, Berlin. Grad. Apprentice with Metropolitan-Vickers, 1933; Lecturer in Electrical Engineering, University of Wales, 1935–42; Commonwealth Fellow, Mass Inst. of Technol., 1938–39; Education Officer to Instn of Electrical Engineers, 1944–47; Lecturer, 1947, and University Reader, 1952, in Electrical Engineering, Imperial Coll., University of London, 1947–56; Dean of Engrg, Univ. of London, 1976–79. Member: Council, IEE, 1948–51, 1958–61 (Chm., Science and Gen. Div. 1964–65). Council, City & Guilds of London Inst., 1952–62; Engineering Adv. Cttee, BBC, 1965–71; Computer Bd for Univs and Res. Councils, 1968–71; Council, University Coll. of N Wales, Bangor, 1976– (Chm., Finance and GP Cttee, 1981–); Chm., Bd of Univ. of London Computer Centre, 1968–79. Hon. DSc Wales, 1985. *Publications:* Power System Analysis (with J. R. Mortlock), 1952; papers in Proc. of Instn of Electrical Engineers. *Recreation:* travel. *Address:* Church Bank, Beaumaris, Anglesey LL58 8AB. *Club:* Athenæum.

DAVIES, Neil; *see* Davies, W. M. N.

DAVIES, Nigel; *see* Davies, Claude N. B.

DAVIES, (Norah) Olwen, MA; Headmistress, St Swithun's School, Winchester, 1973–86; *b* 21 March 1926; *d* of late Rev. and Mrs E. A. Davies. *Educ:* Tregaron County Sch.; Walthamstow Hall, Sevenoaks; Edinburgh Univ. (MA). DipEd Oxon. Staff of Girls' Remand Home, Essex, 1948–50; Russell Hill Sch., Purley, 1950–53; Woodford House, NZ, 1953–57 (Dep. Headmistress); Westonbirt Sch., 1957–65; Headmistress, St Mary's Hall, Brighton, 1965–73. Pres., Girls' Schools Association, 1981–82. Governor: Hurstpierpoint Coll.; Tormead Sch., Guildford; St John's Special Sch., Brighton; St Michael's Sch., Petworth. *Address:* 28 Arle Gardens, Alresford, Hants.

DAVIES, Col Norman Thomas, MBE 1970; JP; Registrar, General Dental Council, since 1981; *b* 2 May 1933; *s* of late Edward Ernest Davies and of Elsie Davies (*née* Scott); *m* 1961, Penelope Mary, *e d* of Peter Graeme Agnew, *qv*; one *s* one *d. Educ:* Holywell; RMA, Sandhurst; Open Univ. (BA 1979). Commnd RA, 1954; Regtl and Staff Appts, Malaya, Germany and UK, 1954–64; ptsc 1966; psc 1967; Mil. Asst to C of S Northern Army Gp, 1968–69; Commanded C Bty RHA and 2IC 3RHA, 1970–72; GSOI (DS), Staff Coll., Camberley, and Canadian Land Forces Comd and Staff Coll., 1972–74; Commanded 4 Field Regt, RA, 1975–77; Mil. Dir of Studies, RMCS, Shrivenham, 1977–80. Mem., EEC Adv. Cttee on the Training of Dental Practitioners, 1983–. JP Hants, 1984. *Recreations:* golf, gardening, wine. *Address:* Lowfields Cottage, London Road, Hartley Wintney, Hants RG27 8HY. *T:* Hartley Wintney 3303.

DAVIES, Olwen; *see* Davies, N. O.

DAVIES, Sir Oswald, Kt 1984; CBE 1973; DCM 1944; JP; Director, AMEC plc (holding company of Fairclough Construction Group and William Press Group), since 1982 (Chairman, 1982–84); *b* 23 June 1920; *s* of George Warham Davies and Margaret (*née* Hinton); *m* 1942, Joyce Eaton; one *s* one *d. Educ:* Central Schs, Sale; Manchester Coll. of Technology. FIHT, FCIOB, FFB; CBIM; FRGS; FRSA. Served War of 1939–45: Sapper, bomb disposal squad, RE, Europe and ME, from 1940 (DCM (ME) 1944); returned to Europe, where involved with his unit in clearance of waterways, port, docks and bridge reconstruction. Dir, 1948–, Jt Man. Dir, 1951, Chm., 1965–83, Fairclough Construction Group plc (formerly Leonard Fairclough Ltd). Director: Wentworth Club Ltd; Wentworth Estates Ltd; Lindgray (Wentworth) Ltd; Fairport Engrg Ltd; Power Securities Ltd; William Press Group, plc; Amec Investments Ltd; Atlantic Services Ltd. JP 1969. *Recreations:* gardening, Rugby football, sport. *Address:* (office) Sandiway House, Northwich, Cheshire CW8 2YA. *T:* Northwich 883885.

DAVIES, Oswald Vaughan L.; *see* Lloyd-Davies.

DAVIES, Patrick Taylor, CMG 1978; OBE 1967; HM Overseas Civil Service, retired; *b* 10 Aug. 1927; *s* of Andrew Taylor Davies and Olive Kathleen Mary Davies; *m* 1959, Marjorie Eileen (*née* Wilkinson); two *d. Educ:* Shrewsbury Sch.; St John's Coll., Cambridge (BA); Trinity Coll., Oxford. Lieut, RA, Nigeria, 1945–48. Colonial Admin. Service, Nigeria, 1952; Permanent Sec., Kano State, 1970; Chief Inspector, Area Courts, Kano State, 1972–79. *Address:* Rose Cottage, Childs Ercall, Salop TF9 2DB. *T:* Childs Ercall 255.

DAVIES, (Percy) Douglas, CB 1981; *b* 17 Sept. 1921; *s* of late Mr and Mrs Thomas Davies; *m* 1947, Renée Margaret Billings; one *s* one *d. Educ:* Liverpool Collegiate School. Clerical Officer, Ministry of Transport, 1938; served Royal Armoured Corps, 1941–46; Chief Executive Officer, Min. of Transport, 1963; Asst Secretary, 1966; Principal Establishment Officer, Under Secretary, Property Services Agency, Dept of the Environment, 1972–81. Chm., Council of Management, London Hostels Assoc., 1983–. *Recreations:* gardening, making things work. *Address:* 37 Byron Avenue, Coulsdon, Surrey CR3 2JS. *T:* 01–660 2789.

DAVIES, Peter; *see* Davies, R. P. H.

DAVIES, Peter Douglas Royston; HM Diplomatic Service; Royal College of Defence Studies, 1986; *b* 29 Nov. 1936; *e s* of Douglas and Edna Davies; *m* 1967, Elizabeth Mary Lovett Williams; one *s* two *d. Educ:* Brockenhurst County High Sch.; LSE (BSc(Econ)). Joined HM Diplomatic Service, 1964; FO, 1964–66; Second Sec., Nicosia, 1966–67; FO, 1967–68; First Sec., Budapest, 1968–71; FCO, 1971–74; Consul (Commercial), Rio de Janeiro, 1974–78; Counsellor (Commercial), The Hague, 1978–82; Dep. High Comr, Kuala Lumpur, 1983–85. *Address:* c/o Foreign and Commonwealth Office, SW1A 2AH. *Club:* Royal Commonwealth Society.

DAVIES, Peter George; Director General, National Association of British and Irish Millers, since 1984; *b* 7 April 1927; *s* of George Llewellyn Davies and Alicia (*née* Galloway); *m* 1952, Norma Joyce Brown; one *s* two *d. Educ:* London School of Economics and Political Science. BSc Econ, 1st Class Hons 1948. Editorial Asst, News Chronicle, 1950–53; Deputy City Editor, The Times, 1953–55; HM Treasury, 1955; Asst Sec., Fiscal Policy Group, 1975–78; Press Sec. to Chancellor of the Exchequer and Head of Information, 1978–80; Under Secretary 1980; seconded to NEDO as Sec. to NEDC and Administrative Dir, 1980–82. Fellow Commoner, Downing College, Cambridge, 1982–83. *Recreations:* walking, music, theatre. *Club:* Travellers'.

DAVIES, Peter Maxwell, CBE 1981; composer; *b* 8 Sept. 1934; *s* of Thomas and Hilda Davies. *Educ:* Leigh Grammar Sch.; Manchester Univ. (MusB (Hons) 1956); Royal Manchester Coll. of Music. FRNCM 1978. Studied with Goffredo Petrassi in Rome (schol. 1957); Harkness Fellow, Grad. Music Sch., Princetown Univ., NJ, 1962. Dir of Music, Cirencester Grammar Sch., 1959–62; lecture tours in Europe, Australia, NZ, USA, Canada and Brazil; Visiting Composer, Adelaide Univ., 1966; Founder and Co-Dir, with Harrison Birtwistle, of Pierrot Players, 1967–70; Prof. of Composition, Royal Northern Coll. of Music, 1975–80; Founder and Artistic Director: The Fires of London, 1971–; St Magnus Fest., Orkney Is, 1977–86; Artistic Dir, Dartington Hall Summer Sch. of Music, 1979–84; Associate Conductor/Composer, Scottish Chamber Orch., 1985–. Pres., Schs Music Assoc., 1983–. Series for Schools Broadcasts, BBC Television. Hon. Member: RAM, 1978; Guildhall Sch. of Music and Drama, 1981; Hon. DMus: Edinburgh, 1979; Manchester, 1983; Bristol, 1984; Hon. DL Aberdeen, 1981. *Compositions* (majority published): 1952: Quartet Movement, for string quartet; 1955: Trumpet Sonata; 1956: Five Pieces for Piano; Stedman Doubles, for clarinet and percussion, rev. 1968; 1957: Clarinet Sonata; St Michael Sonata, for wind instruments; Alma Redemptoris Mater, for wind instruments; 1958: Sextet; Prolation, for orch.; 1959: Five Motets, for soloists, double choir and instruments; Ricercar and Doubles on 'To Many a Well', for instrumental ensemble; Five Klee Pictures, for orch., rev. 1976; William Byrd, Three Dances, arranged for orch.; 1960: O Magnum Mysterium, for unaccompanied voices with two instrumental sonatas and organ fantasia; Five Voluntaries, for orch.; 1961: Ave Maria, Hail Blessed Flower (carol); Te Lucis Ante Terminum, for Voices and instrumental ensemble; String Quartet; 1962: First Fantasia on an In Nomine of John Taverner, for orch. (commnd by BBC); Leopardi Fragments, for soloists and instrumental ensemble; Sinfonia, for chamber orch.; The Lord's Prayer, for unaccompanied voices; Four Carols, for unaccompanied voices; 1963: Veni Sancte Spiritus, for soloists, chorus and orch.; 1964: Second Fantasia on John Taverner's In Nomine, for orch.; Shakespeare Music, for chamber ensemble; Ave, Plena Gracia, for voices with optional organ; 1964–65: Seven In Nomine, for instrumental ensemble; 1965: Ecce Manus Tradentis, for soloists, chorus and instrumental ensemble; The Shepherd's Calendar, for young singers and instrumentalists; Revelation and Fall, for soprano and instruments; Shall I Die for Mannis Sake?, carol for soloists and piano; 1966: Five Carols, for unaccompanied soprano and alto; Notre Dame des Fleurs, for soloists and instrumental ensemble; Solita, for flute with musical box; 1967: Hymnos, for clarinet and piano; Antechrist, for chamber ensemble; Five Little Pieces for Piano; 1968: Missa super l'Homme Armé, for speaker or singer and instrumental ensemble, rev. 1971; Stedman Caters, for instrumental ensemble; Purcell, Fantasia on a Ground and Two Pavanes, realisation for instrumental ensemble; 1969: Eight Songs for a Mad King, for male voice and instrumental ensemble; St Thomas Wake, foxtrot for orch. on a pavane by John Bull (commnd by City of Dortmund); Worldes Blis, for och.; Eram Quasi Agnus, instrumental motet; Gabrielli, Canzona realisation for chamber ensemble; Vesalii Icones, for dancer, 'cello and instrumental ensemble; 1970: Taverner (opera); Points and Dances from Taverner, instrumental dances and keyboard pieces from the opera; Sub Tuam Protectionem, for piano; Ut Re Mi, for piano; 1971: From Stone to Thorn, for mezzo-soprano and instrumental ensemble; Bell Tower, for percussion; Buxtehude, Also Hat Gott Die Welt Geliebet, cantata for soprano and instrumental ensemble; Suite from film, The Devils; Suite from film, The Boyfriend; 1972: Blind Man's Buff, masque for voices, mime and orch.; Fool's Fanfare, for speaker and instrumental ensemble; Hymn to St Magnus, for instrumental ensemble with mezzo-soprano obligate; Tenebrae super Gesualdo, for mezzo-soprano, guiter and instrumental ensemble; Canon In Memoriam Igor Stravinsky, puzzle canon for instrumental ensemble; Lullabye for Ilian Rainbow, for guitar; J. S. Bach, Prelude and Fugue in C Sharp Minor, realisation for instrumental ensemble; Dunstable, Veni Sancte Spiritus—Veni Creator Spiritus, realisation for instrumental ensemble; 1973: Stone Litany—Runes from a House of the Dead, for mezzo-soprano and orch.; Renaissance Scottish Dances, for instrumental ensemble; Si Quis Diliget Me, motet arranged for instrumental ensemble; Purcell, Fantasia on One Note, realisation for instrumental ensemble; 1973–74; Fiddlers at the Wedding, for mezzo-soprano and instrumental ensemble; 1974: Dark Angels, for Voice and guitar; Miss Donnithorne's Maggot, for mezzo-soprano and instrumental ensemble; All Sons of Adam, motet arranged for instrumental ensemble; Psalm 124, motet arranged for instrumental ensemble; J. S. Bach, Prelude and Fugue in C Sharp Major, realisation for instrumental ensemble; 1975: The Door of the Sun, for viola; The Kestrel Paced Round the Sun, for flute; The Seven Brightnesses, for clarinet; Three Studies for Percussion; My Lady Lothian's Lilte, for instrumental ensemble with obligato; Stevie's Ferry to Hoy, for piano; Ave Maris Stella, for chamber ensemble; 1976: The Blind Fiddler, for soprano and chamber ensemble; Three Organ Voluntaries; Kinloche his Fantassie, realisation for instrumental ensemble; Anakreontika (Greek songs); The Blind Fiddler, song cycle for soprano and instrumental ensemble; Symphony No 1; The Martyrdom of St Magnus (chamber opera); 1977: Norn Pater Noster, prayer for voices and organ; Westerlings, for unaccompanied voices; Runes from a Holy Island, for instrumental ensemble; A Mirror of Whitening Light, for instrumental ensemble; Ave Rex Angelorum, for unaccompanied voices or with organ; Our Father Which In Heaven Art, motet arranged for instrumental ensemble; 1978: The Two Fiddlers (opera); Le Jongleur de Notre Dame, masque for mime, baritone, chamber ensemble and children's band; Salome (ballet score); Four Lessons, for two clavichords; Dances from The Two Fiddlers, for instrumental ensemble; 1979: Kirkwall Shopping Songs, for young children; Solstice of Light, for soloists, chorus and organ; Black Pentecost, for soloists and orch.; The Lighthouse (opera); Nocturne, for alto flute; 1980: Cinderella, pantomime opera for young people to perform; Symphony No 2; The Yellow Cake Review, for voice and piano; Farewell to Stromness, piano interlude from The Yellow Cake Review; Yesnaby Ground, piano interlude from The Yellow Cake Review; A Welcome to Orkney, for instrumental ensemble; Little Quartet, string quartet for young musicians; 1981: The Medium, monodrama for mezzo-soprano; Piano Sonata; The Rainbow, for young children to perform; Hill Runes, for guitar; The Bairns of Brugh, for chamber ensemble; Little Quartet No 2, string quartet for young musicians; Tenor Arias from The Martyrdom of St Magnus, for tenor, piano or organ; Lullabye for Lucy, for soloists; Brass Quintet; Seven Songs Home, for unaccompanied children's voices; 1982: Songs of Hoy, masque for children's voices and instruments; Sea Eagle, for horn; Image, Reflection, Shadow, for instrumental ensemble; Sinfonia Concertante, for chamber orch.; Organ Sonata; Tallis, Four Voluntaries, arranged for brass quintet (also arranged for brass band); Gesualdo, Two Motets, arranged for brass quintet (also arranged for brass band); The Pole Star, march for brass quintet (also for brass band); 1983: Birthday Music for John, trio for flute, viola and 'cello; Into the Labyrinth, cantata for tenor and chamber orch.; Sinfonietta Accademica, for chamber orch.; 1984: Agnus Dei, for sopranos, viola and 'cello; Sonatine, for violin and cymbalom; Unbroken Circle, for instrumental ensemble; The Number 11 Bus, music theatre work; Guitar Sonata; One Star, At Last, carol for soloists; Symphony No 3; 1985: An Orkney Wedding, With Sunrise, for orch.; First Ferry to Hoy, for chamber ensemble, children's chorus, percussion and recorders; The Peat Cutters, for brass band and youth choir; Violin Concerto. *Address:* c/o Mrs Judy Arnold, 50 Hogarth Road, SW5.

DAVIES, Maj.-Gen. Philip Middleton, OBE 1975; retired; Joint Managing Director, United Aircraft Industries Ltd, since 1986; *b* 27 Oct. 1932; *s* of Mrs C. H. Allen (*née* Tickler); *m* 1956, Mona Wallace; two *d*. *Educ:* Charterhouse; RMA, Sandhurst. Commnd Royal Scots, 1953; served Korea, Canal Zone, Cyprus, Suez, Berlin, Libya 1st Bn Royal Scots, 1953–63; Staff Coll., 1963; National Defence Coll., 1971; commanded: 1st Bn Royal Scots, 1973–76; 19 Bde/7 Fd Force, 1977–79; RCDS, 1980; comd Land Forces, Cyprus, 1981–83; GOC NW Dist, 1983–86. *Recreations:* fishing, gardening. *Clubs:* Army and Navy, Ebury Court.

DAVIES, Rhys Everson, QC 1981; a Recorder of the Crown Court, since 1980; *b* 13 Jan. 1941; *s* of late Evan Davies and Nancy Caroline Davies; *m* 1963, Katharine Anne Yeates; one *s* one *d*. *Educ:* Cowbridge Grammar School; Neath Grammar School; Victoria University of Manchester. LLB (Hons). Called to the Bar, Gray's Inn, 1964. On Northern Circuit. *Recreations:* music, conversation. *Address:* (chambers) 18 St John Street, Manchester M3 4EA. *T:* 061-834 9843.

DAVIES, Sir Richard Harries, KCVO 1984 (CVO 1982); CBE 1962; BSc, CEng, FIEE; an Extra Equerry to the Duke of Edinburgh, since 1984; *b* 28 June 1916; *s* of Thomas Henry Davies and Minnie Oakley (*née* Morgan); *m* 1st, 1944, Hon. Nan (*d* 1976), *e d* of 1st Baron Macpherson of Drumochter; two *s* two *d*; 2nd, 1979, Mrs Patricia P. Ogier. *Educ:* Porth County Sch.; Cardiff Technical Coll. Scientific Civil Service, 1939–46; British Air Commn, Washington, DC, 1941–45; Vice Pres., Ferranti Electric Inc., New York, 1948–63; Dir, Ferranti Ltd, 1970–76. Duke of Edinburgh's Household: Asst Private Sec., 1977–82; Treasurer, 1982–84. Pres., British Amer. Chamber of Commerce, New York, 1959–62; Vice Pres., Manchester Chamber of Commerce, 1976. *Recreations:* gardening, sailing, amateur radio. *Address:* Haven House, Thorpeness, Suffolk. *T:* Aldeburgh 3603. *Clubs:* Athenæum, Pratt's.

DAVIES, Robert David, CB 1982; CVO 1977; RD 1963; JP; Director, Office of the Premier, Department of the Premier and Cabinet, Western Australia, 1983; Clerk of Executive Council, 1975–83, retired; *b* 17 Aug. 1927; *s* of late William Harold Davies and of Elsie Davies; *m* 1948, Muriel Patricia Cuff; one *s* one *d*. *Educ:* Fremantle Boys High Sch.; Perth Technical Coll. Senior AASA. Defence Service, 1945–47; Asst Commissioner, State Taxation Dept, 1973; Under Sec., Premier's Dept, WA, 1975. Comdr, RANR, 1972. JP 1970. *Recreations:* fishing, sailing. *Address:* 82 Reynolds Road, Mount Pleasant, Western Australia 6153. *T:* 364–1596. *Clubs:* East Fremantle Football, Fremantle Sailing (Western Australia).

DAVIES, Rt. Rev. Robert Edward, CBE 1981; MA, ThD; *b* Birkenhead, England, 30 July 1913; *s* of late R. A. Davies, Canberra; *m* 1953, Helen M., *d* of H. M. Boucher; two *d*. *Educ:* Cessnock High School; Queensland University; St John's Theological College, Morpeth, NSW. Assistant Priest, Christ Church Cathedral, Newcastle, NSW, 1937–41. War of 1939–45: Toc H Army Chaplain, 1941–42; Chaplain, Royal Australian Air Force, Middle East and Mediterranean, 1942–46. Vice-Warden, St John's College, University of Queensland, Brisbane, 1946–48; Archdeacon of Canberra and Rector of Canberra, 1949–53; Archdeacon of Wagga Wagga, NSW, 1953–60; Assistant Bishop of Newcastle and Warden of St John's Theological College, Morpeth, NSW, 1960–63; Bishop of Tasmania, 1963–81. *Recreations:* golf, tennis. *Address:* 12 Elboden Street, Hobart, Tasmania 7000, Australia. *Clubs:* Tasmanian, Naval Military and Air Force of Tas. (Tas.).

DAVIES, Prof. Robert Ernest, FRS 1966; Benjamin Franklin Professor of Molecular Biology and University Professor, University of Pennsylvania, since 1977, and Chairman, Research Advisory Board, Institute for Environmental Medicine, School of Medicine, since 1970; *b* 17 Aug. 1919; *s* of William Owen Davies and Stella Davies; *m* 1961, Helen C. (*née* Rogoff); two step *s*. *Educ:* Manchester Grammar Sch.; Univ. of Manchester and Univ. of Sheffield. BSc(Chem.) Manchester, 1941; MSc Manchester 1942; PhD Sheffield 1949; DSc Manchester 1952; MA Oxon 1956; MA Penn 1971. Temp. Asst Lectr in Chemistry, Univ. of Sheffield. Half-time research (Ministry of Supply, Chemical Defence Research Dept), 1942; full-time research on temp. staff, Medical Research Unit for Research in Cell Metabolism, 1945; apptd to Estab. Staff of MRC, 1947; Hon. Lectr in

Biochemistry, Univ. of Sheffield, 1948–54; Vis. Prof., Pharmakologisches Inst., Univ. Heidelberg, March-May 1954; University of Pennsylvania, 1955–: Prof. of Biochemistry, Sch. of Medicine, 1955–62, Grad. Sch. of Medicine, 1962–70; Prof. of Molecular Biology, 1970–77; Chm., Dept of Animal Biology, Sch. of Vet. Medicine, 1962–73; Chm., Grad. Group Cttee on Molecular Biology, 1962–72. Chm., Benjamin Franklin Professors, 1978–; Mem., Bd of Dirs, Assoc. for Women in Science Educnl Foundn, 1978–. Hon. Life Mem., NY Acad. of Scis. *Publications:* very many: in chemistry, biochemistry, physiolog. and biology journals concerning secretion, muscle contraction, kidneys, etc. *Recreations:* mountaineering, caving, underwater swimming, white water boating. *Address:* Department of Animal Biology, School of Veterinary Medicine, University of Pennsylvania, Philadelphia, Pa 19104, USA. *T:* 215–898–7861; 7053 McCallum Street, Philadelphia, Pa 19119, USA. *Clubs:* Fell and Rock-climbing Club of the English Lake District; Cave Diving Group; Manchester Univ. Mountaineering; Explorers' (New York).

DAVIES, Robert Henry, MBE 1962; DFC 1943; HM Diplomatic Service, retired; *b* 17 Aug. 1921; *s* of John and Lena Davies; *m* 1st, 1945, Marion Ainsworth (marr. diss. 1973); one *s* one *d*; 2nd, 1973, Maryse Deuson. *Educ:* John Bright County Sch., Llandudno. RAF, 1940–46; flew with S African Air Force, N Africa, 1942–43. Joined Min. of Food, 1946; transf. to CRO, 1954; served in India, 1954–57 and Canada, 1959–62; HM Diplomatic Service, 1965; served in Brussels, 1967–70; Consul-Gen. and Counsellor (Admin), Moscow, 1973–75; FCO, 1975–76; Counsellor, Paris, 1976–81. *Recreations:* golf, birdwatching, reading. *Address:* 16 Beechcroft Drive, Guildford, Surrey. *Club:* Bramley Golf.

DAVIES, Prof. Rodney Deane, DSc, PhD, FInstP, FRAS; Professor of Radio Astronomy, University of Manchester, since 1976; *b* 8 Jan. 1930; *s* of Holbin James Davies and Rena Irene (*née* March), Mallala, S Australia; *m* 1953, Valda Beth Treasure; one *s* two *d* (and one *s* decd). *Educ:* Adelaide High Sch.; Univ. of Adelaide (BSc Hons, MSc); Univ. of Manchester (PhD, DSc). Research Officer, Radiophysics Div., CSIRO, Sydney, 1951–53; Univ. of Manchester: Asst Lectr, 1953–56; Lectr, 1956–67; Reader, 1967–76. Visiting Astronomer, Radiophysics Div., CSIRO, Australia, 1963. Member: Internat. Astronomical Union, 1958; Org. Cttee and Working Gps of various Commns; Council, Royal Astronomical Soc., 1972–75, 1978– (Vice-Pres. 1973–75; Sec., 1978–); Bd and various panels and cttees of Astronomy Space and Radio Bd and Science Bd of Science Research Council; British Nat. Cttee for Astronomy, 1974–77. *Publications:* Radio Studies of the Universe (with H. P. Palmer), 1959; Radio Astronomy Today (with H. P. Palmer and M. I. Large), 1963; The Crab Nebula (co-ed with F. G. Smith), 1971; numerous contribs to Monthly Notices of RAS and internat. jls on the galactic and extragalactic magnetic fields, structure and dynamics of the Galaxy and nearby external galaxies, using radio spectral lines, the early Universe. *Recreations:* cricket, gardening, fell-walking. *Address:* University of Manchester, Nuffield Radio Astronomy Laboratories, Jodrell Bank, Macclesfield, Cheshire SK11 9DL. *T:* Lower Withington 71321.

DAVIES, Roger; see Davies, A. R.

DAVIES, (Roger) Peter (Havard), OBE 1978; Director, Anti-Slavery Society, since 1980; *b* 4 Oct. 1919; *s* of Arthur William Davies and Edith Mary Davies (*née* Mealand); *m* 1956, Ferelith Mary Helen Short; two *s* two *d*. *Educ:* Bromsgrove Sch., Worcs; St Edmund Hall, Oxford (MA). Army service, N Africa, Italy, NW Europe, Captain RA (AOP), 1939–46. Joined British Council, 1949; served Hungary, Israel, Sarawak, Finland, Chile, India (Calcutta); Director: Drama and Music Dept, 1965–69; Information Dept, 1974–75; retired, 1980. Chm., Human Rights Cttee, UNA, 1985–; Mem., Exec. Cttee, UNA, 1985–. *Publications:* occasional articles and broadcasts. *Recreations:* family life, music, golf. *Address:* Ley Cottage, Elmore Road, Chipstead, Surrey CR3 3SG. *T:* Downland 53905. *Clubs:* Royal Commonwealth Society; Bengal (Calcutta).

DAVIES, Ronald; MP (Lab) Caerphilly, since 1983; *b* 6 Aug. 1946; *s* of late Ronald Davies; *m* 1981, Christina Elizabeth Rees. *Educ:* Bassaleg Grammar Sch.; Portsmouth Polytechnic; Univ. Coll. of Wales, Cardiff. Schoolteacher, 1968–70; WEA Tutor/Organiser, 1970–74; Further Educn Adviser, Mid-Glamorgan LEA, 1974–83. Councillor, Rhymney Valley DC (formerly Bedwas and Machen UDC), 1969–84 (Vice-Chm.). *Address:* House of Commons, SW1A 0AA. *T:* 01–219 3000.

DAVIES, Rt. Rev. Roy Thomas; see Llandaff, Bishop of.

DAVIES, Rev. Rupert Eric; Warden, John Wesley's Chapel, Bristol, 1976–82, retired; *b* 29 Nov. 1909; *s* of Walter Pierce and Elizabeth Miriam Davies; *m* 1937, Margaret Price Holt; two *s* two *d*. *Educ:* St Paul's Sch.; Balliol Coll., Oxford (Class. Schol.; 1st cl. Hons Mods, Classics, 1930; 2nd cl. Lit. Hum., 1932); Wesley House, Cambridge (1st cl. Theology, Pt II, 1934); BD Cantab 1946; Univ. of Tübingen, Germany, 1934–35 (trav. schol. in Germany). Chaplain, Kingswood Sch., Bath, 1935–47; Methodist Minister, Bristol, 1947–52 and 1973–76; Tutor, Didsbury Coll., Bristol, 1952–67; Principal, Wesley Coll., Bristol, 1967–73. Pres., Methodist Conf., 1970–71. Select Preacher to Univs of: Cambridge, 1962; Oxford, 1969; Mem. Exec. Cttee, World Methodist Council, 1956–76; Mem., Anglican-Methodist Unity Commn, 1965–68; World Council of Churches: Faith and Order Commn, 1965–75; Deleg. to Fourth Assembly, 1968. *Publications:* The Problem of Authority in the Continental Reformers, 1946; Catholicity of Protestantism (ed), 1950; Approach to Christian Education (ed), 1956; John Scott Lidgett (ed), 1957; The Church in Bristol, 1960; Methodists and Unity, 1962; Methodism, 1963, 2nd edn 1985; History of the Methodist Church in Great Britain (ed), vol. I, 1965, vol. II, 1978, vol. III, 1983; We Believe in God (ed), 1968; Religious Authority in an Age of Doubt, 1968; A Christian Theology of Education, 1974; What Methodists Believe, 1976; The Church in Our Times, 1979; (with M. P. Davies) Circles of Community, 1982; (ed) The Testing of the Churches 1932–82, 1982; The Church of England Observed, 1984; (with M. Morgan) Will You Walk a Little Faster?, 1984. *Recreations:* gardening, theatre. *Address:* 6 Elmtree Drive, Bishopsworth, Bristol, Avon BS13 8LY. *T:* Bristol 641087.

DAVIES, Ryland; opera singer; tenor; *b* 9 Feb. 1943; *s* of Gethin and Joan Davies; *m* 1st, 1966, Anne Elizabeth Howells (marr. diss. 1981), *qv*; 2nd, 1983, Deborah Rees; one *d*. *Educ:* Royal Manchester College of Music (Fellow, 1971) (studied with Frederic R. Cox, OBE). Début as Almaviva in The Barber of Seville, WNO, 1964; Glyndebourne Fest. Chorus, 1964–66; has since sung with Royal Opera, Sadler's Wells Opera, WNO, Scottish Opera, at Glyndebourne, and in Brussels, Chicago, NY, San Francisco, Paris, Salzburg and Stuttgart; solo rôles include: Belmonte in Il Seraglio, Fenton in Falstaff, Ferrando in Così Fan Tutte, Flamand in Capriccio; Tamino in The Magic Flute; Essex in Britten's Gloriana; Hylas in The Trojans; Don Ottavio in Don Giovanni; Cassio in Otello; Ernesto in Don Pasquale; Lysander in A Midsummer Night's Dream; title rôle in Werther; Prince in L'Amour des Trois Oranges; Nemorino in L'Elisir d'amore; Alfredo in La Traviata, Pelléas in Pelléas et Melisande, Berlin and Hamburg; Eneas in Esclarmonde, Royal Opera; Jack in The Midsummer Marriage, San Francisco. Many concerts at home with all major British orchestras, and abroad with such orchestras as: Boston Symphony, Cleveland Symphony, Chicago Symphony, Philadelphia, San Francisco, Los Angeles, Bavarian Radio and Vienna Symphony. Principal oratorio rôles include: Bach, B minor Mass; Beethoven: Mass in C; Christus am Olberg; Berlioz, narrator in L'Enfance du Christ; Elgar, St John, in The Kingdom; Handel: Acis, in Acis and Galatea; title rôle, Judas Macoabeus; Messiah; Job, in Saul; Haydn: Nelson Mass; The Seasons; Mendelssohn: Obidiah, in Elijah; Hymn of Praise; Rossini, Messe Solenelle; Schubert, Lazarus; Tippett, Child of Our Time. Has sung in all major religious works including: Missa Solemnis, Verdi's Requiem, Dream of Gerontius, St Matthew Passion, The Creation. Many recordings incl. Il Seraglio, The Trojans, Saul, Cosi Fan Tutte, Thérèse, Monteverdi Madrigals, Idomeneo, Haydn's The Seasons, Messiah, L'Oracolo (Leone), Judas Maccabaeus, Il Matrimonio Segreto (Cimarosa). John Christie Award, 1965. *Recreations:* antiques, art, cinema, sport. *Address:* 71 Fairmile Lane, Cobham, Surrey KT11 2DG.

DAVIES, Sam; *see* Davies, Stanley Mason.

DAVIES, (Stanley) Kenneth, CBE 1951; Chairman, Wire Ropes Ltd, Wicklow; *b* 25 April 1899; 2nd *s* of late Sir John Davies, CBE, JP; *m* 1938, Stephanie Morton (*d* 1979); one *s* one *d*. *Educ:* Christ Coll., Brecon; Blundell's; Royal Military Academy, Woolwich. Commnd RA, 1918; served France and Germany, 1918–19. Chairman and Managing Director: George Elliot & Co. Ltd; Bridgwater Wire Ropes Ltd; Somerset Wire Co. Ltd; Terrells Wire Ropes Ltd; Yacht and Commercial Rigging Co. Ltd; Hartlepool Wire Rope Co.; Excelsior Ropes Ltd (for varying periods between 1929 and 1960, when they were incorp. in British Ropes Ltd, now Bridon Ltd, or in GKN Ltd). Founder Member, Cardiff Aeroplane Club, 1929. Private pilot's licence, 1931–61. Formed Cambrian Air Services Ltd, 1935, Managing Director, 1935–51. Member Cttee Royal Aero Club of United Kingdom, 1935 (Vice-Chm., 1948–51, Chm. 1952–58, Vice-Pres., 1958–); Member Board British European Airways Corporation, 1951–67; Dep. Chairman BEA Helicopters Ltd, 1965–67; Chairman Welsh Advisory Council for Civil Aviation, 1948–60; Chairman Cardiff Airport Consultative Cttee, 1956–63; Member Welsh Cttee of Arts Council of Great Britain, 1954–67; Member Consultative Cttee, Sadler's Wells Trust, 1962–; Chairman of Contemporary Art Society of Wales, 1966–72; Liveryman of the Guild of Air Pilots and Air Navigators; Vice-President, FAI (Fédération Aéronautique Internationale), rep. UK; Member Cttee, Dublin Theatre Festival, 1967; Mem. Ct of Governors, National Theatre of Wales. Life Member: Iron & Steel Institute; S Wales Inst. of Engineers; Royal Agricultural Society; Royal Dublin Society. FRSA; FCIT. Coronation medal, 1953. *Recreations:* aviation and gastronomy (Vice-Pres., Internat. Wine and Food Society). *Address:* Killoughter, Ashford, Co. Wicklow. *T:* Wicklow 4126; Collingdon Road, Cardiff. *T:* 21693. *Clubs:* Athenæum, Brooks's, Naval and Military, Royal Automobile (among remaining 10 longest members); County (Cardiff); Kildare Street and University (Dublin); Bristol Channel Yacht (Swansea).
  See also D. J. Davies.

DAVIES, Stanley Mason, (Sam Davies), CMG 1971; Director, Simonsen & Weel Ltd; Consultant, Alliance International Health Care Trust; *b* 7 Feb. 1919; *s* of late Charles Davies, MBE and Constance Evelyn Davies; *m* 1943, Diana Joan (*née* Lowe); three *d*. *Educ:* Bootle Grammar School. War Service, UK and W Europe, 1939–46; Royal Army Dental Corps, 1939–41 (Sgt); Corps of Royal Engineers, 1941–46 (Staff Captain). Clerical Officer, Min. of Labour, 1936; Exec. Officer, Inland Revenue, 1938; Higher Exec. Officer, Min. of Pensions, 1946–53; Min. of Health, 1953–68; Asst Sec., DHSS, 1968–75; Under Sec., Industries and Exports Div., DHSS, 1975–76. Consultant, Sterling Winthrop Drug, 1977–86. Mem., NY Acad. of Scis. FSAScot. Croix de Guerre (France), 1944. *Recreations:* reading, archæology, philately. *Address:* 31 Leverstock Green Road, Hemel Hempstead, Herts. *T:* Hemel Hempstead 54312. *Club:* Savile.

DAVIES, Stuart Duncan, CBE 1968; BSc; FEng; Hon. FRAeS; Past President, Royal Aeronautical Society, 1972–73 (President, 1971–72); *b* 5 Dec. 1906; *s* of William Lewis Davies and Alice Dryden Duncan; *m* 1935, Ethel Rosalie Ann Radcliffe; one *d*. *Educ:* Westminster City Sch.; London Univ. (BSc Eng.). Vickers (Aviation) Ltd, 1925–31; Hawker Aircraft Ltd, 1931–36; A. V. Roe and Co. Ltd, 1938–55, Chief Designer, 1945–55; with Dowty Group Ltd, 1955–58, as Managing Director of Dowty Fuel System Ltd; Technical Director: Hawker Siddeley Aviation Ltd, 1958–64; Dowty Rotol Ltd, 1965–72. British Gold Medal for Aeronautics, 1958. *Address:* Sheridans, Arun Way, Aldwick Bay, Bognor Regis, W Sussex.

DAVIES, Thomas Glyn, CBE 1966; *b* 16 Aug. 1905; *s* of Thomas Davies, Gwaelod-y-Garth, Cardiff; *m* 1935, Margaret Berry; one *d*. *Educ:* Pontypridd Grammar Sch.; Univ. of Wales, Cardiff (MA). Asst Master, Howard Gardens High Sch., Cardiff, 1927–37; Warden, Educational Settlement, Pontypridd, 1937–43; Director of Education: Montgomeryshire, 1943–58; Denbighshire, 1958–70, retd. Mem. ITA, later IBA, 1970–75. Mem., Court and Council, UC Bangor. Fellow, UC Cardiff, 1981. *Recreations:* travel, music. *Address:* 42 Park Avenue, Wrexham, Clwyd LL12 7AH. *T:* Wrexham 352697.

DAVIES, Trevor Arthur L.; *see* Lloyd Davies.

DAVIES, Walter, OBE 1966; Secretary-General and Chief Executive of The British Chamber of Commerce for Italy since 1961; *b* 7 Dec. 1920; *s* of late William Davies and late Frances Poole; *m* 1947, Alda, *d* of Tiso Lucchetta, Padua; two *d*. *Educ:* St Margaret's Higher Grade Sch., Liverpool; Liverpool Coll. of Commerce. Served War: RA, 1940–41; Scots Guards, 1942–47. Commendatore dell'Ordine al Merito della Repubblica Italiana, 1967. *Recreations:* good food, good company, fishing, motoring. *Address:* Via G. Dezza 27, 20144, Milan, Italy. *T:* Milan 4694391. *Club:* British American (Milan).

DAVIES, Wilfred Horace; Director, Eastern Telecommunications Philippines Inc., since 1974; Trustee, Cable & Wireless Pension Funds, since 1962; *b* 7 March 1917; *s* of late Gerald Edward Davies and Editha Lucy (*née* Sweet-Escott); *m* 1st, Helen Rose Gillam; one *s* one *d*; 2nd, Eva Nancy Berry; two *s*. *Educ:* Aldenham Sch. Cable & Wireless Ltd, 1935: Asst Staff Manager, 1957; Dep. Staff Manager, 1961; Staff Manager, 1962; Dir, 1968–78; Chm., Cable and Wireless Systems (Hong Kong), 1973–78. Chm., Asiadata Ltd (Hong Kong), 1973–78; Chm., Fiji Telecommunications Ltd, 1976–79; Director: Nigeria External Telecommunications Ltd, 1969–73; Sierra Leone External Telecommunications Ltd, 1969–74; E African External Telecommunications Co. Ltd, 1969–74; Oceanic Wireless Network, Inc., Philippines, 1973–78; MBIM. *Recreations:* golf, gardening. *Address:* c/o Cable & Wireless PLC, Mercury House, Theobalds Road, WC1X 8RX. *Clubs:* Royal Commonwealth Society; Exiles (Twickenham).

DAVIES, William Llewellyn M.; *see* Monro Davies.

DAVIES, (William Michael) Neil; Member, Inner London Education Authority, since 1981 (Chairman, 1982–83); *b* 5 Feb. 1931; *s* of William Henry Davies and Hilda Mary (*née* Fielding); *m* 1955, Myra Blanch Clair Smalley; two *s* one *d*. *Educ:* Neath Technical Coll.; Fircroft Coll.; Birmingham Univ. Probation Officer, Birmingham, Monmouthshire and Somerset, 1962–76; Principal Child Care Adviser, Lambeth Bor. Council, 1976–82. Member: Taunton Bor. Council, 1968–74; London Bor. of Bexley, 1978–82. Greater London Council: Mem. for Woolwich W, 1981–86; Vice-Chm., Public Services and Fire Bde Cttee, 1981–82; Chm., Thames Barrier Sub Cttee, Educn Cttee, and London Youth

Cttee, 1981–86; Vice-Chm., Greater London Trng Bd, and Sports Sub Cttee, 1981–86; Mem., Staff Cttee, Arts and Recreation Cttee, Transport Cttee, and Entertainments Licensing Cttee, 1981–86. Member, National Joint Councils: Fire Bde, 1981–; Probation Service, 1981–; Local Authority Bldg Trades, 1980–. Member: Thames Water Authority, 1981–; NEC National Assoc. of Maternal and Child Welfare, 1980–. Contested (Lab.) Ripon, 1979. *Recreations:* sport, music, cooking, walking. *Address:* 49 Gelston Point, Burwell Close, E1 2NR. *Club:* London Welsh Association.

DAVIES, Rev. Dr William Rhys; Principal of Cliff College, Sheffield, since 1983; President of the Methodist Conference, June 1987–June 1988; *b* Blackpool, 31 May 1932; *m* 1955, Barbara; one *s* one *d*. *Educ:* Junior, Central Selective and Grammar schools, Blackpool; Hartley Victoria Methodist Coll., Manchester; Univ. of Manchester. BD London 1955; MA 1959, PhD 1965, Manchester. Junior Rating and Valuation Officer (Clerical), Blackpool Corp., 1950–51. Methodist Circuit Minister: Middleton, Manchester, 1955–60; Fleetwood, 1960–65; Stockton-on-Tees, 1965–66. Sen. Lectr in Religious Studies, Padgate Coll. of Higher Education, and Methodist Minister without pastoral charge on Warrington Circuit, 1966–79; Superintendent Minister, Bradford Methodist Mission, 1979–83. Member of Methodist Committees: Cliff Coll. Gen. Cttee, 1974–77 and 1981–; Faith and Order Cttee, 1975–82; Doctrinal Cttee, 1979–82; Divl Bd for Social Responsibility, 1982–85; Home Mission Bd, 1983–. Co-Editor, Dunamis (renewal magazine for Methodists), 1972–. *Publications:* (with Ross Peart) The Charismatic Movement and Methodism, 1973; Spirit Baptism and Spiritual Gifts in Early Methodism, (USA) 1974; Gathered into One (Archbishop of Canterbury's Lent Book), 1975; (with Ross Peart) What about the Charismatic Movement?, 1980; Rocking the Boat, 1986; (contrib.) A Dictionary of Christian Spirituality, 1983; contribs to jls. *Recreations:* reading, sport (soccer). *Address:* Cliff House, Calver, Sheffield S30 1XG. *T:* Baslow (home) 3262, (office) 2321.

DAVIES, William Rupert R.; *see* Rees-Davies.

DAVIES-SCOURFIELD, Brig. Edward Grismond Beaumont, CBE 1966 (MBE 1951); MC 1945; DL; General Secretary, National Association of Boys Clubs, 1973–82; *b* 2 Aug. 1918; 4th *s* of H. G. Davies-Scourfield and Helen (*née* Newton); *m* 1945, Diana Lilias (*née* Davidson); one *s* one *d*. *Educ:* Winchester Coll.; RMC Sandhurst. Commnd into KRRC, 1938; served War of 1939–45 (despatches 1945); psc; commanded: 3rd Green Jackets (Rifle Bde), 1960–62; Green Jackets Bde, 1962–64; British Jt Services Trng Team (Ghana), 1964–66; British Troops Cyprus and Dhekelia Area, 1966–69; Salisbury Plain Area, 1970–73; retd 1973. DL Hants, 1984. *Recreations:* country pursuits. *Address:* Old Rectory Cottage, Medstead, Alton, Hants GU34 5LX. *T:* Alton 62133. *Clubs:* Army and Navy, Mounted Infantry.

d'AVIGDOR-GOLDSMID, Maj.-Gen. Sir James (Arthur), 3rd Bt *cr* 1934; CB 1975; OBE 1955; MC 1944; *b* 19 Dec. 1912; *yr s* of Sir Osmond d'Avigdor-Goldsmid, 1st Bt, and Alice Lady d'Avigdor-Goldsmid; *S* brother, 1976; unmarried. *Educ:* Harrow; RMC, Sandhurst. 2nd Lieut 4th/7th Royal Dragoon Guards, 1932. Served War of 1939–45, France and Germany (wounded). Commanded: 4th/7th Royal Dragoon Guards, 1950–53; 20th Armoured Brigade Group, 1958–61; Director, Royal Armoured Corps, War Office, subseq. Ministry of Defence, 1962–65; President, Regular Commissions Board, Feb.-Sept. 1965; Director TA and Cadets, 1966–68; Col of 4th/7th Royal Dragoon Guards, 1963–73; Chm., SE TA&VRA, 1974–78; Hon. Col The Mercian Yeomanry, T&AVR, 1972–77. MP (C) Lichfield and Tamworth, 1970–Sept. 1974; Mem., Select Cttee on Estimates, 1971–74. Chairman: Racecourse Security Services Ltd, 1976–80; Tattersall's Cttee, 1980–; Exec. of Governors, Corps of Commissionaires, 1980–; Member: Horserace Betting Levy Bd, 1974–77; Council, Winston Churchill Meml Trust. Comr Royal Hosp. Chelsea, 1972–78. *Heir:* none. *Address:* 101 Mount Street, W1. *T:* 01–499 1989. *Clubs:* Cavalry and Guards, Turf, Jockey.

DAVIGNON, Viscount Etienne; Ambassador of HM the King of the Belgians; Executive Director, Société Générale de Belgique, since 1984; Chairman, Sibeka; Associate, Kissinger Associates; *b* Budapest, 4 Oct. 1932; *m* 1959, Françoise de Cumont; one *s* two *d*. *Educ:* University of Louvain (LLD). Diplomat: Head of Office of Minister for Foreign Affairs, Belgium, 1963; Political Director, Ministry for Foreign Affairs, Belgium, 1969; Chm., Gov. Board, Internat. Energy Agency, 1974. Mem., 1977–84 (with responsibility for internal mkt, customs, union and industl affairs), and Vice-Pres., 1981–84 (with responsibility for industry, energy and research policies), EEC. *Recreations:* tennis, golf, skiing. *Address:* 12 Avenue des Fleurs, 1150 Brussels, Belgium.

DAVIN, Daniel Marcus, (Dan Davin), MBE (mil.) 1945; Oxford Academic Publisher, and Deputy Secretary to Delegates of the Oxford University Press, 1974–78, retired; *b* 1 Sept. 1913; *s* of Patrick and Mary Davin; *m* 1939, Winifred Kathleen Gonley; three *d*. *Educ:* Marist Brothers Sch., Invercargill, NZ; Sacred Heart Coll., Auckland; Otago Univ. (MA); Balliol Coll., Oxford (First in Greats, 1939, MA 1945). Served War: Royal Warwickshire Regt, 1939–40; 2 NZEF, 1940–45; served in Greece and Crete (wounded 1941); Intell. GHQ, ME, 1941–42; NZ Div., N Africa and Italy, 1942–45 (despatches thrice, MBE). With Clarendon Press, 1945–78. Fellow of Balliol Coll., 1965–78, now Emeritus. FRSA. Hon. DLitt Otago Univ., 1984. *Publications: novels:* Cliffs of Fall, 1945; For the Rest of Our Lives, 1947; Roads from Home, 1949; The Sullen Bell, 1956; No Remittance, 1959; Not Here, Not Now, 1970; Brides of Price, 1972; *short stories:* The Gorse Blooms Pale, 1947; Breathing Spaces, 1975; Selected Stories, 1981; *miscellaneous prose:* Introduction to English Literature (with John Mulgan), 1947; Crete (Official History), 1953 (Wellington, War Hist. Br., Dept of Internal Affairs); Writing in New Zealand: The New Zealand Novel (Parts One and Two, with W. K. Davin), 1956; Katherine Mansfield in Her Letters, 1959; Closing Times (Recollections of Julian Maclaren-Ross, W. R. Rodgers, Louis MacNeice, Enid Starkie, Joyce Cary, Dylan Thomas, Itzik Manger), 1975; *editions:* New Zealand Short Stories, 1953; English Short Stories of Today: Second Series, 1958; Katherine Mansfield, Selected Stories, 1963; Short Stories from the Second World War, 1982; (ed jtly) From Oasis to Italy, 1983. *Recreations:* reading, writing, talking. *Address:* 103 Southmoor Road, Oxford OX2 6RE. *T:* Oxford 57311.

DAVIS; *see* Lovell-Davis.

DAVIS, Alan Roger M.; *see* Maryon Davis.

DAVIS, Sir Allan; *see* Davis, Sir W. A.

DAVIS, Andrew Frank; Artistic Director and Chief Conductor, Toronto Symphony, since 1975; *b* 2 Feb. 1944; *m* 1970, Felicity Mary Vincent (marr. diss. 1983); *m* 1984, Nancicarole Monohan. *Educ:* Watford Grammar Sch.; King's Coll., Cambridge (MA, BMus); Accademia di S Cecilia, Rome. Assistant Conductor, BBC Scottish Symphony Orchestra, 1970–72; Asst Conductor, New Philharmonia Orchestra, 1973–77; Principal Guest Conductor, Royal Liverpool Philharmonic Orchestra, 1974–77. Has conducted major US orchestras: New York, Boston, Chicago, Cleveland and LA. Particularly noted for interpretations of Strauss operas; has conducted at: La Scala, Milan, 1985; Metropolitan Opera, NY, 1983 and 1985; Glyndebourne, 1985 and 1986; Royal Opera House, Covent

Gdn, 1986. Toronto Symphony Orchestra tours: US Centres, China, Japan, 1978; Europe, 1983, 1986, incl. London, Helsinki, Bonn, Paris and Edinburgh Fest. Many commercial recordings include: complete Dvorak Symphonies, Philharmonia Orch.; Mendelssohn Symphonies, Bavarian Radio Symphony; Borodin Cycle, Toronto Symphony. *Recreations:* kite flying, the study of mediaeval stained glass. *Address:* c/o Harold Holt Ltd, 31 Sinclair Road, W14 0NS.

DAVIS, Anthony Ronald William James; Editorial Director, New World Publishers Ltd, Middle East Construction and Saudi Arabian Construction, since 1983; *b* 26 July 1931; *e s* of Donald William Davis, Barnes and Mary Josephine Davis (*née* Nolan-Byrne), Templeogue Mill, Co. Dublin; *m* 1960, Yolande Mary June, *o d* of Patrick Leonard, retd civil engr; one *s* two *d* (and one *d* decd). *Educ:* Hamlet of Ratcliffe and Oratory; Regent Street Polytechnic. Joint Services School for Linguists on Russian course as National Serviceman (Army), 1953–55; Architectural Asst, Housing Dept, Mddx County Architect's Dept, 1956–58; Sub-Editor, The Builder, 1959; Editor: Official Architecture and Planning, 1964–70; Building, 1970–74; Director, Building, 1972–77; Editor-in-Chief, New World Publishers Ltd, 1978–83. Member Board: Architecture and Planning Publications Ltd, 1966; Building (Publishers) Ltd, 1972. Mem. Council, Modular Soc., 1970–71. JP Berkshire, 1973–81. *Publications:* contribs to various, architectural and technical. *Recreations:* collecting porcelain, music and dreaming. *Address:* 8 Blake Close, Dowles Green, Wokingham, Berks RG11 1QH. *T:* Wokingham 785046. *Club:* Architecture.

DAVIS, (Arthur) John, RD 1967; FIB; Vice-Chairman, Lloyds Bank, since 1984 (Chief General Manager, 1978–84); *b* 28 July 1924; *s* of Alan Wilfrid Davis and Emily Davis; *m* 1950, Jean Elizabeth Edna Hobbs; one *s* one *d* (and one *d* decd). *Educ:* grammar schs. FIB 1969. Served War, RN, 1942–46. Entered Lloyds Bank, 1941; Jt Gen. Manager, 1973; Asst Chief Gen. Man., 1973; Dep. Chief Gen. Man., 1976. Pres., Inst. of Bankers, 1985–. *Recreations:* gardening, music, country pursuits. *Address:* Little Barley End, Aldbury, Tring, Herts. *T:* Aldbury Common 321. *Clubs:* Naval, Overseas Bankers.

DAVIS, Bette Ruth Elizabeth; Actress; *b* Lowell, Mass, 5 April 1908. *Educ:* Cushing Academy, Ashburnham, Mass. Stage experience in Wild Duck, Broken Dishes, Solid South; entered films, 1930. Pictures she has appeared in: Of Human Bondage, 1934; Border Town; Dangerous (Academy Award of 1935 won 1936); The Petrified Forest, The Golden Arrow, 1936; Marked Woman, Kid Galahad, It's Love I'm After, That Certain Woman, 1937; Jezebel (Academy Award of 1938 won 1939); The Sisters, 1938; Dark Victory, Juarez, The Old Maid, Private Lives of Elizabeth and Essex, 1939; All This and Heaven Too, 1940; The Letter, The Great Lie, The Bride came COD, The Man who came to Dinner, The Little Foxes, 1941; In This our Life, Watch on the Rhine, Old Acquaintance, 1942; Mr Skeffington, 1944; The Corn is Green, 1945; A Stolen Life, Deception, 1946; Winter Meeting, 1948; June Bride, 1948; The Story of a Divorce; All about Eve, 1950; Payment on Demand, 1951; Phone Call from a Stranger, 1952; Another Man's Poison, 1952; The Star, 1953; The Virgin Queen, 1955; Storm Center, 1956; The Catered Affair, 1956; John Paul Jones, 1956; Wedding Breakfast; The Scapegoat, 1959; Pocketful of Miracles, 1961; Whatever Happened to Baby Jane?, 1962; Dead Ringer, 1964; Painted Canvas, 1963; Where Love Has Gone, 1964; Hush . . . Hush, Sweet Charlotte, 1964; The Nanny, 1965; The Anniversary, 1967; Connecting Rooms, 1969; Bunny O'Hare, 1970; Madam Sin, 1971; The Game, 1972; Burnt Offerings, 1977; Death on the Nile, 1978; Watcher In The Woods, 1980. *TV Movies:* Sister Aimee, 1977; The Dark Secret of Harvest Home, 1978; Strangers, The Story of a Mother and Daughter, 1979 (Emmy Award); White Mama, 1980; Skyward, 1980; Family Reunion, 1981; A Piano for Mrs Cimino, 1982; Little Gloria, Happy at Last, 1982; Right of Way, 1983; Hotel, 1983; Murder with Mirrors, 1984; *Plays:* The Night of the Iguana, 1961; Miss Moffitt, 1974. Life Achievement Award, Amer. Film Institute, 1977; Rudolph Valentino Life Achievement Award, 1982; Life Achievement Award, Amer. Acad. of Arts, 1983; Dept of Defense Medal for Distinguished Public Service, 1983; Women in Films Crystal Award, 1983. *Publication:* The Lonely Life, 1963. *Relevant Publication:* Mother Goddam by Whitney Stine, 1975 (footnotes by Bette Davis). *Recreations:* swimming and horseback riding. *Address:* c/o Gottlieb, Schiff, Ticktin & Harris, PC, 555 Fifth Avenue, New York, NY 10017, USA.

DAVIS, Brian; *see* ffolkes, Michael.

DAVIS, Most Rev. Brian Newton; *see* New Zealand, Primate and Archbishop of.

DAVIS, Maj-Gen. Brian William, CB 1985; CBE 1980 (OBE 1974); Director, Royal Ordnance plc, since 1985; *b* 28 Aug. 1930; *s* of late Edward William Davis, MBE, and Louise Jane Davis (*née* Webber); *m* 1954, Margaret Isobel Jenkins; one *s* one *d*. *Educ:* Weston-super-Mare Grammar Sch.; Mons OCS, Aldershot. Commissioned Royal Artillery, 1949; Regtl Duty, 1949–56 and 1960–61, UK/BAOR; Instr-in-Gunnery, 1956–59; Staff Coll. Camberley, 1962; DAA and QMG HQ 7 Armd Bde BAOR, 1963–66; GSO2 SD UN Force, Cyprus, 1966; Regtl Duty, 1967–69; Lt-Col 1969, Directing Staff, Staff Coll. Camberley, 1969–71; CO 32 Lt Regt RA BAOR/England/N Ireland, 1971–74; Col AQ Ops HQ BAOR, 1975; Brig. 1975; CRA 3 Div., 1976–77; RCDS 1978; Chief of Staff N Ireland, 1979–80; Chief of Comdrs-in-Chief Mission to Soviet Forces in Germany, 1981–82; Maj. Gen., 1982; C of S, Logistic Exec. (Army), 1982–83; DGLP (A) (formerly VQMG), MoD, 1983–85, retired. *Recreations:* Rugby (President, RARFC, 1975–78; Dep. Pres., Army Rugby Union, 1984–), cricket, fishing, ornithology. *Address:* c/o Royal Bank of Scotland, Lawrie House, Victoria Road, Farnborough, Hants. *Clubs:* Army and Navy, MCC; Piscatorial Society.

DAVIS, Carl; composer; Associate Conductor, London Philharmonic Orchestra, from Sept. 1987; Principal Conductor, Bournemouth Pops, since 1984; *b* 28 Oct. 1936; *s* of Isadore and Sara Davis; *m* 1971, Jean Boht; two *d*. *Educ:* New England Conservatory of Music; Bard Coll. (BA). *Major TV credits:* The Snow Goose, 1972; World at War, 1973; The Naked Civil Servant, 1973; Our Mutual Friend, 1976; Marie Curie, 1977; Prince Regent, The Old Curiosity Shop, 1979; Hollywood, Oppenheimer, The Sailor's Return, Fair Stood the Wind for France, 1980; The Commanding Sea, Private Schulz, 1981; The Last Night of the Poms, Home Sweet Home, La Ronde, 1982; The Unknown Chaplin, The Tale of Beatrix Potter, 1983; The Far Pavilions, 1984; *scores:* for RSC and National Theatre; *musicals:* The Projector, 1971; Pilgrim, 1975; Cranford, 1976; Alice in Wonderland, 1977; *opera:* Peace, 1978; *TV operas:* The Arrangement, 1967; Orpheus in the Underground, 1976; *West End:* Forty Years On, 1969; Habeas Corpus, 1974; *films:* Napoleon, 1980; The French Lieutenant's Woman (BAFTA Original Film Score Award), The Crowd, 1981; Flesh and the Devil, Show People, How to Make Movies, 1982; Broken Blossoms, The Wind, The Musketeers of Pig Alley, An Unseen Enemy, 1983; Champions, Thief of Baghdad, 1984; King David, The Big Parade, 1985; *ballet:* Dances of Love and Death, 1981; *orchestral compositions:* Lines on London (symphony), 1980 (commnd by Capital Radio); Clarinet Concerto, 1984. Co-founder and partner with Terry Oates of Sundergrade Music Ltd. Mem. BAFTA, 1979–. First winner, BAFTA Award for Original TV Music, 1981. Chevalier de L'Ordre des Arts et des Lettres, 1983.

Publications: sheet music of television themes. *Recreations:* reading, gardening, playing chamber music, cooking. *Address:* c/o Paul Wing, 35 Priory Road, N8. *T:* 01–348 6604.

DAVIS, Sir Charles (Sigmund), Kt 1965; CB 1960; Counsel to the Speaker (European Legislation), (formerly Second Counsel), House of Commons, 1974–83; *b* London, 22 Jan. 1909; *y s* of late Maurice Davis (*b* Melbourne, Australia) and Alfreda Regina Davis; *m* 1940, Pamela Mary, *er d* of late J. K. B. Dawson, OBE, and Phyllis Dawson; two *d*. *Educ:* Trinity Coll., Cambridge. Double 1st Cl. Hons, Law Tripos; Sen. Schol., Exhibitioner and Prizeman of Trinity, 1927–30; MA 1934. Called to the Bar, Inner Temple (Studentship and Certif. of Honour), 1930, and in Sydney, Australia, 1931; practised as barrister in London, 1931–34; entered Legal Branch, Ministry of Health, 1934; held legal posts in various public offices, 1938–46 (Corporal, Home Guard, 1940–45); Asst Solicitor, Min. of Agric. and Fisheries, 1946–55; Prin. Asst Solicitor, MAFF, 1955–57; Legal Adviser and Solicitor, MAFF, and Forestry Commission, 1957–74, retired. Chm. Council, Nat. Soc. for Cancer Relief, 1983–85, Trustee, 1985–. *Recreations:* music (LRAM, ARCM) and much else. *Address:* 43 Wolsey Road, East Molesey, Surrey KT8 9EW.

DAVIS, Mrs Chloë Marion, OBE 1975; Chairman, Consumer Affairs Group of National Organisations, 1973–79; Member: Council on Tribunals, 1970–79; Consumer Standards Advisory Committee of British Standards Institution, 1965–78 (Chairman 1970–73); *b* Dartmouth, Devon, 15 Feb. 1909; *d* of Richard Henry Pound and Mary Jane Chapman; *m* 1928, Edward Thomas Davis (*d* 1983), printer and sometime writer; one *s*. *Educ:* limited formal, USA and England. Various part-time voluntary social and public services from 1929; Birth Control Internat. Information Centre, 1931–38; voluntary activity in bombing etc emergencies, also cookery and domestic broadcasting during War of 1939–45; information service for Kreis Resident Officers, Control Commn for Germany, Berlin, 1946–48; regional Citizens Advice Bureaux office, London Council of Social Service, 1949–55; Sen. Information Officer to Nat. Citizens Advice Bureaux Council, 1956–69. Member: Nat. House-Building Council, 1973–76; Consumer Consultative Cttee, EEC, 1973–76; Exec. Cttee, Housewife's Trust, 1970–77. *Recreations:* reading present history in the morning in newspapers and past history in books in the evening; gardening, walking, talking with friends. *Address:* Auberville Cottage, 246 Dover Road, Walmer, Kent CT14 7NP. *T:* Deal 374038.

DAVIS, Clinton; *see* Davis, S. C.

DAVIS, Sir Colin (Rex), Kt 1980; CBE 1965; Chief Conductor, Bavarian Radio Symphony Orchestra, since 1983; *b* 25 Sept. 1927; *s* of Reginald George and Lillian Davis; *m* 1949, April Cantelo (marr. diss., 1964); one *s* one *d*; *m* 1964, Ashraf Naini; three *s* two *d*. *Educ:* Christ's Hospital; Royal College of Music. Orchestral Conductor, Freelance wilderness, 1949–57; Asst Conductor, BBC Scottish Orchestra, 1957–59. Conductor, Sadler's Wells, 1959, Principal Conductor, 1960–65, Musical Director, 1961–65; Chief Conductor, BBC Symphony Orchestra, 1967–71, Chief Guest Conductor, 1971–75; Musical Dir, Royal Opera House, Covent Garden, 1971–86; Principal Guest Conductor: Boston SO, 1972–84; LSO 1974–84. Artistic Director, Bath Festival, 1969. Conducted at: Metropolitan Opera House, New York, 1969, 1970, 1972; Bayreuth Fest., 1977. Shakespeare Prize, 1984. *Recreations:* anything at all. *Address:* 7A Fitzroy Park, N6 6HS. *Club:* Athenæum.

DAVIS, David; *see* Davis, William Eric.

DAVIS, Derek Alan, CEng; Member, Central Electricity Generating Board, since 1984; *b* 5 Oct. 1929; *s* of Irene Davis (*née* Longstaff) and Sydney George Davis; *m* 1954, Ann Margery Willett; three *s*. *Educ:* private schools; Battersea Polytechnic; London University. BScEng (First Hons) 1950; MIMechE; CBIM. De Havilland Engine Co Ltd: post-graduate apprentice, 1950–52; develt engineer, Gas Turbine Div., 1952–53, Rocket Div., 1953–56; Central Electricity Generating Board: Research Labs, 1956–60; Manager, Mech. and Civil Engineering, 1960–65; Group Head Fuel, 1965, System Econ. Engineer, 1970, System Planning Engineer, 1973–75; Planning Dept; Dir, Resource Planning, later Dir Production, NE Region, 1975–81; Dir Corporate Strategy Dept, 1981–84. *Publications:* articles in tech. and engineering jls. *Recreations:* playing, now watching, sport; gardening, DIY, reading. *Address:* c/o Central Electricity Generating Board, 15 Newgate Street, EC1A 7AU. *T:* 01–634 6742.

DAVIS, Derek Richard; Under Secretary, Gas Division, Department of Energy, since 1985; *b* 3 May 1945; *s* of Stanley Lewis Davis, OBE and Rita Beatrice Rachel (*née* Rosenheim). *Educ:* Clifton Coll., Bristol; Balliol Coll., Oxford (BA 1967). Asst Principal, BoT, 1967; Pvte Sec. to Perm. Sec., DTI, 1971–72; Principal, 1972; Asst Sec., Dept of Energy, 1977; Secretary: Energy Commn, 1977–79; NEDC Energy Task Force, 1981; seconded to NCB, 1982–83. *Address:* 9 Uxbridge Street, W8. *T:* 01–221 3220.

DAVIS, Prof. Derek Russell, MD, FRCP; Norah Cooke Hurle Professor of Mental Health, University of Bristol, 1962–79; *b* 20 April 1914; *s* of late Edward David Darelan Davis, FRCS, and of Alice Mildred (*née* Russell); *m* 1939, Marit, *d* of Iver M. Iversen, Oslo, Norway; one *s* one *d*. *Educ:* Stowe Sch., Buckingham; Clare Coll., Cambridge (major entrance and foundn schol.); Middlesex Hosp. Med. Sch. MA, MD; FRCP. Ho. Phys., Mddx Hosp., 1938; Addenbrooke's Hosp., Cambridge, 1939; Asst Physician, Runwell Hosp., 1939; Mem. Scientific Staff, MRC, 1940; Lectr in Psychopathology, Univ. of Cambridge, 1948; Reader in Clinical Psychology, 1950; Dir, Med. Psychology Research Unit, 1958; Consultant Psychiatrist, United Cambridge Hosps, 1948; Editor, Quarterly Jl of Experimental Psychology, 1949–57. Visiting Professor: Univ. of Virginia, 1958; Univ. of Dundee, 1976; Univ. of Otago, 1977. Fellow, Clare Coll., Cambridge, 1961. Dean of Medicine, Univ. of Bristol, 1970–72. Member: Avon AHA (Teaching), 1974–79; Council of Management, MIND, 1975–; Pres., Fedn of Mental Health Workers, 1972. Adolf Meyer Lectr, Amer. Psychiatric Assoc., 1967. FRCPsych, FBPsS. *Publications:* An Introduction to Psychopathology, 1957, 4th edn 1984; many articles in scientific and med. jls. *Recreations:* Ibsen studies, theatre. *Address:* 9 Clyde Road, Bristol BS6 6RJ. *T:* Bristol 734744.

See also J. D. Russell-Davis.

DAVIS, Hon. Sir (Dermot) Renn, Kt 1981; OBE 1971; Chief Justice, Supreme Court of Gibraltar, 1980–86; *b* 20 Nov. 1928; *s* of Captain Eric R. Davis, OBE and Norah A. Davis (*née* Bingham); *m* 1984, Mary, *widow* of William James Pearce and *d* of late Brig. T. F. K. Howard, DSO, RA. *Educ:* Prince of Wales Sch., Nairobi; Wadham Coll., Oxford (BA Hons). Called to the Bar, Inner Temple, 1953; Daly and Figgis, Advocates, Nairobi, 1953–56; Attorney-General's Chambers, Kenya, 1956–62; Attorney-General, British Solomon Islands Protectorate, and Legal Advr to High Comr for Western Pacific, 1962–73; British Judge, New Hebrides Condominium, 1973–76; Chief Justice, Solomon Islands, 1976–80 and Chief Justice, Tuvalu, 1978–80. *Recreations:* music, walking. *Clubs:* United Oxford & Cambridge University; Muthaiga Country (Nairobi); Royal Gibraltar Yacht.

DAVIS, Sir (Ernest) Howard, Kt 1978; CMG 1969; OBE 1960; Deputy Governor, Gibraltar, 1971–78; *b* 22 April 1918; *m* 1948, Marie Davis (*née* Bellotti); two *s*. *Educ:*

Christian Brothers Schs, Gibraltar and Blackpool; London Univ. (BA 1st cl. hons). Gen. Clerical Staff, Gibraltar, 1936–46; Asst Sec. and Clerk of Councils, 1946–54; seconded Colonial Office, 1954–55; Chief Asst Sec., Estabt Officer and Public Relations Officer (responsible for opening Radio Gibraltar), Gibraltar, 1955–62; Director of Labour and Social Security, 1962–65; Financial and Development Secretary, 1965–71; Acting Governor, various periods, 1971–77. Chairman, Committee of Enquiry: PWD, 1980–81; Electricity Dept, 1982; Chm., Gibraltar Broadcasting Corp., 1982–83. *Recreations:* cricket, gardening, bridge. *Address:* 36 South Barrack Road, Gibraltar. *T:* A.70358.

DAVIS, Godfrey Rupert Carless, CBE 1981; FSA; Secretary, Royal Commission on Historical Manuscripts, 1972–81; *b* 22 April 1917; *s* of late Prof. Henry William Carless Davis and Rosa Jennie Davis (*née* Lindup); *m* 1942, Dorothie Elizabeth Mary Loveband; one *s* two *d*. *Educ:* Highgate Sch.; Balliol Coll., Oxford (MA, DPhil). Rome Scholar in Ancient History, 1938. Army Service, 1939–46, Devon Regt and Intell. Corps, Captain 1942. Dept of MSS, British Museum: Asst Keeper, 1947; Dep. Keeper, 1961–72. FRHistS 1954 (Treas. 1967–74); FSA 1974. *Publications:* Medieval Cartularies of Great Britain, 1958; Magna Carta, 1963; contrib. British Museum Cat. Add. MSS 1926–1950 (6 vols); learned jls. *Address:* 214 Somerset Road, SW19 5JE. *T:* 01-946 7955.

See also R. H. C. Davis.

DAVIS, Harold Sydney, FRCP; retired; Consultant Physician: Royal Free Hospital, London, 1954–73; King Edward VII Hospital, Windsor, 1945–73; Hampstead General Hospital, 1946–73; Florence Nightingale Hospital, London, since 1947; Hon. Physician to the Queen, T&AVR, 1967–68; *b* 6 Aug. 1908; *s* of Harold Adamson Davis and Edith May Davis, Jamaica, WI; *m* 1940, Molly, *d* of Herbert Percy Stimson, London; one *d*. *Educ:* Jamaica Coll., WI; Dulwich Coll., London; Gonville and Caius Coll., Cambridge; Charing Cross Hosp., London (Exhibr). BA 1930, MB, BChir 1935, MA 1936, Cantab.; LRCP, MRCS 1933; MRCP 1936; FRCP 1954. Held usual resident appts in various London hosps, 1933–39. Commissioned into RAMC, March 1939 (Lieut); seconded as Physician, Ashridge Hosp. (EMS), 1940. OC 308 (Co. London) Gen. Hosp. RAMC/AER, 1964 (Col). Examr in Medicine, London Univ.; Lectr in Medicine, Royal Free Hosp. Sch. of Medicine, London Univ., 1962; Mem. Bd of Govs, Royal Free Hosp., 1963. Pres., Eagle Ski Club, 1960–63. *Publications:* contrib. learned jls. *Recreations:* ski-mountaineering, gardening. *Address:* Fingest Hill Cottage, Skirmett, near Henley-on-Thames, Oxon RG9 6TD. *T:* Turville Heath 275. *Clubs:* Ski Club of Gt Britain (Vice-Pres. 1964), Kandahar Ski; Leander (Henley-on-Thames).

DAVIS, Sir Howard; *see* Davis, Sir E. H.

DAVIS, Ivor John Guest, CB 1983; Director, Common Law Institute of Intellectual Property, since 1986; *b* 11 Dec. 1925; *s* of Thomas Henry Davis and Dorothy Annie Davis; *m* 1954, Mary Eleanor Thompson; one *s* one *d*. *Educ:* Devonport High Sch.; HM Dockyard Sch., Devonport. BSc London (ext.). Apprentice, HM Dockyard, Devonport, 1941–45, Draughtsman, 1946–47; Patent Office, Dept of Trade: Asst Examr, 1947; Examr, 1950; Sen. Examr, 1954; Principal Examr, 1967; Superintending Examr, 1972; Asst Comptroller, 1973; Comptroller Gen., Patents, Designs and Trade Marks, 1978. Pres., Administrative Council, European Patent Office, 1981–85. Mem. Governing Bd, Centre d'études de la propriété industrielle, Strasbourg, 1979–85. Mem., Editorial Adv. Bd, World Patent Information Journal, 1979–85. *Recreations:* music, gardening. *Address:* 5 Birch Close, Eynsford, Dartford DA4 0EX.

DAVIS, James Gresham, MA; FCIT; Director, Kleinwort, Benson Ltd, since 1973; *b* 20 July 1928; *s* of Col Robert Davis, OBE, JP and Josephine Davis; *m* 1973, Adriana Johanna Verhoef; three *d*. *Educ:* Bradfield Coll.; Clare Coll., Cambridge (MA). FCIT 1969. Served RN, 1946–49. P&OSN Co., 1952–72: Calcutta, 1953; Kobe, Japan, 1954–56; Hong Kong, 1956–57; Director: P&O Lines, 1967–72; DFDS (UK) Ltd, 1975–; Associated British Ports Plc, 1983–; Transport Develt Gp Plc, 1984–; Vice Chairman: Pearl Cruises of Scandinavia Ltd, 1982–; Harley, Mullion and Co. Ltd (Shipbrokers), 1975–; Mem. Adv. Board: J. Lauritzen A/S, Copenhagen, 1981–; DFDS A/S, Copenhagen, 1981–. President: World Ship Soc., 1969, 1971, 1984, 1985, 1986; Inst. of Freight Forwarders, 1984 and 1985 (Hon. Fellow, 1986); Harwich Lifeboat RNLI, 1984–; World Ship Soc., 1986–; Nat. Waterways Transport Assoc., 1986–; Chairman: Internat. Maritime Industries Forum, 1981–; Friends of the World Maritime Univ., 1985–; pt-time Mem., British Transport Docks Bd, 1981–83; Adviser, Tjaereborg (UK) Ltd, 1985–; Member Council: Missions to Seamen; British Maritime League (Vice-Pres., 1986–); CIT, 1972– (Pres., 1981–82); Marine Soc., 1985–; Internat. Maritime Industries Forum, 1975–; Member: Greenwich Forum; Baltic Exchange, 1973–. FRSA 1986. Hon. FNI. Liveryman, Worshipful Co. of Shipwrights. *Recreations:* golf, family. *Address:* 115 Woodsford Square, W14 8DT. *T:* 01-602 0675; Summer Lawn, Dovercourt, Essex, CO12 4EF. *T:* Harwich 502981. *Clubs:* Hurlingham, Golfers; Harwich & Dovercourt Golf.

DAVIS, John; *see* Davis, A. J.

DAVIS, Prof. John Allen, FRCP; Professor of Paediatrics, and Fellow of Peterhouse, Cambridge University, since 1979; *b* 6 Aug. 1923; *s* of Major H. E. Davis, MC, and Mrs M. W. Davis; *m* 1957, Madeleine Elizabeth Vinnicombe Ashlin (author with D. Wallbridge of Boundary and Space: introduction to the work of D. W. Winnicott, 1981); three *s* two *d*. *Educ:* Blundells Sch., Tiverton (Scholar); St Mary's Hosp. Med. Sch. (Scholar; MB, BS 1946; London Univ. Gold Medal); MSc Manchester, 1968; MA Cantab. FRCP 1967. Army Service, BAOR, 1947–49. House Physician: St Mary's Hosp., 1947; Gt Ormond St Hosp. for Sick Children, 1950; Registrar/Sen. Registrar, St Mary's Paediatric Unit and Home Care Scheme, 1951–57; Sen. Asst Resident, Children's Med. Centre, Boston, Mass, 1953; Nuffield Res. Fellowship, Oxford, 1958–59; Sen. Lectr, Inst. of Child Health, and Reader, Hammersmith Hosp., 1960–67; Prof. of Paediatrics and Child Health, Victoria Univ. of Manchester, 1967–79. Second Vice Pres., RCP, 1986; Member: BPA (former Chm., Academic Bd); Assoc. of Physicians; Chm., Research Cttee, Foundn for Study of Infant Deaths; Past Pres., Eur. Soc. for Pediatric Research. Greenwood Lectr, 1981. Formerly Paediatric Editor of Medicine. *Publications:* Scientific Foundations of Paediatrics (ed and contrib.), 1974 (2nd edn 1981); Place of Birth, 1978; (ed jtly) Parent-Baby Attachment in Premature Infants, 1984; papers in various medical and scientific jls. *Recreations:* collecting and painting watercolours, gardening, reading, music. *Address:* Department of Paediatrics, Addenbrooke's Hospital, Hills Road, Cambridge CB2 2QQ.

DAVIS, John Darelan R.; *see* Russell-Davis, J. D.

DAVIS, Air Chief Marshal Sir John (Gilbert), GCB 1968 (KCB 1964; CB 1953); OBE 1945; psc 1946; idc 1955; RAF, retired; Lieutenant-Governor and Commander-in-Chief of Jersey, 1969–74; *b* 24 March 1911; *e s* of late John Davis, Whitby, Yorks; *m* 1937, Doreen, *d* of Arthur Heaton, Hinckley, Leics; one *s* one *d*. *Educ:* Whitby Grammar Sch.; Queens' Coll., Cambridge, MA 1937. First Commnd RAF, 1934; served Bomber Sqdns 142 and 57, 1934–36; Instructor No 10 Flying Training Sch., 1936–37; Navigation Staff duties, 1938–39; served war of 1939–45 on anti-submarine duties in Mediterranean, Iceland, Azores, UK (seconded to Turkish Air Force as navigation instructor, 1940–41). Instructor RAF Staff Coll., 1948–50; Gp Captain Plans HQ MEAF, 1951–53; OC RAF Station, Topcliffe, 1953–54; Dir of Plans, Air Ministry, 1955–58; SASO, Bomber Command HQ, 1958–59; Air Officer Commanding No 1 Group, Bomber Command, 1959–61; Air Officer Commanding Malta, and Dep. Comdr-in-Chief (Air), Allied Forces Mediterranean, 1961–63; Air Mem. for Supply and Organisation, MoD, 1963–66; Air Officer Commanding-in-Chief: Flying Trng Comd, 1966–68; Trng Comd, 1968–69. Air ADC to the Queen, 1967–69. KStJ 1969. *Recreations:* ornithology, fishing. *Address:* The Stone House, Ruswarp, near Whitby, North Yorks. *Clubs:* Royal Air Force, Union Society (Cambridge).

DAVIS, Sir John (Gilbert), 3rd Bt *cr* 1946; Group Vice-President, Abitibi-Price Inc., Toronto, and Chairman, Abitibi-Price Sales Corporation, New York, since 1983; *b* 17 Aug. 1936; *s* of Sir Gilbert Davis, 2nd Bt, and of Kathleen, *d* of Sidney Deacon Ford; *S* father, 1973; *m* 1960, Elizabeth Margaret, *d* of Robert Smith Turnbull; one *s* two *d*. *Educ:* Oundle School; Britannia RNC, Dartmouth. RN, 1955–56. Joined Spicers Ltd, 1956; emigrated to Montreal, Canada, 1957; joined Inter City Papers and progressed through the company until becoming Pres., 1967; transf. to parent co. in 1976. Director: Abitibi Price Sales Corp.; Gaspesia Paper Co.; Canadian Arthritis Soc. *Recreations:* sports, golf, tennis, squash; music, reading. *Heir:* *s* Richard Charles Davis, *b* 11 April 1970. *Address:* 70 York Mills Road, Toronto, Ont M2P 1B7, Canada. *T:* 222-4916. *Clubs:* Donalda, Toronto (Toronto); Canadian (New York); Kanawaki Golf; Rosedale Golf.

DAVIS, Sir John (Henry Harris), Kt 1971; CVO 1985; Director, The Rank Foundation, since 1953; President, The Rank Organisation plc, Subsidiary and Associated Cos, 1977–83 (Chief Executive, 1962–74; Chairman, 1962–77); Joint President, Rank Xerox, 1972–83 (Joint Chairman 1957–72); *b* 10 Nov. 1906; *s* of Sydney Myering Davis and Emily Harris; *m* 1926, Joan Buckingham; one *s*; *m* 1947, Marion Gavid; two *d*; *m* 1954, Dinah Sheridan (marr. diss. 1965); *m* 1976, Mrs Felicity Rutland. *Educ:* City of London Sch. British Thomson-Houston Group, 1932–38. Joined Odeon Theatres (predecessor of The Rank Organisation Ltd); Chief Accountant, Jan. 1938; Sec., June 1938; Jt Managing Dir, 1942; Man. Dir, 1948–62 and Dep. Chm., 1951–62, The Rank Organisation Ltd. Director: Southern Television Ltd, 1968–76; Eagle Star Insurance Co. Ltd, 1948–82; Chm., Children's Film Foundation, 1951–80; Chm. and Trustee, The Rank Prize Funds, 1972–. Trustee, Westminster Abbey Trust, 1973–85 (Chm., fund raising cttee, Westminster Abbey Appeal, 1973–85). President: The Advertising Assoc., 1973–76; Cinema and Television Benevolent Fund, 1981–83; East Surrey Cons. Assoc., 1982–. FCIS 1939. Commandeur de l'Ordre de la Couronne (Belgium), 1974; KStJ. Hon. DTech Loughborough, 1975. *Recreations:* farming, gardening, reading, travel, music. *Address:* 4 Selwood Terrace, SW7. *Club:* Royal Automobile.

DAVIS, John Michael N.; *see* Newsom Davis.

DAVIS, Leslie Harold Newsom, CMG 1957; *b* 6 April 1909; *s* of Harold Newsom Davis and Aileen Newsom Davis (*née* Gush); *m* 1950, Judith Anne, *d* of L. G. Corney, CMG; one *s* two *d*. *Educ:* Marlborough; Trinity Coll., Cambridge. Apptd to Malayan Civil Service, 1932; Private Sec. to Governor and High Comr, 1938–40; attached to 22nd Ind. Inf. Bde as Liaison Officer, Dec. 1941; interned by Japanese in Singapore, 1942–45; District Officer, Seremban, 1946–47; British Resident, Brunei, 1948; Asst Adviser, Muar, 1948–50; Sec. to Mem. for Education, Fed. of Malaya, 1951–52. Mem. for Industrial and Social Relations, 1952–53; Sec. for Defence and Internal Security, Singapore, 1953–55; Permanent Sec., Min. of Communications and Works, Singapore, 1955–57; Special Rep., Rubber Growers' Assoc. in Malaya, 1958–63. *Recreation:* golf. *Address:* Berrywood, Heyshott, near Midhurst, West Sussex. *Club:* United Oxford & Cambridge University.

DAVIS, Madeline; Regional Nursing Officer, Oxford Regional Health Authority, 1973–83; retired; *b* 12 March 1925; *d* of late James William Henry Davis, JP, and Mrs Edith Maude Davis; *m* 1977, Comdr William Milburn Gibson, RN. *Educ:* Haberdashers' Aske's Hatcham Girls' Sch.; Guy's Hosp. (SRN); British Hosp. for Mothers and Babies, Woolwich; Bristol Maternity Hosp. (SCM). Ward Sister, then Dep. Night Supt, Guy's Hosp., 1949–53; Asst Matron, Guy's Hosp., 1953–57; Admin. Sister then Dep. Matron, St Charles' Hosp., London, 1957–61; Asst Nursing Officer, 1962–68, Chief Regional Nursing Officer, 1968–73, Oxford Regional Hosp. Bd. Formerly Mem., Central Midwives Board. *Recreations:* village community work, theatre, golf. *Club:* North Oxford Golf.

DAVIS, Hon. Sir Maurice, Kt 1975; OBE 1953; QC 1965; Chief Justice of the West Indies Associated States Supreme Court, and of Supreme Court of Grenada, 1975–80; *b* St Kitts, 30 April 1912; *m* Kathleen; one *s* five *d*. Pres., St Kitts Bar Assoc., 1968–75. Mem. Legislature, St Kitts, 1944–57; Mem., Exec. Council, St Kitts; Dep. Pres., Gen. Legislative Council, and Mem., Fed. Exec. Council, Leeward Is. *Recreations:* cricket, football. *Address:* PO Box 31, Basseterre, St Kitts, West Indies.

DAVIS, Dr Michael; Director for Energy Saving, Alternative Sources of Energy, Electricity and Heat, Commission of European Communities, Brussels, since 1981; *b* 9 June 1923; *s* of William James Davis and Rosaline Sarah (*née* May); *m* 1951, Helena Hobbs Campbell, *e d* of Roland and Catherine Campbell, Toronto. *Educ:* UC Exeter (BSc); Bristol Univ. (PhD). CEng, FIMM; CPhys, FInstP. Radar Officer, Flagship, 4th Cruiser Sqdn, British Pacific Fleet, Lieut (Sp. Br.) RNVR, 1943–46 (despatches). Res. Fellow, Canadian Atomic Energy Project, Toronto Univ., 1949–51; Sen. Sci. Officer, Services Electronics Res. Lab., 1951–55; subseq. UKAEA: Commercial Dir and Techn. Adviser, 1956–73; Dir of Nuclear Energy, Other Primary Sources and Electricity, EEC, 1973–81. Chm., OECD Cttee on World Uranium Resources, 1969–73; Dir, NATO Advanced Study Inst., 1971; advised NZ Govt on Atomic Energy, 1967. McLaughlin Meml Lectr, Instn of Engineers of Ireland, 1977. *Publications:* (ed jtly) Uranium Prospecting Handbook, 1972; papers in various sci. jls. *Recreation:* sculpture. *Address:* 200 Rue de la Loi, 1049 Brussels, Belgium. *T:* 235.34.41. *Club:* United Oxford & Cambridge University.

DAVIS, Michael McFarland; Director for Wales, Property Services Agency, Department of the Environment, 1972–77; *b* 1 Feb. 1919; 2nd *s* of Harold McFarland and Gladys Mary Davis; *m* 1942, Aline Seton Butler; three *d*. *Educ:* Haberdashers' Aske's, Hampstead. Entered Air Ministry, 1936. Served War, RAF, 1940–45 (PoW, 1942–45). Private Sec. to Chiefs and Vice-Chiefs of Air Staff, 1945–49, and to Under-Secretary of State for Air, 1952–54; Harvard Univ. Internat. Seminar, 1956; Student, IDC, 1965; Command Sec., FEAF, 1966–69; on loan to Cabinet Office (Central Unit on Environmental Pollution), 1970; transf. to Dept of Environment, 1971. Delegate to UN Conf. on Human Environment, Stockholm, 1972. *Recreations:* doing up old things, music, croquet, wine. *Address:* 3 Sidmount Gardens, Sidmouth, S Devon. *T:* Sidmouth 77123. *Club:* Sidmouth Croquet.

DAVIS, Morris Cael, CMG 1970; MD, FRACP; Consultant Physician, 110 Collins Street, Melbourne; *b* 7 June 1907; *s* of David and Sarah Davis; *m* 1933, Sophia Ashkenasy (*d* 1966); two *s*. *Educ:* Melbourne High Sch.; Univ. of Melbourne. MB, BS (1st cl. hons) Melbourne, 1930; MD 1932; MRCP 1938; FRACP 1946. Univ. of Melbourne: Prosector in Anatomy, 1927; Beaney Schol. in Pathology, 1932–33; Lectr in Pathology, 1933; Lectr in Medicine, Dental Faculty, 1940–63; Bertram Armytage Prize for Med. Res., 1934 and 1942; Fulbright Smith Mundt Schol., 1953–54. Alfred Hosp., Melbourne: Acting Pathologist, 1933–35; Physican to Out-Patients, 1938–46; Phys. to In-Patients, 1946–67; Cons. Phys., 1967–; Foundn Chm., Cardiovascular Diagnostic Service, 1959–67; Dir and Founder, Dept of Visual Aids, 1954–67 (Producer of a number of bedside clinical teaching charts, heart models, cinefilms incl. Routine Examination of the Heart, film strips on mitral stenosis, aortic regurgitation, congenital heart disease, also heart contours of fluoroscopy of heart: all these now in the archives of Monash Univ. Sch. of Medicine, Melbourne); Chm. Drug Cttee, 1960–67. Med. Referee, Commonwealth Dept of Health. Travelled Nuffield Sponsorship, 1954; Litchfield Lectr, Oxford Univ., 1954; Hon. Consultant, Dental Hosp., Melbourne, 1946–. Mem., Curricular Planning Cttee, RMIT; Hon. Pres., Medico-Clerical Soc. of Victoria. Pres., Victorian Friends of Hebrew Univ., Jerusalem, 1953–64; Federal Pres., Australian Friends Hebrew Univ., 1964; Alternate Governor, Hebrew Univ., 1961–63, Governor, Bezalel Acad. of Art and Design, Israel. Founder, Australian Medical Assoc. Arts Group (Pres. 1959–82; creator, twelve fused glass windows in E Melbourne Synagogue, 1977); Hon. Life Pres., Bezalel Fellowship of Arts. Vice-Pres., Aust. Kidney Foundn Appeal, 1971; Mem., Epworth Hosp. Appeal Cttee, 1975–76. *Publications:* History of the East Melbourne Hebrew Congregation 1957–1977, 1977; papers on medicine, medical philosophy and medical educn in Australian Med. Jl, Australian Dental Jl, student jls. *Recreations:* ceramics, painting, music, book collecting, garden. *Address:* 177 Finch Street, Glen Iris, Vic. 3146, Australia. *T:* Melbourne 509.2423.

DAVIS, Nathanael Vining; Chairman of the Board, since 1972, Director since 1947, Alcan Aluminium Limited (President, 1947–72, Chief Executive Officer, 1972–79); *b* 26 June 1915; *s* of Rhea Reineman Davis and Edward Kirk Davis; *m* 1941, Lois Howard Thompson; one *s* one *d. Educ:* Harvard Coll.; London Sch. of Economics. With Alcan group since 1939 with exception of 3 years on active duty with US Navy. Dir, Bank of Montreal, 1961–. *Address:* Alcan Aluminium Ltd, 1188 Sherbrooke Street West, Montreal, Quebec H3A 3G2, Canada. *T:* (514) 848–8000. *Clubs:* Mount Royal, St James's (Montreal); University (New York); The Somerset Club (Boston, Mass).

DAVIS, Prof. Norman, MBE 1945; FBA 1969; Merton Professor of English Language and Literature, University of Oxford, 1959–80; Emeritus Fellow, Merton College, Oxford, since 1980; *b* Dunedin, NZ, 16 May 1913; *s* of James John and Jean Davis; *m* 1944, Magdalene Jamieson Bone (*d* 1983); no *c. Educ:* Otago Boys' High Sch., Dunedin; Otago Univ.; Merton Coll., Oxford. MA NZ 1934; BA Oxon 1936, MA 1944; NZ Rhodes Scholar, 1934. Lecturer in English, Kaunas, Lithuania, 1937; Sofia, Bulgaria, 1938. Government service mainly abroad, 1939–46. Lecturer in English Language, Queen Mary Coll., University of London, 1946; Oriel and Brasenose Colls., Oxford, 1947; Oxford Univ. Lectr in Medieval English, 1948; Prof. of English Language, University of Glasgow, 1949. Hon. Dir of Early English Text Soc., 1957–83. Jt Editor, Review of English Studies, 1954–63. R. W. Chambers Meml Lecturer, UCL, 1971. Hon. DLitt Otago, 1984. *Publications:* Sweet's Anglo-Saxon Primer, 9th edn 1953; The Language of the Pastons (Sir Israel Gollancz Memorial Lecture, British Academy, 1954), 1955; Paston Letters (a selection), 1958; Beowulf facsimile ed. Zupitza, 2nd edn 1959; English and Medieval Studies (ed with C. L. Wrenn), 1962; The Paston Letters (a selection in modern spelling), 1963, rev. edn 1983; Glossary to Early Middle English Verse and Prose (ed J. A. W. Bennett and G. V. Smithers), 1966; rev. edn, Tolkien-Gordon: Sir Gawain, 1967; Non-Cycle Plays and Fragments (EETS), 1970; Paston Letters and Papers of the Fifteenth Century, Part I, 1971, Part II, 1977; (jtly) A Chaucer Glossary, 1979; Non-Cycle Plays and the Winchester Dialogues (facsimiles), 1979; reviews and articles in jls. *Address:* 191b Woodstock Road, Oxford OX2 7AB. *T:* Oxford 59634.

DAVIS, Prof. Ralph Henry Carless, FBA 1975; Professor of Medieval History, University of Birmingham, 1970–84, now Professor Emeritus; *b* 7 Oct. 1918; *s* of late Prof. Henry William Carless Davis and Rosa Jennie Davis; *m* 1949, Eleanor Maud Megaw; two *s. Educ:* Leighton Park Sch.; Balliol Coll., Oxford. Friends' Ambulance Unit, 1939–45. Asst Master, Christ's Hosp., Horsham, 1947–48; Lectr, University Coll., London, 1948–56; Fellow and Tutor, 1956–70, Emeritus Fellow, 1984, Merton Coll., Oxford. Member: Hebdomodal Council, Oxford Univ., 1967–69; Reviewing Cttee on the Export of Arts, 1983–. Pres., Historical Assoc., 1979–82. Editor, History, 1968–78. *Publications:* The Mosques of Cairo, 1944; (ed) The Kalendar of Abbot Samson of Bury St Edmunds, 1954; A History of Medieval Europe, 1957; King Stephen, 1967; (ed with H. A. Cronne) Regesta Regum Anglo-Normannorum, vol. iii, 1968, vol. iv, 1969; The Normans and their Myth, 1976; (ed jtly) The Writing of History in the Middle Ages: essays presented to Richard William Southern, 1981; articles in historical and archæological jls. *Recreations:* travel, archæology, architecture. *Address:* 349 Banbury Road, Oxford OX2 7PL.

See also G. R. C. Davis

DAVIS, Hon. Sir Renn; *see* Davis, Hon. Sir D. R.

DAVIS, Air Vice-Marshal Robert Leslie, CB 1984; RAF, retired 1983; Managing Director, Bodenseewerk Geratetechnik/British Aerospace GmbH, since 1983; *b* 22 March 1930; *s* of Sidney and Florence Davis; *m* 1956, Diana, *d* of Edward William Bryant; one *s* one *d. Educ:* Woolsingham Grammar Sch., Co. Durham; Bede Sch. Collegiate, Sunderland, Co. Durham; RAF Coll., Cranwell. Commnd, 1952; served fighter units, exchange posting, USAF, Staff Coll., OR and Ops appts, MoD, DS Staff Coll., 1953–69; comd No 19 Sqdn, 1970–72; Dep. Dir Ops Air Defence, MoD, 1972–75; comd RAF Leuchars, 1975–77; Comdr RAF Staff, and Air Attaché, British Defence Staff, Washington, DC, 1977–80; Comdr, British Forces Cyprus, and Administrator, Sovereign Base Areas, Cyprus, 1980–83, retired. *Recreations:* golf, antiques, music. *Address:* c/o Lloyds Bank, 54 Fawcett Street, Sunderland, Tyne and Wear.

DAVIS, Sir Rupert C. H.; *see* Hart-Davis.

DAVIS, Stanley Clinton; Member, Commission of the European Communities, since 1985; *b* 6 Dec. 1928; *s* of Sidney Davis; *m* 1954, Frances Jane Clinton Davis (*née* Lucas); one *s* three *d. Educ:* Hackney Downs Sch.; Mercers' Sch.; King's Coll., London University. LLB 1950; admitted Solicitor 1953. Mem. Exec. Council, Nat. Assoc. of Labour Student Organisations, 1949–50. Councillor, London Borough of Hackney, 1959; Mayor of Hackney, 1968. Contested (Lab): Langstone Div. of Portsmouth, 1955; Yarmouth, 1959 and 1964. MP (Lab) Hackney Central, 1970–83; Parly Under-Sec. of State, Dept of Trade, 1974–79; Opposition spokesman on trade, prices and consumer protection, 1979–81, on foreign affairs, 1981–83. Member: Justice; Parly Relations Sub-Cttee of the Law Soc.; Exec. Cttee, Lab. Finance and Industry Gp; APEX; formerly mem., Bd of Deputies of British Jews. Pres., Hackney Br., Multiple Sclerosis Soc.; Vice-Pres., Hackney Assoc. for Disabled; Mem. Rotary Club, Hackney; Hon. Mem. and former Trustee, Merchant Navy and Airline Officers' Assoc. *Recreations:* golf, Association football, reading biographical histories. *Address:* Commission of the European Communities, Rue de la Loi 200, 1049 Brussels, Belgium.

DAVIS, Prof. Stanley Stewart, CChem, FRSC; Lord Trent Professor of Pharmacy, Nottingham University, since 1975; *b* 17 Dec. 1942; *s* of William Stanley and Joan Davis; *m* 1984, Lisbeth Illum; three *s. Educ:* Warwick Sch.; London Univ. (BPharm, PhD, DSc). MPS. Lecturer, London Univ., 1976–80; Sen. Lectr, Aston Univ., 1970–75. Fulbright Scholar, Univ. of Kansas, 1978–79; various periods as visiting scientist to pharmaceutical industry. *Publications:* (co-ed) Radionuclide Imaging in Drug Research, 1982; (co-ed) Microspheres and Drug Therapy, 1984; over 250 research pubns in various scientific jls. *Recreations:* squash, tennis, travel. *Address:* 5 Wortley Hall Close, University Park, Nottingham. *T:* Nottingham 781601.

DAVIS, Steve; snooker player; *b* 22 Aug. 1957; *s* of Harry George Davis and Jean Catherine Davis. *Educ:* Alexander McLeod Primary School and Abbey Wood School, London. Became professional snooker player, 1978; has won numerous championships in UK and abroad; major titles include: UK Professional Champion, 1980, 1981, 1984, 1985; Masters Champion, 1981, 1982; International Champion, 1981, 1983, 1984; World Professional Champion, 1981, 1983, 1984. *Publications:* Steve Davis, World Champion, 1981; Frame and Fortune, 1982; Successful Snooker, 1982. *Recreations:* chess, keep fit, listening to records (jazz/soul), Tom Sharpe books. *Address:* Ground Floor, 1 Arcade Place, South Street, Romford, Essex RM1 1RS. *T:* Romford 24023. *Club:* Matchroom (Romford).

DAVIS, Terence Anthony Gordon, (Terry Davis); MP (Lab) Birmingham, Hodge Hill, since 1983 (Birmingham, Stechford, 1979–83); *b* 5 Jan. 1938; *s* of Gordon Davis and Gladys (*née* Avery), Stourbridge, West Midlands; *m* 1963, Anne, *d* of F. B. Cooper, Newton-le-Willows, Lancs; one *s* one *d. Educ:* King Edward VI Grammar Sch., Stourbridge, Worcestershire; University Coll. London (LLB); Univ. of Michigan, USA (MBA). Company Executive, 1962–71. Motor Industry Manager, 1974–79. Joined Labour Party, 1965; contested (Lab): Bromsgrove, 1970, Feb. and Oct. 1974; Birmingham, Stechford, March 1977. MP (Lab) Bromsgrove, May 1971–Feb. 1974; Opposition Whip, 1979–80; opposition spokesman on the health service and social services, 1980–83, on Treasury and economic affairs, 1983–. Member, Assoc. of Scientific, Technical and Managerial Staffs. Member, Yeovil Rural District Council, 1967–68. *Address:* 5 Hodge Hill Court, Bromford Road, Hodge Hill, Birmingham B36 8AN.

DAVIS, Hon. Sir Thomas (Robert Alexander Harries), KBE 1981; Pa Tu Te Rangi Ariki 1979; Prime Minister, Cook Islands, since 1978; *b* 11 June 1917; *s* of Sidney Thomes Davis and Maryanne Harries; *m* 1940, Myra Lydia Henderson; three *s*; *m* 1979, Pa Tepaeru Ariki. *Educ:* King's Coll., Auckland, NZ; Otago Univ. Med. Sch. (MB, ChB 1945); Sch. of Tropical Medicine, Sydney Univ., Australia (DTM&H 1950); Harvard Sch. of Public Health (Master of Public Health 1952). FRSTM&H 1949. MO and Surg. Specialist, Cook Islands Med. Service, 1945–48; Chief MO, Cook Is Med. Service, 1948–52; Res. Staff, Dept of Nutrition, Harvard Sch. of Public Health, 1952–55; Chief, Dept of Environmental Medicine, Arctic Aero-medical Lab., Fairbanks, Alaska, 1955–56; Res. Physician and Dir, Div. of Environmtl Med., Army Medical Res. Lab., Fort Knox, Ky, 1956–61; Dir of Res., US Army Res. Inst. of Environmtl Med., Natick, 1961–63; Res. Exec., Arthur D. Little, Inc., 1963–71. Involved in biol aspects of space prog., first for Army, later for NASA, 1957–71. Formed Democratic Party, Cook Islands, 1971; private med. practice, Cook Islands, 1974–78. Mem., RSocMed, 1960; twice Pres., Med. and Dental Assoc., Cook Islands. Pres., Avatiu Sports Club. Silver Jubilee Medal, 1977; Order of Merit, Fed. Republic of Germany, 1978. *Publications:* Doctor to the Islands, 1954; Makutu, 1956; over 80 scientific and other pubns. *Recreations:* deep sea fishing, yacht racing, agriculture/planting, amateur radio. *Address:* Prime Minister's Department, Rarotonga, Cook Islands. *Club:* Harvard (Boston, Mass).

DAVIS, William; author, columnist and broadcaster; Editor and Publisher of High Life, since 1973; Chairman, Headway Publications, since 1977; Editorial Director: Executive World, since 1980; Moneycare, since 1983; *b* 6 March 1933; *m* 1967, Sylvette Jouclas. *Educ:* City of London Coll. On staff of Financial Times, 1954–59; Editor, Investor's Guide, 1959–60; City Editor, Evening Standard, 1960–65 (with one year's break as City Editor, Sunday Express); Financial Editor, The Guardian, 1965–68; Editor, Punch, 1968–77; Editor-in-Chief, Financial Weekly, 1977–80. Presenter, Money Programme, BBC TV, 1967–69. Director, Fleet Publishing International, Morgan-Grampian, and Fleet Holdings, 1977–80. *Publications:* Three Years Hard Labour: the road to devaluation, 1968; Merger Mania, 1970; Money Talks, 1972; Have Expenses, Will Travel, 1975; It's No Sin to be Rich, 1976; (ed) The Best of Everything, 1980; Money in the 1980s, 1981; The Rich: a study of the species, 1982; Fantasy: a practical guide to escapism, 1984; The Corporate Infighter's Handbook, 1984; (ed) The World's Best Business Hotels, 1985. *Recreations:* drinking wine, travelling, playing tennis (badly), thinking about retirement. *Address:* Headway Publications, Clareville House, 47 Whitcomb Street, WC2H 7DX. *Clubs:* Garrick, Hurlingham.

DAVIS, Sir (William) Allan, GBE 1985; CA; Senior Partner, Armitage & Norton, London, since 1979 (Partner, 1976); Lord Mayor of London, 1985–86; *b* 19 June 1921; *s* of Wilfred Egwin Davis and Annie Helen Davis; *m* 1944, Audrey Pamela Louch; two *s* one *d. Educ:* Cardinal Vaughan Sch., Kensington. Mem., Inst. of Accountants and Actuaries, Glasgow (now Inst. of Chartered Accountants of Scotland), 1949; ATII. FRSA. Served War, Pilot RNVR FAA, 1940–44. Joined Barclays Bank, 1939; Dunn Wylie & Co.: apprentice, 1944; Partner, 1952; Sen. Partner, 1972–76. Director: Catholic Herald Ltd; Crowning Tea Co. Ltd; Dunkelman & Son Ltd; Fiat Auto (UK) Ltd; Forestry Ltd; Internatio-Muller UK Ltd and UK subsidiaries. Common Councilman, Ward of Queenhithe, 1971–76; Alderman, Ward of Cripplegate, 1976–; Sheriff, City of London, 1982–83. Chairman: Port and City of London Health Cttee and Social Services Cttee, 1974–77; Management Cttee, London Homes for the Elderly, 1975–; Queenhithe Ward Club, 1976–77; Barbican Youth Club, 1979–82; Mem. Court, HAC, 1976–. Hon. Treasurer: City of London Centre, St John Amb. Assoc., 1979–82, 1983–84, Vice-Pres., 1985; Worshipful Co. of Painter-Stainers, 1962– (Liveryman, 1960; Mem. Court, 1962–). Hon. Freeman, Worshipful Co. of Chartered Accountants in England and Wales, 1983–. Governor: Bridewell Royal Hosp., 1976–; Cripplegate Foundn, 1976– (Chm., 1981–); Cardinal Vaughan Meml Sch., 1968–81, 1985–; Lady Eleanor Holles Sch., 1979–; Trustee, Sir John Soane's Mus., 1979–; Patron, Barbican Lawn Tennis Club, 1979–; Vice Pres., Lancia Motor Club. Hon. DSc City, 1985. KCSG 1979; KCHS 1977 (Kt, English Lieutenancy, 1972); KStJ 1986. Comdr, Order of Orange-Nassau, Netherlands, 1982; Order of Merit (Class I), State of Qatar, 1985. *Recreations:* bridge, travel. *Address:* 168 Defoe House, Barbican, EC2Y 8DN. *T:* 01–638 5354. *Clubs:* Oriental, Wig and Pen, City Livery, Players Theatre.

DAVIS, William Eric, (professionally known as **David Davis**), MBE 1969; MA Oxon; LRAM, ARCM; *b* 27 June 1908; *s* of William John and Florence Kate Rachel Davis; *m* 1935, Barbara de Riemer (*d* 1982); one *s* two *d. Educ:* Bishop's Stortford Coll.; The Queen's Coll., Oxford (MA). Schoolmaster, 1931–35; joined BBC as mem. of Children's Hour, 1935. Served with RNVR Acting Temp. Lieut, 1942–46. BBC, 1946–70; Head of Children's Hour, BBC, 1953–61; Head of Children's Programmes (Sound), BBC, 1961–64; Producer, Drama Dept, 1964–70, retired; *Publications:* various songs, etc.

including: Lullaby, 1943; Fabulous Beasts, 1948; Little Grey Rabbit Song Book, 1952; *poetry:* A Single Star, 1973; various speech recordings, including Black Beauty, Just So Stories. *Recreations:* children, cats, growing roses. *Address:* 18 Mount Avenue, W5 2RG. *T:* 01-997 8156. *Club:* Garrick.

DAVIS, Hon. William Grenville, CC (Canada) 1986; PC (Can.) 1982; QC (Can.); barrister and solicitor; Counsel to Tory, Tory, DesLauriers & Binnington, Toronto; Member of the Provincial Parliament, Ontario, 1959–85; Premier of Ontario, Canada, and President of the Council, Ontario, 1971–85; Leader, Progressive Conservative Party, 1971–85; *b* Brampton, Ont., 30 July 1929; *s* of Albert Grenville Davis and Vera M. Davis (*née* Hewetson); *m* 1st, 1953, Helen MacPhee (*d* 1962), *d* of Neil MacPhee, Windsor, Ontario; 2nd, 1963, Kathleen Louise, *d* of Dr R. P. Mackay, California; two *s* three *d*. *Educ:* Brampton High Sch.; University Coll., Univ. of Toronto (BA); Osgoode Hall Law Sch. (grad. 1955). Called to Bar of Ontario, 1955; practised gen. law, Brampton, 1955–59. Elected Mem. (C) Provincial Parlt (MPP) for Peel Riding, 1959, 1963, Peel North Riding, 1967, 1971, Brampton Riding, 1975, 1981. Minister of Educn, 1962–71; also Minister of Univ. Affairs, 1964–71; Special Envoy on Acid Rain, apptd by Prime Minister of Canada, 1985–86. Director: Ford Motor Co. of Canada; Inter-City Gas Corp.; Magna Internat. Inc.; NIKE Canada; Power Corp. of Canada; Seagram Co.; Vice-Chm., Stadium Corp. Ontario. Chm. Exec. Council, True North America's Cup '87. Holds hon. doctorates in Law from eight Ontario Univs: Waterloo Lutheran, W Ontario, Toronto, McMaster, Queen's, Windsor; Hon. Graduate: Albert Einstein Coll. of Med.; Yeshiva Univ. of NY; NUI; Ottawa; Tel Aviv. Amer. Transit Assoc. Man of the Year, 1973. A Freemason. *Publications:* Education in Ontario, 1965; The Government of Ontario and the Universities of the Province (Frank Gerstein Lectures, York Univ.), 1966; Building an Educated Society 1816–1966, 1966; Education for New Times, 1967. *Address:* 61 Main Street South, Brampton, Ontario L6J 1Y7, Canada. *Clubs:* Kiwanis, Shriners, Masons, Albany (Ont.).

DAVIS, William Herbert, BSc; CEng, FIMechE; Deputy Managing Director, British Motor Corporation, 1961–83; *b* 27 July 1919; *s* of William and Dora Davis; *m* 1945, Barbara Mary Joan (*née* Sommerfield); one *d*. *Educ:* Waverley Grammar Sch.; Univ. of Aston in Birmingham (BSc). Austin Motor Co.: Engr Apprentice, 1935–39; Mech. Engr and Section Leader, Works Engrs, 1946–51; Supt Engr, 1951; Asst Production Manager, 1954; Production Manager, 1956; Dir and Gen. Works Manager, 1958. British Motor Corp. Ltd: Dir of Production, 1960; Dep. Managing Dir (Manufacture and Supply), 1961; Dep. Managing Dir, British Leyland (Austin-Morris Ltd), 1968; Chairman and Chief Executive, Triumph Motor Co. Ltd, 1970; Managing Dir, Rover Triumph BLUK Ltd, 1972; Dir (Manufacture), British Leyland Motor Corporation, 1973; Dir, Military Contracts and Govt Affairs, Leyland Cars, 1976–81; Consultant, BL and Land Rover Ltd, 1981–83; Dir, Land Rover Santana (Spain), 1976–83. FIIM, FBIM, SME(USA). *Recreations:* riding, motoring, photography; interests in amateur boxing. *Address:* Arosa, The Holloway, Alvechurch, Worcs. *T:* Redditch 66187.

DAVIS, Most Rev. William Wallace; *b* 10 Dec. 1908; *s* of Isaac Davis and Margaret Dixon; *m* 1933, Kathleen Aubrey Acheson (*d* 1966); two *s* two *d*; *m* 1968, Helen Mary Lynton. *Educ:* Bishop's Univ., Lennoxville, PQ. BA 1931, BD 1934; Deacon, 1932; Priest, 1932; Curate, St Matthew's, Ottawa, 1932–36; Rector, Coaticook, PQ, 1936–38; Rector, St Matthew's, Quebec, 1938–52; Archdeacon of Quebec, 1947–52; Dean of Nova Scotia, and Rector of the Cathedral Church of All Saints, Halifax, NS, 1952–58; Bishop Coadjutor of Nova Scotia, 1958–63; Bishop of Nova Scotia, 1963; Archbishop of Nova Scotia and Metropolitan of Ecclesiastical Province of the Atlantic, Canada, 1972–75. DD University of King's Coll., Halifax, 1954; Hon. DCL Bishop's Univ., Lennoxville, PQ, 1960; Hon. LLD St Francis Xavier Univ., Antigonish, Nova Scotia, 1974. *Address:* Apt 712, 1465 Baseline Road, Ottawa, Ont K2C 3L9, Canada.

DAVIS, Adm. Sir William (Wellclose), GCB 1959 (KCB 1956; CB 1952); DSO 1944, and Bar, 1944; DL; *b* 11 Oct. 1901; *s* of late W. S. Davis, Indian Political Service; *m* 1934, Lady Gertrude Elizabeth Phipps (*d* 1985), 2nd *d* of 3rd Marquis of Normanby; two *s* two *d*. *Educ:* Summerfields, Oxford; Osborne and Dartmouth Naval Colls. Midshipman, 1917; Lieut, 1921; Comdr, 1935; Capt., 1940; Rear-Adm., 1950; Acting Vice-Adm. and Vice-Adm., 1953; Adm. 1956, Dep. Dir of Plans and Cabinet Offices, 1940–42; commanded HMS Mauritius, 1943–44; Dir of Under Water Weapons, Admiralty, 1945–46; Imperial Defence Coll., 1947; Chief of Staff to C-in-C Home Fleet, 1948–49. The Naval Sec., Admiralty, 1950–52; Flag Officer 2nd in Command Mediterranean, 1952–54; Vice-Chief of the Naval Staff, Admiralty, 1954–57; Comdr-in-Chief, Home Fleet, and NATO Comdr-in-Chief, Eastern Atlantic Area, 1958–60; First and Principal Naval ADC to the Queen, 1959–60, retired. Vice-Pres., King George's Fund for Sailors; Member: Royal Institution of GB (Vice-Pres.); Royal United Service Institution; European-Atlantic Group (Vice-Pres.); British Atlantic Cttee; Gloucestershire Community Council; President: Gloucestershire Outward Bound; Gloucestershire County Scouts; Forest of Dean District Scouts; Treasurer, Friends of Gloucester Cathedral; Mem., St Helena Assoc.; Past Chm., Cheltenham Ladies' College and various educational authorities. DL Glos 1963. *Recreations:* fishing, shooting. *Address:* Coglan House, Longhope, Glos. *T:* Gloucester 830282. *Clubs:* Naval and Military; Ends of the Earth.
See also Comdr L. M. M. Saunders Watson.

DAVIS-GOFF, Sir Robert William; *see* Goff.

DAVIS-RICE, Peter; Regional Nursing Officer, North Western Regional Health Authority, since 1973 and Assistant General Manager (Personnel Services), since 1985; *b* 1 Feb. 1930; *s* of Alfred Davis-Rice and Doris Eva (*née* Bates); *m* 1967, Judith Anne Chatterton; one *s* two *d*. *Educ:* Riley High Sch., Hull; Royal Coll. of Nursing, Edinburgh; Harefield Hosp., Mddx; City Hosp., York. SRN; British Tuberculosis Assoc. Cert.; AMBIM; NAdmin(Hosp)Cert. Staff Nurse, Charge Nurse, St Luke's Hosp., Huddersfield, 1954–57; Theatre Supt, Hull Royal Infirmary, 1957–62; Asst Matron (Theatres), Walton Hosp., Liverpool, 1962–66; Matron, Billinge Hosp., Wigan, 1966–69; Chief Nursing Officer, Oldham and District HMC, 1969–73. *Publications:* contrib. Nursing Times. *Recreations:* badminton, tennis, do-it-yourself. *Address:* Riencourt, 185 Frederick Street, Oldham OL8 4DH. *T:* 061–624 2485.

DAVISON, family name of **Baron Broughshane.**

DAVISON, Prof. Alan Nelson, PhD, DSc; FRCPath; Professor of Neurochemistry, Institute of Neurology, University of London, at the National Hospital, Queen Square, and Consulting Neurochemist, National Hospital, since 1971; *b* 6 June 1925; *s* of Alfred N. Davison and Ada E. W. Davison; *m* 1948, Patricia Joyce Pickering; one *s* two *d*. *Educ:* Univ. of Nottingham; Univ. of London (BSc Hons, BPharm; PhD 1954; DSc 1962). FRCPath 1979. Staff of MRC Toxicology Unit, 1950–54; MRC Exchange Fellow, Sorbonne, Paris, 1954; Dept of Pathology, 1957–60, Dept of Biochemistry, 1960–65, Guy's Hosp. Med. Sch. (Reader in Biochem., 1962–65); Prof. of Biochem., Charing Cross Hosp. Med. Sch., 1965–71. Sec., Biochemical Soc., 1968. Chief Editor, Jl of Neurochem., 1970–75; Mem. Editorial Boards: Jl of Pharmacy and Pharmacology, 1960–62; Jl of Neurology, Neurosurgery and Psychiatry, 1965–67; Acta Neuropathologica, 1977–; Brain, 1976–81. Dhole-Eddleston Prize (for most deserving publd work of med. res. appertaining to needs of aged people), 1980. *Publications:* (jtly) Applied Neurochemistry, 1968; (jtly) Myelination, 1970; Biochemistry of Neurological Disease, 1976; Biochemical Correlates of Brain Structure and Function, 1977; The Molecular Basis of Neuropathology, 1981; papers on neurochem. of multiple sclerosis and on ageing and senile dementia. *Recreations:* choral singing, painting. *Address:* Drivers, 54 High Street, Stock, Ingatestone, Essex CM4 9BW. *T:* Stock 840362.

DAVISON, Arthur Clifford Percival, CBE 1974; FRAM 1966; Musical Director and Conductor: Little Symphony of London, since 1964; Virtuosi of England, since 1970; *b* Montreal, Canada; *s* of late Arthur Mackay Davison and Hazel Edith Smith; *m* 1st, 1950, Barbara June Hildred (marr. diss.); one *s* two *d*; 2nd, 1978, Elizabeth Blanche. *Educ:* Conservatory of Music, McGill Univ., Conservatoire de Musique, Montreal; Royal Associated Board Scholar at Royal Acad. of Music, London; later studies in Europe; LRSM 1947; ARCM 1950. A Dir and Dep. Leader, London Philharmonic Orch., 1957–65; Guest Conductor, Royal Danish Ballet, 1964; Asst Conductor, Bournemouth Symphony Orch., 1965–66. Guest Conductor of Orchestras: London Philharmonic; London Symphony; Philharmonia; Royal Philharmonic; BBC Orchs; Birmingham Symphony; Bournemouth Symphony and Sinfonietta; Ulster; Royal Liverpool Philharmonic; New York City Ballet; CBC Radio and Television Orchs; Royal Danish. Founder of Arthur Davison Concerts for Children, 1966; Dir and Conductor, Nat. Youth Orch. of Wales, 1966– (conducted Investiture Week Symphony concert in presence of HRH Prince of Wales, 1969; Guild for Promotion of Welsh Music Award for long and distinguished service, 1976); Mus. Dir, Corralls Concerts, Bournemouth Symphony, 1966–; conducted official Silver Jubilee concert, Fairfield Halls, 1977, and in presence of the Queen and HRH Duke of Edinburgh, Poole Arts Centre, Dorset, 1979; conducted Royal Over-Seas League 70th Anniversary concert, St James's Palace, in presence of HRH Princess Alexandra, 1980. Conductor and Lectr, London Univ., Goldsmiths' Coll., 1971–; Governor and Guest Lectr, Welsh Coll. of Music and Drama, 1973–; Orchestral Dir, Symphony Orchestra, Birmingham Sch. of Music, 1981–. EMI/CFP award for sale of half a million classical records, 1973, Gold Disc for sale of one million classical records, 1977. Tour of Europe recorded for BBC TV. FRSA 1977. Hon. Master of Music, Univ. of Wales, 1974. *Publications:* various articles in musical jls. *Recreations:* reading, theatre-going, fishing, boating on Thames, antiques. *Address:* Glencairn, Shepherd's Hill, Merstham, Surrey RH1 3AD. *T:* Merstham 4434 and 2206. *Clubs:* Savage, Royal Over-Seas League.

DAVISON, Ian Frederic Hay, FCA; Adviser, Arthur Andersen & Co., since 1986; Director: Morgan Grenfell Asset Management Ltd, since 1986, Newspaper Publishing Plc, since 1986; *b* 30 June 1931; *s* of late Eric Hay Davison, FCA, and Inez Davison; *m* 1955, Maureen Patricia Blacker; one *s* two *d*. *Educ:* Dulwich Coll.; LSE (BScEcon); Univ. of Mich. ACA 1956, FCA 1966. Managing Partner, 1966–82, Arthur Andersen & Co., Chartered Accountants; Dep. Chm. and Chief Exec., Lloyd's of London, 1983–86; Mem. Council, Lloyd's, 1983–86. Mem. Council, ICA, 1975–; Chm., Accounting Standards Cttee, 1982–84. Indep. Mem., NEDC for Bldg Industry, 1971–77; Member: Price Commn, 1977–79; Audit Commn, 1983–; Chm., EDC for Food and Drink Manufg Industry, 1981–83. Dept of Trade Inspector, London Capital Securities, 1975–77; Inspector, Grays Building Soc., 1978–79. Trustee, V&A Museum, 1984–; Dir and Trustee, Royal Opera House, 1984–; Chm., Monteverdi Trust, 1979–84. Governor, LSE, 1982–. Councillor and Alderman, London Bor. of Greenwich, 1961–73. *Recreations:* theatre, music, ski-ing. *Address:* 40 Earlham Street, WC2. *Clubs:* Arts, MCC.

DAVISON, Sir John Alec B.; *see* Biggs-Davison.

DAVISON, Rt. Hon. Sir Ronald (Keith), GBE 1978; CMG 1975; PC 1978; **Rt. Hon. The Chief Justice Sir Ronald Davison;** Chief Justice of New Zealand, since 1978; *b* 16 Nov. 1920; *s* of Joseph James Davison and Florence May Davison; *m* 1948, Jacqueline May Carr; one *s* one *d* (and one *s* decd). *Educ:* Auckland Univ. (LLB). Admitted as barrister and solicitor, 1948; QC (NZ) 1963. Chairman: Environmental Council, 1969–74; Legal Aid Bd, 1969–78; Member: Council, Auckland Dist Law Soc., 1960–65 (Pres., 1965–66); Council, NZ Law Soc., 1963–66; Auckland Electric Power Bd (13 yrs); Aircrew Indust. Tribunal, 1970–78. Chm., Montana Wines Ltd, 1971–78; Dir, NZ Insurance Co. Ltd, 1975–78. *Recreations:* golf, fishing, bowls. *Address:* Chief Justice's Chambers, High Court, Wellington, New Zealand. *Clubs:* Wellington; Northern (Auckland, NZ).

DAVSON, Sir Geoffrey Leo Simon, 2nd Bt; *see* Glyn, Sir Anthony, 2nd Bt.

DAVY, Humphrey Augustine A.; *see* Arthington-Davy.

DAWBARN, Sir Simon (Yelverton), KCVO 1980; CMG 1976; HM Diplomatic Service, retired; *b* 16 Sept. 1923; *s* of Frederic Dawbarn and Maud Louise Mansell; *m* 1948, Shelby Montgomery Parker; one *s* two *d*. *Educ:* Oundle Sch.; Corpus Christi Coll., Cambridge. Served in HM Forces (Reconnaissance Corps), 1942–45. Reckitt & Colman (Overseas), 1948–49. Joined Foreign Service, 1949. Foreign Office, 1949–53; Brussels, 1953; Prague, 1955; Tehran, 1957; seconded to HM Treasury, 1959; Foreign Office, 1961; Algiers, 1965; Athens, 1968; FCO, 1971–75. Head of W African Dept and concurrently non-resident Ambassador to Chad, 1973–75; Consul-General, Montreal, 1975–78; Ambassador to Morocco, 1978–82. *Address:* 44 Canonbury Park North, N1 2JT. *T:* 01–226 0659.

DAWE, Donovan Arthur; Principal Keeper, Guildhall Library, London, 1967–73, retired; *b* 21 Jan. 1915; *s* of late Alfred Ernest and Sarah Jane Dawe, Wallington, Surrey; *m* 1946, Peggy Marjory Challen; two *d*. *Educ:* Sutton Grammar Sch. Associate, Library Assoc., 1938. Entered Guildhall Library as junior assistant, 1931. Served with Royal West African Frontier Force in Africa and India, 1941–46. Freeman of City of London and Merchant Taylors' Company, 1953. FRHistS 1954. *Publications:* Skilbecks: drysalters 1650–1950, 1950; 11 Ironmonger Lane: the story of a site in the City of London, 1952; The City of London: a select book list, 1972; Organists of the City of London 1666–1850, 1983; contribs professional literature, Connoisseur, Musical Times, Genealogists' Magazine, etc. *Recreations:* the countryside, local history, musicology. *Address:* 46 Green Lane, Purley, Surrey CR2 3PJ. *T:* 01–660 4218.

DAWE, Roger James, OBE 1970; Deputy Secretary, Department of Employment, since 1985; *b* 26 Feb. 1941; *s* of Harry James and Edith Mary Dawe; *m* 1965, Ruth Day Jolliffe; one *s* one *d*. *Educ:* Hardyes Sch., Dorchester; Fitzwilliam House, Cambridge. BA Cantab. Entered Min. of Labour, 1962; Dept of Economic Affairs, 1964–65; Private Sec. to Prime Minister, 1966–70; Principal, Dept of Employment, 1970; Private Sec. to Secretary of State for Employment, 1972–74; Asst Sec., Dept of Employment, 1974–81; Under Sec., MSC, 1981; Chief Exec., Trng Div., MSC, 1982–84. *Recreations:* tennis, Plymouth Argyle supporter. *Address:* 35 Cromwell Avenue, Bromley, Kent BR2 9AG.

DAWES, Prof. Edwin Alfred, FIBiol; CChem, FRSC; Reckitt Professor and Head of Biochemistry Department, University of Hull, since 1963; *b* 6 July 1925; *s* of late Harold Dawes and Maude Dawes (*née* Barker); *m* 1950, Amy Rogerson; two *s*. *Educ:* Goole

Grammar Sch.; Univ. of Leeds. BSc, PhD, DSc. Asst Lectr, later Lectr, in Biochemistry, Univ. of Leeds, 1947–50; Lectr, later Sen. Lectr, Univ. of Glasgow, 1951–63; Hull University: Dean of Science, 1968–70; Pro-Vice-Chancellor, 1977–80. Visiting Lecturer: Meml Univ., Newfoundland, Dalhousie Univ., 1959; Univ. of Brazil, 1960, 1972; Univ. of S California, 1962; Univ. of Rabat, 1967; Univ. of Göttingen, 1972; Osmania Univ., Hyderabad, 1986; Biochemical Soc. Lectr, Australia and NZ, 1975; Amer. Medical Alumni Lectr, Univ. of St Andrews, 1980–81. Editor, Biochemical Jl, 1958–65; Editor-in-Chief, Jl of Gen. Microbiol., 1976–81; Man. Editor, Fedn of European Microbiol Socs, and Editor-in-Chief, FEMS Microbiology Letters, 1982–. Chm., Scientific Adv. Cttee, Yorks Cancer Res. Campaign, 1978–; Member: Scientific Adv. Cttee, Whyte-Watson-Turner Cancer Res. Trust, 1984–; Scientific Adv. Bd, Microbial Resources Ltd, 1984–. President: Hull Lit. Phil. Soc., 1976–77; British Ring of Internat. Brotherhood of Magicians, 1972–73; Hon. Pres., Scottish Conjurers' Assoc.; Hon. Vice-Pres., Magic Circle (Mem., 1959–). Governor, Pocklington Sch., 1965–74; Member, Court: Leeds Univ., 1974–; Bradford Univ., 1985–. Mem., Hall of Fame and H. A. Smith Literary Award, Soc. Amer. Magicians, 1984; Literary Fellowship, Acad. Magical Arts, USA, 1985. *Publications:* Quantitative Problems in Biochemistry, 1956, 6th edn 1980; (jtly) Biochemistry of Bacterial Growth, 1968, 3rd edn 1982; The Great Illusionists, 1979; Isaac Fawkes: fame and fable, 1979; The Biochemist in a Microbial Wonderland, 1982; Vonetta, 1982; The Barrister in the Circle, 1983; (ed) Environmental Regulation of Microbial Metabolism, 1985; (ed) Enterobacterial Surface Antigens, 1985; Microbial Energetics, 1985; (jtly) The Book of Magic, 1986; numerous papers in scientific jls. *Recreations:* conjuring, book-collecting. *Address:* Dane Hill, 393 Beverley Road, Anlaby, N Humberside HU10 7BQ. *T:* Hull 657998. *Club:* Savage.

DAWES, Prof. Geoffrey Sharman, CBE 1981; FRS 1971; Director of Charing Cross Medical Research Centre, since 1984; *b* 21 Jan. 1918; *s* of Rev. W. Dawes, Thurlaston Grange, Derbyshire; *m* 1941, Margaret Monk; two *s* two *d. Educ:* Repton Sch.; New Coll., Oxford. BA 1939; BSc 1940; BM, BCh 1943; DM 1947. Rockefeller Travelling Fellowship, 1946; Fellow, Worcester Coll., Oxford, 1946–85, Emeritus Fellow, 1985; University Demonstrator in Pharmacology, Oxford, 1947; Foulerton Research Fellow, Royal Society, 1948; Dir, Nuffield Inst. for Medical Research, Oxford, 1948–85. Mem., MRC, 1978–82; Chm., Physiological Systems and Disorders Bd, MRC, 1978–80. Governor of Repton, 1959, Chm., 1971–85. A Vice-Pres., Royal Society, 1976, 1977. FRCOG, FRCP; Hon. FACOG. Max Weinstein Award, 1963; Gairdner Foundation Award, 1966; Maternité Award of European Assoc. Perinatal Medicine, 1976; Virginia Apgar Award, Amer. Acad. of Pediatrics, 1980. *Publications:* Foetal and Neonatal Physiology, 1968; various publications in physiological and pharmacological journals. *Recreation:* fishing. *Address:* 8 Belbroughton Road, Oxford. *T:* Oxford 58131.

DAWES, Ven. Peter Spencer; Archdeacon of West Ham, since 1980; *b* 1928; *s* of Jason Spencer Dawes and Janet Dawes; *m* 1954, Ethel Marrin; two *s* two *d. Educ:* Bickley Hall School; Aldenham School; Hatfield Coll., Durham (BA); Tyndale Hall, Bristol. Assistant Curate: St Andrew's, Whitehall Park, 1954–57; St Ebbe's, Oxford, 1957–60; Tutor, Clifton Theological Coll., 1960–65; Vicar, Good Shepherd, Romford, 1965–80. Examining Chaplain to Bishop of Chelmsford, 1970–; Member General Synod, 1970–, and of Standing Cttee, 1975–. *Address:* 15 Wallenger Avenue, Gidea Park, Romford, Essex RM2 6EP.

DAWICK, Viscount; Alexander Douglas Derrick Haig; *b* 30 June 1961; *s* and *heir* of 2nd Earl Haig, *qv. Educ:* Stowe School. *Address:* Bemersyde, Melrose, Scotland.

DAWKINS, Douglas Alfred; Associate Director, Bank of England, since 1985; *b* 17 Sept. 1927; *s* of Arthur Dawkins and Edith Annie Dawkins; *m* 1953, Diana Pauline (*née* Ormes); one *s* one *d. Educ:* Edmonton County Secondary Sch.; University Coll. London (Rosa Morison Scholar). BA Hons). Entered Bank of England, 1950; Bank for Internat. Settlements, 1953–54; Adviser to Governors, Bank of Libya, 1964–65; Asst Chief of Overseas Dept, 1970; First Dep. Chief of Exchange Control, 1972; Chief of Exchange Control, 1979; Asst Dir, 1980. *Address:* Bank of England, Threadneedle Street, EC2R 8AH.

DAWNAY, family name of **Viscount Downe.**

DAWNAY, Lt-Col Christopher Payan, CBE 1946; MVO 1944; *s* of late Maj.-Gen. Guy P. Dawnay, CB, CMG, DSO, MVO, and Mrs Cecil Dawnay; *m* 1939, Patricia, *d* of Sir Hereward Wake, 13th Bt, CB, CMG, DSO; two *s* two *d. Educ:* Winchester; Magdalen Coll., Oxford. With Dawnay Day & Co. Ltd, Merchant Bankers, 1933–39 and 1946–50. War service with Coldstream Guards and in various staff appointments, 1939–45. Partner, Edward de Stein & Co., Merchant Bankers, 1951–60; Director, Lazard Bros & Co. Ltd, 1960–74; Chairman: Guardian Assurance Co., 1967–68; Guardian Royal Exchange Assurance Co., 1970–74. One of HM Lieutenants, City of London. US Legion of Merit. *Recreations:* fishing, shooting. *Address:* Ropers, Longparish, Andover, Hants. *T:* Longparish 204. *Club:* Brooks's.

See also Captain O. P. Dawnay.

DAWNAY, Hon. George William ffolkes, MC 1944; DL; Coldstream Guards; Director, Barclays Bank Ltd, 1956–79; Local Advisory Director, Barclays Bank Ltd, Norwich, retired 1979; *b* 20 April 1909; *s* of 9th Viscount Downe, CMG, DSO and Dorothy, *o c* of Sir William ffolkes, 3rd Bt; *m* 1945, Rosemary Helen (*d* 1969), *d* of late Lord Edward Grosvenor and of late Lady Dorothy Charteris; two *s* two *d. Educ:* Eton. DL Norfolk, 1961–84. *Address:* Hillington Hall, King's Lynn, Norfolk. *T:* Hillington 600304.

DAWNAY, Captain Oliver Payan, CVO 1953; *b* 4 April 1920; *s* of late Maj.-General Guy Payan Dawnay, CB, CMG, DSO, MVO; *m* 1st, 1944, Lady Margaret Dorothea Boyle (marr. diss. 1962), *y d* of 8th Earl of Glasgow, DSO; two *s* one *d;* 2nd, 1963, Hon. Iris Irene Adele Peake, *e d* of 1st Viscount Ingleby, PC; one *d. Educ:* Eton; Balliol Coll., Oxford. Parliamentary and Press section, Ministry of Economic Warfare, 1939–40. Served War of 1939–45: Coldstream Guards, 1940–46; Adjt 1st Batt., 1943–44 (despatches 1944); seconded to Foreign Office, Conference Dept, 1945–46; demobilised, as Captain, 1946. Messrs Dawnay Day and Co., Merchant Bankers, 1946–50. Private Secretary and Equerry to Queen Elizabeth the Queen Mother, 1951–56; Extra Equerry, 1956–62. Partner, Grieveson, Grant & Co., Stockbrokers, 1961–80. *Address:* Flat 5, 32 Onslow Square, SW7; Wexcombe House, Marlborough, Wilts. *Clubs:* Brooks's, MCC.

See also Lt-Col C. P. Dawnay.

DAWNAY, Vice-Adm. Sir Peter, KCVO 1961 (MVO 1939); CB 1958; DSC 1944; DL; Royal Navy, retired; an Extra Equerry to the Queen since 1958; *b* 14 Aug. 1904; *s* of Maj. Hon. Hugh and Lady Susan Dawnay; *m* 1936, Lady Angela Montagu-Douglas-Scott, *d* of 7th Duke of Buccleuch; one *s* one *d. Educ:* Osborne and Dartmouth. Legion of Merit (USA). In command HMS Saintes and 3rd Destroyer Flotilla, 1950–51; in command HMS Mercury (HM Signal Sch.), 1952–53; in command HMS Glasgow, 1954–56. Deputy Controller of the Navy, Admiralty, 1956–58; Flag Officer, Royal

Yachts, 1958–62; retired, 1962. High Sheriff, Hants, 1973; DL Hants 1975. *Address:* The Old Post Cottage, Wield, Alresford, Hants SO24 9RS. *T:* Alton 63041.

DAWOOD, Nessim Joseph; Arabist and Middle East Consultant; Managing Director, The Arabic Advertising and Publishing Co. Ltd, London, since 1958; Director: Contemporary Translations Ltd, London, since 1962; Bradbury Wilkinson (Graphics) Ltd, 1975; *b* Baghdad, 27 Aug. 1927; 4th *s* of late Yousef Dawood, merchant, and Muzli (*née* Tweg); *m* 1949, Juliet, 2nd *d* of M. and N. Abraham, Baghdad and New York; three *s. Educ:* The American Sch. and Shamash Sch., Baghdad; Iraq State Scholar in England, UC Exeter, 1945–49; Univ. of London, BA (Hons). FIL 1959. Has written and spoken radio and film commentaries. *Publications:* The Muqaddimah of Ibn Khaldun, 1967 (US, 1969); Penguin Classics: The Thousand and One Nights, 1954; The Koran, 1956, 32nd edn 1987; Aladdin and Other Tales, 1957; Tales from The Thousand and One Nights, 1973, 15th edn 1987; Arabian Nights (illus. children's edn), 1978; contribs to specialised and technical English-Arabic dictionaries; translated numerous technical publications into Arabic. *Recreation:* going to the theatre. *Address:* Berkeley Square House, Berkeley Square, W1X 5LE. *T:* 01–409 0953. *Club:* Hurlingham.

DAWS, Dame Joyce (Margaretta), DBE 1975; FRCS, FRACS; Surgeon, Queen Victoria Memorial Hospital, Melbourne, Victoria, Australia, 1958–85; Thoracic Surgeon, Prince Henry's Hospital, Melbourne, since 1975; President, Victorian Branch Council, Australian Medical Association, 1976; *b* 21 July 1925; *d* of Frederick William Daws and Daisy Ethel Daws. *Educ:* Royal School for Naval and Marine Officers' Daughters, St Margaret's, Mddx; St Paul's Girls' Sch., Hammersmith; Royal Free Hosp., London. MB, BS (London) 1949; FRCS 1952, FRACS. Ho. Surg., Royal Free Hosp.; SHMO, Manchester Royal Infirmary; Hon. Surg., Queen Victoria Meml Hosp., Melb., 1958; Asst Thoracic Surg., Prince Henry's Hosp., Melb., 1967–75. Pres., Bd of Management, After-Care Hosp., Melbourne, 1980–85; Chairman: Victorian Nursing Council, 1983–; Academic and Professional Panel, Victoria, for Churchill Fellowship Awards, 1984; Jt Adv. Cttee on Pets in Society, 1984. Hon. Sec., Victorian Br., AMA, 1974. *Recreations:* opera, ballet, theatre, desert travel, protea grower. *Address:* 26 Edwin Street, Heidelberg West, Victoria 3081, Australia. *T:* 452579. *Clubs:* Lyceum, Soroptimist International (Melbourne).

DAWSON, Anthony Michael, MD, FRCP; Physician to the Queen, since 1982 (to the Royal Household, 1974–82); Physician: St Bartholomew's Hospital, since 1965; King Edward VII Hospital for Officers, since 1968; King Edward VII Convalescent Home for Officers, Osborne, since 1975; *b* 8 May 1928; *s* of Leslie Joseph Dawson and Mabel Jayes; *m* 1956, Barbara Anne Baron Forsyth, *d* of late Thomas Forsyth, MB, ChB; two *d. Educ:* Wyggeston Sch., Leicester; Charing Cross Hosp. Med. Sch. MB, BS 1951, MD 1959, London; MRCP 1954, FRCP 1964. Jun. appts, Charing Cross Hosp., Brompton Hosp., Royal Postgrad. Med. Sch., Central Middlesex Hosp., 1951–57; MRC and US Public Health Res. Fellow, Harvard Med. Sch. at Massachusetts Gen. Hosp., 1957–59; Lectr and Sen. Lectr in Medicine, Royal Free Hosp. Med. Sch., 1959–65. Hon. Sec., Assoc. of Physicians of Gt Britain and Ireland, 1973–78, Treasurer 1978–83. Examnr, London and Oxford, MRCP; Censor, RCP, 1977–78, Treasurer, 1985–; Treasurer, St Bartholomew's Hosp. Med. Coll., 1976–79, Vice-Pres., 1979–84; Vice-Chm., Bd of Management, King Edward's Hosp. Fund for London. *Publications:* contrib. med. books and jls. *Recreations:* music, gardening. *Address:* 35 Meadowbank, Primrose Hill Road, NW3 3AY. *T:* 01–722 6601. *Club:* Garrick.

See also J. L. Dawson.

DAWSON, Hon. Sir Daryl (Michael), KBE 1982; CB 1980; **Hon. Mr Justice Dawson;** Justice of the High Court of Australia, since 1982; *b* 12 Dec. 1933; *s* of Claude Charles Dawson and Elizabeth May Dawson; *m* 1971, Mary Louise Thomas. *Educ:* Canberra High Sch.; Ormond Coll., Univ. of Melbourne (LLB Hons); LLM Yale. Sterling Fellow, Yale Univ., 1955–56. QC 1971; Solicitor-General for Victoria, 1974–82. Mem. Council, Univ. of Melbourne, 1976–86; Chm., Australian Motor Sport Appeal Court, 1986– (Mem., 1970–86); Mem., Fédération d'Automobile Appeal Court, 1982–. *Recreation:* squash. *Address:* High Court of Australia, Canberra, ACT, Australia. *Clubs:* Melbourne, Savage, RACV, Beefsteaks (Melbourne).

DAWSON, Sir (Hugh) Michael (Trevor), 4th Bt *cr* 1920, of Edgewarebury; *b* 28 March 1956; *s* of Sir (Hugh Halliday) Trevor Dawson, 3rd Bt; *S* father, 1983. *Heir: b* Nicholas Antony Trevor Dawson, *b* 17 Aug. 1957.

DAWSON, James Gordon, CBE 1981; FEng, FIMechE, FSAE; Consultant; *b* 3 Feb. 1916; *s* of James Dawson and Helen Mitchell (*née* Tawse); *m* 1941, Doris Irene (*née* Rowe) (*d* 1982); one *s* one *d. Educ:* Aberdeen Grammar Sch.; Aberdeen Univ. (BScEng Hons Mech. Eng, BScEng Hons Elect. Eng). Develt Test Engr, Rolls Royce Ltd, Derby, 1942; Chief Engr, Shell Research Ltd, 1946; Technical Dir, Perkins Engines Ltd, 1955; Dir, Dowty Group Ltd, 1966; Man. Dir, Zenith Carburetter Co. Ltd, 1969, Chm., 1977–81. Pres., IMechE, 1979–80. *Publications:* technical papers publd in UK and abroad. *Recreation:* golf. *Address:* Mildmay House, Apethorpe, Peterborough. *T:* Kingscliffe 348. *Club:* Caledonian.

DAWSON, Prof. John Alan; Fraser of Allander Professor of Distributive Studies, University of Stirling, since 1983; *b* 19 Aug. 1944; *s* of Alan and Gladys Dawson; *m* 1967, Jocelyn M. P. Barker; one *s* one *d. Educ:* University College London (BSc, MPhil); University of Nottingham (PhD). Lectr, Univ. of Nottingham, 1967–71; Lectr 1971, Sen. Lectr 1974, Reader, 1981–83, Univ. of Wales, Lampeter. Vis. Lectr, Univ. of Western Australia, 1973; Vis. Res. Fellow, ANU, 1978; Visiting Professor: Florida State Univ., 1982; Chuo Univ., 1986. Mem., Distributive Trades EDC, 1984–. Hon. Sec., Inst. of British Geographers, 1985–. *Publications:* Evaluating the Human Environment, 1973; Man and His World, 1975; Computing for Geographers, 1976; Small Scale Retailing in UK, 1978; Marketing Environment, 1979; Retail Geography, 1980; Commercial Distribution in Europe, 1982; Teach Yourself Geography, 1983; Shopping Centre Development, 1983; Computer Programming for Geographers, 1985; Shopping Centres Policies and Prospects, 1985; articles in Geographical, management and marketing jls. *Recreations:* sport, travel. *Address:* Castle Grove, Callander, Perthshire. *T:* Stirling 73171.

DAWSON, John Leonard, MB, MS; FRCS; Surgeon to the Queen, since 1983; Surgeon: King's College Hospital, since 1964; Bromley Hospital, since 1967; King Edward VII Hospital for Officers, since 1975; *b* 30 Sept. 1932; *s* of Leslie Joseph Dawson and Mabel Annie Jayes; *m* 1958, Rosemary Brundle; two *s* one *d. Educ:* Wyggeston Boys' Grammar Sch., Leicester; King's College Hosp., Univ. of London. MB, BS 1955, MS 1964; FRCS 1958. Served RAMC, 1958–60. Surgeon to Royal Household, 1975–83. Nuffield Scholarship, Harvard Univ., 1963–64; Sir Arthur Sims Travelling Prof., Australasia, 1981. Examiner in Surgery: Univs. of London, 1966–, and Cambridge, 1980–; Soc. of Apothecaries; Primary FRCS, 1974–80; Mem. Ct of Examrs, RCS, 1981–. *Publications:* contribs to surgical text-books and jls on abdominal surgery. *Recreations:* squash, tennis, skiing, gardening, reading. *Address:* 107 Burbage Road, Dulwich, SE21 7AF. *T:* 01–733 3668.

See also A. M. Dawson.

DAWSON, (Joseph) Peter; General Secretary, National Association of Teachers in Further and Higher Education (NATFHE), since 1979; *b* 18 March 1940; *s* of Joseph Glyn and Winifred Olwen Dawson; *m* 1964, Yvonne Anne Charlton Smith; one *s* one *d*. *Educ:* Bishop Gore Grammar Sch., Swansea; University College of Swansea (BSc, DipEd). Assistant Master, Chiswick Grammar Sch., 1962; Field Officer, 1965, Sen. Field Officer, 1966, National Union of Teachers; Asst Sec., 1969, Negotiating Sec., 1974, Assoc. of Teachers in Technical Instns; Negotiating Sec., NATFHE, 1976. Vice-Pres., 1962–64, Sen. Treasurer, 1965–68, National Union of Students. Mem., Teachers' Panel, Teachers' Superannuation Working Party, 1969– (Chm., 1979–). Hon. FCP 1984. *Recreations:* church activities, tennis, cricket. *Address:* NATFHE, Hamilton House, Mabledon Place, WC1H 9BH. *T:* 01–387 6806. *Club:* Surrey County Cricket.

DAWSON, Sir Michael; *see* Dawson, Sir H. M. T.

DAWSON, Ven. Peter; Archdeacon of Norfolk, since 1977; *b* 31 March 1929; *s* of late Leonard Smith and Cicely Alice Dawson; *m* 1955, Kathleen Mary Sansome; one *s* three *d*. *Educ:* Manchester Grammar School; Keble Coll., Oxford (MA); Ridley Hall, Cambridge. Nat. service, Army, 1947–49; University, 1949–52; Theological College, 1952–54. Asst Curate, St Lawrence, Morden, Dio. Southwark, 1954–59; Vicar of Barston, Warwicks, Dio. Birmingham, 1959–63; Rector of St Clement, Higher Openshaw, Dio. Manchester, 1963–68; Rector of Morden, Dio. Southwark, 1968–77, and Rural Dean of Merton, 1975–77. *Recreations:* gardening, politics, the rural community, historical studies. *Address:* Intwood Rectory, Norwich NR4 6TG. *T:* Norwich 51946.

DAWSON, Rev. Peter, OBE 1986; General Secretary, Professional Association of Teachers, since 1980; Methodist Sector Minister, ordained 1985; *b* 19 May 1933; *s* of Richard Dawson and Henrietta Kate Dawson (*née* Trueman); *m* 1957, Shirley Margaret Pentland Johnson; two *d*. *Educ:* Beckenham Technical Sch.; Beckenham Grammar Sch.; London School of Economics (BScEcon); Westminster Coll. (Postgrad. CertEd). Schoolmaster Fellow Commoner, Keble Coll., Oxford, 1969, and Corpus Christi Coll., Cambridge, 1979. Asst Master, Roan Grammar School for Boys, London, 1957–62; Head of Upper School, Sedgehill Sch., London, 1962–67; Second Master, Gateacre Comprehensive Sch., Liverpool, 1967–70; Headmaster, Eltham Green Sch., London, 1970–80. Mem., Burnham Cttee, 1981–. Asst Minister, Queen's Hall Methodist Mission, Derby, 1984–. *Publications:* Making a Comprehensive Work, 1981; Teachers and Teaching, 1984. *Recreations:* reading, golf, family activities. *Address:* (office) Professional Association of Teachers, 99 Friar Gate, Derby DE1 1EZ. *T:* Derby 372337; (home) 3 Lawn Heads Avenue, Littleover, Derby DE3 6DR. *T:* Derby 367615.

DAWSON, Rex Malcolm Chaplin, FRS 1981; PhD, DSc; Deputy Director and Head of Biochemistry Department, Institute of Animal Physiology, Babraham, Cambridge, 1969–84 (Principal Scientific Officer, 1955–69); *b* 3 June 1924; *s* of late James Dawson and Ethel Mary Dawson (*née* Chaplin); *m* 1946, Emily Elizabeth Hodder; one *s* one *d*. *Educ:* Hinckley Grammar Sch.; University Coll., London (BSc 1946, DSc 1960); Univ. of Wales (PhD 1951). MRC Fellowship followed by Beit Meml Fellowship, Neuropsychiatric Res. Centre, Whitchurch Hosp., Cardiff, 1947–52; Betty Brookes Fellow, Dept of Biochemistry, Univ. of Oxford, 1952–55. Vis. Res. Fellow, Harvard Univ., 1959; Vis. Prof., Northwestern Univ., Chicago, 1974. International Lipid Prize, Amer. Oil Chemists' Assoc., 1981. *Publications:* Metabolism and Physiological Significance of Lipids, 1964; Data for Biochemical Research, 1959, 2nd edn 1969; Form and Function of Phospholipids, 1973; numerous papers on structure, turnover and role of phospholipids in cell membranes in various scientific jls. *Recreations:* mercantile marine history, sailing, gardening. *Address:* Kirn House, Holt Road, Langham, Norfolk NR25 7BX. *T:* Binham 396.

DAWSON, Richard Leonard Goodhugh, MB, FRCS; Plastic Surgeon, retired; *b* 24 Aug. 1916; *s* of L. G. Dawson and Freda Hollis; *m* 1945, Betty Marie Freeman-Mathews; two *s*. *Educ:* Bishop's Stortford Coll., Herts; University Coll., London; University College Hospital. MRCS, LRCP 1939; MB London 1940; FRCS 1947; BS London 1948. Royal Army Medical Corps, 1941–46; service in England and Far East (4 years); POW in Japanese hands, 1942–45. Plastic Surgeon: Mt Vernon Centre for Plastic Surgery, Northwood, 1955–82; Royal Free Hosp., London, 1958–76; Royal Nat. Orthopaedic Hosp., Stanmore, 1954–76. Member, British Assoc. Plastic Surgeons (President, 1974). *Publications:* chapters in Operative Surgery, 1957; numerous contributions to Lancet, BMJ, British Journal Plastic Surgery and other journals. *Recreations:* squash, golf, gardening. *Address:* Ford Cottages, Puddle Farm, Sandpit Lane, Bledlow, Bucks. *T:* Princes Risborough 2960.

DAWSON, Air Chief Marshal Sir Walter Lloyd, KCB 1954 (CB 1945); CBE 1943; DSO 1948; *b* 6 May 1902; *s* of late W. J. Dawson, Sunderland; *m* 1927, Elizabeth Leslie (*d* 1975), *d* of late D. V. McIntyre, MA, MB, ChB; one *s* one *d*. Enlisted in RAF as boy mechanic, 1919; commissioned from Cranwell, 1922; Station Comdr St Eval, Coastal Command, 1942–43; Dir, Anti-U-Boat Operations, 1943; Dir of Plans, 1944–46; AOC Levant, 1946–48; Commandant, School of Land/Air Warfare, Old Sarum, 1948–50; idc, 1950–51 (RAF Instructor); Asst Chief of the Air Staff (Policy), 1952–53; Deputy Chief of Staff (Plans and Operations), SHAPE, 1953–56; Inspector-General of RAF, 1956–57; Air Member for Supply and Organisation, 1958–60, retired. Chm., Handley Page, 1966–69 (Vice-Chm., 1964–66). Dir, Southern Electricity Bd, 1961–72. *Address:* Woodlands, Heathfield Avenue, Sunninghill, Berks. *Club:* Royal Air Force.

DAWSON, Wilfred; retired; Under Secretary, Director, Manpower and Management Services, Departments of the Environment and Transport, 1978–80; *b* 11 Jan. 1923; *s* of Walter and Ivy Dawson; *m* 1944, Emily Louise Mayhew; two *d*. *Educ:* Riley High Sch., Hull. Civil Service: Air Min., 1939–49; Min. of Town and Country Planning, 1949; Principal, Min. of Housing and Local Govt, 1963; Asst Sec., DoE, 1970; Under-Sec., DoE, 1974–76; Under Sec., Dept of Transport, 1976–78. *Recreations:* walking, woodworking. *Address:* Reydon Grange, Wangford, Beccles, Suffolk.

DAWSON, William John Richard Geoffrey Patrick, CMG 1980; OBE 1967; HM Diplomatic Service; *b* 21 Sept. 1926; *m* 1956, June Eaton Dangerfield; one *s* one *d*. Served HM Forces, 1942–45; joined FO, 1951; served in British Middle East Office, Tehran, Lomé, Dar es Salaam, 1952–72; FCO, 1972–73; Nairobi, 1973–77; Counsellor, FCO, 1977–86. *Address:* c/o Foreign and Commonwealth Office, SW1.

DAWSON-DAMER, family name of **Earl of Portarlington.**

DAWSON-MORAY, Edward Bruce, CMG 1969; *b* 30 June 1909; *s* of late Alwyn Bruce Dawson-Moray and late Ada (*née* Burlton); *m* 1st, 1933, Ursula Frances (*née* Woodbridge) (marr. diss.); one *s* one *d*; 2nd, Beryl Barber. *Educ:* Cranbrook Sch.; University of London (BA Hons). Housemaster, Chillon Coll., Switzerland, 1938–42. British Legation, Berne, 1942; 3rd Secretary, 1944; 3rd Secretary and Vice-Consul, Rome, 1947–48; Consul: Leopoldville, 1948–50; Detroit, 1950–51; 1st Secretary and Consul, Rangoon, 1952–54; Information Officer and Consul, Naples, 1954–56; Foreign Office, 1956–60; Consul, Casablanca, 1960–63; Chief Establishment Officer, Diplomatic Wireless Service, 1963–69; Principal, Civil Service Dept, 1969–74; retired. Dir, Pre-retirement Training, CSD, 1975–82. Senior Editor, Foreign Office List, 1957–60. *Recreations:* literature, photography, opera, travel. *Address:* 2 Pennypiece, Cleeve Road, Goring-on-Thames, Reading, Berks RG8 9BY. *T:* Goring-on-Thames 873314.

DAWTRY, Sir Alan, Kt 1974; CBE 1968 (MBE (mil.) 1945); TD 1948; Chairman: Sperry Ltd, 1977–86; Sperry (Ireland) Ltd, 1977–86; President, London Rent Assessment Panel, 1979–86; *b* 8 April 1915; *s* of Melancthon and Kate Nicholas Dawtry, Sheffield; unmarried. *Educ:* King Edward VII Sch., Sheffield; Sheffield Univ. (LLB). Served War of 1939–45: commissioned RA; campaigns France, N Africa, Italy (MBE, despatches twice); released with rank of Lt-Col. Admitted Solicitor, 1938; Asst Solicitor, Sheffield, 1938–48; Deputy Town Clerk, Bolton, 1948–52; Deputy Town Clerk, Leicester, 1952–54; Town Clerk, Wolverhampton, 1954–56; Chief Exec. (formerly Town Clerk), Westminster, 1956–77; Hon. Sec., London Boroughs Assoc., 1965–78. Member: Metrication Bd, 1969–74; Clean Air Council, 1960–75; Council of Management, Architectural Heritage Fund, 1977–; CBI Council, 1982–86. Pres., Soc. of Local Authority Chief Execs, 1975–76. FBIM 1975; FRSA 1978. Foreign Orders: The Star (Afghanistan); Golden Honour (Austria); Leopold II (Belgium); Rio Branco (Brazil); Merit (Chile); Legion of Honour (France); Merit (W Germany); the Phœnix (Greece); Merit (Italy); Homayoun (Iran); The Rising Sun (Japan); the Star (Jordan); African Redemption (Liberia); Oaken Crown (Luxembourg); Loyalty (Malaysia); the Right Hand (Nepal); Orange-Nassau (Netherlands); the Two Niles (Sudan); the Crown (Thailand); Zaire (Zaire). *Address:* 901 Grenville House, Dolphin Square, SW1V 3LR. *T:* 01–798 8100.

DAY, Prof. Alan Charles Lynn; Professor of Economics, London School of Economics, University of London, since 1964; *b* 25 Oct. 1924; *s* of late Henry Charles Day, MBE, and of Ruth Day; *m* 1962, Diana Hope Bocking (*d* 1980); no *c*; *m* 1982, Dr Shirley E. Jones. *Educ:* Chesterfield Grammar Sch.; Queens' Coll., Cambridge. Asst Lecturer, then Lecturer, LSE, 1949–54; Economic Adviser, HM Treas., 1954–56; Reader in Economics, London Univ., 1956–64. Ed., National Inst. Econ. Review, 1960–62; Econ. Correspondent, The Observer, intermittently, 1957–81. Economic Adviser on Civil Aviation, BoT, later Dept of Trade and Industry, 1968–72; Economic Adviser, Civil Aviation Authority, 1972–78. Member: Council, Consumers' Assoc., 1963–; Board, British Airports Authority, 1965–68; SE Region Econ. Planning Council, 1966–69; Home Office Cttee on the London Taxicab Trade, 1967–70; Layfield Cttee on Local Govt Finance, 1974–76; Air Transport Users' Cttee, CAA, 1978–79; Home Office Adv. Panel on Satellite Broadcasting Standards, 1982. British Acad. Leverhulme Vis. Prof., Graduate Inst. for International Studies, Geneva, 1971. Governor, LSE, 1971–76, 1977–79, Pro-Director, 1979–83. *Publications:* The Future of Sterling, 1954; Outline of Monetary Economics, 1956; The Economics of Money, 1959; (with S. T. Beza) Wealth and Income, 1960. *Address:* Chart Place, Chart Sutton, Kent. *T:* Maidstone 842236; 9 Bingham Street, N1. *T:* 01–226 8896. *Club:* Reform.

DAY, Bernard Maurice; Assistant Under-Secretary of State (Fleet Support), Ministry of Defence, since 1985; *b* 7 May 1928; *s* of M. J. Day and Mrs M. H. Day; *m* 1956, Ruth Elizabeth Stansfield; two *s* one *d*. *Educ:* Bancroft's Sch.; London School of Economics (BScEcon). Army service, commnd RA, 1946–48. British Electric Traction Fedn, 1950–51; Asst Principal, Air Ministry, 1951; Private Sec. to Air Mem. for Supply and Organisation, 1954–56; Principal, 1956; Cabinet Secretariat, 1959–61; Asst Sec., 1965; Sec., Meteorological Office, 1965–69; Estabt Officer, Cabinet Office, 1969–72; Head of Air Staff Secretariat, MoD, 1972–74; Asst Under Sec. of State, MoD, 1974; Civilian Staff Management, 1974–76; Operational Requirements, 1976–80; Programmes and Budget, 1980–82; Supply and Orgn, Air, 1982–84; Chm., CSSB, 1984–85. Chairman: MoD Branch, First Div. Assoc., 1983–84; MoD Liaison Cttee with CS Benevolent Fund, 1975–84. *Recreations:* swimming, gardening, Parochial Church Council and churchwarden. *Address:* Burfield, Farmleigh Grove, Burwood Park, Walton-on-Thames, Surrey KT12 5BU. *T:* Walton-on-Thames 227416. *Club:* Royal Commonwealth Society.

DAY, Sir Derek, KCMG 1984 (CMG 1973); HM Diplomatic Service; High Commissioner to Canada, since 1984; *b* 29 Nov. 1927; *s* of late Mr and Mrs Alan W. Day; *m* 1955, Sheila Nott; three *s* one *d*. *Educ:* Hurstpierpoint Coll.; Catharine's Coll., Cambridge. Royal Artillery, 1946–48; St Catharine's Coll., 1948–51. Entered HM Foreign Service, Sept. 1951; Third Sec., British Embassy, Tel Aviv, 1953–56; Private Sec. to HM Ambassador, Rome, 1956–59; Second, then First Sec., FO, 1959–62; First Sec., British Embassy, Washington, 1962–66; First Sec., FO, 1966–67; Asst Private Sec. to Sec. of State for Foreign Affairs, 1967–68; Head of Personnel Operations Dept, FCO, 1969–72; Counsellor, British High Commn, Nicosia, 1972–75; Ambassador to Ethiopia, 1975–78; Asst Under-Sec. of State, 1979, Dep. Under-Sec. of State, 1980, and Chief Clerk, 1982–84, FCO. *Address:* c/o Foreign and Commonwealth Office, SW1; Etchinghill, Goudhurst, Kent. *Club:* United Oxford & Cambridge University.

DAY, Graham; *see* Day, J. G.

DAY, John King, TD; MA, BSc; Principal, Elizabeth College, Guernsey, CI, 1958–71; *b* Ipoh, Perak, FMS, 27 Oct. 1909; *s* of Harold Duncan Day, Mining Engineer, and Muriel Edith Day; *m* 1935, Mary Elizabeth Stinton, *er d* of late Tom Stinton, Headmaster of the High Sch., Newcastle-under-Lyme; three *s*. *Educ:* Stamford Sch.; Magdalen Coll., Oxford. Demy 1928–32. Honour School of Natural Science (Chemistry) Class 2. Assistant Master, Kendal Sch., Westmorland, 1932; Asst Master and Housemaster, Gresham's Sch., 1933–57. Served Royal Norfolk Regt (7th Bn) and Military College of Science, 1939–45. *Recreations:* walking, fishing and sketching. *Address:* 1 Pearson's Road, Holt, Norfolk NR25 6EJ. *T:* Holt 713435.

DAY, (Judson) Graham; Chairman and Chief Executive, Rover (formerly BL plc), since 1986; *b* 3 May 1933; *s* of Frank Charles Day and Edythe Grace (*née* Baker); *m* 1958, Leda Ann (*née* Creighton); one *s* two *d*. *Educ:* Queen Elizabeth High Sch., Halifax, NS; Dalhousie Univ., Halifax, NS (LLB). Private practice of Law, Windsor, Nova Scotia, 1956–64; Canadian Pacific Ltd, Montreal and Toronto, 1964–71; Cammell Laird Shipbuilders Ltd, Birkenhead, Eng., 1971–75; Dep. Chm., Organising Cttee for British Shipbuilders and Dep. Chm. and Chief Exec. designate, British Shipbuilders, 1975–76; Prof. of Business Admin and Dir, Canadian Marine Transportation Centre, Dalhousie Univ., NS, 1977–81; Vice-Pres., Shipyards & Marine Devlt, Dome Petroleum Ltd, 1981–83; Chm. and Chief Exec., British Shipbuilders, 1983–86. Director: Misener Hldgs; The Laird Gp plc. Member: Nova Scotia Barristers' Soc.; Law Soc. of Upper Canada; Canadian Bar Assoc. ARINA. *Recreation:* reading. *Address:* c/o Rover, 106 Oxford Road, Uxbridge, Mddx UB5 1EH.

DAY, Lance Reginald; Keeper, Science Museum Library, since 1976; *b* 2 Nov. 1927; *s* of late Reginald and of Eileen Day; *m* 1959, Mary Ann Sheahan; one *s* two *d*. *Educ:* Sherrardswood Sch., Welwyn Garden City; Alleyne's Grammar Sch., Stevenage; Northern Polytechnic and University Coll., London (MSc). Res. Asst, Science Museum Library, 1951–64, Asst Keeper 1964–70; Asst Keeper, Science Museum, Dept of Chemistry, 1970–74; Keeper, Science Museum, Dept of Communications and Electrical Engrg, 1974–76. Sec., Nat. Railway Museum Cttee, 1973–75; Hon. Sec., Newcomen

Soc., 1973–82. *Publications*: reviews and articles. *Recreation*: music. *Address*: 10 Russellcroft Road, Welwyn Garden City, Herts. *T*: Welwyn Garden 322387.

DAY, Lucienne, RDI 1962; in freelance practice, since 1948; Consultant, with Robin Day, to John Lewis Partnership, since 1962; *b* 1917; *d* of Felix Conradi and Dulcie Lilian Duncan-Smith; *m* 1942, Robin Day, *qv*; one *d*. *Educ*: Convent Notre Dame de Sion, Worthing; Croydon School of Art; Royal Coll. of Art. ARCA 1940; FSIAD 1955; Mem. Faculty of Royal Designers for Industry, 1962. Teacher, Beckenham Sch. of Art, 1942–47; began designing full-time, dress fabrics and later furnishing fabrics, carpets, wallpapers, table-linen, 1947 for Edinburgh Weavers, Heal's Fabrics, Cavendish Textiles, Tomkinsons, Wilton Royal, Thos Somerset etc, and firms in Scandinavia, USA and Germany; also china decoration for Rosenthal China, Selb, Bavaria, 1956–68; work for Barbican Art Centre, 1979; currently also designing and making silk wall-hangings (silk mosaics). Work in permanent collections: V&A; Trondheim Museum, Norway; Cranbrook Museum, Michigan, USA; Röhsska Mus., Gothenberg, Sweden (silk mosaics). Member: Rosenthal Studio-line Jury, 1960–68; Cttee, Duke of Edinburgh's Prize for Elegant Design, 1960–63; Council, RCA, 1962–67; RSA Design Bursaries Juries. First Award, Amer. Inst. of Decorators, 1950; Gold Medal, 9th Triennale di Milano, 1951; Gran Premio, 10th Triennale di Milano, 1954; Design Council Awards, 1957, 1960, 1968. *Recreations*: plant collecting in Mediterranean regions, gardening. *Address*: 49 Cheyne Walk, Chelsea, SW3. *T*: 01–352 1455.

DAY, Peter, DPhil; FRS 1986; Lecturer in Inorganic Chemistry, since 1967, Fellow of St John's College, since 1965, Oxford University; *b* 20 Aug. 1938; *s* of Edgar Day and Ethel Hilda Day (*née* Russell); *m* 1964, Frances Mary Elizabeth Anderson; one *s* one *d*. *Educ*: Maidstone Grammar School; Wadham College, Oxford (BA 1961, MA, DPhil 1965). Cyanamid European Research Institute, Geneva, 1962; Junior Research Fellow, 1963–65, Tutor, 1965–, St John's College, Oxford; Departmental Demonstrator, Oxford Univ., 1965–67. Prof. Associé, Univ. de Paris-Sud, 1975; Guest Prof., Univ. of Copenhagen, 1978; Vis. Fellow, ANU, 1980; Senior Research Fellow, SRC, 1977–82. Member: Neutron Beam Res. Cttee, SERC, 1983–; Chemistry Cttee, SERC, 1985–. Corday-Morgan Medal, RSC, 1971; Solid State Chem. Award, RSC, 1986. *Publications*: Physical Methods in Advanced Inorganic Chemistry (ed with H. A. O. Hill), 1968; Electronic States of Inorganic Compounds, 1974; Emission and Scattering Techniques, 1980; Electronic Structure and Magnetism of Inorganic Compounds, vols 1–7, 1972–82; papers in Jl Chem. Soc.; Inorg. Chem. *Recreation*: driving slowly through rural France. *Address*: 16 Blackhall Road, Oxford OX1 3QF. *T*: Oxford 57662.

DAY, Peter Rodney, PhD; Director, Plant Breeding Institute, Trumpington, Cambridge, since 1979; Special Professor of Botany, University of Nottingham, since 1982; Secretary, International Genetics Federation, since 1984; *b* 27 Dec. 1928; *s* of Roland Percy Day and Florence Kate (*née* Dixon); *m* 1950, Lois Elizabeth Rhodes; two *s* one *d*. *Educ*: Birkbeck Coll., Univ. of London (BSc, PhD). John Innes Institute, 1946–63; Associate Prof. of Botany, Ohio State Univ., 1963–64; Chief, Dept of Genetics, Connecticut Agricl Experiment Station, 1964–79. Commonwealth Fund Fellow, 1954; John Simon Guggenheim Meml Fellow, 1973. *Publications*: Fungal Genetics (with J. R. S. Fincham), 1963, 4th edn 1979; Genetics of Host-Parasite Interaction, 1974; contrib. Genetical Research, Genetics, Heredity, Nature, Proc. Nat. Acad. Sci., Phytopathology, etc. *Recreation*: Scottish country dancing. *Address*: Plant Breeding Institute, Maris Lane, Trumpington, Cambridge CB2 2LQ. *T*: Cambridge 840411.

DAY, Sir Robin, Kt 1981; Television and Radio Journalist; *b* 24 Oct. 1923; *s* of late William and Florence Day; *m* 1965, Katherine Ainslie (marr. diss. 1986); two *s*. *Educ*: Bembridge Sch.; St Edmund Hall, Oxford. Military service, 1943–47; commd RA, 1944. Oxford, 1947–51: Union debating tour of American universities, 1949; President Union, 1950; BA Hons (Jurisprudence), 1951; MA. Middle Temple: Blackstone Entrance Scholar, 1951; Harmsworth Law Scholar, 1952–53; called to Bar, 1952. British Information Services, Washington, 1953–54; free-lance broadcaster, 1954–55; BBC Talks Producer (radio), 1955; Newscaster and Parliamentary Correspondent, Independent Television News, 1955–59; columnist in News Chronicle, 1959; ITV programmes, 1955–59: Roving Report (ITN); Tell the People (ITN); Under Fire (Granada); since 1959 BBC TV programmes including: Panorama, Gallery, People to Watch, Daytime, 24 Hours, Midweek, To-night, Sunday Debate, Talk-in, Newsday, Question Time. BBC radio programmes: It's Your Line, 1970–76; Election Call, 1974, 1979, 1983; The World at One, 1979–. Mem. Council, Hansard Soc., 1977– (Chm., 1981–83). Mem., Phillimore Cttee on Law of Contempt, 1971–74. Trustee, Oxford Literary and Debating Union Trust. Contested (L) Hereford, 1959. Hon. LLD Exeter, 1986. Guild of TV Producers' Merit Award, Personality of the Year, 1957; Richard Dimbleby Award for factual television, 1974; Broadcasting Press Guild Award, for Question Time, 1980; RTS Judges' Award for 30 yrs TV journalism, 1985. *Publications*: Television: A Personal Report, 1961; The Case for Televising Parliament, 1963; Day by Day, 1975. *Recreations*: reading, talking, ski-ing. *Address*: c/o BBC TV Studios, Lime Grove, W12. *Clubs*: Garrick, Athenæum, MCC.

DAY, Robin, OBE 1983; RDI 1959; FSIAD 1948; design consultant and freelance designer; *b* 25 May 1915; *s* of Arthur Day and Mary Shersby; *m* 1942, Lucienne Conradi (*see* Lucienne Day); one *d*. *Educ*: Royal Coll. of Art (ARCA). National scholarship to RCA, 1935–39; teacher and lectr for several yrs; Design Consultant: Hille International, 1948–; John Lewis Partnership, 1962–; Barbican Arts Centre, 1968–. Commissions include: seating for Royal Festival Hall, 1951; interior design of Super VC10 and other passenger aircraft for BOAC, 1963–74. Member: Duke of Edinburgh's Cttee for Prize for Elegant Design, 1961, 1970, 1971; juries for many national and internat. indust. design competitions. Governor, London Coll. of Furniture. Many awards for design work, including: 6 Design Centre awards; Gold Medal, Triennale di Milano, 1951, and Silver Medal, 1954; Designs Medal, SIAD, 1957. *Recreations*: mountaineering, skiing. *Address*: 49 Cheyne Walk, Chelsea, SW3 5LP. *T*: 01–352 1455. *Clubs*: Alpine, Alpine Ski, Climbers'.

DAY, Stephen Peter; HM Diplomatic Service; Head of Middle East Department, Foreign and Commonwealth Office, since 1984; *b* 19 Jan. 1938; *s* of Frank William and Mary Elizabeth Day; *m* 1965, Angela Doreen (*née* Waudby); one *s* two *d*. *Educ*: Bancroft's School; Corpus Christi Coll., Cambridge. MA. Entered HMOCS as Political Officer, Western Aden Protectorate, 1961, transf. to FO, 1965; Senior Political Officer, South Arabian Federation, 1964–67; FO, 1967–70; First Sec., Office of C-in-C, Far East, Singapore, 1970–71; First Sec. (Press), UK Mission to UN, NY, 1971–75; FCO, 1976–77; Counsellor, Beirut, 1977–78; Consul-Gen., Edmonton, 1979–81; Ambassador to Qatar, 1981–84. *Recreations*: walking, family. *Address*: c/o Foreign and Commonwealth Office, SW1; 92 West End Lane, Esher, Surrey.

DAY-LEWIS, Séan; Television and Radio Editor, The Daily Telegraph, since 1970; *b* 3 Aug. 1931; *s* of Cecil Day-Lewis, CBE, CLit and Mary Day-Lewis; *m* 1960, Anna Mott; one *s* one *d*. *Educ*: Allhallows Sch., Rousdon, Devon. National Service, RAF, 1949–51. Bridport News, 1952–53; Southern Times, Weymouth, 1953–54; Herts Advertiser, St

Albans, 1954–56; Express and Star, Wolverhampton, 1956–60; The Daily Telegraph, 1960–. Arts Editor, Socialist Commentary, 1966–71; Founder-Chm., Broadcasting Press Guild, 1975; Vice Pres., Bulleid Soc., 1970; Member, BAFTA, 1976. *Publications*: Bulleid: last giant of steam, 1964; C. Day-Lewis: an English literary life, 1980. *Recreations*: being in Devon, listening to J. S. Bach and others, failing at ball games, giving in to temptation. *Address*: 38 Caithness Road, W14 0JA. *T*: 01–602 3221.

DAYKIN, Christopher David, FIA; Directing Actuary (Social Security), Government Actuary's Department, since 1985; *b* 18 July 1948; *s* of John Francis Daykin and Mona Daykin; *m* 1977, Kathryn Ruth (*née* Tingey); two *s* one *d*. *Educ*: Merchant Taylors' Sch., Northwood; Pembroke Coll., Cambridge (BA 1970, MA 1973). FIA 1973. Government Actuary's Department, 1970; VSO, Brunei, 1971; Govt Actuary's Dept, 1972–78; Principal (Health and Social Services), HM Treasury, 1978–80; Govt Actuary's Dept, 1980–, Principal Actuary, 1982–84. Treasurer, Emmanuel Church, Northwood, 1982–; Chm., VSO Harrow and Hillingdon, 1976–. *Publications*: articles and papers on pensions, demography, consumer credit, social security and insurance. *Recreations*: travel, photography, languages. *Address*: 17 Hazeldene Drive, Pinner, Middx HA5 3NJ. *T*: 01–866 9762.

DAYMOND, Douglas Godfrey; Civil Service Commissioner, 1975–80; *b* 23 Nov. 1917; *s* of Samuel Kevern and Minnie Daymond; *m* 1945, Laura Vivien (*née* Selley); one *s* one *d*. *Educ*: Saltash Grammar Sch.; London Univ. LLB Hons 1947. Called to Bar, Gray's Inn, 1952. Inland Revenue, 1935; Customs and Excise, 1939; War Service with Royal Engineers in Egypt, Greece and Crete, POW 1941–45; Inland Revenue, 1947; Asst Sec., Royal Commn on Taxation, 1951–55; Sec., Tithe Redemption Commn, 1959–60; Dep. Dir, CS Selection Bd, 1970; Under-Sec., Civil Service Dept, 1973. *Recreations*: gardening, theatre, music. *Address*: 2 Fenten Park, Saltash, Cornwall. *T*: Saltash 8081; Flat 73, Fort Picklecombe, near Millbrook, Cornwall. *T*: Plymouth 822033.

DAYSH, Prof. George Henry John, CBE 1973; MLitt Oxon; DCL; Deputy Vice-Chancellor of University of Newcastle upon Tyne and Professor of Geography in the University, 1963–66; Emeritus Professor, since Oct. 1966 (Professor of Geography, King's College, University of Durham, Newcastle upon Tyne, 1943–63; Sub Rector, King's College, 1955–63); *b* 21 May 1901; *s* of Alfred John Daysh and Margaret (*née* Campbell); *m* 1927, Sheila Guthrie (*d* 1971), *er d* of Dr A. F. A. Fairweather; one *s* one *d*. *Educ*: Eggars Grammar Sch.; University College, Reading; Wadham Coll., Oxford. Housemaster, Pocklington Sch., E. Yorks, 1924–27; Lecturer in Geography, Bedford Coll., University of London, 1927–29; Lecturer-in-charge, Dept of Geography, 1930–38, Reader of Geography, 1938–43, King's Coll., Newcastle upon Tyne. Seconded for special duties with Dist Comr for special area of Cumberland, 1938; Senior Research Officer, Ministry of Town and Country Planning, 1943–45. Member of Exec. of NE Development Board, 1934–39, Vice-President NE Industrial and Development Assoc.; Chairman Research Cttee of NEIDA; Secretary Commn on Ports of International Geographic Union, 1947–51; Chairman University of Durham Matriculation and Sch. Examination Board, 1953–63. Part-time Member Northern Gas Board, 1956–70. Chairman, Newcastle upon Tyne Hospital Management Cttee, 1968–71. Visiting Prof. Fouad I Univ., 1951. Chairman, Triennial Grants Cttee, University College of Sierra Leone, 1960. Consultant to Cumberland Development Council, 1966–69. Chm., Tyne Tees Television, 1968–71; Dep. Chm., Trident Television Ltd, 1970–72; Dir, Solway Chemicals Ltd. Hon. DCL (Newcastle), 1964. FRSA; FRGS (Victoria Medal 1972). *Publications*: Southampton-Points in its Development, 1928; A Survey of Industrial Facilities of the North-East Coast, 1936 (rev., 1940 and 1949); West Cumberland with Alston-a Survey of Industrial Facilities, 1938 (revised 1951); (ed) Studies in Regional Planning, 1949; (ed) Physical Land Classification of North-East England, 1950; (with J. S Symonds) West Durham, 1953; (ed) A Survey of Whitby, 1958; contribs to Geographical Journal, Geography, Economic Geography, Geographical Review, etc. *Recreations*: gardening, field sports. *Address*: 2 Dunkirk Terrace, Corbridge, Northumberland. *T*: Corbridge-on-Tyne 2154.

DEACON ELLIOTT, Air Vice-Marshal Robert, CB 1967; OBE 1954; DFC 1941; AE 1944 (2 mentions); *b* 20 Nov. 1914; *m* 1948, Grace Joan Willes, Leamington Spa; two *s* one *d*. *Educ*: Northampton. 72 Fighter Sqdn (Dunkirk and Battle of Britain), 1939–41; HQ Fighter Comd, 1942–43; 84 Group 2 ATAF, 1944–46; Air Ministry (OR 5), 1946–48; OC Flying Wing and OC 26 APC in Cyprus, 1948–51; HQ Fighter Comd, Head of Admin. Plans, 1951–54; Army Staff Coll., on Directing Staff, 1954–56; CO, RAF Leconfield, 1956–57; CO, RAF Driffield, 1957–58; Air University USAF, Maxwell AFB, USA, 1958–61; Commandant, Officer and Aircrew Selection Centre, 1962–65; AOC, RAF Gibraltar, 1965–66; AOC, RAF Malta, and Dep. C-in-C (Air), Allied Forces Mediterranean, 1966–68, retd; Bursar, Civil Service Coll., 1969–79. *Recreations*: shooting, photography. *Address*: Wild Rose Cottage, Little London, Andover, Hants SP11 6JE. *T*: Andover 64563. *Club*: Royal Air Force.

DEADMAN, Ronald; Editor, Teachers' World, 1968–76; Member of the Press Council, 1969–75; *s* of Thomas Deadman and Margaret Healey; *m* 1952, Joan Evans; no *c*. *Educ*: Hinguar Street Sch., Shoeburyness; Oakley Coll., Cheltenham. Served RAF, 1937–45. Teaching, 1950–66; Features Editor, The Teacher, 1966–67; Editor, Everyweek, 1967–68. Leverhulme Res. Fellow, 1975–77. Watchkeeper, M/T Aro, River Blackwater, 1977–78; Fishery Bailiff, Barn Elms Reservoir, 1978–79; Fishery Warden, Kempton Park Reservoir, 1980–84. *Publications*: Enjoying English, Bk 1, 1966; Bk 2, 1968; Bk 3 (Contrasts), 1971; Bk 4 (Perception), 1972; (novels for children): The Happening, 1968; Wanderbodies, 1972; The Pretenders, 1972; (ed, short stories) The Friday Story, 1966; Words in Your Ear, vols 1 and 2, 1972; Going My Way, vols 1, 2 and 3, 1973; (with Arthur Razzell) Ways of Knowing, 1977; Grandma George, 1977; Breadwinners, 1978; Firebirds, 1979; (ed) Round the World Folk Tales, Bks 1–12, 1981; English Language Tests, vols 1–3, 1982; contribs to New Statesman, The Times, British Clinical Jl, Guardian, BBC, Where magazine, Education and Training. *Recreation*: brooding. *Address*: Flat 1, Dawley House, 91 Uxbridge Road, Ealing, W5. *T*: 01–840 3627. *Club*: British Legion.

DEAKIN, Maj.-Gen. Cecil Martin Fothergill, CB 1961; CBE 1956; *b* 20 Dec. 1910; *m* 1934, Evelyn (*d* 1984), *e d* of late Sir Arthur Grant, Bt of Monymusk, Aberdeenshire; one *s* one *d*. *Educ*: Winchester Coll. Commissioned into Grenadier Guards, 1931. Served with Regt NW Europe, 1944–45 (despatches). Commanded: 2nd Bn Grenadier Guards, 1945–46; 1st Bn, 1947–50; 32nd Guards Bde, 1953–55; 29th Infantry Bde, 1955–57 (Suez Expedition, despatches); Brigadier, General Staff, War Office, 1957–59; Director of Military Training, 1959; GOC 56th London Div., TA, 1960; Director Territorial Army, Cadets and Home Guard, 1960–62; Commandant of the JSSC, Latimer, 1962–65. *Recreations*: numerous. *Address*: Stocks Farm House, Beenham, Berks. *Club*: Royal Yacht Squadron.

See also Sir A. B. C. Edmonstone, Bt.

DEAKIN, Sir (Frederick) William (Dampier); *see* Deakin, Sir William.

DEAKIN, Michael; Consultant, TV-am (Director of Programmes, 1982–84; Board Member, 1984–85); Director, Griffin Productions Ltd, since 1985; *b* 21 Feb. 1939; *s* of Sir William Deakin, *qv*, and Margaret Hodson (*née* Beatson-Bell). *Educ*: Bryanston; Univ.

d'Aix-Marseille; Emmanuel Coll., Cambridge (MA Hons). Founding Partner, Editions Alecto, Fine Art Publishers, 1960–64; Producer, BBC Radio Current Affairs Dept, 1964–68; Producer, then Editor, Yorkshire Television Documentary Unit, 1968–81. Productions include: Out of the Shadow into the Sun—The Eiger; Struggle for China; The Children on the Hill; Whicker's World—Way Out West; The Japanese Experience; The Good, the Bad and the Indifferent; Johnny Go Home (British Academy Award, 1976); David Frost's Global Village; The Frost Interview—The Shah; Rampton—The Secret Hospital; Painting With Light (co-prodn with BBC); also many others. Founding Mem., TV-am Breakfast Television Consortium, 1980. *Publications:* Restif de la Bretonne—Les Nuits de Paris (critical edn and trans. with Nicholas Deakin), 1968; Gaetano Donizetti—a biography, 1968; (for children) Tom Grattan's War, 1970, 2nd edn 1971; The Children on the Hill, 1972, 9th edn 1982; (with John Willis) Johnny Go Home, 1976; (with Antony Thomas) The Arab Experience, 1975, 2nd edn 1976; Flame in the Desert, 1976; (with David Frost) I Could Have Kicked Myself, 1982, 2nd US edn 1983; (with David Frost) Who Wants to be a Millionaire, 1983; (with David Frost) If You'll Believe That You'll Believe Anything . . ., 1986. *Recreations:* travel, music, books, pictures, motorcycling. *Address:* 6 Glenhurst Avenue, NW5 1PS. *Club:* British Academy of Film and Television Arts.
     See also N. D. Deakin.

DEAKIN, Prof. Nicholas Dampier; Professor of Social Policy and Administration, since 1980, Dean, Faculty of Commerce and Social Science, since 1986, University of Birmingham; *b* 5 June 1936; *s* of Sir (Frederick) William Deakin, *qv* and Margaret Ogilvy Hodson; *m* 1961, Rose Albinia Donaldson, *d* of Baron Donaldson of Kingsbridge, *qv*, and Frances Annesley Donaldson, *qv*; one *s* two *d*. *Educ:* Westminster Sch.; Christ Church Coll., Oxford. BA (1st cl. Hons) 1959, MA 1963, DPhil 1972. Asst Principal, Home Office, 1959–63, Private Sec. to Minister of State, 1962–63; Asst Dir, Nuffield Foundn Survey of Race Relations in Britain, 1963–68; Res. Fellow, subseq. Lectr, Univ. of Sussex, 1968–72; Head of Social Studies, subseq. Head of Central Policy Unit, GLC, 1972–80. Vice-Chm., Social Affairs Cttee, ESRC, 1984–. *Publications:* (ed and trans.) Memoirs of the Comte de Gramont, 1965; Colour and the British Electorate 1964, 1965; Colour, Citizenship and British Society, 1969; (with Clare Ungerson) Leaving London, 1977; (jtly) Government and Urban Poverty, 1983; (ed) Policy Change in Government, 1986; contribs to other vols and learned jls. *Recreations:* reading fiction, music. *Address:* Department of Social Administration, University of Birmingham, PO Box 363, Birmingham B15 2TT; 55 Estria Road, Birmingham B15 2LG. *T:* 021–440 6251. *Club:* British Academy of Film and Television Arts.
     See also M. Deakin.

DEAKIN, Sir William, Kt 1975; DSO 1943; MA; Warden of St Antony's College, Oxford, 1950–68, retired; Hon. Fellow, 1969; *b* 3 July 1913; *e s* of Albert Witney Deakin, Aldbury, Tring, Herts; *m* 1st, 1935, Margaret Ogilvy (marr. diss. 1940), *d* of late Sir Nicholas Beatson Bell, KCSI, KCIE; two *s*; 2nd, 1943, Livia Stela, *d* of Liviu Nasta, Bucharest. *Educ:* Westminster Sch.; Christ Church, Oxford (Hon. Student), 1979). 1st Class, Modern History, 1934; Amy Mary Preston Read Scholar, 1935. Fellow and Tutor, Wadham Coll., Oxford, 1936–49; Research Fellow, 1949; Hon. Fellow, 1961. Served War of 1939–45; with Queen's Own Oxfordshire Hussars, 1939–41; seconded to Special Operations, War Office, 1941; led first British Military Mission to Tito, May 1943. First Secretary, HM Embassy, Belgrade, 1945–46. Hon. FBA, 1980. Russian Order of Valour, 1944; Chevalier de la Légion d'Honneur, 1953; Grosse Verdienstkreuz, 1958; Yugoslav Partisan Star (1st Class), 1969. *Publications:* The Brutal Friendship, 1962; (with G. R. Storry) The Case of Richard Sorge, 1964; The Embattled Mountain, 1971. *Address:* 83330 Le Beausset, Le Castellet Village, Var, France. *Clubs:* White's, Brooks's.
     See also M. Deakin, N. D. Deakin.

DEAKINS, Eric Petro; MP (Lab) Walthamstow, since 1974 (Walthamstow West, 1970–74); *b* 7 Oct. 1932; *er s* of late Edward Deakins and Gladys Deakins. *Educ:* Tottenham Grammar Sch.; London Sch. of Economics. BA (Hons) in History, 1953. Executive with FMC (Meat) Ltd, 1956; General Manager, Pigs Div., FMC (Meat) Ltd, 1969. Parly Under-Sec. of State, Dept of Trade, 1974–76, DHSS, 1976–79. *Publication:* A Faith to Fight For, 1964. *Recreations:* writing, cinema, squash, football. *Address:* House of Commons, SW1. *T:* 01–219 3000.

DEALTRY, Thomas Richard; Managing Director, RBA Management Services Ltd, London and Kuwait, since 1982; *b* 24 Nov. 1936; *s* of George Raymond Dealtry and Edith (*née* Gardner); *m* 1962, Pauline (*née* Sedgwick) (marr. diss. 1982); one *s* one *d*. *Educ:* Cranfield Inst. of Advanced Technol. (MBA). CEng, MIMechE; MInstM. National Service Commn, 1959–61: Temp. Captain 1960. Divl Exec., Tube Investments Ltd, 1967–71; Sen. Exec., Guest, Keen & Nettlefold Gp Corporate Staff, 1971–74; Dir, Simpson-Lawrence Ltd, and Man. Dir, BUKO BV, Holland, 1974–77; Under Sec./Industrial Adviser, Scottish Econ. Planning Dept, 1977–78; Director, Gulf Regional Planning, Gulf Org. for Industrial Consulting, 1978–82. *Recreations:* golf, squash. *Address:* Flat 38, 60 Park Lane, W1. *Club:* The Western (Glasgow).

DEAN, family name of **Baron Dean of Beswick.**

DEAN OF BESWICK, Baron *cr* 1983 (Life Peer), of West Leeds in the County of West Yorkshire; **Joseph Jabez Dean;** *b* 1922. Engineer; formerly Shop Steward, AUEW. Formerly Leader, Manchester City Council. MP (Lab) Leeds West, Feb. 1974–1983; PPS to Minister of State, CSD, 1974–77; an Asst Govt Whip, 1978–79; Labour Party Pairing Whip, 1982–83, 1985–; Labour Party front bench spokesman on employment. Contested (Lab) Leeds West, 1983. *Address:* House of Lords, SW1A 0PW.

DEAN, Anne, (Mrs Stafford Dean); *see* Howells, Anne.

DEAN, Sir (Arthur) Paul, Kt 1985; MP (C) Woodspring, Avon, since 1983 (Somerset North, 1964–83); Deputy Chairman of Ways and Means and Deputy Speaker, since 1982; Company Director; *b* 14 Sept. 1924; *s* of Arthur Percival Dean and Jessie Margaret Dean (*née* Gaunt); *m* 1st, 1957, Doris Ellen Webb (*d* 1979); 2nd, 1980, Peggy Parker. *Educ:* Ellesmere Coll., Shropshire; Exeter Coll., Oxford (MA, BLitt). Former President Oxford Univ. Conservative Assoc. and Oxford Carlton Club. Served War of 1939–45, Capt. Welsh Guards, ADC to Comdr 1 Corps BAOR. Farmer, 1950–56. Resident Tutor, Swinton Conservative Coll., 1957; Conservative Research Dept, 1957–64, Assistant Director from 1962; a Front Bench Spokesman on Health and Social Security, 1969–70; Parly Under-Sec. of State, DHSS, 1970–74; Member: Exec. Cttee, CPA, UK Branch, 1975–; House of Commons Services Select Cttee, 1979–82; House of Commons Chairman's Panel, 1979–82; Chm., Conservative Health and Social Security Cttee, 1979–82. Formerly, Member Governing Body of Church in Wales. *Publications:* contributions to political pamphlets. *Recreation:* fishing. *Address:* Bowman's Batch, Knightcott, Banwell, Weston-super-Mare, Avon; House of Commons, SW1. *Clubs:* St Stephen's Constitutional; Bath and County; Keynsham Conservative.

DEAN, Barbara Florence; Headmistress, Godolphin and Latymer School, Hammersmith, 1974–85; *b* 1 Sept. 1924; *d* of Albert Sidney and Helen Catherine Dean. *Educ:* North

London Collegiate Sch.; Girton Coll., Cambridge (MA); London Inst. of Educn (Teachers' Dipl.). Asst History Mistress, Roedean Sch., 1947–49; Godolphin and Latymer School: Asst History Mistress and Head of Dept, 1949–70; Deputy Headmistress, 1970–73. *Address:* 9 Stuart Avenue, Ealing, W5 3QJ. *T:* 01–992 8324.

DEAN, Brenda; General-Secretary, SOGAT '82, since 1985 (President, 1983–85); Co-Chairman, Women's National Commission, since 1985; *b* 29 April 1943; *d* of Hugh Dean and Lillian Dean. *Educ:* St Andrews Junior Sch., Eccles; Stretford High Sch. for Girls. Admin. Sec., SOGAT, 1959–72; SOGAT Manchester Branch: Asst Sec., 1972–76; Sec., 1976–83; Mem., Nat. Exec. Council, 1977–83. Member: Printing and Publishing Trng Bd, 1974–; Supplementary Benefits Commn, 1976–80; Price Commn, 1977–79; Occupational Pensions Bd, 1983–; Gen. Adv. Council, BBC, 1984–. *Recreations:* sailing, reading, relaxing, thinking! *Address:* SOGAT House, 274/288 London Road, Hadleigh, Essex SS7 2DE.

DEAN, (Cecil) Roy; HM Diplomatic Service, retired; *b* 18 Feb. 1927; *s* of Arthur Dean and Flora Dean (*née* Clare); *m* 1954, Heather Sturtridge; three *s*. *Educ:* Watford Grammar Sch.; London Coll. of Printing and Graphic Arts (diploma). Served RAF, 1945–48, India and Pakistan; Central Office of Information, 1948–58; Second, later First Sec., Colombo, 1958–62; Vancouver, 1962–64; Lagos, 1964–68; FCO, 1968–71; Consul, Houston, 1971, Acting Consul-Gen., 1972–73; FCO, 1973–76; Dir, Arms Control and Disarmament Res. Unit, 1976–83; Dep. High Comr, Accra, 1983–86. Mem., UN Sec.-General's expert group on disarmament instns, 1980–81. Member: RUSI, 1977; Inst. of Public Relations, 1963. Editor: Insight, 1964–68; Arms Control and Disarmament, 1979–83. *Publications:* Peace and Disarmament, 1982; chapter in Ethics and Nuclear Deterrence, 1982; numerous research papers; contribs to learned jls. *Recreations:* crosswords (Times national champion, 1970 and 1979); humour; light verse. *Address:* 14 Blyth Road, Bromley, Kent. *T:* 01–460 8159. *Club:* Royal Commonwealth Society.

DEAN, (Charles) Raymond, QC 1963; **His Honour Judge Dean;** a Circuit Judge (formerly Judge of County Courts), since 1971; *b* 28 March 1923; *s* of late Joseph Irvin Gledhill Dean and late Lilian Dean (*née* Waddington); *m* 1948, Pearl Doreen (*née* Buncall); one *s* one *d*. *Educ:* Hipperholme Grammar Sch.; The Queen's Coll., Oxford (1941–42 and 1945–47). RAF Flying Duties, 1942–45 (Flt Lieut). BA (Jurisprudence) 1947, MA 1948; called to Bar, Lincoln's Inn, 1948; Deputy Chairman, West Riding QS, 1961–65; Recorder: of Rotherham, 1962–65; of Newcastle upon Tyne, 1965–70; of Kingston-upon-Hull, 1970–71. *Recreations:* fishing, motoring, reading, Rugby Union (now non-playing), golf. *Address:* Inner Court, 248A High Street, Boston Spa, Yorks. *T:* Boston Spa 844155. *Club:* Leeds.

DEAN, David Edis; Director of Library Services, British Architectural Library, Royal Institute of British Architects, 1969–83; *b* 18 June 1922; *y s* of Arthur Edis Dean, CBE, MA, MLitt, and Elsie Georgina Musgrave Wood; *m* 1945, Sylvia Mummery Gray. *Educ:* Bryanston; Wadham Coll., Oxford (MA); Reading Univ. (DipEd). Served War, RAF Photographic Interpretation, 1943–46. Schoolmaster, 1950–54; Cataloguer, then Dep. Librarian, Royal Commonwealth Soc., 1954–60; Dep. Librarian, RIBA, 1960–69. FRSA, Hon. FRIBA. *Publications:* English Shopfronts, 1970; The Thirties: recalling the English architectural scene, 1983; The Architect as Stand Designer, 1985; articles, reviews. *Recreations:* book collecting, music, birdwatching. *Address:* 181 Morrell Avenue, Oxford. *T:* Oxford 247029.

DEAN, Eric Walter, CB 1968; CBE 1958; Chairman Member, Surrey and Sussex Rent Assessment Panel, 1968–78; *b* 5 March 1906; *s* of late Thomas W. Dean, London; *m* 1935, Joan Mary, *d* of late L. A. Stanley, Folkestone; one *d*. *Educ:* Forest Sch.; Exeter Coll., Oxford. Called to Bar, Inner Temple, 1931. Solicitors Dept, Board of Trade, 1935–68; Asst Solicitor, 1947–61; Principal Asst Solicitor, 1961–68, retired. *Recreations:* music, horse-racing. *Address:* 31 Hove Manor, Hove Street, Hove, Sussex BN3 2DG. *T:* Brighton 721783.

DEAN, (Frederick) Harold, CB 1976; QC 1979; Chairman, Disciplinary Appeal Committee, Institute of Chartered Accountants, since 1980; *b* 5 Nov. 1908; *o c* of late Frederick Richard Dean and Alice Dean (*née* Baron), Manchester; *m* 1st, 1939, Gwendoline Mary Eayrs Williams (marr. diss., 1966; she *d* 1975); 3rd *d* of late Rev. W. Williams, Kingsley, Staffs; one *s* one *d*; 2nd, 1966, Sybil Marshall Dennis (*d* 1977), *o c* of late Col F. B. M. Chatterton, CMG, CBE; 3rd, 1978, Mary-Rose Lester, *y d* of late Comdr F. L. Merriman, RN. *Educ:* Manchester Grammar Sch.; Manchester Univ. LLB 1930; LLM 1932. Called to Bar, Middle Temple, 1933. Practised on Northern Circuit, 1934–40 and 1945–50. Served in RAFVR, 1940–45 in UK, Iraq, Egypt and E Africa (Sqdn Ldr). AJAG, 1950; DJAG: Far East, 1954–57 and 1962–65; Middle East, 1958–61; Germany, 1967–68; Vice JAG, 1968–72; Judge Advocate General, 1972–79; a Comr, Duke of York's Royal Mil. Sch., 1972–79. *Publication:* Bibliography of the History of Military and Martial Law (in composite vol., Guide to the Sources of British Military History, 1971); (jtly) Royal Forces in Halsbury's Laws of England, 1983. *Recreations:* travel, music, reading. *Address:* The Old Farmhouse, 13 Lower Street, Quainton, Aylesbury, Bucks HP22 4BL. *T:* Quainton 263. *Club:* Athenæum.

DEAN, Sir John (Norman), Kt 1957; *b* 13 Dec. 1899; *s* of late George Dean; *m* 1st, 1922, Ivy Dorothy (marr. diss. 1935), *d* of Ernest William Andrews; one *s* decd; 2nd, 1935, Charlotte Helen Audrey (*d* 1973), *d* of Thomas Atkinson Walker; 3rd, 1974, Isabel Bothwell-Thomson. *Educ:* Felsted; King's Coll., London University. BSc London (Hons Chemistry). Flying Officer, RNAS and RAF, 1916–19. Chairman: The Telegraph Construction and Maintenance Co. Ltd, 1954–61; Submarine Cables Ltd, 1960–63; Asst to President, General Cable Corporation of New York, USA, 1964–69, retd. ARIC; FIRI; Comp. IEE. *Publications:* various, to technical and scientific bodies. *Address:* Kiln Ridge, Ide Hill, Sevenoaks, Kent TN14 6JH. *T:* Ide Hill 245.

DEAN, Joseph (Jolyon); His Honour Judge Joseph Dean; a Circuit Judge, South Eastern Circuit, since 1975; *b* 26 April 1921; *s* of late Basil Dean, CBE; *m* 1962, Hon. Jenefer Mills, *yr d* of late 5th Baron Hillingdon, MC, TD; one *s* two *d*. *Educ:* Elstree Sch.; Harrow Sch.; Merton Coll., Oxford (MA Classics and Law). 51st (Highland) Div., RA, 1942–45. Called to the Bar, Middle Temple, 1947; Bencher 1972. *Publication:* Hatred, Ridicule or Contempt, 1953 (paperback edns 1955 and 1964). *Recreation:* domestic maintenance. *Address:* The Hall, West Brabourne, Ashford, Kent TN25 5LZ.
     See also Winton Dean.

DEAN, Michael, QC 1981; *b* 2 Feb. 1938; *s* of late Henry Ross Dean and Dorothea Alicia Dean; *m* 1967, Diane Ruth Griffiths. *Educ:* Altrincham Co. Grammar Sch.; Univ. of Nottingham. Lectr in Law, Univ. of Manchester, 1959–62; called to the Bar, Gray's Inn, 1962; Northern Circuit, Manchester, 1962–65; Lectr in Law, LSE, 1965–67; practice at the Bar, London, 1968–. *Publications:* articles in various legal periodicals. *Recreations:* conversation, music, theatre, sailing. *Address:* 7 King's Bench Walk, Temple, EC4. *T:* 01–353 3684.

DEAN, Sir Patrick (Henry), GCMG 1963 (KCMG 1957; CMG 1947); Director: Taylor Woodrow, 1969–86 (Consultant since 1986); American Express Asset Management

(UK), since 1983; International Adviser, American Express, since 1969; *b* 16 March 1909; *o s* of late Professor H. R. Dean and Irene, *d* of Charles Arthur Wilson; *m* 1947, Patricia Wallace, *y d* of late T. Frame Jackson; two *s*. *Educ:* Rugby Sch.; Gonville and Caius Coll., Cambridge. Classical Scholar, 1928; First Class Hons, Classical Tripos Part I; Law Tripos Parts 1 and 2, 1929–32; Fellow of Clare Coll., Cambridge, 1932–35; called to the Bar, 1934; Barstow Law Scholar, Inns of Court, 1934; practised at Bar, 1934–39; Asst Legal Adviser, Foreign Office, 1939–45; Head of German Political Dept, FO, 1946–50; Minister at HM Embassy, Rome, 1950–51; Senior Civilian Instructor at Imperial Defence Coll., 1952–53; Asst Under-Secretary of State, Foreign Office, 1953–56; Dep. Under-Secretary of State, Foreign Office, 1956–60; Permanent Representative of the United Kingdom to the United Nations, 1960–64; Ambassador in Washington, 1965–69. Mem., Departmental Cttee to examine operation of Section 2 of Official Secrets Act, 1971. Chairman: Cambridge Petroleum Royalties, 1975–82; English-Speaking Union, 1973–83. Mem., Governing Body, Rugby School, 1939–84 (Chm. 1972–84). Hon. Fellow, Clare Coll. and Gonville and Caius Coll., Cambridge, 1965. Hon. Bencher, Lincoln's Inn, 1965. Hon. LLD Lincoln Wesleyan Univ., 1961, Chattanooga Univ., 1962, Hofstra Univ., 1964, Columbia Univ., 1965, University of South Carolina, 1967, College of William and Mary, 1968. KStJ 1971. *Publications:* various articles and notes in the Law Quarterly Review. *Recreations:* mountains, walking. *Address:* 5 Bentinck Mansions, Bentinck Street, W1. *T:* 01–935 0881. *Club:* Brooks's.

See also Baron Roskill.

DEAN, Sir Paul; *see* Dean, Sir A. P.

DEAN, Dr Paul, CB 1981; Director, National Physical Laboratory, since 1977 (Deputy Director, 1974–76); *b* 23 Jan. 1933; *s* of late Sydney and Rachel Dean; *m* 1961, Sheila Valerie Gamse; one *s* one *d*. *Educ:* Hackney Downs Grammar Sch.; Queen Mary Coll., Univ. of London (Fellow, 1984). BSc, PhD; FInstP, FIMA. National Physical Laboratory: Sen. Sci. Officer, Math. Div., 1957; Principal Sci. Officer, 1963; Sen. Principal Sci. Officer (Individual Merit), 1967; Head of Central Computer Unit, 1967; Supt, Div. of Quantum Metrology, 1969; Under-Sec., DoI (Head of Space and Air Res. and R&D Contractors Divs), 1976–77. Part-time Head, Res. Establts Management Div., DoI, 1979–82; Exec. Dep. Chm., Council of Res. Establts, 1979–82. Mem., Internat. Cttee of Weights and Measures, 1985–. *Publications:* numerous papers and articles in learned jls. *Recreations:* chess, music, bridge. *Address:* Bushy House, Teddington, Middlesex.

DEAN, Peter Henry; free-lance business consultant, since 1985; *b* 24 July 1939; *s* of late Alan Walduck Dean and Gertrude (*née* Bürger); *m* 1965, Linda Louise Keating; one *d*. *Educ:* Rugby Sch.; London Univ. (LLB). Admitted Solicitor, 1962. Joined Rio Tinto-Zinc Corp., 1966; Sec., 1972–74; Dir, 1974–85. Dir, Associated British Ports Holdings, 1982–; Member: British Transport Docks Bd, 1980–82; Monopolies and Mergers Commn, 1982–. Mem., Council of Management, Highgate Counselling Centre, 1985–; Chm., English Baroque Choir, 1985–. *Recreations:* choral singing, ski-ing. *Address:* 52 Lanchester Road, Highgate, N6 4TA. *T:* 01–883 5417.

DEAN, Rt. Rev. Ralph Stanley; Rector, Church of the Redeemer, Greenville, South Carolina, since 1979; *b* London, 1913; *m* 1939, Irene Florence, *er d* of late Alfred Bezzant Wakefield. *Educ:* Roan Sch., Greenwich; Wembley County Sch.; London Coll. of Divinity, BD London 1938; ALCD 1938; MTh 1944. Deacon 1938; Priest 1939; Curate of St Mary, Islington, 1938–41; Curate-in-charge, St Luke, Watford, 1941–45; Chaplain and Tutor, London Coll. of Divinity, 1945–47, Vice-Principal, 1947–51; Principal, Emmanuel Coll., Saskatoon, Canada, 1951–56; Incumbent of Sutherland and Hon. Canon of Saskatoon, 1955–56; Bishop of Cariboo, 1957; Anglican Executive Officer, 1964–69; Archbishop of Cariboo and Metropolitan of British Columbia, 1971–73; Theological Consultant, Christ Church, Greenville, SC, 1973–79. Episcopal Secretary, Lambeth Conference, 1968. Hon. DD: Wycliffe Coll., Toronto, 1953; Emmanuel Coll., Saskatoon, 1957; Anglican Theolog. Coll., Vancouver, 1965; Huron Coll., Ont, 1965; Hon. STD, Hartford Coll., Conn, 1966. *Publications:* In the Light of the Cross, 1961; article on Anglican Communion, Encyclopædia Britannica. *Address:* 601 Wen Wood Circle, Greenville, South Carolina 29607, USA.

DEAN, Raymond; *see* Dean, C. R.

DEAN, Roy; *see* Dean, C. R.

DEAN, Dr William John Lyon, OBE 1959; Chairman, Commission of Enquiry into the Isle of Man Fishing Industry, since 1982; *b* 4 Nov. 1911; *s* of William Dean, Lossiemouth; *m* 1st, 1938, Ellen Maud Mary (*d* 1977), *d* of Charles Weatherill, CBE; two *s* one *d*; 2nd, 1979, Rachel Marian, *e d* of Humphrey and Rebecca Lloyd, Wotton-under-Edge, Glos. *Educ:* Elgin Academy; Aberdeen Univ. (MB, ChB). Served RAF, 1935–43. Gen. med. practice, 1943–66. Provost of Lossiemouth, 1949–58; Chm., Jt CC of Moray and Nairn, 1964–71; Mem. NE Regional Hosp. Bd, 1947–58. Member: Cttee for Scotland and Northern Ireland White Fish Authority, 1954–81; White Fish Authority, 1963–81; Mem., Herring Industry Bd, 1963, Chm. 1971, until dissolution in 1981. *Publication:* Safety at Sea in Fishing Vessels, 1969 (FAO/ILO/WHO). *Recreation:* fishing (lobster, salmon, trout). *Address:* 6 Ravelston Heights, Edinburgh EH4 3LX. *T:* 031–332 9172.

DEAN, Winton (Basil), FBA 1975; author and musical scholar; *b* Birkenhead, 18 March 1916; *e s* of late Basil Dean, CBE, and Esther, *d* of A. H. Van Gruisen; *m* 1939, Hon. Thalia Mary Shaw, 2nd *d* of 2nd Baron Craigmyle; one *s* one adopted *d* (and two *d* decd). *Educ:* Harrow; King's Coll., Cambridge (MA). Translated libretto of Weber's opera Abu Hassan (Arts Theatre, Cambridge) 1938. Served War of 1939–45: in Admiralty (Naval Intelligence Div.), 1944–45. Member: Music Panel, Arts Council, 1957–60, Cttee of Handel Opera Society (London), 1955–60; Council, Royal Musical Assoc., 1965– (Vice-Pres., 1970–). Ernest Bloch Prof. of Music, 1965–66, Regent's Lectr, 1977, Universiy of California (Berkeley); Matthew Vassar Lectr, Vassar Coll., Poughkeepsie, NY, 1979. Member: Management Cttee, Halle Handel Soc., 1979–; Kuratorium, Göttingen Handel Fest., 1981–. Ed, with Sarah Fuller, Handel's opera Julius Caesar (Barber Inst. of Fine Arts, Birmingham), performed 1977. Hon. RAM 1971. *Publications:* The Frogs of Aristophanes (trans. of choruses to music by Walter Leigh), 1937; Bizet (Master Musicians), 1948 (3rd rev. edn, 1975); Carmen, 1949; Introduction to the Music of Bizet, 1950; Franck, 1950; Hambledon *v* Feathercombe, the Story of a Village Cricket Match, 1951; Handel's Dramatic Oratorios and Masques, 1959; Shakespeare and Opera (Shakespeare in Music), 1964; Georges Bizet, His Life and Work, 1965; Handel and the Opera Seria, 1969; Beethoven and Opera (in The Beethoven Companion), 1971; ed, Handel, Three Ornamented Arias, 1976; (ed) E. J. Dent, The Rise of Romantic Opera, 1976; The New Grove Handel, 1982; contributed to Grove's Dictionary of Music and Musicians (5th and 6th edns), New Oxford History of Music and to musical periodicals and learned journals. *Recreations:* cricket, shooting; naval history. *Address:* Hambledon Hurst, Godalming, Surrey. *T:* Wormley 2644.

See also J. J. Dean.

DEANE, family name of **Baron Muskerry.**

DEANE, Dr Basil; Director, Hongkong Academy for Performing Arts, since 1983; *b* 27 May 1928; *s* of Canon Richard A. Deane and Lorna Deane; *m* 1955, Norma Greig; two *s*. *Educ:* Armagh Royal School; The Queen's Univ., Belfast (BA, BMus, PhD). Lecturer in Music, Glasgow Univ., 1953–59; Senior Lectr, Melbourne Univ., 1959–65; Lectr, Nottingham Univ., 1966–68; Prof., Sheffield Univ., 1968–74; Prof. of Music, Manchester Univ., 1975–80; Music Dir, Arts Council, 1980–83. Member of Arts Council, 1977–79 (Chairman, Music Advisory Panel, 1977–79); Chairman of Music Board, Council for Nat. Academic Awards, 1978–80. Hon. FRNCM. *Publications:* Albert Roussel, 1962; Cherubini, 1965; Hoddinott, 1979; contribs to periodicals. *Address:* c/o Academy for Performing Arts, 1 Gloucester Road, Wanchai, Hong Kong.

DEANE, Prof. Phyllis Mary, FBA 1980; Professor of Economic History, University of Cambridge, 1981–82, now Emeritus; Fellow of Newnham College, 1961–83, Honorary Fellow, 1983; *b* 13 Oct. 1918; *d* of John Edward Deane and Elizabeth Jane Brooks; single. *Educ:* Chatham County Sch.; Hutcheson's Girls' Grammar Sch., Glasgow; Univ. of Glasgow. MA Hons Econ. Science Glasgow 1940; MA Cantab; FRHistS. Carnegie Research Scholar, 1940–41; Research Officer, Nat. Inst. of Econ. and Social Research, 1941–45; Colonial Research Officer, 1946–48; Research Officer: HM Colonial Office, 1948–49; Cambridge University: Dept of Applied Econs, 1950–61; Lectr, Faculty of Econs and Politics, 1961–71; Reader in Economic History, 1971–81. Vis. Prof., Univ. of Pittsburgh, 1969. Editor, Economic Jl, 1968–75. Pres., Royal Economic Soc., 1980–82. *Publications:* (with Julian Huxley) The Future of the Colonies, 1945; The Measurement of Colonial National Incomes, 1948; Colonial Social Accounting, 1953; (with W. A. Cole) British Economic Growth 1688–1959, 1962; The First Industrial Revolution, 1965; The Evolution of Economic Ideas, 1978; papers and reviews in econ. jls. *Recreations:* walking, gardening. *Address:* 4 Stukeley Close, Cambridge CB3 9LT.

DEANE, Hon. Sir William (Patrick), KBE 1982; **Hon. Mr Justice Deane;** Justice of the High Court of Australia, since 1982. Called to the Bar of NSW, 1957; QC 1966. Judge, Supreme Court of NSW, 1977, and Judge, Fed. Court of Australia, 1977–82; Pres., Trade Practices Tribunal, 1977–82. *Address:* High Court of Australia, Canberra, ACT 2600, Australia.

DEANE-DRUMMOND, Maj.-Gen. Anthony John, CB 1970; DSO 1960; MC 1942 and Bar, 1945; *b* 23 June 1917; *s* of late Col J. D. Deane-Drummond, DSO, OBE, MC; *m* 1944, Mary Evangeline Boyd; four *d*. *Educ:* Marlborough Coll.; RMA, Woolwich. Commissioned Royal Signals, 1937. War Service in Europe and N Africa; POW, Italy, 1941 (escaped, 1942); Staff Coll., 1945; Bde Major, 3rd Parachute Bde, 1946–47; Instructor, Sandhurst, 1949–51 and Staff Coll., 1952–55; CO, 22 Special Air Service Regt, 1957–60; Bde Comdr, 44 Parachute Bde, 1961–63; Asst Comdt, RMA, Sandhurst, 1963–66; GOC 3rd Division, 1966–68; ACDS (Operations), 1968–70, retired 1971. Col Comdt, Royal Corps of Signals, 1966–71. Director: Paper and Paper Products Industry Trng Bd, 1971–79; Wood Burning Centre, 1980–83. British Gliding Champion, 1957; Pilot, British Gliding Team, 1958, 1960, 1963, 1965. *Publications:* Return Ticket, 1951; Riot Control, 1975. *Recreations:* carpentry and carving, shooting. *Address:* c/o Royal Bank of Scotland, Lombard Street, EC3. *Club:* Special Forces.

DEANS, Rodger William, CB 1977; Regional Chairman, Social Security Appeal Tribunals and Medical Appeal Tribunals (Scotland), since 1984; *b* 21 Dec. 1917; *s* of Andrew and Elizabeth Deans, Perth; *m* 1943, Joan Radley; one *s* one *d*. *Educ:* Perth Academy; Edinburgh Univ. Qual. Solicitor in Scotland, 1939. Served in RA and REME, 1939–46 (Major); Mil. Prosecutor, Palestine, 1945–46; Procurator Fiscal Depute, Edinburgh, 1946–47; entered Office of Solicitor to Sec. of State for Scotland, 1947; Scottish Office: Legal Asst, 1947–50; Sen. Legal Asst, 1951–62; Asst Solicitor, 1962–71; Solicitor to Secretary of State for Scotland and Solicitor in Scotland to HM Treasury, 1971–80. Consultant Editor, Green & Son, Edinburgh, 1981–82; Sen. Chm., Supplementary Benefit Appeal Tribunals (Scotland), 1982–84. *Recreations:* hill walking, travelling, gardening. *Address:* 25 Grange Road, Edinburgh EH9 1UQ. *T:* 031–667 1893. *Clubs:* Royal Commonwealth Society; Scottish Arts (Edinburgh).

DEAR, Geoffrey James, QPM 1982; DL; Chief Constable, West Midlands Police, since 1985; *b* 20 Sept. 1937; *er s* of Cecil William Dear and Violet Mildred (*née* Mackney); *m* 1958, Judith Ann Stocker; one *s* two *d*. *Educ:* Fletton Grammar Sch., Hunts; University Coll., London (LLB). Joined Peterborough Combined Police after cadet service, 1956; 1st Special Course, Staff Coll., Bramshill, 1962–63 (Distinction); Inspector, Mid-Anglia (now Cambridgeshire) Constab., 1965; Bramshill Scholarship, London Univ., 1965–68; Chief Inspector, 1969; Supt, 1970; i/c Cambridge City, 1970–72; 8th Sen. Comd Course, 1971; Asst Chief Constable (Ops), Notts (City and County), 1972–80; seconded as Dir of Comd Training, Bramshill, 1975–77; Metropolitan Police: Dep. Asst Comr, 1980–81; Asst Comr, 1981–85 (Personnel and Trng, 1981–84; Ops, 1984–85). Member: Govt Adv. Cttee on Alcoholism, 1975–78; Council, RUSI, 1982– (Mem. Cttee, 1976–). Lecture tour of Eastern USA univs, 1978; visited Memphis, Tenn, USA to advise on reorganisation of Police Dept, 1979. Vice Chm., London and SE Reg., Sports Council, 1984–85. DL W Midlands, 1985. SBStJ 1982. Queen's Commendation for Brave Conduct, 1979. *Publications:* (contrib.) The Police and the Community, 1975; articles in Police Jl and other pubns. *Recreations:* field sports, Rugby football (Pres., Met. Police RFC, 1983–85), fell-walking, reading, gardening, music. *Address:* West Midlands Police, Lloyd House, Colmore Circus, Queensway, Birmingham B4 6NQ. *T:* 021–236 5000. *Club:* Naval and Military.

DEARE, Ronald Frank Robert; Minister and UK Permanent Representative to UN Food and Agricultural Organisation, Rome, since 1985; *b* 9 Oct. 1927; *s* of late Albert and Lilian Deare; *m* 1952, Iris Mann; one *s*. *Educ:* Wellington Sch., Somerset. RAF Service, 1945–48. CO 1948; Second Sec., UK Commn, Singapore, 1959; CO, 1962; Dept of Technical Cooperation, 1963; Principal, Min. of Overseas Develt, 1965; Private Sec. to Minister of Overseas Develt, 1971; Asst Sec., 1973; Counsellor (Overseas Develt), Washington, and Alternate Exec. Dir, World Bank, 1976–79; Head of W Indian and Atlantic Dept, FCO, 1980–81; Head of Central and Southern Africa Dept, ODA, FCO, 1981–83; Head of Bilateral Co-ord. and Consultancies Dept, ODA, FCO, 1983–84. *Recreations:* reading, gardening. *Address:* c/o Foreign and Commonwealth Office, King Charles Street, SW1A 2AH. *T:* Rome 475–5441.

DEARING, Sir Ronald (Ernest), Kt 1984; CB 1979; Chairman, Post Office Corporation, since 1981; *b* 27 July 1930; *s* of E. H. A. Dearing and M. T. Dearing (*née* Hoyle); *m* 1954, Margaret Patricia Riley; two *d*. *Educ:* Doncaster Grammar Sch.; Hull Univ. (BScEcon); London Business Sch. (Sloan Fellow). Min. of Labour and Nat. Service, 1946–49; Min. of Power, 1949–62; HM Treasury, 1962–64; Min. of Power, Min. of Technology, DTI, 1965–72; Regional Dir, N Region, DTI, 1972–74, and Under-Sec., DTI later Dept of Industry, 1972–76; Dep. Sec. on nationalised industry matters, Dept of Industry, 1976–80; Dep. Chm., Post Office, 1980–81; Chm., NICG, 1983–84. Mem., London Adv. Bd, Nat. and Provincial Building Soc., 1985–; Member, Council: BIM, 1985–; Industrial Soc., 1985–. Mem. Governing Council, London Business Sch., 1985–. Hon. DSc Hull, 1986.

Recreations: gardening, Do it Yourself. *Address:* Post Office Headquarters, 33 Grosvenor Place, SW1X 1PX.

DEARNLEY, Christopher Hugh, MA (Oxon), BMus, FRCO; Organist of St Paul's Cathedral since 1968; *b* 11 Feb. 1930; 3rd *s* of Rev. Charles Dearnley; *m* 1957, Bridget (*née* Wateridge); three *s* one *d. Educ:* Cranleigh Sch., Surrey; Worcester Coll., Oxford. Organ Scholar, Worcester Coll., Oxford, 1948–52. Asst Organist, Salisbury Cathedral, and Music Master, the Cathedral Sch., Salisbury, 1954–57; Organist and Master of the Choristers, Salisbury Cathedral, 1957–67. Pres., Incorporated Assoc. of Organists, 1968–70; Chairman: Friends of Cathedral Music, 1971–; Harwich Festival, 1982–; Percy Whitlock Trust, 1982–. *Publications:* The Treasury of English Church Music, Vol. III, 1965; English Church Music 1650–1750, 1970. *Recreations:* sketching, bicycling, gardening. *Address:* 8B Amen Court, EC4M 7BU.

DEAVE, John James; barrister-at-law; a Recorder of the Crown Court, since 1980; *b* 1 April 1928; *s* of Charles John Deave and Gertrude Debrit Deave; *m* 1958, Gillian Mary, *d* of Adm. Sir Manley Power, *qv*; one *s* one *d. Educ:* Charterhouse; Pembroke Coll., Oxford (MA). Served RA, 2nd Lieut, 1946–48; Pembroke Coll., 1948–51; called to the Bar, Gray's Inn, 1952; in practice at Nottingham, 1957–. *Recreations:* history, gardening. *Address:* (chambers) 24 The Ropewalk, Nottingham. *T:* Nottingham 472581. *Club:* Nottinghamshire United Services.

DEAVIN, Stanley Gwynne, CBE 1971 (OBE 1958); FCA; Chartered Accountant; Chairman, North Eastern Gas Board, 1966–71, retired (Dep. Chairman, 1961–66); *b* 8 Aug. 1905; *s* of Percy John Deavin and Annie (*née* Crayton); *m* 1st, 1934, Louise Faviell (*d* 1982); one *s* one *d*; 2nd, 1982, Hilda Jenkins (*née* Grace). *Educ:* Hymer's Coll., Hull. Firm of Chartered Accountants, 1921–33; Secretary and Accountant, Preston Gas Co., 1933–49; North Western Gas Board: Secretary, 1949–61; Member Board, 1960–61. OStJ. *Recreations:* cricket, Rugby football, theatre. *Address:* 50 Hookstone Drive, Harrogate, North Yorks. *T:* Harrogate 884301.

DeBAKEY, Prof. Michael Ellis, MD, MS; Chancellor, Baylor College of Medicine, since 1979 (Professor of Surgery and Chairman of Department of Surgery since 1948, President, 1969–79, Chief Executive Officer, 1968–69, Baylor University College of Medicine; Vice-President for Medical Affairs, Baylor University, 1968–69); Surgeon-in-Chief, Ben Taub General Hospital, Houston, Texas; Director, National Heart and Blood Vessel Research and Demonstration Center; Consultant in Surgery to various Hospitals etc., in Texas, and to Walter Reed Army Hospital, Washington, DC; *b* 7 Sept. 1908; *s* of Shaker Morris and Raheeja Zorba DeBakey; *m* 1st, 1936, Diana Cooper (*d* 1972); four *s*; 2nd, 1975, Katrin Fehlhaber; one *d. Educ:* Tulane Univ., New Orleans, La, USA (Distinguished Alumnus of Year, 1974). Residency in New Orleans, Strasbourg, and Heidelberg, 1933–36; Instructor, Dept of Surgery, Tulane Univ., 1937–40; Asst Prof. of Surgery, 1940–46; Associate Prof. of Surgery, 1946–48. Colonel Army of US (Reserve). In Office of Surgeon-General, 1942–46, latterly Director Surgical Consultant Div. (Meritorious Civilian Service Medal, 1970). Chairman, President's Commission on Heart Disease, Cancer and Stroke, 1964; US Chm., Task for Mechanical Circulatory Assistance, Jt US-USSR Cttee, 1974; Dir, Cardiovascular Res. and Trng Center, Methodist Hosp. (Houston), 1968–75; Adv. Council, Nat. Heart, Lung, Blood Inst., 1982–86; has served on governmental and university cttees, etc., concerned with public health, research and medical education. Mem. Adv. Editorial Bds: Ann. Surg., 1970–; Coeur, 1969–; Biomedical Materials and Artificial Organs, 1971–; Editor, Jl of Vascular Surgery, 1984–. Member and Hon. Member of medical societies, including: American Assoc. for Thoracic Surgery (Pres. 1959); Hon. Fellow, RCS, 1974; International Cardiovascular Society (Pres. 1959); BMA (Hon. Foreign Corresp. Member 1966); Royal Society Med., London; Acad. of Medical Sciences, USSR; US—China Physicians Friendship Assoc., 1974; Assoc. Internat. Vasc. Surgeons (Pres., 1983). Has received numerous awards from American and foreign medical institutions, and also honorary doctorates; Presidential Medal of Freedom with Distinction; Hektoen Gold Medal, Amer. Med. Assoc., 1970; Merit Order of the Republic, 1st class (Egypt), 1980; The Independence of Jordan Medal, 1st class, 1980; Sovereign Order of the Knights of the Hospital of St John (Denmark), 1980. *Publications:* The Blood Bank and the Technique and Therapeutics of Transfusions, 1942; (with B. M. Cohen) Buerger's Disease, 1962; A Surgeon's Diary of a Visit to China, 1974; The Living Heart, 1977; The Living Heart Diet, 1984; contributions to standard textbooks of medicine and surgery, Current Therapy, and many symposia; Editor, Year Book of General Surgery, etc.; numerous articles in medical journals. *Recreations:* hunting, music. *Address:* Baylor College of Medicine, One Baylor Plaza Avenue, Houston, Texas 77030, USA. *T:* 797–9353; 5323 Cherokee, Houston, Texas 77005, USA. *Clubs:* Cosmos, University Federal (Washington, DC); River Oaks Country (Houston, Texas).

de BASTO, Hon. Gerald Arthur; Hon. Mr Justice de Basto; Judge of the High Court of Hong Kong, since 1982; *b* London, 31 Dec. 1924; *s* of Bernard de Basto and Lucie Marie, *d* of Raoul Melchior Pattard, Paris; *m* 1961, Diana, *d* of Dr Frederick Osborne Busby Wilkinson; two *s. Educ:* Riverview Coll., Sydney, Australia; Univ. of Sydney (LLB). Called to the Bar: Supreme Court of New South Wales and High Court of Australia, 1952; Lincoln's Inn, 1955; called to the Hong Kong Bar, 1957; Chairman, Hong Kong Bar, 1968–70, 1973; QC 1968; Judge of the District Court of Hong Kong, 1973–82; Pres., Deportation Tribunal, 1986–. FRSA 1984. *Recreations:* children, antiques, travel, reading. *Address:* Courts of Justice, Hong Kong; A3401 Tregunter, 14 Tregunter Path, Hong Kong. *T:* 5–220330. *Clubs:* Carlton; Hong Kong, Shek O Country, Royal Hong Kong Jockey (Hong Kong).

de BEER, Esmond Samuel, CBE 1969; FBA 1965; FSA, FRSL, FRHistSoc; historical scholar, specialising in seventeenth-century English history; engaged in editing John Locke correspondence; *b* 15 Sept. 1895; *s* of I. S. de Beer and Emily, *d* of Bendix Hallenstein, Dunedin, NZ. *Educ:* Mill Hill Sch.; New Coll., Oxford (MA); University College, London (MA). Studied under late Sir Charles Firth. A Trustee, National Portrait Gallery, 1959–67. Independent Member, Reviewing Cttee on Export of Works of Art, 1965–70. Fellow University College, London, 1967. Hon. Fellow: New Coll., Oxford; Warburg Inst.; Hon. DLitt (Durham, Oxford); Hon. LittD (Otago). Hon. Vice-Pres., the Historical Association; Pres., Hakluyt Society, 1972–78 (Hon. Vice-Pres., 1966); Vice-Pres., Cromwell Assoc., 1980. *Publications:* first complete edition of Diary of John Evelyn, 1955; (ed) The Correspondence of John Locke, vols I-VII, 1976–82; articles and reviews in learned periodicals, etc. *Address:* Stoke House, Stoke Hammond, Milton Keynes MK17 9BN. *Club:* Athenæum.

DE BENEDETTI, Carlo; Cavaliere del Lavoro, Italy, 1983; Chairman since 1983, and Chief Executive since 1978, Ing. C. Olivetti & Co., SpA; Vice-Chairman/Chief Executive: Compagnie Industriali Riunite, since 1976; Compagnia Finanziaria De Benedetti, since 1985; Chairman, Buitoni, since 1985; Vice-Chairman, Euromobiliare, since 1977; *b* 14 Nov. 1934; *s* of Rodolfo and Pierina Fumel; *m* 1960, Margherita Crosetti; three *s. Educ:* Turin Polytechnic (degree in electrotech. engrg). Chm./Chief Exec., Gilardini, 1972–76; Chief Exec., Fiat, 1976. Vice-Pres., Confindustria, 1983–; Dir, Center for Strategic and Internat. Studies, Washington, 1978–; Member: Internat. Adv. Bd, Morgan Guaranty Trust, NY, 1980–; Internat. Council, INSEAD, Paris, 1983–; Bd of Trustees, Solomon R. Guggenheim Foundn, NY, 1984–; Governor, Atlantic Inst. for Internat. Affairs, Paris, 1982–. Hon. LLD Wesleyan, Conn, 1986. *Publications:* lectures and articles in business jls. *Address:* Ing. C. Olivetti, Via Jervis 77, 10015 Ivrea, Italy. *T:* (0125) 522011.

DEBENHAM, Sir Gilbert Ridley, 3rd Bt, *cr* 1931; *b* 28 June 1906; 2nd *s* of Sir Ernest Ridley Debenham, 1st Bt, JP; *S* brother, Sir Piers Debenham, 2nd Bt, 1964; *m* 1935, Violet Mary, *e d* of late His Honour Judge (George Herbert) Higgins; three *s* one *d. Educ:* Eton; Trinity Coll., Cambridge (BA 1928; BChir 1935). DPM 1946; MRCPsych 1971. *Heir: s* George Andrew Debenham [*b* 10 April 1938; *m* 1969, Penelope Jane, *d* of John David Armishaw Carter; one *s* one *d*]. *Address:* Tonerspuddle Farm, Dorchester, Dorset.

DEBENHAM TAYLOR, John, CMG 1967; OBE 1959; TD 1967; HM Diplomatic Service, retired; *b* 25 April 1920; *s* of John Francis Taylor and Harriett Beatrice (*née* Williams); *m* 1966, Gillian May James; one *d. Educ:* Aldenham School. Eastern Counties Farmers Assoc. Ltd, Ipswich and Great Yarmouth, 1936–39. Commd in RA (TA), Feb. 1939; served War of 1939–46 in Finland, Middle East, UK and SE Asia (despatches, 1946). Foreign Office, 1946; Control Commn for Germany, 1947–49; 2nd Sec., Bangkok, 1950; Actg Consul, Songkhla, 1951–52; Vice-Consul, Hanoi, 1952–53; FO, 1953–54; 1st Sec., Bangkok, 1954–56; FO, 1956–58; Singapore, 1958–59; FO, 1960–64; Counsellor, 1964; Counsellor: Kuala Lumpur, 1964–66; FCO (formerly FO), 1966–69; Washington, 1969–72; Paris, 1972–73; FCO, 1973–77. *Recreations:* walking, reading, history. *Address:* Lloyds Bank, Butler Place, SW1. *Club:* Naval and Military.

de BOER, Anthony Peter, CBE 1982; Chairman, Steel Brothers Holdings PLC, since 1980 (Director, since 1971); Chairman, British Road Federation, since 1972; *b* 22 June 1918; *s* of Goffe de Boer and Irene Kathleen (*née* Grist); *m* 1942, Pamela Agnes Norah Bullock; one *s. Educ:* Westminster School. Served War of 1939–45: RE (AA), 1939–40; Indian Army, 6th Gurkha Rifles, 1940–43; RIASC, 1944–46; Major 1944. Joined Royal Dutch/Shell Gp, 1937: served in China, Sudan, Ethiopia, Egypt, Palestine, 1946–58; Area Co-ordinator, Africa and Middle East, 1959–63; Chm., Shell Trinidad, 1963–64; Man. Dir, Marketing, Shell Mex & BP, 1964–67; Deputy Chairman: Wm Cory & Son, 1968–71; Associated Heat Services Ltd, 1969–76; Chairman: Anvil Petroleum plc (formerly Attock Oil Co.), 1974–85; Tomatin Distillers plc, 1978–85; Channel Tunnel Develts (1981), 1981–84; Director: Nat. Bus Co., 1969–83; Tarmac plc, 1971–83; British Transport Advertising, 1973–83; Internat. Road Fedn, 1974–; Chloride Gp, 1976–85; Burmah Oil plc, 1978–85; The Automobile Pty Ltd, 1984–; Mem. Policy Cttee, Price Waterhouse, 1979–86. Mem., Bd, British Travel Assoc., 1965–67. Vice-Chm., RAC, 1985– (Mem. Cttee, 1984–). Chm., Keep Britain Tidy Gp, 1969–79. Mem. Council, CBI, 1980–83; Mem. Council, Sussex Univ., 1969–; Chm., Indep. Schools Careers Org; Pres., Fuel Luncheon Club, 1967–69; Dir, Brighton and Hove Albion Football Club, 1969–72. Freeman, City of London; Liveryman, Coach Makers' and Coach Harness Makers' Co. FBIM 1970 (Mem. Council 1974). *Recreations:* racing, theatre, gardening. *Address:* Halletts Barn, Ditchling Common, Hassocks, Sussex. *T:* Hassocks 2442. *Clubs:* Royal Automobile, Garrick.

de BONO, Dr Edward Francis Charles Publius; Lecturer in Medicine, Department of Medicine, University of Cambridge, 1976–83; Director of The Cognitive Research Trust, Cambridge, since 1971; Secretary-General, Supranational Independent Thinking Organisation (SITO), since 1983; *b* 19 May 1933; *s* of late Prof. Joseph de Bono, CBE and of Josephine de Bono; *m* 1971, Josephine Hall-White; two *s. Educ:* St Edward's Coll., Malta; Royal Univ. of Malta; Christ Church, Oxford (Rhodes Scholar). BSc, MD Malta; DPhil Oxon; PhD Cantab. Research Asst, Dept of Regius Prof. of Medicine, Univ. of Oxford, 1958–60; Jun. Lectr in Med., Oxford, 1960–61; Asst Dir of Res., Dept of Investigative Medicine, Cambridge Univ., 1963–76. Research Associate: also Hon. Registrar, St Thomas' Hosp. Med. Sch., Univ. of London; Harvard Med. Sch., and Hon. Consultant, Boston City Hosp., 1965–66. TV series: The Greatest Thinkers, 1981; de Bono's Thinking Course, 1982. *Publications:* The Use of Lateral Thinking, 1967; The Five-Day Course in Thinking, 1968; The Mechanism of Mind, 1969; Lateral Thinking: a textbook of creativity, 1970; The Dog Exercising Machine, 1970; Technology Today, 1971; Practical Thinking, 1971; Lateral Thinking for Management, 1971; Beyond Yes and No, 1972; Children Solve Problems, 1972; Eureka!: an illustrated history of inventions from the wheel to the computer, 1974; Teaching Thinking, 1976; The Greatest Thinkers, 1976; Wordpower, 1977; The Happiness Purpose, 1977; The Case of the Disappearing Elephant, 1977; Opportunities: a handbook of business opportunity search, 1978; Future Positive, 1979; Atlas of Management Thinking, 1981; de Bono's Thinking Course, 1982; Tactics: the art and science of success, 1984; Conflicts: a better way to resolve them, 1985; Six Thinking Hats, 1985; Masterthinker's Handbook, 1985; Letters to Thinkers (monthly), 1982–; contribs to Nature, Lancet, Clinical Science, Amer. Jl of Physiology, etc. *Recreations:* travel, toys, thinking. *Address:* L2 Albany, Piccadilly, W1V 9RR. *Club:* Athenæum.

DEBRÉ, Michel Jean-Pierre; Deputy from La Réunion, French National Assembly, since 1963, re-elected 1967, 1968, 1973, 1978, 1981, 1982; *b* 15 Jan. 1912; *s* of late Prof. Robert Debré and Dr Jeanne Debré (*née* Debat-Ponsan); *m* 1936, Anne-Marie Lemaresquier; four *s. Educ:* Lycée Louis-le-Grand; Faculté de Droit de Paris (LLD); Ecole Libre des Sciences Politiques; Cavalry Sch., Saumur. Auditeur, Conseil d'Etat, 1934; French Army, 1939–44; Commissaire de la République, Angers region, 1944–45; Saar Economic Mission, 1947; Secretary-General for German and Austrian Affairs, 1948. Senator from Indre et Loire, 1948, re-elected 1955; Minister of Justice, 1958–59; Prime Minister, 1959–62; Minister of Economic Affairs and Finances, 1966–68; Minister for Foreign Affairs, 1968–69; Minister for National Defence, 1969–73. Member, European Parliament, 1979–80. Mem. from Amboise, Conseil Général of Indre-et-Loire, 1951–70, 1976–82. Mayor of Amboise, 1966–, re-elected 1971, 1977, 1983. Member, Rassemblement pour la République. Officer Légion d'Honneur, Croix de Guerre, Rosette of Résistance, Free French Medal, Medal of Escaped Prisoners. *Publications:* Refaire la France 1944; Demain la Paix, 1945; La Mort de l'Etat Républicain, 1948; La République et son Pouvoir, 1950; La République et ses Problèmes, 1951; Ces Princes qui nous Gouvernent, 1957; Au Service de la Nation, 1963; Jeunesse, quelle France te faut-il?, 1965; Une certaine idée de la France, 1972; Français, choisissons l'espoir, 1979; Lettre ouverte aux Français sur la reconquête de la France, 1980; Peut-on lutter contre le chômage?, 1982; Trois Républiques pour une France (mémoires), vol. 1, 1984. *Recreation:* equitation. *Address:* 20 rue Jacob, 75006 Paris, France.

DEBREU, Prof. Gerard; Professor of Economics, since 1962, and Professor of Mathematics, since 1975, University of California, Berkeley; *b* 4 July 1921; *s* of Camille Debreu and Fernande (*née* Decharne); *m* 1945, Françoise Bled; two *d. Educ:* Ecole Normale Supérieure, Paris; Agrégé de l'Université, Paris, 1946. DSc Univ. de Paris, 1956. Research Associate: Centre National de la Recherche Scientifique, Paris, 1946–48; Cowles Commn for Research in Economics, Univ. of Chicago, 1950–55; Associate Prof. of Economics, Cowles Foundn for Research in Economics, Yale Univ., 1955–61. Fellow, Amer. Acad. of Arts and Sciences, 1970; Pres., Econometric Soc., 1971; Member: Nat. Acad. of Sciences, USA, 1977; Amer. Philos. Soc., 1984; Dist. Fellow, Amer. Economic Assoc.,

1982; For. Associate, French Acad. of Scis, 1984. Hon. degrees: Bonn, 1977; Lausanne, 1980; Northwestern, 1981; Toulouse, 1983. Nobel Prize in Economic Sciences, 1983. Chevalier de la Légion d'Honneur, 1976; Comdr de l'Ordre National du Mérite, 1984. *Publications:* Theory of Value: an axiomatic analysis of economic equilibrium, 1959, 2nd edn 1971 (trans. into French, Spanish, German and Japanese); Mathematical Economics: twenty papers, 1983; contribs to Econometrica, Procs of Nat. Acad. of Sciences, Review of Economic Studies, Economie Appliquée, Procs of Amer. Math. Soc., Internat. Economic Review, Review of Economic Studies, La Décision, Jl of Mathematical Economics, Amer. Economic Review. *Address:* Department of Economics, 250 Barrows Hall, University of California, Berkeley, Calif 94720, USA. *T:* (415) 642–7284.

de BROGLIE, 7th Duc; **Louis Victor de Broglie;** Member of the Institut de France, Académie Française since 1944, Académie des Sciences since 1933; Professor, Faculté des Sciences, Paris, since 1932; Foreign Member Royal Society (London) since 1953; *b* Dieppe, 15 Aug. 1892; *s* of Victor, Duc de Broglie; *S* brother, Maurice, 1960; unmarried. *Educ:* Lycée Janson de Sailly, Paris. Licencié ès Lettres, 1910; Licencié ès Sciences, 1913; served Radio-télégraphie Militaire, 1914–19; Docteur ès Sciences, 1924; Maître de Conférences, Faculté des Sciences, Paris, 1928. Permanent Sec., Académie des Sciences, 1942–75. Prizes include: Nobel Prize for Physics, 1929; Kalinga Prize, 1952. *Publications:* Thèse de doctorat sur la théorie des quanta, 1924; (with Maurice de Broglie) Introduction à l'étude des rayons X et gamma, 1928; La physique nouvelle et les quanta, matiére et lumiére, 1937; Continu et discontinu, 1941; Physique et micro-physique, 1947; Savants et découvertes, 1951; Nouvelles perspectives en microphysique, 1957; Sur les sentiers de la science, 1966; La réinterpretation de la mécanique ondulatoire, 1972; Recherches d'un demi-siècle (souvenirs), 1976; Jalons pour une nouvelle microphysique, 1978. *Address:* 94 Perronet, 92 Neuilly-sur-Seine, France. *T:* Maillot 76.09.

de BROKE; *see* Willoughby de Broke.

de BRUYNE, Dirk, Hon. CBE 1983; Commander, Order of Orange Nassau, 1982; Knight, Order of Netherlands Lion, 1976; Chairman, Algemene Bank Nederland (ABN), Netherlands, since 1983; Deputy Chairman, Ocean Transport & Trading, since 1983; Director, Royal Dutch Petroleum Co., The Hague, since 1982 (President, 1977–82; Managing Director, 1974–77); Chairman, Committee of Managing Directors, Royal Dutch/Shell Group of Companies, 1979–82; *b* Rotterdam, Netherlands, 1 Sept. 1920; *s* of Dirk E. de Bruyne and Maria van Alphen, Rotterdam; *m* 1945, Geertje Straub; one *s* one *d*. *Educ:* Erasmus Univ., Rotterdam (Grad. Econ.). Joined Royal Dutch/Shell Gp of Companies, 1945: served in: The Hague, 1945–55; Indonesia, 1955–58; London, 1958–60 (Dep. Gp Treasurer); The Hague, 1960–62 (Finance Manager); Italy, 1962–65 (Exec. Vice-Pres., Shell Italiana); London, 1965–68 (Regional Co-ordinator: Oil, Africa); Germany, 1968–70 (Pres., Deutsche Shell); Dir of Finance, Shell Petroleum Co. Ltd, 1970; Man. Dir, Royal Dutch/Shell Gp of Cos, 1971–79; Director: Shell Transport & Trading Co. Ltd, 1971–74; Shell Canada Ltd, 1977–; Chm., Shell Oil Co., USA, 1977–82. *Recreations:* swimming, reading. *Address:* Shell Centre, SE1 7NA. *Clubs:* Dutch (London); De Witte (The Hague).

de BRUYNE, Dr Norman Adrian, FRS 1967; FEng 1976; Chairman, Techne Inc., since 1973 (President, 1967–73); *b* 8 Nov. 1904; *s* of Pieter Adriaan de Bruyne and Maud de Bruyne (*née* Mattock); *m* 1940, Elma Lilian Marsh; one *s* one *d*. *Educ:* Lancing Coll.; Trinity Coll., Cambridge. MA 1930, PhD 1930. Fellow of Trinity Coll., Cambridge, 1928–44. Managing Director: Aero Research Ltd, 1934–48; Ciba (ARL) Ltd, 1948–60; Techne (Cambridge) Ltd, 1964–67. Dir, Eastern Electricity Bd, 1962–67. Awarded Simms Gold Medal, RAeS, 1937. FInstP 1944; FRAeS 1955; *Recreation:* inventing. *Address:* 3700 Brunswick Pike, Princeton, New Jersey 08540, USA. *T:* 609–452 9275.

de BUNSEN, Sir Bernard, Kt 1962; CMG 1957; MA Oxon; Principal of Chester College, Chester, 1966–71; *b* 24 July 1907; *s* of late L. H. G. de Bunsen, and late Victoria de Bunsen (*née* Buxton); *m* 1975, Joan Allington Harmston, MBE. *Educ:* Leighton Park Sch.; Balliol Coll., Oxford. Schoolmaster, Liverpool Public Elementary Schools, 1930–34; Asst Director of Education, Wiltshire CC, 1934–38; HM Inspector of Schools, Ministry of Education, 1938–46; Director of Education, Palestine, 1946, until withdrawal of British administration, 1948; Professor of Education, Makerere University College, East Africa, 1948, acting Principal, Aug. 1949, Principal, 1950–64, Hon. Fellow, 1968. Vice-Chancellor of University of East Africa, 1963–65; Chairman: Africa Educational Trust, 1967–; Archbishops' Working Party on Future of Theological Colleges, 1967–68; Africa Bureau, 1971–77; Council for Aid to African Students, 1976–; Vice-President: The Anti-Slavery Soc., 1975–; Royal African Soc., 1977. Hon LLD St Andrews, 1963. *Address:* 3 Prince Arthur Road, NW3. *T:* 01–435 3521.

DE BUTTS, Brig. Frederick Manus, CMG 1967; OBE 1961 (MBE 1943); DL; *b* 17 April 1916; *s* of late Brig. F. C. De Butts, CB, DSO, MC, and K. P. M. O'Donnell; *m* 1944, Evelyn Cecilia, *d* of Sir Walter Halsey, 2nd Bt; one *s* one *d*. *Educ:* Wellington Coll.; Oriel Coll., Oxford. Commissioned into Somerset LI, 1937. Served War of 1939–45, in Middle East, Italy, France and Germany. Staff Coll., 1944; Joint Services Staff Coll., 1954; Bt Lieut-Colonel, 1957; Commanded 3rd Bn Aden Protectorate Levies, 1958–60; Bde Colonel, Light Infantry, 1961–64; Comdr, Trucial Oman Scouts, 1964–67; HQ Home Counties District, Shorncliffe, Kent, 1967–68; Defence Attaché, Cairo, 1968–71; retired 1971; employed on contract as COS (Brig.), MoD, United Arab Emirates, 1971–73; Hon. Brig. 1973. Mem., Dacorum DC, 1976–83. Hon. Dir, Herts Soc., 1981–. County Chm., 1973–76, County Comr, 1976–81, Vice-Pres., 1981–, Herts Scouts; Vice-Pres., Herts Girl Guides, 1981–; Governor, Abbot's Hill School, 1971– (Chm., 1975–84). DL Herts 1975. *Recreations:* tennis, hill-walking. *Address:* The Old Vicarage, Great Gaddesden, Hemel Hempstead, Herts. *T:* Hemel Hempstead 62129.

DEBY, John Bedford; QC 1980; a Recorder of the Crown Court, since 1977; *b* 19 Dec. 1931; *s* of Reginald Bedford Deby and Irene (*née* Slater). *Educ:* Winchester Coll.; Trinity Coll., Cambridge (MA). Called to the Bar, Inner Temple, 1954, Bencher, 1986. *Address:* 11 Britannia Road, Fulham, SW6 2HJ. *T:* 01–736 4976.

de CANDOLE, Eric Armar Vully, CMG 1952; CBE 1950; MA; Sudan Political Service (retired); *b* 14 Sept. 1901; *e s* of late Rev. Armar Corry Vully de Candole, Rector of Ayot Saint Lawrence, Hertfordshire and late Edith Hodgson; *m* 1932, Marian Elizabeth Pender, *d* of Maj. H. Constable Roberts, DSO, MVO; three *s*. *Educ:* Colet Court; Aldenham Sch.; Worcester Coll., Oxford (Exhibitioner). Class II Modern History, 1923, BA 1924, MA 1946. Joined Sudan Political Service, 1923; served in Education Dept as Tutor, Gordon Coll., 1923–27; Acting Warden, 1927–28; Berber, Khartoum and Darfur Provinces as Dist Comr and Magistrate, 1928–36; Resident, Dar Masalit, 1936–44; Bimbashi, SADF, 1940–44; Dep.-Governor, Northern Province, 1944–46; seconded to British Military Administration as Chief Secretary, Cyrenaica, 1946–48; Chief Administrator, Somalia, 1948; Chief Administrator, Cyrenaica, 1948–49; HBM's Resident in Cyrenaica, 1949–51. With Kuwait Oil Co. Ltd, 1952–66, BP Co. Ltd, 1966–69. Order of the Nile, Egypt (4th class), 1934; Order of Istiqlal, Libya (1st class), 1954. *Publications:* articles on Middle East. *Recreations:* gardening, travel. *Address:* Shootwood, Burley, Hants. *T:* Burley 2330.

de CARDI, Beatrice Eileen, OBE 1973; retired 1973, but continuing archæological research in Lower Gulf countries; *b* 5 June 1914; *d* of Edwin Count de Cardi and Christine Berbette Wurrflein. *Educ:* St Paul's Girls' Sch.; University Coll. London (BA). Secretary (later Asst), London Museum, 1936–44; Personal Asst to Representative of Allied Supplies Exec. of War Cabinet in China, 1944–45; Asst UK Trade Comr: Delhi, 1946; Karachi, 1947; Lahore, 1948–49; Asst Sec. (title changed to Sec.), Council for British Archæology, 1949–73. Archæological research: in Kalat, Pakistan Baluchistan, 1948; in Afghanistan, 1949; directed excavations: in Kalat, 1957; at Bampur, Persian Baluchistan, 1966; survey in Ras al-Khaimah (then Trucial States), 1968; Middle East lecture tour for British Council, 1970; survey with RGS's Musandam Expedn (Northern Oman), 1971–72; directed archæological research projects: in Qatar, 1973–74; in Central Oman, 1974–76, 1978; survey in Ras al-Khaimah, 1977, 1982. Winston Churchill Meml Trust Fellowship for work in Oman, 1973. FSA 1950 (Vice-Pres., 1976–80; Dir, 1980–83). *Publications:* Excavations at Bampur, a third millennium settlement in Persian Baluchistan, 1966 (Vol. 51, Pt 3, Anthropological Papers of the American Museum of Natural History), 1970; Archaeological Surveys in Baluchistan 1948 and 1957 (Inst. of Archaeology, Occasional Paper No 8), 1983; contribs to Antiquity, Iran, Pakistan Archæology, East and West, Jl of Oman Studies, Oriens Antiquus. *Recreations:* archæological fieldwork, travel, cooking. *Address:* 1a Douro Place, Victoria Road, W8 5RW. *T:* 01–937 9740.

de CHAIR, Somerset; *b* 22 Aug. 1911; *s* of late Admiral Sir Dudley de Chair, Governor of NSW; *m* 1st, 1932, Thelma Arbuthnot (marr. diss. 1950); one *s* (and one *s* decd); 2nd, 1950, Carmen Appleton (*née* Bowen) (marr. diss. 1958); two *s*; 3rd, 1958, Mrs Margaret Patricia Manlove (*née* Field-Hart) (marr. diss. 1974); one *d*; 4th, 1974, Juliet, Marchioness of Bristol, *o d* of 8th Earl Fitzwilliam, DSC; one *d*. *Educ:* King's Sch., Paramatta, New South Wales; Balliol Coll., Oxford. MP (Nat C) for S. West Norfolk, 1935–45; Parliamentary Private Secretary to Rt Hon. Oliver Lyttelton MP, Minister of Production, 1942–44; MP (C) South Paddington, 1950–51. 2nd Lieut Supp. Res. RHG, 1938; served with Household Cavalry in the Middle East, during Iraqi and Syrian campaigns (wounded), IO to 4th Cavalry Bde, 1940–41; Captain GS (I), 1942; Chairman National Appeal Cttee of UN Assoc., and member of National Exec., 1947–50. *Publications:* The Impending Storm, 1930, and Divided Europe, 1931 (on international situation); Peter Public, 1932 (a political extravaganza); Enter Napoleon, 1935 (a novel); Red Tie in the Morning (a novel), 1937; The Golden Carpet (Iraq Campaign), 1943; The Silver Crescent (Syrian Campaign), 1943; A Mind on the March, 1945; Editor of Napoleon's Memoirs (2 vols), 1945; edited and translated Supper at Beaucaire by Napoleon, 1945; The First Crusade (edited and translated from Gesta Francorum), 1946; The Teetotalitarian State (a novel), 1947; The Dome of the Rock (a novel), 1948; The Millennium (poems), 1949; Julius Caesar's Commentaries (new edn), 1952; The Story of a Lifetime (novel), 1954; The Waterloo Campaign, 1957; Editor of Admiral de Chair's memoirs, The Sea is Strong, 1961; Bring Back the Gods (novel), 1962; Collected Verse, 1970; Friends, Romans, Concubines (novel), 1973; The Star of the Wind (novel), 1974; Legend of the Yellow River (novel), 1979; Buried Pleasure (autobiog). *Address:* Bourne Park, Bishopsbourne, near Canterbury, Kent; St Osyth Priory, St Osyth, Essex; The Lake House, 46 Lake Street, Cooperstown, Otsego County, New York, USA. *Club:* Carlton.

DECIES, 6th Baron *cr* 1812; **Arthur George Marcus Douglas de la Poer Beresford;** Ex-Flying Officer, RAFVR (DFC, USA); *b* 24 April 1915; *s* of 5th Baron Decies and Helen Vivien (*d* 1931), *d* of late George Jay Gould; *S* father, 1944; *m* 1937, Ann Trevor (*d* 1945); *m* 1945, Mrs Diana Galsworthy; one *s* two *d*. *Heir:* *s* Hon. Marcus Hugh Tristram de la Poer Beresford [*b* 5 Aug. 1948; *m* 1st, 1970, Sarah Jane (marr. diss. 1974), *o d* of Col Basil Gunnell, New Romney, Kent; 2nd, 1981, Edel Jeannette, *d* of late Vincent Hendron]. *Address:* c/o Coutts & Co., 1 Old Park Lane, W1Y 4BS.

DE CLERCQ, Willy; MP; Member of the Commission of the European Communities, since 1985; Minister of State, Belgium, since 1985; *b* 8 July 1927; *s* of Frans De Clercq; *m* 1953, Fernande Fazzi; three *c*. *Educ:* Ghent Univ. (Dr en droit 1950); Univ. of Syracuse, USA (MA SocSci 1951). Called to Belgian Bar, 1951; Municipal Councillor, Ghent, 1952–79; Dep. Sec.-Gen., Belgian Liberal Party, 1957; MP Ghent-Eeklo, 1958–; Dep. State Sec., Min. of Budget, 1960; Leader, Parly Lib. Party, 1965; Dep. Prime Minister, 1966–68; created separate Flemish wing of Parly Lib. Party (Chm., 1971–81); Dep. Prime Minister, 1973; Minister of Finance, 1974–77 (Chm., Interim Cttee, IMF; Chm., Bd of Governors, EIB; Governor, World Bank); Dep. Prime Minister and Minister of Finance and Foreign Trade, 1981–85. Mem., European Parlt, 1979–84. Comdr, Order of Leopold; Grand Cross, Order of Leopold II; holds numerous foreign decorations. *Address:* (office) Wetstraat 200, 1049 Brussels, Belgium. *T:* 02/2352530; (home) Cyriel Buyssestraat 12, 9000 Ghent, Belgium.

de CLIFFORD, 27th Baron *cr* 1299; **John Edward Southwell Russell;** *b* 8 June 1928; *s* of 26th Baron de Clifford, OBE, TD, and of Dorothy Evelyn, *d* of late Ferdinand Richard Holmes Meyrick, MD; *S* father, 1982; *m* 1959, Bridget Jennifer, *yr d* of Duncan Robertson, Llangollen, Denbighshire. *Educ:* Eton. *Heir:* *b* Hon. William Southwell Russell [*b* 26 Feb. 1930; *m* 1961, Jean Brodie, *d* of Neil Brodie Henderson; one *s* two *d*]. *Address:* Cliff House, Sheepy, Atherstone, Warwickshire. *Club:* Naval and Military.

de COURCY, family name of **Baron Kingsale.**

de COURCY, Kenneth Hugh; (Duc de Grantmesnil); Chancellor, Order of the Three Orders, since 1977; *b* 6 Nov. 1909; 2nd *s* of late Stephen de Courcy of Co. Galway and Hollinwood Mission (*s* of 8th Duc de Grantmesnil), and late Minnie de Courcy (*née* Schafer), *d* of late Frederick and Sophia Schafer-Andres, Schloss Kyburgh, Kirn am Nahe; *m* 1950, Rosemary Catherine (marr. diss. 1973), *o d* of late Comdr H. L. S. Baker, OBE, RN (retired), Co. Roscommon, Eire; two *s* two *d*. *Educ:* King's College Sch. and by travelling abroad. 2nd Lieut, 3rd City of London Regt (Royal Fusiliers) TA (Regular Army Candidate), 1927. 2nd Lieut Coldstream Guards (Supplementary Reserve), 1930; Lieut and resigned, 1931; Hon. Secretary to late Sir Reginald Mitchell-Banks' unofficial cttee on Conservative policy, 1933; 1934, formed with late Earl of Mansfield, late Viscount Clive, late Lord Phillimore, and with Sir Victor Raikes, KBE, Imperial Policy Group and was Hon. Secretary 1934–39; travelled as Group's chief observer of Foreign Affairs in Europe and America, 1935–39; special visit of enquiry to Mussolini, Doctor Beneš, Dr Schuschnigg, 1936; to King Boris of Bulgaria, etc., 1938; to Italy and King Boris, 1939–40; FCO released 45 secret reports from 1936–40 to PRO, 1972; adviser on War Intelligence to United Steel Companies Ltd, 1944–45. Formerly published monthly serial memoranda on Foreign Affairs and Strategy, (1938–); Proprietor of: Intelligence Digest, 1938–76; The Weekly Review, 1951–76; Director, Ringrone Newspapers Ltd, 1966–68. Editor: Bankers Digest, 1969–72; Special Office Brief, 1973–.Trustee, Marquis de Verneuil Trust, 1971–. Lord of the Manors of Stow-on-the-Wold and Maugersbury, Glos. Hon. Citizen of New Orleans, La, USA, 1950; Hon. Life Mem., Mark Twain Soc., 1977; Companion of Western Europe, 1979. Gave collection of historic documents to Hoover Instn, Stanford Univ., 1983. *Publications:* Review of World Affairs (23 vols since 1938); Mayerling, 1983; Secret Reports of Prime Minister Chamberlain 1938–40, 1984; The Carolingian Crown of France, 1984; various articles on Strategy and Foreign Affairs.

Recreation: climbing. *Address:* Yeomans Cottage, Longborough, Moreton-in-Marsh, Glos; (office) 52 Merrion Square, Dublin 2, Ireland.

de COURCY-IRELAND, Patrick Gault, CVO 1980; HM Diplomatic Service; Consul-General, Jerusalem, since 1984; *b* 19 Aug. 1933; *e s* of late Lawrence Kilmaine de Courcy-Ireland and Elizabeth Pentland Gault; *m* 1957, Margaret Gallop; one *s* three *d*. *Educ:* St Paul's Sch.; Jesus Coll., Cambridge (MA). HM Forces (2nd Lieut), 1952–54. Joined Foreign Service, 1957; Student, ME Centre for Arab Studies, 1957–59; Third, later Second Sec., Baghdad, 1959–62; Private Sec. to HM Ambassador, Washington, 1963; Consul (Commercial), New York, 1963–67; UN (Polit.) Dept, 1967–69; Asst Head of Amer. Dept, 1969–71; First Sec. and Hd of Chancery, Kuwait, 1971–73; Asst Hd of SW Pacific Dept, 1973–76; Hd of Trng Dept and Dir, Diplomatic Serv. Language Centre, FCO, 1976–80; Consul-Gen., Casablanca, 1980–84. *Recreations:* book collecting, opera. *Address:* Foreign and Commonwealth Office, SW1A 2AH. *Clubs:* Athenæum; Hurlingham, MCC.

de COURCY LING, John; Member (C) Midlands Central, European Parliament, since 1979, Vice-Chairman, Development Aid Committee, since 1984; farmer since 1978; External Member of Lloyds, since 1969; *b* 14 Oct. 1933; *s* of Arthur Norman Ling and Veronica de Courcy; *m* 1959, Jennifer Haynes; one *s* three *d*. *Educ:* King Edward's Sch., Edgbaston; Clare Coll., Cambridge. 2nd Lieut, Royal Ulster Rifles, 1956. FO, 1959; 2nd Sec., Santiago, 1963–66; 1st Sec., Nairobi, 1966–69; Chargé d'Affaires, Chad, 1973; Counsellor, HM Embassy, Paris, 1974–77. Left FO to begin politics and farming, 1978; Conservative Chief Whip, European Parlt, 1979–83; Chm., EEC Delegn to Israel, 1979–82. Mem., Exec. Cttee of Nat. Union of Conservative and Unionist Assocs, 1979–83. *Publications:* Do We Need the European Parliament?, 1984; Famine and Surplus, 1985; contribs to The Tablet. *Recreations:* yacht racing, opera, bridge, rough shooting. *Address:* Old Chalford House, Chipping Norton, Oxon. *T:* Chipping Norton 2628. *Clubs:* Beefsteak, Travellers'; Leander; Royal London Yacht (Cowes).

de DENEY, Geoffrey Ivor, CVO 1986; Clerk of the Privy Council, since 1984; *b* 8 Oct. 1931; *s* of Thomas Douglas de Deney and Violet Ivy de Deney (*née* Manwaring); *m* 1959, Diana Elizabeth Winrow; two *s*. *Educ:* William Ellis Sch.; St Edmund Hall, Oxford (MA, BCL); Univ. of Michigan. Home Office: joined, 1956; Asst Principal, 1956–61 (Private Sec. to Parly Under Sec. of State, 1959–61); Principal, 1961–69; Sec. to Graham Hall Cttee on maintenance limits in magistrates' courts; Sec. to Brodrick Cttee on Death Certification and Coroners; Private Sec. to Sec. of State, 1968; Asst Sec., 1969–1978; seconded to Cabinet Office, 1975; Asst Under Sec. of State, 1978–84; Community Programmes and Equal Opportunities Dept, 1978–80; General Dept (and Registrar of the Baronetage), 1980–84. *Recreations:* books, walking. *Address:* 17 Ladbroke Terrace, W11.

DEDIJER, Vladimir, DJur, MA Oxon; Order of Liberation, of Yugoslavia, etc; Yugoslav Author; *b* 4 Feb. 1914; *m* 1944, Vera Krizman; one *s* two *d* (and two *s* decd). *Educ:* Belgrade Univ. Served War from 1941, Tito's Army, Lieut-Colonel; Yugoslav Delegate to Peace Conference, Paris, 1946, and to UN General Assemblies, 1945, 1946, 1948, 1949, 1951, 1952. Member Central Cttee, League of Communists of Yugoslavia, 1952–54, when expelled (defended right of M. Djilas to free speech, 1954; sentenced to 6 months on probation, 1955). Prof. of Modern History, Belgrade Univ., 1954–55. Simon Senior Fellow, Manchester Univ., 1960; Research Fellow, St Antony's Coll., Oxford, 1962–63; Research Associate, Harvard Univ., 1963–64; Visiting Prof.: Cornell Univ., 1964–65; MIT, 1969; Brandeis, 1970; Michigan, 1971, 1973, 1974, 1982–83. Hon. Fellow, Manchester Univ. President International War Crimes Tribunal, 1966; Hon. Pres., Internat. Tribunal on Afghanistan, 1981. Member, Serbian Acad. of Science. *Publications:* Partisan Diary, 1945; Notes from the United States, 1945; Paris Peace Conference, 1948; Yugoslav-Albanian Relations, 1949; Tito, 1952; Military Conventions, 1960; The Beloved Land, 1960; Road to Sarajevo, 1966; The Battle Stalin Lost, 1969; History of Jugoslavia, 1972; History of Spheres of Influence, 1979; Novi prilozi za biografiju Josipa-Broza Tita, 1982 (New Documents for a Biography of J. B. Tito; banned in Army Libraries in Yugoslavia). Contrib. to Acta Scandinavica. *Address:* Sipar 3, 52395 Savudrija, Istria, Yugoslavia. *T:* 053–74–504.

de DUVE, Prof. Christian René Marie Joseph, Grand Cross Order of Leopold II 1975; Professor of Biochemistry, Catholic University of Louvain, since 1951; President, International Institute of Cellular and Molecular Pathology, Brussels, since 1975; Andrew W. Mellon Professor at Rockefeller University, New York, since 1962; *b* England, 2 Oct. 1917; *s* of Alphonse de Duve and Madeleine Pungs; *m* 1943, Janine Herman; two *s* two *d*. *Educ:* Jesuit Coll., Antwerp; Catholic Univ. of Louvain; Med. Nobel Inst., Stockholm; Washington Univ., St Louis. MD 1941, MSc 1946, Agrégé de l'Enseignement Supérieur 1945, Louvain. Lectr, Med. Faculty, Catholic Univ. of Louvain, 1947–51. Vis. Prof. at various univs. Mem. editorial and other bds and cttees; mem. or hon. mem. various learned socs, incl. For. Assoc. Nat. Acad. of Scis (US) 1975. Holds hon. degrees. Awards incl. Nobel Prize in Physiol. or Med., 1974. *Publications:* numerous scientific. *Recreations:* tennis, ski-ing, bridge. *Address:* Le Pré St Jean, 239 rue de Weert, 5988 Nethen (Grez-Doiceau), Belgium. *T:* (010)-866628; 80 Central Park West, New York, NY 10023, USA. *T:* (212)-724–8048.

DEED, Basil Lingard, OBE 1946; TD; MA; Chairman, Oxfordshire County Council, 1983–84; *b* 1909; *s* of late S. G. Deed, Maldon; *m* 1937, Elizabeth Mary, *d* of late S. P. Cherrington, Berkhamsted; four *d*. *Educ:* Haileybury Coll.; Peterhouse, Cambridge. 2nd Class Classical Tripos Part I; 1st class Classical Tripos Part II. Asst Master, Berkhamsted School, 1931–37; Asst Master, Shrewsbury Sch., 1937–47; served War of 1939–45, mostly on General Staff; Lt-Col MEF, 1943; Italy, 1944–45; Headmaster, Stamford Sch., 1947–68. Councillor (Ind.), 1972–85, Vice-Chm., 1981–83, Oxfordshire CC. *Address:* Bendor, Warborough, Oxon. *T:* Warborough 8514. *Club:* Blackwater Sailing.

DEEDES, family name of **Baron Deedes.**

DEEDES, Baron *cr* 1986 (Life Peer), of Aldington in the County of Kent; **William Francis Deedes,** MC 1944; PC 1962; DL; Editor, The Daily Telegraph, 1974–86; *b* 1 June 1913; *s* of (Herbert) William Deedes; *m* 1942, Evelyn Hilary Branfoot; two *s* three *d*. *Educ:* Harrow. Journalist with Morning Post, 1931–37; war correspondent on Abyssinia, 1935. Served war of 1939–45, Queen's Westminsters (12 KRRC). MP (C) Ashford Div. of Kent, 1950–Sept. 1974; Parliamentary Sec., Ministry of Housing and Local Government, Oct. 1954–Dec. 1955; Parliamentary Under-Sec., Home Dept., 1955–57; Minister without Portfolio, 1962–64. DL, Kent, 1962. *Address:* New Hayters, Aldington, Kent. *T:* Aldington 269. *Club:* Carlton.

DEEDES, Maj.-Gen. Charles Julius, CB 1968; OBE 1953; MC 1944; *b* 18 Oct. 1913; *s* of General Sir Charles Deedes, KCB, CMG, DSO; *m* 1939, Beatrice Murgatroyd, Brockfield Hall, York; three *s*. *Educ:* Oratory Sch.; Royal Military Coll., Sandhurst. Served War of 1939–45 (despatches); Asst Military Secretary, GHQ Middle East, 1945; Officer Comdg Glider Pilot Regt, 1948; GSO1 War Office, 1950; Officer Comdg 1st Bn KOYLI, 1954 (despatches); Colonel General Staff, War Office, 1956; Comd 146 Infantry Brigade (TA), 1958; Deputy Director, MoD, 1962; C of S, HQ Eastern Comd, 1965; C of S, HQ Southern Comd, 1968. Colonel of the KOYLI, 1966–68. Dep. Colonel, The Light Infantry (Yorks), 1968–72. Military Cross (Norway), 1940. *Recreations:* riding, tennis. *Address:* Lea Close, Brandsby, York. *T:* Brandsby 239.

DEEGAN, Joseph William, CMG 1956; CVO 1954; KPM; Inspector-General of Colonial Police, 1966–67; *b* 8 Feb. 1899; *s* of John and Sarah Deegan; *m* 1926, Elinor Elsie Goodson; one *s* two *d*. *Educ:* St Paul's and St Gabriel's Schs, Dublin. Army, 1919–25 (seconded to King's African Rifles, 1922–25); Tanganyika Police, 1925–38; Uganda Police, 1938–56 (Commissioner of Police, 1950–56); Dep. Inspector-Gen. of Colonial Police, 1956–61, 1963–65. Colonial Police Medal, 1942; King's Police Medal, 1950. *Address:* Tuffshard, Cuckmere Road, Seaford, East Sussex. *T:* Seaford 894180.

DEELEY, Michael; film producer; *b* 6 Aug. 1932; *s* of John Hamilton-Deeley and Anne Deeley; *m* 1955, Teresa Harrison; one *s* two *d*; *m* 1970, Ruth Stone-Spencer. *Educ:* Stowe. Entered film industry as film editor, 1952; Distributor, MCA TV, 1958–60; independent producer, 1961–63; Gen. Man., Woodfall Films, 1964–67; indep. prod., 1967–72; Man. Director: British Lion Films Ltd, 1973–76; EMI Films Ltd, 1976–77; Pres., EMI Films Inc., 1977–79; Chief Exec. Officer, Consolidated Television Inc. (formerly Consolidated Productions Ltd), 1984–; Dep. Chm., British Screen Adv. Council, 1985–. Member: Prime Minister's Film Industry Working Party, 1975–76; Film Industry Interim Action Cttee, 1977–84. Films include: Robbery; The Italian Job; The Knack; Murphy's War; Conduct Unbecoming; The Man who fell to Earth; The Deer Hunter (Academy Award, Best Picture Producer, 1978); Convoy; Blade Runner. *Address:* Little Island, Osterville, Mass 02655, USA; c/o Pickering Kenyon & Company, 23/24 Great James Street, WC1. *Clubs:* Garrick; Wianno Yacht (Mass).

DEER, Sir (Arthur) Frederick, Kt 1979; CMG 1973; Director, The Mutual Life and Citizens' Assurance Co. Ltd, Australia, 1956–83; *b* 15 June 1910; *s* of Andrew and Maude Deer; *m* 1936, Elizabeth Christine, *d* of G. C. Whitney; one *s* three *d*. *Educ:* Sydney Boys' High Sch.; Univ. of Sydney (BA, LLB, BEc, Hon. DSc Econ.) Admitted to Bar of NSW, 1934. The Mutual Life and Citizens' Assurance Co. Ltd: joined Company, 1930; apptd Manager for S Australia, 1943, and Asst to Gen. Manager, 1954; Gen. Man., 1955–74. Chm., Life Offices' Assoc. for Australasia, 1960–61, 1967–68; Pres., Australian Insurance Inst., 1966. Chm., Cargo Movement Co-ordination Cttee, NSW, 1974–82; Member: Cttee Review of Parly Salaries, NSW, 1971; Admin. Review Council, 1976–82; Fellow, Senate of Univ. of Sydney, 1959–83 (Chm. Finance Cttee of the Univ., 1960–83). Nat. Pres., Australia-Britain Soc., 1973–81; Chm., Salvation Army Sydney Adv. Bd, 1970–83. *Recreations:* golf, tennis. *Address:* 1179 Pacific Highway, Turramurra, NSW 2074, Australia. *T:* 44 2912. *Clubs:* Union, University, Avondale, Elanora (all in Sydney).

DEER, Prof. William Alexander, MSc Manchester, PhD Cantab; FRS 1962; FGS; Emeritus Professor of Mineralogy and Petrology, Cambridge University; Hon. Fellow of Trinity Hall, Cambridge, 1978; *b* 26 Oct. 1910; *s* of William Deer; *m* 1939, Margaret Marjorie (*d* 1971), *d* of William Kidd; two *s* one *d*; *m* 1973, Rita Tagg. *Educ:* Manchester Central High Sch.; Manchester Univ.; St John's Coll., Cambridge. Graduate Research Scholar, 1932, Beyer Fellow, 1933, Manchester Univ.; Strathcona Studentship, St John's Coll., Cambridge, 1934; Petrologist on British East Greenland Expedition, 1935–36; 1851 Exhibition Senior Studentship, 1938; Fellow, St John's Coll., Cambridge, 1939; served War of 1939–45, RE, 1940–45. Murchison Fund Geological Soc. of London, 1945 (Murchison Medal, 1974); Junior Bursar, St John's Coll., 1946; Leader NE Baffin Land Expedition, 1948; Bruce Medal, Royal Society of Edinburgh, 1948; Tutor, St John's Coll., 1949; Prof. of Geology, Manchester Univ., 1950–61; Fellow of St John's Coll., Cambridge, 1961–66, Hon. Fellow, 1969; Prof. of Mineralogy and Petrology, 1961–78, Vice-Chancellor, 1971–73, Cambridge Univ.; Master of Trinity Hall, Cambridge, 1966–75. Percival Lecturer, Univ. of Manchester, 1953; Joint Leader East Greenland Geological Expedition, 1953; Leader British East Greenland Expedition, 1966. Trustee, British Museum (Natural History), 1967–75. President: Mineralogical Soc., 1967–70; Geological Soc., 1970–72; Member: NERC, 1968–71; Marshall Aid Commemoration Commn, 1973–79. Hon. DSc Aberdeen, 1983. *Publications:* books; papers in Petrology and Mineralogy. *Recreations:* walking, bassoon playing. *Address:* 20 Manor Court, Pinehurst, Grange Road, Cambridge.

DEERHURST, Viscount; Edward George William Omar Coventry; *b* 24 Sept. 1957; *s* and *heir* of 11th Earl of Coventry, *qv*.

de FARIA, Antonio Leite, Hon. GCVO 1973; Grand Cross of Christ (Portugal), 1949; Portuguese Ambassador to the Court of St James's, 1968–73; retired; *b* 23 March 1904; *s* of Dr Antonio B. Leite de Faria and Dona Lucia P. de Sequeira Braga Leite de Faria; *m* 1926, Dona Herminia Cantilo de Faria; two *s*. *Educ:* Lisbon University (Faculty of Law). Attaché to Min. of Foreign Affairs, 1926; Sec. to Portuguese Delegn, League of Nations, 1929–30; 2nd Sec., Rio de Janeiro, 1931, Paris, 1933, Brussels, 1934; 1st Sec., London, 1936; Counsellor, London, 1939; Minister to Exiled Allied Govts, London, 1944; Minister to The Hague, 1945; Dir Gen., Political Affairs, and Acting Sec. Gen., Min. of Foreign Affairs, 1947; Ambassador: Rio de Janeiro, 1950; NATO, 1958; Paris, 1959; Rome (Holy See), 1961; London, 1968. Holds many foreign decorations. *Address:* Rua da Horta Seca 11, Lisboa, Portugal. *T:* 32 25 38; Casa do Bom Retiro, S Pedro de Azurem, Guimarães, Portugal. *T:* (053) 416418.

de FERRANTI, Basil Reginald Vincent Ziani; Member (C) Hampshire Central, European Parliament, since 1984 (Hampshire West, 1979–84) (a Vice-President, 1979–82); Chairman, Ferranti plc; *b* 2 July 1930; *yr s* of Sir Vincent de Ferranti, MC, FIEE, and of Dorothy H. C. Wilson; *m* 1st, 1956, Susan Sara, *d* of late Christopher and of Lady Barbara Gore; three *s*; 2nd, 1964, Simone, *d* of late Col and of Mrs H. J. Nangle; one *d*; 3rd, 1971, Jocelyn Hilary Mary, *d* of late Wing Comdr and Mrs A. T. Laing. *Educ:* Eton; Trinity Coll., Cambridge. Served 4th/7th Royal Dragoon Guards, 1949–50. Man., Domestic Appliance Dept, Ferranti Ltd, 1954–57. Contested Exchange Div. of Manchester, Gen. Election, 1955; MP (C) Morecambe and Lonsdale Div. of Lancaster, Nov. 1958–Sept. 1964. Dir of overseas operations, Ferranti Ltd, 1957–62; Parliamentary Sec., Ministry of Aviation, July–Oct. 1962. Dep. Man. Dir, Internat. Computers and Tabulators, Sept. 1963 until Managing Dir, 1964; Dir, International Computers Ltd until 1972. Mem., Economic and Social Cttee, European Communities, 1973–79 (Chm., 1976–78); Chm., European Movement (British Council), 1980–82. Pres., British Computer Soc., 1968–69; Vice-Pres., Kangaroo Gp, 1982–. Hon. DSc City, 1970. *Publications:* In Europe, 1979; contrib. Brit. Computer Soc. Jl, Proc. IFIP, Proc. Royal Instn of GB. *Recreations:* ski-ing, sailing. *Address:* Ferranti plc, Millbank Tower, Millbank, SW1. *T:* 01–834 6611; The Old Manor, Church Lane, Ellisfield, Hants RG25 2QR. *Club:* Royal Yacht Squadron.

See also S. B. J. Z. de Ferranti.

de FERRANTI, Sebastian Basil Joseph Ziani; Chairman, Ferranti plc, 1963–82 (Managing Director, 1958–75; Director 1954); Director: GEC plc, since 1982; National Nuclear Corporation, since 1984; *b* 5 Oct. 1927; *er s* of Sir Vincent de Ferranti, MC, FIEE, and of Dorothy H. C. Wilson; *m* 1st, 1953, Mona Helen, *d* of T. E. Cunningham; one *s* two *d*; 2nd, 1983, Naomi Angela Rae. *Educ:* Ampleforth. 4th/7th Dragoon Guards, 1947–49. Brown Boveri, Switzerland, and Alsthom, France, 1949–50. Dir, British

Airways Helicopters, 1982–84. President: Electrical Research Assoc., 1968–69; BEAMA, 1969–70; Centre for Educn in Science, Educn and Technology, Manchester and region, 1972–. Chm., Internat. Electrical Assoc., 1970–72. Member: Nat. Defence Industries Council, 1969–77; Council, IEE, 1970–73. Trustee, Tate Gallery, 1971–78; Chm., Civic Trust for the North-West, 1978–83; Comr, Royal Commn for Exhibn of 1851, 1984–. Vice-Pres., RSA, 1980–84. Lectures: Granada, Guildhall, 1966; Royal Instn, 1969; Louis Blériot, Paris, 1970; Faraday, 1970–71. Hon. DSc: Salford Univ., 1967; Cranfield Inst. of Technology, 1973. Hon. Fellow, Univ. of Manchester Inst. of Science and Technology. *Address:* Henbury Hall, Macclesfield, Cheshire. *Clubs:* Cavalry and Guards, Pratt's.

See also B. R. V. Z. de Ferranti.

de FONBLANQUE, John Robert; HM Diplomatic Service; Head of Chancery, New Delhi, since 1986; *b* 20 Dec. 1943; *s* of late Maj.-Gen. E. B. de Fonblanque, CB, CBE, DSO and of Elizabeth de Fonblanque; *m* 1984, Margaret Prest; one *s*. *Educ:* Ampleforth; King's College, Cambridge (MA); London School of Economics (MSc). FCO, 1968; Second Sec., Jakarta, 1969; Second, later First Sec., UK Representation to European Community, Brussels, 1972; Principal, HM Treasury, 1977; FCO, 1980; Asst Sec., Cabinet Office, 1983. *Recreation:* mountain walking. *Address:* c/o Foreign and Commonwealth Office, SW1A 2AH.

de FRANCIA, Prof. Peter Laurent; Professor, School of Painting, Royal College of Art, London, 1973–86; *b* 25 Jan. 1921; *s* of Fernand de Francia and Alice Groom. *Educ:* Academy of Brussels; Slade Sch., Univ. of London. Canadian Exhibition Commn, Ottawa, 1951; American Museum, Central Park West, NY, 1952–53; BBC, Television, 1953–55; Teacher, St Martin's Sch., London, 1955–63; Tutor, Royal College of Art, 1963–69; Principal, Dept of Fine Art, Goldsmiths Coll., 1969–72. Work represented in public collections: Tate Gall.; V&A Mus.; Mus. of Modern Art, NY; Arts Council of GB; Graves Art Gall., Sheffield; Mus. of Modern Art, Prague. *Publications:* Fernand Léger, 1969; Léger, 1983. *Address:* 44 Surrey Square, SE17 2JX. *T:* 01–703 8361.

de FREITAS-CRUZ, Joao Carlos Lopes Cardoso; Grand Cross, Order of Prince Henry the Navigator, 1981; Ambassador of Portugal to Spain, since 1984; *b* 27 March 1925; *s* of Jose A. de Freitas-Cruz and Maria A. L. C. de Freitas-Cruz; *m* 1955, Maria de Lourdes Soares de Albergaria; three *s*. *Educ:* Univ. of Lisbon (law degree). Joined Portuguese Foreign Service, 1948; Secretary, Portuguese Embassy, London, 1950–52; Portuguese Delegate to NATO, in Paris, 1952–57; Foreign Office, Lisbon, 1957–59; Sec., Portuguese Embassy, Pretoria, 1959–60; Chargé d'Affaires, Madagascar, 1960–62; Consul-General, New York, 1963–65; Consul-Gen., Salisbury, Rhodesia, 1965–70; Ambassador: to OECD, Paris, 1970–71; in Bonn, 1971–73; Dir-Gen. for Political Affairs, FO, Lisbon, 1973–74; Ambassador, Permanent Representative to NATO, Brussels, 1974–78; Minister for Foreign Affairs, 1978–80; Ambassador to UK, 1980–84. Grand Cross, Order of Merit, Fed. Republic of Germany; Comdr, San Silvester, Holy See; Grand Officer, Légion d'Honneur, France; Grand Cross, Order of Flag, Hungary, and other foreign orders. *Recreations:* golf, hunting, reading. *Address:* Pinar, 1 - Madrid 28006, Spain. *T:* 261–78–00. *Clubs:* Financiero Genova, Real Club Puerta de Hierro.

DE FREYNE, 7th Baron *cr* 1851; **Francis Arthur John French;** Knight of Malta; *b* 3 Sept. 1927; *s* of 6th Baron and Victoria (*d* 1974), *d* of Sir J. Arnott, 2nd Bt; *S* father 1935; *m* 1st, 1954 (marr. diss. 1978); two *s* one *d*; 2nd, 1978, Sheelin Deirdre, *widow* of William Walker Stevenson and *y d* of late Lt-Col H. K. O'Kelly, DSO. *Educ:* Ladycross, Glenstal. *Heir:* *s* Hon. Fulke Charles Arthur John French [*b* 21 April 1957; *m* 1986, Julia Mary, *o d* of Dr James H. Wellard].

de GREY, family name of **Baron Walsingham.**

de GREY, Roger, RA 1969 (ARA 1962); President of the Royal Academy, since 1984; Principal, City and Guilds of London Art School, since 1973; *b* 18 April 1918; *s* of Nigel de Grey, CMG, OBE, and Florence Emily Frances (*née* Gore); *m* 1942, Flavia Hatt (*née* Irwin); two *s* one *d*. *Educ:* Eton Coll.; Chelsea Sch. of Art. Served War of 1939–45: Royal West Kent Yeomanry, 1939–42; RAC, 1942–45 (US Bronze Star, 1945). Lecturer, Dept of Fine Art, King's Coll., Newcastle upon Tyne, 1947–51; Master of Painting, King's Coll., 1951–53; Senior Tutor, later Reader in Painting, Royal Coll. of Art, 1953–73. Treasurer, RA, 1976–84. Pictures in the following public collections: Arts Council; Contemporary Arts Society; Chantrey Bequest; Queensland Gallery, Brisbane; Manchester, Carlisle, Bradford and other provincial galleries. Hon. ARCA, 1959. *Address:* City and Guilds of London Art School, 124 Kennington Park Road, SE11 4DJ; 5 Camer Street, Meopham, Kent. *T:* 2327.

de HAVILLAND, Olivia Mary; actress; *b* Tokyo, Japan, 1 July 1916; *d* of Walter Augustus de Havilland and Lilian Augusta (*née* Ruse) (parents British subjects); *m* 1st, 1946, Marcus Aurelius Goodrich (marr. diss., 1953); one *s*; 2nd, 1955, Pierre Paul Galante (marr. diss. 1979); one *d*. *Educ:* in California; won scholarship to Mills Coll., but career prevented acceptance. Played Hermia in Max Reinhardt's stage production of Midsummer Night's Dream, 1934. *Legitimate theatre* (USA): Juliet in Romeo and Juliet, 1951; Candida, 1951 and 1952; A Gift of Time, 1962. Began film career 1935, Midsummer Night's Dream. Nominated for Academy Award, 1939, 1941, 1946, 1948, 1949; Acad. Award, 1946, 1949; New York Critics' Award, 1948, 1949; San Francisco Critics' Award, 1948, 1949; Women's National Press Club Award for 1950; Belgian Prix Femina, 1957; British Films and Filming Award, 1967; Filmex Tribute, 1978; Amer. Acad. of Achievement Award, 1978. *Important Films:* The Adventures of Robin Hood, 1938; Gone With the Wind, 1939; Hold Back the Dawn, 1941; Princess O'Rourke, 1943; To Each His Own, 1946; The Dark Mirror, 1946; The Snake Pit, 1948; The Heiress, 1949; My Cousin Rachel, 1952; Not as a Stranger, 1955; The Ambassador's Daughter, 1956; Proud Rebel, 1957; The Light in the Piazza, 1961; Lady in a Cage, 1963; Hush . . . Hush, Sweet Charlotte, 1965; The Adventurers, 1969; Pope Joan, 1971; Airport '77, 1976; The Swarm, 1978. Also TV 1966, 1967, 1971; Roots, The Next Generations, 1979; 3 ABC Cable-TV Cultural Documentaries, 1981; Murder is Easy, 1982; Charles & Diana, a Royal Romance, 1982; North and South, Book II, 1986. US Lecture tours, 1971, 1972, 1973, 1974, 1975, 1976, 1978, 1979, 1980. Pres. of Jury, Cannes Film Festival, 1965. Took part in narration of France's BiCentennial Gift to US, Son et Lumière, A Salute to George Washington, Mount Vernon, 19 May 1976; read excerpts from Thomas Jefferson at BiCentennial Service, American Cathedral in Paris, 4 July 1976. Amer. Legion Humanitarian Medal, 1967; Freedoms Foundn Exemplar American Award, 1981. *Publications:* Every Frenchman Has One, 1962; (contrib.) Mother and Child, 1975. *Address:* BP 156–16, 75764 Paris, Cedex 16, France.

de HAVILLAND, Maj.-Gen. Peter Hugh, CBE 1945; DL; *b* 29 July 1904; *s* of late Hugh de Havilland, JP, CA, The Manor House, Gt Horkesley, Essex; *m* 1st, 1930, Helen Elizabeth Wrey (*d* 1976), *d* of late W. W. Otter-Barry, Horkesley Hall, Essex; two *s*; 2nd, 1981, Mrs Angela Hoare. *Educ:* Eton; RMA, Woolwich. 2nd Lieut, RA, 1925; Lieut RHA, 1933–36; Adjt 84th (East Anglian) Field Bde, RA (TA), 1936–38; served War of 1939–45 (despatches thrice, CBE); France, Middle East, N Africa, NW Europe; Brig. i/c Administration, 1 Corps, 1945–47; Dep. Regional Comr, Land Schleswig Holstein, 1948; Dep. Head, UK Deleg. Five Power Military Cttee, 1949; UK Mil. Rep., SHAPE, 1951; Chief of Staff, Northern Comd, 1953–55, retd 1955. DL Essex, 1962. Comdr Order of Leopold II, 1945. *Recreations:* shooting, flying (pilot's licence since 1977). *Address:* Horkesley Hall, Colchester. *T:* Colchester 271 259. *Club:* Army and Navy.

DEHN, Conrad Francis, QC 1968; Barrister; a Recorder of the Crown Court, since 1974; *b* London, 24 Nov. 1926; *o s* of late C. G. Dehn, Solicitor and Cynthia (*née* Fuller: Francyn the painter); *m* 1st, 1954, Sheila (*née* Magan) (marr. diss.); two *s* one *d*; 2nd, 1978, Marilyn, *d* of late Peter Collyer and of Constance Collyer. *Educ:* Charterhouse (Sen. Exhibr); Christ Church, Oxford (Holford Schol.). Served RA, Best Cadet Mons OCTU, 1946, 2nd Lieut 1947. 1st cl. hons PPE Oxon. 1950, MA 1952; Holt Schol., Gray's Inn, 1951; Pres., Inns of Court Students Union, 1951–52. WEA Tutor, 1951–55. Called to Bar, Gray's Inn, 1952; Bencher, 1977. Mem. Governing Body, United Westminster Schs, 1953–57. Chm., Bar Council Working Party on Liability for Defective Products, 1975–77; Mem., Foster Cttee of Inquiry into Operators' Licensing, Dept of Transport, 1978. Chm., Planning Cttee, Senate of Inns of Court and Bar, 1980–83; Mem., Council of Legal Educn, 1981–86. *Publication:* contrib. to Ideas, 1954. *Recreations:* theatre, travel, walking. *Address:* Fountain Court, Temple, EC4Y 9DH. *T:* 01–353 7356. *Club:* Reform.

de HOGHTON, Sir (Richard) Bernard (Cuthbert), 14th Bt *cr* 1611; KM; *b* 26 Jan. 1945; 3rd *s* of Sir Cuthbert de Hoghton, 12th Bt, and of Philomena, *d* of late Herbert Simmons; *S* half-brother, 1978; *m* 1974, Rosanna Stella Virginia (*née* Buratti); one *s* one *d*. *Educ:* Ampleforth College, York; McGill Univ., Montreal (BA Hons); Birmingham Univ. (MA); PhD (USA). Turner & Newall Ltd, 1967–70; international fund management, Vickers Da Costa & Co. Ltd, 1970–77; international institutional brokerage, de Zoete & Bevan & Co., 1977–; estate management, 1978–. Constantinian Order of S George (Naples), 1984. *Recreations:* tennis, shooting, travelling. *Heir:* *s* Thomas James Daniel Adam de Hoghton, *b* 11 April 1980. *Address:* Hoghton Tower, Hoghton, Preston, Lancs. *T:* Hoghton 2986; 22 St Maur Road, SW6. *T:* 01–731 0130.

DEHQANI-TAFTI, Rt. Rev. Hassan Barnaba; Bishop in Iran, since 1961; President-Bishop of the Episcopal Church in Jerusalem and the Middle East, 1976–86; Episcopal Canon of St George's Cathedral, Jerusalem, since 1976; Assistant Bishop of Winchester, since 1982; *b* 14 May 1920; *s* of Muhammad Dehqani-Tafti and Sakinneh; *m* 1952, Margaret Isabel Thompson; three *d* (one *s* decd). *Educ:* Stuart Memorial Coll., Isfahan, Iran; Tehran Univ.; Ridley Hall, Cambridge. Iran Imperial Army, 1943–45; layman in Diocese of Iran, 1945–47; theological coll., 1947–49; Deacon, Isfahan, 1949; Priest, Shiraz, 1950; Pastor: St Luke's Church, Isfahan, 1950–60; St Paul's Church, Tehran, 1960–61. Hon. DD, Virginia Theolog. Seminary, USA, 1981. *Publications:* many books in Persian; in English: Design of my World, 1959; The Hard Awakening, 1981. *Recreations:* Persian poetry (primarily mystical); painting in water colours; walking. *Address:* Sohrab, 1 Camberry Close, Basingstoke, Hants RG21 3AG. *T:* Basingstoke 27457. *Club:* Royal Commonwealth Society.

DE-JA-GOU; *see* Gowda, Deve Javare.

De la BÈRE, Sir Cameron, 2nd Bt *cr* 1953; jeweller, Geneva; *b* 12 Feb. 1933; *s* of Sir Rupert De la Bère, 1st Bt, KCVO, and Marguerite (*d* 1969), *e d* of late Sir John Humphery; *S* father, 1978; *m* 1964, Clairemonde, *o d* of late Casimir Kaufmann, Geneva; one *d*. *Educ:* Tonbridge, and on the Continent. Translator's cert. in Russian. British Army Intelligence Corps, 1951–53. Company director of Continental Express Ltd (subsid. of Hay's Wharf), 1958–64. Engaged in promotion of luxury retail jewellery stores, Switzerland and France, 1965–. Liveryman, Skinners' Co. *Recreations:* riding, swimming, history. *Heir:* *b* Adrian De la Bère, *b* 17 Sept. 1939. *Address:* 1 Avenue Theodore Flournoy, 1207 Geneva, Switzerland. *T:* (022) 86.00.15. *Clubs:* Hurlingham, Société Litéraire (Geneva).

de la BILLIÈRE, Maj.-Gen. Peter Edgar de la Cour, CBE 1983; DSO 1976; MC 1959 and Bar 1966; GOC Wales, since 1985; *b* 29 April 1934; *s* of Surgeon Lieut Comdr Claude Dennis Delacour de Labillière (killed in action, HMS Fiji, 1941) and of Frances Christine Wright Lawley; *m* 1965, Bridget Constance Muriel Goode; one *s* two *d*. *Educ:* Harrow School; Staff College; RCDS. Joined KSLI 1952; commissioned DLI; served Japan, Korea, Malaya (despatches 1959), Jordan, Borneo, Egypt, Aden, Gulf States, Sudan, Oman, Falkland Is; CO 22 SAS Regt, 1972–74; GSO1 (DS) Staff Coll., 1974–77; Comd Bn, Sudan, 1977–78; Dir SAS and Comd, SAS Group, 1978–83; Comd, British Forces Falkland Is and Mil. Comr, 1984–85. Mem. Council, RUSI, 1975–77. *Recreations:* family, squash, down market apiculture, tennis perhaps, small-time farming. *Address:* c/o Coutts & Co., 440 Strand, WC2R 0QS. *Clubs:* Farmers', Special Forces.

DELACOMBE, Maj.-Gen. Sir Rohan, KCMG 1964; KCVO 1970; KBE 1961 (CBE 1951; MBE 1939); CB 1957; DSO 1944; Governor of Victoria, Australia, 1963–74; Administrator of the Commonwealth of Australia on four occasions; *b* 25 Oct. 1906; *s* of late Lieut-Col Addis Delacombe, DSO, Shrewton Manor, near Salisbury; *m* 1941, Eleanor Joyce (CStJ), *d* of late R. Lionel Foster, JP, Egton Manor, Whitby; one *s* one *d*. *Educ:* Harrow; RMC Sandhurst. 2nd Lieut The Royal Scots, 1926; served Egypt, N China, India and UK, 1926–37; active service Palestine, 1937–39 (despatches, MBE); France, Norway, Normandy, Italy, 1939–45; Lieut-Col comd 8th Bn and 2nd Bn The Royal Scots, 1943–45; GSO1, 2nd Infantry Div., Far East, 1945–47; Colonel GS, HQ, BAOR, 1949–50; Brig. Comd 5 Inf. Bde, 1950–53, Germany; Dep. Mil. Sec., War Office, 1953–55; Maj.-Gen. 1956. Col The Royal Scots, 1956–64; GOC 52 Lowland Div. and Lowland District, 1955–58; GOC Berlin (Brit. Sector) 1959–62. Mem. Queen's Body Guard for Scotland, Royal Company of Archers, 1957. Pres., Royal British Legion (Wilts), 1974–85. FRAIA. KStJ, 1963; Freeman, City of Melbourne, 1974. Hon. Col 1st Armoured Regt (Australian Army), 1963–74; Hon. Air Cdre RAAF. LLD *hc* Melbourne; LLD *hc* Monash. *Recreations:* normal. *Address:* Shrewton Manor, near Salisbury, Wilts SP3 4DB. *T:* Shrewton (0980) 620253. *Clubs:* Army and Navy, Victoria Racing (Melbourne).

DELACOURT-SMITH OF ALTERYN, Baroness *cr* 1974 (Life Peer), of Alteryn, Gwent; **Margaret Delacourt-Smith;** *b* 1916; *d* of Frederick James Hando; *m* 1st, 1939, Charles Smith (subsequently Lord Delacourt-Smith, PC) (*d* 1972); one *s* two *d*; 2nd, 1978, Professor Charles Blackton. *Educ:* Newport High School for Girls; St Anne's College, Oxford (MA). *Address:* 56 Aberdare Gardens, NW6 3QD.

DELAFONS, John, CB 1982; Deputy Secretary, Department of the Environment, since 1979; *b* 14 Sept. 1930; *m* 1957, Sheila Egerton; four *d*. *Educ:* Ardingly; St Peter's College, Oxford. 1st cl. Hons English. Asst Principal, Min. of Housing and Local Govt, 1953; Harkness Fellowship, Harvard, 1959–60; Principal Private Sec. to Minister, 1965–66; Department of the Environment: Assistant Sec., 1966–72; Under Sec., 1972–77; Under Sec., Cabinet Office, 1977–79. Bd Mem., English Industrial Estates Corp. 1984–85. Chm., RIPA, 1981–83, Vice Pres., 1985–. *Publication:* Land-Use Controls in the United States (Harvard/MIT), 1962, revd edn 1969. *Address:* Department of the Environment, SW1. *Club:* Athenæum.

de la LANNE-MIRRLEES, Robin Ian Evelyn Stuart; *see* Mirrlees.

de la MARE, Sir Arthur (James), KCMG 1968 (CMG 1957); KCVO 1972; HM Diplomatic Service, retired; *b* 15 Feb. 1914; *s* of late Walter H. de la Mare, Trinity, Jersey,

Channel Islands, and late Laura Vibert Syvret; *m* 1940, Katherine Elisabeth Sherwood; three *d*. *Educ:* Victoria Coll., Jersey; Pembroke Coll., Cambridge. Joined HM Foreign Service, 1936. HM Vice-Consul: Tokyo, 1936–38; Seoul, Korea, 1938–39; USA 1942–43; First Sec., Foreign Service, 1945; HM Consul, San Francisco, 1947–50; HM Embassy, Tokyo, 1951–53; Counsellor, HM Foreign Service, 1953–63; Head of Security Dept, Foreign Office, 1953–56; Counsellor, HM Embassy, Washington, 1956–60; Head of Far Eastern Dept, Foreign Office, 1960–63; Ambassador to Afghanistan, 1963–65; Asst Under-Sec. of State, Foreign Office, 1965–67; High Comr in Singapore, 1968–70; Ambassador to Thailand, 1970–73. Chairman: Anglo-Thai Soc., 1976–82; Royal Soc. for Asian Affairs, 1978–84; Jersey Soc. in London, 1980–86. *Recreation:* gardening. *Address:* 66 Sylvan Road, Exeter, Devon EX4 6HA. *Clubs:* Oriental, Royal Commonwealth Society; Tokyo (Tokyo, Japan).

de la MARE, Prof. Peter Bernard David, MSc NZ; PhD London; DSc London; FRSNZ; Professor of Chemistry, University of Auckland, New Zealand, 1967–82, now Emeritus (Head of Department, 1967–81); *b* 3 Sept. 1920; *s* of late Frederick Archibald and Sophia Ruth de la Mare, Hamilton, NZ; *m* 1945, Gwynneth Campbell, *yr d* of late Alexander and Daisy Gertrude Jolly, Hastings, NZ; two *d*. *Educ:* Hamilton High Sch., Hamilton, NZ; Victoria University Coll. (University of NZ); University Coll., London. BSc NZ, 1941; MSc NZ, 1942; PhD London, 1948; DSc London, 1955. FRSNZ 1970. Agricultural Chemist, NZ Govt Dept of Agriculture, 1942–45; Shirtcliffe Fellow (University of NZ) at University Coll. London, 1946–48; University Coll. London: Temp. Asst Lecturer, 1948; Lecturer, 1949; Reader, 1956; Prof. of Chemistry, Bedford Coll., University of London, 1960–67. Mem., NZ Universities Entrance Bd, 1972–82. Hon. DSc Victoria Univ. Wellington, 1983. Hector Meml Medal, RSNZ, 1985. *Publications:* (with J. H. Ridd) Aromatic Substitution-Nitration and Halogenation, 1959; (with W. Klyne) Progress in Stereochemistry 2, 1958, 3, 1962; (with R. Bolton) Electrophilic Addition to Unsaturated Systems, 1966, 2nd edn 1982; Electrophilic Halogenation, 1976; scientific papers and reviews. *Recreations:* chess, table tennis, stamp collecting, etc. *Address:* 65 Grant's Road, Opotiki, New Zealand.

DELAMERE, 5th Baron *cr* 1821; **Hugh George Cholmondeley;** *b* 18 Jan. 1934; *s* of 4th Baron Delamere, and Phyllis Anne (*d* 1978), *e d* of late Lord George Scott, OBE; *S* father, 1979; *m* 1964, Mrs Ann Willoughby Tinne, *o d* of late Sir Patrick Renison, GCMG and Lady Renison, Mayfield, Sussex; one *s*. *Educ:* Eton; Magdalene Coll., Cambridge. MA Agric. *Heir: s* Hon. Thomas Patrick Gilbert Cholmondeley, *b* 19 June 1968. *Address:* Soysambu, Elmenteita, Kenya.

DELANEY, Francis James Joseph, (Frank); freelance journalist and broadcaster, since 1972; Chairman, National Book League, since 1984; *b* 24 Oct. 1942; 5th *s* of Edward Delaney and Elizabeth Josephine O'Sullivan; *m* 1966, Eilish (*née* Kelliher) (marr. diss. 1980); three *s*. *Educ:* Abbey Schools, Tipperary, Ireland; Rosse Coll., Dublin. Bank of Ireland, 1961–72; journalism, 1972–: includes: broadcasting news with RTE, Dublin; current affairs with BBC Northern Ireland, BBC Radio Four, London, and BBC Television. *Publications:* James Joyce's Odyssey, 1981; Betjeman Country, 1983; The Celts, 1986; sundry criticisms and introductions. *Recreations:* reading, conversation, housewifery, squash, doing nothing. *Address:* 53 Queen's Crescent, NW5 3QG. *Clubs:* Athenæum, Groucho; Hampstead Squash; Dublin United Arts.

DELANEY, Shelagh; playwright; *b* Salford, Lancs, 1939; one *d*. *Educ:* Broughton Secondary Sch. *Plays:* A Taste of Honey, Theatre Royal, Stratford, 1958 and 1959, Wyndhams, 1959, New York, 1960 and 1961, off-Broadway revival, trans. to Broadway, 1981 (Charles Henry Foyle New Play Award, Arts Council Bursary, New York Drama Critics' Award); The Lion in Love, Royal Court 1960, New York 1962. *Films:* A Taste of Honey, 1961 (British Film Academy Award, Robert Flaherty Award); The White Bus, 1966; Charlie Bubbles, 1968 (Writers Guild Award for best original film writing); Dance with a Stranger, 1985 (Prix Film Jeunesse-Etranger, Cannes, 1985). *TV plays:* St Martin's Summer, LWT, 1974; Find Me First, BBC TV, 1979; *TV series:* The House that Jack Built, BBC TV, 1977 (stage adaptation, NY, 1979). *Radio plays:* So Does the Nightingale, BBC, 1980; Don't Worry About Matilda, 1983. FRSL 1985. *Publications:* A Taste of Honey, 1959 (London and New York); The Lion in Love, 1961 (London and New York); Sweetly Sings the Donkey, 1963 (New York), 1964 (London). *Address:* c/o Tessa Sayle, 11 Jubilee Place, SW3 3TE.

de LAROSIÈRE de CHAMPFEU, Jacques (Martin Henri Marie); Chevalier, Legion of Honour, 1977; Chevalier, National Order of Merit, 1970; Managing Director, International Monetary Fund, 1978–86; *b* 12 Nov. 1929; *s* of Robert de Larosière and Hugayte de Champfeu; *m* 1960, France du Bos; one *s* one *d*. *Educ:* Institut d'Etudes Politiques, Paris (L ès L, licencié en droit); Nat. Sch. of Administration, Paris. Inspecteur des Finances, 1958; Inspecteur Général des Finances, 1980; appointments at: Inspectorate-General of Finance, 1961; External Finance Office, 1963; Treasury 1965; Asst Dir, Treasury, 1967; Dep. Dir then Head of Dept, Min. of Economics and Finance, 1971; Principal Private Sec. to Minister of Economics and Finance, 1974; Dir, Treasury, 1974–78. Director: Renault, 1971–74; Banque Nat. de Paris, 1973–78; Air France and French Railways, 1974–78; Société nat. industrielle aérospatiale, 1976–78. Director appointed by Treasury, General Council, Bank of France, 1974–78; Auditor: Crédit national, 1974–78; Comptoir des entrepreneurs, 1973–75; Crédit foncier de France, 1975–78. Vice Pres., Caisse nat. des télécommunications, 1974–78. Chairman: OECD Econ. and Develt Review Cttee, 1967–71; Deputies Group of Ten, 1976–78. *Address:* c/o International Monetary Fund, 700 19th Street NW, Washington, DC 20431, USA. *T:* (202) 623–7000.

de la RUE, Sir Eric (Vincent), 3rd Bt, *cr* 1898; *b* 5 Aug. 1906; *s* of Sir Evelyn Andros de la Rue, 2nd Bt, and Mary Violet (*d* 1959), *e d* of John Liell Francklin of Gonalston, Notts; *S* father 1950; *m* 1st, 1945, Cecilia (*d* 1963), *d* of late Lady Clementine Waring; two *s*; 2nd, 1964, Christine Schellin, Greenwich, Conn, USA; one *s*. *Educ:* Oundle. Served War of 1939–45. Capt. Notts Yeomanry, 1942–45. *Heir: s* Andrew George Ilay de la Rue [*b* 3 Feb. 1946; *m* 1984, Tessa D., *er d* of David Dobson]. *Address:* Caldra, Duns, Scotland. *T:* Duns 83294.

de la TOUR, Frances; actress; *b* 30 July 1944; *d* of Charles de la Tour and Moyra (*née* Fessas); one *s* one *d*. *Educ:* Lycée français de Londres; Drama Centre, London. Royal Shakespeare Company, 1965–71: rôles include Audrey in As You Like It, 1967; Hoyden in The Relapse, 1969; Helena in A Midsummer Night's Dream (Peter Brooks's production), 1971; Belinda in The Man of Mode, 1971; Violet in Small Craft Warnings, Comedy, 1973 (Best Supporting Actress, Plays and Players Award); Ruth Jones in The Banana Box, Apollo, 1973; Isabella in The White Devil, Old Vic, 1976; appearances at Hampstead Theatre, and Half Moon Theatre incl. title rôle in Hamlet, 1979; Stephanie in Duet for One (written by Tom Kempinski), Bush Theatre and Duke of York's, 1980 (Best New Play, and Best Perf. by Actress, Drama Awards, Best Perf. by Actress in New Play, SWET Award, Best Actress, New Standard Award); Jean in Skirmishes, Hampstead, 1982 (also television, 1982); Sonya in Uncle Vanya, Haymarket, 1982; Josie in A Moon for the Misbegotten, Riverside, 1983 (SWET Best Actress award); title rôle in St Joan, Nat. Theatre, 1984; Dance of Death, Riverside, 1985; Sonya and Masha in Chekhov's Women, Lyric, 1985; Brighton Beach Memoirs, NT, 1986. *Films:* include Our Miss Fred, 1972; To the Devil a Daughter, 1976; Rising Damp, 1979 (Best Actress, New Standard British Film Award, 1980). *Television:* Crimes of Passion, 1973; Play for Today (twice), 1973–75; Rising Damp (series), 1974, 1976; Cottage to Let, 1976; Flickers, 1980; Murder with Mirrors, 1984; Duet for One, 1985. *Address:* c/o Saraband Associates, 153 Petherton Road, N5. *T:* 01–359 5136/7.

DE LA WARR, 10th Earl *cr* 1761; **William Herbrand Sackville,** DL; Baron De La Warr, 1299 and 1572; Viscount Cantelupe, 1761; Baron Buckhurst (UK), 1864; *b* 16 Oct. 1921; *e s* of 9th Earl De La Warr, PC, GBE, and Diana (*d* 1966), *d* of late Gerard Leigh; *S* father, 1976; *m* 1946, Anne Rachel, *o d* of Geoffrey Devas, MC, Hunton Court, Maidstone; two *s* one *d*. *Educ:* Eton. Lieut Royal Sussex Regt, 1941–43; Lieut Parachute Regt, 1943; Capt. 1945–46. Contested (C) NE Bethnal Green, 1945; Chm. London Young Conservatives, 1946, Pres. 1947–49. Man. Dir, Rediffusion Ltd, 1974–79 (Dir, 1968–79); Director: British Electric Traction Co. Ltd, 1970–79; Wembley Stadium Ltd, 1972–79; Portals Hldgs Ltd, 1974–; Kent & Sussex Courier, 1982–; Essex Chronicle Series Ltd, 1981–; Chm., Redifon, 1978–79; Dep. Chm., Windsor Television Ltd, 1983–. Pres., Gen. Council and Register of Osteopaths, 1985–. Hon. Col Sussex ACF, 1969–; Vice-Chm., South East TAVR Assoc. (and Chm. Co. of Sussex Cttee), 1968–74 and 1978–83; Chairman: Sussex County Playing Fields Assoc., 1956–71; London and SE Resettlement Cttee for Ex-Regulars, 1969–74. DL East Sussex, 1975. *Heir: s* Lord Buckhurst, *qv*. *Address:* Buckhurst Park, Withyham, East Sussex. *T:* Hartfield 346, (Estate Office) Hartfield 220; 93 Eaton Place, SW1. *T:* 01–235 7990, (office) 01–235 9227. *Clubs:* White's, Pratt's.

See also Hon. T. G. Sackville.

DE LA WARR, Sylvia Countess; Sylvia Margaret Sackville, DBE 1957; *d* of William Reginald Harrison, Liverpool; *m* 1st, 1925, David Patrick Maxwell Fyfe (later Earl of Kilmuir, *cr* 1962, PC, GCVO) (*d* 1967); two *d* (and one *d* decd); 2nd, 1968, 9th Earl De La Warr, PC, GBE (*d* 1976). *Address:* 23 The Priory, Prior Park, Blackheath, SE3.

DELAY, Professeur Jean, Commandeur de la Légion d'Honneur; Grand Officier de l'Ordre national du Mérite; Member of the Académie de Médecine since 1955; Member of the Académie Française, since 1959; *b* Bayonne, Pyrénées Atlantiques, 14 Nov. 1907; *m* 1933, Marie-Madeleine Carrez; two *d*. *Educ:* Faculté de Médecine and Faculté des Lettres Sorbonne. DèsL Sorbonne. Prof. of Mental Diseases, Faculté de Médicine de Paris, 1946–70; Director, L'Institut de Psychologie, Sorbonne, 1951–70. Pres., First Internat. Congress of Psychiatry, 1950. Mem. French Section Unesco. Hon. Member, Royal Society Med.; Mem., Royal Soc. of Sciences of Uppsala; Distinguished Fellow, APA, 1977. Dr hc Univs of Zürich, Montreal and Barcelona. Médaille d'Or, Congrès Mondial de Psycho-Pharmologie, 1971. *Publications:* scientific: Les Dissolutions de la mémoire, 1942; Les Dérèglements de l'humeur, 1946; Les Maladies de la mémoire, 1947; La Psycho-Physiologie humaine, 1945; Aspects de la psychiatrie moderne, 1956; Etudes de psychologie médicale, 1953; Méthodes biologiques, 1950, psychométriques, 1956, chimiothérapiques, 1961, en psychiatrie; Introduction à la médecine psychosomatique, 1961; Abrégé de psychologie, 1962; Les démences tardives, 1962; L'électroencéphalographie clinique, 1966; Le syndrome de Korsakoff, 1969; literary: La Cité grise, 1946; Hommes sans nom, 1948; Les Reposantes, 1947; La Jeunesse d'André Gide (grand prix de la Critique), Vol. 1, 1956, Vol. 2, 1957; Une Amitié (André Gide et Roger Martin du Gard), 1968; La Correspondance de Jacques Copeau et Roger Martin du Gard, 1972; Avant Mémoire: d'une minute à l'autre, vol. 1, 1979, vol. 2, 1980, La Fauconnier, vol. 3, 1982, D'un siècle à l'autre, vol. 4, 1986. *Address:* 53 avenue Montaigne, 75008 Paris. *T:* 4359 77–07.

DELFONT, family name of **Baron Delfont.**

DELFONT, Baron *cr* 1976 (Life Peer), of Stepney; **Bernard Delfont,** Kt 1974; Executive Chairman, First Leisure Corp. (formerly Trusthouse Forte Leisure Ltd), since 1986 (Chairman and Chief Executive, 1980–86); Director: Bernard Delfont Organisation; Blackpool Tower Company; *b* Tokmak, Russia, 5 Sept. 1909; *s* of late Isaac and Olga Winogradsky; *m* Carole Lynne; one *s* two *d*. Entered theatrical management, 1941; has presented over 200 shows in London (and NY), including 50 musicals; also presents summer resort shows; converted London Hippodrome into Talk of the Town Restaurant, 1958. Chief Exec., EMI Ltd, May 1979–Dec. 1980. Past Chief Barker (Pres.), Variety Club of GB, (1969); Life Pres., Entertainment Artistes' Benevolent Fund, for which presented annual Royal Variety Performance, 1958–78; Companion, Grand Order of Water Rats; Member, Saints and Sinners; Pres., Printers Charitable Corp., 1979. *Address:* 7 Soho Street, Soho Square, W1V 5FA. *T:* 01–437 9727.

See also Baron Grade.

DELHI, Archbishop of, (RC), since 1967; **Most Rev. Angelo Fernandes;** Founder Member, Planetary Citizens, 1972; President, World Conference of Religion for Peace, 1970–84, Emeritus President since 1984; *b* 28 July 1913; *s* of late John Ligorio and Evelyn Sabina Fernandes. *Educ:* St Patrick's, Karachi; St Joseph's Seminary, Mangalore; Papal University, Kandy, Ceylon (STL). Secretary to Archbishop Roberts of Bombay, 1943–47; Administrator of Holy Name Cathedral, Bombay, 1947–59; Coadjutor Archbishop of Delhi, 1959–67; Sec. Gen., Catholic Bishops' Conf. of India, 1960–72 (Chm., Justice and Peace Commn, 1986). Member: Vatican Secretariat for Non-Believers, 1966–71; Vatican Justice and Peace Commn, 1967–76; Secretariat of Synod of Bishops, 1971–74, 1980–83; Office of Human Develt of Fedn of Asian Bishops' Confs, 1973–78 (Chm., Exec. Cttee for Ecumenism and Inter-Religious Affairs, Asia, 1985). Hon. DD Vatican, 1959. *Publications:* Apostolic Endeavour, 1962; Religion, Development and Peace, 1971; Religion and the Quality of Life, 1974; Religion and a New World Order, 1976; Towards Peace with Justice, 1981; God's Rule and Man's Role, 1982; Summons to Dialogue, 1983; articles in Clergy Monthly, Vidyajyoti, World Justice, Religion and Society, Social Action, Reality, etc. *Recreations:* music, especially classical, and wide travel on the occasion of numerous meetings in many countries of the world. *Address:* Archbishop's House, Ashok Place, New Delhi 110001, India. *T:* 343457.

DELIGHT, Ven. John David; Archdeacon of Stoke, since 1982; *b* 24 Aug. 1925. *Educ:* Christ's Hospital, Horsham; Liverpool Univ.; Oak Hill Theolog. Coll.; Open Univ. (BA). RNVR (Fleet Air Arm), 1943–46. Curate: Tooting Graveney, 1952–55; Wallington, 1955–58; Travelling Sec., Inter-Varsity Fellowship, 1958–61; Vicar, St Christopher's, Leicester, 1961–69; Chaplain, Leicester Prison, 1965–67; Rector of Aldridge, 1969–82; RD, Walsall, 1981–82. Prebendary of Lichfield Cathedral, 1980–. *Publication:* (contrib.) Families, Facts and Frictions, 1976. *Recreations:* walking, caravanning, music. *Club:* Christ's Hospital.

DE L'ISLE, 1st Viscount, *cr* 1956; **William Philip Sidney,** VC 1944; KG 1968; PC 1951; GCMG 1961; GCVO 1963; Baron De L'Isle and Dudley, 1835; Bt 1806; Bt 1818; Chancellor, Order of St Michael and St George, 1968–84; Governor-General of Australia, 1961–65; *b* 23 May 1909; *o s* of 5th Baron De L'Isle and Dudley and Winifred (*d* 1959), *e d* of Roland Yorke Bevan and Hon. Agneta Kinnaird, 4th *d* of 10th Baron Kinnaird; *S* father, 1945; *m* 1st 1940, Hon. Jacqueline Corinne Yvonne Vereker (*d* 1962), *o d* of late Field Marshal Viscount Gort of Hamsterley, VC, GCB, CBE, DSO, MVO, MC; one *s* four *d*; 2nd 1966, Margaret Lady Glanusk, *widow* of 3rd Baron Glanusk, DSO (whom she *m* 1942). *Educ:* Eton; Magdalene Coll., Cambridge. Commissioned Supplementary Reserve, Grenadier Guards, 1929, and served War of 1939–45 with Regt. MP (C) Chelsea, 1944–45; Parly Sec., Ministry of Pensions, 1945; Sec. of State for Air, Oct. 1951–Dec. 1955. Chairman: Phoenix Assurance Co. Ltd, 1966–78; City Acre Property Trust Ltd; Palmerston Property Development PLC, 1985–; Dir, Radio-Tele-Luxembourg (UK), 1980–. Pres., Freedom Assoc., 1984– (Chm., 1975–84); Dep. Pres., VC and GC Assoc., 1983–; Chairman of Trustees: Churchill Memorial Trust, 1975–; Tower Armouries Mus., 1984–86; Former Trustee: British Museum; Nat. Portrait Gall.; RAF Museum. Hon. Fellow Magdalene Coll., Cambridge, 1955. FCA; Hon. FRIBA. Hon. LLD: Sydney, 1963; Hampden Sydney Coll., Va, 1982. KStJ 1961. *Heir: s* Major Hon. Philip John Algernon Sidney, MBE 1977 [*b* 21 April 1945; *m* 1980, Isobel, *y d* of Sir Edmund Compton, *qv*; one *s* one *d*. Grenadier Guards, 1966–79]. *Address:* Penshurst Place, near Tonbridge, Kent; Glanusk Park, Crickhowell, Brecon.

See also Baron Middleton, Sir E. H. T. Wakefield, Bt.

DELL, David Michael, CB 1986; Deputy Secretary, Department of Trade and Industry, since 1983; *b* 30 April 1931; *s* of late Montague Roger Dell and Aimée Gabrielle Dell; unmarried. *Educ:* Rugby Sch.; Balliol Coll., Oxford (MA). 2nd Lieut Royal Signals, Egypt and Cyprus, 1954–55. Admiralty, 1955–60; MoD, 1960–65; Min. of Technol., 1965–70; DTI, 1970; DoI, 1974, Under Sec., 1976–83.

DELL, Rt. Hon. Edmund, PC 1970; Chairman: Channel Four TV Co., since 1980; Public Finance Foundation, since 1984; *b* 15 Aug. 1921; *s* of late Reuben and Frances Dell; *m* 1963, Susanne Gottschalk. *Educ:* Elementary schls; Owen's Sch., London; Queen's Coll., Oxford (Open Schol.). 1st Cl. Hons Mod. Hist., BA and MA 1947. War Service, 1941–45, Lieut RA (Anti-tank). Lecturer in Modern History, Queen's Coll., Oxford, 1947–49; Executive in Imperial Chemical Industries Ltd, 1949–63. Mem., Manchester City Council, 1953–60. Contested (Lab) Middleton and Prestwich, 1955. Pres., Manchester and Salford Trades Council, 1958–61. Simon Research Fellow, Manchester Univ., 1963–64. MP (Lab) Birkenhead, 1964–79; Parly Sec., Min. of Technology, 1966–67; Jt Parly Under-Sec. of State, Dept of Economic Affairs, 1967–68; Minister of State: Board of Trade, 1968–69; Dept of Employment and Productivity, 1969–70; Paymaster General, 1974–76; Sec. of State for Trade, 1976–78. Chm., Public Accts Cttee, 1973–74 (Acting Chm., 1972–73). Mem., Cttee of Three apptd by European Council to review procedures of EEC, 1978–79. Chm. and Chief Exec., Guinness Peat Gp, 1979–82; Dir, Shell Transport and Trading Co. plc, 1979–. Chairman: Hansard Soc. Commn on Financing of Politics, 1980–81; Working Party on Internat. Business Taxation, Inst. for Fiscal Studies, 1982; Wkg Pty on Company Political Donations (apptd by Hansard Soc. and Constitutional Reform Centre), 1985. Boys' Chess Champion of London, 1936. *Publications:* (ed with J. E. C. Hill) The Good Old Cause, 1949; Brazil: The Dilemma of Reform (Fabian Pamphlet), 1964; Political Responsibility and Industry, 1973; (with B. Biesheuvel and R. Marjolin) Report on European Institutions, 1979; The Politics of Economic Interdependence, 1987; articles in learned journals. *Recreation:* listening to music. *Address:* 4 Reynolds Close, NW11 7EA.

DELL, Dame Miriam (Patricia), DBE 1980 (CBE 1975); JP(NZ); Chairperson, Inter-Church Council on Public Affairs, since 1982; President, International Council of Women, 1979–86 (Vice-President, 1976–79; Hon. President, 1986); *b* 14 June 1924; *d* of Gerald Wilfred Matthews and Ruby Miriam Crawford; *m* 1946, Richard Kenneth Dell; four *d*. *Educ:* Epsom Girls Grammar Sch.; Univ. of Auckland (BA); Auckland Teachers' Coll. (Teachers' Cert. (Secondary Sch.)). Teaching, 1945–47, 1957–58 and 1961–71. Nat. Pres., Nat. Council of Women, 1970–74 (Vice-Pres., 1967–70); Chm., Cttee on Women, NZ, 1974–81. Member: Nat. Develt Council, 1969–74; Cttee of Inquiry into Equal Pay, 1971–72; Nat. Commn for UNESCO, 1974–83; Social Security Appeal Authority, 1974–; Nat. Convenor, Internat. Women's Year, 1975. JP NZ 1975. Jubilee Medal, 1977. *Publications:* Role of Women in National Development, 1970; numerous articles in popular and house magazines, on role and status of women. *Recreations:* gardening, reading, handcrafts, beachcombing. *Address:* 98 Waerenga Road, Otaki, New Zealand. *T:* Otaki 47267; (office) PO Box 12–117, Wellington, New Zealand. *T:* 737623.

DELL, Ven. Robert Sydney; Archdeacon of Derby, since 1973; Canon Residentiary of Derby Cathedral, since 1981; *b* 20 May 1922; *s* of Sydney Edward Dell and Lilian Constance Palmer; *m* 1953, Doreen Molly Layton; one *s* one *d*. *Educ:* Harrow County Sch.; Emmanuel Coll., Cambridge (MA); Ridley Hall. Curate of: Islington, 1948; Holy Trinity, Cambridge, 1950; Asst Chaplain, Wrekin Coll., 1953; Vicar of Mildenhall, Suffolk, 1955; Vice-Principal of Ridley Hall, Cambridge, 1957; Vicar of Chesterton, Cambridge, 1966 (Dir, Cambridge Samaritans, 1966–69). Mem., Archbishops' Commn on Intercommunion, 1965–67; Proctor in Convocation and Mem. Gen. Synod of C of E, 1970–85. Vis. Fellow, St George's House, Windsor Castle, 1981. *Publications:* Atlas of Christian History, 1960; contributor to: Charles Simeon, 1759–1836: essays written in commemoration of his bi-centenary, 1959; Jl of Ecclesiastical History. *Recreations:* reading, walking, travelling. *Address:* 72 Pastures Hill, Littleover, Derby DE3 7BB. *T:* Derby 512700. *Club:* Royal Commonwealth Society.

DELLAL, Jack; Chairman, Allied Commercial Exporters Ltd; *b* 2 Oct. 1923; *s* of Sulman and Charlotte Dellal; *m* 1952, Zehava Helmer; one *s* four *d*. *Educ:* Heaton Moor Coll., Manchester. Chm., Dalton, Barton & Co. Ltd, 1962–72; Dep. Chm., Keyser Ullman Ltd, 1972–74; Chm., Highland Electronics Group Ltd, 1971–76; Director: Anglo African Finance PLC, 1983–; General Tire & Rubber (SA) Ltd, 1983–; Williams, Hunt South Africa Ltd, 1983–. Vice-Pres., Anglo-Polish Conservative Society, 1970–. Officer, Order of Polonia Restituta, 1970. Freeman Citizen of Glasgow, 1971. *Recreations:* lawn tennis, squash, music, art. *Address:* 23 Ilchester Place, W14 8AA. *T:* 01–603 0981; Manor Farm, Brown Candover, Hants. *Clubs:* Royal Thames Yacht, Queen's, Lansdowne, Hurlingham.

DELLOW, John Albert, CBE 1985 (OBE 1979); Assistant Commissioner (Specialist Operations), Metropolitan Police, since 1985; *b* 5 June 1931; *s* of Albert Reginald and Lily Dellow; *m* 1952, Heather Josephine Rowe; one *s* one *d*. *Educ:* William Ellis Sch., Highgate; Royal Grammar Sch., High Wycombe. Joined City of London Police, 1951; seconded Manchester City Police, 1966; Superintendent, Kent County Constabulary, 1966, Chief Supt, 1968; jssc 1969; Asst Chief Constable, Kent Co. Constabulary, 1969; Metropolitan Police: Deputy Assistant Commissioner: Traffic Planning, 1973; Personnel, 1975; No 2 Area, 1978; 'A' Dept Operations, 1979; Inspectorate, 1980; Assistant Commissioner: 'B' Dept, 1982; Crime, 1984. Chairman: Metropolitan Police Museums Adv. Bd; Metropolitan Police History Soc.; Metropolitan Police Climbing, Canoe and Rowing Sections; Cdre, Metropolitan Police Sailing Club. *Recreations:* walking, history, listening to wireless. *Address:* New Scotland Yard, Broadway, SW1H 0BG.

DEL MAR, Norman Rene, CBE 1975; freelance conductor; Artistic Director and Principal Conductor, Aarhus Symfoniorkester, Denmark, since 1985; Conductor and Professor of Conducting, Royal College of Music; *b* 31 July 1919; *m* 1947, Pauline Mann; two *s*. *Educ:* Marlborough; Royal College of Music. Asst Sir Thomas Beecham, Royal Philharmonic Orchestra, 1947; Principal Conductor, English Opera Group, 1949–54; Conductor and Prof. of Conducting, Guildhall Sch. of Music, 1953–60; Conductor: Yorkshire Symphony Orchestra, 1954; BBC Scottish Orchestra, 1960–65; Royal Acad. of Music, 1974–77; Principal Conductor, Acad. of BBC, 1974–77. Artistic Dir, Norfolk and Norwich Triennial, 1979, 1982. Principal Guest Conductor, Bournemouth Sinfonietta, 1983–85. FRCM; FGSM; Hon. RAM. Hon. DMus: Glasgow, 1974; Bristol, 1978; Edinburgh, 1983; Hon. DLitt Sussex, 1977. Audio Award, 1980. *Publications:* Richard Strauss, 3 vols, 1962–72; Mahler's Sixth Symphony: a study, 1980; Orchestral Variations, 1981; Anatomy of the Orchestra, 1981. *Recreations:* writing, chamber music. *Address:* Witchings, Hadley Common, Herts. *T:* 01–449 4836.

DELMAS, Jacques Pierre Michel C.; *see* Chaban-Delmas.

DELORS, Jacques Lucien Jean; President, Commission of the European Economic Community, since 1985; *b* 20 July 1925; *s* of Louis and Jeanne Delors; *m* 1948, Marie Lephaille; one *s* one *d*. *Educ:* Paris Univ. Joined Banque de France, 1945; in office of Chief of Securities Dept, 1950–62, and in Sect. for the Plan and Investments, Conseil Economique et Social, 1959–61; Chief of Social Affairs, Gen. Commissariat of Plan Monnet, 1962–69; Gen. Sec., Interministerial Cttee for Professional Educn, 1969–73; Mem., Gen. Council, Banque de France, 1973–79, and Dir, on leave of absence, 1973–. Special Advr on Social Affairs to Prime Minister, 1969–72. Socialist Party Spokesman on internat. econ. matters, 1976; Minister of the Economy and Finance, 1981–83; Minister of Economy, Finance and Budget, 1983–84. Mem., European Parlt, 1979–81 (Pres., Econ. and Financial Cttee). Associate Prof., Univ. of Paris-Dauphine, 1973–80, Dir, Work and Society Res. Centre, 1975–81. Founder, Club Echange et Projets, 1974. *Publications:* Les indicateurs sociaux, 1971; Changer, 1975; essays, articles and UN reports on French Plan. *Address:* 200 rue de la Loi, 1049 Brussels, Belgium; 93 rue de Rivoli, 75001 Paris, France.

de los ANGELES, Victoria; Cross of Lazo de Dama of Order of Isabel the Catholic, Spain; Condecoracíon Banda de la Orden Civil de Alfonso X (El Sabio), Spain; Opera and Concert-Artiste (singing in original languages), Lyric-Soprano, since 1944; *b* Barcelona, Spain, 1 Nov. 1923; *m* 1948, Enrique Magriñá; two *s*. *Educ:* Conservatorium of Barcelona; University of Barcelona. Studied until 1944 at Conservatorium, Barcelona; first public concert, in Barcelona, 1944; début at Gran Teatro del Liceo de Barcelona, in Marriage of Figaro, 1945; concert tours in Spain and Portugal, 1945 and 1946; winner of first prize at Concours International of Geneva, 1947; Paris Opera first appearance, and début at the Scala, Milan, also South-American concert-tour, 1949; first tour in Scandinavia, first appearance at Covent Garden, and Carnegie Hall Début, 1950; first United States concert tour, and Metropolitan Opera of New York season, 1951. Since 1951 has appeared at the most important opera theatres and concert halls of Europe, South and Central America and Canada; first tour in S Africa, 1953; first tour in Australia, 1956; first appearance, Vienna State Opera, 1957. Opening Festival, Bayreuth, with Tannhäuser, 1961. Gold Medal, Barcelona, 1958; Silver Medal, province of Barcelona, 1959; Medal Premio Roma, 1969, etc. *Address:* c/o Basil Douglas Artists Management, 8 St George's Terrace, NW1 8XJ.

de LOTBINIÈRE, Lt-Col Sir Edmond; *see* Joly de Lotbinière.

DELVE, Sir Frederick (William), Kt 1962; CBE 1942; Chief Officer, London Fire Brigade, 1948–62, retired; Vice-President, Securicor plc, since 1982 (Director and Vice-Chairman, 1962–82); Director, Sound Diffusion plc, 1962–83; *b* 28 Oct. 1902; *s* of Frederick John Delve, Master Tailor, Brighton; *m* 1924, Ethel Lillian Morden (*d* 1980); no *c*. *Educ:* Brighton. Royal Navy, 1918–23; Fire Service since 1923; Chief Officer, Croydon Fire Brigade, 1934–41; Dep. Inspector-in-Chief of NFS, 1941–43; Chief Regional Fire Officer, No 5 London Region, National Fire Service, 1943–48. Pres., Institution of Fire Engineers, 1941–42; King's Police and Fire Services Medal, 1940. *Address:* 53 Ashley Court, Grand Avenue, Hove, East Sussex.

DELVIN, Lord; title borne by eldest son of Earl of Westmeath, *qv*; not at present used.

DELVIN, Dr David George; television and radio broadcaster, writer and doctor; *b* 28 Jan. 1939; *m* Kathleen Sears, SRN, SCM; two *s* one *d*. *Educ:* St Dunstan's Coll.; King's Coll., Univ. of London; King's Coll. Hosp. (MB, BS 1962; psychol medicine, forensic medicine and public health prizes, 1962). LRCP, MRCS 1962; MRCGP 1974; DObstRCOG 1965; DCH 1966; DipVen, Soc. of Apothecaries, 1977; FPA Cert. 1972; FPA Instructing Cert. 1974. Dir, Hosp. Medicine Film Unit, 1968–69. Vice-Chm., Med. Journalists' Assoc., 1982–; Elected Member: GMC, 1979–; Health Cttee of GMC, 1980–. Med. Consultant, FPA, 1981–; Med. Advisor to various BBC and ITV progs, 1974–. Med. Editor, General Practitioner, 1972–; Dr Jekyll Columnist in World Medicine, 1973–82. Cert. of Special Merit, Med. Journalists' Assoc., 1974 and (jtly) 1975. American Medical Writers' Assoc. Best Book Award, 1976. *Publications:* books, articles, TV and radio scripts, short stories, humorous pieces, medical films and videos; papers on hypertension and contraception in BMJ etc. *Recreations:* athletics, opera, orienteering, scuba-diving, hang-gliding (retired hurt). *Address:* c/o Barclays Bank, High Street, Chislehurst, Kent BR7 5AB. *Club:* Royal Society of Medicine.

de MAJO, William Maks, (known as **Willy**), MBE (mil.) 1946; FSIAD; Chairman and Managing Director, W. M. de Majo Associates Ltd, since 1946; Sales Director, Cronmatch Ltd, since 1964; Consultant: Charles Letts & Co. Ltd, John Millar & Sons, Ti-Well Ltd; *b* 25 July 1917; *s* of Maks de Majo and Josefine (*née* Ganz); *m* 1941, Veronica Mary Booker (separated); three *d*. *Educ:* Commercial Academy, Vienna. Chartered Designer. In practice as graphic and industrial designer on continent, 1935–39; news typist and broadcaster with BBC Overseas Service, 1940–41; war service as pilot and liaison officer, Royal Yugoslav Air Force, UK, Africa, ME, 1941–45 (Actg Chief Air Sect.); transf. to RAF, SO SHAEF and CCG HQ, 1945–46; re-established practice London, on demobilisation, 1946. Cons. designer to various nat. and internat. cos; guest lectr on design; co-ordinating designer, Fest. of Britain, 1951 (Ulster farm and factory); guest speaker, Internat. Design Conf., Aspen, Colo, 1953; designer, Baden-Powell Mus., 1961; designer-in-chief and co-ordinator, internat. exhibits, 1950–75; Mem. Jury, Canada Olympic Coins Comp., 1976; work exhibited on 5 continents. Founder and past Pres., Internat. Council of Graphic Design Assocs, 1963–68; Past Mem., Internat. Relations Bd, SIAD. Hon. Member: Assoc. of Graphic Designers, Netherlands, 1959; Assoc. of Swedish Art Dirs and Designers, 1965; Chambre Belges des Graphistes, 1966. SIAD Design Medal, 1969; ZPAP Polish Designers' Assoc. Commemorative Medal, 1983; winner of numerous nat. and internat. design competitions. *Publications:* contrib. Packaging (design of the gift pack), 1959 (Zürich); articles on graphic and industrial design to most leading jls in GB and abroad. *Recreations:* travelling, cooking, fostering good international relations. *Address:* 99 Archel Road, W14 9QL. *T:* 01–385 0394.

de MANIO, Jack, MC 1940; Broadcaster; *b* 26 Jan. 1914; *s* of Jean and Florence de Manio; *m* 1st, 1935, Juliet Gravaeret Kaufmann, New York (marr. diss., 1946); one *s*; 2nd, 1946, Loveday Elizabeth Matthews (*widow*, *née* Abbott). *Educ:* Aldenham. Served War of 1939–45, Royal Sussex Regt; 7th Bn, BEF, 1939–40; 1st Bn, Middle East Forces, 1940–44; Forces Broadcasting, Middle East, 1944–46. Joined Overseas Service, BBC, 1946; BBC

Home Service, 1950; resigned to become freelance, 1964. Presenter BBC programmes: Today, 1958–71; Jack de Manio Precisely, 1971–78; With Great Pleasure, 1971–73; broadcast 1st interview given by HRH The Prince of Wales, 1969; contributor Woman's Hour, 1979–. Assists with fund raising for Assoc. of Friends of Queen Charlotte's and Chelsea Hosp. for Women, 1980–. Radio Personality of Year Award, Variety Club of GB, 1964; Radio Personality Award of Year, British Radio Industries Club, 1971. *Publications:* To Auntie with Love, 1967; Life Begins Too Early, 1970; contribs to Punch and numerous other periodicals. *Recreation:* fishing. *Address:* 105 Cheyne Walk, SW10. *T:* 01–352 0889. *Club:* MCC.

DEMARCO, Richard, OBE 1985; RSW, SSA; Director, The Richard Demarco Gallery Ltd, Edinburgh, since 1966; *b* 9 July 1930; *s* of Carmine Demarco and Elizabeth (*née* Fusco); *m* 1957, Anne Muckle. *Educ:* Holy Cross Academy, Edinburgh; Edinburgh College of Art. National Service, KOSB and RAEC, 1954–56. Art Master, Duns Scotus Academy, Edinburgh, 1956–67; Co-Founder, Traverse Theatre Club; Vice-Chm. and Director, Traverse Art Gall., 1963–67; appointed Dir, Richard Demarco Gall., Melville Crescent, Edinburgh, by co-founders John Martin, Andrew Elliott and James Walker, 1966; introduced contemporary visual arts into official Edinburgh Festival programme with Edinburgh Open 100 Exhibn, 1967; introduced work of 330 internat. artists to UK, mainly through Edinburgh Fest. exhibns, from Canada, 1968, W Germany, 1970, Romania, 1971, Poland, 1972 and 1979, France, 1973, Austria, 1973, Yugoslavia, 1975, Aust. and NZ, 1984, incl. Joseph Beuys, 1970, and Tadeusz Kantor's Cricot Theatre, with prodns of The Water Hen, 1972, Lovelies and Dowdies, 1973, The Dead Class, 1976. Has presented, 1969–, annual programmes of theatre, music and dance prodns, incl. the Freehold Company's Antigone, 1970, the Dublin Project Company's On Baille Strand, 1977. Director: Sean Connery's Scottish Internat. Educn Trust, 1972–74; Edinburgh Arts annual summer sch. and expedns, 1972–. Has directed annual exhib. prog. with Special Unit, HM Prison, Barlinnie, with partic. reference to sculpture of James Boyle, 1974–; directed Edinburgh Fest. Internat. Confs, Towards the Housing of Art in the 21st Century, 1983, Art and the Human Environment, 1984 (also at Dublin Fest.). Was subject of film, Walkabout Edinburgh, dir. by Edward McConnell, 1970; acted in feature films: Long Shot, 1978; That Sinking Feeling, 1980. Has broadcast regularly on television and radio, 1966–; has lectured in over 150 univs, art colls, schools, art galls; as water-colour painter and printmaker is represented in over 1600 public and private collections, incl. Nat. Gall. of Modern Art of Scotland, V&A Museum, Scottish Arts Council. Contributing Editor, Studio International, 1982–. SSA 1964; RWSScot 1966. Gold Order of Merit, Polish People's Republic, 1976. *Publications:* The Artist as Explorer, 1978; The Road to Meikle Seggie, 1978. *Recreations:* exploring: the small and secret spaces in townscape; cathedrals, abbeys, parish churches; coastlines and islands and The Road to Meikle Seggie. *Address:* 29 Frederick Street, Edinburgh EH2 2ND. *T:* 031–225 5879. *Club:* Scottish Arts (Edinburgh).

de MARÉ, Eric, RIBA; writer and photographer; *b* 10 Sept. 1910; *s* of Bror and Ingrid de Maré; *m* 1st, 1936, Vanessa Burrage (*d* 1972); 2nd, 1974, Enid Verity. *Educ:* St Paul's Sch., London; Architectural Assoc., London (Dip.). RIBA 1934. Asst in several arch. practices, 1933–36; in private practice, 1936–40. War Service, survived, with spell in Home Guard designing frondy camouflage. Editor, Architects' Jl, 1942–46; freelance writer and photographer, mostly on architectural, topographical and photographic subjects, 1946–. Has travelled extensively in British Isles, Europe and USA in search of freelance fodder; much lecturing. Hon. Treasurer, Social Credit Party, 1938–46. *Publications:* Britain Rebuilt, 1942; The Canals of England, 1950, 2nd edn 1952; Scandinavia, 1952; Time on the Thames, 1952, 2nd edn 1975; The Bridges of Britain, 1954, 2nd edn 1975; Gunnar Asplund, 1955; Penguin Photography, 1957, 7th edn 1980; London's Riverside: past, present and future, 1958; (with Sir James Richards) The Functional Tradition in Early Industrial Buildings, 1958; Photography and Architecture, 1961; Swedish Cross Cut: the story of the Göta Canal, 1964; London's River: the story of a city, 1964, 2nd edn 1975 (Runner-up for 1964 Carnegie Award); The City of Westminster: heart of London, 1968; London 1851: the year of the Great Exhibition, 1972; The Nautical Style, 1973; The London Doré Saw: a Victorian evocation, 1973; Wren's London, 1975; Architectural Photography, 1975; The Victorian Wood Block Illustrators, 1980 (Yorkshire Post Award for best book on art, 1980); A Matter of Life or Debt, 1983, 4th edn 1986; contrib. Arch. Rev., TLS, Illustrated London News, etc. *Recreations:* talking to friends, reading history, philosophizing, looking at trees, preaching Douglas Social Credit and the Age of Leisure. *Address:* The Old House, Middle Duntisbourne, near Cirencester, Glos GL7 7AR. *T:* Cirencester 3859.

de MARGERIE, Emmanuel; Hon. GCVO; Chevalier de la Légion d'Honneur; Officier de l'Ordre National du Mérite; Commandeur de l'Ordre des Arts et des Lettres; Ambassadeur de France; French Ambassador to Washington, since 1984; *b* 25 Dec. 1924; *s* of Roland de Margerie, *qv*; *m* 1953, Hélène Hottinguer; one *s* one *d*. *Educ:* Lycée Français de Londres; Univ. Aurore, Shanghai; Sorbonne; Institut d'Etudes Politiques, Paris. Ecole Nat. d'Administration, 1949–51; joined Min. of Foreign Affairs, 1951; Sec., French Embassy, London, 1954–59; Moscow, 1959–61; Quai d'Orsay, 1961–67; Minister, Tokyo, 1967–70; Minister, Washington, 1970–72; Dir, European Dept, Quai d'Orsay, 1972–74; Dir Gen. of French Museums, 1975–77; Ambassador: to Madrid, 1978–81; to UK, 1981–84. Grand Cross, Order of Isabel la Católica (Spain), 1980, and various other foreign orders. *Address:* French Embassy, 4101 Reservoir Road NW, Washington, DC 20007, USA. *Clubs:* Beefsteak, Garrick, Travellers', White's.

de MARGERIE, Roland, CVO 1938; Ambassador of France; Hon. Conseiller d'Etat; *b* 6 May 1899; *s* of late P. de Margerie, KBE, French Ambassador in Berlin, 1922–31, and Jeanne Rostand, sister of the Playwright Edmond Rostand, Mem. of the French Academy; *m* 1921, Jenny, *d* of Edmond Fabre-Luce, Vice-Chm. of the Crédit Lyonnais; two *s* one *d*. *Educ:* Sorbonne; Ecole des Sciences Politiques, Paris. Joined Foreign Office, 1917; Lieut 17th Bn of Chasseurs Alpins, 1918–21; Attaché to French Embassy, Brussels, 1921; Sec., Berlin, 1923; 1st Sec. to the French Embassy, London, 1933–39; mem. of the mission attached to their Majesties during their State visit to France, 1938; Counsellor, 1939; Captain 152nd Regt of the Line, Sept. 1939–Feb. 1940; ADC to Gen. Gamelin, Feb.-March 1940; Private Sec. to the Minister for Foreign Affairs, March 1940; French Consul-Gen., Shanghai, 1940–44; Chargé with the office of the French Embassy in Peking, 1944–46. Asst deleg. negotiations for Brussels Pact, 1948; Minister plenipotentiary, 1949; Director-Gen. of Political Affairs, France, 1955; French Ambassador to the Holy See, 1956–59; to Spain, 1959–62; to the Federal Republic of Germany, 1962–65; Conseiller d'Etat, 1965–70. Comdr Legion of Honour; holds various foreign orders. *Address:* 14 rue St Guillaume, 75007 Paris, France. *Club:* Jockey (Paris).

See also Emmanuel de Margerie.

de MAULEY, 6th Baron, *cr* 1838; **Gerald John Ponsonby;** *b* 19 Dec. 1921; *er s* of 5th Baron de Mauley and Elgiva Margaret, *d* of late Hon. Cospatrick Dundas and Lady Cordeaux; *S* father, 1962; *m* 1954, Helen Alice, *d* of late Hon. Charles W. S. Douglas and *widow* of Lieut-Col B. L. L. Abdy Collins, OBE, MC, RE. *Educ:* Eton; Christ Church, Oxford (MA). Served War of 1939–45, France; Lieut Leics Yeo., Captain RA. Called to Bar, Middle Temple, 1949. *Heir:* *b* Col Hon. Thomas Maurice Ponsonby, TD, late Royal Glos Hussars [*b* 2 Aug. 1930; *m* 1956, Maxine Henrietta, *d* of W. D. K. Thellusson; two *s*]. *Address:* Langford House, Little Faringdon, Lechlade, Glos.

de MAYO, Prof. Paul, FRS 1975; FRSC 1971; Professor of Chemistry, University of Western Ontario, since 1959; *b* 8 Aug. 1924; *s* of Nissim and Anna de Mayo; *m* 1949, Mary Turnbull; one *s* one *d*. *Educ:* Univ. of London. BSc, MSc, PhD London; DèsS Paris. Asst Lectr, Birkbeck Coll., London, 1954–55; Lectr, Univ. of Glasgow, 1955–57; Lectr, Imperial Coll., London, 1957–59; Dir, Photochemistry Unit, Univ. of Western Ontario, 1969–72. Chemical Institute of Canada: Merck Lecture Award, 1966; Medal, 1982; E. W. R. Steacie Award for Photochemistry, 1985. Centennial Medal, Govt of Canada, 1967. *Publications:* Mono-and sesquiterpenoids, 1959; The Higher Terpenoids, 1959; (ed) Molecular Rearrangements, 1963; (ed) Rearrangements in Ground and Excited States, vols 1–3, 1980; numerous papers in learned jls. *Address:* 436 St George Street, London, Ontario, Canada. *T:* (office) 679–2473, (home) 679–9026.

DEMERITTE, Richard Clifford; High Commissioner for the Bahamas in London, since 1984; *b* 27 Feb.; *s* of R. H. Demeritte and late Miriam Demeritte (*née* Whitfield); *m* 1966, Ruth Smith; one *s* two *d*. *Educ:* Bahamas Sch. of Commerce; Metropolitan Coll., London; Century Univ., USA. Treasury Department, Bahamas: Asst Accountant, 1967; Accountant, 1969–71; Asst Treasurer, Jan.–Dec. 1972; Dep. Treasurer, 1973–79; Auditor-Gen., 1980–84. Fellow: Corp. of Accountants and Auditors, Bahamas, 1971 (Hon. Fellow, 1983); Assoc. of Internat. Accountants, 1976 (Pres./Chm. Council, 1985–); Certified Gen. Accountant, Canada, 1982; FBIM, 1985. Hon. Life Pres., YMCA (Grand Bahama); Toastmasters Internat. (Grand Bahama). *Recreations:* chess, golf, billiards, weightlifting. *Address:* Bahamas High Commission, 39 Pall Mall, SW1Y 5JG. *T:* 01-930 6967; The Penthouse, Mount Tyndal, Spaniards Road, Hampstead, NW3. *T:* 01-209 0604.

de MILLE, Agnes George, (Mrs W. F. Prude); Choreographer and Author; *b* New York City; *d* of William C. and Anna George de Mille; *m* 1943, Walter F. Prude; one *s*. *Educ:* University of Calif. (AB *cum laude*). Dance concerts USA, England, Denmark, France, 1929–40; Choreographed: Black Crook, 1929; Nymph Errant, 1933; Romeo and Juliet 1936; Oklahoma, 1943, 1980; One Touch of Venus, 1943; Bloomer Girl, 1944; Carousel, 1945; Brigadoon, 1947; Gentlemen Prefer Blondes, 1949; Paint Your Wagon, 1951; The Girl in Pink Tights, 1954; Oklahoma (film), 1955; Goldilocks, 1958; Juno, 1959; Kwamina, 1961; One Hundred and Ten in the Shade, 1963; Come Summer, 1968. Founded and directed Agnes de Mille Dance Theatre, 1953–54. Directed: Allegro, 1947; The Rape of Lucretia, 1948; Out of This World, 1950; Come Summer, 1968; Ballets composed: Black Ritual, 1940; Three Virgins and a Devil, 1941; Drums Sound in Hackensack, 1941; Rodeo, 1942; Tally-Ho, 1944; Fall River Legend, 1948; The Harvest According, 1952; The Rib of Eve, 1956; The Bitter Wierd, 1963; The Wind in the Mountains, 1965; The Four Marys, 1965; The Golden Age, 1966; A Rose for Miss Emily, 1970; Texas Fourth, 1976; A Bridegroom called Death, 1979; Agnes de Mille Heritage Dance Theater, 1973–74; Inconsequentials, 1982, etc. Television shows, for Omnibus, etc. Mem., Nat. Adv. Council of the Arts, 1965–66; Pres., Soc. for Stage Directors and Choreographers, 1966–67. Hon. Degrees: Mills Coll., 1952; Russell Sage College, 1953; Smith Coll., 1954; Northwestern Univ., 1960; Goucher Coll., 1961; University of Calif., 1962; Clark Univ., 1962; Franklin and Marshall Coll., 1966; Western Michigan Univ., 1967; Nasson Coll., 1971; Dartmouth Coll., 1974; Duke Univ., 1975; Univ. of North Carolina, 1980; New York Univ., 1981. New York Critics Award, 1943, 1944, 1945; Antoinette Perry Award, 1962; Handel Medallion, 1976; Kennedy Curtis Award, 1981; and numerous other awards, 1943–58. *Publications:* Dance to the Piper, 1952; And Promenade Home, 1958; To a Young Dancer, 1962; The Book of the Dance, 1963; Lizzie Borden, Dance of Death, 1968; Dance in America, 1970; Russian Journals, 1970; Speak to me, Dance with me, 1973; Where the Wings Grow, 1978; America Dances, 1981; Reprieve, 1981; articles in Vogue, Atlantic Monthly, Good Housekeeping, New York Times, McCall's, Horizon, Esquire. *Club:* Merriewold Country (NY).

DE MOLEYNS; *see* Eveleigh-de-Moleyns.

de MONTEBELLO, (Guy) Philippe (Lannes); Director, Metropolitan Museum of Art, since 1978; *b* 16 May 1936; *s* of Roger Lannes de Montebello and Germaine (*née* Croisset); *m* 1961, Edith Bradford Myles; two *s* one *d*. *Educ:* Harvard Coll. (BA *magna cum laude*); New York Univ., Inst. of Fine Arts (MA). Curatorial Asst, European Paintings, Metropolitan Mus. of Art, 1963; Asst Curator, Associate Curator, MMA, until 1969; Director, Museum of Fine Arts, Houston, Texas, 1969–74; Vice-Director: for Curatorial Affairs, MMA, Jan. 1974–June 1974; for Curatorial and Educnl Affairs, 1974–77; Actg Dir, MMA, 1977–78. Gallatin Fellow, New York Univ., 1981; Hon. LLD: Lafayette Coll., East Pa, 1979; Bard Coll., Annandale-on-Hudson, NY, 1981; Hon. DFA Iona Coll., New Rochelle, NY, 1982. Alumni Achievement Award, New York Univ., 1978. *Publication:* Peter Paul Rubens, 1968. *Address:* 1150 Fifth Avenue, New York, New York 10028, USA. *T:* 289 4475. *Club:* Knickerbocker (New York).

de MONTMORENCY, Sir Arnold (Geoffroy), 19th Bt *cr* 1631; Chairman, Contemporary Review Co. Ltd, since 1962, and Literary Editor since 1960; *b* 27 July 1908; *s* of Prof. James Edward Geoffrey de Montmorency (*d* 1934) and Caroline Maud Saumarez (*d* 1973), *d* of Maj.-Gen. James de Havilland; *S* cousin, 1979; *m* 1949, Nettie Hay Anderson (marr. annulled 1953, remarried 1972), *d* of late William Anderson and Janet Hay, Morayshire; no *c*. *Educ:* Westminster School (Triplett Exhibn); Peterhouse, Cambridge. BA 1930, LLB 1931, MA 1934. Harmsworth Law Scholar. Called to the Bar, 1932. Served War, RASC and staff in ME, Italy and Yugoslavia, 1940–45. Contested (L) Cambridge, 1959, Cirencester and Tewkesbury, 1964. Chm. (pt-time), Industrial Tribunals, 1975–81. Member, RIIA; Pres., Friends of Peterhouse. *Publication:* Integration of Employment Legislation, 1984. *Heir:* none. *Address:* 2 Garden Court, Temple, EC4Y 9BL. *Club:* National Liberal.

de MOURGUES, Prof. Odette Marie Hélène Louise, PhD, DLitt; Palmes Académiques 1964; Ordre National du Mérite 1973; Professor Emerita University of Cambridge; Fellow, Girton College, Cambridge, since 1946; *b* 14 May 1914; *d* of Dr Pierre de Mourgues and Hélène Terle; *m* 1934 (marr. diss. 1943); one *s* decd. *Educ:* Lycée of Le Puy; Univs of Grenoble and Aix-en-Provence. Licence en droit, diplôme d'études supérieures de droit, LèsL, agrégation d'anglais; PhD, DLitt Cantab. Teaching posts, Valence, Digne and Marseille, 1942–45; Asst Lectr, Univ. of Aix-en-Provence, 1944–46; Lectr, Girton Coll., 1946, Lectr in French, 1952–68, Reader, 1968–75, Prof. of French, 1975–80, Univ. of Cambridge. *Publications:* Metaphysical, Baroque and Précieux Poetry, 1953; Le Jugement Avant-dernier (fiction), 1954; L'Hortensia Bleu (fiction), 1956; La Fontaine: Fables, 1960; O Muse, fuyante Proie, 1962; An Anthology of French 17C Poetry, 1966; Racine or the Triumph of Relevance, 1967; Autonomie de Racine, 1967; Two French Moralists: La Rochefoucald and La Bruyère, 1978; articles, contribs to Festschriften, published lectures, and revs. *Recreations:* travel, gardening. *Address:* 1 Marion Close, Cambridge. *T:* Cambridge 356865.

DEMPSEY, Andrew; *see* Dempsey, J. A.

DEMPSEY, (James) Andrew; Assistant Director of Exhibitions, Arts Council of Great Britain, since 1975; *b* 17 Nov. 1942; *s* of James Dempsey, Glasgow; *m* 1966, Grace, *d* of Dr Ian MacPhail, Dumbarton; one *s* one *d. Educ:* Ampleforth Coll.; Glasgow Univ. Whistler Research Asst, Fine Art Dept, Univ. of Glasgow, 1963–65; exhibn work for art dept of Arts Council, 1966–71; Keeper, Dept of Public Relations, V&A, 1971–75. *Address:* 105 Piccadilly, W1.

DEMPSTER, John William Scott; Head of Marine Directorate, Department of Transport, since 1984; *b* 10 May 1938; *s* of late Dr David and Mrs M. C. Dempster; *m* 1965, Ailsa Newman (marr. diss. 1972). *Educ:* Plymouth Coll.; Oriel Coll., Oxford (MA(PPE)). HM Inspector of Taxes, Inland Revenue, 1961–65; Ministry of Transport: Asst Principal, 1965–66; Private Sec. to Parly Sec., 1966–67; Principal, 1967–73; Asst Sec., Property Services Agency, 1973–76; Principal Private Sec. to Sec. of State for the Environment, 1976–77; Asst Sec., 1977–79, Under Sec., 1979–80, Dept of Transport; Principal Estabt and Finance Officer, Lord Chancellor's Dept, 1980–84. *Recreations:* mountaineering, sailing, bridge, Munro collecting. *Address:* Department of Transport, Sunley House, 90–93 High Holborn, WC1V 6LP. *T:* 01–405 6911. *Clubs:* Hampstead Cricket; Fell and Rock Climbing, Swiss Alpine, Royal Southampton Yacht.

DEMPSTER, Nigel Richard Patton; Editorial Executive, Associated Newspapers; Editor, Mail Diary, since 1973; *b* 1 Nov. 1941; *s* of Eric R. P. Dempster and Angela Grace Dempster (*née* Stephens); *m* 1st, 1971, Emma de Bendern (marr. diss. 1974), *d* of Count John de Bendern and Lady Patricia Douglas, *d* of 11th Marquess of Queensberry; 2nd, 1978, Lady Camilla Godolphin Osborne, *o c* of 11th Duke of Leeds and Audrey (who *m* 1955, Sir David Lawrence, Bt, *qv*); one *d. Educ:* Sherborne. Broker, Lloyd's of London, 1958–59; Stock Exchange, 1959–60; PR account exec., Earl of Kimberley Associates, 1960–63; journalist, Daily Express, 1963–71; columnist, Daily Mail, 1971–. London correspondent, Status magazine, USA, 1965–66; contributor to Queen magazine, 1966–70; columnist ('Grovel'), Private Eye magazine, 1969–85. Broadcaster with ABC (USA) and CBC (Canada), 1976–, and with TV-am, 1983–. *Publication:* HRH The Princess Margaret—A Life Unfulfilled (biog.), 1981 (USA and Canada, 1982). *Recreations:* photography, squash, running marathons. *Address:* c/o Daily Mail, Northcliffe House, EC4Y 0JA. *Clubs:* Royal Automobile; Chappaquiddick Beach (Mass, USA).

DENBIGH, 11th Earl of, *cr* 1622 **AND DESMOND, 10th Earl of**, *cr* 1622; **William Rudolph Michael Feilding**; *b* 2 Aug. 1943; *s* of 10th Earl of Denbigh and Verena Barbara, *d* of W. E. Price; *S* father, 1966; *m* 1965, Caroline Judith Vivienne, *o d* of Lt-Col Geoffrey Cooke; one *s* two *d. Educ:* Eton. *Heir: s* Viscount Feilding, *qv. Address:* 21 Moore Park Road, SW6; Newnham Paddox, near Rugby, Warwickshire. *T:* Rugby 832173.

DENBIGH, Prof. Kenneth George, FRS 1965; MA Cantab, DSc Leeds; Principal of Queen Elizabeth College, University of London, 1966–77; Professor Emeritus in the University of London, 1977; Visiting Research Fellow, Chelsea College, since 1980; *b* 30 May 1911; *s* of late G. J. Denbigh, MSc, Harrogate; *m* 1935, Kathleen Enoch; two *s. Educ:* Queen Elizabeth Grammar Sch., Wakefield; Leeds University. Imperial Chemical Industries, 1934–38, 1945–48; Lecturer, Southampton Univ., 1938–41; Ministry of Supply (Explosives), 1941–45; Lecturer, Cambridge Univ., Chemical Engineering Dept, 1948–55; Professor: of Chemical Technology, Edinburgh, 1955–60, of Chemical Engineering Science, London Univ., 1960–61; Courtauld's Prof., Imperial Coll., 1961–66. Dir, Council for Science and Society, 1977–83. Fellow, Imperial Coll., 1976; FKC. Hon. DèsSc Toulouse, 1960; Hon. DUniv. Essex, 1967. *Publications:* The Thermodynamics of the Steady State, 1951; The Principles of Chemical Equilibrium, 1955; Science, Industry and Social Policy, 1963; Chemical Reactor Theory, 1965; An Inventive Universe, 1975; Three Concepts of Time, 1981; (with J. S. Denbigh) Entropy in Relation to Incomplete Knowledge, 1985; various scientific papers. *Address:* 19 Sheridan Road, Merton Park, SW19 3HW.

DENBY, Patrick Morris Coventry, CMG 1982; Assistant Director-General (Treasurer and Financial Comptroller), International Labour Office, Geneva, 1976–81; *b* 28 Sept. 1920; *s* of Robert Coventry Denby and Phyllis Denby (*née* Dacre); *m* 1950, Margaret Joy, *d* of Lt-Col C. L. Boyle; two *d* (and one *d* decd). *Educ:* Bradford Grammar Sch.; Corpus Christi Coll., Oxford (Open Scholar) (Honour Mods, Cl. II, MA). War service with Intelligence Corps, as Temp. Lieut RNVR, and with Foreign Office, 1941–46. Unilever Ltd, UK and Australia: management trainee and product manager, 1946–51; joined International Labour Office, 1951: Professional Officer, 1951; Chief of Budget and Control Div., 1959; Chief of Finance and General Services Dept, Treasurer and Financial Comptroller, 1970; Chm., Investments Cttee; Mem., UN Pension Board, 1971–75. *Recreations:* skiing, mountain walking, squash, tennis. *Address:* c/o Maksud, Case postale 500, 1211 Geneva 22, Switzerland. *Clubs:* United Oxford & Cambridge University; Stokes Poges Lawn Tennis.

DENBY, Sir Richard Kenneth, Kt 1978; DL; President of the Law Society of England and Wales, 1977 (Vice-President, 1976); Consultant, A. V. Hammond & Co., Bradford, since 1985 (Senior Partner, 1972–85); *b* 20 March 1915; *s* of John Henry and Emily Denby; *m* 1939, Eileen (*d* 1974), *d* of M. H. Pickles, CBE; one *s* two *d. Educ:* Ackworth School; Leeds Univ. (LLB). Admitted Solicitor, 1937 (First Cl. Hons and Clifford's Inn Prize). Served War of 1939–45: 2nd Lt, The Green Howards, 1940; AFHQ N Africa, 1942; War Office, DAMS MS1(b), 1944; AMS, Lt-Col Northern Command, 1945 (despatches). Pres., Bradford & Bingley Building Soc., 1982–85; Chairman: Parkland Textile (Holdings) Ltd, 1979–85; Pennine Radio (Bradford Community Radio Ltd), 1975–85. Dir, Opera North Ltd, 1981. Mem., Criminal Injuries Compensation Bd, 1979–. Chm., Mental Health Review Tribunal, NE Region. DL W Yorks, 1982. *Recreations:* fishing, fell-walking. *Address:* 7 Goodwood, Ilkley, W Yorks LS29 0BY. *T:* Ilkley 609076. *Clubs:* Army and Navy, Carlton; Bradford.

DENCH, Judith Olivia, (Judi Dench), OBE 1970; (Mrs Michael Williams); actress (theatre, films and television); *b* 9 Dec. 1934; *d* of Reginald Arthur Dench and Eleanora Olave Dench (*née* Jones); *m* 1971, Michael Williams, *qv*; one *d. Educ:* The Mount Sch., York; Central Sch. of Speech and Drama. *Theatre:* Old Vic seasons, 1957–61: parts incl.: Ophelia in Hamlet; Katherine in Henry V; Cecily in The Importance of Being Earnest; Juliet in Romeo and Juliet; also 1957–61: two Edinburgh Festivals; Paris-Belgium-Yugoslavia tour; America-Canada tour; Venice (all with Old Vic Co.). Subseq. appearances incl.: Royal Shakespeare Co., 1961–62: Anya in The Cherry Orchard; Titania in A Midsummer Night's Dream; Dorcas Bellboys in A Penny for a Song; Isabella in Measure for Measure; Nottingham Playhouse tour of W Africa, 1963; Oxford Playhouse, 1964–65: Irina in The Three Sisters; Doll Common in The Alchemist; Nottingham Playhouse, 1965: Saint Joan; The Astrakhan Coat (world première); Amanda in Private Lives; Variety London Critics' Best Actress of the Year Award for perf. as Lika in The Promise, Fortune, 1967; Sally Bowles in Cabaret, Palace, 1968; Associate Mem., RSC, 1969–; London Assurance, Aldwych, 1970, and New, 1972; Major Barbara, Aldwych, 1970; Bianca in Women Beware Women, Viola in Twelfth Night, doubling Hermione and Perdita in The Winter's Tale, Portia in The Merchant of Venice, the Duchess in The Duchess of Malfi, Beatrice in Much Ado About Nothing, Lady Macbeth in Macbeth,

Adriana in The Comedy of Errors, Regan in King Lear, Imogen in Cymbeline; The Wolf, Oxford and London, 1973; The Good Companions, Her Majesty's, 1974; The Gay Lord Quex, Albery, 1975; Too True to be Good, Aldwych, 1975, Globe, 1976; Pillars of the Community, The Comedy of Errors, Aldwych, 1977; The Way of the World, 1978; Juno and the Paycock, Aldwych, 1980 (Best Actress award, SWET, Evening Standard, Variety Club, and Plays and Players); The Importance of Being Earnest, A Kind of Alaska, Nat. Theatre, 1982; Pack of Lies, Lyric, 1983 (SWET award); Mother Courage, Barbican, 1984; Waste, Barbican and Lyric, 1985. Recital tour of W Africa, 1969; RSC tours: Japan and Australia, 1970; Japan, 1972. *Films:* He Who Rides a Tiger; A Study in Terror; Four in the Morning (Brit. Film Acad. Award for Most Promising Newcomer, 1965); A Midsummer Night's Dream; The Third Secret; Dead Cert; Saigon: Year of the cat; Wetherby; A Room with a View; 84 Charing Cross Road. *Television* appearances include, 1957–: Talking to a Stranger (Best Actress of Year award, Guild of Television Dirs, 1967); Major Barbara; Hilda Lessways; Langrishe, Go Down; Macbeth; Comedy of Errors; On Giant's Shoulders; A Village Wooing; Love in a Cold Climate; Saigon; A Fine Romance (BAFTA Award, 1985); The Cherry Orchard; Going Gently; Mr and Mrs Edgehill; The Browning Version; Make or Break. Awards incl. British and foreign, for theatre, films and TV, incl. BAFTA award for best television actress, 1981. Hon. DLitt Warwick, 1978; DUniv York, 1983. *Recreations:* sewing, drawing, catching up with letters.

DENHAM, 2nd Baron, *cr* 1937, of Weston Underwood; **Bertram Stanley Mitford Bowyer;** PC 1981; 10th Bt, *cr* 1660, of Denham; 2nd Bt, *cr* 1933 of Weston Underwood; Captain of the Gentlemen at Arms (Government Chief Whip in the House of Lords), since 1979; *b* 3 Oct. 1927; *s* of 1st Baron and Hon. Daphne Freeman-Mitford, 4th *d* of 1st Baron Redesdale; *S* father 1948; *m* 1956, Jean, *o d* of Kenneth McCorquodale, Fambridge Hall, White Notley, Essex; three *s* one *d. Educ:* Eton; King's Coll., Cambridge. Mem. Westminster CC, 1959–61. A Lord-in-Waiting to the Queen, 1961–64 and 1970–71; Captain of the Yeomen of the Guard, 1971–74. Opposition Dep. Chief Whip, 1974–78, Opposition Chief Whip, 1978–79. *Publications:* The Man who Lost his Shadow, 1979; Two Thyrdes, 1983. *Recreations:* field sports. *Heir: s* Hon. Richard Grenville George Bowyer, *b* 8 Feb. 1959. *Address:* The Laundry Cottage, Weston Underwood, Olney, Bucks. *T:* Bedford 711535. *Clubs:* White's, Pratt's.

DENHAM, Ernest William; Deputy Keeper of Public Records, Public Record Office, 1978–82; *b* 16 Sept. 1922; *s* of William and Beatrice Denham; *m* 1957, Penelope Agatha Gregory; one *s* one *d. Educ:* City of London Sch.; Merton Coll., Oxford (Postmaster). MA 1948. Naval Intell., UK and SEAC, 1942–45. Asst Sec., Plant Protection Ltd, 1947–49; Asst Keeper 1949, Principal Asst Keeper 1967, Records Admin. Officer 1973, Public Record Office; Lectr in Palaeography and Diplomatic, UCL, 1957–73. *Recreation:* armchair criticism. *Address:* 27 The Drive, Northwood, Mddx. *T:* Northwood 27382.

DENHAM, Captain Henry Mangles, CMG 1945; RN, retired; *b* 9 Sept. 1897; *s* of Henry Mangles Denham and Helen Clara Lowndes; *m* 1924, Estelle Margaret Sibbald Currie; one *s* two *d. Educ:* RN Coll., Dartmouth. Went to sea at beginning of European War, serving at Dardanelles in HMS Agamemnon and destroyer Racoon; occupation of the Rhine in HM Rhine Flotilla; round the world cruise with the Prince of Wales in HMS Renown, 1921; served in Mediterranean for long period largely in HMS Queen Elizabeth and Warspite; at Staff Coll., 1935; Comdr of HMS Penelope, 1936–39. Naval Attaché, Scandinavian Countries, 1940; Naval Attaché, Stockholm, 1940–47; retd list, 1947. *Publications:* The Aegean, 1963, 5th edn, 1983; Eastern Mediterranean, 1964; The Adriatic, 1967; The Tyrrhenian Sea, 1969; The Ionian Islands to Rhodes, 1972; Southern Turkey, the Levant and Cyprus, 1973; Ionian Islands to Anatolian Coast, 1982; Inside the Nazi Ring, 1984. *Recreation:* yachting. *Clubs:* Royal Automobile, Royal Cruising; Royal Yacht Squadron (Cowes).

DENHAM, Maurice; Actor since 1934; *b* 23 Dec. 1909; *s* of Norman Denham and Winifred Lillico; *m* 1936, Margaret Dunn (*d* 1971); two *s* one *d. Educ:* Tonbridge Sch. Hull Repertory Theatre, 1934–36; theatre, radio and television, 1936–39. Served War of 1939–45: Buffs, 1939–43; Royal Artillery, 1943–45; despatches, 1946. Theatre, films, radio and television, 1946–. *Recreations:* painting, conducting gramophone records, golf. *Clubs:* Garrick, Green Room; Stage Golfing.

DENHOLM, Ian; *see* Denholm, J. F.

DENHOLM, John Ferguson, (Ian), CBE 1974; JP; DL; Chairman: Denholm Line Steamers Ltd, since 1974; J. & J. Denholm Ltd, since 1974; Murray Investment Trusts, since 1985; Murray Management Ltd, since 1985; *b* 8 May 1927; *s* of Sir William Lang Denholm, TD; *m* 1952, Elizabeth Murray Stephen; two *s* two *d. Educ:* St Mary's Sch., Melrose; Loretto Sch., Musselburgh. Joined J. & J. Denholm Ltd, 1945. Deputy Chairman: P&O, 1980–85; Murray Johnstone Ltd, 1985–; Director: Fleming Mercantile Investment Trust, 1985–; Murray Cos and Trusts, 1973–; Mem. London Bd, Bank of Scotland, 1982–. Pres., Chamber of Shipping of the UK, 1973–74; Member: Nat. Ports Council, 1974–77; Scottish Transport Gp, 1975–82. Hon. Norwegian Consul in Glasgow, 1975–. DL, 1980, JP, 1984, Renfrewshire. *Recreation:* fishing. *Address:* Newton of Belltrees, Lochwinnoch, Renfrewshire PA12 4JL. *T:* Lochwinnoch 842406. *Clubs:* City of London; Western (Glasgow); Royal Thames Yacht, Royal Yacht Squadron, Royal Northern and Clyde Yacht.

DENINGTON, family name of Baroness Denington.

DENINGTON, Baroness *cr* 1978 (Life Peer), of Stevenage in the County of Hertfordshire; **Evelyn Joyce Denington**, DBE 1974 (CBE 1966); Chairman, Stevenage Development Corporation, 1966–80 (Member, 1950–80); Chairman, Greater London Council, 1975–76; *b* 9 Aug. 1907; *d* of Phillip Charles Bursill and Edith Rowena Bursill; *m* 1935, Cecil Dallas Denington. *Educ:* Blackheath High Sch.; Bedford Coll., London. Journalism, 1927–31; Teacher, 1933–45; Gen. Sec., Nat. Assoc. of Labour Teachers, 1938–47; Member: St Pancras Borough Council, 1945–59; LCC, 1946–65 (Chm. New and Expanding Towns Cttee, 1960–65); GLC, 1964–77 (Chm. Housing Cttee, 1964–67; Dep. Leader (Lab), Opposition, 1967–73; Chm., Transport Cttee, 1973–75); Central Housing Adv. Cttee, 1955–73 (Chm. Sub-Cttee prod. report Our Older Homes); SE Economic Planning Council, 1966–79; Chm., New Towns Assoc., 1973–75. Member: Sutton Dwellings Housing Trust, 1976–82; North British Housing Assoc., 1976–; Sutton (Hastoe) Housing Assoc. Ltd, 1981–; St Edward's Housing Assoc., 1983–. Freeman, City of London. Hon. FRIBA; Hon. MRTPI. *Address:* Weale House, 29 Crescent Grove, Clapham, SW4 7AF. *T:* 01–622 1275.

DENISON, family name of Baron Londesborough.

DENISON, Dulcie Winifred Catherine, (Dulcie Gray), CBE 1983; actress, playwright, authoress; *b* 20 Nov. 1920; *d* of late Arnold Savage Bailey, CBE, and of Kate Edith (*née* Clulow Gray); *m* 1939, Michael Denison, *qv. Educ:* England and Malaya. In Repertory in Aberdeen, 1st part Sorrel in Hay Fever, 1939; Repertory in Edinburgh, Glasgow and Harrogate, 1940; BBC Serial, Front Line Family, 1941; Shakespeare, Regents Park; Alexandra in The Little Foxes, Piccadilly; Midsummer Night's Dream, Westminster,

1942; Brighton Rock, Garrick; Landslide, Westminster, 1943; Lady from Edinburgh, Playhouse, 1945; Dear Ruth, St James's; Wind is 90, Apollo, 1946; on tour in Fools Rush In, 1946; Rain on the Just, Aldwych, 1948; Queen Elizabeth Slept Here, Strand, 1949; The Four-poster, Ambassadors, 1950 (tour of S Africa, 1954–55); See You Later (Revue), Watergate, 1951; Dragon's Mouth, Winter Garden, 1952; Sweet Peril, St James's, 1952; We Must Kill Toni, Westminster; The Diary of a Nobody, Arts, 1954; Alice Through the Looking Glass, Chelsea Palace, 1955, Ashcroft Theatre, Croydon, 1972; appeared in own play, Love Affair, Lyric Hammersmith, 1956; South Sea Bubble, Cape Town, 1956; Tea and Sympathy, Melbourne and Sydney, 1956; South Sea Bubble, Johannesburg, 1957; Double Cross, Duchess, 1958; Let Them Eat Cake, Cambridge, 1959; Candida, Piccadilly and Wyndham's, 1960; Heartbreak House, Wyndham's, 1961; A Marriage Has Been Arranged, and A Village Wooing (Hong Kong); Shakespeare Recital (Berlin Festival); Royal Gambit for opening of Ashcroft Theatre, Croydon, 1962; Where Angels Fear to Tread, Arts and St Martin's, 1963; An Ideal Husband, Strand, 1965; On Approval, St Martin's, 1966; Happy Family, St Martin's, 1967; Number 10, Strand, 1967; Out of the Question, St Martin's, 1968; Three, Fortune, 1970; The Wild Duck, Criterion, 1970; Clandestine Marriage (tour), 1971; Ghosts, York; Hay Fever (tour), 1972; Dragon Variation (tour), 1973; At the End of the Day, Savoy, 1973; The Sack Race, Ambassadors, 1974; The Pay Off, Comedy, 1974, Westminster, 1975; Time and the Conways (tour), 1976; Ladies in Retirement (tour), 1976; The Cabinet Minister (tour), 1977; A Murder is Announced, Vaudeville, 1977; Bedroom Farce, Prince of Wales, 1979; The Cherry Orchard, Exeter, 1980; Lloyd George Knew my Father (tour), 1980; The Kingfisher, Windsor, 1980, Worthing and on tour, 1981; Relatively Speaking (Dinner Theatre Tour, Near and Far East), 1981; A Coat of Varnish, Haymarket, 1982; Cavell, Chichester Fest., 1982; School for Scandal, Haymarket, transf. to Duke of York's, and British Council 50th Anniversary European Tour, 1983; There Goes the Bride (Dinner Theatre tour, Near and Far East), 1985. *Films include:* They were Sisters, 1944; Wanted for Murder, 1945; A Man about the House, 1946; Mine Own Executioner, 1947; My Brother Jonathan, 1947; The Glass Mountain, 1948; The Franchise Affair, 1951; Angels One Five, 1952; There was a Young Lady, 1953; A Man Could Get Killed, 1965. Has appeared in television plays and radio serials; *television series:* Howard's Way, 1985, 1986. Fellow, Linnean Soc., 1984. FRSA. Queen's Silver Jubilee Medal, 1977. *Publications: play:* Love Affair; *books:* Murder on the Stairs; Murder in Melbourne; Baby Face; Epitaph for a Dead Actor; Murder on a Saturday; Murder in Mind; The Devil Wore Scarlet; No Quarter for a Star; The Murder of Love; Died in the Red; The Actor and His World (with Michael Denison); Murder on Honeymoon; For Richer, For Richer; Deadly Lampshade; Understudy to Murder; Dead Give Away; Ride on a Tiger; Stage-Door Fright; Death in Denims; Butterflies on my Mind (TES Senior Information Book Prize, 1978); Dark Calypso; The Glanville Women; Anna Starr. *Recreations:* swimming, butterflies. *Address:* Shardeloes, Amersham, Bucks.

DENISON, Elizabeth Ann Marguerite, (Mrs W. N. Denison); *see* Curnow, E. A. M.

DENISON, John Law, CBE 1960 (MBE 1945); FRCM; Hon. RAM; Hon. GSM; Director, South Bank Concert Halls (formerly General Manager, Royal Festival Hall), 1965–76; Chairman: Arts Educational Schools, since 1977; Royal Concert Committee, St Cecilia Festival, since 1976; Member of Council, RCM, and Associated Board Royal Schools of Music, since 1975; *b* 21 Jan. 1911; *s* of late Rev. H. B. W. and Alice Dorothy Denison; *m* 1st, 1936, Annie Claudia Russell Brown (marriage dissolved, 1946); 2nd, 1947, Evelyn Mary Donald (*née* Moir) (*d* 1958), *d* of John and Mary Scott Moir, Edinburgh; one *d*; 3rd, 1960, Audrey Grace Burnaby (*née* Bowles) (*d* 1970); 4th, 1972, Françoise Charlotte Henriette Mitchell (*née* Garrigues) (*d* 1985). *Educ:* Brighton Coll.; Royal Coll. of Music. Played horn in BBC Symphony, London Philharmonic, City of Birmingham, and other orchestras, 1934–39. Served War of 1939–45; gazetted Somerset Light Inf., 1940; DAA and QMG 214 Inf. Bde and various staff appts, 1941–45 (despatches). Asst Dir, Music Dept, British Council, 1946–48; Music Dir, Arts Council of Great Britain, 1948–65. Chm., Cultural Programme, London Celebrations Cttee, Queen's Silver Jubilee, 1976–78; Hon. Treasurer, Royal Philharmonic Soc, 1977–. Comdr, Order of Lion, Finland, 1976. *Publications:* articles for various musical publications. *Address:* 22 Empire House, Thurloe Place, SW7. *Club:* Army and Navy.

DENISON, (John) Michael (Terence Wellesley), CBE 1983; actor; *b* 1 Nov. 1915; *s* of Gilbert Dixon Denison and Marie Louise (*née* Bain); *m* 1939, Dulcie Gray (*see* D. W. C. Denison). *Educ:* Harrow; Magdalen Coll., Oxford (BA). Dramatic Sch., 1937–38; Westminster Theatre, 1938; Aberdeen Repertory, 1939. First film, 1940. Served War of 1939–45, Royal Signals and Intelligence Corps, 1940–46. Has appeared in following plays: Ever Since Paradise, 1946; Rain on the Just, 1948; Queen Elizabeth Slept Here, 1949; The Four-poster, 1950; Dragon's Mouth, 1952; Sweet Peril, 1952; The Bad Samaritan, 1953; Alice Through the Looking Glass, 1953, 1955 and 1972; We Must Kill Toni, 1954; tour of S Africa, 1954–55; All's Well That Ends Well, Twelfth Night, Merry Wives of Windsor, Titus Andronicus, Stratford-on-Avon, 1955; prod. and acted in Love Affair, 1956; A Village Wooing and Fanny's First Play (Edinburgh and Berlin festivals), 1956; Meet Me By Moonlight, 1957; Let Them Eat Cake, 1959; Candida, 1960; Heartbreak House, 1961; My Fair Lady, (Melbourne); A Village Wooing (Hong Kong); Shakespeare Recital (Berlin Festival), 1962; Where Angels Fear to Tread, 1963; Hostile Witness, 1964; An Ideal Husband, 1965; On Approval, 1966; Happy Family; Number 10, 1967; Out of the Question, 1968; Three, 1970; The Wild Duck, 1970; Clandestine Marriage, 1971; The Tempest, 1972; Twelfth Night, 1972, 1978, 1985; The Dragon Variation (tour), 1973; At the End of the Day, 1973; The Sack Race, 1974; Peter Pan, 1974; The Black Mikado, 1975; The First Mrs Fraser (tour), 1976; The Earl and the Pussycat (tour), 1976; Robert and Elizabeth (tour), 1976; The Cabinet Minister (tour), 1977; The Lady's Not For Burning, Ivanov, 1978; Bedroom Farce, 1979; The Kingfisher (tour), 1980–81; Venus Observed, 1980; Relatively Speaking (Far and Near East tour), 1981; A Coat of Varnish, Captain Brassbound's Conversion, 1982; School for Scandal, 1982, 1983; See How They Run, 1984; There Goes the Bride (Near and Far East tour), 1985; Ring Round the Moon, 1985; The Apple Cart, 1986. *Films include:* My Brother Jonathan, 1947; The Glass Mountain, 1948; Landfall, 1949; The Franchise Affair, 1950; Angels One Five, The Importance of Being Earnest, 1951; The Truth About Women, 1957. Many television appearances including title role Boyd, QC, 1956–61 and 1963. Director: Allied Theatre Productions, 1966–75; Play Company of London, 1970–74; New Shakespeare Company, 1971–. On Council British Actors Equity Assoc., 1949–76 (Vice-Pres. 1952, 1961–63, 1973); Mem. Drama Panel, Arts Council, 1975–78. FRSA. *Publications:* (with Dulcie Gray) The Actor and His World, 1964; memoirs: vol. 1, Overture and Beginners, 1973, vol. 2, Double Act, 1985. DNB articles on Sir Noël Coward and Sir Peter Daubeny, 1983. *Recreations:* golf, painting, watching cricket, gardening, motoring. *Address:* Shardeloes, Amersham, Bucks. *Clubs:* Richmond Golf (Richmond); MCC, Middlesex County Cricket.

DENISON, Michael; *see* Denison, J. M. T. W.

DENISON, William Neil; QC 1980; **His Honour Judge Denison;** a Circuit Judge, since 1985; *b* 10 March 1929; *s* of William George Denison and Jean Brodie; *m*; three *s*; *m* 1981, Elizabeth Ann Marguerite Curnow, *qv*. *Educ:* Queen Mary's Sch., Walsall; Univ. of Birmingham (LLB); Hertford Coll., Univ. of Oxford (BCL). Called to the Bar, Lincoln's Inn, 1952. A Recorder of the Crown Court, 1979–85. *Recreations:* walking, reading rubbish. *Club:* Garrick.

DENISON-PENDER, family name of **Baron Pender.**

DENMAN, family name of **Baron Denman.**

DENMAN, 5th Baron *cr* 1834; **Charles Spencer Denman,** CBE 1976; MC 1942; TD; Bt 1945; *b* 7 July 1916; *e s* of Hon. Sir Richard Douglas Denman, 1st Bt; *S* father, 1957 and to barony of cousin, 1971; *m* 1943, Sheila Anne, *d* of late Lt-Col Algernon Bingham Anstruther Stewart, DSO, Seaforth Highlanders, of Ornockenoch, Gatehouse of Fleet; three *s* one *d*. *Educ:* Shrewsbury. Served War of 1939–45 with Duke of Cornwall's Light Infantry (TA), India, Middle East, Western Desert and Dodecanese Islands; Major, 1943. Contested (C) Leeds Central, 1945. Chairman: Goldfields Mahd adh Dhahab; Arundell House Holdings; Arundell House Securities; Director: Saudi British Bank; Fletcher Challenge Corp.; British Arabian Corp. Formerly Chm., Marine and General Mutual Life Assurance Soc.; formerly Director: C. Tennant Sons & Co. Ltd; British Bank of the Middle East; Consolidated Goldfields Ltd. Chairman, Committee for Middle East Trade, 1971–75 (Mem., 1963–75); Member: Advisory Council of Export Credits Guarantee Department, 1963–68; British National Export Council, 1965; Cttee on Invisible Exports, 1965–67; Lord Kitchener Nat. Meml Fund. Pres., RSAA, 1984–. Chm., Arab British Chamber Charitable Foundn. Chm., Governors of Windlesham House Sch. *Heir: s* Hon. Richard Thomas Stewart Denman, *b* 4 Oct. 1946. *Address:* House of Lords, SW1. *Club:* Brooks's.

DENMAN, Prof. Donald Robert; Professor of Land Economy, 1968–78 and Head of Department of Land Economy, 1962–78, Cambridge University; Fellow of Pembroke College, Cambridge, 1962–78, now Emeritus; *b* 7 April 1911; 2nd *s* of Robert Martyn Denman and Letitia Kate Denman, Finchley; *m* 1941, Jessica Hope, 2nd *d* of Richard H. Prior, Chichester; two *s*. *Educ:* Christ's Coll., Finchley. BSc 1938; MSc 1940; PhD 1945; MA 1948; Hon. DSc 1979; FRICS 1949; Dep. Exec. Off., Cumberland War Agricultural Exec. Cttee, 1939–46; University Lectr, Cambridge Univ., 1948–68. Land Management Cttee of Agricultural Improvement Coun., 1953–60; Member: Church Assembly, 1957–69; Standing Cttee of Istituto de Diritto Agrario Internazionale e Comparato, Florence, 1960–; Nat. Commn of Unesco, 1972–74; Advisor to Min. of Co-operation and Rural Affairs, Iran; Consultant, Internat. Union for Conservation of Nature and Nat. Resources, 1972. Mem. Council, University Coll. at Buckingham, 1973–81. Chm., Commonwealth Human Ecology Council (Mem., 1971–); Mem., Land Decade Educnl Council, 1981–. Patron, Small Farmers' Assoc. Hon. Fellow, Ghana Instn of Surveyors, 1970; Fellow, Royal Swedish Acad. of Forestry and Agriculture, 1971. Gold Medal, RICS, 1972. Distinguished Order of Homayoun of the Imperial Court of Persia, 1974. *Publications:* Tenant Right Valuation: In History and Modern Practice, 1942; Tenant Right Valuation and Current Legislation, 1948; Estate Capital: The Contribution of Landownership to Agricultural Finance, 1957; Origins of Ownership: A Brief History of Landownership and Tenure, 1958; Bibliography of Rural Land Economy and Landownership 1900–1957 (*et al*), 1958; Farm Rents: A Comparison of Current and Past Farm Rents in England and Wales, 1959; (ed and contrib.) Landownership and Resources, 1960; (ed and contrib.) Contemporary Problems of Landownership, 1963; Land in the Market, 1964; (jtly) Commons and Village Greens: A Study in Land Use, Conservation and Management, 1967; (ed and contrib.) Land and People, 1967; Rural Land Systems, 1968; Land Use and the Constitution of Property, 1969; Land Use: An Introduction to Proprietary Land Use Analysis, 1971; Human Environment: the surveyor's response, 1972; The King's Vista (Persian Land reform), 1973; Prospects of Co-operative Planning (Warburton Lecture), 1973; Land Economy: an education and a career (British Assoc. lecture), 1975; The Place of Property, 1978; Land in a Free Society, 1980; The Fountain Principle, 1982; Markets under the Sea?, 1983; numerous monographs, articles and papers in academic and professional jls and nat. press in Britain and abroad. *Recreation:* travel. *Address:* Pembroke College, Cambridge; 12 Chaucer Road, Cambridge. *T:* Cambridge 357725. *Clubs:* Carlton, Farmers'.

DENMAN, Sir George Roy; *see* Denman, Sir Roy.

DENMAN, Sir Roy, KCB 1977 (CB 1972); CMG 1968; Head, Commission of European Communities Delegation in Washington, DC, since 1982; *b* 12 June 1924; *s* of Albert Edward and Gertrude Ann Denman; *m* 1966, Moya Lade; one *s* one *d*. *Educ:* Harrow Gram. Sch.; St John's Coll., Cambridge. War Service 1943–46; Major, Royal Signals. Joined BoT, 1948; Asst Private Sec. to successive Presidents, 1950–52; 1st Sec., British Embassy, Bonn, 1957–60; UK Delegn, Geneva, 1960–61; Counsellor, Geneva, 1965–67; Under-Sec., 1967–70, BoT; Deputy Secretary: DTI, 1970–74; Dept of Trade, 1974–75; Second Permanent Sec., Cabinet Office, 1975–77; Dir-Gen. for External Affairs, EEC Commn, 1977–82. Mem. negotiating delegn with European Communities, 1970–72. Mem., British Overseas Trade Bd, 1972–75. *Address:* 2100 M Street, NW (Suite 707), Washington, DC 20037, USA. *Club:* United Oxford & Cambridge University.

DENMAN, Sylvia Elaine; Pro Assistant Director, Polytechnic of the South Bank, since 1986; *b* Barbados, 16 Sept. 1939; *d* of Alexander Yarde and late Euleen Yarde (*née* Alleyne), Barbados; *m* Hugh Frederick Denman (marr. diss.); one *d*. *Educ:* Queen's College, Barbados; LSE (LLM); called to the Bar, Lincoln's Inn, 1962. Lectr then Sen. Lectr, Oxford Polytechnic, 1965–76; Sen. Lectr and Tutor, Norman Manley Law Sch., Univ. of West Indies, Jamaica, 1977–82; Fulbright Fellow, New York Univ. Sch. of Law, 1982–83; Prin. Equal Opportunities Officer, ILEA, 1983–86. Member: Oxford Cttee for Racial Integration, 1965–76; Oxford, Bucks and Berks Conciliation Cttee, Race Relations Bd, 1965–70; London Rent Assessment Panel, 1968–76 and 1984–; Race Relations Bd, 1970–76; Equal Opportunities Commission, 1975–76; Lord Chancellor's Adv. Cttee on Legal Aid, 1975–76; Trustee, Runnymede Trust, 1985–. *Recreations:* music, theatre, wandering about in the Caribbean. *Address:* 11 Mornington Crescent, NW1 7RH. *T:* 01-387 3537.

DENNELL, Prof. Ralph; Emeritus Professor of Zoology, University of Manchester, 1975; Beyer Professor of Zoology, 1963–74; *b* 29 Sept. 1907; *m* 1932, Dorothy Ethel Howard; no *c*. *Educ:* Leeds Grammar Sch.; University of Leeds. Demonstrator in Zoology, University of Leeds, 1929; Grisedale Research Student, University of Manchester, 1932; Asst Lecturer in Zoology, University of Manchester, 1935; Asst Lecturer in Zoology, and Lecturer in Zoology, Imperial Coll., 1937–46; Reader in Experimental Zoology, 1946–48, Prof. of Experimental Zoology, 1948–63, University of Manchester. *Publications:* papers on crustacea, insect physiology, and arthropod integuments, in various zoological periodicals.

DENNING, Baron (Life Peer) *cr* 1957, of Whitchurch; **Alfred Thompson Denning,** PC 1948; Kt 1944; DL; Master of the Rolls, 1962–82; Hon. Fellow: Magdalen College, Oxford, 1948; Nuffield College, Oxford, 1982; Hon. LLD: Ottawa, 1955; Glasgow, 1959; Southampton, 1959; London, 1960; Cambridge, 1963; Leeds, 1964; McGill, 1967; Dallas, 1969; Dalhousie, 1970; Wales, 1973; Exeter, 1976; Columbia, 1976; Tilburg

(Netherlands), 1977; W Ontario, 1979; British Columbia, 1979; Sussex, 1980; Buckingham, 1983; Nottingham, 1984; Hon. DCL Oxford, 1965; *b* 23 Jan. 1899; *s* of Charles and Clara Denning; *m* 1st, 1932, Mary Harvey (*d* 1941); one *s*; 2nd, 1945, Joan, *d* of J. V. Elliott Taylor, and *widow* of J. M. B. Stuart, CIE. *Educ:* Andover Grammar Sch.; Magdalen Coll., Oxford (Demy). 1st Class Mathematical Moderations; 1st Class Mathematical Final School; 1st Class Final Sch. of Jurisprudence; Eldon Scholar, 1921; Prize Student Inns of Court; called to the Bar, 1923; KC 1938; Judge of the High Court of Justice, 1944; a Lord Justice of Appeal, 1948–57; a Lord of Appeal in Ordinary, 1957–62. Chancellor of Diocese of London, 1942–44; and of Southwark, 1937–44; Recorder of Plymouth, 1944; Bencher of Lincoln's Inn, 1944; Nominated Judge for War Pensions Appeals, 1945–48; Chm. Cttee on Procedure in Matrimonial Causes, 1946–47; Chm., Royal Commission on Historical MSS, 1962–82. Held enquiry into circumstances of resignation of Mr J. D. Profumo, Sec. of State for War, 1963. Chairman: Cttee on Legal Education for Students from Africa, 1960; British Institute of International and Comparative Law, 1959–86. Pres., Birkbeck Coll., 1952–83; Treas., Lincoln's Inn, 1964. Hon. Bencher: Middle Temple, 1972; Gray's Inn, 1979; Inner Temple, 1982. Dimbleby Lectr, BBC TV, 1980. Hon. FBA 1979. Served in RE 1917–19 (BEF France). DL Hants, 1978. *Publications:* Joint Editor of Smith's Leading Cases, 1929; of Bullen and Leake's Precedents, 1935; Freedom under the Law, (Hamlyn Lectures), 1949; The Changing Law, 1953; The Road to Justice, 1955; The Discipline of Law, 1979; The Due Process of Law, 1980; The Family Story, 1981; What Next in the Law, 1982; The Closing Chapter, 1983; Landmarks in the Law, 1984; Leaves from my Library, 1986. *Address:* The Lawn, Whitchurch, Hants RG28 7AS. *T:* 2144. *Club:* Athenæum.

See also Lieut-Gen. Sir R. F. S. Denning.

DENNING, Lt-Gen. Sir Reginald (Francis Stewart), KCVO 1975; KBE 1946; CB 1944; Chairman, SSAFA, 1953–74; Vice-President, Liverpool School of Tropical Medicine, 1967–77; *b* 12 June 1894; 2nd *s* of Charles and Clara Denning, Whitchurch, Hants; *m* 1927, Eileen Violet (OBE 1969), *d* of late H. W. Currie, 12 Hyde Park Place, W2; two *s* one *d*. *Educ:* privately. 2nd Lieut Bedfordshire Regt, 1915; European War, 1914–18 (severely wounded, despatches). Adjutant, 1st Bedfs and Herts Regt, 1922–25; Adjutant, 2 Bedfs and Herts Regt, 1926–29; Student Staff Coll., Camberley, 1929–30; Bt Major, 1934; Bt Lt-Col, 1939; Brig., 1941; Subst. Col, 1942; Acting Maj.-Gen., 1943; Maj.-Gen., 1944; Lieut-Gen., 1949; Maj.-Gen. i/c Administration South-Eastern Command, 1943–44; Principal Administrative Officer to the Supreme Allied Commander, South-East Asia, 1944–46; Chief of Staff, Eastern Command, 1947–49; GOC Northern Ireland, 1949–52; retired pay, 1952. Col, Bedfs and Herts Regt, 1948 3rd East Anglian Regt (16th/44th Foot), 1958, Royal Anglian Regt, 1964–66 (formed Regt, 1964). DL, County of Essex, 1959–68. CStJ 1946; Commander Legion of Merit (USA), 1946. *Recreations:* hunting, polo, riding. *Address:* Delmonden Grange, Hawkhurst, Kent. *T:* 2286. *Clubs:* Army and Navy, MCC.

See also Baron Denning.

DENNINGTON, Dudley, FEng; FICE; FIStructE; FHKIE; Partner, Bullen & Partners, since 1972; *b* 21 April 1927; *s* of John Dennington and Beryl Dennington (*née* Hagon); *m* 1951, Margaret Patricia Stewart; two *d*. *Educ:* Clifton Coll., Bristol; Imperial Coll., London Univ. (BSc). National Service, 2nd Lieut, RE, 1947–49; Sandford Fawcett and Partners, Consulting Engineers, 1949–51; D. & C. Wm Press, Contractors, 1951–52; AMICE 1953; Manager, Design Office, George Wimpey & Co., 1952–65; GLC 1965–72: Asst Chief Engineer, Construction, 1965–67; Chief Engineer, Construction, 1967–70; Traffic Comr and Dir of Development, 1970–72. Mem., Bd for Engineers' Registration, Engrg Council, 1983–. Vis. Prof., King's Coll., London Univ., 1978–. FICE 1966 (Mem. Council, 1975–78 and 1981–); FHKIE 1982; FCGI 1984; FEng 1985. *Recreations:* mathematics, painting. *Address:* 25 Corkran Road, Surbiton, Surrey. *T:* 01–399 2977. *Club:* Reform.

DENNIS, Maj.-Gen. Alastair Wesley, CB 1985; OBE 1973; Secretary, Imperial Cancer Research Fund, since 1985; *b* 30 Aug. 1931; *s* of Ralph Dennis and Helen (*née* Henderson); *m* 1957, Susan Lindy Elgar; one *s* two *d*. *Educ:* Malvern Coll.; RMA, Sandhurst. Commanded 16th/5th The Queen's Royal Lancers, 1971–74; Col GS, Cabinet Office, 1974–75; Comd 20 Armoured Bde, 1976–77; Dep. Comdt, Staff Coll., 1978–80; Director of Defence Policy (B), MoD, Whitehall, 1980–82; Dir, Military Assistance Overseas, MoD, 1982–85. *Recreations:* fishing, golf, gardening. *Address:* c/o Barclays Bank, 2 Market Place, Wallingford, Oxon.

DENNIS, Rt. Rev. John; *see* St Edmundsbury and Ipswich, Bishop of.

DENNIS, Maxwell Lewis, CMG 1971; Chairman, South Australia Totalizator Agency Board, 1973–79; *b* 19 April 1909; *s* of Frank Leonard and Ethel Jane Dennis; *m* 1935, Bernice Abell; one *d* (one *s* decd). *Educ:* Gladstone High Sch., South Australia. FASA. Entered South Australian Public Service, 1924, Public Service Commissioner, 1965; Chm., Public Service Bd, 1968–73; Life Governor, Royal Soc. for the Blind. *Address:* PO Box 79, Glenelg, SA 5045, Australia.

DENNIS, Nigel Forbes; writer; *b* 1912; *s* of Lieut-Col M. F. B. Dennis, DSO, and Louise (*née* Bosanquet); *m* 1st, Mary-Madeleine Massias; 2nd, Beatrice Ann Hewart Matthew; two *d*. *Educ:* Plumtree Sch., S Rhodesia; Odenwaldschule, Germany. Secretary, Nat. Bd of Review of Motion Pictures, NY, 1935–36; Asst Editor and Book Reviewer, The New Republic, NY, 1937–38; Staff Book Reviewer, Time, NY, 1940–58; Dramatic Critic, Encounter, 1960–63; Staff Book Reviewer, Sunday Telegraph, 1961–82; Joint Editor, Encounter, 1967–70. FRSL 1966. *Publications:* Boys and Girls Come out to Play, 1949; Cards of Identity, 1955; Two Plays and a Preface, 1958; Dramatic Essays, 1962; Jonathan Swift, 1964 (RSL Award, 1966); A House in Order, 1966; Exotics (poems), 1970; An Essay on Malta, 1971. *Plays:* Cards of Identity, Royal Court, 1956; The Making of Moo, Royal Court, 1957; August for the People, Royal Court and Edinburgh Festival, 1962; Swansong for Seven Voices (BBC Radio Play), 1985. *Recreation:* gardening. *Address:* c/o A. M. Heath & Co., 40 William IV Street, WC2.

DENNISON, Mervyn William, CBE 1967; MC 1944; DL; *b* 13 July 1914; *er s* of Reverend W. Telford Dennison and Hester Mary (*née* Coulter); *m* 1944, Helen Maud, *d* of Claud George Spiller, Earley, Berks; one *s* one *d*. *Educ:* Methodist Coll., Belfast; Queen's Univ., Belfast (BA); Middle Temple. Called to Bar of Northern Ireland, 1945; Middle Temple, 1964. Served War of 1939–45, with Royal Ulster Rifles and Parachute Regt (POW Arnhem, 1944). Crown Counsel, N Rhodesia, 1947; Legal Draftsman, 1952; Senior Crown Counsel and Parliamentary Draftsman, Federal Govt of Rhodesia and Nyasaland, 1953; Federal Solicitor-Gen., 1959; QC (N Rhodesia) 1960; also Chm. Road Service Bd, N Rhodesia, and Mem. Central African Air Authority. High Court Judge, Zambia, 1961–67. Secretary, Fermanagh CC, NI, 1967–73; Chief Comr, Planning Appeals Commn and Water Appeals Commn, 1973–80; Chm., Industrial Tribunals in N Ireland, 1981–84. Mem. Senate, Queen's Univ., Belfast 1979–. Hon. Col, The Zambia Regt, 1964–66. JP Co. Fermanagh, 1969–73, DL, 1972–. KStJ 1978 (CStJ 1964). *Recreations:* fishing, sailing. *Address:* Creevyloughgare, Saintfield, Ballynahinch, Co. Down BT24 7NB. *T:* Saintfield 510397. *Club:* Harare (Zimbabwe).

DENNISON, Stanley Raymond, CBE 1946; Vice-Chancellor, 1972–79, and Honorary Professor, 1974–79, University of Hull, now Emeritus Professor; Vice-Chairman, Committee of Vice-Chancellors and Principals of the United Kingdom, 1977–79; *b* 15 June 1912; *o s* of late Stanley Dennison and Florence Ann Dennison, North Shields; unmarried. *Educ:* University of Durham; Trinity College, Cambridge. Lecturer in Economics, Manchester University, 1935–39; Professor of Economics, University Coll. of Swansea, 1939–45; Lecturer in Economics, Cambridge Univ., 1945–58; Fellow of Gonville and Caius Coll., 1945–58; Prof. of Economics, Queen's Univ. of Belfast, 1958–61; David Dale Prof. of Economics, Univ. of Newcastle upon Tyne, 1962–72; Pro-Vice-Chancellor, 1966–72. Chief Economic Asst, War Cabinet Secretariat, 1940–46. Member: University Grants Cttee, 1964–68; North Eastern Electricity Board, 1965–72; Review Body on Remuneration of Doctors and Dentists, 1962–70; Verdon Smith Cttee on Marketing and Distribution of Fatstock and Carcase Meat, 1964; Scott Cttee on Land Utilisation in Rural Areas, 1942 (Minority Report); Beaver Cttee on Air Pollution, 1954; Waverley Cttee on Med. Services for the Armed Forces, 1955. Chm. Governors, Royal Grammar Sch., Newcastle upon Tyne, 1969–. Hon. LLD Hull, 1980. *Publications:* The Location of Industry and the Depressed Areas, 1939; (with Sir Dennis Robertson) The Control of Industry, 1960; Choice in Education, 1984; various articles, etc, on economic questions. *Recreation:* music. *Address:* 22 Percy Gardens, Tynemouth, Tyne and Wear NE30 4HQ. *Clubs:* Reform; Northern Counties (Newcastle upon Tyne).

DENNISS, Gordon Kenneth, CBE 1979; Consultant Chartered Surveyor, Eastman & Denniss, Surveyors, since 1983 (formerly Senior Partner); *b* 29 April 1915; *e s* of late Harold W. Denniss; *m* 1939, Violet Fiedler, Montreal; one *s* two *d*. *Educ:* Dulwich Coll.; Coll. of Estate Management. FRICS. Articled to uncle, Hugh F. Thoburn, Chartered Surveyor, Kent, developing building estates, 1935, professional asst 1938; Eastman & Denniss: Junior Partner, 1943; sole principal, 1945. Crown Estate Comr, 1965–71. Farming 2000 acres in E Sussex and Kent. *Recreations:* farming, cricket, fox-hunting, political economy, golf. *Address:* 6 Belgrave Place, Belgravia, SW1. *T:* 01–235 4858; Lodgefield Farm, Blackham, East Sussex. *T:* Fordcombe 276. *Clubs:* Savile, Farmers', MCC; Surrey County Cricket.

DENNISTON, Rev. Robin Alastair; Oxford Publisher and Senior Deputy Secretary to the Delegates, Oxford University Press, since 1984 (Academic and General Publisher, 1980–84); *b* 25 Dec. 1926; *s* of late Alexander Guthrie Denniston, CMG, CBE, head of Govt code and cipher school, and late Dorothy Mary Gilliat; *m* 1950, Anne Alice Kyffin Evans (*d* 1985), *y d* of late Dr Geoffrey Evans, MD, FRCP, consulting Physician at St Bartholomew's Hosp., and late Hon. E. M. K. Evans; one *s* two *d*. *Educ:* Westminster Sch. (King's Schol.; Captain of School, 1945); Christ Church, Oxford (Classical Schol.; 2nd cl. Hons Lit. Hum.). National Service: commnd into Airborne Artillery, 1948. Editor at Collins, 1950–59; Man. Dir, Faith Press, 1959–60; Editor, Prism, 1959–61; Promotion Man., Hodder & Stoughton Ltd, 1960–64, Editorial Dir, 1966, Man. Dir, 1968–72; Dir, Mathew Hodder Ltd (and subsid. cos), 1968–72; Dep. Chm., George Weidenfeld & Nicolson (and subsid. cos), 1973–75; Non-exec. Chm., A. R. Mowbray & Co., 1974–; Dir, Thomson Publications Ltd, 1975–77; also Chm. of Michael Joseph Ltd, Thomas Nelson & Sons (and subsid. cos), George Rainbird Ltd, 1975–77 and Sphere Books, 1975–76; Academic Publisher, OUP, 1978. Student of Christ Church, 1978–. Ordained Deacon, 1978, Priest, 1979; Hon. Curate: Clifton-on-Teme, 1978; New with South Hinksey, 1985. *Publications:* The Young Musicians, 1956; Partly Living, 1967; (ed) Part Time Priests?, 1960. *Recreations:* farming, music, squash. *Address:* The Hope Farm, Clifton-on-Teme, Worcester WR6 6HE. *T:* Upper Sapey 248; 18 Dale Close, Oxford OX1 1TU. *T:* Oxford 44192. *Club:* United Oxford & Cambridge University.

DENNY, Sir Alistair (Maurice Archibald), 3rd Bt, *cr* 1913; *b* 11 Sept. 1922; *er s* of Sir Maurice Edward Denny, 2nd Bt, KBE and Lady Denny (*d* 1982), Gateside House, Drymen, Stirlingshire; *S* father 1955; *m* 1949, Elizabeth *y d* of Sir Guy Lloyd, Bt, *qv*; two *s* (and one *s* decd). *Educ:* Marlborough. Started engineering training with William Denny & Bros. Served War in Fleet Air Arm, 1944–46. Continued engineering training with Alexander Stephen & Sons, Glasgow, and Sulzer Bros., Winterthur, Switzerland; returned to William Denny & Bros, 1948; left, Sept. 1963, when firm went into liquidation. Chm., St Andrews Links Management Cttee, 1980–81. Council Mem., St Leonard's Sch., St Andrews, 1982–. *Recreations:* golf, ski-ing, gardening, photography. *Heir:* *s* Charles Alistair Maurice Denny [*b* 7 Oct. 1950; *m* 1981, Belinda, *yr d* of J. P. McDonald, Walkinstown, Dublin; one *s*]. *Address:* Crombie Cottage, Abercrombie, by St Monans, Fife. *T:* St Monans 631. *Club:* Royal and Ancient Golf (St Andrews).

DENNY, Sir Anthony Coningham de Waltham, 8th Bt, *cr* 1782, of Tralee Castle, Co. Kerry, Ireland; designer; Partner in Verity and Beverley, Architects and Designers (offices in London, Tetbury and Lisbon), since 1959; *b* 22 April 1925; *s* of Rev. Sir Henry Lyttleton Lyster Denny, 7th Bt, and Joan Lucy Dorothy, *er d* of Major William A. C. Denny, OBE; *S* father 1953; *m* 1949, Anne Catherine, *e d* of S. Beverley, FRIBA; two *s* one adopted *d*. *Educ:* Clayesmore Sch. Served War of 1939–45: Middle East, RAF (Aircrew), 1943–47. Anglo-French Art Centre, 1947–50; Mural Painter and Theatrical Designer, 1950–54. Trustee, Waltham Abbey. Hereditary Freeman of City of Cork. FRSA; MSIAD. *Recreations:* architecture and painting. *Heir:* *s* Piers Anthony de Waltham Denny, *b* 14 March 1954. *Address:* Daneway House, Sapperton, Cirencester, Glos. *T:* Frampton Mansell 232.

See also B. L. Denny.

DENNY, Barry Lyttelton, LVO 1979; HM Diplomatic Service; Counsellor, Foreign and Commonwealth Office, seconded to Ministry of Defence, since 1984; *b* 6 June 1928; *s* of Rev. Sir Henry Lyttelton Lyster Denny, 7th Bt, and Joan Lucy Dorothy, *er d* of Major William A. C. Denny, OBE; *m* 1st, 1951 (marr. diss. 1968); one *s* one *d*; 2nd, 1969, Anne Rosemary Jordon, *o d* of Col James F. White, MC; one *d*. *Educ:* Clayesmore Sch.; RMA, Sandhurst. Indian Army Cadet, 1946–47; commnd RA, 1949; retd from HM Forces as Captain (Temp. Major), 1960. Joined Foreign Office, 1962; First Sec., Nicosia, 1964; FO, later FCO, 1966; Kaduna, 1969; FCO, 1972; Vientiane, 1973; FCO, 1975; Kuwait, 1977; Counsellor, Oslo, 1980. Comdr, Order of St Olav (Norway), 1981. *Recreations:* polo, collecting, photography. *Address:* c/o Foreign and Commonwealth Office, SW1A 2AH. *Club:* Army and Navy.

See also Sir A. C. de W. Denny.

DENNY, Margaret Bertha Alice, (Mrs E. L. Denny), OBE 1946; DL; Under Secretary, Ministry of Transport and Civil Aviation, 1957–58; *b* 30 Sept. 1907; *o d* of late Edward Albert Churchard and late Margaret Catherine (*née* Arnold) and step-*d* of late William Ray Lenanton, JP; *m* 1957, Edward Leslie Denny, JP, formerly Chm., William Denny Bros, Shipbuilders, Dumbarton. *Educ:* Dover County Sch.; Bedford Coll. for Women, London Univ. (BA Hons PhD). Entered Civil Service as Principal Ministry of Shipping, 1940; Asst Sec., 1946. Gov., Bedford Coll., University of London. Member: Scottish Adv. Coun. for Civil Aviation, 1958–67; Western Regional Hospital Board, Scotland, 1960–74; Scottish Cttee, Council of Industrial Design, 1961–71; Gen. Advisory Council, BBC, 1962–66; Gen. Nursing Council, Scotland, 1962–78; Board of Management, State Hosp., Carstairs, 1966–76; Exec. Cttee, Nat. Trust for Scotland, 1974– (Mem. Council, 1973–;

Vice-Pres, 1981–); Vice-Chm., Argyll and Clyde Health Bd, 1974–77. County Comr, Girl Guides, Dunbartonshire, 1958–68. DL Dunbartonshire, 1973. Officer, Order of Orange Nassau, 1947. *Address:* Gartochraggan Cottage, Gartocharn, by Alexandria, Dunbartonshire. *T:* Gartocharn 272.

DENNY, Rev. Norwyn Ephraim; Superintendent, Lowestoft and East Suffolk Methodist Church, since 1986; President of the Methodist Conference, 1982–83; *b* 23 Oct. 1924; *s* of Percy Edward James Denny and Dorothy Ann Denny (*née* Stringer); *m* 1950, Ellen Amelia Shaw; three *d*. *Educ.* City of Norwich School; Wesley College, Bristol. BD (Hons), London Univ. Ordained Methodist Minister, 1951; Methodist Minister in Jamaica, 1950–54; Minister in Peterborough, 1955–61; Member of Notting Hill Group (Ecumenical) Ministry, 1961–75; Chm., Liverpool Dist Methodist Church, 1975–86. *Publications:* (with D. Mason and G. Ainger) News from Notting Hill, 1967; Caring, 1976. *Recreations:* gardening, astronomy, association football. *Address:* 8 Corton Road, Lowestoft, Suffolk NR32 4PL. *T:* Lowestoft 3048.

DENNY, William Eric, CBE 1984; QC 1975; a Recorder of the Crown Court, since 1974; *b* 2 Nov. 1927; *s* of William John Denny and Elsie Denny; *m* 1960, Daphne Rose Southern-Reddin; one *s* two *d*. *Educ:* Ormskirk Grammar Sch.; Liverpool Univ. (Pres., Guild of Undergraduates, 1952–53; LLB). Called to the Bar, Gray's Inn, 1953, Bencher, 1985. Lectured at LSE, 1953–58. Chm., Home Secretary's Adv. Bd on Restricted Patients, 1980–85 (Mem., 1979). *Recreations:* music, sailing, gardening. *Address:* 1 Hare Court, Temple, EC4Y 7BE.

DENNYS, Cyril George, CB 1949; MC 1918; retired as Under-Secretary; *b* 25 March 1897; *s* of Lieut-Col A. H. Dennys, IA, and Lena Mary Isabel (*née* Harrison); *m* 1920, Sylvia Maitland (*née* Waterlow) (*d* 1980); two *d* (and one *d* decd). *Educ:* Malvern Coll.; Trinity Coll., Oxford. Served European War, 1914–18, as Lieut, RGA, 1917–18. Entered Ministry of Labour as Asst Principal, 1919; Principal Private Sec. to Minister of Labour, 1938; Asst Sec., 1938; Principal Asst Sec., Ministry of Supply, 1942–45; Under-Secretary: Ministry of Labour, 1946; Ministry of National Insurance, 1946; Ministry of Pensions and National Insurance, 1953; retired 1962. *Address:* 38 Belsize Grove, Hampstead, NW3. *T:* 01–722 3964. *Club:* United Oxford & Cambridge University.

DENNYS, Rodney Onslow, CVO 1982 (MVO 1969); OBE 1943; FSA, FSG; FRSA; Arundel Herald of Arms Extraordinary, since 1982 (Somerset Herald of Arms, 1967–82); *b* 16 July 1911; *s* of late Frederick Onslow Brooke Dennys, late Malayan Civil Service, and Claire (*née* de Paula); *m* 1944, Elisabeth Katharine (served FO 1938–41; GHQ MEF, 1941–44, awarded certificate for outstandingly good service by C-in-C MEF; Allied Forces HQ N Africa, Algiers, 1944, FO 1944–45), *d* of late Charles Henry Greene; one *s* two *d*. *Educ:* Canford Sch.; LSE. Apptd to FO, 1937; HM Legation, The Hague, 1937–40; FO, 1940–41. Commissioned in Intell. Corps, 1941; Lt-Col 1944; RARO, 1946. Reapptd, FO, 1947; 1st Sec. British Middle East Office, Egypt, 1948–50; 1st Sec. HM Embassy: Turkey, 1950–53; Paris, 1955–57; resigned, 1957. Asst to Garter King of Arms, 1958–61; Rouge Croix Pursuivant of Arms, 1961–67. Served on Earl Marshal's Staff for State Funeral of Sir Winston Churchill, 1965, and for the Prince of Wales' Investiture, 1969. Dep. Dir, Heralds' Museum, 1978–83, Dir, 1983–. Advised Queensland Govt on design of first Mace of Qld Leg. Assembly, and in attendance, in Tabard, on Governor of Qld for inauguration of Mace in Qld Parlt, 1978. Mem. Court, Sussex Univ., 1972–77. CPRE, 1972–: Mem., Nat. Exec., 1973–78; Chm., 1972–77, Vice-Pres., 1977, Sussex Br. Dir, Arundel Castle Trustees Ltd; Member: Exec. Cttee, Sussex Historic Churches Trust; Council Harleian Soc. (Chm. 1977–84); Devon Assoc.; Académicien, Académie Internationale d'Héraldique; Mem. Council, Shrievalty Assoc., 1984–. Fellow, Soc. of Genealogists; FRSA. Freeman of City of London; Liveryman and Freeman of Scriveners Co. High Sheriff E Sussex, 1983–84. *Publications:* Flags and Emblems of the World; (jt) Royal and Princely Heraldry of Wales, 1969; The Heraldic Imagination, 1975; Heraldry and the Heralds, 1982; articles in jls on heraldry and kindred subjects. *Recreations:* heraldry, ornithology. *Address:* College of Arms, EC4V 4BT. *T:* 01–248 1912; Heaslands, Steep, near Crowborough, Sussex. *T:* Crowborough 61328. *Clubs:* Garrick, City Livery; Sussex. *See also Graham Greene, Sir Hugh Greene.*

DENSON, John Boyd, CMG 1972; OBE 1965; HM Diplomatic Service, retired; *b* 13 Aug. 1926; *o s* of late George Denson and of Mrs Alice Denson (*née* Boyd); *m* 1957, Joyce Myra Symondson; no *c*. *Educ:* Perse Sch.; St John's Coll., Cambridge. Royal Regt of Artillery, 1944; Intelligence Corps, 1946; Cambridge, 1947–51 (English and Oriental Langs Triposes). Joined HM Foreign (now Diplomatic) Service, 1951. Served in Hong Kong, Tokyo, Peking, London, Helsinki, Washington, Vientiane; Asst Head of Far Eastern Dept, Foreign Office, 1965–68; Chargé d'Affaires, Peking, 1969–71; Royal Coll. of Defence Studies, 1972; Counsellor and Consul-Gen., Athens, 1973–77; Ambassador to Nepal, 1977–83. Gorkha Dakshina Bahu, 1st cl., 1980. *Recreations:* looking at pictures, the theatre, wine. *Address:* Little Hermitage, Pensile Road, Nailsworth, Glos. *T:* Nailsworth 3829. *Club:* Royal Over-Seas League.

DENT, Harold Collett; *b* 14 Nov. 1894; *s* of Rev. F. G. T. and Susan Dent; *m* 1922, Loveday Winifred Martin; one *s* one *d*. *Educ:* Public elementary schs; Kingswood Sch., Bath; London Univ. (external student). Asst Master in secondary schs, 1911–25 (War Service, 1914–19); Head of Junior Dept, Brighton, Hove and Sussex Grammar Sch., 1925–28; first headmaster, Gateway School, Leicester, 1928–31; freelance journalist, 1931–35; asst ed., Book Dept Odhams Press, 1935–40; Ed., The Times Educational Supplement, 1940–51; Educational Correspondent, The Times, 1952–55; Professor of Education and Dir of the Inst. of Education, University of Sheffield, 1956–60; Senior Research Fellow, Inst. of Education, University of Leeds, 1960–62; Asst Dean, Inst. of Education, University of London, 1962–65; Visiting Prof., University of Dublin, 1966; BA; FRSA; Hon. FCP; Hon. FEIS. *Publications:* A New Order in English Education, 1942; The Education Act 1944, 1944; Education in Transition, 1944; To be a Teacher, 1947; Secondary Education for All, 1949; Secondary Modern Schools, 1958; The Educational System of England and Wales, 1961; Universities in Transition, 1961; British Education, 1962; 1870–1970, Century of Growth in English Education, 1970; The Training of Teachers in England and Wales 1700–1975, 1977; Education in England and Wales, 1977. *Recreation:* reading. *Address:* Riccards Spring, Whatlington, Battle, East Sussex.

DENT, Sir John, Kt 1986; CBE 1976 (OBE 1968); Chairman, Civil Aviation Authority, 1982–86; *b* 5 Oct. 1923; *s* of Harry F. Dent; *m* 1954, Pamela Ann, *d* of Frederick G. Bailey; one *s*. *Educ:* King's Coll., London Univ. BSc(Eng), FEng, FRAeS, FIMechE, FIEE, CBIM. Admty Gunnery Estabs at Teddington and Portland, 1944–45; Chief Engr, Guided Weapons, Short Bros & Harland Ltd, Belfast, 1955–60; Chief Engr, Armaments Div., Armstrong Whitworth Aircraft, Coventry, 1961–63; Dir and Chief Engr, Hawker Siddeley Dynamics Ltd, Coventry, 1963–67; Director: Engrg Gp, Dunlop Ltd, Coventry, 1968–76; Dunlop Holdings Ltd, 1970–82; Industrie Pirelli SpA, 1978–81; Dunlop AG, 1979–82; Pirelli Gen. plc, 1980–; Pirelli Ltd, 1985–; Man. Dir, Dunlop Ltd, 1978–82. President: Coventry and District Engrg Employers' Assoc., 1971 and 1972; Engrg Employers' Fedn, 1974–76 (1st Dep. Pres., 1972–74); Inst. of Travel Managers, 1986–; Chm., Nationalized Industries' Chairman's Group, 1984–85. Member: Engineering Industries Council, 1975–76; Review Bd for Government Contracts, 1976–82; Royal Dockyards Policy Bd, 1976–82; NCB, 1980–82. *Recreations:* gardening, fishing, cabinet-making. *Address:* Helidon Grange, Helidon, near Daventry, Northants NN11 6LG.

DENT, Maj.-Gen. Jonathan Hugh Baillie, CB 1984; OBE 1974; Director General, Fighting Vehicles and Engineer Equipment, Ministry of Defence, 1981–85; *b* 19 July 1930; *s* of Joseph Alan Guthrie Dent and Hilda Ina Dent; *m* 1957, Anne Veronica Inglis; one *s* three *d*. *Educ:* Winchester College. Commissioned, Queen's Bays, 1949; regtl and instructional employment in BAOR, UK, Jordan, Libya, 1949–61; Adjt 1958; Adjt Shropshire Yeomanry, 1959–60; Staff trng, RMCS, 1962–63; Staff Coll. Camberley, 1964; Sqdn Comd, Queen's Dragoon Guards, N Ireland and Borneo, 1965–66; MoD (Operational Requirements), 1967–69; Second in Comd, Queen's Dragoon Guards, 1970; Ministry of Defence: MGO Secretariat, 1971–74; Project Manager Chieftain, 1974–76; RCDS 1977; Defence R&D Attaché, British Embassy, Washington, 1978–80. *Recreations:* fishing, bird watching, walking, shooting, classical music. *Address:* c/o Lloyds Bank, 6 Pall Mall, SW1.

DENT, Major Leonard Maurice Edward, DSO 1914; *b* 18 June 1888; *s* of Edward and Mabel P. Dent; *m* 1920, Hester Anita (*d* 1976), *d* of Col Gerard Clark; one *s* two *d* (and two *d* decd). *Educ:* Eton; Trinity Coll., Cambridge, BA. Served European War, 1914–18 (wounded, despatches 4 times, DSO, Chevalier Légion d'Honneur, 1919); Major R of O, retd. Chm. and Man. Dir, Abco Products Ltd, 1936–75. Chm., Berks CC, 1946–58; High Sheriff of Berks, 1948–49. Member: Council, Queen's Coll., London, 1935–83 (Chm., 1953–80); Court, Grocers' Co., 1935–82 (Master, 1935–36); Berks Br., CPRE (Chm., 1950–64); Court, Univ. of Reading (Treas., 1959–63); King's Coll. Hosp. Bd of Governors, 1950–63; Chairman: Belgrave Hosp. for Children, 1947–63; Exec. Cttee, City and Guilds of London Inst., 1937–70; City and Guilds of London Art Sch. Cttee, 1958–70. *Recreations:* photography, music, art collecting (especially Rowlandsons). *Address:* Hillfields, Burghfield Common, near Reading. *T:* Burghfield Common 2495. *Club:* United Oxford & Cambridge University.

DENT, (Robert) Stanley (Gorrell), RWS 1986 (ARWS 1983); RE 1946 (ARE 1935); ARCA (London) 1933; RWA 1954 (ARWA 1951); Principal, Gloucestershire College of Art and Design, 1950–74, retired; *b* 1 July 1909; *o c* of Robert and Phoebe Dent; *m* Doris, *o c* of Clement and Mabel Wenban; two *s*. *Educ:* The Newport Technical Coll.; The Newport, Mon., Sch. of Art and Crafts; Royal College of Art. Runner up in Prix-de-Rome Scholarship, 1935; awarded the British Institution Scholarship in Engraving for the year 1933; Works shown at the Royal Academy, The Royal Scottish Academy, The Royal West of England Academy and other leading Art Exhibitions in GB and abroad, with paintings and etchings in many permanent and private collections, galleries, universities and schools. Ministry of Education Intermediate Assessor, 1957–60. Panel Mem. (Fine Art), National Council for Diplomas in Art and Design, 1962–65; Chief Examiner A Level Art and Design, 1963–76. *Recreations:* river cruising, travel, painting, music, gardening, spectator sports. *Address:* 5 Timbercombe Mews, Little Herberts Road, Charlton Kings, Cheltenham, Glos GL53 8EL. *T:* Cheltenham 524742.

DENT, Robin John; Managing Director, Baring Brothers & Co. Ltd, since 1967; *b* 25 June 1929; *s* of late Rear-Adm. John Dent, CB, OBE; *m* 1952, Hon. Ann Camilla Denison-Pender, *d* of 2nd Baron Pender, CBE; two *d*. *Educ:* Marlborough. Bank of England, 1949–51; joined M. Samuel & Co. Ltd, 1951: Director, 1963–65; Dir, Hill Samuel & Co. Ltd, 1965–67; Dir (London Board), Commercial Banking Co. of Sydney Ltd, 1964–82. Member, London Adv. Cttee, Hong Kong & Shanghai Banking Corp., 1974–81; Dir, TR City of London Trust PLC, 1977–; Mem., Deposit Protection Bd, 1982–85; Dep. Chm., Export Guarantees Adv. Council, 1983–85; Chm., Executive Cttee, British Bankers' Assoc., 1984–85. Mem. Council, Cancer Research Campaign, 1967–; Treasurer, King Edward's Hosp. Fund for London, 1974–. *Address:* 44 Smith Street, SW3 4EP. *T:* 01–352 1234. *Club:* White's.

DENT, Ronald Henry; Chairman, Cape Industries Ltd, 1962–79; *b* 9 Feb. 1913; *s* of late Henry Francis Dent, MA, and Emma Bradley; *m* 1939, Olive May, *d* of late George Wilby, FCA; one *s* one *d*. *Educ:* Portsmouth Grammar Sch. Chartered accountant, 1936. Served War, 1939–45: UK, France, India; War Office, 1942–45. Joined Cape Industries, 1947; Man. Dir, 1957–71. Cancer Research Campaign: Mem. Council, 1965–, Vice-Chm. 1975–83; Chm., Finance Cttee, 1969–75; Chm., Exec. Cttee, 1975–83. Dep. Chm., Finance Cttee, Union Internationale contre le Cancer, Geneva, 1978–; Dir, Internat. Cancer Foundn, 1978–. British Inst. of Management: Fellow 1965; Mem. Council, 1968–77; Mem., Bd of Fellows, 1971–77; Chm. Finance Cttee, and Vice-Chm. of Inst., 1972–76. Mem. Council, UK S Africa Trade Assoc., 1969–80. FRSA. *Recreations:* golf, gardening. *Address:* Badgers Copse, Birtley Green, Bramley, Surrey. *T:* Guildford 893649. *Club:* St George's Hill Golf.

DENT, Stanley; *see* Dent, R. S. G.

DENT-BROCKLEHURST, Mrs Mary, JP; *b* 6 Feb. 1902; *d* of late Major J. A. Morrison, DSO, and late Hon. Mary Hill-Trevor; *m* 1924, Major John Henry Dent-Brocklehurst, OBE (*d* 1949), Sudeley Castle, Glos; three *d* (one *s* decd). *Educ:* at home. JP and CC, 1949, CA 1958, Glos; High Sheriff, County of Gloucester, 1967. *Recreations:* gardening, beekeeping, travelling, archæology. *Address:* Hawling Manor, Andoversford, Cheltenham, Glos GL54 5TA. *T:* Guiting Power 362.

DENTON, Dame Catherine Margaret Mary; *see* Scott, Dame M.

DENTON, Charles; Director, Central Independent Television, since 1981; Chief Executive, Zenith Productions Ltd, since 1984; *b* 20 Dec. 1937; *s* of Alan Charles Denton and Mary Frances Royle; *m* 1961, Eleanor Mary Player; one *s* two *d*. *Educ:* Reading Sch.; Bristol Univ. BA History (Hons). Deckhand, 1960; advertising trainee, 1961–63; BBC TV, 1963–68; freelance television producer with Granada, ATV and Yorkshire TV, 1969–70; Dir, Tempest Films Ltd, 1969–71; Man. Dir, Black Lion Films, 1979–81; ATV: Head of Documentaries, 1974–77; Controller of Programmes, 1977–81; Dir of Progs, Central Indep. TV, 1981–84; Dir, Central Prodns, 1982–84. *Recreations:* walking, music. *Address:* The Garden House, Norman Court, West Tytherley, Hants.

DENTON, Prof. Eric James, CBE 1974; FRS 1964; ScD; Director, Laboratory of Marine Biological Association, Plymouth, since 1974; Member, Royal Commission on Environmental Pollution, 1973–76; *b* 30 Sept. 1923; *s* of George Denton and Mary Anne (*née* Ogden); *m* 1946, Nancy Emily, *d* of Charles and Emily Jane Wright; two *s* one *d*. *Educ:* Doncaster Grammar Sch.; St John's Coll., Cambridge. Biophysics Research Unit, University Coll., London, 1946–48; Lectr in Physiology, University of Aberdeen, 1948–56; Physiologist, Marine Biological Assoc. Laboratory, Plymouth, 1956–74; Royal Soc. Res. Professor, Univ. of Bristol, 1964–74, Hon. Professor, 1975. Fellow, University Coll., London, 1965. Hon. Sec., Physiological Soc., 1963–69. Hon. DSc: Exeter, 1976; Göteborg, 1978. *Publications:* Scientific papers in Jl of Marine Biological Assoc., etc. *Recreation:* gardening. *Address:* Fairfield House, St Germans, Saltash, Cornwall PL12 5LS.

T: St Germans (Cornwall) 30204; The Laboratory, Citadel Hill, Plymouth PL1 2PB. *T:* Plymouth 21761.

DENTON, John Grant, OBE 1977; General Secretary, Anglican Church of Australia, since 1969 (part time until 1977); *b* 16 July 1929; *s* of Ernest Bengrey Denton and Gladys Leonard Stevenson; *m* 1956, Shirley Joan Wise; two *s* two *d*. *Educ:* Camberwell C of E Grammar School, Melbourne. Personnel and Industrial Relations Dept, Mobil Oil (Aust.), 1950–54; Administrative Sec., Dio. of Central Tanganyika, as CMS missionary, 1954–64; Dir of Information, Dio. of Sydney, 1964–69; Registrar, Dio. of Sydney, 1969–77 (part time). Mem., ACC, 1976–84 (Chm., 1980–84). *Recreation:* boating. *Address:* 8 Grayling Road, West Pymble, NSW 2073, Australia. *T:* 498 5424 area code (02).

DENTON, Dame Margaret; *see* Scott, Dame M.

DENTON-THOMPSON, Aubrey Gordon, OBE 1958; MC 1942; *b* 6 June 1920; *s* of late M. A. B. Denton-Thompson; *m* 1944, Ruth Cecily Isaac (*d* 1959); two *s* (one *d* decd); *m* 1961, Barbara Mary Wells. *Educ:* Malvern Coll. Served in RA 1940–44; seconded to Basutoland Administration, 1944; apptd to HM Colonial Service, 1945; transferred to Tanganyika as Asst District Officer, 1947; seconded to Colonial Office, 1948–50, District Officer; seconded to Secretariat, Dar es Salaam, as Asst Sec., 1950; Colonial Sec., Falkland Islands, 1955–60; Dep. Permanent Sec., Ministry of Agriculture, Tanganyika, 1960–62; retired from Tanganyika Civil Service, 1963. Man. Dir, Tanganyika Sisal Marketing Assoc. Ltd, 1966–68 (Sec. 1963); Sen. Agricl Advr, UNDP, 1968–78, and FAO Country Rep.: Korea, 1970–73, Indonesia, 1973–76, Turkey, 1976–78; Sen. Advr to Director General, FAO, Rome, July-Dec. 1978; retd Jan. 1979. Chm., New Forest Conservative Assoc., 1985– (Dep. Chm., 1983–85). *Address:* Octave Cottage, Ramley Road, Pennington, Lymington, Hants.

DENZA, Mrs Eileen, CMG 1984; Legal Counsellor, Foreign and Commonwealth Office, since 1983; *b* 23 July 1937; *d* of Alexander L. Young and Mrs Young; *m* 1966, John Denza; two *s* one *d*. *Educ:* Aberdeen Univ. (MA); Somerville Coll., Oxford (MA); Harvard Univ. (LLM). Called to the Bar, Lincoln's Inn, 1963. Asst Lectr in Law, Bristol Univ., 1961–63; Asst Legal Adviser, FCO (formerly FO), 1963–74; Legal Counsellor, FCO, 1974–80; Counsellor (Legal Adviser), Office of UK Perm. Rep. to European Communities, 1980–83. *Publications:* Diplomatic Law, 1976; contribs to: 5th edn Satow's Guide to Diplomatic Practice; Essays in Air Law; articles in British Yearbook of Internat. Law, Revue du Marché Commun. *Recreation:* music making. *Address:* c/o Foreign and Commonwealth Office, SW1A 2AH.

de OLLOQUI, Dr José Juan; Eminent Ambassador; Chairman, Euro-Latinamerican Bank, since 1982; Director General, Banca Serfin, Mexico, since 1982; *b* 5 Nov. 1931; *m* 1962, Guillermina de Olloqui; three *s* one *d*. *Educ:* Autonomous Univ. of Mexico (LLB 1956, LLD 1979); Univ. of George Washington, Washington, DC (MEc 1970). Official, Bank of Mexico (with license at present), 1951–; Head of Dept of Banking, Currency and Investment, Min. of Finance, 1958–66; Exec. Dir, Interamerican Develt Bank, 1966–71 and also Dep. Dir General for Credit, Min. of Finance, 1966–70; Rep. of Mexico to Exec. Permanent Council of Interamerican Econ. and Social Commn, 1970–71; Chm., Nat. Securities Commn, 1970; Ambassador of Mexico to USA and concurrently Ambassador to Govt of Barbados, 1971–76; Under Sec. of State for Foreign Affairs, 1976–79; Ambassador to UK, 1979–82 and to Ireland, 1980–82. Mem. Bd of Govs, Central Bank, 1984–. Prof. of History of Economic Thought, Faculty of Law, Nat. Autonomous Univ. of Mexico, 1964 (by open competition), Life Prof., 1966 (Mem. Bd of Trustees, 1983–); Prof. of Internat. Law Research, Sch. of Post-Graduate and PhD Candidates, 1983–; Prof., Nat. Autonomous Univ. of Mexico and Universidad Iberoamericana, on Mexico's Econ. Problems, Econ. Theory and History of Econ. Thought. Mem., Bd of several credit instns and official bodies in Mexico, and has represented Mexico, Interamerican Develt Bank and Permanent Council of the Interamerican Econ. and Social Commn at various internat. confs. Pres. and Founder, Miner's Assoc. of Zacatecas, Zac. and Parral, Chihuahua, Mexico, 1963–71. A Vice-Pres., World Food Council. Member: Mexican Lawyer's Bar; Acad. of Political Sciences; Nat. Coll. of Economists; Mexican Acad. of Internat. Law. Dr *hc* in Human Letters St Mary's Coll. 1975. Holds numerous foreign decorations and awards. *Publications:* Mexico fuera de Mexico; Financiamiento Externo y Desarrollo en América Latina; several books, articles and bibliographical reviews on legal and econ. matters. *Address:* Banca Serfin, Avenida 16 de Septiembre 38, 06069 Mexico, DF, Mexico. *T:* 521 9578 and 518 3284.

de PAULA, (Frederic) Clive, CBE 1970; TD 1950 and Clasp 1951; FCA, JDipMA; Chairman, Wessex Sports (Exeter) Ltd, 1984; *b* 17 Nov. 1916; 2nd *s* of late F. R. M. de Paula, CBE, FCA. *Educ:* Rugby Sch.; Spain and France. 2nd Lieut, TA, 1939; Liaison Officer, Free French Forces in London and French Equatorial Africa, 1940; Specially employed Middle East and E Africa, 1941; SOE Madagascar, 1942; comd special unit with 11th E African Div., Ceylon and Burma, 1943; Finance Div., Control Commn, Germany, 1945; demobilised as Major, 1946; Captain 21st Special Air Service Regt (Artists) TA, 1947–56. Joined Robson, Morrow & Co., management consultants, 1946; Partner, 1951; seconded to DEA then to Min. of Technology as an Industrial Adviser, 1967; Co-ordinator of Industrial Advisers to Govt, 1969; returned as Sen. Partner, Robson, Morrow & Co., 1970–71; Man. Dir, Agricultural Mortgage Corp. Ltd, 1971–81; Dir, 1972–83, Dep. Chm., 1978–80, Chm., 1980–83, Tecalemit plc; Non-Exec. Dir, Green's Economiser Group plc, 1972–83. Member: Inst. of Cost & Works Accountants, 1947–72; Council: British Computer Soc., 1965–68; Management Consultants Assoc., 1970–71; BIM, 1971–76; Mem., EDC for Agriculture, 1972–81. Gen. Comr of Income Tax, Winslow Div., Bucks, 1965–82. Vice Pres., Schoolmistresses and Governesses Benevolent Instn, 1982– (Hon. Treas., 1947–81); Chm., Internat. Wine and Food Soc., 1980–83. *Publications:* Accounts for Management, 1954; (ed) F.R.M. de Paula, The Principles of Auditing, 12th edn 1957 (trans. Sinhalese, 1967), (with F.A. Attwood): 15th edn as Auditing: Principles and Practice, 1976, 16th edn 1982; Management Accounting in Practice, 1959 (trans. Japanese, 1960); (with A. W. Willsmore) The Techniques of Business Control, 1973. *Address:* c/o National Westminster Bank PLC, 5 Market Place, Glastonbury, Somerset BA6 9HB.

de PEYER, David Charles; Secretary General, Cancer Research Campaign, since 1984; *b* 25 April 1934; *s* of late Charles de Peyer, CMG and of Flora (*née* Collins); *m* 1959, Ann Harbord. *Educ:* Rendcomb Coll., Cirencester; Magdalen Coll., Oxford (BA PPE). Asst Principal, Min. of Health, 1960; Sec., Royal Commn on NHS, 1976–79; Under Sec., DHSS, 1979–84. *Address:* Cancer Research Campaign, 2 Carlton House Terrace, SW1.

de PEYER, Gervase; Solo Clarinettist; Conductor; Founder and Conductor, The Melos Sinfonia; Founder Member, The Melos Ensemble of London; Director, London Symphony Wind Ensemble; Associate Conductor, Haydn Orchestra of London; solo clarinettist, Chamber Music Society of Lincoln Center, New York, since 1969; Resident Conductor, Victoria International Festival, BC, Canada: Co-founder and Artistic Director, Innisfree Music Festival, Pa, USA; *b* London, 11 April 1926; *m* 1980, Katia Perret Aubry. *Educ:* King Alfred's, London; Bedales; Royal College of Music. Served HM Forces, 1945 and 1946. Principal Clarinet, London Symphony Orchestra, 1955–72. ARCM; Hon. ARAM. Gold Medallist, Worshipful Co. of Musicians, 1948; Charles Gros Grand Prix du Disque, 1961, 1962; Plaque of Honour for recording, Acad. of Arts and Sciences of America, 1962. Most recorded solo clarinettist in world. *Recreations:* travel, cooking, kite-flying, sport, theatre. *Address:* 16 Langford Place, St John's Wood, NW8. *T:* 01–624 4098; 65 Central Park West, New York, NY 10023, USA. *T:* (212) 877 9789.

de PIRO, Alan C. H., QC 1965; FCIArb 1978; **His Honour Judge de Piro;** a Circuit Judge, since 1983; *e s* of late J. W. de Piro; *m* 1947, Mary Elliot (deceased); two *s*; *m* 1964, Mona Addington; one step *s* one step *d*. *Educ:* Repton; Trinity Hall, Cambridge (Sen. Scholar). MA 1947 (Nat. Sci. and Law). Royal Artillery, 1940–45 (Capt.); West Africa. Called to Bar, Middle Temple, 1947; Inner Temple, 1962; Bencher, Middle Temple, 1971; in practice at the Bar, London and Midlands, 1947–83; Deputy Chairman: Beds QS, 1966–71; Warwicks QS, 1967–71; a Recorder of the Crown Court, 1972–83. Member: Gen. Council of the Bar, 1961–65, 1966–70, 1971–73; Senate of the Inns of Court and the Bar, 1976–81; Council Internat. Bar Assoc., 1967–86 (Chm., Human Rights Cttee, 1979–82); Editorial Advisory Cttee, Law Guardian, 1965–73; Law Panel British Council, 1967–74. Vice-Pres., L'Union Internat. des Avocats, 1968–73, Co-Pres., 1969. Legal Assessor, Disciplinary Cttee, RCVS, 1970–83. *Recreations:* conversation, gardening, inland waterways. *Address:* The Toll House, Bascote Locks, near Leamington, Warwicks CV33 0DT; 23 Birmingham Road, Stoneleigh, Warwicks; 3 Temple Gardens, EC4. *Club:* Hawks (Cambridge).

de POSADAS, Dr Luis María; Ambassador of Uruguay to the Court of St James's, since 1983; *b* 25 June 1927; *s* of Dr Gervasio de Posadas Belgrano and Maria Elena Montero; *m* 1952, Sara Mañe-Garzon; one *s* three *d*. *Educ:* Montevideo Univ., Uruguay. Lawyer. Mem., Chamber of Deputies, 1959–63; Sec., National Govt Council, 1963–65; Ambassador to: Spain, 1965–72; USSR, 1972–76; the Argentine, 1978–80; Dir, Dept of Pol Affairs, Min. of Foreign Affairs, Montevideo, 1981–83. Mem., Admin Tribunal of UN, 1981–. Comdr, Legion of Honour, France, 1964; Grand Cross: Order of the Brilliant Star, China, 1962; Order of St Gregory the Great, The Vatican, 1963; Order of Merit, Malta, 1963; Order of Isabel the Catholic, Spain, 1972; Order of May, Argentina, 1978; Grand Officer: Order of the Southern Cross, Brazil, 1963; Order of Merit, Republic of Italy, 1964. *Publications:* works on internat. law. *Recreations:* literature, golf. *Address:* 1 Campden Hill, W8 7AD. *T:* 01–727 6557.

DERAMORE, 6th Baron *cr* 1885; **Richard Arthur de Yarburgh-Bateson,** Bt 1818; Chartered Architect; *b* 9 April 1911; *s* of 4th Baron Deramore and of Muriel Katherine (*née* Duncombe); *S* brother, 1964; *m* 1948, Janet Mary, *d* of John Ware, MD, Askham-in-Furness, Lancs; one *d*. *Educ:* Harrow; St John's Coll., Cambridge. AA Diploma, 1935; MA Cantab 1936; ARIBA 1936. Served as Navigator, RAFVR, 1940–45: 14 Sqdn, RAF, 1942–44 and 1945. County Architect's Dept, Herts, 1949–52. Member: Council, Queen Mary Sch., Duncombe Park, Helmsley, 1977–85; Management Cttee, Purey Cust Nursing Home, York, 1976–84; Manager, Heslington Sch., York, 1965–. Fellow, Woodard Schs (Northern Div.) Ltd, 1978. *Publications:* freelance articles and short stories. *Recreations:* walking, cycling, motoring, water-colour painting. *Heir:* none. *Address:* Heslington House, Aislaby, Pickering, North Yorks YO18 8PE. *Clubs:* Royal Air Force, Royal Automobile.

DE RAMSEY, 3rd Baron *cr* 1887; **Ailwyn Edward Fellowes,** KBE 1974; TD; DL; Captain RA; Lord Lieutenant of Huntingdon and Peterborough, 1965–68 (of Hunts, 1947–65); *b* 16 March 1910; *s* of late Hon. Coulson Churchill Fellowes and Gwendolen Dorothy, *d* of H. W. Jefferson; *S* grandfather, 1925; *m* 1937, Lilah, *d* of Frank Labouchere, 15 Draycott Avenue, SW; two *s* two *d*. Served War of 1939–45 (prisoner, Far East). Pres. Country Landowners' Assoc., Sept. 1963–65. Awarded KBE 1974 for services to agriculture. DL Hunts and Peterborough, 1973, Cambs 1974. *Heir: s* Hon. John Ailwyn Fellowes [*b* 27 Feb. 1942; *m* 1st, 1973, Phyllida Mary (marr. diss. 1983), *d* of Dr Philip A. Forsyth, Newmarket, Suffolk; one *s*; 2nd, 1984, Alison Mary, *er d* of Archibald Birkmyre, Hebron Cottage, West Ilsley Berks; one *s*]. *Address:* Abbots Ripton Hall, Huntingdon. *T:* Abbots Ripton 234. *Club:* Buck's.

See also Lord Ailwyn, Lord Fairhaven.

DERBY, 18th Earl of *cr* 1485; **Edward John Stanley,** MC 1944; DL; Bt 1627; Baron Stanley 1832; Baron Stanley of Preston, 1886; Major late Grenadier Guards; Constable of Lancaster Castle, since 1972; *b* 21 April 1918; *s* of Lord Stanley, PC, MC (*d* 1938), and Sibyl Louise Beatrix Cadogan (*d* 1969), *e d* of Henry Arthur, late Viscount Chelsea, and Lady Meux; *g s* of 17th Earl of Derby, KG, PC, GCB, GCVO; *S* grandfather, 1948; *m* 1948, Lady Isabel Milles-Lade, *yr d* of late Hon. Henry Milles-Lade, and sister of 4th Earl Sondes. *Educ:* Eton; Oxford Univ. Left Army with rank of Major, 1946. President: Merseyside and District Chamber of Commerce, 1972–; Liverpool Chamber of Commerce, 1948–71; NW Area Conservative Assoc., 1969–72. Pro-Chancellor, Lancaster Univ., 1964–71. Lord Lieut and Custos Rotulorum of Lancaster, 1951–68. Alderman, Lancashire CC, 1968–74. Commanded 5th Bn The King's Regt, TA, 1947–51, Hon. Col, 1951–67; Hon. Captain, Mersey Div. RNR, 1955; Hon. Colonel: 1st Bn The Liverpool Scottish Regt, TA, 1964–67; Lancastrian Volunteers, 1967–75; 5th/8th (V) Bn The King's Regt, 1975–; 4th (V) Bn The Queen's Lancashire Regt, 1975–86; Chm., NW of England and IoM TAVR Assoc., 1979–83. President: Rugby Football League, 1948–; Professional Golfers' Assoc., 1964–. DL Lancs 1946. Hon. LLD: Liverpool, 1949; Lancaster, 1972. Hon. Freeman, City of Manchester, 1961. *Heir: nephew* Edward Richard William Stanley, *b* 10 Oct. 1962. *Address:* Knowsley, Prescot, Merseyside L34 4AF. *T:* 051–489 6147; Stanley House, Newmarket, Suffolk. *T:* Newmarket 663011. *Clubs:* White's; Jockey (Newmarket).

DERBY, Bishop of, since 1969; **Rt. Rev. Cyril William Johnston Bowles;** *b* Scotstoun, Glasgow, 9 May 1916; *s* of William Cullen Allen Bowles, West Ham, and Jeanie Edwards Kilgour, Glasgow; *m* 1965, Florence Joan, *d* of late John Eastaugh, Windlesham. *Educ:* Brentwood Sch.; Emmanuel Coll., Jesus Coll. (Lady Kay Scholar) and Ridley Hall, Cambridge. 2nd cl., Moral Sciences Tripos, Pt. I, 1936; 1st cl., Theological Tripos, Pt. I, and BA, 1938; 2nd cl., Theological Tripos, Pt. II, 1939; MA 1941. Deacon 1939, Priest 1940, Chelmsford; Curate of Barking Parish Church, 1939–41; Chaplain of Ridley Hall, Cambridge, 1942–44; Vice-Principal, 1944–51; Principal, 1951–63; Hon. Canon of Ely Cathedral, 1959–63; Archdeacon of Swindon, 1963–69. Entered House of Lords, 1973. Select Preacher: Cambridge, 1945, 1953, 1958, 1963; Oxford, 1961; Dublin, 1961. Exam. Chaplain to Bishop of Carlisle, 1950–63; to Bishops of Rochester, Ely and Chelmsford, 1951–63; to Bishop of Bradford, 1956–61; to Bishop of Bristol, 1963–69. Hon. Canon, Bristol Cathedral, 1963–69; Surrogate, 1963–69; Commissary to Bishop of the Argentine, 1963–69. Mem., Archbishops' Liturgical Commn, 1955–75. Pres., St John's Coll., Durham, 1970–84; Visitor of Ridley Hall, 1979–. *Publications:* contributor: The Roads Converge, 1963; A Manual for Holy Week, 1967; The Eucharist Today, 1974. *Address:* The Bishop's House, 6 King Street, Duffield, Derby DE6 4EU. *T:* (office) Derby 46744; (home) Derby 840132. *Club:* English-Speaking Union.

DERBY, Provost of; *see* Lewers, Very Rev. B. H.

DERBY, Archdeacon of; *see* Dell, Ven. R. S.

DERBYSHIRE, Sir Andrew George, Kt 1986; FRIBA, FSIAD; Chairman: Robert Matthew, Johnson-Marshall & Partners, London; RMJM London Ltd; *b* 7 Oct. 1923; *s* of late Samuel Reginald Derbyshire and late Helen Louise Puleston Derbyshire (*née* Clarke); *m*, Lily Rhodes (*née* Binns), *widow* of late Norman Rhodes; three *s* one *d*. *Educ:* Chesterfield Grammar Sch.; Queens' Coll., Cambridge; Architectural Assoc. MA (Cantab), AA Dip. (Hons). Admty Signals Estabt and Bldg Research Station, 1943–46. Farmer & Dark, 1951–53 (Marchwood and Belvedere power stations); West Riding County Architect's Dept, 1953–55 (bldgs for educn and social welfare). Asst City Architect, Sheffield, 1955–61; responsible for co-ord. of central area redevelt. Mem. Research Team, RIBA Survey of Architects' Offices, 1960–62. Since 1961, as Mem. RM, J-M & Partners, associated with: develt of Univ. of York, Central Lancs New Town, NE Lancs Impact Study, Univ. of Cambridge, West Cambridge Develt and New Cavendish Laboratory, Preston Market and Guildhall, London Docklands Study, Hillingdon Civic Centre, Cabtrack and Minitram feasibility studies, Suez Master Plan Study; Castle Peak Power Stations, and Harbour Reclamation and Urban Growth Study, Hong Kong. Member: RIBA Council, 1950–72, 1975–81 (Senior Vice-Pres., 1980); NJCC, 1961–65; Bldg Industry Communications Res. Cttee, 1964–66 (Chm. Steering Cttee); DoE Planning and Transport Res. Adv. Council, 1971–76; Standing Commn on Energy and the Environment, 1978–. Pt-time Mem., 1973–84, environmental consultant, 1985–, CEGB; Board Member: Property Services Agency, 1975–79; London Docklands Develt Corp., 1984–. Hoffman Wood Prof. of Architecture, Univ. of Leeds, 1978–80; External Prof., Dept of Civil Engineering, Univ. of Leeds, 1981–85. Hon. DUniv York, 1972. FRSA 1981. *Publications:* (jointly) The Architect and his Office, 1962; broadcasts and contribs on auditorium acoustics, building economics, the planning and construction of univs and new towns, also new forms of public transport. *Recreation:* his family. *Address:* 4 Sunnyfield, Hatfield, Herts AL9 5DX. *T:* Hatfield 65903; 42 Weymouth Street, W1A 2BG. *T:* 01–486 4222.

DERHAM, Sir Peter (John), Kt 1980; Chairman, Advisory Board, Commonwealth Scientific and Industrial Research Organization, since 1981; *b* 21 Aug. 1925; *s* of John and Mary Derham; *m* 1950, Averil C. Wigan; two *s* one *d*. *Educ:* Melbourne Church of England Grammar School; Univ. of Melbourne (BSc 1958); Harvard Univ. (Advanced Management Programme). Served RAAF and RAN, 1944–46. Joined Moulded Products (Australasia) Ltd (later Nylex Corp.), 1943; Dir, 1953–82, Sales Dir, 1960, Gen. Manager, 1967, Man. Dir, 1972–80. Chairman: Internat. Pacific Corp. Ltd, later Rothschild Australia Ltd, 1981–85; Robert Bryce & Co. Ltd, 1983–; Australia New Zealand Foundn, 1978–83; Australian Canned Fruits Corp.; DavyMcKee Pacific Pty Ltd, 1984–; Director: Lucas Industries Aust., 1980–84; AMP Soc. (Vic. Br. Bd); Station 3XY Pty; Radio 3XY Pty; Advance Australia Foundn (Jt Chm., Advance Australia America Cup Challenge 1983 Ltd); Enterprise Australia (Dep. Chm., 1975–78). Chairman: Nat. Training Council, 1971–80; Australian Tourist Commn, 1981–85; Member: Manufg Industries Adv. Council, 1971–74; Victorian Econ. Develt Corp., 1981–82. Federal Pres., Inst. of Directors in Australia, 1980–82 (Chm. Victorian Council, 1975–82); Councillor: Yooralla Soc. of Victoria, 1972–79 (Chm. Workshops Cttee, 1972–81); Aust. Industries Develt Assoc., 1975–80; State Councillor, Industrial Design Council, 1967–73, Federal Councillor, 1970–73; Mem. Council, Inst. of Public Affairs, 1971–80; Life Mem., Plastics Inst. of Australia Inc. (Victorian Pres., 1964–66; Nat. Pres., 1971–72); Mem. Board of Advisors, Inst. of Cultural Affairs, 1971–81. Member: Rotary Club of Melbourne (Mem., Bd of Dirs, 1974–75, 1975–76); Victorian State Cttee, Child Accident Prevention Foundn of Australia; Appeal Cttee, Royal Victorian Eye and Ear Hosp.; Bd of Management, Alfred Hosp. and Caulfield Hosp.; Appeal Chm., Victorian Foundn on Alcoholism and Drug Dependence, 1980–; Mem., Melbourne C of E Grammar Sch. Council, 1974–75, 1977–80; Governor, Ian Clunies Ross Meml Foundn, 1979–; Chairman: Trade & Industry Cttee, Victoria's 150th Anniv. Celebration; Police Toy Fund for Underprivileged Children; Pres., Old Melburnians, 1974–75; Life Governor, Assoc. for the Blind. *Recreations:* golf, sailing, tennis and gardening. *Address:* 7 Scotsburn Grove. Toorak, Victoria 3142, Australia. *T:* (03) 209 7809. *Clubs:* Australian, Melbourne (Melbourne); Royal Melbourne Golf, Flinders Golf, Davey's Bay Yacht (Past Commodore), Royal South Yarra Lawn Tennis, Melbourne Cricket.

DERMOTT, William, CB 1984; Under Secretary, Head of Agricultural Science Service, Agricultural Development and Advisory Service, Ministry of Agriculture, Fisheries and Food, 1976–84, retired; *b* 27 March 1924; *s* of William and Mary Dermott; *m* 1946, Winifred Joan Tinney; one *s* one *d*. *Educ:* Univ. of Durham. BSc, MSc. Agricl Chemist, Univ. of Durham and Wye Coll., Univ. of London, 1943–46; Soil Scientist, Min. of Agriculture, at Wye, Bangor and Wolverhampton, 1947–70; Sen. Sci. Specialist, and Dep. Chief Sci. Specialist, MAFF, 1971–76; Actg Dir Gen., ADAS, 1983–84. Pres., British Soc. of Soil Science, 1981–82. *Publications:* papers on various aspects of agricultural chemistry in scientific journals. *Recreations:* gardening, the countryside. *Address:* 22 Chequers Park, Wye, Ashford, Kent. *T:* Wye 812694.

de ROS, 28th Baron *cr* 1264 (Premier Barony of England); **Peter Trevor Maxwell;** *b* 23 Dec. 1958; *s* of Comdr John David Maxwell, RN, and late Georgiana Angela Maxwell, 27th Baroness de Ros; *S* mother, 1983. *Educ:* Headfort School, Kells, Co. Meath; Stowe School, Bucks; Down High School, Co. Down. Upholstered furniture maker. *Recreations:* gardening, travel and sailing. *Heir: sister* Hon. Diana Elizabeth Maxwell, *b* 6 June 1957. *Address:* Old Court, Strangford, Downpatrick, Co. Down, N Ireland. *T:* Strangford 205.

de ROTHSCHILD; *see* Rothschild.

DERRETT, Prof. (John) Duncan (Martin), MA, PhD, DCL, LLD, DD; Professor of Oriental Laws in the University of London, 1965–82, now Emeritus; *b* 30 Aug. 1922; *s* of John West Derrett and Fay Frances Ethel Kate (*née* Martin); *m* 1950, Margaret Esmé Griffiths; four *s* one *d*. *Educ:* Emanuel Sch., London; Jesus Coll., Oxford; Sch. of Oriental and Afr. Studies, London; Inns of Court School of Law. MA 1947, DCL 1966 (Oxon); PhD 1949, LLD 1971, DD 1983 (London). Called to the Bar, Gray's Inn, 1953. Lectr in Hindu Law, SOAS, 1949; Reader in Oriental Laws, 1956, Prof. of Oriental Laws, 1965, Univ. of London; Tagore Prof. of Law, Univ. of Calcutta, 1953 (lectures delivered, 1955); Vis. Professor: Univ. of Chicago, 1963; Univ. of Michigan, 1970; Wilde Lectr in Natural and Compar. Religion, Univ. of Oxford, 1978–81; Japan Soc. Prom. Sci. Fellow and Vis. Prof., Oriental Inst., Univ. of Tokyo, 1982. Mem., editorial bd, Zeitschrift für vergleichende Rechtswissenschaft, 1954, subseq. of Kannada Studies, Bharata Manisha, Kerala Law Times. Mem. Selection Cttee, Fac. of Law, Univs of Dacca and Rajshahi, 1978–. Mem., Stud. Novi Test. Soc., 1971. Barcelona Prize in Comparative Law, 1954; N. C. Sen-Gupta Gold Medal, Asiatic Soc. (Calcutta), 1977. *Publications:* The Hoysalas, 1957; Hindu Law Past and Present, 1957; Introduction to Modern Hindu Law, 1963; Religion, Law and the State in India, 1968; Critique of Modern Hindu Law, 1970; Law in the New Testament, 1970; Jesus's Audience, 1973; Dharmaśāstra and Juridical Literature, 1973; History of Indian Law (Dharmaśāstra), 1973; Henry Swinburne (?1551–1624) Civil Lawyer of York, 1973; Bhāruci's Commentary on the Manusmrti, 1975; Essays in Classical and Modern Hindu Law, vols I-IV, 1976–79; Studies in the New Testament, vols I-IV, 1977–86; The Death of a Marriage Law, 1978; Beiträge zu Indischem Rechtsdenken, 1979; The Anastasis: the Resurrection of Jesus as an Historical Event, 1982; A Textbook for Novices: Jayarakshita's Perspicuous Commentary on the 'Compendium of Conduct', 1983; The Making of Mark, 1985; New Resolutions of Old Conundrums: a fresh insight into Luke's Gospel, 1986; trans. R. Lingat, Classical Law of India, 1973; ed, Studies in the Laws of Succession in Nigeria, 1965; ed, Introduction to Legal Systems, 1968; ed, (with W. D. O'Flaherty) The Concept of Duty in South Asia, 1978; collab. with Yale Edn, Works of St Thomas More, Société Jean Bodin, Brussels, Max Planck Inst., Hamburg, Fritz Thyssen Stiftung, Cologne, Institut für Soziologie, Heidelberg, and Sekai Kyusei Kyo, Atami; contribs to Indian Bar Review, Kastūri (Hubli). *Festschriften:* Indology and Law, 1982; Novum Testamentum, 24, 1982, fasc. 3 and foll. *Recreations:* listening to music, gardening, clocks. *Address:* Half Way House, High Street, Blockley, Moreton-in-Marsh, Glos GL56 9EX. *T:* Blockley 700828.

DERRICK, Patricia, (Mrs Donald Derrick); *see* Lamburn, P.

DERRY AND RAPHOE, Bishop of, since 1980; **Rt. Rev. James Mehaffey;** *b* 29 March 1931; *s* of John and Sarah Mehaffey; *m* 1956, Thelma P. L. Jackson; two *s* one *d*. *Educ:* Trinity College, Dublin (MA, BD); Queen's University, Belfast (PhD). Curate Assistant: St Patrick's, Belfast, 1954–56; St John's, Deptford, London, 1956–58; Minor Canon, Down Cathedral, 1958–60; Bishop's Curate, St Christopher's, Belfast, 1960–62; Incumbent: Kilkeel, Diocese of Dromore, 1962–66; Cregagh, Diocese of Down, 1966–80. *Address:* The See House, Culmore Road, Londonderry. *T:* Londonderry 51206.

DERRY, Thomas Kingston, OBE 1976; Kt, Order of St Olav, Norway, 1981; MA, DPhil Oxon; *b* 5 March 1905; *y s* of late Rev. W. T. Derry, Wesleyan Minister; *m* 1930, Gudny, *e d* of late Hjalmar Wesenberg, Commander of Order of Vasa, Oslo, Norway. *Educ:* Kingswood Sch., Bath; Queen's Coll., Oxford (Bible Clerk and Taberdar). 1st Class, Classical Moderations, 1925; 1st Class, Final Sch. of Modern History, 1927; Senior George Webb Medley Scholar, 1927; Gladstone Prizeman, 1928; Sixth Form Master and Chief History Master, Repton Sch., 1929–37; Headmaster, Mill Hill School, 1938–40; Political Intelligence Dept of Foreign Office, 1941–45 (Chief Intelligence Officer, Scandinavia); Asst Master, St Marylebone Grammar Sch., 1945–65; Visiting Prof., Wheaton Coll., Mass, 1961–62. *Publications:* (with T. L. Jarman) The European World, 1950, rev. and extended edn 1975; The Campaign in Norway (official military history), 1952; A Short History of Norway, 1957; (with T. I. Williams) A Short History of Technology, 1960; The United Kingdom Today, 1961; A Short Economic History of Britain, 1965; (with E. J. Knapton) Europe 1815–1914, 1965; Europe 1914 to the Present, 1966; (with T. L. Jarman and M. G. Blakeway) The Making of Britain, 3 vols, 1956–69; A History of Modern Norway, 1814–1972, 1973; A History of Scandinavia, 1979; (with T. L. Jarman) Modern Britain, 1979. *Address:* Nils Lauritssons vei 27, 0854 Oslo 8, Norway.

DERWENT, 5th Baron *cr* 1881; **Robin Evelyn Leo Vanden-Bempde-Johnstone,** LVO 1957; Bt 1795; Managing Director, Hutchison Whampoa (Europe) Ltd, since 1985; Director: Tanks Consolidated Investments PLC, since 1983; Elbar Industrial PLC, since 1984; Metallurgie Hoboken-Overpelt (Belgium), since 1985; Guidehouse Limited, since 1985; *b* 30 Oct. 1930; *s* of 4th Baron Derwent, CBE and Marie-Louise (*d* 1985), *d* of Albert Picard, Paris; *S* father, 1986; *m* 1957, Sybille, *d* of late Vicomte de Simard de Pitray and of Madame Jeanine Hennessy; one *s* three *d*. *Educ:* Winchester College; Clare Coll., Cambridge (Scholar, MA 1953). 2nd Lieut 1949, 60th Rifles; Lieut 1950, Queen Victoria's Rifles (TA). HM Diplomatic Service, 1954–69; served FO, Paris, Mexico City, Washington. Director, NM Rothschild & Sons, Merchant Bankers, 1969–85. Chevalier de la Légion d'Honneur (France), 1957; Officier de l'Ordre National du Mérite (France), 1978. *Recreations:* shooting, fishing. *Heir: s* Hon. Francis Patrick Harcourt Vanden-Bempde-Johnstone, *b* 23 Sept. 1965. *Address:* Low Hall, Hackness, Scarborough. *T:* Scarborough 82210; 30 Kelso Place, W8 5QG. *T:* 01–937 2826.

DERX, Donald John, CB 1975; with Glaxo Holdings plc, since 1986; *b* 25 June 1928; *s* of John Derx and Violet Ivy Stroud; *m* 1956, Luisa Donzelli; two *s* two *d*. *Educ:* Tiffin Boys' Sch., Kingston-on-Thames; St Edmund Hall, Oxford (BA). Asst Principal, BoT, 1951; seconded to Cabinet Office, 1954–55; Principal, Colonial Office, 1957; Asst Sec., Industrial Policy Gp, DEA, 1965; Dir, Treasury Centre for Admin. Studies, 1968; Head of London Centre, Civil Service Coll., 1970; Under Sec., 1971–72, Dep. Sec., 1972–84, Dept of Employment; Dir, Policy Studies Inst., 1985–86. *Address:* 40 Raymond Road, Wimbledon, SW19 4AP. *T:* 01–947 0682.

DESAI, Prof. Meghnad Jagdishchandra, PhD; Professor of Economics, London School of Economics and Political Science, since 1983; *b* 10 July 1940; *s* of Jagdishchandra and Mandakini Desai; *m* 1970, Gail Graham Wilson; one *s* two *d*. *Educ:* Univ. of Bombay (BA Hons, MA); Univ. of Pennsylvania (PhD 1964). Associate Specialist, Dept of Agricultural Econs, Univ. of Calif, Berkeley, 1963–65; Dept of Econs, London Sch. of Econs and Pol Science: Lectr, 1965–77; Sen. Lectr, 1977–80; Reader, 1980–83. *Publications:* Marxian Economic Theory, 1974; Applied Econometrics, 1976; Marxian Economics, 1979; Testing Monetarism, 1981; (Asst Editor to Prof. Dharma Kumar) The Cambridge Economic History of India 1757–1970, 1983; contrib. Econometrica, Econ. Jl, Rev. of Econ. Studies, Economica, Econ. Hist. Rev. *Address:* London School of Economics and Political Science, Houghton Street, Aldwych, WC2A 2AE.

DESAI, Shri Morarji Ranchhodji, BA; Prime Minister of India, 1977–79; *b* Bhadeli, Gujarat, 29 Feb. 1896; *e s* of Shri Ranchhodji and Smt. Vajiyaben Desai. *Educ:* Wilson Coll., Bombay; Univ. of Bombay. Entered Provincial Civil Service of Govt of Bombay, 1918; resigned to join the Civil Disobedience Campaign of Mahatma Gandhi, 1930; convicted for taking part in the Movement during 1930–34; Sec., Gujarat Pradesh Congress Cttee, 1931–37 and 1939–46; Minister for Revenue, Co-operation, Agriculture and Forests, Bombay, 1937–39; convicted, 1940–41, and detained in prison, 1942–45; Minister for Home and Revenue, Bombay, 1946–52; Chief Minister of Bombay, 1952–56; Mem., 2nd, 3rd and 4th Lok Sabha, 1957–70; Minister of Commerce and Industry, Government of India, 1956–58; Treasurer, All India Congress Cttee, 1950–58; Minister of Finance, Government of India, 1958–63, resigned from Govt (under plan to strengthen Congress) Aug. 1963; Chm., Administrative Reforms Commn, Govt of India, 1966; Dep. Prime Minister and Minister of Finance, Government of India, 1967–69; Chm., Parly Gp, Congress Party (Opposition), 1969–77; elected to 5th Lok Sabha, 1971–79; detained in solitary confinement, 1975–77, under State of Emergency; Founder-Chairman, Janata Party, 1977. Hon. Fellow, College of Physicians and Surgeons, Bombay, 1956; Hon. LLD Karnatak Univ., 1957. *Publications:* books include: A View of the Gita; In My View; A Minister and His Responsibilities (Jawaharlal Nehru Meml Lectures); The Story of My Life (2 vols), 1978; Indian Unity: From Dream to Reality (Patel Meml Lectures); book on Nature Cure. *Recreations:* spinning on Charkha; follower of sport and classical Indian dancing. *Address:* 1 Safdarjung Road, New Delhi 110001, India; Oceana, Marine Drive, Bombay 400020, India.

DE ST JORRE, Danielle Marie-Madeleine J.; *see* Jorre De St Jorre.

de STE. CROIX, Geoffrey Ernest Maurice, DLitt; FBA 1972; Fellow and Tutor in Ancient History, New College, Oxford, 1953–77, Emeritus Fellow, 1977, Hon. Fellow,

1985; *b* 8 Feb. 1910; *s* of Ernest Henry de Ste Croix and Florence Annie (*née* Macgowan); *m* 1st, 1932, Lucile (marr. diss. 1959); one *d* (decd); 2nd, 1959, Margaret Knight; two *s*. *Educ:* Clifton Coll. (to 1925); University Coll. London (1946–50). BA 1st cl. Hons History, London, 1949; MA Oxon, 1953; DLitt Oxon, 1978. Solicitor, 1931. Served War, RAF, 1940–46. Asst Lectr in Ancient Economic History, London Sch. of Economics, and Part-time Lectr in Ancient History, Birkbeck Coll., London, 1950–53. J. H. Gray Lectr, Cambridge Univ., 1972–73; Gregynog Lectr, UCW, Aberystwyth, 1986; Vis. Prof., Univ. of Amsterdam, 1978. *Publications:* The Origins of the Peloponnesian War, 1972; The Class Struggle in the Ancient Greek World, from the Archaic Age to the Arab Conquests, 1981 (Isaac Deutscher Meml Prize, 1982); contributions to: Studies in the History of Accounting, 1956; The Crucible of Christianity, 1969; Studies in Ancient Society, 1974; Debits, Credits, Finance and Profits, 1974; articles and reviews in various learned jls. *Recreations:* listening to music, walking. *Address:* Evenlode, Stonesfield Lane, Charlbury, Oxford OX7 3ER. *T:* Charlbury 810453.

DE SAUMAREZ, 6th Baron *cr* 1831; **James Victor Broke Saumarez;** Bt 1801; *b* 28 April 1924; *s* of 5th Baron de Saumarez and Gunhild (*d* 1985), *d* of late Maj.-Gen. V. G. Balck, Stockholm; *S* father, 1969; *m* 1953, Julia, *d* of late D. R. Charlton, Gt Holland-on-Sea, Essex; twin *s* one *d*. *Educ:* Eton Coll.; Millfield; Magdalene Coll., Cambridge (MA). Farmer; Director, Shrubland Health Clinic Ltd. *Recreations:* swimming, gardening, photography. *Heir:* *s* Hon. Eric Douglas Saumarez [*b* 13 Aug. 1956; *m* 1982, Christine, *yr d* of B. N. Halliday]. *Address:* Shrubland Vista, Coddenham, Ipswich, Suffolk. *T:* Ipswich 830220.

DESCH, Stephen Conway; QC 1980; a Recorder of the Crown Court, since 1979; *b* 17 Nov. 1939; *o s* of Harold Ernest Desch and Gwendolen Lucy Desch; *m* 1973, Julia Beatrice Little; two *d*. *Educ:* Dauntsey's Sch.; Magdalen Coll., Oxford (BCL, MA); Northwestern Univ., Chicago. Called to the Bar, Gray's Inn, 1962; joined Midland Circuit, 1964. Lectr in Law, Magdalen Coll., Oxford, 1963–65. *Publication:* Legal Notes to H. E. Desch: Structural Surveying, 1970. *Recreations:* country pursuits, farming, mountain walking. *Address:* 2 Crown Office Row, Temple, EC4Y 7HJ. *T:* 01–353 9337.

de SILVA, Desmond (George Lorenz); QC 1984; *b* 13 Dec. 1939; *s* of Edmund Frederick Lorenz de Silva, MBE, retired Ambassador, and Esme Gregg Nathanielsz. *Educ:* Dulwich College; Trinity College, Ceylon. Served with 3rd Carabiniers (3rd Dragoon Guards). Called to the Bar: Middle Temple, 1964; Sierra Leone, 1968; The Gambia, 1981. Vice-Chm., Westminster Community Relations Council, 1980–82; Councilman, City of London, 1980–; Main Session Chm., First Internat. Conf. on Human Value, 1981. Member: Home Affairs Standing Cttee, Bow Gp, 1982; Editl Adv. Bd, Crossbow, 1984; Crime and Juvenile Delinquency Study Gp, Centre for Policy Studies, 1983–. Lord of the Manor of Woolstone, Oxon; Member: Governing Council, Manorial Soc. of GB, 1982–; Nat. Cttee for 900th anniv. of Domesday. Liveryman, Fletchers' Co. Vice-Pres., St John Ambulance London (Prince of Wales's) Dist., 1984–; CStJ 1986 (OStJ 1980). *Publication:* (ed) English Law and Ethnic Minority Customs. *Recreations:* politics, shooting, travel. *Address:* 2 Paper Buildings, Temple, EC4; 6 Minera Mews, SW1; Villa Taprobane, Taprobane Island, off Weligama, Sri Lanka. *Clubs:* Carlton, City Livery; Orient (Colombo).

DESIO, Prof. Ardito, Dr rer. nat; FDS; FRGS; FMGS; Professor of Geology (and Past Director of Institute of Geology), at the University of Milan, and of Applied Geology, at the Engineering School of Milan, 1931–72, now Emeritus; *b* Palmanova, Frioul, 18 April 1897; *s* of Antonio Desio and Caterina Zorzella; *m* 1932, Aurelia Bevilacqua; one *s* one *d*. *Educ:* Udine and Florence. Grad. Univ. of Florence in Nat. Sciences, 1920. Asst, University of Pavia, 1923, also Univ. and Engineering Sch., Milan, 1924–25 to 1930–31; Lectr in Phys. Geography, University of Milan, 1929–30 and in Palaeontology there until 1935. Geol Consultant, Edison Co. and Public Power Corp. of Greece, 1948–79. Pres., Italian Geological Cttee, 1966–73. Dir., Rivista Italiana di Paleontologia e Stratigrafia, 1942–; Past Dir., Geologia Tecnica. Past Pres., Ital. Geolog. Soc.; Mem. (Hon. Pres.) Ital. Assoc. of Geologists; Past Pres., Ital. Order of Geologists; Mem., Ital. Order of Journalists; Hon. Member: Ital. Paleont. Soc.; Gesellschaft für Erdkunde zu Berlin, 1941; Italian Geog. Soc., 1955; Faculty of Sciences University of Chile, 1964; Geological Soc. of London, 1964; Indian Paleont. Soc.; Soc. Ital. Progresso delle Scienze, 1978; Ist. per il Medio ed Estremo Oriente, 1979; Assoc. Mineraria Subalpina, 1985; Corresp. Mem., Soc. Géol. Belgique, 1952; Life Mem., Geog. Soc., USA, 1955; Member: Institut d'Egypte, 1936; Accademia Naz. Lincei, 1948; Inst. Lombardo Accad. Scienze Letter, 1949. In 1938 discovered first small deposits of natural oil and gas in subsoil of Libya and Mg-K salt deposit in Marada Oasis; led expedition to K2 (8611 m, 2nd highest peak in the World; reached for 1st time on 31 July 1954), and 18 expeditions in Africa and Asia. Santoro Prize, 1931; Royal Prize, 1934, Royal Acad. Lincei; Gold Medal of the Republic of Pakistan, 1954; Gold Medal of the Sciences, Letters and Arts, of Italy, 1956; Patrons medal of Royal Geog. Soc. of London, 1957; USA Antarctic Service Medal, 1974; Paul Harris Award, Internat. Rotary Club. Kt Grand Cross, Order of Merit, Italy, 1955. *Publications:* about 393, among them: Le Isole Italiane dell'Egeo, 1931; La spedizione geografica Italiana al Karakoram 1929, 1936; scientific reports of his expedn to Libyan Sahara, 7 vols, 1938–42; Le vie delle sete, 1950; Geologia applicata all'ingegneria, 1949, 3rd edn 1973; Ascent of K2, 1956 (11 languages, 15 editions); Geology of the Baltoro Basin (Karakorum), 1970; Results of half-a-century investigation on the glaciers of the Ortler-Cevedale, 1973; La Geologia dell'Italia, 1973; Geology of Central Badakhshan (NE Afghanistan), 1975; Geology of the Upper Shaksgam Valley, Sinkiang, China, 1980; L'Antartide, 1985. *Recreation:* alpinist. *Address:* (office) Dipartimento di Scienze della Terra, Università di Milano, Via Mangiagalli 34, 20133–Milano, Italy. *T:* 292726; (residence) Viale Maino 14, 20129–Milano. *T:* 709845. *Clubs:* Alpine; Internat. Rotary; Panatlon; Himalayan (Hon. Sec. for Italy); Alpino, Touring (Italy); Explorers' (NY); Hon. Member Alpin Français; Excursionista Carioca (Brazil).

DESLONGCHAMPS, Prof. Pierre, PhD; FRS 1983; FRSC 1974; FCIC; Professor of Organic Chemistry, Université de Sherbrooke, Canada, since 1972; *b* 8 May 1938; *s* of Rodolphe Deslongchamps and Madeleine Magnan; *m* 1st, 1960, Micheline Renaud (marr. diss. 1975); two *c*; 2nd, 1976, Shirley E. Thomas (marr. diss. 1983). *Educ:* Univ. de Montréal (BSc Chem., 1959); Univ. of New Brunswick (PhD Chem., 1964). FCIC 1980. Post-doctoral Student with Dr R.B. Woodward, Harvard Univ., USA, 1965; Asst Prof., Univ. de Montréal, 1966; Asst Prof. 1967, Associate Prof. 1968, Univ. de Sherbrooke. Dr *hc:* Univ. Pierre et Marie Curie, Paris, 1983; Bishop's Univ., Univ. de Montréal, and Univ. Laval, 1984; New Brunswick Univ., 1985. A.P. Sloan Fellow, 1970–72; E. W. R. Steacie Fellow, 1971–74. Scientific Prize of Québec, 1971; E. W. R. Steacie Prize (Nat. Scis), NRCC, 1974; Médaille Vincent, ACFAS, 1975; Merck, Sharp and Dohme Lectures Award, CIC, 1976; Canada Council Izaak Walton Killam Meml Scholarship, 1976–77; John Simon Guggenheim Meml Foundn Fellow, 1979; Medáille Pariseau, ACFAS, 1979. *Publications:* Stereoelectronic Effects in Organic Chemistry, 1983; contrib. Tetrahedron, Jl Amer. Chem. Soc., Canadian Jl of Chem., Pure Applied Chem., Synth. Commun., Nouv. Jl Chim., Heterocycles, Jl Molecular Struct., Interface, Aldrichimica Acta, and Bull. Soc. Chim., France. *Recreations:* fishing, hunting, hockey, reading. *Address:* Department of Chemistry, Faculty of Sciences, Université de Sherbrooke, Sherbrooke, PQ J1K 2R1, Canada. *T:* (819) 565–3530; RR 1, McFarland Road, North Hatley, PQ J0B 2C0. *T:* (819) 842–4238.

DESPRÉS, Robert; Chairman of the Board, Atomic Energy of Canada Ltd, since 1980; *b* 27 Sept. 1924; *s* of Adrien Després and Augustine Marmen; *m* 1949, Marguerite Cantin; two *s* two *d*. *Educ:* Académie de Québec (BA 1943); Laval Univ. (MCom 1947); (postgrad. studies) Western Univ. Comptroller, Québec Power Co., 1947–63; Reg. Manager, Administration & Trust Co., 1963–65; Dep. Minister, Québec Dept of Revenue, 1965–69; Pres. and Gen. Man., Québec Health Insurance Bd, 1969–73; Pres., Université du Québec, 1973–78; Pres. and Chief Exec. Officer, National Cablevision Ltd, 1978–80, and Netcom Inc., 1978–. Mem. Board of Directors: Norcen Energy Resources Ltd; Campeau Corporation; Sidbec-Dosco Inc.; Domtar Inc.; Canada Malting Co. Ltd; Manufacturers Life Insurance Co.; Nat. Trust Co.; Sidbec; Canadian Union Insurance Co. Ltd; Corp. Falconbridge Copper; Marshall Drummond McCall Inc.; Netcom Inc.; Flakt Canada Ltd; McNeil, Mantha, Inc.; Bio-Méga Inc.; Wajax Ltd; Réseau de télévision Quatre Saisons Inc.; Disnat Investment Inc.; Canadian Certified General Accountants' Res. Foundn; Council for Canadian Unity; la Soc. du Musée du Séminaire de Québec; Inst de cardiologie de Québec. *Publications:* contrib. Commerce, and Soc. of Management Accountants Revue. *Recreations:* golf, tennis, reading. *Address:* 890 rue Dessane, Québec, Québec G1S 3J8, Canada. *T:* (418) 687–2100. *Clubs:* Mount Royal, Rideau, Cercle Universitaire; Lorette Golf.

DESTY, Prof. Denis Henry, OBE 1983; FRS 1984; FInstPet; *b* 21 Oct. 1923; *s* of Ernest James Desty and Alice Q. R. Desty; *m* 1945, Doreen (*née* Scott); one *s* (one *d* decd). *Educ:* Taunton's Sch., Southampton; University Coll., Southampton (BSc Hons Chemistry, London, 1948). FInstPet 1974. Served War, RAF, 1942–46: Signals Officer, UK and India. Research Centre, British Petroleum Co. Ltd: Physical Chemist, 1948; Gp Leader, 1952; Sen. Chemist, 1962; Sen. Res. Associate, Special Projs, 1965; retd 1982. Res. consultant, technical and indust. orgns, 1982–. Chm., Gas Chromatography Discussion Gp, 1958–68 (Special Parchment Award, 1970). M. S. Tswett Chromatography Medal, USA 1974 and USSR 1978; Award for Combustion Chemistry, RSC, 1980; MacRobert Award, Fellowship of Engrg, 1982. Silver Jubilee Medal, 1977. Editor, Proc. Internat. Gas Chromatography Symposia, 1956 and 1958. *Publications:* about 50 papers and 60 patents. *Recreations:* boating, gliding, camping. *Address:* 16 Albury Road, Burwood Park, Walton-on-Thames, Surrey KT12 5DT. *T:* Walton-on-Thames 229687.

de THIER, Jacques; Grand Officer, Order of Léopold II; Commander, Order of Léopold and Order of the Crown, Belgium; Civic Cross (1914–18); Grand Cross of Royal Victorian Order (Hon. GCVO); Director, Compagnie Financière et de Gestion pour l'Etranger (Cometra), Brussels, 1966–73; Counsellor, Cometra Oil Co.; *b* Heusy, Belgium, 15 Sept. 1900; *m* 1946, Mariette Negroponte (*d* 1973); three step *s*. *Educ:* University of Liège. Doctor of Laws (University of Liège), 1922; Mem. Bar (Liège and Verviers), 1923–29. Attached to Prime Minister's Cabinet, Brussels, 1929–32; entered Diplomatic Service, 1930; Attaché, Belgian Legation, Berlin, 1933; Chargé d'Affaires in Athens, 1935, Teheran, 1936; First Sec., Berlin, 1937–38; First Sec., then Counsellor, Washington, 1938–44; Chargé d'Affaires, Madrid, 1944–46; Asst to Dir-Gen., Polit. Dept, Min. of Foreign Affairs, Brussels, 1947, then Asst Head of Belgian Mission in Berlin; Consul-Gen. for Belgium, NY, 1948–55; Pres., Soc. of Foreign Consuls in New York, 1954; Belgian Ambassador: to Mexico, 1955–58; in Ottawa, 1958–61; Mem. Belgian Delegns to Gen. Assemblies of UN, 1956, 1957, 1959 and 1960; Belg. Rep. to Security Council, Sept. 1960; Belgian Ambassador to Court of St James's, 1961–65, and concurrently Belgian Perm. Rep. to Council of WEU, 1961–65. Hon. Chairman: Soc. Belgo-Allemande; Belgian Nat. Cttee, United World Colls. Holds foreign decorations. *Publications:* articles in La Revue Générale, Brussels: Dans l'Iran d'autrefois, 1979; Souvenirs d'un diplomate belge, Washington, 1938–44, 1981; Pourquoi l'Espagne de Franco n'a pas livré Degrelle, 1983. *Recreation:* golf. *Address:* 38 avenue des Klauwaerts, 1050 Brussels, Belgium. *Clubs:* Anglo-Belgian; Cercle Royal Gaulois, Cercle du Parc, Royal Golf de Belgique (Brussels).

de TRAFFORD, Sir Dermot Humphrey, 6th Bt *cr* 1841; VRD 1963; Director, since 1977, Chairman, since 1982, Low & Bonar plc (Deputy Chairman, 1980–82); Chairman: GHP Group Ltd, 1965–77 (Managing Director, 1961); Calor Gas Holding, since 1974; *b* 19 Jan. 1925; *s* of Sir Rudolph de Trafford, 5th Bt, OBE and June Lady Audley (*née* Chaplin), MBE (*d* 1977); *S* father, 1983; *m* 1st, 1946, Patricia Mary Beeley (marr. diss. 1973); three *s* six *d*; 2nd, 1973, Mrs Xandra Caradini Walter. *Educ:* Harrow Sch.; Christ Church, Oxford (MA). Trained as Management Consultant, Clubley Armstrong & Co. Ltd and Orr & Boss and Partners Ltd, 1949–52; Director: Monks Investment Trust; Imperial Continental Gas Assoc., 1963– (Dep. Chm., 1972–); Petrofina SA, 1971. *Recreations:* golf, ski-ing. *Heir:* *s* John Humphrey de Trafford [*b* 12 Sept. 1950; *m* 1975, Anne, *d* of J. Faure de Pebeyre; one *s* one *d*]. *Address:* 59 Onslow Square, SW7 3LR. *T:* 01–589 2826. *Clubs:* White's, Royal Ocean Racing; Berkshire Golf; Island Sailing.

DEUKMEJIAN, (Courken) George, Jr; Governor of California, since 1983; lawyer; Republican; *b* 6 June 1928; *s* of C. George Deukmejian and Alice (*née* Gairdan); *m* 1957, Gloria M. Saatjian; one *s* two *d*. *Educ:* Watervliet Sch., NY; Siena College (BA 1949); St John's Univ., NY (JD 1952). Admitted to NY State Bar, 1952, Californian Bar, 1956, US Supreme Court Bar, 1970. US Army, 1953–55. Law practice, Calif., 1955; Partner, Riedman, Dalessi, Deukmejian & Woods; Mem., Calif. Assembly, 1963–67; Mem., Calif. Senate (minority leader), 1967–79; Attorney Gen., Calif., 1979–83. *Address:* State Capitol, Sacramento, Calif 95814, USA.

DEUTSCH, André; Co-Chairman and Co-Managing Director, André Deutsch Ltd, since 1984 (Chairman and Managing Director, 1951–84); *b* 15 Nov. 1917; *s* of late Bruno Deutsch and Maria Deutsch (*née* Havas); unmarried. *Educ:* Budapest; Vienna; Zurich. First job in publishing, with Nicholson & Watson, 1942; started publishing independently under imprint of Allan Wingate (Publishers) Ltd, 1945; started André Deutsch Limited, in 1951. Founded: African Universities Press, Lagos, Nigeria, 1962; East Africa Publishing House, Nairobi, Kenya, 1964. *Recreations:* travel preferably by train, ski-ing, publishing, talking. *Address:* 105 Great Russell Street, WC1B 3LJ. *Clubs:* Garrick, Groucho.

de VALOIS, Dame Ninette, CH 1982; DBE 1951 (CBE 1947); Founder and Director of the Royal Ballet, 1931–63 (formerly the Sadler's Wells Ballet, Royal Opera House, Covent Garden, and the Sadler's Wells Theatre Ballet, Sadler's Wells Theatre); Founder of The Royal Ballet School (formerly The Sadler's Wells School of Ballet); *b* Baltiboys, Blessington, Co. Wicklow, 6 June 1898; 2nd *d* of Lieut-Col T. R. A. Stannus, DSO, Carlingford; *m* 1935, Dr A. B. Connell. Prima ballerina the Royal Opera Season Covent Garden (International), May to July 1919 and again in 1928. Première danseuse British National Opera Company, 1918; Mem., The Diaghileff Russian Ballet, 1923–26; choreographic dir to the Old Vic, the Festival Theatre, Cambridge, and The Abbey Theatre, Dublin, 1926–30; Founder of The National Sch. of Ballet, Turkey, 1947. Principal choreographic works: Job, The Rake's Progress, Checkmate, and Don Quixote. Hon. MusDoc London, 1947; Hon. DLitt: Reading, 1951; Oxford, 1955; New Univ. of Ulster, 1979; Hon. DMus: Sheffield, 1955; Durham, 1982; Hon. MusD Trinity Coll.,

Dublin, 1957; Hon. DFA Smith Coll., Mass, USA, 1957; Hon. LLD: Aberdeen, 1958; Sussex, 1975; FRAD 1963. Chevalier of the Legion of Honour, 1950. Gold Albert Medal, RSA, 1964; (jtly) Erasmus Prize Foundn Award (first woman to receive it), 1974; Irish Community Award, 1980. *Publications:* Invitation to the Ballet, 1937; Come Dance with Me, 1957; Step By Step, 1977. *Address:* c/o Royal Ballet School, 153 Talgarth Road, W14.

DEVENPORT, Rt. Rev. Eric Nash; *see* Dunwich, Bishop Suffragan of.

DEVENPORT, Martyn Herbert, MA; Headmaster, Victoria College, Jersey, CI, since Sept. 1967; *b* 11 Jan. 1931; *s* of Horace Devenport and Marjorie Violet (*née* Fergusson); *m* 1957, Mary Margaret Lord; three *s* one *d. Educ:* Maidstone Gram. Sch.; Gonville and Caius Coll., Cambridge. Asst Master at Eton Coll., 1957–67. *Recreations:* photography, squash, sailing. *Address:* Victoria College, Jersey, CI. *T:* 37591.

DEVERELL, Sir Colville (Montgomery), GBE 1963 (OBE 1946); KCMG 1957 (CMG 1955); CVO 1953; retired from Government Service, Nov. 1962; Secretary-General, International Planned Parenthood Federation, 1964–69; *b* 21 Feb. 1907; *s* of George Robert Deverell and Maude (*née* Cooke); *m* 1935, Margaret Wynne, *d* of D. A. Wynne Wilson; three *s. Educ:* Portora Sch., Enniskillen, Ulster; Trinity Coll., Dublin (LLB); Trinity Coll., Cambridge. District Officer, Kenya, 1931; Clerk to Exec. and Legislative Councils, 1938–39; Civil Affairs Branch, E Africa Comd, 1941–46, serving Italian Somaliland, British Somaliland, Ethiopia; Mem. Lord de la Warr's Delegation, Ethiopia, 1944; seconded War Office in connection Italian Peace Treaty, 1946. Sec., Development and Reconstruction Authority, Kenya, 1946; acted as Financial Sec. and Chief Native Comr, 1949; Administrative Secretary, Kenya, 1949; Colonial Sec., Jamaica, 1952–55; Governor and Comdr-in-Chief, Windward Islands, 1955–59; Governor and Comdr-in-Chief, Mauritius, 1959–62. Chm. UN(FP) Mission to India, 1965; Mem., UN Mission on Need for World Population Inst., 1970; Chairman: UN Family Planning Evaluation Mission to Ceylon, 1971; UN Family Planning Assoc. Feasability Mission, Al Azhar Univ., Cairo, 1972. Constitutional Adviser: Seychelles, 1966; British Virgin Islands, 1973. LLD *jure dignitatis,* Dublin, 1964. *Recreations:* cricket, tennis, squash, golf and fishing. *Address:* 46 Northfield End, Henley-on-Thames, Oxon. *Clubs:* East India, Devonshire, Sports and Public Schools; MCC; Nairobi (Kenya).

DEVEREUX, family name of **Viscount Hereford.**

DEVEREUX, Alan Robert, CBE 1980; DL; Director: Scottish Mutual Assurance Society, since 1975; Walter Alexander PLC, since 1980; Solsgirth Investment Trust Ltd, since 1981; Hambros Scotland Ltd, since 1984; Chairman, Hambro Legal Protection (Scotland) Ltd, since 1985; Scottish Advisor, Hambros Bank, since 1984; Chairman, Scottish Tourist Board, since 1980; Member, British Tourist Authority, since 1980; *b* 18 April 1933; *s* of Donald Charles and Doris Louie Devereux; *m* 1959, Gloria Alma Hair (*d* 1985); one *s. Educ:* Colchester School; Clacton County High School; Mid-Essex Technical Coll. CEng, FIProdE, FBIM. Marconi's Wireless Telegraph Co., 1950–56; Halex Div. of British Xylonite Co., 1956–58; Spa Div., Sanitas Trust, 1958–65; Gen. Man., Dobar Engineering, 1965–67; Norcros Ltd, 1967–69; Gp Man. Dir 1969–78, Dep. Chm. 1978–80, Scotcros Ltd; Dir-Gen., Scotcros Europe SA, 1976–79. Dep. Chm. 1975–77, Chm. 1977–79, CBI Scotland; CBI: Council Mem., 1972–; Mem. President's Adv. Cttee, 1979; UK Regional Chm., 1979; Mem., Finance and Gen. Purposes Cttee, 1982–84. Scottish Free Enterprise Award, 1978. Chm., Small Industries Council for Rural Areas of Scotland, 1975–77. Mem., Scottish Development Agency, 1977–82. Chm., Police Dependants' Trust, Scotland. Mem., Les Gastronomes de la Mer. DL Renfrewshire, 1985. FBIM. *Recreations:* reading, work, running for aeroplanes. *Address:* 293 Fenwick Road, Giffnock, Glasgow G46 6UH. *Club:* East India, Devonshire, Sports and Public Schools.

de VERE WHITE; *see* White.

de VESCI, 7th Viscount *cr* 1766; **Thomas Eustace Vesey;** Bt 1698; Baron Knapton, 1750; *b* 8 Oct. 1955; *s* of 6th Viscount de Vesci and Susan Anne (*d* 1986), *d* of late Ronald (Owen Lloyd) Armstrong-Jones, MBE, QC, DL, and of the Countess of Rosse; *S* father, 1983. *Educ:* Eton and Oxford. Assistant Trainer to M. V. O'Brien, 1978–80; Bloodstock Agent in Los Angeles, Calif, 1980–83; returned to family home on death of father to continue bloodstock business, also stud farm, forestry and farming. *Recreations:* horse racing, shooting. *Heir: kinsman* Nicholas Ivo Vesey, *b* 7 Sept. 1954. *Address:* Abbey Leix, Ireland. *T:* Abbeyleix 31162. *Club:* White's.

See also Earl of Snowdon.

DEVESI, Sir Baddeley, GCMG 1980; GCVO 1982; Governor-General of the Solomon Islands, since 1978; Chancellor, University of the South Pacific, since 1980; *b* 16 Oct. 1941; *s* of Mostyn Tagabasoe Norua and Laisa Otu; *m* 1969, June Marie Barley; four *s* three *d. Educ:* St Stephen's Sch., Auckland, NZ; Ardmore Teachers' Coll., Auckland, NZ. MLC and Mem. Exec. Council, 1967–69. Headmaster, St Nicholas Sch., Honiara, 1968; Educn Officer and Lectr, 1970–72; Dist. Officer, 1973; District Comr and Clerk to Malaita Council, 1974; Permanent Secretary, 1976. Dep. Chm., Solomon Islands Broadcasting Corp., 1976. Captain, Solomon Islands team, 2nd South Pacific Games, 1969. Comr, Boy Scouts Assoc., 1968. Hon. DU, 1981. KStJ 1984. *Recreations:* reading, swimming, lawn tennis, cricket, snooker. *Address:* Government House, Honiara, Solomon Islands.

de VIGIER, William Alphonse, Hon. CBE 1978; formerly: Chairman (also founder), Acrow plc; Chairman: Acrow Corp. of America; Acrow Canada; Acrow Misr, Egypt; SOFIM SA, Switzerland; *b* 22 Jan. 1912; *m* 1939, Betty Kendall; two *d. Educ:* La Chataigneraie, Coppet, Switzerland. Board Member: Vigier Cement SA, Switzerland; McConnell Dowell Ltd, Australia; Acrow Peru SA; Acrow India; Acrow Richmond, Canada; Acrow-Carpenter, NZ; Acrow Zimbabwe; Poenamo Ltd, Australia. Mem., British Airways Bd, 1973–78. Knight of Star of the North (Sweden); Grand Commander, Order of Star of Africa. *Recreations:* tennis, skiing, swimming. *Address:* Sommerhaus, Solothurn, Switzerland; Tinkers Lodge, Marsh Lane, Mill Hill, NW7. *Clubs:* East India; Metropolitan (New York).

DE VILLE, Harold Godfrey, (Oscar), CBE 1979; Deputy Chairman, Meyer International plc, since 1985 (Director, since 1984); *b* Derbyshire, 11 April 1925; *s* of Harold De Ville and Anne De Ville (*née* Godfrey); *m* 1947, Pamela Fay Ellis; one *s. Educ:* Burton-on-Trent Grammar Sch.; Trinity Coll., Cambridge (MA). Served RNVR, 1943–46. With Ford Motor Co. Ltd, 1949–65; BICC: Gen. Man., Central Personnel Relations, 1965–70; Dir, 1971–84; Exec. Vice-Chm., 1978–80; Exec. Dep. Chm., 1980–84; Chm., BICC Pension Funds, 1973–84. Director: Phillips Cables Ltd, Canada, 1982–84; Metal Manufacturers Ltd, Australia, 1983–84; Scottish Cables Ltd, S Africa, 1983–84. Mem., BRB, 1985–. Chairman: Iron and Steel EDC, 1984–86; Govt Review of vocational qualifications, 1985–86; Nat. Jt Council for Engrg Construction Industry. Member: Commn on Industrial Relations, 1971–74; Central Arbitration Cttee, 1976–77; Council: Inst. of Manpower Studies, 1971–; ACAS, 1976–; Industrial Soc., 1976–85; CBI, 1977–85 (Chm., CBI Working Parties on Bullock Cttee, 1975–78, on Pay Determination, 1976–78; Member: Employment Policy Cttee, 1974–80; Finance Cttee, 1983–84); BIM, 1982– (Mem., Bd of Companions). Mem. Council, Reading Univ., 1985–. *Recreations:* genealogy, fell-walking. *Address:* Meyer International plc, Villiers House, 41/47 Strand, WC2N 5JG.

de VILLIERS, 3rd Baron, *cr* 1910; **Arthur Percy de Villiers;** *b* 17 Dec. 1911; *s* of 2nd Baron and Adelheid, *d* of H. C. Koch, Pietermaritzburg, Natal; *S* father 1934; *m* 1939, Lovett (marr. diss. 1958), *d* of Dr A. D. MacKinnon, Williams Lake, BC; one *s* two *d. Educ:* Magdalen Coll., Oxford. Barrister, Inner Temple, 1938. Farming in New Zealand. Admitted as a barrister to the Auckland Surpreme Court, 1949. *Heir: s* Hon. Alexander Charles de Villiers, *b* 29 Dec. 1940. *Address:* PO Box 66, Kumeu, Auckland, NZ.

de VILLIERS, Dawid Jacobus, DPhil; Minister of Trade and Industry (formerly Industries, Commerce and Tourism), South Africa, since 1980; *b* 10 July 1940; *m* 1964, Suzaan Mangold; one *s* three *d. Educ:* Univ. of Stellenbosch (BA Hons Philosophy, 1963; BTh, DPhil); Rand Afrikaans Univ. (MA Phil., 1972). Abe Bailey Scholar, 1963–64; Markotter Scholar, 1964. Part-time Lectr in Philosophy, Univ. of Western Cape, 1963–64; Minister of Dutch Reformed Church, Wellington, Cape, 1967–69; Lectr in Philosophy, 1969–72, and Pres. Convocation, 1973–, Rand Afrikaans Univ.; MP for Johannesburg W, 1972–79; Chm., Nat. Party's Foreign Affairs Cttee in Parlt; Ambassador of S Africa to London, 1979–80. Visited: USA on US Leaders Exchange Prog., 1974; UK as guest of Brit. Govt, 1975; Israel as guest of Israeli Govt, 1977. Represented S Africa in internat. Rugby in S Africa, UK, Ireland, Australia, NZ, France and the Argentine, 1962–70 (Captain, 1965–70). State President's Award for Sport, 1968 and 1970; S African Sportsman of the Year, 1968; Jaycee's Outstanding Young Man of the Year Award, 1971. *Recreations:* sports, reading. *Address:* Legal and General Building, Corner of Prinsloo and Pretorius Streets, Private Bag X274, Pretoria 0001, South Africa.

DEVINE, Hon. (Donald) Grant; MLA for Estevan, since 1982; Premier of Saskatchewan, since 1982; Leader, Progressive Conservative Party of Saskatchewan, since 1979; *b* Regina, 5 July 1944; *m* 1966, (Adeline) Chantal Guillaume; two *s* three *d. Educ:* Saskatchewan Univ. (BScA 1967); Alberta Univ. (MSc 1969; MBA 1970); Ohio State Univ. (PhD 1976). Farming, 1962–; marketing specialist, Fed. Govt, Ottawa, 1970–72; Graduate Assistant, Ohio State Univ., 1972–76; Lectr in Agricl Econs, Saskatchewan Univ., 1976–79. Advisor: Food Prices Rev. Bd and Provincial Govts; Sask. Consumers' Assoc. Member: Amer. Econ. Assoc.; Amer. Marketing Assoc.; Amer. Assoc. for Consumer Res.; Canadian Agricl Econs Soc.; Consumers' Assoc. of Canada. *Publications:* contribs to professional jls on retail food pricing and market performance. *Recreations:* golf, ski-ing, baseball. *Address:* Office of the Premier, Legislative Building, 2405 Legislative Drive, Regina S4S 0B3, Canada.

DEVINE, Rt. Rev. Joseph; *see* Motherwell, Bishop of, (RC).

DE VITO, Gioconda; Violinist; Professor of Violin at Accademia Di Santa Cecilia, Rome, 1935; *b* 26 July 1907; *d* of Giacomo and Emilia De Vito (*née* Del Guidice), Martina Franca Puglia, Italy; *m* 1949, James David Bicknell; no *c. Educ:* Conservatorio Di Musica Rossini, Pesaro. Began to play violin at age of 8; final examinations (distinction), Conservatorio Pesaro, 1921; first concert, 1921; first prize, Internat. Competition, Vienna, 1932. World wide musical activities since debut with London Philharmonic Orchestra, 1948, at concert conducted by Victor de Sabata; Royal Philharmonic Soc., 1950; Edinburgh Festival, 1949, 1951, 1953 (took part, 1953, in Festival of the Violin with Yehudi Menuhin and Isaac Stern), and 1960; played at Bath Fest. and Festival Hall with Yehudi Menuhin, 1955; Jury Tchaikowsky Internat. Violin Competition, Moscow, and recitals Moscow and Leningrad, 1958; Soloist, Adelaide Centenary Fest., and toured Australia, 1960; concerts, Buenos Aires, 1961; retired, 1961. Last concerts, Gt Brit., Swansea Festival, Oct. 1961; Continent, Basle Philharmonic, Nov. 1961. Diploma di Medaglia d'Oro del Ministero della Pubblica Istruzione for services to Art, 1957; Academician, Accademia Nazionale di Santa Cecilia, Rome, 1976. *Recreation:* bird watching. *Address:* Flint Cottage, Loudwater, Rickmansworth, Herts. *T:* Rickmansworth 772865; Via Cassia 595, Rome. *T:* 3660937.

DEVITT, Lt-Col Sir Thomas Gordon, 2nd Bt, *cr* 1916; Partner of Devitt & Moore, Shipbrokers; *b* 27 Dec. 1902; *e s* of Arthur Devitt (*d* 1921) *e s* of 1st Bt and Florence Emmeline (*d* 1951), *e d* of late William Forbes Gordon, Manar, NSW; *S* grandfather, 1923; *m* 1st, 1930, Joan Mary (who obtained a divorce, 1936), 2nd *d* of late Charles Reginald Freemantle, Hayes Barton, Pyrford, Surrey; 2nd, 1937, Lydia Mary (marr. diss. 1953), *o d* of late Edward Milligen Beloe, King's Lynn, Norfolk; two *d*; 3rd, 1953, Janet Lilian, *o d* of late Col H. S. Ellis, CBE, MC; one *s* one *d. Educ:* Sherborne; Corpus Christi Coll., Cambridge. 1939–45 War as Lt-Col, Seaforth Highlanders and OC Raiding Support Regt. Royal Order of Phœnix of Greece with swords. Chm. Macers Ltd, 1961–70. Chairman: Board of Governors, The Devitt and Moore Nautical Coll., Pangbourne, 1948–61; Nat. Service for Seafarers, 1948–77. Governor, Sherborne Sch., 1967–75. *Recreations:* shooting, fishing. *Heir: s* James Hugh Thomas Devitt, *b* 18 Sept. 1956. *Address:* 49 Lexden Road, Colchester, Essex CO3 3PY. *T:* Colchester 577958; 5 Rembrandt Close, Holbein Place, SW1. *T:* 01–730 2653. *Club:* MCC.

DEVLIN, family name of **Baron Devlin.**

DEVLIN, Baron (Life Peer) *cr* 1961, of West Wick; **Patrick Arthur Devlin,** PC 1960; Kt 1948; FBA 1963; High Steward of Cambridge University, since 1966; *b* 25 Nov. 1905; *e s* of W. J. Devlin; *m* 1932, Madeleine, *yr d* of Sir Bernard Oppenheimer, 1st Bt; four *s* twin *d. Educ:* Stonyhurst Coll.; Christ's Coll., Cambridge. President of Cambridge Union, 1926. Called to Bar, Gray's Inn, 1929; KC 1945; Master of the Bench, Gray's Inn, 1947; Treasurer of Gray's Inn, 1963. Prosecuting Counsel to the Mint, 1931–39. Legal Dept, Min. of Supply, 1940–42; Junior Counsel to the Ministries of War Transport, Food and Supply, 1942–45; Attorney-Gen., Duchy of Cornwall, 1947–48; Justice of the High Court, Queen's Bench Div., 1948–60; Pres. of the Restrictive Practices Court, 1956–60; a Lord Justice of Appeal, 1960–61; a Lord of Appeal in Ordinary, 1961–64, retd; Chm. Wiltshire QS, 1955–71. A Judge of the Administrative Tribunal of the ILO, 1964–86; Chm., Commn apptd under constn of ILO to examine complaints concerning observance by Greece of Freedom of Assoc. and similar Conventions, 1969–71. Chairman: Cttee of Inquiry into Dock Labour Scheme, 1955–56; Nyasaland Inquiry Commn, 1959; Cttee of inquiry into the port transport industry, 1964–65; Jt Bd for the Nat. Newspaper Industry, 1965–69; Commn of Inquiry into Industrial Representation, 1971–72; Cttee on Identification in criminal cases, 1974–76. Chm., Press Council, 1964–69. Chm. of Council, Bedford Coll., University of London, 1953–59. Pres., British Maritime Law Assoc., 1962–76; Chm. Assoc. Average Adjusters, 1966–67. Hon. LLD: Glasgow 1962; Toronto 1962; Cambridge 1966; Leicester, 1966; Sussex 1966; Durham, 1968; Liverpool, 1970; St Louis, 1980; Hon. DCL Oxon, 1965. *Publications:* Trial by Jury, 1956 (Hamlyn Lectures); The Criminal Prosecution in England (Sherrill Lectures), 1957; Samples of Lawmaking (Lloyd Roberts and other lectures), 1962; The Enforcement of Morals, (Maccabean and other lectures), 1965; The House of Lords and the Naval Prize Bill, 1911 (Rede Lecture), 1968; Too Proud to Fight: Woodrow Wilson's Neutrality, 1974; The Judge (Chorley and other lectures), 1979; Easing the Passing: the trial of Dr John Bodkin Adams, 1985. *Address:* West Wick House, Pewsey, Wilts; Casa da Colina, Praia da Luz, Algarve.

See also Tim Devlin, William Devlin, Sir P. J. M. Kennedy.

DEVLIN, Alexander, OBE 1977; JP; Member, Glenrothes New Town Development Corporation, 1958–78; *b* 22 Dec. 1927; *s* of Thomas Devlin and Jean Gibson; *m* 1949, Annie Scott Gordon. *Educ:* Cowdenbeath St Columba's High Sch.; National Council of Labour Colls (Local Govt and Public Speaking). Member: Fife CC, 1956–74; Fife Regional Council, 1974–78; Chm., Fife Educn Cttee, 1963–78; Vice-Chm., Educn Cttee of Convention of Scottish Local Authorities, 1974–78. Member: Dunning Cttee on Scottish System for Assessment of Pupils after 4 years Secondary Educn, 1974–77; Scottish Sports Council, 1964–74; Manpower Services Commn, 1978–79. JP Fife, 1963. *Address:* 40 Falcon Drive, Glenrothes, Fife KY7 5HP.

DEVLIN, (Josephine) Bernadette; *see* McAliskey, J. B.

DEVLIN, Keith Michael, PhD; **His Honour Judge Devlin;** a Circuit Judge, since 1984; *b* 21 Oct. 1933; *e s* of Francis Michael Devlin and Norah Devlin; *m* 1958, Pamela Gwendoline Phillips; two *s* one *d. Educ:* Price's Sch., Fareham; King's Coll., London Univ. (LLB 1960, MPhil 1968, PhD 1976). Commnd RAOC, 1953. Called to the Bar, Gray's Inn, 1964; Dep. Chief Clerk, Metropolitan Magistrates' Courts Service, 1964–66; various appts as Dep. Metropolitan Stipendiary Magistrate, 1975–79; a Recorder, 1983–84. Brunel University: Lectr in Law, 1966–71; Reader in Law, 1971–84; Associate Prof. of Law, 1984–; Mem., Court, 1985–. Fellow, Netherlands Inst. for Advanced Study in the Humanities and Social Sciences, Wassenaar, 1975–76. Mem., Consumer Protection Adv. Cttee, 1976–81. Magistrates' Association: Mem., 1974–, Vice-Chm., 1984–, Legal Cttee; co-opted Mem. Council, 1980–. JP Inner London (Juvenile Court Panel), 1968–84 (Chm., 1973–84). Jt Founder and Editor, Anglo-Amer. Law Rev., 1972–84. *Publications:* Sentencing Offenders in Magistrates' Courts, 1970; articles in legal jls. *Recreations:* watching cricket, fly-fishing, Roman Britain. *Address:* Crown Court, St Albans, Herts AL1 3XE. *T:* St Albans 34481. *Clubs:* Athenæum, MCC; Hampshire County Cricket.

DEVLIN, Stuart Leslie, CMG 1980; goldsmith, silversmith and designer in London since 1965; Goldsmith and Jeweller by appointment to HM The Queen, 1982; *b* 9 Oct. 1931; *m* 1962, Kim Hose; *m* 1986, Carole Hedley-Saunders. *Educ:* Gordon Inst. of Technology, Geelong; Royal Melbourne Inst. of Technology; Royal Coll. of Art. DesRCA (Silversmith), DesRCA (Industrial Design/Engrg). Art Teacher, Vic. Educn Dept, 1950–58; Royal Coll. of Art, 1958–60; Harkness Fellow, NY, 1960–62; Lectr, Prahran Techn. Coll., Melbourne, 1962; one-man shows of sculpture, NY and Sydney, 1961–64; Inspr Art in Techn. Schs, Vic. Educn Dept, 1964–65; exhibns of silver and gold in numerous cities USA, Australia, Bermuda, Middle East and UK, 1965–. Executed many commns in gold and silver: designed coins for Australia, Singapore, Cayman Is, Gibraltar, IoM, Burundi, Botswana, Ethiopia and Bhutan; designed and made: cutlery for State Visit to Paris, 1972; Duke of Edinburgh trophy for World Driving Championship, 1973; silver to commemorate opening of Sydney Opera House, 1973; Grand National Trophy, 1975, 1976; Australian Bravery Awards, 1975; Regalia for the Order of Australia, 1975–76; Queen's Silver Jubilee Medal, 1977. Freeman, City of London, 1966; Liveryman, 1972, Mem. Ct of Assts, 1986, Goldsmiths' Co. *Recreations:* squash, windsurfing, ham radio. *Address:* 90 St John Street, EC1 4EH. *T:* 01–253 5471.

DEVLIN, Tim; Public Relations Director, Institute of Directors, since 1984; *b* 28 July 1944; 3rd *s* of Rt Hon. Lord Devlin, *qv; m* 1967, Angela Denise, *d* of Mr A. J. G. and late Mrs Laramy; two *s* two *d. Educ:* Winchester Coll.; University Coll., Oxford (Hons degree, History). Feature Writer, Aberdeen Press & Journal, 1966; Reporter, Scotsman, 1967; Educn Reporter, Evening Echo, Watford, 1968–69; Reporter, later News Editor, The Times Educnl Supplement, 1969–71; Reporter, The Times, 1971–73, Educn Corresp., 1973–77; Nat. Dir, ISIS, 1977–84. *Publications:* (with Mary Warnock) What Must We Teach?, 1977; Good Communications Guide, 1980; Independent Schools—The Facts, 1981; Choosing Your Independent School, 1984. *Recreations:* writing, art, tennis, children. *Address:* Institute of Directors, 116 Pall Mall, SW1Y 5ED. *T:* 01-839 1233.

DEVLIN, William; Actor; *b* Aberdeen, 5 Dec. 1911; *y s* of William John Devlin, ARIBA, and Frances Evelyn Crombie; *m* 1936, Mary Casson (marr. diss.); one *d; m* 1948, Meriel Moore (*d* 1981). *Educ:* Stonyhurst Coll.; Merton Coll., Oxford (BA). Sec. OUDS, 1932–33; studied at Embassy Theatre Sch., 1933–34. New Theatre with John Gielgud, 1934–35 (Hamlet and Noah); Old Vic Company, 1935–36 (Peer Gynt, Cassius, Richard III, Leontes, Lear, etc); except for war period has appeared for Old Vic in every year, 1935–53 (Shylock, Macbeth, Claudius, Brutus, Dogberry, Fluellen, etc). Parnell in The Lost Leader, Abbey Theatre, Dublin, 1937; Zola, Clemenceau, Gladstone in biogr. plays about them, 1937–38; Ransom in Ascent of F6 and Seth in Mourning becomes Electra, New Theatre, 1938. Joined HM Forces, Sept. 1939, as a Trooper in Horsed Cavalry; commnd in Royal Wilts Yeom. and served with 8th Army in Africa and Italy for 4' years; released as Major, Nov. 1945. Leading man with Old Vic at Theatre Royal, Bristol, 1945–48. Memorial Theatre, Stratford-on-Avon, seasons 1954 and 1955. First appeared in New York as Bohun, QC in You Never Can Tell, Martin Beck Theatre, 1948; subseq. at Boston as Lear and Macbeth. Played Clemenceau in The Tiger, the first play to be televised in 1936, and has appeared regularly in this medium and also in Sound Broadcasting. Mem., Equity Council, 1957–65. Mem., Monksilver Parish Council, 1967, Chairman 1971, and 1973–74. *Recreations:* golf and fishing. *Address:* Bird's Hill Cottage, Monksilver, Taunton, Som TA4 4JB. *T:* Stogumber 56389.
   See also Baron Devlin.

DEVON, 17th Earl of, *cr* 1553; **Charles Christopher Courtenay,** Bt 1644; RARO Lieutenant (W/Captain) Coldstream Guards; *b* 13 July 1916; *o surv. s* of 16th Earl and Marguerite (*d* 1950), *d* of late John Silva; *S* father, 1935; *m* 1939, Venetia, Countess of Cottenham, *d* of Captain J. V. Taylor; one *s* one *d. Educ:* Winchester; RMC, Sandhurst. Served war of 1939–45 (despatches). *Recreations:* shooting and fishing. *Heir: s* Lord Courtenay, *qv. Address:* Powderham Castle, Exeter. *T:* Starcross 890253.

DEVONPORT, 3rd Viscount *cr* 1917, of Wittington, Bucks; **Terence Kearley,** RIBA, Bt 1908; Baron 1910; Architect, Landscape Architect, and Rural Consultant in private practice, Newcastle upon Tyne, since 1978; *b* 29 Aug. 1944; *s* of 2nd Viscount Devonport and of Sheila Isabel, *e d* of Lt-Col C. Hope Murray; *S* father, 1973; *m* 1968, Elizabeth Rosemary, *d* of late John G. Hopton (marr. diss. 1979); two *d. Educ:* Aiglon Coll., Vaud, Switzerland; Selwyn Coll., Cambridge (MA, DipArch); Newcastle Univ. (BPhil). Chartered Architect, RIBA, ALI. Nuclear Power Group, Dungeness site office, 1963; Fresco restorer, Massada, Israel, 1964; Cambridge Univ., 1964–67 and 1968–70; Waterside and US Pavilion, Expo '70, design teams, with Davis Brody, New York City, 1967–68; Architect, Rehabilitation Div., London Borough of Lambeth, 1971–72; with Barnett Winskell, 1972–75; Newcastle Univ., 1975–77; with Ralph Erskine, Byker, 1977–78. Dir, Chevy Chase Perfumes, 1984–, and various other cos. Mem., National Environment and Land Use Cttee, Timber Growers UK, 1984–. *Recreations:* naturalist, traveller and gourmet; a Turkophile; interests: archæology, shooting and fishing. *Heir: cousin* Chester Dagley Hugh Kearley [*b* 29 April 1932; *m* 1974, Josefa Mesquida]. *Address:* Ray Demesne, Kirkwhelpington, Newcastle upon Tyne NE19 2RG. *Clubs:* Royal Automobile, Beefsteak, Farmers'; Northern Counties (Newcastle upon Tyne).

DEVONS, Prof. Samuel; FRS 1955; Professor of Physics, Columbia University, New York, 1960–85, now Emeritus (Chairman, Dept of Physics, 1963–67); Director, History of Physics Laboratory, Barnard College, Columbia University, 1970–85; *b* 1914; *s* of Rev. David I. Devons and E. Edleston; *m* 1938, Celia Ruth Toubkin; four *d. Educ:* Trinity Coll., Cambridge. BA 1935; MA, PhD 1939. Exhibition of 1851 Senior Student, 1939. Scientific Officer, Senior Scientific Officer, Air Ministry, MAP, and Ministry of Supply, 1939–45. Lecturer in Physics, Cambridge Univ., Fellow and Dir of Studies, Trinity Coll., Cambridge, 1946–49; Prof. of Physics, Imperial Coll. of Science, 1950–55; Langworthy Prof. of Physics and Dir of Physical Laboratories, Univ. of Manchester, 1955–60. Royal Soc. Leverhulme Vis. Prof., Andhra Univ., India, 1967–68; Balfour Vis. Prof., History of Science, Weizmann Inst., Rehovot, Israel, 1973; Racah Vis. Prof. of Physics, Hebrew Univ., Jerusalem, 1973–74. Rutherford Medal and Prize, Inst. of Physics, 1970. *Publications:* Excited States of Nuclei, 1949; (ed) Biology and Physical Sciences, 1969; (ed) High Energy Physics and Nuclear Structure, 1970; contributions to Proc. Royal Society, Proc. Phys. Soc., etc. *Recreations:* plastic arts, travel. *Address:* Lewis Road, Irvington-on-Hudson, NY 10533, USA. *T:* (914) 591–8100.

DEVONSHIRE, 11th Duke of, *cr* 1694; **Andrew Robert Buxton Cavendish,** PC 1964; MC; Baron Cavendish, 1605; Earl of Devonshire, 1618; Marquess of Hartington, 1694; Earl of Burlington, 1831; Baron Cavendish (UK) 1831; Vice-Lord-Lieutenant of the County of Derby since 1957; Chancellor of Manchester University, 1965–86; *b* 2 Jan. 1920; *o surv s* of 10th Duke of Devonshire, KG, and Lady Mary Cecil (*see* Dowager Duchess of Devonshire), *d* of 4th Marquess of Salisbury, KG, GCVO; *S* father, 1950; *m* 1941, Hon. Deborah Vivian Freeman-Mitford, *d* of 2nd Baron Redesdale; one *s* two *d. Educ:* Eton; Trinity Coll., Cambridge. Served War of 1939–45, Coldstream Guards (MC). Contested (C) Chesterfield Div. of Derbyshire, 1945 and 1950. Parliamentary Under-Sec. of State for Commonwealth Relations, Oct. 1960–Sept. 1962; Minister of State, Commonwealth Relations Office, Sept. 1962–Oct. 1964 and for Colonial Affairs, 1963–Oct. 1964. Executive Steward of the Jockey Club, 1966–69. Mem., Horserace Totalisator Board, 1977–86; a Trustee, Nat. Gallery, 1960–68; President: The Royal Hosp. and Home for Incurables, 1954–; Derbyshire Boy Scouts Assoc.; Lawn Tennis Assoc., 1955–61; RNIB, 1979–85; Nat Assoc. for Deaf Children, 1978–; East Midland Area, MENCAP; Building Societies Assoc., 1954–61; Chairman: Grand Council, British Empire Cancer Campaign, 1956–81; Throughbred Breeders' Assoc., 1978–81. Mayor of Buxton, 1952–54. Hon. Col, Manchester and Salford Univs OTC, 1981–85. Hon. LLD: Manchester; Sheffield; Liverpool; Hon. Dr Law, Memorial Univ. of Newfoundland. *Publication:* Park Top: a romance of the Turf, 1976. *Heir: s* Marquess of Hartington, *qv. Address:* Chatsworth, Bakewell, Derbyshire DE4 1PP. *T:* Baslow 2204; 4 Chesterfield Street, W1. *T:* 01-499 5803; Lismore Castle, Co. Waterford, Eire. *T:* Lismore 54288. *Clubs:* Brooks's, Jockey, White's.
   See also Earl of Stockton.

DEVONSHIRE, Dowager Duchess of, (Mary Alice), GCVO 1955; CBE 1946; Mistress of the Robes to The Queen, 1953–66; Chancellor of the University of Exeter, 1956–70; *b* 29 July 1895; *d* of 4th Marquis of Salisbury, KG, PC, GCVO, and Lady Cicely Alice Gore (*d* 1955), 2nd *d* of 5th Earl of Arran; *m* 1917, as Lady Mary Cecil, 10th Duke of Devonshire, KG; one *s* (*see* 11th Duke of Devonshire) two *d* (*er s* killed in action, 1944). *Address:* 107 Eaton Square, SW1W 9AA. *T:* 01–235 8798; Moorview, Edensor, Bakewell, Derbyshire. *T:* Baslow 2204.

DEVONSHIRE, Michael Norman, TD 1969; Master of the Supreme Court, Taxing Office, since 1979; *b* 23 May 1930; *s* of late Norman George Devonshire and late Edith Devonshire (*née* Skinner); *m* 1962, Jessie Margaret Roberts. *Educ:* King's Sch., Canterbury. Military Service, 2nd Lt, RA, served Korea, 1953–55; 4/5 Bn Queen's Own Royal West Kent Regt TA and 7 Bn Queen's Regt TA, 1955–69; retired in rank of Major, 1969. Articled to H. D. Carter, 1948–53; admitted Solicitor, 1953; Partner, Doyle Devonshire Co., 1957–79. Pres., London Solicitors' Litigation Assoc., 1974–76; Mem., Law Soc. Family Law and Contentious Remuneration Cttees, 1969–79. Mem., Recreation and Conservation Cttee, Southern Water Authy, 1984–. Mem., Council, Royal Yachting Assoc., 1978– (Trustee, Seamanship Foundn, 1981–85). *Publication:* (with M. J. Cook and W. H. Elliott) The Taxation of Contentious Costs, 1979. *Recreation:* sailing. *Address:* 17 Chestnut Avenue, Southborough, Tunbridge Wells, Kent. *T:* Tunbridge Wells 28672.

DE VRIES, Peter; writer; *b* Chicago, 27 Feb. 1910; *s* of Joost and Henrietta (*née* Eldersveld) de Vries; *m* 1943, Katinka Loeser; two *s* one *d. Educ:* Calvin College, Michigan (AB); Northwestern University. Editor, community newspaper, Chicago, 1931; free lance writer, 1931–; associate editor Poetry Magazine, 1938; co-editor, 1942; joined editorial staff New Yorker Magazine, 1944. Mem., Amer. Acad. and Inst. of Arts and Letters. *Publications:* No But I saw the Movie, 1952; The Tunnel of Love, 1954; Comfort Me with Apples, 1956; The Mackerel Plaza, 1958; The Tents of Wickedness, 1959; Through the Fields of Clover, 1961; The Blood of the Lamb, 1962; Reuben, Reuben, 1964 (filmed, 1984); Let Me Count the Ways, 1965; The Vale of Laughter, 1967; The Cat's Pajamas and Witch's Milk, 1968 (filmed as Pete and Tillie, 1982); Mrs Wallop, 1970; Into Your Tent I'll Creep, 1971; Without a Stitch in Time, 1972; Forever Panting, 1973; The Glory of the Hummingbird, 1975; I Hear America Swinging, 1976; Madder Music, 1978; Consenting Adults, 1980; Sauce for the Goose, 1981; Slouching Towards Kalamazoo, 1983; The Prick of Noon, 1985; Peckham's Marbles, 1986. *Address:* c/o New Yorker Magazine, 25 W 43rd Street, New York, NY 10036, USA; (home) 170 Cross Highway, Westport, Conn 06880, USA.

DEW, Leslie Robert; Member, Bermuda Insurance Advisory Committee, since 1979; President and Managing Director, Britamco Ltd, 1977–84; President, Insco Ltd, Bermuda (Gulf Oil Corporation Insurance Subsidiaries), 1980–84 (Executive Vice President-Underwriter, 1977–80); Chairman, 1971–77 and formerly Non-Marine Underwriter, Roy J. M. Merrett Syndicates; *b* 11 April 1914; *er s* of Robert Thomas Dew, RHA and Ellen Dora Frampton; *m* 1st, 1939, Vera Doreen Wills (marr. diss. 1956); 2nd, 1956, Patricia Landsberg (*née* Hyde); one *s. Educ:* privately. Underwriting Member of Lloyd's, 1950–; Mem. Cttee of Lloyd's, 1969–72, 1974–77; Dep. Chm. of Lloyd's, 1971, 1975, 1977; Mem. Cttee, Lloyd's Non-Marine Assoc., 1957–77 (Dep. Chm. 1963 and 1965, Chm. 1966); Chm., Lloyd's Common Market Working Gp, 1971–77; Dep. Chm., British Insurers' European Cttee, 1972–77. Binney Award for Civilian Bravery, 1975. *Recreations:* music, reading. *Address:* PO Box WK 457, Warwick 7, Bermuda. *Clubs:* Metropolitan (NY); Royal Bermuda Yacht, Coral Beach and Tennis (Bermuda).

DEW, Prof. Ronald Beresford; Professor Emeritus, University of Manchester Institute of Science and Technology, since 1980; *b* 19 May 1916; *s* of Edwyn Dew-Jones, FCA, and Jean Robertson Dew-Jones, BA, (*née* McInnes); *m* 1940, Sheila Mary Smith, BA; one *s* one *d. Educ:* Sedbergh; Manchester Univ. (LLB); Cambridge Univ. (MA). Barrister-at-Law, Middle Temple, 1965. Lieut, RNVR, 1940–45. Asst Managing Dir, P-E Consulting Gp, 1952–62; Director: Kurt Salmon & Co., 1955–62; S. Dodd & Co., 1957–59. Visiting Prof. of Industrial Administration, Manchester Univ., 1960–63; Head of Dept of Management Sciences, Univ. of Manchester Inst. of Science and Technology, 1963–70 and 1974–77; Prof. of Industrial Administration, Manchester Univ., 1963–67; Prof. of

Management Sciences, 1967–80. Mem. Council, Internat. Univ. Contact for Management Educn, 1966–71; Dir, Centre for Business Research, 1965–69; Dir, European Assoc. of Management Training Centres, 1966–71; Dep. Chm., Manchester Polytechnic, 1970–72; External Examiner, Univs of: Liverpool, 1967–70; Loughborough, 1968–73; Bath, 1970–73; Khartoum (Sudan), 1967–70. Co-Chm., Conf. of Univ. Management Schools (CUMS), 1970–73; Governor: Manchester Coll. of Commerce, 1966–70; Manchester Polytechnic, 1970–76; Member: Council of BIM, 1971–76 (Bd of NW Region, 1966–80); Council of Manchester Business School, 1967–76; Court of Manchester Univ., 1978–80; Trustee, European Foundation for Management Develt, 1975–77; Consultant on organisation and control, to various internat. cos. CBIM, FCA. *Publications:* (co-author) Management Control and Information, 1973; numerous papers in internat. jls, on management control systems. *Recreations:* archaeology, ornithology, bee-keeping, travel. *Address:* University of Manchester Institute of Science and Technology, Department of Management Sciences, Sackville Street, Manchester M60 1QD. *T:* 061–236 3311.

de WAAL, Constant Hendrik, CB 1977; First Parliamentary Counsel since 1987; Barrister-at-law; *b* 1 May 1931; *s* of late Hendrik de Waal and of Elizabeth von Ephrussi; *m* 1964, Julia Jessel; two *s. Educ:* Tonbridge Sch. (scholar); Pembroke Coll., Cambridge (scholar). 1st cl. Law Tripos, 1st cl. LLM. Called to the Bar, Lincoln's Inn, 1953; Buchanan Prize, Cassel Scholar. Fellow of Pembroke Coll., Cambridge, and Univ. Asst Lectr in Law, 1958–60. Entered Parliamentary Counsel Office, 1960; with Law Commission, 1969–71; Parly Counsel, 1971–. *Recreation:* remaining (so far as possible) unaware of current events. *Address:* 62 Sussex Street, SW1.

See also Very Rev. V. A. de Waal.

de WAAL, Rev. Canon Hugo Ferdinand; Principal, Ridley Hall Theological College, Cambridge, since 1978; Hon. Canon of Ely Cathedral, since 1986; *b* 16 March 1935; *s* of Bernard Hendrik and Albertine Felice de Waal; *m* 1960, Brigit Elizabeth Townsend Massingberd-Mundy; one *s* three *d. Educ:* Tonbridge School; Pembroke Coll., Cambridge (MA); Münster Univ., Germany; Ridley Hall, Cambridge. Curate, St Martin's-in-the Bull Ring, Birmingham, 1960; Chaplain, Pembroke Coll., Cambridge, 1964–68; Rector of Dry Drayton, Cambs, 1964–73; with Bar Hill Ecumenical Area, 1967–73; Vicar of St John's, Blackpool Parish Church, 1974–78. *Recreations:* music, tennis and squash, fly-fishing. *Address:* The Principal's Lodge, Ridley Hall, Cambridge CB3 9HG. *T:* Cambridge 58665.

de WAAL, Rev. Victor Alexander; Dean of Canterbury, 1976–86; *b* 2 Feb. 1929; *s* of late Hendrik de Waal and of Elizabeth von Ephrussi; *m* 1960, Esther Aline Lowndes Moir, PhD; four *s. Educ:* Tonbridge School; Pembroke Coll., Cambridge (MA); Ely Theological College. With Phs van Ommeren (London) Ltd, 1949–50; Asst Curate, St Mary the Virgin, Isleworth, 1952–56; Chaplain, Ely Theological Coll., 1956–59; Chaplain and Succentor, King's Coll., Cambridge, 1959–63; Chaplain, Univ. of Nottingham, 1963–69; Chancellor of Lincoln Cathedral, 1969–76. Hon. DD Nottingham, 1983. *Publications:* What is the Church?, 1969; contrib.: Theology and Modern Education, 1965; Stages of Experience, 1965; The Committed Church, 1966; Liturgy Reshaped, 1982. *Recreations:* pottery, fishing. *Address:* Cwm Cottage, Rowlestone, Pontrilas, Hereford HR2 0DP. *T:* Golden Valley 240391.

See also C. H. de Waal.

DEWAR, family name of **Baron Forteviot.**

DEWAR, David Alexander; an Assistant Auditor General, National Audit Office, since 1984; *b* 28 Oct. 1934; *s* of James and Isabella Dewar; *m* 1959, Rosalind Mary Ellen Greenwood; one *s* one *d. Educ:* Leith Academy, Edinburgh. Entered Exchequer and Audit Dept, 1953; Chief Auditor, 1966; Deputy Director of Audit, 1973; Director of Audit, 1977; Dep. Sec. of Dept, 1981. *Recreations:* gardening, golf. *Address:* 85 Orchard Drive, Horsell, Woking, Surrey GU21 4BS. *T:* Woking 5352.

DEWAR, Donald Campbell; MP (Lab) Glasgow, Garscadden, since April 1978; solicitor, with Ross Harper & Murphy, Glasgow; *b* 21 Aug. 1937; *s* of Dr Alasdair Dewar, Glasgow; *m* 1964, Alison McNair (marr. diss. 1973); one *s* one *d. Educ:* Glasgow Acad.; Glasgow Univ. (MA, LLB). MP (Lab) South Aberdeen, 1966–70; PPS to Pres. of Bd of Trade, 1967; Chm., Select Cttee on Scottish Affairs, 1979–81; front bench spokesman on Scottish Affairs, 1980–; Mem., Shadow Cabinet, 1984–. *Address:* 23 Cleveden Road, Glasgow G12 0PQ.

DEWAR, George Duncan Hamilton; chartered accountant; Partner, Peat, Marwick, Mitchell & Co., Glasgow, 1949–81; *b* 11 Sept. 1916; *s* of George Readman Dewar and Elizabeth Garrioch Sinclair Hamilton; *m* 1940, Elizabeth Lawson Potts Lawrie; one *s* one *d. Educ:* High Sch. of Glasgow. Mem. Inst. Chartered Accountants of Scotland (admitted, 1940; Mem. Coun., 1960–65; Vice-Pres., 1969–70; Pres., 1970–71). Mem., Scottish Tourist Bd, 1977–80. *Recreations:* golf, gardening. *Address:* 82 Langside Drive, Glasgow G43 2SX. *T:* 041–637 1734. *Clubs:* Western, Royal Scottish Automobile (Glasgow).

DEWAR, Ian Stewart; JP; Under-Secretary, Welsh Office, 1973–83; Member, South Glamorgan County Council, since 1985; *b* 29 Jan. 1929; *er s* of late William Stewart Dewar and of Eileen Dewar (*née* Godfrey); *m* 1968, Nora Stephanie House; one *s* one *d. Educ:* Penarth County Sch.; UC Cardiff; Jesus Coll., Oxford (MA). RAF, 1947–49. Asst Archivist, Glamorgan County Council, 1952–53. Entered Min. of Labour, 1953; Asst Private Sec. to Minister, 1956–58; Principal, Min. of Labour and Civil Service Commn, 1958–65; Asst Sec., Min. of Labour, Dept of Employment and Commn on Industrial Relations, 1965–70; Asst Sec., Welsh Office, 1970–73. Member, Governing Body: Univ. of Wales, 1985–; Nat. Mus. of Wales, 1985–. JP S Glam, 1985. *Address:* 59 Stanwell Road, Penarth, South Glamorgan. *T:* Cardiff 703255.

DEWAR, Prof. Michael James Steuart, FRS 1960; MA, DPhil Oxon; Robert A. Welch Professor of Chemistry, University of Texas, since 1963; *b* 24 Sept. 1918; *s* of Francis D. Dewar, ICS, and Nan B. Keith; *m* 1944, Mary Williamson; two *s. Educ:* Winchester Coll. (First Scholar); Balliol Coll., Oxford (Brackenbury, Frazer and Gibbs Scholar; Hon. Fellow, 1974). ICI Fellow in Chemistry, Oxford, 1945; Courtaulds Ltd, Fundamental Research Laboratory, 1945–51; Reilly Lecturer at Notre Dame Univ., USA, 1951; Prof. of Chemistry and Head of Dept of Chemistry at Queen Mary Coll., University of London, 1951–59; Prof. of Chemistry, University of Chicago, 1959–63. Visiting Prof. at Yale Univ., USA, 1957. Hon. Sec. Chemical Soc., 1957–59. Harrison Howe Award of Amer. Chem. Soc., 1961; (first) G. W. Wheland Meml Medal, Univ. of Chicago, 1976; Evans Award, Ohio State Univ., 1977; South West Regional Award, Amer. Chem. Soc., 1978; Davy Medal, Royal Soc., 1982; James Flack Norris Award, Amer. Chem. Soc., 1984. Lectures: Tilden, Chem. Soc., 1954; Falk-Plaut, Columbia Univ., 1963; Daines Memorial, Univ. of Kansas, 1963; Glidden Company, Western Reserve Univ., 1964; Marchon Visiting, Univ. of Newcastle upon Tyne, 1966; Glidden Company, Kent State Univ., 1967; Gnehm, Eidg. Tech. Hochschule, Zurich, 1968; Barton, Univ. of Oklahoma, 1969; Kahlbaum, Univ. of Basel, 1970; Benjamin Rush, Univ. of Pennsylvania, 1971; Venable, Univ. of N Carolina, 1971; Foster, State Univ. of NY at Buffalo, 1973; Robinson, Chem. Soc., 1974; Sprague, Univ. of Wisconsin, 1974; Bircher, Vanderbilt Univ., 1976; Faraday, Northern Illinois Univ., 1977; Priestley, Pennsylvania State Univ., 1980; J. Clarence Karcher, Univ. of Oklahoma, 1984; Res. Scholar Lectr., Drew Univ., 1984; Visiting Professor: Arthur D. Little, MIT, 1966; Maurice S. Kharasch, Univ. of Chicago, 1971; Firth, Sheffield, 1972; Dist. Bicentennial, Univ. of Utah, 1976; Pahlavi, Iran, 1977. Fellow, Amer. Acad. of Arts and Sciences, 1966. *Publications:* The Electronic Theory of Organic Chemistry, 1949; Hyperconjugation, 1962; Introduction to Modern Chemistry, 1965; The Molecular Orbital Theory of Organic Chemistry, 1969; Computer Compilation of Molecular Weights and Percentage Compositions, 1970; The PMO Theory of Organic Chemistry, 1975; papers in scientific journals. *Address:* Department of Chemistry, University of Texas, Austin, Texas 78712, USA. *T:* (512) 471–5053.

DEWAR, Robert James, CMG 1969; CBE 1964; Consultant to World Bank, since 1984; *b* 1923; *s* of late Dr Robert Scott Dewar, MA, MB, ChB, Dumbreck, Glasgow, and Mrs Roubaix Dewar, Aberdovey, N Wales; *m* 1947, Christina Marianne, *d* of late Olof August Ljungberger, Stockholm, Sweden; two *s* one *d. Educ:* High Sch. of Glasgow; Edinburgh Univ. (BSc, Forestry); Wadham Coll., Oxford. Asst Conservator of Forests, Colonial Forest Service, Nigeria and Nyasaland, 1944–55; Dep. Chief Conservator of Forests, Nyasaland, 1955–60; Chief Conservator of Forests, Dir of Forestry and Game, Nyasaland (now Malawi), 1960–64; Mem. Nyasaland Legislative Council, 1960. Permanent Secretary, Malawi: Min. of Natural Resources, 1964–67 and 1968–69; Min. of Economic Affairs, 1967–68; retd from Malawi CS, 1969; World Bank: Sen. Agriculturalist, 1969–74; Chief of Agricl Div., Regl Mission for Eastern Africa, 1974–84. Mem. Nat. Development Council, Malawi, 1966–69. *Recreations:* golf, angling. *Address:* 18 Middlebourne Lane, Farnham, Surrey GU10 3NH. *T:* Farnham 713690. *Club:* Royal Commonwealth Society.

DEWAR, His Honour Thomas; a Circuit Judge (formerly Judge of the County Court), 1962–84; Joint President, Council of Circuit Judges, 1980 (Vice-President, 1979); *b* 5 Jan. 1909; *s* of James Stewart Dewar and Katherine Rose Dewar; *m* 1950, Katherine Muriel Johnson; one *s. Educ:* Penarth Intermediate School; Cardiff Technical Coll.; Sch. of Pharmacy, University of London; Birkbeck Coll., University of London. Pharmaceutical Chemist, 1931; BPharm 1931, PhD 1934, BSc (Botany, 1st cl. hons) 1936, London. Called to Bar, Middle Temple, 1939; Blackstone Pupillage Prize, 1939. Admin. staff of Pharmaceutical Soc., 1936–40; Sec., Middx Pharmaceutical Cttee, 1940–41; Asst Dir, Min. of Supply, 1943; Sec., Wellcome Foundation, 1943–45. Mem. of Western Circuit, 1945–62; Judge of the County Court (circuit 59, Cornwall and Plymouth), 1962–65, (circuit 38, Edmonton, etc), 1965–66 (circuit 41, Clerkenwell), 1966–71; Circuit Judge, SE circuit, 1972–83. Presided over inquiry into X-ray accident at Plymouth Hosp., 1962. Mem. Executive Council, Internat. Law Assoc., 1974–. Governor, Birkbeck Coll., 1944–46 and 1971–82. *Publications:* Textbook of Forensic Pharmacy, 1946 and four subsequent editions; scientific papers in Quarterly Jl of Pharmacy and Pharmacology. *Recreations:* horticulture, travel. *Address:* 1 Garden Court, Temple, EC4. *T:* 01–353 3326; Goldenhurst Cottage, Aldington, Kent. *T:* Aldington 420.

de WARDENER, Prof. Hugh Edward, CBE 1982 (MBE (mil.) 1946); MD, FRCP; Professor of Medicine, University of London, Charing Cross Hospital, 1960–81, now Emeritus; Honorary Consultant Physician to the Army, 1975–80; *b* 8 Oct. 1915; *s* of Edouard de Wardener and Becky (*née* Pearce); *m* 1st, 1939, Janet Lavinia Bellis Simon (marr. diss. 1947); one *s*; 2nd, 1947, Diana Rosamund Crawshay (marr. diss. 1954); 3rd, 1954, Jill Mary Foxworthy (marr. diss. 1969); one *d*; 4th, 1969, Josephine Margaret Storey, MBE; two *s. Educ:* Malvern Coll. St Thomas's Hosp., 1933–39; RAMC, 1939–45; St Thomas's Hosp., 1945–60, Registrar, Senior Lecturer, Reader. MRCP 1946, MD 1949, FRCP 1958. Hon. MD, Univ. Pierre et Marie Curie, Paris, 1980. President: Internat. Soc. of Nephrology, 1969–72; Renal Assoc., 1973–76; Mem. Council, Imp. Cancer Res. Fund, 1981. *Publications:* The Kidney: An Outline of Normal and Abnormal Structure and Function, 1958, 5th edn 1986; papers in various scientific journals. *Recreations:* normal and scything. *Address:* 9 Dungarvan Avenue, Barnes, SW15. *T:* 01–878 3130.

DEWDNEY, Duncan Alexander Cox, CBE 1968; Director, The Coverdale Organisation, since 1973; *b* 22 Oct. 1911; *o s* of late Claude Felix Dewdney and Annie Ross Cox; *m* 1935, Ann, *d* of Walter Riley and Emily Sterratt; two *d. Educ:* Bromgrove Sch., Worcs; University of Birmingham (BSc Hons, Cadman Medallist). Served War of 1939–45; RAF, 1940–45 (Wing Comdr); Air Staff appts, Head RE8 Min. of Home Security (R&D Dept). British Petroleum Co., 1932–36; International Assoc. (Pet. Ind.) Ltd, 1936–40; Research Man., Esso Development Co., 1945–51; joined Esso Petroleum Co., 1951; Dir, 1957; Man. Dir, 1963–67; Vice-Chm., 1968. Seconded to NBPI as Jt Dep. Chm., 1965–66, part-time Mem. Bd, 1967–69. Exec. Dir, Rio Tinto Zinc Corporation, 1968–72; Chairman: Irish Refining Co. Ltd, 1958–65; Anglesey Aluminium, 1968–71; RTZ Britain, 1969–72; RTZ Development Enterprises, 1970–72; Dep. Chm., Manpower Services Commn, 1974–77; Dir, Esso Chemicals SA, 1964. Chairman: National Economic Develt Cttee for the Mechanical Engrg Industry, 1964–68; Welsh Industrial Develt Bd, 1972–75; Underwater Training Centre, 1977–79. Legion of Merit, 1945. *Address:* Salters, Harestock, Winchester, Hants. *T:* Winchester 2034. *Club:* Travellers'.

DEWES, Sir Herbert (John Salisbury), Kt 1973; CBE 1954; DL; JP; Chairman, Cheshire County Council, 1968–74; *b* 30 June 1897; *s* of John Hunt Dewes, solicitor, Tamworth, Staffordshire; *m* 1923, Kathleen, *d* of W. Matthews, Nuneaton; two *s. Educ:* Aldenham. County Alderman for Cheshire, 1950; JP 1951, DL 1966, Cheshire. Presidential Award, RSA, 1973. *Address:* 2 Curzon Park North, Chester CH4 8AR. *T:* Chester 679798.

de WET, Dr Carel; South African Ambassador to the Court of St James's, 1964–67 and 1972–77; Director of companies; farmer; *b* Memel, OFS, S Africa, 25 May 1924; *g s* of Gen. Christian de Wet; *m* 1949, Catharina Elizabeth (Rina) Mass, BA; one *s* three *d. Educ:* Vrede High Sch., OFS; Pretoria Univ. (BSc); University of Witwatersrand (MB, BCh). Served at Nat. Hosp., Bloemfontein; subseq. practised medicine at Boksburg, Transvaal, at Winburg, OFS, and, from 1948, at Vanderbijlpark, Transvaal. Mayor of Vanderbijlpark, 1950–53; MP (Nat. Party) for Vanderbijlpark, 1953–64, for Johannesburg West, 1967–72; Mem. various Parly and Nat. Party Cttees, 1953–64; Minister of Mines and Health, Govt of S Africa, 1967–72. *Recreations:* beef ranching, golf, rugby, cricket, hunting, deep sea fishing. *Address:* PO Box 6424, Johannesburg 2000, Republic of South Africa. *T:* (office) 834–1444; (home) 706-6202. *Clubs:* Royal Automobile, East India, Institute of Directors, MCC, Les Ambassadeurs, Eccentric, Wentworth; Here XVII (Cape Town); Constantia (Pretoria); Club RSA, New, Rand Park Golf, Country (Johannesburg); Maccauvlei Country (Vereeniging), Emfuleni Golf (Vanderbijlpark); Brits Golf (Brits, Transvaal).

DEWEY, Sir Anthony Hugh, 3rd Bt, *cr* 1917; JP; *b* 31 July 1921; *s* of late Major Hugh Grahame Dewey, MC (*e s* of 2nd Bt), and of Marjorie Florence Isobell (who *m* 2nd, 1940, Sir Robert Bell, KCSI; he died 1953), *d* of Lieut-Col Alexander Hugh Dobbs; *S* grandfather, 1948; *m* 1949, Sylvia, *d* of late Dr J. R. MacMahon, Branksome Manor, Bournemouth; two *s* three *d.* JP Somerset, 1961. *Heir: s* Rupert Grahame Dewey [*b* 29 March 1953; *m* 1978, Suzanne Rosemary, *d* of late Andrew Lusk, Perthshire; two *s*].

Address: The Rag, Galhampton, Yeovil, Som. *T:* North Cadbury 40213. *Club:* Army and Navy.

DEWEY, Prof. John Frederick, FRS 1985; FGS; Professor of Geology and Fellow of University College, University of Oxford, since 1986; *b* 22 May 1937; *s* of John Edward and Florence Nellie Mary Dewey; *m* 1961, Frances Mary Blackhurst; one *s* one *d. Educ:* Bancroft's School; Queen Mary Coll. and Imperial Coll., Univ. of London (BSc, PhD, DIC, MA). Lecturer: Univ. of Manchester, 1960–64; Univ. of Cambridge, 1964–70; Prof., State Univ. of New York at Albany, 1970–82; Prof. of Geology, Durham Univ., 1982–86. Numerous honours and awards, UK and overseas. *Publications:* contribs to Geol Soc. of America Bulletin, Geol Soc. London Jl, Jl Geophysical Res. and other learned jls. *Recreations:* skiing, cricket, water colour painting, model railways. *Address:* University College, Oxford. *Club:* Athenæum.

DEWHURST, Prof. Sir (Christopher) John, Kt 1977; FRCOG, FRCSE; Professor of Obstetrics and Gynaecology, University of London, at Queen Charlotte's Hospital for Women, 1967–85, now Professor Emeritus; *b* 2 July 1920; *s* of John and Agnes Dewhurst; *m* 1952, Hazel Mary Atkin; two *s* one *d. Educ:* St Joseph's Coll., Dumfries; Manchester Univ. MB, ChB. Surg. Lieut, RNVR, 1943–46. Sen. Registrar, St Mary's Hosp., Manchester, 1948–51; Lectr, Sen. Lectr and Reader, Sheffield Univ., 1951–67. Pres., RCOG, 1975–78. Hon. FACOG 1976; Hon. FRCSI 1977; Hon. FCOG (SA) 1978; Hon. FRACOG 1985. Hon. DSc Sheffield, 1977; Hon. MD Uruguay, 1980. *Publications:* A Student's Guide to Obstetrics and Gynaecology, 1960, 2nd edn 1965; The Gynaecological Disorders of Infants and Children, 1963; (jtly) The Intersexual Disorders, 1969; (ed) Integrated Obstetrics and Gynaecology for Postgraduates, 1972, 3rd edn 1981; (jtly) A General Practice of Obstetrics and Gynaecology, 1977, 2nd edn 1984; Practical Paediatric and Adolescent Gynaecology, 1980; Royal Confinements, 1980; Female Puberty and its Abnormalities, 1984. *Recreations:* cricket, gardening, music. *Address:* 39 Old Slade Lane, Iver, Bucks. *T:* Iver 653395.

DEWHURST, Comdr Ronald Hugh, DSO 1940; RN retired; *b* 10 Oct. 1905; *s* of late Robert Paget Dewhurst, ICS, and late Florence Frances Maud Dewhurst; *m* 1928, Torquilla Macleod Lawrence (*d* 1953); one *s* one *d*; *m* 1954, Marion Isabel Dahm; one *d. Educ:* Abberley Hall; Osborne; Dartmouth. Joined Royal Navy, 1919; served in submarines, 1927–53; commanded HM submarines H. 33, Seahorse, and Rorqual (DSO and two Bars); Amphion, Taciturn, and RN Detention Quarters, 1953–55; retired to New Zealand, 1955. *Recreations:* fishing, bridge. *Address:* 6 Wychwood Crescent, Rotorua, New Zealand.

DEWHURST, Timothy Littleton, MC 1945; Registrar of the High Court of Justice in Bankruptcy, since 1981; *b* 4 March 1920; *s* of late Robert Cyril Dewhurst and Rhoda Joan Dewhurst; *m* 1949, Pandora Laetitia Oldfield (*d* 1984); four *d. Educ:* Stowe Sch.; Magdalen Coll., Oxford (MA). Called to Bar, Lincoln's Inn, 1950. Served with Rifle Brigade, 1941–46, N Africa and Italy (despatches 1944). Mem. Bar Council, 1977–79; Conveyancing Counsel of the Court, 1980–81. *Address:* Thomas More Building, Royal Courts of Justice, Strand, WC2.

de WINTER, Carl; Secretary General, Federation of British Artists, 1978–84; *b* 18 June 1934; *s* of Alfred de Winter; *m* 1958, Lyndall Bradshaw; one *s* one *d. Educ:* Pangbourne. Purser, Orient Line, 1951–60. Art Exhibitions Bureau: PA to Man. Dir, 1961–66; Director, 1967–84; Royal Soc. of Portrait Painters: Asst Sec., 1962–84; Royal Soc. of Miniature Painters, Sculptors and Gravers: Asst Sec., 1964–67; Sec., 1968–84; Royal Soc. of Marine Artists: Asst Sec., 1964–70; Sec., 1971–78; Royal Soc. of British Artists: Asst Keeper, 1969–73; Keeper, 1974–84; Royal Inst. of Oil Painters: Sec., 1973–84; Royal Inst. of Painters in Watercolours: Sec., 1979–84; National Soc. of Painters, Sculptors and Printmakers: Sec., 1973–84; New English Art Club: Sec., 1973–84; United Soc. of Artists: Sec., 1975–81. *Address:* Holbrook Park House, Holbrook, near Horsham, W Sussex RH12 4PW. *T:* Horsham 52431.

de WINTON, Michael Geoffrey, CBE 1960 (OBE 1952); MC 1944; Assistant Legal Secretary to the Law Officers, 1972–80; *b* 17 Oct. 1916; *s* of John Jeffreys de Winton and Ida de Winton; *m* 1948, Ursula Mary, *d* of E. E. Lightwood, MB; two *s* one *d. Educ:* Monmouth School. Admitted Solicitor, 1939. War service, 1939–46: commnd S Wales Borderers, 1940; Company Comdr 2nd Punjab Regt, Indian Army, in India, Middle East and Burma, 1942–45 (despatches twice). Administrative officer, Nigeria, 1946–48; Crown Counsel, 1948–53; called to the Bar, Gray's Inn, 1953; Principal legal draftsman, W Nigeria, 1954; Solicitor General and Permanent Sec. to Min. of Justice, W Nigeria, 1957–61; retired from HM Overseas CS and re-admitted solicitor, 1961; Asst Legal Adviser, Colonial Office, 1961–66, CRO 1967, FCO 1968; Asst Solicitor, Law Officers Dept (Internat. and Commonwealth affairs), 1969; Under Secretary, 1974; retired, 1980. Legal consultant to overseas govts and internat. organizations; Principal Legal Adviser, British Indian Ocean Territory, 1982–83. *Recreations:* music, golf. *Address:* Stable Cottage, Church Walk, Stalbridge, Dorset DT10 2LR. *T:* Stalbridge 62834.

DE WOLF, Vice-Adm. Harry George, CBE 1946; DSO 1944; DSC 1944; *b* 1903; *s* of late Harry George De Wolf, Bedford, NS; *m* 1931, Gwendolen Fowle, *d* of Thomas St George Gilbert, Somerset, Bermuda; one *s* one *d.* Served War of 1939–45. Asst Chief of Naval Staff, Canada, 1944–47; Sen. Canadian Naval Officer Afloat, 1947–48; Flag Officer, Pacific Coast, 1948–50; Vice-Chief of Naval Staff, 1950–52; Chm. of Canadian Joint Staff, Washington, 1953–55; Chief of Naval Staff, Canada, 1956–60, retired. Hon. DSc (M): Royal Military College of Canada, 1966; Royal Roads Mil. Coll., 1980. *Address:* Apt 1006, 200 Rideau Terrace, Ottawa, Ont., Canada; Old Post Office, Somerset, Bermuda.

DEWS, Peter; Theatre and TV Director; *b* 26 Sept. 1929; *er s* of John Dews and Edna (Bloomfield); *m* 1960, Ann Rhodes. *Educ:* Queen Elizabeth Grammar Sch., Wakefield; University Coll., Oxford (MA). Asst Master, Holgate and District Grammar Sch., Barnsley, 1952–53; BBC Midland Region Drama Producer (Radio and TV), 1953–63; Dir, Ravinia Shakespeare Festival, Chicago, 1963–64; Artistic Director: Birmingham Repertory Theatre, 1966–72; Chichester Fest. Theatre, 1978–80. Directed: TV: An Age of Kings, 1960 (SFTA Award 1960); The Spread of the Eagle, 1963; Theatre: As You Like It, Vaudeville, 1967; Hadrian VII, Mermaid, 1968, Haymarket and NY, 1969 (Tony Award 1969); Antony and Cleopatra, Chichester, 1969; Vivat Vivat Regina, Chichester, 1970, Piccadilly and NY, 1972; The Alchemist, Chichester, 1970; Crown Matrimonial, Haymarket, 1972, NY 1973; The Director of the Opera, Chichester, 1973; The Waltz of the Toreadors, Haymarket, 1974; King John, Stratford, Ont, 1974; The Pleasure of His Company, Toronto, 1974; Coriolanus, Tel Aviv, 1975; Othello, Chichester, 1975; Equus, Vancouver, 1975; Number Thirteen Rue de l'Amour, Phœnix, 1976; The Circle, Chichester, transf. to Haymarket, 1976; The Pleasure of His Company, Phœnix, 1976; Man and Superman, Don Juan in Hell, When We Are Married, Ottawa, 1977; Julius Caesar, Chichester, 1977; A Sleep of Prisoners, Chichester Cathedral, 1978; Julius Caesar, A Sleep of Prisoners, Hong Kong Festival, 1979; The Devil's Disciple, The Importance of Being Earnest, Chichester, 1979; Terra Nova, Much Ado About Nothing, Chichester, 1980; Plenty, Toronto, 1981; The Taming of the Shrew, The Comedy of Errors, Stratford, Ont, 1981; Cards on the Table, Vaudeville, 1981; 56 Duncan Terrace, Edmonton, A Midsummer Night's Dream, Plymouth, and Terra Nova, Durban, 1982; Pierewaaien, Arnhem, 1983; Time and the Conways, Chichester, 1983; On The Razzle, Durban, 1983; Romeo and Juliet, Stratford, Ont, and Measure for Measure, Tel Aviv, 1984; Waiting for Godot, and Galileo, Scottish Theatre Co., 1985. *Recreation:* music. *Address:* c/o Larry Dalzell Associates Ltd, 126 Kennington Park Road, SE11 4DJ.

DEXTER, Harold; Organist; Professor, Guildhall School of Music and Drama (Head of General Musicianship Department, 1962–85); Organist, St Botolph's, Aldgate; *b* 7 Oct. 1920; *s* of F. H. and E. Dexter; *m* 1942, Faith Grainger; one *d. Educ:* Wyggeston Grammar Sch., Leicester; Corpus Christi Coll., Cambridge, 1939–41 and 1946. ARCO 1938; College Organ Scholar, 1939; John Stewart of Rannoch Scholar, 1940; FRCO 1940; ARCM 1941. BA, MusB 1942; MA 1946; RCO Choirmaster's Diploma; John Brook Prize, 1946; ADCM, 1948. Royal Navy and RNVR, 1941–46. Organist, Louth Parish Church and Music-Master, King Edward VI Grammar Sch., Louth, 1947–49; Organist, Holy Trinity, Leamington Spa, 1949–56; Music Master, Bablake Sch., Coventry, 1952–56; Master of the Music, Southwark Cathedral, 1956–68. Conductor, Southend Bach Choir, 1980–82. FGSM 1962, FRSCM 1964 (Hon. diplomas). *Address:* 8 Prince Edward Road, Billericay, Essex. *T:* Billericay 52042.

DEXTER, John; Director of Production, 1974–81, Production Adviser, 1981–84, Metropolitan Opera, New York. Actor in repertory, television and radio, until 1957; Associate Dir, National Theatre, 1963. Best Dir of Drama Award, 1975; Shakespeare Prize, 1978. *Plays directed:* 15 plays, 1957–72, Royal Court, incl. The Old Ones, 1972; Pygmalion, Albery, 1974; Valmouth, Chichester Fest., 1982; *National Theatre:* Saint Joan, 1963; Hobson's Choice, Othello, Royal Hunt of the Sun, 1964; Armstrong's Last Goodnight, Black Comedy, 1965; A Bond Honoured, The Storm, 1966; A Woman Killed With Kindness, Tyger, The Good Natur'd Man, 1971; The Misanthrope, Equus, The Party, 1973; Phaedra Britannica, 1975; As You Like It, 1979; The Life of Galileo, 1980; The Shoemakers' Holiday, 1981; *other London theatres:* The Portage to San Cristobal of A. H., Mermaid, 1982; The Devil and the Good Lord, Lyric, Hammersmith, 1984; Gigi, Lyric, 1985; productions by New Theatre Company: The Cocktail Party, Phoenix, 1986; *New York:* Chips With Everything, 1963; Do I Hear a Waltz?, 1965; Black Comedy and White Lies, The Unknown Soldier and His Wife, 1967; Equus, 1974; The Glass Menagerie, 1983; *Los Angeles:* Pygmalian, Ahmanson Th., 1979; *film:* The Virgin Soldiers, 1968; *opera:* Benvenuto Cellini, Covent Garden, 1966; House of the Dead, Boris Godunov, Billy Budd, Ballo in Maschera, I Vespri Siciliani, Hamburg; The Devils of Loudon, Sadler's Wells; La Forza Del Destino, 1975, Paris; L'enfant et les sortilèges, and The Nightingale, Covent Garden, 1983; La Buone Figliola, Buxton Fest., 1985; Nabucco, Zurich, 1986; *opera for Metropolitan, NY:* I Vespri Siciliani, Aida, 1976; Le Prophète, Dialogues of the Carmelites, Lulu, Rigoletto, 1977; Don Pasquale, Billy Budd, The Bartered Bride, 1978; Don Carlo, Rise and Fall of the City of Mahagonny, Die Entführung aus dem Serail, 1979; Le Rossignol, Le Sacre du Printemps, Oedipus Rex (triple bill), 1981; Parade, 1981. *Recreations:* work, garden. *Address:* 142A Portland Road, W11.

DEXTER, Dr Keith, CB 1978; Second Crown Estate Commissioner, since 1983; *b* 3 April 1928; *yr s* of Arthur William Dexter, farmer, and Phyllis Dexter; *m* 1954, Marjorie Billbrough; no *c. Educ:* Dixie Grammar Sch., Market Bosworth; Univs of Nottingham and Illinois. BSc London 1948; MS Illinois 1951; PhD Nottingham 1954; Nat. Diploma in Agric. 1948. ARICS 1986. Asst Agric. Economist, Nottingham Univ., 1948–50; Booth Fellow, Illinois Univ., 1950–51; Fulbright Trav. Schol., 1950–51; Res. Schol. and Agric. Economist, Nottingham Univ., 1951–54; Agric. Economist, Min. of Agriculture, 1954–62; Grade I Adviser, Nat. Agric. Adv. Service, 1962–64; Admin. Staff Coll., Henley, 1963; Sen. Principal Agric. Economist, 1964–68; Dep. Dir of Econs and Statistics, 1968–70; Head of Fatstock Div., 1970–71; Under-Sec. (Meat and Fatstock), MAFF, 1971–75; Dep. Sec. (Agricultural Science) and Dir-Gen., ADAS, 1975–83. Mem., ARC, 1975–84. Mem. Court, Cranfield Inst. of Technology, 1980–; Governor, Coll. of Estate Management, 1984–. Mem. Duke of Edinburgh's 3rd Commonwealth Study Conf., Australia, 1968. *Publications:* (with Derek Barber) Farming for Profits, 1961, 2nd edn 1967; contribs to Jl Agric. Econs. *Recreations:* gardening, fishing. *Address:* Crown Estate Office, 13–15 Carlton House Terrace, SW1Y 5AH. *T:* 01–210 4231. *Club:* Farmers'.

DEXTRAZE, Gen. Jacques Alfred, CC, CBE, CMM, DSO (Bar), CD; Chairman, Canadian National Railways, 1977–82; *b* 15 Aug. 1919; *s* of Alfred and Amanda Dextraze; *m* 1942, Frances Helena Pare; three *s* (and one *s* decd). *Educ:* St Joseph de Berthier; MacDonald Business Coll., Montreal; Univ. of Columbia. With Dominion Rubber Co, 1938–40. Served War of 1939–45: Fusiliers, Mt Royal, 1939–45, Lt-Col and Comdg Officer, 1944–45; Comdg Officer, Hastings and Prince Edward Regt, 1945. With Singer Mfg Co., 1945–50; Manager, Forest Ops, 1947–50. Resumed mil. career as Comdg Officer, 2nd Bn Royal 22e Regt, 1950–52; Chief of Staff HQ, UN ops in Congo, 1963–64; Chief of Personnel, Can. Forces HQ, 1970–72; Chief of Defence Staff, 1972–77, retired. Hon. ADC to the Governor-Gen., 1958. Hon. LLD Wilfred Laurier Univ.; Hon. PhD (Business Admin) Sherbrooke Univ. Cross of Grand Officer, Order of the Crown (Belgium), 1977. *Address:* 467 Crestview Road, Ottawa, Ontario K1H 5G7, Canada.

de YARBURGH-BATESON, family name of **Baron Deramore.**

d'EYNCOURT, Sir John Jeremy Eustace T.; *see* Tennyson d'Eyncourt.

de ZULUETA, Sir Philip Francis; *see* Zulueta.

DHAKA, Archbishop of, (RC), since 1978; **Most Rev. Michael Rozario,** STL; *b* Solepore, Dacca, Bangladesh, 18 Jan. 1926; *s* of Urban Rozario. *Educ:* Little Flower Seminary, Dacca, Bangladesh; St Albert Seminary, Ranchi, India. Jagannath Coll., Dacca, Bangladesh, 1948–50; Univ. of Notre Dame, USA, 1951–53; Urbano Univ., Rome, 1953–57. Ordained priest, 1956; Bishop of Dinajpur, 1968. Pres., Catholic Bishops' Conf. of Bangladesh. *Address:* Archbishop's House, PO Box 3, Dhaka 2, Bangladesh.

DHAVAN, Shanti Swarup; Member, Law Commission of India, 1972–77; *b* 2 July 1905; *m* Shakuntala Kapur, *d* of Malik, Basant Lal Kapur; two *s* one *d. Educ:* Punjab Univ.; Emmanuel Coll., Cambridge. BA, 1st Cl. Hons History, Punjab Univ., 1925. Hist. Tripos 1931, Law Tripos 1932, Cambridge Univ.; Pres., Cambridge Union, 1932. Called to the Bar, Middle Temple, 1934; Advocate of High Court, Allahabad, 1937, and Senior Advocate of Supreme Court of India, 1958; Lecturer in Commercial Law, Allahabad Univ., 1940–54; Senior Standing Counsel of Govt of Uttar Pradesh, 1956–58; Judge of Allahabad High Court, 1958–67; High Commissioner in UK, 1968–69; Governor of West Bengal, 1969–72. Founder-mem. and Sec., Bernard Shaw Soc., formed 1949. Pres. Indo-Soviet Cultural Soc., Uttar Pradesh Sect., 1965–67. Leader of cultural delegation to Soviet Union, 1966. Lal Bahadur Sastri Meml Lectr, Kerala Univ., Trivandrum, 1973; Pres., All-India Ramayana Conf., Trivandrum, 1973. *Publications:* The Legal system and theory of the State in Ancient India, 1962; Doctrine of sovereignty and colonialism, 1962; Secularism in Indian Jurisprudence, 1964; also papers on Indian Judicial system, UNO and Kashmir, and the Nehru Tradition. *Recreations:* study of Indian jurisprudence, journalism. *Address:* 28 Tashkent Marg, Allahabad, Uttar Pradesh, 210001, India.

DHENIN, Air Marshal Sir Geoffrey (Howard), KBE 1975; AFC 1953 and Bar, 1957; GM 1943; MA, MD, DPH; FFCM 1975; FRAeS 1971; Director-General, Medical Services (RAF), 1974–78; *b* 2 April 1918; *s* of Louis Richard Dhenin and Lucy Ellen Dagg; *m* 1946, Claude Andree Evelyn Rabut; one *s* two *d* (and one *s* decd). *Educ:* Hereford Cathedral Sch.; St John's Coll., Cambridge; Guy's Hosp., London. Joined RAF; various sqdn and other med. appts, Bomber Comd, 2nd TAF, 1943–45 (despatches 1945); pilot trng, 1945–46; various med. officer pilot appts, 1946–58; Staff Coll., Bracknell, 1958–59; comd Princess Mary's RAF Hosp. Akrotiri, Cyprus, 1960–63; comd RAF Hosp. Ely, 1963–66; PMO Air Support Comd, 1966 68; Dir of Health and Research, RAF, 1968–70; Dep. DGMS, RAF, 1970–71; PMO Strike Comd, 1971–73. Fellow, Internat. Acad. of Aerospace Medicine, 1972. CStJ 1974. QHP 1970–78. Adviser to Saudi Arabian Nat. Guard, 1978–79. *Publication:* (ed) Textbook of Aviation Medicine, 1978. *Recreations:* golf, ski-ing, sub-aqua. *Address:* Ruxbury Lodge, St Ann's Hill, Chertsey, Surrey. *T:* Chertsey 63624. *Clubs:* Royal Air Force, Wentworth.

DHRANGADHRA, Maharaja Sriraj of Halvad-, His Highness Jhaladhipati Maharana Sriraj Meghrajji III, KCIE 1947; 45th Ruler (dynastic salute of 13 guns), Head of Jhalla–Makhvana Clan; MP for Jhalavad (Gujarat State), 1967–70; *b* 3 March 1923; *s* of HH Maharaja Sriraj Ghanashyamsinhji Saheb, GCIE, KCSI, late Ruler, and HH Maharani Srirajni Anandkunvarba Saheba, Rajmata Saheba; *S* father 1942, assumed government 1943 on termination of political minority; *m* 1943, Princess Brijrajkunvarba Saheba, *d* of HH the Maharaja of Marwar-Jodhpur, GCSI, GCIE, KCVO; three *s. Educ:* Dhrangadhara Rajdham Shala (Palace Sch.) which was translated to UK to become Millfield Sch., Som., 1935; Heath Mount Sch.; Haileybury Coll.; St Joseph's Academy, Dehra Dun; Shivaji Military Sch., Poona; acquired administrative experience at Baroda, then at Dhrangadhra; philosophy course, Christ Church, Oxford, 1952–54; Ruskin Sch. of Drawing; took Diploma in Social Anthropology, 1954–55; research in Indian Sociology, 1955–58 (BLitt Oxon.). FRAS, FRAI; Associate, Royal Historical Soc. Mem. Standing Cttee of Chamber of Princes, 1945–47; as ruler, pursued active policy of social and economic reform, liquidated State debts, promulgated compulsory free primary educn, fundamental rights and local self-government; was prime mover in Confederation of States scheme, 1945; first state in Saurashtra to accept participation in Constituent Assembly of India; signed Instrument of Accession to India, 1947; Uparajpramukh, Actg Rajpramukh and C-in-C of State Forces of United State of Saurashtra, 1948–52; Promoter and Intendant General, Consultation of Rulers of Indian States in Concord for India, 1967. Mem. Gujarat Legislative Assembly (from Dhrangadhra), Feb.–March 1967, resigned. Life Member: Indian Council of World Affairs, 1967; Indian Parly Gp, 1967; CPA, 1967; Linguistic Soc. of India; Numismatic Soc. of India; Heraldry Soc.; WWF. Perm. Pres., Srirajman (Educ.) Trust; Pres., Governing Council, Rajkumar Coll., Rajkot, 1966–; Mem., Ind. Cttee, United World Colls. Patron, Bhandarkar Oriental Res. Inst. *Heir: s* Maharajkumar Shri Sodhsalji, Yuvaraj Saheb of Halvad–Dhrangadhra, *b* 22 March 1944. *Address:* Ajitniwas Palace, Dhrangadhra-Nagar, Jhalavad, Gujarat 363310, India; Dhrangadhra House, Gokhale Road, Poona 16, India; 108/E Malcha Marg, Diplomatic Enclave, New Delhi 110021, India.

DIAMAND, Peter, Hon. CBE 1972; Consultant, Orchestre de Paris, since 1976; *b* 1913; *m* 1st, 1948, Maria Curcio, pianist (marr. diss. 1971); 2nd, Sylvia Rosenberg, violinist (marr. diss. 1979); one *s. Educ:* Schiller–Realgymnasium, Berlin; Berlin Univ. Studied Law and Journalism in Berlin. Left Germany, 1933; became Private Sec. to Artur Schnabel, pianist. Personal Asst to Dir of Netherlands Opera, Amsterdam, 1946, subsequently Artistic Adviser until 1965; Gen. Manager of Holland Festival, 1948–65; Dir, Edinburgh Internat. Festival, 1965–78; Dir and Gen. Manager, RPO, 1978–81. Mem. Board of Netherlands Chamber Orchestra, 1955–77. Hon. LLD Edinburgh, 1972. Knight, Order of Oranje Nassau, Holland, 1959; Grosses Ehrenzeichen fuer Verdienste, Austria, 1964; Medal of Merit, Czechoslovakia, 1966; Commander Italian Republic, 1973; Officier, Ordre des Arts et des Lettres, France, 1985. *Address:* 28 Eton Court, Eton Avenue, NW3. *T:* 01-586 1203.

DIAMOND, family name of **Baron Diamond.**

DIAMOND, Baron *cr* 1970 (Life Peer), of the City of Gloucester; **John Diamond,** PC 1965; FCA; Chairman: Royal Commission on Distribution of Income and Wealth, 1974–79; Industry and Parliament Trust, 1976–82; Trustee, Social Democratic Party, 1981–82, Leader of SDP in House of Lords, since 1982; *b* Leeds, 30 April 1907; *s* of Henrietta and Rev. S. Diamond, Leeds, *m*; two *s* two *d. Educ:* Leeds Grammar Sch. Qualified as Chartered Accountant, 1931, and commenced practice as John Diamond & Co. MP (Lab) Blackley Div. of Manchester, 1945–51, Gloucester, 1957–70; Chief Secretary to the Treasury, 1964–70 (in the Cabinet, 1968–70); formerly PPS to Minister of Works; Deputy Chm. of Cttees, House of Lords, 1974. Chm., Prime Minister's Adv. Cttee on Business Appts of Crown Servants, 1975–. Chm. of Finance Cttee, Gen. Nursing Council, 1947–53; Dir of Sadler's Wells Trust Ltd, 1957–64; Hon. Treas., Fabian Soc., 1950–64. Hon. LLD Leeds, 1978. *Publications:* Socialism the British Way (jtly), 1948; Public Expenditure in Practice, 1975. *Recreations:* golf, ski-ing, music. *Address:* Aynhoe, Doggetts Wood Lane, Chalfont St Giles, Bucks.

DIAMOND, Anthony Edward John; QC 1974; a Recorder of the Crown Court, since 1985; *b* 4 Sept. 1929; *s* of late Arthur Sigismund Diamond, former Master of the Supreme Court, and of Gladys Elkah Diamond (*née* Mocatta); *m* 1965, Joan Margaret Gee; two *d. Educ:* Rugby; Corpus Christi Coll., Cambridge (MA). Served RA, 1947–49. Called to the Bar, Gray's Inn, 1953 (Bencher, 1985). Mem., indep. review body under colliery review procedure, 1985. *Publications:* papers on maritime law. *Recreation:* the visual arts. *Address:* 1 Cannon Place, NW3; 4 Essex Court, Temple, EC4. *T:* 01–583 9191.

DIAMOND, Prof. Aubrey Lionel; Professor of Law and Director, Institute of Advanced Legal Studies, University of London, 1976–84, now Emeritus; Deputy Chairman, Data Protection Tribunal, since 1985; a part-time Chairman of Industrial Tribunals, since 1984; visiting teacher, London School of Economics, since 1984; solicitor; *b* 28 Dec. 1923; *s* of Alfred and Millie Diamond, London; *m* 1955, Dr Eva M. Bobasch; one *s* one *d. Educ:* elementary schs; Central Foundation Sch., London; London Sch. of Economics (LLB, LLM; Hon. Fellow, 1984). Clerical Officer, LCC, 1941–48. Served RAF, 1943–47. Admitted a solicitor, 1951. Sen. Lectr, Law Society's Sch. of Law, 1955–57; Asst Lectr, Lectr and Reader, Law Dept, LSE, 1957–66; Prof. of Law, Queen Mary Coll., Univ. of London, 1966–71, Fellow 1984; Law Comr, 1971–76. Partner in Lawford & Co., Solicitors, 1959–71 (consultant since 1986). Member: Central London Valuation Court, 1956–73; Consumer Advisory Council, BSI, 1961–63; Council, Consumers' Assoc., 1963–71 (Vice-Pres., 1981–84); Consumer Council, 1963–66, 1967–71; Cttee on the Age of Majority, 1965–67; Estate Agents' Council, 1967–70; Council, Law Society, 1976–. Chairman: Social Sciences and the Law Cttee, SSRC, 1977–80; Hamlyn Trust, 1977–; Advertising Adv. Cttee, IBA, 1980–. Pres., Nat. Fedn of Consumer Groups, 1977–81 (Chm., 1963–67); Vice-Pres., Inst. of Trading Standards Administration, 1975–. Visiting Professor: University Coll. Dar es Salaam, Univ. of E Africa, 1966–67; Law Sch., Stanford Univ., 1971; Melbourne Univ., 1977; Univ. of Virginia, 1982; Tulane Univ.,1984. *Publications:* The Consumer, Society and the Law (with Sir Gordon Borrie),

1963 (4th edn, 1981); Introduction to Hire-Purchase Law, 1967 (2nd edn. 1971); (ed) Instalment Credit, 1970; (co-ed) Sutton and Shannon on Contracts (7th edn) 1970; Commercial and Consumer Credit: an introduction, 1982; articles and notes in legal jls and symposia. *Address:* 44 Temple Fortune Hill, NW11 7XS. *T:*01–458 3590.

DIAMOND, Prof. Derek Robin; Professor of Geography with special reference to Urban and Regional Planning, London School of Economics and Political Science, since 1982; *b* 18 May 1933; *s* of John Diamond (Baron Diamond, *qv*) and Sadie Diamond; *m* 1957, Esme Grace Passmore; one *s* one *d. Educ:* Oxford Univ. (MA); Northwestern Univ., Illinois (MSc). Lecturer: in Geography, 1957–65, in Town and Regional Planning, 1965–68, Glasgow Univ.; Reader in Geography, London School of Economics, 1968–82. Editor: Progress in Planning, 1973–; Geoforum, 1974–. *Publication:* Regional Policy Evaluation, 1983. *Recreation:* philately. *Address:* 9 Ashley Drive, Walton-on-Thames, Surrey KT12 1JL. *T:* Walton-on-Thames 223280. *Club:* Geographical.

DIAMOND, Prof. Jack, CBE 1969; Whitworth Scholar, MSc (Cambridge and Manchester); FCGI; FIMechE; Beyer Professor of Mechanical Engineering, Manchester University, 1953–77, now Emeritus; *b* 22 June 1912; *s* of late Alfred John Diamond and Jessie M. Kitchingham; *m* 1943, Iris Evelyn Purvis; three *d. Educ:* Chatham Technical Sch.; Royal Dockyard School, Chatham; City and Guilds Coll., London; St John's Coll., Cambridge. Engineering apprenticeship, HM Dockyard, Chatham, 1928–32; Whitworth Scholar, 1932; BSc, ACGI, Wh. Sch. (sen.), 1935. Research in Heat Transfer, University Eng. labs and St John's, Cambridge, 1935–37; MSc 1937; Univ. Demonstrator in Engineering, Cambridge, 1937–39. RN (temp. Engr Officer), 1939–44. RN Scientific Service on loan to Ministry of Supply in Canada and at AERE, Harwell, 1944–53. Member: Governing Board of Nat. Inst. for Research in Nuclear Science, 1957–60; UGC, 1965–73; NRDC, 1966–71; Council, IMechE, 1958–70 (Vice-Pres. 1967–70); Pres., Section G, British Assoc., 1970. Pro-Vice-Chancellor, Manchester Univ., 1970–77. FCGI 1968. Hon. DSc Heriot-Watt, 1975. *Publications:* various, in engineering publications. *Address:* 5 Chelford Road, Somerford, Congleton, Cheshire CW12 4QD. *Club:* Athenæum.

DIAMOND, (Peter) Michael, MA, FMA; Director, Birmingham City Museums and Art Gallery, since 1980; *b* 5 Aug. 1942; *s* of late William Howard and Dorothy Gladys Diamond; *m* 1968, Anne Marie; one *s* one *d. Educ:* Bristol Grammar Sch.; Queens' Coll., Cambridge (BA Fine Art 1964, MA 1966). Dip. of Museums Assoc. 1968, FMA 1980. Sheffield City Art Galleries: Art Asst, 1965; Keeper, Mappin Art Gall., 1967; Dep. Dir, 1969; City Arts and Museums Officer, Bradford, 1976. Member, Executive Committee: Yorks Arts Assoc., 1977–80; Yorks Sculpture Park, 1978– (Chm., 1978–82); Pres., Yorks Fedn of Museums, 1978–80; Mem., Crafts Council, 1980–84. Mem. Council, Aston Univ., 1983–. *Publications:* numerous exhibition catalogues incl. Victorian Paintings, 1968; Art and Industry in Sheffield 1850–75, 1975; (contrib.) Manual of Curatorship, 1984; articles in Museums Jl. *Recreations:* gardening, DIY, walking, music. *Address:* 40 Jordan Road, Four Oaks, Sutton Coldfield B75 5AB. *T:* 021–308 3287; Birmingham City Museums and Art Gallery, Chamberlain Square, Birmingham B3 3DH.

DIBELA, Sir Kingsford, GCMG 1983 (CMG 1978); Governor-General of Papua New Guinea, since 1983; *b* 16 March 1932; *s* of Norman Dibela and Edna Dalauna; *m* 1952, Winifred Tomolarina; two *s* four *d. Educ:* St Paul's Primary Sch., Dogura. Qualified as primary school teacher; teacher, 1949–63. Pres., Weraura Local Govt Council, 1963–77; MP, PNG, 1975–82; Speaker of Nat. Parlt, 1977–80. *Recreations:* golf, cricket. *Address:* Government House, PO Box 79, Port Moresby, Papua New Guinea. *T:* 214466 (BH). *Club:* Port Moresby Golf.

DICE, Brian Charles; Chief Executive, British Waterways Board, since 1986; *b* 2 Sept. 1936; *s* of late Frederic Charles Dice; *m* 1965, Gwendoline Tazeena Harrison; two *d. Educ:* Clare College, Cambridge; Middle Temple. Cadbury Schweppes, 1960–86; Director, 1979; Managing Director, Schweppes, 1983. *Address:* Stratton Wood, Beaconsfield, Bucks HP9 1HS. *Clubs:* Carlton; Nairobi.

DICK, Air Vice-Marshal Alan David, CB 1978; CBE 1968; AFC 1957; FRAeS 1975; *b* 7 Jan. 1924; *s* of late Brig. Alan MacDonald Dick, CBE, IMS(Retd), and Muriel Angela Dick; *m* 1951, Ann Napier Jeffcoat, *d* of late Col A. C. Jeffcoat, CB, CMG, DSO; two *s* two *d. Educ:* Fettes; Aitchison Coll., Lahore; King's Coll., Cambridge. MA. Joined RAF, 1942; SE Asia Command, 1943–45; Fighter Comd, 1945–46. Central Flying Sch., 1950–53; Empire Test Pilots Sch., 1953; Test Pilot, A&AEE, 1954–57; Fighter Comd, 1957–60; RAF Staff Coll., 1960–63; OC 207 Sqdn, Bomber Comd, 1963–64; Supt of Flying, A&AEE, 1964–68; Strike Comd, 1968–69; IDC 1970; MoD Air Staff, 1971–74; Comdt, A&AEE, 1974–75; Dep. Controller Aircraft/C, MoD(PE), 1975–78. Sec., British Assoc. of Occupational Therapists, 1979–84. *Recreations:* photography, walking, bird watching. *Club:* Royal Air Force.

DICK, Clare L.; *see* Lawson Dick.

DICK, Gavin Colquhoun; student, School of Oriental and African Studies, London University, since 1984; Consultant, Office of Telecommunications, since 1984; *b* 6 Sept. 1928; *s* of late John Dick and Catherine MacAuslan Henderson; *m* 1952, Elizabeth Frances, *e d* of late Jonathan Hutchinson; two *d. Educ:* Hamilton Academy; Glasgow Univ. (MA); Balliol Coll., Oxford (Snell Exhibnr, MA). National Service, 3rd RTR (Lieut), 1952–54. Asst Principal, BoT, 1954, Principal, 1958; UK Trade Comr, Wellington, NZ, 1961–64; Asst Sec., 1967; Jt Sec., Review Cttee on Overseas Representation, 1968–69; Under-Sec., 1975–84, Dept of Industry, 1981–84. Bd Mem., English Industrial Estates Corp., 1982–84. Governor, Coll. of Air Training (Hamble), 1975–80. *Recreation:* words. *Address:* Fell Cottage, Bayley's Hill, Sevenoaks, Kent TN14 6HS. *T:* Sevenoaks 453704. *Club:* United Oxford & Cambridge University.

DICK, Prof. George (Williamson Auchinvole), MD (Edinburgh), DSc (Edinburgh), FRCPE, FRCP, FRCPath, MPH (Johns Hopkins); FIMLS, FIBiol; Emeritus Professor of Pathology, University of London; Chairman, Medical Advisory and Research Consultants Ltd, since 1981; *b* 14 Aug. 1914; *s* of Rev. David Auchinvole Dick and Blanche Hay Spence; *m* 1941, Brenda Marian Cook; two *s* two *d. Educ:* Royal High Sch., Edinburgh; Univ. of Edinburgh; The Johns Hopkins Univ., Baltimore, Md, USA. BSc 1939 (1st Cl. Hons Path.); Vans Dunlop Scholar; Buchanan Medal; MD (Gold Medal) 1949. Asst Pathologist, Royal Infirmary, Edinburgh, 1939–40; Pathologist, RAMC, 1940–46; OC Medical Div. (Lt-Col) (EA Comd), 1945; Pathologist, Colonial Med. Res. Service, 1946–51; Rockefeller Foundn Fellow (Internat. Health Div.), Rockefeller Inst., New York and Johns Hopkins Univ., 1947–48; Res. Fellow, Sch. of Hygiene and Public Health, Johns Hopkins Univ., Baltimore, Md, 1948–49; Scientific Staff, MRC, 1951–54; Prof. of Microbiology, QUB, 1955–65; Dir, Bland-Sutton Inst. and Sch. of Pathology, Middlesex Hosp. Med. Sch., Univ. of London, 1966–73; Bland-Sutton Prof. of Pathology, Univ. of London, 1966–73; Asst Dir, BPMF, and Postgraduate Dean, SW Thames RHA, 1973–81; Prof. of Pathology, Univ. of London, and Hon. Lectr and Hon. Consultant, Inst. of Child Health, 1973–81. Examnr, Med. Schools in UK, Dublin, Nairobi, Kampala, Riyadh, Jeddah; Assessor, HNC and CMS, S London Coll. Pres., Inst. of Med. Laboratory Technology, 1966–76; Member: Mid Downs Health Authority, W Sussex, 1981–84; Jt

Bd of Clinical Nursing Studies, 1982–; Chm., DHSS/Regl Librarians Jt Wking Party. Pres., Rowhook Med. Soc., 1975–. Treasurer, RCPath, 1973–78; Member: RSM; BMA; Internat. Epidemiol. Soc.; Path. Soc. GB and Ireland; Soc. of Scholars, Johns Hopkins Univ., 1979; Alpha Chapter, Delta Omega Hon. Soc., USA, 1981. Liveryman, Worshipful Co. of Apothecaries, 1981–. Singapore Gold Medal, Edinburgh Univ., 1952 and 1958; Laurence Biedl Prize for Rehabilitation, 1958; Sims Woodhead Medal, 1976. *Publications*: Immunisation, 1978, re-issued as Practical Immunisation, 1986; Immunology of Infectious Diseases, 1979; Health on Holiday and other Travels, 1982; papers on yellow fever, Uganda S, Zika and other arbor viruses, Mengovirus, Marburgvirus, etc; encephalitis, poliomyelitis; hepatitis (MHV); multiple sclerosis and EHA (rabies) virus; smallpox, poliomyelitis, whooping cough and combined vaccines; vaccine reactions, immunisation policies, subacute sclerosing panencephalitis etc. *Address*: Waterland, Rowhook, Horsham RH12 3PX. *T*: Slinfold 790549; MARC Ltd, Tripod House, 105/107 Lansdowne Road, Croydon, Surrey CR0 2BN.

See also J. A. Dick.

DICK, James Brownlee, CB 1977; MA, BSc, FInstP, FCIBS, FIOB; consultant; *b* 19 July 1919; *s* of James Brownlee Dick and Matilda Forrest; *m* 1944, Audrey Moira Shinn; two *s*. *Educ*: Wishaw High Sch.; Glasgow Univ. Royal Naval Scientific Service, 1940. Building Research Station, later Building Research Establishment: Physics Div., 1947; Head of User Requirements Div., 1960; Head of Production Div., 1963; Asst Dir, 1964; Dep. Dir, 1969; Dir, 1969–79. Pres., Internat. Council for Building Res., 1974–77. *Publications*: papers in professional and scientific journals. *Recreations*: reading, gardening, golf. *Address*: 4 Murray Road, Berkhamsted, Herts. *T*: Berkhamsted 2580.

DICK, John Alexander, MC 1944; QC (Scotland) 1963; Sheriff Principal of Glasgow and Strathkelvin, 1980–86; *b* 1 Jan. 1920; *y s* of Rev. David Auchinvole Dick and Blanche Hay Spence; *m* 1951, Rosemary Benzie Sutherland; no *c*. *Educ*: Waid Academy, Anstruther; University of Edinburgh. Enlisted in London Scottish, 1940; commissioned Royal Scots, 1942; Italy, 1944; Palestine, 1945–46; released 1946. MA (1st Cl. Hons Economics) 1947, LLB (with distinction) 1949, Univ. of Edinburgh. Called to Scots Bar, 1949; Lecturer in Public Law, Univ. of Edinburgh, 1953–60; Junior Counsel in Scotland to HM Commissioners of Customs and Excise, 1956–63; Comr under Terrorism (N Ireland) Order 1972, 1972–73; Sheriff of the Lothians and Borders at Edinburgh, 1969–78; Sheriff Principal of North Strathclyde, 1978–82. *Recreation*: hill-walking. *Address*: 66 Northumberland Street, Edinburgh EH3 6JE. *T*: 031–556 6081. *Club*: Royal Scots (Edinburgh).

See also Prof. George Dick.

DICK, John Kenneth, CBE 1972; FCA, FRSA; Director: N. M. Rothschild & Sons Ltd, since 1978; N. M. Rothschild (Leasing) Ltd, since 1978; *b* 5 April 1913; *s* of late John Dick and Beatrice May Dick (*née* Chitty); *m* 1942, Pamela Madge, 3rd *d* of late Maurice Salmon and Katie Salmon (*née* Joseph); two *s* (and one *s* decd). *Educ*: Sedbergh. Qual. with Mann Judd & Co., Chartered Accountants, 1936; Partner, Mann Judd & Co., 1947; Mitchell Cotts Group Ltd: Jt Man. Dir, 1957; Sole Man. Dir, 1959–78; Dep. Chm., 1964; Chm., 1966–78; Chm., Hume Holdings Ltd, 1975–80. Mem., Commonwealth Develt Corp., 1967–80; Gov., City of London Soc.; Member: British Nat. Export Cttee, 1968–71; Covent Gdn Mkt Authority, 1976–82; Chm., Cttee for Middle East Trade, 1968–71; Pres., Middle East Assoc., 1976–81 (a Vice-Pres., 1970–76). *Recreation*: golf. *Address*: Overbye, Church Street, Cobham, Surrey KT11 3EG. *T*: (office) 01–280 5000; (home) Cobham (Surrey) 64393. *Club*: Caledonian.

DICK, Kay; writer; *b* 29 July 1915; *o d* of Mrs Kate Frances Dick. *Educ*: Geneva, Switzerland; Lycée Français de Londres, S Kensington. Worked in publishing and bookselling; edited (as Edward Lane) 13 issues of magazine, The Windmill. *Publications*: *fiction*: By the Lake, 1949; Young Man, 1951; An Affair of Love, 1953; Solitaire, 1958; Sunday, 1962; They, 1977 (South-East Arts Literature Prize, 1977); The Shelf, 1984; *non-fiction*: Pierrot, 1960; Ivy and Stevie, 1971; Friends and Friendship, 1974; *edited*: London's Hour: as seen through the eyes of the fire-fighters, 1942; Late Joys at the Players Theatre, 1943; The Mandrake Root, 1946, At Close of Eve, 1947, The Uncertain Element, 1950 (three vols of strange stories); Bizarre and Arabesque (anthology from Edgar Allan Poe), 1967; Writers at Work, 1972. *Recreations*: friends, gardening, walking the dog. *Address*: Flat 5, 9 Arundel Terrace, Brighton, East Sussex BN2 1GA. *T*: Brighton 697243.

DICK, Air Vice-Marshal Ronald; Head of British Defence Staff, Washington, and Defence Attaché, since 1984; *b* Newcastle upon Tyne, 18 Oct. 1931; *s* of Arthur John Craig Dick and Lilian Dick; *m* 1955, Pauline Lomax; one *s* one *d*. *Educ*: Beckenham and Penge County Grammar Sch.; RAF Coll., Cranwell. Commnd 1952; served, 1953–69: No 64 Fighter Sqdn; Flying Instr, No 5 FTS; Central Flying Sch. Examg Wing and Type Sqdn; Flt Comdr, 3615th Pilot Trng Sqdn, USAF, and No IX Bomber Sqdn; Trng (Operational) 2a (RAF), MoD; RAF Staff Coll., Bracknell; Ops B2 (RAF), MoD; Jt Services Staff Coll.; OC No IX Bomber Sqdn, RAF Akrotiri, 1970–72; Staff, RCDS, 1972–74; PSO to Dep. SACEUR, SHAPE, 1974–77; OC RAF Honington, 1978–80; Air Attaché, Washington, DC, 1980–83; Dir of Organization and Estabts, 1983–84, of Organization and Quartering, 1984, RAF. Wright Jubilee Aerobatic Trophy Winner, 1956. *Recreations*: wild life conservation, bird watching, private flying, military history, opera. *Address*: British Embassy, 3100 Massachusetts Avenue NW, Washington, DC 20008, USA. *Club*: Royal Air Force.

DICK, Rear-Adm. Royer Mylius, CB 1951; CBE 1943; DSC 1918; *b* 14 Oct. 1897; *s* of Louis Henry Mylius Dick and Edith Alice Guy; *m* 1928, Agnes Mary Harben; (one *s* killed on active service one *d* decd); *m* 1955, Vera, *widow* of Col Bertram Pott. *Educ*: RN Colls, Osborne and Dartmouth. Midshipman, 1914; at sea, 1914–18 (Falklands, Jutland, North Russia) (DSC); Lieut 1918; Comdr 1933; Capt. 1940; Commodore 1st cl. 1942; Rear-Adm. 1949. Dep. Chief of Staff, Mediterranean Station, 1940–42 (Matapan); British Admty Delegn to Washington, 1942; Chief of Staff, Mediterranean Stn, 1942–44 (despatches twice, CBE); HMS Belfast, 1944–46; Dir Tactical and Staff Duties, Admiralty, 1947–48; Chief of Staff to Flag Officer, Western Europe, 1948–50; Naval ADC to the King, 1949; Flag Officer, Training Sqdn, 1951–52; Standing Group Liaison Officer to North Atlantic Council, 1952–55; Vice-Adm. (Acting), 1953; retired list, 1955. Dep. Comr-in-Chief, 1957–62, Comr-in-Chief, 1962–67, SJAB. Dep. Chm., Horticultural Marketing Council, 1960–63; Chairman: Royal United Service Institution, 1965–67; St John Council for London, 1971–75; a Vice-Pres., Royal UK Beneficent Assoc., 1979. KStJ 1961; Bailiff Grand Cross, Order of Hosp. of St John of Jerusalem, 1967. Officer Legion of Merit (US), 1943; Officer Legion of Honour, 1943; Croix de Guerre avec palme, 1946. *Address*: 15 Dorchester Court, Sloane Street, SW1. *Clubs*: Army and Navy, Royal Automobile.

DICK-LAUDER, Sir Piers Robert; *see* Lauder.

DICKENS, Prof. Arthur Geoffrey, CMG 1974; FBA 1966; Director, Institute of Historical Research and Professor of History in the University of London, 1967–77, now Emeritus Professor; *b* 6 July 1910; *er s* of Arthur James Dickens and Gertrude Helen Dickens (*née* Grasby), both of Hull, Yorks; *m* 1936, Molly (*d* 1978), *er d* of Walter Bygott; two *s*. *Educ*: Hymers Coll., Hull; Magdalen Coll., Oxford. Demy, 1929–32, Senior Demy, 1932–33, of Magdalen Coll.; BA with 1st Class Hons in Mod. Hist., 1932; MA 1936; DLit London, 1965. Fellow and Tutor of Keble Coll., Oxford, 1933–49, Hon. Fellow, 1971; Oxford Univ. Lecturer in Sixteenth Century English History, 1939–49. Served in RA, 1940–45; demobilised as Staff Capt. G. F. Grant Prof. of History, Univ. of Hull, 1949–62; Dep. Principal and Dean of Faculty of Arts, 1950–53; Pro-Vice-Chancellor, 1959–62; Prof. of History, King's Coll., Univ. of London, 1962–67; FKC, 1977. Mem. Senate and Academic Council, Univ. of London, 1974–77. Pres., Ecclesiastical History Soc., 1966–68. Member: Advisory Council on Public Records, 1968–76; Adv. Council on Export of Works of Art, 1968–76; Records Cttee, Essex CC, 1965–71; History of Medicine Adv. Panel, Wellcome Trust, 1974–79; Steering Cttee, Business History Unit, LSE, 1978–85. Chm., Victoria History of the Counties of England, 1967–68. Sec., 1967–73, Chm. and Gen. Sec., 1973–79, British Nat. Cttee of Historical Sciences; Foreign Sec., British Acad., 1969–79 (Vice-Pres., 1971–72); Vice-Pres., British Record Soc., 1978–80; Hon. Vice-President: RHistS, 1977– (Vice-Pres., 1969–73); Historical Assoc., 1977– (Pres., Central London Branch, 1982–); Sec., Anglo-German Group of Historians, 1969–76; Pres., German History Soc., 1979–. Editor, Bulletin of the Inst. of Historical Research, 1967–77. Visiting Prof., Univ. of Rochester, NY, 1953–54; Birkbeck Lectr, Trinity Coll., Cambridge, 1969–70. Fellow, 1954, Vis. Prof., 1972, Folger Library, Washington, DC; Strassberg Vis. Prof., Univ. of Western Australia, 1981; Lectures: James Ford Special, Univ. of Oxford, 1974; Neale, UCL, 1977; Bithell, Inst. of Germanic Studies, 1978; Stenton, Reading, 1980. Hon. Professorial Fellow, Univ. of Wales, Aberystwyth, 1979–. Governor, Highgate Sch., 1976–86. FRHistS 1947; FSA 1962. Medlicott Medal, Historical Assoc., 1985 (first recipient). Hon. DLitt: Kent, 1976; Hull, 1977; Leicester, 1978; Sheffield, 1978; Hon. LittD Liverpool, 1977. Comdr's Cross, Order of Merit, Fed. Repub. of Germany, 1980. *Publications*: Lübeck Diary, 1947; The Register of Butley Priory, 1951; The East Riding of Yorkshire, 1954; Lollards and Protestants, 1959; Thomas Cromwell, 1959; Tudor Treatises, 1960; Clifford Letters, 1962; The English Reformation, 1964; Reformation and Society in 16th Century Europe, 1966; Martin Luther and the Reformation, 1967; (ed jtly) The Reformation in England to the Accession of Elizabeth I, 1967; The Counter-Reformation, 1968; The Age of Humanism and Reformation, 1972, UK edn 1977; The German Nation and Martin Luther, 1974; (ed and contrib.) The Courts of Europe, 1977; Reformation Studies, 1982; (with J. M. Tonkin) The Reformation in Historical Thought, 1985; (Gen. Editor) Documents of Modern History Series, 1966–; (Gen. Editor) A New History of England Series, 1975–; about 60 articles in: English Historical Review, Church Quarterly Review, Yorkshire Archæological Jl, Cambridge Antiquarian Jl, Bodleian Library Record, Archiv für Reformationsgeschichte, Britain and the Netherlands, Victoria County History, York, Trans Royal Hist. Soc., Jl of Ecclesiastical History, Archæological Jl, Encycl. Britannica, Chambers's Encycl., etc. *Festschrift*: Reformation Principle and Practice: essays in honour of A. G. Dickens, ed P. N. Brooks, 1980. *Recreations*: travel, 20th Century British art. *Address*: c/o Institute of Historical Research, Senate House, WC1E 7HU. *Club*: Athenæum.

DICKENS, Geoffrey Kenneth, JP; MP (C) Littleborough and Saddleworth, since 1983 (Huddersfield West, 1979–83); company director, engineering industry; *b* 26 Aug. 1931; *s* of John Wilfred and Laura Avril Dickens; *m* 1956, Norma Evelyn Boothby; two *s*. *Educ*: Park Lane and Byron Court Primary; East Lane Sch., Wembley; Harrow and Acton Technical Colls. Chairman: Sandridge Parish Council, 1968–69; St Albans Rural District Council, 1970–71 (Leader, 1967–70); Councillor, Hertfordshire CC, 1970–75; Hon. Alderman, City and District of St Albans, 1976. Contested (C): Teesside Middlesbrough, Feb. 1974, and Ealing North, Oct. 1974, general elections. Vice-Chm., Assoc. of Conservative Clubs; Vice-Pres., NW Conservative Clubs Council. Royal Humane Soc. Testimonial on Vellum for saving lives, 1972. JP St Albans, later Barnsley, then Oldham, 1968. *Address*: The Sycamores, Greenfield, Saddleworth, Oldham, Lancs OL3 7PB.

DICKENS, James McCulloch York; Chief Personnel Officer, Agricultural and Food Research Council, since 1983; *b* 4 April 1931; *e s* of A. Y. Dickens and I. Dickens (*née* McCulloch); *m* 1st, 1955, M. J. Grieve (marr. diss. 1965); 2nd, 1969, Mrs Carolyn Casey. *Educ*: Shawlands Academy, Glasgow; Newbattle Abbey Coll., Dalkeith, Midlothian; Ruskin Coll. and St Catherine's Coll., Oxford. Administrative Asst, National Coal Board, 1956–58; Industrial Relations Officer, National Coal Board, 1958–65; Management Consultant, 1965–66; MP (Lab) West Lewisham, 1966–70; Asst Dir of Manpower, Nat. Freight Corp., 1970–76; National Water Council: Asst Dir (Ind. Rel.), Manpower Services Div., 1976–80; Dir of Manpower, 1980–82; Dir of Manpower and Trng, 1982–83. *Recreations*: music, theatre, the countryside. *Address*: 64 Woodbastwick Road, Sydenham, SE26 5LH. *T*: 01–778 7446.

DICKENS, Sir Louis (Walter), Kt 1968; DFC 1940; AFC 1938; DL; *b* 28 Sept. 1903; *s* of C. H. Dickens; *m* 1939, Ena Alice Bastable (*d* 1971); one *s* one *d*. *Educ*: Clongowes Wood Coll.; Cranwell Cadet Coll. Bomber Sqdn, 1923–27; Flying Trng, 1927; Egypt, 1932; Personnel, Air Min., 1932–35; subseq. Flying Instructor, Cranwell; Bomber Comd, France, 1940; Flying Instructor, Canada, 1941–42; Bomber Comd, 1943–44; SHAEF France, 1944–45; retired, 1947. Member: Berkshire CC, 1952–74 (Chm., 1965–68, Co. Alderman, 1959–73); Wokingham DC, 1974– (Chm., 1974–76). DL Berks, 1966. *Recreation*: golf. *Address*: Wayford, Bolney Avenue, Shiplake, Henley-on-Thames, Oxon. *Club*: Royal Air Force.

DICKENS, Monica Enid, (Mrs R. O. Stratton), MBE 1981; writer; Founder of The Samaritans, in the USA, Boston, Mass, 1974; *b* 10 May 1915; *d* of late Henry Charles Dickens, Barrister-at-law, and Fanny Runge; *m* 1951, Comdr Roy Olin Stratton (*d* 1985), US Navy; two *d*. *Educ*: St Paul's Girls' Sch., Hammersmith. *Publications*: One Pair of Hands, 1939; Mariana, 1940; One Pair of Feet, 1942; The Fancy, 1943; Thursday Afternoons, 1945; The Happy Prisoner, 1946; Joy and Josephine, 1948; Flowers on the Grass, 1949; My Turn to Make the Tea, 1951; No More Meadows, 1953; The Winds of Heaven, 1955; The Angel in the Corner, 1956; Man Overboard, 1958; The Heart of London, 1961; Cobbler's Dream, 1963; Kate and Emma, 1964; The Room Upstairs, 1966; The Landlord's Daughter, 1968; The Listeners, 1970; The House at World's End, 1970; Summer at World's End, 1971; Follyfoot, 1971; World's End in Winter, 1972; Dora at Follyfoot, 1972; Spring Comes to World's End, 1973; Talking of Horses, 1973; Last Year when I was Young, 1974; The Horse of Follyfoot, 1975; Stranger at Follyfoot, 1976; An Open Book, 1978; The Messenger, 1985; The Ballad of Favour, 1985; Miracles of Courage, 1985; The Haunting of Bellamy 4, 1986. *Recreations*: riding, gardening. *Address*: Lavender Cottage, Brightwalton, Berks RG16 0BY.

DICKENSON, Aubrey Fiennes T.; *see* Trotman-Dickenson.

DICKENSON, Lt-Col Charles Royal, CMG 1965; Postmaster-General of Rhodesia, 1964–68, retired; *b* 17 June 1907; *e s* of Charles Roland and Gertrude Dickenson; *m* 1950, Hendrika Jacoba Margaretha Schippers; two *d*. *Educ*: Shaftesbury Grammar Sch., Dorset. Entered British Post Office as Engineering Apprentice, 1923; British Post Office HQ, 1932–39. Served War in Royal Signals, 1939–45, attaining rank of Lieut-Col. BPO NW Regional HQ as Asst Controller of Telecommunications, 1945–47; BPO HQ, London,

1947–50; loaned to S Rhodesia Govt, 1950–54; Controller of Telecommunications, Ministry of Posts, Federation of Rhodesia and Nyasaland, 1954–57; Regional Controller for N Rhodesia, Fedn of Rhodesia and Nyasaland, 1957–61; Dep. Postmaster-Gen., Rhodesia and Nyasaland, 1961–62; Postmaster-Gen., Rhodesia and Nyasaland, 1962–63. Hon. Mem., S Africa Inst. of Electronic and Radio Engineers (Hon. M(SA) IERE), 1966. ICD, OLM, Rhodesia, 1979. *Recreations:* growing orchids, photography. *Address:* 4600 Gatlin Oaks Lane, Orlando, Florida 32806, USA.

DICKENSON, Joseph Frank, PhD, CEng, FIMechE; Director, North Staffordshire Polytechnic, 1969–86; *b* 26 Nov. 1924; *s* of late Frank Brand Dickenson and late Maud Dickenson (*née* Beharrell); *m* 1948, Sheila May Kingston; two *s* one *d*. *Educ:* College of Technology, Hull. BSc (1st Cl. Hons) Engrg, PhD (both London). Engrg apprenticeship and Jun. Engr's posts, 1939–52; Lectr and Sen. Lectr, Hull Coll. of Technology, 1952–59; Head of Dept of Mechanical Engrg and later Vice-Principal, Lanchester Coll. of Technology, 1960–64; Principal, Leeds Coll. of Technology, 1964–69. *Recreation:* motor cars. *Address:* 5 Byron Walk Mews, Harrogate. *T:* Harrogate 525899.

DICKIE, Brian James; General Administrator, Glyndebourne Festival Opera, since 1981; *b* 23 July 1941; *s* of Robert Kelso Dickie and Harriet Elizabeth (*née* Riddell); *m* 1968, Victoria Teresa Sheldon (*née* Price); two *s* one *d*. *Educ:* Haileybury; Trinity Coll., Dublin. Admin. Asst, Glyndebourne Opera, 1962–66; Administrator, Glyndebourne Touring Opera, 1967–81; Opera Manager, Glyndebourne Fest. Opera, 1970–81. Artistic Dir, Wexford Fest., 1967–73; Artistic Advr, Théâtre Musical de Paris, 1981–. Chm., London Choral Soc., 1978–85; Vice-Chm., TNC, 1980–85 (Chm., TNC Opera Cttee, 1976–85); Vice-Pres., Theatrical Management Assoc., 1983–85. *Address:* Hayes Farmhouse, Barcombe Mills, Lewes, East Sussex. *T:* Barcombe 400275. *Club:* Garrick.

DICKIE, Rev. Edgar Primrose, MC; MA, BD (Edinburgh); BA Oxon; Emeritus Professor of Divinity, St Mary's College, University of St Andrews, since 1967 (Professor, 1935–67, retired); Extra Chaplain to the Queen in Scotland since 1967 (Chaplain, 1956–67, retired); *b* 12 Aug. 1897; *y* and *o surv. s* of William Dickie, editor of Dumfries and Galloway Standard, and Jane Paterson; *m* 1927, Ishbel Graham Holmes, *d* of Andrew Frier Johnston and Magdalene Ross Holmes, Edinburgh. *Educ:* Dumfries Academy; Edinburgh University; Christ Church, Oxford; New Coll., Edinburgh; Marburg; Tübingen. Served with rank of Captain, 3rd and 1/5th KOSB, Palestine, Flanders, France (wounded, MC); mentioned in despatches. MA Edinburgh, First Class Hons in Classics; Vans Dunlop Scholar; BA Oxford, First Class in Literae Humaniores; at New Coll., Edinburgh, Hamilton Scholar; Fullarton Scholar in Hebrew; Tutor in Greek, 1925–26; Hons Diploma; Senior Cunningham Fellow, 1926; Asst Minister, New North Church, Edinburgh; Ordained, 1927; Minister of St Cuthbert's Church, Lockerbie, 1927–33; Minister of St Anne's Church, Corstorphine, Edinburgh, 1933–35; External Examiner in Biblical Criticism, Edinburgh Univ., 1931–34 and 1934–35; in New Testament Greek, New Coll., Edinburgh, 1931–34; in History of Doctrine, Univ. of Manchester, 1939–41; in Ethics, Queen's Univ., Belfast, 1941; in Systematic Theology, Univ. of Aberdeen, 1942; in Theology, Univ. of Glasgow, 1948, Belfast, 1953. Kerr Lectr in 1936–39; Murtle Lectr, Univ. of Aberdeen, 1941; Gen. Supt of work of Church of Scotland in BEF, 1940, and with BLA, 1944–45 (mentioned in despatches). Captain St Andrews Univ. OTC, 1941; Convener, Church of Scotland Youth Cttee, 1945–50. Founder-mem., Studiorum Novi Testamenti Societas, 1937. Pres. Scottish Sunday School Union, 1955–57; Vice-Pres. Scottish Universities Athletic Club. Governor, St Leonards Sch. Hon. DD Edinburgh, 1946; Hon. LLD St Andrews, 1969. Hon. Life Mem., Students' Union, St Andrews; Hon. Blue, Athletic Union, St Andrews. Companion of Merit and Canon, Order St Lazarus of Jerusalem. *Publications:* Psammyforshort: Rex. Imp.: A Nonsense Story, 1928; The New Divine Order, 1930; translation of Karl Heim's Die Neue Welt Gottes; The Seven Words from the Cross, 1931; Spirit and Truth, 1935; translation of Heim's Das Wesen des Evangelischen Christentums; God Transcendent; translation of Heim's Glaube und Denken (3rd edn); Revelation and Response, 1938; One Year's Talks to Children, 1940; Scottish Life and Character, 1942; A Second Year's Talks to Children, 1943; The Paper Boat, 1943; The Obedience of a Christian Man, 1944; Normandy to Nijmegen, 1946; The Fellowship of Youth, 1947; Mister Bannock: A Nonsense Story, 1947; I Promise (Girl Guides), 1949; It was New to me (Church of Scotland), 1949; God is Light: Studies in Revelation and Personal Conviction, 1953; Thou art the Christ, 1954; A Safe Stronghold, 1955; introductory essay to McLeod Campbell The Nature of the Atonement, 1959; The Unchanging Gospel, 1960; The Father Everlasting, 1965; Remembrance, 1966; occasional articles in Punch, The Scots Magazine, and other periodicals. *Recreations:* hill-walking, winter sports. *Address:* Surma, Hepburn Gardens, St Andrews, Fife. *T:* St Andrews 73617.

DICKINS, Aileen Marian, MD, FRCOG; Consultant Gynaecological and Obstetric Surgeon, University College Hospital, London, 1967–83, retired; *b* 17 Nov. 1917; *d* of Arthur George Dickins and Marian Helen Dickins. MD; FRCOG 1958. Obstetrician and Gynaecologist: Windsor Gp of Hosps, 1952–64; Ealing Hosp. and Perivale Maternity Hosp., 1951–82. Jun. Vice Pres., RCOG, 1978–80, Sen. Vice-Pres., 1980–81. FRSM; Mem. Women's Visiting Gynaecological Club. *Publications:* contrib. to BMJ and Jl of Obs and Gyn. of Brit. Commonwealth. *Recreations:* skiing, gardening. *Address:* Driscoll's Cottage, Broughton, near Stockbridge, Hants SO20 8BD.

DICKINS, Basil Gordon, CBE 1952 (OBE 1945); BSc, ARCS, DIC, PhD; Deputy Controller of Guided Weapons, Ministry of Technology, 1966–68; *b* 1 July 1908; *s* of late Basil Dickins; *m* 1st, 1935, Molly Aileen (*d* 1969), *d* of late H. Walters Reburn; 2nd, 1971, Edith, *widow* of Warren Parkinson. *Educ:* Royal Coll. of Science, London. Royal Aircraft Establishment, 1932; Air Min., 1936, later Min. of Aircraft Production; Head of Operational Research Section, HQ Bomber Command, 1941; Asst Scientific Adviser, Air Ministry, 1945; Dir of Tech. Personnel Administration, Min. of Supply, 1948; Dep. Scientific Adviser to Air Ministry, 1952; Dir of Guided Weapons Research and Development, Min. of Supply, 1956; Dir-Gen. of Atomic Weapons, Min. of Supply, 1959; Dir-Gen. of Guided Weapons, Ministry of Aviation, 1962. *Publications:* papers in Proc. Royal Society and Reports and Memoranda of Aeronautical Research Council. *Address:* Villa Caprice, La Folie, Millbrook, Jersey; The Penthouse, Cassandra, Victoria Road, Clifton, Cape Town, South Africa.

DICKINSON, family name of **Baron Dickinson.**

DICKINSON, 2nd Baron *cr* 1930, of Painswick; **Richard Clavering Hyett Dickinson;** *b* 2 March 1926; *s* of late Hon. Richard Sebastian Willoughby Dickinson, DSO (*o s* of 1st Baron) and of May Southey, *d* of late Charles Lovemore, Melsetter, Cape Province, S Africa; *S* grandfather, 1943; *m* 1st, 1957, Margaret Ann (marr. diss. 1980), *e d* of late Brig. G. R. McMeekan, CB, DSO, OBE; two *s*; 2nd, 1980, Rita Doreen Moir. *Heir:* *s* Hon. Martin Hyett Dickinson, *b* 30 Jan. 1961. *Address:* The Stables, Gloucester Road, Painswick, Stroud, Glos. *T:* Painswick 813204.

See also Very Rev. H. G. Dickinson, Hon. P. M. de B. Dickinson.

DICKINSON, Basil Philip Harriman; Under Secretary, Department of the Environment (formerly Ministry of Transport), 1959–74; *b* 10 Sept. 1916; *yr s* of F. H. and I. F. Dickinson; *m* 1941, Beryl Farrow; three *s* one *d*. *Educ:* Cheltenham Coll.; Oriel Coll., Oxford. *Address:* c/o Child & Co., 1 Fleet Street, EC4Y 1BD.

DICKINSON, Sir Ben; *see* Dickinson, Sir S. B.

DICKINSON, Brian Henry Baron; Principal Finance Officer, Ministry of Agriculture, Fisheries and Food, since 1986; *b* 2 May 1940; *s* of Alan Edgar Frederic Dickinson and Ethel Mary Dickinson (*née* McWilliam); *m* 1971, Sheila Minto Lloyd. *Educ:* Leighton Park School, Reading; Balliol College, Oxford (BA). Ministry of Agriculture, Fisheries and Food, 1964; Dept of Prices and Consumer Protection, 1975; MAFF, 1978. *Recreations:* bird-watching, weeding. *Address:* Ministry of Agriculture, Fisheries and Food, 10 Whitehall Place, SW1A 2HH. *T:* 01-233 3339.

DICKINSON, Prof. Christopher John, DM, FRCP; Professor of Medicine and Chairman, Department of Medicine, St Bartholomew's Hospital Medical College, since 1975; *b* 1 Feb. 1927; *s* of Reginald Ernest Dickinson and Margaret Dickinson (*née* Petty); *m* 1953, Elizabeth Patricia Farrell; two *s* two *d*. *Educ:* Berkhamsted School; Oxford University (BSc, MA, DM); University College Hospital Medical College. FRCP 1968. Junior med. posts, UCH, 1953–54; RAMC (Junior Med. Specialist), 1955–56; Registrar and Research Fellow, Middlesex Hosp., 1957–60; Rockefeller Travelling Fellow, Cleveland Clinic, USA, 1960–61; Lectr, then Sen. Lectr and Consultant, UCH and Med. Sch., 1961–75. R. Samuel McLoughlin Vis. Prof., McMaster Univ., Canada, 1970; King Edward Fund Vis. Fellow, NZ, 1972. Sec., European Soc. for Clinical Investigation, 1969–72; Censor, 1978–80, Senior Censor and Vice-Pres., 1982–83, RCP; Chairman: Med. Research Soc., 1983–; Assoc. of Professors of Medicine, 1983–; Mem., MRC, 1986–. *Publications:* Electrophysiological Technique, 1950; Clinical Pathology Data, 1951, 2nd edn 1957; (jtly) Clinical Physiology, 1959, 5th edn 1984; Neurogenic Hypertension, 1965; A Computer Model of Human Respiration, 1977; (jtly) Software for Educational Computing, 1980; papers on hypertension and respiratory physiology. *Recreations:* theatre, opera, playing the organ. *Address:* Griffin Cottage, 57 Belsize Lane, NW3 5AU. *T:* 01-431 1845. *Club:* Garrick.

DICKINSON, Sir Harold (Herbert), Kt 1975; Director: Development Finance Corporation Ltd, since 1979; Australian Fixed Trusts Ltd, since 1979; Chairman, AFT Property Co. Ltd, since 1980; *b* 27 Feb. 1917; *s* of late William James Dickinson and Barwon Venus Clarke; *m* 1946, Elsie May Smith; two *d*. *Educ:* Singleton Public Sch.; Tamworth High Sch.; Univ. of Sydney (LLB, 1st Cl. Hons). Barrister-at-Law. Served War, 2nd AIF HQ 22 Inf. Bde, 1940–45 (despatches); Japanese POW (Sgt). Dept of Lands, NSW, 1933–40; NSW Public Service Bd, 1946–60: Sec. and Sen. Inspector, 1949–60; Chief Exec. Officer, Prince Henry Hosp., 1960–63; NSW Public Service Bd: Mem., 1963–70; Dep. Chm., 1970–71; Chm., 1971–79. Hon. Mem., NSW Univs Bd, 1967–71; Hon. Dir, Prince Henry, Prince of Wales, Eastern Suburbs Teaching Hosps, 1965–75, Chm. of Dirs, 1975–; Governor, NSW Coll. of Law, 1972–77. *Publications:* contribs to administration jls. *Recreation:* sailing. *Address:* 649 Old South Head Road, Rose Bay North, NSW 2030, Australia. *T:* 371–7475. *Clubs:* Union, Rotary (Sydney).

DICKINSON, Very Rev. Hugh Geoffrey; Dean of Salisbury, since 1986; *b* 17 Nov. 1929; *s* of late Hon. Richard Sebastian Willoughby Dickinson, DSO (*o s* of 1st Baron Dickinson) and of May Southey, *d* of late Charles Lovemore; *m* 1963, Jean Marjorie Storey; one *s* one *d*. *Educ:* Westminster School (KS); Trinity Coll., Oxford (MA, DipTh); Cuddesdon Theol Coll. Deacon 1956, priest 1957; Curate of Melksham, Wilts, 1956–58; Chaplain: Trinity Coll., Cambridge, 1958–63; Winchester College, 1963–67; Bishop's Adviser for Adult Education, Diocese of Coventry, 1969–77; Vicar of St Michael's, St Albans, 1977–86. *Recreations:* woodturning, fishing, gardening. *Address:* The Deanery, 7 The Close, Salisbury, Wilts SP1 2EF.

See also Hon. P. M. de B. Dickinson.

DICKINSON, Rt. Rev. John Hubert, MA; Vicar of Chollerton, 1959–71; Hon. Canon in Newcastle Cathedral, 1947–71; *m* 1937, Frances Victoria, *d* of late Rev. C. F. Thorp; two *d*. *Educ:* Jesus Coll., Oxford; Cuddesdon Coll. Deacon, 1925; Priest, 1926; Curate of St John, Middlesbrough, 1925–29; SPG Missionary, South Tokyo, 1929–31; Asst Bishop of Melanesia, 1931–37; Vicar of Felkirk-with-Brierley, 1937–42; Vicar of Warkworth, 1942–59. *Address:* Wingrove, Riding Mill, Northumberland.

DICKINSON, John Lawrence, (Bob), CBE 1973; DL; FCA; Chairman: SKF Steel Ltd, 1974–82; Bofors Cos (UK), 1974–83; General Manager, SKF Holding Co. (Holland), 1975–83; *b* 16 Nov. 1913; *s* of Tom Dickinson and Jennie Louise Dickinson; *m* 1937, Bettine Mary Jenkins; two *d*. *Educ:* Taunton Sch. Qual. as Chartered Accountant, 1937; Chief Accountant, Lucas Industries, 1937–44; SKF (UK) Ltd: Finance Dir and Sec., 1944–62; Sales Dir, 1962–66; Man. Dir, 1967–75, retired. Chairman: Sheffield Twist Drill & Steel Co. Ltd, 1978–81 (Dep. Chm., 1974–78); Weyroc Ltd (subsid. of Swedish Match Co.), 1975–82; British Rail (Eastern) Bd, 1970–81; Mem., National Enterprise Bd, 1975–79; Chm., NEDO Industrial Engines Sector Working Party, 1976–79; Mem. Gen. Council, also Finance and Gen. Purposes Cttee, CBI, until 1977; first Chm., Eastern Regional Council. Dep. Chm., Cranfield Inst., retd 1983. Hon. Life Vice-Pres., Luton and District Chamber of Commerce and Industry. High Sheriff, Bedfordshire, 1972–73, DL Beds 1976–. Gold Medal, Royal Patriots Soc. (Sweden), 1975. *Recreations:* gardening, National Hunt racing. *Address:* Arkle House, Upton End, Shillington, Hitchin, Herts SG5 3PG. *T:* Hitchin 711554.

DICKINSON, Patric (Thomas); poet, playwright and freelance broadcaster; *b* 26 Dec. 1914; *s* of Major A. T. S. Dickinson, 51 Sikhs, FF, IA, and Eileen Constance Kirwan; *m* 1945, Sheila Dunbar Shannon; one *s* one *d*. *Educ:* St Catharine's Coll., Cambridge (Crabtree Exhibitioner). Asst Schoolmaster, 1936–39. Artists' Rifles, 1939–40. BBC, 1942–48 (Feature and Drama Dept); Acting Poetry Editor, 1945–48. Sometime Gresham Prof. in Rhetoric at the City University. Libretti: (for Malcolm Arnold) The Return of Odysseus, 1977; (for Stephen Dodgson) The Miller's Secret, 1973; (for Alan Ridout): Creation, 1973; Good King Wenceslas, 1979. Atlantic Award in Literature, 1948; Cholmondeley Award for Poets, 1973. *Publications: poetry:* The Seven Days of Jericho, 1944; Soldier's Verse (anthology), 1945; Theseus and the Minotaur: play and poems, 1946; Stone in the Midst: play and poems, 1949; (ed) Byron (selected anthology), 1949; A Round of Golf Courses, 1951; The Sailing Race, 1952; The Scale of Things, 1955; (ed with Sheila Shannon) Poems to Remember, 1958; The World I See, 1960; This Cold Universe, 1964; (ed with Sheila Shannon) Poets' Choice: an anthology of English poetry from Spenser to the present day, 1967; (ed) C. Day Lewis, Selections from his Poetry, 1967; Selected Poems, 1968; More Than Time, 1970; A Wintering Tree, 1973; The Bearing Beast, 1976; Our Living John, 1979; Poems from Rye, 1980; Winter Hostages, 1980; (ed and introd) Selected Poems Henry Newbolt, 1981; A Rift in Time, 1982; To Go Hidden, 1984; *translations:* Aristophanes Against War, 1957; The Aeneid of Vergil, 1960; Aristophanes, vols I and II, 1970; *play:* A Durable Fire, 1962; *autobiography:* The Good Minute, 1965. *Recreation:* following golf (Cambridge Blue, 1935). *Address:* 38 Church Square, Rye, East Sussex. *T:* Rye 222194. *Club:* Savile.

DICKINSON, Prof. Peter; composer, pianist; first Professor of Music, University of Keele, 1974–84, now Emeritus; *b* 15 Nov. 1934; *s* of late Frank Dickinson, contact lens specialist, and of Muriel Porter; *m* 1964, Bridget Jane Tomkinson; two *s*. *Educ:* The Leys Sch.; Queens' Coll., Cambridge (organ schol., Stewart of Rannoch schol.; MA); Juilliard Sch. of Music, New York (Rotary Foundn Fellow). LRAM, ARCM; FRCO. Teaching and freelance work in New York, 1958–61, London and Birmingham, 1962–74; founded Centre for American Music, Keele Univ. Concerts, broadcasts and records as pianist, mostly with sister Meriel Dickinson, mezzo soprano, incl. French, American and British works, some specially commissioned, 1960–. Member: Bd, Trinity Coll. of Music, 1984–; Royal Soc. of Musicians, 1985–. FRSA 1981. *Publications: compositions include: orchestral:* Monologue for Strings, 1959; Five Diversions, 1969; Transformations, 1970; Organ Concerto, 1971; Piano Concerto, 1984; *chamber:* String Quartet No 1, 1958; Juilliard Dances, 1959; Fanfares and Elegies, 1967; Translations, 1971; String Quartet No 2, 1975; Hymns, Rags & Blues, 1985; works for solo organ, piano, clavichord, recorder and baryton; *vocal:* Four Auden Songs, 1956; A Dylan Thomas Cycle, 1959; Elegy, 1966; Five Poems of Alan Porter, 1968; Extravaganzas, 1969; An E. E. Cummings Cycle, 1970; Winter Afternoons, 1970; Three Comic Songs (Auden), 1972; Surrealist Landscape (Lord Berners), 1973; Lust (St Augustine), 1974; A Memory of David Munrow, 1977; Reminiscences (Byron), 1979; The Unicorns, 1982; Stevie's Tunes (Stevie Smith), 1984; *choral:* Martin of Tours (Thomas Blackburn), 1966; The Dry Heart (Alan Porter), 1967; Outcry, 1969; Late Afternoon in November, 1975; A Mass of the Apocalypse, 1984; *ballet:* Vitalitas, 1959; *musical drama:* The Judas Tree (Thomas Blackburn), 1965; various church music, music for children and for films; (ed) Twenty British Composers, 1975; Songs and Piano Music by Lord Berners, 1982; contrib. to The New Grove, and various periodicals. *Recreation:* book collecting. *Address:* c/o Novello & Co., 8 Lower James Street, W1R 4DN.

DICKINSON, Hon. Peter Malcolm de Brissac; author; *b* 16 Dec. 1927; *s* of late Hon. Richard Sebastian Willoughby Dickinson and of May Southey (Nancy) Lovemore; *m* 1953, Mary Rose Barnard; two *s* two *d*. *Educ:* Eton; King's Coll., Cambridge (BA). Asst Editor, Punch, 1952–69. Chm., Management Cttee, Soc. of Authors, 1978–80. *Publications: children's books:* The Weathermonger, 1968; Heartsease, 1969; The Devil's Children, 1970 (trilogy republished 1975 as The Changes); Emma Tupper's Diary, 1970; The Dancing Bear, 1972; The Gift, 1973; The Iron Lion, 1973; Chance, Luck and Destiny, 1975; The Blue Hawk, 1976; Annerton Pit, 1977; Hepzibah, 1978; Tulku, 1979 (Whitbread Prize; Carnegie Medal); The Flight of Dragons, 1979; City of Gold, 1980 (Carnegie Medal); The Seventh Raven, 1981; Healer, 1983; Giant Cold, 1984; (ed) Hundreds and Hundreds, 1984; A Box of Nothing, 1985; *TV series,* Mandog (Mandog, by Lois Lamplugh, 1972, is based on this series); *novels:* Skin Deep, 1968; A Pride of Heroes, 1969; The Seals, 1970; Sleep and His Brother, 1971; The Lizard in the Cup, 1972; The Green Gene, 1973; The Poison Oracle, 1974; The Lively Dead, 1975; King and Joker, 1976; Walking Dead, 1977; One Foot in the Grave, 1979; A Summer in the Twenties, 1981; The Last House-party, 1982; Hindsight, 1983; Death of a Unicorn, 1984; Tefuga, 1986. *Recreation:* manual labour. *Address:* 33 Queensdale Road, W11 4SB.

See also Baron Dickinson, Very Rev. H. G. Dickinson.

DICKINSON, Reginald Percy, OBE 1964; retired Under Secretary, Ministry of Defence; *b* 13 Feb. 1914; *s* of Percy and Nellie Dickinson; *m* 1943, Marjorie Ellen Lillistone; two *s*. *Educ:* Grammar school. BScEng London Univ., 1943; FRAeS, CEng. Air Min., Martlesham Heath, 1936; RAE, 1937; Aircraft and Armament Exper. Estabt, 1942: Supt of Performance, 1953, Supt Weapon Systems, 1962; Dir, Aircraft Develt (B), MoD, Project Dir, Lightning, Hercules, Victor, Buccaneer, Hawk etc, 1965–73; Dir Gen. Mil. Aircraft Projects, 1974–75. Chm., Flight Panel, AGARD, 1963–65; Mem., ARC and RAeS Cttees. Alston Medal for achievements in Flight Testing, 1961. *Recreations:* sailing, golf. *Address:* 1A Lingwood Avenue, Mudeford, Christchurch, Dorset BH23 3JS. *T:* Christchurch 482781. *Clubs:* Highcliffe Sailing; Highcliffe Castle Golf.

DICKINSON, Sir Samuel Benson, (Sir Ben Dickinson), Kt 1980; Mining Advisor to South Australian Government, 1975–84; Chairman, South Australian Government Uranium Enrichment Committee, 1979–84; *b* 1 Feb. 1912; *s* of Sydney Rushbrook Dickinson and Margaret Dickinson (*née* Clemes); *m* 1960, Dorothy Joan Weidenhofer; three *s* one *d*. *Educ:* Haileybury College, Melbourne; Univ. of Melbourne. MSc. N Australia Aerial Geological and Geophysical Survey, 1935–36; geologist: Electrolytic Zinc, Mt Lyell, Mt Isa, mining cos, 1937–41; S Australian Geological Survey, 1941–42. Dir of Mines, Govt Geologist, Sec. to Minister of Mines, Dep. Controller, Mineral Production, Chm. Radium Hill Mines, 1943–56; Director: Rio Tinto Mining Co. of Australia, 1956–60; Sir Frank Duval's Gp of Cos, 1960–62; Chief Technical Adviser, Pechiney Australia, 1962–65; Project Manager, Clutha Development Ltd and Daniel K. Ludwig Cos Australia, 1965–75. *Publications:* technical reports for Australian Dept of Mines, Inst. of Mining and Metallurgy and mining jls and bulletins. *Recreations:* golf, bowls. *Address:* PO Box 269, Stirling, SA 5152, Australia. *T:* (08) 339 5135. *Clubs:* Athenæum (Melbourne); American National (Sydney); Naval, Military & Air Force (Adelaide).

DICKINSON, William Michael, MBE 1960; publisher; Managing Director, Africa Research Ltd, since 1966; *b* 13 Jan. 1930; *s* of late Comdr W. H. Dickinson, RN, and Ruth Sandeman Betts; *m* 1971, Enid Joy Bowers; one *s* two *d*. *Educ:* St Edward's Sch., Oxford. Army Service, 1948–51. Colonial and Foreign Service, 1952–65. *Address:* c/o Africa Research Ltd, 1A Summerland Street, Exeter EX1 2AF. *T:* Exeter 215655.

DICKS, Terence Patrick, (Terry); MP (C) Hayes and Harlington, since 1983; Administrative Officer, Greater London Council, since 1971; *b* 17 March 1937; *s* of Frank and Winifred Dicks; *m*; one *s* two *d*. *Educ:* London Sch. of Econs and Pol Science (BScEcon 2.2); Oxford Univ. (DipEcon). Clerk: Imperial Tobacco Co. Ltd, 1952–59; Min. of Labour, 1959–66. Contested (C) Bristol South, 1979. *Address:* House of Commons, SW1A 0AA.

DICKSON, Alexander Graeme, (Alec), CBE 1967 (MBE 1945); MA Oxon; Hon. President, Community Service Volunteers, since 1982 (Hon. Director, 1962–82); *b* 23 May 1914; *y s* of late Norman Dickson and Anne Higgins; *m* 1951, Mora Hope Robertson, artist, author of numerous travel books and biographies. *Educ:* Rugby; New Coll., Oxford. Private Sec. to late Sir Alec Paterson, 1935; editorial staff: Yorkshire Post, 1936–37; Daily Telegraph, 1937–38, Germany; refugee relief, Czechoslovakia, winter 1938–39. Served War of 1939–45: Cameron Highlanders; 1st KAR (Abyssinian Campaign); led E Africa Comd mobile educn unit. Displaced Persons Directorate, Berlin, 1946–48; introd Mass Educn, Gold Coast, 1948–49; founded Man O' War Bay Training Centre, Cameroons and Nigeria, 1950–54; Chief Unesco Mission, Iraq, 1955–56; refugee relief, Austro-Hungarian frontier, winter 1956–57. Founder and first Dir, Voluntary Service Overseas, 1958–62; founded Community Service Volunteers, 1962, developing concept of 'A Year Between' for students, linking curriculum to human needs, promoting tutoring in schools, involving disadvantaged and unemployed young people in social service. Shared experience with US Peace Corps, 1961, 1969; India, 1968, 1972; Hong Kong, 1968, 1974, 1980; Israel, 1970, 1980; Nigeria, 1970, 1975, 1976; Malta, 1971; Nepal, 1972; New Zealand, 1972; Papua New Guinea, 1973; Bahamas, 1975; US Nat. Student Volunteer Program, Washington DC and Alaska, 1975; Ontario, 1975, 1981, 1982, 1983; Sri Lanka, Australia, 1976; Japan, 1976, 1980, 1983; Univ. of the South Pacific, 1978; W Germany, Denmark, 1979; Finland, 1980; Sweden, 1982; Malaysia, 1983. Consultant to Commonwealth Secretariat, 1974–77. Hon. LLD: Leeds, 1970; Bristol, 1980. Niwano Peace Foundn Award, 1982. *Publications:* (with Mora Dickson) A Community Service Handbook, 1967; School in the Round, 1969; A Chance to Serve, 1976; Volunteers, 1983; articles on community development and youth service. *Recreations:* identical with work - involving young people in community service, at home or overseas. *Address:* 19 Blenheim Road, W4. *T:* 01-994 7437; (office) 01-278 6601.

See also M. G. Dickson.

DICKSON, Arthur Richard Franklin, CBE 1974; QC (Belize), 1979; Commissioner for Law Revision, Belize, 1978; *b* 13 Jan. 1913; *m* 1949, Joanna Maria Margaretha van Baardwyk; four *s*. *Educ:* Rusea's Secondary Sch. and Cornwall Coll., Jamaica. Called to the Bar, Lincoln's Inn, 1938. Judicial Service. HM Overseas Judiciary: Jamaica, 1941; Magistrate, Turks and Caicos Islands, 1944–47; Asst to Attorney-Gen., and Legal Draftsman, Barbados, 1947–49; Magistrate, British Guiana, 1949–52; Nigeria, 1952–62: Magistrate, 1952–54; Chief Magistrate, 1954–56; Chief Registrar, High Court, Lagos, 1956–58; Judge of the High Court, Lagos, 1958–62; retired. Temp. appointment, Solicitors Dept, GPO London, 1962–63; served Northern Rhodesia (latterly Zambia), 1964–67; Judge of the High Court, Uganda, 1967–71; Deputy Chm., Middlesex QS, July-Aug., 1971; Chief Justice, Belize, 1973–74; Judge of the Supreme Court, Anguilla (part-time), 1972–76; part-time Chm., Industrial Tribunals, 1972–85. *Publications:* Revised Ordinances (1909–1941) Turks and Caicos Islands, 1944; (ed) Revised Laws of Belize, 1980. *Recreations:* gardening, walking, swimming, riding. *Address:* 14 Meadow Lane, Lindfield, Haywards Heath, West Sussex RH16 2RJ. *T:* Lindfield 4450. *Club:* Royal Commonwealth Society.

DICKSON, Rt. Hon. Brian, PC (Can) 1984; Chief Justice of Canada, since 1984; *b* 25 May 1916; *s* of Thomas and Sarah Elizabeth Dickson (*née* Gibson); *m* 1943, Barbara Melville, *d* of Henry E. Sellers; three *s* one *d*. *Educ:* Regina Collegiate Institute; University of Manitoba; Manitoba Law School. LLB 1938 (Gold Medal). Served with Royal Canadian Artillery, 1940–45 (wounded, despatches); Hon. Lt-Col, 30th Field Regt, Royal Canadian Artillery. Called to the Bar of Manitoba, 1940; practised law with Aikins, MacAulay & Co., 1945–63; Lectr, Manitoba Law Sch., 1948–54; QC (Can) 1953; Court of Queen's Bench, Manitoba, 1963; Manitoba Court of Appeal, 1967; Supreme Court of Canada, 1973; Life Bencher, Law Soc. of Manitoba; Chm., Board of Governors, Univ. of Manitoba, 1971–73; Chancellor of Diocese of Rupert's Land, 1960–71. Hon. Bencher, Lincoln's Inn, 1984. Hon. Prof., Manitoba Univ., 1985. Hon. degrees: St John's Coll.; Univs of Manitoba, Saskatchewan, Ottawa, Queen's, Dalhousie, York. KStJ 1985. *Recreation:* riding. *Address:* Supreme Court Building, Wellington Street, Ottawa, Ont K1A 0J1, Canada; Marchmont, Dunrobin, Ont K0A 1T0. *Club:* Rideau (Ottawa).

DICKSON, Eileen Wadham, (Mrs C. F. Dickson); *d* of John Edward Latton, Librarian to Inner Temple, and Ethel Letitia Baker; *m* 1931, Charles Frederick Dickson, OBE. *Educ:* Convent of the Sacred Heart, Roehampton; Bruges, Belgium. Served War of 1939–45 with WVS and on Executive Council of Stage Door Canteen. Joined Harper's Bazaar, 1949; Fashion Editor, 1951; Editor, 1953–65. *Recreations:* theatre, reading, racing, gardens. *Address:* Grimsdyke, Aldworth, Reading, Berks; 4 Stack House, Ebury Street, SW1.

DICKSON, George, OBE 1974; HM Diplomatic Service; Deputy High Commissioner, Kingston, Jamaica, since 1985; *b* 23 May 1931; *s* of late George James Stark Dickson and of Isobel (*née* Brown). *Educ:* Aberdeen Acad. DSIR, 1952; CRO, 1952–54; Karachi, 1954–56; Penang, 1957–59; Nicosia, 1960–62; Kampala, 1962–66; FCO, 1966–68; Manila, 1968–71; Jakarta, 1971–75; Consul: Stuttgart, 1975–76; Beirut, 1976–79; First Sec. and Head of Chancery, Baghdad, 1979–81; Asst Dir, Internat. Affairs Div., Commonwealth Secretariat, 1981–85. *Recreations:* friends, travel, walking. *Address:* c/o Foreign and Commonwealth Office, SW1A 2AH. *Clubs:* Royal Commonwealth Society, Royal Over-Seas League.

DICKSON, Prof. Gordon Ross; Professor of Agriculture, University of Newcastle upon Tyne, since 1973; Deputy Chairman, Home-Grown Cereals Authority, since 1982; *b* 12 Feb. 1932; *s* of T. W. Dickson, Tynemouth; *m* 1956, Dorothy Stobbs; two *s* one *d*. *Educ:* Tynemouth High Sch.; Durham Univ. BSc (Agric) 1st cl. hons 1953, PhD (Agric) 1958, Dunelm. Tutorial Research Student, Univ. Sch. of Agric., King's Coll., Newcastle upon Tyne, 1953–56; Asst Farm Dir, Council of King's Coll., Nafferton, Stocksfield-on-Tyne, 1956–58; Farms Director for the Duke of Norfolk, 1958–71; Principal, Royal Agric. Coll., Cirencester, 1971–73. Chm., Agricl Wages Bd for England and Wales, 1981–84. *Address:* Faculty of Agriculture, University of Newcastle upon Tyne, Newcastle upon Tyne NE1 7RU; The West Wing, Bolam Hall, Morpeth, Northumberland NE61 3ST.

DICKSON, (Horatio Henry) Lovat, OC 1978; FRSC 1982; writer and publisher; *b* 30 June 1902; *s* of Gordon Fraser Dickson and Josephine Mary Cunningham; *m* 1934, Marguerite Isabella, *d* of A. B. Brodie, Montreal; one *s*. *Educ:* Berkhamsted Sch.; University of Alberta (MA). Lecturer in English, Univ. of Alberta, 1927–29; Associate Editor, Fortnightly Review, 1929–32; Editor of Review of Reviews, 1930–34; Managing Dir of Lovat Dickson Ltd (Publishers), 1932–38; Director: Macmillan & Co. (publishers), 1941–64; Pan Books Ltd, 1946–64; Reprint Soc., 1939–64. Hon. LLD Alberta, 1968; Hon. DLitt: Western Ontario, 1976; York Univ., Toronto, 1981. *Publications:* The Green Leaf, 1938; Half-Breed, The Story of Grey Owl, 1939; Out of the West Land, 1944; Richard Hillary, 1950; two vols of autobiog.: Vol. I, The Ante-Room, 1959; Vol. II, The House of Words, 1963; H. G. Wells, 1969; Wilderness Man, 1973; Radclyffe Hall at the Well of Loneliness, 1975; The Museum-Makers, 1986. *Address:* Apt 808, 21 Dale Avenue, Toronto, Ont M4W 1K3, Canada. *Club:* Arts and Letters (Toronto).

DICKSON, Jennifer (Joan), (Mrs R. A. Sweetman), RA 1976 (ARA 1970); RCA 1978; RE 1965; graphic artist, photographer and painter; *b* 17 Sept. 1936; 2nd *d* of late John Liston Dickson and Margaret Joan Turner, S Africa; *m* 1962, Ronald Andrew Sweetman; one *s*. *Educ:* Goldsmith's College Sch. of Art, Univ. of London; Atelier 17, Paris. Taught at Eastbourne Sch. of Art, 1959–62 (French Govt Schol., to work in Paris under S. W. Hayter). Directed and developed Printmaking Dept, Brighton Coll. of Art, 1962–68; developed and directed Graphics Atelier, Saidye Bronfman Centre, Montreal, 1970–72. Has held appointments of Vis. Artist at following Universities: Ball State Univ., Muncie, Indiana, 1967; Univ. of the West Indies, Kingston, Jamaica, 1968; Univ. of Wisconsin, Madison, 1972; Ohio State Univ., 1973; Western Illinois Univ., 1973; Haystack Mountain Sch. of Crafts, Maine, 1973; Vis. Artist, Queen's Univ., Kingston, Ont., 1977; part-time Instructor of Drawing, 1980–81, 1983, Sessional Instructor, 1980–85, Ottawa Univ. Founder Mem., Brit. Printmakers' Council. Prix des Jeunes Artistes (Gravure), Biennale de Paris, 1963; Major Prize, World Print Competition, San Francisco, 1974; Norwegian Print Biennale Prize, 1981. *Publications:* suites of original prints and photographs: Genesis, 1965; Alchemic Images, 1966; Aids to Meditation, 1967; Eclipse, 1968; Song of Songs, 1969; Out of Time, 1970; Fragments, 1971; Sweet

Death and Other Pleasures, 1972; Homage to Don Juan, 1975; Body Perceptions, 1975; The Secret Garden, 1976; Openings, 1977; Three Mirrors to Narcissus, 1978; Il Paradiso Terrestre, 1980; Il Tempo Classico, 1981; Grecian Odes, 1983; Aphrodite Anadyomene, 1984; The Gardens of Paradise, part 1, 1984, part 2, 1985; Reflected Palaces, 1985. *Address:* 508 Gilmour Street, Ottawa, Ontario K1R 5L4, Canada.

DICKSON, John Abernethy, CB 1970; Director-General and Deputy Chairman, Forestry Commission, 1968–76; *b* 19 Sept. 1915; *yr s* of late John and Williamina Dickson; *m* 1942, Helen Drummond, *o d* of Peter Drummond Jardine; two *d. Educ:* Robert Gordon's Coll., Aberdeen; Aberdeen Univ. MA 1936; BSc (For.) 1938. Joined Forestry Commn, 1938; District Officer, 1940; seconded to Min. of Supply, Home Grown Timber Production Dept, 1940–46; Divisional Officer, 1951; Conservator, 1956; Dir (Scotland), 1963; Comr Harvesting and Marketing, 1965. Director: Economic Forestry (Scotland), 1977–84; Forest Thinnings Ltd, 1979–86 (Chm., 1981–86). Chm., Standing Cttee on Commonwealth Forestry, 1968–76; Vice-Pres., Commonwealth Forestry Assoc., 1975– (Chm., 1972–75). Hon. LLD Aberdeen, 1969. FBIM 1975. *Recreation:* gardening. *Address:* 56 Oxgangs Road, Edinburgh EH10 7AY. *T:* 031–445 1067.

DICKSON, Leonard Elliot, CBE 1972; MC 1945; TD 1951; DL; Solicitor, Dickson, Haddow & Co., 1947–84; *b* 17 March 1915; *s* of Rev. Robert Marcus Dickson, DD, Lanark, and Cordelia Elliot; *m* 1950, Mary Elisabeth Cuthbertson; one *s* one *d. Educ:* Uppingham, Rutland; Univ. of Cambridge (BA 1936); Univ. of Glasgow (LLB 1947). Served War, with 1st Bn Glasgow Highlanders, HLI, 1939–46. Clerk to Clyde Lighthouses Trust, 1953–65. Chm., Lowland TAVR, 1968–70; Vice-Chm. Glasgow Exec. Council, NHS, 1970–74. DL Glasgow, 1963. *Recreations:* travel, gardening. *Address:* Bridge End, Gartmore, by Stirling FK8 3RT. *T:* Aberfoyle 220. *Club:* Royal Scottish Automobile (Glasgow).

DICKSON, Lovat; *see* Dickson, H. H. L.

DICKSON, Murray Graeme, CMG 1961; *b* 19 July 1911; *s* of Norman and Anne Dickson. *Educ:* Rugby; New Coll., Oxford. Prison Service (Borstals), 1935–40. Served War of 1939–45, in Force 136. Entered Colonial Service, 1947; Education Officer, Sarawak, 1947, Deputy Dir of Education, 1952, Dir of Education, 1955–66; retd. Unesco adviser on educl planning to Govt of Lesotho, 1967–68. *Address:* 412 Seddon House, Barbican, EC2.

See also A. G. Dickson.

DICKSON, Prof. Robert Andrew, MA Oxon, MB, ChM; FRCS, FRCSE; Professor and Head of Department of Orthopaedic Surgery, University of Leeds, since 1981; Consultant Surgeon, St James's University Hospital, Leeds, and Leeds General Infirmary, since 1981; *b* 13 April 1943; *s* of Robert Campbell Miller Dickson and Maude Evelyn Dickson; *m* 1980, Ingrid Irene Sandberg; one *s. Educ:* Edinburgh Academy; Edinburgh Univ. (MB, ChB 1967, ChM 1973). FRCSE 1972; Moynihan Medal (Assoc. of Surgeons of GB and Ire.), 1977; FRCS *ad eund.* 1982. Lecturer, Nuffield Dept of Orthopaedic Surgery, Univ. of Oxford, 1972–75; Fellow in Spinal Surgery, Univ. of Louisville, Kentucky, 1975–76; Reader, Nuffield Dept of Orthopaedic Surgery, Univ. of Oxford, 1976–81. Arris and Gale Lectr, and Hunterian Prof., RCS. Fellow, Brit. Orthopaedic Assoc.; Member: Brit. Soc. for Surgery of the Hand; Brit. Orthopaedic Research Soc.; Brit. Scoliosis Soc. *Publications:* Surgery of the Rheumatoid Hand, 1979; Musculo-skeletal disease, 1984; Management of spinal deformities, 1984; papers on scoliosis, spinal surgery, hand surgery, and microsurgery. *Recreations:* squash, music. *Address:* 14A Park Avenue, Leeds LS8 2JH.

DICKSON, Rt. Hon. Robert George Brian; *see* Dickson, Rt. Hon. B.

DICKSON, Dame Violet (Penelope), DBE 1976 (CBE 1964; MBE 1942); *b* Gautby, Lincs, 3 Sept. 1896; *d* of Neville Lucas-Calcraft and Emily Delmar Lindley; *m* 1920, Captain Harold Richard Patrick Dickson, CIE (*d* 1959); one *s* one *d. Educ:* Miss Lunn's High Sch., Woodhall Spa; Les Charmettes, Vevey, Switzerland. Mesopotamia, 1921–22; Quetta, Baluchistan, 1923–24; Bikaner, Rajputana, 1924–28; Bushire, Iran, 1928–29; Kuwait, 1929–. FRZS; Mem.RCAS. *Publications:* Wild Flowers of Kuwait and Bahrain, 1955; Forty Years in Kuwait, 1971. *Recreations:* shooting, riding, tennis, swimming. *Address:* Seef, Kuwait, Arabia. *T:* 432310.

DICKSON, Marshal of the Royal Air Force Sir William (Forster), GCB 1953 (KCB 1952; CB 1942); KBE 1946 (CBE 1945; OBE 1934); DSO 1918; AFC 1922; idc; psa; *b* 24 Sept. 1898; *s* of late C. C. Forster Dickson, Chancery Registrar's Office, Royal Courts of Justice, and of late Agnes Nelson Dickson, Northwood, Mddx; *m* 1932, Patricia Marguerite, *d* of late Sir Walter Allen, KBE; one *d* (and one *d* decd). *Educ:* Bowden House, Seaford; Haileybury Coll. Royal Naval Air Service, 1916–18 (DSO, despatches thrice); transferred to RAF, 1918; Permanent Commn in RAF, 1919; employed on Naval Flying work, 1919–21; Test Pilot, RAE, 1921–22; Air Ministry, 1923–26; No 56 (Fighter) Sqdn, 1926–27; RAF Staff Coll., Andover, 1927–28; posted to India, 1929; served on NW Frontier, 1929–30 and at HQ RAF Delhi (despatches); commanded RAF Station, Hawkinge, and No 25 (Fighter) Squadron, 1935–36; Directing Staff, Staff Coll., 1936–38; Imperial Defence Coll., 1939; Dir of Plans, Air Ministry, 1941–42; commanded Nos 9 and 10 Groups in Fighter Comd, 1942–43; commanded No 83 Group in TAF, 1943–44; commanded Desert Air Force, 1944; Asst Chief of Air Staff (Policy), Air Ministry, 1945–46; Vice-Chief of Air Staff, Air Council, Air Ministry, 1946–48; C-in-C, MEAF, 1948–50; Mem. for Supply and Organisation, Air Council, 1950–52; Chief of the Air Staff, 1953–56; Chm. of the Chiefs of Staff Cttee, 1956–59; Chief of Defence Staff, 1958–59. President: Royal Central Asian Soc., 1961–65; Ex-Services Mental Welfare Soc., 1960–76; Haileybury Soc., 1962; Forces Help Society and Lord Roberts Workshops, 1974–81. Master, The Glass Sellers' Co., 1964. Russian Order of Suvarov, 1944; USA Legion of Merit. *Address:* Foxbriar House, Cold Ash, Newbury, Berks. *Club:* Royal Air Force.

DICKSON MABON, Rt. Hon. Jesse; *see* Mabon, Rt Hon. J. D.

DIEHL, John Bertram Stuart; barrister; a Recorder, since 1984; *b* 18 April 1944; *s* of E. H. S. and C. P. Diehl; *m* 1967, Patricia L. Charman; two *s. Educ:* Bishop Gore Grammar Sch., Swansea; University Coll. of Wales, Aberystwyth (LLB 1965). Called to the Bar, Lincoln's Inn, 1968. Asst Lectr and Lectr in Law, Univ. of Sheffield, 1965–69; in practice on Wales and Chester Circuit, 1969–. *Address:* Angel Chambers, 94 Walter Road, Swansea SA1 5QA. *T:* Swansea 464623.

DIESKAU, Dietrich F.; *see* Fischer-Dieskau.

DIETRICH, Marlene; actress; *b* Berlin, 27 Dec. 1904; *d* of Eduard von Losch and Josephine Felsing; *m* 1924, Rudolph Sieber (*d* 1976); one *d. Educ:* Berlin; Weimar; Max Reinhardt Sch. of Theatre; Stage, Berlin and Vienna; First notable film, The Blue Angel; films in America since 1930, incl. Desire, Destry Rides Again, Foreign Affair, Garden of Allah, Golden Earrings, Rancho Notorious, Scarlet Empress, Shanghai Express, Stage Fright, Witness for the Prosecution, Just a Gigolo; naturalised as an American, 1937; numerous stage appearances in Europe, Great Britain, America and all continents; Special Tony Award, 1967–68. Officier, Légion d'Honneur, 1972; US Medal of Freedom. *Publication:* Marlene Dietrich's ABC, 1962. *Recreation:* tennis.

DIGBY, family name of **Baron Digby.**

DIGBY, 12th Baron (Ire.) *cr* 1620, and 5th Baron (GB) *cr* 1765; **Edward Henry Kenelm Digby,** JP; Lord-Lieutenant, Dorset, since 1984 (Vice Lord-Lieutenant, 1965–84); Captain, late Coldstream Guards; *b* 24 July 1924; *o s* of 11th and 4th Baron Digby, KG, DSO, MC, and Hon. Pamela Bruce, OBE (*d* 1978), *y d* of 2nd Baron Aberdare; *S* father, 1964; *m* 1952, Dione Marian (*see* Lady Digby); two *s* one *d. Educ:* Eton; Trinity Coll., Oxford; RMC. Served War of 1939–45. Capt., 1947; Malaya, 1948–50; ADC to C-in-C: FARELF, 1950–51; BAOR, 1951–52. Chm., W. & J. Tod, 1985– (Dir, 1984–). Director: Brooklyns Westbrick Ltd, 1970–83; C. H. Beazer (Hldgs), 1983–; Kier Internat., 1986–; Cohn Communities Inc., 1986–. Dep. Chm., SW Economic Planning Council, 1972–77. Mem. Council, Royal Agricultural Soc. of England, 1954; Chm., Royal Agricultural Soc. of Commonwealth, 1966–77, Hon. Fellow 1977. Pres., 1976, Vice Pres., 1977, Royal Bath and West Soc. Dorchester Rural District Councillor, 1962–68; Dorset County Councillor, 1966–81 (Vice Chm. CC, 1977); Mem. Dorset Agric. Exec. Cttee. Pres., Wessex Br., Inst. of Dirs; Dep. Pres., Dorset Br., British Red Cross Soc. DL 1957, JP 1959, Dorset. KStJ 1985. *Recreations:* ski-ing, shooting, racing, tennis. *Heir: s* Hon. Henry Noel Kenelm Digby [*b* 6 Jan. 1954; *m* 1980, Susan, *er d* of Peter Watts; one *s*]. *Address:* Minterne, Dorchester, Dorset. *T:* Cerne Abbas 370. *Club:* Pratt's.

See also W. A. Harriman.

DIGBY, Lady; Dione Marian Digby; DL; Member, Wessex Water Authority, since 1983; Director, South West Regional Board, National Westminster Bank, since 1986; *b* 23 Feb. 1934; *d* of Rear-Adm. Robert St Vincent Sherbrooke, VC, CB, DSO, and Rosemary Neville Sherbrooke (*née* Buckley), Oxton, Notts; *m* 1952, Baron Digby, *qv*; two *s* one *d. Educ:* Talindert State Sch., Victoria, Australia; Southover Manor Sch., Lewes, Sussex. Chairman: Dorset Assoc. of Youth Clubs, 1966–73; Dorset Community Council, 1977–79; Standing Conf. of Rural Community Councils and Councils of Voluntary Service SW Region, 1977–79. Councillor (Ind.) W Dorset DC, 1976–86; Mem. Dorset Small Industries Cttee, CoSIRA, 1977 (Chm. 1981). Mem. BBC/IBA Central Appeals Adv. Cttee, 1975–80; Governor, Dorset Coll. of Agriculture, 1978–83; Mem. Council, Exeter Univ., 1981–. Founder Chairman, Hon. Sec., Summer Music Soc. of Dorset, 1963–; Mem. Bath Festival Soc. Council of Management, 1971–81 (Chm. of the Society, 1976–81); Chm. Bath Fest. Friends Trust, 1982–; Member: SW Arts Management Cttee, 1981–86; Arts Council of GB, 1982–86; South Bank Bd, 1985–. DL Dorset, 1983. *Recreations:* music and the arts, skiing, sailing, tennis; interest in local government, politics, history, people. *Address:* Minterne, Dorchester, Dorset DT2 7AU. *T:* Cerne Abbas 370.

DIGBY, Adrian, CBE 1964; MA Oxon; FSA; Keeper, Department of Ethnography, British Museum, 1953–69; excavated Maya site of Las Cuevas, British Honduras, 1957; *b* 13 June 1909; *s* of late William Pollard Digby, FInstP, MIME, MIEE; *m* 1939, Sylvia Mary, *d* of late Arnold Inman, OBE, KC; two *d. Educ:* Lancing; Brasenose Coll., Oxford. Entered British Museum as Asst Keeper, 1932. Hon. Asst Sec. of International Congress of Anthropological and Ethnological Sciences, London, 1934; Hon. Sec. of International Congress of Americanists, Cambridge, 1952. Served in Intelligence Division Naval Staff, Admiralty, 1942–44; Hydrographic Dept, Admiralty, 1944–45. Vis. Prof. in Archaeology, Univ. de Los Andes, Bogota, 1970. Pres. Sect. H of The British Association for the Advancement of Science, 1962; Vice-Pres. Royal Anthropological Inst., 1962–66. *Publications:* Ancient American Pottery (with G. H. S. Bushnell), 1955; Maya Jades, 1964; articles on anthropological subjects in Man and in Chambers's Encyclopædia. *Recreation:* sundials. *Address:* The Paddocks, Eastcombe, Stroud, Glos GL6 7DR. *T:* Gloucester 770409.

DIGBY, George F. Wingfield; retired Keeper Emeritus, Victoria and Albert Museum; *b* 2 March 1911; 2nd *s* of late Col F. J. B. Wingfield Digby, DSO; *m* 1935, Cornelia, *d* of Prof. H. Keitler, University of Vienna; one *s* (decd). *Educ:* Harrow; Trinity Coll., Cambridge; Grenoble Univ.; Sorbonne; Vienna. Asst Keeper, Dept of Textiles, Victoria and Albert Museum, 1934; seconded to Education Office, Jamaica (Jamaica Coll.), 1941–45; Asst Keeper (1st class), Victoria and Albert Museum, 1946; Keeper of Dept of Textiles, 1947–72; retired 1973. *Publications:* The Work of the Modern Potter in England, 1952; Meaning and Symbol in Three Modern Artists, 1955; Symbol and Image in William Blake, 1957; (jtly) History of the West Indian Peoples (4 vols for schools); (part author) The Bayeux Tapestry, 1957; (contributor) Brussels Colloque International: La Tapisserie flamande au XVII-XVIII siècle, 1959; (contributor) Colston Research Soc. Papers: Metaphor and Symbol, 1960; Elizabethan Embroidery, 1963; The Devonshire Hunting Tapestries, 1971; Tapestries, Mediaeval and Renaissance, 1980; (trans. with Cornelia Wingfield Digby) Islamic Carpets and Textiles in the Keir Collection, 1977. *Recreations:* oriental ceramics and contemporary hand-made pottery. *Address:* Raleigh Lodge, Castleton, Sherborne, Dorset DT9 3SA.

See also S. W. Digby.

DIGBY, Very Rev. Richard Shuttleworth Wingfield, MA; Dean of Peterborough, 1966–80, Dean Emeritus since 1980; *b* 19 Aug. 1911; *s* of late Everard George Wingfield Digby and Dorothy (*née* Loughnan); *m* 1936, Rosamond Frances, *d* of late Col W. T. Digby, RE; two *s* one *d. Educ:* Nautical Coll., Pangbourne; Royal Navy; Christ's Coll., Cambridge; Westcott House, Cambridge. BA 1935; MA 1939. Asst Curate of St Andrew's, Rugby, 1936–46. Chaplain to the Forces (4th Cl. Emergency Commn), 1940–45; POW, 1940–45. Vicar of All Saints, Newmarket, 1946–53; Rector of Bury, Lancs, 1953–66; Rural Dean of Bury, 1962–66. Pres. and Chm., Bury Trustee Savings Bank, 1953–66; Dep. Chm., Trustee Savings Bank Assoc., North-West Area, 1965–66. Hon. Canon of Manchester Cath., 1965; Hon. Chaplain to Regt XX, The Lancs Fusiliers, 1965. Chm. CofE Council for Places of Worship, 1976–81. *Recreations:* walking, dry stone walling. *Address:* Byways, Higher Holton, near Wincanton, Somerset. *T:* Wincanton 32137. *Club:* Army and Navy.

DIGBY, Simon Wingfield, TD 1946; DL; MA; *b* 1910; *s* of late Col F. J. B. Wingfield Digby, DSO; *m* 1936, Kathleen Elizabeth, *d* of late Hon. Mr Justice Courtney Kingstone, Toronto, Canada; one *s* one *d. Educ:* Harrow Sch.; Trinity Coll., Cambridge. Delegate to International Studies Conference, 1934. Prospective Conservative Candidate for West Dorset, Jan. 1937–June 1941; MP (U) West Dorset, 1941–Feb. 1974; a Conservative Whip, 1948–51. Barrister-at-law, Inner Temple; served in Army (TA), Aug. 1939–June 1945 in UK and NW Europe; Major, 1943; GSO II. Civil Lord of the Admiralty, 1951–57. Mem. of Empire Parl. Delegn to East Africa, 1948 and Inter-Parliamentary Union Delegation to Chile, 1962. Pres., Wessex Young Conservatives, 1947–50; Sec., Conservative Social Services Cttee, 1947; Chairman: Conservative Forestry Sub-Cttee, 1959–67; Shipping and Shipbuilding Cttee, 1964–74. Member: Coastal Pollution Select Cttee, 1966–68; Select Cttee on Procedure; Public Accounts Cttee. Delegate (C), Council of Europe Assembly and Assembly of WEU, 1968–74 (Leader, 1972–74). Pres., Soc. of Dorset Men, 1972–85. DL Dorset, 1953. Order of Leopold and Order of White Lion.

Medal of Council of Europe Assembly, 1974. *Recreations:* fishing, bloodstock breeding. *Address:* Sherborne Castle, Sherborne, Dorset. *T:* Gillingham 2650; Coleshill House, Coleshill, near Birmingham. *Club:* Carlton.

See also G. F. W. Digby, Sir Rupert Hardy, Bt.

DIGBY, Ven. Stephen Basil W.; *see* Wingfield-Digby.

DIGGINES, Christopher Ewart, CMG 1974; HM Diplomatic Service, retired; British High Commissioner, Port of Spain, Trinidad and Tobago, 1973–77; British High Commissioner (non-resident), Grenada, 1974–77; *b* 2 July 1920; *s* of late Sir William Diggines; *m* 1946, Mary Walls; one *s* one *d.* *Educ:* Haileybury Coll.; Trinity Coll., Oxford. Army, 1940–46. Senior History Master, Birkenhead Sch., 1948–49; apptd to CRO, 1949; Office of the UK High Comr in India (Madras), 1952–56; Canadian National Defence Coll., 1958–59; UK Mission to UN (1st Sec.), 1959–62; British Deputy High Commissioner, Kingston, Jamaica, 1962–64; Foreign and Commonwealth Office (formerly Commonwealth Office), 1964–69; Counsellor (Commercial), Lusaka, 1969–73. *Address:* 115 Middle Street, Deal, Kent. *Clubs:* United Oxford & Cambridge University, Royal Commonwealth Society.

DIGGLE, James, LittD; FBA 1985; University Lecturer in Classics, Cambridge, since 1975; University Orator, since 1982; Fellow of Queens' College, since 1966; *b* 29 March 1944; *s* of James Diggle and Elizabeth Alice Buckley; *m* 1973, Sedwell Mary Chapman, *d* of Rev. Preb. F. A. R. Chapman and K. A. Chapman; three *s.* *Educ:* Rochdale Grammar School; St John's College, Cambridge (Major Scholar; Classical Tripos Pt I, first cl., 1964, Pt II, first cl. with dist., 1965; Pitt Scholar, Browne Scholar, Hallam Prize, Members' Latin Essay Prize, Montagu Butler Prize, Browne Medals for Greek Elegy and Latin Epigram, Porson Prize, First Chancellor's Classical Medal, Craven Student 1965; BA 1965; MA 1969; PhD 1969; LittD 1985). Queens' College, Cambridge: Research Fellow, 1966–67; Official Fellow and Director of Studies in Classics, 1967–; Librarian, 1969–77; Praelector, 1971–73, 1978–; Univ. Asst Lectr in Classics, Cambridge, 1970–75. Hon. Sec., Cambridge Philological Soc., 1970–74 (Jt Editor, Procs, 1970–82); Hon. Treasurer, Classical Jls Bd, 1979–; Jt Editor, Cambridge Classical Texts and Commentaries, 1977–. *Publications:* The Phaethon of Euripides, 1970; (jtly) Flavii Cresconii Corippi Iohannidos, Libri VIII, 1970; (ed jtly) The Classical Papers of A. E. Housman, 1972; (ed jtly) Dionysiaca: nine studies in Greek poetry, presented to Sir Denys Page, 1978; Studies on the Text of Euripides, 1981; Euripidis Fabulae (Oxford Classical Texts), vol. ii 1981, vol. i 1984. *Recreation:* family life. *Address:* Queens' College, Cambridge CB3 9ET. *T:* Cambridge 335511.

DIGNAN, Maj.-Gen. Albert Patrick, CB 1978; MBE 1952; FRCS, FRCSI; Director of Army Surgery and Consulting Surgeon to the Army, 1973–78; Hon. Consultant Surgeon, Royal Hospital, Chelsea, 1973–78; Hon. Consultant in Radiotherapy and Oncology, Westminster Hospital, 1974–78; *b* 25 July 1920; *s* of Joseph Dignan; *m* 1952, Eileen White; two *s* one *d.* *Educ:* Trinity Coll., Dublin (Med. Schol.). MB, BCh, BAO, BA 1943, MA, MD 1968, FRCSI 1947, FRCS 1976. Prof. of Physiol. Prize, TCD. Posts in Dublin, Belfast and Wigan; subseq. NS Sen. Specialist in Surgery, Major RAMC Malaya; Sen. Registrar in Surgery, Bristol Royal Infirmary and Wanstead Hosp.; Sen. Specialist in Surgery, BAOR Mil. Hosps and Consultant Surg., Brit. Mil. Hosps Singapore and Tidworth, 1953–68; Brig., and Consulting Surg., Farelf, 1969–70; Consultant Surg., Mil. Hosp. Tidworth, 1971–72; Consultant Surgeon, Queen Alexandra Mil. Hosp. Millbank, 1972–73; Consultant in Accident and Emergency, Ealing Dist, DHSS, 1978–79. Fellow, Association of Surgeons of GB and Ireland. QHS, 1974–78. *Publications:* papers in Brit. Jl Surgery, BMJ, Jl of RAMC, Postgrad. Med. Jl, Univ. Singapore Med. Soc. Med. Gazette. *Recreations:* gardening, golf. *Address:* 37 Queens Road, Beckenham, Kent BR3 4JJ.

DILHORNE, 2nd Viscount *cr* 1964, of Green's Norton; **John Mervyn Manningham-Buller;** Bt 1866; Baron 1962; Barrister-at-Law; *b* 28 Feb. 1932; *s* of 1st Viscount Dilhorne, PC, and of Lady Mary Lilian Lindsay, 4th *d* of 27th Earl of Crawford, KT, PC; *S* father, 1980; *m* 1955, Gillian Evelyn (marr. diss. 1973), *d* of Colonel George Stockwell; two *s* one *d*; *m* 1981, Dr Eykyn, MB BS, MRCPath. *Educ:* Eton; RMA Sandhurst. Called to the Bar, Inner Temple, 1979. Formerly Lieut, Coldstream Guards. Managing Director, Stewart Smith (LP&M) Ltd, 1970–74. Member, Wilts County Council, 1967–70. Mem., Jt Parly Cttee on Statutory Instruments, 1981–. FTII (Mem. Council, 1967–82). *Heir: s* Hon. James Edward Manningham-Buller, formerly Captain Welsh Guards [*b* 20 Aug. 1956; *m* 1985, Nicola Marion, *e d* of Sven Mackie. *Educ:* Harrow; Sandhurst]. *Address:* 2 Paper Buildings, Temple, EC4. *T:* 01–353 5835; 164 Ebury Street, SW1W 8UP. *T:* 01–730 0913. *Clubs:* Pratt's, Buck's, Beefsteak; Swinley Forest Golf.

DILKE, Sir John Fisher Wentworth, 5th Bt *cr* 1862; *b* 1906; *e s* of Sir Fisher Wentworth Dilke, 4th Bt, and Ethel Clifford (*d* 1959); *S* father, 1944; *m* 1st, 1934, Sheila (marr. diss. 1949), *d* of late Sir William Seeds, KCMG; two *s*; 2nd, 1951, Iris Evelyn, *d* of late Ernest Clark. *Educ:* Winchester; New Coll., Oxford. Foreign Office, 1929; Editorial Staff, The Times, 1936; rejoined Foreign Service, 1939 (economic warfare and shipping); Head of British official wireless news, 1942; Lloyd's, 1944; political corresp., COI, 1945; BBC External Service, 1950. *Heir: s* Charles John Wentworth Dilke, *b* 1937. *Address:* Ludpits, Etchingham, Sussex.

DILKE, Mary Stella F.; *see* Fetherston-Dilke.

DILKS, Prof. David Neville, FRHistS; Professor of International History, University of Leeds, since 1970; *b* Coventry, 17 March 1938; *s* of Neville Ernest Dilks and Phyllis Dilks; *m* 1963, Jill Medlicott; one *s.* *Educ:* Royal Grammar Sch., Worcester; Hertford Coll., Oxford (BA Modern Hist., Class II, 1959); St Antony's Coll., Oxford (Curzon Prizeman, 1960). Research Assistant to: Rt Hon. Sir Anthony Eden (later Earl of Avon), 1960–62; Marshal of the RAF Lord Tedder, 1963–65; Rt Hon. Harold Macmillan, 1964–67; Asst Lectr, then Lectr, in International History, LSE, 1962–70; Vis. Fellow, All Souls' Coll., Oxford, 1973; Chm., Sch. of History, Univ. of Leeds, 1974–79, Dean, Faculty of Arts, 1975–77. Consultant, Sec.-Gen. of the Commonwealth, 1967–75; Chm., Commonwealth Youth Exchange Council, 1968–73. Member: Adv. Council on Public Records, 1977–85; Central Council, 1982–85, Library Cttee, 1982–, Royal Commonwealth Soc.; Acad. Adv. Council, Hughenden Foundn, 1986–. Trustee: Edward Boyle Meml Trust, 1982– (Hon. Sec., 1981–82); Imperial War Museum, 1983–; Lennox-Boyd Meml Trust, 1984–; Nathaniel Trust, 1986–. Chm., Leeds Defence Studies Dining Club. Pres., Worcester Old Elizabethans' Assoc., 1986–87. Liveryman, Goldsmiths' Co., 1984– (Freeman, 1979). Wrote and presented BBC TV series, The Loneliest Job, 1977; interviewer in BBC TV series, The Twentieth Century Remembered, 1982. *Publications:* Curzon in India, Vol. I, 1969, Vol. II, 1970; (ed) The Diaries of Sir Alexander Cadogan, 1971; (contrib.) The Conservatives (ed Lord Butler of Saffron Walden), 1977; (ed and contrib.) Retreat from Power, vol. 1, 1906–1939, Vol. 2, after 1939, 1981; (ed and contrib.) Britain and Canada (Commonwealth Foundn Paper), 1980; (ed and contrib.) The Missing Dimension: governments and intelligence communities in the twentieth century, 1984; Neville Chamberlain, Vol. I: Pioneering and Reform 1869–1929, 1984; reviews and articles in English Historical Rev., Survey, History, Scandinavian Jl of History, etc. *Recreations:* ornithology, painting, railways, Bentley cars. *Address:* Wits End, Long Causeway, Leeds LS16 8EX. *T:* Leeds 673466. *Club:* Royal Commonwealth Society.

DILL, Sir (Nicholas) Bayard, Kt 1955; CBE 1951; JP; Senior Partner, Conyers, Dill & Pearman, Barristers-at-Law, since 1948; *b* 28 Dec. 1905; *s* of Thomas Melville and Ruth Rapalje Dill; *m* 1930, Lucy Clare Dill; two *s.* *Educ:* Saltus Grammar Sch., Bermuda; Trinity Hall, Cambridge. Law Tripos Cantab, 1926. Mem. Colonial Parliament (for Devonshire Parish), 1938–68; Mem. HM Exec. Council, 1944–54; Chairman: Board of Trade, 1935–42, also Bd of Educn, 1940, and Board of Works, 1942–48, Bermuda; St David's Island Cttee, 1940–43; Public Works Planning Commn, 1942–49; Board of Civil Aviation, 1944–63; Bermuda Trade Development Bd, 1957–59; Mem., Legislative Council, Bermuda, 1968–73. Served as Capt., Bermuda Volunteer Engs, 1936–44. Chancellor of Diocese of Bermuda, 1950–84. JP Hamilton, Bermuda, 1949. *Recreations:* sailing, golf. *Address:* Newbold Place, Devonshire, Bermuda. *T:* 2–4463. *Clubs:* Anglo-Belgian; Royal Thames Yacht; Royal Bermuda Yacht (Commodore, 1936–38), Mid-Ocean, Royal Hamilton Amateur Dinghy (Bermuda); India House, Canadian, Cruising of America, Metropolitan (NYC).

DILLAMORE, Ian Leslie, PhD, DSc; FEng 1985; FIM; Director of Technology, INCO Engineered Products Ltd, since 1982; *b* 22 Nov. 1938; *s* of Arthur Leslie Dillamore and Louise Mary Dillamore; *m* 1962, Maureen Birch; two *s.* *Educ:* Birmingham Univ. (BSc, MSc, PhD, DSc). ICI Research Fellow, Birmingham Univ., 1962–63, Lectr in Physical Metallurgy, 1963–69; Head of Phys. Metallurgy, BISRA, 1969–72; Head of Metals Technology Unit, British Steel Corp., 1972–76; Head of Metallurgy Dept, Aston Univ., 1976–81, Dean of Engineering, 1980–81; Director of Research and Development, INCO Europe, 1981–82. Hon. Professor of Metallurgy, Birmingham Univ., 1981–. Mem. Council: Metals Soc., 1980–84; Instn of Metallurgists, 1981–84; Vice-Pres., Inst. of Metals, 1985–; Mem. SRC Metallurgy Cttee, 1972–75, Materials Cttee, 1977–82; Chm., Processing Sub-Cttee, SRC, later SERC, 1979–82; Mem., DTI Non Ferrous Metals Exec. Cttee, 1982–85; Pres. Birmingham Metallurgical Assoc., 1980–81. Sir Robert Hadfield Medal and Prize, Metals Soc., 1976. *Publications:* numerous contribs to metallurgical and engrg jls. *Recreation:* industrial archaeology. *Address:* Wiggin Street, Birmingham B16 0AT. *T:* 021–454 4871.

DILLISTONE, Rev. Canon Frederick William, DD; Fellow and Chaplain, Oriel College, Oxford, 1964–70, Fellow Emeritus, 1970; Canon Emeritus of Liverpool Cathedral since 1964; *b* 9 May 1903; *s* of late Frederick Dillistone; *m* 1931, Enid Mary, *d* of late Rev. Cecil Francis Ayerst; two *s* one *d.* *Educ:* Brighton Coll.; BNC, Oxford (Scholar). BA 1924; BD 1933; DD 1951. Deacon, 1927; Priest, 1928; Vicar of St Andrew, Oxford, 1934–38; Prof. of Theology, Wycliffe Coll., Toronto, 1938–45; Prof. of Theology, Episcopal Theological Sch., Cambridge, Mass, 1947–52; Canon Residentiary and Chancellor of Liverpool Cathedral, 1952–56; Dean of Liverpool, 1956–63. Hulsean Preacher, Cambridge, 1953; Select Preacher, Oxford, 1953–55; Select Preacher, Cambridge, 1960; Stephenson Lectr, Univ. of Sheffield, 1966; Bampton Lectr, Univ. of Oxford, 1968; Vis. Fellow, Clare Hall, Cambridge, 1970; Zabriskie Lectr, Virginia Theol. Seminary, 1971. Asst Editor, Theology Today, 1951–61. Hon. DD: Knox Coll., Toronto, 1946; Episcopal Theological Sch., Cambridge, Mass, 1967; Virginia Theol Seminary, 1979. Chaplain OStJ, 1958. *Publications:* The Significance of the Cross, 1945; The Holy Spirit in the Life of To-day, 1946; Revelation and Evangelism, 1948; The Structure of the Divine Society, 1951; Jesus Christ and His Cross, 1953; Christianity and Symbolism, 1955, repr. 1985; Christianity and Communication, 1956; The Novelist and the Passion Story, 1960; The Christian Faith, 1964; Dramas of Salvation, 1967; The Christian Understanding of Atonement, 1968; Modern Answers to Basic Questions, 1972; Traditional Symbols and the Contemporary World, 1972; Charles Raven: a biography, 1975; C. H. Dodd: a biography, 1977; Into all the World: a biography of Max Warren, 1980; Religious Experience and Christian Faith, 1982; Afire for God: the life of Joe Fison, 1983; The Power of Symbols, 1986; Editor, Scripture and Tradition, 1955; Editor, Myth and Symbol, 1966; contributor to: The Doctrine of Justification by Faith, 1954; A Companion to the Study of St Augustine, 1955; Steps to Christian Understanding, 1958; The Ecumenical Era in Church and Society, 1959; Metaphor and Symbol, 1961; The Theology of the Christian Mission, 1961; Christianity and the Visual Arts, 1964; Mansions of the Spirit, 1966; Christianity in its Social Context, 1967; Studies in Christian History and Interpretation, 1967; Christ for us Today, 1968; Grounds of Hope, 1968; Man, Fallen and Free, 1969; Sociology, Theology and Conflict, 1969; Christ and Spirit in the New Testament, 1973; Religion and Art as Communication, 1974; Theolinguistics, 1981. *Recreation:* gardening. *Address:* 15 Cumnor Rise Road, Oxford OX2 9HD. *T:* Oxford 862071.

DILLON, family name of **Viscount Dillon.**

DILLON, 22nd Viscount *cr* 1622, of Castello Gallen, Co. Mayo, Ireland; **Henry Benedict Charles Dillon;** Count in France, 1711; *b* 6 Jan. 1973; *s* of 21st Viscount Dillon and of Mary Jane, *d* of late John Young, Castle Hill House, Birtle, Lancs; *S* father, 1982. *Heir: uncle* Hon. Richard Arthur Louis Dillon [*b* 23 Oct. 1948; *m* 1975, Hon. Priscilla Frances Hazlerigg, *d* of 2nd Baron Hazlerigg, *qv*; one *s* one *d*].

DILLON, Hon. Sir Brian; *see* Dillon, Hon. Sir G. B. H.

DILLON, C(larence) Douglas; Chairman, US & Foreign Securities Corporation, 1967–84; Managing Director, Dillon, Read & Co. Inc., 1971–83; retired; *b* Geneva, Switzerland, 21 Aug. 1909; *s* of Clarence Dillon; *m* 1st, 1931, Phyllis Ellsworth (*d* 1982); two *d*; 2nd, 1983, Susan Sage. *Educ:* Groton Sch.; Harvard Univ. (AB). Mem., NY Stock Exchange, 1931–36; US and Foreign Securities Corporation and US and International Securities Corporation, 1937–53 (Dir, 1938–53; Pres., 1946–53); Dir, Dillon, Read & Co. Inc., 1938–53 (Chm. of Bd, 1946–53); American Ambassador to France, 1953–57; Under-Sec. of State for Economic Affairs, USA, 1957–59, Under-Sec. of State, USA, 1959–61; Sec. of the Treasury, USA, 1961–65. Served US Naval Reserve, 1941–45 (Lieut-Comdr; Air Medal, Legion of Merit). Dir, Council on Foreign Relations, 1965–78 (Vice-Chm. 1977–78); Pres., Board of Overseers, Harvard Coll., 1968–72; Chm., Rockefeller Foundn, 1971–75; Chm., Brookings Instn, 1971–75. Trustee, Metropolitan Museum of Art (President, 1970–77; Chm., 1977–83). Hon. Dr of Laws: New York Univ., 1956; Lafayette Coll., 1957; Univ. of Hartford, Conn, 1958; Columbia Univ., 1959; Harvard Univ., 1959; Williams Coll., 1960; Rutgers Univ., 1961; Princeton Univ., 1961; University of Pennsylvania, 1962; Bradley Univ., 1964; Middlebury Coll., 1965; Tufts Univ., 1982. *Address:* Far Hills, New Jersey 07931, USA.

DILLON, Rt. Hon. Sir (George) Brian (Hugh), Kt 1979; PC 1982; **Rt. Hon. Lord Justice Dillon;** a Lord Justice of Appeal, since 1982; *b* 2 Oct. 1925; *s* of late Captain George Crozier Dillon, RN; *m* 1954, Alison, *d* of late Hubert Samuel Lane, MC and Dr Isabella Lane, MB, ChB Edin.; two *s* two *d.* *Educ:* Winchester College; New College, Oxford. Called to the Bar, Lincoln's Inn, 1948; QC 1965; a Judge of the High Court of Justice, Chancery Division, 1979–82. *Address:* Royal Courts of Justice, WC2.

DILLON, Sir John (Vincent), Kt 1980; CMG 1974; Ombudsman for Victoria (Commissioner for Administrative Investigations), 1973–80; *b* 6 Aug. 1908; *s* of Roger Dillon and Ellen (*née* Egan); *m* 1935, Sheila Lorraine D'Arcy; three *s* one *d*. *Educ:* Christian Brothers Coll., Melbourne. AASA. Mem. Public Service Bd, 1941–54; Stipendiary Magistrate City Court, 1947–61; Chm., Medical Salaries Cttee, 1959–62; Under-Sec., Chief Sec.'s Dept, Vic, 1961–73; Chm., Racecourses Licences Bd, 1961–73. Hon. LLD Melbourne, 1982. *Recreations:* racing, golf, reading. *Address:* 25 Kelvin Grove, Armadale, Vic 3143, Australia. *Clubs:* Athenæum, Victoria Racing, Victoria Amateur Turf, Moonee Valley Racing, Melbourne Cricket, Metropolitan Golf (Melbourne).

DILLON, Sir Max, Kt 1979; *b* 30 June 1913; *s* of Cyril and Phoebe Dillon; *m* 1940, Estelle Mary Jones; one *s* one *d*. *Educ:* Wesley Coll., Melbourne; Melbourne Univ. (Faculty of Commerce). AASA (Sen.); ACIS; FAIM. General Manager, Cable Makers Australia Pty Ltd, 1957–70; Dep. Man. Dir, Metal Manufactures Ltd Gp, 1970–75. President: Aust. Council of Employer Fedns, 1967–69; Associated Chambers of Manufactures, 1974–77; Confedn of Aust. Industry, 1977–80; Chairman: Nat. Employers Policy Cttee, 1971–73 and 1975–78; Central Industrial Secretariat Council, 1972–77; Productivity Promotion Council, 1971–74; Member: Nat. Labour Adv. Council, 1966–72; Nat. Labour Consultative Council, 1977–80; Exec. Cttee, Aust. Manufacturing Council, 1978–80. *Recreations:* golf, swimming. *Address:* 33 Church Street, Pymble, NSW 2073, Australia. *T:* 44 3160. *Clubs:* Australian, Elanora Country (Sydney).

DILLON, Thomas Michael; QC 1973; **His Honour Judge Dillon;** a Circuit Judge, since 1985; *b* 29 Nov. 1927; *yr s* of Thomas Bernard Joseph Dillon, Birmingham, and Ada Gladys Dillon (*née* Noyes); *m* 1956, Wendy Elizabeth Marshall Hurrell; two *s* one *d*. *Educ:* King Edward's Sch., Aston, Birmingham; Birmingham Univ. (LLB); Lincoln Coll., Oxford (BCL). Called to Bar, Middle Temple, 1952, Master of the Bench 1981. 2nd Lieut, RASC, 1953–54. In practice as barrister, 1954–85; a Recorder, 1972–85; Part-time Chm. of Industrial Tribunals, 1968–74. *Recreations:* reading, listening to music. *Address:* 1 Fountain Court, Birmingham B4 6DR. *T:* 021–236 5721.

DILLWYN-VENABLES-LLEWELYN, Sir John Michael; *see* Venables-Llewelyn.

DILNOT, Mary, (Mrs Thomas Ruffle), OBE 1982; Director, IPC Women's Magazines Group, 1976–81; Editor, Woman's Weekly, 1971–81; *b* 23 Jan. 1921; 2nd *d* of George Dilnot, author, and Ethel Dilnot; *m* 1974, Thomas Ruffle. *Educ:* St Mary's Coll., Hampton. Joined Woman's Weekly, 1939. *Recreations:* home interests, reading, travel, golf. *Address:* 28 Manor Road South, Hinchley Wood, Esher, Surrey.

DIMBLEBY, Bel, (Mrs Jonathan Dimbleby); *see* Mooney, Bel.

DIMBLEBY, David; freelance broadcaster and newspaper proprietor; Chairman: Dimbleby & Sons Ltd, since 1986 (Managing Director, 1966–86); Wandsworth Borough News Ltd, since 1986 (Managing Director, 1979–86); *b* 28 Oct. 1938; *e s* of (Frederick) Richard and Dilys Dimbleby; *m* 1967, Josceline Rose Gaskell (*see* J. R. Dimbleby); one *s* two *d*. *Educ:* Glengorse Sch.; Charterhouse; Christ Church, Oxford (MA); Univs of Paris and Perugia. News Reporter, BBC Bristol, 1960–61; Presenter and Interviewer on network programmes on: religion (Quest), science for children (What's New?), politics (In My Opinion), Top of the Form, etc, 1961–63; Reporter, BBC2 (Enquiry), and Dir films, incl.: Ku-Klux-Klan, The Forgotten Million, Cyprus: Thin Blue Line, 1964–65; worked as asst to his father in family newspaper business at Richmond, Surrey, 1965, being apptd Managing Dir, 1966, on his father's death. Special Correspondent CBS News, New York; documentary film (Texas-England) and film reports for '60 minutes', 1966–; Reporter, BBC1 (Panorama), 1967–69; Commentator, Current Events; Presenter, BBC1 (24 Hours), 1969–72; Yesterday's Men, 1971; Chairman, The Dimbleby Talk-In, 1971–74; films for Reporter at Large, 1973; Presenter: BBC 1 (Panorama), 1974–77, 1980–82; (Nationwide), 1982; (People and Power), 1982–83; (This Week, Next Week), 1984–; Election Campaign Report, 1974; BBC Election and Results programmes, 1979, 1983; film series, The White Tribe of Africa, 1979 (Royal TV Soc. Supreme Documentary Award). *Address:* 14 King Street, Richmond, Surrey TW9 1NF. *Club:* Brooks's.
See also J. Dimbleby.

DIMBLEBY, Jonathan; freelance broadcaster, journalist, and author; *b* 31 July 1944; *s* of Richard and Dilys Dimbleby; *m* 1968, Bel Mooney, *qv*; one *s* one *d*. *Educ:* University Coll. London (BA Hons Philosophy). TV and Radio Reporter, BBC Bristol, 1969–70; BBC Radio, World at One, 1970–71; for Thames TV: This Week, 1972–78; TV Eye, 1979; Jonathan Dimbleby in South America, 1979; for Yorkshire TV: series, Jonathan Dimbleby in Evidence: The Police, 1980; The Bomb, 1980; The Eagle and the Bear, 1981; The Cold War Game, 1982; The American Dream, 1984; Four Years On—The Bomb, 1984; First Tuesday (Associate Editor/Presenter), 1982–86; TV-am: Jonathan Dimbleby on Sunday (Presenter/Editor), 1985–. Dir, TV-am News Ltd. Member: Butler Trust, Richard Dimbleby Cancer Fund; Bd, Internat. Broadcasting Trust, VSO. Sponsor, Centre for Peace Building Studies, Amnesty Internat. SFTA Richard Dimbleby Award, for most outstanding contribution to factual TV, 1974. *Publications:* Richard Dimbleby, 1975; The Palestinians, 1979. *Recreations:* music, sailing, tennis. *Address:* c/o David Higham Associates Ltd, 5 Lower John Street, W1R 4HA.
See also D. Dimbleby.

DIMBLEBY, Josceline Rose; Cookery Editor, Sunday Telegraph, since 1982; *b* 1 Feb. 1943; *d* of late Thomas Josceline Gaskell and of Barbara Montagu-Pollock; *m* 1967, David Dimbleby, *qv*; one *s* two *d*. *Educ:* Cranborne Chase Sch., Dorset; Guildhall School of Music. Contributor, Daily Mail, 1976–78; cookery writer for Sainsbury's, 1978–. André Simon Award, 1979. *Publications:* A Taste of Dreams, 1976, 3rd edn 1984; Party Pieces, 1977; Josceline Dimbleby's Book of Puddings, Desserts and Savouries, 1979, 2nd edn 1983; Favourite Food, 1983, 2nd edn 1984; (for Sainsbury's): Cooking for Christmas, 1978; Family Meat and Fish Cookery, 1979; Cooking with Herbs and Spices, 1979; Curries and Oriental Cookery, 1980; Salads for all Seasons, 1981; Marvellous Meals with Mince, 1982; Festive Food, 1982; Sweet Dreams, 1983; First Impressions, 1984; The Josceline Dimbleby Collection, 1984; Main Attractions, 1985; A Traveller's Tastes, 1986. *Recreations:* singing, travel. *Address:* 14 King Street, Richmond, Surrey TW9 1NF. *T:* 01-940 6668.

DIMECHKIÉ, Nadim, GCVO (Hon.) 1978; business and economic consultant, and Honorary Consultant to the Arab Federation of Chambers of Commerce and Industry, since 1980; *b* Lebanon, 5 Dec. 1919; *s* of Badr and Julia Dimechkié; *m* 1946, Margaret Alma Sherlock; two *s*. *Educ:* American Univ. of Beirut (BA, MA Economics). Deleg., Jt Supply Bd for Syria and Lebanon, 1942–44; Dir Gen., Min. of Nat. Economy, 1943–44; Counsellor, Lebanese Embassy, London, 1944–49; Consul-Gen., Ottawa, 1950; Dir, Economic and Social Dept, Min. of Foreign Affairs, 1951–52; Chargé d'Affaires, Cairo, 1952; Minister, 1953–55; Minister, Switzerland, 1955–57; Ambassador to USA, 1958–62; Dir, Economic Affairs, Min. of Foreign Affairs, 1962–66; Ambassador to UK, 1966–78, and Doyen of the Diplomatic Corps, 1977–78; Ambassador at large, and Senior Adviser on foreign affairs to Foreign Sec., Beirut, 1979–80. Board Member and Consultant: Bank de Credit Populaire Union Nationale, 1985–; Union Foncier et Financing, 1985–; Sterling Drugs Internat., 1985–. Lebanese Order of Cedars, UAR Order of Ismail and Order of Merit; Syrian Order of Merit; Tunisian Order of Merit; Greek Order of Phoenix. *Address:* Ministry of Foreign Affairs, Beirut, Lebanon. *Clubs:* White's, Travellers', Hurlingham, Royal Automobile; Metropolitan, Chevy Chase (Washington); Golf, Aero (Beirut).

DIMMOCK, Peter, CVO 1968; OBE 1961; Vice-President and Consultant, ABC Video Enterprises Division, Capital Cities/ABC Inc, New York; a UK Director: Entertainment and Sports Cable Network, since 1984; Screen Sport cable tv, since 1984; Ambrotel, since 1984; Vice-President, American Broadcasting Companies Worldwide Sales and Marketing TV Sports, and Managing Director, ABC Sports International Inc. (formerly Sports Worldwide Enterprises Ltd), 1978–86; *b* 6 Dec. 1920; *e s* of late Frederick Dimmock, OBE, and of Paula Dimmock (*née* Hudd); *m* 1960, Mary Freya (Polly), *e d* of late Hon. Mr Justice Elwes, OBE, TD; three *d*. *Educ:* Dulwich Coll.; France. TA; RAF pilot, instr, and Air Ministry Staff Officer, 1939–45. After demobilisation became Press Association correspondent; joined BBC as Television Outside Broadcasts Producer and commentator, 1946; produced both studio and outside broadcasts, ranging from documentaries to sporting, theatrical and public events; has produced or commentated on more than 500 television relays, including Olympic Games 1948, Boat Race 1949, first international television relay, from Calais, 1950, King George VI's Funeral, Windsor, 1952. Produced and directed television outside broadcast of the Coronation Service from Westminster Abbey, 1953; first TV State Opening of Parliament, 1958; first TV Grand National, 1960; TV for Princess Margaret's Wedding, 1960. Created BBC Sportsview Unit and introduced new television programme Sportsview, 1954, regular host of this weekly network programme, 1954–64; Gen. Manager and Head of Outside Broadcasts, BBC TV, 1954–72; responsible for Liaison between BBC and Royal Family, 1963–77; Gen. Manager, BBC Enterprises, 1972–77. Sports Adviser, European Broadcasting Union, 1959–72. Mem., Greater London and SE Sports Council, 1972–77; Chm., Sports Develt Panel, 1976–77. Fellow, Royal Television Soc., 1978. *Publications:* Sportsview Annuals, 1954–65; Sports in View, 1964. *Recreations:* flying, winter sports, golf. *Address:* c/o Coutts & Co., 440 The Strand, WC2R 0QS. *T:* 01–636 7366. *Clubs:* Garrick, Turf; Berkshire; Monte Carlo; New York Athletic.

DIMMOCK, Rear-Adm. Roger Charles; Flag Officer, Naval Air Command, since 1987; *b* 27 May 1935; *s* of Frank Dimmock and Ivy Dimmock (*née* Archer); *m* 1958, Lesley Patricia Reid; three *d*. *Educ:* Price's School. Entered Royal Navy, 1953; pilot's wings FAA, 1954, USN, 1955; qualified Flying Instructor, 1959; Master Mariner Foreign Going Cert. of Service, 1979. Served RN Air Sqdns and HM Ships Bulwark, Albion, Ark Royal, Eagle, Hermes, Anzio, Messina, Murray, Berwick (i/c), Naiad (i/c), to 1978; CSO to FO Carriers and Amphibious Ships, 1978–80; Comd RNAS Culrose, 1980–82; Comd HMS Hermes, 1982–83; Dir, Naval Air Warfare, MoD, 1983–84; Naval Sec., 1985–87. Trustee, Fleet Air Arm Museum, 1978–84. Chm., United Services Hockey Club, Portsmouth, 1983–; President: RN Hockey Assoc., 1985–; Denmead and Hambledon Branch, RNLI, 1981–. *Recreations:* hockey (player and umpire), cricket, squash, golf, family, home and garden, RNLI. *Address:* c/o Naval Air Command, Yeovilton, Somerset. *Clubs:* Royal Commonwealth Society; Royal Navy Club of 1765 and 1785.

DIMSON, Gladys Felicia, (Mrs S. B. Dimson), CBE 1976; Member of GLC for Battersea North, 1973–85; Member, Inner London Education Authority, 1970–85; *o d* of late I. Sieve, BA; *m* 1936, Dr S. B. Dimson, *e s* of late Rev. Z. Dimson; one *d*. *Educ:* Laurel Bank Sch., Glasgow; Glasgow Univ.; London Sch. of Economics. Voluntary social worker, mainly in E London, 1950–63; Co-opted Mem., Children's Cttee, LCC, 1958–65; Chm., gp of LCC Children's Homes and of a voluntary Hostel for Girls; Educn Counsellor, Marriage Guidance Council. Member: Home Office Advisory Cttee on Juvenile Delinquency, 1963–65 (Chm. Sub-Cttee on Transition from Sch. to Work); a Youth Employment Cttee, 1960–; Hendon Gp Hosp. Management Cttee, 1965–70; Exec., Greater London Labour Party, 1964–74; Toynbee Housing Soc., 1967– (Chm., 1976–); Council, Toynbee Hall, 1983–; Bd of Governors, Nat. Hosp. for Nervous Diseases, 1976–79; Board of Management, Shelter, 1976– (Trustee, Shelter Housing Aid Centre); London Local Adv. Cttee, IBA, 1979–83; Hampstead DHA, 1981–84; Trustee, Sutton Housing Trust, 1982–; Chm., East London Housing Assoc., 1979–. Mem., GLC Haringey, 1964–67, Wandsworth, 1970–73; (Vice-Chm.) GLC Ambulance Cttee; GLC Housing Cttee; Mem. (co-opted), 1968–70; Labour Spokesman, 1970–73, and 1977–81; Chm., 1973–75, 1981–82. Contested (Lab) Hendon South, at Gen. Election, 1970. Mem., Nat. and London Councils of Nat. Fedn of Housing Assocs, 1980–83. FRSA 1977. *Recreations:* walking in the country, lazing in the sun; reading (incl. thrillers); theatre; watching TV. *Address:* 22a North Gate, Prince Albert Road, St John's Wood, NW8.

DINEEN, Ven. Frederick George K.; *see* Kerr-Dineen.

DINEVOR; *see* Dynevor.

DINGEMANS, Rear-Adm. Peter George Valentin, DSO 1982; Flag Officer Gibraltar, since 1985; *b* 31 July 1935; *s* of Dr George Albert and Marjorie Dingemans; *m* 1961, Faith Vivien Bristow; three *s*. *Educ:* Brighton College. Entered RN 1953; served HM Ships Vanguard, Superb, Ark Royal, 1953–57; qualified Torpedo Anti Submarine specialist, 1961; Comd, HMS Maxton, 1967; RAF Staff Course, 1968; Directorate of Naval Plans, 1971–73; Comd, HMS Berwick, HMS Lowestoft, 1973–74; Staff Asst, Chief of Defence Staff, 1974–76; Captain, Fishery Protection, 1977–79; Comd HMS Intrepid, 1980–83 (incl. service South Atlantic, 1982); Commodore, Amphibious Warfare, 1983–85. Freeman, City of London, 1984; Liveryman, Coach Makers and Coach Harness Makers Co., 1984. *Recreations:* family and friends. *Address:* c/o Lloyds Bank, Steyning, Sussex. *Club:* Naval and Military.

DINGLE, John Thomas, PhD, DSc; Director, Strangeways Research Laboratory, Cambridge, since 1979; Fellow of Corpus Christi College, Cambridge, since 1968; *b* 27 Oct. 1927; *s* of Thomas Henry and Violet Nora Dingle; *m* 1953, Dorothy Vernon Parsons; two *s*. *Educ:* King Edward Sch., Bath; London Univ. (BSc, DSc); Clare Coll., Cambridge (PhD). Royal National Hosp. for Rheumatic Diseases, Bath, 1951–59; Research Fellowship, Strangeways Research Laboratory, Cambridge, 1959–61, MRC External Staff, 1961–79; Head of Tissue Physiology Dept, Strangeways Research Laboratory, 1966, Dep. Dir of the Laboratory, 1970–79. Bursar of Leckhampton, 1972–80, Warden, 1980–. Visiting Professor: of Biochemistry, Royal Free Hosp. Med. Sch., 1975–78; of Rheumatology, New York Univ., 1977. Chm., British Connective Tissue Soc., 1980–; Chm. Editorial Bd, Biochemical Jl, 1975–82. Treas., Cambridge Univ. RFC, 1982–. Heberden Orator and Medalist, 1978; American Orthopaedic Assoc. Steindler Award, 1980. *Publications:* communications to learned jls. *Recreations:* Rugby football (playing member, Bath, Bristol, Somerset RFCs, 1943–57), sailing. *Address:* Corpus Christi College, Cambridge. *T:* Cambridge 359418. *Club:* Hawks (Cambridge).

DINGLE, Prof. Robert Balson, PhD; FRSE; Professor of Theoretical Physics, University of St Andrews, since 1960; *b* 26 March 1926; *s* of late Edward Douglas Dingle and Nora Gertrude Balson; *m* 1958, Helen Glenronnie Munro; two *d*. *Educ:* Bournemouth Secondary Sch.; Cambridge University. PhD 1951. Fellow of St John's Coll., Cambridge,

1948–52; Theoretician to Royal Society Mond Lab., 1949–52; Chief Asst in Theoretical Physics, Technical Univ. of Delft, Holland, 1952–53; Fellow, Nat. Research Council, Ottawa, 1953–54; Reader in Theoretical Physics, Univ. of WA, 1954–60. *Publications:* Asymptotic Expansions: their derivation and interpretation, 1973; contribs to learned journals. *Recreations:* music, local history, gastronomy. *Address:* 6 Lawhead Road East, St Andrews, Fife, Scotland. *T:* St Andrews 74287.

DINGWALL, Baroness; *see* Lucas of Crudwell and Dingwall.

DINGWALL, John James, OBE 1964; HM Inspector of Constabulary for Scotland, 1966–70; *b* 2 Sept. 1907; *s* of late James Dingwall, Bannockburn, Stirling; *m* 1932, Jane Anne (*d* 1980), *d* of late James K. Halliday, Falkirk; two *d. Educ:* Bridge of Allan and Stirling. Stirlingshire Constabulary, 1927–49; Stirling and Clackmannan Police Force, 1949–55; seconded to Directing Staff, Scottish Police Coll., 1953–55; Chief Constable of Angus, 1955–66. *Recreations:* angling, shooting, golf. *Address:* 56 Carlogie Road, Carnoustie, Angus.

DINGWALL, Walter Spender, MA; Secretary, Chichester Diocesan Fund, 1946–61, retired; *b* 14 Dec. 1900; *s* of late Rev. Walter Molyneux Dingwall and Sophia Spender; *m* 1932, Olive Mary Loasby (*d* 1983); no *c. Educ:* Marlborough Coll.; Christ Church, Oxford. Sixth Form Master at St Edward's Sch., Oxford, 1923–37; nine years Bursar of the Sch., ten years Housemaster; Headmaster, Hurstpierpoint Coll., Sussex, 1937–45; Hon. Sec. and Treasurer, Public Schools Bursars' Assoc., 1931–38. Comr of Income Tax, 1962–75. *Address:* 2 Gatehouse Lodge, Terrys Cross, Henfield, BN5 9SX. *T:* Henfield 493350.

DINGWALL-SMITH, Ronald Alfred, CB 1977; *b* 24 Feb. 1917; *m* 1946; one *s* one *d. Educ:* Alleyn's Sch., Dulwich; London School of Economics (evening classes). Entered Civil Service as Clerical Officer, Ministry of Transport, 1934; Exchequer and Audit Dept, 1935–47; Scottish Educn Dept, 1947–65; Scottish Development Dept, 1965–70; Under-Sec. (Principal Finance Officer), Scottish Office, 1970–78. Sen. Res. Fellow, Glasgow Univ., 1979–81. Dir, St Vincent Drilling Ltd, 1979–80. Member: Management Cttee, Hanover (Scotland) Housing Assoc., 1979–; Commn for Local Auth. Accts in Scotland, 1980–85. Governor, Moray Hse Coll. of Educn, Edinburgh, 1980–. *Recreations:* golf, bowls, gardening. *Address:* 3 Frogston Terrace, Edinburgh EH10 7AD. *T:* 031–445 2727. *Club:* Royal Commonwealth Society.

DINSDALE, Richard Lewis; Chairman, West of England Newspapers Ltd, 1969–72; *b* 23 June 1907; *m* 1930, Irene Laverack (*d* 1984); one *d. Educ:* Hull Technical Coll. Joined Hull Daily Mail as reporter, 1926; Editorial posts: Newcastle Evening World; Chief Sub-editor, Manchester Evening News; Dep. Chief Sub-editor, Daily Express, Manchester; Evening News, London; Daily Mirror, 1940–42; War Service, 1942–46; Copy-taster, Daily Mirror, 1946, successively Chief Sub-editor, Dep. Night Editor, Night Editor; Dep. Editor, 1955; seconded Daily Herald as Editorial Adviser, 1961; Dep. Editor, Daily Herald, 1962; Dep. Editor, The Sun, 1964, Editor, 1965–69. *Recreations:* sea fishing, golf. *Address:* 7 Beaulieu Court, Marine Parade, Worthing, W Sussex BN11 3QZ.

DINWIDDY, Thomas Lutwyche; Master of the Supreme Court (Chancery Division), 1958–73; *b* 27 Aug. 1905; *o c* of late Harry Lutwyche Dinwiddy, Solicitor, and late Ethel Maude (*née* McArthur); *m* 1935, Ruth, *d* of late Charles Ernest Rowland Abbott, Barrister-at-Law and Bencher of Lincoln's Inn; three *s. Educ:* Winchester; New Coll., Oxford (BA). Solicitor, Dec. 1930; Partner in Frere Cholmeley & Co., 28 Lincoln's Inn Fields, WC2, 1933–57. Council of Law Soc., 1953–57. Served RA (TA), 1939–45; Staff Coll., Camberley, 1943; demobilised as Major. *Address:* Northolme, 48 Saxmundham Road, Aldeburgh, Suffolk.

DIONISOTTI-CASALONE, Carlo, FBA 1972; Professor of Italian, Bedford College (formerly Bedford College for Women), University of London, 1949–70; *b* 9 June 1908; *s* of Eugenio Dionisotti-Casalone and Carla Cattaneo; *m* 1942, Maria Luisa Pinna-Pintor; three *d* (and one *d* decd). *Educ:* Turin, Italy. Dottore in lettere, Univ. of Turin, 1929; Libero Docente di Letteratura Italiana, Univ. of Turin, 1937; Asst di Letteratura Italiana, Univ. of Rome, 1943; Italian Lectr, Univ. of Oxford, 1947; MA Oxon, 1947. *Publications:* Indici del giornale storico della letteratura italiana (Turin), 1945; Guidiccioni-orazione ai nobili di Lucca (Rome), 1946; Bembo-Savorgnan, Carteggio d'amore (Florence), 1950; Oxford Book of Italian Verse (revised edn), 1952; Bembo, Prose e Rime (Turin), 1960; Geografia e storia della letter. ital. (Turin), 1967; Gli Umanisti e il Volgare (Florence), 1968; Machiavellerie (Turin), 1980. *Address:* 44 West Heath Drive, NW11.

DI PALMA, Vera June, (Mrs Ernest Jones), OBE 1986; FCCA, FTII; Director, Mobile Training Ltd (formerly Mobile Training & Exhibitions Ltd), since 1977; *b* 14 July 1931; *d* of late William Di Palma and of Violet Di Palma; *m* 1972, Ernest Jones. *Educ:* Haverstock Central Sch., London. Accountant in public practice, 1947–64; Taxation Accountant, Dunlop Co., 1964–67; Sen. Lectr in Taxation, City of London Polytechnic, 1967–71; taxation consultant, 1971–80. Pres., Assoc. of Certified Accountants, 1980–81 (Dep. Pres., 1979–80); Public Works Loan Comr, 1978–; Dep. Chm., Air Travel Trust Cttee, 1986–; Mem., VAT Tribunals, 1977–. *Publications:* Capital Gains Tax, 1972, 5th edn 1981; Your Fringe Benefits, 1978. *Recreations:* dog-walking, golf, tennis, gardening. *Address:* Temple Close, Sibford Gower, Banbury, Oxon OX15 5RX. *T:* Swalcliffe 222.

DISBREY, Air Vice-Marshal William Daniel, CB 1967; CBE 1945 (OBE 1943); AFC 1939; *b* London, 23 Aug. 1912; *s* of Horace William Disbrey; *m* 1939, Doreen Alice, *d* of William Henry Ivory, Stevenage; two *d. Educ:* Minchenden Sch. Joined RAF as an Apprentice, 1928; gained Cadetship to RAF Coll., Cranwell, 1931; No 3 Fighter Sqdn, 1933–34; Fleet Air Arm, 1934–37; Engr Specialist Course, Henlow, 1937–39; Engr Officer, No 13 Group HQ, 1940–41; Engr Officer, HQ Fighter Comd, 1941–43; Chief Engr Officer, 2nd TAF, 1943–46; Staff Coll. Course, 1946; CO, No 12 Sch. of Technical Training, 1946–48; Sen. Technical Officer, Royal Indian Air Force, 1948–51; Min. of Supply, 1951–54; Chief Engr Officer, Bomber Comd, 1954–57; Imperial Defence Coll., 1957; Dir of Research and Development, Bombers, Min. of Aviation, 1958–61; Comdt, No 1 Radio Sch., Locking, 1961–64; Dir-Gen. of Engineering (RAF), 1964–67; AO Engineering, Bomber Comd, 1967, Strike Comd, 1968–70, retired. Manager, Tech. Trng Inst., Airwork Services, Saudi Arabia, 1970. CEng; FIMechE; FRAeS. *Recreations:* golf, sailing. *Address:* Old Heatherwode, Buxted, East Sussex. *T:* Buxted 2104. *Club:* Royal Air Force.

DISLEY, John Ivor, CBE 1979; Director: Fleetfoot Ltd, since 1979; London Marathon Ltd, since 1980; Silva UK Ltd; *b* Gwynedd, 20 Nov. 1928; *s* of Harold Disley and Marie Hughes; *m* 1957, Sylvia Cheeseman; two *d. Educ:* Oswestry High Sch.; Loughborough Coll. (Hon. DCL). Schoolmaster, Isleworth, 1951; Chief Instructor, CCPR Nat. Mountaineering Centre, 1955; Gen. Inspector of Educn, Surrey, 1958; Dir, Ski Plan, 1971. Member: Adv. Sports Council, 1964–71; Mountain Leadership Trng Bd, 1965–; Canal Adv. Bd, 1965–66; Internat. Orienteering Fedn, 1972–; Countryside Commn, 1974–77; Water Space Adv. Council, 1976–; Royal Commn on Gambling, 1976–78. Vice-Chm., Sports Council, 1974–82; Chm., Nat. Jogging Assoc., 1978–80. Mem., British athletics team, 1950–59; Brit. record holder steeplechase, 1950–56; Welsh mile record

holder, 1952–57; bronze medal, Olympics, Helsinki, 1952; Sportsman of the Year, 1955; Athlete of the Year, 1955. *Publications:* Tackle Climbing, 1959; Young Athletes Companion, 1961; Orienteering, 1966; Expedition Guide for Duke of Edinburgh's Award Scheme, 1965; Your Way with Map and Compass, 1971. *Recreations:* running games, mountain activities. *Address:* Hampton House, Upper Sunbury Road, Hampton, Mddx TW12 2DW. *T:* 01–979 1707. *Clubs:* Climbers'; Ranelagh Harriers, Southern Navigators.

DISNEY, Harold Vernon, CBE 1956; Manager, Engineering Division, Reactor Group, UK Atomic Energy Authority, 1969–72, retired; *b* 2 July 1907; *s* of Henry Disney and Julia Vernon; *m* 1936, Lucy Quinton; two *d. Educ:* Hallcroft Higher Standard Sch., Ilkeston; Nottingham Univ. Coll. Internat. Combustion, 1931–35; ICI (Alkali), 1935–46. On loan to Min. of Supply (RFF's), 1941–46. Dept of Atomic Energy, 1946–54; UKAEA: Asst Dir, Defence Projects, Industrial Gp, 1954; Dir of Engineering, Industrial Gp, 1958; Man. Dir, Engineering Gp, Risley, 1962. FIMechE 1947. *Recreation:* gardening. *Address:* 63 Vincent Drive, Westminster Park, Chester CH4 7RQ.

DISS, Eileen, (Mrs Raymond Everett), RDI 1978; freelance designer for theatre, film and television, since 1959; *b* 13 May 1931; *d* of Thomas and Winifred Diss; *m* 1953, Raymond Everett; two *s* one *d. Educ:* Ilford County High Sch. for Girls; Central Sch. of Art and Design. MSIAD; FRSA. BBC Television design, 1952–59. Television series and plays: Maigret, 1962–63; The Tea Party, 1964; Up the Junction, 1965; Somerset Maugham, 1969; Uncle Vanya, 1970; The Duchess of Malfi, and Candide, 1972; The Importance of Being Earnest, and Pygmalion, 1973; Caesar and Cleopatra, 1974; Moll Flanders, 1975; Ghosts, and The Winslow Boy, 1976; You Never Can Tell, 1977; The Rear Column, Hedda Gabler, 1980; The Potting Shed, 1981. Television opera: The Merry Widow, 1968; Tales of Hoffmann, 1969; Die Fledermaus, 1971; Falstaff, 1972; The Yeomen of the Guard, 1974. Television films: Cider with Rosie, 1971; Robinson Crusoe, 1974. Theatre: Exiles, 1969; Butley, 1971; The Caretaker, 1972; Otherwise Engaged, 1975; The Apple-cart, 1977; The Rear Column, The Homecoming, 1978; The Hothouse, 1980; Translations, 1981; Quartermaine's Terms, 1981; Incident at Tulse Hill, 1981; Rocket to the Moon, 1982; The Communication Cord, 1983; The Common Pursuit, 1984; Other Places, 1985; The Seagull, 1985; Sweet Bird of Youth, 1985; Circe and Bravo, 1986. National Theatre: Blithe Spirit, 1976; The Philanderer, 1978; Close of Play, When We Are Married, 1979; Watch on the Rhine, 1980; The Caretaker, 1980; Measure for Measure, 1981; The Trojan War Will Not Take Place, 1983. *Films:* Joseph Losey's A Doll's House, 1972; Sweet William, 1978; Harold Pinter's Betrayal, 1982; Secret Places, 1984; 84 Charing Cross Road, 1986. BAFTA Television Design Award, 1962, 1965 and 1974. *Recreations:* cooking, music, cinema. *Address:* 4 Gloucester Walk, W8 4HZ. *T:* 01–937 8794.

DITCHBURN, Robert William, FRS 1962; Professor of Physics, University of Reading, 1946–68, now Emeritus; *b* 14 Jan. 1903; *e s* of William and Martha Kathleen Ditchburn; *m* 1929, Doreen May, *e d* of Arthur Samuel Barrett; one *s* three *d. Educ:* Bootle Secondary Sch.; Liverpool Univ.; Trinity Coll., Cambridge (Entrance and Senior Scholar, Hooper Prizeman, Isaac Newton Student). Fellow of Trinity Coll., Dublin, 1928–46; Prof. of Natural and Experimental Philosophy in Dublin Univ., 1929–46; Temp. Principal Experimental Officer, Admiralty, 1942–45. Mem. of Royal Irish Academy, 1931; Registrar for Social Studies, Trinity Coll., Dublin, 1940–44; Vice-Pres. Physical Soc., 1958; Vice-Pres. Inst. of Physics and Physical Soc., 1960–62. FInstP. Mees Medal, Optical Soc. of America, 1983. *Publications:* Light, 1952; Eye-Movements and Visual Perception, 1973; and scientific papers. *Recreations:* walking, music. *Address:* 9 Summerfield Rise, Goring, Reading RG8 0DS.

DIVER, Hon. Sir Leslie Charles, Kt 1975; President, Legislative Council, Western Australia, 1960–74; Member, Legislative Council (Country Party) for Central Province, Western Australia, 1952–74; *b* Perth, Australia, 4 Nov. 1899; *s* of late J. W. Diver; *m* 1st, 1922, Emma J., *d* of late F. Blakiston; one *s* two *d*; 2nd, 1971, Mrs Thelma May Evans. Farmer and grazier. Chairman: Kellerberrin Road Bd, 1940, 1942–46; Hon. Royal Commn on Retailing of Motor Spirits, 1956. Chm., Sixth Aust. Area Conf., Commonwealth Parly Assoc., 1961; Rep. WA Parlt, Town Planning Adv. Cttee. Warden, State War Meml, 1967–68. *Recreations:* bowls, Australian rules football. *Address:* 48 Sulman Avenue, Salter Point, Como, WA 6152, Australia. *Clubs:* Eastern Districts (Kellerberrin); Manning Memorial Bowling.

DIVERRES, Prof. Armel Hugh; Professor of French and Head of Department of Romance Studies, University College of Swansea, 1974–81, now Emeritus; *b* Liverpool, 4 Sept. 1914; *o s* of late Paul Diverres and Elizabeth (*née* Jones); *m* 1945, Ann Dilys, *d* of late James and Enid Williams; one *s* two *d. Educ:* Swansea Grammar Sch.; University Coll., Swansea; Univ. of Rennes; Sorbonne, Paris. MA (Wales), LèsL (Rennes), Docteur de l'Université de Paris. Fellow of Univ. of Wales, 1938–40; served in RA and Int. Corps, 1940–46, Captain. Asst Lectr in French, 1946–49, Lectr, 1949–54, Univ. of Manchester; Sen. Lectr in French, 1954–57, Carnegie Prof., 1958–74, Dean, Faculty of Arts, 1967–70, Univ. of Aberdeen. Governor: Nat. Mus. of Wales, 1978–81; Centre for Information on Language Teaching and Res., 1977–82; Aberdeen Coll. of Education, 1971–74. Member: CNAA Lang. Board, 1965–78, Cttee for Res., 1975–82, Humanities Bd, 1978–81; Welsh Jt Educn Cttee, 1975–81. Pres., British Br., Internat. Arthurian Soc., 1978–80, Internat. Pres., 1979–81; Pres., Soc. French Stud., 1976–78. Officier des Palmes Académiques, 1971; Chevalier de l'Ordre National du Mérite, 1986. *Publications:* Voyage en Béarn by Froissart (ed), 1953; La Chronique métrique attribuée à Geffroy de Paris (ed), 1956; Chatterton by A. de Vigny (ed), 1967; articles and reviews in learned journals. *Recreation:* hill walking. *Address:* 23 Whiteshell Drive, Langland, Swansea, W Glamorgan. *T:* Swansea 60322.

DIVINE, Arthur Durham, (David Divine), CBE 1976 (OBE 1946); DSM 1940; author and journalist; formerly War Correspondent and Defence Correspondent, Sunday Times (until 1975); *b* 27 July 1904; 2nd *s* of Arthur Henry and Mabel Divine, Cape Town; *m* 1931, Elizabeth Ann, 2nd *d* of Sir Ian MacAlister; two *d. Educ:* Rondebosch High Sch., Cape Town; Kingswood Coll., Grahamstown, S Africa. Cape Times, 1922–26 and 1931–35, where founded daily column of World Comment; has travelled extensively in Europe, Africa, Asia, N and S America, and the Pacific. *Publications:* Sea Loot, 1930; They Blocked the Suez Canal, 1936; The Pub on the Pool, 1938; Tunnel from Calais, 1943, new edn 1975; many other thrillers; The Merchant Navy Fights, The Wake of the Raiders, Behind the Fleets, 1940, in conjunction with Ministry of Information; Destroyer's War, 1942; Road to Tunis, 1944; Navies in Exile, 1944; Dunkirk, 1945, and many boys' books. Under pseudonym of David Rame: Wine of Good Hope, 1939; The Sun Shall Greet Them, 1941. Under name of David Divine: The King of Fassarai, 1950; Atom at Spithead, 1953; The Golden Fool, 1954; Boy on a Dolphin, 1955; The Nine Days of Dunkirk, 1959, new edn 1976; These Splendid Ships, 1960; The Iron Ladies, 1961; The Daughter of the Pangaran, 1963; The Blunted Sword, 1964; The Broken Wing, 1966; The Stolen Seasons, 1967; The Key of England, 1968; The North-West Frontier of Rome, 1969; The Three Red Flares, 1970; Mutiny at Invergordon, 1970; Certain Islands, 1972; The Opening of the World, 1973; *Films:* Atom at Spithead; Boy on a Dolphin; Dunkirk. *Address:* 24 Keats Grove, Hampstead, NW3 2RS. *T:* 01–435 6928.

DIX, Alan Michael, OBE 1985; Director General, Motor Agents' Association Ltd, 1976–85; *b* 29 June 1922; *s* of late Comdr Charles Cabry Dix, CMG, DSO, RN, and Ebba Sievers; *m* 1955, Helen Catherine McLaren; one *s* one *d*. *Educ:* Stenhus Kostskole, Denmark. Escaped Nazi occupied Denmark to Scotland, 1943; joined RAF, commissioned 1944. President, Capitol Car Distributors Inc., USA, 1958–67; Gp Vice-Pres., Volkswagen of America, USA, 1967–68; Man. Dir, Volkswagen (GB) Ltd, London, 1968–72; Pres., Mid Atlantic Toyota Inc., USA, 1972–73; Dir Marketing, British Leyland International, 1973–74; Proprietor, Alan M. Dix Associates, 1974–76. Chm., Motor Agents Pensions Administrators Ltd, 1976–85; Dir, Hire Purchase Information Ltd, 1977–85. Freedom and Livery, Coachmakers' and Coach Harness Makers' Co., 1980. FIMI, FInstM, FIMH, FBIM. King Christian X war medal, 1947. *Publications:* contribs to automotive trade jls. *Recreations:* yachting, photography; the study of professional management (internat. speaker on management and organisation). *Address:* Apartment 1.1, Edifici Hort del Sola, La Massana, Principality of Andorra. *T:* Andorra 35352. *Clubs:* Danish, Royal Air Force, Burkes; Royal Air Force Yacht (Hamble).

DIX, Bernard Hubert; Assistant General Secretary, National Union of Public Employees, 1975–83; *b* 30 March 1925; *s* of Thomas Herbert John Dix and Gertrude Turner; *m* 1979, Eileen Veronica Smith; three *s*; two *s* one *d* by prev. *m*. *Educ:* LCC elem. schs; LSE (TUC Scholar). Engrg industry, 1939–55 (served Army, 1941–47); Deptl Asst, TUC, 1955–63; Res. Officer, NUPE, 1963–75. Member: Health Services Bd, 1976–80; Hotel and Catering Industry EDC, 1973–79; TUC Local Govt Cttee, 1970–83; TUC Hotel and Catering Industry Cttee, 1973–79; Labour Party NEC, 1981–83; Bd of Tribune, 1975–82. Joined Plaid Cymru, 1983. Governor, Ruskin Coll., 1969–84. Associate Fellow, Warwick Univ., 1982–84. *Publications:* (with Alan W. Fisher) Low Pay and How to End It, 1974; (jtly) The Forward March of Labour Halted?, 1981; (contrib.) Y Ddraig Goch; Welsh Nation. *Address:* Pant Tawel, Mynydd Cerrig, Dyfed SA15 5BD. *T:* Pontyberem 870122. *Club:* Mynydd Cerrig Workingman's.

DIX, Geoffrey Herbert, OBE 1979; Secretary-General, The Institute of Bankers, 1971–82; *b* 1 March 1922; *o s* of late Herbert Walter and Winifred Ada Dix; *m* 1945, Margaret Sybil Outhwaite, MA (Cantab) (*d* 1981); one *s*. *Educ:* Watford Grammar Sch.; Gonville and Caius Coll., Cambridge. MA (Mod. langs). Served War, 1942–45: commissioned into Royal Devon Yeomanry; later served with HQ 1st Airborne Corps. Inst. of Export, 1946–51; with Inst. of Bankers, 1951–: Asst Sec., 1956; Under-Sec. 1962; Dep. Sec. 1968. Mem., Jt Cttee for National Awards in Business Studies, 1960–76. *Recreations:* Mozart, theatre. *Address:* 102 Harestone Valley Road, Caterham, Surrey. *T:* Caterham 42837. *Club:* Caterham Players.

DIX, Prof. Gerald Bennett, ARIBA; FRTPI; Lever Professor of Civic Design, University of Liverpool, since 1975; *b* 12 Jan. 1926; *s* of late Cyril Dix and Mabel Winifred (*née* Bennett); *m* 1st, 1956 (marr. diss.); two *s*; 2nd, 1963, Lois Nichols; one *d*. *Educ:* Altrincham Grammar Sch.; Univ. of Manchester (BA (Hons Arch.), DipTP (dist.)); Harvard Univ. (MLA). Studio Asst, 1950–51, Asst Lectr in Town and Country Planning, 1951–53, Manchester Univ.; Asst Architect, 1954; Chief Architect-Planner, Addis Ababa, and chief asst to Sir Patrick Abercrombie, 1954–56; Planning Officer, Singapore, 1957–59; Acting Planning Adviser, 1959; Sen. Research Fellow, Univ. of Science and Technol., Ghana, 1959–63; UN Planning Mission to Ghana, 1962; Planner, later Sen. Planner, BRS/ODM, 1963–65 (adv. missions to W Indies, W Africa, Aden, Bechuanaland, Swaziland, Cyprus); Nottingham University: Lectr, 1966–68; Sen. Lectr, 1968–70; Prof. of Planning, and Dir, Inst. of Planning Studies, 1970–75; Liverpool University: Chm., Fac. of Social and Environmental Studies, 1983–84; Pro Vice-Chancellor, 1984–87. Dir, Cyprus Planning Project, 1967–71; Jt Dir, Alexandria Comprehensive Master Plan Project, 1980–86; adv. visits on planning educn, to Uganda 1971, Nigeria 1972, Sudan 1975, Mexico 1978, Egypt 1980; UK Mem., Adv. Panel on planning Canal towns, Egypt, 1974, and Western Desert, 1975. Member: Professional Literature Cttee, RIBA, 1966–80, 1981– (Chm. 1975–80); Library Management Cttee, 1969–72, 1975–80; Historic Areas Adv. Cttee, English Heritage, 1986–. Vice-Pres., World Soc. for Ekistics, 1975–79. Editorial adviser, Ekistics (journal), 1972–; Chm., Bd of Management, Town Planning Rev., 1976–; (Founder) Editor, Third World Planning Rev., 1978–. FRSA. *Publications:* ed, C. A. Doxiadis, Ecology and Ekistics, 1977, Boulder, Colo, 1978, Brisbane, 1978; numerous planning reports to govts in various parts of world; articles and reviews in Town Planning Rev., Third World Planning Rev., Ekistics, RIBA Jl, Arch. Rev. *Recreations:* photography, listening to music, travel. *Address:* Department of Civic Design, University of Liverpool, PO Box 147, Liverpool L69 3BX. *T:* 051–709 6022; Gamblegate, Meols Drive, West Kirby, Wirral, Merseyside L48 5DE. *T:* 051–632 1390. *Club:* Athenæum.

DIX, Victor Wilkinson, MA, MB, BChir Cantab, FRCS, MRCP, retired; Professor Emeritus, University of London. Assistant Surgeon, The London Hospital, 1930–37; Surgeon, The London Hospital, 1937–64. *Address:* 8 Shandon Close, Tunbridge Wells, Kent. *T:* Tunbridge Wells 30839.

DIXEY, John, OBE 1976; Newspaper Consultant, since 1986; Assistant Managing Director, Mirror Group Newspapers, since 1985; *b* 29 March 1926; *s* of John Dixey and Muriel Doris Dixey; *m* 1948, Pauline Seaden; one *s* one *d*. *Educ:* Battersea Grammar Sch. Served Royal Marines and Royal Fusiliers, 1944–47. Press Telegraphist, Yorkshire Post and Glasgow Herald, 1948–59; Asst to Gen. Sec., Nat. Union of Press Telegraphists, 1959; Labour Officer, Newspaper Soc., 1959–63; Labour Adviser, Thomson Organisation Ltd, 1963–64; Asst Gen. Man., Liverpool Daily Post & Echo, 1964–67; Executive Dir, Times Newspapers, 1967–74; Special Adviser to Man. Dir, Thomson Org., 1974; Dir, Newspaper Publishers Assoc. Ltd, 1975–76; Employment Affairs Advr, IPA, 1977–79; Sec., Assoc. of Midland Advertising Agencies, 1977–79; Production Dir and Bd Mem., The Guardian, 1979–84. Chm., Advertising Assoc. Trade Union Liaison Group; Mem., TUC New Daily Newspaper Advisory Group. Ward-Perkins Vis. Fellow, Pembroke Coll., Oxford, 1978. Former Mem., Printing and Publishing Industry Trng Bd; former Governor, London Coll. of Printing. *Recreations:* cooking, photography. *Address:* 23 West Hill, Sanderstead, Surrey. *T:* 01–657 7940.

DIXEY, Paul (Arthur Groser); Chairman of Lloyd's, 1973, 1974 (Deputy Chairman, 1967, 1969, 1972); *b* 13 April 1915; *e s* of late Neville Dixey, JP (Chairman of Lloyd's, 1931, 1934 and 1936), and Marguerite (*née* Groser); *m* 1939, Mary Margaret Baring, JP, 2nd *d* of late Geoffrey Garrod; four *s* one *d*. *Educ:* Stowe; Trinity Coll., Cambridge. Elected an Underwriting Mem. of Lloyd's, 1938. Served War of 1939–45, Royal Artillery. Member: London Insce market delegn to Indonesia, 1958; Dunmow RDC, 1958–64; Cttee, Lloyd's Underwriters' Assoc., 1962–74; Cttee, Salvage Assoc., 1962–74; Cttee, Lloyd's, 1964–70, 1972–75; Gen. Cttee, Lloyd's Register of Shipping, 1964–; Chm., Salvage Assoc., 1964–65. Chairman: Paul Dixey Underwriting Agencies Ltd, 1973–76; Pieri Underwriting Agencies Ltd, 1976–; Director, Merrett Dixey Syndicates Ltd, 1976–78. Mem. Council, Morley Coll., 1952–62; Chm. Governors, Vinehall Sch., 1966–73. Leader, Barn Boys' Club, 1949–61. Chm., Essex Hunt Cttee, 1981–. *Recreations:* riding, fly-fishing. *Address:* Little Easton Spring, Dunmow, Essex CM6 2JD. *T:* Great Dunmow 2840.

DIXIT, Prof. Avinash Kamalakar; Professor of Economics, Princeton University, USA, since 1981; *b* 8 June 1944; *s* of Kamalakar Ramchandra Dixit and Kusum Dixit (*née* Phadke). *Educ:* Bombay Univ. (BSc); Cambridge Univ. (BA, MA); Massachusetts Inst. of Technology (PhD). Acting Asst Professor, Univ. of California, Berkeley, 1968–69; Lord Thomson of Fleet Fellow and Tutor in Economics, Balliol Coll., Oxford, 1970–74; Professor of Economics, Univ. of Warwick, 1974–80. Res. Fellow, Centre for Economic Policy Res., 1984–. Fellow, Econometric Society, 1977– Co-Editor, Bell Journal of Economics, 1981–83. *Publications:* Optimization in Economic Theory, 1976; The Theory of Equilibrium Growth, 1976; (with Victor Norman) Theory of International Trade, 1980; several articles in professional jls. *Recreations:* listening to music (pre-Schubert only), watching cricket (when possible). *Address:* Department of Economics, Princeton University, Princeton, New Jersey 08544, USA. *T:* (609) 452–4013.

DIXON, family name of **Baron Glentoran.**

DIXON; *see* Graham-Dixon.

DIXON, Dr Bernard; science writer and consultant; *b* Darlington, 17 July 1938; *s* of late Ronald Dixon and Grace Peirson; *m* 1963, Margaret Helena Charlton; two *s* one *d*. *Educ:* Queen Elizabeth Grammar Sch., Darlington; King's Coll., Univ. of Durham; Univ. of Newcastle upon Tyne. BSc, PhD. Luccock Res. Fellow, 1961–64, Frank Schon Fellow, 1964–65, Univ. of Newcastle; Asst Editor, 1965–66, Dep. Editor, 1966–68, World Medicine; Editor, New Scientist, 1969–79. Chm., Cttee, Assoc. of British Science Writers, 1971–72; Member: Soc. for General Microbiology, 1962; Council, BAAS, 1977– (Pres., Section X, 1979; Vice-Pres., 1986–); CSS, 1982–. FIBiol 1982; CBiol 1984. *Publications:* (ed) Journeys in Belief, 1968; What is Science For?, 1973; Magnificent Microbes, 1976; Invisible Allies, 1976; Beyond the Magic Bullet, 1978; (with G. Holister) Ideas of Science, 1984; Man and Medicine, 1986; Engineered Organisms in the Environment; contributor to: Animal Rights—A Symposium, 1979; The Book of Predictions, 1980; Development of Science Publishing in Europe, 1980; Medicine and Care, 1981; Engineered Organisms in the Environment, 1986; numerous articles in scientific and general press on microbiology, and other scientific topics; research papers in Jl of General Microbiology, etc, mostly on microbial biochemistry. *Recreation:* playing Scottish traditional music, collecting old books. *Address:* 7 Warburton Court, Victoria Road, Ruislip Manor, Middlesex HA4 0AN. *T:* Ruislip 632390.

DIXON, Bernard Tunbridge; solicitor; *b* 14 July 1928; *s* of Archibald Tunbridge Dixon and Dorothy Dixon (*née* Cardinal); *m* 1962, Jessie Netta Watson Hastie; one *s* three *d*. *Educ:* Owen's Sch.; University Coll. London (LLB). Admitted Solicitor, 1952 (Edmund Thomas Child Prize); Partner in Dixon & Co., Solicitors, 1952–59; Legal Asst/Sen. Legal Asst with Treasury Solicitor, 1959–67; Sen. Legal Asst with Land Commission, 1967–70; Sen. Legal Asst with Charity Comrs, 1970–74; Dep. Charity Comr, 1975–81; Charity Comr, 1981–84. *Recreation:* photography. *Address:* c/o T. J. Smith & Son, 14 Castle Street, Liverpool L2 0SG.

DIXON, Donald; MP (Lab) Jarrow, since 1979; an Opposition Whip, since 1984; *b* 6 March 1929; *s* of late Christopher Albert Dixon and Jane Dixon; *m* Doreen Morad; one *s* one *d*. *Educ:* Ellison Street Elementary School, Jarrow. Shipyard Worker, 1947–74; Branch Sec., GMWU, 1974–79. Councillor, South Tyneside MDC, 1963–. Mem., Employment Select Cttee; Chm., PLP Shipbuilding Gp; Vice-Chairman: PLP Industries and Trade Gp; Northern Gp of Labour MPs; Sec., Trade Union Gp of Labour MPs. Freeman of Jarrow, 1972. *Recreations:* football, reading. *Address:* 1 Hillcrest, Jarrow NE32 4DP. *T:* Jarrow 897635. *Clubs:* Jarrow Labour; Hastings (Hebburn).

DIXON, Sir (Francis Wilfred) Peter, KBE 1959 (CBE 1952); MB, BS; FRCS; Air Vice-Marshal retired; Consultant in Surgery to the RAF, retired 1966; *b* 4 Oct. 1907; *s* of late Frederick Henry Dixon, New Norfolk, Tas.; *m* 1940, Pamela Ruby, *d* of late Brig. Charles C. Russell, MC, RA (Retd), London; two *s* one *d*. *Educ:* Newman Coll.; Melbourne Univ. MB, BS, Melbourne, 1930; FRCS Ed. 1937; FRCS 1949; DO Oxford, 1936. House Surgeon, St Vincent's Hosp., Melbourne. Joined RAF 1930; Wing-Comdr 1943; served War of 1939–45 (despatches); Aden, Normandy, SW Pacific; Air Cdre 1949; Air Vice-Marshal, 1957. Civilian Consultant in Surgery, RAF, 1966–. Hon. Surgeon to King George VI, 1949–52, to Queen Elizabeth II, 1952–66. Lady Cade Medal, RCS, 1963. *Publications:* contribs to medical journals. *Recreation:* sailing. *Address:* Alde Cottage, Park Road, Aldeburgh, Suffolk IP15 5ER. *T:* Aldeburgh 3772.

DIXON, Prof. Gordon Henry, PhD; FRS 1978; FRSC; Professor of Medical Biochemistry, since 1974, and Head of the Department, since 1983, Faculty of Medicine, University of Calgary; *b* 25 March 1930; *s* of Walter James Dixon and Ruth Nightingale; *m* 1954, Sylvia Weir Gillen; three *s* one *d*. *Educ:* Cambs High Sch. for Boys; Trinity Coll., Cambridge (Open Schol. 1948; BA Hons, MA); Univ. of Toronto (PhD). FRSC 1970. Res. Asst Prof., Dept of Biochem., Univ. of Washington, Seattle, USA, 1954–58; Mem. staff, MRC Unit for res. in cell metabolism, Univ. of Oxford, 1958–59; Univ. of Toronto: Res. Associate, Connaught Med. Res. Lab., 1959–60; Associate Prof., Dept of Biochem., 1960–63; Prof., Dept of Biochem., Univ. of BC, Vancouver, 1963–72; Prof., Biochem. Group, Univ. of Sussex, 1972–74. Vis. Fellow Commoner, Trinity Coll., Cambridge, 1979–80. Pres., Canadian Biochemical Soc., 1982–83; Pres., Pan-American Assoc. of Biochemical Socs, 1987– (Mem. Council, 1981–84; Vice-Pres., 1984–87). Flavelle Medal, RSC, 1980. *Publications:* over 200 pubns in learned jls, incl. Jl Biol Chem., Proc. Nat. Acad. Sci. (US), Nature, and Biochemistry. *Recreations:* skiing, mountain walking, gardening. *Address:* 3424 Underwood Place NW, Calgary, Alberta T2N 4G7, Canada. *T:* 403–282–4394 or 403–220–6022.

DIXON, Guy Holford, JP; Barrister-at-Law; honorary Recorder of Newark-on-Trent, since 1972; *b* 20 March 1902; *s* of late Dr Montague Dixon, Melton Mowbray; unmarried. *Educ:* Abbotsholme Sch., Derbs; Repton Sch.; University Coll., Oxford. BA (History) Oxon, 1925. Called to the Bar, Inner Temple, 1929. Recorder of Newark-on-Trent, 1965–71; Deputy Chairman: Leics QS, 1960–71; Northampton County QS, 1966–71; a Recorder, 1972–75; a Dep. Circuit Judge, 1975–77. Lay Canon, Leicester Cathedral, 1962. JP Leics, 1960. *Recreation:* looking at and collecting pictures. *Address:* The Old Rectory, Brampton Ash, Market Harborough, Leics. *T:* Dingley 200. *Club:* Reform.

DIXON, Jack Shawcross, OBE 1969; HM Diplomatic Service, retired 1976; *b* 8 March 1918; *s* of Herbert Dixon and Helen (*née* Woollacott); *m* 1941, Ida Hewkin; one *d*. *Educ:* Oldham Hulme Grammar Sch.; London Sch. of Economics (BScEcon). Served in Royal Welch Fusiliers and RAOC attached Indian Army, 1940–46. Colonial Office, 1948; entered HM Foreign (subseq. Diplomatic) Service, 1949; FO, 1949; HM Political Agency, Kuwait, 1950; Rep. of Polit. Agent, Mina al Ahmadi, 1951; FO, 1952; 1st Sec., Singapore, 1956; HM Consul, Barcelona, 1959; FO, 1962; 1st Sec., Rome, 1966; FCO, 1971; Head of Treaty and Nationality Dept, FCO, 1973–76. *Recreations:* observing wildlife, photographing butterflies, philately. *Address:* 26 Brook Court, Meads Road, Eastbourne, E Sussex BN20 7PY. *Club:* Royal Commonwealth Society.

DIXON, Sir John George, 3rd Bt cr 1919; b 17 Sept. 1911; s of Sir John Dixon, 2nd Bt and Gwendolen Anne (d 1974), d of Sir Joseph Layton Elmes Spearman, 2nd Bt; S father, 1976; m 1947, Caroline, d of late Charles Theodore Hiltermann; one d. Educ: Cranleigh. Heir: nephew Jonathan Mark Dixon, b 1 Sept. 1949. Address: Avenue des Mousquetaires 19, La Tour de Peilz, Vaud, Switzerland.

DIXON, Jon Edmund, CMG 1975; Under Secretary, Ministry of Agriculture, Fisheries and Food, 1971–85; b 19 Nov. 1928; e s of Edmund Joseph Claude and Gwendoline Alice Dixon; m 1953, Betty Edith Stone; two s one d (and one d decd). Educ: St Paul's Sch., West Kensington; Peterhouse, Cambridge. Natural Sciences Tripos Part I and Part II (Physiology). Asst Principal, Min. of Agric. and Fisheries, 1952; Private Sec. to successive Parliamentary Secretaries, 1955–58; Principal, 1958; Asst Sec., 1966; Under-Sec., 1971; Minister in UK Delegn, subseq. Office of Permanent Rep., to EEC, 1972–75. Publications: contribs to Early Music News; Choral, Organ and String Music: a selection of works by Jon Dixon, 1970–85 (two LPs). Recreations: musical composition, oil painting, building harpsichords, gardening, walking.

DIXON, Prof. Kendal Cartwright, MA, MD, PhD, FRCPath; Professor of Cellular Pathology, University of Cambridge, 1973–78, now Emeritus; Fellow of King's College, Cambridge, since 1937; b 16 Feb. 1911; s of late Prof. Henry H. Dixon, ScD, FRS, Dublin Univ., and Dorothea, d of late Sir John Franks, CB, Blackrock, Co. Dublin; m 1938, Anne, d of late F. D. Darley, Stillorgan, Co. Dublin; one s one d. Educ: St Stephen's Green Sch., Dublin; Haileybury; Trinity Coll., Dublin; King's Coll., Cambridge (Scholar); Dun's Hosp., Dublin; St Bartholomew's Hosp., London. 1st cl. Pt 1 1932, 1st cl. Pt 2 (Biochem.) 1933, Nat. Scis Tripos Cantab; MB, BChir Cantab 1939. Asst to Prof. of Physiol., Dublin Univ., 1936; RAMC, 1940–45, Specialist in Pathology; Univ. of Cambridge: Official Fellow of King's Coll., 1945; Univ. Demonstrator in Chem. Path., 1946, Lectr 1949; Tutor for Advanced Students, King's Coll., 1951–59; Dir of Studies in Medicine, King's Coll., 1959–73; Reader in Cytopathology, 1962–73. Vis. Prof. of Pathology, Columbia Univ., NY, 1978. Mem. European Soc. Pathology. Publications: Cellular Defects in Disease, 1982; chapters in books and articles in med. jls principally on cellular disorder and death, fatty change, and neuronal metabolism. Recreation: the mountains of Kerry. Address: King's College, Cambridge. Club: Kildare Street and University (Dublin).

DIXON, Kenneth Herbert Morley; Chairman, Rowntree Mackintosh plc, since 1981; b 19 Aug. 1929; y s of Arnold Morley Dixon and Mary Jolly; m 1955, Patricia Oldbury Whalley; two s. Educ: Cathedral Sch., Shanghai; Cranbrook Sch., Sydney, Australia; Manchester Univ. (BA(Econ) 1952). Lieut Royal Signals, 1947–49. Calico Printers Assoc., 1952–56; joined Rowntree & Co. Ltd, 1956; Dir, 1970; Chm., UK Confectionery Div., 1973–78; Dep. Chm., 1978–81. Vice-Chm., Legal & General Gp, 1986– (Dir, 1984–). Member: Council, Incorporated Soc. of British Advertisers, 1971–79; Council, Cocoa, Chocolate and Confectionery Alliance, 1972–79; Council, Advertising Assoc., 1976–79; BIM Econ. and Social Affairs Cttee, 1980–; Council, CBI, 1981– (Mem., Companies Cttee, 1979–84; Mem., Employment Policy Cttee, 1983–). Mem. Council, York Univ., 1983–. FRSA; CBIM. Recreations: reading, music, fell walking. Address: Rowntree Mackintosh plc, York YO1 1XY. T: York 53071. Clubs: Reform; Yorkshire (York).

DIXON, Margaret Rumer Haynes; see Godden, Rumer.

DIXON, Michael George, OBE 1964; Chief Passport Officer, Foreign and Commonwealth Office, 1967–80, retired; b 10 March 1920; s of Sidney Wilfrid and Elsie Dixon. Educ: Enfield Grammar Sch. Foreign Office, 1937. HM Forces, 1940–46 (POW, Far East). MInstTM. Recreation: gardening. Address: 9 Ridge Crest, Enfield, Mddx EN2 8JU. T: 01–363 3408.

DIXON, Sir Peter; see Dixon, Sir (F. W.) P.

DIXON, Peter Vibart; Secretary, National Economic Development Council, since 1982; b 16 July 1932; s of late Meredith Vibart Dixon and Phyllis Joan (née Hemingway); m 1955, Elizabeth Anne Howie Davison; three s. Educ: Summer Fields; Radley Coll.; King's Coll., Cambridge (BA Classics and Law 1955, MA 1959). Royal Artillery, 1951–52. Asst Principal, HM Treasury, 1955; Office of Lord Privy Seal, 1956; Treasury, 1956–62: Private Sec. to Economic Sec., 1959; Principal, 1960; Colonial Office, 1963; CS Selection Bd, 1964–65; Treasury, 1965–72; Asst Sec., 1969; Counsellor (Economic), HM Embassy, Washington, 1972–75; Treasury, 1975–82: Press Sec., 1975–78; Under Sec., Industrial Policy, 1978–82. Mem., RIPA (Mem. Council, 1976–82). FRSA 1984. Address: 17 Lauriston Road, Wimbledon SW19 4TJ. T: 01–946 8931.

DIXON, Piers; b 29 Dec. 1928; s of late Sir Pierson Dixon (British Ambassador in New York and Paris) and of Lady (Ismene) Dixon; m 1st, 1960, Edwina (marr. diss. 1973), d of Rt Hon. Lord Duncan-Sandys, qv; two s; 2nd, 1976, Janet (marr. diss. 1981), d of R. D. Aiyar, FRCS, and widow of 5th Earl Cowley; 3rd, 1984, Anne (marr. diss. 1985), d of John Cronin, qv; one s. Educ: Eton (schol.); Magdalene Coll., Cambridge (exhibnr); Harvard Business Sch. Grenadier Guards, 1948. Merchant banking, London and New York, 1954–64; Sheppards and Chase, stockbrokers, 1964–81; Underwriting Mem. of Lloyd's. Centre for Policy Studies, 1976–78. Contested (C) Brixton, 1966; MP (C) Truro, 1970–Sept. 1974; Sec., Cons. Backbenchers' Finance Cttee, 1970–71, Vice-Chm., 1972–74; sponsor of Rehabilitation of Offenders Act, 1974. Publications: Double Diploma, 1968; Cornish Names, 1973. Recreations: tennis, modern history. Address: 22 Ponsonby Terrace, SW1. T: 01–821 6166. Clubs: Beefsteak, Brooks's, Pratt's.

DIXON, Prof. Richard Newland, PhD, ScD; FRS 1986; CChem, FRSC; Professor of Chemistry and Head of Department of Theoretical Chemistry, University of Bristol, since 1969 (Dean of Faculty of Science, 1979–82); b 25 Dec. 1930; s of late Robert Thomas Dixon and Lilian Dixon; m 1954, Alison Mary Birks; one s two d. Educ: The Judd Sch., Tonbridge; King's Coll., Univ. of London (BSc 1951); St Catharine's Coll., Univ. of Cambridge (PhD 1955; ScD 1976). FRSC 1976. Scientific Officer, UKAEA, 1954–56; Res. Associate, Univ. of Western Ontario, 1956–57; Postdoctoral Fellow, NRCC, Ottawa, 1957–59; ICI Fellow, Univ. of Sheffield, 1959–60, Lectr in Chem., 1960–69. Sorby Res. Fellow, Royal Soc., 1964–69. RSC Faraday Council, 1985–. Corday-Morgan Medal, Chemical Soc., 1966; RSC Award for Spectroscopy, 1984. Publications: Spectroscopy and Structure, 1965; Theoretical Chemistry: Vol. 1, 1974, Vol. 2, 1975, Vol. 3, 1978; numerous articles in res. jls of chemistry and physics. Recreations: mountain walking, travel, theatre, concerts. Address: 22 Westbury Lane, Bristol BS9 2PE. T: Bristol 681691; School of Chemistry, The University, Bristol BS8 1TS.

DIXON, Maj.-Gen. Roy Laurence Cayley, CB 1977; MC 1944; Chapter Clerk, College of St George, Windsor Castle, since 1981; b 19 Sept. 1924; s of Lt-Col Sidney Frank Dixon, MC and Edith Mary (Sheena) (née Clark). Educ: Haileybury; Edinburgh Univ. Commnd Royal Tank Regt, 1944; served in armd units and on staff; psc 1956; Instructor, Staff Coll., 1961–64; comd 5th Royal Tank Regt, 1966–67; Royal Coll. of Defence Studies, 1971; Comdr Royal Armd Corps, Germany, 1968–70; qual. helicopter pilot, 1973; Dir, Army Air Corps, 1974–76; Chief of Staff, Allied Forces Northern Europe, 1977–80. Col Comdt, RTR, 1978–83. Publications: articles in mil. jls. Recreations: ski-ing,

sailing, theatre, music. Address: 7 The Cloisters, Windsor Castle, Berks SL4 1NJ. T: Windsor 865538.

DIXON, Stanley; Chairman, Midland-Yorkshire Tar Distillers Ltd, 1968–71; b 12 Aug. 1900; m 1936, Ella Margaret Hogg; two s. Educ: Leeds Grammar Sch.; Queen's Coll., Oxford. Articled to Leather & Veale, Chartered Accountants in Leeds, 1924–27; Manager, Leather & Veale (later Peat, Marwick, Mitchell & Co.), Leeds, 1927–35; Sec., Midland Tar Distillers Ltd, 1935–66; Dir, Midland Tar Distillers Ltd (later Midland-Yorkshire Holdings Ltd), 1943–71. Pres., Inst. of Chartered Accountants in England and Wales, 1968–69. Hon. DSocSc Birmingham, 1972. Publications: The Case for Marginal Costing, 1967; The Art of Chairing a Meeting, 1975. Recreations: Church affairs, gardening and music. Address: 83 Norton Road, Stourbridge, West Midlands DY8 2TB. T: Stourbridge 395672.

DIXON, Group Captain William Michael, CBE 1972; DSO 1943; DFC 1941; AFC 1958; Bursar, Summer Fields School, Oxford, 1975–86; b 29 July 1920; s of late William Michael Dixon; m 1944, Mary Margaret (d 1957), d of late William Alexander Spence, MC, MM; three s. Served War of 1939–45, Bomber Comd; Air Staff, Rhodesian Air Trng Gp, 1946–49; psa 1949; comd No 2 (Bomber) Sqdn RAAF, 1952–55; comd No 192 Sqdn RAF, 1955–58; jssc 1958; comd RAF Feltwell, 1961–63; Sen. Officer Admin No 1 (Bomber) Gp, 1963–66; Sen. Personnel SO HQ Air Support Comd, 1966–68; DCAS, Royal Malaysian Air Force, 1968–73; Dir of Aircraft Projects (RAF), MoD, 1972–75; ADC to the Queen, 1968–73. Recreation: natural history. Address: Lower Farm, Sutton, Oxford OX8 1RX. T: Oxford 881553.

DIXON WARD, Frank, CBE 1979; Executive Director, Royal Society for the Prevention of Cruelty to Animals, since 1982; b 28 June 1922; s of late Cecil Ward, LRAM, and Helen Cecilia Ward, Eastbourne; m 1960, Claire Collasius (d 1985); one s one d. Educ: Eastbourne Grammar School. Solicitor (Hons), 1948. Articled to Town Clerk, Eastbourne, 1940. Served War, Royal Air Force, 1941–46. Solicitor posts, Peterborough, 1948–51, West Ham, 1952–54; Deputy Town Clerk, Hove, 1954–62; Chairman: Local Govt Legal Soc., 1957; Hove Round Table, 1961–62; Mem. Council, Sussex LTA, 1957–62; Town Clerk: Camberwell, 1963–65; Southwark, 1964–70; Chief Exec., Lambeth, 1970–81; Consultant, 1982; Chm., London Rent Assessment Cttees, 1982. Hon. Clerk: South London Housing Consortium, 1965–70; Social Service Cttee, London Boroughs Assoc., 1966–82; Hon. Legal Advr, Age Concern (Gtr London), 1965–82; Member official committees: London Welfare Services, 1963–65; NHS Reorganisation, 1969–74; Homelessness, 1970–72; Citizens Advice Bureaux, 1973–74; Jt Approach to Social Policies, 1975–76. Chm., St Dunstan's College Soc., 1975–78. Recreations: music, lawn tennis. Address: RSPCA, Causeway, Horsham, West Sussex RH12 1HG. T: Horsham 64181. Club: Royal Over-Seas League.

DOBB, Erlam Stanley, CB 1963; TD; b 16 Aug. 1910; m 1937, Margaret Williams; no c. Educ: Ruthin; University Coll. of N Wales. Chartered Surveyor and Land Agent, Anglesey, Denbigh and Merioneth, 1930–35; Asst Land Comr, to Dir, Agricultural Land Service, MAFF, 1935–70; a Dep. Dir-Gen., Agricl Develt and Adv. Service, MAFF, 1971–73; Dir-Gen., 1973–75. Mem., ARC, 1973–75; Vice-Chm., Adv. Council for Agriculture and Horticulture in England and Wales, 1974–75. Trustee, T. P. Price Charity, Markshall Estate, Essex, 1971–84 (Chm. Trustees, 1971–83). Governor, Royal Agricultural College, 1960–75. Royal Welch Fusiliers (TA), 1938–46, Major. FRICS. FRAgS. Publications: professional contributions to journals of learned societies. Recreations: golf, gardening. Address: Churchgate, Westerham, Kent. T: Westerham 62294. Clubs: Farmers'; Crowborough Beacon Golf, Limpsfield Chart Golf.

DOBBING, Prof. John, DSc, FRCP, FRCPath; Professor of Child Growth and Development, Department of Child Health, University of Manchester, and Honorary Consultant, United Manchester Hospitals, 1968–84, now Professor Emeritus; b 14 Aug. 1922; s of Alfred Herbert Dobbing and May Gwendoline (née Cattell); m Dr Jean Sands. Educ: Bootham Sch., York; St Mary's Hosp., London (MSc, MB, BS). DSc Manchester, 1981. FRCPath 1976; FRCP 1981. Lectr in Path. and Gull Student, Guy's Hosp., 1954–61; Sen. Lectr in Physiol., London Hosp., 1961–64; Sen. Lectr, Inst. of Child Health, London, and Hon. Consultant, Hosp. for Sick Children, Gt Ormond Street, 1964–68. Publications: Applied Neurochemistry, 1968; (ed with J. A. Davis) Scientific Foundations of Paediatrics, 1974 (2nd edn 1981); Maternal Nutrition in Pregnancy: eating for two?, 1981; Prevention of Spina Bifida, 1983; pubns on undernutrition and developing brain in scientific literature. Recreations: writing, travel, France and the French. Address: Higher Cliff Farm, via Birch Vale, via Stockport, Cheshire. T: New Mills 43220.

DOBBS, Bernard; see Dobbs, W. B. J.

DOBBS, Prof. (Edwin) Roland, PhD, DSc; Hildred Carlile Professor of Physics, University of London, since 1973, and Head of Department of Physics, Royal Holloway and Bedford New College, since 1985; b 2 Dec. 1924; s of late A. Edwin Dobbs, AMIMechE, and Harriet Dobbs (née Wright); m 1947, Dorothy Helena, o d of late Alderman A. F. T. Jeeves, Stamford, Lincs; two s one d. Educ: Ilford County High Sch.; Queen Elizabeth's Sch., Barnet; University College London. BSc (1st cl. Physics) 1943, PhD 1949; DSc London 1977; FInstP 1964; FIOA 1977. Radar research, Admiralty, 1943–46; DSIR Res. Student, UCL, 1946–49; Lectr in Physics, QMC, Univ. of London, 1949–58; Res. Associate in Applied Maths, 1958–59, Associate Prof. of Physics, 1959–60, Brown Univ., USA; Mem., Gonville and Caius Coll., Cambridge, 1960–; AEI Fellow, Cavendish Lab., Univ. of Cambridge, 1960–64; Prof. and Head of Dept of Physics, Univ. of Lancaster, 1964–73; Bedford College, London University: Head of Dept of Physics, 1973–85; Vice-Principal, 1981–82; Dean, Faculty of Science, 1980–82; Chm., Bd of Studies in Physics, Univ. of London, 1982–85. Member: Physics Cttee, SRC, 1970–73; SERC, 1983–86; Nuclear Physics Bd, SRC, 1974–77. Visiting Professor: Brown Univ., 1966; Wayne State Univ., 1969; Univ. of Tokyo, 1977; Univ. of Delhi, 1983; Cornell Univ., 1984. Pres., Inst. of Acoustics, 1976–78; Hon. Sec., Inst. of Physics, 1976–84. Hon. Fellow, Indian Cryogenics Council, 1977. Publications: Electricity and Magnetism, 1984; Electromagnetic Waves, 1985; research papers on metals and superconductors in Procs of Royal Soc., and on solid state physics and acoustics in Jl of Physics, Physical Rev. Letters, Physical Acoustics, etc. Recreations: travel, theatre, gardening. Address: Royal Holloway and Bedford New College, Egham, Surrey TW20 0EX. Club: Athenæum.

DOBBS, Joseph Alfred, CMG 1972; OBE 1957 (MBE 1945); TD 1945; HM Diplomatic Service, retired; b Abbeyleix, Ireland, 22 Dec. 1914; s of John L. Dobbs and Ruby (née Gillespie); m 1949, Marie, d of Reginald Francis Catton, Sydney; four s. Educ: Worksop Coll.; Trinity Hall, Cambridge (Schol.). Pres., Cambridge Union Soc., 1936. Served War of 1939–45, Major, Royal Artillery (despatches). Joined Foreign Office, 1946; served Moscow, 1947–51, 1954–57 and 1965–68; FO, 1951–54; Delhi, 1957–61; Warsaw, 1961–64; Rome, 1964–65; Consul-Gen., Zagreb, 1969–70; Minister, Moscow, 1971–74. Recreations: riding, gardening. Address: The Coach House, Charlton Musgrove, Wincanton, Somerset BA9 8ES. T: Wincanton 33356.

DOBBS, Mattiwilda; Order of North Star (Sweden), 1954; opera singer (coloratura soprano); Professor, Howard University, Washington, DC, since 1977; *b* Atlanta, Ga, USA; *d* of John Wesley and Irene Dobbs; *m* 1957, Bengt Janzon, retired Dir. of Information, Nat. Ministry of Health and Welfare, Sweden; no *c. Educ:* Spelman Coll., USA (BA); Columbia Univ., USA (MA). Studied voice in NY with Lotte Leonard, 1946–50; special coaching Paris with Pierre Bernac, 1950–52. Marian Anderson Schol., 1948; John Hay Whitney Schol., 1950; 1st prize in singing, Internat. Comp., Geneva Conservatory of Music, 1951. Appeared Royal Dutch Opera, Holland Festival, 1952. Recitals, Sweden, Paris, Holland, 1952; appeared in opera at La Scala, Milan, 1953; Concerts, England and Continent, 1953; Glyndebourne Opera, 1953–54, 1956, 1961; Covent Garden Opera, 1953, 1954, 1956, 1958; command performance, Covent Garden, 1954. Annual concert tours: US, 1954–; Australia, New Zealand, 1955, 1959, 1968; Australia, 1972, 1977; Israel, 1957 and 1959; USSR concerts and opera (Bolshoi Theater), 1959; San Francisco Opera, 1955; début Metropolitan Opera, 1956; there annually, 1956–64. Appearances Hamburg State Opera, 1961–63; Royal Swedish Opera, 1957 and there annually, 1957–73; Norwegian and Finnish Operas, 1957–64. Vis. Prof., Univ. of Texas at Austin, 1973–74; Professor: Univ. of Illinois, 1975–76; Univ. of Georgia, 1976–77. Hon. Dr of Music: Spelman Coll., Atlanta, 1979; Emory Univ., Atlanta, 1980. *Address:* 1101 South Arlington Ridge Road, Apt 301, Arlington, Va 22202, USA.

DOBBS, Captain Richard Arthur Frederick; Lord-Lieutenant of County Antrim, 1975 (HM Lieutenant for County Antrim, 1959–75); *b* 2 April 1919; *s* of Senator Major Arthur F. Dobbs, DL, of Castle Dobbs, and Hylda Louisa Dobbs; *m* 1953, Carola Day, *d* of Christopher Clarkson, Old Lyme, Conn, USA; four *s* one *d. Educ:* Eton; Magdalene Coll., Cambridge (MA). Served War: 2nd Lieut Irish Guards (Supp. Reserve), 1939; Captain 1943. Called to Bar, Lincoln's Inn, 1947; Member, Midland Circuit, 1951–55. *Address:* Castle Dobbs, Carrickfergus, County Antrim, N Ireland. *T:* Whitehead 72238. *Club:* Cavalry and Guards.

DOBBS, Roland; *see* Dobbs, E. R.

DOBBS, (William) Bernard (Joseph); HM Diplomatic Service, retired; Ambassador to Laos (Lao People's Democratic Republic), 1982–85; *b* 3 Sept. 1925, *s* of late William Evelyn Joseph Dobbs and Maud Clifford Dobbs (*née* Bernard); *m* 1952, Brigid Mary Bilitch; one *s* one *d. Educ:* Shrewsbury Sch.; Trinity Coll., Dublin (BA Hons Mod. History). Served Rifle Bde/7th Gurkha Rifles, 1943–47 (Captain). Forbes Forbes Campbell and Co. Ltd, 1952–56; Examiner, Patent Office, 1957–61; British Trade Commission, 1961–65: Lagos, 1961–64; Freetown, 1964–66; HM Diplomatic Service: Freetown, London, Rangoon, Milan, Kinshasa, Vientiane, 1965–85. *Recreations:* reading, walking, writing. *Clubs:* Royal Automobile; Kildare Street and University (Dublin).

DOBEREINER, Peter Arthur Bertram; golf correspondent, The Observer, since 1965; *b* 3 Nov. 1925; *s* of Major Arthur Dobereiner and Dorothy (*née* Hassall); *m* 1951, Betty Evelyn Jacob; two *s* two *d. Educ:* King's College, Taunton; Lincoln College, Oxford. RNVR 1942. Asst Manager, Parry & Co. (Madras), 1946; various newspaper appts, 1949–: East Essex Gazette, Oxford Times, News Chronicle, Daily Express, Daily Mail, The Guardian. Hon. Mem., Amer. Soc. of Golf Course Architects. Screen Writers Guild Award (jtly) (That Was the Week That Was), 1962; MacGregor writing awards, 1977, 1981; Donald Ross award, 1985. *Publications:* The Game With a Hole In It, 1970, 3rd edn 1973; The Glorious World of Golf, 1973, 3rd edn 1975; Stroke, Hole or Match?, 1976; Golf Rules Explained, 1980, 6th edn 1985; For the Love of Golf, 1981; Tony Jacklin's Golf Secrets, 1982; Down the Nineteenth Fairway, 1982; The World of Golf, 1982; (ed) The Golfers, 1982; The Book of Golf Disasters, 1983; The Fifty Greatest Post-War Golfers, 1985; Arnold Palmer's Complete Book of Putting, 1986. *Recreation:* golf. *Address:* Chelsfield Hill House, Pratts Bottom, Orpington, Kent BR6 7SL. *T:* Farnborough (Kent) 53849. *Clubs:* West Kent Golf; Hon. Ballybunion (Ireland).

DOBLE, Denis Henry; HM Diplomatic Service; Deputy High Commissioner, Calcutta, since 1985; *b* 2 Oct. 1936; *s* of Percy Claud Doble and Dorothy Grace (*née* Petley); *m* 1975, Patricia Ann Robinson; one *d* one *s. Educ:* Dover Grammar School; New College, Oxford (MA Modern Hist.). RAF, 1955–57. Colonial Office, 1960–64; Asst Private Sec. to Commonwealth and Colonial Sec., 1963–64; HM Diplomatic Service, 1965; First Sec., Brussels, 1966–68, Lagos, 1968–72; S. Asian Dept, FCO, 1972–75; First Sec. (Economic), Istanbul, 1975–78; Head of Chancery, Lima, 1978–82; E African Dept, FCO, 1982–84; Actg Dep. High Comr, Bombay, 1985. SBStJ. *Recreations:* travel, cinema, cricket, tennis, colonial history. *Address:* c/o Foreign and Commonwealth Office, SW1. *Clubs:* MCC; Bengal, Tollygunge, Calcutta (Calcutta).

DOBLE, John Frederick, OBE 1981; HM Diplomatic Service; Consul General, Edmonton, since 1985; *b* 30 June 1941; *s* of Comdr Douglas Doble, RN and Marcella (*née* Cowan); *m* 1975, Isabella Margaret Ruth, *d* of Col. W. H. Whitbread, *qv*; one *d. Educ:* Sunningdale; Eton (Scholar); RMA Sandhurst; Hertford College, Oxford. 17th/21st Lancers, 1959–69 (Captain); attached Lord Strathcona's Horse (Royal Canadians), 1967–69; joined HM Diplomatic Service, 1969; Arabian Dept, FCO, 1969–72; Beirut, 1972–73; UK deleg. to NATO, Brussels, 1973–77; Commonwealth Coordination Dept, FCO, 1977–78. Maputo, 1978–81; Inf. Dept, FCO, 1981–83; attached Barclays Bank International, 1983–85. *Recreations:* manual labour, horse and water sports, history. *Address:* c/o Foreign and Commonwealth Office, SW1A 2AH. *Clubs:* Royal Commonwealth Society; Poplar, Blackwall and District Rowing.

DOBREE, John Hatherley, MS, FRCS; Consulting Ophthalmic Surgeon, St Bartholomew's Hospital, London, EC1 (Consultant 1956); Honorary Ophthalmic Surgeon, North Middlesex Hospital, N18 (Senior Ophthalmic Surgeon 1947); *b* 25 April 1914; *s* of Hatherley Moor Dobree, OBE, and Muriel Dobree (*née* Hope); *m* 1941, Evelyn Maud Smyth; two *s. Educ:* Victoria Coll., Jersey; St Bartholomew's Hosp. MS London 1947; FRCS 1950. House Physician, Metropolitan Hosp., E8, 1938–39; House Surgeon, Western Ophthalm. Hosp., 1940. Served in RAMC, 1940–46, in MEF, as RMO and Ophthalmic Specialist. Chief Asst, Eye Dept, St Bartholomew's Hosp., 1946–51. FRSocMed (Past Sec., Sect. of Ophthalmology); Vice-Pres. and Past Hon. Sec. Ophthalmological Soc. of UK; Dep. Master, Oxford Ophth. Congress, 1976. *Publications:* The Retina, vol. x, in Sir Stewart Duke-Elder's System of Ophthalmology, 1967; (with E. S. Perkins) Differential Diagnosis of Fundus Conditions, 1971; (with E. Boulter) Blindness and Visual Handicap, the Facts, 1982. *Recreations:* archaeology, walking. *Address:* 113 Harley Street, W1. *T:* 01–935 9189; 2 Nottingham Terrace, NW1. *T:* 01–486 6227.

DOBROSIELSKI, Marian, PhD Zürich; Banner of Labour, 1st Class 1975 (2nd Class 1973); Knight Cross of the Order of Polonia Restituta, 1964; Professor of Philosophy, Warsaw University, since 1974; Ambassador *ad personam*, since 1973; *b* 25 March 1923; *s* of Stanislaw and Stefania Dobrosielski; *m* 1950; one *d. Educ:* Univ. of Zürich; Univ. of Warsaw. Served in Polish Army in France, War of 1939–45. With Min. of Foreign Affairs, 1948–81; Polish Legation, Bern, 1948–50; Head of Section, Min. of Foreign Affairs, 1950–54; Asst Prof., Warsaw Univ. and Polish Acad. of Sciences, 1954–57; Mem. Polish delegn to UN Gen. Assembly, 1952, 1953, 1958, 1966, 1972, 1976. First Sec., Counsellor, Polish Embassy in Washington, 1958–64; Min. of Foreign Affairs: Counsellor

to Minister, 1964–69; Acting Dir, Research Office, 1968–69; Polish Ambassador to London, 1969–71; Dir, Polish Inst. of Internat. Affairs, 1971–80; Dep. Minister of Foreign Affairs, 1978–81. Univ. of Warsaw: Associate Prof., 1966; Vice-Dean of Faculty of Philosophy, 1966–68; Dir, Inst. of Philosophy, 1971–73 (Chm. Scientific Council, 1969). Chm., Editorial Bd of Studia Filozoficzne, 1968–69; Sec., Polish Philos. Soc., 1955–57 and 1965–69. Mem. Polish United Workers Party (Sec. Party Org., Univ. of Warsaw, 1956–57, 1968–69); Chm., Polish Cttee for European Security and Co operation, 1973–79 (Vice-Chm., 1971–73); Vice-Chm., Cttee on Peace Research, Polish Acad. of Scis, 1984–. Hon. Vice-Pres., Scottish-Polish Cultural Assoc., Glasgow, 1969–71; Chm., Polish delegn to: 2nd stage Conf. on Security and Co-operation in Europe, 1973–75; CSCE Belgrade Meeting, 1977–78; CSCE Meeting, Madrid, 1980–81. *Publications:* A Basic Epistemological Principle of Logical Positivism, 1947; The Philosophical Pragmatism of C. S. Peirce, 1967; On some contemporary problems: Philosophy, Ideology, Politics, 1970; (trans. and introd) Selection of Aphorisms of G. C. Lichtenberg, Oscar Wilde, Karl Kraus, M. von Ebner-Eschenbach, Mark Twain, C. Norwid, 1970–85; On the Theory and Practice of Peaceful Coexistence, 1976; Belgrad 77, 1978; Chances and Dilemmas, 1980; The Crisis in Poland, 1984; numerous articles on philosophy and internat. problems in professional jls. *Recreation:* tennis. *Address:* Kozia Street 9–14, Warszawa, Poland.

DOBRY, George Leon Severyn, CBE 1977; QC 1969; **His Honour Judge George Dobry;** a Circuit Judge, since 1980; *b* 1 Nov. 1918; *m* 1st, 1948, Margaret Headley Smith (*d* 1978), *e d* of late Joseph Quartus Smith, JP, Bardfield, Saling, Essex; two *d*; 2nd, 1982, Rosemary Anne Alexander, *d* of Charles Edward Wilson Sleigh, Bridge of Allan, Stirlingshire. *Educ:* Edinburgh Univ. (MA). Served War of 1939–45: Army, 1939–42; Air Force, 1942–46. Called to Bar, Inner Temple, 1946; Bencher 1977. A Recorder of the Crown Court, 1977–80. Mem. Council, Justice, 1956–68. Adviser to Sec. of State for Environment and Sec. of State for Wales on Develt Control, 1973–75; Mem., Docklands Jt Cttee, 1974–76. *Publications:* Woodfall's Law of Landlord and Tenant, 25th edition (one of the Editors), 1952; Blundell and Dobry, Town and Country Planning, 1962; Blundell and Dobry Planning Appeals and Inquiries, 1962, 3rd edn, 1982; Hill and Redman, Landlord and Tenant (Cons. Editor), 16th edn, 1976; Review of the Development Control System (Interim Report), 1974 (Final Report), 1975; (ed jtly) Development Gains Tax, 1975; (Gen. Editor) Encyclopedia of Development Law, 1976. *Address:* 40 Chester Row, SW1W 8JP. *T:* 01–730 7335; Great Lodge, Great Bardfield, near Braintree, Essex CM7 4QD. *T:* Great Dunmow 810776. *Clubs:* Garrick, Travellers'.

DOBSON, Maj.-Gen. Anthony Henry George, CB 1968; OBE 1953; MC 1944; BA Cantab; *b* 15 Dec. 1911; *s* of late Col Arthur Curtis Dobson, DSO, Royal Engineers, and late Susanna (*née* Oppenheim); *m* 1945, Nellie Homberger; two *s* two *d. Educ:* Cheltenham Coll.; Royal Military Academy, Woolwich; Clare Coll., Cambridge. Commissioned Royal Engineers, 1931; hons degree (mech. science), Cambridge, 1934; service in UK, 1934–37; seconded to RAF for survey duties, Iraq, 1938–39. Served War of 1939–45: Middle East (Egypt, Turkey, Iraq), 1939–42; Prisoner of War, Italy, 1942–43; interned in Switzerland after escape, 1944; North-West Europe (Holland and Germany), 1945. Germany, 1945–50; Manpower planning Dept, War Office, 1950–53; in comd, Engineer Regt, Hong Kong, 1953–56; Engr branch, War Office, 1956–59; Chief Engr, HQ Eastern Comd, UK, 1959–62; DQMG, HQ BAOR, 1962–64; Chief Engr, HQ North AG/BAOR, 1964–67, retd. Lt-Col 1945; Col 1956; Brig. 1959; Maj.-Gen. 1964. Planning Inspectorate, DoE, 1969–78. *Recreations:* travel, gardening. *Address:* Ramillies, Compton Way, Moor Park, Farnham, Surrey. *T:* Runfold 2350. *Clubs:* Army and Navy, Ski Club of Great Britain; Kandahar Ski; International Lions.

DOBSON, Christopher Selby Austin, CBE 1976; FSA; Librarian, House of Lords, 1956–77; *b* 25 Aug. 1916; *s* of late Alban Tabor Austin Dobson, CB, CVO, CBE; *m* 1941, Helen Broughton (*d* 1984), *d* of late Capt. E. B. Turner, Holyhead; one *d* (one *s* decd). *Educ:* Clifton Coll.; Emmanuel Coll., Cambridge (BA). With National Council of Social Service, 1938–39. Served War of 1939–45, Lieut Middx Regt (despatches). Asst Principal (Temp.), Ministry of Education, 1946–47; Asst Librarian, House of Lords, 1947–56. *Publication:* (ed) Oxfordshire Protestation Returns 1641–42, 1955. *Recreations:* collecting books, stamps, etc. *Address:* Loxbeech, Mount Street, Battle, Sussex. *T:* Battle 4409. *Clubs:* Roxburghe; (Hon.) Rowfant (Cleveland).

DOBSON, Sir Denis (William), KCB 1969 (CB 1959); OBE 1945; QC 1971; Clerk of the Crown in Chancery and Permanent Secretary to the Lord Chancellor, 1968–77; *b* 17 Oct. 1908; *s* of late William Gordon Dobson, Newcastle upon Tyne; *m* 1st, 1934, Thelma (marr. diss. 1947), *d* of Charles Swinburne, Newcastle upon Tyne; one *s* one *d*; 2nd, 1948, Mary Elizabeth, *d* of J. A. Allen, Haywards Heath; two *s* one *d. Educ:* Charterhouse; Trinity Coll., Cambridge (MA, LLB). Solicitor, 1933. Served in RAF, 1940–45 (Desert Air Force, 1942–45). Called to the Bar, Middle Temple, 1951; Bencher, 1968. Dep. Clerk of the Crown in Chancery and Asst Permanent Sec. to Lord Chancellor, 1954–68. Mem., Adv. Council on Public Records, 1977–83. *Address:* 50 Egerton Crescent, SW3. *T:* 01–589 7990. *Club:* Athenæum.

DOBSON, Frank Gordon; MP (Lab) Holborn and St Pancras, since 1983 (Holborn and St Pancras South, 1979–83); *b* 15 March 1940; *s* of James William and Irene Shortland Dobson, York; *m* 1967, Janet Mary, *d* of Henry and Edith Alker; three *c. Educ:* Dunnington County Primary Sch., York; Archbishop Holgate's Grammar Sch., York; London School of Economics (BScEcon). Administrative jobs with Central Electricity Generating Bd, 1962–70, and Electricity Council, 1970–75; Asst Sec., Commn for Local Administration (local Ombudsman's office), 1975–79. Member, Camden Borough Council, 1971–76 (Leader of Council, 1973–75); Chm., Coram's Fields and Harmsworth Meml Playground, 1977–. NUR sponsored MP; front bench spokesman on educn, 1981–83, on health, 1983–. Chm., NHS Unlimited, 1981–. Member: Exec., Chile Solidarity Campaign, 1979–; Nat. Cttee, Anti Apartheid Movement, 1980–. Governor, LSE, 1986–. *Address:* 22 Great Russell Mansions, Great Russell Street, WC1. *T:* 01–242 5760. *Club:* Covent Garden Community Centre.

DOBSON, Sir Patrick John H.; *see* Howard-Dobson.

DOBSON, Sir Richard (Portway), Kt 1976; President, BAT Industries Ltd, 1976–79; *b* 11 Feb. 1914; *s* of Prof. J. F. Dobson; *m* 1946, Emily Margaret Carver; one step *d. Educ:* Clifton Coll.; King's Coll., Cambridge. Flt-Lt, RAF, 1941–45 (Pilot). Joined British American Tobacco Co. Ltd, 1935: served in China, 1936–40; China, Rhodesia and London, 1946–76: Dir, 1955; Dep. Chm., 1962; Vice-Chm., 1968; Chm., 1970–76. Director: Molins Ltd, 1970–84; Commonwealth Development Finance, 1974–79; Exxon Corporation (USA), 1975–84; Davy Corp. Ltd, 1975–85; Foseco Minsep, 1976–85; Lloyds Bank International, 1976–84; Chm., British Leyland Ltd, 1976–77. Chm., British-North American Res. Assoc., 1976–80. *Publication:* China Cycle, 1946. *Recreations:* fly fishing, golf. *Address:* 16 Marchmont Road, Richmond upon Thames, Surrey. *T:* 01–940 1504. *Clubs:* United Oxford & Cambridge University; Richmond Golf.

DOBSON, Susan, (Sue); Editor, Woman and Home, since 1982; *b* 31 Jan. 1946; *d* of Arthur and Nellie Henshaw; *m* 1966, Michael Dobson (marr. diss. 1974). *Educ:* convent schs; BA Hons CNAA. From 1964, a glorious collection of women's magazines, including

Femina and Fair Lady in S Africa, working variously as fashion, cookery, beauty, home and contributing editor, editor at SA Institute of Race Relations and editor of Wedding Day and Successful Slimming in London, with breaks somewhere in between in PR and doing research into the language and learning of children. *Publication*: The Wedding Day Book, 1981. *Recreations*: relaxing, reading, travelling, exploring. *Address*: The Cottage, Knotts Lane, St Margarets-at-Cliffe, Kent CT15 6BH. *T*: (office) 01–261 5423.

DOCHERTY, Dr Daniel Joseph, JP; General Medical Practitioner, since 1949; *b* 24 Oct. 1924; *s* of Michael Joseph Docherty and Ellen Stewart; *m* 1952, Dr Rosemary Catherine Kennedy; eight *s* two *d*. *Educ*: St Aloysius' Coll.; Anderson Coll. of Medicine; Glasgow Univ. LRCP, LRCS, LRFPS. MO, King's Flight, RAF Benson, 1950; pt-time Examng MO, DHSS, 1982–. Glasgow Town Councillor, 1959–75; Sen. Magistrate, City of Glasgow, 1964–65; Chm. of Police Cttee, 1967–68; Chm. of Educn Cttee, 1971–74. Mem., MSC, 1974–77; Chm. in Scotland, Job Creation Programme, 1975–78. Member: Strathclyde Univ. Ct, 1971–72; Glasgow Univ. Ct, 1972–74; Council, Open Univ., 1972–75. JP Glasgow, 1961. *Recreation*: travel. *Address*: 26 Newlands Road, Glasgow G43 2JE. *T*: 041–632 5031; Govan Health Centre, 295 Langlands Road, Glasgow G51 4BJ. *T*: 041–440 1212.

DOCKER, Rt. Rev. Ivor Colin; *see* Horsham, Bishop Suffragan of.

DODD, Air Vice-Marshal Frank Leslie, CBE 1968; DSO 1944; DFC 1945; AFC 1944 and Bars, 1955 and 1958; AE 1945; Administrator, MacRobert Trusts, 1974–85; *b* 5 March 1919; *s* of Frank H. Dodd and Lillian (*née* Willis); *m* 1942, Joyce L. Banyard; one *s* three *d*. *Educ*: King Edward VI Sch., Stafford; Reading University. RAFVR, 1938; CFS course and Flying Instructor, 1940–44; No 544 Sqdn (photo-reconnaissance), 1944–46; CO 45 Sqdn (Beaufighters), 1947–48; CFS Staff and HQ Flying Trng Comd, 1948–52; pfc 1952–53; Chief Instructor CFS, 1953–55; psc 1955; CO 230 OCU Waddington (Vulcans),1955–59; Gp Captain Trng HQ Bomber Comd, 1959–61; CO RAF Coningsby (Vulcans), 1961–63; idc 1964; AOC and Comdt CFS, 1965–68; MoD (Dir Estabs), 1968–70. Dir Gen., Linesman Project, 1970–74, retired. *Recreations*: golf, music, photography. *Address*: c/o Barclays Bank, Market Square, Stafford. *Club*: Royal Air Force.

DODD, Rev. Harold, MB, ChM (Liverpool), FRCS, LRCP; Hon. Curate, All Soul's Church, W1, 1970–81, retired; Emeritus Surgeon to: St Mary's Hospital Group, Paddington; King George Hospital, Ilford; Royal Hospital, Richmond; Royal London Homoeopathic Hospital; *b* 13 March 1899; *e s* of Alfred Ledward Dodd and Annie Elizabeth Marshall; *m* 1945, Mary, *yr d* of late R. H. Bond; one *s*. *Educ*: University of Liverpool; Guy's Hosp. RAF (pilot), 1917–19; MB, ChB (Distinction in Surgery) Liverpool, 1922, O. T. Williams Prizeman for 1923; House Surgeon, House Physician, Surgical Tutor and Registrar, Liverpool Royal Infirmary, 1923–26; Asst Medical Superintendent, St Luke's Hosp., Chelsea, 1926–28; Resident Medical Officer, Royal Northern Hosp., N7, 1928–30. Past Pres., Assoc. of Consultants and Specialists of Reg. Bd Hosps. Fellow, Assoc. of Surgeons of Great Britain; FRSM (Ex-Pres. Section of Proctology). *Publications*: (with F. B. Cockett) Pathology and Surgery of the Veins of the Lower Limb, 1956, 2nd edn, 1976; surgical papers in medical journals. *Address*: 8 Park Close, Ilchester Place, W14 8ND. *T*: 01–602 3024.

DODD, Prof. James Munro, DSc, PhD; FRS 1975; FRSE; Professor of Zoology, University College of North Wales, 1968–81, now Emeritus; Leverhulme Emeritus Fellowship, 1982–83; *b* 26 May 1915; *m* 1951, Margaret Helen Ingram Macaulay (*née* Greig), BSc (Aberdeen), PhD (Harvard); three *s*. *Educ*: The White House Sch., Brampton, Cumberland; Univ. of Liverpool. BSc hons (Cl. 1) 1937; DipEd 1938. PhD St Andrews, 1953; DSc St Andrews, 1968. Biology Master, Cardigan Grammar Sch., 1938–40. Royal Air Force (Navigator and Staff Navigator), 1940–46. Asst in Zoology, Univ. of Aberdeen, 1946–47; Lectr in Zoology, Univ. of St Andrews, in charge of Gatty Marine Laboratory, 1947–57; Reader in Zoology, Univ. of St Andrews, and Dir of Gatty Marine Laboratory, 1957–60; Prof. of Zoology, Leeds Univ., 1960–68. Chm., British Nat. Cttee for Biology, 1976–81 (Chm., Zoology Sub-Cttee, 1972–76). Member Council: Freshwater Biol Assoc.; Scottish Marine Biol Assoc. Assessor, ARC, 1981–82. Trustee, BM (Natural History), 1975–82. Royal Society Representative: Internat. Trust for Zool Nomenclature; Court, Univ. of Wales. Hon. Member: British Soc. for Endocrinology; European Soc. for Comparative Endocrinol. FRSE 1957. Editor in Chief, General and Comparative Endocrinology, 1973–78; Associate Editor: Proceedings of the Royal Soc., series B; Philosophical Trans of the Royal Soc., series B, 1978–83, 1985–. Frink Medal, Zool Soc. of London, 1982. *Publications*: contributor to Marshall's Physiology of Reproduction (3rd and 4th edns), The Thyroid Gland, The Pituitary Gland, The Ovary, and to zoological and endocrinological jls. *Recreations*: fishing, photography, music. *Address*: Weirglodd Wen, Bulkeley Road, Bangor, Gwynedd LL57 2BP.

DODD, Kenneth Arthur, (Ken Dodd), OBE 1982; professional entertainer, comedian, singer and actor, since 1957; *b* 1931; *s* of Arthur and late Sarah Dodd; unmarried. *Educ*: Holt High Sch., Liverpool. Frequently appears at the Palladium, London, etc. Pantomime, Robinson Crusoe, Coventry Theatre, 1969–70; Malvolio in Twelfth Night, Liverpool, 1971; HaHa, Liverpool, 1973; Aladdin, Coventry, 1982. *Relevant publication*: How Tickled I Am: Ken Dodd, by Michael Billington, 1977. *Recreations*: racing, soccer, reading. *Address*: 76 Thomas Lane, Knotty Ash, Liverpool L14 5NX.

DODD, William Atherton, CMG 1983; Consultant: University of London Institute of Education, since 1983; University College, Cardiff, since 1983; *b* 5 Feb. 1923; *s* of Frederick Dodd and Sarah Atherton; *m* 1949, Marjorie Penfold; two *d*. *Educ*: Chester City Grammar Sch.; Christ's Coll., Cambridge (MA, CertEd). Served War, 1942–45: Captain, 8 Gurkha Rifles. Sen. History Master, Ipswich Sch., 1947–52; Educn Officer, Dept of Educn, Tanganyika, 1952–61; Sen. Educn Officer, Min. of Educn, Tanzania, 1961–65; Lectr, Dept of Educn in Developing Countries, Univ. of London Inst. of Educn, 1965–70; Educn Adviser, ODM, 1970–77; Chief Educn Advr, 1978–83, and Under Sec. (Educn Div.), 1980–83, ODA; UK Mem., Unesco Exec. Bd, 1983–85. *Publications*: A Mapbook of Exploration, 1965; Primary School Inspection in New Countries, 1968; Education for Self-Reliance in Tanzania, 1969; (with J. Cameron) Society, Schools and Progress in Tanzania, 1970; (ed) Teacher at Work, 1970; (with C. Criper) Report on the Teaching of the English Language in Tanzania, 1985. *Recreations*: walking, music, cricket. *Address*: 20 Bayham Road, Sevenoaks, Kent TN13 3XD. *T*: Sevenoaks 454238. *Clubs*: MCC; Sevenoaks Vine.

DODD, Rev. William Harold Alfred; *see* Dodd, Harold.

DODDERIDGE, Morris, CBE 1974 (OBE 1962); British Council Representative, Rome, 1970–75, retired; *b* 17 Oct. 1915; *s* of Reginald William Dodderidge and Amy Andrew; *m* 1941, Esme Williams; two *s* one *d*. *Educ*: Hertford Grammar Sch.; King's Coll., London; Inst. Educn, London. BA 1st cl. hons English 1937; Brewer Prize for Lit.; Teachers Dip. 1938; DipEd 1952. Asst Master, Hele's Sch., Exeter, 1938–40. War of 1939–45, Royal Signals; served N Africa, Italy, Austria (Captain, despatches). Joined British Council, 1946: Dir of Studies, Milan, 1947–53; Rep., Norway, 1953–57; Teaching of English Liaison Officer, 1957–59; Dir, Recruitment Dept, 1959–64; Controller:

Recruitment Div., 1964–66; Overseas Div. A, 1966–67; Home Div. I, 1967–68; Appts Div., 1968–70. *Publications*: Man on the Matterhorn, 1940; (with W. R. Lee) Time for a Song, 1965. *Recreations*: golf, swimming. *Address*: River Cottage, Church Street, Presteigne, Powys LD8 2BU. *T*: Presteigne 267609.

DODDS, Denis George, CBE 1977; LLB (London); CompIEE; Solicitor; Chairman, British Approval Service for Electricity Cables Ltd, since 1982; *b* 25 May 1913; *s* of Herbert Yeaman Dodds and Violet Katharine Dodds; *m* 1937, Muriel Reynolds Smith; two *s* three *d*. *Educ*: Rutherford Coll., Newcastle upon Tyne; King's Coll., Durham Univ. Asst Solicitor and Asst Town Clerk, Gateshead, 1936–41. Served Royal Navy (Lieut RNVR), 1941–46. Dep. Town Clerk and Dep. Clerk of the Peace, City of Cardiff, 1946–48; Sec., S Wales Electricity Board, 1948–56; Chief Industrial Relations Officer, CEA and Industrial Relations Adviser, Electricity Council, 1957–59; Dep. Chm., 1960–62, Chm., 1962–77, Merseyside and N Wales Electricity Bd; Chairman: Merseyside Chamber of Commerce and Industry, 1976–78; Port of Preston Adv. Bd, 1978; Assoc. of Members of State Industry Boards, 1976–. Member: CBI Council for Wales, 1960–78; NW Economic Planning Council, 1971; Dir, Development Corporation for Wales, 1970–83. Mem., Nat. Adv. Council for Employment of the Disabled, 1978–. *Recreations*: music and gardening. *Address*: Corners, 28 Grange Park, Westbury on Trym, Bristol BS9 4BP. *T*: Bristol 621440.

DODDS, George Christopher Buchanan, CMG 1977; Assistant Under-Secretary of State, Ministry of Defence, 1964–76; *b* 8 Oct. 1916; *o* s of George Hepple Dodds and Gladys Marion (*née* Ferguson), Newcastle upon Tyne; *m* 1944, Olive Florence Wilmot Ling; no *c*. *Educ*: Rugby; Gonville and Caius Coll., Cambridge (BA). Entered Secretary's Dept, Admiralty, 1939; Royal Marines, 1940–41; Private Sec. to Sec. of the Admiralty, 1941–43; Asst Private Sec. to Prime Minister, June-Aug. 1944; Asst Sec., 1951; idc, 1959. *Recreations*: bird-watching, walking, golf, bridge. *Address*: 5 Bryanston Square, W1. *T*: 01–262 2852. *Club*: Royal Mid-Surrey Golf.

DODDS, James Pickering, CB 1954; Under-Secretary, Department of Health and Social Security, 1968–73; *b* 7 Feb. 1913; *s* of James Thompson and Elizabeth Fingland Dodds; *m* 1942, Ethel Mary Gill; two *d*. *Educ*: Queen Elizabeth's Grammar Sch., Darlington; Jesus Coll., Cambridge. Entered Ministry of Health, 1935; Nuffield Home Civil Service Travelling Fellowship, 1950; Under-Sec., 1951; Dir of Establishments and Orgn, 1965–68. *Address*: 17 Herne Road, Oundle, Peterborough PE8 4BS.

DODDS, Sir Ralph (Jordan), 2nd Bt *cr* 1964; *b* 25 March 1928; *o s* of Sir (Edward) Charles Dodds, 1st Bt, MVO, FRS, and Constance Elizabeth (*d* 1969), *o d* of late J. T. Jordan, Darlington; *S* father; 1973; *m* 1954, Marion, *er d* of late Sir Daniel Thomas Davies, KCVO; two *d*. *Educ*: Winchester; RMA, Sandhurst. Regular commission, 13/18th Royal Hussars, 1948; served UK and abroad; Malaya, 1953 (despatches); resigned, 1958. Underwriting Member of Lloyd's, 1964. *Address*: Picton House, Thames Ditton, Surrey. *Clubs*: Cavalry and Guards, Hurlingham.

DODDS-PARKER, Sir (Arthur) Douglas, Kt 1973; MA (Oxford); company director since 1946; *b* 5 July 1909; *o s* of A. P. Dodds-Parker, FRCS, Oxford; *m* 1946, Aileen, *d* of late Norman B. Coster and late Mrs Alvin Dodd, Grand Detour, Ill., USA; one *s*. *Educ*: Winchester; Magdalen Coll., Oxford. BA in Modern History, 1930; MA 1934. Entered Sudan Political Service, 1930; Kordofan Province, 1931–34; Asst Private Sec. to Governor-General, Khartoum, 1934–35; Blue Nile Province, 1935–38; Public Security Dept, Khartoum, 1938–39; resigned 1938; joined Grenadier Guards, 1939; employed on special duties, March 1940; served in London, Cairo, East African campaign, North Africa, Italy and France, 1940–45; Col, 1944 (despatches, French Legion of Honour, Croix de Guerre). MP (C): Banbury Div. of Oxon, 1945–Sept. 1959; Cheltenham, 1964–Sept. 1974; Jt Parly Under-Sec. of State for Foreign Affairs, Nov. 1953–Oct. 1954, Dec. 1955–Jan. 1957; Parly Under-Sec. for Commonwealth Relations, Oct. 1954–Dec. 1955. Chairman: British Empire Producers Organisation; Joint East and Central Africa Board, 1947–50; Conservative Commonwealth Council, 1960–64; Cons. Parly Foreign and Commonwealth Cttee, 1970–73; Europe Atlantic Gp, 1976–79; Delegate to Council of Europe, North Atlantic and W European Assemblies, 1965–72; Mem., British Parly Delegn to European Parlt, Strasbourg, 1973–75. Mem., Regtl Bd, FANY, 1945–. Freeman, City of London, 1983. *Publications*: Setting Europe Ablaze, 1983; Political Eunuch, 1986. *Address*: 9 North Court, Great Peter Street, SW1; The Lighthouse, West Port, New York 12993, USA. *Clubs*: Carlton, Special Forces (Pres., 1977–81); Leander, Institute of Directors.

DODGE, John V.; Senior Editorial Consultant, Encyclopædia Britannica, since 1972; Chairman, Board of Editors, Encyclopædia Britannica Publishers, since 1977; *b* 25 Sept. 1909; *s* of George Dannel Dodge and Mary Helen Porter; *m* 1935, Jean Elizabeth Plate; two *s* two *d*. *Educ*: Northwestern Univ., Evanston, Ill., USA; Univ. of Bordeaux, Bordeaux, France. Free-lance writer, 1931–32; Editor, Northwestern Alumni News and official publications of Northwestern Univ., 1932–35; Exec. Sec., Northwestern Univ. Alumni Assoc., 1937–38; Asst Editor, Encyclopædia Britannica, and Associate Editor, Britannica Book of the Year, 1938–43. US Army, 1943–46 (Intelligence). Associate Editor, Ten Eventful Years and Asst Editor, Encyclopædia Britannica, 1946–50; Editor, Britannica World Language Dictionary, 1954; Managing Editor, Encyclopædia, 1950–60; Executive Editor, 1960–64; Senior Vice-Pres., Editorial, 1964–65; Senior Editorial Consultant, 1965–70; Vice-Pres., Editorial, 1970–72. Conseiller Editorial, Encyclopædia Universalis (Paris), 1968–; Editorial Advisor: Britannica Internat. Encyclopædia (in Japanese), Tokyo, 1969–; Enciclopedia Mirador (Rio de Janeiro) and Enciclopedia Barsa (Mexico City), 1974–. *Address*: 3851 Mission Hills Road, Northbrook, Ill 60062, USA. *T*: (312) 272–0254.

DODSON, family name of Baron Monk Bretton.

DODSON, Sir Derek (Sherborne Lindsell), KCMG 1975 (CMG 1963); MC 1945; HM Diplomatic Service, retired; Special Representative of Secretary of State for Foreign and Commonwealth Affairs, since 1981; *b* 20 Jan. 1920; *e* and *o* surv. *s* of late Charles Sherborne Dodson, MD, and Irene Frances Lindsell; *m* 1952, Julie Maynard Barnes; one *s* one *d*. *Educ*: Stowe; RMC Sandhurst. Commissioned as 2nd Lieut in Royal Scots Fusiliers, 1939, and served in Army until Feb. 1948. Served War of 1939–45 (MC): India, UK, Middle East, and with Partisans in Greece and N Italy. Mil. Asst to Brit. Comr, Allied Control Commn for Bulgaria, July 1945–Sept. 1946; GSO 3, War Office, Oct. 1946–Nov. 1947; apptd a Mem. HM Foreign Service, 1948; 2nd Sec., 1948; Acting Vice-Consul at Salonika, Sept. 1948; Acting Consul Gen. there in 1949 and 1950; Second Sec., Madrid, 1951; promoted First Sec., Oct. 1951; transferred to Foreign Office, Sept. 1953; apptd Private Sec. to Minister of State for Foreign Affairs, 1955; First Sec. and Head of Chancery, Prague, Nov. 1958; Chargé d'Affaires there in 1959, 1960, 1961, 1962; promoted and apptd Consul at Elisabethville, 1962; Transf. FO and apptd Head of the Central Dept, 1963; Counsellor, British Embassy, Athens, 1966–69; Ambassador: to Hungary, 1970–73; to Brazil, 1973–77; to Turkey, 1977–80. Chm., Beaver Guarantee Ltd, 1984–86; Dir, Benguela Rly Co., 1984–. Chm., Anglo-Turkish Soc., 1982–. Mem., Bd of Governors, United World College of the Atlantic, 1982–. Order of the Southern Cross, Brazil.

Recreations: shooting, fishing, walking. *Address:* 47 Ovington Street, SW3. *T:* 01–589 5055; Gable House, Leadenham, Lincoln. *T:* Loveden 72212. *Clubs:* Boodle's, Travellers'.

DODSON, Robert North; *see* North, R.

DODSWORTH, Geoffrey Hugh, FCA, JP; Chairman, Oceanic Financial Services, since 1985; Deputy Chairman, Oceanic Finance Corporation, since 1985; *b* 7 June 1928; *s* of late Walter J. J. Dodsworth and Doris M. Baxter; *m* 1st, 1949, Isabel Neale (decd); one *d*; 2nd, 1971, Elizabeth Ann Beeston; one *s* one *d*. *Educ:* St Peter's Sch., York. MP (C) Herts SW, Feb. 1974–Oct. 1979, resigned. Mem. York City Council, 1959–65; JP York 1961, later JP Herts. Dir, Grindlays Bank Ltd, 1976–80; Chief Exec., Grindlay Brandts Ltd, 1977–80; Pres. and Chief Exec., Oceanic Finance Corp., 1980–85. *Recreation:* riding. *Address:* Well Hall, Well, Bedale, N Yorks DL8 2PX. *T:* Bedale 70223. *Club:* Carlton.

DODSWORTH, Sir John Christopher S.; *see* Smith-Dodsworth.

DODWELL, Prof. Charles Reginald, MA, PhD, LittD; FBA 1973; FRHistS, FSA; Pilkington Professor of History of Art and Director of Whitworth Gallery, University of Manchester, since 1966; *b* 3 Feb. 1922; *s* of William Henry Walter and Blanche Dodwell; *m* 1942, Sheila Juliet Fletcher; one *s* one *d*. *Educ:* Gonville and Caius Coll., Cambridge (MA, PhD, LittD). Served War, Navy, 1941–45. Research Fellow, Caius Coll., 1950–51. Sen. Research Fellow, Warburg Inst., 1950–53; Lambeth Librarian, 1953–58; Fellow, Lectr, Librarian, Trinity Coll., Cambridge, 1958–66. Visiting scholar, Inst. of Advanced Studies, Princeton, USA, 1965–66. *Publications:* The Canterbury School of Illumination, 1954; Lambeth Palace, 1958; The Great Lambeth Bible, 1959; The St Albans Psalter (section 2) 1960; Theophilus: De Diversis Artibus, 1961; Reichenau Reconsidered, 1965; Painting in Europe 800–1200, 1971; Early English Manuscripts in Facsimile, vol. xviii (section 2), 1972; Anglo-Saxon Art: a new perspective, 1982; articles in Burlington Magazine, Gazette des Beaux Arts, Atti del 18 Congresso Internazionale di studi sull'alto medioevo (Spoleto), Jumièges, Congrès Scientifique du 13 Centenaire, l'Archéologie, etc. *Recreations:* badminton, table-tennis. *Address:* The Old House, 12 Park Road, Cheadle Hulme, Cheshire SK8 7DA. *T:* 061–485 3923.

DOGGART, George Hubert Graham; Headmaster, King's School, Bruton, 1972–85; *b* 18 July 1925; *e s* of late Alexander Graham Doggart and Grace Carlisle Hannan; *m* 1960, Susan Mary, *d* of R. I. Beattie, Eastbourne; one *s* two *d*. *Educ:* Winchester; King's Coll., Cambridge. BA History, 1950; MA 1955. Army, 1943–47 (Sword of Honour, 161 OCTU, Mons, 1944); Coldstream Guards. On staff at Winchester, 1950–72 (exchange at Melbourne C of E Grammar Sch., 1963); Housemaster, 1964–72. HMC Schools rep. on Nat. Cricket Assoc., 1964–75; President: English Schools Cricket Assoc., 1965–; Quidnuncs, 1983–; Cricket Soc., 1983–; Member: Cricket Council, 1968–71, 1972, 1983–; MCC Cttee, 1975–78, 1979–81, 1982– (Pres., 1981–82). Captain, Butterflies CC, 1986–. *Publication:* (ed) The Heart of Cricket: memoir of H. S. Altham, 1967. *Recreations:* literary and sporting (captained Cambridge v Oxford at cricket, Association football, rackets and squash, 1949–50; played in Rugby fives, 1950; played for England v W Indies, two tests, 1950; captained Sussex, 1954). *Address:* 19 Westgate, Chichester, West Sussex PO19 3ET. *Clubs:* MCC, Lord's Taverners', Hawks (Cambridge).

DOGGART, James Hamilton, MA, MD, FRCS; Consulting Surgeon, Moorfields, Westminster and Central Eye Hospital and Hospital for Sick Children, Great Ormond Street; Past Chairman, British Orthoptic Board; FRSM; Livery of the Society of Apothecaries of London; Ophthalmological Society, Société belge d'Ophtalmologie, Société française d'Ophtalmologie; Hon. Member: Australian, NZ and Peruvian Ophthalmological Societies; Oto-Neuro-Ophth. Soc. of the Argentine; Canadian Ophthalmological Society; formerly: Lecturer, Institute of Ophthalmology; Examiner: for British Orthoptic Board; (in Fellowship of Ophthalmology) RCSI; Faculty of Ophth. representative on Council of RCS; Examiner in Ophthalmology, Royal Coll. of Surgeons and Physicians, University of Belfast, and for FRCS, 1954–60; formerly Pres. and Mem. Council, Faculty of Ophthalmologists and Fellow and Councillor, Hunterian Society; Hon. Secretary, Editorial Committee, British Journal Ophthalmology; surgeon-oculist in London, 1929–72; *b* 22 Jan. 1900; *s* of late Arthur Robert Doggart, Bishop Auckland; *m* 1st, 1928, Doris Hilda Mennell; one *d*; 2nd, 1938, Leonora Sharpley Gatti; one *s*. *Educ:* Bishop's Stortford Coll.; King's Coll., Cambridge (Scholar); St Thomas's Hospital. Surg. Sub-Lt, RNVR, 1918; Schol., King's Coll., Cambridge, 1919–22; Mem. Anglo-American Physiological Exped. to Andes, 1921; Ophth. Ho. Surg., St Thomas's Hosp., 1923–24; Ho. Surg., Casualty Officer, Royal Northern Hosp., 1925–26; appts at Royal Westminster Ophthalmic Hosp.: Clinical Asst, Refraction Asst, Chief Clin. Asst and Pathologist, 1926–30; appts at Moorfields Eye Hosp.: Clin. Asst, Refraction Asst, Chief Clin. Asst, 1927–34, Asst Med. Officer to Physico-Therapy Dept, 1930–31, Lang Research Schol., 1930–33; Clin. Asst, London Hosp., 1929–34; Ophth. Surg., East Ham Memorial Hosp., 1930–31; appts at St George's Hosp.: Asst Ophth. Surg., 1931–46, Ophth. Surg., 1946–49; Lectr in Ophthalmology, St George's Hosp. Med. Sch., University of London, 1931–49; Ophth. Surg., Lord Mayor Treloar Hosp., 1932–37; Asst Surgeon, Central London Ophthalmic Hosp., 1934–38; Ophth. Surg., Hosp. for Sick Children, Great Ormond Street, 1936–63; Lectr in Ophth., Inst. of Child Health, 1936–63; Hon. Secretary: Section of Ophthalmology, RSM, 1935–37; Ophthalmological Soc., 1939–40, 1946–47. Chm., Cttee of Horatian Soc., 1965–69. Sq/Ldr, W/Cdr, RAF, Med. Br., 1940–45. CStJ 1962. *Publications:* Diseases of Children's Eyes, 1947, 2nd edn, 1950; Children's Eye Nursing, 1948; Ocular Signs in Slit-Lamp Microscopy, 1949; Ophthalmic Medicine, 1949; Chapters in: Moncrieff's Nursing of Sick Children, 1948; Garrod Batten and Thursfield's Diseases of Children, 1949; Stallard's Modern Practice in Ophthalmology, 1949; Berens' Diseases of the Eye, 1949; Parsons and Barling's Diseases of Children, 1954; Treves and Rogers' Surgical Applied Anatomy, 1952; Gaisford and Lightwood's Pædiatrics for the Practitioner, 1955; Thérapeutique Médicale Oculaire; articles in British Encyclopædias of Medical and Surgical Practice; papers in Brit. Jl Ophth., etc. *Recreations:* walking, reading. *Address:* Albury Park, Albury, Guildford, Surrey. *T:* Shere 3289. *Clubs:* English-Speaking Union; Hawks (Cambridge).

DOGGETT, Frank John, CB 1965; retired; Deputy Chairman, UKAEA, 1971–76; Director, National Nuclear Corporation, 1973–76; *b* 7 Jan. 1910; *s* of Frank Hewitt and Charlotte Doggett; *m* 1st, 1940, Clare Judge (*d* 1956); one *d*; 2nd, 1957, Mary Battison. *Educ:* Mathematical Sch., Rochester; University of London (LLB). Inland Revenue, 1929; Air Ministry, 1938; MAP, 1940; MOS, 1946, Under-Sec., 1957–59; Under-Sec., Min. of Aviation, 1959–66, Dep. Sec., 1966–67; Dep. Sec. (A), Min. of Technology, 1967–70; Under-Sec., Dept of Trade and Industry, 1970–71. *Address:* The Jays, Ridgeway Road, Dorking, Surrey. *T:* Dorking 885819.

DOHA, Aminur Rahman S.; *see* Shams-ud Doha, A. R.

DOIG, Very Rev. Dr Andrew Beveridge; *b* 18 Sept. 1914; *s* of George and Hannah Doig; *m* 1st, 1940, Nan Carruthers (*d* 1947); one *d*; 2nd, 1950, Barbara Young; one *s* one *d*. *Educ:* Hyndland Secondary Sch., Glasgow; Glasgow Univ. (MA, BD; Hon. DD 1974); Union Theol Seminary, New York (STM). Ordained, 1938; Church of Scotland Missionary to Nyasaland, 1939–63; service included: Dist Missionary and Sec. of Mission Council; Sen. Army Chaplain, E Africa Comd, 1941–45; Mem., Legislative Council; Mem., Adv. Cttee on African Educn, and Coll. Council, Univ. of Rhodesia and Nyasaland; Regional Sec., Nyasaland and N Rhodesia; seconded to represent African interests in Fed. Parlt, Rhodesias and Nyasaland, 1953–58; Gen. Sec., Synod of Ch. of Central Africa (Presbyterian), 1958–63; Minister, St John's and King's Park, Dalkeith, Scotland, 1963–72; Gen. Sec., National Bible Soc. of Scotland, 1972–82; Moderator of the Gen. Assembly of the Church of Scotland, 1981–82. *Address:* The Eildons, Moulin, Pitlochry. *T:* Pitlochry 2892.

DOIG, Peter Muir; *b* 27 Sept. 1911; *m* 1938, Emily Scott; two *s*. *Educ:* Blackness Sch., Dundee. Served RAF, 1941–46. Sales Supervisor with T. D. Duncan Ltd, Bakers, Dundee, until 1963. Mem., TGWU; joined Labour Party, 1930; Mem. of Dundee Town Council, 1953–63, Hon. Treasurer, 1959–63. Contested (Lab) S Aberdeen, 1959; MP (Lab) Dundee West, Nov. 1963–1979. *Recreation:* chess. *Address:* 2 Westwater Place, Wormit, Fife.

DOIG, Ralph Herbert, CMG 1974; CVO 1954; *b* 24 Feb. 1909; *s* of late William and Rose Doig; *m* 1937, Barbara Crock; two *s* four *d*. *Educ:* Guildford Grammar Sch.; University of Western Australia (BA, DipCom). Entered Public Service of WA, 1926; Private Sec. to various Premiers, 1929–41; Asst Under-Sec., Premier's Dept, 1941; Under-Sec., Premier's Dept, and Clerk of Executive Council, Perth, Western Australia, 1945–65; Public Service Comr, W Australia, 1965–71; Chm., Public Service Board, WA, 1971–74. State Director: visit to Western Australia of the Queen and the Duke of Edinburgh, 1954; visit of the Duke of Edinburgh for British Empire and Commonwealth Games, 1962; visit of the Queen and the Duke of Edinburgh, 1963. *Recreation:* bowls. *Address:* 27 Marine Terrace, Sorrento, WA 6020, Australia. *T:* 448–4347.

DOISY, Prof. Edward A.; Professor Emeritus of Biochemistry and Director Emeritus of Edward A. Doisy Department of Biochemistry, St Louis University School of Medicine, since 1965; *b* Hume, Ill., 13 Nov. 1893; *s* of Edward Perez and Ada Alley Doisy; *m* 1st, 1918, Alice Ackert (*d* 1964); four *s*; 2nd, 1965, Margaret McCormick. *Educ:* Univ. of Illinois (AB 1914, MS 1916); Harvard (PhD 1920). Hon. ScD: Yale, 1940; Washington, 1940; Chicago, 1941; Central Coll., 1942; Illinois, 1960; Gustavus Adolphus Coll., 1963; Hon. Dr, Paris, 1945; Hon. LLD, St Louis, 1955. Asst in Biochemistry, Harvard Medical Sch., 1915–17; Army Service, 1917–19; Instructor, Associate and Associate Prof. in Biochemistry, Washington Univ. Sch. of Medicine, 1919–23; Prof. of Biochemistry and Chm. of Dept, St Louis Univ. Sch. of Medicine, 1923–65, Distinguished Service Prof., 1951–65. Member: American Soc. of Biological Chemists (Pres. 1943–45); American Chem. Soc.; Endocrine Soc. (Pres. 1949–50); American Assoc. for the Advancement of Science; Soc. for Experimental Biology and Medicine (Pres. 1949–51); National Academy of Sciences; American Philosophical Soc.; Amer. Acad. Arts and Sci.; Pontifical Acad. of Sci.; Foundation or Memorial Lectr at New York, Kansas, Pittsburgh, Chicago, Cleveland, Minnesota, Rochester; several medals and awards; shared the Nobel Prize in Physiology and Medicine for 1943 with Dr Henrik Dam. *Publications:* more than 100 papers in medical and scientific journals. *Recreations:* golf, hunting and fishing. *Address:* Apt 4b, Colonial Village Apartments, Webster Groves, Mo 63119, USA; St Louis University School of Medicine, 1402 South Grand Boulevard, St Louis, Missouri 63104. *T:* 664–9800 ext. 121.

DOLBY, Ray Milton, PhD; engineering company executive; electrical engineer; Owner and Chairman, Dolby Laboratories Inc., San Francisco and London, since 1965; *b* Portland, Ore, 18 Jan. 1933; *s* of Earl Milton Dolby and Esther Eufemia (*née* Strand); *m* 1966, Dagmar Baumert; two *s*. *Educ:* San Jose State Coll.; Washington Univ.; Stanford Univ. (Beach Thompson award, BS Elec. Engrg); Pembroke Coll., Cambridge (Marshall schol., 1957–60, Draper's studentship, 1959–61, NSF Fellow, 1960–61; PhD Physics 1961; Fellow, 1961–63; research in long-wave length x-rays, 1957–63; Hon. Fellow 1983). Electronic technician/jun. engr, Ampex Corp., Redwood City, Calif, 1949–53. Served US Army 1953–54. Engr, 1955–57; Sen. Engr, 1957; UNESCO Advr, Central Sci. Instruments Org., Punjab, 1963–65; Cons., UKAEA, 1962–63. Inventions, research, pubns in video tape rec., x-ray microanalysis, noise reduction and quality improvements in audio and video systems; patentee. Fellow: Audio Engrg Soc. (Silver Medal, 1971; Governor, 1972–74, 1979–84; Pres., 1980–81); Brit. Kinematograph, Sound, TV Soc.; Soc. Motion Picture, TV Engrs (S. L. Warner award, 1978; Alexander M. Poniatoff Gold Medal, 1982; Progress Medal, 1983). MIEEE; Tau Beta Pi. Other Awards: Emmy (for contrib. to Ampex video recorder), 1957; Trendsetter, Billboard, 1971; Lyre, Inst. High Fidelity, 1972; Emile Berliner Assoc. Maker of Microphone award, 1972; Top 200 Execs Bi-Centennial, 1976; Sci. and Engrg, Acad. of Motion Picture Arts and Scis, 1979. Trustee, Univ. High Sch., San Francisco, 1978–84; Mem., Marshall Scholarships Selection Cttee, 1979–85; Dir, San Francisco Opera; Governor, San Francisco Symphony. *Recreations:* yachting, skiing. *Address:* (home) 3340 Jackson Street, San Francisco, Calif 94118, USA. *T:* (415) 563–6947; (office) 100 Portrero Avenue, San Francisco, Calif 94103. *T:* (415) 558–0200.

DOLCI, Danilo; Coordinator, Centro Studi e Iniziative, since 1958 (Founder); *b* Sesana, Trieste, 1924; *s* of Enrico Dolci and Mely Kontely. *Educ:* University of Rome; University of Milan. Came to Sicily to work for improvement of social conditions, 1952; arrested and tried for non-violent "reverse strike" to find work for unemployed, 1958. Mem. Internat. Council of War Resisters' International, 1963. Hon. DPhil, Univ. of Berne, 1968; Lenin Peace Prize, 1958; Gold Medal, Accademia Nazionale dei Lincei, 1969; Sonning Prize, 1971; Etna Taormina Poetry Prize, 1975; Viareggio Internat. Prize, 1979. *Publications:* Banditi a Partinico, 1955; Inchiesta a Palermo, 1956; Spreco, 1960; Racconti siciliani, 1963; Verso un mondo nuovo, 1964 (trans. A New World in the Making, 1965); Chi Gioca Solo, 1966; Chissá se i pesci piangono (documentazione di un'esperienza educativa), 1973; Non esiste il silenzio, 1974; Esperienze e riflessioni, 1974; Creatura di creature, 1983; Palpitare di nessi, 1985; The World is One Creature. *Address:* Centro Studi, Largo Scalia 5, Partinico (PA), Italy. *T:* 781905; Centro di formazione, Trappeto (PA). *T:* 788 312.

DOLE, Bob; *see* Dole, R. J.

DOLE, John Anthony; Controller of HM Stationery Office, and the Queen's Printer of Acts of Parliament, since 1987; *b* 14 Oct. 1929; *s* of Thomas Stephen Dole and Winifred Muriel (*née* Henderson); *m* 1952, Patricia Ivy Clements; two *s*. *Educ:* Bideford Grammar Sch.; Berkhamsted Sch. Air Ministry: Exec. Officer, 1950; Higher Exec. Officer, 1959; Principal, 1964; Ministry of Transport: Principal, 1965; Asst Sec. (Roads Programme), 1968; Administrator of Sports Council, 1972–75; Under Sec., Freight Directorate, 1976–78; Dir, Senior Staff Management, Depts of the Environment and Transport, 1978–82; Controller of Supplies, PSA, DoE, 1982–84; Controller of the Crown Suppliers, 1984–86. FInst PS 1986. *Publications: plays:* Cat on the Fiddle, 1964; Shock Tactics, 1966; Lucky for Some, 1968; Once in a Blue Moon, 1972; Top Gear, 1976. *Recreations:* writing, philately. *Address:* 240 Upton Road South, Bexley, Kent DA5 1QS. *Club:* Gresham.

DOLE, Robert Joseph, (Bob Dole); Purple Heart; United States Senator, since 1968; Majority Leader, United States Senate, since 1985; *b* 22 July 1923; *s* of Doran and Bina Dole; *m* 1975, Elizabeth Hanford; one *d*. *Educ:* Univ. of Kansas (AB); Washburn

Municipal Univ. (LLB). Served US Army, 1943–48; Platoon Ldr, 10th Mountain Div., Italy; wounded and decorated twice for heroic achievement; Captain. Kansas Legislature, 1951–53; Russell County Attorney, Kansas, 1953–61; US House of Representatives, 1960–68. *Address:* Office of the Majority Leader, United States Senate, Washington, DC 20510, USA. *T:* (202) 224-3135.

DOLL, Sir Richard; *see* Doll, Sir W. R. S.

DOLL, Prof. Sir (William) Richard (Shaboe), Kt 1971; OBE 1956; FRS 1966; DM, MD, FRCP, DSc; Hon. Consultant, Imperial Cancer Research Fund Cancer Epidemiology Unit, Radcliffe Infirmary, Oxford, since 1983; first Warden, Green College, Oxford, 1979–83; *b* Hampton, 28 Oct. 1912; *s* of Henry William Doll and Amy Kathleen Shaboe; *m* 1949, Joan Mary Faulkner, MB, BS, MRCP, DPH; one *s* one *d. Educ:* Westminster Sch.; St Thomas's Hosp. Med. Sch.; London. MB, BS 1937; MD 1945; FRCP 1957; DSc London 1958. RAMC, 1939–45. Appts with Med. Research Council, 1946–69; Mem. Statistical Research Unit, 1948; Dep. Dir, 1959; Dir, 1961–69. Hon. Associate Physician, Central Middlesex Hosp., 1949–69; Teacher in Medical Statistics and Epidemiology, University Coll. Hosp. Med. Sch., 1963–69; Regius Prof. of Medicine, Oxford Univ., 1969–79. Member: MRC, 1970–74; Royal Commn on Environmental Pollution, 1973–79; Standing Commn on Energy and the Environment, 1978–81; Scientific Council of Internat. Cancer Research Agency, 1966–70 and 1975–78; Council, Royal Society, 1970–71 (a Vice-Pres., 1970–71); Chairman: Adverse Reaction Sub-Cttee, Cttee on Safety of Medicines, 1970–77; UK Co-ordinating Cttee on Cancer Research, 1972–77. Hon. Lectr London Sch. of Hygiene and Tropical Med., 1956–62 (Hon. Fellow 1982); Milroy Lectr, RCP, 1953; Marc Daniels Lectr, RCP, 1969; Harveian Orator, RCP, 1982; William Julius Mickle Fellow, Univ. of London, 1955. Hon. Foreign Member: Norwegian Acad. of Scis, Amer. Acad. of Arts and Scis. Hon DSc: Newcastle, 1969; Belfast, 1972; Reading, 1973; Newfoundland, 1973; Hon. DM Tasmania, 1976. David Anderson Berry Prize (jt), RSE 1958; Bisset Hawkins Medal, RCP, 1962; UN award for cancer research, 1962; Gairdner Award, Toronto, 1970; Buchanan Medal, Royal Soc., 1972; Presidential award, NY Acad. Sci., 1974; Prix Griffuel, Paris, 1976; Gold Medal, RIPH&H, 1977; Mott Award, Gen. Motors' Cancer Res. Foundn, 1979; Bruce Medal, Amer. Coll. of Physicians, 1981; National Award, Amer. Cancer Soc., 1981; Gold Medal, BMA, 1983; Conrad Röntgen prize, Accademia dei Lincei, 1984; Johann-Georg-Zimmermann Prize, Hanover, 1985; Royal Medal, Royal Soc., 1986. *Publications:* Prevention of Cancer: pointers from epidemiology, 1967; (jtly) Causes of Cancer, 1982; articles in scientific journals on aetiology of lung cancer, leukaemia and other cancers, also aetiology and treatment of peptic ulcer, effects of ionizing radiations, oral contraceptives; author (jt) Med. Research Council's Special Report Series, 1951, 1957, 1964. *Recreations:* food and conversation. *Address:* 12 Rawlinson Road, Oxford.

DOLLERY, Prof. Colin Terence, FRCP; Professor of Clinical Pharmacology at Royal Postgraduate Medical School, University of London, since 1965; *b* 14 March 1931; *s* of Cyril Robert and Thelma Mary Dollery; *m* 1958, Diana Myra (*née* Stedman); one *s* one *d. Educ:* Lincoln Sch.; Birmingham Univ. (BSc, MB,ChB); FRCP 1968. House officer: Queen Elizabeth Hosp., Birmingham; Hammersmith Hosp., and Brompton Hosp., 1956–58; Hammersmith Hospital: Med. Registrar, 1958–60; Sen. Registrar and Tutor in Medicine, 1960–62; Consultant Physician, 1962–; Lectr in Medicine at Royal Postgrad. Med. Sch., 1962–65. Member: MRC, 1982–84; UGC, 1984–. Hon. Mem., Assoc. of Amer. Physicians, 1982. Chevalier de l'Ordre National du Mérite (France), 1976. *Publications:* The Retinal Circulation, 1971 (New York); numerous papers in scientific jls concerned with high blood pressure and drug action. *Recreations:* travel, amateur radio, work. *Address:* 101 Corringham Road, NW11 7DL. *T:* 01–458 2616. *Club:* Athenæum.

DOLLEY, Christopher; Chairman: Damis Group Ltd, since 1971; Vinopoly Ltd, since 1980; *b* 11 Oct. 1931; *yr s* of late Dr Leslie George Francis Dolley and of Jessie, Otford, Kent; *m* 1966, Christine Elizabeth Cooper; three *s. Educ:* Bancrofts Sch.; Corpus Christi Coll., Cambridge. Joined Unilever, 1954; with Unilever subsidiaries, 1954–62: G. B. Ollivant Ltd, 1954–59; United Africa Co., 1959–62. Joined Penguin Books Ltd as Export Manager, 1962; became Dir, 1964, Man. Dir, 1970–73, Chm., 1971–73; Dir for Book Develt, IPC, 1973–77. Exec. Vice-Pres., Penguin Books Inc., Baltimore, 1966; Director: Penguin Publishing Co., 1969–73 (Jt Man. Dir, 1969); Pearson Longman Ltd, 1970–73; The Hamlyn Group, 1971–81; Farvise Ltd, 1976–80. Mem., Nat. Film Finance Corp., 1971–81; Dir, Nat. Film Trustee Corp., 1971–81. *Publication:* (ed) The Penguin Book of English Short Stories, 1967. *Recreations:* golf, gardening, collecting. *Address:* Elm Place, 54 St Leonards Road, Windsor, Berkshire SL4 3BY. *T:* Windsor 66961. *Clubs:* Savile; 14 West Hamilton Street (Baltimore, Md).

DOLLING, Francis Robert; Chairman, Barclays International, since 1985; Director, Barclays Bank PLC (Deputy Chairman, 1983–85); Chairman, Barclays Merchant Bank Ltd, 1980–85; *b* 21 Jan. 1923; *s* of Frederick George Dolling and Edith Lilian Auriel; *m* 1949, Maisie Alice Noquet; two *d. Educ:* Tottenham County School. Served RAF, 1940–47. Joined Barclays Bank DCO, 1947; served in various overseas territories; Managing Director, Barclays National Bank Ltd, South Africa, 1974; Director and Sen. General Manager, Barclays Bank Internat. Ltd, and Director, Barclays Bank Ltd, 1976; Vice-Chm., Barclays Bank, 1980–83. *Recreations:* gardening, golf. *Address:* Rowan Cottage, The Ridgway, Pyrford, Surrey. *T:* Byfleet 43362. *Club:* Royal Automobile.

DOLMETSCH, Carl Frederick, CBE 1954; Director of Haslemere Festival since 1940; specialist and authority on early music and instruments; recording artist in England and America; *b* 23 Aug. 1911; *s* of Arnold Dolmetsch and Mabel Johnston; *m;* one *s* two *d* (and one *s* decd). *Educ:* privately. Began studying music with Arnold Dolmetsch at age of 4; first performed in public at 7, first concert tour at 8, first broadcast on violin and viol, 1925, at 14 years of age; virtuoso recorder-player at 15. Toured and broadcast in America, 1935 and 1936; recorder recitals, Wigmore Hall, Feb. and Nov. 1939, and annually, 1946–; toured and broadcast on radio and TV in Holland, 1946; Italy and Switzerland, 1947; Sweden, 1949; New Zealand, 1953; France, 1956; America, 1957; Switzerland, Austria, Germany, Holland, 1958; Belgium, America, 1959; Sweden, Austria, Germany, 1960; Australia, 1965; Colombia, 1966; France, Sweden, 1967; Alaska, Canada and Italy, 1969; Japan, 1974; Denmark, 1983; Colombia, 1984; Italy, 1985; America (yearly), 1961–. Frequent broadcasts in this country and abroad. Chm. and Man. Dir, Arnold Dolmetsch Ltd, 1963–78; Chm., Dolmetsch Musical Instruments, 1982–. Musical Dir of Soc. of Recorder Players, 1937; Musical Dir, Dolmetsch Internat. Summer School, 1970–; Mem. Incorporated Soc. of Musicians; Mem. Art Workers' Guild, 1953; Patron Early Music Soc., University of Sydney. Hon. Fellow of Trinity Coll. of Music, 1950. Hon. DLitt University of Exeter, 1960. Hon. Fellow London Coll. of Music, 1963. *Publications:* Recorder Tutors, 1957, 1962, 1970, 1977; edited and arranged numerous publications of 16th-, 17th- and 18th-century music; contrib. to many music jls. *Recreations:* ornithology, natural history. *Address:* Jesses, Haslemere, Surrey GU27 2BS. *T:* Haslemere 3818.

DOLTON, David John William; Assistant General Manager, National Employers Mutual General Insurance Association Ltd, since 1979; *b* 15 Sept. 1928; *e s* of Walter William and Marie Frances Duval Dolton; *m* 1959, Patricia Helen Crowe (marr. diss.

1985); one *s* one *d; m* 1986, Rosalind Jennifer Chivers. *Educ:* St Lawrence Coll., Ramsgate. FCIS, FBIM, FIPM, MInstAM. Various appointments in Delta Metal Co. Ltd, 1950–76, incl. Commercial Director, Extrusion Division, and Director of Administration and Personnel, Rod Division, 1967–76; Chief Exec., Equal Opportunities Commn, 1976–78. Governor, The Queen's Coll., Birmingham, 1974–. Reader, Dio. Gloucester. Liveryman, Worshipful Co. of Gold and Silver Wyre Drawers. *Recreations:* music, reading, formerly mountaineering, now mountain and hill walking, swimming, travel. *Address:* 85 Corinium Gate, Cirencester, Glos GL7 2PX. *T:* Cirencester 67739.

DOMB, Prof. Cyril, PhD; FRS 1977; Professor of Physics, Bar-Ilan University, since 1981; *m* Shirley Galinsky; three *s* three *d. Educ:* Hackney Downs Sch.; Pembroke Coll., Cambridge. Major Open Schol., Pembroke Coll., 1938–41; Radar Research, Admiralty, 1941–46; MA Cambridge, 1945; Nahum Schol., Pembroke Coll., 1946; PhD Cambridge, 1949; ICI Fellowship, Clarendon Laboratory, Oxford, 1949–52; MA Oxon, 1952; University Lecturer in Mathematics, Cambridge, 1952–54; Prof. of Theoretical Physics, KCL, 1954–81; FKC 1978. Max Born Prize, Inst. of Physics and German Physical Soc., 1981. *Publications:* (ed) Clerk Maxwell and Modern Science, 1963; (ed) Memories of Kopul Rosen, 1970; Phase Transitions and Critical Phenomena, (ed with M.S. Green) vols 1 and 2, 1972, vol. 3, 1974, vols 5a, 5b, 6, 1976, (ed with J. L. Lebowitz) vols 7 and 8, 1983, vol. 9, 1984; (ed with A. Carmell) Challenge, 1976; articles in scientific journals. *Recreation:* walking. *Address:* Department of Physics, Bar-Ilan University, Ramat-Gan, Israel; 28 St Peter's Court, Queens Road, NW4.

DOMINGO, Placido; tenor singer, conductor; *b* Madrid, 21 Jan. 1941; *s* of Placido Domingo and Pepita (*née* Embil), professional singers; *m* Marta Ornelas, lyric soprano; three *s. Educ:* Instituto, Mexico City; Nat. Conservatory of Music, Mexico City. Operatic début, Monterrey, as Alfredo in La Traviata, 1961; with opera houses at Dallas, Fort Worth, Israel, to 1965; NY City Opera, 1965–; débuts: at NY Metropolitan Opera, as Maurizio in Adriana Lecouvreur, 1968; at La Scala, title role in Ernani, 1969; at Covent Garden, Cavaradossi in Tosca, 1971. Has conducted in Vienna, Barcelona, NY and Frankfurt; début as conductor in UK, Covent Garden, 1983. *Films:* La Traviata, 1983; Carmen, 1984; Otello, 1986; appears on TV, makes recordings, throughout USA and Europe. FRCM; FRNCM. Officer, Legion of Honour, 1983; Medal of City of Madrid. *Publication:* My First Forty Years (autobiog.), 1983. *Recreations:* piano, swimming. *Address:* c/o Stafford Law Associates, 26 Mayfield Road, Weybridge, Surrey KT13 8XB.

DOMINIAN, Dr Jacobus, FRCPEd, FRCPsych; DPM; Senior Consultant Psychiatrist, Central Middlesex Hospital, since 1965; *b* 25 Aug. 1929; *s* of Charles Joseph Dominian and Mary Dominian (*née* Scarlatou); *m* 1955, Edith Mary Smith; four *d. Educ:* Lycée Leonin, Athens; St Mary's High Sch., Bombay; Stamford Grammar Sch., Lincs; Cambridge Univ.; Oxford Univ. MA, MB BChir (Cantab). Postgraduate work in medicine, various Oxford hosps, 1955–58, Maudsley Hosp. (Inst. of Psychiatry), 1958–64; training as psychiatrist at Maudsley Hosp.; Cons. Psychiatrist, Central Middlesex Hosp., 1965–; Dir, Marital Research Centre, 1971–. Hon. DSc Lancaster, 1976. *Publications:* Psychiatry and the Christian, 1961; Christian Marriage, 1967; Marital Breakdown, 1968; The Church and the Sexual Revolution, 1971; Cycles of Affirmation, 1975; Depression, 1976; Authority, 1976; (with A. R. Peacocke) From Cosmos to Love, 1976; Proposals for a New Sexual Ethic, 1977; Marriage, Faith and Love, 1981; Make or Break, 1984; The Capacity to Love, 1985; contribs to Lancet, BMJ, the Tablet, TLS. *Recreations:* enjoyment of the theatre, music, reading and writing. *Address:* Pefka, The Green, Croxley Green, Rickmansworth, Herts WD3 3JA. *T:* Rickmansworth 720972.

DOMOKOS, Dr Mátyás; Hungarian Ambassador to the Court of St James's, since 1984; *b* 28 Oct. 1930; *m* 1956, Irén Beretyán; one *d. Educ:* Karl Marx Univ. of Econs, Budapest. Foreign trading enterprises, 1954–57; Commercial Sec., Damascus and Trade Comr, Khartoum, 1958–61; various posts in Ministry for Foreign Trade, 1961–74; Ambassador to UN, Geneva, 1974–79; Head of Dept of Internat. Organisations, Ministry of Foreign Affairs, 1979–84. *Recreations:* gardening, chess. *Address:* Hungarian Embassy, 35 Eaton Place, SW1. *T:* 01-235 7191.

DON-WAUCHOPE, Sir P. G.; *see* Wauchope.

DONALD, Alan Ewen, CMG 1979; HM Diplomatic Service; Ambassador to Republic of Indonesia, since 1984; *b* 5 May 1931; 2nd *s* of Robert Thomson Donald and Louise Turner; *m* 1958, Janet Hilary Therese Blood; four *s. Educ:* Aberdeen Grammar Sch.; Fettes Coll., Edinburgh; Trinity Hall, Cambridge. BA, LLM. HM Forces, 1949–50. Joined HM Foreign Service, 1954: Third Sec., Peking, 1955–57; FO, 1958–61: Private Sec. to Parly Under-Sec., FO, 1959–61; Second, later First Sec., UK Delegn to NATO, Paris, 1961–64; First Sec., Peking, 1964–66; Personnel Dept, Diplomatic Service Admin. Office, later FCO, 1967–71; Counsellor (Commercial), Athens, 1971–73; Political Advr to Governor of Hong Kong, 1974–77; Ambassador to: Republics of Zaire, Burundi and Rwanda, 1977–80; People's Republic of the Congo, 1978–80; Asst Under-Sec. of State (Asia and the Pacific), FCO, 1980–84. *Recreations:* music, military history, water colour sketching, films, gentle golf. *Address:* c/o Foreign and Commonwealth Office, SW1A 2AH. *Clubs:* United Oxford & Cambridge University; Aula (London/Cambridge).

DONALD, Dr Alastair Geoffrey, OBE 1982; FRCGP, FRCPE; General Medical Practitioner, since 1952; Assistant Director, Edinburgh Postgraduate Board for Medicine, since 1970; Regional Adviser in General Practice, SE Scotland, since 1972; *b* 24 Nov. 1926; *s* of Dr Pollok Donald and Henrietta Mary (*née* Laidlaw); *m* 1952, Patricia Ireland; two *s* one *d. Educ:* Edinburgh Academy; Corpus Christi Coll., Cambridge (MA); Edinburgh Univ. (MB, ChB); Member: Cambridge and Edinburgh Univs Athletic Teams, RAF Medical Branch, 1952–54; general medical practice, Leith and Cramond (Edin.), 1954–; Lectr, Dept of General Practice, Univ. of Edinburgh, 1960–70. Royal College of General Practitioners: Vice-Chm. of Council, 1976–77, Chm., 1979–82; Chm., Bd of Censors, 1979–80; past Chm. and Provost, SE Scotland Faculty. Chairman: UK Conf. of Postgrad. Advisers in Gen. Practice, 1978–80; Jt Cttee on Postgrad. Trng for Gen. Practice, 1982–85; Radio Doctor, BBC (Scotland), 1976–78. Chm., Scottish Cttee, ASH. Chm. Court of Directors, Edinburgh Acad., 1978–85 (Dir, 1955–); President: Edinburgh Academical Club, 1978–81; Rotary Club of Leith, 1957–58. James Mackenzie Lectr, RCGP, 1985. James Mackenzie Medal, RCPE, 1983. *Publications:* contribs to medical jls. *Recreations:* golf, family life, reading The Times. *Address:* 30 Cramond Road North, Edinburgh EH4 6JE. *T:* 031–336 3824. *Clubs:* Hawks (Cambridge); University of Edinburgh Staff (Edinburgh).

DONALD, Craig Reid Cantlie, CMG 1963; OBE 1959; *b* 8 Sept. 1914; *s* of Rev. Francis Cantlie and Mary Donald, Lumphanan, Aberdeenshire; *m* 1945, Mary Isabel Speid; one *d. Educ:* Fettes; Emmanuel Coll., Cambridge (Scholar). BA 1937, MA 1947. Administrative Officer, Cyprus, 1937. Military Service, 1940–46, Lieut-Col. Commissioner, Famagusta, 1948. Registrar, Cooperative Societies, 1951; Deputy Financial Sec., Uganda, 1951; Sec. to the Treasury, 1956–63. Bursar, Malvern Coll., 1964–79. *Recreation:* country pursuits. *Address:* 55 Geraldine Road, Malvern WR14 3NU. *T:* Malvern 61446. *Club:* Travellers'. *See also* I. G. Gilbert.

DONALD, Prof. Ian, CBE 1973 (MBE 1946); MD; FRCSGlas; FRCOG; FCOG(SA); Regius Professor of Midwifery, University of Glasgow, 1954–76, now Emeritus Professor; Hon. Research Consultant, National Maternity Hospital, Dublin, since 1977; *b* 27 Dec. 1910; British; *m* 1937, Alix Mathilde de Chazal Richards; four *d. Educ:* Warriston Sch., Moffat; Fettes Coll., Edinburgh; Diocesan Coll., Rondebosch, Cape. BA Cape Town, 1930; MB, BS London, 1937; MD London, 1947; MRCOG 1947; FRCOG 1955; FRCSGlas 1958; FCOG(SA) 1967; Hon. FACOG 1976. Served War of 1939–45 with Royal Air Force (Medical), 1942–46 (despatches). Reader in Obstetrics and Gynæcology, St Thomas's Hosp. Medical Sch., 1951; Reader, University of London, Inst. of Obstetrics and Gynæcology, 1952; Leverhulme Research Scholar, 1953; Blair Bell Memorial Lecturer, RCOG, 1954. Hon. FRCOG 1982; Hon. FRCR 1983; Hon. FRCP Glas 1984. Hon. DSc: London, 1981; Glasgow, 1983. Eardley Holland Gold Medal, 1970; Blair Bell Gold Medal, RSM, 1970; Victor Bonney Prize, RCS, 1970–72; MacKenzie Davidson Medal, BIR, 1975. Order of Flag with Gold Star, Yugoslavia, 1982. *Publications:* Practical Obstetric Problems, 1955, 5th edn 1979; articles on respiratory disorders in the newborn, in Lancet and Jl of Obst. and Gynæc. Brit. Empire, and on ultrasonics in diagnosis, in Lancet. *Recreations:* sailing, music, painting. *Address:* Cobblers Row, East End, Paglesham, Essex SS4 2ER. *T:* Canewdon 616.

DONALD, Air Marshal Sir John (George), KBE 1985 (OBE 1972); Deputy Surgeon General (Operations), Ministry of Defence, and Director General, Royal Air Force Medical Services, 1985–86; *b* 7 Nov. 1927; *s* of John Shirran Donald and Janet Knox (*née* Napier); *m* 1954, Margaret Jean Walton; one *s* two *d. Educ:* Inverurie Acad.; Aberdeen Univ. (MB, ChB 1951); DTM&H Edin 1964; MRCGP 1971, FRCGP 1977; MFCM 1972, FFCM 1985; MFOM 1982 (AFOM 1980); FRCPE 1986. Commnd RAF, 1953; Senior Medical Officer: Colombo, Ceylon, 1954–57; RAF Stafford, 1957–60; RAF Waddington, 1960–63; student, RAF Staff Coll., 1965; SMO, HQ AFCENT, France and Holland, 1966–68; Dep. Dir, Medical Personnel (RAF), 1969–72; OC, The Princess Mary's RAF Hosp., Akrotiri, Cyprus, 1972–76; OC, RAF Hosp., Ely, 1976–78; PMO, RAF Germany, 1978–81; PMO, RAF Strike Comd, 1981–84; Dir-Gen., RAF Med. Services, 1984–85. QHS, 1983–86. CStJ 1984. *Recreations:* golf, skiing, camping, ornithology. *Address:* Curzon House, Drews Park, Knotty Green, Beaconsfield, Bucks HP9 2TT. *T:* Beaconsfield 4621. *Club:* Royal Air Force.

DONALD, Prof. Kenneth William, OBE 1983; DSC 1940; MA, MD, DSc, FRCP, FRCPE, FRSE; Professor of Medicine, University of Edinburgh, 1959–76, now Emeritus Professor; Senior Physician, Royal Infirmary, Edinburgh; Physician to the Queen in Scotland, 1967–76; *b* 25 Nov. 1911; *s* of Col William Donald, MC, RA and Julia Jane Donald, Sandgate; *m* 1942, Rêthe Pearl, *d* of D. H. Evans, Regents Park. *Educ:* Cambridge Univ.; St Bartholomew's Hosp. Kitchener Scholar and State Scholar, 1930; Senior Scholar, Emmanuel Coll., Cambridge, 1933. Served with Royal Navy, 1939–45: Senior MO, 1st and 5th Flotilla of Destroyers; Senior MO, Admiralty Experimental Diving Unit. Chief Asst, Med. Prof. Unit and Cattlin Research Fellow, St Bartholomew's Hosp., 1946–48; Rockefeller Travelling Research Fellow, Columbia Univ., 1948–49; Senior Lecturer in Medicine, Inst. Diseases of the Chest, Brompton Hosp., 1949–50; Reader in Medicine, Univ. of Birmingham and Physician, Queen Elizabeth Hosp., Birmingham, 1950–59. Scientific Consultant to the Royal Navy. Physician to the Royal Navy in Scotland. Medical Consultant to Scottish Dept of Home and Health; Member: Commonwealth Scholarship Commn; Medical Sub-Cttee, UGC; RN Personnel Research Cttee (Chm.) of MRC; Scottish Adv. Cttee on Med. Research; Council and Scientific Adv. Cttee, British Heart Foundn; Scottish Gen. Nursing Council; Chairman: Under-Water Physiology Sub-Cttee of MRC; Adv. Gp to Sec. of State for Scotland on Health Care Aspects of Industrial Developments in North Sea. Governor, Inst. of Occupational Medicine, Edinburgh. *Publications:* contribs to scientific and medical jls concerning normal and abnormal function of the lungs, the heart and the circulation and high pressure physiology in relation to diving and submarines, drowning, resuscitation. *Recreations:* reading, theatre, fishing. *Address:* Nant-y-Celyn, Cloddiau, Welshpool, Powys SY21 9JE. *T:* Welshpool 2859. *Club:* Athenæum.

DONALDSON, family name of **Baron Donaldson of Kingsbridge.**

DONALDSON OF KINGSBRIDGE, Baron *cr* 1967 (Life Peer), of Kingsbridge; **John George Stuart Donaldson,** OBE 1943; retired farmer; *b* 9 Oct. 1907; *s* of Rev. S. A. Donaldson, Master of Magdalene, Cambridge, and Lady Albinia Donaldson (*née* Hobart-Hampden); *m* 1935, Frances Annesley Lonsdale (*see* F. A. Donaldson); one *s* two *d. Educ:* Eton; Trinity Coll., Cambridge. Pioneer Health Centre, Peckham, 1935–38; Road Transport, 1938–39. Royal Engineers, 1939–45. Farmed in Glos, and later Bucks. Member: Glos Agric. Exec. Cttee, 1953–60; SE Regional Planning Council, 1966–69. Parly Under-Sec. of State, NI Office, 1974–76; Minister for the Arts, DES, 1976–79. Joined SDP, 1981. Hon. Sec. Nat. Assoc. Discharged Prisoners Aid Socs, 1961; Chairman: Nat. Assoc. for the Care and Resettlement of Offenders, 1966–74; Bd of Visitors, HM Prison, Grendon, 1963–69; Consumer Council, 1968–71; EDC for Hotel and Catering Industry, 1972–74; Nat. Cttee Family Service Units, 1968–74; Cttee of Enquiry into conditions of service for young servicemen, 1969; Assoc. of Arts Instns, 1980–83; Confedn of Art and Design Assocs, 1982–84; British Fedn of Zoos, 1970–74; Pres., RSPB, 1975–80. Director: Royal Opera House, Covent Garden, 1958–74; Sadler's Wells, 1963–74; British Sugar Corp., 1966–74. *Recreations:* music in general, opera in particular. *Address:* 17 Edna Street, SW11 3DP. *Clubs:* Brooks's, Garrick.
See also N. D. Deakin.

DONALDSON OF KINGSBRIDGE, Lady; *see* Donaldson, Frances Annesley.

DONALDSON, David Abercrombie, RSA 1962 (ARSA 1951); RP 1964; RGI 1977; Painter; Head of Painting School, Glasgow School of Art, 1967–81; Her Majesty's Painter and Limner in Scotland, since 1977; *b* 29 June 1916; *s* of Robert Abercrombie Donaldson and Margaret Cranston; *m* 1st, 1942, Kathleen Boyd Maxwell; one *s*; 2nd, 1949, Maria Krystyna Mora-Szorc; two *d. Educ:* Coatbridge Sec. Sch.; Glasgow Sch. of Art. Travelling Scholarship, 1938. Joined Staff of Glasgow Sch. of Art, 1940. Paintings in private collections in America and Europe and public collections in Scotland. Sitters include: The Queen, 1968; Sir Hector Hetherington; Dame Jean Roberts; Sir John Dunbar; Lord Binning; Rev. Lord McLeod; Mrs Winifred Ewing; Miss Joan Dickson; Earl of Haddo; Sir Samuel Curran; Roger Ellis. Hon. LLD Strathclyde, 1971. *Recreations:* music, cooking. *Address:* 5 Cleveden Drive, Glasgow G12 0SU. *T:* 041–334 1029; 7 Chelsea Manor Studios, Flood Street, SW3. *T:* 01–352 1932. *Club:* Art (Glasgow).

DONALDSON, David Torrance; QC 1984; *b* 30 Sept. 1943; *s* of Alexander Walls Donaldson and Margaret Merry Bryce. *Educ:* Glasgow Academy; Gonville and Caius College, Cambridge (Maj. Schol.; MA); University of Freiburg i. Br., West Germany (Dr jur). Fellow, Gonville and Caius College, Cambridge, 1965–69. Called to the Bar, Gray's Inn, 1968. *Address:* 2 Hare Court, Temple, EC4. *T:* 01–583 1770.

DONALDSON, Sir Dawson, KCMG 1967; BSc; CEng, FIEE; Chairman, Commonwealth Telecommunications Board, 1962–69, retired; *b* 29 Dec. 1903; *s* of Dawson Donaldson and Ada M. Gribble; *m* 1928, Nell Penman; two *s* two *d. Educ:* Auckland Grammar Sch.; New Zealand Univ. New Zealand Post and Tels Dept, 1922–62; Executive Engineer, 1928–48; Superintending Engineer, 1948–54; Dep. Dir Gen., 1954–60; Dir Gen., 1960–62. *Recreations:* bowls and garden. *Address:* 2 Ridd Crescent, Karori, Wellington, New Zealand.

DONALDSON, Dame (Dorothy) Mary, GBE 1983; JP; Lord Mayor of London for 1983–84; Alderman, City of London Ward of Coleman Street, since 1975; *b* 29 Aug. 1921; *d* of late Reginald George Gale Warwick and Dorothy Alice Warwick; *m* 1945, Rt Hon. Sir John Francis Donaldson, *qv*; one *s* two *d. Educ:* Portsmouth High Sch. for Girls (GPDST); Wingfield Morris Orthopædic Hosp.; Middlesex Hosp., London. SRN 1946. Chairman: Women's Nat. Cancer Control Campaign, 1967–69; Voluntary Licensing Authy for Human In Vitro Fertilisation and Embryol., 1985–; Vice-Pres., British Cancer Council, 1970; Member: NE Met. Regional Hosp. Bd, 1970–74; NE Thames RHA, 1976–81. Governor: London Hosp., 1971–74; Gt Ormond Street Hosp. for Sick Children, 1978–80; Member: Cities of London and Westminster Disablement Adv. Cttee, 1974–79; Inner London Educn Authority, 1968–71; City Parochial Foundn, 1969–75; Cttee, Royal Humane Soc., 1968–83; Cttee, AA, 1985–; Vice-Pres., Counsel and Care for the Elderly, 1980–; Pres., British Assoc. of Cancer United Patients, 1985–. Governor: City of London Sch. for Girls, 1971–83; Berkhamsted Schools, 1976–80; Mem., Governing Body, Charterhouse Sch., 1980–85; Mem., Court of Common Council, 1966–75, Sheriff, 1981–82, HM Lieutenant, 1983, City of London; Mem. Guild of Freemen, City of London, 1970, Mem. Court 1983–; Liveryman, Gardeners' Co., 1975; Hon. Freeman, Shipwrights' Co., 1985. JP Inner London, 1960; Mem., Inner London Juvenile Court Panel, 1960–65. Hon. Mem., CIArb, 1981; Hon. Fellow, Girton Coll., Cambridge, 1983. Hon. DSc City, 1983. DStJ 1984. Freedom, City of Winnipeg, 1968. Order of Oman, 1982; Order of Bahrain, 1984. Grand Officier, Ordre Nat. du Mérite, 1984. *Recreations:* gardening, sailing, geriatric ski-ing. *T:* (home) 01–637 9658. *Clubs:* Reform, City Livery, Royal Cruising; Royal Lymington Yacht, Bar Yacht.

DONALDSON, Air Cdre Edward Mortlock, CB 1960; CBE 1954; DSO 1940; AFC 1941 (and bar 1947); Air Correspondent, The Daily Telegraph, 1961–79; *b* 22 Feb. 1912; *s* of C. E. Donaldson, Malay Civil Service; *m* 1st, 1936, Winifred Constant (marr. diss., 1944); two *d*; 2nd, 1944, Estellee Holland (marr. diss., 1956); one *s*; 3rd, 1957, Anne, Sofie Stapleton (marr. diss., 1982). *Educ:* King's Sch., Rochester; Christ's Hosp., Horsham; McGill Univ., Canada. Joined RAF, 1931; 3 Sqdn, Upavon, Kenley and Sudan until 1936; won RAF air firing trophy, 1933 and 1934; Flight Comdr, 1 Sqdn, 1936–38; led flight aerobatic team, Hendon and Zürich, 1937; Flight-Lieut 1936; Sqdn Leader 1938; Comdr, 151 Squdn, 1938–40, Battle of Britain; Chief Instructor, 5 Flying Training Sch., 1941; Wing Comdr, 1940; went to US to build four air Gunnery Schs, 1941, and teach USAF combat techniques; Group Capt., 1942; Mem. USAF Board and Directing Staff at US Sch. of Applied Tactics, 1944; Comdr RAF Station, Colerne, RAF first jet station, 1944; in comd RAF Station, Milfield, 1946; in comd RAF High Speed Flight, 1946; holder of World's Speed Record, 1946; SASO, No. 12 Group, 1946–49; in comd Air Cadet Corps and CCF, 1949–51; in comd RAF Station, Fassberg, Germany, 1951–54; Joint Services Staff Coll., 1954; Dir of Operational Training, Air Ministry, 1954–56; Air Cdre, 1954; Dep. Comdr Air Forces, Arabian Peninsular Command, 1956–58; Commandant, Royal Air Force Flying Coll., Manby, 1958–61; retd. Legion of Merit (US), 1948. *Recreations:* shooting, sailing, golf. *Address:* 3 Fair Oak Court, Tower Close, Alverstoke, Gosport PO12 2TX; Suite Royal 4011, El Palmar, Denia, Alicante, Spain. *Clubs:* Royal Air Force; Island Sailing (Cowes).

DONALDSON, Frances Annesley, (Lady Donaldson of Kingsbridge); *b* 13 Jan. 1907; *d* of Frederick Lonsdale and Leslie Lonsdale (*née* Hoggan); *m* 1935, John George Stuart Donaldson (*see* Lord Donaldson of Kingsbridge); one *s* two *d. Publications:* Approach to Farming, 1941, 6th edn 1946; Four Years' Harvest, 1945; Milk Without Tears, 1955; Freddy Lonsdale, 1957; Child of the Twenties, 1959; The Marconi Scandal, 1962; Evelyn Waugh: portrait of a country neighbour, 1967; Actor Managers, 1970; Edward VIII, 1974 (Wolfson History Award, 1975); King George VI and Queen Elizabeth, 1977; Edward VIII: the road to abdication, 1978; P. G. Wodehouse, 1982; The British Council: the First Fifty Years, 1984. *Recreations:* gardening, golf. *Address:* 17 Edna Street, SW11 3DP. *T:* 01-223 0259.
See also N. D. Deakin.

DONALDSON, Prof. Gordon, FRSE 1978; FBA 1976; Professor of Scottish History and Palæography, University of Edinburgh, 1963–79, now Professor Emeritus; Historiographer to HM the Queen in Scotland, since 1979; *b* 13 April 1913; *s* of Magnus Donaldson and Rachel Hetherington Swan. *Educ:* Royal High Sch., Edinburgh; Universities of Edinburgh and London. Asst in HM Gen. Register House, Edinburgh, 1938; Lecturer in Scottish History, University of Edinburgh, 1947, Reader, 1955. Birkbeck Lectr, Cambridge, 1958. Member: Royal Commission on the Ancient and Historical Monuments of Scotland, 1964–82; Scottish Records Adv. Council, 1964–; President: Scottish Ecclesiological Soc., 1963–65; Scottish Church History Soc., 1964–67; Scottish History Soc., 1968–72; Scottish Record Soc., 1981–. Editor, Scottish Historical Review, 1972–77. Hon. DLitt Aberdeen, 1976. *Publications:* The Making of the Scottish Prayer Book of 1637, 1954; A Source Book of Scottish History, 1952–61; Register of the Privy Seal of Scotland, vols v-viii, 1957–82; Shetland Life under Earl Patrick, 1958; Scotland: Church and Nation through sixteen centuries, 1960, 2nd edn, 1972; The Scottish Reformation, 1960, repr. 1972; Scotland—James V to James VII, 1965, repr. 1971; The Scots Overseas, 1966; Northwards by Sea, 1966, repr. 1978; Scottish Kings, 1967, repr. 1977; The First Trial of Mary Queen of Scots, 1969; Memoirs of Sir James Melville of Halhill, 1969; (comp.) Scottish Historical Documents, 1970; Mary Queen of Scots, 1974; Who's Who in Scottish History, 1974; Scotland: The Shaping of a Nation, 1974, 2nd edn 1980; Dictionary of Scottish History, 1977; All the Queen's Men, 1983; Isles of Home, 1983; Sir William Fraser, 1985; Scottish Church History, 1985; contribs to Scottish Historical Review, English Historical Review, Transactions of Royal Historical Society, etc. *Address:* 6 Pan Ha', Dysart, Fife KY1 2TL. *T:* Kirkcaldy 52685.

DONALDSON, Rt. Hon. Sir John (Francis), Kt 1966; PC 1979; Master of the Rolls, since 1982; *b* 6 Oct. 1920; *er s* of late Malcolm Donaldson, FRCS, FRCOG, and late Evelyn Helen Marguerite Maunsell; *m* 1945, Dorothy Mary (*see* Dame Mary Donaldson); one *s* two *d. Educ:* Charterhouse; Trinity Coll., Cambridge (Hon. Fellow, 1983); MA Oxon 1982. Sec. of Debates, Cambridge Union Soc., 1940; Chm. Federation of University Conservative and Unionist Assocs, 1940; BA (Hons) 1941; MA 1959. Commissioned Royal Signals, 1941; served with Guards Armoured Divisional Signals, in UK and NW Europe, 1942–45; and with Military Government, Schleswig-Holstein, 1945–46; Hon. Lieut-Col, 1946. Called to Bar, Middle Temple, 1946; Harmsworth Law Scholar, 1946; Bencher 1966; Treas. 1986; Mem. Gen. Council of the Bar, 1956–61, 1962–66, Junior Counsel to Registrar of Restrictive Trading Agreements, 1959–61; QC 1961; Dep. Chm., Hants QS, 1961–66; Mem. Council on Tribunals, 1965–66; Judge of the High Court, Queen's Bench Div., 1966–79; Pres., Nat. Industrial Relations Court, 1971–74; a Lord Justice of Appeal, 1979–82. Mem. Croydon County Borough Council, 1949–53. President: Carthusian Soc., 1978–82; British Maritime Law Assoc., 1979– (Vice-Pres.,

1969–78); British Insurance Law Assoc., 1979–81 (Dep. Pres., 1978–79); British Records Assoc., 1982–; Chairman: Adv. Council on Public Records, 1982–; Magna Carta Trust, 1982–. FCIArb 1980 (Pres., 1980–83). Hon. Member: Assoc. of Average Adjusters, 1966 (Chm., 1981); Grain and Feed Trade Assoc., 1979; Liverpool Cotton Assoc., 1979. Governor, Sutton's Hosp. in Charterhouse, 1981–84. Visitor: UCL, 1982–; Nuffield Coll., Oxford, 1982–. Hon. Freeman, Worshipful Co. of Drapers, 1984. DU Essex, 1983; Hon. LLD Sheffield, 1984. *Publications:* Jt Ed., Lowndes and Rudolf on General Average and the York-Antwerp Rules (8th edn), 1955, (9th edn), 1964 and (10th edn), 1975; contributor to title Insurance, in Halsbury's Laws of England (3rd edn), 1958. *Recreations:* sailing, do-it-yourself. *Address:* Royal Courts of Justice, Strand, WC2. *T:* 01–936 6002; (home) 01–637 9658. *Clubs:* Royal Cruising, Bar Yacht, Royal Lymington Yacht.

DONALDSON, Dame Mary; *see* Donaldson, Dame D. M.

DONALDSON, Patricia Anne; *see* Hodgson, P. A.

DONALDSON, Prof. Simon Kirwan, DPhil; FRS 1986; Wallis Professor of Mathematics, and Fellow of St Anne's College, University of Oxford, since 1985; *b* 20 Aug. 1957. *Educ:* Sevenoaks Sch., Kent; Pembroke Coll., Cambridge (BA 1979); Worcester Coll., Oxford (DPhil 1983). Jun. Res. Fellow, All Souls Coll., Oxford, 1983–85. *Publications:* papers in mathematical jls. *Recreation:* sailing. *Address:* St Anne's College, Oxford.

DONALDSON, Timothy Baswell, CBE 1973; PhD; Governor, Central Bank of the Bahamas, since 1974; *b* 2 Jan. 1934; *s* of late Rev. Dr T. E. W. Donaldson and of M. B. Donaldson; *m* 1957, Donna Ruth Penn; two *s*. *Educ:* Fisk Univ., Tennessee (BA Hons); Univ. of Minnesota; Columbia Univ.; Pacific Northwestern Univ. (PhD). FIB. Lectr in Maths, Fisk Univ., 1957–58; Sen. Master, Clarendon Coll., Jamaica, 1959–61; Headmaster, Prince Williams High Sch., 1961–63; Sen. Inspector, Bahamas Min. of Educn, 1963–64; Asst Sec., 1964–66, Controller of Exchange, 1966–68, Min. of Finance, Bahamas; Manager, 1968–70, Chm., 1970–74, Bahamas Monetary Authority. Alternate Governor for Bahamas: IMF; Caribbean Develt Bank; Director: Intercontinental Diversified Corp.; Grand Bahama Port Authority; Morgan Guaranty Trust (Bahamas) Ltd; Bahamas Intenational Trust; Chm., Bahamas Hotel Employers Pension Fund. Chm., Duke of Edinburgh Awards Scheme, Nassau; Treasurer, Bahamas Assoc. for Mentally Retarded; Founder Mem., Rotary Club of E Nassau (Past Sec. and Vice Pres.). Mem., Bd of Trustees, Fisk Univ.; Founder Pres., Bahamas Br., Guild of Graduates; Pres., Gym Tennis Club. Pres. and Hon. Fellow, Bahamas Inst. of Bankers; FIB; Associate, Inst. of Dirs. Delta Chapter, Phi Beta Kappa, 1977. Hon. LLD London Inst. for Applied Research, 1972. *Publications:* numerous articles on international finance in periodicals and journals. *Recreations:* tennis, swimming. *Address:* (office) PO Box N 7112, Nassau, Bahamas. *T:* 22193; (home) PO Box ES-5116, Nassau, Bahamas. *T:* 43259.

DONALDSON, Rear-Adm. Vernon D'Arcy; *b* 1 Feb. 1906; *s* of Adm. Leonard Andrew Boyd Donaldson, CB, CMG, and of Mary Mitchell, *d* of Prof. D'Arcy Thompson, Queen's Coll., Galway; *m* 1946, Joan Cranfield Monypenny of Pitmilly, (The Lady Pitmilly) (*d* 1986), *d* of James Egerton Howard Monypenny. *Educ:* RN Colls, Osborne and Dartmouth. Entered Royal Navy, Sept. 1919; Midshipman, 1923; Sub-Lieut 1927, Lieut 1928; specialised in Torpedoes and served as Torpedo Officer in HMS Vernon, 8th Dest. Flot., China Stn, and HMS Glorious; Comdr Dec. 1939, and served in Plans Div. Admlty, as exec. officer HM Ships Birmingham and Frobisher in Eastern Fleet, and on staff of C-in-C Eastern Fleet; Capt. Dec. 1944. Asst-Dir, TASW Div., Naval Staff, 1945–47; Naval Attaché, China, 1948–49; commanded HMS Gambia, 1950–51; Dir TASW div., Naval Staff, 1952–54; ADC to the Queen, 1953–54; Dep. Chief of Supplies and Transport, Admiralty (acting Rear-Adm.), 1955–57; retired, 1957. *Address:* 36 Knox Court, Knox Place, Haddington, East Lothian EH41 4EB.

DONCASTER, Bishop Suffragan of, since 1982; **Rt. Rev. William Michael Dermot Persson;** *b* 27 Sept. 1927; *s* of Leslie Charles Grenville Alan and Elizabeth Mercer Persson; *m* 1957, Ann Davey; two *s* one *d*. *Educ:* Monkton Combe School; Oriel Coll., Oxford (MA); Wycliffe Hall Theological Coll. National service, Army, 1945–48; commissioned, Royal Signals. Deacon 1953, priest 1954; Curate: Emmanuel, South Croydon, 1953–55; St John, Tunbridge Wells, 1955–58; Vicar, Christ Church, Barnet, 1958–67; Rector, Bebington, Cheshire, 1967–79; Vicar, Knutsford with Toft, 1979–82. *Recreations:* gardening, writing poetry. *Address:* Bishop's Lodge, Hooton Roberts, Rotherham S65 4PF.

DONCASTER, Archdeacon of; *see* Carnelley, Ven. Desmond.

DONEGALL, 7th Marquess of, *cr* 1791; **Dermot Richard Claud Chichester,** LVO 1986; Viscount Chichester and Baron of Belfast, 1625; Earl of Donegall, 1647; Earl of Belfast, 1791; Baron Fisherwick (GB), 1790; Baron Templemore, 1831; Hereditary Lord High Admiral of Lough Neagh; late 7th Queen's Own Hussars; Standard Bearer, Honourable Corps of Gentlemen at Arms, 1984–86 (one of HM Bodyguard, since 1966); *b* 18 April 1916; 2nd *s* of 4th Baron Templemore, PC, KCVO, DSO, and Hon. Clare Meriel Wingfield, 2nd *d* of 7th Viscount Powerscourt, PC Ireland (she *d* 1969); *S* father 1953, and to Marquessate of Donegall, 1975; *m* 1946, Lady Josceline Gabrielle Legge, *y d* of 7th Earl of Dartmouth, GCVO, TD; one *s* two *d*. *Educ:* Harrow; RMC, Sandhurst. 2nd Lt 7th Hussars, 1936; Lt 1939; served War of 1939–45 in Middle East and Italy (prisoner); Major, 1944; retired, 1949. *Recreations:* hunting, shooting, fishing. *Heir:* *s* Earl of Belfast, *qv*. *Address:* Dunbrody Park, Arthurstown, Co. Wexford, Eire. *T:* Waterford 89104. *Clubs:* Cavalry and Guards; Kildare Street and University (Dublin).

DONEGAN, Rt. Rev. Horace W(illiam) B(aden), Hon. CBE 1957; DD; *b* Matlock, Derbyshire, England, 17 May 1900; *s* of Horace George Donegan and Pembroke Capes Hand. *Educ:* St Stephen's, Annandale, NY; Oxford University, England; Harvard Divinity School; Episcopal Theological Seminary, Rector, Christ Church, Baltimore, 1929–33; Rector, St James' Church, NYC, 1933–47; Suffragan Bishop of New York, 1947–49; Bishop Coadjutor of New York, 1949–50. Bishop of New York, 1950–72. Vice-Pres., Pilgrims, USA; President: St Hilda's and St Hugh's Sch., NY; House of Redeemer, NY; Episcopal Actors Guild, NY; Chaplain, Veterans of Foreign Wars; Episcopal Visitor: Sisters of St Helena; Community of the Holy Spirit; Trustee: St Luke's Hosp., NY; Episcopal Sch., NY; Contemporary Club, NY. Award, Conf. of Christians and Jews; Medal of City of New York; Medal of Merit, St Nicholas Society, NY; Citation, NY Hospital Assoc.; Harlem Arts & Culture Award. Churchill Fellow, Westminster Coll., Fulton, Mo. Hon. degrees: DD: New York Univ., 1940; Univ. of South, 1949; Trinity, 1950; Bard, 1957; King's Univ., Halifax, 1958; Berkley Divinity School, New Haven, Conn., 1969; STD: Hobart, 1948; General Theological Seminary, 1949; Columbia Univ., 1960; DCL Nashotah, 1956; Sub Prelate OStJ, 1956; Grand Cross St Joanikije, 1956; Legion of Honour, France, 1957; Silver Medal of Red Cross of Japan, 1959; Holy Pagania from Armenian Church, 1960; Grand Kt, Order of St Denys of Zante (Greece), 1959. *Publications:* articles in religious publications. *Recreations:* golf, swimming, painting. *Address:* Manhattan House, 200 E 66th Street, New York, NY 10021, USA. *Clubs:* Athenæum, Royal Automobile, American, Kennel (London); Union, Union League, Pilgrims, Century Association, Columbia Faculty, Tuxedo Park (all of New York).

DONERAILE, 10th Viscount *cr* 1785 (Ire.); **Richard Allen St Leger;** Baron Doneraile, 1776; Food Marketing Analyst since 1974; *b* 17 Aug. 1946; *s* of 9th Viscount Doneraile and of Melva, Viscountess Doneraile; *S* father, 1983; *m* 1970, Kathleen Mary Simcox, Churchtown, Mallow, Co. Cork; one *s* one *d*. *Educ:* Orange Coast College, California; Mississippi Univ. Served US Army. Air Traffic Control specialist; antiquarian book appraiser, 1970–73. *Recreations:* outdoor sports, skiing, golf, sailing. *Heir:* *s* Hon. Nathaniel Warham Robert St John St Leger, *b* 13 Sept. 1971. *Address:* 405 Eve Circle, Placentia, California 92670, USA. *Club:* Yorba Linda Country (California).

DONIACH, Prof. Israel, MD (London); FRCPath 1963; FRCP 1968; Professor of Morbid Anatomy in University of London, London Hospital, 1960–76, now Emeritus Professor; Hon. Lecturer in Histopathology, St Bartholomew's Hospital Medical School, since 1976; *b* 9 March 1911; *yr s* of late Aaron Selig and late Rahel Doniach; *m* 1933, Deborah Abileah; one *s* (one *d* decd). *Educ:* University Coll. and Hosp., London. Asst Pathologist, St Mary's Hosp., London, 1935–37; Clinical Pathologist and Cancer Research Asst, Mount Vernon Hosp., Northwood, 1937–43; Senior Lecturer in Morbid Anatomy, Postgraduate Medical Sch. of London, 1943–59, Reader, 1959–60. *Publications:* papers in morbid anatomy and experimental pathology in various journals. *Address:* 25 Alma Square, NW8 9PY. *T:* 01–286 1617.

DONKIN, Alexander Sim; HM Diplomatic Service, retired; Counsellor (Administration), UK Mission to United Nations, and Deputy Consul-General, New York, 1977–82; *b* 14 July 1922; *s* of Matthew Henderson Donkin and Margaret Donkin; *m* 1944, Irene Florence (*née* Willis); two *d*. *Educ:* Monkwearmouth Sch., Co. Durham. Served War, RAF, 1941–46; Sqdn Ldr. Civil Service, 1947–66; HM Diplomatic Service, 1966; FCO, 1966–70; Washington, 1970–74; FCO, 1974–77. *Recreations:* music, walking, photography. *Address:* 1 Amberley Road, Eastbourne, East Sussex.

DONKIN, Air Cdre Peter Langloh, CBE 1946; DSO 1944; retired; *b* 19 June 1913; *s* of Frederick Langloh and Phyllis Donkin; *m* 1941, Elizabeth Marjorie Cox; two *d*. *Educ:* Sherborne; RAF Coll., Cranwell. Commissioned RAF, 1933; No. 16 Sqdn, 1933–38; British Mission in Poland, 1939; CO 225 Sqdn, 1940; CO 239 Sqdn, 1941–42; CO 35 Wing, 1943–44; Sch. Land Air Warfare, 1945; HQ, RAF Levant, 1946; RCAF Staff Coll., 1948–49; Exchange USAF, 1950; CO, RAF Chivenor, 1951–53; Air Attaché, Moscow, 1954–57; Asst Chief of Staff, HQ Allied Air Forces, Central Europe, 1957–58; idc, 1959; AOC, RAF, Hong Kong, 1960–62. *Recreations:* shooting, yachting. *Address:* Coombe Cross Cottage, Templecombe, Som. *Club:* Carlton.

DONKIN, Dr Robin Arthur, FBA 1985; Lecturer in the Geography of Latin America, since 1971 and Fellow of Jesus College, since 1972, University of Cambridge; *b* Morpeth, 28 Oct. 1928; *s* of Arthur Donkin and Elizabeth Jane Kirkup; *m* 1970, Jennifer Gay Kennedy; one *d*. *Educ:* Univ. of Durham (BA 1950; PhD 1953); MA Cantab 1971. Lieut, Royal Artillery, 1953–55 (Egypt). King George VI Meml Fellow, Univ. of California, Berkeley, 1955–56; Asst Lectr, Dept of Geography, Univ. of Edinburgh, 1956–58; Lectr, Dept of Geography, Univ. of Birmingham, 1958–70; Tutor, Jesus Coll., Cambridge, 1975–. Leverhulme Research Fellow, 1966; Vis. Associate Prof. of Geography, Univ. of Toronto, 1969; field work in Middle and S America, NW Africa. *Publications:* The Cistercian Order in Europe: a bibliography of printed sources, 1969; Spanish Red: cochineal and the Opuntia cactus, 1977; The Cistercians: studies in the geography of medieval England and Wales, 1978; Agricultural Terracing in the Aboriginal New World, 1979; Manna: an historical geography, 1980; The Peccary, 1985; The Muscovy Duck, 1986; articles in geographical, historical and anthropological jls. *Address:* Jesus College, Cambridge; 13 Roman Hill, Barton, Cambridge. *T:* Comberton 2572.

DONLEAVY, James Patrick; author; *b* 23 April 1926; *m* Valerie Heron (marr. diss.); one *s* one *d*; *m* Mary Wilson Price; one *s* one *d*. *Educ:* schs in USA; Trinity Coll., Dublin. *Publications:* The Ginger Man (novel), 1955; Fairy Tales of New York (play), 1960; What They Did In Dublin With The Ginger Man (introd. and play), 1961; A Singular Man (novel), 1963 (play, 1964); Meet My Maker The Mad Molecule (short stories), 1964; The Saddest Summer of Samuel S (novella), 1966 (play, 1967); The Beastly Beatitudes of Balthazar B (novel), 1968 (play, 1981); The Onion Eaters (novel), 1971; The Plays of J. P. Donleavy, 1972; A Fairy Tale of New York (novel), 1973; The Unexpurgated Code: a complete manual of survival and manners, 1975; The Destinies of Darcy Dancer, Gentleman (novel), 1977; Schultz (novel), 1980; Leila (novel), 1983; De Alfonce Tennis: the superlative game of eccentric champions, its history, accoutrements, rules, conduct and regimen (sports manual), 1984; Ireland, in all her Sins and in some of her Graces, 1986. *Address:* Levington Park, Mullingar, Co. Westmeath, Ireland.

DONNE, David Lucas; Chairman: Asda-MFI, since 1986 (Director, since 1984); Crest Nicholson, since 1973; Steetley, since 1983 (Deputy Chairman, 1979–83); *b* 17 Aug. 1925; *s* of late Dr Cecil Lucas Donne, Wellington, NZ, and of Marjorie Nicholls Donne; *m* 1st, 1957, Jennifer Margaret Duncan (*d* 1975); two *s* one *d*; 2nd, 1978, Clare, *d* of Maj. F. J. Yates. *Educ:* Stowe; Christ Church, Oxford (MA Nat. Science). Called to the Bar, Middle Temple, 1949. Studied Business Admin, Syracuse Univ., 1952–53; Charterhouse Group, 1953–64; William Baird, 1964–67. Chm., Dalgety, 1977–86 (Dep. Chm., 1975–77); Dir, Royal Trust of Canada, 1972–. Member: Bd, British Coal (formerly NCB), 1984–; Royal Opera House Develt Land Trust, 1985–. Chm., Hellenic Travellers' Club. *Recreations:* shooting, gun dogs, opera, sailing. *Address:* 21 Hertford Square, W1. *Club:* Royal Thames Yacht.

DONNE, Hon. Sir Gaven (John), KBE 1979; Chief Justice: of Nauru, since 1985; of Tuvalu, since 1986; *b* 8 May 1914; *s* of Jack Alfred Donne and Mary Elizabeth Donne; *m* 1946, Isabel Fenwick, *d* of John Edwin Hall; two *s* two *d*. *Educ:* Palmerston North Boys' High Sch.; Hastings High Sch.; Victoria Univ., Wellington; Auckland Univ. (LLB New Zealand). Called to the Bar and admitted solicitor, 1938. Military Service, 2nd NZEF, Middle East and Italy, 1941–45. Stipendiary Magistrate, NZ, 1958–75; Puisne Judge, Supreme Court of Western Samoa, 1970–71; Chief Justice, Western Samoa, 1972–75, Mem. Court of Appeal of Western Samoa, 1975–82; Judge, High Court of Niue, 1973; Chief Justice of the Cook Islands, 1975–82, and of Niue, 1974–82; Queen's Rep. in the Cook Islands, 1982–84. Hon. Counsellor, Internat. Assoc. of Youth Magistrates, 1974–. Member: Takapuna Bor. Council, 1957–58; Auckland Town Planning Authority, 1958; Bd of Governors, Westlake High Sch., 1957–58. Grand Cross 2nd Cl., Order of Merit of Fed. Republic of Germany, 1978. *Recreations:* golf, fishing, walking. *Address:* Meneng Drive, Nauru, Central Pacific. *T:* 3465; RD4, Otaramarae, Lake Rotoiti, Rotorua, New Zealand. *T:* Okere Falls 861. *Club:* University (Auckland).

DONNE, Sir John (Christopher), Kt 1976; Chairman, National Health Service Training Authority, 1983–86; *b* 19 Aug. 1921; *s* of late Leslie Victor Donne, solicitor, Hove, and Mabel Laetitia Richards (*née* Pike); *m* 1945, Mary Stuart (*née* Seaton); three *d*. *Educ:* Charterhouse. Royal Artillery, 1940–46 (Captain); served Europe and India. Solicitor, 1949; Notary Public; Consultant, Donne Mileham & Haddock; Pres., Sussex Law Soc.,

1969–70. Chairman: SE (Metropolitan) Regional Hosp. Bd, 1971–74; SE Thames RHA, 1973–83. Governor, Guy's Hosp., 1971–74, Guy's Hosp. Med. Sch., 1974–; Dep. Chm., RHA Chairmen, 1976–78 (Chm., 1974–76); Mem., Gen. Council, King Edward's Hosp. Fund for London, 1972– (Mem., Management Cttee, 1978–84); a Governing Trustee, Nuffield Provincial Hosp. Trust, 1975–; Dir, Nuffield Health and Soc. Services Fund, 1976–. Member: Council, Internat. Hosp. Fedn, 1979–85; Council, Inst. for Med. Ethics (formerly Soc. for Study of Medical Ethics), 1980–; Court of Univ. of Sussex, 1979–. FRSA 1985; FRSocMed 1985. Mem. Ct of Assts, Hon. Company of Broderers, 1979– (Master, 1983–84). Mem., Editorial Bd, Jl Medical Ethics, 1977–79. *Recreations:* genealogy, gardening, photography, listening to music. *Address:* The Old School House, Acton Burnell, Shrewsbury SY5 7PG. *T:* Acton Burnell 647. *Clubs:* Army and Navy, Pilgrims, MCC; Butterflies, Sussex Martlets.

DONNER, Frederic Garrett; Chairman of the Board of Trustees, Alfred P. Sloan Foundation, 1968–75, retired; Director, General Motors Corporation, 1942–74 (Chairman, 1958–67); *b* 1902; *s* of Frank Donner and Cornelia (*née* Zimmerman); *m* 1929, Eileen Isaacson; one *d* (and one *s* decd). *Educ:* University of Michigan, Ann Arbor, Michigan, USA. General Motors Corporation, 1926; Dir, Communications Satellite Corporation, 1964–77; Trustee, Sloan-Kettering Inst. for Cancer Research, NY, 1964–75. Holds hon. doctorates and foreign decorations. *Address:* 40 West Elm Street, Apt 5D, Greenwich, Conn 06830, USA. *Clubs:* Links, University (NY City); North Hempstead Country (Long Island, NY).

DONNER, Sir Patrick William, Kt 1953; MA; DL; *b* 1904; *s* of late Ossian Donner and Violet Marion McHutchen, Edinburgh; *m* 1938, Hon. Angela Chatfield (*d* 1943), *er d* of 1st Baron Chatfield, GCB, OM, KCMG, CVO, Admiral of the Fleet; *m* 1947, Pamela *y d* of Rear Adm. Herbert A. Forster, MVO; one *s* two *d*. *Educ:* abroad and Exeter Coll., Oxford. Studied Imperial development and administration, 1928–30; MP (C) West Islington, 1931–35; Basingstoke Div. of Hants, 1935–55; Hon. Sec., India Defence League, 1933–35; Parliamentary Private Sec. to Sir Samuel Hoare, Home Sec., 1939; Mem. Advisory Cttee on Education in the Colonies; Parliamentary Private Sec. to Col Oliver Stanley, Sec. of State for the Colonies, 1944; Dir, National Review Ltd, 1933–47; Mem. Executive Council Joint East and Central African Board, 1937–54. Volunteered RAFVR 1939; served at HQ Fighter Command; Acting Sqdn Leader, 1941. Chm. Executive Cttee of the Men of the Trees, 1959–62. Mem., Art Panel of the Arts Council, 1963–66. High Sheriff of Hants, 1967–68; DL Hants 1971. *Publication:* Crusade: a life against the calamitous twentieth century, 1985. *Recreations:* music, travel, landscape gardening. *Address:* Hurstbourne Park, Whitchurch, Hants. *T:* Whitchurch 2230.

DONNISON, Prof. David Vernon; Professor of Town and Regional Planning, Glasgow University, since 1980; *b* 19 Jan. 1926; *s* of F. S. V. Donnison, *qv*; *m*; two *s* two *d*. *Educ:* Marlborough Coll., Wiltshire; Magdalen Coll., Oxford. Asst Lecturer and Lecturer, Manchester Univ., 1950–53; Lecturer, Toronto Univ., 1953–55; Reader, London Sch. of Economics, 1956–61; Prof. of Social Administration, 1961–69; Dir, Centre for Environmental Studies, 1969–75. Chairman: Public Schs Commission, 1968–70; Supplementary Benefits Commn, 1975–80. Hon. Doctorates: Bradford, 1973; Hull, 1980; Leeds, Southampton, 1981. *Publications:* The Neglected Child and the Social Services, 1954; Welfare Services in a Canadian Community, 1958; Housing since the Rent Act, 1961; The Government of Housing, 1967; An Approach to Social Policy, 1975; Social Policy and Administration Revisited, 1975; (with Paul Soto) The Good City, 1980; The Politics of Poverty, 1982; (with Clare Ungerson) Housing Policy, 1982. *Address:* 12 Holyrood Crescent, Glasgow G20 6HJ. *T:* 041–334 2827.

DONNISON, Frank Siegfried Vernon, CBE 1943; Indian Civil Service (retired); *b* 3 July 1898; *s* of Frank Samuel and of Edith Donnison; *m* 1923, Ruth Seruya Singer, MBE, JP (*d* 1968); one *s* one *d*. *Educ:* Marlborough Coll.; Corpus Christi Coll., Oxford. Served with Grenadier Guards, 1917–19; ICS (Burma), 1922; Chief Sec. to Govt of Burma, 1946; military service, Burma, 1944–45 (despatches). Historian, Cabinet Office, Historical Section, 1949–66. *Publications:* Public Administration in Burma, 1953; British Military Administration in the Far East, 1943–46, 1956; Civil Affairs and Military Government, North-West Europe, 1944–46, 1961; Civil Affairs and Military Government, Central Organization and Planning, 1966; Burma, 1970. *Recreation:* music. *Address:* Lower Cross Farmhouse, East Hagbourne, Didcot OX11 9LD. *T:* Didcot 3314. *Club:* East India, Devonshire, Sports and Public Schools.

See also Professor D. V. Donnison.

DONOGHUE, Prof. Denis, MA, PhD; literary critic; Henry James Professor of Letters, New York University, since 1979; *b* 1928. *Educ:* University College, Dublin. BA 1949, MA 1952, PhD 1957; MA Cantab 1965. Admin. Office, Dept of Finance, Irish Civil Service, 1951–54. Asst Lectr, Univ. Coll., Dublin, 1954–57; Coll. Lectr, 1957–62; Visiting Schol., Univ. of Pennsylvania, 1962–63; Coll. Lectr, Univ. Coll., Dublin, 1963–64; University Lectr, Cambridge Univ., 1964–65; Fellow, King's Coll., Cambridge, 1964–65; Prof. of Modern English and American Literature, University Coll., Dublin, 1965–79. Mem. Internat. Cttee of Assoc. of University Profs of English. Mem. BBC Commn to monitor the quality of spoken English on BBC Radio, 1979. Reith Lectr, BBC, 1982. *Publications:* The Third Voice, 1959; Connoisseurs of Chaos, 1965; (ed jtly) An Honoured Guest, 1965; The Ordinary Universe, 1968; Emily Dickinson, 1968; Jonathan Swift, 1969; (ed) Swift, 1970; Yeats, 1971; Thieves of Fire, 1974; (ed) W. B. Yeats, Memoirs, 1973; Sovereign Ghost: studies in Imagination, 1978; Ferocious Alphabets, 1981; contribs to reviews and journals. *Address:* New York University, 19 University Place, New York, NY 10003, USA; Gaybrook, North Avenue, Mount Merrion, Dublin, Ireland.

DONOHOE, Peter Howard; pianist; *b* 18 June 1953; *s* of Harold Donohoe and Marjorie Donohoe (*née* Travis); *m* 1980, Elaine Margaret Burns; one *d*. *Educ:* Chetham's School of Music, Manchester; Leeds Univ.; Royal Northern Coll. of Music; Paris Conservatoire. BMus; GRNCM, ARCM; Hon. FRNCM 1983. Professional solo pianist, 1974–; London début, 1978; concert tours in Europe, USA, Canada, Australia, Asia, USSR; regular appearances at Royal Festival Hall, Barbican Hall, Queen Elizabeth Hall, Henry Wood Promenade concerts, 1979–; numerous TV and radio broadcasts, UK and overseas; recordings include music by Rachmaninov, Stravinsky, Prokofiev, Britten, Messiaen, Muldowney. Competition finalist: British Liszt, London, 1976; Liszt-Bartok, Budapest, 1976; Leeds International Piano, 1981; winner, Internat. Tschaikovsky competition, Moscow, 1982. *Recreations:* jazz, golf, helping young musicians, clock collecting. *Address:* c/o Harold Holt Ltd, 31 Sinclair Road, W14 0NS. *T:* 01–603 4600.

DONOUGHMORE, 8th Earl of, *cr* 1800; **Richard Michael John Hely-Hutchinson;** Baron Donoughmore, 1783; Viscount Hutchinson (UK), 1821; *b* 8 Aug. 1927; *er s* of 7th Earl of Donoughmore and of Dorothy Jean (MBE 1947), *d* of late J. B. Hotham; *S* father, 1981; *m* 1951, Sheila, *o c* of late Frank Frederick Parsons and Mrs Learmond Perkins; four *s*. *Educ:* Winchester; New College, Oxford (MA; BM, BCh). *Heir:* *s* Viscount Suirdale, *qv*. *Address:* The Manor House, Bampton, Oxon. *Clubs:* Hurlingham; Kildare Street and University (Dublin); Jockey (Paris).

DONOUGHUE, family name of **Baron Donoughue**.

DONOUGHUE, Baron *cr* 1985 (Life Peer), of Ashton in the County of Northamptonshire; **Bernard Donoughue;** Director, Kleinwort, Benson Ltd, since 1986; Head of Research, Kleinwort Grieveson Securities, since 1986; *b* 1934; *s* of late Thomas Joseph Donoughue and of Maud Violet Andrews; *m* 1959, Carol Ruth Goodman; two *s* two *d*. *Educ:* Secondary Modern Sch. and Grammar Sch., Northampton; Lincoln Coll. and Nuffield Coll., Oxford. MA, DPhil (Oxon). FRHistS. Henry Fellow, Harvard, USA. Mem., Editorial Staff: The Economist, Sunday Times, Sunday Telegraph. Sen. Res. Officer, PEP, 1960–63; Lectr, Sen. Lectr, Reader, LSE, 1963–74; Sen. Policy Advr to the Prime Minister, 1974–79; Development Dir, Economist Intelligence Unit, 1979–81; Asst Editor, The Times, 1981–82; Partner and Head of Res. and Investment Policy, Grieveson, Grant & Co., 1983–86. Member: Sports Council, 1965–71; Commn of Enquiry into Association Football, 1966–68; Ct of Governors, LSE, 1968–74, 1982–; Civil Service Coll. Adv. Council, 1976–79; Adv. Bd, Wissenschaftzentrum, Berlin, 1978–; Bd of Nene Coll., Northampton, 1979–; Bd, Centre for European Policy Studies, Brussels, 1982–; Council, Campaign for Freedom of Information, 1984–; Council, Employment Inst., 1985–. Chm. Exec., London Symphony Orch., 1979–. Associate Mem., Nuffield Coll., Oxford, 1982–; Mem., Sen. Common Room, Lincoln Coll., Oxford, 1985–; Internat. Fellow, Roosevelt Center for Policy Studies, Washington, DC, 1982–83. *Publications:* (ed jtly) Oxford Poetry, 1956; Wage Policies in the Public Sector, 1962; Trade Unions in a Changing Society, 1963; British Politics and the American Revolution, 1964; (with W. T. Rodgers) The People into Parliament, 1966; (with G. W. Jones) Herbert Morrison: portrait of a politician, 1973. *Recreations:* politics, economics, music, the Gay Hussar. *Address:* 7 Brookfield Park, NW5.

DONOVAN, Charles Edward; Managing Director, Personnel, and Member, British Gas Corporation, since 1981; *b* 28 Jan. 1934; *s* of Charles and Sarah Donovan; *m* 1963, Robina Evelyn (*née* Anderson); three *s*. *Educ:* Camphill Sch., Paisley; Scottish Coll. of Commerce; Royal Technical Coll., Glasgow (now Univ. of Strathclyde). MIPM. Personnel Officer: HQ, BEA, 1962; London and SE, Richard Costain Ltd, Constr. and Civil Engrs, 1963; Sen. Personnel Officer, Engrg, W Midlands Gas Bd, 1966; Southern Gas, 1970–77: Personnel Manager, 1973; Personnel Dir, 1975; Dir, Indust. Relations, British Gas, 1977. *Recreations:* sailing, hill walking, reading. *Address:* British Gas Corporation, Rivermill House, 152 Grosvenor Road, SW1V 3JL.

DONOVAN, Prof. Desmond Thomas; Yates-Goldsmid Professor of Geology and Head of Department of Geology, University College, London, 1966–82; Hon. Curator, Wells Museum, Somerset, 1982–85; *b* 16 June 1921; *s* of T. B. Donovan; *m* 1959, Shirley Louise Saward; two *s* one *d*. *Educ:* Epsom Coll.; University of Bristol. BSc 1942; PhD 1951; DSc 1960. Asst Lectr in Geology, University of Bristol, 1947; Lectr in Geology, Bristol, 1950; Prof. of Geology, University of Hull, 1962. Pres., Palaeontographical Soc., 1979–84. *Publications:* Stratigraphy: An Introduction to Principles, 1966; (ed) Geology of Shelf Seas, 1968; papers on fossil cephalopods, Jurassic stratigraphy, Pleistocene deposits, marine geology. *Address:* 52 Willow Road, NW3 1TP. *T:* 01-794 8626. *Club:* Athenæum.

DONOVAN, Hedley (Williams); *b* 24 May 1914; *s* of Percy Williams Donovan and Alice Dougan Donovan; *m* 1941, Dorothy Hannon (*d* 1978); two *s* one *d*. *Educ:* University of Minnesota; Hertford Coll., Oxford (Hon. Fellow, 1977). BA (*magna cum laude*) Minn., 1934; BA Oxon. 1936. US Naval Reserve, active duty, 1942–45 (Lieut-Comdr). Reporter, Washington Post, 1937–42; Writer and Editor, 1945–53, Managing Editor, 1953–59, Fortune; Editorial Dir, Time Inc., 1959–64, Editor in Chief, 1964–79, Consultant, 1979–84. Trustee: Nat. Humanities Center; Asia Soc.; Aerospace Corp. Mem., Council on Foreign Relations; Senior Advisor to the President, 1979–80. Fellow, Faculty of Govt, Harvard Univ., 1981–. Fellow, Amer. Acad. of Arts and Sciences. Phi Beta Kappa; Rhodes Scholar. Hon. LittD: Pomona Coll., 1966; Mount Holyoke, 1967; Boston, 1968; Hon DHL: South-Western at Memphis, 1967; Rochester, 1968; Transylvania, 1979; Hon LLD: Carnegie-Mellon, 1969; Lehigh, 1976; Allegheny Coll., 1979. *Publication:* Roosevelt to Reagan: a reporter's encounters with nine Presidents, 1985. *Address:* Harbor Road, Sands Point, NY 11050, USA. *Clubs:* University, Century, (both New York); Metropolitan, 1925 F Street (Washington DC); Manhasset Bay Yacht (Long Island); Sands Point Golf.

DONOVAN, Ian Edward, FCMA; Member since 1985, and Group Director, Finance and Central Services, since 1986, Civil Aviation Authority; *b* 2 March 1940; *s* of John Walter Donovan and Ethel Moyneux; *m* 1969, Susan Betty Harris; two *s*. *Educ:* Leighton Park, Reading. FCMA 1985. Gen. Factory Manager, Lucas CAV, 1969–72; Finance Man., Lucas Girling, 1972–78; Finance Director: Lucas Girling, Koblenz, 1978–81; Lucas Electrical Ltd, 1982–84. *Recreations:* sailing, gardening, music. *Address:* Lawn Farm, Church Lane, Tibberton, Droitwich, Worcs WR9 7NW.

DOOGE, Prof. James Clement Ignatius; Professor of Civil Engineering, University College, Dublin, 1970–81, and since 1982; Leader of the Irish Senate, since 1983; *b* 30 July 1922; *s* of Denis Patrick Dooge and Veronica Catherine Carroll; *m* 1946, Veronica O'Doherty; two *s* three *d*. *Educ:* Christian Brothers' Sch., Dun Laoghaire; University Coll., Dublin (BE, BSc 1942, ME 1952); Univ. of Iowa (MSc 1956). FICE; FASCE. Jun. Civil Engr, Irish Office of Public Works, 1943–46; Design Engr, Electricity Supply Bd, Ireland, 1946–58; Prof. of Civil Engrg, UC Cork, 1958–70; Minister for Foreign Affairs, Ireland, 1981–82. President: ICEI, 1968–69 (Hon. FICEI; Kettle Premium and Plaque, 1948; Mullins Medal, 1951, 1962); Internat. Assoc. for Hydrologic Scis, 1975–79; Member: Exec. Bureau, Internat. Union for Geodesy and Geophysics, 1979–87; Gen. Cttee, ICSU, 1980–86 (Sec. Gen., 1980–82). Fellow, Amer. Geophysical Union (Horton Award, 1959); MRIA. Hon. DrAgrSc Wageningen, 1978; Hon. DrTech. Lund, 1980. Internat. Prize for Hydrology, 1983. *Address:* University College, Earlsfort Terrace, Dublin 2, Ireland.

DOOKUN, Sir Dewoonarain, Kt 1984; Chairman and Managing Director, Mauritius Cosmetics Ltd, since 1966; *b* 7 Dec. 1929; *s* of Jadoonath Dookun; *m* 1959, Henriette Keupp; two *s*. *Educ:* St Joseph College; Univ. of Edinburgh. Manufacturing, marketing, business administration and accounts, Mainz, West Germany; founder of: Mauritius Cosmetics, 1966; Paper Converting Co., 1967; Jet Industries, 1967; FDG Garments Industries, 1968; Agri-Pac, 1979; Deramann, 1979; Gumboots Manufacturers, 1976; DG Rubber, 1979; Elite Textiles, 1982; Deodan Textile, 1984. *Recreations:* reading, walking, golf. *Address:* Queen Mary Avenue, Floreal, Mauritius. *T:* 86-2361; *telex:* 4239 Dookun IW. *Clubs:* Institute of Directors; Mauritius Gymkhana; Swastika.

DOOLITTLE, Lt-Gen. James H.; Hon. KCB 1945; Trustee, 1963–69 (Chairman of Executive Committee and Vice-Chairman, Board of Trustees, 1965–69), Aerospace Corporation; Chairman of Board, Space Technology Laboratories, Inc., 1959–62; Director: Mutual of Omaha Insurance Co.; United Benefit Life Insurance Co.; Tele-Trip Co., Inc.; *b* 14 Dec. 1896; *s* of Frank H. Doolittle and Rosa C. Shephard; *m* 1917, Josephine E. Daniels; two *s*. *Educ:* University of California (AB); MIT (MS, ScD). US Army Air Force, 1917–30; Manager, Aviation Dept, Shell Oil Co., 1930–40; USAAF, 1940–45. Dir, Shell Oil Company, 1946–67 (Vice-Pres., 1946–59). *Publications:* various scientific.

Recreations: shooting, fishing. *Address:* 8545 Carmel Valley Road, Carmel, Calif 93923, USA.

DORAN, John Frederick, CEng, FInstGasE, MInstM; Chairman, East Midlands Gas Region, 1974–77; *b* 28 July 1916; *s* of Henry Joseph and Clara Doran; *m* 1940, Eileen Brotherton; two *s*. *Educ:* Wandsworth Technical Coll.; Wimbledon Technical Coll. Served War, Fleet Air Arm, 1943–46. Various appts Gas Light & Coke Co. (subseq. North Thames Gas Bd), 1935–53; Dist Manager, Hornsey Dist, North Thames Gas Bd, 1953; Regional Sales Manager, North Western Div., North Thames Gas Bd, 1955–57. Southern Gas Board: Regional Sales and Service Manager, Southampton Region and Dorset and Bournemouth Regions, 1957–65; Marketing Manager, 1965–67; Commercial Manager, 1968–69; Commercial Dir, 1970–71; Commercial Dir and Bd Mem., 1971–73. Dep. Chm., East Midlands Gas Region, 1973. Founder, John Doran Gas Museum, Leicester. *Publications:* technical papers to Instn Gas Engrs. *Recreations:* golf, gardening. *Address:* 14 Oberfield Road, Brockenhurst, Hants SO42 7QF. *T:* Lymington 23185.

DORÁTI, Antal, Hon. KBE 1983; composer and conductor; Conductor Laureate for life: Royal Philharmonic Orchestra, 1978 (Principal Conductor, 1975–78); Detroit Symphony Orchestra, 1981 (Musical Director, 1977–81); Stockholm Philharmonic, 1981; *b* Budapest, 9 April 1906; *s* of Alexander Doráti and Margit (*née* Kunwald); *m* 1st, 1929, Klara Korody; one *d*; 2nd, 1971, Ilse von Alpenheim. *Educ:* Royal Academy of Music, Budapest; University of Vienna. Conductor: Royal Opera House, Budapest, 1924–28; Münster State Opera, 1929–32; Musical Director: Ballet Russe de Monte Carlo, 1932–40; Ballet Theatre, NY, 1940–42; New Opera Co., NY, 1942–43; Musical Dir and Conductor: Dallas Symph. Orch., 1944–49; Minneapolis Symph. Orch., 1944–60; Chief Conductor: BBC Symphony Orchestra, 1963–66; Stockholm Philharmonic Orch., 1966–74; Musical Dir, Nat. Symphony Orch., Washington, DC, 1970–77. Guest conductor of major orchestras of the world, Salzburg, Holland, Venice, Lucerne, Berlin Festivals, etc; London Symphony, New Philharmonia, London Philharmonic, Royal Philharmonic, Israel Philharmonic orchestras, etc. Holder of 26 recording awards in America and Europe. DrMus: Macalister Coll., St Paul, 1958; George Washington Univ., 1975; Dr (hc) Humanities: Maryland, 1976; Wayne State Univ., Detroit, 1982. Member: Swedish Acad., 1967; Royal Swedish Academy of the Arts; Hon. Prof., Music Acad., Budapest, 1981. Comdr, Order of Vasa; Chevalier of Arts and Letters, France; Order of Letters and Arts, Austria; Order of the Flag, Hungary. Compositions include: The Way (dramatic cantata); Symphony I; Missa Brevis; The two enchantments of Li-Tai-Pe; String Quartet; Cello Concerto; Nocturne and Capriccio for oboe and strings; Magdalena (ballet); Seven Pictures for Orch.; Madrigal Suite; String Octet; Largo Concertato for String Orch.; 'Chamber-Music', Song Cycle for Sopr. and small orch.; Night Music for flute and small orch.; Variations on a theme of Bartok for piano, Piano Concerto; Threni for String Orch.; American Serenades for String Orch.; Öt Ének; Divertimento for Oboe and Orch.; The Voices (song cycle) for bass voice and Orch.; In the Beginning (five meditations) for baritone, oboe, cello and percussion; Sonata for Assisi for two flutes; String Quartet; Five Pieces for Oboe; Three Studies for Mixed Choir; Of God, Man and Machine for Mixed Choir; Four Choruses for Female Choir; Duo Concertante for Oboe and Piano; The Chosen (opera); Querela Pacis (fantasy for orch.); Triptych for Oboe, Oboe d'amore and English Horn with string orch. *Publication:* Notes of Seven Decades, 1979. *Recreations:* painting sketching, reading, art collecting.

DORCHESTER, Area Bishop of; Rt. Rev. Conrad John Eustace Meyer; appointed Bishop Suffragan of Dorchester, 1979, Area Bishop, 1985; *b* 2 July 1922; *s* of William Eustace and Marcia Meyer; *m* 1960, Mary Wiltshire; no *c*. *Educ:* Clifton Coll.; Pembroke Coll., Cambridge; Westcott House. BA 1946, MA 1948. Served War of 1939–45: Royal Navy (commissioned from lower deck), 1942–46. Lieut (S) RNVR, post war, until apptd Chaplain, RNVR, 1950–54. Deacon, 1948; Priest, 1949; Asst Curate: St Francis, Ashton Gate, Bristol, 1948–51; Kenwyn, Truro, 1951; Falmouth Parish Church, 1954; Vicar of Devoran, Truro, 1956–65; Diocesan Youth Chaplain, 1956; Asst Dir of Religious Educn, 1958; Diocesan Sec. for Educn, 1960–69; Archdeacon of Bodmin, 1969–79; Hon. Canon of Truro, 1966–79; Examining Chaplain to Bishop of Truro, 1973–79. Hon. Diocesan Sec., Nat. Soc., 1960–69. Mem. Governing Body, SPCK, 1972–; Chairman: Grants Cttee, SPCK, 1973–; Federation of Catholic Priests, 1976–79; Church Union Exec. Cttee, 1979–84; Joint Group on Funerals at Cemeteries and Crematoria, 1980–. Fellow, Woodard Corp. of Schools, 1967; Provost, Western Div., Woodard Corp., 1970–; Hon. FICD. *Recreations:* swimming, walking, military history, civil defence, archaeology. *Address:* 151 Wroslyn Road, Freeland, Oxford OX7 2HR. *Club:* Royal Commonwealth Society.

DORE, Ronald Philip, FBA 1975; Visiting Professor, Imperial College of Science and Technology, University of London, 1982; *b* 1 Feb. 1925; *s* of Philip Brine Dore and Elsie Constance Dore; *m* 1957, Nancy Macdonald; one *s* one *d*. *Educ:* Poole Grammar Sch.; SOAS, Univ. of London (BA). Lectr in Japanese Instns, SOAS, London, 1951; Prof. of Asian Studies, Univ. of BC, 1956; Reader, later Prof. of Sociol., LSE, 1961 (Hon. Fellow, 1980); Fellow IDS, 1969–82; Asst Dir, Technical Change Centre, 1982–86. Hon. Foreign Mem., Amer. Acad. of Arts and Scis, 1978. *Publications:* City Life in Japan, 1958; Land Reform in Japan, 1959, 2nd edn 1984; Education in Tokugawa Japan, 1963, 2nd edn 1983; (ed) Aspects of Social Change in Modern Japan, 1967; British Factory, Japanese Factory, 1973; The Diploma Disease, 1976; Shinohata: portrait of a Japanese village, 1978; (ed with Zoe Mars) Community Development, Comparative Case Studies in India, The Republic of Korea, Mexico and Tanzania, 1981; Energy Conservation in Japanese Industry, 1982; Flexible Rigidities: structural adjustment in Japan, 1986. *Address:* 157 Surrenden Road, Brighton, East Sussex. *T:* Brighton 501370.

DORKING, Suffragan Bishop of, since 1986; **Rt. Rev. David Peter Wilcox;** *b* 29 June 1930; *s* of John Wilcox and Stella Wilcox (*née* Bower); *m* 1956, Pamela Ann Hedges; two *s* two *d*. *Educ:* Northampton Grammar School; St John's Coll., Oxford (2nd cl. Hons Theol., MA); Lincoln Theological Coll. Deacon 1954, priest 1955; Asst Curate, St Peter's, St Helier, Morden, Surrey, 1954–56; Asst Curate, University Church, Oxford and SCM Staff Secretary in Oxford, 1956–59; on staff of Lincoln Theological Coll., 1959–64; USPG Missionary on staff of United Theological Coll., Bangalore, and Presbyter in Church of S India, 1964–70; Vicar of Great Gransden with Little Gransden, dio. Ely, 1970–72; Canon Residentiary, Derby Cathedral and Warden, E Midlands Joint Ordination Training Scheme, 1972–77; Proctor in Convocation, 1973–77; Canon Emeritus, Derby Cathedral, 1977; Principal of Ripon College, Cuddesdon and Vicar of All Saints', Cuddesdon, 1977–85. *Recreations:* walking, music, art. *Address:* 13 Pilgrims Way, Guildford, Surrey GU4 8AD. *T:* Guildford 570829.

DORKING, Archdeacon of; *see* Hogben, Ven. P. G.

DORMAN, Lt-Col Sir Charles (Geoffrey), 3rd Bt *cr* 1923; MC 1942; *b* 18 Sept. 1920; *o s* of Sir Bedford Lockwood Dorman, 2nd Bart, CBE and Lady Constance Phelps Dorman (*née* Hay), (*d* 1946); *S* father 1956; *m* 1954, Elizabeth Ann (marr. diss. 1972), *d* of late George Gilmour Gilmour-White, OBE; one *d*. *Educ:* Rugby Sch.; Brasenose Coll., Oxford (MA). Commissioned, 1941; served with 3rd The King's Own Hussars at Alamein (MC) and in Italian Campaign; Commissioned to 13th/18th Royal Hussars (QMO), 1947; GSO1, 1961–70; retired. *Recreation:* gliding. *Heir: cousin* Philip Henry Keppel Dorman, *b* 19 May 1954. *Address:* Hutton Grange Cottage, Great Rollright, Chipping Norton, Oxon OX7 5SN. *T:* Hook Norton 737535.

DORMAN, Sir Maurice Henry, GCMG 1961 (KCMG 1957; CMG 1955); GCVO 1961; DL; MA; Chairman, Swindon District Health Authority (formerly of Wiltshire Area Health Authority), since 1972; Chairman, West of England (formerly Ramsbury) Building Society, since 1983 (Director since 1972; Vice-Chairman, 1981–83); *b* 7 Aug. 1912; *s* of late John Ehrenfried and late Madeleine Louise Dorman; *m* 1937, Florence Monica Churchward Smith, DStJ 1968; one *s* three *d*. *Educ:* Sedbergh Sch.; Magdalene Coll., Cambridge. Administrative Officer, Tanganyika Territory, 1935; Clerk of Councils, Tanganyika, 1940–45; Asst to the Lt-Governor, Malta, 1945; Principal Asst Sec., Palestine, 1947; Seconded to Colonial Office as Asst Sec., Social Services Dept, 1948; Dir of Social Welfare and Community Develt, Gold Coast, 1950; Colonial Sec., Trinidad and Tobago, 1952–56; Actg Governor of Trinidad, 1954, 1955; Governor, Comdr-in-Chief and Vice-Adm., Sierra Leone, 1956–61, after independence, Governor-Gen., 1961–62; Governor and Comdr-in-Chief, Malta, 1962–64, after independence, Governor-Gen., 1964–71. Dep. Chm., Pearce Commn on Rhodesia, 1971–72; Chm., British observers of Zimbabwe independence elecns, 1980. Chm., Swindon HMC, 1972–74. Vice Pres., Badminton Sch., 1966– (Chm. Bd of Govs, 1975–81); Life Governor, Monkton Combe Sch., 1984–. A Trustee, Imperial War Museum, 1972–85; Venerable Order of St John of Jerusalem: Almoner, 1972–75; Lord Prior, 1980–86; Mem., Chapter-Gen. Chief Comdr, St John Ambulance, 1975–80. DL Wilts 1978. Hon. DCL Durham, 1962; Hon. LLD Royal Univ. Malta, 1964. GCStJ 1978 (KStJ 1957). Gran Croce Al Merito Melitense (Soc. Ordine Militaire di Malta), 1966. *Recreations:* once sailing, squash, and sometimes golf. *Address:* The Old Manor, Overton, Marlborough, Wilts. *T:* Lockeridge 600; 42 Lennox Gardens, SW1. *T:* 01–584 8698. *Clubs:* Athenæum; Casino Maltese (Valletta).

See also R. B. Dorman.

DORMAN, Richard Bostock, CBE 1984; HM Diplomatic Service, retired; High Commissioner to Vanuatu, 1982–85; *b* 8 Aug. 1925; *s* of late John Ehrenfried and late Madeleine Louise Dorman; *m* 1950, Anna Illingworth; one *s* two *d*. *Educ:* Sedbergh Sch.; St John's Coll., Cambridge. Army Service (Lieut, S Staffs Regt), 1944–48; Asst Principal, War Office, 1951; Principal, 1955; transferred to Commonwealth Relations Office, 1958; First Sec., British High Commission, Nicosia, 1960–64; Dep. High Commissioner, Freetown, 1964–66; SE Asia Dept, FO, 1967–69; Counsellor, Addis Ababa, 1969–73; Commercial Counsellor, Bucharest, 1974–77; Counsellor, Pretoria, 1977–82. *Address:* 67 Beresford Road, Cheam, Surrey. *T:* 01–642 9627. *Club:* Royal Commonwealth Society.

See also Sir M. H. Dorman.

DORMAND, John Donkin; MP (Lab) Easington since 1970; *b* 27 Aug. 1919; *s* of Bernard and Mary Dormand; *m* 1963, Doris Robinson; one step *s* one step *d*. *Educ:* Bede Coll., Durham; Loughborough Coll.; Univs of Oxford and Harvard. Teacher, 1940–48; Education Adviser, 1948–52 and 1957–63; District Education Officer, Easington RDC, 1963–70. An Asst Govt Whip, 1974; a Lord Comr of HM Treasury, 1974–79; Chm., PLP, 1981–. *Recreations:* music, sport.

DORMER, family name of **Baron Dormer.**

DORMER, 16th Baron *cr* 1615; **Joseph Spencer Philip Dormer;** Bt 1615; landowner and farmer; *b* 4 Sept. 1914; *s* of 14th Baron Dormer, CBE, and Caroline May (*d* 1951), *y d* of Sir Robert Cavendish Spencer Clifford, 3rd Bt; *S* brother, 1975. *Educ:* Ampleforth; Christ Church, Oxford. Formerly Captain, Scots Guards; served War of 1939–45. Consultant, Thomas Comely & Sons Ltd. Pres., Warwick and Leamington Conservative Assoc., 1983–. Formerly Mem. Council, West Midlands Area Conservative Assoc. Hon. Vice-Pres., Worcs Br., Grenadier Gds Assoc. *Heir: cousin* Geoffrey Henry Dormer [*b* 13 May 1920; *m* 1st, 1947, Janet (marr. diss. 1957), *yr d* of James F. A. Readman; two *d*; 2nd, 1958, Pamela, *d* of late Wallace Levick Simpson; two *s*]. *Address:* Grove Park, Warwick. *Club:* Cavalry and Guards.

DORNHORST, Antony Clifford, CBE 1977; MD, FRCP; Professor of Medicine, St George's Hospital Medical School, 1959–80; Civilian Consultant in Aviation Medicine to RAF, since 1973; *b* 2 April 1915; *s* of Ernst Dornhorst and Florence, *née* Partridge; *m* 1946, Helen Mary Innes; three *d*. *Educ:* St Clement Danes Sch.; St Thomas's Hosp. Medical Sch. MB BS London 1937; MD London 1939; FRCP 1955. Junior Appointments, St Thomas' Hosp., 1937–39. Served with RAMC, mostly in Mediterranean theatre, 1940–46. Reader in Medicine, St Thomas's Hosp. Medical Sch., 1949–59. Member: MRC, 1973–77; SW Thames RHA, 1974–82. *Publications:* papers in various journals on normal and abnormal physiology. *Recreation:* music. *Address:* 8 Albert Place, W8. *T:* 01–937 8782.

DORR, Noel; Ambassador of Ireland to the Court of St James's, since 1983; *b* Limerick, 1933; *m* 1983, Catriona Doran. *Educ:* St Nathy's Coll., Ballaghaderreen; University Coll., Galway (BA, BComm, HDipEd); Georgetown Univ., Washington, DC (MA). Asst Inspector of Taxes, 1958–60; entered Dept of Foreign Affairs, 1960; Third Sec., 1960–62; Third Sec., Brussels, 1962–64; First Sec., Washington, 1964–70; First Sec., Dept of For. Affairs, 1970–72; Counsellor (Press and Inf.), Dept of For. Affairs, 1972–74; Asst Sec., Political Div., and Political Dir, 1974–77, Dep. Sec. and Political Dir, 1977–80; Perm. Rep. of Ireland to UN, New York, 1980–83; Rep of Ireland, Security Council, 1981–82. *Address:* Irish Embassy, 17 Grosvenor Place, SW1X 7HR. *T:* 01–235 2171. *Clubs:* Athenæum, Garrick, Royal Automobile.

DORRELL, Ernest John; Secretary, Headmasters' Conference, 1975–79; General Secretary, Secondary Heads Association, 1978–79 (Secretary, Incorporated Association of Headmasters, 1975–77); *b* 31 March 1915; *s* of John Henry Whiting Dorrell and Amy Dorrell (*née* Roberts); *m* 1940, Alwen Irvona Jones; one *s* one *d*. *Educ:* Taunton Sch.; Exeter Coll., Oxford (Exhibr). Hon. Mods and Lit. Hum., MA. Served with 71 Field Regt and HQ 46 Div. RA, 1940–46. Asst Master, Dauntsey's Sch., 1937–40 and 1946–47; Admin. Asst, WR Educn Dept, 1947; Dep. Dir of Educn, Oxfordshire CC, 1950; Dir of Educn, Oxfordshire CC, 1970; Report on Educn in St Helena, 1974. *Recreations:* walking, travel, golf. *Address:* Swan Cottage, Shillingford, Oxford. *T:* Warborough 8342.

DORRELL, Stephen James; MP (C) Loughborough, since 1979; *b* 25 March 1952; *s* of Philip Dorrell; *m* 1980, Penelope Anne Wears, *y d* of Mr and Mrs James Taylor, Windsor. *Educ:* Uppingham; Brasenose Coll., Oxford. BA 1973. RAFVR, 1971–73. Chm., family's Industrial Clothing Co. Personal asst to Rt Hon. Peter Walker, MBE, MP, Feb. 1974; contested (C) Kingston-upon-Hull East, Oct. 1974; PPS to the Secretary of State for Energy, 1983–. Sec., Cons. Backbench Trade Cttee, 1980–81. Bd Mem., Christian Aid, 1985–. *Recreations:* aviation, reading. *Address:* House of Commons, SW1.

DORSET, Archdeacon of; *see* Walton, Ven. G. E.

DORWARD, William, OBE 1977; Commissioner for Hong Kong Commercial Affairs, United States, since 1983; *b* 25 Sept. 1929; *s* of Alexander and Jessie Dorward; *m* 1960, Rosemary Ann Smith; one *s*. *Educ:* Morgan Academy, Dundee. Colonial Office, 1951–53;

Commerce and Industry Dept, Hong Kong Govt, 1954–74; Counsellor (Hong Kong Affairs) UK Mission, Geneva, 1974–76; Hong Kong Government: Dep. Dir of Commerce and Industry, 1974–77; Comr of Industry and Customs, 1977–79; Dir of Trade, Industry and Customs, 1979–82, Sec. for Trade and Industry, 1982–83; Mem. Legislative Council, 1979–83. *Address:* Apartment 12G, River Tower, 420 East 54th Street, New York, NY 10022, USA; 38 Bingham Terrace, Dundee, Scotland. *Clubs:* Carlton; Hong Kong; Metropolitan (NY).

DOS SANTOS, Sir Errol Lionel, Kt 1946; CBE 1939; Consultant, Alstons Ltd; *b* 1 Sept. 1890; *s* of Solomon and Margaret dos Santos; *m* 1st, 1915; one *s* one *d*; 2nd, 1939, Enid Hilda Jenkin, Bath, England; two *d*. *Educ:* St Mary's Coll., Trinidad. Entered Trinidad Civil Service as a junior clerk in the Treasury; Financial Sec., 1941; Colonial Sec., 1947; retired from Colonial Service, 1948. Dir, Alstons Ltd, 1948, Chm. 1953–61. *Address:* Flat 3, 7 Bryanston Square, W1. *Clubs:* MCC; Union, Queen's Park Cricket, Portuguese (Trinidad).

DOSSER, Prof. Douglas George Maurice; Professor of Economics, University of York, 1965–81; retired, 1981; *b* 3 Oct. 1927; *s* of George William Dosser; *m* 1954, Valerie Alwyne Elizabeth, *d* of Leslie Jack Lindsey; three *d*. *Educ:* Latymer Upper School; London School of Economics. Lecturer in Economics, Univ. of Edinburgh, 1958–62; Vis. Prof. of Economics, Univ. of Washington, Seattle, 1960; Vis. Res. Prof. of Economics, Columbia Univ., NY, 1962; Reader in Economics, Univ. of York, 1963–65. *Publications:* Economic Analysis of Tax Harmonisation, 1967; (with S. Han) Taxes in the EEC and Britain, 1968; (with F. Andic) Theory of Economic Integration for Developing Countries, 1971; European Economic Integration and Monetary Unification, 1973; (with K. Hartley) The Collaboration of Nations, 1981; articles in Economic Jl, Economica, Rev. of Economic Studies. *Recreations:* art and antiques.

DOSSOR, Rear-Adm. Frederick, CB 1963; CBE 1959; *b* 12 March 1913; *s* of John Malcolm Dossor and Edith Kate Brittain; *m* 1951, Pamela Anne Huxley Newton; two *d*. *Educ:* Hymers Coll., Hull; Loughborough Coll. BSc(Eng.) London; FIEE. Post Graduate Apprentice and Junior Engineer, Metropolitan Vickers Electrical Co., Manchester, 1935–39; Dept of Dir of Electrical Engineering, Admiralty, 1939–50; Electrical Specialisation, Royal Navy, 1950–65; Chief Staff Officer (Technical), staff of Comdr-in-Chief, Portsmouth, 1961–63; Polaris Project Officer in the Ministry of Technology, 1963–67; Dir of Hovercraft, DTI (formerly Min. of Technology), 1968–71. Retired from Royal Navy, 1965. *Recreation:* gardening. *Address:* 1a Lynch Road, Farnham, Surrey. *Club:* Royal Commonwealth Society.

DOTRICE, Roy; actor (stage, films and television); *b* 26 May 1925; *m* 1946, Kay Newman, actress; three *d*. *Educ:* Dayton and Intermediate Schs, Guernsey, CI. Served War of 1939–45: Air Gunner, RAF, 1940; PoW, 1942–45. Acted in Repertory, 1945–55; formed and directed Guernsey Theatre Co., 1955; Royal Shakespeare Co., 1957–65 (Caliban, Julius Caesar, Hotspur, Firs, Puntila, Edward IV, etc); World War 2½, New Theatre, London, 1966; Brief Lives, Golden Theatre, New York, 1967; Latent Heterosexual and God Bless, Royal Shakespeare Co., Aldwych, 1968; Brief Lives (one-man play), Criterion, 1969 (over 400 perfs, world record for longest-running solo perf.), toured England, Canada, USA, 1973, Mayfair, 1974 (over 150 perfs); Broadway season, 1974; Australian tour, 1975; Peer Gynt, Chichester Festival, 1970; One At Night, Royal Court, 1971; The Hero, Edinburgh, 1970; Mother Adam, Arts, 1971; Tom Brown's Schooldays, Cambridge, 1972; The Hollow Crown, seasons in USA 1973 and 1975, Sweden 1975; Gomes, Queen's, 1973; The Dragon Variation, Duke of York's, 1977; Australian tour with Chichester Festival, 1978; Passion of Dracula, Queen's, 1978; Oliver, Albery, 1979; Mister Lincoln (one-man play on Abraham Lincoln), Washington, NY and TV special, 1980, Fortune, 1981; A Life, NY, 1980–81; Henry V, and Falstaff in Henry IV, American Shakespeare Theatre, Stratford, Conn, 1981; Murder in Mind, Strand, 1982; Winston Churchill (one-man play), USA 1982 (also CBS TV); Kingdoms, NY, 1982; The Genius, Los Angeles, 1984 (Dramalogue Best Perf. Award); Down an Alley, Dallas, 1984; Great Expectations, Old Vic, 1985; Enemy of the People, NY, 1985; Hay Fever, NY and Washington, 1986; *films include:* Heroes of Telemark, Twist of Sand, Lock up Your Daughters, Buttercup Chain, Tomorrow, One of Those Things, Nicholas and Alexandra, Amadeus, Corsican Brothers, The Eliminators. *Television:* appearances in: Dear Liar, Brief Lives, The Caretaker (Emmy award), Imperial Palace, Misleading Cases, Clochemerle, Dickens of London, Stargazy on Zummerdown, Family Reunion (USA), Tales of the Gold Monkey (USA), etc. TV Actor of the Year Award, 1968; Tony Nomination for A Life, 1981. *Recreations:* fishing, riding. *Club:* Garrick.

DOUBLEDAY, John Vincent; sculptor since 1968; *b* 9 Oct. 1947; *s* of Gordon V. and Margaret E. V. Doubleday; *m* 1969, Isobel J. C. Durie; three *s*. *Educ:* Stowe; Goldsmiths' College School of Art. *Exhibitions include:* Waterhouse Gallery, 1968, 1969, 1970, 1971; Galerie Sothmann, Amsterdam, 1969, 1971, 1979; Richard Demarco Gallery, Edinburgh, 1973; Laing Art Gallery, Newcastle, Bowes Museum, Barnard Castle, 1974; Pandion Gallery, NY, Aldeburgh Festival, 1983; *works include:* Baron Ramsey of Canterbury, 1974; King Olav of Norway, 1975; Prince Philip, Duke of Edinburgh, Earl Mountbatten of Burma, Golda Meir, 1976; Ratu Sukuna, 1977; Regeneration, 1978; Maurice Bowra, 1979; Charlie Chaplin (Leicester Square), Lord Olivier, Mary and Child Christ, 1981; Caduceus (Harvard, Mass), Lord Feather (TUC Congress House), Isambard Kingdom Brunel (two works), Charlie Chaplin (Vevey), 1982; Beatles (Liverpool), Dylan Thomas, Phoenix, 1984; Royal Marines Commando Meml, Lympstone, Devon, 1986; *works in public collections:* Ashmolean Mus., British Mus., Herbert F. Johnson Mus., USA, Tate Gall., V & A, Nat. Mus. of Wales. *Recreations:* cross country skiing, fishing. *Address:* Lodge Cottage, Great Totham, Maldon, Essex CM9 8BX. *T:* Maldon 892085.

DOUEK, Ellis Elliot, FRCS; Consultant Otologist since 1970, and Chairman, Hearing Research Group, since 1974, Guy's Hospital; *b* 25 April 1934; *s* of Cesar Douek and Nelly Sassoon; *m* 1964, Nicole Galante; two *s*. *Educ:* English School, Cairo; Westminster Medical School. MRCS, LRCP 1958; FRCS 1967. House appts, St Helier Hosp., 1959, and Whittington Hosp., 1963; nat. service, RAMC, 1960–62; ENT Registrar, Royal Free Hosp., 1966; Sen. Registrar, King's College Hosp., 1968. Mem., MRC working party on Hearing Research, 1975; MRC Rep. to Europ. Communities on Hearing Res., 1980; UK Rep. to Europ. Communities on Indust. Deafness, 1983. Dalby Prize for hearing research, RSM, 1978. *Publications:* Sense of Smell—Its Abnormalities, 1974; Eighth Nerve, in Peripheral Neuropathy, 1975; Olfaction, in Scientific Basis of Otolaryngology, 1976; Cochlear Implant, in Textbook of ENT, 1980; papers on hearing and smell. *Recreations:* drawing and painting; studying history. *Address:* (home) 24 Reynolds Close, NW11. *T:* 01–455 6047; 97 Harley Street, W1. *T:* 01–935 7828. *Club:* Athenæum.

DOUGAL, Malcolm Gordon; HM Diplomatic Service; Deputy High Commissioner and Head of Chancery, Canberra, since 1986; *b* 20 Jan. 1938; *s* of Eric Gordon Dougal and Marie (*née* Wildermuth); *m* 1964, Elke (*née* Urban); one *s*. *Educ:* Ampleforth Coll., Yorkshire; The Queen's Coll., Oxford (MA Mod. History). National Service in Korea and Gibraltar with Royal Sussex Regt, 1956–58; Oxford, 1958–61; Contracts Asst, De Havilland Aircraft, Hatfield, 1961–64; Asst to Export Manager, Ticket Equipment Ltd (Plessey), 1964–66; Export Manager, Harris Lebus Ltd, 1967–69; entered HM Diplomatic Service, 1969; Foreign Office, 1969–72; 1st Secretary (Commercial): Paris, 1972–76; Cairo, 1976–79; Foreign Office, 1979–81; Consul Gen., Lille, 1981–85. *Recreations:* natural history, walking, books, sport, wine. *Address:* c/o Foreign and Commonwealth Office, Whitehall, SW1.

DOUGAN, (Alexander) Derek; Chairman and Chief Executive, Wolverhampton Wanderers' Football Club, 1982–85, *b* 20 Jan. 1938; *s* of John and Josephine Dougan; *m* 1963, Jutta Maria; two *s*. *Educ:* Mersey Street primary sch., Belfast; Belfast Technical High School. Professional footballer with: Distillery, NI, 1953–57; Portsmouth, 1957–59; Blackburn Rovers, 1959–61; Aston Villa, 1961–63; Peterborough, 1963–65; Leicester, 1965–67; Wolverhampton Wanderers, 1967–75. Represented N Ireland at all levels, from schoolboy to full international, more than 50 times. Chm., PFA, 1970–78. Chief Exec., Kettering Town FC, 1975–78; Sports Presenter, Yorkshire Television. *Publications:* Attack! (autobiog.), 1969; The Sash He Never Wore (autobiog.), 1972; The Footballer (novel), 1974; On the Spot (football as a profession), 1974; Doog (autobiog.), 1980; How Not to Run Football, 1981; (with Patrick Murphy) Matches of the Day 1958–83, 1984. *Recreations:* watching football, playing squash. *Address:* Bayern House, 40 Keepers Lane, Codsall, Wolverhampton, West Midlands.

DOUGAN, Dr David John; Director, Crafts Council, since 1984; *b* 26 Sept, 1936; *s* of William John Dougan and Blanche May; *m* 1st, 1959, Eileen Ludbrook (marr. diss. 1985); one *s*; 2nd, 1986, Barbara Taylor; one *d*. *Educ:* Durham Univ. (BA, MA); City Univ. (PhD). Reporter, Tyne Tees Television, 1963; presenter, BBC, 1966; Director, Northern Arts, 1970. *Publications:* History of North East Shipbuilding, 1966; Great Gunmaker, 1968; Shipwrights Trade Union, 1971. *Recreations:* theatre, crafts, running. *Address:* 2 Lee Terrace, Blackheath, SE3 9TZ. *T:* 01-318 4164. *Club:* Athenæum.

DOUGHERTY, Maj.-Gen. Sir Ivan Noel, Kt 1968; CBE 1946; DSO 1941 (bar, 1943); ED; *b* Leadville, NSW, 6 April 1907; *m* 1936, Emily Phyllis Lofts; two *s* two *d* (and one *d* decd). *Educ:* Leadville Primary Sch.; Mudgee High Sch.; Sydney Teachers' Coll.; Sydney Univ. (BEc). NSW Education Dept: Asst Teacher, 1928–32; Dep. Headmaster, 1933–39; Headmaster, 1946–47; Dist Inspector of Schs, 1948–53; Staff Inspector 1953–55. Commissioned Sydney Univ. Regt, 1927. Capt. 1931; Unattached List, 1932–34; transf. to 33/41 Bn. 1934; Major, 1938; Command, 33rd Bn, 1938; Lieut-Col 1939. Served War of 1939–45 (DSO and Bar, CBE, despatches thrice); Australian Imperial Force, Second-in-Command, 2/2 Inf. Bn, 1939–40; Commanded 2/4 inf. Bn (Libya, Greece, Crete campaigns), 1940–42; Brig. 1942; commanded 23 Bde, 1942; commanded 21 Bde, South-West Pacific, 1942–45; R of O, 1946–47; commanded 8th Bde, Austr. Mil. Forces, 1948–52; Maj.-Gen., 1952; commanded 2nd Div., 1952–54; Citizen Military Forces Member, Australian Mil. Bd, 1954–57; R of O, 1957–64; Retired List, 1964. Hon. ADC to Governor-Gen. of Australia, 1949–52; Hon. Col, Australian Cadet Corps, Eastern Command, 1964–70; Representative Hon. Col, Australian Cadet Corps, 1967–70. Dir of Civil Defence for NSW, 1955–73. Mem. Council, Nat. Roads and Motorists' Assoc., 1969–79. Mem. Senate, 1954–74, Dep. Chancellor, 1958–66, Hon. LLD 1976, Univ. of Sydney. *Address:* 4 Leumeah Street, Cronulla, NSW 2230, Australia. *T:* 523–5465.

DOUGHTY, George Henry; General Secretary, Technical and Supervisory Section, Amalgamated Union of Engineering Workers, 1971–74, retired; Member, Central Arbitration Committee, 1976–85; *b* 17 May 1911; British; *m* 1941, Mildred Dawson; two *s*. *Educ:* Handsworth Tech. Sch.; Aston Technical Coll. Draughtsman; trained at General Electric Co., Birmingham, 1927–32; employed as Design Draughtsman: English Electric, Stafford 1932–33; GEC Birmingham, 1934–46. With Draughtsmen's & Allied Technician's Assoc., 1946–71, General Secretary, 1952–71. Member: Gen. Council of TUC, 1968–74; Independent Review Cttee, 1976–; Chm., EDC for Electrical Engrg, 1974–82. Mem., Royal Commn on Distribution of Income and Wealth, 1974–78. Industrial Relns Advr, SIAD, 1977–. *Publications:* various technical and Trade Union publications. *Recreation:* photography. *Address:* Short Way, Whitton, Twickenham, Middx TW2 7NU. *T:* 01–894 0299.

DOUGHTY, William Roland; Chairman, North West Thames Regional Health Authority, since 1984; Deputy Chairman, Britannia Refined Metals Ltd, since 1982 (Director, since 1978); Director, Meyer International PLC, since 1983; *b* 18 July 1925; *s* of Roland Gill Doughty and Gladys Maud Doughty (*née* Peto); *m* 1952, Patricia Lorna Cooke; three *s*. *Educ:* Headstone Sch.; Acton Technical Coll.; Trinity Coll., Dublin (MA); Harvard Business Sch. (AMP). Metal Box Co. Ltd, 1953–66; Molins Ltd, 1966–69, Dir, 1967; Cape Industries, 1969–84, Dir, 1972, Man. Dir, 1980–84. Member: SE Economic Planning Council, 1966–79 (Chm., Industry and Employment Cttee, 1972–79); CBI Council, 1975– (Chm., London Region, 1981–83). Founder and Chm., Assoc. for Conservation of Energy, 1981–85, Pres., 1985–. Governor: SE Tech. Coll., 1967–69; Gt Ormond St Hosp. for Sick Children, 1978–; Mem., Gen. Council, King Edward's Hosp. Fund for London, 1984–. CBIM; FRSA. *Recreations:* cricket, theatre, golf, horse riding. *Address:* Sun Hollow, North Park, Gerrards Cross, Bucks SL9 8JL. *Clubs:* American, MCC, Middlesex County Cricket.

DOUGLAS, family name of **Viscount Chilston, Earl of Morton,** and **Marquess of Queensberry.**

DOUGLAS AND CLYDESDALE, Marquess of; Alexander Douglas-Hamilton; *b* 31 March 1978; *s* and *heir* of Duke of Hamilton, *qv*.

DOUGLAS, Prof. Alexander Stuart; Regius Professor of Medicine, University of Aberdeen, 1970–85, now Emeritus; *b* 2 Oct. 1921; *s* of late Dr R. Douglas, MOH for Moray and Nairn; *m* 1954, Christine McClymont Stewart; one *s* one *d*. *Educ:* Elgin Academy, Morayshire. Mil. Service, RAMC, 1945–48 (despatches 1947). Research Fellow, Radcliffe Infirmary, Oxford, and Postgrad. Med. Sch., London, 1951–53; Lectr, Sen. Lectr and Reader in Medicine, Univ. Dept of Med., Royal Infirmary, Glasgow, 1953–64; Hon. Consultant status, 1957; Prof. of Med., Univ. of Glasgow, 1964–70; secondment to Univ. of East Africa with hon. academic rank of Prof., 1965; Hon. Consultant Physician in Administrative Charge of wards, Royal Infirmary, Glasgow, 1968–70. *Publications:* scientific papers on blood coagulation, etc. *Recreations:* curling, travel. *Address:* Department of Medicine, Aberdeen Royal Infirmary, Foresterhill, Aberdeen AB9 2ZB. *T:* Aberdeen 681818 (ext 3349).

DOUGLAS, Arthur John Alexander, CMG 1965; OBE 1962; Assistant Secretary, Overseas Development Administration, Foreign and Commonwealth Office, (formerly Ministry of Overseas Development), 1975–80; *b* 31 May 1920; *s* of Alexander and Eileen Douglas; *m* 1948, Christine Scott Dyke; two *d*. *Educ:* Dumfries Academy; Edinburgh Univ. Royal Navy, 1940–45. District Officer, Basutoland, 1946; Seconded Colonial Office, 1957; Administration Sec., Bechuanaland, 1959; Government Sec. and Chief Sec. 1962–65; Dep. Commissioner for Bechuanaland, 1965–66; ODM, then ODA, 1967–80, retired. *Address:* 13 Pickers Green, Lindfield, West Sussex RH16 2BS. *Club:* Royal Commonwealth Society.

DOUGLAS, Prof. Charles Primrose, FRCOG; Professor of Obstetrics and Gynæcology, University of Cambridge, since 1976; Fellow, Emmanuel College, Cambridge, since 1979; *b* 17 Feb. 1921; *s* of Dr C. Douglas, Ayr, Scotland; *m* 1948, Angela Francis; three *s* one *d*. *Educ:* Loretto Sch.; Peterhouse; Edinburgh Univ. Surg. Lieut RNVR, 1944–47. Registrar and Sen. Registrar, Victoria Infirmary, Glasgow, 1950–59; William Waldorf Astor Foundn Fellow, 1957; Visiting Fellow, Duke Univ., NC, 1957; Sen. Lectr, Univ. of the West Indies, 1959–65; Prof. of Obst. and Gyn., Royal Free Hosp. Sch. of Medicine, 1965–76. Member: Bd of Governors, Royal Free Hosp., 1972–74; Camden and Islington AHA, 1974–76, Cambridge AHA, 1981–82; Cambridge DHA, 1983–. Mem., Council, RCOG, 1980–86. Hon. FACOG, 1983. *Publications:* contribs to BMJ, Amer. Heart Jl, Jl of Obst. and Gynæc. of Brit. Commonwealth, etc. *Recreations:* travel, art. *Address:* Old Mill House, Linton Road, Balsham, Cambs CB1 6HA. *Club:* United Oxford & Cambridge University.

DOUGLAS, Sir Donald (Macleod), Kt 1972; MBE 1943; ChM St Andrews, MS Minn, FRCSE; FRCS; FRSE 1973; Surgeon to the Queen in Scotland, 1965–76; an Extra Surgeon to the Queen in Scotland, since 1977; Professor of Surgery, University of Dundee (formerly Queen's College), 1951–76, Emeritus Professor, 1977; Surgeon, Ninewells Hospital, Dundee, 1951–76; *b* 28 June 1911; *s* of William Douglas and Christina Broom; *m* 1945, Margaret Diana Whitley; two *s* two *d*. *Educ:* Madras Coll.; Universities of St Andrews and Minnesota. Commonwealth Fellow in Surgery, Mayo Clinic, University of Minnesota, USA, 1937–39; First Asst in Surgery, British Postgraduate Medical Sch., 1939–40; RAMC, 1941–45; Reader in Experimental Surgery, University of Edinburgh, 1945–51; Asst Surgeon, Edinburgh Municipal Hospitals, 1945; formerly Surgeon, Royal Infirmary, Dundee. Assoc. Asst Surgeon, Royal Infirmary, Edinburgh. Dean of Faculty of Medicine, Univ. of Dundee, 1969–70. President: RCSE, 1971–73; Assoc. of Surgeons of GB and Ireland, 1964; Surgical Research Soc. of GB, 1966–69; Harveian Soc., 1974. Trustee, Thalidomide Trust, 1973– (Chm., Health and Welfare). Hon. FACS, 1972; Hon. FRCS (SA), 1972; Hon. FRCSI, 1973. Hon. DSc St Andrews, 1972. *Publications:* Wound Healing, 1965; The Thoughtful Surgeon, 1970; Surgical Departments in Hospitals, 1971. *Address:* The Whitehouse of Nevay, Newtyle, Angus. *T:* Newtyle 315.

DOUGLAS, Sir (Edward) Sholto, Kt 1977; Solicitor of the Supreme Court of Queensland, since 1934; *b* 23 Dec. 1909; *s* of Hon. Mr Justice E. A. Douglas and Annette Eileen Power; *m* 1939, Mary Constance Curr. *Educ:* St Ignatius Coll., Riverview, Sydney. Queensland Law Society Incorporated: Mem. Council, 1954–76; Actg Pres., 1960; Pres., 1962–64; Mem., Statutory Cttee, 1976–81; Member: Legal Assistance Cttee, Qld, 1965–80; Solicitors' Bd, 1969–75; Exec. Mem., Law Council of Aust., 1973–75. President: Taxpayers Assoc. of Qld, 1955–58; Federated Taxpayers of Aust., 1957–58; Mem. Adv. Cttee, Terminating and Permanent Building Socs, 1966–77. Pres., Qld Div., Nat. Heart Foundn, 1976–77 (Vice-Pres., 1966–75); Vice-Pres., RSPCA, 1965–86; Chm., Management Cttee, Currumbin Bird Sanctuary and Wildlife Reserve, 1978–80. *Recreations:* racing, gardening. *Address:* 81 Markwell Street, Hamilton, Brisbane, Qld 4007, Australia. *T:* 268.2759. *Clubs:* Queensland, Brisbane (Pres. 1965), Tattersalls, Royal Queensland Golf, Queensland Turf, Tattersalls Racing, Brisbane Amateur Turf (all Brisbane).

DOUGLAS, Gavin Stuart, RD 1970; QC (Scot.) 1971; *b* 12 June 1932; *y s* of late Gilbert Georgeson Douglas and Rosena Campbell Douglas. *Educ:* South Morningside Sch.; George Heriot's Sch.; Edinburgh Univ. MA 1953, LLB 1955. Qual. as Solicitor, 1955; nat. service with RN, 1955–57. Admitted to Faculty of Advocates, 1958; Sub-editor (part-time), The Scotsman, 1957–61; Mem. Lord Advocate's Dept in London (as Parly Draftsman), 1961–64; returned to practice at Scots Bar, 1964; Junior Counsel to BoT, 1965–71; Counsel to Scottish Law Commn, 1965–; Hon. Sheriff in various sheriffdoms, 1965–71; a Chm. of Industrial Tribunals, 1966–78; Counsel to Sec. of State for Scotland under Private Legislation Procedure (Scotland) Act 1936, 1969–75, Sen. Counsel under that Act, 1975–. Mem., Lothian Health Bd, 1981–85. Mem. Bd, Leith Nautical Coll., 1981–84. Editor, Session Cases, 7 vols, 1976–82. *Recreations:* golf, ski-ing. *Address:* Parliament House, Parliament Square, Edinburgh EH1 1RF. *Club:* University Staff (Edinburgh).

DOUGLAS, Henry Russell, FJI; Legal Manager, News Group Newspapers, since 1976; *b* Bishopbriggs, Lanarkshire, 11 Feb. 1925; 2nd *s* of late Russell Douglas and Jeanie Douglas Douglas (*née* Drysdale); *m* 1951, Elizabeth Mary, *d* of late Ralph Nowell, CB; two *s* three *d*. *Educ:* various Scottish and English Grammar Schools; Lincoln Coll., Oxford (MA Hons). Served RNVR, 1943–46 (Sub-Lt, submarines). Merchant Navy, 1946–47; Oxford Univ., 1947–50; Liverpool Daily Post, 1950–69; The Sun, 1969–76. Inst of Journalists, 1956: Fellow, 1969; Pres., 1972–73; Chm. of Executive, 1973–76; Member: Press Council, 1972–80; Council, Newspaper Press Fund; Founder Mem. and Treasurer, Media Society, 1973. *Recreations:* chess, travel, history. *Address:* Austen Croft, 31 Austen Road, Guildford, Surrey. *T:* Guildford 576960. *Club:* United Oxford & Cambridge University.

DOUGLAS, James Murray, CBE 1985; Director-General, Country Landowners Association, since 1970; *b* 26 Sept. 1925; *s* of Herbert and Amy Douglas, Brechin; *m* 1950, Julie Kemmner; one *s* one *d*. *Educ:* Morrison's Acad., Crieff; Aberdeen Univ. (MA); Balliol Coll., Oxford (BA). Entered Civil Service, 1950; Treasury, 1960–63; Asst Sec., Min. of Housing and Local Govt, 1964; Sec. to Royal Commn on Local Govt, 1966–69; Vice-Pres., Confedn of European Agriculture, 1971; Mem., Econ. Develt Cttee for Agriculture, 1972; Sec., European Landowning Orgns Gp, 1972–. *Publications:* various articles on local govt and landowning. *Address:* 1 Oldfield Close, Bickley, Kent. *T:* 01–467 3213. *Club:* United Oxford & Cambridge University.

DOUGLAS, Kenneth, CEng, FRINA; Managing Director, Austin and Pickersgill Ltd, 1958–69, and 1979–83; Chairman, Kenton Shipping Services, Darlington, 1968–83; Member, Tyne and Wear Residuary Body, Department of the Environment, since 1985; *b* 28 Oct. 1920; British; *m* 1942, Doris Lewer; one *s* two *d*. *Educ:* Sunderland Technical Coll. (Dip. Naval Architecture). CEng, FRINA. Dep. Shipyard Manager, Vickers Armstrong Naval Yard, Newcastle-upon-Tyne, 1946–53; Dir and Gen. Manager, Wm Gray & Co. Ltd, West Hartlepool, 1954–58; Man. Dir, Upper Clyde Shipbuilders Ltd, Chm., Simons Lobnitz Ltd and Chm., UCS Trng Co., 1969–72; Dep. Chm., Govan Shipbuilders, 1971–73; Chm., Douglas (Kilbride) Ltd, 1972–77; Chm. and Man. Dir, Steel Structures Ltd, 1974–76; Shiprepair Marketing Dir, British Shipbuilders, 1978–79. Fellow, Sunderland Poly., 1980 (Chm. of Governors, 1982–). *Recreations:* fishing, golf. *Address:* 7 Birchfield Road, Sunderland, Tyne and Wear; Monks Cottage, Romaldkirk, Barnard Castle, Co. Durham. *Clubs:* Sunderland; Ashbrooke.

DOUGLAS, Margaret Elizabeth; Chief Assistant to the Director General, BBC, since 1983; *b* 22 Aug. 1934; *d* of Thomas Mincher Douglas and Dorothy Jones. *Educ:* Parliament Hill Grammar Sch., London. Joined BBC as sec., 1951; subseq. researcher, dir and producer in Current Affairs television, working on Panorama, Gallery, 24 Hours and on special progs with Lord Avon and Harold Macmillan; Editor, Party Conf. coverage, 1972–83. *Recreations:* watching politics and football. *Address:* BBC, Broadcasting House, W1A 1AA. *T:* 01–580 4468.

DOUGLAS, Prof. Mary; Avalon Foundation Professor in the Humanities, Northwestern University, 1981–85, Professor Emeritus, since 1985; Visiting Professor, Princeton University, since 1986; *b* 25 March 1921; *d* of Gilbert Charles Tew and Phyllis Twomey; *m* 1951, James A. T. Douglas, OBE; two *s* one *d*. *Educ:* Sacred Heart Convent, Roehampton; Univ. of Oxford (MA, BSc, PhD). Returned to Oxford, 1946, to train as anthropologist; fieldwork in Belgian Congo, 1949–50 and 1953; Lectr in Anthropology, Univ. of Oxford, 1950; Univ. of London, 1951–78, Prof. of Social Anthropology, UCL, 1970–78. Res. Scholar, Russell Sage Foundn, NY, 1977–81. Hon. Dr of Letters, Univ. of Uppsala, 1986. *Publications:* The Lele of the Kasai, 1963; Purity and Danger, 1966; Natural Symbols, 1970; Implicit Meanings, 1976; (with Baron Isherwood) The World of Goods: towards an anthropology of consumption, 1979; Evans-Pritchard, 1980; (with Aaron Wildavsky) Risk and Culture, 1982; In the Active Voice, 1982; Risk Acceptability, 1986. *Address:* 22 Hillway, Highgate, N6 6QA; (Feb.-June) Department of Religion, Princeton University, NJ 08544, USA. *Club:* United Oxford & Cambridge University.

DOUGLAS, Richard Giles; MP (Lab and Co-op) Dunfermline West, since 1983 (Dunfermline, 1979–83); *b* 4 Jan. 1932; *m* 1954, Jean Gray, *d* of Andrew Arnott; two *d*. *Educ:* Co-operative College, Stanford Hall, Loughborough; Univ. of Strathclyde. Engineer (Marine); Mem. AUEW. Tutor organiser in Adult Educn, Co-operative movement, 1957; Sectional Educn Officer, Scotland, 1958–61; Lectr in Economics, Dundee Coll. of Technol., 1964–70. Contested (Lab): South Angus, 1964, Edinburgh West, 1966, Glasgow Pollok, March 1967; (Lab and Co-op) Clackmannan and E Stirlingshire, Oct. 1974; MP (Lab and Co-op) Clackmannan and E Stirlingshire, 1970–Feb. 1974. Hon. Lectr, Strathclyde, 1980–. Hon. Mem., Univ. of Strathclyde Staff Club. *Address:* Braehead House, High Street, Auchtermuchty, Fife.

DOUGLAS, Sir Robert (McCallum), Kt 1976; OBE 1956; President, Robert M. Douglas Holdings PLC, since 1980 (Director, since 1930; Chairman, 1952–77); *b* 2 Feb. 1899; *s* of John Douglas and Eugenia McCallum; *m* 1927, Millicent Irene Tomkys Morgan (*d* 1980); one *s* one *d*. *Educ:* Terregles Sch.; Dumfries Academy. Served Army, 1916–19. Served 10 years with civil engineering contracting co., 1920–30; founded Douglas Group of Companies, 1930. Mem., MPBW Midland Regional Jt Adv. Cttee, 1940–46. Federation of Civil Engineering Contractors: Chm., Midland Section, 1942–43 and 1947–48; Chm. Council, 1948–49; Pres., 1958–60. Patron, Staffs Agric. Soc. Hon. DSc Aston, 1977. *Recreations:* shooting, farming. *Address:* Dunstall Hall, Barton-under-Needwood, Burton-on-Trent, Staffordshire DE13 8BE. *T:* Barton-under-Needwood 2471. *Clubs:* Caledonian; Birmingham (Birmingham).

DOUGLAS, Hon. Roger Owen; MP (Lab) Manurewa, New Zealand, since 1969; Minister of Finance, since 1984; *b* 5 Dec. 1937; *s* of Norman and Jenny Douglas; *m* 1961, Glennis June Anderson; one *s* one *d*. *Educ:* Auckland Grammar Sch.; Auckland Univ. (Accountancy Degree). Company Sec. and Acct; Cabinet Minister, 1972–75; Minister in Charge of Inland Revenue Dept and Minister in Charge of Friendly Societies, 1984–. *Publications:* There's Got to be a Better Way, 1981; papers on NZ economy: An Alternative Budget, 1980; Proposal for Taxation, 1981. *Recreations:* cricket, rugby, reading. *Address:* 15 Wheturangi Road, Green Lane, Auckland, New Zealand. *T:* Auckland 545-603.

DOUGLAS, Ronald Albert Neale, DFC 1944; JP; Agent General for Western Australia in London, 1982–86; *b* 18 Sept. 1922; *s* of Edwyn William Albert Douglas and Kate Maria Douglas; *m* 1st, 1944 (marr. diss. 1966); one *s* one *d*; 2nd, Pamela Joy Carroll; one *s*. *Educ:* Albany High Sch., WA. Served War, RAAF, 1941–46 (Sqdn Ldr). Joined Shell Co. of Australia, 1938; sales rep., 1946–50; various appts, incl. Aviation Manager and Dist Manager, WA and NSW, 1950–60; appts with Shell Cos, France and USA, 1960–61; Sales Man., WA, 1961–65; Commercial Man., Shell Malaysia, 1965–66; Marketing Man., Shell Singapore, 1966–67; Retail Man., Vic/Tas, 1967–71; Chm.'s Rep. and Commercial Man., Shell Gp of Cos in WA, 1971–82. JP WA, 1982. *Recreations:* cricket, golf, fishing, farming. *Address:* 12 Jarrad Street, Cottesloe, Perth, WA 6011, Australia. *T:* 384 9986. *Clubs:* Weld, West Australian, Royal Aero (Perth); Lake Karrinyup Country (WA).

DOUGLAS, Prof. Ronald Walter, DSc, FInstP, FSGT; Professor of Glass Technology, University of Sheffield, 1955–75; *b* 28 March 1910; *s* of John H. P. and A. E. Douglas; *m* 1933, Edna Maud Cadle; two *s*. *Educ:* Latymer Upper Sch.; Sir John Cass Coll., London. Mem., Research Staff, Research Laboratories of General Electric Company, 1927–55. Pres., Internat. Commn on Glass, 1972–75. *Publications:* (with S. Frank) A History of Glassmaking, 1972; many papers on the physics of glass and semiconductors. *Address:* Burford Lea, Eymore, West Hill, Ottery St Mary, Devon.

DOUGLAS, Sir Sholto; *see* Douglas, Sir E. S.

DOUGLAS, Rt. Hon. Sir William (Randolph), KCMG 1983; Kt 1969; PC 1977; Chief Justice of Barbados, since 1965; *b* Barbados, 24 Sept. 1921; *e s* of William P. Douglas and Emily Frances Douglas (*née* Nurse); *m* 1951, Thelma Ruth (*née* Gilkes); one *s* one *d*. *Educ:* Bannatyne Sch. and Verdun High Sch., Verdun, Que., Canada; McGill Univ. (BA, Hons); London Sch. of Economics (LLB). Private Practice at Barbados Bar, 1948–50; Dep. Registrar, Barbados, 1950; Resident Magistrate, Jamaica, 1955; Asst Attorney-Gen., Jamaica, 1959; Solicitor-Gen., Jamaica, 1962; Puisne Judge, Jamaica, 1962. Chm., Commonwealth Caribbean Council of Legal Education, 1971–77; Mem., ILO Cttee of Experts on the Application of Conventions and Recommendations, 1975–; Dep. Judge, ILO Administrative Tribunal, 1982–; Judge, Inter-Amer. Develt Bank Administrative Tribunal, 1983–. President: Barbados Assoc. for the Blind and Deaf; UN Assoc. of Barbados; Barbados Boy Scouts Assoc. *Address:* Leland, Pine Gardens, St Michael, Barbados. *T:* 429–2030. *Club:* Barbados Yacht.

DOUGLAS, Prof. William Wilton, MD; FRS 1983; Professor of Pharmacology, Yale University School of Medicine, New Haven, USA, since 1968; *b* 15 Aug. 1922; *s* of Thomas Hall James Douglas and Catherine Dorward (*née* Wilton); *m* 1954, Jeannine Marie Henriette Dumoulin; two *s*. *Educ:* Glasgow Acad.; Univ. of Glasgow (MB, ChB 1946, MD 1949). Resident House Surgeon: Glasgow Western Infirm., 1946; Law Hosp., Carluke, 1947; Demonstr in Physiology, Univ. of Aberdeen, 1948; served RAMC, 1949–50: Chemical Defence Res. Estab., Porton Down, Wilts (Major); Mem. Staff, National Inst. for Med. Res., Mill Hill, 1950–56; Prof. of Pharmacol., Albert Einstein Coll. of Medicine, New York, 1956–68. *Publications:* papers on cellular mechanisms of secretion in Jl of Physiol., Brit. Jl of Pharmacol., Nature, and Science. *Recreations:* yachting, skiing. *Address:* 76 Blake Road, Hamden, Conn 06517, USA. *T:* (203) 776–8696.

DOUGLAS-HAMILTON, family name of **Duke of Hamilton and Brandon** and **Earl of Selkirk.**

DOUGLAS-HAMILTON, Lord James Alexander; MP (C) Edinburgh West since Oct. 1974; *b* 31 July 1942; 2nd *s* of 14th Duke of Hamilton, and *b* of 15th Duke of Hamilton, *qv*; *m* 1974, Hon. Priscilla Susan Buchan, *d* of Baron Tweedsmuir, *qv* and late Baroness Tweedsmuir of Belhelvie, PC; four *s* (incl. twins). *Educ:* Eton College; Balliol Coll., Oxford (MA, Mod. History; Oxford Boxing Blue, 1961; Pres., Oxford Univ.

Cons. Assoc., 1963; Pres., Oxford Union Soc., 1964); Edinburgh Univ. (LLB, Scots Law). Advocate at Scots Bar, 1968. Town Councillor, Murrayfield-Cramond, Edinburgh, 1972. Scottish Conservative Whip, 1977; a Lord Comr of HM Treasury, and Govt Whip for Scottish Cons. Mems, 1979–81; PPS to Malcolm Rifkind, 1983– (Foreign Office Minister, 1983–86, Sec. of State for Scotland, 1986–). Captain Cameronian Co., 2 Bn Low Vols RARO, 1972. Hon. Pres., Scottish Amateur Boxing Assoc., 1975–; President: Royal Commonwealth Soc. in Scotland, 1979–; Scottish Council, UNA, 1981–. *Publications:* Motive for a Mission: The Story Behind Hess's Flight to Britain, 1971; The Air Battle for Malta: the diaries of a fighter pilot, 1981; Roof of the World: man's first flight over Everest, 1983. *Recreations:* golf, forestry. *Address:* 12 Quality Street Lane, Davidsons Mains, Edinburgh EH4 5BU. *T:* 031–336 4213; Ryvra, 3 Fidra Road, North Berwick, East Lothian. *T:* North Berwick 2918. *Clubs:* New (Edinburgh); Hon. Company of Edinburgh Golfers.

DOUGLAS-HOME, family name of **Baroness Dacre** and **Baron Home of the Hirsel.**

DOUGLAS-HOME, Hon. David Alexander Cospatrick; Director, Morgan Grenfell & Co. Ltd, since 1974; *b* 20 Nov. 1943; *o s* of Baron Home of the Hirsel, *qv*; *heir* to Earldom of Home; *m* 1972, Jane Margaret, *yr d* of Col J. Williams-Wynne, *qv*; two *d*. *Educ:* Eton College; Christ Church, Oxford (BA 1966). Director: Morgan Grenfell Egyptian Finance Co. Ltd, 1975–77; Morgan Grenfell (Asia) Ltd, 1978–82 (Dep. Chm., 1979–82); Morgan Grenfell (Scotland) Ltd, 1978–; Arab Bank Investment Co., 1979–; Agricultural Mortgage Corp., 1979–; Arab-British Chamber of Commerce, 1975–84; Economic Forestry Group, 1981–. Chm., Committee for Middle East Trade, 1986– (Mem., 1973–75). Governor, Ditchley Foundn, 1977–. *Recreations:* outdoor sports. *Address:* 99 Dovehouse Street, SW3. *T:* 01–352 9060. *Club:* Turf.

DOUGLAS-HOME, Hon. William; *see* Home.

DOUGLAS-MANN, Bruce Leslie Home; Solicitor, in practice since 1954; Member: Management Committee, Notting Hill Housing Trust, since 1985; Board, Shelter, since 1974; *b* 23 June 1927; *s* of late Leslie John Douglas-Mann, MC and of Alice Home Douglas-Mann; *m* 1955, Helen Tucker; one *s* one *d*. *Educ:* Upper Canada Coll., Toronto; Jesus Coll., Oxford. Leading Seaman, RN, 1945–48; Oxford, 1948–51. Admitted solicitor, 1954. Contested (Lab): St Albans, 1964; Maldon, 1966; MP North Kensington, 1970–74, Merton, Mitcham and Morden, 1974–May 1982, resigned (Lab 1970–81, Ind 1981, SDP Jan.-May 1982); contested (SDP): Merton, Mitcham and Morden, June 1982; Mitcham and Morden, 1983; Prospective Parly Cand. (SDP), Mitcham and Morden, 1983–. Chairman: PLP Housing and Construction Gp, 1974–79; PLP Environment Gp, 1979–81 (Vice-Chm., 1972–79); Parly Select Cttee on Environment, 1979–82. Vice-Pres., Soc. of Lab. Lawyers, 1980–81 (Chm., 1974–80). Mem., Kensington or Kensington and Chelsea Borough Council, 1962–68. Chm., Arts Council Trust for Special Funds, 1981–. *Publications:* pamphlets: (ed) The End of the Private Landlord, 1973; Accidents at Work—Compensation for All, 1974. *Address:* 33 Furnival Street, EC4A 1JQ. *T:* 01–405 7216.

DOUGLAS MILLER, Robert Alexander Gavin; Chairman and Managing Director, Jenners (Princes St Edinburgh) Ltd; Chairman, Clarkson Puckle (Scotland) Ltd; Director: Kennington Leasing Ltd; Chamber Developments Ltd; *b* 11 Feb. 1937; *s* of F. G. Douglas Miller and Mora Kennedy; *m* 1963, Judith Madeleine Smith; three *s* one *d*. *Educ:* Harrow; Oxford Univ. (MA). 9th Lancers, 1955–57; Oxford, 1958–61. Treasurer, Queen's Body Guard for Scotland (Royal Company of Archers). Pres., Edinburgh Chamber of Commerce & Manufacturers, 1985–; Mem. Council, Assoc. of Scottish Salmon Fishery Bds. Chm., Outreach Trust. Governor, Fettes Coll. *Recreations:* shooting, fishing. *Address:* Bavelaw Castle, Balerno, Midlothian. *T:* 031–449 3972. *Club:* New (Edinburgh).
See also Ian MacArthur.

DOUGLAS-PENNANT, family name of **Baron Penrhyn.**

DOUGLAS-SCOTT-MONTAGU, family name of **Baron Montagu of Beaulieu.**

DOUGLAS-WILSON, Ian, MD, FRCPE; Editor of the Lancet, 1965–76; *b* 12 May 1912; *o s* of late Dr H. Douglas-Wilson; *m* 1939, Beatrice May, *e d* of late R. P. Bevan; one *s* two *d*. *Educ:* Marlborough Coll.; Edinburgh Univ. MB ChB 1936; MD (commended) Edinburgh 1938; FRCP Edinburgh 1945. Served with RAMC, 1940–45 (temp. Major). House-physician, Royal Infirmary, Edinburgh, 1937; joined the Lancet staff, 1946; Asst Ed., 1952–62; Dep. Ed., 1962–64. Corresp. Mem., Danish Soc. of Int. Med., 1965. Dr (*hc*) Edinburgh, 1974. *Address:* 14 St Matthew's Drive, Bickley, Bromley, Kent. *T:* 01–467 1703.

DOUGLAS-WITHERS, Maj.-Gen. John Keppel Ingold, CBE 1969; MC 1943; *b* 11 Dec. 1919; *s* of late Lt-Col H. H. Douglas-Withers, OBE, MC, FSA, and late Mrs V. G. Douglas-Withers; *m* 1945, Sylvia Beatrice Dean, Croydon, Surrey; one *s* one *d*. *Educ:* Shrewsbury Sch.; Christ Church, Oxford. Diploma in French, Univ. of Poitiers, 1938; Associate of Inst. of Linguists, in French and German, 1939. Commissioned into RA, 1940; Service in UK, Iraq, Western Desert, N Africa and Italy, 1940–45. Instr in Gunnery, Sch. of Artillery, Larkhill, 1945–47; service in Canal Zone, 1948–49; attended Staff Coll., Camberley, 1950; Staff appt in WO (Mil. Ops), 1951–53; service in The King's Troop, RHA, 1954–55; Instr, Staff Coll., Camberley, 1956–58; Battery Comdr, G Bty, Mercers Troop, RHA, 1959–60; Staff appt in WO (Mil. Sec. Dept), 1961; commanded 49 Field Regt in BAOR and Hong Kong, 1962–64; student at IDC, 1965; Comd 6 Inf. Bde in BAOR, 1966–67; Chief of Staff, 1st Brit. Corps, 1968–69; GOC SW District, 1970–71; Asst Chief of Personnel and Logistics, MoD, 1972–74; retired 1974. Col Comdt, RA, 1974–82. Asst Dir and Gp Personnel Man., Jardine Matheson & Co. Ltd, Hong Kong, 1974–80; Matheson & Co. Ltd, London, 1980–. MPIM (Hong Kong), 1976. *Recreations:* golf, history, military music, gardening. *Address:* c/o Australia and New Zealand Banking Group, 55 Gracechurch Street, EC3V 0BN. *Clubs:* East India, Devonshire, Sports and Public Schools; MCC.

DOULTON, Alfred John Farre, CBE 1973 (OBE 1946); TD 1954; psc 1943; MA Oxon; Head of Statistical Team and Comptroller, Independent Schools Information Service, 1974–80, Consultant, 1980–81; *b* 9 July 1911; *s* of H. V. Doulton, Housemaster, Dulwich Coll., and Constance Jessie Farre, Dulwich; *m* 1940, Vera Daphne, *d* of A. R. Wheatley, Esher; four *s* one *d*. *Educ:* Dulwich Coll.; Brasenose Coll., Oxford (Classical Scholar). Asst Master, Uppingham School, 1934–40. Served War, 1940–46 (despatches twice); DAAG 11 Army Group, 1944; active service, Burma, Malaya, Java, 1945–46; DAQMG 4 Corps, AA&QMG 23 Indian Division, 1945–46. Burma Star, Far East and GS Medal with Java Clasp. Head of Classics and Housemaster of The Lodge, Uppingham Sch., 1946; Headmaster, Highgate Sch., 1955–74. Vice-Chm., HMC, 1967 (Hon. Treasurer, 1964–74). Alderman, Haringey, 1968–71 (Vice-Chm. Educn Cttee). Mem., Governing Bodies Assoc., 1977–80. Vice-Chm. and Chm. Finance Cttee, Kelly Coll.; Trustee, Uppingham Sch., 1966–85. Mem., Indep. Schools Careers Orgn Council, 1978–81. *Publications:* The Fighting Cock, 1951; Highgate School 1938–1944: the story of a wartime evacuation, 1976. *Recreations:* music, cricket, books, dinghy sailing, ornithology. *Address:* Field Cottage, Salcombe, Devon TQ8 8JS. *T:* Salcombe 2316. *Clubs:* Athenæum, MCC.

DOUNE, Lord; John Douglas Stuart; *b* 29 Aug. 1966; *s* and *heir* of 20th Earl of Moray, *qv*. *Educ:* Loretto School, Musselburgh. *Address:* Doune Park, Doune, Perthshire; Darnaway Castle, Forbes, Moray.

DOURO, Marquess of; Arthur Charles Valerian Wellesley; Member (C) Surrey West, European Parliament, since 1984 (Surrey, 1979–84); Chairman, Deltec Securities (UK) Ltd; Director: Eucalyptus Pulp Mills; Transatlantic Insurance Holdings; *b* 19 Aug. 1945, *s* and *heir* of 8th Duke of Wellington, *qv*; *m* 1977, Antonia von Preussen, *d* of late Prince Frederick of Prussia and of Lady Brigid Ness; one *s* one *d*. *Educ:* Eton; Christ Church, Oxford. Dep. Chm., Thames Valley Broadcasting, 1975–84; Dir., Antofagasta and Bolivia Railway Co., 1977–80. Contested (C) Islington N, Oct. 1974; Mem., Basingstoke Borough Council, 1978–79. Kt Comdr, Order of Isabel the Catholic (Spain), 1986. *Heir:* *s* Earl of Mornington, *qv*. *Address:* Apsley House, Piccadilly, W1V 9FA; The Old Rectory, Stratfield Saye, Reading RG7 2DA.

DOVE, Arthur Allan, CEng, FIGasE; Chairman, South Eastern Region, British Gas Corporation, since 1982; *b* 20 May 1933; *s* of William Joseph Dove and Lucy Frances Dove; *m* 1958, Nancy Iris Powell; two *s* one *d*. *Educ:* Taunton's Sch., Southampton; King's Coll. and London Sch. of Econs and Pol. Science, Univ. of London (BSc; AKC 1954). CEng, FIGasE 1974; MIS 1962. Asst Statistician, 1958, Marketing Officer, 1961, Southern Gas; Controller of Sales and Marketing, Scottish Gas, 1965; Commercial Sales Manager, Gas Council, 1969; Dep. Chm., South Eastern Gas, 1973. *Recreations:* photography, walking. *Address:* South Eastern Gas, Katharine Street, Croydon, Surrey CR9 1JU. *T:* 01–688 4466.

DOVE, Sir Clifford (Alfred), Kt 1967; CBE 1960 (MBE 1944); ERD 1963; FCIT; Chairman, British Transport Docks Board, 1970–71; Director-General and Member, Mersey Docks and Harbour Board, Liverpool, 1965–69 (General Manager, 1962); Member: National Ports Council, 1967–71; Council Institute of Transport, 1963–66 (Vice-President, 1964–65); Chairman Merseyside and District Section, Institute of Transport, 1964–65; Council, Dock and Harbour Authorities Assoc., 1970–71 (Executive Committee, 1962–69, Chairman, 1965–67, Vice-President, 1971); *b* 1 Dec. 1904; *e s* of Frederick George Dove and Beatrice Dove (*née* Warren); *m* 1936, Helen Taylor, *d* of Captain James Wilson; no *c*. *Educ:* Russell Sch.; West Ham Municipal Coll.; London School of Economics. Joined Port of London Authority, 1921; Asst Port Director, Calcutta, 1945–46; Asst to Gen. Manager, Tees Conservancy Comrs, 1947–52; Gen. Manager, Ports, Nigeria and British Cameroons, 1952–54; Chm. and Gen. Manager, Nigeria Ports Authority, 1954–61; Mem. Nigeria Railway Corp., 1955–61; Mem. Nigeria Coal Corp., 1956–61; Comr of St John, Nigeria, 1956–61; Vice-Chm., Nat. Stadium Board of Nigeria, 1959–61; First Chm., Inst. of Transport, Nigeria Sect., 1959–61. Member: NW Economic Planning Council, 1965–69; Economic Develt Cttee for Movement of Exports, 1965–69; Exec. Cttee, Nat. Assoc. of Port Employers, 1968–69. Served War, 1939–46 (despatches, MBE): enlisted RE as 2nd Lieut, 1939; BEF, 1940; Middle East, 1941–44; Military Dock Supt., Alexandria, 1942–44; Dep. Asst Director of Transportation, MEF, 1944; AQMG (Movements) India and Embarkation Comdt, Calcutta, 1946; Demob., as Lt-Col. Joined Suppl. Reserve, 1947; retd, 1956, as Lt-Col. OStJ 1956. FRSA 1967. *Publication:* (with late A. H. J. Bown) Port Operation and Administration, 1950. *Recreation:* golf. *Clubs:* East India, Devonshire, Sports and Public Schools; Royal Lymington Yacht.

DOVER, Suffragan Bishop of, since 1980; **Rt. Rev. Richard Henry McPhail Third;** *b* 29 Sept. 1927; *s* of Henry McPhail and Marjorie Caroline Third; *m* 1966, Helen Illingworth; two *d*. *Educ:* Alleyn's Sch.; Reigate Grammar Sch.; Emmanuel Coll., Cambridge (BA 1950, MA 1955); Lincoln Theological Coll. Deacon 1952, priest 1953; Southwark; Curate: S Andrew, Mottingham, 1952–55; Sanderstead (in charge of St Edmund, Riddlesdown), 1955–59; Vicar of Sheerness, 1959–67; Vicar of Orpington, 1967–76; RD of Orpington, 1973–76; Hon. Canon of Rochester, 1974–76; Proctor in Convocation, 1975–76 and 1980–85; Bishop Suffragan of Maidstone, 1976–80. *Recreations:* music, walking. *Address:* Upway, St Martin's Hill, Canterbury, Kent CT1 1PR. *T:* Canterbury 464537.

DOVER, Den; MP (C) Chorley, since 1979; *b* 4 April 1938; *s* of Albert and Emmie Dover; *m* 1959, Anne Marina Wright; one *s* one *d*. *Educ:* Manchester Grammar Sch.; Manchester Univ. BSc Hons. CEng, MICE. John Laing & Son Ltd, 1959–68; National Building Agency: Dep. Chief Executive, 1969–70; Chief Exec., 1971–72; Projects Dir, Capital and Counties Property Co. Ltd, 1972–75; Contracts Manager, Wimpey Laing Iran, 1975–77. Director of Housing Construction, GLC, 1977–79. Member, London Borough of Barnet Council, 1968–71. Mem., Commons Select Cttee on Transport, 1979–. *Recreations:* cricket, hockey, golf; Methodist. *Address:* 166 Furzehill Road, Boreham Wood, Herts. *T:* 01–953 5945; 30 Countess Way, Euxton, Chorley, Lancs.

DOVER, Sir Kenneth James, Kt 1977; DLitt; FRSE 1975; FBA 1966; Chancellor, University of St Andrews, since 1981; *b* 11 March 1920; *o s* of P. H. J. Dover, London, Civil Servant; *m* 1947, Audrey Ruth Latimer; one *s* one *d*. *Educ:* St Paul's Sch. (Scholar); Balliol Coll., Oxford (Domus Scholar); Gaisford Prize, 1939; 1st in Classical Hon. Mods., 1940; Ireland Scholar, 1946; Cromer Prize (British Academy), 1946; 1st in Lit. Hum., Derby Scholar, Amy Mary Preston Read Scholar, 1947; Harmsworth Sen. Scholar, Merton Coll., 1947 (Hon. Fellow, 1980); DLitt Oxon 1974. Served War of 1939–45: Army (RA), 1940–45; Western Desert, 1941–43, Italy, 1943–45 (despatches). Fellow and Tutor, Balliol Coll., 1948–55 (Hon. Fellow, 1977); Prof. of Greek, 1955–76, Dean of Fac. of Arts, 1960–63, 1973–75, Univ. of St Andrews; Pres., Corpus Christi Coll., Oxford, 1976–86. Vis. Lectr, Harvard, 1960; Sather Prof. of Classical Literature, Univ. of California, 1967; Prof.-at-large, Cornell Univ., 1984–. President: Soc. for Promotion of Hellenic Studies, 1971–74; Classical Assoc., 1975; Jt Assoc. of Classical Teachers, 1985. Pres., British Acad., 1978–81. For. Hon. Mem., Amer. Acad. of Arts and Sciences, 1979; For. Mem., Royal Netherlands Acad. of Arts and Sciences, 1979. Hon. LLD: Birmingham, 1979; St Andrews, 1981; Hon. DLitt: Bristol, 1980; London, 1980; St Andrews, 1981; Durham, 1984; Hon. LittD Liverpool, 1983. *Publications:* Greek Word Order, 1960; Commentaries on Thucydides, Books VI and VII, 1965; (ed) Aristophanes' Clouds, 1968; Lysias and the Corpus Lysiacum, 1968; (with A. W. Gomme and A. Andrewes) Historical Commentary on Thucydides, vol. IV, 1970, vol. V, 1981; (ed) Theocritus, select poems, 1971; Aristophanic Comedy, 1972; Greek Popular Morality in the Time of Plato and Aristotle, 1974; Greek Homosexuality, 1978; (ed) Plato, Symposium, 1980; (ed and co-author) Ancient Greek Literature, 1980; The Greeks, 1980 (contrib., The Greeks, BBC TV series, 1980); articles in learned journals; Co-editor, Classical Quarterly, 1962–68. *Recreations:* historical linguistics, country walking. *Address:* 49 Hepburn Gardens, St Andrews, Fife. *Club:* Athenæum.

DOW, Christopher; *see* Dow, J. C. R.

DOW, Harold Peter Bourner; QC 1971; *b* 28 April 1921; *s* of late Col H. P. Dow and P. I. Dow; *m* 1943, Rosemary Merewether, *d* of late Dr E. R. A. Merewether, CB, CBE, FRCP; two *s* one *d*. *Educ:* Charterhouse; Trinity Hall, Cambridge (MA). Served RAF (Air Crew), 1941–42. Min. of Supply, 1943–45. Barrister, Middle Temple, 1946.

Publications: Restatement of Town and Country Planning, 1947; National Assistance, 1948; Rights of Way (with Q. Edwards), 1951; ed, Hobsons Local Government, 1951 and 1957 edns. *Recreations:* music, painting. *Address:* The Priory, Brandeston, near Woodbridge, Suffolk. *T:* Earl Soham 244.

DOW, (John) Christopher (Roderick), FBA 1982; Visiting Fellow, National Institute of Economic and Social Research, since 1984; *b* 25 Feb. 1916; *s* of Warrender Begernie and Amy Langdon Dow; *m* 1960, Clare Mary Keegan; one *s* three *d*. *Educ:* Bootham Sch., York; Brighton, Hove and Sussex Grammar Sch.; University College London, Fellow 1973. Economic Adviser, later Senior Economic Adviser, HM Treasury, 1945–54; on staff, and Dep. Dir, National Inst. for Economic and Social Research, 1954–62; Treasury, 1962–63; Asst Sec.-Gen., OECD, Paris, 1963–73; Exec. Dir, Bank of England, 1973–81; an Advr to the Governor of the Bank of England, 1981–84. *Publications:* The Management of the British Economy, 1945–1960, 1964; Fiscal Policy for a Balanced Economy (jointly), 1968. Various articles in learned jls. *Club:* Reform.

DOWD, Ronald, AO 1976; voice consultant; tenor; *b* Sydney, Australia, 23 Feb. 1914; *s* of Robert Henry Dowd and Henrietta (*née* Jenkins); *m* 1938, Elsie Burnitt Crute (English born); one *s* one *d*. *Educ:* Sydney. Prior to Army service in Australia, New Guinea and the Celebes, was a bank officer. Upon discharge, adopted full-time singing and performed for various opera organisations and Australian Broadcasting Commission in the Commonwealth. Came to UK for Sadler's Wells, 1956, and returned to Australia by arrangement with Elizabethan Theatre Trust; then rejoined Sadler's Wells, 1959, remaining for a year. Since then has been fully engaged in concerts and opera singing with leading conductors and organisations, including Royal Opera House. Toured NZ and Australia for Australian Broadcasting Commission, 1964; toured Continent with Sadler's Wells, 1963 and 1965; with Aust. Opera Co., 1972–78. Chm., opera panel, Australian Council for the Arts, 1973–; Mem., Sydney Cultural Council, 1982. *Address:* 171 Albion Street, Surrey Hills, NSW 2010, Australia. *Club:* Savage (London).

DOWDALLS, Hon. Sheriff Edward Joseph; Principal, Coatbridge Technical College, since 1973; *b* 6 March 1926; *s* of late Alexander Dowdalls and Helen Dowdalls; *m* 1953, Sarah Quinn; one *s*. *Educ:* Our Lady's High Sch., Motherwell; Glasgow Univ. (BSc). Member, Coatbridge Town Council, 1958, Provost, 1967. Mem., Scottish Economic Planning Council, 1968–71; Chm., Lanarkshire Area Health Bd, 1977–81 (Mem., 1974–81). Hon. Sheriff, S Strathclyde and Galloway, 1975–. *Recreations:* reading, watching sport. *Address:* 72 Drumpellier Avenue, Coatbridge, Lanarkshire ML5 1JS. *Clubs:* Drumpellier Cricket, Drumpellier Rugby (Coatbridge).

DOWDEN, Richard George; journalist, The Times, since 1980; *b* 20 March 1949; *s* of Peter Dowden and Eleanor Dowden; *m* 1976, Penny Mansfield; two *d*. *Educ:* St George's Coll., Weybridge, Surrey; London Univ. (BA History). Volunteer Teacher, Uganda, 1971–72; Asst Sec., Justice and Peace Commn, 1973–76; Editor, Catholic Herald, 1976–79. *Address:* 7 Highbury Grange, N5.

DOWDING, family name of **Baron Dowding.**

DOWDING, 2nd Baron *cr* 1943, of Bentley Priory; **Derek Hugh Tremenheere Dowding;** Wing Commander, RAF, retired; *b* 9 Jan. 1919; *s* of (Air Chief Marshal) 1st Baron Dowding, GCB, GCVO, CMG, and Clarice Maud (*d* 1920), *d* of Captain John Williams, IA; *S* father, 1970; *m* 1st, 1940, Joan Myrle (marr. diss. 1946), *d* of Donald James Stuart, Nairn; 2nd, 1947, Alison Margaret (marr. diss. 1960), *d* of Dr James Bannerman, Norwich and *widow* of Major R. M. H. Peebles; two *s*; 3rd, 1961, Odette L. M. S. Hughes, *d* of Louis Joseph Houles. *Educ:* Winchester; RAF College, Cranwell. Served War of 1939–45, UK and Middle East; in comd No 49 (B) Sqdn, 1950; Wing Commander, 1951. Gen. Sec., Sea Cadet Assoc. (formerly Navy League), 1977–. *Heir: s* Hon. Piers Hugh Tremenheere Dowding, *b* 18 Feb. 1948. *Address:* c/o Lloyds Bank, 6 Pall Mall, SW1.

DOWDING, Michael Frederick, CBE 1973; Chairman, Michael Dowding Associates Ltd, consulting engineers; *b* 19 Nov. 1918; *s* of late Guy Francis Dowding and of Frances Constance Dowding (*née* Bragger); *m* 1947, Rosemary, *d* of Somerville Hastings, MS, FRCS; one *s* two *d*. *Educ:* Westminster; Magdalene Coll., Cambridge. MA Cantab. CEng, FIMechE; FIM. Served War, 1939–45, Major RA (despatches, 1945). Joined Davy & United Engineering Co., 1946: Man. Dir, 1961–64; Chm., Davy Ashmore International, 1964–70; Dir, Davy Ashmore Ltd, 1962–72. Mem., Finnish British Technological Cttee, 1969. Vice-Pres., Iron and Steel Inst., 1965; Pres., The Metals Soc., 1978–79. Commander, Knights of Finnish Lion, 1st Class, 1969. *Publications:* various technical papers to Iron and Steel Inst. and foreign metallurgical socs. *Recreations:* painting, shooting, fishing. *Address:* 27 Old Palace Lane, Richmond, Surrey TW9 1PQ. *T:* 01-940 1782; Bod Isaf, Aberdaron, Gwynedd. *Clubs:* Brooks's, MCC.

DOWELL, Anthony (James), CBE 1973; Senior Principal, since 1967, Director, since 1986, Royal Ballet, Covent Garden (Assistant to Director, 1984–85; Associate Director, 1985–86); *b* 16 Feb. 1943; *s* of late Catherine Ethel and Arthur Henry Dowell; unmarried. *Educ:* Hampshire Sch., St Saviour's Hall, Knightsbridge; Royal Ballet Sch., White Lodge, Richmond, Surrey; Royal Ballet Sch., Barons Court. Joined Opera Ballet, 1960; 1st Company, for Russian Tour, 1961; created The Dream, 1964; Italian Tour, 1965; promoted Principal Dancer, 1966; Eastern Europe Tour, 1966; Japanese Tour, 1975; created Shadow Play, 1967; American Tours and Metropolitan Opera House, New York, 1968, 1969, 1972; created: Pavane, 1973; Manon, 1974. *Principal roles with Royal Ballet include:* La Fête Etrange, 1963; Napoli, 1965; Romeo and Juliet, 1965; Song of the Earth, 1966; Card Game, Giselle, Swan Lake, 1967; The Nutcracker, Cinderella, Monotones, Symphonic Variations, new version of Sleeping Beauty, Enigma Variations, Lilac Garden, 1968; Raymonda Act III, Daphnis and Chloe, La Fille Mal Gardée, 1969; Dances at a Gathering, 1970; La Bayadère, Meditation from Thaïs, Afternoon of a Faun, Anastasia, 1971; Triad, Le Spectre de la Rose, Giselle, 1972; Agon, Firebird, 1973; Manon, 1974; Four Schumann Pieces, Les Sylphides, 1975; Four Seasons, 1975; Scarlet Pastorale, 1976; Rhapsody, 1981; A Month in the Country, The Tempest, Varii Capricci, 1983. Guest Artist with Amer. Ballet Theater, 1977–79; *performed in:* The Nutcracker; Don Quixote; Other Dances; *created:* Contredanses; Solor in Makarova's La Bayadère; Fisherman in Le Rossignol (Ashton's choreography), NY Metropolitan Opera, 1981. Narrator in A Wedding Bouquet (first speaking role), Joffrey Ballet, 1977; guest appearances with Nat. Ballet of Canada (The Dream, Four Schumann Pieces), 1979 and 1981; Anthony Dowell Ballet Gala, Palladium, 1980 (for charity); narrated Oedipus Rex, NY Metropolitan Opera, 1981. *Television performances:* La Bayadère (USA); Swan Lake, Cinderella, Sleeping Beauty, A Month in the Country, The Dream, Les Noces (all BBC); All the Superlatives (personal profile), Omnibus, BBC. Dance Magazine award, NY, 1972. *Recreations:* painting, paper sculpture, theatrical costume design. *Address:* Royal Opera House, Covent Garden, WC2.

DOWELL, Prof. John Derek, FRS 1986; Professor of Elementary Particle Physics, University of Birmingham, since 1980; *b* 6 Jan. 1935; *s* of William Ernest Dowell and Elsie Dorothy Dowell (*née* Jarvis); *m* 1959, Patricia Clarkson; one *s* one *d*. *Educ:* Coalville Grammar Sch., Leics; Univ. of Birmingham (BSc, PhD). Research Fellow, Univ. of Birmingham, 1958–60; Res. Associate, CERN, Geneva, 1960–62; Lectr, 1962–70, Sen. Lectr, 1970–75, Reader, 1975–80, Univ. of Birmingham. Vis. Scientist, Argonne Nat. Lab., USA, 1968–69; Scientific Associate, CERN, Geneva, 1973–74, 1985–. *Publications:* numerous, in Phys. Letters, Nuovo Cimento, Nuclear Phys., Phys. Rev., Proc. Royal Soc., and related literature. *Recreations:* piano, amateur theatre, squash, ski-ing. *Address:* 57 Oxford Road, Moseley, Birmingham B13 9ES; EP Division, CERN, 1211 Geneva 23, Switzerland.

DOWER, E. L. G.; *see* Gandar Dower.

DOWLING, Kenneth, CB 1985; Deputy Director of Public Prosecutions, 1982–85; *b* 30 Dec. 1933; *s* of Alfred and Maria Dowling; *m* 1957, Margaret Frances Bingham; two *d*. *Educ:* King George V Grammar Sch., Southport. Called to the Bar, Gray's Inn, 1960. RAF, 1952–54. Immigration Branch, Home Office, 1954–61; joined DPP Dept: Legal Asst, 1961; Sen. Legal Asst, 1966; Asst Solicitor, 1972; Asst Dir, 1976; Princ. Asst Dir, 1977. *Recreations:* reading, golf. *Address:* c/o 4–12 Queen Anne's Gate, SW1H 9AZ. *T:* 01-213 6026.

DOWLING, Rt. Rev. Owen Douglas; *see* Canberra and Goulburn, Bishop of.

DOWLING, Prof. Patrick Joseph, PhD; FEng 1981; British Steel Corporation Professor of Steel Structures, Imperial College of Science and Technology, University of London, since 1979; Head of Engineering Structures Section, since 1981, and of Civil Engineering Department, since 1985, Imperial College; Founder Partner, Chapman and Dowling, Consulting Engineers, since 1981; *b* 23 March 1939; *s* of John Dowling and Margaret McKittrick, Dublin; *m* 1966, Grace Carmine Victoria Lobo, *d* of Palladius Lobo and Marcilia Moniz, Zanzibar; one *s* one *d*. *Educ:* Christian Brothers Sch., Dublin; University Coll., Dublin (BE NUI 1960); Imperial Coll. of Science and Technol., London (PhD 1968). DIC 1961; FRINA 1985 (MRINA 1976); FIStructE 1978; FICE 1979. Demonstr in Civil Engrg, UC Dublin, 1960–61; Post-grad. studies, Imperial Coll., London, 1961–65; Bridge Engr, British Constructional Steelwork Assoc., 1965–68; Res. Fellow, 1968–74 and Reader in Structural Steelwork, 1974–79, Imperial Coll., London. Chm., Eurocode 3 (Steel Structures) Drafting Cttee, 1981–84. Instn of Structural Engineers: Oscar Faber Award, 1971; Henry Adams Medal, 1976; Guthrie Brown Medal, 1979; Oscar Faber Medal, 1985; Telford Premium, ICE, 1976; Gustave Trasenster Medal, Assoc. des Ingénieurs sortis de l'Univ. de Liège, 1984. Editor, Jl of Constructional Steel Research, 1980–. *Publications:* Steel Plated Structures, 1977; Buckling of Shells in Offshore Structures, 1982; technical papers on elastic and inelastic behaviour and design of steel and composite land-based and offshore structures. *Recreations:* travelling, sailing, reading, the enjoyment of good company. *Address:* Imperial College of Science and Technology, SW7 2BU. T: 01-589 5111. *Club:* Chelsea Arts.

DOWN AND CONNOR, Bishop of, (RC), since 1982; **Most Rev. Cahal Brendan Daly;** *b* 1917. *Educ:* St Malachy's, Belfast; Queen's Univ., Belfast (BA Hons, Classics, MA); St Patrick's, Maynooth (DD); Institut Catholique, Paris (LPh). Ordained, 1941. Lecturer in Scholastic Philosophy, Queen's Univ., Belfast, 1946–62; Reader, 1962–67; consecrated Bishop, 1967; Bishop of Ardagh and Clonmacnois, 1967–82. *Publications:* Morals, Law and Life, 1962; Natural Law Morality Today, 1965; Violence in Ireland and Christian Conscience, 1973; Theologians and the Magisterium, 1977; Peace the Work of Justice, 1979; chapters in: Prospect for Metaphysics, 1961; Intellect and Hope, 1968; New Essays in Religious Language, 1969; Understanding the Eucharist, 1969. *Address:* Bishop's House, Lisbreen, Somerton Road, Belfast BT15 4DE.

DOWN AND DROMORE, Bishop of, since 1986; **Rt. Rev. Gordon McMullan;** *b* 1934; *m* 1957, Kathleen Davidson; two *s*. *Educ:* Queen's Univ., Belfast (BSc Econ 1961, PhD 1971); Ridley Hall, Cambridge. ACIS 1957. Dipl. of Religious Studies (Cantab) 1978. Deacon 1962, priest 1963, dio. Down; Curate of Ballymacarrett, 1962–67; Central Adviser on Christian Stewardship to Church of Ireland, 1967–70; Curate of St Columba, Knock, Belfast, 1970–71; Rector of St Brendan's, East Belfast, 1971–76; Rector of St Columba, Knock, Belfast, 1976–80; Archdeacon of Down, 1979–80; Bishop of Clogher, 1980–86. *Address:* The See House, 32 Knockdene Park South, Belfast BT5 7AB.

DOWN, Sir Alastair (Frederick), Kt 1978; OBE 1944 (MBE 1942); MC 1940; TD 1951; Chairman, The Burmah Oil Co. PLC, 1975–83 (Chief Executive, 1975–80); *b* 23 July 1914; *e s* of Frederick Edward Down and Margaret Isobel Down (*née* Hutchison); *m* 1947, Bunny Mellon; two *s* two *d*. *Educ:* Edinburgh Acad.; Marlborough Coll. Commissioned in 7th/9th Bn, The Royal Scots (TA), 1935. CA 1938. Joined British Petroleum Co. Ltd in Palestine, 1938. Served War of 1939–45 (despatches twice, MC, MBE, OBE, Kt Comdr, Order of Orange Nassau, with swords, 1946): Middle East, N Africa, Italy and Holland, with Eighth Army and 1st Canadian Army as Lt-Col and full Col. Rejoined BP, in Iran, 1945–47; Head Office, 1947–54; Canada, 1954–62 (Chief Rep. of BP in Canada, 1954–57; Pres., BP Group in Canada, 1957–62); Pres. BP Oil Corp., 1969–70; Man. Dir, 1962–75 and Dep. Chm., 1969–75, British Petroleum Co. Ltd; Director: TRW Inc., USA, 1977–86; Scottish American Investment Co. Ltd, 1980–85; Royal Bank of Canada, 1981–85; Chairman: British-North American Res. Assoc., 1980–84; London American Energy NV, 1981–85. Member: Review Body for pay of doctors and dentists, 1971–74; Television Adv. Cttee, 1971–72; Council, Marlborough Coll., 1979– (Chm. Council, 1982–); Hon. Treasurer, Field Studies Council, 1977–81. FRSA 1970; FBIM 1972; JDipMA (Hon.), 1966. Hambro British Businessman of the Year Award, 1980; Cadman Meml Medal, Inst. of Petroleum, 1981. *Recreations:* shooting, golf, fishing. *Address:* Stockleigh House, Stockleigh Pomeroy, near Crediton, Devon; 15 Rutland Gate, SW7. *Club* Carlton.

DOWN, Antony Turnbull L.; *see* Langdon-Down.

DOWN, Barbara Langdon; *see* Littlewood, Lady (Barbara).

DOWNE, 11th Viscount, *cr* 1680; **John Christian George Dawnay;** Bt 1642; Baron Dawnay of Danby (UK) *cr* 1897; DL; *b* Wykeham, 18 Jan. 1935; *s* of 10th Viscount Downe, OBE and Margaret Christine (*d* 1967), *d* of Christian Bahnsen, NJ; *S* father, 1965; *m* 1965, Alison Diana, *d* of I. F. H. Sconce, MBE; one *s* one *d*. *Educ:* Eton Coll.; Christ Church, Oxford. 2nd Lieut, Grenadier Guards, 1954–55. Non-marine broker at Lloyd's, 1957–65. Director: Brookdeal Electronics Ltd, 1962–; Dawnay Faulkner Associates Ltd, 1968–; Mill Feed Holdings Ltd, 1978–; George Rowney & Co. Ltd, 1978–, etc. Mem., N Yorks CC, 1973–85. President: Yorkshire Rural Community Council, 1979–; Aston Martin Owners Club, 1980–; Chairman: Friends of the Nat. Railway Museum, 1977–; York Technology Ltd, 1980–. Trustee, Science Mus., 1984–. DL N Yorks, 1981. *Publications:* contributions to various journals. *Recreation:* linear circuit design. *Heir: s* Hon. Richard Henry Dawnay, *b* 9 April 1967. *Address:* Wykeham Abbey, Scarborough, North Yorks. *T:* Scarborough 862404, *Telex:* 527192; 5 Douro Place, W8. *T:* 01-937 9449. *Clubs:* Pratt's, Cavalry and Guards'.

DOWNER, Dr Martin Craig; Chief Dental Officer and Under Secretary, Department of Health and Social Security, since 1983; *b* 9 March 1931; *s* of Dr Reginald Lionel Ernest

Downer and Mrs Eileen Maud Downer (*née* Craig); *m* 1961, Anne Catherine (*née* Evans); four *d*. *Educ:* Shrewsbury Sch.; Univ. of Liverpool; Univ. of Manchester (PhD 1974); Univ. of London. LDSRCS 1958; DDPH RCS 1969. Dental Officer, St Helens Local Authority, 1959–59; gen. dental practice, 1959–64; Dental Officer, Bor. of Haringey, 1964–67; Principal Dental Officer, Royal Bor. of Kensington and Chelsea, 1967–70; Res. Fellow in Dental Health, Univ. of Manchester, 1970–74; Area Dental Officer, Salford HA (also Hon. Lectr, Univ. of Manchester), 1974–79; Chief Dental Officer, SHHD (also Hon. Sen. Lectr, Univs of Edinburgh and Dundee), 1979–83. *Publications:* papers in learned jls in gen. field of community dental health, incl. epidemiology and biostatistics, clin. trials and trial methodology, inf. systems, health services res., and econs of dental care. *Recreations:* music, reading, cookery, natural history, vintage aviation, walking. *Address:* Department of Health and Social Security, Alexander Fleming House, Elephant and Castle, SE1 6BY.

DOWNES, George Robert, CB 1967; Director of Studies, Royal Institute of Public Administration, since 1972; *b* 25 May 1911; *o s* of late Philip George Downes; *m* Edna Katherine Millar; two *d*. *Educ:* King Edward's Grammar School, Birmingham; Grocers', London. Entered GPO, 1928; Assistant Surveyor, 1937; Asst Principal, 1939. Served War of 1939–45: RNVR, in destroyers, 1942–45. Principal, GPO, 1946; Principal Private Sec. to: Lord President of the Council, 1948–50, Lord Privy Seal, 1951; Assistant Secretary, 1951; Imperial Defence College, 1952; Deputy Regional Director, GPO London, 1955; Dir, London Postal Region, 1960–65; Dir of Postal Services, 1965–67; Dir, Operations and Overseas, PO, 1967–71. *Recreations:* music, gardening. *Address:* Orchard Cottage, Frithsden, Berkhamsted, Herts HP4 1NW.

DOWNES, George Stretton, CBE 1976; Deputy Receiver for the Metropolitan Police District, 1973–76; retired; *b* London, 2 March 1914; *e s* of late George and Rosalind S. Downes; *m* 1939, Sheilah Gavigan; two *s* two *d*. *Educ:* Cardinal Vaughan Sch., Kensington. Joined Metropolitan Police Office, 1934; Secretary, 1969. *Recreations:* golf, gardening. *Address:* 9 Browning Road, Fetcham, Leatherhead, Surrey KT22 9HN.

DOWNES, Prof. (John) Kerry, FSA; Professor of History of Art, University of Reading, since 1978; *b* 8 Dec. 1930; *s* of Ralph William Downes, *qv*; *m* 1962, Margaret Walton. *Educ:* St Benedict's, Ealing; Courtauld Institute of Art. BA, PhD London. Library, Courtauld Inst. of Art, 1954–58; Librarian, Barber Inst. of Fine Arts, Univ. of Birmingham, 1958–66; Lectr in Fine Art, Univ. of Reading, 1966–71, Reader, 1971–78. Vis. Lectr, Yale Univ., 1968. Mem., Royal Commission on Historical Monuments (England), 1981–; Pres., Soc. of Architectural Historians of GB, 1984–. *Publications:* Hawksmoor, 1959, 2nd edn 1979; English Baroque Architecture, 1966; Hawksmoor, 1969; Christopher Wren, 1971; Whitehall Palace, in Colvin and others, History of the King's Works, V, 1660–1782, 1976; Vanbrugh, 1977; The Georgian Cities of Britain, 1979; Rubens, 1980; The Architecture of Wren, 1982; contribs to Burlington Magazine, Architectural History, Architectural Rev., TLS, etc. *Recreations:* drawing, making music, learning electronics, procrastination. *Address:* Department of History of Art, University of Reading, London Road, Reading RG1 5AQ. *T:* Reading 875234.

DOWNES, M. P.; *see* Panter-Downes.

DOWNES, Ralph (William), CBE 1969; Organist, Brompton Oratory, 1936–78, now Organist Emeritus; Curator-Organist, Royal Festival Hall, since 1954; *b* 16 Aug. 1904; *s* of James William and Constance Edith Downes; *m* 1929, Agnes Mary (*née* Rix) (*d* 1980); one *s*. *Educ:* Derby Municipal Secondary Sch. (Scholar); Royal College of Music, London (Schol.); Keble Coll., Oxford. ARCM 1925, MA 1931, BMus 1935. Asst Organist, Southwark Cathedral, 1924; Organ Scholar, Keble Coll., 1925–28; Director of Chapel Music and Lecturer, Princeton Univ., USA, 1928–35; Organ Prof., RCM, 1954–75. Organ Curator to LCC, 1949. Consultant to: the Corporation of Croydon, 1960; Cardiff City Council (St David's Hall), 1977; Designer and Supervisor of organs in: Buckfast Abbey, 1952; Royal Festival Hall, 1954; Brompton Oratory, 1954; St John's Cathedral, Valletta, Malta, 1961; St Albans Cathedral, 1963, 1981; Fairfield Halls, 1964; Paisley Abbey, 1968; Gloucester Cathedral, 1971, and others. Recitals and performances in: Aldeburgh, 1948–76, Belgium, France, Germany, Holland, Italy, Switzerland, also radio and TV. Jury mem., organ festivals, Amsterdam, Haarlem, Munich, St Albans. Received into the Catholic Church, 1930. Hon. RAM 1965; Hon. FRCO 1966; FRCM 1969. KSG 1970. *Publications:* Baroque Tricks (Adventures with the Organ Builders), 1983; miscellaneous articles on the organ, compositions for keyboard and chorus. *Address:* 9 Elm Crescent, Ealing, W5 3JW. *T:* 01–567 6330.
See also J. K. Downes.

DOWNEY, Anne Elisabeth; Her Honour Judge Downey; a Circuit Judge, since 1986; *b* 22 Aug. 1936; *d* of John James Downey and Ida May Downey. *Educ:* Notre Dame Convent, Liverpool; Liverpool Univ. LLB (Hons.). Called to the Bar, Gray's Inn, 1958. A Recorder, 1980–86. *Recreations:* antiques, reading. *Address:* Copperfield, 4 Pine Walk, Prenton, Merseyside. *T:* 051–608 2404.

DOWNEY, Sir Gordon (Stanley), KCB 1984 (CB 1980); Comptroller and Auditor General, since 1981; *b* 26 April 1928; *s* of Stanley William and Winifred Downey; *m* 1952, Jacqueline Goldsmith; two *d*. *Educ:* Tiffin's Sch.; London Sch. of Economics (BSc(Econ)). Served RA, 1946–48. Ministry of Works, 1951; entered Treasury, 1952; Asst Private Sec. to successive Chancellors of the Exchequer, 1955–57; on loan to Ministry of Health, 1961–62; Asst Sec., 1965, Under-Sec., 1972, Head of Central Unit, 1975; Dep. Sec., Treasury, 1976–81; on loan as Dep. Head, Central Policy Review Staff, Cabinet Office, 1978–81. *Recreations:* reading, visual arts. *Address:* Chinley Cottage, 1 Eaton Park Road, Cobham, Surrey KT11 2JG. *T:* Cobham 67878. *Club:* Army and Navy.

DOWNEY, Air Vice-Marshal John Chegwyn Thomas, CB 1975; DFC 1945, AFC; Deputy Controller of Aircraft (C), Ministry of Defence, 1974–75, retired; *b* 26 Nov. 1920; *s* of Thomas Cecil Downey and Mary Evelyn Downey; *m* Diana, (*née* White); one *s* two *d*. *Educ:* Whitgift Sch. Entered RAF 1939; served War of 1939–45 in Coastal Command (DFC 1945 for his part in anti-U-boat ops). Captained Lincoln Aries III on global flight of 29,000 miles, during which London-Khartoum record was broken. RAF Farnborough 1956–58; commanded Bomber Comd Develt Unit 1959–60; head of NE Defence Secretariat, Cyprus, 1960–62; Comd RAF Farnborough, 1962–64; a Dir, Op. Requirements (RAF) MoD, 1965–67; IDC, 1968; Comdt, RAF Coll. of Air Warfare, Manby, Jan./Oct. 1969; Comdr Southern Maritime Air Region, 1969–71; Senior RAF Mem., RCDS, 1972–74. *Publications:* Management in the Armed Forces: an anatomy of the military profession, 1977; (contrib.) Yearbook of World Affairs, 1983; contribs to The Listener, and Armed Forces. *Recreation:* sailing. *Address:* c/o Lloyds Bank, 6 Pall Mall, SW1. *Club:* Royal Air Force.

DOWNEY, William George, CB 1967; *b* 3 Jan. 1912; *s* of late William Percy Downey; *m* 1936, Iris, *e d* of late Ernest Frederick Pickering; three *d*. *Educ:* Southend Grammar Sch. ACWA 1935, ACA 1937, FCA 1960. Ministry of Aircraft Production, 1940; Ministry of Supply, 1946 (Director of Finance and Administration, Royal Ordnance Factories, 1952–57); Ministry of Aviation, 1959; Under-Secretary, 1961; Chm., Steering Gp, Develt Cost Estimation, 1964–66; Min. of Technology, 1967, Min. of Aviation Supply, 1970; DTI, 1971; Management Consultant to Procurement Exec., MoD, 1972–74; Under Sec., NI Office, 1974–75; Dir, Harland and Wolff, 1975–81; Consultant to CAA, 1976–79, to Dept of Energy, 1980. *Address:* Starvelarks, Dawes Heath Road, Rayleigh, Essex. *T:* Rayleigh 774138.

DOWNIE, Prof. Allan Watt, FRCP 1982; FRS 1955; Professor of Bacteriology, Liverpool University, 1943–66, now Emeritus Professor; *b* 5 Sept. 1901; *s* of William Downie, Rosehearty, Aberdeenshire; *m* 1936, Nancy McHardy; one *s* two *d*. *Educ:* Fraserburgh Academy, Aberdeen Univ. MB, ChB, Aberdeen Univ., 1923; MD, 1929; DSc, 1937. Lecturer Aberdeen Univ., 1924–26, Manchester Univ., 1927–34; Senior Freedom Research Fellow, London Hospital, 1935–39; Member Scientific Staff, Nat. Institute Medical Research, 1939–43. Voluntary Asst, Rockefeller Inst. Med. Research, New York City, USA, 1934–35. Vis. Prof., Medical Sch., Univ. of Colorado, Denver, 1966–69, 1971, 1973. Founder Fellow, RCPath. Hon. LLD Aberdeen Univ., 1956. *Publications:* (Jt) Virus and Rickettsial Diseases of Man, 1950; numerous articles in scientific journals. *Recreations:* golf, fishing, ornithology. *Address:* 10 College Close, Birkdale, Merseyside. *T:* Southport 67269.
See also Sir Christopher Hewetson.

DOWNIE, Prof. Robert Silcock; Professor of Moral Philosophy, Glasgow University, since 1969; *b* 19 April 1933; *s* of late Robert Mackie Downie and late Margaret Barlas Downie; *m* 1958, Eileen Dorothea Flynn; three *d*. *Educ:* The High Sch. of Glasgow; Glasgow Univ.; The Queen's Coll., Oxford. MA, first cl. hons, Philosophy and Eng. Lit., Glasgow, 1955; Russian linguist, Intelligence Corps, 1955–57; Ferguson Schol., 1958; BPhil Oxford Univ., 1959. Glasgow University: Lectr in Moral Philosophy, 1959; Sen. Lectr in Moral Philosophy, 1968; Stevenson Lectr in Med. Ethics, 1985–. Vis. Prof. of Philosophy, Syracuse Univ., NY, USA, 1963–64. FRSE 1986. *Publications:* Government Action and Morality, 1964; Respect for Persons (jt), 1969; Roles and Values, 1971; Education and Personal Relationships (jt), 1974; Values in Social Work (jt), 1976; (jt) Caring and Curing, 1980; Healthy Respect, 1986; contribs to: Mind, Philosophy, Analysis, Aristotelian Society, Political Studies. *Recreation:* music. *Address:* Department of Moral Philosophy, University of Glasgow G12 8QQ. *T:* 041–339 8855.

DOWNING, Dr Anthony Leighton; Consultant, Binnie & Partners, Consulting Engineers, since 1986 (Partner, 1973–86); *b* 27 March 1926; *s* of Sydney Arthur Downing and Frances Dorothy Downing; *m* 1952, Kathleen Margaret Frost; one *d*. *Educ:* Arnold Sch., Blackpool; Cambridge and London Universities. BA Cantab. 1946; BSc Special Degree 2 (1) Hons. London, 1950; DSc London 1967. Joined Water Pollution Research Lab., 1946; seconded to Fisheries Research Lab., Lowestoft, 1947–48; granted transfer to Govt Chemist's Lab., 1948; returned to WPRL as Scientific Officer, 1950; subsequently worked mainly in field of biochemical engrg; Dir, Water Pollution Res. Lab., 1966–73. Vis. Prof., Imperial Coll. of Science and Technology, 1978–82. FIChemE 1975; FIWPC 1965 (Pres., 1979); FIBiol 1965; Hon. FIPHE 1965; FIWES 1975. FRSA. *Publications:* papers in scientific and technical journals. *Recreations:* golf, gardening. *Address:* 2 Tewin Close, Tewin Wood, Welwyn, Herts. *T:* Bulls Green 474. *Clubs:* United Oxford & Cambridge University; Knebworth Golf.

DOWNING, David Francis, PhD; Head, Land Systems Group, British Defence Staff, British Embassy, Washington, since 1983; *b* 4 Aug. 1926; *e s* of late Alfred William Downing, ARCO, and of Violet Winifred Downing; *m* 1948, Margaret Joan Llewellyn; one *s* one *d*. *Educ:* Bristol Grammar Sch.; Univ. of Bristol (BSc 1952, PhD 1955). Served Coldstream Gds and Royal Welch Fusiliers, 1944–48 (Lieut RWF, 1947). Student Mem. of delegn from Brit. univs to Soviet univs, 1954; Eli Lilley Res. Fellow, Univ. of Calif, LA, and Fulbright Travel Scholarship, 1955–56; Long Ashton Res. Stn, Univ. of Bristol, 1957–58; Chem. Def. Estab., 1958–63; Def. Res. Staff, Washington, 1963–66; Chem. Def. Estab., 1966–68; Counsellor (Scientific), British High Commn, Ottawa, 1968–73; Head, Management Services, RARDE, 1973–75, and Head, Pyrotechnics Br., 1975–78; Counsellor (Scientific), British Embassy, Moscow, 1978–81; Asst Dir, Resources and Programmes B, MoD, 1981–83. Mem. Council, Internat. Disaster Inst., 1982. FRSA 1969. *Publications:* Psychotomimetic Compounds (monograph), in, Psychopharmacological Agents, 1964; scientific papers, mainly in Jl of Chem. Soc., and Qly Revs of Chem. Soc. *Recreations:* music, Arctic art, travel, bird watching, skiing. *Address:* c/o Foreign and Commonwealth Office, SW1; 13 The Close, Salisbury, Wilts SP1 2EB. *T:* Salisbury 23910. *Club:* Army and Navy.

DOWNING, Henry Julian; HM Diplomatic Service, retired; *b* 22 March 1919; *o s* of Henry Julian Downing and Kate Avery; *m* 1951, Ruth Marguerite Ambler. *Educ:* Boys' High Sch., Trowbridge; Hertford Coll., Oxford. Indian Civil Service (Madras) 1941–47. Joined HM Foreign Service, 1947; 2nd Secretary, Madras and Dacca, 1947–50; Foreign Office, 1950–52; 1st Secretary (Commercial), Istanbul, 1952–56; Foreign Office, 1956–58; 1st Secretary and Head of Chancery, Kabul, 1958–62; Foreign Office, 1963–65; HM Consul-General, Lourenço Marques, 1965–69; Head of Claims Dept, 1969–71, of Migration and Visa Dept, 1971–73, FCO; Consul-Gen., Cape Town, 1973–77. *Recreations:* swimming, walking, bird watching. *Address:* 8b Greenaway Gardens, Hampstead, NW3. *T:* 01–435 2593. *Club:* United Oxford & Cambridge University.

DOWNS, Sir Diarmuid, Kt 1985; CBE 1979; FRS 1985; FEng, FIMechE; Chairman, Ricardo Consulting Engineers plc, since 1976 (Managing Director, 1976–84); *b* 23 April 1922; *s* of John Downs and Ellen McMahon; *m* 1951, Mary Carmel Chillman; one *s* three *d*. *Educ:* Gunnersbury Catholic Grammar Sch.; City Univ., London (BScEng). CEng, FIMechE 1961. Ricardo Consulting Engineers Ltd, 1942–: Head, Petrol Engine Dept, 1947; Dir, 1957; Man. Dir, 1967. Mem., Adv. Council for Applied R&D, 1976–80; Member: SERC, 1981–85 (Chm., Engineering Bd); Design Council, 1981–; Bd of Dirs, Soc. of Automotive Engineers Inc., 1983–. President: Fédération Internationale des Sociétés d'Ingénieurs des Techniques de L'Automobile, 1978 (Vice-Pres., 1975); IMechE, 1978–79 (Vice-Pres., 1971–78); Assoc. of Indep. Contract Res. Organisations, 1975–77; Section G, British Assoc. for Advancement of Science, 1984; Royal Commn for Exhibn of 1851. Mem. Council: City Univ., 1980–82; Surrey Univ., 1983–. Hon. DSc: City, 1978; Cranfield Inst. of Technol., 1981. James Alfred Ewing Medal, ICE, 1985; Medal, Internat. Fedn of Automobile Engrs' and Technicians' Assocs, 1986. *Publications:* paper on internal combustion engines in British and internat. engrg jls and conf. proc. *Recreation:* theatre. *Address:* The Downs, 143 New Church Road, Hove, East Sussex BN3 4DB. *T:* Brighton 419357. *Clubs:* St Stephen's Constitutional; Hove (Hove).

DOWNS, Mrs George Wallingford; *see* Tureck, Rosalyn.

DOWNS, Leslie Hall, CBE 1942; MA Cantab; FIMechE; Chairman, 1936–71, Rose, Downs & Thompson Ltd, Old Foundry, Hull, retired; former Chairman, Rose Downs (Holdings) Ltd, Hull; *b* 6 June 1900; *s* of late Charles Downs, Hull and Bridlington; *m* 1930, Kathleen Mary Lewis; three *d*. *Educ:* Abbotsholme Sch., Derbys; Christ's Coll., Cambridge (Scholar, BA, 1922, MA, 1927). European War, Artists' Rifles; served engineering apprenticeship and subsequently employed in various positions with Rose, Downs & Thompson Ltd; former Chm., Barnsley Canister Co. Ltd; former Vice-Chm.,

Davy-Ashmore Ltd; former Director: Blundell-Permoglaze (Holdings) Ltd; Ashmore Benson Pease & Co. Ltd; Power Gas Corp. Ltd. Past President Hull Chamber of Commerce and Shipping; Custodian Trustee, Hull Trustee Savings Bank; Former Treasurer and Member of Council, Hull Univ., retd 1976. Hon. DSc Hull Univ. *Recreations:* fly-fishing, cabinet making, reading. *Address:* King's Mill, Driffield, North Humberside. *T:* Driffield 43204; Rowling End Farm, Newlands, Keswick, Cumbria. *T:* Braithwaite 335.

DOWNSHIRE, 7th Marquess of, *cr* 1789; **Arthur Wills Percy Wellington Blundell Trumbull Sandys Hill;** Viscount Hillsborough, Baron Hill, 1717; Earl of Hillsborough, Viscount Kilwarlin, 1751; Baron Harwich (Great Britain), 1756; Earl of Hillsborough and Viscount Fairford, 1772; Hereditary Constable of Hillsborough Fort; late Lieut Berks Yeomanry; *b* 7 April 1894; *s* of 6th Marquess and Katherine, 2nd *d* of Hon. Hugh Hare, Forest House, Bracknell, Berks, and *g d* of 2nd Earl of Listowel; *S* father, 1918; *m* 1953, Mrs Noreen Gray-Miller (*d* 1983), *d* of late William Barraclough. *Heir: nephew* (Arthur) Robin Ian Hill [*b* 10 May 1929; *m* 1957, Hon. Juliet Mary Weld-Forester, *d* of 7th Baron Forester, and of Marie Louise Priscilla, CStJ, *d* of Sir Herbert Perrott, 6th Bt, CH, CB; two *s* one *d*]. *Address:* 81 Onslow Square, SW7.

DOWNSIDE, Abbot of; *see* Roberts, Rt Rev. D. J.

DOWNWARD, Maj.-Gen. Peter Aldcroft, CB 1979; DSO 1967; DFC 1952; Director, Oxley Developments Co. Ltd, since 1984; *b* 10 April 1924; *s* of late Aldcroft Leonard and Mary Downward; *m* 1st, 1953, Hilda Hinckley Wood (*d* 1976); two *s*; 2nd, 1980, Mrs Mary Boykett Procter (*née* Allwork). *Educ:* King William's Coll., Isle of Man. Enlisted 1942; 2nd Lieut, The South Lancashire Regt (Prince of Wales's Volunteers), 1943; served with 13th Bn (Lancs) Parachute Regt, NW Europe, India, Far East, 1944–46, Greece and Palestine, 1947; transf. to Glider Pilot Regt, 1948; Berlin Airlift, 1949, Korea, 1951–53; 1st Bn The South Lancs Regt (PWV) in Egypt and UK, 1953–54; instructor at Light Aircraft Sch., 1955–56; RAF Staff Coll., 1958; War Office, 1959–60; BAOR, 1961–63; Brigade Major 127 Bde, 1964; Comd 4th Bn The East Lancs Regt, 1965–66; Comd 1st Bn The Lancs Regt (PWV), Aden, 1966–67; Allied Forces N Europe, Oslo, 1968–69; instructor, Sch. of Infantry, 1970–71; Comd Berlin Inf. Bde. 1971–74; Comdt, Sch. of Infantry, 1974–76; GOC West Midland District, 1976–78; Lt-Governor and Sec., The Royal Hosp., Chelsea, 1979–84. Col, The Queen's Lancashire Regt, 1978–83; Col Comdt, The King's Division, 1979–83; Hon. Col, Liverpool Univ. OTC, 1980–. Chm., Museum of Army Flying, 1984–; President: British Korean Veterans Assoc., 1986–; Assoc. of Service Newspapers, 1986–. *Recreations:* sailing, skiing, shooting. *Address:* c/o Lloyds Bank, 37 Market Place, Warminster, Wilts BA12 9BD.

DOWNWARD, Sir William (Atkinson), Kt 1977; JP; Lord-Lieutenant of Greater Manchester, since 1974; Councillor, Manchester City Council, 1946–75; Alderman, Manchester, 1971–74; *b* 5 Dec. 1912; *s* of late George Thomas Downward; *m* 1946, Enid, *d* of late Ald. Charles Wood. *Educ:* Manchester Central High Sch.; Manchester Coll. of Technology. Dir, Royal Exchange Theatre Co., 1976–; Chairman: Manchester Overseas Students Welfare Conf., 1972–; Peterloo Gall., 1974–. Mem. Court of Governors: Manchester Univ., 1969–; Salford Univ., 1974–. Hon. LLD Manchester, 1977. Hon. RNCM 1982; FRSA 1978. Lord Mayor of Manchester, 1970–71; DL Lancs, 1971; JP Manchester, 1973. KStJ 1974. *Address:* 23 Kenmore Road, Northenden, Manchester M22 4AE. *T:* 061–998 4742; 061–247 3478.

DOWSETT, Prof. Charles James Frank, MA, PhD Cantab; FBA 1977; Calouste Gulbenkian Professor of Armenian Studies, University of Oxford, and Fellow of Pembroke College, Oxford, since 1965; *b* 2 Jan. 1924; *s* of late Charles Aspinall Dowsett and Louise, *née* Stokes; *m* 1949, Friedel, *d* of Friedrich Lapuner, Kornberg, E Prussia. *Educ:* Owen's Sch.; St Catherine's Society, Oxford, 1942–43; Peterhouse, Cambridge (Thomas Parke Scholar), 1947–50 (Mod. and Mediaeval Languages Tripos, Part I, 1st Class Russian, 1st Class German, 1948, Part II, Comparative Philology, 1st Class with distinction, 1949). Treasury Studentship in Foreign Languages and Cultures, 1949–54. Ecole Nationale des Langues Orientales Vivantes, Univ. de Paris, 1950–52 (diplôme d'arménien); Ecole des Langues Orientales Anciennes, Institut Catholique de Paris, 1950–53 (diplôme de géorgien); Lecturer in Armenian, School of Oriental and African Studies, University of London, 1954; Reader in Armenian, 1965. Vis. Prof., Univ. of Chicago, 1976. Member: Council, RAS, 1972–76; Philological Soc., 1973–77. *Publications:* The History of the Caucasian Albanians by Movses Dasxuranci, 1961; The Penitential of David of Ganjak, 1961; (with J. Carswell) Kütahya Armenian Tiles, vol. 1, The Inscribed Tiles, 1972; (contrib.) Iran and Islam: Vladimir Minorsky Memorial Volume, 1971; (contrib.) Hayg Berberian Memorial Volume, 1985; articles in Bulletin of the School of Oriental and African Studies, Le Muséon, Revue des Etudes Arméniennes, The Geographical Journal, W. B. Henning Memorial Volume, 1970, etc; translations from Flemish (Felix Timmermans' Driekoningentryptiek: "A Christmas Triptych", 1955, Ernest Claes' De Witte: "Whitey", 1970); as Charles Downing (children's books): Russian Tales and Legends, 1956; Tales of the Hodja, 1964; Armenian Folktales and Fables, 1972. *Address:* Oriental Institute, Pusey Lane, Oxford. *Club:* United Oxford & Cambridge University.

DOWSON, Maj.-Gen. Arthur Henley, CB 1964; CBE 1961 (OBE 1945); Director-General, Ordnance Survey, 1961–65, retired; *b* 7 Dec. 1908; *s* of late Kenneth Dowson and Beatrice Mary (*née* Davis); *m* 1933, Mary Evelyn, *d* of Col. A. J. Savage, DSO; one *d*. *Educ:* Haileybury; RMA; King's Coll., Cambridge (BA). Commissioned in RE, 1928; War Service in NW Europe, N Africa, Italy. Director of Military Survey, War Office and Air Ministry, 1957. ADC to the Queen, 1958–61; Maj-Gen. 1961. Chm., Norfolk Broads Consortium Cttee, 1966–71. FRICS 1949. Bronze Star (USA) 1945. *Address:* Flint Cottage, Stanhoe, King's Lynn, Norfolk PE31 8PT.

DOWSON, Prof. Duncan, FEng; Professor of Engineering Fluid Mechanics and Tribology, since 1966, and Director of The Institute of Tribology, Department of Mechanical Engineering, since Dec. 1967, Leeds University; *b* 31 Aug. 1928; *o s* of Wilfrid and Hannah Dowson, Kirkbymoorside, York; *m* 1951, Mabel, *d* of Mary Jane and Herbert Strickland; one *s* (and one *s* decd). *Educ:* Lady Lumley's Grammar Sch., Pickering, Yorks; Leeds Univ. (BSc Mech Eng. 1950; PhD 1952; DSc 1971). FEng 1982; FIMechE; Fellow ASME 1973; Fellow ASLE 1983. Research Engineer, Sir W. G. Armstrong Whitworth Aircraft Co., 1953–54; Univ. of Leeds: Lecturer in Mechanical Engineering, 1954; Sen. Lecturer, 1963; Reader, 1965; Prof. 1966; Pro-Vice-Chancellor, 1983–85. Chm., Tribology Group Cttee, IMechE, 1967–69. James Clayton Fund Prize (jtly), IMechE, 1963; Thomas Hawksley Gold Medal, IMechE, 1966; Gold Medal, British Soc. of Rheology, 1969; Nat. Award, ASLE, 1974; ASME Lubrication Div. Best Paper Awards (jt), 1975, 1976; ASME Melville Medal (jt), 1976; James Clayton Prize, IMechE, 1978; ASME Mayo D. Hersey Award, 1979; Tribology Gold Medal, IMechE, 1979. Hon. DTech Chalmers Univ. of Technology, Göteborg, 1979. *Publications:* Elastohydrodynamic Lubrication—the fundamentals of roller and gear lubrication (jtly), 1966, 2nd edn 1977; History of Tribology, 1979; (jtly) An Introduction to the Biomechanics of Joints and Joint Replacement, 1981; (jtly) Ball Bearing Lubrication: The Elastohydrodynamics of Elliptical Contacts, 1981; papers on tribology and bio-medical engrg, published by: Royal Society; Instn of Mech. Engineers; Amer. Soc. of Mech. Engineers; Amer. Soc. of Lubrication Engineers. *Recreations:* travel, astronomy, photography. *Address:* 23 Church Lane, Adel, Leeds LS16 8DQ. *T:* Leeds 678933.

DOWSON, Graham Randall; Chairman, since 1984, and Chief Executive, Teltech Ltd; *b* 13 Jan. 1923; *o s* of late Cyril James Dowson and late Dorothy Celia (*née* Foster); *m* 1954, Fay Weston (marr. diss. 1974); two *d*; *m* 1975, Denise Shurman. *Educ:* Alleyn Court Sch.; City of London Sch.; Ecole Alpina, Switzerland. Served War of 1939–45 (1939–43 and Africa Stars, Atlantic and Defence Medals, etc); RAF, 1941–46 (Pilot, Sqdn-Ldr). Sales, US Steel Corporation (Columbia Steel), Los Angeles, 1946–49; Sales and Senior Commentator, Mid South Network (MBS), radio, US, 1949–52; Dir, Rank Organization Ltd, 1960–75, Chief Exec., 1974–75; Chairman: Erskine House Investments, 1975–83; Mooloya Investments, 1975–78; Pincus Vidler Arthur Fitzgerald Ltd, 1979–83; Marinex Petroleum, 1981–83; Deputy Chairman: Nimslo European Hldgs, 1978–; Nimslo International Ltd, 1981–; Nimslo Ltd, 1979– (Dir, 1978); Director: A. C. Nielsen Co., Oxford, 1953–58; Carron Co. (Holdings) Ltd, 1976–; Carron Investments Ltd, 1976–; RCO Holdings PLC (formerly Barrowmill Ltd), 1979–; Nimslo Corp., 1978–; Filmbond plc, 1985–. Chm., 1972–84, Pres., 1984–, European League for Econ. Co-operation (British Section). Vice-Pres., 1974–, Dep. Chm., 1974–, NPFA; Chm., Migraine Trust, 1985–; Patron, Internat. Centre for Child Studies. Liveryman, Distillers' Co. FInstD 1957; FBIM 1969; FInstM 1971. *Recreation:* sailing. *Address:* 193 Cromwell Tower, Barbican, EC2Y 8DD. *T:* 01–588 0396. *Clubs:* Brooks's, Carlton, City Livery, Royal Air Force, Saints and Sinners, Thirty; Royal London Yacht (Ex-Commodore), Royal Cork Yacht, Royal Southern Yacht.

DOWSON, Sir Philip (Manning), Kt 1980; CBE 1969; ARA 1979; MA; ARIBA, FSIAD; a Senior Partner, Ove Arup Partnership, since 1969; Partner, Arup Associates; *b* 16 Aug. 1924; *m* 1950, Sarah Crewdson; one *s* two *d*. *Educ:* Gresham's Sch.; University Coll., Oxford; Clare Coll., Cambridge; Architectural Association. AA Dip. Lieut, RNVR, 1943–47. Member: Royal Fine Art Commn, 1971–; Craft Adv. Cttee, 1972–75. Governor, St Martin's Sch. of Art, 1975–82. Trustee: The Thomas Cubitt Trust, 1978–; Royal Botanic Gdns, Kew, 1983–; Royal Armouries, 1984–. Royal Gold Medal for Architecture, 1981. *Recreation:* sailing. *Address:* 2–4 Dean Street, W1V 6QB. *T:* 01–734 8494; 1 Pembroke Studios, Pembroke Gardens, W8. *Club:* Garrick.

DOYLE, Bernard; *see* Doyle, F. B.

DOYLE, Brian André; Judge, Botswana Court of Appeal, 1973–79; *b* 10 May 1911; *s* of John Patrick Doyle, ICS and Louise Doyle (*née* Renard); *m* 1937, Nora (*née* Slattery); one *s* one *d*. *Educ:* Douai Sch.; Trinity Coll., Dublin. BA, LLB. British Univs and Hosps Boxing Champion, 1929, 1930, 1931 (Flyweight), 1932 (Bantamweight); Irish Free State Army Boxing Champion, 1930 (Flyweight). Called to Irish Bar, 1932; Magistrate, Trinidad and Tobago, 1937; Resident Magistrate, Uganda, 1942; Solicitor-Gen., Fiji, 1948; Attorney-Gen., Fiji, 1949; KC (Fiji), 1950, later QC; Attorney-Gen., N Rhodesia, 1956; Minister of Legal Affairs and Attorney-Gen., Northern Rhodesia (Zambia, 1964), 1959–65, retired as minister, 1965; Chm., Local Govt Service Commn, Zambia, 1964; Justice of Appeal, 1965; Chief Justice and Pres., Supreme Court of Zambia, 1969–75. Dir, Law Develt Commn, Zambia, 1976–79; Chm., Delimitation Commn, Botswana, 1981–82. *Recreations:* fishing, golf. *Address:* 41 Choumert Square, Peckham Rye, SE15 4RE. *Clubs:* Lusaka, Chainama Hills Golf; Dulwich and Sydenham Hill Golf.

DOYLE, (Frederick) Bernard; Chief Executive, Welsh Water Authority, since 1983; *b* 17 July 1940; *s* of James Hopkinson Doyle and Hilda Mary Doyle (*née* Spotsworth); *m* 1963, Ann Weston; two *s* one *d*. *Educ:* St Bede's Coll.; Univ. of Manchester (BSc Hons); Harvard Business Sch., 1965–67 (MBA). CEng, FICE. Resident Civil Engineer with British Rail, 1961–65; Management Consultant with Arthur D. Little Inc., 1967–72; Booker McConnell Ltd: Secretary to Executive Cttee, 1973; Director, Engineering Div., 1973–76; Chairman, General Engineering Div., 1976–78; Chm. and Chief Exec., Booker McConnell Engineering, and Director, Booker McConnell, 1978–81; Chief Exec., SDP, 1981–83. *Recreations:* sport, theatre, reading, travel. *Address:* Cwm Uchaf, Crai, Sennybridge, Powys LD3 8YN. *T:* Sennybridge 703.

DOYLE, Air Comdt Dame Jean (Lena Annette) C.; *see* Conan Doyle.

DOYLE, Sir John (Francis Reginald William Hastings), 5th Bt, *cr* 1828; *b* 3 Jan. 1912; *s* of Col Sir Arthur Havelock James Doyle, 4th Bt, and Joyce Ethelreda (*d* 1961), 2nd *d* of Hon. Greville Howard; *S* father, 1948; *m* 1947, Diana (*d* 1980), *d* of late Col Steel, Indian Army; one *d*. *Educ:* Eton; RMC Sandhurst. Served Palestine, 1938 (medal with clasp); War of 1939–45, in France, Italy, Greece; Major, Cameronians and Royal Irish Fusiliers; retired, 1950. *Address:* Glebe House, Camolin, Co. Wexford.

DOYLE, Prof. William, DPhil; FRHistS; Professor of History, University of Bristol, since 1986; *b* 4 March 1942; *s* of Stanley Joseph Doyle and Mary Alice Bielby; *m* 1968, Christine Thomas. *Educ:* Bridlington Sch.; Oriel Coll., Oxford (BA 1964; MA, DPhil 1968). FRHistS 1976. University of York: Asst Lectr, 1967; Lectr, 1969; Sen. Lectr, 1978; Prof. of Modern History, Univ. of Nottingham, 1981–85. Vis. Professor: Univ. of S Carolina, 1969–70; Univ. de Bordeaux III, 1976. *Publications:* The Parlement of Bordeaux, 1974; The Old European Order 1660–1800, 1978; Origins of the French Revolution, 1980; The Ancien Régime, 1986; contribs to Past and Present, Historical Jl, French Historical Studies, Studies on Voltaire. *Recreations:* books, decorating, travelling about. *Address:* School of History, University of Bristol, 13 Woodland Road, Bristol BS8 1TB. *T:* Bristol 303429. *Club:* United Oxford & Cambridge University.

DOYLE, William Patrick, PhD; CBIM; Managing Director, Exploration and Production, Texaco Ltd, since 1981; *b* 15 Feb. 1932; *s* of James W. Doyle and Lillian I. Doyle (*née* Kime); *m* 1957, Judith A. Gosha; two *s* one *d* (and one *s* decd). *Educ:* Seattle Univ. (BS 1955); Oregon State Univ. (PhD 1959). CBIM 1981 (FBIM 1980); MInstD 1982. Texaco, USA: Chemist, 1959; Res. Supervisor, 1966; Asst to Vice Pres. of Petrochemicals, 1968; Asst to Sen. Vice Pres. of Supply and Distribn, 1971; Asst Manager, Producing, 1972; Asst Regional Man., Marketing, 1974; Dep. Man. Dir, Texaco Ltd, 1977. Pres., UK Offshore Operators Assoc., 1985 (Vice Pres., 1984). *Publications:* contrib. Jl of Amer. Chem. Soc. *Recreations:* tennis, music, theatre. *Address:* 1 Knightsbridge Green, SW1X 7QJ. *T:* 01–584 5000.

D'OYLY, Sir Nigel Hadley Miller, 14th Bt *cr* 1663, of Shottisham, Norfolk; *b* 6 July 1914; *s* of Sir Hastings Hadley D'Oyly, 11th Bt, and Evelyn Maude, *d* of George Taverner Miller; *S* half-brother, 1986; *m* 1940, Dolores (*d* 1971), *d* of R. H. Gregory; one *s* two *d*. *Educ:* Radley; RMA Sandhurst. Formerly Major, Royal Scots; served War of 1939–45, Hong Kong, France and War Office. *Heir: s* Hadley Gregory D'Oyly [*b* 29 May 1956; *m* Emma Dent].

DRABBLE, Margaret, (Mrs Michael Holroyd), CBE 1980; author; *b* 5 June 1939; 2nd *d* of His Honour J.F. Drabble, QC and late Kathleen Marie Bloor; *m* 1st, 1960, Clive Walter Swift (marr. diss. 1975); two *s* one *d*; 2nd, 1982, Michael Holroyd, *qv*. *Educ:* The Mount Sch., York; Newnham Coll., Cambridge. Lives in London. Chm., Nat. Book

League, 1980–82 (Dep. Chm., 1978–80). E. M. Forster Award, Amer. Acad. of Arts and Letters, 1973. Hon DLitt Sheffield, 1976. *Publications:* A Summer Birdcage, 1962; The Garrick Year, 1964; The Millstone, 1966 (filmed, as A Touch of Love, 1969); Wordsworth, 1966; Jerusalem the Golden, 1967; The Waterfall, 1969; The Needle's Eye, 1972; (ed with B. S. Johnson) London Consequences, 1972; Arnold Bennett, a biography, 1974; The Realms of Gold, 1975; (ed) The Genius of Thomas Hardy, 1976; (ed jtly) New Stories 1, 1976; The Ice Age, 1977; For Queen and Country, 1978; A Writer's Britain, 1979; The Middle Ground, 1980; (ed) The Oxford Companion to English Literature, 5th edn, 1985. *Address:* c/o A. D. Peters, 10 Buckingham Street, WC2.

DRAIN, Geoffrey Ayrton, CBE 1981; JP; General Secretary, National and Local Government Officers Association, 1973–83; Visiting Professor, Imperial College of Science and Technology, since 1983; *b* 26 Nov. 1918; *s* of late Charles Henry Herbert Drain, MBE, and Ann Ayrton; *m* 1950, Dredagh Joan Rafferty (marr. diss. 1959); one *s*. *Educ:* Preston Grammar Sch.; Bournemouth Sch.; Skipton Grammar Sch.; Queen Mary Coll., Univ. of London (BA, LLB; Fellow, QMC, 1980). Called to Bar, Inner Temple, 1955. Served War, 1940–46. Asst Sec., Inst. of Hosp. Administrators, 1946–52; Exec., Milton Antiseptic Ltd, 1952–58; Dep. Gen.-Sec., NALGO, 1958–73; Mem. Gen. Council, TUC, 1973–83; Pres., Nat. Fedn. of Professional Workers, 1973–75; Staff Side Sec., Health Service Admin. and Clerical Staffs Whitley Council, 1962–72; Comr, Crown Prosecution Service Staff Commn, 1985–. Director: Bank of England, 1978–86; Collins-Wilde, 1985– (Dep. Chm.); Ferguson and Partners (Dep. Chm.); Home Bridging PLC (Chm.). Member: NW Metropolitan Regional Hosp. Bd and N London Hosp. Management Cttee, 1967–74; Lord Chancellor's Adv. Cttee on Legal Aid, 1974–76; Layfield Cttee of Inquiry into Local Govt Finance, 1974–76; NEDO Sector Working Party for Paper and Board Ind., 1976– (Chm.); Insolvency Law Review Cttee, 1976–82; Council, Industrial Soc., 1974–83; Energy Commn, 1977–79; NEDC, 1977–83; Central Arbitration Cttee, 1977–; Cttee on Finance for Industry, 1978–83; Engrg Council, 1981–83; Exec. Cttee, Public Services Internat., 1981–; Employment Appeal Tribunal, 1982–; Audit Commn, 1983–; Appeals Panel, Nat. Assoc. of Security Dealers and Investment Managers, 1985–. Dir, Co-operative Press Ltd, 1983–84. Member: Bd, Volunteer Centre, (Treas.) 1977–; British-North American Cttee, 1978–84; Franco British Council, 1978–; Trilateral Commn, 1979–; Jt Hon. Treasurer, European Movement, 1979–83, Dep. Chm., 1983–; Trustee: Community Projects Foundn, 1974–; Trident Trust, 1979–. Mem., Goldsmiths' Coll. Delegacy, 1985–. Hampstead Borough Councillor, 1956–58; contested (Lab), Chippenham, 1950; JP N Westminster, 1966. Freeman of City of London and Liveryman of Coopers' Company. *Publication:* The Organization and Practice of Local Government, 1966. *Recreations:* cricket, football, walking, studying birds, bridge. *Address:* Flat 3, Centre Heights, Swiss Cottage, NW3 6JG. *T:* 01–722 2081. *Clubs:* Reform, MCC.

DRAKE, Antony Elliot, CBE 1967 (OBE 1945); *b* 15 June 1907; *s* of Francis Courtney Drake and Mabel Grace (*née* Drake); *m* 1935, Moira Helen Arden Wall; one *s* one *d*. *Educ:* Aldenham Sch.; New Coll., Oxford. Indian Civil Service, 1930; Bihar and Orissa, 1931–37; seconded to Indian Political Service, 1937; served Rajputana, 1937–39; Baluchistan, 1939–43; Mysore (Sec. to Resident), 1943–46; Rajkot (Political Agent, E Kathiawar), 1946–47; appointed to Home Civil Service, HM Treasury, 1947; Asst Sec., 1950; on loan to UK Atomic Energy Authority as Principal Finance Officer, 1957; transferred permanently to UKAEA, 1960; Finance and Programmes Officer, 1964–69; retd, 1969. Member: Hosp. Management Cttee, Royal Western Counties Hosp. Group, 1970–74; Reg. Fisheries Adv. Cttee, SW Water Authority, 1975–86. *Recreation:* fishing. *Address:* Badgers, Windmill Lane, West Hill, Ottery St Mary, Devon. *Club:* Flyfishers'.

DRAKE, Sir (Arthur) Eric (Courtney), Kt 1970; CBE 1952; DL; *b* 29 Nov. 1910; *e s* of Dr A. W. Courtney Drake; *m* 1st, 1935, Rosemary Moore; two *d*; 2nd, 1950, Margaret Elizabeth Wilson; two *s*. *Educ:* Shrewsbury; Pembroke Coll., Cambridge (MA; Hon. Fellow 1976). With The British Petroleum Co. Ltd, 1935–75, Chm., 1969–75, Dep. Chm., P&O Steam Navigation Co., 1976–81. Pres., Chamber of Shipping, 1964; Hon. Mem., General Council of British Shipping, 1975–; Member: Gen. Cttee, Lloyd's Register of Shipping, 1960–81; MoT Shipping Adv. Panel, 1962–64; Cttee on Invisible Exports, 1969–75; Bd of Governors, Pangbourne Nautical Coll., 1958–69; Court of Governors, London Sch. of Economics and Political Science, 1963–74; Governing Body of Shrewsbury Sch., 1969–83; Cttee of Management, RNLI, 1975–85; Life Mem., Court of City Univ., 1969–; Pres., City and Guilds Insignia Award Assoc., 1971–75; Hon. Petroleum Adviser to British Army, 1971–. Hon. Mem., Honourable Co. of Master Mariners, 1972; Hon. Elder Brother of Trinity House, 1975. Vice Pres., Mary Rose Trust, 1984– (Chm., 1979–83). Freeman of City of London, 1974; one of HM Lieutenants, City of London. DL Hants, 1983. Hon. DSc Cranfield, 1971; Hon. Fellow, UMIST, 1974. Hambro British Businessman of the Year award, 1971; Cadman Meml Medal, Inst. of Petroleum, 1976. Comdr, Ordre de la Couronne, Belgium, 1969; Kt Grand Cross of Order of Merit, Italy, 1970; Officier, Légion d'Honneur, 1972; Order of Homayoun, Iran, 1974; Comdr, Ordre de Leopold, Belgium, 1975. *Address:* The Old Rectory, Cheriton, Alresford, Hants. *T:* Bramdean 334. *Clubs:* London Rowing; Royal Yacht Squadron, Leander, Royal Cruising.

DRAKE, Sir Eric; *see* Drake, Sir A. E. C.

DRAKE, Hon. Sir (Frederick) Maurice, Kt 1978; DFC 1944; **Hon. Mr Justice Drake;** a Judge of the High Court of Justice, Queen's Bench Division, since 1978; *b* 15 Feb. 1923; *o s* of late Walter Charles Drake and Elizabeth Drake; *m* 1954, (Alison) May, *d* of late W. D. Waterfall, CB; two *s* three *d*. *Educ:* St George's Sch., Harpenden; Exeter Coll., Oxford. MA Hons 1948. Served War of 1939–45, RAF 96 and 255 Squadrons. Called to Bar, Lincoln's Inn, 1950, QC 1968, Bencher, 1976. Dep. Chm., Beds QS, 1966–71; a Recorder of the Crown Court, 1972–78; Dep. Leader, Midland and Oxford Circuit, 1975–78, Presiding Judge, 1979–83. Standing Senior Counsel to RCP, 1972–78. Judge of Pensions Appeals Tribunal, 1985–. Vice-Chm., Parole Bd, England and Wales, 1985–86 (Mem., 1984–86). Chm. Governors, Aldwickbury Prep. Sch. (Trust), 1969–80; Governor, St George's Sch., Harpenden, 1975–79. Hon. Alderman, St Albans DC, 1976–. *Recreations:* music, gardening, sea-fishing, countryside. *Address:* The White House, West Common Way, Harpenden, Herts. *T:* Harpenden 2329; Royal Courts of Justice, Strand, WC2.

DRAKE, Jack Thomas Arthur H.; *see* Howard-Drake.

DRAKE, Sir James, Kt 1973; CBE 1962; Director, Fairclough Construction Group Ltd (formerly Leonard Fairclough Ltd), 1972–77; *b* 27 July 1907; *s* of James Drake and Ellen (*née* Hague); *m* 1937, Kathleen Shaw Crossley; two *d*. *Educ:* Accrington Grammar Sch.; Owens Coll.; Manchester Univ. (BSc). FEng, FICE, FIMunE, PPInstHE. Jun. Engrg Asst, Stockport Co. Borough, 1927–30; Sen. and Chief Engrg Asst, Bootle Co. Borough, 1930–37; Blackpool Co. Borough: Dep. Engr and Surveyor, 1937–38; Borough Engr and Surveyor, 1938–45; County Surveyor and Bridgemaster, Lancs CC, 1945–72 (seconded to Min. of Transport as Dir of NW Road Construction Unit, 1967–68). Hon. Fellow, Manchester Polytechnic, 1972. Hon. DSc Salford, 1973. *Publications:* Road Plan for Lancashire, 1949; Motorways, 1969. *Recreation:* golf. *Address:* 11 Clifton Court, St Annes-on-Sea, Lancs. *T:* St Annes 721635. *Clubs:* Royal Automobile; Royal Lytham and St Annes Golf.

DRAKE, Brig. Dame Jean Elizabeth R.; *see* Rivett-Drake.

DRAKE, John Edmund Bernard, CBE 1973; DSC 1945; *b* 15 Nov. 1917; *s* of late D. H. C. Drake, CIE; *m* 1942, Pauline Marjory Swift; three *s*. *Educ:* Blundells Sch.; Exeter Coll., Oxford (BA). Served War, RNVR. Executive, Burmah-Shell, India, 1945–57; Gen. Manager, Shell Co of Ceylon, 1955; Overseas Staff Manager, Burmah Shell, 1957–62; Gen. Manager Personnel, Shell Mex and BP, 1962–69; Special Advr on Personnel Management to CS, 1970–73; Partner, Tyzack & Partners Ltd, 1974–81. *Recreations:* travel, sailing, reading, music. *Address:* Farm House, Coldharbour Lane, Hildenborough, Kent. *T:* Hildenborough 832102.

DRAKE, John Gair; Chief Registrar and Chief Accountant, Bank of England, since 1983; *b* 11 July 1930; *s* of John Nutter Drake and Anne Drake; *m* 1957, Jean Pamela Bishop; one *s* one *d*. *Educ:* University College School; The Queen's College, Oxford; Oxford Centre for Management Studies. MA; Cert. of Management Studies. Joined Bank of England, 1953; editor, Quarterly Bulletin, 1971; Asst Chief Cashier, 1973; Management Development Manager, 1974; Dep. Chief, Economic Intell. Dept, 1977; Dep. Chief Cashier and Dep. Chief, Banking Dept, 1980. *Recreations:* eclectic, including sport, history, reading. *Address:* Bank of England, New Change, EC4M 9AA. *T:* 01–601 4444. *Club:* Chaldon Cricket.

DRAKE, Hon. Sir Maurice; *see* Drake, Hon. Sir F. M.

DRAKE-BROCKMAN, Hon. Sir Thomas Charles, Kt 1979; DFC 1944; Senator (Country Party) for West Australia, 1958–78; *b* 15 May 1919; *s* of R. J. Drake-Brockman; *m* 1st, 1942, Edith Sykes (marr. diss.); one *s* four *d*; 2nd, 1972, Mary McGinnity. *Educ:* Guildford Grammar School. Farmer, 1938; RAAF 1941. Minister for Air, 1969–72; Minister for Administrative Services and Minister for Aboriginal Affairs, Nov.-Dec. 1975; Dep. Pres. of the Senate, 1965–69, 1976–78. Gen. Pres., Nat. Country Party (WA) Inc., 1978–81; Federal Pres., Nat. Country Party of Aust., 1978–81. Former Wool President and Exec. Mem., WA Farmers' Union; Vice-Pres., Aust. Wool and Meat Producers' Fedn, 1956–57. State Pres., Australia-Britain Soc., 1982–. *Address:* 80 Basildon Road, Lesmurdie, WA 6076, Australia.

DRAPER, Alan Gregory; Senior Lecturer, Defence Procurement, Royal Military College of Science, since 1986; *b* 11 June 1926; *e s* of late William Gregory Draper and Ada Gertrude (*née* Davies); *m* 1st, 1953, Muriel Sylvia Cuss, FRSA (marr. diss.); three *s*; 2nd, 1977, Jacqueline Gubel; one *d*. *Educ:* Leeds Grammar Sch.; The Queen's Coll., Oxford (Scholar 1944; MA 1951). RNVR, 1945; Sub-Lt, 1946–47. Admiralty: Asst Principal, 1950; Private Sec. to Civil Lord of the Admiralty, 1953–55; MoD, 1957–60; Head of Polit. Sect., Admiralty 1960–64; First Sec., UK Delegn to NATO, 1964–66; Asst Sec., MoD, 1966; Counsellor, UK Delegn to NATO, 1974–77; Chm., NATO Budget Cttees, 1977–81; Royal Ordnance Factories: Personnel Dir, 1982–84; Dir Gen., Personnel, 1984; Dir, Management/Career Develt, Royal Ordnance plc, 1985. MIPM 1985. *Recreations:* reading, travel, tennis, indifferent golf. *Address:* c/o Royal Military College of Science, Shrivenham, Swindon SN6 8LA. *Club:* Naval.

DRAPER, Gerald Carter, OBE 1974; Chairman, Draper Associates Ltd, since 1982; Deputy Chairman, Hoverspeed, since 1984; *b* 24 Nov. 1926; *s* of Alfred Henderson Draper and Mona Violanta (*née* Johnson); *m* 1951, Winifred Lilian Howe; one *s* three *d*. *Educ:* Univ. of Dublin, Trinity Coll. (MA). FInstM, FCIT. Joined Aer Lingus, 1947; Advertising and PR Manager, 1950; Commercial Man., Central Afr. Airways, 1959; British European Airways: Advertising Man., 1964; Asst Gen. Man. (Market Develt), 1966; Gen. Man. and Dir, Travel Sales Div., 1970; British Airways: Dir, Travel Div., 1973; Marketing Dir, 1977; Dir, Commercial Ops, 1978; Mem. Bd, 1978–82; Man. Dir, Intercontinental Services Div., 1982. Chairman: British Air Tours Ltd, 1978–82; Silver Wing Surface Arrangements Ltd, 1971–82; Deputy Chairman: Trust Houses Forte Travel Ltd, 1974–82; ALTA Ltd, 1977–82; Member Board: Internat. Aeradio Ltd, 1971–82; British Airways Associated Cos Ltd, 1972–82; British Intercontinental Hotels Ltd, 1976–82; Communications Strategy Ltd, 1984–; AGB Travel Research Internat. Ltd, 1984–. Chm., Outdoor Advertising Assoc., 1985–. Liveryman, Co. of Marketors, 1978. FRSA 1979. Chevalier de l'Ordre du Tastevin, 1980; l'Officier de l'Ordre des Coteaux de Champagne, 1982. *Recreations:* shooting, golf. *Address:* Old Chestnut, Onslow Road, Burwood Park, Walton-on-Thames, Surrey. *Clubs:* Livery; Burhill Golf (Weybridge).

DRAPER, Col Gerald Irving Anthony Dare, OBE 1965; a Chairman of Industrial Tribunals, since 1965; Barrister-at-law; *b* 30 May 1914; *o s* of late Harold Irving Draper and Florence Muriel Short; *m* 1951, Julia Jean, *e d* of late Captain G. R. Bald, RN. *Educ:* privately, and by late Hubert Brinton; King's Coll., London Univ. (Law Prizeman, 1933; LLB Hons 1935); LLM London 1938. Admitted Solicitor, 1936; called to the Bar, Inner Temple, 1946. Irish Guards, Ensign and Subaltern, 1941–44; seconded to Judge-Advocate-General's Office, 1945–48; Mil. Prosecutor (War Crimes Trials, Germany), 1945–49; Legal Advr, Directorate of Army Legal Staff, 1950–56; retd as Col, 1956. Lectr in Internat. Law, 1956, Reader, 1964, Univ. of London; Reader, 1967–76, Prof. of Law, 1976–79, Univ. of Sussex; Professor Emeritus, 1979. Vis. Prof., Cairo, 1965; Titular Prof., Internat. Inst. of Humanitarian Law, S Remo, 1976; Lionel Cohen Lectr, Hebrew Univ., Jerusalem, 1972; Vis. Lectr at UK Staff Colls, and Defence Acads, Vienna, Hamburg, Newport RI, and Tokyo. UK Deleg., Internat. Red Cross Confs, 1957–73; Legal Advr to UK Delegn, Diplomatic Conf. on Law of War, 1974–77. Mem., Medico-Juridical Commn, Monaco, 1977. Fellow of NATO, 1958. Hon. Mem., Faculty of US Army Judge-Advocate-General Sch. of Mil. Law. Mem. Editorial Bd, British Year Book of Internat. Law. *Publications:* Red Cross Conventions, 1958; Hague Academy Lectures, 1965, 1979; Civilians and NATO Status of Forces Agreement, 1966; (with HRH Prince Hassan) A Study on Jerusalem, 1979; (with HRH Prince Hassan) Palestinian Self-determination, 1981; articles in learned journals, incl. British Year Book of Internat. Law, Internat. Affairs, Internat., Comp. Law Qly, The Month, Acta Juridica. *Recreations:* Egyptology, history of Penitentials; (for leisure) sitting in the sun. *Address:* 16 Southover High Street, Lewes, Sussex. *T:* Lewes 2387; 2 Hare Court, Temple, EC4. *Clubs:* Beefsteak; Cercle de la Terrasse (Geneva).

DRAPER, (John Haydn) Paul; Senior Planning Inspector, Department of Environment, 1977–86, retired; *b* 14 Dec. 1916; *o c* of late Haydn Draper, clarinet player, and Nan Draper; *m* 1941, Nancy Allum, author and journalist; one *s* one *d* (and one *d* decd). *Educ:* LCC primary sch.; Bancroft's Sch.; University Coll. London. Engr in Post Office, 1939–48; Royal Signals, Signalman to Major, Middle East, N Africa, Sicily, NW Europe (despatches), 1940–46; MoT, 1948–64 and 1968–70; Jt Principal Private Sec. to Minister, 1956–58; Asst Sec., 1959; Counsellor (Shipping), British Embassy, Washington, 1964–67; BoT, 1967–68; Under-Sec., 1968; DoE, 1970–74; Senior Planning Inspector, 1973–74; Resident Chm., Civil Service Selection Bd, 1975–76. *Address:* 24 Gordon Mansions, Huntley Street, WC1E 7HF.

DRAPER, Michael William; Secretary, Diocese of Bath and Wells, since 1978; b 26 Sept. 1928; s of late John Godfrey Beresford Draper and Aileen Frances Agatha Draper (née Masefield); m 1952, Theodora Mary Frampton, o d of late Henry James Frampton; one s two d. Educ: St Edward's Sch., Oxford. FCA. Chartered Accountant, 1953; various posts in England, Ireland, Burma, Nigeria, Unilever Ltd, 1953–64; joined Civil Service, 1964; Principal, Min. of Power, 1964; Asst Sec., 1972, Under Sec., 1976–78, DHSS. Recreations: mountain walking, church affairs. Address: The Old Deanery, Wells, Somerset.

DRAPER, Paul; see Draper, J. H. P.

DRAPER, Peter Sydney; Under Secretary, Director of Defence Services II, Property Services Agency, Department of the Environment, since 1985; b 18 May 1935; s of late Sydney George Draper and Norah Draper; m 1959, Elizabeth Ann (née French); three s. Educ: Haberdashers' Aske's; Regent Polytechnic Sch. of Management (Dip. in Management Studies). AMBIM 1966. Joined GCHQ, Cheltenham, 1953; Min. of Transport, 1956–70; Principal, 1969; DoE, 1970–: Directorate of Estate Management Overseas, PSA, 1970; Asst Sec., 1975; Head of Staff Resources Div., 1975–78; Asst Dir, Home Regional Services, 1978–80; RCDS, 1981; Dir, Eastern Reg., PSA, 1982–84. Recreations: squash, golf, walking. Address: Langdale, 22 Brewery Road, Pampisford, Cambs CB2 4EN. T: Cambridge 835949. Clubs: Civil Service; Saffron Walden Golf.

DRAPER, Prof. Ronald Philip, PhD; Regius Chalmers Professor of English, University of Aberdeen, since 1986; b 3 Oct. 1928; s of Albert William and Elsie Draper; m 1950, Irene Margaret Aldridge; three d. Educ: Univ. of Nottingham (BA, PhD). Educn Officer, RAF, 1953–55. Lectr in English, Univ. of Adelaide, 1955–56; Lectr, Univ. of Leicester, 1957–68, Sen. Lectr, 1968–73; Prof., Univ. of Aberdeen, 1973–86. Publications: D. H. Lawrence, 1964, 3rd edn 1984; (ed) D. H. Lawrence, The Critical Heritage, 1970, 3rd edn 1986; (ed) Hardy, The Tragic Novels, 1975, 6th edn 1985; (ed) George Eliot, The Mill on the Floss and Silas Marner, 1977, 3rd edn 1984; (ed) Tragedy, Developments in Criticism, 1980; Lyric Tragedy, 1985; The Winter's Tale, Text and Performance, 1985; (ed) Hardy, The Pastoral Novels, 1987; articles and reviews in Critical Qly, Essays in Criticism, Etudes Anglaises, English Studies, Jl of D. H. Lawrence Soc., MLR, New Lit. Hist., Notes and Queries, Revue des Langues Vivantes, Rev. of English Studies, Shakespeare Qly, Studies in Short Fiction, Thomas Hardy Annual, Thomas Hardy Jl. Recreations: reading, listening to music. Address: 50 Queen's Road, Aberdeen AB1 6YE. T: Aberdeen 318735.

DRAYCOTT, Douglas Patrick, MA Oxon; QC 1965; a Recorder, since 1972 (Recorder of Shrewsbury, 1966–71); b 23 Aug. 1918; s of George Draycott and Mary Ann Draycott (née Burke); m Elizabeth Victoria Hall (marr. diss. 1974); two s three d; m 1979, Margaret Jean Brunton (née Speed). Educ: Wolstanton Grammar Sch.; Oriel Coll., Oxford (MA). War Service: Royal Tank Regiment and General Staff, 1939–46. Barrister, Middle Temple, 1950, Master of the Bench, 1972. Joined Oxford Circuit, 1950; Leader, Midland and Oxford Circuit, 1979–83. Recreation: cruising on inland waterways. Address: 1 Essex Court, Temple, EC4Y 9AR. T: 01–353 6717; Devereux Chambers, Devereux Court, Strand, WC2R 3JJ. T: 01–353 1974; 11 Sir Harry's Road, Edgbaston, Birmingham B15 2UY. T: 021–440 1050; 5 Fountain Court, Steelhouse Lane, Birmimgham, B4 6DR. T:021–236 5771.

DRAYCOTT, Gerald Arthur; a Recorder of the Crown Court, since 1972; b 25 Oct. 1911; s of Arthur Henry Seely Draycott and Maud Mary Draycott; m 1939, Phyllis Moyra Evans; two s one d. Educ: King Edward's Sch., Stratford-on-Avon. FCII. Called to Bar, Middle Temple, 1938. Served in RAF, 1939–46 (Sqdn Ldr; despatches). Practised at Bar, SE Circuit, 1946–. Chairman: Eastern Rent Assessment Panel, 1965–77; Nat. Insurance Tribunal, Norwich, 1970–84; E Anglia Med. Appeal Tribunal, 1978–84. Address: Nethergate House, Saxlingham Nethergate, Norwich NR15 1PB. T: Hempnall 224; Octagon House, Colegate, Norwich; 5 King's Bench Walk, Temple, EC4Y 7DN. Club: Norfolk County (Norwich).

DRAYSON, Robert Quested, DSC 1943; MA; b 5 June 1919; s of late Frederick Louis Drayson and late Elsie Mabel Drayson; m 1943, Rachel, 2nd d of Stephen Spencer Jenkyns; one s two d. Educ: St Lawrence Coll., Ramsgate; Downing Coll., Cambridge. Univ. of Cambridge: 1938–39, 1946–47; History Tripos, BA 1947, MA 1950. Served RNVR, 1939–46; Lieut in command HM Motor Torpedo Boats. Asst Master and Housemaster, St Lawrence Coll., 1947–50; Asst Master, Felsted Sch., 1950–55; Headmaster, Reed's Sch., Cobham, 1955–63; Headmaster of Stowe, 1964–79; Resident Lay Chaplain to Bishop of Norwich, 1979–84; Lay Reader, 1979. Member: HMC Cttee, 1973–75; Allied Schools Council, 1980–; Gen. Council, S Amer. Missionary Soc. (and Chm. Selection Cttee), 1980–. Governor, St Lawrence Coll. FRSA 1968. Recreations: hockey (Cambridge Blue, 1946, 1947; Kent XI (Captain), 1947–56; England Final Trial, 1950); golf, walking. Address: Three Gables, Linkhill, Sandhurst, Kent TN18 5PQ. T:Sandhurst 447. Club: Hawks (Cambridge).

DRESCHFIELD, Ralph Leonard Emmanuel, CMG 1957; b 18 March 1911; s of late Henry Theodore and Jessie Mindelle Dreschfield; unmarried. Educ: Merchiston Castle Sch.; Trinity Hall, Cambridge (BA). Called to Bar, 1933; entered Colonial Service, 1938, and apptd resident Magistrate, Uganda; served in War of 1939–45, in 4th King's African Rifles; Crown Counsel, Uganda, 1948; Solicitor-Gen., Uganda, 1949; QC 1950; Attorney-Gen., Uganda, 1951–62. Chm. Trustees of Uganda National Parks, 1952–62. Sec., Community Council of Essex, 1963–76. Parly Counsel, Law Reform, Bermuda, 1976–79. Recreation: yachting. Address: 5 Fairhaven Court, West Mersea, Colchester, Essex. Clubs: Royal Ocean Racing, Bar Yacht, Little Ship; West Mersea Yacht.

DREVER, James; Principal and Vice-Chancellor, University of Dundee, 1967–78; b 29 Jan. 1910; s of late Prof. James Drever; m 1936, Joan Isabel Mackay Budge; one s one d. Educ: Royal High Sch., Edinburgh; Universities of Edinburgh (MA Hons Philosophy, 1932) and Cambridge (MA Moral Science Tripos, 1934). LLD Dundee, 1979. FRSE. Asst, Dept of Philosophy, Edinburgh, 1934–38; Lecturer in Philosophy and Psychology, King's Coll., Newcastle, 1938–41; Royal Navy, 1941–45; Prof. of Psychology, Univ. of Edinburgh, 1944–66. Visiting Professor, Princeton Univ., 1954–55. Editor, British Journal of Psychology, 1954–58; President: British Psychological Soc., 1960–61; Internat. Union of Scientific Psychology, 1963–66. Member: Cttee on Higher Education, 1961–63; SSRC, 1965–69; Adv. Council, Civil Service Coll., 1973–; Oil Develt Council for Scotland, 1973–77; Perm. Cttee of Conf. of European Rectors, 1975–78; Chm., Advisory Council on Social Work, in Scotland, 1970–74. Dir, Grampian Television Ltd, 1973–80. Publications: papers and reviews. Address: East Ardblair, 494 Perth Road, Dundee DD2 1LR.

DREW, Sir Arthur (Charles Walter), KCB 1964 (CB 1958); Chairman: Voluntary Welfare Work Council, since 1979; Queen Mary College, University of London, since 1982; Ancient Monuments Advisory Committee, since 1984; Administrator, J. Paul Getty Jr Charitable Trust, since 1986; b 2 Sept. 1912; er s of late Arthur Drew, Mexico City, and Louise Schulte-Ummingen; m 1943, Rachel, er d of late G. W. Lambert, CB; one s three d. Educ: Christ's Hospital; King's Coll., Cambridge. Asst Principal, War Office,

1936; Private Sec. to successive Secs of State for War, 1944–49; IDC, 1949; International Staff, NATO, 1951–53; Dep. Under Sec. of State, Home Office, 1961–63; last Permanent Under-Sec. of State, War Office, 1963–64; Permanent Under-Sec. of State (Army), MoD, 1964–68; Perm. Under-Sec. of State (Administration), MoD, and Mem., Admiralty, Army (from 1964) and Air Force Boards, 1968–72. Chairman: Museums and Galls Commn (formerly Standing Commn on Museums and Galls, 1978–84 (Mem., 1973–84); Ancient Monuments Bd for England, 1978–84; Pres., Museums Assoc., 1984–86; Trustee: British Museum (Natural History), 1972–83; British Museum, 1973–86; Imperial War Museum, 1973–84; Nat. Army Museum, 1975–; RAF Museum, 1976–; Member: Council, Nat. Trust, 1974–84; Historic Houses Assoc., 1981–84; Science Mus. Adv. Council, 1981–84; Council, Zool Soc., 1982–; Historic Buildings Council, 1982–84; Historic Buildings and Monuments Commn, 1984–. Master, Drapers' Co., 1977–78. JP 1963, 1973–83, Richmond. Coronation Medal, 1953. Recreation: following Baedeker. Address: 2 Branstone Road, Kew, Surrey TW9 3LB. T: 01–940 1210. Club: Reform.

DREW, Brig. Cecil Francis, DSO 1918; b 1890; o s of late Albert Francis Drew, JP of Foston, Farnham Royal, Bucks; m 1915, Elizabeth Seymour Hawker (d 1983); one s (and one s decd). Educ: Highgate and Royal Milit. Acad.; Joined The Cameronians, 1910; served European War (despatches twice, DSO); temp. Lt-Col, 1917–19; Brevet Lt-Col, 1932; Lt-Col, 1936; Col, 1938; Brigadier, 1939; GSO 3, War Office, 1919–22; GSO 3, Scottish Command, 1924; DAA and QMG Highland Area, 1925–27; DAQMG South China Command, 1927–28; GSO 51st (Highland) Division, 1929–33; commanded 1st Bn The Cameronians, 1936–38; AAG War Office, 1938–39; Comd East Lancs Area, 1939–40; Comd 183 Inf. Brigade, 1940–42; Brigadier i/c Administration, 1st Corps District, 1942; AAG Southern Command, 1943; Gen. Staff, GHQ Home Forces, 1944–45; retired pay, 1945. JP Bucks, 1949. Address: Gatehouse Cottages, Framfield, near Uckfield, East Sussex. Club: Army and Navy.

DREW, Charles Edwin, LVO 1952; VRD 1960; FRCS; Hon. Consultant Thoracic Surgeon: St George's Hospital (Surgeon, 1954–79); Westminster Hospital (Surgeon, 1951–82); Hon. Consulting Thoracic Surgeon, King Edward VII Hospital, Midhurst; b 1916; s of Edwin Frank Drew, Croydon; m 1950, Doreen, d of Frederick James Pittaway, Stocksfield, Northumberland; one s one d. Educ: Westminster City Sch.; King's Coll., London. MB, BS London 1941; MRCS, LRCP 1941; FRCS 1946. Served War of 1939–45, RNVR (Surgeon-Comdr 1957). Formerly: Chief Asst and Surg. Registrar, Westminster Hosp.; Chief Surgical Asst, Brompton Hosp.; Civilian Consultant in Thoracic Surgery to RN; Hon. Consultant in Thoracic Surgery to Army. Mem. Soc. Thoracic Surgeons; FRSocMed. Publications: papers in med. jls. Address: The Cottage, 24 Dover Park Drive, Roehampton, SW15 5BG. T: 01–788 7030.

DREW, Sir Ferdinand (Caire), Kt 1960; CMG 1951; FASA; Under-Treasurer, South Australia and Chairman State Grants Committee, 1946–60, retired; b Adelaide, S Aust., 1 May 1895; s of late Charles H. Drew, Adelaide; m 1934, Chrissie A., d of George M. McGowan; one s two d. Educ: Rose Park Public Sch.; Muirden Coll. Asst Auditor-Gen., 1936–39; Asst Under-Treasurer, 1939–46. Chm. Supply and Tender Board, 1943–49; Mem. Industries Development Cttee, 1942–49; Board Member: State Bank of South Australia, 1948–73 (Dep. Chm. 1963); Adelaide Steamship Co. Ltd, 1962–70; Cellular Aust. Ltd, 1948–59; Director: Unit Trust of SA; United Insurance Co. Ltd; Chrysler Aust. Ltd, 1963–74; Chm., Board of Electricity Trust, South Australia, 1949–70 (Mem., 1949–74). Address: 614 Anzac Highway, Glenelg East, SA 5045, Australia.

DREW, Prof. George Charles, MA; London University Professor of Psychology, University College, 1958–79, now Professor Emeritus; Honorary Fellow, 1979; b 10 Dec. 1911; e s of George Frederick Drew; m 1936, Inez Annie, d of F. Hulbert Lewis; one s one d. Educ: St George's Sch., Bristol; Bristol, Cambridge and Harvard Univs. Viscount Haldane of Cloan studentship, Cambridge, 1935–36; Rockefeller Fellowship, Harvard Univ., 1936–38; Rockefeller Research Fellowship, Cambridge, 1938–42; Psychological Adviser, Air Ministry, 1942–46; Lecturer in Psychology, University of Bristol, 1946–49, Reader, 1949–51, Prof. of Psychology, 1951–58. Mem. Science Research Council, 1965–67. Vis. Prof., University of Calif, Berkeley, USA, 1967–68. C. S. Myers Lectr, 1973. Founder Mem., Exper. Psych. Soc., 1946 (Pres. 1950–51, 1959–60); Pres., British Psych. Soc., 1962–63; Pres. and Chm., Org. Cttee, 19th Internat. Congress of Psychology, 1969. Dean of Science, UCL, 1973–76. Publications: articles on animal behaviour, learning, vision, and other psychological problems, in various British and American journals.

DREW, Harry Edward, CB 1970; Director, Quality Audit and Advisory Services, since 1973; b 18 Jan. 1909; 2nd s of W. H. Drew and F. E. Drew (née Brindley), Gillingham, Kent; m 1937, Phyllis (née Flippance) (decd); one s. Educ: Wesleyan Sch., Gillingham; RAF Apprentice Sch., Flowerdown, RAF, 1924–37; Air Min. Research Stn, Bawdsey, 1937; Works Man., Radio Prodn Unit, Woolwich, Min. of Supply, 1943; Officer i/c, Research Prototype Unit, W. Howe, Bournemouth, Min. of Aircraft Prodn, 1946; Asst Dir, 1951, Dir, 1959, Electronic Prodn, Min. of Supply, London; Dir of Techn. Costs, Min. of Aviation, London, 1964; Dir-Gen. of Quality Assurance, Min. of Technology, 1966–70; Chief Exec., Defence Quality Assurance Bd, MoD, 1970–72. FIProdE 1951; Hon. FIERE 1985 (Mem. Charter Council; Pres., 1981–83); Hon. FIIM 1981 (Nat. Chm., 1966–68, Vice-Pres., 1969–79, Pres., 1979–81). Hon. CGIA 1974. Past Master, Worshipful Co. of Scientific Instrument Makers, 1980– (Master, 1978–79). Publications: papers on training and quality and reliability. Recreations: photography, reading, gardening. Address: 18 Marten's Close, Shrivenham, Swindon, Wilts SN6 8BA. Clubs: Civil Service, City Livery.

DREW, Jane Beverly, FRIBA; architect; Partner in firm of Fry Drew and Partners, since 1946; b 24 March 1911; m 1st; two d; 2nd, 1942, Edwin Maxwell Fry, qv. Educ: Croydon. Was in partnership with J. T. Alliston, 1934–39; independent practice, 1939–45; in partnership with Maxwell Fry, 1945–. Asst Town Planning Adviser to Resident Minister, West African Colonies, 1944–45; Senior Architect to Capital project of Chandigarh, Punjab, India, 1951–54; Beamis Prof. Mass Inst. of Techn., Jan.-June, 1961; Vis. Prof. of Architecture, Harvard, Feb-March 1970; Bicentennial Prof., Utah Univ., 1976. Completed work includes housing, hospitals, schools, and colleges in UK, West Africa, including Univs in Nigeria, Middle East and India; a section of Festival of Britain, 1951; town planning, housing and amenity buildings in Iran, W Africa and India. Past Pres., Architectural Association (1969). Hon. FAIA 1978; Hon. FNIA 1985. Hon LLD Ibadan, 1966; DUniv Open Univ., 1973. Publications: (with Maxwell Fry) Architecture for Children, 1944; (with Maxwell Fry and Harry Ford) Village Housing in the Tropics, 1945; (Founder Editor, 1945–) Architects' Year Book; (with Maxwell Fry) Architecture in the Humid Tropics; Tropical Architecture, 1956; (with Maxwell Fry) Architecture and the Environment, 1976. Recreations: reading, writing, friends. Address: West Lodge, Cotherstone, Barnard Castle, Co. Durham DH12 9PF. T: Teesdale 50217. Club: Institute of Contemporary Arts.

DREW, Joanna Marie, CBE 1985; Director of Art, Arts Council of Great Britain, since 1978; b Naini Tal, India, 28 Sept. 1929; d of Brig. Francis Greville Drew, CBE, and Sannie Frances Sands. Educ: Dartington Hall; Edinburgh Univ. (MA Hons Fine Art); Edinburgh

Coll. of Art (DA). Arts Council of GB, 1952–: Asst Dir of Exhibns, 1970; Dir of Exhibns, 1975. Mem. Council, RCA, 1979–82. Chevalier, l'Ordre des Arts et Lettres, 1979. *Address:* Arts Council of Great Britain, 105 Piccadilly, W1V 0AU.

DREW, John Alexander, CB 1957; *b* 19 July 1907; *s* of Charles Edward Drew, Okehampton, Devon, and Ethel Margaret Drew; *m* 1930, Edith Waud Marriott; two *s* (and one *s* decd). *Educ:* Gram. Sch., Okehampton. Entered CS, 1928; Secretaries' Office, HM Customs and Excise, 1935–40; employed on special duties, 1940–45; Asst Sec., Cabinet Office, 1945–48; Bd of Trade, 1948–50, Asst Under-Sec. of State, Ministry of Defence, 1951–67, retired, 1967. US Medal of Freedom with Bronze Palm, 1946. *Address:* 28 Montague Avenue, Sanderstead, Surrey. *T:* 01–657 3264.

DREW, Lt-Gen. Sir (William) Robert (Macfarlane), KCB 1965 (CB 1962); CBE 1952 (OBE 1940); KStJ 1977 (CStJ 1965); FRCP; company director, since 1977; *b* 4 Oct. 1907; *s* of late William Hughes Drew and Ethel Macfarlane; *m* 1934, Dorothy, *d* of late Alfred E. Dakingsmith, Bowral, NSW; one *s* (one *d* decd). *Educ:* Sydney Gram. Sch.; Sydney Univ. MB, BS, BSc Sydney, 1930; DTM&H (Eng.), 1938; MRCP 1938; FRCP 1945; FRCPEd, 1966; FRACP, 1966; Hon. FACP 1966; Hon. FRCS 1970. Joined RAMC, 1931; first House Physician appointed at Postgrad. Med. Sch., London, 1935; served India, France (Dunkirk), Iraq, MELF; MO, War Cabinet Offices, 1943–46; Consulting Physician to the Army, 1959–60; Commandant, Royal Army Medical Coll., 1960–63; Dir of Medical Services, British Army of the Rhine, 1963–64; Dir-Gen., Army Medical Services, 1965–69. Dep. Dir, British Postgraduate Med. Fedn, 1970–76 (Mem. Governing Body, 1954–56, 1967–69). QHP, 1959–69. Leishman Prize, Royal Army Medical Coll., 1938; Goulstonian Lecturer, RCP, 1946; Mitchener Medallist, RCS, 1955; Lettsomian Lecturer, Medical Soc., London, 1961. Prof. Medicine, Royal Faculty of Med., Baghdad, 1946–52; Lectr Westminster Med. Sch., 1954–59; Pres. Clin. Section, Royal Society of Medicine, 1968–70. Hon. Sec. and later Councillor: Royal Society of Tropical Medicine and Hygiene (Pres., 1971–73); Med. Soc. of London (Pres., 1967–68); Australia and NZ Med. Assoc. (Chm.); Councillor: Royal Society of Medicine; RCP (Vice-Pres., 1970–71); Hunterian Soc.; Mem. Bd of Governors: Hospital for Sick Children, Gt Ormond Street, London; Moorfields Eye Hosp.; Royal Sch. for Daughters of Officers of the Army; Member: Assoc. Physicians Gt Britain and Ireland; Exec. Cttee, Forces Help Soc.; Control Bd, Army Benevolent Fund; Bd, Kennedy Inst. of Rheumatology; Cttee, St John Ophthalmic Hospital of Jerusalem; Cttee of Management, Sir Oswald Stoll Foundn; Mem. Council, Royal Blind Soc., NSW, 1978–; Mem., Aust. Soc. of Genealogists, 1978–. Life Member: Dunkirk Veterans Assoc.; Officers' Pension Soc.; HM Comr, The Royal Hosp., Chelsea, 1965–69 and 1970–76. Orator: York Med. Soc., 1963; Harrogate Med. Soc., 1963; Hunterian, Hunterian Soc., 1966. FRSA 1965. Extraordinary Mem., Assoc. of Clin. Pathologists; Hon. Member: Sydney Univ. Med. Soc., 1965; Anglo-German Med. Soc., 1970; Vice-Pres., Australia-Iraq Friendship Assoc., 1982–. Trustee, Commonwealth Philharmonic Orch. Trust, 1974–; Mem. Aust. Ctte, Australian Musical Foundn in London, 1985. Mem. Chapter-Gen., Order of St John, 1977–84. Comdr Order of El-Rafidain (Iraq), 1951. *Publications:* Roll of Medical Officers in the British Army 1660–1960, 1968; articles in medical journals. *Recreations:* travel, gardening. *Address:* c/o Royal Bank of Scotland, 22 Whitehall, SW1; 5B and 5C Wakefield, 26–28 Etham Avenue, Darling Point, NSW 2027, Australia. *Clubs:* Army and Navy; Australian (Hon. Librarian, 1983–), Royal Sydney Golf (Sydney).

DREWITT, (Lionel) Frank; Managing Director, Harrods Ltd, since 1984; *b* 24 Sept. 1932; *s* of William and Jeanne Drewitt; *m* 1959, Doris Else Heybrok; three *d*. *Educ:* London Univ. (Bsc Econ). FCA. National Service, 1951–53. Wells & Partners, later Thornton Baker, 1956–64; Chartered Accountant, 1961; joined Harrods Store group, 1964; positions incl. Asst Internal Auditor, Chief Accountant, Company Sec., Asst Man. Dir. *Recreation:* cottages. *Address:* 23 Hertford Avenue, East Sheen, SW14. *T:* 01–876 9348.

DREWRY, Dr David John; Director, Scott Polar Research Institute, University of Cambridge, since 1984; *b* 22 Sept. 1947; *s* of late Norman Tidman Drewry and of Mary Edwina Drewry (*née* Wray); *m* 1971, Gillian Elizabeth (*née* Holbrook). *Educ:* Havelock School, Grimsby; Queen Mary Coll., Univ. of London (BSc 1st cl. hons 1969); Emmanuel College, Cambridge (PhD 1973). FRGS 1972. Queen Mary Coll. E Greenland Expdn, 1968; UK-US Antarctic Expdns, 1969–70 and 1971–72; Cambridge E Greenland Expdn, 1972; Sir Henry Strakosh Fellow, 1974; UK-US Antarctic Expdns, 1974–75, 1977–78 (leader), 1978–79 (leader); Sen. Res. Asst, Univ. of Cambridge, 1978–83; leader, UK-Norwegian Svalbard Expdns, 1980, 1983, 1985; Asst Dir of Research, Univ. of Cambridge, 1983. Member: Young Explorers Trust Council, 1973–79; British Nat. Cttee Antarctic Res., 1973–79, 1982–; UK Nat. Remote Sensing Centre, 1981–; Transantarctic Assoc., 1982–; RGS Expdns Cttee, 1982–; Council, Internat. Glaciological Soc., 1980–82; ESA Experts Team, 1981–; Hon. Sec., Arctic Club, 1976–83; UK alternate deleg., Sci. Cttee on Antarctic Res., 1985–. US Antarctic Service Medal, 1979; Cuthbert Peek Award, RGS, 1979. *Publications:* Antarctica: glaciological and geophysical folio, 1983; Glacial Geologic Processes, 1985; papers on polar glaciology, geophysics, remote sensing in learned jls. *Recreations:* music, book collecting, walking. *Address:* Scott Polar Research Institute, University of Cambridge, Lensfield Road, Cambridge CB2 1ER. *T:* Cambridge 356445. *Clubs:* Geographical, Antarctic, Arctic.

DREYER, Adm. Sir Desmond (Parry), GCB 1967 (KCB 1963; CB 1960); CBE 1957; DSC; JP; DL; *b* 6 April 1910; *yr s* of late Adm. Sir Frederic Dreyer, GBE, KCB; *m* 1st, 1934, Elisabeth (*d* 1958), *d* of late Sir Henry Chilton, GCMG; one *s* one *d* (and one *s* decd); 2nd, 1959, Marjorie Gordon, *widow* of Hon. R. G. Whiteley. Served War of 1939–45 (DSC). Cdre First Class, 1955. Chief of Staff, Mediterranean, 1955–57; Asst Chief of Naval Staff, 1958–59; Flag Officer (Flotillas) Mediterranean, 1960–61; Flag Officer Air (Home), 1961–62; Comdr, Far East Fleet, 1962–65; Second Sea Lord, 1965–67; Chief Adviser (Personnel and Logistics) to Sec. of State for Defence, 1967–68. Principal Naval ADC to the Queen, 1965–68. Gentleman Usher to the Sword of State, 1973–80. Member: Nat. Bd for Prices and Incomes, 1968–71; Armed Forces Pay Review Body, 1971–79. President: RN Benevolent Trust, 1970–78; Officers' Pension Soc., 1978–84; Regular Forces Employment Assoc., 1978–82; Not Forgotten Assoc., 1973–. JP 1968, High Sheriff, 1977–78, DL 1985, Hants. *Recreations:* fishing, golf. *Address:* Brook Cottage, Cheriton, near Alresford, Hants SO24 0QA. *T:* Bramdean 215. *Club:* Army and Navy.

DREYFUS, John Gustave, FIOP; typographical consultant and historian; *b* 15 April 1918; *s* of late Edmond and Marguerite Dreyfus; *m* 1948, Irène Thurnauer; two *d* (one *s* decd). *Educ:* Oundle Sch.; Trinity Coll., Cambridge (MA). FIOP 1977. Served War, Army, 1939–45. Joined Cambridge University Press as graduate trainee, 1939; Asst Univ. Printer, 1949–56; Typographical Adviser, 1956–82; Typographical Adviser to Monotype Corp., 1955–82; European Consultant to Limited Editions Club, USA, 1956–77; Dir, Curwen Press, 1970–82; Sandars Reader in Bibliography, Univ. of Cambridge, 1979–80. Helped plan exhibn, Printing and the Mind of Man, 1963 (also designed catalogues). Pres., Assoc. Typographique Internationale, 1968–73 (organised internat. congresses for Assoc.); Chm., Printing Historical Soc., 1974–77 (org. Caxton Internat. Congress, 1976). FRSA. Sir Thomas More Award, Univ. of San Francisco, 1979; Laureate, Amer. Printing Historical Soc., 1984; Frederic W. Goudy Award, Rochester Inst. of Technology, NY, 1984. *Publications:* The Survival of Baskerville's Punches, 1949; The Work of Jan van Krimpen, 1952; (ed series) Type Specimen Facsimiles, 1963–71; Italic Quartet, 1966; (ed with François Richaudeau) La Chose Imprimée (French encyc. on printing), 1977; A History of the Nonesuch Press, 1981; French Eighteenth Century Typography, 1982; contrib. The Library. *Recreations:* travel, theatre-going. *Address:* 38 Lennox Gardens, SW1X 0DH. *T:* 01–584 3510. *Club:* Garrick.

DREYFUS, Pierre; Grand Officier, Légion d'Honneur; Conseiller à la Présidence de la République, since 1982; *b* Paris, 18 Nov. 1907; *s* of Emmanuel Dreyfus, Banker, and Madeleine (*née* Bernard); *m* 1936, Laure Ullmo; one *d*. *Educ:* Lycée Janson-de-Sailly; Faculty of Law, Univ. of Paris (Dip., Dr of Law). Inspector-Gen. of Industry and Commerce, Chief of Gen. Inspectorate, and Dir of Cabinet to Minister of Industry and Commerce, M Robert Lacoste, 1947–49; Pres., Commn of Energy of the Plan, and Dir of the Cabinet to Minister of Industry and Commerce, M Bourgès-Maunoury, 1954. President: Houillères de Lorraine, 1950–55; Charbonnages de France, 1954; Société des Aciers Fins de l'Est, 1955. President Director-General, Régie Nationale des Usines Renault, 1955–75; Pres., Renault-Finance, 1976–80; Minister for Industry, 1981–82. *Address:* 12 rue Duroc, 75007 Paris, France.

DRIDAN, Julian Randal, CMG 1955; retired; Chairman, Electricity Trust of South Australia, 1970–76 (Member, 1953–76); *b* 24 Nov. 1901; *s* of Sydney John Dridan and Eliza Gundry Dridan; *m* 1925, Ivy Viola Orr; two *d*. *Educ:* South Australian Sch. of Mines; University of Adelaide (BE). Entered service with Govt of S Australia, 1923; construction of locks and weirs on River Murray, 1923–34; District Engineer, 1934–44; Deputy Engineer-in-Chief, 1946; Engineer-in-Chief, 1949; Dir and Engineer-in-Chief, 1960–66. Mem. River Murray Commission, 1947–66. Coronation Medal, 1953; Jubilee Medal, 1978. *Recreations:* bowls, fishing. *Address:* 555 Fullarton Road, Mitcham, South Australia 6032. *Club:* Rotary (Adelaide).

DRIELSMA, Claude Dunbar H.; *see* Hankes Drielsma.

DRINAN, Adam; *see* Macleod, Joseph T. G.

DRING, Lt-Col Sir (Arthur) John, KBE 1952; CIE 1943; JP; DL; *b* 4 Nov. 1902; *s* of late Sir William Dring, KCIE; *m* 1934, Marjorie Wadham (*d* 1943); two *d*; *m* 1946, Alice Deborah, *widow* of Maj.-Gen. J. S. Marshall, CB, DSO, OBE, and *o d* of late Maj.-Gen. Gerald Cree, CB, CMG. *Educ:* Winchester Coll.; RMC, Sandhurst. Joined Guides Cavalry, 1923; Indian Political Service, 1927; Asst Private Sec. to Viceroy, 1930–32; Deputy Commissioner, Dera Ismail Khan, 1935–36; Sec. to Governor, NWFP, 1937–40; Political Agent, South Waziristan, 1940–42 (despatches); Sec. to NWFP Govt Development Depts; Revenue Commissioner, NWFP; Chief Sec. NWFP, 1947; Prime Minister of Bahawalpur, 1948–52; Adviser to Governor of Gold Coast on Togoland Plebiscite, 1955–56. Adviser to Governor-Gen. of Nigeria and the Governor of the Northern Region for the N & S Cameroons Plebiscite, 1959. JP 1954, DL 1973, Hants. *Recreations:* riding and gardening. *Address:* Ava Cottage, Purbrook, Hants. *T:* Waterlooville 3000.

DRING, (Dennis) William, RA 1955 (ARA 1944); RWS; *b* 26 Jan. 1904; *s* of William Henry Dring; *m* 1931, Grace Elizabeth Rothwell; one *s* two *d*. *Educ:* Slade Sch. of Fine Art. Portrait and landscape painter; during the war official war artist to Ministry of Information, Admiralty, and Air Ministry. *Address:* Windy Ridge, Compton, Winchester, Hants. *T:* Twyford, Hants 712181.

DRING, Lieut-Col Sir John; *see* Dring, Lieut-Col Sir A. J.

DRING, Richard Paddison; Editor of Official Report (Hansard), House of Commons, 1972–78; *b* 6 Nov. 1913; *s* of late Fred Dring and late Florence Hasleham Dring, East Sheen; *m* 1939, Joan Wilson, St Albans; one *s*. *Educ:* St Paul's School. Served Army, 1942–46. Herts Advertiser, 1932; Press Association, 1936; Official Report (Hansard), House of Commons, 1940: Asst Editor, 1954; Dep. Editor, 1970. *Recreation:* golf. *Address:* 24 Vicarage Drive, SW14 8RX. *T:* 01–876 2162. *Club:* Richmond Golf.

DRING, William; *see* Dring, D. W.

DRINKALL, John Kenneth, CMG 1973; HM Diplomatic Service, retired; High Commissioner to Jamaica, and Ambassador (non-resident) to Haiti, 1976–81; *b* 1 Jan. 1922; *m* 1961, Patricia Ellis; two *s* two *d*. *Educ:* Haileybury Coll.; Brasenose Coll., Oxford. Indian Army, 1942–45. Entered HM Foreign Service, 1947; 3rd Sec., Nanking, 1948; Vice-Consul, Tamsui, Formosa, 1949–51; Acting Consul, 1951; Foreign Office, 1951–53; 1st Sec., Cairo, 1953–56; Foreign Office, 1957–60; 1st Sec., Brasilia, 1960–62; Foreign Office, 1962–65. Appointed Counsellor, 1964; Counsellor: Nicosia, Cyprus, 1965–67; British Embassy, Brussels, 1967–70; FCO, 1970–71; Canadian Nat. Defence Coll., 1971–72; Ambassador to Afghanistan, 1972–76. *Recreations:* lawn tennis, golf, racquets and squash. *Address:* Bolham House, Tiverton, Devon EX16 7RA. *Clubs:* Royal Automobile, All England Lawn Tennis.

DRINKROW, John; *see under* Hardwick, Michael.

DRINKWATER, John Muir; QC 1972; a Recorder of the Crown Court, since 1972; a Commissioner of Income Tax, since 1983; *b* 16 March 1925; *s* of late Comdr John Drinkwater, OBE, RN (retd); *m* Jennifer Marion, *d* of Edward Fitzwalter Wright, Morley Manor, Derbs; one *s* four *d*. *Educ:* RNC Dartmouth. HM Submarines, 1943–47; Flag Lieut to C-in-C Portsmouth and First Sea Lord, 1947–50; Lt-Comdr 1952; invalided 1953. Called to Bar, Inner Temple, 1957, Bencher, 1979. Mem., Parly Boundary Commn for England, 1977–80. Mem. Bd, British Airports Authy, 1985–. Life Mem. Council, SPAB, 1982. Governor, St Mary's Hosp., 1960–64. *Recreations:* swimming, reading, travel. *Address:* Meysey Hampton Manor, Cirencester, Glos GL7 5JS. *T:* Poulton 366; 27 Kilmaine Road, SW6. *T:* 01–381 1279; Lohitzun, 64120 St Palais, France. *Clubs:* Garrick, Pratt's.

DRISCOLL, James; Director, Nationalised Industries' Chairmen's Group, since 1976; Chairman and Managing Director, Woodcote Consultants Ltd, since 1980; *b* 24 April 1925; *s* of Henry James Driscoll and Honorah Driscoll; *m* 1955, Jeanne Lawrence Williams, BA, CertEd; one *s* one *d*. *Educ:* Coleg Sant Illtyd, Cardiff; University Coll., Cardiff. BA (1st Cl. Hons). Chm., Welsh Young Conservatives, 1948–49; Nat. Dep. Chm., Young Conservatives, 1950; Dep. Chm., Univ. Cons. Fedn, 1949–50; Dep. Chm., NUS, 1951–53. Vice-Chm., European Youth Campaign, 1951–53. Contested (C) Rhondda West, 1950. Asst Lectr, UC Cardiff, 1950–53; Council of Europe Res. Fellowship, 1953. Joined British Iron and Steel Fedn, 1953; various econ. and internat. posts; Econ. Dir and Dep. Dir-Gen., 1963–67; various posts, British Steel Corporation, 1967–80; Man. Dir, Corporate Strategy, 1971–76, Adviser, 1976–80. Member: Grand Council, FBI, 1957–65; CBI Council, 1970–; Observer, NEDC, 1977–. Chm., Econ. Studies Cttee, Internat. Iron and Steel Inst., 1972–74. Mem., Court of Governors, UC, Cardiff, 1970– (Fellow). FREcon S; FRSA. *Publications:* various articles and pamphlets on econ. and internat. affairs, esp. steel affairs, European integration, wages policy and financing of world steel investment. *Recreations:* travel, reading. *Address:* Foxley Hatch, Birch Lane, Purley, Surrey CR2 3LH. *T:* 01-668 4081.

DRISCOLL, Dr James Philip, CEng; Associate Director, Coopers & Lybrand Associates, since 1985; *b* 29 March 1943; *s* of Reginald Driscoll and Janetta Bridget Driscoll; *m* 1969, Josephine Klapper, BA; two *s* two *d*. *Educ:* St Illtyd's Coll., Cardiff; Birmingham Univ. (BSc 1964; PhD 1972); Manchester Business Sch. MIChemE 1975; MIGasE 1975; MInstF 1975. Taught at St Illtyd's Coll., Cardiff, 1964; res. posts with Joseph Lucas, Solihull, 1968–69; British Steel Corporation: res. posts, 1969–70; Commercial posts, 1971–79, incl. Manager, Divl Supplies, 1973; Reg. Manager, BSC (Industry), 1979–82; Dir, S Wales Workshops, 1980–82; Industrial Dir, Welsh Office, 1982–85. *Publications:* various technical papers. *Recreations:* family, sport. *Address:* 6 Cory Crescent, Wyndham Park, Peterston-super-Ely, S Glam. *T:* Peterston-super-Ely 760372. *Clubs:* Cardiff Athletic, Peterston Football (Cardiff).

DRIVER, Sir Antony (Victor), Kt 1986; Chairman, South West Thames Regional Health Authority, since 1982; Chairman, Hoogovens (UK) Ltd, since 1985; *b* London, 20 July 1920; *s* of late Arthur William Driver and Violet Clementina Driver (*née* Browne); *m* 1948, Patricia (née Tinkler); three *s*. *Educ:* King's Coll., Univ. of London (BScEng Hons); Dip., Graduate Sch. of Industrial Admin., Carnegie-Mellon Univ., Pittsburgh. CEng; FIMechE, FInstPet; FBIM. In oil industry withShell-Mex and BP Ltd, until 1975, and BP Oil Ltd, 1976–80: seconded to British Petroleum Co. Ltd, as Marketing Manager, N Europe, 1969–71; General Manager, Sales, 1971–78; Director, Personnel and Admin., 1979–80. Non-executive director: Candles Ltd, 1976–80; Rockwool Ltd, 1978–80; Baxter Fell & Co. Ltd, 1980–85; Director: Inst. of Cancer Research, 1981–; Oil Industries Club Ltd, 1981–. Liveryman, Tallow Chandlers' Co., 1977–; Freeman, City of London. *Recreations:* travel, gardening, wine, pyrotechnics. *Address:* Winterdown, Holmbury St Mary, Dorking, Surrey RH5 6NL. *T:* Dorking 730238.

DRIVER, Sir Arthur (John), Kt 1962; JP; *b* 1900; *s* of Percy John Driver, East Sheen, and Mary Amelie Driver; *m* 1937, Margaret, *d* of Hugh Semple McMeekin, Carnmoney, Northern Ireland; one *s* one *d*. Served in Royal Air Force, 1918. Pres. of Law Soc., 1961–62. Mem. Council, and Hon. Dep. Kt Principal, Imperial Soc. of Knights Bachelor. Hon. LLD University of Buckingham, 1983. JP Supplementary List. *Address:* Frogmore Cottage, East Clandon, Surrey. *Club:* Reform.

DRIVER, Bryan, FCIT 1976; Chairman, since 1985 and Managing Director, since 1982, Freightliners Ltd; *b* 26 August 1932; *s* of Fred and Edith Driver; *m* 1955, Pamela Anne (*née* Nelson); two *d*. *Educ:* Wath-upon-Dearne Grammar School. Joined British Railways (Junior Clerk), 1948; Royal Air Force, 1950–52; management training with BR, 1958–59; posts in London, Doncaster, Newcastle, 1959–69; Divisional Operating Manager, Norwich, 1969–71, Liverpool Street, 1971–72; Divisional Manager, West of England, 1972–75, South Wales, 1975–77; Dep. Gen. Manager, Eastern Region, 1977–82. *Recreations:* cricket, Rugby football, golf. *Address:* Riverdslea, 4 Shilton Garth Close, Old Earswick, York. *T:* York 762848. *Clubs:* Savile, MCC.

DRIVER, Charles Jonathan, MPhil; Headmaster, Berkhamsted School, since 1983; *b* 19 Aug. 1939; *s* of Rev. Kingsley Ernest Driver and Phyllis Edith Mary (*née* Gould); *m* 1967, Ann Elizabeth Hoogewerf; two *s* one *d*. *Educ:* St Andrews Coll., Grahamstown; Univ. of Cape Town (BA Hons, BEd, STD); Trinity Coll., Oxford (MPhil). Pres., National Union of S African Students, 1963–64; Asst Teacher, Sevenoaks Sch., 1964–65 and 1967–68; Housemaster, Internat. Sixth Form Centre, Sevenoaks Sch., 1968–73; Dir of Sixth Form Studies, Matthew Humberstone Sch., 1973–78; Res. Fellow, Univ. of York, 1976; Principal, Island Sch., Hong Kong, 1978–83. Member: HMC; Soc. of Authors; Royal Soc. of Arts; FRSA. *Publications:* Elegy for a Revolutionary (novel), 1968; Send War in Our Time, O Lord (novel), 1969; Death of Fathers (novel), 1972; A Messiah of the Last Days (novel), 1974; I Live Here Now (poems), 1979; (with Jack Cope) Occasional Light (poems), 1979; Patrick Duncan (biog.), 1980. *Recreations:* long-distance running (marathons), reading, writing, reviewing, broadcasting, Rugby, family. *Address:* Wilson House, Berkhamsted School, Berkhamsted, Herts HP4 2BE. *T:* (school) Berkhamsted 3236, (Wilson House) Berkhamsted 4827.

DRIVER, Christopher Prout; writer and broadcaster; Food and Drink Editor, The Guardian, since 1984; *b* 1 Dec. 1932; *s* of Dr Arthur Herbert Driver and Elsie Kathleen Driver (*née* Shepherd); *m* 1958, Margaret Elizabeth Perfect; three *d*. *Educ:* Dragon Sch., Oxford; Rugby Sch.; Christ Church, Oxford (MA). Friends Ambulance Unit Internat. Service, 1955–57; Reporter, Liverpool Daily Post, 1958–60; Reporter, 1960–64, Features Editor, 1964–68, The Guardian; Editor, Good Food Guide, 1969–82. Member: Christian Aid Bd, 1972–84; Highgate URC, 1962–. *Publications:* A Future for the Free Churches?, 1962; The Disarmers: a study in protest, 1964; The Exploding University, 1971; The British at Table 1940–1980, 1983; (jtly) Pepys at Table, 1984; Twelve Poems, 1985; (contrib.) More Words, 1977; (published and co-ed) Shaftesbury, 1983; contribs on various topics to New Society, Listener, London Rev. of Books and other serious jls. *Recreations:* cooking, playing violin and viola, fellwalking, accumulating books as reader, reviewer and dealer. *Address:* 6 Church Road, Highgate, N6 4QT. *T:* 01-340 5445; The Book in Hand, 17 Bell Street, Shaftesbury, Dorset.

DRIVER, Sir Eric (William), Kt 1979; retired; Chairman, Mersey Regional Health Authority, 1973–82; Chairman, National Staff Committee, (Works), 1979–82; *b* 19 Jan. 1911; *s* of William Weale Driver and Sarah Ann Driver; *m* 1st, 1938, Winifred Bane; two *d*; 2nd, 1972, Sheila Mary Johnson. *Educ:* Strand Sch., London; King's Coll., London Univ. (BSc). FICE. Civil Engr with ICI Ltd, 1938–73, retd as Chief Civil Engr Mond Div. *Recreations:* dinghy sailing (racing), hill walking, gardening, travel. *Address:* Chapel House, Crowley, Northwich, Cheshire CW9 6NX. *Clubs:* Royal Yachting Association; Budworth Sailing.

DRIVER, Olga Lindholm; *see* Aikin, O. L.

DRIVER, Thomas; General Secretary, National Association of Teachers in Further and Higher Education, 1976–77, retired; *b* 9 Sept. 1912; *s* of Joseph and Eliza Driver; *m* 1936, Thora Senior (*d* 1985); one *s* one *d*. *Educ:* Sheffield Univ. (BA, DipEd). FEIS 1977. Barnsley Central Sch., 1937–42; Keighley Jun. Techn. Sch., 1942–45; Barnsley Techn. Sch., 1945–47; Doncaster Coll. of Technology, 1947–68. Gen. Sec., Assoc. of Teachers in Technical Institutions, 1969–76. Hon. Fellow: Polytechnic of City of Sheffield, 1976; NE London Polytechnic, 1978. *Recreations:* walking, reading. *Address:* 20 Farndale Road, Doncaster, S Yorks DN5 8SH.

DROGHEDA, 11th Earl of, *cr* 1661 (Ireland); **Charles Garrett Ponsonby Moore,** KG 1972; KBE 1964 (OBE 1946); Baron Moore of Mellifont, 1616; Viscount Moore, 1621; Baron Moore of Cobham (UK), 1954; Chairman of the Financial Times Ltd, 1971–75 (Managing Director, 1945–70); *b* 23 April 1910; *o s* of 10th Earl of Drogheda, PC, KCMG; *S* father, 1957; *m* 1935, Joan, *o d* of late William Henry Carr; one *s*. *Educ:* Eton; Trinity Coll., Cambridge. 2nd Lieut Royal Artillery (TA), 1939; Captain 1940. On staff of Ministry of Production, 1942–45. Chairman: Newspaper Publishers' Assoc., 1968–70; Royal Opera House, Covent Garden Ltd, 1958–74. Pres., Institute of Directors, 1975–76. Trustee: British Museum, 1974–77; St John's, Smith Square. Chm., London Celebrations Cttee, Queen's Silver Jubilee, 1977. Chm., Royal Ballet Sch. 1978–82. Chairman: Henry Sotheran, 1977–; Clifton Nurseries, 1979–. Director: Times Newspapers Hldgs Ltd, 1981–; Earls Court & Olympia Ltd. Governor, Royal Ballet. Commander: Legion of Honour (France), 1960; Ordine al Merito (Italy), 1968; Grand Officier de l'Ordre de Léopold II (Belgium), 1974. *Publications:* Double Harness (memoirs), 1978; (jtly) Covent Garden Album, 1981. *Heir:* *s* Viscount Moore, *qv*. *Address:* Parkside House, Englefield Green, Surrey. *Club:* White's.

See also Sir Richard Latham, Bt.

DROMGOOLE, Jolyon; MA Oxon; Director (Council Secretariat), Institution of Civil Engineers, since 1985; Deputy Under-Secretary of State (Army), Ministry of Defence, 1984–85; *b* 27 March 1926; 2nd *s* of Nicholas and Violet Dromgoole; *m* 1956, Anthea, *e d* of Sir Anthony Bowlby, 2nd Bt, *qv*; five *d* (incl. triplets). *Educ:* Christ's Hospital; Dulwich Coll.; University Coll., Oxford, 1944. 2nd Cl. Hons (History), MA. Entered HM Forces, 1944; commissioned 14/20 King's Hussars, 1946. University Coll., 1948–50. Entered Administrative Cl., Civil Service; assigned to War Office, 1950; Private Sec. to Permanent Under-Sec., 1953; Principal, 1955; Private Sec. to Sec. of State, 1964–65; Asst Sec., 1965; Command Sec., HQ FARELF, Singapore, 1968–71; Royal Coll. of Defence Studies, 1972; Under-Sec., Broadcasting Dept, Home Office, 1973–76; Asst Under-Sec. of State, Gen. Staff, 1976–79, Personnel and Logistics, 1979–84, MoD. *Recreations:* polo, literature. *Address:* 13 Gladstone Street, SE1 6EY. *T:* 01-928 2162; Montreal House, Barnsley, Glos. *T:* Bibury 331. *Clubs:* Athenæum, Royal Commonwealth Soc.

DROMGOOLE, Lesley Faye, (Mrs Nicholas Dromgoole); *see* Collier, L. F.

DROMORE, Bishop of, (RC), since 1976; **Most Rev. Francis Gerard Brooks,** DD, DCL; *b* Jan. 1924. Priest, 1949. Formerly President, St Colman's Coll., Violet Hill, Newry. *Address:* Bishop's House, Newry, Co. Down, N Ireland BT35 6PN.

DRONFIELD, Ronald; Chief Insurance Officer for National Insurance, Department of Health and Social Security, 1976–84, retired; *b* 21 Dec. 1924; *m* 1966, Marie Renie (*née* Price). *Educ:* King Edward VII Sch., Sheffield; Oriel Coll., Oxford. RN, 1943–46. Entered Min. of National Insurance, 1949; Principal Private Sec. to Minister of Pensions and Nat. Insurance, 1964–66; Cabinet Office, 1970–71. *Recreation:* reading, biography. *Address:* Market Towers (Room 1304), 1 Nine Elms Lane, SW8 5NQ. *T:* 01-720 2188.

DRONKE, (Ernst) Peter (Michael), FBA 1984; Fellow of Clare Hall, since 1964, and Reader in Medieval Latin Literature, since 1979, University of Cambridge; *b* 30 May 1934; *s* of Senatspräsident A. H. R. Dronke and M. M. Dronke (*née* Kronfeld); *m* 1960, Ursula Miriam (*née* Brown); one *d*. *Educ:* Victoria University, NZ (MA 1st Cl. Hons 1954); Magdalen College, Oxford (BA 1st Cl. Hons 1957; MA 1961); MA Cantab 1961. Research Fellow, Merton Coll., Oxford, 1958–61; Lectr in Medieval Latin, Univ. of Cambridge, 1961–79. Guest Lectr, Univ. of Munich, 1960; Guest Prof., Centre d'Etudes Médiévales, Poitiers, 1969; Leverhulme Fellow, 1973; Guest Prof., Univ. Autónoma, Barcelona, 1977; Vis. Fellow, Humanities Res. Centre, Canberra, 1978; Vis. Prof. of Medieval Studies, Westfield Coll., 1981–86. W. P. Ker Lectr, Univ. of Glasgow, 1976; Matthews Lectr, Birkbeck Coll., 1983. Corresp. Fellow, Real Academia de Buenas Letras, 1976. Hon. Pres., Internat. Courtly Literature Soc., 1974. Co-Editor, Mittellateinisches Jahrbuch, 1977–. *Publications:* Medieval Latin and the Rise of European Love-Lyric, 2 vols, 1965–66; The Medieval Lyric, 1968; Poetic Individuality in the Middle Ages, 1970; Fabula, 1974; Abelard and Heloise in Medieval Testimonies, 1976; (with Ursula Dronke) Barbara et antiquissima carmina, 1977; (ed) Bernardus Silvestris, Cosmographia, 1978; Introduction to Francesco Colonna, Hypnerotomachia, 1981; Women Writers of the Middle Ages, 1984; The Medieval Poet and his World, 1984; Dante and Medieval Latin Traditions, 1986; (ed) A History of Twelfth-Century Western Philosophy, 1987; essays in learned jls and symposia. *Recreations:* music, film, Brittany. *Address:* 6 Parker Street, Cambridge. *T:* Cambridge 359942.

DRUCKER, Prof. Peter (Ferdinand); writer and consultant; Clarke Professor of Social Science, Claremont Graduate School, Claremont, Calif, since 1971; Professorial Lecturer in Oriental Art, Claremont Colleges, since 1980; *b* 19 Nov. 1909; *s* of Adolph B. Drucker and Caroline (*née* Bond); *m* 1937, Doris Schmitz; one *s* three *d*. *Educ:* Austria, Germany, England. Investment banker, London, 1933–36; newspapers, 1937–41; Professor of Philosophy and Politics, Bennington Coll., Bennington, Vt, USA, 1942–49; Prof. of Management, NY Univ., 1950–72. Management Consultant (internat. practice among businesses and govts) (as well as Professorships), 1948–. Holds fifteen hon. doctorates from Univs in Belgium, GB, Japan, Switzerland, USA. Hon. FBIM; FAAAS; Fellow: Amer. Acad. of Management; Internat. Acad. of Management. Order of Sacred Treasure, Japan; Grand Cross, Austria. *Publications:* End of Economic Man, 1939; Future of Industrial Man, 1942; Concept of Corporation, 1946; The New Society, 1950; Practice of Management, 1954; America's Next Twenty Years, 1959; Landmarks of Tomorrow, 1960; Managing for Results, 1964; The Effective Executive, 1966; The Age of Discontinuity, 1969; Technology, Management and Society, 1970; Men, Ideas and Politics, 1971; The New Markets . . . and other essays, 1971; Management: tasks, responsibilities, practices, 1974; The Unseen Revolution: how pension fund socialism came to America, 1976; Adventures of a Bystander, 1979; Managing in Turbulent Times, 1980; Toward the New Economics, 1981; The Changing World of the Executive (essays), 1982; Innovation and Entrepreneurship, 1985; The Frontiers of Management, 1986; *novels:* The Last of All Possible Worlds, 1982; The Temptation to Do Good, 1984. *Recreations:* mountaineering; Japanese history and paintings. *Address:* 636 Wellesley Drive, Claremont, Calif 91711, USA. *T:* (714) 621–1488.

DRUMALBYN, 1st Baron, *cr* 1963; **Niall Malcolm Stewart Macpherson,** PC 1962; KBE 1974; *b* 3 Aug. 1908; 3rd *s* of late Sir T. Stewart Macpherson, CIE, LLD, Newtonmore, Inverness-shire and Lady (Helen) Macpherson, K-i-H (*née* Cameron); *m* 1st; *m* Margaret Phyllis (*d* 1979), *d* of late J. J. Runge and late Norah Cecil Runge, OBE, (she *m* 2nd, Dr T. A. Ross); two *d* (and one *d* decd); 2nd, 1985, Mrs Rita Edmiston. *Educ:* Edinburgh Academy; Fettes Coll.; Trinity Coll., Oxford (Scholar). First Class Honour Mods. 1929; First Class Litt Hum. 1931; MA; Rugby Football Blue, 1928. Business training with J. & J. Colman Ltd; Manager Turkish branch, 1933–35; Export branch, London, 1936–39. Commissioned Queen's Own Cameron Highlanders, TA June 1939: Staff Coll., 1942; Temp. Major 1942; MP (Nat L) 1945–50 (Nat L and U), 1950–63, Dumfriesshire. Scottish Whip, 1945–55; Chm., Commonwealth Producers' Organisation, 1952–55, Pres., 1967–70. Dep. Pres., Assoc. of British Chambers of Commerce, 1970. Member BBC General Advisory Council, 1950–55. Joint Under-Sec. of State for Scotland, 1955–60; Parly Sec., Board of Trade, 1960–62; Minister of Pensions and National Insurance, 1962–63; Minister of State, BoT, 1963–64; Minister without Portfolio, 1970–74. Chairman: Advertising Standards Authority, 1965–70, and 1974–77; Assoc. of Conservative Peers, 1975–80. *Heir:* none. *Address:* Claytons, Beeches Hill, Bishop's Waltham, Southampton SO3 1FU. *Club:* Royal Automobile.

See also R. T. S. Macpherson.

DRUMLANRIG, Viscount; Sholto Francis Guy Douglas; *b* 1 June 1967; *s* and *heir* of 12th Marquess of Queensberry, *qv*.

DRUMMOND, family name of **Earl of Perth.**

DRUMMOND, Lieut-Gen. Sir Alexander; *see* Drummond, Lieut-Gen. Sir W. A. D.

DRUMMOND, Maj.-Gen. Anthony John D.; *see* Deane-Drummond.

DRUMMOND, David Classon, FIBiol; Senior Agricultural Scientist with special responsibilities for Research and Development, Agricultural Science Service, Agricultural Development Advisory Service, Ministry of Agriculture, Fisheries and Food, since 1985; *b* 25 July 1928; *s* of Roger Hamilton Drummond and Marjorie Holt Drummond; *m* 1952, Barbara Anne, *d* of late Prof. Alfred Cobban; three *d. Educ:* St Peter's Sch., York; University Coll., London (BSc 1952); Pennsylvania State Univ., USA (Kellogg Fellow; MS 1962). FIBiol 1975. Project Manager, FAO, UN, Karachi, 1971–72; Head of Rodent Res. Dept, and Officer i/c Tolworth Lab., Agricl Sci. Service, MAFF, 1974–82; Head of Biol. Div., and Officer i/c Slough Lab., Agricl Sci. Service, MAFF, 1982–85. *Publications:* scientific papers and reviews mainly concerned with rodent biology and control and develt of agricl and urban rat control programmes. *Recreations:* travel, gardening, history of rat catching. *Address:* 32 Compton Crescent, Chessington, Surrey KT9 2HB.

DRUMMOND, Dame (Edith) Margaret, DBE 1966 (OBE 1960); MA; Director of the Women's Royal Naval Service, 1964–67; *b* 4 Sept. 1917; *d* of Prof. Robert James Drummond and Marion (*née* Street). *Educ:* Park Sch., Glasgow; Aberdeen Univ. Joined WRNS, April 1941 and progressed through various ranks of the Service. *Recreations:* gardening, reading, concerts and friends. *Address:* Somersham Cottage, Saxlingham, Holt, Norfolk. *Club:* University Women's.

DRUMMOND, John Richard Gray; writer and broadcaster; Controller of Music, BBC, since 1985; *b* 25 Nov. 1934; *s* of late Captain A. R. G. Drummond and Esther (*née* Pickering), Perth, WA. *Educ:* Canford; Trinity Coll., Cambridge (MA History). RNVR, 1953–55. BBC Radio and Television, 1958–78, latterly as Asst Head, Music and Arts. Programmes produced incl.: Tortelier Master Classes, 1964; Leeds Piano Comp., 1966 (1st Prize, Prague Fest., 1967); Diaghilev, 1967; Kathleen Ferrier, 1968; Music Now, 1969; Spirit of the Age, 1975; The Lively Arts, 1976–78. Dir, Edinburgh Internat. Fest., 1978–83. Chairman: Nat. Dance Co-ordinating Cttee; Kensington Soc.; Vice-Chm., British Arts Fests Assoc., 1981–83; Mem. various adv. councils and cttees concerning music and dance; Governor, Royal Ballet. FRSA. *Publications:* (with Joan Bakewell) A Fine and Private Place, 1977; (with N. Thompson) The Turn of Dance?, 1984. *Recreations:* conversation, looking at architecture, browsing in bookshops. *Address:* 61c Campden Hill Court, W8 7HL. *T:* 01-937 2257. *Club:* New (Edinburgh).

DRUMMOND, Maldwin Andrew Cyril; JP; DL; farmer and author; Member, Countryside Commission, since 1980; *b* 30 April 1932; *s* of late Maj. Cyril Drummond, JP, DL, and Mildred Joan Quinnell; *m* 1st, 1955, Susan Dorothy Cayley (marr. diss. 1977); two *d*; 2nd, 1978, Gillian Turner Laing; one *s. Educ:* Eton Coll.; Royal Agricl Coll., Cirencester; Univ. of Southampton (Cert. in Environmental Sci., 1972). 2nd Lieut, Rifle Bde, 1950–52; Captain, Queen Victoria's, later Queen's, Royal Rifles (TA), retd 1967. Verderer of New Forest, 1961–, now Sen. Elected Verderer; Chm., New Forest Consultative Panel, 1982–. Member: Southampton Harbour Bd, 1967; British Transport Docks Bd, Southampton, 1968–74; Southern Water Authority, 1984–. Chairman: Sail Training Assoc., 1967–72; Maritime Trust, 1979–; Cutty Sark Soc., 1979–; Ships Preservation Trust, 1979–; Vice-Pres., 1983–, and Chm. Boat Cttee, 1983–, RNLI; Trustee, World Ship Trust, 1980–; Chm., Hampshire Bldgs Preservation Trust, 1986–. Mem., New Forest RDC, 1957–66; Hampshire: County Councillor, 1967–75; JP 1964; DL 1975; High Sheriff, 1980–81. *Publications:* Conflicts in an Estuary, 1973; Tall Ships, 1976; Salt-Water Places, 1979; (with Paul Rodhouse) Yachtsman's Naturalist, 1980; (with Philip Allison) The New Forest, 1980; The Riddle, 1985. *Recreations:* cruising under sail and wondering about the sea. *Address:* Cadland House, Fawley, Southampton SO4 1AA. *T:* (office) Fawley 892039, (home) Fawley 891543; Wester Kames Castle, Port Bannatyne, Isle of Bute. *T:* Rothesay 3983. *Clubs:* White's, Pratt's, Royal Cruising; Royal Yacht Squadron (Cowes); Leander (Henley).

DRUMMOND, Dame Margaret; *see* Drummond, Dame E. M.

DRUMMOND, Rev. Norman Walker, MA; BD; Headmaster, Loretto School, since 1984; *b* 1 April 1952; *s* of late Edwin Payne Drummond and of Jean (*née* Walker); *m* 1976, Lady Elizabeth Helen Kennedy, *d* of 7th Marquess of Ailsa, *qv*; one *s* two *d. Educ:* Merchiston Castle Sch.; Fitzwilliam Coll., Cambridge (MA Law); New Coll., Univ. of Edinburgh (BD). Ordained as Minister of the Church of Scotland, and commnd to serve as Chaplain to HM Forces in the Army, 1976; Chaplain: Depot, Parachute Regt and Airborne Forces, 1977–78; 1st Bn The Black Watch (Royal Highland Regt), 1978–82; to the Moderator of the Gen. Assembly of the Church of Scotland, 1980; Fettes Coll., 1982–84. Cambridge Univ. Rugby Blue, 1971; Captain: Scottish Univs XV, 1974; Army XV and Combined Services XV, 1976–77. *Publication:* The First Twenty-five Years: official history of The Black Watch Kirk Session, 1979. *Recreations:* Rugby football, cricket, golf, curling, traditional jazz, Isle of Skye. *Address:* Pinkie House, Loretto School, Musselburgh, East Lothian, Scotland. *T:* 031-665 3108. *Clubs:* MCC, Free Foresters; New (Edinburgh); Hawks (Cambridge).

DRUMMOND, Lieut-Gen. (Retd) Sir (William) Alexander (Duncan), KBE 1957 (CBE 1951; OBE 1945); CB 1954; SPk 1969; Director-General, Army Medical Services, War Office, 1956–61 (Deputy Director-General, 1954–56); late RAMC; *b* 16 Sept. 1901. *Educ:* Dundee Univ. MRCS, LRCP 1924; DLO Eng. 1932; FRCS 1947. Formerly: Registrar, Throat, Nose and Ear Hospital, Golden Square; Registrar, Throat, Nose and Ear Dept, Charing Cross Hosp. Served War of 1939–45 (despatches five times, OBE). Col Comdt RAMC, 1961–66. Formerly HM Comr, Royal Hospital, Chelsea. KStJ, 1959. Hon. LLD: Birmingham, 1959; Punjab, 1960. *Publications:* contributions to medical journals. *Address:* c/o Grindlay's Bank, 13 St James's Square, SW1; Chase Lodge, 27 Clapham Common North Side, SW4.

DRUMMOND, William Norman; Under Secretary (formerly Deputy Secretary), Department of Economic Development (formerly Department of Commerce), Northern Ireland, since 1979; *b* 10 July 1927; *s* of Thomas and Martha Drummond, Lurgan; *m* 1958, Pamela Joyce Burnham; two *d. Educ:* Lurgan Coll.; Queen's Univ. Belfast (BSc (Hons)). Physicist, Iraq Petroleum Co., Kirkuk, Iraq, 1950–54; Reed's Sch., Cobham, 1954–57; Northern Ireland Civil Service, 1957–; Dep. Sec., Dept of Manpower Services, NI, 1974–79. *Recreations:* gardening, reading. *Address:* Magheralave Park East, Lisburn, Northern Ireland. *T:* Lisburn 4104.

DRUON, Maurice Samuel Roger Charles; Officier de la Légion d'Honneur; Commandeur des Arts et Lettres; author; Member of the French Academy since 1966, Permanent Secretary, since 1986; Member: French Parliament (Paris), 1978–81; Assembly of Council of Europe, 1978–81; European Parliament, 1979–80; Franco-British Council, since 1972; *b* Paris, 23 April 1918; *s* of René Druon de Reyniac and Léonilla Jenny Samuel-Cros; *m* 1968, Madeleine Marignac. *Educ:* Lycée Michelet and Ecole des Sciences Politiques, Paris. Ecole de Cavalerie de Saumur, aspirant, 1940; joined Free French Forces, London, 1942; Attaché Commissariat à l'Intérieur et Direction de l'Information, 1943; War Correspondent, 1944–45; Lieut de réserve de cavalerie. Journalist, 1946–47; Minister for Cultural Affairs, France, 1973–74. Awarded Prix Goncourt, 1948, for novel Les Grandes Familles; Prix de Monaco, 1966. Member: Acad. of Morocco, 1980; Athènes' Acad., 1981; Pres., Franco-Italian Assoc., 1985–. Commandeur du Phénix de Grèce; Grand Officer de l'Ordre de l'Honneur de Grèce; Grand Officier du Mérite de l'Ordre de Malte; Commandeur de l'Ordre de la République de Tunisie; Grand Officier du Lion du Sénégal; Grand Croix du Mérite de la République Italienne; Grand Croix de l'Aigle Aztèque du Mexique; Grand Officier Ouissam Alaouite (Morocco); Commandeur du Mérite de Monaco. *Publications:* Lettres d'un Européen, 1944; La Dernière Brigade (The Last Detachment), 1946 (publ. in England 1957); Les Grandes Familles, La Chute des Corps, Rendez-Vous aux Enfers, 1948–51 (trilogy publ. in England under title The Curtain falls, 1959); La Volupté d'Etre (Film of Memory), 1954 (publ. in England 1955); Les Rois Maudits (The Accursed Kings), 1955–60 (six vols: The Iron King, The Strangled Queen, The Poisoned Crown, The Royal Succession, The She-Wolf of France, The Lily and the Lion, publ. in England 1956–61); Tistou les pouces verts (Tistou of the green fingers), 1957 (publ. in England 1958); Alexandre le Grand (Alexander the God), 1958 (publ. in Eng. 1960); Des Seigneurs de la Plaine- (The Black Prince and other stories), 1962 (publ. in Eng. 1962); Les Mémoires de Zeus I (The Memoirs of Zeus), 1963 (in Eng. 1964); Bernard Buffet, 1964; Paris, de César à Saint Louis (The History of Paris from Caesar to St Louis), 1964 (in Eng. 1969); Le Pouvoir, 1965; Les Tambours de la Mémoire, 1965; Le Bonheur des Uns, 1967; L'Avenir en désarroi, 1968; Vézelay, colline éternelle, 1968; Nouvelles lettres d'un Européen, 1970; Une Eglise qui se trompe de siècle, 1972; La Parole et le Pouvoir, 1974; Oeuvres complètes, 25 vols, 1973–79; Quand un roi perd la France (Les Rois Maudits 7), 1977; Attention la France!, 1981; Réformer la Démocratie, 1982; *plays:* Mégarée, 1942; Un Voyageur, 1953; La Contessa, 1962; *song:* Le Chant des Partisans (with Joseph Kessel and Anna Marly), 1943 (London). *Recreations:* riding, travel. *Address:* 73 rue de Varenne, 75007 Paris, France; Abbaye de Faise, Les Artigues de Lussac, 33570 Lussac, France.

DRURY, (Alfred) Paul (Dalou), PPRE; etcher and painter; Principal, Goldsmiths' College School of Art, 1967–69, retired; *b* London, 14 Oct. 1903; *s* of late Alfred Drury, RA; *m* 1937, Enid Marie, painter, *o c* of late Victor Solomon; one *s. Educ:* King's Coll. Sch.; Bristol Grammar Sch.; Westminster Sch.; Goldsmiths' Coll. Sch. of Art (British Institution Scholarship in Engraving, 1924). Served War, 1939–45; Plaster (Orthopaedic) Dept, Queen Mary's Hosp., Roehampton. Since 1923 has exhibited etchings, paintings and drawings at the Royal Academy, galleries in England, and prints at representative exhibitions of British Art in Paris, Vienna, Florence, Stockholm, Buenos Aires, Tokyo, etc., and in Canada and the USA; etchings and drawings acquired by the Print Room, British Museum, Ashmolean, Imperial War Museum, Contemporary Art Soc., Boston, USA, and by various museums and galleries in the provinces and abroad. Fellow, Royal Soc. of Painter-Etchers and Engravers, 1926, President, 1970–75. Mem., Faculty of Engraving, British Sch. at Rome, 1948–74. Governor, West Surrey Coll. of Art, 1969–74. *Recreations:* music, writing. *Address:* Rangers Cottage, Nutley, Uckfield, East Sussex TN22 3LL. *T:* Nutley 2857. *Club:* Arts.

DRURY, Allen Stuart; Author; *b* Houston, Texas, 2 Sept. 1918; *s* of Alden M. and Flora A. Drury. *Educ:* Stanford Univ. (BA). Served with US Army, 1942–43. Ed., The Tulare (Calif) Bee, 1939–41; county ed., The Bakersfield Californian, Bakersfield, Calif, 1941–42; United Press Senate Staff, Washington, DC, 1943–45; freelance correspondent, 1946; Nation Ed., Pathfinder Magazine, Washington, DC, 1947–53; National Staff, Washington Evening Star, 1953–54; Senate Staff, New York Times, 1954–59. Mem., National Council on the Arts (apptd by Pres. Reagan), 1983–. Sigma Delta Chi Award for Editorial Writing, 1942; Hon. LitD, Rollins Coll., Winter Park, Fla, 1961. *Publications:* Advise and Consent, 1959 (Pulitzer Prize for Fiction, 1960); A Shade of Difference, 1962; A Senate Journal, 1963; That Summer, 1965; Three Kids in a Cart, 1965; Capable of Honor, 1966; "A Very Strange Society", 1967; Preserve and Protect, 1968; The Throne of Saturn, 1971; Courage and Hesitation: inside the Nixon administration, 1972; Come Nineveh, Come Tyre, 1973; The Promise of Joy, 1975; A God Against the Gods, 1976; Return to Thebes, 1977; Anna Hastings, 1977; Mark Coffin, USS, 1978; Egypt: the eternal smile, 1980; The Hill of Summer, 1981; Decision, 1983; The Roads of Earth, 1984; Pentagon, 1986. *Address:* c/o Doubleday & Co., 245 Park Avenue, New York, NY 10167, USA. *Clubs:* Cosmos, University, National Press (Washington, DC); Bohemian (San Francisco).

DRURY, Charles Mills, OC 1981; CBE 1946 (MBE 1942); DSO 1944; ED 1956; Chairman, National Capital Commission, Canada, since 1978; *b* 17 May 1912; *s* of Victor Montague Drury, Montreal, and Pansy Jessie Mills, Ottawa; *m* 1939, Jane Ferrier Counsell (decd); two *s* two *d. Educ:* Bishops Coll. Sch., Lennoxville, Quebec; Royal Military Coll. of Canada, Kingston, Ontario; McGill Univ., Montreal (BCL); University of Paris, France. Practised at law, 1936–39; served War of 1939–45, Canadian Army (final rank Brig.). Chief of UNNRA Mission to Poland, 1945–46; Dept of External Affairs, Canada, 1947–48; Dep. Minister of National Defence, Canada, 1949–55; Pres. and Man. Dir, Provincial Transport Co., 1955–60; Pres., Avis Transport of Canada Ltd, 1960–62; MP, Montreal St Antoine-Westmount, 1962–78; Minister, Dept of Defence Production, and Minister of Industry, 1963–68; Pres., Treasury Bd, 1968–74; Minister of Public Works, Canada, and Minister of State for Science and Technol., 1974–76; responsible for Nat. Res. Council of Canada, 1963–76. Chevalier de la Légion d'Honneur (France), 1946; Order of Polonia Restituta (Poland), 1946. *Address:* (office) 161 Laurier Street West, Ottawa, Ont. K1P 6J6, Canada. *Club:* St James (Montreal).

DRURY, Rev. John Henry; Dean, since 1981, and Fellow, since 1982, King's College, Cambridge; *b* 23 May 1936; *s* of Henry and Barbara Drury; *m* 1972, (Frances) Clare Nineham, *d* of Rev. Prof. D. E. Nineham, *qv*; two *d. Educ:* Bradfield; Trinity Hall and Westcott House, Cambridge. MA (Hist. Pt 1, Cl. 1; Theol. Pt 2, Cl. 2/1). Curate, St John's Wood Church, 1963; Chaplain of Downing Coll., Cambridge, 1966; Chaplain and Fellow of Exeter Coll., Oxford, 1969; Res. Canon of Norwich Cathedral and Examining Chaplain to Bp of Norwich, 1973–79, Vice-Dean of Norwich, 1978; Fleck Resident in Religion, Bryn Mawr Coll., USA, 1978; Lectr in Religious Studies, Sussex Univ., 1979–81. Examining Chaplain to Bp of Chichester, 1980–82. Mem., Doctrine Commn for C of E, 1978–82. Jt Editor, Theology, 1976–86. *Publications:* Angels and Dirt, 1972; Luke, 1973; Tradition and Design in Luke's Gospel, 1976; The Pot and The Knife, 1979; The Parables in the Gospels, 1985; articles and reviews in Jl of Theol. Studies, Theology, Expository Times, TLS. *Recreations:* Mozart, gardening, reading. *Address:* King's College, Cambridge CB2 1ST.

DRURY, Michael; *see* Drury, V. W. M.

DRURY, Paul; *see* Drury, A. P. D.

DRURY, Prof. (Victor William) Michael, OBE 1978; FRCGP; Professor of General Practice, University of Birmingham, since 1980; President, Royal College of General

Practitioners, since 1985; *b* 5 Aug. 1926; *s* of Leslie and Beatrice Drury; *m* 1950, Joan (*née* Williamson); three *s* one *d*. *Educ:* Bromsgrove Sch.; Univ. of Birmingham (MB ChB Hons); MRCS LRCP 1949; FRCGP 1970 (MRCGP 1963). Ho. Surg., Birmingham Gen., 1949–50; RSO, Kidderminster, 1950–51; Major, RAMC, 1951–53; Principal in Gen. Practice, Bromsgrove, 1953; Nuffield Trav. Fellow, 1965; Clarkson Sen. Clin. Tutor, Univ. of Birmingham, 1973–80. Lectures: James MacKenzie, 1983, Eli Lilley, 1984; Sir David Bruce, 1985; Gale, 1986. Royal College of General Practitioners: Mem. Council, 1971–85 (Vice-Chm. 1980); Chm., Practice Org., 1966–71, Cttee and Res. Div., 1983–85. Member: Cttee on Safety of Medicines (Adverse Drug Reaction), 1975–79; Prescription Pricing Authy, 1981–86; DHA, 1981–85; Res. Cttee, RHA, 1982–86; Civilian Advr in Gen. Practice to Army, 1984. Mem., Ct of Liverpool Univ., 1980–; Mem., GMC, 1984–. *Publications:* Introduction to General Practice, 1974; Treatment, 1978; Medical Secretaries Handbook, 5th edn 1986; various chapters in books on Drug Safety, Gen. Practice, etc; res. articles in Lancet, BMJ, Brit. Jl of Surgery, Jl RCGP. *Recreations:* gardening, reading, bridge, talking and listening. *Address:* Rossall Cottage, Church Hill, Belbroughton, near Stourbridge DY9 0DT. *T:* Belbroughton 730224.

DRYDEN, Sir John (Stephen Gyles), 8th and 11th Bt *cr* 1795 and 1733; *b* 26 Sept. 1943; *s* of Sir Noel Percy Hugh Dryden, 7th and 10th Bt, and of Rosamund Mary, *e d* of late Stephen Scrope; *S* father, 1970; *m* 1970, Diana Constance, *o d* of Cyril Tomlinson, Highland Park, Wellington, NZ; one *s* one *d*. *Educ:* Oratory School. *Heir: s* John Frederick Simon Dryden, *b* 26 May 1976. *Address:* Spinners, Fairwarp, Uckfield, Sussex.

DRYSDALE WILSON, John Veitch, CEng, FIMechE, FInstPet; Deputy Secretary, Institution of Mechanical Engineers, since 1979; *b* 8 April 1929; *s* of Alexander Drysdale Wilson and Winifred Rose (*née* Frazier); *m* 1954, Joan Lily, *e d* of Mr and Mrs John Cooke, Guildford; one *s* one *d*. *Educ:* Solihull School; Guildford Technical Coll. Dennis Bros Ltd, Guildford: Engineer Apprentice, 1946–50; MIRA Research Trainee, 1949–50; Jun. Designer, 1950–51. National Service Officer, REME, 1951–53, Captain on Staff of CREME, 6th Armd Div. Management Trainee, BET Fedn, 1953–55; Technical Sales Engr, subseq. Head of Mechanical Laboratories, Esso Petroleum Co. Ltd, 1955–66; Chief Engr, R&D, Castrol Ltd, subseq. Burmah Oil Trading Ltd and Edwin Cooper Ltd, 1966–77; Projects and Res. Officer, Instn of Mechanical Engineers, 1977–79. Dir, Mechanical Engineering Publications Ltd, 1979–. Freeman, Worshipful Co. of Engrs, 1986. ACIArb; MInstE; MSAE; MBIM. *Publications:* numerous papers to learned societies in USA and Europe on subjects related to engine lubrication. *Recreations:* travel, gardening, horology. *Address:* Institution of Mechanical Engineers, 1 Birdcage Walk, SW1. *T:* 01–222 7899. *Club:* East India.

DUBLIN, Archbishop of, and Primate of Ireland, since 1985; **Most Rev. Donald Arthur Richard Caird;** *b* Dublin, 11 Dec. 1925; *s* of George Robert Caird and Emily Florence Dreaper, Dublin; *m* 1963, Nancy Ballantyne, *d* of Prof. William Sharpe, MD, and Gwendolyn Hind, New York, USA; one *s* two *d*. *Educ:* Wesley Coll., Dublin, 1935–44; Trinity Coll., Dublin Univ., 1944–50. Sen. Exhibn, TCD, 1946; elected Schol. of the House, TCD, 1948; 1st cl. Moderatorship in Mental and Moral Science, 1949; Prizeman in Hebrew and Irish Language, 1946 and 1947; Lilian Mary Luce Memorial Prize for Philosophy, 1947; BA 1949; MA and BD 1955; HDipEd 1959. Curate Asst, St Mark's. Dundela, Belfast, 1950–53; Chaplain and Asst Master, Portora Royal Sch., Enniskillen, 1953–57; Lectr in Philosophy, University Coll. of St. David's, Lampeter, 1957; Rector, Rathmichael Parish, Shankill, Co. Dublin, 1960–69; Asst Master, St Columba's Coll., Rathfarnham, Co. Dublin, 1960–67; Dept Lectr in Philosophy, Trinity Coll., Dublin, 1962–63; Lectr in the Philosophy of Religion, Church of Ireland Theol Coll., Dublin, 1964–70; Dean of Ossory, 1969–70; Bishop of Limerick, Ardfert and Aghadoe, 1970–76; Bishop of Meath and Kildare, 1976–85. Fellow of St Columba's Coll., Dublin, 1971. Mem., Bord na Gaeilge, 1974. *Publications:* The Predicament of Natural Theology since the Criticism of Kant, in Directions, 1970 (Dublin). *Recreations:* swimming, tennis. *Address:* The See House, 17 Temple Road, Milltown, Dublin 6.

DUBLIN, Archbishop of, and Primate of Ireland, (RC), since 1984; **Most Rev. Kevin McNamara,** DD; *b* 10 June 1926; *s* of Patrick and Eileen McNamara. *Educ:* St Flannan's Coll., Ennis; St Patrick's Coll., Maynooth (BA, DD); Univ. of Munich; BA NUI. Prof. of Dogmatic Theology 1954–76, Vice-Pres. 1968–76, St Patrick's Coll., Maynooth; Bishop of Kerry, 1976–84. Mem., Internat. Dialogue Commn, Roman Catholics/Disciples of Christ; Chm., Episcopal Commn for Doctrine of Irish Bishops' Conf.; Consultor, Pontifical Council for the Family. Chairman: Bd of Govs and Trustees, St Vincent's Hosp., Fairview; Cttee of Management, Our Lady's Hosp. for Sick Chidren, Crumlin; Nat. Maternity Hosp., Holles Street; Bd of Management, Mater Hosp.; Mem. Cttee of Management, Jervis St Hosp. *Publications:* (ed and contrib.) Mother of the Redeemer, 1959; (ed and contrib.) Christian Unity, 1962; (jtly) Truth and Life, 1968; (ed. and jt author) Vatican II: Constitution on the Church—A Theological and Pastoral Commentary, 1968; Sacrament of Salvation—Studies in the Mystery of Christ and the Church, 1977; regular contribs to Irish Theolog. Quarterly, Irish Eccles. Record, The Furrow, etc; popular series of booklets on religious subjects. *Recreations:* reading and walking. *Address:* Archbishop's House, Drumcondra, Dublin 9. *T:* 37 37 32.

DUBLIN, Auxiliary Bishop of, (RC); *see* Dunne, Most Rev. Patrick.

DUBLIN, (Christ Church), Dean of; *see* Salmon, Very Rev. T. N. D. C.

DUBLIN, (St Patrick's), Dean of; *see* Griffin, Very Rev. V. G. B.

du BOULAY; *see* Houssemayne du Boulay.

DU BOULAY, Prof. Francis Robin Houssemayne, FBA 1980; Emeritus Professor of Mediæval History in the University of London, 1982; *b* 19 Dec. 1920; *er s* of late Philip Houssemayne Du Boulay and Mercy Tyrrell (*née* Friend); *m* 1948, Cecilia Burnell Matthews; two *s* one *d*. *Educ:* Christ's Hospital; Phillip's Academy, Andover, Mass., USA; Balliol Coll., Oxford. Williams Exhibitioner at Balliol Coll., 1939; Friends' Ambulance Unit and subsequently Royal Artillery, 1940–45; MA 1947; Asst lecturer at Bedford Coll., 1947, Lecturer, 1949; Reader in Mediæval History, in University of London, 1955, Prof., 1960–82. Hon. Sec., RHistS, 1961–65. *Publications:* The Register of Archbishop Bourgchier, 2 vols, 1953–55; Medieval Bexley, 1961; Documents Illustrative of Medieval Kentish Society, 1964; The Lordship of Canterbury, 1966; An Age of Ambition, 1970; (ed jtly) The Reign of Richard II, 1972; Germany in the later Middle Ages, 1983; Legion, and other poems, 1983; various essays and papers on late medieval subjects, English and German, in specialist journals and general symposia. *Address:* Broadmead, Riverhead, Sevenoaks, Kent TN13 3DE.

DUBOWITZ, Prof. Victor, MD, PhD; FRCP; Professor of Paediatrics, University of London, at the Royal Postgraduate Medical School, since 1972; Consultant Paediatrician, Hammersmith Hospital, since 1972; Co-Director, Jerry Lewis Muscle Research Centre, Royal Postgraduate Medical School, since 1975; *b* 6 Aug. 1931; *s* of late Charley and Olga Dubowitz (*née* Schattel); *m* 1960, Dr Lilly Magdalena Suzanne Sebok; four *s*. *Educ:* Beaufort West Central High Sch., S Africa; Univ. of Cape Town (BSc, MB, ChB, 1954; MD 1960). PhD Sheffield, 1965; DCH 1958; FRCP 1972. Intern, Groote Schuur Hosp., Cape Town, 1955; Sen. House Officer, Queen Mary's Hosp. for Children, Carshalton, 1957–59; Res. Associate in Histochem., Royal Postgrad. Med. Sch., 1958–59; Lectr in Clin. Path., National Hosp. for Nervous Diseases, Queen Square, London, 1960; Lectr in Child Health, 1961–65, Sen. Lectr, 1965–67, and Reader, 1967–72, Univ. of Sheffield; Res. Associate, Inst. for Muscle Diseases, and Asst Paediatrician, Cornell Med. Coll., New York, 1965–66. Several lectureships and overseas vis. professorships. Comdr, Order of Constantine the Great, 1980. Arvo Ylppö Gold Medal, Finland, 1982; Baron ver Heyden de Lancey Prize, Med. Art Soc., 1980 and 1982. *Publications:* Developing and Diseased Muscle: a histochemical study, 1968; The Floppy Infant, 1969, 2nd edn 1980; (with M. H. Brooke) Muscle Biopsy: a modern approach, 1973, 2nd edn 1985; (with L. M. S. Dubowitz) Gestational Age of the Newborn: a clinical manual, 1977; Muscle Disorders in Childhood, 1978; (with L. M. S. Dubowitz) The Neurological Assessment of the Preterm and Full-term Newborn Infant, 1981; chapters in books and articles in learned jls on paediatric topics, partic. muscle disorders and newborn neurology. *Recreation:* sculpting. *Address:* 25 Middleton Road, Golders Green, NW11 7NR. *T:* 01–455 9352.

DuBRIDGE, Lee A(lvin); *b* 21 Sept. 1901; *s* of Frederick A. and Elizabeth Browne DuBridge; *m* 1st, 1925, Doris May Koht (*d* 1973); one *s* one *d*; 2nd, 1974, Arrola B. Cole. *Educ:* Cornell Coll., Mt Vernon, Ia (BA); University of Wisconsin (MA, PhD). Instructor in Physics, University of Wisconsin, 1925–26; Nat. Research Council Fellow at Calif. Inst. Tech., 1926–28; Asst Prof. Physics, Washington Univ. (St Louis, Mo.), 1928–33; Assoc. Prof., Washington Univ., 1933–34; Prof. of Physics and Dep. Chm., University of Rochester (NY), 1934–46; Dean of Faculty, University of Rochester, 1938–42; on leave from University of Rochester, 1940–45, as Dir of Radiation Lab. of Nat. Def. Research Comm. at MIT, Cambridge; Pres., California Inst. of Techn., Pasadena, 1946–69, Pres. Emeritus, 1969–; Science Adviser to President of USA, 1969–70. Hon. ScD: Cornell Coll.; Mt Vernon, Iowa, 1940; Weslyan Univ., Middletown, Conn., 1946; Polytechnic Inst. of Brooklyn, New York, 1946; University of Brit. Columbia, Can., 1947; Washington Univ., St Louis, Mo, 1948; Occidental Coll., 1952; Maryland, 1955; Columbia, 1957; Indiana, 1957; Wisconsin, 1957; Pennsylvania Mil. Coll., Chester, Pa, 1962; DePauw, Indiana, 1962; Pomona Coll., Claremont, Calif., 1965; Carnegie Inst. of Techn., Pittsburgh, 1965; Hon. LLD: California, 1948; Rochester, 1953; Southern California, 1957; Northwestern, 1958; Loyola, Los Angeles, 1963; Notre Dame, Indiana, 1967; Illinois Inst. Technology, 1968; Hon. LHD: University Judaism, Los Angeles, 1958; Redlands, 1958; Hon. DCL, Union Coll., Schenectady, NY, 1961; Hon. DSc: Rockefeller Institute, NY, 1965; Tufts Univ., 1969; Syracuse Univ., 1969; Rensselaer Polytech. Inst., 1970. King's Medal, 1946; Research Corp. Award, 1947; Medal for Merit of US Govt, 1948, Golden Key Award, 1959; Leif Erikson Award, 1959; Arthur Noble Award, 1961; Golden Plate Award, 1973; Vannevar Bush Award, 1982. *Publications:* Photoelectric Phenomena (with A. L. Hughes), 1932; New Theories of Photoelectric Effect (Paris), 1934; Introduction to Space, 1960; articles in various scientific and other journals. *Address:* 1730 Homet Road, Pasadena, Calif 91106, USA. *T:* 818 793–1683. *Clubs:* Sunset (Los Angeles); Bohemian (San Francisco).

DUBS, Alfred; MP (Lab) Battersea, since 1983 (Wandsworth, Battersea South, 1979–83); *b* Prague, Czechoslovakia, Dec. 1932; *m*; one *s* one *d*. *Educ:* LSE. BSc (Econs). Local govt officer. Mem., Westminster CC, 1971–78; Chm., Westminster Community Relns Council, 1972–77; Mem., Kensington, Chelsea and Westminster AHA, 1975–78. Member: NALGO; GMWU; Co-operative Party. Contested (Lab) Cities of London and Westminster, 1970, Hertfordshire South, Feb. and Oct. 1974; Mem., Home Affairs Select Cttee, 1981–83 (Mem., Race Relations and Immigration Sub-Cttee, 1981–83); opposition front bench spokesman on home affairs, 1983–. *Recreation:* walking in the Lake District. *Address:* House of Commons, SW1.

DU CANE, John Peter, OBE 1964; Director: Amax Inc., since 1966; Ultramar Plc, since 1983; *b* 16 April 1921; *s* of Charles and Mathilde Du Cane; *m* 1945, Patricia Wallace (*née* Desmond); two *s*. *Educ:* Canford Sch., Wimborne. Pilot, Fleet Air Arm, RN, 1941–46. De Beers Consolidated Mines, 1946–54; Sierra Leone Selection Trust, 1955–63; Director: Consolidated African Selection Trust, 1963–81; Selection Trust Ltd, 1966–81 (Man. Dir, 1975–80; Chm., 1978–81); BP International Ltd, 1981; Chief Exec., BP Minerals Internat. Ltd, 1980–81; Director: Australian Consolidated Minerals Pty, 1981–85 (Dep. Chm., 1983–85); Austamax Resources Ltd, 1984–85 (Dep. Chm., 1984–85). FRSA. *Recreations:* sailing, fishing. *Address:* 20 Jameson Street, W8 7SH.

du CANN, Col Rt. Hon. Sir Edward (Dillon Lott), KBE 1985; PC 1964; MP (C) Taunton Division of Somerset since Feb. 1956; Chairman, Lonrho Plc, since 1984 (Director, since 1972; Joint Deputy Chairman, 1983–84); *b* 28 May 1924; *er s* of late C. G. L. du Cann, Barrister-at-Law, and Janet (*née* Murchie); *m* 1962, Sallie Innes, *e d* of late James Henry Murchie, Caldy, Cheshire; one *s* two *d*. *Educ:* Colet Court; Woodbridge Sch.; St John's Coll., Oxford (MA, Law). Served with RNVR, 1943–46. Contested West Walthamstow Div., Gen. Election, 1951; Contested Barrow-in-Furness Div., Gen. Election, 1955. Vice-Pres., Somerset and Wilts Trustee Savings Bank, 1956–75; Founder, Unicorn Group of Unit Trusts, 1957; Chairman: Barclays Unicorn Ltd and associated cos, 1957–72; Keyser Ullman Holdings Ltd, 1970–75; Cannon Assurance Ltd, 1972–80. Chm., Association of Unit Trust Managers, 1961. Mem., Lord Chancellor's Adv. Cttee on Public Records, 1960–62; Joint Hon. Sec.: UN Parly Group, 1961–62; Conservative Parly Finance Group, 1961–62; Mem., Select Cttee on House of Lords Reform, 1962; Economic Sec. to the Treasury, 1962–63; Minister of State, Board of Trade, 1963–64; Founder Chairman: Select Cttee on Public Expenditure, 1971–73; All-Party Maritime Affairs Parly Gp, 1984–; Mem., Select Cttee on Privilege, 1972–; Chairman: Select Cttee on Public Accounts, 1974–79; 1922 Cttee, 1972–84; Liaison Cttee of Select Cttee Chairmen, 1974–83; (founder) Select Cttee on Treasury and Civil Service Affairs, 1979–83; (first) Public Accounts Commn, 1984–; Cons. Party Organisation, 1965–67; Burke Club, 1968–79. President: (founder) Anglo-Polish Cons. Soc., 1972–74; Nat. Union of Conservative and Unionist Assocs, 1981–82; Vice-Chm., British American Parly Gp, 1978–81. Jt Leader, British-American Parly Gp delegns to USA, 1978, 1980; Leader, Jt British Parly Gp delegn to China, IPU, 1982. Dir, James Beattie Ltd, 1965–79; Vice-Pres., British Insurance Brokers Assoc., 1978–; Patron, Assoc. of Insurance Brokers, 1974–77. Visiting Fellow, Univ. of Lancaster Business School, 1970–82. Mem., Panel of Judges, Templeton Foundn, 1984–. Commodore, 1962, Admiral, 1974, House of Commons Yacht Club. Hon. Col, 155 (Wessex) Regt, RCT (Volunteers), 1972–82, Hon. Life Mem., Instn of RCT, 1983. Lecturer, broadcaster. Elected first Freeman of Taunton Deane Borough, 1977. *Publications:* Investing Simplified, 1959; articles on financial and international affairs (incl. The Case for a Bill of Rights, How to Bring Government Expenditure within Parliamentary Control, A New Competition Policy, etc). *Recreations:* travel, gardening, sailing. *Address:* 9 Tufton Court, Tufton Street, SW1. *T:* 01–222 1922; Cothay Barton, Greenham, Wellington, Somerset. *Clubs:* Carlton, Pratt's; Royal Thames Yacht.

See also R. D. L. Du Cann.

Du CANN, Richard Dillon Lott, QC 1975; a Recorder of the Crown Court, since 1982; *b* 27 Jan. 1929; *yr s* of late C. G. L. Du Cann; *m* 1955, Charlotte Mary Sawtell; two *s* two *d. Educ:* Steyning Grammar Sch.; Clare Coll., Cambridge. Called to Bar, Gray's Inn, 1953; Bencher, 1980; Treasury Counsel, Inner London QS, 1966–70; Treasury Counsel, Central Criminal Court, 1970–75. Chairman: Criminal Bar Assoc., 1977–80; Bar of England and Wales, 1980–81. *Publications:* (with B. Hayhoe) The Young Marrieds, 1954; The Art of the Advocate, 1964. *Address:* 29 Newton Road, W2 5AF. *T:* 01–229 3859.

See also Col Rt Hon. Sir E. D. L. du Cann.

DUCAT, David; Chairman, The Metal Box Co. Ltd., 1967–70, retired (Managing Director 1949–66; Vice-Chairman 1952–66; Deputy Chairman 1966–67); *b* 1 June 1904; *s* of William John and Amy Ducat; *m* 1933, Hilary Mildred Stokes; three *s* one *d. Educ:* Merchant Taylors' Sch.; Gonville and Caius Coll., Cambridge (MA). ACIS 1935. Min. of Production, 1942–45. British Tin Box Manufacturers Fedn: Chm., 1952–61; Vice-Chm., 1961–69. Mem. Court of Assts, Merchant Taylors' Co., 1956– (Master, 1964). Vice-Pres., British Inst. of Management (Council Chm., 1966–68); Mem. Coun., City University, 1966–71. FCIS 1967. *Address:* Morar, 16 Sandy Lodge Road, Moor Park, Rickmansworth, Herts. *T:* Rickmansworth 773562.

DUCAT-AMOS, Air Comdt Barbara Mary, CB 1974; RRC 1971; Matron-in-Chief, Princess Mary's Royal Air Force Nursing Service, 1972–78, and Director of Royal Air Force Nursing Service, 1976–78; Nursing Sister, Medical Department, Cable and Wireless plc, 1978–85; *b* 9 Feb. 1921; *d* of late Captain G. W. Ducat-Amos, Master Mariner, and late Mrs M. Ducat-Amos. *Educ:* The Abbey Sch., Reading; St Thomas's Hosp., London (The Nightingale Trng Sch.). SRN 1943; CMB Pt 1 1948. PMRAFNS, 1944–47: served in RAF Hosps, UK and Aden; further training; nursing in S Africa and SW Africa, 1948–52; rejoined PMRAFNS, 1952: served in RAF Hosps as General Ward and Theatre Sister, UK, Germany, Cyprus, Aden and Changi (Singapore); Matron 1967; Sen. Matron 1968; Principal Matron 1970. QHNS 1972–78. Chm., Girls' Venture Corps, 1982–. CStJ 1975. *Recreations:* music, theatre, travel. *Address:* c/o Barclays Bank, King Street, Reading, Berks RG1 2HD. *Club:* Royal Air Force.

DUCCI, Dr Roberto, Grand Cross, Italian Order of Merit; Ambassador of Italy to the Court of St James's, 1975–80; Professor of Political Science, Rome University, since 1982; *b* 8 Feb. 1914; *s* of Gino Ducci and Virginia Boncinelli; *m* 1951, Wanda Matyjewicz; two *s. Educ:* Univ. of Rome (Dr of Law). Entered Foreign Service, 1937; served: Ottawa, 1938; Newark, NJ, 1940; Italian Delegn to Peace Conf., 1946; Warsaw, 1947; Rio de Janeiro, 1949; Italian Delegn to NATO and OEEC, 1950–55; Chm., Drafting Cttee, Rome Treaties, 1956–57; Asst Dir, General Economic Affairs, 1955–57; Ambassador to Finland, 1958–62; Head, Italian Delegn to Brussels, UK-EEC Conf., 1961–63; Dep. Dir-Gen. for Political Affairs, 1963–64; Ambassador to: Yugoslavia, 1964–67; Austria, 1967–70; Director-General for Political Affairs, 1970–75. Counsellor of State, 1980–84, Hon. Pres. Sect. Council of State, 1984. Mem. Bd, European Investment Bank, 1958–68; Chm., Press Agency Italia, 1984. *Publications:* Prima Età di Napoleone, 1933; Questa Italia, 1948; L'Europa Incompiuta, 1971; D'Annunzio Vivente, 1973; Contemporanei, 1976; L'Innocenza (poems), 1978; 24 Hours at No 4 Grosvenor Square, 1979; Il Libro di Musica (poems), 1981; I Capintesta, 1982; Candidato a Morte, 1983; numerous political essays and articles. *Recreations:* riding, collecting frail things. *Address:* Via Belsiana 35, 00187 Rome, Italy. *Club:* Circolo della Caccia (Rome).

duCHARME, Gillian Drusilla Brown; Headmistress, Benenden School, since 1985; *b* 23 Jan. 1938; *d* of Alfred Henry Brown and Alice Drusilla Grant; *m* 1969, Jean Louis duCharme (marr. diss.). *Educ:* Girton College, Cambridge. BA 1960, MA 1964. Visitors' Dept, British Council, London and Oxford, 1964–66; Chm., French Dept and Head of Upper Sch., Park Sch., Brookline, Mass, 1969–77; Dir of Admissions, Concord Acad., Concord, Mass, 1977–80; Headmistress, The Town Sch., New York City, 1980–85. *Recreations:* tennis, cross-country skiing, cycling, theatre, film, travel. *Address:* Benenden School, Benenden, Kent TN17 4AA. *T:* Benenden 240592.

DUCHÊNE, Louis-François; author; *b* 17 Feb. 1927; *s* of Louis Adrien Duchêne and Marguerite Lucienne Duchêne (*née* Lainé); *m* 1952, Anne Margaret Purves; one *d. Educ:* St Paul's Sch.; London Sch. of Economics. Leader writer, Manchester Guardian, 1949–52; Press attaché, High Authority, European Coal and Steel Community, Luxembourg, 1952–55; Correspondent of The Economist, Paris, 1956–58; Dir, Documentation Centre of Action Cttee for United States of Europe (Chm. Jean Monnet), Paris, 1958–63; Editorial writer, The Economist, London, 1963–67. Director: Internat. Inst. for Strategic Studies, 1969–74; European Res. Centre, Sussex Univ., 1974–82. *Publications:* (ed) The Endless Crisis, 1970; The Case of the Helmeted Airman, a study of W. H. Auden, 1972; New Limits on European Agriculture, 1985. *Address:* 3 Powis Villas, Brighton, East Sussex BN1 3HD. *T:* Brighton 29258.

DUCIE, 6th Earl of *cr* 1837; **Basil Howard Moreton;** Baron Ducie, 1763; Baron Moreton, 1837; *b* 15 Nov. 1917; *s* of Hon. Algernon Howard Moreton (2nd *s* of 4th Earl) (*d* 1951), and Dorothy Edith Annie, *d* of late Robert Bell; *S* uncle 1952; *m* 1950, Alison May, *d* of L. A. Bates, Pialba, Queensland; three *s* one *d. Heir: s* Lord Moreton, *qv. Address:* Tortworth House, Tortworth, Wotton-under-Edge, Glos.

DUCK, Leslie; Director, Financing of the Budget, Commission of the European Communities, Brussels, 1982–85; *b* 14 Jan. 1935; *s* of John Robert Duck and Elizabeth Duck; *m* 1st, 1961, Maureen Richmond (marr. diss. 1980); ons *s* one *d*; 2nd, 1981, Catherina von Tscharner; two step *s. Educ:* Acklam Hall Grammar Sch., Middlesbrough; Leeds Univ. National Service, 2nd Lieut Green Howards, 1955–57. Joined Civil Service (HM Customs and Excise), 1958; Principal, 1965; seconded to Secretariat, EFTA, Geneva, 1967–70; HM Treasury, 1970–72; Asst Sec., 1972; HM Customs and Excise, 1972–73; Head of Div., Taxation Directorate, Commn of Eur. Communities, Brussels, 1973–82. *Recreations:* sailing, skiing, music, reading. *Address:* chemin du Beau-Soleil 8, 1206 Geneva, Switzerland. *T:* 46.66.23.

DUCKER, Herbert Charles, BSc London; NDA; Field Officer Groundnut Research, under the Federal Ministry of Agriculture, Rhodesia and Nyasaland, now retired; *b* 13 May 1900; *s* of Charles Richard and Gertrude Louise Ducker; *m* 1925, Marjorie, *y d* of late Charles Tuckfield, AMICE; two *s* one *d. Educ:* Kingston Grammar Sch., Kingston-on-Thames; South-Eastern Agricultural Coll., Wye; Imperial Coll. of Science, South Kensington. British Cotton Industry Research Assoc. Laboratories; Asst Cotton Specialist, Nyasaland, 1922; Cotton Specialist, Empire Cotton Growing Corporation, Nyasaland, 1925–56; Superintendent-Curator of the National Botanic Gardens, Salisbury, Southern Rhodesia, under the Federal Ministry of Agriculture, of Rhodesia and Nyasaland, 1957. *Publications:* Annual Reports on Cotton Research work 1925–55, carried out in Nyasaland; articles on cotton growing. *Recreation:* fishing. *Address:* Pleasant Ways, MP 13, Mount Pleasant, Harare, Zimbabwe. *Club:* Royal Over-Seas League.

DUCKHAM, Prof. Alec Narraway, CBE 1950 (OBE 1945); Professor of Agriculture, University of Reading, 1955–69; *b* 23 Aug. 1903; *e s* of Alexander Duckham, FCS, and Violet Ethel Duckham (*née* Narraway); *m* 1932, Audrey Mary Polgreen (*d* 1969), St Germans, Cornwall; one *s* two *d. Educ:* Oundle Sch.; Clare Coll., Cambridge. MA (Hons) Cantab.: Cambridge Dip. Agric. Sci. (dist. in Animal Husbandry), 1926; FIBiol; Silver Research Medallist, Royal Agricultural Society, England, 1926. Research and Advisory work on Animal Husbandry at Cambridge, Aberdeen, Belfast, 1927–39. Chm. Home and Overseas Agric. Supplies Cttees and Dir of Supply Plans Div., Min. of Food, 1941–45. Agric. Attaché, Brit. Embassy, Washington, and Agric. Adviser to UK High Comr, Ottawa, 1945–50. Asst Sec. to Min. of Agriculture and Fisheries, 1950–54. Liaison Officer (SE Region), to the Minister of Agriculture, Fisheries and Food, 1965–70. Vice-Chm., Alex. Duckham and Co. Ltd, 1945–68. *Publications:* Animal Industry in the British Empire, 1932; American Agriculture, 1952 (HMSO); The Fabric of Farming, 1958; Agricultural Synthesis: The Farming Year, 1963; (with G. B. Masefield) Farming Systems of the World, 1970; (ed with J. G. W. Jones and E. H. Roberts) Food Production and Consumption, 1976. *Recreations:* painting and music. *Address:* Little Park House, Brimpton, Berks. *Club:* Royal Automobile.

DUCKMANTON, Sir Talbot (Sydney), Kt 1980; CBE 1971; General Manager, Australian Broadcasting Commission, 1965–82 (Deputy General Manager, 1964–65); *b* 26 Oct. 1921; *s* of Sydney James Duckmanton; *m* 1947, Florence Simmonds (decd); one *s* three *d*; *m* 1984, Carolyn, *d* of late R. Pumfrey. Joined Australian Broadcasting Commission, 1939. War Service: AIF and RAAF. President: Asia-Pacific Broadcasting Union, 1973–77; Commonwealth Broadcasting Assoc., 1975–82. *Address:* PO Box E148, St James, Sydney, NSW 2000, Australia. *Clubs:* Legacy, Australian, Tattersalls (Sydney).

DUCKWORTH, Arthur; *see* Duckworth, G. A. V.

DUCKWORTH, Brian Roy; His Honour Judge Duckworth; a Circuit Judge, since 1983; *b* 26 July 1934; *s* of Roy and Kathleen Duckworth; *m* 1964, Nancy Carolyn Holden; three *s* one *d. Educ:* Sedbergh Sch.; Worcester Coll., Oxford (MA). Called to Bar, Lincoln's Inn, 1958; a Recorder of the Crown Court, 1972–83; Member: Northern Circuit; Bar Council, 1979–82. Councillor, Blackburn RDC, 1960–74 (Chm. 1970–72). *Recreations:* golf, gardening, motor sport. *Address:* c/o The Crown Court, Lancaster Road, Preston. *T:* Preston 23431. *Clubs:* St James's (Manchester); Pleasington Golf.

DUCKWORTH, Eric; *see* Duckworth, W. E.

DUCKWORTH, (George) Arthur (Victor), JP; *b* 3 Jan. 1901; *e s* of Major A. C. Duckworth of Orchardleigh Park, Frome; *m* 1927, Alice, 3rd *d* of John Henry Hammond, New York; three *d*; *m* 1945, Elizabeth, *o d* of Alfred Ehrenfeld, Bridgeham Farm, Forest Green, Surrey; two *d*; *m* 1968, Mary, *y d* of Archdeacon Edmund Hope, and *widow* of Captain K. Buxton. *Educ:* Eton; Trinity Coll., Cambridge (BA). MP (C) Shrewsbury Div. of Salop, 1929–45; Parliamentary Private Sec. to Rt Hon. Sir Geoffrey Shakespeare, 1932–39. Served War of 1939–45, 36th (Middlesex) AA Bn RA, 1939–41. CC Somerset, 1949–64; JP Somerset, 1957. *Address:* Orchardleigh Park, Frome, Somerset BA11 2PH. *T:* Frome 830306. *Clubs:* Travellers', Garrick.

DUCKWORTH, John Clifford; FEng 1975; FIEE, FInstP, FInstE; Chairman: Lintott Control Equipment Ltd, since 1980; BVT Ltd, since 1983; Focom Ltd, since 1983; *b* 27 Dec. 1916; *s* of late H. Duckworth, Wimbledon, and of Mrs A. H. Duckworth (*née* Woods); *m* 1942, Dorothy Nancy Wills; three *s. Educ:* KCS, Wimbledon; Wadham Coll., Oxford (MA). FIEE 1957; FInstP 1957; SFInstE 1957. Telecommunications Research Establishment, Malvern: Radar Research and Development, 1939–46; National Research Council, Chalk River, Ont., 1946–47; Atomic Energy Research Establishment, Harwell, 1947–50; Ferranti Ltd: Chief Engineer, Wythenshawe Laboratories, 1950–54; Nuclear Power Engineer, Brit. Electricity Authority, 1954–58; Central Electricity Authority, 1957–58; Chief Research and Development Officer, Central Electricity Generating Board, 1958–59; Man. Dir., Nat. Research Devel Corp., 1959–70. Pres., Institute of Fuel, 1963–64; Vice-Pres., Parliamentary and Scientific Cttee, 1964–67. Chm., Science Mus. Adv. Council, 1972–84; Trustee, Science Mus., 1984–. Vice-Pres., IEE, 1974–77. Dir, Rank Organisation, 1980–. *Recreations:* swimming, colour photography, cartography. *Address:* Suite 33, 140 Park Lane, W1. *Club:* Athenæum.

DUCKWORTH, Major Sir Richard Dyce, 3rd Bt, *cr* 1909; *b* 30 Sept. 1918; *s* of Sir Edward Dyce Duckworth, 2nd Bt, and Cecil Gertrude, *y d* of Robert E. Leman; *S* father, 1945; *m* 1942, Violet Alison, *d* of Lieut-Col G. B. Wauchope, DSO; two *s. Educ:* Marlborough Coll. Started business in 1937, retired 1969. *Recreations:* sailing, golf, squash, shooting. *Heir: s* Edward Richard Dyce Duckworth [*b* 13 July 1943; *m* 1976, Patricia, *o d* of Thomas Cahill]. *Address:* Dunwood Cottage, Shootash, Romsey, Hants. *T:* Romsey 513228.

DUCKWORTH, Prof. Roy, MD; FRCS, FDSRCS, FRCPath; Professor of Oral Medicine, University of London, since 1968; Head, Department of Oral Medicine, since 1968, and Dean, from Oct. 1986, The London Hospital Medical College; Consultant in Oral Medicine to The London Hospital, since 1965; *b* Bolton, 19 July 1929; *s* of Stanley Duckworth and Hilda Evelyn Moores; *m* 1953, Marjorie Jean Bowness, Flimby; two *s* one *d. Educ:* King George V Sch., Southport; Univ. of Liverpool (BDS; MD 1964); Univ. of London. FDSRCS 1957; FRCPath 1973. Served RAF Dental Br., 1953–55. Nuffield Fellow, RPMS and Guy's Hosp. Dental Sch., 1959–61; The London Hosp. Med. College: Sen. Lectr in Oral Medicine, 1961; Reader in Oral Medicine, 1965; Dean of Dental Studies, 1969–75. Dean, Faculty of Dental Surgery, RCS, 1983–86. Civil Consultant: in Dental Surg., to Army, 1977–; in Oral Medicine and Oral Path., to RN, 1982–; Temp. Consultant, WHO, 1973–; British Council Visitor, 1977–. Vis. Prof. in many countries. Pres., Soc. of Periodontology, 1972–73; Pres., British Soc. for Oral Medicine, 1986–87. Member: Adv. Council on Misuse of Drugs, 1977–85; Medicines Commn, 1980–83; Council, Fédération Dentaire Internationale, 1981–; GDC, 1984–; Standing Dental Adv. Cttee, DHSS, 1984–. Scientific Adviser, British Dental Jl, 1975–82; Editor, Internat. Dental Jl, 1981–. *Publications:* contrib. professional jls. *Recreation:* sailing. *Address:* Department of Oral Medicine, The London Hospital Medical College, Turner Street, E1 2AD. *T:* 01-377 7065.

DUCKWORTH, (Walter) Eric, PhD; FEng, FIM, FInstP, FIS; Managing Director, Fulmer Research Institute, since 1969; *b* 2 Aug. 1925; *s* of Albert Duckworth and Rosamund (*née* Biddle); *m* 1949, Emma Evans; one *s. Educ:* Cambridge Univ. (MA, PhD). Research Manager, Glacier Metal Co., 1955; Asst Director, BISRA, 1966; Chm., Yarsley Technical Centre, 1973–; Director: Ricardo Consulting Engineers plc, 1978–85; H. Darnell Ltd, 1982–; Fleming Technol. Investment Trust plc, 1984–. Chm., Council of Science and Technology Insts, 1977–78; first Charter Pres., Instn of Metallurgists, 1974–75; Pres., Assoc. of Contract Res. Organisations, 1978–79; Hon. Treas., Metals Soc., 1981–84; Chm., Professional Affairs Bd, Inst. of Metals, 1985–. Member: Res. and Technol. Cttee, 1979–, and Indust. Policy Cttee, 1983–, CBI; Engrg Council Nominations Cttee, 1983–85; Engrg Bd, SERC, 1985–. Chm., Christian Nationals Evangelism Commn, 1974–; Trustee, Comino Foundn, 1981–; Vice-Pres., St Mary's Hosp. Med. Sch., 1976–; Mem. Court, Brunel Univ., 1978–85. Liveryman: Worshipful Co. of Scientific Instrument Makers; Co. of Engineers; Freeman, City of London. First Edwin Liddiard Meml Lectr, London Metallurgical Soc. of Inst. of Metals, 1982. Hon. DTech Brunel, 1976; DUniv Surrey, 1980. Editor, Materials and Design, 1978–. *Publications:* A Guide to Operational Research, 1962, 3rd edn 1977; Statistical Techniques in Technological Research, 1968;

Electroslag Refining, 1969; Manganese in Ferrous Metallurgy, 1976; circa 100 contribs to learned and other jls on many topics. *Recreations*: gardening, photography, changing other people's attitudes. *Address*: Orinda, Church Lane, Stoke Poges, Bucks SL2 4NZ. *T*: Fulmer 2181.

du CROS, Sir Claude Philip Arthur Mallet, 3rd Bt *cr* 1916; *b* 22 Dec. 1922; *s* of Sir (Harvey) Philip du Cros, 2nd Bt, and of Dita, *d* of late Sir Claude Coventry Mallet, CMG; *S* father, 1975; *m* 1st, 1953, Mrs Christine Nancy Tordoff (marr. diss. 1974), *d* of late F. R. Bennett, Spilsby, Lincs; one *s*; 2nd, Mrs Margaret Roy Cutler (marr. diss. 1982), *d* of late R. J. Frater, Gosforth, Northumberland. *Heir*: *s* Julian Claude Arthur Mallet du Cros [*b* 23 April 1955; *m* 1984, Patricia, *o d* of Gerald Wyatt, Littlefield School, Liphook]. *Address*: Long Meadow, Ballaugh Glen, IoM.

DUDBRIDGE, Bryan James, CMG 1961; retired from HM Overseas Civil Service, Nov. 1961; Deputy Director, formerly Associate Director, British Council of Churches Department of Christian Aid, 1963–72; *b* 2 April 1912; *o s* of late W. Dudbridge, OBE, and of Anne Jane Dudbridge; *m* 1943, Audrey Mary, *o d* of late Dr and Mrs Heywood, Newbury; two *s* one *d*. *Educ*: King's Coll. Sch., Wimbledon; Selwyn Coll., Cambridge. Appointed to Colonial Administrative Service as Cadet in Tanganyika, 1935; Asst Dist Officer, 1937; Dist Officer, 1947; Sen. Dist Officer, 1953; Actg Provincial Commr, Southern Province; Administrative Officer (Class IIA), 1955, and Actg Provincial Commissioner (Local Government); Provincial Commissioner, Western Province, 1957; Minister for Provincial Affairs, 1959–60, retd. *Publications*: contrib. Journal of African Administration, and Tanganyika Notes and Records. *Recreations*: natural history, wildfowl. *Address*: Red Rock Bungalow, Elm Grove Road, Topsham, Exeter EX3 0EJ. *T*: Topsham 4468. *Club*: Royal Commonwealth Society.

DUDBRIDGE, Prof. Glen, PhD; FBA 1984; Professor of Chinese, and Fellow of Magdalene College, University of Cambridge, since 1985; *b* 2 July 1938; *s* of George Victor Dudbridge and Edna Kathleen Dudbridge (*née* Cockle); *m* 1965, Sylvia Lo (Lo Fung-young); one *s* one *d*. *Educ*: Bristol Grammar School; Magdalene College, Cambridge (MA, PhD); New Asia Institute of Advanced Chinese Studies, Hong Kong. MA Oxon. Research Fellow, Magdalene College, Cambridge, 1965; Lectr in Modern Chinese, 1965–85 and Fellow, Wolfson Coll., 1966–85, Univ. of Oxford. Visiting Professor: Yale Univ., 1972–73; Univ. of California, Berkeley, 1980. *Publications*: The Hsi-yu chi: a study of antecedents to the sixteenth century Chinese novel, 1970; The Legend of Miao-shan, 1978; The Tale of Li Wa: study and critical edition of a Chinese story from the ninth century, 1983; contribs to Asia Major, Harvard Jl of Asiatic Studies, New Asia Jl. *Address*: Magdalene College, Cambridge CB3 0AG.

DUDGEON, Alastair; *see* Dudgeon, J. A.

DUDGEON, Air Vice-Marshal Antony Greville, CBE 1955; DFC 1941; *b* 6 Feb. 1916; *s* of late Prof. Herbert William Dudgeon, Guy's Hosp. and Egyptian Government Service; *m* 1942, Phyllis Margaret, *d* of late Group Capt. John McFarlane, OBE, MC, AFC, Lowestoft, Suffolk; one *s* one *d*. *Educ*: Eton; RAF Cranwell; Staff Coll., Flying Coll.; Polytechnic London. RAF Service, 1933–68, in UK, Europe, Near, Middle and Far East, USA; personnel work, training, operations, flight safety, organisation of new formations, liaison with civilian firms and youth organisations; NATO Staff; 6 command appointments; 3,500 hours as pilot. Manager, Professional Staff Services, McKinsey & Co., Paris, 1968–78; representative, France, Grangersol Ltd, 1978–81. *Publications*: A Flying Command (under pen-name Tom Dagger), 1962; The Luck of the Devil, 1985 (autobiog. 1934–41); several stories contributed to Blackwood's Magazine and to The Aeroplane Monthly. *Recreations*: writing, photography, swimming; languages (French, Egyptian). *Address*: 43 Winchendon Road, SW6 5DH. *Club*: Royal Air Force.

DUDGEON, Prof. (John) Alastair, CBE 1977; MC 1942 and Bar 1943; TD 1947; DL; Consultant Microbiologist, Hospital for Sick Children, Great Ormond Street, 1960–81, Honorary Consulting Microbiologist, 1982; Professor of Microbiology, Institute of Child Health, University of London, 1972–81, Emeritus Professor 1982; *b* 9 Nov. 1916; *yr s* of late Prof. L. S. Dudgeon; *m* 1st, 1945, Patricia Joan Ashton (*d* 1969); two *s*; 2nd, 1974, Joyce Kathleen Tibbetts. *Educ*: Repton Sch.; Trinity Coll., Cambridge; St Thomas's Hosp., London. MB, BCh 1944; MA, MD Cantab 1947; FRCPath 1967; MRCP 1970; FRCP 1974. Served in London Rifle Bde and 7th Bn Rifle Bde, 1936–43; transf. to RAMC, 1944; Specialist in Pathology RAMC, 1945; served TA and TAVR, 1947–58; Col RAMC (TA), retd. Asst Pathologist, St Thomas's Hosp., 1947; Asst Pathologist, 1948, Hon. Consultant Virologist, 1953, Hosp. for Sick Children, Gt Ormond St; Sen. Lectr, St George's Hosp. Med. Sch., 1953; Head of Virus Research, Glaxo Labs, 1958. Mem. Cttee of Management, 1966–81, Dean, 1974–81, Inst. of Child Health (Univ. of London); Mem. Bd of Governors, Hosp. for Sick Children, Gt Ormond St, 1962–69 and 1970–81. Hon. Consultant in Pathology to Army, 1977–81. Chm., Res. Funds Cttee, Inst. of Child Health; Mem. Council, British Heart Foundn, 1982–. Mem. Court of Assts, 1974, Sen. Warden, 1984–85, Master, 1985–86, Soc. of Apothecaries of London. DL Greater London, 1973. OStJ 1958. *Publications*: Modern Trends in Paediatrics (contrib.); Immunization Procedures for Children; Viral Infections of the Fetus and Newborn (co-author). *Recreation*: sailing. *Address*: Cherry Orchard Cottage, Bonnington, Ashford, Kent TN25 7AZ. *T*: Aldington 310. *Clubs*: Army and Navy; Aldeburgh Yacht.

DUDLEY, 4th Earl of, *cr* 1860; **William Humble David Ward**; Baron Ward, 1644; Viscount Ednam, 1860; *b* 5 Jan. 1920; *e s* of 3rd Earl of Dudley, MC, TD, and Rosemary Millicent, RRC (*d* 1930), *o d* of 4th Duke of Sutherland; *S* father, 1969; *m* 1st, 1946, Stella (marr. diss., 1961), *d* of M. A. Carcano, KCMG, KBE; one *s* twin *d*; 2nd, 1961, Maureen Swanson; one *s* five *d*. *Educ*: Eton; Christ Church, Oxford. Joined 10th Hussars, 1941, Adjt, 1944–45; ADC to Viceroy of India, 1942–43. Served War of 1939–45 (wounded). Director: Baggeridge Brick Co. Ltd; Tribune Investment Trust Ltd. *Heir*: *s* Viscount Ednam, *qv*. *Address*: 6 Cottesmore Gardens, W8; Vention House, Putsborough, N Devon. *Clubs*: White's, Pratt's; Royal Yacht Squadron.

DUDLEY, Baroness (14th in line), *cr* 1439–1440 (called out of abeyance, 1916); **Barbara Amy Felicity Hamilton**; *b* 23 April 1907; *o d* of 12th Baron Dudley and Sybil Augusta (*d* 1958), *d* of late Rev. Canon Henry William Coventry; *S* brother, 1972; *m* 1929, Guy Raymond Hill Wallace (*d* 1967), *s* of late Gen. Hill Wallace, CB, RHA; three *s* one *d*; *m* 1980, Charles Anthony Crosse Hamilton. *Recreations*: floral water-colours (has exhibited Royal Watercolour Society, Conduit St); gardening. *Heir*: *e s* Hon. Jim Anthony Hill Wallace [*b* 9 Nov. 1930; *m* 1962, Nicola Jane, *d* of Lt-Col Philip William Edward Leslie Dunsterville; two *s*]. *Address*: Hill House, Kempsey, Worcestershire. *T*: Worcester 820253.

DUDLEY, Bishop Suffragan of, since 1977; **Rt. Rev. Anthony Charles Dumper**; *b* 4 Oct. 1923; *s* of Charles Frederick and Edith Mildred Dumper; *m* 1948, Sibylle Anna Emilie Hellwig; two *s* one *d*. *Educ*: Surbiton Grammar School; Christ's Coll., Cambridge (MA); Westcott House, Cambridge. Relief Worker, Germany, 1946–47; ordained, 1947; Curate, East Greenwich, 1947–49; Vicar of South Perak, Malaya, 1949–57; Archdeacon of North Malaya, 1955–64; Vicar of Penang, Malaya, 1957–64; Dean of St Andrew's

Cathedral, Singapore, 1964–70; Vicar of St Peter's, Stockton on Tees, and Rural Dean of Stockton, 1970–77. *Publication*: Vortex of the East, 1963. *Recreations*: walking, gardening. *Address*: Bishop's House, Halesowen Road, Cradley Heath, West Midlands. *T*: 021–550 3407.

DUDLEY, Prof. Hugh Arnold Freeman, FRCSE, FRCS, FRACS; Professor of Surgery, St Mary's Hospital, London, since 1973; *b* 1 July 1925; *s* of W. L. and Ethel Dudley; *m* 1947, Jean Bruce Lindsay Johnston; two *s* one *d*. *Educ*: Heath Grammar Sch., Halifax; Edinburgh and Harvard Univs. MB, ChB Edin. 1947; ChM (Gold Medal and Chiene Medal) Edin. 1958; FRCSE 1951; FRACS 1965; FRCS 1974. Lecturer in Surgery, Edinburgh Univ., 1954–58; Sen. Lectr, Aberdeen Univ., 1958–63; Foundation Prof. of Surgery, Monash Univ., Melbourne, 1963–72. President: Surgical Res. Soc. of Australasia, 1968; Biol. Engrg Soc. of GB, 1978–80; Surgical Res. Soc. of GB, 1981–82. Chairman: Med. Writers Gp, Soc. of Authors, 1980–83; Editorial Board of Br. Jl of Surgery and of Br. Jl Surgery Soc. Ltd. *Publications*: Principles of General Surgical Management, 1958; Access and Exposure in Abdominal Surgery, 1963; (jtly) Guide to House Surgeons in the Surgical Unit, 5th edn 1974, 7th edn 1982; (ed) Rob and Smiths Operative Surgery, 1976–; Hamilton Bailey's Emergency Surgery, 1977; Communication in Medicine and Biology, 1977; (ed) Aid to Clinical Surgery, 1978, 3rd edn 1984; papers in med. jls. *Recreations*: accidentally and unintentionally annoying others; surgical history. *Address*: Academic Surgical Unit, St Mary's Hospital, W2 1NY. *T*: 01–927 1169; Broombrae, Glenbuchat, Aberdeenshire. *T*: Glenkindie 341.

DUDLEY, Prof. Norman Alfred, CBE 1977; PhD; FEng; Lucas Professor of Engineering Production, 1959–80, Emeritus Professor 1981, University of Birmingham; Head of Department of Engineering Production and Director of Lucas Institute of Engineering Production, 1956–80; Chartered Engineer; *b* 29 Feb. 1916; *s* of Alfred Dudley; *m* 1940, Hilda Florence, *d* of John Miles; one *s* two *d*. *Educ*: Kings Norton Grammar Sch.; Birmingham Coll. of Technology. BSc London, PhD Birmingham. FEng 1981. Industrial training and appts: H. W. Ward & Co. Ltd, 1932–39; Imperial Typewriter Co. Ltd, 1940–45; Technical Coll. Lectr, 1945–52; Sen. Lectr, Wolverhampton and Staffs, 1948–52; Lectr in Eng. Prod., 1952, Reader, 1956, University of Birmingham. Chm., Manufacturing Processes Div., Birmingham Univ. Inst. for Advanced Studies in Engineering Sciences, 1965–68. Director: Birmingham Productivity Services Ltd; West Midlands Low Cost Automation Centre. Member: SRC Manufacturing Technol. Cttee; SRC and DoI Teaching Company Cttee, 1977–80. Chm., Cttee of Hds of Univ. Depts of Production Studies, 1970–80. Governor: Dudley and Staffs Tech. Coll., and Walsall and Staffs Tech. Coll., 1955–60; Letchworth Coll. of Technol., 1964–66. Member: Council, West Midlands Productivity Assoc.; Council Internat. Univ. Contact for Management Education, 1957; Council, Instn of Prod. Engineers, 1959–61 (Chm., Research Cttee, 1965–66; Viscount Nuffield Meml Lectr, 1969); UK Delegn to UNCSAT Geneva, 1963; W Midlands Economic Planning Council, 1970–78; Adv. Panel on Economic Develt, West Midlands Metropolitan CC, 1976–77; Council, Nat. Materials Handling Centre. Pres., Midlands Operational Research Soc., 1966–80. Mem., Ergonomics Res. Soc.; Emeritus Mem., Internat. Inst. of Production Engrg Research. FBIM; Hon. FIProdE. Hon. Member: Japanese Industrial Management Assoc.; Internat. Foundn of Prodn Research. Hon. DTech Loughborough, 1981. Editor, International Journal of Production Research, 1961–80. J. D. Scaife Medal, 1958. *Publications*: Work Measurement: Some Research Studies, 1968; (co-ed) Production and Industrial Systems, 1978; various papers on Engineering Production. *Address*: 37 Abbots Close, Knowle, Solihull, West Midlands. *T*: Knowle 5976.

DUDLEY, William Stuart; Associate Designer of the National Theatre, since 1981; *b* 4 March 1947; *s* of William Dudley and Dorothy Stacey. *Educ*: Highbury Sch., London; St Martin's School of Art; Slade School of Art. DipAD, BA Fine Art; UCL Postgrad. Dip. Fine Art. First production, Hamlet, Nottingham Playhouse, 1970; subseq. prodns include: The Duchess of Malfi and Man is Man, Royal Court, 1971; *National Theatre*, 1971–: Tyger, 1974; The Good-Natured Man, 1974; The Passion, 1977; Lavender Blue, 1977; The World Turned Upside Down, Has Washington Legs?, 1978; Dispatches, Lost Worlds, Lark Rise, Candleford, Undiscovered Country (SWET award, Designer of the Year, 1980), 1979; Good Soldier Schweyk, 1982; Cinderella, 1983; The Mysteries, Real Inspector Hound/The Critic, 1985 (Laurence Olivier (formerly SWET) Award, Designer of the Year, 1985); Futurists, 1986; *Royal Court*: Live Like Pigs, 1972; Merry-Go-Round, 1973; Magnificence, 1975; The Fool, 1975; Small Change, 1976; Hamlet, 1980; *RSC*: Twelfth Night, 1974; Ivanov, 1976; That Good Between Us, 1977; Richard III, The Party, Today, 1984; Merry Wives of Windsor, 1985; A Midsummer Night's Dream, 1986; *West End*: Mutiny, Piccadilly, 1985; *Opera*: WNO: Il barbiere di Siviglia, 1976; Metropolitan, NY: Billy Budd, 1978; Glyndebourne: Die Entführung aus dem Serail, 1980; Il barbiere di Siviglia, 1981; Royal Opera: Les Contes d'Hoffman (sets), 1980, 1986; Don Giovanni, 1981; Bayreuth: Der Ring des Nibelungen, 1983; Des Rosenkavalier, 1984. *Recreation*: playing the concertina. *Address*: 39 Ulundi Road, SE3. *T*: 01–858 8711.

DUDLEY-SMITH, Rt. Rev. Timothy; *see* Thetford, Bishop Suffragan of.

DUDLEY-WILLIAMS, Sir Rolf (Dudley), 1st Bt, *cr* 1964; *b* 17 June 1908; *s* of Arthur Williams, Plymouth; assumed and adopted surname of Dudley-Williams, by Deed Poll, 1964; *m* 1940, Margaret Helen, *er d* of F. E. Robinson, OBE, AMIMechE; two *s*. *Educ*: Plymouth Coll.; Royal Air Force Coll., Cranwell. Gazetted, 1928, Flying Officer, 1930; Central Flying Sch., 1933, invalided from service, 1934. Founded Power Jets Ltd, 1936, to develop Whittle system of jet propulsion; Managing Dir, 1941. Mem. Council Soc. of British Aircraft Constructors, 1944; Companion Royal Aeronautical Society, 1944. Contested (C) Brierley Hill, 1950. MP (C) Exeter, 1951–66; PPS to Sec. of State for War, 1958; PPS to Minister of Agriculture, 1960–64. Chm., Western Area of National Union of Conservative Assocs, 1961–64. *Heir*: *s* Alastair Edgcumbe James Dudley-Williams [*b* 26 Nov. 1943; *m* 1972, Diana Elizabeth Jane, twin *d* of R. H. C. Duncan; three *d*]. *Address*: The Old Manse, South Petherton, Som. *T*: South Petherton 40143. *Club*: Royal Air Force.

DUDMAN, George Edward, CB 1973; *b* 2 Dec. 1916; *s* of William James Dudman and Nora Annie (*née* Curtis); *m* 1955, Joan Doris, *d* of late Frederick John Eaton; one *s* one *d*. *Educ*: Merchant Taylors' Sch., London; St John's Coll., Oxford (MA); Churchill Coll., Cambridge, 1982–84. Royal Artillery, 1940–46; Control Commn, Germany, 1946–49. Called to Bar, Middle Temple, 1950. Law Officers' Dept, 1951; Legal Sec., Law Officers' Dept, 1958; Legal Advr, DES, 1965–77; Editor, Statutes in Force, 1977–81. *Recreations*: painting, gardening, cooking, playing chess, studying philosophy. *Address*: 10 Viga Road, Grange Park, N21. *T*: 01–360 5129.

DUFF, Rt. Hon. Sir (Arthur) Antony, GCMG 1980 (KCMG 1973; CMG 1964); CVO 1972; DSO 1944; DSC; PC 1980; Deputy Secretary, Cabinet Office, since 1980; *b* 25 Feb. 1920; *s* of late Adm. Sir Arthur Allen Morison Duff, KCB; *m* 1944, Pauline Marion, *d* of Capt. R. H. Bevan, RN, and *widow* of Flt-Lieut J. A. Sword; one *s* two *d* (and one step *s*). *Educ*: RNC, Dartmouth. Served in RN, 1937–46. Mem., Foreign (subseq. Diplomatic) Service, 1946; 3rd Sec., Athens, Oct. 1946; 2nd Sec., 1948; 2nd Sec., Cairo, 1949; 1st Sec.,

1952; transferred Foreign Office, Private Sec. to Minister of State, 1952; 1st Sec., Paris, 1954; Foreign Office, 1957; Bonn, 1960; Counsellor, 1962; British Ambassador to Nepal, 1964–65; Commonwealth Office, 1965–68; FCO, 1968–69; Dep. High Comr, Kuala Lumpur, 1969–72; High Comr, Nairobi, 1972–75; Dep. Under-Sec. of State, 1975–80, Dep. to Perm. Under-Sec. of State, 1976–80, FCO. Dep. Governor, Southern Rhodesia, 1979–80. *Address:* c/o National Westminster Bank, 17 The Hard, Portsea, Hants. *Club:* Army and Navy.

DUFF, Patrick Craigmile, CMG 1982; *b* 6 Jan. 1922; *o s* of late Archibald Craigmile Duff, ICS, and Helen Marion (*née* Phillips); *m* 1st, 1947, Pamela de Villeneuve Graham (*osp*); 2nd, 1950, Elizabeth Rachel, *d* of late Rt Rev. R. P. Crabbe (Bishop of Mombasa, 1936–53) and Mrs Crabbe; two *d. Educ:* Wellington Coll., Berks; New Coll., Oxford (MA 1946). War service, 1941–42. HMOCS, 1942–63: Tanganyika; Kenya; CRO, 1964–65; ODM/ODA, 1966–74; Head, West Indian and Atlantic Dept, FCO, 1975–80; Head, British Develt for E Africa, FCO, 1980–82. *Recreations:* making music, fell walking, ball games. *Address:* 6 Christchurch Road, Winchester, Hants SO23 9SR. *T:* Winchester 65200. *Club:* Royal Commonwealth Society.

DUFF, Patrick William; Fellow of Trinity College, Cambridge; *b* 21 Feb. 1901; 3rd *s* of J. D. Duff, Fellow of Trinity College, Cambridge, and Laura, *d* of Sir William Lenox-Conyngham, KCB. *Educ:* Winchester; Trinity Coll., Cambridge; Munich Univ.; Harvard Law Sch. 1st Class, Classical Tripos Parts I and II; Craven and Whewell Scholar; Tancred Scholar of Lincoln's Inn; Fellow of Trinity, 1925; Lecturer, 1927; Tutor, 1938; Senior Tutor, 1945; Dean of Coll., 1950; Vice-Master, 1960. Regius Prof. of Civil Law, Cambridge, 1945–68. Barrister-at-Law, 1933. Cambridge Borough Councillor, 1947–51. Fellow of Winchester Coll., 1948–76; Warden, 1959–62. Pres. Soc. of Public Teachers of Law, 1957–58. Hon. Bencher of Lincoln's Inn, 1959. *Publications:* The Charitable Foundations of Byzantium (in Cambridge Legal Essays presented to Doctor Bond, Prof. Buckland and Prof. Kenny), 1926; The Personality of an Idol (in Cambridge Law Journal), 1927; Delegata Potestas Non Potest Delegari (in Cornell Law Quarterly), 1929; Personality in Roman Private Law, 1938; Roman Law Today (in Tulane Law Review), 1947. *Recreation:* scouting. *Address:* Trinity College, Cambridge.

DUFF, Col Thomas Robert G.; *see* Gordon-Duff.

DUFF GORDON, Sir Andrew (Cosmo Lewis), 8th Bt, *cr* 1813; *b* 17 Oct. 1933; *o s* of Sir Douglas Duff Gordon, 7th Bt and Gladys Rosemary (*d* 1933), *e d* of late Col Vivien Henry, CB; *S* father, 1964; *m* 1st, 1967, Grania Mary (marr. diss. 1975), *d* of Fitzgerald Villiers-Stuart, Ireland; one *s*; 2nd, 1975, Eveline Virginia, BA, *d* of S. Soames, Newbury; three *s. Educ:* Repton. Served with Worcs Regiment and 1st Bn Ches Regt, 1952–54. Mem. of Lloyd's, 1962–. *Recreations:* golf, shooting, skiing. *Heir: s* Cosmo Henry Villiers Duff Gordon, *b* 18 June 1968. *Address:* Downton House, Walton, Presteigne, Powys. *T:* New Radnor 223; 27 Cathcart Road, SW10. *Clubs:* City University; Kington Golf; Sunningdale Golf.

DUFFERIN AND AVA, 5th Marquess of, *cr* 1888; **Sheridan Frederick Terence Hamilton-Temple-Blackwood;** Baron Dufferin and Clandeboye, Ireland, 1800; Baron Clandeboye, UK, 1850; Earl of Dufferin, Viscount Clandeboye, 1871; Earl of Ava, 1888, and a Bt; *b* 9 July 1938; *o s* of 4th Marquess (killed in action, 1945) and Maureen (she *m* 1948, Major Desmond Buchanan, MC, from whom she obtained a divorce, 1954; *m* 1955, John Cyril Maude, QC), 2nd *d* of late Hon. (Arthur) Ernest Guinness; *S* father, 1945; *m* 1964, Serena Belinda Rosemary, *d* of Group Capt. (Thomas) Loel Evelyn Bulkeley Guinness, *qv. Educ:* Eton Coll.; Christ Church, Oxford. Trustee: Wallace Collection, 1973–; Nat. Gall., 1981–. Dir, Arthur Guinness PLC, 1979–. *Address:* 4 Holland Villas Road, W14. *T:* 01–603 8910; Clandeboye, Co. Down, Northern Ireland.

DUFFUS, Sir Herbert (George Holwell), Kt 1966; *b* 30 Aug. 1908; *e s* of William Alexander Duffus, JP, and Emily Henrietta Mary (*née* Holwell); *m* 1939, Elsie Mary (*née* Hollinsed); no *c. Educ:* Cornwall Coll., Jamaica. Admitted as Solicitor: Jamaica, 1930, England, 1948. Resident Magistrate, Jamaica, 1946–58; Called to the Bar, Lincoln's Inn, 1956; acted as Puisne Judge, Jamaica, 1956–58; Puisne Judge, Jamaica, 1958–62; Judge of Appeal, Jamaica, 1962–64; Pres. Court of Appeal, 1964–67; Chief Justice of Jamaica, 1968–73; Acting Governor General of Jamaica, 1973. Chairman: Commn of Enquiry into Prisons of Jamaica, 1954; Commn of Enquiry into the administration of justice and police brutality in Grenada, WI, 1974; Police Service Commission (Jamaica), 1958–68. Sole Commissioner, Enquiries into: Maffesanti Affair, 1968; Operations of Private Land Developers in Jamaica, 1975–76; Barbados Govt's Private Enterprises, 1977–78. Pres., Boy Scouts Assoc., Jamaica, 1967–70. Chancellor of the Church (Anglican) in Jamaica, 1973–76. *Address:* 6 Braywick Road, PO Box 243, Kingston 6, Jamaica. *T:* 92–70171.

DUFFY, (Albert Edward) Patrick, PhD; MP (Lab) Sheffield, Attercliffe, since 1970; *b* 17 June 1920. *Educ:* London Sch. of Economics (BSc(Econ.), PhD); Columbia Univ., Morningside Heights, New York, USA. Served War of 1939–45, Royal Navy, incl. flying duties with FAA. Lecturer, University of Leeds, 1950–63, 1967–70. Visiting Professor: Drew Univ., Madison, NJ, 1966–70; Amer. Grad. Sch. of Internat. Business, 1982–. Contested (Lab) Tiverton Division of Devon, 1950, 1951, 1955. MP (Lab) Colne Valley Division of Yorks, 1963–66; PPS to Sec. of State for Defence, 1974–76; Parly Under-Sec. of State for Defence (Navy), MoD, 1976–79; opposition spokesman on defence, 1979–80, 1983–84. Chairman: PLP Economic and Finance Gp, 1965–66, 1974–76; Trade and Industry Sub-Cttee of Select Cttee on Expenditure, 1972–74; PLP Defence Cttee, 1984; Vice-Chairman: PLP Defence Gp, 1979–84; Anglo-Irish Gp, 1979–. Mem., N Atlantic Assembley, 1979– (Chm., Defence Co-op. sub-cttee, 1983–). *Publications:* contrib. to Economic History Review, Victorian Studies, Manchester School, Annals of Amer. Acad. of Pol. and Soc. Sci., etc. *Address:* 153 Bennetthorpe, Doncaster, South Yorks. *Clubs:* Naval; Trades and Labour (Doncaster).

DUFFY, Antonia Susan, (Mrs P. J. Duffy); *see* Byatt, A. S.

DUFFY, Most Rev. Joseph; *see* Clogher, Bishop of, (RC).

DUFFY, Maureen Patricia; author; *b* 1933; *o c* of Grace Rose Wright. *Educ:* Trowbridge High Sch. for Girls; Sarah Bonnell High Sch. for Girls; King's College, London (BA). FRSL 1985. Chairman: Greater London Arts Literature Panel, 1979–81; Authors Lending and Copyright Soc., 1982–; Vice-Chm., British Copyright Council, 1981–86; Pres., Writers' Guild of GB, 1985– (Jt Chm., 1977–78); Co-founder, Writers' Action Group; Vice-Pres., Beauty Without Cruelty. *Publications:* That's How It Was, 1962; The Single Eye, 1964; The Microcosm, 1966; The Paradox Players, 1967; Lyrics for the Dog Hour (poetry), 1968; Wounds, 1969; Rites (play), 1969; Love Child, 1971; The Venus Touch, 1971; The Erotic World of Faery, 1972; I want to Go to Moscow, 1973; A Nightingale in Bloomsbury Square (play), 1974; Capital, 1975; Evesong (poetry), 1975; The Passionate Shepherdess, 1977; Housespy, 1978; Memorials of the Quick and the Dead (poetry), 1979; Inherit the Earth, 1980; Gorsaga, 1981; Londoners: an elegy, 1983; Men and Beasts, 1984; Collected Poems 1949–84, 1985; Change (novel), 1987; *visual art:* Prop art exhibn (with Brigid Brophy, *qv*), 1969. *Address:* 18 Fabian Road, SW6 7TZ. *T:* 01–385 3598.

DUFFY, Patrick; *see* Duffy, A. E. P.

DUFFY, Peter Clarke, QPM 1979; Director General, Federation Against Copyright Theft, since 1985; *b* Hamilton, Scotland, 10 May 1927; *s* of Hugh Duffy and Margaret Archibald; *m* 1958, S. M. Joyce (marr. diss.); one *s* two *d. Educ:* Our Lady's High Sch., Motherwell. MInstAM 1983. Served Army, Western Arab Corps, Sudan Defence Force, 1945–48 (War Medal). Joined Metropolitan Police, 1949; Criminal Investigation Dept, 1954; Comdr, New Scotland Yard, 1976–83; Dir, Investigations, Fedn Against Copyright Theft, 1983–85. *Recreations:* golf, living. *Address:* Federation Against Copyright Theft, St Margaret's House, 19–23 Wells Street, W1P 3FP. *Club:* Royal Automobile.

DUFTY, Arthur Richard, CBE 1971; FSA; Master of the Armouries in HM Tower of London, 1963–76; *b* 23 June 1911; *s* of T. E. Dufty, and Beatrice (*née* Holmes); *m* 1937, Kate Brazley (*née* Ainsworth); one *s* two *d. Educ:* Rugby; Liverpool School of Architecture. War service in RN. On staff of Royal Commn on Historical Monuments, 1937–73, Sec. and Gen. Editor 1962–73, with responsibility for Nat. Monuments Record, inc. Nat. Buildings Record, 1964–73. Pres., Soc. of Antiquaries, 1978–81; Member: Ancient Monuments Bd for England, 1962–73 and 1977–80; Council for Places of Worship, 1976–81; Council, Nat. Army Museum, 1963–83; Royal Commn on Historical Monuments, 1975–85. Vice-Chm., Cathedrals Advisory Commission, 1981–. Chairman: British Cttee, Corpus Vitrearum Medii Aevi, 1970–84 (sponsored by British Acad.); London Dio. Adv. Cttee, 1973–84; Standing Cttee on Conservation of West Front of Wells Cathedral, 1974–85. Trustee: Coll. of Arms Trust, 1978–; Marc Fitch Fund, 1978–. Directed, for Soc. of Antiquaries, repair and rehabilitation of Kelmscott, William Morris's home in Oxfordshire, 1964–67. Hon. Freeman, Armourers and Brasiers' Co., 1974. Hon. Mem., Art Workers' Guild, 1977. ARIBA 1935–74; FSA 1946. London Conservation Award, GLC, 1984. *Publications:* Kelmscott: an illustrated guide, 1970; Morris Embroideries: the prototypes, 1985; ed 5 RCHM Inventories and 5 occasional publications; Intr. Vol. to Morris's Story of Cupid and Psyche, 1974. *Recreations:* viewing sales; taking pleasure in Victoriana and Art Nouveau; music. *Address:* 46 Trafalgar Court, Farnham, Surrey. *Clubs:* Athenæum, Arts, Naval.

DUGARD, Arthur Claude, CBE 1969; Chairman, Cooper & Roe Ltd, 1952–79, retired (formerly Joint Managing Director); *b* 1 Dec. 1904; *s* of Arthur Thomas Turner Dugard, Nottingham; *m* 1931, Christine Mary Roe, Nottingham; two *s. Educ:* Oundle Sch., Northants. Joined Cooper & Roe Ltd, Knitwear manufacturers, 1923 (Dir, 1936; Man. Dir, 1947). President: Nottingham Hosiery Manufrs Assoc., 1952–53; Nat. Hosiery Manufrs Fedn, 1959–61; Nottingham Chamber of Commerce, 1961–62. First Chm., CBI North Midland Regional Council, 1965–66; Chm. British Hosiery & Knitwear Export Gp, 1966–68; Mem. East Midlands Economic Planning Council, 1967–72. Liveryman, Worshipful Co. of Framework Knitters, 1949–. *Recreation:* golf. *Address:* 16 Hollies Drive, Edwalton, Nottingham NG12 4BZ. *T:* Nottingham 233217.

DUGDALE, family name of **Baron Crathorne.**

DUGDALE, Mrs John; *see* Dugdale, K. E. H.

DUGDALE, John Robert Stratford; Lord-Lieutenant of Salop, since 1975; *b* 10 May 1923; 2nd *s* of Sir William Francis Stratford Dugdale, 1st Bt, and Margaret, 2nd *d* of Sir Robert Gordon Gilmour, 1st Bt; *m* 1956, Kathryn Edith Helen (*see* K. E. H. Dugdale); two *s* two *d. Educ:* Eton; Christ Church, Oxford. Chm., Telford Develt Corp., 1971–75. KStJ 1976. *Recreation:* sleeping. *Address:* Tickwood Hall, Much Wenlock, Salop. *T:* Telford 882644. *Clubs:* Brooks's, White's.

See also Sir William Dugdale, Bt.

DUGDALE, Kathryn Edith Helen, (Mrs John Dugdale), DCVO 1984 (CVO 1973); JP; a Lady-in-Waiting to the Queen, since 1985; *b* 4 Nov. 1923; *d* of Rt Hon. Oliver Stanley, PC, MC, MP and Lady Maureen Vane-Tempest Stewart; *m* 1956, John Robert Stratford Dugdale, *qv*; two *s* two *d. Educ:* many and varied establishments. Served with WRNS. Temp. Woman of the Bedchamber to The Queen, 1955–60, Extra Woman of the Bedchamber 1960–72; Woman of the Bedchamber, 1972–85. Chm., Shropshire Community Council. JP Salop, 1964. Employee of Greater London Fund for the Blind. *Recreations:* gardening, reading. *Address:* Tickwood Hall, Much Wenlock, Salop. *T:* Telford 882644.

See also M. C. Stanley.

DUGDALE, Norman, CB 1974; Chairman, Belfast Voluntary Welfare Society, since 1985; Member of the Board, British Council, since 1986; Permanent Secretary, Department (formerly Ministry) of Health and Social Services, Northern Ireland, 1970–84; *b* 6 Feb. 1921; *yr s* of William and Eva Dugdale, Burnley, Lancs; *m* 1949, Mary Whitehead. *Educ:* Burnley Grammar Sch.; Manchester Univ. (BA). Asst Principal, Bd of Trade, 1941; Min. of Commerce, NI, 1948; Asst Sec., Min. of Health and Local Govt, NI, 1955; Sen. Asst Sec., Min. of Health and Local Govt, NI, 1964; Second Sec., Min. of Health and Social Services, 1968. Governor, Nat. Inst. for Social Work, London, 1965–84; Mem. Court, NUU, 1971–84. Hon. DLitt NUU, 1983. *Publications: poems:* The Disposition of the Weather, 1967; A Prospect of the West, 1970; Night-Ferry, 1974; Corncrake in October, 1978; Running Repairs, 1983; contribs to various literary periodicals. *Recreations:* procrastinating; next week-end.

DUGDALE, Peter Robin; Managing Director, Guardian Royal Exchange Assurance plc, since 1978; Chairman, Trade Indemnity plc, since 1980; *b* 12 Feb. 1928; *s* of Dr James Norman Dugdale and Lilian (*née* Dolman); *m* 1957, Esmé Cyraine, *d* of L. Norwood Brown; three *s. Educ:* Canford; Magdalen Coll., Oxford (MA). Joined Union Insurance Soc. of Canton, Hong Kong, 1949; merged with Guardian Assurance, London, 1960; Marine and Aviation Underwriter, 1965; Pres., Guardian Insurance Company of Canada, 1973; Gen. Man., Guardian Royal Exchange, 1976; Chm., Aviation and General Insurance Co. Ltd, 1982–84. Chm., British Insurance Assoc., 1981–82. CBIM 1984. *Address:* Trentham House, Emsworth, Hants PO10 7BH. *T:* Emsworth 372934.

DUGDALE, Sir William (Stratford), 2nd Bt *cr* 1936; CBE 1982; MC 1943; JP; DL; *b* 29 March 1922; *er s* of Sir William Francis Stratford Dugdale, 1st Bt, and Margaret, 2nd *d* of Sir Robert Gordon Gilmour, 1st Bt, of Liberton and Craigmillar; *S* father, 1965; *m* 1st, 1952, Lady Belinda Pleydell-Bouverie (*d* 1961), 2nd *d* of 6th Earl of Radnor; one *s* three *d*; 2nd, 1967, Cecilia Mary, *e d* of Sir William Malcolm Mount, 2nd Bt, *qv*; one *s* one *d. Educ:* Eton; Balliol Coll., Oxford. Served War of 1939–45, Grenadier Guards (Captain). Admitted as Solicitor, 1949. Dir, Phoenix Assurance Co., 1968–85. Mem., Warwicks County Council, 1964–76; Chairman: Severn Trent Water Authority, 1974–83; National Water Council, 1982–83; Birmingham Diocesan Board of Finance, 1979–. Steward, Jockey Club, 1985–. Governor, Lady Katherine Leveson's Hosp., Temple Balsall. High Steward, Stratford upon Avon, 1977. JP 1951, DL 1955, High Sheriff 1971, Warwicks. *Heir: s* William Matthew Stratford Dugdale, *b* 22 Feb. 1959. *Address:* Blyth Hall, Coleshill, near Birmingham. *T:* Coleshill 62203; Merevale Hall, Atherstone. *T:* Atherstone 3143; 24 Bryanston Mews West, W1. *T:* 01–262 2510. *Clubs:* Brooks's, White's, MCC; Jockey (Newmarket).

See also J. R. S. Dugdale, Baron Hazlerigg.

DUGGAN, Gordon Aldridge; HM Diplomatic Service; Consul-General and Commercial Counsellor, Zürich, Director of British Export Promotion in Switzerland, and Consul-General, Liechtenstein, since 1985, b 12 Aug. 1937; s of Joseph Nathan Duggan and Elizabeth Aldridge; m 1969, Erica Rose Anderssen; one s two d. Educ: Liverpool Collegiate Sch.; Lincoln Coll., Oxford. BA, BPhil. FO, 1963–66; Canberra, 1966–69; FCO, 1969–72; Information Officer, Bonn, 1972–74; Head of Chancery, Jakarta, 1974–76; Canberra, 1976–79; FCO, 1979–80; Commercial and Economic Counsellor, Lagos, 1981–84. Recreations: armchair sport, jazz, theatre, walking, countryside. Address: c/o Foreign and Commonwealth Office, King Charles Street, SW1.

DUGGAN, Rt. Rev. John Coote; b 7 April 1918; s of Rev. Charles Coote Whittaker Duggan, BD and Ella Thackeray Duggan (née Stritch); m 1948, Mary Elizabeth Davin; one s one d (and one d decd). Educ: High School, Dublin; Trinity Coll., Dublin (Schol.). Moderator (1st cl.)Men. and Moral Sci., 1940; Bernard Prize, Div. Test. (2nd cl.); BA 1940; BD 1946. Deacon 1941; Priest 1942. Curate Asst: St Luke, Cork, 1941–43; Taney, Dublin, 1943–48; Hon. Clerical Vicar, Christ Church Cath., 1944–48; Incumbent: Portarlington Union, Kildare, 1948–55; St Paul, Glenageary, Dublin, 1955–69; Westport and Achill Union, Tuam, 1969–70; Archdeacon of Tuam, 1969–70; Bishop of Tuam, Killala and Achonry, 1970–85. Exam. Chaplain to Archbp of Dublin, 1958–69; Examiner in BD Degree, Univ. of Dublin, 1960–69. Editor, Irish Churchman's Almanack, 1958–69. Publications: A Short History of Glenageary Parish, 1968. Recreation: fishing. Address: 15 Beechwood Lawn, Rochestown Avenue, Dun Laoghaire, Co. Dublin. Club: Kildare Street and University (Dublin).

DUGMORE, Rev. Prof. Clifford William, DD; Member, Advisory Editorial Board, The Journal of Ecclesiastical History, since 1979 (Editor, 1950–78); British Member of Editorial Board of Novum Testamentum, 1956–76; b 9 May 1909; s of late Rev. Canon William Ernest Dugmore, MA, RD, and late Frances Ethel Dugmore (née Westmore); m 1st, 1938, Ruth Mabel Archbould Prangley (d 1977); one d; 2nd, 1979, Kathleen Mary Whiteley. Educ: King Edward VI Sch., Birmingham (foundation scholar); Exeter Coll., Oxford; Queens' Coll., Cambridge. Oxford: BA (Hons Sch. of Oriental Studies), 1932; MA and James Mew Rabbinical Hebrew Scholar, 1935; BD 1940; DD 1957. Cambridge: BA (by incorporation) 1933; MA 1936; Norrisian Prizeman 1940; Select Preacher 1956; Hulsean Lecturer, 1958–60. Deacon 1935, Priest 1936; Asst Curate of Holy Trinity, Formby, 1935–37; Sub-Warden St Deiniol's Library, Hawarden, 1937–38; Rector of Ingestre-with-Tixall, 1938–43; Chaplain of Alleyn's Coll. of God's Gift, Dulwich, 1943–44; Rector of Bredfield and Dir of Religious Education, dio. St Edmundsbury and Ipswich, 1945–47; Sen. Lecturer in Ecclesiast. Hist., University of Manchester, 1946–58; Tutor to Faculty of Theology, 1958; Prof. of Ecclesiastical History, King's Coll., Univ. of London, 1958–76, Emeritus Prof., 1976–. Chm. of British Sous-Commission of Commission Internationale d'Histoire Ecclésiastique, 1952–62; Pres. of the Ecclesiastical History Soc., 1963–64; Mem. of the Senate, 1964–71, Proctor in Convocation, 1970–75, Dean, Univ. Faculty of Theology, 1974–76, University of London. Permission to officiate, Dio. of Guildford, 1966–. FKC 1965; FRHistS 1970. Publications: Eucharistic Doctrine in England from Hooker to Waterland, 1942; The Influence of the Synagogue upon the Divine Office, 1944 (2nd edn 1964); (ed) The Interpretation of the Bible 1944 (2nd edn 1946); The Mass and the English Reformers, 1958; Ecclesiastical History No Soft Option, 1959. Contributor to: Chambers's Encyclopædia, 1950 (Advisory Editor, 1960–); Weltkirchenlexikon 1960; Studia Patristica IV, 1961; Neotestamentica et Patristica, 1962; The English Prayer Book, 1963; A Companion to the Bible, 2nd revised edn, 1963; Studies in Church History I, 1964 (also ed); Studies in Church History II, 1965; Eucharistic Theology then and now, 1968; Man and his Gods, 1971; Aspects de l'Anglicanisme, 1974; Thomas More: through many eyes, 1978; Gen. Editor, Leaders of Religion, 1964–76; articles and reviews in Journal of Theological Studies, Journal of Ecclesiastical History, Theology, History, etc. Recreations: motoring and philately. Address: 77 The Street, Puttenham, Surrey GU3 1AT. T: Guildford 810460.

DUGUID, Andrew Alexander; Under Secretary, Department of Trade and Industry, since 1985; b 22 June 1944; s of Wing Comdr (retd) Alexander Gordon Duguid and Dorothy Duguid (née Duder); m 1967, Janet Hughes; two s one d. Educ: Whitby Dist High Sch.; Ashbury Coll., Ottawa; Sidcot Sch.; LSE (BSc Econs); Univ. of Lancaster (MA Marketing). Res. Assistant, Brunel Univ., 1967–69; Marketing Executive: Interscan Ltd, 1969–72; Ogilvy Benson and Mather, 1972–73; joined DTI as Principal, 1973; Prin. Pvte Sec. to Sec. of State for Industry, 1977–79; Asst Sec., seconded to Prime Minister's Policy Unit, 1979; returned to set up Policy Planning Unit, Dept of Industry, later DTI, 1982. Non-exec. Dir, Kingsway Public Relations, 1982–85. Publication: (with Elliott Jaques) Case Studies in Export Organisation, 1971. Recreations: tennis, ski-ing, walking, canoeing. Address: 1 Binden Road, W12 9RJ. T: 01–743 7435. Club: Hartswood.

DUGUID, Prof. James Paris, CBE 1979; MD, BSc; FRCPath; Professor of Bacteriology, University of Dundee, 1967–84; Consultant, Tayside Health Board, 1963–84; b 10 July 1919; s of late Maj.-Gen. David Robertson Duguid, CB, and Mary Paris; m 1944, Isobel Duff; one s three d. Educ: Edinburgh Academy; Univ. of Edinburgh (MB ChB Hons 1942; BSc 1st Cl. Hons 1943; MD (Gold Medal) 1949); FRCPath 1966. Lectr, Sen. Lectr and Reader, Univ. of Edinburgh, 1944–62; Prof. of Bacteriology, Univ. of St Andrews, 1963–67; Director of Postgrad. Medical Educn, Univ. of Dundee, 1968–71, Dean of Faculty of Medicine, 1971–74, Mem. Univ. Court, 1977–81. Cons. Adviser in Microbiology, Scottish Home and Health Dept, 1967–85, Mem. Adv. Cttee on Medical Research, 1967–71; Member: Eastern Regional and Tayside Health Bds, 1967–77; Adv. Cttee on Laboratory Services, Scottish Health Serv. Council, 1967–74 (Chm., Epidemiology Sub-cttee, 1966–71); Scottish Health Services Planning Council, 1974–77 (Member: Adv. Cttee on New Developments in Health Care, 1976–84; Scientific Services Adv. Gp, 1975–79; Chm., Microbiology and Clin. Immunology Cttees, 1975–77); Jt Cttee on Vaccination and Immunisation, Health Services Councils, 1967–74; GMC, 1975–81; Council for Professions Supp. to Medicine, 1978–86. Asst Editor: Jl of Pathology and Bacteriology, 1959–68; Jl of Medical Microbiology, 1968–71. Publications: co-ed, Medical Microbiology, 11th edn 1969, 12th edn 1973, 13th edn 1978; scientific papers on bacterial fimbriae, adhesins, biotyping and phylogeny, airborne infection, and the action of penicillin. Recreations: gardening, atheism. Address: 69 Dalkeith Road, Dundee DD4 7HF. T: Dundee 44856; Hillside, Glenborrodale, Argyll.

du HEAUME, Sir (Francis) Herbert, Kt 1947; CIE 1943; OBE 1932; KPM 1924; Indian Police Medal; b 27 May 1897; s of George du Heaume, OBE; m 1923, Blanche Helen Learmonth Tainsh (d 1981); two s. Served European War, 1914–18, Captain, 15th London Regt; joined Indian Police, 1920; Principal, Police Training Sch., Punjab, 1934–42; Deputy Inspector-Gen. of Police, 1942–47. Address: c/o Grindlay's Bank, 13 St James's Square, SW1.

DUKE, family name of **Baron Merrivale.**

DUKE, Cecil Howard Armitage; Director of Establishments and Organisation, Ministry of Agriculture, Fisheries and Food, 1965–71; b 5 May 1912; s of late John William Duke and Gertrude Beatrice (née Armitage); m 1939, Eleanor Lucy (née Harvie); one s one d.

Educ: Selhurst Gram. Sch.; LSE. RNVR, 1942–45 (Corvettes). Entered Civil Service, 1929; Asst Princ., 1940; Princ., 1945; Private Sec. to Lord Presidents of the Council, 1951–53; Asst Sec., Land Drainage Div. and Meat Div., 1953; Under-Sec., 1965. Recreations: walking, gardening, watching Sussex cricket. Address: 22 Fairways Road, Seaford, East Sussex. T: Seaford 894338.

DUKE, Maj.-Gen. Sir Gerald (William), KBE 1966 (CBE 1945); CB 1962; DSO 1945; DL; b 12 Nov. 1910; e s of late Lieut-Col A. A. G. Duke, Indian Army; m 1946, Mary Elizabeth (d 1979), er d of late E. M. Burn, Church Stretton; one s one d. Educ: Dover Coll.; RMA Woolwich; Jesus Coll., Cambridge. Commissioned RE, 1931; served Egypt and Palestine, 1936–39; War of 1939–45, in Western Desert and Italy; BGS Eighth Army, 1944; North West Europe, Brig. Q (Movements), 21st Army Group, 1944; CRE 49th Div., 1945. Chief Engineer, Malaya Comd, 1946; idc 1948; Mil. Attaché, Cairo, 1952–54; Comdt Sch. of Mil. Engineering, 1956–59. Commodore Royal Engineer Yacht Club, 1957–60. DPS, WO, 1959–62; Engineer-in-Chief (Army), 1963–65; retired. Col Comdt, RE, 1966–75. Chm., SS&AFA, Kent, 1973–85; Pres., Scout Assoc., Kent, 1974–; Vice-Pres., Hockey Assoc., 1965–. Governor of Dover Coll. FICE. DL Kent, 1970. Recreations: sailing, golf. Address: Little Barnfield, Hawkhurst, Kent TN18 4PX. T: Hawkhurst 3214. Clubs: Royal Ocean Racing; Rye Golf.

DUKE, Rt. Rev. Michael Geoffrey H.; see Hare Duke.

DUKE, Neville Frederick, DSO 1943; OBE 1953; DFC and Two Bars, 1942, 1943, 1944; AFC 1948; MC (Czech) 1946; Managing Director, Duke Aviation; Technical Adviser and Consultant Test Pilot; b 11 Jan. 1922; s of Frederick and Jane Duke, Tonbridge, Kent; m 1947, Gwendoline Dorothy Fellows. Educ: Convent of St Mary and Judds Sch., Tonbridge, Kent. Joined Royal Air Force (cadet), 1940, training period, 1940; 92 Fighter Sqdn, Biggin Hill, 1941; Desert Air Force: 112 Fighter Sqdn, Western Desert, 1941–42, 92 Fighter Sqdn, Western Desert, 1943, Chief Flying Instructor, 73 Operational Training Unit, Egypt, 1943–44, Commanding 145 Sqdn Italy (Fighter), 1944, 28 enemy aircraft destroyed. Hawker Aircraft Ltd test flying, 1945; Empire Test Pilots Sch., 1946; RAF high speed flight, 1946 (world speed record); test flying Aeroplane and Armament Experimental Estab., Boscombe Down, 1947–48; resigned from RAF as Sqdn Leader, 1948; test flying Hawker Aircraft Ltd, 1948; Commanding 615 (County of Surrey) Sqdn, Royal Auxiliary Air Force, Biggin Hill, 1950; Chief Test Pilot, Hawker Aircraft Ltd, 1951–56 (Asst Chief, 1948–51). FRSA 1970; ARAeS 1948. World records: London-Rome, 1949; London-Karachi, 1949; London-Cairo, 1950. World Speed Record, Sept. 1953. Closed Circuit World Speed Record, 1953. Gold Medal Royal Danish Aero Club, 1953; Gold Medal, Royal Aero Club, 1954; two De la Vaux Medals, FAI, 1954; Segrave Trophy, 1954; Queen's Commendation, 1955. Member: RAF Escaping Soc.; United Service & Royal Aero Club (Associate); Royal Aeronautical Soc. FRSA. Publications: Sound Barrier, 1953; Test Pilot, 1953; Book of Flying, 1954; Book of Flight, 1958; The Crowded Sky (anthology), 1959. Recreations: sporting flying, yachting. Address: Everton Grange, Lymington, Hants. Clubs: Royal Air Force; Royal Cruising, Royal Naval Sailing, Royal Lymington Yacht.

DUKES, Alan M.; TD (FG) Kildare, since 1981; Minister for Justice, Republic of Ireland, since 1986; b 22 April 1945; s of James and Rita Dukes; m 1968, Fionnuala Corcoran; two d. Educ: Colaiste Mhuire, Dublin; University College Dublin (MA). Chief Economist, Irish Farmers' Assoc., 1967–72; Dir, Irish Farmers' Assoc., Brussels, 1973–76; Personal Advr to Comr of European Communities, 1977–80. Minister for Agriculture, 1981–82; opposition spokesman on agric., March-Dec. 1982; Minister for Finance. Governor: EIB, 1982–86; IMF. Address: Department of Justice, 72–76 St Stephen's Green, Dublin 2. T: 789711.

DUKES, Justin Paul; Managing Director, Channel Four Television Company Ltd, since 1981; b 19 Sept. 1941; s of John Alexander Dukes and Agnes Dukes; two s one d. Educ: King's Coll., Univ. of Durham. Dir, Financial Times Ltd, 1975–81; Chairman: Financial Times (Europe) Ltd and Fintel Ltd, 1978–81; C. S. & P. International Inc., NY, 1980–83. Pres., Inst. of Information Scientists, 1982–83; Mem. Council, Foundn for Management Educn, 1979–. Member: British Screen Adv. Council; Nat. Electronics Council. Trustee, Internat. Inst. of Communications. FRTS 1986; FRSA 1986. Recreations: changing institutions, walking. Address: c/o Channel Four Television Co. Ltd, 60 Charlotte Street, W1P 2AX.

DULBECCO, Dr Renato; Distinguished Research Professor, since 1977, Senior Clayton Foundation Investigator, since 1979, The Salk Institute for Biological Studies; b Italy, 22 Feb. 1914; USA citizen; s of late Leonardo Dulbecco and late Maria Virdia; m 1963, Maureen R. Muir; one s two d. Educ: Univ. of Turin Medical Sch. (MD). Assistente, Univ. of Turin: Inst. Pathology, 1940–46; Anatomical Inst., 1946–47; Res. Assoc., Indiana Univ., 1947–49; Sen. Res. Fellow, 1949–52, Assoc. Prof., 1952–54, Prof. 1954–63, California Inst. Technology; Vis. Prof., Rockefeller Inst., 1962; Royal Soc. Vis. Prof. at Univ. of Glasgow, 1963–64; Resident Fellow, Salk Inst., Calif, 1963–72, Fellow, 1972–77; Imperial Cancer Research Fund: Asst Dir of Res., 1972–74; Dep. Dir of Res., 1974–77; Prof. of Pathology and Medicine, Univ. of Calif San Diego Med. Sch., 1977–81. MNAS; Member: Fedn of Amer. Scientists; Amer. Assoc. for Cancer Research; Cancer Center, Univ. of Calif at San Diego; Bd of Scientific Counselors, Dept of Cancer Etiology, NCI; Amer. Acad. of Arts and Scis; Internat. Physicians for Prevention of Nuclear War, Inc.; Pres., Amer.-Ital. Foundn for Cancer Res. Trustee: Amer.-Italian Foundn for Cancer Res.; La Jolla Country Day School. Foreign Member: Academia dei Lincei, 1969; Royal Society, 1974; Hon. Mem., Accademia Ligure di Scienze a Lettere. Has given many lectures to learned instns. Hon. DSc Yale, 1968; Hon. LLD Glasgow, 1970; hc Dr Med., Vrije Universiteit Brussel, Brussels, 1978; Hon. DSc Indiana, 1984. (Jtly) Nobel Prize for Physiology or Medicine, 1975; numerous other prizes and awards. Publications: (jtly) Microbiology, 1967; numerous in sci. jls. Recreation: music. Address: The Salk Institute, PO Box 85800, San Diego, Calif 92138, USA. Club: Athenæum.

DULVERTON, 2nd Baron, cr 1929, of Batsford; **Frederick Anthony Hamilton Wills,** CBE 1974; TD; DL; Bt 1897; MA Oxon; b 19 Dec. 1915; s of 1st Baron Dulverton, OBE, and Victoria May, OBE (d 1968), 3rd d of Rear-Adm. Sir Edward Chichester, 9th Bt, CB, CMG; S father, 1956; m 1st, 1939, Judith Betty (marr. diss. 1960; she d 1983), e d of late Lieut-Col Hon. Ian Leslie Melville, TD; two s two d; 2nd, 1962, Ruth Violet, o d of Sir Walter Farquhar, 5th Bt. Educ: Eton; Magdalen Coll., Oxford (MA; Waynflete Fellow, 1982). Commissioned Lovat Scouts (TA), 1935; Major, 1943. President: Timber Growers' Orgn Ltd, 1976–78; Bath and West and Southern Counties Agric. Soc., 1973; British Deer Soc., 1973; Three Counties Agric. Soc., 1975; Gloucestershire Trust for Nature Conservation, 1979–; Member, Red Deer Commn, 1972–; Chairman: Forestry Cttee of GB, 1978–80; Dulverton Trust, 1956–; Trustee, Wildfowl Trust; former Trustee, World Wildlife Fund (UK); Hon. Pres., Timber Growers UK, 1983–. Joint Master: N Cotswold Foxhounds, 1950–56; Heythrop Foxhounds, 1967–70. DL Gloucester, 1979. Commander, Order of Golden Ark (Netherlands), 1985. Heir: s Hon. (Gilbert) Michael Hamilton Wills [b 2 May 1944; m 1980, Rosalind van der Velde-Oliver; one s one d]. Address: Batsford Park, Moreton-in-Marsh, Glos. T: 50303; Fassfern,

Kinlocheil, Fort William, Inverness-shire. *T:* Kinlocheil 232. *Clubs:* Boodles's, Pratt's, Army and Navy.

DULY, Surgeon Rear-Adm. (D) Philip Reginald John, CB 1982; OBE 1971; Director of Naval Dental Services, 1980–83; *b* 3 April 1925; *s* of Reginald and Minnie Duly; *m* 1948, Mary Walker Smith; two *s* one *d. Educ:* The London Hospital. LDSRCS 1947. Joined Royal Navy, Surgeon Lieut(D), 1948; Officer in Charge, Dental Training, 1965–70; Asst to Director of Naval Dental Services, 1970–72; Director of Dental Trng and Research, 1972–76; Comd Dental Surgeon to Flag Officer Naval Air Comd, 1976–77; to C-in-C Naval Home Comd, 1977–80. Chairman of Examiners, General Dental Council Central Examining Board for Dental Hygienists, 1977–80. QHDS 1978–83. FRSM. *Recreations:* music, esp. church organ playing; DIY repairs on lost causes. *Address:* 13 The Avenue, Alverstoke, Gosport, Hants PO12 2JS. *T:* Gosport 580532. *Club:* Army and Navy.

DULY, Sidney John, MA; Consultant on the carriage of goods by sea; *b* London, 30 Oct. 1891; *s* of Henry Charles Duly; *m* 1916, Florence (*d* 1980), *d* of William George Smith. *Educ:* St Olave's Gram. Sch.; Corpus Christi Coll., Cambridge; Berlin Univ. (Advanced Physics under Rector Professor Max Planck until 1914). Till 1941 Head of the Dept for the Scientific Study of Commercial Products, City of London Coll. Visited Pacific Coast of N America for Furness Withy, to find cause of rusting of canned goods on voyage home, 1926; further voyages of investigation in 1927, 1929, 1930, 1932, 1933, 1934, 1935, 1936 and 1937. Mem., Shaef OKL Party to take surrender of and interrogate German Air Force Gen. Staff in Berchtesgaden and Chesham. A Governor, City of London College, 1950–70. Dir, Cargocaire Ltd, 1946–60. *Address:* 34 Sheldon Court, Bath Road, Worthing, West Sussex.

DUMAS, Roland; Chevalier de la Légion d'Honneur; Croix de Guerre (1939–45); Croix du Combattant Volontaire; Deputy for the Dordogne; Minister for External Relations, France, 1984–86; *b* Limoges, Haute-Vienne, 23 Aug. 1922; *s* of Georges Dumas and Elisabeth (*née* Lecanuet); *m* 1964, Anne-Marie Lillet; two *s* one *d. Educ:* Lycée de Limoges; Faculté de Droit de Paris; Univ. of London; Ecole de langues orientales de Paris. LLL; Diplomas in Advanced Studies in Laws; in Political Science, Paris, and London School of Economics. Counsel, Court of Appeal, Paris; journalist; Sen. Political Dir, Journal Socialiste Limousin; Political Dir of weekly, La Corrèze Républicaine et Socialiste; Deputy: UDSR, Haute Vienne, 1956–58; FGDS, Corrèze, 1967–68; Socialiste de la Dordogne, 1981–83; Minister for European Affairs, 1983–84; Govt spokesman, 1984. Grand Cross, Order of Isabel (Spain), 1982. *Publications:* J'ai vu vivre la Chine, 1960; Les Avocats, 1970; Le Droit de l'Information et de la Presse, 1981; Plaidoyer pour Roger Gilbert Lecomte, 1985. *Recreation:* tennis. *Address:* 28 rue de Bièvre, 75005 Paris, France.

du MAURIER, Dame Daphne, DBE 1969; **(Lady Browning);** writer; *b* 1907; 2nd *d* of late Sir Gerald du Maurier; *m* 1932, Lieut-Gen. Sir Frederick A. M. Browning, GCVO, KBE, CB, DSO (*d* 1965); one *s* two *d. Educ:* privately; in Paris. Began writing short stories and articles in 1928; first novel appeared 1931. *Publications:* The Loving Spirit, 1931; I'll Never Be Young Again, 1932; The Progress of Julius, 1933; Gerald, a Portrait, 1934; Jamaica Inn, 1936; The du Mauriers, 1937; Rebecca, 1938; Frenchman's Creek, 1941; Hungry Hill, 1943; The King's General, 1946; The Parasites, 1949; My Cousin Rachel, 1951; The Apple Tree, 1952; Mary Anne, 1954; The Scapegoat, 1957; The Breaking Point, 1959; The Infernal World of Branwell Brontë, 1960; Castle Dor (continuation of MS left by late Sir Arthur Quiller-Couch (Q)), 1962; The Glassblowers, 1963; The Flight of the Falcon, 1965; Vanishing Cornwall, 1967; The House on the Strand, 1969; Not After Midnight, 1971; Rule Britannia, 1972; Golden Lads: a study of Anthony Bacon, Francis and their Friends, 1975; The Winding Stair: Francis Bacon, his Rise and Fall, 1976; The Rendezvous and other stories, 1980; The Rebecca Notebook and Other Memories, 1981; *autobiography:* Growing Pains, 1977; *drama:* The Years Between, 1945; September Tide, 1948; *edited:* The Young George du Maurier, 1951. *Recreations:* walking and swimming. *Address:* Kilmarth, Par, Cornwall.
See also Viscount Montgomery of Alamein, Gen. Sir P. J. H. Leng.

DUMBELL, Dr Keith Rodney; Senior Specialist in Microbiology, Medical School, University of Cape Town, since 1982; *b* 2 Oct. 1922; *s* of late Stanley Dumbell and Dorothy Ellen (*née* Hewitt); *m* 1st, 1950, Brenda Margaret (*née* Heathcote) (*d* 1971); two *d*; 2nd, 1972, Susan (*née* Herd); two *s. Educ:* Wirral Gram. Sch.; University of Liverpool, MB, ChB 1944; MD (Liverpool), 1950. FRCPath 1975. Asst Lecturer, Dept of Bacteriology, University of Liverpool, 1945–47; Mem. of Scientific Staff, MRC, 1947–50; Junior Pathologist, RAF, 1950–52; Asst in Pathology and Microbiology, Rockefeller Inst. for Medical Research (Dr Peyton Rous' laboratory), 1952–53; Lecturer in Bacteriology, University of Liverpool, 1952–58; Senior Lecturer, 1958–64; Prof. of Virology, Univ. of London at St Mary's Hosp. Med. Sch., 1964–81. *Publications:* articles in various medical and scientific journals. *Address:* Department of Medical Microbiology, Medical School, Observatory, Cape, 7925, South Africa.

DUMBUTSHENA, Hon. Enoch; Hon. Mr Justice Dumbutshena; Chief Justice of Zimbabwe, since 1984; *b* 25 April 1920; *s* of late Job Matabasi Dumbutshena and of Sarah Dumbutshena; *m* 1st, 1948, Alphosina (*née* Mahlangu) (marr. diss.); one *s* one *d*; 2nd, 1964, Miriam Masango; one *s* two *d. Educ:* Univ. of South Africa (BA, BEd, UED). Called to the Bar, Gray's Inn, 1963. Teacher, 1946–56; journalist, 1956–59; barrister, Southern Rhodesia, 1963–67; Zambia: founded Legal Aid Scheme, 1967–70; private practice, 1970–78; Zimbabwe: private practice, 1978–80; Judge of High Court, 1980; Judge President, 1983. Chm., Art Printers Employees Trust, Harare; Pres., Boy Scouts; Trustee, Omay Develt Trust, Harare. Gov., Arundel Sch., Harare; Trustee: Chisipite Jun. Sch., Harare; Dhaniko Sch., Harare. *Publication:* Zimbabwe Tragedy, 1986. *Recreations:* mountain climbing (average height), reading, formerly tennis. *Address:* PO Box CH70, Chisipite, Harare, Zimbabwe. *T:* (office) 724778, (residence) 884147. *Club:* Harare.

DUMFRIES, Earl of; John Colum Crichton-Stuart; *b* 26 April 1958; *s* and *heir* of 6th Marquess of Bute, *qv.* British Formula Three Champion, 1984; European Formula Three Championship runner-up, 1984; Formula One Ferrari test driver, 1985; JPS Lotus Grand Prix Driver, 1986. *Address:* Mount Stuart, Rothesay, Isle of Bute. *T:* Rothesay 2730.

DUMMETT, (Agnes Margaret) Ann; Director, Runnymede Trust, since 1984; *b* 4 Sept. 1930; *d* of Arthur William Chesney and Kitty Mary Chesney; *m* 1951, Michael Anthony Eardley Dummett, *qv;* three *s* two *d* (and one *s* one *d* decd). *Educ:* Guildhouse Sch., Pimlico; Ware Grammar Sch. for Girls; Somerville Coll., Oxford (MA). Pres., Oxford Univ. Liberal Club, 1949. Community Relations Officer, Oxford, 1966–69; teaching in further education, 1969–71; Research Worker: Inst. of Race Relations, 1971–73; Runnymede Trust, 1975, 1977; Jt Council for the Welfare of Immigrants, 1978–84. *Publications:* A Portrait of English Racism, 1973; Citizenship and Nationality, 1976; A New Immigration Policy, 1978; (with Ian Martin) British Nationality: a guide to the new law, 1982; (ed) Towards a Just Immigration Policy, 1986; (with Andrew Nichol) British Nationality and Immigration, 1987; chapters in: Justice First (with Michael Dummett), 1969; Colloque de la Société Française pour le Droit International, 1979; Moral Philosophy, 1979; numerous articles and pamphlets. *Recreations:* walking about

cities, theatregoing, popular music. *Address:* 54 Park Town, Oxford OX2 6SJ. *T:* Oxford 58698. *Club:* Royal Commonwealth Society.

DUMMETT, George Anthony, FEng, FIChemE; Chairman, Council of Engineering Institutions, 1976–77 (Vice-Chairman, 1975); *b* 13 Oct. 1907; *s* of George Herbert Dummett and Gertrude (*née* Higgins); *m* 1st, 1931, Peggy Schaeffer; 2nd, 1939, Ursula Margarete Schubert; two *s* one *d. Educ:* Rugby Sch.; Birmingham Univ.; Pembroke Coll., Cambridge, MA. Research in phys. chem., Cambridge Univ., 1930–32; Research Asst, Thorncliffe Coal Distillation Ltd, 1932–35; APV Co. Ltd (then Aluminium Plant and Vessel Co. Ltd): Technical Res. Asst, 1935; Laboratory Man., 1943; Chem. Engrg Dept Man., 1948; Scientific Man., 1949; Res. Dir, 1956; Dep. Man. Dir, 1965–72; Dir, APV (Holdings) Ltd, 1962–72; Dep. Chm., APV Internat., 1965–72. Chm., Res. Cttee, FBI, 1958–65; Pres., IChemE, 1968–69, Hon. Fellow, 1981. Fellow, Fellowship of Engineering, 1977. Chm., European Fedn Chemical Engrng, 1977–78. Hon. Member: Soc. de Chimie Ind., 1969; Dechema, 1976. *Publications:* From Little Acorns: a history of the APV company, 1981; numerous papers on chemical and biochemical engrg, metallurgy, etc. *Recreations:* music, mountaineering, gardening, stamp collecting. *Address:* Gowans, Possingworth Close, Cross-in-Hand, Heathfield, Sussex TN21 0TL. *T:* Heathfield 2085. *Clubs:* Alpine, Climbers.
See also M. A. E. Dummett.

DUMMETT, Michael Anthony Eardley; Wykeham Professor of Logic in the University of Oxford, and Fellow of New College, Oxford, since 1979; *b* 27 June 1925; *s* of George Herbert Dummett and Iris Dummett (*née* Eardley-Wilmot); *m* 1951, Ann Chesney (*see* A. M. A. Dummett); three *s* two *d* (one *s* one *d* decd). *Educ:* Sandroyd Sch.; Winchester Coll. (1st Schol.); Christ Church, Oxford. Major hist. schol. (Ch. Ch.), 1942. Served in Army, 1943–47: in RA and Intell. Corps (India, 1945, Malaya, 1946–47, Sgt). Ch. Ch., Oxford, 1947–50, First Class Hons, PPE, 1950. Asst Lectr in Philosophy, Birmingham Univ., 1950–51; Commonwealth Fund Fellow, Univ. of California, Berkeley, 1955–56; Reader in the Philosophy of Mathematics, Univ. of Oxford, 1962–74; All Souls College, Oxford: Fellow, 1950–79, Senior Research Fellow, 1974–79; Sub-Warden, 1974–76; Emeritus Fellow, 1980. Vis. Lectr, Univ. of Ghana, 1958; Vis. Professor: Stanford Univ., several occasions, 1960–66; Univ. of Minnesota, 1968; Princeton Univ., 1970; Rockefeller Univ., 1973; William James Lectr in Philosophy, Harvard Univ., 1976; Alex. von Humboldt-Stiftung Vis. Res. Fellow, Münster Univ., 1981. Founder Mem., Oxford Cttee for Racial Integration, 1965 (Chm., Jan.-May 1966); Member: Exec. Cttee, Campaign Against Racial Discrimination, 1966–67; Legal and Civil Affairs Panel, Nat. Cttee for Commonwealth Immigrants, 1966–68; Chairman: Jt Council for the Welfare of Immigrants, 1970–71 (Vice-Chm., 1967–69, 1973–75); unofficial cttee of enquiry into events in Southall 23 April 1979, 1979–80; shadow board, Barclays Bank, 1981–82. FBA 1968–84. Hon. PhD Nijmegen, 1983; For. Hon. Mem., Amer. Acad. of Arts and Scis, 1985. *Publications:* Frege: philosophy of language, 1973, 2nd edn 1981; The Justification of Deduction, 1973; Elements of Intuitionism, 1977; Truth and other Enigmas, 1978; Immigration: where the debate goes wrong, 1978; Catholicism and the World Order, 1979; The Game of Tarot, 1980; Twelve Tarot Games, 1980; The Interpretation of Frege's Philosophy, 1981; Voting Procedures, 1984; contributions to: Mind and Language, 1975; Truth and Meaning, 1976; Studies on Frege, 1976; Contemporary British Philosophy, 1976; Meaning and Use, 1979; Perception and Identity, 1979; Perspectives on the Philosophy of Wittgenstein, 1981; Approaches to Language, 1983; Frege: tradition and influence, 1984; contrib. entry on Frege, to Encyclopedia of Philosophy (ed P. Edwards), 1967; (with Ann Dummett) chapter on Rôle of the Government, in Justice First (ed L. Donnelly), 1969; preface to R. C. Zaehner, The City Within the Heart, 1980; articles in: Aristotelian Soc. Proceedings, Philos. Review, Synthese, Inquiry, Econometrica, Jl of Symbolic Logic, Zeitschrift für mathematische Logik, Dublin Review, New Blackfriars, Clergy Review, Jl of Warburg and Courtauld Insts, Jl of Playing-Card Soc. *Recreations:* listening to the blues, investigating the history of card games, reading science fiction. *Address:* 54 Park Town, Oxford. *T:* Oxford 58698. *Club:* Royal Commonwealth Society.
See also G. A. Dummett.

DUMPER, Rt. Rev. Anthony Charles; *see* Dudley, Bishop Suffragan of.

DUNALLEY, 6th Baron *cr* 1800; **Henry Desmond Graham Prittie;** Lt-Col (retired) late The Rifle Brigade; *b* 14 Oct. 1912; *er s* of 5th Baron Dunalley, DSO, and Beatrix Evelyn (*d* 1967), *e d* of late James N. Graham of Carfin, Lanarkshire; *S* father, 1948; *m* 1947, Philippa, *o d* of late Hon. Philip Cary; two *s* one *d. Educ:* Stowe; RMC, Sandhurst. Retd 1953. *Recreation:* fishing. *Heir: s* Hon. Henry Francis Cornelius Prittie [*b* 30 May 1948; *m* 1978, Sally Louise, *er d* of Ronald Vere; one *s* two *d*]. *Address:* Church End House, Swerford, Oxfordshire. *Clubs:* Kildare Street and University (Dublin); Christchurch (NZ) (Hon. Mem.).

DUNBAR, Alexander Arbuthnott; farmer; *b* 14 March 1929; *yr s* of Sir Edward Dunbar, 9th Bt; *m* 1965, Elizabeth Susannah, *d* of Rev. Denzil Wright; one *s* one *d. Educ:* Wellington Coll., Berks; Pembroke Coll., Cambridge (MA); Edinburgh Sch. of Agriculture, 1980–81. Mil. Service, Lieut QO Cameron Highlanders, 1947–49. Called to the Bar, Inner Temple, 1953. Joined ICI, 1954: Asst Sec., Wilton Works, 1959–63. Joined North Eastern Assoc. for the Arts, 1963, Sec. 1964, Dir 1967; Director: Northern Arts Assoc., 1967–69; UK and British Commonwealth Branch, Calouste Gulbenkian Foundn, 1970–71; Scottish Arts Council, 1971–80. *Publications:* contribs to various jls. *Recreations:* art, theatre, ski-ing, running. *Address:* Pitgaveny, Elgin, Moray IV30 2PQ.

DUNBAR of Northfield, Sir Archibald (Ranulph), 11th Bt *cr* 1700; *b* 8 Aug. 1927; *er s* of Sir (Archibald) Edward Dunbar, 9th Bt (by some reckonings 10th Bt) and Olivia Douglas Sinclair (*d* 1964), *d* of Maj.-Gen. Sir Edward May, KCB, CMG; *S* father, 1969; *m* 1974, Amelia Millar Sommerville, *d* of Horace Davidson; one *s* two *d. Educ:* Wellington Coll.; Pembroke Coll., Cambridge; Imperial Coll. of Tropical Agriculture, Trinidad. Mil. Service, 2nd Lt, Cameron (att. Gordon) Highlanders, 1945–48. Entered Colonial Agricultural Service, Uganda, as Agricultural Officer, 1953; retired, 1970. *Publications:* A History of Bunyoro-Kitara, 1965; Omukama Chwa II Kabarega, 1965; The Annual Crops of Uganda, 1969; various articles in Uganda Jl. *Recreations:* cross-country running, model railway. *Heir: s* Edward Horace Dunbar, Younger of Northfield, *b* 18 March 1977. *Address:* The Old Manse, Duffus, Elgin, Scotland. *T:* Hopeman 830270. *Club:* New (Edinburgh).

DUNBAR, Charles, CB 1964; Director, Fighting Vehicles Research and Development Establishment, Ministry of Defence, 1960–67; *b* 12 Jan. 1907; *s* of John Dunbar, Barrow-in-Furness, Lancs; *m* 1933, Mary Alice (*née* Clarke), Barnes, SW; two *d. Educ:* Grammar Sch., Barrow-in-Furness; Manchester Univ. (MSc). National Physical Laboratory, Dept of Scientific and Industrial Research, 1929–43; Tank Armament Research Establishment, Min. of Supply, 1943–47; Fighting Vehicles Research and Development Establishments, 1947–67, retired. *Publications:* contribs to learned journals. *Recreations:* golf, fishing. *Address:* Cedar Lodge, 2 Freemans Close, Stoke Poges, Bucks.
See also Peter Graham.

DUNBAR, Sir David H.; see Hope-Dunbar.

DUNBAR of Durn, Sir Drummond Cospatrick Ninian, 9th Bt, cr 1697; MC 1943; Major Black Watch, retired; b 9 May 1917; o s of Sir George Alexander Drummond Dunbar, 8th Bt and Sophie Kathleen (d 1936), d of late J. Benson Kennedy; S father, 1949; m 1957, Sheila Barbara Mary, d of John B. de Fonblanque, London; one s. Educ: Radley Coll.; Worcester Coll., Oxford. BA 1938. Served War of 1939–45, Middle East, Sicily, Normandy (wounded twice, MC). Retired pay, 1958. Heir: s Robert Drummond Cospatrick Dunbar, Younger of Durn [b 17 June 1958. Educ: Harrow; Christ Church, Oxford; BA 1979]. Address: Town Hill, Westmount, Jersey, Channel Islands. Club: Naval and Military.

DUNBAR of Mochrum, Sir Jean Ivor, 13th Bt cr 1694; b 4 April 1918; s of Sir Adrian Ivor Dunbar of Mochrum, 12th Bt and Emma Marie (d 1925), d of Jean Wittevrongel; S father, 1977; m 1944, Rose Jeanne (marr. diss. 1979), d of Henry William Hertsch; two s one d. Formerly Sergeant, Mountain Engineers, US Army. Recreation: horsemanship. Heir: s Captain James Michael Dunbar, DDS, US Air Force [b 17 Jan. 1950; m 1978, Margaret Jacobs].

DUNBAR, John Greenwell; Secretary, Royal Commission on the Ancient and Historical Monuments of Scotland, since 1978; b 1 March 1930; o s of John Dunbar and Marie Alton; m 1974, Elizabeth Mill Blyth. Educ: University College Sch., London; Balliol Coll., Oxford (MA). FSA, FSAScot. Joined staff of Royal Commission on the Ancient and Historical Monuments of Scotland, 1953; Mem., Ancient Monuments Board for Scotland, 1978. Vice-President: Soc. for Medieval Archaeology, 1981–86; Soc. of Antiquaries of Scotland, 1983–86. Lindsay-Fischer Lectr, Oslo, 1985. Hon. FRIAS. Publications: The Historic Architecture of Scotland, 1966, revd edn 1978; (ed with John Imrie) Accounts of the Masters of Works 1616–1649, 1982; numerous articles in archaeological jls, etc. Recreations: reading, gardening. Address: Patie's Mill, Carlops, By Penicuik, Midlothian EH26 9NF. T: West Linton 60250. Club: New (Edinburgh).

DUNBAR of Hempriggs, Dame Maureen Daisy Helen, (Lady Dunbar of Hempriggs), Btss (8th in line) cr 1706 (NS); b 19 Aug. 1906; d of Courtenay Edward Moore and Janie King Moore (née Askins); m 1940, Leonard James Blake (assumed the name of Dunbar, in lieu of Blake, on claiming succession to the Hempriggs baronetcy after death of kinsman, Sir George Cospatrick Duff-Sutherland-Dunbar, 7th Bt, in 1963; claim established and title recognised by Lyon Court, 1965); one s one d. Educ: Headington Sch.; Royal Coll. of Music. LRAM 1928. Music teacher at: Monmouth Sch. for Girls, 1930–33; Oxford High Sch., 1935–40; Malvern Coll., 1957–68. Heir: (to mother's Btcy) s Richard Francis Dunbar of Hempriggs, younger [b 8 Jan. 1945 (assumed the name of Dunbar, 1965); m 1969, Elizabeth Margaret Jane Lister; two d]. Address: 51 Gloucester Street, Winchcombe, Cheltenham, Glos. T: Cheltenham 602122; Ackergill Tower, Wick, Caithness. T: Wick 2812.

DUNBAR-NASMITH, Rear-Adm. David Arthur, CB 1969; DSC 1942; retired 1972; Member: British Waterways Board, since 1980; Vice-Lord-Lieutenant, Morayshire, since 1980; Chairman, Moray and Nairn Newspaper Co., since 1982; b 21 Feb. 1921; e s of late Admiral Sir Martin Dunbar-Nasmith, VC, KCB, KCMG, DL, and of late Justina Dunbar-Nasmith, CBE, DStJ; m 1951, Elizabeth Bowlby; two s two d. Educ: Lockers Park; RNC, Dartmouth. To sea as Midshipman, 1939. War Service, Atlantic and Mediterranean, in HM Ships Barham, Rodney, Kelvin and Petard. In comd: HM Ships Haydon 1943, Peacock 1945–46, Moon 1946, Rowena 1946–48, Enard Bay 1951, Alert 1954–56, Berwick, and 5th Frigate Squadron, 1961–63; Commodore, Amphibious Forces, 1966–67. RN and Joint Service Staff Colls, 1948–49; Staff of Flag Officer 1st Cruiser Squadron, 1949–51; NATO HQ, SACLANT, 1952–54 and SACEUR, 1958–60; Dir of Defence Plans, Min. of Defence, 1963–65; Naval Secretary, 1967–70; Flag Officer, Scotland and N Ireland, 1970–72. Comdr 1951; Capt. 1958; Rear-Adm. 1967. Member: Highlands and Islands Develt Bd, 1972–83 (Dep. Chm., 1972–81; Chm., 1981–82); Countryside Commn for Scotland, 1972–76; N of Scotland Hydro-Electric Bd, 1982–85. Mem. Queen's Body Guard for Scotland (Royal Company of Archers), 1974–; Gentleman Usher of the Green Rod to the Order of the Thistle, 1979–. DL Moray, 1974. Recreations: sailing, ski-ing and shooting. Address: Glen of Rothes, Rothes, Moray. T: Rothes 216. Clubs: New (Edinburgh); Royal Ocean Racing.
  See also J. D. Dunbar-Nasmith.

DUNBAR-NASMITH, Prof. James Duncan, CBE 1976; RIBA; PPRIAS; FRSA; FRSE; Professor and Head of Department of Architecture, Heriot-Watt University and Edinburgh College of Art, since 1978; Partner, The Law & Dunbar-Nasmith Partnership, architects, Edinburgh and Forres (founded 1957); b 15 March 1927; y s of late Adm. Sir Martin Dunbar-Nasmith, VC, KCB, KCMG, DL and of late Justina Dunbar-Nasmith, CBE, DStJ. Educ: Lockers Park; Winchester. Trinity Coll., Cambridge (BA); Edinburgh Coll. of Art (DA). ARIBA 1954. Lieut, Scots Guards, 1945–48. President: Royal Incorporation of Architects in Scotland, 1971–73; Edinburgh Architectural Assoc., 1967–69. Member: Council, RIBA, 1967–73 (a Vice-Pres., 1972–73; Chm., Bd of Educn, 1972–73); Council, ARCUK, 1976–84 (Vice-Chm., Bd of Educn, 1977); Royal Commn on Ancient and Historical Monuments of Scotland, 1972–; Ancient Monuments Bd for Scotland, 1969–83 (interim Chm., 1972–73); Historic Buildings Council for Scotland, 1966–; Dep. Chm., Edinburgh Internat. Festival, 1981–85; Trustee: Scottish Civic Trust, 1971–; Theatres Trust, 1983–. Recreations: music, theatre, ski-ing, sailing. Address: 16 Dublin Street, Edinburgh EH1 3RE. T: 031–556 8631. Clubs: Royal Ocean Racing; New (Edinburgh).
  See also D. A. Dunbar-Nasmith.

DUNBOYNE, 28th Baron by Summons, 18th Baron by Patent; **Patrick Theobald Tower Butler; His Honour The Lord Dunboyne**; a Circuit Judge, 1972–86; b 27 Jan. 1917; e s of 27th Baron Dunboyne and Dora Isolde Butler (d 1977), e d of Comdr F. F. Tower; S father, 1945; m 1950, Anne Marie, d of late Sir Victor Mallet, GCMG, CVO; one s three d. Educ: Winchester; Trinity Coll., Cambridge (MA). Pres. of Cambridge Union. Lieut Irish Guards (Suppl. Res.); served European War, 1939–44 (King's Badge) (prisoner, then repatriated); Foreign Office, 1945–46. Barrister-at-Law, Middle Temple (Harmsworth Scholar), Inner Temple, South-Eastern Circuit, King's Inns, Dublin. In practice 1949–71. Recorder of Hastings, 1961–71; Dep. Chm., Quarter Sessions: Mddx, 1963–65; Kent, 1963–71; Inner London 1971–72. Commissary Gen., Diocese of Canterbury, 1959–71. Pres., 1971–, Fellow 1982, Irish Genealogical Res. Soc.; Founder Hon. Sec., Bar Lawn Tennis Soc., 1950 (Vice-Pres. 1963–), and of Irish Peers Assoc., 1963–71; Pres., Wireless Telegraphy Appeal Tribunal for Eng. and Wales, 1967–70. Publications: The Trial of J. G. Haigh, 1953; (with others) Cambridge Union, 1815–1939, 1953; Butler Family History, 1966. Recreations: rowing, lawn tennis, chess. Heir: s Hon. John Fitzwalter Butler [b 31 July 1951; m 1975, Diana Caroline, yr d of Sir Michael Williams, KCMG; one s three d]. Address: 36 Ormonde Gate, SW3 4HA. T: 01–352 1837. Clubs: Irish; International Lawn Tennis of Great Britain (Vice-Pres., Pres. 1973–83) and (hon.) of Australia, France, Germany, Monaco, Netherlands and USA; Forty Five Lawn Tennis (Pres.); All England Lawn Tennis (Wimbledon); Pitt, Union (Cambridge).

DUNCAN, Prof. Archibald Alexander McBeth, FBA 1985; Professor of Scottish History and Literature, Glasgow University, since 1962; b 17 Oct. 1926; s of Charles George Duncan and Christina Helen McBeth; m 1954, Ann Hayes Sawyer, d of W. E. H. Sawyer, Oxford; two s one d. Educ: George Heriot's Sch.; Edinburgh Univ.; Balliol Coll., Oxford. Lecturer in History, Queen's Univ., Belfast, 1951–53; Lecturer in History, Edinburgh Univ., 1953–61; Leverhulme Research Fellow, 1961–62. Clerk of Senate, Glasgow Univ., 1978–83. Mem., Royal Commn on the Ancient and Historical Monuments of Scotland, 1969–. Publications: Scotland: The Making of the Kingdom, 1975; (ed and revised) W. Croft Dickinson's Scotland from the Earliest Times to 1603, 3rd edn 1977. Address: 17 Campbell Drive, Bearsden, Glasgow G61 4NF.

DUNCAN, Prof. Archibald Sutherland, DSC 1943; FRCSE, FRCPE, FRCOG; Executive Dean of the Faculty of Medicine and Professor of Medical Education, Edinburgh University, 1966–76, now Emeritus; b 17 July 1914; y s of late Rev. H. C. Duncan, K-i-H, DD and late Rose Elsie Edwards; m 1939, Barbara, d of late John Gibson Holliday, JP, Penrith, Cumberland. Educ: Merchiston Castle Sch.; Edinburgh Univ. MB, ChB Edinburgh, 1936. Resident hosp. appts in Edinburgh and London, 1936–41. Served RNVR Surg. Lieut-Comdr (surg. specialist), 1941–45 (DSC). Temp. Cons. in Obst. and Gynæc., Inverness, 1946; Lectr in Univ. and part-time Cons. Obstetr. and Gynæcol., Aberdeen, 1946–50; Sen. Lectr, University of Edinburgh and Obstetr. and Gynæcol. to Western Gen. Hosp., Edinburgh 1950–53; Prof. of Obstetrics and Gynæcology in the Welsh National Sch. of Medicine, Univ. of Wales, 1953–66; Cons. Obstetrician and Gynæcologist, United Cardiff Hosps, 1953–66; Advisor in Obstetrics and Gynæcology to Welsh Hosp. Board, 1953–66. Member: Clin. Res. Bd of MRC, 1965–69; Council, RCSE, 1968–73; GMC, 1974–78; Lothian Health Bd, 1977–83 (Vice-Chm., 1981–83). Chm., Scottish Council on Disability, 1977–80. Vice-Pres., Inst. of Medical Ethics, 1985–. Hon. Pres., Brit. Med. Students Assoc., 1965–66. Mem. Court, Edinburgh Univ., 1979–83; Hon. Pres., Graduates' Assoc., Edinburgh Univ., 1986. Mem., James IV Assoc. of Surgeons; Hon. Mem., Alpha Omega Alpha Honor Med. Soc. Hon. MD Edinburgh, 1984. Associate Editor, British Jl of Medical Education, 1971–75; Consulting Editor, Jl of Medical Ethics, 1975–81. Publications: (ed jtly) Dictionary of Medical Ethics, 1977, 2nd edn 1981; contribs on scientific and allied subjects in various med. jls and books. Recreations: mountains, photography. Address: 1 Walker Street, Edinburgh EH3 7JY. T: 031–225 7657. Club: New (Edinburgh).

DUNCAN, Brian Arthur Cullum, CB 1972; CBE 1963 (MBE 1949); QC 1972; Judge Advocate General of the Forces, 1968–72; b 2 Feb. 1908; yr s of late Frank Hubert Duncan, LDS, RCS, and late Edith Jane Duncan (née Cullum); m 1934, Irene Flora Templeman (d 1983), o c of late John Frederick Templeman and late Flora Edith Templeman; two s two d. Educ: Queens' Coll., Cambridge (MA). Called to the Bar, Lincoln's Inn, 1931. Practised South Eastern Circuit, Central Criminal Court, North London Sessions, and Herts and Essex Sessions. Commissioned RAF, April 1940; relinqd commn, 1950 (Wing Comdr). Joined JAG's Dept, 1945. Dep. Judge Advocate Gen. (Army and RAF): Middle East, 1950–53; Germany, 1954–57; Far East, 1959–62; Vice Judge Advocate Gen., 1967–68. Address: Culverlands, Neville Park, Baltonsborough, Glastonbury, Som.

DUNCAN, David Francis; HM Diplomatic Service, retired; b 22 Feb. 1923; s of late Brig. William Edmonstone Duncan, CVO, DSO, MC, and Mrs Magdalene Emily Duncan (née Renny-Tailyour). Educ: Eton; Trinity Coll., Cambridge. Served War, RA, 1941–46 (despatches). Entered Foreign (later Diplomatic) Service, 1949; Foreign Office, 1949–52; Bogotá, 1952–54; UK Delegn to ECSC, Luxembourg, 1954–55; FO, 1955–58; Baghdad, 1958; Ankara, 1958–60; FO, 1960–62; Quito, 1962–65; Phnom Penh, 1965 (as Chargé d'Affaires); FO (later Foreign and Commonwealth Office), 1965–70; Islamabad, 1970–71; Counsellor, UK Delegn to Geneva Disarm. Conf., 1971–74; Ambassador to Nicaragua, 1974–76; retired 1976. Recreations: walking, photography, travel. Address: 8 Eaton Mews South, SW1W 9HP. T: 01–235 7761.

DUNCAN, Rev. Denis Macdonald, MA, BD; Director: Highgate Counselling Centre, since 1969; The Churches' Council for Health and Healing, since 1982; Managing Director, Arthur James Ltd (Publishers), since 1983; b 10 Jan. 1920; s of late Rev. Reginald Duncan, BD, BLitt and late Clarice Ethel (née Hodgkinson); m 1942, Henrietta Watson McKenzie (née Houston); one s one d. Educ: George Watson's Boys' Coll., Edinburgh; Edinburgh Univ.; New Coll., Edinburgh. Minister of: St Margaret's, Juniper Green, Edinburgh, 1943–49; Trinity Duke Street Parish Church, Glasgow, 1949–57; Founder-editor, Rally, 1956–67; Managing Editor, British Weekly, 1957–70 (Man. Dir, 1967–70); Man. Dir, DPS Publicity Services Ltd, 1967–74; broadcaster and scriptwriter, Scottish Television, 1963–68; concert promotion at Edinburgh Festival and elsewhere, 1966–; Concert series "Communication through the Arts" poetry/music anthologies (with Benita Kyle), 1970–. Associate Dir and Trng Supervisor, Westminster Pastoral Foundn, 1971–79; Chm., Internat. Cttee of World Assocs of Pastoral Care and Counselling, 1977–79; Moderator of the Presbytery of England, Church of Scotland, 1984. FIBA (FIICS) 1976. Publications: (ed) Through the Year with William Barclay, 1971; (ed) Through the Year with Cardinal Heenan, 1972; (ed) Daily Celebration, vol. 1, 1972, vol. 2, 1974; Marching Orders I, 1973; (ed) Every Day with William Barclay, 1973; (ed) Through the Year with J. B. Phillips, 1974; Marching On, 1974; Here is my Hand, 1977; Creative Silence, 1980; A Day at a Time, 1980; Love, the Word that Heals, 1981; The Way of Love, 1982; Victorious Living, 1982. Recreations: cricket, badminton. Address: 1 Cranbourne Road, N10 2BT. T: 01–883 1831. Club: Arts.

DUNCAN, George; Chairman, Lloyds Bowmaker Finance Ltd (formerly Lloyds and Scottish plc), since 1976 (Director since 1973); Director, Lloyds Bank Plc, since 1982; Chairman: Allied Steel and Wire (Holdings) Ltd, since 1986; Household Mortgage Corporation Plc, since 1986; b 9 Nov. 1933; s of William Duncan and Catherine Gray Murray; m 1965, Frauke Ulrike Schnuhr; one d. Educ: Holloway County Grammar Sch.; London Sch. of Economics (BSc(Econ)); Wharton Sch.; Univ. of Pennsylvania (MBA). Mem., Inst. of Chartered Accountants (FCA); CBIM. Chief Executive, Truman Hanbury Buxton and Co. Ltd, 1967–71; Chief Executive, Watney Mann Ltd, 1971–72; Vice-Chm., Internat. Distillers and Vintners Ltd, 1972. Director: BET plc, 1981–; Haden plc, 1974–85 (Dep. Chm., 1984–85); TR City of London Trust PLC, 1977–; Associated British Ports PLC, 1986–; Whessoe PLC, 1986–; Newspaper Publishing plc, 1986–. Chm., CBI Companies Cttee, 1980–83; Mem., CBI President's Cttee, 1980–83. Freeman, City of London, 1971. Recreations: opera, tennis, skiing. Address: c/o Lloyds Bowmaker Finance Ltd, 9/13 Grosvenor Street, W1X 9FB. T: 01–491 3236.

DUNCAN, George Alexander; Fellow Emeritus of Trinity College, Dublin, since 1967; b 15 May 1902; s of Alexander Duncan and Elizabeth Linn; m 1932, Eileen Stone, MSc, d of William Henry Stone and Sarah Copeland; one d. Educ: Ballymena Academy; Campbell Coll., Belfast; Trinity Coll., Dublin; University of North Carolina. BA, LLB 1923, MA 1926; Research Fellow on the Laura Spelman Rockefeller Memorial Foundation, 1924–25; Prof. of Political Economy in the University of Dublin, 1934–67; Registrar of TCD, 1951–52, and Bursar, 1952–57; Pro-Chancellor, Univ. of Dublin, 1965–72. Leverhulme Research Fellow, 1950; Visiting Fellow, Princeton Univ., 1963–64. Mem. of IFS Commissions of Inquiry into Banking, Currency and Credit, 1934–38; Agriculture,

1939; Emigration and Population, 1948. Planning Officer (temp.) in Ministry of Production, London, 1943–45; Economic Adviser to British National Cttee of Internat. Chambers of Commerce, 1941–47. Vice-Pres., Royal Dublin Society; Life Mem., Mont Pelerin Soc.; Mem., Bd of Visitors, National Museum of Ireland. Formerly Member: Irish National Productivity Cttee; Council Irish Management Inst.; Exec. Bd, Dublin Economic Research Inst.; Internat. Inst. of Statistics. *Publications:* numerous papers in the economic periodicals. *Recreations:* travel, walking. *Address:* 7 Braemor Park, Churchtown, Dublin 14. *T:* Dublin 970442. *Club:* Kildare Street and University (Dublin).

DUNCAN, Dr George Douglas; Regional Medical Officer, East Anglian Regional Health Authority, 1973–85; *s* of late George Forman Duncan and of Mary Duncan (*née* Davidson); *m* 1949, Isobel (*née* Reid); two *s* one *d. Educ:* Robert Gordon's Coll., Aberdeen; Aberdeen Univ. MB, ChB 1948, DPH 1952, FFCM 1972. Various hosp. appts; Asst MOH Stirlingshire, Divisional MO Grangemouth, 1953–57; Asst Sen. MO, Leeds RHB, 1957–60; Dep. Sen. Admin. MO, Newcastle RHB, 1960–68; Sen. Admin. MO, East Anglian RHB, 1968–73. Member: Nat. Nursing Staff Cttee and Nat. Staff Cttee for Nurses and Midwives, 1970–74; PHLS Bd, 1973–75; Central Cttee for Community Medicine, 1974–81; Chm., English Regl MOs Gp, 1981–83; Vice-Pres., FCM RCP, 1979–83. QHP 1984–86. Hon. MA Cambridge, 1986. *Address:* 12 Storey's Way, Cambridge CB3 0DT. *T:* Cambridge 63427.

DUNCAN, Sir James (Blair), Kt 1981; Chairman, since 1975, and Chief Executive, since 1970, Transport Development Group; *b* 24 Aug. 1927; *s* of late John Duncan and Emily MacFarlane Duncan; *m* 1974, Dr Betty Psaltis, San Francisco. *Educ:* Whitehill Sch., Glasgow. Qualified as Scottish Chartered Accountant. Joined Transport Development Group, 1953; Dir, 1960; Mem., LTE (part-time), 1979–82. Scottish Council: Mem. 1976–, and Chm. 1982–; London Exec. Cttee; Vice Pres., 1983–. Confedn of British Industry: Mem. Council, 1980–82; Mem. 1979–, and Chm. 1983–, London Region Roads and Transportation Cttee; Mem., Transport Policy Cttee, 1983–. London Chamber of Commerce: Mem. Council, 1982–; Mem., Gen. Purposes Cttee, 1983–; Dep. Chm., 1984–86; Pres., 1986–. Pres., IRTE, 1984–. FCIT (Pres., 1980–81; Spurrier Meml Lectr, 1972; Award of Merit, 1973; Herbert Crow Medal, 1978); CBIM; FRSA 1977. *Publications:* papers on transport matters. *Recreations:* travel, reading, walking, swimming, theatre. *Address:* 17 Kingston House South, Ennismore Gardens, SW7. *T:* 01–589 3545. *Club:* Caledonian.

DUNCAN, Prof. James Playford, ME Adelaide, DSc Manchester; Professor of Mechanical Engineering, University of British Columbia, 1966–84, now Emeritus; Adjunct Professor, University of Victoria, since 1984; *b* 10 Nov. 1919; *s* of late Hugh Sinclair Duncan and late Nellie Gladys Duncan; *m* 1942, Jean Marie Booth; three *s* one *d. Educ:* Scotch Coll., Adelaide; University of Adelaide, S Australia. Executive Engineer, Richards Industries Ltd, Keswick, S Australia, 1941–46; Senior Physics Master, Scotch Coll., Adelaide, 1946–47; Lecturer in Mechanical Engineering, University of Adelaide, 1948–49, Senior Lecturer, 1950–51 and 1953–54; Turbine Engineer, Metropolitan Vickers Electrical Co., Trafford Park, Manchester, 1952; Turner and Newall Research Fellow, University of Manchester, 1955; Lecturer in Mechanical Engineering, University of Manchester, 1956; Prof. of Mechanical Engineering, University of Sheffield, 1956–66. *Publication:* Sculptured Surfaces in Engineering and Medicine, 1983. *Recreations:* sailing, flautist. *Address:* 25 Oceanview Road, PO Box 137, Lions Bay, BC V0N 2E0, Canada. *T:* (604) 921–7191.

DUNCAN, James Stuart, CMG 1946; Hon. Air Commodore; company director; *b* 1893; *m* 1936, Victoria Martinez Alonso, Cordoba, Spain; one *s* two *d. Educ:* Coll. Rollin, Paris. Joined Massey-Harris Ltd, Berlin, 1909; went to Canada, 1911. Served with UK Forces in 1914–18 War, rising to be Capt. and Adjutant of 180th Brigade 16th Irish Divisional Artillery. Apptd Gen. Manager Massey-Harris Co., 1936; Pres. 1941; Chm. and Pres. 1949 until his resignation in 1956. Apptd Actg Dep. Minister of Defence for Air, 1940, when he took over leadership of Brit. Commonwealth Air Trg Plan; declined invitation of Prime Minister, in summer 1940, to join Federal Cabinet as Minister of Air. Chm., Combined Agricl & Food Cttee of UNRRA, 1941–42; Mem. Nat. Res. Council, Ottawa, during War Years. Past Chm.: Toronto Bd of Trade, Toronto Community Chest, Canadian Council of Internat. Chambers of Commerce, Montreal; Hon. Pres., Toronto section, "Free Fighting French"; Chm. Dollar Sterling Trade Council, 1949–61. First Canadian chosen by Nat. Sales Exec. Organization as "Canadian Businessman of the Year," 1956; Chm., Nat. Conf. on Engrg, Sci. and Tech. Manpower, NB, 1956; organizer and Dep. Chm. Canadian Trade Mission to the UK, 1957. On accepting Chairmanship of Hydro-Electric Power Commn of Ont., Nov. 1956, resigned from bd of many Canadian cos incl. Argus Corp. Ltd, Canada Cement, Ltd, Canadian Bank of Commerce, Internat. Nickel of Canada, Ltd, Page-Hersey Tubes; resigned from Chmship Hydro-Electric Power Commn of Ont., 1961. Upon establishing residence in Bermuda, Aug. 1961, resigned from Gov., University Toronto; Chm., Dollar Sterling Trade Coun.; Chm., Australian-Canadian Assoc.; Dir, Industrial Foundn on Educn; Dir, Atomic Energy of Canada, Ltd; Chm., Royal Conservatory of Music Cttee. Hon. LLD, Dartmouth Coll., NH, USA, 1957. Chevalier, French Legion of Honour; Croix de Lorraine; King Haakon VII Cross of Liberation. *Publications:* Russia's Bid for World Supremacy, 1955; The Great Leap Forward, 1959; Russia Revisited, 1960; In The Shadow of the Red Star, 1962; A Businessman Looks at Red China, 1965; Not a One-Way Street (autobiography), 1971. *Address:* Somerset House, Paget, Bermuda. *Clubs:* York (Toronto); Royal Bermuda Yacht (Bermuda); Sotogrande (Spain).

DUNCAN, Ven. John Finch; Archdeacon of Birmingham, since 1985; *b* 9 Sept. 1933; *s* of John and Helen Maud Duncan; *m* 1965, Diana Margaret Dewes; one *s* two *d. Educ:* Queen Elizabeth Grammar School, Wakefield; University Coll., Oxford; Cuddesdon Coll. MA (Oxon). Curate, St John, South Bank, Middlesbrough, 1959–61; Novice, Society of St Francis, 1961–62; Curate, St Peter, Birmingham, 1962–65; Chaplain, Univ. of Birmingham, 1965–76; Vicar of All Saints, Kings Heath, Birmingham, 1976–85. Chm., Copec Housing Trust, 1970–. *Recreations:* golf, convivial gatherings. *Address:* 122 Westfield Road, Edgbaston, Birmingham B15 3JQ. *T:* 021-454 3402. *Club:* Harborne Golf (Birmingham).

DUNCAN, John Spenser Ritchie, CMG 1967; MBE 1953; HM Diplomatic Service, retired; High Commissioner in the Bahamas, 1978–81; *b* 26 July 1921; *s* of late Rev. J. H. Duncan, DD; *m* 1950, Sheila Conacher, MB, ChB, DObstRCOG; one *d. Educ:* George Watson's Boys' Coll.; Glasgow Acad.; Dundee High Sch.; Edinburgh Univ. Entered Sudan Political Service, 1941. Served in HM Forces, 1941–43. Private Sec. to Governor-Gen. of the Sudan, 1954; Dep. Adviser to Governor-Gen. on Constitutional and External Affairs, 1955; appointed to Foreign (subseq. Diplomatic) Service, 1956; seconded to Joint Services Staff Coll., 1957; Political Agent, Doha, 1958; Dep. Dir-Gen., British Information Services, New York, 1959–63; Consul-Gen., Muscat, 1963–65; Head of Personnel Dept, Diplomatic Service, 1966–68; Minister, British High Commn, Canberra, 1969–71; High Comr, Zambia, 1971–74; Ambassador to Morocco, 1975–78. *Publications:* The Sudan: A Record of Achievement, 1952; The Sudan's Path to Independence, 1957. *Address:* 9

Blackford Road, Edinburgh EH9 2DT. *Club:* New (Edinburgh).
See also K. P. Duncan.

DUNCAN, Dr Kenneth Playfair, CB 1985; FRCP; FRCPE; Assistant Director (Biomedical Sciences), National Radiological Protection Board, since 1985; *b* 27 Sept. 1924; *s* of late Dr J. H. Duncan, MA, BPhil, DD, and H. P. Duncan (*née* Ritchie); *m* 1950, Dr Gillian Crow, MB, ChB; four *d. Educ:* Kilmarnock Acad.; Glasgow Acad.; Dundee High Sch.; St Andrews Univ. BSc, MB, ChB; DIH. FFOM 1978. House Surg., Dundee Royal Infirmary, 1947; RAMC, 1948–50; Gen. Practice, Brighton, 1950–51; Area MO, British Rail, 1951–54; Chief Medical Officer: SW Gas Bd, 1954–58; UKAEA, 1958–69; Head of Health and Safety, BSC, 1969–75; Dir of Medical Services, HSE, 1975–82; Dep. Dir-Gen., HSE, 1982–84. External Examiner in Occupational Health, Univ. of Dundee, 1970–74; Examiner in Occupational Health, Soc. of Apothecaries, 1974–79. Vis. Prof., London Sch. of Hygiene and Tropical Medicine, 1977–82. Mem., MRC, 1975–83; Mem., IHAC, 1960–74. Pres., Soc. of Occupational Medicine, 1970. *Publications:* contrib. medical and scientific jls on radiological protection and gen. occupational health topics. *Recreation:* gardening. *Address:* Westfield, Steeple Aston, Oxon OX5 3SD. *T:* Steeple Aston 40277.
See also J. S. R. Duncan.

DUNCAN, Malcolm McGregor, WS; Chief Executive, City of Edinburgh District Council, since 1980; *b* 23 Jan. 1922; *s* of Rev. Reginald Duncan, BD, BLitt, and Clarice Ethel (*née* Hodgkinson); *m* 1954, Winifred Petrie (*née* Greenhorn); two *s* one *d. Educ:* George Watson's Coll., Edinburgh; Edinburgh Univ. (MA 1942; LLB 1948). Admitted Writer to the Signet, 1949. Served RAFVR, Flt Lieut. 1942–46. Edinburgh Corporation, 1952; Depute Town Clerk, 1971; Director of Administration, City of Edinburgh District Council, 1975–80. *Recreations:* playing golf, watching other sports, listening to music. *Address:* City Chambers, High Street, Edinburgh EH1 1YJ. *T:* 031–225 2424.
See also Rev. D. M. Duncan.

DUNCAN, Michael John Freeman; HM Diplomatic Service; Regional Director, Research Department, Foreign and Commonwealth Office, since 1983; *b* 9 Jan. 1926; *s* of late John Colley Duncan and of Blanche (*née* Freeman); *m* 1964, Sally Ilbert Crosse; one *s* one *d. Educ:* Hurstpierpoint (Scholar); Christ Church, Oxford (Scholar; MA); Ecole Nationale des Langues Orientales, Paris (Diplôme des Langues Slaves). Entered HM Diplomatic Service, 1951; Attaché, Moscow, 1949; FO, 1951; Germany, 1952; FO, 1954; Moscow, 1959; FO, 1961; UN Disarmament Conf., Geneva, 1964; FO, 1966; Caracas, 1969; FCO, 1973; Counsellor, Moscow, 1982–83. Order of St Cecilia, Estado de Miranda, Venezuela, 1972. *Publications:* Ilf and Petrov, 1964; *translations:* Trotsky Papers, 1964; Paustovsky, Story of a Life, 1964; Lydia Ginzburg, Within the Whirlwind, 1981; various articles. *Recreations:* reading, linguistics, mushrooms, gardening. *Address:* c/o Foreign and Commonwealth Office, SW1; Whin Cottage, St Michaels Drive, Otford, Sevenoaks, Kent TN14 5SA.

DUNCAN, Maj.-Gen. Nigel William, CB 1951; CBE 1945; DSO 1945; DL; *b* 27 Nov. 1899; *s* of George William and Edith Duncan, Earlston, Guildford; *m* 1928, Victoria Letitia Troyte, *d* of late Capt. J. E. Acland, Wollaston House, Dorchester, Dorset; three *d. Educ:* Malvern Coll.; RMC Sandhurst. 2nd Bn The Black Watch, 1919; transf. Royal Tank Corps, 1923; Captain, 1931; Major, 1938; Lieut-Col, 1940; Col, 1943; Brig. 30 Armoured Bde, 1943, 2nd Armoured Bde, 1946; Comdr Royal Armoured Corps Centre, 1947; Maj.-Gen., 1949; Dir Royal Armoured Corps, WO, 1949–52; retired pay, 1952. Col Comdt Royal Tank Regt, 1952–58. Lieut-Governor Royal Hospital, Chelsea, 1953–57. DL Dorset, 1959. *Address:* Marley House, Winfrith Newburgh, Dorchester DT2 8JR. *Club:* Army and Navy.

DUNCAN, Sean Bruce; a Recorder of the Crown Court, since 1984; *b* 21 Dec. 1942; *s* of Joseph Alexander Duncan and Patricia Pauline Duncan; *m* 1974, Dr Diana Bowyer Courtney; three *s* one *d. Educ:* Shrewsbury Sch.; St Edmund Hall, Oxford (MA). Called to the Bar, Inner Temple, 1966; Northern Circuit (Hon. Sec., Circuit Cttee, 1985–). Served with Cheshire Yeomanry (TA), 1963–68 (Lieut). Chairman: Old Swan Boys Club, Liverpool, 1974–79; Liverpool Youth Organisations Cttee, 1977–83; Vice-Chm., Liverpool Council of Voluntary Service, 1982–. *Recreations:* farming, sport, music. *Address:* South Alton, 22 Rose Mount, Oxton, Birkenhead L43 5SW. *T:* 051-653 6545. *Clubs:* Liverpool Racquet; Royal Liverpool Golf; Liverpool Ramblers AFC (Vice Pres.); Royal Chester Rowing.

DUNCAN, Stanley Frederick St Clare, CMG 1983; HM Diplomatic Service; High Commissioner in Malta, since 1985; *b* 13 Nov. 1927; *yr s* of late Stanley Gilbert Scott and Louisa Elizabeth Duncan; *m* 1967, Jennifer Jane Bennett; two *d. Educ:* Latymer Upper Sch. FRGS. India Office, 1946; CRO, 1947; Private Sec. to Parly Under-Sec. of State, 1954; Second Sec., Ottawa, 1954–55; Brit. Govt Information Officer, Toronto, 1955–57; Second Sec., Wellington, 1958–60; First Sec., CRO, 1960; seconded to Central African Office, 1962–64; Mem., Brit. Delegn to Victoria Falls Conf. on Dissolution of Fedn of Rhodesia and Nyasaland, 1963; First Sec., Nicosia, 1964–67; FCO, 1967–70; FCO Adviser, Brit. Gp, Inter-Parly Union, 1968–70; Head of Chancery and First Sec., Lisbon, 1970–73; Consul-General and subsequently Chargé d'Affaires in Mozambique, 1973–75; Counsellor (Political), Brasilia, 1976–77; Head of Consular Dept, FCO, 1977–80; Canadian Nat. Defence Coll., 1980–81; Ambassador to Bolivia, 1981–85. Officer, Military Order of Christ (Portugal), 1973. *Recreations:* countryside pursuits. *Address:* c/o Foreign and Commonwealth Office, SW1.

DUNCAN MILLAR, Ian Alastair, CBE 1978; MC; CEng, MICE; JP, DL; Director, Macdonald Fraser & Co. Ltd, Perth, 1961–85; Member, Royal Company of Archers (Queen's Body Guard for Scotland), since 1956; *b* 22 Nov. 1914; *s* of late Sir James Duncan Millar and Lady Duncan Millar (*née* Forester Paton); *m* 1945, Louise Reid McCosh; two *s* two *d. Educ:* Gresham's Sch., Holt; Trinity Coll., Cambridge (MA). Served with Corps of Royal Engineers, 1940–45 (Major; wounded; despatches): 7th Armoured Div., N Africa and Normandy; 51 (Highland) Div., France and Germany. Contested Parly Elections (L): Banff, 1945; Kinross and W Perthshire, 1949 and 1963. Depute Chm., North of Scotland Hydro-Electric Bd, 1970–72 (Mem., 1957–72). Chm., United Auctions (Scotland) Ltd, 1967–74. Dir, Hill Farming Research Organisation, 1966–78; Chm., Consultative Cttee to Sec. of State for Scotland under 1976 Freshwater and Salmon Fisheries Act, 1981–. Mem. Ct, Dundee Univ., 1975–78. Perth CC, 1945–75: Chm. Planning Cttee, 1954–75; Convener, 1970–75; Chm. Jt CC of Perth and Kinross, 1970–75; Tayside Regional Council: Councillor and Chm., 1974–75; Convener, 1975–78. DL 1963, JP 1952, Perthshire. *Recreations:* studying and catching salmon, shooting, meeting people. *Address:* Remony, Aberfeldy, Perthshire. *T:* Kenmore 209. *Club:* Royal Golfing Society (Perth).

DUNCAN-SANDYS, family name of **Baron Duncan-Sandys.**

DUNCAN-SANDYS, Baron *cr* 1974 (Life Peer); **Duncan Edwin Duncan-Sandys,** CH 1973; PC 1944; Founder, Civic Trust and President, since 1956; President, Lonrho Ltd, since 1984 (Chairman 1972–84); *b* 24 Jan. 1908; *o s* of Captain George Sandys, formerly MP for Wells, and Mildred, *d* of Duncan Cameron, Ashburton, New Zealand; *m* 1st,

1935, Diana (marr. diss. 1960; she *d* 1963), *d* of late Rt Hon. Sir Winston Churchill; one *s* two *d*; 2nd, 1962, Marie-Claire, *d* of Adrien Schmitt, Paris, and formerly Viscountess Hudson; one *d*. *Educ:* Eton; Magdalen Coll., Oxford (MA). Entered Diplomatic Service, 1930; served in Foreign Office and British Embassy, Berlin; MP (C) Norwood Div. of Lambeth, 1935–45, Streatham, 1950–Feb. 1974; Political Columnist of Sunday Chronicle, 1937–39; Member Nat. Exec. of Conservative Party, 1938–39; Commissioned in [illegible] Army (Royal Artillery), 1937; Co-founder, Air Raid Protection Inst. (later [illegible] 1938; served in Expeditionary Force in Norway, 1940; Lt-Col [illegible]e, 1941; Financial Sec. to War Office, 1941–43; Parly Sec., [illegible]e for armament production, 1943–44; Chm., War Cabinet [illegible]an flying bombs and rockets, 1943–45; Minister of Works, [illegible] Oct. 1951–Oct. 1954; Minister of Housing and Local Govt, [illegible]er of Defence, Jan. 1957–Oct. 1959; Minister of Aviation, [illegible]ary of State for Commonwealth Relations, July 1960–Oct. [illegible]ate for the Colonies, July 1962–Oct. 1964. Founded European [illegible]ternational Executive until 1950; Chm., Parly Council of [illegible]–51 (Pres. of Honour, European Movement, 1980–); Mem. [illegible]l of Europe and of WEU, 1950–51, 1965– (Leader British Dele[illegible]uropa Nostra, 1969–84 (Hon. Life Pres., 1984); Chm. British Section, F[illegible]uncil, 1972–78; Chm. Internat. Organising Cttee, European Architectura[illegible]ar, 1975. Mem., Gen. Adv. Council, BBC, 1947–51. Director, Ashanti Goldf[illegible]ration, 1947–51 and 1966–72. Vice-Pres., Assoc. of District Councils, 1979–. [illegible]ce-Pres., Nat. Chamber of Trade, 1951–. Hon. MRTPI, 1956; Hon. FRIBA, 1968. M[illegible]n. of Magic Circle. Freeman of Bridgetown, Barbados, 1962. Grand Cross, Order of Merit, Italy, 1960; Order of Sultanate of Brunei, 1973; Medal of Honour, City of Paris, 1974; Gold Cup of European Movement, 1975; Goethe Gold Medal, Hamburg Foundn, 1975; Grand Cross of Order of Crown, Belgium, 1975; Commandeur, Légion d'Honneur, France, 1979; Grand Cross, Order of Merit, Fed. Rep. of Germany, 1981. *Publications:* European Movement and the Council of Europe, 1949; The Modern Commonwealth, 1961. *Recreation:* abstract painting. *Address:* Flat T, 12 Warwick Square, SW1. *T:* 01–834 5886. *Club:* Pratt's.

See also J. G. W. Sandys, Maj.-Gen. K. Perkins.

DUNCOMBE, family name of **Baron Feversham.**

DUNCOMBE, Sir Philip (Digby) Pauncefort-, 4th Bt *cr* 1859; DL; one of HM Body Guard, Honorable Corps of Gentlemen-at-Arms, since 1979; *b* 18 May 1927; *o s* of Sir Everard Pauncefort-Duncombe, 3rd Bt, DSO, and Evelyn Elvira (*d* 1986), *d* of Frederick Anthony Denny; *S* father, 1971; *m* 1951, Rachel Moyra, *d* of Major H. G. Aylmer; one *s* two *d*. *Educ:* Stowe. 2nd Lieut, Grenadier Guards, 1946; served in Palestine, 1947–48; Malaya, 1948–49; Cyprus, 1957–59; Hon. Major, retired 1960, Regular Army Reserve. County Comdt, Buckinghamshire Army Cadet Force, 1967–70. DL Bucks 1971. *Heir: s* David Philip Henry Pauncefort-Duncombe, *b* 21 May 1956. *Address:* Great Brickhill Manor, Milton Keynes, Bucks MK17 9BE. *T:* Great Brickhill 205. *Club:* Cavalry and Guards.

DUNCOMBE, Roy, VRD 1957; Chairman, Anglia Building Society, since 1985; *b* 7 June 1925; *s* of Joseph William Duncombe and Gladys May Duncombe (*née* Reece); *m* 1946, Joan Thornley Pickering; one *s* two *d*. *Educ:* Hinckley Grammar School. RNR, 1943–68 (Lt-Comdr (A); Pilot, Fleet Air Arm). Financial Dir, Ferry Pickering Group, 1965–85. *Recreations:* walking, swimming, boating, ornithology. *Address:* Westways, Market Bosworth, Nuneaton, Warwickshire CV13 0LQ. *T:* Market Bosworth 291728. *Club:* Naval and Military.

DUNCUMB, Dr Peter, FRS 1977; Director and General Manager, TI Group (formerly Tube Investments) Research Laboratories, since 1979 (Assistant Director, 1972–79); *b* 26 Jan. 1931; *s* of late William Duncumb and of Hilda Grace (*née* Coleman); *m* 1955, Anne Leslie Taylor; two *s* one *d*. *Educ:* Oundle Sch.; Clare Coll., Cambridge (BA 1953, MA 1956, PhD 1957). DSIR Res. Fellow, Cambridge Univ., 1957–59; Res. Scientist and Gp Leader, Tube Investments Res. Labs, 1959–67, Head, Physics Dept, 1967–72. Hon. Mem., Microbeam Analysis Soc. of America, 1973. C. V. Boys Prize, Inst. of Physics, 1966. *Publications:* numerous on electron microscopy and analysis in Jl of Inst. of Physics. *Recreations:* hill walking, family genealogy. *Address:* 5 Woollards Lane, Great Shelford, Cambridge. *T:* Cambridge 843064.

DUNDAS, family name of **Viscount Melville,** and of **Marquess of Zetland.**

DUNDAS, Lord; Robin Lawrence Dundas; *b* 5 March 1965; *s* and *heir* of Earl of Ronaldshay, *qv*. *Educ:* Harrow. *Recreations:* shooting, skiing, tennis. *Address:* Copt Hewick Hall, Ripon, North Yorks. *Club:* Slainte Mhah.

DUNDAS, Group Captain Hugh Spencer Lisle, CBE 1977; DSO 1944 and Bar 1945; DFC 1941; RAF retired; DL; Chairman: BET Public Limited Company, since 1982 (Managing Director, 1973–82, Deputy Chairman, 1981–82); Thames Television Ltd, since 1981 (Director, since 1968); *b* 22 July 1920; *s* of late Frederick James Dundas and Sylvia Mary (*née* March-Phillipps); *m* 1950, Hon. Enid Rosamond Lawrence, 2nd *d* of 1st Baron Oaksey and 3rd Baron Trevethin; one *s* two *d*. *Educ:* Stowe. Joined 616 (S Yorks) Sqdn AAF 1939; served in UK Fighter Comd Sqdn, 1939–43; N Africa, Malta, Sicily, Italy, 1943–46; perm. commn 1944; comd 244 Wing, Italy, 1944–46 (Gp Captain; despatches 1945); retd 1947. Comd 601 (Co. London) Sqdn RAuxAF, 1947–50. Beaverbrook Newspapers, 1948–60: various editorial and managerial posts; joined Exec. Staff, Rediffusion Ltd, 1961: Dir, 1966; Dep. Man. Dir, 1968; Man. Dir 1970–74. Chairman: Humphries Hldgs Ltd, 1975–77; Redifon Ltd, 1970–78; Rediffusion plc, 1978–85; A-R Television PLC (formerly Rediffusion Television Ltd), 1978–85 (Dep. Chm., 1970–78); BET Omnibus Services PLC, 1978–85; BET Investments Ltd, 1978–85; Dir, BET Leisure Holdings Ltd, 1973–85. Vice-Chm. (Air) South East, TAVRA, 1973–83; Mem. Council, and Finance and General Purposes Cttee, RAF Benevolent Fund, 1976–; Mem. Council, Nat. Soc. for Cancer Relief, 1976– (Trustee). DL Surrey, 1969. *Address:* 55 Iverna Court, W8 6TU. *T:* 01–937 0773; The Schoolroom, Dockenfield, Farnham, Surrey. *T:* Frensham 2331. *Clubs:* White's, Royal Air Force.

DUNDEE, 12th Earl of, *cr* 1660 (Scotland); **Alexander Henry Scrymgeour;** Viscount Dudhope and Lord Scrymgeour, 1641 (Scotland); Lord Inverkeithing, 1660 (Scotland); Lord Glassary (UK), 1954; Hereditary Royal Standard-Bearer for Scotland; *b* 5 June 1949; *s* of 11th Earl of Dundee, PC, and of Patricia Katherine, *d* of late Col Lord Herbert Montagu Douglas Scott; *S* father, 1983; *m* 1979, Siobhan Mary, *d* of David Llewellyn, Gt Somerford, Wilts; one *s* two *d*. *Educ:* Eton; St Andrews Univ. Contested (C) Hamilton, by-election May 1978. *Heir: s* Lord Scrymgeour, *qv*. *Address:* Farm Office, Birkhill, Cupar, Fife. *Clubs:* White's; New (Edinburgh).

DUNDEE (St Paul's Cathedral), Provost of; *see* Sanderson, Very Rev. P. O.

DUNDERDALE, Comdr Wilfred Albert, CMG 1942; MBE 1920; RNVR, retired; *b* 24 Dec. 1899; *s* of late Richard Albert Dunderdale, Shipowner, and Sophie Dunderdale; *m* 1952, Dorothy Brayshaw Hyde (*d* 1978); *m* 1980, Deborah, *d* of Eugene B. Jackson, Boston, Mass and *widow* of Harry McJ. McLeod. Trained as Naval Architect, 1914–17; served with Mediterranean Fleet, 1918–22 (despatches twice); Lieut RNVR, 1920; transferred to British Embassy, Constantinople, 1922–26; Paris, 1926–40; Comdr, 1939. Russian Order of St Anne; Polonia Restituta; French Legion of Honour (Officer); French Croix de Guerre with palm; United States Legion of Merit (Officer). *Address:* Castlefield, Bletchingley, Surrey RH1 4LB. *T:* Godstone 843121. *Clubs:* Boodle's; Royal Harwich Yacht (Harwich).

DUNDONALD, 15th Earl of, *cr* 1669; **Iain Alexander Douglas Blair Cochrane;** Lord Cochrane of Dundonald, 1647; Lord Cochrane of Paisley and Ochiltree, 1669; Managing Director, Arthurstone Development Company Ltd, since 1985; *b* 17 Feb. 1961; *s* of 14th Earl of Dundonald and Aphra Farquhar (*d* 1972), *d* of late Comdr George Fetherstonhaugh; *S* father, 1986. *Educ:* Wellington College; RAC Cirencester. DipREM. *Recreations:* shooting, fishing, skiing, sailing. *Address:* Lochnell Castle, Ledaig, Argyll.

DUNEDIN, Bishop of, since 1976; **Rt. Rev. Peter Woodley Mann;** *b* 25 July 1924; *s* of Edgar Allen and Bessie May Mann; *m* 1955, Anne Victoria Norman; three *d*. *Educ:* Prince Alfred Coll., Adelaide; St John's Coll., Auckland (Fellow); Univ. of London (BD). Deacon, Dio. Waiapu, 1953; priest, 1954; Curate: Waiapu Cathedral, 1953–55; Rotorua, 1955–56; Vicar: Porangahau, 1956–61; Dannevirke, 1961–66; Vicar of Blenheim and Archdeacon of Marlborough, 1966–71; Vicar of St Mary's and Archdeacon of Timaru, 1971–75; Vicar of St James' Lower Hutt, 1975–76. *Recreations:* tennis, athletics. *Address:* Bishop's House, 10 Claremont Street, Roslyn, Dunedin, NZ. *T:* 772694.

DUNGEY, Prof. James Wynne, PhD; Professor of Physics, Imperial College, University of London, 1965–84; *b* 30 Jan. 1923; *s* of Ernest Dungey and Alice Dungey; *m* 1950, Christine Scotland (*née* Brown); one *s* one *d*. *Educ:* Bradfield; Magdalene Coll., Cambridge (MA, PhD). Res. Fellow, Univ. of Sydney, 1950–53; Vis. Asst Prof., Penn State Coll., 1953–54; ICI Fellow, Cambridge, 1954–57; Lectr, King's Coll., Newcastle upon Tyne, 1957–59; Sen. Principal Scientific Officer, AWRE, Aldermaston, 1959–63; Res. Fellow, Imperial Coll., London, 1963–65. Fellow, Amer. Geophysical Union, 1973. Chapman Medal, RAS, 1982. *Publications:* Cosmic Electrodynamics, 1958; papers on related topics. *Recreations:* music, sailing. *Address:* Long Roof, Leverett's Lane, Walberswick, Southwold, Suffolk. *T:* Southwold 722242.

DUNGLASS, Lord (courtesy title used by heirs to Earldom of Home before title was disclaimed); *see under* Douglas-Home, Hon. D. A. C.

DUNHAM, Sir Kingsley (Charles), Kt 1972; FRS 1955; FRSE; PhD Dunelm, 1932; SD Harvard, 1935; FGS; FEng; Hon. FIMM; Director, Institute of Geological Sciences, 1967–75; *b* Sturminster Newton, Dorset, 2 Jan. 1910; *s* of Ernest Pedder and Edith Agnes Dunham; *m* 1936, Margaret, *d* of William and Margaret Young, Choppington, Northumberland; one *s*. *Educ:* Durham Johnston Sch.; Hatfield Coll., Durham Univ.; Adams House, Harvard Univ. Temporary Geologist, New Mexico Bureau of Mines, 1934; HM Geological Survey of Great Britain; Geologist, 1935–45; Senior Geologist 1946; Chief Petrographer, 1948; Prof. of Geology, Univ. of Durham, 1950–66, Emeritus, 1968–; Sub-Warden of Durham Colls, 1959–61. Miller Prof., University of Ill., 1956. Director: Weardale Minerals Ltd, 1982–; Blackdene Minerals Ltd, 1983–. Member: Council, Royal Society, 1965–66 (Foreign Sec., a Vice-Pres., 1971–76; Royal Medal, 1970); Council for Scientific Policy (Min. of Ed. & Sci.), 1965–66. President: Instn Mining and Metallurgy, 1963–64 (Gold Medal, 1968); Yorks Geological Soc., 1958–60 (Sorby Medal, 1964); Internat. Union of Geological Sciences, 1969–72; Geological Soc. of London, 1966–68 (Council 1949–52, 1960–64; Bigsby Medal, 1954; Murchison Medal, 1966; Wollaston Medal, 1976); BAAS, 1972–73; Mineralogical Soc., 1975–77. NE Region, Inst. of Geologists, 1981–; Friends of Killhope, 1985–. Institution of Geology: Founder Mem., 1976; Fellow, 1985; Aberconway Medal, 1986. Trustee, British Museum (Natural History), 1963–66. Member Geology-Geophysics Cttee (NERC) 1965–70; Chairman: Internat. Geol. Correlation Project (IUGS-UNESCO), 1973–76; Council for Environmental Science and Engineering, 1973–75. Mem. Council and UK Rep., 1972–77, Hon. Scholar, 1977, Internat. Inst. for Applied Systems Analysis, Laxenburg, Vienna. Pres., Durham Univ. Soc., 1973–75. Founder Fellow, Fellowship of Engineering, 1976. Hon. Member: Royal Geol Soc. Cornwall (Bolitho Medal 1972); Geol. Soc. of India, 1972; Hon. Foreign Fellow, Geol. Soc. of America; Corr. Foreign Mem., Austrian Acad. of Scis, 1971; Hon. Foreign Member: Société Géologique de Belge, 1974; Bulgarian Geological Soc., 1975. Fellow, Imperial Coll., 1976. Hon. DSc: Dunelm, 1946; Liverpool, 1967; Birmingham, 1970; Illinois, 1971; Leicester, 1972; Michigan, 1973; Canterbury, 1973; Edinburgh, 1974; Exeter, 1975; Hull, 1978; Hon. ScD Cantab, 1973; DUniv Open, 1982. Haidinger Medaille der Geologischen Bundesanstalt, 1976; von Buch Medal, Deutsche Geologische Gesellschaft, 1981. Hon. Citizen of Texas, 1975. *Publications:* Geology of the Organ Mountains, 1935; Geology of the Northern Pennine Orefield, Vol. 1, 1948, Vol. 2 (with A. A. Wilson), 1985; (as Editor) Symposium on the Geology, Paragenesis and Reserves of the Ores of Lead & Zinc, 2nd edn, 1950; Fluorspar, 1952; Geology of Northern Skye (with F. W. Anderson) 1966; (with W. C. C. Rose) Geology and Hermatite Deposits of South Cumbria, 1977; articles in Quarterly Jl of Geological Soc., Mineralogical Magazine, Geological Magazine, American Mineralogist, etc. *Recreations:* music (organ and pianoforte); gardening. *Address:* Charleycroft, Quarryheads Lane, Durham DH1 3DY. *T:* Durham 48977. *Club:* Geological Society's.

DUNICAN, Peter Thomas, CBE 1977; FEng, FICE, FIStructE, FIEI; Consultant, Ove Arup Partnership, since 1984 (Chairman and Director, 1977–84); Director, The Arup Partnerships, since 1977 (Chairman, 1977–85); Chairman, National Building Agency, 1978–82 (part-time Director, 1964–82); *b* 15 March 1918; *s* of Peter Dunican and Elsie Alice McKenzie; *m* 1942, Irene May Jordan; two *s* one *d* (and one *d* decd). *Educ:* Central Sch., Clapham; Battersea Polytechnic. FICE 1971, FIStructE 1959, FIEI 1970. Asst, S. H. White & Son, Civil Engineers, 1936–43; Structural Engr, Ove Arup & Partners, Consulting Engineers, 1943–49, Sen. Partner 1956–78. Instn of Structural Engineers: Mem. Council, 1964–78; Vice-Pres., 1971–77; Pres., 1977–78. Member: LCC Adv. Cttee on London Bldg Act and Byelaws, 1957; Min. of Housing Working Party to revise Model Bldg Byelaws, 1960; Bldg Regulations Adv. Cttee, 1962–65; Council, Architect. Assoc., 1968–69; Chm., Ground and Structures Res. Cttee, BRE, 1979–83. Univ. Science and Technol. Bd of Science Research Council: Mem., Aeronaut. and Civil Eng Cttee, 1968–71; Mem., National Jt Consultative Cttee, 1974–77; Chm., Jt Bldg Gp, 1973–76. FEng 1978 (Mem. Council, 1983–). *Publications:* professional, technical and philosophical papers to jls dealing with construction industry in general and struct. eng in particular. *Recreations:* working in the garden and going to to the opera. *Address:* Charlwood House, Legsheath Lane, East Grinstead, W Sussex RH19 4JW. *T:* Sharpthorne 810088. *Clubs:* Athenæum, Danish.

DUNITZ, Prof. Jack David, FRS 1974; Professor of Chemical Crystallography at the Swiss Federal Institute of Technology (ETH), Zürich, since 1957; *b* 29 March 1923; *s* of William Dunitz and Mildred (*née* Gossman); *m* 1953, Barbara Steuer; two *d*. *Educ:* Hillhead High Sch., Glasgow; Hutcheson's Grammar Sch., Glasgow; Glasgow Univ. (BSc, PhD). Post-doctoral Fellow, Oxford Univ., 1946–48, 1951–53; California Inst. of

Technology, 1948–51, 1953–54; Vis. Scientist, US Nat. Insts of Health, 1954–55; Sen. Res. Fellow, Davy Faraday Res. Lab., Royal Instn, London, 1956–57. Overseas Fellow, Churchill Coll., Cambridge, 1968; Vis. Professor: Iowa State Univ., 1965; Tokyo Univ., 1967; Technion, Haifa, 1970; Hill Vis. Prof., Univ. of Minnesota, 1983; Fairchild Distinguished Scholar, CIT, 1985; Lectures: British Council, 1965; Treat B. Johnson Meml, Yale Univ., 1965; 3M Univ. of Minnesota, 1966; Reilly, Univ. Notre Dame, US, 1971; Kelly, Purdue Univ., 1971; Gerhard Schmidt Meml, Weizmann Inst. of Sci., 1973; George Fisher Baker, Cornell Univ., 1976; Centenary, Chem. Soc., 1977; Appleton, Brown Univ., 1979; H. J. Backer, Gröningen Univ., 1980; Havinga, Leiden Univ., 1980; Karl Folkers, Wisconsin Univ., 1981; A. L. Patterson Meml, Inst. for Cancer Res., Philadelphia, 1983. For. Mem., Royal Netherlands Acad. of Arts and Sciences, 1979; Mem., Leopoldina Acad., 1979; Fellow AAAS, 1981. Tishler Award, Harvard Univ., 1985; Paracelsus Prize, Swiss Chem. Soc., 1986. Jt Editor, Perspectives in Structural Chemistry, 1967–71; Mem. Editorial Bd: Helvetica Chimica Acta, 1971–85; Structure and Bonding, 1971–81. *Publications:* X-ray Analysis and the Structure of Organic Molecules, 1979; papers on various aspects of crystal and molecular structure in Acta Crystallographica, Helvetica Chimica Acta, Jl Chem. Soc., Jl Amer. Chem. Soc., etc. *Recreation:* walking. *Address:* (office) Organic Chemistry Laboratory, ETH, Universitätstrasse 16, CH-8092 Zürich, Switzerland. *T:* CH (01) 256 2892; (home) Obere Heslibachstrasse 77, 8700 Küsnacht, Switzerland. *T:* CH (01) 9101723.

DUNKEL, Arthur; Director General, General Agreement on Tariffs and Trade (GATT), since 1980; *b* 28 Aug. 1932; *s* of Walter Dunkel and Berthe Lerch; *m* 1957, Christiane Müller-Serda; one *s* one *d*. *Educ:* Univ. of Lausanne (LèsSc écon. et comm.). Federal Office for external economic affairs, 1956: successively Head of sections for OECD matters, 1960; for cooperation with developing countries, 1964; for world trade policy, 1971; Permanent Representative of Switzerland to GATT, with rank of Minister, 1973; Delegate of Federal Council for Trade Agreements, rank of Ambassador, 1976; in this capacity, head of Swiss delegations to multilateral (GATT, UNCTAD, UNIDO, etc) and bilateral negotiations in the fields of trade, development, commodities, transfer of technology, industrialisation, agriculture, etc. Dr *hc* rer. pol. Fribourg, 1980. *Publications:* various articles and studies in economic, commercial, agricl and development fields. *Address:* GATT, Centre William Rappard, 154 rue de Lausanne, 1211 Geneva 21, Switzerland.

DUNKELD, Bishop of, (RC), since 1981; **Rt. Rev. Vincent Logan;** *b* 30 June 1941; *s* of Joseph Logan and Elizabeth Flannigan. *Educ:* Blairs College, Aberdeen; St Andrew's Coll., Drygrange, Melrose. Ordained priest, Edinburgh, 1964; Asst Priest, St Margaret's, Davidson's Mains, Edinburgh, 1964–66; Corpus Christi Coll., London, 1966–67 (DipRE); Chaplain, St Joseph's Hospital, Rosewell, Midlothian, 1967–77; Adviser in Religious Education, Archdiocese of St Andrews and Edinburgh, 1967; Parish Priest, St Mary's, Ratho, 1977–81; Episcopal Vicar for Education, Archdiocese of St Andrews and Edinburgh, 1978. *Address:* Bishop's House, 29 Roseangle, Dundee DD1 4LS. *T:* Dundee 24327.

DUNKERLEY, George William, MC 1942; Chairman, Oil and Pipelines Agency, since 1985; Director, STC plc, since 1985; *b* 14 June 1919; *s* of Harold and Eva Dunkerley; *m* 1947, Diana Margaret Lang; two *s*. *Educ:* Felsted School, Essex. FCA. War Service, 1940–46, with RA (The Northumberland Hussars) in N Africa, Sicily, Northern Europe; Major. With Peat Marwick Mitchell & Co., 1948–85, Dep. Senior Partner (UK), 1982–85. *Recreations:* gardening, forestry, travel. *Address:* Smallfield Place, Smallfield, Horley, Surrey RH6 9JN. *T:* Smallfield 2073. *Clubs:* Lansdowne, Royal Ocean Racing.

DUNKLEY, Christopher; journalist and broadcaster; Television Critic, Financial Times, since 1973; *b* 22 Jan. 1944; 2nd *s* of Robert Dunkley and Joyce Mary Dunkley (*née* Turner); *m* 1967, Carolyn Elizabeth, *e d* of late Col A. P. C. Lyons; one *s* one *d*. *Educ:* Haberdashers' Aske's (expelled). Various jobs, incl. theatre flyman, cook, hospital porter, 1961–63; general reporter, then cinema and theatre critic, Slough Observer, 1963–65; feature writer and news editor, UK Press Gazette, 1965–68; night news reporter, then mass media correspondent and TV critic, The Times, 1968–73. Frequent radio broadcaster, 1963–, esp. on Kaleidoscope, Critics' Forum, Meridian, LBC; Presenter, Feedback, Radio 4, 1986–. Occasional television presenter/script writer/chairman; series incl. Edition, Real Time, In Vision (all BBC2), Whistle Blowers, and Panorama: The Television Revolution (BBC1). Critic of the Year, British Press Awards, 1976. *Publications:* Television Today and Tomorrow: Wall to Wall Dallas?, 1985; many articles in The Listener, Television World, Stills, Electronic Media, Telegraph Magazine, etc. *Recreations:* motorcycling, reading in secondhand bookshops, collecting almost everything, especially dictionaries, tin toys, Victorian boys' books. *Address:* 38 Leverton Street, NW5 2PG. *T:* 01-485 7101.

DUNKLEY, Captain James Lewis, CBE 1970 (OBE 1946); RD 1943; Marine Manager, P&O Lines, 1971–72 (Marine Superintendent, 1968–71); *b* 13 Sept. 1908; *s* of William E. Dunkley, Thurlaston Grange, Warwickshire; *m* 1937, Phyllis Mary Cale; one *d*. *Educ:* Lawrence Sheriff Sch., Rugby; Thames Nautical Training Coll., HMS Worcester. Junior Officer, P&O Line, 1928; Captain, 1954; Cdre, 1964. RNR: Sub-Lt, 1931; Comdr, 1951; Captain, 1956. Master, Honourable Co. of Master Mariners, 1970. *Recreations:* gardening, collecting. *Address:* 1 Collindale Gardens, Clacton-on-Sea, Essex. *T:* Clacton 813950. *Club:* City Livery.

DUNLAP, Air Marshal Clarence Rupert, CBE 1944; CD; RCAF retired; *b* 1 Jan. 1908; *s* of late Frank Burns Dunlap, Truro, Nova Scotia; *m* 1935, Hester, *d* of late Dr E. A. Cleveland, Vancouver, BC; one *s*. *Educ:* Acadia Univ.; Nova Scotia Technical Coll. Joined RCAF 1928 as Pilot Officer; trained as pilot and specialised in aerial survey; later specialised in armament; Dir of Armament, RCAF HQ Ottawa on outbreak of War; commanded: RCAF Station, Mountain View, Ont., Jan.-Oct. 1942; RCAF Station, Leeming, Yorks, Dec. 1942–May 1943; 331 Wing NASAF, Tunisia, May-Nov. 1943; 139 Wing TAF, Nov. 1943–Feb. 1945; 64 Base, Middleton St George, Feb.-May 1945; Dep., AMAS, AFHQ, Ottawa, 1945–48; Air Mem. for Air Plans, AFHQ, Ottawa, 1948–49; AOC North-West Air Command, Edmonton, Alberta, 1949–51; Commandant of National Defence Coll., Kingston, Ont., 1951–54; Vice Chief of the Air Staff, AFHQ, Ottawa, 1954–58; Dep. Chief of Staff, Operations, SHAPE, Paris, 1958–62; Chief of Air Staff, AFHQ, Ottawa, 1962–64; Dep. C-in-C, N Amer. Air Def. Comd, 1964–67. Hon. DCL Acadia Univ., 1955; Hon. DEng Nova Scotia Technical Coll., 1967. *Address:* 203–1375 Newport Avenue, Victoria, BC V8S 5E8, Canada. *Clubs:* Union (Victoria); Victoria Golf; Royal Ottawa Golf (Ottawa).

DUNLEATH, 4th Baron, *cr* 1892; **Charles Edward Henry John Mulholland,** TD; DL; MPA; Chairman: Dunleath Estates Ltd; Ulster & General Holdings Ltd; *b* 23 June 1933; *s* of 3rd Baron Dunleath, CBE, DSO, and of Henrietta Grace, *d* of late Most Rev. C. F. D'Arcy, Archbishop of Armagh; *S* father, 1956; *m* 1959, Dorinda Margery, *d* of late Lieut-Gen. A. E. Percival, CB, DSO and Bar, OBE, MC. *Educ:* Eton; Cambridge Univ. Served with 11th Hussars, 1952–53, with N Irish Horse, 1954–69, Lt-Col 1967–69; Captain, Ulster Defence Regt, 1971–73; Lt-Col, NIH, RARO, 1973–, Hon. Col 1981–86. Member (Alliance): N Down, NI Assembly, 1973–75; N Down, NI Constitutional Convention, 1975–76; resigned from Alliance Party, 1979, rejoined 1981; Mem. (Alliance) for N Down, and Asst Speaker, NI Assembly, 1982–86. Mem., Ards Borough Council, 1977–81 (Independent 1979–81). Chairman: Carreras Rothmans of NI, 1974–84; NI Independent Television Ltd, 1979–83; Dir, Northern Bank Ltd, 1974–. Governor of BBC for N Ireland, 1967–73; Mem. Admin. Council, King George's Jubilee Trust, 1974–75; President: Royal Ulster Agric. Soc., 1973–76; Lagan Coll., 1982–86. DL Co. Down, 1964. *Recreations:* vintage motoring, mixtures and mutations, steam, B flat cornet. *Heir: cousin* Major Sir Michael Mulholland, Bt, *qv*. *Address:* Ballywalter Park, Newtownards, Co. Down, Northern Ireland. *T:* Ballywalter 203. *Club:* Cavalry and Guards.

DUNLEAVY, Philip, CBE 1983 (OBE 1978); JP; Leader, Cardiff City Council, 1974–76 and 1979–82; Lord Mayor of Cardiff, 1982–83; *b* 5 Oct. 1915; *s* of Michael and Bridget Dunleavy; *m* 1936, Valerie Partridge; two *s* two *d*. *Educ:* St Cuthbert's Sch., Cardiff. Served War, TA (Sgt), 1939–46. Post Office, 1930–39 and 1946–75 (Executive Officer, 1960–75). Member: Cardiff City Council, 1962–83; South Glamorgan County Council, 1974–81. JP 1960. *Recreations:* youth, conservation, local historical research, local govt political activity. *Address:* 35 Merches Gardens, Grangetown, Cardiff CF1 7RF.

DUNLOP, Rear-Adm. Colin Charles Harrison, CB 1972; CBE 1963; DL; Director General: Cable Television Association, 1974–83; National Television Rental Association, 1974–83; *b* 4 March 1918; *s* of late Engr Rear-Adm. S. H. Dunlop, CB; *m* 1941, Moyra Patricia O'Brien Gorges; two *s* (and one *s* decd). *Educ:* Marlborough Coll. Joined RN, 1935; served War of 1939–45 at sea in HM Ships Kent, Valiant, Diadem and Orion; subseq. HMS Sheffield, 1957–59; Sec. to 1st Sea Lord, 1960–63; comd HMS Pembroke, 1964–66; Programme Evaluation Gp, MoD, 1966–68; Director, Defence Policy (A), MoD, 1968–69; Comdr, British Navy Staff, Washington, 1969–71; Chief Naval Supply and Secretariat Officer, 1970–74; Flag Officer, Medway, and Port Adm., Chatham, 1971–74, retd 1974. DL Kent 1976. *Recreations:* cricket, country pursuits. *Address:* Chanceford Farm, Sand Lane, Frittenden, near Cranbrook, Kent. *T:* Frittenden 242. *Clubs:* Army and Navy; MCC, I Zingari, Free Foresters, Incogniti, RN Cricket, Band of Brothers.

DUNLOP, Prof. Douglas Morton; Professor of History, Columbia University, New York, 1963–77, now Emeritus; *b* 25 Feb. 1909; *o s* of Rev. H. Morton Dunlop and Helen Oliver, *e d* of W. D. Dunn; *m* 1948, Margaret Sinclair, *y d* of Major A. R. Munro, TD, Hillend, Edinburgh. *Educ:* Glasgow Academy; Glasgow Univ.; University Coll., Oxford. Scholar, 1928–32; Vans Dunlop Scholar in Medicine, Edinburgh Univ., 1933; Trinity Coll., Glasgow, 1934–37; Brown Downie Fellow, 1937; Maclean Scholar, 1937 and 1938; University of Bonn, 1937–39; BA Oxon 1939, MA 1960. Trinity Hall, Cambridge (MA) 1950; DLitt Glasgow, 1955. Travelled in Turkey and Syria, 1938; Syria (Jabal Ansariyah), 1939; Asst to Prof. of Hebrew, Glasgow Univ., 1939–46. NFS 1942–44. Asst to Prof. of Oriental Langs, 1947–48, Lectr in Semitic Langs, 1948–50, St Andrews Univ.; Mem. CCG, 1948; Lectr in Islamic History, Cambridge Univ., 1950–62. Visiting Prof. of History, Columbia Univ., 1962–63. FRAS; FIAL. *Publications:* The History of the Jewish Khazars, 1954; The Fusul al-Madani (Aphorisms of the Statesman) of al-Farabi, 1961; Arabic Science in the West, 1965; Arab Civilization to AD 1500, 1971; The Muntakhab Siwan al-Hikmah of Abu Sulaiman al-Sijistani, 1979; original papers and reviews in British and foreign Orientalist publications, and articles in encyclopædias. *Recreations:* hill-walking, Scottish history. *Address:* 46 Owlstone Road, Cambridge. *T:* 354147. *Club:* Royal and Ancient Golf (St Andrews).

DUNLOP, Sir (Ernest) Edward, Kt 1969; CMG 1965; OBE 1947; Consultant Surgeon; Consultant, Royal Melbourne Hospital, since 1967; *b* Wangaratta, Australia, 12 July 1907; *s* of James Henry and Alice Emily Maud Dunlop; *m* 1945, Helen Raeburn Ferguson, *d* of Mephan Ferguson; two *s*. *Educ:* Benalla High Sch.; Victorian Coll. of Pharmacy, Melbourne; Ormond Coll., Melbourne Univ.; St Bartholomew's, London. Qual. in Pharmacy, Gold Medallist, 1928; MB, BS Melbourne Univ., 1st Cl. Hons and Exhibn 1934; MS Melbourne 1937; FRCS 1938; FRACS 1947; FACS 1964. Membre Titulaire, Internat. Soc. of Surgeons, 1963–; Mem., James IV Assoc. of Surgeons, 1971–. Ho. Surg. and Registrar, Royal Melbourne Hosp., 1935–36; Royal Children's, Melbourne, 1937; Brit. Post-Grad. Med. Sch., Hammersmith, 1938; Specialist Surgeon, EMS London, St Mary's, Paddington, 1939. Served War, 1939–46 (despatches, OBE); RAAMC (Capt. to Col), Europe. Middle East and Far East. Hon. Surg. Royal Melbourne Hosp., 1946, Senior Hon. Surg. 1964–67; Hon. Surg. Victorian Eye and Ear Hosp., 1949, Hon. Life Governor, 1967; Cons. Surg., Peter MacCallum Clinic, Cancer and Repatriation Dept. Colombo Plan Adviser, Thailand and Ceylon 1956, India 1960–64; Team Leader, Australian Surgical Team, South Vietnam, 1969; CMO, British Phosphate Commn, 1974–81. Pres., Victorian Anti-Cancer Council, 1980–83 (Vice-Pres., 1966–74, Chm. Executive, 1975–80); Vice-Pres., Internat. Soc. of Surgeons, 1981–83. Mem., Internat. Med. Scis Acad., 1981–. Sir Edward Dunlop Res. Foundn, Heidleberg Repatriation Hosp., launched 1985; Dunlop/Boon Pong Medical Exchange Foundn, Australia–Thailand, launched 1986. Cecil Joll Prize and Lectr, RCS 1960; Gordon Taylor Lectr, Malaysia, 1978; Chapman Meml Lecture and Medal, Australian Instn of Engineers, 1978. Pres. Aust.-Asian Assoc., Victoria, 1965–; Pres. Ex-POW and Relatives Assoc., Victoria, 1946–; Hon. Life Mem., RSL, 1979; Chm., Prime Minister's POW Relief Fund; President: Australian Ex-POW Assoc., 1971–73; Victorian Foundn on Alcoholism and Drug Dependence; Chm., Adv. Cttee on Drug Educn, Victorian Min. of Health, 1970, 1977; Patron, Australian Foundn on Alcoholism and Drug Dependency; Mem., Standing Cttee on Health Problems of Alcohol, Nat. Health and Medical Res. Council, 1973. Pres., Melbourne Council for Overseas Students, 1982–85; Member: Council, Ormond Coll.; Cttee, Nurses' Meml Centre, Melbourne; Exec., Vict. Red Cross Soc.; Victorian Cttee, Queen's Jubilee Appeal, 1977; Dir, Queen Elizabeth II Silver Jubilee Trust for Young Australians, 1977–; Vice-President: 3rd Asian Pacific Congress of Gastroenterology, 1968; Melbourne Scots Soc., 1974–77. Vice Pres., Victorian Rugby Union, 1946–. Gov., Aust. Adv. Council of Elders, 1983–. Hon. Mem., Assoc. of Surgeons of India, 1974. Hon. Fellow: Pharmaceutical Soc. of Victoria, 1946; AMA, 1973; Coll. of Surgeons of Sri Lanka, 1985. Hon. DSc (Punjab), 1966. Freedom of City, Wanganui, NZ, 1962. KSJ 1982. Australian of the Year Award, 1977. *Publications:* Carcinoma of the Oesophagus; Reflections upon Surgical Treatment, 1960; Appendix of Into the Smother, 1963; The War Diaries of Sir Edward ("Weary") Dunlop, 1986; contribs to med. and surg. jls. *Recreations:* farming, travelling, golf; Rugby Union football (Blue, Aust. Caps 1932–34, British Barbarians 1939); formerly boxing (Blue). *Address:* (home) 605 Toorak Road, Toorak, Victoria 3142, Australia. *T:* 20 4749; (professional) 14 Parliament Place, East Melbourne, Victoria 3002, Australia. *T:* 63 1214. *Clubs:* Melbourne, Naval and Military, Peninsula Golf, Melbourne Cricket (Melbourne); Barbarian Football.

DUNLOP, Frank, CBE 1977; Director, Edinburgh International Festival, since 1983; *b* 15 Feb. 1927; *s* of Charles Norman Dunlop and Mary Aarons. *Educ:* Kibworth Beauchamp Grammar Sch.; University Coll., London (Fellow, 1979). BA Hons, English. Postgrad. Sch. in Shakespeare, at Shakespeare Inst., Stratford-upon-Avon; Old Vic Sch., London. Served with RAF before going to University. Director: (own young theatre co.) Piccolo

Theatre, Manchester, 1954; Arts Council Midland Theatre Co., 1955; Associate Dir, Bristol Old Vic, 1956; Dir, Théâtre de Poche, Brussels, 1959–60; Founder and Dir, Pop Theatre, 1960; Dir, Nottingham Playhouse, 1961–63; New Nottingham Playhouse, 1963–64; (dir.) The Enchanted, Bristol Old Vic Co., 1955; (wrote and dir.) Les Frères Jaques', Adelphi, 1960; Director: London Première, The Bishop's Bonfire, Mermaid, 1960; Schweyk, Mermaid, 1963; The Taming of the Shrew, Univ. Arts Centre, Oklahoma, 1965; Any Wednesday, Apollo, 1965; Too True to be Good, Edinburgh Fest., also Strand and Garrick, 1965; Saturday Night and Sunday Morning, Prince of Wales, 1966; The Winter's Tale and The Trojan Women, Edin. and Venice Festivals, also Cambridge Theatre, London, 1966; The Burglar, Vaudeville, 1967; Getting Married, Strand, 1967; A Midsummer Night's Dream and The Tricks of Scapin, Edin. Fest. and Saville Theatre, London, 1967; A Sense of Detachment, Royal Court, 1972; Sherlock Holmes, Aldwych, 1974, NY 1974; Habeas Corpus, NY 1975; The New York Idea, The Three Sisters, NY 1977; The Devil's Disciple, LA and NY, 1978; The Play's the Thing, Julius Caesar, NY, 1978; The Last of Mrs Cheyney, USA, 1978; Rookery Nook, Birmingham and Her Majesty's, 1979; Camelot, USA, 1980; Sherlock Holmes, Norwegian Nat. Th., Oslo, 1980; Lolita, NY, 1981; *National Theatre:* Assoc. Dir, 1967–71 and Admin. Dir, 1968–71; productions: *Nat. Theatre:* Edward II (Brecht and Marlowe); Home and Beauty; Macrune's Guevara; The White Devil; Captain of Kopenick; *Young Vic:* Founder, 1969; Mem. Bd, 1969–; Dir, 1969–78 and 1980–83; Consultant, 1978–80; productions: (author and Dir) Scapino 1970, 1977, NY 1974, LA 1975, Australia 1975, Oslo 1975; The Taming of the Shrew, 1970, 1977; The Comedy of Errors, 1971; The Maids, Deathwatch, 1972; The Alchemist, 1972; Bible One, 1972; French Without Tears, 1973; Joseph and the Amazing Technicolor Dreamcoat (Roundhouse and Albery Theatre), 1973, NY 1976; Much Ado About Nothing, 1973; Macbeth, 1975; Antony and Cleopatra, 1976; King Lear, 1980; Childe Byron, 1981; Masquerade, 1982; *for Théâtre National de Belgique:* Pantagleise, 1970; Antony and Cleopatra, 1971; Pericles, 1972. Mem., Arts Council Young People's Panel, 1968. Governor, Central School of Arts and Crafts, 1970. Hon. Fellow of Shakespeare Inst. Hon. Dr of Theatre, Philadelphia Coll. of Performing Arts, 1978. *Recreations:* reading and looking. *Address:* c/o Edinburgh International Festival, 44 Chandos Place, WC2.

DUNLOP, Gordon; *see* Dunlop, N. G. E.

DUNLOP, Rev. Canon Ian Geoffrey David, FSA; Canon and Chancellor of Salisbury Cathedral, since 1972; *b* 19 Aug. 1925; *s* of late Walter N. U. Dunlop and Marguerite Irene (*née* Shakerley); *m* 1957, Deirdre Marcia, *d* of late Dr Marcus Jamieson; one *s* one *d*. *Educ:* Winchester Coll.; New Coll., Oxford (MA); Strasbourg Univ. (Diploma); Lincoln Theol Coll. FSA 1965. Served Irish Guards, 1944–46 (Lieut). Curate, Hatfield, 1956–60; Chaplain, Westminster Sch., 1960–62; Vicar of Bures, Suffolk, 1962–72. Member: Gen. Synod, 1975–85; Cathedrals' Adv. Commn, 1981–86. Trustee, Historic Churches Preservation Trust, 1969–. *Publications:* Versailles, 1956, 2nd edn 1970; Palaces and Progresses of Elizabeth I, 1962; Châteaux of the Loire, 1969; Companion Guide to the Ile de France, 1979, 2nd edn 1985; Cathedrals Crusade, 1981; Royal Palaces of France, 1985; Thinking It Out, 1986; weekly column in Church Times. *Recreations:* painting, bird watching. *Address:* 24 The Close, Salisbury, Wilts SP1 2EH. *T:* Salisbury 336809. *Club:* Army and Navy.

DUNLOP, John; *b* 20 May 1910; *s* of Martin T. and Agnes Dunlop, Belfast; *m* 1st, 1936, Ruby Hunter; two *s* (and one *s* decd); 2nd, 1970, Joyce Campbell. *Educ:* primary sch. and techn. college. Apprentice multiple grocers, 1926; assumed management, 1934; acquired own business, 1944. Mem. (VULC), Mid-Ulster, NI Assembly, 1973–74. MP (UUUP) Mid-Ulster, 1974–83. Civil Defence Medal and ribbon 1945. *Recreations:* music, choral singing, amateur soccer. *Address:* Turnaface Road, Moneymore, Magherafelt, Co. Londonderry BT45 7YP. *T:* Moneymore 48594.

DUNLOP, (Norman) Gordon (Edward); Finance Director, British Airways, since 1983 (Chief Financial Officer, 1982–83); *b* 16 April 1928; *s* of Ross Munn Dunlop, CA and May Dunlop; *m* 1952, Jean (*née* Taylor); one *s* one *d*. *Educ:* Trinity Coll., Glenalmond. CA 1951, Scotland. Thomson McLintock & Co., Glasgow, 1945–56; De Havilland and Hawker Siddeley Aviation Companies, 1956–64; Commercial Union Assce Co. Ltd, 1964–77, Chief Exec., 1972–77; Dir, Inchcape Berhad, Singapore, 1979–82. *Recreations:* gardening, fishing, ski-ing, ballet. *Address:* 28 Brunswick Gardens, W8 4AL. *T:* 01–221 5059. *Clubs:* Caledonian, Buck's.

DUNLOP, Richard B.; *see* Buchanan-Dunlop.

DUNLOP, Sir Thomas, 3rd Bt, *cr* 1916; Partner, Thomas Dunlop & Sons, Ship & Insurance Brokers, Glasgow, since 1938; *b* 11 April 1912; *s* of Sir Thomas Dunlop, 2nd Bt; *S* father, 1963; *m* 1947, Adda Mary Alison, *d* of T. Arthur Smith, Lindsaylands, Biggar, Lanarks; one *s* one *d* (and one *d* decd). *Educ:* Shrewsbury; St John's Coll., Cambridge (BA). Chartered Accountant, 1939. Former Chm., Savings Bank of Glasgow. Member: Cttee of Princess Louise Scottish Hosp., Erskine; Vice-Pres., Royal Alfred Seafarers' Soc. OStJ 1965. *Recreations:* shooting, fishing, golf. *Heir: s* Thomas Dunlop, *b* 22 April 1951. *Address:* The Corrie, Kilmacolm, Renfrewshire. *T:* Kilmacolm 3239. *Club:* Western (Glasgow).

DUNLOP, Sir William (Norman Gough), Kt 1975; JP; Managing Director, Dunlop Farms Ltd; *b* 9 April 1914; *s* of Norman Matthew Dunlop and Alice Ada Dunlop (*née* Gough); *m* 1940, Ruby Jean (*née* Archie); three *s* three *d*. *Educ:* Waitaki Boys' High Sch. Farmer in Canterbury, NZ. President: Federated Farmers, NZ, 1973–74; Coopworth Sheep Soc., NZ, 1971–74; Member: Agriculture Adv. Council, NZ, 1970–74; Immigration Adv. Council, NZ, 1971–; Transport Adv. Council, NZ, 1971–76; Chairman: Neurological Foundn (Canterbury), 1975–; Lincoln Coll. Foundn, 1977–; Dep. Chm., NZ Meat and Wool Board Electoral Coll., 1973; Director: Rural Bank & Finance Corp., NZ, 1974–81; New Zealand Light Leathers, 1973–80. Trustee: Todd Foundn, 1973–81; Lincoln Coll. Foundn, 1977– (Chm. Bd). Internat. Visitors Award, US Dept of State, 1971. JP 1972. *Recreations:* music, gardening. *Address:* 242 Main Road, Monks Bay, Christchurch 8, New Zealand. *T:* Christchurch 849056. *Club:* Canterbury (Christchurch).

DUNLUCE, Viscount; *see under* Antrim, 14th Earl of (who succeeded 1977, but is still known as Viscount Dunluce).

DUNMORE, 11th Earl of, *cr* 1686; **Kenneth Randolph Murray;** Viscount Fincastle, Lord Murray of Blair, Moulin and Tillemett, 1686; retired; *b* 6 June 1913; *s* of Arthur Charles Murray (*d* 1964) (*g g s* of 4th Earl), and Susan Maud (*d* 1922), *d* of Edward Richards, Tasmania; *S* brother, 1981; *m* 1938, Margaret Joy (*d* 1976), *d* of late P. D. Cousins, Burnie, Tasmania; two *s*. *Educ:* Tasmanian State School. Sgt, 12th/50th Bn, AIF, 1939–45. Former Post-master, Tasmania. Past Master, Tamar Valley Masonic Lodge 42 Tasmanian Constitution, 1957–58. Patron: NSW Combined Scottish Soc.; Exeter RSL Bowls Club. JP Beaconsfield, Tasmania, 1963. *Recreation:* lawn bowls. *Heir: s* Viscount Fincastle, *qv*. *Address:* Gravelly Beach, Tasmania, Australia. *T:* 944275. *Club:* Exeter RSL (Exeter, Tasmania).

DUNN, Douglas Eaglesham, FRSL; poet and short-story writer; full-time writer since 1971; *b* 23 Oct. 1942; *s* of William Douglas Dunn and Margaret McGowan; *m* 1st, 1964, Lesley Balfour Wallace (*d* 1981); 2nd, 1985, Lesley Jane Bathgate. *Educ:* Univ. of Hull (BA). Writer-in-residence, Duncan of Jordanstone Coll. of Art, 1986–87. FRSL 1981. *Publications:* Terry Street, 1969 (Somerset Maugham Award, 1972); The Happier Life, 1972; (ed) New Poems, 1972–73, 1973; Love or Nothing, 1974 (Geoffrey Faber Meml Prize, 1976); (ed) A Choice of Byron's Verse, 1974; (ed) Two Decades of Irish Writing, 1975 (criticism); (ed) The Poetry of Scotland, 1979; Barbarians, 1979; St Kilda's Parliament, 1981 (Hawthornden Prize, 1982); Europa's Lover, 1982; (ed) A Rumoured City: new poets from Hull, 1982; (ed) To Build a Bridge: celebration of Humberside in verse, 1982; Elegies, 1985 (Whitbread Poetry Prize, 1985; Whitbread Book of the Year Award, 1986); Secret Villages, 1985 (short stories); contrib. to Glasgow Herald, New Yorker, TLS, etc. *Recreations:* playing the clarinet and saxophone, listening to jazz music, gardening. *Address:* c/o Faber & Faber Ltd, 3 Queen Square, WC1N 3AU.

DUNN, Air Marshal Sir Eric (Clive), KBE 1983; CB 1981; BEM 1951; Chief Engineer, Royal Air Force, 1983–86, retired; *b* 27 Nov. 1927; *s* of W. E. and K. M. Dunn; *m* 1951, Margaret Gray; three *d*. *Educ:* Bridlington Sch. CEng, FRAeS; CBIM; FIIM. RAF aircraft apprentice, 1944–47; commnd Engr Br., 1954; Staff Coll., 1964; Jt Services Staff Coll., 1967; Sen. Engrg Officer, RAF Boulmer, 1968; MoD, 1969–70; Comd Electrical Engr, NEAF, 1971–72; Dir of Engrg Policy (RAF), 1973–75; RCDS, 1976; AO Wales, and Stn Comdr RAF St Athan, 1977; Air Officer Maintenance, RAF Support Comd, 1977–81; Air Officer Engineering, HQ Strike Comd, 1981–83. *Recreations:* golf, sailing. *Address:* Headlands Cottage, Babcary, Somerton, Somerset TA11 7EQ. *Club:* Royal Air Force.

DUNN, Lt-Col Sir (Francis) Vivian, KCVO 1969 (CVO 1954; MVO 1939); OBE 1960; FRAM; RM Retd; *b* 24 Dec. 1908; *s* of Captain William James Dunn, (Paddy), MVO, MC, Director of Music, Royal Horse Guards, and Beatrice Maud Dunn; *g s* of Sgt Thomas Dunn, Band Sgt, 1st Bn 33rd (W Riding) Regt of Foot (over a century in succession in military music); *m* 1938, Margery Kathleen Halliday; one *s* two *d*. *Educ:* Peter Symonds Coll.; Winchester; Konservatorium der Musik, Cologne; Royal Acad. of Music. ARAM 1932, FRAM 1953. Played with Queen's Hall Prom. Orch., 1927, BBC Symph. Orch., 1930 (founder mem., 1st violin section). Lieut RM and Director of Music, 1931; addtl duties in cypher work, War of 1939–45; with HMS Vanguard for Royal Tour of S Africa, 1947; toured Canada and USA, 1949; Lt-Col and Principal Director of Music, RM, 1953; Royal Tour of Commonwealth countries, 1953; retired 1968. Liveryman, 1956 and Mem. Court, Worshipful Co. of Musicians, 1981–. Hon. Mem., Amer. Bandmasters' Assoc., 1969; Pres., International Military Music Soc., 1977–. EMI Golden Disc Award, 1969. Guest conductor with principal British orchestras and at Univs in Canada and USA; composer and arranger of ceremonial music for RM. *Address:* 16 West Common, Haywards Heath, Sussex RH16 2AH. *T:* Haywards Heath 412987. *Clubs:* Army and Navy, MCC.

DUNN, Col George Willoughby, CBE 1959; DSO 1943 and Bar 1944; MC 1943; TD 1949; DL; Consultant, Thornton Oliver, WS, Arbroath; former Partner, Clark & Oliver, Solicitors, Arbroath; former Chairman: The Alliance Trust; The Second Alliance Trust; Member of Queen's Body Guard for Scotland (Royal Company of Archers); *b* 27 March 1914; *s* of Willoughby Middleton Dunn, coal owner, Lanarkshire; *m* 1944, Louise Wilson, *er d* of Alexander Stephen MacLellan, LLD, ship builder and engr, Glasgow; two *d*. *Educ:* Trinity Coll., Glenalmond; Glasgow Univ. BL 1937; Solicitor, 1937. Served War of 1939–45 with 51st Highland Div., Middle East, N Africa, Sicily and NW Europe; Col late TA The Black Watch. Chm., Royal British Legion Scotland, 1971–74. DL Angus 1971. *Recreations:* golf, fishing. *Address:* David's Hill, St Vigeans, Arbroath, Angus DD11 4RG. *T:* Arbroath 72538. *Clubs:* Naval and Military; New (Edinburgh); Royal and Ancient (St Andrews).

DUNN, John Churchill; broadcaster, host of own daily radio programme; *b* 4 March 1934; *s* of late John Barrett Jackson Dunn and of Dorothy Dunn (*née* Hiscox); *m* 1958, Margaret Jennison; two *d*. *Educ:* Christ Church Cathedral Choir School, Oxford; The King's School, Canterbury. Nat. Service, RAF, 1953–55. Joined BBC as studio manager, External Service, 1956; announcer/newsreader, Gen. Overseas Service, 1958, Domestic Services, 1959; worked all radio networks before joining Light Programme/Radio 2, and subseq. freelance; *radio series include:* Just For You; Housewives' Choice; Music Through Midnight; Roundabout; Jazz at Night; Saturday Sport; Sunday Sport; 4th Dimension; Breakfast Special; It Makes Me Laugh; Nat. and European Brass Band Championships; Light Music Festivals; The John Dunn Show, 1972–; numerous TV appearances. TV and Radio Industries Club Personality of the Year, 1971, 1984, 1986; Variety Club of GB Radio Personality of the Year, 1983. *Publication:* John Dunn's Curious Collection, 1982. *Recreations:* music, skiing, wine. *Address:* c/o Jo Gurnett Personal Management, 45 Queen's Gate Mews, SW7 5QN. *T:* 01–584 7642.

DUNN, Hon. Lydia Selina, CBE 1983 (OBE 1978); JP; MLC; MEC; Director, John Swire & Sons (HK) Ltd, since 1978; Executive Director, Swire Pacific Ltd, since 1982; Director: Hong Kong and Shanghai Banking Corporation, since 1981; Cathay Pacific Airways Ltd, since 1985; Chairman, Hong Kong Trade Development Council, since 1983; *b* 29 Feb. 1940; *d* of Yenchuen Yeh Dunn and Chen Yin Chu. *Educ:* St Paul's Convent Sch., Hong Kong; Univ. of Calif, Berkeley (BS). Swire & Maclaine: Exec. Trainee, 1963; Dir, 1973; Man. Dir, 1976; Chm., 1982; also chm. and dir of subsid. cos. Director: Mass Transit Rly Corp., 1979–85; Kowloon-Canton Rly Corp., 1982–84; Mem. Adv. Bd, Volvo Internat., 1985–. MLC, 1976–, Sen. Unofficial MLC, 1985– (Mem., Finance Cttee, 1976–); MEC, 1982–. Member: Transport Adv. Cttee, 1977–80; Econ. Review Cttee, 1978–83; Gen. Cttee, Fedn of Hong Kong Industries, 1978–83 (Chm., Textile Cttee, 1980–81); Land Develt Policy Cttee, 1981–83; Gen. Cttee, Hong Kong Gen. Chamber of Commerce, 1983–85; Chm., Special Cttee on Land Supply, 1980–83. Member Council: Trade Policy Res. Centre, London, 1980–; Hong Kong Chinese Univ., 1978– (Hon. Treasurer, 1982–85; Chm., Finance Cttee, 1983–85). Member: Hong Kong Br., Hong Kong Assoc. UK, 1983–; Internat. Council, Asia Soc., 1986–; WWF Hong Kong, 1982–85. Chm., Prince Philip Dental Hosp., 1981–. Patron, Assoc. of Chairmen of Tung Wah Gp of Hosps, 1986–87. JP Hong Kong, 1976. Hon. LLD Chinese Univ. of Hong Kong, 1984. *Publication:* In the Kingdom of the Blind, 1983. *Recreation:* collection of antiques. *Address:* John Swire & Sons (HK) Ltd, 5th Floor, Swire House, 9 Connaught Road C, Hong Kong. *Clubs:* Hong Kong, Hong Kong Country; World Trade Centre.

DUNN, Air Marshal Sir Patrick Hunter, KBE 1965 (CBE 1950); CB 1956; DFC 1941; FRAeS; *b* 31 Dec. 1912; *s* of late William Alexander Dunn, Ardentinny, Argyllshire; *m* 1939, Diana Ledward Smith; two *d*. *Educ:* Glasgow Academy; Loretto; Glasgow Univ. Commissioned, 1933, Pre-war service in flying boats; as flying instructor 500 (County of Kent) Sqdn, AAF; with the Long Range Development Unit and as instructor at the Central Flying Sch. War service included command of 80 and 274 Fighter Squadrons and 71 OTU, all in Middle East (1940–42); at Air Ministry, and in Fighter Command, Sector Commander, 1945–46. Post-war service in Air Ministry, 1947–48; Malaya, 1949–50; NATO Defence Coll., 1950–52; Fighter Command, 1953–56; ADC to the Queen, 1953–58. AOC and Commandant, RAF Flying Coll., 1956–58; Deputy Air Sec., 1959–61; AOC No. 1 Group, Bomber Command, 1961–64; AOC-in-Chief, Flying Training Command, 1964–66; retired from RAF, 1967. Director i/c Management Services, British Steel Corp., 1967–68; resigned to become Dep. Chm., British Eagle Internat. Airlines Ltd; Chm., Eagle Aircraft Services, 1969; Aviation Consultant, British Steel Corporation, 1969–76. Mem. Council, Air League, 1968–73 and 1975–79 (Dep. Chm., 1972–73; Chm., Defence Cttee, 1968–73); Mem., British Atlantic Cttee, 1976–. Dir, Gloucester, Coventry, Cricklewood and Kingston Industrial Trading Estates, 1969–75 and 1977–81. A Trustee and Governor of Loretto, 1959–81; President: Fettesian-Lorettonian Club, 1972–75; Lorettonian Soc., 1980–81; Mem. Cttee, Assoc. of Governing Bodies of Public Schs, 1976–79. *Recreations:* tennis, sailing, shooting. *Address:* Little Hillbark, Cookham Dean, Berks. *Clubs:* Royal Air Force, Hurlingham.

See also Sir N. J. D. Marsden, Bt.

DUNN, Richard Johann; Managing Director, Thames Television PLC, since 1985; Chairman: Euston Films Ltd, since 1985; Cosgrove Hall Ltd, since 1985; Thames Television International Ltd, since 1985; *b* 5 Sept. 1943; *s* of late Major Edward Cadwalader Dunn, MBE, TD, and of Gudlaug Johannesdóttir; *m* 1972, Virginia Gregory Gaynor, USA; two *s*. *Educ:* Forest Sch.; St John's Coll., Cambridge (state schol.; MA Eng. Lit., Fine Arts). Founder and Chm., Lady Margaret Players, 1965; Teacher in Jizan, Saudi Arabia, 1965–66; Eothen Films, 1966–67; Writer and Producer, Associated British Pathe, 1967–70; Exec. Producer, EMI Special Films Unit, 1970–72; Man. Dir, Swindon Viewpoint Ltd, cable community television service, 1972–76; Founder and first Chm., Community Communications Gp, 1976; Asst to Lord Delfont, EMI Film and Th. Corp., 1976–77; joined Thames Television as asst to Jeremy Isaacs, 1978, Dir of Prodn, 1981–85; Director: ITN, 1985–; Ind. TV Publications Ltd, 1985–; Grand Central Films Inc., 1985–; Ind. TV Cos Assoc., 1985–; Thames Valley Broadcasting PLC, 1985–; Broadcasters Audience Research Board Ltd, 1986–. Mem., then Chm., Film and Video Panel, GLAA, 1978–82; Chairman: Battersea Arts Centre, 1984–; Dir, Internat. Council of Nat. Acad. of Television Arts and Scis, NY, 1985–; Governor, Forest Sch., 1986–. *Recreations:* theatre, sports, reading. *Address:* 14 Bolingbroke Grove, Wandsworth Common, SW11 6EP. *T:* 01–673 1966. *Clubs:* Royal Automobile; Hawks (Cambridge).

DUNN, Robert John; MP (C) Dartford, since 1979; Parliamentary Under Secretary of State, Department of Education and Science, since 1983; *b* July 1946; *s* of Robert and Doris Dunn, Swinton, Lancs; *m* 1976, Janet Elizabeth Wall, BD, *d* of Denis Wall, Dulwich; two *s*. *Educ:* State schs. Senior Buyer, J. Sainsbury Ltd, 1973–79. Councillor, London Borough of Southwark, 1974–78 (Opposition Minority Gp spokesman on Housing and Finance Matters). Vice-Pres., Eccles Conservative Assoc., 1974–; contested (C): Eccles, Gen. Elections, Feb. and Oct. 1974; adopted as Parly Candidate (C) Dartford, 1975. Jt Sec., Conservative backbench Educn Cttee, 1980–81; Mem., Parly Select Cttee on the Environment, 1981–82; PPS to Parly Under-Secs of State at DES, 1981–82, to Paymaster General and Chancellor of the Duchy of Lancaster, 1982–83. President: Dartford Young Conservatives, 1976–; Kent Gp Young Conservatives, 1982–85; SE Area Educn Adv. Cttee, 1982–; Dartford Soc., 1982–; Dartford branch, Kent Assoc. for the Disabled, 1983–; Vice-Pres., SE Area Fedn of Cons. Students, 1981–. *Recreations:* canvassing; American politics. *Address:* House of Commons, SW1A 0AA. *T:* 01–219 5209. *Clubs:* Carlton; Dartford Rotary (Hon. Mem.).

DUNN, Rt. Hon. Sir Robin Horace Walford, Kt 1969; MC 1944; PC 1980; a Lord Justice of Appeal, 1980–84; *b* 16 Jan. 1918; *s* of late Brig. K. F. W. Dunn, CBE, and of Ava, *d* of Brig.-Gen. H. F. Kays, CB; *m* 1941, Judith, *d* of late Sir Gonne Pilcher, MC; one *s* one *d* (and one *d* decd). *Educ:* Wellington; Royal Military Academy, Woolwich (Sword of Honour). First Commissioned, RA, 1938; RHA, 1941; Staff Coll., 1946; retired (hon. Major), 1948. Served War of 1939–45; France and Belgium, 1939–40; Western Desert and Libya, 1941–42; Normandy and NW Europe, 1944–45 (wounded thrice, despatches twice, MC); Hon. Col Comdt, RA, 1980–84, Hon. Col 1984–. Called to Bar (Inner Temple), 1948; Master of the Bench, Inner Temple, 1969. Western Circuit, Junior Counsel to Registrar of Restrictive Trading Agreements, 1959–62; QC 1962; Judge of the High Court of Justice, Family Division (formerly Probate, Divorce and Admiralty Division), 1969–80; Presiding Judge, Western Circuit, 1974–78. Treas., Gen. Council of the Bar, 1967–69 (Mem., 1959–63); Chm. Betting Levy Appeal Tribunal, 1964–69; Dep. Chm., Somerset QS, 1965–71; Mem., Lord Chancellor's Cttee on Legal Educn, 1968–69. *Recreation:* hunting. *Address:* Lynch Mead, Allerford, Somerset. *T:* Minehead 862509.

DUNN, Prof. Thomas Alexander; Professor of Literature and Head of Department of English Studies, University of Stirling, since 1966; *b* 6 March 1923; *s* of James Symington Dunn and Elizabeth Taylor; *m* 1947, Joyce Mary Armstrong; two *s* one *d*. *Educ:* Dumfries Academy; Edinburgh Univ. (MA, PhD). Served War, Pilot, Fleet Air Arm, Sub-Lt (A) RNVR, 1942–45. Univ. of Ghana, 1953, Prof., 1960; Prof., Univ. of Lagos, 1964–65; Visiting Prof., Univ. of Western Ontario, 1965–66; University of Stirling: Mem., Academic Council, 1966–, Univ. Court, 1968–72; Chm., Board of Studies for Arts, 1975–81; Chm., MacRobert Arts Centre, 1973–82. Member: Inter-Univ. Council for Higher Educn Overseas, 1967–75; Scottish Univs Council on Entrance, 1968–74, 1979–81; Consultative Cttee on the Curriculum, 1968–76. Member: Scottish Arts Council, 1969–76; Arts Council of Gt Britain, 1971–73; Broadcasting Council for Scotland, 1972–76; Films of Scotland, 1972–82; Chairman: Univs Cttee on Scottish Literature, 1970–; Drama Cttee, 1972–76; Grants to Publishers Panel, 1975–78; Pres., Assoc. for Scottish Literary Studies, 1972–76; UKNC Unesco, Culture Cttee, 1983–85. *Publications:* Philip Massinger: the man and the playwright, 1957; (with D. E. S. Maxwell) Introducing Poetry, 1966; Massinger and Field: The Fatal Dowry, 1969; (ed) Universitas (Ghana), 1955–63; (ed) Fountainwell Drama Texts. *Recreations:* gardening, theatre and arts generally. *Address:* Coney Park, 121 Henderson Street, Bridge of Allan, Stirling FK9 4RQ. *T:* Stirling 833373. *Club:* Stirling and County (Stirling).

DUNN, Sir Vivian; *see* Dunn, Sir F. V.

DUNN, William Francis N.; *see* Newton Dunn.

DUNN, William Hubert, QC 1982; a Recorder of the Crown Court, since 1980; *b* 8 July 1933; *s* of William Patrick Millar Dunn and Isabel (*née* Thompson); *m* 1971, Maria Henriqueta Theresa d'Arouje Perestrello de Moser; one *s* one *d*. *Educ:* Rockport, Co. Down, N Ireland; Winchester Coll.; New Coll., Oxford (Hons degree PPE) (Half-Blue fencing 1954–55). 2nd Lieut, Life Guards, 1956–57; Household Cavalry Reserve of Officers, 1957–64. Cholmondeley Scholar, Lincoln's Inn, 1958, called to Bar, 1958; Local Govt Commissioner, 1963; a Deputy Circuit Judge, 1972. *Recreations:* hunting, travel, literature. *Address:* 19 Clarendon Street, SW1. *T:* 01–834 5578; Tudor Hall, Holywood, Co. Down, N Ireland. *T:* Holywood 3139. *Club:* Boodle's.

DUNNE, Irene, (Mrs F. D. Griffin), Hon. Doctor of Music, Hon. LLD; *b* Louisville, Kentucky, USA, 20 Dec. 1904; *d* of Joseph A. Dunne and Adelaide A. Henry; *m* 1927, Dr Francis D. Griffin (*d* 1965); one *d*. *Educ:* Loretta Academy, St Louis, Mo., USA; Chicago Musical Coll., Chicago. Acted in the original Show Boat, 1929. Entered motion pictures, 1931; first film Cimarron. Films include: Back Street, Awful Truth, Roberta, Anna and the King of Siam, Life with Father, I Remember Mama, The Mudlark (as Queen Victoria), Never a Dull Moment. Laetare Medal, University of Notre Dame. Mem. Defence Advisory Cttee, US, to advise on welfare matters in the women's services, 1951; Mem. US Delegation to United Nations 12th Gen. Assembly. *Recreation:* golf. *Address:* 461 North Faring Road, Moment, Los Angeles, Calif 90077, USA.

DUNNE, Most Rev. Patrick, DD; Auxiliary Bishop of Dublin, (RC) and titular Bishop of Nara since 1946; Parish Priest of St Mary's Haddington Road, Dublin; Dean of the Metropolitan Chapter; Vicar-General; *b* Dublin, 3 June 1891. *Educ:* Holy Cross Coll., Clonliffe, Dublin; Irish Coll., Rome. Ordained in Rome, 1913; Sec. to Archbishops of Dublin, 1919–43; Parish Priest, Church of the Holy Family, Aughrim Street, Dublin, 1943–47; Domestic Prelate, 1943. *Address:* St Mary's, Haddington Road, Dublin.

DUNNE, Thomas Raymond, JP; HM Lord-Lieutenant, County of Hereford and Worcester, since 1977; *b* 24 Oct. 1933; *s* of Philip Dunne, MC, and Margaret Walker; *m* 1957, Henrietta Crawley; two *s* two *d*. *Educ:* Eton; RMA Sandhurst. Served Army, 1951–59: Royal Horse Guards. Herefordshire CC, 1962–68. Pres., 3 Counties Agric. Soc., 1977; National Vice Pres., Royal British Legion, 1982–. Dir, West Regional Bd, Central TV, 1981–. Chm., N Hereford Conservative Assoc., 1968–74. High Sheriff 1970, DL 1973, Herefordshire; JP Hereford and Worcester, 1977. KStJ 1978. *Address:* Gatley Park, Leinthall Earls, Leominster, Herefordshire HR6 9TT.

DUNNET, Prof. George Mackenzie, OBE 1986; DSc; Regius Professor of Natural History, University of Aberdeen, since 1974; *b* 19 April 1928; *s* of John George and Christina I. Dunnet; *m* 1953, Margaret Henderson Thomson; one *s* two *d*. *Educ:* Peterhead Academy; Aberdeen Univ. BSc (1st cl. hons) 1949; PhD 1952; DSc 1984. Research Officer, CSIRO, Australia, 1953–58; Lectr in Ecology, Dir Culterty Field Stn, Univ. of Aberdeen, 1958–66, Sen. Lectr 1966–71; Sen. Research Fellow, DSIR, NZ, 1968–69; Prof. of Zoology, Univ. of Aberdeen, 1971–74. Member: Red Deer Commn, 1975–80; Scottish Adv. Cttee of Nature Conservancy Council, 1979–84; Chairman: Shetland Oil Terminal Environment Adv. Gp, 1977–; Adv. Cttees on Protection of Birds, 1979–81. Pres., British Ecological Soc., 1980 81. FRSE 1970; FIBiol 1974; FRSA 1981. *Publications:* contrib. Ibis, Jl Animal Ecology, Jl Applied Ecol., Aust. Jl Zool., CSIRO Wildl. Res. *Recreations:* hill walking, photography. *Address:* Whinhill, Inverebrie, Ellon, Aberdeenshire AB4 9PT. *T:* Schivas 215. *Club:* Royal Commonwealth Society.

DUNNETT, Alastair MacTavish; Director: Thomson Scottish Petroleum Ltd (Chairman, 1972–79); Scottish Television, 1975–79; Member Executive Board, The Thomson Organisation Ltd, 1973–78; *b* 26 Dec. 1908; *s* of David Sinclair Dunnett and Isabella Crawford MacTavish; *m* 1946, Dorothy Halliday; two *s*. *Educ:* Overnewton Sch.; Hillhead High Sch., Glasgow. Commercial Bank of Scotland, Ltd, 1925; Co-founder of The Claymore Press, 1933–34; Glasgow Weekly Herald, 1935–36; The Bulletin, 1936–37; Daily Record, 1937–40; Chief Press Officer, Sec. of State for Scotland, 1940–46; Editor, Daily Record, 1946–55; Editor, The Scotsman, 1956–72; Man. Dir, The Scotsman Publications Ltd, 1962–70, Chm., 1970–74. Smith-Mundt Scholarship to USA, 1951. Governor, Pitlochry Festival Theatre, 1928–84. Member: Scottish Tourist Board, 1956–69; Press Council, 1959–62; Council of Nat. Trust for Scotland, 1962–69; Council of Commonwealth Press Union, 1964–78; Edinburgh Univ. Court, 1964–66; Edinburgh Festival Council, 1967–80. Hon. LLD Strathclyde, 1978. *Publications:* Treasure at Sonnach, 1935; Heard Tell, 1946; Quest by Canoe, 1950, repr. 1967, as It's Too Late in the Year; Highlands and Islands of Scotland, 1951; The Donaldson Line, 1952; The Land of Scotch, 1953; (as Alec Tavis) The Duke's Day, 1970; (ed) Alistair Maclean Introduces Scotland, 1972; No Thanks to the Duke, 1978; Among Friends (autobiog.), 1984; *plays:* The Original John Mackay, Glasgow Citizens, 1956; Fit to Print, Duke of York's, 1962. *Recreations:* sailing, riding, walking. *Address:* 87 Colinton Road, Edinburgh EH10 5DF. *T:* 031–337 2107. *Clubs:* Caledonian; Scottish Arts, New (Edinburgh).

DUNNETT, Denzil Inglis, CMG 1967; OBE 1962; HM Diplomatic Service, retired; *b* 21 Oct. 1917; *s* of late Sir James Dunnett, KCIE and late Annie (*née* Sangster); *m* 1946, Ruth Rawcliffe (*d* 1974); two *s* one *d*. *Educ:* Edinburgh Acad.; Corpus Christi Coll., Oxford. Served with RA, 1939–45. Diplomatic Service: Foreign Office, 1947–48; Sofia, 1948–50; Foreign Office, 1950–53; UK Delegn to OEEC, Paris, 1953–56; Commercial Sec., Buenos Aires, 1956–60; Consul, Elisabethville, 1961–62; Commercial Counsellor, Madrid, 1962–67; seconded to BoT, 1967–70; Counsellor, Mexico City, 1970–73; Ambassador to Senegal, Mauritania, Mali and Guinea, 1973–76, and to Guinea-Bissau, 1975–76; Diplomatic Service Chm., CS Selection Bd, 1976–77. London Rep., Scottish Develt Agency, 1978–82. *Recreations:* golf, music. *Address:* 11 Victoria Grove, W8 5RW. *T:* 01–584 7523. *Club:* Caledonian.

DUNNETT, Jack; President, Football League, 1981–86; (Member, Management Committee, since 1977); *b* 24 June 1922; *m* 1951; two *s* three *d*. *Educ:* Whitgift Middle Sch., Croydon; Downing Coll., Cambridge (MA, LLB). Served with Cheshire Regt, 1941–46 (Capt.). Admitted Solicitor, 1949. Middlesex CC, 1958–61; Councillor, Enfield Borough Council, 1958–61; Alderman, Enfield Borough Council, 1961–63; Councillor, Greater London Council, 1964–67. MP (Lab) Central Nottingham, 1964–74, Nottingham East, 1974–83; former PPS to: Minister of State, FCO; Minister of Transport. Mem. FA Council, 1977–, Vice-Pres., 1981–; Mem., Football Trust, 1982–; Chm., Notts County FC, 1968–. *Recreation:* watching professional football. *Address:* Whitehall Court, SW1A 2EP. *T:* 01–839 6962.

DUNNETT, Sir (Ludovic) James, GCB 1969 (KCB 1960; CB 1957); CMG 1948; Permanent Under-Secretary of State, Ministry of Defence, 1966–74; *b* 12 Feb. 1914; *s* of late Sir James Dunnett, KCIE; *m* 1st, 1944, Olga Adair (*d* 1980); no *c*; 2nd, 1984, Lady Clarisse Grover. *Educ:* Edinburgh Acad.; University Coll., Oxford. Entered Air Ministry, 1936; Private Sec. to Permanent Sec., 1937–44; transferred to Ministry of Civil Aviation, 1945; Under Sec., 1948; Under Sec., Min. of Supply, 1951, Deputy Sec., 1953; Deputy Sec., Min. of Transport, 1958; Permanent Secretary: Min. of Transport, 1959–62; Min. of Labour, 1962–66. Mem., SSRC, 1977–82. Visiting Fellow, Nuffield Coll., Oxford, 1964–72. Chm., Internat. Maritime Industries Forum, 1976 79; Pres., Inst. of Manpower Studies, 1977–80; Trustee, Charities Aid Foundn. *Recreation:* golf. *Address:* 85 Bedford Gardens, W8. *T:* 01–727 5286. *Club:* Reform.

DUNNING, John Ernest Patrick, CBE 1973; retired; Director, Rocket Propulsion Establishment, Westcott, 1955–72; *b* 19 Sept. 1912; *s* of late Rev. E. M. Dunning, MA, sometime Rector of Cumberworth and Denby Dale, Yorks; *m* 1939, Mary Meikle Robertson. *Educ:* Wheelwright Gram. Sch., Dewsbury; Downing Coll., Cambridge (Exhibr, MA). 1st cl. hons Mech. Scis Tripos, 1935. Blackstone Ltd, Stamford, 1935–37; Bristol Aeroplane Co. Ltd (Engines), 1937–38; Armstrong Whitworth Securities Ltd (Kadenacy Dept), 1938 40; RAE, 1940–50; Asst Dir, Min. of Supply, 1950–55; Dir, Engine Research, Min. of Supply, 1955. FRAeS, FIMechE; FRSA. *Publications:* scientific and technical papers. *Address:* 24 Coombe Hill Crescent, Thame, Oxon. *T:* Thame 3893. *Club:* North Oxford Golf.

DUNNING, Prof. John Harry, PhD; Professor of International Investment and Business Studies, since 1974 and Head of Department of Economics since 1964, University of Reading; *b* 26 June 1927; *m* 1st, 1948, Ida Teresa Bellamy (marr. diss. 1975); one *s*; 2nd, 1975, Christine Mary Brown. *Educ:* Lower Sch. of John Lyon, Harrow; University Coll. London (BSc (Econ); PhD). Research Asst, University Coll. London, 1951–52; Lectr and Sen. Lectr, Univ. of Southampton, 1952–64; Prof. of Economics, Univ. of Reading, 1964–74. Visiting Prof.: Univ. of Western Ontario, Canada; Univ. of California (Berkeley), 1968–69; Boston Univ., USA, 1976; Stockholm Sch. of Economics, 1978; HEC, Univ. of Montreal, Canada, 1980; Walker-Ames Prof., Univ. of Washington, Seattle, 1981; Seth Boyden Distinguished Prof., Rutgers Univ., 1987. Consultant to UN, 1974– and OECD, 1975–. Member: SE Economic Planning Council, 1966–68; Chemicals EDC, 1968–77; UN Study Gp on Multinational Corps, 1973–74. Chm., Economists Advisory Gp Ltd. Fellow, Acad. of Internat. Business. Hon. PhD Uppsala, 1975. *Publications:* American Investment in British Manufacturing Industry, 1958; (with C. J. Thomas) British Industry, 1963; Economic Planning and Town Expansion, 1963; Studies in International Investment, 1970; (ed) The Multinational Enterprise, 1971; (with E. V. Morgan) An Economic Study of the City of London, 1971; (ed) International Investment, 1972; (ed) Economic Analysis and the Multinational Enterprise, 1974; US Industry in Britain, 1976; (with T. Houston) UK Industry Abroad, 1976; International Production and the Multinational Enterprise, 1981; (ed with J. Black) International Capital Movements, 1982; (with J. Stopford) Multinationals: Company Performance and Global Trends, 1983; (with R. D. Pearce) The World's Largest Industrial Companies 1962–83, 1985; (ed) Multinational Enterprises, Economic Structure and International Competitiveness, 1985; Japanese Participation in British Industry, 1986; (with J. Cantwell) World Dirctory of Statistics on International Direct Investment and Production, 1986; numerous articles in learned and professional jls. *Address:* University of Reading, Whiteknights Park, Reading, Berks. *T:* Reading 875123. *Club:* Athenæum.

DUNNING, Joseph, CBE 1977; Chairman, Lothian Health Board, 1983–84; Principal, Napier College of Commerce and Technology, Edinburgh, 1963–81, retired; *b* 9 Oct. 1920; *s* of Joseph and Elizabeth Ellen Dunning; *m* 1948, Edith Mary Barlow (*d* 1972); one *s* one *d*. *Educ:* London University (BSc Hons); Durham University (MEd); Manchester College of Technology (AMCT). Metallurgical Industry and lecturing, 1936–56; Principal, Cleveland Technical College, 1956–63. MA Open Univ.; FEIS. Hon. DEd CNAA, 1983. *Recreations:* silversmithing, photography. *Address:* 50 Frogston Terrace, Edinburgh EH10 7AE. *Club:* New (Edinburgh).

DUNNING, Sir Simon (William Patrick), 3rd Bt, *cr* 1930; *b* 14 Dec. 1939; *s* of Sir William Leonard Dunning, 2nd Bt, and of Kathleen Lawrie, *d* of J. P. Cuthbert, MC; *S* father, 1961; *m* 1975, Frances Deirdre Morton, *d* of Major Patrick Lancaster; one *d*. *Educ:* Eton. *Recreation:* shooting. *Address:* Low Auchengillan, Blanefield, by Glasgow. *T:* Blanefield 70323. *Clubs:* Turf; Western (Glasgow).

DUNNINGTON-JEFFERSON, Sir Mervyn (Stewart), 2nd Bt *cr* 1958; Company Director, since 1968; *b* 5 Aug. 1943; *s* of Sir John Alexander Dunnington-Jefferson, 1st Bt, DSO, and of Frances Isobel, *d* of Col H. A. Cape, DSO; *S* father, 1979; *m* 1971, Caroline Anna, *o d* of J. M. Bayley; one *s* two *d*. *Educ:* Eton College. Joined Charrington & Co. Ltd (Brewers), 1961; left in 1968 to become joint founder and director of Hatton Builders Ltd, specialising in building contracting and property development. *Recreations:* sport—cricket, skiing, golf, etc. *Heir:* *s* John Alexander Dunnington-Jefferson, *b* 23 March 1980. *Address:* 7 Bolingbroke Grove, SW11 6ES. *T:* 01–675 3395. *Clubs:* MCC, Queen's.

DUNPARK, Hon. Lord; Alastair McPherson Johnston, TD; BA, LLB; FSAScot; a Senator of the College of Justice in Scotland and Lord of Session, since 1971; *b* 15 Dec. 1915; *s* of late Rev. A. M. Johnston, BD, Stirling; *m* 1939, Katharine Margaret (Bunty) (*d* 1983), *d* of Charles Mitchell, Chislehurst; three *s*; *m* 1984, Kathleen Macfie, *widow* of John S. Macfie, WS. *Educ:* Merchiston Castle Sch.; Jesus Coll., Cambridge; Edinburgh Univ. RA (TA), 1939–46 (despatches); Staff Coll., Haifa, 1943; Major 1943. Mem. of Faculty of Advocates, 1946; QC (Scotland), 1958. Sheriff of Dumfries and Galloway, 1966–68; Mem., Scottish Law Commn, 1968–71. Chairman: The Cockburn Assoc. (Edinburgh Civic Trust), 1969–74; Royal Artillery Assoc., E of Scotland District, 1946–60, Scottish Region, 1962–78; Edinburgh Marriage Guidance Council, 1969–72 (Pres., 1973–); Council, St George's Sch. for Girls, Edinburgh, 1973–; Edinburgh Legal Dispensary, 1961–. Hon. Fellow, Dept of Law, Edinburgh Univ., 1969. *Publications:* Jt Editor, 3rd edn of Walton's Law of Husband and Wife, 1951; Jt Editor, 7th edn of Gloag and Henderson's Introduction to Law of Scotland, 1968. *Recreations:* golf, walking. *Address:* 8 Heriot Row, Edinburgh EH3 6HU. *T:* 031–556 4663. *Club:* New (Edinburgh).

DUNPHIE, Maj.-Gen. Sir Charles (Anderson Lane), Kt 1959; CB 1948; CBE 1942; DSO 1943; *b* 20 April 1902; *s* of late Sir Alfred Dunphie, KCVO, Rotherfield Greys, Oxon; *m* 1st, 1931, Eileen (*d* 1978), *d* of late Lieut-Gen. Sir Walter Campbell, KCB, KCMG, DSO; one *s* one *d*; 2nd, 1981, Susan, *widow* of Col P. L. M. Wright. *Educ:* RN Colls Osborne and Dartmouth; RMA Woolwich. Commissioned into RA, 1921; served War of 1939–45 (wounded, despatches); Brig. RAC, 1941; Comdr 26 Armoured Bde, 1942–43; Dep. Dir RAC, War Office, 1943–45; Temp. Maj.-Gen., Dir Gen. Armoured Fighting Vehicles 1945–48; retired 1948. Joined Vickers Ltd, 1948; Chm., 1962–67. One of HM's Honourable Corps of Gentlemen-at-Arms, 1952–62. US Legion of Merit (Commander); US Silver Star. *Address:* Roundhill, Wincanton, Somerset. *Club:* Army and Navy.

DUNPHY, Rev. Thomas Patrick, SJ; Parish Priest, Corpus Christi, Boscombe, since 1980; *b* Donnybrook, Dublin, 17 Aug. 1913; *o s* of Thomas Joseph Dunphy and Agnes Mary (*née* Rogers), Dublin. *Educ:* Wimbledon Coll. Joined Soc. of Jesus, 1932; Priest, 1946. Headmaster of St John's (preparatory sch. of Beaumont Coll.), 1949–64; Rector, Beaumont Coll., 1964–67; Socius to the Provincial of the Society of Jesus, 1967–71; Rector, Stonyhurst Coll., 1971–77; Vicar for Religious Sisters in Devon and Dorset, 1977–79; Spiritual Father, St Mary's Hall, Stonyhurst, 1979–80. *Address:* Corpus Christi, 757 Christchurch Road, Boscombe, Bournemouth BH7 6AN. *T:* Bournemouth 425286.

DUNRAVEN and MOUNT-EARL, 7th Earl of, *cr* 1822; **Thady Windham Thomas Wyndham-Quin;** Baron Adare, 1800; Viscount Mountearl, 1816; Viscount Adare, 1822; Bt 1871; *b* 27 Oct. 1939; *s* of 6th Earl of Dunraven and Mount-Earl, CB, CBE, MC, and Nancy, *d* of Thomas B. Yuille, Halifax County, Va; *S* father 1965; *m* 1969, Geraldine, *d* of Air Commodore Gerard W. McAleer, CBE, MB, BCh, DTM&H, Wokingham; one *d*. *Educ:* Ludgrove; Le Rosey. *Heir:* none. *Address:* Kilcurly House, Adare, Co. Limerick, Ireland. *T:* Limerick 94201. *Club:* Kildare Street and University (Dublin).

See also Sir F. G. W. Brooke, Bt.

DUNROSSIL, 2nd Viscount, *cr* 1959; **John William Morrison,** CMG 1981; HM Diplomatic Service; Governor and Commander-in-Chief of Bermuda, since 1983; *b* 22 May 1926; *e s* of William Shepherd Morrison, 1st Viscount Dunrossil, GCMG, MC, PC, QC; *S* father, 1961; *m* 1st, 1951, Mavis (marr. diss. 1969), *d* of A. Ll. Spencer-Payne, LRCP, MRCS, LDS; three *s* one *d*; 2nd, 1969, Diana Mary Cunliffe, *d* of C. M. Vise; two *d*. *Educ:* Fettes; Oxford. Royal Air Force, 1945–48, Flt-Lieut (Pilot). Joined Commonwealth Relations Office, 1951; Asst Private Sec. to Sec. of State, 1952–54; Second Sec., Canberra, 1954–56; CRO, 1956–58; First Sec. and Acting Deputy High Commissioner, Dacca, East Pakistan, 1958–60; First Sec., Pretoria/Capetown, 1961–64; FO, 1964–68; seconded to Intergovernmental Maritime Consultative Org., 1968–70; Counsellor and Head of Chancery, Ottawa, 1970–74; Counsellor, Brussels, 1975–78; High Comr in Fiji, and High Comr (non-resident) to Republic of Nauru and to Tuvalu, 1978–82; High Comr, Bridgetown, Antigua, Barbuda, Dominica, Grenada, St Vincent and the Grenadines, and British Govt Rep. to WI Associated States, 1982–83. Liveryman, Merchant Taylor's Co. *Heir:* *s* Hon. Andrew William Reginald Morrison, *b* 15 Dec. 1953. *Address:* Government House, Hamilton, Bermuda. *Clubs:* Royal Air Force, Royal Commonwealth Society.

DUNSANY, 19th Baron of, *cr* 1439; **Randal Arthur Henry Plunkett;** Lieut-Col (retd) Indian Cavalry (Guides); *b* 25 Aug. 1906; *o s* of 18th Baron Dunsany, DL, LittD, and Rt Hon. Beatrice, Lady Dunsany (*d* 1970); *S* father, 1957; *m* 1st, 1938, Mrs Vera Bryce (from whom he obtained a divorce, 1947), *d* of Señor G. De Sà Sottomaior, São Paulo, Brazil; one *s*; 2nd, 1947, Sheila Victoria Katrin, *widow* of Major John Frederick Foley, Baron de Rutzen, DL, JP, CC, Welsh Guards (killed in action, 1944), *o d* of Sir Henry Philipps, 2nd Bt; one *d*. *Educ:* Eton. Joined the 16th/5th Lancers (SR), 1926; transferred to the Indian Army, 1928, Guides Cavalry, Indian Armoured Corps, retired, 1947. *Heir:* *s* Hon. Edward John Carlos Plunkett [*b* 10 Sept. 1939. *Educ:* Eton; Slade Sch. of Fine Art]. *Address:* (Seat) Dunsany Castle, Co. Meath, Ireland. *T:* 046–25198. *Clubs:* Beefsteak, Cavalry and Guards; Kildare Street and University (Dublin).

DUNSTAN, (Andrew Harold) Bernard, RA 1968 (ARA 1959); RWA; painter; *b* 19 Jan. 1920; *s* of late Dr A. E. Dunstan; *m* 1949, Diana Maxwell Armfield; three *s*. *Educ:* St Paul's; Byam Shaw Sch.; Slade Sch. Has exhibited at RA since 1945. Many one-man exhibitions; now exhibits regularly at Agnews, Bond St. Pictures in public collections include London Museum, Bristol Art Gall., Nat. Gall. of NZ, Arts Council, Nat. Portrait Gall., and many in private collections. Mem., New English Art Club; Hon. Sec., Artists' General Benevolent Instn, 1984–; Pres., Royal West of England Acad., 1980–84. *Publications:* Learning to Paint, 1970; Painting in Progress, 1976; Painting Methods of the Impressionists, 1976. *Recreations:* music, walking in London. *Address:* 10 High Park Road, Kew, Richmond, Surrey TW9 4BH. *T:* 01–876 6633.

DUNSTAN, Hon. Donald Allan, AC 1979; QC 1965; Chairman, Victorian Tourism Commission, since 1982; National President, Australian Freedom from Hunger Campaign, since 1982; *b* 21 Sept. 1926; of S Australian parents; *m* 1st, 1949, Gretel Ellis (marr. diss.); two *s* one *d*; 2nd, 1976, Adele Koh (*d* 1978). *Educ:* St Peter's Coll. and Univ. of Adelaide, S Australia. MHA (Labor) South Australia, for Norwood, 1953–79; Attorney-Gen. of S Australia, 1965; Premier, Treasurer, Attorney-Gen. and Minister of Housing, 1967–68; Leader of Opposition, 1968–70; Premier, Treasurer, 1970–79. Freeman of City of Georgetown, Penang, 1973. *Publication:* Felicia: the political memoirs of Don Dunstan, 1983. *Address:* c/o Victorian Tourism Commission, World Trade Centre, corner of Spencer and Flinders Street, Melbourne, Vic 3005, Australia; 59 Gipps Street, East Melbourne, Vic 3002.

DUNSTAN, Lt-Gen. Sir Donald (Beaumont), KBE 1980 (CBE 1969; MBE 1954); CB 1972; Governor of South Australia, since 1982; *b* 18 Feb. 1923; *s* of late Oscar Reginald Dunstan and Eileen Dunstan; *m* 1948, Beryl June Dunningham; two *s*. *Educ:* Prince Alfred Coll., South Australia; RMC, Duntroon. Served War of 1939–45: Regimental and Staff appts in SW Pacific Area, 1942–45. Served in Korea, 1954; Instructor: RMC Duntroon, 1955–56, 1963; Staff Coll., Queenscliff, 1958; Staff Coll., Camberley, 1959–60; Dep. Comdr 1 Task Force, Vietnam, 1968–69; Comdr, 10th Task Force, Holsworthy, NSW, 1969; idc 1970; Commander Aust. Force, Vietnam, 1971; Chief of Materiel, 1972–74; GOC Field Force Comd, 1974–77; CGS, 1977–82. Hon. Col, Royal S Aust. Regt, 1982; Hon. Air Cdre, RAAF, 1982. KStJ 1982. *Recreations:* golf, fishing. *Address:* Government House, Adelaide, SA 5000, Australia. *Club:* Australian (Sydney).

DUNSTAN, Rev. Prof. Gordon Reginald; F. D. Maurice Professor of Moral and Social Theology, King's College, London, 1967–82, now Emeritus; Honorary Research Fellow, University of Exeter, since 1982; Chaplain to the Queen, since 1976; *b* 25 April 1917; *yr s* of late Frederick John Menhennet and Winifred Amy Dunstan (*née* Orchard); *m* 1949, Ruby Maud (*née* Fitzer); two *s* one *d*. *Educ:* Plymouth Corp. Gram. Sch.; University of Leeds; College of the Resurrection, Mirfield. BA, 1st cl. Hist., 1938, Rutson Post-Grad. Schol. 1938, MA w dist. 1939, Leeds Univ.; FSA 1957; FKC 1974. Deacon 1941, priest 1942; Curate, King Cross, Halifax, 1941–45; Huddersfield, 1945–46; Sub Warden, St Deiniol's Library, Hawarden, 1945–49; Vicar of Sutton Courtney with Appleford, 1949–55; Lecturer, Wm Temple Coll., 1947–49; Ripon Hall, Oxford, 1953–55; Minor Canon, St George's Chapel, Windsor Castle, 1955–59; Westminster Abbey, 1959–67; Canon Theologian, Leicester Cathedral, 1966–82, Canon Emeritus, 1982–. Sec., C of E Council for Social Work, 1955–63; Sec., Church Assembly Jt Bd of Studies, 1963–66; Editor of Crucible, 1962–66; Editor of Theology, 1965–75; Dep. Priest in Ordinary to the Queen, 1959–64, Priest in Ordinary, 1964–76; Select Preacher: University of Cambridge 1960, 1977; Leeds, 1970; Hulsean Preacher, 1977. Lectures: Prideaux, Univ. of Exeter, 1968; Moorhouse, Melbourne, 1973; Stephenson, Sheffield, 1980. Gresham's Prof. in Divinity, City Univ., 1969–71. Mem. Council, Canterbury and York Soc., 1950–85 (Vice-Pres., 1985–). Mem. or Sec. cttees on social and ethical problems; Vice-Pres., 1965–66, and Chm. Brit. Cttee, of Internat. Union of Family Organizations, 1964–66; Vice-Pres., London Medical Gp and Inst. of Medical Ethics, 1985– (Mem., 1967–82); Member: Adv. Gp on Transplant Policy, Dept of Health, 1969; Council of Tavistock Inst. of Human Relations (Vice-Pres., 1977–82), and Inst. of Marital Studies, 1969–; Adv. Gp on Arms Control and Disarmament, FCO, 1970–74; Adv. Cttee on Animal Experiments, Home Office, 1975–; Council, Advertising Standards Auth., 1981–; MRC/RCOG Voluntary Licensing Authority, 1985–. Pres., Open Section, RSM, 1976–78 (Hon. FRSM 1985). Pres., Devon and Cornwall Record Soc., 1984–87 (Vice Pres., 1976–84); Vice-Pres., UFAW, 1985–. Hon. DD Exeter, 1973; Hon. LLD Leicester, 1986. *Publications:* The Family Is Not Broken, 1962; The Register of Edmund Lacy, Bishop of Exeter 1420–1455, 5 vols, 1963–72; A Digger Still, 1968; Not Yet the Epitaph, 1968; The Sacred Ministry, 1970; The Artifice of Ethics, 1974; A Moralist in the City, 1974; (ed) Duty and Discernment, 1975; (ed jtly) Consent in Medicine, 1983. *Recreations:* small islands, *domus* and *rus*. *Address:* 9 Maryfield Avenue, Exeter EX4 6JN. *T:* Exeter 214691.

DUNSTAN, Ivan, PhD; CChem, FRSC; Director-General, British Standards Institution, since 1986; *b* 27 Aug. 1930; *s* of Edward Ernest and Sarah Kathleen Dunstan; *m* 1955, Monica Jane (*née* Phillips); two *s* one *d*. *Educ:* Falmouth Grammar Sch.; Bristol Univ. (BSc). Joined Scientific Civil Service, working at Explosives Research and Development Estabt, Waltham Abbey, 1954; became Supt of Gen. Chemistry Div., 1967; Warren Spring Laboratory (DTI) as Dep. Dir (Resources), 1972–74; Dir, Materials Quality Assurance, MoD (PE), 1974–79; Dir, Bldg Res. Estabt, DoE, 1979–83; Standards Dir, BSI, 1983–86. *Publications:* research papers on analytical and synthetic chem.; contribs to Annual Reports on Progress of Applied Chem., and to encyclopaedia, etc. *Recreations:*

sailing, tennis, badminton, gardening. *Address:* 5 Aldock, Welwyn Garden City, Herts AL7 4QF. *T:* Welwyn Garden 22272. *Club:* Naval and Military.

DUNSTER, (Herbert) John, CB 1979; Director, National Radiological Protection Board, since 1982; *b* 27 July 1922; *s* of Herbert and Olive Grace Dunster; *m* 1945, Rosemary Elizabeth, *d* of P. J. Gallagher; one *s* three *d*. *Educ:* University Coll. Sch.; Imperial College of Science and Technology (ARCS, BSc). Scientist, UK Atomic Energy Authority, 1946–71; Asst Dir, Nat. Radiological Protection Bd, 1971–76; Dep. Dir Gen., HSE, 1976–82. Member: Internat. Commn on Radiological Protection, 1977–; Sci. and Tech. Cttee, Euratom, 1982–; Sci. Adv. Cttee, IAEA, 1982–. *Publications:* numerous papers in technical jls. *Recreations:* music, photography. *Address:* 5 Shoe Lane, East Hagbourne, Oxon.

DUNTZE, Sir John Alexander, 7th Bt *cr* 1774, of Tiverton, Devon; Mechanical Engineer, retired; *b* 13 Nov. 1909; *s* of John Alexander Ralph Duntze (*d* 1950) and Carrie Fairchild Godfrey (*d* 1927); *S* kinsman, Sir George Edwin Douglas Duntze, 6th Bt, CMG, 1985; *m* 1935, Emily Ellsworth, *d* of Elmer E. Harlow, New Bedford, Mass, USA. *Educ:* Pratt Inst., Brooklyn, NY (grad. 1930, Industrial Mech. Engrg). With R. T. Vanderbilt Co., Rubber Lab., E Norwalk, Conn, 1931–40; Mem. NY Rubber Gp of Amer. Chem. Soc.; Federal Tel. & Radio (IT&T), Transformer Div., Belville, NJ, 1941–44; Mem. Amer. Soc. of Mil. Engrs; Dictaphone Corp., Bridgeport, Conn, 1944–59; two patents bearing his name assigned to company on equipment used in sound recording and reproduction (method of rubber sealing for use in tropical humidity and Magnetic Sheet Machine); Perkin-Elmer Corp., Instrument Div., Norwalk, Conn, 1962–69 (a Sen. Manfg Engr); Manager of Engineering, Connecticut Engineering & Instrument Corp., Norwalk, Conn (optical equipment for US govt), 1975–78. Chief Officer, Westport Aux. Police, 1951–60. *Recreations:* German language; old musical shows, scores, recordings and revivals; steam locomotive "buff". *Heir: cousin* Daniel Evans Duntze [*b* 4 April 1926; *m* 1954, Marietta Welsh; one *s* two *d*]. *Address:* St John's Place, Westport, Conn 06880, USA. *T:* 1–203–227–6954.

DUNWICH, Viscount; Robert Keith Rous; *b* 17 Nov. 1961; *s* and *heir* of Earl of Stradbroke, *qv*.

DUNWICH, Bishop Suffragan of, since 1980; **Rt. Rev. Eric Nash Devenport;** *b* 3 May 1926; *s* of Joseph and Emma Devenport; *m* 1954, Jean Margaret Richardson; two *d*. *Educ:* Kelham Theological Coll. BA (Open Univ.). Curate, St Mark, Leicester, 1951–54; St Matthew, Barrow-in-Furness, 1954–56; Succentor, Leicester Cathedral, 1956–59; Vicar of Shepshed, 1959–64; Oadby, 1964–73; Proctor in Convocation, 1964–80; Hon. Canon of Leicester Cathedral, 1973–80; Leader of Mission, Diocese of Leicester, 1973–80. Chaplain, Worshipful Company of Framework Knitters, 1964–80. *Recreation:* theatre. *Address:* 94 Henley Road, Ipswich, Suffolk IP1 4NJ. *T:* Ipswich 58394.

DUNWOODY, Gwyneth (Patricia); MP (Lab) Crewe and Nantwich, since 1983 (Crewe, Feb. 1974–1983); *b* 12 Dec. 1930; *d* of late Morgan Phillips and of Baroness Phillips, *qv*; *m* 1954, Dr John Elliott Orr Dunwoody, *qv* (marr. diss. 1975); two *s* one *d*. MP (Lab) Exeter, 1966–70; Parly Sec. to BoT, 1967–70; Mem., European Parlt, 1975–79; Front Bench Spokesman on Foreign Affairs, 1980, on Health Service, 1980–83, on Transport, 1984–85; Parly Campaign Co-ordinator, 1983–. Mem., Labour Party NEC, 1981–. Dir, Film Production Assoc. of GB, 1970–74. *Address:* The Mount, Manor Avenue, Crewe, Cheshire.

DUNWOODY, Dr John (Elliott Orr), CBE 1986; general practitioner; Chairman, Bloomsbury District Health Authority, since 1982; *b* 3 June 1929; *s* of Dr W. O. and late Mrs F. J. Dunwoody; *m* 1st, 1954, Gwyneth Patricia (*née* Phillips), *qv* (marr. diss. 1975); two *s* one *d*; 2nd, 1979, Evelyn Louise (*née* Borner). *Educ:* St Paul's Sch.; King's Coll., London Univ.; Westminster Hosp. Med. Sch. MB, BS London; MRCS, LRCP 1954. House Surgeon, Westminster (Gordon) Hosp., 1954; House Physician, Royal Berks Hosp., 1954–55; Sen. House Physician, Newton Abbot Hosp., 1955–56; Family Doctor and Medical Officer, Totnes District Hosp, 1956–66; MO, Staff Health Service, St George's Hosp., 1976–77. MP (Lab) Falmouth and Camborne, 1966–70; Parly Under-Sec., Dept of Health and Social Security, 1969–70. Vice-Chm., 1974–77, Chm., 1977–82, Kensington, Chelsea and Westminster AHA (T). Member: Exec. Cttee, British Council, 1967–69; Council, Westminster Med. Sch., 1974–82; (co-opted) Social Services Cttee, Westminster City Council, 1975–78; Nat. Exec. Council, FPA, 1979–, Dep. Chm., 1980, Chm., 1981–. Council Mem., UCL, 1982–. Hon. Dir, Action on Smoking and Health, 1971–73. Governor, Pimlico Sch., 1972–75. *Publication:* (jtly) A Birth Control Plan for Britain, 1972. *Recreations:* travel, cooking. *Address:* 9 Cautley Avenue, SW4. *T:* 01–673 7471.

DUNWORTH, John Vernon, CB 1969; CBE 1955; President, International Committee of Weights and Measures, Sèvres, France, 1975–85; *b* 24 Feb. 1917; *o c* of late John Dunworth and Susan Ida (*née* Warburton); *m* 1967, Patricia Noel Boston; one *d*. *Educ:* Manchester Grammar Sch.; Clare Coll., Cambridge; Denman Baynes Research Studentship, 1937, Robins Prize, 1937; MA, PhD; Twisden Studentship and Fellowship, Trinity Coll., 1941. War Service: Ministry of Supply on Radar Development, 1939–44; National Research Council of Canada, on Atomic Energy Development, 1944–45. Univ. Demonstrator in Physics, Cambridge, 1945. Joined Atomic Energy Research Establishment, Harwell, 1947; Dir, NPL, 1964–76. Alternate United Kingdom Member on Organising Cttee of UN Atoms for Peace Confs in Geneva, 1955 and 1958. Pres., 1975–85, Vice-Pres., 1968–75, Internat. Cttee of Weights and Measures; Mem., Manx Telecommunications Commn, 1985. Fellow Amer. Nuclear Soc. 1960. Chm., British Nuclear Energy Soc., 1964–70; Vice-President, Institute of Physics: Physical Soc., 1966–70. CEng 1966. Comdr (with Star), Order of Alfonso X el Sabio, Spain, 1960. *Address:* The Warbuck, Kirk Michael, Isle of Man. *T:* Kirk Michael 359. *Club:* Athenæum.

DU PLESSIS, Barend Jacobus; Minister of Finance, Republic of South Africa, since 1984; MP (National Party) Florida, since 1974; *b* 19 Jan. 1940; *s* of late Jan Hendrik and of Martha J. W. (*née* Botha); *m* 1962, Antoinette (*née* Van Den Berg); three *s* one *d*. *Educ:* Potchefstroom Univ. for Christian Higher Educn (BSc); Potchefstroom Teachers' Trng Coll. (THED). Mathematics Teacher, Hoër Seunskool Helpmekaar, Johannesburg and Johannesburg Technical Coll., 1962; Engineering Div., Data Processing and Admin. Sec., SABC, 1962–68; Systems Engineering and Marketing in Banking and Finance, IBM (SA), 1968–74. Dep. Minister of Foreign Affairs and Information, 1982; Minister of Educn and Trng, 1983; Member: Parly study gps on finance, econ. affairs, foreign affairs and educn, 1974–82; Secret Cttee on Public Accounts, 1976–82. *Address:* Private Bag X115, Pretoria, 0001, Republic of S Africa. *T:* (012) 260261.

du PLESSIS, Prof. Daniel Jacob, FRCS; Vice-Chancellor and Principal, University of the Witwatersrand, 1978–83; *b* 17 May 1918; *s* of D. J. du Plessis and L. du Plessis (*née* Carstens); *m* 1946, Louisa Susanna Wicht; two *s*. *Educ:* Univ. of Cape Town (MB ChB; Hon. MD, 1986); Univ. of the Witwatersrand (ChM). Served, SA Medical Corps, 1942–46. Postgraduate study, 1947–51; Surgeon and Lectr, Univ. of Cape Town, 1952–58; Prof. of Surgery, Univ. of the Witwatersrand, 1958–77 (Hon. LLD, 1984). Hon. FACS 1974; Hon. Fellow: Assoc. of Surgeons of GB and Ireland, 1979; Amer. Surgical Assoc., 1981; Hon. FCSSA 1982. Hon. Life Vice-President: Assoc. of Surgeons of S Africa; Surgical Res. Soc. of Southern Africa. Paul Harris Fellowship, Rotary Club, Orange Grove, Johannesburg, 1984. *Publications:* Principles of Surgery, 1968, 2nd edn 1976; Synopsis of Surgical Anatomy, 10th edn (with A. Lee McGregor), 1969, 12th edn (with G. A. G. Decker) 1986; numerous articles in learned jls on surgical topics, espec. on diseases of parotid salivary gland and gastric ulcers. *Address:* 17 Chateau Road, Richmond, Johannesburg, 2092, South Africa.

DUPPA-MILLER, John Bryan Peter; *see* Miller, J. B. P. D.

DUPPLIN, Viscount; Charles William Harley Hay, BA; Associate at Credit Suisse First Boston Ltd, since 1985; *b* 20 Dec. 1962; *s* and *heir* of 15th Earl of Kinnoull, *qv*. *Educ:* Summer Fields; Eton; Christ Church, Oxford (Scholar). *Recreations:* cricket, skiing, philately, night clubs. *Address:* 15 Carlyle Square, SW3. *T:* 01–634 3512. *Clubs:* Turf, Lansdowne.

du PRÉ, Jacqueline, OBE 1976; British violoncellist; *b* 1945; *m* 1967, Daniel Barenboim, *qv*. *Educ:* studied with William Pleeth both privately and at Guildhall Sch. of Music, with Paul Tortelier in Paris, and with Rostropovich in Moscow. Concert début at Wigmore Hall at age of sixteen, followed by appearances on the continent and with principal English orchestras and conductors. Soloist in London and at Bath and Edinburgh Festivals. N American début, 1965. Continued studies in Moscow with Rostropovitch, 1966, returning later to USSR as soloist with BBC Symphony Orchestra. Toured N America, and appeared New York and at World Fair, Montreal; subseq. concerts, major musical centres, 1967. Awarded Suggia Gift at age of ten; Gold medal, Guildhall Sch. of Music, and Queen's Prize, 1960; City of London Midsummer Prize, 1975; Musician of the Year Award, Incorporated Soc. of Musicians, 1980; FGSM, 1975; FRCM, 1977; Hon. FRAM, 1974. Hon. Fellow, St Hilda's Coll., Oxford, 1984. Hon. DMus: London, 1979; Sheffield, 1980; Leeds, 1982; Durham, 1983; Oxford, 1984; Hon. DLit Salford, 1978; DUniv Open, 1979. *Address:* c/o Harold Holt Ltd, 31 Sinclair Road, W14 0NS.

DUPREE, Sir Peter, 5th Bt *cr* 1921; *b* 20 Feb. 1924; *s* of Sir Victor Dupree, 4th Bt and of Margaret Cross; *S* father, 1976; *m* 1947, Joan, *d* of late Captain James Desborough Hunt. *Heir: cousin* Thomas William James David Dupree, *b* 5 Feb. 1930. *Address:* Great Seabrights, Galley Wood, near Chelmsford, Essex.

DUPUCH, Hon. Sir (Alfred) Etienne (Jerome), Kt 1965; OBE 1949; KCSG, OTL, CHM; Editor, 1919–72, Contributing Editor since 1972, The Tribune, Nassau, Bahamas; *b* Nassau, 16 Feb. 1899; *s* of Leon Edward Hartman Dupuch, Founder of The Tribune, and Elizabeth Harriet Saunders Dupuch; *m* 1928, Marie Plouse, USA; three *s* three *d*. *Educ:* Boys' Central Sch., Nassau; St John's Univ., Collegeville, Minn, USA. Served War, 1914–18, Eastern and Western Fronts, BWI Regt; Rep. for Inagua and Mayaguana, House of Assembly, Bahamas, 1925–42; Eastern District, New Providence, 1949–56; MLC, 1960–64; Mem. Senate, 1964–68. Mem., US Nat. Adv. Bd, Amer. Security Council, 1981. Board Member: ES-U, Miami; United World Colls, NY. Hon. Member: East Nassau Rotary Club; Coral Gables Rotary Club; Lions Club, Pennsylvania. Hon. LittD, Hon. LLD. IAPA Award for breaking down racial discrimination in Bahamas, 1956; IAPA Award for successful defence of Freedom of Press, 1969; Citation from Associated Press N American Editors' Assoc. for outstanding coverage of fire on SS Yarmouth Castle, 1965; Paul Harris Award for work in social services (Rotary Club of Lucaya, Freeport); listed in Guinness Book of Records as longest serving editor in history of journalism. Has RSA medal and several decorations from governments of three nations. Kt, SMO Malta, 1977. *Publications:* We Call Him Friend (tribute to Rt Hon. Lord Beaverbrook), 1961; The Tribune Story, 1967; A Salute to Friend and Foe, 1981. *Address:* Camperdown Heights, PO Box N-3207, Nassau, Bahamas; 700 Coral Way, Coral Gables, Florida, USA. *Clubs:* East India, Devonshire, Sports and Public Schools; The Admirals of the Florida Fleet; Country (Coral Gables, Fla).

DURACK, Dame Mary, (Mrs Horrie Miller), DBE 1978 (OBE 1966); novelist and historian; *b* 20 Feb. 1913; *d* of Michael Patrick Durack and Bessie Ida Muriel (*née* Johnstone); *m* 1938, Captain H. C. Miller (decd); two *s* two *d* (and two *d* decd). *Educ:* Loreto Convent, Perth. Formerly: lived at Argyle and Ivanhoe Stns, E Kimberley; mem. staff, West Australian Newspapers Ltd. Member: Aust. Soc. of Authors; National Trust; Royal Western Aust. Hist. Soc.; Kuljak Playwrights Inc. Formerly Exec. Mem., Aboriginal Cultural Foundn. Dir, Aust. Stockman's Hall of Fame. Emeritus Fellow, Literature Bd of Aust., 1983; Hon. Life Member: WA Br., Fellowship of Aust. Writers (Pres., 1958–63); Internat. PEN, Australia. Commonwealth Lit. Grant, 1973, 1977 and Australian Research Grants Cttee Grant, 1980 and 1984. Hon. DLitt Univ. of WA, 1978. Alice Award, Soc. of Women Writers (Australia), 1982. *Publications:* (E Kimberley District stories illus. by sister, Elizabeth Durack): All-about, 1935; Chunuma, 1936; Son of Djaro, 1938; The Way of the Whirlwind, 1941, new edn 1979; Piccaninnies, 1943; The Magic Trumpet, 1944; (with Florence Rutter) Child Artists of the Australian Bush, 1952; (novel) Keep Him My Country, 1955; (family documentary) Kings in Grass Castles, 1959; To Ride a Fine Horse, 1963; The Courteous Savage, 1964 (new edn as Yagan of the Bibbulmun, 1976); Kookanoo and Kangaroo, 1963; An Australian Settler, 1964 (pub. Australia, A Pastoral Emigrant); The Rock and the Sand, 1969; (with Ingrid Drysdale) The End of Dreaming, 1974; To Be Heirs Forever, 1976; Tjakamarra—boy between two worlds, 1977; Sons in the Saddle, 1983; *plays:* The Ship of Dreams, 1968; Swan River Saga, 1972; scripts for ABC drama dept; libretto for opera, Dalgerie (music by James Penberthy), 1966; six dramatised Kookanoo stories on tape and record, 1973. *Address:* 12 Bellevue Avenue, Nedlands, WA 6009, Australia. *T:* 386–1117.

DURAND, Rev. Sir (Henry Mortimer) Dickon (Marion St George), 4th Bt *cr* 1892; Rector, Youghal Union of Parishes, Co. Cork, since 1982; *b* 19 June 1934; *s* of Lt-Comdr Mortimer Henry Marion Durand, RN (*y s* of 1st Bt) (*d* 1969), and Beatrice Garvan-Sheridan, *d* of Judge Sheridan, Sydney, NSW; *S* uncle, 1971; *m* 1971, Stella Evelyn, *d* of Captain C. C. L'Estrange; two *s* two *d*. *Educ:* Wellington College; Sydney University; Salisbury Theological College. Curate: All Saints, Fulham, 1969–72; St Leonard's, Heston, 1972–74. Curate-in-Charge, St Benedict's, Ashford, Mddx, 1975–79; Bishop's Curate, Kilbixy Union of Parishes, Co. Westmeath, 1979–82. *Recreations:* heraldry, philately, model railways, printing, militaria, painting, poetry, travel. *Heir: s* Edward Alan Christopher Percy Durand, *b* 21 Feb. 1974. *Address:* The Rectory, Youghal, Co. Cork, Ireland.

DURAND, Victor Albert Charles, QC 1958; *s* of Victor and Blanche Durand; *m* 1935, Betty Joan Kirchner (*d* 1986); one *s* one *d*. *Educ:* Howard High Sch. (Kitchener Scholar). LLB, BSc, AMInstCE. Served War 1939–45 with RE. Called to Bar, Inner Temple, 1939, Bencher, 1985. Dep. Chm., Warwicks QS, 1961. *Address:* Queen Elizabeth Building, Temple, EC4Y 9BS.

DURANT, Robert Anthony Bevis, (Tony Durant); MP (C) Reading West, since 1983 (Reading North, Feb. 1974–1983); a Lord Commissioner of HM Treasury, since 1986; *b* 9 Jan. 1928; *s* of Captain Robert Michael Durant and Mrs Violet Dorothy Durant (*née*

Bevis); *m* 1958, Audrey Stoddart; two *s* one *d*. *Educ:* Dane Court Prep. Sch., Pyrford, Woking; Bryanston Sch., Blandford, Dorset. Royal Navy, 1945–47. Coutts Bank, Strand, 1947–52; Cons. Party Organisation, 1952–67 (Young Cons. Organiser, Yorks; Cons. Agent, Clapham; Nat. Organiser, Young Conservatives). PPS to Sec. of State for Transport and to Sec. of State for Employment, 1983–84; Asst Govt Whip, 1984–86. Mem., Select Cttee Parly Comr (Ombudsman), 1973–83; Mem., Council of Europe, 1981–83; Chairman: All Party Gp on Widows and One Parent Families, 1977–85; Cons. Nat. Local Govt Adv. Cttee, 1981–84; Vice-Chm., Parly Gp for World Govt, 1979–84. Former Consultant: The Film Production Association of Great Britain Ltd; Delta Electrical Div. of Delta Metal Co. Ltd; Allied Industrial Designers. Mem., Inland Waterways Adv. Council, 1975–84. Dir, British Industrial Scientific Film Assoc., 1967–70. *Recreations:* boating, golf. *Address:* Hill House, Surley Row, Caversham, Reading RG4 8ND.

DURBIN, Prof. James; Professor of Statistics, University of London (London School of Economics), since 1961; *b* 30 June 1923; *m* 1958, Anne Dearnley Outhwaite; two *s* one *d*. *Educ:* St John's Coll., Cambridge. Army Operational Research Group, 1943–45. Boot and Shoe Trade Research Assoc., 1945–47; Dept of Applied Economics, Cambridge, 1948–49; Asst Lectr, then Lecturer, in Statistics, London Sch. of Economics, 1950–53; Reader in Statistics, 1953–61. Visiting Professor: Univ. of North Carolina, 1959–60; Stanford Univ., 1960; Johns Hopkins Univ., 1965–66; Univ. of Washington, 1966; ANU, 1970–71; Univ. of Calif, Berkeley, 1971; Univ. of Cape Town, 1978; UCLA, 1984. Member: ESRC, 1983– (Chm., Res. Resources and Methods Cttee, 1982–85); Internat. Statistical Inst., 1955 (Pres., 1983–85); Bd of Dirs, Amer. Statistical Assoc., 1980–82 (Fellow, 1960); Fellow, Inst. of Mathematical Statistics, 1958; Fellow, Econometric Soc., 1967; Royal Statistical Society: Vice Pres., 1969–70 and 1972–73; Pres. 1986–87; Guy Medal in Bronze, 1966, in Silver, 1976. *Publications:* Distribution Theory for Tests based on the Sample Distribution Function, 1973; articles in statistical journals, incl. Biometrika, Jl of Royal Statistical Society, etc. *Recreations:* skiing, mountain walking, travel, opera, theatre. *Address:* 31 Southway, NW11. *T:* 01–458 3037.

DURBIN, Leslie, CBE 1976; MVO 1943; silversmith; *b* 21 Feb. 1913; *s* of late Harry Durbin and of Lillian A. Durbin; *m* 1940, Phyllis Ethel Durbin (*see* Phyllis E. Ginger); one *s* one *d*. *Educ:* Central Sch. of Arts and Crafts, London. Apprenticed to late Omar Ramsden, 1929–39; full-time schol., 1938–39, travelling schol., 1939–40, both awarded by Worshipful Co. of Goldsmiths. Started working on own account in workshop of Francis Adam, 1940–41. RAF, Allied Central Interpretation Unit, 1941–45. Commissioned by Jt Cttee of Assay Offices of GB to design Silver Jubilee Hall Mark; designed regional variants of pound coin for Royal Mint, 1983. Retrospective exhibn, Leslie Durbin, 50 years of Silversmithing, Goldsmiths' Hall, 1982. Hon. LLD Cambridge, 1963. Council of Industrial Design Awards for Silver for the 70's.

DURBRIDGE, Francis (Henry); playwright and author; *b* 25 Nov. 1912; *s* of late Francis and Gertrude Durbridge; *m* 1940, Norah Elizabeth Lawley; two *s*. *Educ:* Bradford Grammar Sch.; Wylde Green Coll.; Birmingham Univ. After period in stockbroker's office, began to write (as always intended); short stories and plays for BBC; many subseq. radio plays, including Promotion, 1933; created character of Paul Temple. Entered Television with The Broken Horseshoe, 1952 (the first adult television serial); other serials followed; Portrait of Alison, 1954; My Friend Charles, 1955; The Other Man, 1956; The Scarf 1960; The World of Tim Frazer (Exec. Prod.), 1960–61; Melissa, 1962; Bat Out of Hell, 1964; Stupid Like a Fox, 1971; The Doll, 1976; Breakaway, 1980. The television serials have been presented in many languages, and are continuing; novels, based on them, have been published in USA, Europe, etc. The European Broadcasting Union asked for a radio serial for an internat. market (La Boutique, 1967, broadcast in various countries); German, French and Italian productions, 1971–72. Films include two for Korda and Romulus, 1954–57. Stage plays: Suddenly at Home, 1971; The Gentle Hook, 1974; Murder With Love, 1976; House Guest, 1980; Nightcap, 1983; Murder Diary, 1986. *Publications:* include contribs to newspapers and magazines, at home and abroad. *Recreations:* family, reading, travel. *Address:* 4 Fairacres, Roehampton Lane, SW15 5LX.

DURHAM, 6th Earl of, *cr* 1833; Baron Durham, 1828; Viscount Lambton, 1833; peerages disclaimed, 1970; *see under* Lambton.

DURHAM, Baron; a subsidiary title of Earldom of Durham (disclaimed 1970), used by Hon. Edward Richard Lambton, *b* 19 Oct. 1961, *heir* to disclaimed Earldom.

DURHAM, Bishop of, since 1984; **Rt. Rev. David Edward Jenkins;** *b* 26 Jan. 1925; *er s* of Lionel C. Jenkins and Dora (*née* Page); *m* 1949, Stella Mary Peet; two *s* two *d*. *Educ:* St Dunstan's Coll., Catford; Queen's Coll., Oxford (MA). EC, RA, 1943–45 (Captain). Priest, 1954. Succentor, Birmingham Cath. and Lectr, Queen's Coll., 1953–54; Fellow, Chaplain and Praelector in Theology, Queen's Coll., Oxford, 1954–69; Dir, Humanum Studies, World Council of Churches, Geneva, 1969–73 (Consultant, 1973–75); Dir, William Temple Foundn, Manchester, 1973–78 (Jt Dir, 1979–); Prof. of Theology, Univ. of Leeds, 1979–84. Exam. Chaplain to Bps of Lichfield, 1956–69, Newcastle, 1957–69, Bristol, 1958–84, Wakefield, 1978–84, and Bradford, 1979–84; Canon Theologian, Leicester, 1966–82, Canon Emeritus, 1982–. Bampton Lectr, 1966; Hale Lectr, Seabury-Western, USA, 1970; Moorhouse Lectr, Melbourne, 1972; Cadbury Lectr, Birmingham Univ., 1974; Lindsay Meml Lectr, Keele Univ., 1976; Heslington Lectr, York Univ., 1980; Drummond Lectr, Stirling Univ., 1981; Hibbert Lectr, Hibbert Trust, 1985. Jt Editor, Theology, 1976–82. *Publications:* Guide to the Debate about God, 1966; The Glory of Man, 1967; Living with Questions, 1969; What is Man?, 1970; The Contradiction of Christianity, 1976; contrib. Man, Fallen and Free, 1969, etc. *Recreations:* music, reading, walking. *Address:* Auckland Castle, Bishop Auckland, Co. Durham DL14 7NR.

DURHAM, Dean of; *see* Baelz, Very Rev. P. R.

DURHAM, Archdeacon of; *see* Perry, Ven. M. C.

DURHAM, Sir Kenneth, Kt 1985; Chairman, Woolworth Holdings plc, since 1986 (non-executive Deputy Chairman, 1985–86); *b* 28 July 1924; *s* of late George Durham and Bertha (*née* Aspin); *m* 1946, Irene Markham; one *s* one *d*. *Educ:* Queen Elizabeth Grammar Sch., Blackburn; Univ. of Manchester (Hatfield Schol.; BSc Hons, Physics). Flight Lieut, RAF, 1942–46. ARE, Harwell, 1950; Unilever: joined Res. Lab., Port Sunlight, 1950, Head of Lab., 1961; Head, Res. Lab., Colworth, Bedford, 1965; assumed responsibility for animal feed interests, 1970; Chm., BOCM Silcock Ltd, 1971; Dir, Unilever Ltd, 1974, Vice-Chm., 1978, Chm., 1982–86; Dir, Unilever NV, 1974–86. Board Member: British Aerospace, 1980–; Delta PLC, 1984–; Dir, Morgan Grenfell Hldgs, 1986–. Chairman: Food, Drink and Packaging Machinery EDC, NEDO, 1981–86; Trade Policy Res. Centre, 1982–; Industry and Commerce Liaison Cttee, Royal Jubilee Trusts, 1982–; Economic and Financial Policy Cttee, CBI, 1983–; Priorities Bd for Govt Agricl Depts and AFRC, 1984–; Member: British-N America Cttee, 1982–; British Shippers Council, 1982–; Bd, British Exec. Service Overseas, 1982–86; Euro. Adv. Council, Utd Technologies Corp., 1983–; Adv. Cttee, Chase Manhattan Bank, 1983–; Adv. Cttee, CVCP, 1984–; Governing Body, ICC UK, 1984–; ACARD, 1984–; European Adv. Council, Air Products and Chemicals Inc., 1985–; European Adv. Council, NY Stock Exchange, 1985–; Council for Industry and Higher Educn, 1985–; Adv. Panel, Science Policy Res. Unit, Sussex Univ., 1985–; Adv. Bd, Industrial Res. Labs, Durham Univ., 1985–; President: Centre for World Develt Educn, 1985–; ABCC, 1986–. Attended Harvard Advanced Management Program, 1962; Member: Council, PSI, 1978–; Council, Royal Free Hosp. Sch. of Med., 1984–; Council, RHBNC, 1985–. Vice-President: Liverpool Sch. of Tropical Medicine, 1982–; Opportunities for the Disabled, 1982–; Help the Aged, 1986–; Trustee: Leverhulme Trust, 1974–; Civic Trust, 1982–. Governor: London Business Sch., 1982–; NIESR, 1983–. CBIM 1978; FIGD 1983. Hon. LLD Manchester, 1984; Hon. DSc Loughborough, 1984. Comdr, Order of Orange Nassau (Netherlands), 1985. *Publications:* Surface Activity and Detergency, 1960; various scientific papers. *Recreations:* walking, golf. *Address:* c/o Woolworth Holdings plc, North West House, 119 Marylebone Road, NW1 5PX. *T:* 01–724 7749. *Club:* Athenæum.

DURIE, Sir Alexander (Charles), Kt 1977; CBE 1973; Vice-President, The Automobile Association, since 1977 (Director-General, 1964–77); *b* 15 July 1915; *er s* of late Charles and Margaret Durie (*née* Gardner), Shepton Mallet, Somerset; *m* 1941, Joyce, *o c* of late Lionel and Helen Hargreaves (*née* Hirst), Leeds and Bridlington, Yorks; one *s* one *d*. *Educ:* Queen's Coll., Taunton. Joined Shell-Mex and BP Ltd, 1933. Served War of 1939–45, Royal Artillery; Gunnery Staff Course (IG), 1941; Lieut-Col 1945. Dir Shell Co. of Australia Ltd, 1954–56; Dir, 1962, Man. Dir, 1963–64, Shell-Mex and BP Ltd; Director: Mercantile Credit Co. Ltd, 1973–80; Thomas Cook Group Ltd, 1974–79; Private Patients Plan Ltd, 1977–; H. Clarkson (Holdings) Ltd, 1978–85; Chelsea Building Soc., 1979–. Mem. Council, Motor and Cycle Trades Benevolent Fund, 1959–73; Vice-Pres. British Assoc. of Industrial Editors, 1959–71; Gen. Commissioner of Income Tax, 1960–85; Member Govt Inquiries into: Civilianisation of Armed Forces, 1964; Cars for Cities, 1964; Road Haulage Operators' Licensing, 1978. FBIM, 1959, Council Mem., 1962–73, Chm. Exec. Cttee, 1962–65, Vice-Chm. Council, 1962–67, Chm., Bd of Fellows, 1970–73 (Verulam Medal 1973); Member: Nat. Road Safety Adv. Council, 1965–68; Adv. Council on Road Res., 1965–68; Brit. Road Fedn Ltd, 1962– (Vice-Pres., 1978); Council, Internat. Road Fedn Ltd, London, 1962–64; Marketing Cttee, BTA, 1970–77; Adv. Cttee on Traffic and Safety, TRRL, 1973–77; Vice-Pres., Alliance Internationale de Tourisme, 1965–71, Pres., 1971–77; Chm., Indep. Schs Careers Orgn, 1969–73 (Vice-Pres., 1973–); Governor: Ashridge Coll., 1963–78 (Vice Pres., 1978–); Queen's Coll., Taunton, 1969–83. Chm. Council, Imperial Soc. of Knights Bachelor, 1986– (Mem., 1978–); Pres., Surrey CCC, 1984–85 (Mem. Cttee, 1970–80; Vice-Pres., 1980–84, 1985–); Vice-Pres., Hampshire CCC, 1984–. Freeman of City of London and Liveryman, Worshipful Co. of Paviors, 1965. FCIT; Hon. FInstHE 1969. Spanish Order of Touristic Merit Silver Medal, 1977. *Recreations:* cricket, golf, racing. *Address:* The Garden House, Windlesham, Surrey GU20 6AD. *T:* Bagshot 72035. *Clubs:* MCC, Carlton; Royal and Ancient; Berkshire Golf.

DURIE, David Robert Campbell; Under Secretary, Shipbuilding and Electrical Engineering Division, Department of Trade and Industry, since 1985; *b* 21 Aug. 1944; *s* of Frederick Robert Edwin Durie and Joan Elizabeth Campbell Durie (*née* Learoyd); *m* 1966, Susan Frances Weller; three *d*. *Educ:* Fettes Coll., Edinburgh; Christ Church, Oxford (MA Physics). Asst Principal, 1966, Pvte Sec. to Perm. Sec., 1970, Min. of Technology; Principal, DTI, 1971; First Sec., UK Delegn to OECD, 1974; Dept of Prices and Consumer Protection, 1977; Asst Sec., 1978; Dept of Trade, 1979; Cabinet Office, 1982; DTI, 1984. *Recreations:* running slowly, cycling, theatre, family. *Address:* 62 Burlington Avenue, Kew Gardens, Richmond, Surrey TW9 4DH. *T:* 01–876 2288.

DURKIN, Air Marshal Sir Herbert, KBE 1976; CB 1973; MA; CEng, FIEE, FRAeS; CBIM; Controller of Engineering and Supply (RAF), 1976–78; *b* 31 March 1922; *s* of Herbert and Helen Durkin, Burnley, Lancs; *m* 1951, Dorothy Hope, *d* of Walter Taylor Johnson, Burnley; one *s* two *d*. *Educ:* Burnley Grammar Sch.; Emmanuel Coll., Cambridge (MA). Commissioned into Tech. Br., RAF, Oct. 1941. Served War, with No 60 Gp, until 1945. India, 1945–47, becoming ADC to AOC-in-C India; Central Bomber Estabt, 1947–50; Sqdn Ldr, 1950; Atomic Weapons Research Estabt, 1950–52; RAF Staff Coll., 1953; Chief Signals Officer, AHQ, Iraq, 1954–56; Wing Comdr, Chief Instr of Signals Div. of RAF Tech. Coll., 1956–58; Air Ministry, 1958–60; jssc, 1961; HQ, 2 ATAF, 1961–63; Gp Capt 1962; Sen. Tech. Staff Officer, HQ Signals Command, 1964–65; Comdt, No 2 Sch. of Tech. Trg, Cosford, 1965–67; Air Cdre, 1967; Director of Eng (Policy), MoD, 1967–69; IDC, 1970; AOC No 90 Group, RAF, 1971–73; Dir-Gen. Engineering and Supply Management, 1973–76. Pres., IEE, 1980 (Dep. Pres., 1979). FBIM. *Recreation:* golf. *Address:* Willowbank, Drakes Drive, Northwood, Middlesex HA6 2SL. *T:* Northwood 23167. *Club:* Royal Air Force.

DURRANDS, Prof. Kenneth James, DGS (Birm), MSc, CEng, FIMechE, FIEE, FIProdE; Rector, The Polytechnic, Queensgate, Huddersfield, since 1970 (Professor, 1985); *b* 24 June 1929; *s* of A. I. Durrands, Croxton Kerrial; *m* 1956 (marr. diss. 1971), one *s*. *Educ:* King's Sch., Grantham; Nottingham Technical Coll.; Birmingham Univ. Min. of Supply Engrg Apprentice, ROF, Nottingham, 1947–52; Techn. Engr, UKAEA, Risley, 1954–58; Lecturer in Mechanical and Nuclear Engrg, Univ. of Birmingham, 1958–61; Head of Gen. Engrg Dept, Reactor Engrg Lab., UKAEA, Risley, 1961–67; Mem. Council, IMechE, 1963–66; Visiting Lecturer, Manchester Univ., 1962–68; Technical Dir, Vickers Ltd, Barrow Engrg Works, 1967–70. Member: DoI Educn and Training Cttee, 1973–75 (Chm., 1975–80); DoI Garment & Allied Industries Requirements Bd, 1975–79 (Chm. Computer Cttee, 1975–79); BEC Educn Cttee, 1975–79; BEC Business Studies Bd, 1976–79; Inter-Univ. and Polytech. Council, 1978–81; British Council: Higher Educn Cttee, 1981–; Engrg and Technology Adv. Cttee, 1981–; CICHE, 1985–; Hon. Sec./Treas., Cttee of Dirs of Polytechnics, 1970–79. Educn Comr, MSC, 1986–. Member: Council and Court, Leeds Univ., 1970–; Court, Bradford Univ., 1973–. *Publications:* technical and policy papers. *Recreations:* gardening, squash rackets. *Address:* Church Cottage, Croxton Kerrial, Grantham, Lincolnshire. *Club:* Athenæum.

DURRANT, Maj.-Gen. James Thom, CB 1945; DFC 1941; City Councillor, Johannesburg, 1969–77; *b* 1913; *s* of late J. C. Durrant, Hertford and Johannesburg; *m* 1970, Margaret, *d* of late Archie White, Johannesburg. Commanded a group in Air Command, South-East Asia, 1945; Dir-Gen. South African Air Force, 1947–51; retired, 1952. *Address:* 71 First Avenue East, Parktown North, Johannesburg, South Africa.

DURRANT, Sir William Henry Estridge, 7th Bt, *cr* 1784; JP (NSW); *b* 1 April 1901; *s* of Sir William Durrant, 6th Bt; *S* father 1953; *m* 1927, Georgina Beryl Gwendoline (*d* 1968), *d* of Alexander Purse, Kircubbin, Co. Down, N Ireland; one *s* one *d*. Served War of 1939–45 (Pacific Area). NSW Registrar, Australian Inst. of Company Dirs, 1959. *Heir:* *s* William Alexander Estridge Durrant [*b* 26 Nov. 1929; *m* 1953, Dorothy (BA), *d* of Ronal Croker, Quirindi, NSW; one *s* one *d*]. *Address:* Woodside Gardens, Yardley Avenue, Waitara, NSW 2077, Australia.

DURRELL, Gerald Malcolm, OBE 1983; Zoologist and Writer since 1946; regular contributor to BBC Sound and TV Services; *b* Jamshedpur, India, 7 Jan. 1925; *s* of Lawrence Samuel Durrell, Civil Engineer, and Louisa Florence Dixie; *m* 1st, 1951,

Jacqueline Sonia Rasen (marr. diss. 1979); no *c*; 2nd, 1979, Lee Wilson McGeorge. *Educ:* by Private Tutors, in France, Italy, Switzerland and Greece. Student Keeper, Whipsnade, 1945–46; 1st Animal Collecting Expedition, British Cameroons, 1947–48; 2nd Cameroon Expedition, 1948–49; Collecting trip to British Guiana, 1949–50; began writing, script writing and broadcasting, 1950–53; trip with wife to Argentine and Paraguay, 1953–54; filming in Cyprus, 1955; 3rd Cameroon Expedition with wife, 1957; Trans-Argentine Expedition, 1958–59; Expedition in conjunction with BBC Natural History Unit, Sierra Leone, 1965; collecting trip to Mexico, 1968; Aust. Expedn, 1969–70; expedns to Mauritius, 1976 and 1977, Assam, 1978, Mexico, 1979, Madagascar, 1981. Founder and Hon. Director: Jersey Zoological Park, 1958; Jersey Wildlife Preservation Trust, 1964. Founder Chm. SAFE Internat. USA, 1972. FZS; (Life) FIAL; FRGS; FRSL 1972; MBOU; MIBiol. Hon. LHD Yale, 1977. *Films for TV:* 1st series, 1956; Two in the Bush, 1962; Catch Me a Colobus, 1966; Animal People-Menagerie Manor, 1967; Garden of the Gods, 1967; The Stationary Ark, 1976; The Ark on the Move, 1981; The Amateur Naturalist (series), 1983. *Publications:* The Overloaded Ark, 1953, Three Singles to Adventure, 1954; The Bafut Beagles, 1954; The New Noah, 1955; The Drunken Forest, 1956; My Family and Other Animals, 1956; Encounters with Animals, 1958; A Zoo in my Luggage, 1960; The Whispering Land, 1961; Island Zoo, 1961; Look at Zoos, 1961; My Favourite Animal Stories, 1962; Menagerie Manor, 1964; Two in the Bush, 1966; Rosy is My Relative, 1968; The Donkey Rustlers, 1968; Birds, Beasts and Relatives, 1969; Fillets of Plaice, 1971; Catch Me a Colobus, 1972; Beasts in My Belfry, 1973; The Talking Parcel, 1974; The Stationary Ark, 1976; Golden Bats and Pink Pigeons, 1977; The Garden of the Gods, 1978; The Picnic & Suchlike Pandemonium, 1979; The Mockery Bird, 1981; The Amateur Naturalist, 1982; How to Shoot an Amateur Naturalist, 1984; (with Lee Durrell) Durrell in Russia, 1986; contribs to Zoo Life, etc. *Recreations:* reading, riding, filming, photography, drawing, swimming, study of the History and Maintenance of Zoological Gardens. *Address:* Jersey Zoo Park, Les Augres Manor, Trinity, Jersey, Channel Isles. *T:* Central 61949.

See also Lawrence G. Durrell.

DURRELL, Lawrence George, FRSL 1954; lately Director of Public Relations, Government of Cyprus; *b* 27 Feb. 1912; *m* 1937, 1947 and 1960; one *d* (and one *d* decd). *Educ:* College of St Joseph, Darjeeling, India; St Edmund's Sch., Canterbury. Formerly: Foreign Service Press Officer, Athens and Cairo; Press Attaché, Alexandria; Dir of Public Relations, Dodecanese Islands; Press Attaché, Belgrade, Yugoslavia; Dir of British Council Institutes of Kalamata, Greece, and Cordoba, Argentina. Mellon Lectr in Humanities, Calif. Inst. of Technology, Pasadena, 1975. *Publications:* (novel, under pseudonym Charles Norden) Panic Spring, 1937; The Black Book, 1938 (France and USA), 1973 (England); Private Country (poetry), 1943; Prospero's Cell, 1945; (trans) Four Greek Poets, 1946; Cities, Plains and People, 1946; Cefalu, 1947 (republished as The Dark Labyrinth, 1958); On Seeming to Presume, 1948; (trans) Pope Joan, 1948; Sappho (verse play), 1950; Reflections on a Marine Venus, 1953; The Tree of Idleness, 1955; Selected Poems, 1956; Bitter Lemons, 1957 (Duff Cooper Memorial Prize); White Eagles Over Serbia (juvenile), 1957; The Alexandria Quartet: Justine, 1957, Balthazar, 1958 (Prix du Meilleur Livre Etranger, Paris), Mountolive, 1958, Clea, 1960; Esprit de Corps, 1957; Stiff Upper Lip, 1958; (ed) The Best of Henry Miller, 1960; Collected Poems, 1960, new edn with additions and revisions, 1968; An Irish Faustus (verse play), 1963; The Ikons, 1966; The Revolt of Aphrodite: Tunc, 1968, Nunquam, 1970; Spirit of Place: letters and essays on travel, 1969; The Red Limbo Lingo: a poetry notebook for 1968–70, 1971; Vega and other poems, 1973; The Avignon Quintet: Monsieur, or the Prince of Darkness, 1974 (James Tait Black Memorial Prize), Livia or Buried Alive, 1978, Constance or Solitary Practices, 1982; Sebastian or Ruling Passions, 1983; Quinx or the Ripper's Tale, 1985; The Best of Antrobus, 1975; Selected Poems, 1976; Sicilian Carousel, 1976; The Greek Islands, 1978; Collected Poems, 1980; Smile in the Mind's Eye, 1980; Antrobus Complete, 1985. *Recreation:* travel. *Address:* c/o Grindlay's Bank, 13 St James's Square, SW1.

See also Gerald M. Durrell.

DÜRRENMATT, Friedrich; Swiss author and playwright; *b* Konolfingen, Switzerland, 5 Jan. 1921; *s* of Reinhold Dürrenmatt, pastor, and Hulda (*née* Zimmermann); *m* 1946, Lotti Geissler; one *s* two *d*. *Educ:* Gymnasium, Bern; University of Bern; University of Zürich. Prix Italia, 1958; Schillerpreis, 1960; Grillparzer-Preis, 1968; Kunstpreis, Bern, 1969. Hon DLitt, Temple Univ. Philadelphia, 1969; Dr (*hc*): Hebrew Univ. of Jerusalem, 1977; Univ. of Nice, 1977; Univ. of Neuchâtel, 1981. Buber-Rosenzweig Medaille, Frankfurt, 1977. *Publications: plays:* Es steht geschrieben, 1947; Der Blinde, 1948; Romulus der Grosse, 1949; Die Ehe des Herrn Mississippi (The Marriage of Mr Mississippi), 1952 (produced New York, Fools Are Passing Through, 1958; filmed, 1961); Nächtliches Gespräch mit einem verachteten Menschen, 1952; Ein Engel kommt nach Babylon (An Angel Comes to Babylon), 1953; Der Besuch der alten Dame, 1956 (The Visit, produced New York, 1958, London, 1960) (Eng. trans., by Patrick Bowles, publ. 1962); Frank V-Oper einer Privatbank, 1959; Die Physiker, 1962 (prod. Aldwych Theatre, London as The Physicists, 1963); The Meteor (prod. Aldwych Theatre, London, 1966); Die Wiedertäufer, 1967; Die Panne (The Deadly Game, prod. Savoy Theatre, 1967; Die Panne Komödie, 1979); König Johann, nach Shakespeare, 1968; Play Strindberg, 1969; Titus Andronicus, nach Shakespeare, 1970; Porträt eines Planeten, 1970 (Portrait of a Planet, prod London, 1973); Komödien, I, II, III, 1972; Der Mitmacher, 1973; Die Frist, 1977; Achterloo, 1983; *plays for radio:* Der Doppelgänger; Der Prozess um des Esels Schatten; Nächtliches Gespräch; Stranitzki und der Nationalheld; Herkules und der Stall des Augias; Das Unternehmen der Wega; Die Panne; Abendstunde im Spätherbst; *essays and criticism:* Theater-Schriften und Reden I, II (Eng. trans., Writings on Theatre and Drama, 1977); Theater-probleme; Gerechtigkeit und Recht; Friedrich Schiller, Rede; Sätze aus Amerika, 1970; Gespräch mit Heinz Ludwig Arnold, 1976; Zusammenhänge: Essay über Israel, 1976; Der Mitmacher: ein Komplex, 1976; Frankfurter Rede, 1977; Friedrich Dürrenmatt, Lesebuch, 1978; Einstein-Vortrag, 1979; Stoffe I-III, 1981; *novels:* Pilatus, 1949; Der Nihilist, 1950; Die Stadt (short stories), 1952; Der Richter und sein Henker, 1952 (Eng. trans. by Therese Pol, The Judge and His Hangman, 1955); Der Verdacht, 1953 (Eng. trans. as The Quarry, by Eva H. Morreale), 1962; Grieche sucht Griechin, 1955; Die Panne, 1956 (Eng. trans. by R. and C. Winston, The Dangerous Game, 1960); Das Versprechen, 1958 (Eng. trans. by R. and C. Winston, The Pledge, 1959); Der Sturz, 1971; Justiz, 1986. *Recreations:* painting and astronomy. *Address:* Pertuis du Sault 34, Neuchâtel, Switzerland.

du SAUTOY, Peter Francis, CBE 1971 (OBE 1964); *b* 19 Feb. 1912; *s* of late Col E. F. du Sautoy, OBE, TD, DL; *m* 1937, Phyllis Mary (Mollie), *d* of late Sir Francis Floud, KCB, KCSI, KCMG; two *s*. *Educ:* Uppingham (Foundn Schol.); Wadham Coll., Oxford (Sen. Class. Schol.). MA, 1st cl. Lit. Hum. Dept of Printed Books, British Museum, 1935–36; Asst Educn Officer, City of Oxford, 1937–40; RAF, 1940–45; joined Faber & Faber Ltd, 1946; Dir, Dec. 1946; Vice-Chm., 1960–71; Chm., 1971–76, editorial consultant, 1977–; Chm., Faber and Faber (Publishers) Ltd, 1971–76; Mem. Bd, Faber Music Ltd, 1966– (Chm., 1971–76, Vice Chm., 1977–81); Trustee, Yale Univ. Press, London, 1984– (Mem. Bd, 1977–84). Mem. Council, Publishers Assoc., 1957–63, 1965–77 (Pres., 1967–69); Mem. Exec. Cttee, Internat. Publishers Assoc., 1972–76; Pres., Groupe des Editeurs de Livres de la CEE, 1973–75. Official visits on behalf of Publishers Assoc. and British Council to Australia, USSR, Finland, Hungary, Nigeria, China. Mem. Council, Aldeburgh Foundn Ltd, 1976– (Vice-Chm., 1977–80; Dep. Chm., 1982–); Pres., Ipswich and Suffolk Book League, 1986– (Vice-Pres., 1982–85); Hon. Treasurer, The William Blake Trust, 1959–83; Trustee: The James Joyce Estate; The Alison Uttley Estate. Liveryman, Stationers' Co., 1973; Freeman, City of London, 1973. *Publications:* various articles on publishing. *Address:* 31 Lee Road, Aldeburgh, Suffolk. *T:* Aldeburgh 2838. *Club:* Garrick.

DUTHIE, Prof. Herbert Livingston, MD; FRCS, FRCSEd; Provost of the Welsh National School of Medicine, University of Wales, since 1979; *b* 9 Oct. 1929; *s* of Herbert William Duthie and Margaret McFarlane Livingston; *m* 1959, Maureen McCann; three *s* one *d*. *Educ:* Whitehill Sch., Glasgow; Univ. of Glasgow (MB, ChB 1952; MD Hons 1962; ChM Hons 1959). FRCSEd 1956; FRCS 1957. Served RAMC, 1954–56. Sen. House Officer, Registrar, and Lectr in Surgery, Western Infirmary, Glasgow, 1956–59; Rockefeller Travelling Fellow, Mayo Clinic, Rochester, Minn, USA, 1959–60; Lectr in Surg., Univ. of Glasgow, 1960–61; Sen. Lectr in Surg., Univ. of Leeds, 1961–63, Reader, 1964; Prof. of Surg., Univ. of Sheffield, 1964–79 (Dean, Faculty of Medicine, 1976–78). Pres., Surgical Res. Soc., 1978–80; Mem., GMC, 1976–, Treasurer 1981–. *Publications:* articles on gastroenterological topics. *Address:* 86 Dan-y-Bryn Avenue, Radyr, Cardiff CF4 8DQ. *T:* Cardiff 843472. *Club:* Army and Navy.

DUTHIE, Prof. Robert Buchan, CBE 1984; MA Oxon, MB, ChM; FRCSE, FRCS; Nuffield Professor of Orthopædic Surgery, Oxford University; Professorial Fellow, Worcester College, Oxford; Surgeon, Nuffield Orthopædic Centre, Oxford; Civilian Consultant Adviser in Orthopaedic Surgery to Royal Navy, since 1978; *b* 4 May 1925; 2nd *s* of late James Andrew Duthie and late Elizabeth Jean Duthie, Edinburgh; *m* 1956, Alison Ann Macpherson Kittermaster, MA; two *s* two *d*. *Educ:* Aberdeen Grammar Sch.; King Edward VI Gram. Sch., Chelmsford; Heriot-Watt Coll., Edinburgh; University of Edinburgh Med. Sch. Robert Jones Prize 1947, MB, ChB 1948, ChM (with dist.) (Gold Medal for Thesis) 1956, University of Edinburgh; FRCSE 1953. Ho. Surg. Royal Infirmary, 1948–49; Ho. Phys., Western Gen. Hosp., Edinburgh, 1949. Active service in Malaya, RAMC, 1949–51. Registrar, Royal Infirmary, Edinburgh, 1951–53; David Wilkie Res. Schol. of University of Edinburgh, 1953–; Res. Fellow of Scottish Hosps Endowment Research Trust, Edinburgh, 1953–56; Res. Fellow, Nat. Cancer Inst., Bethesda, USA, 1956–57; Extern. Mem. of MRC in Inst. of Orthopædics, London and Sen. Registrar, 1957–58; Prof. of Orthopædic Surg., University of Rochester Sch. of Medicine and Dentistry and Orthopædic Surg.-in-Chief, University of Rochester Med. Centre, 1958–66. Consultant Adviser in Orthopaedics and Accident Surgery to DHSS, 1971–80. Mem., Royal Commn on Civil Liability and Compensation for Personal Injury, 1973–78; Chairman: Adv. Cttee of Res. in Artificial Limbs and Appliances, DHSS, 1975; Working Party on Orthopaedic Services to Sec. of State for Social Services, 1980–81. Governor, Oxford Sch. for Boys. Fellow Brit. Orthopædic Assoc. (Pres., 1983–84); Member: Internat. Soc. for Orthopædic Surgery and Traumatology; Orthopædic Research Soc.; Inter-urban Orthopædic Club: Internat. Orthopædic Club. Amer. Rheumatism Assoc.; Hon. Member: Portuguese Soc. of Orthopaedic Surgery and Traumatology; Japanese Orthopaedic Assoc.; Corresp. Mem., Assoc. of Orthopaedic Surgery and Traumatology, Yugoslavia. Hon. DSc Rochester, NY, 1982. President's Prize, Soc. Internat. de Chirurgie, 1957. Commander, SMO, Malta. *Publications:* (co-author) Textbook of Orthopædic Surgery, 7th edn, 1982; contribs to med. and surg. jls relating to genetics, histochemistry, transplantation, pathology, neoplasia of musculo-skeletal tissues, and clinical subjects. *Recreations:* family, tennis. *Address:* Nuffield Orthopædic Centre, Headington, Oxford; Barna Brow, Harberton Mead, Headington, Oxford. *T:* 62745.

DUTHIE, Robert Grieve, CBE 1978; CA; Chairman, Scottish Development Agency, since 1979; Chairman: Blacks Travel Agency Ltd, since 1967; Insight International Tours Ltd, since 1979; Bruntons (Musselburgh) PLC, since 1984; Director: British Assets Trust PLC, since 1977; Edinburgh American Asset Trust, since 1977; Royal Bank of Scotland plc, since 1978; Insight Group plc, since 1983; Investors Capital Trust PLC, since 1985; *b* 2 Oct. 1928; *s* of George Duthie and Mary (*née* Lyle); *m* 1955, Violetta Noel Maclean; two *s* one *d*. *Educ:* Greenock Academy. Apprentice Chartered Accountant with Thomson Jackson Gourlay & Taylor, CA, 1946–51 (CA 1952); joined Blacks of Greenock, 1952: Man. Dir, 1962; Chm., Black & Edgington Ltd, 1972–83. Chm., Greenock Provident Bank, 1974; Dir, Greenock Chamber of Commerce, 1967–68; Tax Liaison Officer for Scotland, CBI, 1976–79. Member: Scottish Telecommunications Bd, 1972–77; E Kilbride Develt Corp., 1976–78; Clyde Port Authority, 1971–83 (Chm., 1977–80); Council, Inst. of Chartered Accountants of Scotland, 1973–78; Scottish Econ. Council, 1980–. Chm., Made Up Textiles Assoc. of GB, 1972; Pres., Inverkip Soc., 1966; Mem. of Council, Royal Caledonian Curling Club, 1985–. Commissioner: Queen Victoria Sch., Dunblane, 1972–; Scottish Congregational Ministers Pension Fund, 1973–; Treasurer, Nelson Street Evangelical Union Congregational Church, Greenock, 1970–. Hon. LLD Strathclyde, 1984. CBIM 1976; FRSA 1983. *Recreations:* curling, golf. *Address:* Fairhaven, Finnart Street, Greenock PA16 8JA. *T:* Greenock 22642. *Club:* Greenock (Greenock).

DUTTON, James Macfarlane; HM Diplomatic Service, retired; *b* 3 June 1922; *s* of late H. St J. Dutton and Mrs E. B. Dutton; *m* 1958, Jean Mary McAvoy; one *s*. *Educ:* Winchester Coll.; Balliol Coll., Oxford. Dominions Office, 1944–46; Private Sec. to Permanent Under Sec., 1945; Dublin, 1946–48; CRO, 1948–50; Asst Private Sec. to Sec. of State, 1948; 2nd Sec., New Delhi, 1950–53; CRO, 1953–55; 1st Sec., Dacca and Karachi, 1955–58, Canberra, 1958–62; Head of Constitutional and Protocol Dept, CRO, 1963–65; Canadian Nat. Defence Coll., 1965–66; Dep. High Comr and Counsellor (Commercial), Colombo, 1966–70; Head of Rhodesia Econ. Dept, FCO, 1970–72; attached CSD, 1972–73; seconded to: British Electrical & Allied Manufacturers Assoc. (Dir, Overseas Affairs), 1973–74; Wilton Park and European Discussion Centre, 1974–75; Consul-Gen., Gothenburg, 1975–78. *Recreations:* golf, trout-fishing. *Address:* Cockerhurst, Tyrrells Wood, Leatherhead, Surrey KT22 8QH.

DUTTON, Reginald David Ley; *b* 20 Aug. 1916; *m* 1951, Pamela Jean (*née* Harrison); two *s* one *d*. *Educ:* Magdalen Coll. Sch., Oxford. Joined OUP; subseq. joined leading British advertising agency, London Press Exchange (now Lopex Ltd), 1937. During War of 1939–45 served in Royal Navy. Returned to agency after his service; there, he worked on many of major accounts; Dir, 1954; Man. Dir and Chief Exec., 1964–71; Chm., 1971–76; retired 1976. Pres. Inst. Practitioners in Advertising, 1969–71; Chm., Jt Ind. Council for TV Advertising Research, 1973–75; Mem. Council, BIM, 1970–74; FIPA 1960. Councillor, Canterbury CC, 1976–77. *Recreations:* fishing, amateur radio. *Address:* Butts Fold, Stalham Road, Hoveton, Norwich. *T:* Wroxham 3145.

DUVAL, Sir (Charles) Gaetan, Kt 1981; QC 1975; barrister; Deputy Prime Minister and Minister of Justice, Mauritius, since 1983; *b* 9 Oct. 1930. *Educ:* Royal Coll., Curepipe; Faculty of Law, Univ. of Paris. Called to the Bar, Lincoln's Inn. Entered politics, 1958; Member: Town Council, Curepipe, 1960, re-elected 1963 (Chm., 1960–61, 1963–68); Legislative Council, Curepipe, 1960, re-elected, 1963; Municipal Council, Port Louis, 1969 (Mayor, 1969–71; Lord Mayor, 1971–74, 1981); Minister of Housing, 1964–65; Leader, Parti Mauritien Social Démocrate, 1966–; first MLA for Grand River NW and

Port-Louis West, 1967; Minister of External Affairs, Tourism and Emigration, 1969–73; Leader of Opposition, 1973–76, 1982. Comdr, Legion of Honour, France, 1973; Grand Officer, Order of the Lion, Senegal, 1973. *Address:* Place Foch, Port-Louis, Mauritius.

DUVAL, Sir Gaetan; *see* Duval, Sir C. G.

DUXBURY, Air Marshal Sir (John) Barry, KCB 1986; CBE 1981 (MBE 1967); Air Officer Commanding No 18 Group, RAF, and Commander Maritime Air Eastern Atlantic and Channel, since 1986; *b* 23 Jan. 1934; *s* of Lloyd Duxbury and Hilda Robins; *m* 1954, Joan Leake; one *s*. *Educ:* Lancashire County Grammar Schs. Commnd 1954; served Maritime Sqdns, Aeroplane and Armament Exptl Estab., Canadian Forces Staff Coll., and Central Tactics and Trials Orgn, 1955–70; CO 201 Sqdn, 1971; PSO to CAS, 1971–74; CO RAF St Mawgan, 1976–77; Sec., Chiefs of Staff Cttee, 1978–80; RAF Dir, RCDS, 1982; Air Sec. (RAF), 1983–85. ADC to the Queen, 1977. *Recreations:* painting, photography. *Address:* c/o Lloyds Bank, Cox's & King's Branch, 6 Pall Mall, SW1Y 5NH. *Club:* Royal Air Force.

DWIGHT, Reginald Kenneth; *see* John, E. H.

DWORKIN, Paul David, FSS; Director of Statistics, Department of Employment, since 1983; *b* 7 April 1937; *s* of Louis and Rose Dworkin; *m* 1959, Carole Barbara Burke; two *s*. *Educ:* Hackney Downs Grammar Sch., London; LSE (BScEcon 1958). FSS 1969. E Africa High Commn, Dar es Salaam, Tanganyika, 1959; E African Common Services Org., Nairobi, Kenya, 1961; Asst Statistician, BoT, 1962, Stat. 1965; Chief Statistician: DTI, 1972; Dept of Employment, 1977; Under Secretary: Depts of Trade and Industry, 1977–81; Central Statistical Office, 1982–83. *Recreations:* golf, skiing, theatre. *Address:* 17 Cornbury Road, Edgware, Mddx. *T:* 01–952 2673. *Clubs:* Civil Service; Ski Club of Great Britain; Stanmore Golf.

DWORKIN, Prof. Ronald Myles, FBA 1979; Professor of Jurisprudence, Oxford University, since 1969; Fellow of University College, Oxford, since 1969; *b* 11 Dec. 1931; *s* of David Dworkin and Madeline Talamo; *m* 1958, Betsy Celia Ross; one *s* one *d*. *Educ:* Harvard Coll.; Oxford Univ.; Harvard Law Sch. Legal Sec. to Judge Learned Hand, 1957–58; Associate, Sullivan & Cromwell, New York, 1958–62; Yale Law School: Associate Prof. of Law, 1962–65; Prof. of Law, 1965–68; Wesley N. Hohfeld Prof. of Jurisprudence, 1968–69. Vis. Prof. of Philosophy, Princeton Univ., 1974–75; Prof. of Law, NY Univ. Law Sch., 1975–; Prof.-at-Large, Cornell Univ., 1976–; Vis. Prof. of Philosophy and Law, Harvard Univ., 1977, Vis. Prof. of Philosophy, 1979–82. Member: Council, Writers & Scholars Educnl Trust, 1982–; Programme Cttee, Ditchley Foundn, 1982–. Co-Chm., US Democratic Party Abroad, 1972–76. Fellow, Amer. Acad. of Arts and Scis, 1979. Hon. LLD: Williams Coll., 1981; John Jay Coll. of Criminal Justice, 1983. *Publications:* Taking Rights Seriously, 1977; (ed) The Philosophy of Law, 1977; A Matter of Principle, 1985; Law's Empire, 1986; several articles in legal and philosophical jls. *Address:* University College, Oxford. *Clubs:* Garrick; Oxford American Democrats (Oxford).

DWYER, Most Rev. George Patrick, MA, DD, PhD; former Archbishop of Birmingham; *b* 25 Sept. 1908; *s* of John William and Ima Dwyer. *Educ:* St Bede's Coll., Manchester; Ven. English Coll., Rome; Christ's Coll., Cambridge. PhD 1929, DD 1934, Gregorian Univ., Rome; ordained Priest, 1932; BA Mod. and Med. Lang. Trip. Cambridge (Lady Margaret Scholar, Christ's Coll.). Teaching, St Bede's, Manchester, 1937–47; Catholic Missionary Society, 1947; Editor of Catholic Gazette, 1947–51; Superior, Catholic Missionary Society, 1951–57; Bishop of Leeds, 1957–65; Archbishop of Birmingham, 1965–81; Apostolic Administrator, 1981–82. Pres., RC Bishops' Conference of England and Wales, 1976–79. Hon. Fellow, St Edmund's House, Univ. of Cambridge, 1980. Hon. DLitt: Keele, 1979; Warwick, 1980. *Publications:* The Catholic Faith, 1954; Mary-Doctrine for Everyman (with Rev. T. Holland, DD), 1956. *Address:* St Paul's Convent, Selly Park, Birmingham B29 7LL.

DWYER, Air Vice-Marshal Michael Harington, CB 1961; CBE 1955; retired; *b* 18 Sept. 1912; *s* of late M. H. Dwyer, Royal Garrison Artillery; *m* 1936, Barbara, *d* of late S. B. Freeman, CBE; one *s* one *d*. *Educ:* Oundle Sch. Entered RAF, 1931; served India, 1933–36; UK and NW Europe, 1939–45; Middle East, 1949–51; Air Officer Commanding No 62 Group, 1954–56; SASO No 3 Group, RAF, 1956–57; Student at Imperial Defence Coll., 1958; Air Officer Commanding No 3 Group, 1959–61; AOA, HQ Bomber Command, 1961–65; Regional Dir of Civil Defence, North-West Region, 1966–68. Chm., Harington Carpets, 1973–74. *Address:* Island House, Rambledown Lane, West Chiltington, Sussex.

DYDE, John Horsfall, CBE 1970 (OBE 1957); Chairman, Eastern Gas Board, 1959–69; *b* 4 June 1905; *m* 1930, Ethel May Hewitt; two *s*. *Educ:* Scarborough High Sch.; University of Leeds (MSc). Engineer and Manager, North Middlesex Gas Co., 1937–42; prior to nationalisation was Engineer and Gen. Manager of Uxbridge, Maidenhead, Wycombe & District Gas Co. and Slough Gas & Coke Co.; also Technical Director of group of undertakings of the South Eastern Gas Corp. Ltd; Dep.-Chm., Eastern Gas Board, 1949. President: Western Junior Gas Assoc., 1935–36; Southern Assoc. of Gas Engineers and Managers, 1949–50; Institution of Gas Engineers, 1951–52; British Road Tar Association. CEng, FIChemE; Hon. FIGasE. *Recreations:* golf, fishing. *Address:* Stable End, Thellusson Lodge, Aldeburgh, Suffolk. *T:* Aldeburgh 3148.

DYE, Maj.-Gen. Jack Bertie, CBE 1968 (OBE 1965); MC; Vice Lord-Lieutenant of Suffolk, since 1983; Director, Volunteers, Territorials and Cadets, 1971–74; Major-General late Royal Norfolk Regiment; *b* 1919. Served War of 1939–45 (MC). Brigadier, 1966; psc. Commanded South Arabian Army, 1966–68; GOC Eastern District, 1969–71. Col Comdt, The Queen's Division, 1970–; Col, Royal Anglian Regt, 1976–82 (Dep. Col, 1974–76). DL Suffolk, 1979.

DYER, Charles; playwright and novelist; actor-director (as Raymond Dyer); *b* 7 July 1928; *s* of James Sidney Dyer and Florence (*née* Stretton); *m* 1959, Fiona Thomson, actress; three *s*. *Educ:* Queen Elizabeth's Sch., Barnet. *Plays:* Clubs Are Sometimes Trumps, 1948; Who On Earth!, 1951; Turtle in the Soup, 1953; The Jovial Parasite, 1954; Single Ticket Mars, 1955; Time, Murderer, Please, and Poison In Jest, 1956; Wanted—One Body!, 1958; Prelude to Fury, 1959 (also wrote theme music); Rattle of A Simple Man, 1962 (also in Berlin, Paris, NY, Rome and London), 1981; Staircase, 1966 (for RSC; also in NY, Paris (1968, 1982 and 1986), Amsterdam, Berlin, Rome); Mother Adam, Paris, Berlin, 1970, London, 1971, 1973, NY, 1974; The Loving Allelujah, 1974; Circling Dancers, 1979; Lovers Dancing, 1981, 1983; Futility Rites, 1981; as R. Kraselchik: Red Cabbage and Kings, 1960 (also wrote theme music); *screenplays:* Rattle, 1964; Insurance Italian Style, 1967; Staircase, 1968; Brother Sun and Sister Moon, 1970. Also directed plays for the stage and television. *Acted in: plays:* Worm's Eye View, 1948; Room For Two, 1955; Dry Rot, 1958; *films:* Cuptie Honeymoon, 1947; Britannia Mews, 1949; Road Sense, 1950; Off The Record, 1952; Pickwick Papers, 1952; Dockland Case, 1953; Strange Case of Blondie, 1953; Naval Patrol, 1959; Loneliness of the Long Distance Runner, 1962; Mouse On The Moon, 1962; Knack, 1964; Rattle of A Simple Man, 1964; How I Won The War, 1967; Staircase, 1968; *television:* Charlie in Staircase, BBC, 1986; *television series:* Hugh and I, 1964. *Publications:* (as Charles Dyer): plays: Wanted—One Body!, 1961; Time, Murderer, Please, 1962; Rattle Of A Simple Man, (Fr.) 1963; Staircase, 1966; Mother Adam, 1970; The Loneliness Trilogy, 1972; Hot Godly Wind, 1973; novels: Rattle Of A Simple Man, 1964; Charlie Always Told Harry Almost Everything, 1969 (USA and Europe, 1970); The Rising of our Herbert, 1972. *Recreations:* amateur music and carpentry. *Address:* Old Wob, Gerrards Cross, Bucks.

DYER, Sir Henry Peter Francis S.; *see* Swinnerton-Dyer.

DYER, Lois Edith, OBE 1984; MCSP; (First) Adviser in Physiotherapy, Department of Health and Social Security, 1976–85; *b* 18 March 1925; *d* of Richard Morgan Dyer and Emmeline Agnes (*née* Wells). *Educ:* Middlesex Hospital. Variety of posts as physiotherapist in Britain, Southern, Central and North Africa, 1948–71; extensive travel world wide, visiting and lecturing at national and internat. conferences. First Physiotherapist Member, NHS Health Adv. Service, 1971; first non-medical Chm., Chartered Society of Physiotherapy, 1972–75; Hon. Life Vice-Pres., S African Soc. of Physiotherapy. Editor-in-Chief, Physiotherapy Practice, 1985–. *Publications:* Care of the Orthopaedic Patient (jtly), 1977; numerous papers in professional jls. *Recreations:* music, country pursuits, bird watching, bridge, ecology, conservation. *Address:* Garden Flat, 6 Belsize Grove, NW3 4UN. *T:* 01–722 1794.

DYER, Mark; His Honour Judge Dyer; a Circuit Judge, since 1977; *b* 20 Nov. 1928; *er s* of late Maj.-Gen. G. M. Dyer, CBE, DSO, and of Evelyn Mary (*née* List); *m* 1953, Diana, *d* of Sir Percy Lancelot Orde, CIE; two *d*. *Educ:* Ampleforth Coll.; Christ Church, Oxford (MA). 2nd Lieut, Royal Scots Greys, 1948–49; The Westminster Dragoons (2nd CLY) TA, 1950–58, Captain. Called to the Bar, Middle Temple, 1953; Mem., Gen. Council of the Bar, 1965–69. Dep. Chm., Isle of Wight QS, 1971. A Recorder of the Crown Court, 1972–77. *Address:* Furbelow House, 17 King Street, The Green, Richmond, Surrey. *Club:* Cavalry and Guards.

DYER, Simon, FCA; Managing Director 1983-Aug. 1987, Director General from Aug. 1987, Automobile Association; *b* 19 Oct. 1939; *s* of late Maj.-Gen. G. M. Dyer, CBE, DSO, and of Evelyn Dyer; *m* 1967, Louise Gay Walsh; two *d*. *Educ:* Ampleforth Coll., Univ. of Paris; Univ. of Oxford (MA Jurisprudence). FCA 1967. Coopers and Lybrand, 1963–67; Automobile Association, 1967–: Dir, 1973; Asst Man. Dir, 1977. *Recreations:* gardening, tennis, ski-ing. *Address:* 2 Broomfield Road, Kew, Surrey TW9 3HR. *Club:* Cavalry and Guards.
See also M. Dyer.

DYER-SMITH, Rear-Adm. John Edward, CBE 1972; Director-General Aircraft (Naval), Ministry of Defence, 1970–72, retired; *b* 17 Aug. 1918; *s* of Harold E. Dyer-Smith and Emily Sutton; *m* 1940, Kathleen Powell; four *s* one *d*. *Educ:* Devonport High Sch.; RN Engineering Coll.; Imperial Coll. of Science. Served War of 1939–45: Engineer Officer, HMS Prince of Wales, 1940–41; Asst Fleet Engr Officer, Eastern Fleet, 1942–43; HMS Illustrious, 1943. Various MAP and Min. of Aviation appts, 1946–54; Head of Naval Air Dept, RAE, 1957–61; Dir of RN Aircraft/Helicopters, Min. of Aviation, 1961–64; Defence and Naval Attaché, Tokyo, 1965–67; Superintendent, RN Aircraft Yard, Belfast, 1968–70. *Recreation:* travel. *Address:* Nutmeg Cottage, Saint Cross Back Street, Winchester SO23 9SB. *T:* Winchester 69198; Casa Gomila, Alcaufar, Menorca.

DYKE, Sir Derek William H.; *see* Hart Dyke.

DYKES, Dr David Wilmer; Director, National Museum of Wales, since 1986; *b* 18 Dec. 1933; *s* of late Captain David Dykes, OBE and Jenny Dykes; *m* 1967, Margaret Anne (*née* George); two *d*. *Educ:* Swansea Grammar Sch.; Corpus Christi Coll., Oxford (MA); PhD (Wales). FSA; FRHistS; FRNS (Parkes-Weber Prize, 1954). Commnd RN, 1955–58. Civil Servant, Bd of Inland Revenue, 1958–59; administrative appts, Univ. of Bristol and Univ. Coll. of Swansea, 1959–63; Dep. Registrar, Univ. Coll. of Swansea, 1963–69; Registrar, Univ. of Warwick, 1969–72; Sec., Nat. Museum of Wales, 1972–86, Acting Dir, 1985–86. Mem., Bd of Celtic Studies; Member Governing Body: Univ. Coll. Cardiff; Univ. Coll. Swansea. Liveryman, Worshipful Co. of Tin Plate Workers, 1985; Freeman, City of London, 1985. *Publications:* museum publications and articles and reviews in numismatic, historical and other jls. *Recreations:* numismatics, writing, gardening. *Address:* National Museum of Wales, Cathays Park, Cardiff CF1 3NP. *T:* Cardiff 397951. *Clubs:* Athenæum, United Oxford & Cambridge University; Cardiff and County (Cardiff); Bristol Channel Yacht (Swansea).

DYKES, Hugh John; MP (C) Harrow East since 1970; Associate Member, Quilter, Hilton, Goodison, Stockbrokers, since 1978; *b* 17 May 1939; *s* of Richard Dykes and Doreen Ismay Maxwell Dykes; *m* 1965, Susan Margaret Dykes (*née* Smith); three *s*. *Educ:* Weston super Mare Grammar Sch.; Pembroke Coll. Cambridge. Partner, Simon & Coates, Stockbrokers, 1968–78. Dir, Dixons Stores Far East Ltd, 1985–. Contested (C) Tottenham, Gen. Elec., 1966. PPS: to three Parly Under-Secs of State for Defence, 1970; to Parly Under-Sec. of State in Civil Service Dept attached to Cabinet Office, 1973; Mem., European Parlt, Strasbourg, 1974. Chm., Cons. Parly European Cttee, 1979–80 (Vice-Chm., 1974–79); Vice-Pres., Cons. Gp for EEC, 1982– (Chm., 1978–81). Joint Hon. Sec., European Movement, 1982–. Mem., Wider Share Ownership Council; Research Sec., Bow Gp, 1965; Chm., Coningsby Club, 1969. Governor: Royal Nat. Orthopaedic Hosp., 1975–82; N London Collegiate Sch., 1982–. *Publications:* (ed) Westropp's "Invest £100", 1964, and Westropp's "Start Your Own Business", 1965; many articles and pamphlets on political and financial subjects. *Recreations:* music, theatre, swimming, travel. *Address:* House of Commons, SW1. *T:* 01–219 3000. *Clubs:* Garrick, Carlton, Beefsteak.

DYKES BOWER, S(tephen) E(rnest), MA; FRIBA; FSA; Surveyor of the Fabric of Westminster Abbey, 1951–73, now Emeritus; Consulting Architect, Carlisle Cathedral, 1947–75; *b* 18 April 1903; 2nd *s* of Ernest Dykes Bower, MD; unmarried. *Educ:* Cheltenham Coll.; Merton Coll., Oxford (Organ Schol.); Architectural Assoc. Sch. of Architecture. Private practice as architect since 1931, work chiefly domestic and ecclesiastical. Architect for: New High Altar, Baldachino and American Memorial Chapel, St Paul's Cathedral (with W. Godfrey Allen); enlargement of Bury St Edmunds Cathedral; Cathedral Library and Bishop's Palace, Exeter; completion of Lancing Coll. Chapel; re-building of Gt Yarmouth Parish Church; St Vedast, Foster Lane, EC; and other churches in London and country; work in Canterbury, Winchester, Norwich, Ely, Gloucester, Wells, Oxford, Carlisle, Peterborough and other cathedrals, Oxford and Cambridge Colls, Public Schs, Halls of City Livery Cos, etc. Lay Canon of St Edmundsbury Cathedral, 1979–84. Pres., Ecclesiological Soc., 1983–. Hon. RCO. *Publications:* papers and addresses on architectural subjects. *Address:* Quendon Court, Quendon, near Saffron Walden, Essex. *T:* Rickling 242. *Clubs:* Athenæum, United Oxford & Cambridge University.

DYMOKE, Rear-Adm. Lionel Dorian, CB 1974; *b* 18 March 1921; *s* of Henry Lionel Dymoke and Dorothy (*née* Briscoe); *m* 1st, 1952, Patricia Pimlott (*d* 1968); one *s*; 2nd, 1970, Iris Hemsted (*née* Lamplough). *Educ:* Nautical Coll., Pangbourne. Entered Royal Navy, 1938; Comdr 1953; Captain 1961; Rear-Adm. 1971; retired 1976. *Address:* 3 Woodland Place, Bath, Avon. *T:* Bath 64228.

DYMOND, Charles Edward, CBE 1967; JP; HM Diplomatic Service, retired; *b* 15 Oct. 1916; *s* of Charles George Dymond and Dora Kate Dymond (*née* Gillingham); *m* 1945, Dorothy Jean Peaker; two *s* two *d. Educ:* Tiverton Grammar Sch.; Exeter Univ. BSc (Econ) London. Royal Artillery, 1939–46; BoT Regional Div., 1946; Trade Commn Service, 1951; Trade Comr, Johannesburg, 1951; Cape Town, 1955; Nairobi, 1957; Sen. Trade Comr, Lagos, 1963–64; Counsellor (Commercial), Lagos, 1965–66; Counsellor i/c, British High Commn, Auckland, 1967–73; Comr for Pitcairn Island, 1970–72; Consul-General, Perth, 1973–76. JP Western Australia, 1980. *Address:* PO Box 15, Sawyers Valley, WA 6074, Australia.

DYNEVOR, 9th Baron *cr* 1780; **Richard Charles Uryan Rhys;** *b* 19 June 1935; *s* of 8th Baron Dynevor, CBE, MC; *S* father, 1962; *m* 1959, Lucy (marr. diss. 1978), *d* of Sir John Rothenstein, *qv*; one *s* three *d. Educ:* Eton; Magdalene Coll., Cambridge. *Heir: s* Hon. Hugo Griffith Uryan Rhys, *b* 19 Nov. 1966. *Address:* Flat 2, 17 Sheffield Terrace, W8. *T:* 01–727 7439.

DYSART, Countess of (11th in line), *cr* 1643; **Rosamund Agnes Greaves;** Baroness Huntingtower, 1643; *b* 15 Feb. 1914; *d* of Major Owain Greaves (*d* 1941), RHG, and Wenefryde Agatha, Countess of Dysart (10th in line); *S* mother, 1975. *Heir: sister* Lady Katherine Grant of Rothiemurchus [*b* 1 June 1918; *m* 1941, Colonel John Peter Grant of Rothiemurchus, MBE; one *s* one *d*]. *Address:* Bryn Garth, Grosmont, Abergavenny, Gwent.

DYSON, Rev. Anthony Oakley, DPhil; Samuel Ferguson Professor of Social and Pastoral Theology, Manchester University, since 1980; *b* 6 Oct. 1935; *s* of Henry Oakley Leslie Dyson and Lilian Dyson; *m* 1960, Edwina Anne Hammett; two *s. Educ:* William Hulme's Grammar Sch., Manchester; Univs of Cambridge (BA 1959, MA 1963) and Oxford (MA, BD 1964, DPhil). 2nd Lieut, West Yorks Regt, 1954–56; Emmanuel Coll., Cambridge, 1956–59; Exeter Coll., Oxford and Ripon Hall, Oxford, 1959–61; Curate of Putney, Dio. Southwark, 1961–63; Chaplain of Ripon Hall, Oxford, 1963–69; Principal of Ripon Hall, 1969–74; Canon of St George's Chapel, Windsor Castle, 1974–77; Custodian, 1975–77; Lectr in Theology, Univ. of Kent, 1977–80. Licensed to Officiate Dio. Oxford, 1965–75, Dio. Canterbury, 1978–80, Dio. Chester, 1980–, Dio. Manchester, 1980–. Examng Chaplain to Bishop of Carlisle; Select Preacher, Univ. of Oxford, 1971; University Preacher, Cambridge, 1985; Lectures: Hensley Henson, Univ. of Oxford, 1972–73; Pollock, Halifax, NS, 1973; Shann, Hong Kong, 1983. Associate Dir, Centre for the Study of Religion and Society, Canterbury, 1978–80. Hon. MA (Theol) Manchester, 1982. Editor: The Teilhard Review, 1966–72; The Modern Churchman, 1982–. *Publications:* Existentialism, 1965; Who is Jesus Christ?, 1969; The Immortality of the Past, 1974; We Believe, 1977; contribs to Evolution Marxism and Christianity, 1967; What Kind of Revolution?, 1968; A Dictionary of Christian Theology, 1969, 2nd edn 1983; The Christian Marxist Dialogue, 1969; Teilhard Reassessed, 1970; Oxford Dictionary of the Christian Church, 2nd edn, 1974; Education and Social Action, 1975; Ernst Troeltsch and the Future of Theology, 1976; The Language of the Church in Higher and Further Education, 1977; England and Germany: studies in theological diplomacy, 1981; The Nature of Religious Man, 1982; A New Dictionary of Christian Theology, 1983; The Church of England and Politics, 1986; contrib. Theology, The Modern Churchman, Study Encounter, The Month, Contact, TLS, Bull. of John Rylands Library, Studia Theologica, etc. *Recreations:* literature, sport. *Address:* Department of Theological Studies, Faculty of Theology, University of Manchester, Manchester M13 9PL. *T:* 061–273 3333 (ext. 3545); 33 Danesmoor Road, West Didsbury, Manchester M20 9JT. *T:* 061–434 5410.

DYSON, Fred; General Secretary, National Union of Dyers, Bleachers and Textile Workers, 1973–79; *b* 28 Sept. 1916; *s* of James Dyson and Jane Anne Dyson (*née* Ashwood); *m* 1946, Beatrice Lilian (*née* Goepel); one *d. Educ:* Nields Council School. MIWP. Served with RAFVR, 1940–46. Woollen Spinner, 1934–39 and 1946–53; National Union of Dyers, Bleachers and Textile Workers: Organiser, 1953; Work Study Officer, 1958; No 4 District Sec., Manchester Area, 1970; Asst Gen. Sec., 1972. Mem. TUC General Council, 1975–79. Member: Garment and Allied Industries Requirements Bd, 1976–79; Industrial Injuries Adv. Council, 1977–81; Central Arbitration Cttee, 1976–79; Industrial Disputes Tribunals, 1974–86; Council, British Textile Confedn, 1973–79; co-opted Mem., Northumberland Co. Highways and Transport Cttee, 1981–; Governor: Tweedmouth First Sch., 1981–; Tweedmouth Middle Sch., 1981–. *Recreations:* landscape painting, swimming. *Address:* 6 Lindisfarne Gardens, Berwick-upon-Tweed, Northumberland TD15 2YA. *T:* Berwick 2176. *Clubs:* Slaithwaite Working Men's (Slaithwaite); Shipley Trades Hall (Shipley); Lidgett Green Working Men's (Bradford).

DYSON, Prof. Freeman John, FRS 1952; Professor, School of Natural Sciences, Institute for Advanced Study, Princeton, New Jersey, since 1953; *b* 15 Dec. 1923; *s* of late Sir George Dyson, KCVO; *m* 1st, 1950, Verena Esther (*née* Huber) (marr. diss. 1958); one *s* one *d*; 2nd, 1958, Imme (*née* Jung); four *d. Educ:* Winchester; Cambridge; Cornell University. Operational research for RAF Bomber Command, 1943–45. Fellow of Trinity Coll., Cambridge, 1946–50; Commonwealth Fund Fellow at Cornell and Princeton, USA, 1947–49; Mem. of Institute for Advanced Study, Princeton, USA, 1949–50; Professor of Physics, Cornell Univ., Ithaca, NY, USA, 1951–53. Mem. of National Academy of Sciences (USA), 1964. Lorentz Medal, Royal Netherlands Acad. of Sciences, 1966; Hughes Medal, Royal Soc., 1968; Max Planck Medal, German Physical Soc., 1969. *Publications:* Disturbing the Universe, 1979; Weapons and Hope, 1984; Origins of Life, 1986; contrib. to The Physical Review, Annals of Mathematics, etc. *Address:* School of Natural Sciences, Institute for Advanced Study, Olden Lane, Princeton, NJ 08540, USA.

DYSON, Dr James, FRS 1968; Deputy Chief Scientific Officer, National Physical Laboratory, 1975–76; retired 1976; *b* 10 Dec. 1914; *s* of George Dyson and Mary Grace (*née* Bateson); *m* 1st, Ena Lillian Turner (marr. diss. 1948); one *d*; 2nd, 1948, Marie Florence Chant (*d* 1967); 3rd 1975, Rosamund Pearl Greville Shuter. *Educ:* Queen Elizabeth Sch., Kirkby Lonsdale; Christ's Coll., Cambridge. BA 1936; MA 1960; ScD 1960. Student Apprentice, BT-H Co., Rugby, 1936–39; Research Engr, BT-H Co., Rugby, 1939–46; Consultant (Optics), AEI Research Lab., Aldermaston, 1946–63; Supt, Div. of Mech. and Optical Metrology, NPL, 1963–74. FInstP 1960; Hon. Fellow Royal Microscopical Soc., 1969. *Publications:* Interferometry, 1969; papers on applied optics in learned jls. *Recreations:* astronomy, mechanical occupations, music, people, deploring the motor-car and Women's Lib. *Address:* 6 Rectory Close, Tadley, Basingstoke, Hants RG26 6PH.

DYSON, John Anthony, QC 1982; a Recorder, since 1986; *b* 31 July 1943; *s* of Richard and Gisella Dyson; *m* 1970, Jacqueline Carmel Levy; one *s* one *d. Educ:* Leeds Grammar Sch.; Wadham Coll., Oxford (Open Classics Scholar; MA). Harmsworth Law Scholar, 1968, called to Bar, Middle Temple, 1968. *Recreations:* piano playing, gardening, walking. *Address:* 10 Essex Street, Outer Temple, WC2R 3AA. *T:* 01–240 6981.

DYSON, John Michael; Master of the Supreme Court of Judicature (Chancery Division) since 1973; *b* 9 Feb. 1929; *s* of late Eric Dyson, Gainsborough and Hope Patison (*née* Kirkland). *Educ:* Bradfield Coll.; Corpus Christi Coll., Oxford. 2nd Lieut, Royal Tank Regt, 1948. Admitted Solicitor, 1956; Partner, Field Roscoe & Co., 1957 (subseq. Field Fisher & Co. and Field Fisher & Martineau). *Address:* 20 Keats Grove, NW3 2RS. *T:* 01–794 3389. *Club:* United Oxford & Cambridge University.

DYSON, Richard George; Director, Commonwealth Development Finance Co. Ltd, 1968–81; *b* 17 July 1909; 2nd *s* of late Charles Dyson and late Ellen Gwendoline Dyson (*née* Barrington-Ward), Huddersfield, Yorks; *m* 1940, Lorna Marion, *d* of late H. H. Elkin, Alexandria, Egypt, and Port Lincoln, Australia; four *s* (two *d* decd). *Educ:* Charterhouse (Sen. Schol.); Christ Church, Oxford (Open Classical Exhibn). MA 1st cl. Hons in Hon. Mods and Greats. Joined Barclays Bank Ltd, 1933; transf. to Barclays Bank DCO, 1936; served overseas in Egypt, Sudan and E Africa until 1945; apptd an Asst Gen. Manager, 1951, a Gen. Manager, 1959, a Vice-Chm., 1967, and the Dep. Chm., 1968–76 (Bank renamed Barclays Bank International Ltd, 1971); Dir, Barclays Bank Ltd, 1972–80; Dep. Chm., Antony Gibbs Holdings Ltd, 1976–80; Chm., Lombard Assoc., 1962–63. Vice-Pres. Council, Inst. of Bankers, 1974– (Mem. 1963–74, Dep. Chm. 1970, Pres. 1972–74); Governor: Sutton's Hosp. in Charterhouse, 1968–84; Charterhouse Sch., Godalming, 1968–84. FIB 1960. *Recreations:* cricket, gardening. *Address:* Brickfields, Chobham, Surrey. *T:* Chobham 8150. *Clubs:* MCC; Free Foresters.

DYSON, Prof. Roger Franklin, PhD; Professor and Director of Adult and Continuing Education, University of Keele, since 1976; *b* 30 Jan. 1940; *s* of John Franklin Dyson and Edith Mary Jobson; *m* 1964, Anne Greaves; one *s* one *d. Educ:* Counthill Grammar Sch., Oldham; Keele Univ. (BA Hons 1st cl. Hist. and Econs, 1962); Leeds Univ. (PhD 1971). Asst Lectr, 1963, Lectr, 1966, Adult Educn Dept, Leeds Univ.; Dep. Dir and Sen. Lectr in Ind. Relations, Adult Educn Dept, Keele Univ., 1974. Consultant Advr on Ind. Relations to Sec. of State, DHSS, 1979–81. Chm., N Staffs HA, 1982–86. Mem., RSocMed; FRSA 1980. Editor, Health Services Manpower Review, 1975–. *Publications:* contribs to BMJ. *Recreations:* gardening, gastronomy. *Address:* Elendil, Newcastle Road, Ashley Heath, Market Drayton TF9 4PH. *T:* Ashley 2906. *Club:* Carlton.

DYVIG, Peter; Comdr, Order of the Dannebrog, 1986; Ambassador of Denmark to the Court of St James's, since 1986; *b* 23 Feb. 1934; *m* 1959, Karen Dyvig (*née* Møller); one *s* one *d. Educ:* Copenhagen Univ. (grad. in Law). Entered Danish For. Service, 1959; bursary at Sch. of Advanced Internat. Studies, Washington, 1963–64; First Secretary: Danish Delegn to NATO, Paris, 1965–67; Brussels, 1967–69; Min. of For. Affairs, Copenhagen, 1969–74; Minister Counsellor, Washington, 1974–76; Ambassador, Asst Under-Sec. of State, Min. of For. Affairs, Copenhagen, 1976–79; Dep. Under-Sec. for Pol. Affairs, 1980; Perm. Under-Sec. of State for Pol. Affairs, 1981–86. *Address:* Royal Danish Embassy, 55 Sloane Street, SW1X 9SR. *T:* 01–235 1255. *Club:* Hurlingham.

E

EABORN, Prof. Colin, PhD, DSc (Wales); FRS 1970; FRSC; Professor of Chemistry, University of Sussex, since 1962; *b* 15 March 1923; *s* of Tom Stanley and Caroline Eaborn; *m* 1949, Joyce Thomas. *Educ:* Ruabon Grammar Sch., Denbighshire; Univ. Coll. of N Wales, Bangor. Asst Lecturer, 1947, Lecturer, 1950, and Reader 1954, in Chemistry, Univ. of Leicester. Research Associate, Univ. of California at Los Angeles, 1950–51; Robert A. Welch Visiting Scholar, Rice Univ., Texas, 1961–62; Erskine Fellow, Univ. of Canterbury (NZ), 1965; Pro-Vice Chancellor (Science), Univ. of Sussex, 1968–72; Dist. Prof., New Mexico State Univ., 1973; Canadian Commonwealth Fellow, Univ. of Victoria, BC, 1976; R. A. Welch Vis. Lectr, Texas, 1983. Hon. Sec., Chemical Society, 1964–71, Vice-Pres., Dalton Div., 1971–75: Mem. Council, Royal Soc., 1978–80; Chm., British Cttee on Chemical Educn, 1967–69; Mem., Italy/UK Mixed Commn, 1972–. F. S. Kipping Award, Amer. Chem. Soc., 1964; Organometallic Award, Chem. Soc., 1975; Ingold Lectureship and Medal, Chem. Soc., 1976. *Publications:* Organosilicon Compounds, 1960; Organometallic Compounds of the Group IV Elements, Vol. 1, Part 1, 1968; numerous publications, mainly in Jl of Chem. Soc. and Jl of Organometallic Chemistry (Regional Editor). *Address:* School of Chemistry and Molecular Sciences, University of Sussex, Brighton BN1 9QJ. *T:* Brighton 606755.

EADEN, Maurice Bryan, CBE 1983; HM Diplomatic Service, retired; Consul General, Amsterdam, 1980–83; *b* 9 Feb. 1923; *s* of William Eaden and Florence Ada Eaden (*née* Hudson); *m* 1947, Nelly Margaretha Dorgelo; three *s*. *Educ:* Bemrose Sch., Derby. Served Army, 1942–47. Foreign Office, 1947; Vice-Consul, Leopoldville, 1955; First Secretary (Commercial): Addis Ababa, 1958; Beirut, 1963; FO, 1967; First Sec. (Commercial), Bombay, 1970; Counsellor (Administration), Brussels, 1972–75; Consul-Gen., Karachi, 1975–79. *Recreations:* walking in Derbyshire; languages. *Address:* New Houses, Cressbrook, Buxton, Derbyshire. *T:* Tideswell 871404. *Club:* Royal Commonwealth Society.

EADIE, Alexander, BEM 1960; JP; MP (Lab) Midlothian since 1966; *b* 23 June 1920; *m* 1941; one *s*. *Educ:* Buckhaven Senior Secondary Sch. Coal-miner from 1934. Chm., Fife County Housing Cttee, 9 yrs; Chm., Fife County Educn Cttee, 18 mths; Governor, Moray House Teachers' Training Coll., Edinburgh, 5 years; Exec. Committee: Scottish Council of Labour Party, 9 yrs; NUM Scottish Area, 2 yrs; Mem., Eastern Regional Hosp. Bd (Scotland), 14 yrs. Contested Ayr, 1959 and 1964; Former PPS to Miss M. Herbison, MP, Minister of Social Security, and Mem. of Parly Select Cttee on Scottish Affairs; Opposition Front Bench Spokesman on Energy (incl. N Sea Oil), 1973–74; Parly Under-Sec. of State, Dept of Energy, 1974–79; No 2 Shadow Front Bench Spokesman on Energy, 1985–86. Chm., Parly Labour Party Power and Steel Gp; Sec., Miners' Parly Gp; Vice-Chm., Parly Trade Union Group. JP Fife, 1951. *Recreations:* bowling, gardening. *Address:* Balkerack, The Haugh, East Wemyss, Fife. *T:* Buckhaven 3636.

EADIE, Douglas George Arnott, FRCS; Consultant Surgeon: The London Hospital, since 1969; King Edward VII Hospital, London, since 1978; *b* 16 June 1931; *s* of Dr Herbert Arnott Eadie and Hannah Sophia (*née* Wingate); *m* 1957, Gillian Carlyon Coates; two *s* two *d*. *Educ:* Epsom Coll.; London Hosp. Med. Coll. (MB BS; MS). Jun. Specialist in Surgery and Captain RAMC, Far East Land Forces, 1957–60; Hugh Robertson Exchange Fellow, Presbyterian St Luke's Hosp., Chicago, 1962; Surgical Registrar, London Hosp., 1963–67. Cons. to Royal Masonic Hosp., 1980–82; Hon. Cons., Osborne House, IoW, 1980. Chm. of Council, Medical Protection Soc., 1976–83 (Mem. Council, 1974). Examiner in Surgery: Soc. of Apothecaries of London, 1976–80; Univ. of London, 1976–84. Mem. Ct of Assts, Soc. of Apothecaries, 1980; rep. on GMC, 1983–. FRSM 1956. *Publications:* contribs to med. jls on topics relating to vascular disease. *Recreations:* golf, gardening, shooting. *Address:* 18 Upper Wimpole Street, W1. *T:* 01-487 3285; 7 Hillsleigh Road, W8 7LH. *T:* 01-229 5242. *Clubs:* Athenæum, MCC.

EADIE, Mrs Ellice (Aylmer), CBE 1966; Standing Counsel to General Synod of Church of England, 1972–80; *b* 30 June 1912; *d* of late Rt Rev. R. T. Hearn, LLD, sometime Bishop of Cork, and of late Dr M. E. T. Hearn, MD, FRCPI; *m* 1946, John Harold Ward Eadie. *Educ:* Cheltenham Ladies' Coll.; St Hugh's Coll., Oxford. Called to Bar, Gray's Inn, 1936. Flt Officer, WAAF, 1941–46. Parliamentary Counsel Office, 1949–72, Parly Counsel, 1968–72. *Address:* 74 Roebuck House, Palace Street, SW1E 5BD. *T:* 01–828 6158.

EADY, family name of **Baron Swinfen.**

EADY, David, QC 1983; a Recorder, since 1986; *b* 24 March 1943; *s* of late Thomas William Eady and of Kate Eady; *m* 1974, Catherine, *yr d* of J. T. Wiltshire, Streatley, Berks; one *s* one *d*. *Educ:* Brentwood Sch.; Trinity Coll., Cambridge (Exhibnr; Pt I Moral Science Tripos, Pt II Law Tripos; MA, LLB). Called to the Bar, Middle Temple, 1966, in practice, South Eastern Circuit. *Publication:* The Law of Contempt (with A. J. Arlidge, QC), 1982. *Recreations:* music, gardening. *Address:* 1 Brick Court, Temple, EC4Y 9BY. *T:* 01-353 8845; Goodshill House, Tenterden, Kent TN30 6UN. *T:* Tenterden 3644.

EAGERS, Derek; Under-Secretary, Department of Trade and Industry (formerly Department of Trade), 1975–84; *b* 13 Sept. 1924; *s* of late Horace Eagers and Florence (*née* Green); *m* 1953, Hazel Maureen Henson; two *s*. *Educ:* King Edward VII Sch., Sheffield; Brasenose Coll., Oxford. RNVR, 1943–47. Min. of Fuel and Power, 1949; UK Atomic Energy Authority, 1955–57; British Embassy, Washington, 1958–60; Principal Private Sec. to successive Ministers of Power, 1963–65; Petroleum Counsellor, Washington, 1966–68; Min. of Power (subseq. Min. of Technology, Dept of Trade and Industry), 1969; Dept of Industry, 1974. *Recreation:* concealing his true ignorance of cricket, gardening and railway history. *Address:* Bryniau Golau, Llangower, Bala, Gwynedd LL23 7BT. *T:* Bala 520517.

EAGGER, Brig. Arthur Austin, CBE 1944 (OBE 1940), TD 1945; *b* 14 March 1898; *s* of Edward and Elsie Eagger; *m* 1st, 1935, Kate Mortimer Hare (*d* 1946); three *s*; 2nd, 1948, Barbara Noel Hare. *Educ:* Aberdeen Univ. (MB ChB 1922). Lieut 6th Bn Gordon Hldrs. Commissioned RAMC (TA), 1928; late DDMS 1 Airborne Corps. Medical Dir, Slough Industrial Health Service, retired 1963, Consultant 1963–79. Bronze Star (USA), 1945. *Publications:* Industrial Resettlement (Proc. RSM), 1952; Health in the Factory (Jl Royal Institute of Public Health and Hygiene), 1953; Venture in Industry, 1965. *Address:* 1 Underwood Close, Dawlish, Devon EX7 9RY. *T:* Dawlish 864597.

EAGLES, Lt-Col Charles Edward James; Member, HM Body Guard of the Honourable Corps of Gentlemen at Arms, since 1967, Standard Bearer, since 1986 (Harbinger, 1981–86); *b* 14 May 1918; *o s* of late Major C. E. C. Eagles, DSO, RMLI and Esmé Field; *m* 1941, Priscilla May Nicolette, *d* of late Brig. A. F. B. Cottrell, DSO, OBE; one *s* three *d*. *Educ:* Marlborough Coll. 2nd Lieut RM, 1936; served: HMS Sussex, Mediterranean and S Atlantic, 1938–40; Mobile Naval Base Def. Orgn, UK, ME, Ceylon and India, 1940–43; 1 HAA Regt RM, India, UK and NW Europe, 1943–45; Asst Mil. Sec., 1945; Amphibious Trng Wing, 1945–47; Staff of Maj.-Gen. RM, Portsmouth, 1947–50; HMS Devonshire, 1951–52; RN Staff Course, 1952; DS, Amphibious Warfare Sch., 1952–55; HMS Afrikander, SO (Intell.), S Atlantic, 1955–57; Dep. Dir, PRORM, 1957–59; CSO, Plymouth Gp, 1960; AAG, Staff of CGRM, 1960–62; Dir, PRORM, 1962–65; retd 1965; Civil Service, MoD, 1965–83. *Recreations:* shooting, genealogy. *Address:* Fallowfield, Westwell, Ashford, Kent TN25 4LQ. *T:* Charing 2552. *Club:* Army and Navy.

EAGLESHAM, Eric John Ross, MA, BEd, LLB; Professor of Education, Durham University, 1947–66, retired; Professor Emeritus, 1966; *b* 29 Oct. 1905; 3rd *s* of late Reverend David Eaglesham, Chapelknowe, Canonbie, Dumfriesshire; *m* 1957, Nancy, *yr d* of late J. F. Rintoul; three *s* one *d*. *Educ:* Dumfries Acad.; Edinburgh Univ., 1923–27, 1930–31. Asst Teacher, Gretna Sch., 1927–30; Asst Teacher, Lockerbie Academy, 1931–35; Lecturer, Education Dept, Manchester Univ., 1936–38; Master of Method, Jordanhill Training Centre, Glasgow, 1938–40; RAF, rank Flight Lieut, on planning staff of Air Ministry dealing with questions of International Law, 1941–42; Principal Master of Method, Jordanhill Training Centre, Glasgow, 1942–43; Depute Dir of Studies, Jordanhill Training Centre, 1944–46. *Publications:* From School Board to Local Authority, 1956; Morant on the March (Yearbook of Education), 1957; The Foundations of Twentieth Century Education in England, 1967; articles in various learned journals. *Address:* Westfield, Gelt Road, Brampton, Cumbria.

EAGLETON, Guy Tryon; *b* 1 July 1894; *s* of late John Eagleton and of Violet Marion Eagleton; *m* 1947, Amy Rubina Gothard; no *c*. *Educ:* Aldenham Sch. Solicitor, 1919; Asst Clerk Haberdashers' Company, 1925; Clerk of the Haberdashers' Company, 1931–50, retired. *Address:* Bradbourne Residential Home, Bradbourne Road, Sevenoaks, Kent TN13 2DD. *T:* Sevenoaks 454781. *Club:* Royal Blackheath Golf (Captain General, Sen. Past Captain).

EAGLING, Wayne John; Senior Principal, Royal Ballet, since 1975; *s* of Eddie and Thelma Eagling. *Educ:* P. Ramsey Studio of Dance Arts; Royal Ballet Sch. Has danced lead rôles in major classics including Sleeping Beauty, Swan Lake, Cinderella; first rôle created for him was Young Boy in Triad, 1972; subsequent created rôles include: Solo Boy in Gloria; Ariel in The Tempest; Woyzeck in Different Drummer. Choreographed: The Hunting of the Snark by Michael Batt; Frankenstein, The Modern Prometheus, for Royal Ballet, 1985; choreographed, produced and directed various galas. *Publication:* (with Ross MacGibbon and Robert Jude) The Company We Keep, 1981. *Recreations:* golf, scuba diving, tennis, antique cars. *Address:* Royal Opera House, Covent Garden, WC2.

EAKER, Gen. Ira Clarence, Hon. KCB 1945; Hon. KBE 1943; DSM, US Army (2 Oak Leaf Clusters), US Navy; DFC (Oak Leaf Cluster); Silver Star; Legion of Merit; Wright Brothers Trophy, 1977; Special Congressional Gold Medal, 1979; *b* Field Creek, Texas, 13 April 1896; *s* of Y. Y. Eaker and Dona Lee; *m* Ruth Huff Apperson; no *c*. *Educ:* South Eastern State Teachers' Coll., Durant, Okla; University of Southern California; Columbia Univ., 2nd Lieut of Infantry, Regular Army, 1917; Capt. 1920; Major, 1935; Lieut-Col (temp.) 1937; Lieut-Col 1940; Col (temp.), 1941; Brig.-Gen. (temp.) Jan. 1942; Maj.-Gen. (temp.) Sept. 1942; Lieut-Gen. (temp.) 1943; permanent Brig.-Gen. RA 1944; Gen. 1985. Served in Philippines, 1919–22; pilot of one of planes of Pan-American Flight round South America, 1926–27 (DFC); chief pilot of Airplane Question Mark on refuelling endurance flight, 1929, establishing a new world flight endurance record (Oak Leaf Cluster for DFC). In command of VIII Bomber Command in European Theatre of Operations, 1942; commanded Eighth Air Force, 1942–44 and also US Army Air Forces in UK, 1943–44; comd. Mediterranean Allied Air Forces in Italy, 1944; Dep. Comdg Gen. Army Air Forces and Chief of Air Staff, US, 1945–47; retired 1947. Vice-President: Hughes Tool Co., 1947–57; Douglas Aircraft, 1957–61. Founding Pres., US Strategic Inst., 1972 (Vice-Chm., 1974). Author, syndicated weekly column on subjects in nat. security area, 1962–. DSM 1981, awarded by USAF for exceptionally meritorious service, 1957–81. French Legion of Honour (Grand Officer) and many other foreign decorations. *Publications:* (with Gen. Arnold); Army Flyer, This Flying Game, Winged Warfare. *Address:* 2202 Decatur Place, Washington, DC 20008, USA.

EALES, Victor Henry James, CEng, MIMechE; Founder and Director, Parkultra Ltd, since 1984; Director of Weapons Production and Quality (Naval), 1980–81, and Head of Naval Weapons Professional and Technical Group, 1979–81, Ministry of Defence; *b* 11 Dec. 1922; *s* of William Henry and Frances Jean Eales; *m* 1949, Elizabeth Gabrielle Irene

James; two *s* one *d. Educ:* Wimbledon Central Sch.; Guildford Technical Coll.; Portsmouth Polytechnic. Ministry of Defence: Asst Director, Weapons Production (Naval), 1970; Dep. Director, Surface Weapons Projects (Naval), 1975; Director, Weapons Production (Naval), 1979. *Recreation:* golf. *Address:* 11 Penrhyn Avenue, East Cosham, Portsmouth, Hants PO6 2AX.

EAMES, Eric James, JP; Lord Mayor of Birmingham, 1974–75, Deputy Lord Mayor, 1975–76; *b* Highley, Shropshire, 13 April 1917; *s* of George Eames; *m* (marr. diss.); one *s. Educ:* Highley Sch., Highley, Shropshire. Member (Lab): Birmingham City Council, 1949–; W Midlands CC, 1974–77. Mem., Governing Board, Internat. Center for Information Co-operation and Relationship among World's Major Cities; Governor, Harper Adams Agric. Coll. JP Birmingham, 1972. *Recreations:* gardening, do-it-yourself enthusiast. *Address:* 78 Westley Road, Acocks Green, Birmingham B27 7UH. *T:* 021–706 7629.

EAMES, Most Rev. Robert Henry Alexander; *see* Armagh, Archbishop of, and Primate of All Ireland.

EARDLEY-WILMOT, Sir John (Assheton), 5th Bt *cr* 1821; MVO 1956; DSC 1943; Staff of Monopolies Commission, 1967–82; *b* 2 Jan. 1917; *s* of Commander Frederick Neville Eardley-Wilmot (*d* 1956) (*s* of 3rd Bt) and Dorothy Little (*d* 1959), formerly of Brooksby, Double Bay, Sydney; *S* uncle, 1970; *m* 1939, Diana Elizabeth, *d* of Commander Aubrey Moore, RN, and Mrs O. Bassett; one *s* one *d. Educ:* Stubbington; RNC, Dartmouth. Motor Torpedo Boats, 1939–43; served HMS Apollo, 1944; HMS Fencer, 1945–46; RN Staff Course, 1950; Commander 1950; HMS Opossum, 1951–53; Cabinet Office, 1954–57; Admiralty, 1958–67; retired 1967, as Deputy Director Naval Administrative Planning. MBIM 1978; FRSA 1970. Freeman, City of London (by Redemption). Norwegian War Medal. *Recreation:* fishing. *Heir: s* Michael John Assheton Eardley-Wilmot [*b* 13 Jan. 1941; *m* 1971, Wendy, *y d* of A. J. Wolstenholme; two *s* one *d*]. *Address:* 41 Margravine Gardens, W6. *T:* 01–748 3723.

EARL, Christopher Joseph, MD, FRCP; Physician to: Neurological Department, Middlesex Hospital, since 1971; National Hospital, Queen Square, since 1958; Moorfields Eye Hospital, since 1959; Consultant Neurologist, King Edward VII Hospital for Officers, since 1966 and Hospital of St John and St Elizabeth, since 1967; Civil Consultant in Neurology, Royal Air Force, since 1976; *b* 20 Nov. 1925; *s* of Christopher and Winifred Earl, Ashbourne, Derbyshire; *m* 1951, Alma Patience Hopkins, Reading; two *s* three *d. Educ:* Cotton Coll.; Guy's Hosp. House phys. and house surg., Guy's Hosp., and MO, RAF, 1948–50. Lecturer in Chemical Pathology, Guy's Hosp., 1950–52; Research Fellow, Harvard Med. Sch., and Neurological Unit, Boston City Hosp., 1952–54; Resident MO, Nat. Hosp., Queen Square, 1954–56; Chief Asst, Neurological Dept, Guy's Hosp., 1956–58; Physician, Neurological Dept, London Hosp., 1961–71. Dir, Medical Sickness Annuity & Life Assce Soc. Ltd, 1981–. Hon. Dir of Photography, Royal Society of Medicine, 1967–73. Hon. Sec., Assoc. British Neurologists, 1968–74. Vice-Pres., Med. Defence Union; Chm., Cttee on Neurology, RCP. Corresp. Mem., Amer. Neurological Assoc. *Publications:* Papers in learned jls on Biochemistry and Neurology. *Recreation:* reading history. *Address:* 23 Audley Road, Ealing, W5. *T:* 01–997 0380; 149 Harley Street, W1N 1HG. *Club:* Garrick.

EARL, Eric Stafford; Clerk to the Worshipful Company of Fishmongers, since 1974; *b* 8 July 1928; *s* of late Alfred Henry Earl and Mary Elizabeth Earl; *m* 1951, Clara Alice Alston. *Educ:* SE Essex Technical Coll.; City of London Coll. Served with RA, 1946–48. Joined Fishmongers' Co. 1948: Accountant, 1961–68; Asst Clerk, 1969–73; Actg Clerk, 1973–74; Liveryman, 1977. Clerk to Governors of Gresham's Sch., 1974–; Hon. Sec., Shellfish Assoc. of GB, 1974–; Secretary: Atlantic Salmon Research Trust Ltd, 1974–; City and Guilds of London Art School Ltd, 1974–; Jt Hon. Sec., Central Council for Rivers Protection, 1974–; Hon. Asst River Keeper of River Thames, 1968–; Chm., Nat. Anglers' Council, 1983–85; Mem. Council, Anglers' Co-operative Assoc, 1974–. Director: Hulbert Property Co. Ltd, 1975–; Hulbert Property Holdings Ltd, 1975–. Hon. Freeman, Watermen's Co., 1984. *Recreations:* fishing, gardening, tennis, cricket. *Address:* Dolphins, Watling Lane, Thaxted, Essex CM6 2RA. *T:* Thaxted 758. *Club:* Flyfishers'.

EARLE, Air Chief Marshal Sir Alfred, GBE 1966 (KBE 1961; CBE 1946); CB 1956; *b* 1907; *s* of late Henry Henwood Earle, and Mary Winifred Earle, Beaworthy, Devon; *m* 1st, 1934, Phyllis Beatrice (*d* 1960), *o d* of W. J. Rice, Watford; one *s* one *d*; 2nd, 1961, Rosemary (*d* 1978), *widow* of Air Vice-Marshal F. J. St G. Braithwaite, and *d* of late G. Grinling Harris, Clifford's Inn; 3rd, 1979, Mrs Clare Newell, *widow* of Rev. Gp Captain Ivor Newell and *d* of Dr Thomas Yates, DD. *Educ:* Shebbear Coll., Beaworthy, Devon. Graduated from Royal Air Force Coll., Cranwell, 1929. Served in Bomber Squadrons in United Kingdom and Iraq and as instructor at RAF Sch. of Photography, 1930–38; psa 1939; Training Command, 1940; Air Ministry, in Directorate of Plans, 1941–42; Comd No 428 RCAF Sqdn and stations in Bomber Comd, 1942–43; Offices of War Cabinet and Minister of Defence (attended Cairo and Yalta Confs), 1943–45; AOC No 300 Transport Grp (Austr.) and No 232 Transport Grp (Far East), 1945–46; Directing Staff, RAF Staff Coll., 1946–49; idc 1950; Comd RAAF Staff Coll., 1951–53; Air Ministry, Dir of Policy (Air Staff), 1954; Asst Chief of Air Staff (Policy), 1955–57; AOC No 13 Group, 1957–59; Deputy Chief of Defence Staff, 1960–62; AOC-in-C, Technical Training Command, 1962–64; Vice-Chief of Defence Staff, 1964–66; retd 1966; Dir Gen. of Intelligence, Min. of Defence, 1966–68. Chm., Waveney DC, 1974–76. *Recreation:* gardening. *Address:* 3 Buttermere Gardens, Alresford, Hants. *Club:* Royal Air Force.

EARLE, Arthur Frederick; management and economic consultant, since 1983; *b* Toronto, 13 Sept. 1921; *s* of Frederick C. Earle and Hilda M. Earle (*née* Brown); *m* 1946, Vera Domini Lithgow; two *s* one *d. Educ:* Toronto; London Sch. of Economics (BSc (Econ.), PhD; Hon. Fellow 1980). Royal Canadian Navy (Rating to Lieut Comdr), 1939–46. Canada Packers Ltd, 1946–48; Aluminium Ltd cos in British Guiana, West Indies and Canada, 1948–53; Treas., Alumina Jamaica Ltd, 1953–55; Aluminium Union, London, 1955–58; Vice-Pres., Aluminium Ltd Sales Inc., New York, 1958–61; Dir, 1961–74, Dep. Chm., 1961 65, Man. Dir, 1963–65, Hoover Ltd; Principal, London Graduate Sch. of Business Studies, 1965–72. Pres., Internat. Investment Corp. for Yugoslavia, 1972–74; Pres., Boyden Consulting Group Ltd, 1974–82; Associate, 1974–82, Vice-Pres., 1975–82, Boyden Associates, Inc.; Advisor to the Pres., Canada Develt Investment Corp., 1983–; Director: Rio Algom Ltd, 1983–; National Sea Products Ltd, 1984–; Bathpaul Ltd, UK, 1984–; Monkwells Ltd, UK, 1984. Member: Commn of Enquiry, Jamaican Match Industry, 1953; Consumer Council, 1963–68; NEDC Cttee on Management Educn, Training and Develt, 1967–69; NEDC for Electrical Engineering Industry. Chm., Canadian Assoc. of Friends of LSE, 1975–. Dir, Nat. Ballet of Canada, 1982–. Governor: Ashridge Management Coll., 1962–65; LSE, 1968; NIESR, 1968–74; Governor and Mem. Council, Ditchley Foundn, 1967. Fellow, London Business Sch., 1973; Hon. Fellow, LSE, 1979. Thomas Hawksley Lecture, IMechE, 1968. *Publications:* numerous, on economics and management. *Recreations:* hill climbing, model ship building. *Address:* PO Box 752, Niagara-on-the-Lake, Ont. L0S 1J0, Canada. *T:* (416) 468–3119. *Club:* National (Toronto).

EARLE, Lt-Col Charles, DSO 1945; OBE 1943; jssc; psc; *b* 23 Nov. 1913; *s* of late Col Maxwell Earle, CB, CMG, DSO; *m* 1st, 1939, Marguerite (marr. diss., 1956), 2nd *d* of Herbert Carver; one *s* two *d*; 2nd, 1957, Fenella, *o d* of late H. C. Whitehouse. *Educ:* Wellington; RMC. Grenadier Guards, 1933; Lt-Col 1953, Retired 1958. Sec.-Gen., Internat. Cargo Handling Assoc., 1961–72. Served War of 1939–45 in NW Europe, Africa and Italy. Adjt RMA Sandhurst, 1948. Croix de Guerre with palm, France, 1943. *Address:* 3 The Tithe Barn, Queen Camel, Yeovil, Somerset BA22 7NF. *T:* Marston Magna 850937.

EARLE, Ven. E(dward) E(rnest) Maples; Archdeacon of Tonbridge, 1953–76, Archdeacon Emeritus since 1977; Vicar of Shipbourne, Kent, since Nov. 1959; *b* 22 Dec. 1900; 2nd *s* of Ernest William Earle and Lilian Geraldine Earle (*née* Hudson); *m* 1966, Mrs Jocelyn Mary Offer, *widow* of Canon C. J. Offer. *Educ:* London Coll. of Divinity; St John's Coll., Durham University (LTh, MA). Vicar of: St John, Bexley, 1936–39; Rainham (Kent), 1939–44; Secretary Rochester Diocesan Reorganisation Cttee, 1944–52, Great Appeal Cttee, etc., 1944–49; Hon. Canon, Rochester Cathedral, 1949; Rector of Chatham, 1950–52; Proctor in Convocation, 1950–53. Rector of Wrotham 1952–59. *Recreations:* artistic and architectural interests. *Address:* The Vicarage, Shipbourne, Kent. *T:* Plaxtol 810478.

EARLE, Sir George; *see* Earle, Sir H. G. A.

EARLE, Very Rev. George Hughes, SJ; MA; Superior of the English Province of the Society of Jesus, since 1981; *b* 20 Sept. 1925; *s* of late Lieut-Col F. W. Earle, DSO, JP, Morestead House, Winchester, and late Marie Blanche Lyne-Stivens. *Educ:* Pilgrims' Sch., Winchester; Westminster Sch.; Peter Symonds' Sch., Winchester; Balliol Coll., Oxford. Served with RAF, 1943–47. Joined Soc. of Jesus, 1950. Taught at Beaumont Coll., 1955–57, and Stonyhurst Coll., 1962–63; Headmaster, Stonyhurst Coll., 1963–72; Superior of Southwell House, 1972–75; Educnl Asst to Provincial, 1972–75; Co-editor, The Way, 1974–78; Rector of St Aloysius, Glasgow, 1978–81. *Recreations:* none; wasting time. *Address:* 114 Mount Street, W1Y 6AH.

EARLE, Sir (Hardman) George (Algernon), 6th Bt *cr* 1869; *S* father, 1979; *m*; one *s* one *d. Heir: s.*

EARLE, Ion, TD 1946; Assistant to the Directors, Clive Discount Co., 1973–81, retired; *b* 12 April 1916; *s* of late Stephen Earle and of E. Beatrice Earle (*née* Blair White); *m* 1946, Elizabeth Stevens, US citizen; one *s* one *d. Educ:* Stowe Sch.; University Coll., Oxford; Université de Grenoble. Federation of British Industries, Birmingham, 1938–51, London, 1952–60; Chief Executive, Export Council for Europe, 1960–64; Dep. Dir-Gen., BNEC, 1965–71 (Dir, 1964–65); Head of Personnel, Kleinwort Benson Ltd, 1972. Royal Artillery, TA, 1939–46 (Major). *Recreations:* golf, tennis, gardening. *Address:* 69 Sea Avenue, Rustington, West Sussex BN16 2DP. *T:* Rustington 773350. *Club:* Royal Wimbledon Golf.

EARLE, Joel Vincent, (Joe); Keeper, Far Eastern Department, Victoria and Albert Museum, since 1982; *b* 1 Sept. 1952; *s* of James Basil Foster Earle and Mary Isabel Jessie Weeks; *m* 1980, Sophia Charlotte Knox; two *s. Educ:* Westminster Sch.; New Coll., Oxford (BA 1st Cl. Hons Chinese). Res. Asst, Far Eastern Dept, V&A Museum, 1974–77, Asst Keeper 1977–82. *Publications:* An Introduction to Netsuke, 1980, 2nd edn 1982; An Introduction to Japanese Prints, 1980; (contrib.) Japan Style, 1980; (contrib.) The Great Japan Exhibition, 1981; (trans.) The Japanese Sword, 1983; The Toshiba Gallery: Japanese art and design, 1986. *Address:* 123 Middleton Road, E8 4LL. *T:* 01–254 5178.

EARLE, Rev. John Nicholas Francis, (Rev. Nick Earle); Headmaster, Bromsgrove School, 1971–85; *b* 14 Nov. 1926; *s* of John William Arthur Earle and Vivien Constance Fenton (*née* Davies); *m* 1959, Ann Veronica Lester; one *s* two *d. Educ:* Winchester Coll.; Trinity Coll., Cambridge. 1st cl. Maths Tripos pt 2, 1st cl. Theol. Tripos pt 1; MA. Deacon, 1952; Priest, 1953. Curate, St Matthew, Moorfields, 1952–57; PARS Fellow, Union Theol Seminary, New York, 1957–58; Lectr, St Botolph, Aldgate, 1958–61; Asst Master, Dulwich Coll., 1961–71. *Publications:* What's Wrong With the Church?, 1961; Culture and Creed, 1967; Logic, 1973. *Recreations:* travel, gardening. *Address:* 1 Red Post Hill, Post Mead, SE21.

EARLES, Prof. Stanley William Edward, PhD, DScEng; CEng, FIMechE; Professor of Mechanical Engineering and Head of Department of Mechanical Engineering, King's College, University of London, since 1976; *b* 18 Jan. 1929; *s* of late William Edward Earles and Winnifred Anne Cook; *m* 1955, Margaret Isabella Brown; two *d. Educ:* King's Coll., Univ. of London (BScEng, PhD, DScEng, AKC). CEng, FIMechE 1976. Nuffield Apprentice, Birmingham, 1944–50; King's Coll., Univ. of London, 1950–53; Scientific Officer, Royal Naval Scientific Service, 1953–55; Queen Mary Coll., Univ. of London: Lectr in Mech. Eng, 1955–69; Reader in Mech. Eng, 1969–75; Prof. of Mech. Eng, 1975–76. James Clayton Fund prize, IMechE, 1967; Engineering Applied to Agriculture Award, IMechE, 1980. *Publications:* papers and articles in Proc. IMechE, Jl of Mech. Eng Science, Jl of Sound and Vibration, Wear, Proc. ASME and ASLE, and Eng. *Recreations:* squash rackets, real tennis, gardening. *Address:* Woodbury, Church Lane, Wormley, Broxbourne, Herts EN10 7QF. *T:* Hoddesdon 464616.

EARNSHAW, (Thomas) Roy, CBE 1978 (OBE 1971); consultant and lecturer; *b* 27 Feb. 1917; *s* of Godfrey Earnshaw and Edith Annie (*née* Perry); *m* 1953, Edith Rushworth; two *d. Educ:* Marlborough Coll., Liverpool. MIEx; AICS. Served War, Army, 1940–46: Major Lancs Fusiliers. Shipbroking, Liverpool, 1933–39; appts with subsid. cos of Turner & Newall Ltd: Turner Brothers Asbestos Co. Ltd, Rochdale (mainly Export Sales Manager), 1939–40 and 1946–53; Dir, AM&FM Ltd, Bombay, 1954–59; Export Dir, Ferodo Ltd, Chapel-en-le-Frith, 1959–66; Dir and Gen. Man. of Div., TBA Industrial Products Ltd, Rochdale, 1966–76; British Overseas Trade Board: Mem. Adv. Council, 1975–82; Export Year Advr, 1976–77; Export United Advr, 1978–83. Director: Actair Holdings Ltd, 1979–83; Actair Internat. Ltd, 1979–83; Unico Finance Ltd, 1979–81. Formerly: Pres., Rochdale Chamber of Commerce; Chm., NW Region Chambers of Commerce; UK Delegate to European Chambers of Commerce, London Economic Adviser to Merseyside CC, 1980–82. Vis. Fellow, Henley Management Coll. (formerly ASC), 1981–. FRSA. *Recreations:* gardening, oil painting, hill walking, cycling. *Address:* 89 St Andrews Road, Henley-on-Thames, Oxon RG9 1PN. *T:* Henley-on-Thames 576620. *Clubs:* Rotarian, Leander (Henley-on-Thames).

EASMON, Prof. Charles Syrett Farrell, MD, PhD; Fleming Professor of Medical Microbiology, St Mary's Hospital Medical School, University of London, since 1984; *b* 20 Aug. 1946; *s* of Dr McCormack Charles Farrell Easmon and Enid Winifred Easmon; *m* 1977, Susan Lynn (*née* Peach). *Educ:* Epsom Coll.; St Mary's Hospital Med. Sch. (Open Schol.; MB BS; MD); PhD London. MRCPath. Pathology trng, St Bartholomew's Hosp., 1970–71; St Mary's Hospital Medical School: Research Asst, 1971; Lectr, 1973; Sen. Lectr, 1976; Reader and Actg Head of Dept, 1980; Personal Chair, 1983. *Publications:* (ed) Medical Microbiology, vol. 1 1982, vols 2 and 3 1983, vol. 4 1984; (ed) Infections in the Immunocompromised Host, 1983; (ed) Staphylococci and Staphylococcal Infections,

1983; numerous papers in learned jls. *Recreations:* music, history, gardening. *Address:* 21 Cranes Park Avenue, Surbiton, Surrey KT5 8BS.

EASON, Henry, CBE 1967; JP; a Vice-President of the Institute of Bankers, 1969–75, and Consultant with special reference to overseas relationships, 1971–74 (Secretary-General, 1959–71); *b* 12 April 1910; *s* of late H. Eason and F. J. Eason; *m* 1939 (at Hexham Abbey), Isobel, *d* of Wm Stevenson; one *s* two *d. Educ:* Yarm (Schol.); King's Coll., University of Durham. BCom (with distinction). Barrister-at-law, Gray's Inn. Served Lloyds Bank until 1939; Asst Sec., Institute of Bankers, 1939. Served War of 1939–45 and until 1946, with Royal Air Force (Wing Commander, despatches twice). Asst Dir, Military Gov. (Banking), NW Europe, 1944–46; United Nations Adviser (Banking) to Pakistan Govt, 1952; Deputy Sec., Institute of Bankers, 1956; Governor, City of London Coll., 1958–69; Mem., British National Cttee, Internat. Chamber Commerce, 1959–74. Director: Internat. Banking Summer Sch., Christ Church, Oxford, 1961, 1964, 1970; Cambridge Banking Seminar, Christ's Coll., Cambridge, 1968 and 1969. Editor, Jl Inst. of Bankers, 1959–71. Hon. Fellow, Inst. of Bankers, 1971. JP Bromley 1967. Gen. Comr of Income Tax, Bromley, 1973–76. *Publications:* contributions to professional journals. *Recreations:* golf, walking, gardening, world travel. *Address:* 12 Redgate Drive, Hayes Common, Bromley BR2 7BT. *T:* 01–462 1900. *Clubs:* Gresham; Overseas Bankers; Langley Park Golf.

EASON, His Honour Robert Kinley; HM's First Deemster, Clerk of the Rolls and Deputy Governor of the Isle of Man, 1974–80; *b* 12 April 1908; 2nd *s* of Henry Alexander Eason and Eleanor Jane Eason (*née* Kinley); *m* 1937, Nora Muriel, *d* of Robert Raisbeck Coffey, Douglas, IOM. *Educ:* Douglas High Sch.; King William's Coll., IOM; University Coll. London. LLB (Hons). Called to Bar, Gray's Inn, 1929; Advocate, Manx Bar, 1930. High Bailiff and Chief Magistrate, Isle of Man, 1961–69; HM's Second Deemster, IOM, 1969–74. Chairman: Criminal Injuries Compensation Tribunal, IOM, 1969–74; IOM Income Tax Appeal Comrs, 1974–80; IOM Unit Trust Tribunal, 1968–74; Tourist (IOM) Appeal Tribunal, 1969–74; Tynwald Arrangements Cttee, 1974–80; Chm. of Trustees: Cunningham House Scout and Guide Headquarters, 1964–; Ellan Vannin Home, 1971–; Trustee, Manx Marine Soc., 1974–. President: Ellynyn Ny Gael, 1974–; IOM Anti-Cancer Assoc., 1969–; Wireless Telegraphy Appeal Bd for IOM, 1971–80; Legion Players, 1971–81; SS&AFA, IOM Br., 1973–; Licensing Appeal Court, 1969–74; King William's College Soc., 1978–80; past Pres., IOM Soc. for Prevention of Cruelty to Animals. Queen's Silver Jubilee Medal, 1977. *Recreation:* organ music. *Address:* Greenacres, Highfield Drive, Baldrine, Lonan, Isle of Man. *T:* Laxey 781622. *Clubs:* Ellan Vannin, Manx Automobile (Douglas).

EASSON, Rt. Rev. Edward Frederick; *b* 29 July 1905; *s* of Edward Easson and Ada Jessie Easson (*née* Betsworth); *m* 1937, Mary Forbes Macdonald; two *s. Educ:* Morgan Academy, Dundee; St Andrews Univ.; Edinburgh Theological College. Maths and Science Master at Lasswade Secondary School, 1929–31; Assistant Curate of St Peter's, Lutton Place, 1933–36, with charge of St Aidan's, Craigmillar, 1936–39; Rector of St Peter's, Peterhead, and Chaplain to HM Prison, 1940–48; Diocesan Inspector of Schools, 1945–55; Canon of St Andrew's Cathedral, Aberdeen, 1946; Rector of St Devenick's, Bieldside, 1948–56; Dean of Aberdeen and Orkney, 1953–56; Bishop of Aberdeen and Orkney, 1956–72. Hon. DD St Andrews, 1962. *Address:* 25 Corbiehill Avenue, Davidsons Mains, Edinburgh EH4 5DX.

EAST, David Albert, QPM 1982; Chief Constable, South Wales Constabulary, since 1983; *b* 5 June 1936; *s* of Albert East and Florence Emily East; *m* 1957, Gloria (*née* Swinden); one *d. Educ:* King Alfred Grammar Sch., Wantage, Berks; University Coll. London (LLB Hons). Berks Constabulary, 1958–65 (constable to sergeant); First Special Course, Police Coll., Bramshill, 1962 (Johnson Prize and Cert. of Distinction); Inspector, York City Police, 1965–68; UCL, 1965–68; Metropol. Police Chief Inspector to Chief Supt, 1968–75; Eight Sen. Comd Course, Bramshill, 1971; Asst Chief Constable, Avon and Somerset Constab., 1975–78; RCDS, 1978; Dep. Chief Constable, Devon and Cornwall Constab., 1978–82, Chief Constable, 1982–83; seconded to Cyprus, 1981 and to Singapore, 1982. OStJ 1985. Police Long Service and Good Conduct Medal, 1980. *Recreations:* Rugby, cricket. *Address:* Police Headquarters, Cowbridge Road, Bridgend, Mid Glam CF31 3SR.

EAST, Frederick Henry, CB 1976; FEng 1984; FIEE, FRAeS; consulting engineer and company director; Deputy Secretary, and Chief Weapon System Engineer (Polaris), Ministry of Defence, 1976–80, retired; *b* 15 Sept. 1919; *s* of Frederick Richard East; *m* 1942, Pauline Isabel Veale Horne (*d* 1972). *Educ:* Skinners' Company's Sch., Tunbridge Wells; University Coll., Exeter (Visc. St Cyres Schol., Tucker and Franklin Prize, 1939). BSc London 1940; MInstP. Joined Research Dept, Min. of Aircraft Production, 1940; various appts in RAE, 1942–57; Asst Dir of Air Armament Research and Develt, Min. of Supply/Aviation, 1957–62; Head of Weapon Project Gp, RAE, 1962–67; Student, IDC, 1968; Asst Chief Scientific Adviser (Projects), MoD, 1969–70; Dir, Royal Armament Res. and Develt Establishment, 1971–75. Reader, C of E, 1969–; Mem., Candidates Cttee, ACCM, 1981–. *Publications:* contrib. to: Application of Critical Path Techniques, 1968; official reports, and articles in jls. *Address:* 2 Beacon Rise, Sevenoaks, Kent. *T:* Sevenoaks 453942. *Club:* Athenæum.

EAST, Gerald Reginald Ricketts; Civil Service Commissioner, 1974–78, retired; Chairman, Incorporated Froebel Educational Institute, since 1979; *b* 17 Feb. 1917; *s* of late R. B. East and Dora East (*née* Ricketts); *m* 1944, Anna Elder Smyth; one *s* two *d. Educ:* Peter Symonds' Sch.; St Edmund Hall, Oxford. Goldsmiths' Company's Exhibnr; MA 1945. Royal Artillery, 1939–46; Control Commn for Germany, 1946–47; Asst Principal, War Office, Oct. 1947; Private Sec. to Under-Sec. of State for War, 1949; Directing Staff Imperial Defence Coll., 1952–54; Private Sec. to Sec. of State for War, 1954–55; Asst Sec. (Inspector of Establishments), 1958; Comd Sec., BAOR, 1961–64; Asst Sec. (Establishments), MoD, 1965–70; Asst Under-Sec. of State, MoD, 1970–74. *Address:* 43 Manor Road North, Esher, Surrey KT10 0AA. *T:* 01–398 2446.

EAST, Grahame Richard, CMG 1961; Special Commissioner of Income Tax, 1962–73; *b* 1908; 2nd *s* of William Robert and Eleanor East; *m* 1937, Cynthia Mildred, *d* of Adam Louis Beck, OBE; two *s* two *d. Educ:* Bristol Grammar Sch.; Corpus Christi Coll., Oxford. Asst Master, Royal Belfast Academical Institution, Belfast, 1929; Inland Revenue Dept, Secretaries Office, 1930, Asst Sec., 1941. *Address:* 44 Devonshire Road, Sutton, Surrey. *T:* 01–642 0638.

EAST, John Anthony, OBE 1982; Chief Executive, English Tourist Board, since 1985; *b* 25 May 1930; *s* of John East and Jessie Mary East; *m* 1st, 1957, Barbara Collins; two *s* one *d;* 2nd, 1982, Susan Finch; one *d. Educ:* Bromley Grammar School. Reuter's, 1954–58; Notley Advertising, 1958–60; Director: French Government Tourist Office, 1960–70; English Tourist Bd, 1970–. *Publications:* History of French Architecture, 1968; Gascony and the Pyrenees, 1969; articles on France and French architecture. *Recreations:* walking, gardening, studying things French. *Address:* The Knott, Springfield Lane, Colgate, Sussex.

EAST, Kenneth Arthur, CMG 1971; HM Diplomatic Service, retired; Ambassador to Iceland, 1975–81; *b* 9 May 1921; *s* of H. F. East; *m* 1946, Katherine Blackley; two *s* three

d. Educ: Taunton's Sch.; Southampton Univ. Served HM Forces, 1942–46. India Office/Commonwealth Relations Office, 1946–50; Asst Private Sec. to Sec. of State; First Secretary: Ottawa, 1950–53; Colombo, 1956–60; Head of East and General Africa Dept, CRO, 1961–63; Head of Personnel Dept, CRO, 1963–64; Counsellor, Diplomatic Service Administration, 1965; Counsellor and Head of Chancery, Oslo, 1965–70; Minister, Lagos, 1970–74. *Club:* Royal Commonwealth Society.

EAST, Sir (Lewis) Ronald, Kt 1966; CBE 1951; retired as Chairman, State Rivers and Water Supply Commission, Victoria (1936–65) and as Commissioner, River Murray Commission, Australia (1936–65); *b* 17 June 1899; *s* of Lewis Findlay East, ISO, Evansford, Vic., Australia and Annie Eleanor (*née* Burchett) Brunswick, Vic.; *m* 1927, Constance Lilias Keil, MA, Kilwinning, Ayrshire; three *d. Educ:* Scotch Coll., Melbourne; Melbourne Univ. BCE (Melbourne) 1922; MCE (Melbourne) 1924. Mem., Snowy Mountains Coun., until 1965; Pres., Instn of Engrs, Austr., 1952–53; Mem. Coun., Instn of Civil Engrs, 1960–62; Vice-Pres., Internat. Commn on Irrigation and Drainage, 1959–62. Hon. Fellow, Instn of Engineers, Australia, 1969; FRHSV 1983. Kernot Memorial Medal, University of Melbourne, 1949; Peter Nicol Russell Memorial Medal, Instn of Engineers, Australia, 1957. Hon. DEng Melbourne, 1981. *Publications:* River Improvement, Land Drainage and Flood Protection, 1952; A South Australian Colonist of 1836 and his Descendants, 1972; The Kiel Family and related Scottish Pioneers, 1974; More Australian Pioneers: the Burchetts and related families, 1976; (ed) The Gallipoli Diary of Sergeant Lawrence, 1981; many technical papers on water conservation and associated subjects in Proc. Instn Engs, Austr., Proc. Instn Civil Engrs, Amer. Soc. Civil Engrs and other jls. *Recreation:* handicrafts (model engineering). *Address:* 57 Waimarie Drive, Mt Waverley, Victoria 3149, Australia. *T:* Melbourne 277–4315.

EAST, Sir Ronald; *see* East, Sir L. R.

EAST, Ronald Joseph; Chairman, Wettern Brothers plc, since 1981; Director, Amstrad Consumer Electronics plc, since 1980; *b* 17 Dec. 1931; *s* of Joseph William and Marion Elizabeth Emma East; *m* 1955, Iris Joyce Beckwith; two *d. Educ:* Clare Coll., Cambridge Univ. (MA). Engineering Apprenticeship, Ford Trade Sch., Ford Motor Co. Ltd, 1945–52. Troop Comdr, RA (Lieut), 1953–55. Managerial posts in economics, product planning, finance, and engineering areas of Ford Motor Co. Ltd, 1959–65; Guest, Keen & Nettlefolds Ltd: Corporation Staff Dir of Planning, 1965–70; Planning Exec., Automotive and Allied Products Sector, 1972–73; Chairman: GKN Castings Ltd, 1974–77; GKN Kent Alloys Ltd, 1974–77; GKN Shotton Ltd, 1974–77. Dir, GKN (UK) Ltd, 1974–77; Corporate Staff Dir, Group Supplies, GKN Ltd, 1976–77. Dir, Programme Analysis and Review (PAR) and Special Advisor to Chief Sec. to the Treasury, 1971–72. *Recreations:* walking, ski-ing, ethnology, dramatic art. *Address:* The Waldrons, Feckenham, Worcs. *T:* Astwood Bank 2486.

EAST, William Gordon; Professor of Geography in the University of London at Birkbeck College, 1947–70, now Emeritus Professor; *b* 10 Nov. 1902; *s* of George Richard East and Jemima (*née* Nicoll); *m* 1934, Dorothea Small; two *s* two *d. Educ:* Sloane Sch., Chelsea; Peterhouse, Cambridge. Open scholarship in History, 1921, and research studentship, 1924, at Peterhouse. BA (Hons), Cambridge Univ. (History), 1924. MA 1928; Thirlwall Prizeman of Cambridge Univ., 1927. Asst in historical geography, London Sch. of Economics, 1927; temp. administrative officer in Ministry of Economic Warfare and Foreign Office, 1941–45; Reader in Geography in University of London, 1946. Visiting Professor: Univ. of Minnesota, 1952; Univ. of California, Los Angeles, 1959–60; Univ. of Michigan, 1966–67; Univ. of Wisconsin, 1969–70; Univ. of Saskatchewan, 1971. Myres Memorial Lectr, Oxford Univ., 1970–71. Mem., RGS Council, 1956–59; Pres., Inst. of British Geographers, 1959. Murchison Award, RGS, 1972. *Publications:* The Union of Moldavia and Wallachia, 1859, 1929, repr. 1973; An Historical Geography of Europe, 1935; The Geography Behind History, 1938; Mediterranean Problems, 1940; (ed jtly) The Changing Map of Asia, 1950, 1971; (Jt) The Spirit and Purpose of Geography, 1951; (ed jtly) The Changing World, 1956; (ed) The Caxton Atlas, 1960; (ed) Regions of The British Isles, 1960–; The Soviet Union, 1963, 2nd edn 1976; (jt) Our Fragmented World, 1975; contributions to journals of geography, history and foreign affairs. *Address:* Wildwood, Danes Way, Oxshott, Surrey. *T:* Oxshott 2351.

EAST ANGLIA, Bishop of, (RC), since 1976; **Rt. Rev. Alan Charles Clark;** *b* 9 Aug. 1919; *s* of William Thomas Durham Clark and Ellen Mary Clark (*née* Compton). *Educ:* Westminster Cathedral Choir Sch.; Ven. English Coll., Rome, Italy. Priest, 1945; Curate, St Philip's, Arundel, 1945–46; postgrad. studies, Rome, 1946–48; Doctorate in Theol., Gregorian Univ., Rome, 1948; Tutor in Philosophy, English Coll., Rome, 1948–53, Vice-Rector, 1954–64; Parish Priest, St Mary's, Blackheath, SE3, 1965–69; Auxiliary Bishop of Northampton, 1969–76; Titular Bishop of Elmham, 1969–76. *Peritus* at Vatican Council, 1962–65; Jt Chm., The Anglican/Roman Catholic Internat. Commn, 1969–81 (Lambeth Cross); Chm., Dept for Mission and Unity, Bishops' Conf. of Eng. and Wales, 1984–; Co-Moderator, Jt Working Group of RC Church and WCC, 1984–. Freeman, City of London, 1969. *Recreation:* music. *Address:* The White House, 21 Upgate, Poringland, Norwich NR14 7SH. *T:* Framingham Earl 2202.

EASTAUGH, Rt. Rev. Cyril; *see* Easthaugh.

EASTAUGH, Rt. Rev. John (Richard Gordon); *see* Hereford, Bishop of.

EASTCOTT, Harry Hubert Grayson, MS; FRCS; FRCOG; Consulting Surgeon, St Mary's Hospital; Consultant in Surgery and Vascular Surgery to the Royal Navy, 1957–82, now Emeritus; Consultant Surgeon, King Edward VII Hospital for Officers, since 1965; *b* 17 Oct. 1917; *s* of Harry George and Gladys Eastcott; *m* 1941, Doreen Joy, *e d* of Brenchley Ernest and Muriel Mittell; four *d. Educ:* Latymer Sch.; St Mary's Hosp. Medical School and Middlesex Hospital Medical Sch., University of London; Harvard Med. Sch. War of 1939–45, Junior surgical appts and service as Surgeon Lieut, RNVR up till 1946. Surg. Lieut Comdr RNVR, London Div., until 1957. MRCS; LRCP; MB, BS (Hons), 1941; FRCS 1946; MS (London), 1951. Sen. Registrar, 1950 as Hon. Cons. to St Mary's and Asst Dir Surgical Unit; Research Fellow in Surgery, Harvard Med. Sch., and Peter Bent Brigham Hosp., Boston, Mass, 1949–50; recognised teacher, 1953, and Examr, 1959, in surgery, University of London; Cons. Surgeon, St Mary's Hosp. and Lectr in Surgery, St Mary's Hosp. Med. Sch., 1955–82; Surgeon, Royal Masonic Hosp., 1964–80; Hon. Surg., RADA, 1959–; External Examr in Surgery: Queen's Univ., Belfast, 1964–67; Cambridge Univ., 1968–; Univ. of Lagos, Nigeria, 1970–71. Editorial Sec., British Jl of Surgery, 1972–78. Royal College of Surgeons: Hunterian Prof., 1953; Mem. Court of Examrs, 1964–70; Mem. Council, 1971–83; Bradshaw Lectr, 1980; Vice-Pres., 1981–83; Cecil Joll Prize, 1984; RCS Visitor to RCOG Council, 1972–80. FRSocMed (Hon. Sec., Section of Surgery, 1963–65, Vice-President, 1966, Pres., 1977; Pres., United Services Section, 1981–83). Fellow Medical Soc. of London (Hon. Sec., 1962–64, Vice-Pres. 1964, Pres., 1976, Fothergill Gold Medal, 1974). Pres., Assoc. of Surgeons of GB and Ireland, 1982–83. Mem., Soc. Apothecaries, 1967. Hon. FACS, 1977; Hon. FRACS, 1978; Hon. Fellow: Amer. Surgical Assoc., 1981; Stroke Council, 1981; Hon. Mem., Purkinje Med. Soc., Czechoslovakia, 1984. Editor, Brit. Jl of Surg., 1973–79. *Publications:* Arterial

Surgery, 1969, 2nd edn 1973; various articles on gen. and arterial surgery, and on tissue transplantation and preservation, Lancet, Brit. Jl of Surg., etc.; contrib. chap. of peripheral vascular disease, Med. Annual, 1961–80; various chaps in textbooks on these subjects. *Recreations:* music, travel, and a lifelong interest in aeronautics. *Address:* 4 Upper Harley Street, NW1 4PN. *T:* 01–935 2020. *Club:* Garrick.

EASTER, Bertie Harry, CMG 1944; CBE 1936 (MBE 1927); BA; retired as Resident Tutor, Windward Islands, for University College of the West Indies (Extra-Mural Studies); *b* 4 June 1893; *s* of Samuel and Lucy Elizabeth Easter; *m* 1930, Hazel Marie Swabey; one *s*. *Educ:* Christ's Coll., Finchley. Head Master, St Mary's Coll., St Lucia and Secondary Sch., Grenada; Dir of Education, Grenada; Acting Colonial Sec. (or Administrator), Grenada, Jamaica; Dir of Education, Jamaica, 1932–48; Information Officer and Officer i/c Broadcasting, 1939; served European War, Royal Naval Div. and Scots Guards (Lieut). Emeritus Pres., St Lucia Archæol and Hist. Soc. *Address:* Castries, St Lucia, West Indies.

EASTHAM, Kenneth; MP (Lab) Manchester, Blackley, since 1979; *b* 11 Aug. 1927; *s* of late James Eastham; *m* 1951, Doris, *d* of Albert Howarth. Planning engr, GEC, Trafford Park. Mem., Manchester CC, 1962–80 (Dep. Leader 1975–79); Chairman: Planning Cttee, 1971–74; Educn Cttee, 1978–79); Mem., NW Econ. Planning Council, 1975–79. *Address:* House of Commons, SW1; 12 Nan Nook Road, Manchester M23 9BZ.

EASTHAM, Hon. Sir (Thomas) Michael, Kt 1978; **Hon. Mr Justice Eastham;** a Judge of the High Court of Justice, Family Division, since 1978; *b* 26 June 1920; *y s* of late His Hon. Sir Tom Eastham, QC; *m* 1942, Mary Pamela, *o d* of late Dr H. C. Billings; two *d*. *Educ:* Harrow; Trinity Hall, Cambridge. Served with Queen's Royal Regiment, 1940–46 (Capt.). Called to the Bar, Lincoln's Inn, 1947, Bencher, 1972. QC 1964. Recorder: of Deal, 1968–71; of Cambridge, 1971; Hon. Recorder of Cambridge, 1972; a Recorder of the Crown Court, 1972–78. Inspector, Vehicle and General Insurance Company, 1971. *Address:* 7a Porchester Terrace, W2. *T:* 01–723 0770. *Club:* Garrick.

EASTHAUGH, Rt. Rev. Cyril, MC 1917; MA (Oxon); *b* 22 Dec. 1897; *y s* of late Robert Wilgress Eastaugh; adopted spelling of Easthaugh, 1983; *m* 1948, Lady Laura Mary Palmer, *d* of 3rd Earl of Selborne, PC, CH; one *s* two *d*. *Educ:* Christ Church, Oxford; Cuddesdon College. Served European War, 1914–18, S Staffs Regt. Chaplain, Cuddesdon Coll., 1930–34; Vice-Principal, 1934–35; Vicar of St John the Divine, Kennington, 1935–49; Suffragan Bishop of Kensington, 1949–61; Bishop of Peterborough, 1961–72. Hon. Canon of Southwark, 1945; Proctor in Convocation, 1943. Chaplain and Sub-Prelate of the Order of St John of Jerusalem, 1961–. *Address:* Blackmoor House, Liss, Hants. *T:* Bordon 3777.

EASTICK, Brig. Sir Thomas (Charles), Kt 1970; CMG 1953; DSO 1942; ED 1939; CSS 1946; KCSA 1975; Chairman, Standing Committee, "Call to the People of Australia", 1951–54; President, El Alamein Group (SA), 1946–60; Chairman of Trustees, Poppy Day Fund (Inc.), 1950–77; President of Australia Day Council, S Australian Branch (Federal), 1962–65 and 1976–78; Chairman of Trustees, Services Cemeteries Trust; Deputy Chairman, World War II Fund; *b* 3 May 1900; *s* of Charles William Lone and Agnes Ann Eastick; *m* 1925, Ruby Sybil Bruce; five *s*. *Educ:* Goodwood Sch., Australia. Senior Cadets, 1914–18; Citizen Forces, 1918 (Artillery); Lieut 1922, Capt. 1926, Major 1930, Lieut-Col 1939. Served War of 1939–45 (despatches, ED, DSO); raised and commanded 2/7 Aust. Fd Regt 1940–43; Middle East, Alamein; Brig., CRA 7 Aust. Div., 1943; CRA 9 Aust. Div., 1944; Comdr Kuching Force, 1945; took Japanese surrender and relieved Kuching Prisoner Compound; administered comd 9 Aust. Div., Dec. 1945–Feb. 1946, when Div. disbanded. Hon. ADC to Governor-Gen. of Australia, 1950–53; Mem., Betting Control Board, 1954–65; State Pres. Returned Sailors, Soldiers and Airmen's Imperial League of Australia, S Australia, 1950–54–61–72; Comdr HQ Group Central Command, 1950–54. Pres., SA Womens Meml Playing Fields, 1954–80. Col Comdt, Royal Australian Artillery, 1955–60. Pres. Engine Reconditioners Assoc. of Austr., 1958–61. FAIM. Rotary Club of Adelaide Service Award, 1969–70. *Recreation:* photography. *Address:* c/o Dr B. C. Eastick, PO Box 163, Gawler, SA 5118, Australia.

EASTMAN, Ven. Derek Ian Tennent, MC 1945; Archdeacon Emeritus, Diocese of Oxford, since 1985; Canon of St George's Chapel, Windsor, 1977–85; *b* 22 Jan. 1919; *s* of Archibald Tennent Eastman and Gertrude Towler Eastman (*née* Gambling); *m* 1949, Judith Mary, *e d* of Canon Philip David Bevington Miller; three *s* one *d*. *Educ:* Winchester; Christ Church, Oxford; Cuddesdon Theol. Coll. BA 1941; MA 1946. Coldstream Guards, 1940–46; Guards Armoured Div., Temp. Major. Cuddesdon Theol. Coll., 1946–48; Deacon 1948; Priest 1949; Asst Curate, Brighouse, 1948–51; Priest-in-Charge, St Andrew's, Caversham, 1951–56; Vicar: Headington, Oxford, 1956–64; Banbury, 1964–70; Archdeacon of Buckingham, and Vicar of Chilton and Dorton, 1970–77. Proctor in Convocation for Dio. of Oxford, 1964–70. Mem., General Synod, 1975–77. *Recreations:* sea fishing, painting. *Address:* 43 Clay Lane, Beaminster, Dorset DT8 3BX. *T:* Beaminster 862443.

EASTON, David John; HM Diplomatic Service; Counsellor (Political), New Delhi, since 1986; *b* 27 March 1941; *o s* of Air Cdre Sir James Easton, *qv*; *m* 1964, Alexandra Julie, *er d* of K. W. Clark, London, W8; two *s* two *d*. *Educ:* Stone House, Broadstairs; Stowe (Exhbnr); Balliol Coll., Oxford (Trevelyan Schol.; BA Hons Jurisprudence 1963, MA 1973). Apprentice, United Steel Cos, Workington, 1960. TA, 1959–65; 2nd Lieut, Oxford Univ. OTC, 1962; Lieut, Inns of Court and City Yeo., 1964. Entered Foreign Office, 1963; Third Sec., Nairobi, 1965–66; Second Sec., UK Mission to UN, Geneva, 1967–70; MECAS, Lebanon, 1970–72; First Sec., FCO, 1972–73; First Sec. (Information), Tripoli, 1973–77; Defence Dept, FCO, 1977–80; First Sec. (Chancery), later Political Counsellor, Amman, 1980–83; Counsellor, FCO, 1984–86. Director, Internat. Community Sch. (Jordan) Ltd, 1980–83 (Chm. 1981–83). *Recreations:* swimming, tennis, travel, antiques and antiquities. *Address:* c/o Foreign and Commonwealth Office, King Charles Street, SW1A 2AH; British High Commission, Chanakyapuri, New Delhi 110021, India. *T:* 601371.

EASTON, Admiral Sir Ian, KCB 1975; DSC 1946; Commandant, Royal College of Defence Studies, 1976–77; retired 1978; *b* 27 Nov. 1917; *s* of Walter Easton and Janet Elizabeth Rickard; *m* 1st, 1943, Shirley Townend White (marr. diss.); one *s* one *d*; 2nd, 1962, Margharetta Elizabeth Martinette Van Duyn de Sparwoude; one *d*. *Educ:* The Grange, Crowborough; RNC, Dartmouth. Entered Royal Navy, 1931, and, as an actg Sub-Lt, qualified as a pilot, 1939. During War of 1939–45 served as pilot in HM Ships Glorious, Ark Royal and Formidable and as Direction Officer HMS Indefatigable; Comdr, 1952; Naval Staff Coll., 1953; on staff of BJSM, Washington, 1955–57; Staff Direction Officer, on Staff of Flag Officer Aircraft Carriers, 1957–59; JSSC, 1959; Captain, 1960; Asst Dir of Tactical and Weapons Policy Div., 1960–62; two years exchange service with RAN, in command of HMAS Watson, 1962–64; Naval Asst to Naval Member of Templer Cttee, 1965; Dir of Naval Tactical and Weapons Policy Div., 1966–68; Comdg Officer of HMS Triumph, Far East, 1968–69; Asst Chief of the Naval Staff (Policy), 1969–71; Flag Officer, Admiralty Interview Bd, 1971–73; Head of British Defence Staff and Defence Attaché, Washington, 1973–75. *Recreations:* boats, books, gardening. *Address:*

Causeway Cottage, Freshwater, Isle of Wight. *T:* Freshwater 2775. *Club:* Royal Solent Yacht (Yarmouth, IoW).

EASTON, Air Cdre Sir James (Alfred), KCMG 1956; CB 1952; CBE 1945; RAF retired; *b* 11 Feb. 1908; *s* of late W. C. Easton, Winchester; *m* 1st, 1939, Anna Mary (*d* 1977), *d* of Lieut-Col J. A. McKenna, Ottawa; one *s* one *d*; 2nd, 1980, Jane Walker, *d* of late Dr J. S. Leszynski and *widow* of Mr William M. Walker Jr, both of Detroit. *Educ:* Peter Symonds' Sch., Winchester; RAF Coll., Cranwell. Joined RAF 1928; served NWF India, 1929–32; Egypt, 1935–36, and Canada, 1937–39, as Air Armament Adviser to Dept of National Defence; despatches, 1940; Group Capt., 1941; Air Cdre, 1943; Dir in Air Staff Branch, Air Ministry, 1943–45, and then in RAF Delegation, Washington; retired, 1949; attached Foreign Office, 1945–58; HM Consul-Gen., Detroit, 1958–68. Res. Consultant on Trade Develt of Great Lakes Area, USA, 1968–71; Dep. Chm., Host Cttee for 1974 World Energy Conf., 1972–75; Associate Mem., Overseas Advisory Associates Inc., Detroit, 1975–82. Officer Legion of Merit (US). *Publication:* The Transportation of Freight in the Year 2000, 1970. *Recreations:* travel and travel literature, gardening, golf. *Address:* 390 Chalfonte Avenue, Grosse Pointe Farms, Mich 48236, USA. *Clubs:* Royal Air Force; Country, Detroit, Grosse Pointe (Detroit).

See also D. J. Easton.

EASTON, John Francis; Under-Secretary (Legal), Solicitor's Office, Inland Revenue, since 1980; *b* 20 Aug. 1928; *s* of Rev. Cecil Gordon Easton and Nora Gladys Easton (*née* Hall); *m* 1960, Hon. Caroline Ina Maud, *e d* of 9th Baron Hawke; one *s* one *d*. *Educ:* City of London Sch.; Keble Coll., Oxford (MA). Called to Bar, Middle Temple, 1951. National Service, RASC, 1951–53. Joined Inland Revenue Solicitor's Office, 1955. Member, General Synod of Church of England, 1970–75; Licensed Diocesan Reader, dio. of St Albans, 1969–. *Recreations:* Church affairs, foreign languages, swimming. *Address:* The Old Hall, Barley, Royston, Herts SG8 8JA. *T:* Barkway 368.

EASTON, Robert William Simpson, CBE 1980; CEng, FIMechE, FIMarE, FRINA; FRSA; Chairman and Managing Director, Yarrow Shipbuilders Ltd, since 1979; Chairman, Clyde Port Authority, since 1983; *b* 30 Oct. 1922; *s* of James Easton and Helen Agnes (*née* Simpson); *m* 1948, Jean, *d* of H. K. Fraser and Jean (*née* Murray); one *s* one *d*. *Educ:* Royal Technical Coll., Glasgow. Fairfield Shipbuilding Co., 1939–51; Yarrow Shipbuilders Ltd: Manager, 1951; Director, 1965; Dep. Managing Director, 1970; Managing Director, 1977; Main Board Director, Yarrow & Co. Ltd, 1970–77. Vice Pres., Clyde Shipbuilders, 1972–79; Dir, Genships (Canada), 1979–80; Mem. Council, RINA, 1983–. Member, Worshipful Company of Shipwrights, 1982–. *Recreations:* walking, sailing, golf, gardening. *Address:* Springfield, Stuckenduff, Shandon, Dunbartonshire, Scotland G84 8NW. *T:* Rhu 820677. *Clubs:* Caledonian; RNVR (Glasgow).

EASTWOOD, Basil Stephen Talbot; HM Diplomatic Service; Counsellor, Khartoum, since 1984; *b* 4 March 1944; *s* of Christopher Gilbert Eastwood, CMG and of Catherine Emma (*née* Peel); *m* 1970, Alison Faith Hutchings; four *d*. *Educ:* Eton (KS); Merton College, Oxford. Entered Diplomatic Service, 1966; Middle East Centre for Arab Studies, 1967; Jedda, 1968; Colombo, 1969; Cairo, 1972; Cabinet Office, 1976; FCO, 1978; Bonn, 1980. *Recreation:* theatre. *Address:* c/o Foreign and Commonwealth Office, SW1A 2AH.

EASTWOOD, (George) Granville, OBE 1973; General Secretary, Printing and Kindred Trades Federation, 1958–73; *b* 26 June 1906; *s* of George and Anne Eastwood, *m* 1st, 1934, Margaret Lambert (*d* 1967); no *c*; 2nd, 1971, Elizabeth Gore Underwood (*d* 1981). *Educ:* Burnley; Compositor, Burnley, 1927; Asst Sec., Printing and Kindred Trades Fedn, 1943–58. Workpeople's Sec., HMSO Deptl Whitley Council, 1958–73; Jt Secretary: Printing and Allied Trades Jt Industrial Council, 1958–66; Jt Bd for Nat. Newspaper Industry, 1965–67. Member: Council, Printing Industry's Research Assoc., 1958–73; City and Guilds of London Inst., 1958–73; Council, Inst. of Printing, 1961–76; ILO Printing Conf., Geneva, 1963; Econ. Develt Cttee for Printing and Publishing, 1966–72; Printing and Publishing Industry Trng Bd, 1968–74; Industrial Arbitration Bd, 1973–76; Editorial Adv. Bd, Ind. Relns Digest, 1973–; DHSS Community Health Council, 1974–76; Advisory, Conciliation and Arbitration Service Panel, 1976–80; toured USA and Europe with EDC Jt Mission, 1968. Governor: Chelsea Sch. of Art, 1963–71; Nat. Heart Hosp., Brompton Hosp. and London Chest Hosp., 1969–76. *Publications:* George Isaacs, 1952; Harold Laski, 1977. *Recreations:* reading, gardening. *Address:* 16 The Vineries, Enfield, Mddx EN1 3DQ. *T:* 01-363 2502.

EASTWOOD, Sir John (Bealby), Kt 1975; DL; Chairman, Adam Eastwood & Sons Ltd, Builders, since 1946; *b* 9 Jan. 1909; *s* of William Eastwood and Elizabeth Townroe Eastwood (*née* Bealby); *m* 1st, 1929, Constance Mary (*née* Tilley) (*d* 1981); two *d*; 2nd, 1983, Mrs Joan Mary McGowan (*d* 1986). *Educ:* Queen Elizabeth's Grammar Sch., Mansfield. Civil Engr and Contractor, 1925; founded W. & J. B. Eastwood Ltd, 1945. DL Notts, 1981. OStJ 1972. *Recreations:* shooting, horse-racing, golf, cricket. *Address:* Hexgreave Hall, Farnsfield, Newark, Notts. *Club:* Farmers'.

EASTWOOD, John Stephen; Regional Chairman of Industrial Tribunals, Nottingham Region, since 1983; *b* 27 April 1925; *s* of Rev. John Edgar Eastwood and Elfreda Eastwood; *m* 1949, Nancy (*née* Gretton); one *s* two *d*. *Educ:* Denstone College, Uttoxeter. Solicitor. RN (Coder), 1943–46. Articles, and Asst Sol. to Leics CC, 1946–50; Asst Sol., Salop CC, 1950–53; Sen. Asst Sol., Northants CC, 1953–58; Partner, Wilson & Wilson, Solicitors, Kettering, 1958–76; Chm., Industrial Tribunals, 1976–83; Asst Recorder, 1983–. *Recreations:* music, painting, photography, walking, gardening, exploring British Isles, grandchildren. *Address:* 20 Gipsy Lane, Kettering, Northants NN16 8TY. *T:* Kettering 85612.

EASTWOOD, Noel Anthony Michael, MA; CEng, MRAeS; Chairman, InterData Group, since 1981; *b* 7 Dec. 1932; *s* of Edward Norman Eastwood and Irene Dawson; *m* 1965, Elizabeth Tania Gresham Boyd, *d* of Comdr Thomas Wilson Boyd, CBE, DSO and Irene Barbara Gresham; three *s*. *Educ:* The Leys School, Cambridge; Christ's College, Cambridge. Lieut RA, 1951–53; Pilot Officer, RAFVR, 1954–57; de Havilland Aircraft Co., 1956–60; RTZ Group, 1960–61; AEI Group, 1961–64; Director: Charterhouse Development, 1964–69; Charterhouse Japhet, 1969–79 (Pres., Charterhouse Japhet Texas, 1974–77); Charterhouse Middle East, 1975–79; Wharton Crane & Hoist, 1967–70 (Chm.); Daniel Doncaster & Son, 1971–81; The Barden Corp., 1971–82; Hawk Publishing (UAE), 1981–; Oryx Publishing (Qatar), 1981–; Falcon Publishing (Bahrain), 1981–84; Caribbean Publishing, 1981–84; IDP InterData (Australia), 1984–. Mem. London Cttee, Yorkshire & Humberside Development Assoc., 1975–. Sec., RAeS, 1983. *Recreations:* vintage sportscars, family picnics, desert travel. *Address:* Palace House, Much Hadham, Herts SG10 6HW. *T:* Much Hadham 2409. *Club:* Royal Thames Yacht.

EASTWOOD, Dr Wilfred, PhD; FEng, FICE, FIStructE, FIMechE; Senior Partner, Eastwood and Partners, Consulting Engineers, since 1972; *b* 15 Aug. 1923; *s* of Wilfred Andrew Eastwood and Annice Gertrude Eastwood; *m* 1947, Dorothy Jean Gover; one *s* one *d*. Road Research Laboratory, 1945–46; University of Manchester, 1946–47; University of Aberdeen, 1947–53; University of Sheffield, 1954–70: Head, Dept of Civil

Engrg, 1964–70; Dean, Faculty of Engrg, 1967–70. Pres., IStructE, 1976–77; Chairman: CEI, 1983–84; Commonwealth Engrg Council, 1983–85. Hon. DEng Sheffield, 1983. *Publications:* papers in Proc. ICE and Jl IStructE, etc. *Address:* 242 Abbeydale Road South, Sheffield S17 3LL. *T:* 364645.

EATES, Edward Caston, CMG 1968; LVO 1961; QPM 1961; CPM 1956; Commissioner, The Royal Hong Kong Police, 1967–69, retired; re-employed at Foreign and Commonwealth Office, 1971–76; *b* London, 8 April 1916; *o s* of late Edward Eates and Elizabeth Lavinia Issac Eates (*née* Caston); *m* 1941, Maureen Teresa McGee; no *c*. *Educ:* Highgate Sch.; King's Coll., London (LLB). Asst Examr, Estate Duty Office, 1935. Army, 1939–46 (RAC): Western Desert and NW Europe; Adjt 2nd Derby Yeo., 1943; Temp. Maj. 1944; Staff Coll. Quetta (sc), 1945. Apptd to Colonial Police Service, Nigeria, 1946; Sen. Supt, Sierra Leone, 1954; Comr, The Gambia, 1957; Asst Comr, 1963, Dep. Comr, 1966, Hong Kong. *Recreations:* cricket and association football (inactive); travel, motoring. *Address:* Banjul, Toadpit Lane, Ottery St Mary, Devon. *T:* Ottery St Mary 2838. *Clubs:* Royal Commonwealth Society, East India; Surrey County Cricket.

EATHER, Maj.-Gen. Kenneth William, CB 1947; CBE 1943; DSO 1941; Executive Director, Water Research Foundation of Australia, 1958–79; *b* 1901; *m* 1st, 1924, Adeline Mabel, *d* of Gustavus Lewis; one *s* one *d*; 2nd, 1968, Kathleen, *d* of M. F. Carroll. Served War of 1939–45; AMF, Middle East and SW Pacific (despatches, DSO, CBE). *Address:* 6 Edensor Road, Epping, NSW 2121, Australia. *T:* 8691131. *Club:* Imperial Service (Sydney).

EATON, Air Vice-Marshal Brian Alexander, CB 1969; CBE 1959; DSO and Bar, DFC, American Silver Star; Regional Executive, Canberra Rolls-Royce Ltd, since 1974; *b* Launceston, Tas, 15 Dec. 1916; *s* of S. A. Eaton; *m* 1952, Josephine Rumbles; one *s* two *d*. *Educ:* Carey Grammar Sch., Melbourne; RAAF Coll., Pt Cook. Served war of 1939–45: Co 3 Sqdn N Africa-Medit., 1943, CO 239 Wing RAF Italy, 1944–45. UK, 1945–46; OC 81 Fighter Wing, Japan, 1948; OC BCAIR, 1948–49; OC 78 Wing Malta, 1952–54; Dir of Ops, RAAF HQ, 1955; OC Williamtown RAAF and Comdt Sch. of Land-Air Warfare, 1957–58; Dir Joint Service Plans, 1959–60; Imp. Defence Coll., 1961; Dir-Gen. of Operational Requirements, 1962; Deputy Chief of Air Staff, 1966–67; AOC HQ 224 Mobile Group (RAF) Far East Air Force, Singapore, 1967–68; Chief of Staff HQFEAF, 1968–69; Air Mem. for Personnel, Dept of Air, Canberra, 1969–73; AOC Operational Comd, RAAF, 1973–74. *Recreations:* shooting, fishing. *Address:* 125 Mugga Way, Red Hill, ACT 2603, Australia. *Club:* Commonwealth (Canberra).

EATON, James Thompson, TD 1963; Lord-Lieutenant, City of Londonderry, since 1986; *b* 11 Aug. 1927; *s* of late J. C. Eaton, DL, and Mrs E. A. F. Eaton, MBE; *m* 1954, Lucy Edith Smeeton, OBE 1986; one *s* one *d*. *Educ:* Campbell Coll., Belfast; Royal Technical Coll., Glasgow. Man. Dir, Eaton & Co. Ltd, 1965–80. Member: Londonderry Develt Commn, 1969–73 (Chm., Educn Cttee, 1969–73); Londonderry Port and Harbour Comrs, 1977– (Vice Chm., 1985). Served North Irish Horse (TA), 1950–67 (Second in Comd, 1964–67). High Sheriff, Co. Londonderry, 1982. *Recreations:* military history, gardening. *Address:* Ballyowen House, Londonderry, Northern Ireland. *T:* Londonderry 860372.

EATON, Peter; owner of the largest antiquarian bookstore in England; *b* 24 Jan. 1914; *m* 1st, Ann Wilkinson; 2nd, Valerie Carruthers; two *s*; 3rd, Margaret Taylor; two *d*. *Educ:* elementary sch.; Municipal Sch. (later Coll.) of Technology, Manchester Univ. (expelled). Born in London at 8 York Gate, Regent's Park; advertised for adoption in Nursing Times, Feb. 1914; brought up in Rochdale, where became apprentice printer; became a tramp; in London, later helped found now defunct Domestic Workers Union; advised on start of Tribune newspaper; mem. of Labour Party for 40 yrs; Conscientious Objector, tried at Royal Courts of Justice, 1939; voluntarily joined London Rescue Squad for duration of War and helped Bomb Disposal Squad; started bookselling in Portobello Road when it was predominantly a fruit and vegetable market, 1945; bought Queen Victoria's books from Kensington Palace (now in Victoria State Library, Australia); bought part or all of libraries of Bernard Shaw, H. G. Wells, Marie Stopes and R. H. Tawney; formed many important collections of books, incl. world's largest collection of books on the atom (now in Texas Univ.). Travelled in many parts of the world, incl. Alaska, India and African jungles; FRGS 1950. *Publications:* Marie Stopes: a bibliographical list of her books, 1977; History of Lilies, 1982; articles in trade jls. *Recreations:* taking the dog for a walk, watching my wife play tennis. *Address:* Lilies, Weedon, Aylesbury, Bucks HP22 4NS. *T:* Aylesbury 641393.

EAYRS, Prof. John Thomas, PhD, DSc; Sands Cox Professor of Anatomy, University of Birmingham, 1968–77; *b* 23 Jan. 1913; *e s* of late Thomas William Eayrs, AMICE, and late Florence May (*née* Clough); *m* 1941, Frances Marjorie Sharp; one *s* two *d*. *Educ:* King Edward's, Birmingham; University of Birmingham. In industry until 1938. War service: Pte Royal Warwicks Regt, 1939–40; 2nd Lieut Manchester Regt, 1940; Lieut 1940; Capt. 1941; Major 1942; Worcester Regt, 1943; sc Staff Coll., Camberley, 1944. University of Birmingham: Peter Thompson Prize, 1947; John Barritt Melson Memorial Gold Medal, 1947; Lectr in Anatomy, 1948; Bertram Windle Prize, 1950; Sen. Lectr 1955; Research Fellow, Calif. Inst. of Technology, 1956–57; Reader in Comparative Neurology, Birmingham, 1958; Henry Head Research Fellow, Royal Society, London, 1957–62; Prof. of Neuroendocrinology, Birmingham, 1961; Fitzmary Prof. of Physiology, London Univ., 1963–68. Governor, King Edward's Foundn, Birmingham, 1968–77. *Publications:* Scientific Papers dealing with developmental neuroendocrinology and behaviour in Jl Endocrin., Jl Anat. (London), Anim. Behav., etc. *Recreations:* cruising, foreign travel and languages. *Address:* 51 Old Street, Upton upon Severn, Worcs; Penllyn Dyfi, Aberangell, Powys.

EBAN, Abba; a Member of the Knesset, since 1959; Minister of Foreign Affairs, Israel, 1966–74; *b* 2 Feb. 1915, Cape Town, SA; *s* of Avram and Alida Solomon; *m* 1945, Susan Ambache; one *s* one *d*. *Educ:* Cambridge Univ. (MA). Res. Fellow and Tutor for Oriental Languages, Pembroke Coll., Cambridge, 1938. Liaison officer of Allied HQ with Jewish population in Jerusalem, 1942–44; Chief Instructor, Middle East Arab Centre, Jerusalem, 1944–46; Jewish Agency, 1946–47; Liaison Officer with UN Special Commn on Palestine, 1947; UN: Representative of provisional govt of Israel, 1948; Permanent rep., 1949–59; Vice-Pres., General Assembly, 1953; Ambassador to USA, 1950–59; Minister without Portfolio, 1959–60; Minister of Educn and Culture, 1960–63; Dep. Prime Minister, 1963–66. Pres., Weizmann Inst. of Science, 1958–66; Vice-Pres., UN Conf. on Science and Technology in Advancement of New States, 1963; Mem., UN Adv. Cttee on Science and Technology for Develt. Fellow: World Acad. of Arts and Sciences; Amer. Acad. of Arts and Sciences. Hon. Doctorates include: New York; Boston; Maryland; Cincinnati; Temple; Brandeis; Yeshiva. *Publications:* The Modern Literary Movement in Egypt, 1944; Maze of Justice, 1946; Social and Cultural Problems in the Middle East, 1947; The Toynbee Heresy, 1955; Voice of Israel, 1957; Tide of Nationalism, 1959; Chaim Weizmann: a collective biography, 1962; Reality and Vision in the Middle East (Foreign Affairs), 1965; Israel in the World, 1966; My People, 1968; My Country, 1972; An Autobiography, 1978; The New Diplomacy: international affairs in the modern age, 1983; Heritage, Civilisation and the Jews, 1985; articles in English, French, Hebrew and Arabic. *Address:* The Knesset, Jerusalem, Israel.

EBBISHAM, 2nd Baron, *cr* 1928, of Cobham, Surrey; **Rowland Roberts Blades,** Bt, *cr* 1922; TD; MA; *b* 3 Sept. 1912; *o s* of 1st Baron Ebbisham, GBE, and Margaret (MBE 1943, Officer Legion of Honour, OStJ) (*d* 1965), *d* of Arthur Reiner, Sutton, Surrey; *S* father, 1953; *m* 1949, Flavia Mary, *y d* of Charles Meade, Pen y lan, Meifod, Montgomeryshire; three *d*. *Educ:* Winchester; Christ Church, Oxford (MA). Served War of 1939–45; Lieut 98th (Surrey and Sussex Yeo.) Field Regt, RA. Master, Mercers' Co., 1963; Common Councilman, City of London, 1947–83; Chm., City Lands Cttee, and Chief Commoner, Corp. of London, 1967–68; one of HM Lieutenants, City of London, 1966–. President: London Chamber of Commerce, 1958–61; Assoc. of British Chambers of Commerce, 1968–70; British Importers' Confedn, 1978–81; Mem., European Trade Cttee, BOTB, 1973–82; Hon. Treasurer, BPIF, 1971–81; Director: Williams, Lea Ltd; Chm., Anglo-Dal Ltd. Vice-Pres. The London Record Society. Captain, Surrey II XI, 1946–54. Hon. DSc City Univ., 1984. Order of Yugoslav Flag with gold wreath, 1976; Comdr, Order of Orange-Nassau, Netherlands, 1982. *Address:* St Ann's, Church Street, Mere, Wiltshire BA12 6DS. *T:* Mere 860376. *Club:* MCC.

EBERHART, Richard (Ghormley); Professor Emeritus of English and Poet in Residence, Dartmouth College, USA; Florida Ambassador of the Arts, since 1984; *b* Austin, Minn, 5 April 1904; *s* of late Alpha La Rue Eberhart and late Lena Eberhart (*née* Lowenstein); *m* 1941, Helen Elizabeth Butcher, Christ Church, Cambridge, Mass; one *s* one *d*. *Educ:* Dartmouth Coll., USA (AB); St John's Coll., Cambridge Univ., England (BA, MA); Harvard Univ. Grad. Sch. of Arts and Sciences. Taught English, 1933–41, also tutor to son of King Prajadhipok of Siam for a year. Served War in USN Reserve finishing as Lieut-Comdr, 1946; subseq. entered Butcher Polish Co., Boston, Mass, as Asst Man., finishing as Vice-Pres. (now Hon. Vice-Pres. and Mem. Bd of Directors). Founder (and first Pres.) Poets' Theatre Inc., Cambridge, Mass, 1950. Called back to teaching, 1952, and has served as Poet in Residence, Prof., or Lecturer at University of Washington, University of Conn., Wheaton Coll., Princeton, and in 1956 was apptd Prof. of English and Poet in Residence at Dartmouth Coll. Class of 1925 Chair, 1968 (being absent as Consultant in Poetry to the Library of Congress, 1959–61). Visiting Professor: Univ. of Washington, 1967, Jan.-June 1972; Columbia Univ., 1975; Distinguished Vis. Prof., Florida Univ., 1974– (President's Medallion, 1977); Regents Prof., Univ. of California, Davis, 1975; First Wallace Stevens Fellow, Timothy Dwight Coll., Yale, 1976. Shelley Memorial Prize; Bollingen Prize, 1962; Pulitzer Prize, 1966; Fellow, Acad. of Amer. Poets, 1969 (Nat. Book Award, 1977). Advisory Cttee on the Arts, for the National Cultural Center (later John F. Kennedy Memorial Center), Washington, 1959; Member: Amer. Acad. and Inst. of Arts and Letters, 1960; Nat. Acad. of Arts and Sciences, 1967; Amer. Acad. of Arts and Letters, 1982; Elliston Lecturer on Poetry, University of Cincinnati, 1961. Poet Laureate of New Hampshire, 1979–84. Apptd Hon. Consultant in American Letters, The Library of Congress, 1963–66, reapptd, 1966–69. Hon. Pres., Poetry Soc. of America, 1972. Participant, Poetry International, London, 1973; Exhibn, Dartmouth Coll. Library, 1984. Hon. LittD: Dartmouth Coll., 1954; Skidmore Coll., 1966; Coll. of Wooster, 1969; Colgate Univ., 1974; St Lawrence Univ., 1985; Hon. DHL, Franklin Pierce, 1978. Phi Beta Kappa poem, Harvard, 1967; Hon. Mem., Alpha Chapter, Mass, 1967; New York Qly Poetry Day Award, 1980; Sarah Josepha Hale Award, Richards Library, Newport, NH, 1982; Robert Frost Medal, Poetry Soc. of America, 1986. Diploma, World Acad. of Arts and Culture, Republic of China, 1981. Richard Eberhart Day: 14 July 1982, RI; 14 Oct. 1982, Dartmouth; Eberhart at Eighty, celebration at Univ. of Florida, 4–6 April 1984. *Publications:* (concurrently in England and America): A Bravery of Earth, 1930; Reading the Spirit, 1936; Selected Poems, 1951; Undercliff, Poems, 1946–53, also Great Praises, 1957; Collected Poems, 1930–60, 1960; Collected Verse Plays, 1962 (USA); The Quarry, 1964; Selected Poems, 1930–65, New Directions, 1965; Thirty One Sonnets, 1967 (USA); Shifts of Being, 1968; Fields of Grace, 1972 (Nat. Book Award nominee, 1973); Poems to Poets, 1975; Collected Poems 1930–1976, 1976, 1930–86, 1986; To Eberhart from Ginsberg: a letter about 'Howl', 1956, 1976; Of Poetry and Poets (criticism), 1979; Ways of Light, 1980 (USA); Survivors, 1980 (USA); Four Poems, 1980; New Hampshire/Nine Poems, 1980; Chocorua, 1981 (USA); Florida Poems, 1981 (USA); The Long Reach, 1984 (USA); Recorded Readings of his Poetry, 1961, 1968; four documentary films, 1972, 1975, 1986, 1987; *Festschriften:* (in New England Review, 1980) Richard Eberhart: A Celebration; (in Negative Capability, 1986) Richard Eberhart. *Recreations:* swimming, cruising, tennis, flying 7–ft kites. *Address:* 5 Webster Terrace, Hanover, New Hampshire 03755, USA. *Clubs:* Century (New York); Buck's Harbor Yacht (S Brooksville, Maine); Signet (Harvard).

EBERLE, Adm. Sir James (Henry Fuller), GCB 1981 (KCB 1979); Director, Royal Institute of International Affairs, since 1984; writer on international affairs and security; *b* 31 May 1927; *s* of late Victor Fuller Eberle and of Joyce Mary Eberle, Bristol; *m* 1950, Ann Patricia Thompson, Hong Kong; one *s* two *d*. *Educ:* Clifton Coll.; RNC Dartmouth and Greenwich. Served War of 1939–45 in MTBs, HMS Renown, HMS Belfast; subseq. in Far East; qual. Gunnery Specialist 1951; Guided Missile Develt and trials in UK and USA, 1953–57; Naval Staff, 1960–62; Exec. Officer, HMS Eagle, 1963–65; comd HMS Intrepid, 1968–70; Asst Chief of Fleet Support, MoD (RN), 1971–74; Flag Officer Sea Training, 1974–75; Flag Officer Carriers and Amphibious Ships, 1975–77; Chief of Fleet Support, 1977–79; C-in-C, Fleet, and Allied C-in-C, Channel and Eastern Atlantic, 1979–81; C-in-C, Naval Home Comd, 1981–82, retired 1983. Vice-Pres., RUSI, 1979. Freeman: Bristol, 1946; London, 1982. *Publications:* Management in the Armed Forces, 1972; Jim, First of the Pack, 1982. *Recreations:* hunting (Master of Britannia Beagles), tennis (Pres., RN Lawn Tennis Assoc.). *Address:* c/o RIIA, Chatham House, SW1Y 4LE. *Clubs:* Farmers'; Society of Merchant Venturers (Bristol); All England Lawn Tennis.

EBERT, Peter; Producer; *b* 6 April 1918; *s* of Carl Ebert, CBE, and Lucie Oppenheim; *m* 1st, 1944, Kathleen Havinden; two *d*; 2nd, 1951, Silvia Ashmole; five *s* three *d*. *Educ:* Salem Sch., Germany; Gordonstoun, Scotland. BBC Producer, 1948–51; 1st opera production, Mefistofele, Glasgow, 1951; Mozart and Rossini guest productions: Rome, Naples, Venice, 1951, 1952, 1954, 1955: Wexford Festival: 12 prods, 1952–65; 1st Glyndebourne Fest. prod., Ariecchino, 1954, followed by Seraglio, Don Giovanni, etc.; 1st Edinburgh Fest. prod., Forza del Destino, 1955; Chief producer: Hannover State Opera, 1954–60; Düsseldorf Opera, 1960–62; directed opera class, Hannover State Conservatory, 1954–60; Head of Opera studio, Düsseldorf, 1960–62. Guest productions in Europe, USA, Canada. TV productions of Glyndebourne operas, 1955–64; 1st TV studio prod., 1963; Opera Adviser to BBC TV, 1964–65; Dir of Productions, 1965–77, Gen. Administrator, 1977–80, Scottish Opera Co. First drama prod., The Devils, Johannesburg, 1966; first musical, Houdini, London, 1966. Dir, Opera Sch., University of Toronto, 1967–68; Intendant: Stadttheater, Augsburg, 1968–73; Stadttheater Bielefeld, 1973–75; Staatstheater Wiesbaden, 1975–77. Hon. DMus St Andrews, 1979. *Recreation:* raising a family. *Address:* Ades House, Chailey, East Sussex. *T:* Newick 2441.

EBERTS, John David, (Jake); Founder, 1976, and Chief Executive, 1976–83 and since 1985, Goldcrest Films and Television Ltd; *b* 10 July 1941; *s* of Edmond Howard Eberts and Elizabeth Evelyn MacDougall; *m* 1968, Fiona Louise Leckie; two *s* one *d*. *Educ:* McGill Univ. (BChemEng 1962); Harvard Univ. (MBA 1966). Project Engr, l'Air Liquide, Paris, 1962–64; Marketing Manager, Cummins Engine Co., Brussels, 1966–68; Vice Pres., Laird Inc., NY, 1968–71; Managing Director: Oppenheimer and Co. Ltd, London, 1971–76; Pres., Embassy Communications International, 1984–85. *Recreations:* tennis, skiing, photography. *Address:* 107 Oakwood Court, W14. *T:* 01–602 2919. *Club:* Queen's.

EBOO PIRBHAI, Diwan Sir; Kt 1952; OBE 1946; Director of Companies; *b* 25 July 1905; *m* 1925, Kulsambai; two *s* three *d* (and one *s* decd). *Educ:* Duke of Gloucester Sch., Nairobi. Representative of HH The Aga Khan. Member, Nairobi City Council, 1938–43. MLC Kenya, 1952–60; Member of various other official bodies; Past President Central Muslim Association; President Aga Khan Supreme Council, Africa, Europe, Canada and USA. Given title of Count, 1954 and title of Diwan, 1983, both created by HH The Aga Khan. Brilliant Star of Zanzibar, 1956; Order of Crescent Cross of the Comores, 1966. *Address:* PO Box 40898, Nairobi, Kenya. *T:* (home) 767133; (office) 338177. *Clubs:* Reform, Lansdowne, Royal Commonwealth Society; Nairobi, Muthaiga (Kenya).

EBRAHIM, Sir (Mahomed) Currimbhoy, 4th Bt, *cr* 1910; BA, LLB, Advocate, Pakistan; Member, Standing Council of the Baronetage, 1961; *b* 24 June 1935; *o s* of Sir (Huseinali) Currimbhoy Ebrahim, 3rd Bt, and Alhaja Lady Amina Khanum, *d* of Alhaj Cassumali Jairajbhoy; *S* father 1952; *m* 1958, Dur-e-Mariam, *d* of Minuchehir Ahmud Ghulamaly Nana; three *s* one *d*. *Recreations:* tennis (Karachi University No 1, 1957, No 2, 1958), cricket, table-tennis, squash, reading (literary), art, poetry writing, debate, quotation writing. *Heir:* *s* Zulfiqar Ali Currimbhoy Ebrahim, *b* 5 Aug. 1960.

EBRINGTON, Viscount; Charles Hugh Richard Fortescue; *b* 10 May 1951; *s* and *heir* of 7th Earl Fortescue, *qv*; *m* 1974, Julia, *er d* of Air Commodore J. A. Sowrey; three *d*. *Address:* Ebrington Manor, Chipping Campden, Glos.

EBSWORTH, Ann Marian; Her Honour Judge Ebsworth; a Circuit Judge, since 1983; *b* 19 May 1937; *d* of Arthur E. Ebsworth, OBE, BEM, RM (retd) and late Hilda Mary Ebsworth. *Educ:* Notre Dame Convent, Worth, Sussex; Portsmouth High Sch., GPDST; London Univ. BA Hons (History). Called to Bar, Gray's Inn, 1962; a Recorder of the Crown Court, 1978–83. *Recreations:* Italian travel, medieval history, needlework. *Address:* 33 Warren Drive, Wallasey, Cheshire. *T:* 051–639 1579. *Club:* Royal Commonwealth Society.

EBURNE, Sir Sidney (Alfred William), Kt 1983; MC 1944; Senior Crown Agent and Chairman of the Crown Agents for Oversea Governments and Administrations, 1978–83; *b* 26 Nov. 1918; *s* of Alfred Edmund Eburne and Ellen Francis Eburne; *m* 1942, Phoebe Freda (*née* Beeton Dilley); one *s* one *d*. *Educ:* Downhills School. Served War, 1939–46; Captain, RA. Joined Morgan Grenfell & Co. Ltd, 1946; Director: Morgan Grenfell & Co. Ltd, 1968–75; Morgan Grenfell Holdings Ltd, 1971–75; Peachey Property Corp. Ltd, 1983; Crown Agents: Dir of Finance, 1975; Man. Dir, 1976. Governor, Peabody Trust, 1984. *Recreations:* golf, travelling. *Address:* Motts Farm, Eridge, East Sussex. *Club:* Carlton.

EBURY, 6th Baron, *cr* 1857; **Francis Egerton Grosvenor;** *b* 8 Feb. 1934; *s* of 5th Baron Ebury, DSO and Ann Acland-Troyte; *heir-pres.* to 7th Earl of Wilton, *qv*; *S* father 1957; *m* 1st, 1957, Gillian Elfrida (Elfin) (marr. diss. 1962), *d* of Martin Soames, London; one *s*; 2nd, 1963, Kyra (marr. diss. 1973), *d* of late L. L. Aslin; 3rd, 1974, Suzanne Jean, *d* of Graham Suckling, Christchurch, NZ; one *d*. *Educ:* Eton. *Recreation:* angling. *Heir:* *s* Hon. Julian Francis Martin Grosvenor, *b* 8 June 1959. *Address:* 8B Branksome Tower, 3 Tregunter Path, Hong Kong. *Clubs:* Melbourne, Melbourne Savage (Melbourne).

ECCLES, family name of **Viscount Eccles.**

ECCLES, 1st Viscount, *cr* 1964; 1st Baron, *cr* 1962; **David McAdam Eccles,** CH 1984; KCVO 1953; PC 1951; MA Oxon; Chairman, British Library Board, 1973–78; *b* 18 Sept. 1904; *s* of late W. McAdam Eccles, FRCS and Anna Coralie, *d* of E. B. Anstie, JP; *m* 1st, 1928, Sybil (*d* 1977), *e d* of Viscount Dawson of Penn, PC, GCVO, KCB, KCMG; two *s* one *d*; 2nd, 1984, Mrs Donald Hyde, Somerville, NJ. *Educ:* Winchester, New Coll., Oxford. Joined Ministry of Economic Warfare, Sept. 1939; Economic Adviser to HM Ambassadors at Madrid and Lisbon, 1940–42; Ministry of Production, 1942–43. MP (C) Chippenham Div. of Wilts, 1943–62; Minister of Works, 1951–54; Minister of Education, 1954–57; Pres. of the Board of Trade, 1957–59; Minister of Education, Oct. 1959–July 1962; Paymaster-General, with responsibility for the arts, 1970–73. Trustee, British Museum, 1963–, Chm. of Trustees, 1968–70. Dir, Courtaulds, 1962–70. Chm., Anglo-Hellenic League, 1967–70. Pres., World Crafts Council, 1974–78. Hon. Fellow, RIBA. *Publications:* Half-Way to Faith, 1966; Life and Politics: A Moral Diagnosis, 1967; On Collecting, 1968; By Safe Hand: Letters of Sybil and David Eccles 1939–42, 1983. *Heir:* *s* Hon. John Dawson Eccles, *qv*. *Address:* Dean Farm, Chute, near Andover, Hants; *T:* Chute Standen 210; 6 Barton Street, SW1. *T:* 01–222 1387. *Clubs:* Brooks's, Roxburghe; Knickerbocker, Grolier (New York).

ECCLES, Sir John Carew, Kt 1958; FRS 1941; FRSNZ; FAA; *b* 27 Jan. 1903; *s* of William James and Mary Eccles; *m* 1st, 1928, Irene Frances Miller (marr. diss. 1968); four *s* five *d*; 2nd, 1968, Helena Táboříková. *Educ:* Melbourne Univ.; Magdalen Coll., Oxford. Melbourne University: 1st class Hons MB, BS 1925; Victoria Rhodes Scholar, 1925. Univ. of Oxford: Christopher Welch Scholar; 1st class Hons Natural Science (Physiology), 1927; MA 1929; DPhil 1929; Gotch Memorial Prize, 1927; Rolleston Memorial Prize, 1932. Junior Res. Fellow, Exeter Coll., Oxford, 1927–32; Staines Med. Fellow, Exeter Coll., 1932–34; Fellow and Tutor of Magdalen Coll., and Univ. Lectr in Physiology, 1934–37; Dir, Kanematsu Memorial Inst. of Pathology, Sydney, 1937–44; Prof. of Physiology: Univ. of Otago, Dunedin, NZ, 1944–51; ANU, Canberra, 1951–66; Mem., Inst. for Biomedical Res., Chicago, 1966–68; Dist. Prof. and Head of Res. Unit of Neurobiology, Health Sci. Faculty, State Univ. of NY at Buffalo, 1968–75, now Dist. Prof. Emeritus. Lectures: Waynflete, Magdalen Coll., Oxford, 1952; Herter, Johns Hopkins Univ., 1955; Ferrier, Royal Soc., 1959; Sherrington, Liverpool Univ., 1966; Patten, Indiana Univ., 1972; Pahlavi, Iran, 1976; Gifford, Edinburgh, 1978, 1979; Carroll, Georgetown, 1982. Pres., Australian Acad. of Science, 1957–61. Member: Pontifical Acad. of Science; Deutsche Akademie der Naturforscher Leopoldina. Foreign Hon. Member: Amer. Acad. of Arts and Sciences; Amer. Philosophical Soc.; Amer. Neurological Soc.; Accademia Nazionale dei Lincei. Hon. Life Mem., New York Acad. of Sciences, 1965; Foreign Associate, Nat. Acad. of Sciences; For. Mem., Max-Planck Soc. Hon. Fellow: Exeter Coll., Oxford, 1961; Magdalen Coll., Oxford, 1964; Amer. Coll. of Physicians, 1967. Hon. ScD Cantab; Hon. DSc: Oxon; Tasmania; British Columbia; Gustavus Adolphus Coll., Minnesota; Marquette Univ., Wisconsin; Loyola, Chicago; Yeshiva, NY; Fribourg; Georgetown, Washington DC; Hon. LLD Melbourne; Hon. MD: Charles Univ., Prague; Torino. (Jointly) Nobel Prize for Medicine, 1963; Baly Medal, RCP, 1961; Royal Medal, Royal Soc., 1962; Cothenius Medal, Deutsche Akademie der Naturforscher Leopoldina, 1963. *Publications:* (jtly) Reflex Activity of Spinal Cord, 1932; Neuro-physiological Basis of Mind, 1953; Physiology of Nerve Cells, 1957; Physiology of Synapses, 1964; (jtly) The Cerebellum as a Neuronal Machine, 1967; The Inhibitory Pathways of the Central Nervous System, 1969; Facing Reality, 1970; The Understanding of the Brain, 1973; (jtly) Molecular Neurobiology of the Mammalian Brain, 1977, 2nd edn 1986; (jtly) The Self and Its Brain, 1977; The Human Mystery, 1979; (jtly) Sherrington, his Life and Thought, 1979; The Human Psyche, 1980; (jtly) The Wonder of Being Human: our brain, our mind, 1984; papers in Proc. Royal Soc., Jl of Physiology, Jl of Neurophysiology, Experimental Brain Research. *Recreations:* walking, European travel. *Address:* Ca' a la Gra', CH 6611 Contra (Locarno), Ticino, Switzerland. *T:* 093–672931.

ECCLES, Hon. John Dawson, CBE 1985; General Manager, Commonwealth Development Corporation, since 1985 (Member, 1982–85); Chairman, Board of Trustees, Royal Botanic Gardens, Kew, since 1983; *b* 20 April 1931; *er s* and *heir* of 1st Viscount Eccles, *qv*; *m* 1955, Diana Catherine, *d* of late Raymond Sturge; one *s* three *d*. *Educ:* Winchester Coll.; Magdalen Coll., Oxford (BA). Director: Glynwed International plc, 1972–; Investors in Industry plc, 1974–; Chairman: Head Wrightson & Co. Ltd, 1964–77 (Man. Dir, 1968–77); The Nuclear Power Gp Ltd, 1968–74; Davy Internat. Ltd, 1977–81; Chamberlin & Hill plc, 1982–. Mem., Monopolies and Mergers Commn, 1976–85 (Dep. Chm., 1981–85). *Address:* 6 Barton Street, SW1P 3NG. *T:* 01-222 7559; Moulton Hall, Richmond, N Yorks DL10 6QH. *T:* Barton 77227. *Club:* Brooks's.

ECCLES-WILLIAMS, Hilary a'Beckett, CBE 1970; Vice-President, West Midlands Conservative Council, since 1985 (Deputy Chairman, 1982–85); *b* 5 Oct. 1917; *s* of late Rev. Cyril Eccles-Williams and Hermione (*née* Terrell); *m* 1941, Jeanne, *d* of W. J. Goodwin; two *s* four *d*. *Educ:* Eton; Brasenose Coll., Oxford (MA). Served War of 1939–45, Major RA (anti-tank). Consul: for Nicaragua, 1951–59; for Cuba, 1952–60; for Costa Rica, 1964–; for Bolivia, 1965–82. Chairman of companies; Chm., 1978–82, non-exec. Dir, 1982–, Rabone Petersen; has travelled 900,000 miles on export business. Chairman: Brit. Export Houses Assoc., 1958–59; Guardians of Birmingham Assay Office, 1979– (Guardian, 1970–); President: Birmingham Chamber of Commerce, 1965–66; Assoc. of Brit. Ch. of Commerce (93 Chambers), 1970–72. Comr of Income Tax, 1966–70. Chairman: Birmingham Cons. Assoc., 1976–79 (Pres., 1979–84); W Midlands Metropolitan Co. Co ordinating Cttee, Cons. Party, 1980–86; European Parlt constituency of Birmingham S Cons. Assoc., 1978–82 (Pres., 1982–84); Latin Amer. Gp, Cons. Foreign and Overseas Council, 1986–; President: Eur. Parlt constituency of Birmingham E Cons. Assoc., 1984–; Anglo-Asian Cons. Soc., 1984–; Mem., National Union Exec. Cttee, Cons. Party, 1975–85. Mem., Brit. Hallmarking Council, 1976–; Pres., Birmingham Consular Assoc., 1973–74; Chairman: Asian Christian Colls Assoc., 1960–66; Brit. Heart Foundn, Midland Counties, 1973–74; Governor, Birmingham Univ., 1966; Liveryman, Worshipful Co. of Glaziers, 1974; Hon. Captain, Bolivian Navy, 1969. Numerous TV appearances. *Recreations:* sailing, golf. *Address:* 36 St Bernard's Road, Solihull, West Midlands B92 7BB. *T:* 021–706 0354. *Clubs:* Olton Mere Sailing; North Warwickshire Golf.

ECCLESHARE, Colin Forster; publisher; formerly London Manager, Cambridge University Press; Founder Member, PuMA (Publishers Management Advisers), since 1984; *b* 2 May 1916; *yr s* of Albert and Mary Alice Eccleshare, Derby; *m* 1942, Elizabeth, *e d* of late H. S. Bennett, FBA, and Joan Bennett; one *s* two *d* (and one *d* decd). *Educ:* Bemrose Sch., Derby; St Catharine's Coll., Cambridge (MA). Joined Cambridge Univ. Press, 1939. War Service, 1940–46; commissioned RE; Captain Survey Directorate, War Office, 1944; Major, HQ, ALFSEA, 1945. Rejoined Cambridge Univ. Press, 1946; Asst London Manager, 1948; London Manager, 1963–72; Dir Group Projects, 1972–77. Publishing Consultant, British Library, 1977. Acting Sec., Athlone Press, Univ. of London, 1978–79. Director: Educational Associates Ltd (Hong Kong); John Wiley & Sons Ltd, 1979–85. Mem. Council, Publishers Assoc., 1965–71; Treasurer, 1971–73; Pres., 1973–75; Vice Pres., 1975–77. Member: Publishers' Advisory Cttee, British Council, 1964–85; Bd, Book Development Council, 1968–70 and 1975–79 (Chm., 1975–77); Exec. and Internat. Cttees, Internat. Publishers' Assoc., 1975–77; Groupe des Editeurs du Livre de la CEE, 1973–75; Adv. Cttee, British Library Bibliographical Services Div., 1975–78; British Nat. Bibliography Res. Fund Cttee, 1978–85; UK Nat. Commn UNESCO, 1978–85; Chairman: Other-Media Cttee, Internat. Scientific, Technical and Medical Publishers, Soc. of Bookmen, 1977–80. Missions (for Publishers Assoc., BDC, Brit. Council) to: Hungary, USSR, 1964; Philippines, Japan, 1968; Pakistan, 1971; USSR, Australia, 1974; Saudi Arabia, 1976; Israel, 1977. *Publications:* The Society of Bookmen: an informal history, 1984; regular contributor to The Bookseller, 1950–62. *Address:* 4 Branch Hill, NW3. *T:* 01–794 3496; Tyddyn Pandy, Barmouth. *T:* Barmouth 280315. *Club:* Garrick.

ECCLESTON, Harry Norman, OBE 1979; PRE 1975 (RE 1961; ARE 1948); RWS 1975 (ARWS 1964); Artist Designer at the Bank of England Printing Works, 1958–83; *b* 21 Jan. 1923; *s* of Harry Norman Eccleston and Kate Pritchard, Coseley, Staffs; *m* 1948, Betty Doreen Gripton; two *d*. *Educ:* Sch. of Art, Bilston; Coll. of Art, Birmingham; Royal College of Art. ATD 1947; ARCA (1st Class) 1950. Studied painting until 1942. Served in Royal Navy, 1942–46; Temp. Commn, RNVR, 1943. Engraving Sch., Royal College of Art, 1947–51; engraving, teaching, free-lance graphic design, 1951–58. Pres., Royal Soc. of Painter-Etchers and Engravers, 1975–. *Recreation:* reading. *Address:* 110 Priory Road, Harold Hill, Romford, Essex. *T:* Ingrebourne 40275. *Club:* Arts.

ECCLESTONE, Jacob Andrew; Deputy General Secretary, National Union of Journalists, since 1981; *b* 10 April 1939; *s* of Alan Ecclestone and late Delia Reynolds Abraham; *m* 1966, Margaret Joan Bassett; two *s* one *d*. *Educ:* High Storrs Grammar Sch., Sheffield; Open Univ. (BA). Journalism: South Yorkshire Times, 1957–61; Yorkshire Evening News, 1961–62; The Times, 1962–66, 1967–81. Member: Nat. Exec., NUJ, 1977 (Vice-Pres. 1978, Pres., 1979); Press Council, 1977–80; Exec., Nat. Council for Civil Liberties, 1982–. *Recreations:* gardening, climbing, music. *Address:* 40 Chatsworth Way, SE27 9HN. *T:* 01–670 8503.

ECHLIN, Sir Norman David Fenton, 10th Bt, *cr* 1721; Captain 14/1st Punjab Regiment, Indian Army; *b* 1 Dec. 1925; *s* of Sir John Frederick Echlin, 9th Bt, and Ellen Patricia (*d* 1971), *d* of David Jones, JP, Dublin; *S* father, 1932; *m* 1953, Mary Christine, *d* of John Arthur, Oswestry, Salop. *Educ:* Masonic Boys' School, Dublin. *Heir:* none. *Address:* Nartopa, 36 Marina Avenue, Appley, Ryde, IoW.

ECKERSLEY, Sir Donald (Payze), Kt 1981; OBE 1977; farmer, since 1946; Inaugural President, National Farmers' Federation of Australia, 1979–81; *b* 1 Nov. 1922; *s* of Walter Roland Eckersley and Ada Gladys Moss; *m* 1949, Marjorie Rae Clarke; one *s* two *d*. *Educ:* Muresk Agricl Coll. (Muresk Diploma in Agriculture). Aircrew, RAAF, 1940–45. Pres., Milk Producers' Assoc., 1947–50; Farmers' Union of WA: Executive, 1962–67; Pres., Milk Sect., 1965–70; Vice-Pres., 1969–72; Gen. Pres., 1972–75; Pres., Australian Farmers' Fedn, 1975–79; Austr. Rep., Internat. Fedn of Agric., 1979–81. Pres., Harvey Shire Council, 1970–79; Director: Chamberlain John Deere, 1980–; Br. Bd. Australian Mutual Provident Soc., 1983–. Chairman: Leschenault Inlet Management Authority, 1977–; Artificial Breeding Bd of WA, 1981–; Member: WA Waterways Commn, 1977–; Nat. Energy Adv. Cttee, 1979–; Comr, WA State Housing Commn, 1982–. Mem., Senate, Univ. of WA, 1981–. Mem., Harvey Rotary Club. JP WA, 1982–86. WA Citizen of

Year award, 1976; Man of Year, Austr. Agriculture, 1979. *Publication:* (contrib.) Farm Focus: the '80s, 1981. *Recreations:* golf, fishing. *Address:* Korijedale, Harvey, WA 6220, Australia. *T:* 097–291472. *Clubs:* Weld (Perth); Harvey Golf.

ECKERSLEY, Thomas, OBE 1948; RDI 1963; AGI; graphic designer; Head of Department of Design, London College of Printing, 1958–76; *b* Sept. 1914; *s* of John Eckersley and Eunice Hilton; *m* Daisy Eckersley; three *s*; *m* 1966, Mary Kessell, painter. *Educ:* Salford Sch. of Art. Free-lance Graphic Designer for London Transport, Shell Mex, BBC, GPO, MOI, Unicef, CoID and other leading concerns since 1936. Work exhibited in Sweden, USA, Paris, Hamburg, Lausanne, Milan, Amsterdam; permanent collections of work in V&A Museum, Imperial War Museum, London Transport Museum, Nat. Gall. of Australia and Museum of Modern Art, USA. One-man exhibitions: Soc. of Artists and Designers, 1976; Camden Arts Centre, British Arts Centre, Yale, 1980; Peel Park Gall., Salford, Edinburgh, 1981; Newcastle upon Tyne Polytechnic Gall., 1983; London Transport Museum, 1985; Maidstone Coll. of Art, 1985; Oxford Polytechnic, 1986. Mem. of Alliance Graphique Internationale; Hon. Fellow, Manchester Coll. of Art and Design; FSTD. *Publications:* contribs to Graphis, Gebrauchsgraphik, Form und Technik, Art and Industry, Print Design and Production, Penrose Annual; *relevant publication:* F. H. K. Henrion, Top Graphic Designers, 1983. *Recreation:* cricket. *Address:* 53 Belsize Park Gardens, NW3. *T:* 01–586 3586.

ECKERSLEY-MASLIN, Rear Adm. David Michael, CB 1984; Director General, NATO Communications and Information Systems Agency, Brussels, since 1986; *b* Karachi, 27 Sept. 1929; *e s* of Comdr C. E. Eckersley-Maslin, OBE, RN, Tasmania, and Mrs L. M. Lightfoot, Bedford; *m* 1955, Shirley Ann, *d* of Captain and Mrs H. A. Martin; one *s* one *d*. *Educ:* Britannia Royal Naval Coll. Qual. Navigation Direction Officer, 1954; rcds 1977. Far East Malayan Campaign, 1950–53; Australian Navy, 1954–56; BRNC Dartmouth, 1959–61; commanded HM Ships Eastbourne, Euryalus, Fife and Blake, 1966–76; Captain RN Presentation Team, 1974; Dir, Naval Operational Requirements, 1977–80; Flag Officer Sea Training, 1980–82; ACDS (CIS), 1982–84; Asst Dir (CIS), IMS, NATO, Brussels, 1984–86. Naval Gen. Service Decoration, Palestine, 1948, and Malaya, 1951. *Recreations:* tennis, squash, cricket. *Address:* Dunningwell, Hall Court, Shedfield, near Southampton SO3 2HL. *T:* Wickham 832350. *Clubs:* MCC, Royal Commonwealth Society.

EDDEN, Alan John, CMG 1957; HM Diplomatic Service, retired; *b* 2 Dec. 1912; *s* of late Thomas Frederick Edden and Nellie Shipway; *m* 1939, Pauline Klay; one *s*. *Educ:* Latymer Sch., Edmonton; Gonville and Caius Coll., Cambridge (Exhibitioner). Served at HM Legation, Bangkok, 1935; Batavia, 1938; Foreign Office, 1939; HM Legation, Bangkok, 1940; HM Legation, Tehran, 1942; Kermanshah, 1944; with SHAEF, May 1945; Actg Consul-Gen. Amsterdam, June 1945; Foreign Office, Oct. 1945; HM Embassy, Warsaw, 1948; Brit. Information Services, New York, 1951; FO, 1953; Counsellor, Foreign Office, 1954–58; Counsellor, HM Embassy, Beirut, 1958–62; HM Consul-Gen., Durban, 1962–66; HM Ambassador to: Cameroon, Central African Republic, Gabon and Chad, 1966–70; Equatorial Guinea, 1969–70; Lebanon, 1970–71. *Recreation:* music. *Address:* 4 Ridgewood, 328 Ridge Road, Durban, South Africa.

EDDEN, Vice-Adm. Sir (William) Kaye, KBE 1960 (OBE 1944); CB 1956; DL; *b* 27 Feb. 1905; *s* of late Major H. W. Edden, The Cameronians, and late Mrs H. W. Edden (*née* Neilson); *m* 1936, Isobel Sybil Pitman (*d* 1970), Bath, *g d* of Sir Isaac Pitman; one *s*. *Educ:* Royal Naval Colls, Osborne and Dartmouth. Comdr, 1938; Admiralty, 1938–40; served War of 1939–45: HMS London, 1941–42; Staff C-in-C, Eastern Fleet, 1942–44 (OBE); Capt. 1944, Admty, 1944–47; RNAS Yeovilton, 1947–49; Capt. (D) 6th Destroyer Sqdn, and HMS Battleaxe, 1949–51; Admiralty, 1951–53; Rear-Adm. 1954; Commandant, Jt-Services Staff Coll., Latimer, 1953–56; Flag Officer Commanding Fifth Cruiser Sqdn and Flag Officer Second-in-Command, Far East Station, 1956–57; Vice-Adm. 1957; Admiral Commanding Reserves, 1958–60, retd 1960. DL West Sussex, 1977. *Address:* Littlecroft, Old Bosham, West Sussex PO18 8LR. *T:* Bosham 573119. *Club:* Army and Navy.

EDDERY, Patrick James John; jockey (retained by M. V. O'Brien and J. Tree); *b* 18 March 1952; *s* of Jimmy and Josephine Eddery; *m* 1978, Carolyn Jane (*née* Mercer). Rode for Peter Walwyn, 1972–80; Champion Jockey, 1974, 1975, 1976, 1977; Champion Jockey in Ireland, 1982; won the Oaks, 1974, 1979, the Derby, on Grundy, 1975; Prix de l'Arc de Triomphe, 1980, 1985; St Leger on Moon Madness, 1986. *Recreations:* swimming, golf, snooker. *Address:* Musk Hill Farm, Lower Winchendon, Aylesbury, Bucks HP18 0DT. *T:* Haddenham 290282. *Club:* The Subscription Rooms (Newmarket).

EDDEY, Prof. Howard Hadfield, CMG 1974; FRCS, FRACS, FACS; Foundation Professor of Surgery, University of Melbourne, at Austin Hospital and Repatriation General Hospital, 1967–75, now Emeritus; also Dean of Austin Hospital and Repatriation General Hospital Clinical School, 1971–75; *b* Melbourne, 3 Sept. 1910; *s* of Charles Howard and Rachel Beatrice Eddey; *m* 1940, Alice Paul; two *s* one *d*. *Educ:* Melbourne Univ.; St Bartholomew's Hosp. Med. Sch. BSc, MB BS, 1934; FRCS 1938; FRACS 1941; FACS 1964; Hallet Prize of RCS of Eng., 1938. Served War, 1941–45: AAMC, Major and Surgical Specialist; served in PoW camps: Changi (Singapore); Sandakan and Kuching (Borneo). Hon. Surgeon: Prince Henry Hosp., Melbourne, 1946–47; Alfred Hosp., Melbourne, 1947; Royal Melbourne Hosp., 1947–67; Cons. Surg., 1967, Royal Melbourne and Royal Women's Hosps; Peter MacCallum Clinic. Mem. AMA, 1935; Mem., Faculty of Med., Univ. of Melbourne, 1950–75 (Mem. Convocation, 1965–67); Indep. Lectr in Surgical Anatomy, Univ. of Melb., 1950–65; Dean, Royal Melb. Hosp. Clin. Sch., 1965–67; Colombo Plan Visitor to India, 1960–65; Cons. in Surg., Papuan Med. Coll., 1965–68; Mem. Cancer Inst. Bd, 1958–67; Mem. Med. and Sci. Cttee, Anti-Cancer Council of Vic., 1958–67; Chm., Melb. Med. Postgrad. Cttee, 1963–71; Vice-Pres., Aust. Postgrad. Fedn in Med., 1965–71 (Life Governor, 1972). Mem. Council, RACS, 1967–75 (Mem. Bd of Examrs, 1958–75, Chm. Bd, 1968–73; Hon. Librarian, 1968–75). Mem. Med. Bd of Vic., 1968–77; Mem. Austin Hosp. Bd of Management, 1971–77 (Vice-Pres., 1975–77; Life Governor, 1977). Hunterian Prof., RCS, 1960; Vis. Prof. of Surg., 1962, External Examr in Surg., 1970, Univ. of Singapore; Leverhulme Fellow, Univ. of Melb., 1974; Vis. Prof. of Surg., Univ. of Hong Kong, 1974. Howard Eddey Medal, named in 1972 by RACS and awarded to most successful cand., Part I exam (surgery) for FRACS in SE Asia, in recognition of dist. service to RACS. Hon. Surgeon to HRH Prince Charles on his visit to Victoria, 1974. Melbourne and Australian Universities Lacrosse Blue. *Publications:* many, in sci. jls, particularly in relation to diseases of salivary glands and cancer of mouth. *Recreations:* travel, gardening. *Address:* (home) 2/34 High Street, Kew, Vic 3101, Australia. *T:* 861–8214; (office) 24 Collins Street, Melbourne, Australia. *T:* 654–2917. *Clubs:* Naval and Military (Melbourne), Melbourne Cricket.

EDDINGTON, Paul (Clark); actor; *b* 18 June 1927; *s* of Albert Clark Eddington and Frances Mary (*née* Roberts); *m* 1952, Patricia Scott; three *s* one *d*. *Educ:* Holy Child Convent, Cavendish Sq., W1; Friends (Quaker) Sch., Sibford Ferris, Banbury, Oxon; RADA. First appearance on stage with ENSA, 1944; joined Birmingham Repertory Th., 1945; has played with several other rep. theatres during subseq. 30 years; first appearance in West End in The 10th Man, Comedy Th., 1961; first (and only, so far) appearance in New York in A Severed Head, 1964; joined National Theatre to play in revival of Who's Afraid of Virginia Woolf?, 1981; Noises Off, Savoy, 1982; Lovers Dancing, Albery, 1983; Forty Years On, Queen's, 1984; Jumpers, Aldwych, 1985. Many TV appearances, including series, The Good Life, Yes Minister and Yes, Prime Minister. Mem. Council, Equity, 1972–75; Governor, Bristol Old Vic Theatre Trust, 1975–84. *Recreations:* listening to music, reading, washing up, lying down and thinking what ought to be done in the garden. *Address:* c/o ICM Ltd, 388/396 Oxford Street, W1N 9HE. *T:* 01–629 8080. *Club:* Garrick.

EDDLEMAN, Gen. Clyde Davis; DSM with oak leaf cluster (US); Silver Star; Legion of Merit; Bronze Star; Philippines Distinguished Service Star; Vice-Chief of Staff, US Army, 1960–62; *b* 17 Jan. 1902; *s* of Rev. W. H. Eddleman and Janie Eddleman (*née* Tureman); *m* 1926, Lorraine Heath; one *s* (and one *s* decd). *Educ:* US Military Academy, West Point, New York. Commissioned 2nd Lieut of Infantry upon graduation from US Military Academy, 1924. Advanced, through the ranks, and reached grade of Gen. 1959. Comdr, Central Army Group (NATO), and C-in-C, US Army, Europe, at Heidelberg, Germany, 1959–60. Knight Commander's Cross, Order of Merit (Germany); Kt Grand Cross of the Sword (Sweden). *Recreations:* hunting, fishing. *Address:* 1101 S Arlington Ridge Road 802, Arlington, Va 22202, USA.

EDDY, Prof. Alfred Alan; Professor of Biochemistry, University of Manchester Institute of Science and Technology since 1959; *b* 4 Nov. 1926; Cornish parentage; *s* of late Alfred and Ellen Eddy; *m* 1954, Susan Ruth Slade-Jones; two *s*. *Educ:* Devonport High Sch.; Open scholarship Exeter Coll., Oxford, 1944; BA 1st Class Hons, 1949. ICI Research Fellow, 1950; DPhil 1951. Joined Brewing Industry Research Foundation, Nutfield, 1953. *Publications:* various scientific papers. *Address:* Larchfield, Buxton Road, Disley, Cheshire.

EDE, Jeffery Raymond, CB 1978; Keeper of Public Records, 1970–78; *b* 10 March 1918; *e s* of late Richard Arthur Ede; *m* 1944, Mercy, *d* of Arthur Radford Sholl; one *s* one *d*. *Educ:* Plymouth Coll.; King's Coll., Cambridge (MA). Served War of 1939–45, Intell. Corps (despatches); GSO2 HQ 8 Corps District, BAOR, 1945–46. Asst Keeper, Public Record Office, 1947–59; Principal Asst Keeper, 1959–66; Dep. Keeper, 1966–69. Lectr in Archive Admin., Sch. of Librarianship and Archives, University Coll., London, 1956–61; Unesco expert in Tanzania, 1963–64. Chm., British Acad. Cttee on Oriental Documents, 1972–78; Vice Pres., Internat. Council on Archives, 1976–78. Pres., Soc. of Archivists, 1974–77. FRHistS 1969. Hon. Mem., L'Institut Grand-Ducal de Luxembourg, 1977. Freeman: Goldsmiths' Company, 1979; City of London, 1979. *Publications:* Guide to the Contents of the Public Record Office, Vol. II (major contributor), 1963; articles in archival and other professional jls. *Recreations:* theatre, countryside. *Address:* Palfreys, East Street, Drayton, Langport, Som TA10 0JZ. *T:* Langport 251314.

EDEL, (Joseph) Leon; Citizens Professor of English, University of Hawaii, 1970–78, now Emeritus; *b* 9 Sept. 1907; *e s* of Simon Edel and Fanny (*née* Malamud), Pittsburgh, Pa; *m* 1st, 1935, Bertha Cohen (marr. diss. 1950); 2nd, 1950, Roberta Roberts (marr. diss. 1979); 3rd, 1980, Marjorie Sinclair; no *c*. *Educ:* McGill Univ., Montreal (BA 1927, MA 1928); Univ. of Paris (Docteur-ès-Lettres 1932). Served with US Army in France and Germany, 1943–47: Bronze Star Medal (US), 1945; Chief of Information Control, News Agency, US Zone, 1946–47. Asst Prof., Sir George Williams Coll., Montreal, 1932–34; miscellaneous writing and journalism, 1934–43; Christian Gauss Seminar in Criticism, Princeton Univ., 1951–52; New York University: Vis. Prof., 1952–53; Associate Prof., 1953–55; Prof. of English, 1955–66; Henry James Prof. of English and American Letters, 1966–72. Guggenheim Fellow, 1936–38, 1965–66; Alexander Lectures, Toronto, 1956; Vis. Professor: Indiana, 1954; Hawaii, 1955, 1969, 1970; Harvard, 1959–60; Purdue, 1970; Centenary Vis. Prof., Toronto, 1967; Vernon Vis. Prof. in Biography, Dartmouth, 1977. Pres., US Center of PEN, 1957–59. Pres., Hawaii Literary Arts Council, 1978–79. Fellow, Amer. Acad. of Arts and Sciences, 1959; Bollingen Fellow, 1959–61. Member: Nat. Inst. of Arts and Letters, 1964– (Sec., 1965–67); Amer. Acad. of Arts and Letters, 1972; Council, Authors' Guild, 1965–68 (Pres., 1969–70). FRSL 1970. Hon. Member: W. A. White Psychiatric Inst., 1966; Amer. Acad. Psychoanalysis, 1975. Hon. DLitt: McGill, 1963; Union Coll., Schenectady, 1963; Univ. of Saskatchewan, 1983. Nat. Inst. of Arts and Letters Award, 1959; US Nat. Book Award for non-fiction, 1963; Pulitzer Prize for biography, 1963; AAAL Gold Medal for biography, 1976; Hawaii Literary Arts Award, 1978; Nat. Arts Club Medal for Literature, 1981; Nat. Book Critics Circle Award (Biography), 1985. *Publications:* James Joyce: The Last Journey, 1947; (ed) The Complete Plays of Henry James, 1949; (with E. K. Brown) Willa Cather, 1953; The Life of Henry James: The Untried Years, 1953, The Conquest of London, 1962, The Middle Years, 1963, The Treacherous Years, 1969, The Master, 1972, rev. edn in 2 vols, 1978, rewritten, rev. into 1 vol., Henry James, a life, 1985; The Psychological Novel, 1955; (ed) Selected Letters of Henry James, 1956; Literary Biography, 1957; (with Dan H. Laurence) A Bibliography of Henry James, 1957; (ed) The Complete Tales of Henry James, 12 vols, 1962–65; (ed) The Diary of Alice James, 1964; (ed) Literary History and Literary Criticism, 1965; Thoreau, 1970; (ed) Henry James: Stories of the Supernatural, 1971; (ed) Harold Goddard Alphabet of the Imagination, 1975; (ed) Henry James Letters: vol. I, 1843–1875, 1975; vol. II, 1875–1883, 1980; vol. III, 1883–1895, 1981; vol. IV, 1895–1916, 1984; (ed) Edmund Wilson: The Twenties, 1975; Bloomsbury: A House of Lions, 1979; (ed) Edmund Wilson: The Thirties, 1980; Stuff of Sleep and Dreams (essays), 1982; (ed) Edmund Wilson: The Forties, 1983; Writing Lives: Principia Biographica, 1984; (ed) Edmund Wilson: The Fifties, 1986; (ed with Lyall H. Powers) The Complete Notebooks of Henry James, 1986. *Recreations:* music, swimming. *Address:* c/o William Morris Agency, 1350 Avenue of the Americas, New York, NY 10019, USA. *Clubs:* Athenæum; Century (New York).

EDELL, Stephen Bristow; Partner, Crossman Block and Keith (Solicitors), since 1983; *b* 1 Dec. 1932; *s* of late Ivan James Edell and late Hilda Pamela Edell; *m* 1958, Shirley Ross Collins; two *s* one *d*. *Educ:* St Andrew's Sch., Eastbourne; Uppingham. LLB London. Legal Mem., RTPI. Commnd RA, 1951. Articled to father, 1953; qual. Solicitor 1958; Partner, Knapp-Fishers (Westminster), 1959–75; Law Comr, 1975–83. Mem. Cttee, 1973–, Vice-Pres., 1980–82, Pres., 1982–83, City of Westminster Law Soc. Oxfam: Mem. Property Cttee, 1984–; Mem. Council, 1985–. Makers of Playing Cards' Company: Liveryman, 1955–; Mem., Ct of Assts, 1978–; Sen. Warden, 1980–81; Master, 1981–82. FRSA. *Publications:* Inside Information on the Family and the Law, 1969; The Family's Guide to the Law, 1974; articles in Conveyancer, Jl of Planning and Environmental Law, and newspapers. *Recreations:* family life; music, opera, theatre; early astronomical instruments; avoiding gardening; interested in problems of developing countries. *Address:* The Old Farmhouse, Twineham, Haywards Heath, Sussex. *T:* Hurstpierpoint 832058. *Club:* City Livery.

EDELMAN, Prof. Gerald Maurice, MD, PhD; Vincent Astor Distinguished Professor of Biochemistry, The Rockefeller University, New York, since 1974; *b* NYC, 1 July 1929; *s* of Edward Edelman and Anna Freedman; *m* 1950, Maxine Morrison; two *s* one *d*. *Educ:* Ursinus Coll. (BS); University of Pennsylvania (MD); The Rockefeller University (PhD). Med. Hse Officer, Massachusetts Gen. Hosp., 1954–55; Asst Physician, Hosp. of

The Rockefeller Univ., 1957–60; The Rockefeller University: Asst Prof. and Asst Dean of Grad. Studies, 1960–63; Associate Prof. and Associate Dean of Grad. Studies, 1963–66; Prof., 1966–74. Trustee, Rockefeller Brothers Fund, 1972–82; Associate, Neurosciences Res. Program, 1965– (Scientific Chm., 1980–; Dir, Neurosciences Inst., 1981–). Mem., Adv. Bd, Basel Inst. Immunology, 1970–77 (Chm., 1975–77); Mem., Bd Governors, Weizmann Inst. of Science, 1971–; non-resident Fellow and Mem. Bd Trustees, Salk Inst. for Biol. Studies, 1973–85; Member: Biophysics and Biophys. Chem. Study Section, Nat. Insts of Health, 1964–67; Sci. Council, Center for Theoretical Studies, 1970–72; Bd of Overseers, Faculty Arts and Scis, Univ. of Pa, 1976–83; Board of Trustees, Carnegie Inst. of Washington (Mem., Adv. Cttee). Member: Nat. Acad. Scis; Amer. Acad. Arts Scis; Amer. Philosophical Soc.; Fellow: NY Acad. Scis; NY Acad. of Medicine; Member: Amer. Soc. Biol Chemists; Amer. Assoc. Immunologists; Genetics Soc. of America; Harvey Soc. (Pres., 1975–76); Amer. Chem. Soc.; Amer. Soc. Cell Biol.; Soc. for Developmental Biol.; Sigma XI; Alpha Omega Alpha; Amer. Assoc. for the Advancement of Sci.; Council of Foreign Relations. Hon. Member: Pharmaceutical Soc. of Japan; Japanese Biochem. Soc.; Foreign Mem., Academie des Sciences, Institut de France. Spencer Morris Award, Univ. of Pennsylvania, 1954; Eli Lilly Award in Biol Chem., Amer. Chem. Soc., 1965; Annual Alumni Award, Ursinus College, 1969; (jtly) Nobel Prize in Physiology or Medicine, 1972; Albert Einstein Commemorative Award, Yeshiva Univ., 1974; Buchman Meml Award, Caltech, 1975; Rabbi Shai Shacknai Meml Prize in Immunology and Cancer Res., Hebrew Univ. Hadassah Med. Sch., 1977; Regents Medal of Excellence, New York State, 1984. Hon. DSc: Pennsylvania, 1973; Gustavus Adolphus Coll., Minn., 1975; Hon. ScD: Ursinus Coll., 1974; Williams Coll., 1976; Hon. MD Univ. Siena, Italy, 1974. *Recreation:* music. *Address:* Department of Developmental and Molecular Biology, The Rockefeller University, 1230 York Avenue, New York, NY 10021, USA.

EDEN, family name of **Barons Auckland, Eden of Winton** and **Henley.**

EDEN OF WINTON, Baron *cr* 1983 (Life Peer), of Rushyford in the County of Durham; **John Benedict Eden;** Bt (E) 1672 and Bt (GB) 1776; PC 1972; Chairman, Wonderworld plc; Deputy Chairman, Central & Sheerwood PLC (Chairman, 1984–85); Director: Associated Book Publishers PLC; Lady Eden's Schools Ltd; *b* 15 Sept. 1925; *s* of Sir Timothy Calvert Eden, 8th and 6th Bt and Patricia, *d* of Arthur Prendergast; *S* father, 1963; *m* 1st, 1958, Belinda Jane (marr. diss. 1974), *o d* of late Sir John Pascoe; two *s* two *d*; 2nd, 1977, Margaret Ann, Viscountess Strathallan. Lieut Rifle Bde, seconded to 2nd KEO Goorkha Rifles and Gilgit Scouts, 1943–47. Contested (C) Paddington North, 1953; MP (C) Bournemouth West, Feb. 1954–1983. Mem. House of Commons Select Cttee on Estimates, 1962–64; Vice-Chm., Conservative Parly Defence Cttee, 1963–66 (formerly: Chm., Defence Air Sub-Cttee; Hon. Sec., Space Sub-Cttee); Vice-Chm., Aviation Cttee, 1963–64; Additional Opposition Front Bench Spokesman for Defence, 1964–66; Jt Vice-Chm., Cons. Parly Trade and Power Cttee, 1966–68; Opposition Front Bench Spokesman for Power, 1968–70; Minister of State, Min. of Technology, June-Oct. 1970; Minister for Industry, DTI, 1970–72; Minister of Posts and Telecommunications, 1972–74; Mem., Expenditure Cttee, 1974–76; Chairman: House of Commons Select Cttee on European Legislation, 1976–79; Home Affairs Cttee, 1981–83. Vice-Chm., Assoc. of Conservative Clubs Ltd, 1964–67, Vice-Pres., 1970–; President: Wessex Area Council, Nat. Union of Conservative and Unionist Assocs, 1974–77; Wessex Area Young Conservatives, 1978–80. UK Deleg. to Council of Europe and to Western European Union, 1960–62; Mem., NATO Parliamentarians' Conf., 1962–66. Chm., Royal Armouries, 1986–. Pres., Independent Schs Assoc., 1969–71; a Vice-Pres., Nat. Chamber of Trade, 1974–86. Hon. Vice-Pres., Nat. Assoc. of Master Bakers, Confectioners & Caterers, 1978–82. *Heir* (to baronetcies only): *s* Hon. Robert Frederick Calvert Eden, *b* 30 April 1964. *Address:* 41 Victoria Road, W8; Knoyle Place, East Knoyle, Salisbury, Wilts. *Clubs:* Boodle's, Pratt's.

EDEN, Conrad W., TD; DMus Lambeth 1973; BMus Oxon; Hon. FRCO; retired 1974; *m* 1943, Barbara L., *d* of late Rev. R. L. Jones, Shepton Mallet. *Educ:* Wells Cath. Sch.; Rugby; RCM; St John's Coll., Oxford. Organist, Wells Cathedral, 1933–36; Durham Cathedral, 1936–74. *Address:* The Vale, Highmore Road, Sherborne, Dorset. *T:* Sherborne 813488.

EDEN, Edward Norman, CB 1980; Consultant; Under Secretary, Metrology, Quality Assurance, Safety and Standards Division, Department of Trade, retired 1982; *b* 5 Nov. 1921; *o s* of late Edward Eden and late Eva Eunice Eden; *m* 1st, 1967, Madge Nina Savory (*d* 1969); 2nd, 1974, Norma Veronica Berringer. *Educ:* Bancroft's Sch.; University Coll. London (BSc(Eng), PhD). Served RN, 1941–46. Senior Scientific Officer, Min. of Fuel and Power, 1953, Senior Principal Scientific Officer 1965, DCSO 1967–71; Head, Fuel Policy Planning Unit, Min. of Technology, later DTI, 1969–71; Under Sec., Metrology, Quality Assurance, Safety and Standards Div., DTI, later Dept of Prices and Consumer Protection, later Dept of Trade, 1971–81. Chairman: Working Party on Metrological Control Systems, 1976–77; Cttee on Metrological Control of Equipment for Use for Trade, 1984–85. *Publications:* Report, Metrological Control Systems, 1977; Report, Metrological Control of Equipment for Use for Trade, 1985; articles in learned jls. *Recreations:* walking, bird watching, odd-jobbing. *Address:* 13 Allison Grove, Dulwich, SE21 7ER. *T:* 01-693 7267.

EDEN, Prof. Richard John, OBE 1978; Professor of Energy Studies, since 1982 and Head of Energy Research Group, since 1974, Cavendish Laboratory, University of Cambridge; Fellow of Clare Hall, Cambridge, since 1966; Chairman, Cambridge Energy Research Ltd, since 1985; *b* 2 July 1922; *s* of James A. Eden and Dora M. Eden; *m* 1949, Elsie Jane Greaves; one *s* one *d* and one step *d*. *Educ:* Hertford Grammar Sch.; Peterhouse, Cambridge. BA 1943, MA 1948, PhD 1951. War service, 1942–46, Captain REME, Airborne Forces. Cambridge Univ.: Bye-Fellow, Peterhouse, 1949–50; Stokes Student, Pembroke Coll., 1950–51; Clare Coll.: Research Fellow, 1951–55; Official Fellow, 1957–66; Dir of Studies in Maths, 1951–53, 1957–62; Royal Soc. Smithson Res. Fellow, 1952–55; Mem., Princeton Inst. for Advanced Study, 1954, 1959, 1973; Sen. Lectr in Physics, Univ. of Manchester, 1955–57; Lectr in Maths, Univ. of Cambridge, 1957–64 (Stokes Lectr, 1962); Reader in Theoretical Physics, Cambridge, 1964–82; Head of High Energy Theoretical Physics Gp, Cavendish Lab., Cambridge, 1964–74; Vis. Scientist: Indiana Univ., 1954–55; Univ. of California, Berkeley, 1960, 1967; Vis. Professor: Univ. of Maryland, 1961, 1965; Columbia Univ., 1962; Scuola Normale Superiore, Pisa, 1964; Univ. of Marseilles, 1968; Univ. of California, 1969. Member: UK Adv. Council on Energy Conservation, 1974–83; Eastern Electricity Bd, 1985–; Energy Adviser to UK NEDO, 1974–75. Syndic, CUP, 1984–. Smiths Prize, Univ. of Cambridge, 1949; Maxwell Prize and Medal, Inst. of Physics, 1970. *Publications:* (jtly) The Analytic S Matrix, 1966; High Energy Collisions of Elementary Particles, 1967; Energy Conservation in the United Kingdom (NEDO report), 1975; Energy Prospects (Dept of Energy report), 1976; World Energy Demand to 2020 (World Energy Conf. report), 1977; (jtly) Energy Economics, 1981; (jtly) Electricity's Contribution to UK Energy Self Sufficiency, 1984; (jtly) UK Energy, 1984; papers and review articles on nuclear physics and theory of elementary particles. *Recreations:* painting, reading, gardening, travel. *Address:* Cavendish Laboratory, Cambridge. *T:* Cambridge 337231; 6 Wootton Way, Cambridge. *T:* Cambridge 355591.

EDES, (John) Michael, CMG 1981; HM Diplomatic Service; Head, UK Delegation to Conference on Security and Disarmament in Europe, Stockholm, since 1983; *b* 19 April 1930; *s* of late Lt-Col N. H. Edes and Mrs Louise Edes; *m* 1978, Angela Mermagen; two *s*. *Educ:* Blundell's Sch.; Clare Coll., Cambridge (Scholar; BA); Yale Univ. (MA). HM Forces, 1948–49; Mellon Fellow, Yale Univ., 1952–54; FO, 1954; MECAS, 1955; Dubai, 1956–57; FO, 1957–59 (Moscow, 1959); Rome, 1959–61; FO, 1961–62; UK Delegn to Conf. on Disarmament, Geneva, 1962–65 (UK Mission to UN, NY, 1963); FO, 1965–68; Cabinet Office, 1968–69; FCO, 1969–71; Ambassador to Yemen Arab Republic, 1971–73; Mem., UK Delegn to CSCE, Geneva, 1973–74; FCO, 1974–77; RIIA, 1977–78; Paris, 1978–79; Ambassador to Libya, 1980–83. *Recreations:* listening to music, gardening. *Address:* c/o Foreign and Commonwealth Office, SW1. *Clubs:* Athenæum; Hawks (Cambridge).

EDEY, Prof. Harold Cecil, BCom (London), FCA; Professor of Accounting, London School of Economics, University of London, 1962–80, now Emeritus; *b* 23 Feb. 1913; *s* of Cecil Edey and Elsie (*née* Walmsley); *m* 1944, Dilys Mary Pakeman Jones; one *s* one *d*. *Educ:* Croydon High Sch. for Boys; LSE. Chartered Accountant, 1935. Commnd in RNVR, 1940–46. Lectr in Accounting and Finance, LSE, 1949–55; Reader in Accounting, Univ. of London, 1955–62; Pro-Dir, LSE, 1967–70. Mem., UK Adv. Coun. on Educn for Management, 1961–65; Mem., Academic Planning Bd for London Grad. Sch. of Business Studies, and Governor, 1965–71; Chm., Arts and Social Studies Cttee, CNAA, 1965–71, and Mem. Council, 1965–73; Chm., Bd of Studies in Econs, 1966–71, Mem. Senate, 1975–80, University of London; Mem. Council, Inst. of Chartered Accountants in England and Wales, 1969–80. Hon. Freeman, 1981, Hon. Liveryman, 1986, Co. of Chartered Accountants in England and Wales. Hon. Professor, UCW, Aberystwyth, 1980–; Patron, Univ. of Buckingham, 1984–. Hon. LLD CNAA, 1972. Bard of the Cornish Gorsedd, 1933. *Publications:* (with A. T. Peacock) National Income and Social Accounting, 1954; Business Budgets and Accounts, 1959; Introduction to Accounting, 1963; (with B. S. Yamey and H. Thomson) Accounting in England and Scotland 1543–1800, 1963; (with B. V. Carsberg) Modern Financial Management, 1969; (with B. S. Yamey) Debits, Credits, Finance and Profits, 1974; (with L. H. Leigh) The Companies Act 1981, 1981; Accounting Queries, 1982; articles in various jls. *Address:* 10 The Green, Southwick, Brighton BN4 4DA.

EDGCUMBE, family name of **Earl of Mount Edgcumbe.**

EDGE, Geoffrey; New Initiatives Co-ordinator, COPEC Housing Trust, since 1984; *b* 26 May 1943; single. *Educ:* London Sch. of Econs (BA); Birmingham Univ. Asst Lectr in Geography, Univ. of Leicester, 1967–70; Lectr in Geog., Open Univ., 1970–74. Bletchley UDC, 1972–74 (Chm. Planning Sub-cttee 1973–74); Milton Keynes District Councillor, 1973–76 (Vice-Chm. Planning Cttee, 1973–75); Mem. Bucks Water Bd, 1973–74. MP (Lab) Aldridge-Brownhills, Feb. 1974–1979; PPS to Minister of State for Educn, Feb.-Oct. 1974, 1976–79, to Minister of State, Privy Council Office, Oct. 1974–76. Research Fellow, Dept of Planning Landscape, Birmingham Polytechnic, 1979–80; Senior Research Fellow: Preston Polytechnic, 1980–81; NE London Polytechnic, 1982–84. Hon. Res. Fellow, Birmingham Polytechnic, 1980–81. Chm., W Midlands Enterprise Bd; Member: W Midlands CC, 1981–86 (Chm., Econ. Develt Cttee); Walsall Met. Bor. Council, 1983– (Chm., Econ. Develt and Property Cttee). *Publications:* (ed jtly) Regional Analysis and Development, 1973; Open Univ. booklets on industrial location and urban development. *Recreations:* music, reading, touring. *Address:* 18 Harringworth Court, Lichfield Road, Shelfield, Walsall, W Midlands; 31 Dudley Road West, Tividale, Warley, W Midlands. *T:* 021-557 3858. *Club:* Walsall Wood Labour (Walsall).

EDGE, Maj.-Gen. Raymond Cyril Alexander, CB 1968; MBE 1945; FRICS 1949; FRGS; Director General, Ordnance Survey, 1965–69, retired; *b* 21 July 1912; *s* of Raymond Clive Edge and Mary (*née* Masters); *m* 1st, 1939, Margaret Patricia (*d* 1982), *d* of William Wallace McKee; one *s* one *d*; 2nd, 1983, Audrey Anne, *d* of Sir Lewis Richardson, 1st Bt, CBE, and *widow* of Jonathan Muers-Raby. *Educ:* Cheltenham Coll.; RMA; Caius Coll., Cambridge (BA). Commissioned in RE, 1932. Served in India, Royal Bombay Sappers and Miners and Survey of India, 1936–39. War Service in India, Burma (despatches), and Malaya. Lt-Col 1951; Col 1954; Dir (Brig.) Ordnance Survey, 1961; Maj.-Gen. 1965. Col Comdt, RE, 1970–75 (Representative Col Comdt, 1974). Mem., Sec. of State for the Environment's Panel of Independent Inspectors, 1971–82. Chairman: Assoc. British Geodesists, 1963–65; Geodesy Sub-Cttee, Royal Soc., 1968–75; Field Survey Assoc., 1968–70. Pres., Section E, British Assoc., 1969. Member: Council, RGS, 1966–69; Council, RICS, 1966–72 (Vice-Pres. 1970–72); Land Surveyors Council (Chm. 1970–72). *Publications:* contrib. A History of the Ordnance Survey, 1980; various papers on geodetic subjects in Bulletin Géodesique and other publications. *Recreation:* music. *Address:* Brook Farm, North Curry, near Taunton, Som TA3 6DJ. *T:* North Curry 490444. *Club:* Army and Navy.

EDGE, William, (3rd Bt *cr* 1937); *S* father, 1984. *Heir: s* Edward Knowles Edge. Does not use the title and his name is not on the Official Roll of Baronets.

EDGEWORTH-JOHNSTONE, Maj.-Gen. Ralph, CBE 1947; *b* 23 Nov. 1893; *s* of Ralph William Johnstone; *m* 1933, Cecily Margaret Thorp. *Educ:* France and Germany. Enlisted Fort Garry Horse, 1914; served European War, 1914–18 (wounded twice); commissioned Royal North'd Fusiliers, 1915. Retired, 1938, to join Public Relations Directorate War Office; Asst Dir, Lieut-Col, 1940; Dep. Dir, Brig., 1944; Dir, Maj.-Gen., 1946–52. *Address:* c/o Lloyds Bank, 6 Pall Mall, SW1.

EDGEWORTH JOHNSTONE, Robert; *see* Johnstone.

EDIE, His Honour Thomas Ker; a Circuit Judge, South Eastern Circuit, 1972–84; *b* 3 Oct. 1916; *s* of H. S. Ker Edie, Kinloss, Morayshire; *m* 1945, Margaret, *d* of Rev. A. E. Shooter, TD; four *s* one *d*. *Educ:* Clifton; London Univ. Called to Bar, Gray's Inn, 1941. Metropolitan Magistrate, 1961–70; Dep. Chm. Middlesex QS, 1970–71. *Address:* Worfield Lodge, Pennington Road, Southborough, Kent.

EDINBURGH, Bishop of, since 1986; **Rt. Rev. Richard Frederick Holloway;** *b* 26 Nov. 1933; *s* of Arthur and Mary Holloway; *m* 1963, Jean Elizabeth Kennedy, New York; one *s* two *d*. *Educ:* Kelham Theol Coll.; Edinburgh Theol Coll.; Union Theol Seminary, New York (STM); BD (London). Curate, St Ninian's, Glasgow, 1959–63; Priest-in-charge, St Margaret and St Mungo's, Glasgow, 1963–68; Rector, Old St Paul's, Edinburgh, 1968–80; Rector, Church of the Advent, Boston, Mass, USA, 1980–84; Vicar, St Mary Magdalen's, Oxford, 1984–86. *Publications:* Let God Arise, 1972; New Vision of Glory, 1974; A New Heaven, 1978; Beyond Belief, 1982; Signs of Glory, 1983; The Killing, 1984; (ed) The Anglican Tradition, 1984; Paradoxes of Christian Faith and Life, 1984; The Sidelong Glance, 1985; The Way of the Cross, 1986; Seven to Flee, Seven to Follow, 1987. *Recreations:* running, long-distance walking, reading, going to the cinema, listening to music. *Address:* 30 Kingsburgh Road, Murrayfield, Edinburgh. *T:* 031-337 7010.

EDINBURGH, Dean of; *see* Hardy, Very Rev. B. A.

EDINBURGH, (St Mary's Cathedral), Provost of; *see* Crosfield, Very Rev. G. P. C.

EDIS, Richard John Smale; HM Diplomatic Service; Counsellor, United Kingdom Disarmament Delegation, Geneva, since 1984; *b* 1 Sept. 1943; *s* of Denis Edis and Sylvia (*née* Smale); *m* 1971, Geneviève Cérisoles; three *s. Educ:* King Edward's Sch., Birmingham (schol.); St Catharine's Coll., Cambridge (Exhibnr; MA). British Centre, Stockholm, 1965–66; entered HM Diplomatic Service, 1966; FO, 1966–68; Third, later Second Sec., Nairobi, 1968–70; Second, later First Sec., Lisbon, 1971–74; FCO, 1974–77; First Sec., UK Mission to UN, New York, 1977–80; Asst Head of Southern African Dept, FCO, 1981–82; Counsellor 1982; on secondment to Home CS, 1982–84. Officer, Military Order of Christ, Portugal, 1973. *Recreations:* sport, reading. *Address:* c/o Foreign and Commonwealth Office, SW1A 2AH. *Club:* Travellers'.

EDMENSON, Sir Walter Alexander, Kt 1958; CBE 1944; DL; shipowner; *b* 1892; 2nd *s* of late Robert Robson Edmenson; *m* 1918, Doris Davidson (*d* 1975); one *d* (and one *s* killed in action, 1940). Served European War, 1914–18, RFA (despatches). Min. of War Transport Rep., N Ireland, 1939–45. President: The Ulster Steamship Co. Ltd; G. Heyn & Sons Ltd; Director: Clyde Shipping Co.; The Belfast Banking Co. Ltd, 1946–70; The North Continental Shipping Co. Ltd, 1946–70; The Belfast Bank Executor & Trustee Co. Ltd, 1946–70; Commercial Insurance Co. of Ireland Ltd, 1964–72; Member Board: BEA, 1946–63; Gallaher Ltd, 1946–66. Chm., N Ireland Civil Aviation Adv. Council, 1946–61; Member: Bd, Ulster Transport Authority, 1948–64; Council, Chamber of Shipping, 1943–73; Lloyd's Register of Shipping, 1949–74; Belfast Harbour Comr, 1940–61; Irish Lights Comr. DL Belfast, 1951. Amer. Medal of Freedom with Palms, 1945. *Address:* 101 Bryansford Road, Newcastle, Co. Down. *T:* Newcastle (Co. Down) 22769.

EDMOND, Prof. John Marmion, PhD; FRS 1986; Professor of Marine Geochemistry, Massachusetts Institute of Technology, since 1970; *b* 27 April 1943; *s* of Andrew John Shields Edmond and late Christina Marmion Edmond; *m* 1978, Massoudeh Vafai; one *s. Educ:* Univ. of Glasgow (BSc 1st class Hons, Pure Chemistry, 1965); Univ. of California at San Diego, Scripps Instn of Oceanography (PhD, Marine Chemistry, 1970). Massachusetts Institute of Technology: Asst Prof., 1970; Associate Prof., 1975; Full Prof., 1981. Mackelwane Award, Amer. Geophysical Union, 1976. *Publications:* over 80 scientific papers in professional jls. *Recreations:* reading, gardening. *Address:* 21 Robin Hood Road, Arlington, Mass 02174, USA. *T:* 617 253 5739.

EDMONDS, Charles; *see* Carrington, C. E.

EDMONDS, David Albert; Chief Executive, Housing Corporation, since 1984; *b* 6 March 1944; *s* of Albert and Gladys Edmonds; *m* 1966, Ruth Beech; two *s* two *d. Educ:* Helsby County Grammar School; University of Keele. BA Hons Political Institutions and History. Asst Principal, Min. of Housing and Local Govt, 1966–69; Private Sec. to Parly Sec., MHLG and DoE, 1969–71; Principal, DoE, 1971–73; Observer, CSSB, 1973–74; Vis. Fellow, Centre for Metropolitan Planning and Research, Johns Hopkins Univ., 1974–75; Private Sec. to Perm. Sec., DoE, 1975–77; Asst Sec., DoE, 1977–79; Principal Private Sec. to Sec. of State, DoE, 1979–83; Under Sec., Inner Cities Directorate, DoE, 1983–84. Mem., Exec. Cttee, Internat. New Town Assoc., 1983–. Chm., New Society, 1986–; Mem. Editl Adv. Bd, Building, 1986–87. *Recreations:* films, cricket, walking, visiting France, golf. *Address:* 61 Cottenham Park Road, West Wimbledon, SW20 0DR. *T:* 01–946 3729. *Clubs:* Wimbledon Park Golf; Wimbledon Wanderers Cricket.

EDMONDS, John Christopher, CMG 1978; CVO 1971; HM Diplomatic Service, retired; *b* 23 June 1921; *s* of late Captain A. C. M. Edmonds, OBE, RN, and late Mrs. Edmonds; *m* 1st, 1948, Elena Tornow (marr. diss., 1965); two *s*; 2nd, 1966, Armine Williams. *Educ:* Kelly College. Entered Royal Navy, 1939; psc, 1946. Staff: of NATO Defence Coll., Paris, 1953–55; of C-in-C Home Fleet, 1956–57 (Comdr, 1957); of Chief of Defence Staff, 1958–59. Entered Diplomatic Service, 1959; Foreign Office, 1959–60; 1st Secretary (Commercial), Tokyo, 1960–62; FO, 1963–67; 1st Secretary and Head of Chancery, Ankara, 1967–68; Counsellor: Ankara, 1968–71; Paris, 1972–74; Head of Arms Control and Disarmament Dept, FCO, 1974–77; Leader, UK Delegn to Comprehensive Test Ban Treaty Negotiations, Geneva, with personal rank of Ambassador, 1978–81. Vis. Fellow in Internat. Relations, Reading Univ., 1981–. *Recreations:* golf, gardening, travel. *Address:* North Lodge, Sonning, Berks RG4 0ST. *Club:* Army and Navy.

EDMONDS, John Walter; General Secretary, General, Municipal, Boilermakers and Allied Trade Union (formerly General and Municipal Workers' Union), since 1986; *b* 28 Jan. 1944; *s* of Walter and Rose Edmonds; *m* 1967, Linden (*née* Callaby); two *d. Educ:* Brunswick Park Primary; Christ's Hosp.; Oriel Coll., Oxford (BA 1965, MA 1968). General and Municipal Workers' Union: Res. Asst, 1966; Dep. Res. Officer, 1967; Reg. Officer, 1968; Nat. Industrial Officer, 1972. Dir, National Building Agency, 1978–82. Mem., Royal Commn on Environmental Pollution, 1979–. Gov., LSE, 1986–. *Recreations:* carpentry, cabinet making. *Address:* 50 Graham Road, Mitcham, Surrey. *T:* 01–648 9991.

EDMONDS, Robert Humphrey Gordon, CMG 1969; MBE 1944; HM Diplomatic Service, retired; *b* 5 Oct. 1920; *s* of late Air Vice-Marshal C. H. K. Edmonds, CBE, DSO; *m* 1st, 1951, Georgina Combe (marr. diss.); four *s*; 2nd, 1976, Mrs Enid Balint, *widow of* Dr Michael Balint. *Educ:* Ampleforth; Brasenose Coll., Oxford. Pres., Oxford Union, 1940. Served Army, 1940–46; attached to Political Div., Allied Commn for Austria, 1945–46. Entered Foreign Service, Dec. 1946; served Cairo, 1947; FO, 1949; Rome, 1953; Warsaw, 1957; FO, 1959; Caracas, 1962; FO, CO and FCO, 1966–69; Minister, Moscow, 1969–71; High Comr, Nicosia, 1971–72; Vis. Fellow, Glasgow Univ., 1973–74; Asst Under Sec. of State, FCO, 1974–77; Fellow, Woodrow Wilson Internat. Centre for Scholars, Washington, 1977; retd 1978. Adviser, Kleinwort Benson, 1978–83. *Publications:* Soviet Foreign Policy: the Brezhnev years, 1983; Setting the Mould: the United States and Britain 1945–1950, 1986. *Address:* 43 North Road, Highgate Village, N6; Hill Cottage, Street, Som. *Club:* Turf.

EDMONDS, Sheila May, MA, PhD; Fellow, and Lecturer in Mathematics, Newnham College, Cambridge, 1945–82 (Vice-Principal, 1960–81); Fellow Emerita, Newnham College, since 1982; *b* 1 April 1916; *d* of Harold Montagu Edmonds and Florence Myra Edmonds. *Educ:* Wimbledon High Sch.; Newnham Coll., Cambridge. Research Student of Westfield Coll., 1939–40, and of Newnham Coll., 1940–41; Research Fellow of Newnham Coll., 1941–43; Asst Lecturer, Newnham Coll., 1943–45. *Publications:* papers in mathematical journals. *Recreations:* travel, photography. *Address:* 5 Cross Lane Close, Orwell, Royston, Herts SG8 5QW. *T:* Cambridge 207789.

EDMONDS, Winston Godward, CBE 1966; ERD 1945; Managing Director, Manchester Ship Canal Co., 1961–70; *b* 27 Nov. 1912; *s* of Wilfred Bell Edmonds and Nina (*née* Godward); *m* 1940, Sheila Mary (*née* Armitage); one *s. Educ:* Merchant Taylors'. Joined LNER, first as traffic apprentice and then in various positions, 1930–46; Manchester Ship Canal Co.: Commercial Manager, 1947–58; Manager, 1959–61. *Recreations:* golf, philately. *Address:* Herons Wood, 22 Castlegate, Prestbury, Cheshire SK10 4AZ. *T:* Prestbury 828966.

EDMONDSON, family name of Baron Sandford.

EDMONDSON, Anthony Arnold; His Honour Judge Edmondson; a Circuit Judge (formerly County Court Judge and Commissioner, Liverpool and Manchester Crown Courts), since 1971; *b* 6 July 1920; *s* of late Arnold Edmondson; *m* 1947, Dorothy Amelia Wilson, Gateshead-on-Tyne; three *s* one *d. Educ:* Liverpool Univ. (LLB Hons); Lincoln Coll., Oxford (BCL Hons). Served RA (Adjutant), 1940–44; RAF (Pilot), 1944–46; thereafter RA (TA) and TARO. Called to the Bar, Gray's Inn, 1947; William Shaw Schol. 1948; practised on Northern Circuit, 1948–71; Chairman, Liverpool Dock Labour Bd Appeal Tribunal, 1955–66; Mem. Court of Liverpool Univ., 1960–. Dep. Chm., Lancashire QS, 1970–71; Pres., S Cumbria Magistrates' Assoc., 1977–; JP Lancs, 1970. *Recreations:* walking, fishing. *Address:* County Sessions House, Preston, Lancs.

EDMONDSON, Leonard Firby; Executive Council Member, Amalgamated Union of Engineering Workers, 1966–77; *b* 16 Dec. 1912; *s* of Arthur William Edmondson and Elizabeth Edmondson; unmarried. *Educ:* Gateshead Central Sch. Served apprenticeship as engr, Liner Concrete Machinery Co. Ltd, Newcastle upon Tyne, 1929–34; worked in a number of engrg, ship-bldg and ship-repairing firms; shop steward and convener of shop stewards in several firms. AUEW: Mem., Tyne Dist Cttee, 1943–53; Tyne Dist Sec., 1953–66. CSEU: Mem., Exec. Council, 1966–78; Pres., 1976–77. Member: Shipbldg Industry Trng Bd, 1966–79; Council, ACAS, 1976–78; Royal Commn on Legal Services, 1976–79; Council on Tribunals, 1978–84; Cttee of Inquiry into Prison Services, 1978–79; Gen. Council of TUC, 1970–78. Mem., Birtley Canine Soc. *Recreation:* exhibiting Shetland sheep dogs. *Address:* 6 Kenwood Gardens, Low Fell, Gateshead, Tyne and Wear NE9 6PN. *T:* Low Fell 4879167. *Clubs:* Northern Counties Shetland Sheep Dog; Manors Social (Newcastle-upon-Tyne).

EDMONSTONE, Sir Archibald (Bruce Charles), 7th Bt *cr* 1774; *b* 3 Aug. 1934; *o* surv. *s* of Sir Charles Edmonstone, 6th Bt, and Gwendolyn Mary, *d* of late Marshall Field and Mrs Maldwin Drummond; *S* father, 1954; *m* 1st, 1957, Jane (marr. diss. 1967), *er d* of Maj.-Gen. E. C. Colville, CB, DSO; two *s* one *d*; 2nd, 1969, Juliet Elizabeth, *d* of Maj.-Gen. C. M. F. Deakin, *qv*; one *s* one *d. Educ:* St Peter's Court; Stowe Sch. *Heir: s* Archibald Edward Charles Edmonstone, *b* 4 Feb. 1961. *Address:* Duntreath Castle, Blanefield, Stirlingshire.

See also Sir A. R. J. B. Jardine, Captain Sir C. E. McGrigor.

EDMONTON, Area Bishop of, since 1984; **Rt. Rev. Brian John Masters;** *b* 17 Oct. 1932; *s* of Stanley William and Grace Hannah Masters; unmarried. *Educ:* Collyers School, Horsham; Queens' Coll., Cambridge (MA 1955); Cuddesdon Theological Coll. Lloyds broker, 1955–62. Asst Curate, S Dunstan and All Saints, Stepney, 1964–69; Vicar, Holy Trinity with S Mary, Hoxton, N1, 1969–82; Bishop Suffragan of Fulham, 1982–84. Chm. Exec. Cttee, Church Union, 1984–. *Recreations:* theatre, squash. *Address:* 13 North Audley Street, W1Y 1WF. *T:* 01-629 3891. *Club:* United Oxford & Cambridge University.

EDMONTON (Alberta), Archbishop of, (RC), since 1973; **Most Rev. Joseph Neil MacNeil;** *b* 15 April 1924; *s* of John Martin MacNeil and Kate MacNeil (*née* MacLean). *Educ:* St Francis Xavier Univ., Antigonish, NS (BA 1944); Holy Heart Seminary, Halifax, NS; Univs of Perugia, Chicago and St Thomas Aquinas, Rome (JCD 1958). Priest, 1948; pastor, parishes in NS, 1948–55; Chancery Office, Antigonish, 1958–59; admin. dio. Antigonish, 1959–60; Rector, Antigonish Cathedral, 1961; Dir of Extension Dept, St Francis Xavier Univ., Antigonish, 1961–69; Vice-Pres., 1962–69; Bishop of St John, NB, 1969–73. Pres., Canadian Conf. of Catholic Bishops, 1979–81 (Vice-Pres., 1977–79). Chancellor, Univ. of St Thomas, Fredericton, NB, 1969. Founding Mem., Inst. for Res. on Public Policy, 1968–80; Mem., Bd of Dirs, The Futures Secretariat, 1981–. *Address:* 10044 113th Street, Edmonton, Alberta T5K 1N8, Canada.

EDMONTON (Alberta), Bishop of, since 1980; **Rt. Rev. Edwin Kent Clarke,** DD. *Educ:* Bishop's Univ., Lennoxville (BA 1954, LST 1956); Union Seminary, NY (MRE 1960); Huron Coll., Ontario (DD). Deacon 1956, priest 1957, Ottawa. Curate of All Saints, Westboro, 1956–59; Director of Christian Education, Diocese of Ottawa, 1960–66; Rector of St Lambert, Montreal, 1966–73; Diocesan Sec., Diocese of Niagara, 1973–76; Archdeacon of Niagara, 1973–76; Bishop Suffragan of Niagara, 1976–79. *Address:* 10033 84th Avenue, Edmonton, Alberta T6E 2G6, Canada.

EDMUND-DAVIES, family name of Baron Edmund-Davies.

EDMUND-DAVIES, Baron *cr* 1974 (Life Peer), of Aberpennar, Mid Glamorgan; **Herbert Edmund Edmund-Davies,** PC 1966; Kt 1958; a Lord of Appeal; Life Governor and Fellow, King's College, London University; Hon. Fellow, Exeter College, Oxford; *b* 15 July 1906; 3rd *s* of Morgan John Davies and Elizabeth Maud Edmunds; *m* 1935, Eurwen Williams-James; three *d. Educ:* Mountain Ash Grammar Sch.; King's Coll., London; Exeter Coll., Oxford. LLB (London) and Postgraduate Research Scholar, 1926; LLD London, 1928; BCL (Oxon) and Vinerian Scholar, 1929; called to Bar, Gray's Inn, 1929; QC 1943; Bencher, 1948; Treasurer, 1965; Lecturer and Examiner, London School of Economics, 1930–31; Army Officers' Emergency Reserve, 1938; Infantry OCTU; commissioned in Royal Welch Fusiliers, 1940; Lt-Col; later seconded to JAG's Dept; Asst Judge Advocate-General, 1944–45; Recorder of Merthyr Tydfil, 1942–44; of Swansea, 1944–53; of Cardiff, 1953–58; Chm., QS for Denbighshire, 1953–64; Judge of High Court of Justice, Queen's Bench Division, 1958–66; a Lord Justice of Appeal, 1966–74; a Lord of Appeal in Ordinary, 1974–81; Foreign Office Observer, Cairo espionage trials, 1957. Chairman: Transport Users' Consultative Cttee for Wales, 1959–61; Lord Chancellor's Cttee on Limitation of Actions, 1961; Tribunal of Inquiry into Aberfan Disaster, 1966; Council of Law Reporting 1967–72; Home Secretary's Criminal Law Revision Cttee, 1969–77; Home Sec's Police Inquiry Cttee, 1977–79. Mem., Royal Commn on Penal Reform, 1964–66. President: London Welsh Trust/London Welsh Assoc., 1982–; University College of Swansea, 1965–75; Hon. Standing Counsel, Univ. of Wales, 1947–57; Pro-Chancellor, Univ. of Wales, 1975–85. Hon. Life Member, Canadian Bar Assoc.; CIBA Foundn Trustee; Fellow, Royal Soc. of Medicine. Hon. LLD Wales, 1959. *Publications:* Law of Distress for Rent and Rates, 1931; miscellaneous legal writings. *Address:* House of Lords, SW1; 5 Gray's Inn Square, WC1. *Clubs:* Reform; Cardiff and County (Cardiff); City (Chester); Bristol Channel Yacht.

EDMUNDS, Christopher Montague, MusD; *b* 26 Nov. 1899; 2nd *s* of Charles Edmunds; *m* 1923, Kathleen, *d* of Arthur Vaughan-Jones; one *s* one *d. Educ:* King Edward VI Sch., Camp Hill, Birmingham; Birmingham Univ.; Manchester Univ.; Birmingham Sch. of Music. 1st Cl. Hons BMus Birmingham, 1922; MusD, Manchester, 1936. Theory Teacher and Dir of opera class, Birmingham Sch. of Music, 1928–45; Principal, Birmingham Sch. of Music, 1945–56; Fellow Birmingham Sch. of Music; Fellow Trinity Coll. of Music (Mem. Corp. and Examiner, 1940–78). *Publications:* compositions include: The Blue Harlequin (opera); chamber and orchestral music; vocal and instrumental music; Romance, 1946 (pianoforte and orchestral work, commissioned by BBC). *Recreation:* gardening. *Address:* Tanyard Cottage, Stonegate, Whixley, N Yorks. *T:* Green Hammerton 30766.

EDNAM, Viscount; William Humble David Jeremy Ward; *b* 27 March 1947; *s* and *heir* of Earl of Dudley, *qv* and of Stella Viscountess Ednam, *d* of M. A. Carcano, KCMG, KBE; *m* 1st, 1972, Sarah (marr. diss. 1976), *o d* of Sir Alastair Coats, Bt, *qv*; 2nd, 1976, Debra Louise (marr. diss. 1980), *d* of George Robert and Marjorie Elvera Pinney; one *d*. *Educ:* Eton; Christ Church, Oxford. *Address:* Rowlandson Ground, near Coniston, Cumbria. *T:* Coniston 397.

EDWARD, David Alexander Ogilvy, CMG 1981; QC (Scotland) 1974; Salvesen Professor of European Institutions, University of Edinburgh, since 1985; *b* 14 Nov. 1934; *s* of J. O. C. Edward, Travel Agent, Perth; *m* 1962, Elizabeth Young McSherry; two *s* two *d*. *Educ:* Sedbergh Sch.; University Coll., Oxford; Edinburgh Univ. Sub-Lt RNVR (Nat. Service); HMS Hornet, 1956–57. Admitted Advocate, 1962; Clerk of Faculty of Advocates, 1967–70, Treasurer, 1970–77. Trustee, Nat. Library of Scotland, 1966–; Pres., Consultative Cttee of Bars and Law Societies, EEC, 1978–80; Mem. Law Adv. Cttee, British Council; Specialist Advr, H of L Select Cttee on EC, 1985 and 1986. Distinguished Cross, First Class, Order of St Raymond of Penafort, Spain, 1979. *Publications:* The Professional Secret, Confidentiality and Legal Professional Privilege in the EEC, 1976; (with P. A. Leach) Guide to the Legal Profession in Europe; articles in legal jls. *Address:* Centre of European Governmental Studies, Old College, South Bridge, Edinburgh EH8 9YL; 32 Heriot Row, Edinburgh EH3 6ES; Ardargie Cottage, Forgandenny, Perth PH2 9DJ.*Clubs:* Athenæum; New (Edinburgh).

EDWARDES, family name of **Baron Kensington.**

EDWARDES, Sir Michael (Owen), Kt 1979; Non-Executive Chairman, since 1982, and acting Chief Executive, since 1985, Chloride Group PLC; Chairman, Stabilization Ltd, since 1984; Non-Executive Director: Hill Samuel Group PLC, since 1980; Standard Securities, since 1984; Minerals and Resources Corp., since 1984; Director, Gooding Group Ltd, since 1983; *b* 11 Oct. 1930; *s* of Denys Owen Edwardes and Audrey Noel (*née* Copeland); *m* 1958, Mary Margaret (*née* Finlay); three *d*. *Educ:* St Andrew's Coll., Grahamstown, S Africa; Rhodes Univ., Grahamstown (BA; Hon. LLD). Employed Chloride Group Ltd, 1951–81; Chm., 1974–77; non-exec. Dep. Chm., 1977–82; Chm. and Chief Exec., BL Ltd (formerly British Leyland), 1977–82; Chairman: Mercury Communications Ltd, 1982–83; ICL PLC, 1984; Chm. and Chief Exec., Dunlop Hldgs, 1984–85. Non-Exec. Dir, Internat. Management Develt Inst., Washington, 1978–. Member: CBI Council, 1974–81; CBI President's Cttee, 1981–; Nat. Enterprise Bd, 1975–77; Queen's Award for Industry Review Cttee, 1975. CBIM (a Vice-Chm., 1977–80); Pres., Comité des Constructeurs d'Automobiles du Marché Commun (CCMC), 1979–80. Hon. FIMechE, 1981. *Publication:* Back From the Brink, 1983. *Recreations:* sailing, squash, water ski-ing, tennis. *Address:* Chloride Group PLC, 52 Grosvenor Gardens, SW1W 0AU. *Clubs:* Royal Automobile; Jesters; Rand (Johannesburg).

EDWARDES JONES, Air Marshal (Retd) Sir (John) Humphrey, KCB 1957 (CB 1954); CBE 1943; DFC 1940; AFC 1941; retired 1961; *b* 15 Aug. 1905; *s* of late G. M. Edwardes Jones, KC and G. R. Johnston; *m* 1935, Margaret Rose Graham; one *s* one *d*. *Educ:* Brighton Coll.; Pembroke Coll., Cambridge. Entered RAF, Sept. 1926; served in Egypt, 4 Flying Training Sch. and 208 Sqdn, 1930–35; Commanded: No 213 Fighter Sqdn, 1937–40; No 56 Op. Trg Unit, 1940; Nos 60 and 58 OTU's, 1941; Exeter Fighter Sector, 1942; No 323 Fighter Wing, Algiers, Nov. 1942; AOC, No 210 Group, Algiers, 1943; idc 1950; Dir of Plans, Air Ministry, 1951. Commandant, Sch. of Land/Air Warfare, RAF, Old Sarum, Wilts, 1955–57; Comdr-in-Chief, 2nd Tactical Air Force, and Comdr, 2nd Allied Tactical Air Force, 1957–61. Legion of Honour (French), 1946. *Recreation:* golf. *Address:* Old Marks, Holtye, Sussex TN8 7ED. *T:* Cowden 317. *Club:* Royal Air Force.

EDWARDS, family name of **Baron Chelmer.**

EDWARDS, (Alfred) Kenneth, MBE 1963; Deputy Director-General, Confederation of British Industry, since 1982; *b* 24 March 1926; *s* of late Ernest Edwards and Florence Edwards (*née* Branch); *m* 1949, Jeannette Lilian, *d* of David Speeks, MBE; one *s* two *d*. *Educ:* Latymer Upper Sch.; Magdalene Coll., Cambridge; University Coll. London (BScEcon). Served RAF, 1944–47; RAF Coll., Cranwell, 1945, FO (Pilot). Entered HMOCS, Nigeria, 1952; Provincial Administration, Warri and Benin, 1952–54; Lagos Secretariat, 1954; Sen. Asst Sec., Nigerian Min. of Communications and Aviation, 1959; retired, 1962. Secretary, British Radio Equipment Manufrs' Assoc., 1962; Gp Marketing Manager, Thorn Elec. Industries Ltd, 1965; Internat. Dir, Brookhirst Igranic Ltd (Thorn Gp), 1967; Gp Marketing Dir, Cutler Hammer Europa, 1972; Dep. Chm., BEAMA Overseas Trade Cttee, 1973; Chief Exec., BEAMA, 1976–82. CBI: Member: Council, 1974, 1976–82; Finance and Gen. Purposes Cttee, 1977–82; Vice-Chm., Eastern Reg. Council, 1974; Chm., Working Party on Liability for Defective Products, 1978–82; Mem., President's Cttee, 1979–82. Member: Elec. Engrg EDC, 1976; Council, Elec. Res. Assoc. Ltd, 1976–82; Exec. Cttee, Organisme de Liaison des Industries Metalliques Européennes (ORGALIME), 1976–82; BSI Bd, 1978–82, 1984– (Chm., British Electrotechnical Cttee and Electrotechnical Divisional Council, 1981–); BOTB, 1982–; Salvation Army Adv. Bd (London), 1982–; BTEC, 1983–; BBC Consultative Gp on Indust. and Business Affairs, 1983 ; President: Eur. Cttee for Electrotechnical Standardisation (CENELEC), 1977–79; Liaison Cttee for Electrical and Electronic Industries, ORGALIME, 1979–82 (Chm., 1980–82); Mem. Exec. Cttee, 1982–, and Chm. Finance Cttee, 1983–, Union des Industries de la Communauté Européenne (UNICE). Mem. Court, Cranfield Inst. of Technol., 1970–75. FRSA 1985. *Publications:* contrib. technical jls; lectures and broadcasts on industrial subjects. *Recreations:* music, books, walking. *Address:* Confederation of British Industry, Centre Point, 103 New Oxford Street, WC1. *Clubs:* Athenæum, Royal Automobile, Royal Air Force.

EDWARDS, Andrew John Cumming; Under Secretary, European Community Group, HM Treasury, since 1985; *b* 3 Nov. 1940; *s* of John Edwards and Norah Hope Edwards (*née* Bevan); *m* 1969, Charlotte Anne Chilcot (separated 1985); one *s* two *d*. *Educ:* Fettes Coll., Edinburgh; St John's Coll., Oxford (MA); Harvard Univ. (AM, MPA). Asst master, Malvern Coll., 1962–63; HM Treasury: Asst Principal, 1963–67; Pvte Sec. to Jt Perm. Sec., 1966–67; Principal, 1967–75; Harkness Fellow, Harvard Univ., 1971–73; Asst Sec., 1975–83; RCDS, 1979; Asst Sec., DES, 1983–85. Gov., British Inst. of Recorded Sound, 1974–79; Sec., Develt Bd, Royal Opera House, 1984–. Conductor, Acad. of St Mary's, Wimbledon, 1981–. *Publications:* Nuclear Weapons, the balance of terror, the quest for peace, 1986; articles on European Community Budget. *Recreations:* music, writing, reading, walking. *Address:* 15 Highbury Road, SW19 7PR. *T:* 01–946 7312.

EDWARDS, Brig. Arthur Bertie Duncan, CBE 1943; MC; *b* 29 April 1898; *s* of Joseph Arthur Edwards, Portsmouth, and Rosa May Duncan, Isle of Wight; *m* 1925, Clara Elizabeth, 3rd *c* of late Edmund Barkworth, JP, Seaton, Devon; three *s*. *Educ:* RMA Woolwich. 2nd Lieut RE 1916; Capt. 1926; Major 1935; Lt-Col 1942; Temp. Col 1943, Temp. Brig. 1943; Col 1945; Brig. 1949. Served France, 1917–18 (BWM and VM); India, 1918–19; Iraq, 1919–20 (MC, BGS with Iraq clasp); India, 1920–22; England, 1922–35; Malta, 1935–39; England, 1939–40; France, 1940 (despatches); Greece, 1940–41; Libya, 1941; CRE Eighth Army Troops Engineers, Libya and Egypt, 1941–42 (despatches twice, OBE, North African Star); Dep. Chief Engineer, N Delta Defences, Egypt, 1942; Chief Engineer, Malta, 1942–43 (CBE); Chief Engineer, British Troops in Egypt, 1943; No 13 CE Works (Construction), Middle East, 1943–44; Engineer Adviser, AA Command, England, 1944; Dep. Dir Works 21 Army Group BLA and BAOR, 1944–48 (despatches; Kt Comdr of Orange-Nassau with swords); Chief Engineer, Eastern Command, United Kingdom, 1948–51; retired, 1951. *Address:* c/o Lloyds Bank, 6 Pall Mall, SW1.

EDWARDS, Arthur Frank George; Vice-Chairman, Thames Water Authority, 1973–83; *b* 27 March 1920; *o s* of Arthur Edwards and Mabel (Elsie) Edwards; *m* 1946, Joyce May Simmons; one *s* one *d*. *Educ:* West Ham Grammar Sch.; Garnett Coll., London; West Ham Coll. of Technology. CEng, FIChemE, MSE; Hon. FIWM. Various posts with Ever Ready (GB) Ltd, 1936–50; Prodn Man., J. Burns & Co. Ltd, 1950–53; various lectrg posts, 1954–65; Organiser for science and techn. subjects, London Boroughs of Barking and Redbridge, 1965–82. Member: West Ham Co. Borough Council, 1946–65; Newham Council, 1964–86 (Mayor, 1967–68); GLC, 1964–86 (Dep. Chm., 1970–71; Chm., Public Services Cttee, 1973–77); Chm. of Governors, NE London Polytechnic, 1972–. Mem., Fabian Soc. *Recreations:* reading, Association football (watching West Ham United). *Address:* 18 Wanstead Park Avenue, E12 5EN. *T:* 01–633 5086. *Club:* West Ham Supporters'.

EDWARDS, Brian; Regional General Manager, Trent Regional Health Authority, since 1984; *b* 19 Feb. 1942; *s* of John Albert Edwards and Ethel Edwards; *m* 1964, Jean (*née* Cannon); two *s* two *d*. *Educ:* Wirral Grammar Sch. Jun. Administrator, Clatterbridge Hosp., 1958–62; Dep. Hosp. Sec., Cleaver Hosp., 1962–64; National Trainee, Nuffield Centre, Leeds, 1964–66; Administrator, Gen. Infirmary, Leeds, 1966–67; Hosp. Sec., Keighley Victoria Hosp., 1967–68; Administrator, Mansfield HMC, 1969–70; Lectr, Univ. of Leeds, 1970–72; Dep. Gp Sec., Hull A HMC, 1972–74; Dist Administrator, Leeds AHA(T), 1974–76; Area Administrator, Cheshire AHA, 1976–81; Regional Administrator, Trent RHA, 1981–84. Vis. Lectr, Health Care Studies, Univ. of Leeds, 1973–. Adviser to WHO, 1982–; Chairman: NHS Manpower Planning Adv. Gp, 1983–86; Regional Gen. Managers Gp, 1986 . Dir, Mercia Publications Ltd. Inst. of Health Service Administrators: Mem., 1964–; Pres., 1982–83; Mem. Editorial Cttee, Health Care in the UK: its organisation and management, 1982–. Jt Editor, Health Services Manpower Review, 1970–. *Publications:* Si Vis Pacem—preparations for change in the NHS, 1973; Profile for Change, 1973; Bridging in Health, Planning the Child Health Services, 1975; Industrial Relations in the NHS: managers and industrial relations, 1979; Manpower Planning in the NHS, 1984; Employment Policies for Health Care, 1985; conf. papers presented in UK, Norway, Germany, USA, India and USSR; contrib. prof. jls. *Recreations:* golf, stage management. *Address:* 3 Royal Croft Drive, Baslow, Derbyshire DE4 1SN. *T:* Baslow 3459.

EDWARDS, Charles Harold, FRCP; Dean of St Mary's Hospital, Paddington, 1973–79; *b* 1913; *m* 1959; one *s* two *d*. *Educ:* Blundell's Sch., Tiverton; Guy's Hosp. Med. Sch. MRCS 1937; LRCP 1937; MRCP 1946; FRCP 1961. Formerly: Resident Medical Appts, Guy's Hosp.; Resident Med. Officer, Nat. Hosp., Queen Square; Neurological Registrar, St Mary's Hosp., Paddington; Consultant Physician, Dept Nervous Diseases, St Mary's Hosp., 1954–78; Consultant Neurologist: Royal Nat. Throat, Nose and Ear Hosp., 1955–78; King Edward VII Hosp., Windsor, 1952–78; Canadian Red Cross Meml Hosp., Taplow, 1952–78; Maidenhead Hosp., 1952–78. Co-ordinator, Special Progs, Wellcome Trust, 1979–85. Mem., British Assoc. of Neurologists, 1952–; FRSocMed. *Publications:* Neurology of Ear, Nose and Throat, 1973; Neurological Section: Synopsis of Otolaryngology, 1967; Scott-Brown, Diseases of Ear, Nose and Throat, 1971; contrib. Qly Jl Medicine, Lancet, etc. *Recreations:* words, gardening. *Address:* Cardinal House, The Green, Hampton Court, Surrey. *T:* 01–979 6922. *Club:* Garrick.

EDWARDS, (Charles) Marcus; His Honour Judge Marcus Edwards; a Circuit Judge, since 1986; *b* 10 Aug. 1937; *s* of John Basil Edwards, *qv*; *m* 1st, 1963, Anne Louise Stockdale (*d* 1970), *d* of Sir Edmund Stockdale, Bt, *qv*; 2nd, 1975, Sandra Wates (*née* Mouroutsos); one *d* and three step *d*. *Educ:* Dragon Sch., Oxford; Rugby Sch.; Brasenose Coll., Oxford (scholar; BA Jurisprudence). Trooper, RAC, 1955; 2nd Lieut, Intelligence Corps, Cyprus, 1956–57. HM Diplomatic Service, 1960–65; Third Sec., 1960, Spain, 1961, FO, 1961–62, South Africa and High Commn Territories, 1962–63, Laos, 1964; Second Sec., FO, 1965, resigned. Called to the Bar, Middle Temple, 1962; practised, London, 1966–86; Mem., Midland and Oxford Circuit; a Recorder, 1985–86. *Recreations:* gardening, walking, talking, food and drink. *Address:* Melbourne House, South Parade, W4 1JU. *T:* 01-995 9146. *Club:* Beefsteak.

EDWARDS, Sir Christopher (John Churchill), 5th Bt *cr* 1866; *b* 16 Aug. 1941; *s* of Sir (Henry) Charles (Serrell Priestley) Edwards, 4th Bt and of Lady (Daphne) Edwards (*née* Birt); *S* father, 1963; *m* 1972, Gladys Irene Vogelgesang; two *s*. *Educ:* Frensham Heights, Surrey; Loughborough, Leics. Managing Dir, Kelsar Corp., California. *Heir: s* David Charles Priestley Edwards, *b* 22 Feb. 1974. *Address:* 5110 Glen Verde Drive, Bonita, California 92002, USA. *T:* 714–267–3873.

EDWARDS, Sir Clive; *see* Edwards, Sir J. C. L.

EDWARDS, David; Director, John Laing plc; Secretary, Legal Aid, The Law Society, 1976–86, and Deputy Secretary-General 1982–86; *b* 27 Oct. 1929; *s* of Col Cyril Edwards, DSO, MC, DL and Jessie Edwards; *m* 1966, Gay Clothier; two *s* one *d*. *Educ:* Felsted Sch.; Trinity Hall, Cambridge (MA, LLM). Called to the Bar, Middle Temple, 1952; Harmsworth Scholar, Middle Temple, 1955; admitted Solicitor, 1958. Partner, E. Edwards Son & Noice, 1959–75. Chm., Offshore Racing Council, 1970–78; Dep. Chm., Royal Yachting Assoc., 1976–81. *Recreation:* sailing. *Address:* Olivers, Colchester, Essex CO2 0HJ. *Clubs:* Royal Ocean Racing; Royal Yacht Squadron (Cowes).

See also Baron Chelmer, J. T. Edwards.

EDWARDS, (David) Elgan (Hugh); barrister; a Recorder of the Crown Court (Wales and Chester Circuit), since 1983; *b* 6 Dec. 1943; *s* of Howell and Dilys Edwards; *m* 1982, Carol Anne Smalls; two *s* one *d*. *Educ:* Rhyl Grammar Sch.; University Coll. of Wales, Aberystwyth (LLB Hons 1966; Pres., Students Union, 1967). Called to the Bar, Gray's Inn, 1967. Conservative Parly Candidate: Merioneth, 1970; Stockport South, Feb. 1974. Sheriff, City of Chester, 1977–78. *Recreations:* reading, swimming, golf. *Address:* 1 Lea Hall Mews, Lea-by-Backford, near Chester. *Club:* City, Grosvenor, Eaton Golf (Chester).

EDWARDS, Very Rev. David Lawrence; Provost of Southwark Cathedral since 1983; *b* 20 Jan. 1929; *s* of late Lawrence Wright and Phyllis Boardman Edwards; *m* 1st, 1960, Hilary Mary (*née* Phillips) (marr. diss. 1984); one *s* three *d*; 2nd, 1984, Sybil, *d* of Michael and Kathleen Falcon. *Educ:* King's Sch., Canterbury; Magdalen Coll., Oxford. Lothian Prize, 1951; 1st cl. hons Mod. Hist., BA 1952; MA 1956. Fellow, All Souls Coll., Oxford, 1952–59. Deacon, 1954; Priest, 1955. On HQ staff of Student Christian Movement of Gt Brit. and Ireland, 1955–66; Editor and Man. Dir, SCM Press Ltd, 1959–66; Gen. Sec. of Movt, 1965–66. Curate of: St John's, Hampstead, 1955–58; St Martin-in-the-Fields, 1958–66; Fellow and Dean of King's College, Cambridge, 1966–70; Asst Lectr in

Divinity, Univ. of Cambridge, 1967–70; Rector of St Margaret's, Westminster, 1970–78; Canon of Westminster, 1970–78; Sub-Dean, 1974–78; Speaker's Chaplain, 1972–78; Dean of Norwich, 1978–82. Exam. Chaplain: to Bp of Manchester, 1965–73; to Bp of Durham, 1968–72; to Bp of Bradford, 1972–78; to Bp of London, 1974–78; to Archbishop of Canterbury, 1975–78. Hulsean Lectr, 1967; Six Preacher, Canterbury Cathedral, 1969–76. Chairman: Churches' Council on Gambling, 1970–78; Christian Aid, 1971–78. *Publications:* A History of the King's School, Canterbury, 1957; Not Angels But Anglicans, 1958; This Church of England, 1962; God's Cross in Our World, 1963; Religion and Change, 1969; F. J. Shirley: An Extraordinary Headmaster, 1969; The Last Things Now, 1969; Leaders of the Church of England, 1971; What is Real in Christianity?, 1972; St Margaret's, Westminster, 1972; The British Churches Turn to the Future, 1973; Ian Ramsey, Bishop of Durham, 1973; Good News in Acts, 1974; What Anglicans Believe, 1974; Jesus for Modern Man, 1975; A Key to the Old Testament, 1976; Today's Story of Jesus, 1976; The State of the Nation, 1976; A Reason to Hope, 1978; Christian England: vol 1, Its story to the Reformation, 1981; vol. 2, From the Reformation to the Eighteenth Century, 1983; vol. 3, From the Eighteenth Century to the First World War, 1984; The Futures of Christianity, 1987; (ed) The Honest to God Debate, 1963; (ed) Collins Children's Bible, 1978. *Address:* Provost's Lodging, 51 Bankside, SE1 9JE. *T:* 01–928 6414. *Club:* Athenæum.
See also M. G. Falcon.

EDWARDS, David Michael; HM Diplomatic Service; Counsellor (Legal Adviser), UK Mission to UN, New York, and HM Embassy, Washington, since 1985; *b* 28 Feb. 1940; *s* of Ernest William Edwards and Thelma Irene Edwards; *m* 1966, Veronica Margaret Postgate; one *s* one *d*. *Educ:* The King's Sch., Canterbury; Univ. of Bristol. LLB Hons. Admitted to Roll of Solicitors, 1964. Solicitor of Supreme Court, 1964–67; Asst Legal Adviser, Foreign Office, 1967; Legal Adviser: British Military Govt, Berlin, 1972; British Embassy, Bonn, 1974; Legal Counsellor, 1977; Dir, Legal Div., IAEA, Vienna (on secondment), 1977–79; Legal Counsellor, FCO, 1979; Agent of the UK Govt in cases before European Commn and Court of Human Rights, 1979–82. *Recreations:* reading, walking, gardening. *Address:* c/o Foreign and Commonwealth Office, King Charles Street, SW1A 2AH. *Club:* Royal Over-Seas League.

EDWARDS, Donald Isaac, CBE 1965 (OBE 1958); Managing Director, Independent Television News, 1968–71; *b* 27 Sept. 1904; *s* of late Isaac Edwards, Bolton, Lancs; *m* 1930, Enid Bent; two *s*. *Educ:* Bolton Sch.; Emmanuel Coll., Cambridge (MA). Tillotsons Newspapers, 1926–28; Daily News, 1928–30; Allied Newspapers, 1930–33; Daily Telegraph, 1933–39; BBC: Asst European News Editor, 1940–42; European News Editor, 1942–45; Correspondent in India, 1946; Dir, European News, 1946–48; Head of External Services, News Dept, 1948–58; Editor, News, 1958–60; News and Current Affairs, 1960–67; Gen. Man., Local Radio Development, 1967–68. *Publications:* The Two Worlds of Donald Edwards (autobiography), 1970; contribs to various books on journalism and broadcasting. *Recreations:* gardening, music, chess, walking. *Address:* Spindles, Miles Lane, Cobham, Surrey. *T:* Cobham 62257.

EDWARDS, Douglas John; Consultant, Argyll Foods Ltd (formerly Louis C. Edwards & Sons (Manchester) Ltd), 1979–84 (Joint Chairman and Managing Director, 1966–79); Chairman and Managing Director, Imexport Meats Ltd, since 1979; *b* 18 March 1916; *s* of Louis Edwards and Catherine Edwards; *m* 1st, 1941, Emmeline H. Haslam (*d* 1964); two *s*; 2nd, 1973, Valerie Barlow-Hitchen. *Educ:* De La Salle Coll., Salford. Served in Grenadier Guards, 1940–45. Member of Lloyd's, 1965–: Joined Manchester Conservative Party, 1947; Mem. Manchester City Council, 1951–74; Alderman, 1967–74; Lord Mayor of City of Manchester, 1971–72; Greater Manchester Metropolitan CC, 1974–78; High Sheriff, 1975–76. President: Manchester Cttee, Grenadier Guards Assoc., 1968–81 (Life Mem.); Greater Manchester Youth Assoc., 1973–80; Chairman: Manchester Br., Variety Club of GB, 1969–70; Northern Cttee, Hotel and Catering Benev. Assoc., 1976–81. Governor: De La Salle Teacher Training Coll., Greater Manchester, 1972–81; De La Salle Coll., Salford, 1972–81. DL Greater Manchester, 1979–81. Freeman and Liveryman, Makers of Playing Cards Co., 1974. Polonia Restituta, First Cl., 1972. KHS 1986. *Recreations:* golf, sailing, shooting. *Address:* Apt 10A, The Marbella, 250 South Ocean Boulevard, Boca Raton, Florida 33432, USA. *T:* (305) 392–8203. *Clubs:* Carlton; Royal Thames Yacht; Lloyd's Yacht; Lancs County Cricket (Life Mem.); Cheshire Polo; Altrincham Rifle; Antibes Yacht; St Francis Yacht (USA) (Hon. Mem.).

EDWARDS, Prof. Edward George, PhD, BSc, FRSC; Vice-Chancellor and Principal, University of Bradford, 1966–78, Hon. Professor, since 1978; Principal of Bradford Institute of Technology, 1957–66; *b* 18 Feb. 1914; *m* 1940, Kathleen Hewitt; two *s* two *d*. *Educ:* Cardiff High Sch.; University of South Wales; Cardiff Coll. of Technology. Lecturer in Chemistry, University of Nottingham, 1938–40; Research Chemist (ICI Ltd), 1940–45; Head of Dept of Chemistry and Applied Chemistry, Royal Technical Coll., Salford, 1945–54; Principal, Coll. of Technology, Liverpool, 1954–57. Hon. DTech Bradford, 1980; Fellow, University Coll., Cardiff, 1981. *Publications:* Higher Education for Everyone, 1982; various research papers in chemical jls; articles and papers on higher educn, technological innovation, university planning. *Recreations:* philosophy, music, walking, travel. *Address:* Corner Cottage, Westwood Drive, Ilkley, West Yorks. *T:* Ilkley 607112.

EDWARDS, Elgan; *see* Edwards, D. E. H.

EDWARDS, Frederick Edward, RD 1968 and Clasp, 1977; Director of Social Work, Strathclyde Region, since 1976; *b* 9 April 1931; *s* of Reginal Thomas Edwards and Jessie Howard Simpson; *m* 1957, Edith Jocelyn Price; two *s* one *d*. *Educ:* St Edward's Coll., Liverpool; Univ. of Glasgow (Dip. Applied Soc. Studies 1965). BA Open Univ., 1973. FBIM; FISW. Merchant Navy Deck Officer, 1948–58; Perm. Commn, RNR, 1953, Lt-Comdr 1963; sailed Barque Mayflower to USA, 1957. Morgan Refractories, 1958–60; Probation Service, Liverpool, 1960–69; Dir of Social Work: Moray and Nairn, 1969–74; Grampian, 1974–76. Member: Scottish Marriage Guidance Council, 1970– (Chm., 1980–83); Scottish Council on Crime, 1972–75; Adv. Council on Social Work, 1976–81. *Publications:* articles in social work jls. *Recreations:* sailing, natural history, reading. *Address:* Tigh na Bealach, Empress Road, Rhu, Dunbartonshire G84 8LT. *T:* Rhu 820365.

EDWARDS, Gareth Owen; QC 1985; a Recorder of the Crown Court, since 1978; *b* 26 Feb. 1940; *s* of Arthur Wyn Edwards and Mair Eluned Edwards; *m* 1967, Katharine Pek Har Goh; two *s* one *d*. *Educ:* Herbert Strutt Grammar Sch., Belper; Trinity Coll., Oxford (BA,BCL). Called to the Bar, Inner Temple, 1963; Army Legal Service, 1963–65; Commonwealth Office, 1965–67. Practised, Wales and Chester Circuit, 1967–. *Recreations:* climbing, chess. *Address:* 58 Lache Lane, Chester CH4 7LS. *T:* Chester 677795. *Club:* Army and Navy.

EDWARDS, Gareth Owen, MBE 1975; Welsh Rugby footballer; Director of Engineering Company in S Wales; *b* 12 July 1947; *s* of Granville and Anne Edwards; *m* 1972, Maureen Edwards; two *s*. *Educ:* Pontardawe Tech. Sch.; Millfield Sch.; Cardiff College of Educn. Rugby Football: 1st cap for Wales, 1967 (*v* France); Captain of Wales on 13 occasions; youngest Captain of Wales (at 20 years), 1968; British Lions Tours: 1968, 1971, 1974; Barbarians, 1967–78. Member of Cardiff RFC, 1966–; a record 53 consecutive caps, to 1978; retired, 1978. *Publications:* Gareth: an autobiography, 1978; (jtly) Rugby Skills, 1979; Rugby Skills for Forwards, 1980. *Recreations:* fishing, golf. *Address:* 211 West Road, Nottage, Porthcawl, Mid-Glamorgan CF36 3RT. *T:* Porthcawl 5669.

EDWARDS, Geoffrey, CEng, FICE, FRICS, FCIArb, MConsE, FASCE; Chairman, GEP International Ltd (formerly GEP Consulting Group), since 1966; Westfield Trust Ltd, since 1966; Principal, Edwards Newstead, since 1967; *b* 28 April 1917; *s* of Frank Edwards, boot and shoe manufr, and Gladys Evelyn, *d* of Joseph Downes, mining engr; *m* 1st, 1943, Barbara Henrietta Edwards (*d* 1959); no *c*; 2nd, 1960, Pauline Nancy (*d* 1984), *d* of Walter James Edwards, boot and shoe manufr, and Anne Evelyn Gully; two *d*; 3rd, 1984, Joan Hibberd, PhD. *Educ:* private prep. sch.; St Brendan's Coll., Clifton, Bristol; Merchant Venturers/Bristol Univ. FRICS 1951; CEng, FICE 1956; FCIArb 1976. Defence works, 1939–43; Civil Engr, BOAC, W Africa, 1943–45; various appts, BOAC, 1945–66, incl. Gen. Man. Properties and Services, and Mem. of Exec. Management. Dir and Dep. Chm., N Surrey Water Co., 1962–78; Dir and Dep. Chm., Sutton Dist Water Co., 1970–73; Chm., Thames Water Authority, 1978–83; Founder Chm., Surveyors Holdings Ltd, 1980–82; Mem., National Water Council, 1978–83. Chm., Westminster Chamber of Commerce, 1982–84; formerly Member: Council, RICS; Airport Engrg Bd, ICE; Council, Nat. Fedn of Housing Assocs. Freeman and Liveryman, City of London; Liveryman: Worshipful Co. of Plumbers; Worshipful Co. of Engineers. Founder Chm., World Airports Confs; broadcaster on airport subjects; Founder Chm., World Water Congresses, 1983 and 1986. Underwriting name, Lloyd's of London. Former Steward, Henley Royal Regatta. *Publications:* papers, and contribs to technical jls on airport and water matters. *Recreations:* swimming, shooting, farming. *Address:* 402 Drake House, Dolphin Square, SW1V 3NN. *T:* 01–834 9929; Coldharbour Farm, Wick, near Bristol BS15 5RJ. *T:* Abson 2212. *Clubs:* City Livery, Farmers'.

EDWARDS, Geoffrey Francis, CBE 1975 (OBE 1968; MBE 1956); TD; HM Diplomatic Service, retired; *b* 28 Sept. 1917; *s* of late Oliver and Frances Margaret Edwards, Langley, Bucks; *m* 1st, 1949, Joyce Black (*d* 1953); one *d*; 2nd, 1961, Johanna Elisabeth Franziska Taeger. *Educ:* Brighton Coll. Joined Pixley & Abell, Bullion Brokers, 1936. Commissioned RA (TA), June 1939; served with 117 Fd Regt and 59 (Newfoundland) Heavy Regt RA in NW Europe, 1939–45; joined Control Commn for Germany, 1945; joined British Military Govt, Berlin, 1949; Economic Adviser, 1956; Consul-General, Berlin, 1966–75. Ernst Reuter Silver Plaque, Berlin, 1975. *Recreations:* gardening, fishing, golf. *Address:* Whitegates, Mathon Road, Colwall, near Malvern, Worcs WR13 6ER.

EDWARDS, George, FFARCS; Consulting Anæsthetist: St George's, General Lying-in (St Thomas'), Samaritan (St Mary's) and Queen Charlotte's Hospitals; *b* 14 Jan. 1901; *m* 1934, Jean Lilian Smith, MD; one *s*. *Educ:* Royal Grammar Sch., Worcester; St George's Hospital (Johnson Anatomy Prize). MRCS, LRCP 1926; DA, RCP and S 1936; FFARCS 1948. RAMC, 1941–44; Lt-Col. Adviser in Anæsthetics, BNAF and CMF. Hon. Mem. (Pres. 1945–46), Sect. Anæsthetics, RSocMed. Mem. of Bd of Faculty of Anæsthetists, RCS, 1948–54; first Hewitt Lectr, RCS, 1950; first Snow Memorial Lectr, Assoc. of Anæsthetists, 1958. *Publications:* articles in medical journals. *Address:* Davenham, Graham Road, Malvern, Worcester WR14 2HY. *T:* Malvern 64338.

EDWARDS, Sir George (Robert), OM 1971; Kt 1957; CBE 1952 (MBE 1945); FRS 1968; FEng; DL; now retired; Chairman, British Aircraft Corporation Ltd, 1963–75; Pro-Chancellor, University of Surrey, 1964–79, now Pro-Chancellor Emeritus; *b* 9 July 1908; *m* 1935, Marjorie Annie (*née* Thurgood); one *d*. *Educ:* S West Essex Tech. Coll.; London Univ. (BScEng). Gen. engineering, 1928–35; joined Design Staff, Vickers-Aviation Ltd, Weybridge, 1935; Experimental Manager, Vickers-Armstrongs Ltd, Weybridge Works, 1940. Chief Designer, Weybridge Works, 1945; Dir, Vickers Ltd, 1955–67. Pres., Royal Aeronautical Soc., 1957–58; Vice-Pres., Royal Society of Arts, 1958–61. Mem., Royal Instn, 1971–. Pres., Surrey CCC, 1979 (Vice-Pres., 1974). DL Surrey, 1981. FEng; Hon. Fellow: RAeS 1960; IMechE; Manchester Coll. of Science and Technology; Hon. FAIAA. Hon. DSc: Southampton, 1962; Salford, 1967; Cranfield Inst. of Technology, 1970; City Univ., 1975; Stirling, 1979; Surrey, 1979; Hon. DSc(Eng) London, 1970; Hon. LLD Bristol, 1973. George Taylor Gold Medal, 1948; British Gold Medal for Aeronautics, 1952; Daniel Guggenheim Medal, 1959; Air League Founders Medal, 1969; Albert Gold Medal (RSA), 1972; Royal Medal, Royal Soc., 1974. *Publications:* various papers and lectures in Jl RAeS, Amer. Inst. of Aeronautical Sciences and Amer. Soc. of Automotive Engrs. *Recreation:* painting. *Address:* Albury Heights, White Lane, Guildford, Surrey. *T:* Guildford 504488. *Clubs:* Athenæum; Royal Air Force Yacht.

EDWARDS, Harold Clifford, CBE 1945; MS, FRCS, FRCOG, FACS (Hon.); Honorary Colonel RAMC; Consulting Surgeon to King's College Hospital; Emeritus Lecturer, and Director, Department of Surgery, King's College Hospital Medical School, 1956–70, Fellow 1983; Surgeon to Royal Masonic Hospital, 1956–70; Consulting Surgeon to King Edward VII Hospital for Officers, 1956–70; St Saviour's Hospital; Consultant Adviser in Surgery to the Minister of Health, 1956–70; Surgeon Emeritus to the Evelina Hospital for Children; *b* 15 Aug. 1899; *s* of William Evans Edwards and Mary Selina Jones; *m* 1926, Ida Margaret Atkinson Phillips (*d* 1981); two *s*. *Educ:* University Coll., Cardiff; King's College Hospital, London. Served in Royal Engineers, 1917–19; entered University Coll., Cardiff, 1919; MRCS, LRCP, MB, BS 1923; FRCS 1926; MS London Univ., 1928; Hon. Surgeon to King's Coll. Hosp., 1928, and to Evelina Hosp. for Children, 1931; Robert Jones Gold Medal for an Essay upon Injuries to Muscles and Tendons, 1930, and Jacksonian Prize of RCS for a Dissertation on Diverticula of the Intestine, 1932; Hunterian Prof., RCS, 1934; Consulting Surg. Southern Comd, England, 1942–44; Consulting Surg., Central Mediterranean Forces, 1944–46; late Dean of King's College Hosp. Medical Sch. Past Master, Worshipful Soc. of Apothecaries. Mem. Court of Examiners, 1931–60, and Mem. Council, 1955–71, RCS (past Vice-Pres.). Examiner in Surgery, Univs of London, Cambridge, Wales, Birmingham, Dublin and Bristol. Chm., Armed Forces Adv. Cttee on Postgraduate Med. and Dental Officers, 1971–75; President: British Soc. of Gastroenterology, 1961; Assoc. of Surgeons of Gt Brit. and Ireland, 1962; FRCOG 1971; Hon. Fellow: American Surgical Assoc.; Assoc. of Surgeons of W Africa; Assoc. of Surgeons of West Indies; Mem. Académie de Chirurgie. Former Editor of GUT the British Jl of Gastro-enterology. Hon. Gold Medal, RCS, 1972; Eric Farquharson Award, RCSE, 1978. *Publications:* Surgical Emergencies in Children, 1935; Diverticula and Diverticulitis of the Intestine, 1939; Recent Advances in Surgery, 1954; papers in BMJ, Lancet, etc. *Recreation:* gardening. *Address:* 17 Grange Court, Pinehurst, Grange Road, Cambridge CB3 9BD. *T:* Cambridge 69512. *Club:* Athenæum.
See also Prof. J. H. Edwards.

EDWARDS, Iorwerth Eiddon Stephen, CMG 1973; CBE 1968; MA, LittD; FBA 1962; Keeper of Egyptian Antiquities, British Museum, 1955–74; *b* 21 July 1909; *s* of late Edward Edwards, Orientalist, and Ellen Jane (*née* Higgs); *m* 1938, Elizabeth, *y d* of late Charles Edwards Lisle; one *d* (one *s* decd). *Educ:* Merchant Taylors'; Gonville and Caius Coll., Cambridge (Major Scholar). Merchant Taylors' Sch. Exhibitioner and John Stewart of Rannoch Univ. Scholar, Cambridge, 1928; 1st Cl. Oriental Languages Tripos (Arabic and Hebrew), Parts I and II, 1930–31; Mason Prize, Tyrwhitt Scholarship and Wright Studentship, 1932. Entered Dept of Egyptian and Assyrian Antiquities, British Museum, 1934; seconded to Foreign Office; attached to British Embassies, Cairo and Baghdad, and to Secretariat, Jerusalem, 1942–45. T. E. Peet Prize, Liverpool Univ., 1947. Visiting Prof., Brown Univ., Providence, RI, USA, 1953–54. Glanville Meml Lectr, Cambridge Univ., 1980. Pioneered and chose objects for Tutankhamun Exhibition, London, 1972. Mem., Unesco-Egyptian Min. of Culture Archaeol. Cttee for saving monuments of Philae, 1973–80. Vice-Pres. Egypt Exploration Soc.; Mem. of German Archæological Inst.; Associate Mem., Inst. of Egypt; Mem., Cttee of Visitors of Metropolitan Museum of Art, NY; Corres. Mem., Fondation Egyptologique Reine Elisabeth. *Publications:* Hieroglyphic Texts in the British Museum, Vol. VIII, 1939; The Pyramids of Egypt, 1947, 3rd edn 1985; Hieratic Papyri in the British Museum, 4th Series (Oracular Amuletic Decrees of the Late New Kingdom), 1960; The Early Dynastic Period in Egypt, 1964; Joint Editor of The Cambridge Ancient History (3rd edn), vols I-III, 1970–86; Treasures of Tutankhamun (Catalogue of London exhibn), 1972; Treasures of Tutankhamun (Catalogue of US exhibn), 1976; Tutankhamun's Jewelry, 1976; Tutankhamun: his tomb and its treasures, 1976; articles in Journal of Egyptian Archæology and other scientific periodicals. *Recreations:* golf, gardening. *Address:* Dragon House, The Bullring, Deddington, Oxon OX5 4TT. *T:* Deddington 38481. *Club:* Athenæum.

EDWARDS, Jack Trevor, CBE 1985; CEng, FICE; FCIT; Consultant, Freeman Fox & Partners, since 1986 (Senior Partner, 1979–86); *b* 23 June 1920; *s* of late Col Cyril Ernest Edwards, DSO, MC, JP, and Jessie Boyd; *m* 1959, Josephine, (Sally), *d* of late S. W. Williams; one *d. Educ:* Felsted Sch.; City and Guilds Coll., Imperial Coll. London (BScEng, FCGI). RAF Armament and Airfield Construction Branches, Sqdn Ldr, 1941–46. Civil Engr on hydro-electric and thermal power stations, James Williamson and Partners, 1946–50; Freeman Fox & Partners: Engineer, 1951–64; Partner, 1965–79; special field: civil engrg and building works associated with thermal power stations and railways at home and overseas; major projects: Hong Kong Mass Transit Railway, opened 1980; Baghdad and Taipei Metros; Engineer to Dean and Chapter of St Paul's Cathedral. Mem. Council, British Consultants Bureau, 1979–85 (Chm., 1982–83). Liveryman, Worshipful Co. of Painter-Stainers, 1969–. *Publications:* contrib. Proc. Instn of Civil Engrs. *Recreation:* sailing. *Address:* Keepers, 77 Brentwood Road, Ingrave, Brentwood, Essex CM13 3NU. *T:* Brentwood 810285. *Clubs:* St Stephen's Constitutional, Royal Cruising, Royal Burnham Yacht.

See also Baron Chelmer, D. Edwards.

EDWARDS, Prof. James Griffith, DM, FRCP, FRCPsych; Professor of Addiction Behaviour, Institute of Psychiatry, University of London, since 1979; Hon. Director, Addiction Research Unit, since 1970; Hon. Consultant, Bethlem and Maudsley Hospitals, since 1967; *b* 3 Oct. 1928; *yr s* of late Dr J. T. Edwards and late Constance Amy (*née* McFadyean); *m* 1st, 1969, Evelyn Morrison (marr. diss. 1981); one *s* one *d* (and one *d* decd); 2nd, 1981, Frances Susan Stables. *Educ:* Andover Grammar Sch.; Balliol Coll., Oxford (MA; Theodore Williams Schol. in Anatomy); St Bartholomew's Hosp. (Kirkes Schol. and Gold Medal); DM Oxford, 1966; DPM London, 1962; FRCP 1976; FRCPsych 1976. Served RA, 1948–49 (2nd Lieut). Jun. hosp. appts, King George, Ilford, St Bartholomew's, Hammersmith and Maudsley Hosps, 1956–62; Inst. of Psychiatry: res. worker, 1962; Lectr, 1966; Sen. Lectr, 1967; Reader, 1973. Chm., Royal Coll. of Psych. Special Cttee on Drug Dependence, 1983– (on Alcohol and Alcoholism, 1975–78); Medical Dir, Alcohol Educn Centre, 1980–83; Member: Home Office Working Party on Drunkenness Offenders, 1967–70; WHO Expert Adv. Cttee on Drug Dependence, 1969–; DoE Cttee on Drinking and Driving, 1974–75; Home Office Adv. Council on Misuse of Drugs, 1972–; DHSS Adv. Cttee on Alcoholism, 1975–78; ESRC (formerly SSRC), 1981–; Consultant Advr on Alcoholism, DHSS, 1986–. Trustee, Community Drug Proj., 1967–. Steven's Lectr and Gold Medallist, RSM, 1971; Dent Lectr, King's Coll., 1980; Roche Vis. Prof., Aust. and NZ, 1982. Jellinek Meml Award, 1980. Editor, British Jl of Addiction, 1978–. *Publications:* Unreason in an Age of Reason, 1971; (jtly) Alcohol Control Policies, 1975; (ed jtly) Drugs in Socio-Cultural Perspective, 1980; (jtly) Opium and the People, 1981; Treatment of Drinking Problems, 1982; articles in jls on scientific and policy aspects of alcohol and drug dependence. *Recreations:* chess, looking at pictures, frequenting junk shops. *Address:* 32 Crooms Hill, SE10 8ER. *T:* 01–858 5631. *Club:* Athenæum.

See also J. M. McF. Edwards.

EDWARDS, James Keith O'Neill, (Jimmy Edwards), DFC 1945; MA (Cantab); MFH; *b* 23 March 1920; *s* of late Prof. R. W. K. Edwards and late Mrs P. K. Edwards; *m* 1958, Valerie Seymour (marr. diss. 1969). *Educ:* St Paul's Cathedral Choir Sch.; King's Coll. Sch., Wimbledon; St John's Coll., Cambridge. Served War of 1939–45, in RAF, 1940–46. Windmill Theatre, London, 1946; Adelphi Theatre, 1950–51, 1952–54, 1954–55 and 1960–61; *Radio and Television:* Take It From Here, BBC, 1948–59; Does The Team Think?, BBC, 1957–77; Whack-O!, BBC Television, 1957–61 and 1971–72; Seven Faces of Jim, 1961–62; Six More Faces of Jim, 1962–63; Bold as Brass, 1964; John Jorrocks, Esq., BBC-2, 1966; Fosset Saga, ATV, 1969; The Glums, LWT, 1979. *Films:* Three Men in a Boat, 1957; Bottoms Up, 1960; Nearly a Nasty Accident, 1961; The Plank, 1979; Rhubarb, 1980; It's Your Move, 1982. *Stage:* Big Bad Mouse, Shaftesbury, 1966–68, Prince of Wales, 1971; Halfway up the Tree, Queen's, 1968; Maid of the Mountains, Palace, 1972; Hulla Baloo, Criterion, 1972; Doctor in the House, 1978; Oh Sir James, 1979; Oliver!, Toronto, 1983. Lord Rector of Aberdeen Univ., 1951–54. *Publications:* Take It From Me, 1952; Oh Sir James (play), 1979; Six of the Best (Memoirs), 1984. *Recreations:* foxhunting, polo, flying, squash, brass bands. *Address:* Riven Oak, Mill Lane, Fletching, Uckfield, East Sussex TN22 3SR. *Club:* Savile.

EDWARDS, James Valentine, CVO 1978; MA; *b* 4 Feb. 1925; *s* of late Captain Alfred Harold Edwards, OBE, and Mrs Eleanor Edwards; *m* Barbara, *d* of late Sir John Hanbury-Williams, CVO, and Lady Hanbury-Williams; two *d*, and one step *s* one step *d. Educ:* St Edmund's, Hindhead; Radley; Magdalen Coll., Oxford (MA). Served RN, 1943–47. Oxford, 1943 and 1947–49. *Address:* Long Sutton House, Long Sutton, near Langport, Som. *T:* Long Sutton 284. *Clubs:* MCC, Free Foresters.

EDWARDS, John; Editor, Yorkshire Post, since 1969; *b* 2 Jan. 1932; *s* of late Arthur Leonard Edwards; *m* 1st, 1954, Nancy Woodcock (*d* 1978); one *s* one *d*; 2nd, 1979, Brenda Rankin; one *d. Educ:* Wolverhampton Municipal Grammar School. Entered journalism, Wolverhampton Chronicle; subseq. worked on newspapers and magazines in Fleet Street and provinces; from 1961, Yorkshire Post: Dep. Night Editor, Business Editor, Asst Editor and Dep. Editor. Dir, Yorkshire Post Newspapers Ltd. *Address:* 1 Edgerton Road, West Park, Leeds LS16 5JD.

EDWARDS, John Basil, CBE 1972; JP; Chairman, Magistrates Association, 1976–79; *b* 15 Jan. 1909; *s* of Charles and Susan Edwards; *m* 1935, Molly Patricia Philips (*d* 1979); one *s* two *d. Educ:* King's Sch., Worcester; Wadham Coll., Oxford (BA Hons Jurisprudence, MA). Commnd Royal Warwickshire Regt (RE) TA, 1938. Admitted Solicitor, 1933. Worcester CC, 1936; Mayor of Worcester, 1947–49; Alderman, City of Worcester, 1948. Magistrates Association: Mem. Council, 1960; Chm., Worcestershire Br., 1960–66; Hon. Treasurer, 1968–70; Dep. Chm., 1970–76. Mem., James Cttee on Distribution of Criminal Business, 1973–75. Chm., Worcester Three Choirs Festival, 1947–72. Freeman, City of London. Liveryman: Haberdashers Company; Distillers Company. JP Worcs 1940; Chm., Worcester City Justices, 1951–79. *Recreation:* gardening. *Address:* 21 Britannia Square, Worcester. *T:* Worcester 29933.

See also C. M. Edwards.

EDWARDS, John Braham Scott, MA (Oxon); **His Honour Judge John Edwards;** a Circuit Judge, since 1977; *b* Bristol, 29 March 1928; *s* of late Lewis Edwards and late Hilda Edwards (*née* Scott); *m* 1963, Veronica Mary, *d* of late Lt-Col Howard Dunbar (killed in action, 1942), and of Mrs Brodie Good; one *s* two *d. Educ:* Royal Masonic Schools, Bushey; Merton Coll., Oxford. National service, Army, 1946–48. Teaching Fellow, Univ. of Chicago Law Sch., 1952–53. Called to the Bar, Middle Temple, 1954; Bencher 1973. A Recorder of the Crown Court, 1972–77. Hon. Secretary-Gen. of Internat. Law Assoc., 1960–85. Churchwarden, St Anne's, Kew, 1973–83. *Recreations:* history, golf, gardening. *Address:* c/o Treasury, Middle Temple, EC4Y 9AT. *T:* (home) 01–940 8734. *Club:* Roehampton.

EDWARDS, John Charles, JP; Lord Mayor of Cardiff, 1980–81; *b* 3 April 1925; *s* of John Robert Edwards and Elsie Florence Edwards; *m* 1946, Cynthia Lorraine Bushell; one *s* two *d. Educ:* Lansdowne Road Sch., Cardiff. Served War of 1939–45, RM (1939–45 Star, France and Germany Star, War Medal 1939–45); TA, 1948–62, RASC (TEM). Postal Exec. Officer, GPO. Mem., S Glam CC, 1974–78; Dep. Lord Mayor, Cardiff, 1978–79. Freeman of City of London, 1981. JP S Glam, 1979. Mem., St John's Council for S Glam; OStJ 1980. *Recreations:* athletics, football. *Address:* 61 Cosmeston Street, Cathays, Cardiff CF2 4LQ. *T:* Cardiff 21506. *Clubs:* Civil Service; United Services Mess; Cardiff Athletic.

EDWARDS, Sir (John) Clive (Leighton), 2nd Bt *cr* 1921; *b* 1916; *s* of 1st Bt and Kathleen Ermyntrude (*d* 1975) *d* of late John Corfield, JP; *S* father, 1922. *Educ:* Winchester Coll. Volunteered and served in the Army, 1940–46. *Recreations:* motoring, gardening. *Heir:* none. *Address:* Milntown, Lezayre, Ramsey, Isle of Man.

EDWARDS, John Coates; HM Diplomatic Service; Deputy High Commissioner, Nairobi, Kenya, since 1984; *b* 25 Nov. 1934; *s* of Herbert John Edwards and late Doris May Edwards; *m* 1959, Mary Harris; one *s* one *d. Educ:* Skinners' Co. Sch., Tunbridge Wells, Kent; Brasenose Coll., Oxford (MA). Military Service, 1953–55: Lieut, RA. Asst Principal: Min. of Supply, 1958; Colonial Office, 1960; Private Sec. to Parly Under Sec. of State for the Colonies, 1961; Principal: Nature Conservancy, 1962; Min. of Overseas Develt, 1965; First Sec. (Develt), and UK Perm. Rep. to ECAFE, Bangkok, Thailand, 1968; Asst Sec., Min. of Overseas Develt, 1971; Head of E Africa Develt Div., Nairobi, Kenya, 1972; Asst Sec., Min. of Overseas Develt, 1976; Head of British Develt Div. in the Caribbean, Barbados, and UK Dir, Caribbean Develt Bank, 1978; Hd, West Indian and Atlantic Dept, FCO, 1981–84. *Address:* c/o Foreign and Commonwealth Office, SW1. *Clubs:* Royal Commonwealth Society; Muthaiga Country (Nairobi).

EDWARDS, Prof. John Hilton, FRCP; FRS 1979; Professor of Genetics, University of Oxford, since 1979; *b* 26 March 1928; *s* of H. C. Edwards, *qv*; *m* 1953, Felicity Clare, *d* of Dr C. H. C. Toussaint; two *s* two *d. Educ:* Univ. of Cambridge (MB, BChir). FRCP 1972. MO, Falkland Islands Dependency Survey, 1952–53; Mem., MRC Unit on Population Genetics, Oxford, 1958–60; Geneticist, Children's Hosp. of Philadelphia, 1960–61; Lectr, Sen. Lectr, and Reader, Birmingham Univ., 1961–67; Hon. Consultant Paediatrician, Birmingham Regional Bd, 1967; Vis. Prof. of Pediatrics, Cornell Univ., and Sen. Investigator, New York Blood Center, 1967–68; Consultant, Human Genetics, Univ. of Iceland, 1967–; Prof. of Human Genetics, Birmingham Univ., 1969–79. *Publications:* Human Genetics, 1978; scientific papers. *Recreations:* gliding, skiing. *Address:* 78 Old Road, Headington, Oxford. *Club:* Athenæum.

EDWARDS, John Lionel; retired civil servant; *b* 29 Aug. 1915; *s* of Rev. Arthur Edwards and Constance Edwards; *m* 1948, Cecily Miller; one *s* two *d. Educ:* Marlborough; Corpus Christi Coll., Oxford. Entered Scottish Office, 1938. Served War, (Army), 1940–45. Min. of Labour, 1945: Principal Private Sec. to Minister of Labour, 1956; Asst Sec., 1956; Sec., NEDC, 1968–71; Under-Sec., Dept of Employment, 1971–75; Certification Officer for Trade Unions and Employers' Assocs, 1976–81. *Address:* Little Bedwyn, The Ridgway, Pyrford, Surrey. *T:* Byfleet 43459. *Club:* United Oxford & Cambridge University.

EDWARDS, (John) Michael (McFadyean), CBE 1986; QC 1981; Provost, City of London Polytechnic, since 1981; *b* 16 Oct. 1925; *s* of Dr James Thomas Edwards and Constance Amy Edwards, *yr d* of Sir John McFadyean; *m* 1st, 1952, Morna Joyce Piper (marr. diss.); one *s* one *d*; 2nd, 1964, Rosemary Ann Moore; two *s. Educ:* Andover Grammar Sch. (schol.); University Coll., Oxford (BCL, MA). Called to the Bar, Middle Temple, 1949; Asst Parly Counsel, HM Treasury, 1955–60; Dep. Legal Advr and Dir of certain subsid. cos, Courtaulds Ltd, 1960–67; British Steel Corporation: Dir, Legal Services, 1967–71; Man. Dir, BSC (Internat.) Ltd, 1967–81; Chm. and Man. Dir, BSC (Overseas Services) Ltd, 1973–81; Director: Bell Gp Internat., 1982–; TVW (UK) Ltd, 1982–; Bell Resources Ltd (Australia), 1983–; Product Innovation Ltd, 1984–. Member: Overseas Projects Bd, 1973–81; E European Trade Council, 1973–81; Student Educn Adv. Gp, ICA, 1982–; Appeal Cttee, Assoc. of Certified Accountants, 1983–; Member: Bar Council, 1971–79, 1980–83; Senate of Inns of Court and Bar, 1974–79, 1980–83; Council of Legal Educn, 1985; Vice-Pres., Bar Assoc. for Commerce, Finance and Industry, 1980–82 (Chm., 1972–74). Chm., Eastman Dental Hosp., 1983– (Governor, 1981–83); ICC Mem., Acad. Council, Inst. of Internat. Business Law and Practice, Paris, 1982–; Chm., Management Cttee, Inst. of Dental Surgery, Univ. of London, 1984–. Chm. Council, Regional Opera Trust, (Kent Opera), 1983– (Mem. 1981–). CBIM (Mem. Council, 1978–81, 1982–); Fellow, Inst. of Dirs; FRSA; FCIArb, 1984. Freeman, City of London; Mem. Court, Ironmongers' Co. *Recreations:* listening to music, vernacular architecture, local history. *Address:* City of London Polytechnic, 117–119 Houndsditch, EC3A 7BU. *T:* 01–283 1030. *Clubs:* Garrick, City of London.

See also J. G. Edwards.

EDWARDS, Rear Adm. John Phillip, CB 1984; LVO 1972; CEng, FIMechE 1982; Domestic Bursar and Fellow of Wadham College, Oxford, since 1984; *b* 13 Feb. 1927; *s* of Robert Edwards and Dilys (*née* Phillips); *m* 1951, Gwen Lloyd Bonner; three *d. Educ:* Brynhyfryd Sch., Ruthin, Clwyd; HMS Conway; Royal Naval Engrg Colls, Keyham and Manadon. MA 1984. FBIM 1980. Served, 1948–72: HMS Vengeance, Mauritius, Caledonia, Torquay, Lion, Diamond, Defender, HMCS Stadacona, and HMY Britannia; Mechanical Trng Estab., Portsmouth; Personnel Panel; Staff of C-in-C Fleet; SOWC; Dep. Dir, RN Staff Coll., 1972–74; Asst Dir, Dir Gen. Ships, 1974–76; RCDS, 1977; Captain of Portland Naval Base, 1978–80; Dir Gen., Fleet Support Policy and Services, 1980–83. Comdr 1964, Captain 1971, Rear Adm. 1980. Mem. (non-exec.), Welsh Office Health Policy Bd, 1985–. President: Oxford Royal Naval Assoc., 1984; Midland Naval Officers Assoc., 1985; Vice-Pres., N Oxfordshire SSAFA, 1984. Freeman: Co. of Engineers, 1984; City of London, 1984. Hon. FISTC 1976. *Recreations:* golf, tennis. *Address:* Wadham College, Oxford OX1 3PN. *Club:* Royal Commonwealth Society.

EDWARDS, Joseph Robert, CBE 1963; JP; Chairman: Penta Motors Ltd, Reading, since 1978; Canewdon Consultants plc, Southend-on-Sea, since 1986; Deputy Chairman, Martin Electrical Equipment (Theale) Ltd, since 1979; Director: CSE Aviation Ltd, since 1973; Creative Industries Group Inc., Detroit, since 1985; *b* 5 July 1908; *y s* of late Walter Smith Edwards and Annie Edwards, Gt Yarmouth; *m* 1st, 1936, Frances Mabel Haddon Bourne (*d* 1975); three *s* one *d*; 2nd, 1976, Joan Constance Mary Tattersall. *Educ*: High Sch., Great Yarmouth. Joined Austin Motor Co., Birmingham, 1928; Hercules factory, 1939; rejoined Austin Motor Co., 1941; Gen. Works Manager, 1951; Local Dir, 1953; Works Dir, 1954; Dir of Manufacturing, British Motor Corp., 1955; Managing Director: British Motor Corp., 1966–68; Pressed Steel/Fisher Ltd, 1956–67; Dep. Chm., Harland & Wolff Ltd, 1968–70, Chm. 1970; Dep. Chm., Associated Engrg, 1969–78; Dir, BPC Ltd, 1973–81; Vice-Chm., Lucas (Industries) Ltd, 1976–79. Pres., Motor Industry Research Assoc. Mem., Commn on Industrial Relations to 1974. JP Oxford, 1964. Hon. MA Oxon, 1968. *Recreation*: golf. *Address*: Flat 16, Shoreacres, Banks Road, Sandbanks, Poole, Dorset BH13 7QH. *T*: Canford Cliffs 709315. *Clubs*: Royal Motor Yacht; Parkstone Golf.

EDWARDS, Julie Andrews; *see* Andrews, J.

EDWARDS, Kenneth; *see* Edwards, A. K.

EDWARDS, Dr Kenneth John Richard; Secretary General of Faculties, University of Cambridge, 1984–Sept. 1987; Fellow, St John's College, Cambridge, 1971–Sept. 1987; Vice-Chancellor, University of Leicester, from Sept. 1987; *b* 12 Feb. 1934; *s* of John and Elizabeth May Edwards; *m* 1958, Janet Mary Gray; two *s* one *d*. *Educ*: Market Drayton Grammar Sch.; Univ. of Reading (BSc 1st class 1958); University Coll. of Wales, Aberystwyth (PhD 1961). Nat. Service, RAF, 1952–54. Fellow, Univ. of California, 1961–62; ARC Fellow, Welsh Plant Breeding Station, Aberystwyth, 1962–63, Sen. Sci. Officer, 1963–66; Cambridge University: Lectr in Genetics, 1966–84; Head of Dept of Genetics, 1981–84; St John's College: Lectr, 1971–84; Tutor, 1980–84. Vis. Lectr in Genetics, Univ. of Birmingham, 1965; Vis. Prof., INTA, Buenos Aires, 1973; Leverhulme Res. Fellow, Univ. of California, 1973. *Publications*: Evolution in Modern Biology, 1977; articles on genetics in sci. jls. *Recreations*: music, gardening. *Address*: (until Sept. 1987) 10 Sedley Taylor Road, Cambridge CB2 2PW. *T*: Cambridge 245680; (from Sept. 1987) Knighton Hall, Leicester. *T*: Leicester 706677.

EDWARDS, Hon. Sir Llewellyn (Roy), Kt 1984; Chairman, World Expo 88 Authority, since 1983; *b* 2 Aug. 1935; *s* of Roy Thomas Edwards and Agnes Dulcie Gwendoline Edwards; *m* 1958, Leone Sylvia Burley; two *s* one *d*. *Educ*: Raceview State Sch.; Silkstone State Sch.; Ipswich Grammar Sch.; Univ. of Queensland (MB, BS 1965). Qualified Electrician, 1955. RMO and Registrar in Surgery, Ipswich Hosp., 1965–68; gen. practice, Ipswich, 1968–74. MLA (L) Ipswich, Qld Parlt, 1972–83; Minister for Health, Qld, 1974–78; Dep. Premier and Treasurer, Qld, 1978–83; Dep. Med. Supt, Ipswich Hosp., 1983–85. FRACMA 1984. *Recreations*: tennis, walking. *Address*: 211 Edwards Street, Flinders View, Ipswich, Qld 4305, Australia. *T*: 07 2888333. *Clubs*: Brisbane (Brisbane, Qld); Cricketers, United Services (Qld), Ipswich (Ipswich, Qld).

EDWARDS, Malcolm John, CBE 1985; Commercial Director, British Coal (formerly National Coal Board), since 1985; Member of the Board, British Coal, since 1986; *b* 25 May 1934; *s* of John J. Edwards and Edith (*née* Riley); *m* 1967, Yvonne, *d* of Mr and Mrs J. A. W. Daniels, Port Lincoln, S Australia; two *s*. *Educ*: Alleyn's Sch., Dulwich; Jesus Coll., Cambridge (MA). Joined NCB as trainee, 1956; Industrial Sales Manager, 1962; Dir of Domestic and Industrial Sales, 1969; Dir Gen. of Marketing, 1973; Jt Chm., Solid Fuel Adv. Service, 1984; responsible for coal utilisation R & D, 1984–; Director: British Fuel Co., 1985–; Inter Continental Fuels, 1985–. *Publication*: (with J. J. Edwards) Medical Museum Technology, 1959. *Recreations*: book collecting, arts and crafts movement, music, gardening. *Address*: Lodge Farm, Moot Lane, Downton, Salisbury, Wilts SP5 3LN.

EDWARDS, Marcus; *see* Edwards, C. M.

EDWARDS, Sir Martin Llewellyn, Kt 1974; DL; Solicitor; Consultant with Edwards, Geldard & Shepherd, Cardiff; *b* 21 May 1909; *s* of Charles Ernest Edwards, Solicitor, and Annie Matilda Edwards (*née* Llewellyn); *m* 1936, Dorothy Ward Harrap; one *s* two *d* (and one *d* decd). *Educ*: Marlborough Coll.; Lincoln Coll., Oxford (MA). Admitted Solicitor, 1934. Commnd in RAuxAF, 1937; served 614 (Glamorgan Sqdn RAuxAF, UK), 1937–41; 241 Sqdn, 1941–42; RAF Staff Coll., 1942; Wing Comdr Desert Air Force, HQ Iraq, Persia, and Air Defences Eastern Med., 1942–43; Mem. Directing Staff, ME Jt Staff Coll., Haifa, 1944; Station Comdr, RAF Amman, 1944–45. Mem. Council and Gen. Purposes and Finance Cttees, Glamorgan T&AFA, 1946–68 (Vice-Chm., Air, 1961–68). Mem. Council, Law Society, 1957 (Vice-Pres. 1972–73, Pres., 1973–74; Chm., Educn and Trng Cttee, 1966–69). Pres., Associated Law Socs of Wales, 1960–62; Pres., Incorporated Law Soc. for Cardiff and District, 1969–70. Member: Lord Chancellor's Cttee on Legal Educn, 1967–71. Council, UWIST, 1969–79; Drinking and Driving Cttee, DoE, 1974–76; part-time Chm., Industrial Tribunals, 1975–78. Governor, Coll. of Law, 1967–80 (Chm. of Governors, 1969–72). DL Glamorgan, 1961. *Recreations*: walking, gardening, photography. *Address*: Pentwyn Farm, Graig Llwyn Road, Lisvane, Cardiff CF4 5RP. *T*: Cardiff 751813. *Club*: Army and Navy.

EDWARDS, Michael; *see* Edwards, J. M. McF.

EDWARDS, Rt. Hon. Nicholas; *see* Edwards, Rt Hon. R. N.

EDWARDS, Norman L.; *see* Lloyd-Edwards.

EDWARDS, Owen; Director, Sianel 4 Cymru, (Welsh Fourth Channel Authority), since 1981; *b* 26 Dec. 1933; *m* 1958, Shân Emlyn; two *d*. *Educ*: Leighton Park, Reading; Lincoln Coll., Oxford (MA). Cataloguer, Nat. Library of Wales, 1958–60; BBC Wales: Compère, TV Programme Heddiw, 1961–66; Programme Organiser, 1967–70; Head of Programmes, 1970–74; Controller, 1974–81. Chm., Assoc. for Film and TV in Celtic Countries, 1983–85; Vice-Chm., Royal Nat. Eisteddfod of Wales, 1985. *Recreations*: swimming, walking. *Address*: (office) Sianel 4 Cymru, Sophia Close, Cardiff CF1 9XY. *T*: Cardiff 43421; (home) Coed-y-Pry, 3 Llandennis Avenue, Cyncoed, Cardiff. *T*: Cardiff 751469.

EDWARDS, Prof. Philip Walter, PhD; FBA 1986; King Alfred Professor of English Literature, University of Liverpool, since 1974; *b* 7 Feb. 1923; *er s* of late R. H. Edwards, MC, and late Mrs B. Edwards; *m* 1st, 1947, Hazel Margaret (*d* 1950), *d* of late Prof. C. W. and Mrs E. R. Valentine; 2nd, 1952, Sheila Mary, *d* of R. S. and Mrs A. M. Wilkes, Bloxwich, Staffs; three *s* one *d*. *Educ*: King Edward's High Sch., Birmingham; Univ. of Birmingham. MA, PhD Birmingham; MA Dublin. Royal Navy, 1942–45 (Sub-Lieut RNVR). Lectr in English, Univ. of Birmingham, 1946–60; Commonwealth Fund Fellow, Harvard Univ., 1954–55; Prof. of English Lit., TCD, 1960–66; Fellow of TCD, 1962–66; Prof. of Lit., Univ. of Essex, 1966–74; Pro-Vice-Chancellor, Liverpool Univ., 1980–83. Visiting Professor: Univ. of Michigan, 1964–65; Williams Coll., Mass, 1969; Otago Univ., NZ, 1980; Visiting Fellow: All Souls Coll., Oxford, 1970–71; Huntington Liby, Calif., 1977, 1983. *Publications*: Sir Walter Ralegh, 1953; (ed) Kyd, The Spanish Tragedy,

1959; Shakespeare and the Confines of Art, 1968; (ed) Pericles Prince of Tyre, 1976; (ed with C. Gibson) Massinger, Plays and Poems, 1976; Threshold of a Nation, 1979; (ed jtly) Shakespeare's Styles, 1980; (ed) Hamlet Prince of Denmark, 1985; Shakespeare: a writer's progress, 1986; numerous articles on Shakespeare and literature of his time in Shakespeare Survey, Proc. British Acad., etc. *Recreation*: hill walking. *Address*: 12 South Bank, Oxton, Birkenhead L43 5UP. *T*: 051–652 6089.

EDWARDS, Quentin Tytler, QC 1975; **His Honour Judge Quentin Edwards;** a Circuit Judge, since 1982; Chancellor, Diocese of Blackburn, since 1977, Diocese of Chichester, since 1978; *b* 16 Jan. 1925; *s* of Herbert Jackson Edwards and Juliet Hester Edwards; *m* 1948, Barbara Marian Guthrie; two *s* one *d*. *Educ*: Bradfield Coll.; Council of Legal Educn. Royal Navy, 1943–46. Called to Bar, Middle Temple, 1948; Bencher, 1972. A Recorder of the Crown Court, 1974–82. Licensed Reader, Dio. of London, 1967; Member: Legal Adv. Commn of General Synod of Church of England, 1973; Dioceses Commn, 1978–. Hon. MA (Archbp of Canterbury), 1961. *Publications*: (with Peter Dow) Public Rights of Way and Access to the Countryside, 1951; (with K. Macmorran, et al) Ecclesiastical Law, 3rd edn, Halsbury's Laws of England, 1955; What is Unlawful?, 1959; (with J. N. D. Anderson, et al) Putting Asunder, 1966. *Recreations*: the open air; the table; architecture. *Address*: c/o The Treasury, Middle Temple, EC4. *Club*: Athenæum.

EDWARDS, Robert; MP (Lab and Co-op) Wolverhampton South East, since 1974 (Bilston, 1955–74); National Officer of Transport and General Workers' Union, 1971–76; *b* 16 Jan. 1905; *m* 1933, Edith May Sandham (*d* 1970); one *s*. *Educ*: Council Schs and Technical Coll. Served with Republicans in Spain during Spanish civil war. Chm. delegns to Russia, 1926 and 1934. Mem. Liverpool City Council, 1929–32; Nat. Chm., ILP, 1943–48; Founder Pres., Socialist Movement for United States of Europe. Contested (ILP) Chorley 1935, Stretford 1939 and Newport 1945. Gen. Sec., Chemical Workers' Union, 1947–71; Chm., Chem. Section, ICF, 1971–. Vice-President: British Section European League for Economic Co-operation; Economic Research Council; Council of Europe, 1969–70; Dep. Leader, British Delgn to Council of Europe, and Chm., Defence Cttee, WEU Assembly, 1968–; Leader, British Delegn, N Atlantic Assembly, 1968–69. Pres., Industrial Common Ownership Movement, 1970–. Chm., Parly Gp for Industrial Common Ownership, 1976–; Mem., European Parlt, 1977–79. Editor, The Chemical Worker. Trustee, Scott Bader Commonwealth, 1969. Hon. Fellow, Wolverhampton Polytechnic, 1986. *Publications*: Chemicals—Servant or Master, 1947; Study of a Master Spy, 1962; Multinationals and the Trade Unions, 1978; One Year in the European Parliament, 1979. *Address*: House of Commons, SW1.

EDWARDS, Prof. Robert Geoffrey, FRS 1984; Professor of Human Reproduction, Cambridge University, since 1985; Fellow, Churchill College, Cambridge; Scientific Director, Bourn Hall Clinic, Cambridgeshire; *b* 27 Sept. 1925; *s* of Samuel and Margaret Edwards; *m* 1956, Ruth Eileen Fowler; five *d*. *Educ*: Manchester Central High Sch.; Univs of Wales and Edinburgh. PhD (Edin); DSc (Wales); MA (Cantab). Service in British Army, 1944–48; commnd 1946. UC North Wales, Bangor, 1948–51; Univ. of Edinburgh, 1951–57; Res. Fellow at California Inst. of Tech., 1957–58; Scientist at Nat. Inst. of Medical Research, Mill Hill, NW7, 1958–62; Glasgow Univ. 1962–63; in Dept of Physiology, Cambridge Univ. 1963–; Ford Foundation Reader in Physiology, 1969–85. Chm., European Soc. of Human Reproduction and Embryology, 1984–. Vis. Scientist: in Johns Hopkins Hosp., Baltimore, 1965; Univ. of N Carolina, 1966; Vis. Prof., Free Univ., Brussels, 1984. Hon. FRCOG 1985; Hon. MRCP 1986. Hon. Mem. French Soc. for Infertility, 1983. Life Fellow, Australian Fertility Soc., 1985. Hon. Citizen of Bordeaux, 1985. Hon. DSc Hull, 1983. Spanish Fertility Soc. Gold Medal, 1985. Chief Editor, Human Reproduction, 1986–. *Publications*: A Matter of Life (with P. C. Steptoe), 1980; Conception in the Human Female, 1980; (with C. R. Austin) Mechanisms of Sex Differentiation in Animals and Man; (with J. M. Purdy) Human Conception in Vitro, 1982; (with J. M. Purdy and P. C. Steptoe) Implantation of the Human Embryo, 1985; (with M. Seppälä) In Vitro Fertilisation and Embryo Transfer, 1985; editor of several scientific textbooks on reproduction; numerous articles in scientific and medical jls, organiser of conferences, etc. *Recreations*: farming, politics, music. *Address*: Duck End Farm, Dry Drayton, Cambridge. *T*: Crafts Hill 80602.

EDWARDS, Robert John, CBE 1986; Deputy Chairman, Mirror Group Newspapers, 1985–86 (Senior Group Editor, 1984–85); *b* 26 Oct. 1925; *m* 1st, 1952, Laura Ellwood (marr. diss. 1972); two *s* two *d*; 2nd, 1977, Brigid Segrave. *Educ*: Ranelagh Sch., Bracknell. Editor, Tribune, 1951–54; Dep. Editor, Sunday Express, 1957–59; Man. Editor, Daily Express, 1959–61; Editor: Daily Express, 1961, 1963–65; Evening Citizen, Glasgow, 1962–63; Sunday People, 1966–72; Sunday Mirror, 1972–84; Dir, Mirror Group Newspapers, 1976–86. *Address*: 74 Duns Tew, Oxford OX5 4JL. *T*: (0869) 40417. *Clubs*: Reform, Kennel, Variety Club of Great Britain; Royal Southern Yacht.

EDWARDS, Robert Septimus Friar, CVO 1964; CBE 1963; *b* 21 Oct. 1910; *y s* of late Augustus C. Edwards and of Amy Edwards; *m* 1946, Janet Mabel Wrigley; one *s* two *d*. *Educ*: Hereford Cathedral Sch. Chief Engineering Asst, Hereford, until 1936; Min. of Transport, Highway Engineering, 1936–43; Principal, Min. of War Transport, 1943; Mem. British Merchant Shipping Mission, Washington, DC, 1944–46. Sec. Gen. Internat. Conf. on Safety of Life at Sea, 1948; Principal Private Sec. to Minister of Transport, 1949–51; Shipping Attaché, British Embassy, Washington, DC, 1951–54; Dir of Sea Transport, 1954–57; Gen. Manager, London Airports, 1957–63; Gen. Manager, 1967–69, Dir-Gen., 1969–71; Mersey Docks and Harbour Board. Chm., Morris & David Jones Ltd, 1973–74. Called to the Bar, Middle Temple, 1941. *Address*: Bryn-y-Groes, Nannerch, Clwyd CH7 5QS. *T*: Mold 740018.

EDWARDS, Robin Anthony, CBE 1981; Partner with Dundas & Wilson, CS (formerly Davidson & Syme, WS), since 1965; *b* 7 April 1939; *s* of Alfred Walton Edwards and Ena Annie Ruffell; *m* 1963, Elizabeth Alexandra Mackay; one *s* one *d*. *Educ*: Daniel Stewart's Coll., Edinburgh; Edinburgh Univ. (MA, LLB (distinction), Cl. Medallist). Former Lectr in Conveyancing, Edinburgh Univ.; Admitted Member, WS Society, 1964; Mem. Council, Law Society of Scotland, 1969–, Vice-Pres., 1978–79, Pres., 1979–80 (youngest Pres. ever, at that time). *Recreations*: golf, travel. *Address*: 12 Barnton Gardens, Edinburgh EH4 6AF. *T*: 031–336 3272.

EDWARDS, Rt. Hon. (Roger) Nicholas; PC 1979; MP (C) Pembroke since 1970; Secretary of State for Wales, since 1979; *b* 25 Feb. 1934; *s* of late (H. C.) Ralph Edwards, CBE, FSA, and Marjorie Ingham Brooke; *m* 1963, Ankaret Healing; one *s* two *d*. *Educ*: Westminster Sch.; Trinity Coll., Cambridge, 1954–57; read History: BA 1957, MA, 1968. Member of Lloyds, 1965–. Opposition spokesman on Welsh affairs, 1975–79. Hon. Fellow, UC, Cardiff. *Publications*: articles and reviews in The Connoisseur and other jls. *Recreations*: fishing, gardening, collecting English drawings. *Address*: House of Commons, SW1A 0AA. *Clubs*: Carlton; Cardiff and County.

EDWARDS, Dr Roger Snowden, CBE 1964; JP; Chairman, Gas Industry Training Board, 1965–74, retired; *b* 19 Dec. 1904; *s* of late Herbert George Edwards and late Margaret Alice Edwards; *m* 1935, Eveline Brunton, MBE; two *s* one *d*. *Educ*: Enfield Grammar Sch.; Imperial Coll. of Science. Junior Staff, Imperial Coll. of Science, 1925–28;

Physicist, British Xylonite Co., 1928–29; Physicist, Boot Trade Research Association, 1929–39; Dir, Co-operative Wholesale Soc., 1939–49. Chairman: Council of Industrial Design, 1947–52 (Mem., 1944–47); NE Gas Board, 1949–66; Mem., Gas Council, 1966–70. JP Harrogate, 1960; Surrey, 1966. *Recreation:* golf. *Address:* 23 Manor Way, Letchworth, Herts SG6 3NL.

EDWARDS, Prof. Ronald Walter, DSc; FIBiol, FIWPC; Professor and Head of Department of Applied Biology, University of Wales Institute of Science and Technology, since 1968; *b* 7 June 1930; *s* of Walter and Violet Edwards. *Educ:* Solihull Sch., Warwicks; Univ. of Birmingham (BSc, DSc). FIBiol 1965; FIWPC 1981. Biologist, Freshwater Biol Assoc., 1953–58; Sen., Principal, and Sen. Principal Scientific Officer, Water Pollution Res. Lab., 1958–68. Dep. Chm., Welsh Water Authority, 1983– (Mem., 1974–84); Natural Environment Res. Council, 1970–73 and 1982–85. *Publications:* (co-ed) Ecology and the Industrial Society, 1968; (co-ed) Conservation and Productivity of Natural Waters, 1975; (with Dr M. Brooker) The Ecology of the River Wye, 1982; about 70 papers in learned jls. *Recreations:* music, collecting Staffordshire pottery. *Address:* Department of Applied Biology, University of Wales Institute of Science and Technology, King Edward VII Avenue, Cardiff CF1 3NU. *Club:* Royal Commonwealth Society.

EDWARDS, Prof. Sir Samuel Frederick, (Sir Sam Edwards), Kt 1975; FRS 1966; Cavendish Professor of Physics, Cambridge University, since 1984 (John Humphrey Plummer Professor, 1972–84); Fellow, Caius College, since 1972; Chief Scientific Adviser, Department of Energy, since 1983; *b* 1 Feb. 1928; *s* of Richard and Mary Jane Edwards, Manselton, Swansea; *m* 1953, Merriell E. M. Bland; one *s* three *d*. *Educ:* Swansea Grammar Sch.; Caius Coll., Cambridge (MA, PhD); Harvard University. Inst. for Advanced Study, Princeton, 1952; Univ. of Birmingham, 1953; Univ. of Manchester, 1958, Prof. of Theoretical Physics, 1963–72. Chm., SRC, 1973–77. UK Deleg. to NATO Science Cttee, 1974–79; Mem., Planning Cttee, Max-Planck Gesellschaft, 1974–77. Vice-Pres., Institute of Physics, 1970–73 (Mem. Council, 1967–73); Mem. Council, Inst. of Mathematics and its Applications, 1976– (Vice-Pres., 1979, Pres., 1980–81). Member: Physics Cttee, SRC, 1968–73 (Chm. 1970–73); Polymer Cttee, SRC, 1968–73; Science Bd, SRC, 1970–73; Council, European Physical Soc., 1969–71 (Chm., Condensed Matter Div., 1969–71); UGC, 1971–73; Defence Scientific Adv. Council, 1973– (Chm., 1977–80); Metrology and Standards Req. Bd, Dept of Industry, 1974–77; Chm., Adv. Council on R&D, Dept of Energy, 1983– (Mem., 1974–77); Member Council: European R&D (EEC), 1976–80; Royal Soc., 1982–83 (a Vice-Pres., 1982–83); Chm., Council, BAAS, 1977–82. Non-exec. Director: Lucas Industries, 1981–; Steetley plc, 1985–. FInstP; FIMA; FRSC. Hon. DTech Loughborough, 1975; Hon. DSc: Salford, Edinburgh, 1976; Bath, 1978; Birmingham, 1986. Maxwell Medal and Prize, Inst. of Physics, 1974; High Polymer Physics Prize, Amer. Phys. Soc., 1982; Davy Medal, Royal Soc., 1984; Gold Medal, Inst. of Maths, 1986. *Publications:* Technological Risk, 1980; (with M. Doi) Theory of Polymer Dynamics, 1986; contribs to learned jls. *Address:* 7 Penarth Place, Cambridge CB3 9LU. *T:* Cambridge 66610. *Club:* Athenæum.

EDWARDS, Stewart Leslie, CMG 1967; Under-Secretary, Department of Trade, retired; *b* 6 Nov. 1914; *s* of late Walter James and Lilian Emma Edwards; *m* 1940, Dominica Jeanne Lavie, *d* of Joseph Lavie and Jeanne Jauréguiberry; two *s*. *Educ:* King's Sch., Canterbury; Corpus Christi Coll., Cambridge (Foundn Scholar). BA 1936; MA 1943. Appointed to War Office, 1937. Military service, 1942–44. Called to the Bar, Inner Temple, 1947. Seconded from War Office to OEEC, 1948–51; Board of Trade, 1951–65; Minister (Economic), Bonn, 1965–70; Under-Sec., DTI later Dept of Trade, 1970–74. *Recreations:* music, reading, hill-walking, wine. *Address:* B51 Résidence La Pastourelle, Bât. A, 20 Avenue Daniel-Hedde, 17200 Royan, France. *T:* 46392203.

EDWARDS, Vero C. W.; *see* Wynne-Edwards.

EDWARDS, William (Henry); solicitor; *b* 6 Jan. 1938; *s* of Owen Henry Edwards and S. Edwards; *m* 1961, Ann Eleri Rogers; one *s* three *d*. *Educ:* Sir Thomas Jones' Comprehensive Sch.; Liverpool Univ. LLB. MP (Lab) Merioneth, 1966–Feb. 1974; contested (Lab) Merioneth, Oct. 1974; Prospective Parly Cand. (Lab), Anglesey, 1981–83. Mem., Historic Building Council for Wales, 1971–76. Editor, Solicitors Diary. *Recreations:* golf, Association football (from the terraces). *Address:* Hope House, Lombard Street, Dolgellau, Gwynedd.

EDWARDS, William Philip Neville, CBE 1949; *b* 5 Aug. 1904; *s* of late Neville P. Edwards, Orford, Littlehampton, Sussex; *m* 1st, 1931, Hon. Sheila Cary (*d* 1976), 2nd *d* of 13th Viscount Falkland; two *s*; 2nd, 1976, Joan, *widow* of Norman Mullins. *Educ:* Rugby Sch.; Corpus Christi Coll., Cambridge; Princeton Univ., USA (Davison Scholar). Joined Underground Electric group of companies, 1927; shortly afterwards appointed Sec. to Lord Ashfield, Chm. of Board; First Sec. of Standing Jt Cttee of Main Line Railway Companies and of LPTB, 1933; Officer of Board as Personal Asst to Gen. Manager of Railways, 1937; Outdoor Supt of Railways, 1938; Public Relations Officer of Board, 1939; Asst to Chm. of Supply Council of Min. of Supply, 1941–42; Head of Industrial Information Div. of Min. of Production and Alternate Dir of Information of British Supply Council in N America, 1943–45; Dir of Overseas Information Div. of BoT, 1945–46; Head of British Information Services in USA, 1946–49. A Dir, Confedn of British Industry (previously FBI), 1949–66; Man. Dir, British Overseas Fairs Ltd, 1959–66, Chm., 1966–68. UK Associate Dir, Business International SA, 1968–75; Chm., Public Relations (Industrial) Ltd, 1970–75. Chevalier (1st class) of Order of Dannebrog (Denmark), 1955; Commander of Order of Vasa (Sweden), 1962. *Recreations:* golf, gardening. *Address:* Four Winds, Kithurst Lane, Storrington, Sussex RH20 4LP. *Club:* Carlton.

EDWARDS-JONES, Ian, QC 1967; The Banking Ombudsman, since 1985; *b* 17 April 1923; *o s* of late Col H. V. Edwards-Jones, MC, DL, Swansea, Glam; *m* 1950, Susan Vera Catharine McClintock, *o d* of E. S. McClintock and of Mrs A. MacRossie; three *s*. *Educ:* Rugby Sch.; Trinity Coll., Cambridge (BA). Capt., RA, N Africa, Italy, Palestine, 1942–47. Called to Bar, Middle Temple, Lincoln's Inn, 1948, Bencher, Lincoln's Inn, 1975. A Social Security (formerly Nat. Insurance) Comr, 1979–85. *Recreations:* fishing, shooting, photography. *Address:* 7 Stone Buildings, Lincoln's Inn, WC2A 3SZ. *T:* 01–405 3886/7; Office of the Banking Ombudsman, Citadel House, 5/11 Fetter Lane, EC4A 1BR. *T:* 01–583 1395. *Clubs:* United Oxford & Cambridge University; Bar Yacht.

EDWARDS-MOSS, Sir John (Herbert Theodore), 4th Bt *cr* 1868; *b* 24 June 1913; *s* of late Major John Edwards-Moss and Dorothy Kate Gwyllyam, *e d* of late Ven. Henry William Watkins, DD; *S* uncle, Sir Thomas Edwards-Moss, 3rd Bt, 1960; *m* 1951, Jane Rebie, *d* of Carteret John Kempson; five *s* one *d*. *Educ:* Downhouse, Rottingdean. *Heir:* *s* David John Edwards-Moss, *b* 2 Feb. 1955. *Address:* Ruffold Farm, Cranleigh, Surrey.

EELES, Air Cdre Henry, CB 1956; CBE 1943; retired as Director of Administrative Plans, Air Ministry, 1959; *b* 12 May 1910; *yr s* of Henry Eeles, Newcastle upon Tyne; *m* 1st, 1940, Janet (*d* 1960), *d* of Major J. H. Norton; two *s* one *d*; 2nd, 1963, Pamela Clarice, *d* of Comdr G. A. Matthew, Royal Navy. *Educ:* Harrow. Entered RAF Coll., 1929; Commnd Dec. 1930; Sqdn Ldr 1938; Group Capt. 1949; Air Cdre 1955. Comdt RAF Coll. and AOC RAF Cranwell, 1952–56. *Address:* The Cottage, Sutton Veny, Warminster, Wilts.

EFFINGHAM, 6th Earl of, *cr* 1837; **Mowbray Henry Gordon Howard;** 16th Baron Howard, of Effingham, *cr* 1554; *b* 29 Nov. 1905; *er s* of 5th Earl and Rosamond Margaret, *d* of late E. H. Hudson; *S* father, 1946; *m* 1st, 1938, Manci Maria Malvina Gertler (marr. diss. 1946); 2nd, 1952, Gladys Irene Kerry (marr. diss. 1971); 3rd, 1972, (Mabel) Suzanne Mingay Cragg, *d* of late Maurice Jules-Marie Le Pen, Paris, and *widow* of Wing Comdr Francis Talbot Cragg. *Educ:* Lancing. Served War 1939–45, RA and 3rd Maritime Reg. *Recreations:* shooting, fishing, philately. *Heir:* *n* Lt-Comdr David Peter Mowbray Algernon Howard, RN [*b* 29 April 1939; *m* 1964, Anne Mary Sayer (marr. diss. 1975); one *s*]. *Address:* House of Lords, SW1.

EGAN, Sir John Leopold, Kt 1986; Chairman and Chief Executive, Jaguar plc, since 1985; *b* 7 Nov. 1939; *m* 1963, Julia Emily Treble; two *d*. *Educ:* Bablake Sch., Coventry; Imperial Coll., London Univ., 1958–61 (BSc Hons; FIC 1985); London Business Sch., London Univ., 1966–68 (MScEcon). Petroleum Engineer, Shell International, 1962–66; General Manager, Al-Delco Replacement Parts Operation, General Motors Ltd, 1968–71; Managing Director, Leyland Cars Parts Div., Parts and Service Director, Leyland Cars, BLMC, 1971–76; Corporate Parts Director, Massey Ferguson, 1976–80; Chm. and Chief Exec., Jaguar Cars Ltd, 1980–85. *Recreations:* music, squash, tennis. *Address:* Jaguar plc, Brown's Lane, Coventry CV5 9DR. *T:* Coventry 402121. *Club:* Warwick Boat.

EGDELL, Dr John Duncan; Regional Medical Officer, Mersey Regional Health Authority, since 1977; *b* 5 March 1938; *s* of John William Egdell and Nellie (*née* Thompson); *m* 1963, Dr Linda Mary Flint; two *s* one *d*. *Educ:* Clifton Coll.; Univ. of Bristol. MB, ChB (Bristol) 1961; DipSocMed (Edin.) 1967; FFCM 1979 (MFCM 1973). Ho. Phys. and Ho. Surg., Bristol Gen. Hosp., 1961–62; gen. practice, 1962–65; Med. Administration: with Newcastle Regional Hosp. Bd, 1966–69; with South Western Regional Hosp. Bd, 1969–74; Regional Specialist in Community Med., South Western Regional Health Authority, 1974–76; Regional Medical Postgrad. Co-ordinator, Univ. of Bristol, 1973–76; Hon. Lectr in Community Health, Univ. of Liverpool, 1980–. *Recreations:* delving into the past; investigating the obscure. *Address:* 8 Kingsmead Road North, Oxton, Birkenhead, Merseyside L43 6TB. *T:* 051–653 7810.

EGELAND, Leif; *b* 19 Jan. 1903; *s* of late J. J. Egeland, Consul for Norway in Natal, and Ragnhild Konsmo; *m* 1942, Marguerite Doreen (*d* 1984), *d* of late W. J. de Zwaan, Waterkloof, Pretoria; one *d*. *Educ:* Durban High Sch.; Natal University Coll.; Oxford Univ. MA English Lang. and Literature, Natal Univ. Coll.; MA, Hons BA, Jurisprudence, BCL Oxon; Rhodes Scholar (Natal), Trinity Coll., Oxford, 1924–27; official Fellow in Law and Classics, Brasenose Coll., 1927–30 (Hon.Fellow, 1984); Harmsworth Scholar, Middle Temple, 1927–30; Barrister, Middle Temple, 1930, bencher, 1948; Hon. LLD Cambridge, 1948. Admitted as Advocate of Supreme Court of S Africa, 1931; Vice-Consul for Norway, Natal, 1931–44; MP (House of Assembly) for Durban (Berea), 1933–38, for Zululand, 1940–43; SA Minister to Sweden, 1943, to Holland and Belgium, 1946. Served War of 1939–45, as AJAG, in UDF, 1940–43; Middle East with 6th Armoured Div. of UDF, 1943. SA Delegate to San Francisco Conf., 1945, to 1st Gen. Assembly of UN, London, 1946, to Final Assembly of League of Nations, 1946; SA delegate and Pres. of Commn on Italian Political and Territorial Questions at Peace Conf., Paris, 1946. High Comr in London for the Union of South Africa, 1948–50; Consultant to Standard General Insurance Co. Ltd. Hon. Pres., South Africa Inst. of Internat. Affairs; Chm., Smuts Memorial Trust; Life Trustee, South Africa Foundn. Hon. Pres., SA Guide-dogs Assoc. for the Blind. FRSA 1948. *Recreations:* tennis, bridge. *Address:* 11 Fricker Road, Illovo, Johannesburg, S Africa. *Clubs:* Rand, Inanda (S Africa).

EGERTON, family name of **Duke of Sutherland** and **Earl of Wilton.**

EGERTON, Maj.-Gen. David Boswell, CB 1968; OBE 1956; MC 1940; *b* 24 July 1914; *s* of Vice-Admiral W. de M. Egerton, DSO, and late Anita Adolphine (*née* David); *m* 1946, Margaret Gillian, *d* of Canon C. C. Inge; one *s* two *d*. *Educ:* Stowe; RMA Woolwich. Commissioned Royal Artillery, Aug. 1934; served in India, 1935–39; ops in Waziristan, 1937; France and Belgium, 1940 (MC); Egypt 1942, Italy 1944 (wounded). Technical Staff course, RMCS, 1946; BJSM, Washington, DC, 1950–52; Asst Chief Engineer in charge of ammunition development, Royal Armament R&D Estabt, 1955–58; idc 1959; Army Mem., Defence Research Policy Staff, 1959–62; Comdt, Trials Estabt Guided Weapons, RA, 1962–63; Army Mem., Air Defence Working Party, 1963–64; Dir-Gen. of Artillery, Army Dept, 1964–67; Vice-Pres., Ordnance Board, 1967–69, President, 1969–70; retired 1970. Col Comdt, RA, 1970–74. Gen. Sec., Assoc. of Recognised Eng. Lang. Schs, 1971–79. *Recreations:* gardening, travel. *Address:* Campion Cottage, Cheselbourne, Dorchester. *T:* Milborne St Andrew 641. *Club:* Army and Navy.

EGERTON, Sir John Alfred Roy, (Jack Egerton), Kt 1976; Alderman and Deputy Mayor, Gold Coast City Council; *b* Rockhampton, 11 March 1918; *s* of J. G. Egerton, Rockhampton; *m* 1940, Moya, *d* of W. Jones; one *s*. *Educ:* Rockhampton High Sch.; Mt Morgan High Sch.; Australian Admin. Staff Coll. A Union Exec. Officer, 1941–76; Federal Officer of Boilermakers' Union, 1951–66 (Vice-Pres. Fed. Council; rep. Union in China, 1956); Official, Metal Trades Fedn, 1951–67; Mem., ACTU Interstate Exec., 1969; former Pres., Qld Trades and Labor Council. Aust. Rep. ILO Congresses, Geneva: 1960, 1966, 1968, 1974; Qld Rep. to ACTU Congress and ALP Fed. Conf.; Pres., ALP Qld Exec., 1968–76 (Mem. Qld Central Exec., 1958); Mem., Fed. Exec. of ALP, 1970, Sen. Vice-Pres. 1972. Director: Qantas Airways Ltd, 1973–; Mary Kathleen Uranium; SGIO Building Soc.; Beenleigh Rum. Member: Duke of Edinburgh Study Conf. Cttee, 1967–74; Griffith Univ. Council. *Recreations:* reading, Rugby League (Vice-Pres. and Dir, Qld), golf, trotting. *Address:* Gold Coast City Centre, Bundall Road, Southport, Qld 4215, Australia. *Clubs:* NSW and Queensland League, Virginia Golf, Albion Park Trotting.

EGERTON, Sir Philip John Caledon G.; *see* Grey Egerton.

EGERTON, Sir Seymour (John Louis), GCVO 1977 (KCVO 1970); Director, Coutts & Co., Bankers, 1947–85 (Chairman, 1951–76); *b* 24 Sept. 1915; *s* of late Louis Egerton and Jane, *e d* of Rev. Lord Victor Seymour; unmarried. *Educ:* Eton. Served War of 1939–45, in Grenadier Guards. Governor, St George's Hosp., 1958–73. Treasurer, Boy Scouts' Assoc., 1953–64; Vice-Pres., Corporation of the Church House, 1954–81. Sheriff of Greater London, 1968. *Address:* Flat A, 51 Eaton Square, SW1. *T:* 01–235 2164. *Clubs:* Boodle's, Beefsteak, Pratt's.

EGERTON, Stephen Loftus, CMG 1978; HM Diplomatic Service; Ambassador to Saudi Arabia, since 1986; *b* 21 July 1932; *o s* of late William le Belward Egerton, ICS, and late Angela Doreen Loftus Bland; *m* 1958, Caroline, *er d* of Major and Mrs E. T. E. Cary-Elwes, Laurel House, Bergh Apton, Norfolk; one *s* one *d*. *Educ:* Summer Fields; Eton; Trinity Coll., Cambridge. BA 1956, MA 1960. 2nd Lieut, 60th Rifles (KRRC), 1952–53. Entered Foreign Service, 1956; Middle East Centre for Arab Studies, Lebanon, 1956–57; Political Officer and Court Registrar, Kuwait, 1958–61; Private Sec. to Parliamentary Under-Secretary, FO, 1961–62; Northern Dept, FO, 1962–63; Oriental Sec. and later also Head of Chancery, Baghdad, 1963–67; First Sec., UK Mission to the UN, New York,

1967–70; Asst Head of Arabian and Near Eastern Depts, FCO, 1970–72; Counsellor and Head of Chancery, Tripoli, 1972–73; Head of Energy Dept, FCO, 1973–77; Consul-Gen., Rio de Janeiro, 1977–80; Ambassador to Iraq, 1980–82; Asst Under-Sec. of State, FCO, 1982–85. *Recreations:* topiary, argument. *Address:* c/o Foreign and Commonwealth Office, SW1. *Clubs:* Brooks's; Greenjackets.

EGGAR, Timothy John Crommelin, (Tim); MP (C) Enfield North, since 1979; Parliamentary Under-Secretary of State, Foreign and Commonwealth Office, since 1985; *b* 19 Dec. 1951; *s* of late John Drennan Eggar and of Pamela Rosemary Eggar; *m* 1977, Charmian Diana Minoprio; one *s* one *d*. *Educ:* Winchester Coll.; Magdalene Coll., Cambridge (MA). Called to the Bar, Inner Temple, 1976. European Banking Co., 1975–83. Chm., Cambridge Univ. Cons. Assoc., 1972; Vice-Chm., Fedn of Cons. Students, 1973–74. Prospective Parly Candidate, Enfield N, 1975–79; PPS to Minister for Overseas Develt, 1982–85. *Recreations:* skiing, village cricket, simple gardening. *Address:* 117 Fentiman Road, SW8 1JZ. *T:* 01–735 2194. *Clubs:* Bush Hill Park Conservative, Enfield Highway Conservative, Ponders End Conservative, North Enfield Conservative, Enfield Town Conservative.

EGGINTON, Anthony Joseph; Director of Engineering, Science and Engineering Research Council, since 1983; *b* 18 July 1930; *s* of Arthur Reginald Egginton and Margaret Anne (*née* Emslie); *m* 1957, Janet Leta, *d* of late Albert and Florence Herring; two *d*. *Educ:* Selhurst Grammar Sch., Croydon; University Coll., London. BSc 1951. Res. Assoc., UCL, 1951–56; AERE Harwell (Gen. Physics Div.), 1956–61; Head of Beams Physics Gp, NIRNS Rutherford High Energy Lab., 1961–65; Head of Machine Gp, SRC Daresbury Nuclear Physics Lab., 1965–72; Head of Engrg Div., 1972–74, Dir of Engineering and Nuclear Physics, 1974–78, Dir of Science and Engrg Divs, 1978–83, SRC. *Publications:* papers and articles in jls and conf. proceedings on particle accelerators and beams. *Recreations:* sport, cinema, music. *Address:* Witney House, West End, Witney, Oxon OX8 6NQ. *T:* Witney 3502.

EGGLESTON, Anthony Francis, OBE 1968; Headmaster, Campion School, Athens, since 1983; *b* 26 Jan. 1928; *s* of late J. F. Eggleston and late Mrs J. M. Barnard, Harrow, Middx; *m* 1957, Jane Morison Buxton, JP, *d* of late W. L. Buxton, MBE and Mrs F. M. M. Buxton, Stanmore, Middx; one *s* two *d*. *Educ:* Merchant Taylors' Sch., Northwood (Schol.); St John's Coll., Oxford (Sir Thomas White Schol.). BA 1949, MA 1953; 2nd cl. hons Chemistry. National Service, 1950–52; 2nd Lieut, RA, Suez Canal Zone. Asst Master, Cheltenham Coll., 1952–54; Sen. Science Master, English High Sch., Istanbul, 1954–56; Asst Master, Merchant Taylors' Sch., Northwood, 1956–62; Principal, English Sch., Nicosia, 1962–68; Headmaster, Felsted Sch., 1968–82. *Recreation:* looking at buildings. *Address:* PO Box 65009, 15410 - Psychico, Greece. *T:* Athens 8133883; Garden House, Chester Place, Norwich NR2 3DG. *T:* Norwich 616025.

EGGLESTON, Prof. Harold Gordon; Professor of Pure Mathematics in London University and Head of Department of Mathematics, at Royal Holloway College, 1966–81; *b* 27 Nov. 1921; 2nd *s* of H. T. and E. M. Eggleston, Bents Green, Sheffield; *m* 1955, Elizabeth, *o d* of F. R. and C. A. W. Daglish, Beamish, County Durham; two *s* one *d*. *Educ:* High Storrs Grammar Sch., Sheffield; Trinity Coll., Cambridge. Lecturer and Senior Lecturer, University Coll. of Swansea, 1948–53; Lecturer, University of Cambridge, 1953–58; Prof. of Mathematics, University of London at Bedford Coll., 1958–66. *Publications:* Problems in Euclidean Space, 1957; Convexity, 1958; Elementary Real Analysis, 1962. *Address:* Tacoma, High Street, Great Shelford, Cambs.

EGGLESTON, Prof. James Frederick; Professor of Education, University of Nottingham, 1972–84, now Emeritus; *b* 30 July 1927; *s* of Frederick James and Anne Margaret Eggleston; *m* 1956, Margaret Snowden; three *s* two *d*. *Educ:* Appleby Grammar Sch.; Durham Univ. (King's Coll., Newcastle upon Tyne). BSc Hons Zoology; DipEd; FIBiol 1975. School teacher, 1953–64, Head of Biol., later Head of Sci., Hinckley Grammar Sch.; Res. Fellow, Res. Unit for Assessment and Curriculum Studies, Leicester Univ. Sch. of Educn, 1964; team leader, later consultant, Nuffield Sci. Teaching Project, 1964–68; Lectr in Educn, Leicester Univ. Sch. of Educn, 1966; apptd to Colls and Curriculum Chair of Educn, Nottingham Univ., 1973, Dean of Educn, 1975–81. *Publications:* A Critical Review of Assessment Procedures in Secondary School Science, 1965; Problems in Quantitative Biology, 1968; (with J. F. Kerr) Studies in Assessment, 1970; (jtly) A Science Teaching Observation Schedule, 1975; (jtly) Processes and Products of Science Teaching, 1976; contributions to: The Disciplines of the Curriculum, 1971; The Art of the Science Teacher, 1974; Frontiers of Classroom Research, 1975; Techniques and Problems of Assessment, 1976; articles in professional jls. *Recreations:* fell walking, golf, photography. *Address:* The Mount, Bown's Hill, Crich, near Matlock, Derbys DE4 5DG. *T:* Ambergate 2870.

EGGLESTON, Hon. Sir Richard (Moulton), Kt 1971; Consultant, Faculty of Law, Monash University, 1974–83 (Chancellor, 1975–83); *b* Hampton, Vic, Australia, 8 Aug. 1909; *s* of late John Bakewell Eggleston and Elizabeth Bothwell Eggleston (*née* McCutcheon); *m* 1934, Marjorie, *d* of late F. E. Thom; one *s* three *d*. *Educ:* Wesley Coll., Melbourne; Univ. of Melbourne (LLB). Barrister, 1932–41 and 1945–60. Staff of Defence Dept, 1942–45; Indep. Lectr in Equity, Melbourne Univ., 1940–49; KC 1950. Judge: Supreme Ct of Norfolk Is, 1960–69; Supreme Ct of ACT, 1960–74; Commonwealth Industrial Ct, 1960–74; Pres., Trade Practices Tribunal, 1966–74. Dir, Barclays Australia Ltd, 1974–80. Hon. Treas., Victorian Bar Council, 1953–56 (Chm., 1956–58); Mem., Bd of Aust. Elizabethan Theatre Trust, 1961–67; Fellow, Queen's Coll., Univ. of Melbourne, 1964–; Pro-Chancellor, ANU, 1968–72. Chm., Company Law Adv. Cttee, 1967–73. FASSA 1981; Hon. FIArbA, 1977. Hon. LLD: Melbourne, 1973; Monash, 1983. *Publication:* Evidence, Proof and Probability, 1978, 2nd edn, 1983. *Recreations:* painting, golf, billiards, music. *Address:* 3 Willow Street, Malvern, Vic 3144, Australia. *Clubs:* Australian (Melbourne); Commonwealth (Canberra).

EGGLESTON, Prof. Samuel John, BScEcon, MA, DLitt; FCP; Chairman of the Department of Education, University of Warwick, since 1985; *b* 11 Nov. 1926; *s* of Edmund and Josephine Eggleston, Dorchester; *m* 1957, Greta, *d* of James and Alice Patrick, Hereford; two *s* two *d*. *Educ:* Chippenham Grammar Sch.; LSE (BScEcon 1957); Univ. of London Inst. of Educn (MA 1965). Univ. of Keele, DLitt 1977. Teacher, Suffolk and Worcs, 1950–54; Leverhulme Scholarship, LSE, 1954–57; Teacher, Beds, and Headteacher, Oxfordshire, 1957–60; Lectr, Loughborough Coll. of Educn, 1960–63; Lectr, later Sen. Lectr, Leicester Univ., 1963–67; Keele University: Prof. and Head of Dept of Educn, 1967–84; Chm., Bd of Soc. Scis, 1976–79; Chm., Higher Degree and Res. Cttee, 1981–84. Vis. Commonwealth Fellow, Canada, 1973–74. Director: DES Res. Project, Structure and Function of Youth Service, 1968–74; Schs Council Project, Design and Craft Educn, 1968–74; DES Research Projects: Training for Multi-Racial Educn, 1978–80; Minority Gp Adolescence, 1981–84. Chm., Council of Europe Workshop on Multi-Cultural Higher Educn, 1981–86; Member: Schs Council Working Party, Whole Curriculum, 1970–74; Council of Europe Working Party, Diversif. of Tertiary Educn, 1972–78; Cheshire Educn Cttee, 1981–83; Council, Eur. Inst. of Educn and Social Policy, 1983–; Educnl Res. Bd, SSRC, 1973–77; Panel on Public Disorder and Sporting Events, SSRC, 1976–77; In-Service Educn Bd and Art Design Cttee, CNAA, 1977–85; Assessment of Performance Unit, DES, Co-ord. Cttee, 1975–80, Consultative Cttee, 1980–; Res. Consultancy Cttee, DES, 1981–83; Arts Council Cttee on Trng for the Arts, 1982–. Editor: Studies in Design Education and Craft, 1968–; Sociological Rev., 1982– (Chm., Editorial Bd, 1970–82); Chm., Editorial Bd, European Jl of Educn (formerly Paedagogica Europaea), 1976– (Editor in Chief, 1968–76); Founding Chm., Editorial Bd, Multicultural Teaching, 1982–. *Publications:* The Social Context of the School, 1967; (with G. N. Brown) Towards an Education for the 21st Century, 1969; (ed with A. R. Pemberton) International Perspectives of Design Education, 1973; (ed) Contemporary Research in the Sociology of Education, 1974; Adolescence and Community, 1976; New Developments in Design Education, 1976; The Sociology of the School Curriculum, 1977; The Ecology of the School, 1977; (ed) Experimental Education in Europe, 1978; Teacher Decision Making in the Classroom, 1979; School Based Curriculum Development, 1980; Work Experience in Secondary Schools, 1982; Education for Some, 1986; articles in books and jls, incl. Sociol., Brit. Jl of Sociol., New Soc., Educnl Res., Brit. Jl of In-Service Educn, Brit. Jl of Teacher Educn, Res. Intelligence. *Recreations:* work in design and craft, skiing, riding, travel, gardening. *Address:* Hallaton House, Whitmore Heath, Newcastle under Lyme, Staffs ST5 5JA. *T:* Whitmore 680483.

EGGLETON, Anthony, CVO 1970; Federal Director, Liberal Party of Australia, since 1975; *b* 30 April 1932; *s* of Tom and Winifred Eggleton; *m* 1953, Mary Walker, Melbourne; two *s* one *d*. *Educ:* King Alfred's Sch., Wantage. Journalist, Westminster Press Group, 1948–50; Editorial Staff, Bendigo Advertiser, Vic, 1950–51; Australian Broadcasting Commn, 1951–60 (Dir of ABC-TV News Coverage, 1956–60); Dir of Public Relations, Royal Australian Navy, 1960–65; Press Sec. to Prime Ministers of Australia, 1965–71 (Prime Ministers Menzies, Holt, Gorton, McMahon); Commonwealth Dir of Information, London, 1971–74; Special Advr to Leader of Opposition, and Dir of Communications, Federal Liberal Party, 1974–75; Govt Campaign Dir, Federal Elections, 1975, 1977, 1980, 1983, 1984. Exec. Sec., Pacific Democrat Union, 1982–84, 1985–. Australian Public Relations Inst.'s 1st Award of Honour, 1968. *Address:* c/o Parliament House, Canberra, ACT 2600, Australia. *T:* 732564. *Clubs:* (Foundn Pres.) National Press (Canberra), Commonwealth (Canberra).

EGLINGTON, Charles Richard John; Director, Akroyd & Smithers plc, since 1978; *b* 12 Aug. 1938; *s* of Richard Eglington and Treena Margaret Joyce Eglington. *Educ:* Sherborne. Mem. Council, Stock Exchange, 1975–86, Dep. Chm., 1981–84 (Chairman: Quotations Cttee, 1978–81; Property and Finance Cttee, 1983–86). Governor: Sherborne Sch., 1980–; Twyford Sch., 1984–. *Recreations:* golf, cricket. *Address:* Austin Friars House, EC2N 2EE. *T:* 01–588 4535. *Clubs:* MCC; Royal and Ancient Golf (St Andrews); Walton Heath Golf; Rye Golf.

EGLINTON and WINTON, 18th Earl of, *cr* 1507; **Archibald George Montgomerie;** Lord Montgomerie, 1448; Baron Seton and Tranent, 1859; Baron Kilwinning, 1615; Baron Ardrossan (UK), 1806; Earl of Winton (UK), 1859; Hereditary Sheriff of Renfrewshire; Managing Director, since 1972, a Deputy Chairman, since 1980, Gerrard & National plc; *b* 27 Aug. 1939; *s* of 17th Earl of Eglinton and Winton and Ursula, *er d* of Hon. Ronald Watson, Edinburgh; *S* father, 1966; *m* 1964, Marion Carolina, *o d* of John Dunn-Yarker; four *s*. *Educ:* Eton. *Heir:* *s* Lord Montgomerie, *qv*. *Address:* The Dutch House, West Green, Hartley Wintney, Hants.

EGLINTON, Prof. Geoffrey, PhD, DSc; FRS 1976; Professor of Organic Geochemistry, University of Bristol, since 1973; *b* 1 Nov. 1927; *s* of Alfred Edward Eglinton and Lilian Blackham; *m* 1955, Pamela Joan Coupland; two *s* one *d*. *Educ:* Sale Grammar Sch.; Manchester Univ. (BSc, PhD, DSc). Post-Doctoral Fellow, Ohio State Univ., 1951–52; ICI Fellow, Liverpool Univ., 1952–54; Lectr, subseq. Sen. Lectr and Reader, Glasgow Univ., 1954–67; Sen. Lectr, subseq. Reader, Bristol Univ., 1967–73. Mem., NERC, 1984–. Hon. Fellow, Plymouth Polytechnic, 1981. Gold Medal for Exceptional Scientific Achievement, NASA, 1973; Hugo Müller Silver Medal, Chemical Soc., 1974; Alfred Treibs Gold Medal, Geochem. Soc., 1981; Coke Medal, Geol Soc. of London, 1985. *Publications:* Organic Geochemistry: methods and results, 1969; contrib. Nature, Geochim. Cosmochim. Acta, Phytochem., Chem. Geol., Sci. American. *Recreations:* gardening, walking, sailing. *Address:* Oldwell, 7 Redhouse Lane, Bristol BS9 3RY. *T:* Bristol 683833. *Club:* Rucksack (Manchester).

EGMONT, 11th Earl of, *cr* 1733; **Frederick George Moore Perceval;** Bt 1661; Baron Perceval, 1715; Viscount Perceval, 1722; Baron Lovell and Holland (Great Britain), 1762; Baron Arden, 1770; Baron Arden (United Kingdom), 1802; *b* 14 April 1914; *o s* of 10th Earl and Cecilia (*d* 1916), *d* of James Burns Moore, Montreal; *S* father, 1932; *m* 1932, Ann Geraldine, *d* of D. G. Moodie; one *s* one *d* (and two *s* decd). *Heir:* *s* Viscount Perceval, *qv*. *Address:* Two-dot Ranch, Nanton, Alberta, Canada.

EGREMONT, 2nd Baron *cr* 1963, **AND LECONFIELD,** 7th Baron *cr* 1859; **John Max Henry Scawen Wyndham;** *b* 21 April 1948; *s* of John Edward Reginald Wyndham, MBE, 1st Baron Egremont and 6th Baron Leconfield, and of Pamela, *d* of late Captain the Hon. Valentine Wyndham-Quin, RN; *S* father, 1972; *m* 1978, Caroline, *er d* of A. R. Nelson, Muckairn, Taynuilt, Argyll, and Hon. Lady Musker; one *s* three *d*. *Educ:* Eton; Christ Church, Oxford (MA Modern History). *Publications:* The Cousins, 1977 (Yorkshire Post First Book Award); Balfour: a life of Arthur James Balfour, 1980; The Ladies' Man (novel), 1983; Dear Shadows (novel), 1986. *Heir:* *s* Hon. George Ronan Valentine Wyndham, *b* 31 July 1983. *Address:* Petworth House, Petworth, West Sussex GU28 0AE. *T:* Petworth 42447.

EHRMAN, John Patrick William, FBA 1970; historian; *b* 17 March 1920; *o s* of late Albert and Rina Ehrman; *m* 1948, Elizabeth Susan Anne, *d* of late Vice-Adm. Sir Geoffrey Blake, KCB, DSO; four *s*. *Educ:* Charterhouse; Trinity Coll., Cambridge (MA). Served Royal Navy, 1940–45. Fellow of Trinity Coll., Cambridge, 1947–52; Historian, Cabinet Office, 1948–56; Lees Knowles Lectr, Cambridge, 1957–58; James Ford Special Lectr, Oxford, 1976–77. Hon. Treas., Friends of the National Libraries, 1960–77; Trustee of the Nat. Portrait Gall., 1971–85; Member: Reviewing Cttee on Export of Works of Art, 1970–76; Royal Commn on Historical Manuscripts, 1973–; Chm., Adv. Cttee to British Library Reference Div., 1975–84; Panizzi Foundn Selection Council, 1983–; Vice-Pres., Navy Records Soc., 1968–70, 1974–76. FSA 1958; FRHistS. *Publications:* The Navy in the War of William III, 1953; Grand Strategy, 1943–5 (2 vols, UK Official Military Histories of the Second World War), 1956; Cabinet Government and War, 1890–1940, 1958; The British Government and Commercial Negotiations with Europe, 1783–1793, 1962; The Younger Pitt, vol. 1, The Years of Acclaim, 1969, vol. 2, The Reluctant Transition, 1983. *Address:* The Mead Barns, Taynton, near Burford, Oxfordshire OX8 5UH. *Clubs:* Army and Navy, Beefsteak, Garrick.

EIGEN, Manfred; Director at Max-Planck-Institut für biophysikalische Chemie, Göttingen, since 1964; *b* 9 May 1927; *s* of Ernst and Hedwig Eigen; *m* 1952, Elfriede Müller; one *s* one *d*. *Educ:* Göttingen Univ. Dr rer. nat. (Phys. Chem.) 1951. Research Asst, Inst. für physikal. Chemie, Göttingen Univ., 1951–53; Asst, Max-Planck-Institut für physikal. Chemie, 1953; Research Fellow, Max-Planck-Gesellschaft, 1958; Head of separate dept of biochemical kinetics, Max-Planck-Inst., 1962. Andrew D. White Prof. at Large, Cornell Univ., 1965; Hon. Prof., Technische Hochschule Braunschweig, 1965. For. Hon. Mem., Amer. Acad. of Arts and Sciences, 1964; Mem. Leopoldina, Deutsche Akad. der Naturforscher, Halle, 1964; Mem., Akad. der Wissenschaften, Göttingen, 1965; Hon. Mem., Amer. Assoc. Biol Chemists, 1966; For. Assoc., Nat. Acad. of Scis, Washington, 1966; For. Mem., Royal Soc., 1973. Dr of Science *hc*, Washington, Harvard and Chicago Univs, 1966. Has won prizes, medals and awards including Nobel Prize for Chemistry (jointly), 1967. *Publications:* numerous papers in Z. Elektrochem., Jl Phys Chem., Trans Faraday Soc., Proc. Royal Soc., Canad. Jl Chem., ICSU Rev., and other learned jls. *Address:* Max-Planck-Institut für biophysikalische Chemie, Karl-Friedrich Bonhoeffer Institut, Postfach 2841, D3400 Göttingen-Nikolausberg, Germany.

EILLEDGE, Elwyn Owen Morris, FCA; Senior Partner, Ernst & Whinney, Chartered Accountants, since 1986; *b* 20 July 1935; *s* of Owen and Mary Elizabeth Eilledge; *m* 1962, Audrey Ann Faulkner Ellis; one *s* one *d*. *Educ:* Merton College, Oxford. BA, MA; FCA 1968. Articled with Farrow, Bersey, Gain, Vincent & Co. (now Dearden Farrow), 1959–66; Whinney Murray & Co. (now Ernst & Whinney), Liberia, 1966–68; Ernst & Whinney: Audit Manager, Hamburg, 1968–71; Partner, London, 1972; Managing Partner, London office, 1983–86; Dep. Sen. Partner, 1985. *Recreations:* gardening, swimming, tennis, listening to classical music. *Address:* (office) Becket House, 1 Lambeth Palace Road, SE1 7EU. *T:* 01–928 2000. *Clubs:* Brooks's, Gresham.

EILON, Prof. Samuel, FEng; Professor and Head of Department of Management Science (formerly Management Engineering Section), Imperial College of Science and Technology, University of London, since 1963; Director, Amey Roadstone Corporation, since 1974; *b* 13 Oct. 1923; *s* of Abraham and Rachel Eilon; *m* 1946, Hannah Ruth (*née* Samuel); two *s* two *d*. *Educ:* Reali Sch., Haifa; Technion, Israel Inst. of Technology, Haifa; Imperial Coll., London. PhD 1955, DSc(Eng) 1963, London. Founder FEng, FIMechE, FIProdE. Engr, Palestine Electric Co. Ltd, Haifa, 1946–48; Officer, Israel Defence Forces, 1948–52; CO of an Ordnance and workshop base depot (Major); Res. Asst, Imperial Coll., 1952–55; Lectr in Production Engrg, Imperial Coll., 1955–57; Associate Prof. in Industrial Engrg, Technion, Haifa, 1957–59; Reader, and Head of Section, Imperial Coll., 1959–63; Consultant and Lectr, European Productivity Agency, Paris, 1960–62. Professorial Research Fellow, Case Western Reserve Univ., Cleveland, Ohio, 1967–68. Vis. Fellow, University Coll., Cambridge, 1970–71. Dir, Campari International, 1978–80. Past Mem. of several cttees of IProdE and DES. Member Council: Operational Res. Soc., 1965–67; Inst. of Management Scis, 1970–72, 1980–82. Adviser, P-E Consulting Gp, 1961–71; Principal and Dir, Spencer Stuart and Associates, 1971–74; consultant to numerous industrial cos. Chief Editor, OMEGA, Internat. Jl of Management Science, 1972– ; Deptl Editor, Management Science, 1969–77. CBIM; Hon. FCGI 1978. Two Joseph Whitworth Prizes for papers, IMechE, 1960; Silver Medal, ORS, 1982. *Publications:* Elements of Production Planning and Control, 1962; Industrial Engineering Tables, 1962; (jtly) Exercises in Industrial Management, 1966; (jtly) Industrial Scheduling Abstracts, 1967; (jtly) Inventory Control Abstracts, 1968; (jtly) Distribution Management, 1971; Management Control, 1971, 2nd edn 1979; (jtly) Applications of Management Science in Banking and Finance, 1972; (jtly) Applied Productivity Analysis for Industry, 1976; Aspects of Management, 1977, 2nd edn 1979; The Art of Reckoning: analysis of performance criteria, 1984; Management Assertions and Aversions, 1985; numerous scientific papers. *Recreations:* theatre, tennis, walking. *Address:* Department of Management Science, Imperial College, Exhibition Road, SW7 2BX. *T:* 01–589 5111. *Club:* Athenæum.

EKIN, Maj.-Gen. Roger Gillies, CIE 1946; IA, retired; *b* 18 Nov. 1895; *yr s* of T. C. Ekin, MInstCE; *m* 1st, 1923, Phyllis Marian (*d* 1967), *er d* of Maj.-Gen. Sir Henry Croker, KCB, CMG; one *s* two *d*; 2nd, 1972, Mona de Hamel (*d* 1979), *widow* of Etienne Bruno de Hamel. *Educ:* Westminster; RMC Sandhurst. First Commissioned, 1914; Palestine campaign, 1916–19; on Operations in Waziristan, 1920–21; Operations NWFP, 1930; Brevet Lt-Col 1936; Comdt 5th Bn FF Rifles, 1937–40; Comd Kohat Bde Ahmedzal Ops, 1940; Col 1939; Comdt Tactical Sch., India, 1940–41; Comd 46 Inf. Bde, Burma campaign, 1941–42; Nowshera Bde, 1942–45; Kohat (Independent) Bde, 1945–46. Despatches five times. GOC Bihar and Orissa Area, India, 1946–47; retired, 1947; Sec., Hereford Diocesan Board of Finance, 1947–61. *Address:* c/o Lloyds Bank, 6 Pall Mall, SW1Y 5NH.

EKLUND, Dr (Arne) Sigvard; Director General (now Emeritus), International Atomic Energy Agency, Vienna, 1961–81; *b* Kiruna, Sweden, 1911; *m* 1941, Anna-Greta Johansson; one *s* two *d*. *Educ:* Uppsala Univ., Sweden (DSc). Assoc. Prof. in Nuclear Physics, Royal Inst. of Technology, Stockholm, 1946–56; Dir of Research, later Reactor development Div., AB Atomenergi, 1950–61. Conference Sec.-Gen., 2nd Internat. UN Conf. on Peaceful Uses of Atomic Energy, 1958. Fellow, Amer. Nuclear Soc., 1961; Member: Royal Swedish Acad. of Engineering Sciences, 1953; Royal Swedish Acad. of Sciences, 1972; Hon. Member: British Nuclear Energy Soc., 1963; European Nuclear Soc., 1982. For. Associate, Nat. Acad. of Engineering, USA, 1979. Dr *hc*: Univ. of Graz, 1968; Acad. of Mining and Metallurgy, Cracow, 1971; Univ. of Bucarest, 1971; Chalmers Inst. of Technol., Gothenberg, 1974; Buenos Aires, Budapest, Columbia and Moscow Univs, 1977; Dresden Technical and Yon-sei, Seoul Univs, 1978; Nat. Agrarian Univ. of La Molina, Peru, 1979; Royal Inst. of Technol., Stockholm, 1980. (Jointly) Atoms for Peace Award, 1968; Golden Medal of Honour, Vienna, 1971; Henry DeWolf Smyth Nuclear Statesman Award, 1976; Exceptional Service Award, Amer. Nuclear Soc., 1980. Hon. Senator, Univ. of Vienna, 1977. Kt Comdr, Order of North Star, Sweden, 1971; Das Grosse Goldene Ehrenzeichen am Bande für Verdienste, Austria, 1981; Das Grosse Verdienstkreuz mit Stern und Schulterband, FRG, 1981; Aquila Azteca en el Grado de Banda, Mexico, 1981. Comdr, Order of St Gregory, bestowed by His Holiness Pope John Paul II, 1982. *Publications:* Studies in Nuclear Physics, 1946 (Sweden); articles on peaceful uses of nuclear energy. *Address:* Krapfenwaldgasse 48, 1190–Vienna, Austria.

ELAM, His Honour Henry; a Circuit Judge (formerly Deputy Chairman of the Court of Quarter Sessions, Inner London), 1953–76; barrister-at-law; *b* 29 Nov. 1903; *o s* of Thomas Henry Elam, 33 Sackville Street, W1; *m* 1st, 1930, Eunice (*d* 1975), *yr d* of J. G. Matthews, 41 Redington Road, NW3; one *d*; 2nd, 1975, Doris A. Horsford. *Educ:* Charterhouse; Lincoln Coll., Oxford (MA). Called to Bar, Inner Temple, 1927; Western Circuit; Junior Prosecuting Counsel to the Treasury, Central Criminal Court, 1937; late Dep. Judge Advocate, RAF; Recorder of Poole, 1941–46; 2nd Junior Prosecuting Counsel, 1942–45; 1st Junior, 1945–50; 3rd Senior, Jan.-March 1950; 2nd Senior, 1950–53; Recorder of Exeter, 1946–53; Dep. Chm., West Kent QS, 1947–53. *Recreation:* flyfishing. *Address:* Clymshurst, Burwash Common, East Sussex. *T:* Burwash 883335.

ELAM, (John) Nicholas; Consul-General, Montreal, since 1984; *b* 2 July 1939; *s* of John Frederick Elam, OBE and Joan Barrington Elam (*née* Lloyd); *m* 1967, Florence Helen, *d* of P. Lentz; two *s* one *d*. *Educ:* Colchester Royal Grammar Sch.; New Coll., Oxford (schol.). Frank Knox Fellow, Harvard Univ., 1961–62. Entered HM Diplomatic Service, 1962; FO, 1962–64; Pretoria and Cape Town, 1964–68; Treasury Centre for Admin. Studies, 1968–69; FCO, 1969–71; First Sec., Bahrain, 1971; Commercial Sec., Brussels, 1972–76; FCO, 1976–79, Dep. Head of News Dept, 1978–79; Counsellor and Dep. British Govt Rep., Salisbury, 1979; Dep. High Comr, Salisbury (later Harare), 1980–84. *Recreations:* fine arts, travel. *Address:* c/o Foreign and Commonwealth Office, SW1A 2AH.

ELATH, Eliahu, PhD; President Emeritus, Hebrew University, Jerusalem; Israeli diplomatist; Chairman, Board of Governors, Israel Afro-Asian Institute; *b* 30 July 1903; *s* of Menachem and Rivka Epstein (Elath); *m* 1931, Zehava Zalel. *Educ:* Hebrew Univ., Jerusalem; American Univ., Beirut, Lebanon. Reuter's Corresp. in Syria and Lebanon, 1931–34. Mem. Political Dept of Jewish Agency for Palestine in Jerusalem, 1934–45; Dir Political Office of Jewish Agency for Palestine in Washington, 1945–48; Special Representative of Provisional Govt of Israel in USA, 1948; Ambassador of Israel to USA, 1948–50; Minister of Israel, 1950–52, Ambassador, 1952–59, to the Court of St James's. Pres., Israel Oriental Soc. Vice-Pres., Jewish Colonization Assoc. (ICA). Hon. PhD: Brandeis; Wayn; Hebrew Union Coll.; Dropsie Coll., USA. *Publications:* The Bedouin, Their Customs and Manners, 1933; Trans-Jordan, 1934; Israel and her Neighbours, 1960; The Political Struggle for Inclusion of Elath in the Jewish State, 1967; San Francisco Diary, 1971; British Routes to India, 1971; Zionism and the Arabs, 1974; Zionism and the UN, 1977; The Struggle for Statehood, 1982; contribs to Quarterly of Palestine Exploration Fund, Jl of Royal Central Asian Society, Encyclopædia Britannica. *Address:* 17 Bialik Street, Beth Hakerem, Jerusalem, Israel. *T:* 524615.

ELBORNE, Sydney Lipscomb, MBE 1918; Chairman of Hunts Quarter Sessions, 1947–63; *b* 6 July 1890; *e s* of late William Elborne, MA, Wootton House, Peterborough; *m* 1925, Cavil Grace Mary (*d* 1984), *d* of late George E. Monckton, Fineshade Abbey, Northants; one *s* one *d*. *Educ:* King's Sch., Peterborough; Trinity Coll. Cambridge (MA). Asst Inspector of High Explosives (Technical), The Royal Arsenal, Woolwich, 1914–18; called to Bar, Inner Temple, 1919; Mem. Midland Circuit; Mem. Gen. Council of the Bar, 1940–47; Asst Recorder of Birmingham, 1953. Mem. Hunts CC, 1930–45; JP Hunts, 1932. Pres. Soc. of Chairmen and Dep. Chm. of Quarter Sessions, 1955. Mem. Mr Justice Austen Jones's Cttee on County Court procedure, 1947; formerly Trustee and Mem. Council, Northants Record Soc.; formerly Trustee of Peterborough Museum Soc. and Maxwell Art Gallery; Mem. Area Cttee (No 11) Legal Aid, 1950–69. Contested (C) Leicester (Bosworth Div.), 1929 and Manchester (Ardwick), by-election, 1931. Formerly FGS, ARIC. *Address:* Water Newton, Peterborough. *T:* Peterborough 233223. *Club:* Carlton.

ELCOAT, Rev. Canon George Alastair; Priest-in-charge of Tweedmouth, Berwick-upon-Tweed, since 1981; Chaplain to The Queen, since 1982; Rural Dean of Norham, since 1982; *b* 4 June 1922; *s* of George Thomas Elcoat and Hilda Gertrude Elcoat. *Educ:* Tynemouth School; Queen's College, Birmingham. Served RAF, 1941–46. Asst Master, Newcastle Cathedral Choir School, 1947–48. Deacon 1951, priest 1952; Asst Curate, Corbridge, 1951–55; Vicar: Spittal, 1955–62; Chatton with Chillingham, 1962–70; Sugley, 1970–81; RD, Newcastle West, 1977–81; Hon. Canon, Newcastle, 1979–. *Recreations:* fell walking, photography, gardening, music. *Address:* The Vicarage, Main Street, Tweedmouth, Berwick-upon-Tweed, Northumberland TD15 2AW. *T:* Berwick-upon-Tweed 306409.

ELDER, David Renwick, MC 1940; CA; *b* 4 Jan. 1920; *s* of John Kidd Elder and Mary Kinnear Swanley; *m* 1947, Kathleen Frances Duncan; two *s* two *d*. *Educ:* Dundee High School. Served 1939–46, The Black Watch (RHR) and Sea Reconnaissance Unit (Major). Royal Dutch Shell Group, 1948–71; Ocean Transport & Trading Ltd, 1971–80 (Dep. Chm., 1975–80; Chm., Ocean Inchcape, 1974–80); Director: Letraset International Ltd, 1975; Capital & Counties Property Ltd, 1979–; Whessoe Ltd, 1980–. *Recreation:* golf. *Address:* Green Hedges, Lake Road, Virginia Water, Surrey. *T:* Wentworth 2134. *Clubs:* Wentworth Golf (Virginia Water); Panmure Golf (Carnoustie).

ELDER, Mark Philip; Music Director, English National Opera, since 1979; *b* 2 June 1947; *s* of John and Helen Elder; *m* 1980, Amanda Jane Stein; one *d*. *Educ:* Bryanston Sch.; Corpus Christi Coll., Cambridge (Music Scholar, Choral Scholar; BA, MA). Music staff, Wexford Festival, 1969–70; Chorus Master and Asst Conductor, Glyndebourne, 1970–71; music staff, Covent Garden, 1970–72; Staff Conductor, Australian Opera, 1972–74; Staff Conductor, ENO, 1974, Associate Conductor, 1977; Principal Guest Conductor, London Mozart Players, 1980–83; Principal Guest Conductor, BBC Symphony Orchestra, 1982–85. *Address:* c/o London Coliseum, St Martin's Lane, WC2.

ELDER-JONES, His Honour Thomas; retired Circuit Judge (formerly Judge of County Courts), 1953–76; *b* 4 Oct. 1904; *o s* of late David Jones, JP, Foxcote Grange, Andoversford, shipowner, and late Anne Amelia (Roberts); *m* 1948, Hon. Diana Katherine Taylor (*née* Russell) (*d* 1978), *o d* of 25th Baron de Clifford; one adopted *d* one step *s*. *Educ:* Shrewsbury; Trinity Coll., Oxford (MA). Barrister-at-law, Inner Temple, 1927. Served 1939–43, 2nd Royal Gloucestershire Hussars, retired, rank of Hon. Major. Sec. National Reference Tribunal for Coal Mining Industry, 1943–53; Judge of County Courts Circuit 34 (Brentford and Uxbridge), 1953–57, Circuit 52 (Bath-Swindon), 1957–76. At Bar practised in Common Law and Coal Mining matters. *Recreation:* fox-hunting. *Address:* The Dower House, Somerford Keynes, Cirencester, Glos. *T:* Cirencester 861296.

ELDERFIELD, Maurice; Chairman: Midland Industrial Leasing Ltd, since 1979; Saga Ltd, since 1979; Sheldon & Partners Ltd, since 1981; Chairman and Chief Executive, Berfield Associates Ltd, since 1980; *b* 10 April 1926; *s* of Henry Elderfield and Kathleen Maud Elderfield; *m* 1953, Audrey June (*née* Knight); one *s* three *d*. *Educ:* Southgate Grammar Sch. FCA. Fleet Air Arm, 1944–47. Thomson, Kingdom & Co., Chartered Accountants (qual. 1949), 1947–49; Personal Asst to Man. Dir, Forrestell, Land, Timber & Railway Co., 1949–57; Group Chief Accountant, Stephens Group, 1957–60; various posts, Segas, culminating in Board Mem. and Dir for Finance, 1960–73; Dir of Finance, Southern Water Authority, 1973–75; PO Board Mem. for Finance and Corporate Planning, 1975–76; Dir of Finance, Ferranti Ltd, 1977; Finance Mem., British Shipbuilders, 1977–80. Chairman: Throgmorton Trust, 1972–84; Throgmorton Investment Management, 1981–84; Capital for Industry Ltd, 1980–84. *Recreations:* golf, tennis, squash. *Address:* Hadleigh, Cansiron Lane, Ashurst Wood, Sussex RH19 3SD; (office) The Square, Forest Row, Sussex RH18 5NB. *Club:* Gravetye Manor Country.

ELDIN-TAYLOR, Kenneth Roy, CVO 1955; *b* 27 Sept. 1902; *s* of late Thomas Taylor, Welbourn, Lincoln; *m* 1st, 1926, Katharine Mary (*d* 1984), *er d* of late Frederick Ernest Taylor, FRCS, LRCP, Brancaster, Norfolk; three *s*; 2nd, 1985, Mrs Nellie Gladys Midgley. *Educ:* Lincoln School; Selwyn College, Cambridge (BA, LLM, Exhibitioner and Univ. Squire Law Schol.). Called to the Bar, Lincoln's Inn, 1970. Solicitor for Affairs of HM Duchy of Lancaster, 1942–67; Chm., Industrial Appeals Tribunals, 1967–74; Sec., Diocesan Conf., 1966–68; former Member of Council, British Records Association; Chairman: Portsmouth Diocesan Parsonages Bd; Clergy Sustentation Fund. *Recreations:* literature, rowing, racing. *Address:* 5 Yardley Court, Milton Road, Harpenden, Herts. *T:* Harpenden 60164. *Clubs:* Leander; Royal Naval and Royal Albert Yacht (Portsmouth).

ELDON, 5th Earl of, *cr* 1821; **John Joseph Nicholas Scott;** Baron Eldon 1799; Viscount Encombe 1821; *b* 24 April 1937; *s* of 4th Earl of Eldon, GCVO, and Hon. Magdalen Fraser, OBE (*d* 1969), *d* of 16th Baron Lovat; *S* father, 1976; *m* 1961, Comtesse Claudine de Montjoye-Vaufrey et de la Roche, Vienna; one *s* two *d. Educ:* Ampleforth; Trinity Coll., Oxford. 2nd Lieut Scots Guards (National Service). Lieut AER. *Heir: s* Viscount Encombe, *qv. Address:* 2 Coach House Lane, Wimbledon, SW19.

ELDRIDGE, Eric William, CB 1965; OBE 1948; Consultant with Lee and Pembertons, solicitors, since 1971; *b* 15 April 1906; *o s* of late William Eldridge; *m* 1936, Doris Margaret Kerr; one *s* one *d. Educ:* Millfields Central Sch.; City of London Coll. Admitted Solicitor (Hons), 1934. Chief Administrative Officer, Public Trustee Office, 1955–60; Asst Public Trustee, 1960–63; Public Trustee, 1963–71. *Address:* Old Stocks, Gorelands Lane, Chalfont St Giles, Bucks. *T:* Chalfont St Giles 2159.

ELDRIDGE, John Barron; Chairman, Matthews Wrightson Holdings Ltd, 1971–77; *b* 28 May 1919; *s* of William John Eldridge and Jessie Winifred (*née* Bowditch); *m* 1940, Marjorie Potier; one *s* two *d. Educ:* Lancing Coll. FIA 1950. Dir, Matthews Wrightson Holdings Ltd, 1964. Croix de Guerre 1944. *Address:* Castleton, Warwicks Bench Road, Guildford, Surrey. *T:* Guildford 62687.

ELDRIDGE, Lt-Col William James, OBE (mil.) 1944; DL; Vice Lord-Lieutenant, Isle of Wight, since 1986; *b* 14 Feb. 1917; *s* of R. J. Eldridge; *m* 1941, Joan Cecily, *d* of late F. W. Fidgeon and of D. M. Fidgeon; one *s* three *d. Educ:* Sherborne School. Served War, 2nd Lieut, Royal Hampshire Regt, 1940–41; various Staff appts until GSO1 (Ops): 10 Corps, 1944; AFHQ Greece, 1945–46. Solicitor (Partner), James Eldridge & Sons, IoW, 1947–83. *Recreation:* gardening. *Address:* Cypress Cottage, St John's Road, Newport, Isle of Wight. *T:* Newport 522722.

ELEK, Prof. Stephen Dyonis, MD, DSc; FRCP; Professor of Medical Microbiology in the University of London, 1957–74, now Emeritus; Consultant Bacteriologist, St George's Hospital, SW1, 1948–73; *b* 24 March 1914; *s* of Dezso and Anna Elek; *m* Sarah Joanna Hall; three *d. Educ:* Lutheran High Sch., Budapest, Hungary; St George's Hosp. Med. Sch., Univ. of London. MB, BS 1940; MD 1943; PhD 1948; DPH 1943; DSc 1958; MRCP 1960; FRCPath 1964. Clinical Pathologist, Maida Vale Hosp. for Nervous Diseases, 1946–47; Laking-Dakin Fellow, 1942–43; Fulbright Fellow, Harvard Medical Sch., 1956. Member: Pathological Soc. of Great Britain; American Society for Microbiology; New York Academy of Sciences; Soc. of Gen. Microbiology, etc. Editor, Jl of Medical Microbiology, 1972–74. Introduced immuno-diffusion as a new analytical tool in serology, 1948. *Publications:* Staphylococcus pyogenes and its Relation to Disease, 1959; scientific papers relating to diphtheria, leprosy, vaccination against mental retardation due to CM Virus infection during pregnancy, etc, in Lancet, BMJ, Jl Path. and Bact., Brit. Jl Exper. Path. *Recreations:* sculpting, walking. *Address:* Avenue de Cour 155, 1007 Lausanne, Switzerland. *T:* 26.58.14. *Club:* Athenæum.

ELEY, Prof. Daniel Douglas, OBE 1961; ScD, PhD Cantab; MSc, PhD Manchester; FRS 1964; Professor of Physical Chemistry, University of Nottingham, 1954–80, now Emeritus; Dean of Faculty of Pure Science, 1959–62; *b* 1 Oct. 1914; *s* of Daniel Eley and Fanny Allen Eley, *née* Ross; *m* 1942, Brenda May Williams, MA, MB, BChir (Cantab), 2nd *d* of Benjamin and Sarah Williams, Skewen, Glam; one *s. Educ:* Christ's Coll., Finchley; Manchester Univ.; St John's Coll., Cambridge. Manchester Univ.: Woodiwiss Schol. 1933, Mercer Schol. 1934, Darbishire Fellow 1936, PhD 1937; PhD, 1940, ScD 1954, Cambridge. Bristol Univ.: Lectr in Colloid Chemistry, 1945; Reader in Biophysical Chemistry, 1951. Leverhulme Emeritus Fellow, 1981. Lectures: Reilly, Univ. of Notre Dame (USA), 1950; Royal Aust. Chem. Inst., 1967; Sir Jesse Boot Foundn, Nottingham Univ., 1955, 1981; Sir Eric Rideal, Soc. of Chem. Industry, 1975. Mem. Council of Faraday Soc., 1951–54, 1960–63; Vice-Pres., 1963–66. Corresp. Mem., Bavarian Acad. of Sciences, 1971. Meetings Sec., British Biophysical Soc., 1961–63, Hon. Sec., 1963–65, Hon. Mem., 1983. Scientific Assessor to Sub-Cttee on Coastal Pollutions, House of Commons Select Cttee on Science and Technology, 1967–68. Medal of Liège Univ. 1950. *Publications:* (ed) Adhesion, 1961; papers in Trans Faraday Soc., Proc. Royal Soc., Jl Chem. Soc., Biochem. Jl, etc. *Recreations:* hill walking, gardening, ski-ing. *Address:* Brooklands, 35 Brookland Drive, Chilwell, Nottingham NG9 4BD; Chemistry Department, Nottingham University, University Park, Nottingham NG7 2RD.

ELEY, Sir Geoffrey (Cecil Ryves), Kt 1964; CBE 1947; Member of the Court, University of Essex, since 1967; *b* 18 July 1904; *s* of late Charles Cuthbert Eley, JP, VMH, East Bergholt Place, Suffolk, and of Ethel Maxwell Eley (*née* Ryves); *m* 1937, Penelope Hughes, *d* of late Adm. Sir Frederick Wake-Walker, KCB, CBE; two *s* two *d. Educ:* Eton; Trinity Coll., Cambridge (BA 1925; MA 1933); Harvard Univ. (Davison Scholar), 1925–26. On Editorial Staff of Financial News, 1926–28; banking, finance and brokerage in England, France, Switzerland and the USA, 1928–32; London Manager of Post and Flagg, members of New York Stock Exchange, 1932–39; Naval Intelligence Div., Admiralty, 1939–40; Capital Issues Cttee, 1940–41; Min. of Supply as Dir of Contracts in charge of Capital Assistance to Industry, 1941–46; Min. of Supply as Dir of Overseas Disposals, 1946–47. Mem., London Electricity Bd, 1949–59. Chairman: British Drug Houses Ltd, 1948–65; Richard Crittall Holdings Ltd, 1948–68; Dep. Chm. and Chm., Brush Group, 1953–58; Chairman: Richard Thomas & Baldwin's Ltd, 1959–64; Thomas Tilling Ltd, 1965–76 (Dir, 1950–76); Heinemann Group of Publishers Ltd, 1965–76; Dep. Chm., British Bank of the Middle East, 1952–77 (Dir, 1950–77); Vice-Chm., BOC International Ltd, 1964–76 (Dir, 1959–76); Director: Bank of England, 1949–66; Equity & Law Life Assurance Soc., 1948–80. Leader, UK Trade Mission to Egypt, Sudan and Ethiopia, 1955. Vice-Pres., Middle East Assoc., 1962–85. Member: Cttee, Royal UK Benevolent Assoc., 1957–85; Council, Friends of Tate Gall., 1977–85. High Sheriff, Co. of London, 1954–55; High Sheriff of Greater London, 1966. *Recreations:* gardening, the arts, foreign travel. *Address:* 27 Wynnstay Gardens, Allen Street, W8 6UR. *T:* 01–937 0797; The Change House, Great Yeldham, Essex CO9 4PT. *T:* Great Yeldham 237260. *Clubs:* Brooks's, Beefsteak.

ELEY, John L.; *see* Lloyd-Eley.

ELFER, David Francis, QC 1981; a Recorder of the Crown Court, since 1978; *b* 15 July 1941; *s* of George and Joy Elfer; *m* 1958, Karin Ursula Strub; two *s. Educ:* St Bede's Coll., Manchester; Emmanuel Coll., Cambridge (MA). Called to the Bar, Inner Temple, 1964; Western Circuit. *Recreation:* music. *Address:* (home) Monks Park, Luddington Avenue, Virginia Water, Surrey. *T:* Wentworth 3168; (chambers) 1 Paper Building, Temple, EC4Y 7EP.

ELGIN, 11th Earl of, *cr* 1633, **AND KINCARDINE,** 15th Earl of, *cr* 1647; **Andrew Douglas Alexander Thomas Bruce,** KT 1981; CD 1981; DL; JP; Baron Bruce of Kinloss, 1604, Baron Bruce of Torry, 1647; Baron Elgin (UK), 1849; 37th Chief of the Name of Bruce; late Scots Guards; Brigadier of Royal Company of Archers, HM Body Guard for Scotland; Hon. Colonel, Elgin Regiment, Canada; *b* 17 Feb. 1924; *e s* of 10th Earl of Elgin, KT, CMG, TD and Hon. Katherine Elizabeth Cochrane (DBE 1938), *er d* of 1st Baron Cochrane of Cults; *S* father, 1968; *m* 1959, Victoria, *o d* of Dudley Usher, MBE

and Mrs Usher of Larach Bhan, Kilchrennan, Argyll; three *s* two *d. Educ:* Eton; Balliol College, Oxford (BA Hons, MA Hons). Served War of 1939–45 (wounded). Director: Nationwide Building Soc. (Scottish Bd); Royal Highland and Agricultural Soc., 1973–75; Pres., Scottish Amicable Life Assurance Soc., 1975–. Chm., Nat. Savings Cttee for Scotland, 1972–78; Mem., Scottish Postal Bd, 1980–. Lord High Comr, Gen. Assembly of Church of Scotland, 1980–81. County Cadet Commandant, Fife, 1952–65. Hon. Col, 153(H) Regt RCT(V), TAVR, 1976–86. JP 1951, DL 1955, Fife. Grand Master Mason of Scotland, 1961–65. Brigade Pres. of the Boys' Brigade, 1966–85; Pres., Royal Caledonian Curling Club, 1968–69. Hon. LLD: Dundee, 1977; Glasgow, 1983; Hon. DLitt St Mary's, Halifax, NS. Freeman: Bridgetown, Barbados; Regina; Port Elgin; Winnipeg; St Thomas, Ont; Moose Jaw. *Heir: s* Lord Bruce, *qv. Address:* Broomhall, Dunfermline KY11 3DU. *T:* Limekilns 872222. *Clubs:* Beefsteak, Caledonian, Pratt's; New (Edinburgh); Royal Scottish Automobile (Pres.) (Glasgow).

ELGOOD, Captain Leonard Alsager, OBE 1919; MC 1915; DL; JP; FRSE; Director, The Distillers Co. Ltd, 1943–60; Chairman, United Glass Ltd, 1951–61; Director, Royal Bank of Scotland, 1946–66, Extraordinary Director, 1966–68; Chairman of Committee on Natural Resources of Scotland (Scottish Council for Development and Industry), 1958–62; *b* 13 Dec. 1892; *s* of late William Alsager Elgood, Dundee, and late Mrs Elgood; *m* 1917, Jenny Coventry Wood (*d* 1984), *d* of late R. A. Harper Wood and late Mrs Wood, Perth; two *s. Educ:* Dundee High Sch. Served with the Black Watch (Capt.), 1914–19 (despatches thrice); retd, 1919. Chartered Accountant, 1919; Sec., John Dewar & Sons Ltd, Perth, 1936; Sec., The Distillers Co. Ltd, 1939. DL 1948, JP 1943, County of the City of Edinburgh. *Address:* 16 Cumlodden Avenue, Edinburgh EH12 6DR. *T:* 031–337 6919.

EL HASSAN, Sayed Abdullah; *see* Hassan.

ELIAS, Gerard, QC 1984; a Recorder of the Crown Court, since 1984; *b* 19 Nov. 1944; *s* of Leonard Elias and Patricia Elias, JP; *m* 1970, Elisabeth Kenyon; three *s. Educ:* Cardiff High School; Exeter University. LLB; Barrister; called to the Bar, Inner Temple, 1968; Wales and Chester Circuit; Asst Comr, Boundary Commission for Wales, 1981–83, 1985–. *Recreations:* music, cricket. *Address:* 13 The Cathedral Green, Llandaff, Cardiff, South Glamorgan CF5 2EB. *T:* Cardiff 562635. *Club:* Cardiff and County.

ELIAS, Dr Taslim Olawale, GCON 1983; CFR 1963; NNMA 1979; QC 1961; Judge, International Court of Justice, since 1976 (Vice-President, 1979–82, President, 1982–85); *b* Lagos, 11 Nov. 1914; *s* of Momolesho Elias Frowoshere; *m* 1959, Ganiat Yetunde Elias; three *s* two *d. Educ:* Igbobi Coll., Lagos; University Coll. London (BA, LLM, PhD; Fellow, 1983; Hon. DSc Econ, 1983). Inst. of Advanced Legal Studies, London. Called to the Bar, Inner Temple, 1947 (Hon. Bencher 1982). Simon Res. Fellow, Manchester Univ., 1951–53; Oppenheim Res. Fellow, Oxford, 1954–60. Federal Attorney-Gen. and Minister of Justice, Nigeria, 1960–66; Attorney-Gen., 1966–72; Mem., Fed. Exec. Council, 1967–72; Comr for Justice, 1967–72; Prof. and Dean of Faculty of Law, Univ. of Lagos, 1966–72; Chief Justice of Supreme Court, 1972–75. Vis. Prof., Delhi Univ., 1956. Sen. Gen. Editor, Nigerian Law Jl, 1967–73. Member: Internat. Law Commn, UN, 1961–76 (Chm. 1970); Executive: Inst. of Human Rights, Strasbourg, 1969; Internat. Commn of Jurists, 1975–. Mem., Delegn to Nigerian Constitutional Conf., London, 1958; Chm., UN Cttee of Constitnl Experts to draft Congo Constitution, 1961–62; Mem., Expert Cttee drafting OAU Charter, 1963. President: World Assoc. of Judges, 1975; Nigerian Soc. of Internat. Law; Chm., African Inst. of Internat. Law. Chm., Governing Council, Nigerian Inst. of Internat. Affairs, 1972–; Governor, SOAS, 1958–61; Mem., Governing Council, Univ. of Nigeria, 1959–66; Member: Inst. of Internat. Law, 1969–; Council of Management, British Inst. of Internat. and Comparative Law, 1983–; Hon. Fellow, Nigerian Inst. of Advanced Legal Studies, 1981; Hon. Member: Amer. Soc. of Internat. Law, 1973; Soc. of Public Teachers of Law, 1981. Hon. LLD: Dakar, 1964; Ahmadu Bello, 1972; Ife, 1974; Howard, 1975; Jodhpur, 1976; Hull, 1980; Dalhousie, Halifax, 1983; Nairobi, 1983; Manchester, 1984; Buckingham, 1986; Hon. DSc (Econ.) London, 1983. Hon. DLitt: Ibadan, 1969; Nigeria (Nsukka), 1973; Lagos 1974. World Jurist Award, 1973; Nigerian Nat. Merit Award, 1979. *Publications:* Nigerian Land Law and Custom, 1951; Nigerian Legal System, 1954; Makers of Nigerian Law, 1956; Nature of African Customary Law, 1956, 2nd edn 1962; (jtly) British Legal Papers, 1958; The Impact of English Law upon Nigerian Customary Law, 1960; Government and Politics in Africa, 1961, 2nd edn 1963; Ghana and Sierra Leone: development of their laws and constitutions, 1962; British Colonial Law: a comparative study, 1962; (jtly) International Law in a Changing World, 1963; Nigeria: development of its laws and constitution, 1965; (jtly) Sovereignty within the Law, 1965; (jtly) African Law: adaptation and development, 1965; (jtly) Law, Justice and Equity, 1967; (jtly) Nigerian Prison System, 1968; (jtly) Nigerian Press Law, 1969; Problems concerning the Validity of Treaties, 1971; Nigerian Magistrate and the Offender, 1972; Law and Social Change in Nigeria, 1972; Africa and the Development of International Law, 1972; Law in a Developing Society, 1973; Modern Law of Treaties, 1974; Judicial Process in Commonwealth Africa, 1976; New Horizons in International Law, 1979; Africa before the World Court, 1981; (jtly) International Law: teaching and practice, 1982; The International Court of Justice and Some Contemporary Problems, 1983; (jtly) Essays in International Law in Honour of Judge Manfred Lachs, 1984; (jtly) Encyclopedia of Public International Law, 1984; (jtly) Essays on Third World Perspectives in Jurisprudence; (jtly) Africa and the West: the legacies of Empire, 1986; contribs to legal jls. *Address:* c/o International Court of Justice, Peace Palace, The Hague, Netherlands; (home) 20 Ozumba Mbadiwe Street, Victoria Island, Lagos, Nigeria. *T:* 612389.

ELIBANK, 14th Lord *cr* 1643 (Scotland); **Alan D'Ardis Erskine-Murray;** Bt (Nova Scotia) 1628; personnel consultant; Deminex UK Oil and Gas, since 1981; *b* 31 Dec. 1923; *s* of Robert Alan Erskine-Murray (*d* 1939) and Eileen Mary (*d* 1970), *d* of late John Percy MacManus; *S* cousin, 1973; *m* 1962, Valerie Sylvia, *d* of late Herbert William Dennis; two *s. Educ:* Bedford Sch.; Peterhouse, Cambridge (MA Law). Barrister-at-Law. RE, 1942–47; Cambridge Univ., 1947–49; Practising Barrister, 1949–55; Shell International Petroleum Co., 1955–80. *Recreations:* golf, tennis. *Heir: s* Master of Elibank, *qv. Address:* The Coach House, Charters Road, Sunningdale, Ascot, Berks SL5 9QB. *T:* Ascot 22099. *Club:* MCC.

ELIBANK, Master of; Hon. Robert Francis Alan Erskine-Murray; student; *b* 10 Oct. 1964; *s* and *heir* of 14th Lord Elibank, *qv. Educ:* The Grove, Harrow School; Reading Univ. *Recreations:* judo, soccer, tennis and photography.

ELIOT, family name of **Earl of St Germans.**

ELIOT, Lord; Peregrine Nicholas Eliot; *b* 2 Jan. 1941; *o s* of 9th Earl of St Germans, *qv*, and of late Helen Mary, *d* of late Lieut-Col Charles Walter Villiers, CBE, DSO, and Lady Kathleen Villiers; *m* 1964, Hon. Jacquetta Jean Frederika Lampson, *d* of 1st Baron Killearn and Jacqueline Aldine Lesley (*née* Castellani); three *s. Educ:* Eton. *Recreation:* mucking about. *Heir: s* Hon. Jago Nicholas Aldo Eliot, *b* 24 March 1966. *Address:* Port Eliot, St Germans, Cornwall. *Clubs:* Pratt's; Cornish Club 1768.

ELIOT, Ven. Canon Peter Charles, MBE 1945; TD 1945; Archdeacon of Worcester, 1961–75; now Archdeacon Emeritus; Residentiary Canon, Worcester Cathedral, 1965–75; now Canon Emeritus; *b* 30 Oct. 1910; *s* of late Hon. Edward Granville Eliot and late Mrs Eliot; *m* 1934, Lady Alethea Constance Dorothy Sydney Buxton, *d* of 1st and last Earl Buxton, PC, GCMG, and late Countess Buxton; no *c*. *Educ:* Wellington Coll.; Magdalene Coll., Cambridge. Commissioned in Kent Yeomanry (Lt-Col Comdg, 1949–52), 1933. Admitted Solicitor, 1934; Partner in City firm until 1953. Studied at Westcott House, Cambridge, 1953–54; made Deacon to serve in Parish of St Martin-in-the-Fields, London, 1954; Priest, 1955; Vicar of Cockermouth, 1957–61; Rural Dean of Cockermouth and Workington, 1960–61; Vicar of Cropthorne with Charlton, 1961–65. *Recreations:* amateur acting, sketching, sight-seeing, gardening. *Address:* The Old House, Kingsland, Leominster, Herefordshire HR6 9QS. *T:* Kingsland 285. *Club:* Travellers'.

ELIOTT OF STOBS, Sir Arthur Francis Augustus Boswell, 11th Bt *cr* 1666; Chief of the Clan Elliot; *b* 2 Jan. 1915; *s* of Sir Gilbert Alexander Boswell Eliott, 10th Bt, and Dora Flournoy Adams Hopkins (*d* 1978), Atlanta, Georgia, USA; *S* father, 1958; *m* 1947, Frances Aileen, *e d* of late Sir Francis McClean, AFC; one *d*. *Educ:* Harrow; King's Coll., Cambridge. BA 1936, MA 1949. 2nd Lieut, King's Own Scottish Borderers (TA), 1939, Major, 1944. Served in East Africa and Burma with King's African Rifles, 1941–45. Member of Queen's Body Guard for Scotland, Royal Company of Archers. FSAScot 1986. *Publication:* The Elliots, the story of a Border Clan, 1974. *Address:* Redheugh, Newcastleton, Roxburghshire. *T:* Liddesdale 213. *Clubs:* New (Edinburgh); Leander.

ELKAN, Prof. Walter; Professor, and Head of Department of Economics, Brunel University, since 1978; *b* Hamburg, 1 March 1923; *s* of Hans Septimus Elkan and Maud Emily (*née* Barden); *m* Susan Dorothea (*née* Jacobs) (marr. diss. 1982); one *s* two *d*. *Educ:* Frensham Heights; London Sch. of Economics. BSc (Econ), PhD. Army, 1942–47; Research Asst, LSE, 1950–53; Sen. Res. Fellow, E African Inst. of Social Research, 1954–58; Vis. Res. Assoc., MIT and Lectr, N Western Univ., 1958; Lectr in Econs, Makerere UC, 1958–60; Lectr in Econs, Durham Univ., 1960; Prof. of Econs, 1966–78, and rotating Head of Dept, 1968–78, Durham Univ. Vis. Res. Prof., Nairobi Univ., 1972–73. Member: Council, Overseas Develt Inst.; Econ. and Social Cttee, EEC, 1982–; Bd of Management, Sch. of Hygiene and Trop. Med., 1982–86; Econ. and Social Cttee for Overseas Res., 1977–; Associate, Inst. of Development Studies. Former Pres., African Studies Assoc.; former Member: Northern Economic Planning Council; REconS. Sometime consultant to Govts of Basutoland, Mauritius, Solomon Is, Fiji, Kenya and others. *Publications:* An African Labour Force, 1956; Migrants and Proletarians, 1960; Economic Development of Uganda, 1961; Introduction to Development Economics, 1973; articles mainly on contemp. African econ. history in econ. and other social science jls; ILO, UNESCO, IBRD and British Govt reports. *Recreation:* music. *Address:* Economics Department, Brunel University, Uxbridge, Mddx UB8 3PH. *T:* Uxbridge 56461.

ELKES, Prof. Joel, MD, ChB; FACP, FAPA; Distinguished Service Professor Emeritus, The Johns Hopkins University, since 1975; Professor of Psychiatry, University of Louisville, 1980–84, now Emeritus (Director, Division of Behavioral Medicine, 1982); *b* 12 Nov. 1913; *s* of Dr Elchanan Elkes and Miriam (*née* Malbin); *m* 1943, Dr Charmian Bourne; one *d*; *m* 1975, Josephine Rhodes, MA. *Educ:* private schools; Lithuania and Switzerland; St Mary's Hosp., London; Univ. of Birmingham Med. Sch. (MB, ChB 1947; MD Hons 1949). MRCS, LRCP 1941. University of Birmingham: Sir Halley Stewart Research Fellow, 1942–45; Lectr, Dept of Pharmacology, 1945–48; Senior Lectr and Actg Head of Dept, 1948–50; Prof. and Chm., Dept of Experimental Psychiatry, 1951–57; Clinical Professor of Psychiatry, George Washington Univ. Med. Sch., Washington, 1957–63; Chief of Clinical Neuropharmacology Research Center, Nat. Inst of Mental Health, Washington, 1957–63; Dir, Behavioral and Clinical Studies Center St Elizabeth's Hosp., Washington, 1957–63; Henry Phipps Prof. and Dir, Dept of Psychiatry and Behavioural Scis, Johns Hopkins Univ. Sch. of Medicine, and Psychiatrist-in-Chief, Johns Hopkins Hosp., 1963–74; Samuel McLaughlin Prof.-in-residence, McMaster Univ., 1975; Prof. of Psychiatry, McMaster Univ., 1976–80. Dir, Foundns Fund for Research in Psychiatry, 1964–68; Consultant, WHO, 1957. Vis. Fellow, New York Univ. and New England Med. Center, Boston, 1950; Benjamin Franklin Fellow, RSA, 1974. Lectures: Harvey, 1962; Salmon, 1963; Jacob Bronowski Meml, 1978, etc. President: (first) Amer. Coll. of Neuropsychopharmacology, 1962; Amer. Psychopathological Assoc., 1968; Chm., Foundns Fund Prize Bd for Res. in Psychiatry, 1977–81; Dir, Inst. for Advancement of Health, 1982. Formerly Member: Council, Internat. Collegium N Psychopharm; Central Council, Internat. Brain Research Organisation, UNESCO (Chm., Sub-Cttee on Educn); RSM. Life Fellow, Amer. Psych. Assoc.; Charter Fellow, RCPsych, GB; Fellow: Amer. Acad. of Arts and Scis; Amer. Coll. of Psychiatry; Amer. Coll. of Neuropsychopharmacol; Amer. Acad. of Behavioral Medicine Res. and Soc. of Behavioral Medicine; Fellow and Mem. Exec. Cttee, World Acad. of Art and Sci., 1985; Member: Physiological Soc., GB; Pharmacological Soc., GB; Amer. Soc. for Pharmacology and Experimental Therapeutics; New York Acad. of Science; Sigma Xi; Scientific Assoc.; Acad. of Psychoanalysis. Distinguished Practitioner, Nat. Acads of Practice, 1985. *Publications:* papers to various jls and symposia. *Recreation:* painting. *Address:* Department of Psychiatry, University of Louisville, Louisville, Ky 40292, USA. *Clubs:* Cosmos (Washington); West Hamilton, Johns Hopkins (Baltimore).

ELKIN, Alexander, CMG 1976; international law consultant; *b* Leningrad (St Petersburg), 2 Aug. 1909; *o c* of Boris and Anna Elkin; *m* 1937, Muriel Solomons, Dublin. *Educ:* Grunewald Gymnasium and Russian Academic Sch., Berlin; Univs of Berlin, Kiel and London. DrJur Kiel 1932, LLM London 1935. Called to the Bar, Middle Temple, 1937; practised at English Bar, 1937–39; BBC Monitoring Service, 1939–42; war-time govt service, 1942–45; Associate Chief, Legal Service, UN Interim Secretariat, London, 1945–46; Asst Dir, UN European Office, Geneva, 1946–48; Legal Adviser to UNSCOB, Salonica, 1948; Dep. Legal Adviser, later Legal Adviser, OEEC (OECD 1960–), Paris, 1949–61; UNECA Legal Consultant, formation of African Develt Bank and Econ. Council for Africa, 1962–64; Actg Gen. Counsel of ADB, 1964–65; UNDP Legal Consultant, formation of Caribbean Develt Bank, 1967–68; Special Adviser on European Communities Law, FCO, 1970–79. Legal consultancies for: WHO, 1948; IBRD, 1966; W Afr. Regional Gp, 1968; OECD, 1975. Lectured: on Europ. payments system and OEEC/OECD activs, Univ. of the Saar, 1957–60, and Univ. Inst. of Europ. Studies, Turin, 1957–65; on drafting of treaties, UNITAR Seminars, The Hague, Geneva and NY, for legal advisers and diplomats, 1967–84; on language and law, Univ. of Bath, 1979–; Univ. of Bradford, 1979–84. Hon. Vis. Prof., Bradford Univ., 1982–84. Mem., RIIA. Ford Foundn Leadership Grant, 1960. *Publications:* contrib. European Yearbook, Jl du Droit Internat., Revue Générale de Droit Internat. Public, Survey of Internat. Affairs 1939–1946, Travaux pratiques de L'Institut de Droit Comparé de la Faculté de Droit de Paris, etc. *Recreations:* reading, visiting art collections, travel. *Address:* 140 Hamilton Terrace, NW8; 22 Old Buildings, Lincoln's Inn, WC2. *Club:* Travellers'.

ELKIN, Sonia Irene Linda, OBE 1981 (MBE 1966); Director for Regions and Smaller Firms, Confederation of British Industry, since 1985; *b* 15 May 1932; *d* of Godfrey Albert Elkin and Irene Jessamine Archibald. *Educ:* Beresford House Sch., Eastbourne. Association of British Chambers of Commerce, 1950–66: Overseas Director, 1956–66; Lloyds Bank Overseas Dept, 1966–67; Confederation of British Industry, 1967–: Head of West European Dept, 1967–72; Head of Regional and Smaller Firms Dept, 1972–73; Dep. Director, Regions and Smaller Firms, 1973–79; Director: for Smaller Firms, 1979–83; for Regions, 1983–85. Commissioner, Manpower Services Commission, 1982–85. *Publications:* What about Europe?, 1967; What about Europe Now?, 1971. *Address:* Confederation of British Industry, Centre Point, 103 New Oxford Street, WC1A 1DU. *Club:* United Oxford & Cambridge University (Lady Associate).

ELKINGTON, Reginald Geoffrey, CB 1962; *b* 24 Dec. 1907; *s* of Harold and Millicent Elkington; *m* 1935, Bertha Phyllis, *d* of William and Bertha Dyason; one adopted *s* one adopted *d*. *Educ:* Battersea Grammar Sch.; Fitzwilliam Coll., Cambridge. Inland Revenue, 1929–42; Min. of Supply, 1942–57 (Under-Sec., 1954); DSIR, 1957–65; Principal Establishment Officer, Min. of Technology, 1964–67; retired from Civil Service, 1967; Estabt Officer (part-time), Monopolies Commn, 1968–73. Sec., AERE Harwell, 1948–51. *Recreations:* gardening, crossword solving. *Address:* Maranwood, Highfield Road, West Byfleet, Surrey. *T:* Walton-on-Thames 343766.

ELLACOMBE, Air Cdre John Lawrence Wemyss, CB 1970; DFC 1942 (Bar 1944); FBIM; *b* Livingstone, N Rhodesia, 28 Feb. 1920; *s* of Dr Gilbert H. W. Ellacombe; *m* 1951, Wing Officer Mary Hibbert, OBE, WRAF; one *s* two *d*. *Educ:* Diocesan Coll., Rondebosch, Cape. War of 1939–45: RAF, 1939; Fighter Comd and Two ATA Force, 1940–45 (Pilot, Battle of Britain). Aden, 1946–48; RAF Staff Coll., 1948–49; Fighter Command, 1949–57; BJSM, Washington, 1959. JSSC, 1959–60; Gp Captain, CO RAF Linton on Ouse, to Nov 1962; CFE, to Aug. 1965; Defence Operational Analysis Estabt, West Byfleet, 1965–68; Air Cdre, Commander Air Forces Gulf, 1968–70; Dir of Ops (Air Defence and Overseas), MoD (Air), 1970–73; St Thomas' Hospital: Dir, Scientific Services, 1973–80; Administrator to Special Trustees, 1980–85. *Recreations:* photography, golf, cricket. *Address:* 33 The Drive, Northwood, Middlesex HA6 1HW. *Club:* Royal Air Force.

ELLEN, Eric Frank, QPM 1980; LLB; CBIM; Director: International Chamber of Commerce International Maritime Bureau, since 1981; Counterfeiting Intelligence Bureau, since 1985; *b* London, 30 Aug. 1930; *s* of late Robert Frank Ellen and of Jane Lydia Ellen; *m* 1949, Gwendoline Dorothy Perkins; one *s* one *d*. *Educ:* Wakefield Central Sch., East Ham; Holborn Coll. of Law, Univ. of London (LLB Hons, London Univ. Certificate in Criminology). CBIM (FBIM 1978). Joined PLA Police, 1951; Sgt 1956; Inspector 1961; Chief Insp. 1972; Supt and Chief Supt 1973; attended 11th Sen. Comd Course, Bramshill Police Coll., 1974; Dep. Chief Constable 1975; Chief Constable, 1975–80. Adviser on security to Ports Div. of Dept of Environment; advised Barbados Govt on formation of Barbados Port Authy Police Force, 1983; reviewed port security at Jeddah and Dammam. Sec., Internat. Assoc. of Airport and Seaport Police, 1980– (Pres., 1977–78 and 1978–79); Founder, Chm. and Life Mem., EEC Assoc. of Airport and Seaport Police, 1975–78; Chm., Panel on Maritime Fraud, Commonwealth Secretariat, 1982–; Consultant, Commercial Crime Unit. Member: Internat. Assoc. of Ports and Harbours Standing Cttee on Legal Protection of Port Interests, 1977–79 (Chm., Sub-Cttee on Protection of Ports against Sabotage and Terrorism, 1977–79); Cttee of Conservative Lawyers, 1985–; Shipbrokers Cttee on Maritime Fraud; British Acad. of Forensic Sciences; Hon. Soc. of Middle Temple. Police Long Service and Good Conduct Medal, 1974. Freeman of the City of London, 1978. Police Medal Republic of China, 1979. *Publications:* (co-author) International Maritime Fraud, 1981; professional articles on marine fraud and counterfeiting, terrorism, piracy and port policing (has lectured on these topics at seminars in over 40 countries). *Recreations:* golf, swimming. *Address:* Maritime House, 1 Linton Road, Barking, Essex IG11 8HG. *T:* 01-591 3000. *Club:* Wig and Pen.

ELLEN, Patricia Mae Hayward; *see* Lavers, P. M.

ELLENBOROUGH, 8th Baron *cr* 1802; **Richard Edward Cecil Law;** Director, Towry Law & Co., since 1958; *b* 14 Jan. 1926; *s* of 7th Baron and Helen Dorothy, *o d* of late H. W. Lovatt; *S* father, 1945; *m* 1953, Rachel Mary, *o d* of late Major Ivor Hedley; three *s*. *Educ:* Eton Coll.; Magdalene Coll., Cambridge. Pres., Nat. Union of Ratepayers' Associations, 1960–. *Heir:* *s* Captain the Hon. Rupert Edward Henry Law, Coldstream Guards [*b* 28 March 1955; *m* 1981, Hon. Grania, *d* of Baron Boardman, *qv*; one *s* one *d*]. *Address:* Withypool House, Observatory Close, Church Road, Crowborough, East Sussex TN6 1BN. *T:* Crowborough 63139. *Clubs:* Gresham, Turf.

ELLERTON, Geoffrey James, CMG 1963; MBE 1956; Chairman, Local Government Boundary Commission for England, since 1983; *b* 25 April 1920; *er s* of late Sir Cecil Ellerton; *m* 1946, Peggy Eleanor, *d* of late F. G. Watson; three *s*. *Educ:* Highgate Sch.; Hertford Coll., Oxford (MA). Military Service, 1940–45. Apptd Colonial Administrative Service as District Officer, Kenya, 1945. Acted as Minister for Internal Security and Defence, 1960 and 1962. Retired as Permanent Sec., Prime Minister's Office and Sec. to the Cabinet, at time of Kenya's Independence, Dec. 1963. Sec. to the Maud and Mallaby Cttees on Management and Staffing in Local Government, 1964. Joined Elder Dempster Lines, 1965, Chm., 1972–74; an Exec. Dir, Ocean Transport & Trading Ltd, 1972–80; Dir, Overseas Containers Ltd, 1975–80; Chm., Globe Management Ltd, 1981–83; Dir, Globe Investment Trust PLC, 1983–86. Member: Council, Liverpool Univ., 1974–78; Council, Hakluyt Soc., 1984–. *Recreations:* music, reading. *Address:* Briar Hill House, Broad Campden, Chipping Campden, Glos. *T:* Evesham 841003. *Clubs:* Brooks's, Beefsteak, MCC; Nairobi.

ELLES, family name of **Baroness Elles.**

ELLES, Baroness *cr* 1972 (Life Peer), of the City of Westminster; **Diana Louie Elles;** Member (C) Thames Valley, European Parliament, since 1979; Bureau Member, European Democratic Group, since 1979, and Vice President, since 1982, European Parliament; *b* 19 July 1921; *d* of Col Stewart Francis Newcombe, DSO and Elisabeth Chaki; *m* 1945, Neil Patrick Moncrieff Elles, *qv*; one *s* one *d*. *Educ:* private Schs, England, France and Italy; London University (BA Hons). Served WAAF, 1941–45. Barrister-at-law. Care Cttee worker in S London, 1956–72. UK Delegn to UN Gen. Assembly, 1972; Mem., UN Sub-Commn on Prevention of Discrimination and Protection of Minorities, 1973–75; UN special rapporteur on Human Rights, 1973–75; Mem., British delegn to European Parlt, 1973–75. Mem., Cripps Cttee on legal discrimination against women; Chm., Sub-cttee of Women's Nat. Adv. Cttee (Conservative Party) on one-parent families (report publ. as Unhappy Families); Internat. Chm., European Union of Women, 1973–79; Chm., Cons. Party Internat. Office, 1973–78; Opposition front bench spokesman, 1975–79. Vice-Pres., UK Assoc. of European Lawyers, 1985–. Governor, British Inst. Florence, 1986–. *Publications:* The Housewife and the Common Market (pamphlet), 1971; Human Rights of Aliens, 1980. *Address:* 75 Ashley Gardens, SW1; Villa Fontana, Ponte del Giglio, Lucca, Italy.

ELLES, James Edmund Moncrieff; Member (C) Oxford and Buckinghamshire, European Parliament, since 1984; *b* 3 Sept. 1949; *s* of N. P. M. Elles, *qv* and Baroness Elles, *qv*; *m* 1977, Françoise Le Bail; one *s* one *d*. *Educ:* Ashdown House; Eton College;

Edinburgh University. External Relations Div., EEC, 1976–80; Asst to Dep. Dir Gen. of Agriculture, EEC, 1980–84. Mem., Budget and Agriculture Cttee, European Parlt. *Address:* c/o European Parliament, 97–113 Rue Belliard, 1040 Brussels, Belgium; Conservative Centre, Church Street, Amersham, Bucks HP7 0BD. *Club:* Royal and Ancient Golf (St Andrews).

ELLES, Neil Patrick Moncrieff; Chairman, Value Added Tax Appeals Tribunal, since 1972; *b* 8 July 1919; *s* of Edmund Hardie Elles, OBE and Ina Katharine Hilda Skene; *m* 1945, Diana Louie Newcombe (*see* Baroness Elles); one *s* one *d*. *Educ:* Eton; Christ Church, Oxford (MA). War Service, RAF, 1939–45. Called to the Bar, Inner Temple, 1947; Sec., Inns of Court Conservative and Unionist Taxation Cttee, 1957–71; Mem., Special Study Gp, Commn on Law of Competition, Brussels, 1962–67. *Publications:* The Law of Restrictive Trade Practices and Monopolies (with Lord Wilberforce and Alan Campbell), 1966; Community Law through the Cases, 1973. *Recreations:* fishing, listening to music, the cultivation of vines. *Address:* 75 Ashley Gardens, SW1. *T:* 01–828 0175; Villa Fontana, Ponte del Giglio, Lucca, Italy. *Clubs:* Flyfishers', MCC.

ELLES, Robin Jamieson, CBE 1974 (OBE 1945; MBE 1942); JP; County Director, Dunbartonshire British Red Cross Society, 1968–80; *b* 4 Jan. 1907; *er s* of late Bertram Walter Elles, Malayan Civil Service, and late Jean Challoner Elles; *m* 1932, Eva Lyon Scott Elliot (*d* 1984), *d* of Lt-Col William Scott Elliot; one *s*. *Educ:* Marlborough Coll.; Trinity Hall, Cambridge. BA 1928, MA 1950. Sudan Political Service, 1929–34; J. & P. Coats Ltd, India and China, 1935–40; Army, 1940–45: OETA Abyssinia, 1941; Sudan Defence Force, 1942–45, Libya and Tripolitania, Temp. Lt-Col Comdg 10 SDF Inf. Bn, 1944–45; J. & P. Coats Ltd, Personnel, 1946–66, retd 1966. Chm. of Governors, Paisley Coll. of Technology, 1966–76 (Governor, 1950–76); Chairman: Scottish Adv. Cttee, Nat. Youth Employment Council, 1962–71; Nat. Youth Employment Council, 1971–74. JP Dunbartonshire, 1952. *Publications:* various papers. *Recreations:* fishing, rowing (Cambridge Blue, 1927 and 1929; rowed for Leander, 1929). *Address:* Rogart, Garelochhead, Dunbartonshire. *T:* Garelochhead 810304. *Club:* Leander (Henley-on-Thames).

ELLINGWORTH, Richard Henry; HM Diplomatic Service, retired; *b* 9 March 1926; *s* of Vincent Ellingworth; *m* 1952, Joan Mary Waterfield; one *s* three *d*. *Educ:* Uppingham; Aberdeen Univ.; Magdalen Coll., Oxford (Demy). Served War of 1939–45: RA, and Intelligence Corps, 1944–47. Oxford, 1947–50 (first Lit. Hum.); HM Embassy, Japan, 1951–55; FO, 1955–59; HM Embassy: Belgrade, 1959–63; Japan, 1963–68 (Olympic Attaché, 1964); Head of Oil Dept., FCO, 1969–71; Research Associate, Internat. Inst. for Strategic Studies, 1971–72; Counsellor, Tehran, 1972–75; seconded to Dept of Energy, 1975–77. Course Dir (European Training), Civil Service Coll., 1978–83. Mem., Farningham Parish Council, 1979–83; pt-time Agent, Sevenoaks Liberal Assoc., 1983–84; Hon. Organiser, Farmingham, Royal British Legion, 1982–. *Publications:* (with A. N. Gilkes) An Anthology of Oratory, 1946; Japanese Economic Policy and Security, 1972. *Recreations:* gardening, music. *Address:* 20A Maunsel Street, SW1P 2QN. *T:* 01-828 4650.

ELLIOT; *see* Elliot-Murray-Kynynmound, family name of Earl of Minto.

ELLIOT; *see* Scott-Elliot.

ELLIOT, family name of **Baroness Elliot of Harwood.**

ELLIOT OF HARWOOD, Baroness *cr* 1958 (Life Peer); **Katharine Elliot,** DBE 1958 (CBE 1946); JP; *b* 15 Jan. 1903; *d* of Sir Charles Tennant, 1st Bt, Innerleithen, Peeblesshire, and late Mrs Geoffrey Lubbock; *m* 1934, Rt Hon. Walter Elliot, PC, CH, MC, FRS, LLD, MP (*d* 1958); no *c*. *Educ:* Abbot's Hill, Hemel Hempstead; Paris. Chairman: Nat. Assoc. of Mixed Clubs and Girls' Clubs, 1939–49; Adv. Cttee on Child Care for Scotland, 1956–65; Women's Nat. Adv. Cttee of Conservative Party, 1954–57; Nat. Union of Conservative and Unionist Assocs, 1956–67; Carnegie UK Trust, 1965– (Trustee, 1940–86); Consumer Council, 1963–68. Chm., Lawrie & Symington Ltd, Lanark, 1958–75. Member: Women's Consultative Cttee, Dept of Employment and Productivity (formerly Min. of Labour), 1941–51, 1958–70; Home Office Adv. Cttee on Treatment of Offenders, 1946–62; King George V Jubilee Trust, 1936–68; NFU. UK Delegate to Gen. Assembly of UN, New York, 1954, 1956 and 1957. Contested (C) Kelvingrove Div. of Glasgow, March 1958. Roxburghshire: CC 1946–75 (Vice-Convener, 1974); JP 1968–. Farms in Roxburghshire. FRSA 1964. Hon. LLD: Glasgow, 1959; Selly Oak Colls, Birmingham, 1986. Grand Silver Cross, Austrian Order of Merit, 1963. *Publication:* Tennants Stalk, 1973. *Recreations:* foxhunting, golf, music. *Address:* Harwood, Bonchester Bridge, Hawick, Roxburghshire TD9 9TL; 17 Lord North Street, Westminster, SW1P 3LD. *T:* 01–222 3230.

ELLIOT, Sir Gerald Henry, Kt 1986; FRSE; Chairman, Christian Salvesen plc, since 1981; *b* 24 Dec. 1923; *s* of late Surg. Captain J. S. Elliot, RN, and Magda Salvesen; *m* 1950, Margaret Ruth Whale; two *s* one *d*. *Educ:* Marlborough Coll.; New Coll., Oxford (BA PPE 1948). FRSE 1978. Captain FF Rifles, Indian Army, 1942–46. Christian Salvesen Ltd, 1948–, Dep. Chm. and Man. Dir, 1973–81. Dir, Scottish Provident Instn, 1971–, Chm., 1983–; Chairman: Chambers and Fargus, 1975–79; Scottish Br., RIIA, 1973–77 (Sec., 1963–73); FAO Fishery Industries Develt Gp, 1971–76; Forth Ports Authority, 1973–79; Scottish Arts Council, 1980–86. Chm., Scottish Unit Managers Ltd, 1984–. Sec., National Whaling Bd, 1953–62; Mem., Nat. Ports Council, 1978–81. Mem. Court, Edinburgh Univ., 1984–. Consul for Finland in Edinburgh, 1957–. Kt 1st Cl., Order of White Rose of Finland, 1975. *Publications:* papers on national and internat. control of whaling and fishing and on arts administration. *Address:* 39 Inverleith Place, Edinburgh EH3 5QD.

ELLIOT, Prof. Harry, CBE 1976; FRS 1973; Senior Research Fellow at Imperial College, London, since 1981; Emeritus Professor of Physics, University of London; Professor of Physics at Imperial College, London, 1960–80 (Assistant Director of Physics Department, 1963–71); *b* 28 June 1920; *s* of Thomas Elliot and Hannah Elizabeth (*née* Littleton), Weary Hall, Cumberland; *m* 1943, Betty Leyman; one *s* one *d*. *Educ:* Nelson Sch., Wigton; Manchester Univ. MSc, PhD. Served War, Signals Branch, RAF, incl. liaison duties with USN, 1941–46. Manchester Univ.: Asst Lectr in Physics, 1948–49; Lectr in Physics, 1949–54; Imperial Coll.: Lectr in Physics, 1954–56; Sen. Lectr in Physics, 1956–57; Reader in Physics, 1957–60. Member: Science Research Council, 1971–77; Council, Royal Soc., 1978–79; Science Adv. Cttee, ESA, 1979–. Hon. Prof., Universitad Mayor de San Andres, 1957; Hon. ARCS, 1965. Fellow, World Acad. of Arts and Scis, 1978. Holweck Prize and Medal, Inst. of Physics and Société Française de Physique, 1976. *Publications:* papers on cosmic rays, solar physics and magnetospheric physics in scientific jls; contrib. scientific reviews and magazine articles. *Recreation:* painting. *Address:* The Blackett Laboratory, Imperial College, SW7 2BZ. *T:* 01–589 5111 (ext. 2301).

ELLIOT, Sir John, Kt 1954; High Sheriff of Greater London, 1970–71; *b* London, 6 May 1898; 2nd *s* of R. D. Blumenfeld; assumed Christian name as surname by Deed Pole, 1922; *m* 1924, Elizabeth, *e d* of late Dr A. S. Cobbledick; one *s* one *d*. *Educ:* Marlborough; Sandhurst. European War in 3rd Hussars; after four years in journalism joined former Southern Rly, 1925, in charge public relations (first in UK). Visited USA, Canada, frequently; Deputy General Manager, Southern Rly, 1937, Gen. Manager, 1947; Chief Regional Officer, Southern Region, British Railways, 1948–49. London Midland Region, Euston, 1950–51; Chairman: Railway Exec., 1951–53; London Transport, 1953–59; Pullman Car Co., 1959–63; Thos. Cook & Son Ltd, 1959–67; Willing & Co. Ltd, 1959–70; London and Provincial Poster Group Ltd, 1965–71. Director: Commonwealth Development Corp., 1959–66; Railway Air Services, Channel Islands Airways, 1933–48; Thomas Tilling Ltd, 1959–70; British Airports Authority, 1965–69; Cie Internationale des Wagons-Lits, 1960–71. Vice-Pres., Internat. Union of Railways (UIC), 1947 and 1951–53. Formerly Col. (Comdg) Engineer and Railway Staff Corps, Royal Engineers, 1956–63. Visited Australia, 1949 (at invitation of Govt of Victoria, to report on rail and road transport), 1966, 1970, and E Africa, 1969 (on transport study (World Bank)). FInstT (Pres., 1953–54). Mem. Société de l'histoire de Paris, 1958–74. Officier, Légion d'Honneur; American Medal of Freedom. *Publications:* The Way of the Tumbrils (Paris during the Revolution), 1958; Where our Fathers Died (Western Front 50 years after), 1964; On and Off the Rails, 1982; regular newspaper feature, Speaking of That . . .; book reviews in Daily Telegraph and Sunday Times; many papers on transport. *Recreations:* military history, gardening, cricket (Vice-Pres. Essex CCC). *Address:* 3 Duchess of Bedford House, Duchess of Bedford Walk, W8 7QL. *Clubs:* Cavalry and Guards, MCC.

ELLIOT, Captain Walter, DSC 1944; RN Retd; *b* 17 Feb. 1910; *s* of John White Elliot and Frances Hampson; *m* 1936, Thelma Pirie Thomson; four *d*. *Educ:* HMS Conway; Royal Naval Coll. Joined RN, 1929; specialised in Naval Aviation. Served War of 1939–45 (DSC, despatches); retired, 1958. Took Economics Degree, London Univ., 1958 (BSc Econ). In business, 1958–60. MP (C) Carshalton and Banstead, 1960–Feb. 1974. *Recreations:* fencing, fishing, tennis.

ELLIOT-MURRAY-KYNYNMOUND, family name of **Earl of Minto.**

ELLIOT-SMITH, Alan Guy, CBE 1957; *b* 30 June 1904; *s* of late F. Elliot-Smith; *m* 1939, Ruth Kittermaster; no *c*. *Educ:* Charterhouse; Oriel Coll., Oxford. Hons Mod. Lang. Sch., 1925; Asst Master, Harrow Sch., 1925–40; Headmaster, Cheltenham Coll., 1940–51; Mem., Harrow UDC, 1933–36; Deleg. to Inst. of Pacific Relations Conf., Calif., 1936; lectured to German teachers on Education, 1947 and 1948; lectured to Service units in the Middle East, 1949; Head-master of Victoria Coll., Cairo, 1952–56; Representative in Nigeria of the West Africa Cttee, 1957–58; Headmaster, Markham Coll., Lima, Peru, 1960–63. *Recreations:* travel, reading. *Address:* Bevois Mount, Rowsley Road, Eastbourne, Sussex.

ELLIOTT, family name of **Baron Elliott of Morpeth.**

ELLIOTT OF MORPETH, Baron *cr* 1985 (Life Peer), of Morpeth in the County of Northumberland and of the City of Newcastle-upon-Tyne; **Robert William Elliott;** Kt 1974; DL; Vice-Chairman, Conservative Party Organisation, 1970–74; *b* 11 Dec. 1920; *s* of Richard Elliott; *m* 1956, Jane Morpeth; one *s* four *d* (of whom two are twin *d*). *Educ:* Morpeth Grammar Sch. Farmer, 1939–, at Low Heighley, Morpeth, Northumberland. MP (C) Newcastle-upon-Tyne North, March 1957–1983; Parliamentary Private Secretary: to joint Parliamentary Secs, Ministry of Transport and Civil Aviation, April 1958–Oct. 1959; to Under-Sec., Home Office, Nov. 1959–60; to Minister of State, Home Office, Nov. 1960–61; to Sec. for Technical Co-operation, 1961–63; Asst Govt Whip (unpaid), 1963–64; Opposition Whip, 1964–70; Comptroller of the Household, June-Sept. 1970. Chm., Select Cttee on Agric., Fisheries and Food, 1980–83. DL Northumberland, 1985. *Address:* Lipwood Hall, Haydon Bridge, Northumberland. *T:* Haydon Bridge 777. *Clubs:* Carlton; Northern Counties (Newcastle upon Tyne).

ELLIOTT, Hon. Lord; Walter Archibald Elliott, MC 1943; Chairman, Scottish Land Court, since 1978; President, Lands Tribunal for Scotland, since 1971; *b* 6 Sept. 1922; 2nd *s* of late Prof. T. R. Elliott, CBE, DSO, FRS, Broughton Place, Broughton, Peeblesshire; *m* 1954, Susan Isobel Mackenzie Ross, Kaimend, North Berwick; two *s*. *Educ:* Eton; Trinity Coll., Cambridge; Edinburgh Univ. Active service in Italy and North West Europe with 2nd Bn Scots Guards, 1943–45; captured and escaped, Salerno landings (MC); demobilised, Staff Capt., 1947. Barrister-at-law, Inner Temple, 1950; Advocate at Scottish Bar, 1950; QC (Scotland) 1963. Standing Junior Counsel to Accountant of Court and later to Minister of Aviation. Brigadier, Royal Company of Archers (Queen's Body Guard for Scotland). *Publications:* articles in legal periodicals. *Recreations:* gardening, travelling. *Address:* Morton House, Fairmilehead, Edinburgh. *T:* 031–445 2548. *Clubs:* New, Arts (Edinburgh).

ELLIOTT, Dr Charles Kennedy; Physician to HM the Queen, 1980–86; *b* 1919; *e s* of late Charles Harper Elliott and Martha Elliott; *m* 1949, Elizabeth Margaret Kyle. *Educ:* Campbell Coll., Belfast; Trinity Coll., Dublin (BA, 1941; MA 1970; MB, BCh 1942). MRCGP; MLCO, MFHom, AFOM RCP. Sir Patrick Dun's Hosp., Dublin, 1943; Captain, RAMC, attached SEAC, 1944; General practitioner, Wisbech, 1949–69; Editor, Rural Medicine, 1969–72; Clinical Asst, Royal London Homoeopathic Hosp., 1973–81; Sub Dean, Faculty of Homoeopathy, 1976–79; Area Surgeon, Cambridgeshire St John Ambulance, 1974–81; Chm., Organizing Cttee, VI Internat. Congress Rural Medicine, Cambridge, 1975; Pres., Internat. Assoc. of Agricl Medicine and Rural Health, 1972–78; Trustee: Rehabilitation Trust of Gt Britain, 1977–; Inst. for Complementary Medicine, 1982–. SBStJ 1970; Chevalier de l'Ordre Militaire et Hospitalier de St Lazare de Jerusalem, 1975. *Publications:* (ed jtly) Classical Homoeopathy, 1986; articles in internat. med. pubns and nat. jls. *Recreations:* heraldry, history. *Address:* West Walton, Wisbech, Cambridgeshire PE14 7EU. *T:* Wisbech 780269. *Club:* Royal Society of Medicine.

ELLIOTT, Rev. Dr Charles Middleton; Senior Consultant, Overseas Development Institute, since 1986; Visiting Professor in Theology, King's College London, since 1986; *b* 9 Jan. 1939; *s* of Joseph William Elliott and Mary Evelyn Elliott; *m* 1962, Hilary Margaret Hambling; three *s* (one *d* decd). *Educ:* Repton; Lincoln and Nuffield Colls, Oxford (MA, DPhil). Deacon, 1964; priest, 1965. Lectr in Econs, Univ. of Nottingham, 1963–65; Reader in Econs, Univ. of Zambia, 1965–69; Asst Sec., Cttee on Society, Develt and Peace, Vatican and World Council of Churches, 1969–72; Sen. Lectr in Develt Econs, Univ. of E Anglia, 1972–73; Dir, Overseas Develt Gp, UEA, 1973–77; Minor Canon, Norwich Cathedral, 1974–77; Prof. of Develt Policy and Planning, and Dir, Centre of Develt Studies, Univ. of Wales, 1977–82; Director of Christian Aid, 1982–84; Asst Gen. Sec., BCC, 1982–84; Benjamin Meaker Prof., Bristol Univ., 1985–86. G. E. M. Scott Fellow, Univ. of Melbourne, 1984–85; Hon. Vis. Prof. of Christian Ethics, Univ. of Edinburgh, 1985–. Chm., Indep. Gp on British Aid, 1981–. *Publications:* The Development of Debate, 1972; Inflation and the Compromised Church, 1973; Patterns of Poverty in the Third World, 1975; Praying the Kingdom: an introduction to political spirituality, 1985; (Biennial Collins Prize for Religious Lit., 1984/85); articles in Jl of Develt Studies, Econ. Hist. Rev., Theology, World Health Forum and in Proc. Royal Soc. *Recreations:* sailing, fly-fishing, walking, chatting to rural craftsmen. *Address:* 119 Fentiman Road, Kennington, SW8.

ELLIOTT, David Murray; Minister and Deputy UK Permanent Representative to the European Communities, Brussels, since 1982; *b* 8 Feb. 1930; *s* of late Alfred Elliott, ISM, and Mabel Kathleen Emily Elliott (*née* Murray); *m* 1956, Ruth Marjorie Ingram; one *d* (one *s* decd). *Educ:* Bishopshalt Grammar Sch.; London Sch. of Economics and Political Science (BScEcon); Kitchener Scholar. National Service, RAF, 1951–54; Gen. Post Office, 1954–57; seconded to Federal Ministry of Communications, Nigeria, 1958–62; GPO, 1962–69; Asst Secretary: Min. of Posts and Telecommunications, 1969–74; Dept of Industry, 1974–75; Counsellor at UK Representation to the European Communities, Brussels, 1975–78; Under Sec., Cabinet Office, 1978–82. *Recreation:* reading The Times. *Address:* c/o Foreign and Commonwealth Office, SW1. *Club:* International Château Ste-Anne (Brussels).

ELLIOTT, Denholm Mitchell; actor, stage and films; *b* 31 May 1922; *m* 1954, Virginia McKenna (marr. diss. 1957; she *m* 1957, Bill Travers); *m* 1962, Susan Robinson; one *s* one *d*. *Educ:* Malvern. *Plays:* The Guinea-Pig, Criterion, 1946; Venus Observed, St James's, 1949; Ring Round the Moon, Martin Beck, New York, 1950; Sleep of Prisoners, St Thomas's, Regent Street, 1950; Third Person, Criterion, 1951; Confidential Clerk, Lyric, 1954; South, Arts, 1955; Who Cares, Fortune, 1956; Camino Real, Phœnix, 1957; Traveller Without Luggage, Arts, 1958; The Ark, Westminster, 1959; Stratford-on-Avon Season, 1960; Write Me a Murder, Belasco Theatre, New York, 1961; The Seagull, The Crucible, Ring Round the Moon, Nat. Repertory Co., New York, 1963–64; Come as You Are, New, 1970; Chez Nous, Globe, 1974; The Return of A. J. Raffles, Aldwych, 1975; Heaven and Hell, Greenwich, 1976; The Father, Open Space, 1979; TV plays. *Films:* Sound Barrier, 1949; The Cruel Sea, 1952; They Who Dare, 1953; Pacific Destiny, 1955; Scent of Mystery, 1959; Station Six Sahara, 1962; Nothing But the Best, 1963; King Rat, 1964; The High Bright Sun, 1964; You Must Be Joking, 1965; Alfie, 1966; Here we go round the Mulberry Bush, 1967; The Seagull, 1968; Too Late the Hero, 1969; Madame Sin, 1972; A Doll's House, 1973; The Apprenticeship of Duddy Kravitz, 1974; Russian Roulette, 1976; Sweeney II, Saint Jack, The Hound of the Baskervilles, Zulu Dawn, A Game for Vultures, Cuba, 1978; Bad Timing, Sunday Lovers, 1980; Brimstone and Treacle; Trading Places, 1982; The Missionary, The Wicked Lady, 1983; A Private Function, 1984; Defence of the Realm, A Room with a View, 1986. Has awards, London and New York, incl. BAFTA Best TV Actor, New Standard Best Film Actor, 1981, BAFTA Best Supporting Film Actor, 1984, 1985, 1986. *Recreations:* ski-ing, golf. *Address:* c/o London Management, 235 Regent Street, W1. *Club:* Garrick.

ELLIOTT, Frank Abercrombie, MD, FRCP; Emeritus Professor of Neurology, University of Pennyslvania, since 1979; Director, Elliott Neurology Centre, Pennsylvania Hospital, Philadelphia, since 1975; *b* 18 Dec. 1910; *s* of Arthur Abercrombie Elliott and Kathleen Gosselin; *m* 1st, 1940, Betty Kathleen Elkington; two *d*; 2nd, 1970, Mrs Josiah Marvel (*née* Hopkins). *Educ:* Rondebosch; Univ. of Cape Town. Univ. entrance schol., 1928; Lewis Memorial schol., 1930–34; MB, ChB Cape Town, with Hons and Gold Medal; Hiddingh Travelling Fellowship, 1936–39. House Surg. and House Phys. to professorial units, Cape Town; House Physician, British Postgrad. Sch. of Medicine and Nat. Hosp. for Nervous Diseases, London; Resident MO, Nat. Heart Hosp. RAMC, 1943–48, Lt-Col; Adviser in Neurology, India and War Office. FRCP 1948; FACP 1973. Physician to Charing Cross Hosp., 1947–58; to Moorfields Eye Hospital, 1949–58; Prof. of Neurology, Univ. of Pennsylvania, 1963–78. Lecturer and Examiner, London Univ. Member: Assoc. of British Neurologists; Assoc. of British Physicians; Internat. Soc. of Internal Medicine; Am. Acad. of Neurology; Philadelphia Neurological Soc. *Publications:* (ed) Clinical Neurology, 1952; Clinical Neurology, 1964 (2nd edn, 1971); papers on neurological subjects and the origins of aggressive behaviour. *Address:* Pennsylvania Hospital, Philadelphia, Pa 19107, USA. *Club:* Philadelphia.

ELLIOTT, Frank Alan; Under Secretary, Department of Health and Social Services, Northern Ireland, since 1981; *b* 28 March 1937; *s* of Frank Elliott and Doreen Allen; *m* 1964, Olive Lucy O'Brien; one *s* two *d*. *Educ:* Royal Belfast Academical Inst.; Trinity Coll., Dublin (BA (Mod.) 1st cl.). Entered NI Civil Service, 1959; Principal, Min. of Health, 1966, Asst Sec., 1971; Sen. Asst Sec., Dept of Health and Social Services, 1975. *Recreations:* music and the arts, motoring. *Address:* Department of Health and Social Services, Dundonald House, Upper Newtownards Road, Belfast, Northern Ireland. *T:* Belfast 650111.

ELLIOTT, George, FRICS; Senior Partner, Edmond Shipway and Partners, since 1985; *b* 20 Aug. 1932; *s* of Harry Elliott and Nellie Elizabeth Elliott; *m* 1958, Winifred Joan; one *s* one *d*. *Educ:* Sir George Monoux Grammar Sch.; SW Essex Technical Coll. FRICS 1966. Founder Partner, Edmond Shipway, 1963; Chief Exec., British Urban Develt Services Unit, 1975–78. *Recreation:* travel. *Address:* Flat 8.6, Stirling Court, Marshall Street, W1V 1LQ. *T:* 01–437 3133. *Club:* Carlton.

ELLIOTT, Harold William, CBE 1967; *b* 24 Nov. 1905; *s* of late W. J. Elliott and Ellen Elliott; *m* 1st, 1929, Mary Molyneux (marr. diss. 1935); one *s* one *d*; 2nd, 1937, Betty (*d* 1976), *d* of late C. J. Thumling; one *s*; 3rd, 1978, Helen Bridget, *y d* of Sir Lionel Faudel-Phillips, 3rd Bt, and *widow* of 5th Earl of Kilmorey. *Educ:* Brighton Coll. Apprenticed to Adolf Saurer, AG Arbon, Switz., 1924; joined Pickfords Ltd, 1926. Mem., Road and Rail Central Conf., 1938; Transport Adv. Cttee, Food Defence Plans Dept, BoT, 1939; Asst Divisional Food Officer (Transport), London, 1940; Controller of Road Transport, Min. of Supply, 1941; Mem., Salvage Bd; Dir of Transport, Middle East Supply Centre, Cairo, 1943–44; Mem., Road Haulage Central Wages Bd and Vice-Chm., Meat Transport Organisation Ltd, 1945; Gen. Man., Hay's Wharf Cartage Co. Ltd, Pickfords Ltd and Carter Paterson & Co. Ltd, 1947; Chief Officer (Freight), Road Transport Exec.; Mem., Coastal Shipping Adv. Cttee, 1948; Mem. Bd of Management, Brit. Road Services, and Dir, Atlantic Steam Navigation Co. Ltd, 1959; Man. Dir, Pickfords Ltd, 1963–70, Chm., 1970. Vice-Pres., CIT, 1970–71; Life Mem., Road Haulage Assoc. Trustee, Sutton Housing Trust, 1971–79; Chm., Holmwood Common Management Cttee, 1971–79; Governor, Brighton Coll., 1955 (Chm. Governors, 1974–78; a Vice Patron, 1980). Liveryman, Worshipful Co. of Carmen, 1939–84; Freeman, City of London, 1939. *Address:* Ombla, Moushill Lane, Milford, Godalming, Surrey GU8 5BH. *T:* Godalming 20723.

ELLIOTT, Sir Hugh (Francis Ivo), 3rd Bt *cr* 1917; OBE 1953; Editor, Technical Publications, and Research Consultant, International Union for Conservation of Nature, 1970–80, retired; *b* 10 March 1913; *er s* of Sir Ivo Elliott, 2nd Bt; *S* father, 1961; *m* 1939, Elizabeth Margaret, *er d* of A. G. Phillipson; one *s* two *d*. *Educ:* Dragon Sch.; Eastbourne Coll.; University Coll., Oxford. Tanganyika Administration, 1937; Administrator, Tristan da Cunha, 1950–52; Permanent Sec., Min. of Natural Resources, Tanganyika, 1958; retired, 1961. Commonwealth Liaison Officer for International Union for Conservation of Nature, 1961–66; acting Sec.-Gen., 1962–64, Sec.-Gen., 1964–66, Sec. Ecology Commn, 1966–70. Trustee, British Museum (Natural History), 1971–81; Hon. Sec., British Ornithologists' Union, 1962–66, Vice-Pres. 1970–73, Pres., 1975–79; Chm., British Nat. Sect., Internat. Council for Bird Preservation, 1980–81. Comdr, Order of Golden Ark (Netherlands), 1980. *Publications:* (ed) Proc. 2nd World Conf. on Nat. Parks, Yellowstone, 1972; (jtly) Herons of the World, 1978; contributor to Ibis and various ornithological and conservation jls. *Recreations:* ornithology, travel. *Heir:* *s* Clive Christopher Hugh Elliott, PhD [*b* 12 Aug. 1945; *m* 1975, Marie-Thérèse, *d* of H. Ruttimann; two *s*]. *Address:* 173 Woodstock Road, Oxford OX2 7NB. *T:* Oxford 55469.

ELLIOTT, Hugh Percival, CMG 1959; retired, 1967; *b* 29 May 1911; *s* of late Major P. W. Elliott, IA; *m* 1951, Bridget Rosalie (*d* 1981), *d* of late Rev. A. F. Peterson. *Educ:* St Lawrence Coll., Ramsgate; Hertford Coll., Oxford. Joined Colonial Administrative Service, Nigeria, 1934; seconded Colonial Office, 1946; Supervisor, Colonial Service Courses, London, 1948–50; Senior District Officer, 1954; Permanent Sec., 1956; Adviser, Govt of Eastern Nigeria, 1962–67. Many visits to Ethiopia, Kenya, Rhodesia etc, to support the initiatives for Moral Re-Armament by African friends, 1968–78. CON, 1964 (Comdr, Order of the Niger, Nigeria). *Publications:* Darkness and Dawn in Zimbabwe, 1978; Dawn in Zimbabwe, 1980. *Address:* 14 Eldon Avenue, Shirley, Croydon, Surrey.

ELLIOTT, Maj.-Gen. James Gordon, CIE 1947; retd; *b* 6 April 1898; *s* of late Dr William Elliott, Welshpool, Montgomeryshire; *m* 1931, Barbara Eleanor (*d* 1979), *y d* of William Douglas, Malvern; one *s* one *d*. *Educ:* Blundell's Sch. Commissioned, Indian Army, 1916; 1st Punjab Regt, 1922; GSO2 Staff Coll., Quetta, 1935–37; Dir Military Training, India, 1942–43; Bde Comdr, 1943–44; Dep. Welfare Gen., India, 1945–46; Dep. Sec. (Mil.), Defence Cttee, India, 1947–48; retired 1948. *Publications:* Administrative Aspect of Tactics and Training, 1938; The Story of the Indian Army, 1939–45, 1965; The Frontier 1839–1947, 1968; Field Sports in India 1800–1947, 1973; India, 1976. *Recreations:* gardening, fishing. *Address:* 13 Barnfield Avenue, Exmouth, Devon. *Club:* Naval and Military.

ELLIOTT, Prof. James Philip, PhD; FRS 1980; Professor of Theoretical Physics, University of Sussex, since 1969; *b* 27 July 1929; *s* of James Elliott and Dora Kate Smith; *m* 1955, Mavis Rosetta Avery; one *s* two *d*. *Educ:* University College, Southampton; London External degrees: BSc 1949, PhD 1952. Senior Scientific Officer, AERE Harwell, 1951–58; Vis. Associate Prof., Univ. of Rochester, USA, 1958–59; Lecturer in Mathematics, Univ. of Southampton, 1959–62; Reader in Theoretical Physics, Univ. of Sussex, 1962–69. Fellow of former Physical Soc. *Publications:* Symmetry in Physics, 1979; contribs include: The Nuclear Shell Model, Handbuch der Physik, vol 39, 1957; many papers, mostly published in Proc. Roy. Soc. and Nuclear Phys. *Recreations:* gardening, sport and music. *Address:* 36 Montacute Road, Lewes, Sussex BN7 1EP. *T:* Lewes 474783.

ELLIOTT, John Dorman; Chairman and Chief Executive, Elders IXL Ltd, since 1985; Federal Treasurer, Liberal Party of Australia, since 1985; *b* 3 Oct. 1941; *s* of Frank Faithful Elliott and Anita Caroline Elliott; *m* 1965, Lorraine Clare (*née* Golder); two *s* one *d*. *Educ:* Carey Baptist Grammar School, Melbourne; BCom (Hons) 1962, MBA Melbourne 1965. With BHP, Melbourne, 1963–65; McKinsey & Co., 1966–72; formed consortium and raised $30 million to acquire Henry Jones (IXL), and became Man. Dir, 1972; Elder Smith Goldsbrough Mort merged with Henry Jones (IXL) to form Elders IXL, 1981; Elders IXL acquired Carlton & United Breweries, 1983, largest takeover in Aust. history. *Recreations:* football, tennis, Royal tennis. *Address:* 546 Toorak Road, Toorak, Vic 3142, Australia. *T:* 20 3682. *Clubs:* Melbourne, Australian, Savage; Royal Melbourne Tennis.

ELLIOTT, Prof. John Huxtable, FBA 1972; Professor of History, Institute for Advanced Study, Princeton, NJ, since 1973; *b* 23 June 1930; *s* of Thomas Charles Elliott and Janet Mary Payne; *m* 1958, Oonah Sophia Butler. *Educ:* Eton College; Trinity College, Cambridge (MA, PhD). Fellow of Trinity Coll., Cambridge, 1954–67; Asst Lectr in History, Cambridge Univ., 1957–62; Lectr in History, Cambridge Univ., 1962–67; Prof. of History, KCL, 1968–73. Wiles Lectr, QUB, 1969; Trevelyan Lectr, Cambridge Univ., 1982–83. Corresp. Fellow, Real Academia de la Historia, Madrid, 1965; Fellow, Amer. Acad. Arts and Scis, 1977. Mem., Amer. Philosophical Soc., 1982; Corresponding Member: Hispanic Soc. of America, 1975; Real Academia Sevillana de Buenas Letras, 1976. Dr *hc* Universidad Autónoma de Madrid, 1983. Leo Gershoy Award, Amer. Hist. Assoc., 1985. Visitante Illustre de Madrid, 1983; Comdr, Order of Alfonso X El Sabio, 1984. *Publications:* The Revolt of the Catalans, 1963; Imperial Spain, 1469–1716, 1963; Europe Divided, 1559–1598, 1968; The Old World and the New, 1492–1650, 1970; ed (with H. G. Koenigsberger) The Diversity of History, 1970; (with J. F. de la Peña) Memoriales y Cartas del Conde Duque de Olivares, 2 vols, 1978–80; (with Jonathan Brown) A Palace for a King, 1980; Richelieu and Olivares, 1984; The Count-Duke of Olivares, 1986. *Address:* The Institute for Advanced Study, Princeton, NJ 08543, USA; 73 Long Road, Cambridge CB2 2HE. *T:* Cambridge 841 332.

ELLIOTT, Mark; HM Diplomatic Service; Under Secretary on secondment to Northern Ireland Office, since 1985; *b* 16 May 1939; *s* of William Rowcliffe Elliott, *qv*, and Karin Tess Elliott, (*née* Classen); *m* 1964, Julian Richardson; two *s*. *Educ:* Eton Coll. (King's Scholar); New Coll., Oxford. HM Forces (Intell. Corps), 1957–59. FO, 1963; Tokyo, 1965; FCO, 1970; Private Sec. to Perm. Under-Sec. of State, 1973–74; First Sec. and Head of Chancery, Nicosia, 1975–77; Counsellor, 1977–81, Head of Chancery, 1978–81, Tokyo; Hd of Far Eastern Dept, FCO, 1981–85. *Recreations:* photography, walking, music. *Address:* c/o Foreign and Commonwealth Office, SW1.

ELLIOTT, Dr Michael, CBE 1982; FRS 1979; Visiting Research Chemist, University of California, Berkeley, since 1986; *b* 30 Sept. 1924; *s* of Thomas William Elliott and Isobel Constance (*née* Burnell); *m* 1950, Margaret Olwen James; two *d*. *Educ:* Skinners Co.'s Sch., Tunbridge Wells, Kent; The Univ., Southampton (BSc, PhD); King's Coll., Univ. of London (DSc; FKC 1984). FRSC. Postgrad. res., University Coll., Southampton, 1945–46, and King's Coll., Univ. of London, 1946–48; Rothamsted Experimental Station: Organic Chemist, Dept of Insecticides and Fungicides, 1948–85; SPSO 1971–79; DCSO 1979–83 (Hd of Dept of Insecticides and Fungicides, 1979–83, and Dep. Dir, 1980–83); Hon. Scientist and Consultant, Chemistry of Insecticides, 1983–85. Vis. Lectr, Div. of Entomology, Univ. of Calif at Berkeley, 1969 and 1974; Vis. Prof., Imperial Coll. of Sci. and Tech., 1978–. Hon. DSc Southampton, 1985. Burdick and Jackson Internat. Award for Res. in Pesticide Chemistry, 1975; Holroyd Medal and Lectureship, Soc. of Chem. Ind., 1977; John Jeyes Medal and Lectureship, Chem. Soc., 1978; Mullard Medal, Royal Soc., 1981; Grande Médaille de la Société Française de Phytiatrie et de Phytopharmacie, 1983; Fine Chemicals and Medicinals Gp Award, RSC, 1984. *Publications:* Synthetic Pyrethroids, 1977; papers on chemistry of insecticides and relation of chemical structure with biological activity; chapters in books on insecticides. *Recreations:* photography, designing insecticides. *Address:* Pesticide Chemistry and Toxicology Laboratory, Department of Entomological Sciences, 115 Wellman Hall, University of California, Berkeley, Calif 94720, USA. *T:* (415) 642-5424. *Club:* Camera.

ELLIOTT, Michael Alwyn; Director of Administration, Denton, Hall, Burgin and Warrens, Solicitors, since 1985; *b* 15 July 1936; *s* of W. A. Edwards and Mrs J. B. Elliott (assumed stepfather's name); *m* Caroline Margaret McCarthy; two *s* one *d*. *Educ:* Raynes Park Grammar School. Journalist, 1955–59; Public Relations, Avon Rubber Co. Ltd, 1959–63; Marketing Executive, then Assistant Corporate Planning Manager, CPC International, 1963–68; Kimberly-Clark Ltd: Product Manager, 1968; Marketing Manager, 1969; Marketing and Development Manager, 1975; General Manager, 1976; Director, 1977; Gen. Administrator, Nat. Theatre, 1979–85. Member: Executive Council,

Soc. of West End Theatre, 1980–85; Bd of Management, British Theatre Assoc., 1985–. *Recreations:* acting, golf, walking, tennis. *Address:* 149 Forest Road, Tunbridge Wells, Kent TN2 5EX. *T:* Tunbridge Wells 30615. *Club:* Reform.

ELLIOTT, Michael Norman; Member (Lab) London West, European Parliament, since 1984; *b* 3 June 1932. *Educ:* Brunel College of Technology. Formerly res. chemist in food industry. Mem., Ealing Borough Council, 1964–86 (former Leader of Council and Chm., Educn Cttee). Mem. CND. *Address:* 358 Oldfield Lane North, Greenford, Middx UB6 8PT. *T:* 01–578 1303.

ELLIOTT, Sir Norman (Randall), Kt 1967; CBE 1957 (OBE 1946); MA; Chairman of the Electricity Council, 1968–72; Chairman, Howden Group, 1973–83; Director: Newarthill & McAlpine Group, since 1972; Slumberger Ltd, since 1977; *b* 19 July 1903; *s* of William Randall Elliott and Catherine Dunsmore; *m* 1963, Phyllis Clarke. *Educ:* privately; St Catharine's Coll., Cambridge. Called to the Bar, Middle Temple, 1932 (J. J. Powell Prizeman, A. J. Powell Exhibitioner). London Passenger Transport Board; London and Home Counties Joint Electricity Authority; Yorkshire Electric Power Co.; 21 Army Group: first as CRE (Royal Engineers) then, as Col, Deputy Dir of Works, 21 Army Group (OBE); Chief Engineer and Manager, Wimbledon Borough Council; Gen. Manager and Chief Engineer, London and Home Counties Joint Electricity Authority and sometime Chm. and Dir, Isle of Thanet Electric Supply Co., and Dir, James Howden & Co. Ltd; Chairman: S-E Electricity Bd, 1948–62; S of Scotland Electricity Bd, 1962–67; Member: Brit. Electricity Authority, 1950 and 1951; Central Electricity Authority, 1956 and 1957; Electricity Council, 1958–62; N of Scotland Hydro-Electric Bd, 1965–69. *Publication:* Electricity Statutes, Orders and Regulations, 1947, rev. edn 1951. *Recreations:* ball games and the theatre. *Address:* 3 Herbrand Walk, Cooden, East Sussex. *Clubs:* Athenæum; Western (Glasgow); Royal Northern Yacht.

ELLIOTT, Oliver Douglas; British Council Representative in Yugoslavia, 1979–85; *b* 13 Oct. 1925; *y s* of late Walter Elliott and Margherita Elliott, Bedford; *m* 1954, Patience Rosalie Joan Orpen; one *s*. *Educ:* Bedford Modern Sch.; Wadham Coll., Oxford (MA); Fitzwilliam House, Cambridge. Served RNVR (Sub-Lt), 1944–47. Colonial Educn Service, Cyprus, 1953–59; joined British Council, 1959; served Lebanon, 1960–63; Dep. Rep., Ghana, 1963; Dir, Commonwealth I Dept, 1966; Dir, Service Conditions Dept, 1970; Dep. Educn Advr, India, 1973; Representative in Nigeria, 1976–79. *Recreation:* golf.

ELLIOTT, Sir Randal (Forbes), KBE 1977 (OBE 1976); President, New Zealand Medical Association, 1976; *b* 12 Oct. 1922; *s* of Sir James Elliott and Lady (Ann) Elliott (*née* Forbes), MBE; *m* 1949, Pauline June Young; one *s* six *d*. *Educ:* Wanganui Collegiate Sch.; Otago Univ. MB, ChB (NZ), 1947; DO, 1953; FRCS, FRACS. Group Captain, RNZAF. Ophthalmic Surgeon, Wellington Hospital, 1953–. Chm. Council, NZ Med. Assoc. KStJ 1978. *Publications:* various papers in medical jls. *Recreations:* sailing, skiing, mountaineering. *Address:* 88 The Terrace, Wellington, New Zealand. *T:* 721–375. *Club:* Wellington (NZ).

ELLIOTT, Robert Anthony K.; *see* Keable-Elliott.

ELLIOTT, Air Vice-Marshal Robert D.; *see* Deacon Elliott.

ELLIOTT, Prof. Roger James, FRS 1976; Wykeham Professor of Physics, Oxford University, since 1974; Fellow of New College, Oxford, since 1974; *b* Chesterfield, 8 Dec. 1928; *s* of James Elliott and Gladys Elliott (*née* Hill); *m* 1952, Olga Lucy Atkinson; one *s* two *d*. *Educ:* Swanwick Hall Sch., Derbyshire; New Coll., Oxford (MA, DPhil). Research Fellow, Univ. of California, Berkeley, 1952–53; Research Fellow, UKAEA, Harwell, 1953–55; Lectr, Reading Univ., 1955–57. Fellow of St John's College, Oxford, 1957–74; University Reader, Oxford, 1964–74; Senior Proctor, 1969; Delegate, Oxford Univ. Press, 1971–. Chm., Computer Bd for Univs and Research Councils, 1983–. Physical Sec. and Vice-Pres., Royal Soc., 1984–. Visiting Prof., Univ. of California, Berkeley, 1961; Miller Vis. Prof., Univ. of Illinois, Urbana, 1966; Vis. Dist. Prof., Florida State Univ., 1981. Hon. DSc Paris, 1983. Maxwell Medal, Inst. of Physics, 1968. *Publications:* Magnetic Properties of Rare Earth Metals, 1973; Solid State Physics and its Applications (with A. F. Gibson), 1973; papers in Proc. Royal Soc., Jl Phys., Phys. Rev., etc. *Address:* 11 Crick Road, Oxford OX2 6QL. *T:* Oxford 53281. *Club:* Athenæum.

ELLIOTT, Sir Ronald (Stuart), Kt 1981; Director: Brambles Industries Ltd, since 1981; Australian Board, International Commodities Clearing House Ltd, since 1981; International Board, Security Pacific National Bank, USA, since 1983; Security Pacific Australia Ltd, since 1985; *b* 29 Jan. 1918; *s* of Harold J. W. Elliott and Mercedes E. Manning; *m* 1944, Isabella Mansbridge Boyd; one *s* one *d*. *Educ:* C of E Grammar Sch., Ballarat, Victoria. ABIA; FAIM. Commonwealth Banking Corporation: Sec., 1960–61; Dep. Manager for Queensland, 1961–63; Chief Manager, Foreign Div., 1963–64; Chief Manager, Queensland, 1964–65; Gen. Manager, Commonwealth Develt Bank of Australia, 1966–75; Dep. Man. Dir, 1975–76, Man. Dir, 1976–81, Commonwealth Banking Corp.; Chm., Australian European Finance Corp. Ltd, 1976–81. Mem., Sci. and Industry Forum, Australian Acad. of Sci., 1978–81. Dir., Australian Opera, 1980–; Mem., Australian Film Develt Corp., 1970–75. *Recreations:* golf, reading, music, particularly opera. *Address:* 56 Milray Avenue, Wollstonecraft, NSW 2065, Australia. *T:* 432734. *Clubs:* Union, Australian Golf (Sydney) (Pres., 1982–).

ELLIOTT, Sydney Robert; Editor of the Daily Herald, 1953–57; *b* 31 Aug. 1902; *o* surv. *s* of Robert Scott Elliott and Helen Golden; *m* 1927, Janet Robb Johnston; two *s* one *d* (one *s* decd). *Educ:* Govan High Sch., Glasgow. Managing Editor, Reynolds News, 1929; Editor, Evening Standard, 1943; Political Adviser, Daily Mirror, 1945; Managing Dir, The Argus and Australian Post, Melbourne, 1949; Gen. Manager, Daily Herald, 1952. Collaborated with author of George Wigg by Lord Wigg, 1972. *Publications:* Life of Sir William Maxwell, 1922; Co-operative Storekeeping; Eighty Years of Constructive Revolution, 1925; England, Cradle of Co-operation, 1937. *Address:* 5 Frognal Close, Hampstead, NW3. *T:* 01–435 4149.

ELLIOTT, Walter Archibald; *see* Elliott, Hon. Lord.

ELLIOTT, Sir William; *see* Elliott, Sir R. W.

ELLIOTT, William Rowcliffe, CB 1969; Senior Chief Inspector, Department of Education and Science, 1968–72, retired; *b* 10 April 1910; *s* of Thomas Herbert Elliott and Ada Elliott (*née* Rowcliffe); *m* 1937, Karin Tess, *d* of Ernest and Lilly Classen; one *s*. *Educ:* St Paul's Sch.; The Queen's Coll., Oxford. Schoolmaster, 1933–36; HM Inspector of Schools: in Leeds, 1936–39; in Leicestershire, 1940–44; in Liverpool, 1944–48; Staff Inspector: for Adult Education, 1948–55; for Secondary Modern Education, 1955–57; Chief Inspector for Educational Developments, 1957–59; for Secondary Educn, 1959–66; Dep. Sen. Chief Insp., 1966–67. Pres., Section L, British Assoc., 1969; Mem., Oxfam Governing Council, 1974–80. Chm. of Governors, Friends' Sch., Saffron Walden, 1982–84. Governor of The Retreat, York, 1984–. *Publications:* Monemvasia, The Gibraltar of Greece, 1971; Chest-tombs and 'tea caddies' by Cotswold and Severn, 1977. *Recreations:* village life, photography, gardenage, cyclamen and clematis growing. *Address:* Astwick House, Farthinghoe, Brackley, Northants. *T:* Banbury 710388. *Club:* Royal Over-Seas League.

See also Mark Elliott.

ELLIOTT-BINNS, Edward Ussher Elliott, CB 1977; Under-Secretary, Scottish Home and Health Department, 1966–78; *b* 24 Aug. 1918; *e s* of Leonard and Anna Elliott-Binns; *m* 1942, Katharine Mary McLeod, *d* of late Dr J. M. Caie; one *d*. *Educ:* Harrow; King's Coll., Cambridge. Served with Army, 1939–46; Leics Regt and Special Forces (Major). Asst Principal, Scottish Home Dept, 1946; Principal, 1948; Asst Sec., Royal Commn on Capital Punishment, 1949–53; Private Sec. to Minister of State, Scottish Office, 1956–57; Asst Sec., 1957. *Address:* 22 Wilton Road, Edinburgh EH16 5NX. *T:* 031–667 2464. *Club:* Special Forces.

See also Sir P. J. Harrop.

ELLIS; *see* Scott-Ellis.

ELLIS, Andrew Steven, OBE 1984; Secretary-General, Liberal Party, since 1985; *b* 19 May 1952; *s* of Peter Vernon Ellis and Kathleen Dawe; *m* 1975, Patricia Ann Stevens. *Educ:* Trinity Coll., Cambridge (BA Mathematics); Univ. of Newcastle upon Tyne (MSc Statistics); Newcastle upon Tyne Polytechnic (BA Law). Proprietor, Andrew Ellis (Printing and Duplicating), Newcastle upon Tyne, 1973–81; freelance Election Agent/Organizer, 1981–84; Consultant Nat. Agent, Welsh Liberal Party, 1984–. Contested (L): Newcastle upon Tyne Central, Oct. 1974, Nov. 1976, 1979; Boothferry, 1983; Leader, Liberal Gp, Tyne & Wear CC, 1977–81; Vice-Chm., Liberal Party, 1980–86. *Publications:* Algebraic Structure (with Terence Treeby), 1971; Let Every Englishman's Home Be His Castle, 1978. *Recreation:* travel. *Address:* Liberal Party Organization, 1 Whitehall Place, SW1A 2HE. *T:* 01–839 4092; 32 North Parade, Aberystwyth, Ceredigion. *T:* Aberystwyth 617686. *Club:* National Liberal.

ELLIS, Arthur John, CBE 1986; Chairman since 1984, and Chief Executive Officer since 1969, Fyffes Group Ltd; Chairman, Intervention Board for Agricultural Produce, since 1986; *b* 22 Aug. 1932; *s* of Arthur Ellis and Freda Jane Ellis; *m* 1956, Rita Patricia Blake; two *s* one *d*. *Educ:* Chingford Jun. High Sch.; South West Essex Technical Coll. FCCA; FCMA; FCIS; MBCS. Joined Fyffes Gp Ltd as qual. accountant in Finance and Admin Dept, 1954; Chief Financial Officer, 1965; Financial Dir, 1967. *Recreations:* golf, reading, gardening. *Address:* 38 Forest View, Chingford, E4 7AU. *T:* 01–529 7503. *Clubs:* Reform, Farmers', Lansdowne.

ELLIS, Arthur Robert Malcolm, DL; **His Honour Judge Ellis;** a Circuit Judge (formerly Judge of County Courts), since 1971; *b* 27 June 1912; *s* of David and Anne Amelia Ellis, Nottingham; *m* 1938, Brenda Sewell (*d* 1983); one *d*. *Educ:* Nottingham High Sch. Admitted Solicitor, 1934; called to the Bar, Inner Temple, 1953. Chm., Nottingham Council of Social Service, 1950–55; Dep. Chm., E Midland Traffic Area, 1955–71; Chm., Ministry of Pensions and National Insurance Tribunal, Sutton-in-Ashfield, Notts, 1961–64, resigned; Chm., Min. of Pensions and Nat. Insce Tribunal, Notts, 1964–71; Chm., Medical Appeals Tribunal, 1971–76. Chm., Notts QS, 1963–71 (Dep.-Chm., 1962–63); Chm., Derbyshire QS, 1966–71 (Dep.-Chm., 1965–66). DL Notts, 1973. *Recreations:* golf, bridge. *Address:* Byways, 5 Manvers Grove, Radcliffe-on-Trent, Notts NG12 2FT. *Clubs:* United Services (Nottingham); Royal Over-Seas League (Nottingham Branch).

ELLIS, Bryan James; Chairman, Civil Service Selection Board, since 1986; *b* 11 June 1934; *s* of late Frank and Renée Ellis; *m* 1960, Barbara Muriel Whiteley; one *s* one *d*. *Educ:* Merchant Taylors' Sch.; St John's Coll., Oxford (MA). Sec., Oxford Union Soc., 1956. Joined Civil Service, entering Min. of Pensions and National Insurance (subseq. Min. of Social Security and DHSS) as Asst Principal, 1958; Principal 1963; Asst Sec. 1971; Under Sec., 1977. Chm., Assoc. of First Div. Civil Servants, 1983–85. Chm., Trustees of Leopardstown Park Hosp., Dublin, 1979–84. *Recreations:* walking, theatre and cinema, bridge. *Address:* 6 Crutchfield Lane, Walton-on-Thames, Surrey KT12 2QZ. *T:* Walton 228664. *Club:* MCC.

ELLIS, Carol Jacqueline, (Mrs Ralph Gilmore), QC 1980 (practises as Miss Ellis); JP (sits as Mrs Gilmore); Editor, The Law Reports and Weekly Law Reports, since 1976; *b* 6 May 1929; *d* of Ellis W. Ellis and Flora Bernstein; *m* 1957, Ralph Gilmore; two *s*. *Educ:* Abbey Sch., Reading; La Ramée, Lausanne; Univ. of Lausanne; University Coll. London (LLB). Called to the Bar, Gray's Inn, 1951; supernumerary law reporter for The Times, other law reports and legal jls, 1952; law reporter to The Law Reports and Weekly Law Reports, 1954; Asst Editor, Weekly Law Reports, 1969; Managing Editor, The Law Reports and Weekly Law Reports, 1970. JP W Central Div. Inner London, 1972–. *Recreations:* travel, music, theatre. *Address:* 11 Old Square, Lincoln's Inn, WC2. *T:* 01–405 5243/3930.

ELLIS, (Dorothy) June; Headmistress, The Mount School, York, 1977–86; *b* 30 May 1926; *d* of Robert Edwin and Dora Ellis. *Educ:* La Sagesse, Newcastle upon Tyne; BSc Pure Science, Durham; DipEd Newcastle upon Tyne. Assistant Mistress: Darlington High Sch., 1947–49; Rutherford High Sch., 1949–50; La Sagesse High Sch., 1950–53; Housemistress, 1953–61, Sen. Mistress, 1961–64, St Monica's Sch.; Dep. Head, Sibford Sch., 1964–77. *Recreations:* walking, gardening, home-making. *Address:* Willowside, Swerford, Oxford OX7 4BQ.

ELLIS, Rear-Adm. Edward William, CB 1974; CBE 1968; *b* 6 Sept. 1918; *s* of Harry L. and Winifred Ellis; *m* 1945, Dilys (*née* Little); two *s*. Joined RN, 1940; War service afloat in HM Ships Broadwater and Eclipse, and liaison duties in USS Wichita and US Navy destroyer sqdn; psc 1952; Staff of Flag Officer Flotillas, Mediterranean, 1954–55; Sec. to 4th Sea Lord, 1956–58; Sec. to C-in-C South Atlantic and South America, 1959–60; HM Ships Bermuda and Belfast, 1960–62; Head of C-in-C Far East Secretariat, 1963–65; Sec. to C-in-C Portsmouth and Allied C-in-C Channel, 1965–66; Sec. to Chief of Naval Staff and 1st Sea Lord, 1966–68; Cdre RN Barracks Portsmouth, 1968–71; Adm. Pres., RNC Greenwich, 1972–74. Comdr 1953; Captain 1963; Rear-Adm. 1972. Private Sec. to Lord Mayor of London, 1974–82. Freeman of the City of London, 1974; Liveryman, Shipwrights' Co., 1980. OStJ 1981. Commander, Royal Order of Danebrog, 1974. *Recreations:* fishing, gardening. *Address:* South Lodge, Minstead, Lyndhurst, Hants. *Club:* Army and Navy.

ELLIS, Prof. Harold, MA, MCh, DM, FRCS; Professor of Surgery, University of London, since 1962; Hon. Consultant Surgeon, Westminster Hospital, since 1962; *b* 13 Jan. 1926; *s* of Samuel and Ada Ellis; *m* 1958, Wendy Mae Levine; one *s* one *d*. *Educ:* Queen's Coll. (State Scholar and Open Scholar in Natural Sciences), Oxford; Radcliffe Infirmary, Oxford. BM, BCh, 1948; FRCS, MA, 1951; MCh 1956; DM 1962. House Surgeon, Radcliffe Infirmary, 1948–49; Hallett Prize, RCS, 1949. RAMC, 1949–51. Res. Surgical Officer, Sheffield Royal Infirm., 1952–54; Registrar, Westminster Hosp., 1955; Sen. Registrar and Surgical Tutor, Radcliffe Infirm., Oxford, 1956–61; Sen. Lectr in Surgery, Westminster Hosp., 1961–62. Hon. Consultant Surgeon to the Army, 1978–. Mem. Council, RCS, 1974–86. Member: Association of Surgeons; British Soc. of Gastroenterol.;

Surgical Research Soc.; Council: RSocMed; British Assoc. of Surgical Oncology; Associé étranger, L'Academie de Chirurgie, Paris, 1983. *Publications:* Clinical Anatomy, 1960; Anatomy for Anaesthetists, 1963; Lecture Notes on General Surgery, 1965; Principles of Resuscitation, 1967; History of the Bladder Stone, 1970; General Surgery for Nurses, 1976; Intestinal Obstruction, 1982; Notable Names in Medicine and Surgery, 1983; Famous Operations, 1984; Maingot's Abdominal Operations, 1985; numerous articles on surgical topics in medical journals. *Recreation:* medical history. *Address:* 16 Bancroft Avenue, N2. *T:* 01–348 2720.

ELLIS, Herbert; *see* Ellis, W. H. B.

ELLIS, Humphry Francis, MBE 1945; MA; writer; *b* 1907; 2nd *s* of late Dr John Constable Ellis, Metheringham, Lincs and Alice Marion Raven; *m* 1933, Barbara Pauline Hasseldine; one *s* one *d*. *Educ:* Tonbridge Sch.; Magdalen Coll., Oxford (Demy). 1st cl. Hon. Mods, 1928; 1st cl. Lit. Hum., 1930. Asst Master, Marlborough Coll., 1930–31. Contributor to Punch, 1931–68; Editorial staff, 1933; Literary and Dep. Ed., 1949–53. Privilege Mem., RFU, 1952–. Served War of 1939–45 in RA (AA Command). *Publications:* So This is Science, 1932; The Papers of A. J. Wentworth, 1949; Why the Whistle Went (on the laws of Rugby Football), 1947; Co-Editor, The Royal Artillery Commemoration Book, 1950; Editor, Manual of Rugby Union Football, 1952; Twenty Five Years Hard, 1960; Mediatrics, 1961; A. J. Wentworth, BA (Retd), 1962; The World of A. J. Wentworth, 1964 (re-issued as A. J. Wentworth, BA, 1980); Swansong of A. J. Wentworth, 1982; A Bee in the Kitchen, 1983; contribs to The New Yorker. *Recreation:* fishing. *Address:* Hill Croft, Kingston St Mary, Taunton, Somerset. *T:* Kingston St Mary 264. *Clubs:* Garrick, MCC.

ELLIS, John; *b* Hexthorpe, Doncaster, 22 Oct. 1930; *s* of George and Hilda Ellis; *m* 1953, Rita Butters; two *s* two *d*. *Educ:* Rastrick Gram. Sch., Brighouse. Laboratory technician, Meteorological Office, 1947–63; Vice-Chm., Staff side, Air Min. Whitley Council, 1961–63; Member Relations Offr, Co-op. Retail Services, Bristol/Bath Region, 1971–74. Mem., Easthampstead RDC, 1962–66; Mem., Bristol City Council, 1971–74. Contested (Lab) Wokingham, 1964; MP (Lab) Bristol North-West, 1966–70, Brigg and Scunthorpe, Feb. 1974–1979; PPS to Minister of State for Transport, 1968–70; an Asst Govt Whip, 1974–76. JP, North Riding Yorks, 1960–61. *Recreations:* gardening, cricket. *Address:* 102 Glover Road, Scunthorpe, South Humberside.

ELLIS, John, CB 1985; Head of Royal Armament Research and Development Establishment, Chertsey, 1984–85, retired; *b* 9 Jan. 1925; *s* of Frank William and Alice Ellis; *m* 1958, Susan Doris (*née* Puttock). *Educ:* Leeds Univ. BSc, 1st cl. hons. Mech. Eng; CEng, MIMechE. Hydro-Ballistic Research Estabt, Admty, 1945–47; David Brown & Sons Ltd, Huddersfield, 1948; RAE, Min. of Supply (Structures Dept, Armament Dept, Weapons Dept), 1948–68; MVEE (formerly FVRDE), MoD, 1968–84; Dir, MVEE, Chertsey, 1978–84, when MVEE and RARDE amalgamated. *Recreations:* motoring, golf. *Address:* Well Diggers, 1 and 2 New Cottages, New Pond Road, Compton, Guildford, Surrey. *T:* Godalming 7788.

ELLIS, Sir John (Rogers), Kt 1980; MBE 1943; MA, MD, FRCP; Physician, 1951–81, Consulting Physician, since 1981, The London Hospital; President, Medical Protection Society, since 1985; *b* 15 June 1916; 3rd *s* of late Frederick William Ellis, MD, FRCS; *m* 1942, Joan, *d* of late C. J. C. Davenport; two *s* two *d*. *Educ:* Oundle Sch.; Trinity Hall, Cambridge; London Hosp. Served RNVR, 1942–46, Mediterranean and Far East, Surg-Lieut. Gen. Practice, Plymouth, 1946; Sen. Lectr, Med. Unit, London Hosp., 1948–51; Sub-Dean, London Hosp. Med. Coll., 1948–58, Vice-Dean, 1967–68, Dean, 1968–81, Fellow, 1986; Asst Registrar, RCP, 1957–61, Mem. Council 1969–72, Streatfield Schol., 1957; Physician to Prince of Wales Gen. Hosp., 1958–68; PMO (part-time), Min. of Health, 1964–68. Mem., City and E London AHA, 1974–81; Vice-Chm., Newham DHA, 1981–85. Member: UGC's Med. Sub-cttee, 1959–69; WHO Expert Adv. Panel on Health Manpower, 1963–82; Jt Bd of Clinical Nursing Studies, 1969–74; formerly Member: Porritt (Med. Services) Cttee; Royal Commn on Med. Educn; UK Educn Cttee, RCN. Sec., Assoc. for Study of Med. Educn, 1956–71, Vice-Pres., 1971–. Lectures: Goulstonian, RCP, 1956; Wood-Jones, Univ. of Manchester, 1960; Porter, Univ. of Kansas, 1960; Sir Charles Hastings, BMA, 1964; Anders, Coll. of Physicians, Pa, 1965; Adams, RCSI, 1965; Shattuck, Massachusetts Med. Soc., 1969; Shorstein, 1979, 1981, Sprawson, 1980, 1985, London Hosp. Med. Coll.; Visiting Lecturer: Assoc. of Amer. Med. Colls, 1957, 1960 and 1963; Ghana Acad. of Sciences, 1967. Corr. Mem., Royal Flemish Acad. of Medicine; Hon. Member: Royal Swedish Med. Soc.; AOA Honor Med. Soc., USA; Sect. of Med. Educn, RSocMed (former Pres.). Member Bd of Governors: Atlantic Coll.; Court, Univ. of Essex; Chm., Cttee of Management, Inst. of Educn, Univ. of London, 1984–; formerly Member Bd of Governors: Inst. of Psychiatry; Bethlem Royal and Maudsley Hosps; London Hosp.; British Postgrad. Med. Fedn; Queen Mary Coll.; CARE for Mentally Handicapped. Former examr in Med., Univs of Birmingham, Bristol, Cambridge, E Africa, London, Nairobi, Ireland, Newcastle upon Tyne, St Andrews. Editor, British Jl of Medical Education, 1966–75. Hon. Fellow: QMC, 1985; London Hosp. Med. Coll., 1986. Hon. MD Uppsala, 1977. *Publications:* articles on medical education in medical and scientific journals. *Recreations:* painting, gardening. *Address:* Little Monkhams, Monkhams Lane, Woodford Green, Essex. *T:* 01–504 2292.

ELLIS, Prof. John Romaine; Consultant to National Highway Traffic Safety Administration, US Department of Transportation; Adjunct Professor, Ohio State University; *b* 30 Sept. 1922; *m* 1947, Madelaine Della Blaker; one *s* one *d*. *Educ:* Tiffin Sch., Kingston-on-Thames. Royal Aircraft Establishment, 1944–56; Fairey Aviation Company, 1946–48; Royal Military Coll. of Science, Shrivenham, near Swindon, Wilts, 1949–60; Prof. of Automobile Engrg, 1960–82, and Dir, 1960–76, Sch. of Automotive Studies, Cranfield. *Recreations:* golf, tennis, music. *Address:* Summercourt, Lower Road, Edington, Wilts BA13 4QN; Vehicle Research & Test Center, PO Box 37, East Liberty, Ohio 43311, USA.

ELLIS, Dr Jonathan Richard, FRS 1985; Senior Staff Physicist, CERN, Geneva, since 1973; *b* 1 July 1946; *s* of Richard Ellis and Beryl Lilian Ellis (*née* Ranger); *m* 1985, Maria Mercedes Martinez Rengifo. *Educ:* Highgate Sch.; King's Coll., Cambridge. BA; PhD. Postdoctoral research, SLAC, Stanford, 1971–72; Richard Chase Tolman Fellow, Caltech, 1972–73; Staff Mem., CERN, Geneva, 1973–. Maxwell Medal, Inst. of Physics, 1982. *Recreations:* movies, hiking in the mountains, horizontal jogging. *Address:* 5 Chemin du Ruisseau, Tannay, 1295 Mies, Vaud, Switzerland. *T:* (41) (22) 76-48-58.

ELLIS, Joseph Stanley, CMG 1967; OBE 1962; Head of News Department, Commonwealth Office, 1967; retired; *b* 29 Nov. 1907; *m* 1933, Gladys Harcombe (*d* 1983); one *s*. *Educ:* Woodhouse Grove, Bradford; University Coll., University of London. Journalist, Manchester Evening News, 1930–40; Publications Div., Min. of Inf., 1941–45; Seconded to Dominions Office for service in Australia until 1949. Central Office of Information, 1949–51; Regional Information Officer, Karachi, 1952; Dir, British Information Services: Pakistan, 1953–55; Canberra, Australia, 1955–58; Kuala Lumpur, Malaya, 1958–62; Head, Information Services Dept, Commonwealth Office, 1962–66. *Recreation:* cricket. *Address:* Downview Close, Hindhead, Surrey.

ELLIS, June; *see* Ellis, D. J.

ELLIS, Laurence Edward, MA; Rector, The Edinburgh Academy, since 1977; *b* 21 April 1932; *s* of Dr and Mrs E. A. Ellis; *m* 1961, Elizabeth Ogilvie; two *s* one *d*. *Educ:* Winchester Coll.; Trinity Coll., Cambridge (MA). AFIMA. 2/Lieut Rifle Bde, 1950–52. Marlborough Coll., 1955–77 (Housemaster, 1968). FRSA. *Publications:* (part-author) texts on school maths, statistics, computing, and calculating; articles in jls. *Recreations:* Lay Reader; writing, music, woodwork. *Address:* 50 Inverleith Place, Edinburgh EH3 5QB. *T:* (office) 031–556 4603.

ELLIS, Mary; actress; singer; authoress; *b* New York City, 15 June 1901; *m* 1st, L. A. Bernheimer (decd); 2nd (marr. diss.); 3rd, Basil Sydney (marr. diss.); 4th, J. Muir Stewart Roberts (decd). *Educ:* New York. Studied art for three years; studied singing with Madame Ashforth. First Stage appearance, Metropolitan Opera House, New York, in Sœur Angelica, 1918; with Metropolitan Opera House, 1918–22; first appearance dramatic stage, as Nerissa in Merchant of Venice, Lyceum, New York, 1922; was the original Rose Marie (in the musical play, Rose Marie), Imperial, 1924; The Dybbuk, New York, 1925–26; Taming of the Shrew, 1927, and many New York leads followed; first appearance on London stage, as Laetitia in Knave and Quean, Ambassadors', 1930; in following years alternated between London and US. From 1932–39: London: Strange Interlude, 1932; Double Harness, 1933; Music in the Air, 1934; Glamorous Night, Drury Lane, 1935; Innocent Party, St James's, 1937; 2 years, Hollywood, 1936–37; Dancing Years, Drury Lane, 1939. From 1939–43: doing hospital welfare work and giving concerts for troops. Re-appeared on stage as Marie Foret in Arc de Triomphe, Phœnix, London, 1943; Old Vic (at Liverpool Playhouse), 1944 (Ella Rentheim in John Gabriel Borkman; Linda Valaine in Point Valaine; Lady Teazle in The School for Scandal); Maria Fitzherbert in The Gay Pavilion, Piccadilly, 1945; Season at Embassy: Mrs Dane's Defence, also tour and première of Ian Hay's Hattie Stowe, 1946–47; post-war successes include: Playbill, Phœnix, 1949; Man in the Raincoat, Edinburgh, 1949; If this be Error, Hammersmith, 1950. Stratford-on-Avon Season, 1952: Volumnia in Coriolanus. London: After the Ball (Oscar Wilde-Noel Coward), Globe, 1954–55; Mourning Becomes Electra, Arts, 1955 56; Dark Halo, Arts, 1959; Look Homeward Angel, Pembroke Theatre, Croydon, 1960; Phœnix, 1962. First appeared in films, in Bella Donna, 1934; films, 1935–38; (Hollywood) Paris in the Spring; The King's Horses; Fatal Lady; Glamorous Night; Gulliver's Travels, 1961; Silver Cord (revival), Yvonne Arnaud, Guildford, 1971; Mrs Warren's Profession, Yvonne Arnaud, Guildford, 1972. Has made several major television appearances; Television plays, 1956–: Shaw's Great Catherine, Van Druten's Distaff Side and numerous others. Theatre lectures in USA, 1977. Has small hideaway in Swiss mountains, where she writes, paints and gets fresh air. *Publication:* Those Dancing Years (autobiog.), 1982; Moments of Truth, 1986. *Recreations:* painting, travel, writing. *Address:* c/o Chase Manhattan Bank, Woolgate House, Coleman Street, EC2.

ELLIS, Maxwell (Philip), MD, MS, FRCS; Dean of the Institute of Laryngology and Otology, University of London, 1965–71; Consulting Surgeon, Royal National Throat, Nose and Ear Hospital; Consulting Ear, Nose and Throat Surgeon, Central Middlesex Hospital; *b* 28 Feb. 1906; *s* of Louis Ellis; *m* 1st, 1935, Barbara Gertrude Chapman (*d* 1977); 2nd, 1979, Mrs Clarice Adler. *Educ:* University Coll., London (Exhibitioner), Fellow 1975; University Coll. Hosp. (Bucknill Exhbnr). Liston and Alexander Bruce Gold Medals, Surgery and Pathology, UCH, 1927–29. MB, BS (London), Hons Medicine, 1930; MD 1931; FRCS 1932; MS 1937; Geoffrey Duveen Trav. Student, Univ. of London, 1934–36; Leslie Pearce Gould Trav. Schol., 1934, Perceval Alleyn Schol. (Surg. research), 1936, UCH; Hunterian Prof., RCS, 1938. RAFVR, 1940–45 (Wing-Comdr). FRSM, also Mem. Council; Past Pres., Section of Otology; Trustee, Hon. Fellow and Mem. Council, Med. Soc. London (Hon. Sec. 1961–63; Pres., 1970–71); Hon. Member: Assoc. of Otolaryngologists of India; Salonika Soc. of Otolaryngology; Athens Soc. of Otolaryngology; Corresp. Mem., Société Française d'Oto-Rhino-Laryngologie; Hon. Corresp. Mem., Argentine Soc. of Otolaryngology. Lectr on Diseases of Ear, Nose and Throat, Univ. of London, 1952–. *Publications:* Modern Trends in Diseases of the Ear, Nose and Throat (Ed. and part author), 1954, 2nd edn 1971; Operative Surgery (Rob and Smith), Vol. 8 on Diseases of the Ear, Nose and Throat (Ed. and part author), 1958; 2nd edn 1969; Clinical Surgery (Rob and Smith), Vol. 11, Diseases of the Ear, Nose and Throat (Ed. and part author), 1966; Sections in Diseases of the Ear, Nose and Throat (Ed. Scott-Brown), 1952, new edns 1965, 1971; Sections in Cancer, Vol. 4 (Ed. Raven), 1958; Section in Modern Trends in Surgical Materials (Ed. Gillis), 1958; papers in various medical and scientific jls. *Recreations:* golf, gardening; formerly bridge and squash rackets. *Address:* 48 Townshend Road, NW8. *T:* 01–722 2252. *Clubs:* Royal Automobile; Sunningdale Golf.

ELLIS, Norman David; Under Secretary, British Medical Association, since 1980 (Senior Industrial Relations Officer, 1978–82); *b* 23 Nov. 1943; *s* of late George Edward Ellis and late Annie Elsie Scarfe; *m* 1966, Valerie Ann Fenn, PhD; one *s*. *Educ:* Minchenden Sch.; Univ. of Leeds (BA); MA (Oxon), PhD. Research Officer, Dept of Employment, 1969–71; Leverhulme Fellowship in Industrial Relations, Nuffield Coll., Oxford, 1971–74; Gen. Sec., Assoc. of First Division Civil Servants, 1974–78. *Publications:* (with W. E. J. McCarthy) Management by Agreement, 1973; Employing Staff, 1984; various contribs to industrial relations literature; contribs to BMJ. *Recreations:* reading, railways, swimming. *Address:* 33 Foxes Dale, SE3 9BH. *T:* 01–852 6244.

ELLIS, Osian Gwynn, CBE 1971; harpist; Professor of Harp, Royal Academy of Music, London, since 1959; *b* Ffynnongroew, Flints, 8 Feb. 1928; *s* of Rev. T. G. Ellis, Methodist Minister; *m* 1951, Rene Ellis Jones, Pwllheli; two *s*. *Educ:* Denbigh Grammar Sch.; Royal Academy of Music. Has broadcast and televised extensively. Has given recitals/concertos all over the world; shared poetry and music recitals with Dame Peggy Ashcroft, Paul Robeson, Burton, C. Day-Lewis, etc. Mem., Melos Ensemble; solo harpist with LSO. Former Mem., Music and Welsh Adv. Cttees, British Council. Works written for him include Harp Concertos by Hoddinott, 1957 and by Mathias, 1970; Jersild, 1972; Gian Carlo Menotti, 1977; William Schuman, 1978; from 1960 worked with Benjamin Britten who wrote for him Harp Suite in C (Op. 83) and (for perf. with Sir Peter Pears) Canticle V, Birthday Hansel, and folk songs; accompanies Sir Peter Pears on recital tours, Europe and USA, 1974–; records concertos, recitals, folk songs, etc. Film, The Harp, won a Paris award; other awards include Grand Prix du Disque and French Radio Critics' Award. FRAM 1960. Hon. DMus Wales, 1970. *Address:* 90 Chandos Avenue, N20. *T:* 01–445 7896.

ELLIS, Raymond Joseph; MP (Lab) Derbyshire North East, since 1979; *b* 17 Dec. 1923; *s* of Harold and Ellen Ellis; *m* 1946, Cynthia (*née* Lax); four *c*. *Educ:* elementary school; Sheffield Univ.; Ruskin Coll., Oxford. Coal miner, 1938–79. National Union of Mineworkers: Branch Secretary, Highmoor, 1959–79; Pres., Derbyshire Area, 1972–79. Councillor, South Yorkshire CC, 1976–79. *Address:* Oakdene, 3 The Villas, Mansfield Road, Wales Bar, Kiveton, Sheffield S31 8RL.

ELLIS, Prof. Reginald John, PhD; FRS 1983; Professor of Biological Sciences, University of Warwick, since 1976; SERC Senior Research Fellow, since 1983; *b* 12 Feb. 1935; *s* of

Francis Gilbert Ellis and Evangeline Gratton Ellis; *m* 1963, Diana Margaret Warren; one *d*. *Educ:* Highbury County Sch.; King's Coll., London (BSc, PhD). ARC Fellow, Univ. of Oxford, 1961–64; Lectr in Botany and Biochemistry, Univ. of Aberdeen, 1964–70; Sen. Lectr, 1970–73, Reader, 1973–76, Dept of Biol Sciences, Univ. of Warwick. Mem. EMBO, 1986–. Tate & Lyle Award (for contribs to plant biochem.), 1980. *Publications:* 100 papers in biochem. jls. *Recreations:* photography, cycling, archery. *Address:* 44 Sunningdale Avenue, Kenilworth, Warwicks CV8 2BZ. *T:* Kenilworth 56382.

ELLIS, (Robert) Thomas; *b* 15 March 1924; *s* of Robert and Edith Ann Ellis; *m* 1949, Nona Harcourt Williams; three *s* one *d*. *Educ:* Universities of Wales and Nottingham. Works Chemist, ICI, 1944–47; Coal Miner, 1947–55; Mining Engineer, 1955–70; Manager, Bersham Colliery, N Wales, 1957–70. MP Wrexham, 1970–83 (Lab, 1970–81; SDP, 1981–83). Contested (SDP) Clywd South West, 1983. Mem., European Parlt, 1975–79. *Publication:* Mines and Men, 1971. *Recreations:* golf, reading, music. *Address:* Whitehurst House, Whitehurst, Chirk, Wrexham. *T:* Chirk 773462.

ELLIS, Ven. Robin Gareth; Archdeacon of Plymouth, since 1982; Vicar of Yelverton, since 1982; *b* 8 Dec. 1935; *s* of Walter and Morva Ellis; *m* 1964, Anne Ellis (*née* Landers); three *s*. *Educ:* Worksop Coll., Notts; Pembroke Coll., Oxford (BCL, MA). Curate of Swinton, 1960–63; Asst Chaplain, Worksop Coll., 1963–66; Vicar of Swaffham Prior and Reach, and Asst Director of Religious Education, Diocese of Ely, 1966–74; Vicar of S Augustine, Wisbech, 1974–82. *Recreations:* cricket, theatre, prison reform. *Address:* S Paul's Vicarage, Yelverton, Devon. *T:* Yelverton 852362.

ELLIS, Roger Henry, MA; FSA; FRHistS; Secretary, Royal Commission on Historical Manuscripts, 1957–72; *b* 9 June 1910; *e s* of late Francis Henry Ellis, Debdale Hall, Mansfield; *m* 1939, Audrey Honor, *o d* of late H. Arthur Baker, DL; two *d*. *Educ:* Sedbergh (scholar); King's College, Cambridge (scholar, Augustus Austen Leigh Student). 1st Cl. Class. Tripos, Pts I and II. Asst Keeper, Public Record Office, 1934; Principal Asst Keeper, 1956. Served War of 1939–45: Private, 1939; Major, 5th Fusiliers, 1944; Monuments, Fine Arts and Archives Officer in Italy and Germany, 1944–45. Lectr in Archive Admin, Sch. of Librarianship and Archives, University Coll. London, 1947–57. Mem. London Council, British Inst. in Florence, 1947–55; Hon. Editor, British Records Assoc., and (first) Editor of Archives, 1947–57, Chm. Council, 1967–73, Vice-Pres., 1971–. Vice-Pres., Business Archives Council, 1958–; Member: Adv. Council on Export of Works of Art, 1964–72; Jt Records Cttee of Royal Soc. and Historical MSS Commn, 1968–76; ICA Cttee on Sigillography, 1962–77; Pres., Soc. of Archivists, 1964–73. A Manager, 1973–76, a Vice-Pres., 1975–76, Royal Instn. Corresp. Mem., Indian Historical Records Commn. *Publications:* Catalogue of Seals in the Public Record Office: Personal Seals, vol. I, 1978, vol. II, 1981, Monastic Seals, vol. I, 1986; Ode on St Crispin's Day, 1979; Walking Backwards, 1986; opuscula and articles in British and foreign jls on care and use of archives and MSS. *Recreations:* poetry, travel, the arts, gardening (unskilled). *Address:* Cloth Hill, 6 The Mount, Hampstead, NW3. *Club:* Athenæum.

ELLIS, Roger Wykeham, CBE 1984; Graduate Recruitment Manager, Barclays Bank, since 1986; *b* 3 Oct. 1929; *s* of Cecil Ellis, solicitor, and Pamela Unwin; *m* 1964, Margaret Jean Stevenson; one *s* two *d*. *Educ:* St Peter's Sch., Seaford; Winchester Coll.; Trinity Coll., Oxford (Schol., MA). Royal Navy, 1947–49. Asst Master, Harrow Sch., 1952–67, and Housemaster of the Head Master's House, 1961–67; Headmaster of Rossall Sch., 1967–72; Master of Marlborough College, 1972–86. Member: Harrow Borough Educn Cttee, 1956–60; Wilts County Educn Cttee, 1975–86. Governor: Campion Sch., Athens, 1981–; Cheam Sch., 1975–; Hawtreys Sch., 1975–86; Sandroyd Sch., 1982–86; Fettes Coll., 1983–; St Edward's Sch., Oxford, 1985–. Chm., HMC, 1983. *Recreations:* golf, fishing. *Address:* 18 North Avenue, Ealing, W13 8AP.

ELLIS, Sir Ronald, Kt 1978; FEng, FIMechE; FCIT; Director, International Group, Allegheny International, 1981–86; *b* 12 Aug. 1925; *s* of William Ellis and Besse Brownbill; *m* 1st, 1956, Cherry Hazel Brown (*d* 1978); one *s* one *d*; 2nd, 1979, Myra Ann Royle. *Educ:* Preston Grammar Sch.; Manchester Univ. (BScTech Hons 1949). FIMechE 1949; FCIT 1975; FEng 1981. Gen. Man., BUT Ltd, 1954; Gen. Sales and Service Man., 1962, Gen. Man., 1966, Leyland Motors Ltd; Man. Dir, British Leyland Truck and Bus, 1968; Dir, British Leyland Motor Corp. Ltd, 1970. Head of Defence Sales, MoD, 1976–81. Chm., Bus Manufacturers Hldg Co., 1972–76. Dir of corp. develt, Wilkinson Sword Gp, 1981–82; Pres. and Man. Dir, Industrial Div., Allegheny International, 1982–85. Director: Yarrow & Co., 1981–; Redman Heenan Internat., 1981–86. Vice-Pres., SMMT, 1972–73; Dir, ROFs, 1976–81. Governor, UMIST, 1970–, Vice-Pres., 1983–, Hon. Fellow, 1981. Pres., Manchester Technology Assoc., 1982. Liveryman, Engineers' Co., 1984–; Freeman, City of London, 1984. FRSA; CBIM 1984. *Recreations:* fishing, sailing. *Address:* Allenview Cottage, Witchampton, near Wimborne, Dorset; 12 Seaton Close, Lynden Gate, Putney Heath, SW15 3TJ. *Clubs:* Turf, Royal Thames Yacht; Royal Naval Sailing Assoc., Poole Harbour Yacht.

ELLIS, Tom; *see* Ellis, R. T.

ELLIS, Vivian, CBE 1984; Lt-Comdr RNVR; composer, author; President, Performing Right Society, since 1983 (Deputy President, 1975–83); *s* of Harry Ellis and Maud Isaacson. *Educ:* Cheltenham Coll. (Musical Exhibition). Commenced his career as concert pianist after studying under Myra Hess; studied composition at the Royal Academy of Music; first song published when fifteen; his first work for the theatre was the composition of additional numbers for The Curate's Egg, 1922; contributed to The Little Revue and The Punch Bowl Revue, 1924; to Yoicks, Still Dancing, and Mercenary Mary, and composer of By the Way, 1925; to Just a Kiss, Kid Boots, Cochran's Revue, My Son John, Merely Molly and composer of Palladium Pleasures, 1926; to Blue Skies, The Girl Friend, and Clowns in Clover, 1927; to Charlot, 1928; and composer of Peg o' Mine, Will o' The Whispers, Vogues and Vanities, 1928; to A Yankee at the Court of King Arthur, The House that Jack Built, and (with Richard Myers) composer of Mister Cinders, 1929, new production, Fortune Theatre, 1983; part-composer of Cochran's 1930 Revue, and composer of Follow a Star and Little Tommy Tucker, 1930; part-composer of Stand Up and Sing, and Song of the Drum (with Herman Finck), and composer of Folly to be Wise, and Blue Roses, 1931; part-composer of Out of the Bottle, 1932; composer of Cochran's revue Streamline, 1934; Jill Darling, 1935; music and lyrics of Charlot Revue, The Town Talks, 1936; Hide and Seek, 1937; The Fleet's Lit Up, Running Riot, Under Your Hat, 1938; composer (to Sir A. P. Herbert's libretto) Cochran light operas: Big Ben, 1946; Bless the Bride, 1947 (new prodn, 1985); Tough at the Top, 1949; Water Gipsies, 1955; music and lyrics of And So To Bed, 1951; music for The Sleeping Prince, 1953; music and lyrics of Listen to the Wind, 1954; Half in Earnest (musical adaptation of The Importance of Being Earnest), 1958; composer of popular songs, inc. Spread a Little Happiness and This is My Lovely Day; many dance items; Coronation Scot; also music for the films Jack's the Boy, Water Gipsies, 1932; Falling for You, 1933; Public Nuisance No 1, 1935; Piccadilly Incident, 1946, etc. Ivor Novello Award for outstanding services to British music, 1973; Ivor Novello Award for Lifetime Achievement in British Music, 1983. Vivian Ellis Prize instituted by PRS in collab. with GSMD, to celebrate his 80th birthday. *Publications: novels:* Zelma; Faint Harmony; Day Out; Chicanery; *travel:* Ellis in Wonderland; *autobiography:* I'm on a See-Saw; *humour:* How to Make your Fortune on the Stock Exchange; How to Enjoy Your Operation; How to Bury Yourself in the Country; How to be a Man-about-Town; Good-Bye, Dollie; contrib: The Rise and Fall of the Matinée Idol; Top Hat and Tails: biography of Jack Buchanan; The Story and the Song; *for children:* Hilary's Tune; Hilary's Holidays; The Magic Baton; *song book:* Vivian Ellis: a composer's jubilee, 1982. *Recreations:* gardening, painting, operations. *Club:* Garrick.

ELLIS, Wilfred Desmond, OBE 1952; TD; Customer Service and Conversion Manager, Gas Council, 1968–73; Lay Member, Press Council, 1969–76; *b* 7 Nov. 1914; 2nd *s* of late Bertram V. C. W. Ellis and late Winifred Dora Ellis; *m* 1947, Effie Douglas, JP, *d* of late Dr A. Barr, Canonbie, Scotland; one *s* two *d*. *Educ:* Temple Grove; Canford. Commissioned as 2nd Lt, Middlesex Regt, 1937. Served War of 1939–45 at home and NW Europe with Middlesex Regt (despatches, 1944). Rejoined TA, 1947, retiring as Dep. Comdt 47 (L) Inf. Bde, 1962; County Comdt, Mddx Army Cadet Force, 1958–62; ADC to the Queen, 1966–69. Joined Gas Industry, 1932; Uxbridge, Maidenhead, Wycombe & Dist. Gas Co. until War of 1939–45; returned to Company until nationalisation; served with North Thames Gas Bd in various appts until joining Gas Council Research Station, Watson House, 1963, as Asst, and then Dep. Dir; transf. to Gas Council, 1966, as Manager, Conversion Executive. DL (Greater London), 1964–79. Fellow, Inst. of Marketing. *Recreations:* shooting, local affairs. *Address:* Lea Barn, Winter Hill, Cookham Dean, Berkshire SL6 9TW. *T:* Maidenhead 4230.

ELLIS, Dr (William) Herbert (Baxter), AFC 1954; Industrial Medical Consultant: Plessey Co., since 1981; Telephone Manufacturing Co., since 1980; Wellworthy, since 1979; Medical Adviser, Department of Health and Social Security; County Surgeon, Gloucestershire, St John Ambulance Brigade, since 1979; Underwriting Member of Lloyd's; *b* 2 July 1921; *er s* of William Baxter Ellis and Georgina Isabella Ellis (*née* Waller); *m* 1st, 1948, Margaret Mary Limb (marr. diss.); one *s* one *d*; 2nd, 1977, Mollie Marguerite Clarke. *Educ:* Oundle Sch.; Durham Univ. (MD, BS). Royal Navy, 1945–59: Surg. Comdr, Fleet Air Arm Pilot. Motor industry, 1960–71; research into human aspects of road traffic accidents, 1960–71; Dir-Gen., Dr Barnardo's, 1971–73; dir of various companies. Part-time Mem., Employment Medical Adv. Service, 1973–81. OStJ 1981. Gilbert Blane Medal, RCP, 1954. *Publications:* Physiological and Psychological Aspects of Deck Landings, 1954; various on the human factor in industrial management. *Recreations:* walking, observing humanity. *Address:* The Manor House, Compton Abdale, near Cheltenham, Glos GL54 4DR. *T:* Withington 247. *Clubs:* Army and Navy, Naval and Military.

ELLIS-REES, Hugh Francis, CB 1986; Regional Director, West Midlands Regional Office, Departments of the Environment and Transport, since 1981 (also East Midlands Regional Office, 1981–83); *b* 5 March 1929; *s* of late Sir Hugh Ellis-Rees, KCMG, CB and Lady (Eileen Frances Anne) Ellis-Rees; *m* 1956, Elisabeth de Mestre Gray; three *s* one *d*. *Educ:* Ampleforth Coll.; Balliol Coll., Oxford. Served Grenadier Guards, 1948–49. Joined War Office, 1954; transf. to DoE, 1970; Cabinet Office, 1972–74; Under Sec., DoE, 1974. Non-exec. Dir, Redland Aggregates Ltd, 1984–. *Recreation:* squash. *Address:* The Gabled House, Burford, Oxford OX8 4QY.

ELLISON, Prof. Arthur James, DSc(Eng); CEng, FIMechE, FIEE; Professor of Electrical and Electronic Engineering, and Head of Department, The City University, London, 1972–85, now Professor Emeritus; *b* 15 Jan. 1920; *s* of late Lawrence Joseph and Elsie Beatrice Ellison, Birmingham; *m* 1st, 1952, Marjorie Cresswell (*d* 1955); 2nd, 1963, Marian Elizabeth Gumbrell; one *s* one *d*. *Educ:* Solihull Sch., Warwicks; Birmingham Central Tech. Coll. (now Univ. of Aston); Northampton Polytechnic (now City Univ.), as ext. student of Univ. of London BSc(Eng) (1st Cl. Hons); DSc(Eng). Sen. MIEEE. Design Engr, Higgs Motors, Birmingham, 1938–43; Tech. Asst, RAE, 1943–46; Graduate apprentice with British Thomson-Houston Co., Rugby, 1946, Design Engr, 1947–58; Lectr, Queen Mary Coll. (Univ. of London), 1958–65, Sen. Lectr, 1965–72. Visiting Prof., MIT, USA, 1959; lecture tour of Latin Amer. for Brit. Council, 1968; Hon. Prof., Nat. Univ. of Engrg, Lima, Peru, 1968; numerous overseas lectures and conf. contribs. Ext. Examiner to many UK and overseas univs and polytechnics; Founder and Chm., biennial Internat. Conf. on Elec. Machines, 1974–84 (Pres. of Honour). Consultant to industrial cos and nationalised industry on elec. machines, noise and vibration problems; Director: Landspeed, 1975–; Landspeed University Consultants, 1975–82; Landspeed International, 1975–; Cotswold Research, 1983–. Pres., Soc. for Psychical Research, 1976–79, 1981–84; Chm., Theosophical Res. Centre, 1976–. Member: Council, IEE, 1981–84; Bd, Eta Kappa Nu Assoc., USA, 1984–86 (Hon. Mem.); Trustee, Res. Council for Complementary Med., 1983–. *Publications:* Electromechanical Energy Conversion, 1965, 2nd edn 1970; Generalized Electric Machines, 1967; Generalized Electric Machine Set Instruction Book (AEI), 1963, 2nd edn 1968; (jtly) Machinery Noise Measurement, 1985; ed, Proc. Queen Mary Coll. Conf., The Teaching of Electric Machinery Theory, 1961; jt ed, Proc. Queen Mary Coll. Conf., Design of Electric Machines by Computer, 1969; contrib. Psychism and the Unconscious Mind, 1968; contrib. Intelligence Came First, 1975; numerous papers in engrg and sci. jls on elec. machines, noise and vibration, future guided land transport (IEE premium, 1964); also papers in Jl Soc. for Psych. Res. *Recreations:* reading, meditation, psychical research, travel. *Address:* 10 Foxgrove Avenue, Beckenham, Kent BR3 2BA. *T:* 01–650 3801; Department of Electrical Engineering, The City University, EC1V 0HB. *T:* 01–253 4399. *Club:* Athenæum.

ELLISON, Rt. Rev. and Rt. Hon. Gerald Alexander, KCVO 1981; PC 1973; *b* 19 Aug. 1910; *s* of late Preb. John Henry Joshua Ellison, CVO, Chaplain in Ordinary to the King, Rector of St Michael's, Cornhill, and of Sara Dorothy Graham Ellison (*née* Crum); *m* 1947, Jane Elizabeth, *d* of late Brig. John Houghton Gibbon, DSO; one *s* two *d*. *Educ:* St George's, Windsor; Westminster Sch.; New Coll., Oxford (Hon. Fellow, 1974); Westcott House, Cambridge. Curate, Sherborne Abbey, 1935–37; Domestic Chaplain to the Bishop of Winchester, 1937–39; Chaplain RNVR, 1940–43 (despatches); Domestic Chaplain to Archbishop of York, 1943–46; Vicar, St Mark's Portsea, 1946–50; Hon. Chaplain to Archbishop of York, 1946–50; Canon of Portsmouth, 1950; Examining Chaplain to Bishop of Portsmouth, 1949–50; Bishop Suffragan of Willesden, 1950–55; Bishop of Chester, 1955–73; Bishop of London, 1973–81; Vicar General of Diocese of Bermuda, 1983–84. Dean of the Chapels Royal, 1973–81; Prelate, Order of the British Empire, 1973–81; Prelate, Imperial Soc. of Knights Bachelor, 1973–85; Episcopal Canon of Jerusalem, 1973–81. Select Preacher: Oxford Univ., 1940, 1961, 1972; Cambridge Univ., 1957. Chaplain, Master Mariners' Company, 1946–73; Chaplain, Glass Sellers' Company, 1951–73; Chaplain and Sub-Prelate, Order of St John, 1973–. Hon. Chaplain, RNR. Mem. Wolfenden Cttee on Sport, 1960; Chairman: Bd of Governors, Westfield Coll., Univ. of London, 1953–67; Council of King's Coll., London, 1973–80 (FKC 1968; Vice-Chm. newly constituted Council, 1980–); Governor, Sherborne Sch., 1982–85. Chm., Archbishop's Commn on Women and Holy Orders, 1963–66; Mem., Archbishop's Commn on Church and State, 1967; President: Actors' Church Union, 1973–81; Pedestrians Assoc. for Road Safety, 1964–75; Nat. Fedn of Housing Assocs, 1981–. Hon. Bencher Middle Temple, 1976. Freeman, Drapers' Co.; Hon. Liveryman: Merchant

Taylors' Co.; Glass Sellers' Co.; Painter Stainers' Co.; Mem., Master Mariners' Co. Chm., Oxford Soc., 1973–85. A Steward of Henley Regatta. *Publications:* The Churchman's Duty, 1957; The Anglican Communion, 1960. *Recreations:* oarsmanship, walking, music, watching television, tapestry, reading. *Address:* Billeys House, 16 Long Street, Cerne Abbas, Dorset. *T:* Cerne Abbas 247. *Clubs:* Army and Navy; Leander.

ELLISON, John Harold, VRD 1948; **His Honour Judge Ellison;** a Circuit Judge, since 1972; Chancellor of the Dioceses of Salisbury and Norwich, since 1955; *b* 20 March 1916, *s* of late Harold Thomas Ellison, MIMechE, and late Mrs Frances Amy Swithinbank, both of Woodspeen Grange, Newbury; *m* 1952, Margaret Dorothy Maud, *d* of late Maynard D. McFarlane, Sun City, Arizona; three *s* one *d*. *Educ:* Uppingham Sch.; King's Coll., Cambridge (MA). Res. Physicist, then Engr, Thos Firth & John Brown Ltd, Sheffield; Lieut, RE, TA (49th WR) Div., 1937–39; Officer in RNVR, 1939–51 (retd as Lt-Comdr): Gunnery Specialist, HMS Excellent, 1940; Sqdn Gunnery Officer, 8 Cruiser Sqdn, 1940–42; Naval Staff, Admty, 1942–44; Staff Officer (Ops) to Flag Officer, Western Mediterranean, 1944–45. Called to Bar, Lincoln's Inn, 1948; practised at Common Law Bar, 1948–71. Pres., SW London Br., Magistrates' Assoc. Governor, Forres Sch. Trust, Swanage. FRAS. *Publications:* (ed) titles Allotments and Smallholdings, and Courts, in Halsbury's Law of England, 3rd edn, and Allotments and Smallholdings, 4th edn. *Recreations:* organs and music, sailing, ski-ing, shooting. *Address:* Goose Green House, Egham, Surrey TW20 8PE. *Club:* Bar Yacht; Ski Club of GB, Kandahar Ski.

ELLISON, Sir Ralph Henry C.; *see* Carr-Ellison, Sir R. H.

ELLMAN, Louise Joyce; Leader, Lancashire County Council, since 1981 (Chairman, 1981–85; Leader, Labour Group, since 1977); *b* 14 Nov. 1945; *d* of late Harold and Annie Rosenberg; *m* 1967, Geoffrey David Ellman; one *s* one *d*. *Educ:* Manchester High Sch. for Girls; Hull Univ. (BA Hons); York Univ. (MPhil). Lectr, Salford Coll. of Technology, 1970–73; Counsellor, Open Univ., 1973–76. Member: Lancs CC, 1970–; W Lancs DC, 1974–; Local Govt Adv. Cttee, Labour Party's NEC, 1977–; Regl Exec., NW Labour Party, 1985–. Contested (Lab) Darwen, 1979. Vice-Chm., Lancashire Enterprises Ltd, 1981–; Founder Mem., NW Co-op. Develt Agency, 1979–. Youngest mem., Lancs CC, 1970; youngest mem. and first woman to be Chm., 1981. *Recreations:* reading, travel. *Address:* 153 Birleywood, Digmoor, Skelmersdale, Lancs. *T:* Skelmersdale 23669. *Club:* Upholland Labour (Skelmersdale).

ELLMAN-BROWN, Hon. Geoffrey, CMG 1959; OBE 1945; FCA 1950 (ACA 1934); *b* 20 Dec. 1910; *s* of John and Violet Ellman-Brown; *m* 1936, Hilda Rosamond Fairbrother; two *s* one *d*. *Educ:* Plumtree Sch., S Rhodesia. Articled to firm of Chartered Accountants in London, 1929–34; final Chartered Accountant exam. and admitted as Mem. Inst. of Chartered Accountants of England and Wales, 1934. In Rhodesia Air Force (rising to rank of Group Capt.), 1939–46. Resumed practice as Chartered Accountant, 1946–53. Entered S Rhodesia Parliament holding ministerial office (Portfolios of Roads, Irrigation, Local Government and Housing), 1953–58; re-entered Parliament, 1962, Minister of Finance; re-elected, 1962–65, in Opposition Party. Pres. Rhodesia Cricket Union, 1950–52; Mem. S African Cricket Board of Control, 1951–52. Chairman: African Distillers Ltd; Rothmans of Pall Mall (Zimbabwe) Ltd; The Zimbabwe Sugar Assoc.; Sugar Sales (Private) Ltd; Industrial Promotion Corp. Central Africa Ltd; C. T. Bowring and Associates (Pvt) Ltd; Bowmakers (CA) (Pvt) Ltd; Director: RAL Merchant Bank Ltd; Hippo Valley Estates Ltd; Freight Services Ltd. *Recreations:* cricket, golf, shooting, fishing. *Address:* PO Box 8426, Harare, Zimbabwe. *T:* 706381. *Clubs:* Harare, Royal Harare Golf (Harare, Zimbabwe); Ruwa Country.

ELLMANN, Richard, MA Oxon; PhD Yale; FBA 1979; Woodruff Professor, Emory University, since 1982; Extraordinary Fellow, Wolfson College, Oxford, since 1984; *b* Highland Park, Michigan, 15 March 1918; *s* of James Isaac Ellmann and Jeanette (*née* Barsook); *m* 1949, Mary Donahue; one *s* two *d*. *Educ:* Highland Park High Sch.; Yale Univ. (MA, PhD); Trinity Coll., Dublin (LittB). Served War of 1939–45, Office of Strategic Services, USNR, 1943–46. Instructor at Harvard, 1942–43, 1947–48; Briggs-Copeland Asst Prof. of Eng. Composition, Harvard, 1948–51; Prof. of English, Northwestern Univ., 1951, Franklin Bliss Snyder Prof., 1963–68; Prof. of English, Yale, 1968–70; Goldsmiths' Prof. of English Lit. and Fellow, New Coll., Oxford Univ., 1970–84. Rockefeller Fellow, 1946–47; Guggenheim Fellow, 1950, 1957, 1970; Kenyon Review Fellow Criticism, 1955–56; Fellow, Sch. of Letters, Indiana Univ., 1956, 1960; Senior Fellow, 1966–72; Frederick Ives Carpenter Vis. Prof., Univ. of Chicago, 1959, 1968, 1975, 1976, 1977; Grantee, Nat. Endowment for the Humanities, 1977–78. Mem., US-UK Educnl Commn, 1970–. Mem. Editorial Committee: Publications of the Modern Language Assoc., 1968–73; American Scholar, 1968–74. FRSL; Fellow, Amer. Acad. and Inst.; National Book Award, 1960. Hon. DLitt: NUI, 1976; Boston Coll., 1979; Emory Univ., 1979; Northwestern, 1980; McGill, 1986; Hon. PhD Gothenburg, 1978; Hon. DHL Rochester, 1981. *Publications:* Yeats: The Man and the Masks, 1948; The Identity of Yeats, 1954; James Joyce: a biography, 1959 (Nat. Book Award for non-fiction, 1960), revd edn 1982 (Duff Cooper Meml Prize, James Tait Black Prize, 1983); Eminent Domain, 1967; Ulysses on the Liffey, 1972; Golden Codgers, 1973; The Consciousness of Joyce, 1977; James Joyce's Hundredth Birthday, 1982; Oscar Wilde at Oxford, 1984; W. B. Yeats's Second Puberty, 1985; Samuel Beckett: Nayman of Noland, 1986; Four Dubliners: Wilde, Yeats, Joyce and Beckett, 1986; Edited: Selected Writings of Henri Michaux (trans.), 1951; My Brother's Keeper, by Stanislaus Joyce, 1958; (with others) Masters of British Literature, 1958; Arthur Symons: The Symbolist Movement in Literature, 1958; (with Ellsworth Mason) The Critical Writings of James Joyce, 1959; Edwardians and late Victorians, 1959; (with Charles Feidelson, Jr) The Modern Tradition, 1965; Letters of James Joyce (Vols II and III), 1966; James Joyce: Giacomo Joyce, 1968; The Artist as Critic: Oscar Wilde, 1970; Oscar Wilde: twentieth century views, 1970; (with Robert O'Clair) Norton Anthology of Modern Poetry, 1973; Selected Letters of James Joyce, 1975; New Oxford Book of American Verse, 1976; (with Robert O'Clair) Modern Poems, 1976; Oscar Wilde, The Picture of Dorian Gray and Other Writings, 1982. *Address:* 39 St Giles', Oxford OX1 3LW. *Clubs:* Athenæum; Signet (Harvard); Elizabethan (Yale).

ELLSWORTH, Robert; President, Robert Ellsworth & Co. Inc., since 1977; Deputy Secretary of Defense, 1976–77; *b* 11 June 1926; *s* of Willoughby Fred Ellsworth and Lucile Rarig Ellsworth; *m* 1956, Vivian Esther Sies; one *s* one *d*. *Educ:* Univs of Kansas (BSME) and Michigan (JD). Active service, US Navy, 1944–46, 1950–53 (Lt-Comdr). Mem. United States Congress, 1961–67; Asst to President of US, 1969; Ambassador and Permanent Representative of US on N Atlantic Council, 1969–71; Asst Sec. of Defense (Internat. Security Affairs), 1974–75. Mem. Council, IISS, 1973– (Vice-Chm. 1981–). Licensed Lay Reader, Episcopal Dio. of Washington. Hon. LLD: Ottawa, 1969; Boston, 1970. *Recreations:* tennis, ski-ing, swimming. *Address:* 24020 Old Hundred Road, Dickerson, Md 20842, USA. *Clubs:* Brook (New York); Cosmos, Army and Navy (Washington).

ELLWOOD, Air Marshal Sir Aubrey (Beauclerk), KCB 1949 (CB 1944); DSC; DL; *b* 3 July 1897; *s* of late Rev. C. E. Ellwood, Rector of Cottesmore, Rutland, 1888–1926; *m* 1920, Lesley Mary Joan Matthews (*d* 1982); one *s* one *d* (and one *s* decd). *Educ:* Cheam Sch.; Marlborough Coll. Joined Royal Naval Air Service, 1916; permanent commission RAF 1919. Served India 1919–23 and 1931–36 in RAF; RAF Staff Coll., Air Min., Army Co-operation Comd variously, 1938–42; AOC No. 18 Group RAF, 1943–44; Temp. Air Vice-Marshal, 1943; SASO HQ Coastal Comd RAF, 1944–45; Actg Air Marshal, 1947; a Dir-Gen. of Personnel, Air Ministry, 1945–47. Air Marshal, 1949; AOC-in-C, Bomber Command, 1947–50; AOC in C, Transport Command, 1950–52; retired, 1952. Governor and Commandant, The Church Lads' Brigade, 1954–70. DL Somerset, 1960. *Recreations:* riding, fishing, music. *Address:* The Old House, North Perrott, Crewkerne, Somerset.

ELMES, Dr Peter Cardwell; Director, Medical Research Council Pneumoconiosis Unit, Llandough Hospital, Penarth, 1976–81, retired from MRC 1982; Consultant in Occupational Lung Diseases, since 1976; *b* 12 Oct. 1921; *s* of Florence Romaine Elmes and Lilian Bryham (*née* Cardwell); *m* 1957, Margaret Elizabeth (*née* Staley); two *s* one *d*. *Educ:* Rugby; Oxford Univ. (BM, BCh 1945); Western Reserve Univ., Cleveland, Ohio (MD 1943). MRCP 1951. Mil. Service, RAMC, 1946–48. Trng posts, Taunton and Oxford, 1948–50; Registrar, then Sen. Registrar in Medicine, Hammersmith Hosp., 1950–58; Dept of Therapeutics, Queen's Univ., Belfast: Sen. Lectr, 1959–63; Reader, 1963–67; Prof. of Therapeutic Sciences, 1967–71; Whitla Prof. of Therapeutics and Pharmacology, 1971–76. Member: Medicines Commn, 1976–79; Industrial Injuries Adv. Council, 1982–; Indep. Scientific Cttee on Smoking and Health, 1982–. *Publications:* contrib. med. jls on chronic chest disease, treatment and control of infection, occupational lung disease asbestosis, and mesothelioma. *Recreation:* working on house and garden. *Address:* Dawros House, St Andrews Road, Dinas Powys, South Glamorgan CF6 4HB. *T:* Dinas Powys 512102.

ELMSLIE, Maj.-Gen. Alexander Frederic Joseph, CB 1959; CBE 1955; psc; CEng; FIMechE; FCIT; *b* 31 Oct. 1905; *er s* of Captain A. W. Elmslie, RAEC and Florence Edith Elmslie (*née* Kirk); *m* 1931, Winifred Allan Wright; one *d* one *s*. *Educ:* Farnham Grammar Sch.; RMC Sandhurst; Staff Coll., Camberley. Commissioned in Royal Army Service Corps, 29 Jan. 1925, and subsequently served in Shanghai, Ceylon, E Africa and Singapore; Lieutenant 1927; Captain 1935; served War of 1939–45 (despatches) in Madagascar, India and Europe; Major, 1942; Lt-Col 1948; Temp. Brig.1944; Brig. 1953; Maj.-Gen. 1958. Dep. Dir of Supplies and Transport, War Office, 1953–55; Dir of Supplies and Transport, GHQ Far East Land Forces, 1956–57; Inspector, RASC, War Office, 1957–60, retired. Chairman Traffic Commissioners: NW Traffic Area, 1962–64; SE Traffic Area, 1965–75. Hon. Col 43 (Wessex) Inf. Div. Coln, RASC, TA, 1960–64; Col Comdt, RASC, 1964–65; Col Comdt, Royal Corps of Transport, 1965–69. Fellow, Royal Commonwealth Soc. *Address:* 9 Stanmer House, Furness Road, Eastbourne, E Sussex.

ELPHIN, Bishop of, (RC), since 1971; **Most Rev. Dominic Joseph Conway;** *b* 1 Jan. 1918; *s* of Dominic Conway and Mary Hoare. *Educ:* Coll. of the Immaculate Conception, Sligo; Pontifical Irish Coll., Pontifical Lateran Univ., Pontifical Angelicum Univ., Gregorian Univ. (all in Rome); National Univ. of Ireland. BPh, STL, DEcclHist, Higher Diploma Educn. Missionary, Calabar Dio., Nigeria, 1943–48; Professor: All Hallows Coll., Dublin, 1948–49; Summerhill Coll., Sligo, 1949–51; Spiritual Dir, 1951–65, Rector, 1965–68, Irish Coll., Rome; Sec.-Gen., Superior Council of the Propagation of the Faith, Rome, 1968–70; Auxiliary Bishop of Elphin, 1970–71. *Address:* St Mary's, Sligo, Ireland. *T:* 2670.

ELPHINSTONE, family name of **Lord Elphinstone.**

ELPHINSTONE, 18th Lord *cr* 1509; **James Alexander Elphinstone;** Baron (UK) 1885; *b* 22 April 1953; *s* of Rev. Hon. Andrew Charles Victor Elphinstone (*d* 1975) (2nd *s* of 16th Lord) and of Hon. Mrs Andrew Elphinstone (*see* Jean Mary Woodroffe); *S* uncle, 1975; *m* 1978, Willa, 4th *d* of Major David Chetwode, Upper Slaughter, Cheltenham; three *s*. *Educ:* Eton Coll.; Royal Agricultural Coll., Cirencester. ARICS 1979. *Heir:* *s* Master of Elphinstone, *qv*. *Address:* Drumkilbo, Meigle, Blairgowrie, Perthshire. *T:* Meigle 216. *Clubs:* Turf, White's.

ELPHINSTONE, Master of; Hon. Alexander Mountstuart Elphinstone; *b* 15 April 1980; *s* and *heir* of 18th Lord Elphinstone, *qv*.

ELPHINSTONE, Sir Douglas; *see* Elphinstone, Sir M. D. W.

ELPHINSTONE of Glack, Sir John, 11th Bt *cr* 1701, of Logie Elphinstone and Nova Scotia; consultant Land Agent; *b* 12 Aug. 1924; *s* of Thomas George Elphinston (*d* 1967), and of Gladys Mary Elphinston, *d* of late Ernest Charles Lambert Congdon; *S* uncle, 1970; *m* 1953, Margaret Doreen, *d* of Edric Tasker; four *s*. *Educ:* Eagle House, Sandhurst, Berks; Repton; Emmanuel College, Cambridge (BA). Lieut, Royal Marines, 1942–48. Chartered Surveyor; Land Agent with ICI plc, 1956–83. Past Pres., Cheshire Agricultural Valuers' Assoc.; Past Chm., Land Agency and Agric. Div., Lancs, Cheshire and IoM Branch, RICS; Mem., Lancs River Authority, 1970–74. *Recreations:* shooting, ornithology, cricket. *Heir:* *s* Alexander Elphinston [*b* 6 June 1955; *m* 1986, Ruth, *er d* of Rev. Robert Dunnett]. *Address:* Pilgrims, Churchfields, Sandiway, Northwich, Cheshire. *T:* Sandiway 883327.

ELPHINSTONE, Sir (Maurice) Douglas (Warburton), 5th Bt *cr* 1816; TD 1946; retired, 1973; *b* 13 April 1909; *s* of Rev. Canon Maurice Curteis Elphinstone (4th *s* of 3rd Bt) (*d* 1969), and Christiana Georgiana (*née* Almond); *S* cousin, 1975; *m* 1943, Helen Barbara, *d* of late George Ramsay Main; one *s* one *d*. *Educ:* Loretto School, Musselburgh; Jesus Coll., Cambridge (MA). FFA; FRSE. Actuary engaged in Life Assurance companies until 1956 (with the exception of the war); Member of Stock Exchange, London, 1957–74. War service with London Scottish and Sierra Leone Regt, RWAFF, mainly in W Africa and India. *Publications:* technical papers mainly in Trans Faculty of Actuaries and Jl Inst. of Actuaries. *Recreation:* gardening. *Heir:* *s* John Howard Main Elphinstone, *b* 25 Feb. 1949. *Address:* West Dene, 10 The Green, Houghton, Carlisle CA3 0LW. *T:* Carlisle 23297.

ELRINGTON, Christopher Robin, FSA, FRHistS; Editor, Victoria History of the Counties of England, since 1977; *b* 20 Jan. 1930; *s* of Brig. Maxwell Elrington, DSO, OBE, and Beryl Joan (*née* Ommanney); *m* 1951, Jean Margaret (*née* Buchanan), RIBA; one *s* one *d*. *Educ:* Wellington Coll., Berks; University Coll., Oxford (MA); Bedford Coll., London (MA). FSA 1964; FRHistS 1969. Asst to Editor, Victoria County History, 1954; Editor for Glos, 1960; Dep. Editor, 1968. British Acad. Overseas Vis. Fellow, Folger Shakespeare Library, Washington DC, 1976. Mem., Adv. Bd for Redundant Churches, 1982–; Pres., Bristol and Glos Archaeol Soc., 1984–85. Hon. Gen. Editor, 1962–72, Pres., 1983–, Wilts Record Soc. *Publications:* Divers Letters of Roger de Martival, Bishop of Salisbury, 2 vols, 1963, 1972; Wiltshire Feet of Fines, Edward III, 1974; articles in Victoria County History and in learned jls. *Address:* 34 Lloyd Baker Street, WC1X 9AB. *T:* 01-837 4971.

EL SAWI, Amir; Ambassador of the Democratic Republic of the Sudan to the Court of St James's, 1976–82; *b* 1921; *m* 1946, El Sura Mohamed Bella; three *s* six *d*. *Educ:* University

Coll., Khartoum; Univ. of Bristol. Min. of Interior, 1944–49; Admin. Officer, Merowi Dist., Northern Province, 1950–51; Asst Dist Comr, Kosti Dist, Blue Nile Prov., 1951–53; Asst Sudan Agent, Cairo, 1953–55; Dist Comr, Gadaraf Dist, Kassala Prov., 1955–56; Asst Permanent Sec., Min. of Foreign Affairs, 1956–58, Min. of Interior, 1958–59; Dep. Governor, Northern Prov., 1959–60; Dep. Perm. Sec., Min. of Interior, 1960–64, Perm. Sec., 1964–70; Perm. Sec., Min. of Civil Service and Admin. Reform, 1971–73; Dep. Minister and Doyen of Sudan Civil Service, 1973–76. *Recreations:* swimming, tennis. *Address:* c/o Ministry of Foreign Affairs, Khartoum, Sudan.

ELSDEN, Sidney Reuben, BA, PhD (Cambridge); Professor of Biology, University of East Anglia, 1965–85; *b* 13 April 1915; *er s* of late Reuben Charles Elsden, Cambridge; *m* 1st, 1942, Frances Scott Wilson (*d* 1943); 2nd, 1948, Erica Barbara Scott, *er d* of late Grahame Scott Gardiner, Wisbech, Cambs; twin *s. Educ:* Cambridge and County High Sch. for Boys; Fitzwilliam House, Cambridge (Exhibn, Goldsmiths' Co.). Lecturer, Biochemistry, University of Edinburgh, 1937–42; Mem. Scientific Staff of ARC Unit for Animal Physiology, 1943–48; Sen. Lectr in Microbiology, 1948–59, West Riding Prof. of Microbiology, 1959–65, Sheffield Univ.; Hon. Dir, ARC Unit for Microbiology, Univ. of Sheffield, 1952–65; Dir, ARC Food Research Inst., 1965–77. Visiting Prof. of Microbiology, Univ. of Illinois, Urbana, Ill, USA, 1956. Pres., Soc. for General Microbiology, 1969–72, Hon. Mem. 1977. Hon. DSc Sheffield, 1985. *Publications:* contribs to scientific jls on metabolism of micro-organisms. *Recreations:* gardening, angling. *Address:* 26a The Street, Costessey, Norwich NR8 5DB.

ELSE, John, MBE 1946; TD 1946; Regional Chairman of Industrial Tribunals, Eastern Region, Bury St Edmunds, 1980–84; *b* 9 Aug. 1911; *s* of late Mr and Mrs A. G. Else; *m* 1937, Eileen Dobson; one *d. Educ:* Cowley Sch., St Helens; Liverpool Univ. (LLB 1930). Admitted as solicitor, 1932. Commnd TA, 1932; served War: UK and BEF, 1939–41 (despatches, 1940); Iraq, 1942; India, 1942–45 (ADS GHQ, 1944–45). Practised in St Helens, London and Birmingham, 1932–39; Partner, Beale & Co., London and Birmingham, 1946–61; Mem., Mental Health Review Tribunal, 1960–61; Chm., Traffic Comrs and Licensing Authority for Goods Vehicles, W Midlands Traffic Area, 1961–72; Indust. Tribunals Chm., Birmingham, 1972–76, Cambridge, 1976–80. *Recreations:* photography, gardening. *Address:* The Cottage, Long Lane, Fowlmere, Royston, Herts SG8 7TA. *T:* Fowlmere 367.

ELSMORE, Sir Lloyd, Kt 1982; OBE 1977; JP; Mayor of Manukau City, since 1968; *b* 16 Jan. 1913; *s* of George and Minnie Elsmore; *m* 1935, Marie Kirk; two *s* two *d. Educ:* Greymouth High Sch. Commenced grocery business on own account, 1933; President: Grocers' Assoc., 1949, 1950, 1952, Life Member, 1954; NZ Grocers' Federation, 1955, Life Member, 1959. Mem., Auckland Harbour Bd, 1971–83. Local Body involvement, 1953–; Mayor of Ellerslie Borough Council, 1956–62. *Recreations:* boating, fishing, gardening. *Address:* 18 Sanctuary Point, Pakuranga, New Zealand. *T:* 567–025. *Club:* Rotary (Pakuranga).

ELSOM, Cecil Harry, CBE 1976; Consultant (formerly Senior Partner), Elsom Pack & Roberts, Architects; *b* 17 Jan. 1912; *s* of Julius Israelson and Leah Lazarus; name changed by deed poll to Elsom, 1930; *m* 1940, Gwyneth Mary Buxton Hopkin; two *s. Educ:* Upton Cross Elem. Sch.; West Ham Polytechnic; Northern Polytechnic Architectural School. FRIBA. Started practice by winning competition for town hall, Welwyn Garden City, 1933; partner in Lyons Israel & Elsom, 1936; won two more competitions, Town Hall, Consett, Co. Durham and Health Clinic in Bilston, Staffs. Served with Ordnance Corps, RE, 1940–46, ending war as Captain. Began new practice, as Sen. Partner, Elsom Pack & Roberts, 1947. Works include housing, schools and old people's homes for GLC, Lambeth BC and Westminster CC; office buildings and flats for Church Commissioners, Crown Estate Commissioners, BSC, LWT (Eternit Prize for offices, Victoria St, 1977); stores in Wolverhampton, Guildford and London for Army & Navy Stores; town centres in Slough, Chesterfield, Derby and Tamworth (three Civic Trust Awards, four Commendations). Adviser to DoE on Lyceum Club, Liverpool; Assessor for Civic Trust Awards, 1980. Pres., Nightingale House Old People's Home, 1973–. Liveryman, Worshipful Co. of Painter-Stainers, 1965, of Clockmakers, 1979. FSA 1979; FFOB 1969. *Recreations:* horology, model yacht racing. *Address:* 21 Douglas Street, SW1P 4PE. *T:* 01–834 4411. *Club:* Royal Automobile.

ELSTEIN, David Keith; Director of Programmes, Thames Television PLC, since 1986; *b* 14 Nov. 1944; *s* of late Albert Elstein and Millie Cohen; *m* 1978, Jenny Conway; one *s. Educ:* Haberdashers' Aske's; Gonville and Caius Coll., Cambridge (BA, MA). BBC: The Money Programme, Panorama, Cause for Concern, People in Conflict, 1964–68; Thames Television: This Week, The Day Before Yesterday, The World At War, 1968–72; London Weekend Television: Weekend World, 1972; Thames Television, 1972–82: This Week (ed., 1974–78); Exec. Producer, Documentaries; founded Brook Prodns, 1982; Exec. Producer, A Week in Politics, 1982–86; Exec. Producer, Concealed Enemies, 1983; Man. Dir, Primetime Television, 1983–86. *Recreations:* theatre, cinema, bridge, politics, reading. *Address:* Thames Television, 306 Euston Road, NW1 3BB. *T:* 01–387 9494.

ELSTOB, Peter (Frederick Egerton); Vice-President: International PEN, since 1981 (Secretary-General, 1974–81); English PEN, since 1978; Managing Director: Archive Press Ltd, since 1964 (co-founder 1963); Yeast-Pac Co. Ltd, since 1970 (co-founder and Director, 1938–70); writer and entrepreneur; *b* London, 22 Dec. 1915; *e s* of Frederick Charles Elstob, chartered accountant, RFC, and Lillian Page, London; *m* 1st, 1937, Medora Leigh-Smith (marr. diss. 1953); three *s* one *d* (and one *d* decd); 2nd, 1953, Barbara Zacheisz; one *s* one *d. Educ:* private schs, London, Paris, Calcutta; state schs, NY and NJ; Univ. of Michigan, 1934–35. Reporter, salesman, tourist guide, 1931–36; volunteer, Spanish Civil War, 1936 (imprisoned and expelled); RTR, 1940–46 (despatches); with A. B. Eiloart: founded Yeast-pac Co. Ltd; bought Arts Theatre Club, London, 1941; founded Peter Arnold Studios (artists' and writers' colony, Mexico), 1951–52, and Archives Designs Ltd, 1954–62; Director: MEEC Prodns (Theatre), 1946–54; Peter Arnold Properties, 1947–61; City & Suffolk Property Ltd, 1962–70; ABC Expedns, 1957–61; Manager, Small World Trans-Atlantic Balloon Crossing, 1958–59. Chm., Dorking Divl Lab. Party, 1949–50. Bulgarian Commemorative Medal, 1982. *Publications:* (autobiog.) Spanish Prisoner, 1939; (with A. B. Eiloart) The Flight of the Small World, 1959; novels: Warriors for the Working Day, 1960; The Armed Rehearsal, 1964; Scoundrel, 1986; military history: Bastogne the Road Block, 1968; The Battle of the Reichswald, 1970; Hitler's Last Offensive, 1971; Condor Legion, 1973; (ed) The Survival of Literature, 1979; (ed series) PEN International Books; PEN Broadsheet, 1977–82. *Recreations:* playing the Stock Exchange unsuccessfully, travelling. *Address:* Burley Lawn House, Burley Lawn, Ringwood, Hants BH24 4AR. *T:* Burley 3406; 212 Stapleton Hall Road, N4 4QR. *Clubs:* Savage, Garrick, PEN, Society of Authors; Authors Guild (New York).

ELSTON, Christopher David; Adviser (Asia and Australasia), Bank of England, since 1983; *b* 1 Aug. 1938; *s* of Herbert Cecil Elston and Ada Louisa (*née* Paige); *m* 1964, Jennifer Isabel Rampling; one *s* two *d. Educ:* University Coll. Sch., Hampstead; King's Coll., Cambridge (BA Classics, 1960, MA 1980); Yale Univ. (MA Econs, 1967). Bank of

England, 1960–; seconded to Bank for Internat. Settlements, Basle, Switzerland, 1969–71; Private Sec. to Governor of Bank of England, 1974–76; Asst to Chief Cashier, 1976–79; seconded to HM Diplomatic Service, as Counsellor (Financial), British Embassy, Tokyo, 1979–83. *Recreations:* serious music, photography, walking, cricket, squash. *Address:* c/o Bank of England, Threadneedle Street, EC2R 8AH. *T:* 01–601 4444.

ELSTUB, Sir St John (de Holt), Kt 1970; CBE 1954; BSc, FEng, FIMechE, FInstP; Chairman, IMI plc, 1972–74 (Managing Director, 1962–74); *b* 16 June 1915; *s* of Ernest Elstub and Mary Gertrude (*née* Whitaker); *m* 1939, Patricia Arnold; two *d. Educ:* Rugby Sch.; Manchester Univ. Joined ICI, Billingham, 1936. Served War of 1939–45 as RAF Bomber Pilot; Supt, Rocket Propulsion Dept, Ministry of Supply, 1945. Joined ICI Metals Div., 1947, Prod. Dir, 1950, Man. Dir, 1957, Chm., 1961; Director: Royal Insurance Co., 1970–76; The London & Lancashire Insurance Co., 1970–76; The Liverpool, London & Globe Insurance Co., 1970–76; British Engine Insurance Ltd, 1970–84; Rolls Royce Ltd, 1971–85; Averys Ltd, 1974–79; Hill Samuel Group Ltd, 1974–82; Regional Dir, W Midlands and Wales, Nat. Westminster Bank Ltd, 1974–79; Dir, TI Gp PLC, 1974–85, Dep. Chm., 1979–85. Past Pres., British Non-Ferrous Metals Federation. Chm., Jt Government/Industry Cttee on Aircraft Industry, 1967–69; Member: Plowden Cttee on Aircraft Industry, 1964–65; Engrg Industry Trng Bd, 1964–72; Midlands Electricity Bd, 1966–75; Review Bd for Govt contracts, 1969–75; Pres., IMechE, 1974–75. A Guardian, Birmingham Assay Office; Governor, Administrative Staff Coll., Henley, 1962–74; Mem. Council, Univ. of Aston in Birmingham, 1966–72 (Vice-Chm. 1968–72); Life Governor, Univ. of Birmingham. Hon. DSc Univ. of Aston in Birmingham, 1971. Verulam Medal, Metals Soc., 1975. *Recreations:* landscape gardening, travel, DIY, old motor cars. *Address:* Haynes Green Farm, Broadwas-on-Teme, Worcester WR6 5NX. *T:* Knightwick 21116. *Club:* Army and Navy.

ELTIS, Walter Alfred; Economic Director, National Economic Development Office, since 1986; Fellow and Tutor in Economics, Exeter College, Oxford, since 1963; *b* 23 May 1933; *s* of Rev. Martin Eltis and Mary (*née* Schnitzer); *m* 1959, Shelagh Mary, *d* of Rev. Preb. Douglas Owen; one *s* two *d. Educ:* Wycliffe Coll.; Emmanuel Coll., Cambridge (BA Econs 1956; MA 1960). Nuffield Coll., Oxford. Nat. Service, Navigator, RAF, 1951–53. Res. Fellow, Exeter Coll., Oxford, 1958–60; Lectr in Econs, Exeter and Keble Colls, Oxford, 1960–63. Vis. Reader in Econs, Univ. of WA, 1970; Visiting Professor: Univ. of Toronto, 1976–77; European Univ., Florence, 1979. Econ. Consultant, NEDO, 1963–66. Gov., Wycliffe Coll., 1972–. Gen. Ed., Oxford Economic Papers, 1975–81. *Publications:* Economic Growth: analysis and policy, 1966; Growth and Distribution, 1973; (with R. Bacon) The Age of US and UK Machinery, 1974; (with R. Bacon) Britain's Economic Problem: too few producers, 1976, 2nd edn 1978; The Classical theory of Economic Growth, 1984; contribs to econ. jls. *Recreations:* chess, music. *Address:* Danesway, Jarn Way, Boars Hill, Oxford OX1 5JF. *T:* Oxford 735440. *Club:* Reform.

ELTON, family name of **Baron Elton.**

ELTON, 2nd Baron *cr* 1934, of Headington; **Rodney Elton,** TD 1970; *b* 2 March 1930; *s* of 1st Baron Elton and of Dedi (*d* 1977), *d* of Gustav Hartmann, Oslo; *S* father, 1973; *m* 1958, Anne Frances (divorced, 1979), *e d* of late Brig. R. A. G. Tilney, CBE, DSO, TD; one *s* three *d*; *m* 1979, S. Richenda Gurney, *y d* of late Sir Hugh Gurney, KCMG, MVO, and Lady Gurney. *Educ:* Eton; New Coll., Oxford (MA). Farming, 1954–74. Assistant Master, Loughborough Grammar Sch., 1962–67; Assistant Master, Fairham Comprehensive School for Boys, Nottingham, 1967–69; Lectr, Bishop Lonsdale College of Education, 1969–72. Cons. Whip, House of Lords, Feb. 1974–76, an Opposition spokesman, 1976–79; Parly Under Sec. of State, NI Office, 1979–81, DHSS, 1981–82, Home Office, 1982–84; Minister of State: Home Office, 1984–85; DoE, 1985–86. Formerly Director: Andry Montgomery Ltd; Overseas Exhibition Services Ltd; Building Trades Exhibition Ltd. Dep. Sec., Cttee on Internat. Affairs, Synod of C of E, 1976–78. Mem. Boyd Commn to evaluate elections in Rhodesia, 1979. Late Captain, Queen's Own Warwickshire and Worcs Yeo.; late Major, Leics and Derbys (PAO) Yeo. Lord of the Manor of Adderbury, Oxon. *Heir: s* Hon. Edward Paget Elton, *b* 28 May 1966. *Address:* House of Lords, SW1. *Clubs:* Pratt's, Beefsteak, Cavalry and Guards.

ELTON, Arnold, CBE 1982; MS; FRCS; Consultant Surgeon: Northwick Park Hospital and Clinical Research Centre, since 1970; British Airways, since 1981; *b* 14 Feb. 1920; *s* of late Max Elton and of Ada Elton; *m* 1952, Billie Pamela Briggs; one *s. Educ:* University Coll. London (exhibnr; MB BS 1943); UCH Med. Sch. (MS 1951); Jun. and Sen. Gold Medal in Surgery. LRCP 1943; MRCS 1943, FRCS 1946. House Surg., House Physician and Casualty Officer, UCH, 1943–45; Sen. Surgical Registrar, Charing Cross Hosp., 1947–51 (Gosse Res. Schol.); Consultant Surgeon: Harrow Hosp., 1951–70; Mount Vernon Hosp., 1960–70. First Chm., Med. Staff Cttee, Chm., Surgical Div. and Theatre Cttee, Mem., Ethical Cttee, Northwick Park Hosp. Mem., Govt Wkg Party on Breast Screening for Cancer. Examiner: GNC; RCS, 1971–83; Surgical Tutor, RCS, 1970–82. Nat. Chm., Cons. Med. Soc., 1973–; Mem., Cons. Central Council and Nat. Exec. Cttee, 1976–. Mem., Professional Cttee, RADAR, 1976–; Founder Mem., British Assoc. of Surgical Oncology; Mem. Ct of Patrons, RCS, 1986–. Fellow: Assoc. of Surgeons of GB; Hunterian Soc.; FRSocMed; FICS; Associate Fellow, British Assoc. of Urological Surgeons. Liveryman: Apothecaries' Soc.; Carmen's Co. Jubilee Medal, 1977. *Publications:* contribs to med. jls. *Recreations:* tennis, music. *Address:* 22 St Stephen's Close, Avenue Road, NW8 6DB. *T:* 01–722 4222; 101 Harley Street, W1N 1DF. *T:* 01-935 4101. *Clubs:* Carlton, Royal Automobile.

ELTON, Sir Charles (Abraham Grierson), 11th Bt *cr* 1717; *b* 23 May 1953; *s* of Sir Arthur Hallam Rice Elton, 10th Bt, and of Lady Elton; *S* father, 1973. *Address:* Clevedon Court, Somerset BS21 6QU.

ELTON, Charles Sutherland, FRS 1953; Director, Bureau of Animal Population, Department of Zoological Field Studies, 1932–67, and Reader in Animal Ecology, Oxford University, 1936–67; Senior Research Fellow, Corpus Christi College, Oxford, 1936–67, Hon. Fellow since Oct. 1967; *b* 29 March 1900; *s* of late Oliver Elton; *m* 1st, 1928, Rose Montague; no *c*; 2nd, 1937, Edith Joy, *d* of Rev. Canon F. G. Scovell; one *s* one *d. Educ:* Liverpool Coll.; New Coll., Oxford. First Class Hons Zoology, Oxford, 1922; served as Ecologist on Oxford Univ. Expedition to Spitsbergen, 1921, Merton Coll. Arctic Expedition, 1923, Oxford Univ. Arctic Expedition, 1924 and Oxford Univ. Lapland Expedition, 1930. Founding Mem., Oxford Univ. Exploration Club, 1927; Mem. Nature Conservancy, 1949–56. Vis. Fellow, Smithsonian Inst., 1968. Hon. Member: NY Zoo Soc., 1931; Chicago Acad. of Scis, 1946; Wildlife Soc., 1949; British Ecol Soc., 1960; Ecol Soc. of Amer., 1961 (and as Eminent Ecologist, 1982); Amer. Soc. of Mammalogists, 1973; Inst. of Biology, 1983. Foreign Hon. Mem., Amer. Acad. of Arts and Sciences, 1968. Murchison Grant, RGS, 1929; Linnean Soc. Gold Medal, 1967; Darwin Medal, Royal Soc., 1970; John and Alice Tyler Ecology Award, 1976; Edward W. Browning Achievement Award, for Conserving the Environment, 1977. *Publications:* Animal Ecology, 1927; Animal Ecology and Evolution, 1930; The Ecology of Animals, 1933; Exploring the Animal World, 1933; Voles, Mice and Lemmings, 1942; The Ecology of Invasions by Animals and Plants, 1958; The Pattern of Animal Communities, 1966.

Recreations: natural history, gardening, reading. *Address:* 61 Park Town, Oxford OX2 6SL. *T:* Oxford 57644.

ELTON, Prof. Sir Geoffrey (Rudolph), Kt 1986; LittD; PhD; FBA 1967; Regius Professor of Modern History, Cambridge, since 1983; Fellow of Clare College, Cambridge, since 1954; *b* 17 Aug. 1921; changed name to Elton under Army Council Instruction, 1944; *er s* of late Prof. Victor Ehrenberg, PhD; *m* 1952, Sheila Lambert; no *c. Educ:* Prague; Rydal Sch. London External BA (1st Cl. Hons) 1943; Derby Student, University Coll. London, 1946–48, PhD 1949; LittD Cantab 1960. Asst Master, Rydal Sch., 1940–43. Service in E Surrey Regt and Int. Corps (Sgt), 1944–46. Asst in History, Glasgow Univ., 1948–49; Univ. Asst Lectr, Cambridge, 1949–53, Lectr, 1953–63, Reader in Tudor Studies, 1963–67, Prof. of English Constitutional History, 1967–83. Visiting Amundson Prof., Univ. of Pittsburgh, Sept.-Dec. 1963; Vis. Hill Prof., Univ. of Minnesota, 1976. Lectures: Ford's, Oxford, 1972; Wiles, Belfast, 1972; Hagey, Waterloo, 1974. Publications Sec., British Acad., 1981–. Member: Adv. Council on Public Records, 1977–85; Library and Inf. Services Council, 1986–. FRHistS 1954 (Pres., 1972–76); Founder and Pres., List & Index Soc., 1965–; President: Selden Soc., 1983–85; Ecclesiastical Hist. Soc., 1983–84. Fellow, UCL, 1978. Hon. DLitt: Glasgow, 1979; Newcastle, 1981; Bristol, 1981; London, 1985. For. Mem., Amer. Acad. Arts and Scis, 1975; Hon. Mem., American Historical Assoc., 1982. *Publications:* The Tudor Revolution in Government, 1953; England under the Tudors, 1955; (ed) New Cambridge Modern History, vol. 2, 1958, new edn 1975; Star Chamber Stories, 1958; The Tudor Constitution, 1960; Henry VIII: an essay in revision, 1962; Renaissance and Reformation (Ideas and Institutions in Western Civilization), 1963; Reformation Europe, 1963; The Practice of History, 1967; The Future of the Past, 1968; The Sources of History: England 1200–1640, 1969; Political History: Principles and Practice, 1970; Modern Historians on British History 1485–1945: a critical bibliography 1945–1969, 1970; Policy and Police: the enforcement of the Reformation in the age of Thomas Cromwell, 1972; Reform and Renewal, 1973; Studies in Tudor and Stuart Politics and Government: papers and reviews, 1946–1972, 2 vols, 1974, vol. 3, 1973–1981, 1983; Reform and Reformation: England 1509–1558, 1977; The History of England (inaug. lecture), 1984; (with R. W. Fogel) Which Road to the Past?, 1984; F. W. Maitland, 1985; contribs to English Hist. Review, Econ. Hist. Rev., History, Hist. Jl, Times Lit. Supplement, Listener, NY Review of Books, etc. *Recreations:* squash rackets, joinery, gardening, and beer. *Address:* Clare College, Cambridge; Faculty of History, West Road, Cambridge. *T:* Cambridge 337733.
See also L. R. B. Elton.

ELTON, George Alfred Hugh, CB 1983; biochemist; Scientific Adviser, British Food Manufacturing Industries Research Association, since 1986; *b* 25 Feb. 1925; *s* of Horace and Violet Elton; *m* 1951, Theodora Rose Edith Kingham; two *d. Educ:* Sutton County Sch.; London Univ. (evening student). BSc 1944, PhD 1948, DSc 1956; CChem 1974, FRSC (FRIC 1951); FIFST 1968; FIBiol 1976; CBiol 1984. Mem. Faculty of Science, and Univ. Examnr in Chemistry, Univ. of London, 1951–58; Dir, Fog Res. Unit, Min. of Supply, 1954–58; Reader in Applied Phys. Chemistry, Battersea Polytechnic, 1956–58; Dir, British Baking Industries Res. Assoc., 1958–66; Dir, Flour Milling and Baking Res. Assoc., 1967–70; Ministry of Agriculture, Fisheries and Food: Chief Sci. Adviser (Food), 1971–85; Head of Food Science Div., 1972–73; Dep. Chief Scientist, 1972; Under-Sec. 1974; Chief Scientist (Fisheries and Food), 1981–85. Vis. Prof., Surrey Univ., 1982–. Chairman: National Food Survey Cttee, 1978–85; Adv. Bd, Inst. of Food Res. (Bristol), 1985–; Scientific Governor, British Nutrition Foundn; Member: Cttee on Medical Aspects of Food Policy, 1971–85; UK Delegn, Tripartite Meetings on Food and Drugs, 1971–85; AFRC (formerly ARC), 1981–85; NERC, 1981–85; Fisheries Res. and Develt Bd, 1982–85; Adv. Bd for Research Councils, 1981–84; EEC Scientific Cttee for Food, 1985–; Council, Chemical Soc., 1972–75. Co-inventor, Chorleywood Bread Process (Queen's Award to Industry 1966); Silver Medallist, Royal Soc. of Arts, 1969. Hon. DSc Reading, 1984. *Publications:* research papers in jls of various learned societies. *Recreation:* golf. *Address:* Green Nook, Bridle Lane, Loudwater, Rickmansworth, Herts WD3 4JH. *Clubs:* Savage, MCC.

ELTON, John; *see* Elton, P. J.

ELTON, Air Vice-Marshal John Goodenough, CB 1955; CBE 1945; DFC 1940; AFC 1935; *b* 5 May 1905; *s* of late Rev. George G. Elton, MA Oxon; *m* 1st, 1927, Helen Whitfield (marr. diss.); one *s*; 2nd, 1949, Francesca Cavallero. *Educ:* St John's, Leatherhead. Entered RAF, 1926; service in UK, 1926–31; Singapore, 1932–35 (AFC); Irak, 1939. Served War of 1939–45 (despatches twice, DFC, CBE); CO 47 Sqdn, Sudan, 1940; HQ, ME, Cairo, 1941; comd in succession Nos 242, 238 and 248 Wings, N Africa, 1942; CO RAF Turnberry, Scotland, 1943; CO RAF Silloth, Cumberland, 1944; AOA, HQ Mediterranean Allied Coastal Air Force, 1945–46; idc 1947; Dep. Dir, Air Min., 1948; RAF Mem., UK Delegn, Western Union Military Cttee, 1949–50; Comdt, Sch. of Tech. Training, Halton, 1951; Air Attaché, Paris, 1952; Air Officer i/c Administration, HQ Bomber Comd, 1953–56; Chief of Staff to the Head of British Jt Services Mission, Washington, DC, 1956–59; retired, 1959. *Address:* 64 Lexham Gardens, W8. *Club:* Royal Air Force.

ELTON, Prof. Lewis Richard Benjamin, MA, DSc; FInstP, FIMA, FRSA; Professor of Science Education, since 1971, and Associate Head, Department of Educational Studies, since 1983, University of Surrey; *b* 25 March 1923; *yr s* of late Prof. Victor Leopold Ehrenberg, PhD, and Eva Dorothea (*née* Sommer); *m* 1950, Mary, *d* of late Harold William Foster and Kathleen (*née* Meakin); three *s* one *d. Educ:* Stepanska Gymnasium, Prague; Rydal Sch., Colwyn Bay; Christ's Coll., Cambridge (Exhibr); Univ. Correspondence Coll., Cambridge, and Regent Street Polytechnic; University Coll. London (Univ. Research Studentship). BA 1945, Certif.Ed 1945, MA 1948, Cantab; BSc (External) 1st Cl. Hons Maths 1947, PhD 1950, London. Asst Master, St Bees Sch., 1944–46; Asst Lectr, then Lectr, King's Coll., London, 1950–57; Head of Physics Dept: Battersea Coll. of Technology, 1958–66; Univ. of Surrey, 1966–69; Prof. of Physics, Surrey, 1964–71; Hd, Inst. of Educnl Develt (formerly Educnl Technol.), Surrey Univ., 1967–84. Research Associate: MIT, 1955; Stanford Univ., 1956; Niels Bohr Inst., Copenhagen, 1962; Vis. Professor: Univ. of Washington, Seattle, 1965; UCL, 1970–77; Univ. of Sydney, 1971; Univ. of Sao Paulo, 1975; Univ. of Science, Malaysia, 1978, 1979; Univ. of Malaya, 1982, 1983; Member: Governing Body, Battersea Coll. of Technology, 1962–66; Council, Univ. of Surrey, 1966–67, 1981–83; Council for Educational Technology of UK, 1975–81; Army Educn Adv. Bd, 1976–80; Convener, Standing Conf. of Physics Profs, 1971–74; Chairman: Governing Council, Soc. for Research into Higher Educn, 1976–78. Vice-Pres., Assoc. for Educnl and Trng Technology, 1976–. Fellow, Amer. Physical Soc., 1978. *Publications:* Introductory Nuclear Theory, 1959, 2nd edn 1965, Spanish edn 1964; Nuclear Sizes, 1961, Russian edn 1962; Concepts in Classical Mechanics, 1971; (with H. Messel) Time and Man, 1978; contribs to sci. jls on nuclear physics, higher education, science educn and educnl technology. *Recreation:* words. *Address:* 107 Farnham Road, Guildford, Surrey GU2 5PF. *T:* Guildford 576548.
See also Sir G. R. Elton.

ELTON, (Peter) John, MC 1944: Director: Hill Samuel Group Ltd, since 1976; British Alcan Aluminium (formerly Alcan Aluminium (UK) Ltd), since 1962; Consolidated Goldfields, since 1977; *b* 14 March 1924; 2nd *s* of Sydney George Elton; *m* 1948, Patricia Ann Stephens; two *d. Educ:* Eastbourne Coll.; Clare Coll., Cambridge. Indian Army: 14th Punjab Regt, 1942–45 (twice wounded). Hons Degree, Econs and Law, Cambridge. Man. Dir, Alcan Aluminium (UK) Ltd, 1967–74, Exec. Chm. 1974–76, non-Exec. Chm., 1976–78; Chairman: Alcan Booth Industries Ltd, 1968–76; Alcan (UK) Ltd, 1967–76; Director: Alcan Aluminium Ltd, 1972–77; Spillers, 1978–80. *Recreations:* sailing, shooting. *Address:* Salternshill Farm, Buckler's Hard, Beaulieu, Hants. *T:* Buckler's Hard 206. *Clubs:* Bucks, Royal Yacht Squadron (Cowes).

ELVEDEN, Viscount; Arthur Edward Rory Guinness; *b* 10 Aug. 1969; *s* and *heir* of Earl of Iveagh, *qv.*

ELVIN, Herbert Lionel; Emeritus Professor of Education; Director of the University of London Institute of Education, 1958–73 (Professor of Education in Tropical Areas, 1956–58); Director, Department of Education, UNESCO, Paris, 1950–56; *b* 7 Aug. 1905; *e s* of late Herbert Henry Elvin; *m* 1934, Mona Bedortha, *d* of Dr C. S. S. Dutton, San Francisco; one *s. Educ:* elementary schs; Southend High Sch.; Trinity Hall, Cambridge (1st Class Hons, History and English; Hon. Fellow, 1980). Commonwealth Fellow, Yale Univ., USA, Fellow of Trinity Hall, Cambridge, 1930–44; Temporary Civil Servant (Air Min., 1940–42, MOI, 1943–45); Principal, Ruskin Coll., Oxford, 1944–50. Parliamentary candidate (Lab), Cambridge Univ., 1935; Formerly: Pres., English New Education Fellowship; Pres., Council for Education in World Citizenship; Chm., Commonwealth Educn Liaison Cttee. Member: Cttee on Higher Education; Govt of India Educn Commn; University Grants Cttee, 1946–50; Central Advisory Council for Education (England) and Secondary School Examinations Council. *Publications:* Men of America (Pelican Books), 1941; An Introduction to the Study of Literature (Poetry), 1949; Education and Contemporary Society, 1965; The Place of Commonsense in Educational Thought, 1977; (ed) The Educational Systems in the European Community, 1981. *Recreations:* most games indifferently; formerly athletics (half-mile, Cambridge *v* Oxford, 1927). *Address:* 4 Bulstrode Gardens, Cambridge. *T:* Cambridge 358309.

ELVIN, Violetta, (Violetta Prokhorova), (Signora Fernando Savarese); ballerina; a prima ballerina of Sadler's Wells Ballet, Royal Opera House, London (now The Royal Ballet), 1951–56; Director, Ballet Company, San Carlo Opera, Naples, since 1985; *b* Moscow, 3 Nov. 1925; *d* of Vassilie Prokhorov, engineer, and Irena Grimouzinskaya, former actress; *m* 1st, 1944, Harold Elvin (divorced 1952), of British Embassy, Moscow; 2nd, 1953, Siegbert J. Weinberger, New York; 3rd, 1959, Fernando Savarese, lawyer; one *s. Educ:* Bolshoi Theatre Sch., Moscow. Trained for ballet since age of 8 by: E. P. Gerdt, A. Vaganova, M. A. Kojuchova. Grad, 1942, as soloist; made mem. Bolshoi Theatre Ballet; evacuated to Tashkent, 1943; ballerina Tashkent State Theatre; rejoined Bolshoi Theatre at Kuibishev again as soloist, 1944; left for London, 1945. Joined Sadler's Wells Ballet at Covent Garden as guest-soloist, 1946; later became regular mem. Has danced all principal rôles, notably, Le Lac des Cygnes, Sleeping Beauty, Giselle, Cinderella, Sylvia, Ballet Imperial, etc. Danced four-act Le Lac des Cygnes, first time, 1943; guest-artist Stanislavsky Theatre, Moscow, 1944, Sadler's Wells Theatre, 1947; guest-prima ballerina, La Scala, Milan, Nov. 1952–Feb. 1953 (Macbeth, La Gioconda, Swan Lake, Petrouchka); guest artist, Cannes, July 1954; Copenhagen, Dec. 1954; Teatro Municipal, Rio de Janeiro, May 1955 (Giselle, Swan Lake, Les Sylphides, Nutcracker, Don Quixote and The Dying Swan); Festival Ballet, Festival Hall, 1955; guest-prima ballerina in Giselle, Royal Opera House, Stockholm (Anna Pavlova Memorial), 1956; concluded stage career when appeared in Sleeping Beauty, Royal Opera House, Covent Garden, June 1956. *Appeared in films:* The Queen of Spades, Twice Upon a Time, Melba. Television appearances in Russia and England. Has toured with Sadler's Wells Ballet, France, Italy, Portugal, United States and Canada. *Recreations:* reading, painting, swimming. *Address:* Marina di Equa, 80066 Seiano, Bay of Naples, Italy. *T:* 081–879 8520.

ELWES, Captain Jeremy Gervase Geoffrey Philip; Vice Lord-Lieutenant of Humberside, since 1984; *b* 1 Sept. 1921; *s* of Rev. Rolf Elwes, OBE, MC; *m* 1955, Clare Mary Beveridge; four *s. Educ:* Avisford Sch.; Ampleforth Coll.; RMC Sandhurst. Joined Lincolnshire Regt, 1940; commissioned KRRC 1941; served until 1946, S Africa, Middle East, 8th Army, Yugoslavia, Southern Albania (despatches), Dalmatia and Greece; Moulton Agricultural Coll., 1947; farmer, 1949–; founder Dir, Linvend Ltd, 1960–, later J. S. Linder Ltd; founder Dir, Universal Marine Ltd, 1965–71; founder, Elwes Enterprises, 1970–; co-founder and Chm., Euro-Latin Commercial Co. Ltd, 1971; founder Dir, Euro-Latin Aviation Ltd, 1975–. Opened country park to the public, Conservation Year, 1970; Mem., BBC Northern Adv. Council, 1966–69; Vice-Chm., BBC Radio Humberside, 1970–73; founder Chm., Lincs and Humberside Arts and Heritage Assoc., 1964–69; Pres., Lincs Branch, CPRE, 1957–; Mem. Council, Vice-Pres. and Steward, Lincs Agric. Soc., 1964–; Mem., Lincs Branch Exec., CLA, 1966–69; founder Chm., Shrievalty Assoc. of GB, 1971–; joint founder, Scarbank Trust Charity, 1978–; Mem., Brigg and Scunthorpe Cons. Assoc. Exec. Cttee, 1948–73; Mem., Brigg RDC, 1957–73, Lindsey CC, 1961–71; High Sheriff, Lincs, 1969, DL Lincs 1969, later Humberside. *Recreations:* the arts and countryside. *Address:* Elsham Hall, near Brigg, South Humberside DN20 0QZ. *T:* Barnetby (0652) 688738.

ELWES, Jeremy Vernon, CBE 1984; Personnel Director, Business Press International Ltd, since 1982; *b* 29 May 1937; *s* of late Eric Vincent Elwes and of Dorothea Elwes (*née* Bilton); *m* 1963, Phyllis Marion Relf, 2nd *d* of George Herbert Harding Relf and late Rose Jane Relf (*née* Luery); one *s. Educ:* Wirral Grammar Sch.; Bromley Grammar Sch.; City of London Coll. ACIS 1963. Technical Journalist, Heywood & Co., 1958–62; Accountant and Co. Sec., Agricultural Press, 1962–70; Sec. and Dir, East Brackland Hill Farming Development Co., 1967–70; IPC Business Press: Pensions Officer, 1966–70; Divl Personnel Manager, 1970–73; Manpower Planning Manager, 1973–78; Exec. Dir (Manpower), 1978–82. Chairman: Cons. Political Centre Nat. Adv. Cttee, 1981–84; Cons. SE Area, 1986–; Member: Nat. Union Exec. Cttee; Gen. Purposes Cttee; Cons. Group for Europe. Chm. of Governors, Walthamstow Hall; Vice-Chm. of Governors, Wildernesse Sch. for Boys; Governor, Eltham College. Member Judge, Internat. Wine and Spirit Competition; Maître des Cérémonies, Ordre des Chevaliers Bretvins (Dailliage de GB). *Recreations:* wine and food, reading, walking (with dog). *Address:* Crispian Cottage, Weald Road, Sevenoaks, Kent TN13 1QQ. *T:* Sevenoaks 454208. *Clubs:* Carlton, St Stephen's Constitutional.

ELWORTHY, family name of **Baron Elworthy.**

ELWORTHY, Baron *cr* 1972 (Life Peer); **Marshal of the Royal Air Force Samuel Charles Elworthy,** KG 1977; GCB 1962 (KCB 1961; CB 1960); CBE 1946; DSO 1941; LVO 1953; DFC 1941; AFC 1941; *b* 23 March 1911; *e s* of late P. A. Elworthy, Gordon's Valley, Timaru, New Zealand; *m* 1936, Audrey (*d* 1986), *o d* of late A. J. Hutchinson, OBE; three *s* one *d. Educ:* Marlborough; Trinity Coll., Cambridge (MA). Commissioned in RAFO 1933, transferred to Auxiliary Air Force (600 Sqdn), 1934; called to Bar, Lincoln's Inn, 1935, Hon. Bencher 1970; permanent commission in RAF, 1936; War Service in Bomber Comd; Acting Air Cdre, 1944; Air Vice-Marshal, 1957; Air Marshal, 1960; Air Chief Marshal, 1962; Marshal of the RAF, 1967. Comdt RAF

Staff Coll., Bracknell, 1957–59; Deputy Chief of Air Staff, 1959–60; C-in-C, Unified Command, Middle East, 1960–63; Chief of Air Staff, 1963–67; Chief of the Defence Staff, 1967–71. Constable and Governor, Windsor Castle, 1971–78; Lord-Lieutenant of Greater London, 1973–78. Chairman: Royal Commn for the Exhibition of 1851, 1971–78; King Edward VII Hospital for Officers, 1971–78; Royal Over-Seas League, 1971–76. Sometime Governor: Bradfield Coll.; Wellington Coll.; Marlborough Coll. Hon. Freeman, Skinners' Co., 1968–, Master 1973–74. KStJ 1976. Retired to live in NZ, 1978. *Address:* Gordon's Valley, RD2, Timaru, South Canterbury, New Zealand. *Clubs:* Royal Air Force; Leander; South Canterbury (NZ); Christchurch (NZ).

ELWORTHY-JARMAN, Air Cdre Lance Michael, DFC 1940; RAF (retired); Director, Engineering Industries Association, 1958–73, retired; *b* 17 Aug. 1907; *s* of Hedley Elworthy and Mary Elizabeth Jarman (*née* Chatterway-Clarke); *m* 1940, Elizabeth Evelyn Litton-Puttock (*d* 1978); one *s* one *d. Educ:* Christchurch High Sch., NZ; Canterbury Coll., Univ. of NZ. Commissioned, RAF, 1929; No 12 Bomber Sqdn, Andover, 1930; No 14 Bomber Sqdn, Amman, 1931; Officers' Engineering Course, Henlow, 1932–35; RAF, Abukir, Atbara, Sudan, Cairo, 1935–38; Maintenance Command, 1938. Served War of 1939–45: Nos 214 and 9 Bomber Sqdns, 1939; Chief Flying Instructor, Nos 11–20 and 23 Operational Training Units, 1940; CO, No 27 OTU, Lichfield, 1941; SASO, No 93 Bomber Gp, 1942; CO, RAF Stations, Kidlington and Wyton, 1943; SASO, No 205 Gp, Italy, 1945, qualified as Pathfinder; OC RAF Stations, Oakington and Abingdon, 1947; Senior Officer Administration, RAF, No 42 Gp, 1949; OC, RAF Jet Training Stations, Full Sutton and Merryfield, 1951; Chief of Staff, Royal Pakistan Air Force, 1952; attached Nellis Air Force Base to test T33 and F86E, 1953; official observer, atomic explosions at Yucca Flat and Nevada, 1955; AO Defence Research Policy Staff, Cabinet Office, 1955–56; RAF Rep., Commonwealth Conf. on Defence Sci., Canada; AOA, NATO, Channel and Atlantic Commands, 1957; retired from RAF, 1958. CEng, MIMechE, AFRAeS, MBIM, MAIE. *Publications:* Editor, Engineering Industries Jl. *Recreation:* sailing; lectr, offshore and ocean navigation; examr, RYA/DTI yachtmaster certificate. *Address:* Merryfield, 9 Newenham Road, Lymington, Hants. *T:* Lymington 74577. *Clubs:* Royal Air Force, Royal Ocean Racing; RAF Yacht (Hamble); Royal New Zealand Yacht Squadron.

ELWYN-JONES, family name of **Baron Elwyn-Jones.**

ELWYN-JONES, Baron *cr* 1974 (Life Peer), of Llanelli and Newham; **Frederick Elwyn-Jones,** PC 1964; CH 1976; Kt 1964; Lord High Chancellor of Great Britain, 1974–79; a Lord of Appeal, since 1979; *b* 24 Oct. 1909; *s* of Frederick and Elizabeth Jones, Llanelli, Carmarthenshire; *m* 1937, Pearl Binder; one *s* two *d. Educ:* Llanelli Grammar Sch.; University of Wales, Aberystwyth; Gonville and Caius Coll., Cambridge (Scholar, MA, Pres. Cambridge Union); Hon. Fellow, 1976. Called to Bar, Gray's Inn, 1935, Bencher, 1960, Treasurer, 1980; QC 1953; QC (N Ireland) 1958; Hon. Bencher, Inn of Court of N Ireland, 1981. Major RA (TA); Dep. Judge Advocate, 1943–45. MP (Lab) Plaistow Div. of West Ham, 1945–50, West Ham South, 1950–74, Newham South 1974; PPS to Attorney-Gen., 1946–51; Attorney General, 1964–70. Recorder: of Merthyr Tydfil, 1949–53; of Swansea, 1953–60; of Cardiff, 1960–64; of Kingston-upon-Thames, 1968–74. Member of British War Crimes Executive, Nuremberg, 1945. UK Observer, Malta Referendum, 1964. Mem., Inter-Departmental Cttee on the Court of Criminal Appeal, 1964. Mem. of Bar Council, 1956–59. President: University Coll., Cardiff, 1971–; Mental Health Foundn, 1980–. FKC, 1970. Hon. LLD: University of Wales, 1968; Ottawa Univ., 1975; Columbia Univ., NY, 1976; Warsaw, 1977; Univ. of Philippines, 1979; Law Soc. of Upper Canada, 1982. Hon. Freeman: Llanelli; London. *Publications:* Hitler's Drive to the East, 1937; The Battle for Peace, 1938; The Attack from Within, 1939; In My Time (autobiog.), 1983. *Recreation:* travelling. *Address:* House of Lords, SW1.

ELY, 8th Marquess of, *cr* 1801; **Charles John Tottenham;** Bt 1780; Baron Loftus, 1785; Viscount Loftus, 1789; Earl of Ely, 1794; Baron Loftus (UK), 1801; Headmaster, Boulden House, Trinity College School, Port Hope, Ontario, 1941–81; *b* 30 May 1913; *s* of G. L. Tottenham, BA (Oxon), and Cécile Elizabeth, *d* of J. S. Burra, Bockhanger, Kennington, Kent; *g s* of C. R. W. Tottenham, MA (Oxon), Woodstock, Newtown Mount Kennedy, Co. Wicklow, and Plâs Berwyn, Llangollen, N Wales; *S* cousin, 1969; *m* 1st, 1938, Katherine Elizabeth (*d* 1975), *d* of Col W. H. Craig, Kingston, Ont; three *s* one *d*; 2nd, 1978, Elspeth Ann, *o d* of late P. T. Hay, Highgate. *Educ:* Collège de Genève, Internat. Sch., Geneva; Queen's Univ., Kingston, Ont (BA). Career as Schoolmaster. *Recreation:* gardening. *Heir: e s* Viscount Loftus, *qv. Address:* Trinity College School, Port Hope, Ontario L1A 3W2, Canada. *T:* 885 5209; 20 Arundel Court, Jubilee Place, SW3. *T:* 01–352 9172. *Club:* University (Toronto).

ELY, Bishop of, since 1977; **Rt. Rev. Peter Knight Walker,** DD; *b* 6 Dec. 1919; *s* of late George Walker and Eva Muriel (*née* Knight); *m* 1973, Mary Jean, JP 1976, *yr d* of late Lt-Col J. A. Ferguson, OBE. *Educ:* Leeds Grammar Sch. (Schol.); The Queen's Coll., Oxford (Hastings schol.; Cl. 2 Classical Hon. Mods. 1940, Cl. 1 Lit. Hum. 1947; MA Oxon 1947; Hon. Fellow, 1981); Westcott House, Cambridge. MA Cantab by incorporation, 1958; Hon. DD Cantab, 1978. Served in RN (Lieut, RNVR), 1940–45. Asst Master: King's Sch., Peterborough, 1947–50; Merchant Taylors' Sch., 1950–56. Ordained, 1954; Curate of Hemel Hempstead, 1956–58; Fellow, Dean of Chapel and Lectr in Theology, Corpus Christi Coll., Cambridge, 1958–62 (Asst Tutor, 1959–62), Hon. Fellow, 1978; Principal of Westcott House, Cambridge, 1962–72; Commissary to Bishop of Delhi, 1962–66; Hon. Canon of Ely Cathedral, 1966–72; Bishop Suffragan of Dorchester, and Canon of Christ Church, Oxford, 1972–77. Select Preacher: Univ. of Cambridge, 1962, 1967 (Hulsean), 1986; Univ. of Oxford, 1975, 1980; Examining Chaplain to Bishop of Portsmouth, 1962–72. A Governor, St Edward's Sch., Oxford. Chm., Hosp. Chaplaincies Council, 1982–86. *Publications:* contrib. to: Classical Quarterly; Theology, etc. *Address:* The Bishop's House, Ely, Cambs CB7 4DW. *T:* Ely 2749. *Club:* Cambridge County.

ELY, Dean of; *see* Patterson, Very Rev. W. J.

ELY, Archdeacon of; *see* Walser, Ven. David.

ELYAN, Prof. Sir (Isadore) Victor, Kt 1970; Professor of Law, and Dean of the Faculty of Law, Durban-Westville University, 1973–77, retired; Chief Justice of Swaziland, 1965–70, retired; *b* 5 Sept. 1909; *s* of Jacob Elyan, PC, JP and Olga Elyan; *m* 1939, Ivy Ethel Mabel Stuart-Weir (*d* 1965); no *c*; *m* 1966, Rosaleen Jeanette O'Shea. *Educ:* St Stephen's Green Sch., Dublin; Trinity Coll., Dublin Univ. BA 1929, LLB 1931, MA 1932, TCD. Admitted a Solicitor of Supreme Court of Judicature, Ireland, 1930; Barrister-at-Law, King's Inns 1949, Middle Temple, 1952. Resident Magistrate, HM Colonial Legal Service, Gold Coast, 1946–54; Senior Magistrate, 1954–55; Judge of Appeal of the Court of Appeal for Basutoland, the Bechuanaland Protectorate and Swaziland, 1955–66; Judge, High Courts of Basutoland and the Bechuanaland Protectorate, 1955–65; on occasions acted as Judge between 1953 and 1955, Gold Coast; as Justice of Appeal, West African Court of Appeal; and as Chief Justice of Basutoland, the Bechuanaland Protectorate and Swaziland, also Pres. Court of Appeal, during 1956, 1961 and 1964; Judge of Appeal:

Court of Appeal for Botswana, 1966–70; Court of Appeal for Swaziland, 1967–70; Court of Appeal, Lesotho, 1968–70. Served War, 1942–46; attached to Indian Army, 1944–46; GSO2 Military Secretary's Branch (DAMS), 1945–46 in rank of Major. Mem., Internat. Adv. Bd, The African Law Reports, 1969. *Publications:* Editor, High Commission Territories Law Reports, 1956, 1957, 1958, 1959, 1960. *Recreation:* sailing. *Address:* PO Box 3052, Durban, Natal, South Africa.

ELYSTAN-MORGAN, family name of Baron Elystan-Morgan.

ELYSTAN-MORGAN, Baron *cr* 1981 (Life Peer), of Aberteifi in the County of Dyfed; **Dafydd Elystan Elystan-Morgan;** Barrister-at-Law; a Recorder of the Crown Court, since 1983; *b* 7 Dec. 1932; *s* of late Dewi Morgan and late Mrs Olwen Morgan; *m* 1959, Alwen, *d* of William E. Roberts; one *s* one *d. Educ:* Ardwyn Grammar Sch., Aberystwyth; UCW, Aberystwyth. LLB Hons Aberystwyth, 1953. Research at Aberystwyth and Solicitor's Articles, 1953–57; admitted a Solicitor, 1957; Partner in N Wales (Wrexham) Firm of Solicitors, 1958–68; Barrister-at-law, Gray's Inn, 1971. MP (Lab) Cardiganshire, 1966–Feb. 1974; Chm., Welsh Parly Party, 1967–68, 1971–74; Parly Under-Secretary of State, Home Office, 1968–70; front-bench spokesman on Home Affairs, 1970–72, on Welsh Affairs, 1972–74, on Legal and Home Affairs, House of Lords, 1981–. Contested (Lab): Cardigan, Oct. 1974; Anglesey, 1979. Pres., Welsh Local Authorities Assoc., 1967–73. *Address:* Carreg Afon, Dolau, Bow Street, Dyfed.

ELYTIS, Odysseus; Order of the Phoenix, 1965; Grand Commander, Order of Honour, 1979; poet; *b* Crete, 2 Nov. 1911; *y c* of Panayiotis and Maria Alepoudelis. *Educ:* Athens Univ. (Law); Sorbonne (Lettres). First publication, 1940; Broadcasting and Program Director, National Broadcasting Inst., 1945–47 and 1953–54; Administrative Board, Greek National Theatre, 1974–76. President, Admin. Board, Greek Broadcasting and Television, 1974. Hon. DLitt: Salonica, 1976; Sorbonne, 1980; Hon. DLit London, 1981. First National Prize in Poetry, 1960; Nobel Prize for Literature, 1979; Benson Silver Medal, RSL, 1981. *Publications:* Orientations, 1940; Sun the First, 1943; The Axion Esti, 1959; Six, but one remorses for the Sky, 1960; The Light Tree, 1971; The Monogram, 1972; Villa Natacha, 1973; The Painter Theophilos, 1973; The Open Book, 1974; The Second Writing, 1976; Maria Nefeli, 1978; Selected Poems, 1981; Three Poems, 1982; Journal of an Unseen April, 1984; Saphfo, 1984. *Address:* Skoufa Street 23, Athens, Greece. *T:* 3626458.

EMANUEL, Aaron, CMG 1957; Consultant to OECD, 1972–83; *b* 11 Feb. 1912; *s* of Jack Emanuel and Jane (*née* Schaverien); *m* 1936, Ursula Pagel; two *s* one *d. Educ:* Henry Thornton Sch., Clapham; London Sch. of Economics (BSc Econ.). Economist at International Institute of Agriculture, Rome, 1935–38; Board of Trade, 1938; Ministry of Food, 1940; Colonial Office, 1943; Ministry of Health, 1961; Dept. of Economic Affairs, 1965; Under Secretary: Min. of Housing and Local Govt, 1969; Dept of the Environment, 1970–72. Chm., West Midlands Econ. Planning Bd, 1968–72; Vis. Sen. Lectr, Univ. of Aston in Birmingham, 1972–75. *Publication:* Issues of Regional Policies, 1973. *Address:* 119 Salisbury Road, Moseley, Birmingham B13 8LA. *T:* 021–449 5553.

EMANUEL, Richard Wolff, MA, DM Oxon, FRCP; Physician to Department of Cardiology, Middlesex Hospital, since 1963; Lecturer in Cardiology, Middlesex Hospital Medical School since 1963; Physician to National Heart Hospital since 1963; Lecturer to Institute of Cardiology since 1963; Civil Consultant in Cardiology, Royal Air Force, since 1979; *b* 13 Jan. 1923; *s* of Prof. and Mrs J. G. Emanuel, Birmingham; *m* 1950, Lavinia Hoffmann; three *s. Educ:* Bradfield Coll.; Oriel Coll., Oxford; Middlesex Hospital. House Appts at Middx Hospital, 1948 and 1950. Captain RAMC, 1948–50; Med. Registrar, Middx Hosp., 1951–52; Sen. Med. Registrar, Middx Hosp., 1953–55; Sen. Med. Registrar, Nat. Heart Hosp., 1956–58; Fellow in Med., Vanderbilt Univ., 1956–57; Sen. Med. Registrar, Dept of Cardiology, Brompton Hosp., 1958–61; Asst Dir, Inst. of Cardiology and Hon. Asst Physician to Nat. Heart Hosp., 1961–63. Advr in Cardiovascular Disease to Sudan Govt, 1969–. Vis. Lecturer: Univ. of Med. Sciences and Chulalongkorn Univ., Thailand; Univ. of the Philippines; Univ. of Singapore; Univ. of Malaya; Khartoum Univ.; St Cyre's Lectr, London, 1968; Ricardo Molina Lectr, Philippines, 1969. Has addressed numerous Heart Socs in SE Asia. Member: British Cardiac Soc., 1955– (Asst Sec., 1966–68; Sec., 1968–70; Mem. Council, 1981–85); Chest, Heart and Stroke Assoc., 1978–. FACC; Hon. Fellow, Philippine Coll. of Cardiology; Hon. Mem., Heart Assoc. of Thailand. Member: Brit. Acad. of Forensic Sciences (Med.); Cardiological Cttee, RCP 1967–85 (Sec., 1972–79; Chm., 1979–85); Assoc. of Physicians of GB and Ireland. Mem., Editl Cttee, British Heart Journal, 1964–72. *Publications:* various articles on diseases of the heart in British and American jls. *Recreations:* XVIIIth century glass, fishing. *Address:* 6 Upper Wimpole Street, W1M 7TD. *T:* 01–935 3243; 6 Lansdowne Walk, W11. *T:* 01–727 6688; Canute Cottage, Old Bosham, near Chichester, West Sussex. *T:* Bosham 3318. *Club:* Oriental.

EMBLING, John Francis, CB 1967; Deputy Under-Secretary of State, Department of Education and Science, 1966–71; *b* 16 July 1909; *m* 1940, Margaret Gillespie Anderson; one *s. Educ:* University of Bristol. Teaching: Dean Close, 1930; Frensham Heights, 1931; Lecturer: Leipzig Univ., 1936; SW Essex Technical Coll., 1938 (Head of Dept, 1942); Administrative Asst, Essex LEA, 1944; Ministry of Education: Principal, 1946; Asst Secretary, 1949; Under-Secretary of State for Finance and Accountant-General, Dept of Education and Science, 1960–66. Research Fellow in Higher Educn, LSE, 1972–73, Univ. of Lancaster, 1974–76. Mem. Council, Klagenfurt Univ., 1972–. Grand Cross, Republic of Austria, 1976. *Address:* Fern Hill, Start Lane, Whaley Bridge, Derbyshire SK12 7BP. *T:* Whaley Bridge 3433.

EMBREY, Derek Morris, OBE 1986; CEng, FIEE, FIMechE, FIERE, MIGasE; Group Technical Director, AB Electronic Products Group PLC, since 1973; *b* 11 March 1928; *s* of Frederick and Ethel Embrey; *m* 1951, Frances Margaret Stephens; one *s* one *d. Educ:* Wolverhampton Polytechnic. Chief Designer (Electronics), Electric Construction Co. Ltd, 1960–65, Asst Manager Static Plant, 1965–69; Chief Engineer, Abergas Ltd, 1969–73. Member: Engineering Council, 1982–86; Welsh Industrial Develt Adv. Bd, 1982–85; NACCB, 1985–; Council, IERE, 1984– (Vice Pres., 1985–); National Electronics Council, 1985–; Council, UWIST, Cardiff; Welsh Adv. Bd, 1986–. Visiting Professor, Univ. of Technology, Loughborough, 1978–84 (External Examr, Dept of Mechanical Engrg, 1984–); Lectr, 'State of the Art' conferences. *Publications:* contribs to various jls. *Recreations:* power flying, gliding, music, archaeology. *Address:* 102 Mill Road, Lisvane, Cardiff CF4 5UG. *T:* Cardiff 758473. *Clubs:* Royal Air Force; Birmingham Electric.

EMECHETA, Buchi; writer and lecturer, since 1972; *b* 21 July 1944; *d* of Alice and Jeremy Emecheta; *m* 1960, Sylvester Onwordi; two *s* three *d. Educ:* Methodist Girls' High Sch., Lagos, Nigeria; London Univ. (BSc Hons Sociol.). Librarian, 1960–69; Student, 1970–74; Youth Worker and Res. Student, Race, 1974–76; Community Worker, Camden, 1976–78. Visiting Prof., 11 Amer. univs, incl. Penn. State, Pittsburgh, UCLA, Illinois at Urbana-Champaign, 1979; Sen. Res. Fellow and Vis. Prof. of English, Univ. of Calabar, Nigeria, 1980–81; lectured: Yale, Spring 1982; London Univ., 1982–. Proprietor, Ogwugwn Afo Publishing Co. Included in twenty 'Best of Young British', 1983. Member: Arts Council of GB, 1982–83; Home Sec.'s Adv. Council on Race, 1979–. *Publications:* In the Ditch, 1972; Second Class Citizen, 1975; The Bride Price, 1976; The Slave Girl, 1977; The Joys of Motherhood, 1979; Destination Biafra, 1982; Naira Power, 1982; Double Yoke, 1982; The Rape of Shavi, 1983; Head Above Water (autobiog.), 1984; *for children:* Titch the Cat, 1979; Nowhere to Play, 1980; The Moonlight Bride, 1981; The Wrestling Match, 1981; contribs to New Statesman, TLS, The Guardian, etc. *Recreations:* gardening, going to the theatre, listening to music, reading. *Address:* 7 Briston Grove, Crouch End, N8 9EX. *T:* 01–340 3762. *Club:* Africa Centre.

EMELEUS, Prof. Harry Julius, CBE 1958; FRS 1946; MA, DSc; Professor of Inorganic Chemistry, University of Cambridge, 1945–70; now Professor Emeritus; Fellow of Sidney Sussex College, Cambridge; Fellow of Imperial College, London; *b* 22 June 1903; *s* of Karl Henry Emeleus and Ellen Biggs; *m* 1931, Mary Catherine Horton; two *s* two *d.* *Educ:* Hastings Grammar Sch.; Imperial Coll., London. 1851 Exhibition Senior Student, Imperial Coll. and Technische Hochschule, Karlsruhe, 1926–29; Commonwealth Fund Fellow, Princeton Univ., 1929–31; Member of Staff of Imperial Coll., 1931–45. President: Chemical Society, 1958; Royal Institute of Chemistry, 1963–65. Trustee, British Museum, 1963–72. Hon. Fellow, Manchester Institute of Science and Technology. Hon. Member: Austrian, Finnish, Indian, Bangladesh and French Chemical Societies; Finnish Scientific Academy; Gesellschaft Deutscher Chemiker; Royal Academy of Belgium; Akad. Naturf. Halle; Akad. Wiss. Göttingen; Austrian Acad. of Scis; Acad. of Scis in Catania; Spanish Royal Society for Physics and Chemistry. Hon. Doctor: Ghent; Kiel; Lille; Paris; Tech. Hoch. Aachen; Marquette; Kent. Lavoisier Medal, French Chem. Society; Stock Medal, Gesellschaft Deutscher Chemiker; Davy Medal, Royal Society, 1962. *Publications:* scientific papers in chemical journals. *Recreation:* fishing. *Address:* 149 Shelford Road, Trumpington, Cambridge CB2 2ND. *T:* Cambridge 840374.

EMELEUS, Prof. Karl George, CBE 1965; MA, PhD; FInstP; MRIA; Professor of Physics, Queen's University, Belfast, 1933–66; *b* 4 Aug. 1901; *s* of Karl Henry Emeleus and Ellen Biggs; *m* 1928, Florence Mary Chambers; three *s* one *d.* *Educ:* Hastings Grammar Sch.; St John's Coll., Cambridge. Fellow, Amer. Physical Soc. Hon. ScD Dublin; Hon. DSc: NUI; Queen's Univ., Belfast, 1983; Ulster, 1986. *Address:* c/o Queen's University of Belfast, Belfast BT7 1NN.

EMERSON, Michael Ronald, MA; FCA; Director for Macroeconomic Analyses and Policies, Directorate-General II, Commission of the European Communities, Brussels, since 1981; *b* 12 May 1940; *s* of James and Priscilla Emerson; *m* 1966, Barbara Brierley; one *s* two *d.* *Educ:* Hurstpierpoint Coll.; Balliol Coll., Oxford (MA (PPE)). Price Waterhouse & Co., London, 1962–65; Organisation for Economic Cooperation and Development, Paris: several posts in Develt and Economics Depts, finally as Head of General Economics Div., 1966–73; EEC, Brussels: Head of Division for Budgetary Policy, Directorate-General II, 1973–76; Economic Adviser to President of the Commission, 1977; Dir for Nat. Economies and Economic Trends, EEC, 1978–81. Fellow, Centre for Internat. Affairs, Harvard Univ., 1985–86. *Publications:* contribs to various economic jls and edited volumes on internat. and European economics. *Address:* 50 rue Clement Delpierre, 1310 La Hulpe, Belgium. *T:* 02.354.3730.

EMERSON, Dr Peter Albert, FRCP; Consultant Physician, Westminster Hospital, since 1959; Civilian Consultant Physician in Chest Diseases to RN, since 1974; *b* 7 Feb. 1923; *s* of Albert Emerson and Gwendoline (*née* Davy); *m* 1947, Ceris Hood Price; one *s* one *d.* *Educ:* The Leys Sch., Cambridge; Clare Coll., Univ. of Cambridge (MA); St George's Hosp., Univ. of London (MB, BChir 1947; MD 1954). FRCP 1964; Hon. FACP 1975. House Physician, St George's Hosp., 1947; RAF Med. Bd, 1948–52 (Sqdn Leader); Registrar, later Sen. Registrar, St George's Hosp. and Brompton Hosp., London, 1952–57; Asst Prof. of Medicine, Coll. of Medicine, State Univ. of New York, Brooklyn, USA, 1957–58; Dean, Westminster Medical Sch., London, 1981–84. Hon. Consultant Phys., King Edward VII Hosp., Midhurst, 1969–. Royal Coll. of Physicians: Asst Registrar, 1965–71; Procensor and Censor, 1978–80; Vice-Pres. and Sen. Censor, 1985–86; Mitchell Lectr, 1969. *Publications:* Thoracic Medicine, 1981; articles in med. jls and chapters in books on thoracic medicine and the application of decision theory to clinical medicine. *Recreations:* tennis, restoring old buildings. *Address:* 3 Halkin Street, Belgrave Square, SW1 7DJ. *T:* 01–235 8529. *Club:* Royal Air Force.

EMERTON, Audrey C., CStJ; SRN, SCM, RNT; Regional Nursing Officer, since 1973 and Director, Administration, Personnel and Training, since 1985, South East Thames Regional Health Authority; Chairman, UK Central Council for Nursing, Midwifery and Health Visiting, since 1985. Formerly: Chief Nursing Officer, Tunbridge Wells and Leybourne HMC; Principal Nursing Officer, Education, Bromley HMC; Senior Tutor, Experimental 2 year and 1 year Course, St George's Hosp., SW1. Kent County Commissioner, St John Ambulance Brigade. Pres., Assoc. of Nurse Administrators, 1979–82. Chm., English Nat. Bd for Nursing, Midwifery and Health Visiting, 1983. *Address:* SE Thames Regional Health Authority, Thrift House, Collington Avenue, Bexhill-on-Sea, Sussex TN39 3NQ. *T:* Bexhill-on-Sea 222555.

EMERTON, Rev. Prof. John Adney, FBA 1979; Regius Professor of Hebrew, Cambridge, since 1968; Fellow of St John's College, since 1970; Honorary Canon, St George's Cathedral, Jerusalem, since 1984; *b* 5 June 1928; *s* of Adney Spencer Emerton and Helena Mary Emerton; *m* 1954, Norma Elizabeth Bennington; one *s* two *d.* *Educ:* Minchenden Grammar Sch., Southgate; Corpus Christi Coll., Oxford; Wycliffe Hall, Oxford. BA (1st class hons Theology), 1950; 1st class hons Oriental Studies, 1952; MA 1954. Canon Hall Jun. Greek Testament Prize, 1950; Hall-Houghton Jun. Septuagint Prize, 1951, Senior Prize, 1954; Houghton Syriac Prize, 1953; Liddon Student, 1950; Kennicott Hebrew Fellow, 1952. Corpus Christi Coll., Cambridge, MA (by incorporation), 1955; BD 1960; DD 1973. Deacon, 1952; Priest, 1953. Curate of Birmingham Cathedral, 1952–53; Asst Lecturer in Theology, Birmingham Univ., 1952–53; Lecturer in Hebrew and Aramaic, Durham Univ., 1953–55; Lecturer in Divinity, Cambridge Univ., 1955–62; Reader in Semitic Philology and Fellow of St Peter's Coll., Oxford, 1962–68. Visiting Professor: of Old Testament and Near Eastern Studies, Trinity Coll., Toronto Univ., 1960; of Old Testament, Utd Theol Coll., Bangalore, 1986; Fellow, Inst. for Advanced Studies, Hebrew Univ. of Jerusalem, 1982–83. Select Preacher before Univ. of Cambridge, 1962, 1971, 1986. Sec., Internat. Orgn for the Study of the Old Testament, 1971–; Pres., Soc. for OT Study, 1979. Mem. Editorial Bd, Vetus Testamentum, 1971–. Hon. DD Edinburgh, 1977. *Publications:* The Peshitta of the Wisdom of Solomon, 1959; The Old Testament in Syriac: Song of Songs, 1966; (ed) Studies in the Historical Books of the Old Testament, 1979; (ed) Prophecy: essays presented to Georg Fohrer, 1980; Editor, Congress Volumes (International Organization for Study of the Old Testament): Edinburgh 1973, 1974; Göttingen 1977, 1978; Vienna 1980, 1981; Salamanca 1983, 1985; articles in Journal of Semitic Studies, Journal of Theological Studies, Theology, Vetus Testamentum, Zeitschrift für die Alttestamentliche Wissenschaft. *Address:* 34 Gough Way, Cambridge CB3 9LN.

EMERY, Prof. Alan Eglin Heathcote; MD, PhD, DSc; FRSE, FRCP, FRCPE; Professor of Human Genetics, University of Edinburgh and Hon. Consultant Physician, Lothian Health Board, 1968–83, now Emeritus Professor and University Fellow; Visiting Fellow, Green College, Oxford; *b* 21 Aug. 1928; *s* of Harold Heathcote Emery and Alice Eglin; *m* 1st, 1952, Alys Mary Townsend (marr. diss. 1972); 2nd, 1973, Dr Rosalind Doris Skinner; three *s* three *d.* *Educ:* Manchester Univ.; Johns Hopkins Univ., Baltimore (PhD). MD, DSc; FRIPHH 1965; FRCPE 1970; MFCM 1974; FRSE 1972; FLS 1985. Formerly: Resident in Medicine and Surgery, Manchester Royal Infirmary; Fellow in Medicine, Johns Hopkins Hosp., Baltimore, 1961–64; Reader in Medical Genetics, Univ. of Manchester, 1964–68 and Hon. Consultant in Medical Genetics, United Manchester Hosps. Vis. Prof., Univs of NY, 1968, Heidelberg, 1972, Hyderabad, 1975, California (UCLA), 1980, Padua, 1984 and Medical Coll., Peking, 1985. Lectures: Harveian, 1970; Woodhull, Royal Instn, 1972. Pres., British Clinical Genetics Soc., 1980–83; Council Mem., British Genetic Soc. Hon. Fellow, Muscular Dystrophy Assoc. of Brazil, 1982. Nat. Foundn (USA) Internat. Award for Research, 1980. *Publications:* Elements of Medical Genetics, 1968, 6th edn 1983; Methodology in Medical Genetics, 1976, 2nd edn 1986; Recombinant DNA—an introduction, 1984; editor: Modern Trends in Human Genetics, vol. 1, 1970, vol. 2, 1975; Antenatal Diagnosis of Genetic Disease, 1973; Registers for the Detection and Prevention of Genetic Disease, 1976; Principles and Practice of Medical Genetics, 1983; Psychological Aspects of Genetic Counselling, 1984; numerous scientific papers. *Recreations:* writing poetry, marine biology, oil painting. *Address:* 1 Eton Terrace, Edinburgh EH4 1QE. *T:* 031–343 2262. *Clubs:* Athenæum; Scottish Arts (Edinburgh).

EMERY, Rt. Rev. Anthony Joseph; *see* Portsmouth, Bishop of, (RC).

EMERY, Eleanor Jean, CMG 1975; HM Diplomatic Service, retired; *b* 23 Dec. 1918; *d* of Robert Paton Emery and Nellie Nicol Wilson. *Educ:* Western Canada High Sch., Calgary, Alberta; Glasgow Univ. MA Hons in History, 1941. Dominions Office, 1941–45; Asst Private Sec. to Sec. of State, 1942–45; British High Commn, Ottawa, 1945–48; CRO, 1948–52; Principal Private Sec. to Sec. of State, 1950–52; First Sec., British High Commn, New Delhi, 1952–55; CRO, 1955–58; First Sec., British High Commn, Pretoria/Cape Town, 1958–62; Head of South Asia Dept, CRO, 1962–64; Counsellor, British High Commn, Ottawa, 1964–68; Head of Pacific Dependent Territories Dept, FCO, 1969–73; High Comr, Botswana, 1973–77. Chm., UK Botswana Soc., 1984–. Governor, Commonwealth Inst., 1980–85. *Recreations:* walking, gardening. *Address:* 17 Winchmore Drive, Cambridge CB2 2LW. *Club:* Royal Commonwealth Society.

See also J. M. Zachariah.

EMERY, Fred; Presenter, Panorama, BBC TV, 1978–80 and since 1982; *b* 19 Oct. 1933; *s* of Frederick G. L. Emery and Alice May (*née* Wright); *m* 1958, E. Marianne Nyberg; two *s.* *Educ:* Bancroft's Sch.; St John's Coll., Cantab (MA). RAF fighter pilot, 266 & 234 Squadrons, National Service, 1953. Radio Bremen, 1955–56; joined The Times, 1958, Foreign Correspondent, 1961; served in Paris, Algeria, Tokyo, Indonesia, Vietnam, Cambodia, Malaysia and Singapore until 1970; Chief Washington Corresp., 1970–77; Political Editor, 1977–81; Home Editor, 1981–82; Exec. Editor (Home and Foreign), 1982. *Recreations:* skiing, hill walking, tennis. *Address:* 5 Woodsyre, SE26 6SS. *T:* 01–761 0076. *Club:* Garrick.

EMERY, George Edward, CB 1980; Director General of Defence Accounts, Ministry of Defence, 1973–80, retired; *b* 2 March 1920; *s* of late Frederick and Florence Emery; *m* 1946, Margaret (*née* Rice); two *d.* *Educ:* Bemrose Sch., Derby. Admiralty, 1938; Min. of Fuel and Power, 1946; Min. of Supply, 1951; Min. of Aviation, 1959; Min. of Technology, 1967; Principal Exec. Officer, 1967; Asst Sec., Min. of Aviation Supply, 1970; Ministry of Defence: Asst Sec., 1971; Exec. Dir, 1973; Under-Sec., 1973. *Recreations:* amateur dramatics, gardening. *Address:* 3 The Orchard, Freshford, Bath BA3 6EW. *T:* Limpley Stoke 3561.

EMERY, Joan Dawson, (Mrs Jack Emery); *see* Bakewell, J. D.

EMERY, Joyce Margaret; *see* Zachariah, J. M.

EMERY, Sir Peter (Frank Hannibal), Kt 1982; MA; FInstPS; MP (C) Honiton, since 1967 (Reading, 1959–66); *b* 27 Feb. 1926; *s* of late F. G. Emery, Highgate; *m* 1st, 1954 (marr. diss.); one *s* one *d*; 2nd, 1972, Elizabeth, *y d* of late G. J. R. Monnington; one *s* one *d.* *Educ:* Scotch Plains, New Jersey, USA; Oriel Coll., Oxford. Joint Founder and First Secretary of the Bow Group. Parliamentary Private Secretary in Foreign Office, War Dept and Min. of Labour, 1960–64; Jt Hon. Secretary, 1922 Cttee, 1964–65; Opposition Front Bench Spokesman for Treasury, Economics and Trade, 1964–66; Parliamentary Under-Secretary of State: DTI, 1972–74; Dept of Energy, 1974; Member: Select Cttee on Industry and Trade, 1979–; Select Cttee on Procedure, 1982– (Chm., 1983). Jt Vice-Chm., Conservative Finance Cttee, 1970–72; Chairman: Cons. Housing and Construction Cttee, 1974–75. Member, Delegation to CPA Conference: Westminster, 1961; Canada, 1962; Fiji, 1981; Leader, Delegn to Kenya, 1977; Delegate: Council of Europe and WEU, 1962–64, 1970–72; North Atlantic Assembly, 1983– (Chm., Science and Technology Cttee, 1985–). Chm., Shenley Trust Services Ltd; Director: Property Growth Insurance, 1966–72; Phillips Petroleum-UK Ltd, 1963–72; Institute of Purchasing and Supply, 1961–72; Secretary-General, European Federation of Purchasing, 1962–72; Chairman, Consultative Council of Professional Management Organisations, 1968–72. *Recreations:* sliding down mountains, tennis, cricket, golf and bridge (Capt., H of C team, 1984–). *Address:* Tytherleigh Manor, near Axminster, Devon. *T:* South Chard 20309; 15 Tufton Court, Tufton Street, SW1. *T:* 01–222 6666; (office) 01–437 6666. *Clubs:* Carlton, Portland, Turf; Leander (Henley-on-Thames).

EMERY-WALLIS, Frederick Alfred John, FSA; Leader, Hampshire County Council, since 1975 (County Councillor, since 1973; Vice-Chairman, 1975–76); Chairman, Southern Tourist Board, since 1976; *b* 11 May 1927; *o s* of Frederick Henry Wallis and Lillian Grace Emery Coles; *m* 1960, Solange, *o d* of William Victor Randall, London, and Albertine Beaupère, La Guerche-sur-l'Aubois; two *d.* *Educ:* Blake's Academy, Portsmouth. Royal Signals SCU4 (Middle East Radio Security), 1945–48. Portsmouth City Council, 1961–74; Lord Mayor, 1968–69; Alderman, 1969–74. Chm., ACC Recreation Cttee, 1982–85. Chairman: Portsmouth Develt and Estates Cttee, 1965–74; Portsmouth Papers Editorial Bd, 1966–82; S Hampshire Plan Adv. Cttee, 1969–74; Portsmouth South Cons. and Unionist Assoc., 1971–79, 1982–85; Portsmouth Record Series Adv. Panel, 1982–; Hampshire Archives Trust, 1986–; Member: Economic Planning Council for the South East, 1969–74; British Library Adv. Council, 1979–84, 1986–; Council, British Records Assoc., 1979–; Library and Information Services Council, 1980–83; Mary Rose Develt Trust, 1980–; Arts Council of GB Reg. Adv. Cttee, 1984–. Vice-Chm., Portsmouth Polytechnic, 1967–75; Pres., Hampshire Field Club, 1971–74. Vice-Pres., Mottisfont Soc., 1978–. Pres., Portsmouth YMCA, 1978–. Hon. Fellow, Portsmouth Polytechnic, 1972. FSA 1980. Hon. FRIBA 1985. *Publications:* various publications concerning history and develt of Portsmouth and Hampshire. *Recreations:* book collecting, music. *Address:* Froddington, Craneswater Park, Portsmouth. *T:* Portsmouth 731409.

EMETT, Rowland, OBE 1978; FSIAD; artist and inventor; *b* 1906; *m* 1941, Mary; one *d.* Contributor to Punch for many years. In 1951 The Far Twittering to Oyster Creek Railway forsook the pages of Punch and appeared full-blown and passenger-carrying at

The Festival Gardens, for The Festival of Britain. The impact of this led to a succession of large three-dimensional, Gothick-Kinetic, fully-working inventions of ever-increasing complexity, which have been exhibited all over the world. Constructed the Edwardian inventions for the film Chitty Chitty, Bang Bang, 1968. Built his first permanent construction The Rhythmical Time Fountain, for the City of Nottingham Victoria Centre, 1974. The fully-working three-dimensional inventions include: the Exploratory Moon-probe Lunacycle "Maud"; the Borg Warner Vintage Car of the Future, permanently in the Museum of Science and Industry, Chicago; SS Pussiewillow II, personal air-and-space vehicle, commnd by and housed in Nat. Mus. of Air and Space, Smithsonian Instn, Washington DC. The Featherstone Kite Openwork Basket-weave Gentleman's Flying Machine, together with seven other inventions, have been acquired by Ontario Science Centre, Toronto. Pussiewillow III, a celestial cats'-cradle, commnd by Basildon New Town. Dawn Flight: mist clearing, mallard rising, and the early Up Slow Surprised, acquired by Tate Gallery for permanent collection, 1985. *Publications:* collections from Punch incl. Home Rails Preferred, Engines Aunties and Others, and Saturday Slow; The Early Morning Milk Train, 1978; Alarms and Excursions, 1978; two signed limited-edn prints, 1978. *Address:* Wild Goose Cottage, 113 East End Lane, Ditchling, Hassocks, West Sussex BN6 8UR. *T:* Hassocks 2459; Nell Gwynn House, Sloane Avenue, SW3 3AX.

EMLYN, Viscount; Colin Robert Vaughan Campbell; *b* 30 June 1962; *s* and *heir* of Earl Cawdor, *qv. Educ:* Eton; St Peter's College, Oxford. Member, James Bridal Meml Soc., London.

EMLYN JONES, John Hubert, CBE 1986 (MBE (mil.) 1941); FRICS; JP; Member of the Lands Tribunal, since 1968; *b* 6 Aug. 1915; *s* of late Ernest Pearson Jones and Katharine Cole Jones (*née* Nicholas); *m* 1954, Louise Anne Montague, *d* of late Raymond Ralph Horwood Hazell; two *s* one *d. Educ:* Dulwich. FRICS 1939. Served War, RE, 1939–46: Major 1943. Partner, Rees-Reynolds and Hunt, and Alfred Savill & Sons, Chartered Surveyors, 1950–68. President: Rating Surveyors Assoc., 1965–66 (Hon. Mem. 1968); Climbers' Club, 1966–69 (Hon. Mem. 1970); Alpine Club, 1980–82. Mem. Council, RICS, 1964–69. Mem. Bureau, 1964–72, Treasurer 1967–69, Fédération Internationale des Géomètres; Mem. Council, Rainer Foundn, 1965–85 (Chm. 1968–71). Mem., expedns to Himalayas: Annapurna, 1950; Ama Dablam, 1959 (Leader). High Sheriff, Bucks, 1967–68, JP 1968. *Publications:* articles and revs in mountaineering jls. *Recreations:* mountaineering, music. *Address:* Ivinghoe Manor, Leighton Buzzard, Beds. *T:* Cheddington 668202. *Clubs:* Garrick, Alpine.

EMMERSON, Rt. Rev. Ralph; an Assistant Bishop, Diocese of Ripon, since 1986; *b* 7 June 1913; *s* of Thomas and Alys Mary Emmerson; *m* 1942, Ann Hawthorn Bygate (*d* 1982); no *c. Educ:* Leeds Grammar Sch.; King's Coll., London (BD, AKC); Westcott House, Cambridge. Leeds Educn Authority Youth Employment Dept, 1930–35; Curate, St George's, Leeds, 1938–41; Priest-in-Charge, Seacroft Estate, 1941–48; Rector of Methley and Vicar of Mickletown, 1949–56; Vicar of Headingley, 1956–66; Hon. Canon of Ripon Cath., 1964; Residentiary Canon and Canon Missioner for Dio. Ripon, 1966–72; Bishop Suffragan of Knaresborough, 1972–79; Asst Bishop, Dio. Wakefield, 1980–86. *Address:* Flat 1, 15 High Saint Agnesgate, Ripon HG4 1QR. *T:* Ripon 701626.

EMMET, Dorothy Mary, MA Oxon, Cantab and Manchester; *b* 1904; *d* of late Rev. C. W. Emmet, Fellow of University Coll., Oxford, and late Gertrude Julia Emmet (*née* Weir). *Educ:* St Mary's Hall, Brighton; Lady Margaret Hall, Oxford. Classical Exhibitioner, Lady Margaret Hall, Oxford, 1923; Hon. Mods Class I, 1925; Lit. Hum. Class I, 1927. Tutor, Maesyrhaf Settlement, Rhondda Valley, 1927–28 and 1931–32; Commonwealth Fellow, Radcliffe Coll., Cambridge, Mass, USA, 1928–30; Research Fellow, Somerville Coll., Oxford, 1930–31; lecturer in Philosophy, Armstrong Coll., Newcastle upon Tyne, 1932–38 (now Newcastle Univ.); lecturer in Philosophy of Religion, University of Manchester, 1938–45; Reader in Philosophy, 1945–46; Prof. of Philosophy, University of Manchester, 1946–66; Prof. Emeritus, 1966. Stanton Lecturer in Philosophy of Religion, University of Cambridge, 1950–53. Visiting Professor: Barnard Coll., Columbia Univ., New York, 1960–61; Univ. of Ibadan, Nigeria, 1974. President Aristotelian Society, 1953–54. Dean of the Faculty of Arts, University of Manchester, 1962–64. Hon. Fellow, Lady Margaret Hall, Oxford. Fellow, Lucy Cavendish Coll., Cambridge, 1967, Emeritus Fellow, 1981. Hon. DLitt: Glasgow, 1974; Leicester, 1976. *Publications:* Whitehead's Philosophy of Organism, 1932, 2nd edn 1982; Philosophy and Faith, 1936; The Nature of Metaphysical Thinking, 1945; Function, Purpose and Powers, 1958, 2nd edn 1972; Rules, Roles and Relations, 1966; (ed with Alasdair MacIntyre) Sociological Theory and Philosophical Analysis, 1970; The Moral Prism, 1979; The Effectiveness of Causes, 1984; contributions to philosophical journals. *Recreations:* gardening, reading. *Address:* 11 Millington Road, Cambridge.
See also Prof. R. C. Wilson.

EMMETT, Bryan David; Under Secretary, since 1980, and Head, Oil Division, since 1986, Department of Energy; *b* 15 Feb. 1941; *m* 1960, Moira (*née* Miller); one *s. Educ:* Tadcaster Grammar Sch. Clerical Officer, Min. of Labour, and National Service, 1958–59; Exec. Officer, War Dept, 1959–64; Asst Principal, MOP, 1965–69 (Asst Private Sec. to Ministers of Power, 1968–69); Principal, Electricity Div., DTI, 1969–74; Department of Energy: Principal, and Private Sec. to Minister of State, 1974–75; Asst Sec., and Principal Private Sec. to Sec. of State for Energy, 1975–76; Asst Sec., Petroleum Engrg Div., 1977–80; Under Sec., and Principal Estab. Officer, 1980–81; Principal Estab. and Finance Officer, 1981–82; Chief Exec., Employment Div., MSC, 1982–85; Head, Energy Policy Div., Dept of Energy, 1985–86. *Recreations:* National Hunt racing, hacking, golf. *Address:* Department of Energy, Thames House South, Millbank, SW1P 4QJ.

EMMETT, Harold Leslie; Assistant Under-Secretary of State, Ministry of Defence, 1972–79; *b* 20 Sept. 1919; 4th *s* of Alfred and Charlotte Emmett (*née* Frith); *m* 1943, Phyllis Mabel (*née* Tranah); three *s* one *d. Educ:* Gillingham Grammar Sch., Kent. Joined Civil Service (Admiralty), 1938; transf. to War Office, 1948; Principal, 1951; Asst Sec., 1960; Command Sec., HQ BAOR, 1964–67; Imperial Defence College, 1968; seconded to Home Office for service with New Scotland Yard, 1969–70. *Recreation:* golf. *Address:* 9 Oakdale Road, Tunbridge Wells, Kent. *T:* Tunbridge Wells 22658.

EMMS, David Acfield, MA; Director, London House for Overseas Graduates, since 1987; *b* 16 Feb. 1925; *s* of late Archibald George Emms and Winifred Gladys (*née* Richards); *m* 1950, Pamela Baker Speed; three *s* one *d. Educ:* Tonbridge Sch.; Brasenose Coll., Oxford. BA Hons Mod. Langs Oxford, 1950, Diploma in Education, 1951; MA 1954. Rugby football, Oxford *v* Cambridge, 1949, 1950. Served War of 1939–45, RA, 1943–47. Undergraduate, 1947–51; Asst Master, Uppingham Sch. (Head of Mod. Languages Dept, CO, CCF Contingent), 1951–60; Headmaster of: Cranleigh School, 1960–70; Sherborne School, 1970–74; Master, Dulwich Coll., 1975–86. Chm., HMC, 1984; Vice-Pres., ISCO, 1973–. Dep. Chm., E-SU; Mem. Council, City Univ., 1986–; Governor: St Felix Sch., Southwold; Brambletye; Feltonfleet Sch., Cobham. President: Alleyn Club, 1985; Brasenose Soc., 1987. Mem. Council, Fairbridge Soc., 1984–. Freeman, City of London; First Warden, Skinners' Co. *Publication:* HMC Schools and British Industry, 1981. *Recreations:* radical gardening, sailing. *Address:* London House, Mecklenburgh Square,

WC1N 2AB; Seaforth, Spinney Lane, Itchenor, W Sussex. *T:* Chichester 512585. *Clubs:* East India, Devonshire, Sports and Public Schools; Vincent's (Oxford); Itchenor Sailing.

EMMS, John Frederick George, FIA; a Deputy Chairman, Commercial Union Assurance Company Ltd, since 1983 (Vice-Chairman, 1979–83); *b* 2 Sept. 1920; *s* of late John Stanley Emms and Alice Maud Emms (*née* Davies); *m* 1942, Margaret Alison Hay; one *s* one *d* (and one *s* decd). *Educ:* Harrow County Sch.; Latymer Upper Sch. FIA. Served War RA/RCS, 1939–46. Joined Commercial Union Assurance Co. Ltd, 1938; Investment Manager, 1968–70; Chief Investment Manager, 1970–72; Dir, 1972; Exec. Dir, 1974; Chief General Manager, 1977–82. Director: Barclays Bank UK, 1981–; British Technol. Gp., 1979–85. Mem., NEB, 1979–. Mem., British Red Cross Finance Cttee, 1973–. Mem. Adv. Panel, British Coal (formerly NCB) Superannuation and Pension Schemes, 1973–; Chm. Trustees, PO Staff Superannuation Scheme, 1983–86. *Recreations:* sport, reading. *Address:* 7 Eastglade, Pinner, Middlesex HA5 3AN. *T:* 01–868 6151.

EMPEY, Most Rev. Walton Newcombe Francis; *see* Meath and Kildare, Bishop of.

EMPSON, Adm. Sir (Leslie) Derek, GBE 1975; KCB 1973 (CB 1969); Rear-Admiral of the United Kingdom, since 1984; Consultant, THORN EMI (formerly EMI) plc, since 1976; *b* 29 Oct. 1918; *s* of Frank Harold Empson and Madeleine Norah Empson (*née* Burge); *m* 1958, Diana Elizabeth Kelly; one *s* one *d. Educ:* Eastbourne Coll.; Clare Coll., Cambridge (Class. Exhibn). Athletics Blue, 1939; BA 1940. Joined Royal Navy for pilot duties, 1940; commd as Sub-Lieut (A) RNVR, 1940; flew as Fleet Air Arm pilot, 1940–45; perm. commn in RN, 1944; Naval Asst to First Sea Lord, 1957–59; Comd HMS Eagle, 1963–65; Imp. Def. Coll., 1966; Flag Officer, Aircraft Carriers, 1967–68; Asst Chief of Naval Staff (Operations and Air), 1968–69; Comdr, Far East Fleet, 1969–71; Second Sea Lord and Chief of Naval Personnel, 1971–74; C-in-C Naval Home Comd and FO Portsmouth Area, 1974–75; Flag ADC to The Queen, 1974–75. Comdr 1952; Captain 1957; Rear-Adm. 1967; Vice-Adm. 1970; Adm. 1972. Chm. of Governors, Eastbourne Coll., 1972–. *Address:* Deepdale, Hambledon, Hants. *T:* Hambledon 451. *Clubs:* MCC, Naval; Hawks (Cambridge), Achilles.

EMSLIE, family name of **Baron Emslie.**

EMSLIE, Baron *cr* 1980 (Life Peer), of Potterton in the District of Gordon; **George Carlyle Emslie,** PC 1972; MBE 1946; Lord Justice-General of Scotland and Lord President of the Court of Session, since 1972; *b* 6 Dec. 1919; *s* of late Alexander and Jessie Blair Emslie; *m* Lilias Ann Mailer Hannington; three *s. Educ:* The High School of Glasgow; The University of Glasgow (MA, LLB). Commissioned A&SH, 1940; served War of 1939–45 (despatches): North Africa, Italy, Greece, Austria, 1942–46; psc Haifa, 1944; Brigade Major (Infantry), 1944–46. Advocate, 1948; Advocate Depute (Sheriff Courts), 1955; QC (Scotland) 1957; Sheriff of Perth and Angus, 1963–66; Dean of Faculty of Advocates, 1965–70; Senator of Coll. of Justice in Scotland and Lord of Session, 1970–72. Chm., Scottish Agricultural Wages Bd, 1969–73; Mem., Council on Tribunals (Scottish Cttee), 1962–70. Hon. Bencher: Inner Temple, 1974; Inn of Court of N Ireland, 1981. Hon. LLD Glasgow, 1973. *Recreation:* golf. *Address:* 47 Heriot Row, Edinburgh EH3 6EX. *T:* 031–225 3657. *Clubs:* Caledonian; New (Edinburgh); The Honourable Company of Edinburgh Golfers.

EMSLIE, Prof. Ronald Douglas, FDSRCS; Dean of Dental Studies, Guy's Hospital Medical and Dental Schools, 1968–80, retired; Professor of Periodontology and Preventive Dentistry, University of London, 1970–80, now Emeritus; *b* 9 March 1915; *s* of late Alexander G. H. Emslie and Elizabeth Spence; *m* 1951, Dorothy, *d* of William A. Dennis, Paris, Ill, USA; four *s. Educ:* Felsted Sch.; Guy's Hosp. Dental Sch., London (BDS); Univ. of Illinois, Chicago (MSc). FDSRCS Eng., 1950; DRD (Edin), 1978. Served War: Surg. Lt (D) RNVR, 1943–46; Surg. Lt Comdr (D) RNVR, 1946. Half-time Asst in Dept of Preventive Dentistry, Guy's Hosp., 1946–48, also in private practice with Mr E. B. Dowsett; Research Fellow, Univ. of Illinois, Chicago, 1948–49; Head of Dept of Preventive Dentistry, Guy's Hosp., 1949–55; Reader in Preventive Dentistry, Univ. of London (Guy's Hosp. Dental Sch.), 1956–62; Prof. of Preventive Dentistry, Univ. of London (Guy's Hosp. Dental Sch.), 1963–70. Pres., Brit. Soc. of Periodontology, 1959–60; Chm., Dental Health Cttee of BDA, 1963–69; Member: Internat. Dental Fedn; Internat. Assoc. for Dental Research; Dental Educn Adv. Council (Chm., 1978–80); Bd of Faculty of Dental Surgery, RCS, 1966–81 (Vice-Dean, 1976–77); Fluoridation Soc. (Chm. 1970–80); Bd of Studies in Dentistry, Univ. of London (Chm., 1975–77). Past Pres., Odontological Section, RSM; Vis. Lectr, Univ. of Illinois, 1956; Nuffield Grant to study dental aspects of facial gangrene, in Nigeria, Sept.-Dec. 1961; Sci. Advr, Brit. Dental Jl, 1961–80 (Sci. Asst Ed., 1951–61); Consultant in Periodontology to RN, 1971–80. Fellow, BDA. *Publications:* various contribs to dental literature. *Recreations:* tennis, sailing, old motor cars. *Address:* Little Hale, Woodland Way, Kingswood, Surrey KT20 6NW. *T:* Mogador 832662.

EMSON, Air Marshal Sir Reginald (Herbert Embleton), KBE 1966 (CBE 1946); CB 1959; AFC 1941; Inspector-General of the Royal Air Force, 1967–69; *b* 11 Jan. 1912; *s* of Francis Reginald Emson, Hitcham, Buckinghamshire; *m* 1934, Doreen Marjory, *d* of Hugh Duke, Holyport, Maidenhead, Berkshire; two *s* two *d. Educ:* Christ's Hospital; RAF Coll., Cranwell. Joined RAF, 1931; served War of 1939–45 in Aeroplane Armament Establishment Gunnery Research Unit, Exeter; Fighter Command Headquarters and Central Fighter Establishment. Director, Armament Research and Development (Air), Ministry of Supply, 1950–59; Commander RAF Staff and Air Attaché, British Defence Staffs, Washington, 1961–63; Asst Chief of Air Staff (Operational Requirements), 1963–66; Dep. Chief Air Staff, 1966–67. Group Captain, 1943; Air Commodore, 1958; Air Vice-Marshal, 1962; Air Marshal (Acting), 1966. *Address:* Vor Cottage, Holyport, Maidenhead, Berks. *T:* Maidenhead 21992. *Club:* Royal Air Force.

ENCOMBE, Viscount; John Francis Thomas Marie Joseph Columba Fidelis Scott; *b* 9 July 1962; *s* and *heir* of 5th Earl of Eldon, *qv.*

ENDERBY, Prof. John Edwin, FRS 1985; Director-Adjoint, Institut Laue-Langevin, Grenoble, since 1985; H. O. Wills Professor of Physics, University of Bristol, since 1981; *b* 16 Jan. 1931; *s* of Thomas Edwin Enderby and Rheita Rebecca Hollinshead (*née* Stather); *m*; one *s* three *d. Educ:* Chester Grammar Sch.; London Univ. (BSc, PhD). Lecturer in Physics: Coll. of Technology, Huddersfield, 1957–60; Univ. of Sheffield, 1960–67; Reader in Physics, Univ. of Sheffield, 1967–69; Prof. in Physics and Head of the Dept, Univ. of Leicester, 1969–76; Prof. of Physics, Bristol Univ., 1976–. Visiting Fellow, Battelle Inst., 1968–69; Vis. Prof., Univ. of Guelph, Ont., 1978. Member: Physics Cttee, SRC, 1974–77; Neutron Beam Res. Cttee, SRC, 1974–80 (Chm., 1977–80). Mem. Council, Institut Laue-Langevin, Grenoble, 1973–80. FInstP 1970 (Chm., SW Br., 1979–). Associate Editor, Philosophical Magazine, 1975–81. *Publications:* (jointly): Physics of Simple Liquids, 1968; Amorphous and Liquid Semiconductors, 1974; many publications on the structure and properties of liquids in: Phil. Mag. Adv. Phys, Jl Phys, Proc. Royal Soc., etc. *Recreations:* gardening, watching Association football. *Address:* Institut Laue-Langevin, Avenue des Martyrs, 156X-38042 Grenoble, France; H. H. Wills Physics Laboratory, Tyndall Avenue, Bristol BS8 1TL. *T:* Bristol 24161.

ENDERBY, Kenneth Albert; General Manager, Runcorn Development Corporation, 1978–81; *b* 7 Aug. 1920; *s* of Albert William Enderby and Frances Enderby; *m* 1946, Mary Florence; one *s* two *d*. *Educ:* Nottingham High Sch.; London Univ. (BSc Econs). IPFA. Served War, Royal Corps of Signals (TA), 1939–46: BEF, MEF, CMF (mentioned in despatches, 1944); Captain. Local Govt Finance: Nottingham, 1936–51; Buckingham, 1951–53; Chief Auditor, City of Sheffield, 1953–56; Dep. City Treasurer, Coventry, 1956–64; Chief Finance Officer, Runcorn Develt Corp., 1964–78. *Recreations:* gardening, camping, fresh air, zymology. *Address:* Four Winds, 2 Helmeth Road, Church Stretton, Salop SY6 7AS. *T:* Church Stretton 722328.

ENDERBY, Col Samuel, CVO 1977; DSO 1943; MC 1939; JP; *b* 15 Sept. 1907; *s* of Col Samuel Enderby and Mary Cuninghame; *m* 1936, Pamela, *e d* of Major Charles Beck Hornby, DSO; two *s* one *d*. *Educ:* Uppingham Sch.; RMC Sandhurst. Regular soldier, commissioned 5th Fusiliers, 1928. Served War, 1939–46: MEF, CMF, comd 2/4th KOYLI and 2/5 Leicester Regt; Commandant, Sch. of Infantry: ACRE, 1945–46; Netheravon, 1947–48; comd, 7th Bn Royal Northumberland Fusiliers, 1949; retd 1949. JP 1956; High Sheriff of Northumberland, 1968. Mem., Hon. Corps of Gentlemen at Arms, 1954–77, Standard Bearer, 1976–77. *Address:* The Riding, Hexham, Northumberland. *T:* Hexham 2250. *Club:* Army and Navy.

ENFIELD, Viscount; William Robert Byng; *b* 10 May 1964; *s* and *heir* of 8th Earl of Strafford, *qv*. *Educ:* Winchester Coll.; Durham Univ. *Address:* Abbotts Worthy House, Abbotts Worthy, Winchester, Hants.

ENGESET, Jetmund, FRCSE; FRCSG; Senior Lecturer in Surgery, University of Aberdeen, since 1974; Surgeon to the Queen in Scotland, since 1985; *b* 22 July 1938; *s* of Arne K. Engeset and Marta Engeset; *m* 1966, Anne Graeme (*née* Robertson); two *d*. *Educ:* Slemdal and Ris Skole, Oslo, Norway; Oslo University; Aberdeen University (MB ChB, ChM Hons). House Officer (Surgical and Medical), Aberdeen Royal Infirmary, 1964–65; Aberdeen University: Res. Assistant, Dept of Surgery, 1965–67; Surgical Registrar, 1967–70; Lectr in Surgery, 1970–74; Head of Dept of Surgery, 1982–85 (seconded to Salgrenska Hosp. Surgical Unit, Gothenburg, Sweden, 1972–74). *Publications:* papers on microcirculation, vascular surgery, organ preservation and tissue transplantation. *Recreations:* skiing, angling, squash, gardening. *Address:* Pine Lodge, 315 North Deeside Road, Milltimber, Aberdeen, Aberdeenshire. *T:* Aberdeen 733753.

ENGHOLM, Sir Basil Charles, KCB 1968 (CB 1964); Director, Sadlers Wells Theatre Trust, since 1975; *b* 2 Aug. 1912; *o s* of late C. F. G. Engholm; *m* 1936, Nancy, *er d* of Lifford Hewitt, St Anthony, Rye; one *d*. *Educ:* Tonbridge Sch.; Sorbonne, Paris; Sidney Sussex Coll., Cambridge (Law Tripos, MA). Member of Gray's Inn; Metal business, New York, 1933–34; entered Ministry of Agriculture and Fisheries, 1935; War of 1939–45: part-time NFS; Principal Private Secretary to Minister of Agriculture and Fisheries, 1943–45; Asst Secretary, 1945; Under-Secretary, 1954; Fisheries Secretary, 1960–62; Dep. Secretary, 1964–67; Permanent Sec., MAFF, 1968–72. Dir, Comfin Ltd, 1973–85 (Consultant, 1985–86). Gov., BFI, 1978–81 (Chm., 1978–81); Trustee, Theatre Trust, 1977–84. *Recreations:* reading, painting, opera, ballet, films, looking at pictures. *Address:* 93 Meadway, NW11. *T:* 01–455 3975. *Club:* United Oxford & Cambridge University.

ENGLAND, Frank Raymond Wilton; *b* 24 Aug. 1911; *s* of Joseph and Florence England; *m*; one *d*. *Educ:* Christ's Coll., Finchley. Served War, Pilot, RAF, 1941–45. Apprenticeship with Daimler Co. Ltd, Hendon, 1927–32; Racing Mechanic to: Sir Henry Birkin, Whitney Straight, ERA Ltd, Richard Seaman, B. Bira, 1932–38; Service Engr, Service Dept Supt, Alvis Limited, 1938–40. Service Manager, Jaguar Cars Ltd, 1946–56; Service Dir, 1956–61; Asst Man. Dir, 1961–66; Dep. Man. Dir, 1966–67; Jt Man. Dir, 1967; Dep. Chm., 1968; Chm. and Chief Executive, 1972; retd as Chm., Jan. 1974. *Recreation:* motor sport. *Address:* 196 Gmundnerberg, 4813 Altmünster, Austria. *T:* 07612 88316. *Clubs:* Royal Air Force, British Racing Drivers'.

ENGLAND, Glyn, BSc(Eng); FEng, FIEE, FIMechE, CBIM; Director, F. H. Lloyd (Holdings) plc, since 1982; Consultant: World Bank; Commission of the European Communities; Chairman, Council for Environmental Conservation, since 1983; *b* 19 April 1921; *m* 1942, Tania Reichenbach; two *d*. *Educ:* Penarth County Sch.; Queen Mary Coll., London Univ. (BSc (Eng)); London School of Economics. Department of Scientific and Industrial Research, 1939. War service, 1942–47. Chief Ops Engr, CEGB, 1966–71; Dir-Gen., SW Region, 1971–73; Chm., SW Electricity Bd, 1973–77; part-time Mem., 1975–77, Chm., 1977–82, CEGB. Mem., British Nat. Cttee, World Energy Conf., 1977–82; Vice-Pres., Internat. Union of Producers and Distributors of Electrical Energy, 1981–82. Chm., Dartington Inst., 1985–. Sometime Labour Mem., Herts CC; Mem. Council, Magistrates' Assoc. JP Welwyn, Herts, 1962–71. Hon. DSc Bath, 1981. *Publications:* (with Rex Savidge) Landscape in the Making; papers on: Clean Air, Conservation of Water Resources, Economic Growth and the Electricity Supply Industry, Security of Electricity Supplies, Planning for Uncertainty, Railways and Power (IMechE Tritton Lecture). *Recreation:* actively enjoying the countryside. *Address:* Woodbridge Farm, Ubley, Bristol BS18 6PX. *T:* Blagdon 62479.

ENGLE, Sir George (Lawrence Jose), KCB 1983 (CB 1976); QC 1983; First Parliamentary Counsel, 1981–86; *b* 13 Sept. 1926; *o s* of late Lawrence Engle; *m* 1956, Irene, *d* of late Heinz Lachmann; three *d*. *Educ:* Charterhouse (scholar); Christ Church, Oxford (Marjoribanks and Dixon schols, MA). Served RA, 1945–48 (2nd Lt, 1947). Firsts in Mods and Greats; Cholmeley Schol., Lincoln's Inn, 1952. Called to Bar, Lincoln's Inn, 1953, Bencher, 1984. Joined Parly Counsel Office, 1957; seconded as First Parly Counsel, Fedn of Nigeria, 1965–67; Parly Counsel, 1970–80; Second Parly Counsel, 1980–81; with Law Commn, 1971–73. Pres., Commonwealth Assoc. of Legislative Counsel, 1983–86. *Publications:* Law for Landladies, 1955; contributor to: Ideas, 1954; O Rare Hoffnung, 1960; The Oxford Companion to English Literature, 1985. *Recreations:* book-hunting, oriental and Islamic pots, bricolage. *Address:* 32 Wood Lane, Highgate, N6. *T:* 01–340 9750.

ENGLEHART, Robert Michael; QC 1986; *b* 1 Oct. 1943; *s* of G. A. F. and K. P. Englehart; *m* 1971, Rosalind Mary Foster; one *s* two *d*. *Educ:* St Edward's Sch., Oxford; Trinity Coll., Oxford (MA); Harvard Law School (LLM); Bologna Centre (Dip. in Internat. Relns). Assistente, Univ. of Florence, 1968. Called to the Bar, Middle Temple, 1969; practising barrister, 1969–. *Publication:* (contrib.) Il Controllo Giudiziario: a comparative study of civil procedure, 1968. *Recreations:* shooting, cricket, windsurfing. *Address:* 2 Hare Court, Temple, EC4Y 7BH. *T:* 01–583 1770. *Club:* MCC.

ENGLISH, Cyril; Director since 1978, and Chief General Manager, 1981–85, Nationwide Building Society; *b* 18 Feb. 1923; *s* of Joseph and Mary Hannah English; *m* 1945, Mary Brockbank; two *d*. *Educ:* Ashton-under-Lyne Grammar School. ALCM; CBIM. Joined Nationwide Building Society, 1939; Asst Secretary, 1961; Asst General Manager, 1967; General Manager, 1971; Deputy Chief General Manager, 1974. *Recreations:* golf, music. *Address:* Ashton Grange, Cedar Drive, Pangbourne, Berks. *T:* Pangbourne 3841. *Club:* Calcot Park Golf (Reading).

ENGLISH, Sir Cyril (Rupert), Kt 1972; retired; Director-General, City and Guilds of London Institute, 1968–76; *b* 19 April 1913; *m*; two *s*. *Educ:* Northgate Sch., Ipswich. BScEng Ext. London, 1934. Technical teacher, 1935–39. Served Royal Navy, 1939–46, Lieut-Commander (E). HM Inspector of Schools, 1946–55; Staff Inspector (Engineering), 1955–58; Chief Inspector of Further Education, in connection with Industry and Commerce, 1958–65; Senior Chief Inspector, Dept of Education and Science, 1965–67. Member, Anglo-American Productivity Team, 1951; attended Commonwealth Education Conferences, Delhi, 1962, Ottawa, 1964. Chairman: British Assoc. for Commercial and Industrial Educn, 1970–71, 1971–72; RAF Educn Adv. Cttee; Member: Services Colleges Cttee, 1965–66; Adv. Bd, RAF Coll., Cranwell; Academic Adv. Council, Royal Defence Acad.; Bd of Dirs, Industrial Training Service; Central Training Council; CTC Gen. Policy Cttee; Nat. Adv. Council for Educn in Industry and Commerce; Council for Tech. Educn and Training for Overseas Countries (Bd Mem., Chm. Educn Cttee); Reg. Adv. Council for Technol. Educn (London and Home Counties); Schools Science and Technology Cttee; Educn Cttee, IMechE; Associated Examining Bd; Cttee of Inquiry into Training of Teachers (James Cttee); Standing Conf. on Schs' Science and Technology; Cttee on Regular Officer training (Army). Vice-Pres., Soc. Electronic and Radio Technicians, 1972–74, Pres., 1975. Governor, Imperial Coll. FIMechE; FIProdE; FIMarE. Hon. Fellow, Inst. of Road Transport Engrs, 1971. Hon. Fellow, Manchester Polytechnic, 1976. Hon. DTech Brunel, 1970; Hon. DSc Loughborough, 1973; DUniv Open, 1974. *Address:* 12 Pineheath Road, High Kelling, Holt, Norfolk.

ENGLISH, Sir David, Kt 1982; Editor: Daily Mail, since 1971; Mail on Sunday, 1982; Vice-Chairman, Associated Newspapers Group, since 1986; *b* 26 May 1931; *m* 1954, Irene Mainwood; one *s* two *d*. *Educ:* Bournemouth Sch. Daily Mirror, 1951–53; Feature Editor, Daily Sketch, 1956; Foreign Correspondent: Sunday Dispatch, 1959; Daily Express, 1960; Washington Correspdt, Express, 1961–63; Chief American Correspdt, Express, 1963–65; Foreign Editor, Express, 1965–67; Associate Editor, Express, 1967–69; Editor, Daily Sketch, 1969–71. Mem. Bd, Assoc. of British Editors, 1985–. *Publication:* Divided They Stand (a British view of the 1968 American Presidential Election), 1969. *Recreations:* reading, ski-ing, boating. *Address:* Daily Mail, EC4Y 0JA. *T:* 01–353 6000. *Clubs:* Press, Royal Temple Yacht.

ENGLISH, Rev. Donald; General Secretary, Methodist Church Division of Home Mission, since 1982; Moderator, Free Church Federal Council, 1986–87; President of the Methodist Conference, 1978–79; *b* 20 July 1930; *s* of Robert and Ena Forster English; *m* 1962, Bertha Forster Ludlow; two *s*. *Educ:* Consett Grammar Sch.; University Coll., Leicester; Wesley House, Cambridge. BA London; DipEd Leicester; MA Cantab. Education Officer, RAF, 1953–55; Travelling Sec., Inter-Varsity Fellowship, 1955–58; Asst Tutor, Wesley Coll., Headingley, 1960–62; ordained into Methodist Ministry, 1962; New Testament Tutor, Trinity Coll., Umuahia, E Nigeria, 1962–66; Circuit Minister, Cullercoats, Northumberland, 1966–72; Tutor in Historical Theology, Hartley Victoria Coll., Manchester (Lord Rank Chair), 1972–73; Tutor in Practical Theol. and Methodism, Wesley Coll., Bristol (Lord Rank Chair), 1973–82. Member, World Methodist Exec., 1976–; Vice-Chm., World Methodist Council Exec., 1986–. Hon. DD Asbury, USA, 1979. *Publications:* Evangelism and Worship, 1971; God in the Gallery, 1975; Christian Discipleship, 1977; Windows on the Passion, 1978; From Wesley's Chair: Presidential Addresses, 1979; Why Believe in Jesus?: evangelistic reflections for Lent, 1986; contrib. Expository Times, Epworth Rev., Themelios, Proc. World Methodist Council. *Recreations:* gardening, reading. *Address:* 44 Anne Boleyn's Walk, Cheam, Surrey. *T:* 01–643 3679.

ENGLISH, Gerald; Director, Opera Studio, Victorian College for the Arts, Melbourne, since 1977; *b* 6 Nov. 1925; *m* 1954, Jennifer Ryan; two *s* two *d*; *m* 1974, Linda Jacoby; one *s*. *Educ:* King's Sch., Rochester. After War service studied at Royal College of Music and then began career as lyric tenor; subsequently travelled in USA and Europe, appeared at Sadler's Wells, Covent Garden and Glyndebourne and recorded for major gramophone companies; Professor, Royal Coll. of Music, 1960–77. *Address:* c/o Victorian College for the Arts, 234 St Kilda Road, Melbourne, Vic 3003, Australia.

ENGLISH, Michael; *b* 24 Dec. 1930; *s* of late William Agnew English; *m* 1976, Carol Christine Owen; one *s* one *d*. *Educ:* King George V Grammar Sch., Southport; Liverpool Univ. (LLB). Joined Labour Party, 1949; Rochdale County Borough Council, 1953–65 (Chairman Finance Cttee until 1964). Member, official parliamentary panel NUGMW. Employed until 1964 as Asst Manager of department concerned with organisation and methods in subsidiary of large public company. Contested (Lab) Shipley Div., WR Yorks, 1959; MP (Lab) Nottingham West, 1964–83. Parliamentary Private Secretary, Board of Trade, 1966–67; Chairman: Parly Affairs Gp of Parly Lab. Party, 1970–76; Gen. Sub-Cttee of House of Commons Expenditure Cttee, 1974–79; Chm., E Midlands Gp, PLP, 1976–78; formerly Mem., Chairmen's Panel, Treasury and Civil Service, Procedure (Finance) and Sound Broadcasting Cttees, House of Commons. Chm., E Midlands Regional Lab. Party, 1979–80. *Recreation:* reading history. *Address:* 12 Denny Crescent, Kennington, SE11.

ENGLISH, Terence Alexander Hawthorne, FRCS; Consultant Cardiothoracic Surgeon, Papworth and Addenbrooke's Hospitals, Cambridge, since 1973; Director, Papworth Heart Transplant Research Unit, since 1980; *b* 3 Oct. 1932; *s* of late Arthur Alexander English and Mavis Eleanor (*née* Lund); *m* 1963, Ann Margaret, *e d* of late Frederick Mordaunt Dicey and Ann Gwendoline (*née* Smartt); two *s* two *d*. *Educ:* Hilton Coll., Natal; Witwatersrand Univ. (BSc(Eng) 1954); Guy's Hosp. Med. Sch. (MB, BS 1962). FRCSE 1967, FRCS 1967. House appointments, Guy's Hosp., 1962–63; Demonstrator, Anatomy Dept, Guy's Hosp., 1964–65; Surgical Registrar: Bolingbroke Hosp., 1966; Brompton Hosp., 1967–68; Res. Fellow, Dept of Surgery, Univ. of Alabama, 1969; Sen. Registrar, Brompton, National Heart and London Chest Hosps, 1968–72. Mem., Specialists Adv. Cttee in Cardiothoracic Surgery, 1980–. Member: British Cardiac Soc., 1973–; British Transplantation Soc., 1980–; Soc. of Thoracic and Cardiovascular Surgeons, 1972– (Exec. Council, 1975–77); Thoracic Soc., 1971– (Exec. Council, 1978–81). Member Council: RCS, 1981–; British Heart Foundn; Mem., GMC, 1983–; President: Internat. Soc. of Heart Transplantation, 1984–85; Soc. of Perfusionists of GB and Ireland, 1985–86. Capt., Guy's Hosp. RFC, 1959–60. Hon. MA Cantab, 1977. *Publications:* chapter on Surgery of the Thorax and Heart in Bailey and Love's Short Practice of Thoracic Surgery, 1980; numerous articles in medical jls on matters relating to the practice of cardiac and thoracic surgery. *Recreations:* reading, music, walking, tennis. *Address:* 19 Adams Road, Cambridge CB3 9AD. *T:* Cambridge 68744.

ENGLISH, Terence Michael; a Metropolitan Stipendiary Magistrate, since 1986; *b* 3 Feb. 1944; *s* of John Robert English and Elsie Letitia English; *m* 1966, Ivy Joan Weatherley; one *s* one *d*. *Educ:* St Ignatius' Coll., London N15; London Univ. (external LLB 1967). Admitted Solicitor of the Supreme Court, 1970. Assistant, Edmonton PSD, 1962–71; Dep. Clerk to Justices, Bullingdon, Bampton E, Henley and Watlington PSDs, 1972–76; Clerk to the Justices: Newbury and Hungerford and Lambourn PSDs, 1977–85; Slough and Windsor PSDs, 1985–86. *Recreations:* golf, philately. *Address:* 3 Beckett Close, Wokingham, Berks RG11 1YZ. *T:* Wokingham 782888.

ENNALS, family name of **Baron Ennals.**

ENNALS, Baron *cr* 1983 (Life Peer), of Norwich in the County of Norfolk; **David Hedley Ennals;** PC 1970; Chairman: United Nations Association, since 1984; Ockenden Venture; National Association for Mental Health (MIND), since 1984 (Campaign Director, 1970–73); Gandhi Foundation, since 1984; *b* 19 Aug. 1922; *s* of A. F. Ennals, 8 Victoria Terrace, Walsall, Staffs; *m* 1st, 1950, Eleanor Maud Caddick (marr. diss. 1977); three *s* one *d*; 2nd 1977, Katherine Gene Tranoy. *Educ:* Queen Mary's Grammar School, Walsall; Loomis Inst., Windsor, Conn, USA. Served with HM Forces, 1941–46: Captain, RAC. Secretary, Council for Education in World Citizenship, 1947–52; Secretary, United Nations Association, 1952–57; Overseas Sec., Labour Party, 1957–64. MP (Lab): Dover, 1964–70; Norwich North, Feb. 1974–1983; PPS to Minister of Overseas Development, 1964; Parly Under-Sec. of State, Army, 1966–67; Parly Under-Sec., Home Office, 1967–68; Minister of State: DHSS, 1968–70; FCO, 1974–76; Sec. of State for Social Services, 1976–79. Chm., Parly Food and Health Forum, 1985–. Contested (Lab) Norwich North, 1983. Chm., John Bellers Ltd, 1972–74. Chairman: Anti-Apartheid Movement, 1960–64; Campaign for Homeless and Rootless, 1972–74; Peter Bedford Trust, 1984–; Children's Medical Trust, 1984–; Pres., Coll. of Occupational Therapy, 1984–. Patron, Nat. Soc. of Non Smokers; Gov., Ditchley Foundn. *Publications:* Strengthening the United Nations, 1957; Middle East Issues, 1958; United Nations Peace Force, 1960; United Nations on Trial, 1962; Out of Mind, 1973. *Address:* 47 Brookfield, Highgate West Hill, N6.

See also J. A. F. Ennals, M. Ennals.

ENNALS, John Arthur Ford; Member, South Buckinghamshire District Council, since 1983; Director, United Kingdom Immigrants Advisory Service, 1970–83; *b* Walsall, 21 July 1918; *e s* of Arthur Ford Ennals, MC, and Jessie Edith Ennals (*née* Taylor); one *s* one *d*. *Educ:* Queen Mary's Grammar Sch., Walsall; St John's Coll., Cambridge. MA (History and Psychology). Rotary Travelling Schol. to USA, 1935. Pres., British Univs League of Nations Soc., and Cttee, Cambridge Union, 1938–39. Lectr for British Council, Roumania and Yugoslavia, 1939–40; War Corresp., Greece, Yugoslavia, Albania, 1941; on staff of British Embassy, Madrid, 1941–42, and Foreign Office, 1942–43. Served War: Egypt, Italy and Yugoslavia, 1943–45. Contested (Lab): Walsall South, 1955, 1959; Thames Valley, European Parly elecns, 1979. Secretary-Gen., World Fedn of UN Assocs, 1946–56; Gen.-Sec. and Tutor in Internat. Relations, Ruskin Coll., Oxford, 1956–66; Dir-Gen., UN Assoc., 1966–70 (Vice-Pres., 1978–); Hon. Pres., World Fedn of UN Assocs, 1977–; Member: OXFAM Exec., 1965–75; Exec. Council, Assoc. of Supervisory Staffs, Executives and Technicians, 1960–69. Trustee, Assoc. of Scientific Technical and Managerial Staffs, 1969–; Chm., Anti-Apartheid Movement, 1968–76; Member: Community Relations Cttee, Baptist Union, 1971–82; Community and Race Relations Unit, British Council of Churches, 1971–79; Exec. Cttee, British Refugee Council, 1981–83. Chm., British-Yugoslav Soc., 1982–. Parish Councillor: Kidlington, 1961–67; Hedgerley, 1976–. Yugoslav Star with Golden Wreath, 1984. *Recreations:* travelling in Europe, Asia, Africa and the Americas; walking in Wales; tennis, cricket. *Address:* 3 Village Lane, Hedgerley, Bucks SL2 3UY. *T:* (home) Farnham Common 4302. *Club:* India.

See also Baron Ennals, M. Ennals.

ENNALS, Kenneth Frederick John, CB 1983; Deputy Secretary, Finance and Local Government, Department of the Environment, since 1985; *b* 10 Jan. 1932; *s* of Ernest Ennals and Elsie Dorothy Ennals; *m* 1958, Mavis Euphemia; one *s* two *d*. *Educ:* Alleyn's Sch., Dulwich; LSE. Joined Export Credits Guarantee Dept, 1952; Principal, DEA, 1965–69; Min. of Housing and Local Govt, later DoE, 1969; Asst Sec., 1970, Under Sec., 1976–80, DoE; Dep. Sec., Depts of the Environment and Transport, 1980–84. *Recreations:* reading, architecture, dog-walking. *Address:* St Anthony's, Tuesley Lane, Godalming, Surrey. *T:* Godalming 7239. *Club:* Royal Commonwealth Society.

ENNALS, Martin; international human rights consultant; Founding President, Human Rights International Documentation and Information System (HURIDOCS), since 1982; Secretary-General, International Alert, since 1985; Director (ad interim), Article 19; *b* 27 July 1927; *s* of A. Ford Ennals and Jessie E. Ennals (*née* Taylor); *m* 1951, Jacqueline B. Ennals (*née* Morris); one *s* one *d*. *Educ:* Queen Mary's Sch., Walsall; London Sch. of Economics. BScEcon (Internat. Relations). UNESCO, 1951–59; Gen. Sec., National Council for Civil Liberties, 1960–66; Information Officer, Nat. Cttee for Commonwealth Immigrants, 1966–68 (resigned in protest at Govt's Commonwealth Immigration Act, 1968); Sec. Gen., Amnesty International (Nobel Peace Prize, 1977), 1968–80; Head of Police Cttee Support Unit, GLC, 1982–85. Joint Chm., Human Rights Network UK. *Recreations:* escapist television and ski-ing. *Address:* 90 Borough High Street, E1; 157 Southwood Lane, N6. *T:* 01–340 8629.

See also Baron Ennals, J. A. F. Ennals.

ENNISKILLEN, 6th Earl of, *cr* 1789; **David Lowry Cole,** MBE 1955; Baron Mountflorence, 1760; Viscount Enniskillen, 1776; Baron Grinstead (UK), 1815; farmer, Kenya and N Ireland; *b* 10 Sept. 1918; *er s* of Hon. Galbraith Lowry Egerton Cole (*d* 1929) (3rd *s* of 4th Earl of Enniskillen) and Lady Eleanor Cole (*d* 1979), *d* of 2nd Earl of Balfour; *S* uncle, 1963; *m* 1st, 1940, Sonia Mary Syers (from whom he obtained a divorce, 1955; she *d* 1982); one *s* one *d*; 2nd, 1955, Nancy Henderson MacLennan, former American Vice Consul. *Educ:* Eton; Trinity Coll., Cambridge. BA Agric. 1940. Served War of 1939–45, Captain Irish Guards: Kenya Emergency, 1953–55, Provincial Comdt, Kenya Police Reserve (MBE). MLC for North Kenya, 1961–63. Formerly: Member Kenya Meat Commn; Member Exec., Kenya National Farmers Union; Vice-Chairman Kenya Stockowners Council; Member Exec., Kenya Board of Agriculture; Member Board: Land and Agric. Bank of Kenya; East African Diatomite Syndicate Ltd. Captain, Ulster Defence Regt, 1971–73. Mem., Fermanagh CC, 1963–69; DL 1963–78, JP 1972–78, Co. Fermanagh. *Recreations:* shooting, golf, fishing. *Heir:* *s* Viscount Cole, *qv*. *Address:* House of Lords, SW1A 0PW; PO Box 30100, Nairobi, Kenya. *Clubs:* Carlton, Turf; Muthaiga Country (Nairobi); Mombasa (Kenya).

See also Sir J. H. Muir, Bt.

ENNISMORE, Viscount; Francis Michael Hare; *b* 28 June 1964; *s* and heir of 5th Earl of Listowel, *qv*. *Address:* 7 Constable Close, Wildwood Road, NW11.

ENRICI, Most Rev. Domenico, JCD; former Apostolic Nuncio; *b* 9 April 1909; *s* of late Domenico Enrici and Maria Dalmasso Enrici. *Educ:* Diocesan Seminary, Cuneo; Pontifical Gregorian Univ. and Pontifical Ecclesiastical Academy, Rome. Ordained, 1933; parochial work in Dio. Cuneo, 1933–35. Served at various Apostolic Nunciatures and Delegations: Ireland, 1938–45; Egypt, 1946–48; Palestine and Jordan, 1948–53; Formosa, Free China, 1953–55; apptd Titular Archbp of Ancusa, 1955; Apostolic Internuncio to Indonesia, 1955–58; Apostolic Nuncio to Haiti and Apostolic Delegate to West Indies, 1958–60; Apostolic Internuncio to Japan, 1960–62; Apostolic Delegate to Australia, New Zealand and Oceania, 1962–69; Apostolic Delegate to GB and Gibraltar, 1969–73; Pro-Pres., Pontifical Ecclesiastical Acad., 1974–75; Delegate for Pontifical Representations, 1973–79; retired, 1979. Commander, Order of the Nile (Egypt), 1948; Order of the Sacred Treasure,

1st class (Japan), 1962; Assistant to the Pontifical Throne, Vatican City, 1979. *Publication:* Mistero e Luce (Mystery and Light), 1984. *Address:* Via Senatore Toselli, 8, 12100 Cuneo, Italy. *T:* (0171) 51120.

ENRIGHT, Dennis Joseph; freelance writer; *b* 11 March 1920; *s* of late George and Grace Enright; *m* 1949, Madeleine Harders; one *d*. *Educ:* Leamington Coll.; Downing Coll., Cambridge. MA Cantab; DLitt Alexandria. Lecturer in English, University of Alexandria, 1947–50; Organising Tutor, University of Birmingham Extra-Mural Dept, 1950–53; Vis. Prof., Kōnan Univ., Japan, 1953–56; Vis. Lecturer, Free University of Berlin, 1956–57; British Council Professor, Chulalongkorn Univ., Bangkok, 1957–59; Prof. of English, Univ. of Singapore, 1960–70; Hon. Prof. of English, Univ. of Warwick, 1975–80. Dir, Chatto and Windus, 1974–82. Co-Editor, Encounter, 1970–72. FRSL 1961. Cholmondeley Poetry Award, 1974; Queen's Gold Medal for Poetry, 1981. Hon. DLitt Warwick, 1982; DUniv. Surrey, 1985. *Publications: poetry:* The Laughing Hyena, 1953; Bread Rather Than Blossoms, 1956; Some Men Are Brothers, 1960; Addictions, 1962; The Old Adam, 1965; Unlawful Assembly, 1968; Selected Poems, 1969; Daughters of Earth, 1972; The Terrible Shears, 1973; Rhyme Times Rhyme (for children), 1974; Sad Ires, 1975; Paradise Illustrated, 1978; A Faust Book, 1979; Collected Poems, 1981; Instant Chronicles, 1985; *novels:* Academic Year, 1955; Heaven Knows Where, 1957; Insufficient Poppy, 1960; Figures of Speech, 1965; *novels for children:* The Joke Shop, 1976; Wild Ghost Chase, 1978; Beyond Land's End, 1979; *criticism:* The Apothecary's Shop, 1957; English Critical Texts (co-editor), 1962; Conspirators and Poets, 1966; Shakespeare and the Students, 1970; Man is an Onion, 1972; (ed) A Choice of Milton's Verse, 1975; Samuel Johnson: Rasselas, 1976; (ed) The Oxford Book of Contemporary Verse 1945–1980, 1980; A Mania for Sentences, 1983; (ed) Fair of Speech: the uses of euphemism, 1985; The Alluring Problem: an essay on irony; *travel:* The World of Dew: Japan, 1955; Memoirs of a Mendicant Professor, 1969; *translation:* The Poetry of Living Japan (co-editor), 1957; *anthology:* (ed) The Oxford Book of Death, 1983; contributor to: Scrutiny, Encounter, Observer, TLS, etc. *Recreations:* reading, writing, television, listening to music. *Address:* 35A Viewfield Road, SW18.

ENRIGHT, Derek Anthony; EEC delegate in Guinea Bissau, since 1985; *b* 2 Aug. 1935; *s* of Lawrence and Helen Enright; *m* 1963, Jane Maureen (*née* Simmons); two *s* two *d*. *Educ:* St Michael's Coll., Leeds; Wadham Coll., Oxford (BA, DipEd). Head of Classics, John Fisher Sch., Purley, Surrey, 1959–67; Dep. Head of St Wilfrid's, North Featherstone, W Yorks, 1967–79. Mem. (Lab) Leeds, Eur. Parlt, 1979–84; Brit. Labour Group Spokesman on third world affairs and women's rights, 1979–84. Contested (Lab) Kent East, European elecn, 1984. *Publications:* reports on: fishing agreements in West Africa; EEC relations with non ACP developing countries; Namibia after independence. *Recreations:* reading the Guardian, entertaining the family, walking the dogs. *Address:* The Hollies, 112 Carleton Road, Pontefract, W Yorks. *T:* Pontefract 702096; Service Valise Diplomatique, rue de la Loi 200, 1049 Brussels, Belgium.

ENSOM, Donald, FRICS, FCIArb; Consultant, Debenham Tewson & Chinnocks, Chartered Surveyors, since 1986 (Partner, 1962–86); *b* 8 April 1926; *s* of Charles R. A. W. Ensom and Edith (*née* Young); *m* 1951, Sonia (*née* Sherrard); one *s* one *d*. *Educ:* Norbury Manor Sch., Croydon. Qualified as Chartered Surveyor, 1951; FRICS 1958; FCIArb 1970. Served RA, 1943–47. Partner, Nightingale, Page & Bennett/Debenham Tewson & Chinnocks (after merger), 1958–86. Chm., Bldg Conservation Trust, 1981–83; Hon. Sec., RICS, 1983–. *Recreations:* reading, opera and music, caravanning, canals. *Address:* Saxons, 102 Grange Road, Cambridge CB3 9AA. *Clubs:* East India, Royal Over-Seas League, Chartered Surveyors (1913), Pyramus and Thisbe.

ENSOR, (Alick Charles) David; solicitor, journalist and author; *b* 27 Nov. 1906; *s* of Charles William Ensor, MRCS, LRCP, and Helen Margaret Creighton Ensor; *m* 1st, 1932, Norah Russell (marr. diss.); one *s* two *d*; 2nd, 1944, Frances Vivienne Mason. *Educ:* Westminster Sch. Solicitor, 1928; Prosecuting Solicitor, Newcastle upon Tyne, 1932; Prosecuting Solicitor, Metropolitan Police, 1935; Law Lecturer, Police Coll., Hendon, 1935; Deputy Clerk of Peace, Middlesex, 1937; Clerk of Peace, London, 1938. War service with Army in France, Africa, Far East, 1939–44. Practised as Solicitor in Brussels, 1945–47. Retired from Law and farmed in Dorset, 1948. MP (Lab) Bury and Radcliffe, 1964–70; PPS to Ministers of Agriculture. Mem., Select Cttee on Estimates, 1964–69; Chairman: Private Bill Cttee, 1967–70; House of Commons Catering Cttee, 1969–70; Anglo-Soviet Parly Cttee and other Gps; Leader of many delegations all round the world including Mauritius, Pakistan, Spain and GDR. Has broadcast regularly for radio and television since 1957. Films include: The Trials of Oscar Wilde; The Pot Carriers; Death and the Sky Above. TV Series, The Verdict is Yours. Vice-Pres., Mark Twain Soc. of America, 1977–. Has travelled extensively in Eastern Europe, Middle and Far East. *Publications:* Thirty Acres and a Cow, 1955; I was a Public Prosecutor, 1958; Verdict Afterwards, 1960; With Lord Roberts through the Khyber Pass, 1963; contributions to Local Government Law in England and Wales, Journal of Criminal Law. *Recreation:* studying French history. *Address:* L'Etoile d'Or, 66701 Argelès-sur-Mer, France.

ENSOR, David; see Ensor, A. C. D.

ENSOR, David, OBE 1986; Managing Director, Croydon Advertiser Ltd, 1979–85; *b* 2 April 1924; *s* of Rev. William Walters and Constance Eva Ensor; *m* 1947, Gertrude Kathleen Brown; two *s*. *Educ:* Kingswood Sch., Bath; London Coll. of Printing. Served Royal Signals, 1942–46, Captain; ADC to GOC Bengal Dist. Managing Director: George Reveirs, 1947–59; Charles Skipper & East, 1959–69; Knapp Drewett & Sons, 1969–79; Chairman: Methodist Newspaper Co., 1975–; Methodist Publishing House, 1981–. Member: Council, Newspaper Soc., 1979–; Press Council, 1982–. Pres., London Printing Industries Assoc., 1976. Vice-Pres., Methodist Conf., 1981. *Address:* Milborne Lodge, Dinton Road, Fovant, Salisbury, Wilts SP3 5JW. *T:* Fovant 521.

ENSOR, George Anthony; Partner, Rutherfords, Solicitors, Liverpool, since 1962; a Recorder of the Crown Court, since 1983; *b* 4 Nov. 1936; *s* of George and Phyllis Ensor; *m* 1968, Jennifer Margaret Caile, MB, ChB; two *d*. *Educ:* Malvern College; Liverpool University (LLB). Solicitor, 1961 (Atkinson Conveyancing Medal, 1962; Rupert Bremner Medal, 1962). Deputy Coroner, City of Liverpool, 1966–; part-time Chairman, Industrial Tribunals, 1975–; President, Liverpool Law Society, 1982. Dir, Liverpool FC, 1985–. *Recreation:* golf. *Address:* 23 Far Moss Road, Blundellsands, Liverpool L23 8TG. *T:* 051–924 5937. *Clubs:* Artists (Liverpool); Formby Golf.

ENSOR, Michael de Normann, CMG 1980; OBE 1958; *b* 11 June 1919; *s* of Robert Weld Ensor and Dr Beatrice Ensor; *m* 1945, Mona Irene Blackburn; two *s*. *Educ:* Bryanston School; St. John's Coll., Oxford. Military service, 1940; Colonial Service, Gold Coast/Ghana Civil Service, 1940–58; Secretary, Foundation for Mutual Assistance in Africa South of the Sahara, 1958–64; Dept of Technical Cooperation/Min. of Overseas Development/Overseas Development Administration, 1964–80: Head, East Africa Development Division, 1975–80; Chm., Paragon Management Co., 1983–86. *Address:* Flat 1, 12 The Paragon, Blackheath, SE3 0NZ. *T:* 01–852 5345. *Clubs:* Travellers', Royal Blackheath Golf; Karen (Kenya).

ENSOR WALTERS, P. H. B.; *see* Walters.

ENTERS, Angna; mime; dancer; painter; sculptor; author; dramatist; composer; choreographer; scene and costume designer for the theatre; *b* NYC, US, 28 April 1907; *o c* of Edward Enters and Henriette Gasseur-Styleau; *m* Louis Kalonyme. *Educ:* privately and self-educated in US; Europe; Egypt; Greece. Theatre début New York, 1924, presenting in solo performance a new theatre form in which she combined for the first time the arts of mime, dance, music, costume, scenic design; originated phrase dance-mime now in Amer. dictionaries; first performer to be presented in a theatrical performance, 1943, by Metropolitan Museum of Art, NYC; presented for her 25th Broadway (NY) season, 1959; a nationwide television broadcast, in US, presented a composite portrait of her work in theatre, painting, writing, 1959. London début, St Martin's Theatre, 1928; many subseq. British seasons including television. Paris début, 1929; Am. Rep. in Internat. Theatre Season presented by C. B. Cochran, Queen's Theatre, 1931. Rep. Am. Nat. Theatre and Acad., at Internat. Arts Festival, Berlin, and tour of W Germany. Guggenheim Foundation Fellowships, 1934 and 1935 (research in Greece, Egypt, Near East). Début exhibn of painting, NY, 1933, many subseq. Début exhibn of paintings in London, Eng., 1934 and subseq. Début exhibn of sculpture, New York, 1945; subseq. one-woman shows of painting and sculpture in US and Canada. Works are in Metropolitan Museum of Art, New York, etc. Painted mural, modern Penthouse Theatre of University of Washington, Seattle, 1950. Rep. in Exhibns, NY Museum of Modern Art, 1953. First work in Ceramics exhibited in New York and Los Angeles, 1953. Lecture tours US, 1954–. Prof. of Acting, Baylor Univ., Waco, Texas, and Director of plays, Dallas Theatre Center, Dallas, Texas, 1961–62. Fellow: Center for Advanced Studies, Wesleyan Univ., Middletown, Conn, 1962–; Pennsylvania State Univ., 1970. Films based on her original stories: Lost Angel, Tenth Avenue Angel, Silly Girl, 1944–47; You Belong to Me, 1950. Created and staged Commedia dell' Arte (play within play seq.) in film Scaramouche, 1951; Dir, also designer of stage settings and costumes, for play, Yerma, by G. Lorca (Broadway, NY, etc.), 1958. Plays produced: Love Possessed Juana, 1946; The Unknown Lover-A Modern Psyche, 1947. *Publications:* First Person Plural (self-illustr.), 1937, new edn 1978; Love Possessed Juana (self-scored and illustr. play), 1939; Silly Girl (self-illustr. autobiog.), 1944; Among the Daughters (novel), 1955 (publ. London, 1956, as A Thing of Beauty); Artist's Life (self-illustrated), 1957; Artist's Life (publ. London, 1959); (trans. with L. Kalonyme) Chantecler, by E. Rostand, 1960; Angna Enters on Mime, 1965; also illustrated Best American Short Stories of 1945; article on Pantomime, Encyclopædia Britannica.

ENTWISTLE, Sir (John Nuttall) Maxwell, Kt 1963; Consultant Solicitor and Notary; Director of companies; Under-writing Member of Lloyd's since 1964; *b* 8 Jan. 1910; *s* of Isaac and Hannah Entwistle; *m* 1940, Jean Cunliffe McAlpine, *d* of late Dr John and Amy Margaret Penman; two *s*. *Educ:* Merchant Taylors' Sch., Great Crosby. Solicitor, 1931; Notary Public, 1955. Liverpool City: Councillor, 1938; Alderman, 1960; Leader of Liverpool City Council, when initiated preparation of develt plan for City centre. Councillor, Cumbria County, 1979–82. Chairman: Merseyside Development Cttee; Mersey Tunnel Cttee, 1961–63; Abbeyfield Liverpool Soc. Ltd, 1970–75; Council of Management, League of Welldoers, 1972–74. Mem., Liverpool Univ. Court and Council, 1955–64. President: Edge Hill Liverpool Conservative Assoc., 1963–71; Liverpool Clerks Assoc., 1964–78. Merchant Taylors' School: Chm., Appeal Cttee, 1969–74; Pres., Old Boys' Assoc., 1969–70; Governor, 1969–75. *Recreations:* gardening, shooting. *Address:* Stone Hall, Sedbergh, Cumbria. *T:* Sedbergh 20700.

EÖTVÖS, Peter; composer and conductor; *m* 1968, Piroska Molnar; one *s*; *m* 1976, Pi-Hsien Chen; one *d*. *Educ:* Musik Hochschule, Budapest; Musik Hochschule, Cologne. Composer from age 16, chamber music, electronic music, film music, theatre music; conductor and musical director, Ensemble Intercontemporain, Paris, 1979–; principal guest conductor, BBC Symphony Orchestra, 1985–. *Recreations:* walking, pipe smoking, jazz. *Address:* c/o Allied Artists, 42 Montpelier Square, SW7 1JZ. *T:* 01–589 6243.

EPHRAUMS, Maj.-Gen. Roderick Jarvis, CB 1977; OBE 1965; DL; Major-General Royal Marines, Commando Forces, 1976–78, retired; *b* 12 May 1927; *s* of Hugh Cyril Ephraums and Elsie Caroline (*née* Rowden); *m* 1955, Adela Mary (*née* Forster); two *s* one *d*. *Educ:* Tonbridge. Commnd 2nd Lieut, RM, 1945; HMS Mauritius, 1946–48; 3 Commando Bde, RM, 1952–54; Staff Coll., Camberley, 1960; Bde Major, 3 Commando Bde, 1962–64; CO, 45 Commando RM, 1969–71; Royal Coll. of Defence Studies, 1972; Comdr, 3 Commando Bde, 1973–74; NATO Defense Coll., Rome, 1975. A Col Comdt, RM, 1985–. DL Angus, 1985. FBIM 1979. *Recreations:* painting, gardening. *Club:* Army and Navy.

EPSTEIN, Prof. (Michael) Anthony, CBE 1985; FRS 1979; Professor of Pathology, 1968–85 (now Emeritus), and Head of Department, 1968–82, University of Bristol; Hon. Consultant Pathologist, Bristol Health District (Teaching), 1968–82; *b* 18 May 1921; *yr s* of Mortimer and Olga Epstein; *m* 1950, Lisbeth Knight; two *s* one *d*. *Educ:* St Paul's Sch., London; Trinity Coll., Cambridge (Perry Exhibr, 1940); Middlesex Hosp. Medical Sch. MA, MD, DSc, PhD; FRCPath. Ho. Surg., Middlesex Hosp., London, and Addenbrooke's Hosp., Cambridge, 1944; Lieut and Captain, RAMC, 1945–47; Asst Pathologist, Bland Sutton Inst., Mddx Hosp. Med. Sch., 1948–65, with leave as: Berkeley Travelling Fellow, 1952–53; French Govt Exchange Scholar at Institut Pasteur, Paris, 1952–53; Vis. Investigator, Rockefeller Inst., NY, 1956. Reader in Experimental Pathology, Mddx Hosp. Med. Sch., 1965–68; Hon. Consultant in Experimental Virology, Mddx Hosp., 1965–68. Major lectures: Edgar Allen Meml, Yale Univ., 1960; Kettle Meml, Royal Coll. of Pathologists, 1971; Distinguished Scientist Series, Tulane Univ., 1972; Sydney Watson Smith, RCPE, 1973; Collège de France, Paris, 1975; Long Fox Meml, Bristol, 1976; Chinese Acad. of Medical Scis, Peking, 1977; A. B. Pearson Oration, NZ Soc. of Pathologists, 1978; Korner Meml, Sussex Univ., 1980; Nat. Sci. Res. Foundn, Athens, 1981; Senate Guest, Welsh Nat. Sch. of Medicine, Cardiff, 1981; Wade Foundn, Southampton Univ., 1982; Almroth Wright, St Mary's Hosp. Med. Sch., 1983; Adami, Univ. of Liverpool, 1984; Special, US NIH, 1984; 20th Annual Guest, Leukaemia Res. Fund, 1984; Walter Hubert, British Assoc. Cancer Res., 1986; Henderson Meml, PHLS CAMRE, 1986; Florey, Royal Soc., 1986. Member: Cttee, Pathological Soc. of GB and Ire., 1969–72; Council, and Vice-Pres., Pathology Section of RSM, 1966–72; Study Gp on Classification of Herpes Viruses, of Internat. Commn for Nomenclature of Viruses, 1971–; Scientific Adv. Bd, Harvard Med. Sch.'s New England Regional Primate Center, 1972–; Cancer Research Campaign MRC Jt Cttee, 1973–77, 1982–86 (Chm. 1983–86); Cttee, British Soc. for Cell Biology, 1974–77; MRC, 1982–86 (Mem. 1979–84, Chm. 1982–84, Cell Bd; Mem., 1984–85, Chm., 1985–, Tropical Medicine Res. Bd); Council, Royal Soc., 1983–85; Medical and Scientific Panel, Leukaemia Research Fund, 1982–85; Scientific Adv. Cttee, Lister Inst., 1984–; Foreign Sec., Royal Soc., 1986–. Discovered in 1964 a new human herpes virus, now known as Epstein-Barr virus, which causes infectious mononucleosis and is also causally implicated in some forms of human cancer (Burkitt's lymphoma and nasopharyngeal carcinoma). Paul Ehrlich and Ludwig Darmstaedter Prize and Medal of W German Paul Ehrlich Foundn, 1973; Markham Skerrit Prize, 1977; (jtly) Bristol-Myers Award, NY, 1982. Mem. d'honneur, Belgian Soc. for Cancer Res., 1979. Hon. Prof., Zhongshan Med. Coll., Guangzhou, 1981. Hon. Fellow, Queensland Inst. of Med. Research, 1983; Hon. FRCP 1986; Hon. MD Edinburgh, 1986. Leeuwenhoek Prize Lectr, Royal Soc., 1983; Prix Griffuel, Assoc. pour la recherche sur le cancer, Paris, 1986. *Publications:* over 205 scientific papers in internat. jls on tumour cell structure, viruses, tumour viruses, Burkitt's lymphoma, and the EB virus. Jt Founder Editor, The Internat. Review of Experimental Pathology (vols 1–28, 1962–86); (ed jtly) The Epstein-Barr Virus, 1979; (ed jtly) The Epstein-Barr Virus: recent advances, 1986. *Address:* Nuffield Department of Clinical Medicine, University of Oxford, John Radcliffe Hospital, Oxford OX3 9DU. *T:* Oxford 817623.

EREAUT, Sir (Herbert) Frank (Cobbold), Kt 1976; Bailiff of Jersey, 1975–85; Judge of the Court of Appeal of Guernsey, since 1976; Director, Standard Chartered Bank (CI), since 1986; *b* 6 May 1919; *s* of Herbert Parker Ereaut and May Julia Cobbold, *m* 1942, Kathleen FitzGibbon; one *d*. *Educ:* Tormore Sch., Upper Deal, Kent; Cranleigh Sch., Surrey; Exeter Coll., Oxford. BA 1946, MA 1966. RASC, 1940–46: N Africa, Italy and NW Europe; 2nd Lieut 1940; Lieut 1941; Captain 1943. Called to Bar, Inner Temple, 1947; Solicitor-General, Jersey, 1958–62, Attorney-General, 1962–69; Dep. Bailiff of Jersey, 1969–74. KStJ 1983 (CStJ 1978). *Recreations:* music, gardening. *Address:* Les Cypres, St John, Jersey, Channel Islands. *T:* Jersey 22317.

EREMIN, Prof. Oleg, MD, FRCSE, FRACS; Regius Professor of Surgery, University of Aberdeen, since 1985; *b* 12 Nov. 1938; *s* of Theodor and Maria Eremin; *m* 1963, Jennifer Mary Ching; two *s* one *d*. *Educ:* Christian Brothers' Coll., St Kilda, Melbourne; Univ. of Melbourne. MB BS 1964; MD 1985. FRACS 1971; FRCSE 1983. Clinical posts: Royal Melbourne Hosp., 1965–72; Norfolk and Norwich Hosps, 1972–74; Research Asst-Associate, Dept of Pathology, Univ. of Cambridge, 1974–80; Sen. Lectr, Dept Clinical Surgery, Univ. of Edinburgh, 1981–85. *Publications:* articles in surgical, oncological and immunological jls. *Recreations:* music, sport, reading. *Address:* 3 The Chanonry, Old Aberdeen. *T:* Aberdeen 44065.

ERICKSON, Prof. Charlotte Joanne; Paul Mellon Professor of American History, University of Cambridge, since 1983; Fellow of Corpus Christi College, Cambridge; *b* 22 Oct. 1923; *d* of Knut Eric Erickson and Lael A. R. Johnson; *m* 1952, G. L. Watt; two *s*. *Educ:* Augustana Coll., Rock Island, Ill (BA 1945); Cornell Univ., Ithaca, NY (MA 1947; PhD 1951). Instructor in History, Vassar Coll., Poughkeepsie, NY, 1950–52; Research Fellow, NIESR, 1952–55; Lillian Gilmore Fellow, Cornell Univ., April-Sept. 1954; Asst Lectr, 1955, Lectr, 1958, Sen. Lectr, 1966, Reader, 1975, Prof., 1979–82, in Economic History, London School of Economics. Guggenheim Fellow, Washington, DC, 1966–67; Sherman Fairchild Distinguished Scholar, Calif Inst. of Technology, 1976–77. Hon. DHumLet Augustana College, 1977. *Publications:* British Industrialists, Steel and Hosiery 1850–1950, 1958; American Industry and the European Immigrant 1860–1885, 1969; Invisible Immigrants, The Adaptation of English and Scottish Immigrants in Nineteenth Century America, 1972; articles in professional jls and collective works. *Recreations:* music, gardening. *Address:* Corpus Christi College, Cambridge CB2 1RH; 8 High Street, Chesterton, Cambridge.

ERICKSON, Prof. John, FRSE 1982; FBA 1985; Professor of Politics (Defence Studies), University of Edinburgh, since 1969; *b* 17 April 1929; *s* of Henry Erickson and Jessie (*née* Heys); *m* 1957, Ljubica (*née* Petrović); one *s* one *d*. *Educ:* South Shields High Sch.; St John's Coll., Cambridge (MA). Research Fellow, St Antony's Coll., Oxford, 1956–58; Lectr, Dept of History, St Andrews Univ., 1958–62; Lectr, Sen. Lectr and Reader, Dept of Government, Univ. of Manchester, 1962–67; Visiting Prof., Russian Research Center, Univ. of Indiana, 1967; Reader, Lectr in Higher Defence Studies, Univ. of Edinburgh, 1967. Vis. Prof., Texas A&M Univ., 1981. Pres., Assoc. of Civil Defence and Emergency Planning Officers, 1981–. *Publications:* The Soviet High Command 1918–1941, 1962; Storia dello Stato Maggiore Sovietico, 1963; ed, The Military-Technical Revolution, 1966; ed, The Armed Services and Society, 1970; Soviet Military Power, 1971; The Road to Stalingrad, 1975; (ed) Soviet Military Power and Performance, 1979; The Road to Berlin, 1983. *Recreations:* military models and music. *Address:* 13 Ravelston House Road, Edinburgh EH4 3LP. *T:* 031–332 1787. *Club:* Edinburgh University Staff, Scottish Arts (Edinburgh).

ERKIN, Feridun Cemal, Hon. GBE 1967; Minister of Foreign Affairs, Turkey, 1962–65; *b* 1899, *m* Madame Mukaddes Feridun Erkin (*d* 1955). *Educ:* Galatasaray Lyceum, Istanbul; Faculty of Law, University of Paris. First Sec., London, 1928–29; Chief of Section, Ankara, 1930–33; Counsellor and Chargé d'Affaires, Berlin, 1934–35; Consul-Gen., Beirut, 1935–37; Dir-Gen., Econ. Dept, Min. of Foreign Affairs, 1937; Dir-Gen., Polit. Dept, 1939; Asst Sec.-Gen., 1942; Deleg, UN Conf. San Francisco, 1945; Sec.-Gen. of Min., 1945; Chm. Turkish Delegn, final session of League of Nations, 1946; Ambassador to Italy, 1947–48; to USA, 1948–55; to Spain, 1955–57; to France, 1957–60; to the Court of St James's, 1960–62. Lately Senator. Turkish Governor to Internat. Banks, 1954; Mem. Internat. Diplomatic Academy, 1949–; Mem. Inst. of France, 1959–. Holds Grand Cross of several foreign Orders, including Grand Cross of the Legion of Honour of France. *Publications:* The Turkish-Soviet relations and the Problem of the Straits, 1968 (French and Turkish edns); articles in daily papers and journals. *Recreation:* classical music. *Address:* Ayaspaşa, Sarayarkasi Sok 24/9, Istanbul, Turkey.

ERLEIGH, Viscount; Julian Michael Rufus Isaacs; *b* 26 May 1986; *s* and *heir* of Marquess of Reading, *qv*.

ERNE, 6th Earl of, *cr* 1789; **Henry George Victor John Crichton,** JP; Baron Erne 1768; Viscount Erne (Ireland), 1781; Baron Fermanagh (UK), 1876; Lord Lieutenant of Co. Fermanagh, Northern Ireland, since 1986; *b* 9 July 1937; *s* of 5th Earl and Lady Katharine Cynthia Mary Millicent (Davina) Lytton (who *m* 1945, Hon. C. M. Woodhouse, *qv*), *yr d* of 2nd Earl of Lytton, KG, PC, GCSI, GCIE; *S* father, 1940; *m* 1958, Camilla Marguerite (marr. diss. 1980), *er d* of late Wing-Comdr Owen G. E. Roberts, and of Mrs Roberts, 30 Groom Place, Belgrave Square, SW1; one *s* four *d*; *m* 1980, Mrs Anna Carin Hitchcock (*née* Bjork). *Educ:* Eton. Page of Honour to the Queen, 1952–54 (to King George VI, 1952). Lieut, North Irish Horse, 1959–66. Member: Royal Ulster Agricultural Society; Royal Forestry Society. DL, JP Co. Fermanagh. *Recreations:* sailing, fishing, shooting. *Heir:* *s* Viscount Crichton, *qv*. *Address:* Crom Castle, Newtown Butler, Co. Fermanagh. *T:* Newton-butler 208; 10 Kylestrome House, Cundy Street Flats, Ebury Street, SW1. *Clubs:* White's; Lough Erne Yacht.

ERRINGTON, Viscount; Evelyn Rowland Esmond Baring; Managing Director, Inchcape (China) Limited (formerly Manager, China Trading Division, Inchcape Far East Ltd), since 1979; *b* 3 June 1946; *e s* of 3rd Earl of Cromer, *qv*; *m* 1971, Plern Isarangkun Na Ayudhya, *e d* of late Dr Charanphat Isarangkun Na Ayudhya, Thailand. *Educ:* Eton. Director: Lai Tong Trading Co. Ltd; The Motor Transport Co. of Guangdong & Hong Kong Ltd (China); Alternate Dir, Cluff Oil (Hong Kong) Ltd. Mem. Council, St John Ambulance Assoc., Hong Kong. *Address:* GPO Box 56, Hong Kong; 7B Bowen Road, Hong Kong. *T:* 5–236426, (office) 5–8931066. *Clubs:* Turf, Oriental; Siam Society; Hong Kong, Royal Hong Kong Yacht (Hong Kong).

ERRINGTON, Col Sir Geoffrey (Frederick), 2nd Bt *cr* 1963; Chairman: EAL International Ltd, since 1985; Executive Appointments Ltd, since 1982 (Director, since 1979); Guy Redmayne & Partners Ltd, since 1982 (Director, since 1979); Moore, Wingate Ltd, since 1982; *b* 15 Feb. 1926; *er s* of Sir Eric Errington, 1st Bt, JP, and Marjorie (*d* 1973), *d* of A. Grant Bennett; *S* father, 1973; *m* 1955, Diana Kathleen Forbes, *o d* of late E. Barry Davenport, Edgbaston, Birmingham; three *s. Educ:* Rugby Sch.; New Coll., Oxford. psc 1958. GSO 3 (Int.), HQ 11 Armd Div., 1950–52; GSO 3, MI3 (b), War Office, 1955–57; Bde Major 146 Inf. Bde, 1959–61; Coy Comdr, RMA Sandhurst, 1963–65; Military Assistant to Adjutant-General, 1965–67; CO 1st Bn, The King's Regt, 1967–69; GSO 1, HQ 1st British Corps, 1969–71; Col. GS, HQ NW District, 1971–74; AAG MI (Army), MoD, 1974–75; retired 1975. Col, The King's Regt, 1975–86; Chm., The King's and Manchester Regts Assoc., 1971–86; Dir, Personnel Services, British Shipbuilders, 1977–78; Employer Bd Mem., Shipbuilding ITB, 1977–78. Freeman, City of London, 1980. Liveryman, Coachmakers' and Coach Harness Makers' Co. *Recreations:* sailing, skiing. *Heir: s* Robin Davenport Errington, *b* 1 July 1957. *Address:* Stone Hill Farm, Sellindge, Ashford, Kent TN25 6AJ. *T:* Sellindge 3191; 203A Gloucester Place, NW1 6BU. *Clubs:* Boodle's, Army and Navy.
See also S. G. Errington.

ERRINGTON, Sir Lancelot, KCB 1976 (CB 1962); Second Permanent Secretary, Department of Health and Social Security, 1973–76; *b* 14 Jan. 1917; *e s* of late Major L. Errington; *m* 1939, Katharine Reine, *o d* of late T. C. Macaulay; two *s* two *d. Educ:* Wellington Coll.; Trinity Coll., Cambridge. Entered Home Office, 1939. Served RNVR, 1939–45. Transferred to Ministry of National Insurance, 1945; Principal Private Sec. to Minister of National Insurance, 1951; Asst Sec., 1953; Under-Sec., 1957–65; Cabinet Office, 1965–68; Min. of Social Security, 1968; Asst Under-Sec. of State, DHSS, 1968–71, Dep. Under-Sec. of State, 1971–73. *Recreation:* sailing. *Address:* St Mary's, Fasnacloich, Appin, Argyll. *T:* Appin 331.

ERRINGTON, Richard Percy, CMG 1955; Chartered Accountant (FCA), retired; *b* 17 May 1904; 2nd *s* of Robert George Errington and Edna Mary Errington (*née* Warr); *m* 1935, Ursula, *d* of Henry Joseph Laws Curtis and Grace Barton Curtis (*née* Macgregor); one *d. Educ:* Sidcot Sch. Asst Treasurer, Nigeria Government, 1929–37; Colonial Administrative Service: Nigeria, 1937–46; Nyasaland, 1946–48; Financial Sec. to Govt of Aden Colony (also Mem. Bd of Trustees of Port of Aden), 1948–51; Chm., Aden Port Trust, 1951–60. Mem. Governor's Exec. Council, Aden, 1948–58. Unofficial Mem. Aden Colony Legislative Council, 1951–60 (Official Mem., 1948–51). Chairman: Aden Soc. for the Blind, 1951–60; Aden Lab. Advisory Bd, 1951–57. Area Comr, St John Amb. Bde, 1964–71. SBStJ, 1965. *Recreation:* walking. *Address:* Whitecliffs, Wodehouse Road, Old Hunstanton, Norfolk PE36 6JD. *T:* Hunstanton 2356.

ERRINGTON, Stuart Grant; JP; Chairman and Chief Executive, Mercantile Credit Co. Ltd, since 1985; *b* 23 June 1929; *yr s* of Sir Eric Errington, 1st Bt and late Marjorie Lady Errington; *m* 1954, Anne, *d* of late Eric and Eileen Baedeker; two *s* one *d. Educ:* Rugby; Trinity College, Oxford (MA). National Service, 2nd Lieut Royal Artillery, 1947–49. Ellerman Lines, 1952–59; Astley Industrial Trust, 1959–70; Exec Dir, 1970, Man. Dir, 1977, Mercantile Credit Co. Chairman: Equipment Leasing Assoc., 1976–78; European Fedn of Leasing Assocs, 1978–80; Finance Houses Assoc., 1982–84; Dir., Barclays Merchant Bank, Barclays Bank UK, 1979–. JP Windsor Forest, 1970. *Recreations:* fishing, golf, splitting logs, avoiding telephones. *Address:* 203 Gloucester Place, NW1. *T:* 01–242 7022. *Club:* Army and Navy.

ERRITT, Michael John Mackey; Assistant Director, Central Statistical Office, Cabinet Office, since 1985; *b* 15 Feb. 1931; *s* of William Albert Erritt, MBE, and Anna Erritt; *m* 1957, Marian Elizabeth Hillock; two *s. Educ:* St Andrews Coll., Dublin; Prince of Wales Sch., Nairobi; Queen's Univ., Belfast. BSc(Econ). Research Officer, Science and Industry Cttee, 1953; Asst Statistician, Central Statistical Office, 1955; Statistician: Board of Trade, 1960; Treasury, 1964; Board of Trade, 1967; Chief Statistician: Inland Revenue, 1968; Central Statistical Office, 1973; Depts of Industry, Trade and Prices and Consumer Protection, 1975; MoD, 1979; Asst Under-Sec. of State (Statistics), MoD, 1981. *Publications:* articles in official, academic and trade jls. *Address:* Green Tiles, 14 Brook Lane, Lindfield, Sussex RH16 1SG. *T:* Haywards Heath 413391.

ERROLL, 24th Earl of, *cr* 1452; **Merlin Sereld Victor Gilbert Hay;** Lord Hay, 1429; Baron of Slains, 1452; Bt 1685; 28th Hereditary Lord High Constable of Scotland, *cr* 1314; Celtic title, Mac Garadh Mor; 33rd Chief of the Hays (from 1171); Senior Great Officer, Royal Household in Scotland; computer consultant; *b* 20 April 1948; *er s* of 23rd Countess of Erroll and Sir Iain Moncreiffe of that Ilk, 11th Bt, CVO, QC; *S* mother, 1978 (and to baronetcy of father, 1985); *m* 1982, Isabelle Astell, *o d* of T. S. Astell Hohler, *qv*; one *s. Educ:* Eton; Trinity College, Cambridge. Page to the Lord Lyon, 1956. Lieut, Atholl Highlanders, 1974. OStJ 1977. Member, Queen's Body Guard for Scotland, Royal Company of Archers, 1978. *Recreations:* skiing, climbing, TAVR. *Heir: s* Lord Hay, *qv. Address:* Wolverton Farm, Basingstoke, Hants RG26 5SX. *Clubs:* White's, Pratt's; Puffin's (Edinburgh).

ERROLL OF HALE, 1st Baron, *cr* 1964; **Frederick James Erroll,** PC 1960; MA, FIEE; FIMechE; Chairman, Bowater Corporation, 1973–84; *b* 27 May 1914; *s* of George Murison Erroll, engineer, and Kathleen Donovan Edington, both of Glasgow and London; *m* 1950, Elizabeth, *o d* of R. Sowton Barrow, Exmouth, Devon. *Educ:* Oundle Sch.; Trinity Coll., Cambridge. Engineering Apprenticeship, 1931–32; Cambridge Univ., 1932–35; Engineer at Metropolitan-Vickers Electrical Co. Ltd, Manchester, 1936–38; Commissioned into 4th County of London Yeomanry (Sharpshooters), TA, 1939; technical appointments in connection with Tank Construction and Testing, 1940–43; service in India and Burma, 1944–45; Col 1945. MP (C) Altrincham and Sale, 1945–64. A Dir of Engineering and Mining Companies until April 1955; Parly Sec., Min. of Supply, April 1955–Nov. 1956; Parly Sec., BoT, 1956–58; Economic Sec. to the Treasury, Oct. 1958–59; Minister of State, BoT, 1959–61; Pres., BoT, 1961–63; Minister of Power, 1963–64. Mem., H of L Select Cttee on Science and Technology, 1985–. Pres., Consolidated Gold Fields, 1982– (Chm., 1976–82); Chairman: Bowater Corporation Ltd; Whessoe plc, 1970–; ASEA Ltd, 1965–84; Fläkt Ltd, 1971–85; Gen. Advr, ASEA, Sweden, 1965–. Member: Council Inst. Directors, 1949–55, and 1965– (Chm. Council, 1973–76, Pres., 1976–84, Chancellor, 1984–); NEDC, 1962–63. President: London Chamber of Commerce, 1966–69; Hispanic and Luso-Brazilian Councils, 1969–73; British Export Houses Assoc., 1969–72; British Exec. Service Overseas, 1972–85; UK South Africa Trade Assoc., 1979–84; World Travel Market, 1986–; Vice-President: Inst. of Marketing, 1983–; Automobile Assoc., 1986– (Chm., 1974–86). Dep. Chm., Decimal Currency Board, 1966–71; Chm., Cttee on Liquor Licensing, 1971–72; Pres., Electrical Research Assoc., 1971–74. Trustee, Westminster Abbey Trust, 1978–. FRSA 1971. *Heir:* none. *Address:* House of Lords, SW1. *Club:* Carlton.

ERSHAD, Lt-Gen. Hussain Muhammad; President of Bangladesh, since 1983; President of the Council of Ministers, since 1982; Minister of Defence, Establishment, Health and Population Control, since 1986; *b* 1 Feb. 1930; *s* of late Makbul Hussain, Advocate, and of Mojida Begum; *m* 1956, Begum Raushad Ershad; one *s* one adopted *d. Educ:* Carmichael Coll., Rangpur; Dhaka Univ. (BA 1st Div.). Staff Course, Defence Service Command and Staff Coll., Quetta, Pakistan, 1966; War Course, National Defence Coll., New Delhi, India, 1975. Infantry Regimental Service, 1953–58; Adjt, E Bengal Regimental Centre (Basic Inf. Trng Centre), 1960–62; E Pakistan Rifles, 1962–65; Bde Major/Dep. Asst Adjt and Quarter Master General, 1967–68; CO, Inf. Bn, 1969–71; Adjt General, Bangladesh Army, 1973–74; Dep. Chief of Army Staff, Bangladesh Army, Chm., Coordination and Control Cell for National Security, 1975–78; Chief of Army Staff, Bangladesh Army, 1978–86; C-in-C, Bangladesh Armed Forces, and Chief Martial Law Administrator, Bangladesh, 1982–86. Chm., National Sports Control Bd. *Publications:* poems in Bengali contributed occasionally to literary jls. *Address:* Office of the President, Bangabhaban, Dhaka, Bangladesh. *Club:* Kurmitola Golf (Dhaka).

ERSKINE; *see* St Clair-Erskine.

ERSKINE, family name of **Earls of Buchan** and **Mar and Kellie,** and of **Baron Erskine of Rerrick.**

ERSKINE OF RERRICK, 2nd Baron *cr* 1964; **Iain Maxwell Erskine;** Bt 1961; professional photographer; Director: Debenham Group; Consultancy Holdings plc; *b* 22 Jan. 1926; *o s* of 1st Baron Erskine of Rerrick, GBE, and of Henrietta, *d* of late William Dunnett, Caithness; *S* father, 1980; *m* 1st, Marie Elisabeth (later Countess of Caledon) (marr. diss. 1964), *d* of Major Burton Allen, Benvhier House, Ballachulish; no *c*; 2nd, 1974, Maria Josephine, *d* of late Dr Josef Klupt and of Mona Lilias Klupt, Richmond, Surrey; three *d. Educ:* Harrow. Served War of 1939–45: 2nd Lieut Grenadier Guards, 1945. ADC, RMA, Sandhurst, 1951–52; Comptroller to Governor-Gen. of New Zealand, 1960–61; retd as Major, 1963. PRO to Household Bde, 1964–66. Chm., Orgn of Professional Sales Agents. Life Mem., Nat. Trust of Scotland; Mem. Cttee and Life Mem., Royal Photographic Soc.; Mem. Cttee and Dir, De Haviland Aircraft Museum (British Aerospace), Salisbury Hall, Herts. MInstM, MIPR; FInstD, 1967–75. Chevalier, Chaîne des Rôtisseurs. Chevalier, Legion of Honour. OStJ. *Recreations:* fishing, flying (qualified pilot, Chm. Guards Flying Club), good food, photography. *Heir:* none. *Address:* House of Lords, SW1. *Clubs:* Caledonian, Special Forces.

ERSKINE, Lord; James Thorne Erskine; Community Service Supervisor, Inverness, since 1983; *b* 10 March 1949; *s* and *heir* of 13th Earl of Mar and 15th Earl of Kellie, *qv*; *m* 1974, Mrs Mary Mooney, *yr d* of Dougal McD. Kirk. *Educ:* Eton; Moray House Coll. of Education, 1968–71. Page of Honour to the Queen, 1962, 1963. Community Service Volunteer, York, 1967–68; Community Worker, Richmond-Craigmillar Parish Church, Edinburgh, 1971–73; Sen. Social Worker, Family and Community Services, Sheffield District Council, 1973–76; Social Worker: Grampian Regional Council, Elgin, 1976–77, Forres, 1977–78; Highland Regional Council, Aviemore, 1979; HM Prison, Inverness, 1979–81; Inverness, Aug.-Dec. 1981; Community Worker, Merkinch Centre, Inverness, Jan.-July 1982. Pilot Officer, RAuxAF, 1979, attached to 2622 Highland Sqdn, RAuxAF Regt; Flying Officer, RAuxAF, 1982–85. *Recreations:* hill walking, railways, gardening, cycling, service with RNXS. *Address:* Claremont House, Alloa, Clackmannanshire. *T:* Alloa 212020; Dumyat, Drummond Crescent, Inverness. *T:* Inverness 220280. *Club:* New (Edinburgh).

ERSKINE, Sir David; *see* Erskine, Sir T. D.

ERSKINE, Ralph, CBE 1978; architect; own practice (in Sweden since 1939; also at Byker, Newcastle upon Tyne); *b* 24 Feb. 1914; *s* of late George and Mildred Erskine; *m* 1939, Ruth Monica Francis; one *s* two *d. Educ:* Friends' Sch., Saffron Walden, Essex; Regent Street Polytechnic (architecture). ARIBA 1936; AMTPI 1938; SAR 1965. Won number of prizes in arch. comps in Sweden; one year's study at Academy for Fine Arts, Sweden, 1945. *Work executed:* town plans; workers' houses; co-operative housing and industrial housing; flats; hostels; factories; ski-hotel; shopping centre; school; town hall; hall of residence at Clare Coll., Cambridge; churches; housing estates at Newmarket and Killingworth; Allhuset and Sports hall; clearance scheme, Byker, Newcastle upon Tyne; design of new town, Resolute Bay, Canada; University Library, Stockholm. Lecturing: in America, Canada, Japan and many countries in Europe. Hon. Dr, Lund Univ., Sweden, 1975; Hon. DLitt, Heriot-Watt Univ., 1982. For. Mem., Royal Acad. of Arts, Sweden, 1972; Hon. Mem., Bund Deutscher Architekten, 1983. Hon Fellow of AIA, 1966; SAR's Kasper Sahlin prize for 1971 and 1981; Ytong Prize, 1974; Guld medal, Litteris et Artibus, 1980; Canadian Gold Medal, RAIC, 1983; Wolf Prize for Architecture, 1984. *Publications:* for several arch. magazines, on building in northern climates, etc. *Relevant publication:* Ralph Erskine, by Mats Egelius, 1978. *Recreations:* ski-ing, skating, swimming, yachting, ice yachting. *Address:* Gustav III's väg, Drottningholm, Sweden. *T:* 7590352.

ERSKINE, Sir (Thomas) David, 5th Bt, *cr* 1821; JP; Vice Lord-Lieutenant, Fife Region, since 1981; Convener, Fife County Council, 1970–73; *b* 31 July 1912; *o surv. s* of Sir Thomas Wilfred Hargreaves John Erskine, 4th Bt, and late Magdalen Janet, *d* of Sir Ralph Anstruther, 6th Bt of Balcaskie; *S* father, 1944; *m* 1947, Ann, *er d* of late Lt-Col Neil Fraser-Tytler, DSO, MC, and of Christian Helen Fraser-Tytler, CBE, *qv*; two *s* (and one *d* decd). *Educ:* Eton; Magdalene Coll., Cambridge. Employed by Butterfield & Swire, London and China, in 1934 and served with them in China, 1935–41. Joined HM Forces in India and commissioned into Indian Corps of Engineers. Served with them in Mid-East, India and Malaya, being demobilised in 1945 with rank of Major. JP Fife, 1951; DL Fife, 1955–81. *Heir: s* Thomas Peter Neil Erskine [*b* 28 March 1950; *m* 1972, Catherine, *d* of Col G. H. K. Hewlett; two *s* two *d*]. *Address:* West Newhall House, Kingsbarns, Fife. *T:* Crail 50228. *Club:* New (Edinburgh).

ERSKINE, Thomas Ralph, CB 1986; First Legislative Draftsman, Northern Ireland, since 1979; *b* 14 Oct. 1933; *m* 1966, Patricia Joan Palmer; one *s* one *d. Educ:* Campbell College; Queen's University, Belfast. Called to the Bar, Gray's Inn, 1962. *Publications:* contribs to Cryptologia, Annals of the History of Computing and to legal periodicals. *Recreations:* skiing, cycling. *Address:* Office of the Legislative Draftsmen, Parliament Buildings, Belfast BT4 3SW. *T:* Belfast 63210.

ERSKINE-HILL, Henry Howard, PhD; FBA 1985; Fellow of Pembroke College, since 1980, and Reader in Literary History, since 1984, Cambridge University; *b* 19 June 1936; *s* of Henry Erskine-Hill and Hannah Lilian Poppleton. *Educ:* Ashville Coll.; Nottingham Univ. (BA, PhD); MA Cantab. University of Wales, Swansea: Tutor, 1960; Asst Lectr, 1961; Lectr in Eng. Lit., 1962; Sen. Fellow, 1964–65; University of Cambridge: Lectr in English, 1969–84; Fellow, 1969–80, Tutor, 1970–76, Jesus Coll.; Tutor for Graduates, Pembroke Coll., 1983–84. Taught at British Council seminars in Britain, 1962–69; invited lectr, univs of Alberta, Adelaide, Berkeley (Calif), Bristol, Davis (Calif), Essex, Flinders (S Australia), Liverpool, London, Monash, Nantes, Oxford, Saskatchewan, Stanford, Singapore, Wales (Swansea), Victoria (BC), Warwick, W Australia and York; also at David Nichol Smith Seminar, Canberra, Inter-Univ. Centre, Dubrovnik, Inst. of Hist. Res., London, and Herzog-August Library, Wolfenbüttel. *Publications:* (ed) Alexander Pope: Horatian Satires and Epistles, 1964; Pope: The Dunciad, 1972; The Social Milieu of Alexander Pope, 1975; (ed with Anne Smith) The Art of Alexander Pope, 1978; (ed with Graham Storey) Revolutionary Prose of the English Civil War, 1983; The Augustan Idea, 1983; contributions to: Renaissance and Modern Essays, ed G. R. Hibbard, 1966; English Drama: forms and Development, ed Marie Axton and Raymond Williams, 1977; Ideology and Conspiracy, ed Eveline Cruickshanks, 1982; jls incl. Essays in Criticism, Eighteenth-Century Studies, Jl of the Warburg and Courtauld Insts, Rev. of English Studies, Renaissance and Modern Studies. *Recreation:* fell walking. *Address:* Pembroke College, Cambridge CB2 1RF. *T:* Cambridge 338100. *Club:* United Oxford & Cambridge University.

ERSKINE-HILL, Sir Robert, 2nd Bt, *cr* 1945; Member of the Royal Company of Archers, Queen's Body Guard for Scotland; Chartered Accountant; Director, Life Association of Scotland, since 1951 (Chairman, 1960–86); *b* 6 Feb. 1917; *er s* of Sir Alexander Galloway Erskine-Hill, 1st Bt, KC, DL, and Christian Hendrie, MBE (*d* 1947), *o d* of John Colville, MP, Cleland, Lanarkshire; *S* father, 1947; *m* 1942, Christine Alison, *o d* of late Capt. (A) Henry James Johnstone of Alva, RN; two *s* two *d*. *Educ:* Eton; Trinity Coll., Cambridge (BA). Served War of 1939–45, in RNVR. Partner, Chiene & Tait, CA, Edinburgh, 1946–80. *Heir: s* Alexander Roger Erskine-Hill, [*b* 15 Aug. 1949; *m* 1984, Sarah Anne Sydenham Clarke, *er d* of late Dr R. J. Sydenham Clarke and of Mrs Charles Clarke; one *s* one *d*]. *Address:* Quothquhan Lodge, Biggar, Lanarkshire. *T:* Tinto 332.

ERSKINE-LINDOP, Audrey Beatrice Noël; novelist; *b* London; *d* of late Lt-Col A. H. Erskine-Lindop, MC, and Ivy Monck-Mason; *m* 1945, Dudley Gordon Leslie, scriptwriter and playwright. *Educ:* Convent of Our Lady of Lourdes, Hatch End, Middx; Blackdown Sch., Wellington, Somerset. Started career in Worthing Repertory Company; became scriptwriter (England and Hollywood). Books have been published in numerous countries. Freeman of City of London, 1954. *Plays:* Beware of Angels (in collaboration with Dudley Leslie), prod Westminster Theatre, 1959; Let's Talk Turkey, prod 1955. *Publications:* In Me My Enemy, 1948; Soldiers' Daughters Never Cry, 1949; The Tall Headlines, 1950; Out of the Whirlwind, 1951; The Singer Not the Song, 1953 (Book Society choice; filmed, 1961); Details of Jeremy Stretton, 1955; The Judas Figures, 1956; I Thank a Fool, 1958; The Way to the Lantern, 1961; Nicola, 1964; I Start Counting, 1966 (Prix Roman Policier, France, 1968); Sight Unseen, 1969; Journey into Stone, 1973; The Self-Appointed Saint, 1975. *Recreations:* history (particularly collecting relics of favourite historical characters); anything to do with birds and cats; very fond of the wilder type of countryside. *Address:* Southcliffe Cottage, Sandrock Road, Niton Undercliff, IoW PO38 2NQ. *T:* Niton 730291.

ERSKINE-MURRAY, family name of **Lord Elibank.**

ERVINE-ANDREWS, Lieut-Col Harold Marcus, VC 1940; East Lancashire Regiment, retired; *b* 29 July 1911; *s* of late C. C. Ervine-Andrews, New Ross, Wexford, Southern Ireland; *m* 1st, 1939, Betty (decd), *er d* of R. I. Torrie; one *s* one *d*; 2nd, 1981, Margaret Gregory. *Educ:* Stonyhurst Coll.; Royal Military Coll., Sandhurst. 2nd Lieut East Lancs Regt, 1932; Captain 1940; Temp. Major, 1940; War Subst. Major, 1942; Temp. Lieut-Col 1942; served with RAF during North-West Frontier of India Operations, 1936–37 (medal and two clasps, despatches) and NW Frontier, 1938–39; served in France with BEF (VC); attached to RAF in UK, 1940; on loan to Australian Military Forces, 1941; attached RAAF, 1942; GSO 1 Air HQ Allied Land Forces in South-West Pacific Area, 1943; commanding No. 61 Carrier-Borne Army Liaison Section, 1944; SALO in 21st Aircraft Carrier Squadron (East Indies), 1945; Lieut-Col Commanding No. 18 Infantry Holding Bn, 1946; attached to The Army Mobile Information Unit, 1948; Asst Dir of Public Relations to BAOR, 1951, as a Lieut-Col; retired pay, 1952. *Address:* Treveor Cot, Gorran, St Austell, Cornwall PL26 6LW. *T:* Mevagissey 842140.

ESAKI, Leo; IBM Fellow since 1967; Manager, Device Physics, IBM T. J. Watson Research Center, since 1962; *b* 12 March 1925; *s* of Soichiro Esaki and Niyoko Ito; *m* 1959, Masako Araki; one *s* two *d*. *Educ:* Univ. of Tokyo. MS 1947, PhD 1959. Sony Corp., Japan, 1956–60; IBM Research, 1960–. Director: IBM-Japan, 1976–; Yamada Science Foundn, 1976–. Research in tunnelling in semiconductor junctions which led to the discovery of the tunnel diode, now working on man-made semiconductor superlattice in search of predicted quantum mechanical effect. Sir John Cass sen. vis. res. fellow, London Poly, 1982. Councillor-at-Large, Amer. Phys. Soc., 1971; Dir, Amer. Vacuum Soc., 1972; Mem., Japan Academy, 1975; For. Associate, Nat. Acad. of Sciences, USA, 1976; For. Associate, Nat. Acad. of Engineering, USA, 1977; Corresp. Mem., Academia Nacional De Ingenieria, Mexico, 1978. Nishina Meml Award, 1959; Asahi Press Award, 1960; Toyo Rayon Foundn Award, 1961; Morris N. Liebmann Meml Prize, 1961; Stuart Ballantine Medal, Franklin Inst., 1961; Japan Academy Award, 1965; (jtly) Nobel Prize for Physics, 1973; (jtly) Internat. Prize for New Materials, Amer Physical Soc, 1985. Order of Culture, Japan, 1974; Science Achievement Award, US-Asia Inst., 1983. *Publications:* numerous papers in learned jls. *Address:* IBM Thomas J. Watson Research Center, PO Box 218, Yorktown Heights, New York 10598, USA. *T:* (914) 945–2342.

ESCHENBACH, Christoph; pianist and conductor; Principal Guest Conductor, London Philharmonic Orchestra, since 1981; *b* 20 Feb. 1940. *Educ:* Hamburg Conservatory; State Music Conservatory, Cologne. Winner: Internat. Piano Competition, Munich, 1962; Concours Clara Haskil, 1965. Canadian début, Montreal Expo, 1967; US début, Cleveland Orch., 1969; has toured Europe, N and S America, USSR, Israel, Japan; and has performed as pianist with leading orchs incl. Concertgebouw Amsterdam, Orch. de Paris, London Symphony, Berlin Philharmonic, and Cleveland Orch.; festivals incl. Salzburg, Lucerne, Bonn, and Aix-en-Provence. Chief Conductor, Tonhalle Orch., Zürich, and Artistic Dir, Tonhalle-Gesellschaft, Zürich, 1982–86; guest appearances with NY Philharmonic, Boston Symphony, Chicago Symphony, Cleveland Orch., Pittsburgh Symphony, Los Angeles Philharmonic, London Symphony, BBC Philharmonia, Berlin Philharmonic, Bavarian Radio Symphony Munich, Munich Philharmonic, Vienna Symphonic, Czech Philharmonic and New Japan Philharmonic. *Address:* c/o Columbia Artists Management Inc., 165 West 57th Street, New York, NY 10019, USA.

ESCRITT, (Charles) Ewart, OBE 1970; MA; Secretary, Oxford University Appointments Committee, 1947–70; Fellow, Keble College, Oxford, 1965–70; *b* 26 Aug. 1905; *s* of late Rev. Charles Escritt; *m* 1939, Ruth Mary, *d* of late T. C. Metcalf; two *s* one *d*. *Educ:* Christ's Hospital; Keble Coll., Oxford. Asst Master, Bromsgrove Sch., 1928; Staff of Tootal Broadhurst Lee Co. Ltd, 1933–46. Served War of 1939–45: 42 Div. RASC (TA), 1939; 18 Div. RASC, Capt. 1940; POW, Singapore and Thailand, 1942–45. *Recreation:* Japanese studies. *Address:* 32 Portland Road, Oxford. *T:* Oxford 57072.

ESCRITT, Maj.-Gen. Frederick Knowles, CB 1953; OBE 1943; MRCS; late RAMC, retired Nov. 1953; *b* 29 Nov. 1893; *s* of Harold Teal Escritt; *m* 1931, Elsa Alfrida, *d* of Director Larssen, Stockholm; one *d*. *Educ:* Dulwich Coll.; Guy's Hosp. MRCS, LRCP, 1918. Joined RAMC, Aug. 1918 (1914–15 Star, British War and Victory Medals). Served War of 1939–45 (Gen. Service Iraq, 1939–45 Star, Burma Star, Defence and War Medals, 1939–45). ADMS Eastern and 14 Armies, 1942–45; DDMS 1 Corps Dist, BAOR, 1945–47; Inspector of Training, AMS, 1950–51; DDMS, Eastern Command, 1951–53. QHS, 1952–53. Order of St John (Officer Brother), 1952.

ESDAILE, Philippa Chichele, DSc, FLS; Reader in Biology, University of London, and Head of Biology Department, King's College of Household and Social Science, 1921–51; *b* 1888; *y d* of late George Esdaile, Manchester and late Georgina, *d* of George Doswell, Somerset. *Educ:* Manchester High Sch. for Girls. Graduated Univ. of Manchester, 1910; Research Fellow of University of Manchester and University Coll., Reading; Acting Head of Zoology Dept, Bedford Coll., University of London, 1915–20; Senior Lecturer in Zoology, Birkbeck Coll., University of London, 1920–21; Vice-Pres. of Linnean Soc. of London, 1932–33; Member: Makerere-Khartoum Education Commission, 1937; Advisory Committee on Education, Colonial Office, 1933–38; Committee on Nutrition in the Colonial Empire, Econ. Adv. Coun., 1933; Federation of Univ. Women; Crosby Hall. Formerly Member: Coun. of Girls' Public Day Sch. Trust, Ltd; Governing Body of Hatfield Sch., Herts. *Publications:* Economic Biology for Students of Social Science, Parts 1 and 2; various scientific papers. *Address:* St Audrey's, Church Street, Old Hatfield, Herts. *T:* Hatfield 61990.

ESDALE, Mrs G. P. R.; *see* Lindop, Patricia J.

ESER, Prof. Dr Günter Otto; Director General, International Air Transport Association, Montreal/Geneva, since 1985; *b* 10 Sept. 1927; *s* of Ernst Eser and Martha Siering; *m* 1976, Florida Huisman; two *s*. *Educ:* Bonn Univ.; Federal Acad. of Finance, Siegburg; Harvard (Management Programme). Auditor, Fed. German Min. of Finance, 1953–55; Lufthansa German Airlines, 1955–84: Head, Persian subsidiary, Teheran; Head, Munich Dist Office for Southern Germany; Sales Manager, Germany; Gen. Man., N and Central America; Mem., Chief Exec. Bd. Member: Adv. Bd, Europäische Reiseversicherung, 1978–; Adv. Bd, Amer. Univ., 1982–. Associate Prof., Pace Univ., NY, 1978–. Bundesverdienstkreuz 1st Class (FRG), 1985; Commendatore Officiale (Italy), 1967. *Recreations:* trekking, ocean-fishing, literature, music. *Address:* c/o IATA, PO Box 160, 1216 Cointrin-Geneva, Switzerland. *T:* Geneva 983366.

ESHER, 4th Viscount, *cr* 1897; Baron *cr* 1885; **Lionel Gordon Baliol Brett,** CBE 1970; MA; PPRIBA; DistTP; Rector and Vice-Provost, Royal College of Art, 1971–78; *b* 18 July 1913; *o s* of 3rd Viscount Esher, GBE; *S* father, 1963; *m* 1935, Christian, *e d* of late Col Ebenezer Pike, CBE, MC; five *s* one *d*. *Educ:* Eton (Scholar); New Coll., Oxford (Scholar); BA (1st Class), 1935; Hon. Fellow, 1980; RIBA Ashpitel Prizeman, 1939. Served War in RA, 1940–45; France and Germany, 1944–45 (despatches); Major. Architect Planner, Hatfield New Town, 1949–59; major housing projects: Hatfield, Stevenage, Basildon; consultant architect: Downside Abbey; Maidenhead Town Centre; Abingdon Town Centre; Portsmouth City Centre; York City Centre; Santiago, Chile and Caracas, Venezuela (both for UNDP); principal buildings include: (with Francis Pollen): High Comr's House, Lagos; 82 and 190 Sloane St, London; Pall Mall Ct, Manchester; Downside Sch. extensions; Exeter Coll., and Oxenford Hall, Oxford; (with Teggin & Taylor) Civic Offices, Portsmouth. Lecture tours: USA 1953; India, 1954; Australia, 1959; S America, 1970. Governor, Museum of London, 1970–77; Member: Royal Fine Art Commn, 1951–69; Adv. Bd for Redundant Churches (Chm., 1977–83); Advisory Council, Victoria and Albert Museum, 1967–72; Arts Council of GB, 1972–77 (Chm., Art Panel); Environment Panel, British Rail, 1977–85; National Trust (Chm., Thames and Chilterns Reg., 1979–83); Vice-Pres., RIBA, 1958–59, 1962–63, 1964–65; Pres., 1965–67; Trustee, Soane Museum, 1976–. Hon. DLitt Strathclyde Univ., 1967; Hon. DUniv York, 1970; Hon. DSc Edinburgh, 1981. Hon. Fellow: Amer. Inst. of Architects, 1967; Portsmouth Polytechnic, 1984; Hon. FSIAD, 1975. *Publications:* Houses, 1947; The World of Architecture, 1963; Landscape in Distress, 1965; York: a study in conservation, 1969; Parameters and Images, 1970; (with Elisabeth Beazley) Shell Guide to North Wales, 1971; A Broken Wave, 1981; The Continuing Heritage, 1982; Our Selves Unknown (autobiog.), 1985. *Recreation:* landscapes. *Heir: s* Hon. Christopher Lionel Baliol Brett [*b* 23 Dec. 1936; *m* 1st, 1962, Camilla Charlotte (marr. diss. 1970), *d* of Sir (Horace) Anthony Rumbold, 10th Bt, KGMG, KCVO, CB; one *s* two *d*; 2nd, 1971, Valerie Harrington; two *s* twin *d*]. *Address:* Christmas Common Tower, Watlington, Oxford. *Club:* Arts.

See also Sir Martyn G. Beckett, Sir Evelyn Shuckburgh.

ESKDAILL, Lord; Walter John Francis Montagu Douglas Scott; *b* 2 Aug. 1984; *s* and *heir* of Earl of Dalkeith, *qv*.

ESMONDE, Sir John Henry Grattan, 16th Bt *cr* 1629; SC; **His Honour Judge Esmonde;** Circuit Court Judge, Western Circuit, since 1977; *b* 27 June 1928; *s* of Sir Anthony Charles Esmonde, 15th Bt, and of Eithne Moira Grattan, *y d* of Sir Thomas Grattan Esmonde, 11th Bt; *S* father, 1981; *m* 1957, Pamela Mary, *d* of late Francis Stephen Bourke, FRCPI; three *s* two *d*. *Educ:* Blackrock College, Dublin; University Coll., Dublin; King's Inns, Dublin. BComm, NUI. Member of the Irish Bar, 1949; Senior Counsel, 1971. TD (Fine Gael) Wexford, 1973–77. *Heir: s* Thomas Francis Grattan Esmonde, *b* 14 Oct. 1960. *Address:* 6 Nutley Avenue, Dublin 4. *T:* Dublin 693040. *Club:* Galway County.

ESPIE, Sir Frank (Fletcher), Kt 1979; OBE 1971; FTS, FIMM, MAIMM, MAIME; Deputy Chairman, CRA Ltd, 1974–79 (Director, 1968; non-executive Director, 1979–85); *b* 8 May 1917; *s* of late Frank Fancett Espie and Laura Jean Espie; *m* 1941, Madeline Elizabeth Robertson (decd); one *s* three *d*; *m* 1985, Jean Primrose Angove. *Educ:* St Peter's Coll., Adelaide; Univ. of Adelaide (BEng). FTS 1978; FIMM 1958. Bougainville Copper Ltd: Gen. Man., 1965; Man. Dir, 1969; Chm., 1971–79; Dir, 1979–85. Director: ICI Aust. Ltd, 1979–; Tubemakers of Australia, 1980–; Westpac Banking Corporation, 1981–; Woodside Petroleum, 1981–. Member: Exec. Cttee, Aust. Mining Industry Council, 1973–81 (Pres., 1978–80); Chm., National Petroleum Adv. Cttee, 1979–; Council: Australasian Inst. of Mining and Metallurgy (Pres., 1975; Inst. Medal, 1980); Aust. Acad. of Technological Scis. *Recreations:* swimming, golf. *Address:* 31 The Righi, South Yarra, Vic 3141, Australia. *T:* (03) 266.2062. *Clubs:* Melbourne, Athenæum, Royal Melbourne Golf (Melbourne); Union (Sydney); Adelaide (Adelaide).

ESPINOSA, Dr Augusto; Senator of the Republic of Colombia, 1958–74 and since 1978; *b* 5 June 1919; *m* 1944, Myriam de Espinosa; three *s*. *Educ:* Universidad Nacional, Colombia (Dr in Law and Pol Scis, 1942). Manager, Banco de Bogotá, Bucaramanga, 1943–46; Gen. Man., Agriculture, Industrial and Mining Credit Bank, 1959–61. Deputy and Pres., Deptl Assembly of Santander, 1943; Councillor and Pres. of Council of Bucaramanga, 1945–47; Mem., House of Representatives, 1947–51 and 1974–78; Minister of Agriculture, 1958–59; Pres. of Senate, 1963–64; Ambassador to UN and Perm. Colombian Rep., UN, 1970–73; Ambassador to UK, 1982–84. Pres., First Commn of the Senate, 1982. Grand Cross, Order of Merit, France, 1964. *Publications:* El Pensamiento Económico y Político en Colombia (The Economic and Political Thought in Colombia), 1942; essays and articles in leading Colombian newspapers and magazines. *Recreations:* reading, writing; fond of dogs. *Clubs:* Jockey, Country (Bogotá, Colombia).

ESPLEN, Sir William Graham, 2nd Bt, *cr* 1921; former Shipowner; *b* 29 Dec. 1899; *s* of 1st Bt and Laura Louise (*d* 1936), *d* of late John Dickinson, Sunderland; *S* father, 1930; *m* 1928, Aline Octavia (marr. diss. 1951), *y d* of late A. Octavius Hedley; one *s*. *Educ:* Harrow; Cambridge. Joined Royal Naval College, Keyham, 1918; retired, 1922.

Recreation: fishing. *Heir: s* John Graham Esplen [*b* 4 Aug. 1932; *m* 1956, Valerie Joan, *yr d* of Maj.-Gen. A. P. Lambooy, CB, OBE, and late Doris Lambooy; one *s* three *d*]. *Address:* c/o Alldens Cottage, Thorncombe Street, Bramley, Surrey GU5 0NA.

ESPLIN, Air Vice-Marshal Ian (George), CB 1963; OBE 1946; DFC 1943; retired (voluntarily) 1965; *b* 26 Feb. 1914; *s* of late Donald Thomas Esplin and Emily Freame Esplin; *m* 1944, Patricia Kaleen Barlow; one *s* one *d. Educ:* Sydney Univ.; Oxford Univ. BEc 1936; MA 1939. Rowing Blue, 1934 and 1935. NSW Rhodes Schol., 1937. Entered RAF from Oxford, 1939. Served War of 1939–45, as Pilot in Night-Fighters; destroyed three enemy aircraft at night; also served at CFS and in HQ, SEAC; Air Min. (Policy), 1945; Comd Desford, 1947; Dep. Senior Personnel Staff Officer, HQ Reserve Comd, 1948; Directing Staff, RAF Staff Coll., 1950–51; Comd first Jet All Weather Wing, Germany (No 148), 1952–54; Flying Coll. Course, 1954; Dep. Dir of Operational Requirements, Air Min., 1955–58; Comd RAF Wartling, 1958–60; Dir of Operational Reqts, 1960–62; Comdr, RAF Staff and Air Attaché, Washington, DC, 1963–65; Dean, Air Attaché Corps, 1964–65. *Recreations:* golf, tennis, swimming. *Address:* c/o National Westminster Bank, West End Office, 1 St James's Square, SW1. *Clubs:* Vincent's (Oxford); Leander (Henley-on-Thames).

ESQUIVEL, Rt Hon. Manuel; PC 1986; Prime Minister of Belize, since 1984; Member, House of Representatives, since 1984; Leader, United Democratic Party, since 1982; *b* 2 May 1940; *s* of John and Laura Esquivel; *m* 1971, Kathleen Levy; one *s* two *d. Educ:* Loyola Univ., New Orleans (BSc Physics); Bristol Univ. (Cert Ed.). Instructor in Physics, St John's Coll., Belize City, 1967–82. Member: Belize City Council, 1974–80; Nat. Senate, 1979–84. Chm., Utd Democratic Party, 1976–82. Hon. DHL Loyola Univ., 1986. *Recreation:* electronics. *Address:* Office of the Prime Minister, Belmopan, Belize. *T:* Belmopan 08-2346.

ESSAAFI, M'hamed, Grand Officier, Order of Tunisian Republic, 1963; United Nations Disaster Relief Co-ordinator, since 1982; *b* 26 May 1930; *m* 1956, Hedwige Klat; one *s* one *d. Educ:* Sadiki Coll., Tunis; Sorbonne, Paris. Secretariat of State for For. Affairs, 1956; 1st Sec., Tunisian Embassy, London, 1956; 1st Sec., Tunisian Embassy, Washington, 1957; Secretariat of State for For. Affairs, Tunis: Dir of Amer. Dept, 1960; America and Internat. Confs Dept, 1962; Ambassador to London, 1964–69; Ambassador to Moscow, 1970–74; Ambassador to Bonn, 1974–76; Sec.-Gen., Ministry of Foreign Affairs, Tunis, 1969–70 and 1976–78; Ambassador to Belgium and EEC, 1978–79; Permanent Rep. of Tunisia to the UN, and Special Rep. of the Sec.-Gen., 1980–81, Chef de Cabinet 1982. *Address:* United Nations, Room 140, Palais des Nations, CH-1211 Geneva 10, Switzerland.

ESSAME, Enid Mary, MA Cantab; Headmistress of Queenswood School, 1943–71; 2nd *d* of Oliver Essame. *Educ:* Wyggeston Gram. Sch., Leicester; Girls' High Sch., Newark; Newnham Coll., Cambridge (Hist. Tripos, 1928); King's Coll., University of London (Certificate of Education, 1929). Mary Ewart Travelling Scholar, Newnham Coll., 1934–35; AM in Education, American Univ., Washington, DC, USA, 1935. Asst Headmistress Queenswood Sch., 1935–43. British Council lecturer, India and Pakistan, 1953, Nigeria, 1961. Governor, Chorleywood Coll. for Girls with Little or No Sight, 1962. Hon. Sec. Assoc. of Headmistresses of Boarding Schools, Pres. 1962–64. Chm., Assoc. of Ind. and Direct Grant Schools. Bd Mem., Schoolmistresses and Governesses Benevolent Instn, 1974–; Hon. Adviser, Nat. Assoc. for Gifted Children, 1974–. Governor: St Helen's Sch., Northwood; Channing Sch., Highgate; Trustee, Stormont Sch., Potters Bar. Mem., Overseas Grants Cttee, Help the Aged, 1981. JP Herts 1952–76. *Address:* 4 Elmroyd Avenue, Potters Bar, Herts. *T:* Potters Bar 53255. *Clubs:* Royal Over-Seas League, Arts Theatre.

ESSAYAN, Michael, QC 1976; *b* 7 May 1927; *s* of late Kevork Loris Essayan and Rita Sirvarte (*née* Gulbenkian); *m* 1956, Geraldine St Lawrence Lee Guinness, *d* of K. E. L. Guinness, MBE; one *s* one *d. Educ:* France; Harrow; Balliol Coll., Oxford (1st Cl. Class. Hon. Mods 1949, 1st Cl. Lit. Hum. 1951, MA). Served with RA, 1945–48 (Palestine, 1947–48). Iraq Petroleum Co., London and ME, 1951–56. Called to the Bar, Middle Temple 1957 (Bencher 1983), joined Lincoln's Inn *ad eundem* 1958. Mem., Bd of Administration, Calouste Gulbenkian Foundn, Lisbon, 1981–. *Publications:* The New Supreme Court Costs (with M. J. Albery, QC), 1960; (ed with Hon. Mr Justice Walton) Adkin's Landlord and Tenant, 15th, 16th, 17th and 18th edns. *Recreations:* wine and wife. *Address:* 6 Chelsea Square, SW3. *T:* 01–352 6786; 9 Old Square, Lincoln's Inn, WC2. *T:* 01–405 4682. *Club:* Brooks's.

ESSEN, Louis, OBE 1959; FRS 1960; DSc, PhD; retired; *b* 6 Sept. 1908; *s* of Fred Essen and Ada (*née* Edson); *m* 1937, Joan Margery Greenhalgh; four *d. Educ:* High Pavement Sch., Nottingham; London Univ. (Ext.). BSc 1928, PhD 1941, DSc 1948, London. Joined the National Physical Laboratory, 1929; Senior Principal Scientific Officer, 1956–60; Deputy Chief Scientific Officer, 1960–72. Charles Vernon Boys Prize, Phys. Soc. 1957; Tompion Gold Medal, Clockmakers' Company, 1957; Wolfe Award, 1959; A. S. Popov Gold Medal, USSR Acad. of Sciences, 1959. Hon. FUMIST, 1971. *Publications:* Velocity of Light and Radio Waves, 1969; The Special Theory of Relativity, 1971; scientific papers. *Recreations:* walking, gardening, music. *Address:* High Hallgarth, 41 Durleston Park Drive, Great Bookham, Surrey KT23 4AJ. *T:* Bookham 54103.

ESSER, Robin Charles; Editor, Sunday Express, since 1986; *b* 6 May 1935; *s* of late Charles and Winifred Eileen Esser; *m* 1959, Irene Shirley Clough (decd); two *s* two *d*; 1981, Tui (*née* France); one *s. Educ:* Wheelwright Grammar School, Dewsbury; Wadham College, Oxford (BA Hons, MA). Edited Oxford Univ. newspaper, Cherwell, 1954. Commissioned, King's Own Yorkshire Light Infantry, 1956. Freelance reporter, 1957–60; Daily Express: Staff Reporter, 1960; Editor, William Hickey Column, 1963; Features Editor 1965; New York Bureau, 1969; Northern Editor, 1970; Exec. Editor, 1985; Consultant Editor, Evening News, 1977. *Publications:* The Hot Potato, 1969; The Paper Chase, 1971. *Recreations:* lunching, sailing, talking, reading. *Address:* Sunday Express, Fleet Street, EC4. *T:* 01–353 8000. *Club:* Kennel.

ESSERY, David James; Under Secretary, Department of Agriculture and Fisheries for Scotland, since 1985; *b* 10 May 1938; *s* of Lawrence and Edna Essery; *m* 1963, Nora Sim; two *s* one *d. Educ:* Royal High Sch., Edinburgh. Entered Dept of Health for Scotland, 1956; Private Sec. to Minister of State, Scottish Office, 1968; Principal, Scottish Develt Dept, 1969; Assistant Secretary: Scottish Economic Planning Dept, 1976; Scottish Develt Dept, 1981–85. *Recreations:* reading, music, cricket, squash. *Address:* 41 Minto Street, Edinburgh EH9 2BR. *T:* 031–667 5533. *Club:* Royal Commonwealth Society.

ESSEX, 10th Earl of, *cr* 1661; **Robert Edward de Vere Capell;** Baron Capell, 1641; Viscount Malden, 1661; *b* 13 Jan. 1920; *s* of Arthur Algernon de Vere Capell (*d* 1924) and Alice Mabel (*d* 1951), *d* of James Currie, Wimbledon; *S* kinsman, 1981; *m* 1942, Doris Margaret, *d* of George Frederick Tomlinson, Morecambe; one *s.* Heir: *s* Viscount Malden, *qv. Address:* 2 Novak Place, Torrisholme, Morecambe, Lancs.

ESSEX, Francis; author, producer and composer; *b* 24 March 1929; *s* of Harold and Beatrice Essex-Lopresti; *m* 1956, Jeanne Shires; two *s. Educ:* Cotton Coll., N Staffs. Light Entertainment Producer, BBC Television, 1954–60; Sen. Prod., ATV Network Ltd,

1960–65; Controller of Progs, Scottish Television, 1965–69; ATV Network Ltd: Prodn Controller, 1969–76; Mem., Bd of Dirs, 1974; Dir of Production, 1976–81. Wrote and presented, The Bells of St Martins, St Martin's Theatre, 1953; devised and directed, Six of One, Adelphi, 1964; *television film scripts include:* Shillingbury Tales; Silent Scream; The Elizabethan Suite; The Blarney Boys; Cuffy series; *musical script:* Percy French; *scores:* Luke's Kingdom; The Seas Must Live; The Lightning Tree; Maddie With Love, etc; writer of plays and songs. Fellow, Royal Television Soc., 1974. British Acad. Light Entertainment Award, 1964, and Leonard Brett Award, 1964, 1981. *Publications:* Shillingbury Tales, 1983; Skerrymor Bay, 1984. *Recreations:* blue-water sailing, gardening. *Address:* Punta Vista, Aldea de las Cuevas, Benidoleig, Prov. de Alicante, Spain.

ESSEX, Francis William, CMG 1959; retired from HMOCS; *b* 29 June 1916; *s* of Frank Essex; *m* 1947, Marjorie Muriel Joyce Lewis; two *s. Educ:* Royal Grammar Sch., High Wycombe; Reading Univ.; Exeter Coll., Oxford. Joined Colonial Administrative Service, Sierra Leone, 1939; Asst District Commissioner, 1942; District Commissioner, 1948; Principal, HM Treasury, 1951; Dep. Financial Sec., Sierra Leone, 1953; Financial Sec., British Guiana, 1956–60; Financial Sec. to High Comr for Basutoland, Bechuanaland and Swaziland, 1960–64; Counsellor, British Embassy, South Africa, 1964–65; Sec. for Finance and Development, later Permanent Sec., Min. of Finance, Commerce and Industry, Swaziland, 1965–68; Principal, ODM, 1968–76. Mem., Pearce Commn on Rhodesian opinion, 1971–72. Short term British Technical Co-operation assignments, British Virgin Is, 1977, Tuvalu, 1978 and 1979, Antigua and Barbuda, 1981. *Address:* Undermoor, Broomhill, Chagford, Devon.

ESSEX-CATER, Dr Antony John, LRCP, MRCS; FFCM; FRAI; Medical Officer of Health, States of Jersey, Channel Islands, since 1974; Venereologist, General Hospital, Jersey, since 1974; Chairman, National Association for Maternal and Child Welfare, since 1975; *b* 28 Sept. 1923; *s* of Herbert Stanley Cater and Helen Marjorie Essex; *m* 1947, Jane Mary Binning; three *s* one *d. Educ:* Solihull Sch.; King's Coll., Univ. of London; Charing Cross Hosp.; School of Hyg. and Trop. Med., Univ. of London. Bygott Postgrad. Schol., Univ. of London, 1952–53. DPH, DIH, DCH; FRSH; AFOM. Medical Br., RAF, 1948–50. Dep. MOH, Swansea, 1953–58; Admin. MOH, Birmingham, 1958–61; Dep. MOH, Manchester, 1961–68; County MOH, Monmouthshire, 1968–74. Part-time Lectr in Child Health, Univ. of Birmingham, 1958–61; Council of Europe Medical Fellow, 1968. Mem. Exec. Cttee 1958, Vice-Chm. 1969, Nat. Assoc. for Maternal and Child Welfare; Member: Public Health Lab. Services Bd, 1969–75; Steering Cttee, Nat. Health Service Reorganization (Wales), 1971–72; Founder Fellow and Mem. First Bd, Fac. of Community Med., Royal Colls of Physicians of UK, 1972–73. Member: BMA; Med. Soc. for Study of Venereal Diseases. *Publications:* Synopsis of Public Health and Social Medicine, 1960, 2nd edn 1967; Manual of Public Health and Community Medicine, 3rd edn 1979; numerous papers on medical and allied subjects. *Recreations:* literary, music, sport. *Address:* Honfleur, La Vallette, Mont Cambrai, St Lawrence, Jersey, CI. *T:* Jersey 72438. *Club:* Society of Authors.

ESSLIN, Martin Julius, OBE 1972; Professor of Drama, Stanford University, California (for two quarters annually), since 1977; *b* 8 June 1918; *s* of Paul Pereszlenyi and Charlotte Pereszlenyi (*née* Schiffer); *m* 1947, Renate Gerstenberg; one *d. Educ:* Gymnasium, Vienna; Vienna Univ.; Reinhardt Seminar of Dramatic Art, Vienna. Joined BBC, 1940; Producer and Scriptwriter, BBC European Services, 1941–55; Asst Head, BBC European Productions Dept, 1955; Asst Head, Drama (Sound), BBC, 1961; Head of Drama (Radio), BBC, 1963–77. Awarded title Professor by Pres. of Austria, 1967; Vis. Prof. of Theatre, Florida State Univ., 1969–76. Hon. DLitt Kenyon Coll., Ohio, 1978. *Publications:* Brecht, A Choice of Evils, 1959; The Theatre of the Absurd, 1962; (ed) Beckett (anthology of critical essays), 1965; Harold Pinter, 1967; The Genius of the German Theatre, 1968; Reflections, Essays on Modern Theatre (NY), 1969 (UK, as Brief Chronicles, 1970); The Peopled Wound: the plays of Harold Pinter, 1970, rev. edn as Pinter: a study of his plays, 1973, 4th edn as Pinter: the Playwright, 1982; (ed) The New Theatre of Europe, 1970; Artaud, 1976; An Anatomy of Drama, 1976; (ed) Illustrated Encyclopaedia of World Theatre, 1977; Mediations, Essays on Brecht, Beckett and the Media, 1981; The Age of Television, 1982. *Recreations:* reading, book collecting. *Address:* 64 Loudoun Road, NW8. *T:* 01–722 4243; Ballader's Plat, Winchelsea, Sussex. *T:* Rye 226 392; c/o Department of Drama, Stanford University, Stanford, Calif. 94305, USA. *Club:* Garrick.

ESSWOOD, Paul Lawrence Vincent; singer (counter-tenor); Professor, Royal Academy of Music, since 1985; *b* West Bridgford, Nottingham, 6 June 1942; *s* of Alfred Walter Esswood and Freda Garratt; *m* 1966, Mary Lillian Cantrill, ARCM; two *s. Educ:* West Bridgford Grammar Sch.; Royal Coll. of Music (ARCM). Lay-Vicar, Westminster Abbey, 1964–71. Prof., RCM, 1973–85; Specialist in baroque performance; has made recordings of Bach, Handel, Purcell, Monteverdi, Cavalli, etc; first broadcast, BBC, 1965; co-founder: Pro Cantione Antiqua; A Cappella Male Voice Ensemble for Performance of Old Music, 1967; operatic debut in Cavalli's L'Erismena, Univ. of California, Berkeley, 1968; debut at La Scala, Milan with Zurich Opera in L'Incoronazione di Poppea and Il Ritorno d'Ulisse, 1978; Scottish Opera debut in Dido and Aeneas, 1978; world premieres: Penderecki's Paradise Lost, Chicago Lyric Opera, 1979; Philip Glass's Echnaton, Stüttgart Opera, 1984; performed in major festivals: Edinburgh, Leeds Triennial, English Bach, Vienna, Salzburg, Zurich, Hamburg, Berlin, Naples, Israel, Lucerne, Flanders, Wexford, Holland. *Recreations:* philately, sports, aquariology. *Address:* 6 Gowan Avenue, SW6 6RF. *T:* 01–736 3141.

ESTES, Elliott M.; retired as President and Chief Operating Officer, General Motors Corporation, Detroit, USA; *b* Mendon, Mich. Joined Gen. Motors Corp., 1956; Exec. Vice-Pres., Ops and Staff Dir, 1972–74; Pres. and Chief Operating Officer, 1974–80. Director: Kellogg Co. Inc.; Owens-Illinois Inc.; Communications Satellite Corp. *Address:* c/o General Motors Corporation, 3044 West Grand Boulevard, Detroit, Mich 48202, USA.

ESTEY, Willard Zebedee; Hon. Mr Justice Estey; Justice of the Supreme Court of Canada, since 1977; *b* 10 Oct. 1919; *s* of James Wilfred Estey and Muriel Baldwin Estey; *m* 1946, Marian Ruth McKinnon; three *s* one *d. Educ:* Univ. of Saskatchewan (BA, LLB); Harvard Law Sch. (LLM). Mem., Bar of Sask., 1942 and of Ont, 1947; QC Ont 1960. Prof., Coll. of Law, Univ. of Sask., 1946–47; Lectr, Osgoode Hall Law Sch., 1947–51. Practised law, Toronto, 1947–72. Pres., Canadian Bar Assoc., Ont, 1972. Mem. Court of Appeal, 1973, and Chief Justice of High Court, Supreme Court of Ont, 1975; Chief Justice of Ontario, 1976. Commissioner: Steel Profits Inquiry, Royal Commn of Inquiry, 1974; Air Canada Inquiry, 1975; Inquiry into certain banking operations, 1985–86. Hon. LLD: Wilfrid Laurier Univ., Waterloo, Ont, 1977; Univ. of Toronto, 1979; Univ. of W Ont, 1980; Law Soc. of Upper Canada, 1981; Univ. of Saskatchewan, 1984. *Address:* Supreme Court of Canada, Ottawa, Ont K1A 0J1, Canada.

ETCHELLS, (Dorothea) Ruth, MA, BD; Principal, St John's College with Cranmer Hall, University of Durham, since 1979; *b* 17 April 1931; *d* of late Walter and Ada Etchells. *Educ:* Merchant Taylor's School for Girls, Crosby, Liverpool; Universities of Liverpool (MA) and London (BD). Head of English Dept, Aigburth Vale High Sch.,

Liverpool, 1959; Lectr in English, 1963, Sen. Lectr in English and Resident Tutor, 1965, Chester College of Education; Trevelyan College, Univ. of Durham: Resident Tutor and part-time Lectr in English, 1968; Vice Principal, 1972; Sen. Lectr, 1973. Examining Chaplain to Bishop of Bath and Wells, 1984–. Member: Council of Univ. of Durham, 1985–; Gen. Synod, 1985–; Doctrine Commn, 1986–; Bishop's Council and Standing Cttee of Diocesan Synod; Panel of Reference, Assoc. of Christian Teachers; Panel of Reference, Christians in The Arts; Panel of Reference, Traidcraft; Principals' Rep., ACCM Finance and Grants Cttee; Governing Bodies, Dame Allan's Schools and Monkton Combe School; Trustee, Anvil, 1983–. *Publications:* Unafraid To Be, 1969; The Man with the Trumpet, 1970; A Model of Making, 1983; Evidences for the Cross, 1987. *Recreations:* friends, quiet, country walking, London. *Address:* 12 Dunelm Court, South Street, Durham City. *T:* (College) Durham 69113.

ETHERINGTON-SMITH, (Raymond) Gordon (Antony), CMG 1962; HM Diplomatic Service, retired; *b* 1 Feb. 1914; *o s* of late T. B. Etherington-Smith and Henriette de Pitner; *m* 1950, Mary Elizabeth Besly; one *s* three *d*. *Educ:* Downside; Magdalen Coll., Oxford; Sch. of Oriental and African Studies, London Univ. Entered FO, 1936. Served at: Berlin, 1939; Copenhagen, 1939–40; Washington, 1940–42; Chungking, 1943–45; Kashgar, 1945–46; Moscow, 1947; Foreign Office, 1947–52; Holy See, 1952–54; Counsellor, Saigon, 1954–57; The Hague, 1958–61; Office of UK Commissioner-Gen. for South-East Asia, Singapore, 1961–63; Ambassador to Vietnam, 1963–66; Minister, and Dep. Commandant, Berlin, 1966–70; Ambassador to Sudan, 1970–74. *Recreations:* physical and mental exercise. *Address:* The Old Rectory, Melbury Abbas, Shaftesbury, Dorset SP7 0DZ. *T:* Shaftesbury 3105. *Club:* Oriental.

ETHERTON, Ralph, MA; Barrister-at-Law; *b* 11 Feb. 1904; *o s* of late Louis Etherton and Bertha Mary, *d* of late John Bagge; *m* 1944, Johanne Patricia, *y d* of late Gerald Cloherty, Galway, Ireland; one *s* one *d*. *Educ:* Charterhouse; Trinity Hall, Cambridge. Called to Bar, Inner Temple, 1926, and joined Northern Circuit, practised at Common Law Bar until 1939; Municipal Reform Candidate LCC election, N Camberwell 1931, and W. Fulham 1937; served in RAFVR (Special Duties), Flt Lt, 1940–42; MP (Nat. C) for Stretford div. of Lancs, 1939–45; contested (Nat. C) Liverpool (Everton div.), 1935, Stretford div. of Lancs, 1945; engaged in commerce and farming, since 1945. Chm. of Coningsby Club, 1933–34; Mem. of Parliamentary Delegation to Australia and New Zealand, 1944. *Recreations:* travel, riding. *Address:* Greentree Hall, Balcombe Forest, W Sussex RH17 6JZ. *T:* Balcombe 319. *Clubs:* Carlton, Pratt's.

ETIANG, Paul Orono, BA London; an Assistant Secretary-General, Organisation of African Unity, Addis Ababa, since 1978; *b* 15 Aug. 1938; *s* of late Kezironi Orono and Adacat Ilera Orono; *m* 1967, Zahra Ali Foum; two *s* two *d*. *Educ:* Makerere Univ. Coll. Uganda Admin. Officer, 1962–64; Asst Sec., Foreign Affairs, 1964–65; 3rd Sec., 1965–66, 2nd Sec., 1966–67, Uganda Embassy, Moscow; 1st Sec., Uganda Mission to UN, New York, 1968; Counsellor, 1968–69, High Commissioner, 1969–71, Uganda High Commission, London; Chief of Protocol and Marshal of the Diplomatic Corps, Uganda, 1971; Permanent Sec., Uganda Min. of Foreign Affairs, 1971–73; Minister of State for Foreign Affairs, 1973; Minister of State in the President's office, 1974; Minister of Transport and Communications, July 1976, of Transport, Communications and Works, Mar. 1977, of Transport and Works, 1978. *Recreations:* chess, classical music, billiards. *Address:* Organisation of African Unity, PO Box 3243, Addis Ababa, Ethiopia.

ETON, Robert; *see* Meynell, L. W.

ETTLINGER, Prof. Leopold David; Professor of History of Art, University of California, Berkeley, 1970–80; *b* 20 April 1913; *s* of Dr Emil Ettlinger, University Librarian, and Dora (*née* Beer); *m* 1st, 1939, Amrei (*née* Jacoby) (*d* 1955); 2nd, 1959, Madeline (*née* Noirot); 3rd, 1973, Helen (*née* Shahrokh). *Educ* Stadtgymnasium Halle; Universities of Halle and Marburg. Social Worker for Refugee Children from Germany, 1938–41; Asst Master, King Edward VI Grammar Sch., Five Ways, Birmingham, 1941–48; Asst Curator, Photographic Collection, Warburg Institute, University of London, 1948–51; Curator of Photographic Collection, 1951–56; Lectr, Warburg Inst., 1956–59; Durning Lawrence Prof. of History of Art, Univ. of London, 1959–70. Fellowship, Inst. for Advanced Study, Princeton, 1956; Vis. Professor: Yale Univ., 1963–64; Univ. of Calif, Berkeley, 1969; Univ. of Bonn, 1975–76, 1981–82, 1984–85; Univ. of Victoria, BC, 1980; Stanford Univ., 1983–85; Univ. of Melbourne, 1983; Kress Prof., Nat. Gall. of Art, Washington DC, 1980–81; Johnson Prof., Middlebury Coll., 1982; Scholar-in-Residence, Univ. of Puget Sound, Tacoma, Washington, 1986. FSA 1962–. British Academy award, 1963. *Publications:* (with R. G. Holloway) Compliments of the Season, 1947; The Art of the Renaissance in Northern Europe, in New Cambridge Modern History, Vol. I, 1957; Kandinsky's "At Rest", 1961; Art History Today, 1961; The Sistine Chapel before Michelangelo: Religious Imagery and Papal Politics, 1965; (with Helen S. Ettlinger) Botticelli, 1976; Antonio and Piero Pollaiuolo, 1978; (with Helen S. Ettlinger) Raphael, 1987; contribs to Journal of Warburg and Courtauld Insts, Burlington Magazine, Architectural Review, Connoisseur, Italian Studies and other jls. *Address:* 23 Royal Close, Ealing, W5.

ETZDORF, Hasso von; *b* 2 March 1900; *s* of Rüdiger von Etzdorf-Neumark and Agnes Maria Lorentz; *m* Katharina Otto-Margonin. *Educ:* Universities of Berlin, Göttingen, Halle (LLD). German Foreign Office, 1928; served in Berlin, Tokyo, Rome, Genoa (Consul-Gen.); Dep. Head, German Office for Peace Questions, Stuttgart, 1947–50; FO, Bonn, 1950–53; Head of German Delegn at Interim Cttee for Eur. Def. Community in Paris, rank of Minister, 1953; Dep. Sec.-Gen., WEU, London, 1955; Ambassador of German Federal Republic to Canada, 1956–58; Dep. Under-Sec. and Head of Western Dept, FO, Bonn, 1958–61; Ambassador of German Fed. Rep. to Court of St James's, 1961–65. GCVO (Hon.) 1964; Order of Merit with Star, Federal Republic of Germany, 1957. *Address:* Eichtling, D-8018 Grafing bei München, Germany. *T:* Glonn (08093) 1402. *Clubs:* Travellers'; Anglo-Belgian.

EURICH, Richard Ernst, OBE 1984; RA 1953 (ARA 1942); Artist (Painter); *b* Bradford, 14 March 1903; *s* of late Professor Frederick Wm Eurich; *m* 1934, Mavis Llewellyn Pope; two *d* (one *s* decd). *Educ:* St George's Sch., Harpenden; Bradford Grammar Sch. Studied art at Bradford Sch. of Arts and Crafts, and Slade Sch., London; held One Man Show of drawings at Goupil Gallery in 1929, and several exhibitions of paintings at Redfern Gallery; exhibited at Royal Academy, New English Art Club and London Group; Retrospective Exhibitions: Bradford, 1951; Bradford, Glasgow, London (Fine Art Soc.), Southampton, 1980–81; works purchased by Contemporary Art Soc. and Chantrey Bequest; Painting, Dunkirk Beach 1940, purchased for Canadian Government; Official War Artist, 1941–45; representative works in various public galleries. *Recreations:* music and gardening. *Address:* Appletreewick, Dibden Purlieu, Southampton. *T:* Hythe (Hants) 842291.

EUSTACE, Sir (Joseph) Lambert, GCMG 1985; GCVO 1985; Governor-General, St Vincent and the Grenadines, since 1985; *b* 28 Feb. 1908; *s* of Reynold Lambert Eustace and Beatrice Alexandrine Eustace (*née* St Hilaire); *m* 1945, Faustina Eileen Gatherer; one *s* one *d* (and one *d* decd). *Educ:* St Vincent Grammar School. Founded Intermediate High Sch., 1926; teacher of English, Maths and French, incl. latterly at St Vincent Grammar Sch., 1926–52; Manager, St Vincent Cotton Ginnery, 1952–59; Manager of own factory (oil, soap and feeds), 1959–66; MP South Leeward, 1966–71; Speaker, House of Assembly, 1972–74. Deleg. to overseas confs, 1957–74. *Recreations:* reading, gardening, woodwork. *Address:* Government House, Montrose, St Vincent and the Grenadines, West Indies. *T:* 61401.

EUSTON, Earl of; James Oliver Charles FitzRoy, MA, FCA; *b* 13 Dec. 1947; *s* and *heir* of 11th Duke of Grafton, *qv*; *m* 1972, Lady Clare Kerr, BA, *d* of Marquess of Lothian, *qv*; one *s* four *d*. *Educ:* Eton; Magdalene Coll., Cambridge (MA). Dir, Smith St Aubyn & Co. (Holdings) plc, 1980–; Exec. Dir, Enskilda Securities, 1982–. *Heir:* *s* Viscount Ipswich, *qv*. *Address:* 6 Vicarage Gardens, W8; The Racing Stables, Euston, Thetford, Norfolk.

EVAN-COOK, John Edward, JP; *b* 25 Oct. 1902; 2nd *s* of late Evan Cook, JP, of London; *m* 1928, Winifred Elizabeth (*d* 1985), *d* of Joseph Samuel Pointon; no *c*. *Educ:* Westminster City Sch. Served War, 1940–46, Major, RAOC. Adviser on Packaging, War Office, 1940–46. Vice-Chm. London District Rotary, 1950–52; Pres. Rotary Club of Camberwell, 1948. Chairman: Bd of Visitors, HM Prison, Brixton, 1967–73; Evan-Cook Group (retd); Inst. of Packaging (Nat. Chm., 1954, President, 1954–57); Min. of Labour & Nat. Service Local Disablement Cttee, 1959–67. Estates Governor, Dulwich, 1973–. Chief Scouts' Medal of Merit, 1962; Silver Acorn, 1968. Past Master, Worshipful Company of Paviors; Liveryman: Worshipful Co. of Carmen; Worshipful Co. of Farmers. Sheriff of London, 1958–59; Common Councilman, City of London, 1960–66 and 1972–77. JP City of London, 1950. Order of Homayoun, 3rd Class (Iran); Grand Cross of Merit, Order of Merit (Federal Republic of Germany). *Address:* Paxhill Park, Ardingly Road, Lindfield, West Sussex RH16 2RB. *T:* Lindfield 3210. *Clubs:* City Livery (Pres., 1964–65), United Wards, Royal Automobile, Bentley Drivers', Institute of Advanced Motorists.

EVANS; *see* Carey Evans.

EVANS; *see* Parry-Evans and Parry Evans.

EVANS, family name of **Barons Evans of Claughton** and **Mountevans.**

EVANS OF CLAUGHTON, Baron *cr* 1978 (Life Peer), of Claughton in the County of Merseyside; **(David Thomas) Gruffydd Evans;** JP; President of the Liberal Party, 1977–78; Liberal Party Spokesman in House of Lords on Local Government and Housing; *b* 9 Feb. 1928; *s* of John Cynlais Evans and Nellie Euronwy Evans; *m* 1956, Moira Elizabeth (*née* Rankin); one *s* three *d*. *Educ:* Birkenhead Prep. Sch.; Birkenhead Sch.; Friars Sch., Bangor; Univ. of Liverpool (LLB 1949). Solicitors' final exam., 1952. Pilot Officer, RAF, 1952–54. Hon. Sec., Lancs, Cheshire and N West Liberal Fedn, 1956–60; Chm., Nat. League of Young Liberals, 1960–61. Councillor: Birkenhead CBC, 1957–74; Wirral BC, 1973–78 (Leader Lib. Gp, 1973–77); Merseyside CC, 1973–81 (Leader Lib. Gp, 1977–81); introduced Leasehold Reform Bill, 1981. Chairman: Nat. Exec. 1965–68, Assembly Cttee 1971–74, Gen. Election Cttee of the Liberal Party, 1977–79 and 1983; Pres., Welsh Liberal Party, 1986– (Vice-Pres., 1979–86). Dir, Granada TV, 1985–. Mem. Court, Liverpool Univ., 1977–83; Governor Birkenhead Sch., 1974–78; Chairman: Birkenhead Council of Voluntary Service, 1964–73; Abbeyfield Soc. (Birkenhead), 1970–74; Liverpool Luncheon Club, 1980–81; Marcher Sound Radio, 1980–. JP Wirral, 1960. *Publications:* booklets: Local Finance for Local Government, 1981; Power and Responsibility to Local Government, 1982. *Recreations:* golf; Welsh Rugby; Liverpool FC. *Address:* Sunridge, 69 Bidston Road, Claughton, Birkenhead, Merseyside L43 6TR. *T:* 051–652 3425. *Clubs:* National Liberal, MCC; Oxton Cricket, Birkenhead Squash Racquets, Wirral Ladies' Golf (Birkenhead).

EVANS, A. Briant; Hon. Consulting Gynæcological Surgeon, Westminster Hospital and Chelsea Hospital for Women; Hon. Consulting Obstetric Surgeon, Queen Charlotte's Maternity Hospital; *b* 26 June 1909; *e s* of late Arthur Evans, OBE, MD, MS, FRCS; *m* 1939, Audrey Marie, *er d* of late Roland Eveleigh Holloway; three *s*. *Educ:* Westminster Sch.; Gonville and Caius Coll., Cambridge; Westminster Hosp. MA, MB, BCh Cantab; FRCS; FRCOG. Sometime Examiner in Obstetrics to Univs of Cambridge and London and to Royal College of Obstetricians and Gynæcologists. Temp. Lieut-Col RAMC, served in Egypt, Italy and Austria; OC No. 9 Field Surgical Unit. *Address:* Stocks, Radnage, near High Wycombe, Bucks HP14 4DW. *T:* Radnage 3460. *Club:* Army and Navy.

EVANS, Albert; *b* 10 June 1903; *s* of Moses Richard Evans; *m* 1929, Beatrice Joan, *d* of F. W. Galton. *Educ:* LCC Sch.; WEA. MP (Lab) West Islington, Sept. 1947–Feb. 1950, South-West Islington, 1950–70; retired; Member: Islington Borough Council, 1937–47; LCC, 1946–49. *Address:* Abbey Lodge, 3 Hooks Hill Road, Sheringham, Norfolk.

EVANS, Alfred Thomas, (Fred Evans); BA; *b* 24 Feb. 1914; *s* of Alfred Evans, Miner, and Sarah Jane Evans; *m* 1939, Mary (*née* O'Marah); one *s* two *d*. *Educ:* Primary and Grammar Schs; University of Wales. Head of Dept, Grammar Sch., Bargoed, Glam, 1937–49; Headmaster, Bedlinog Secondary Sch., Glam, 1949–66; Headmaster, Lewis Boys Grammar Sch., Pengam, Mon, 1966–68. Contested (Lab) Leominster, 1955, Stroud, 1959; MP (Lab) Caerphilly, July 1968–1979. Organising Agent, Caerphilly Constituency Labour Party, 1962–66. Chm., Welsh Parly Lab. Party, 1977; a Chm., Private Bills Cttee, 1975. *Address:* 8 Dilwyn Avenue, Hengoed, Mid Glam CF8 7AG. *T:* Hengoed 812069. *Clubs:* Aneurin Labour (Caerphilly); Labour (Bargoed).

EVANS, Alun; *see* Evans, T. A.

EVANS, Alun S.; *see* Sylvester-Evans.

EVANS, Anthony; *see* Evans, D. A.

EVANS, Sir Anthony (Adney), 2nd Bt, *cr* 1920; *b* 5 Aug. 1922; *s* of Sir Walter Harry Evans, 1st Bt, and Margaret Mary, *y d* of late Thomas Adney Dickens; *S* father 1954; married; two *s* one *d*. *Educ:* Shrewsbury; Merton Coll., Oxford. *Club:* Leander (Henley).

EVANS, Hon. Sir Anthony (Howell Meurig), Kt 1985; RD 1968; **Hon. Mr Justice Evans;** a Judge of the High Court of Justice, Queen's Bench Division, since 1984; a Judge of the Commercial Court, 1984; *b* 11 June 1934; *s* of late His Honour David Meurig Evans and Joy Diedericke Sander; *m* 1963, Caroline Mary Fyffe Mackie, *d* of late Edwin Gordon Mackie; one *s* two *d*. *Educ:* Bassaleg Sec. Grammar Sch., Mon; Shrewsbury Sch.; St John's Coll., Cambridge. Nat. Service, RNVR, 1952–54 (Lt-Comdr RNR). BA 1957, LLB 1958, Cantab. Called to Bar, Gray's Inn, 1958 (Arden Scholar and Birkenhead Scholar; Bencher, 1979); QC 1971; a Recorder, 1972–84; a Presiding Judge, Wales and Chester Circuit, 1986. Hon. Mem. Melbourne, Vic, Bar, 1985. Hon. Fellow, Internat. Acad. of Trial Lawyers, 1985; FCIArb 1986. *Publication:* (Jt Editor) The Law of the Air (Lord McNair), 1964. *Recreations:* sailing, music. *Address:* c/o Royal Courts of Justice, Strand, WC2. *Clubs:* Cardiff & County; Royal Lymington Yacht.

EVANS, Prof. Anthony John, PhD, FLA; University Librarian, since 1964 and Professor in Department of Library and Information Studies, since 1973, Loughborough University of Technology; *b* 1 April 1930; *s* of William John and Marion Audrey (*née* Young); *m* 1954, Anne (*née* Horwell); two *d*. *Educ:* Queen Elizabeth's Hosp., Bristol; Sch. of Pharmacy and University College, Univ. of London. BPharm, PhD. Lectr in Pharm. Eng. Sci., Sch. of Pharmacy, Univ. of London, 1954–58; Librarian, Sch. of Pharmacy, Univ. of London, 1958–63; Dean, Sch. of Educnl Studies, Loughborough Univ. of Technology, 1973–76. Pres., IATUL, 1970–75 (Bd Mem. and Treasurer, 1968–70; Hon. Life Mem., 1976–); Mem. Exec. Bd, IFLA, 1983– (Treas., 1985–; Consultative Cttee, 1968–76; Standing Cttee on Sci. and Tech. Libraries, 1977–); ASLIB: Vice-Pres., 1985–; Mem. Council, 1970–80, 1985–; Internat. Relations Cttee, 1974–85; Annual Lecture, 1985; BSI: Mem. Bd, 1984; Chm., Documentation Standards Cttee, 1980– (Mem., 1976–); Member: Inf. Systems Council, 1980–86; Automation and Inf. Technologies Council, 1986–. Member: Adv. Cttee, Sci. Ref. Library, 1975–83; Vice-Chancellors and Principals Cttee on Libraries, 1972–77; Jt UNESCO/ICSU Cttee for establishment of UNISIST, 1968–71; Internat. Affairs Sub-Cttee, LA, 1985–; Adv. Council to Bd of Dirs of Engineering Information Inc., USA, 1986–; Chm., Adv. Gp on Documentation Standards, ISO, 1983–85; consultancy work for British Council, UNESCO, UNIDO, World Bank in African and Asian countries. *Publications:* (with D. Train) Bibliography of the tabletting of medicinal substances, 1964, suppl. 1965; (with R. G. Rhodes and S. Keenan) Education and training of users of scientific and technical information, 1977; articles in librarianship and documentation. *Recreations:* travel, sport, model railways. *Address:* 78 Valley Road, Loughborough, Leics LE11 3QA. *T:* Loughborough 215670. *Club:* Royal Commonwealth Society.

EVANS, (Arthur) Mostyn; General Secretary, Transport and General Workers Union, 1978–85; Member, TUC General Council, 1977–85; *b* 13 July 1925; *m* 1947, Laura Bigglestone; two *s* three *d* (and one *s* decd). *Educ:* Cefn Coed Primary Sch., S Wales; Church Road Secondary Modern Sch., Birmingham. District Officer, Birmingham, Chem. and Eng. Industries, 1956; Regional Officer, Midlands, 1960; Nat. Officer, Eng., 1966; National Secretary: Chem., Rubber, and Oil Industries, 1969; Engineering Industries, 1969; (Automotive Section), TGWU, 1969–73; Nat. Organiser, TGWU, 1973–78. Part-time Mem., Nat. Bus Co., 1976–78; Member: BOTB, 1978–79; NEDC, 1978–84; Exec., ITF, 1980–; Council, ACAS, 1982–; Pres., ICEF, 1982– (Vice-Pres., 1980–82). *Recreation:* music. *Address:* 6 Highland Drive, Hemel Hempstead, Herts. *T:* Hemel Hempstead 157503.

EVANS, Sir Athol (Donald), KBE 1963 (CBE 1954; MBE 1939); retired as Secretary for Home Affairs, Government of the Federation of Rhodesia and Nyasaland (Sept. 1953–Dec. 1963); *b* 16 Dec. 1904; *s* of Henry Evans; *m* 1931, Catherine Millar Greig; one *s* two *d*. *Educ:* Graeme Coll. and Rhodes Univ., Grahamstown, S Africa (BA, LLB). Joined S Rhodesia Public Service, 1928: consecutively Law Officer, Legal Adviser, Mem. of Public Services Board, and Sec. for Internal Affairs. Chairman of: Board of Trustees, National Gallery of Zimbabwe; Zimbabwe National Trust; Nat. Council for Care of Aged. Past District Governor, Rotary International. Gold Cross of St Mark (Greece), 1962. *Recreations:* tennis, shooting. *Address:* 8 Harvey Brown Avenue, Harare, Zimbabwe. *T:* 725164.

EVANS, Briant; *see* Evans, A. B.

EVANS, Rt. Rev. Bruce Read; *see* Port Elizabeth, Bishop of.

EVANS, Sir Charles; *see* Evans, Sir R. C.

EVANS, Charles; *see* Evans, W. C.

EVANS, Rev. Prof. Christopher Francis, MA; Professor of New Testament Studies, King's College, London, 1962–77, now Emeritus Professor, University of London; *b* 7 Nov. 1909; 2nd *s* of Frank and Beatrice Evans; *m* 1941, Elna Mary (*d* 1980), *d* of Walter and Elizabeth Burt; one *s*. *Educ:* King Edward's Sch., Birmingham; Corpus Christi Coll., Cambridge. Asst Curate, St Barnabas, Southampton, 1934–38; Tutor Schol. Canc. Linc., 1938–44; Chaplain and Divinity Lecturer, Lincoln Training Coll., 1944–48; Chaplain, Fellow and Lecturer in Divinity, Corpus Christi Coll., Oxford, 1948–58, Emeritus Fellow, 1977; Lightfoot Prof. of Divinity in the University of Durham and Canon of Durham Cathedral, 1959–62; Vis. Fellow, Trevelyan Coll., Durham, 1982–83. Select Preacher, University of Oxford, 1955–57; Proctor in Convocation for University of Oxford, 1955–58; Exam. Chaplain: to Bishop of Bristol, 1948–58; to Bishop of Durham, 1958–62; to Archbishop of Canterbury, 1962–74; to Bishop of Lichfield, 1969–75. FKC, 1970. Hon. DLitt Southampton, 1977. *Publications:* Christology and Theology, 1961; The Lord's Prayer, 1963; The Beginning of the Gospel, 1968; Resurrection and the New Testament, 1970; (ed jtly) The Cambridge History of the Bible: vol. I, From the Beginnings to Jerome, 1970; Is 'Holy Scripture' Christian?, 1971; Explorations in Theology 2, 1977; contribs to Journal of Theological Studies, Theology and Religious Studies, to Studies in the Gospels and to Christian Faith and Communist Faith. *Recreation:* fishing. *Address:* 4 Church Close, Cuddesdon, Oxford. *T:* Wheatley 4406; 5 The Square, Clun, Craven Arms, Salop.

EVANS, Colin Rodney; Assistant Under Secretary of State, Ministry of Defence, Deputy Director (Vehicles) and Head of Royal Armament Research and Development Establishment, Chertsey, since 1985; *b* 5 June 1935; *s* of John Evans and Annie (*née* Lawes); *m* 1963, Jennifer MacIntosh; two *d*. *Educ:* Bridlington Sch.; Woolwich Polytechnic; Imperial Coll., London. BSc(Eng); HND; MIMechE. Scientific Officer, ARDE (now RARDE), 1959–60; Lectr, RNC, Greenwich, 1960–61; Scientific Officer, then Sen. Scientific Officer and PSO, ARDE, 1961–69; SO to Chief Scientist (Army), MoD, 1969–71; British Defence Staff, Washington, 1971–73; SPSO, RARDE, 1973–79; Dep. Dir, Scientific and Technical Intell., MoD, 1979–81; seconded to Sir Derek Rayner's study team on efficiency in govt, 1981; RCDS, 1982; Dep. Dir (1), RARDE, 1983–84. *Recreations:* squash, tennis, bird watching, stamp collecting. *Address:* 75 Culverden Park, Tunbridge Wells, Kent TN4 9QS. *T:* Tunbridge Wells 45835.

EVANS, David; Director-General, National Farmers' Union, since 1985 (Deputy Director-General, 1984–85); *b* 7 Dec. 1935; *yr s* of William Price Evans and Ella Mary Evans; *m* 1960, Susan Carter Connal, *yr d* of late Dr John Connal and Antoinette Connal; one *s* one *d*. *Educ:* Welwyn Garden City Grammar Sch.; University Coll. London (BScEcon). Joined Min. of Agriculture, Fisheries and Food, 1959; Private Sec. to Parliamentary Sec. (Lords), 1962–64; Principal, 1964; Principal Private Sec. to Ministers, 1970–71; Asst Sec., 1971; seconded to Cabinet Office, 1972–74; Under-Sec., MAFF, 1976–80; joined NFU as Chief Economic and Policy Adviser, 1981. *Address:* 6 Orchard Rise, Kingston upon Thames, Surrey KT2 7EY. *T:* 01–942 7701.

EVANS, Dr David Alan Price, FRCP; Director of Medicine, Riyadh Armed Forces Hospital, Saudi Arabia, since 1983; *b* 6 March 1927; *s* of Owen Evans and Ellen (*née* Jones). *Educ:* Univ. of Liverpool (MD, PhD, DSc); Johns Hopkins Univ. House Physician, House Surg. and Med. Registrar, United Liverpool Hosps; Fellow, Dept of Medicine, Johns Hopkins Hosp., 1958–59; Lectr 1960–62, Sen. Lectr 1962–68, Personal Chair, 1968–72, Dept of Medicine, Univ. of Liverpool; Prof. and Chm., Dept of Medicine and Dir, Nuffield Unit Medical Genetics, Univ. of Liverpool, 1972–83; Cons. Physician, Royal Liverpool Hosp. (formerly Royal Liverpool Infirmary) and Broadgreen Hosp., Liverpool, 1965–83. Life Mem., Johns Hopkins Soc. of Scholars, 1972. *Publications:* medical and scientific, principally concerned with genetic factors determining responses to drugs. *Recreation:* country pursuits. *Address:* 28 Montclair Drive, Liverpool L18 0HA. *T:* 051–722 3112; Pen-yr-Allt, Paradwys, Llangristiolus, Bodorgan, Gwynedd LL62 5PD. *T:* Bodorgan 840346.

EVANS, (David) Anthony; QC 1983; a Recorder of the Crown Court, since 1980; *b* 15 March 1939; *s* of Thomas John Evans, MD and May Evans; *m* 1974, Angela Bewley, *d* of John Clive Bewley, JP and Cynthia Bewley; two *d*. *Educ:* Clifton Coll., Bristol; Corpus Christi Coll., Cambridge (BA). Called to the Bar, Gray's Inn, 1965; practised at the Bar, Swansea, 1965–84. *Recreations:* sport of all kinds. *Address:* Carey Hall, Neath, W Glamorgan. *T:* Neath 3859; 3 Paper Buildings, Temple, EC4. *T:* 01–353 8192. *Clubs:* Turf, MCC; Cardiff and County (Cardiff).

EVANS, Ven. David Eifion; Archdeacon of Cardigan, 1967–79; *b* 22 Jan. 1911; *e s* of John Morris Evans, Borth, Cards, Dyfed; *m* 1st, 1941, Iris Elizabeth Gravelle (*d* 1973); one *s*; 2nd, 1979, Madeleine Kirby. *Educ:* Ardwyn, Aberystwyth; UCW, Aberystwyth; St Michael's Coll., Llandaff. BA 1932; MA 1951. Deacon, 1934; Priest, 1935. Curate: Llanfihangel-ar-Arth, 1934–36; Llanbadarn Fawr, 1936–40; Chaplain to the Forces, 1940–45; Vicar, Llandeloy with Llanrheithan, 1945–48; Penrhyncoch, 1948, with Elerch, 1952–57; St Michael, Aberystwyth, 1957–67; Rural Dean, Llanbadarn Fawr, 1957–67; Chaplain, Anglican Students, 1966–67; Canon of St David's Cathedral (Caerfai), 1963–67; Chaplain, Earl of Lisburne, 1967–69; Vicar: Llanafan with Llanwnnws, 1967–69; Newcastle Emlyn, 1969–. Member: Governing Body of Church in Wales, 1956–; Representative Body of Church in Wales, 1967–79; Court of Governors, and Council, UCW, Aberystwyth, 1958–; Sub-Visitor, St David's Univ. Coll., Lampeter, 1972–79. *Publications:* contributions to: Llên Cymru Yn Y Bedwaredd Ganrif Ar Bymtheg, 1968; Jl of Hist. Soc. of Church in Wales and other Welsh Church periodicals. *Recreation:* reading. *Address:* 31 Bryncastell, Bow Street, Dyfed. *T:* Aberystwyth 828747.

EVANS, Prof. (David) Ellis, DPhil; FBA 1983; Jesus Professor of Celtic, University of Oxford, and Fellow of Jesus College, since 1978; *b* Llanfynydd, 23 Sept. 1930; *yr s* of David Evans and Sarah Jane (*née* Lewis); *m* 1957, Sheila Mary, *er d* of David and Evelyn Jeremy; two *d*. *Educ:* Llandeilo Grammar Sch.; University Coll. of Wales, Aberystwyth, and University Coll., Swansea (Hon. Fellow, 1985) (BA Wales, 1st cl. Hons Greek, Latin and Welsh, 1952; MA Wales, 1954); Jesus Coll., Oxford (Meyricke Grad. Scholar, 1952–54; DPhil 1962, MA 1978). University Coll. of Swansea: Asst Lectr in Welsh, 1957; Lectr, 1960; Reader, 1968; Actg Head, Dept of Welsh, 1973; Prof. of Welsh Lang. and Lit. and Head of Dept of Welsh, 1974; Chm., Faculty of Medieval and Modern Langs, Oxford Univ., 1985–86. Curator, Taylor Instn, Oxford, 1979–86. Sir John Rhys Meml Lectr, British Acad., 1977; Rudolf Thurneysen Meml Lectr, Univ. of Bonn, 1979; O'Donnell Lectr, Univ. of Wales, 1980; G. J. Williams Meml Lectr, UC Cardiff, 1986. Pres. and Organizing Sec., Seventh Internat. Congress of Celtic Studies, Oxford, 1983; President: Cymdeithas Dafydd ap Gwilym, 1978–; Irish Texts Soc., 1983– (Mem. Council, 1978–); Vice President: Clwyd Place-Name Council, 1984–; N Amer. Congress of Celtic Studies, Ottawa, 1986. Chairman: Welsh Dialect Studies Group, 1977–80; Council for Name Studies of GB and Ireland, 1980–84 (Mem. Council, 1962–); Member: Bd of Celtic Studies, Univ. of Wales, 1968–; Court and Council, National Library of Wales, 1974–; Internat. Cttee of Onomastic Sciences, 1975–; Welsh Arts Council, 1981–; Royal Commn on Ancient and Hist. Monuments in Wales, 1984–; Court, University of Wales, 1978–; Court, UC Swansea, 1980–; Court and Council, University Coll. of Wales, Aberystwyth, 1981–85; Court, UC Cardiff, 1983–; UNESCO Internat. Cttee for the Study of Celtic Cultures, 1984– (Provisional Cttee, 1981–83); Council, Hon. Soc. Cymmrodorion, 1984–. Governor, Christ's Coll., Brecon, 1979–. Hon. Mem., Druidic Order of Gorsedd of Bards, 1976–; Correspondent étranger, Etudes celtiques, 1982–. Editor, Lang. and Lit. Section, Bull. of Bd of Celtic Studies, 1972–; Mem. Editorial Bd: Geiriadur Prifysgol Cymru/A Dictionary of the Welsh Language, 1973–; Nomina, 1980–85; Welsh Acad. English-Welsh Dictionary, 1981–; Mem. Adv. Bd, Jl of Celtic Studies, 1978–. *Publications:* Gaulish Personal Names: a study of some continental Celtic formations, 1967; (contrib.) Swansea and its Region, ed W. G. V. Balchin, 1971; (contrib.) Homenaje a Antonio Tovar, 1972; (contrib.) The Anatomy of Wales, ed R. Brinley Jones, 1972; Gorchest y Celtiaid yr Hen Fyd, 1975; Cofiant Agricola, Rheolwr Prydain, 1975; Termau Gwleidyddiaeth, 1976; (contrib.) Indogermanisch und Keltisch, ed K. H. Schmidt, 1977; (contrib.) Aufstieg und Niedergang der römischen Welt, ed H. Temporini and W. Haase, 1983; (contrib.) Proc. 6th Internat. Congress of Celtic Studies, Galway (1979), 1983; (ed) Proc. 7th Internat. Congress of Celtic Studies, Oxford (1983), 1986; contrib. colloquia; articles and revs in British Book News, Bull. Bd of Celtic Studies, Class. Rev., Etudes celtiques, History, Jl of Welsh Bibliog. Soc., Llên Cymru, Medium Aevum, Onoma, Proc. of British Acad., Studia Celtica, Y Traethodydd, Trans Hon. Soc. Cymmrodorion, Trivium, Welsh Hist. Rev., Year's Work in Mod. Lang. Studies, and Zeitschrift celt. Phil. *Recreations:* music, walking. *Address:* Jesus College, Oxford. *T:* Oxford 249511.

EVANS, Air Chief Marshal Sir David (George), GCB 1979 (KCB 1977); CBE 1967 (OBE 1962); Military Adviser to British Aerospace, since 1983; Bath King of Arms, since 1985; *b* Windsor, Ont, Canada, 14 July 1924; *s* of William Stanley Evans, Clive Vale, Hastings, Sussex; *m* 1949, Denise Marson Williamson-Noble, *d* of late Gordon Till, Hampstead, London; two *d* (and two step *s*). *Educ:* Hodgson Sch., Toronto, Canada; North Toronto Collegiate. Served War, as Pilot, in Italy and NW Europe, 1944–45. Sqdn Pilot, Tactics Officer, Instructor, 1946–52; Sqdn Comdr, Central Flying Sch., 1953–55; RAF Staff Coll. course, 1955; OC No 11 (F) Sqdn, in Germany, 1956–57; Personal Staff Officer to C-in-C, 2nd Allied TAF, 1958–59; OC Flying, RAF, Coltishall, 1959–61; Coll. of Air Warfare course, 1961; Air Plans Staff Officer, Min. of Defence (Air), 1962–63; OC, RAF Station, Gutersloh, Germany, 1964–66; IDC, 1967; AOC, RAF Central Tactics and Trials Organisation, 1968–70; ACAS (Ops), 1970–73; AOC No 1 (Bomber) Group, RAF, 1973–76; Vice-Chief of Air Staff, 1976–77; C-in-C, RAF Strike Command, and UK NATO Air Forces, 1977–80; VCDS (Personnel and Logistics), 1981–83. Non-exec. Dir, NAAFI, 1984– (Pres. Council, 1981–83). Queen's Commendation for Valuable Service in the Air (QCVSA), 1955. CBIM 1978 (Mem. Bd of Companions, 1983–). *Recreations:* rep. RAF at Rugby football and winter sports (President: RAF Winter Sports Assoc.; Combined Services Winter Sports Assoc.); has rep. Gt Brit. at Bobsleigh in World Championships, Commonwealth Games and, in 1964, Olympic Games. *Address:* Royal Bank of Canada, 2 Cockspur Street, SW1. *Club:* Royal Air Force.

EVANS, Sir David (Lewis), Kt 1958; OBE 1947; BA, BLitt, Hon. DLitt Wales; Keeper of Public Records, Jan. 1959–Oct. 1960, retired (Deputy Keeper of the Records, 1954–58); Commissioner, Historical MSS Commission, 1954–80; *b* 14 Aug. 1893; *s* of Rev. David Evans and Margaret Lewis; *m* 1923, Marie Christine (*d* 1966), *d* of Edwin Austin, JP; two *d*. *Educ:* Bridgend County Sch.; University Coll. of Wales, Aberystwyth; Jesus Coll., Oxford. Lieut, Duke of Wellington's Regt, 1915–19, France and Belgium (despatches). Entered Public Record Office, 1921; Principal Asst Keeper, 1947. Lectr, Administrative

History and Archive Administration, Sch. of Librarianship and Archives, University Coll. London, 1947–54. FRHistS (Vice-Pres. 1956–60); Council, Hon. Soc. of Cymmrodorion; Member: Advisory Council on Public Records, 1959–65; History and Law Cttee, Bd of Celtic Studies; Exec Committee: Internat. Council on Archives, 1953–68 (Vice-Pres. 1956–60); Pres. 4th Internat. Congress of Archivists, Stockholm, 1960; Governor: British Film Institute, 1961–64; Nat. Library of Wales, 1961– (Council, 1962–80); Nat. Museum of Wales, 1965–. *Publications:* Flintshire Ministers' Accounts, 1328–1352, 1929; History of Carmarthenshire: Chapter on Later Middle Ages, 1935; (part author) Notebook of John Smibert, Painter, Mass Hist. Soc., 1969; articles, reviews, in Cymmrodorion Transactions, Eng. Hist. Review, Nat. Lib. of Wales Jl, Virginia Hist. Soc. Trans, etc. *Address:* Whitegates, Stratton-on-the-Fosse, Somerset. *Club:* National Liberal.

EVANS, David M.; *see* Moule-Evans.

EVANS, David Marshall, QC 1981; a Recorder of the Crown Court, since 1984; *b* 21 July 1937; *s* of Robert Trevor and Bessie Estelle Evans; *m* 1961, Alice Joyce Rogers; two *s. Educ:* Liverpool Coll.; Trinity Hall, Cambridge (MA, LLM); Law Sch., Univ. of Chicago (JD). Called to the Bar, Gray's Inn, 1964. Teaching Fellow, Stanford University Law Sch., 1961–62; Asst Professor, Univ. of Chicago Law Sch., 1962–63; Lectr in Law, University Coll. of Wales, Aberystwyth, 1963–65; joined Northern Circuit, 1965. *Recreations:* walking, photography, visual arts, bird-watching, motorsport. *Address:* 5 Essex Court, Temple, EC4Y 9AH. *T:* 01–353 4363. *Club:* Athenæum (Liverpool).

EVANS, David Milne; Cabinet Office, 1977–81; *b* 8 Aug. 1917; *s* of Walter Herbert Evans, MSc and Florence Mary Evans (née Milne); *m* 1946, Gwynneth May (née Griffiths), BA. *Educ:* Charterhouse (Scholar); Gonville and Caius Coll., Cambridge (Schol.; Wrangler, Math. Tripos). Administrative Class, Home Civil Service (War Office), 1939. Served in Army (Major, RA), 1940–45. Asst Sec., 1954; Imp. Def. Coll., 1954; Asst Under-Sec. of State, MoD, 1967–77 (Under-Sec., CS Dept, 1972). Coronation Medal, 1953; Silver Jubilee Medal, 1977. *Address:* 1 Church Rise, Walston Road, Wenvoe, Cardiff, South Glamorgan CF5 6DE. *T:* Cardiff 597129.

EVANS, David Philip, CBE 1968; MSc, PhD, FRSC; Principal, Glamorgan Polytechnic, Treforest, Pontypridd, Glam, 1970–72; *b* 28 Feb. 1908; *s* of D. C. and J. Evans, Port Talbot, Glam; *m* 1938, Vura Helena (née Harcombe); one *s. Educ:* Port Talbot County Grammar Sch.; University Coll., Cardiff (Fellow, 1981). Lectr in Chemistry, Cardiff Technical Coll., 1934–44; Principal: Bridgend Technical Coll., Glam, 1944–52; Glamorgan Coll. of Technology, Treforest, 1952–70. Hon. Fellow, Polytechnic of Wales, 1984. *Publications:* numerous papers in various chemical jls. *Recreations:* fishing, gardening, music. *Address:* Tree Tops, St Bride's Road, Ewenny Cross, Ewenny, Bridgend, Mid Glam. *T:* Bridgend 61354.

EVANS, Rt. Rev. David Richard John; *see* Peru, Bishop of.

EVANS, Prof. Dennis Frederick, FRS 1981; Professor in Inorganic Chemistry, Imperial College, London, since 1981; *b* 27 March 1928; *s* of George Frederick Evans and Gladys Martha Taylor. *Educ:* Nottingham High Sch.; Lincoln Coll., Oxford (open scholar); Gibbs Univ. Scholar, 1949; MA, DPhil. ICI Res. Fellow, Oxford, 1952–53 and 1954–56; Res. Associate, Univ. of Chicago, 1953–54; Lectr in Inorganic Chemistry, Imperial Coll., London, 1956–63, Sen. Lectr, 1963–64, Reader, 1964–81. *Publications:* articles in various scientific jls. *Recreations:* wine, travel. *Address:* 64A Cathcart Road, SW10. *T:* 01–352 6540.

EVANS, Eben, OBE 1976; Controller, Books Division, British Council, 1976–80; *b* 1 Nov. 1920; *s* of John Evans and Mary Evans; *m* 1946, Joan Margaret Howells; two *s* two *d. Educ:* Llandovery Grammar Sch.; University Coll. of Wales, Aberystwyth (BA 1948). Served War, 1941–46 (Army, Captain). Appointed to British Council, 1948; Cardiff, 1948–55; Thailand, 1955–59; Gambia, 1959–62; Ghana, 1962–64; Personnel Dept, London, 1964–68; Representative: Algeria, 1968–73; Yugoslavia, 1973–76. *Recreations:* walking, music. *Address:* Gorddinog Isaf, Llanfairfechan, Gwynedd.

EVANS, Rt. Rev. Edward Lewis, BD, MTh; *b* 11 Dec. 1904; *s* of Edward Foley Evans and Mary (née Walker). *Educ:* St Anselm's, Croydon; Tonbridge Sch.; Bishops' Coll., Cheshunt. BD London 1935, MTh 1938. Deacon, 1937; priest 1938; Curate of St Mary's, Prittlewell, Essex, 1937–39; Warden of St Peter's, Theological Coll., Jamaica, 1940–49; Rector, Kingston Parish Church, Jamaica, 1949–52; Rector of Woodford and Craigton, 1952–57; Archdeacon of Surrey, Jamaica, 1950–57; Bishop Suffragan of Kingston, 1957–60; Bishop of Barbados, 1960–71. *Publication:* A History of the Diocese of Jamaica, 1977. *Address:* Bungalow 1, Terry's Cross, Woodmancote, Henfield, Sussex BN5 9SX.

EVANS, Edward Stanley Price, FRTPI; City Planning Officer, Liverpool, 1974–84, retired; *b* 13 April 1925; *s* of late Bernard James Reuben Evans and of Nellie Evans; *m* 1948, Eva Magdalena Emma Fry; one *s* (and one *s* decd). *Educ:* Wolverhampton Grammar Sch.; Nottingham Coll. of Art and Crafts (DipTP). FRTPI 1966 (MTPI 1954). Chief Town Planning Officer, Norwich, 1957; City Planning Officer, Nottingham, 1966. Member: DoE Environmental Bd, 1977–79; DoE Panel of Local Plan Inspectors; Management Cttee, Young Persons Housing Assoc. FRSA. *Recreations:* travel, gardening, bridge (social). *Address:* Willow Cottage, The Ridgeway, Heswall, Wirral, Merseyside L60 8NB. *T:* 051–342 4546.

EVANS, Ven. Eifion; *see* Evans, Ven. D. E.

EVANS, Ellis; *see* Evans, D. E.

EVANS, Emrys; *see* Evans, W. E.

EVANS, Prof. (Emyr) Estyn, CBE 1970; Emeritus Professor of Geography, and Hon. Fellow, Institute of Irish Studies, Queen's University of Belfast; Leverhulme Emeritus Fellow, 1970–72; *b* 29 May 1905; 4th *s* of Rev. G. O. and Elizabeth Evans, Shrewsbury; *m* 1931, Gwyneth Lyon, *e d* of Prof. Abel Jones, Aberystwyth; four *s. Educ:* Welshpool County Sch.; University Coll. of Wales, Aberystwyth. BA Geography and Anthropology, 1925, MA 1931, DSc 1939. Independent Lecturer in Geography, QUB, 1928–44; Reader, 1944–45; Prof., 1945–68; Dir, Inst. of Irish Studies, 1965–70; Dean of the Faculty of Arts, 1951–54; Mem. of Senate. Tallman Visiting Professor: Bowdoin Coll., Maine, 1948–49; Visiting Professor: Indiana Univ., 1964; Louisiana State Univ., 1969. Mem., Historic Monuments Council (NI) (former Chm.); former Mem. Adv. Council, Republic of Ireland; first President: Ulster Folk Life Soc.; Ulster Archæological Soc.; Ulster Architectural Heritage Soc.; former Chm. of Trustees, Ulster Folk and Transport Museum and Trustee, Ulster Museum; Hon. Mem. and former Vice-Pres., Prehistoric Soc. Former Member: Executive Cttee, NI Council of Social Service; NI Tourist Bd; Pres. Sect. E 1958 and Sect. H 1960, Brit. Assoc. for the Advancement of Science (first Chm. NI Area Cttee); Sir James Frazer Memorial Lectr, 1961; Sir Everard im Thurn Memorial Lectr, 1966; Wiles Lectr, 1971. Chm., Northern Ireland Government Cttee on Itinerants; Vice-Chm., Cttee on Nature Conservation. FSA; MRIA; Hon. MRTPI; Hon. Life Mem., Royal Dublin Soc., 1981. Hon. ScD Bowdoin, 1949; Hon. LittD Dublin, 1970; Hon. LLD QUB, 1973; Hon. DLitt: NUI, 1975; Wales, 1977; Hon. DSc NUU 1980. Victoria

Medal, RGS, 1973. Hons Award, Assoc. of Amer. Geographers, Pa, 1979. *Publications:* France, A Geographical Introduction, 1937; (joint) Preliminary Survey of the Ancient Monuments of Northern Ireland, 1940; Irish Heritage, 1942; A Portrait of Northern Ireland (Festival of Britain) 1951; Mourne Country, 1951, rev. edn 1967; Lyles Hill: A Late Neolithic Site in County Antrim, 1953; Irish Folk Ways, 1957; Prehistoric and Early Christian Ireland, 1966; (ed) Facts from Gweedore, 1971; The Personality of Ireland (Wiles Lectures), 1973, revd edn 1981; The Personality of Wales (BBC Wales Annual Lecture), 1973; (ed) Harvest Home: the last sheaf, 1975; (ed) Ireland's Eye, the photographs of R. J. Welch, 1977; The Irishness of the Irish (essays), 1986; papers in scientific journals. *Address:* 98A Malone Road, Belfast. *T:* 668510. *Club:* Ulster Arts (Hon. Member) (Belfast).

EVANS, Ena Winifred; Headmistress, King Edward VI High School for Girls, Birmingham, since 1977; *b* 19 June 1938; *d* of Frank and Leonora Evans. *Educ:* The Queen's Sch., Chester; Royal Holloway Coll., Univ. of London (BSc); Hughes Hall, Cambridge (CertEd). Asst Mistress, Bolton Sch. (Girls' Div.), 1961–65; Bath High School (GPDST): Head of Mathematics Dept, 1965–72; Second Mistress, 1970–72; Dep. Head, Friends' Sch., Saffron Walden, 1972–77. *Recreation:* music. *Address:* King Edward VI High School for Girls, Edgbaston Park Road, Birmingham B15 2UB. *T:* 021–472 1834.

EVANS, Ven. Eric; *see* Evans, Ven. T. E.

EVANS, Prof. Estyn; *see* Evans, Prof. Emyr E.

EVANS, Fabyan Peter Leaf; a Recorder, since 1985; barrister; *b* 10 May 1943; *s* of Peter Fabyan Evans and Catherine Elise Evans; *m* 1977, Karen Myrtle (née Balfour), *g d* of 1st Earl Jellicoe; two *s* one *d. Educ:* Clifton College. Called to the Bar, Inner Temple, 1969. *Recreations:* sailing, thinking about sailing. *Address:* 6 King's Bench Walk, Temple, EC4Y 7DR. *T:* 01-583 0410. *Clubs:* Brooks's, MCC, Roehampton; Newport Boat (Newport, Pembs).

EVANS, Sir Francis Loring G.; *see* Gwynne-Evans.

EVANS, Fred; *see* Evans, Alfred T.

EVANS, Frederick Anthony, CVO 1973; General Secretary, The Duke of Edinburgh's Award Scheme, 1959–72 (Adviser for the Handicapped, 1972–84); *b* 17 Nov. 1907; *s* of Herbert Anthony Evans, mining engineer, and Pauline (née Allen); *m* 1934, Nancy (née Meakin); two *s* one *d. Educ:* Charterhouse; Corpus Christi, Cambridge. Manager Doondu Coffee Plantation, Kenya, 1927–31; Colonial Service, 1934; Asst District Officer, Nigeria, 1935–39; Provincial Commissioner and Asst Colonial Sec., Gambia, 1940–47; Colonial Sec., Nassau, Bahamas, 1947–51; Acting Governor, 1950; Permanent Sec., Gold Coast (later Ghana), 1951–57. Dir, Anglo-Gambian Archæological Expedition, 1965–66. *Publication:* The State Apartments at Buckingham Palace: a souvenir, 1985. *Recreations:* golf, ski-ing. *Address:* Bamber Cottage, Saintbury Hill, Froyle, Hants. *Club:* Royal Commonwealth Society.

EVANS, Lt-Gen. Sir Geoffrey (Charles), KBE 1954 (CBE 1945); CB 1946; DSO 1941 (bars 1942, 1944); retired, 1957; *b* 13 March 1901; *s* of late Col C. R. Evans, DSO; *m* 1928, Ida Louise, *d* of late H. R. Sidney; no *c. Educ:* Aldenham Sch.; Royal Military Coll., Sandhurst. 2nd Lieut The Royal Warwickshire Regt, 1920; Adjutant: 1st Bn, 1926–29; 7th Bn (TA), 1934–35; Staff Coll., 1936–37. Served War of 1939–45 (despatches five times): Bde Major, N Africa and Eritrea, 1940–41; OC 1st Bn Royal Sussex Regt, N Africa, 1941–42; Comdt Staff Coll., Quetta, 1942; Brig. Comd., India, 1943; Brig., Gen. Staff 4 Corps, Burma, 1943–44; Bde Commander, Burma, 1944; GOC 5 and 7 Indian Divs, Burma, 1944–45; GOC Allied Land Forces, Siam, 1945–46; GOC 42 (Lancs) Div. and North-West District, 1947–48; Dir of Military Training War Office, 1948–49; GOC 40 Div., Hong Kong, 1949–51; Temp. Comd. (Lt-Gen.), British Forces, Hong Kong, 1951–52; Asst Chief of Staff (Org. and Trng), Supreme HQ, Allied Powers, Europe, 1952–53; GOC-in-C, Northern Command, 1953–57; retired. Hon. Col 7th Bn The Royal Warwickshire Regt, 1959–64. A Vice-Pres., Nat. Playing Fields Assoc.; Chairman: London and Middlesex Playing Fields Association, 1959–70; Anglo-Thai Soc., 1967–71. Comr, Royal Hosp., Chelsea, 1968–76. DL Greater London, 1970–76. *Publications:* The Desert and the Jungle, 1959; (with A. Brett-James) Imphal, 1962; The Johnnies, 1964; Slim as Military Commander, 1969; Tannenberg 1410:1914, 1971; Kensington, 1975; contrib. chapters: The Decisive Battles of the 20th Century, 1975; War Lords, 1976; articles for Purnell's History of the Second World War, History Today, The Field, The Antique Collector, reviews. *Address:* 11 Wellington Square, SW3.

EVANS, George Ewart; author, lecturer, and broadcaster, since 1948; *b* 1 April 1909; *s* of William and Janet Evans, Abercynon, Glamorgan; *m* 1938, Florence Ellen Knappett; one *s* three *d. Educ:* Abertaf Sch.; Mountain Ash Grammar Sch.; UC Cardiff. BA Hons Classics Wales, 1930; DipEd 1931. Writer of short stories, verse, radio and film scripts; specialized in history and folk life of the village. Univ. of Essex: Major Burrows Lectr, 1972; Vis. Fellow, 1973–78; Hon. DU 1982; Hon. DLitt Keele, 1983. Pres., Section H (Anthropology), British Assoc. for Advancement of Science, Swansea, 1971. *Publications:* The Voices of the Children, 1947; Ask the Fellows who Cut the Hay, 1956; (ed) Welsh Short Stories, 1959; The Horse in the Furrow, 1960; The Pattern Under the Plough, 1966; The Farm and the Village, 1969; Where Beards Wag All, 1970; (with David Thomson) The Leaping Hare, 1972; Acky, 1973; The Days That We Have Seen, 1975; Let Dogs Delight, 1975; From Mouths of Men, 1976; Horse Power and Magic, 1979; The Strength of the Hills (autobiography), 1983. *Recreations:* walking, gardening, watching Rugby football. *Address:* 19 The Street, Brooke, Norwich NR15 1JW. *T:* Brooke 50518.

See also Matthew Evans, David Gentleman.

EVANS, George James; Sheriff of Glasgow and Strathkelvin at Glasgow, since 1983; *b* 16 July 1944; *s* of Colin Evans and Caroline Catherine Kennedy MacPherson Harris; *m* 1973, Lesley Jean Keir Cowie; two *d. Educ:* Ardrossan Acad.; Glasgow Univ. (MA Hons). Edinburgh Univ. (LLB). Advocate, 1973; Standing Jun. Counsel, Dept of Energy, Scotland, 1982. *Publications:* contribs to legal periodicals. *Recreations:* reading, music, Cuban vegetation, swimming, country rambles. *Address:* 14 Dalkeith Avenue, Glasgow G41 5BJ. *T:* 041-427 3709.

EVANS, Sir Geraint Llewellyn, Kt 1969; CBE 1959; Opera Singer; Principal Baritone, Royal Opera House, Covent Garden, 1948–84; *b* 16 Feb. 1922; *m* 1948, Brenda Evans Davies; two *s. Educ:* Guildhall Sch. of Music. Has sung at: Royal Opera House, Covent Garden (since 1948) Glyndebourne Festival Opera; Vienna State Opera; La Scala, Milan; Metropolitan Opera, New York; San Francisco Opera; Lyric Opera, Chicago; Salzburg Festival Opera; Edinburgh Festival Opera; Paris Opera; Teatro Colon, Buenos Aires; Mexico City Opera; Welsh Nat. Opera; Scottish Opera; Berlin Opera; Teatr Wielki, Warsaw. Director: Harlech Television Ltd; Buxton Arts Festival Ltd. President: Guild for Promotion of Welsh Music; Friends of the WNO; Vice-Pres., Kidney Research Unit for Wales Foundn. Mem., Gorsedd of Bards, Royal Nat. Eisteddfod of Wales; Patron, Churchill Theatre, Bromley; Governor, University Coll. of Wales, Aberystwyth. FGSM

1960; FRNCM 1978; FRCM 1981; FRSA 1984; Fellow: University Coll., Cardiff, 1976; Jesus Coll., Oxford, 1979. Hon. Freeman, City of London, 1984. Hon. DMus: Wales, 1965; Leicester, 1969; Oxford, 1985; CNAA 1980; London 1982. Hon. RAM 1969. Worshipful Company of Musicians Sir Charles Santley Meml Award, 1963; Harriet Cohen Internat. Music Award (Opera Medal), 1967; Fidelio Medal, Internat. Assoc. of Opera Dirs, 1980; San Francisco Opera Medal, 1981; Soc. of Cymmrodorion Medal, 1984. *Publication:* (with Noël Goodwin) Sir Geraint Evans: a knight at the opera, 1984. *Recreations:* rugby, sailing. *Address:* 17 Highcliffe, 32 Albemarle Road, Beckenham, Kent.

EVANS, Godfrey; *see* Evans, T. G.

EVANS, Gwynfor; Honorary President, Plaid Cymru, since 1982 (President, 1945–81, Vice-President, 1943–45); *b* 1 Sept. 1912; *s* of Dan Evans and Catherine Mary Richard; *m* 1941, Rhiannon Prys Thomas; four *s* three *d. Educ:* Gladstone Road Elementary Sch.; County Sch., Barry; University of Wales, Aberystwyth; St John's Coll., Oxford. Qual. Solicitor, 1939. Hon. Sec. Heddychwyr Cymru (Welsh Pacifist movement), 1939–45; Chm. Union of Welsh Independents, 1954. MP (Plaid Cymru) Carmarthen, July 1966–1970 and Oct. 1974–1979. Contested (Plaid Cymru) Carmarthen, 1979 and 1983. Member: Carmarthen CC, 1949–74; Ct of Govs, University of Wales and UC, Aberystwyth; Council Univ. of Wales, and UC Aberystwyth. Past Mem. Welsh Broadcasting Council. Hon. LLD Wales, 1973; Soc. of Cymmrodorion Medal, 1984. *Publications:* Plaid Cymru and Wales, 1950; Rhagom i Ryddid, 1964; Aros Mae, 1971; Wales can Win, 1973; Land of My Fathers, 1974; A National Future for Wales, 1975; Diwedd Prydeindod, 1981; Bywyd Cymro, 1982. *Address:* Talar Wen, Pencarreg, Llanybydder, Dyfed. *T:* Llanybydder 480907.

EVANS, Harold Matthew; Vice-President and Senior Editor, Weidenfeld & Nicolson, New York, since 1986; Editorial Director, US News and World Report, since 1984; *b* 28 June 1928; *s* of late Frederick and late Mary Evans; *m* 1st, 1953, Enid (marr. diss. 1978), *d* of late John Parker and of Susan Parker; one *s* two *d*; 2nd, 1981, Christina Hamley Brown, *d* of George H. Brown, San Pedro de Alcantara, Spain; one *s. Educ:* St Mary's Road Central Sch., Manchester; Durham Univ. BA 1952, MA Dunelm 1966. Ashton-under-Lyne, Lancs, Reporter Newspapers, 1944–46 and 1949; RAF, 1946–49; Durham Univ., 1949–52; Manchester Evening News, 1952; Commonwealth Fund Fellow in Journalism, Chicago and Stanford Univs, USA, 1956–57; Asst Ed, Manchester Evening News, 1958–61; Ed., Northern Echo, 1961–66; Editor-in-Chief, North of England Newspaper Co., 1963–66; Sunday Times: Chief Asst to Editor, 1966; Managing Editor, 1966; Editor, 1967–81; Editor, The Times, 1981–82. Member, Executive Board: Times Newspapers Ltd, 1968–82 (Mem. Main Bd, 1978); International Press Inst., 1974–80; Director: The Sunday Times Ltd, 1968–82; Times Newspapers Ltd, 1978–82; Editor-in-Chief, Atlantic Monthly Press, NY, 1984–86. Writer and Presenter, Evans on Newspapers, BBC TV, 1981. Hon. Vis. Prof. of Journalism, City Univ., 1978–; Vis. Prof., Inst. of Public Affairs, Duke Univ., N Carolina, 1984. Hon. FSIAD. Internat. Editor of the Year, 1975; Gold Medal Award, Inst. of Journalists, 1979; Editor of the Year, 1982. DUniv Stirling, 1982. *Publications:* The Active Newsroom, 1961; Editing and Design (five volumes): vol. 1, Newsman's English, 1972; vol. 5, Newspaper Design, 1973; vol. 2, Newspaper Text, 1974; vol. 3, Newspaper Headlines, 1974; vol. 4, Pictures on a Page, 1977; Good Times, Bad Times, 1983; (jointly): We Learned To Ski, 1974; The Story of Thalidomide, 1978; (ed) Eye Witness, 1981; How We Learned to Ski, 1983; Front Page History, 1984. *Recreations:* running, table-tennis, chess, ski-ing. *Address:* c/o Weidenfeld & Nicolson, 10 E 53rd Street, New York, NY 10022, USA. *Clubs:* Garrick, Royal Automobile; Century (New York).

EVANS, Sir Haydn T.; *see* Tudor Evans.

EVANS, Maj.-Gen. Henry Holland, CB 1972; *b* Harrogate, 18 Nov. 1914; *o s* of Major H. Evans; *m* 1939, Norah Mary, *d* of F. R. Lawson, Wolstanton, Staffs; one *s* one *d. Educ:* King James Grammar Sch., Almondbury, near Huddersfield; Manchester Univ. Commissioned Duke of Wellington's Regt (TA), 1936; Regular Army Commission in AEC, 1939; Officer Instructor, Duke of York's Royal Mil. Sch., 1939–41; Staff Officer: 43 (Wessex) Div., 1942–45; War Office, 1945–48; Chief Educn Officer, Malta and Libya, 1948–51; various RAEC appts, incl. Headmaster DYRMS and Chief Inspector of Army children's schools, to 1963; CEO, Northern Comd, 1963–65; CEO, BAOR, 1965–68; Dir of Army Educn, 1969–72. Sec., Council for Accreditation of Corresp. Colls, 1973–75. Mem., Sevenoaks Town Council, 1973–77. *Address:* c/o Royal Bank of Scotland, Whitehall, SW1.

EVANS, Prof. (Henry) John; Director, Medical Research Council Clinical and Population Cytogenetics Unit, Edinburgh, since 1969; *b* 24 Dec. 1930; *s* of David Evans and Gwladys Evans (*née* Jones); *m* 1st, 1957, Gwenda Rosalind (*née* Thomas) (*d* 1974); 2nd, 1976, Roslyn Rose (*née* Angell); four *s. Educ:* Llanelli Boys Grammar Sch.; UCW, Aberystwyth (BSc, PhD 1955). FIBiol. Res. Scientist, MRC Radiobiology Unit, Harwell, 1955–65, Head of Cell Biology Section, 1962–65; Vis. Fellow, Brookhaven Nat. Laboratory, Brookhaven, NY, USA, 1960–61; Prof. of Genetics, Univ. of Aberdeen, 1965–69. Chm., Assoc. Radiation Research, 1970–72; Cttee on Biological Effects of Ionizing Radiation, US Nat. Acad. Sci., 1972; Mem., MRC Biological Res. Bd, 1968–72; Council Mem., MRC, 1978–82. Member: DHSS Cttee, Mutagenicity of Foods and Chemicals, 1978–; Nat. Radiology Protection Bd, 1982–; Sci. Council, Internat. Agency for Research on Cancer, 1982–86 (Chm., 1985–86); Scientific Cttee, CRC, 1983–; Chief Scientist Cttee, SHHD, 1983–; Council, Imperial Cancer Res. Fund, 1985–; Cttee on Med. Aspects of Radiation in the Environment, DHSS, 1985–; Scientific Rev. Cttee, Alberta Heritage Foundn for Med. Res., 1986–. FRSE. Hon. Prof., Univ. of Edinburgh; Vis. Prof., Kyoto Univ., Japan, 1981. Hon. Fellow: UK Clinical Cytogenetics Soc., 1984; UK Environmental Mutagen Soc., 1984. Lilly Prize, RCPE, 1985. *Publications:* papers on radiation cytology, mutagenesis, chromosome structure and human cytogenetics in various internat. jls; editor of various books and jls in the field of genetics and radiobiology. *Recreations:* golf, music, fishing. *Address:* 45 Lauder Road, Edinburgh EH9 1UE. *T:* 031–667 2437. *Club:* Royal Commonwealth Society.

EVANS, Hubert John Filmer, CMG 1958; LLD; HM Diplomatic Service, retired; Central Asian Research Centre, 1965–70; *b* 21 Nov. 1904; *y s* of late Harry Evans and late Edith Gwendoline Rees; *m* 1948, Marjory Maureen Filmer (*née* Carrick), *widow* of Col R. A. M. Tweedy. *Educ:* City of London Sch.; Jesus Coll., Oxford (Classical Scholar); Montpellier. Studied oriental languages with Ross, Minorsky, and in the East. Entered Indian Civil Service, 1928; served as Magistrate in various districts of United Provinces, 1929–37; Deputy Commissioner of Delhi, and Pres., Delhi Municipal Council, 1938–42; Sec. Delhi Administration, 1942–45; Collector of Agra, 1945–47; appointed to Foreign Service, 1947; at the Foreign Office, 1948–50; Financial Adviser to Persian Gulf Residency, 1950–51; Consul-Gen. at Meshed, 1951; in Latin America, 1952–54; Consul-Gen., Rotterdam, 1955–56; HM Ambassador to Korea, 1957–61. Hon. Sec., Royal Central Asian Soc. and Chm. Ed. Board 1965–70. Hon. MRAS; Hon. LLD Korea, 1960; Freedom of Seoul, 1960. *Publications:* Islam in Iran (trans. from Russian), 1955; various in oriental jls. *Recreations:* the Persian Poets, and travel. *Address:* Manoir d'Arlette, Fatouville, 27210 Beuzeville, France; Le Vert Feuillage, Honfleur, France. *Club:* Athenæum.

EVANS, Huw Prideaux; Under Secretary, HM Treasury, since 1980; *b* 21 Aug. 1941; *s* of late Richard Hubert Evans and of Kathleen Annie Evans; *m* 1966, Anne (*née* Bray); two *s. Educ:* Cardiff High Sch.; King's Coll., Cambridge (MA); London Sch. of Econs and Polit. Science (MSc). Economist: HM Treasury, 1964–72; European Commn, 1972–73; Asst Econ. Sec., Hong Kong Govt, 1973–75; Sen. Econ. Adviser (Econ. Forecasting), HM Treasury, 1976–79. *Recreations:* cinema, opera. *Address:* c/o HM Treasury, Parliament Street, SW1. *T:* 01–233 4297.

EVANS, Hywel Eifion, CB 1974; Welsh Secretary, Ministry of Agriculture, Fisheries and Food, 1968–75; *b* 24 Jan. 1910; *s* of late Gruffydd Thomas and Winnifred Evans, Felin Rhydhir, Pwllheli, Caernarvonshire; *m* 1st, 1939, Mary Elizabeth (*d* 1977), *d* of late Richard and Hannah Jones, Gilfach, Glanywydden, Llandudno; one *s* one *d*; 2nd, 1978, Mrs Mair Lloyd Jones, *d* of late David Lloyd and Amelia Davies, Ceinfan, Narbeth, Dyfed. *Educ:* Pwllheli Grammar Sch.; University Coll. of North Wales, Bangor. BSc (Hons) (Agric.). Research Asst, Dept of Agricultural Economics, UCW, Aberystwyth, 1934–40; Dist and Dep. Exec. Officer, Leicester WAEC, 1940–46; County Advisory Officer: Radnor AEC, 1946–47; Carmarthen AEC, 1947–57; Dep. Regional Dir, Nat. Agricl Advisory Service for Wales, 1957–59, Regional Dir, 1959–66; Dep. Dir, Nat. Agricl Adv. Service (London), 1967–68. FRAgS, 1972. *Publications:* articles on agricultural, economic and sociological topics in Welsh Jl of Agriculture, Agriculture, and other jls. *Recreations:* idling, fishing, shooting. *Address:* Llawryglyn, Lôn Tyllyd, Llanfarian, Aberystwyth, Wales. *Club:* Farmers'.

EVANS, Sir Hywel (Wynn), KCB 1976 (CB 1972); Deputy Chairman, Prince of Wales Committee, since 1986; Permanent Secretary, Welsh Office, 1971–80; *b* 30 May 1920; *s* of late Dr T. Hopkin Evans, MusDoc and Adelina Evans; *m* 1949, Jessie Margaret Templeton; one *d. Educ:* Liverpool Collegiate Sch.; Liverpool Univ. RA and Intell. Corps, 1940–46 (despatches). Joined Min. of Labour, as Asst Principal, 1947; seconded to FO, 1952–54; Commonwealth Fellow, 1957–58; Private Sec. to Ministers of Labour, 1959–60; Sec., NEDC, 1964–68; Asst Under-Sec. of State, Welsh Office, 1968–71. Chm., Welsh Arts Council, 1981–86; Mem., Arts Council of GB, 1981–86. Member: Court of Govs: Nat. Mus. of Wales, 1981–; Court, Univ. of Wales, 1985–; Council, WNO, 1986–; Gorsedd of Bards of Wales. US Bronze Star, 1945. *Publication:* Governmental Regulation of Industrial Relations, 1960 (USA). *Recreations:* opera, watching rugby. *Address:* Coed-yr-Iarll, St Fagans, Cardiff, S Wales CF5 6DU. *T:* Cardiff 565214.

EVANS, James; Managing Director and Chief Executive, 1985–86, and Chairman, 1986, International Thomson Organisation plc; *b* 27 Nov. 1932; *s* of Rex Powis Evans and Louise Evans; *m* 1961, Jette Holmboe; two *d. Educ:* Aldenham School; St Catharine's College, Cambridge (MA). Called to the Bar, Gray's Inn, 1959; admitted Solicitor, 1972. Commissioned 26th Field Regt RA, 1951–53. Legal Dept, Kemsley Newspapers Ltd, 1956–59; practised at Bar, 1959–65; Legal Adviser: Thomson Newspapers Ltd, 1965–73; Times Newspapers Ltd, 1967–73; Sec. and Mem. Exec. Bd, 1973–78, Dir, 1978–86, Thomson Organisation Ltd; Dir, 1977–81, Chm., 1980–81, Times Newspapers Ltd; Chm., Thomson Withy Grove Ltd, 1979–84; Dir, 1978, Jt Dep. Man. Dir, 1982–84, International Thomson Organisation; Chm. and Chief Exec., Thomson Regional Newspapers Ltd, 1982–84; Director: Press Assoc., 1983–; Reuters, 1984–. Mem. Council, Newspaper Soc., 1984–. Mem., Home Office Deptl Cttee on Official Secrets Act (Franks Cttee), 1971. *Recreations:* infrequent. *Address:* The Quadrangle, 180 Wardour Street, W1. *T:* 01–437 9787. *Club:* Garrick.

EVANS, James Donald; Special Correspondent, Westminster Press Ltd, 1983–86; Acting Editor, UK Press Gazette, 1986; *b* 12 Nov. 1926; *yr s* of Arthur Evans and Isabella McKinnon Evans; *m* 1946, Freda Bristow; two *s* three *d. Educ:* Royal Grammar Sch., High Wycombe. Jun. Reporter, Bucks Free Press, 1943–45; Army, 1945–48; Chief Reporter, Maidenhead Advertiser, 1948–50; Northern Echo: District Chief Reporter, 1950–60; Industrial Corresp., 1961–65; Industrial Editor, 1965–66; Editor and Editor-in-Chief, 1966–82; Dir, North of England Newspapers, 1971–82. *Recreations:* driving, reading. *Address:* 81 Defoe House, Barbican, EC2Y 8DN. *T:* 01-638 5412. *Clubs:* National Liberal, Presscala.

EVANS, Col J(ames) Ellis, CBE 1973 (OBE 1952); TD 1947; JP; Lord-Lieutenant of Clwyd, 1979–85; *b* 6 Aug. 1910; *s* of James William Evans and Eleanor Evans, MBE, JP; unmarried. *Educ:* Epworth Coll., Rhyl. Chartered Accountant (FCA). Joined TA, 1937; served War of 1939–45, RA: France, 1940; N Africa, 1941–44; Italy, 1944–45; comd 384 Light Regt RA (RWF), TA, 1947–52; Dep. CRA, 53 (Welsh) Div., 1953–57; Chm. Denbigh and Flint TA Assoc., 1961–68; Chm., Wales and Mon TA&VRA, 1971–74 (Vice-Chm., 1968–71); Pres., Wales TA&VRA, 1981–85. Mem., Prestatyn UDC, 1939–74 (Chm. 1947); Mayor, Prestatyn Town Council, 1974–75. Clwyd, formerly Flintshire: JP 1951; DL 1953; High Sheriff, 1970–71; Vice-Lieut, 1970–74, Vice Lord-Lieut, 1977–79. Chm., North Wales Police Authority, 1976–78. *Recreations:* lawn tennis (played for Wales and Lancashire, 1936–48), gardening. *Address:* Trafford Mount, Gronant Road, Prestatyn, Clwyd. *T:* Prestatyn 4119. *Clubs:* East India, Devonshire, Sports and Public Schools; City (Chester).

EVANS, Jeremy David Agard; Director, Britoil plc, since 1982; *b* 20 June 1936; *s* of Arthur Burke Agard Evans and Dorothy (*née* Osborne); *m* 1964, Alison Mary (*née* White); one *s* two *d. Educ:* Whitgift Sch.; Christ's Coll., Cambridge (BA Hons). Ministry of Power: Asst Principal, 1960–64 (Private Sec. to Parly Sec., 1963–64); Principal, 1964–69; Sloan Fellow, London Business Sch., 1969–70; Principal, 1970–73, and Private Sec. to Minister for Industry, 1971–73, DTI; Asst Sec., DTI, 1973, Dept of Energy, 1974 (first Dep. Dir of Offshore Supplies Office, 1973); seconded as Sec. to BNOC on its foundn, 1976–78; a Man. Dir, 1978; Man. Dir Corporate Develt, and Sec., 1980–82, Mem. Bd 1981–82. *Recreations:* opera, skiing, walking. *Address:* Dormans House West, Dormans Park, East Grinstead, West Sussex RH19 2LY. *T:* Dormans Park 518.

EVANS, John; MP (Lab) St Helens, North, since 1983 (Newton, Feb. 1974–1983); Member, National Executive Committee of the Labour Party, since 1982; *b* 19 Oct. 1930; *s* of late James Evans, miner and Margaret (*née* Robson); *m* 1959, Joan Slater; two *s* one *d. Educ:* Jarrow Central School. Apprentice Marine Fitter, 1946–49 and 1950–52; Nat. Service, Royal Engrs, 1949–50; Engr, Merchant Navy, 1952–55; joined AUEW, 1952; joined Labour Party, 1955; worked in various industries as fitter, ship-building and repairing, steel, engineering, 1955–65, 1968–74. Mem. Hebburn UDC, 1962, Leader 1969, Chm. 1972; Sec./Agent Jarrow CLP, 1965–68, resigned. An Asst Govt Whip, 1978–79; Opposition Whip, 1979–80; PPS to Leader of Labour Party, 1980–83; opposition spokesman on employment, 1983–. Mem., European Parlt, 1975–78; Chm., Regional Policy, Planning and Transport Cttee, European Parlt, 1976–78. Political Sec., Nat. Union of Labour and Socialist Clubs. *Recreations:* watching football, reading, gardening. *Address:* 6 Kirkby Road, Culcheth, Warrington, Cheshire WA3 4BS. *T:* Culcheth 766322. *Clubs:* Labour (Earlestown and Cadishead); Daten (Culcheth).

EVANS, Prof. John; *see* Evans, Prof. H. J.

EVANS, Dr John; *see* Evans, Dr N. J. B.

EVANS, Maj.-Gen. John Alan Maurice; Commandant, Royal Military College of Science, Shrivenham, since 1985; *b* 13 Feb. 1936; *s* of John Arthur Mortimer Evans and Margaret (*née* Lewis); *m* 1958, Shirley Anne May; one *s* one *d*. *Educ*: Grammar schs in Wales and England; RMA Sandhurst; Trinity Coll., Cambridge (MA). Various Staff and RE appointments; CO, 22 Engr Regt, 1976–78; Comd, Berlin Inf. Bde, 1980–82; RCDS, 1983. *Recreations*: music, reluctant DIY, travel. *Address*: c/o Midland Bank, 29 High Street, Camberley GU15 3RE.

EVANS, Prof. John Davies, FBA 1973; Director, University of London Institute of Archæology, and Professor of Archæology in the University of London, since 1973; *b* 22 Jan. 1925; *o s* of Harry Evans and Edith Haycocks; *m* 1957, Evelyn Sladdin. *Educ*: Liverpool Institute High Sch. (open schol. in English to Pemb. Coll.); Pembroke Coll., Cambridge. War Service, 1943–47. BA 1948, MA 1950, PhD 1956, LittD 1979; Dr *hc* Lyon 2, 1983. Fellow of British Institute of Archæology at Ankara, 1951–52; Research Fellow of Pembroke Coll., Cambridge, 1953–56; Prof. of Prehistoric Archæology, London Univ., 1956–73. President: Prehistoric Soc., 1974–78; Council for British Archæology, 1979–82; Member: Permanent Council, Internat. Union of Prehistoric and Protohistoric Scis, 1975– (Pres., 1982–86); Royal Commn on Historical Monuments (England), 1985–; Chm., Area Archaeol Adv. Cttee for SE England, 1975–79. FSA 1955 (Dir, 1975–80, 1983–84, Pres., 1984–); Mem., German Archaeological Inst., 1979– (Corr. Mem., 1968–79). *Publications*: Malta (Ancient Peoples and Places Series), 1959; (with Dr A. C. Renfrew) Excavations at Saliagos, near Antiparos, 1968; The Prehistoric Antiquities of the Maltese Islands, 1971; papers and reports in archæological journals. *Recreations*: walking, listening to music. *Address*: Institute of Archæology, Gordon Square, WC1H 0PY.

EVANS, John Field, QC 1972; **His Honour Judge Evans**; a Circuit Judge, since 1978; *b* 27 Sept. 1928; 2nd *s* of late John David Evans, Llandaff, and Lucy May Evans (*née* Field). *Educ*. Cardiff High Sch.; Exeter Coll., Oxford (MA). Pilot Officer, RAF, 1948–49. Called to Bar, Inner Temple, 1953; Dep. Chm., Worcestershire QS, 1964–71; a Recorder of the Crown Court, 1972–78. *Recreation*: golf. *Clubs*: Army and Navy; Vincent's (Oxford).

EVANS, John G.; *see* Grimley Evans.

EVANS, John Isaac Glyn; Director of Weapons Production (Naval), Ministry of Defence, 1970–79; *b* 1 April 1919; *s* of William Evans; *m* 1943, Hilda Garratt Evans (*née* Lee); two *s* one *d*. *Educ*: Ystalyfera Grammar Sch.; University Coll., Swansea (BSc Physics, BSc Elec. Engineering). Engineer, GEC, 1940–41. Served War, Captain REME, 1941–46. Development Engineer, GEC, 1946–50; Works Group Engineer, Admiralty, 1950–53; main grade, 1953–59; senior grade, 1959–64; superintending grade, 1964–67; Dep. Dir, 1967–70. FIEE. *Recreations*: tennis, badminton, cricket. *Address*: 16 Woodland Grove, Claverton Down, Bath, Avon.

EVANS, John Kerr Q.; *see* Quarren Evans.

EVANS, John Marten Llewellyn, CBE 1956 (MBE 1945); JP; Official Solicitor to the Supreme Court of Judicature, 1950–70; *b* 9 June 1909; *s* of late Marten Llewellyn Evans, Solicitor, and Edith Helena (*née* Lile); *m* 1943, Winifred Emily, *y d* of late Austin Reed; one *s* one *d*. *Educ*: Rugby Sch.; Trinity Coll., Oxford. Admitted Solicitor, 1935; Legal Asst to the Official Solicitor, 1937. Served War of 1939–45, Major RA. Senior Legal Asst to the Official Solicitor, 1947; Asst Master in Lunacy, 1950. Vice-Chm., Austin Reed Group Ltd, 1969–77. Master of Worshipful Company of Cutlers, 1967–68. JP City of London, 1969. *Recreations*: the theatre, cricket, golf, tennis. *Address*: The Paddock, Waltham St Lawrence, Reading, Berks.

EVANS, Rev. Canon John Mascal; *b* 17 May 1915; *s* of Rev. Edward Foley Evans and Mary Evans; *m* 1941, Mary Elizabeth (*née* Rathbone); three *s* two *d*. *Educ*: St John's Sch., Leatherhead; Brasenose Coll., Oxford; Wells Theological Coll. Asst Curate, St Martin's, Epsom, 1938; Perpetual Curate, Stoneleigh, Epsom, 1942, All Saints, Fleet, 1952; Vicar, St Mary, Walton-on-Thames, 1960–68; Archdeacon of Surrey, 1968–80; Hon. Canon of Guildford, 1963–80, Canon Emeritus, 1980–; Mem. of Ridgeway Team Ministry, Dio. Salisbury, 1980–84. Member: General Synod of C of E, 1977–80; C of E Pensions Bd, 1977–85; Council of Cremation Soc., 1969–80. *Recreations*: outdoor sports, fishing. *Address*: 60 Swan Meadow, Pewsey, Wilts.

EVANS, John Robert, CC 1978; MD, DPhil, FRCP, FRCP (C), FACP; Chairman and Chief Executive Officer, Allelix Inc. (Biotechnology), Mississauga, Ont, since 1983; *b* 1 Oct. 1929; *s* of William Watson Evans and Mary Thompson; *m* 1954, Gay Glassco; four *s* two *d*. *Educ*: Univ. of Toronto (MD); Oxford Univ. (Rhodes Schol.) (Dphil). FRCP 1980. Jr interne, Toronto Gen. Hosp., 1952–53; Hon. Registrar, Nat. Heart Hosp., London, 1955; Asst Res.: Sunnybrook Hosp., Toronto, 1956; Toronto Gen. Hosp., 1957; Ontario Heart Foundn Fellow, Hosp. for Sick Children, Toronto, 1958; Chief Res. Physician, Toronto Gen. Hosp., 1959; Research Fellow, Baker Clinic Research Lab., Harvard Med. Sch., 1960; Markle Schol. in Acad. Med., Univ. of Toronto, 1960–65; Associate, Dept of Med., Faculty of Med., Univ. of Toronto, 1961–65; Asst Prof., 1965–66; Dean, Faculty of Med., McMaster Univ., 1965–72, Vice-Pres., Health Sciences, 1967–72; Pres., Univ. of Toronto, 1972–78; Dir, Dept of Population, Health and Nutrition, IBRD, Washington DC, 1979–83. Member: Council RCP (Can.), 1972–78; Inst. of Medicine, Nat. Acad. Sci., USA, 1972– (Mem. Council, 1976–80); Adv. Cttee Med. Res., WHO, 1976–80; Trustee, Rockefeller Foundn. Director: Dominion Foundries and Steel Ltd; Canadian Corporate Management Co. Ltd; Royal Bank of Canada; Torstar Ltd; Alcan Aluminium Ltd (Montreal); Southam Inc. (Toronto). Hon. LLD: McGill, 1972; Dalhousie, 1972; McMaster, 1972; Queen's, 1974; Wilfred Laurier, 1975; York, 1977; Yale, 1978; Toronto, 1980; Hon. DSc: Meml Univ. of Newfoundland, 1973; Montreal, 1977; Hon. DU Ottawa, 1978; Hon. DHL Johns Hopkins, 1978. *Recreations*: ski-ing, fishing, farming. *Address*: 58 Highland Avenue, Toronto, Ontario M4W 2A3, Canada.

EVANS, John Roger W.; *see* Warren Evans

EVANS, (John) Wynford; Chairman, South Wales Electricity Board, since 1984; *b* 3 Nov. 1934; *s* of late Gwilym Everton and Margaret Mary Elfreda Evans; *m* 1957, Sigrun Brethfeld; three *s*. *Educ*: Llanelli Grammar Sch.; St John's Coll., Cambridge (MA). FBCS; FRSA; CBIM. Served RAF (Flying Officer), 1955–57. IBM, 1957–58; NAAFI, W Germany, 1959–62; Kayser Bondor, 1962–63; various posts, inc. Computer and Management Services Manager, S Wales Electricity Bd, 1963–76; ASC, Henley, 1968; Dep. Chm., London Electricity Bd, 1977–84. Member: Milton Keynes IT Adv. Panel, 1982–84; Welsh Regional Council, CBI, 1984–; Chm., SE Wales Cttee, Industry Year 1986. Member: Hon. Soc. of Cymmrodorion, 1978; Court, Cranfield Inst. of Technol., 1980–; Civic Trust Bd for Wales, 1984–; Nat. Trust Cttee for Wales, 1985–. *Recreations*: fishing, cross-country ski-ing, golf. *Address*: South Wales Electricity Board, St Mellons, Cardiff CF3 9XW. *T*: Cardiff 792111. *Clubs*: Flyfishers', London Welsh; Cardiff and County, Radyr Golf (Cardiff).

EVANS, John Yorath Gwynne; Deputy Director (Air), Royal Aircraft Establishment, 1972–76, retired; *b* 10 Feb. 1922; *s* of Randell and Florence Evans, Carms; *m* 1948, Paula Lewis, *d* of late Roland Ford Lewis; two *s* one *d*. *Educ*: UCW Aberystwyth. Royal Aircraft Estabt, 1942; attached to RAF, Germany, 1945–46; Supt Wind Tunnels, RAE Bedford, 1958, Head of Aerodynamics Dept, RAE, 1971. *Publications*: contrib. various sci. and techn. jls. *Recreations*: sailing, travel, reading. *Address*: Rushmoor Cottage, Tilford, Farnham, Surrey. *T*: Frensham 2275.

EVANS, Rt. Rev. Kenneth Dawson; Assistant Bishop of Guildford, since 1986; *b* 7 Nov. 1915; *s* of late Dr Edward Victor Evans, OBE; *m* 1939, Margaret, *d* of J. J. Burton; one *s*. *Educ*: Dulwich Coll.; Clare Coll., Cambridge. Ordained, 1938; Curate of: St Mary, Northampton, 1938–41; All Saints', Northampton, 1941–45; Rector of Ockley, 1945–49; Vicar of Dorking, 1949–63; Archdeacon of Dorking and Canon Residentiary of Guildford Cathedral, 1963–68; Bishop Suffragan of Dorking, 1968–85. Hon. Canon of Guildford, 1955–63 and 1979–85. Mem., Bishop's Finance Commn, 1957. *Address*: 3 New Inn Lane, Burpham, Guildford, Surrey. *T*: Guidford 67978.

EVANS, Laurence James, CBE 1977; HM Diplomatic Service, retired; *b* 16 Dec. 1917; *s* of Albert Victor and Margaret Evans; *m* 1940, Clare Mary (*née* Kolb); one *d*. *Educ*: Alsop High Sch., Liverpool; Univ. of Liverpool (BA Hons, French); Univ. of Rennes (Diploma). Reader in the Faculté des Lettres, Univ. of Rennes, 1938–39. HM Forces (Intell. Corps), 1939–45. Foreign Office, Asst Principal, 1946–47; Bd of Inland Revenue (HM Inspector of Taxes), 1947–49; rejoined Foreign Service and apptd to Brussels, 1950–51; HM Vice-Consul, Khorramshahr, 1951–52; FO, 1952–54; Second Sec. and Vice-Consul, Ciudad Trujillo, Dominican Republic, 1954–57 (Chargé d'Affaires, 1955 and 1957); FO, 1957–63 (Asst Head of Communications, 1959); HM Consul, New York, 1963–66; Asst Head of Personnel Dept (Ops), DSAO, 1966–69; HM Consul-Gen., Geneva, 1969–73; HM Consul-General at Barcelona and Andorra, 1973–77; Doyen, Barcelona Consular Corps, 1974–76, Hon. Doyen, 1976–77; Staff Assessor, FCO, 1978–82. *Recreation*: music. *Address*: 16 Oakhurst Rise, Carshalton Beeches, Surrey SM5 4AG. *T*: 01-643 3023. *Clubs*: Royal Commonwealth Society, Civil Service.

EVANS, Lloyd Thomas; AO 1979; DSc, DPhil; FRS 1976; FAA; Chief Research Scientist, Commonwealth Scientific and Industrial Research Organization Division of Plant Industry, Canberra, Australia; *b* 6 Aug. 1927; *s* of C. D. Evans and G. M. Fraser; *m* 1954, Margaret Honor Newell; two *s* one *d* (and one *d* decd). *Educ*: Wanganui Collegiate Sch., NZ; Univ. of NZ (BSc, MAgrSc, DSc); Univ. of Oxford (DPhil). FAA 1971. Rhodes Scholar, Brasenose Coll., Oxford, 1950–54; Commonwealth Fund Fellow, Calif Inst. of Technol., 1954–56; res. scientist, CSIRO Div. of Plant Industry, Canberra, 1956–. National Acad. of Sciences (USA) Pioneer Fellow, 1963; Overseas Fellow, Churchill Coll., Cambridge, 1969–70; Vis. Fellow, Wolfson Coll., Cambridge, 1978. President: ANZAAS, 1976–77; Aust. Acad. of Science, 1978–82. Hon. LLD Canterbury, 1978. *Publications*: Environmental Control of Plant Growth, 1963; The Induction of Flowering, 1969; Crop Physiology, 1975; Daylength and the Flowering of Plants, 1976; Wheat Science: today and tomorrow, 1981; more than 100 scientific papers in jls. *Address*: 3 Elliott Street, Canberra, ACT 2601, Australia. *T*: Canberra 477815.

EVANS, Matthew; Managing Director since 1972 and Chairman since 1981, Faber & Faber Ltd; *b* 7 Aug. 1941; *s* of George Ewart Evans, *qv* and Florence Ellen Evans; *m* 1966, Elizabeth Amanda (*née* Mead); two *s*. *Educ*: Friends' Sch., Saffron Walden; London Sch. of Econs and Polit. Science (BScEcon). Bookselling, 1963–64; Faber & Faber, 1964–. Chairman: National Book League, 1982–84; English Stage Company, 1984–; Member: Council, Publishers Assoc., 1978–84; Franco-British Soc., 1981–. Governor, BFI, 1982–. *Recreation*: cricket. *Address*: 3 Canonbury Place, N1 2NQ. *T*: 01-226 0320.

EVANS, Maurice; Legion of Merit (US) 1945; Actor-manager; *s* of Alfred Herbert Evans, JP (Dorset). *Educ*: Grocers' Company Sch. Commenced theatrical career at Festival Theatre, Cambridge; later in a series of plays at Wyndham's, London; made his first successes in John van Druten's Diversion and R. C. Sherriff's Journey's End; following several years of appearances in West End became leading man at the Old Vic, where he was seen as Hamlet, Richard II, Petruchio, Benedick, etc.; went to America, 1936, to play Romeo to Katharine Cornell's Juliet; also appeared as the Dauphin in St Joan, Napoleon in St Helena. Produced and played title role Richard II, New York City, 1937; uncut Hamlet, 1938–39; produced and played Falstaff in Henry IV (Part 1), 1939; appeared as Malvolio in Twelth Night with Helen Hayes, 1940–41; produced and played title role in Macbeth, New York City, 1941–42; in each play toured provinces extensively. Went on a lecture tour in aid of British War Relief, 1941. Captain US Army, 1942; disch. with rank of Major, 1945. Played Hamlet in own GI version, 1945–46, New York; 1946–47, in provinces (acting version published Doubleday & Co., 1947). Produced and starred in Man and Superman, New York, 1947–48, establishing record New York run for play of Bernard Shaw; toured provinces, 1948–49; produced, and co-starred with Edna Best in Terence Rattigan's Browning Version, 1949; starred in Shaw's The Devil's Disciple, New York, and toured provinces, 1950; revived Richard II at NY City Center, 1951; starred in Dial 'M' for Murder, New York, 1952–54, and toured provinces, 1954; starred in Shaw's The Apple Cart, New York and provinces, 1956–57; produced and starred in Shaw's Heartbreak House, New York, 1959–60; starred in Tenderloin (musical), New York, 1960–61; The Aspern Papers, New York, 1961–62; with Helen Hayes in Shakespeare Revisited, A Program For Two Players, at Stratford (USA) and on tour, 1962–63; Holiday, Los Angeles, 1980; On Golden Pond, Florida, 1981; produced The Teahouse of the August Moon (Pulitzer-Critics' prize), 1953; No Time for Sergeants, 1955; Artistic Supervisor, New York City Center Theatre Company, 1949–51. Made first American picture 1950, co-starring with Ethel Barrymore in Kind Lady; also made Androcles and the Lion, Warlord, Jack of Diamonds, Planet of the Apes, Rosemary's Baby, Thin Air, Planet of the Apes Revisited, and, in England, Gilbert and Sullivan, 1952 and Macbeth, 1960. Became United States citizen, 1941. Hon. doctorates: Univ. of Hawaii; Lafayette Coll., Penn.; Brandeis Univ. *Address*: c/o Charles H. Renthal & Co., 20 East 46th Street, New York, NY 10017, USA. *Clubs*: Oriental; Players (New York).

EVANS, Michael; *see* Evans, T. M.

EVANS, Michael Nordon, CMG 1964; Permanent Secretary, Ministry of Health and Housing, Kenya, 1960–64, retired; *b* 27 April 1915; *s* of late Christmas and Lilian Margaret Louise Evans, Tunbridge Wells; *m* 1st, 1939, Mary Stockwood; one *d*; 2nd, 1951, Mary Josephine Suzette van Vloten; one *d*. *Educ*: Eastbourne Coll.; Queens' Coll., Cambridge. Apptd District Officer in Colonial Administrative Service, Kenya, 1939; African Courts Officer, Kenya, 1953; Dep. Commissioner for Local Government, 1954; Permanent Sec., 1958. *Recreation*: tennis. *Address*: Hugon Lodge, 13 Hugon Road, Claremont, Cape, 7700, Republic of South Africa. *Clubs*: Hawks (Cambridge); Nairobi (Kenya).

EVANS, Mostyn; *see* Evans, Arthur M.

EVANS, Dr (Noel) John (Bebbington), CB 1980; Deputy Secretary, Department of Health and Social Security, 1977–84; *b* 26 Dec. 1933; *s* of William John Evans and Gladys Ellen (*née* Bebbington); *m* 1st, 1960, Elizabeth Mary Garbutt (marr. diss.); two *s* one *d*; 2nd, 1974, Eileen Jane McMullan. *Educ:* Hymers Coll., Hull; Christ's Coll., Cambridge (scholar; 1st cl., Nat. Sci. Tripos); Westminster Medical Sch., London; London Sch. of Hygiene and Tropical Med. (Newsholme prize, Chadwick Trust medal and prize). MA, MB, BChir; FRCP, DPH (Dist.), FFCM. Called to Bar, Gray's Inn, 1965. House officer posts at: Westminster, Westminster Children's, Hammersmith, Central Middlesex and Brompton Hosps, 1958–60; Medical Registrar and Tutor, Westminster Hosp., 1960–61; Asst MoH, Warwickshire CC, 1961–65; Dept of Health and Social Security (formerly Min. of Health), 1965–84, DCMO 1977–82; Sir Wilson Jameson Travelling Fellowship, 1966. Chm., Welsh Cttee on Drug Misuse, 1986–; Member: Nat. Biological Standards Bd, 1975–; Welsh Cttee, Countryside Commn, 1985–. *Publications:* The Organisation and Planning of Health Services in Yugoslavia, 1967; contribs to med. jls. *Recreations:* canals, photography. *Address:* Athelstan, Grosmont, Abergavenny, Gwent NP7 8LW. *T:* Golden Valley 240616.

EVANS, Prof. Peter Angus, DMus; FRCO; Professor of Music, University of Southampton, since 1961; *b* 7 Nov. 1929; *y s* of Rev. James Mackie Evans and Elizabeth Mary Fraser; *m* 1953, June Margaret Vickery. *Educ:* West Hartlepool Grammar Sch.; St Cuthbert's Soc., University of Durham. BA (1st cl. hons Music), 1950; BMus, MA 1953; DMus 1958; FRCO 1952. Music Master, Bishop Wordsworth's Sch., Salisbury, 1951–52; Lecturer in Music, University of Durham, 1953–61. Conductor, Palatine Opera Group, 1956–61; Conductor, Southampton Philharmonic Soc., 1965–. *Publications:* Sonata for Oboe and Piano, 1953; Three Preludes for Organ, 1955; Edns of 17th Century Chamber Music, 1956–58; The Music of Benjamin Britten, 1979; contributor to Die Musik, in Geschichte und Gegenwart, to A Concise Encyclopædia of Music, 1958, to New Oxford History of Music, 1974, and to New Grove Dictionary of Music, 1981; writer and reviewer, especially on contemporary music. *Address:* 9 Bassett Close, Southampton. *T:* Southampton 768125.

EVANS, Dr Philip Rainsford, CBE 1968; Physician-Paediatrician to the Queen, 1972–76; Physician, The Hospital for Sick Children, Great Ormond Street, 1946–75; *b* 14 April 1910; 2nd *s* of Charles Irwin Evans, headmaster of Leighton Park Sch., and Katharine Evans; *m* 1935, Dr Barbara Dorothy Fordyce Hay-Cooper; three *s* one *d*. *Educ:* Sidcot Sch., Winscombe, Som; Leighton Park Sch., Reading; Manchester University. BSc 1930, MSc 1941, MB, ChB 1933, MD 1941, Manchester; MRCP 1935, FRCP 1945, London. Rockefeller Travelling Research Fellow, 1937–38; Asst Pædiatrician, Johns Hopkins Hosp., Baltimore, 1938–39; Asst Physician to Children's Dept, King's Coll. Hosp., London, 1939–46; Dir, Dept of Paediatrics, Guy's Hosp., 1946–71; Dir, British Tay-Sachs Foundn, 1971–74. Served War of 1939–45, RAMC, N Africa and Italy, 1942–46 (despatches); Hon. Col AMS. Editor, Archives of Disease in Childhood, 1947–54. Hon. Mem., British, French and American Pædiatric Socs. Member, Cttee on Milk Composition, 1957–59, Ministry of Agriculture, Fisheries and Food. FRSM (Pres., Section of Pædiatrics, 1968–69, Section of Comparative Medicine, 1982–83); Hon. Sec. British Pædiatric Assoc., 1954–59; Hon. Consultant to the Army in Pædiatrics, 1962–66; formerly Visiting Prof., Makerere, Saigon, Sheffield, Beirut; late Examr Universities of Bristol, Leeds, Birmingham, Cambridge, Jordan, and RCP; Mem. Council, RCP, 1962–65; Censor, RCP, 1972–74. (Jointly) Dawson Williams Prize, BMA, 1969. *Publications:* (joint) Infant Feeding and Feeding Difficulties, 1954; Jt Editor, Garrod, Batten and Thursfield's Diseases of Children, 1953; original papers in med. journals. *Recreations:* painting and paintings. *Address:* 24 Abbey Road, NW8 9AX. *T:* 01–624 1668.

EVANS, Phyllis Mary Carlyon, MA; Headmistress, St Swithun's School, Winchester, 1952–73; *b* 17 April 1913; *d* of L. L. C. Evans, late Headmaster of Swanbourne House Sch., Bletchley, Bucks, and of Mrs M. Evans (*née* Gore-Browne). *Educ:* Wycombe Abbey Sch., Bucks; St Hugh's Coll., Oxford. Lit Hum, 1935. Classics mistress, St Mary's, Calne, 1935–39; Yates Theology Scholar St Hugh's Coll., Oxford, 1939–40; Degree in Theology, 1940; MA 1940. Senior Classics mistress, The Alice Ottley Sch., Worcester, 1940–45; Head Mistress, Wellington Diocesan Sch. for Girls, Marton, New Zealand, 1946–51. Representative of Winchester Diocese in Church Assembly, 1957–70; Lay Reader. *Address:* April Cottage, 13 St Swithun's Street, Winchester.

EVANS, Raymond John Morda, MA, PhD; JP; Headmaster, Silcoates School, 1960–78; *b* 1 Oct. 1917; 2nd *s* of late Rev. J. Morda Evans, Congregational Minister; *m* 1942, Catherine Mair Gernos Davies, *er d* of late Rev. J. Gernos Davies, Congregational Minister; one *s* two *d* (and one *s* decd). *Educ:* Silcoates Sch., near Wakefield; (Casberd Scholar) St John's Coll., Oxford. BA Oxon (Mod. Langs), 1939, MA 1942; MA, PhD London (Russian Lang. and Lit.), 1959. Dauntsey's Sch., 1939–40; Intelligence Corps (Captain), 1940–46; Leeds Grammar School, 1946–52; Head of Dept of Modern Languages, Royal Naval Coll., Greenwich, 1952–60. *Publications:* contrib. to Slavonic and Eastern European Review, and to Mariners' Mirror. *Recreation:* swimming. *Address:* 16 Kepstorn Road, West Park, Leeds LS16 5HL.

EVANS, Prof. Rhydwyn Harding, CBE 1958; MSc, DSc Manchester, PhD Leeds; FICE, FIMechE, FIStructE, MSocCE France, Hon. MIPlantE; Professor of Civil Engineering and Administrative Head of Engineering Departments, University of Leeds, 1946–68, Emeritus Professor, 1968; *b* 9 Oct. 1900; *s* of late David Evans, Tygwyn, Pontardulais, Glam; *m* 1929, Dilys Elizabeth, *o c* of late George Rees, Welsh Poet and Hymnologist, and Kate Ann Rees, London; one *s*. *Educ:* Llanelly Grammar Sch.; University of Manchester. Mercantile Marine, 1918–20. BSc top 1st class Graduate Prizeman, 1923; MSc 1928; PhD 1932; DSc 1943. Demonstrator, Asst Lecturer, Lecturer, Senior Lecturer and later Reader in Civil Engineering, University of Leeds, 1926–46; Dean, Faculty of Tech. University of Leeds, 1948–51; Pro-Vice-Chancellor, University of Leeds, 1961–65. Lectures: Unwin Meml ICE, 1960; first George Hondros Meml, WA, 1970. IStructE: Vice-Pres., 1948–49; Chm., Yorks Br., 1940–41, 1955–56 and 1958–59 (Yorkshire Br. Prize, 1946–47 and 1950–51); ICE: Chm. Yorks Assoc., 1942–43 and 1952–53; Mem. Council, 1949–52; Mem., Joint Matriculation Bd, Manchester, 1949–68; Chm., Leeds Univ. Min. of Labour and NS Bd, 1949–60; first Chm., Trng Consultative Cttee, Cement and Concrete Assoc., 1966–73. Consulting Editor in Civil Engineering: McGraw-Hill Book Co. (UK) Ltd, 1975–; Pitman Ltd, 1978–. Hon. Mem., Concrete Soc., 1970. Hon. DèsSc Ghent, 1953; Hon. DTech Bradford, 1971. Rugby Engrg Soc. Student's Prize, 1925; Telford Premiums, 1942–43–44; Medal, Ghent Univ., 1949, 1953; George Stephenson Gold Medal, 1956; Institution of Water Engineers, Instn Premium, 1953; Reinforced Concrete Assoc. Medal, 1961; Instn of Struct. Engrs: Research Diploma, 1965; Certif. of Commendation, 1970; Henry Adams Award, 1971. *Publications:* Prestressed Concrete (with E. W. Bennett), 1962; Concrete Plain, Reinforced Prestressed, Shell (with C. B. Wilby), 1963; Reinforced and Prestressed Concrete (with F. K. Kong), 1975 (2nd edn. 1980); (jtly) Handbook of Structural Concrete, 1983; papers on elasticity and plasticity of concrete and other building materials; strain and stress distribution in reinforced concrete beams and arches; pre-stressed concrete; extensibility, cracking and tensile stress-strain of concrete; bond stresses; shear stresses; combined bending and shear stresses; torsional stresses; preflexed pre-stressed concrete beams; lightweight aggregate concrete; vibration and pressure moulding of concrete in Journals of Institutions of Civil, Struct. and Water Engineers, Concrete Soc., Philosophical Magazine, Engineer, Engineering, Civil Engineering and Public Works. *Recreations:* motoring, travel, gardening. *Address:* 23 Christopher Rise, Pontlliw, Swansea, West Glamorgan SA4 1EN. *T:* Gorseinon 891961.

EVANS, Sir Richard (Mark), KCMG 1984 (CMG 1978); HM Diplomatic Service; Ambassador to the People's Republic of China, since 1984; *b* 15 April 1928; *s* of late Edward Walter Evans, CMG; *m* 1973, Rosemary Grania Glen Birkett; two *s*. *Educ:* Dragon Sch., Oxford; Repton Sch.; Magdalen Coll., Oxford. BA (Oxon) 1949. Joined HM Foreign (now Diplomatic) Service: Third Sec., London, 1952–55; Third Sec., Peking, 1955–57; Second Sec., London, 1957–62; First Sec.: Peking, 1962–64; Berne, 1964–68; London, 1968–70; Counsellor, 1970; Head of Near Eastern Dept, FCO, 1970–72, Head of Far Eastern Dept, 1972–74; Fellow, Centre for Internat. Affairs, Harvard Univ., 1974–75; Commercial Counsellor, Stockholm, 1975–77; Minister (Economic), Paris, 1977–79; Asst Under-Sec. of State, 1979–82, Dep. Under-Sec. of State, 1982–83, FCO. *Recreations:* travel, reading, music. *Address:* c/o Foreign and Commonwealth Office, SW1A 2AH. *Club:* United Oxford & Cambridge University.

EVANS, Robert; Chief Executive and Member of the Board, British Gas Corporation, since 1983; *b* 28 May 1927; *s* of Gwilym Evans and Florence May Evans; *m* 1950, Lilian May (*née* Ward); one *s* one *d*. *Educ:* Old Swan Coll.; Blackburn Coll.; City of Liverpool Coll. (Tech.); Liverpool Univ. D. Napier & Son Ltd, 1943–49; North Western Gas Bd, 1950–56; Burmah Oil Co. (Pakistan), 1956–62; Dir of Engrg, Southern Gas Bd, 1962–72; Dep. Dir (Ops), Gas Council, 1972; Dir of Operations, British Gas, 1972–75; Dep. Chm., North Thames Gas, 1975–77; Chm., E Midlands Gas Region, 1977–82; Man. Dir, Supplies, British Gas Corp., 1982–83. Pres., Instn of Gas Engrs, 1981–82. *Recreations:* motoring, reading, golf. *Address:* British Gas Corporation, Rivermill House, 152 Grosvenor Road, SW1V 3JL.

EVANS, Sir (Robert) Charles, Kt 1969; MA, FRCS; Principal, University College of North Wales, 1958–84; Vice-Chancellor, University of Wales, 1965–67, and 1971–73; *b* 19 Oct. 1918; *o s* of late R. C. Evans and Mrs Charles Evans; *m* 1957, Denise Nea Morin; three *s*. *Educ:* Shrewsbury Sch.; University Coll., Oxford. BM, BCh Oxon 1943; MA Oxon 1947; FRCS 1949. RAMC, 1943–46 (despatches). Surgical Registrar, United Liverpool Hosps, and Liverpool Regional Hosps, 1947–57. Hunterian Prof., Royal College Surg. Eng., 1953. Dep. Leader, Mt Everest Expedition, 1953; Leader, Kangchenjunga Expedition, 1955; Pres., Alpine Club, 1967–70; Mem. Council, Royal Geog. Society, 1960–61. Hon. DSc Wales, 1956. Cullum Medal, American Geog. Soc., 1954; Livingstone Medal, Scottish Geog. Soc., 1955; Founder's Medal, Royal Geog. Society, 1956. *Publications:* Eye on Everest, 1955; On Climbing, 1956; Kangchenjunga—The Untrodden Peak, 1956; articles in Alpine Journal, Geographical Journal, etc. *Address:* Ardincaple, Capel Curig, N Wales. *Club:* Alpine.

EVANS, Robert John Weston, PhD; FBA 1984; Research Fellow, Brasenose College, since 1968 and University Lecturer in Modern History of East-Central Europe, since 1969, Oxford; *b* 7 Oct. 1943; *s* of Thomas Frederic and Margery Evans (*née* Weston), Cheltenham; *m* 1969, Kati Róbert; one *s* one *d*. *Educ:* Dean Close School; Jesus College, Cambridge (BA 1st Cl. with distinction 1965, PhD 1968). Mem., Inst. for Advanced Study, Princeton, 1981–82. Jt Editor, English Historical Review, 1985–. *Publications:* Rudolf II and his World, 1973; The Wechel Presses, 1975; The Making of the Habsburg Monarchy, 1979 (Wolfson Literary Award for History, 1980). *Recreations:* music, walking, natural (and unnatural) history. *Address:* Brasenose College, Oxford. *T:* Oxford 248641; 83 Norreys Road, Cumnor, Oxford.

EVANS, Maj.-Gen. Robert Noel, CB 1981; Postgraduate Dean and Commandant, Royal Army Medical College, 1979–81; *b* 22 Dec. 1922; *s* of William Evans and Norah Moynihan; *m* 1950, Mary Elizabeth O'Brien; four *s* one *d*. *Educ:* Christian Brothers Sch., Tralee, Co. Kerry; National University of Ireland (MB, BCh, BAO 1947). DTM&H 1961; FFARCS 1963. Commnd RAMC 1951; Consultant Anaesthetist, 1963; CO BMH Rinteln, 1969–71; ADMS 4th Div., 1971–73; DDMS HQ BAOR, 1973–75; Comdt, RAMC Trng Centre, 1975–77; DMS, HQ BAOR, 1977–79; QHP 1976–81. Col Comdt, RAMC, 1981–. MFCM 1978. OStJ 1978. *Recreations:* gardening, walking, music. *Address:* 32 Folly Hill, Farnham, Surrey. *T:* Farnham 726938.

EVANS, Roger W.; *see* Warren Evans.

EVANS, Roy Lyon; General Secretary, Iron and Steel Trades Confederation, since 1985; *b* 13 Aug. 1931; *s* of David Evans and Sarah (*née* Lyon); *m* 1960, Brenda Jones; one *s* two *d*. *Educ:* Gowerton Grammar Sch., Swansea. Employed in Tinplate Section of Steel Industry, 1948. Iron and Steel Trades Confederation: Divl Organiser, NW Area, 1964–69; Divl Organiser, W Wales Area, 1969–73; Asst Gen. Sec., 1973–85. Jt Sec., Jt Industrial Council for the Slag Industry, 1975–85; Member: Jt Accident Prevention Adv. Cttee, 1974– (Chm., 1983); NEC of Labour Party, 1981–84. *Recreations:* reading, walking. *Address:* Swinton House, 324 Gray's Inn Road, WC1X 8DD. *T:* 01–837 6691.

EVANS, Russell Wilmot, MC 1945; Director, Eagle Star Holdings, since 1982; *b* 4 Nov. 1922; *s* of William Henry Evans and Ethel Williams Wilmot; *m* 1956, Pamela Muriel Hayward; two *s* one *d*. *Educ:* King Edward's Sch., Birmingham; Birmingham Univ. LLB Hons. Served HM Forces, 1942–47; commnd Durham LI, 1942, Major, 1945. Admitted Solicitor, Birmingham, 1949; Solicitor with Shakespeare & Vernon, Birmingham, 1949–50; Asst Sec., Harry Ferguson, 1951; Sec., Massey-Ferguson (Hldgs) and UK subsids, 1955–62; Dir, gp of private cos in construction industry, 1962–67; joined Rank Organisation, 1967: Dep. Sec., 1967–68; Sec., 1968–72; Dir, 1972–83; Man. Dir, 1975–82; Dep. Chm., 1981; Chm., 1982–83; Dir, principal subsid. and associated cos incl. Rank Xerox, 1975–83; Fuji Xerox, 1976–83; Chm., Rank City Wall, 1976–83. *Recreations:* tennis, squash, photography. *Address:* Walnut Tree, Roehampton Gate, SW15 5JR. *T:* 01–876 2433. *Clubs:* English-Speaking Union, Roehampton (Dir 1971–, Chm., 1984–).

EVANS, Very Rev. Sydney Hall, CBE 1976; Dean of Salisbury, 1977–86; *b* 23 July 1915; *s* of William and Winifred Evans; *m* 1941, Eileen Mary (*née* Evans); two *s* one *d*. *Educ:* Bristol Grammar Sch.; St Chad's Coll., Durham. MA 1940, BD 1945, Durham. Deacon 1939, priest 1940; Curate of Bishop Auckland, Co. Durham, 1939–41; Curate of Ferryhill, Co. Durham, 1941–43. Chaplain RAFVR, 1943–45. Chaplain and Lecturer, King's Coll., London, 1945–48; Warden of King's Coll. post-graduate coll. at Warminster, 1948–56; Dean of King's Coll., London, 1956–77; Hon. Canon of Southwark, 1959–77; Preacher of Gray's Inn, 1960–77; formerly Exam. Chaplain to Bishops of Southwark, Chelmsford, Truro, Durham, London. Public Orator, Univ. of London, 1972–74. FKC 1955. Hon. Bencher, Gray's Inn, 1977. Hon. DD: Lambeth, 1978; London, 1978. *Recreations:* walking and bird-watching. *Address:* 18 Cripstead Lane, St Cross, Winchester.

EVANS, (Thomas) Alun; HM Diplomatic Service; Counsellor, Foreign and Commonwealth Office, since 1982; *b* 8 June 1937; *s* of late Thomas Evans and Mabel Elizabeth (*née* Griffiths); *m* 1964, Bridget Elisabeth, *d* of Peter Lloyd, *qv* and Nora Kathleen

Williams (*née* Patten); three *s*. *Educ:* Shrewsbury Sch.; University Coll., Oxford (MA). Army, 1956–58. Entered HM Foreign Service, 1961; Third Sec., Rangoon, 1962–64; Second Sec., Singapore, 1964–66; FO, 1966–70; First Sec., Geneva, 1970–74; FCO, 1974–79; Counsellor, Pretoria, 1979–82. *Recreations:* music, fishing. *Address:* c/o Foreign and Commonwealth Office, SW1A 2AH. *Club:* Royal Commonwealth Society.

EVANS, Ven. (Thomas) Eric; Archdeacon of Cheltenham, since 1975; Residentiary Canon of Gloucester Cathedral, since 1969; *b* 1928; *s* of late Eric John Rhys Evans and Florence May Rogers; *m* 1957, Linda Kathleen Budge; two *d*. *Educ:* St David's Coll., Lampeter (BA); St Catherine's Coll., Oxford (MA); St Stephen's House, Oxford. Ordained, 1954; Curate, Margate Parish Church, 1954–58; Sen. Curate, St Peter's, Bournemouth, 1958–62; first Dir, Bournemouth Samaritans; Diocesan Youth Chaplain, dio. Gloucester, 1962–69; Wing Chaplain, ATC, 1963–69; Hon. Chaplain: Gloucester Coll. of Educn, 1968–75; Gloucestershire Constabulary, 1977–. Chm., Glos Trng Cttee, 1967–69; Proctor in Convocation and Mem. Gen. Synod of C of E, 1970–; a Church Comr, 1978– (Mem., Bd of Governors, 1978–, Assets Cttee, 1985–). Canon Missioner, dio. Gloucester, 1969–75; Chairman: House of Clergy, dio. Gloucester, 1979–82; Bd of Social Responsibility, dio. Gloucester, 1982–83; Glos Assoc. for Mental Health, 1983–85 (Vice-Chm., 1965–78); Glos Diocesan Adv. Cttee, 1984–. Mem. Exec. Cttee, 1975–, Chm., 1981–, Council for the Care of Churches (formerly Council for Places of Worship). Dir, Ecclesiastical Insurance Office Ltd, 1979–. Mem. Council, Cheltenham Ladies' College, 1982–. *Recreation:* travel, esp. Middle East. *Address:* 9 College Green, Gloucester. *T:* Gloucester 20620. *Clubs:* Carlton; Downhill Only (Wengen).

EVANS, (Thomas) Godfrey, CBE 1960; public relations officer; *b* Finchley, 18 Aug. 1920; *s* of A. G. L. Evans; *m* 1973, Angela Peart; one *d*. *Educ:* Kent Coll., Canterbury. Joined Kent County Staff at age of 16. First kept wicket for England in Test *v* India, 1946; first overseas Test tour, Australia and New Zealand, 1946–47; has also played in Test matches in W Indies and S Africa. Has played in 91 Test matches (world record 1959); dismissed 218 batsmen in Test cricket from behind the stumps, 88 more than Oldfield, the previous record-holder, and retained the record until 1976; the first wicket-keeper to have dismissed more than 200 victims and scored over 2000 runs in Test cricket; held world record for not conceding a bye while 1,054 runs were scored in a Test series (Australia, 1946); holds record for longest Test innings without scoring (95 minutes *v* Australia, Adelaide, 1947); holds jointly, with Charles Barnett, record for fastest score before lunch in a Test match (98 *v* India, Lord's, 1952); in making 47 in 29 minutes was three runs off the fastest 50 in Test cricket (*v* Australia, Old Trafford, 1956); first Englishman to tour Australia with MCC four times after War of 1939–45. *Publications:* Behind the Stumps, 1951; Action in Cricket, 1956; The Gloves Are Off, 1960; Wicket Keepers of the World, 1984. *Recreations:* real tennis, golf, squash. *Address:* 51 Delaware Mansions, Delaware Road, W9. *Club:* MCC (Hon. Life Mem.).

EVANS, Thomas Henry, CBE 1957; DL; LLM; Clerk of the Peace, Clerk of the County Council, and Clerk to Lieutenancy for Staffordshire, 1942–72; Clerk of Staffordshire Magistrates Courts Committee, 1952–72; Clerk of Staffordshire County and Stoke-on-Trent Police Authority, 1968–72; *b* 1907; *s* of late Henry Evans, Bootle, Lancs. *Educ:* Merchant Taylors' Sch., Crosby, Lancs; University of Liverpool (LLM). Admitted Solicitor, 1930. Asst Solicitor with Surrey County Council, 1930–35; Asst County Solicitor and later Dep. Clerk of Staffs County Council, 1935–42. Member: Cttee on Consolidation of Highway Law, 1958; Interdepartmental Cttee (Streatfeild) on business of Criminal Courts, 1958; Nat. Advisory Coun. on Training of Magistrates, 1964–73. DL Staffs, 1947. *Publication:* contributor to Macmillan's Local Government Law and Administration. *Address:* 108 Holland Road, Hove, East Sussex.

EVANS, (Thomas) Michael, QC 1973; **His Honour Judge Michael Evans;** a Circuit Judge, since 1979; *b* 7 Sept. 1930; *s* of late David Morgan Evans, Barrister, and of Mary Gwynydd Lloyd; *m* 1957, Margaret Valerie Booker; one *s* four *d*. *Educ:* Brightlands Prep. Sch., Newnham, Glos; Marlborough Coll., Wilts; Jesus Coll., Oxford (MA (Juris.)). Called to the Bar, Gray's Inn, 1954; Wales and Chester Circuit, 1955; a Recorder of the Crown Court, 1972–79. Legal Chm., Mental Health Review Tribunal for Wales, 1970. *Recreations:* golf, sailing. *Address:* The Old Rectory, Reynoldston, Gower, Swansea. *T:* Reynoldston 329.

EVANS, Dr Trevor John; General Secretary, Institution of Chemical Engineers, since 1976; *b* 14 Feb. 1947; *o s* of Evan Alban Evans and Margaret Alice Evans (*née* Hilton); *m* 1973, Margaret Elizabeth (*née* Whitham); two *s* one *d*. *Educ:* King's Sch., Rochester; University Coll., London (BSc (Eng) 1968, PhD 1972); CEng, FIChemE, FBIM. Res. Officer, CSIR, Pretoria, 1968–69; Ford Motor Co., Aveley, Essex, 1972–73; Institution of Chemical Engineers: Asst Sec., Technical, 1973–75; Dep. Sec., 1975–76. Member: Bd, Council of Science and Technology Institutes, 1976–; Exec. Cttee, Commonwealth Engineers Council, 1976–; Jt Hon. Sec., European Fedn of Chem. Engrg, 1976–. *Publications:* scientific papers and general articles in Chemical Engrg Science, The Chem. Engr, etc. *Recreations:* photography, the theatre, travel. *Address:* The Institution of Chemical Engineers, 12 Gayfere Street, SW1. *T:* 01–222 2681.

EVANS, Sir Vincent; *see* Evans, Sir W. V. J.

EVANS, William, MD, DSc, FRCP; Consulting Physician: to Cardiac Department, London Hospital; to National Heart Hospital; and to Institute of Cardiology; Consulting Cardiologist to Royal Navy, 1946–67; Hon. Cardiologist to Royal Society of Musicians; *b* 24 Nov. 1895; *s* of late Eben Evans, Tregaron, Cardiganshire; *m* 1936, Christina (*d* 1964), *d* of late John Lessels Downie, Kirkcaldy. *Educ:* University Coll. of Wales, Aberystwyth; London Hospital; London Univ., MB, BS (London) 1925, hons in Surgery; MD (London) 1927; FRCP 1937; DSc (London) 1944; K. E. D. Payne Prize in Pathology, 1927; Hutchinson Triennial Prize in Clinical Surgery, 1929; Liddle Triennial Prize in Pathology, 1931; Sydney Body Gold Medal, 1954; Strickland Goodall Lect., 1942; Finlayson Lect., 1947; St Cyres Lect., 1952; Gerrish Milliken Lect., University of Philadelphia, 1954; First Rufus Stolp Memorial Lect., University of Evanston, Ill., 1954; Carbutt Memorial Lect., 1957; Schorstein Lect., 1961; Wiltshire Lect., 1961. First Leonard Abrahamson Memorial Lecture, Royal College of Surgeons in Ireland, Dublin, 1963; Sir Thomas and Lady Dixon Lecture, Belfast, 1965. Formerly Asst Dir to Medical Unit, Paterson Medical Officer and Chief Asst to Cardiac Dept, London Hosp. Served European War, 1914–18, Combatant Officer, Lancs Fusiliers, and Battalion Education Officer. Hon. DSc (Wales), 1961. Mem. American Heart Assoc.; Hon. Mem. British Cardiac Soc.; Hon. Mem. Soc. of Phys. in Wales; Hon. FRSM. Guest Lecturer at Centenary Meetings of Royal Melbourne Hospital, 1948. High Sheriff of Cardiganshire, 1959. Hon. Mem. Order of Druids, 1960. *Publications:* Student's Handbook of Electrocardiography, 1934; Cardiography (2nd edn, 1954); Cardiology (2nd edn, 1956); Cardioscopy, 1952; Diseases of the Heart and Arteries, 1964; Journey to Harley Street, 1969; Diary of a Welsh Swagman, 1975; various papers on medical and cardiological subjects in Quarterly Jl of Med., Lancet, BMJ and Brit. Heart Jl. *Recreations:* fishing, gardening, farming. *Address:* Bryndomen, Tregaron, Dyfed, West Wales. *T:* Tregaron 404.

EVANS, William Campbell, OBE 1976; General Manager, Redditch Development Corporation, 1976–79; *b* 13 Jan. 1916; *s* of Frank Randolph Evans and Elizabeth Evans; *m* 1939, Sarah A. Duckworth; one *s* one *d*. *Educ:* Calday Grange Grammar Sch., West Kirby, Cheshire; Bury High Sch., Bury, Lancs. IPFA; FCA. Served RASC and RE, 1939–42. Local Govt Finance: Bury, 1932–38; Newton-le-Willows, Lancs, 1938–39 and 1942–44; Wolverhampton, 1944–53; Dep. Borough Treas., Northampton, 1953–58; Borough Treas., West Bromwich, 1958–64; Chief Finance Officer, Redditch Develt Corp., 1965–76. Mem. Council, IMTA/CIPFA, 1969–79, Vice-Pres., 1976–77, Pres., 1977–78. *Recreations:* gardening, music, watching sport.

EVANS, Prof. (William) Charles, PhD; FRS 1979; FRSC, FIBiol; Professor and Head, Department of Biochemistry and Soil Science, University College of North Wales, Bangor, 1951–79, now Emeritus; *b* 1 Oct. 1911; *s* of Robert and Elizabeth Evans; *m* 1942, Dr Irene Antice Woods; three *s* one *d*. *Educ:* Caernarfon Higher Grade and County Schs; University Coll. of N Wales, Bangor (John Hughes Entrance Scholar; 1st Cl. Hons Chemistry, 1932; MSc Org. Chem., 1934); Med. Sch., Univ. of Manchester (Platt Physiol Scholar; PhD Physiol., 1936). FRIC 1948; FIBiol 1955. Demonstr in Biochem., Sch. of Medicine, Univ. of Leeds, 1937, Dir of Blood Transfusion Labs, 1940; res. staff, Inoculation Dept (Wright-Fleming Inst.), St Mary's Hosp. Med. Sch., London, 1944; Special Lectr in Biochem. and Animal Health, University Coll., Aberystwyth, 1946. *Publications:* contrib. to Jl Chem. Soc., Biochem. Jl, Nature, MRC Reports, Brit. Jl Exp. Path., Brit. Vet. Jl, and Bot. Jl Linnean Soc. *Recreations:* cross country and middle distance running (when younger), farming and out-of-door pursuits, Rugby football. *Address:* Cae Ocyn, Llangaffo, Ynys Mon, Gwynedd LL60 6LY; Department of Biochemistry and Soil Science, University College of North Wales, Deiniol Road, Bangor. *T:* Bangor 351151, ext. 411.

EVANS, (William) Emrys, CBE 1981; Senior Regional Director, Wales, Midland Bank Ltd, 1976–84; *b* 4 April 1924; *s* of late Richard and Mary Elizabeth Evans; *m* 1946, Mair Thomas; one *d*. *Educ:* Llanfair Caereinion County Sch. FIB. Served War, RN, 1942–46 (despatches 1944). Entered Midland Bank Ltd, 1941; Asst Gen. Manager (Agric.), 1967–72; Reg. Dir, S Wales, 1972–74; Reg. Dir, Wales, 1974–76. Chairman: Welsh Cttee for Economic and Industrial Affairs, 1984–; Midland Bank Adv. Council for Wales, 1984–. Director: Develt Corp. for Wales, 1973–77; Welsh Industrial Develt Adv. Bd, 1975–; Develt Bd for Rural Wales, 1976–; Royal Welsh Agricl Soc., 1973–; Mem. Council, CBI, Wales, 1975– (Chm., 1979–81). Pres., Royal Nat. Eisteddfod of Wales, 1980–83. Vice President: Tenovus Cancer Res. Unit, 1980–; Kidney Res. Unit for Wales Foundn, 1980–; Trustee: Catherine and Lady Grace James Foundn, 1973–; John and Rhys Thomas James Foundn, 1973–; Welsh Sports Trust, 1980– (Vice Chm.); Llandovery Coll., 1982–; Member: Council for the Welsh Lang,, 1973–78; Design Council Wales Adv. Cttee, 1981–; Prince of Wales Cttee, 1982–. Treasurer: Congregational Church in Wales, 1975–; Mansfield Coll., Oxford, 1977–; Member Council, and Governor: UC Swansea, 1972– (Chm. Council, 1982–); UC Aberystwyth, 1979–; Governor, UC Cardiff, 1981–84; Mem., Ct and Council, Univ. of Wales, 1980. Hon. LLD Wales, 1983. FRSA 1982. High Sheriff, S Glamorgan, 1985–86.*Recreations:* golf, gardening, music. *Address:* Maesglas, Pen-y-turnpike, Dinas Powis, S Glam CF6 4HH. *T:* Cardiff 512985. *Club:* Cardiff and County (Cardiff).

EVANS, William Ewart; Judge of the High Court of Lesotho, 1967–73 (Acting Chief Justice, 1968); Judge of High Court of Northern Rhodesia and of the Rhodesia and Nyasaland Court of Appeal, 1953–62; *b* 24 May 1899; *s* of late John William Evans and Catherine Evans, Swansea, S Wales; *m* 1919, Agnes May Wilson (*d* 1981); one *s* four *d*. *Educ:* Swansea Grammar Sch. Served European War, 1917–19, in King's Royal Rifle Corps and Royal Army Service Corps. Called to Bar, 1934; practised on South Wales Circuit; Colonial Legal Service, 1938; acted in various judicial capacities; Resident Magistrate, Lusaka, Livingstone, N'Dola, Broken Hill, and Luanshya, 1940. *Recreation:* gardening. *Address:* 1 Van Riebeeck Street, Bedford, Cape Province, South Africa.

EVANS, Sir (William) Vincent (John), GCMG 1976 (KCMG 1970; CMG 1959); MBE 1945; QC 1973; Barrister-at-Law; a Judge of the European Court of Human Rights, since 1980; *b* 20 Oct. 1915; *s* of Charles Herbert Evans and Elizabeth (*née* Jenkins); *m* 1947, Joan Mary Symons; one *s* two *d*. *Educ:* Merchant Taylors' Sch., Northwood; Wadham Coll., Oxford (Hon. Fellow 1981). 1st Class Hons, Jurisprudence, 1937; BCL, 1938; MA, 1941; elected Cassel Scholar, Lincoln's Inn, 1937; called to Bar, Lincoln's Inn, 1939 (Hon. Bencher, 1983). Served in HM Forces, 1939–46. Legal Adviser (Lt-Col) to British Military Administration, Cyrenaica, 1945–46; Asst Legal Adviser, Foreign Office, 1947–54; Legal Counsellor, UK Permanent Mission to the United Nations, 1954–59; Legal Counsellor, FO, 1959–60; Dep. Legal Adviser, FO, 1960–68; Legal Adviser, FCO, 1968–75, retired. Chm., Bryant Symons & Co. Ltd, 1964–85. Chm., European Cttee on Legal Cooperation, Council of Europe, 1969–71; UK Rep. Council of Europe Steering Cttee on Human Rights, 1976–80 (Chm., 1979–80); Mem., Human Rights Cttee set up under Internat. Covenant on Civil and Political Rights, 1977–84 (Vice-Chm., 1979–80); Mem., Adv. Bd, Centre for Internat. Human Rights Law, Univ. of Essex; Member: Council of Management, British Inst. of Internat. and Comparative Law; Diplomatic Service Appeals Bd, 1976–; Exec. Cttee, David Davies Memorial Inst. of Internat. Studies, 1984–; Sch. Cttee, Merchant Taylor's Co., 1985–. Pres., Old Merchant Taylors' Soc., 1984–85. DUniv Essex, 1986. *Recreation:* gardening. *Address:* (home) 4 Bedford Road, Moor Park, Northwood, Mddx. *T:* Northwood 24085; (office) 2 Hare Court, Temple, EC4. *T:* 01–353 0076. *Club:* Athenæum.

EVANS, Wynford; *see* Evans, J. W.

EVANS-ANFOM, Emmanuel, FRCSE 1955; Commissioner for Education and Culture, Ghana, 1978; Member, Council of State, 1979; *b* 7 Oct. 1919; *m* 1952, Leonora Francetta Evans; three *s* one *d*. *Educ:* Achimota School; Edinburgh University (MB; ChB; DTM&H). House Surgeon, Dewsbury Infirmary, 1948–49; Medical Officer, Gold Coast Medical Service, 1950–56, Specialist Surgeon, 1956–67; Senior Lecturer, Ghana Medical School, 1966–67; Vice-Chancellor, Univ. of Science and Technology, Kumasi, 1967–74. Mem., WHO Expert Panel on Med. and Paramed. Educn, 1972–; Chm., Nat. Council for Higher Educn, 1974–78; Chm., Med. and Dental Council. Titular Mem., Internat. Assoc. Surgeons; Past President: Ghana Medical Assoc.; Assoc. of Surgeons of W Africa; FICS. Fellow, Ghana Acad. Arts and Sciences, 1971. Chm., Ghana Hockey Assoc. Hon. DSc Salford, 1974. *Publication:* Aetiology and Management of Intestinal Perforations, Ghana Med. Jl, 1963. *Recreations:* hockey, music, art. *Address:* PO Box M135, Accra, Ghana.

EVANS-BEVAN, Sir Martyn Evan, 2nd Bt *cr* 1958; *b* 1 April 1932; *s* of Sir David Martyn Evans-Bevan, 1st Bt, and of Eira Winifred, *d* of late Sidney Archibald Lloyd Glanley; *S* father, 1973; *m* 1957, Jennifer Jane Marion, *d* of Robert Hugh Stevens; four *s*. *Educ:* Uppingham. Entered family business of Evan Evans Bevan and Evans Bevan Ltd, 1953; High Sheriff of Breconshire, 1967; Liveryman, Worshipful Co. of Farmers; Freeman, City of London. *Recreations:* shooting and fishing. *Heir:* *s* David Gawain Evans-Bevan, *b* 16 Sept. 1961. *Address:* Felinnewydd, Llandefalle, Brecon, Powys. *Club:* Carlton.

EVANS-FREKE, family name of **Baron Carbery.**

EVANS-LOMBE, Edward Christopher, QC 1978; a Recorder of the Crown Court, since 1982; *b* 10 April 1937; *s* of Vice-Adm. Sir Edward Evans-Lombe, KCB, and Lady Evans-Lombe; *m* 1964, Frances Marilyn MacKenzie; one *s* three *d*. *Educ:* Eton; Trinity Coll., Cambridge (MA). National Service, 1955–57: 2nd Lieut Royal Norfolk Regt. Called to the Bar, Inner Temple, 1963, Bencher, 1985. Standing Counsel to Dept of Trade in Bankruptcy matters, 1971. Chm., Agricultural Land Tribunal, S Eastern Region, 1983–. *Recreations:* fishing, falconry, forestry. *Address:* Marlingford Hall, Norwich *T:* Norwich 880319. *Club:* Norfolk (Norwich).

EVE, family name of **Baron Silsoe.**

EVELEIGH, Rt. Hon. Sir Edward Walter, PC 1977; Kt 1968; ERD; MA; a Lord Justice of Appeal, 1977–85; *b* 8 Oct. 1917; *s* of Walter William and Daisy Emily Eveleigh; *m* 1940, Vilma Bodnar; *m* 1953, Patricia Helen Margaret Bury; two *s* (and one *s* decd). *Educ:* Peter Symonds; Brasenose Coll., Oxford (Hon. Fellow 1977). Commissioned in the Royal Artillery (Supplementary Reserve), 1936; served War of 1939–45 (despatches, 1940). Called to Bar, Lincoln's Inn, 1945, Bencher 1968; QC 1961. Recorder of Burton-on-Trent, 1961–64, of Gloucester, 1964–68; Chm., QS, County of Oxford, 1968–71 (Dep. Chm., 1963–68); a Judge of the High Court of Justice, Queen's Bench Div., 1968–77; Presiding Judge, SE Circuit, 1971–76. Mem., General Council of the Bar, 1965–67. Mem., Royal Commn on Criminal Procedure, 1978–80; Chm., Statute Law Soc., 1985–. President: British-German Jurists' Assoc., 1974–85; Bar Musical Soc., 1980–. Hon. Citizen: Texas, 1980; Austin, 1985; Dallas, 1985. *Address:* Royal Courts of Justice, Strand, WC2. *Club:* Garrick.

EVELEIGH, Air Vice-Marshal Geoffrey Charles, CB 1964; OBE 1945; RAF retired; *b* 25 Oct. 1912; *s* of Ernest Charles Eveleigh, Henley-on-Thames; *m* 1939, Anthea Josephine, *d* of F. H. Fraser, Ceylon; one *s* one *d*. *Educ:* Brighton Coll.; RAF Coll., Cranwell. Joined RAF, 1932; served War of 1939–45 in Bomber Command and No 2 Group; Dep. Chief of Air Staff, Royal New Zealand Air Force, 1955–57; Air Commodore, 1957; Dir-Gen. of Signals, Air Ministry, 1959–61; Air Vice-Marshal, 1961; Air Officer, Administration, Fighter Command, 1961–64; retd 1965. *Address:* Cán Tirana, PO Box 20, Puerto de Pollensa, Mallorca, Spain. *Club:* Royal Air Force.

EVELEIGH-DE-MOLEYNS, family name of **Baron Ventry.**

EVELING, Walter Raphael Taylor, CBE 1960; Chartered Surveyor, retired, 1968; Deputy Chief Valuer, Inland Revenue, 1965–68 (Assistant Chief Valuer, 1951); *b* 8 March 1908; *s* of late Raphael Eveling, Hampstead Garden Suburb; *m* 1935, Annie Ferguson Newman, Belfast; one *s*. *Educ:* Paradise House Sch., Stoke Newington. Joined the Valuation Office, Inland Revenue, 1935. FRICS. *Address:* 12 Cooil Ny Marrey, Waterloo Road, Ramsey, Isle of Man.

EVELYN, (John) Michael, CB 1976; Assistant Director of Public Prosecutions, 1969–76, retired (Under-Secretary, 1972); *b* 2 June 1916; *s* of Edward Ernest Evelyn and Kate Rosa Underwood. *Educ:* Charterhouse; Christ Church, Oxford (MA). Called to Bar, 1939. Army service, 1939–46. Dept of Dir of Public Prosecutions, 1946–76. *Publications:* (under pseudonym Michael Underwood): Murder on Trial, 1954; Murder Made Absolute, 1955; Death on Remand, 1956; False Witness, 1957; Lawful Pursuit, 1958; Arm of the Law, 1959; Cause of Death, 1960; Death by Misadventure, 1960; Adam's Case, 1961; The Case against Phillip Quest, 1962; Girl Found Dead, 1963; The Crime of Colin Wise, 1964; The Unprofessional Spy, 1965; The Anxious Conspirator, 1965; A Crime Apart, 1966; The Man who Died on Friday, 1967; The Man who Killed Too Soon, 1968; The Shadow Game, 1969; The Silent Liars, 1970; Shem's Demise, 1970; A Trout in the Milk, 1971; Reward for a Defector, 1973; A Pinch of Snuff, 1974; The Juror, 1975; Menaces, Menaces, 1976; Murder with Malice, 1977; The Fatal Trip, 1977; Crooked Wood, 1978; Anything but the Truth, 1978; Smooth Justice, 1979; Victim of Circumstance, 1979; A Clear Case of Suicide, 1980; Crime upon Crime, 1980; Double Jeopardy, 1981; Hand of Fate, 1981; Goddess of Death, 1982; A Party to Murder, 1983; Death in Camera, 1984; The Hidden Man, 1985; Death at Deepwood Grange, 1986; The Uninvited Corpse, 1987. *Recreations:* writing, reading, opera, cinema, travel. *Address:* 100 Ashdown, Eaton Road, Hove, Sussex BN3 3AR. *Clubs:* Garrick, Detection.

EVENNETT, David Anthony; MP (C) Erith and Crayford, since 1983; *b* 3 June 1949; *s* of Norman Thomas Evennett and Irene Evennett; *m* 1975, Marilyn Anne Smith; two *s*. *Educ:* Buckhurst Hill County High School for Boys; London School of Economics and Political Science. BSc (Econ) Upper Second Hons, MSc (Econ). School Master, Ilford County High School for Boys, 1972–74; Marine Insurance Broker, Lloyd's, 1974–81; Mem., LLoyds, 1976–; Lloyds Underwriter, 1981–. Redbridge Borough Councillor, 1974–78. Contested (C) Hackney South and Shoreditch, 1979. Mem., Select Cttee on Educn, Science and the Arts, 1986–. Sec., H of C Motor Club, 1985–. *Recreations:* reading, history, theatre and cinema. *Address:* House of Commons, SW1A 0AA. *Clubs:* Carlton; Priory Conservative (Belvedere).

EVERARD, Maj.-Gen. Sir Christopher E. W.; *see* Welby-Everard.

EVERARD, Sir Robin (Charles), 4th Bt *cr* 1911; Management Consultant, since 1976; *b* 5 Oct. 1939; *s* of Sir Nugent Henry Everard, 3rd Bt and Frances Audrey (*d* 1975), *d* of J. C. Jesson; *S* father, 1984; *m* 1963, Ariel Ingrid, *d* of late Col Peter Cleasby-Thompson, MBE, MC; one *s* two *d*. *Educ:* Sandroyd School; Harrow; RMA Sandhurst. Short service commn, Duke of Wellington's Regt, 1958–61. Money Broker; Managing Director, P. Murray-Jones, 1962–76; Consultant, 1976–86. *Heir:* *s* Henry Peter Charles Everard, *b* 6 Aug. 1970. *Address:* Church Farm, Shelton, Long Stratton, Norwich NR15 2SB.

EVERARD, Timothy John, CMG 1978; HM Diplomatic Service; Ambassador to German Democratic Republic, since 1984; *b* 22 Oct. 1929; *s* of late Charles M. Everard and late Monica M. Everard (*née* Barford); *m* 1955, Josiane Romano; two *s* two *d*. *Educ:* Uppingham Sch.; Magdalen Coll., Oxford. BA (Mod. Langs). Banking: Barclays Bank DCO, 1952–62, in Egypt, Sudan, Kenya, Congo (Manager for Congo). Entered Foreign (later Diplomatic) Service: First Sec., FO, 1962–63; First Sec., Commercial, Bangkok, 1964–66; resigned to take up directorship in Ellis & Everard Ltd, 1966–67. Rejoined Foreign and Commonwealth Office, Oct. 1967: First Sec., FO, 1967–68; Bahrain, 1969–72 (First Sec. and Head of Chancery, HM Political Residency); seconded to Northern Ireland Office, FCO, April-Aug. 1972; Consul-Gen., then Chargé d'Affaires, Hanoi, 1972–73; Economic and Commercial Counsellor, Athens, 1974–78; Commercial Counsellor, Paris, 1978–81; Minister, Lagos, 1981–84. *Recreations:* golf, tennis, sailing. *Address:* c/o Foreign and Commonwealth Office, SW1; Leagues, Stonecross, Crowborough, East Sussex. *T:* Crowborough 3278. *Club:* Reform.

EVERED, David Charles; Director of the Ciba Foundation, since 1978; *b* 21 Jan. 1940; *s* of late Thomas Charles Evered and Enid Christian Evered; *m* 1964, Anne Elizabeth Massey Lings, (Kit), *d* of John Massey Lings, Manchester; one *s* two *d*. *Educ:* Cranleigh Sch., Surrey; Middlesex Hosp. Med. Sch. (BSc 1961, MB 1964, MRCP 1967, MD 1971). Junior hospital appointments, London and Leeds, 1964–70; First Asst in Medicine, Wellcome Sen. Res. Fellow and Consultant Physician, Univ. of Newcastle upon Tyne and Royal Victoria Infirmary, 1970–78. Member: British Library Medical Information Review Panel, 1978–80; Council, St George's Hosp. Med. Sch. 1983–; Cttee, Assoc. of Med. Res. Charities, 1981–84; Vice-Pres., Science Cttee, Louis Jeantet Fondation de Médecine, 1984–; Public Understanding of Science Cttee, Royal Soc., 1986–; Media Resource Service Adv. Cttee, NY, 1986–. FRCP 1978; FIBiol 1978; FRSM; Scientific Fellow, Zool Soc. of London (Mem. Council, 1985–). Member: Soc. for Endocrinology; Eur. Thyroid Assoc. (Mem. Exec. Cttee, 1977–81, Sec.-Treas., 1983–); Amer. Thyroid Assoc.; Med. Res. Soc.; Hague Club (Sec., 1981–83). *Publications:* Diseases of the Thyroid, 1976; (with R. Hall and R. Greene) Atlas of Clinical Endocrinology, 1979; (with M. O'Connor) Collaboration in Medical Research in Europe, 1981; numerous papers on medicine, education and science policy. *Recreations:* reading, history, tennis, sailing. *Address:* 41 Portland Place, W1N 4BN. *T:* 01–636 9456; Keswick, 17 Cumberland Road, Kew, Surrey TW9 3HJ. *T:* 01–940 1579. *Club:* Roehampton.

EVEREST, David Anthony, PhD; FRSC; Chief Scientist, Environmental Protection Group, since 1979, and Director of Science Research Policy, since 1983, Department of the Environment; *b* 18 Sept. 1926; *s* of George Charles and Ada Bertha Everest; *m* 1956, Audrey Pauline (*née* Sheldrick); three *s*. *Educ:* John Lyon Sch., Harrow; University Coll. London (Bsc, PhD). Lecturer in Chemistry, Battersea Polytechnic, 1949–56; Sen. Scientific Officer, 1956–58, PSO, 1958–64, National Chemical Laboratory; SPSO, 1964–70, Dep. Chief Scientific Officer, 1970–77, National Physical Laboratory; DCSO, RTP Div., Dept of Industry, 1977–79. *Publications:* Chemistry of Beryllium, 1962; section on Beryllium in Comprehensive Inorganic Chemistry, 1972; papers in Inorganic Chemistry, Extractive Metallurgy and Material Science. *Recreations:* astronomy, reading, walking. *Address:* Talland, Chorleywood Road, Chorleywood, Herts WD3 4ER. *T:* Rickmansworth 773253.

EVERETT, Christopher Harris Doyle, JP; MA; Headmaster, Tonbridge School, since 1975; *b* 20 June 1933; *s* of Alan Doyle Everett, MS, FRCS, and Annabel Dorothy Joan Everett (*née* Harris); *m* 1955, Hilary (Billy) Anne (*née* Robertson); two *s* two *d*. *Educ:* Winchester College; New College, Oxford. MA (Class. Mods and Lit. Hum.). Grenadier Guards, Nat. Service, 1951–53. HM Diplomatic Service, 1957–70: posts included Beirut, Washington and Foreign Office; Headmaster, Worksop Coll., 1970–75. Vice-Chm., HMC, 1987– (Chm., 1986). JP, Tonbridge and W Malling, 1976. *Recreations:* reading, walking, tennis. *Address:* School House, Tonbridge, Kent.

EVERETT, Douglas Hugh, MBE 1946; FRS 1980; Leverhulme Professor of Physical Chemistry, University of Bristol, 1954–82, now Emeritus; Dean of Faculty of Science, 1966–68; Pro-Vice-Chancellor, 1973–76; *b* 26 Dec. 1916; *e s* of late Charles Everett and Jessie Caroline; *m* 1942, Frances Elizabeth Jessop; two *d*. *Educ:* Grammar Sch., Hampton-on-Thames; University of Reading; Balliol Coll., Oxford. Wantage Scholar, Reading Univ., 1935–38; Kitchener Scholar, 1936–39; BSc, 1938; Ramsay Fellow, 1939–41; DPhil 1942. Special Scientific Duties, WO, 1942–45. ICI Fellow, Oxford Univ., 1945–47; Chemistry Lecturer, Dundee Univ. Coll., 1947; MA 1947; Fellow, Lecturer and Tutor, Exeter Coll., Oxford, 1947–48; Prof. of Chemistry, Dundee Univ. Coll., University of St Andrews, 1948–54. Chm., Internat. Union of Pure and Applied Chemistry Commn on Colloid and Surface Chemistry, 1969–73. FRSE 1950; DSc 1956. Mem., Building Research Board, DSIR, 1954–61; a Vice-Pres., Faraday Soc., 1958–61, 1963–65, 1968–70, Pres., 1976–78; Mem. Chemical Soc. Council, 1961–64, 1972–74 (Tilden Lectr, 1955; Award in Colloid and Surface Chemistry, 1971); Pres., Section B, BAAS, 1979–80; a Vice-Pres. and Gen. Sec., BAAS, 1983–; Pres.-elect, Internat. Assoc. of Colloid and Interface Scientists, 1986. *Publications:* Introduction to Chemical Thermodynamics, 1959, 2nd edn, 1971; papers on Physical Chemistry in scientific jls. *Recreations:* walking, painting. *Address:* School of Chemistry, The University, Bristol BS8 1TS.

EVERETT, Eileen, (Mrs Raymond Everett); *see* Diss, E.

EVERETT, Oliver William, LVO 1980; Librarian, Windsor Castle and Assistant Keeper of The Queen's Archives, since 1985; *b* 28 Feb. 1943; *s* of Charles Everett, DSO, MC and Judy Rothwell; *m* 1965, Theffania Vesey Stoney; two *s* two *d*. *Educ:* Felsted Sch.; Christ's Coll., Cambridge; Fletcher Sch. of Law and Diplomacy, Mass, USA. HM Diplomatic Service, 1967–81: First Sec., New Delhi, 1969–73; Head of Chancery, Madrid, 1980–81; Asst Private Sec. to HRH The Prince of Wales, 1978–80; Private Sec. to HRH The Princess of Wales, 1981–83, and Comptroller to The Prince and Princess of Wales, 1981–83; Dep. Librarian, Windsor Castle, 1984. *Recreations:* skiing, real tennis, rackets. *Address:* Garden House, Windsor Castle, Berks. *T:* Windsor 868286; The East Wing, Kirtlington Park, Oxon. *T:* Bletchington 50589. *Club:* Ski Club of Great Britain.

EVERETT, Thomas Henry Kemp; Special Commissioner of Income Tax, since 1983; *b* 28 Jan. 1932; *s* of late Thomas Kemp Everett and Katharine Ida Everett (*née* Woodward); *m* 1954, June (*née* Partridge); three *s*. *Educ:* Queen Elizabeth's Hospital, Bristol; Univ. of Bristol. LLB Hons 1957. Solicitor (Hons), admitted 1960; Partner, Meade-King & Co., 1963–83. Clerk to General Commissioners, Bedminster Div., 1965–83. Chairman: Service 9, 1972–75; Bristol Council of Voluntary Service, 1975–80; St Christopher's Young Persons' Residential Trust, 1976–83; Vice-Chm., Governors of Queen Elizabeth's Hosp., 1980–; Mem., Governing Council, St Christopher's School, Bristol, 1983; Hon. Treasurer, Rowberrow PCC; Mem., Axbridge Deanery Synod. *Recreations:* music, reading, walking, squash. *Address:* Dolebury Cottage, Dolberrow, Churchill, near Bristol BS19 5NS. *T:* Churchill 852329.

EVERITT, Anthony Michael; Deputy Secretary-General, Arts Council of Great Britain, since 1985; *b* 31 Jan. 1940; *s* of late Michael Anthony Hamill Everitt and Simone Dolores Cathérine (*née* de Vergriette; she *m* 2nd, John Brunel Cohen). *Educ:* Cheltenham Coll.; Corpus Christi Coll., Cambridge (BA Hons English, 1962). Lectured variously at National Univ. of Iran, Teheran, SE London Coll. of Further Educn, Birmingham Coll. of Art, and Trent Polytechnic, 1963–72; The Birmingham Post: Art Critic, 1970–75; Drama Critic, 1974–79; Features Editor, 1976–79; Director: Midland Gp Arts Centre, Nottingham, 1979–80; E Midlands Arts Assoc., 1980–85. Chairman: Ikon Gall., Birmingham, 1976–79; Birmingham Arts Lab., 1977–79; Vice-Chm., Council of Regional Arts Assocs, 1984–85; Mem., Drama Panel, 1974–78, and Regional Cttee, 1979–80, Arts Council of GB. *Publications:* Abstract Expressionism, 1974; contribs to Financial Times, Studio Internat., etc. *Address:* 74 Cambray Road, SW12 0EP.

EVERS, Claude Ronald; MA; Headmaster of Sutton Valence School, 1953–67; *b* 17 Jan. 1908; *s* of late C. P. Evers (formerly housemaster at Rugby Sch.); *m* 1935, Marjorie Janet Ironside Bruce; four *s*. *Educ:* Rugby; Trinity Coll., Oxford. Asst Master, Wellington Coll., 1931–35; Asst Master, Rugby Sch., 1936–40; Headmaster of Berkhamsted Sch., 1946–53. Warden of Pendley Residential Centre of Adult Education, 1967–73. War service (Royal Warwicks Regt), 1940–45. Old Stager. *Publication:* Rugby (Blackie's Public School Series), 1939. *Address:* 20 Richmond Court, Osmond Road, Hove BN3 1TD. *T:* Brighton 723721.

EVERSLEY, David Edward Charles, PhD; social researcher; *b* 22 Nov. 1921; *s* of Dr Otto Eberstadt and Dela Morel; *m* 1st, 1945, Edith Wembridge (*d* 1978); one *s* three *d*;

2nd, 1986, Barbara Rojo. *Educ:* Goethe-Gymnasium, Frankfurt/Main; Leighton Park Sch., Reading; London Sch. of Economics. BSc (Econ) (London), PhD (Birmingham). Asst Lectr, Lectr, then Reader, in Economic (and then Social) Hist., Univ. of Birmingham, 1949–66. Dir, W Midlands Social and Polit. Res. Unit, 1962–65; Reader in Population and Regional Studies, Univ. of Sussex, 1966; Dir, Social Research Unit, Univ. of Sussex, 1967–69; Prof., 1969. Hon. Sec., Midlands New Towns Soc., 1958–62; Chief Planner (Strategy), Greater London Council, 1969–72; Centre for Environmental Studies, 1972–76; Sen. Res. Fellow, PSI, 1976–81; Vivien Stewart Bursar, Dept of Land Economy, Univ. of Cambridge, 1981–82. Visiting Professor of Demography, Univ. of California at Berkeley, 1965; Bartlett Sch. of Architecture and Planning, University Coll. London, 1976–79; Dept of Town and Country Planning, QUB, 1984–85; Vis. Schol., Population Reference Bureau, Washington, 1986. Mem., W Midlands Economic Planning Coun., 1965–66; Corr. Mem., German Acad. for Urban and Regional Planning, 1972–; Pres., Commn sur la Démographie Historique, Internat. Congress of Hist. Sciences, 1965–70. Chm., Regional Studies Assoc., 1972–75, Vice-Chm., 1975–. Chm., Social Responsibility Council, Society of Friends (Quakers), 1972–75; Pres., British Soc. for Population Studies, 1981–83. Hon. MRTPI 1978, Mem. Council, 1979–. *Publications:* Rents and Social Policy, 1955; Social Theories of Fertility and the Malthusian Debate, 1959, new US edn 1975; (with D. Keate) The Overspill Problem in the West Midlands, 1958; (ed and contrib. with D. V. Glass) Population in History, 1965; (with Lomas and Jackson) Population Growth and Planning Policy, 1965; (with F. Sukdeo) The Dependants of the Coloured Commonwealth Population of England and Wales, 1969; (ed and contrib. with D. Donnison) London: urban patterns, problems and policies, 1973; The Planner in Society, 1973; A Question of Numbers?, 1973; (ed and contrib. with J. Platts) Public Resources and Private Lives, 1976; (ed and contrib. with Alan Evans) The Inner City, Industry and Employment, 1980; (ed and contrib. with W. Koellmann) Population Change and Social Planning, 1982; Religion and Employment in Northern Ireland, 1987; numerous chapters in collected vols; contribs to Victoria History of the Counties of England; articles in jls of history, demography and planning. *Recreations:* walking, talking, working. *Address:* Hummerstons, Cottered, Buntingford, Herts SG9 9QP. *T:* Cottered 354.

EVERSON, Sir Frederick (Charles), KCMG 1968 (CMG 1956); *b* 6 Sept. 1910; *s* of Frederick Percival Everson, *m* 1937, Linda Mary Clark (*d* 1984); two *s* one *d* (and one *s* decd). *Educ:* Tottenham County Sch., Middlesex. BSc (Econ.) London. Entered Civil Service, July 1928; Consular Service, Dec. 1934. Chief Administrative Officer, British Embassy, Bonn, Germany, 1953–56; Ambassador to El Salvador, 1956–60; Commercial Counsellor, British Embassy, Stockholm, 1960–63; Minister (Economic), British Embassy, Paris, 1963–68. *Address:* 8 Gainsborough Court, College Road, Dulwich, SE21 7LT. *T:* 01–693 8125.

EVERSON, John Andrew; HM Chief Inspector of Schools, Secondary Education, Department of Education and Science, since 1981; *b* 26 Oct. 1933; *s* of Harold Leslie Everson and Florence Jane Stone; *m* 1961, Gilda Ramsden; two *s*. *Educ:* Tiffin Boys' Sch., Kingston-upon-Thames; Christ's Coll., Cambridge (MA); King's Coll., London (PGCE). Teacher: Haberdashers' Aske's Sch., Elstree, 1958–65; City of London Sch., 1965–68; Schools Inspectorate, DES, 1968–. *Publications:* (with B. P. FitzGerald) Settlement Patterns, 1968; (with B. P. FitzGerald) Inside the City, 1972. *Recreations:* opera, walking, theatre, chess. *Address:* Department of Education and Science, Elizabeth House, York Road, SE1 7PH. *T:* 01–934 9803.

EVERY, Sir John (Simon), 12th Bt, *cr* 1641; *b* 24 April 1914; *er s* of Sir Edward Oswald Every, 11th Bt and Lady (Ivy Linton) Every (*d* 1976); *S* father, 1959; *m* 1st, 1938, Annette Constance (marr. diss., 1942), *o c* of late Major F. W. M. Drew, Drewscourt, Co. Cork; 2nd, 1943, Janet Marion, *d* of John Page, Blakeney, Norfolk; one *s* two *d*. *Educ:* Harrow. Served War of 1939–45. Capt., Sherwood Foresters. Business Co. Dir, 1945–60, Dir of private companies. *Recreations:* cricket, tennis, shooting. *Heir:* *s* Henry John Michael Every [*b* 6 April 1947; *m* 1974, Susan Mary, *er d* of Kenneth Beaton, Hartford, Hunts; three *s*]. *Address:* Egginton, near Derby. *T:* Etwall 2245. *Club:* MCC.

EVETTS, Lt-Gen. Sir John (Fullerton), Kt 1951; CB 1939; CBE 1937; MC; *b* 30 June 1891; *s* of late Lieut-Col J. M. Evetts, Tackley Park, Oxon; *m* 1916, Helen Phyllis (*d* 1980), *d* of late Captain C. A. G. Becher, Burghfields, Bourton on the Water, Glos; one *s*. *Educ:* Temple Grove; Lancing; Royal Military Coll., Sandhurst; Staff Coll., Camberley. Entered Army, 1911; joined The Cameronians (Scottish Rifles); served European War, 1914–18 (MC, despatches); Lieut 1913; Captain 1915; temp. Major Machine Gun Corps, 1916; Bt-Major 1929; Substantive, 1929; Bt Lt-Col 1931; Substantive Lt-Col Royal Ulster Rifles, 1934; Col 1935; Maj.-Gen. 1941; employed with Iraq Army, 1925–28; DAAG War Office, 1932; Commander British Troops in Palestine, 1935; GSO1 Palestine, 1936; Brig. Comd. 16th Inf. Bde, Palestine and Trans-Jordan, 1936–39 (despatches); BGS, HQ, Northern Command, India, 1939–40; Comdr Western (Indept) Dist, India, 1940–41; Divl Comdr, 1941 (despatches); Asst CIGS, 1942; Senior Military Adviser to Minister of Supply, 1944–46; retired pay, 1946; Head of British Ministry of Supply Staff in Australia, 1946–51, and Chief Executive Officer Joint UK-Australian Long Range Weapons, Board of Administration, 1946–49. Managing Dir, 1951–58, Chm., 1958–60, Rotol Ltd and Brit. Messier. OStJ. Legion of Merit (US), 1943. *Address:* Pepper Cottage, Kemerton, near Tewkesbury, Glos. *Club:* Army and Navy.

EWANS, Martin Kenneth, CMG 1980; HM Diplomatic Service; High Commissioner to Nigeria, since 1986; *b* 14 Nov. 1928; *s* of late John Ewans; *m* 1953, Mary Tooke; one *s* one *d*. *Educ:* St Paul's; Corpus Christi Coll., Cambridge (major scholar, MA). Royal Artillery, 1947–49, 2nd Lt. Joined Commonwealth Relations Office, 1952; Second Sec., Karachi, 1954–55; First Sec.: Ottawa, 1958–61; Lagos, 1962–64; Kabul, 1967–69. Counsellor, Dar-es-Salaam, 1969–73; Head of East African Dept, FCO, 1973–77; Minister, New Delhi, 1978–82; Diplomatic Service Chm., Civil Service Selection Bd, 1982; Sen. Civilian Instructor, RCDS, 1982–83; High Commissioner in Harare, Zimbabwe, 1983–85. *Recreation:* bird watching. *Address:* c/o Foreign and Commonwealth Office, SW1. *Club:* Royal Commonwealth Society.

EWART, Gavin Buchanan, FRSL; freelance writer (poet), since 1971; *b* 4 Feb. 1916; *s* of George Arthur Ewart and Dorothy Hannah (*née* Turner); *m* 1956, Margaret Adelaide Bennett; one *s* one *d*. *Educ:* Wellington Coll.; Christ's Coll., Cambridge (BA Hons 1937, MA 1942). FRSL 1981. Salesman, Contemporary Lithographs, 1938; served War, Royal Artillery, 1940–46; Production Manager, Editions Poetry, London, 1946; British Council, 1946–52; Advertising copywriter in London advertising agencies, 1952–71. Cholmondeley Award for Poetry, 1971. *Publications:* Poems and Songs, 1939; Londoners, 1964; Pleasures of the Flesh, 1966; The Deceptive Grin of the Gravel Porters, 1968; The Gavin Ewart Show, 1971; Be My Guest!, 1975; No Fool Like An Old Fool, 1976; Or Where a Young Penguin Lies Screaming, 1978; All My Little Ones, 1978; The Collected Ewart 1933–1980, 1980, 2nd edn 1982; The New Ewart, 1982; More Little Ones, 1983; Other People's Clerihews, 1983; The Ewart Quarto, 1984; The Young Pobble's Guide to His Toes, 1985. *Recreations:* reading, listening to music. *Address:* 57 Kenilworth Court, Lower Richmond Road, SW15 1EN. *T:* 01–788 7071.

EWART, Sir (William) Ivan (Cecil), 6th Bt, *cr* 1887; DSC 1945; JP; Administrator, Ngora Freda Carr Hospital, Uganda (Association of Surgeons of East Africa), since 1985; *b* 18 July 1919; *s* of late Major William Basil Ewart (*y s* of late Frederick William Ewart, 7th *s* of 1st Bt); *S* kinsman (Sir Talbot Ewart, 5th Bt), 1959; *m* 1948, Pauline Chevallier (*d* 1964), *e d* of late Wing Comdr Raphael Chevallier Preston, OBE, AFC, JP, Abbey Flat, Bellapais, Kyrenia, Cyprus; one *s* two *d*. *Educ:* Radley. Joined Ulster Div., RNVR, 1938. Served War of 1939–45; Lieut, RNVR; service in Coastal Forces (Motor Torpedo-Boats), 1939–42 (DSC); POW, Germany, 1942–45. Chairman: William Ewart & Son Ltd, Linen Manufacturers, 1968–73 (Dir, 1954–73); William Ewart Investments Ltd, Belfast, 1973–77; Ewart New Northern Ltd, Belfast, 1973–77; E Africa Resident Rep., Royal Commonwealth Soc. for the Blind, 1977–84. Pres., NI Chamber of Commerce and Industry, 1974. A Northern Ireland Delegate to the Duke of Edinburgh's Study Conf. on the Human Problems of Industrial Communities within the Commonwealth and Empire, Oxford, 1956; Pres., Church of Ireland's Young Men's Soc., 1951–61 and 1975–77; Chm. Flax Spinners Assoc., 1961–66; Pres., Oldpark Unionist Assoc., 1950–68. Belfast Harbour Comr, 1968–77. High Sheriff for County Antrim, 1976. *Recreations:* travel, gliding. *Heir:* *s* William Michael Ewart, *b* 10 June 1953. *Address:* PO Box 40870, Nairobi, Kenya. *T:* 501634; Hill House, Hillsborough, Co. Down, N Ireland BT26 6AE. *T:* Hillsborough 683000. *Clubs:* Naval; Ulster Reform (Belfast); Nairobi.

EWART-BIGGS, family name of **Baroness Ewart-Biggs.**

EWART-BIGGS, Baroness *cr* 1981 (Life Peer), of Ellis Green in the County of Essex; **(Felicity) Jane Ewart-Biggs;** *d* of Major Basil Randall; *m* 1960, Christopher Ewart-Biggs, CMG, OBE (HM Diplomatic Service) (*d* 1976); one *s* two *d*. *Educ:* Downe House School, Cold Ash, Newbury, Berks. Lived in Algiers, Brussels, Paris and Dublin, 1960–76, during husband's service overseas. In 1976, established Christopher Ewart-Biggs Memorial Literary Prize, designed to promote better understanding between people of Britain and Ireland and closer co-operation between partners of the European Community. Labour Party spokesman on Home Affairs, 1983. Hon. DLitt, New Univ. of Ulster, 1978. *Publication:* Pay, Pack and Follow, 1984. *Recreations:* travel, discussion and international affairs. *Address:* 31 Radnor Walk, SW3 4BP.

EWART EVANS, George; *see* Evans, G. E.

EWART JAMES, His Honour William Henry; a Circuit Judge, 1974–83; *b* 15 Dec. 1910; *e s* of Rev. David Ewart James; *m* 1941, Esmé Vivienne, *y d* of Edward Lloyd, Liverpool and Gresford; two *s* one *d*. *Educ:* Bishop's Stortford Coll.; Worcester Coll., Oxford. MA (Mod. Hist.). Private Sec. to J. H. Morgan, KC, Counsel to the Indian Princes, 1936; Asst. Sec. European Gp, Bengal Legislature, 1937–38; travelled Far East and America, 1936–39. Served War: in Grenadier Guards, Royal Welch Fusiliers and 1st Airborne Div., Sept. 1939–Dec. 1945. Called to the Bar, 1948; Counsel to the Post Office, Western Circuit, 1957–70; Dep. Chm., Devon QS, 1968–71; a Recorder of the Crown Court, 1972–74. Mem., Hants CC, 1952–74; Alderman, 1965; Chm., Local Govt Cttee, 1963–74. *Recreations:* travel, butterflies. *Address:* Springfield, Greywell, Basingstoke, Hants. *T:* Odiham 2644.

EWBANK, Hon. Sir Anthony (Bruce), Kt 1980; **Hon. Mr Justice Ewbank;** Judge of the High Court of Justice, Family Division, since 1980; *b* 30 July 1925; *s* of late Rev. Harold Ewbank and Gwendolen Ewbank (*née* Bruce); *m* 1958, Moya McGinn; four *s* one *d*. *Educ:* St John's Sch., Leatherhead; Trinity Coll., Cambridge, Natural Sciences Tripos (MA). RNVR, 1945–47 and 1951–56. Called to Bar, Gray's Inn, 1954; Bencher, 1980. Junior Counsel to Treasury in Probate matters, 1969; QC 1972; a Recorder of the Crown Court, 1975–80. Chm., Family Law Bar Assoc., 1978–80. *Recreations:* walking, sailing, swimming. *Address:* Royal Courts of Justice, Strand, WC2.

EWBANK, Prof. Inga-Stina; Professor of English Literature, University of Leeds, since 1985; *b* 13 June 1932; *d* of Gustav and Ingeborg Ekeblad; *m* 1959, Roger Ewbank; one *s* two *d*. *Educ:* Högre Allänna Läroverket för Flickor, Gothenburg; Univs of Carleton (BA), Gothenburg (Fil.kand.), Sheffield (MA) and Liverpool (PhD). William Noble Fellow, Univ. of Liverpool, 1955–57; Res. Fellow at Shakespeare Inst., Univ. of Birmingham, 1957–60; Univ. of Liverpool: Asst Lectr, 1960–63; Lectr, 1963–70; Sen. Lectr, 1970–72; Reader in English Literature, Bedford Coll., Univ. of London, 1972–74, Hildred Carlile Prof., 1974–84. Vis. Lectr, Univ. of Munich, 1959–60; Vis. Assoc. Prof., Northwestern Univ., 1966, Vis. Prof., Harvard Univ., 1974. *Publications:* Their Proper Sphere: A Study of the Brontë Sisters as Early-Victorian Female Novelists, 1966; Shakespeare, Ibsen and the Unspeakable (Inaugural Lecture), 1975; chapter in, A New Companion to Shakespeare Studies, 1971; (with Peter Hall) Ibsen's John Gabriel Borkman: An English Version, 1975; (ed with Philip Edwards and G. K. Hunter) Shakespeare's Styles, 1980; chapters in other books; contrib. Shakespeare Survey, Ibsen Yearbook, Rev. Eng. Studies, Mod. Lang. Rev., English Studies, etc. *Recreations:* same as work: reading, theatre; children. *Address:* 19 Woodfield Road, Ealing, W5. *T:* 01–997 2895.

EWBANK, Michael Henry, CBE 1980; Director, Ewbank Preece Ltd, since 1983; *b* 5 May 1930; *s* of Charles Henry Preston Ewbank and Doris Minnie Ewbank; *m* 1959, Julia Ann Bartley (*d* 1986); three *s* one *d*. *Educ:* Stowe School; City and Guilds Coll., London Univ. BSc, ACGI, CEng, FIChemE. Royal Navy, 1951–53; S/Lt RNR. Technical Engineer, Ewbank and Partners Ltd, 1953–57; Dir, 1957; Dep. Chm. 1965; Chm., 1969. Chairman: British Consultants' Bureau, 1974–76; ME Assoc., 1981–82; Pres., European Cttee of Consulting Firms (CEBI), 1976–78. Director: Associated Nuclear Services, 1984–; Ewbank Preece Gp Ltd, 1986–; Offshore Certification Bureau, 1986–. *Recreations:* riding, skiing. *Address:* Oakwood, Clayhill Road, Leigh, Reigate, Surrey. *T:* Dawes Green 354.

EWBANK, Ven. Walter Frederick; Archdeacon Emeritus and Canon Emeritus of Carlisle Cathedral; *b* Poona, India, 29 Jan. 1918; *er s* of late Sir Robert Benson Ewbank, CSI, CIE, and Frances Helen, *d* of Rev. W. F. Simpson; *m* 1st, 1941, Ida Margaret, 3rd *d* of late John Haworth Whitworth, DSO, MC, Inner Temple; three *d*; 2nd, 1976, Mrs Josephine Alice Williamson, MD, ChB, FRCOG. *Educ:* Shrewsbury Sch.; Balliol Coll., Oxford. Classical Scholar of Balliol, 1936; 1st, Classical Hon. Mods, 1938; 2nd, Hon. Sch. of Theology, 1946; BA and MA 1946; Bishops' Coll., Cheshunt, 1946; BD 1952. Friends' Ambulance Unit, 1939–42; Deacon, 1946; Priest, 1947; Asst Curate, St Martin's, Windermere, 1946–49; Dio. Youth Chaplain and Vicar of Ings, 1949–52; Chap. to Casterton Sch. and Vicar of Casterton, 1952–62; Domestic Chap. to Bp of Carlisle and Vicar of Raughtonhead, 1962–66; Vicar of St Cuthbert's, Carlisle, and Chap. to Corporation, 1966–71; Rural Dean of Carlisle, 1970–71; Archdeacon of Westmorland and Furness and Vicar of Winster, 1971–77; Archdeacon of Carlisle, 1977–84; Administrator of Church House, Carlisle and Chm., Diocesan Glebe Cttee, 1977–84; Canon Residentiary of Carlisle Cathedral, 1977–82; Hon. Canon, 1966–77 and 1982–84. Proctor in Convocation and Mem. Ch Assembly, 1957–70; Member: Canon Law Standing Commn, 1968–70; Faculty Jurisdiction Commn, 1979–83; Diocesan Dir: of Ordinands, 1962–70; of Post Ordination Trng, 1962–66; Vice-Chm., Diocesan Synod, 1970–79; Chm., Diocesan Board of Finance, 1977–82. Chm., Carlisle Tithe Barn Restoration Cttee, 1968–70. Winter War Remembrance Medal (Finland), 1940.

Publications: Salopian Diaries, 1961; Morality without Law, 1969; Charles Euston Nurse-A Memoir, 1982; Thomas Bloomer—A Memoir, 1984; Poems of Cumbria and of the Cumbrian Church, 1985; articles in Church Quarterly Review. *Recreation:* classical studies. *Address:* High Rigg, Castle Sowerby, Hutton Roof, Penrith, Cumbria CA11 0XY. *Club:* Royal Over-Seas League.

See also A. C. Renfrew.

EWEN, Peter; Chartered Accountant; *b* 4 June 1903; *s* of Alexander H. and Elizabeth Ewen, Liverpool; *m* 1932, Janet Howat (*née* Allan) (*d* 1982); two *d*. *Educ:* Merchant Taylors, Crosby, Qualified as Chartered Accountant, 1927; after 4 years in India joined Allan Charlesworth & Co., 1931; Partner, 1938; Senior Partner, 1953; retired, 1969. Dir of companies; Chm., Westinghouse Brake and Signal Co. Ltd, 1962–74. *Address:* Kestor, Moretonhampstead, Devon. *T:* Moretonhampstead 307. *Club:* Oriental.

EWENS, John Qualtrough, CMG 1971; CBE 1959; QC 1983; First Parliamentary Counsel, Commonwealth of Australia, 1948–72; *b* 18 Nov. 1907; *er s* of L. J. Ewens, Adelaide; *m* 1935, Gwendoline, *e d* of W. A. Wilson, Adelaide; two *s*. *Educ:* St Peter's Coll., Adelaide; Univ. of Adelaide. LLB 1929. Barrister and Solicitor, S Australia, 1929. Legal Asst, Attorney-General's Dept, Commonwealth of Australia, 1933; Sen. Legal Officer, 1939; Asst Parly Draftsman, 1945; Principal Asst Parly Draftsman, 1948; First Parly Counsel (formerly called Parly Draftsman), 1948–72; Actg Solicitor-Gen. and Actg Sec., Commonwealth of Australia Attorney-Gen.'s Dept, numerous occasions, 1953–70. Mem. Council: Canberra UC, 1945–60; Australian Nat. Univ., 1960–75; Mem., Australian Law Reform Commn, 1978–80; Consultant (Legislative Drafting): Norfolk Island Admin, 1979–; Australian Law Reform Commn, 1980–. *Publications:* articles in legal periodicals. *Recreations:* reading, music, bowls. *Address:* 57 Franklin Street, Forrest, ACT 2603, Australia. *T:* Canberra 95 9283. *Club:* University House (Canberra).

EWER, Prof. Tom Keightley, OBE 1978; HDA; BVSc; PhD; MRCVS; Professor of Animal Husbandry, Bristol University, 1961–77, now Emeritus; retired; *b* 21 Sept. 1911; *s* of William Edward Frederick Ewer and Maria Louisa Wales; *m* 1st, 1937, Iva Rosalind Biddle; three *s*; 2nd, 1959, Margaret June Fischer; three *d* one step *s* two step *d*. *Educ:* Fowey Grammar Sch.; Sydney Univ. (BVSc); Cambridge Univ. (PhD). Veterinary research with NZ Govt, 1938–45; Senior Lecturer, Univ. of NZ, 1945–47; Wellcome Research Fellow, University of Cambridge, 1947–50; Prof. of Animal Husbandry, University of Queensland, 1950–61; Prof. of Animal Resources, King Faisal Univ., Saudi Arabia, 1978–80. *Publications:* Practical Animal Husbandry, 1982; contrib. to scientific publications, on animal nutrition and veterinary education. *Recreation:* music. *Address:* Oakridge, Winscombe, Avon BS25 1LZ. *T:* Winscombe 3279.

EWIN, Sir David Ernest Thomas F.; *see* Floyd Ewin.

EWING; *see* Orr-Ewing and Orr Ewing.

EWING, Vice-Adm. Sir Alastair; *see* Ewing, Vice-Adm. Sir R. A.

EWING, Harry; MP (Lab) Falkirk East, since 1983 (Stirling and Falkirk, Sept. 1971–1974, Stirling, Falkirk and Grangemouth, 1974–83); *b* 20 Jan. 1931; *s* of Mr and Mrs William Ewing; *m* 1954, Margaret Greenhill; one *s* one *d*. *Educ:* Fulford Primary Sch., Cowdenbeath; Beath High Sch., Cowdenbeath. Contested (Lab) East Fife, 1970. Parly Under-Sec. of State, Scottish Office, 1974–79. Mem., Union of Post Office Workers. *Recreations:* bowls, gardening. *Address:* 16 Robertson Avenue, Leven, Fife. *T:* Leven 26123.

EWING, Margaret Anne; administrator; *b* 1 Sept. 1945; *d* of John and Peggie McAdam; *m* 1983, Fergus Stewart Ewing. *Educ.* Univs of Glasgow and Strathclyde. MA Glasgow 1967, BA Hons Strathclyde 1973. Asst Teacher, Our Lady's High, Cumbernauld, 1968–70; St Modan's High, Stirling: Special Asst Teacher, 1970–73; Principal Teacher, Remedial Educn, 1973–74. MP (SNP) East Dunbartonshire, Oct. 1974–1979; contested (SNP) Strathkelvin and Bearsden, 1983. Sen. Vice-Chm., SNP, 1984. *Recreations:* the arts in general, folk music in particular. *Address:* Speedwell, Buchanan Castle Estate, Drymen, Glasgow G63 0HX.

EWING, Vice-Adm. Sir (Robert) Alastair, KBE 1962; CB 1959; DSC 1942; *b* 10 April 1909; *s* of Major Ian Ewing and Muriel Adèle Child; *m* 1st, 1940, Diana Smeed (*d* 1980), *d* of Major Harry Archer, DSO; one *s;* 2nd, 1984, Anne, *d* of Captain C. G. Chichester, DSO, RN and *widow* of Comdr Henry Wilkin. *Educ:* Royal Naval Coll., Dartmouth. In command of Destroyers during War of 1939–45; NATO Standing Group Staff, 1950–51; Imperial Defence Coll., 1952; in command of HMS Vanguard, 1953–54; Dir of Naval Staff Coll., Greenwich, 1954–56; Naval Sec. to First Lord of the Admiralty, 1956–58; Flag Officer Flotillas (Mediterranean), 1958–60; Adm. Commanding Reserves and Inspector of Recruiting, 1960–62; retd list, 1962. *Address:* 19 Reyntions View, Odiham, Hants. *T:* Odiham 3509. *Clubs:* Army and Navy; Royal Yacht Squadron.

EWING, Mrs Winifred Margaret; Member (SNP) European Parliament, since 1975, elected for Highlands and Islands, 1979 and 1984; *b* 10 July 1929; *d* of George Woodburn and Christina Bell Anderson; *m* 1956, Stewart Martin Ewing; two *s* one *d*. *Educ:* Queen's Park Sen. Sec. Sch.; University of Glasgow (MA, LLB). Qual. as Solicitor, 1952. Lectr in Law, Scottish Coll. of Commerce, 1954–56; Solicitor, practising on own account, 1956–. Sec., Glasgow Bar Assoc., 1961–67, Pres., 1970–71. MP (Scottish Nationalist) for Hamilton, Nov. 1967–70; MP (SNP) Moray and Nairn, Feb. 1974–1979; contested (SNP) Orkney and Shetland, 1983. Vice-President: Scottish National Party, 1968–; Renewal and Democratic Alliance. Chm., Cttee on Youth, Culture, Educn, Information and Sport, Europ. Parlt, 1984–. Mem., Exec. Cttee, Scottish Council for Develt and Industry, 1972–. Pres., Glasgow Central Soroptimist Club, 1966–67. *Address:* 52 Queen's Drive, Glasgow G42 8DD. *T:* 041–423 1765.

EWUSIE, Prof. Joseph Yanney; Professor of Biology, University of Swaziland, since 1984; *b* 18 April 1927; *s* of Samuel Mainsa Wilson Ewusie and Elizabeth Dickson; *m* 1959, Stella Turkson; four *s*. *Educ:* Winneba Anglican Sch.; Mfantsipim Sch.; University Coll. of the Gold Coast; Univ. of Cambridge. BSc (London), PhD (Cantab). Lectr in Botany, Univ. of Ghana, 1957–62; Gen. Sec. (Chief Exec.), Ghana Academy of Sciences (highest learned and res. org. in Ghana), 1963–68; Univ. of Cape Coast: Associate Prof. of Botany, 1969–72, Prof., 1973–79; Head, Dept of Botany, 1969–73; Dean, Faculty of Science, 1971–74; Pro-Vice Chancellor, 1971–73; Vice Chancellor, 1973–78; Sec.-Gen., Pan African Inst. for Development, 1980–83. Vis. Prof., Univ. of Nairobi, 1979–80; Prof., Ahmadu Bello Univ., Nigeria, 1980. Mem. Exec. Cttee, ICSU, 1964–67. Member: Bimillenium Foundn, Washington DC, 1984–; NY Acad. of Sciences, 1984–. FWA 1963; Dipl. of Merit, Internat. Acad. of Science, Letters and Arts, Rome, 1968; Dipl. of Honour, Internat. Inst. of Community Service, 1975; Ghana Scientist of the Year, Ghana Science Assoc., 1985. Medal (Govt of Hungary) for internat. understanding between Ghana and Hungary, 1964. *Publications:* School Certificate Biology for Tropical Schools, 1964, 4th edn 1974; Tropical Biological Drawings, 1973; Elements of Tropical Ecology, 1980. *Address:* Department of Biology, University of Swaziland, Kwaluseni Campus, P/Bag Kwaluseni, Kingdom of Swaziland.

EXETER, 7th Marquess of, *cr* 1801; **William Martin Alleyne Cecil;** Baron Burghley, 1571; Earl of Exeter, 1605; *b* 27 April 1909; 2nd *s* of 5th Marquess of Exeter, KG, CMG and Hon. Myra Rowena Sibell Orde-Powlett, *d* of 4th Baron Bolton; *S* brother, 1981; *m* 1st, 1934, Edith Lilian De Csanady (*d* 1954); one *s*; 2nd, 1954, Lillian Jane Johnson; one *d* (and one *d* decd). *Educ:* Royal Naval Coll., Dartmouth. *Publications:* Being Where You Are, 1974; On Eagles' Wings, 1977; Beyond Belief, 1986. *Heir: s* Lord Burghley, *qv*. *Address:* PO Box 8, 100 Mile House, British Columbia V0K 2E0, Canada. *T:* 604–395–2323.

EXETER, Bishop of, since 1985; **Rt. Rev. (Geoffrey) Hewlett Thompson;** *b* 14 Aug. 1929; *o s* of late Lt-Col R. R. Thompson, MC, RAMC; *m* 1954, Elisabeth Joy Fausitt, BA (Oxon), *d* of late Col G. F. Taylor, MBE and Dr Frances Taylor; two *s* two *d*. *Educ:* Aldenham Sch.; Trinity Hall, Cambridge (MA); Cuddesdon Theol College. 2nd Lieut, Queen's Own Royal West Kent Regt, 1948–49 (Nat. Service). Ordained 1954. Curate, St Matthew, Northampton, 1954; Vicar: St Augustine, Wisbech, 1959; St Saviour, Folkestone, 1966; Bishop Suffragan of Willesden, 1974. Chm., Community and Race Relations Unit, BCC, 1980–84 (Vice-Chm., 1976–80). *Recreations:* fell walking, reading, gardening, music. *Address:* The Palace, Exeter EX1 1HY. *T:* Exeter 72362. *Club:* United Oxford & Cambridge University.

EXETER, Dean of; *see* Eyre, Very Rev. R. M. S.

EXETER, Archdeacon of; *see* Richards, Ven. John.

EXMOUTH, 10th Viscount *cr* 1816; **Paul Edward Pellew;** Bt 1796 (Pellew of Treverry); Baron 1814; *b* 8 Oct. 1940; *s* of 9th Viscount Exmouth and Maria Luisa, Marquesa de Olias (Spain, *cr* 1652; *S* 1940), *d* of late Luis de Urquijo, Marques de Amurrio, Madrid; *S* father, 1970; *m* 1st, 1964 (marr. diss. 1974); one *d*; 2nd, 1975, Rosemary Countess of Burford; twin *s*. *Educ:* Downside. Mem. Cons. Party, House of Lords. Mem., Inst. of Dirs. *Heir: er twin s* Hon. Edward Francis Pellew, *b* 30 Oct. 1978. *Address:* Canonteign, near Exeter, Devon.

EXTON, Clive; scriptwriter and playwright; *b* 11 April 1930; *s* of late J. E. M. Brooks and Marie Brooks (*née* Rolfe); *m* 1951, Patricia Fletcher Ferguson (marr. diss. 1957); two *d*; *m* 1957, Margaret Josephine Reid; one *s* two *d*. *Educ:* Christ's Hospital. *TV plays:* No Fixed Abode, 1959; The Silk Purse; Where I Live; Some Talk of Alexander; Hold My Hand, Soldier; I'll Have You to Remember; The Big Eat; The Trial of Doctor Fancy; Land of my Dreams; The Close Prisoner; The Bone Yard; Are You Ready for the Music?; The Rainbirds; Killers (series); Stigma; Henry Intervenes; The Crezz (series); Dick Barton—Special Agent (series). *Stage play:* Have You Any Dirty Washing, Mother Dear?. *Films:* Night Must Fall; Isadora; Entertaining Mr Sloane; Ten Rillington Place; Running Scared; Doomwatch; The House in Nightmare Park; The Awakening. *Publications:* No Fixed Abode (in Six Granada Plays, anthol.), 1960; Have You Any Dirty Washing, Mother Dear? (in Plays of the Year, vol. 37), 1970. *Address:* c/o A. D. Peters & Co., 10 Buckingham Street, WC2.

EXTON, Rodney Noel, JP; MA; Director, Independent Schools Careers Organization, since 1978; *b* 28 Dec. 1927; *s* of Noel Exton and Winifred (*née* Stokes); *m* 1961, Pamela Sinclair (*née* Hardie); two step *s* two step *d*. *Educ:* Clifton Coll.; Lincoln Coll., Oxford (MA Mod. Langs); Corpus Christi Coll., Cambridge (PGCE). FInstD. Served Royal Hampshire Regt, 1946–48. Asst Master, Eton, 1951–52; Internat. Research Fund Schol. to USA, 1952; Asst Master, Mill Hill Sch., 1953–63; Royal Commonwealth schol. to Australia, 1959–60; Headmaster, Reed's Sch., 1964–77; Walter Hines Page schol. to USA, 1971. Vice-Chm., British Atlantic Educn Cttee, 1972–78; UK Delegate to Atlantic Treaty Assoc. Conferences: Copenhagen, 1976; Hamburg, 1979; Madeira, 1980; London, 1981; Chm., Exec. Cttee, GAP, 1982–. Man. Dir, Exton Hotels Co. Ltd, 1966–80. Hampshire County Cricket XI, 1946. JP Surrey, 1968. *Recreations:* collecting old lithographs, guitar-playing. *Address:* 12A Princess Way, Camberley, Surrey GU15 3SP. *T:* Camberley 21188. *Clubs:* East India, Devonshire, Sports and Public Schools, MCC; Royal Mid-Surrey Golf; Vincent's (Oxford).

EXTON-SMITH, Prof. Arthur Norman, CBE 1981; MD; FRCP; Director, Geriatric Neurophysiology Unit, Whittington Hospital, London; Professor of Geriatric Medicine, University College Hospital Medical School, London, 1973–84; *b* 7 Jan. 1920; *s* of Arthur and Ethel Exton-Smith; *m* 1951, Jean Barbara Belcher; one *s* one *d*. *Educ:* Nottingham High Sch.; Pembroke Coll., Cambridge (MA, MD). FRCP 1964. Consultant Physician: Whittington Hosp., London, 1951–65; UCH, 1965–73. Lord Cohen of Birkenhead Medal, British Soc. for Res. in Ageing, 1984; Moxon Medal, RCP, 1984; Dhole-Eddlestone Meml Prize, British Geriatrics Soc., 1986. *Publications:* Medical Problems of Old Age, 1955; Geriatrics (with P. W. Overstall), 1979; (ed with M. Weksler) Practical Geriatric Medicine, 1986; contrib. Lancet, BMJ. *Address:* 6 North Grove, Highgate, N6 4SL. *T:* 01–341 4433.

EYERS, Patrick Howard Caines, CMG 1985; LVO 1966; HM Diplomatic Service; Ambassador to the Republic of Zaire, to the People's Republic of the Congo, to the Republic of Rwanda, and to the Republic of Burundi, since 1985; *b* 4 Sept. 1933; *s* of late Arthur Leopold Caines Eyers and Nora Lilian Eyers; *m* 1960, Heidi, *d* of Werner Rüsch, Dipl. Ing, and Helene (*née* Feil); two *s* one *d*. *Educ:* Clifton Coll.; Gonville and Caius Coll., Cambridge (BA Hons 1957); Institut Universitaire de Hautes Etudes Internationales, Geneva. RA, 1952–54. Asst Editor, Grolier Soc. Inc., New York, 1957; HM Foreign (now Diplomatic) Service, 1959; ME Centre for Arabic Studies, 1960; Dubai, 1961; Brussels, 1964; FO, 1966; Aden, 1969; Abidjan, 1970; British Mil. Govt, Berlin, 1971; FCO, 1974; Counsellor, Bonn, 1977; Head, Republic of Ireland Dept, FCO, 1981; RCDS, 1984. Officer, Order of Leopold, Belgium, 1966. *Recreations:* music, skiing, sailing. *Address:* c/o Foreign and Commonwealth Office, SW1. *Clubs:* Ski of GB, Kandahar Ski, Hurlingham.

EYRE, Hon. Dean Jack; New Zealand High Commissioner to Canada, 1968–73 and 1976–80; *b* Westport, NZ, 1914; *m*; two *s* one *d*. *Educ:* Hamilton High Sch.; Auckland University Coll. Served War of 1939–45, Lieut in RNVR. Electrical importer and manufacturer. MP (Nat) North Shore, 1949–66; Minister of Customs, Industries and Commerce, 1954–57; Minister of Social Security and Tourist and Health Resorts, 1956–57; Minister of Housing, State Advances and Defence, New Zealand, 1957; Minister in Charge of Police, 1960–63; Minister of Defence, 1960–66; Minister i/c Tourism, 1961–66. *Recreations:* yachting, fishing. *Address:* 517 Wilbrod Street, Ottawa, Ontario K1N 5R6, Canada. *Clubs:* Royal New Zealand Yacht Squadron, Northern, Officers (Auckland); Wellington (Wellington); Royal Ottawa Golf.

EYRE, Graham Newman, QC 1970; a Recorder of the Crown Court, since 1975; *b* 9 Jan. 1931; *s* of Newman Eyre; *m* 1954, Jean Dalrymple Walker; one *s* three *d*. *Educ:* Marlborough Coll.; Trinity Coll., Cambridge. BA 1953, LLB 1954, MA 1958. Council Prizewinner, 1954. Called to Bar, Middle Temple, 1954, Harmsworth Law Schol., 1955, Bencher, Middle Temple, 1979; Mem., Lincoln's Inn, 1971; Head of Chambers, 1981. Inspector, The London Airports Inquiries, 1981–84. *Publications:* Rating Law and Valuation, 1963; contrib. Jl Planning Law. *Address:* Walberton House, Walberton,

Arundel, West Sussex BN18 0PJ; Casa de Monte, 4 Campo Alto, Calahonda, Mijas Costa, Marbella, Spain; 8 New Square, Lincoln's Inn, WC2A 3QP. *Club*: Athenæum.

EYRE, Maj.-Gen. Sir James (Ainsworth Campden Gabriel), KCVO 1986 (CVO 1978); CBE 1980 (OBE 1975); General Officer Commanding London District and Major General Commanding Household Division, 1983–86; *b* 2 Nov. 1930; *s* of Edward Joseph Eyre and Hon. Dorothy Elizabeth Anne Pelline (*née* Lyon-Dalberg-Acton); *m* 1967, Monica Ruth Esther Smyth; one *s* one *d*. *Educ*: Harvard Univ. (BA, LLB). Commissioned RHG, 1955; Commanding Officer, The Blues and Royals, 1970–73; GSO 1 HQ London District, 1973–75; Officer Commanding Household Cavalry and Silver Stick, 1975–78; Col GS HQ Northern Ireland, 1978–80; Sec., Chiefs of Staff Cttee, MoD, 1980–82; Dir of Defence Programmes Staff (Concepts), MoD, 1982–83. *Recreations*: racing, shooting. *Address*: Bockhampton Manor, Lambourn, Berks RG16 7LX. *Club*: Turf.

EYRE, Sir Reginald (Edwin), Kt 1984; MP (C) Birmingham Hall Green, since May 1965; *b* 28 May 1924; *s* of late Edwin Eyre; *m* 1978, Anne Clements; one *d*. *Educ*: King Edward's Camp Hill Sch., Birmingham; Emmanuel Coll., Cambridge (MA). Midshipman and Sub-Lieut, RNVR, War of 1939–45. Admitted a Solicitor, 1950; Senior Partner, Eyre & Co., solicitors, Birmingham. Hon. Consultant, Poor Man's Lawyer, 1948–58. Contested (C) Birmingham (Northfield) 1959; Conservative Political Centre: Chm., W Midlands Area, 1960–63; Chm., National Advisory Cttee, 1964–66; Opposition Whip, 1966–70; a Lord Comr of the Treasury, June-Sept. 1970; Comptroller of HM Household, 1970–72; Parliamentary Under-Secretary of State: DoE, 1972–74; Dept of Trade, 1979–82; Dept of Transport, 1982–83. A Vice Chm., Cons. Party Organisation, 1975–79; Chm., Cons. Parly Urban Affairs Cttee, 1983–84. *Publication*: Hope for our Towns and Cities, 1977. *Address*: 45 Aylesford Street, SW1; 1041 Stratford Road, Birmingham B28 8AS. *Clubs*: Carlton; Birmingham (Birmingham).

EYRE, Richard Charles Hastings; theatre, film and TV director; Associate Director, National Theatre, since 1981; *b* 28 March 1943; *m* 1973, Susan Elizabeth Birtwistle; one *d*. *Educ*: Sherborne Sch.; Peterhouse, Cambridge (BA). Asst Dir, Phoenix Theatre, Leicester, 1966; Lyceum Theatre, Edinburgh: Associate Dir, 1967–70; Dir of Productions, 1970–72; freelance director: Liverpool, 7:84 Co., West End; tours for British Council: W Africa, 1971; SE Asia, 1972; Artistic Dir, Nottingham Playhouse, 1973–78; Prod./Dir, Play for Today, BBC TV, 1978–80; Director: The Churchill Play, Nottingham, 1974; Comedians, Old Vic and Wyndhams, 1976; Touched, Nottingham, 1977; Hamlet, Royal Court, 1980; Edmond, Royal Court, 1985; National Theatre: Guys and Dolls (SWET Director of the Year, 1982, Standard Best Director, 1982), The Beggar's Opera, and Schweyk in the Second World War, 1982; The Government Inspector, 1985; Futurists, 1986. Films: The Ploughman's Lunch (Evening Standard Award for Best Film, 1983), Loose Connections, 1983; Laughterhouse, 1984, released as Singleton's Pluck, USA, 1985 (TV Prize, Venice Film Fest.). Films for TV: The Imitation Game, Pasmore, 1980; Country, 1981; The Insurance Man, 1986; Past Caring, 1986. Directed premières of plays by Trevor Griffiths, David Hare, Howard Brenton, Ken Campbell, John McGrath, Barrie Keeffe, Stephen Lowe, Ann Jellicoe, Charles Wood, Adrian Mitchell, Henry Livings, Ian McEwan. STV Awards for Best Production, 1969, 1970 and 1971. *Address*: c/o Curtis Brown, 162–168 Regent Street, W1R 5TA. *T*: 01–437 9700.

EYRE, Very Rev. Richard Montague Stephens; Dean of Exeter, since 1981; *b* 1929; *s* of Montague Henry and Ethel Mary Eyre; *m* 1963, Anne Mary Bentley; two *d*. *Educ*: Charterhouse; Oriel Coll. and St Stephen's House, Oxford. MA Oxon. Deacon 1956, priest 1957; Curate, St Mark's Church, Portsea, 1956–59; Tutor and Chaplain, Chichester Theological Coll., 1959–62; Chaplain, Eastbourne Coll., 1962–65; Vicar of Arundel, 1965–73; Vicar of Good Shepherd, Brighton, 1973–75; Archdeacon of Chichester, 1975–81; Treasurer of Chichester Cathedral, 1978–81. *Recreations*: golf, music, travel, gardening. *Address*: The Deanery, Exeter, Devon. *T*: Exeter 72697.

EYRE, Ronald; freelance theatre and television director; writer; *b* 13 April 1929; *s* of Christopher Eyre and Mabel Smith. *Educ*: Queen Elizabeth Grammar Sch., Wakefield, Yorks; University Coll., Oxford (MA English Lang. and Lit.). English Master, Queen Elizabeth Grammar Sch., Blackburn, 1952–54; Sen. English Master, Bromsgrove Sch., 1954–56; Producer, BBC Television, 1956–64. *Theatre Director*: *RSC*: Much Ado About Nothing, 1971; London Assurance, London, 1972 and New York, 1974; The Marquis of Keith, 1974; Saratoga, 1978; Othello, 1979; The Winter's Tale, 1981; *West End*: Enjoy; Three Months Gone, 1970 (also Royal Court); Voyage Round My Father, 1971; Habeas Corpus, 1973; The Secret Policeman's Other Ball, 1981; Hobson's Choice, 1982; Messiah, 1983; A Patriot for Me, 1983; When We Are Married, 1986; *Theatre Royal, Stratford East*: Widower's Houses, 1965; *Hampstead Theatre Club*: Events While Guarding the Bofors Gun, 1966; Bakke's Night of Fame, 1968; *Royal Court*: Veterans, 1972; A Pagan Place, 1972; *Chichester Festival Theatre and Haymarket Theatre*: A Patriot for Me, 1983; *National Theatre*: Saint Joan, 1984; *Stratford, Ontario*: The Government Inspector, 1985. *Opera Producer*: Beatrice and Benedict, Buxton, 1980 (also translator); Mussorgsky's Marriage, Nexus Opera, 1981; Falstaff, Los Angeles and Covent Garden, 1982 and Teatro Communale, Florence, 1983, new prodn, Covent Garden, 1984; Jason, Buxton, 1984 (also translator). *Playwright*: theatre: Something's Burning, 1973; television: I'm not Stopping, 1963; A Crack in the Ice, 1964 (theatre, 1966); Bruno, 1965; The Single Passion, 1967; The Glory of Llewellyn Smiley, 1967. Writer and Presenter, The Long Search, BBC, 1977. *Publication*: Ronald Eyre on The Long Search, 1979. *Address*: c/o L. Dalzell, 126 Kennington Park Road, SE11 4DJ. *T*: 01–735 2294.

EYRES MONSELL, family name of **Viscount Monsell.**

EYSENCK, Prof. Hans Jurgen, PhD, DSc; Professor of Psychology, University of London, Institute of Psychiatry, 1955–83, Professor Emeritus, since 1983; Director, Psychological Department, Maudsley Hospital, 1946–83; *b* 4 March 1916; *s* of Eduard Anton and Ruth Eysenck; *m* 1st, 1938, Margaret Malcolm Davies; one *s*; 2nd, 1950, Sybil Bianca Giuletta Rostal; three *s* one *d*. *Educ*: school in Germany, France and England; Univ. of London. BA 1938, PhD 1940, DSc 1964. Senior Research Psychologist, Mill Hill Emergency Hosp., 1942–46; Reader in Psychology, Univ. of London (Inst. of Psychiatry), 1950–54; Visiting Prof., Univ. of Pennsylvania, 1949–50; Visiting Prof., Univ. of California, Berkeley, 1954. *Publications*: Dimensions of Personality, 1947; The Scientific Study of Personality, 1952; The Structure of Human Personality, 1953; Uses and Abuses of Psychology, 1953; The Psychology of Politics, 1954; Sense and Nonsense in Psychology, 1957; Dynamics of Anxiety and Hysteria, 1957; Perceptual Processes and Mental Illness, 1957; (ed) Handbook of Abnormal Psychology, 1960, 2nd edn, 1972; (ed) Behaviour Therapy and the Neuroses, 1960; (ed) Experiments in Personality, 1960; (ed) Experiments with Drugs, 1963; (ed) Experiments in Behaviour Therapy, 1964; (ed) Experiments in Motivation, 1964; Crime and Personality, 1964; Causes and Cures of Neurosis, 1965; Fact and Fiction in Psychology, 1965; Smoking, Health and Personality, 1965; The Biological Basis of Personality, 1968; Personality Structure and Measurement, 1969; Race, Intelligence and Education, 1971; Psychology is about People, 1972; (ed) Readings in Introversion-Extraversion, 3 vols, 1971; (ed) Lexikon der Psychologie, 3 vols, 1972; The Measurement of Intelligence, 1973; The Inequality of Man, 1973; (ed jtly) The Experimental Study of Freudian Theories, 1973; (ed jtly) Encyclopaedia of Psychology, 1973; (with Glenn Wilson) Know Your Own Personality, 1975; (ed) Case Studies in Behaviour Therapy, 1976; Sex and Personality, 1976; (with S. B. G. Eysenck) Psychoticism as a Dimension of Personality 1976; You and Neurosis, 1977; Die Zukunft der Psychologie, 1977; (with D. K. B. Nias) Sex, Violence and the Media, 1978; The Structure and Measurement of Intelligence, 1979; (with Glenn Wilson) The Psychology of Sex, 1979; The Causes and Effects of Smoking, 1980; (with M. W. Eysenck) Mindwatching, 1981; (ed) A Model for Personality, 1981; (with J. Kamin) Intelligence: the battle for the mind, 1981 (US as The Intelligence Controversy, 1981); (with D. K. B. Nias) Astrology: Science or Superstition?, 1982; Personality, Genetics and Behaviour, 1982; (ed) A Model for Intelligence, 1982; (with Carl Sargent) Explaining the Unexplained, 1982; I Do: your guide to happy marriage, 1983; (with Carl Sargent) Know your own psi-Q, 1984; (with M. W. Eysenck) Personality and Individual Differences, 1985; Decline and Fall of the Freudian Empire, 1985; Editor-in-Chief: Behaviour Research and Therapy, 1963–78; Personality and Individual Differences, 1980–; (ed) International Monographs of Experimental Psychology; some 800 articles in British, American, German, Spanish and French Jls of Psychology. *Recreations*: walking, tennis, chess, detective stories, squash. *Address*: 10 Dorchester Drive, SE24.

EYTON, Anthony John Plowden, ARA 1976; ARWS 1985; RWA 1984; NEAC 1985; Part-time Lecturer, Camberwell School of Art, since 1956; Visiting Teacher, Royal Academy Schools, since 1963; *b* 17 May 1923; *s* of late Captain John Seymour Eyton, ICS, author, and of Phyllis Annie Tyser; *m* 1960, Frances Mary Capell, MA (marr. diss.); three *d*. *Educ*: Twyford Sch.; Canford Sch.; Dept of Fine Art, Reading Univ.; Camberwell Sch. of Art (NDD). Served War, 1939–45, Cameronians (Scottish Rifles), Hampshire Regt, and Army Educn Corps. Abbey Major Scholarship in Painting, 1950–51. Elected Mem., London Gp, 1958. One Man Exhibitions: St George's Gall., 1955; Galerie de Seine, 1957; New Art Centre, 1959, 1961, 1968; New Grafton Gall., 1973; William Darby Gall., 1975; Newcastle Polytechnic Art Gall., 1978; Browse and Darby, 1978, 1981, 1985; Retrospective Exhibn, S London Art Gall., Towner Art Gall., Eastbourne, and Plymouth Art Gall., 1981; Hong Kong and the New Territories exhibn, Imperial War Museum, 1983 (subsequent to commission); work included in British Painting 1945–77, RA. Work in public collections: Tate Gall.; Arts Council; Plymouth Art Gall.; Towner Art Gall., Eastbourne; Carlisle Art Gall.; DoE; RA; Government Picture Coll.; BR; Contemp. Art Soc. Fellowship awarded by Grocers' Co. (for work and travel in Italy), 1974. Hon. Mem., Pastel Soc., 1986. Prize, John Moore's Exhibn, Liverpool, 1972; First Prize, Second British Internat. Drawing Biennale, Middlesbrough, 1975; Charles Wollaston Award, RA, 1981. *Recreation*: gardening. *Address*: 166 Brixton Road, SW9 6AU.

EZARD, Clarence Norbury, CBE 1954 (OBE 1942); Retired as Ambassador to Costa Rica; *b* 6 Oct. 1896; *m* 1936, Olive Lillian Vaneus. *Educ*: Carlisle Grammar Sch.; Emmanuel Coll., Cambridge. Probationer Vice-Consul in General Consular Service, 1924; Acting Vice-Consul, Havana, 1926; Chargé d'Affaires, May-Oct. 1928; Sec. to Special Mission at Inauguration of Pres. of Republic of Cuba, with Temp. rank of 3rd Sec. in Diplomatic Service, 1929; Subst. rank of Vice-Consul, 1929; Vice-Consul at Bogotá, 1930; local rank of 2nd Sec. in Dipl. Service, 1930; in charge of Consulate at Havana, March-June 1931, of Legation April-June 1931. Transferred to New York, 1932, to Piræus, 1934. Acting Consul at Athens, 1935 and 1936; Consul at Beira, 1938; Montevideo, 1945, with rank of Consul and 1st Sec.; Consul-Gen., Gdansk, 1946; Consul-Gen., Haifa, 1949; Minister to Costa Rica, 1953; Ambassador to Costa Rica, 1956; retired, 1957. *Address*: Three Fields, Mayfield, East Sussex. *Club*: Carlton.

EZEILO, Prof. James Okoye Chukuka, CON 1979; PhD; Professor of Mathematics, University of Nigeria; *b* 17 Jan. 1930; *s* of Josiah Ezeilo and Janet Ezeilo; *m* 1960, Phoebe Uchechuku; two *s* two *d*. *Educ*: Dennis Memorial Grammar Sch., Onitsha; University Coll., Ibadan (MSc London); Queens' Coll., Cambridge (PhD). University of Ibadan: Lectr in Maths, 1958–62; Sen. Lectr in Maths, 1962–64; Prof. of Maths, 1964–66; University of Nigeria: Prof. of Maths, 1966–75, 1980–; Vice-Chancellor, 1975–78. Vice-Chancellor, Bayero Univ., Nigeria, 1978–79. Benedict Dist. Prof. of Maths, Carleton Coll., 1979; Vis. Prof. of Maths, Howard Univ., 1979–80. Pres., Nigerian Math. Assoc., 1972–74, 1984–; Mem., Nigerian Council for Science and Technol., 1970–75; Foundation Mem., Nigerian Acad. of Sciences. *Publications*: numerous papers on differential equations in math. jls. *Recreation*: gardening. *Address*: Department of Mathematics, University of Nigeria, Nsukka, Nigeria. *Clubs*: Athenæum; Rotary (Nsukka) (Charter Pres.).

EZRA, family name of **Baron Ezra.**

EZRA, Baron *cr* 1983 (Life Peer), of Horsham in the County of West Sussex; **Derek Ezra;** Kt 1974; MBE 1945; Chairman, Associated Heat Services plc, since 1966; Industrial Adviser, Morgan Grenfell & Co. Ltd, since 1982; *b* 23 Feb. 1919; *s* of David and Lillie Ezra; *m* 1950, Julia Elizabeth Wilkins. *Educ*: Monmouth Sch.; Magdalene Coll., Cambridge (MA, Hon. Fellow, 1977). Army, 1939–47. Joined NCB, 1947; representative of NCB at Cttees of OEEC and ECE, 1948–52; Mem. of UK Delegn to High Authority of European Coal and Steel Community, 1952–56; Dep. Regional Sales Manager, NCB, 1956–58; Regional Sales Manager, 1958–60; Dir-Gen. of Marketing, NCB, 1960–65; NCB Bd Mem., 1965–67; Dep. Chm., 1967–71; Chm., 1971–82. Chairman: J. H. Sankey & Son Ltd, 1977–82; Petrolex PLC, 1982–85; Director: British Fuel Co., 1966–82; Solvay SA, 1979–; Redland PLC, 1982–; Supervisory Bd, Royal Boskalis Westminster NV, 1982–85. Chm., NICG, 1972 and 1980–81; President: Nat. Materials Handling Centre, 1979; Coal Industry Soc., 1981–86 (Chm., 1961); W European Coal Producers' Assoc., 1976–79; BSI, 1983–; Vice-Pres., BIM, 1978 (Chm., 1976–78); Chm., British Iron and Steel Consumers' Council, 1983–86; Member: BOTB, 1972–82 (Chm., European Trade Cttee); Cons. Cttee, ECSC, 1973–82 (Pres., 1978–79); Adv. Council for Energy Conservation, 1974–79; Adv. Bd, Petrofina SA, 1982–; Internat. Adv. Bd, Creditanstalt Bankverein, 1982; Energy Commn, 1977–79; Ct of Governors, Administrative Staff Coll., 1971–82; Internat. Adv. Bd, Banca Nazionale del Lavoro, 1984; Governor, London Business Sch., 1973–82. Chm., Keep Britain Tidy Gp, 1979–85. Chm., Throgmorton Trust, 1984–. Hon. DSc Cranfield, 1979; Hon. LLD Leeds, 1982. Bronze Star (USA), 1945; Grand Officer, Italian Order of Merit, 1979; Comdr, Luxembourg Order of Merit, 1981; Officer of Légion d'Honneur, 1981. *Publications*: Coal and Energy, 1978; The Energy Debate, 1983. *Address*: House of Lords, Westminster, SW1. *T*: 01-219 3180.

F

FABER, Julian Tufnell; Chairman: Willis Faber Ltd, 1972–77; Cornhill Insurance plc, since 1986 (Director, since 1972); *b* 6 April 1917; *s* of late Alfred and Edith Faber; *m* 1944, Lady (Ann) Caroline, *e d* of Earl of Stockton, *qv*, and late Lady Dorothy Macmillan; four *s* one *d. Educ:* Winchester; Trinity Coll., Cambridge. Joined Willis, Faber & Dumas Ltd, 1938. Served Welsh Guards (Major 2nd Bn), 1939–45. Director: Willis, Faber & Dumas Ltd, 1952; Willis, Faber & Dumas (Agencies) Ltd, 1965; Taisho Marine & Fire Insurance Co. (UK) Ltd, 1972 (Chm.); Willis Faber (Middle East) SAL, 1973; Morgan Grenfell Ltd, 1974–77; Allianz International Insurance Co., 1974. Mem. Bd of Governors, Summer Fields Sch., Oxford. Member: MCC Cttee, 1981–84; Kent CCC Cttee, 1977–84. *Address:* 3 Chester Square, SW1. *T:* 01–730 6474; Fisher's Gate, Withyham, E Sussex. *Clubs:* White's, City of London, MCC.

FABER, Prof. Michael Leslie Ogilvie; Director, Institute of Development Studies, Sussex University, since 1982; *b* 12 Aug. 1929; *s* of George and Kathleen Faber; *m* 1956, Diana Catriona Howard; two *s* twin *d. Educ:* Avon Old Farms, USA; Eton; Magdalen Coll., Oxford (MA); Univ. of Michigan. MA Cantab. Served 11th Hussars, PAO, Germany, 1948–49. Merchant Seaman, 1953–54. Claims Adjuster, Amer. Internat. Underwriters, Japan and Korea, 1954; Foreign Correspondent for Sunday Times, Observer, and Economist in FE, ME, N and Central Africa, 1954–60; Lectr in Econs, UCRN, 1958–60; community develt worker with Danilo Dolci in Sicily, 1961; Lectr in Econs, UWI, 1962–63; Sen. Economist and Under-Sec., Govt of Zambia, 1964–67; Dept of Applied Econs, Cambridge, 1968; Overseas Develt Gp, UEA, 1969–78; Dir, Tech. Assistance Gp, Commonwealth Secretariat, 1972–75 and 1978–82. Mem. Council, Overseas Develt Inst., 1982–. Leader, UNDP/IBRD Mission to PNG, 1972; specialist negotiator of resource agreements. *Publications:* Economic Structuralism and its Relevance, 1965; (with J. Potter) Towards Economic Independence, 1971; (ed with Dudley Seers) The Crisis in Economic Planning, 1972; (with R. Brown) Mining Agreements: law and policy, 1977; (with R. Brown) Changing the Rules of the Game, 1980. *Address:* The Combe, Glynde, Lewes, Sussex BN8 6RP. *Club:* Lewes Golf.

FABER, Sir Richard (Stanley), KCVO 1980; CMG 1977; FRSL; HM Diplomatic Service, retired; Ambassador to Algeria, 1977–81; *b* 6 Dec. 1924; *er s* of late Sir Geoffrey Faber and of Enid, *d* of Sir Henry Erle Richards, KCSI, KC; unmarried. *Educ:* Westminster Sch.; Christ Church, Oxford (MA). RNVR, 1943–46. 1st cl. Lit. Hum. Oxon; Pres., Oxford Union Soc., 1949. Joined HM Foreign (subseq. Diplomatic) Service, 1950; service in FO and in Baghdad, Paris, Abidjan, Washington; Head of Rhodesia Political Dept, FCO, 1967–69; Counsellor: The Hague, 1969–73; Cairo, 1973–75; Asst Under Sec. of State, FCO, 1975–77. *Publications:* Beaconsfield and Bolingbroke, 1961; The Vision and the Need: Late Victorian Imperialist Aims, 1966; Proper Stations: Class in Victorian Fiction, 1971; French and English, 1975; The Brave Courtier (biog. of Sir William Temple), 1983; High Road to England, 1985. *Address:* Flat 3, 110 Highgate Hill, N6. *Club:* Travellers'.
See also T. E. Faber.

FABER, Thomas Erle, PhD; Chairman, Faber & Faber (Publishers) Ltd, since 1977 (Director since 1969); Lecturer in Physics, University of Cambridge, since 1959; Fellow of Corpus Christi College, Cambridge, since 1953; *b* 25 April 1927; *s* of Sir Geoffrey Faber; *m* 1st, 1959, Penelope (*d* 1983), *d* of Clive Morton, actor; two *s* two *d*; 2nd, 1986, Dr Elisabeth van Houts. *Educ:* Oundle Sch.; Trinity Coll., Cambridge (MA, PhD). Univ. of Cambridge: Res. Fellow, Trinity Coll., 1950–53; Univ. Demonstr, 1953–58; Armourers' and Brasiers' Fellow, 1958–59. Treasurer, Corpus Christi Coll., 1963–76. *Publications:* Introduction to the Theory of Liquid Metals, 1972; papers on superconductivity, liquid metals and liquid crystals. *Recreations:* walking, shooting. *Address:* The Old Vicarage, Thompson's Lane, Cambridge CB5 8AQ. *T:* Cambridge 356685.
See also Sir R. S. Faber.

FABIAN, Prof. Andrew Christopher; Royal Society Research Professor, Institute of Astronomy, University of Cambridge, since 1982; Fellow of Darwin College, Cambridge, since 1983; *b* 20 Feb. 1948; *s* of John Archibald and Daphne Monica Fabian; *m* 1971, Diane Marie Owen; one *s* one *d. Educ:* Daventry Grammar Sch.; King's Coll., London (BSc Physics); University Coll. London (PhD). SRC post doctoral research asst, University Coll. London, 1972–73; Institute of Astronomy, Cambridge: SRC post doctoral Fellow, 1973–75; SRC PDRA, 1975–77; Radcliffe Fellow in Astronomy, 1977–81. *Publications:* contribs to Monthly Notices RAS, Astrophys. Jl, Nature, etc. *Address:* 84 De Freville Avenue, Cambridge CB4 1HU. *T:* Cambridge 311968.

FABIUS, Laurent; Prime Minister of France, 1984–86; Deputy for Seine Maritime, National Assembly, 1978–81, re-elected 1981, 1986; *b* 20 Aug. 1946; *s* of André Fabius and Louise Fabius (*née* Mortimer); *m* 1981, Françoise Castro; two *s. Educ:* Lycée Janson-de-Sailly; Lycée Louis-le-Grand; Ecole Normale Supérieure, Paris; Institut d'Etudes Politiques, Paris; Ecole Nationale d'Administration. Conseil d'Etat, 1973–81; First Deputy Mayor, Grand-Quevilly, 1977–81; Nat. Sec., Parti Socialiste (responsible for the press), 1979–81; Junior Minister, Ministry of Economy and Finance (responsible for the budget), 1981–83; Minister of Industry and Research, 1983–84. Mem., Conseil d'Etat, 1981–. Pres., Regional Council, Haute Normandie, 1981–. *Publications:* La France inégale, 1975; Le Coeur du Futur, 1985. *Address:* Assemblée Nationale, 75007 Paris, France; 15 place du Panthéon, 75005 Paris, France.

FACER, Roger Lawrence Lowe; Assistant Under-Secretary of State, Ministry of Defence, since 1984; *b* 28 June 1933; *s* of late John Ernest Facer and Phyllis Facer; *m* 1960, Ruth

Margaret, *o d* of late Herbert Mostyn Lewis, PhD, Gresford, Clwyd; three *d. Educ:* Rugby; St John's Coll., Oxford (MA). HM Forces, 2nd Lieut, East Surrey Regt, 1951–53. War Office, 1957; Asst Private Sec. to Secretary of State, 1958; Private Sec. to Permanent Under-Sec., 1958; Principal, 1961; Cabinet Office, 1966; Ministry of Defence, 1968–: Private Sec. to Minister of State (Equipment), 1970; Asst Sec., 1970; Internat. Inst. for Strategic Studies, 1972–73; Counsellor, UK Delegn, MBFR Vienna, 1973–75; Private Sec. to Sec. of State for Defence, 1976–79; Asst Under-Sec. of State, 1979–81; Under Sec., Cabinet Office, 1981–83; Rand Corporation, Santa Monica, USA, 1984. *Publications:* Weapons Procurement in Europe—Capabilities and Choices, 1975; Conventional Forces and the NATO Strategy of Flexible Response, 1985; articles in Alpine Garden Soc. Bulletin. *Recreations:* Alpine gardening, hill-walking, opera. *Address:* c/o Ministry of Defence, Whitehall, SW1.

FACK, Robbert; Commander, Order of Orange-Nassau, 1979; Chevalier, Order of Netherlands Lion 1971; Netherlands diplomat, retired; Ambassador of the Netherlands to the Court of St James's, 1976–82; also, concurrently, Ambassador to Iceland, 1976–82; *b* 1 Jan. 1917; *m* 1943, Patricia H. Hawkins; four *s. Educ:* Univ. of Amsterdam. Military service, 1937–45. Min. of Foreign Affairs, The Hague, 1945–46; New York (UN), 1946–48; Min. of Foreign Affairs, 1948–50; Rome, 1950–54; Canberra, 1954–58; Bonn, 1958–63; Min. of Foreign Affairs, 1963–68; Ambassador-at-large, 1968–70; Perm. Rep. to UN, New York, 1970–74. Holds various foreign decorations. *Publication:* Gedane Zaken (Finished Business), (reminiscences), 1984. *Address:* Widden Hill House, Horton, near Bristol BS17 6QU. *Club:* Dutch.

FAGE, Prof. John Donnelly, MA, PhD; Professor of African History, 1963–84, now Emeritus, Pro-Vice-Chancellor, 1979–84, and Vice-Principal 1981–84, University of Birmingham; *b* 3 June 1921; *s* of late Arthur Fage, CBE, FRS, and Winifred Eliza Donnelly; *m* 1949, Jean, *d* of late Frederick Banister; one *s* one *d. Educ:* Tonbridge Sch.; Magdalene Coll., Cambridge (scholar, MA, PhD). Served War, Pilot with RAFVR (Flt Lt), 1941–45. Bye-Fellow, Magdalene Coll., Cambridge, 1947–49; Lectr and Sen. Lectr, Univ. Coll. of the Gold Coast, 1949–55; Prof. of History, 1955–59, and Dep. Principal, 1957–59; Lectr in African History, SOAS, Univ. of London, 1959–63. Visiting Prof., Univ. of Wisconsin, Madison, 1957, and Smith Coll., Northampton, Mass, 1962; Dir, Centre of West African Studies, Univ. of Birmingham, 1963–82; Dep. Dean, Faculty of Arts, 1973–75, Dean, 1975–78; Founding Hon. Sec., African Studies Assoc. of the UK, 1963–66 (Vice-Pres. 1967–68, Pres. 1968–69); Council Mem., Internat. African Inst., 1965–75, and Consultative Dir, 1975–80; Member: UNESCO Scientific Cttee for Gen. History of Africa, 1971–80; Culture Adv. Cttee of UK Nat. Commn for UNESCO, 1967–85 (Chm., 1978–85); Coordinating Council of Area Studies Associations (Vice-Chm. 1980–84, Chm., 1984–); FRHistS. Hon. Fellow, SOAS, Univ. of London. Editor (with Roland Oliver), The Jl of African History, 1960–73; Gen. Editor (with Roland Oliver), The Cambridge History of Africa, 8 vols, 1975–86. *Publications:* An Introduction to the History of West Africa, 1955, 3rd edn 1962; An Atlas of African History, 1958, 2nd edn, 1978; Ghana, a Historical Interpretation, 1959; A Short History of Africa (with Roland Oliver), 1962, 6th edn 1986; A History of West Africa, 1969; (ed) Africa Discovers Her Past, 1970; (ed with Roland Oliver) Papers on African Prehistory, 1970; A History of Africa, 1978; articles in historical and Africanist jls. *Recreations:* doing things to houses and gardens. *Address:* 17 Antringham Gardens, Birmingham B15 3QL. *T:* 021–455 0020; Hafod Awel, Pennal, Machynlleth, Powys SY20 9DP. *Club:* Athenæum.

FAGG, Bernard Evelyn Buller, MBE 1962; MA; FSA; FMA; Curator, Pitt Rivers Museum, Oxford, 1963–75; *b* 8 Dec. 1915; *s* of late W. P. Fagg and Mrs L. Fagg; *m* 1942, Mary Catherine, *d* of G. W. Davidson; one *s* two *d* (and two *s* decd). *Educ:* Dulwich Coll.; Downing Coll., Cambridge. Nigerian Admin. Service, 1939–47. War service with West African Engineers, East African Campaign, 1939–43. Dept of Antiquities, Republic of Nigeria, 1947–63 (Dir, 1957–63); Lincoln Coll., Oxford, 1964; Fellow of Linacre Coll., 1965–75, Emeritus Fellow, 1976. *Publications:* Nok terracottas, 1977; contribs to learned jls. *Address:* 45 Woodstock Road, Oxford. *T:* 54875. *Club:* Leander.

FAGG, William Buller, CMG 1967; ethnologist, tribal art historian and consultant; Keeper, Ethnography Department (from 1972 the Museum of Mankind), British Museum, 1969–74 (Deputy Keeper, 1955–69); *b* 28 April 1914; *s* of late William Percy Fagg and late Lilian Fagg. *Educ:* Dulwich Coll.; Magdalene Coll., Cambridge. Sir Wm Browne's Medal for Latin Epigram; Montagu Butler Prize for Latin Hexameters; BA Classics, 1936; Archaeology and Anthropology, 1937; MA 1939. Asst Keeper Dept of Ethnography, BM, 1938; seconded to Bd of Trade, Industries and Manufactures Dept, 1940–45. Royal Anthropological Institute: Hon. Sec., 1939–56; Mem. Council, 1966–69, 1972–75, 1976–79; Vice-Pres., 1969–72; Patron's Medal, 1966; Hon. Editor, Man: A Monthly Record of Anthropological Science, 1947–65, Hon. Librarian, 1976–. Chm., UK Cttee for First World Festival of Negro Arts, Dakar, 1966; Trustee: UK African Festival Trust, 1973–77; Chm., African Fine Art Gallery Trust, 1974–; Consulting Fellow in African Art, Museum of Primitive Art, NY, 1957–. Consultant on Tribal Art to Christies, 1974–. Fieldwork: Nigeria and Congo, 1949–50; Nigeria, 1953, 1958–59, 1971, 1974, 1981; Cameroon, 1966; Mali, 1969. Organised and arranged many loan exhibns including: Nigerian Art (Arts Council), London, Manchester, Bristol, 1960, Munich, Basel, 1961; African Art, Berlin Festival, 1964, Musée des Arts Décoratifs, Paris, 1964–65; African Sculpture, Nat. Gall. of Art, Washington, DC, Kansas City Art Gall., and Brooklyn Museum, 1970. FRSA (Silver-Medallist, 1951). Member: Reindeer Council of UK; Royal African Soc.; RIIA; Internat. African Inst.; Museums Assoc.; African Studies Assoc.; China Soc.; ICA; Assoc. of Art Historians. Leadership Award, Arts Council of African Studies Assoc., USA, 1986. *Publications:* The Webster Plass Collection of African Art, British Museum, 1953; (with E. Elisofon) The Sculpture of Africa, 1958; Afro-Portuguese

Ivories, 1959; Nigerian Images, 1963 (awarded P. A. Talbot Prize, 1964, and grand prize for best work on African art at World Festival of Negro Arts, Dakar, 1966); (with Margaret Plass) African Sculpture: An Anthology, 1964; Tribes and Forms in African Art, 1966; African Tribal Sculptures, 2 vols, 1967; Arts of Western Africa, Arts of Central Africa (UNESCO), 1967; African Tribal Images (The Katherine White Reswick Collection of African Art), 1968; African Sculpture (Washington, DC), 1970; Miniature Wood Carvings of Africa, 1970; The Tribal Image: wooden figure sculpture of the world, 1970; African Sculpture from the Tara Collection, 1971; (ed) The Living Arts of Nigeria, 1971; Eskimo Art in the British Museum, 1972, Yoruba Beadwork, 1980; Masques d'Afrique, 1980; African Majesty: from grassland and forest, 1981; Yoruba Sculpture of West Africa, 1982; numerous exhibn catalogues, articles in Man, etc. *Recreations:* photography (esp. of art, incl. ancient churches), listening to music, cycling, travel, geopolitics. *Address:* 6 Galata Road, Barnes, SW13 9NQ. *T:* 01-748 6620. *Club:* Travellers'.

FAGGE, Sir John William Frederick, 11th Bt, *cr* 1660; *b* 28 Sept. 1910; *s* of late William Archibald Theodore Fagge (*b* of 9th Bt) and Nellie (*d* 1924), *d* of H. T. D. Wise; *S* uncle, 1940; *m* 1940, Ivy Gertrude, *d* of William Edward Frier, 15 Church Lane, Newington, Kent; one *s* one *d*. *Heir:* *s* John Christopher Fagge, *b* 30 April 1942. *Address:* 26 The Mall, Faversham, Kent.

FAINT, John Anthony Leonard; UK Alternate Executive Director to International Bank for Reconstruction and Development. Washington, since 1986; *b* 24 Nov. 1942; *s* of Thomas Leonard Faint and Josephine Rosey Faint (*née* Dunkerley); *m* 1978, Elizabeth Theresa Winter. *Educ:* Chigwell Sch.; Magdalen Coll., Oxford (BA LitHum 1965); MA Development Economics, Fletcher Sch., Mass, 1969. Ministry of Overseas Development (later Overseas Development Administration), London, 1965–71 (study leave in Cambridge, Mass, 1968–69); First Secretary (Aid), Blantyre, Malawi, 1971–73; ODM/ODA, London, 1974–80; Head of SE Asia Develt Div., Bangkok, 1980–83; Head of Finance Dept, ODA, FCO, 1983–86. *Recreations:* music, bridge, chess, squash. *Address:* UK Delegation to IMF/IBRD, Washington DC, USA.

FAIR, Donald Robert Russell, OBE (mil.) 1945; Board Member, Central Electricity Generating Board, 1975–77; *b* 26 Dec. 1916; *s* of Robert Sidney Fair and Mary Louie Fair; *m* 1941, Patricia Laurie Rudland; one *s*. *Educ:* Roan Sch., Blackheath; King's Coll., London Univ. (BSc, AKC). CEng, FInstE; CPhys, FInstP. Served War of 1939–45, RAF (Wing Comdr; despatches 1944; USAAF Commendation 1944). Lectr, RMA Sandhurst, 1948–50; UK AEA, 1950–62; Central Electricity Generating Bd, 1962–77. *Recreations:* sailing, cricket. *Address:* Rozelle, St James' Close, Birdham, Chichester, Sussex PO20 7HE. *T:* Birdham 512711. *Club:* Island Sailing.

FAIRBAIRN, Sir Brooke; *see* Fairbairn, Sir J. B.

FAIRBAIRN, David; Metropolitan Stipendiary Magistrate since 1971; Deputy Circuit Judge, since 1972; *b* 9 Aug. 1924; *s* of Ernest Hulford Fairbairn and late Iva May Fairbairn; *m* 1946, Helen Merriel de la Cour Collingwood, *d* of Harold Lewis Collingwood; two *s* two *d*. *Educ:* Haileybury Coll.; Trinity Hall, Cambridge (MA). Served War of 1939–45, Lieut, RNVR, in Mediterranean. Called to Bar, Middle Temple, 1949; Central Criminal Court Bar Mess; South Eastern Circuit; Herts and Essex QS; Dep. Chm., Surrey QS, 1969–71. Liveryman, Gold and Silver Wyre Drawers' Company, 1957–. *Recreations:* golf, tennis, country life. *Address:* Wollards Farm, Mayes Green, Ockley, Dorking, Surrey.

FAIRBAIRN, Hon. Sir David Eric, KBE 1977; DFC 1944; Australian Ambassador to the Netherlands, 1977–80; *b* 3 March 1917; *s* of Clive Prell Fairbairn and Marjorie Rose (*née* Jowett); *m* 1945, Ruth Antill (*née* Robertson); three *d*. *Educ:* Geelong Grammar Sch.; Cambridge Univ. (MA). MP (L) Commonwealth of Australia, 1949–75; Minister: for Air, 1962–64; for Nat. Develt, 1964–69; for Educn and Science, March–Aug. 1971; for Defence, 1971–72. *Recreations:* golf, tennis. *Address:* 86 Dominion Circuit, Deakin, ACT 2600, Australia. *T:* 733245. *Clubs:* Leander (Henley); Hawks (Cambridge); Melbourne (Melbourne); Commonwealth (Canberra); Albury (Albury).

FAIRBAIRN, David Ritchie; Managing Director, James Martin Associates UK Ltd; Director, British Standards Institution, since 1986; *b* 4 July 1934; *s* of G. F. Fairbairn; *m* 1958, Hon. Susan Hill, *d* of Baron Hill of Luton, *qv*; one *s* two *d*. *Educ:* Mill Hill Sch.; Gonville and Caius Coll., Cambridge (BAEcon). FBCS; FIDPM, FInstD. President, Cambridge Union Soc. Overseas Marketing Manager, Arthur Guinness Son & Co. Ltd, 1960; President, Guinness-Harp Corp., New York, 1964; Marketing Dir, Guinness Overseas Ltd, 1969; Man. Dir, Dataset Ltd (ICL), 1970; Manager, Retail and Distribution Sector, International Computers Ltd, 1975; Dir of Marketing, EMI Medical Ltd, 1976; Dir, Nat. Computing Centre, 1980–86. Pres., Inst. of Data Processing Management, 1982– (Vice-Pres., 1980–82). Vice-Chm., Parly IT Cttee, 1982. Member, Monopolies and Mergers Commn, 1985–. *Recreations:* sailing, water-skiing. *Address:* 11 Oak Way, West Common, Harpenden, Herts AL5 2RU. *T:* Harpenden 5820.

FAIRBAIRN, Douglas Chisholm, CIE 1945; CBE 1956; MA; retired; formerly Director, Thomas Hamling & Co. Ltd, St Andrew's Dock, Hull; *b* 1904; *s* of late Rev. R. T. and Mrs Fairbairn; *m* 1938, Agnes, *d* of late Rev. William amd Mrs Arnott; two *s*. *Educ:* George Heriot's, Edinburgh; Edinburgh Univ. (MA). Formerly: Secretary Bengal Chamber of Commerce and Industry, Calcutta, 1938–56, also in that capacity Sec. Associated Chambers of Commerce of India; Chm., Hull Fishing Vessel Owners and Hull Fishing Industry Associations, 1957–62. JP, City and County of Kingston-upon-Hull, 1966–71. *Recreation:* gardening. *Address:* Vikings, 29 Hampden Hill, Beaconsfield, Bucks HP9 1BP. *T:* Beaconsfield 4670.

FAIRBAIRN, Douglas Foakes, CBE 1971; Chairman, Springwood Cellulose Company Ltd, since 1983; Director, Town and Commercial Property Services Ltd, since 1986; *b* 9 Oct. 1919; *s* of William and Florence Fairbairn; *m* 1947, Gertrude Betty Buswell; two *s*. *Educ:* John Lyon Sch., Harrow; Royal School of Mines, Imperial Coll., London Univ. BSc (Hons), ARSM. Served War, RAF (Sqdn Ldr), 1940–46. Commonwealth Development Corp., 1949–; Regional Controller: Central Africa, 1959–66; West Africa, 1966–71. Dir, Bank of Rhodesia and Nyasaland, 1961–63; Chm., Central African Airways, 1964–68; Mem., Central African Power Corp., 1961–77; Co-ordinator of Operations, Commonwealth Develt Corp., 1971–83. *Recreation:* golf. *Address:* 11 Portland Terrace, The Green, Richmond, Surrey TW9 1QQ. *T:* 01-948 1921. *Club:* Richmond Golf.

FAIRBAIRN, Sir (James) Brooke, 6th Bt *cr* 1869, of Ardwick; *b* 10 Dec. 1930; *s* of Sir William Albert Fairbairn, 5th Bt, and of Christine Renée Cotton, *d* of late Rev. Canon Robert William Croft; *S* father, 1972; *m* 1960, Mary Russell, *d* of late William Russell Scott, MB, ChB, FFARCS; two *s* one *d*. *Educ:* Stowe. Proprietor of J. Brooke Fairbairn & Co., textile converters and wholesalers dealing in furnishing fabrics. *Heir:* *s* Robert William Fairbairn, *b* 10 April 1965. *Address:* Barkway House, Bury Road, Newmarket, Suffolk CB8 7BT. *T:* Newmarket 662733; J. Brooke Fairbairn & Co., The Railway Station, Newmarket CB8 9BA. *T:* Newmarket 665766. *Club:* City Livery.

FAIRBAIRN of Fordell, Nicholas Hardwick, QC(Scot.) 1972; MP (C) Perth and Kinross, since 1983 (Kinross and Perthshire West, Oct. 1974–1983); Baron of Fordell; *b* 24 Dec. 1933; *s* of William Ronald Dodds Fairbairn, DPsych, and Mary Ann More-Gordon of Charleton and Kinnaber; *m* 1st, 1962, Hon. Elizabeth Mary Mackay (marr. diss. 1979), *e d* of 13th Baron Reay; three *d* (and one *s* one *d* decd); 2nd, 1983, Suzanne Mary Wheeler. *Educ:* Loretto; Edinburgh Univ.; MA, LLB. Author, farmer, painter, poet, TV and radio broadcaster, journalist, dress-designer, landscape gardener, bon viveur and wit. Called to Scots Bar 1957. Cons. Candidate, Central Edinburgh, 1964, 1966. HM Solicitor Gen. for Scotland, 1979–82. Comr of Northern Lighthouses, 1979–82. Mem., Council of World Population Crisis, 1968–70. Founder and Hon. Pres., Soc. for Preservation of Duddingston Village; Mem., Edinburgh Festival Council, 1971–. Chairman: Traverse Theatre, 1964–72; Edinburgh Brook Adv. Centre, 1968–75; Waverley Broadcasting Co., 1973–74; Dir, Ledlanet Nights, 1960–73. Chm., Scottish Soc. for Defence of Literature and the Arts. Pres., Dysart and Dundonald Pipe Band. Private exhibns throughout Britain since 1960, and in public exhibns. KLJ; KStJ; FSAScot. Hon. Fellow, Internat. Acad. of Trial Lawyers, 1984. *Publication:* contrib., Alistair Maclean Introduces Scotland, 1972. *Recreations:* serving queens, restoring castles, debunking bishops, entertaining knights, befriending pawns. *Address:* Fordell Castle, By Dunfermline, Fife. *Clubs:* Puffins, Beefsteak, Chatham Dining; New (Edinburgh).

FAIRBAIRN, Sir Robert, Kt 1975; JP; Chairman, Clydesdale Bank plc, 1975–85 (Director, 1967–85; General Manager, 1958–71; Vice-Chairman, 1971–75); *b* 25 Sept. 1910; *s* of late Robert Fairbairn and Christina Fairbairn; *m* 1939, Sylvia Lucinda, *d* of late Rev. Henry Coulter; two *s* one *d*. *Educ:* Perth Academy. Joined service of The Clydesdale Bank at Perth, 1927; Beckett & Whitehead Prizeman, Inst. of Bankers, 1934; Midland Bank, 1934. Lt-Comdr (S) RNVR, 1939–46. Asst Gen. Manager, Clydesdale & North of Scotland Bank, 1951. Chm., Clydesdale Bank Industrial Finance Ltd, 1981–85; Director: Commercial Union Assurance Group (Local Board), 1958–85; Midland Bank Finance Corp. Ltd, 1967–74; Clydesdale Bank Finance Corp. Ltd, 1967–85; Clydesdale Bank Insurance Services Ltd, 1970–85; Newarthill Ltd; Midland Bank Ltd, 1975–85; Chairman: Scottish Computer Services Ltd, 1971–85; Scottish Amicable Life Assce Soc., 1976–78 (Dir to 1981); A Dir, British Nat. Oil Corp., 1976–79. Glasgow Chamber of Commerce (Vice-Pres., 1970–76). Pres., Inst. of Bankers in Scotland, 1961–63; Vice-Pres., Scottish Economic Soc. (Pres. 1966–69); Chairman: Scottish Industrial Develt Advisory Bd, 1972–81; Cttee of Scottish Bank General Managers, 1963–66; Vice-Chm., Inst. of Fiscal Studies (Scotland), 1976–85; Vice-Pres., British Bankers Assoc., 1966–68; Member: Scottish Council (Develt and Industry), Vice-Pres., 1967–68; Scottish Council of CBI. Chm., Cystic Fibrosis Research Investment Trust plc, 1981–85. FIB, FIB (Scot); FRSA; CBIM; Hon. FSIAD. JP Glasgow, 1962. *Recreations:* golf, fishing. *Address:* The Grange, Hazelwood Road, Bridge of Weir, Renfrewshire. *T:* Bridge of Weir 2102. *Clubs:* Caledonian, MCC; Western (Glasgow); Corinthian Casuals; Royal and Ancient (St Andrews).

FAIRBANKS, Douglas (Elton), (Jr), KBE 1949; DSC 1944; Captain, USNR, retired; actor, writer, producer, company director; Chairman, Fairtel, Inc. (US), since 1946; formerly Chairman, Douglas Fairbanks Ltd; Director or Special Consultant: Fairbanks Co. Inc.; Norlantic Development; Boltons Trading; Alcoa Inc.; Dougfair Corp. (US); Scripto Pens Ltd (US and UK), 1952–73; Golden Cycle and subsidiaries, 1965–73; Rambagh Palace Hotel, Ltd (Jaipur, India); Cavalcade Film Co. Ltd (UK), etc; *b* New York City, 9 Dec. 1909; *s* of Douglas Elton Fairbanks, Denver, Colorado, and Anna Beth Sully, Providence, RI; *m* 1st, 1929, Lucille Le Sueur (Joan Crawford) (marr. diss. 1933); 2nd, 1939, Mary Lee Epling, Keystone, W Virginia; three *d*. *Educ:* Bovée Sch., Knickerbocker Greys, Collegiate Mil. Sch., NY; Pasadena Polytechnic, Harvard Mil. Sch., Los Angeles; tutored privately in London and Paris. Began career as film actor, 1923, on stage 1927. Organised own producing company, UK, 1935. Studied painting and sculpture, Paris, 1922–24; began writing, professionally, 1928; articles, fiction and essays on public affairs, etc., 1936–. Vice-Pres. Franco-British War Relief and National Vice-Pres. Cttee "Defend America by Aiding the Allies", 1939–40; Presidential Envoy, Special Mission to Latin America, 1940–41; one-time Consultant to Office of the Presidency (Washington, DC); Lieut (jg), USNR, 1941; promoted through grades to Capt., 1954. National Chm., CARE Cttee, 1947–50; Nat. Vice-Pres. Amer. Assoc. for the UN, 1946–60; Pres. Brit.-Amer. Alumni Assoc. 1950; Bd Gov., English-Speaking Union of the US, 1949–60; Nat. Chm., Amer. Relief for Korea, 1950–54; Trustee, Edwina Mountbatten Trust; Mem., Bd of Dirs, Mountbatten Meml Trust (US); Mem. Bd of Dirs, Amer. Friends of RSC and RSC Trust; Dir, Shakespeare Globe Theater; Mem. Council, American Museum in Brit.; a Governor and Exec. Cllr, Royal Shakespeare Theatre; United World Colleges, 1951–; Governor, Ditchley Foundations; Co-Chm., US Capitol Bicentenary 1776–1976; Guild of St Bride's Church, Fleet Street, EC; Mem., Counoil on Foreign Relations (NY); US Naval Mem., US Mil. Delegn, SEATO Conf., 1971; Mem., Bd of Dirs, Pilgrims Soc. of US, 1985–; Vis. Fellow, St Cross Coll., Oxford; MA Oxon; Senior Churchill Fellow, Westminster Coll., Fulton, Mo; Hon. DFA Westminster Coll., Fulton, Mo, USA; Hon. LLD Univ. of Denver, Colo; Silver Star Medal (US); Legion of Merit ("Valor" clasp) (US), Special Naval Commendation (US), KJStJ 1950 (Hon. Dep. Chancellor, Amer. Friends, Order of St John), etc; Officer Legion of Honour (Fr.), Croix de Guerre with Palm (Fr.); Knight Comdr Order of George I (Greece); Knight Grand Officer, Order del Merito (Chile); Grand Officer, Order of Merit (Italy); Comdr Order of Orange Nassau (Neth.); Officer of: Orders of Crown (Belg.), of Star of Italy, Cross of Mil. Valour (Italy), Southern Cross (Brazil); Grand Comdr Order of Merit (West Germany); Hon. Citizen and National Medal of Korea, etc. *Films include:* Stella Dallas; Little Caesar; Outward Bound; Morning Glory; Catherine the Great; The Amateur Gentleman; The Prisoner of Zenda; Gunga Din; The Corsican Brothers; Sinbad the Sailor; The Exile; The Fighting O'Flynn; State Secret; The Young in Heart; Having Wonderful Time; The Rage of Paris; The Joy of Living; L'Athlète Malgré Lui (French); A Woman of Affairs; Lady in Ermine; Stephen Steps Out; The Barker; Chances; The Life of Jimmy Dolan; Mimi; Angels Over Broadway. *Plays include:* Young Woodley; Romeo and Juliet; The Jest; Man in Possession; The Winding Journey; Moonlight is Silver; My Fair Lady; The Pleasure of his Company; The Secretary Bird; Present Laughter; Sleuth; The Youngest; The Dummy; Towards the Light; produced over 160 TV plays, acted in over 50; also recordings etc. *Publications:* short stories, poems, articles, to periodicals. *Relevant publications:* Knight Errant, by Brian Connell; The Fairbanks Album, by Richard Schickel; The Fourth Musketeer, by Letitia Fairbanks-Milner. *Recreations:* swimming, tennis, golf, travel. *Address:* The Beekman, 575 Park Avenue, New York, NY 10021, USA; The Vicarage, 448 North Lake Way, Palm Beach, Florida 33480, USA; (office) Inverness Corporation, 545 Madison Avenue, New York, NY 10022, USA. *Clubs:* White's, Naval and Military, Garrick, Beefsteak; Puffin's (Edinburgh); Brook, Knickerbocker, Century (NY); Metropolitan (Washington, DC); Raquet (Chicago); Myopia Hunt (Hamilton, Mass) (Hon. Mem.).

FAIRCLOUGH, Anthony John; Acting Director-General for the Environment, Consumer Protection and Nuclear Safety, Commission of the European Communities, since 1985; *b* 30 Aug. 1924; *m* 1957, Patricia Monks; two *s*. *Educ:* St Philip's Grammar Sch., Birmingham; St Catharine's Coll., Cambridge. Scholar 1944, BA Cantab 1945, MA

1950. Ministry of Aircraft Production and Ministry of Supply, 1944–48; Colonial Office, 1948; Secretary, Nyasaland Commn of Inquiry, 1959; Private Secretary to Minister of State for Commonwealth Relations and for the Colonies, 1963–64; Assistant Secretary, 1964; Head of Pacific and Indian Ocean Dept, Commonwealth Office (formerly Colonial Office), 1964–68; Head of W Indian Dept, FCO, 1968–70; Head of New Towns 1 Div., DoE, 1970–72; Under-Sec., 1973; Head of Planning, Minerals and Countryside Directorate, 1973, of Planning, Sport and Countryside Directorate, 1973–74; Dir, Central Unit on Environmental Pollution, 1974–78; Dir, Internat. Transport, Dept of Transport, 1978–81; Dir for the Environment, EEC, 1981–85. Senior UK Commissioner at Sessions of South Pacific Commn, 1965–67; Minister's Deputy, European Conf. of Mins of Transport, 1978–81; Chm., Environment Cttee, OECD, 1976–79; British Channel Tunnel Co., 1978–81; British Co-Chm., Jt UK/USSR Cttee established under UK/USSR Agreement on cooperation in field of Environmental Protection, 1974–78; Member: Royal Soc.'s British Nat. Cttee on Problems of Environment, 1974–78; EDC for Internat. Freight Movement, 1978–80; Governing Body, Chiswick Sch., 1973–79. FRSA. *Address:* 6 Cumberland Road, Kew, Richmond, Surrey TW9 3HQ; 12 Résidence Balderic, 32 Quai aux Briques, 1000 Brussels, Belgium. *Club:* Civil Service.

FAIRCLOUGH, Hon. Ellen Louks, OC 1979; PC (Can.) 1957; FCA 1965; Chairman, Hamilton Hydro Electric Commission, since 1978; Member of Progressive Conservative Party, Canada; *b* Hamilton, Ont, 28 Jan. 1905; *d* of Norman Ellsworth Cook and Nellie Bell Louks; *m* 1931, David Henry Gordon Fairclough; one *s*. *Educ:* Hamilton Public and Secondary Schs. Certified Public Accountant, public practice, 1935–57. Hamilton City Council, Alderman, 1946–49; Controller, 1950. Elected to House of Commons as Progressive Conservative mem. for Hamilton West, 1950; re-elected at gen. elections, 1953, 1957, 1958, 1962, defeated in 1963 election. Sec. of State for Canada, 1957–58; Minister of Citizenship and Immigration, 1958–62; Postmaster-Gen., 1962–63. Patron, Huguenot Soc. of Canada, 1969–; Chancellor, Royal Hamilton College of Music, 1978–80. Mem. Bd, Ontario Bicentennial Commn, 1983–84; Hon. Treas. and Exec. Dir, Chedoke-McMaster Hosps Foundn, 1982–; Patron, United Empire Loyalists Assoc., Hamilton Br., 1980–. Ontario Govt Bldg named Ellen Fairclough Bldg, 1982. LLD (*hc*), McMaster Univ., 1975. *Recreations:* music, reading and photography. *Address:* 25 Stanley Avenue, Hamilton, Ont, Canada. *T:* Hamilton 522–5248.

FAIRCLOUGH, John Whitaker, CEng, FIEE, FBCS; Chief Scientific Adviser to Cabinet Office, since 1986; *b* 23 Aug. 1930; *m* Margaret Ann; two *s* one *d*. *Educ:* Manchester Univ. (BScTech). Ferranti, 1954; IBM: Poughkeepsie Lab., US, 1957; Hursley Lab., UK, 1958; Director of Development, IBM UK Ltd, 1964; Asst Gen. Manager and Dir Data Processing IBM UK, 1968; Dir, Raleigh Development Lab., USA, 1970; System Develt Div. Vice Pres., Raleigh, USA, 1972; System Communication Div. Vice Pres. and Man. Dir, Director of Development, Hursley Lab., UK, 1974; System Product Div. Vice Pres. and Man. Dir, Hursley Lab., UK, 1982; Dir of Manufacturing & Development, IBM UK Ltd, and Chm, IBM UK Laboratories Ltd, 1983. Mem., Engineering Council, 1982–. Hon. DSc Southampton, 1983. *Recreations:* gardening, carpentry. *Address:* The Old Blue Boar, St John's Street, Winchester, Hants.

FAIRCLOUGH, Wilfred, RE; RWS; ARCA (London); Assistant Director, Kingston Polytechnic, and Head of the Division of Design, 1970–72, retired; Principal of Kingston College of Art, Surrey, 1962–70; *b* 13 June 1907; *s* of Herbert Fairclough and Edith Amy Milton; *m* 1936, Joan Cryer; one *s* one *d*. *Educ:* Royal College of Art, London, 1931–34 (Diploma 1933); British Sch. at Rome, Italy, 1934–37; Rome Scholar in Engraving, 1934–37. Army and Royal Air Force, 1942–46. Rome Scholarships, Faculty of Engraving, 1951 (Chm., 1964–73); Leverhulme Research Award, 1961. RE 1946 (ARE 1934); RWS 1968 (ARWS 1961). Chairman: Assoc. of Art Instns, 1965–66; Assessors, Vocational Courses of Surrey CC. *Work in public and private collections: paintings:* Min. of Supply; Min. of Works; Surrey CC; Scottish Modern Art Assoc.; Beaumont Coll.; *drawings:* British Museum; V&A Museum; Arts Council; Contemporary Art Soc.; Wye Coll., London Univ.; English Electric Co.; Art Galls at Blackburn, Kingston-upon-Thames, Worthing; Graves Art Gall., Sheffield; Atkinson Art Gall., Southport; *prints:* British Museum, V&A Museum; Ashmolean Museum, Oxford; Contemporary Art Soc.; British Sch. at Rome; South London Art Gall.; Stoke Educn Authority; Wye Coll., London Univ.; Gottenburg Museum; Print Collectors Club. *Publications:* work reproduced: Recording Britain; Londoners' England; Royal Academy Illustrated; Studio; Fine Prints of the Year; Print Collectors Quarterly; illustrated article, Leisure Painter, 1969; paintings, drawings and prints. *Address:* 12 Manorgate Road, Kingston-upon-Thames, Surrey.

FAIREY, Michael John; Director of Planning and Information, National Health Service Management Board, Department of Health and Social Security, since 1984; *b* 20 Sept. 1933; *s* of late Ernest John Saunder Fairey and Lily Emily (*née* Pateman); *m* 1958, Audrey Edwina Kermode; two *s* one *d*. *Educ:* Queen Elizabeth's Sch., Barnet; Jesus Coll., Cambridge (MA). Deputy House Governor, The London Hosp., 1962, House Governor 1972; Regional Administrator, NE Thames RHA, 1973. *Publications:* various articles in med. and computing jls. *Recreations:* church music, history of medieval exploration, Rugby football. *Address:* 42B Oakleigh Park South, N20 9JN. *Club:* Athenæum.

FAIRFAX, family name of **Lord Fairfax of Cameron.**

FAIRFAX OF CAMERON, 14th Lord *cr* 1627; **Nicholas John Albert Fairfax;** *b* 4 Jan. 1956; *e s* of 13th Lord and of Sonia, *yr d* of late Capt. Cecil Gunston, MC; *S* father, 1964; *m* 1982, Annabel, *er d* of late Nicholas and of Sarah Gilham Morriss; two *s*. *Educ:* Eton; Downing Coll., Cambridge (LLB in international law subjects, 1981). Called to the Bar, Gray's Inn, 1977. *Recreations:* watersports, skiing, tennis. *Heir:* *s* Hon. Edward Nicholas Thomas Fairfax, b 20 Sept. 1984. *Address:* 6 Crescent Grove, SW4. *T:* 01–622 1650. *Club:* Queen's.

FAIRFAX, Sir Vincent Charles, Kt 1971; CMG 1960; Company Director and Pastoralist, Australia; *b* 26 Dec. 1909; *s* of late J. H. F. Fairfax; *m* 1939, Nancy, *d* late Dr C. B. Heald, CBE, FRCP; two *s* two *d*. *Educ:* Geelong Church of England Grammar Sch., Australia; Brasenose Coll., Oxford Univ. (BA). Staff, John Fairfax & Sons Pty Ltd, 1933; Advertising Manager, 1937–38. Major, Australian Imperial Forces, 1940–46. Director: John Fairfax & Sons Pty Ltd, 1946–53; John Fairfax Ltd (Publishers, Sydney Morning Herald), 1956; Chm. Australian Sectn, Commonwealth Press Union, 1950–73; Chm., Stanbroke Pastoral Co. Pty Ltd, 1964–82; Director: Bank of NSW, 1953–82; Australian Mutual Provident Soc., 1956–82 (Chm. 1966–82); Chief Comr Scout Assoc., for NSW, 1958–68, for Australia, 1969–73; Pres., Nat. Council, Scout Assoc. of Australia, 1977; Dep. Pres., Royal Agric. Society of Commonwealth, 1966; Mem. C of E Property Trust, 1950–71; Trustee, Walter and Eliza Hall Trust, 1953–; Mem. Council: Art Gall. Soc. of NSW, 1953–69; Royal Flying Doctor Service, 1954–71; Royal Agric. Society of NSW, 1956 (Pres., 1970–79, Vice-Patron, 1979); Mem., Glebe Administration Bd, 1962–73; Rector's Warden, St Mark's, Darling Point, 1948–71. *Recreations:* tennis, golf, trout fishing. *Address:* Elaine, 550 New South Head Road, Double Bay, Sydney, NSW 2000, Australia. *T:* 327. 1416. *Clubs:* Leander; Commonwealth (Canberra); Melbourne (Melbourne); Union, Royal Sydney Golf (Sydney); Queensland (Brisbane).

FAIRFAX, Sir Warwick (Oswald), Kt 1967; MA; Director: John Fairfax & Sons Ltd (The Sydney Morning Herald, The Sun Herald, The Sun, The Australian Financial Review, The National Times, and other publications); Vice President, Australian Elizabethan Theatre Trust; owns Harrington Park; *b* 1901; *o s* of Sir James Oswald Fairfax, a Proprietor and Dir of John Fairfax and Sons, Ltd, and Mabel, *d* of Capt. Francis Hixson, RN; *m* 1928, Marcie Elizabeth, *o d* of David Wilson, Barrister of Sydney; one *s* one *d*; *m* 1948, Hanné Anderson, 2nd *d* of Emil Bendixsen, Copenhagen; one *d*; *m* 1959, Mary, *o d* of Kevin Wein; one *s*. *Educ:* Geelong Grammar Sch., St Paul's Coll., Sydney Univ.; Balliol Coll., Oxford. 2nd Class Hons in Sch. of Philosophy, Politics and Economics; joined staff of John Fairfax and Sons, Ltd, 1925; Dir, 1927; Managing Dir 1930; Cttee of One with admin. and management powers, 1970–76; Chairman of Dirs, 1956–76. Plays: A Victorian Marriage, Vintage for Heroes, The Bishop's Wife, performed Sydney, 1951, 1952, 1956. *Publications:* Men, Parties, and Policies, 1943; The Triple Abyss: towards a modern synthesis, 1965; ed, A Century of Journalism (The Sydney Morning Herald), 1931. *Recreations:* the arts, philosophy, motoring and vintage cars. *Address:* John Fairfax & Sons Ltd, Box 506, GPO Sydney, Australia; Fairwater, 560 New South Head Road, Double Bay, Sydney, NSW 2028, Australia; Harrington Park, Narellan, NSW 2567. *Clubs:* Carlton, Oriental, Australian, Union, Pioneers, Royal Sydney Yacht Squadron (Sydney).

FAIRFAX-LUCY, Sir Edmund (John William Hugh Cameron-Ramsay-), 6th Bt *cr* 1836; painter; *b* 4 May 1945; *s* of Sir Brian Fulke Cameron-Ramsay-Fairfax-Lucy, 5th Bt and of Hon. Alice Caroline Helen Buchan, *o d* of 1st Baron Tweedsmuir, PC, GCMG, GCVO, CH; *S* father, 1974; *m* 1986, Lady Lucinda, *d* of Viscount Lambton, *qv*. *Educ:* City and Guilds of London Art Sch.; Royal Academy Schs of Art. *Heir:* *cousin* Duncan Cameron Cameron-Ramsay-Fairfax-Lucy, FCA [*b* 18 Sept. 1932; *m* 1964, Janet Barclay, *o d* of P. A. B. Niven; one *s* one *d*]. *Address:* Charlecote Park, Warwick.

FAIRGRIEVE, Sir (Thomas) Russell, Kt 1981; CBE 1974; TD 1959; JP; Director: William Baird and Co. PLC, 1975–79, and since 1982; Hall Advertising Ltd, since 1982; *b* 3 May 1924; *s* of late Alexander Fairgrieve, OBE, MC, JP, and Myma Margaret Fairgrieve; *m* 1954, Millie Mitchell; one *s* three *d*. *Educ:* St Mary's Sch., Melrose; Sedbergh School. Major 8th Gurkha Rifles (Indian Army), 1946. Major, KOSB, 1956. Man. Dir, Laidlaw & Fairgrieve Ltd, 1958; Dir, Joseph Dawson (Holdings) Ltd, 1961. Selkirk County and Galashiels Town Councillor, 1949; Pres., Scottish Conservative Assoc., 1965, Vice-Chm., 1971; Chm., Conservative Party in Scotland, 1975–80. MP (C) Aberdeenshire West, Feb. 1974–83; Parly Under Sec. of State, Scottish Office, 1979–81. JP Selkirkshire, 1962. *Recreation:* golf. *Address:* Pankalan, Boleside, Galashiels, Selkirk TD1 3NX. *T:* Galashiels 2278. *Clubs:* Carlton; New (Edinburgh); Royal and Ancient (St Andrews).

FAIRHALL, Hon. Sir Allen, KBE 1970; FRSA; Member, House of Representatives, 1949–69; *b* 24 Nov. 1909; *s* of Charles Edward and Maude Fairhall; *m* 1936, Monica Clelland, *d* of James and Ellen Ballantyne; one *s*. *Educ:* East Maitland Primary and High Sch.; Newcastle Tech. Inst. Founded commercial broadcasting stn 2KO, 1931; Supervising Engr, Radio and Signals Supplies Div., Min. of Munitions, 1942–45; Pres., Austr. Fedn of Commercial Broadcasting Stns, 1942–43. Mem. Australian Delegn to UN Gen. Assembly, 1954; Minister for Interior and Works, 1956–58; Minister for Supply, 1961–66; Minister for Defence, 1966–69. Mem. Newcastle CC, 1941. Hon. DSc Univ. of Newcastle, 1968. *Recreations:* amateur radio; deep sea fishing. *Address:* 7 Parkway Avenue, Newcastle, NSW 2300, Australia. *T:* 2.2295. *Clubs:* Tattersall's, National (Sydney); Newcastle (Newcastle).

FAIRHAVEN, 3rd Baron *cr* 1929 and 1961 (new creation); **Ailwyn Henry George Broughton;** JP; Vice Lord-Lieutenant, Cambridgeshire, 1977–85; *b* 16 Nov. 1936; *s* of 2nd Baron Fairhaven and Hon. Diana Rosamond (*d* 1937), *o d* of late Captain Hon. Coulson Fellowes; *S* father, 1973; *m* 1960, Kathleen Patricia, *d* of Col James Henry Magill, OBE; four *s* two *d*. *Educ:* Eton; RMA, Sandhurst. Royal Horse Guards, 1957–71. Mem., Jockey Club, 1977– (Steward, 1981–82, Sen. Steward, 1985–). DL Cambridgeshire and Isle of Ely, 1973; JP South Cambridgeshire, 1975. CStJ 1983. *Recreations:* shooting, cooking. *Heir:* *s* Hon. James Henry Ailwyn Broughton, *b* 25 May 1963. *Address:* Anglesey Abbey, Cambridge. *T:* Cambridge 811746. *Club:* Turf.

FAIRLEY, Alan Brand; Deputy Chairman of Grand Metropolitan Hotels Ltd, 1970–73; First President of Mecca Ltd since 1972; *b* Edinburgh, *s* of James Fairley and Jane Alexander; *m* 1942, Roma Josephine Haddow; one *d*. *Educ:* George Watson's Coll., Edinburgh. Joined family catering business (Fairleys of Edinburgh) from college, 1919; opened Dunedin dance hall where broadcast bands and cabaret artists, 1923; opened Piccadilly Club (first night club in Glasgow), internat. stars and bands, 1926; formed a number of Scottish cos to run dance halls, 1934–37; partnership with Carl Heimann to run dance halls all over UK, 1936 (until his death, 1968). Served War of 1939–45, Army Catering Corps, 1940–45, Major. Acquired lease of Café de Paris, London, 1943, and re-opened it, 1948, presenting Noel Coward, Marlene Dietrich, Maurice Chevalier and many others. Created Mecca Ltd, now notable for its promotion of Miss World, TV Come Dancing and Carl-Alan award for outstanding contributions to ballroom dancing, after the Christian names of its founders; Jt Chm. with Carl Heimann, Mecca Ltd, 1952, Chm. Mecca Ltd 1968; Mecca Ltd merged with Grand Metropolitan Hotels Ltd, 1970. Member: Variety Club of Great Britain and Réunion des Gastronômes (both in London). *Recreations:* swimming, golf. *Address:* 5 Mount Rule House, Braddan, Isle of Man. *T:* Marown 852702. *Club:* Saints and Sinners.

FAIRLEY, Prof. Barker, OC 1979; MA Leeds, PhD Jena; Hon. LittD: Leeds; Waterloo (Canada); Toronto; Carleton; York (Canada); Western; Hon. LLD Alberta; RCA 1980; FRSC; Emeritus Professor of German in University College, University of Toronto; *b* Barnsley, Yorks, 21 May 1887; *s* of Barker and Charlotte Fairley; *m* 1914, Margaret Adele Keeling (*d* 1968), Bradford, Yorks; one *d*. *Educ:* Universities of Leeds and Jena. Lektor in English at University of Jena, 1907–10; Lecturer in German at University of Alberta, 1910; Henry Simon Prof. of German Language and Literature, Manchester Univ., 1932–36. Corresp. Fellow, British Acad., 1971. *Publications:* Charles M. Doughty, 1927; Goethe as revealed in his Poetry, 1932; A Study of Goethe, 1947; Goethe's Faust, 1953; Heinrich Heine, An Interpretation, 1954; Wilhelm Raabe, an Introduction to his Novels, 1961; (trans.) Goethe, Faust, 1970; Poems of 1922, 1972. *Address:* 90 Willcocks Street, Toronto, Canada. *Club:* Arts and Letters (Toronto).

FAIRLIE, Professor Alison (Anna Bowie), FBA 1984; Emeritus Professor of French, University of Cambridge, since 1980 (Professor, 1972–80), and Professorial Fellow, Girton College, since 1972; *b* 23 May 1917; *e d* of Rev. Robert Paul Fairlie, MA, Minister of the Church of Scotland, and of Florence A. A. Wilson. *Educ:* Ardrossan Acad.; Dumfries Acad.; Penrhos Coll.; St Hugh's Coll. Oxford; Sorbonne. BA 1st Cl. in Final Hons Sch. of Medieval and Mod. Langs, Oxon; MA, DPhil (Oxon). Doctoral Research: in Paris, 1938–40 (interruptions for voluntary war-work); in Oxford, 1940–42; Temp. Admin. Officer, Foreign Office, 1942–44; Lectr in French, Girton Coll., 1944–67; Staff Fellow and Dir of Studies in Mod. Langs, Girton Coll., 1946–67; Univ. Lectr in French, Cambridge, 1948–67, Reader in French, 1967–72. Vice-Pres., Soc. for French Studies,

1965–66 and 1968–69, Pres., 1966–68; Mem. Council, 1969–, Vice Pres., 1983–, Assoc. Internationale des Etudes françaises; Member: Editorial Bd, French Studies, 1972–80, Adv. Bd 1980–; Adv. Bd, Romance Studies, 1982–. Hon. Fellow, St Hugh's Coll., Oxford, 1972. *Publications*: Leconte de Lisle's Poems on the Barbarian Races, 1947; Baudelaire: Les Fleurs du Mal, 1960 (repr. 1975); Flaubert: Madame Bovary, 1962 (repr. 1976); Imagination and Language, 1981; (ed jtly) Baudelaire, Mallarmé, Valéry—New Essays in honour of Lloyd Austin, 1982; contrib.: to Acta of colloquia, on Baudelaire, Constant, Flaubert, Nerval, etc.; to presentation vols; to learned jls in France, England, Italy, USA, Australia, etc. *Recreations*: reading, travel. *Address*: 11 Parker Street, Cambridge CB1 1JL. *T*: Cambridge 358465.

FAIRLIE, Hugh, OBE 1984; MA, MEd; *b* 14 Dec. 1919; *s* of Thomas and Joanna Fairlie; *m* 1947, Jemima Peden; two *s*. *Educ*: Univ. of Edinburgh. MA (Hons Maths and NatPhil); MEd (Dist.). FEIS. Teacher, Maybole Carrick Academy, 1947–49; Asst Director of Education: Morayshire, 1949–52; Fife, 1952–57; Depute Dir of Educn, 1957–64, Dir of Educn, 1964–75, Renfrewshire; Lectr, Jordanhill Coll. of Educn, 1975–82. Chairman: Scottish Council for Research in Education, 1978–84; Renfrew District Arts Guild, 1980–. FEIS 1975. *Recreations*: golf, gardens. *Address*: 26 Thornly Park Avenue, Paisley, Scotland PA2 7SE. *T*: 041–884 2494. *Clubs*: Royal Over-Seas League; Paisley Burns; Western Gailes Golf.

FAIRLIE-CUNINGHAME, Sir William Henry, 16th Bt *cr* 1630, of Robertland, Ayrshire; *b* 1 Oct. 1930; *s* of Sir William Alan Fairlie-Cuninghame, 15th Bt, MC, and Irene Alice (*d* 1970), *d* of Henry Margrave Terry; *S* father, 1981; *m* 1972, Janet Menzies, *d* of late Roy Menzies Saddington; one *s*. *Heir*: *s* Robert Henry Fairlie-Cuninghame, *b* 19 July 1974. *Address*: 29A Orinoco Street, Pymble, NSW 2073, Australia.

FAIRTLOUGH, Gerard Howard; Chief Executive, Celltech Ltd, since 1980; *b* 5 Sept. 1930; *s* of Maj.-Gen. Eric V.H.Fairtlough, DSO, MC, and A. Zoë Fairtlough (*née* Barker); *m* 1954, Elizabeth A. Betambeau; two *s* two *d*. *Educ*: Cambridge Univ. (BA Biochemistry, Pt II). Royal/Dutch Shell Group, 1953–78; Managing Director, Shell Chemicals UK Ltd, 1973–78. Divisional Director, NEB, 1978–80. *Recreations*: walking, Yoga. *Address*: 5 Belmont Grove, SE13 5DW. *T*: 01–852 4904.

FAIRWEATHER, Brig. Claude Cyril, CB 1967; CBE 1965 (OBE 1944); TD 1944; JP; Vice Lord-Lieutenant, County of Cleveland, 1977–82; Chairman, North of England TA&VRA, 1968–71; *b* 17 March 1906; *s* of Nicholas Fairweather, Middlesborough; *m* 1930, Alice Mary, *e d* of late Sir William Crosthwaite; one *s* one *d*. *Educ*: St Peter's Sch., York. 2nd Lieut, Royal Corps of Signals, 1928; Lt-Col 1941; Col 1943; Brig. 1945. Chm., North Riding T&AFA, 1950–53 and 1962–68; Member: TA Advisory Cttee and TA Exec. Cttee, 1968–71. Chm., St John Council, N Yorks (Vice-Pres., N Yorks St John Amb. Bde); Hon. Col, 34 (N) Signal Regt (V), 1967–75; Chairman: N Riding Co. Cadet Cttee, 1947–52; St Luke's Hosp. Man. Cttee, Middlesborough, 1959–74; Cleveland AHA, 1973–76. Retd Company Dir. Hon. Trust Representative for Cleveland, Royal Jubilee Trusts, 1977–81. DL 1949, JP 1963, NR Yorks. KStJ 1978. *Recreations*: golf, cricket, Rugby football. *Address*: The White Lodge, Hutton Rudby, Yarm, Cleveland TS15 0HY. *T*: Stokesley 700598. *Clubs*: Army and Navy; Cleveland (Middlesborough); Royal and Ancient (St Andrews).

FAIRWEATHER, Dr Frank Arthur; Environmental Safety Officer, Research Division, Unilever House, since 1982; *b* 2 May 1928; *s* of Frank and Maud Harriet Fairweather; *m* 1953, Christine Winifred Hobbs; two *s*. *Educ*: City of Norwich Sch.; Middlesex Hospital. MB, BS 1954; MRCPath 1963, FRCPath 1975; FIBiol 1972. Clinical house appts, Ipswich Gp of Hosps, 1955–56; Pathologist, Bland Sutton Inst. of Pathology, and Courtauld Inst. of Biochem., Middlesex Hosp., Soho Hosp. for Women, 1956–60; Jt Sen. Registrar in Histopathology, Middlesex and West Middlesex Hosps, 1961–62; Chief Med. Adviser and Cons. Pathologist, Benger Labs, 1962–63; Chief Pathologist, British Industrial Biological Res. Assoc., Carshalton, and Hon. Sen. Lectr, RCS, 1963–65; Associate Res. Dir, Wyeth Labs, Taplow, 1965–69; Sen. Med. Officer, DHSS, and Principal Med. Officer, Cttee on Safety of Medicines, 1969–72; SPMO, DHSS, 1972–82. Member: Expert Panels on Environmental Pollution, Food Toxicology, and Safety, to WHO; EEC Scientific Cttee for Food, 1976– (Chm., Sci. Cttee for Cosmetology); Consultant Adviser in Toxicology to DHSS, 1978–81; Dir, DHSS Toxicological Lab., St Bartholomew's Hosp., 1978–82, Hon. Dir, 1982–84; Hon. Lectr in Path., Middlesex Hosp., 1972–; Hon. Prof. of Toxicology, Dept of Biochemistry, Univ. of Surrey, 1978; Hon. Prof. of Toxicology and Pathology, Sch. of Pharmacy, Univ. of London, 1982. QHP, 1977–80. *Publications*: various toxicological and medical papers. *Recreations*: angling, gardening, painting. *Address*: 394 London Road, Langley, Slough, Berks SL3 7HX.

FAIRWEATHER, Patrick Stanislaus, CMG 1986; HM Diplomatic Service; Ambassador to Angola, since 1985; *b* 17 June 1936; *s* of John George Fairweather and Dorothy Jane (*née* Boanus); *m* 1962, Maria (*née* Merica); two *d*. *Educ*: Ottershaw Sch., Surrey; Trinity Coll., Cambridge (Hons History). National Service in Royal Marines and Parachute Regt, 1955–57. Entered FCO, 1965; 2nd Secretary, Rome, 1966–69; FCO, 1969–70; 1st Secretary (Economic), Paris, 1970–73; FCO, 1973–75; 1st Sec. and Head of Chancery, Vientiane, 1975–76; 1st Sec., UK Representation to EEC, Brussels, 1976–78; Counsellor (Economic and Commercial), Athens, 1978–83; Head of European Community Dept (Internal), FCO, 1983–85. *Recreations*: travel, gardening, photography, dinghy sailing. *Address*: c/o Foreign and Commonwealth Office, SW1A 2AH.

FAITH, (Irene) Sheila; JP; Dental Surgeon; Member (C) Cumbria and Lancashire North, European Parliament, since 1984; *b* 3 June 1928; *yr d* of late I. Book; *m* 1950, Dennis Faith. *Educ*: Central High School, Newcastle upon Tyne; Durham Univ. LDS 1950. Member: Northumberland CC, 1970–74; Newcastle City Council, 1975–77. Vice-Chm., Jt Consultative Cttee on Educn for District of Newcastle during local govt reorganisation, 1973–74. Contested (C) Newcastle Central, Oct. 1974; MP (C) Belper, 1979–83. Member: Select Cttee on Health and Social Services, 1979–83; Cttee on Unopposed Bills, 1980–83; Sec., Conservative backbench Health and Social Services Cttee, 1982–83; Eur. Parlt Transport and Regl Develt Cttees. Member: Exec. Cttee, Cons Medical Soc., 1981–84; British-American Parly Gp; CPA; IPU; UN Parly Gp; the European Movement, Parly and Scientific Cttee; Parly Maritime Gp; Sen. Vice-Chm., Swiss Delegation, 1985–. Has served as Chm. or Mem. several school governing bodies and Manager of Community Homes. JP: Northumberland County, 1972–74; Newcastle upon Tyne, 1974–78; Inner London, 1978–. *Recreations*: reading, music. *Address*: 4 William Cobbett House, Scarsdale Place, W8; Office No 1, The Square, Milnthorpe, Cumbria LA7 7QJ; Pinewood Cottage, Sedgwick, near Kendal, Cumbria LA8 0JP.

FAITHFULL, family name of **Baroness Faithfull.**

FAITHFULL, Baroness *cr* 1975 (Life Peer), of Wolvercote, Oxfordshire; **Lucy Faithfull,** OBE 1972; *b* 26 Dec. 1910; *d* of Lt Sydney Leigh Faithfull, RE (killed 1916) and late Elizabeth Adie Faithfull (*née* Algie); unmarried. *Educ*: Talbot Heath Sch. (formerly Bournemouth High Sch.). Social Science Dipl., Birmingham Univ., 1933; Family case work training (Charity Welfare Organisation, now Family Welfare Assoc.), 1936, and Cert. in Child Care, 1969. Club Leader and Sub-Warden, Birmingham Settlement, 1932–35; Asst Organiser, Child Care, LCC Education Dept, 1935–40; Regional Welfare Officer (Evacuation Scheme), Min. of Health, 1940–48; Inspector in Children's Br., Home Office, 1948–58; Oxford City Council: Children's Officer, 1958–70; Director of Social Services, 1970–74; retired, 1974. Chm. Cttee, New Approaches to Juvenile Crime, 1980–; Mem. Council and Exec. Finance Cttee, Dr Barnardo's, 1975–; Mem. Council, Caldecott Community Kent Sch. for Maladjusted Children, 1979–; Trustee and Mem. Cttee, Dessel Leigh Sch. for Maladjusted Children, 1975. Hon. MA Oxford, 1974; Hon. DLitt Warwick, 1978. *Recreations*: friends, travel, garden. *Address*: 303 Woodstock Road, Oxford OX2 7NY. *T*: Oxford 55389.

FAKLEY, Dennis Charles, OBE 1973; retired; *b* 20 Nov. 1924; *s* of Charles Frederick and Ethel May Fakley; *m* 1976, Louise Grace Swindell. *Educ*: Chatham House Grammar Sch., Ramsgate; Queen Mary Coll., Univ. of London (BSc Special Physics). Royal Naval Scientific Service, 1944–63; Min. of Defence, 1963–84. *Recreations*: reading, cricket. *Address*: 14 Coval Gardens, SW14 7DG. *T*: 01–876 6856.

FALCON, Michael Gascoigne, CBE 1979; JP, DL; Chairman: Pauls & Whites PLC, 1976–85 (Director since 1973); Eastern Counties Regional Board, Lloyds Bank Ltd, since 1979 (Director, since 1972); Norwich Union Insurance Group, since 1981 (Director, since 1963; Vice Chairman, 1979–81); Norwich Winterthur Holdings Ltd, since 1984; *b* 28 Jan. 1928; *s* of late Michael Falcon and Kathleen Isabel Frances Gascoigne; *m* 1954, April Daphne Claire Lambert; two *s* one *d*. *Educ*: Stowe Sch., Bucks; Heriot-Watt Coll., Edinburgh. National Service, Grenadier Gds and Royal Norfolk Regt, 1946–48. Head Brewer and Jt Man. Dir, E. Lacon & Co. Ltd, Great Yarmouth, 1952–68; Exec. Dir, Edgar Watts, Willow Merchants, 1968–73; Chm., National Seed Develt Orgn Ltd, 1972–82; Director: Securicor (East) Ltd, 1969–72; Lloyds Bank UK Management Ltd, 1979–85; Matthew Brown plc, 1981–; National Bus Properties Ltd, 1983–. Trustee, E Anglian Trustee Savings Bank, 1963–75. Mem., Norwich Prison Bd of Visitors, 1969–82. JP 1967, High Sheriff 1979, DL 1981, Co. of Norfolk; High Steward, Great Yarmouth, 1984. CStJ 1986. *Recreation*: country pursuits. *Address*: Keswick Old Hall, Norwich, Norfolk NR4 6TZ. *T*: Norwich 54348; Kirkgate, Loweswater, Cockermouth, Cumbria. *Clubs*: Norfolk (Norwich); Royal Norfolk and Suffolk Yacht (Lowestoft).

See also Ven. D. L. Edwards.

FALCON, Norman Leslie, FRS 1960; *b* 29 May 1904; 2nd *s* of late Thomas Adolphus Falcon, MA, RBA; *m* 1938, Dorothy Muriel, 2nd *d* of late F. G. Freeman, HM Consular Service; two *s* one *d*. *Educ*: Exeter Sch.; Trinity Coll., Cambridge (Sen. Exhibitioner 1925, Natural Science Tripos Pt I 1925, 1st cl., Part II 1927, 1st cl.; MA Cantab). Joined Anglo-Persian Oil Company as geologist, 1927; FGS, FRGS, 1927; Geological Exploration in Persia, UK and elsewhere, 1927–40. Served War of 1939–45, Intelligence Corps, 1940–45. Rejoined Anglo-Iranian Oil Company as Geologist on Head Office staff, 1945; Chief Geologist, 1955–65, Geological Adviser, 1965–72, British Petroleum Co Ltd. FInstPet, 1959; Geological Soc. of London: Mem. Council, 1954–58, 1967–71; Foreign Sec. 1967–70; Murchison Medal, 1963; Royal Geographical Society: Mem. Council, 1966–69; Vice-Pres. 1973; Founder's Medal, 1973. Mem., NERC, 1968–71. Hon. Mem., American Assoc. Petroleum Geologists, 1973. Bronze Star Medal (USA), 1945. *Publications*: geological papers. *Recreations*: outdoor pursuits. *Address*: The Downs, Chiddingfold, Surrey. *T*: Wormley 3101.

FALCONER, Prof. Alexander Frederick, VRD; BLitt, MA; FRSL; Professor of English in the University of St Andrews, 1955–78; *s* of Alexander W. Falconer and Emily Henrietta Carlow Falconer. *Educ*: Universities of Glasgow, St Andrews and Oxford (Magdalen Coll.). Lecturer, St Salvator's Coll., St Andrews, 1935–39. Served in Home and Eastern Fleets, rank of Lieut, and Lt-Comdr RNVR, 1940–45. Senior Lecturer in Univ. of St Andrews, 1946. Mem. of group of editors for Boswell's correspondence at Yale, 1952–. Folger Fellow, 1958. Jt Gen. Editor, Percy Letters Series, 1964. Naval Officer i/c, St Andrews Univ. Unit, RNR. Trustee, Nat. Library of Scotland, 1956–. Mem., Royal Inst. of Navigation. *Publications*: A. Spir, Right and Wrong (trans.), 1954; The Percy Letters, Vol. IV, 1954, Vol. VI, 1960; Shakespeare and the Sea, 1964; A Glossary of Shakespeare's Sea and Naval Terms, 1965; articles and reviews. *Address*: 6 Alexandra Place, St Andrews. *T*: St Andrews 73457. *Clubs*: Naval, Mayfair.

See also Peter S. Falconer.

FALCONER, Prof. Douglas Scott, FRS 1973; FRSE 1972; *b* 10 March 1913; *s* of Gerald Scott Falconer and Lillias Harriet Gordon Douglas; *m* 1942, Margaret Duke; two *s*. *Educ*: Edinburgh Academy; Univ. of St Andrews (BSc); Univ. of Cambridge (PhD. ScD). Scientific Staff of Agricultural Research Council, 1947–68; Prof. of Genetics, Univ. of Edinburgh, and Dir, ARC Unit of Animal Genetics, 1968–80. *Publications*: Introduction to Quantitative Genetics, 1960, 2nd edn 1981; Problems on Quantitative Genetics, 1983; papers in scientific jls. *Recreations*: music, walking, sailing. *Address*: Institute of Animal Genetics, West Mains Road, Edinburgh EH9 3JN. *T*: 031–667 1081.

FALCONER, Hon. Sir Douglas (William), Kt 1981; MBE 1946; **Hon. Mr Justice Falconer;** a Judge of the High Court of Justice, Chancery Division, since 1981; *b* 20 Sept. 1914; *s* of late William Falconer, S Shields; *m* 1941, Joan Beryl Argent, *d* of late A. S. Bishop, Hagley, Worcs; one *s* one *d*. *Educ*: South Shields; King's Coll., Durham Univ.; BSc (Hons) Physics, 1935. Served War of 1939–45 (Hon. Major): commissioned E Yorks Regt, 1939. Called to Bar, Middle Temple, 1950, Bencher 1972; QC 1967. Apptd to exercise appellate jurisdiction of BoT, later DoT, under Trade Marks Act, 1970–81; Member: of Departmental Cttee to review British trade mark law and practice, 1972–73; Standing Adv. Cttee on Patents, 1975–79; Standing Adv. Cttee on Trade Marks, 1975–79; Senate of Four Inns of Court, 1973–74; Senate of Four Inns of Court and the Bar, 1974–77; Chm., Patent Bar Assoc., 1971–80. *Publications*: (Jt Editor) Terrell on the Law of Patents (11th and 12th edns), 1965 and 1971. *Recreations*: music, theatre. *Address*: Royal Courts of Justice, Strand, WC2; Ridgewell House, West Street, Reigate, Surrey. *T*: Reigate 44374.

FALCONER, Peter Serrell, FRIBA, FRSA; Founder of The Falconer Partnership, Architects and Consultants, and of Handling Consultants Ltd, Stroud and Johannesburg; *b* 7 March 1916; *s* of Thomas Falconer, FRIBA, and Florence Edith Falconer; presumed heir to the Barony (1206) and Lordship (1646) of Halkerton, vacant since 1966; *m* 1941, Mary Hodson; three *s* one *d*. *Educ*: Bloxham Sch., Banbury. Commenced practice in Stroud, as partner in Ellery Anderson Roiser & Falconer, 1944; Sen. Partner of Peter Falconer and Partners, 1959–82 (with br. office in Adelaide, SA, 1970). Specialist in materials handling and industrial architecture; Mem., Materials Handling Inst. *Publications*: Building and Planning for Industrial Storage and Distribution, 1975; contributor to: Architectural Review; Architects' Jl; Material Handling magazines. *Recreations*: restoring historic buildings, garden planning, motor sport. *Address*: St Francis, Lammas Park, Minchinhampton, Stroud, Glos. *T*: Brimscombe 882188.

FALETAU, 'Inoke Fotu; Director, Commonwealth Foundation, since 1985; *b* 24 June 1937; 2nd *s* of 'Akau'ola Sateki Faletau and Celia Lyden; *m* 'Evelini Ma'ata Hurrell; three *s* three *d*. *Educ*: St Peter's, Cambridge, NZ; Tonga High Sch.; Auckland Grammar Sch.;

UC Swansea; Manchester Univ. Joined Tonga Civil Service, 1958; Asst Sec., Prime Minister's Office, 1965; Sec. to Govt, 1969; seconded to Univ. of South Pacific, 1971; Sec. to Govt, 1972; High Comr, UK, 1972–82; Ambassador to: France, 1972–82; Germany, 1976–82; Belgium, Luxembourg, Netherlands, EEC, 1977–82; USA, 1979–82; USSR, 1980–82; Denmark, 1981–82; Dir. Management Develt Programme, Commonwealth Secretariat, 1983–84. *Recreations:* Rugby, tennis, reading, bridge, fishing. *Address:* Commonwealth Foundation, Marlborough House, Pall Mall, SW1Y 5HY. *Clubs:* Royal Over-Seas League; Nuku'alofa Yacht and Motor Boat.

FALK, Sir Roger (Salis), Kt 1969; OBE (mil.) 1945; CBIM; Vice President, Sadler's Wells Foundation and Trust, since 1986 (Chairman, 1976–86); *b* 22 June 1910; *s* of Lionel David Falk; *m* 1938, Margaret Helen (*née* Stroud) (*d* 1958); one *s* two *d*. *Educ:* Haileybury (Life Governor, 1971–; Council Mem., 1978–); Geneva Univ. Gen. Manager's Office, Rhodesia Railways, Bulawayo, 1931; D. J. Keymer & Co: Manager in Bombay and Calcutta, 1932–35; Dir, 1935–49; Managing Dir, 1945–49; Vice-Chm., 1950; formerly: Dir, P-E International Ltd (Chm., 1973–76); Chm., London Bd, Provincial Insurance Co. Ltd. Shoreditch Borough Council, 1937–45. Dir-Gen. British Export Trade Research Organisation (BETRO) from 1949 until disbandment. Chairman: Furniture Development Council, 1963–82; Central Council for Agric. and Hort. Cooperation, 1967–75; British European Associated Publishers, 1976–79; Action for Dysphasic Adults (ADA), 1982–85 (Vice-Pres., 1985–); Dep. Chm., Gaming Bd, 1978–81; Member: Council of Industrial Design, 1958–67; Monopolies and Mergers Commn, 1965–80; Council, RSA, 1968–74; Council, Imp. Soc. of Knights Bachelor, 1979–; Pres., Design and Industries Assoc., 1971–72. Served War of 1939–45, RAFVR; Wing-Comdr, 1942. Hon. DLitt City Univ. *Publication:* The Business of Management, 1961, 5th rev. edn 1976. *Recreations:* writing, music, reading, theatre. *Address:* 603 Beatty House, Dolphin Square, SW1. *T:* 01–828 3752. *Clubs:* Garrick, MCC.

FALKENDER, Baroness *cr* 1974 (Life Peer), of West Haddon, Northants; **Marcia Matilda Falkender,** CBE 1970; Personal and Political Secretary to Lord Wilson of Rievaulx, since 1956; *b* March 1932; *d* of Harry Field. *Educ:* Northampton High School; Queen Mary Coll., Univ. of London. BA Hons Hist. Secretary to Gen. Sec., Labour Party, 1955–56. Member: Prime Minister's Film Industry Working Party, 1975–76; Interim Cttee on Film Industry, 1977–82; British Screen Adv. Council, 1985–. Dir, Peckham Building Soc., 1986–. Political columnist, 'Mail on Sunday', 1982–. *Publications:* Inside Number 10, 1972; Downing Street in Perspective, 1983. *Address:* 3 Wyndham Mews, Upper Montagu Street, W1.

FALKINER, Lt-Col Sir Terence (Edmond Patrick), 8th Bt of Annmount, Cork, *cr* 1778; DL; late Coldstream Guards; retired 1956; *b* 17 March 1903; *s* of 7th Bt and Kathleen (*d* 1948), *e d* of Hon. Henry Robert Orde-Powlett, 2nd *s* of 3rd Baron Bolton; *S* father, 1917; *m* 1925, Mildred, *y d* of Sir John Cotterell, 4th Bt; two *s* three *d*. *Educ:* St Anthony's, Eastbourne; The Oratory Sch., Edgbaston. DL, Herefordshire, 1965. KStJ. *Heir:* *s* Edmond Charles Falkiner [*b* 24 June 1938; *m* 1960, Janet Iris, *d* of Arthur E. B. Darby, Bromyard, Herefordshire; two *s*]. *Address:* c/o Edmond Falkiner, 111 Wood Street, Barnet, Herts EN5 4BX. *T:* 01–440 2426.

FALKINGHAM, Ven. John Norman; Warden, Community of the Holy Name, 1969–85; *b* 9 Feb. 1917; 2nd *s* of Alfred Richard Falkingham and Amy Grant (*née* Macallister); *m* 1947, Jean Dorothy Thoren; two *d*. *Educ:* Geelong Gram. Sch., Corio, Vic.; Trinity Coll., Univ. of Melbourne. BA (Hons) Melbourne 1940; ThL (1st Cl. Hons), ThD 1978, Australian Coll. of Theol.; prizes for Divinity and Biblical Greek. Deacon, 1941; Priest, 1942. Curate of Holy Trinity, Surrey Hills, Vic., 1941–44; Chaplain, Trinity Coll., Univ. of Melbourne, 1944–50; Incumbent, St Paul's, Caulfield, Vic., 1950–61. Exam. Chaplain to Archbishop of Melbourne, 1947–61; Lectr in Theol. Faculty, Trinity Coll., Melbourne, 1950–60; Canon of St Paul's Cath., Melbourne, 1959–61; Dean of Newcastle, NSW, 1961–75; Rector of St Paul's, Manuka, ACT, 1975–82; Canon of St Saviour's Cath., Goulburn, 1976–81; Archdeacon of Canberra, 1981–82, Archdeacon Emeritus, 1982. Sec., Liturgical Commn of Gen. Synod, 1966–78; Mem. Bd of Delegates, Aust. Coll. of Theology, 1962–; Lecturer: Canberra Coll. of Ministry, 1975–84; St Mark's Library, Canberra, 1982–; Chm., Bd of Dirs, Canberra C of E Girls' Grammar Sch., 1983–. *Publications:* articles in various jls. *Recreation:* walking. *Address:* 4 Serra Place, Stirling, ACT 2611, Australia.

FALKLAND, 15th Viscount *cr* 1620 (Scot.), of Falkland, Co. Fife; **Lucius Edward William Plantagenet Cary;** Lord Cary 1620; *b* 8 May 1935; *s* of 14th Viscount Falkland, and of Constance Mary, *d* of late Captain Edward Berry; *S* father, 1984; *m* 1962, Caroline Anne, *o d* of late Lt-Comdr Gerald Butler, DSC, RN, and late Mrs Patrick Parish; one *s* two *d* (and one *d* decd). *Educ:* Wellington Coll.; Alliance Française, Paris. Late 2nd Lieut 8th Hussars. Export marketing consultant, formerly Chief Executive, C. T. Bowring Trading (Holdings) Ltd. Mem., SDP; H of L Select Cttee on Overseas Trade, 1984–85. *Recreations:* golf, cinema. *Heir:* *s* Master of Falkland, *qv*. *Address:* 137 Sabine Road, SW11 5LU. *Clubs:* Brooks's, Turf; Sunningdale Golf.

FALKLAND, Master of; Hon. Lucius Alexander Plantagenet Cary; 2nd Lieut, 2nd Battalion, Scots Guards; *b* 1 Feb. 1963; *s* and *heir* of 15th Viscount Falkland, *qv*. *Educ:* Loretto School; RMA Sandhurst. *Recreation:* ski-ing. *Address:* Shutelake Farm, Butterleigh, Cullompton, Devon.

FALKNER, Sir (Donald) Keith, Kt 1967; Hon. DMus Oxon, 1969; FRCM; Hon. RAM; Hon. GSM; Hon. FTCL; Hon. FLCM; Director, Royal College of Music, 1960–74, Vice President, since 1984; professional singer; *b* Sawston, Cambs, 1900; *y s* of late John Charles Falkner; *m* 1930, Christabel Margaret, *o d* of Thomas Fletcher Fullard, MA; two *d*. *Educ:* New Coll. Sch.; Perse Sch.; Royal College of Music; Berlin, Vienna, Paris. Has sung at all principal festivals in England, and many European cities; toured USA eight times, including concerts with Boston Symphony, New York Philharmonic, Cincinnati, St Louis, and Philadelphia Orchestras; toured: South Africa, 1935, 1939, 1955, 1962, 1974; Canada in 1953; New Zealand in 1956; starred in three Warner Bros musicals, 1937–39. British Council Music Officer for Italy, 1946–50. Prof. of the Dept of Music at Cornell Univ., USA, 1950–60. An Artistic Dir, King's Lynn Fest., 1981–83. FRSA 1979. Hon. Mem., Assoc. Européene des Conservatoires de Musique, Académies, et Musikhochschulen, 1976. Served European War, 1914–18, in RNAS, 1917–19; War of 1939–45, RAFVR, 1940–45. Editor, Voice, 1983–. *Recreations:* cricket, golf, lawn tennis, squash rackets, walking. *Address:* Low Cottages, Ilketshall St Margaret, Bungay, Suffolk. *T:* Bungay 2573. *Clubs:* Athenæum, Royal Automobile, MCC; Norfolk (Norwich).

FALKUS, Hugh Edward Lance; naturalist, independent writer, film director, broadcaster; *b* 15 May 1917; *s* of James Everest Falkus and Alice Musgrove. *Educ:* The East Anglian Sch. (Culford Sch.). Served War of 1939–45 (Fighter Pilot). TV films include: Salmo—the Leaper; (with Niko Tinbergen) Signals for Survival (Italia Prize, 1969; Amer. Blue Ribbon, New York Film Fest., 1971); Highland Story; The Gull Watchers; The Signreaders; The Beachcombers; The Riddle of the Rook (Venice Film Festival, 1972); Tender Trap; Self-Portrait of a Happy Man. Cherry Kearton Medal and Award, RGS, 1982. *Publications:* Sea Trout Fishing, 1962, 2nd edn 1975, revised 2nd edn 1981; The Stolen Years, 1965, 2nd edn 1979; (with Niko Tinbergen) Signals for Survival, 1970; (with Fred Buller) Freshwater Fishing, 1975, new edn 1978; (jtly) Successful Angling, 1977; Nature Detective, 1978; (with Joan Kerr) From Sydney Cove to Duntroon, 1982; Master of Cape Horn, 1982; Salmon Fishing, 1984. *Recreations:* fishing, shooting, sailing. *Address:* Cragg Cottage, near Ravenglass, Cumbria CA18 1RT. *T:* Ravenglass 247.

FALL, Brian James Proetel, CMG 1984; HM Diplomatic Service; Director, Cabinet of the Secretary General of NATO, since 1984; *b* 13 Dec. 1937; *s* of John William Fall, Hull, Yorkshire, and Edith Juliette (*née* Proetel); *m* 1962, Delmar Alexandra Roos; three *d*. *Educ:* St Paul's Sch.; Magdalen Coll., Oxford; Univ. of Michigan Law Sch. Joined HM Foreign (now Diplomatic) Service, 1962; served in Foreign Office UN Dept, 1963; Moscow, 1965; Geneva, 1968; Civil Service Coll., 1970; FO Eastern European and Soviet Dept and Western Organisations Dept, 1971; New York, 1975; Harvard Univ. Center for Internat. Affairs, 1976; Counsellor, Moscow, 1977–79; Head of Energy, Science and Space Dept, FCO, 1979–80; Head of Eastern European and Soviet Dept, FCO, 1980–81; Prin. Private Sec. to Sec. of State for Foreign and Commonwealth Affairs, 1981–84. *Address:* c/o Foreign and Commonwealth Office, King Charles Street, SW1A 2AH. *Club:* Travellers'.

FALLA, Paul Stephen; *b* 25 Oct. 1913; *s* of Norris Stephen Falla and Audrey Frances Stock, Dunedin, New Zealand; *m* 1958, Elizabeth Shearer; one *d*. *Educ:* Wellington and Christ's Colls, NZ; Balliol Coll., Oxford (Scholar). Appointed to Foreign Office, 1936; served HM Embassies, Warsaw, 1938–39, Ankara, 1939–43, Tehran, 1943; Foreign Office, 1943–46; UK Delegation to UN, New York, 1946–49; Foreign Office, 1949–67 (Dep. Dir of Research, 1958–67). Member: Exec. Cttee, Translators' Assoc., Soc. of Authors, 1971–73 (Vice-Chm., 1973); Council, Inst. Linguists, 1975–81 (FIL 1984); Cttee, Translators' Guild, 1975–81. Scott Moncrieff prize, 1972 and 1981; Schlegel-Tieck Prize, 1983. *Publications:* (ed) The Oxford English-Russian Dictionary, 1984; about 45 book translations from various languages, 1967–. *Recreations:* reading (history, philosophy, poetry, language matters). *Address:* 63 Freelands Road, Bromley, Kent BR1 3HZ. *T:* 01–460 4995. *Club:* Travellers'.

FALLE, Sir Sam, KCMG 1979 (CMG 1964); KCVO 1972; DSC 1945; HM Diplomatic Service, retired; *b* 19 Feb. 1919; *s* of Theodore and Hilda Falle; *m* 1945, Merete Rosen; one *s* three *d*. *Educ:* Victoria Coll., Jersey, CI. Served Royal Navy, 1937–48; joined Foreign (subseq. Diplomatic) Service, 1948; British Consulate, Shiraz, Iran, 1949–51; British Embassy, Tehran, 1952; British Embassy, Beirut, 1952–55; FO, 1955–57; British Embassy, Baghdad, 1957–61; Consul-Gen., Gothenburg, 1961–63; Head of UN Dept, FO, 1963–67; with Lord Shackleton's mission to Aden 1967; Deputy High Comr, Kuala Lumpur, 1967–69; Ambassador to Kuwait, 1969–70; High Comr, Singapore, 1970–74; Ambassador to Sweden, 1974–77; High Comr in Nigeria, 1977–78; Delegate, Commn of the European Communities, Algiers, 1979–82; carried out evaluation of EEC aid to Zambia, 1983–84. Kt Grand Cross, Order of Polar Star, Sweden, 1975. *Recreations:* swimming, ski-ing, jogging. *Address:* Slättna, 57030 Mariannelund, Sweden.

FALLON, Hazel Rosemary; *see* Counsell, H. R.

FALLON, Ivan Gregory; Deputy Editor, Sunday Times, since 1984; *b* 26 June 1944; *s* of Padraic and Dorothea Fallon; *m* 1967, Susan Mary Lurring; one *s* two *d*. *Educ:* St Peter's Coll., Wexford; Trinity Coll., Dublin (BBS). Irish Times, 1964–66; Thomson Provincial Newspapers, 1966–67; Daily Mirror, 1967–68; Sunday Telegraph, 1968–70; Deputy City Editor, Sunday Express, 1970–71; Sunday Telegraph, 1971–84: City Editor, 1979–84. Member: Council, Univ. of Buckingham, 1982–; Council of Governors, United Med. and Dental Schs of Guy's and St Thomas's Hosps, 1985–; Trustee: Project Trust, 1984–; Generation Trust, Guy's Hosp., 1985–. *Publication:* DeLorean: the rise and fall of a dream-maker (with James L. Srodes), 1983. *Recreations:* squash, tennis. *Address:* Clare Cottage, Mill Street, East Malling, Kent ME19 6BU. *T:* West Malling 843091. *Clubs:* Beefsteak, Royal Automobile.

FALLON, Martin; *see* Patterson, Harry.

FALLON, Michael; MP (C) Darlington, since 1983; *b* 14 May 1952; *s* of Martin Fallon, OBE, FRCSI and Hazel Fallon; *m* 1986, Wendy Elizabeth, *e d* of Peter H. Payne, Holme-on-Spalding Moor, Yorks. *Educ:* St Andrews Univ. (MA Hons 1974). European Educnl Res. Trust, 1974–75; Opposition Whips Office, House of Lords, 1975–77; EEC Officer, Cons. Res. Dept, 1977–79; Jt Man. Dir, European Consultants Ltd, 1979–81. Sec., Lord Home's Cttee on future of House of Lords, 1977–78; Assistant to Baroness Elles, 1979–83. Pres., Darlington YCs. Lectr on trade and industry, foreign affairs and EEC matters. *Publications:* The Quango Explosion (jtly), 1978; Sovereign Members?, 1982; The Rise of the Euroquango, 1982; contribs to journals. *Recreation:* squash. *Address:* House of Commons, SW1A 0AA. *T:* 01–219 3000. *Clubs:* Darlington Conservative, Junior Unionist (Darlington).

FALLON, Peter, QC 1971; **His Honour Judge Fallon;** a Circuit Judge, since 1979; *b* 1 March 1931; *s* of Frederick and Mary Fallon; *m* 1st, 1955, Zina Mary (*née* Judd); one *s* two *d*; 2nd, 1980, Hazel Rosemary Counsell, *qv*. *Educ:* Leigh Grammar Sch.; St Joseph's Coll., Blackpool; Bristol Univ. (LLB Hons). Called to Bar, Gray's Inn, 1953. Commissioned in RAF for three years. A Recorder of the Crown Court, 1972–79. *Publications:* Crown Court Practice: Sentencing, 1974; Crown Court Practice: Trial, 1978; contrib. Proc. RSM. *Recreations:* golf, fishing, painting. *Address:* The Crown Court, The Guildhall, Bristol BS1 2HI.

FALLOWS, Albert Bennett, FRICS; Chief Valuer, Inland Revenue Valuation Office and Commissioner of Inland Revenue, since 1984; *b* 7 Dec. 1928; *s* of Bennett and May Fallows; *m* 1955, Maureen James; two *d*. *Educ:* Leek High School. Private practice, surveying, 1945–56; Stoke City Council, 1956–58; Staffs County Council, 1958–62; District Valuer's Office, Kidderminster, 1962–68; Chief Valuer's Office, 1968–73; District Valuer, Basingstoke, 1973–75; Superintending Valuer, Liaison Officer, DoE/Dept of Transport, 1975–77; Board of Inland Revenue: Superintending Valuer, North West, Preston, 1977–80; Asst Chief Valuer, 1980–83; Dep. Chief Valuer, 1983. *Recreation:* golf. *Address:* 110 Whitedown Lane, Alton, Hants. *T:* Alton 82818. *Club:* Blackmoor Golf.

FALLSIDE, Prof. Frank, PhD; CEng, FIWES; Professor of Information Engineering, since 1983, and Fellow of Trinity Hall, since 1962, University of Cambridge; *b* 2 Jan. 1932; *s* of William Thomas Fallside, Leith and Daisy Helen Janet Kinnear Madden, Edinburgh; *m* 1958, Maureen Helen Couttie, Edinburgh; two *s* one *d*. *Educ:* George Heriot's Sch., Edinburgh; Edinburgh Univ. (BSc); PhD Wales; MA Cantab. MIEE 1968; CEng, FIWES 1983. Engr, English Electric Co., 1957–58; Cambridge University: Sen. Asst in Res., 1958–61; Lectr in Engrg, 1961–72; Reader in Electrical Engrg, 1972–83; Tutor for grad. students, Trinity Hall, 1966–72. Director: Cambridge Water Co., 1969–; Cambridge Microprocessor Courses, 1979–; Eastcam Systems, 1983–. *Publications:* (ed with W. A. Woods) Computer Speech Processing, 1985; various tech. papers in engrg and speech science. *Recreations:* sailing, maritime history. *Address:* 37 Earl Street, Cambridge CB1 1JR. *T:* Cambridge 353966.

FALMOUTH, 9th Viscount, *cr* 1720; **George Hugh Boscawen;** 26th Baron Le Despencer, 1264; Baron Boscawen-Rose, 1720; Lord-Lieutenant of Cornwall, since 1977; *b* 31 Oct. 1919; 2nd but *e* surv. *s* of 8th Viscount; *S* father, 1962; *m* 1953, Elizabeth Price Browne; four *s*. *Educ:* Eton Coll.; Trinity Coll., Cambridge. Served War, 1939–46, Italy. Capt., Coldstream Guards. DL Cornwall, 1968. *Heir: s* Hon. Evelyn Arthur Hugh Boscawen [*b* 13 May 1955; *m* 1977, Lucia Vivian-Neal, *e d* of R. W. Vivian-Neal; one *s* one *d*]. *Address:* Tregothnan, Truro, Cornwall; Buston, Hunton, Kent. *Clubs:* Athenæum, Army and Navy.

See also Hon. R. T. Boscawen.

FALVEY, Sir John (Neil), KBE 1976; QC 1970; barrister, Fiji; *b* 16 Jan. 1918; *s* of John Falvey and Adela Falvey; *m* 1943, Margaret Katherine, *d* of Stanley Weatherby; three *s* two *d* (and one *d* decd). *Educ:* Eltham and New Plymouth Convent Schs; Whangarei High Sch.; Otago Univ. (BA); Auckland Univ. (LLB). Colonial Admin. Service (incl. mil. service, Fiji and Gilbert and Ellice Is), 1940–48; private legal practice, 1949–70. Mem., Legislative Council, 1953–72; Attorney-General, 1970–77; Senator and Leader of Govt Business, 1972–79. Hon. Danish Consul, 1950–70. Chevalier (First Cl.), Royal Order of Dannebrog, 1968. *Recreation:* golf. *Address:* PO Box 1056, Suva, Fiji. *T:* 315–817. *Clubs:* Fiji, Defence, Fiji Golf.

FANE, family name of **Earl of Westmorland.**

FANE, Harry Frank Brien, CMG 1967; OBE 1957 (MBE 1945); Department of Employment and Productivity, retired 1968; *b* 21 Aug. 1915; *s* of late Harry Lawson Fane and Edith (*née* Stovold); *m* 1947, Stella, *yr d* of late John Hopwood; two *d*. *Educ:* William Ellis Sch.; Birkbeck Coll., London. Joined Ministry of Labour, 1933. HM Forces, 1940–45: Major, Royal Corps of Signals (despatches); served in N Africa, Italy and Austria. British Embassy, Washington: First Sec. (Labour), 1950–56; Counsellor (Labour), 1960–66. Regional Controller, Dept of Employment and Productivity (formerly Min. of Labour), Birmingham, 1966–68. *Address:* 40 Winterbourne Road, Solihull, West Midlands B91 1LU.

FANE TREFUSIS, family name of **Baron Clinton.**

FANNER, Peter Duncan; His Honour Judge Fanner; a Circuit Judge, since 1986; *b* 27 May 1926; *s* of late Robert William Hodges Fanner, solicitor, and Doris Kitty Fanner; *m* 1949, Sheila Eveline England; one *s* one *d*. *Educ:* Pangbourne Coll. Admitted Solicitor of the Supreme Court, 1951 (holder Justices' Clerks' Society's prize). Served War of 1939–45, Pilot in Fleet Air Arm, Lieut (A) RNVR, 1944–47. Asst Clerk to Bromley Justices, 1947–51; Dep. Clerk to Gore Justices, 1951–56; Clerk to Bath Justices, 1956 72; Metropolitan Stipendiary Magistrate, 1972–86; a Dep. Circuit Judge, 1974–80; a Recorder, 1980–86. Mem. Council of Justices' Clerks' Society, 1966–72; Assessor Mem. of Departmental Cttee on Liquor Licensing, 1971–72. Chm., Bath Round Table, 1963–64. *Publications:* Stone's Justices' Manual; contrib. to Justice of the Peace, The Magisterial Officer, The Lawyer's Remembrancer. *Recreations:* travel, railways. *Address:* Bristol Crown Court, Guildhall, Bristol. *T:* Bristol 211681.

FANSHAWE OF RICHMOND, Baron *cr* 1983 (Life Peer), of South Cerney in the County of Gloucestershire; **Anthony Henry Fanshawe Royle,** KCMG 1974; *b* 27 March 1927; *s* of Sir Lancelot Royle, KBE; *m* 1957, Shirley Worthington; two *d*. *Educ:* Harrow; Sandhurst. Captain, The Life Guards (Germany, Egypt, Palestine and Transjordan), 1945–48; 21st Special Air Service Regt (TA), 1948–51. MP (C) Richmond, 1959–83; Parliamentary Private Secretary: to Under-Sec. of State for the Colonies, 1960; to Sec. of State for Air, 1960–62; to Minister of Aviation, 1962–64; Vice-Chm., Cons. Parly Foreign Affairs Cttee, 1965–67; Tory Opposition Whip, 1967–70; Parly Under-Sec. of State for Foreign and Commonwealth Affairs, 1970–74. Vice-Chm., Cons. Party Orgn, 1979–84 (Chm., Internat. Office, 1979–84). Mem., Assembly of Council of Europe and WEU, 1965. Esteemed Family Order (1st cl.), Brunei, 1975. *Address:* The Chapter Manor, South Cerney, Gloucestershire. *Clubs:* Pratt's, White's, Brooks's.

See also T. L. F. Royle.

FANSHAWE, Maj.-Gen. George Drew, CB 1954; DSO 1944; OBE 1944; *b* 27 Sept. 1901; *s* of Lt-Col Edward Cardwell Fanshawe; *m* 1934, Dorothy Elizabeth Norman-Walker; one *s* one *d*. *Educ:* Tonbridge. 2nd Lieut, RFA, 1922, Lieut 1924. RHA 1928; Capt. 1935; Adjt Herts Yeomanry, 1935; Brigade-Maj., RA, 1939, CO 1942; CRA, 3 Div., 1945; 5th Anti-Aircraft Bde, 1949; Comdr 1st Anti-Aircraft Group, 1952–55; retired 1955. BRA Southern Comd, 1950. Col Comdt, Royal Artillery, 1956–66 (Representative Col Comdt, 1961–62). High Sheriff, Wilts, 1961–62; Alderman, Wilts CC. CStJ. Order of Merit (US). *Address:* Farley Farm, Farley, Wilts. *T:* Farley 202. *Club:* Army and Navy.

FANSHAWE, Captain Thomas Evelyn, CBE 1971; DSC 1943; RN retd; Captain of the Sea Cadet Corps, 1972–81; *b* 29 Sept. 1918; *s* of Rev. Richard Evelyn Fanshawe and Mrs Isobel Fanshawe (*née* Prosser Hale); *m* 1944, Joan Margaret Moxon; one *s* two *d*. *Educ:* Dover Coll.; Nautical Coll., Pangbourne. FRHS. Served 1939–45 in destroyers and frigates and comdg HMS Clover (DSC, despatches 1943 and 1944); HM Ships Ocean, Constance and Phoenix, 1945–51; comd HM Ships: Zest and Obedient, 1951–54; Loch Insh, 1955–57; Temeraire, 1957–59; Tyne, 1959–61; NATO Defence Coll. and Liaison Officer with C-in-C Southern Europe, 1961–64; comd HMS Plymouth and Captain (D) 29th Escort Sqdn, 1964–66; Sen. Naval Officer Persian Gulf and Comdr Naval Forces Gulf, 1966–68 (Cdre); SBNO and Naval Attaché, S Africa (Cdre), 1969–71; ADC to the Queen, 1970–71; retd 1971. Cmdr 1955; Captain 1961. *Recreations:* gardening, golf, general interest in sport. *Address:* Freshwater House, Stroud, Petersfield, Hants. *T:* Petersfield 2430. *Clubs:* Naval, MCC; Royal Naval (Portsmouth).

FANTONI, Barry Ernest; novelist, broadcaster, cartoonist, jazz musician; Member of editorial staff of Private Eye, since 1963; Diary cartoonist, The Times, since 1983; Director, Barry Fantoni Merchandising Co Ltd, since 1985; *b* 28 Feb. 1940; *s* of Peter Nello Secondo Fantoni and Sarah Catherine Fantoni; *m* 1972, Teresa Frances Reidy. *Educ:* Archbishop Temple Sch.; Camberwell Sch. of Arts and Crafts (Wedgwood Scholar). Cartoonist of The Listener, 1968–; contrib. art criticism to The Times, 1973–77; record reviewer, Punch, 1976 77; designer of film and theatre posters and illustrator of book jackets; mural for Queen Elizabeth II Conf. Centre, London, 1985; film and television actor; presenter and writer, Barry Fantoni's Chinese Horoscopes, BBC Radio 4 series, 1986. One-man shows: Woodstock Gall., London, 1963; Comara Gall., LA, 1964; Brunel Univ., 1974; two-man shows (with Peter Fantoni): Langton Gall., London, 1977; Annexe Gall., London, 1978; Katherine House Gall., 1983; Fulford Cartoon Gall., 1983; New Grafton Gall., 1985; work exhibited: AIA Gall., London, 1958, 1961 and 1964; D and AD Annual Exhibn, London, 1964; Royal Acad. Summer Exhibn, 1963 (as Stuart Harris, with William Rushton), 1964, 1975 and 1978 (with Richard Napper); Tate Gall., 1973; Bradford Print Biennale, 1974; National Theatre, 1977; Browse and Darby, 1977; Gillian Jason Gall., 1983; Three Decades of Art Schools, RA, 1983. Musical compositions include: popular songs (also popular songs with Marianne Faithfull and with Stanley Myers); The Cantors Crucifixion (musical improvisation for 13 instruments), 1977; (with John Wells) Lionel (musical), 1977. Male TV Personality of the Year, 1966. Editor, St Martin's Review, 1969–74; weekly columnist on Chinese Horoscopes, Sunday Today, 1986. *Publications:* (with Richard Ingrams) Private Pop Eye, 1968; (as Old Jowett, with Richard Ingrams) The Bible for Motorists, 1970; Tomorrow's Nicodemus, 1974; (as Sylvie Krin, with Richard Ingrams) Love in the Saddle, 1974; Private Eye Cartoon Library 5, 1975; (as E. J. Thribb, with Richard Ingrams) So Farewell Then . . . and Other Poems, 1978; Mike Dime, 1980; (as Sylvie Krin, with Richard Ingrams) Born to be Queen, 1981; Stickman, 1982; (ed) Colemanballs, 1982; (ed) Colemanballs 2, 1984; The Times Diary Cartoons, 1984; Barry Fantoni's Chinese Horoscope, 1985; *illustrations for:* How To Be a Jewish Mother, 1966; The BP Festivals and Events in Britain, 1966; (with George Melly) The Media Mob, 1980. *Recreations:* snooker, road running, animal welfare. *Address:* c/o Fraser & Dunlop, 91 Regent Street, W1R 8RV. *Club:* Chelsea Arts (Chm., 1978–80).

FARIDKOT, Col HH Farzand-i-Saadat Nishan Hazrrat-i-Kaisar-i-Hind, Raja Sir Har Indar Singh Brar Bans Bahadur, Ruler of, KCSI 1941; *b* 29 Jan. 1915; *S* father as Raja, 1919; *m* 1933. *Educ:* Aitchison Chiefs Coll., Lahore. Full Ruling Powers, 1934; is one of Ruling Princes of India; Hon. Col Sikh LI; Hon. Col Bengal Engineer Group; MLA Pepsu LA. Salute, 11 guns. Formerly Mem. National Defence Council of India and of Standing Cttee of Chamber of Princes. Past Grand Master (Hon.), 1974, OSM 1971, Grand Lodge of India; Dist. Grand Master for N India, 1977, United Grand Lodge of England. *Address:* Faridkot, Punjab, India.

FARINGDON, 3rd Baron *cr* 1916; **Charles Michael Henderson;** Bt 1902; Partner, Cazenove and Company, since 1968; Chairman, Witan Investment Company plc, since 1980; *b* 3 July 1937; *s* of Hon. Michael Thomas Henderson (*d* 1953) (2nd *s* of Col Hon. Harold Greenwood Henderson, CVO, and *g s* of 1st Baron) and Oonagh Evelyn Henderson, *er d* of late Lt-Col Harold Ernest Brassey; *S* uncle, 1977; *m* 1959, Sarah Caroline, *d* of J. M. E. Askew, *qv*; three *s* one *d*. *Educ:* Eton College; Trinity College, Cambridge (BA). Treasurer, Nat. Art Collection Fund, 1984–. Chm. Bd of Governors, Royal Marsden Hosp., 1980–85. *Heir: s* Hon. James Harold Henderson, *b* 14 July 1961. *Address:* Buscot Park, Faringdon, Oxon; Barnsley Park, Cirencester, Glos.

FARLEY, Prof. Francis James Macdonald, FRS 1972; Visiting Senior Research Physicist, Yale University, since 1984; Professor Emeritus, Royal Military College of Science (Dean, 1967–82); Visiting Professor, since 1982, Hon. Fellow, 1986, Trinity College, Dublin; *b* 13 Oct. 1920; *er s* of late Brig. Edward Lionel Farley, CBE, MC; *m* 1945, Josephine Maisie Hayden; three *s* one *d*; *m* 1977, Margaret Ann Pearce. *Educ:* Clifton Coll.; Clare Coll., Cambridge. MA 1945; PhD 1950; ScD Cantab 1967; FInstP. Air Defence Research and Development Establishment, 1941–45 (first 3cm ground radar, Doppler radar); Chalk River Laboratories, 1945–46; Research Student, Cavendish Lab., Cambridge, 1946–49; Auckland Univ. Coll., NZ, 1950–57; attached AERE, 1955; CERN, Geneva, 1957–67 (muon g-2 experiment). Vis. Lectr, Univ. of Bristol, 1965–66; Vis. Scientist, CERN, 1967– (muon storage ring, tests of relativity); Vis. Professor: Swiss Inst. of Nuclear Research, 1976–77; Reading, 1982–. Rep. NZ at UN Conf. on Atomic Energy for Peaceful Purposes, 1955. Governor: Clifton Coll.; Welbeck Coll., 1970–82; Mem. Court, Univ. of Bath, 1974–82. Hon. Mem., Instn of Royal Engineers. FRSA. Hughes Medal, Royal Soc., 1980. *Publications:* Elements of Pulse Circuits, 1955; Progress in Nuclear Techniques and Instrumentation, Vol. I, 1966, Vol. II, 1967, Vol. III 1968; scientific papers on nuclear physics, electronics, high energy particle physics, wave energy. *Recreations:* gliding (FAI gold and diamond); ski-ing, windsurfing. *Address:* Le Masage, chemin de Saint Pierre, 06620 Le Bar sur Loup, S France.

FARLEY, Henry Edward; Group Deputy Chief Executive, Royal Bank of Scotland Group, since 1986; *b* 28 Sept. 1930; *s* of William and Frances Elizabeth Farley; *m* 1955, Audrey Joyce Shelvey; one *s* one *d*. *Educ:* Harrow County Sch. for Boys. FIB 1966. Entered National Bank, 1947; Dir and Head of UK Banking, Williams & Glyn's Bank, 1981; Chairman: Williams & Glyn's Bank (IOM) Ltd, 1973–76; Joint Credit Card Co. Ltd, 1982–84; Mem. Bd, Mastercard International Inc., 1982–84; Director: Royal Bank of Scotland Group plc, 1985–; Royal Bank of Scotland, 1985– (Man. Dir, 1985–86); Charterhouse Japhet, 1985–; Charterhouse Development, 1985–. Mem. Council, Inst. of Bankers, 1985–. *Publications:* The Clearing Banks and Housing Finance, 1983; Competition and Deregulation: branch networks, 1984; The Role of Branches in a Changing Environment, 1985. *Recreations:* all forms of rough sport, travel, modern literature. *Address:* 13 Montagu Square, W1. *Clubs:* Wig and Pen; St James (Manchester).

FARLEY, Prof. Martyn Graham, CEng, FRAeS, FIMechE, FIProdE; CBIM; Professor of Management Sciences, Royal Military College of Science, Shrivenham, since 1975 (Head of Department of Management Sciences, 1975–84); Vice Chairman, School of Management and Mathematics, RMCS Faculty of Cranfield Institute of Technology, since 1984; *b* 27 Oct. 1924; *s* of Herbert Booth Farley and Hilda Gertrude (*née* Hendey); *m* 1948, Freda Laugharne; two *s* one *d*. *Educ:* Merchant Venturers Tech. Coll., Bristol; Bristol Aeroplane Co. Tech. Coll. CEng, FRAeS 1968; FIMechE 1969; FIProdE 1975; CBIM 1980. Engine Div., Bristol Aeroplane Co.: Design Apprentice, 1939–45; Engine Design, 1945–46; Develt Engr, 1946–51; Bristol Aero Engines Ltd: Sen. Designer, Gas Turbine Office, 1951–55; Asst Chief Develt Engr, 1955–59; Bristol Siddeley Engines: Asst Chief Mech. Engr, 1959–62; Chief Develt Engr, Small Engines Div., 1962–65, Chief Engr, 1965–67; Small Engines Div., Rolls-Royce: Chief Engr, 1967–68; Gen. Works Manager, 1968–72; Manufg and Prodn Dir, 1972–74; HQ Exec. to Vice-Chm. of Rolls-Royce (1971) Ltd, 1974–75. Chm., British Management Data Foundn, 1978–. Royal Aeronautical Society: Mem. Council, 1972–; Vice Pres., 1980–83; Pres., 1983–84; Dir, Aeronautical Trusts, 1975–. Vice Pres., Instn of Indust. Engrs, 1981; Pres., IProdE, 1984–85 (Mem. Council, 1973–, Chm. Council, 1978–80, Vice-Pres., 1982–83); Founder Chm., Alliance of Manufg and Management Orgns, 1981–; Member: Chartered Engr Bd, CEI, 1977–; Sen. Awards Cttee, CGLI, 1979–; (Pres., CGIA Assoc., 1984); Guggenheim Medal Bd of Award, 1983; Court, Brunel Univ., 1977–80, Loughborough Univ., 1977–, Cranfield Inst. of Technol., 1977–, Bath Univ., 1983–; Hon. Mem. Council, CGLI, 1985–. Designer and Project Co-ordinator, EITB Mnfg Fellowships, 1977–. Hon. CGIA, 1981; Hon. Fellow, Indian IProdE, 1979; Hon. Member: Amer. Inst. of Indust. Managers, 1979; Australian Inst. of Indust. Engrs, 1981; Amer. Soc. Mfg Engrs, 1985. Mem., Co. of Coachmakers and Coach Harness Makers. Internat. Archimedes Award, Amer. Soc. of Prof. Engrs, 1979; Internat. Award, LA Council of Engrs and Scientists, 1981; First Shuttle Contributions Medal, 1981; Educn Award, ASME, 1983; Amer. Instn Advanced Engr Medal, 1984. *Publications:* various articles and technical pubns; proc. conferences. *Address:* Royal Military College of Science, Shrivenham, Swindon, Wilts SN6 8LA. *T:* Shrivenham 782551, ext. 592. *Club:* Athenæum.

FARMAR, Hugh William, MVO 1973; Clerk to the Drapers' Company, 1952–73; Member of the Court of the Company since 1974; Governor, Queen Mary College, University of London, 1952–83 (Treasurer 1952–73), Hon. Fellow, 1967; *b* 6 June 1908; *o s* of late Col H. M. Farmar, CMG, DSO, and Violet, *y d* of late Sir William Dalby and Hyacinthe Wellesley; *m* 1944, Constantia, *o d* of late Rt Hon. Sir Horace Rumbold, 9th Bt, GCB, and late Etheldred, Lady Rumbold, CBE; two *s*. *Educ:* Eton; Balliol Coll., Oxford. 2nd class clerk, Charity Commn, 1937; RAFVR, 1939–46 (on staff, Resident

Minister, Accra, 1942–43; Asst Private Sec. to Sec. of State for Air 1945–46). Principal clerk, Charity Commn, 1946. Hon. LLD William and Mary Coll., Virginia, 1968. *Publications:* The Cottage in the Forest, 1949; A Regency Elopement, 1969; articles and broadcasts on travel and country subjects. *Recreations:* country pursuits. *Address:* Wasing Old Rectory, Aldermaston, Reading, Berks. *T:* Tadley 4873. *Clubs:* Brooks's, Pratt's.

See also Sir Henry Rumbold, Bt, Lord Swinfen.

FARMBROUGH, Rt. Rev. David John; *see* Bedford, Bishop Suffragan of.

FARMER, Prof. Edward Desmond; Louis Cohen Professor of Dental Surgery, 1957–82, Director of Post-Graduate Dental Studies, 1972–77, Dean of the Faculty of Medicine, 1977–82, and Pro-Vice-Chancellor, 1967–70, University of Liverpool; *b* 15 April 1917; *s* of late S. R. and L. M. Farmer; *m* 1942, Mary Elwood Little; one *s* two *d*. *Educ:* Newcastle-under-Lyme High Sch.; Univ. of Liverpool (1936–41); Queens' Coll., Cambridge (1948–50). MA Cantab, 1955; MDS Liverpool, 1951; FDSRCS 1952; MRCPath 1967, FRCPath 1968; Hon. FRCR 1981. RNVR, Surgeon Lieut (D), 1942–45; Lectr in Parodontal Diseases, Univ. of Liverpool, 1950–57; Nuffield Fellow, 1948–50. Hon. Cons. Dent. Surg. to Bd of Governors of United Liverpool Hosps and Liverpool AHA (Teaching), formerly Liverpool Regional Hosp. Bd. Member Council: Brit. Soc. of Periodontology, 1954–59 (Pres. 1957–58); RSM, Odonto. Sect., 1965–68. Member: Central Cttee and Exec., Hosp. Dental Service, 1964–76; Negotiating Cttee of Central Cttee for Hosp. Medical Services, 1968–76; Bd of Govs, United Liverpool Hosps, 1968–71; UGC Dental Sect., 1968–77; Conf. and Exec., Dental Post-Grad. Deans, 1972–77; Cttee of Dental Teachers and Res. Workers Gp, BDA, 1974–79; Liverpool AHA(T) (and Chm., Regional Dental Cttee), 1975–77; RHA, 1977–82; Faculty of Dental Surgery, RCS, 1974–82; Dental Cttee of Medical Defence Union; Council, Medical Insurance Agency; Exec., Teaching Hospitals Assoc.; Chm., Commn of Dental Educn, Fedn Dentaire Internat., 1977–79 (Vice-Chm., 1974–77); Alternate, Dental Adv. Cttee to EEC, 1980–83; NW Cancer Research Exec. Cttee, 1982–; President: NW Br. BDA, 1967–68; Hospitals' Gp, BDA, 1972–73; Assoc. for Dental Educn in Europe, 1976–78; British Soc. of Oral Medicine, 1982–83; Pres., Odontological Section, RSM, 1983–84. Chairman: Merseyside Conf. for Overseas Students, 1983–; Age Concern, Liverpool, 1984–. *Publications:* (with F. E. Lawton) Stones' Oral and Dental Diseases, 5th edn, 1966; papers in Proceedings Royal Society Med., Jl of Gen. Microbiology, Brit. Med. Jl, Dental Practitioner; Internat. Dental Jl. *Recreations:* golf, gardening, painting and enjoyment of the countryside. *Address:* Heath Moor, Beacon Lane, Heswall, Merseyside L60 0DG. *T:* 051–342 3179.

FARMER, Frank Reginald, OBE 1967; FRS 1981; *b* 18 Dec. 1914; *s* of Frank Henry Farmer and Minnie Godson; *m* 1939, Betty Smart; one *s* two *d*. *Educ:* St John's Coll., Cambridge (BA). Kestner Evaporator & Engineering Co., 1936–46; Director, Safety Reliability Directorate, Atomic Energy Authority (formerly Dept of Atomic Energy), 1947–79, retired. Editor, Reliability Engineering, 1980–. FInstP 1965; Hon. FSE 1974; Foreign Associate, Nat. Acad. of Engineers, USA, 1980. Churchill Gold Medal, 1974. *Publication:* Nuclear Reactor Safety, 1977. *Recreations:* golf, books. *Address:* The Long Wood, Lyons Lane, Appleton, Warrington WA4 5ND. *T:* Warrington 62503.

FARMER, Sir George; *see* Farmer, Sir L. G. T.

FARMER, George Wallace; Vice President, Immigration Appeal Tribunal, since 1982; *b* 4 June 1929; *s* of George Lawrence Farmer and Blanche Amy (*née* Nicholls); *m* 1961, Patricia Mary Joyce; three *d*. *Educ:* The Lodge, Barbados; Harrison Coll., Barbados. Called to the Bar, Middle Temple, 1950. Private practice, Barbados, 1950–52; Magistrate, Barbados, 1952–56; Resident Magistrate, Uganda, 1956–63, Sen. Resident Magistrate, 1963–64; Dir of Public Prosecutions, Uganda, 1964–65; attached to Cottle Catford & Co., Solicitors, Barbados, 1965–67; Legal Manager, Road Transport Industry Trng Bd, 1967–70; Adjudicator, Immigration Appeals, 1970–82. *Recreations:* allotments (Britain), beach cricket (Barbados). *Address:* 40 South Croxted Road, West Dulwich, SE21 8BD. *T:* 01–670 4828.

FARMER, Hugh Robert Macdonald, CB 1967; *b* 3 Dec. 1907; *s* of late Charles Edward Farmer and late Emily (*née* Randolph); *m* 1st, 1934, Penelope Frances (*d* 1963), *d* of late Capt. Evelyn Boothby, RN; one *s* three *d*; 2nd, 1966, Jean, *widow* of Peter Bluett Winch. *Educ:* Cheam Sch.; Eton Coll.; New Coll., Oxford. House of Commons: Asst Clerk, 1931; Sen. Clerk, 1943; Clerk of Private Bills and Taxing Officer, and Examr of Petitions for Private Bills, 1958–60; Clerk of Cttees, 1960–65; Clerk/Administrator, 1965–72, retired 1972. *Recreations:* golf, gardening. *Address:* Grayswood Cottage, Haslemere, Surrey. *T:* Haslemere 3129. *Club:* MCC.

FARMER, Sir (Lovedin) George (Thomas), Kt 1968; LLD, MA, FCA, JDipMA; Coordinator, Rover and Triumph, 1972–73; Chairman: Rover Co. Ltd, 1963–73; Zenith Carburettor Co. Ltd, 1973–77; Deputy Chairman, British Leyland Motor Corporation, 1971–73; *b* 13 May 1908; *m* 1st, 1938, Editha Mary Fisher (*d* 1980); no *c*; 2nd, 1980, Muriel Gwendoline Mercer Pinfold. *Educ:* Oxford High Sch. 2nd Vice-Chm. and Mem. Adv. Cttee, Metalurgica de Santa Ana, Madrid, 1963–74; Director: Empresa Nacional de Automcamiones, 1968–73; ATV Network Ltd, 1968–75; Rea Brothers (Isle of Man) Ltd, 1976–; Aero Designs (Isle of Man) Ltd, 1979–. President: Birmingham Chamber of Commerce, 1960–61; Soc. of Motor Manufrs and Traders, 1962–64 (Dep. Pres., 1964–65; Chm., Exec. Cttee, 1968–72); Past Member: Advisory Council, ECGD (Board of Trade); UK Committee of Federation of Commonwealth and British Chambers of Commerce; Past Vice-Pres., West Midlands Engineering Employers' Assoc.; Governor, Chm. Finance Cttee, Dep. Chm. Executive Council (Chm., 1966–75), Royal Shakespeare Theatre; Pres., Loft Theatre, Leamington Spa. Pro-Chancellor, Birmingham Univ., 1966–75; Hon. LLD Birmingham, 1975. Past Pres., Automobile Golfing Soc. Mem., Worshipful Co. of Coach and Coach Harness Makers. *Recreations:* theatre, golf, fishing. *Address:* Longridge, The Chase, Ballakillowey, Colby, Isle of Man. *T:* Port St Mary 832603. *Club:* Royal and Ancient (St Andrews).

FARMER, Robert Frederick, OBE 1985; General Secretary, Institute of Journalists, since 1962; Member of Council, Media Society, since 1982 (Secretary, 1973–82); *b* 19 Aug. 1922; *s* of Frederick Leonard Farmer and Gladys Farmer (*née* Winney); *m* 1958, Anne Walton. *Educ:* Saltley Grammar Sch., Birmingham. FCIS. Served War of 1939–45, Royal Armoured Corps, 1941–52 (commissioned 3rd Carabiniers, despatches, Burma campaign). Secretariat: Instn of Plant Engineers, 1952–59; Instn of Civil Engineers, 1959–62. Consultative Mem., Press Council, 1962–; Mem., Cttee on Defamation, 1971–75. *Recreations:* cookery, walking, archaeology. *Address:* Institute of Journalists, Bedford Chambers, Covent Garden, WC2E 8HA. *T:* 01 836 6541. *Club:* National Liberal.

FARNCOMBE, Charles Frederick, CBE 1977; FRAM; Musical Director: Handel Opera Society, since 1955; Royal Court Theatre, Drottningholm, Sweden, since 1968; *b* 29 July 1919; *o s* of Harold and Eleanor Farncombe, both of London; *m* 1963, Sally Mae (*née* Felps), Riverside, Calif, USA; one *d*. *Educ:* London Univ., 1936–40 (Archibald Dawnay Scholarship in Civil Engrg, 1936) (BSc Hons (Eng) 1940); Royal Sch. of Church Music, 1947–48; Royal Academy of Music, 1948–51 (RAM, Mann Prize). Civil Engr to John Mowlem & Co, 1940–42. Served War, 1942–47, as Captain in REME, in 21st Army Gp. Free Lance Conductor: formed Handel Opera Soc. (with encouragement of late Prof. Dent), 1955; Chief Conductor, Royal Court Theatre, Drottningholm, Sweden, 1970–79; Chief Guest Conductor, Badisches Staatstheater, Karlsruhe, 1979–. AMICE, 1945 (resigned later); FRAM 1963 (ARAM 1962). Hon DMus Columbus Univ., Ohio, USA, 1959. Gold Medal of the Friends of Drottningholm, 1971; Hon. Fellow Royal Swedish Academy of Music, 1972. Kt Comdr, Order of North Star, Sweden, 1982. *Recreations:* cajoling singers, swimming, cottage on Offa's Dyke. *Address:* c/o Royal Bank of Scotland, 127 High Holborn, WC1V 6PQ.

FARNDALE, Gen. Sir Martin (Baker), KCB 1983 (CB 1980); Commander-in-Chief, BAOR, and Commander, Northern Army Group, since 1985; *b* Alberta, Canada, 6 Jan. 1929; *s* of Alfred Farndale and Margaret Louise Baker; *m* 1955, Margaret Anne Buckingham; one *s*. *Educ:* Yorebridge Grammar Sch., Yorks. Joined Indian Army, 1946; RMA, Sandhurst, 1947; commnd RA, 1948; Egypt, 1949; 1st RHA, 1950–54 (Germany from 1952); HQ 7 Armoured Div., 1954–57; Staff College, 1959; HQ 17 Gurkha Div., Malaya, 1960–62; MoD, 1962–64; comd Chestnut Troop 1st RHA, Germany and Aden, 1964–66; Instructor, Staff Coll., 1966–69; comd 1st RHA, UK, N Ire., Germany, 1969–71; MoD, 1971–73; comd 7th Armoured Bde, 1973–75. Dir, Public Relations (Army), 1976–78; Dir of Mil. Ops, MoD (Army), 1978–80; Comdr 2nd Armoured Div., BAOR, 1980–83; Comdr 1st (British) Corps, BAOR, 1983–85. Colonel Commandant: Army Air Corps, 1980–; RA, 1982–. Hon. Colonel: 3rd Bn Yorkshire Volunteers TA, 1983–; 1st RHA, 1985–. *Publications:* The Story of the Royal Artillery 1914–18, 1976; articles for British Army Rev. and Jl RA. *Recreations:* military history, gardening. *Address:* c/o Lloyds Bank, Cox's and King's Branch, 6 Pall Mall, SW1. *Club:* East India, Devonshire, Sports and Public Schools.

FARNHAM, 12th Baron, *cr* 1756; **Barry Owen Somerset Maxwell;** Bt (Nova Scotia) 1627; Chairman: Brown, Shipley & Co. Ltd (Merchant Bankers), since 1984 (Director, since 1959); Brown, Shipley Holdings Ltd, since 1976; Avon Rubber Co., since 1978; Assistant Grand Master, United Grand Lodge of England, since 1982; *b* 7 July 1931; *s* of Hon. Somerset Arthur Maxwell, MP (died of wounds received in action, 1942), and Angela Susan (*d* 1953), *o d* of late Capt. Marshall Owen Roberts; *S* grandfather 1957; *m* 1959, Diana Marion, *er d* of Nigel Gunnis; two adopted *d*. *Educ:* Eton; Harvard Univ. *Heir:* *b* Hon. Simon Kenlis Maxwell [*b* 12 Dec. 1933; *m* 1964, Karol Anne, *d* of Maj.-Gen. G. E. Prior-Palmer, CB, DSO, and Katherine Edith Bibby; two *s* one *d* (of whom one *s* one *d* are twins)]. *Address:* 11 Earl's Court Gardens, SW5 0TD; Farnham, Co. Cavan. *Clubs:* Boodle's; Kildare Street and University (Dublin).

FARNINGHAM, Alexander Ian, DSC; Managing Director, Industrial Relations and Personnel, British Shipbuilders, 1977–80; *b* 3 Nov. 1923; *s* of Alexander Farningham and Janet Leask Broadley; *m* 1st, 1949, Lois Elizabeth Halse (marr. diss. 1981); one *s* two *d*; 2nd, 1981, Susan Wyllie. *Educ:* Glebelands Primary Sch., Dundee; Morgan Academy, Dundee; St Andrews Univ. (MA). Mem., RYA. *Recreations:* walking, birdwatching, photography, sailing. *Address:* South Lodge, Whitehouse, near Tarbert, Argyll PA29 6XR. *T:* Whitehouse (Argyll) 221. *Clubs:* Cruising Association; Royal Northern and Clyde Yacht (Rhu); Clyde Cruising; Tarbert (Loch Fyne) Sailing.

FARNSWORTH, John Windsor; Chairman, East Midlands Economic Planning Board, 1965–72; *b* 5 May 1912; *yr s* of late Arthur Claude and Annie Farnsworth, Derby; *m* 1938, Betty Mary Bristow; two *s*. *Educ:* Hanley High Sch.; Balliol Coll., Oxford; Univ. of Birmingham. Asst Comr, Nat. Savings Cttee, 1935; transf. to Min. of Nat. Insurance, 1948; Regional Controller, N Midland Region, Min. of Pensions and Nat. Insurance, 1961; transf. to Dept of Economic Affairs, 1965; Min. of Housing and Local Govt, later Dept of the Environment, 1969. Pres., Nottingham and E Mids Group, Royal Inst. of Public Administration, 1966–68. *Recreations:* painting, foreign travel. *Address:* 143 Melton Road, West Bridgford, Nottingham. *T:* Nottingham 231937.

FARQUHAR, Charles Don Petrie, JP; DL; Area Manager, Community Industry, since 1972; engineer; *b* 4 Aug. 1937; *s* of late William Sandeman Farquhar and Annie Preston Young Farquhar; *m*; two *d*. *Educ:* Liff Road and St Michael's Primary Schs, Dundee; Stobswell Secondary Sch., Dundee. Served with Royal Engineers (Trng NCO); subseq. supervisory staff, plant engrg. Mem., Labour Party Parly Panel; City Councillor, Dundee, 1965–75 (ex-Convener, Museums, Works and Housing Cttees); Lord Provost and Lord Lieutenant of City of Dundee, 1975–77. Chm., Dundee Dist Licensing Bd, Dundee Dist Licensing Cttee, 1984–. JP Dundee, 1974; DL Dundee, 1977. *Recreations:* fresh-water angling, gardening, caravanning, numismatics, do-it-yourself. *Address:* 15 Sutherland Crescent, Dundee DD2 2HP. *T:* Dundee 610666/643127, (office) Dundee 21980/27024.

FARQUHAR, Sir Michael (Fitzroy Henry), 7th Bt *cr* 1796, of Cadogan House, Middlesex; farmer; *b* 29 June 1938; *s* of Sir Peter Walter Farquhar, 6th Bt, DSO, OBE, and Elizabeth Evelyn (*d* 1983), *d* of Francis Cecil Albert Hurt; *S* father, 1986; *m* 1963, Veronica Geraldine Hornidge; two *s*. *Educ:* Eton; Royal Agricultural College. *Recreations:* fishing, shooting. *Heir:* *s* Charles Walter Fitzroy Farquhar, *b* 21 Feb. 1964. *Address:* Manor Farm, West Kington, Chippenham, Wilts. *T:* Castle Combe 782671. *Club:* White's.

FARQUHARSON of Invercauld, Captain Alwyne Arthur Compton, MC 1944; JP; Head of Clan Farquharson; *b* 1 May 1919; *er s* of late Major Edward Robert Francis Compton, JP, DL, Newby Hall, Ripon, and Isle of Mull, and Sylvia, *y d* of A. H. Farquharson; recognised by Lord Lyon King of Arms as Laird of Invercauld (16th Baron of Invercauld; *S* aunt 1941), also as Chief of name of Farquharson and Head of Clan, since 1949; assumed (surname) Compton as a third fore-name and assumed surname of Farquharson of Invercauld, by warrant granted in Lyon Court, Edinburgh, 1949; *m* 1949, Frances Strickland Lovell, *d* of Robert Pollard Oldham, Seattle, Washington, USA. *Educ:* Eton; Magdalen Coll., Oxford. Joined Royal Scots Greys, 1940. Served War, 1940–45, Palestine, N Africa, Italy, France (wounded); Captain 1943. County Councillor, Aberdeenshire, 1949–75, JP 1951. *Address:* Invercauld, Braemar, Aberdeenshire. *T:* Braemar 213.

See also R. E. J. Compton.

FARQUHARSON of Whitehouse, Captain Colin Andrew, FRICS; chartered surveyor and land agent; Vice Lord Lieutenant of Aberdeenshire, since 1983; JP; *b* 9 Aug. 1923; *s* of late Norman Farquharson of Whitehouse; *m* 1948, Jean Sybil Mary (*d* 1985), *d* of late Brig.-Gen. J. G. H. Hamilton of Skene, DSO, JP, DL; two *d* (and one *d* decd). *Educ:* Rugby. FLAS 1956, FRICS 1970. Served Grenadier Guards, 1942–48: ADC to Field Marshal Sir Harold Alexander (later (1st) Earl Alexander of Tunis), 1945. Member, Queen's Body Guard for Scotland (Royal Company of Archers), 1964–. Chartered surveyor and land agent in private practice in Aberdeenshire, 1953–; Director, MacRobert Farms (Douneside) Ltd, 1971–. Member, Bd of Management for Royal Cornhill Hosps, 1962–74; Chm., Gordon Local Health Council, 1975–81; Mem., Grampian Health Bd, 1981–. DL 1966, JP 1969, Aberdeenshire. *Recreations:* shooting, fishing, farming. *Address:* Whitehouse, Alford, Aberdeenshire AB3 8DP. *Clubs:* MCC; Royal Northern and University (Aberdeen).

See also Master of Arbuthnott.

FARQUHARSON, Hon. Sir Donald (Henry), Kt 1981; **Hon. Mr Justice Farquharson;** Judge of the High Court of Justice, Queen's Bench Division, since 1981; *b* 1928; *yr s* of Charles Anderson Farquharson, Logie Coldstone, Aberdeenshire, and Florence Ellen Fox; *m* 1960, Helen Mary, *er d* of Comdr H. M. Simpson, RN (retd), Abbots Brow, Kirkby Lonsdale, Westmorland; three *s* (one *d* decd). *Educ:* Royal Commercial Travellers Sch.; Keble Coll., Oxford (MA). Called to Bar, Inner Temple, 1952; Bencher, 1979. Dep. Chm., Essex QS, 1970; a Recorder of the Crown Court, 1972–81; QC 1972; Presiding Judge, SE Circuit, 1985–. A Legal Assessor to GMC and GDC, 1978–81; Chm., Disciplinary Cttee of Bar, 1983–85; Mem., Judicial Studies Bd, 1984–85. *Recreations:* opera, walking. *Address:* Royal Courts of Justice, Strand, WC2A 2LL.

FARQUHARSON, Sir James (Robbie), KBE 1960 (CBE 1948; OBE 1944); retired, and is now farming; *b* 1 Nov. 1903; *s* of Frank Farquharson, Cortachy, Angus, Scotland, and Agnes Jane Robbie; *m* 1933, Agnes Binny Graham; two *s*. *Educ:* Royal Technical College, Glasgow; Glasgow Univ. BSc Glasgow 1923. Asst Engineer, LMS Railway, 1923–25; Asst Engineer, Kenya and Uganda Railway, 1925–33; Senior Asst Engineer, Kenya and Uganda Railway, 1933–37; Asst to Gen. Manager, Tanganyika Railways, 1937–41; Chief Engineer, Tanganyika Railways, 1941–45; General Manager, Tanganyika Railways, 1945–48; Deputy General Manager, East African Railways, 1948–52; Gen. Manager, Sudan Railways, 1952–57; Gen. Manager, East African Railways and Harbours, 1957–61; Asst Crown Agent and Engineer-in-Chief of Crown Agents for Overseas Governments and Administrations, 1961–65. Chm., Millbank Technical Services Ordnance Ltd, 1973–75. *Publication:* Tanganyika Transport, 1944. *Recreation:* cricket. *Address:* Kinclune, by Kirriemuir, Angus, Scotland. *T:* Kingoldrum 210. *Club:* Nairobi (Kenya).

FARQUHARSON, Robert Alexander, CMG 1975; HM Diplomatic Service, retired; *b* 26 May 1925; *s* of late Captain J. P. Farquharson, DSO, OBE, RN, and late Mrs Farquharson (*née* Prescott-Decie); *m* 1955, Joan Elizabeth, *o d* of Sir (William) Ivo Mallet, *qv*; two *s* one *d* (and one *s* decd). *Educ:* Harrow; King's Coll., Cambridge. Served with RNVR, 1943–46. Joined Foreign (now Diplomatic) Service, 1949; 3rd Sec., Moscow, 1950; FO, 1952; 2nd Sec., Bonn, 1955; 1st Sec., Panama, 1958; Paris, 1960; FO, 1964; Counsellor, Dir of British Trade Develt, S Africa, 1967; Minister, Madrid, 1971; Consul-Gen., San Francisco, 1973; Ambassador to Yugoslavia, 1977–80. *Address:* The Old Rectory, Tollard Royal, Wilts. *Clubs:* Naval and Military, Flyfishers'.

FARQUHARSON-LANG, William Marshall, CBE 1970; Member, National Health Service (Scotland) Staff Commission, 1972–77; *b* 2 July 1908; *s* of late Very Rev. Marshall B. Lang, DD, sometime Moderator, Gen. Assembly of Church of Scotland, and Mary Eleanor Farquharson Lang; *m* 1937, Sheila Clive Parker; one *d*. *Educ:* Edinburgh Acad.; Edinburgh Univ. (MA); London Univ. Sudan Political Service (Educn), 1931–55; Dep. Dir of Educn (Sudan Govt), 1950–55. Mem., 1959, Chm., 1965–72, NE Regional Hosp. Board; Vice-Chm., Scottish Health Services Council, 1964–66; Chm., Cttee on Admin. Practice of Hosp. Bds in Scotland, 1966; Rector's Assessor and Mem., Aberdeen Univ. Court, 1965–76. Mem., Kincardine CC, 1956–59. Laird of Finzean, Aberdeenshire, 1938–61. Hon. LLD Aberdeen, 1972. Coronation Medal, 1953. Sudan Republic Medal, 1977. *Recreations:* fishing, country activities. *Address:* Balnahard House, Finzean, Aberdeenshire. *T:* Feughside 270. *Club:* New (Edinburgh).

FARR, Dennis Larry Ashwell, Hon. DLitt; FRSA, FMA; Director, Courtauld Institute Galleries, since 1980; *b* 3 April 1929; *s* of late Arthur William Farr and Helen Eva Farr (*née* Ashwell); *m* 1959, Diana Pullein-Thompson (writer), *d* of Captain H. J. Pullein-Thompson, MC, and Joanna (*née* Cannan); one *s* one *d*. *Educ:* Luton Grammar Sch.; Courtauld Inst. of Art, London Univ. (BA, MA). Asst Witt Librarian, Courtauld Inst. of Art, 1952–54; Asst Keeper, Tate Gallery, 1954–64; Curator, Paul Mellon Collection, Washington, DC, 1965–66; Sen. Lectr in Fine Art, and Dep. Keeper, University Art Collections, Univ. of Glasgow, 1967–69; Dir, City Museums and Art Gallery, Birmingham, 1969–80. Fred Cook Meml Lecture, RSA, 1974. Hon. Art Adviser, Calouste Gulbenkian Foundation, 1969–73; Member: British Council Fine Arts Adv. Cttee, 1971–80; Wright Cttee on Provincial Museums and Galleries, 1971–73; Museums Assoc. Council, 1971–74 (Vice-Pres., 1978–79, 1980–81; Pres., 1979–80); Art Panel, Arts Council, 1972–77; ICOM(UK) Exec. Bd, 1976–85; Cttee, Victorian Soc., 1980; Exec. Cttee, Assoc. of Art Historians, 1981– (Chm. of Assoc., 1983–86); History of Art and Design Bd, CNAA, 1981–; Trustee, Birmingham Mus. and Art Gall. Appeal Fund, 1980– (Chm. Trustees, 1978–80). FRSA 1970; FMA 1972. Hon. DLitt Birmingham, 1981. JP Birmingham, 1977–80. Gen. Editor, Clarendon Studies in the History of Art, 1985–. *Publications:* William Etty, 1958; Catalogue of the Modern British School Collection, Tate Gallery (with M. Chamot and M. Butlin), 1964; British Sculpture since 1945, 1965; New Painting in Glasgow, 1968; Pittura Inglese 1660–1840, 1975; English Art 1870–1940, 1978, 2nd edn 1984; (contrib.) British Sculpture in the Twentieth Century, 1981; (with W. Bradford) The Courtauld Collection (catalogue for exhibns in Tokyo and Canberra), 1984; (with W. Bradford) The Northern Landscape (exhibn catalogue, New York), 1986; (contrib.) In Honor of Paul Mellon, Collector and Benefactor, 1986; articles in: Apollo, Burlington Magazine, TLS, etc. *Recreations:* riding, reading, foreign travel. *Address:* 12 Blandford Road, Bedford Park, W4 1DU. *T:* 01–995 6400; The Cottage, Longborough, Moreton-in-Marsh, Glos GL56 0QD. *Clubs:* Athenæum, Institute of Contemporary Arts.

See also Denis Cannan.

FARR, Sir John (Arnold), Kt 1984; MP (C) Harborough Division of Leicestershire since 1959; Member of Lloyd's; *b* 25 Sept. 1922; *er s* of late Capt. John Farr, JP, and Mrs M. A. Farr, JP; *m* 1960, Susan Ann, *d* of Sir Leonard Milburn, 3rd Bt, and of Joan Lady Milburn, Guyzance Hall, Acklington, Northumberland; two *s*. *Educ:* Harrow. RN, 1940–46 serving in Mediterranean and S Atlantic; Lieut-Comdr RNVR. Executive Dir, Home Brewery and Apollo Productions Ltd, 1950–55. Contested Ilkeston, General Election, 1955. Sec., Cons. Parly Agric. Cttee, 1970–74, Vice-Chm., 1979–; Sec., Parly Conservation Cttee, 1972–. Member: Exec. Cttee, UK Branch CPA, 1972–74; UK Delegn to WEU and Council of Europe, 1973–78 (Vice-Chm., Cttee on Agric.); Chairman: Anglo-Irish Parly Gp, 1977–80; Parly Knitwear Ind. Gp, 1980–; British-Zimbabwe Parly Gp, 1980–. Vice-Pres., Shooting Sports Trust, 1972–; Chm., British Shooting Sports Council, 1977–. *Recreations:* cricket and shooting. *Address:* Shortwood House, Lamport, Northants. *T:* Maidwell 260; 11 Vincent Square, Westminster, SW1; Tanrago, Beltra, Co. Sligo. *T:* Sligo 72106. *Clubs:* Boodle's, MCC.

FARR, Air Vice-Marshal Peter Gerald Desmond, CB 1968; OBE 1952; DFC 1942; retired; Director, Brain Research Trust, 1973–83; *b* 26 Sept. 1917; *s* of late Gerald Farr and Mrs Farr (*née* Miers); *m* 1949, Rosemarie (*d* 1983), *d* of late R. S. Haward; two *s* one *d*. *Educ:* Tonbridge Sch. Commnd in RAF, 1937; served War of 1939–45, Middle East, India and Burma; OC, No. 358 Sqdn, 1944–45; OC, RAF Pegu, 1945–46; OC, 120 Sqdn, 1950–51; Dep. Dir, Jt Anti-Submarine Sch., 1952–54; OC, RAF Idris, 1954–55; Directing Staff, Jt Services Staff Coll., 1959; SASO, Malta, 1960–63; OC, RAF Kinloss, 1963–64; Air Officer Administration: RAF Germany, 1964–68; Strike Comd, 1969–72. *Recreations:* golf, fishing, music. *Address:* c/o Lloyds Bank, Great Missenden, Bucks. *Club:* Royal Air Force.

FARRANCE, Roger Arthur; Member, Electricity Council, since 1979; *b* 10 Nov. 1933; *s* of Ernest Thomas Farrance and Alexandra Hilda May (*née* Finch); *m* 1956, Kathleen Sheila (*née* Owen); one *d*. *Educ:* Trinity School of John Whitgift, Croydon; London School of Economics (BScEcon). FIPM. HM Inspector of Factories, Manchester, Doncaster and Walsall, 1956–64; Asst Sec., West of England Engineering Employers' Assoc., Bristol, 1964–67; Industrial Relations and Personnel Manager, Foster Wheeler John Brown Boilers Ltd, 1967–68; Dep. Director, Coventry and District Engineering Employers' Assoc., also Coventry Management Trng Centre, 1968–75; Dep. Industrial Relations Adviser (Negotiating), Electricity Council, 1975–76; Industrial Relations Adviser, Electricity Council, 1976–79. Member Council: ACAS, 1983–; CBI, 1983–. OStJ 1983. *Recreations:* photography, music. *Address:* 7 Melville Avenue, Wimbledon, SW20 0NS. *T:* 01–946 9650. *Club:* Royal Automobile.

FARRAND, Prof. Julian Thomas, LLD; a Law Commissioner, since 1984; Professor of Law, Victoria University of Manchester, since 1968; *b* 13 Aug. 1938; *s* of J. and E. A. Farrand; *m* 1957, Winifred Joan Charles; one *s* two *d*. *Educ:* Haberdashers' Aske's Sch.; University Coll. London (LLB 1957, LLD 1966). Admitted Solicitor, 1960. Asst Lectr, then Lectr, KCL, 1960–63; Lectr, Sheffield Univ., 1963–65; Reader in Law, QMC, 1965–68; Dean, Faculty of Law, Manchester Univ., 1970–72, 1976–78. Chairman: Rent Assessment Panel, Gtr Manchester and Lancs Area, 1973– (Vice-Pres., 1977–84); Supplementary Benefit Appeals Tribunal, 1977–80; Nat. Insce Local Tribunal, 1980–83; Social Security Appeal Tribunal, 1983–; Govt Conveyancing Cttee, 1984–85. *Publications:* (ed with Dr J. Gilchrist Smith) Emmet on Title, 15th edn 1967 to 19th edn (as sole editor) 1986; Contract and Conveyance, 1963–64, 4th edn 1983; (ed) Wolstenholme and Cherry, Conveyancing Statutes, 13th edn (vols 1–6) 1972; The Rent Acts and Regulations, 1978, 2nd edn (with A. Arden) 1981. *Recreations:* chess, France. *Address:* 69 Trinity Court, Gray's Inn Road, WC1.

FARRANDS, Dr John Law, CB 1982; FTS, CEng; FInstP, FAIP; Chairman, Overseas Telecommunications Commission Research and Development Board, since 1983; Chairman, Australian Institute of Marine Science, since 1982; Director, Quest Investment, since 1986; consultant to companies and government, since 1982; *b* 11 March 1921; *s* of Harold Rawlings Farrands and Hilda Elizabeth (*née* Bray); *m* 1946, Jessica (*née* Ferguson); three *s* one *d* (and one *s* decd). *Educ:* Melbourne Univ. (BSc); London Univ. (PhD); Imperial Coll. of Science and Technol. (DIC, CEng). FTS 1976; FInstP 1957; FAIP 1962. Served RAEME, AIF, 1941 (Captain). Scientific Adviser to Mil. Bd, 1957; Chief Supt, Aeronautical Res. Labs, 1967; Chief Def. Scientist, 1971; Permanent Head, Dept of Science and Environment, later Dept of Science and Technol., 1977–82. Leader, Aust. Delegn to UNCSTD, 1980. Cllr, Nat. Energy Res., Develt and Demonstration Council, 1978–83. Dir, Interscan Australia, 1980–84. *Publications:* (jtly) Changing Disease Patterns and Human Behaviour, 1981; articles in scientific and engrg jls. *Recreations:* fishing, music. *Address:* 20 The Boulevard, Glen Waverley, Vic 3150, Australia. *T:* (03) 232–8195. *Clubs:* Commonwealth (Canberra); Sciences, Naval and Military (Melbourne).

FARRANT, Maj.-Gen. Ralph Henry, CB 1964; retd; Chairman, Royal National Lifeboat Institution, 1975–79; *b* 2 Feb. 1909; *s* of late Henry Farrant, MICE, Rye, Sussex; *m* 1932, Laura Bonella (*d* 1984), *d* of late Lieut-Col G. Clifford M. Hall, CMG, DSO; two *d*. *Educ:* Rugby; RMA, Woolwich. 2nd Lieut, RA 1929; Field and Mountain Artillery till 1938. War of 1939–45: Tech. Appts in Min. of Defence (1) and HQ, MEF, 3rd British Inf. Div., 1944. Lieut-Col 1950, Min. of Supply; Col 1954; Brig. 1957; Dir of Munitions, Brit. Jt Services Mission, Washington, 1955–58; Sen. Mil. Officer, Armament R&D Estabt, 1958–61; Maj.-Gen. 1961; Vice-Pres., Ordnance Board, 1961–63; Pres. of Ordnance Bd, War Office, 1963–64. Yachtsman's Award, RYA, 1973. *Recreation:* sailing. *Address:* 3 Meadow View Close, Wareham, Dorset. *Clubs:* Army and Navy, Royal Yacht Squadron, Royal Motor Yacht, Royal Ocean Racing, Royal Artillery Yacht.

FARRAR, Bernard; City Treasurer, Birmingham City Council, since 1986; *b* 30 June 1930; *s* of Charles Newton and Edith Ethel Farrar; *m* 1963, Sheila Mary Moore (*d* 1982); one *d*. *Educ:* County Commercial College, Wednesbury. IPFA 1963; FRVA 1986. Borough of Tipton, 1950–58; County Borough of Smethwick, 1958–65; City of Birmingham, 1965–73; W Midlands County Council, 1973–76; Asst City Treasurer, 1976–82, Dep. City Treasurer, 1982–86, City of Birmingham. *Recreations:* visits to theatres and concerts, gardening, walking, DIY. *Address:* Council House, Birmingham B3 3AB. *T:* 021–235 3803.

FARRAR, Rex Gordon, LVO 1975; HM Diplomatic Service, retired; Consul-General and Director of Trade Promotion, Osaka, Japan, 1980–85; *b* 22 Aug. 1925; *s* of late John Percival Farrar and Ethel Florence Farrar (*née* Leader); *m* 1978, Masako (*née* Ikeda); one *s* one *d*. *Educ:* Latymer's Sch., Edmonton; London Univ. (BA Hons History). Served Royal Navy, 1944–47. Joined HM Diplomatic Service, 1947; served, New Orleans, 1953–57; Jakarta, 1960–63; Caracas, 1964–68; San Salvador, 1968–71; Tokyo, 1971–75; Rangoon, 1978–80. *Recreations:* golf, tennis, studying Japanese. *Address:* 2 Lexham Garden Mews, Kensington W8. *T:* 01–370 7729. *Club:* Kobe (Japan).

FARRAR-HOCKLEY, Gen. Sir Anthony Heritage, GBE 1982 (MBE 1957); KCB 1977; DSO 1953 and bar 1964; MC 1944; author (military history); Commander-in-Chief Allied Forces Northern Europe, 1979–82; ADC General to the Queen, 1981–83; retired 1983; *b* 8 April 1924; *s* of late Arthur Farrar-Hockley; *m* 1945, Margaret Bernadette Wells (*d* 1981); two *s* (and one *s* decd); *m* 1983, Linda Wood. *Educ:* Exeter Sch. War of 1939–45 (despatches, MC): enlisted under-age in ranks of The Gloucestershire Regt and served until Nov. 1942; commissioned into newly forming 1st Airborne Div., campaigning in Greece, Italy, S France, to 1945 (despatches 1943). Palestine, 1945–46; Korea, 1950–53 (despatches 1954); Cyprus and Port Said, 1956; Jordan, 1958; College Chief Instructor, RMA Sandhurst, 1959–61; commanded parachute bn in Persian Gulf and Radfan campaign, 1962–65; Principal Staff Officer to Dir of Borneo Ops, 1965–66; Comdr, 16 Parachute Bde, 1966–68; Defence Fellowship, Exeter Coll., Oxford, 1968–70 (BLitt); DPR (Army), 1970; Comdr, Land Forces, N Ireland, 1970–71; GOC 4th Div., 1971–73; Dir, Combat Development (Army), 1974–77; GOC SE District, 1977–79. Colonel Commandant: Prince of Wales's Div., 1974–80; Parachute Regt, 1977–83; Col, The Gloucestershire Regt, 1978–84. *Publications:* The Edge of the Sword, 1954; (ed) The Commander, 1957; The Somme, 1964; Death of an Army, 1968; Airborne Carpet, 1969; War in the Desert, 1969; General Student, 1973; Goughie: the Life of General Sir Hubert Gough, GCB, GCMG, KCVO, 1975. *Recreations:* cricket, badminton, sailing, walking. *Address:* Pye Barn, Moulsford, Oxon. *Club:* Savage.

FARRELL, Arthur Denis, CMG 1970; *b* 27 Jan. 1906; *s* of Joseph Jessop Farrell, CBE; *m* 1953, Margaret Madeline (*née* Cox); one *s*. *Educ:* St Paul's Sch.; Balliol Coll., Oxford. Sixth Form (Classical) Master, Sedbergh Sch., 1929–30, Bradford Grammar Sch., 1930–36; called to the Bar, Middle Temple, 1937; Sixth Form (Classical) Master, Bedford Sch., 1939–41; served RAF, 1941–46. Squadron-Leader; Crown Counsel, Singapore, 1947–51: Legal Draftsman, Fedn of Malaya, 1951–56; Solicitor-Gen., Fedn of Malaya,

1956–58; QC 1957; Puisne Judge, Kenya, 1958–69 (Acting Chief Justice, 1968). Chm., Med. Appeal Tribunals, 1974–78. Coronation Medal, 1953. *Recreations*: golf, photography, music. *Address*: 64 East Avenue, Bournemouth, Dorset. *T*: Bournemouth 761878.

FARRELL, James; Procurator Fiscal, South Strathclyde, Dumfries and Galloway (formerly Lanarkshire) at Airdrie, 1955–75; Solicitor; *s* of Thomas Farrell and Margaret Farrell (*née* Quigley); *m* 1952, Margaret Clare O'Brien; one *s* three *d*. *Educ*: Our Lady's High Sch., Motherwell; St Patrick's Coll., Armagh, N Ireland; Glasgow Univ. (BL). In private practice as a solicitor, prior to joining Procurator Fiscal Service of the Crown. In latter capacity, Prosecutor for the Crown in the Sheriff Court, leading evidence at inquiries, there, into circumstances of death, particularly in suspicious, sudden and unexplained circumstances, fatal accidents, and where the public interest generally is involved; precognition and preparation of cases for High Court of Justiciary, and investigation relating to estates where the Crown may have to intervene as Ultimus Haeres, etc. *Recreations*: golf, bridge, gardening, photography, motoring, walking. *Address*: Clairville, 4 Belleisle Avenue, Uddingston, Glasgow G71 7AP. *T*: Uddingston 813385. *Club*: St Mungo's Academy FP Centenary (Glasgow).

FARRELL, James Aloysius; Sheriff of Lothian and Borders of Edinburgh, since 1986; *b* 14 May 1943; *s* of James Stoddart Farrell and Harriet Louise McDonnell; *m* 1967, Jacqueline Allen; two *d*. *Educ*: St Aloysius College; Glasgow University (MA); Dundee University (LLB). Admitted to Faculty of Advocates, 1974; Advocate-Depute, 1979–83; Sheriff: Glasgow and Strathkelvin, 1984; S Strathclyde, Dumfries and Galloway, 1985. *Recreations*: sailing, hillwalking, cycling. *Address*: 73 Murrayfield Gardens, Edinburgh. *T*: 031–337 2884.

FARRELL, M. J.; *see* Keane, M. N.

FARRELL, Michael Arthur; General Secretary, Amateur Athletics Association, since 1982; *b* 27 April 1933; *s* of Herbert and Marjorie Farrell; *m* 1st, 1957, Myra Shilton (*d* 1973); two *d*; 2nd, 1976, Beryl Browne. *Educ*: Beverley Grammar Sch., Yorks; Holly Lodge Grammar Sch., Birmingham. Design Draughtsman, 1949–51; Nat. Service, RASC, 1951–53; Planning Engineer, 1953–61; Representative, 1961–74; Sales Manager, Lillywhites Cantabrian, 1974–80; Sales Executive, En-Tout-Cas, 1980–82. *Recreations*: painting, walking, cycling. *Address*: Amateur Athletic Association, Francis House, Francis Street, SW1P 1DL. *T*: 01–828 9326.

FARRELL, Terence, (Terry Farrell), OBE 1978; Partner in Terry Farrell Partnership, since 1980; *b* 12 May 1938; *s* of Thomas and Mary Farrell (*née* Molly Maguire); *m* 1st, 1960, Angela Rosemarie Mallam; two *d*; 2nd, 1973, Susan Hilary Aplin; two *s* one *d*. *Educ*: St Cuthbert's Grammar Sch., Newcastle; Durham Univ. (BArch, 1st class hons); Univ. of Pennsylvania (MArch, MCP). ARIBA 1963; MRTPI 1970; FSIAD 1981. Harkness Fellow, Commonwealth Fund, USA, 1962–64. Partner in Farrell Grimshaw Partnership, 1965–80. Major projects include: Headquarters and studios for TVam and Limehouse Productions; greenhouses for Clifton Nurseries; Craft Council Galleries; Henley Royal Regatta Headquarters. *Publications*: articles in numerous British and foreign jls; *relevant publication*: (monograph) Terry Farrell, by Academy Editions, 1984. *Recreations*: walking, swimming. *Address*: 8 Paddington Street, W1M 4DN. *T*: 01–487 2641.

FARRELL, Timothy Robert Warwick; Organist, Liberal Jewish Synagogue, St John's Wood, since 1975; *b* 5 Oct. 1943; *m* 1975, Penelope Walmsley-Clark; one *s*. *Educ*: Diocesan Coll., Cape Town; Royal Coll. of Music, London, etc. FRCO, ARCM (piano and organ). Asst Organist, St Paul's, Knightsbridge, 1962–66; Asst Organist, St Paul's Cath., 1966–67; Sub-organist, Westminster Abbey, 1967–74; Organ Tutor at Addington Palace, RSCM, 1966–73; Organist, Choirmaster and Composer, HM Chapels Royal, 1974–79. Broadcaster, gramophone records, etc. *Recreations*: golf, walking, sailing. *Address*: Didcroft, Toat, Pulborough, W Sussex RH20 1BZ.

FARRER, Brian Ainsworth; QC 1978; **His Honour Judge Farrer**; a Circuit Judge, since 1985; *b* 7 April 1930; *s* of A. E. V. A. Farrer and Gertrude (*née* Hall); *m* 1960, Gwendoline Valerie (*née* Waddoup), JP; two *s* one *d*. *Educ*: King's Coll., Taunton; University Coll., London (LLB). Called to the Bar, Gray's Inn, 1957. A Recorder, 1974–85. Mem. Cttee, Normid Housing Assoc., 1977–. *Recreations*: golf, music, chess, bridge. *Address*: Shutt Cross House, Walsall Wood Road, Aldridge, West Midlands WS9 8QT; Ardudwy Cottage, Ty Ardudwy, Aberdovey, Gwynedd. *Club*: Aberdovey Golf.

FARRER, Sir (Charles) Matthew, KCVO 1983 (CVO 1973); Private Solicitor to the Queen, since 1965; Partner in Messrs Farrer & Co, Solicitors, since 1959; *b* 3 Dec. 1929; *s* of Sir (Walter) Leslie Farrer, KCVO, and late Hon. Lady Farrer; *m* 1962, Johanna Creszentia Maria Dorothea Bennhold; one *s* one *d*. *Educ*: Bryanston Sch.; Balliol Coll., Oxford (MA). Hon. Treasurer, British Inst. of Archaeology, Ankara. *Recreations*: travel, reading. *Address*: 6 Priory Avenue, Bedford Park, W4 1TX. *T*: 01–994 6052. *Club*: United Oxford & Cambridge University.

FARRER, David John; QC 1986; a Recorder, since 1983; *b* 15 March 1943; *s* of John Hall Farrer and Mary Farrer; *m* 1969, Hilary Jean Bryson; two *s* one *d*. *Educ*: Queen Elizabeth's Grammar Sch., Barnet; Downing Coll., Cambridge (MA, LLB). Called to the Bar, Middle Temple, 1967; in practice, 1968–. Contested (L): Melton, 1979; Rutland and Melton, 1983. *Recreations*: tennis, cricket, Liberal Party politics. *Address*: The Grange, Hoby, Melton Mowbray, Leics LE14 3DT. *T*: Rotherby 232. *Club*: National Liberal.

FARRER, Margaret Irene, OBE 1970; Chairman of Central Midwives Board, 1973–79; *b* 23 Feb. 1914; *e d* of Alfred and Emblyn Farrer. *Educ*: Poltimore Coll., Exeter; UCH London. SRN, SCM, DN (London), MTD, RST. Midwifery Tutor, General Lying-in Hosp., 1942–49; Matron: St Mary's Hosp., Croydon, 1949–56; Forest Gate Hosp., 1956–71; Chief Nursing Officer, Thames Gp, 1971–74. Member: Central Midwives Bd, 1952–; Central Health Services Council, 1963–74; NE Metropolitan Regional Hosp. Bd, 1969–74; NE Thames Regional Health Authority, 1973–76; Editorial Bd, Midwife and Health Visitor; Hon. Treas., Royal Coll. of Midwives, 1967–76. *Recreations*: gardening, walking. *Address*: Coombe Brook, Dawlish, South Devon. *T*: Dawlish 863323.

FARRER, Sir Matthew; *see* Farrer, Sir C. M.

FARRER-BROWN, Leslie, CBE 1960; Consultant; Director: Nuffield Foundation, 1944–64; Alliance Building Society, 1969–83 (Chairman, 1975–81); *b* 2 April 1904; *er s* of late Sydney and Annie Brown; *m* 1928, Doris Evelyn (*d* 1986), *o d* of late Herbert Jamieson; two *s*. *Educ*: LSE (BSc Econ.), Hon. Fellow 1975; Gray's Inn (Barrister-at-Law, 1932). Asst Registrar, LSE, 1927–28; on Administrative Staff, Univ. of London, 1928–36; Sec., Central Midwives Bd, 1936–45; seconded to Min. of Health, 1941–44. Pres., Surrey and Sussex Rent Assessment Panel, 1965–76. Sec., Interdepartmental Cttee on Med. Schs, 1942–44. Chairman: Malta Med. Services Commn, 1956; Highgate Juvenile Court, 1952–61; Highgate Court, 1961–65; Nat. Council of Social Service, 1960–73; Centre for Educational Television Overseas, 1962–70; Overseas Visual Aid Centre, 1958–70; Voluntary Cttee on Overseas Aid and Develt, 1965–76; Centre for Information on Language Teaching, 1966–72; Cttee for Res. and Develt in Modern Languages, 1964–70; Rhodesia Med. Sch. Cttee; Univ. of London Inst. of Child Health, 1966–76; Inst. of Race Relations, 1968–72. Member: Colonial Adv. Med. Cttee, 1946–61; Colonial Social Science Res. Council, 1954–61; Med. Educn Cttee of UGC, 1945–52; Rating of Charities Cttee, 1958–59; Adv. Council, BBC, 1956–65; Court of Governors, LSE; Chm. Council and Sen. Pro-Chancellor, Univ. of Sussex, 1976–80. Trustee, Nuffield Provincial Hospitals Trust, 1955–67; UK Governor, Commonwealth Foundn, 1966–. JP: Middx, 1947–65; East Sussex, 1966–81. Hon. FDSRCS. Hon. LLD: Birmingham; Witwatersrand; Sussex; Hon. DSc Keele. *Publication*: (jt) A Short Textbook on Public Health and Social Services. *Recreations*: travel, painting. *Address*: Dale House, Keere Street, Lewes, East Sussex. *Clubs*: Athenæum, Royal Commonwealth Society (Life Vice-Pres., 1969).

FARRIMOND, Herbert Leonard, CBE 1977; Coordinator, Public Affairs, Associated Octel Company Ltd, since 1982; Chairman, H. L. Farrimond & Associates Ltd, since 1978; *b* 4 Oct. 1924; *s* of late George and Jane Farrimond, Newcastle upon Tyne; *m* 1951, Patricia Sara (*née* McGrath); one *s*. *Educ*: St Cuthbert's Grammar Sch., Newcastle upon Tyne; Durham Univ. BA (Hons) Politics and Economics. Australian Dept of Labour and Nat. Service, 1948–50; Imperial Chemical Industries Ltd, and Imperial Metal Industries Ltd, 1950–68; Upper Clyde Shipbuilders Ltd, 1968–69; Dir of Personnel, Dunlop Ltd, 1969–72; Mem., British Railways Bd, 1972–77. Director: British Rail Engineering Ltd; British Rail Shipping and Internat. Services Div.; Transmark Ltd (Chm.); Portsmouth and Sunderland Newspapers Ltd, 1978–80; Chm., British Transport Hotels, 1976–78. Adviser to industrial and commercial cos, 1978–. Mem. Council, Advisory, Conciliation and Arbitration Service, 1974–78. Part-time Mem., British Waterways Bd, 1980–82. Governor, British Transport Staff Coll. Ltd, 1972–77. FCIT; FIPM. *Recreations*: golf, gardening, music. *Address*: 9 Ardgare, Shandon, Helensburgh, Dunbartonshire. *T*: Helensburgh 820803. *Clubs*: Royal Scottish Automobile (Glasgow); Royal Northern and Clyde Yacht (Rhu).

FARRINGTON, Sir Henry Francis Colden, 7th Bt, *cr* 1818; RA retired; *b* 25 April 1914; *s* of Sir Henry Anthony Farrington, 6th Bt, and Dorothy Maria (*d* 1969), *o d* of Frank Farrington; *S* father, 1944; *m* 1947, Anne, *e d* of late Major W. A. Gillam, DSO; one *s* one *d*. *Educ*: Haileybury. Retired from Army, 1960 (Major; now Hon. Col). *Heir*: *s* Henry William Farrington, ARICS [*b* 27 March 1951; *m* 1979, Diana Donne Broughton, *yr d* of Geoffrey Broughton, Somerset; one *s*]. *Address*: Higher Ford, Wiveliscombe, Taunton, Somerset TA4 2RL. *T*: Wiveliscombe 23219.

FARRIS, Hon. John Lauchlan; Chief Justice of British Columbia and Administrator of Province of British Columbia, 1973–79; *b* 5 Sept. 1911; *s* of late Senator John Wallace de Beque Farris, QC and late Dr Evlyn Fenwick Farris; *m* 1933, Dorothy Colledge; one *s* two *d*. *Educ*: Univ. of British Columbia (BA); Harvard Law Sch. (LLB). Lectured on commercial law, Univ. of British Columbia, 1945–55. KC (Canada) 1950. Past Pres., Vancouver Bar Assoc.; Past Chm. of Bd of Governors, Crofton House Sch.; Past Pres., Harvard Club of Vancouver; Pres., Canadian Bar Assoc., 1971–72 (Past Vice-Pres. for BC); Fellow, Amer. Coll. of Trial Lawyers. Hon. Member: Amer. Bar Assoc.; Manitoba Bar Assoc.; Law Soc. of Saskatchewan. Senior Partner, Farris Farris Vaughan Wills & Murphy, until 1973. *Recreations*: boating, woodworking. *Address*: 1403 Angus Drive, Vancouver, BC V6H 1V2, Canada. *T*: (604) 738–1264. *Clubs*: Vancouver (Vancouver); Union (Victoria); Royal Vancouver Yacht, West Vancouver Yacht.

FARROW, Christopher John; an Assistant Director, Bank of England, since 1983; *b* 29 July 1937; *s* of late Thomas and Evangeline Dorothea Farrow; *m* 1961, Alison Brown; one *s* one *d*. *Educ*: Cranleigh Sch.; King's Coll., Cambridge (BA). Board of Trade, 1961; Harkness Fellowship and visiting scholar, Stanford Univ., USA, 1968–69; Private Sec. to Pres. of BoT and Minister for Trade, 1970–72; Dept of Trade and Industry, 1972–74; Cabinet Office, 1975–77; Dept of Industry, 1977–83; on secondment to Kleinwort Benson, 1982–83. Mem., Engrg Council, 1984–86. *Recreation*: gardening. *Address*: Bank of England, EC2R 8AH.

FARROW, Mia (Villiers); actress; *b* 9 Feb. 1945; *d* of John Villiers Farrow and Maureen O'Sullivan; *m* 1970, André Previn (marr. diss. 1979), *qv*; three *s* two *d*. *TV series*: Peyton Place, 1965; *films*: Secret Ceremony, 1968; Rosemary's Baby, 1969; John and Mary, 1970; The Public Eye, 1972; The Great Gatsby, 1974; Full Circle, Death on the Nile, A Wedding, 1978; Hurricane, 1980; A Midsummer Night's Sex Comedy, 1982; Zelig, 1983; Broadway Danny Rose, 1984; The Purple Rose of Cairo, 1985; Hannah and her Sisters, 1986; *stage*: The Importance of Being Earnest, NY, 1963; Mary Rose, Shaw, 1973; The Three Sisters, Greenwich, 1974; The House of Bernarda Alba, Greenwich, 1974; Peter Pan, 1975; The Marrying of Ann Leete, RSC, 1975; The Zykovs, Ivanov, RSC, 1976; A Midsummer Night's Dream, Leicester, 1976; Romantic Comedy, NY, 1979. David Donatello Award, Italy, 1969; Best Actress awards: French Academy, 1969; San Sebastian, 1969; Rio de Janeiro, 1970. *Address*: Bridgewater, Conn, USA.

FARTHING, (Richard) Bruce (Crosby); Deputy Director-General, General Council of British Shipping, 1980–83; Rapporteur, Sea Transport Commission, International Chamber of Commerce, since 1976; Consultant Director, International Association of Dry Cargo Shipowners, since 1984; *b* 9 Feb. 1926; *s* of late Col Herbert Hadfield Farthing and late Marjorie Cora (*née* Fisher); *m* 1959, Anne Brenda Williams (marr. diss.), LLB, barrister, *d* of late Thomas Williams, solicitor; one *s* one *d*. *Educ*: Alleyns Sch., (Dulwich and Rossall) St Catharine's Coll., Cambridge (MA). Commissioned RA and RHA, 1944–48. Called to Bar, Inner Temple, 1954; Govt Legal Service, 1954–59; joined Chamber of Shipping of the United Kingdom, 1959; Asst General Manager, 1966; Secretary, Cttee of European Shipowners and Cttee of European National Shipowners' Assocs, 1967–74; Secretary-General, Council of European and Japanese National Shipowners' Assocs (CENSA), 1974–76; Director, General Council of British Shipping, 1976–80. Trustee, Nautical Museums Trust, 1983–. Mem. Court of Common Council (Aldgate Ward), 1982–. Pres., Aldgate Ward Club, 1985 (Vice-Pres., 1984); Governor: City of London Sch., 1983–; SOAS, 1985–. FBIM. *Publication*: ed, Vol. 20, Aspinalls Maritime Law Cases, 1961. *Recreations*: sailing, music, golf. *Address*: 44 St George's Drive, SW1V 4BT. *Clubs*: MCC, Incogniti Cricket, Royal Ocean Racing; Rye Golf.

FARVIS, Prof. William Ewart John, CBE 1978 (OBE 1972); BSc, BSc(Eng), CEng, FIEE, FRSE; engineering consultant; Professor Emeritus of Electrical Engineering, University of Edinburgh (Professor, 1961–77); *b* 12 Dec. 1911; *o s* of late William Henry Farvis and Gertrude Anne Farvis; *m* 1939, Margaret May Edmonstone Martin; one *s* one *d*. *Educ*: Queen Elizabeth's Hosp., Bristol; Bristol and London Univs. Lectr, University Coll., Swansea, 1937–40 and 1945–48; Air Ministry, Telecommunications Res. Estab., 1940–45; Lectr/Sen. Lectr, Edinburgh Univ., 1948–61, Prof. and Head of Dept of Electrical Eng., 1961–77, Chairman, Sch. of Engineering Sci. 1972–75. Mem., British Nat. Cttee for Radio Science, 1960–66; Science Research Council: Mem., Electrical and Systems Cttee, 1968–72; Engineering Board, 1972–75 and 1976–81; Polytechnics Cttee, 1975–78; Chm., Solid-state Devices Panel, 1972–75; Electrical and Systems Cttee 1972–75; Advanced Ground Transport Panel 1975–80; Mem. Council, 1976–81. Mem. Council, IEE, 1972–75 and 1976–79; Editor, Microelectronics Journal, 1976–78.

Recreation: music. *Address:* 14 Cluny Terrace, Edinburgh EH10 4SW. *T:* 031-447 4939. *Club:* Athenæum.

FARWELL, Rt. Rev. Gerard Victor; Abbot of Worth, since 1965; Abbot President of English Benedictine Congregation, 1967–85; *b* 15 Oct. 1913; 3rd *s* of late Frederick Arthur Farwell and Monica Mary Quin. *Educ:* St Benedict's, Ealing. Entered Downside Abbey, 1932; Housemaster at Downside Sch., 1946–48; Bursar at Worth, 1950–57; Prior of Worth, 1957–65. *Address:* Worth Abbey, Crawley, West Sussex RH10 4SB.

FATAYI-WILLIAMS, Hon. Atanda, GCON 1983; CFR 1980; Chief Justice of Nigeria, 1979–83; *b* 22 Oct. 1918; *s* of Alhaji Issa Williams and Alhaja Ashakun Williams; *m* 1948, Irene Violet Lofts; three *s*. *Educ:* Methodist Boys' High Sch., Lagos, Nigeria; Trinity Hall, Cambridge (BA 1946, LLB 1947, MA 1949; Hon. Fellow 1983). Called to the Bar, Middle Temple, 1948. Private practice, Lagos, 1948–50; Crown Counsel, Lagos, 1950–55; Dep. Comr for Law Revision, Western Nigeria, 1955–58; Chief Registrar, High Court of Western Nigeria, 1958–60; High Court Judge, 1960–67; Justice of Appeal, Western State Court of Appeal, 1967–69; Justice, Supreme Court of Nigeria, 1969–79. Mem., Council of State, 1983–84. Chairman: Ports Arbitration Bd, 1971; All Nigeria Law Reports Cttee, 1972–75; Body of Benchers, 1979–80; Legal Practitioners' Privileges Cttee, 1979–83; Federal Judicial Service Commn, 1979–83; Judiciary Consultative Cttee, 1979–83; National Archives Cttee, 1979–83; Bd of Trustees, The Van Leer Nigerian Educn Trust, 1973–85; Crescent Bearers, Lagos, 1978–84; Council of Legal Educn, 1984–. Member: Nigerian Inst. of Internat. Affairs, 1972–; National Museum Soc., Lagos, 1972–. Trustee, Nigerian Youth Trust, 1979–84. Hon. Fellow, Nigerian Inst. of Advanced Legal Studies, 1983; Life FRSA 1949. *Publications:* (ed) Western Nigeria Law Reports, 1955–58; (with Sir John Verity) Revised Laws of the Western Region of Nigeria, 1959; Sentencing Processes, Practices and Attitudes, as seen by an Appeal Court Judge, 1970; Faces, Cases and Places (autobiog.), 1983. *Recreations:* reading, swimming, walking, speed-boats. *Address:* 8 Adetokunbo Ademola Street, Victoria Island, Lagos, Nigeria. *T:* Lagos 611315. *Clubs:* Athenæum, United Oxford & Cambridge University; Metropolitan, Motor Boat (Lagos).

FATCHETT, Derek John; MP (Lab) Leeds Central, since 1983; *b* 22 Aug. 1945; *s* of Herbert and Irene Fatchett; *m* 1969, Anita Bridgens (*née* Oakes); two *s*. *Educ:* Monks Road Primary School; Lincoln School; Birmingham University (LLB); LSE (MSc). Research Officer, LSE, 1968–70; Research Fellow, University College, Cardiff, 1970–71; Lectr in Industrial Relations, Univ. of Leeds, 1971–83. *Publications:* (jtly) Workers Participation in Management, 1972; (jtly) Worker Participation: industrial control and performance, 1974; (jtly) The Worker Directors, 1976; articles in learned jls. *Recreations:* gardening, cricket, jogging. *Address:* 130 Bradford Road, Wakefield, Yorks. *T:* Wakefield 375291.

FATEH, Abul Fazal Muhammad Abul; Ambassador of Bangladesh at Algiers, 1977–82; *b* 28 Feb. 1926; *s* of Abdul Gafur and Zohra Khatun; *m* 1956, Mahfuza Banu; two *s*. *Educ:* Dacca, Bangladesh. MA (English Lit.); special course, LSE, 1949–50. Carnegie Fellow in Internat. Peace, 1962–63. Entered Pakistan Foreign Service, 1949; 3rd Secretary: Paris, 1951–53; Calcutta, 1953–56; 2nd Sec., Washington, DC, 1956–60; Dir, Min. of Foreign Affairs, Karachi, 1961–65; 1st Sec., Prague, 1965–66; Counsellor, New Delhi, 1966–67; Dep. High Comr for Pakistan, Calcutta, 1968–70; Ambassador of Pakistan, Baghdad, 1971; Adviser to Actg President of Bangladesh, July, 1971; Foreign Sec., Bangladesh, Jan. 1972; Ambassador of Bangladesh to France and Spain, 1972–75; Permanent Deleg. to UNESCO, 1972–76; High Comr for Bangladesh in London, 1976–77. Leader, Bangladesh Delegation: Commonwealth Youth Ministers' Conf., Lusaka, 1973; Meeting of UN Council on Namibia, Algiers, 1980; Ministerial Meeting of Non-aligned Countries Co-ordination Bureau on Namibia, Algiers, 1981. Chm., Commonwealth Human Ecology Council Symposium, 1977; Hon. Rep. of Royal Commonwealth Soc. in Bangladesh, 1985–. *Address:* 21 Dhanmondi Residential Area, Road No 8, Dhaka, Bangladesh.

FATT, Prof. Paul, FRS 1969; Professor of Biophysics, University College, London, since 1976 (Reader, 1956–76), Fellow 1973. *Publications:* papers in various scientific jls. *Address:* Department of Biophysics, University College, Gower Street, WC1. *T:* 01-387 7050, ext. 283.

FAULDS, Andrew Matthew William; MP (Lab) Warley East, since 1974 (Smethwick, 1966–74); *b* 1 March 1923; *s* of late Rev. Matthew Faulds, MA, and of Doris Faulds; *m* 1945, Bunty Whitfield; one *d*. *Educ:* George Watson's, Edinburgh; King Edward VI Grammar Sch., Louth; Daniel Stewart's, Edinburgh; High Sch., Stirling; Glasgow Univ. Three seasons with Shakespeare Memorial Co., Stratford-upon-Avon; BBC Repertory Co.: Jet Morgan in Journey into Space (BBC). Has appeared in over 35 films and many TV and radio performances. Parliamentary Private Secretary: to Minister of State for Aviation, Min. of Technology, 1967–68; to Postmaster General, 1968–69; Opposition spokesman for the Arts, 1970–73, 1979–82; Chairman: British br., Parly Assoc. for Euro-Arab Cooperation, 1974–; All-Party Parly Heritage Gp; Member: British Delegn to Council of Europe and WEU, 1975–80; Exec. Cttee, GB China Centre, 1976–; Exec. Cttee, Franco-British Council, 1978–; Exec. Cttee, IPU, (British Section), 1983–. *Recreation:* cosseting his constituents. *Address:* 14 Albemarle Street, W1. *T:* 01-499 7589.

FAULKNER OF DOWNPATRICK, Lady; Lucy (Barbara Ethel) Faulkner, CBE 1985; *b* 1 July 1925; *d* of William John Forsythe and Jane Ethel Sewell; *m* 1951, Arthur Brian Deane Faulkner (MP (NI) 1949–73; PC 1959; *cr* Baron Faulkner of Downpatrick, 1977) (killed in a hunting accident, 1977); two *s* one *d*. *Educ:* Aubrey House; Bangor Collegiate Sch.; Trinity College Dublin. BA (Hons History). Journalist, Belfast Telegraph, 1947; Personal Secretary to Sir Basil Brooke, Prime Minister of N Ireland, 1949. Nat. Governor for NI, BBC, 1978–85; Chm., Broadcasting Council for NI, 1981–85; Researcher, 1977, Trustee 1980–, Ulster Historical Foundation; Member: Cttee, Irish Museums Trust, 1984–; NI Tourist Bd, 1985–; Governor, Belfast Library and Soc. for Promoting Knowledge, 1982–. *Recreations:* hunting and dressage, oil painting, genealogy. *Address:* Toberdoney, Farranfad, Downpatrick BT30 8NH. *T:* Seaforde 712.

FAULKNER, Hon. Arthur James; MP (Labour) for Roskill, NZ, since 1957; President, New Zealand Labour Party, since 1976; *b* Auckland, NZ, 1921; *m* 1945, May Cox; two *s* three *d*. *Educ:* Otahuhu District High Sch., NZ. Served War of 1939–45 with RAF as Spitfire pilot in UK, N Africa and Europe. Formerly a credit manager. Labour Party organiser for North Island, 1952–57. Contested (Lab) Franklin, 1951; North Shore, 1954. Parliamentary experience on Select Cttees on Defence, Foreign Affairs, Statutes Revision, Local Govt Convener of Labour Caucus Cttees on Defence and Foreign Affairs. Fact-finding missions to South-East Asia, 1963 and 1967; travelled to Europe and UK to discuss EEC matters, 1969. Minister of Defence, Minister i/c War Pensions and Rehabilitation, 1972–74; Minister of Labour and State Services, 1974–75. *Recreations:* fishing, boating, aviation. *Address:* 1 Inverness Avenue, Mt Roskill, Auckland, New Zealand.

FAULKNER, David Ewart Riley, CB 1985; Deputy Under-Secretary of State, Home Office, since 1982; *b* 23 Oct. 1934; *s* of Harold Ewart and Mabel Faulkner; *m* 1961, Sheila Jean Stevenson; one *s* one *d*. *Educ:* Manchester Grammar Sch.; Merchant Taylors' Sch., Northwood; St John's Coll., Oxford (MA Lit Hum). Home Office: Asst Principal, 1959; Private Sec. to Parly Under-Sec. of State, 1961–63; Principal, 1963; Jt Sec. to Inter-Party Conf. on House of Lords Reform, 1968; Private Sec. to Home Sec., 1969–70; Asst Sec., Prison Dept, 1970, Establishment Dept, 1974, Police Dept, 1976; Asst Under-Sec. of State, 1976; Under Sec., Cabinet Office, 1978–80; Asst Under-Sec. of State, Dir of Operational Policy, Prison Dept, Home Office, 1980–82. *Recreations:* railways, birds. *Address:* Home Office, 50 Queen Anne's Gate, SW1.

FAULKNER, Dennis; *see* Faulkner, J. D. C.

FAULKNER, Prof. Douglas, WhSch, BSc, PhD; FEng, FRINA, FIStructE, MSNAME; RCNC; Head of Department of Naval Architecture and Ocean Engineering, University of Glasgow, since 1973; *b* 29 Dec. 1929; *s* of Vincent and Florence Faulkner; *m* 1954, Jenifer Ann Cole-Adams; three *d*. *Educ:* Sutton High Sch., Plymouth; HM Dockyard Technical Coll., Devonport; RNC, Greenwich. Aircraft Carrier Design, 1955–57; Production Engrg, 1957–59; Structural Research at NCRE, Dunfermline, 1959–63; Asst Prof. of Naval Construction, RNC, Greenwich, 1963–66; Structural Adviser to Ship Dept, Bath, 1966–68; Naval Construction Officer att. to British Embassy, Washington DC, 1968–70, and Mem. Ship Research Cttee, Nat. Acad. of Scis, 1968–71; Res. Associate and Defence Fellow, MIT, 1970–71; Structural Adviser to Ship Dept, Bath, and to the Merrison Box Girder Bridge Cttee, 1971–73. UK Rep., Standing Cttee, Internat. Ship Structures Congress, 1973–85. Chm., Conoco-ABS cttee producing a design code for Tension Leg Platforms offshore, 1981–83; Dir, Veritec Ltd, 1985–. FRSA 1983. *Publications:* chapters in Ship Structural Design Concepts (Cornell Maritime Press), 1975; papers related to structural design of ships, in Trans RINA, Jl of Ship Res., Behaviour of Offshore Structures, etc. *Recreations:* hill walking, swimming, music, chess. *Address:* 57 Bellshaugh Place, Glasgow G12 0PF. *T:* 041-357 1748.

FAULKNER, Sir Eric (Odin), Kt 1974; MBE 1945; Director, Lloyds Bank Ltd, 1968–84 (Chairman, 1969–77); Advisory Director, Unilever, 1978–84; *b* 21 April 1914; *s* of late Sir Alfred Faulkner, CB, CBE; *m* 1939, Joan Mary, *d* of Lt-Col F. A. M. Webster; one *s* one *d*. *Educ:* Bradfield; Corpus Christi Coll., Cambridge (Hon. Fellow, 1975). Joined Glyn, Mills & Co., 1936. Served War of 1939–45, Royal Artillery and Leics Yeomanry; Staff Coll.; Bde Major RA, GSO2; commanded 91 Field Regt RA. Rejoined Glyn, Mills & Co., 1946; Local Dir, 1947–50; Exec. Dir, 1950–68; Dep. Chm., 1959–63; Chm., 1963–68. Chm., Cttee of London Clearing Bankers, 1972–74. Pres., British Bankers' Assoc., 1972–73, 1980–84. Director: Union Discount Co. of London Ltd, 1949–70 (Chm., 1959–70); Hudsons Bay Co., 1950–70 (Dep. Governor, 1952–56); Vickers Ltd, 1957–79. Chairman: Industrial Soc., 1973–76; City Communications Organisation, 1976–79. Warden of Bradfield Coll., 1965–84; Trustee, Winston Churchill Meml Trust, 1973–84. *Recreations:* fishing and walking; formerly cricket and Association football (CUAFC XI 1935). *Address:* Chart Cottage, Seal Chart, Kent.

FAULKNER, Hugh (Branston), OBE 1980; Director: Asthma Research Council, and Asthma Society, since 1983; Help the Aged, from formation, 1961–83; *b* Lutterworth, 8 June 1916; *s* of Frank and Ethel Faulkner; *m* 1954, Anne Carlton Milner; one *s* one *d*. *Educ:* Lutterworth Grammar Sch. ACIS. Educn Administration, City of Leicester, 1936–46; Organising Sec., Fellowship of Reconciliation, 1946–54; business and charity career from 1954. Hon. Dir and later Dir, Voluntary and Christian Service, 1954–79; a Director: Helpage International Ltd, 1966–83; Help the Aged Housing Appeal, 1975–83. Christian peace delegate to USSR, 1952, followed by lecture tour in USA, 1953, on internat. relations; deleg. and speaker, UN World Assembly on Ageing, Vienna, 1982. Mem., Council for Music in Hospitals, 1983–. Trustee: Phyllis Trust; Lester Trust; Andrews Pension Trust; Voluntary and Christian Service; Committee Member: Help the Aged Housing Assoc., 1966–; Voluntary and Christian Service Housing Assoc., 1980–. *Recreations:* music, gardening. *Address:* Longfield, 4 One Tree Lane, Beaconsfield, Bucks. *T:* Beaconsfield 4769. *Club:* National Liberal.

FAULKNER, Dr Hugh Charles, FRCGP; Consultant to Regional Health Authority, Tuscany and to Unità Sanitaria Locale del Chianti; Editorial Board, Salute e Territorio; Hon. Lecturer in Social Medicine, Bedford College, University of London, since 1976; Medical Secretary, Medical Practitioners' Union (ASTMS), and Medical Editor of Medical World, 1971–76; *b* 22 Sept. 1912; *s* of Frank Whitehead Faulkner and Emily Maud Knibb; *m*; one *s* two *d*. *Educ:* Oundle Sch.; London Hosp. MRCS, LRCP, FRCGP 1979. Boys' Club Manager, 1932–35; qual. MRCS, LRCP, 1943. Served War, RAMC, 1944–46. Gen. Practitioner, 1948–76. Mem. Council of Medical Practitioners' Union, 1948–76. Mem., Ordine dei Medici (Firenze), 1981. *Publications:* Medicina di Base in due paesi, Gran Bretagna e l'URSS, 1977; articles in Medical World, Lancet, etc. *Recreation:* attacking the Establishment. *Address:* La Galera, Passo del Sugame, Greve-in-Chianti, Firenze, Italy.

FAULKNER, (James) Dennis (Compton), CBE 1980; VRD 1960; Chairman, Ladybird (NI) Ltd, since 1963; *b* 22 Oct. 1926; *s* of James and Nora Faulkner; *m* 1952, Janet Cunningham; three *d*. *Educ:* College of St Columba, Co. Dublin. Served RNVR, 1946–71. Chairman: Belfast Collar Co. Ltd, 1957–63; Belfast Savings Bank, 1960–61; NI Devlt Agency, 1978–82; Board Member: Gallaher NI, 1980– (Chm., 1982–); Northern Bank Ltd, 1983–. Farming, 1946–. *Recreations:* sailing, hunting, shooting, ocean racing. *Address:* Ringhaddy House, Killinchy, Co. Down, Northern Ireland. *T:* Killinchy 541114. *Clubs:* Royal Ocean Racing, Royal Cruising; Cruising Club of America (New York).

FAULKNER, John Richard Hayward; Head of Artistic Planning, National Theatre, since 1983; *b* 29 May 1941; *s* of Richard Hayward Ollerton and Lilian Elizabeth (*née* Carrigan); *m* 1970, Janet Gill (*née* Cummings); two *d* two step *d*. *Educ:* Archbishop Holgate's Sch., York; Keble Coll., Oxford (BA). Worked with a number of theatre companies, Prospect Productions, Meadow Players, Century Theatre, Sixty-Nine Theatre Co., Cambridge Theatre Co., toured extensively, UK, Europe, Indian Sub-Continent, Australia, 1960–72; Drama Director: Scottish Arts Council, 1972–77; Arts Council of GB, 1977–83. *Recreations:* intricacies and wildernesses. *Address:* 33 Hadley Gardens, Chiswick W4 4NU. *T:* 01-995 3041.

FAULKNER, Most Rev. Leonard Anthony; *see* Adelaide, Archbishop of, (RC).

FAULKNER, Sir Percy, KBE 1964; CB 1950; Controller of HM Stationery Office and Queen's Printer of Acts of Parliament, 1961–67; *b* 11 May 1907; *s* of Thomas Faulkner and Margaret A. Faulkner (*née* Hood); *m* 1933, Joyce Rosemary Lois MacDonogh; one *s* one *d*. *Educ:* Royal Belfast Academical Institution; Trinity Coll., Dublin. Entered Ministry of Transport, 1930; Dep. Sec. (Inland Transport), 1957; Dep. Sec. (Shipping), 1958–61; Chm. British Cttee on Prevention of Pollution of the Sea by Oil, 1953–57; rep. UK at various international conferences on shipping matters, 1947–60. *Address:* Highfield, 11 Green Lane, Aspley Guise, Beds MK17 8EN. *Club:* Athenæum.

FAULKS, Peter Ronald, MC 1943; **His Honour Judge Faulks;** a Circuit Judge, since 1980; *b* 24 Dec. 1917; *s* of late M. J. Faulks and A. M. Faulks (*née* Ginner); *m* 1949, Pamela Brenda, *d* of Peter Lawless; two *s*. *Educ:* Tonbridge; Sidney Sussex Coll., Cambridge (MA). Served War of 1939–45, Duke of Wellington's Regt, Dunkirk, N Africa, Anzio, etc; Major 1943; wounded 3 times. Admitted a solicitor, 1949. A Recorder of the Crown Court, 1972–80. Dep. Chm., Agricultural Land Tribunal (SE England), 1972–80; Pres., Berks, Bucks and Oxon Law Soc., 1976–77. *Recreation:* country life. *Address:* Downs Cottage, Westbrook, Boxford, Newbury, Berks. *T:* Boxford 382. *Clubs:* MCC, Farmers'.

FAURE, Edgar (Jean); de l'Académie Française; President, National Assembly, France, 1973–78; Member, European Parliament, since 1979; *b* Béziers, 18 Aug. 1908; *s* of Jean-Baptiste Faure and Claire Faure (*née* Lavit); *m* 1931, Lucie Meyer (*d* 1977); two *d*; *m* 1980, Marie-Jeanne Vuez. *Educ:* Ecole de Langues Orientales, Paris. Advocate, Paris Court of Appeal, 1929; Dir of Legislative Services to the Presidency, Council of French Cttee of Nat. Liberation, 1943–44; Asst Deleg. to War Crimes Trials, Nuremberg, 1945; Deputy for the Jura (Radical-Socialist), 1946–58; Mayor of Port-Lesney (Jura), 1947–70; Pres., General Council of the Jura, 1949–67; Secretary of Finance, 1949–50; Minister of Budget, 1950–51; Minister of Justice, 1951–52; Prime Minister, Jan.-Feb. 1952; Pres, Commn of Foreign Affairs of Nat. Assembly, 1952–53; Minister of Finance and Economic Affairs, 1953–54; Minister of Foreign Affairs, Jan.-Feb. 1955; Prime Minister, Feb. 1955–Jan. 1956; Minister of Finance, May-June 1958; Senator for the Jura, 1959–66; Deputy for Doubs, 1966–72, 1973–; Prof. of Law, Univ. of Dijon, 1962–66; Minister of Agriculture, 1966–68; Minister of Education, 1968–69; Dir of Research, Faculty of Law, Besançon, 1970–72; Pres., Internat. Commn of Develt of Educn, 1971–72; Mayor of Pontarlier, 1971; Minister of State for Social Affairs, 1972–73; Pres., Regional Council, Franche-Comté, 1974–; Senator from Doubs, 1980. *Publications:* La politique française du pétrole, 1939; M Langois n'est pas toujours égal à lui-meme (novel), 1950; Le serpent et la tortue (study of China), 1957; La disgrace du Turgot, 1961; Etude sur la capitation de Dioclétian d'après le panégyrique VIII, Prévoir le present, 1966; Philosophie d'une réforme, 1969; L'âme du combat (essay), 1970; Ce que je crois, 1971; Apprendre à être (Rapport de la Commission internationale sur le développement de l'éducation, Unesco), 1972; Pour un nouveau contrat social, 1973; La Banqueroute de Law, 1978; (memoirs) Avoir toujours raison . . . c'est un grand tort, vol. 1, 1982 (Prix Cazes, 1983). *Address:* 134 rue de Grenelle, 75007 Paris, France; Ermitage de Beaulieu, 77350 France.

FAUVELLE, Major Michael Henry; barrister-at-law; a Recorder of the Crown Court, since 1979; a Chairman since 1983, Deputy President since 1984, Pensions Appeal Tribunals; Lord Chancellor's Legal Visitor, since 1983; *b* 12 Aug. 1920; *s* of Victor Edmond Fauvelle and Brigid Mary Fauvelle (*née* Westermann); *m* 1964, Marie-Caroline, *e d* of Count and Countess Stanislas d'Orsetti, Château de la Grènerie, Jarzé, France; one *s* one *d*. *Educ:* Stonyhurst Coll.; Royal Military Coll., Sandhurst. Commissioned, 2/Lieut The South Lancashire Regt, 1939, T/Major 1944; active service in N Africa, Italy and Palestine (wounded three times, arguably five); Staff employment as GSO 3 (Ops), Gibraltar, 1947; Staff Captain Q HQ Palestine, 1947–48; Staff Captain A HQ BMM to Greece and HQ 2 Inf. Bde, 1948–50; Adjt 1st Bn, 1951; Major 1952; retired, 1953. Called to the Bar, Lincoln's Inn, 1955; Western Circuit and Hampshire Sessions, 1955–; Dep. Recorder, Oxford, Bournemouth and Reading, 1971. *Address:* Tadley Cottage, Wherwell, Hampshire SP11 7JU. *T:* Chilbolton 217; 17 Carlton Crescent, Southampton SO9 5AL. *T:* Southampton 36036. *Clubs:* Hampshire (Winchester); Home Guard (Wherwell, Hants).

FAVELL, Anthony Rowland; MP (C) Stockport, since 1983; *b* 29 May 1939; *s* of Arnold Rowland Favell and Hildegard Favell; *m* 1966, Susan Rosemary Taylor; one *s* one *d*. *Educ:* St Bees School, Cumbria; Sheffield University (LLB). Solicitor. *Recreations:* music, gardening, hill walking, squash, windsurfing, local community interests. *Address:* Skinners Hall, Edale, Sheffield S30 2ZE. *T:* Hope Valley 70281. *Club:* Lansdowne.

FAWCETT, Colin, QC 1970; *b* 22 Nov. 1923; *s* of late Frank Fawcett, Penrith; *m* 1952, Elizabeth Anne Dickson; one *s* one *d*. *Educ:* Sedbergh. Commnd Border Regt, 1943. Called to Bar, Inner Temple, 1952, Bencher, 1978. Mem., Criminal Injuries Compensation Bd, 1983–. *Recreations:* fishing, music. *Address:* Fairings, Valley Way, Gerrards Cross, Bucks. *T:* Gerrards Cross 883999.

FAWCETT, Sir James (Edmund Sandford), Kt 1984; DSC 1942; QC 1985; President, European Commission of Human Rights, 1972–81 (Member, 1962–84); *b* 16 April 1913; *s* of Rev. Joseph Fawcett and Edith Fawcett; *m* 1937, Frances Beatrice, 2nd *d* of late Dr E. A. Lowe; one *s* four *d*. *Educ:* Rugby Sch.; New Coll., Oxford. Called to the Bar, 1938. Fellow of All Souls Coll., Oxford, 1938. Served War of 1939–45, Royal Navy. Asst Legal Adviser to FO, 1945–50 (to UK Delegn to UN and British Embassy, Washington, 1948–50); Gen. Counsel, IMF, 1955–60; Fellow of All Souls Coll., Oxford, 1960–69; Dir of Studies, RIIA, 1969–73; Prof. of Internat. Law, King's Coll., London, 1976–80, Emeritus Professor 1980. Mem., Inst. of Internat. Law, 1973–; Chm., British Inst. of Human Rights, 1977–81. Pres., UK Immigrants Advisory Service, 1985–. *Publications:* British Commonwealth in International Law, 1963; International Law and the Uses of Outer Space, 1968; The Law of Nations (Penguin), 1968; The Application of the European Convention on Human Rights, 1969; International Economic Conflicts, 1977; Law and Power in International Relations, 1981; Outer Space: new perspectives, 1984; numerous articles. *Recreations:* astronomy, piano. *Address:* Field House, Combe, Newbury, Berks.

FAWCETT, John Harold, CMG 1986; HM Diplomatic Service; Ambassador to Bulgaria, since 1986; *b* 4 May 1929; *yr s* of late Comdr Harold William Fawcett, OBE, RN, and of late Una Isobel Dalrymple Fawcett (*née* Gairdner); *m* 1961, Elizabeth Shaw; one *s*. *Educ:* Radley (Scholar); University Coll., Oxford (Scholar). 1st cl. Hon. Mods 1951, 2nd cl. Lit. Hum. 1953. Nat. Service, RN (Radio Electrician's Mate), 1947–49. British Oxygen Co., 1954–63 (S Africa, 1955–57). Entered Foreign Service, 1963; FO, 1963–66; 1st Sec. (Commercial), Bombay, 1966–69; 1st Sec. and Head of Chancery, Port-of-Spain, 1969–70; Asst, Caribbean Dept, FCO, 1971–72; Head of Icelandic Fisheries Unit, Western European Dept, FCO, 1973; Amb. to Democratic Republic of Vietnam, 1974; Head of Chancery, Warsaw, 1975–78; Dep. High Comr, Wellington, 1978–86; Counsellor (Commercial and Economic, 1978–83, Political and Economic, 1983–86), and Head of Chancery 1983–85, Wellington. *Recreations:* walking, gardening. *Address:* c/o Foreign and Commonwealth Office, SW1. *Clubs:* Athenæum, Brooks's, Savile; Royal Bombay Yacht.

FAWCUS, Maj.-Gen. Graham Ben; Chief, Joint Services Liaison Organisation, Bonn, since 1986; *b* 17 Dec. 1937; *s* of late Col Geoffrey Arthur Ross Fawcus, RE and Helen Sybil Graham (*née* Stronach); *m* 1966, Diana Valerie, *d* of Dr P. J. Spencer-Phillips of Bildeston, Suffolk; two *s* one *d*. *Educ:* Wycliffe College; RMA Sandhurst (Sword of Honour); King's College, Cambridge (BA 1963, MA 1968). Commissioned RE, 1958; served UK, Cyprus, BAOR, MoD; OC 39 Field Squadron RE, BAOR, 1973–74; MoD, 1975–76; GSO1 (DS), Staff College, 1977–78; CO 25 Engineer Regt, BAOR, 1978–81; Cabinet Office, 1981; Comdt, RSME, 1982–83; ACOS, HQ 1 (Br) Corps, 1984–85. *Recreations:* ski-ing, windsurfing, tennis, Scottish country dancing, furniture restoration. *Address:* c/o Lloyds Bank, Cox & King's Branch, 6 Pall Mall, SW1Y 5NH.

FAWCUS, Sir (Robert) Peter, KBE 1964 (OBE 1957); CMG 1960; Overseas Civil Service, retd; *b* 30 Sept. 1915; *s* of late A. F. Fawcus, OBE; *m* 1943, Isabel Constance (*née* Ethelston); one *s* one *d*. *Educ:* Charterhouse; Clare Coll., Cambridge. Served RNVR, 1939–46. Joined Colonial Service (District Officer, Basutoland), 1946; Bechuanaland Protectorate: Govt Sec., 1954; Resident Commissioner, 1959; HM Commissioner, 1963–65; retd 1965. *Address:* Dochart House, Killin, Perthshire.

FAWCUS, Simon James David; His Honour Judge Fawcus; a Circuit Judge, since 1985; *b* 12 July 1938; *s* of late Ernest Augustus Fawcus and of Jill Shaw; *m* 1966, Joan Mary (*née* Oliphant); one *s* four *d*. *Educ:* Aldenham Sch.; Trinity Hall, Cambridge (MA). Called to the Bar, Gray's Inn, 1961; in practice on Northern Circuit, 1962–85; a Recorder, 1980–85. *Recreations:* real tennis and other lesser sporting activities, music (listening). *Address:* 601 Royal Exchange, Manchester M2 7EB. *T:* 061–834 9560. *Clubs:* MCC; Manchester Tennis and Racket, Big Four (Manchester and Hong Kong); Wilmslow Golf.

FAWKES, Sir Randol (Francis), Kt 1977; Attorney-at-Law, since 1948; *b* 20 March 1924; *s* of Edward Ronald Fawkes and Mildred Fawkes (*née* McKinney); *m* 1951, Jacqueline Fawkes (*née* Bethel); three *s* one *d*. *Educ:* public schools in the Bahamas. Called to the Bar, Bahamas, 1948. A founder: Citizen Cttee, 1949; People's Penny Savings Bank, 1951. Elected Mem. (Progressive Liberal Party), House of Assembly, 1956; promoted law establishing Labour Day as Public Holiday, 1961. Founder, and Pres. 1955–, Bahamas Fedn of Labour (led 19 day general strike which resulted in major labour and political reforms, 1958). Represented Labour Party at constitutional confs in London, 1963 and 1968; addressed UN Cttee of 24 on preparation of Bahamas for independence, 1966. *Publications:* You Should Know Your Government, 1949; The Bahamas Government, 1962; The New Bahamas, 1966; The Faith That Moved The Mountain: a memoir of a life and the times, 1977. *Recreations:* swimming, music, Bible tract writing. *Address:* PO Box N-7625, John F. Kennedy Drive, Nassau, NP, Bahamas. *T:* (office) 809–32–34053; (home) 809–32–34855.

FAWKES, Wally; cartoonist, since 1945; *b* 21 June 1924; *m* 1st, 1949, Sandra Boyce-Carmichelle; one *s* two *d*; 2nd, 1965, Susan Clifford; one *s* one *d*. *Educ:* Sidcup Central Sch.; Sidcup Sch. of Art; Camberwell Sch. of Art. Came from Vancouver, BC, to England, 1931. Joined Daily Mail, 1945; started Flook strip, 1949, transferred to The Mirror, 1984. Political cartoons for: Spectator, 1959–; Private Eye, and New Statesman, 1965–; Observer, and Punch, 1971–; Today, 1986–. Co-Founder, Humphrey Lyttelton Band, 1948. *Publications:* World of Trog, 1977; Trog Shots, 1984; collections of Flook strips. *Recreations:* playing jazz (clarinet and soprano saxophone), cooking, cricket. *Address:* 44 Laurier Road, NW5 1SG. *T:* 01–267 2979. *Clubs:* MCC, Middlesex County Cricket.

FAY, His Honour Edgar Stewart, QC 1956; FCIArb; a Circuit Judge (formerly an Official Referee of the Supreme Court of Judicature), 1971–80; *b* 8 Oct. 1908; *s* of late Sir Sam Fay; *m* 1st, Kathleen Margaret, *e d* of late C. H. Buell, Montreal, PQ, and Brockville, Ont; three *s*; 2nd, Jenny Julie Henriette, *yr d* of late Dr Willem Roosegaarde Bisschop, Lincoln's Inn; one *s*. *Educ:* Courtenay Lodge Sch.; McGill Univ.; Pembroke Coll., Cambridge (MA). Called to Bar, Inner Temple, 1932; Master of the Bench, 1962. FCIArb 1981. Recorder: of Andover, 1954–61; of Bournemouth, 1961–64; of Plymouth, 1964–71; Dep. Chm., Hants QS, 1960–71. Member: Bar Council, 1955–59, 1966–70; Senate of Four Inns of Court, 1970–72. Chm., Inquiry into Crown Agents, 1975–77. *Publications:* Why Piccadilly?, 1935; Londoner's New York, 1936; Discoveries in the Statute Book, 1937; The Life of Mr Justice Swift, 1939; Official Referees' Business, 1983. *Address:* Knox End, Ashdon, Saffron Walden, Essex. *T:* Ashdon 275; 13 Egbert Street, NW1. *T:* 01–586 0725. *Club:* Reform.

FAY, John David, CMG 1985; Director for Publications Policy, Organisation for Economic Co-operation and Development, Paris, 1980–84; *b* 5 July 1919; *s* of late Stanley John Fay and Muriel Etrenne (*née* Nicholson); *m* 1949, Valerie Joyce Stroud; one *s* two *d*. *Educ:* Stowe Sch.; King's Coll., Cambridge (Minor Scholar; BA 1941, 1st Cl. both parts Historical Tripos; MA 1983). BoT, London, 1941–46 (Asst Private Sec. to Pres., 1944–46); Washington, 1946–48; Internat. Secretariat of OECD (formerly OEEC), Paris, 1949–84: Head of Country Studies Div., 1952; Dir, Econs Br., 1957; Dep. Head of Econs and Statistics Dept, 1958, Head of Dept, 1975. *Publications:* extensive unsigned contribs to OEEC and OECD econ. pubns; editorials for Internat. Herald Tribune. *Recreations:* gardening, gastronomy, helping economists to write English. *Address:* 31 avenue du Cardinal de Retz, 78600 Maisons-Laffitte, France. *T:* 3962 27 28. *Club:* Athenæum.

FAYRER, Sir John (Lang Macpherson), 4th Bt *cr* 1896; clerical officer; *b* 18 Oct. 1944; *s* of Sir Joseph Herbert Spens Fayrer, 3rd Bt, DSC, and Helen Diana Scott (*d* 1961), *d* of late John Lang; *S* father, 1976. *Educ:* Edinburgh Academy; Scottish Hotel School, Univ. of Strathclyde. *Heir:* none. *Address:* Overhailes, Haddington, East Lothian.

FEA, William Wallace; Director, Guest, Keen & Nettlefolds Ltd, 1958–72 (Deputy Chairman, 1968–72); *b* Cordova, Argentina, 3 Feb. 1907; *s* of Herbert Reginald Fea and Hilda Florence Fea (*née* Norton); *m* 1935, Norah Anne, *d* of Richard Festing; one *s* (and one *s* decd). *Educ:* Cheltenham Coll. (scholar); Brasenose Coll., Oxford (scholar); BA. ACA 1932; FCA. Mem., Council, Inst. of Chartered Accountants, 1953–71; Mem. Council, BIM, 1969–73; Management Cttee, AA, 1971–77. *Recreations:* (now geriatric) shooting, lawn tennis, listening to music. *Address:* The Lowe, Worfield, near Bridgnorth, Salop. *T:* Worfield 241. *Clubs:* Lansdowne; Edgbaston Priory (Birmingham).

FEARN, John Martin, CB 1976; Secretary, Scottish Education Department, 1973–76, retired; *b* 24 June 1916; *s* of William Laing Fearn and Margaret Kerr Fearn; *m* 1947, Isobel Mary Begbie, MA, MB, ChB; one *d*. *Educ:* High Sch. of Dundee; Univ. of St Andrews (MA); Worcester Coll., Oxford. Indian Civil Service, Punjab, 1940–47; District Magistrate, Lahore, 1946; Scottish Home Dept, 1947; Asst Sec., 1956; Under-Sec., 1966; Under-Sec., Scottish Educn Dept, 1968. *Recreation:* golf. *Address:* 31 Midmar Gardens, Edinburgh EH10 6DY. *T:* 031–447 5301. *Club:* New (Edinburgh).

FEARN, (Patrick) Robin, CMG 1983; HM Diplomatic Service; Assistant Under Secretary of State (Americas), Foreign and Commonwealth Office, since 1986; *b* 5 Sept. 1934; *s* of Albert Cyprian Fearn and Hilary (*née* Harrison); *m* 1961, Sorrel Mary Lynne Thomas; three *s* one *d*. *Educ:* Ratcliffe Coll.; University Coll., Oxford (BA Hons, Mod. Langs). Nat. Service, Intelligence Corps, 1952–54. Overseas marketing, Dunlop Rubber Co. Ltd, 1957–61; entered Foreign Service, 1961; FO, 1961–62; Third, later Second Sec., Caracas, 1962–64; Havana, 1965; First Sec., Budapest, 1966–68; FCO, 1969–72; Head of Chancery, Vientiane, 1972–75; Asst Head of Science and Technol. Dept, FCO, 1975–76; Counsellor, Head of Chancery and Consul Gen., Islamabad, 1977–79; Head of S America Dept, FCO, 1979–82; Head of Falkland Islands Dept, FCO, 1982; RCDS, 1983; Ambassador to Cuba, 1984–86. *Recreations:* tennis, golf, reading, family life. *Address:* c/o Foreign and Commonwealth Office, SW1; 17 Durham Terrace, W2. *T:* 01–229 0479; 14 Gastard, Corsham, Wilts. *T:* Corsham 713067.

FEARNLEY SCARR, J. G.; *see* Scarr.

FEATHERSTONE, Hugh Robert, CBE 1984 (OBE 1974); FCIS, FCIT; Director-General, Freight Transport Association, 1969–84; *b* 31 March 1926; *s* of Alexander Brown Featherstone and Doris Olive Martin; *m* 1948, Beryl Joan Sly; one *s* one *d*. *Educ:* Minchenden Sch., Southgate, London. FCIS 1956; FCIT 1970. Served War, RNVR, 1943–46 (Sub-Lt). Assistant Secretary: Nat. Assoc. of Funeral Dirs, 1946–48; Brit. Rubber

Develt Bd, 1948–58; Asst Sec. 1958–60, Sec. 1960–68, Traders Road Transport Assoc. *Publications:* contrib. to jls concerned with transport and admin. *Recreations:* golf, gardening, languages, travel. *Address:* 5 Rossdale, Tunbridge Wells, Kent. *T:* Tunbridge Wells 30063.

FEAVER, Rt. Rev. Douglas Russell; *b* 22 May 1914; *s* of late Ernest Henry Feaver, Bristol; *m* 1939, Katharine, *d* of late Rev. W. T. Stubbs; one *s* two *d*. *Educ:* Bristol Grammar School; Keble College, Oxford (Scholar; 1st cl. Hons. Mod. History, 1935; 1st Cl. Hons. Theology, 1937; Liddon Student, 1935–37; MA); Wells Theological College. Deacon 1938, priest 1939, St Albans; Curate, St Albans Abbey, 1938–42. Chaplain, RAFVR, 1942–46. Canon and Sub-Dean of St Albans, 1946–58; Chaplain to St Albans School, 1946–58; Proctor in Convocation, 1951–58; Examining Chaplain to Bp of St Albans, 1948–58, to Bp of Portsmouth, 1960–72; Vicar of St Mary's, Nottingham and Rural Dean of Nottingham, 1958–72; Hon. Canon of Southwell, 1958–72; Treasurer, 1959–69; Proctor in Convocation for Southwell, 1970–72; Bishop of Peterborough, 1972–84. Chairman of Trent House Boys' Probation Hostel, 1967–72; Governor of Nottingham Bluecoat School, 1958–72. *Publications:* reviews and articles in Church Times. *Recreation:* conferences not attended. *Address:* 10 Spens Avenue, Gough Way, Cambridge CB3 9LS.

FEDIDA, Sam, OBE 1980; independent consultant, information systems; inventor of Prestel, viewdata system (first public electronic information service); *b* 1918; *m* 1942, Joan Iris Druce. Served Royal Air Force, Radar Officer, 1940–46. Became Asst Dir of Research, The English Electric Company; started research for the Post Office, 1970; Prestel first in use 1979, as public service; MacRobert Award, Council of Engineering Instns, 1979; Prestel sold in Europe, USA, Far East. *Address:* Constable Cottage, 23 Brook Lane, Felixstowe, Suffolk.

FEENY, Max Howard; barrister; *b* 5 Nov. 1928; *s* of late Howard Raymond John Feeny and Frances Kate Feeny (*née* Muspratt); *m* 1952, June Elizabeth (*née* Camplin) (*d* 1986); three *s* four *d*. *Educ:* Stonyhurst Coll.; Oratory Sch.; Univ. of Birmingham (LLB). Called to Bar, Inner Temple, 1953. A Recorder of the Crown Court, 1972–78. Senior Lectr, Inst. of Professional Legal Studies, Queen's Univ. of Belfast, 1982–. Mem., Council of Legal Educn (NI), 1983–. *Recreation:* gardening. *Address:* 28 Hampton Grove, Belfast BT7 3DG; Urlee, Lisselton, near Listowel, Co. Kerry, Eire.

FEHILY, Rt. Rev. Mgr Thomas Francis, Canon; Principal RC Chaplain (Army), 1973–77; *b* 16 Nov. 1917; *s* of late Patrick and Mary Fehily, Ballineen, Co. Cork. *Educ:* Capuchin Franciscan Coll., Rochestown, Co. Cork; St Kieran's Coll., Kilkenny. Ordained, 1942; Motherwell Dio., 1943–53. Commissioned Army Chaplain, 1953; served: Germany, 1953–56; Malaya, 1956–59; Germany and Berlin, 1959–63; RMA, Sandhurst, 1963–66. Senior Chaplain: NI, 1966–67; Singapore, 1967–69; HQ 1 Br. Corps, 1969–71; Western Command, 1971; Northern Command, 1972–73. Canon of Motherwell Cathedral Chapter, 1984. *Recreations:* fishing, golf. *Address:* St John's, Blackwood, Kirkmuirhill, Lanarkshire ML11 9RZ.

FEHR, Basil Henry Frank, CBE 1979; Chairman and Managing Director, Frank Fehr & Co. Ltd London and group of companies, since 1957; Chairman: Fehr Bros Inc. New York and group of companies, since 1970; Colyer Fehr Holdings Pty Ltd, Sydney, since 1984; *b* 11 July 1912; *s* of Frank E. Fehr, CBE and Jane (*née* Poulter); *m* 1st, 1936, Jane Marner (*née* Tallent) (marr. diss. 1951); two *s* one *d*; 2nd, 1951, Greta Constance (*née* Bremner) (marr. diss. 1971); one *d* one step *d*; 3rd, 1974, Anne Norma (*née* Cadman); one *d*. *Educ:* Rugby Sch.; Neûchatel Ecole de Commerce, Switzerland. Served War, 1939–45: HAC, later Instr, Gunnery Sch. of Anti-Aircraft, RA; retd Major. Joined father in family firm, Frank Fehr & Co., 1934; Partner, 1936; Governing Dir, Frank Fehr & Co. London, 1948; Pres., Fehr Bros (Manufactures) Inc. New York, 1949. Chairman: Cocoa Assoc. of London, 1952; London Commodity Exchange, 1954; London Oil and Tallow Trades Assoc., 1955; Copra Assoc. of London, 1957; Inc. Oilseed Assoc. 1958; United Assocs Ltd, 1959. Elected to Baltic Exchange, 1936; Dir, Baltic Mercantile and Shipping Exchange, 1963–69 and 1970–, Vice Chm. 1973–75, Chm. 1975–77. Jurat of Liberty of Romney Marsh, 1979. *Recreations:* sports generally, farming. *Address:* Slodden Farm, Dymchurch, Romney Marsh, Kent. *T:* Dymchurch 2241; 64 Queen Street, EC4R 1ER. *T:* 01–248 5066. *Clubs:* City Livery, Aldgate Ward, MCC, Royal Automobile; Ski Club of Great Britain; West Kent Cricket; Littlestone Golf.

FEIBUSCH, Hans; painter, mural painter, lithographer, sculptor, writer; *b* 15 Aug. 1898; *s* of Dr Carl Feibusch and Marianne Ickelheimer; *m* 1935, Sidonie (*d* 1963), *e d* of D. Gestetner. *Educ:* Frankfurt a/M and Munich Univs. Studied at the Berlin Academy, at Paris Art Schs, in Florence and Rome; received German State award and grant in 1931; pictures in German Public Galleries; work banned and destroyed by Nazis in 1933; since then in London; large mural paintings in churches: St Wilfred's, Brighton; St Elizabeth's, Eastbourne; St Martin's, Dagenham; St John's, Waterloo Road, SE1; St Ethelburga's, Bishopsgate; St Alban's, Holborn; Town Hall, Dudley; Civic Centre, Newport, Mon; Chichester Cathedral; Chichester Palace; Parish Churches, Egham, Goring, Wellingborough, Welling, Preston, Plumstead, Eltham, Portsmouth, Bexley Heath, Wembley, Merton, Southwark, Harrow, Exeter, Battersea, Rotherhithe, Plymouth, Coventry, Christchurch Priory, Bournemouth, Christ Church, St Laurence, Sydney, Portmeirion, Bath; West London Synagogue; statues: St John the Baptist, St John's Wood Church; Christ, Ely Cathedral; Risen Christ, St Alban's Church EC1; 80th birthday exhibn by GLC, Holland Park, 1978. 6 one-man exhibns, incl. Berlin 1980; retrospective exhibn 1925–85, Historisches Museum, Frankfurt, 1986. Much portrait and figure sculpture, 1975–. Dr of Letters, Lambeth, 1985. German Cross of Merit, 1967. *Publications:* Mural Painting, 1946; The Revelation of Saint John, 1946. *Recreations:* music and poetry. *Address:* 30 Wadham Gardens, NW3. *Club:* Athenæum.

FEILDEN, Sir Bernard (Melchior), Kt 1985; CBE 1976 (OBE 1969); FRIBA 1968 (ARIBA 1949); Consultant, Feilden and Mawson, Chartered Architects (Partner, 1956–77); Member, Cathedrals Advisory Commission for England, since 1981; *b* 11 Sept. 1919; *s* of Robert Humphrey Feilden, MC, and Olive Feilden (*née* Binyon); *m* 1949, Ruth Mildred Bainbridge; two *s* two *d*. *Educ:* Bedford Sch. Exhibr, Bartlett Sch. of Architecture, 1938. Served War of 1939–45: Bengal Sappers and Miners. AA Diploma (Hons), 1949; Bratt Colbran Schol., 1949. Architect, Norwich Cathedral, 1963–77; Surveyor to the Fabric: York Minster, 1965–77; St Paul's Cathedral, 1969–77; Dir, Internat. Centre for the Preservation and Restoration of Cultural Property, Rome, 1977–81. Hoffman Wood Prof. of Architecture, Leeds Univ., 1973–74. Mem., Ancient Monuments Bd (England), 1964–77; Mem. Council, RIBA, 1972–77; President: Ecclesiastical Architects' and Surveyors' Assoc., 1975–77; Guild of Surveyors, 1976–77. FSA 1969; FRSA 1973. Corresp. Mem., Architectes en Chef, France. DUniv York, 1973. *Publications:* The Wonder of York Minster, 1976; Introduction to Conservation, 1979; Conservation of Historic Buildings, 1982; articles in Architectural Review, Chartered Surveyor, AA Quarterly. *Recreations:* painting, sailing, fishing, photography. *Address:*

Stiffkey Old Hall, Stiffkey, near Wells-on-Sea, Norfolk NR23 1QJ. *T:* Bingham (Norfolk) 585. *Club:* English-Speaking Union.
See also G. B. R. Feilden.

FEILDEN, Geoffrey Bertram Robert, CBE 1966; MA Cantab; FRS 1959; Founder FEng 1976, FIMechE, Hon. FIStructE; CBIM; Principal Consultant, Feilden Associates Ltd, since 1981; *b* 20 Feb. 1917; *s* of Robert Humphrey Feilden, MC, and Olive Feilden (*née* Binyon); *m* 1st, Elizabeth Ann Gorton; one *s* two *d*; 2nd, Elizabeth Diana Angier (*née* Lloyd). *Educ:* Bedford Sch.; King's Coll., Cambridge (Scholar). Lever Bros. and Unilever Ltd, 1939–40; Power Jets Ltd, 1940–46; Ruston and Hornsby Ltd, 1946–59; Chief Engineer, Turbine Dept, 1949; Engineering Dir, 1954; Man. Dir, Hawker Siddeley Brush Turbines Ltd, and Dir of Hawker Siddeley Industries Ltd, 1959–61; Gp Technical Dir, Davy-Ashmore Ltd, 1961–68; Dep. Dir Gen., British Standards Instn, 1968–70, Dir Gen. 1970–81. Director: Averys Ltd, 1974–79; Plint & Partners Ltd, 1982–. Member: Cttees and Sub-Cttees of Aeronautical Research Council, 1947–62; BTC Res. Adv. Council, 1956–61; Council for Sci. and Indust. Res. of DSIR, 1961–65; Design Council (formerly CoID), 1966–78 (Dep. Chm., 1977–78); Central Adv. Council for Science and Technology, 1970–71; Vis. Cttee to RCA, 1968–84 (Chm., 1977–84); Res. Develt and Engrg Cttee, Industrial Develt Bd for NI, 1983–; Pres., European Cttee for Standardisation, 1977–79. Member, Royal Society Delegation: to USSR, 1965; Latin America, 1968; People's Republic of China, 1975; Leader, BSI Delegn to People's Republic of China, 1980. Technical Adviser to Govt of India, 1968. DSIR Visitor to Prod. Engineering Res. Assoc. of Gt Brit., 1957–65, and to Machine Tool Industry Res. Assoc., 1961–65. Member Council: Royal Society (a Vice-Pres., 1967–69); IMechE, 1955–61, 1969–80; Univ. of Surrey, 1977–78. Trustee: Maurice Lubbock Meml Fund, 1973–; Smallpeice Trust, 1981–. Hon. DTech Loughborough, 1970; Hon. DSc QUB, 1971. MacRobert Award for innovation (jt winner), 1983. *Publications:* Gas Turbine Principles and Practice (contributor), 1955; First Bulleid Memorial Lecture (Nottingham Univ.), 1959; Report, Engineering Design, 1963 (Chm. of Cttee); numerous papers and articles on engineering subjects. *Recreations:* sailing, ski-ing, driving kitchen and garden machines. *Address:* Verlands, Painswick, Glos GL6 6XP. *T:* Painswick 812112. *Club:* Athenæum.
See also Sir B. M. Feilden.

FEILDEN, Sir Henry (Wemyss), 6th Bt *cr* 1846; *b* 1 Dec. 1916; *s* of Col Wemyss Gawne Cunningham Feilden, CMG (*d* 1943) (3rd *s* of 3rd Bt) and Winifred Mary Christian (*d* 1980), *d* of Rev. William Cosens, DD; *S* cousin, Sir William Morton Buller Feilden, 5th Bt, 1976; *m* 1943, Ethel May, 2nd *d* of John Atkinson, Annfield Plain, Co. Durham; one *s* two *d*. *Educ:* Canford Sch.; King's Coll., London. Served War, RE, 1940–46. Clerical Civil Service, 1960–79. *Recreations:* watching cricket, reading. *Heir:* *s* Henry Rudyard Feilden, BVetSc, MRCVS [*b* 26 Sept. 1951; *m* 1982, Anne Shepperd; one *s*]. *Address:* Little Dene, Heathfield Road, Burwash, Etchingham, East Sussex TN19 7HN. *T:* Burwash 882205. *Club:* MCC.

FEILDING, family name of **Earl of Denbigh.**

FEILDING, Viscount; Alexander Stephen Rudolph Feilding; *b* 4 Nov. 1970; *s* and heir of Earl of Denbigh and Desmond, qv.

FEINSTEIN, Prof. Charles Hilliard, PhD; FBA 1983; Professor of Economic and Social History, University of York, since 1978 (Head of Department of Economic and Related Studies, 1981–86); *b* 18 March 1932; *s* of Louis and Rose Feinstein; *m* 1st, 1958, Ruth Loshak; one *s* three *d*; 2nd, 1980, Anne Digby. *Educ:* Parktown Boys' High Sch., Johannesburg; Univ. of Witwatersrand (BCom 1950); Fitzwilliam Coll., Cambridge (PhD 1958). CA (SA) 1954. Research Officer, Dept of Applied Econs, Univ. of Cambridge, 1958–63; Univ. Lectr in Faculty of Econs, Cambridge, 1963–78; Fellow of Clare Coll., Cambridge, 1963–78; Sen. Tutor, Clare Coll. 1969–78. Harvard University: Vis. Res. Fellow, Russian Res. Centre, 1967–68; Vis. Fac. Mem., Dept of Econ., 1986–87; Vis. Lectr, Univ. of Delhi, 1972. Mem. Council: Royal Economic Soc., 1980–; Economic History Soc., 1980–86; Mem., Economic Affairs Cttee, SSRC, 1982–86 (Chm., 1985–86). Governor, NIESR, 1985–. Man. Editor, The Economic Jl, 1980–86. *Publications:* Domestic Capital Formation in the United Kingdom 1920–1938, 1965; (ed) Socialism, Capitalism and Economic Growth, Essays presented to Maurice Dobb, 1967; National Income, Expenditure and Output of the United Kingdom 1855–1965, 1972; (ed) York 1831–1981, 1981; (jtly) British Economic Growth 1856–1973, 1982; (ed) The Managed Economy: Essays in British Economic Policy and Performance since 1929, 1983. *Recreations:* reading, buying books. *Address:* 48 Marygate, York YO3 7BH.

FELDBERG, Wilhelm Siegmund, CBE 1963; MD Berlin; MA Cantab; FRS 1947; FRCP 1978; Professor Emeritus; Personal Grant Holder, National Institute for Medical Research, London, since 1967; Hon. Lecturer, University of London, since 1950; *b* 19 Nov. 1900; *m* 1925, Katherine (*d* 1976), *d* of late Karl Scheffler; one *d* (and one *s* decd); *m* 1977, Kim O'Rourke (*d* 1981). Reader in Physiology, Cambridge Univ., until 1949; Head of Physiology and Pharmacology Division, National Institute for Medical Research, London, 1949–65 (Hon. Head of Division, 1965–66); Head, Lab. of Neuropharmacology, Nat. Inst. for Med. Res., 1966–74. Lectures: Dunham, Harvard, 1953; Evarts Graham Meml, Washington Univ., St Louis, USA, 1961; Aschoff Meml, Freiburg Univ., 1961; Dixon Meml, RSM, 1964; William Withering, 1966; Nat. Research Council of Canada/Nuffield Foundn, 1970–71; Ferrier, Royal Soc., 1974; Sherrington, 1980. Hon. Member: Br. Pharmacol. Soc.; RSM; Physiol. Soc.; Soc. française d'allergie; Deutsche Phys. Gesell.; Deutsche Pharm. Gesell.; Berliner Medizinische Gesell.; Berliner Phys. Gesell. Hon. MD: Freiburg, Berlin, Cologne, Würzburg, Heidelberg, Liège; Hon. DSc: Bradford, 1973; London, 1979; Hon. LLD: Glasgow, 1976; Aberdeen, 1977. Grand Cross, Order of Merit of German Federal Republic, 1961. Baly Medal, 1963; Schmiedeberg Plakette, 1969; Stöhr Medal, 1970; Royal Medal, Royal Soc., 1983. *Publications:* Histamin (with E. Schilf); A Pharmacological Approach to the Brain from its Inner and Outer Surface, 1963; articles in med. and scientific jls. *Recreations:* antique furniture, women's fashions. *Address:* National Institute for Medical Research, Mill Hill, NW7 1AA. *T:* 01–959 3666; Lavenham, 74 Marsh Lane, Mill Hill, NW7 4NT. *T:* 01–959 5545.

FELDMAN, Sir Basil, Kt 1982; Chairman, Watchpost Ltd, since 1983, and other companies; Chairman, National Union of Conservative Party, 1985–86 (Vice-Chairman, 1982–85); *b* 23 Sept. 1926; *s* of Philip and late Tilly Feldman; *m* 1952, Gita Julius; two *s* one *d*. *Educ:* Grocers' School. National Union of Conservative and Unionist Associations, Greater London area: Dep. Chm., 1975–78; Chm., 1978–81; Pres., 1981–; Mem. Nat. Union Exec. Cttee, 1975–; Jt Nat. Chm., Cons. Party's Impact 80s Campaign, 1982–; Member: Policy Gp for London, 1975–81, 1984–; Nat. Campaign Cttee, 1976 and 1978; Adv. Cttee on Policy, 1981–; Cttee for London, 1984–; Vice-Pres., Greater London Young Conservatives, 1975–77; President: Richmond and Barnes Cons. Assoc., 1976–84; Hornsey Cons. Assoc., 1978–82; Patron, Hampstead Cons. Assoc., 1981–. Contested GLC Elections, Richmond, 1973; Member: GLC Housing Management Cttee, 1973–77; GLC Arts Cttee, 1976–81. Mem., Free Enterprise Loan Soc., 1977–84. Chairman: Martlet Services Gp Ltd, 1973–81; Solport Ltd, 1980–85; Dir, Young Entrepreneurs Fund, 1985–. Underwriting Mem. of Lloyds, 1979–. Membre Consultatif, Institut Internat. de Promotion et de Prestige, Geneva (affiliated to Unesco), 1978–. Member: Post Office

Users National Council, 1978–81 (Mem., Tariffs Sub-Cttee, 1980–81); Job Opportunities Task Force (NEDO), 1985–; English Tourist Board, 1986–; Chm., Clothing EDC (NEDO), 1978–85. Chm., Better Made in Britain Campaign, 1983–. *Publications:* Some Thoughts on Jobs Creation (for NEDO), 1984; Constituency Campaigning: a guide for Conservative Party workers; several other Party booklets and pamphlets. *Recreations:* golf, tennis, theatre, opera, travel. *Club:* Carlton.

FELDSTEIN, Prof. Martin Stuart; Professor, Harvard University, since 1969; *b* 25 Nov. 1939; *m* Kathleen Foley; two *d. Educ:* Harvard Coll. (AB *summa cum laude* 1961); Oxford Univ. (BLitt 1963, MA 1964, DPhil 1967). Nuffield College, Oxford University: Research Fellow, 1964–65; Official Fellow, 1965–67; Lectr in Public Finance, Oxford Univ., 1965–67; Harvard University: Asst Professor, 1967–68; Associate Professor, 1968–69. President, National Bureau of Economic Research, 1977–82; Chm., Council of Economic Advrs, 1982–84. *Publications:* (ed) The American Economy in Transition, 1980; Hospital Costs and Health Insurance, 1981; Inflation, Tax Rules, and Capital Formation, 1983; Capital Taxation, 1983. *Address:* Department of Economics, Harvard University, Cambridge, Mass 02138, USA.

FELL, Sir Anthony, Kt 1982; *b* 18 May 1914; *s* of Comdr David Mark Fell, RN; *m* 1938, June Warwick; one *s* one *d. Educ:* New Zealand. Contested (C) Brigg, 1948, South Hammersmith, 1949 and 1950. MP (C) Yarmouth, Norfolk, 1951–66 and 1970–83. *Address:* 11 Denny Street, SE11 4UX.

FELL, Charles Percival, LLD; Hon. Director, Royal Trustco Ltd; Hon. Governor, McMaster University (Chancellor, 1960–65); *b* Toronto, 1894; *s* of I. C. Fell and Sarah (Branton) Fell, both of Toronto, Ont.; *m* 1st, Grace E. Matthews; three *s*; 2nd, 1976, Marjorie Jane Montgomery. *Educ:* University of Toronto Schs; McMaster Univ. Associated with Dillon, Read & Co., NY, 1921–24; Dominion Securities Corp., Toronto, 1925–29; Chm. Canadian group, Investment Bankers Assoc. of America, 1928. Pres., Empire Life Assurance Co., 1934–68. Mem. Bd of Referees (Excess Profits Tax Act, Canada), Ottawa, 1940–45. Pres., Art Gall. of Toronto, 1950–53; Chm., Bd of Trustees, Nat. Gall. of Canada, Ottawa, 1953–59. Coronation Medal, Canada, 1953. Hon. LLD McMaster Univ., 1957. *Address:* 123 Cheltenham Avenue, Toronto, Ontario M3N 1R1, Canada. *T:* 416 4851356. *Clubs:* York, Toronto, Granite (Toronto).

FELL, David; Permanent Secretary, Department of Economic Development, Northern Ireland, since 1984; *b* 20 Jan. 1943; *s* of Ernest Fell and Jessie (*née* McCreedy); *m* 1967, Sandra Jesse (*née* Moore); one *s* one *d. Educ:* Royal Belfast Academical Instn; The Queen's University of Belfast (BSc: Pure and Applied Mathematics, also (1st Cl. Hons) Physics). Sales Manager, Rank Hovis McDougall Ltd, 1965–66; Teacher, 1966–67; Research Associate, 1967–69; Civil Servant, 1969–: Dept of Agriculture (NI), 1969–72; Dept of Commerce (NI), 1972–82 (Under Secretary, 1981); Under Secretary, Dept of Economic Development (NI), 1982; Dep. Chief Exec., Industrial Develt Bd for NI, 1982–84. *Recreations:* music, reading, Rugby Union. *Address:* Department of Economic Development, Netherleigh, Massey Avenue, Belfast BT4 2JP. *Club:* Old Instonians (Belfast).

FELL, Richard Taylor; HM Diplomatic Service; First Secretary and Head of Chancery, Kuala Lumpur, since 1983; *b* 11 Nov. 1948; *s* of late Eric Whineray Fell and of Margaret Farrer Fell (*née* Taylor); *m* 1981, Claire Gates; one *s. Educ:* Bootham Sch., York; Bristol Univ. (BSc); Univ. of London (MA). Joined HM Diplomatic Service, 1971; Ottawa, 1972–74; Saigon, 1974–75; Vientiane, 1975; First Sec. and Chargé d'Affaires *ai*, Hanoi, 1979; First Sec., UK Delegn to NATO, 1979–83. *Recreations:* antiques, reading, sport. *Address:* c/o Foreign and Commonwealth Office, SW1.

FELL, Robert, CB 1972; CBE 1966; JP; Commissioner of Banking and Deposit-taking companies, Hong Kong, since 1984; *b* 6 May 1921; *s* of Robert and Mary Ann Fell, Cumberland; *m* 1946, Eileen Wicks; two *s* one *d. Educ:* Whitehaven Grammar School. War Office, 1939; military service, 1940–46 (despatches); BoT, 1947; Trade Comr, Qld, 1954–59; Asst Sec., Tariff Div., 1961; Commercial Counsellor, Delhi, 1961–66; Under-Sec. i/c export promotion, 1967–71; Sec., ECGD, 1971–74; Chief Exec., The Stock Exchange, 1975–82; Comr for Securities, Hong Kong, 1981–84. Mem., British Overseas Trade Board, 1972–75; Pres., City Branch, BIM, 1976–82. FRSA. JP 1985. *Recreations:* Rugby football (watching), gardening. *Address:* Dalegarth, Guildown Avenue, Guildford, Surrey. *T:* Guildford 572204. *Club:* Travellers'.

FELLGETT, Prof. Peter Berners, PhD; FRS 1986; Professor of Cybernetics, University of Reading, 1965–Sept. 1987; *b* 11 April 1922; *s* of Frank Ernest Fellgett and Rose, (Rowena), (*née* Wagstaffe); *m* 1947, Janet Mary, *o d* of late Prof. G. E. Briggs, FRS and Mrs Nora Briggs; one *s* two *d. Educ:* The Leys Sch., Cambridge; Univ. of Cambridge (BA 1943, MA 1947, PhD 1952). Isaac Newton Student, Cambridge Observatories, 1950–51; Lick Observatory, Calif, 1951–52; Cambridge Observatories, 1952–59; Royal Observatory, Edinburgh, 1959–65. *Publications:* approx. 75 pubns in learned jls and 32 gen. articles. *Recreations:* making musical instruments, high quality audio, gardening, fun-running, not being interrupted and not being hurried. *Address:* Department of Cybernetics, 3 Earley Gate, Whiteknights, PO Box 238, Reading RG6 2AL. *T:* Reading 65758; 48 Northcourt Avenue, Reading RG2 7HQ. *T:* Reading 871612.

FELLINI, Federico; film director since 1950; *b* 20 Jan. 1920; *s* of late Urbano Fellini and Ida Barbiani; *m* 1943, Giulietta Masina. *Educ:* Bologna, Italy. Journalist, 1937–39; radio-author, scenario writer, etc, 1939–42. Has gained many prizes and awards in every part of the world including four "Oscars" (1957, 1958, 1964, 1975) for films La Strada, Le Notti di Cabiria, 8½ and Amarcord. Films include: (as Assistant Director and writer) Quarta Pagina, 1942; Roma Città Aperta, 1944–45; Paisà, 1946; Il Delitto di Giovanni Episcopo, 1947; In Nome della Legge, 1948–49; La Città si Defende, 1951; Il Brigante di Tacca di Lupo, 1953; San Francesco Giullare di Dio, 1954; Fortunella, 1956; (as Director) Luci del Varietà, 1950; Lo Sceicco Bianco, 1952; I Vitelloni, 1953; Agenzia Matrimoniale, 1953; La Strada, 1954; Il Bidone, 1955; Cabiria, 1957; La Dolce Vita, 1960; The Temptation of Dr Antonio, 1962; 8½, 1963 (foreign awards); Giulietta Degli Spiriti, 1965; Never Bet the Devil Your Head, 1968; Director's Blocknotes, 1969; Satyricon, 1969; The Clowns, 1970; Fellini's Roma, 1972; Amarcord, 1974; Casanova, 1976; Orchestra Rehearsal, 1979; La citta delle donne, 1980; E la nave vá, 1983; Ginger and Fred, 1986. *Publications:* Amarcord (trans. Nina Rootes), 1974; Quattro film, 1975. *Address:* 141a Via Margutta 110, Rome, Italy.

FELLOWES, family name of **Barons Ailwyn** and **De Ramsey.**

FELLOWES, Robert, LVO 1983; Deputy Private Secretary to the Queen, since 1986 (Assistant Private Secretary, 1977–86); *b* 11 Dec. 1941; *s* of Sir William Fellowes, KCVO; *m* 1978, Lady Jane Spencer, *d* of Earl Spencer, *qv*; one *s* two *d. Educ:* Eton. Scots Guards (short service commission), 1960–63. Director, Allen Harvey & Ross Ltd, Discount Brokers and Bankers, 1968–77. *Recreations:* cricket, golf, shooting. *Clubs:* White's, Pratt's, MCC.

FELLOWS, Derek Edward, FIA; Chief Actuary, Prudential Assurance Co. Ltd, since 1981; *b* 23 Oct. 1927; *s* of Edward Frederick Fellows and Gladys Fellows; *m* 1948, Mary Watkins; two *d. Educ:* Mercers' Sch. FIA 1956. Entered Prudential Assurance Co. Ltd, 1943; Gp Pensions Manager, 1973–81; Man. Dir, Gp Pension Div., 1984–; Dir, Prudential Corp. plc, 1985–. Mem., Occupational Pensions Bd, 1974–78. FPMI 1976; Vice Pres., Inst. of Actuaries, 1980–83. *Publications:* contrib. Jl of Inst. of Actuaries. *Recreations:* music, gardening. *Address:* 20 Fairbourne, Cobham, Surrey KT11 2BT. *T:* Cobham 65488.

FELLS, Prof. Ian, FEng; Professor of Energy Conversion, University of Newcastle upon Tyne, since 1975; *b* 5 Sept. 1932; *s* of late Dr Henry Alexander Fells, MBE and Clarice Fells, Sheffield; *m* 1957, Hazel Denton Scott; four *s. Educ:* King Edward VII School, Sheffield; Trinity College, Cambridge. MA, PhD. FInstE, CChem, FRSC, FIChemE; FEng 1979. Chief Wireless Officer, British Troops in Austria, 1951–52; Lectr and Dir of Studies, Dept of Fuel Technology and Chem. Engineering, Univ. of Sheffield, 1958–62; Reader in Fuel Science, King's Coll., Univ. of Durham, 1962; Public Orator, Univ. of Newcastle upon Tyne, 1970–73. Allerdale Wylde Lectr, 1986. Pres., Inst. of Energy, 1978–79; Member: Sci. Consultative Gp, BBC, 1976–81; Electricity Supply Res. Council, 1979–; Exec., David Davies Inst. of Internat. Affairs, 1975–; Trustee, Northern Sinfonia Orch., 1984–. Hatfield Meml Prize, 1974; Beilby Meml Medal and Prize, 1976. Participator in TV series: Young Scientist of the Year; The Great Egg Race; Men of Science; Earth Year 2050. *Publications:* Energy for the Future, 1973; contribs to professional jls. *Recreations:* sailing, guitar, energy conversation. *Address:* Department of Chemical Engineering, The University, Newcastle upon Tyne NE1 7RU. *T:* Tyneside 2328511; (home) Tyneside 2855343. *Club:* Naval and Military.

FENBY, Eric William, OBE 1962; Professor of Harmony, Royal Academy of Music, 1964–77; *b* 22 April 1906; *s* of late Herbert Henry and Ada Fenby; *m* 1944, Rowena Clara Teresa Marshall; one *s* one *d. Educ:* Municipal Sch., Scarborough; privately. Amanuensis to Frederick Delius, 1928–34; Mus. Adv. Boosey & Hawkes, 1936–39; début as composer, BBC Promenade Concerts, 1942. Captain, RAEC Sch. of Educn, Cuerdon Hall, 1942–45. Mus. Dir, N Riding Coll. of Educn, 1948–62; Artistic Dir, Delius Centenary Festival, 1962; Pres. Delius Soc., 1964–; Chm., Composers' Guild of Great Britain, 1968, Mem. Council, 1970. Visiting Prof. of Music and Composer in Residence, Jacksonville Univ., Fla, USA, 1968. Mem. Cttee of Management, Royal Philharmonic Soc., 1972. FRCM 1985. Hon. Member: RAM, 1965; Royal Philharmonic Soc., 1984; Hon. DMus Jacksonville, 1978; Hon. DLitt Warwick, 1978; Hon. DLitt Bradford, 1978. *Publications:* Delius as I Knew Him, 1936, rev. edn 1966; a further rev. edn, 1981, packaged with own recordings of all works dictated to him by Delius, known as The Fenby Legacy; Menuhin's House of Music, 1969; Delius, 1971. *Recreations:* walking, chess. *Address:* 35 Brookfield, Highgate West Hill, N6. *T:* 01–340 5122. *Club:* Royal Academy of Music.

FENDALL, Prof. Neville Rex Edwards, MD; Professor of International Community Health, School of Tropical Medicine, University of Liverpool, 1971–81, now Emeritus Professor; Visiting Professor of Public Health, Boston University, since 1982; Adjunct Professor of Community Health, University of Calgary, since 1983; *b* 9 July 1917; *s* of Francis Alan Fendall and Ruby Inez Matthews; *m* 1942, Margaret Doreen (*née* Beynon). *Educ:* University College Hosp. (MD, BSc); London Sch. of Hygiene and Tropical Med. (DPH); FFCM. Colonial Medical Service, 1944–64, Dir of Med. Services, Kenya; Staff Mem., Rockefeller Foundn, 1964–66; Regional Dir, Population Council Inc., New York, 1966–71. Mem., Panel of Experts, WHO, 1957–83; Consultant: World Bank; UN Fund for Population Activities; ODM; Cento; Internat. Develt Res. Centre, Canada; APHA; USAID; Overseas govts. Visiting Lecturer: Harvard, 1966–83; Inst. of Tropical Medicine, Marseilles; Univ. of Glasgow; Univ. of Bradford; Vis. Consultant, Univ. of Hawaii; Commonwealth Foundn Travelling Lectr, 1976. Gold Medal, Mrigendra Medical Trust, Nepal, 1983. *Publications:* Auxiliaries in Health Care, 1972 (English, French, Spanish edns); (with J. M. Paxman and F. M. Shattock) Use of Paramedicals for Primary Health Care in the Commonwealth, 1979; (with F. M. Shattock) Restraints and Constraints to Development, 1983; Selected Papers, 1986; contribs on primary health care, epidemiology, in various jls. *Recreations:* gardening, travel. *Address:* Berwyn, North Close, Bromborough, Wirral L62 2BU. *T:* 051–334 2193. *Clubs:* Royal Commonwealth Society; Athenæum (Liverpool).

FENDER, Prof. Brian Edward Frederick, CMG 1985; Vice-Chancellor, University of Keele, since 1985; *b* 15 Sept. 1934; *s* of late George Clements and of Emily Fender; *m* 1st, 1956; one *s* three *d*; 2nd, 1986, Ann Linscott. *Educ:* Carlisle Grammar Sch.; Sale County Grammar Sch.; Imperial College London (ARCS, BSc 1956; DIC, PhD 1959); MA Oxon 1963; CChem, FRSC. Research Instructor, Univ. of Washington, Seattle, 1959–61; Senior Research Fellow, Nat. Chem. Lab. (now NPL), 1961–63; University of Oxford: Dept Demonstrator in Inorganic Chemistry, 1963–65; Lectr, 1965–84; Senior Proctor, 1975–76; Mem., Hebdomadal Council, 1977–80; St Catherine's College: Fellow, 1963–84 (Hon. Fellow 1986); Sen. Tutor, 1965–69; Chm., Management Cttee, Oxford Colls Admissions Office, 1973–80. Inst. Laue-Langevin, Grenoble: Asst Dir, 1980–82; Dir, 1982–85; Mem., Steering Cttee, 1974–77; Mem., Scientific Council, 1977–80. Mem., SERC, 1985–; Chairman: Science Board, SERC, 1985– (Mem., 1974–77); Neutron Beam Res. Cttee, 1974–77 (Mem., 1969–71); Science Planning Group for Rutherford Lab. Neutron Scattering Source, 1977–80. Mem. Council, Chem. Soc., 1973–76. *Publications:* scientific articles on neutron scattering and solid state chemistry. *Recreation:* visiting France. *Address:* The Clock House, University of Keele, Keele, Staffs ST5 5BG. *T:* Newcastle (Staffs) 628394. *Club:* Athenæum.

FENECH-ADAMI, Dr Edward; MP Malta, since 1969; Leader of Opposition and Leader of Nationalist Party, 1977–81 and since 1982; *b* Birkirkara, Malta, 7 Feb. 1934; *s* of late Luigi Fenech-Adami and Josephine (*née* Pace); *m* 1965, Mary (*née* Sciberras); four *s* one *d. Educ:* St Aloysius Coll., Malta; Royal Univ. of Malta (BA 1955, LLD 1958). Entered legal practice in Malta, 1958. Mem. Nat. Exec., Nationalist Party, 1961, Asst Gen. Sec., 1962–75, Chm., Gen. Council and Admin. Council, 1975–77; Shadow Minister for Labour and Social Services, 1971–77. Vice-Pres., European Union of Christian Democrat Parties, 1979–. Editor, Il-Poplu, 1962–69. *Address:* Partit Nazzjonalista, Pietá, Malta. *T:* (356) 623641/2/3. *Telex:* 1941 Litho.

FENHALLS, Richard Dorian; Chairman, Henry Ansbacher & Co. Ltd, since 1985; Group Executive Director, Henry Ansbacher Holdings PLC, since 1985; *b* 14 July 1943; *s* of Roydon Myers and Maureen Rosa Fenhalls; *m* 1967, Angela Sarah Allen; one *s* one *d. Educ:* Hilton Coll., Univ. of Natal (BA); Christ's Coll., Cambridge (MA, LLM). Attorney, S Africa, 1969. Goodricke & Son, Attorney, S Africa, 1969–70; Citibank, 1970–72; Senior Vice President: Marine Midland Bank, 1972–77; American Express Bank, 1977–81; Dep. Chm. and Chief Exec., Guinness Mahon & Co. Ltd, 1981–85. *Recreations:* sailing, ski-ing. *Address:* 15 St James's Gardens, W11 4RE. *Clubs:* Royal Ocean Racing, Ski Club of Great Britain; Campden Hill Lawn Tennis; Royal Southern Yacht (Hamble).

FENN, Nicholas Maxted, CMG 1980; HM Diplomatic Service; Ambassador in Dublin, since 1986; *b* 19 Feb. 1936; *s* of Rev. Prof. J. Eric Fenn and Kathleen (*née* Harrison); *m*

1959, Susan Clare (*née* Russell); two *s* one *d*. *Educ:* Kingswood Sch., Bath; Peterhouse, Cambridge (MA). Pilot Officer, RAF, 1954–56. Third Sec., British Embassy, Rangoon, 1959–63; Asst Private Sec. to Sec. of State for Foreign and Commonwealth Affairs, 1963–67; First Secretary: British Interests Sect., Swiss Embassy, Algiers, 1967–69; Public Relations, UK Mission to UN, NY, 1969–72; Dep. Head, Energy Dept, FCO, 1972–75; Counsellor, Peking, 1975–77; Head of News Dept and FCO Spokesman, 1979–82; Spokesman to last Governor of Rhodesia, 1979–80; Ambassador, Rangoon, 1982–86. *Recreation:* sailing. *Address:* c/o Foreign and Commonwealth Office, SW1; Applecroft, Chainhurst, Marden, Tonbridge, Kent TN12 9SS. *T:* Hunton 438. *Club:* United Oxford & Cambridge University.

FENNELL, (John) Desmond (Augustine), OBE 1982; QC; *b* 17 Sept. 1933; *s* of late Dr A. J. Fennell, Lincoln; *m* 1966, Susan Primrose, *d* of late J. M. Trusted; one *s* two *d*. *Educ:* Ampleforth; Corpus Christi Coll., Cambridge. Served with Grenadier Guards, 1956–58. Called to the Bar, Inner Temple, 1959, Bencher, 1983; Dep. Chm., Bedfordshire QS, 1971; a Recorder of the Crown Court, 1972–; QC 1974; Leader, Midland and Oxford Circuit, 1983–; a Judge of the Courts of Appeal of Jersey and Guernsey, 1984–. Chm., Buckingham Div. Cons. Assoc., 1976–79 (Pres., 1983–). *Address:* 2 Crown Office Row, Temple, EC4Y 7HJ. *T:* 01–353 1365; Lawn House, Winslow, Buckingham MK18 3AJ. *T:* Winslow 2464. *Clubs:* Boodle's, Pilgrims.

FENNELL, Prof. John Lister Illingworth, MA, PhD Cantab; FRSL; Professor of Russian, Oxford University, 1967–85; Emeritus Fellow of New College, Oxford (Fellow, 1967); *b* 30 May 1918; *s* of Dr C. H. Fennell and Sylvia Mitchell; *m* 1947, Marina Lopukhin; one *s* one *d*. *Educ:* Radley Coll.; Trinity Coll., Cambridge. FRSL 1980; FRHistS. Served with Army, 1939–45. Asst Lectr, Dept of Slavonic Studies, Cambridge Univ., 1947–52; Reader in Russian and Head of Dept of Slavonic Languages, Nottingham Univ., 1952–56; Lectr in Russian, Oxford Univ., 1956–67, Fellow and Praelector in Russian, University Coll., Oxford, 1964–67. Vis. Lectr, Harvard Univ., 1963–64; Visiting Professor: Univ. of Calif at Berkeley, 1971, 1977; Virginia Univ., 1974; Bonsall and Kratter Vis. Prof., Stanford Univ., 1982–83; Univ. of Texas at Austin, 1986. Organiser, 3rd Internat. Conf. of Historians of Muscovy, Oxford, 1975. Joint Editor: Oxford Slavonic Papers; Russia Mediaevalis. *Publications:* The Correspondence between Prince A. M. Kurbsky and Ivan IV, 1955; Ivan the Great of Moscow, 1961; The Penguin Russian Course, 1961; Pushkin, 1964; Kurbsky's History of Ivan IV, 1965; The Emergence of Moscow, 1968; (ed jtly) Historical Russian Reader, 1969; (ed) Nineteenth Century Russian Literature, 1973; (with A. Stokes) Early Russian Literature, 1974; (ed jtly) The Cambridge Encyclopaedia of Russia and the Soviet Union, 1982; The Crisis of Medieval Russia, 1983; Cambridge Modern History, Vol. II, Chap. 19; articles in Slavonic and East European Review, Jahrbücher für Geschichte Osteuropas, etc. *Recreation:* music. *Address:* 8 Canterbury Road, Oxford. *T:* Oxford 56149.

FENNER, Prof. Frank John, CMG 1976; MBE 1944; FRCP 1967; FRS 1958; FAA 1954; Visiting Fellow, John Curtin School of Medical Research, Australian National University, since 1983 (University Fellow, 1980–82); *b* 21 Dec. 1914; *s* of Charles and Emma L. Fenner; *m* 1944, Ellen Margaret Bobbie Roberts; one *d* (and one *d* decd). *Educ:* Thebarton Technical High Sch.; Adelaide High Sch.; Univ. of Adelaide. MB, BS (Adelaide) 1938; MD (Adelaide) 1942; DTM (Sydney) 1940. Served as Medical Officer, Hospital Pathologist, and Malariologist, AIF, 1940–46; Francis Haley Research Fellow, Walter and Eliza Hall Inst. for Medical Research, Melbourne, 1946–48; Rockefeller Foundation Travelling Fellow, 1948–49; Prof. of Microbiology, 1949–73, Dir, John Curtin Sch. of Med. Research, 1967–73, Prof. of Environmental Studies and Dir, Centre for Resource and Environmental Studies, 1973–79, ANU; Overseas Fellow, Churchill Coll., Cambridge, 1962–63. Fogarty Schol., Nat. Insts of Health, USA, 1973–74, 1982–83. Chm., Global Commn for Certification of Smallpox Eradication, WHO, 1978–80. For. Associate, Nat. Acad. of Scis, USA, 1977; David Syme Prize, Univ. of Melbourne, 1949; Harvey Lecture, Harvey Soc. of New York, 1957; Royal Society: Leeuwenhoek Lecture, 1961, Florey Lecture, 1983; Australian Acad. of Science: Matthew Flinders Lecture, 1967; Burnet Lecture, 1985. Hon. MD Monash, 1966. Mueller Medal, Australian and New Zealand Assoc. for the Advancement of Science, 1964; Britannica Australia Award for Medicine, 1967; ANZAC Peace Award, 1980; ANZAAS Medal, 1980. *Publications:* The Production of Antibodies (with F. M. Burnet), 1949; Myxomatosis (with F. N. Ratcliffe), 1965; The Biology of Animal Viruses, 1968, 2nd edn 1974; Medical Virology (with D. O. White), 1970, 3rd edn 1986; Classification and Nomenclature of Viruses, 1976; (with A. L. G. Rees) The Australian Academy of Science: the First Twenty-five Years, 1980; numerous scientific papers, dealing with virology, epidemiology, bacteriology, and environmental problems. *Recreations:* gardening, tennis, fishing. *Address:* 8 Monaro Crescent, Red Hill, Canberra, ACT 2603, Australia. *T:* 95–9176.

FENNER, Dame Peggy, DBE 1986; MP (C) Medway, since 1983 (Rochester and Chatham, 1970–Sept. 1974 and 1979–83); *b* 12 Nov. 1922; *m* 1940, Bernard Fenner; one *d*. *Educ:* LCC School, Brockley; Ide Hill, Sevenoaks. Contested (C) Newcastle-under-Lyme, 1966; Parly Sec., MAFF, 1972–74 and 1981–86; Mem., British Delegn to European Parlt, Strasbourg, 1974. Member: West Kent Divisional Exec. Educn Cttee, 1963–72; Sevenoaks Urban District Council, 1957–71 (Chairman, 1962 and 1963); Exec. of Kent Borough and Urban District Councils Assoc., 1967–71; a Vice-Pres, Urban District Councils Assoc., 1971. *Recreations:* reading, travel, theatre, gardening. *Address:* 12 Star Hill, Rochester, Kent. *T:* Medway 42124.

FENNESSY, Sir Edward, Kt 1975; CBE 1957 (OBE 1944); BSc; FIEE, FRIN; Chairman: Biochrom, since 1978; British Medical Data Systems, since 1981; Deputy Chairman, L.B.K. Instruments Ltd, since 1978; *b* 17 Jan. 1912; *m* 1st, 1937, Marion Banks (*d* 1983); one *s* one *d*; 2nd, 1984, Leonora Patricia Birkett, *widow* of Trevor Birkett. *Educ:* Univ. of London. Telecommunications Research, Standard Telephones and Cables, 1934–38; Radar Research, Air Min. Research Station, Bawdsey Manor, 1938. War of 1939–45: commissioned RAFVR, 1940; Group Captain, 1945; staff No 60 Group, RAF, 1940–45; resp. for planning and construction radar systems for defence of UK, and Bomber Ops. Joined Bd of The Decca Navigator Co., 1946; Managing Director: Decca Radar Ltd, 1950–65; The Plessey Electronics Group, 1965–69. Chairman: British Telecommunications Research Ltd, 1966–69; Electronic Engineering Assoc., 1967–68; Man. Dir, Telecommunications, 1969–77, and Dep. Chm., 1975–77, Post Office Corp. Chm., IMA Microwave Products Ltd, 1979–83. Pres., Royal Institute of Navigation, 1975–78. DUniv Surrey, 1971. *Recreations:* sailing, golf. *Address:* Northbrook, Littleford Lane, Shamley Green, Surrey. *T:* Guildford 892444. *Clubs:* Royal Air Force; Island Sailing.

FENNEY, Roger Johnson, CBE 1973 (MBE (mil.) 1945); Chairman, Special Trustees, Charing Cross Hospital, since 1980; *b* 11 Sept. 1916; *s* of James Henry Fenney and Annie Sarah Fenney; *m* 1942, Dorothy Porteus; two *d*. *Educ:* Cowley Sch., St Helens; Univ. of Manchester (BA Admin 1939). Served War, 1939–46: Gunner to Major, Field Artillery; served N Africa and Italy (mentioned in despatches). Secretary, Central Midwives Board, 1947–82; Governor, Charing Cross Hosp., 1958–74 (Chm., Clinical Res. Cttee, 1970–80; Mem. Council, Med. Sch., 1970–80); Governor, Hammersmith Hosp., 1956–74; Chm., W London Hosp., 1957–68; First Nuffield Fellow for Health Affairs, USA, 1968; Dep. Chm., Kennedy Inst. of Rheumatol., 1970–77. Member: Exec., Arthritis and Rheumatism Council, 1978–; Ealing, Hammersmith and Hounslow AHA, 1974–79; Field Dir, Jt Study Gp (FIGO/ICM), Accra, Yaounde, Nairobi, Dakar, San José and Bogotá, 1972–76. *Address:* 11 Gilray House, Gloucester Terrace, W2 3DF. *T:* 01–262 8313; Chiltern Cottage, Lower Assendon, Henley-on-Thames, Oxon.

FENNING, Frederick William; Deputy Director, Atomic Energy Research Establishment, 1979–84, retired; *b* 14 Dec. 1919; *s* of Thomas and Lilian Fenning; *m* 1949, Eileen Mary Lyttle; one *s* two *d*. *Educ:* Clacton; Cambridge Univ. BA (Hons). Min. of Aircraft Production, 1940; Min. of Supply, Tube Alloys Project, Cambridge, 1942; Montreal, 1943; Chalk River, Ontario, 1945; AERE, Harwell, 1946–58; Chief Physicist, Risley, 1958; Dir, Reactor Technology, Risley, 1960–66; Dep. Dir, Harwell, 1966–77; Dir of Atomic Energy Technical Unit, UKAEA, 1977–79. *Recreations:* gardening, general DIY. *Address:* 21 St Peter's Hill, Caversham, Reading, Berks RG4 7AX. *T:* Reading 472302.

FENTON, Dr Alexander, CBE 1986; Research Director, National Museums of Scotland, since 1985; *b* 26 June 1929; *s* of Alexander Fenton and Annie Stirling Stronach; *m* 1956, Evelyn Elizabeth Hunter; two *d*. *Educ:* Turriff Academy; Aberdeen Univ. (MA); Cambridge Univ. (BA); Edinburgh Univ. (DLitt). Senior Asst Editor, Scottish National Dictionary, 1955–59; Asst Keeper, Nat. Museum of Antiquities of Scotland, 1959–75, Dep. Keeper, 1975–78, Director, 1978–85. Mem., Ancient Monuments Bd for Scotland, 1979–. Member: Royal Gustav Adolf Acad., Uppsala, Sweden, 1978; Royal Danish Acad. of Scis and Letters, 1979; Jury, Europa Preis für Volkskunst (FVS Foundation, Hamburg) 1975–. Co-editor, Tools and Tillage (Copenhagen), 1968–; Editor, Review of Scottish Culture, 1984–. *Publications:* The Various Names of Shetland, 1973, 2nd edn 1977; Scottish Country Life, 1976, 2nd edn 1978; (trans.) S. Steensen Blicher, En Landsbydegns Dagbog (The Diary of a Parish Clerk, 1976); The Island Blackhouse, 1978; The Northern Isles: Orkney and Shetland, 1978; (with B. Walker) The Rural Architecture of Scotland, 1981; The Shape of the Past, 2 vols, 1985; (trans.) S. Weöres, Ha a Világ Rigó Lenne (If All the World were a Blackbird), 1985; numerous articles in learned jls. *Address:* 132 Blackford Avenue, Edinburgh EH9 3HH. *T:* 031–667 5456. *Club:* New (Edinburgh).

FENTON, Air Cdre Harold Arthur, CBE 1946; DSO 1943; DFC 1942; BA; AFRAeS; *b* Gallegos, Patagonia, Argentine, 9 Feb. 1909; *s* of Dr E. G. Fenton, FRCSI, DPH, Co. Sligo and J. Ormsby, Glen Lodge, Ballina, Co. Mayo; *m* 1935, H. de Carteret; no *c*. *Educ:* Sandford Park Sch.; Trinity Coll., Dublin (BA 1927). Joined RAF 1928. Served India, 1930–33. Flying Instructor at Air Service Training Ltd, Hamble, until outbreak of war. During war commanded: Fighter Sqdn, Battle of Britain; Fighter Wing, and Fighter Group, Western Desert and Libya; Fighter Sector, London Area. Finished war as Senior Staff Officer, Germany (83 Group) (despatches thrice). Managing Dir, Deccan Airways Ltd, Hyderabad, Deccan, until 1947; Gen. Manager of Airways Training Ltd, 1947–48; Operations Manager, BOAC, 1949–52; Managing Dir, Peter Jones, 1952–58. *Recreation:* gardening. *Address:* Le Vallon, St Brelade, Jersey, Channel Islands. *T:* 41172.

FENTON, James Martin, FRSL; writer; *b* 25 April 1949; *s* of Rev. Canon J. C. Fenton, *qv* and Mary Hamilton (*née* Ingoldby). *Educ:* Durham Choristers Sch.; Repton Sch.; Magdalen Coll., Oxford (MA). FRSL 1983. Asst Literary Editor, 1971, Editorial Asst, 1972, New Statesman; freelance correspondent in Indo-China, 1973–75; Political Columnist, New Statesman, 1976–78; German Correspondent, The Guardian, 1978–79; Theatre Critic, Sunday Times, 1979–84; Chief Book Reviewer, The Times, 1984–86. *Publications:* Our Western Furniture, 1968; Terminal Moraine, 1972; A Vacant Possession, 1978; A German Requiem, 1980; Dead Soldiers, 1981; The Memory of War, 1982; (trans.) Rigoletto, 1982; You Were Marvellous, 1983; (ed) The Original Michael Frayn, 1983; Children in Exile, 1984; Poems 1968–83, 1985; (trans.) Simon Boccanegra, 1985; The Fall of Saigon, in Granta 15, 1985; James Fenton in the Philippines, 1986; The Snap Revolution, in Granta, 1986. *Address:* 1 Bartlemas Road, Oxford OX4 1XU. *T:* Oxford 726797; c/o A. D. Peters & Co. Ltd, 10 Buckingham Street, WC2N 6BU.

FENTON, Rev. Canon John Charles; Canon of Christ Church, Oxford, since 1978; *b* 5 June 1921; *s* of Cornelius O'Connor Fenton and Agnes Claudine Fenton. *Educ:* S Edward's Sch., Oxford; Queen's Coll., Oxford (BA 1943, MA 1947, BD 1953); Lincoln Theol Coll. Deacon 1944, priest 1945. Asst Curate, All Saints, Hindley, Wigan, 1944–47; Chaplain, Lincoln Theol Coll., 1947–51, Sub-Warden, 1951–54; Vicar of Wentworth, Yorks, 1954–58; Principal: Lichfield Theol Coll., 1958–65; S Chad's Coll., Durham, 1965–78. *Publications:* Preaching the Cross, 1958; The Passion according to John, 1961; Crucified with Christ, 1961; Saint Matthew (Pelican Commentaries), 1963; Saint John (New Clarendon Bible), 1970; What was Jesus' Message?, 1971; (with M. Hare Duke) Good News, 1976; contrib. Theol., and Jl of Theol Studies. *Recreations:* walking, camping, gardening. *Address:* Christ Church, Oxford. *T:* Oxford 243887.

FENWICK, John James, DL; Chairman, Fenwick Ltd, since 1979 (Deputy Chairman, 1972–79; Managing Director, 1972–82); Director, Northern Rock Building Society, since 1984; *b* 9 Aug. 1932; *e s* of James Frederick Trevor Fenwick; *m* 1957, Muriel Gillian Hodnett; three *s*. *Educ:* Rugby Sch.; Pembroke Coll., Cambridge (MA). Chairman: Northumberland Assoc. of Youth Clubs, 1966–71; Retail Distributors Assoc., 1977–79; Vice Chm., National Assoc. of Citizens Advice Bureaux, 1971–79; Regional Dir, Northern Bd, Lloyds Bank, 1982–85. Member: Newcastle Diocesan Bd of Finance, 1964–69; Retail Consortium Council, 1976–79; Post Office Users' Nat. Council, 1980–82; Civic Trust for NE, 1979–. Governor: Royal Grammar Sch., Newcastle upon Tyne, 1975–; Moorfields Eye Hosp., 1981–86; Royal Shakespeare Theatre, 1985–. DL Tyne and Wear, 1986. *Recreations:* travel, shooting, theatre. *Address:* 49 Perrymead Street, SW6 3SN; 35 Osborne Road, Newcastle upon Tyne NE2 2AH. *Clubs:* Garrick, MCC; Northern Counties (Newcastle upon Tyne).

FENWICK, Robert George, CBE 1975; QPM 1969; HM Inspector of Constabulary, 1967–77; *b* 1913; *s* of late George R. F. Fenwick, Horton Grange, Northumberland; *m* 1943, Eileen Winifreda, *d* of late James Carstairs Dodds, Buenos Aires. *Educ:* Dame Allan's Sch. Barrister-at-Law, Gray's Inn, 1951. Metropolitan Police, 1934–59; seconded to Foreign Office for duties in São Paulo, Brazil, 1957–58; Directing Staff, Police Coll., 1959–60; Asst Chief Constable, Glos, 1960–62; Chief Constable, Shropshire, 1962–67. Adviser to Qatar State Police, 1972–77. *Address:* Ebor House, Kingsland, Shrewsbury, Shropshire. *T:* Shrewsbury 4158.

FERENS, Sir Thomas (Robinson), Kt 1957; CBE 1952; *b* 4 Jan. 1903; *e s* of late J. J. T. Ferens, Hull; *m* 1934, Jessie (*d* 1982), *d* of P. G. Sanderson, Hull and Scarborough; two *d*. *Educ:* Rydal; Leeds Univ. (BSc Eng). *Recreation:* fly-fishing. *Address:* Sunderlandwick, Driffield, North Humberside. *T:* Driffield 42323.

FERGUS, Most Rev. James, DD; *b* Louisburgh, Co. Mayo, 23 Dec. 1895. *Educ:* St Jarlath's College, Tuam; and at Maynooth. Ordained priest, 1920; studied Dunboyne; Curate, Glenamaddy, 1921, Tuam, 1924; Archbishop's secretary, 1926; Administrator,

Westport, 1943; Parish Priest, Ballinrobe, 1944; Bishop of Achonry, 1947–76, retired 1977. *Address*: Ballaghaderreen, Co. Roscommon, Eire.

FERGUSON, Ernest Alexander; Deputy Chairman, Central Arbitration Committee, since 1977; *b* 26 July 1917; *s* of William Henry and Lilian Ferguson; *m* 1940, Mary Josephine Wadsworth; two *s*. *Educ*: Priory Sch., Shrewsbury; Pembroke Coll., Cambridge (Scholar, 1935–39; MA 1944). Served War, RA (Captain), 1940–45. Entered Ministry of Labour, 1945; Principal, 1948; Asst Sec., 1962; Under-Sec. and Accountant-Gen., Dept of Employment, 1973–77. Chm., Central Youth Employment Executive, 1967–69; Sec. to NEDC, 1971–73. *Recreations*: sport, hill walking, reading. *Address*: 164 Balcombe Road, Horley, Surrey. *T*: Horley 785254. *Club*: Civil Service.

FERGUSON, John, FIAL; FRSA; President, The Selly Oak Colleges, Birmingham, 1979–86; *b* 2 March 1921; *s* of Prof. Allan and Dr Nesta Ferguson; *m* 1950, Elnora Dixon; no *c*. *Educ*: Bishop's Stortford Coll.; St John's Coll., Cambridge. BD 1st cl. hons London, 1944; BA 1st cl. hons with double distinction Class. Tripos Cantab, 1947; Henry Carrington and Bentham Dumont Koe Studentship, 1947; Denny Studentship, 1947; Kaye Prize, 1951 (for essay in early Church History). Civil Defence, 1941–45; Master at Bishop's Stortford Coll., 1945–46; Lectr in Classics, King's Coll., Newcastle upon Tyne, 1948–53; Sen. Lectr in Classics, Queen Mary Coll., London, 1953–56; Prof. of Classics, Univ. of Ibadan, 1956–66 (Dean, Faculty of Arts, 1958–59, 1960–61); Hill Vis. Prof. 1966–68, Prof. 1968–69, Univ. of Minnesota; Old Dominion Vis. Prof. Humanities, Hampton Inst., Va, 1968–69. Dean and Dir of Studies in Arts, Open Univ., 1969–79 (Dep. Chm. of Senate, 1969–74). Vis. Prof., Univ. of Florida, 1977; Ohio Wesleyan Univ., 1978. Lectures: Emily Hobhouse Meml, Cape Town, 1961; Alex Wood Meml, Cambridge, 1971; Kinchin Smith Meml, London, 1972; Herbert Collins Meml, Southampton, 1976; Lady Ardilaun, Dublin, 1976; Rodes-Helm, Bowling Green, Ky, 1977; Montgomery, UK, 1977–79; Carpenter, Delaware, Ohio, 1978; Apothecaries, London, 1983; Dacorum, Hemel Hempstead, 1983; Noel-Baker Meml, London, 1983; Chavasse, Oxford, 1985; Doris Hansen, Cardiff, 1985. Chm. 1953–56, Vice-Chm. 1969–78, Fellowship of Reconciliation; Trustee, UNA, 1984– (Vice-Chm., 1978–80; Chm., 1980–84); British Council of Churches: Chm., Educn Dept, 1971–74; Community Affairs Div., 1974–78; Chairman: British and Foreign Schools Soc., 1975–86; Birmingham Jt Cttee for Adult Educn Inf. and Advice Services, 1979–86; Mem. Council, Prospect Hall, 1978–86; Governor, Queen's Coll., Birmingham; Vice-Chm., Christian Social and Economic Res. Foundn; President: Friends' Guild of Teachers, 1978–79; London Soc. for Study of Religion, 1978–80; Vice-President: Orbilian Soc., 1973– (Pres., 1972); Nat. Peace Council; Hon. Life Vice-Pres., Assoc. for Reform of Latin Teaching. Chm., Weoley Hill Cricket Club. Hon. Mem., Mark Twain Soc., and Kt of Mark Twain. *Publications*: The Enthronement of Love, 1950; (ed) Studies in Christian Social Commitment, 1954; Pelagius, 1956; (jtly) Letters on Pacifism, 1956; Christian Faith for Today, 1956; The UN and the World's Needs, 1957; (ed) Plato Republic X, 1957; Moral Values in the Ancient World, 1958; (jtly) The Emergent University, 1960; (ed) Studies in Cicero, 1962; Foundations of the Modern World, 1963; (jtly) The Enduring Past, 1965; (jtly) Nigeria under the Cross, 1965; Ibadan Verses, 1966; (ed) Ibadan Versions, 1967; The Wit of the Greeks and Romans, 1968; Christian Byways, 1968; (jtly) Africa in Classical Antiquity, 1969; Socrates: A Source-Book, 1970; Religions of the Roman Empire, 1970; American Verses, 1971; Some Nigerian Church Founders, 1971; Sermons of a Layman, 1972; The Place of Suffering, 1972; A Companion to Greek Tragedy, 1972; Aristotle, 1972; The Heritage of Hellenism, 1973; The Politics of Love, 1973; (ed) War and the Creative Arts, 1973; (rapporteur) Non-violent Action: a Christian appraisal, 1973; Clement of Alexandria, 1974; Utopias of the Classical World, 1975; The Open University from Within, 1975; Danilo Dolci, 1975; An Illustrated Encyclopaedia of Mysticism and the Mystery Religions, 1976; O My People, 1977; War and Peace in the World's Religions, 1977; Religions of the World, 1978; (jtly) Political and Social Life in the Great Age of Athens, 1978; (ed) Juvenal The Satires, 1979; Greek and Roman Religion: a source book, 1980; Jesus in the Tide of Time, 1980; The Arts in Britain in World War I, 1980; Callimachus, 1980; (ed) Christianity, Society and Education, 1981; Gods Many and Lords Many, 1981; (jtly) Rome: the Augustan Age, 1981; Disarmament: The Unanswerable Case, 1982; Hymns of a Layman, 1982; (ed) Euripides, Hippolytus, 1984; Catullus, 1985; some 25 course-unit books for the Open Univ.; *plays*: The Camp, 1956; The Trial, 1957; The Road to Heaven, 1958; Job, 1961; Editor, Nigeria and the Classics, Vols I-IX; Jt Editor, Reconciliation Quarterly; Sen. Editor, Selly Oak Jl, 1984–86; numerous articles on classical subjects, theology, internat. affairs and literature; also some hymns. *Recreations*: cricket, fell-walking, book-hunting, church architecture, drama, opera, conducting madrigals, travelling in the Graeco-Roman world. *Address*: 102 Oakfield Road, Selly Park, Birmingham B29 7ED. *T*: 021–472 1922. *Clubs*: Penn; MCC; Union (Cambridge).

FERGUSON, John Alexander; HM Senior Chief Inspector of Schools in Scotland, since 1981; *b* 16 Oct. 1927; *s* of George Ferguson and Martha Crichton Dykes; *m* 1953, Jean Stewart; two *s* one *d*. *Educ*: Royal Coll. of Science and Technology, Univ. of Glasgow (BSc Hons, Diploma). Teacher, Airdrie Central Sch., 1950–51; Lectr, 1951–55, Head of Dept of Engrg, 1955–61, Coatbridge Technical Coll.; HM Inspector of Schs, 1961–72, Asst Sec., 1972–75, Scottish Educn Dept; HM Depute Sen. Chief Inspector of Schs, 1975–81. *Recreations*: tennis, badminton, bridge. *Address*: 28 Esslemont Road, Edinburgh EH16 5PY. *T*: 031–667 5881. *Clubs*: Craigmillar Park Lawn Tennis, Carlton Bridge (Edinburgh).

FERGUSON, John McIntyre, CBE 1976; FEng 1978, FIEE, FIMechE, FITE; engineering consultant, since 1973; *b* 16 May 1915; *s* of Frank Ferguson and Lilian (*née* Bowen); *m* 1941, Margaret Frances Tayler; three *s*. *Educ*: Armstrong Coll., Durham Univ. BScEng (1st Cl. Hons). English Electric Co., Stafford: Research, 1936; Chief Engr, 1953; Dir Engrg, Heavy Electric Products, 1965; Dir of Engrg, GEC Power Engrg Co., 1969. Member: Metrication Bd, 1969–76; Science Res. Council, 1972–76; UGC, 1977–82. President: IEE, 1977–78; IEETE, 1979–81. Hon. DSc Birmingham, 1983. *Recreations*: golf, sailing. *Address*: Leacroft, 19 St John's Road, Stafford ST17 9AS. *T*: Stafford 3516. *Club*: Royal Commonwealth Society.

FERGUSON, Sir Neil Edward J.; *see* Johnson-Ferguson.

FERGUSON, Richard; QC 1986; QC (NI) 1973; SC (Ireland) 1983; *b* 22 Aug. 1935; *o s* of late Wesley Ferguson and Edith Ferguson (*née* Hewitt); *m*; three *s* one *d*. *Educ*: Methodist Coll., Belfast; Trinity Coll., Dublin (BA); Queen's Univ. of Belfast (LLB). Called to NI Bar, 1956, to Bar of England and Wales, Gray's Inn, 1972; Vice-Chm., Bar Council of NI, 1983; Chm., NI Mental Health Review Tribunal, 1973–84. MP (OU) S Antrim, 1969–70. Chm., NI Mountain Trng Bd, 1974–82; Mem., Irish Sports Council, 1981–83. Governor, Methodist Coll., Belfast, 1978–. FRGS 1980. *Recreations*: playing at being a farmer, drinking Guinness. *Address*: 1 Crown Office Row, EC4Y 7HH; Sandhill House, Derrygonnelly, Co. Fermanagh. *T*: 612. *Clubs*: London Irish Rugby Football, North of Ireland Rugby Football and Cricket (Belfast); Kildare Street and University (Dublin).

FERGUSON DAVIE, Rev. Sir (Arthur) Patrick, 5th Bt *cr* 1641 and *re-created* 1847 for General Henry Ferguson, husband of Juliana, *d* of Sir John Davie, 8th Bt of Creedy; TD 1954; Liturgical Adviser to the Anglican Province of Jerusalem and the Middle East, 1976–84; *b* 17 March 1909; *s* of late Lt-Col Arthur Francis Ferguson Davie, CIE, DSO (3rd *s* of 3rd Bt), and late Eleanor Blanche Daphne, *d* of late C. T. Naylor (she *m* 1918, Major J. H. W. Knight-Bruce, who *d* 1951; she *d* 1964); *S* uncle, 1947; *m* 1949, Iris Dawn Cable-Buller, *o d* of Capt. and Hon. Mrs Buller, Downes, Crediton; one *s*. *Educ*: Wellington Coll.; Lincoln Coll., Oxford (MA). Ely Theological Coll., 1932–34; Deacon, 1934, Priest, 1935. Asst Curate, Littleham-cum-Exmouth, 1934–37; St Augustine's, Kilburn, NW6, 1938–39; CF (TA), 1937–45; Hon. CF 1945; served with 4th Bn Devonshire Regt in UK and Gibraltar, 1939–43; CMF, N Africa and Italy, 1943–45; Vicar of St John's Torquay, 1945–48; Rural Dean of Cadbury, 1966–68; Hon. Chaplain to Bishop of Exeter, 1949–73. *Publication*: The Bishop in Church, 1961. *Heir*: *s* Antony Francis Ferguson Davie, *b* 23 March 1952. *Address*: Skalatos House, PO Box 129, Girne, Mersin 10, Turkey. *Club*: United Oxford & Cambridge University.

FERGUSON-SMITH, Prof. Malcolm Andrew, FRS 1983; FRSE 1978; Professor of Medical Genetics, University of Glasgow, since 1973; Director, West of Scotland Medical Genetics Service; *b* 5 Sept. 1931; *s* of John Ferguson-Smith, MA, MD, FRCP and Ethel May (*née* Thorne); *m* 1960, Marie Eva Gzowska; one *s* three *d*. *Educ*: Stowe Sch.; Univ. of Glasgow (MB ChB 1955). MRCPath 1966, FRCPath 1978; MRCPGlas 1972, FRCPGlas 1974. Registrar in Lab. Medicine, Dept of Pathology, Western Infirmary, Glasgow, 1958–59; Fellow in Medicine and Instructor, Johns Hopkins Univ. Sch. of Medicine, 1959–61; Lectr, Sen. Lectr and Reader in Med. Genetics, Univ. of Glasgow, 1961–73; Hon. Consultant: in Med. Paediatrics, Royal Hosp. for Sick Children, Glasgow, 1966–73; in Clin. Genetics, Yorkhill and Associated Hosps, 1973–. Pres., Clinical Genetics Soc., 1979–81. Bronze Medal, Univ. of Helsinki, 1968; Mem., Johns Hopkins Univ. Soc. of Scholars, 1983. Editor, Prenatal Diagnosis, 1980–. *Publications*: (ed) Early Prenatal Diagnosis, 1983; (jtly) Essential Medical Genetics, 1984; papers on cytogenetics, gene mapping, human genetics and prenatal diagnosis in med. jls. *Recreations*: swimming, sailing, fishing. *Address*: Duncan Guthrie Institute of Medical Genetics, Yorkhill, Glasgow G3 8SJ. *T*: 041–339 6996; 5 Hamilton Drive, Glasgow G12 8DN. *T*: 041–339 5720.

FERGUSSON, Adam (Dugdale); Special Adviser on European Affairs, Foreign and Commonwealth Office, since 1985; *b* 10 July 1932; *yr s* of Sir James Fergusson of Kilkerran, 8th Bt, LLD, FRSE, and of Frances Dugdale; *m* 1965, Penelope, *e d* of Peter Hughes, Furneaux Pelham Hall; two *s* two *d*. *Educ*: Eton; Trinity Coll., Cambridge (BA History, 1955). Glasgow Herald, 1956–61: Leader-writer, 1957–58; Diplomatic Corresp., 1959–61; Statist, 1961–67: Foreign Editor, 1964–67; Feature-writer for The Times on political, economic and environmental matters, 1967–77. European Parliament: Member (C) West Strathclyde, 1979–84; Spokesman on Political Affairs for European Democratic Gp, 1979–82; Vice-Chm., Political Affairs Cttee, 1982–84; Mem., Jt Cttee of ACP/EEC Consultative Assembly, 1979–84; contested (C) London Central, European elecn, 1984. Vice-Pres., Pan-European Union, 1981–; Mem., Scotland Says No Referendum Campaign Cttee, 1978–79. *Publications*: Roman Go Home, 1969; The Lost Embassy, 1972; The Sack of Bath, 1973; When Money Dies, 1975; various pamphlets; articles in national and internat. jls and magazines. *Address*: 15 Warwick Gardens, W14 8PH. *T*: 01–603 7900; Ladyburn, Maybole, Ayrshire. *T*: Crosshill 206. *Club*: Travellers'.

FERGUSSON of Kilkerran, Sir Charles, 9th Bt *cr* 1703; *b* 10 May 1931; *s* of Sir James Fergusson of Kilkerran, 8th Bt, and Frances, *d* of Edgar Dugdale; *S* father, 1973; *m* 1961, Hon. Amanda Mary Noel-Paton, *d* of Lord Ferrier, *qv*; two *s*. *Educ*: Eton; Edinburgh and East of Scotland Coll. of Agriculture (Scottish Diploma in Agric.). *Heir*: *s* Adam Fergusson, *b* 29 Dec. 1962. *Address*: c/o Messrs Dundas & Wilson, CS, 25 Charlotte Square, Edinburgh EH2 4EZ.

FERGUSSON, Ewen Alastair John; HM Diplomatic Service; Deputy Under Secretary of State (Middle East and Africa), Foreign and Commonwealth Office, since 1984; *b* 28 Oct. 1932; *er s* of late Sir Ewen MacGregor Field Fergusson; *m* 1959, Sara Carolyn, *d* of late Brig-Gen. Lord Esmé Gordon Lennox, KCVO, CMG, DSO and *widow* of Sir William Andrew Montgomery-Cuninghame, 11th Bt; one *s* two *d*. *Educ*: Rugby; Oriel Coll., Oxford (MA). Played Rugby Football for Oxford Univ., 1952 and 1953, and for Scotland, 1954. 2nd Lieut, 60th Rifles (KRRC), 1954–56. Joined Foreign (now Diplomatic) Service, 1956; Asst Private Sec. to Minister of Defence, 1957–59; British Embassy, Addis Ababa, 1960; FO, 1963; British Trade Development Office, New York, 1967; Counsellor and Head of Chancery, Office of UK Permanent Rep. to European Communities, 1972–75; Private Sec. to Foreign and Commonwealth Sec., 1975–78; Asst Under Sec. of State, FCO, 1978–82; Ambassador to S Africa, 1982–84. Governor, Rugby Sch., 1985–. *Address*: c/o Foreign and Commonwealth Office, SW1. *Club*: Royal Automobile.

FERGUSSON, Ian Victor Lyon; *b* 22 Jan. 1901; *y s* of late Rev. Dr John Moore Fergusson; *m* 1927, Hannah Grace (*née* Gourlay) (*d* 1978); three *s* one *d*. *Educ*: Berkhamsted Sch. Joined Evans Medical Ltd. (then Evans Sons Lescher & Webb Ltd), 1919; Dir, 1927; Man. Dir, 1941; Chm. and Man. Dir, Evans Medical Ltd, 1943–62; Dir, Glaxo Group Ltd, 1961–62; Dir, Carless Capel & Leonard Ltd, 1964–72. Pres., Chemists Federation, 1940–41; Chm., Assoc. British Pharmaceutical Industry, 1946–47. Mem., Liverpool Regional Hospital Board, 1958–61. *Recreations*: fishing, gardening. *Address*: Orchard Lodge, Avon Dassett, Leamington Spa, Warwickshire CV33 0AY. *T*: Farnborough 228.

FERGUSSON, James David, CB 1982; *b* 14 Jan. 1923; *s* of James Thomson Fergusson and Agnes Eva Fergusson; *m* 1946, Jean Barbara Debnam; two *s* one *d*. *Educ*: Montrose Acad.; St Andrews Univ. (BSc). Temp. Experimental Officer, Admiralty, 1943–47; Patent Office Examining Staff, 1947–69; Asst Comptroller, Patent Office, 1969–83. *Address*: 42 Cedar Avenue, Chelmsford, Essex CM1 2QH. *T*: Chelmsford 355774.

FERGUSSON, Sir James H. H. C.; *see* Colyer-Fergusson.

FERMAN, James Alan; Secretary, British Board of Film Censors, since 1975; *b* New York, 11 April 1930; *m* 1956, Monica Sophie (*née* Robinson); one *s* one *d*. *Educ*: Great Neck High Sch., NY; Cornell Univ. (BA Hons); King's Coll., Cambridge (MA Hons). Actor and univ. lectr until 1957; author/adaptor, Zuleika (musical comedy), Saville Theatre, 1957; Television Director: ABC, 1957–59; ATV, 1959–65; freelance, chiefly at BBC, 1965–75; drama series incl.: The Planemakers, Probation Officer, Emergency Ward 10; plays incl.: The Pistol, Who's A Good Boy Then? I Am, Kafka's Amerika, Death of a Private, Before the Party, Chariot of Fire, When the Bough Breaks, Terrible Jim Fitch; documentaries incl.: Decisions of Our Time, The Four Freedoms, CURE; stage productions incl.: Three Sisters, Mooney and His Caravans, This Space Is Mine; wrote and dir., Drugs and Schoolchildren, film series for teachers and social workers. Lectr in Community Studies, Polytechnic of Central London, 1973–76 (Dir and Chm., Community Mental Health Prog. in assoc. with MIND); Educn Adviser, Standing Conf. on Drug Abuse; Vice-Pres., Assoc. for Prevention of Addiction. *Recreations*: reading and hill-walking. *Address*: The Fairhazel Co-operative, Canfield Gardens, NW6; British Board of Film Censors, 3 Soho Square, W1. *T*: 01–437 2677.

FERMOR, Patrick Michael Leigh, DSO 1944; OBE (mil.) 1943; author; Hon. Citizen of Herakleion, Crete, 1947, Gytheion, Laconia, 1966, and of Kardamyli, Messenia, 1967;

b 11 Feb. 1915; *s* of late Sir Lewis Leigh Fermor, OBE, FRS, DSc, and Eileen, *d* of Charles Taaffe Ambler; *m* 1968, Hon. Joan Eyres-Monsell, *d* of 1st Viscount Monsell, PC, GBE. *Educ:* King's Sch., Canterbury. After travelling for four years in Central Europe, Balkans and Greece, enlisted in Irish Guards, 1939; 2nd Lieut, "I" Corps, 1940; Lieut, British Mil. Mission, Greece, 1940; Liaison Officer, Greek GHQ, Albania; campaigns of Greece and Crete; 2 years in German occupied Crete with Cretan Resistance, commanded some minor guerilla operations; Major 1943; team-commander in Special Allied Airborne Reconnaissance Force, N Germany, 1945. Dep.-Dir British Institute, Athens, till middle 1946; travelled in Caribbean and Central American republics, 1947–48. Corres. Mem., Athens Acad., 1980. *Publications:* The Traveller's Tree (Heinemann Foundation Prize for Literature, 1950, and Kemsley Prize, 1951); trans. Colette, Chance Acquaintances, 1952; A Time to Keep Silence, 1953; The Violins of Saint Jacques, 1953; Mani, 1958 (Duff Cooper Meml Prize; Book Society's Choice); (trans.) The Cretan Runner (George Psychoundakis), 1955; Roumeli, 1966; A Time of Gifts, 1977 (W. H. Smith & Son Literary Award, 1978); Between the Woods and the Water, 1986. *Recreation:* travel. *Address:* c/o Messrs John Murray, 50 Albemarle Street, W1. *Clubs:* White's, Travellers', Pratt's, Beefsteak, Special Forces, Puffins.

FERMOR-HESKETH, family name of **Baron Hesketh.**

FERMOY, 6th Baron *cr* 1856; **Patrick Maurice Burke Roche;** *b* 11 Oct. 1967; *s* of 5th Baron Fermoy and of Lavinia Frances Elizabeth, *o d* of late Captain John Pitman; *S* father, 1984. *Educ:* Eton. *Heir: b* Hon. (Edmund) Hugh Burke Roche, *b* 1972. *Address:* Axford House, Axford, near Marlborough, Wilts.

FERMOY, Dowager Lady; Ruth Sylvia; (Rt. Hon. Ruth Lady Fermoy), DCVO 1979 (CVO 1966); OBE 1952; JP; Woman of the Bedchamber to Queen Elizabeth the Queen Mother since 1960 (an extra Woman of the Bedchamber, 1956–60); *b* 2 Oct. 1908; *y d* of late W. S. Gill, CB, Dalhebity, Bieldside, Aberdeenshire; *m* 1931, Edmund Maurice Burke Roche, 4th Baron Fermoy (*d* 1955); two *d* (one *s* decd). JP Norfolk, 1944. Freedom of King's Lynn, 1963. Hon. RAM 1968; FRCM 1983. Hon. MusD Univ. of East Anglia,1975.

FERNANDES, Most Rev. Angelo; *see* Delhi, Archbishop of, (RC).

FERNANDO, Most Rev. Nicholas Marcus; *see* Colombo, Archbishop of, (RC).

FERNEYHOUGH, Brian John Peter; composer; Principal Composition Teacher, Royal Conservatory, The Hague, Holland, since 1986; *b* 16 Jan. 1943; *s* of Frederick George Ferneyhough and Emily May (*née* Hopwood); *m* 1st, 1967, Barbara Joan Pearson; 2nd, 1980, Elke Schaaf; 3rd, 1984, Carolyn Steinberg. *Educ:* Birmingham Sch. of Music; RAM; Sweelinck Conservatory, Amsterdam; Musikakademie, Basle. Mendelssohn Schol., 1968; Stipend: City of Basle, 1969; Heinrich-Strobel-Stiftung des Südwestfunks, 1972; Composition teacher, Musikhochschule, Freiburg, 1973–86 (Prof., 1978–86). Guest Artist, Artists' Exchange Scheme, Deutsche Akad. Austauschdienst, Berlin, 1976–77; Lectr, Darmstadt Summer Sch., 1976– (Comp. course co-ordinator, 1984, 1986); Guest Prof., Royal Conservatory, Stockholm, 1981–83, 1985; Vis. Prof., Univ. of Chicago, 1986; Master Class, Civica Scuola di Musica di Milano, 1985–. Mem., ISCM Internat. Jury, 1977. Prizes, Gaudeamus Internat. Comp., 1968, 1969; First Prize, ISCM Internat. Comp., Rome, 1974; Koussevitsky Prize, 1978. Chevalier, l'Ordre des Arts et des Lettres, 1984. *Compositions include:* Sonatas for String Quartet, 1967; Epicycle, for 20 solo strings, 1968; Firecycle Beta, for large orch. with 5 conductors, 1971; Time and Motion Studies I–III, 1974–76; Unity Capsule, for solo flute, 1975; Funérailles, for 7 strings and harp, 1978; La Terre est un Homme, for orch., 1979; 2nd String Quartet, 1980; Lemma-Icon-Epigram, for solo piano, 1981; Carceri d'Invenzione, for various ensembles, 1981–86. *Publications:* collected writings in Quaderni della Civica Scuola di Musica, numero speciale (Italian lang.), 1984. *Recreations:* reading, wine, cats. *Address:* Urbanstrasse 14, D-7800 Freiberg, German Federal Republic. *T:* 0761–3 54 18.

FERNS, Prof. Henry Stanley, MA, PhD Cantab; Professor of Political Science, University of Birmingham, 1961–81, now Emeritus Professor; *b* Calgary, Alberta, 16 Dec. 1913; *er s* of Stanley and Janie Ferns; *m* 1940, Helen Maureen, *d* of John and Eleanor Jack; three *s* one *d*. *Educ:* St John's High Sch., Winnipeg; Univ. of Manitoba; Trinity Coll., Cambridge. Research Scholar, Trinity Coll., Cambridge, 1938. Secretarial staff of Prime Minister of Canada, 1940; Asst Prof. of History and Government, Univ. of Manitoba, 1945; Fellow, Canadian Social Science Research Council, 1949; Lectr in Modern History and Government, Univ. of Birmingham, 1950; successively Sen. Lectr, Head of Dept and Prof. of Political Science, Dean, Faculty of Commerce and Social Sci., 1961–65. Pres., Bd of Dirs, Winnipeg Citizens' Cooperative Publishing Co. Ltd, 1946–48; Member of various Conciliation Boards appointed by Minister of Labour of Govt of Manitoba, 1947–49. Past Pres., British Assoc. of Canadian Studies. Hon. DLitt Buckingham, 1983. *Publications:* (with B. Ostry) The Age of McKenzie King: The Rise of the Leader, 1955 (Toronto and London), 2nd edn 1976; Britain and Argentina in the Nineteenth Century, 1960 (Oxford); Towards an Independent University, 1969; Argentina, 1969; The Argentine Republic 1516–1971, 1973; The Disease of Government, 1978; How Much Freedom for Universities?, 1982; Reading from Left to Right, 1983; (with K. W. Watkins) What Politics is About, 1985; articles in learned jls. *Recreations:* journalism, idling and pottering about. *Address:* 1 Kesteven Close, Sir Harry's Road, Birmingham B15 2UT. *T:* 021–440 1016.

FERNYHOUGH, Ven. Bernard; Archdeacon of Oakham, since 1977; Canon Residentiary of Peterborough Cathedral, since 1977; *b* 2 Sept. 1932; *s* of Edward and Edith Fernyhough; *m* 1957, Freda Malkin; one *s* one *d*. *Educ:* Wolstanton Grammar Sch.; Saint David's Coll., Lampeter (BA 1953). Precentor, Trinidad Cathedral, 1955–61; Rector of Stoke Bruerne with Grafton Regis and Alderton, 1961–67; Vicar of Ravensthorpe with East Haddon and Holdenby, 1967–77; Rural Dean: Preston, 1965–67; Haddon, 1968–70; Brixworth, 1971–77; Non-Residentiary Canon, Peterborough Cathedral, 1974–77. *Address:* 18 Minster Precincts, Peterborough. *T:* Peterborough 62762.

FERNYHOUGH, Rt. Hon. Ernest, PC 1970; *b* 24 Dec. 1908; British; *m* 1934, Ethel Edwards; one *s* one *d* (and one *s* decd). *Educ:* Wood Lane Council Sch. Full-time official, Union of Shop, Distributive and Allied Workers, 1936–47. MP (Lab) Jarrow, May 1947–1979; PPS to the Prime Minister, 1964–67; Jt Parly Under-Sec. of State, Dept of Employment and Productivity (formerly Min. of Labour), 1967–69. Freeman, Borough of Jarrow, 1972. *Address:* 35 Edwards Road, Lache Park, Chester.

FEROZE, Sir Rustam Moolan, Kt 1983; MD; FRCS, FRCOG; Consultant Obstetrician and Gynæcologist, King's College Hospital; Consulting Obstetrician and Gynæcologist: Queen Charlotte's Maternity Hospital; Chelsea Hospital for Women; *b* 4 Aug. 1920; *s* of Dr J. Moolan-Feroze; *m* 1947, Margaret Dowsett; three *s* one *d*. *Educ:* Sutton Valence Sch.; King's Coll. Hospital, London. MRCS, LRCP 1943; MB, BS 1946; MRCOG 1948; MD (Obst. & Dis. Wom.) London 1952; FRCS 1952; FRCOG 1962. Dean, Inst. of Obstetrics and Gynæcology, Univ. of London, 1954–67. Senr Registrar: Chelsea Hosp. for Women, and Queen Charlotte's Maternity Hosp., London, 1953–54; Hosp. for Women, Soho Square, and Middlesex Hosp., 1950–53; Resident Medical Officer, Samaritan Hosp. for Women, 1948. Pres., RCOG, 1981–84. *Publications:* contribs to medical jls and to Integrated Obstetrics and Gynaecology for Postgraduates, 1976. *Recreation:* Bonsai. *Address:* 127 Harley Street, W1. *T:* 01–935 8157. *Clubs:* Royal Automobile, Rugby.

FERRALL, Sir Raymond (Alfred), Kt 1982; CBE 1969; director, various public and private companies; *b* 27 May 1906; *s* of Alfred C. Ferrall and Edith M. Ferrall; *m* 1931, Lorna, *d* of P. M. Findlay; two *s* two *d*. *Educ:* Launceston C of E Grammar Sch. Chairman: Launceston Bank for Savings, 1976–82; Tasmanian Colls of Advanced Educn, 1977–81; Launceston C of E Grammar Sch. Bd, 1956–73; Master Warden, Port of Launceston Authority, 1960–80. Captain, Tasmanian Cricket team, 1934; Vice Captain, Tasmanian Amateur Football team, 1932. Freeman, City of Launceston, 1981. Queen's Silver Jubilee Medal, 1977. *Publications:* Partly Personal, 1976; Idylls of the Mayor, 1978; Notable Tasmanians, 1980; The Age of Chiselry, 1981; The Story of the Port of Launceston, 1984; A Proud Heritage, 1985. *Recreations:* writing, print collecting, sailing. *Address:* 135 High Street, Launceston, Tas 7250, Australia. *T:* 31 6081. *Clubs:* Launceston, Northern, Tamar Yacht (Tasmania).

FERRANTI; *see* de Ferranti.

FERRAR, William Leonard; Principal, Hertford College, Oxford, 1959–64; *b* 21 Oct. 1893; *s* of George William Parsons and Maria Susannah Ferrar; *m* 1923, Edna O'Hara (*d* 1986); one *s*. *Educ:* Queen Elizabeth's Hospital, Bristol; Bristol Grammar Sch.; Queen's Coll., Oxford. Open Mathematical Schol., Queen's, 1912; Univ. Junior Math. Schol., 1914; Sen. Schol., 1922; MA Oxon 1920; DSc Oxon 1947. Served European War, 1914–18, in ranks, Artillery and Intelligence, 1914–19. Lecturer, University Coll. of N Wales, Bangor, 1920–24; Sen. Lecturer, Edinburgh, 1924–25; Fellow, Hertford Coll., Oxford, 1925–59, Bursar, 1937–59. Formerly mem. Hebdomadal Council, Gen. Board and the Chest, Oxford Univ.; Sec., London Math. Soc., 1933–38. *Publications:* Convergence, 1938; Algebra, 1941; Higher Algebra for Schools, 1945, Part II, 1948; Finite Matrices, 1951; Differential Calculus, 1956; Integral Calculus, 1958; Mathematics for Science, 1965; Calculus for Beginners, 1967; Advanced Mathematics for Science, 1969; various research papers, 1924–37. *Address:* 21 Sunderland Avenue, Oxford OX2 8DT.

FERRARI, Enzo; President and Managing Director of Ferrari Automobili SpA Sefac, 1940–77; *b* Modena, 20 Feb. 1898; *s* of Alfredo Ferrari and Adalgisa Bisbini; *m* 1923, Laura Garello; one *s* decd. *Educ:* State sch.; Professional Institute of Technology. Started as tester, Turin, 1918; later with CMN, Milan; tester, driver, sales executive, Alfa Romeo, 1920–39; subsequently Dir, Alfa Corse; Pres. and Managing Dir of Scuderia Ferrari, later of Auto Avio Construzione Ferrari, 1940–60. Builder of racing, sports and gran turismo cars in factory built at Maranello in 1943 and reconstructed in 1946. Commendatore, 1928; Cavaliere del Lavoro, 1952. Hon. doctorate in engineering, Bologna, 1960. *Publication:* Le mie gioie terribili (autobiog.). *Address:* viale Trento Trieste 31, Modena, Italy. *T:* 24081–24082; (office) Maranello, Modena, Italy. *T:* 91161–91162.

FERRER, José Vicente; actor, director and producer, USA; *b* 8 Jan. 1912; *s* of Rafael Ferrer and Maria Providencia (*née* Cintrón); *m* 1st, 1938, Uta Hagen (marr. diss. 1948); one *d*; 2nd, 1948, Phyllis Hill (marr. diss. 1953); 3rd, 1953, Rosemary Clooney (marr. diss. 1967); three *s* two *d*; 4th, Stella Daphne Magee. *Educ:* Princeton Univ. AB (architecture), 1933. First appearance, The Periwinkle, Long Island show-boat, 1934; Asst Stage Manager Summer Theatre Stock Co., NY, 1935; first appearance NY stage, 1935; A Slight Case of Murder, 1935; Boy Meets Girl, 1935; Spring Dance, Brother Rat, 1936; In Clover, 1937; Dir Princeton Univ. Triangle Club's Fol-de-Rol, 1937; How To Get Tough About It, Missouri Legend, 1938; Mamba's Daughters, Key Largo, 1939; first star rôle, Lord Fancourt Babberley, Charley's Aunt, 1940; producer and dir, The Admiral Had A Wife, 1941; staged and co-starred, Vickie, 1942; Let's Face It, 1943; played Iago to Paul Robeson's Othello, Theatre Guild, 1943, 1944, 1945; producer and dir Strange Fruit, 1945; Play's The Thing, Richard III, Green Goddess, 1946; producer and star, Cyrano, 1946; Design For Living, Goodbye Again, 1947; Gen. dir to NY Theatre Co., City Centre, 1948; Silver Whistle, Theatre Guild, 1948; produced, directed and appeared in Twentieth Century, 1950; produced, directed, Stalag 17; The Fourposter, 1951; producer, dir and appeared in The Shrike, 1952; The Chase, 1952; staged My 3 Angels, 1953; dir and co-author, Oh Captain, 1958; producer, dir, and starred in, Edwin Booth, 1959; dir, The Andersonville Trial, 1960; starred in, The Girl Who Came to Supper, 1963–64; Man of La Mancha, 1966; dir, Cyrano de Bergerac, Chichester, 1975; *Films include:* Joan of Arc, 1947; Whirlpool, 1949; Crisis, Cyrano, 1950; Anything Can Happen, 1951; Moulin Rouge, 1952; Miss Sadie Thompson (Rain), Caine Mutiny, 1953; Deep in My Heart, 1955; Cockleshell Heroes, The Great Man, 1957; The High Cost of Loving, I Accuse, The Shrike (Dir, starred), 1958; Return to Peyton Place (Dir), 1962; State Fair (Dir), 1963; Nine Hours to Rama, Lawrence of Arabia, 1963; Cyrano et D'Artagnan, Train 349 From Berlin, The Greatest Story Ever Told, 1964; Ship of Fools, Enter Laughing, 1966; The Fifth Musketeer, 1976; Fedora, 1977; The Amazing Captain Nemo, 1979; The Big Brawl, 1980; A Midsummer Night's Sex Comedy, 1981; To Be Or Not To Be, Dune, 1983. Pres., Players Club, NY, 1983–. Mem., Acad. of Arts and Scis of Puerto Rico, 1974. Holds hon. degrees. Various awards for acting, etc, since 1944, include American Academy of Arts and Letters Gold Medal, 1949; Academy Award, 1950 (Best Actor, Cyrano); Theatre Hall of Fame, 1981; Ambassador of the Arts, State of Florida, 1983; Hispanic Heritage Festival Don Quixote Award, Florida, 1984; National Medal of Arts, 1985. *Recreations:* tennis, golf. *Address:* PO Box 616, Miami, Florida 33133, USA.

FERRERS, 13th Earl *cr* 1711; **Robert Washington Shirley;** Viscount Tamworth 1711; Bt 1611; PC 1982; DL; High Steward of Norwich Cathedral, since 1979; Chairman, Royal Commission on Historical Monuments (England), since 1984; *b* 8 June 1929; *o s* of 12th Earl Ferrers and Hermione Morley (*d* 1969); *S* father, 1954; *m* 1951, Annabel Mary, *d* of late Brig. W. G. Carr, CVO, DSO; two *s* three *d*. *Educ:* Winchester Coll.; Magdalene Coll., Cambridge. MA (Agric.). Lieut Coldstream Guards, 1949 (as National Service). A Lord-in-waiting, 1962–64, 1971–74; Parly Sec., MAFF, 1974; Jt Dep. Leader of the Opposition, House of Lords, 1976–79; Dep. Leader of House of Lords, 1979–83; Minister of State, MAFF, 1979–83. Mem., Armitage Cttee on political activities of civil servants, 1976–. Chm., TSB of Eastern England, 1977–79; Mem., TSB Central Bd, 1977–79; Director: Central TSB, 1978–79; TSB Trustcard Ltd, 1978–79; Norwich Union Insurance Group, 1975–79 and 1983–. Dir, Economic Forestry Gp, 1985–; Chm., British Agricl Export Council, 1984–; Mem. Council, Food From Britain, 1984–. Mem. of Council, Hurstpierpoint Coll., 1959–68; Dir, Chatham Historic Dockyard Trust, 1984–. DL Norfolk, 1983. *Heir: s* Viscount Tamworth, *qv*. *Address:* Ditchingham Hall, Norfolk. *Club:* Beefsteak.

FERRIE, Maj.-Gen. Alexander Martin, CBE 1971; RAMC retired; *b* 30 Nov. 1923; *s* of late Archibald Ferrie and Elizabeth Ferrie (*née* Martin). *Educ:* Glasgow Academy; Univ. of Glasgow (MB ChB). MFCM 1974. Commissioned RAMC, 1947; Commanding Officer, Queen Alexandra Military Hospital, Millbank, 1973–75; Director of Medical Supply, Min. of Defence, 1975–77; Dep. Dir of Medical Services, UKLF, and Inspector of

Trng, TA Medical Services, 1977–81; QHS 1978–83; DMS, UKLF, 1981–82; Comdt, RAMC Trng Gp, and PMO, UKLF, 1982–83. *Recreation:* gardening. *Address:* c/o Barclays Bank, 31b Western Road, Hove, Sussex BN3 1AD.

FERRIER, Baron *cr* 1958, of Culter (Life Peer); **Victor Ferrier Noel-Paton,** ED; DL; *b* Edinburgh, 1900; *s* of late F. Noel-Paton, Dir-Gen. of Commercial Intelligence to the Govt of India; *m* 1932, Joane Mary (*d* 1984), *d* of late Sir Gilbert Wiles, KCIE, CSI; one *s* three *d*. *Educ:* Cargilfield and The Edinburgh Academy. Served RE, 1918–19, Indian Auxiliary Force (Major, ED), 1920–46, and IARO. Commercial and Industrial Management, Bombay, 1920–51; one time Dir and Chm. of a number of Cos in India and UK; Pres., Bombay Chamber of Commerce. Mem., Legislative Council, Bombay, 1936 and Hon. ADC to Governor of Bombay; Past Chairman: Federation of Electricity Undertakings of India; Indian Roads and Transport Develt Assoc., Bombay. A Dep. Speaker and Chm. of Cttees, House of Lords, 1970–73. Mem. of Royal Company of Archers. DL, Lanarks, 1960. *Recreations:* field sports. *Address:* Kilkerran, Maybole, Ayrshire KA19 7SJ. *T:* Crosshill 515. *Clubs:* Cavalry and Guards, Beefsteak; New (Edinburgh).

See also Sir Charles Fergusson Bt.

FERRIER, Prof. Robert Patton, FRSE 1977; Professor of Natural Philosophy, University of Glasgow, since 1973; *b* 4 Jan. 1934; *s* of William McFarlane Ferrier and Gwendoline Melita Edwards; *m* 1961, Valerie Jane Duncan; two *s* one *d*. *Educ:* Glebelands Sch. and Morgan Academy, Dundee; Univ. of St Andrews (BSc, PhD). MA Cantab, FInstP. Scientific Officer, AERE Harwell, 1959–61; Res. Assoc., MIT, 1961–62; Sen. Asst in Res., Cavendish Lab., Cambridge, 1962–66; Fellow of Fitzwilliam Coll., Cambridge, 1965–73; Asst Dir of Res., Cavendish Lab. 1966–71; Lectr in Physics, Univ. of Cambridge, 1971–73; Guest Scientist, IBM Res. Labs San José, Calif, 1972–73. Chm., SERC Semiconductor and Surface Physics Sub-Cttee, 1979–. *Publications:* numerous papers in Phil. Mag., Jl Appl. Physics, Jl Physics, etc. *Recreations:* do-it-yourself, golf, reading crime novels. *Address:* Glencoe, 31 Thorn Road, Bearsden, Dunbartonshire G61 4BS. *T:* (office) 041–330 5388.

FERRIS, *see* Grant-Ferris, family name of Baron Harvington.

FERRIS, Francis Mursell, TD 1965; QC 1980; barrister; *b* 19 Aug. 1932; *s* of Francis William Ferris and Elsie Lilian May Ferris (*née* Mursell); *m* 1957, Sheila Elizabeth Hester Falloon Bedford; three *s* one *d*. *Educ:* Bryanston Sch.; Oriel Coll., Oxford. BA (Modern History) 1955, MA 1979. Served RA, 1951–52; 299 Field Regt (RBY QOOH and Berks) RA, TA 1952–67, Major 1964. Called to the Bar, Lincoln's Inn, 1956; Practice at Chancery Bar, 1958–. Member: Bar Council, 1966–70; Senate of Inns of Court and the Bar, 1979–82; Standing Counsel to Dir Gen. of Fair Trading, 1966–80. *Recreation:* gardening. *Address:* White Gables, Shiplake, Oxfordshire; 13 Old Square, Lincoln's Inn, WC2A 3UA. *T:* 01–242 6105. *Club:* Marlow Rowing.

FERRIS, Paul Frederick; author and journalist; *b* 15 Feb. 1929; *o c* of late Frederick Morgan Ferris and of Olga Ferris; *m* 1953, Gloria Moreton; one *s* one *d*. *Educ:* Swansea Gram. Sch. Staff of South Wales Evening Post, 1949–52; Womans Own, 1953; Observer Foreign News Service, 1953–54. *Publications: novels:* A Changed Man, 1958; Then We Fall, 1960; A Family Affair, 1963; The Destroyer, 1965; The Dam, 1967; Very Personal Problems, 1973; The Cure, 1974; The Detective, 1976; Talk to Me About England, 1979; A Distant Country, 1983; *non-fiction:* The City, 1960; The Church of England, 1962; The Doctors, 1965; The Nameless: abortion in Britain today, 1966; Men and Money: financial Europe today, 1968; The House of Northcliffe, 1971; The New Militants, 1972; Dylan Thomas, 1977; Richard Burton, 1981; Gentlemen of Fortune: the world's investment bankers, 1984; (ed) The Collected Letters of Dylan Thomas, 1986; *television plays:* The Revivalist, 1975; Dylan, 1978; Nye, 1982; The Extremist, 1984; The Fasting Girl, 1984; contribs to The Observer. *Address:* c/o Curtis Brown Ltd, 162–168 Regent Street, W1. *T:* 01–437 9700.

FERRIS, Rt. Rev. Ronald Curry; *see* Yukon, Bishop of.

FERRY, Alexander, MBE 1977; General Secretary, Confederation of Shipbuilding and Engineering Unions, since 1978; Member of Board, Harland and Wolff plc, Shipbuilders and Engineers, Belfast, since 1984; *b* 14 Feb. 1931; *s* of Alexander and Susan Ferry; *m* 1958, Mary O'Kane McAlaney; one *s* two *d* (and one *s* decd). *Educ:* St Patrick's High, Senior Secondary, Dunbartonshire. Apprentice Engineer, 1947–52; served Royal Air Force, 1952–54; Engineer, 1954–64; full-time officer, AUEW, 1964–78. Part-time Mem., Monopolies and Mergers Commn, 1986–. *Publication:* The Red Paper on Scotland (co-author), 1975. *Recreation:* golf. *Address:* 190 Brampton Road, Bexley Heath, Kent. *T:* 01–303 5338.

FERSHT, Prof. Alan Roy, MA, PhD; FRS 1983; Wolfson Research Professor of the Royal Society, in the Department of Chemistry, Imperial College of Science and Technology, London, since 1978; *b* 21 April 1943; *s* of Philip and Betty Fersht; *m* 1966, Marilyn Persell; one *s* one *d*. *Educ:* Sir George Monoux Grammar Sch.; Gonville and Caius Coll., Cambridge (MA, PhD). Res. Fellow, Brandeis Univ., 1968; Scientific Staff, MRC Lab. of Molecular Biology, Cambridge, 1969–77; Fellow, Jesus Coll., Cambridge, 1969–72; Eleanor Roosevelt Fellow, Stanford Univ., 1978. Lectures: Smith Kline & French, Berkeley, 1984; Edsall, Harvard, 1984; B. R. Baker, Univ. of California at Santa Barbara, 1986. Mem., EMBO, 1980–. Essex County Jun. Chess Champion, 1961; Pres., Cambridge Univ. Chess Club, 1964 (Half Blue, 1965). FEBS Anniversary Prize, 1980; Novo Biotechnology Prize, 1986. *Publications:* Enzyme Structure and Mechanism, 1977, 2nd edn 1984; papers in scientific jls. *Recreations:* chess, horology. *Address:* Department of Chemistry, Imperial College of Science and Technology, SW7 2AY. *T:* 01–589 5111; 37 Home Park Road, SW19 7HS. *T:* 01–947 2616.

FESSEY, Mereth Cecil, CB 1977; Director, Business Statistics Office, 1969–77, retired; *b* Windsor, Berks, 19 May 1917; *s* of late Morton Fessey and Ethel Fessey (*née* Blake), Bristol; *m* 1945, Grace Lilian, *d* of late William Bray, Earlsfield, London; one *s* two *d*. *Educ:* Westminster City Sch.; LSE, Univ. of London. London Transport, 1934; Army, 1940; Min. of Transport, 1947; Board of Trade, 1948; Statistician, 1956; Chief Statistician, 1965. Statistical Adviser to Syrian and Mexican Govts, 1979. Chm. of Council, Inst. of Statisticians, 1970–73; Vice Pres. and Mem., Council, Royal Statistical Soc., 1974–78; Chm., Cttee of Librarians and Statisticians, LA/Royal Stat. Soc., 1978–. Hon. FLA 1984. *Publications:* articles and papers in: Economic Trends; Statistical News; Jl of Royal Statistical Soc.; The Statistician; Annales de Sciences Economiques Appliquées, Louvain; etc. *Recreations:* chess, walking. *Address:* Undy House, Undy, Gwent NP6 3BX. *T:* Magor 880478.

FETHERSTON-DILKE, Mary Stella, CBE 1968; RRC 1966; Organiser, Citizens' Advice Bureau, 1971–83, retired; *b* 21 Sept. 1918; *d* of late B. A. Fetherston-Dilke, MBE. *Educ:* Kingsley Sch., Leamington Spa; St George's Hospital, London (SRN). Joined QARNNS, 1942; Matron-in-Chief, QARNNS, 1966–70, retired. OStJ 1966. *Recreation:* antiques. *Address:* 12 Clareville Court, Clareville Grove, SW7.

FEUILLÈRE, Edwige; Officier de la Légion d'Honneur; Commandeur des Arts et Lettres; French actress; *b* 29 Oct.; *m* (divorced). *Educ:* Lycée de Dijon; Conservatoire National de Paris. *Plays include:* La Dame aux camélias, 1940–42, 1952–53; Sodome et Gomorrhe, 1943; L'Aigle a deux têtes, 1946; Partage de midi, Pour Lucrèce, La Parisienne, Phèdre, Lucy Crown, Constance, Rodogune, 1964; La Folle de Chaillot, 1965–66; Delicate Balance; Sweet Bird of Youth; Le bâteau pour Lipaïa, 1971; Léovardia, 1984–85. *Films include:* L'Idiot, 1946; L'Aigle a deux têtes, 1947; Olivia, 1950; Le Blé en herbe, 1952; En cas de malheur, 1958; La vie à deux, 1958; Les amours célèbres, 1961; Le crime ne paye pas, 1962; La chair de l'orchidée, 1975. *Publications:* Les Feux de la Mémoire, 1977; Moi, La Clairon: biographie romancée de Mlle Clairon, 1984. *Address:* 19 rue Eugène Manuel, 75016 Paris, France.

FEVERSHAM, 6th Baron *cr* 1826; **Charles Antony Peter Duncombe;** free-lance journalist; *b* 3 Jan. 1945; *s* of Col Antony John Duncombe-Anderson and G. G. V. McNalty; *S* (to barony of) *kinsman*, 3rd Earl of Feversham (the earldom having become extinct), 1963; *m* 1st, 1966, Shannon (*d* 1976), *d* of late Sir Thomas Foy, CSI, CIE; two *s* one *d*; 2nd, 1979, Pauline, *d* of John Aldridge, Newark, Notts; one *s*. *Educ:* Eton; Middle Temple. Chairman: Yorkshire Arts Assoc., 1969–80; Standing Conf. of Regional Arts Assocs, 1969–76; Trustees, Yorkshire Sculpture Park, 1981–. Governor, Leeds Polytechnic, 1969–76. Pres., Soc. of Yorkshiremen in London, 1974; Pres., The Arvon Foundn, 1976–86. Pres., Yorks and Cleveland Local Councils Assoc., 1977–. *Publications:* A Wolf in Tooth (novel), 1967; Great Yachts, 1970. *Heir: s* Hon. Jasper Orlando Slingsby Duncombe, *b* 14 March 1968. *Address:* Beckdale House, Helmsley, York.

FEYNMAN, Prof. Richard (Phillips); Professor of Physics, California Institute of Technology, Pasadena, Calif, since 1951; *b* 11 May 1918; *s* of Melville Feynman and Lucille (*née* Phillips); *m* 1960, Gweneth Howarth, Ripponden, Yorks; one *s* one *d*. *Educ:* MIT; Princeton Univ. Los Alamos, N Mex. Atomic Bomb Project, 1943–46; Cornell Univ., 1946–51. Mem. Brazilian Acad. of Sciences; Fellow (Foreign), Royal Soc., London, 1965. Einstein Award, 1954; Nobel Prize for Physics (jointly), 1965; Oersted Medal, 1972; Niels Bohr Internat. Gold Medal, 1973. *Publications:* The Feynman Lectures in Physics, 1963; The Character of Physical Law, 1965; Statistical Mechanics, 1972; Photon-Hadron Interactions, 1972; Surely You're Joking, Mr Feynman, 1985; QED: the strange theory of flight and matter, 1985; papers in scientific journals on quantum electrodynamics, liquid helium, theory of beta-decay, quantum chromodynamics. *Recreations:* Mayan Hieroglyphics, opening safes, playing bongo drums, drawing, biology experiments, computer science (none done well). *Address:* 2475 Boulder Road, Altadena, Calif 91001, USA. *T:* 213–797–1262.

FFITCH, George Norman; Managing Director, London Broadcasting Company and Independent Radio News, 1979–85; *b* 23 Jan. 1929; *s* of late Robert George Ffitch; *m* 1958, Pamela Mary Lyle; one *s* one *d*. *Educ:* state schools and London Univ. Industrial Correspondent, Political Correspondent and Output Editor, Independent Television News, 1955–62; interviewer and presenter, ITV, 1962–67; Political Editor and an Asst Editor, The Economist, 1967–74; Associate Editor, Daily Express, 1974–76; columnist and broadcaster, 1976–79. *Recreation:* playing at playing golf. *Address:* 7 St Mary Abbots Terrace, W14 8NX. *T:* 01–602 3494. *Club:* Reform.

FFOLKES (ffolkes), Michael, (Brian Davis), FSIAD 1966; freelance artist; *b* 6 June 1925; *s* of late Walter Lawrence Davis, MSIAD, and of Elaine Rachel Bostock; *m* 1st, 1952, Miriam Boxer (marr. diss. 1971); two *s*; 2nd, 1972, Irene Ogilvy Kemp (marr. diss. 1978); one *d*. *Educ:* Leigh Hall Coll., Essex; St Martin's School of Art, 1941–43; Chelsea School of Art, 1946–49 (ND Painting 1948). Served Royal Navy, 1943–46. First drawing in Punch, 1943, and regular contributor, 1946–; Illustrator: Daily Telegraph's Way of the World, 1955–; Punch film column, 1961–72, 1978–; Member, Punch Table, 1978–. Drawings appear in The New Yorker, Playboy, Private Eye, Reader's Digest; exhibitor: Royal Academy, Leicester Galls, Arthur Jeffress Gall., The Workshop; drawings in V&A and BM; has illustrated over fifty books. *Publications:* ffanfare, 1953; How to Draw Cartoons, 1963; Mini Art, 1968; Private Eye Cartoon Library, 1976; ffolkes' ffauna, 1977; ffolkes' Companion to Mythology, 1978; ffundamental ffolkes, 1985. *Recreations:* walking, cinema, music, collecting illustrated books. *Address:* 186 Shaftesbury Avenue, WC2H 8BA. *T:* 01–240 1841. *Clubs:* Savage, Toby, Omar Khayyam.

FFOLKES, Sir Robert (Francis Alexander), 7th Bt *cr* 1774; *b* 2 Dec. 1943; *o s* of Captain Sir (Edward John) Patrick (Boschetti) ffolkes, 6th Bt, and Geraldine (*d* 1978), *d* of late William Roffey, Writtle, Essex; *S* father, 1960. *Educ:* Stowe Sch.; Christ Church, Oxford. *Address:* Coast Guard House, Morston, Holt, Norfolk NR25 7BH. *Club:* Turf.

FFORDE, John Standish; Director: Halifax Building Society, since 1984; Mercantile House Holdings plc, since 1984; Chairman, The Joint Mission Hospital Equipment Board Ltd, since 1985 (Director, since 1981); *b* 16 Nov. 1921; 4th *s* of late Francis Creswell Fforde and late Cicely Creswell; *m* 1951, Marya, *d* of late Joseph Retinger; three *s* one *d*. *Educ:* Rossall Sch.; Christ Church, Oxford (1st cl. Hons PPE). Served RAF, 1940–46. Prime Minister's Statistical Branch, 1951–53; Fellow, Nuffield Coll., Oxford, 1953–56; entered Bank of England, 1957; Dep. Chief, Central Banking Information Dept, 1959–64; Adviser to the Governors, 1964–66; Chief Cashier, 1966–70; Exec. Dir (Home Finance), 1970–82; Advr to the Governors, 1982–84; offical historian, 1984–. *Publications:* The Federal Reserve System, 1945–49, 1953; An International Trade in Managerial Skills, 1957. *Recreations:* travel, walking.

FFOWCS WILLIAMS, Prof. John Eirwyn; Rank Professor of Engineering (Acoustics), University of Cambridge, and Professorial Fellow, Emmanuel College, Cambridge, since 1972; *b* 25 May 1935; *m* 1959, Anne Beatrice Mason; two *s* one *d*. *Educ:* Friends Sch., Great Ayton; Derby Techn. Coll.; Univ. of Southampton. BSc; MA, ScD Cantab, PhD Southampton. CEng, FRAeS, FInstP, FIMA, FInstAcoust, Fellow Acoustical Soc. of America, FAIAA. Engrg Apprentice, Rolls-Royce Ltd, 1951–55; Spitfire Mitchell Meml Schol. to Southampton Univ., 1955–60; Aerodynamics Div., NPL, 1960–62; Bolt, Beranek & Newman Inc., 1962–64; Reader in Applied Maths, Imperial Coll. of Science and Technology, 1964–69; Rolls Royce Prof. of Theoretical Acoustics, Imperial Coll., 1969–72. Exec. Consultant, Rolls Royce Ltd, 1969–; Chm., Topexpress Ltd, 1979–. Chm., Noise Research Cttee, ARC, 1969–76. Corresp. Mem., INCE/USA. AIAA Aero-Acoustics Medal, 1977; Rayleigh Medal, Inst. of Acoustics, 1984. *Publications:* (with A. P. Dowling) Sound and Sources of Sound, 1983; (with C. F. Ross) Anti-Sound, 1986; articles in Philosophical Trans Royal Soc., Jl of Fluid Mechanics, Jl IMA, Jl of Sound Vibration, Annual Reviews of Fluid Mechanics, Random Vibration, Financial Times; (jtly) film on Aerodynamic Sound. *Recreations:* friends and cigars. *Address:* 298 Hills Road, Cambridge CB2 2QG. *T:* Cambridge 248275. *Clubs:* Athenæum, Danish.

FFRANGCON-DAVIES, Gwen; Actress; *b* 25 Jan. 1891; *d* of David Ffrangcon-Davies, the famous singer, and Annie Frances Rayner. *Educ:* South Hampstead High Sch.; abroad. First London success The Immortal Hour, 1922; created the part of Eve in Shaw's Back to Methuselah; principal successes, Tess, in Tess of the D'Urbervilles, Elizabeth Barrett, in The Barretts of Wimpole Street, Anne of Bohemia, in Richard of Bordeaux. Played Lady Macbeth to Macbeth of John Gielgud, Piccadilly, 1942. Appeared, in association with

Marda Vanne, in leading parts in various plays in S Africa, 1943–46. Returned to England, 1949; played in Adventure Story, St James's, 1949; Stratford Festival, 1950, as Katherine in King Henry VIII; Portia in Julius Cæsar, Regan in King Lear (again Katherine, Old Vic. 1953); Madame Ranevsky in The Cherry Orchard, Lyric, 1954; Aunt Cleofe in Summertime, Apollo, 1955; Rose Padley in The Mulberry Bush, Royal Court, 1956; Agatha in The Family Reunion, Phoenix, 1956; Miss Madrigal in The Chalk Garden, Haymarket, 1957; Mrs Callifer in The Potting Shed, Globe Theatre, 1958; Mary Tyrone in Long Day's Journey into Night, Edinburgh Fest. and Globe, 1958; Queen Isolde in Ondine, Aldwych, 1961, Queen Mother in Becket, Aldwych, 1961; Hester Bellboys in A Penny for a Song, Aldwych, 1962; Beatrice in Season of Goodwill, Queen's, 1964; Amanda in The Glass Menagerie, Haymarket, 1965; Uncle Vanya, Royal Court, 1970; *Films:* The Burning, 1967; Leo the Last, 1969. Numerous radio and TV plays. *Recreation:* gardening. *Address:* c/o Larry Dalzell, 126 Kennington Park Road, SE11 4DS.

FFRENCH, family name of **Baron ffrench.**

FFRENCH, 8th Baron *cr* 1798; **Robuck John Peter Charles Mario ffrench;** Bt 1779; *b* 14 March 1956; *s* of 7th Baron ffrench and of Sonia Katherine, *d* of late Major Digby Cayley; *S* father, 1986. *Educ:* Blackrock, Co. Dublin; Ampleforth College, Yorks. *Heir: uncle* John Charles Mary Joseph Francis ffrench [*b* 5 Oct. 1928; *m* 1963, Sara-Primm, *d* of James A. Turner; three *d*]. *Address:* Castle ffrench, Ballinasloe, Co. Galway, Ireland. *T:* Roscommon 4226.

FFRENCH-BEYTAGH, Canon Gonville Aubie; Rector of St Vedast-alias-Foster, London, since 1974; Hon. Canon of Johannesburg, since 1972 and of Canterbury, since 1973; *b* 26 Jan. 1912; *s* of Leo Michael and Edith ffrench-Beytagh; unmarried. *Educ:* Monkton Combe Sch., Bath; Bristol Grammar Sch.; St Paul's Theol Coll., Grahamstown (LTh). Priest 1939. Tramp and casual labourer, New Zealand, 1929–33; clerk in Johannesburg, 1933–36; Parish Priest and Diocesan Missioner, Johannesburg Dio., 1939–54; Dean of Salisbury, Rhodesia, 1955–65; Dean of Johannesburg, 1965–72; detained, tried, convicted and sentenced to 5 yrs imprisonment under SA Terrorism Act, 1971–72; conviction and sentence quashed by Appellate Div. and returned to England, 1972. *Publications:* Encountering Darkness, 1973; Encountering Light, 1975, Facing Depression, 1978; A Glimpse of Glory, 1986. *Recreations:* drink, companionship and science fiction. *Address:* St Vedast's Rectory, Foster Lane, EC2. *T:* 01–606 3998.

FFYTCHE, Timothy John, FRCS; Surgeon–Oculist to HM Household, since 1980; Ophthalmic Surgeon to St Thomas's Hospital, since 1973; Consultant Ophthalmologist, Moorfields Eye Hospital, since 1975; Consultant Ophthalmic Surgeon to King Edward VIIth Hospital for Officers, since 1980; *b* 11 Sept. 1936; *s* of Louis ffytche and Margaret (*née* Law); *m* 1961, Bärbl, *d* of Günther Fischer; two *s*. *Educ:* Lancing Coll.; St George's Hosp., London. MB, BS; DO 1961; FRCS 1968. Registrar, Moorfields Eye Hosp., 1966–69; Wellcome Lectr, Hammersmith Hosp., 1969–70; Sen. Registrar, Middlesex Hosp., 1970–73. Sec., OSUK, 1980–82. Mem., Medical Adv. Bd, LEPRA, 1982–; Vice-Pres., Ophthalmol Sect., RSocMed, 1985–; UK rep. to Internat. Fedn of Ophthalmic Socs, 1985–; Adv. Cttee to Internat. Council of Ophthalmology, 1985–. Clayton Meml Lectr, LEPRA, 1984. Editorial Committee: Ophthalmic Literature, 1968–; Transactions of OSUK, 1984–. *Publications:* articles on retinal diagnosis and therapy, retinal photography and the ocular complications of leprosy, in The Lancet, British Jl of Ophthalmol., Trans OSUK, Proc. Roy. Soc. Med., Leprosy Review and other specialist jls. *Recreations:* travel, swimming, cricket, occasional fishing. *Address:* 149 Harley Street, W1N 2DE; (home) 1 Wellington Square, SW3 4NJ.

FICKLING, Benjamin William, CBE 1973; FRCS, FDS RCS; Honorary Consultant Dental Surgeon, since 1974, formerly Dental Surgeon: St George's Hospital, SW1, 1936–74; Royal Dental Hospital of London, 1935–74; Mount Vernon Centre for Plastic and Jaw Surgery (formerly Hill End), 1941–74; *b* 14 July 1909; *s* of Robert Marshall Fickling, LDS RCS, and Florence (*née* Newson); *m* 1943, Shirley Dona, *er d* of Albert Latimer Walker, FRCS; two *s* one *d*. *Educ:* Framlingham; St George's Hosp. Royal Dental Hospital. William Brown Senior Exhibition, St George's Hosp., 1929; LDS RCS, 1932; MRCS, LRCP, 1934; FRCS 1938; FDS, RCS 1947, MGDS RCS 1979. Lectures: Charles Tomes, RCS, 1956; Everett Magnus, Melbourne, 1971; Webb-Johnson, RCS, 1978. Examiner (Chm.), Membership in Gen. Dental Surgery, 1979–83; formerly Examiner: in Dental Surgery, RCS; Univ. of London and Univ. of Edinburgh. Dean of Faculty of Dental Surgery, 1968–71, and Mem. Council, Royal College of Surgeons, 1968–71 (Vice-Dean, 1965; Colyer Gold Medal, 1979); Fellow Royal Society of Medicine (Pres. Odontological Section, 1964–65); Pres., British Assoc. of Oral Surgeons, 1967–68; Mem. GDC, 1971–74. Director: Med. Sickness Annuity and Life Assurance Soc. Ltd; Permanent Insurance Co. Ltd; Medical Sickness Finance Corp. Ltd. Civilian Dental Consultant to RN, 1954–76. *Publications:* (joint) Injuries of the Jaws and Face, 1940; (joint) Chapter on Faciomaxillary Injuries and Deformities in British Surgical Practice, 1951. *Address:* Linksview, Linksway, Northwood, Mddx. *T:* Northwood 22035. *Club:* Ski Club of Great Britain.

FIDDES, James Raffan, QC (Scot.) 1965; Sheriff of South Strathclyde, Dumfries and Galloway at Hamilton, since 1977; *b* 1 Feb. 1919; *er s* of late Sir James Raffan Fiddes, CBE; *m* 1954, Edith Margaret (*d* 1979), 2nd *d* of late Charles E. Lippe, KC. *Educ:* Aberdeen Gram. Sch.; Glasgow Univ. (MA, 1942; LLB 1948); Balliol Coll., Oxford, (BA 1944). Advocate, 1948. *Address:* 23 South Learmonth Gardens, Edinburgh EH4 1EZ. *T:* 031–332 1431. *Club:* Scottish Arts (Edinburgh).

FIDLER, Alwyn G. Sheppard, CBE 1963; MA, BArch, DipCD, FRIBA, FRTPI; architect and town planning consultant; *b* 8 May 1909; *e s* of late W. E. Sheppard Fidler and Phoebe M. Williams; *m* 1936, Margaret (*d* 1977), *d* of Capt. J. R. Kidner, Newcastle upon Tyne; one *s*. *Educ:* Holywell Gram. Sch.; University of Liverpool; British Sch. at Rome. Tite Finalist, 1930; studied in USA, 1931; Victory Schol., 1933; Rome Schol. in Architecture, 1933–35. Chief Architect: Land Settlement Assoc., 1937; Barclays Bank Ltd, 1938; Sen. Tech. Intelligence Officer, Min. of Home Security, 1940–46; Chief Archt, Crawley New Town, 1947–52 (Housing Medals of Min. of Housing and Local Govt in 1951, 1952 and 1954); City Archt of Birmingham, 1952–64 (Distinction in Town Planning, 1955, for work at Crawley and Birmingham Redevelopment Areas); private practice, 1964–74. Council Mem., 1953–62, 1963–75, Vice-Pres., 1958–60, Chm. Practice Cttee, 1958–62, Treasurer, 1974–75, External Examr in Architecture, 1958–, RIBA. Pres. City and Borough Architects Soc., 1956–58; Chm. Exec. Cttee, British Sch. at Rome, 1972– (Chm., Fac. of Architecture, 1958–72). Mem., Royal Commn for the Exhibn of 1851. Chm. ARC of UK, 1960–63; Mem. Jt Consultative Cttee of Architects, Quantity Surveyors and Builders, 1958–61; Mem. Birmingham and Five Counties Architectural Assoc. (Mem. Council, 1956–, Vice-Pres., 1960–62, Pres., 1962–64); Chm. Assoc. of Building Centres, 1964–72; Member Council: Building Centre Gp, 1971–81; Royal Albert Hall, 1974–; Gov., Coll. of Estate Management, 1965–72; Mem. SE Regional Adv. Cttee to Land Commn, 1967–70. Mem. or past Mem., of many other councils and cttees. *Publications:* contrib. to professional jls. *Recreations:* travel and gardening. *Address:* 1 Burnham Drive, Reigate, Surrey RH2 9HD. *T:* Reigate 43849.

FIDLER, Jan; Ambassador of the Czechoslovak Socialist Republic to the Court of St James's, since 1986; *b* 14 May 1927; *s* of Marie and Josef Fidler; *m* 1950, Alena (*née* Oulehlová); two *s*. *Educ:* Higher School of Economics. Manager in woollen industry, 1950–60; Min. of Foreign Affairs, 1960–63; Second Sec., Stockholm, 1963–67; Min. of Foreign Affairs, 1967–70; Counsellor, Helsinki, 1970–77; Head, Office of First Dep. Minister, 1977–80; Minister Counsellor, Warsaw, 1980–83; Chief of Diplomatic Protocol, Min. of Foreign Affairs, 1984–86. Holder of State distinctions. *Address:* 70 Redington Road, NW3. *T:* 01–229 1255.

FIDLER, Michael M., JP; President, General Zionist Organisation of Great Britain, since 1973; Founder and National Director, Conservative Friends of Israel, since 1974; Founder and International Director, All Party Friendship with Israel Group, European Parliament, since 1979; Chairman, International Organisation Commission, World Jewish Congress, since 1975; business consultant; Managing Director, Wibye Ltd, since 1968; *b* 10 Feb. 1916; *s* of Louis Fidler and Golda Fidler (*née* Sherr); *m* 1939, Maidie (*née* Davis); one *s* one *d*. *Educ:* Salford Grammar Sch.; Salford Royal Tech Coll. Cllr, Borough of Prestwich, 1951–63; Mayor, 1957–58; Alderman, 1963–74. Pres., Middleton, Prestwich and Whitfield Div. Cons. Assoc., 1965–69; Chm., Divl Educn Exec. (Prestwich, Whitfield and Radcliffe), Lancs CC, 1967–69. MP (C) Bury and Radcliffe, June 1970–Oct. 1974; Sec., Canadian Gp of Cons. Commonwealth Overseas Cttee, 1970–71; Treasurer, Parly Migraine Gp, 1970–74. Lectr, Extra Mural Dept, Manchester Univ., 1966–. Man. Director: H. & L. Fidler Ltd, 1941–70; Michael Lewis Ltd, 1942–70. Member: Grand Council, CBI, 1965–67; Nat. Exec., Nat. Assoc. of British Manufacturers, 1953–65. President: Fedn of Jewish Youth Socs of Gt Britain and Ireland, 1951–; Manchester Union of Jewish Socs, 1964–; Council of Manchester and Salford Jews, 1966–68 (Hon. Sec., 1950–53; Hon. Treasurer, 1953–55; Vice-Pres., 1954–60); Holy Law Congregation, Manchester, 1967–70 (Life Vice-Pres., 1977–84, Life Pres., 1984–); Bd of Deputies of British Jews, 1967–73; Cons. Friends of Israel, Redbridge Area Council, 1982–85; Vice-President: Children and Youth Aliyah Cttee for Gt Britain, 1968–81; Mizrachi, Hapoel-Hamizrachi Fedn of Gt Britain and Ireland, 1968–78; Hillel Foundn of Gt Britain, 1968–; Life Vice-President: Manchester Jewish Bd of Guardians, 1967–; Manchester Jewish Social Services, 1967–; Vice-Chairman: World Conf. on Jewish Educn, 1968–75; World Conf. of Jewish Organisations, 1967–73; Member Exec. Cttee: Council of Christians and Jews, Manchester Branch, 1966–; World Meml Foundn for Jewish Culture, 1968–80; World Conf. on Jewish Material Claims against Germany, 1968–80. Patron, All Party Parly Cttee for release of Soviet Jewry, 1971–74. Governor: Stand Grammar Schools, 1955–74; Inst. of Contemporary Jewry, Hebrew Univ. of Jerusalem, 1967–73; St Peter's RC Grammar Sch., 1968–80; Bury Grammar Schools, 1970–74. President: British Parks Lawn Tennis Assoc., 1952–59; SE Lancs Amateur Football League, 1966–67; Prestwich Heys Amateur Football Club, 1965–; Member: House of Commons Motor Club, 1970–74; Parly Flying Club, 1971–74. JP Co. Lancs, 1958. FRGS, FRAS, FREconS, FIAI. *Publications:* One Hundred Years of the Holy Law Congregation, 1964; articles. *Recreations:* politics, travel, reading, filming, foreign affairs, education. *Address:* 51 Tavistock Court, Tavistock Square, WC1H 9HG. *T:* 01–387 4925; 1 Woodcliffe Lodge, Sedgley Park Road, Prestwich, Manchester M25 8JX. *T:* 061–773 1471; Lower Ground Floor, 45 Westbourne Terrace, W2 3UR. *T:* 01–262 2493. *Clubs:* Embassy; Milverton Lodge (Manchester).

FIDLER-SIMPSON, John Cody; *see* Simpson.

FIELD, Brig. Anne, CB 1980; Chairman, Greater London Regional Board, Lloyds Bank Plc, since 1985 (Regional Director, 1982–85); Deputy Controller Commandant, Women's Royal Army Corps since 1984 (Director, 1977–82); Hon. ADC to the Queen, 1977–82; *b* 4 April 1926; *d* of Captain Harold Derwent and Annie Helena Hodgson. *Educ:* Keswick Sch.; St George's, Harpenden; London Sch. of Economics. Joined ATS, 1947; commissioned: ATS, 1948; WRAC, 1949; Lt-Col, 1968; Col, 1971. Freeman, City of London, 1981. CBIM (FBIM 1978). *Address:* c/o Lloyds Bank Plc, 6 Pall Mall, SW1Y 5NH. *Club:* Lansdowne.

FIELD, Arnold, OBE 1965; Air Traffic Services and Systems Consultant; Joint Field Commander, National Air Traffic Services, 1974–77; *b* 19 May 1917; *m* 1943, Kathleen Dulcie Bennett; one *s* one *d*. *Educ:* Sutton Coldfield Royal Sch.; Birmingham Technical Coll. RAF, 1940–46 (Sqdn Ldr). Civil Air Traffic Control Officer, 1946; Centre Supt, Scottish Air Traffic Control Centre, 1954; Centre Supt, London Air Traffic Control Centre, 1957; Divisional Air Traffic Control Officer, Southern Div., 1963; Dir, Civil Air Traffic Ops, 1969. Master, Guild of Air Traffic Control Officers, 1958; Pres., Internat. Fedn of Air Traffic Control Officers, 1970. *Publications:* The Control of Air Traffic, 1981; International Air Traffic Control, 1985; From Take-off to Touchdown—A Passenger's Guide, 1984; articles in Interavia, Times Supplement, Flight, Controller. *Recreations:* vintage cars, boating. *Address:* Footprints, Stoke Wood, Stoke Poges, Bucks. *T:* Farnham Common 2710. *Club:* Bentley Drivers (Long Crendon).

FIELD, Edward John; HM Diplomatic Service; Counsellor, UK Mission to the United Nations, New York, since 1984; *b* 11 June 1936; *s* of Arthur Field, OBE, MC, TD, and late Dorothy Agnes Field; *m* 1960, Irene Sophie du Pont Darden; one *s* one *d*. *Educ:* Highgate Sch.; Corpus Christi Coll., Oxford; Univ. of Virginia. Courtaulds Ltd, 1960–62; FCO, 1963–: 2nd, later 1st Sec., Tokyo, 1963–68; Amer. Dept, FCO, 1968–70; Cultural Attaché, Moscow, 1970–72; 1st Sec. (Commercial), Tokyo, 1973–76; Asst Head, S Asian Dept, FCO, 1976–77; Dept of Trade, 1977–79 (Head, Exports to Japan Unit); Counsellor: (Commercial), Seoul, 1980–83; at Harvard Univ., 1983–84. *Recreations:* tennis, squash, riding, listening to music. *Address:* c/o Foreign and Commonwealth Office, SW1.

FIELD, Frank; MP (Lab) Birkenhead, since 1979; *b* 16 July 1942; *s* of late Walter and of Annie Field. *Educ:* St Clement Danes Grammar Sch.; Univ. of Hull (BSc (Econ)). Teacher: at Southwark Coll. for Further Education, 1964–68; at Hammersmith Coll. for Further Education, 1968–69. Director: Child Poverty Action Gp, 1969–79; Low Pay Unit, 1974–80. Mem., Hounslow BC, 1964–68. Contested (Lab) Buckingham S, 1966. *Publications:* (ed, jtly) Twentieth Century State Education, 1971; (ed, jtly) Black Britons, 1971; (ed) Low Pay, 1973; Unequal Britain, 1974; (ed) Are Low Wages Inevitable?, 1976; (ed) Education and the Urban Crisis, 1976, (ed) The Conscript Army: a study of Britain's unemployed, 1976; (jtly) To Him Who Hath: a study of poverty and taxation, 1976; (with Ruth Lister) Wasted Labour, 1978 (Social Concern Book Award); (ed) The Wealth Report, 1979; Inequality in Britain: freedom, welfare and the state, 1981; Poverty and Politics, 1982; The Wealth Report—2, 1983; (ed) Policies against Low Pay, 1984; The Minimum Wage: its potential and dangers, 1984. *Recreation:* book collecting. *Address:* House of Commons, SW1. *T:* 01–219 5193.

FIELD, Dr Ian Trevor; Deputy Secretary, British Medical Association, since 1985; *b* 31 Oct. 1933; *s* of late Major George Edward Field, MBE, IA, and Bertha Cecilia Field; *m* 1960, Christine Mary Osman, JP; three *s*. *Educ:* Shri Shivaji School, Poona; Bournemouth School; Guy's Hosp. Med. School. MB, BS, FFCM. Royal Engineers, 1952–54; Med. Sch., 1954–60; house posts, 1960–62; general practice, 1962–64; Asst Sec., later Under Sec., BMA, 1964–75; SMO, 1975–78, SPMO/Under Sec., 1978–85, DHSS, (Internat. Health and Communicable Disease Control, later NHS Regional Orgn); Chief Med. and Health Services Advr, ODA, 1978–83. Member: Council, Liverpool Sch. of Trop. Med., 1979–83; Bd of Management, London Sch. of Hygiene and Trop. Med., 1979–83; Council, Royal Vet. Coll., 1982–; WHO Global Adv. Cttee on Malaria Control, 1979–82 (Chm., 1981). *Publications:* contribs to medical jls. *Recreations:* military history, watching cricket and rugby. *Address:* 10 Rockwells Gardens, Dulwich Wood Park, SE19 1HW. *T:* 01–670 5877.

FIELD, John, CBE 1967; ARAD; Artistic Director, British Ballet Organisation, since 1984; *b* 22 Oct. 1921; *m* 1958, Anne Heaton. *Educ:* Wheatley Boys' Sch., Doncaster. Sadler's Wells Ballet Co., 1939; RAF, 1942–46; Principal, Sadler's Wells Ballet Co., 1947–56; Resident Dir, Sadler's Wells Theatre Ballet, 1956–57; Asst Dir, 1957–70, Co-Dir, July-Dec. 1970, Royal Ballet Co.; Dir of Ballet, La Scala, Milan, 1971–74; Artistic Dir, 1975–76, Dir, 1976–79, Royal Acad. of Dancing; Artistic Dir, 1979–81, Director, 1982–84, London Festival Ballet. *Address:* c/o Yorkshire Bank, 56 Cheapside, EC2P 2BA.

FIELD, Marshall Hayward, CBE 1985; Consultant Partner, Bacon & Woodrow, since 1986; Consultant, Marketing of Investments Board Organising Committee, since 1985; President, Institute of Actuaries, since 1986; *b* 19 April 1930; *s* of Harold Hayward Field and Hilda Maud Field; *m* 1960, Barbara Evelyn Harris; two *d. Educ:* Dulwich College. FIA 1957. With Pearl Assce, 1948–58; Phoenix Assurance: Actuary, 1964–85; Gen. Manager, 1972–85; Dir, 1980–85. Dir, TSB Trust Co. Ltd, 1985–. Institute of Actuaries: Hon. Sec., 1975–77; Vice-Pres., 1979–82; Vice Pres., International Actuarial Assoc., 1984–; Chm., Life Offices' Assoc., 1983–85. Mem., Fowler Inquiry into Provision for Retirement, 1984. Mem., Dulwich Picture Gall. Cttee; Dep. Chm., Dulwich College Estates Governors, 1985–; Governor, James Allen's Girls' School. *Recreations:* theatre, architecture. *Address:* Low Cross, 35 Woodhall Drive, SE21 7HJ.

FIELD, William James; *b* 22 May 1909; *s* of late Frederick William Field, Solicitor; unmarried. *Educ:* Richmond County Sch.; London Univ.; abroad. Joined Labour Party, 1935; Parliamentary Private Sec. to Sec. of State for War, May-Oct. 1951 (to Under-Sec. for War, 1950–51); Chm. South Hammersmith Divisional Labour Party, 1945–46; contested Hampstead Div., General Election, 1945; MP (Lab) North Paddington, Nov. 1946–Oct. 1953. Mem. Hammersmith Borough Council, 1945–53, and Leader of that Council, 1946–49; a Vice-Pres. of Assoc. of Municipal Corporations, 1952–53; for several years, mem. Metropolitan Boroughs' Standing Joint Cttee and of many local govt bodies. Volunteered for Army, Sept. 1939 and served in ranks and as officer in Intelligence Corps and RASC.

FIELD-FISHER, Thomas Gilbert, TD 1950; QC 1969; a Recorder of the Crown Court, since 1972; *b* 16 May 1915; *s* of Caryl Field-Fisher, Torquay; *m* 1945, Ebba, *d* of Max Larsen, Linwood, USA. *Educ:* King's Sch., Bruton; Peterhouse, Cambridge. BA 1937, MA 1942. Called to Bar, Middle Temple, 1942, Bencher, 1976. Served Queen Victoria's Rifles, KRRC, 1939–47; BEF 1940 (POW; despatches). Judge Advocate Gen.'s Dept, 1945–47 (i/c War Crimes Dept, CMF); joined Western Circuit, 1947. Mem., Bar Council, 1962–66; Deputy Chairman: SW Agricultural Land Tribunal, 1967–82; Cornwall QS, 1968–71; Chm., Maria Colwell Inquiry, 1973–74. Vice-Chm., London Council of Social Service, 1966–79; Vice-Pres., London Voluntary Service Council, 1979–. Mem., Home Secretary's Adv. Cttee on Animal Experiments, 1980–. Chairman: Dogs' Home, Battersea, 1982–; Assoc. of British Dogs' Homes, 1985–. Pres., Cornwall Magistrates' Assoc., 1985–. *Publications:* Animals and the Law, 1964; Rent Regulation and Control, 1967; contribs to Halsbury's Laws of England, 3rd and 4th edns, Law Jl, and other legal publications. *Recreations:* tennis, dogs, collecting watercolours, gardening. *Address:* 38 Hurlingham Court, SW6. *T:* 01–736 4627; 2 King's Bench Walk, Temple, EC4. *T:* 01–353 1746. *Clubs:* Hurlingham, International Lawn Tennis of Great Britain.

FIELDEN, Frank, MA (Dunelm); Secretary, Royal Fine Art Commission, 1969–79; *b* 3 Oct. 1915; *s* of Ernest and Emma Fielden, Greenfield, Yorks; *m* 1939, Margery Keeler; two *d. Educ:* University of Manchester. Graduated, 1938. Served 1939–45 with Royal Engineers (Special Forces), France, N Africa, Italy, Germany. Town Planning Officer to Nigerian Government, 1945–46; Lecturer and Sen. Lectr, University of Durham, 1946–59; Prof. of Architecture, Univ. of Strathclyde, 1959–69. Mem., Royal Fine Art Commn for Scotland, 1965–69. RIBA Athens Bursar, 1950, Bronze Medallist 1960. Chairman: Soc. of Architectural Historians of Great Britain, 1965–67; Richmond Soc., 1971–74. *Publications:* articles in professional journals and national press. *Recreations:* music, gardening. *Address:* 28 Caledonian Road, Chichester, W Sussex PO19 2LQ.

FIELDGATE, Alan Frederic Edmond, CMG 1945; *b* 20 Nov. 1889; *m* 1915, Dorothy Alice Thomas. *Educ:* Worcester Coll., Oxford (BA). Asst District Commissioner, Gold Coast Colony, 1915; District Commissioner, 1922; Provincial Commissioner, 1934–46. *Address:* Olde Court, Higher Lincombe Road, Torquay, Devon.

FIELDHOUSE, Arnold; *see* Fieldhouse, R. A.

FIELDHOUSE, Bill; *see* Fieldhouse, W.

FIELDHOUSE, Prof. David Kenneth; Vere Harmsworth Professor of Imperial and Naval History, Cambridge University, since 1981; Fellow, Jesus College, Cambridge, since 1981; *b* 7 June 1925; *s* of Rev. Ernest Fieldhouse and Clara Hilda Beatrice Fieldhouse; *m* 1952, Sheila Elizabeth Lyon; one *s* two *d. Educ:* Dean Close Sch., Cheltenham; Queen's Coll., Oxford (MA, DLitt). War Service: RN, Sub-Lt (A), 1943–47. History master, Haileybury Coll., 1950–52; Lectr in Modern History, Univ. of Canterbury, NZ, 1953–57; Beit Lectr in Commonwealth History, Oxford Univ., 1958–81; Fellow, Nuffield Coll., Oxford, 1966–81. *Publications:* The Colonial Empires, 1966, 2nd edn 1982; The Theory of Capitalist Imperialism, 1967, 2nd edn 1969; Economics and Empire, 1973, 2nd edn 1984; Unilever Overseas, 1978; Colonialism 1870–1945, 1981; Black Africa 1945–80, 1986. *Recreations:* music, farming, golf, writing fiction. *Address:* Jesus College, Cambridge. *T:* Cambridge 68611.

FIELDHOUSE, Sir Harold, KBE 1949 (OBE 1934); CB 1947; Secretary, National Assistance Board, 1946–59, retired; Member of Letchworth Garden City, Welwyn Garden City and Hatfield Corporations, retired; *b* Leeds, Yorks, 18 Aug. 1892; *e s* of Frank and Mary Ellen Fieldhouse; *m* 1922, Mabel Elaine Elliott, Conisborough, Yorks; two *s. Educ:* Armley Higher Grade Sch., Leeds. Asst Clerk, Leeds Board of Guardians, 1909–30; Public Assistance Officer, City of Leeds, 1930–34; Regional Officer, Asst Sec. and Under-Sec. Assistance Board, 1934–46. Liveryman, Clockmakers' Co., 1959. *Recreations:* golf, bridge, music, reading. *Address:* 5 Gayton Court, Harrow, Mddx. *T:* 01–427 0918. *Clubs:* City Livery; Grim's Dyke Golf, West Hill Golf.

See also Sir J. D. E. Fieldhouse.

FIELDHOUSE, Admiral of the Fleet Sir John (David Elliott), GCB 1982 (KCB 1980); GBE 1982; Chief of the Defence Staff, since 1985; *b* 12 Feb. 1928; *s* of Sir Harold Fieldhouse, *qv; m* 1953, Margaret Ellen Cull; one *s* two *d. Educ:* RNC Dartmouth. MINucE. Midshipman, E Indies Fleet, 1945–46; entered Submarine Service, 1948; comd HMS Acheron, 1955; CO HMS Dreadnought, 1964–66; Exec. Officer, HMS Hermes,

1967; Captain SM10 (Polaris Sqdn), 1968–70; Captain HMS Diomede, 1971; Comdr, Standing Naval Force Atlantic, 1972–73; Dir, Naval Warfare, 1973–74; Flag Officer, Second Flotilla, 1974–76; Flag Officer, Submarines, and Comdr Submarine Force, E Atlantic Area, 1976–78; Controller of the Navy, 1979–81; C-in-C Fleet, and Allied C-in-C, Channel and Eastern Atlantic, 1981–82; Chief of Naval Staff and First Sea Lord, 1982–85. First and Principal Naval ADC to the Queen, 1982–85. Liveryman: Shipwrights' Co., 1982–; Glovers' Co., 1983–; Freeman, Clockmakers' Co., 1984. *Recreations:* home, family and friends.

FIELDHOUSE, (Richard) Arnold; building contractor; *b* 1 Aug. 1916; *m* 1952. *Educ:* elem. sch. Elected to Manchester City Council for Levenshulme Ward, 1946: served as Leader of City Council, Chm. Policy Cttee, and Chm. Finance Cttee. Elected to Greater Manchester County Council for Levenshulme Elect. Div., 1973: Leader of Conservative Opposition, 1973–77; Mem., Policy Cttee; Leader of Council, 1977–81. *Recreations:* gardening, sailing. *Address:* Tudor Cottage, Macclesfield Road, Prestbury, Cheshire SK10 4BH. *T:* Prestbury 828272.

FIELDHOUSE, William, (Bill Fieldhouse), CBE 1978; Director, Fort Howard International, since 1984; *b* 1 Jan. 1932; *o c* of Joseph Fieldhouse and Elsie Broadbent; *m* 1st, 1953, Joan Lomax; one *s* one *d*; 2nd, 1978, Torunn Hassel; one *d* (and one *d* decd). *Educ:* Wallsend Grammar Sch.; Rutherford Coll., Newcastle upon Tyne. CEng; MIMechE 1967. Parsons Marine, 1949–53; Cunard, 1953–56; Allis-Chalmers, 1956–65; Tarmac, 1965–67; Peter Dixon, 1967–69; Letraset, 1969–81 (Chm., 1973–81); Director: UBM, 1978–80; Carrington Viyella, 1979–83 (Chm., 1980–83); Dalgety, 1980–83; Consoltex Inc., 1981–83 (Chm., 1982–83); Vantona Viyella, 1983 (Dep. Chm., 1983); Aquanautics, 1984. FRSA 1975. *Recreations:* hunting, skiing, tennis. *Address:* Fort Howard International, Chesterfield House, 385 Euston Road, NW1 3AU. *Club:* Royal Automobile.

FIELDING, Sir Colin Cunningham, Kt 1986; CB 1981; Controller of Research and Development Establishments, Research and Nuclear Programmes, Ministry of Defence, 1982–86; *b* 23 Dec. 1926; *s* of Richard Cunningham and Sadie Fielding; *m* 1953, Gillian Aerona (*née* Thomas); one *d. Educ:* Heaton Grammar Sch., Newcastle upon Tyne; Durham Univ. BSc Hons Physics. British Scientific Instruments Research Assoc., 1948–49; RRE Malvern, 1949–65; Asst Dir of Electronics R&D, Min. of Technology, 1965–68; Head of Electronics Dept, RRE Malvern, 1968–73; RCDS, 1973–74; Dir of Scientific and Technical Intelligence, MoD, 1975–77; Dir, Admiralty Surface Weapons Estabt, 1977–78; Dep. Controller, R&D Estabts and Res. A, and Chief Scientist (RN), MoD, 1978–80; Dep. Chief of Defence Procurement (Nuclear), and Dir, AWRE, MoD, 1980–82. *Publications:* papers in Proc. IEE, Proc. IERE, Nature. *Recreations:* yachting, tennis, music. *Address:* Cheviots, Rosemount Drive, Bickley, Kent.

FIELDING, Fenella Marion; actress; *b* London, 17 Nov. 1934. *Educ:* North London Collegiate School. Began acting career in 1954; *plays include:* Cockles and Champagne, Saville, 1954; Pay the Piper, Saville, 1954; Jubilee Girl, Victoria Palace, 1956; Valmouth, Lyric, Hammersmith, 1958, Saville, 1959, and Chichester Fest., 1982; Pieces of Eight, Apollo, 1959; Five Plus One, Edinburgh Fest., 1961; Twists, Arts, 1962 (Best Revue Performance of the Year in Variety); Doctors of Philosophy, New Arts, 1962; Luv, New Arts, 1963; So Much to Remember—The Life Story of a Great Lady, Establishment, transf. to Vaudeville, 1963; Let's Get a Divorce, Mermaid, transf. to Comedy, 1966; The Beaux Stratagem and The Italian Straw Hat, Chichester Fest., 1967; The High Bid, Mermaid, 1967; Façade, Queen Elizabeth Hall, 1970; Colette, Ellen Stewart, NY, 1970 (first appearance in NY); Fish Out of Water, Greenwich, 1971; The Old Man's Comforts, Open Space, 1972; The Provok'd Wife, Greenwich, 1973; Absurd Person Singular, Criterion, 1974, transf. to Vaudeville, 1975; Fielding Convertible, Edinburgh Fest., 1976; Jubilee Jeunesse, Royal Opera House, 1977; Look After Lulu, Chichester Fest., transf. to Haymarket, 1978; A personal Choice, Edinburgh Fest., 1978; Fenella on Broadway, W6, Studio, Lyric, Hammersmith, 1979; Valmouth, Chichester, 1982; Wizard of Oz, Bromley, 1983; The Jungle Book, Adelphi, 1984; *films include:* Drop Dead, Darling; Lock Up Your Daughters; Carry On Screaming; Carry On Regardless; Doctor in Clover; Doctor in Distress; Doctor in Trouble; No Love for Johnnie; Robin Hood; *television series:* That Was The Week That Was; A Touch of Venus; Ooh La La; Stories from Saki; Dean Martin and the Gold-Diggers; Comedy Tonight; Rhyme and Reason; numerous appearances in UK and USA. *Recreations:* reading, diarising. *Address:* c/o Hamper Neafsey Associates, 193 Wardour Street, W1. *T:* 01–734 1827.

FIELDING, Frank Stanley, OBE 1966; HM Diplomatic Service, retired; Deputy Consul-General, Toronto, 1975–78; *b* 21 Dec. 1918; *s* of John Edgar Fielding and Anne; *m* 1944, Lela Coombs; one *s. Educ:* St Albans Sch.; UCL; King's Coll., London. Diploma in Journalism. HM Forces, 1940–46. Control Commn for Germany, 1946–48; Third Sec., Brit. Embassy, Vienna, 1948–50; Second Sec., Brit. Embassy, Beirut, 1950–55; Vice Consul, Cleveland, 1955–56; First Secretary: Brit. Embassy, Djakarta, 1956–60; FO, 1960–62; Consul (Commercial), Cape Town, 1962–65; First Sec., Brit. Embassy, Pretoria, 1965–68; Consul, NY, 1968–69; Dep. High Comr, Brisbane, 1969–72; Counsellor (Commercial), Singapore, 1972–75. *Recreations:* golf, fishing. *Address:* 28 Berkeley Square, Havant, Hants. *T:* Havant 482540.

FIELDING, Gabriel, (Alan Gabriel Barnsley); Professor of English, Washington State University, 1967–81, now Professor Emeritus; *b* 25 March 1916; *s* of late George Barnsley, Clerk in Holy Orders, and Katherine Mary (*née* Fielding-Smith), a descendant of Henry Fielding, the novelist; *m* 1943, Edwina Eleanora Cook, Storrington, Sussex; three *s* two *d. Educ:* St Edward's Sch., Oxford; Trinity Coll., Dublin; St George's Hospital, London. BA, TCD, 1939. MRCS (Eng.), LRCP (London) 1942. Served with RAMC, 1943–46 (Capt.). Dep. Medical Officer, HM Training Establishment, Maidstone, Kent, 1954–64. Appointed Author in Residence (Prof. of English) to Washington State Univ., USA, 1966–67. Hon. DLitt Gonzaga Univ., Spokane, Washington, 1967. *Publications: poetry:* The Frog Prince and Other Poems, 1952; Twenty-Eight Poems, 1955; Songs without Music, 1979; *novels:* Brotherly Love, 1954; In the Time of Greenbloom, 1956, repr. 1984; Eight Days, 1958; Through Streets Broad and Narrow, 1960, repr. 1986; The Birthday King (W. H. Smith Prize for Literature, 1964; St Thomas More Gold Medal, USA, 1964), 1963, repr. 1985; Gentlemen in Their Season, 1966; Pretty Doll-Houses, 1979; The Women of Guinea Lane, 1986 (USA 1986); *short stories:* New Queens for Old (a novella and nine stories), 1972 (Governor's Literary Award, Washington State, 1972). *Recreations:* my home, painting, cold river swimming, my daily journal, walking. *Address:* 945 Monroe Street, Pullman, Washington 99163, USA.

FIELDING, Ven. Harold Ormandy; Archdeacon of Rochdale, 1972–82; Archdeacon Emeritus since 1982; Vicar of St Peter, Bolton, 1965–83; *b* 13 Nov. 1912; *s* of Harold Wolstencroft and Florence Ann Fielding; *m* 1939, Elsie Whillance; three *s* one *d. Educ:* Farnworth Grammar Sch.; Magdalene Coll., Cambridge (MA); Ripon Hall, Oxford. Curate: St Mary, Leigh, 1936–40; St Paul, Walkden, 1940–44; Vicar of St James, New Bury, 1944–65; Hon. Canon of Manchester, 1965–72; Rural Dean of Bolton, 1965–72. *Address:* 6 High Meadows, Bromley Cross, Bolton BL7 9AR. *T:* Bolton 594650.

FIELDING, Leslie; Director-General for External Relations, Commission of the European Communities, 1982–87; Vice-Chancellor, University of Sussex, from Oct. 1987; *b* 29 July 1932; *o s* of late Percy Archer Fielding and of Margaret (*née* Calder Horry); *m* 1978, Dr Sally P. J. Harvey, MA, PhD, FRHistS, Fellow of St Hilda's Coll., Oxford; one *s* one *d*. *Educ*: Queen Elizabeth's Sch., Barnet; Emmanuel Coll., Cambridge (1st Cl. Hons, historical tripos pt II; hon. bac. scholar; MA); School of Oriental and African Studies, London. Served with Royal Regt of Artillery, 1951–53. Entered HM Diplomatic Service, 1956; served in: Tehran, 1957–60; Foreign Office, 1960–64; Phnom Penh (Chargé d'Affaires), 1964–66; Paris, 1967–70; FCO, 1970–73; Counsellor and Dep. Head of Planning Staff, 1973. Seconded for service with European Commn in Brussels, 1973; Dir (External Relns Directorate Gen.), 1973–77; permanent transfer 1979; Head of Delegn of Commn to Japan, 1978–82. Vis. Fellow, St Antony's Coll., Oxford, 1977–78 (MA). Admitted to office of Reader by Bishop of Exeter, 1981. *Recreation*: life in the country. *Address*: 200 rue de la Loi, 1049 Brussels, Belgium; (from Oct. 1987) University of Sussex, Sussex House, Falmer, Brighton BN1 9RH. *Club*: Travellers'.

FIELDS, Terence; MP (Lab) Liverpool, Broad Green, since 1983; *b* 8 March 1937; *s* of late Frank Fields; *m* 1962, Maureen Mongan; two *s* two *d*. Served RAMC, 1955–57. Fireman, Merseyside County Fire Bde, 1957–83. Vice-Chm., Bootle Constit. Lab. Party; former Mem., NW Regl Exec. Cttee, Lab. Party. *Address*: House of Commons, SW1; 20 John Hunter Way, Bootle, Merseyside L30 5RJ.

FIELDSEND, John Charles Rowell; Member, Court of Appeal of St Helena, Falkland Islands and British Antarctic Territory, since 1985; Chief Justice (non-resident), Turks and Caicos Islands, since 1985; Principal Legal Adviser (non-resident), British Indian Ocean Territory, since 1984; *b* 13 Sept. 1921; *s* of C. E. Fieldsend, MC, and Phyllis (*née* Brucesmith); *m* 1945, Muriel Gedling; one *s* one *d*. *Educ*: Michaelhouse, Natal; Rhodes University Coll., Grahamstown, SA (BA 1942, LLB 1947). Served RA, 1943–45. Called to the Bar, S Rhodesia, 1947; advocate in private practice, 1947–63; QC S Rhodesia, 1959; Pres., Special Income Tax Court for Fedn of Rhodesia and Nyasaland, 1958–63; High Court Judge, S Rhodesia, 1963, resigned 1968; Asst Solicitor, Law Commn, 1968–78, Sec., 1978–80; Chief Justice of Zimbabwe, 1980–83. *Recreations*: home-making, travel. *Address*: Great Dewes, Ardingly, Sussex.

FIENNES; *see* Twisleton-Wykeham-Fiennes.

FIENNES, family name of **Baron Saye and Sele.**

FIENNES, Sir Maurice (Alberic Twisleton-Wykeham-), Kt 1965; CEng; FIMechE; Engineering and Industrial Consultant; Chairman and Managing Director of Davy-Ashmore Ltd, 1961–69; Associate Consultant, L. H. Manderstam & Partners Ltd, 1977–80; *b* 1 March 1907; *s* of Alberic Arthur Twisleton-Wykeham-Fiennes and Gertrude Theodosia Pomeroy Colley; *m* 1st, 1932, Sylvia Mabel Joan (marr. diss., 1964), *d* of late Major David Finlay, 7th Dragoon Guards. two *s* three *d*; 2nd, 1967, Erika Hueller von Huellenried, *d* of late Dr Herbert Hueller, Vienna. *Educ*: Repton; Armstrong Coll., Newcastle upon Tyne. Apprenticeship with Ransomes and Rapier Ltd, Ipswich; joined Sir W. G. Armstrong, Whitworth & Co Ltd (Engineers), Newcastle-upon-Tyne, 1930; with The United Steel Companies Ltd, 1937, first as Commercial Asst to Managing Dir, then in charge Gun Forgings and Gun Dept at Steel Peech & Tozer; Gen. Works Dir, Brush Electrical Engineering Co. Ltd, 1942; Managing Dir, Davy and United Engineering Co. Ltd, 1945; Managing Dir, Davy-Ashmore Ltd, 1960. Steel Industry Advr for UN Industrial Develt Orgn to Govt of Peru, 1974–75; Engineering Advisor for World Bank to Venezuelan Investment Fund, 1976–77. Mem. Economic Develt Cttee for Mech. Eng, 1964–67; Pres. of Iron and Steel Institute, 1962–63; Chairman: Athlone Fellowships Cttee, 1966–71; Overseas Scholarships Bd, CBI, 1970–76; Mem., Reserve Pension Bd, 1974–75. Governor, Yehudi Menuhin School, 1969–84. *Recreations*: music, grandchildren. *Address*: 11 Heath Rise, Kersfield Road, Putney Hill, SW15 3HF. *T*: 01-785 7489. *Clubs*: Carlton, Naval and Military.

FIENNES, Very Rev. Hon. Oliver William Twisleton-Wykeham-; Dean of Lincoln, since 1969; *b* 17 May 1926; *yr s* of 20th Baron Saye and Sele, OBE, MC, and Hersey Cecilia Hester, *d* of late Captain Sir Thomas Dacres Butler, KCVO; *m* 1956, Juliet, *d* of late Dr Trevor Braby Heaton, OBE; two *s* two *d*. *Educ*: Eton; New College, Oxford; Cuddesdon College. Asst Curate, New Milton, Hants, 1954; Chaplain, Clifton College, Bristol, 1958; Rector of Lambeth, 1963. ChStJ 1971. *Address*: The Deanery, Lincoln. *T*: Lincoln 23608.

FIENNES, Sir Ranulph Twisleton-Wykeham-, 3rd Bt, *cr* 1916; *b* 7 March 1944; *s* of Lieut-Col Sir Ranulph Twisleton-Wykeham-Fiennes, DSO, 2nd Bt (died of wounds, 1943) and Audrey Joan, *yr d* of Sir Percy Newson, 1st Bt; *S* father 1944; *m* 1970, Virginia Pepper. *Educ*: Eton. Liveryman, Vintners' Company, 1960. French Parachutist Wings, 1965. Lieut, Royal Scots Greys, 1966, Captain 1968 (retd 1970). Attached 22 SAS Regt, 1966, Sultan of Muscat's Armed Forces, 1968 (Dhofar Campaign Medal, 1969; Sultan's Bravery Medal, 1970). T&AVR 1971, Captain RAC. Leader of British expeditions: White Nile, 1969; Jostedalsbre Glacier, 1970; Headless Valley, BC, 1971; (Towards) North Pole, 1977; Transglobe (first surface journey around the world's polar axis), 1979–82, reached South Pole, 15 Dec. 1980, reached North Pole, 11 April 1982; PUNS Expedition which reached 84°48′N (Furthest North Unsupported record), on 16 April 1986. Hon. DSc Loughborough, 1986. Livingstone Gold Medal, RSGS, 1983; Explorers' Club of New York Medal (and Hon. Life Membership), 1983; Founder's Medal, RGS, 1984. *Film*: (cameraman) To the Ends of the Earth, 1983. *Publications*: A Talent for Trouble, 1970; Ice Fall in Norway, 1972; The Headless Valley, 1973; Where Soldiers Fear To Tread, 1975; Hell on Ice, 1979; To the Ends of the Earth, 1983; (with Virginia Fiennes) Bothie, the Polar Dog, 1984. *Recreations*: langlauf, photography. *Heir*: none. *Address*: Robins, Lodsworth, Petworth, West Sussex. *T*: Lodsworth 363.

FIFE, 3rd Duke of, *cr* 1900; **James George Alexander Bannerman Carnegie**; *b* 23 Sept. 1929; *o s* of 11th Earl of Southesk, *qv*, and Princess Maud (*d* 1945); *S* aunt, Princess Arthur of Connaught (Dukedom of Fife), 1959; *m* 1956, Hon. Caroline Cicely Dewar (marr. diss. 1966; she *m* 1980, Gen. Sir Richard Worsley), *er d* of 3rd Baron Forteviot, *qv*; one *s* one *d*. *Educ*: Gordonstoun. Nat. Service, Scots Guards (Malayan Campaign), 1948–50. Royal Agricultural College. Clothworkers' Company, and Freeman City of London. Pres. of ABA, 1959–73, Vice-Patron, 1973; a Vice-Patron, Braemar Royal Highland Soc.; a Vice-Pres., British Olympic Assoc. *Heir*: *s* Earl of Macduff, *qv*. *Address*: Elsick House, Stonehaven, Kincardineshire AB3 2NT. *Club*: Turf.

FIFE, His Honour Ian Braham, MC 1945; TD (2 bars) 1946; a Circuit Judge (formerly County Court Judge), 1965–82 (Judge of Bromley County Court, 1969–82); *b* 10 July 1911; *o s* of late Donald Fulford Fife and Muriel Alice Fife (*née* Pitt); *m* 1947, Pauline, *e d* of T. R. Parsons and Mrs Winifred Parsons, CBE, Cambridge; two *s* two *d*. *Educ*: Monkton Combe Sch. Served, Royal Fusiliers, 1939–47. Called to Bar, Inner Temple, 1948; Mem. Bar Council, 1960–64; Deptl Cttee on Mechanical Recording of Court Proceedings, 1964–70. A Conservator of Wimbledon and Putney Commons, 1982–. *Publications*: The Offices, Shops and Railway Premises Act, 1963; Agriculture (Safety, Health and Welfare); Redgrave's Factories Acts (edns 20–22); Redgrave's Offices and Shops (edns 1–2); Redgrave's Health and Safety in Factories (edns 1–2); Health and Safety at Work, 1st edn; contrib. Halsbury's Laws of England, 3rd and 4th edns; Atkin's Court Forms. *Address*: 2 Castello Avenue, Putney, SW15. *T*: 01-788 6475.

FIFOOT, Erik Richard Sidney, MC 1945; MA; ALA; Bodley's Librarian, and Professorial Fellow of Exeter College, Oxford, 1979–81; *b* 14 June 1925; *s* of Cecil Herbert Stuart Fifoot and Hjördis (*née* Eriksen); *m* 1949, Jean, *o d* of Lt Col J. S. Thain, two *d*. *Educ*: Berkhamsted Sch.; Oxford Univ. (MA); London Univ. (DipLibr). HM Coldstream Guards, 1943–46. Leeds University Library: Asst Librarian, 1950–52; Sub-Librarian, 1952–58; Dep. Librarian, Nottingham Univ., 1958–60; Librarian, Univ. of Edinburgh, 1960–79. Chm., Standing Conf. of Nat. and Univ. Libraries, 1979–81; Mem., Exec. Bd, Internat. Fedn of Library Assocs and Instns, 1979–83. Founder and dir, Three Rivers Books Ltd, 1981–. *Publications*: A Bibliography of Edith, Osbert and Sacheverell Sitwell, 1963, 2nd edn 1971; articles and reviews in library, architectural and educnl jls, symposia, and encycl. *Address*: Mill Green, Bampton, Oxon OX8 2HF.

FIFOOT, Paul Ronald Ninnes, CMG 1978; HM Diplomatic Service; Deputy Legal Adviser, Foreign and Commonwealth Office, since 1984; *b* 1 April 1928; *o s* of late Ronald Fifoot, Cardiff; *m* 1952, Erica, *er d* of late Richard Alford, DMD; no *c*. *Educ*: Monkton House Sch., Cardiff; Queens' Coll., Cambridge. BA 1948, MA 1952. Military Service, 1948–50, RASC (2nd Lieut 1949). Called to Bar, Gray's Inn, 1953; Crown Counsel, Tanganyika, 1953; Asst to the Law Officers, 1960; Legal Draftsman (later Chief Parliamentary Draftsman), 1961; retd from Tanzania Govt Service, 1966; Asst Legal Adviser, Commonwealth Office, 1966; Legislative Counsel, Province of British Columbia, 1967; Asst Legal Adviser, Commonwealth (later Foreign and Commonwealth) Office, 1968; Legal Counsellor, 1971; Agent of the UK Govt in cases before the European Commn and Court of Human Rights, 1971–76; Counsellor (Legal Advr), UK Mission to UN, NY, 1976–79; Legal Counsellor, FCO, 1979–84. Dep. Leader, UK Delegation to 3rd UN Conference on the Law of the Sea, 1981–82; Leader, UK Delegation to Preparatory Commn for Internat. Sea Bed Authority, 1983–84. *Address*: c/o Foreign and Commonwealth Office, SW1.

FIGG, Sir Leonard (Clifford William), KCMG 1981 (CMG 1974); HM Diplomatic Service, retired; *b* 17 Aug. 1923; *s* of late Sir Clifford Figg and late Lady (Eileen) Figg (*née* Crabb); *m* 1955, Jane Brown, *d* of Judge Harold Brown; three *s*. *Educ*: Charterhouse; Trinity Coll., Oxford. RAF, 1942–46 (Flt-Lt). HM Diplomatic Service, 1947; served in: Addis Ababa, 1949–52; FO, 1952–58; Amman, 1958–61; FO, 1961–67; Counsellor, 1965; Deputy Consul-General, Chicago, 1967–69; DTI, 1970–73; Consul General and Minister, Milan, 1973–77; Asst Under Sec. of State, FCO, 1977–80; Ambassador to Ireland, 1980–83. Mem. Council, Cooperation Ireland, 1985–. A Vice-Chm., British Red Cross Soc., 1983–. Pres., Aylesbury Divnl Conservative Assoc., 1985–. *Recreations*: field sports. *Address*: c/o Foreign and Commonwealth Office, SW1. *Club*: Brooks's.

FIGGESS, Sir John (George), KBE 1969 (OBE 1949); CMG 1960; a director of Christie, Manson and Woods Ltd, 1973–82; *b* 15 Nov. 1909; *e s* of Percival Watts Figgess and Leonora (*née* McCanlis); *m* 1948, Alette, *d* of Dr P. J. A. Idenburg, The Hague; two *d*. *Educ*: Whitgift Sch. In business in Japan, 1933–38. Commissioned, Intelligence Corps, 1939; Staff Coll., 1941; served with Intelligence Corps, India/Burma Theatre, 1942–45. Attached to UK Liaison Mission, Japan, 1945; Asst Mil. Adviser (Lt-Col), UKLM, Tokyo, 1947–52; GSO1, War Office (MI Directorate), 1953–56; Military Attaché, Tokyo, 1956–61; Information Counsellor, British Embassy, Tokyo, 1961–68; Comr Gen. for Britain, World Exposition, Osaka, Japan, 1968–70. Mem., Expert Adv. Council, Percival David Foundn of Chinese Art, 1984–. *Publications*: (with Fujio Koyama) Two Thousand Years of Oriental Ceramics, 1960; The Heritage of Japanese Ceramics, 1973; contrib. to Oriental Art, Far Eastern Ceramic Bulletin, etc. *Address*: The Manor House, Burghfield, Berks. *Club*: Army and Navy.

FIGGIS, Anthony St John Howard; HM Diplomatic Service; Head of Eastern European Department, Foreign and Commonwealth Office, since 1986; *b* 12 Oct. 1940; *s* of Roberts Richmond Figgis and Philippa Maria Young; *m* 1964, Miriam Ellen Hardt; two *s* one *d*. *Educ*: Rugby Sch.; King's Coll., Cambridge (Mod Langs). Joined HM Foreign (later Diplomatic) Service, 1962; Third Sec., Belgrade, 1963–65; Commonwealth Office, 1965–68; Second Sec., Polit. Residency, Bahrain, 1968–70; FCO, 1970–71; First Sec. (Commercial), Madrid, 1971–74; FCO, 1974–79; CSCE delegn, Geneva, 1974–75; FCO, 1975–79; Madrid: Head of Chancery, 1979–80; Commercial Counsellor, 1980–82; Counsellor, Belgrade, 1982–85. *Recreations*: fly-fishing, tennis, music (piano). *Address*: c/o Foreign and Commonwealth Office, SW1A 2AH. *Club*: Roehampton.

FIGGIS, Arthur Lenox; His Honour Judge Figgis; a Circuit Judge (formerly Judge of County Courts), since 1971; *b* 12 Sept. 1918; *s* of late Frank Fernesley Figgis and late Frances Annie Figgis; *m* 1953, Alison, *d* of late Sidney Bocher Ganthony and late Doris Ganthony; two *s* three *d*. *Educ*: Tonbridge; Peterhouse, Cambridge (MA). Served War, 1939–46, Royal Artillery. Barrister-at-Law, Inner Temple, 1947. *Recreations*: walking (with dog); rifle shooting half-blue, 1939, and shot for Ireland (Elcho Shield), 1935–39. *Address*: Wallis Wood Farm, Ockley, Surrey. *T*: Oakwood Hill 268.

FIGGURES, Sir Frank (Edward), KCB 1970 (CB 1966); CMG 1959; *b* 5 March 1910; *s* of Frank and Alice Figgures; *m* 1st, 1941, Aline (*d* 1975), *d* of Prof. Hugo Frey; one *s* one *d*; 2nd, 1975, Ismea, *d* of George Napier Magill and *widow* of Jack Barker. *Educ*: Rutlish Sch.; New Coll., Oxford. Harmsworth Senior Scholar, Merton Coll., Oxford, 1931; Henry Fellow, Yale Law Sch., 1933; Called to Bar, Lincoln's Inn, 1936; Military Service (RA), 1940–46; Joined HM Treasury, 1946; Dir of Trade and Finance, OEEC, 1948–51; Under-Sec., HM Treasury, 1955–60; Sec.-Gen. to EFTA, 1960–65; Third Secretary, Treasury, 1965–68; Second Permanent Secretary, 1968–71; Dir-Gen., NEDO, 1971–73; Chm., Pay Bd, 1973–74. Dir, Julius Baer Bank Internat. Ltd, 1975–81; Mem. Adv. Bd, London Br., Julius Baer, Zurich, 1982–84. Chairman: Central Wagon Co. Ltd, 1976; BBC Gen. Adv. Council, 1978–82. Hon. DSc Aston 1975. *Address*: 9 Main Street, Barrowden, Oakham, Rutland. *Club*: Reform.

FIGURES, Sir Colin (Frederick), KCMG 1983 (CMG 1978); OBE 1969; HM Diplomatic Service; Deputy Secretary, Cabinet Office, since 1985; *b* 1 July 1925; *s* of Frederick and Muriel Figures; *m* 1956, Pamela Ann Timmis; one *s* two *d*. *Educ*: King Edward's Sch., Birmingham; Pembroke Coll., Cambridge (MA). Served Worcestershire Regt, 1943–48. Joined Foreign Office, 1951; attached Control Commn, Germany, 1953–56; Amman, 1956–58; FCO, 1958–59; Warsaw, 1959–62; FCO, 1962–66; Vienna, 1966–69; FCO, 1969–. *Recreations*: watching sport, gardening, beachcombing. *Address*: c/o Foreign and Commonwealth Office, SW1. *Clubs*: United Oxford & Cambridge University; Old Edwardians (Birmingham).

FILBY, Ven. William Charles Leonard; Archdeacon of Horsham, since 1983; *b* 21 Jan. 1933; *s* of William Richard and Dorothy Filby; *m* 1958, Marion Erica Hutchison; four *s* one *d*. *Educ*: Ashford County Grammar School; London Univ. (BA); Oak Hill Theological Coll. Curate, All Souls, Eastbourne, 1959–62; Curate-in-charge, Holy Trinity, Knaphill,

1962–65; Vicar, Holy Trinity, Richmond-upon-Thames, 1965–71; Vicar, Bishop Hannington Memorial Church, Hove, 1971–79; Rector of Broadwater, 1979–83; RD of Worthing, 1980–83; Hon. Canon of Chichester Cathedral, 1981–83. Proctor in Convocation, 1975–; Chm., Redcliffe Missionary Trng Coll., Chiswick, 1970–; Mem., Keswick Convention Council, 1973–; Pres., Chichester Diocesan Evangelical Union, 1978–84; Chairman: Diocesan Stewardship Cttee, 1983–; Sussex Churches Broadcasting Cttee, 1984–; Bishops Advr for Hosp. Chaplains, 1986–. Governor: St Mary's Hall, Brighton, 1984–; W Sussex Inst. of Higher Educn, 1985–. *Recreations:* sport, music. *Address:* The Archdeaconry, Itchingfield, Sussex. *T:* Slinfold 790315.

FILER, Albert Jack, CB 1954; Past President, Brick Development Association Ltd; *b* 14 Aug. 1898; 2nd *s* of Albert James Shephard Filer and Jessie (*née* Marrison); *m* 1923, Violet D., *o d* of late Edward T. Booth, Bexhill, Sussex; one *d. Educ:* County Secondary Sch., Holloway, N. Entered Civil Service, 1914, Office of Works. Served European War of 1914–18 in Civil Service Rifles. Principal, 1940, Min. of Works, Asst Sec., 1943, Under Sec., 1948; Gen. Manager, Directorate Gen. of Works, 1958–60, retired from Civil Service, 1960. *Address:* 1 Heatherwood, Midhurst, West Sussex. *T:* Midhurst 2816.

FILLEUL, Peter Amy, MA; Head Master, William Hulme's Grammar School, Manchester, 1974–Aug. 1987; *b* 7 Aug. 1929; *s* of J. C. Filleul and L. A. Mundy; *m* 1963, Elizabeth Ann Talbot; one *s* one *d. Educ:* Victoria Coll., Jersey; Bedford Sch.; (Exhibnr) Exeter Coll., Oxford (MA, DipEd). Royal Air Force, 1952–55. Portsmouth GS, 1955–65; Stationers' Company's Sch., 1965–68; Cardiff High Sch. (Head Master), 1969–74. *Recreations:* rifle shooting, fishing. *Address:* 254 Wilbraham Road, Manchester M16 8PR. *T:* 061–226 2058; (from Aug. 1987) Petit Coin, Route des Genets, St Brelade, Jersey, CI.

FILON, Sidney Philip Lawrence, TD; Librarian and Secretary to the Trustees, National Central Library, 1958–71, retired; *b* 20 Sept. 1905; *s* of late Prof. L. N. G. Filon, FRS and late Anne Godet; *m* 1st, 1939, Doris Schelling; one *d*; 2nd, 1959, Liselotte Florstedt; one *d. Educ:* Whitgift Sch.; University Coll., London (BSc). Sch. of Librarianship, University Coll., London, 1929–30; FLA 1931. National Central Library, 1930–39. Military service, 1939–45. Dep. Librarian, National Central Library, 1946–58. Mem., Library Advisory Council (England), 1966–71. *Publication:* The National Central Library: an experiment in library cooperation, 1977. *Address:* 107 Littleheath Road, Selsdon, Surrey.

FINCASTLE, Viscount; Malcolm Kenneth Murray; *b* 17 Sept. 1946; *er s* and *heir* of Earl of Dunmore, *qv*; *m* 1970, Joy Anne, *d* of A. Partridge; one *s* one *d* (both adopted). *Educ:* Launceston Technical High School (Board A Certificate). Electrical Technical Officer, Dept of Aviation. *Recreation:* flying (Tow Master for Soaring Club of Tasmania). *Address:* PO Box 100E, East Devonport, Tasmania 7310, Australia. *Club:* Soaring Club of Tasmania.

FINCH, Stephen Clark; Assistant Coordinator, Information Systems Administration, The British Petroleum Company plc, since 1984; *b* 7 March 1929; *s* of Frank Finch and Doris Finch (*née* Lloyd), Haywards Heath; *m* 1975, Sarah Rosemary Ann Griffith Griffin; two *d. Educ:* Ardingly; Sch. of Signals; RMCS. FInstAM; FBIM. Commnd Royal Signals 1948; served Korea, UK and BAOR; retired 1968. Joined British Petroleum Co. Ltd, 1968: Gp Telecommunications Manager, 1968–81; Sen. Adviser, Regulatory Affairs, 1981–84. Member: Adv. Panel on Licensing Value Added Network Services, 1982–; Monopolies and Mergers Commn, 1985–. Member: Inst. of Administrative Management, 1968– (Mem. Council, 1981–84; Medallist, 1985); Telecommunications Managers Assoc., 1968– (Exec. Cttee, 1971–; Chm., 1981–84; Regulatory Affairs Exec., 1984–). *Publications:* occasional contribs to learned jls. *Recreations:* sailing, skiing, swimming, opera. *Address:* c/o Lloyds Bank, Boltro Road, Haywards Heath, W Sussex RH16 1BY. *T:* (office) 01–920 7788. *Club:* National.

FINCH HATTON, family name of **Earl of Winchilsea and Nottingham.**

FINCH-KNIGHTLEY, family name of **Earl of Aylesford.**

FINCHAM, Prof. John Robert Stanley, FRS 1969; FRSE 1978; Arthur Balfour Professor of Genetics, University of Cambridge, since 1984; Professorial Fellow, Peterhouse, Cambridge, since 1984; *b* 11 Aug. 1926; *s* of Robert Fincham and Winifred Emily Fincham (*née* Western); *m* 1950, Ann Katherine Emerson; one *s* three *d. Educ:* Hertford Grammar Sch.; Peterhouse, Cambridge. BA 1946, PhD 1950, ScD 1964. Bye-Fellow of Peterhouse, 1949–50; Lectr in Botany, University Coll., Leicester, 1950–54; Reader in Genetics, Univ. of Leicester, 1954–60; Head of Dept of Genetics, John Innes Inst., 1960–66; Prof. of Genetics, Leeds Univ., 1966–76; Buchanan Prof. of Genetics, Univ. of Edinburgh, 1976–84. Vis. Associate Prof. of Genetics, Massachusetts Inst. of Technology, 1960–61. Pres., Genetical Soc., 1978–81. Editor, Heredity, 1971–78. *Publications:* Fungal Genetics (with P. R. Day), 1963, 4th edn, 1979; Microbial and Molecular Genetics, 1965; Genetic Complementation, 1966; Genetics, 1983; papers in Biochemical Jl, Jl Gen. Microbiol., Jl Biol. Chem., Heredity, Jl Molecular Biol., Genet. Res. *Recreation:* listening to music. *Address:* 10 Guest Road, Cambridge; Department of Genetics, Downing Street, Cambridge.

FINDLAY, Alexander, MBE 1983; Chairman, Lothian Health Board, 1983–86; *b* 9 May 1926; *s* of Alexander and Margaret Findlay; *m* 1951, Margaret Webster Aitken Milne; two *s. Educ:* Harris Academy, Dundee. Telecoms engineer, 1942–57; Telecoms executive, 1957–84. Mem., Mental Welfare Commn for Scotland, 1986–. Chief Scout's Award for services to Scouting, 1978. *Recreations:* golf, travel. *Address:* 54 Rullion Road, Penicuik, Midlothian. *T:* Penicuik 73443. *Club:* Royal Commonwealth Society.

FINDLAY, Ian Herbert Fyfe; Chairman, Lloyd's, 1978 and 1979 (Deputy Chairman, 1977); *b* 5 Feb. 1918; *s* of Prof. Alexander Findlay, CBE, Aberdeen, and Alice Mary (*née* de Rougemont); *m* 1950, Alison Mary Ashby; two *s* one *d. Educ:* Fettes Coll., Edinburgh. Served War, Royal Artillery, 1939–46. Mem. of Lloyd's, 1946. Chm., Price Forbes (Holdings) Ltd, 1967; Dep. Chm., Sedgwick Forbes Holdings Ltd, 1972, Chm., 1974–77. Mem. Cttee, Lloyd's Insurance Brokers Assoc., 1961–65 and 1966–69; Chm., Non-Marine Cttee, 1967–68; Chm. of Assoc., 1969–70; Mem., Cttee of Lloyd's, 1971–74, 1976–79; Chm., British Insurance Brokers Assoc., 1980–82. Trustee, St George's English Sch., Rome, 1980–; Chm., Guide Dogs for the Blind, 1981–; Governor, Brighton Coll., 1981–. *Recreations:* golf, postal history. *Address:* 24 Forest Ridge, Keston Park, Kent BR2 6EQ. *T:* Farnborough (Kent) 52993. *Clubs:* City of London; Royal and Ancient Golf (St Andrews); Royal St George's (Sandwich); Addington (Surrey).

FINDLAY, Prof. John Niemeyer, FBA 1956; Borden Parker Bowne Professor of Philosophy, Boston University, since 1978 (University Professor of Philosophy, since 1972); *b* 25 Nov. 1903; 2nd *s* of J. H. L. Findlay, Pretoria, South Africa; *m* 1941, Aileen May, *d* of G. S. Davidson, Wellington, NZ; one *s* one *d* (and one *d* decd). *Educ:* Boys' High Sch., Pretoria; Transvaal Univ. Coll.; Balliol Coll., Oxford (Rhodes Scholar, 1st Lit. hum.); University of Graz. Lecturer in Philosophy, Transvaal University Coll., 1927–33; Prof. of Philosophy, University of Otago, NZ, 1934–44; Prof. of Philosophy, Rhodes University Coll., Grahamstown, S Africa, 1945; Prof. of Philosophy, Natal University Coll., 1946–48; Prof. of Philosophy, King's Coll., Newcastle upon Tyne, Univ. of Durham, 1948–51; University Prof. of Philosophy, King's Coll., Univ. of London, 1951–66. Gifford Lecturer, Univ. of St Andrews, 1964–66. Prof. of Philosophy, Univ. of Texas, 1966–67; Clark Prof. of Moral Philosophy and Metaphysics, Yale Univ., 1967–72. Fellow, Amer. Acad. of Arts and Scis, 1978. FKC 1970. *Publications:* Meinong's Theory of Objects and Values, 1933, new edn, 1963; Hegel: A Re-Examination, 1958; Values and Intentions, 1961; Language, Mind and Value, 1963; The Discipline of the Cave, 1965; The Transcendence of The Cave, 1967; trans. Husserl, Logische Untersuchungen, 1969; Axiological Ethics, 1970; Ascent to the Absolute: metaphysical papers and lectures, 1970; Plato's Written and Unwritten Doctrines, 1974; Plato and Platonism, 1978; Kant and the Transcendental Object, 1981; Wittgenstein: a critique, 1984; Studies in the Philosophy of J. N. Findlay, ed Cohen, Martin and Westphal, replies and autobiog. by J. N. Findlay, 1985; articles in Mind, Philosophy, Philosophy and Phenomenological Research, Proc. of the Aristotelian Soc., etc. *Address:* 14 Lambolle Road, NW3; 96 Bay State Road, Boston, Mass 02215, USA. *Club:* Royal Commonwealth Society.

FINER, Prof. Samuel Edward, FBA 1982; Gladstone Professor of Government and Public Administration, University of Oxford, 1974–82, now Professor Emeritus; *b* 22 Sept. 1915; *y s* of Max and Fanny Finer, 210a Green Lanes, N4; *m* 1st, 1949, Margaret Ann (marr. diss. 1975), 2nd *d* of Sir Andrew McFadyean; two *s* one *d*; 2nd, 1977, Dr Catherine J. Jones, 2nd *d* of T. P. Jones, Prestatyn. *Educ:* Holloway Sch., London; Trinity Coll., Oxford. BA (Oxon) 1st Class Hons Mod. Greats, 1937; 1st Cl. Hons Mod. Hist., 1938; MA (Oxon) 1946, DLitt 1979; Sen. George Webb-Medley Schol., 1938–40. Served War, 1940–46; Capt. Royal Signals, 1945. Lecturer in Politics, Balliol Coll., Oxford, 1946–49; Junior Research Fellow, Balliol Coll., Oxford, 1949–50; Prof. of Political Institutions, University of Keele, 1950–66; Prof. of Government, Univ. of Manchester, 1966–74; Dep. Vice-Chancellor, University of Keele, 1962–64. Visiting Prof. and Faculty Mem., Institute of Social Studies, The Hague, Netherlands, 1957–59. Visiting Prof. in Government: Cornell Univ., 1962; Hebrew Univ., Jerusalem, 1969; Simon Fraser Univ., BC, 1976; Europ. Univ. Inst., Florence, 1977; Stanford Univ., 1979; Hong Kong Univ., 1980; Vis. Schweitzer Prof., Columbia Univ., 1982. Chm. Political Studies Assoc. of UK, 1965–69; FRHistSoc. DU Essex, 1982. *Publications:* A Primer of Public Administration, 1950; The Life and Times of Sir Edwin Chadwick, 1952; (with Sir John Maud) Local Government in England and Wales, 1953; Anonymous Empire—a Study of the Lobby in Britain, 1958, 2nd edn 1966; Private Industry and Political Power, 1958; (with D. J. Bartholomew and H. B. Berrington) Backbench Opinion in the House of Commons, 1955–59, 1961; The Man on Horseback: The Rôle of The Military in Politics, 1962, 2nd edn 1976; Great Britain, in Modern Political Systems: Europe, ed Macridis and Ward, 1963, 1968, 1972, 1980; (ed) Siéyès: What is the Third Estate, 1963; Pareto: Sociological Writings, 1966; Comparative Government, 1970; Adversary Government and Electoral Reform, 1975; Five Constitutions, 1979; Britain's Changing Party System, 1980. *Recreation:* oil-painting. *Address:* All Souls College, Oxford; 48 Lonsdale Road, Oxford. *T:* Oxford 58060.

FINESTEIN, Israel, MA; QC 1970; **His Honour Judge Finestein;** a Circuit Judge, since 1972; *b* 29 April 1921; *y c* of late Jeremiah Finestein, Hull; *m* 1946, Marion Phyllis, *er d* of Simon Oster, Hendon, Mddx. *Educ:* Kingston High School, Hull; Trinity Coll., Cambridge (Major Scholar and Prizeman). MA 1946. Called to the Bar, Lincoln's Inn, 1953. Pres., Jewish Hist. Soc. of England. *Publications:* Short History of the Jews of England, 1956; Sir George Jessel, 1959, etc. *Recreation:* reading history. *Address:* 18 Buttermere Court, Boundary Road, NW8.

FINGERHUT, John Hyman; Consultant to the Pharmaceutical and Allied Industries; *b* 2 Nov. 1910; *s* of late Abraham Fingerhut and Emily (*née* Rowe); *m* 1950, Beatrice Leigh, FCA; two *s* two *d. Educ:* Manchester Grammar Sch.; Manchester Univ. FBOA 1931; Hon. FPS 1971. Pharmaceutical Chemist, 1932. Served with RAC and Infantry, France, Mauritius and E Africa, 1942–46; commnd Royal Pioneer Corps, transf. to Queen's Royal Regt (seconded King's African Rifles); demobilised as Captain. Merck Sharp & Dohme Ltd: medical rep., 1937–42; Sales Man., 1946; Dep. Man. Dir, 1957; Man. Dir, 1963; Chm., 1967–72; Consultant, 1972–77; Regional Dir, Merck Sharp & Dohme International, 1967–72; Chm., Thomas Morson & Son Ltd, 1967–72; Mem., ABPI Working Party on Resale Price Maintenance, 1970; Associate: Bracken Kelner and Associates Ltd, 1976; Key Pharmaceutical Appointments, 1978. Admin. Staff Coll., Henley, 1960. Mem., New Southgate Group Hosp. Management Cttee, 1972–74. Associate Mem., Faculty of Homœopathy, 1974. *Recreations:* music, reading, gardening, washing up. *Address:* 76 Green Lane, Edgware, Mddx HA8 7QA. *T:* 01–958 6163.

FINGLAND, Sir Stanley (James Gunn), KCMG 1979 (CMG 1966); HM Diplomatic Service, retired; High Commissioner to Kenya, 1975–79; UK Permanent Representative to the UN Environment Programme 1975–79, and to UN Centre for Human Settlements, 1979; *b* 19 Dec. 1919; *s* of late Samuel Gunn Fingland and late Agnes Christina (*née* Watson); *m* 1946, Nellie (*née* Lister); one *s* one *d. Educ:* Royal High Sch., Edinburgh. TA 1938. War service, 1939–46 as Major, Royal Signals; served N Africa, Sicily, Italy, Egypt. Commonwealth Relations Office, 1948–; British High Commission, India, 1948–51; Australia, 1953–56; Adviser on Commonwealth and External Affairs to Governor-Gen., Nigeria, 1958–60; British High Commission, Nigeria, 1960; Adviser on Commonwealth and External Affairs to Governor-Gen., Fedn of The W Indies, 1960–61, and to the Governor of Trinidad and Tobago, 1962; British Dep. High Commissioner: Trinidad and Tobago, 1962–63; Rhodesia, 1964–66; High Comr, Sierra Leone, 1966–69; Asst Under-Sec. of State, FCO, 1969–72; Ambassador to Cuba, 1972–75. *Recreation:* fishing.

FINGLETON, David Melvin; Metropolitan Stipendiary Magistrate, since 1980; *b* 2 Sept. 1941; *s* of Laurence Fingleton and Norma Phillips (*née* Spiro); *m* 1975, Clare, *yr d* of late Ian Colvin. *Educ:* Aldwickbury Sch., Harpenden; Stowe Sch. (Schol.); University Coll., Oxford (Exhibnr; BA Hons Modern History, MA). Called to Bar, Middle Temple, 1965; South Eastern Circuit. Music Correspondent, Contemporary Review, 1969–; Opera and Ballet Critic, Tatler and Bystander, 1970–78; Stage Design Corresp., Arts Review, 1976–; Associate Editor, Music and Musicians, 1977–80; Music Critic: Evening News, 1979–80; Daily Express, 1982–. *Publications:* Kiri, 1982; articles in Contemp. Rev., Tatler and Bystander, Music and Musicians, Arts Rev., Evening News, Daily Express. *Recreation:* listening to and writing about music. *Address:* Highbury Corner Magistrates' Court, 51 Holloway Road, N7 8JA. *T:* 01–607 6757. *Clubs:* Garrick, MCC.

FINGRET, Peter; Metropolitan Stipendiary Magistrate, since 1985; *b* 13 Sept. 1934; *s* of late Iser and Irene Fingret; *m* 1st, 1960, June Moss (marr. diss. 1980); one *s* one *d*; 2nd, 1980, Dr Ann Lilian Mary Hollingworth (*née* Field). *Educ:* Leeds Modern Sch.; Leeds Univ. (LLB Hons). President, Leeds Univ. Union, 1957–58. Admitted Solicitor, 1960. Partner: Willey Hargrave & Co., Leeds, 1964–75; Fingret, Paterson & Co., Leeds, 1975–82. Stipendiary Magistrate for Co. of Humberside sitting at Kingston-upon-Hull, 1982–85. Councillor, Leeds City Council, 1967–72; Member: Court, Univ. of Leeds, 1975–85; Cttee, Leeds Internat. Piano Competition, 1981–. *Recreations:* golf, music, theatre. *Address:* Dairy Cottage, 313 Petersham Road, Petersham, Richmond, Surrey TW10 7DB. *T:* 01-948 7852; 6 Stable Yard, Herring House, Holy Island, Northumberland. *Clubs:* Royal Society of Medicine; Leeds; Moor Allerton Golf (Leeds).

FINKELSTEIN, Prof. Ludwik, MSc; FEng 1986; CPhys, FIEE, FInstP, FInstMC; Professor of Measurement and Instrumentation, since 1980, and Dean of the School of Electrical Engineering and Applied Physics, since 1984, The City University; *b* 6 Dec. 1929; *s* of Adolf and Amalia Finkelstein; *m* 1957, Mirjam Emma, *d* of Dr Alfred and Dr Margarethe Wiener; two *s* one *d*. *Educ:* Univ. of London (MSc). Physicist, Technical Staff, Electronic Tubes Ltd, 1951–52; Scientist, Instrument Br., NCB Mining Res. Estabt, 1952–59; Northampton Coll., London, and City University, London: Lectr, 1959–61; Sen. Lectr, 1961–63; Principal Lectr, 1963–67; Reader, 1967–70; Prof. of Instrument and Control Engineering, 1970–80; Head of Dept of Systems Science, 1974–79. Visiting Prof., Delft Univ. of Technology, 1973–74. Pres., Inst. of Measurement and Control, 1980 (Vice-Pres., 1972–75, 1977–79; Hartley Silver Medal, 1980); Chm., Management and Design Div., IEE, 1984–85 (Management and Design Divl Premium (jtly), 1984). *Publications:* papers in learned jls and conference proc. *Recreations:* books, conversation, Jewish studies. *Address:* The City University, Northampton Square, EC1V 0HB. *T:* 01-253 4399; 9 Cheyne Walk, Hendon NW4 3QH. *T:* 01-202 6966.

FINLAISON, Brig. (retd) Alexander Montagu, CBE 1957; DSO 1944; *b* 14 March 1904; *s* of Maj.-Gen. J. B. Finlaison, CMG, late Royal Marines, Dedham, Essex; *m* 1935, Monica Mary Louisa, *d* of T. W. Donald, Grendon, Stirling; one *d* (and one *d* decd). *Educ:* RN Colls Osborne and Dartmouth; RMC Sandhurst. Commissioned Cameronians (Scottish Rifles), 1924; seconded Sudan Defence Force, 1932–38; served War of 1939–45; Greece, Crete, Sicily, Italy; commanded 2nd Wiltshires, 2nd Cameronians, 17 Infantry Brigade, Italy, 1943–44; BGS, HQ Scottish Command, 1954–57; ADC to the Queen, 1955–57; retired, 1957; Commandant, Queen Victoria Sch., Dunblane, 1957–64. *Address:* Gledenholm, Ae, Dumfries DG1 1RF. *T:* Parkgate 242. *Club:* Naval and Military.

FINLAY, Alexander William; retired; *b* 28 Nov. 1921; *s* of late Robert Gaskin Finlay and late Alice Finlay; *m* 1949, Ona Margaret Lewis; no *c*. *Educ:* Tottenham County School. Flt-Lt RAF, 1941–47; various posts, BOAC and British Airways, 1947–78, Planning Dir, 1971–78, retd. Chm., Soc. for Long Range Planning, 1978–79; Mem. Council, Sussex Trust for Nature Conservation, 1982–; Trustee, Charitable Trust, 1983–. FCIT. *Recreations:* conservation, photography, gardening. *Address:* 12 Hunters Way, Chichester, West Sussex PO19 4RB. *Club:* Royal Air Force.

FINLAY, Maj.-Gen. Charles Hector, CB 1966; CBE 1958 (OBE 1942); retired; Trustee, Returned Services League of Australia, since 1985 (Hon. National Treasurer, 1969–84); *b* 6 Oct. 1910; 3rd *s* of Frank J. Finlay and Margaret A. Stephenson; *m* 1935, Helen M., *d* of Arthur P. and Edith M. Adams; two *s*. *Educ:* Sydney; RMC Duntroon, Australia. Graduated RMC, 1931; Light Horse and Cavalry service, 1931–39; ADC to Gov.-Gen., 1932–35; with 14th/20th Hussars, India, 1935–36. Served War of 1939–45; Western Desert, Syria, New Guinea, Philippines, Borneo; Comd 2/24 Inf. Bn, 1942–43. Exchange duty, Canada, 1946–49; DMI, 1950–53; Comd Aust. Component BCFK, 1953–54; attended Imperial Def. Coll., 1955; Aust. Army Rep., London, 1956–57; Quartermaster Gen. AMF, 1957–62; Commandant Royal Military Coll., Duntroon, Australia, 1962–67. Hon. Col, Australian Intelligence Corps, 1973–77. *Recreation:* cricket. *Address:* 89 Buxton Street, Deakin, ACT 2600, Australia. *Clubs:* Naval and Military (Melbourne); Commonwealth (Canberra).

FINLAY, Frank, CBE 1984; actor; *b* Farnworth, Lancs, 6 Aug. 1926; *s* of Josiah Finlay; *m* 1954, Doreen Shepherd; two *s* one *d*. *Educ:* St Gregory the Great, Farnworth; RADA (Sir James Knott Schol.). *Stage:* repertory, 1950–52 and 1954–57; Belgrade, Coventry, 1958; Epitaph for George Dillon, NY, 1958; Royal Court, 1958, 1959–62: Sugar in the Morning; Sergeant Musgrave's Dance; Chicken Soup with Barley, Roots, I'm Talking About Jerusalem; The Happy Haven; Platonov; Chips with Everything, Royal Court, transf. to Vaudeville Theatre, 1962 (Clarence Derwent Best Actor Award); Chichester Festival, 1963: St Joan; The Workhouse Donkey; with National Theatre Co. 1963–70: St Joan, 1963; Willie Mossop in Hobson's Choice, and Iago in Othello (both also Chichester Fest., 1964, Berlin and Moscow, 1965), The Dutch Courtesan (also Chichester Fest.), 1964; Giles Corey in The Crucible, Dogberry in Much Ado About Nothing, Mother Courage, 1965; Joxer Daly in Juno and the Paycock, Dikoy in The Storm, 1966; Bernard in After Haggerty, Aldwych, Criterion, Jesus Christ in Son of Man, Leicester Theatre and Round House (first actor ever to play Jesus Christ on stage in English theatre), 1970; Kings and Clowns (musical), Phoenix, 1978; Filumena, Lyric, 1978, US tour, 1979–80, and NY, 1980; The Girl in Melanie Klein, 1980; The Cherry Orchard, tour and Haymarket, 1983; Mutiny (musical), Piccadilly, 1985; *with National Theatre Co.:* Peppino in Saturday, Sunday, Monday, 1973; Sloman in The Party, 1973; Freddy Malone in Plunder, Ben Prosser in Watch It Come Down, Josef Frank in Weapons of Happiness, 1976; Amadeus, 1982; *films include*, 1962–: The Longest Day, Private Potter, The Informers, A Life for Ruth, Loneliness of the Long Distance Runner, Hot Enough for June, The Comedy Man, The Sandwich Man, A Study in Terror, Othello (nominated for Amer. Acad. award; best actor award, San Sebastian, 1966), The Jokers, I'll Never Forget What's 'Is Name, The Shoes of the Fisherman, Deadly Bees, Robbery, Inspector Clouseau, Twisted Nerve, Cromwell, The Molly Maguires (in Hollywood), Assault, Victory for Danny Jones, Gumshoe, Shaft in Africa, Van Der Valk and the Girl, Van Der Valk and the Rich; Van Der Valk and the Dead; The Three Musketeers; The Ring of Darkness, The Wild Geese, The Thief of Baghdad, Sherlock Holmes—Murder by Decree; Enigma; Return of the Soldier; The Ploughman's Lunch, 1982; La Chiave (The Key), Italy, 1983; Sakharov, 1983; Christmas Carol, Arch of Triumph, 1919, 1984; Lifeforce, 1985; *TV appearances include:* Julius Caesar, Les Misérables, This Happy Breed, The Lie (SFTA Award), Casanova (series), The Death of Adolf Hitler, Don Quixote (SFTA Award), Voltaire, Merchant of Venice, Bouquet of Barbed Wire (series) (Best Actor Award), 84 Charing Cross Road, Saturday Sunday Monday, Count Dracula, The Last Campaign, Napoleon in Betzi, Dear Brutus, Tales of the Unexpected, Tales from 1001 Nights, Aspects of Love—Mona; In the Secret State. *Address:* c/o Al Parker Ltd, 55 Park Lane, W1. *Club:* Garrick.

FINLAY, Sir Graeme Bell, 1st Bt, *cr* 1964; ERD; Barrister-at-Law; Sous Juge d'Instruction and Assistant Judge of Petty Debts Court for Jersey, 1972–77; *b* 29 Oct. 1917; *yr s* of late James Bell Pettigrew Finlay and late Margaret Helena, *d* of John Euston Davies, JP, Portskewett House, nr Chepstow, Mon.; *m* 1953, June Evangeline, *y d* of Col Francis Collingwood Drake, OBE, MC, DL, late 10th Royal Hussars, Harlow, Essex; one *s* two *d*. *Educ:* Marlborough; University College, London. Served War of 1939–45, 2nd Lieut S Wales Borderers (suppl. res.), 1939; 7th (Croix de Guerre) Bn, 24th Regt (Beach Divs), 1940–41; seconded to 5th Royal Gurkha Rifles (Frontier Force), 1942–45; Martial Law Officer, Upper Sind Force (Hur Rebellion), 1943; Acting Major and DAAG, HQ, NW Army, 1945. Hon. Captain, The Royal Regt of Wales. Called to Bar, Gray's Inn, 1946 (Lord Justice Holker Sen. Exhibr); pupil of Lord Hailsham of St Marylebone; President of Hardwicke Society, 1950–51. Presided over first televised joint debate between Oxford and Cambridge Union Societies, 1950. Contested (C) Ebbw Vale, General Election, 1950; MP (C) Epping Division of Essex, 1951–64; Parliamentary Private Secretary to Rt Hon. Iain Macleod, Minister of Health, 1952–55; Asst Whip (unpaid), 1957–59; Lord Commissioner of the Treasury, 1959–60; Vice-Chamberlain of the Household, 1960–64; Mem., Parly Delegn to Russia, 1960; a Deputy Judge of County Courts, later Circuit Judge, 1967–72; a Dep. Chm., Agricultural Land Tribunal (SE Region), 1971–72. *Publications:* (jt author) Proposals for an Administrative Court, 1970; frequent contributor to Justice of the Peace and Local Government Review. *Recreations:* reading history and painting. *Heir:* *s* David Ronald James Bell Finlay, *b* 16 Nov. 1963. *Address:* La Campagne, Rozel, Jersey, CI. *T:* Jersey 51194; 4 Paper Buildings, Temple, EC4. *T:* 01-353 3366.

FINLAY, Ian; *see* Finlay, W. I. R.

FINLAY, John Alexander Robertson, QC 1973; **His Honour Judge Finlay;** a Circuit Judge, since 1976; *b* 9 Nov. 1917; *o s* of late Rev. John Adamson Finlay, MA and Mary Hain Miller; *m* 1941, Jane Little Hepburn, (Sheena), CBE (*d* 1985); one *s* two *d* (and one *d* decd). *Educ:* High Sch. of Glasgow; Glasgow Univ. (Foulis Schol., John Clerk Schol.); Queen's Coll., Oxford (Schol.). Caird Medal, Melville Medal, MA 1st cl. Philosophy Glasgow, 1939; BA 2nd cl. Jurisprudence 1946, MA 1959, Oxon. Served in RN, 1940–46: Seaman 1940; commnd 1941; Lieut RNVR 1942. Called to Bar, Middle Temple, 1946 (Harmsworth Schol., Bencher, 1971. Recorder of the Crown Court, 1975–76; Acting Deemster, IoM Court of Appeal, 1975; periodically Judge of High Ct, Chancery Div., 1976–; Judge, Bromley County Ct, 1982–. Member: Bar Council, 1970–74; Senate of Inns of Ct and the Bar, 1984–; Hon. Sec., Council of HM Circuit Judges, 1986–. Chm., Crosby Hall, 1975–76. Member: Law Guardian Editorial Adv. Cttee, 1971–72; Renton Cttee on Preparation of Legislation, 1973–75. *Recreations:* music, sailing, garden labour, thinking. *Address:* Thornhill, Golf Road, Bickley, Bromley, Kent. *T:* 01-467 3637; 16 Old Buildings, Lincoln's Inn, WC2. *Clubs:* Athenæum; Medway Yacht.

FINLAY, Thomas Aloysius; Hon. Mr Justice Finlay; Chief Justice of Ireland, since 1985; *b* 17 Sept. 1922; *s* of Thomas A. Finlay and Eva Finlay; *m* 1948, Alice Blayney; two *s* three *d*. *Educ:* Xavier Sch., Dublin; Clongowes Wood Coll.; University Coll. Dublin. BA Legal and Political Science, NUI. Called to the Bar, King's Inns, 1944; Hon. Bencher, Middle Temple, 1986. Mem., Dáil Éireann, 1954–57; Sen. Counsel, 1961; Judge of the High Court, 1972, Pres. of the High Court, 1974. *Recreations:* fishing, shooting, conversation. *Address:* 22 Ailesbury Drive, Dublin 4. *T:* 693395.

FINLAY, (William) Ian (Robertson), CBE 1965; MA; HRSA; Director of the Royal Scottish Museum, 1961–71 (Keeper of the Department of Art and Ethnography, 1955–61); Professor of Antiquities to the Royal Scottish Academy, since 1971; *b* Auckland, New Zealand, 2 Dec. 1906; *s* of William R. Finlay and Annie M. Somerville; *m* 1933, Mary Scott, *d* of late W. Henderson Pringle, barrister-at-law; two *s* one *d*. *Educ:* Edinburgh Academy; Edinburgh Univ. Joined staff of Royal Scottish Museum, 1932; Deputy Regional Officer for Scotland, Ministry of Information, 1942–44; Vice-Chairman, Scottish Arts Council, 1967; Secretary, Royal Fine Art Commission for Scotland, 1953–61. Guest of State Department in US, 1960. Freeman of City of London; Member of Livery, Worshipful Company of Goldsmiths, London; Mem., Edinburgh Festival Council, 1968–71. FRSA 1971. *Publications:* Scotland, World To-Day Series, 1945; Scottish Art (for British Council), 1945; Art in Scotland, 1948; Scottish Crafts, 1948; The Scottish Tradition in Silver (Saltire booklet), 1948; Scottish Architecture (for schools), 1951; Treasures in Edinburgh, 1951; Scotland, Young Traveller Series, 1953; A History of Scottish Gold and Silver Work, 1956; Scotland, 1957; The Lothians, 1960; The Highlands, 1963; The Young Robert Louis Stevenson, 1965; The Lowlands, 1967; Celtic Art: an introduction, 1973; The Central Highlands, 1976; Priceless Heritage: the future of museums, 1977; Columba, 1979; articles, reviews and broadcast talks on art and general subjects. *Address:* Currie Riggs, Balerno, Midlothian. *T:* Balerno 3249.

FINLAY-MAXWELL, David Campbell, PhD; CEng, MIEE; FTI, FSDC; Chairman and Managing Director, John Gladstone & Co. (Engineering) Ltd, and John Gladstone & Co. Ltd, since 1948; *b* 2 March 1923; *s* of Luke Greenwood Maxwell and of Lillias Maule Finlay; *m* 1954, Constance Shirley Hood; one *s* one *d*. *Educ:* St Paul's; Heriot-Watt/Edinburgh Univ. (Electronic and Control Engrg). CEng 1950; MIEE 1950; FTI 1974; FSDC 1985. PhD Leeds, 1983. Major Royal Signals, 1945. Harvard Univ. Advanced Management Programme, 1968. Chairman: Manpower Working Party, NEDO, 1970–73; Wool Industries Res. Assoc., 1974–77; Textile Res. Council, 1977–82; Wool Textile EDC, 1977–79, UK Rep., Consultative Cttee for R&D, Brussels, 1979–84. Dir, Wool Foundn (Internat. Wool Secretariat), 1985–. Member: Council, Textile Inst., 1972–74; British Textile Council, 1977–85; Textile Industry and Dyeing Adv. Cttee, Leeds Univ. Council, 1974–; Soc. of Dyers and Colourists, 1950–. Pres., Comitextil Sci. Res. Cttee, Brussels. Hon. Lectr, Leeds Univ. Dir/Vice-Chm., Sound Recording Bd of Dirs, RNIB (also Mem., Scientific Develt Sub Cttee); Hon. Organiser for UK, Technical Volunteer Helpers for Blind. *Recreations:* radio propagation, satellite tracking. *Address:* John Gladstone & Co. Ltd, Wellington Mills, Huddersfield HD3 3HJ. *T:* Huddersfield 653437; Folly Hall House, Cross Lane, Kirkburton, Huddersfield HD8 0ST. *T:* Huddersfield 604546. *Clubs:* Special Forces; Royal Scottish Automobile (Glasgow).

FINLAYSON; *see* Gordon-Finlayson.

FINLAYSON, Maj.-Gen. Forbes; *see* Finlayson, Maj.-Gen. W. F.

FINLAYSON, George Ferguson, CMG 1979; CVO 1983; HM Diplomatic Service, retired; *b* 28 Nov. 1924; *s* of late G. B. Finlayson; *m* 1st, 1951, Rosslyn Evelyn (*d* 1972), *d* of late E. N. James; one *d*; 2nd, 1982, Anthea Perry. *Educ:* North Berwick High Sch. Royal Air Force, 1943–47. Apptd HM Foreign (later Diplomatic) Service, 1949; 2nd Sec. (Inf.), HM Embassy, Rangoon, 1952–54; FO, 1955–59; First Sec., 1959; HM Consul, Algiers, 1959–61; First Sec., HM Embassy, Bamako, 1961–63; HM Consul (Commercial), New York, 1964–68; Counsellor, 1968; Counsellor (Commercial), British High Commn, Singapore, 1969–72; Head of Trade Relations and Exports Dept, FCO, 1972–73; Counsellor (Commercial) Paris, 1973–78; Consul-General: Toronto, 1978–81; Los Angeles, 1981–84. *Recreations:* travel, walking, tennis, swimming. *Address:* 141b Ashley Gardens, SW1. T: 01-834 6227; 49 Westgate, North Berwick, East Lothian. *T:* North Berwick 2522. *Club:* Oriental.

FINLAYSON, Maj.-Gen. (William) Forbes, OBE 1955; Director, Army Dental Service, 1966–70; *b* 12 Oct. 1911; *s* of late Lieut-Colonel W. T. Finlayson, OBE, Army Dental Corps, Edinburgh; *m* Anne McEwen, *d* of Walter Stables Smith, Peebles; one *s* one *d*. *Educ:* George Heriot's Sch., Edinburgh; Royal College of Surgeons, Edinburgh; FDSRCSE 1970. LDS 1933. Lieut, Army Dental Corps, 1935; Captain 1936; Major 1945; Lieut-Colonel 1952; Colonel 1959; Maj.-General 1966. Served in: UK, 1935–39, 1945–50, 1955–59, 1963–70; Far East, 1939–45 (POW); BAOR, 1950–52, 1959–63; MELF, 1952–55. QHDS, 1966–70. CStJ 1970. *Recreations:* Rugby football, golf, tennis, walking. *Address:* 9 Oldlands Hall, Heron's Ghyll, near Uckfield, Sussex TN22 3DA.

FINLEY, Michael John; Executive Director, Periodical Publishers Association, since 1983; *b* 22 Sept. 1932; *s* of late Walter Finley and of Grace Marie Butler; *m* 1955, Sheila Elizabeth Cole; four *s*. *Educ:* King Edward VII Sch., Sheffield. Editor, 1964–69, Sheffield Morning Telegraph (formerly Sheffield Telegraph); Chief Editorial Exec., 1969–72, Editorial Dir, 1972–79, and Dir and Gen. Man., 1979–82, Kent Messenger Gp. Hon. Mem. and Past Chm., Parly and Legal Cttee, Guild of British Newspaper Editors. Chm.,

Inst. of Dirs (Kent branch), 1980–83. Member: BBC Regional Adv. Council, 1967–69; BBC Gen. Adv. Council, 1971–77; Exec. Cttee, Internat. Fedn of Periodical Publishers, 1983–; Bd, Fedn of Periodical Publishers in EEC, 1984–. Governor, Cranbrook Sch., 1978–. *Publication:* contrib. Advertising and the Community, 1968. *Recreations:* tennis, rugby (spectator), snooker. *Address:* Golford Place, Cranbrook, Kent.

FINLEY, Sir Peter (Hamilton), Kt 1981; OBE 1974; DFC 1944; FCA; Chairman: Boral Ltd, since 1976; Email Ltd, since 1974; Hygienic Lily Ltd, since 1971; Avery Aust. Ltd, since 1972; Custom Credit Corporation Ltd, since 1973; Deputy Chairman, Cadbury Schweppes Aust. Ltd, since 1971; Director, National Australia Bank, since 1970; *b* 6 Dec. 1919; *s* of Cecil Aubert Finley and Evelyn Finley (*née* Daniels); *m* 1947, Berenice Mitchell Finley (*née* Armstrong); one *s* one *d. Educ:* The King's Sch., Parramatta. Served RAAF with RAF Bomber Command and RAAF SW Pacific Area, 1941–45. With W. V. Armstrong & Co., Chartered Accountants, 1946–48, Peat, Marwick, Mitchell & Co. (formerly Smith Johnson & Co.), 1949–55, P. H. Finley & Co., 1955–72, when virtually ceased practice. Director: Amalgamated Wireless Australasia Ltd, 1974– (Dep. Chm., 1978–); Burns Philp & Co. Ltd, 1980–; Sir Robert Menzies Meml Trust, 1979–. *Recreations:* cricket, tennis, gardening. *Address:* (business) 6 O'Connell Street, Sydney, NSW 2000, Australia. *T:* 235 1972; (home) 50 Treatts Road, Lindfield, NSW 2070. *T:* 46 5319. *Clubs:* Australian (Sydney); Melbourne (Melbourne).

FINNEY, Albert; actor, stage and film; film director; Associate Artistic Director, English Stage Company, since 1972; a Director, United British Artists, since 1983; *m* 1957, Jane Wenham, actress (marr. diss.); one *s*; *m* 1970, Anouk Aimée (marr. diss.). *Stage:* London appearance in The Party, New, 1958; Cassio in Othello, and Lysander, Stratford-on-Avon, 1959; subsequently in: The Lily White Boys, Royal Court, 1960; Billy Liar, Cambridge Theatre, 1960; Luther, in Luther: Royal Court Theatre and Phoenix Theatre, 1961–62; New York, 1963; Armstrong in Armstrong's Last Goodnight, Miss Julie and Black Comedy, Chichester, 1965, Old Vic, 1966; A Day in the Death of Joe Egg, NY, 1968; Alpha Beta, Royal Court and Apollo, 1972; Krapp's Last Tape, Royal Court, 1973; Cromwell, Royal Court, 1973; Chez Nous, Globe, 1974; Uncle Vanya, and Present Laughter, Royal Exchange, Manchester, 1977; Orphans, Hampstead, tranf. to Apollo, 1986; *National Theatre:* Love for Love, 1965; Much Ado About Nothing, 1965; A Flea in Her Ear, 1966; Hamlet, 1975; Tamburlaine, 1976; The Country Wife, 1977; The Cherry Orchard, Macbeth, Has "Washington" Legs?, 1978; *Directed for stage:* The Freedom of the City, Royal Court, 1973; Loot, Royal Court, 1975; *Directed for stage and appeared in:* The Biko Inquest, Riverside, 1984; Serjeant Musgrave's Dance, Old Vic, 1984; *Films include:* Saturday Night and Sunday Morning; Tom Jones; Night Must Fall; Two for the Road; Charlie Bubbles (also Director); Scrooge; Gumshoe; Alpha Beta; Murder on the Orient Express; Wolfen; Loophole; Looker; Shoot the Moon; Annie; The Dresser; Under the Volcano; John Paul II (TV film). Hon. LittD: Sussex, 1965; Salford, 1979. *Address:* c/o ICM, 388/396 Oxford Street, W1N 9HE.

FINNEY, Prof. David John, CBE 1978; MA, ScD Cantab; FRS 1955; FRSE; Professor of Statistics, University of Edinburgh, 1966–84; Director, Agricultural and Food Research Council (formerly Agricultural Research Council) Unit of Statistics, 1954–84; *b* Latchford, Warrington, 3 Jan. 1917; *e s* of late Robert G. S. Finney and late Bessie E. Whitlow; *m* 1950, Mary Elizabeth Connolly; one *s* two *d. Educ:* Lymm and Manchester Grammar Schools; Clare Coll., Cambridge; Galton Laboratory, Univ. of London. Asst Statistician, Rothamsted Experimental Station, 1939–45; Lecturer in the Design and Analysis of Scientific Experiment, University of Oxford, 1945–54; Reader in Statistics, University of Aberdeen, 1954–63, Professor, 1963–66. United Nations FAO expert attached to Indian Council of Agricultural Research, 1952–53. Scientific Consultant, Cotton Research Corporation, 1959–75. Chm., Computer Bd for Univs and Research Councils, 1970–74 (Mem., 1966–74); Member: Adverse Reactions Sub-Cttee, Cttee on Safety of Medicines, 1963–81; BBC General Adv. Council, 1969–76; Visiting Prof. of Biomathematics, Harvard Univ., 1962–63; President of Biometric Society, 1964–65 (Vice-President, 1963, 1966); Fellow: Royal Statistical Soc. (Pres., 1973–74); American Statistical Assoc.; Mem. Internat. Statistical Inst.; Hon. Fellow Eugenics Society; Hon. Mem., Société Adolphe Quetelet. Weldon Memorial Prize, 1956. Dr *hc*, Faculté des Sciences Agronomiques de l'Etat à Gembloux, Belgium, 1967; Hon.DSc: City,1976; Heriot-Watt, 1981. *Publications:* Probit Analysis, 1947 (3rd edn 1971); Biological Standardization (with J. H. Burn, L. G. Goodwin), 1950; Statistical Method in Biological Assay, 1952 (3rd edn 1978); An Introduction to Statistical Science in Agriculture, 1953 (4th edn 1972); Experimental Design and its Statistical Basis, 1955; Tecnica y Teoria en el diseño de Experimentos, 1957; An Introduction to the Theory of Experimental Design, 1960; Statistics for Mathematicians: An Introduction, 1968; Statistics for Biologists, 1980. Numerous papers in statistical and biological journals. *Recreations:* travel (active), music (passive), and the 3 R's. *Address:* 43 Cluny Drive, Edinburgh EH10 6DU. *T:* 031–447 2332.

FINNEY, James; Chairman, Staff Commission for Education and Library Boards, 1981–85; Permanent Secretary, Department of Manpower Services for Northern Ireland, 1976–80, retired; *b* 21 Jan. 1920; *s* of James and Ellen Finney, Co. Armagh; *m* 1956, Barbara Ann Bennett, Wargrave, Berks; one *s* three *d. Educ:* Royal Belfast Academical Instn; Trinity Coll., Dublin Univ. BA 1st cl. Mods 1942. Royal Engrs, 1943–46. Min. of Educn for N Ireland, 1946–76. *Recreation:* gardening. *Address:* Honeypots, Ballyhanwood Road, Dundonald, Belfast, N Ireland. *T:* Dundonald 3428.

FINNEY, Jarlath John; His Honour Judge Finney; a Circuit Judge, since 1986; *b* Hale, Cheshire, 1 July 1930; *s* of late Victor Harold Finney, MA, and Aileen Rose Finney (*née* Gallagher), Dorking, Surrey; *m* 1957, Daisy Emöke, *y d* of late Dr Matyas Veszy, formerly of Budapest; two *s* two *d. Educ:* Wimbledon College; Gray's Inn. Served, 2nd Lieut, 8th Royal Tank Regt, 1953–55 (Lieut 1955). Called to Bar, Gray's Inn, 1953; Member, SE Circuit, 1955–86; a Recorder, 1980–86. Member, Panel of Counsel for HM Customs and Excise before VAT Tribunals, 1973–86. *Publications:* Gaming, Lotteries, Fundraising and the Law, 1982; articles. *Recreations:* wild flowers, books, walking in the country. *Address:* c/o Ground Floor, 1 Essex Court, Temple, EC4Y 9AR. *T:* 01–353 5362. *Club:* Wig and Pen.

FINNISTON, Sir (Harold) Montague, (Sir Monty), Kt 1975; BSc, PhD; FRS 1969; FRSE 1978; FEng 1983; business consultant since 1980; Chairman: H. M. Finniston Ltd, since 1980; KCA Drilling PLC, since 1983; Taddale Investments PLC, since 1983; Clyde Cablevision, since 1983; Finance for Housing Ltd (formerly Building Trust Management Co.), since 1981; Sherwood International, since 1984; Industrial Technology Securities Ltd, since 1984; Engineering Council Award Company, since 1984; Information Technology Training Accreditation Council, since 1985; Director: Cluff Oil PLC, since 1976; Caledonian Heritable Estates Ltd, since 1982; British Nutrition Foundation, since 1982; Combined Capital Ltd, since 1983; *b* 15 Aug. 1912; *s* of late Robert and Esther Finniston; *m* 1936, Miriam Singer; one *s* one *d. Educ:* Allan Glen's Sch., Glasgow; Glasgow Univ.; Royal College of Science and Technology, Glasgow. Lecturer in Metallurgy, Royal College of Science and Technology, 1933–35; Metallurgist, Stewart & Lloyds, 1935–37; Chief Research Officer, Scottish Coke Research Cttee, 1937–40; Metallurgist, RN Scientific Service, 1940–46; seconded to Ministry of Supply, Chalk River, Canada,

1946–47; Chief Metallurgist, UKAEA, Harwell, 1948–58; Man. Director, International Research and Development Co. (Chm. 1968–77), and Technical Director, C. A. Parsons & Co. Ltd, 1959–67; Chairman: Cryosystems Ltd; System Computors Ltd; Electronics Association of the North-East; Director, C. A. Parsons & Co. Ltd; Mem. Board of Thorn-Parsons Co. Ltd and Northern Economic Planning Council, 1963–67; Dep. Chm. (Technical), BSC, 1967–71; Dep. Chm. and Chief Executive, 1971–73, Chm., 1973–76, BSC; Director: Sears Holdings Ltd, 1976–79; GKN PLC, 1976–83; Bodycote Internat. PLC, 1980–84; Barmel Associates, 1981–82; Unimedia Ltd, 1983; Chairman: Sears Engrg Ltd, 1976–79; Anderson Strathclyde PLC, 1980–83; Drake & Scull Holdings, 1980–83; Butterfield-Harvey, 1981–84; Future Technology Systems, 1981–85; Metal Sciences (Holdings) PLC, 1983–85. Member: Council British Non-Ferrous Metals Research Assoc., 1965–72 (Vice-Chm. 1969–72; Chm. Research Board, 1965–70); NRDC, 1963–73; NEDC, 1973–76; Advisory Council, R&D (Fuel and Power), Dept of Trade and Industry (formerly Ministry of Power), 1965–74; SRC University Science and Technology Board, 1965–67; NPL Steering Cttee, 1966–68; Iron and Steel Adv. Cttee, 1969–73; Academic Adv. Cttee, Cranfield Inst. of Technology, 1970–75; BBC Science Consultative Group, 1971–74; Chairman: Policy Studies Inst. (formerly PEP), 1975–84 (Exec. Cttee 1968–74); Council, Scottish Business Sch., 1976–; Govt Cttee of Inquiry into engineering profession, 1977–79; Building EDC, 1980–; Prison Reform Trust, 1981–; President: Ironbridge Gorge Mus. Develt Trust, 1977–81; Inst. of Metals, 1967–68; Metals Soc., 1974–75 (Hon. Mem., 1980); Inst. Metallurgists, 1975–76; ASLIB, 1976–78 (Vice-Pres., 1974–76); Inst. of Management Services, 1977–82; Design and Industries Assoc., 1978–84; Indust. Market Res. Assoc., 1982–; Indust. Bldg Bureau, 1983–; ABCC, 1980–83; BISFA, 1980; IMGTechE, 1984–; British Export Houses Assoc., 1984–; Assoc. of Project Managers, 1984–; Engineering Industries Assoc., 1984–; Vice Pres., Iron and Steel Inst., 1968–73; Gen. Sec., BAAS, 1970–73 (Life Mem.); Mem., Soc. of Chem. Industry, 1974. A Vice-Pres., Royal Soc., 1971–72. Mem., Court of Assts, Worshipful Co. of Tinplate Workers, 1974–. Lectures: Dunn Meml, 1968; 19th Hatfield Meml, 1968; 18th Coal Science, BCURA, 1969; Edward Williams, 1970; Andrew Laing, 1970; Cockcroft, UMIST, 1975; Thomas Graham, Harold Moore, R. W. Mann, Marlow (Scotland), Colquhoun, 1976; Edwards Meml, 1977; ASM-TMS/AIME Distinguished, Chicago, 1977; 3rd Cantor, RSA, 1978; John Simmons, 1978; Lillian Gilbreth, 1978; Mason, 1979; Thomson, 1979; Lubbock Meml, 1979; Wilfrid Fish, 1980; Willis Jackson, 1980; Alfred Herbert, 1980; Massey Ferguson Meml, 1981; Barnett Shine, 1981; Conn Meml, 1981; Thomas Harrison, 1985. Governor, Carmel Coll., 1973– (Chm., 1980–82). Vis. Fellow, Univ. of Lancaster, 1970–. Pro-Chancellor, Surrey Univ., 1978–85; Chancellor, Stirling Univ., 1978–; Mem. Council, King's Coll. London (KQC), 1985–. ARTC; FIM; FInstP; FIChemE; FBIM; life FRSA; MRI 1978. Hon. Member: American Iron and Steel Inst., 1974; Japan Iron and Steel Inst., 1975 (Tawara Gold Medal, 1975); Indian Inst. of Metals, 1976; Smeatonian Soc. of Civil Engrs, 1977. Hon. Fellow: UMIST, 1973; Sunderland Polytech., 1975; Imp. Coll. of Science and Technology, 1979; St Cross Coll., Oxford, 1981. Hon. FSIAD, 1984; Hon. FIED, 1985. Hon. DSc: Strathclyde, 1968; Aston, 1971; City, 1974; Cranfield, 1976; Bath, 1977; Sussex, 1981; Open, 1982; DUniv: Surrey, 1969; Stirling, 1979; Hon. DCL Newcastle, 1976; Hon. DEng Liverpool, 1978; Hon. LLD: Glasgow, 1978; Hull, 1980; Hon. DMet Sheffield, 1979; Hon. DSc(Eng) QUB, 1985. Bessemer Medal, Metals Soc., 1974; Silver Medal, Inst. Sheet Metal Engrg, 1975; Eichner Medal, Soc. Française de Metallurgie, 1976; A. A. Griffiths Silver Medal, Material Sci. Club, 1976; Glazebrook Medal, Inst. of Physics, 1976. *Publications:* Editor: Metallurgy of the Rarer Metals, 1954–; Progress in Nuclear Energy, 1954–; Structural Characteristics of Materials, 1971; various scientific papers. *Recreations:* reading, writing and spectator interest in sport. *Address:* (office) 6 Manchester Square, W1A 1AU. *T:* 01–486 3658; Flat 72, Prince Albert Court, 33 Prince Albert Road, NW8. *T:* 01–722 8197. *Club:* Athenæum.

FINSBERG, Sir Geoffrey, Kt 1984; MBE 1959; JP; MP (C) Hampstead and Highgate, since 1983 (Hampstead, 1970–83); *b* 13 June 1926; *o s* of late Montefiore Finsberg, MC, and May Finsberg (*née* Grossman); *m* 1969, Pamela Benbow Hill. *Educ:* City of London Sch. National Chm., Young Conservatives, 1954–57; Mem., Exec. Cttee, Nat. Union of Cons. and Unionist Assocs, 1953–79 (Mem. Exec. Cttee, Greater London Area, 1949–79); a Vice-Chm., Conservative Party Organisation, 1975–79 and 1983–. Borough Councillor: Hampstead, 1949–65; Camden, 1964–74 (Leader, 1968–70). Chairman: Gtr London Area Cons. Local Govt Cttee, 1972–75. Opposition spokesman on Greater London, 1974–79; Mem. Exec., 1922 Cttee, 1974–75; Member, Select Cttee on Expenditure, 1970–79; Parly Under Sec. of State, DoE, 1979–81, DHSS, 1981–83; Mem., Parly Assembly of Council of Europe and of WEU, 1983–. Controller of Personnel and Chief Industrial Relations Adviser, Great Universal Stores, 1968–79; Dep. Chm., South East Reg. Bd, TSB, 1984–. Vice-Pres., Assoc. of Municipal Corporations, 1971–74 (Dep. Chm., 1969–71); Member: Post Office Users Nat. Council, 1970–77; Council, CBI, 1968–79 (Chm., Post Office Panel). FIPM 1975. Patron, Maccabi Assoc. of GB. Governor, Univ. Coll. Sch. JP Inner London, 1962. *Recreations:* bridge, reading. *Address:* House of Commons, SW1A 0AA. *T:* (home) 01–435 5320.

FINTRIE, Lord; James Alexander Norman Graham; *b* 16 Aug. 1973; *s* and *heir* of Marquis of Graham, *qv.*

FIRMSTON-WILLIAMS, Peter, OBE 1979; Chairman: Covent Garden Market Authority, since 1982; Flowers and Pot Plants Association, since 1985; *b* 30 Aug. 1918; *s* of late Geoffrey and Muriel Firmston-Williams; *m* Margaret Beaulah; one *s* one *d. Educ:* Harrow. Served War, Infantry, Green Howards Regt, 1939–45 (Captain). J. Lyons & Co. Ltd, 1945–53; Marketing Director, United Canners Ltd, 1953–55; Associated British Foods Ltd, Director, Store Operations, Fine Fare, 1958–61; Fitch Lovell Ltd, Man. Dir, Key Markets Ltd, 1962–71; Associated Dairies Group Ltd, Man. Dir, ASDA Stores, and Dir, Associated Dairies, 1971–81, retired; Director: Woolworth Hdgs (formerly Paternoster Stores) (Dep. Chm., 1982–85); Bredero Properties Ltd. Chm., Retail Consortium, 1984–86. *Recreations:* golf, water skiing, gardening. *Address:* Oak House, 12 Pembroke Road, Moor Park, Northwood, Mddx. *T:* Northwood 23052; 30 Rowland Place, Northwood, Mddx. *T:* Northwood 24535.

FIRNBERG, David; Chairman, The Networking Centre Ltd, since 1985; Managing Director, Eosys Ltd, since 1980; *b* 1 May 1930; *s* of L. B. Firnberg and K. L. E. Firnberg; *m* 1957, Sylvia Elizabeth du Cros; one *s* three *d. Educ:* Merchant Taylors' Sch., Northwood. FBCS; MIInfSc. Went West, 1953–56; Television Audience Measurement Ltd, 1956–59; ICT/ICL, 1959–72; David Firnberg Associates Ltd, 1972–74; Dir, Nat. Computing Centre Ltd, 1974–79. President: UK Assoc. of Project Managers, 1978–84; British Computer Soc., 1983–84. *Publications:* Computers Management and Information, 1973; Cassell's Spelling Dictionary, 1984. *Address:* The Great House, Buckland Common, Tring, Herts HP23 6NX. *T:* Cholesbury 448. *Clubs:* Institute of Directors, Wig and Pen.

FIRTH, Andrew Trevor; Regional Chairman, Industrial Tribunals, Yorkshire/ Humberside, since 1982 (Chairman, Industrial Tribunals, 1972–82); *b* 4 June 1922; *s* of Seth Firth and Amy Firth; *m* 1946, Nora Cornforth Armitage; one *s* two *d. Educ:* Prince Henry's Grammar Sch.; Leeds Univ. (LLB). Served RA, 6th Airborne Div., Normandy,

1944, Lieut; Intelligence Officer, Potsdam Conf., 1945, Captain; Rhine Army Coll., 1946, Major. Partner, later Sen. Partner, Barret Chamberlain & McDonnell, Solicitors, Harrogate, Otley, Leeds, 1948–72. Pres., Harrogate and Dist Law Soc., 1965–66; Area Chm., Law Soc. Legal Aid Cttee, Yorkshire, 1969–72. Bronze Star Medal, USA, 1945. *Recreations:* Chippendale Soc. (Chm.), golf, grandchildren. *Address:* Chevin Close, Birdcage Walk, Otley, West Yorkshire. *Clubs:* Leeds (Leeds); Otley Golf.

FIRTH, Arthur Percival; Assistant Editor, Daily Mail, since 1982; *b* 13 Aug. 1928; *s* of Arthur and Florence Firth; *m* 1957, Joyce Mary (*née* Fairclough); two *d*. *Educ:* Arnold Sch., Blackpool. Reporter, Lancashire Evening Post, 1950–58; Sub-Editor, Daily Herald, 1959; Daily Express: Sub-Editor, 1960; Night Editor, 1969–72; Northern Editor, 1972–78; Dep. Editor, 1978–80; Editor, 1980–81. *Recreations:* golf, fishing, cricket. *Address:* Greshams, Layters Way, Gerrards Cross, Bucks SL9 7QY. *T:* (office) 01–353 6000.

FIRTH, Maj.-Gen. Charles Edward Anson, CB 1951; CBE 1945; DSO 1943; *b* 9 Oct. 1902; *s* of late Major E. W. A. Firth, Indian Army; *m* 1933, Mary Kathleen (*d* 1977), *d* of late Commander W. St J. Fraser, RN; two *s*. *Educ:* Wellington Coll., Berks; RMC Sandhurst. 2nd Lieut The Gloucestershire Regt, 1923; Lieut, 1925; Captain, 1935; Staff Coll., 1936–37; War Office, 1938–40; Major, 1940; Middle East: Temp. Lieut-Colonel; AA and QMG 50 Div., 1941–42; OC 1st Royal Sussex Regt in Middle East, 1942–43; Temp. Brigadier, 7th Indian Infantry Bde, 1943; Comd 167 Infantry Bde, 1943–44 (Italy); Comd 21 Tank Bde, 1944 (N. Africa); Comd 2 Infantry Bde, 1944 (Italy); Comdr and Dep. Comdr British Military Mission to Greece, 1944–45. Colonel 1946; War Office, 1946–48; Comd Area Troops, Berlin (British Sector), 1948–50; Maj.-General, 1950; Comd East Anglian Dist, 1950; GOC Salisbury Plain Dist, 1951–53; Director of Personal Services, War Office, 1953–56. Colonel The Gloucestershire Regt, 1954–64; first Colonel Comdt, Military Provost Staff Corps, 1956–61. Governor, Dauntsey's Sch., 1961–77 (Vice-Chairman, 1965–77). Grand Commander Order of the Phoenix (Greek), 1946. *Recreations:* gardening, writing, fishing. *Address:* Garden Cottage, Church Street, Great Bedwyn, Marlborough, Wilts SN8 3PF. *T:* Marlborough 870270. *Club:* Army and Navy.

FIRTH, David Colin; Headmaster, Cheadle Hulme School, since 1977; *b* 29 Jan. 1930; *s* of Jack and Muriel Firth; *m* 1954, Edith Scanlan; three *s* one *d*. *Educ:* Rothwell Grammar Sch.; Sheffield Univ. (BSc, DipEd). Royal Signals, 1952–54; Stand Grammar Sch., 1954–57; East Barnet Grammar Sch., 1957–61; Bristol Grammar Sch., 1961–73; The Gilberd Sch., 1973–77. *Publications:* A Practical Organic Chemistry, 1966; Elementary Thermodynamics, 1969; (jtly) Introductory Physical Science, 1971. *Recreations:* cricket, fell walking, talking about gardening. *Address:* Cheadle Hulme School, Claremont Road, Cheadle Hulme, Cheadle, Cheshire SK8 6EF.

FIRTH, Edward Michael Tyndall, CB 1951; *b* 17 Feb. 1903; *s* of Edward H. Firth, Sheffield; *m* 1929, Eileen Marie (*d* 1982), *d* of Edward Newman, Hove; two *s*. *Educ:* King Edward VII Sch., Sheffield; University College, Oxford. Classical Scholar, 1922–26. Inland Revenue, 1926; Ministry of Health, 1945; Under Secretary, 1947–58; Registrar General, 1958–63. *Address:* 65 Middle Way, Oxford.

FIRTH, Mrs Joan Margaret, PhD; Under-Secretary, Community Services Division, Department of Health and Social Security, since 1986; *b* 25 March 1935; *d* of Ernest Wilson and Ann (*née* Crowther); *m* 1955, Kenneth Firth. *Educ:* Lawnswood High Sch., Leeds; Univ. of Leeds (1st Cl. BSc Colour Chemistry; PhD Dyeing of Wool). Research Asst, Leeds Univ., 1958–60; Head of Science, Selby High Sch., 1960–62; Sen. Lecturer in General Science, Elizabeth Gaskell Coll., Manchester, 1962–66; Lectr in Organic Chemistry, Salford Univ., 1966–67; joined Civil Service as Direct Entry Principal, 1967; Asst Sec., 1974; Under-Sec., DHSS, 1981. *Publications:* contrib. Jl Textile Inst., 1958. *Recreations:* eating, walking, Open University. *Address:* 2 Stratton Court, Devonshire Road, Hatch End, Mddx HA5 4NA. *T:* 01–428 7204.

FIRTH, Rt. Rev. Peter James; *see* Malmesbury, Bishop Suffragan of.

FIRTH, Prof. Sir Raymond (William), Kt 1973; MA; PhD; FBA 1949; Professor of Anthropology, University of London, 1944–68, now Emeritus; *b* 25 March 1901; *s* of late Wesley Hugh Bourne Firth and Marie Elizabeth Jane Cartmill; *m* 1936, Rosemary, *d* of late Sir Gilbert Upcott, KCB; one *s*. *Educ:* Auckland Grammar Sch.; Auckland University College; London School of Economics (Hon. Fellow, 1970). Anthropological research in British Solomon Islands, including one year on Tikopia, 1928–29; Lecturer in Anthropology, University of Sydney, 1930–31; Acting Professor of Anthropology, University of Sydney, 1931–32; Lecturer in Anthropology, London School of Economics, 1932–35; Reader, 1935–44; Hon. Secretary Royal Anthropological Institute, 1936–39 (President 1953–55); Research in peasant economics and anthropology in Malaya, as Leverhulme Research Fellow, 1939–40; served with Naval Intelligence Division, Admiralty, 1941–44; Secretary of Colonial Social Science Research Council, Colonial Office, 1944–45; Fellow, Center for Advanced Study in the Behavioral Sciences, Stanford, 1958–59; Prof. of Pacific Anthropology, Univ. of Hawaii, 1968–69. Visiting Professor: British Columbia, 1969; Cornell, 1970; Chicago, 1971; Graduate Center, City Univ. of New York, 1971; Univ. of California, Davis 1974, Berkeley 1977; Auckland, 1978. Life Pres., Assoc. of Social Anthropologists, 1975. Foreign Hon. Member American Academy of Arts and Sciences, 1963; Hon. Member Royal Society, NZ, 1964; Foreign Member: American Philosophical Society, 1965; Royal Soc., NSW; Royal Danish Academy of Sciences and Letters, 1966; Internat. Union of Anthropol and Ethnol Sciences, 1983. Social research surveys: W Africa, 1945; Malaya, 1947; New Guinea, 1951; Tikopia, 1952, 1966; Malaya, 1963. Hon. degrees: DPh Oslo, 1965; LLD Michigan, 1967; LittD East Anglia, 1968; Dr Letters ANU, 1969; DHumLett Chicago, 1968; DSc British Columbia, 1970; DLitt Exeter, 1972; DLit Auckland, 1978; PhD Cracow, 1984; DSc Econ London, 1984. *Publications:* The Kauri Gum Industry, 1924; Primitive Economics of the New Zealand Maori, 1929 (new edn, 1959); Art and Life In New Guinea, 1936; We, The Tikopia: A Sociological Study of Kinship in Primitive Polynesia, 1936; Human Types, 1938 (new edn, 1975); Primitive Polynesian Economy, 1939 (new edn, 1964); The Work of the Gods in Tikopia, 1940 (new edn, 1967); Malay Fishermen: Their Peasant Economy, 1946 (enlarged edn, 1966); Elements of Social Organization, 1951 (new edn 1971); Two Studies of Kinship in London (ed.), 1956; Man and Culture: An Evaluation of the Work of Malinowski (ed.), 1957; Social Change in Tikopia, 1959; History and Traditions of Tikopia, 1961; Essays on Social Organization and Values, 1964; (with B. S. Yamey) Capital Saving and Credit in Peasant Societies, 1964; Tikopia Ritual and Belief, 1967; Rank and Religion in Tikopia, 1970; (with J. Hubert and A. Forge) Families and Their Relatives, 1970; Symbols Public and Private, 1973; Tikopia-English Dictionary, 1985. *Recreations:* Romanesque art, early music. *Address:* 33 Southwood Avenue, N6 5SA. *Club:* Athenæum.

FIRTH, Tazeena Mary; designer; *b* 1 Nov. 1935; *d* of Denis Gordon Firth and Irene (*née* Morris). *Educ:* St Mary's, Wantage; Chatelard Sch. Theatre Royal, Windsor, 1954–57; English Stage Co., Royal Court, 1957–60; partnership in stage design with Timothy O'Brien estabd 1961; output incl.: The Bartered Bride, The Girl of the Golden West, 1962; West End prodns of new plays, 1963–64; London scene of Shakespeare Exhibn, 1964; Tango, Days in the Trees, Staircase, RSC, and Trafalgar at Madame Tussaud's, 1966; All's Well that Ends Well, As You Like It, Romeo and Juliet, RSC, 1967; The Merry Wives of Windsor, Troilus and Cressida (also Nat. Theatre, 1976), The Latent Heterosexual, RSC, 1968; Pericles (also Comédie Française, 1974), Women Beware Women, Bartholomew Fair, RSC, 1969; 1970: Measure for Measure, RSC; Madame Tussaud's in Amsterdam; The Knot Garden, Royal Opera; 1971: Enemies, Man of Mode, RSC; 1972: La Cenerentola, Oslo; Lower Depths, The Island of the Mighty, RSC; As You Like It, OCSC; 1973: Richard II, Love's Labour's Lost, RSC; 1974: Next of Kin, NT; Summerfolk, RSC; The Bassarids, ENO; 1975: John Gabriel Borkman, NT; Peter Grimes, Royal Opera (later in Paris); The Marrying of Ann Leete, RSC; 1976: Wozzeck, Adelaide Fest.; The Zykovs, RSC; The Force of Habit, NT; 1977: Tales from the Vienna Woods, Bedroom Farce, NT; Falstaff, Berlin Opera; 1978: The Cunning Little Vixen, Göteborg; Evita, London (later in USA, Australia, Vienna); A Midsummer Night's Dream, Sydney Opera House; 1979: Peter Grimes, Göteborg; The Rake's Progress, Royal Opera; Turandot, Vienna State Opera, 1983. Designed independently: The Two Gentlemen of Verona, RSC, 1969; Occupations, RSC, 1971; The Rape of Lucretia, Karlstad, 1982; Katherina Ismailova, Göteborg, 1984; La Traviata, Umeå, The Trojan Woman, Göteborg, and Bluebeard's Castle, Copenhagen, 1985. (Jtly) Gold Medal for Set Design, Prague Quadriennale, 1975. *Recreation:* sailing. *Address:* 33 Lansdowne Gardens, SW8 2EQ. *T:* 01–622 5384.

FISCHER, Annie; Hungarian Pianist; *b* Budapest, 1914; *m* Aladár Toth (decd). *Educ:* Franz Liszt Landemusikhochschule, Budapest. Studied under Arnold Székely and Ernst von Dohnanyi. Concert Début, Budapest, at age of eight (performed Beethoven's C Major Concerto), 1922; began international career as a concert pianist, Zurich, 1926; toured and played in most European Music centres, 1926–39. Concert pianist, Sweden, during War of 1939–45. Returned to Hungary after War and has made concert tours to all parts of the world. Hon. Prof., Acad. of Music, Budapest, 1965. Awarded 1st prize, Internat. Liszt Competition, Budapest, 1933; Kossuth Prizes 1949, 1955, 1965. Eminent Artist; Red Banner, Order of Labour, 1974. *Address:* c/o Harrison/Parrott Ltd, 12 Penzance Place, W11 4PA.

FISCHER, Prof. Ernst Otto; Professor of Inorganic Chemistry, Munich University (Techn); *b* Munich, 10 Nov. 1918; *s* of Prof. Karl T. Fischer and Valentine (*née* Danzer); unmarried. *Educ:* Tech. Univ., Munich. Dip. Chem., 1949; Dr rer. nat., 1952, Habilitation 1954. Associate Prof. of Inorganic Chem., Univ. of Munich, 1957, Prof. 1959, Prof. and Dir, Inorganic Chem. Inst., Tech. Univ., Munich, 1964. Member: Bavarian Acad. of Sciences; Akad. deutscher Naturforscher Leopoldina, 1969; Austrian Acad. of Scis, 1976; Accad. dei Lincei, Italy, 1976; Göttingen Akad. der Wissenschaften, 1977; Soc. of German Chemists, etc; Centennial For. Fellow, Amer. Chem. Soc., 1976. Hon. Dr rer. nat.: Munich, 1972; Erlangen, 1977; Veszprem, 1983; Hon. DSc Strathclyde, 1975. Has received many prizes and awards including the Nobel Prize for Chemistry, 1973 (jointly with Prof. Geoffrey Wilkinson) for their pioneering work, performed independently, on the chem. of organometallic "sandwich compounds". *Publications:* (with H. Werner) Metall-pi-Komplexe mit di- und oligoolefinischen Liganden, 1963 (trans. as Metal pi-Complexes Vol. 1, Complexes with di- and oligo-olefinic Ligands, 1966–); numerous contribs to learned jls on organometallic chem., etc. *Recreations:* art, history, travel. *Address:* 16 Sohnckestrasse, 8 Munich-Solln, West Germany.

FISCHER-DIESKAU, Dietrich; baritone; *b* Berlin, 28 May 1925; *s* of Dr Albert Fischer-Dieskau; *m* 1949, Irmgard Poppen (*d* 1963); three *s*. *Educ:* High Sch., Berlin; Music Academy, Berlin. First Baritone, Städtische Oper, Berlin, 1948–78, Hon. Mem., 1978–; Mem., Vienna State Opera, 1957–63. Extensive Concert Tours of Europe and USA; soloist in Festivals at Edinburgh, Salzburg, Bayreuth, Vienna, Berlin, Munich, Holland, Luzern, Prades, etc. Opera roles include: Wolfram, Jochanaan, Almaviva, Marquis Posa, Don Giovanni, Falstaff, Mandryka, Wozzeck, Danton, Macbeth, Hans Sachs. Many recordings. Prof., Music Acad., Berlin, 1983; Member: Acad. of Arts, Berlin; Acad. of Fine Arts, Munich; Hon. RAM, 1972; Honorary Member: Wiener Konzerthausgesellschaft, 1962; Königlich-Schwedische Akad., 1972; Acad. Santa Cecilia, Rome; Royal Philharmonic Soc., 1985. Hon. DMus Oxford, 1978; Dr *hc:* Sorbonne, 1980; Yale, 1980. Kunstpreis der Stadt Berlin, 1950; Internationaler Schallplattenpreis, since 1955 nearly every year; Orfeo d'oro, 1955 and 1966; Bayerischer Kammersänger, 1959; Edison Prize, 1961, 1964, 1966, 1970; Naras Award, USA, 1962; Mozart-Medaille, Wien, 1962; Berliner Klammersänger, 1963; Electrola Award, 1970; Léonie Sonning Music Prize, Copenhagen, 1975; Golden Gramophone Award, Germany, 1975; Ruckert-Preis, Schweinfurth, 1979; President's Prize, Charles Gros Acad., Paris, 1980; Ernst Von Siemen Prize, 1980; Artist of the Year, Phonoakademie, Germany, 1980. Bundesverdienstkreuz (1st class), 1958; Grosses Verdienstkreuz, 1974. *Publications:* Texte Deutscher Lieder, 1968 (The Fischer-Dieskau Book of Lieder, 1976); Auf den Spuren der Schubert-Lieder, 1971; Wagner und Nietzsche, 1974; Robert Schumann—Wort und Musik, 1981.

FISH, Anthony, PhD; Managing Director, Sittingbourne Research Centre, Shell Research Ltd, since 1985; *b* 18 Feb. 1937; *s* of Leonard and Enid Irene Towrass Fish; *m* 1959, Yvonne Angela Stock. *Educ:* Chesterfield Sch.; Queens' Coll., Cambridge (MA); Imperial College of Science and Technology (PhD). Asst Lectr, Imperial Coll., 1960–63; Lectr, Hatfield Coll., 1963–64; Shell companies in UK, 1964; secondment to Central Policy Rev. Staff, Cabinet Office, 1970–71; Dir, Shell Toxicology Laboratory, 1978–80; Shell Internat. Petroleum Co. Ltd, 1980–85. Corday-Morgan Medalist, RSC, 1964. *Publications:* papers in Proc. Royal Soc., Trans Faraday Soc., Jl Chem. Soc., Internat. Symposia on Combustion, Qly Revs Chem. Soc., Jl Catalysis, Angewandte Chemie. *Recreations:* horse racing, ornithology, painting, opera. *Address:* Shell Research Ltd, Sittingbourne, Kent ME9 8AG. *T:* Sittingbourne 24444. *Club:* Newbury Race.

FISH, Francis, BPharm, PhD; FPS; Dean, School of Pharmacy, University of London, since 1978; *b* 20 April 1924; *s* of William Fish and Phyllis (*née* Griffiths); *m* 1949, Hilda Mary Brown; two *s*. *Educ:* Houghton-le-Spring Grammar Sch.; Technical Coll., Sunderland (now Sunderland Polytechnic). BPharm (London) 1946; PhD (Glasgow) 1955. FPS 1946. Asst Lectr, 1946–48, Lectr, 1948–62, Royal Coll. of Science and Technology, Glasgow; University of Strathclyde: Sen. Lectr, 1962–69; Reader in Pharmacognosy and Forensic Science, 1969–76; Personal Prof., 1976–78; Dean, Sch. of Pharmaceutical Sciences, 1977–78; Supervisor, MSc course in Forensic Science, 1966–78. Mem. Editorial Bd, Jl Pharm. Pharmacol., 1964–70 and 1975–78. Member: Pharm. Soc. Cttee on Pharmacognosy, 1963–74; British Pharm. Codex Pharmacognosy Sub-Cttee A, 1968–73; Brit. Pharm. Conf. Sci. Cttee, 1973–78; Brit. Pharmacopoeia Pharmacognosy Panel, 1974–77; Council, Forensic Science Soc., 1974–77 (Vice-Pres., 1981–82); Professional and Gen. Services Cttee, Scottish Council on Alcoholism, 1976–78; Herbal Sub-Cttee, Cttee on Safety of Medicines, 1978–80; British Pharmacopœia Commn, 1980–; Cttee on Safety of Medicines, 1980–83; Univ. of London Senate, 1981–; DHSS Standing Pharmaceutical Adv. Cttee, 1982–; UGC Panel on Studies Allied to Medicine, 1982– (Chm., 1984–); Nuffield Foundn Cttee of Inquiry into Pharmacy, 1983–86; Cttee on Review of Medicines, 1984–; UGC Medical Subcttee, 1984–. Mem., Governing Body, Wye College, 1985–. *Publications*: (with J. Owen Dawson) Surgical Dressings, Ligatures and Sutures, 1967; research pubns and review articles in Pharmaceut., Phytochem. and Forensic Sci. jls. *Recreations*: theatre, winemaking. *Address*: School of Pharmacy, University of London, 29–39 Brunswick Square, WC1N 1AX. *T*: 01–837 7651.

FISH, Hugh, CBE 1984 (OBE 1971); Chairman: Natural Environment Research Council, since 1985 (Member, 1976–84); Water Technology Transfer Ltd, since 1984; Member, Management Board, British National Space Centre, since 1986; *b* 6 Jan. 1923; *s* of Leonard Mark and Millicent Fish; *m* 1943, Nancy, *o d* of William and Louise Asquith; two *s* one *d*. *Educ*: Rothwell Grammar Sch.; Leeds Univ. (BSc). War Service, 1942–46, RNVR (Lieut). Chemist, W Riding Rivers Bd, 1949–52; Pollution and Fisheries Inspector, Essex River Bd, 1952–65; River Conservator, Essex River Authy, 1965–69; Chief Purification Officer, Thames Conservancy, 1969–74; Thames Water Authority: Dir of Scientific Services, 1974–78; Chief Exec., 1978–84; Mem., 1983–85. Member of Council: IWES, 1975– (Pres. 1984); Freshwater Biol Assoc., 1972–74. FRSC, FIPHE, FInstWPC, FIWES. *Publications*: Principles of Water Quality Management, 1973; contribs to various jls on natural science of water. *Recreations*: gardening, water sports, inventions, theatre. *Address*: Red Roofs, Shefford Woodlands, near Newbury, Berks. *T*: Great Shefford 369.

FISH, John; formerly Under-Secretary, Head of Establishment General Services Division, Department of Industry, 1973–80; *b* 16 July 1920; *m* 1948, Frances; two *s*. *Educ*: Lincoln School. Entered Customs and Excise, 1937; Exchequer and Audit Dept, 1939; War service, Pilot in RAF, 1940–46; Exchequer and Audit Dept, 1946; BoT, 1949; Principal, 1950; Min. of Materials, 1951; Volta River Preparatory Commn, Accra, 1953; BoT, 1956; Asst Sec., 1960; Min. of Health, 1962; BoT, 1965; DTI, 1970; Under-Sec., 1973; Dept of Industry, 1974. *Address*: The Green, Stockton, near Rugby, Warwicks CV23 8JF. *T*: Southam 2833. *Club*: Civil Service.

FISHER, family name of **Baron Fisher** and **Baroness Fisher of Rednal.**

FISHER, 3rd Baron, *cr* 1909, of Kilverstone; **John Vavasseur Fisher,** DSC 1944; JP; Director, Kilverstone Latin-American Zoo and Wild Life Park, since 1973; *b* 24 July 1921; *s* of 2nd Baron and Jane (*d* 1955), *d* of Randal Morgan, Philadelphia, USA; *S* father, 1955; *m* 1st, 1949, Elizabeth Ann Penelope (marr. diss. 1969), *yr d* of late Herbert P. Holt, MC; two *s* two *d*; 2nd, 1970, Hon. Mrs Rosamund Anne Fairbairn, *d* of 12th Baron Clifford of Chudleigh. *Educ*: Stowe; Trinity Coll., Cambridge. Member: Eastern Gas Bd, 1962–71; East Anglia Economic Planning Council, 1971–77. DL Norfolk, 1968–82; JP Norfolk, 1970. *Heir*: *s* Hon. Patrick Vavasseur Fisher [*b* 14 June 1953; *m* 1977, Lady Karen Carnegie, *d* of Earl of Northesk, *qv*; one *s* three *d*]. *Address*: Kilverstone Hall, Thetford, Norfolk. *T*: Thetford 2222. *Club*: Naval.

See also Baron Clifford of Chudleigh.

FISHER OF REDNAL, Baroness *cr* 1974 (Life Peer), of Rednal, Birmingham; **Doris Mary Gertrude Fisher,** JP; Member of the European Parliament, 1975–79; Member, Warrington and Runcorn (formerly Warrington) Development Corporation, since 1974; *b* 13 Sept. 1919; *d* of late Frederick J. Satchwell, BEM; *m* 1939, Joseph Fisher (*d* 1978); two *d*. *Educ*: Tinker's Farm Girls Sch.; Fircroft Coll.; Bournville Day Continuation Coll. Member: Birmingham City Council, 1952–74; Labour Party, 1945–; UNESCO study group; Nat. Pres. Co-operative Women's Guild, 1961–62. Contested Ladywood, Birmingham, 1969 by-election; MP (Lab) Birmingham, Ladywood, 1970–Feb. 1974. Member: Gen. Medical Council, 1974–79; New Towns Staff Commn, 1976–79; Birmingham Civic Housing Assoc. Ltd, 1982–; Vice-Pres., Assoc. of Municipal Authorities. Guardian, Birmingham Assay Office, 1979–; Chm. Governors, Baskerville Special Sch., 1981–. JP Birmingham 1961. Hon. Alderman, 1974, Birmingham District Council. *Recreations*: swimming, walking. *Address*: 60 Jacoby Place, Priory Road, Birmingham B5 7UW. *T*: 021–471 2003.

FISHER, Alan Wainwright; General Secretary, National Union of Public Employees, 1968–82; *b* 20 June 1922; *s* of Thomas Wainwright Fisher and Ethel Agnes Fisher; *m* 1958, Joyce Tinniswood (marr. diss. 1976); two *s* one *d*; *m* 1978, Ruth Woollerton. *Educ*: Primary and Secondary Schools in Birmingham. National Union of Public Employees: Junior Clerk, 1939; Midlands Divisional Officer, 1953; Asst General Secretary, 1962. Mem., TUC Gen. Council, 1968–82; Chm., TUC, 1980–81. Member: Nat. Jt Council for Local Authorities, Services, 1956– (Chm., 1971–72); Ancillary Staffs Council (Sec. 1965–79) and Gen. Council (Chm. 1966–69) of Whitley Councils for Health Services; Potato Marketing Bd, 1969–70; Bd, Centre for Educnl Develt Overseas (Governor 1970–); Bd, BOAC, 1970–72; BAB, 1972–82; London Electricity Bd, 1970–80; Nat. Radiological Protection Bd, 1971; Med. Adv. Cttee, Health and Safety Commn, 1977–; Governor, Henley Administrative Staff Coll., 1977–. *Recreation*: seismography. *Address*: Plas Farchynys, Bontddu, Gwynedd. *T*: Bontddu 643.

FISHER, Anne; *see* Fisher, Phyllis Anne.

FISHER, Arthur J.; *see* Jeddere-Fisher.

FISHER, Major (Hon.) Charles Howard Kerridge, MC 1918; JP; Director of property companies, since 1960; *b* 21 Dec. 1895; *s* of late Charles Henry Fisher, Westbury, Wilts; *m* 1923, Ethel Mary (*d* 1958), *d* of Sidney Redcliffe Chope, JP, Bideford, Devon; one *s* one *d*; *m* 1967, Gertrude Elizabeth, JP, *widow* of William Walter Symper, Harrow. *Educ*: Trowbridge High Sch., Wiltshire. Served European War, 1914–18 (MC); with Hon. Artillery Company and RA in Belgium and France; War of 1939–45: Home Guard and Army Welfare Officer; Hon. Major 1958. Manufacturer ladies' clothing, 1923–59, when retired (Company Dir). Member Acton Borough Council, 1940–45 (Educn Cttee, 1945–65). JP 1947, DL 1961–79, Middlesex (now London). First High Sheriff of Greater London, 1965. Lord Lieutenant's Representative for Acton, 1958–70 (now London Borough of Ealing, 1965–71); Dep. Chairman, Willesden Petty Sessional Division, 1962–69. General Comr of Income Tax, 1965–69. Freeman, City of London, 1947; Liveryman, Haberdashers' Company, 1948; Patron, Local Cadets; Pres., Boy Scouts Assoc.; Vice-President: Acton Branch, British Legion; NW County Met. Area British Legion. Member, War Pension Cttee, Ealing, 1940 (Vice-Chairman 1960). Queen's Jubilee Medal. *Recreations*: local social activities. *Address*: Arunshead Farm, Green Lane, Shamley Green, Guildford GU5 0RD. *Club*: City Livery.

FISHER, Desmond (Michael); Editor and Managing Director, Nationalist and Leinster Times, Carlow, since 1985; *b* 9 Sept. 1920; *e s* of Michael Louis Fisher and Evelyn Kate Shier; *m* 1948, Margaret Elizabeth Smyth; three *s* one *d*. *Educ*: St Columb's Coll., Derry; Good Counsel Coll., New Ross, Co. Wexford; University Coll., Dublin (BA (NUI)). Asst Editor, Nationalist and Leinster Times, Carlow, 1945–48; Foreign Editor, Irish Press, Dublin, 1948–51; Economic Correspondent, Irish News Agency, Dublin, 1951–54; London Editor, Irish Press, 1954–62; Editor, Catholic Herald, 1962–66; Radio Telefis Eireann: Dep. Head of News, 1967–73; Head of Current Affairs, 1973–75; Dir of Broadcasting Develt, 1975–83. *Publications*: The Church in Transition, 1967; Broadcasting in Ireland, 1978; The Right to Communicate: a status report, 1981; The Right to Communicate: a new human right, 1983; contributor to The Economist, The Furrow,

Irish Digest and to various Irish, US and foreign magazines. *Address*: Louvain 22, Dublin 14. *T*: 884608.

FISHER, Donald; County Education Officer, Hertfordshire, since 1974; *b* 20 Jan. 1931; *s* of John Wilfred and Mabel Fisher; *m* 1953, Mavis Doreen (*née* Sutcliffe); one *s* two *d*. *Educ*: Heckmondwike Grammar Sch.; Christ Church, Oxford (MA). Teacher, Hull GS, 1954–59; Admin. Asst, Cornwall LEA, 1959–61; Asst Educn Officer, W Sussex LEA, 1961–64; Headmaster: Helston GS, 1964–67; Midhurst GS, 1967–72; Dep. Educn Officer, W Sussex LEA, 1972–74. Chm., Assoc. of Educn Officers, 1982; Pres., Soc. of Educn Officers, 1984; Member: Business and Technician Educn Council, 1980–; Jt Bd, Certificate of Pre-Vocational Educn, 1983–; Schs Curriculum Develt Cttee, 1983–. *Publications*: (contrib). Educational Administration, 1980; articles and book reviews in Education. *Recreation*: reading. *Address*: 74 The Ryde, Hatfield, Herts AL9 5DN. *T*: Hatfield 71428.

FISHER, Doris G.; *b* 1907; *d* of Gathorne John Fisher, Pontypool. *Educ*: Farringtons, Chislehurst; Royal Holloway Coll., University of London (BA Hons (English) 1929, (French) 1931); Sorbonne. Senior English Mistress, Maidenhead County Gram. Sch. 1934–39; Second Mistress, Dover County Grammar Sch., 1945; Headmistress of Farringtons, Chislehurst, Kent, 1946–57, retired. Lecturer at Westminster Training Coll., 1957–59; Lecturer at Avery Hill Training Coll., 1959–62. *Address*: 9 The Ridgeway, Newport, Gwent NP9 5AF.

FISHER, Dudley Henry, IPFA; Chairman, Wales Region, British Gas Corporation, since 1974; *b* 22 Aug. 1922; *s* of Arthur and Mary Fisher; *m* 1st, 1946, Barbara Lilian Sexton (*d* 1984); one *s* two *d*; 2nd, Jean Mary Livingstone Miller, *d* of late Dr Robert Brown Miller, Cowbridge, S Glam. *Educ*: City of Norwich Sch. Various accountancy positions in Local Govt and Eastern Electricity Bd, 1938–53. War service, RAF, 1942–46 (Flt Lt). Northern Gas Bd, 1953; Wales Gas Board: Asst Chief Accountant, Dep. Chief Accountant, Chief Accountant, Dir of Finance, 1956–69; Dep. Chm., 1970. Member: Adv. Cttee on Local Govt Audit, 1979–82; Audit Commn for Local Authorities in England and Wales, 1983–; Broadcasting Council for Wales, 1986–; Hon. Treasurer, British National Cttee, 1980–, and Chm., Admin. Cttee, 1986–, World Energy Conf. Mem. Council, UC Cardiff, 1983–. *Recreations*: golf, gardening, reading. *Address*: Norwood Edge, 8 Cyncoed Avenue, Cardiff CF2 6SU. *Club*: Cardiff and County (Cardiff).

FISHER, Rt. Rev. Edward George K.; *see* Knapp-Fisher.

FISHER, Elisabeth Neill; a Recorder of the Crown Court, since 1982; *b* 24 Nov. 1944; *d* of Kenneth Neill Fisher and Lorna Charlotte Honor Fisher. *Educ*: Oxford High Sch. for Girls (GPDST); Cambridge Univ. (MA). Called to the Bar, Inner Temple, 1968. Mem. Senate, 1983–. *Address*: 1 Fountain Court, Steelhouse Lane, Birmingham B4 6DR. *T*: 021–236 5721.

FISHER, Hon. Francis Forman, CBE 1980; MC 1944; Principal, Wolsey Hall, Oxford, since 1980; Master of Wellington College, 1966–80; *b* 25 Sept. 1919; 2nd *s* of late Most Rev. and Rt Hon. Lord Fisher of Lambeth, GCVO; unmarried. *Educ*: Repton; Clare Coll., Cambridge (MA). Commissioned, The Sherwood Foresters, 1940; served War of 1939–45, Middle East, and Western Desert (POW Tobruk, 1942); escaped from Italy and returned to England, 1943; demobilised, rank of Capt., 1946 (MC); returned to Cambridge, 1946; Asst Master, Repton Sch., 1947–54; Housemaster, 1948–54; Warden of St Edward's Sch., Oxford, 1954–66. Incorporated MA Oxford Univ. through Christ Church, 1955. Chm., Headmaster's Conf., 1973. Governor: Repton Sch.; Oundle Sch.; St Catherine's Sch.; Dragon Sch.; Caldicott and Horris Hill Prep. Schs; Chairman of Governors: Mount House Sch.; Greycotes Sch. Dir, Ecclesiastical Insurance Office Ltd, 1981–; Chm., GAP Activities Ltd, 1982–. *Recreations*: cricket, hockey (rep. CUHC *v* Oxford, 1947), and other games. *Address*: New Barn, Cassington Road, Yarnton, Oxford. *T*: Kidlington 6717. *Clubs*: East India, Devonshire, Sports and Public Schools; Hawks (Cambridge).

See also Hon. Sir Henry A. P. Fisher.

FISHER, Francis George Robson, MA Oxon; Deputy Secretary, Headmasters' Conference and Secondary Heads' Association, 1982–86; *b* 9 April 1921; *s* of late John Henry Fisher and Hannah Clayton Fisher; *m* 1965, Sheila Vernon, *o d* of late D. Dunsire and Mrs H. E. Butt; one *s*. *Educ*: Liverpool Coll. (Schol.); Worcester Coll., Oxford (Classical Exhibitioner). Served War of 1939–45; Capt. in Ayrshire Yeomanry, North Africa and Italy, 1942–45. Kingswood Sch., Bath, 1948–59, Housemaster and Sen. English Master, 1950–59; Headmaster, Bryanston Sch., 1959–74; Chief Master, King Edward's Sch., Birmingham, and Head Master, Schs of King Edward VI in Birmingham, 1974–82. Chairman: HMC Direct Grant Sub-Cttee, 1979–80; HMC Assisted Places Sub-Cttee, 1981. Life Governor, Liverpool Coll., 1969–; Governor: Harrow Sch., 1982–; Bromsgrove Sch., 1985–; Kelly Coll., Tavistock, 1985–. *Recreations*: music, reading, sailing. *Address*: Craig Cottage, Lower Street, Dittisham, S Devon TQ6 0HY. *T*: Dittisham 309.

FISHER, Prof. Frederick Jack, MA; Professor of Economic History, London School of Economics, University of London, 1954–75; *b* 22 July 1908; *s* of A. H. Fisher, Southend-on-Sea; *m* 1943, Barbara Vivienne, *d* of J. E. Whisstock, Southend-on-Sea; one *s* one *d*. *Educ*: Southend High Sch.; London Sch. of Economics. MA. Served RAF, 1941–46. Asst Lecturer and Lecturer in Economic History, London Sch. of Economics, 1935–47; Reader in Economic History, 1947–54. FRHistS. Wiles' Lectr, QUB, 1973. Hon. DLitt Exeter, 1983. *Publications*: (ed) Essays in the Economic and Social History of Tudor and Stuart England, 1961; (ed) Calendar of Manuscripts of Lord Sackville of Knole, vol II, 1966; contrib. Economica, Economic History Review. *Address*: 22 Lyndale Avenue, NW2.

FISHER, Fredy; *see* Fisher, M. H.

FISHER, Sir George Read, Kt 1967; CMG 1961; Mining Engineer; President, MIM Holdings Ltd, 1970–75; *b* 23 March 1903; *s* of George Alexander and Ellen Harriett Fisher; *m* 1st, 1927, Eileen Elaine Triggs (*d* 1966); one *s* three *d*; 2nd, 1973, Marie C. Gilbey. *Educ*: Prince Alfred Coll., Adelaide; Adelaide Univ. (BE). Formerly Gen. Manager of Operations for Zinc Corporation Ltd, Broken Hill, NSW; Chm., Mount Isa Mines Ltd, 1953–70. *Recreations*: shooting and bowling. *Address*: GPO Box 2236, Brisbane, Qld 4001, Australia. *Clubs*: Queensland, Brisbane (Brisbane).

FISHER, Harold Wallace; Director, 1959–69, and Vice-President, 1962–69, Exxon Corporation, formerly Standard Oil Company (New Jersey) New York, retired; *b* 27 Oct. 1904; *s* of Dean Wallace Fisher and Grace Cheney Fisher; *m* 1930, Hope Elisabeth Case; one *s*. *Educ*: Massachusetts Institute of Technology (BSc). Joined Standard Oil Company (NJ), 1927; Dir Esso Standard Oil Co. and Pres. Enjay Co. Inc., 1945. Resided in London, 1954–59. UK Rep. for Standard Oil Co. (NJ) and Chm. of its Coordination Cttee for Europe, 1954–57; Joint Managing Dir, Iraq Petroleum Co. Ltd and Associated Companies, 1957–59. Mem., Marine Bd, Nat. Acad. of Engineering, 1971–74; Vice-Chm., Sloan-Kettering Inst. for Cancer Research, 1974–75 (Chm., 1970–74); Mem., MIT Corp. Develt Cttee, 1975–; Vice-Chm., and Chm. Exec. Cttee, Community Blood

Council of Greater New York, 1969–71. Hon. DSc 1960, Clarkson Coll. of Technology, Nat. Acad. of Engrg. *Publications:* various patents and technical articles relating to the Petroleum Industry. *Recreations:* golf, photography, horology. *Address:* 68 Goose Point Lane, PO Box 1792, Duxbury, Mass 02331, USA. *Clubs:* Pilgrims, American; University (New York); Duxbury Yacht.

FISHER, Hon. Sir Henry (Arthur Pears), Kt 1968; President, Wolfson College, Oxford, 1975–85, Hon. Fellow, 1985; *b* 20 Jan. 1918; *e s* of late Lord Fisher of Lambeth, PC, GCVO, *m* 1948, Felicity, *d* of late Eric Sutton; one *s* three *d. Educ:* Marlborough; Christ Church, Oxford (Schol.); Gaisford Greek Prose Prize, 1937; 1st Cl. Hon. Mods 1938; BA 1942; MA 1943. Served Leics Regt, 1940–46; Staff Coll., Quetta, 1943; GSO2, 1943–44. GSO1 HQ 14th Army, 1945. Hon. Lieut-Col 1946 (despatches). Fellow of All Souls Coll., 1946–73, Emeritus, 1976–, Estates Bursar, 1961–66, Sub-Warden, 1965–67. Barrister, Inner Temple, 1947, Bencher, 1966; QC 1960; Recorder of Canterbury, 1962–68; a Judge of the High Court of Justice, Queen's Bench Div., 1968–70; Director: J. Henry Schroder Wagg & Co. Ltd, 1970–75; Schroder International Ltd, 1973–75; Thomas Tilling plc, 1970–83; Equity and Law Life Assurance Soc. plc, 1975–. Mem., Gen. Council of the Bar, 1959–63, 1964–68, Vice-Chm., 1965–66, Chm., 1966–68; Vice-Pres., Senate of the Four Inns of Court, 1966–68; Vice-Pres., Bar Assoc. for Commerce, Finance and Industry, 1973–. Pres., Howard League, 1983–; Chairman: Cttee of Inquiry into Abuse of the Social Security System, 1971; City Cttee on Company Law, 1974–76; Cttee of Inquiry into self-regulation at Lloyd's, 1979–80; Appeal Cttee, Panel on Take-overs and Mergers, 1981–; Jt Commn on the Constitution (set up by Social Democratic and Liberal Parties), 1981–83; Investment Management Regulatory Orgn, 1986–. Conducted inquiry into Confait case, 1976–77. Member: Private Internat. Law Cttee, 1961–63; Coun. on Tribunals, 1962–65; Law Reform Cttee, 1963–66; Council, Marlborough Coll., 1967–83 (Chm., 1977–82); BBC Programmes Complaints Commn, 1972–79; Governing Body, Imperial Coll., 1973– (Chm., 1975–); Trustee, Pilgrim Trust, 1965– (Chm., 1979–83). Hon. mem., Lloyd's, 1983. Hon. Fellow, Darwin Coll., Cambridge, 1984. Hon. LLD Hull, 1979. *Recreations:* music, walking. *Address:* Garden End, SN8 1LA; (professional) 1 Hare Court, Temple, EC4. *T:* 01-353 3171. *Club:* Travellers'.
See also Hon. F. F. Fisher.

FISHER, Rev. James Atherton; *b* 1 May 1909; *s* of Rev. Legh Atherton Fisher and Beatrice Edith Fisher; *m* 1938, Joan Gardiner Budden; two *s* one *d. Educ:* Haileybury; Sidney Sussex Coll., Cambridge (Scholar); 1st cl. Theological Tripos Pts I and II (Senior Scofield Prize); Cuddesdon Theological Coll; BA 1932, MA 1945; Deacon 1933; Priest, 1934; Asst Curate: St Matthew's, Oxhey, 1933–36; The Priory Church, Dunstable, 1936–39; Chaplain of Bedford Sch., 1939–43; Vicar of St Paul's, Peterborough, 1943–53; Religious Broadcasting Asst, BBC, 1953–58; Chaplain of St Christopher's Coll., Blackheath, 1954–58; Chaplain of Heathfield Sch., Ascot, 1959–64. Canon of St George's, Windsor, 1958–78; Treasurer, 1962–77; Founder Mem., Council of St George's House, Windsor Castle, 1966–78 (resp. for Clergy trng, 1966–74). *Address:* 32 High Lawn, Devizes, Wilts. *T:* Devizes 4254.
See also P. A. Fisher.

FISHER, James Neil; Partner, Theodore Goddard & Co., Solicitors, 1951–83, Senior Partner, 1980–83; *b* 27 May 1917; *s* of Henry John Fisher and Ethel Marie Fisher; *m* 1953, Elizabeth Mary Preston, *d* of late Bishop Arthur and Mrs Nancy Preston; one *s* two *d. Educ:* Harrow Sch.; Balliol Coll., Oxford (MA). Served War, Royal Signals, 1940–46 (Major 1945; despatches). Admitted solicitor, 1949. Rochester Diocesan Adv. Cttee for the Care of Churches, 1984. *Recreations:* the piano, walking, reading. *Address:* Ridge Lea, Oak Avenue, Sevenoaks, Kent TN13 1PR. *Club:* City University.

FISHER, John Mortimer, CMG 1962; HM Diplomatic Service, retired; *b* 20 May 1915; *yr s* of late Capt. Mortimer Fisher (W Yorks Regt) and Mrs M. S. Fisher (*née* Bailey); *m* 1949, Helen Bridget Emily Caillard; two *s. Educ:* Wellington; Trinity Coll., Cambridge. Entered Consular (subseq. Diplomatic) Service, 1937; Probationer Vice-Consul, Bangkok, 1938; served at Casablanca, 1942, Naples, 1944; 1st Sec. in Foreign Office, 1946, Mexico City, 1949; Detroit, Mich., USA, 1952; Counsellor in charge of British Information Services, Bonn, 1955; an Inspector in HM Foreign Service, 1959; Counsellor and Consul-Gen. at Bangkok, 1962; Consul-General, Düsseldorf, 1966–70; part-time Course Dir (Eur. Trng), Civil Service Coll., 1971–85; *Address:* The North Garden, Treyford, Midhurst, West Sussex. *T:* Harting 448.

FISHER, Ven. Leslie Gravatt; Archdeacon of Chester and Canon Residentiary of Chester Cathedral, 1965–75; Vice-Dean, 1973–75; Archdeacon Emeritus since 1975; *b* 18 Aug. 1906; *m* 1935, Dorothy Minnie, (*née* Nash); two *d. Educ:* Hertford Grammar Sch.; London Coll. of Divinity. ALCD 1933. Deacon, 1933; Priest 1934. Curate of Emmanuel, Northwood, 1933–36; Vicar of St Michael and All Angels, Blackheath Park, 1936–39; Rector of Bermondsey, 1939–47; Curate-in-charge, Christ Church, Bermondsey, 1942–47; Chap., Bermondsey Med. Mission Hosp., 1946–47; Home Sec., CMS, and Licensed Preacher, Diocese of Southwark, 1947–; License to Officiate, Bromley, Dio. of Rochester, 1948–. Chm., Church Information Cttee, 1966–75. *Recreations:* music and photography. *Address:* 14 Lamb Park, Chagford, Newton Abbot, Devon. *T:* Chagford 3308.

FISHER, Mrs Margery Lilian Edith; free-lance writer, editor of review journal; *b* 21 March 1913; *d* of late Sir Henry Turner, and late Edith Rose; *m* 1936, James Maxwell McConnell Fisher (*d* 1970); three *s* three *d. Educ:* Rangi Ruru Sch., Christchurch, NZ; Amberley House Sch., NZ; Somerville Coll., Oxford (1st Cl. Hons English; MA, BLitt). Taught English at Queen Anne's Sch., Caversham, and Oundle Sch., 1939–45; coach for university scholarships and entrance exams; some broadcasting (BBC) of book reviews, free-lance lectr; Editor and proprietor of Growing Point (private jl reviewing children's books); Children's Books Editor, Sunday Times. Eleanor Farjeon Award, 1966; May Arbuthnot Award, USA, 1970. *Publications:* (with James Fisher) Shackleton, a biography, 1957; Intent upon Reading (criticism), 1961, rev. edn 1964; Field Day (novel), 1951; Matters of Fact, 1972; Who's Who in Children's Books, 1975; The Bright Face of Danger (criticism), 1986; Classics (monograph), 1986; articles in Review of English Studies. *Recreations:* music, gardening. *Address:* Ashton Manor, Northampton NN7 2JL. *T:* Roade 862277.

FISHER, Mark; MP (Lab) Stoke-on-Trent Central, since 1983; an Opposition Whip, since 1985; *b* 29 Oct. 1944; *m* 1971, Ingrid Geach; two *s* two *d. Educ:* Eton College; Trinity College, Cambridge. MA. Documentary film producer and script writer, 1966–75; Principal, Tattenhall Centre of Education, 1975–83. Chairman: PLP Educn Cttee, 1984–85; PLP Arts Cttee, 1984–85; Vice-Chm., PLP Treasury Cttee, 1983–84. Contested (Lab) Leek, 1979. Staffordshire County Councillor, 1981– (Chm., Libraries Cttee, 1981–83). *Address:* 8 Bakewell Street, Penkhull, Stoke-on-Trent. *T:* Stoke-on-Trent 46757.

FISHER, Maurice; RCNC; General Manager, HM Dockyard, Rosyth, 1979–83; *b* 8 Feb. 1924; *s* of William Ernest Fisher and Lily Edith (*née* Hatch); *m* 1955, Stella Leslie Sumsion; one *d. Educ:* St Luke's Sch., Portsmouth; Royal Dockyard Sch., Portsmouth; Royal Naval Coll., Greenwich. Constructor-in-Charge, HM Dockyard, Simonstown, 1956–60; Staff of Director of Naval Construction, 1960–63; Staff of C-in-C Western Fleet, 1963–65; Dep. Supt, Admiralty Experiment Works, Haslar, 1965–68; Dep. Prodn Manager, HM Dockyard, Devonport, 1968–72; Personnel Manager, HM Dockyard, Portsmouth, 1972–74; Planning Manager, 1974–77, Prodn Manager, 1977–79, HM Dockyard, Devonport. *Recreation:* game fishing. *Address:* Waterside, The Street, Chilompton, Bath BA3 4EN.

FISHER, Max Henry, (Fredy Fisher); Director, S. G. Warburg & Co. Ltd, since 1981; *b* 30 May 1922; *s* of Fritz and Sophia Fischer; *m* 1952, Rosemary Margaret Maxwell; two *s* one *d. Educ:* Fichte-Gymnasium, Berlin; Rendcomb Coll.; Lincoln Coll., Oxford. FO Library, working on German War Documents project, 1949–56; Vis. Lectr, Melbourne Univ., 1956; Financial Times, 1957–80, Editor, 1973–80. Director: Commercial Union Assurance Co., 1981–; Booker McConnell, 1981–. Governor, LSE, 1981–. *Publication:* (ed with N. R. Rich) The Holstein Papers. *Recreations:* reading, listening to music. *Address:* 16 Somerset Square, Addison Road, W14 8EE. *T:* 01–603 9841. *Club:* Reform.

FISHER, Rt. Rev. Brother Michael, SSF, **(Reginald Lindsay Fisher);** Minister-General, Society of Franciscans, since 1985; Assistant Bishop, Diocese of Ely, since 1985; *b* 6 April 1918; *s* of late Reginald Watson Fisher and Martha Lindsay Fisher. *Educ:* Clapham Central School; Bolt Court; Westcott House, Cambridge. Member, Society of St Francis, 1942. Deacon 1953, priest 1954, dio. Ely; Licence to officiate: Diocese of Ely, 1954–62; Newcastle, 1962–67; Sarum, 1967–79. Minister Provincial, SSF, 1967–79. Bishop Suffragan of St Germans, 1979–85; Bishop to HM Prisons, 1985. MA Lambeth, 1978. *Recreations:* poetry, music, cinema; people. *Address:* 15 Botolph Lane, Cambridge, Cambs CB2 3RD. *T:* Cambridge 353903.

FISHER, Prof. Michael Ellis, FRS 1971; Horace White Professor of Chemistry, Physics and Mathematics, since 1973, Chairman, Department of Chemistry, 1975–78, Cornell University; *b* 3 Sept. 1931; *s* of Harold Wolf Fisher and Jeanne Marie Fisher (*née* Halter); *m* 1954, Sorrel Castillejo; three *s* one *d. Educ:* King's Coll., London. BSc 1951, PhD 1957, FKC 1981. Flying Officer (Educn), RAF, 1951–53; London Univ. Postgraduate Studentship, 1953–56; DSIR Sen. Research Fellow, 1956–58. King's Coll., London: Lectr in Theoretical Physics, 1958–62; Reader in Physics, 1962–64; Prof. of Physics, 1965–66; Prof. of Chemistry and Maths, Cornell Univ., 1966–73. Guest Investigator, Rockefeller Inst., New York, 1963–64; Vis. Prof. in Applied Physics, Stanford Univ., 1970–71; Walter Ames Prof., Univ. of Washington, 1977; Vis. Prof. of Physics, MIT, 1979; Sherman Fairchild Disting. Scholar, CIT, 1984; Vis. Prof. in Theoretical Physics, Oxford, 1985. Lectures: Buhl, Carnegie-Mellon, 1971; 32nd Richtmyer Meml, 1973; 17th Fritz London Meml, 1975; Morris Loeb, Harvard, 1979; H. L. Welsh, Toronto, 1979; Bakerian, Royal Soc., 1979; Welch Foundn, Texas, 1979; Alpheus Smith, Ohio State Univ., 1982; Laird Meml, Univ. of Western Ontario, 1983; Fries, Rensselaer Polytechnic Inst., NY, 1984; Amos de-Shalit Meml, Weizmann Inst., Rehovoth, 1985; Cherwell-Simon, Oxford, 1985. John Simon Guggenheim Memorial Fellow, 1970–71, 1978–79; Fellow, Amer. Acad. of Arts and Scis, 1979; For. Associate, National Acad. of Sciences, USA, 1983. Hon. FRSE 1986. Irving Langmuir Prize in Chemical Physics, Amer. Phys. Soc., 1970; Award in Phys. and Math. Scis, NY Acad. of Scis, 1978; Guthrie Medal, Inst. of Physics, 1980; Wolf Prize in Physics, State of Israel, 1980; Michelson-Morely Award, Case-Western Reserve Univ., 1982; James Murray Luck Award, National Acad. of Sciences, USA, 1983; Boltzmann Medal, Internat. Union of Pure and Applied Physics, 1983. *Publications:* Analogue Computing at Ultra-High Speed (with D. M. MacKay), 1962; The Nature of Critical Points, (Univ. of Colorado) 1964, (Moscow) 1968; contribs to Proc. Roy. Soc., Phys. Rev., Jl Sci. Insts, Jl Math. Phys., Arch. Rational Mech. Anal., Jl Chem. Phys., Rept Prog. Phys., Rev. Mod. Phys., Physica, etc. *Recreations:* Flamenco guitar, travel. *Address:* Baker Laboratory, Cornell University, Ithaca, New York 14853, USA. *T:* (607) 255 4205.

FISHER, Nancy Kathleen; *see* Trenaman, N. K.

FISHER, Sir Nigel (Thomas Loveridge), Kt 1974; MC 1945; MA (Cambridge); *b* 14 July 1913; *s* of late Comdr Sir Thomas Fisher, KBE, Royal Navy and of late Lady Shakespeare; step *s* of Rt Hon. Sir Geoffrey Shakespeare, 1st Bt; *m* 1935, Lady Gloria Vaughan (marr. diss. 1952), *e d* of 7th Earl of Lisburne; one *s* one *d*; *m* 1956, Patricia, *o d* of late Lieut-Col Sir Walter Smiles, CIE, DSO, DL, MP (*see* Lady Fisher). *Educ:* Eton; Trinity Coll., Cambridge. Served War of 1939–45; volunteered Welsh Guards and commissioned as 2nd Lieut 1939; Hook of Holland, Boulogne, 1940 (despatches); Capt., 1940; Major, 1944; N West Europe, 1945 (wounded, MC). Mem., National Executive Cttee of Conservative Party, 1945–47 and 1973–83; contested Chislehurst (N Kent), Gen. Election, 1945. MP (C): Herts, Hitchin, 1950–55; Surbiton, 1955–74; Kingston-upon-Thames, Surbiton, 1974–83. Mem. British Parl. Deleg. to Sweden, 1950, W Indies 1955, Malta 1966, Canada 1966, Uganda 1967, special mission to St Kitts, Anguilla, 1967. Parly Private Sec. to Minister of Food, 1951–54, to Home Sec., 1954–57; Parly Under-Sec. of State for the Colonies, July 1962–Oct. 1963; Parly Under-Sec. of State for Commonwealth Relations and for the Colonies, 1963–64; Opposition Spokesman for Commonwealth Affairs, 1964–66. Treasurer, CPA, 1966–68 (Vice-Chm., 1975–76; Treasurer 1977–79, Dep. Chm., 1979–83, UK Branch). Mem. Exec., 1922 Cttee, 1960–62, 1969–83. Pres., British Caribbean Assoc. Member: British Bd of African Medical Research Foundn; Surbiton Conservative Assoc. Granted Freedom of Kingston-upon-Thames, 1983. *Publications:* Iain Macleod, 1973; The Tory Leaders, 1977; Harold Macmillan, 1982. *Recreations:* reading, writing, walking. *Address:* 45 Exeter House, Putney Heath, SW15; St George's Court, St George's Bay, Malta, GC. *Club:* MCC.

FISHER, Mrs O. H.; *see* Anderson, Marian.

FISHER, Patricia, (Lady Fisher); Founder and Co-Chairman, Women Caring Trust; *b* 5 April 1921; *d* of late Lieut-Col Sir W. D. Smiles, CIE, DSO, DL, MP for N Down; *m* 1st, 1941, Capt. Neville M. Ford (marr. diss., 1956), 2nd *s* of late Dr Lionel Ford, Headmaster of Harrow and Dean of York; two *d*; 2nd, 1956, Sir Nigel Fisher, *qv. Educ:* privately and abroad. MP (UU) North Down (unopposed return), April 1953–55 (as Mrs Patricia Ford). *Recreations:* sailing, travel. *Address:* 45 Exeter House, Putney Heath, SW15.
See also W. M. J. Grylls.

FISHER, (Phyllis) Anne; Headmistress, Wycombe Abbey School, 1962–74; *b* 8 March 1913; *d* of Rev. L. A. Fisher, Rector of Higham on the Hill, Nuneaton, and Beatrice Fisher (*née* Eustace). *Educ:* Sch. of St Mary and St Anne, Abbots Bromley; Bristol Univ. BA History Hons, 1938. Senior History Mistress: St Helen's, Northwood, 1938–41; St Anne's Coll., Natal, SA, 1941–44; Headmistress, St Winifred's Sch., George, SA, 1944–45; Joint Headmistress, St George's, Ascot, 1946–49; Headmistress, Limuru Girls' Sch., Limuru, Kenya, 1949–57; Headmistress, Arundel Sch., Salisbury, Rhodesia, 1957–61. *Recreations:* study of old churches, the history of painting. *Address:* 7 Selwyn House, Selwyn Road, Eastbourne BN21 2LF. *Clubs:* Royal Commonwealth Society, Landsdowne.
See also J. A. Fisher.

FISHER, Rear-Adm. Ralph Lindsay, CB 1957; DSO 1940; OBE 1941; DSC 1943; *b* 18 June 1903; *s* of F. Lindsay Fisher, CBE, one-time Pres. Inst. of Chartered Accountants, and Ethel Owen Pugh, Caernarvon; *m* 1934, Ursula Carver, Torquay; five *d. Educ:* Osborne and Dartmouth. First went to sea, 1920; Commanded: HMS Wakeful, 1940 (Dunkirk, DSO); Musketeer, 1943–45 (sinking of Scharnhorst, DSC); Solebay, 1947–48; Indefatigable, 1952–54. Naval Staff Course, 1934; Jt Services Staff Coll., 1949; Flag Officer Ground Trng (Home Air Comd), 1954–57. Retd, 1957. *Recreation:* sailing. *Address:* Scotnish Cottage, by Lochgilphead, Argyll. *T:* Tayvallich 646. *Clubs:* Naval and Military, Royal Cruising.
See also Baron Spens.

FISHER, Prof. Reginald Brettauer, CBE 1966; Professor of Biochemistry, University of Edinburgh, 1959–76, Dean of Faculty of Medicine, 1972–75; engaged in research, Medical Research Council, 1976–79, and postgraduate teaching, since 1976; *b* 13 Feb. 1907; *s* of late Joseph Sudbury and Louie Fisher; *m* 1929, Mary, *d* of late C. W. Saleeby; one *s* three *d. Educ:* King Edward VII Sch., Sheffield; St John's Coll., Oxford. MA, DPhil (Oxon), 1933. University Demonstrator in Biochemistry, Oxford, 1933–59; Rockefeller Travelling Fellow, 1939; Research Officer (on secondment), Min. of Home Security, 1942; Air Ministry, 1943–45; Consultant, US War Dept, 1945. Member: Physiological Soc.; Royal Society of Medicine. *Publications:* Protein Metabolism, 1954; contributions to: Biochem. Jl; Jl Physiol.; Jl Biol. Chem.; Am. Jl Physiol., etc. *Address:* University Laboratory of Physiology, Parks Road, Oxford.

FISHER, Richard Colomb; HM Diplomatic Service, retired; *b* Hankow, 11 Nov. 1923; *s* of Comdr Richard Fisher, RN and late Phillipa (*née* Colomb), Lee-on-Solent; *m* 1946, Edwine Kempers; two *s. Educ:* RNC Dartmouth. Joined Navy, 1937; to sea as Midshipman, 1941; War Service in submarines, 1943–45, Far East; flying trng, 1946–47; specialised in navigation/direction, 1948; Comdr 1958; retd from RN and joined Diplomatic Service, 1969; 1st Sec., Bonn, 1970–73; Commercial Counsellor, Warsaw, 1973–76, Rome, 1976–79. *Recreations:* history, languages. *Address:* c/o National Westminster Bank, Osborne Road, Southsea, Hants.

FISHER, Sylvia Gwendoline Victoria; Principal Soprano, Royal Opera House, London; *d* of John Fisher and Margaret Fisher (*née* Frawley); *m* 1954, Ubaldo Gardini (marr. diss.). *Educ:* St Joseph's Coll., Kilmore, Australia; Conservatorium of Music, Melbourne. Won "Sun" Aria Competition, Melbourne, 1936; International Celebrity Concert in Australia, 1947; tour of Australia, 1955. Operatic Debut in Cadmus and Hermione, 1932; Covent Garden Debut in Fidelio (Leonora), 1948. Appeared in: Rome (Sieglinde), 1952; Cagliari (Isolde), 1954; Bologna (Gutrune), 1955; Covent Garden (Brunnhilde), 1956; Frankfurt Opera House (in Der Rosenkavalier), 1957, etc. *Recreations:* gardening and rare books on singing.

FISHER, Thomas Gilbert F.; *see* Field-Fisher.

FISHLOCK, Dr David Jocelyn, OBE 1983; Science Editor, Financial Times, since 1967; *b* 9 Aug. 1932; *s* of William Charles Fishlock and Dorothy Mary Turner; *m* 1959, Mary Millicent Cosgrove; one *s. Educ:* City of Bath Boys' Sch. (now Beechen Cliff Sch.); Bristol Coll. of Technol. National Service, REME, 1955–58. Westinghouse Brake & Signal Co. Ltd, 1948–55; McGraw-Hill, 1959–62; New Scientist, 1962–67. Glaxo Travelling Fellow, 1978. Hon. DLitt Salford, 1982. Chemical Writer of the Year Award, BASF, 1982; Worthington Pump Award, 1982. Silver Jubilee Medal, 1977. *Publications:* The New Materials, 1967; Man Modified, 1969; The Business of Science, 1975; The Business of Biotechnology, 1982; (with Elizabeth Antêbi) La Genie de la Vie, 1985. *Recreations:* writing, reading, listening to people with something to say. *Address:* Traveller's Joy, Copse Lane, Jordans, Bucks HP9 2TA. *T:* Chalfont St Giles 3242. *Club:* Athenæum.

FISHLOCK, Trevor; journalist and author; roving foreign correspondent, The Daily Telegraph, since 1986; *b* 21 Feb. 1941; *m* 1978, Penelope Symon. *Educ:* Churcher's Coll., Petersfield; Southern Grammar Sch., Portsmouth. Portsmouth Evening News, 1957–62; freelance and news agency reporter, 1962–68; The Times: Wales and W England staff correspondent, 1968–77; London and foreign staff, 1978–80; S Asia correspondent, Delhi, 1980–83; New York correspondent, 1983–86. Fellow, World Press Inst., St Paul, Minnesota, 1977–78. Mem., Council for the Welsh Language, 1973–77. David Holden Award for foreign reporting, British Press Awards, 1983. *Publications:* Wales and the Welsh, 1972; Talking of Wales, 1975; Discovering Britain: Wales, 1979; Americans and Nothing Else, 1980; India File, 1983; The State of America, 1986; Indira Gandhi (for children), 1986. *Recreation:* sailing. *Address:* c/o The Daily Telegraph, Fleet Street, EC4.

FISKE, Dudley Astley; education consultant; *b* 16 June 1929; *s* of Tom Fiske and late Barbara Fiske; *m* 1958, Patricia Elizabeth, *d* of late Donald MacIver and of Helen MacIver, Weybridge; two *s* one *d. Educ:* Berkhamsted Sch.; Merton Coll., Oxford (MA). Asst Master, Barnard Castle Sch., 1953–56; Asst Tutor, Oxford Univ. Dept of Educn, 1956–58; Admin. Asst, East Sussex, 1959–60; Asst Educn Officer, Berkshire, 1961–65; Dep. Educn Officer, Leeds, 1965–68; Chief Educn Officer, Manchester, 1968–82; Educn Officer, AMA, 1983. Pres., Educnl Develt Assoc., 1969–74; Mem., Business Educn Council, 1974–80; President: British Educnl Equipment Assoc., 1973–74; Soc. of Educn Officers, 1978; Commonwealth Educn Fellow in Australia, 1974. *Address:* Farthings, High Street, Hook Norton, Oxon OX15 5NF. *T:* Hook Norton 737613. *Club:* Royal Commonwealth Society.

FISON, Sir Guy; *see* Fison, Sir R. G.

FISON, Sir (Richard) Guy, 4th Bt *cr* 1905; DSC 1944; Chairman, Fine Vintage Wines PLC, since 1985; *b* 9 Jan. 1917; *er s* of Sir William Guy Fison, 3rd Bt; *S* father, 1964; *m* 1952, Elyn Hartmann; one *s* one *d. Educ:* Eton; New Coll., Oxford. Served RNVR, 1939–45. Entered Wine Trade, 1948; Master of Wine, 1954; Dir, Saccone & Speed Ltd, 1952–82; Chairman: Saccone & Speed Internat., 1979–82; Percy Fox & Co. Ltd, 1982–83; Wine Develt Bd, 1982–83; Pres., Wine and Spirit Assoc., 1977–78. Hon. Freeman, 1976, Renter Warden, 1981–82, Upper Warden, 1982–83, Master, 1983–84, Vintners' Co. *Heir: s* Charles William Fison, *b* 6 Feb. 1954. *Address:* Wingate, Long Sutton, Basingstoke, Hants. *T:* Long Sutton 576. *Club:* MCC.

FISTOULARI, Anatole; Principal Conductor of London Philharmonic Orchestra, 1943, now guest conductor; *b* Kiev, Russia, 20 Aug. 1907; obtained British nationality, 1948; *s* of Gregor and late Sophie Fistoulari; *m* 1942, Anna Mahler (marr. diss., 1956); one *d*; 1957, Mary Elizabeth, *y d* of late James Lockhart, Edinburgh. *Educ:* Kiev, Berlin, and Paris. Conducted first concert at age of 7 at Opera House in Kiev and later all over Russia; at 13 gave concerts in Germany and Holland; at 24 conducted Grand Opera Russe in Paris at the Châtelet Theatre with Colonne Orchestra and Chaliapine with whom he then toured France and Spain; then conducted the Ballet de Monte-Carlo with Massine in Drury Lane and Covent Garden before the War; toured with same company all over America, France, and Italy; in England in 1941 started opera production of Sorotchinsky Fair by Moussorgsky; March 1942 gave first Symphony Concert with London Symphony Orchestra and later conducted it regularly at Cambridge Theatre; first concert with London Philharmonic Orchestra in Bristol, Jan. 1943; concert engagements in numerous countries, from 1949. Founder, 1946, and Principal Conductor, London Internat. Orch. Guest conductor for Sadler's Wells Ballet, Royal Opera House, Covent Garden and NY Metropolitan Opera House, 1955; on tour with London Philharmonic Orchestra, to Moscow, Leningrad, Paris, 1956. Has made recordings for several firms. *Recreation:* listening to good concerts. *Address:* Flat 4, 65 Redington Road, NW3. *Club:* Savage.

FITCH, Douglas Bernard Stocker, FRICS; Director, Land and Water Service, Agricultural Development and Advisory Service, Ministry of Agriculture, Fisheries and Food, since 1980; *b* 16 April 1927; *s* of William Kenneth Fitch and Hilda Barrington; *m* 1952, Joyce Vera Griffiths; three *s. Educ:* St Albans Sch.; Royal Agricl Coll. (Dip. 1951). FRICS 1977. Served Army, RE, 1944–48. Joined Land Service, MAFF, 1951; Divl Surveyor, Guildford, 1971; Regional Surveyor, SE Reg., 1979. Former Mem. Gen. Council, and Mem., Land Agency and Agric. Divl Council, RICS; Mem., Bd of Governors, 1981, Chm., Academic Bd, 1986–, Royal Agricl Coll. *Recreations:* golf, re-building old cars, allotmenteering. *Address:* Ministry of Agriculture, Fisheries and Food, Great Westminster House, Horseferry Road, SW1P 2AE. *T:* 01–216 6281; 71 Oasthouse Crescent, Hale, Farnham, Surrey GU9 0NP. *T:* Farnham 716742. *Clubs:* Farmers', Civil Service.

FITCH, Marcus Felix Brudenell, (Marc), CBE 1977; FSA; Founder, Marc Fitch Fund, 1956; *b* 5 Jan. 1908; *s* of Hugh Bernard Fitch and Bertha Violet (*née* James). *Educ:* Repton; Vienna and Geneva. FSA 1952. Served Intel. Corps, Belgian Congo, Eritrea and GHQ ME, 1940–46. Chm., Soc. of Genealogists, 1956. Founded English Surnames Survey, Leicester Univ., 1965; with Dame Joan Evans estabd Stratigraphical Mus., Knossos, 1966; founded Fitch Archaeological Lab., Athens, 1974; assisted rural re-foundn of St Catherine's British Embassy Sch., Athens, 1974. Master, Tallow Chandlers' Co., 1957. Associate Mem., All Souls Coll., Oxford, 1973. Hon. Fellow, St Cross Coll., Oxford, 1981. Hon. FBA 1978. Hon. DLitt Leicester, 1973. *Publications:* ed 10 vols for British Record Soc., 1959–86. *Clubs:* Athenæum, Garrick, Royal Automobile.

FITCH, Admiral Sir Richard (George Alison), KCB 1985; Second Sea Lord, Chief of Naval Personnel and Admiral President, Royal Naval College, Greenwich, since 1986; *b* 2 June 1929; *s* of Edward William Fitch and Agnes Jamieson Fitch; *m* 1969, Kathleen Marie-Louise Igert; one *s. Educ:* Royal Naval College, Dartmouth. Seagoing appointments, 1946–66; HMS Berwick in Command, 1966–67; Staff of Flag Officer, Second in Command, Far East Fleet, 1967–69; Directorate of Naval Plans, MoD, 1969–71; RCDS 1972; HMS Apollo in Command, 1973–74; Naval Asst to First Sea Lord, 1974–76; HMS Hermes in Command, 1976–78; Dir of Naval Warfare, 1978–80; Naval Secretary, 1980–83; Flag Officer, Third Flotilla and Comdr Anti-Submarine Group Two, 1983–85. Liveryman, Coachmakers' and Coach Harness Makers' Co. CBIM. *Recreations:* gardening, philately, following sport. *Address:* West Hay, 32 Sea Lane, Middleton-on-Sea, West Sussex PO22 7RT. *T:* Middleton-on-Sea 2361. *Clubs:* Royal Commonwealth Society; Middleton Sports.

FITCH, Rodney Arthur, FSIAD 1976; design consultant; Founder, 1971, major shareholder, Deputy Chairman, Creative Director and Joint Managing Director, Fitch and Company (Design Consultants) PLC (largest design company in Europe); *b* 19 Aug. 1938; *s* of Arthur and Ivy Fitch; *m* 1965, Janet Elizabeth, *d* of Sir Walter Stansfield, CBE, MC, QPM; one *s* four *d. Educ:* Willesden Polytechnic, Sch. of Building and Architecture; Central School of Arts and Crafts (Theatre, TV Design); Hornsey School of Art (Interior and Furniture Design). Trainee designer, Hickman Ltd, 1956–58; National Service, RAPC, 1958–60; Charles Kenrick Associates, 1960–62; Conran Design Gp Ltd, 1962–69; C.D.G. (Design Consultants) Ltd, 1969–71; thereafter, Fitch and Company, a multi-discipline design practice engaged on a wide range of UK and overseas projects from offices in London. Governor, St Martin's College of Art, 1976–. Vice-Pres., 1982–, Hon. Sec., 1984–, SIAD; Past Pres., Designers and Art Dirs Assoc., 1983. FRSA 1976. *Publications:* regular contributor to design publications. *Recreations:* horse riding, tennis, music, theatre, his family. *Address:* 5 Hanway Place, W1. *T:* 01–580 3060.

FITCHEW, Geoffrey Edward; Director-General (for Banking, Financial Services and Company Law), Directorate-General XV, European Commission, Brussels, since 1986; *b* 22 Dec. 1939; *s* of Stanley Edward Fitchew and Elizabeth Scott; *m* 1966, Mary Theresa Spillane; two *s. Educ:* Uppingham School; Magdalen Coll., Oxford (MA); London Sch. of Economics (MScEcon). Asst Principal, HM Treasury, 1964; Private Sec. to Minister of State, 1968–69; Principal, 1969; Gwilym Gibbon Research Fellow, Nuffield Coll., Oxford, 1973–74; Asst Sec., Internat. Finance Div., HM Treasury, 1975–77; Counsellor (Economics and Finance), UK Perm. Rep. to EEC, 1977–80; Asst Sec., HM Treasury, 1980–83; Under Sec., HM Treasury, 1983–86. *Recreations:* tennis, squash. *Address:* Directorate-General XV, Commission of the European Community, 6 Square de Meeus, Brussels, Belgium.

FITT, family name of **Baron Fitt.**

FITT, Baron *cr* 1983 (Life Peer), of Bell's Hill in the County of Down; **Gerard Fitt;** *b* 9 April 1926; *s* of George Patrick and Mary Ann Fitt; *m* 1947, Susan Gertrude Doherty; five *d* (and one *d* decd). *Educ:* Christian Brothers' Sch., Belfast. Merchant Seaman, 1941–53; various positions, 1953–. Councillor, later Alderman, Belfast Corp., 1958–81; MP (Eire Lab), Parlt of N Ireland, Dock Div. of Belfast, 1962–72; Mem. (SDLP), N Belfast, NI Assembly, 1973–75, NI Constitutional Convention, 1975–76; Dep. Chief Exec., NI Exec., 1974; elected MP (Repub. Lab) Belfast West, 1966, a founder and Leader, Social Democratic and Labour Party, and MP (SDLP), 1970–79, when resigned Leadership; MP (Socialist), 1979–83. Contested (Socialist) Belfast West, 1983. *Recreation:* full-time politics. *Address:* House of Lords, SW1A 0PW.

FITT, Robert Louis, CMG 1975; FEng; *b* 9 Aug. 1905; *s* of late R. F. Fitt; *m* 1936, Elsie Ockleshaw, *d* of late William Ockleshaw, Liverpool; one *s. Educ:* Launceston and Barnstaple Grammar Schs; City and Guilds Coll., London. BSc; FCGI. Engineer with Sudan Govt, 1927–31; with Mott Hay & Anderson, on Mersey Tunnel and London Underground Extensions, 1931–39. Joined Sir Alexander Gibb & Partners, 1939; Partner, 1946; retired, 1978; responsible for industrial develts, irrigation works, water supplies, thermal and hydro-electric power projects, airports, and economic develt surveys, in countries incl. UK, Iran, Iraq, Sudan, Argentina, Kenya, Tanzania, Swaziland, Rhodesia, Australia and Jamaica. Chm., Assoc. of Consulting Engineers, 1961–62; Vice-Pres., Middle East Assoc., 1972, Pres., Internat. Fedn of Consulting Engrs (FIDIC), 1972–74. FEng, FICE (Vice-Pres., 1976–78). Order of Homayoun, Iran, Third Class, 1955. *Recreations:* gardening, golf. *Address:* 27 Longdown Lane North, Ewell, Surrey KT17 3HY. *T:* 01–393 1727.

FITTALL, Betty Daphne C.; *see* Callaway-Fittall.

FITTER, Richard Sidney Richmond; author and naturalist; *b* 1 March 1913; *o s* of Sidney and Dorothy Fitter; *m* 1938, Alice Mary (Maisie) Stewart, *e d* of Dr R. S. Park, Huddersfield; two *s* one *d. Educ:* Eastbourne Coll.; LSE. BSc(Econ). Research staff: PEP, 1936–40; Mass-Observation, 1940–42; Operational Research Section, Coastal Command, 1942–45; Sec., Wild Life Cons. Special Cttee of Hobhouse Cttee on Nat. Parks, 1945–46;

Asst Editor, The Countryman, 1946–59; Open Air Corresp., The Observer, 1958–66; Dir, Intelligence Unit, Council for Nature, 1959–63; Editor, Kingfisher, 1965–72. Chm., Fauna and Flora Preservation Soc., 1983– (Hon. Secretary, 1964–81); Member: Species Survival Commn (formerly Survival Service Commn), Internat. Union for Cons. of Nature, 1963– (Chm., Steering Cttee, 1975–); Conservation Adv. Cttee, World Wildlife Fund Internat., 1977–79; Scientific Authority for Animals, DoE, 1965–81; Trustee, World Wildlife Fund, UK, 1977–83; Past Pres., Berks, Bucks and Oxfordshire Naturalists' Trust; Chm., Council for Nature, 1979; Hon. Sec., Falkland Is Foundn, 1980–82; Minister's Representative, Southern Council for Sport and Recreation, 1980–82; formerly Hon. Treasurer and Hon. Sec., British Trust for Ornithology; Chm., Gen. Purposes Cttee, Royal Soc. for Protection of Birds; Editor, The London Naturalist; and council or cttee mem. of numerous nat. history and conservation bodies. Scientific FZS. Officier, Order of the Golden Ark, The Netherlands, 1978. *Publications:* London's Natural History, 1945; London's Birds, 1949; Pocket Guide to British Birds, 1952; Pocket Guide to Nests and Eggs, 1954; (with David McClintock) Pocket Guide to Wild Flowers, 1956; The Ark in Our Midst, 1959; Six Great Naturalists, 1959; Guide to Bird Watching, 1963; Wildlife in Britain, 1963; Britain's Wildlife: rarities and introductions, 1966; (with Maisie Fitter) Penguin Dictionary of Natural History, 1967; Vanishing Wild Animals of the World, 1968; Finding Wild Flowers, 1972; Birds of Britain and Europe, with North Africa and the Middle East, 1972; (with A. Fitter and M. Blamey) Flowers of Britain and Northern Europe, 1974; The Penitent Butchers, 1979; (with M. Blamey) Handguide to the Wild Flowers of Britain and Northern Europe, 1979; (with M. Blamey) Gem Guide to Wild Flowers, 1980; (with N. Arlott and A. Fitter) The Complete Guide to British Wildlife, 1981; (ed with Eric Robinson) John Clare's Birds, 1982; (with A. Fitter and J. Wilkinson) Collins Guide to the Countryside, 1984; (with A. Fitter and A. Farrer) Grasses, Sedges, Rushes and Ferns of Britain and Northern Europe, 1984; (ed) The Wildlife of the Thames Counties, 1985. *Recreations:* botanising, observing wild and human life, exploring new habitats, reading. *Address:* Drifts, Chinnor Hill, Oxford OX9 4BS. *T:* Kingston Blount 51223. *Club:* Athenæum.

FITZALAN-HOWARD, family name of **Lady Herries of Terregles** and of **Duke of Norfolk.**

FITZALAN-HOWARD, Maj.-Gen. Lord Michael, GCVO 1981 (KCVO 1971; MVO 1952); CB 1968; CBE 1962; MC 1944; DL; Her Majesty's Marshal of the Diplomatic Corps, 1972–81; *b* 22 Oct. 1916; 2nd *s* of 3rd Baron Howard of Glossop, MBE, and Baroness Beaumont (11th in line), OBE; *b* of 17th Duke of Norfolk, *qv*; granted title and precedence of a Duke's son, 1975; *m* 1st, 1946, Jean (*d* 1947), *d* of Sir Hew Hamilton-Dalrymple, 9th Bt; one *d*; 2nd, 1950, Margaret, *d* of Capt. W. P. Meade-Newman; four *s* one *d*. *Educ:* Ampleforth Coll.; Trinity Coll., Cambridge. Joined Scots Guards, 1938. Served in: North West Europe, 1944–45; Palestine, 1945–46; Malaya, 1948–49; Egypt, 1952–53; Germany, 1956–57 and 1961–66; Commander Allied Command Europe Mobile Forces (Land), 1964–66; Chief of Staff, Southern Command, 1967–68; GOC London Dist, and Maj.-Gen. comdg The Household Division, 1968–71. Col: The Lancs Regt (Prince of Wales's Volunteers), 1966–70; The Queen's Lancashire Regiment, 1970–78; Colonel of The Life Guards, 1979–; Gold Stick to the Queen, 1979–; Joint Hon. Col, Cambridge Univ. OTC, 1968–71. Chm. Council, TAVR Assocs, 1973–81, Pres., 1981–84; Patron, Council, TA&VRA, 1984–. DL Wilts, 1974. Freeman, City of London, 1985. *Address:* Fovant House, Fovant, Salisbury, Wilts. *T:* Fovant 617. *Club:* Buck's.

FITZCLARENCE, family name of **Earl of Munster.**

FITZER, Herbert Clyde, CB 1971; OBE 1958; Head of Royal Naval Engineering Service, 1970–71, Director of Engineering (Ships), Navy Department, Ministry of Defence, 1968–71, retired; *b* 3 Nov. 1910; *s* of Herbert John Fitzer; *m* 1938, Queenie Stent; one *d*. *Educ:* Portsmouth Royal Dockyard Sch.; RNC Greenwich; London Univ. 1st cl. hons BSc (Eng) London, 1932; Greenwich Professional Certif. in Electrical Engrg, 1933. CEng, FIEE 1959. Asst Elec. Engr, Admty, 1936; Sheerness Dockyard, 1938; Elec. Engr, Submarine Design, Admty, 1939; Shore Estabs, 1945; Suptg Elec. Engr, Submarine Design, 1950; Asst Dir of Elec. Engrg, Ships Power Systems, 1961; Polaris Project, 1963; Dep. Dir of Elec. Engrg, 1966. Licensed Lay Reader, Dio. Bath and Wells. *Publication:* Christian Flarepath, 1956. *Address:* Rosefield, Sway Road, Lymington SO4 8LR. *T:* Lymington 73238.

FitzGEORGE-BALFOUR, Gen. Sir (Robert George) Victor, KCB 1968 (CB 1965); CBE 1945; DSO 1950; MC 1939; DL; Chairman, National Fund for Research into Crippling Diseases, since 1975; *b* 15 Sept. 1913; *s* of Robert S. Balfour and Iris (*née* FitzGeorge), 47 Wilton Crescent, SW1; *m* 1943, Mary (Diana), *er d* of Rear-Adm. Arthur Christian, 3 Sloane Gardens, SW3; one *s* one *d*. *Educ:* Eton; King's Coll., Cambridge (BA). Commissioned 2nd Lieut Coldstream Guards, 1934; Palestine, 1936; Middle East, 1937–43; France and NW Germany, 1944–46; commanded 2nd Bn Coldstream Guards, Malaya, 1948–52; idc 1955; Chief of Staff to Governor of Cyprus, 1956; Commanded 1st Guards Brigade, 1957; Chief of Staff, HQ Southern Comd, 1962–63; Dir of Military Operations, Ministry of Defence, 1964–66; Senior Army Instructor, IDC, 1966–68; Vice-Chief of the General Staff, 1968–70; UK Mil. Representative, NATO, 1971–73. ADC (Gen.), 1972–73. Col Comdt, HAC, 1976–84. DL West Sussex, 1977. Knight Commander of the Order of Orange Nassau with swords (Netherlands), 1946. *Address:* The Old Rectory, West Chiltington, West Sussex. *T:* West Chiltington 2255. *Club:* Army and Navy.

FITZGERALD, family name of **Duke of Leinster.**

FITZGERALD, Charles Patrick; Professor of Far Eastern History, Australian National University, 1953–67, now Emeritus; Visiting Fellow, Department International Relations, Australian National University, 1968–69; *b* 5 March 1902; *s* of Dr H. Sauer; *m* 1941, Pamela Knollys (*d* 1980); two *d* (and one *d* decd). *Educ:* Clifton. China, 1923–27, 1930–32, 1936–38, 1946–50. Leverhulme Fellowship for Anthropological Research in South-West China. DLitt ANU 1968. *Publications:* Son of Heaven, 1932; China, a Cultural History, 1935; The Tower of Five Glories, 1941; (with George Yeh) Introducing China, 1948; Revolution in China, 1951 (revised version (Penguin) as The Birth of Communist China, 1965); The Empress Wu, 1955; Flood Tide in China, 1958; Barbarian Beds: the origin of the chair in China, 1965; A Concise History of Eastern Asia, 1965; The Third China, Chinese Communities in SE Asia, 1965; Des Mantchous à Mao Tse-tong, 1968; History of China, 1969; Communism Takes China, 1970; The Southern Expansion of the Chinese People: Southern Fields and Southern Ocean, 1972; Mao Tsetung and China, 1976; Ancient China, 1978; Why China?, 1985. *Address:* 4 St Paul's Street, Randwick, NSW 2031, Australia. *Club:* Savile.

FITZ-GERALD, Desmond John Villiers, (29th Knight of Glin); Irish Agent, Christie, Manson & Woods Ltd, since 1975; *b* 13 July 1937; *s* of Desmond Windham Otho Fitz-Gerald, 28th Knight of Glin (*d* 1949), and Veronica (who *m* 2nd, 1954, Ray Milner, CC (Canada), QC, Edmonton, Alta, and Qualicum Beach, Vancouver Island, BC), 2nd *d* of late Ernest Amherst Villiers, MP, and of Hon. Elaine Augusta Guest, *d* of 1st Baron Wimborne; *m* 1st, 1966, Louise Vava Lucia Henriette (marr. diss. 1970), *d* of the Marquis de la Falaise, Paris; 2nd, 1970, Olda Ann, *o d* of T. V. W. Willes, 39 Brompton Sq., SW3; three *d*. *Educ:* Stowe Sch.; University of British Columbia (BA 1959); Harvard Univ. (MA 1961). FSA 1970. Asst Keeper, 1965–72, Dep. Keeper, 1972–75, Dept of Furniture and Woodwork, V&A. Director: Irish Georgian Foundn, 1974–; Irish Architecture Archive, 1975–; Historic Irish Tourist Houses Assoc., 1977– (Chm., 1982–86); Castletown Foundn, 1979–; Irish Landowners Convention, 1983–. Vice-Pres., Irish Georgian Soc.; Member: Heritage Gardens Cttee, An Taisce (Irish National Trust), 1978–; Steering Cttee, Internat. Union of Historic Houses Assocs, 1981–; Irish Historic Properties Cttee, 1982–. *Publications:* (ed) Georgian Furniture, 1969; (with Maurice Craig) Ireland Observed, a handbook to the buildings and antiquities, 1970; The Music Room from Norfolk House, 1972; (with Edward Malins) Lost Demesnes: Irish Landscape Gardening 1660–1845, 1976; (with Anne Crookshank) The Painters of Ireland, 1978; Irish Furniture, 1978; Catalogues: Irish Houses and Landscapes (jointly), 1963; Irish Architectural Drawings (jointly), 1965; Irish Portraits 1660–1860 (jointly), 1969; Mildred Anne Butler (jointly), 1981; articles and reviews on architecture and the decorative arts in many Art periodicals. *Address:* Glin Castle, Glin, Co. Limerick, Ireland. *TA:* Knight Glin. *T:* Listowel 34173 and 34112; 52 Waterloo Road, Dublin 4. *T:* Dublin 680585. *Clubs:* Beefsteak, White's; Kildare Street and University (Dublin).

FITZGERALD, Rev. (Sir) Edward Thomas, 3rd Bt *cr* 1903; a Roman Catholic priest; *b* 7 March 1912; *S* father, Sir John Joseph Fitzgerald, 2nd Bt, 1957, but does not use title. *Heir: b* Rev. Daniel Patrick Fitzgerald, *b* 28 June 1916.

FITZGERALD, Frank, PhD; FEng 1977; Managing Director, Technical, British Steel Corporation, and Chairman, British Steel Corporation (Overseas Services) Ltd, since 1981; *b* 11 Nov. 1929; *s* of George Arthur Fitzgerald and Sarah Ann (*née* Brook); *m* 1956, Dorothy Eileen Unwin; two *s* one *d*. *Educ:* Barnsley Holgate Grammar Sch.; Univ. of Sheffield (BScTech; PhD). FInstE, FIChemE. Ministry of Supply, RAE, Westcott, Bucks, 1955; United Steel Cos, Swinden Laboratories, Rotherham, 1960–68; British Steel Corporation, 1968–: Process Res. Manager, Special Steels Div., 1970; Head Corporate Advanced Process Laboratory, 1972; Director, R&D, 1977. Hadfield Medal, Iron and Steel Inst., for work on application of combustion and heat transfer science to industrial furnaces, 1972. *Publications:* papers in learned jls on heat and mass transfer and metallurgical processes. *Recreation:* rock climbing and mountaineering. *Clubs:* Alpine; Climbers'.

FITZGERALD, Garret, PhD; Barrister-at-Law; Member of the Dáil (TD) (FG) for Dublin South East, since 1969; Taoiseach (Prime Minister of Ireland), June 1981–March 1982 and since Dec. 1982; *b* Dublin, 9 Feb. 1926; *s* of late Desmond FitzGerald (Minister for External Affairs, Irish Free State, 1922–27, and Minister for Defence, 1927–32) and Mabel FitzGerald (*née* McConnell); *m* 1947, Joan, *d* of late Charles O'Farrell; two *s* one *d*. *Educ:* St Brigid's Sch., Bray; Coláiste na Rinne, Waterford; Belvedere Coll., University Coll., and King's Inns, Dublin. Called to the Bar, 1946. Research and Schedules Manager, Aer Lingus (Irish Air Lines), 1947–58; Rockefeller Research Asst, Trinity Coll., Dublin, 1958–59; College Lectr, Dept of Political Economy, University Coll., Dublin, 1959–73. Member: Seanad Eireann (Irish Senate), 1965–69; Dáil Cttee on Public Accounts, 1969–73; Minister for Foreign Affairs, Ireland, 1973–77; Leader and President, Fine Gael Party, 1977–; Leader of the Opposition, 1977–June 1981, and March-Dec. 1982. President: Council of Ministers, EEC, Jan.–June 1975; European Council, July–Dec. 1984; Irish Council of Eur. Movement, 1977–81 and March–Dec. 1982; Mem., Internat. Exec. Cttee of Eur. Movement, 1972–73 and 1977–81; Vice-Pres., Eur. People's Party, Eur. Parlt. Mem., Oireachtas Library Cttee, 1965–69; Governor, Atlantic Inst. of Internat. Relations, Paris, 1972–73 and 1977–81; Mem., Senate of National Univ. of Ireland. Formerly: Irish Correspondent of BBC, Financial Times, Economist and other overseas papers; Economic Correspondent, Irish Times; also Past Managing Dir, Economist Intelligence Unit of Ireland; Economic Consultant to Fedn of Irish Industries and Construction Industry Fedn, and Rep. Body for Guards; Past Member: Exec. Cttee and Council, Inst. of Public Admin; Council, Statistical and Social Inquiry, Soc. of Ireland; Senate Electoral Law Commn; Workmen's Compensation Commn; Transport Advisory Cttee for Second Programme; Cttee on Industrial Organisation; Gen. Purposes Cttee of Nat. Industrial Economic Council. Lectures: Radcliffe, Warwick Univ., 1979; Richard Dimbleby, BBC, 1982. Hon. LLD: New York, 1974; St Louis, 1974. *Publications:* State-sponsored Bodies, 1959; Planning in Ireland, 1968; Towards a New Ireland, 1972; Unequal Partners (UNCTAD), 1979; Estimates for Baronies of Minimum Level of Irish Speaking Amongst Successive Decennial Cohorts 1771–1781 to 1861–1871, 1984. *Address:* Department of Taoiseach, Government Buildings, Upper Merrion Street, Dublin 2, Ireland. *Club:* Royal Irish Yacht (Dun Laoghaire).

FitzGERALD, Sir George (Peter Maurice), 5th Bt *cr* 1880; 23rd Knight of Kerry; MC 1944; Major, Army, retired; *b* 27 Feb. 1917; *s* of Sir Arthur Henry Brinsley FitzGerald, 4th Bt, and Mary Eleanor (*d* 1967), *d* of late Capt. Francis Forester; *S* father 1967; *m* 1939, Angela Dora Mitchell; one *s* one *d*. *Educ:* Harrow; RMC, Sandhurst. Commnd into Irish Guards, 1937; 2nd in comd, 1st Bn, 1944; 2nd in comd, 2nd Bn, 1946; retired, 1948. *Heir: s* Adrian James Andrew Denis FitzGerald, *b* 24 June 1940. *Address:* Collin's Farm House, 55 High Street, Durrington, Salisbury, Wilts SP4 8AQ. *Club:* Army and Navy.

FITZGERALD, Brig. (retd) Gerald Loftus, CBE 1956; DSO 1945; *b* 5 May 1907; *s* of late Col D. C. V. FitzGerald, MC, Nairobi Kenya; *m* 1937, Mary Stuart, *d* of late Charles E. Mills, Holbrook, Suffolk; one *s* one *d*. *Educ:* Wellington Coll.; Royal Military Academy, Woolwich. Commissioned 2nd Lieut RA, 1926; Regimental duty UK and overseas, 1926–39; staff and regimental duty in UK and NW Europe during War of 1939–45. Brit. Mil. Mission to Greece, 1946–48; Chief Instructor, Officer Cadet Sch., 1949–50; Brit. Joint Services Mission, Washington, USA, 1951–52; Comdr Trg Bde, RA, 1953–55; Dep. Dir, War Office, 1956–58; retired pay, 1959. OStJ 1982. Order of Leopold (with Palm), Belgium, 1945; Croix de Guerre (with Palm), 1945. *Recreations:* field sports, travel. *Club:* Army and Navy.

FitzGERALD, Michael Frederick Clive, QC 1980; *b* 9 June 1936; *s* of Sir William James FitzGerald, *qv*, and Mrs E. J. Critchley; *m* 1966, Virginia Grace Cave; one *s* three *d*. *Educ:* Downside; Christ's Coll., Cambridge, 1956–59 (MA). 2nd Lieut 9th Queen's Royal Lancers, 1954–56. Called to the Bar, Middle Temple, 1961. *Recreations:* fishing, shooting. *Address:* East Lymden, Ticehurst, Sussex TN5 7JB. *Clubs:* Athenæum, Special Forces.

FITZGERALD, Prof. Patrick John; Professor of Law, Carleton University, Ottawa, since 1971; *b* 30 Sept. 1928; *s* of Dr Thomas Walter and Norah Josephine Fitzgerald; *m* 1959, Brigid Aileen Judge; two *s* one *d*. *Educ:* Queen Mary's Grammar Sch., Walsall; University Coll., Oxford. Called to the Bar, Lincoln's Inn, 1951; Ontario Bar, 1984. Fellow, Trinity Coll., Oxford, 1956–60. Professor of Law: Leeds Univ., 1960–66; Univ. of Kent at Canterbury, 1966–71. Visiting Prof., University of Louisville, 1962–63. Consultant, Law Reform Commn of Canada, 1973–. *Publications:* Criminal Law and Punishment, 1962; Salmond on Jurisprudence (12th edn), 1966; This Law of Ours, 1977; Looking at Law, 1979. *Recreations:* music, golf, bridge. *Address:* 207 Belmont Avenue, Ottawa, Canada.

FITZGERALD, Penelope Mary, (Mrs Desmond Fitzgerald); writer; *b* 1916; *d* of E. V. Knox and Christina Hicks; *m* 1941, Desmond Fitzgerald, MC; one *s* two *d*. *Educ:* Wycombe Abbey; Somerville Coll., Oxford (BA). *Publications:* Edward Burne-Jones, 1975; The Knox Brothers, 1977; The Golden Child, 1977; The Bookshop, 1978; Offshore, 1979 (Booker Prize); Human Voices, 1980; At Freddie's, 1982; (ed) William Morris's unpublished Novel on Blue Paper, 1982; Charlotte Mew and her Friends, 1984 (Rose Mary Crawshay Prize, 1985); Innocence, 1986. *Recreations:* listening, talking, growing orange and lemon trees. *Address:* c/o Wm Collins, 8 Grafton Street, W1X 3LA.

FitzGERALD, Sir William James, Kt 1944; MC; QC 1936; *b* Cappawhite, Co. Tipperary, May 1894; *s* of late Joseph FitzGerald, MB, Cappawhite; *m* 1st, 1933, Erica (marr. diss. 1946), *d* of F. J. Clarke, Chikupi Ranch, Northern Rhodesia; one *s*; 2nd, Cynthia Mary Mangnall, *d* of late W. Foster, OBE, Jerusalem; one step *s*. *Educ:* Blackrock Coll.; Trinity Coll., Dublin (Hon. LLD 1960). Served European War, Durham Light Infantry and XV Corps Mounted Troops (MC and Croix de Guerre); BA 1919; Barrister-at-Law, King's Inns, Dublin, 1922, and Middle Temple; Nigerian Administrative Service, 1920; Police Magistrate, Lagos, 1921; Crown Counsel, Nigeria, 1924; Solicitor-Gen., N Rhodesia, 1932; Attorney-Gen., N Rhodesia, 1933; Palestine, 1937–43; Chief Justice of Palestine, 1944–48. Pres. Lands Tribunal, 1950–65. *Address:* 47 Sussex Square, Brighton, Sussex. *Club:* Athenæum.

See also M. F. C. FitzGerald.

FITZGERALD, William Knight, CBE 1981; JP; DL; Convener, Tayside Regional Council, since 1978; *b* 19 March 1909; *e s* of John Alexander Fitzgerald and Janet Fitzgerald; *m* 1st, 1938, Elizabeth (*d* 1980), *d* of Alexander Grant; three *s*; 2nd, 1984, Margaret Eleanor Bell. *Educ:* Robertson Grammar Sch., S Africa. Assessor, Dundee Repertory Theatre, 1967–77; Member: Tayside Economic Consultative Group, 1970–77; Dundee Harbour Trust, 1970–73; University Court, Dundee, 1970–; Dundee Town Council, 1956; City Treasurer, 1967–70; Lord Provost of Dundee, and Lord Lieutenant of County of the City of Dundee, 1970–73; Chairman: Tay Road Bridge Joint Board, 1970–73 and 1975–; Dundee High Sch. Directors, 1970–73; Vice-Chairman: Dundee Coll. of Art and Technology, 1970–75; Scottish Council on Alcoholism, 1972–; E Scotland Water Bd, 1973–75. President: Convention of Scottish Local Authorities, 1979–82; Dundee Bn, Boys' Brigade. Dundee: JP 1948; DL 1974. Hon. LLD Dundee, 1981. *Recreations:* gardening, reading. *Address:* Morven, Roxburgh Terrace, Dundee DD2 1NZ. *T:* 68475. *Club:* University (Dundee).

FitzGIBBON, Louis Theobald Dillon; Comte Dillon in France; political writer; *b* 6 Jan. 1925; *s* of Comdr Francis Lee-Dillon FitzGibbon, RN, and Kathleen Clare (*née* Atchison), *widow* of Hon. Harry Lee-Dillon; *m* 1st, 1950, Josephine Miriam Maud (*née* Webb) (marr. diss.); 2nd, 1962, Madeleine Sally (*née* Hayward-Surry) (*d* 1980); one *s* two *d*; 3rd, 1980, Joan Elizabeth Jevons. *Educ:* St Augustine's Abbey Sch.; Royal Naval Coll., Dartmouth. Royal Navy, 1942–54 (incl. War of 1939–45); Polish interpreter's course, 1950–52. Dir, De Leon Properties Ltd, 1954–72. Solicitor's articled clerk, 1960–63; Anglo-Polish Conf., Warsaw, 1963. Personal Asst to the then Rt Hon. Duncan Sandys, MP (later Lord Duncan-Sandys), 1967–68; Gen. Sec., British Council for Aid to Refugees, 1968–72; United Nations (UNHCR) Mission to South Sudan, 1972–73; Dir of a medical charity, 1974–76; Exec. Officer, Nat. Assoc. for Freedom, 1977–78; Gen. Sec. of a trade assoc., 1978–80; missions to: Somalia, 1978, 1980–81; Sudan and Egypt, 1982; Sudan, German Parlt, Somalia and European Parlt, 1984. Member: RIIA, 1982; Anglo-Somali Soc.; Ethiopian Soc.; UN Assoc. Won first Airey Neave Meml Scholarship (proj. on Somalia), 1981. Hon. Secretary: Katyn Memorial Fund, 1971–77; British Horn of Africa Council, 1984. Area Pres., St John Amb. Brigade (Hants East), 1974–76. Holds SMO Malta (Kt of Honour and Devotion and Officer of Merit). Polish Gold Cross of Merit, 1969; Order of Polonia Restituta (Polish Govt in Exile) (Officer, 1971; Comdr, 1972; Kt Comdr, 1976); Katyn Meml Medal Bronze, USA, 1977; Leaureate van de Arbeid, Netherlands, 1982. *Publications:* Katyn—A Crime without Parallel, 1971; The Katyn Cover-up, 1972; Unpitied and Unknown, 1975; Katyn—Triumph of Evil (Ireland), 1975; The Katyn Memorial, 1976; Katyn Massacre (paper) 1977, 2nd edn 1979; Katyn (USA), 1979; Katyn Horror (in German), 1979; The Betrayal of the Somalis, 1982 (commnd by Somali Govt in Arabic, French, German and Italian, 1984); Straits and Strategic Waterways in the Red Sea, 1984; Ethiopia Hijacks the Hijack, 1985; The Evaded Duty, 1985; reports on: Soviet Influence behind the Tripartite Pact of Aden, 1982; Sudan, 1984; contribs to internat. and nat. jls and publications, inc. Sudanow (Khartoum) and Heegan (Mogadishu). *Recreations:* travelling, politics, writing, reading, history, languages, refugee problems, Horn of Africa affairs, Islamic matters, *pro deo*. *Address:* Flat 2, 8 Portland Place, Brighton BN2 1DG. *T:* Brighton 685661. *Club:* Beefsteak.

FitzHARRIS, Viscount; James Carleton Harris; *b* 19 June 1946; *o s* and *heir* of 6th Earl of Malmesbury, *qv*; *m* 1969, Sally Ann, *yr d* of Sir Richard Newton Rycroft, *qv*; three *s* two *d*. *Educ:* Eton; Queen's Coll., St Andrews (MA). *Heir:* *s* Hon. James Hugh Carleton Harris, *b* 29 April 1970. *Address:* Heather Row Farm House, Nately Scures, Basingstoke, Hants RG27 9JP. *T:* Hook 3138.

FITZHERBERT, family name of **Baron Stafford.**

FitzHERBERT, Giles Eden, CMG 1985; HM Diplomatic Service; Minister, HM Embassy, Rome, since 1983; *b* Dublin, 8 March 1935; *e s* of late Captain H. C. FitzHerbert, Irish Guards, and Sheelah, *d* of J. X. Murphy; *m* 1962, Margaret Waugh (*d* 1986); two *s* three *d*. *Educ:* Ampleforth Coll.; Christ Church Oxford; Harvard Business Sch. 2nd Lieut, 8th King's Royal Irish Hussars, 1957–58. Vickers da Costa & Co., 1962–66. First Secretary: Foreign Office, 1966; Rome, 1968–71; FCO, 1972–75; Counsellor: Kuwait, 1975–77; Nicosia, 1977–78; Head of Eur. Community Dept (Ext.), FCO, 1978–82; on sabbatical leave, LSE, 1982; Inspector, FCO, 1983. Contested (L) Fermanagh and South Tyrone, Gen. Elect., 1964. *Address:* Cove House, Cove, Tiverton, Devon. *Clubs:* Beefsteak; Kildare Street and University (Dublin).

FitzHERBERT, Sir John (Richard Frederick), 8th Bt, *cr* 1784; TD; *b* 15 Sept. 1913; *s* of Ven. Henry E. FitzHerbert, sometime Archdeacon of Derby, and Hon. Margaret Elinor (*d* 1957), *d* of 3rd Baron Heytesbury; *S* uncle, Sir William FitzHerbert, 7th Bt, 1963; *m* 1957, Kathleen Anna Rees; no *c*. *Educ:* Charterhouse; Royal Agricultural Coll., Cirencester. Served War of 1939–45, Sherwood Foresters (TA). FLAS 1950; FRICS 1970. *Heir:* *nephew* Richard Ranulph FitzHerbert, *b* 2 Nov. 1963. *Address:* Tissington Hall, Ashbourne, Derbyshire. *T:* Parwich 246. *Club:* Derby County (Derby).

FITZHERBERT-BROCKHOLES, Michael John, JP; Vice Lord-Lieutenant of Lancashire, since 1977; *b* 12 June 1920; *s* of John William Fitzherbert-Brockholes and Eileen Agnes; *m* 1950, Mary Edith Moore; four *s*. *Educ:* The Oratory Sch.; New Coll., Oxford. Scots Guards, 1940–46. Mem., Lancs CC, 1968–; Chm., Educn Cttee, 1977–81. JP 1960, DL 1975, Lancs. KSG 1978. *Recreation:* gardening. *Address:* Claughton Hall, Garstang, near Preston, Lancs. *T:* Brock 40286.

FitzHUGH, James, QC 1973; **His Honour Judge FitzHugh;** a Circuit Judge, since 1976; *b* 2 April 1917; *s* of T. J. FitzHugh and S. FitzHugh (formerly Jocelyn); *m* 1955, Shelagh (*née* Bury), *d* of R. W. and B. Bury, Lytham St Annes. *Educ:* St Bede's Coll., Manchester; Manchester Univ. (BA (Admin)); London Univ. (LLB). Commissioned in Supplementary Reserve of Officers, RA, 1938; War of 1939–45: Captain, GSO. Called to Bar, Gray's Inn, and became a Member of Northern Circuit, 1948. *Recreations:* travel, golf. *Address:* 186 St Leonard's Road East, St Annes on the Sea, Lytham St Annes, Lancs. *T:* St Annes 723068. *Clubs:* St James's (Manchester); Royal Lytham and St Annes Golf.

FITZ-MAURICE, family name of **Earl of Orkney.**

FITZMAURICE; *see* Mercer Nairne Petty-Fitzmaurice, family name of Marquess of Lansdowne.

FITZMAURICE, Lt-Col Sir Desmond FitzJohn, Kt 1946; CIE 1941; late RE; *b* 17 Aug. 1893; *s* of John Day Stokes Fitzmaurice, ICS, Tralee, Co. Kerry; *m* 1926, Nancy (*d* 1975), *d* of Rev. John Sherlock Leake, Grayswood, Surrey; one *s* three *d*. *Educ:* Bradfield; RMA, Woolwich; Cambridge Univ. Joined RE, 1914. Served in France, Belgium and Italy, European War, 1914–18 (despatches); Instructor, RMA Woolwich, 1918–20; Cambridge Univ., 1920–22; Instructor, Sch. of Military Engineering, Chatham, 1923, 1924; hp list, 1925; Deputy Mint Master, Bombay, 1929–30; Calcutta, 1931–32; Deputy Master, Security Printing, India, 1932; Master Security Printing and Controller of Stamps, India, 1934; retired. *Address:* Lincombe Lodge, Fox Lane, Boars Hill, Oxford OX1 5DN.

See also G. J. Milton-Thompson.

FitzPATRICK, Air Cdre David Beatty, CB 1970; OBE 1953; AFC 1949 and Bar, 1958; *b* 31 Jan. 1920; *s* of late Comdr D. T. FitzPatrick, RN and Beatrice Anne Ward; *m* 1941, Kathleen Mary Miles; one *d*. *Educ:* Kenilworth Coll., Exeter; Midhurst. Commnd RAF, 1938; served War of 1939–45, Atlantic, Mediterranean and Far East theatres; comd No 209 Sqdn (Far East), 1944; (GD Pilot) Sqdn flying duty, 1945–52; cfs, pfc and GW Specialist, RAF Henlow, 1952–57; GW (Trials) Project Officer, Min. of Supply, 1957–59; Base Comdr Christmas Island, 1959–60 (British Nuclear Trials); NATO Def. Coll., and jssc, 1960–61; Dep. Dir (Ops) Air Staff, 1961–64; comd RAF Akrotiri and Nicosia, 1964–66; Dir of (Q) RAF, MoD, 1966–69; attached NBPI for special duty, 1969; Dir, Guided Weapons (Trials and Ranges), Min. of Technology, 1969–72; Dir, Guided Weapons Trials, MoD (PE), 1972–74; retd RAF, 1975; Head, teaching dept of indep. sch., 1975–85, retd. FBIM 1970; FRMetS 1984; MRAeS 1971. *Recreations:* swimming (Life Vice-Pres., Royal Air Force Swimming Assoc.), deep-sea fishing, cricket. *Address:* Whistledown, 38 Courts Mount Road, Haslemere, Surrey. *T:* Haslemere 4589. *Clubs:* Royal Air Force; Naval, Military and Air Force (Adelaide).

FITZPATRICK, Gen. Sir (Geoffrey Richard) Desmond, GCB 1971 (KCB 1965; CB 1961); DSO 1945; MBE 1943; MC 1939; *b* 14 Dec. 1912; *o s* of late Brig.-Gen. Sir Richard Fitzpatrick, CBE, DSO, and Lady (G. E.) Fitzpatrick; *m* 1944, Mary Sara, *o d* of Sir Charles Campbell, 12th Bt; one *s* one *d*. *Educ:* Eton; RMC Sandhurst. Commissioned The Royal Dragoons, 1932. Served in Palestine, 1938–39 (MC); War of 1939–45 (despatches, MBE, DSO); in Middle East, Italy, NW Europe. Bt. Lieut-Col 1951; Col 1953; ADC to the Queen, 1959; Maj.-Gen. 1959; Asst Chief of Defence Staff, Ministry of Defence, 1959–61; Dir Mil. Ops, War Office, 1962–64; Chief of Staff, BAOR, 1964–65; Lt-Gen. 1965; GOC-in-C, N Ire., 1965–66; Vice-Chief of Gen. Staff, 1966–68; Gen. 1968; C-in-C, BAOR, and Commander N Army Gp 1968–70; Dep. Supreme Allied Comdr, Europe, 1970–73; ADC (General) to the Queen, 1970–73. Lieutenant-Governor and C-in-C, Jersey, 1974–79. Col, The Royal Dragoons, 1964–69; Dep. Col., 1969–74, Col, 1979–, The Blues and Royals, and Gold Stick to the Queen, 1979–; Col Comdt, RAC, 1971–74. *Address:* Belmont, Otley, Suffolk IP6 9PF. *Clubs:* Cavalry and Guards; Royal Yacht Squadron.

FITZPATRICK, James Bernard, CBE 1983; JP; DL; Chairman: Mersey Docks and Harbour Company, since 1984; Liverpool Health Authority, since 1986; *b* 21 April 1930; *s* of late B. A. Fitzpatrick and Mrs J. E. Fitzpatrick; *m* 1965, Rosemary, *d* of late Captain E. B. Clark, RD and bar, RNR (Croix de Guerre avec Palme, Polish Golden Cross of Merit with Swords), and late Mrs K. E. Clark, Claughton; one *s* one *d*. *Educ:* Bootle Grammar Sch.; London Univ. (LLB). Admitted Solicitor, 1962; FCIT 1973 (AMInstT 1954, by examination); CBIM. Joined Mersey Docks and Harbour Bd, 1951: various management posts from 1965; Personnel and Industrial Relns Dir, 1971, on formation of Mersey Docks and Harbour Co.; Jt Man. Dir, 1974; Dep. Chief Exec., 1975; Man. Dir and Chief Exec., 1977. Dir, Plan Invest Group plc, 1984–. Chairman: Nat. Assoc. of Port Employers, 1979–82 (Vice-Chm., 1973–79); Employers' Assoc. of Port of Liverpool, 1974–83; Member: Liverpool Dock Labour Bd, 1974–76 (Chm., 1976); Exec. Council, British Ports Assoc., 1976– (Dep. Chm., 1985–); Nat. Dock Labour Bd, 1978–84; Vice Pres., Inst. of Materials Handling, 1978. FIMH. JP Liverpool 1977. DL Merseyside, 1985. *Recreations:* fell walking, gardening, music, reading. *Address:* 30 Abbey Road, West Kirby, Merseyside. *T:* 051–625 9612; Pierhead, Liverpool L3 1BZ. *T:* 051–200 7003. *Clubs:* Oriental, Pilgrims.

FITZPATRICK, Air Marshal Sir John (Bernard), KBE 1984; CB 1982; Royal Air Force, retired; Independent Panel Inspector, Departments of the Environment and Transport, since 1986; *b* 15 Dec. 1929; *s* of Joseph Fitzpatrick and Bridget Fitzpatrick; *m* 1954, Gwendoline Mary Abbott; two *s* one *d*. *Educ:* St Patrick's School, Dungannon, N Ireland; Royal Air Force College, Cranwell. Officer Commanding: No 81 Sqdn, 1966–68; No 35 Sqdn, 1971–72; Group Captain Plans to AOC No 18 Gp, 1973; OC, RAF Scampton, 1974–75; RCDS, 1976; Dir of Ops (Strike), RAF, 1977–79; SASO, HQ Strike Command, 1980–82; Dir Gen. of Organisation, RAF, 1982–83; AOC No 18 Gp, RAF, and Comdr Maritime Air Eastern Atlantic and Channel, 1983–86. *Recreations:* golf, reading, carpentry. *Address:* c/o Lloyds Bank, 23 Market Place, Fakenham, Norfolk NR21 9BT. *Club:* Royal Air Force.

FITZPATRICK, John Ronald; Solicitor and Parliamentary Officer, Greater London Council, 1977–85, Consultant, 1985–86; *b* 22 Sept. 1923; *s* of Henry Fitzpatrick and Mary Lister; *m* 1952, Beryl Mary Newton; two *s* one *d*. *Educ:* St Bede's Coll., Manchester; Univ. of Manchester (LLB). Admitted Solicitor, 1947; LMRTPI 1951. Asst Solicitor: Burnley, 1947; Stockport, 1948–51; Asst/Principal Asst Solicitor, Mddx CC, 1951–65; Asst Clerk/Asst Dir-Gen., GLC, 1965–69; Asst Dir, 1969–72, Dir, 1972–77, Planning and Transportation, GLC. *Recreations:* golf, bridge. *Address:* Courtlands, 2 Langley Grove, New Malden, Surrey. *T:* 01–942 8652.

FitzROY, family name of **Duke of Grafton** and of **Southampton Barony.**

FitzROY, Charles; late 2nd Lieutenant Royal Horse Guards and Pioneer Corps; *b* 3 Jan. 1904; *o s* of 4th Baron Southampton, OBE, and late Lady Hilda Mary Dundas, *d* of 1st Marquess of Zetland; *S* father, 1958, as 5th Baron Southampton, but disclaimed his title for life, 16 March 1964; *m* 1st, 1927, Margaret (*d* 1931), *d* of Prebendary H. Mackworth Drake, Vicar of Paignton; one *s*; 2nd, 1940, Mrs Joan Leslie (marr. diss., 1944); 3rd, 1951, Rachel Christine, *d* of Charles Zaman, Lille, France. *Educ:* Harrow. Served Royal Horse Guards, 1923–25; re-employed, 1940, with RA, Pioneer Corps, 1941. Joint-master, Grove Fox-hounds, 1930–32. *Heir:* (*to disclaimed barony*): *s* Hon. Charles James FitzRoy [*b* 12

Aug. 1928; *m* 1951, Pamela Anne, *d* of E. Henniker, Maidenhead, Berks; one *s* one *d* (and one *s* decd)]. *Address:* Preluna Hotel, Sliema, Malta.

FitzROY NEWDEGATE, family name of **Viscount Daventry**.

FITZSIMMONS, Rt. Hon. William Kennedy, PC (N Ireland) 1965; JP; *b* 31 Jan. 1909; *m* 1935, May Elizabeth Lynd; two *d*. *Educ:* Skegoniell National Sch.; Belfast Techn. Sch. Mem., Belfast City and Dist Water Comrs, 1948–57 (Chm. 1954–55); Pres., Duncairn Unionist Assoc.; N Ireland Parliament: MP, Duncairn Div. of Belfast, 1956–72; Dep. Govt Whip, 1961–63; Parl. Secretary, Min. of Commerce, 1961–65; Min. of Home Affairs, 1963–64; Min. of Develt, 1964–65; Min. of Education, 1965–66 and 1968–69; Minister of Development, 1966–68; Minister of Health and Social Services, 1969–72. MRSH; JP Belfast, 1951. *Address:* 4 Tudor Oaks, Holywood, Co. Down, Northern Ireland BT18 0PA.

FITZWALTER, 21st Baron, *cr* 1295; **(Fitzwalter) Brook Plumptre,** JP; Hon. Captain, The Buffs; *b* 15 Jan. 1914; *s* of late George Beresford Plumptre, Goodnestone, Canterbury, Kent; *S* uncle, 1943 (FitzWalter Barony called out of abeyance in his favour, 1953); *m* 1951, Margaret Melesina, *yr d* of (Herbert) William Deedes, JP, Galt, Hythe, Kent; five *s*. *Educ:* Diocesan Coll., Rondebosch, Cape; Jesus Coll., Cambridge. Served War of 1939–45, with the Buffs (Royal East Kent Regt) in France, Belgium, UK and India; attached RIASC, as Capt. JP Kent, 1949. Landowner and farmer; succeeded to family estate, 1943. *Heir: s* Hon. Julian Brook Plumptre, *b* 18 Oct. 1952. *Address:* Goodnestone Park, Canterbury, Kent. *T:* Nonington 840218.

FLACK, Bertram Anthony, CMG 1979; HM Diplomatic Service, retired; *b* 3 Feb. 1924; *y s* of Dr F. H. Flack and Alice Cockshut, Nelson, Lancs; *m* 1948, Jean W. Mellor; two *s* two *d*. *Educ:* Epsom Coll.; Liverpool Univ. (LLB Hons). Enlisted Gren. Gds, 1942; commissioned E Lancashire Regt, 1943; served in NW Europe (Captain). Joined Foreign Service, 1948; served Karachi, 1948–50; Alexandria, 1950–52; Stockholm, 1955–58; Accra, 1958–61; Johannesburg, 1964–67; Dep. High Comr, E Pakistan, 1967–68; Inspector, Diplomatic Service, 1968–70; Head of Communications Dept, FCO, 1971–73; Commercial Counsellor, Stockholm, 1973–75; Canadian Nat. Defence Coll., 1975–76; Dep. High Comr, Ottawa, 1976–79; High Comr, Repub. of Uganda, 1979–80. *Recreations:* cricket, golf. *Address:* Ripple Cottage, Douglas Street, Castletown, Isle of Man.

FLAGG, Rt. Rev. John William Hawkins; General Secretary, South American Missionary Society, since 1986; *b* 16 April 1929; *s* of Wilfred John and Emily Flagg; *m* 1954, Marjorie Lund; two *s* four *d*. *Educ:* All Nations Christian Coll.; Clifton Theological Coll. Agricultural missionary, Chile, 1951; Chaplain and Missionary Superintendent, St Andrew's, Asunción, Paraguay, 1959–64; Archdeacon, N Argentine, 1964–69; Diocesan Bishop of Paraguay and N Argentine, 1969–73; Bishop of Peru and Bolivia, 1973; Bishop, Diocese of Peru, 1977; Asst Bishop, Diocese of Liverpool, 1978–86; Vicar, St Cyprian's with Christ Church, Edge Hill, 1978–85; Priest-in-Charge of Christ Church, Waterloo, 1985–86. Member of Anglican Consultative Council, 1974–79; Presiding Bishop of Anglican Council of South America (CASA), 1974–77. *Address:* South American Missionary Society, Allen Gardiner House, Pembury Road, Tunbridge Wells, Kent TN2 3QU. *T:* Tunbridge Wells 38647.

FLAHIFF, His Eminence Cardinal George Bernard, CC (Canada) 1974; CSB, DD; Former Archbishop of Winnipeg; *b* Paris, Ontario, 26 Oct. 1905; *s* of John James Flahiff and Eleanor (*née* Fleming). *Educ:* St Michael's Coll. (BA); St Basil's Seminary; University of Strasbourg; Ecole des Chartes and Ecole des Hautes Etudes, Paris, 1931–35; Professor of Mediæval History, University of Toronto Graduate School and Pontifical Institute of Mediæval Studies, 1935–54; Superior General, Basilian Fathers, 1954–61; Archbishop of Winnipeg, 1961–82. Cardinal, 1969. Member: Sacred Congregation of Religious, Rome, 1967; Société de l'Ecole des Chartes (Paris); American Catholic Historical Society; Mediæval Academy of America. Hon. LLD: St John Fisher Coll., Rochester, NY, 1964; Seattle, 1965; Notre Dame, 1969; Manitoba, 1969; Windsor, 1970; Toronto, 1972; Hon. DD: Winnipeg, 1972; St Francis Xavier, 1973; Laval, 1974; Univ. of St Thomas, Houston, 1977. *Address:* 81 St Mary Street, Toronto, Ontario M5S 1J4, Canada.

FLANDERS, Dennis, RWS 1976 (ARWS 1970); RBA 1970; artist: townscapes and landscapes in pencil and water-colour; *b* 2 July 1915; *s* of late Bernard C. Flanders, ARAM (pianist), and Jessie Marguarite Flanders, ARMS (artist); *m* 1952, Dalma J. Darnley, *o d* of late J. Darnley Taylor and of Mrs Joan Darnley Taylor; one *s* one *d*. *Educ:* Merchant Taylors' Sch.; Regent Street Polytechnic; St Martin's Art Sch.; Central Sch. of Arts and Crafts, Princess Louise Gold Medal at age of 7. Mem. of St Paul's Watch, 1940–42; Royal Engineers, 1942–46. Occasional drawings for Daily Telegraph and other journals; series of drawings for Yorkshire Post, 1949; Birmingham Post, 1950–51; "Famous Streets," Sunday Times, 1952–53; Special artist to the Illustrated London News, 1956–64. Water-colours (reproduced as prints) of: RMA Sandhurst; Police Coll., Bramshill; St Edward's Sch., Oxford; Glencorse Barracks, Midlothian. Drawings in private collections and Nat. War Collection (1939–45), Guildhall Library, Bank of England, Nat. Library of Wales, and Museums at Exeter, York, Lincoln, Kensington, St Marylebone, Walthamstow, Wolverhampton, and Bury, Lancs. Exhibitor: RA and in provinces: one-man shows: London, 1947, 1951, 1953, 1955, 1964, 1967, 1986; Bedford, 1965, 1966, 1985; Boston (Lincs), 1966; Southport, 1969; Buxton-Lammas, Norfolk, 1972; Worthing, 1972; Cambridge, 1980; York, 1981; Fine Art Soc., London and Edin., 1984; George's Art Bookshop, Bristol, 1985. Member: Art Workers Guild (Master 1975); Soc. for Protection of Ancient Buildings. Freeman: City of London, 1970; Painter Stainers' Co., 1970. Lord Mayor's Art Award, 1966. *Publications: illustrations:* Bolton Abbey, 1947; Chelsea by Richard Edmonds, 1956; Soho for East Anglia by Michael Brander, 1963; A Westminster Childhood by John Raynor, 1973; The Twelve Great Livery Companies of London, 1973; (artist and author) Dennis Flanders' Britannia, 1984. *Recreations:* walking, riding, reading Who's Who. *Address:* 51 Great Ormond Street, WC1. *T:* 01–405 9317; Baker's Cross House, Cranbrook, Kent. *T:* Cranbrook 712018.

FLANNERY, Martin Henry; MP (Lab) Hillsborough, Sheffield, since Feb. 1974; *b* 2 March 1918; *m* 1949; one *s* two *d*. *Educ:* Sheffield Grammar Sch.; Sheffield Teachers' Trng College. Served with Royal Scots, 1940–46. Teacher, 1946–74 (Head Teacher, 1969–74). Chairman: Tribune Group, 1980–81; PLP's NI Cttee; Consultant MP for NUT. *Recreations:* music, rambling. *Address:* 53 Linaker Road, Sheffield S6 5DS.

FLATHER, Gary Denis; QC 1984; a Recorder, since 1986; *b* 4 Oct. 1937; *s* of Denis and Joan Flather; *m* Shreela Flather, *qv*; two *s*. *Educ:* Oundle Sch.; Pembroke Coll., Oxford (MA). Called to the Bar, Inner Temple, 1962. National Service, Second Lieut 1st Bn York and Lancaster Regt, 1956–58; Lieut Hallamshire Bn, TA, 1958–61. Asst Parly Boundary Comr, 1982–; Asst Recorder, 1983–86. Mem., Panel of Chairmen: for ILEA Teachers' Disciplinary Tribunal, 1974– (Chm., Disciplinary ILEA Tribunal, William Tyndale Jun. Sch. teachers, 1976); for Disciplinary Tribunal for London Polytechnics, 1982–; Vice-Chm., Community Council for Berks, 1985–. Escort to the Mayor of the Royal Borough of Windsor and Maidenhead, 1986–87. *Recreations:* travel, gardening, music, coping with multiple sclerosis. *Address:* Lamb Building, Temple, EC4Y 7AS. *T:* 01–353 6701. *Club:* Oriental.

FLATHER, Mrs Shreela, JP; Member, Commission for Racial Equality, 1980–86; Councillor, Royal Borough of Windsor and Maidenhead, since 1976 (first ethnic minority woman Councillor in UK), Mayor, 1986–87 (first Asian woman to hold this office); *b* India; *m* Gary Flather, *qv*; two *s*. *Educ:* University Coll. London (LLB). Called to the Bar, Inner Temple, 1962. Infant Teacher, ILEA, 1965–67; Teacher of English as a second lang., Altwood Comp. Sch., Maidenhead, 1968–74, Broadmoor Hosp., 1974–78. Member: Police Complaints Bd, 1982–85; Lord Chancellor's Legal Aid Adv. Cttee, 1985–; Cttee of Inquiry (Rampton, later Swann Cttee) into Educn of Children from Ethnic Minority Gps, 1979–85; Cons. Women's Nat. Cttee (formerly Cons. Women's Nat. Adv. Cttee), 1978–; Exec. Cttee, Anglo-Asian Cons. Soc., 1979–83; Bd of Visitors, Holloway Prison, 1981–83; HRH Duke of Edinburgh's Inquiry into British Housing, 1984–85; Management Cttee, Maidenhead CAB; Pres., Cambs Chilterns and Thames Rent Assessment Panel, 1983–; Trustee, Berks Community Trust. Governor: Altwood Comp. Sch., 1978–86; Slough Coll. of Higher Educn, 1984. Formerly: Vice-Chm. and Founder Mem., Maidenhead Community Relns Council; Mem., W Metrop. Conciliation Cttee, Race Relns Bd, 1973–78; Sec./Organiser, Maidenhead Ladies Asian Club, 1968–78; started New Star Boys' Club for Asian Boys and Summer Sch. Project for Asian children, Maidenhead; prepared English Teaching Scheme for Asian adults 'Stepping Stones'. JP Maidenhead, 1971. *Recreations:* travel, cinema. *Address:* Triveni, Ascot Road, Maidenhead, Berks. *T:* Maidenhead 25408. *Club:* Oriental.

FLATLEY, Derek Comedy, FJI; Public Affairs Correspondent, Southend Evening Echo, since 1970; *b* 16 Oct. 1920; *m* 1959, Valerie Eve Stevens; one *d*. *Educ:* Grammar sch. Trained West Essex Gazette, 1936. Served War of 1939–45: Household Cavalry, 1945. Army newspaper unit, Southend Standard, 1947; Chief Reporter, 1949. Mem., Press Council, 1968–72; Mem. Council (rep. Essex), Inst. of Journalists, 1957– (Pres. 1966–67); also Chairman: Salaries and Conditions Bd of the Inst., 1958–67; Estabt Cttee, 1963–65; Exec., 1967–70. Fellow, Inst. of Journalists, 1962–. *Recreations:* football, cricket, tennis. *Address:* Windyridge House, 22 Earls Hall Avenue, Southend-on-Sea, Essex. *T:* Southend-on-Sea 343485.

FLAVELL, Geoffrey, FRCS; FRCP; Hon. Consulting Thoracic Surgeon to: The London Hospital; Chelmsford and Harlow Districts Health Authorities; Whipps Cross Hospital; *b* 23 Feb. 1913; *o* surviving *s* of late W. A. Flavell, JP, of Wellington, NZ; *m* 1943, Joan Margaret, *o d* of S. Ewart Adams, Hawkwell, Essex; no *c*. *Educ:* Waitaki; Otago; University of New Zealand; St Bartholomew's Hospital, London. Qualified in medicine, 1937; House appts, St Bartholomew's Hosp., 1937–39; Resident Surgical Officer, Brompton Hosp., 1940–41. Surgeon Specialist, RAF, 1942, O/C Surgical Divs RAF Gen. Hosps, Carthage and Algiers, 1943; RAF Gen. Hosp., Cairo; Adviser in Surgery RAF Med. and Middle East Command, 1944; retired rank of Wing Comdr, 1958. Consultant Thoracic Surgeon, British Legion Hosp., and to LCC, 1946; Senior Registrar to London Hosp., 1947; Sen. Surgeon, Dept of Cardiovascular and Thoracic Surgery, London Hosp., 1950–78 (Chm., Surgical Div., 1974–77); Mem., Faculty of Med., Univ. of London, 1953–; Consultant Thoracic Surgeon, Royal Masonic Hosp., 1957–78; Sen. Thoracic Surgeon, Broomfield Hosp., 1947–78. Visiting Thoracic Surgeon to: Whipps Cross Hosp.; St Margaret's Hosp., Epping; Harold Wood Hosp.; Harts Hosp.; Oldchurch Hosp., Romford. Consultant, Qatar Govt, 1969–. Chm., Adv. Cttee on Cardiothoracic Surgery to NE Thames RHA, 1970–78; Sen. Mem., Soc. of Thoracic Surgeons of GB and Ireland. Touring Lectr for British Council, Middle and Far Eastern Univs, 1961; Ivor Lewis Lectr, N Mddx Hosp., 1978. Liveryman, Hon. Soc. of Apothecaries; Freeman, City of London. *Publications:* Introduction to Chest Surgery, 1957; Basic Surgery (Thoracic section), 1958; The Oesophagus, 1963; many contribs to surgical textbooks and med. jls; various articles on travel, wine and food, in lay periodicals. *Recreations:* history; architecture; literature and art; indulging the senses. *Address:* Belfield House, Weymouth, Dorset DT4 9RD. *T:* Weymouth 784013. *Club:* Royal Air Force.

FLAVELL, Dr Richard Anthony, FRS 1984; President, Biogen Research Corporation since 1982; Principal Research Officer, Biogen Group, since 1984; *b* 23 Aug. 1945; *s* of John T. and Iris Flavell; *m* Ellen Anna (*née* Haije); two *s*. *Educ:* Dept of Biochemistry, Univ. of Hull (PhD 1970); Univ. of Amsterdam (Royal Soc. Eur. Fellow); Univ of Zürich (Post-doctoral Fellow). Wetenschappelijk Medewerker, Univ. of Amsterdam, 1973–79; Head, Lab. of Gene Structure and Expression, NIMR, Mill Hill, 1979–82. Mem., EMBO, 1978–. Anniversary Prize, FEBS, 1980; Colworth Medal, Biochem. Soc., 1980. *Publications: chapters in:* Handbook of Biochemistry and Molecular Biology ed Fasman, 3rd edn 1976; McGraw-Hill Yearbook of Science and Technology, 1980; Eukaryotic Genes: their structure, activity and regulation, ed jtly with it Maclean and Gregory, 1983; articles in Biochem. Jl, Biochim. Biophys. Acta, Jl of Cell. Sci., Eur. Jl of Biochem., Jl of Mol. Biol., Nature, Nucl. Acids Res., Gene, Cell, Proc. Nat. Acad. Sci., Biochem. Soc. Trans, Trends in Biochem. Scis, EMBO Jl; contrib. Proceedings of symposia. *Recreations:* tennis, squash, sailing. *Address:* Biogen Research Corporation, 14 Cambridge Center, Cambridge, Mass 02142, USA. *T:* (617) 864–8900.

FLAVELLE, Sir (Joseph) David (Ellsworth), 3rd Bt *cr* 1917; *b* 9 Nov. 1921; *s* of Sir (Joseph) Ellsworth Flavelle, 2nd Bt, and of Muriel, *d* of William Norman McEachren; *S* father, 1977; *m* 1942, Muriel Barbara, *d* of Reginald Morton; three *d*. *Address:* Waterlot, 1420 Watersedge Road, Clarkson, Ontario L5J 1A4, Canada.

FLAXEN, David William; Assistant Director (Under Secretary), Central Statistical Office, since 1983; *b* 20 April 1941; *s* of late William Henry Flaxen and Beatrice Flaxen (*née* Laidlow); *m* 1969, Eleanor Marie Easton; two *d*. *Educ:* Manchester Grammar Sch.; Brasenose Coll., Oxford (BA Physics); University Coll. London (DipStat). Teacher, Leyton County High School for Boys, 1963; cadet statistician, 1963–64; statistical posts, Central Statistical Office and Min. of Labour, 1964–71; United Nations Adviser: Swaziland, 1971–72; Ghana, 1985–86; Statistician, Dept of Employment, 1973–75; Chief Statistician: Dept of Employment, 1975–76; Central Statistical Office, 1976–77 and 1981–83; Inland Revenue, 1977–81. *Publications:* contribs to articles in Physics Letters, Economic Trends, Dept of Employment Gazette, etc. *Recreations:* bridge, wine, cooking, music. *Address:* 65 Corringham Road, NW11 7BS. *T:* 01–458 5451.

FLECKER, James William, MA; Headmaster, Ardingly College, since 1980; *b* 15 Aug. 1939; *s* of Henry Lael Oswald Flecker, CBE, and Mary Patricia Flecker; *m* 1967, Mary Rose Firth; three *d*. *Educ:* Marlborough Coll.; Brasenose Coll., Oxford (BA, now MA Lit. Hum., 1962). Asst Master: Sydney Grammar Sch., 1962–63; Latymer Upper Sch., 1964–67; (and later Housemaster), Marlborough Coll., 1967–80. *Recreations:* hockey, cricket, flute playing, children's operas. *Address:* Ardingly College, Haywards Heath, West Sussex RH17 6SQ. *T:* Ardingly 892577.

FLEET, Kenneth George; Executive Editor (Finance and Industry), The Times, since 1983; *b* 12 Sept. 1929; *s* of late Fred Major Fleet and Elizabeth Doris Fleet; *m* 1953, (Alice) Brenda, *d* of late Captain H. R. Wilkinson, RD, RNR and Mrs Kathleen Mary Wilkinson; three *s* one *d*. *Educ:* Calday Grange Grammar Sch., Cheshire; LSE (BScEcons). Jl of

Commerce, Liverpool, 1950–52; Sunday Times, 1955–56; Dep. City Editor, Birmingham Post, 1956–58; Dep. Financial Editor, Guardian, 1958–63; Dep. City Editor, Daily Telegraph, 1963; City Editor, Sunday Telegraph, 1963–66; City Editor, Daily Telegraph, 1966–77; Editor, Business News, Sunday Times, 1977–78; City Editor, Sunday Express, 1978–82; City Editor-in-Chief, Express Newspapers plc, 1982–83. Dir, Young Vic, 1976–83; Chm., Chichester Fest. Theatre, 1985– (Dir, 1984–). Wincott Award, 1974. *Publication:* The Influence of the Financial Press, 1983. *Recreations:* theatre, books, sport. *Address:* c/o The Times, 1 Virginia Street, E1 9XN. *Clubs:* MCC, Lord's Taverners; Sussex CC; Chigwell Golf.

FLEET, Stephen George, PhD; FInstP; Registrary, University of Cambridge, since 1983; Vice Master, Downing College, Cambridge, since 1985 (Fellow since 1974; Bursar, 1974–83; President, 1983–85); *b* 28 Sept. 1936; *er s* of late George Fleet and of Elsie Fleet, Lewes, Sussex. *Educ:* Brentwood Sch.; Lewes County Grammar Sch.; St John's Coll., Cambridge (Scholar; MA; PhD 1962). FInstP 1972. Res. Physicist, Mullard Res. Labs, Surrey, 1961–62; Univ. of Cambridge: Demonstr in Mineralogy, 1962–67; Lectr in Mineralogy, 1967–83; Fellow, Fitzwilliam House, 1963–66; Fellow, Fitzwilliam Coll., 1966–73 (Jun. Bursar, 1967–73; Dir of Studies in Physical Sciences, 1971–74); Mem., Council of Senate, 1975–82; Mem., Financial Bd, 1979–83; Pres., Fitzwilliam Soc., 1977. Trustee, Mineralogical Soc. of GB, 1977–. Chm., Foundn of Edward Storey, 1984–. *Publications:* res. pubns in scientific jls. *Recreations:* books, music, history of Sussex. *Address:* Downing College, Cambridge CB2 1DQ. *T:* Cambridge 59491. *Club:* Athenæum.

FLEISCHMANN, Prof. Martin, FRS 1986; FRSC 1980; Research Professor, Department of Chemistry, University of Southampton, since 1983; *b* 29 March 1927; *s* of Hans Fleischmann and Margarethe Fleischmann (*née* Srb); *m* 1950, Sheila Flinn; one *s* two *d*. *Educ:* Worthing High School; Imperial College of Science and Technology. ARCS 1947; BSc 1948; PhD 1951. ICI Fellow, King's College, Univ. of Durham, 1952–57; Lectr, then Reader, Univ. of Newcastle upon Tyne, 1957–67; Electricity Council Faraday Prof. of Electrochemistry, Univ. of Southampton, 1967–77; Senior Fellowship, SERC, 1977–82. Pres., Internat. Soc. of Electrochemistry, 1970–72; Palladium Medal, US Electrochemical Soc., 1985. *Publications:* numerous papers and chapters in books. *Recreations:* ski-ing, walking, music, cooking. *Address:* Bury Lodge, Duck Street, Tisbury, Wilts SP3 6LJ. *T:* Tisbury 870384.

FLEMING, Sir Charles (Alexander), KBE 1977 (OBE 1964); FRS 1967; Honorary Fellow, Research School of Earth Sciences, Victoria University of Wellington, since 1986; Research Associate, National Museum of New Zealand, since 1983; Chief Palæontologist, New Zealand Geological Survey, Department of Scientific and Industrial Research, 1953–77; *b* 9 Sept. 1916; *s* of Geo. H. Fleming, Auckland, NZ; *m* 1941, Margaret Alison, *d* of S. G. Chambers, Auckland; three *d*. *Educ:* King's Coll., Auckland; University of Auckland. Boyhood interest in birds and shell-collecting led to participation in Auckland Mus. expedns, 1933–35; student fieldwork on birds of NZ and Chatham Is (basis of papers publ. 1939); Asst Geologist, NZ Geol Survey, 1940; subseq. Palæontologist and Sen. Palæontologist. Overseas service as coastwatcher, Auckland Is, 1942–43. Pres., Ornithol. Soc. NZ, 1948–49; NZ Delegate: Internat. Geol Congresses, 1948, 1960; British Commonwealth Conf. on Geology and Mineral Resources, 1948; Mem. Bd of Trustees: Nat. Art Gall. and National (formerly Dominion) Mus., 1954–76 (Chm., Mus. Council, 1972–75); Nat. Library, 1971–72; NZ Fauna Protection Adv. Council; NZ Nat. Commn for Unesco, 1966–70; Nat. Parks Authority, 1970–81; Environmental Council, 1970–73. President: Internat. Paleont. Union (Oceania Filial), 1964–68; Aust. and NZ Assoc. for Advancement of Science, 1968–70. FRSNZ 1952 (Pres. 1962–66); Fellow, Art Galls and Museums Assoc. of NZ, 1956; Corresp. Fellow, American Ornithologists' Union, 1962; Hon. FGS 1967; For. Mem., Amer. Philosophical Soc., 1973; Hon. FZS 1979; Sen. ANZAC Fellow, 1979. Several scientific prizes and awards. *Publications:* (ed) Checklist of New Zealand Birds, 1953; trans. Hochstetter's Geology of New Zealand, 1959; Marwick's Illustrations of New Zealand Shells, 1966; The Geological History of New Zealand and its Life, 1979; George Edward Lodge: Unpublished Bird Paintings, 1982; geol and palæontol bulletins; about 300 research papers on mollusca, cicadas, birds, geology, palæontology, biogeography. *Recreations:* recorded music, natural history. *Address:* Balivean, 42 Wadestown Road, Wellington, NZ. *T:* Wellington 737–288.

FLEMING, Ven. David; Archdeacon of Wisbech, since 1984; Vicar of Wisbech St Mary, since 1985; Hon. Canon of Ely Cathedral, since 1982; *b* 8 June 1937; *s* of John Frederick Fleming and Emma (*née* Casey); *m* 1966, Elizabeth Anne Marguerite Hughes; three *s* one *d*. *Educ:* Hunstanton County Primary School; King Edward VII Grammar School, King's Lynn; Kelham Theological Coll. National Service with Royal Norfolk Regt, 1956–58. Deacon 1963; Asst Curate, St Margaret, Walton on the Hill, Liverpool, 1963–67; priest 1964; attached to Sandringham group of churches, 1967–68; Vicar of Great Staughton, 1968–76; Chaplain of HM Borstal, Gaynes Hall, 1968–76; RD of St Neots, 1972–76; RD of March, 1977–82; Vicar of Whittlesey, 1976–85; Priest-in-Charge of Pondersbridge, 1983–85. Chm. of House of Clergy, Ely Diocesan Synod, 1982–85. *Recreations:* tennis, chess, extolling Hunstanton. *Address:* The Vicarage, Church Road, Wisbech St Mary, Wisbech, Cambs PE13 4RN. *T:* Wisbech 81596. *Club:* Whittlesey Rotary.

FLEMING, Hon. Donald Methuen, PC (Canada) 1957; QC (Ontario) 1944; *b* Exeter, Ont., 23 May 1905; *s* of Louis Charles and Maud Margaret Wright Fleming; *m* 1933, Alice Mildred Watson, Toronto; two *s* one *d*. *Educ:* public schools and Collegiate Inst., Galt; Univ. of Toronto (BA, LLB); Osgoode Hall Law Sch. Called to Bar, Ontario, 1928; subsequently practised in Toronto, 1928–57; Counsel to Blake, Cassels and Graydon, Barristers and Solicitors, Toronto, 1963–67. MP for Toronto-Eglinton, 1945–63; Minister of Finance and Receiver-General, 1957–62; Minister of Justice and Attorney-General of Canada, 1962–63. A Governor, Internat. Bank and IMF, 1957–63; Chairman: Commonwealth Finance Ministers' Conf., Mont Tremblant, Province of Quebec, 1957; Commonwealth Trade and Economic Conf., Montreal, 1958; OECD, 1961, 1962; Leader: delegn of Canadian Ministers to meetings of US-Canada Jt Trade and Economic Cttee, Washington, 1957, 1960, 1961 (Chm. Ottawa meeting, 1959, 1962), and meeting of Canada-Japan Jt Cttee of Ministers, Tokyo, 1963; Canadian delegn to OEEC Confs, Paris, 1960; Canadian delegate: NATO Conf. of Heads of Govt, Paris, 1957; NATO Ministerial Confs, 1958, 1959, 1961; Commonwealth Parly Confs, London, 1948, Ottawa, 1952, Nairobi, 1954. Has taken part in numerous parly, political, municipal and civic welfare activities and in church affairs. Man. Dir, Bank of Nova Scotia Trust Cos; General Counsel to Bank of Nova Scotia in Bahamas, 1968–80; Chm., M&G (Cayman) Ltd. Mem. Senate, 1944–48, Bd of Governors, 1964–68, Univ. of Toronto. Past Pres., Toronto YMCA. Hon. Mem., Canadian Legion; Hon. Life Mem., Canadian Bar Assoc. DCL hc Bishop's Univ., 1960; LLD hc Waterloo Lutheran Univ., 1967. *Publications:* So Very Near (political memoirs), 2 vols, 1985; numerous works and articles on legal subjects; contribs to legal periodicals including Canadian Encyclopedic Digest, Canadian Bar Review, Canadian Abridgement, etc. *Recreations:* all branches of sport. *Address:* 21 Country Lane, Willowdale, Toronto, Ont M2L 1E1, Canada. *Clubs:* Canadian (Pres., 1964), Empire, Granite, National, Queen's, Rosedale Golf, Toronto Cricket (Toronto).

FLEMING, Ian, RSA 1956 (ARSA 1947); RSW 1947; RWA 1975; Head, Gray's School of Art, Aberdeen, 1954–71, retired; *b* 19 Nov. 1906; *s* of John and Catherine Fleming; *m* 1943, Catherine Margaret Weetch; one *s* two *d*. *Educ:* Hyndland Sch., Glasgow; Glasgow Sch. of Art. Lectr, Glasgow Sch. of Art, 1931–48; Warden, Patrick Allen-Fraser Art Coll., Hospitalfield, Arbroath, 1948–54. Chm., Peacock Printmakers Workshop (Aberdeen), 1973–86. Hon. LLD Aberdeen, 1984. *Recreation:* anything Scottish. *Address:* 15 Fonthill Road, Aberdeen. *T:* 580680.

FLEMING, Rear-Adm. Sir John, KBE 1960; DSC 1944; Director of the Naval Education Service, 1956–60; *b* 2 May 1904; *s* of late James Fleming; *m* 1930, Jean Law (*d* 1986), *d* of late James Stuart Gillitt, South Shields; no *c*. *Educ:* Jarrow Grammar Sch.; St John's Coll., Cambridge. BA 1925, MA 1957. Entered RN as Instructor Lieut, 1925; Instr Lieut-Comdr, 1931; Instr Comdr, 1939; Instr Capt., 1950; Instr Rear-Adm., 1956. Asst Dir Naval Weather Service, 1945, Dep. Dir, 1947; Fleet Instructor Officer and Fleet Meteorological Officer, Home Fleet, 1950; Command Instructor Officer, The Nore, 1951; Education Dept, Admiralty, 1952. *Recreation:* gardening. *Address:* Mullion Cottage, Tanners Lane, Haslemere, Surrey. *T:* Haslemere 2412.

FLEMING, John, FRSL; writer; *b* 12 June 1919; *s* of Joseph Fleming and Elizabeth Stawart. *Educ:* Rugby Sch.; Trinity Coll., Cambridge (BA). FRSL 1963. Editor of Style & Civilisation, Art in Context, and, Architect and Society, for Penguin Books, 1964–. *Publications:* Robert Adam and his Circle in Edinburgh and Rome, 1962; (with Sir Nikolaus Pevsner and Hugh Honour) The Penguin Dictionary of Architecture, 1966, 3rd rev. edn 1980; (with Hugh Honour) The Penguin Dictionary of Decorative Arts, 1977; (with Hugh Honour) A World History of Art, 1982 (Mitchell Prize, 1982), rev. edn 1987 (US edn, The Visual Arts: a history). *Recreation:* gardening. *Club:* Travellers'.

FLEMING, John Bryden; retired; *b* 23 June 1918; *s* of W. A. Fleming, advocate, and Maria MacLeod Bryden; *m* 1942, Janet Louise Guthrie (*d* 1981); one *s* three *d*. *Educ:* Edinburgh Academy; Univs of Edinburgh and London. MA Hons Geog. Edinburgh, BScEcon London. Army, 1940–46, RASC and REME. Planning Officer, Dept of Health for Scotland, 1946; Principal, 1956; Asst Sec., Scottish Develt Dept, 1963, Under Sec., 1974–78; Sec., Scottish Special Housing Assoc., 1978–83. *Recreation:* gardening. *Address:* 10 Fettes Row, Edinburgh EH3 6SE. *T:* 031–557 4625. *Clubs:* Royal Commonwealth Society; Scottish Arts (Edinburgh).

FLEMING, John Marley; Vice President, Sales, General Motors, Europe, since 1986; *b* 4 April 1930; *s* of David A. Fleming and Mary L. Fleming (*née* Marley); *m* 1961, Jeanne (*née* Retelle); one *s* two *d*. *Educ:* Harvard Coll., Cambridge, Mass, USA (BA); Harvard Business Sch., Boston, Mass (MBA). Lieut US Navy, 1952–55. Dist Manager, Frigidaire Sales Corp., 1957–63; Sales Promotion Manager, Ford Motor Co., 1963–68; Vice-Pres., J. Walter Thompson Co., 1969; Dir of Marketing, Oldsmobile Div., GMC, 1970–76; Dir of Sales, Adam Opel AG, West Germany, 1977–79; Dir of Commercial Vehicles, 1980–81, and Chm. and Man. Dir, 1982–85, Vauxhall Motors Ltd. *Recreations:* ski-ing, sailing, golf. *Address:* Fischerhaus, Seestrasse 842/44, 8706 Meilen, Switzerland. *Clubs:* Harvard Business School of London; Harpenden Golf.

FLEMING, Rt. Rev. Launcelot; *see* Fleming, Rt Rev. W. L. S.

FLEMING, Raylton Arthur; Liaison Officer, United Nations University, World Institute for Development Economics Research, Helsinki, since 1984; *b* 1925; *s* of Arthur and Evelyn Fleming; *m* 1967, Leila el Doweini; one *s*. *Educ:* Worksop Coll. Associate Producer, World Wide Pictures Ltd, 1952; Head of Overseas Television Production, Central Office of Information, 1957; Dep. Dir, Films/Television Div., COI, 1961; Asst Controller (Overseas) COI, 1968; Actg Controller (Overseas), 1969; Dir, Exhibns Div. COI, 1971; Controller (Home), COI, 1972–76; Controller (Overseas), COI, 1976–78; Dir of Inf., UN Univ., Japan, 1978–83; Dir, UN Univ. Liaison Office, NY, 1983–84. *Recreations:* music, opera. *Address:* World Institute for Development Economics Research, Annankatu 42, 00100 Helsinki, Finland.

FLEMING, Rt. Rev. (William) Launcelot (Scott), KCVO 1976; DD (Lambeth); MA (Cambridge), MS (Yale); FRSE; *b* 7 Aug. 1906; *y s* of late Robert Alexander Fleming, MD, LLD; *m* 1965, Jane, *widow* of Anthony Agutter. *Educ:* Rugby Sch.; Trinity Hall and Westcott House, Cambridge; Yale Univ. Commonwealth Fund Fellow, Yale Univ., 1929–31; Deacon, 1933; Priest, 1934; Expeditions to Iceland and Spitzbergen, 1932 and 1933; Chaplain and Geologist, British Graham Land Expedition to the Antarctic, 1934–37; Polar Medal, 1935–37; Examining Chaplain to Bishop of Southwark, 1937–49, to Bishop of St Albans, 1940–43, to Bishop of Hereford, 1942–49; Fellow and Chaplain, Trinity Hall, Cambridge, 1933–49, Dean, 1937–49; Director of Scott Polar Research Institute, Cambridge, 1947–49; Bishop of Portsmouth, 1949–59; Bishop of Norwich, 1959–71; Dean of Windsor, 1971–76; Register, Order of the Garter, 1971–76; Domestic Chaplain to the Queen, 1971–76. Chaplain RNVR, HMS King Alfred, 1940; HMS Queen Elizabeth, 1940–43; HMS Ganges, 1943–44; Director of Service Ordination Candidates, 1944–46. Chairman: Church of England Youth Council, 1950–61; Archbishops' Advisers for Needs and Resources, 1963–73. Parly Gp for World Govt: Vice-Chm., 1969–71; Chm., Associate Members, 1971–76. Member: Council, Univ. of E Anglia, 1964–71; Royal Commn on Environmental Pollution, 1970–73; Chairman of Governors, Portsmouth Grammar Sch., 1950–59; Canford Sch., 1954–60; Mem., Governing Body, United World Coll. of the Atlantic; a Visitor, Bryanston Sch., 1984– (Governor, 1946–83); President: Young Explorers Trust, 1976–79; Trident Trust, 1983– (Trustee, 1972–); Trustee, Prince's Trust, 1976–83. Hon. Chaplain, RNR (RNVR 1950). Hon. Fellow, Trinity Hall, Cambridge, 1956; Hon. Vice-President, Royal Geographical Society, 1961. Hon. DCL Univ. of East Anglia, 1976. *Address:* Tithe Barn, Poyntington, near Sherborne, Dorset DT9 4LF. *T:* Corton Denham 479.

FLEMINGTON, Rev. William Frederick, MA Oxon, BD Cantab; Principal of Wesley House, Cambridge, 1955–67; held Greenhalgh Chair of New Testament Language and Literature, Wesley House, Cambridge, 1937–67, retired; *b* 24 May 1901; *er s* of Rev. William Frederick Flemington and Annie Mary Geden Bate; *m* 1930, Ethel Phyllis Goodenough, *er d* of Rev. John Henry Doddrell; one *s* one *d*. *Educ:* Liverpool Coll.; Jesus Coll., Oxford (Exhibitioner, 2nd Cl. Classical Hon. Mods, 2nd Cl. Lit. Hum.); Jesus Coll., Fitzwilliam Coll. and Wesley House, Cambridge (Carus Greek Testament Prize; 1st Cl. Theological Tripos, Pt II, Sect. 2, New Testament). Entered Wesleyan Methodist Ministry, 1925; Asst Tutor, Handsworth Coll., Birmingham, 1926–30; Minister in Stourbridge Circuit (Cradley), 1930–33; West Bromwich Circuit, 1933–37; Tutor, Wesley House, 1937–55. Select Preacher, Cambridge Univ., 1944, 1950, 1954. Pres. of Cambridge Theological Soc., 1963–65. *Publications:* The New Testament Doctrine of Baptism, 1948; contributor to Prayer and Worship, 1945; articles and reviews in Expository Times and Jl of Theological Studies. *Recreations:* walking, reading. *Address:* 204 Chesterton Road, Cambridge.

FLEMMING, John Stanton; Economic Adviser to the Governor, Bank of England, since 1984; *b* 6 Feb. 1941; *s* of Sir Gilbert Nicolson Flemming, KCB, and of Virginia Coit; *m* 1963, Jean Elizabeth (*née* Briggs); three *s* one *d*. *Educ:* Rugby Sch.; Trinity and Nuffield Colls, Oxon. BA Oxon 1962, MA 1966. Lecturer and Fellow, Oriel Coll., Oxford, 1963–65; Official Fellow in Economics, 1965–80, Emeritus Fellow, 1980, and Bursar,

1970–79, Nuffield Coll., Oxford. Chief Adviser, Bank of England, 1980–84. Member: Nat. Freight Corp., 1978–80; Council, Royal Economic Soc., 1980–; Adv. Bd on Research Councils, 1986–; Chm., Economic Affairs Cttee, SSRC, 1981–84. Associate Editor: Oxford Economic Papers, 1970–73; Review of Economic Studies, 1973–76; Editor, Economic Jl, 1976–80. *Publications:* Inflation, 1976; contrib. economic jls. *Address:* Bank of England, Threadneedle Street, EC4. *T:* 01-601 4963.

FLESCH, Michael Charles, QC 1983; *b* 11 March 1940; *s* of Carl and late Ruth Flesch; *m* 1972, Gail Schrire; one *s* one *d*. *Educ:* Gordonstoun Sch.; University College London (LLB 1st Cl. Hons). Called to the Bar, Gray's Inn, 1963 (Lord Justice Holker Sen. Schol.). Bigelow Teaching Fellow, Univ. of Chicago, 1963–64; Lectr (part-time) in Revenue Law, University Coll. London, 1965–82. Practice at Revenue Bar, 1966–. Chm., Taxation and Retirement Benefits Cttee, Bar Council, 1985–. Governor of Gordonstoun Sch., 1976–. *Publications:* various articles, notes and reviews concerning taxation, in legal periodicals. *Recreation:* all forms of sport. *Address:* (home) 38 Farm Avenue, NW2. *T:* 01–452 4547; (chambers) Gray's Inn Chambers, Gray's Inn, WC1. *T:* 01–242 2642. *Clubs:* Arsenal FC, Middlesex CCC, Brondesbury Lawn Tennis and Cricket.

FLETCHER, family name of **Baron Fletcher.**

FLETCHER; *see* Aubrey-Fletcher, family name of Baroness Braye.

FLETCHER, Baron *cr* 1970 (Life Peer), of Islington; **Eric George Molyneux Fletcher,** PC 1967; Kt 1964; LLD London; Solicitor, Consultant to Denton, Hall & Burgin, Gray's Inn and Paris; *b* 26 March 1903; *s* of late Clarence George Eugene Fletcher, Town Clerk of Islington; *m* 1929, Bessie Winifred, *d* of late James Butt, Enfield; two *s* one *d*. *Educ:* Radley; University of London, LLB London, 1923; Admitted Solicitor, 1924; BA London, 1926; LLD London, 1932; FSA 1954; FRHistS. MP (Lab) East Islington, 1945–70; Minister without Portfolio, 1964–66; Chairman of Ways and Means and Deputy Speaker, House of Commons, 1966–68. Mem. LCC for South Islington, 1934–49 (Chm. Finance Cttee); formerly Mem. Exec. Cttee Fabian Soc.; Dep. Chm., Associated British Picture Corp., 1946–64; Commissioner for Public Works Loans, 1946–55; Senator of London Univ., 1946–50 and 1956–74; Mem. Exec. Cttee, Grotius Soc.; Pres. of Selden Soc., 1967–70; Chm., Management Cttee, Inst. of Archaeology, 1968–73; Governor: Birkbeck Coll., 1934–62 (Hon. Fellow, 1983); London Sch. of Economics; Member: Evershed Cttee on Practice and Procedure of Supreme Court; Church Assembly, 1962; Commission on Church and State, 1951; Advisory Council on Public Records, 1959–64; Royal Commission on Historical Manuscripts, 1966–; Statute Law Cttee, 1951–76. A Trustee of the British Museum, 1968–77. Chm., Advisory Bd for Redundant Churches, 1969–74. Pres. British Archæological Assoc., 1960–63. *Publications:* The Students' Conflict of Laws, 1928 (with late E. Leslie Burgin); The Carrier's Liability, 1932; Benedict Biscop (Jarrow Lecture), 1981; miscellaneous articles on legal historical, and archæological subjects. *Recreations:* golf, swimming. *Address:* 90 Chancery Lane, WC2. *T:* 01–242 1212; The Barn, The Green, Sarratt, Rickmansworth, Herts WD3 6BP. *T:* King's Langley 65385. *Club:* Athenæum.

FLETCHER, Alan Gerard, RDI 1972; FSIAD; designer; Partner, Pentagram Design; *b* Nairobi, Kenya, 27 Sept. 1931; *s* of Bernard Fletcher and Dorothy Murphy; *m* 1956, Paola Biagi; one *d*. *Educ:* Christ's Hosp. Sch.; Central Sch. of Arts and Crafts; Royal Coll. of Art (ARCA); Sch. of Architecture and Design, Yale Univ. (Master of Fine Arts). FSIAD 1964. Designer, Fortune Magazine, New York, 1958–59; freelance practice, London, 1959–62; Partner: Fletcher Forbes Gill, 1962–65; Crosby Fletcher Forbes, 1965–72; Partner, Pentagram, 1972–. Pres., Designers and Art Dirs Assoc., 1973; Internat. Pres., Alliance Graphique Internat., 1982–85. Served on design competition juries for: Designers and Art Dirs Assoc. Exhibns, London; Internat. poster Biennale, Warsaw; Annual Awards for Newspaper Design, London; Art Dirs Club, Toronto; European Illustration, London; Common Market EEC symbol, Brussels; Amer. Inst. of Graphic Arts. Designers and Art Dirs Assoc. Gold Award for Design, 1974, and President's Award for Outstanding Contribn to Design, 1977; One Show Gold Award for Design, New York, 1974; Design Medal, SIAD, 1983. *Publications:* (jtly) Graphic Design: a visual comparison, 1963; (jtly) A Sign Systems Manual, 1970; (jtly) Identity Kits, 1971; (jtly) Living by Design, 1978; (also illus.) Was Ich Sah, 1967. *Address:* Pentagram, 11 Needham Road, W11 2RP. *T:* 01–229 3477.

FLETCHER, Alan Philip; QC 1984; *b* 28 June 1914; *s* of late Philip Cawthorne Fletcher, MC and Edith Maud Fletcher; *m* 1945, Annette Grace Wright; three *s* one *d*. *Educ:* Marlborough College; Trinity College, Oxford. MA; hockey blue, 1936 and 1937. War service, Army, England and India, 1939–45, ending as acting Lt-Col; called to the Bar, Inner Temple, 1940; bencher; Junior Counsel, Inland Revenue (Rating Valuation), 1969–84; Leader, Barnet London Borough Council, 1965–73. *Recreations:* walking, golf, architectural and garden history. *Address:* 8 New Square, Lincoln's Inn, WC2. *T:* 01–242 4986.

See also R. A. Fletcher.

FLETCHER, Hon. Sir Alan (Roy), Kt 1972; Minister for Education and Cultural Activities, Queensland, 1968–74, retired 1975; MLA (Country Party) for Cunningham, Queensland, 1953–74; *b* Pittsworth, 26 Jan. 1907; *s* of Alexander Roy Fletcher, Pittsworth, and Rosina Wilhemina (*née* McIntyre); *m* 1934, Enid Phair, *d* of James Thompson, Ashburton, NZ; two *s* two *d*. *Educ:* Irongate State Sch.; Scots Coll., Warwick, Qld. Pittsworth Shire: Councillor, 1945–57, Chm., 1949–57. Speaker, Legislative Assembly, Qld, 1957–60; Minister for Lands, 1960–68. Dir, Queensland Co-op. Milling Assoc., 1951–65. Member: Presbyterian Schs Council, Warwick, 1951– (Chm., 1958–61); Council, Darling Downs Inst. of Advanced Educn, 1975–. Pres., Old Boys' Assoc., Scots Coll., Warwick, 1948–. *Recreations:* shooting, croquet. *Address:* 3/11 Beresford Street, Pittsworth, Queensland 4356, Australia. *T:* 076–931–091.

FLETCHER, Alexander MacPherson; MP (C) Edinburgh Central, since 1983 (Edinburgh North, Nov. 1973–1983); *b* 26 Aug. 1929; *s* of Alexander Fletcher and Margaret Muirhead; *m* 1950, Christine Ann Buchanan; two *s* one *d*. *Educ:* Greenock High School. Chartered Accountant, 1956. Marketing Exec., internat. co., 1956–64; Man. Dir, 1964–71; private practice as Chartered Accountant, 1971–. Mem. East Kilbride Develt Corp., 1971–73. Opposition front bench spokesman on Scottish Affairs, 1977–79; Parly Under Sec. of State, Scottish Office, 1979–83, DTI, 1983–85. Mem., European Parlt, 1976–77. Contested (C) West Renfrewshire, 1970. Elder, Cramond Kirk. *Recreations:* golf, music. *Address:* House of Commons, SW1. *Clubs:* Royal Automobile; New (Edinburgh).

FLETCHER, Ann Elizabeth Mary, (Mrs Michael Fletcher); *see* Leslie, A. E. M.

FLETCHER, Dr Archibald Peter; Research Physician, Upjohn International Inc., Brussels, since 1979; *b* 24 Dec. 1930; *s* of Walter Archibald Fletcher and Dorothy Mabel Fletcher; *m* 1972, Patricia Elizabeth (*née* Marr); three *s* two *d*. *Educ:* Kingswood Sch.; London Hosp. Med. Coll.; St Mary's Hosp. Med. Sch., London Univ. MB, BS; PhD (Biochemistry). Sen. Lectr in Chemical Pathology, St Mary's Hosp., London, 1961–69; Head of Biochemistry, American Nat. Red Cross, USA, 1970–73; Med. Dir, Upjohn, Scandinavia; PMO, Medicines Div., DHSS, 1977; Med. Assessor to Cttee on Safety of Medicines; Chief Sci. Officer and SPMO, DHSS, 1978–79. *Publications:* numerous papers in scientific and medical journals on glycoproteins, physical chemistry and metabolism of blood cells. *Recreations:* gardening, golf. *Address:* Hall Corner Cottage, Little Maplestead, Halstead, Essex. *T:* Halstead 5465.

FLETCHER, Augustus James Voisey, OBE 1977; GM 1957; HM Diplomatic Service; Foreign and Commonwealth Office, since 1982; *b* 23 Dec. 1928; *s* of James Fletcher and Naomi Fletcher (*née* Dudden); *m* 1956, Enyd Gwynne Harries; one *s* one *d*. *Educ:* Weston-super-Mare Grammar Sch.; Oriental Language Institute, Malaya. Colonial Service, Palestine, 1946–48, Malaya, 1948–58; Min. of Defence, 1958–64; FCO, 1964–: Hong Kong (seconded HQ Land Forces), 1966–70; FCO, 1970–73; Hong Kong, 1973–76; FCO, 1976–79; Counsellor, New Delhi, 1979–82. *Recreations:* trout fishing, walking, food/wine, theatre. *Address:* c/o Foreign and Commonwealth Office, SW1. *Clubs:* Travellers', Royal Commonwealth Society.

FLETCHER, Charles Montague, CBE 1952; MD, FRCP, FFCM; Physician to Hammersmith Hospital, 1952–76; Professor of Clinical Epidemiology, University of London at Royal Postgraduate Medical School, 1973–76 (Reader, 1952–73), now Professor Emeritus; *b* 5 June 1911; *s* of late Sir Walter Morley Fletcher, FRS and late Mary Frances Fletcher (*née* Cropper); *m* Louisa Mary Sylvia Seely, *d* of 1st Baron Mottistone; one *s* two *d*. *Educ:* Eton Coll.; Trinity Coll., Cambridge (Sen. Schol.; rowed in Univ. Boat, 1933); St Bartholomew's Hospital. MA 1936, MD 1945, Cantab; MRCP 1942; FRCP 1947; FFCM 1974. Michael Foster Research Student, Trinity Coll., 1934–36; Nuffield Res. Student, Oxford, 1940–42. Asst Phys., EMS, 1943–44; Dir, MRC Pneumoconiosis Res. Unit, 1945–52; Sec., MRC Cttee on Bronchitis Res., 1954–76. Royal Coll. of Physicians: Mem. Council, 1959–62; 2nd Vice Pres., 1975; Sec., Cttee on Smoking and Health, 1961–71; Goulstonian Lectr, 1947; Bissett Hawkins Gold Medal, 1969. WHO Consultant: Pulmonary Heart Disease, 1960; Chronic Bronchitis, 1962; Smoking and Health, 1970. Mem., Central Health Services Council and Standing Med. Adv. Cttee, 1966–76; Vice-Chm., Health Educn Council, 1967; Chairman, Action on Smoking and Health (ASH), 1971–78, Pres., 1979. Introd. many TV med. programmes incl. Hurt Mind, 1955, Your Life in Their Hands, 1958–65, Television Doctor, 1969–70. *Publications:* Communication in Medicine, 1973; Natural History of Chronic Bronchitis and Emphysema, 1976; many papers on: first use of penicillin, 1941; dust disease of lungs, 1946–55; bronchitis and emphysema, 1952–76. *Recreations:* music, gardening, beekeeping. *Address:* 24 West Square, SE11 4SN. *T:* 01–735 8753; 2 Coastguard Cottages, Newtown, IoW PO30 4PA. *T:* Calbourne 321. *Club:* Brooks's.

FLETCHER, Geoffrey Bernard Abbott, MA Cantab; *b* Hampstead, 28 Nov. 1903; *s* of J. Alexander Fletcher and Ursula Constance, *d* of William Richard Rickett and *cousin* of Rt Honourable Sir Joseph Compton-Rickett, MP. *Educ:* Rugby Sch.; King's Coll., Cambridge (Senior Scholar), First Class, Classical Tripos, Part I, 1924; First Class Classical Tripos, Part 2, 1926; Prendergast Student, 1926; Asst Lectr in Classics, University of Leeds, 1927–28; Lectr in Greek, University of Liverpool, 1928–36; Prof. of Classics in the University of Durham, King's Coll., Newcastle upon Tyne, 1937–46, Prof. of Latin, 1946–63; Prof. of Latin, University of Newcastle upon Tyne, 1963–69, now Emeritus Prof. Examiner in Greek, University of Leeds, 1940–42; Examiner in Latin, Queen's Univ., Belfast, 1949–51, University of Wales, 1954–56, Bristol, 1961–63; Dean of Faculty of Arts, University of Durham, 1945–47; Public Orator, University of Durham, 1956–58. *Publications:* an appendix on Housman's Poetry in Housman, 1897–1936, by Grant Richards, 1941; Annotations on Tacitus, 1964; many contributions to classical and other periodicals, British and foreign, and to co-operative works. *Recreations:* music, reading, art galleries, walking, travel. *Address:* Thirlmere Lodge, Elmfield Road, Gosforth, Newcastle upon Tyne NE3 4BB. *T:* Tyneside (091) 2852873. *Club:* Athenæum.

FLETCHER, Geoffrey Scowcroft; artist and author; *o s* of Herbert Fletcher and Annie Talence Fletcher; *m* 1953, Mary Jean Timothy. *Educ:* University Coll., London Univ. (Dip. in Fine Art). Abbey Major Schol., British Sch. at Rome, 1948. Drawings appeared in Manchester Guardian, 1950; London drawings and articles featured in The Daily Telegraph, 1958–. Author of television features on unusual aspects of London; has been instrumental in saving a number of metropolitan buildings from demolition. Drawings and paintings in various public and private collections in England and abroad, incl. exhibn of paintings and drawings in possession of Islington Council, 1972, 1978, and exhibn of drawings and paintings acquired by Bolton Art Gall., 1981; Geoffrey Fletcher Room, decorated with the artist's drawings, opened Selfridge Hotel, London, 1973. Designed enamel box for St Paul's Cathedral Appeal, 1972; exhbn of drawings, Miles Gall., St James's, 1980; exhibn, East End Drawings and Paintings, Limehouse, 1984. *Publications:* The London Nobody Knows (filmed, 1968), 1962; Down Among the Meths Men, 1966; Geoffrey Fletcher's London, 1968; City Sights, 1963; Pearly Kingdom, 1965; London's River, 1966; Elements of Sketching, 1966 (Amer. edn, 1968); London's Pavement Pounders, 1967; London After Dark, 1969; Changing London (Drawings from The Daily Telegraph), 1969; The London Dickens Knew, 1970; London Souvenirs, 1973; Paint It In Water Colour, 1974; Italian Impressions, 1974; Sketch It In Black and White, 1975; Daily Telegraph Series: London Prints, 1975, London Colour Prints, 1978, London Portraits, 1978, London at My Feet, 1979; London Alleys, 1980. *Address:* c/o The Daily Telegraph, Fleet Street, EC4.

FLETCHER, Sir James Muir Cameron, Kt 1980; FCA; President, Fletcher Challenge Ltd, Wellington, New Zealand; Chairman, Pacific Steel Ltd; Director: Hikurangi Forest Farms Ltd; Security Pacific Regional Holdings Ltd; *b* Dunedin, NZ, 25 Dec. 1914; *s* of Sir James Fletcher; *m* 1942, Margery Vaughan, *d* of H. H. Gunthorp; three *s*. *Educ:* Waitaki Boys' High School; Auckland Grammar School. South British Insurance Co., 1931–37; then Fletcher Construction Co. and Fletcher Holdings. *Address:* Fletcher Challenge Ltd, Private Bag, Auckland, New Zealand; 2 Crescent Road, Parnell, Auckland, NZ.

FLETCHER, James Thomas, CBE 1967; (first) Chairman, North Yorkshire County Council, 1973–77 (formerly North Riding of Yorkshire County Council, 1957–73); *b* 3 Dec. 1898; *s* of Thomas Fletcher; *m* 1933, A. Walburn; two *s* one *d*. *Educ:* St John's Sch., Whitby. Mayor of Borough of Redcar, 1944; Chm., S Tees-side Hosp. Man. Cttee, 1958–74; Mem., N Riding Yorks. CC, 1934. *Address:* The Barns, 1A The Lane, Mickleby, Saltburn, Cleveland TS13 5LU.

FLETCHER, Major John Antony, MBE (mil.) 1953; RA retired; Chairman, Association of Care-Takers and Care-Seekers; *b* 4 May 1918; *s* of Alexander Ernest Fletcher and Abbie (*née* Wheeler); *m* 1st, 1951, Elizabeth Cross (marr. diss. 1979); one *s* three *d*; 2nd, 1980, Susan Mary Brown. *Educ:* Cheltenham Coll. Jun. Sch.; Abingdon Sch.; RMA, Woolwich; Army and RAF Staff Colls (psc, pac). 2nd Lieut, RA, 1938; war service, Malta, Middle East, Malaya and Burma; Korea Commonwealth Div.; retired 1960; Sec., Inst. of Road Transport Engrs, 1963–85. Secretariat, Powell Duffryn Gp, 1960–63. Hon. FIRTE 1985. *Publications:* article in Gunner Jl; eight letters (out of twelve!) to The Times. *Recreations:* being ex!: ex-playing mem., MCC; ex-Stragglers of Asia; ex-Sherringham and many other golf clubs. *Address:* Milford Cottage, 10 Cudnall Street, Charlton Kings, Cheltenham, Glos.

FLETCHER, John Edwin; His Honour Judge Fletcher; a Circuit Judge, since 1986; *b* 23 Feb. 1941; *s* of Sidney Gerald Fletcher and Celia Lane Fletcher. *Educ:* St Bees Sch., Cumbria; Clare Coll., Cambridge (MA). Called to the Bar, Inner Temple, 1964; Midland and Oxford Circuit, 1965–; a Recorder, 1983–86. Mem. Panel of Chairmen, Medical Appeal Tribunals, 1981–. *Recreations:* fell walking, philately, music. *Address:* (professional) 4 Fountain Court, Steelhouse Lane, Birmingham B4 6DR. *T:* 021–236 3476.

FLETCHER, Sir John Henry Lancelot A.; *see* Aubrey-Fletcher.

FLETCHER, (Leopold) Raymond; journalist; *b* 3 Dec. 1921; *s* of Leopold Raymond Fletcher, Ruddington, Notts; *m* 1st, 1947, Johanna Klara Elisabeth (*d* 1973), *d* of Karl Ising, Berlin; 2nd, 1977, Dr Catherine Elliott, *widow* of Jasper Fenn. *Educ:* abroad. Served 1941–48 in Indian and British forces. Former Columnist on The Times and contributor to other journals at home and abroad. MP (Lab) Ilkeston, 1964–83. Vice-Pres., Assembly of Council of Europe, 1974–76; Leader, UK Delegn to Council of Europe and WEU, 1974–76; Leader, Socialist Gp in Council of Europe, 1974–76. Founder and Council Mem., Airship Assoc. *Publication:* Sixty Pounds a Second on Defence, 1963. *Recreation:* theatre. *Address:* 304 Frobisher House, Dolphin Square, SW1V 3LX; Brooklands, Ilkeston Road, Heanor, Derbyshire DE7 7DT.

FLETCHER, Leslie; General Manager (Chief Executive Officer) Williams Deacon's Bank Ltd, 1964–70, Director, 1966–70, retired; *b* 30 Jan. 1906; *s* of late Edward Henry and Edith Howard Fletcher; *m* 1934, Helen, *d* of Frank Turton; one *s* one *d*. *Educ:* City Gram. Sch., Chester; Manchester Univ. (BA Com). Entered Williams Deacon's Bank Ltd 1922; Asst Gen. Man., 1957; Dep. Gen. Man., 1961. Fellow and Mem. Council, Inst. of Bankers. *Recreations:* lawn tennis, golf. *Address:* Mote Cottage, Burley, near Ringwood, Hants. *T:* Burley 2291.

FLETCHER, Sir Leslie, Kt 1983; DSC 1945; FCA; Deputy Chairman, Standard Chartered PLC, since 1983 (Director since 1972); *b* 14 Oct. 1922; *s* of Ernest and Lily Fletcher; *m* 1947, Audrey Faviell Jackson; one *s* one *d*. *Educ:* Nether Edge Secondary Sch., Sheffield. FCA 1952. Served War, RNVR (FAA), 1942–46 (Lieut). Helbert Wagg & Co. Ltd (subseq. J. Henry Schroder Wagg & Co. Ltd), 1955–71, Dir 1966–71; Chm., Glynwed Internat., 1971–86; Director: RMC Group, 1983–; The Rank Organisation, 1984–. Mem. Council, CBI, 1976–. *Recreations:* gardening, golf, photography. *Address:* 33–36 Gracechurch Street, EC3V 0AX. *T:* 01–623 8711. *Clubs:* Brooks's, MCC, Royal Automobile; Royal & Ancient Golf (St Andrews).

FLETCHER, Comdt Marjorie Helen (Kelsey); Director, Women's Royal Naval Service, since 1986; ADC to the Queen, since 1986; *b* 21 Sept. 1932; *d* of Norman Farler Fletcher and Marie Amelie Fletcher (*née* Adams). *Educ:* Avondale Grammar Sch.; Sutton Coldfield High Sch. for Girls. Solicitor's Clerk, 1948–53; joined WRNS as Telegraphist, 1953; progressively, 3rd Officer to Chief Officer, 1956–76; Supt, 1981; served in Secretarial, Careers Advisor, Intelligence and Staff appts; ndc 1979; Directing Staff, RN Staff Coll., 1980–81; psc 1981; Internat. Mil. Staff, NATO HQ, 1981–84; Asst Dir, Dir Naval Staff Duties, 1984–85. *Recreations:* reading, needlework, entertaining, cookery, fishing, collecting paintings. *Address:* 97b Kennington Park Road, Kennington, SE11 4JJ. *T:* 01–735 4717.

FLETCHER, Sir Norman Seymour, Kt 1977; agriculturalist and pastoralist, Western Australia; *b* Sydney, 20 Sept. 1905; *s* of Thomas Fletcher, Nottingham and Ivy Jeffrey, Goulburn, NSW. Established the Dirk Brook Stud at Keysbrook in 1948 and pioneered the introduction to WA of the Hereford cattle breed. AASA. Past Pres., Western Australia Royal Agricultural Soc.; has given outstanding service to the agricultural and pastoral industries in WA for 30 years; worked hard for advancement and development of cattle and meat industry, both in the southern areas of WA and in the Kimberleys. *Address:* Unit 1, Haddon Place, 39 The Esplanade, South Perth, WA 6151, Australia. *Clubs:* Weld, Western Australian (Perth).

FLETCHER, Paul Thomas, CBE 1959; FEng; Deputy President, British Standards Institution, since 1982 (Chairman, 1979–82); Consulting Engineer: National Nuclear Corporation; BGE 6, Tokyo; *b* 30 Sept. 1912; *s* of Stephen Baldwin Fletcher and Jessie Carrie; *m* 1941, Mary Elizabeth King; three *s*. *Educ:* Nicholson Inst., Stornaway, Isle of Lewis; Maidstone Grammar Sch.; Medway Techn. Coll. BSc(Eng); FEng, FICE, FIMechE, FIEE. Served 3-year apprenticeship with E. A. Gardner & Sons Ltd, Maidstone, remaining for 7 years; joined Min. of Works, 1939, initially in Test Br. of Engrg Div., later with responsibility for variety of engrg services in public bldgs and Govt factories and for plant and equipment for Govt civilian and service res. estabts; Chief Mech. and Elec. Engr, 1951. On formation of UKAEA in 1954, became Dep. Dir of Engrg in Industrial Gp, later Engrg Dir and Dep. Man. Dir; Dir, United Power Co., 1961; Man. Dir, GEC (Process Engrg) Ltd, 1965; Man. Dir, 1971–76, Dep. Chm., 1976–84, Atomic Power Constructions Ltd. Chm., Pressure Vessels Quality Assurance Bd, 1977–. President: IMechE, 1975–76; ITEME, 1979–81, 1985–87. *Publications:* papers to IMechE. *Recreations:* photography, motoring. *Address:* 26 Foxgrove Avenue, Beckenham, Kent BR3 2BA. *T:* 01–650 5563.

FLETCHER, Air Chief Marshal Sir Peter Carteret, KCB 1968 (CB 1965); OBE 1945; DFC 1943; AFC 1952; aerospace consultant, since 1983; Director, Corporate Strategy and Planning, British Aerospace, 1977–82, retired; Director, Airbus Industry Supervisory Board, 1979–82; *b* 7 Oct. 1916; *s* of F. T. W. Fletcher, Oxford (sometime tobacco farmer, Southern Rhodesia), and Dora Clulee, New Zealand; *m* 1940, Marjorie Isobel Kotze; two *d*. *Educ:* St George's Coll., Southern Rhodesia; Rhodes Univ., S Africa. SR Law Dept, 1937. Served War of 1939–45: SR Air Force, 1939; trans. to RAF, 1941; commanded 135 and 258 Fighter Sqdns and RAF Station Belvedere. Directing Staffs at: RAF Staff Coll., 1945–46; Jt Services Staff Coll., 1946–48; Imp. Defence Coll., 1956–58; Mem. Jt Planning Staff, 1951–53; comdg RAF Abingdon, 1958–60; Dep. Dir Jt Planning Staff, 1960–61; Dir of Opl Requirements (B), Air Min., 1961–63; Asst Chief of Air Staff (Policy and Plans), 1964–66; AOC, No 38 Group, Transport Command, 1966–67; VCAS, 1967–70; Controller of Aircraft, Min. of Aviation Supply (formerly Min. of Technology), 1970–71; Air Systems Controller, Defence Procurement Executive, MoD, 1971–73; Dir, Hawker Siddeley Aviation Ltd, 1974–77. *Recreations:* books, travel. *Address:* Woodlands, Sandy Lane, Tilford, Surrey GU10 2ET. *T:* Frensham 2897.

FLETCHER, Raymond; *see* Fletcher, L. R.

FLETCHER, Robin Anthony, OBE 1984; DSC 1944; DPhil; Warden of Rhodes House Oxford, since 1980; Professorial Fellow, Trinity College, Oxford, since 1980; *b* 30 May 1922; *s* of Philip Cawthorne Fletcher, MC, and Edith Maud Fletcher (*née* Okell); *m* 1950, Jinny May (*née* Cornish); two *s*. *Educ:* Marlborough Coll.; Trinity Coll., Oxford (MA, DPhil). Served Royal Navy (Lieut RNVR), 1941–46. University Lecturer in Modern Greek, 1949–79; Domestic Bursar, Trinity Coll., Oxford, 1950–74; Senior Proctor, 1966–67; Member, Hebdomedal Council, 1967–74. Represented England at hockey, 1949–55 and GB, 1952 Olympic Games (Bronze Medal). *Publications:* Kostes Palamas, Athens, 1984; various articles. *Recreations:* sport, music. *Address:* Rhodes House, Oxford. *T:* Oxford 55745. *Clubs:* Naval; Vincent's (Oxford).
See also A. P. Fletcher.

FLETCHER-COOKE, Sir Charles (Fletcher), Kt 1981; QC 1958; *b* 5 May 1914; *yr s* of late Capt. C. A. and Gwendolen May Fletcher-Cooke; *m* 1959, Diana Lady Avebury (whom he divorced, 1967), *d* of late Capt. Edward King and of Mrs J. St Vincent Hand; no surv. *c*. *Educ:* Malvern Coll. (Scholar); Peterhouse, Cambridge (Schol., MA 1940). FCIArb 1981. Pres., Cambridge Union, 1936; Editor, The Granta, 1936. Called to Bar through Lincoln's Inn, 1938 (1st Class Hons, Bar Final Examination; Studentship and Certificate of Honour), Bencher 1969. Mem. Senate, Four Inns of Court, 1970–74. Served War of 1939–45, in Naval Intelligence Div. and on Joint Intelligence Staff, with rank of Lieut-Comdr, RNVR. MP (C) Darwen, Lancs, 1951–83; Joint Parly Under-Sec. of State, Home Office, 1961–63; Chm., Select Cttee on Parly Comr for Admin, 1974–77. Legal Adviser to British Delegation, Danube Conf., Belgrade, 1948; Deleg. to Consultative Assembly of Council of Europe, 1954–55; Mem., European Parlt, 1977–79. Mem., Statute Law Cttee, 1955–61, 1970–83. Dato SPMB, Brunei, 1978. *Publications:* (with others) The Rule of Law; (with M. J. Albery) Monopolies and Restrictive Trade Practices. *Recreation:* fishing. *Address:* The Red House, Clifton Hampden, Oxon. *T:* Clifton Hampden 7754; 2 Paper Buildings, Temple, EC4. *T:* 01–353 1853. *Clubs:* Garrick, Pratt's.
See also Sir John Fletcher-Cooke.

FLETCHER-COOKE, Sir John, Kt 1962; CMG 1952; MA Oxon; *b* 8 Aug. 1911; *er s* of late Charles Arthur and Gwendolen May Fletcher-Cooke; *m* 1st, 1936, Louise Brander (marr. diss. 1948); one *s*; 2nd, 1949, Alice Egner (marr. diss. 1971), Washington, DC; one *s* one *d*; 3rd, 1977, Marie-Louise, *widow* of Louis Vicomte Fournier de la Barre. *Educ:* Malvern Coll. (Barham Schol.); University of Paris (Diplomé, degré supérieur); Oxford Univ. (Kitchener Scholar, Senior Exhibitioner, St Edmund Hall). First Cl. Hons Politics, Philosophy and Economics; economic research, Oxford Univ., 1933; Asst Principal, Colonial Office, 1934; Private Sec. to successive Permanent Under-Secs of State for the Colonies, 1937; Officer Malayan CS, 1937; Asst Sec., FMS, 1938; special duty, FMS, 1939; Magistrate, Singapore, 1939; Sec., Foreign Exchange Control, Malaya, 1939; Dist Officer, FMS, 1940. Served with RAF as intelligence officer, FO, 1942–46; Prisoner of War in Japan, 1942–45. Attached to Colonial Office for special duty and accompanied Constitutional Comr to Malta, 1946; Under-Sec. to Govt of Palestine, 1946–48; Mem. Exec. Council, Palestine, 1947; Special Rep. for Palestine at UN discussions on Palestine, 1948; UK rep. on Special Cttee and later on Trusteeship Council UN, Geneva and Lake Success, 1948–50; Counsellor (Colonial Affairs), Perm. UK Deleg. to UN, New York, 1949–51; Colonial Adviser to UK Deleg. to UN Gen. Assembly, 1948–50 and alternate UK deleg. to UN Gen. Assembly 1949; Colonial Sec., Cyprus, 1951–55. Acted as Governor of Cyprus for various periods, 1951–55. Attached Colonial Office for Special Duty (temp.), 1956; Minister for Constitutional Affairs, Tanganyika, 1956–59; Chief Sec. to the Govt of Tanganyika, 1959–60. Special Rep. of Tanganyika at Ghana Independence Celebrations, 1957, at Economic Commission for Africa, Addis Ababa, 1959, and at Trusteeship Council, UN, New York, 1957, 1958, 1959, 1960 and 1961. Acted as Governor of Tanganyika for various periods, 1959–61; Dep. Governor, Tanganyika, 1960–61. Visiting Prof. (African Affairs) University of Colorado, Boulder, USA, 1961–62, 1966, and 1973–74; Fellow, African Studies Assoc., NY, 1961–. Mem. Constituencies Delimitation Commn for Kenya, 1962; Mem. Exec. Cttee, Overseas Employers' Federation, 1963–67. Contested (C) Luton, Nov. 1963. MP (C) Test Div. of Southampton, 1964–66. Mem. Councils of Royal Commonwealth Society and of United Society for Propagation of the Gospel, 1964–67. Vice-Chm., Internat. Team to review structure and organisation of FAO, Rome, 1967. Dir, Programmes in Diplomacy, Carnegie Endowment for International Peace, New York, 1967–69. Mission for British Govt to Anglo-French Condominium of New Hebrides, 1969. Chm., various Civil Service Commn Selection Boards, 1971–. *Publications:* The Emperor's Guest, 1942–45, 1971, 3rd edn 1982 (also issued as Talking Book for the Blind, 1982; original diaries donated to Imperial War Museum, 1982); (contrib.) Parliament as an Export, 1966; short stories and contribs to many periodicals. *Recreation:* building dry Cotswold stone walls. *Address:* c/o Lloyds Bank, Stock Exchange Branch, 111 Old Broad Street, EC2N 1AU. *Clubs:* Travellers', Royal Commonwealth Society.
See also Sir Charles Fletcher-Cooke.

FLETCHER-VANE, family name of **Baron Inglewood.**

FLEW, Prof. Antony Garrard Newton; part-time Distinguished Research Fellow, Social Philosophy and Policy Center, Bowling Green State University, Ohio, since 1986; Emeritus Professor, University of Reading, since 1983; *b* 11 Feb. 1923; *o s* of Rev. Dr R. N. Flew; *m* 1952, Annis Ruth Harty; two *d*. *Educ:* St Faiths Sch., Cambridge; Kingswood Sch., Bath; Sch. of Oriental and African Studies, London; St John's Coll., Oxford (John Locke Schol., MA); DLitt Keele, 1974. Lectr: Christ Church, Oxford, 1949–50; Univ. of Aberdeen, 1950–54; Prof. of Philosophy: Univ. of Keele, 1954–71; Univ. of Calgary, 1972–73; Univ. of Reading, 1973–82; (part-time) York Univ., Toronto, 1983–85. Many temp. vis. appts. Gavin David Young Lectr, Adelaide, 1963; Gifford Lectr, St Andrews, 1986. A Vice-Pres., Rationalist Press Assoc., 1973–; Chm., Voluntary Euthanasia Soc., 1976–79. Fellow, Acad. of Humanism, 1983–. *Publications:* A New Approach to Psychical Research, 1953; Hume's Philosophy of Belief, 1961; God and Philosophy, 1966; Evolutionary Ethics, 1967; An Introduction to Western Philosophy, 1971; Crime or Disease?, 1973; Thinking About Thinking, 1975; The Presumption of Atheism, 1976; Sociology, Equality and Education, 1976; A Rational Animal, 1978; Philosophy: an introduction, 1979; The Politics of Procrustes, 1981; Darwinian Evolution, 1984; Thinking About Social Thinking, 1985; Hume, Philosopher of Moral Science, 1986; articles in philosophical and other jls. *Recreations:* walking, climbing, house maintenance. *Address:* (Jan.-May) Social Philosophy and Policy Center, Bowling Green State University, Bowling Green, Ohio 43403, USA; 26 Alexandra Road, Reading, Berks RG1 5PD. *T:* Reading 61848. *Club:* Union Society (Oxford).

FLINDALL, Jacqueline; JP; Associate Consultant, PA Management Consultants, since 1986; Consultant (part-time), Royal College of Nursing, since 1986; *b* 12 Oct. 1932; *d* of Henry and Lilian Flindall. *Educ:* St Davids Sch., Ashford, Mddx; University Coll. Hosp., London (DipN). SRN, SCM, UCH, 1950–54; Midwifery, St Luke's Mat. Hosp., Guildford and Watford, 1955; exchange student, Mount Sinai Hosp., NY, 1956; Ward Sister and Clinical Teacher, UCH, 1957–63; Asst Matron, Wexham Park Hosp., 1964–66; Dep. Supt of Nursing, Prince of Wales and St Anne's, 1967–69; Chief Nursing Officer: Northwick Park Hosp., 1969–73; Oxfordshire HA, 1973–83; Regional Nursing Officer, Wessex RHA, 1983–85. Pres., UCH Nurses' League, 1983–. County Welfare Officer, St John, Wiltshire, 1984–. Mem., RCN; Hon. FRCN 1983. JP Oxford, 1982. *Publications:* contribs to nursing press. *Recreation:* painting. *Address:* Greenways Cottage, Cowesfield Green, Whiteparish, near Salisbury, Wiltshire SP5 2QS. *T:* Whiteparish 836. *Club:* Royal College of Nursing.

FLINT, Prof. David, TD, MA, BL, CA; Professor of Accountancy, 1964–85, (Johnstone Smith Chair, 1964–75), and Vice-Principal, 1981–85, University of Glasgow; *b* 24 Feb.

1919; s of David Flint, JP, and Agnes Strang Lambie; m 1953, Dorothy Mary Maclachlan Jardine; two s one d. Educ: Glasgow High Sch.; University of Glasgow. Served with Royal Signals, 1939–46, Major (despatches). Awarded distinction final examination of Institute of Chartered Accountants of Scotland, 1948. Lecturer, University of Glasgow, 1950–60; Dean of Faculty of Law, 1971–73. Partner, Mann Judd Gordon & Co. Chartered Accountants, Glasgow, 1951–71. Hon. Pres. Glasgow Chartered Accountants Students Soc., 1959–60; Chm., Assoc. of Univ. Teachers of Accounting (now British Accounting Assoc.), 1969. Mem. Council, Scottish Business Sch., 1971–77; Vice-Pres., Scottish Economic Soc., 1977–; Vice-Pres., Inst. of Chartered Accountants of Scotland, 1973–75, Pres., 1975–76; Pres., European Accounting Assoc., 1983–84; Member: Management and Ind. Rel. Cttee, SSRC, 1970–72 and 1978–80; Commn for Local Authy Accounts in Scotland, 1978–80. Publication: A True and Fair View in Company Accounts, 1982. Recreation: golf. Address: 3 Merrylee Road, Newlands, Glasgow G43 2SH. T: 041–637 3060.

FLINT, Percy Sydney George, (Pip); Member, Monopolies and Mergers Commission, since 1986; b 23 May 1921; s of Percy Benjamin Flint and Nellie Kate Flint; m 1946, Joyce Marjorie Peggy Papworth; two d. Educ: Sir George Monoux Grammar School; Emmanuel College, Cambridge. Called to the Bar, Inner Temple, 1955. Royal Signals (Major), 1941–47; Colonial Administrative Service and HMOCS, Nigeria, 1948–61; Imperial Chemical Industries, 1961–85 (Secretary, 1981–85). Address: Courtlands, Kippington Road, Sevenoaks, Kent TN13 2LH. T: Sevenoaks 455638. Club: Athenæum.

FLINT, Rachael H.; see Heyhoe Flint, R.

FLOOD, Prof. John Edward, OBE 1986; DSc, PhD; CEng, FIEE, FIERE; Professor of Electrical Engineering, since 1965, and Head of Department of Electrical and Electronic Engineering, 1967–81 and since 1983, University of Aston in Birmingham; b 2 June 1925; s of Sydney E. Flood and Elsie G. Flood; m 1949, Phyllis Mary Groocock; two s. Educ: City of London Sch.; Queen Mary Coll., Univ. of London (BSc 1945; PhD 1951; DSc 1965). CEng, FIEE 1959; FIERE 1967. Admiralty Signals Estab., 1944–46; Standard Telephone and Cables Ltd, 1946–47; PO Res. Stn, 1947–52; Siemens Brothers Ltd, 1952–57; Chief Engr, Advanced Develt Labs, AEI Telecommunications Div., 1957–65; Dean, Faculty of Engrg, 1971–74, and Sen. Pro-Vice-Chancellor, 1981–83, Univ. of Aston in Birmingham. Chairman: IEE Professional Gp on Telecommunications, 1974–77; IEE S Midland Centre, 1978–79; Univs Cttee on Integrated Sandwich Courses, 1981–82; BSI Cttee on Telecommunications, 1981–; Member: British Electrotechnical Council, 1981–86; Monopolies and Mergers Commn, 1985–. Liveryman, Engineers' Co., 1985. CGIA 1962. Publications: Telecommunication Networks, 1975; papers in scientific and technical jls; patents. Recreations: swimming, wine-making. Address: 60 Widney Manor Road, Solihull, West Midlands B91 3JQ. T: 021–705 3604. Club: Royal Over-Seas League.

FLOREY, Prof. Charles du Vé; Professor of Community Medicine, University of Dundee, since 1983; b 11 Sept. 1934; s of Howard Walter Florey and Ethel Mary Florey; m 1966, Susan Jill Hopkins; one s one d. Educ: Univ. of Cambridge (MD); Yale Univ. (MPH). FFCM 1977. Instructor, 1965, Asst Prof., 1966–69, Yale Univ. School of Medicine; Mem. Scientific Staff, MRC, Jamaica, 1969–71; St Thomas's Hospital Medical School, London: Sen. Lectr, 1971–78; Reader, 1978–81; Prof., 1981–83. Publications: (with S. R. Leeder) Methods for Cohort Studies of Chronic Airflow Limitation, 1982; (with others) Introduction to Community Medicine, 1983. Recreations: photography, sailing, walking, computing. Address: Ninewells Hospital and Medical School, Dundee DD1 9SY. T: Dundee 60111.

FLOUD, Mrs Jean Esther, CBE 1976; MA, BSc(Econ); Principal, Newnham College, Cambridge, 1972–83, Hon. Fellow, 1983; b 3 Nov. 1915; d of Annie Louisa and Ernest Walter McDonald; m 1938, Peter Castle Floud, CBE (d 1960; s of late Sir Francis Floud, KCB, KCSI, KCMG; formerly Keeper of Circulation, Victoria and Albert Museum); two d (one s decd). Educ: public elementary and selective secondary schools; London School of Economics (BScEcon), Hon. Fellow, 1972. Asst Dir of Educn, City of Oxford, 1940–46; Teacher of Sociology in the University of London (London School of Economics and Inst. of Educn), 1947–62; Official Fellow of Nuffield College, Oxford, 1963–72, Hon. Fellow, 1983; Hon. Fellow, Darwin Coll., Cambridge, 1986. Member: Franks Commission of Inquiry into the University of Oxford, 1964–66; University Grants Cttee, 1969–74; Social Science Research Council, 1970–73; Exec. Cttee, PEP, 1975–77; Adv. Bd for the Res. Councils, 1976–81; Council, Policy Studies Inst., 1979–83. Hon. LittD Leeds, 1973; Hon. DLitt City, 1978. Publications: (with A. H. Halsey and F. M. Martin) Social Class and Educational Opportunity, 1956; (with Warren Young) Dangerousness and Criminal Justice, 1981; papers and reviews in sociological jls. Recreations: books, music. Address: White Lodge, Osler Road, Old Headington, Oxford.

FLOUD, Prof. Roderick Castle; Professor of Modern History, Birkbeck College, University of London, since 1975; b 1 April 1942; s of late Bernard Francis Castle Floud, MP and Ailsa (née Craig); m 1964, Cynthia Anne (née Smith); two d. Educ: Brentwood Sch.; Wadham Coll., Oxford; Nuffield Coll., Oxford. MA, DPhil. Asst Lectr in Economic History, UCL, 1966–69; Lectr in Economic History, Univ. of Cambridge and Fellow of Emmanuel Coll., Cambridge, 1969–75. Vis. Prof. of European History and of Economics, Stanford Univ., Calif, 1980–81. Research Associate, Nat. Bureau of Economic Research, USA, 1978–; Research Programme Dir, Centre for Economic Policy Research, 1983–; Mem., Lord Chancellor's Adv. Council on Public Records, 1978–84. Publications: An Introduction to Quantitative Methods for Historians, 1973, 2nd edn 1980; (ed) Essays in Quantitative Economic History, 1974; The British Machine Tool Industry 1850–1914, 1976; (ed) The Economic History of Britain since 1700, 1981; (ed) The Power of the Past, 1984; articles in Economic History Review, Social Science History, etc. Recreations: camping, walking, music. Address: Birkbeck College, Malet Street, WC1E 7HX. T: 01–631 6283; 21 Savernake Road, NW3 2JT. T: 01–267 2197.

FLOWER, family name of Viscount Ashbrook.

FLOWER, Antony John Frank, (Tony), MA, PhD; General Secretary, Tawney Society, since 1982; Director, Research Institute for Economic and Social Affairs, since 1982; b 2 Feb. 1951; s of late Frank Robert Edward Flower and of Dorothy Elizabeth (née Williams). Educ: Chipping Sodbury Grammar Sch.; Univ. of Exeter (BA Hons Philosophy and Sociology, MA Sociology); Univ. of Leicester (PhD Mass Communications). Graphic Designer, 1973–76; Fund-raiser, Royal Devon and Exeter Hosp., 1981–82; Co-ordinator, Argo Venture, 1984–, Dir, Argo Trust, 1986–; Dir, Healthline Health Inf. Service, 1986–. Founder Mem., SDP, 1981; Mem., Council for Social Democracy, 1982–84. Editor, Tawney Journal, 1982–. Recreations: photography and drawing (several published), carpentry, collecting. Address: 18 Victoria Park Square, E2 9PF. T: 01–981 6719.

FLOWER, Group Capt. Arthur Hyde, CBE 1939; b Bemboka, NSW, 13 Dec. 1892; s of late Thomas Flower; m 1924, Nina Joan Castleden Whitby (d 1976); no c; m 1977, Margaret June, d of late Cecil Vernon Wickens, Adelaide, SA. Educ: Tilba, NSW. Served with AIF, Egypt and France, 1915–16; transferred to Royal Flying Corps, 1917; served in

No. 42 Squadron, France and Italy, 1917–1918 (French Croix de Guerre with palm); Egypt and Turkey, 1920–23; Egypt, 1926–31 and 1934–36; Palestine, 1937–38 (CBE, despatches); France, Sept. 1939–May 1940; England, 1940–42; SWP Area, Aug. 1942–Nov. 1944; retired May 1945; returned to Australia, 1948. Comdr Order of Leopold (Belgium). Recreations: shooting, golf. Address: Garden Cottage, 188 Longwood Road, Heathfield, SA 5153, Australia.

FLOWER, Desmond John Newman, MC 1944; Editorial Consultant, Sheldon Press, 1973–85, Chairman, Cassell & Co. Ltd, 1958–71; President, Cassell Australia Ltd, 1965–71; b London, 25 Aug. 1907; o s of late Sir Newman Flower; m 1st, 1931, Margaret Cameron Coss (marr. diss., 1952); one s; 2nd, 1952, Anne Elizabeth Smith (marr. diss. 1972); one s two d. Educ: Lancing; King's Coll., Cambridge. Entered Cassell & Co. 1930; Dir, 1931; Literary Dir, 1938; Dep.-Chm., 1952; Chm. Cassell & Co. (Holdings) Ltd, 1958–70. Served War of 1939–45 (despatches, MC); commissioned 1941, 5 Bn Argyll and Sutherland Highlanders later 91 (A&SH) A/T-Regt. Chm., the Folio Society, 1960–71; Liveryman, Stationers' Co. Président des Comités d'Alliance Française en Grande Bretagne, 1963–72. Officier de la légion d'honneur, 1972 (Chevalier 1950). DLitt (hc) University of Caen, 1957. Publications: founder and editor (with A. J. A. Symons) Book Collector's quarterly, 1930–34; ed, Complete Poetical Works of Ernest Christopher Dowson, 1934; compiled (with Francis Meynell and A. J. A. Symons) The Nonesuch Century, 1936; (with A. N. L. Munby) English Poetical Autographs, 1938; The Pursuit of Poetry, 1939; Voltaire's England, 1950; History of 5 Bn Argyll and Sutherland Highlanders, 1950; (with James Reeves) The War, 1939–1945, 1960; (with Henry Maas) The Letters of Ernest Dowson, 1967; New Letters of Ernest Dowson, 1984; numerous translations, inc. Saint Simon, Voltaire, Maupassant, Morand. Recreation: book collecting. Address: 187 Clarence Gate Gardens, NW1 6AR. T: 01–262 4690. Club: Royal and Ancient (St Andrews).

FLOWER, Rear-Adm. Edward James William, CB 1980; Director, Post-Design (Ships), Ministry of Defence (Navy), 1977–80, retired; b 1923; m; three d. Joined RN, 1941; served in HM Ships Norfolk, Duke of York, Liverpool, Whitby, Urchin and Tenby; Canadian Nat. Defence Coll., 1966; Fleet Marine Engineering Officer, Western Fleet, 1967–69; commanded RN Nuclear Propulsion Test and Trng Estab., 1970–71; MoD (Navy), 1971–75; Flag Officer Portsmouth, and Port Admiral, Portsmouth, 1975–76; Dir of Engrg (Ships), MoD, 1976–77. Address: Fairmount, Hinton Charterhouse, Bath.

FLOWERS, family name of Baron Flowers.

FLOWERS, Baron cr 1979 (Life Peer), of Queen's Gate in the City of Westminster; Brian Hilton Flowers, Kt 1969; FRS 1961; Vice-Chancellor, University of London, since 1985; b 13 Sept. 1924; o s of late Rev. Harold J. Flowers, Swansea; m 1951, Mary Frances, er d of late Sir Leonard Behrens, CBE; two step s. Educ: Bishop Gore Grammar Sch., Swansea; Gonville and Caius Coll. (Exhibitioner), Cambridge (MA); Hon. Fellow, 1974; University of Birmingham (DSc). Anglo-Canadian Atomic Energy Project, 1944–46; Research in nuclear physics and atomic energy at Atomic Energy Research Establishment, Harwell, 1946–50; Dept of Mathematical Physics, University of Birmingham, 1950–52; Head of Theoretical Physics Div., AERE, Harwell, 1952–58; Prof. of Theoretical Physics, 1958–61, Langworthy Prof. of Physics, 1961–72, Univ. of Manchester; Rector of Imperial Coll. of Sci. and Technol., 1973–85. Chairman: Science Research Council, 1967–73; Royal Commn on Environmental Pollution, 1973–76; Standing Commn on Energy and the Environment, 1978–81; Univ. of London Working Party on future of med. and dent. teaching resources, 1979–80; Cttee of Vice-Chancellors and Principals, 1983–85; Mem., Select Cttee on Science and Technology, H of L, 1980–. President: Inst. of Physics, 1972–74; European Science Foundn, 1974–80; Nat. Soc. for Clean Air, 1977–79. Chm., Computer Bd for Univs and Research Councils, 1966–70. A Managing Trustee, Nuffield Foundn, 1982–. Founder Mem., SDP, 1981. FInstP 1961; Hon. FCGI, 1975; Hon. MRIA (Science Section), 1976; Hon. FIEE, 1975; Sen. Fellow, RCA, 1983; Hon. Fellow, UMIST, 1985; Corresp. Mem., Swiss Acad. of Engrg Sciences. MA Oxon, 1956; Hon. DSc: Sussex, 1968; Wales, 1972; Manchester, 1973; Leicester, 1973; Liverpool, 1974; Bristol, 1982; Oxford, 1985; Hon. DEng Nova Scotia, 1983; Hon. ScD Dublin, 1984; Hon. LLD Dundee, 1985. Rutherford Medal and Prize, IPPS, 1968; Chalmers Medal, Chalmers Univ. of Technol., Sweden, 1980. Officier de la Légion d'Honneur, 1981 (Chevalier, 1975). Publications: (with E. Mendoza) Properties of Matter, 1970; contribs to scientific periodicals on structure of the atomic nucleus, nuclear reactions, science policy, energy and the environment. Recreations: music, walking, computing, painting, gardening. Address: Senate House, Malet Street, WC1E 7HU. T: 01–636 8000.

FLOYD, Sir Giles (Henry Charles), 7th Bt cr 1816; Director, Burghley Estate Farms, since 1958; b 27 Feb. 1932; s of Sir John Duckett Floyd, 6th Bt, TD, and of Jocelin Evadne (d 1976), d of late Sir Edmund Wyldbore Smith; S father, 1975; m 1st, 1954, Lady Gillian Moyra Katherine Cecil (marr. diss. 1978), 2nd d of 6th Marquess of Exeter, KCMG; two s; 2nd, 1985, Judy Sophia Lane, er d of W. L. Tregoning, CBE, and late D. M. E. Tregoning. Educ: Eton College. High Sheriff of Rutland, 1968. Heir: er s David Henry Cecil Floyd [b 2 April 1956; m 1981, Caroline, d of John Beckly, Manor Farm, Bowerchalke, Salisbury, Wilts; one d]. Address: Tinwell Manor, Stamford, Lincs. T: Stamford 62676. Clubs: Turf, Farmers'.

FLOYD, John Anthony; Chairman: Christie Manson & Woods Ltd, 1974–85; Christies International Ltd, since 1976; b 12 May 1923; s of Lt-Col Arthur Bowen Floyd, DSO, OBE; m 1948, Margaret Louise Rosselli; two d. Educ: Eton. Served King's Royal Rifle Corps, 1941–46. Address: 26 Park Village East, NW1 7PZ. T: 01–387 6311. Clubs: Boodle's, White's, MCC.

FLOYD EWIN, Sir David Ernest Thomas, Kt 1974; LVO 1954; OBE 1965; MA; Lay Administrator, 1939–44, Registrar and Receiver, 1944–78, Consultant to the Dean and Chapter, since 1978, St Paul's Cathedral; Notary Public; Chairman: Tubular Barriers Ltd, since 1978; Stonebert Ltd and subsidiaries; b 17 Feb. 1911; 7th s of late Frederick P. Ewin and Ellen Floyd; m 1948, Marion Irene, d of William R. Lewis; one d. Educ: Eltham. MA (Lambeth) 1962. Freeman, City of London, 1948; Member of Court of Common Council for Ward of Castle Baynard (Dep., 1972–); Vice-Pres., Castle Baynard Ward Club (Chm. 1962); Chm., Corp. of London Gresham Cttee, 1975–76; Member: Lord Mayor and Sheriffs Cttee, 1976, 1978, 1984; Court of Assts, Hon. Irish Soc., 1976–79; Surrogate for Province of Canterbury; Trustee: City Parochial Foundn, 1967– (Chm., Pensions Cttee, 1978–); St Paul's Cathedral Trust, 1978–; Temple Bar Trust, 1979–; Dep. Chm., City of London's Endowment Trust for St Paul's Cathedral, 1982–. Hon. Dir, British Humane Assoc.; Governor and Member of Court: Sons of the Clergy Corp.; St Gabriel's Coll., Camberwell, 1946–72. Past Master: Scriveners Co.; Guild of Freemen of the City of London; Liveryman, Wax Chandlers Co.; Gold Staff Officer at Coronation of HM Queen Elizabeth, 1953. KStJ 1970 (OStJ 1965). Publications: A Pictorial History of St Paul's Cathedral, 1970; The Splendour of St Paul's, 1973; numerous papers and articles. Recreations: tennis, gardening, fishing. Address: St Augustine's House, 4 New Change, EC4M 9AB. T: 01–248 0683; Chapter House, St Paul's Churchyard, EC4. T: 01–248

2705; Silver Springs, Stoke Gabriel, South Devon. *T:* Stoke Gabriel 264. *Clubs:* City Livery, Guildhall.

FLOYER, Prof. Michael Antony, MD; FRCP; Professor of Medicine, since 1974, Dean, since 1982, The London Hospital Medical College; Hon. Consultant Physician, since 1958, Consultant in charge of Emergency and Accident Department, since 1975, The London Hospital; *b* 28 April 1920; *s* of Comdr William Antony Floyer, RN and Alice Rosalie Floyer (*née* Whitehead); *m* 1946, Lily Louise Frances Burns; two *s* one *d*. *Educ:* Sherborne Sch.; Trinity Hall, Cambridge; The London Hosp. Med. Coll. MA; MB, BCh; MD; FRCP 1963. RAF Medical Service, Sqdn Leader, RAF Hosps, Karachi and Cawnpore, 1946–48. The London Hospital: House Officer, 1944–45; Registrar in Medicine, 1945–46, Hon. Registrar, 1948–51; Hon. Sen. Registrar, 1951–58; The London Hospital Medical College: Lectr in Medicine, 1948–51; Sen. Lectr, 1951–67; Asst Dir, Medical Unit, 1953–; Reader in Medicine, 1967–74; Acting Dean, 1982–83; seconded to Nairobi Univ., Kenya, as Prof. of Medicine, 1973–75. Oliver-Sharpey Prize, RCP, 1980. *Publications:* chapters in books and papers in scientific jls on the aetiology and mechanism of hypertension and on the physiology of the interstitial fluid space. *Recreations:* wild places and wild things. *Address:* The London Hospital Medical College, E1 2AD. *T:* 01–377 8800; Dukes Cottage, Willingale, Ongar, Essex. *T:* Willingdale 86270.

FLUTE, Prof. Peter Thomas, TD 1970; MD; FRCP, FRCPath; Postgraduate Medical Dean, South West Thames Regional Health Authority and Assistant Director, British Postgraduate Medical Federation, since 1985; *b* 12 Aug. 1928; *s* of Rev. Richard Prickett Flute and Katie Flute (*née* Click); *m* 1951, Ann Elizabeth Harbroe, *d* of late G. John Wright; two *s* two *d*. *Educ:* Southend High Sch.; King's College London; KCH Med. Sch. (Ware Prize; MB, BS; MRCS). KCH, 1951–52; RAMC, 1952–54; Demonstrator in Pathology, KCH Med. Sch., 1955–56; Elmore Res. Student, Dept of Medicine, Cambridge, 1957–58; Lectr, 1958–62, Sen. Lectr, 1962–68, Reader, 1968–72, Dept of Haematology, KCH Med. Sch.; Hon. Consultant in Haematology, KCH, 1966–72; Prof. of Haematology, St George's Hosp. Med. Sch. and Hon. Consultant, St George's Hosp., 1972–85. RAMC T&AVR: Pathologist, 24 Gen. Hosp., 1955–58, 308 Gen. Hosp., 1958–67; OC 380 Blood Supply Unit, 1967–73, Hon. Col, 1977–82; Hon. Consultant to the Army in Haematology, 1977–. Mem., Mid-Downs DHA, 1984–. Royal College of Pathologists: Mem. Council, 1981–84; Exec. Cttee, 1982–84; SW Thames Regional Adviser in Postgraduate Educn, 1975–85; Royal College of Physicians: Mem., Cttee of Haematology, 1981–; Jt Cttee on Higher Med. Training; Mem., Specialist Adv. Cttee on Haematology, 1977–83; Sec., 1978–83; British Soc. for Haematology: Mem., 1960–; Cttee, 1975–87; Associate Sec., 1977–81; Sec., 1981–83; Pres., 1985–86; Section of Pathology, Royal Society of Medicine: Mem. Council, 1964–68; Sec., 1972–76; Pres., 1978. Mem., Editorial Bd, British Jl of Haematology, 1971–81. *Publications:* chapters and contribs on thrombosis and blood diseases to med. and sci. jls. *Recreations:* mountain walking, reading. *Address:* 31 Eversley Road, Upper Norwood, SE19 3PY. *T:* 01–653 1759.

FLYNN, Prof. Frederick Valentine, MD (Lond), FRCP, FRCPath; Professor of Chemical Pathology in University of London at University College School of Medicine, since 1970, and Consultant Chemical Pathologist to University College Hospital, London, since 1960; Civil Consultant in Chemical Pathology to Royal Navy, since 1978; *b* 6 Oct. 1924; *e s* of Frederick Walter Flynn and Jane Laing Flynn (*née* Valentine); *m* 1955, Catherine Ann, *o d* of Dr Robert Walter Warrick and Dorothy Ann Warrick (*née* Dimock); one *s* one *d*. *Educ:* University Coll. London; University Coll. Hosp. Med. Sch. (Fellow, UCL, 1974). Obstetric Ho. Surg. and various posts, incl. Research Asst and Registrar, Dept of Clin. Pathology, UCH, 1947–60; Associate in Clin. Path., Pepper Laboratory of Clin. Medicine, Univ. of Pennsylvania, and British Postgrad. Med. Fedn Travelling Fellow, 1954–55. Chairman: Assoc. of Clin. Pathologists Working Party on Data Processing in Laboratories, 1964–67; Assoc. of Clin. Biochemists Sci. and Technical Cttee, 1968–70; Dept of Health's Adv. Gp on Scientific and Clinical Applications of Computers, 1971–76; Organising Cttee for 1st, 2nd and 3rd Internat. Confs on Computing in Clinical Labs, 1972–80; Research Cttee, NE Thames RHA, 1984–; Member: Min. of Health Lab. Equipment and Methods Adv. Gp, 1966–71; Min. of Technol. Working Party on Lab. Instrumentation, 1966–67; BMA Working Party on Computers in Medicine, 1968–69; Dept of Health's Adv. Cttee on Med. Computing, 1969–76, and Laboratory Develts Adv. Gp, 1972–75; MRC Working Party on Hypogammaglobulinaemia, 1959–70; MRC Adv. Panel on Applications for Computing Facilities, 1973–; NW Thames RHA Sci. Cttee, 1973–74; Med. Cttee, Sir Jules Thorn Charitable Trust, 1983–. Mem. Council, 1968–72, Vice-Pres., 1971–72, Section of Path., RSM; Royal Coll. of Pathologists: Mem. Council, 1973–75 and 1984–87; Vice-Pres., 1975–78; Treas., 1978–83; Chm., Panel of Examrs in Chem. Path., 1972–82. *Publications:* numerous contribs to med. and sci. books and jls. *Recreations:* photography, carpentry, gardening. *Address:* 20 Oakleigh Avenue, Whetstone, N20 9JH. *T:* 01–445 0882.

FLYNN, John Gerrard; HM Diplomatic Service; Counsellor, Madrid, since 1982; *b* 23 April 1937; *s* of Thomas Flynn and late Mary Chisholm; *m* 1973, Drina Anne Coates; one *s* one *d*. *Educ:* Glasgow Univ. (MA). Foreign Office, 1965; Second Sec., Lusaka, 1966; First Sec., FCO, 1968; seconded to Canning House as Asst Dir-Gen., 1970; First Sec. (Commercial) and Consul, Montevideo, 1971; FCO, 1976; Chargé d'Affaires, Luanda, 1978; Counsellor and Consul-Gen., Brasilia, 1979. *Recreations:* walking, golf. *Address:* c/o Foreign and Commonwealth Office, SW1. *Club:* Travellers'.

FLYNN, Most Rev. Thomas; *see* Achonry, Bishop of, (RC).

FOAKES, Prof. Reginald Anthony; Professor of English, University of California at Los Angeles, since 1983; *b* 18 Oct. 1923; 2nd *s* of William Warren Foakes and Frances (*née* Poate); *m* 1951, Barbara, *d* of Harry Garratt, OBE; two *s* two *d*. *Educ:* West Bromwich Grammar Sch.; Birmingham Univ. (MA, PhD). Fellow of the Shakespeare Inst., 1951–54; Lectr in English, Durham Univ., 1954–62; Sen. Lectr, 1963–64; University of Kent at Canterbury: Prof. of Eng. Lit., 1964–82, now Emeritus Prof. of Eng. and Amer. Lit.; Dean, Faculty of Humanities, 1974–77. Commonwealth Fund (Harkness) Fellow, Yale Univ., 1955–56; Visiting Professor: University Coll., Toronto, 1960–62; Univ. of California, Santa Barbara, 1968–69; UCLA, 1981. *Publications:* (ed) Shakespeare's King Henry VIII, 1957; The Romantic Assertion, 1958; (ed with R. T. Rickert) Henslowe's Diary, 1961; (ed) The Comedy of Errors, 1962; (ed) The Revenger's Tragedy, 1966; (ed) Macbeth and Much Ado About Nothing, 1968; Romantic Criticism, 1968; Coleridge on Shakespeare, 1971; Shakespeare, the Dark Comedies to the Last Plays, 1971; (ed) The Henslowe Papers, 2 vols, 1977; Marston and Tourneur, 1978; (ed) A Midsummer Night's Dream, 1984; Illustrations of the English Stage 1580–1642, and Visitor's Guide, 1985; (ed) S. T. Coleridge, Lectures 1808–19: On Literature, 2 vols, 1986. *Address:* Department of English, University of California at Los Angeles, 405 Hilgard Avenue, Los Angeles, Calif 90024, USA.

FOALE, Air Cdre Colin Henry; Pilot to the Committee for Aerial Photography, University of Cambridge, since 1981; *b* 10 June 1930; *s* of late William Henry Foale and Frances M. (*née* Muse); *m* 1954, Mary Katherine Harding, Minneapolis, USA; two *s* one *d*. *Educ:* Wolverton Grammar Sch.; RAF Coll., Cranwell. 1951–74: 13 Sqdn Pilot, Egypt; 32 Sqdn Flt Comdr; Fighter Flt, RAF Flying Coll., Manby; Officer and Aircrew Selection, Hornchurch; OC 73 Sqdn, Cyprus (Sqdn Ldr); Staff Coll., Bracknell; Air Staff, HQ RAF Germany (Wing Comdr); Jt Services Staff Coll., Latimer; OC 39 Sqdn, Malta; SO Flying, MoD (PE) (Gp Captain); Stn Comdr, Luqa, Malta, 1974–76; RCDS, 1977 (Air Cdre); Dir of Public Relations (RAF), 1977–79; retired at own request, for business and writing, 1979. Trng Advr to Chm., Conservative Party, 1980–81. FBIM, FIWM. *Recreations:* sailing, swimming, flying, canoeing, music, drama, writing. *Address:* St Catharine's College, Cambridge; 37 Pretoria Road, Cambridge. *Club:* Royal Air Force.

FOCKE, Paul Everard Justus; QC 1982; a Recorder, since 1986; *b* 14 May 1937; *s* of Frederick Justus Focke and Muriel Focke; *m* 1973, Lady Tana Marie Alexander, *er d* of 6th Earl of Caledon; two *d*. *Educ:* Downside; Exeter Coll., Oxford; Trinity Coll., Dublin. National Service, 1955–57; Territorial Army, 1957–66, Cheshire Yeomanry (Captain). Called to the Bar, Gray's Inn, 1964, to the Bar of NSW and to the NZ Bar, 1982. QC NSW 1984. *Recreations:* travelling, aeroplanes. *Address:* (chambers) 1 Mitre Court Buildings, Temple, EC4. *T:* 01–353 0434; (home) 7 Cheyne Walk, SW3. *T:* 01–351 0299. *Clubs:* Turf, Beefsteak, Cavalry and Guards.

FODEN, Air Vice-Marshal Arthur, CB 1964; CBE 1960; BSc; CEng; FIEE; Consultant, Electronic Systems, since 1985; *b* 19 April 1914; *s* of Henry Foden, Macclesfield, Cheshire; *m* 1938, Constance Muriel Foden (*née* Corkill); one *s* one *d*. *Educ:* Manchester Univ. Electronic Engineer, 1935–37; Education Officer, Royal Air Force, 1937–39; Signals Officer, Royal Air Force, 1939; Dep. Dir, Signals Staff, Min. of Def., 1964–67; Asst Chief of Defence Staff (Signals), 1967–69, retired; Director: (C), Govt Communications HQ, 1969–75; Racal Comsec, 1975–85. *Recreations:* gardening, music. *Address:* Ravenglass, Wargrave, Berks. *T:* Wargrave 2589.

FODEN-PATTINSON, Peter Lawrence; a Deputy Chairman of Lloyd's, 1976; *b* 14 June 1925; *s* of late Hubert Foden-Pattinson; *m* 1956, Joana Pryor (*née* Henderson); one *s*. *Educ:* Downside. Irish Guards, 1943–47. Lloyd's, 1942–: Underwriting Mem., 1956; Mem., Cttee of Lloyd's, 1973–76; Mem., Cttee of Lloyd's Non-Marine Assoc., 1965, Chm. 1971, Dep. Chm. 1970 and 1972. *Recreations:* boating, music. *Address:* 123 Pier House, Cheyne Walk, SW3 5HM. *T:* 01–351 1313. *Club:* Royal Yacht Squadron.

FOGARTY, Christopher Winthrop, CB 1973; Deputy Secretary, Overseas Development Administration, Foreign and Commonwealth Office, (formerly Ministry of Overseas Development), 1976–81; *b* 18 Sept. 1921; *s* of late Philip Christopher Fogarty, ICS, and late Hilda Spenser Fogarty; *m* 1961, Elizabeth Margaret Ince (*d* 1972). *Educ:* Ampleforth Coll.; Christ Church, Oxford. War Service (Lieut RA), 1942–45. Asst Principal, 1946, Principal, 1949, HM Treasury; Permanent Sec., Min. of Finance of Eastern Nigeria, 1956; Asst Sec., HM Treasury, 1959, Under-Sec., 1966; Treasury Rep., S Asia and FE, 1967–72; Dep. Sec., HM Treasury, and Dir, European Investment Bank, 1972–76. *Address:* 7 Hurlingham Court, Ranelagh Gardens, SW6 3SH. *Clubs:* Royal Commonwealth Society, Travellers'; Royal Selangor Golf.

See also M. P. Fogarty.

FOGARTY, Michael Patrick; Director, Institute for Family and Environmental Research, 1981–84; *b* 3 Oct. 1916; *s* of late Philip Christopher Fogarty, ICS, and Mary Belle Pye, Galway; *m* 1939, Phyllis Clark; two *s* two *d*. *Educ:* Ampleforth Coll.; Christ Church, Oxford. Lieut RA, 1940 (wounded, Dunkirk). Nuffield Coll., 1941–51 (Fellow, 1944); Montague Burton Prof. of Industrial Relations, University Coll. of S Wales and Mon, 1951–66; Dir and Prof., Econ. and Social Res. Inst., Dublin, 1968–72; Centre for Studies in Social Policy: Sen. Fellow, 1973; Dep. Dir, 1977–78; Dep. Dir, PSI, 1978–82. Also held posts in Administrative Staff Coll., Oxford Institute of Statistics, Nat. Institute of Economic and Social Research, Ministry of Town and Country Planning, and as Asst Editor, The Economist. Chairman: Cttee on Industrial Relations in the Electricity Supply Bd (Ireland), 1968–69; Banks Inquiry, 1970–71; Member: Commn on the Status of Women (Ireland), 1970–72; Commn on Insurance Industry (Ireland), 1970–72; Cttee on Aid to Political Parties, 1975–76. Pres., Newman Assoc., 1957–59; Chm., Catholic Social Guild, 1959–63; Mem., Social Welfare Commn, RC Bishops' Conf. (E&W); Vice-Pres. Assoc. of University Teachers, 1964–66. Prospective Parly candidate (Lab) Tamworth, 1938–44; Parliamentary Candidate (L): Devizes, 1964 and 1966; Abingdon, Feb. and Oct. 1974. Vice-Pres. of the Liberal Party, 1964–66. Contested (L) Thames Valley, European Parlt, 1979. District Councillor, Vale of White Horse, 1973–; CC Oxfordshire, 1981– (Vice-Chm., 1985–86; Chm., 1986–87). Hon. Dr of Political and Social Science, Louvain, 1963. *Publications:* Prospects of the Industrial Areas of Great Britain, 1945; Plan Your Own Industries, 1947; (ed) Further Studies in Industrial Organisation, 1948; Town and Country Planning, 1948; Economic Control, 1955; Personality and Group Relations in Industry, 1956; Christian Democracy in Western Europe, 1820–1953, 1957; The Just Wage, 1961; Under-Governed and Over-Governed, 1962; The Rules of Work, 1963; Company and Corporation—One Law?, 1965; Companies Beyond Jenkins, 1965; Wider Business Objectives, 1966; A Companies Act 1970?, 1967; (with Allen, Allen and Walters) Women in Top Jobs, 1971; (with Rapoport and Rapoport) Sex, Career and Family, 1971; Women and Top Jobs: the next move, 1972; Irish Entrepreneurs Speak For Themselves, 1974; Forty to Sixty, 1975; Company Responsibility and Participation—A New Agenda, 1975; Pensions—where next?, 1976; (with Eileen Reid) Differentials for Managers and Skilled Manual Workers in the UK, 1980; Retirement Age and Retirement Costs, 1980; (with Allen and Walters) Women in Top Jobs 1968–79, 1981; (ed) Retirement Policy: the next fifty years, 1982. *Recreations:* swimming, walking. *Address:* Red Copse, Boars Hill, Oxford.

See also C. W. Fogarty.

FOGDEN, Michael Ernest George; Under Secretary, Manpower Policy, Department of Employment, since 1984; *b* 30 May 1936; *s* of late George Charles Arthur and of Margaret May Fogden; *m* 1957, Rose Ann Diamond; three *s* one *d*. *Educ:* High Sch. for Boys, Worthing. Nat. Service, RAF, 1956–58. Ministry of Pensions and National Insurance, later Department of Health and Social Security: Clerical Officer, 1958–59; Exec. Officer, 1959–67, Private Sec. to Parly Sec., 1967–68; Asst Private Sec. to Sec. of State for Social Services, 1968–70; Principal, 1970–76; Asst Sec., 1976–83; Under Sec., 1983–84. Chm., First Div. Assoc. of Civil Servants, 1980–83. *Recreations:* gardening, wine making, talking. *Address:* 59 Mayfield Avenue, Orpington, Kent BR6 0AH. *T:* Orpington 77395. *Club:* Royal Commonwealth Society.

FOGEL, Prof. Robert W.; Charles R. Walgreen Professor of American Institutions, University of Chicago, since 1981; *b* 1 July 1926; *s* of Harry G. Fogel and Elizabeth (*née* Mitnik); two *s*. *Educ:* Cornell, Columbia and Johns Hopkins Univs. AB Cornell 1948; AM Columbia 1960; PhD Johns Hopkins 1963. Instructor, Johns Hopkins Univ., 1958–59; Asst Prof., Univ. of Rochester, 1960–64; Assoc. Prof., Univ. of Chicago, 1964–65; Prof., Econs and History, Univ. of Chicago, 1965–75, Univ. of Rochester, 1968–75. Taussig Research Prof., Harvard Univ., 1973–74; Pitt Prof. of Amer. History and Instns, Cambridge Univ., 1975–76; Harold Hitchings Burbank Prof. of Econs and Prof. of History, Harvard Univ., 1975–81. President: Economic History Assoc., 1977–78;

Soc. Sci. Hist. Assoc., 1980–81. FRHistS 1975. Phi Beta Kappa, 1963; Arthur H. Cole Prize, 1968; Schumpeter Prize, 1971; Bancroft Prize, 1975; Fellow: Econometric Soc., 1971; Amer. Acad. of Arts and Sciences, 1972; Nat. Acad. of Sciences, 1973; Amer. Assoc. for the Advancement of Science, 1978; FRHistS 1974. *Publications:* The Union Pacific Railroad: a case in premature enterprise, 1960; Railroads and American Economic Growth: essays in econometric history, 1964 (Spanish edn 1972); (jtly) The Reinterpretation of American Economic History, 1971 (Italian edn 1975); (jtly) The Dimension of Quantitative Research in History, 1972; (jtly) Time on the Cross: The Economics of American Negro Slavery, 1974 (Japanese edn 1977, Spanish edn 1981); Ten Lectures on the New Economic History, 1977; (jtly) Which Road to the Past? Two Views of History, 1983; numerous papers in learned jls. *Address:* (home) 5321 S University Avenue, Chicago, Illinois 60615, USA; (office) 1101 E 58th Street, Chicago, Illinois 60637, USA.

FOGG, Alan; Chairman, Royal Philanthropic Society, since 1982; former Director, PA International; *b* 19 Sept. 1921; *o s* of John Fogg, Dulwich; *m* 1948, Mary Marsh; two *s* one *d*. *Educ:* Repton; Exeter Coll., Oxford (MA, BSc). Served with RN, 1944–47. *Publications:* (with Barnes, Stephens and Titman) Company Organisation: theory and practice, 1970; various papers on management subjects. *Recreations:* travel, gardening. *Address:* Albury Edge, Merstham, Surrey. *T:* Merstham 2023. *Club:* United Oxford & Cambridge University.

FOGG, Albert, CBE 1972; DSc; *b* 25 Feb. 1909; *o s* of late James Fogg, Bolton. *Educ:* Manchester University. Scientific staff, National Physical Laboratory, 1930–46; first Dir, Motor Industry Research Assoc., 1946–64; Director: Leyland Motor Corporation, 1964–68; British Leyland Motor Corporation Ltd, 1968–74; ENASA (Spain), 1965–74; retired. Hon. DSc Southampton, 1979. Inst. of Mechanical Engineers: T. Bernard Hall Prize, 1945 and 1955; Starley Premium, 1956; James Clayton Prize, 1962; Viva Shield and Gold Medal, Worshipful Company of Carmen, 1962. *Publications:* numerous papers in jls of scientific socs and professional instns. *Address:* 4 Brownsea View Close, Lilliput, Poole, Dorset. *T:* Poole 708788.

FOGG, Cyril Percival, CB 1973; Director, Admiralty Surface Weapons Establishment, Ministry of Defence (Procurement Executive), 1973–75, retired; *b* 28 Nov. 1914; *s* of Henry Fogg and Mabel Mary (*née* Orton); *m* 1st, 1939, Margaret Amie Millican (*d* 1982); two *d*; 2nd, 1983, June Adele McCoy. *Educ:* Herbert Strutt Sch., Belper; Gonville and Caius Coll., Cambridge (MA, 1st cl. Mechanical Sciences Tripos). Research Staff, General Electric Co., 1936–37; various positions in Scientific Civil Service from 1937 with Air Ministry, Ministries of Aircraft Production, Supply, Aviation and Technology. Head of Ground Radar Dept, RRE Malvern, 1956–58; Dir Electronics R&D (Ground), 1959–63; Imperial Defence Coll., 1961; Dir of Guided Weapons Research, 1963–64; Dir-Gen. of Electronics R&D, Min. of Aviation, 1964–67; Dep. Controller of Electronics, Min. of Technology, later MoD (Procurement Executive), 1967–72. *Address:* 10 Miles Cottages, Taylors Lane, Old Bosham, Chichester, West Sussex PO18 8QG.

FOGG, Prof. Gordon Elliott, CBE 1983; FRS 1965; Professor and Head of the Department of Marine Biology, University College of North Wales, Bangor, 1971–85, now Professor Emeritus; *b* 26 April 1919; *s* of Rev. L. C. Fogg; *m* 1945, Elizabeth Beryl Llechid-Jones; one *s* one *d*. *Educ:* Dulwich Coll.; Queen Mary Coll., London; St John's Coll., Cambridge. BSc (London), 1939; PhD (Cambridge), 1943; ScD (Cambridge), 1966. Sea-weed Survey of British Isles, 1942; Plant Physiologist, Pest Control Ltd, 1943–45; successively Asst Lectr, Lectr and Reader in Botany, University Coll., London, 1945–60; Rockefeller Fellow, 1954; Prof. of Botany, Westfield Coll., Univ. of London, 1960–71. Trustee: BM (Natural Hist.), 1976–85; Royal Botanic Gardens, Kew, 1983–. Member: Royal Commn on Environmental Pollution, 1979–85; NERC, 1981–82. Royal Soc. Leverhulme Vis. Prof., Kerala, 1969–70; Leverhulme Emeritus Fellow, 1986. Botanical Sec., Soc. for Experimental Biology, 1957–60; President: British Phycological Soc., 1961–62; International Phycological Soc., 1964; Inst. of Biology, 1976–77; Chm. Council, Freshwater Biol Assoc., 1974–85; Joint Organizing Sec., X International Botanical Congress. Visiting research worker, British Antarctic Survey, 1966, 1974, 1979; Biological Gen. Sec., British Assoc., 1967–72, Pres., Section K, 1973. Fellow, QMC, 1976. Hon. LLD Dundee, 1974. *Publications:* The Metabolism of Algae, 1953; The Growth of Plants, 1963; Algal Cultures and Phytoplankton Ecology, 1965, 3rd edn (with B. Thake), 1986; Photosynthesis, 1968; (jointly) The Blue-green Algae, 1973; papers in learned jls. *Recreations:* water colour painting, walking. *Address:* Bodolben, Llandegfan, Menai Bridge, Gwynedd. *T:* Menai Bridge 712916. *Club:* Athenæum.

FOGGON, George, CMG 1961; OBE 1949 (MBE 1945); Director, London Office, International Labour Organisation, 1976–82, retired; *b* 13 Sept. 1913; *s* of Thomas Foggon, Newcastle upon Tyne; *m* 1st, 1938, Agnes McIntosh (*d* 1968); one *s*; 2nd, 1969, Audrey Blanch. Joined Min. of Labour, 1930. Served War of 1939–45 (MBE), Wing-Comdr, RAFVR, 1941–46. Seconded to FO, 1946; on staff of Mil. Gov., Berlin, 1946–49; Principal, CO, 1949; Asst Sec., W African Inter-Territorial Secretariat, Gold Coast (now Ghana), 1951–53; Comr of Labour, Nigeria, 1954–58; Labour Adviser: to Sec. of State for Colonies, 1958–61; to Sec. for Techn. Co-op., 1962–64; to Min. of Overseas Development, 1965–66; Overseas Labour Advr, FO later FCO, 1966–76, retd. *Recreations:* walking, photography. *Address:* 8 Churton Place, SW1. *T:* 01–828 1492. *Clubs:* Athenæum, Oriental.

FOLDES, Andor; international concert pianist since 1933; Head of Piano Master Class, Conservatory, Saarbrücken, 1957–65; *b* Budapest, Hungary, 21 Dec. 1913; *s* of Emil Foldes and Valerie Foldes (*née* Ipolyi); *m* 1940, Lili Rendy (writer); no *c*. *Educ:* Franz Liszt Academy of Music, Budapest. Started piano playing at 5; first appeared with Budapest Philh. Orch. at 8; studied with Ernest von Dohnanyi, received Master Diploma (Fr. Liszt Acad. of Music, Budapest), 1932. Concerts all over Europe, 1933–39; US debut (NBC Orch.), 1940; toured US extensively, 1940–48. US citizen since 1948. Concerts, since, all over the world, incl. three recitals in Peking, 1978. Grand Prix du Disque, Paris, for Bartok Complete Works (piano solo), 1957. Beethoven concerts, Bonn Festival and throughout Europe. Recordings of all Beethoven Sonatas, and works of Mozart and Schubert. Order of Merit, First Class, 1956, Gr. Cross, 1964 (Germany); Commandeur, Mérite Culturel et Artistique (City of Paris), 1968; Medaille d'Argent de la Ville de Paris, 1971. *Publications:* Keys to the Keyboard, 1950; Cadenzas to Mozart Piano Concertos (W Germany); Is there a Contemporary Style of Beethoven-playing?, 1963; various piano compositions. *Relevant publication:* Wolf-Eberhard von Lewinski, Andor Foldes, 1970. *Recreations:* collecting art, reading, writing on musical subjects; swimming, hiking. *Address:* 8704 Herrliberg, Zürich, Switzerland.

FOLDES, Prof. Lucien Paul; Professor of Economics, University of London, at London School of Economics and Political Science, since 1979; *b* 19 Nov. 1930; *s* of Egon and Marta Foldes. *Educ:* Bunce Court Sch.; Monkton Wyld Sch.; London School of Economics (BCom, MScEcon, DBA). National Service, 1952–54. LSE: Asst Lecturer in Economics, 1954–55; Lectr, 1955–61; Reader, 1961–79. Rockefeller Travelling Fellow, 1961–62. *Publications:* articles in Rev. of Economic Studies, Economica, Jl of Mathematical Economics, and others. *Recreation:* mathematical analysis. *Address:* London School of Economics, Houghton Street, WC2A 2AE. *T:* 01–405 7686.

FOLEY, family name of **Baron Foley.**

FOLEY, 8th Baron *cr* 1776; **Adrian Gerald Foley;** *b* 9 Aug. 1923; *s* of 7th Baron and Minoru (*d* 1968), *d* of late H. Greenstone, South Africa; *S* father, 1927; *m* 1st, 1958, Patricia Meek (marr. diss. 1971); one *s* one *d*; 2nd, 1972, Ghislaine Lady Ashcombe. *Heir:* *s* Hon. Thomas Henry Foley, *b* 1 April 1961. *Address:* c/o Marbella Club, Marbella, Malaga, Spain. *Club:* White's.

FOLEY, Rt. Rev. Brian Charles; Former Bishop of Lancaster; *b* Ilford, 25 May 1910. *Educ:* St Cuthbert's Coll., Ushaw; English College and Gregorian Univ., Rome. Priest, 1937; Assistant Priest, Shoeburyness; subseq. Assistant Priest, Romford; Parish Priest, Holy Redeemer, Harold Hill, and Holy Cross, Harlow. Canon of Brentwood Diocese, 1959. Bishop of Lancaster, 1962–85. President: Catholic Record Society, 1964–80; Catholic Archive Soc., 1979–. *Address:* Nazareth House, Ashton Road, Lancaster LA1 5AQ. *T:* Lancaster 382748.

FOLEY, Johanna Mary, (Jo), (Mrs D. F. C. Quigley); Editor, Observer Magazine, since 1986; *b* 8 Dec. 1945; *d* of John and Monica Foley; *m* 1973, Desmond Francis Conor Quigley. *Educ:* St Joseph's Convent, Kenilworth; Manchester Univ. (BA Jt Hons English and Drama, 1968). Woman's Editor, Walsall Observer, 1968; Reporter, Birmingham Post, 1970; English Teacher, Monkwick Secondary Modern Sch., Colchester, and More House Sch., London, 1972–73; Dep. Beauty Editor, Woman's Own, 1973; launched and edited magazine, Successful Slimming, 1976; Sen. Asst Editor, Woman's Own, 1978; Woman's Editor, The Sun, 1980; Editor, Woman, 1982; Exec. Editor (Features), The Times, 1984–85; Man. Editor, The Mirror, 1985–86. Editor of the Year, British Soc. of Magazine Editors, 1983. *Publication:* The Pick of Woman's Own Diets, 1979. *Recreations:* eating, reading, cinema, ballet. *Address:* The Observer, 8 St Andrew's Hill, EC4V 5JA.

FOLEY, Maurice (Anthony); Deputy Director General, Directorate General for Development, Commission of the European Communities, since 1973; *b* 9 Oct. 1925; *s* of Jeremiah and Agnes Foley; *m* 1952, Catherine, *d* of Patrick and Nora O'Riordan; three *s* one *d*. *Educ:* St Mary's Coll., Middlesbrough. Formerly: electrical fitter, youth organiser, social worker. Member: ETU, 1941–46; Transport and General Workers Union, 1948–; Royal Arsenal Co-operative Soc. MP (Lab), West Bromwich, 1963–73; Joint Parliamentary Under-Sec. of State, Dept of Economic Affairs, 1964–66; Parly Under-Secretary: Home Office, 1966–67; Royal Navy, MoD, 1967–68; FCO, 1968–70. *Address:* Commission of the European Communities, 200 rue de la Loi, 1049 Brussels, Belgium.

FOLEY, Sir Noel; *see* Foley, Sir T. J. N.

FOLEY, Rt. Rev. Ronald Graham Gregory; *see* Reading, Area Bishop of.

FOLEY, Sir (Thomas John) Noel, Kt 1978; CBE 1967; Chairman: CSR Ltd, 1980–84; Allied Manufacturing and Trading Industries (AMATIL) Ltd, 1955–79 (retired); President, Westpac Banking Corporation, since 1982 (Chairman, 1980–87; Chairman, Bank of New South Wales, 1978–82); Founding President, World Wildlife Fund, Australia, 1978–80; *b* 1914; *s* of late Benjamin Foley, Brisbane. *Educ:* Brisbane Grammar Sch., Queensland; Queensland Univ. (BA, BCom). *Address:* c/o Westpac Banking Corporation, 60 Martin Place, Sydney, NSW 2000, Australia.

FOLEY, Most Rev. William J.; *see* Perth (Australia), Archbishop of.

FOLEY-BERKELEY, family name of **Baroness Berkeley.**

FOLJAMBE, family name of **Earl of Liverpool.**

FOLKESTONE, Viscount; William Pleydell-Bouverie; *b* 5 Jan. 1955; *s* and *heir* of 8th Earl of Radnor, *qv*. *Educ:* Harrow; Royal Agricultural Coll., Cirencester. *Address:* Round House, Charlton All Saints, Salisbury, Wilts. *T:* Salisbury 330295.

FOLLETT, Prof. Brian Keith, PhD, DSc; FRS 1984; Professor of Zoology and Head of Department, University of Bristol, since 1978; *b* 22 Feb. 1939; *s* of Albert James Follett and Edith Annie Follett; *m* 1961, Deb (*née* Booth); one *s* one *d*. *Educ:* Bournemouth Sch.; Univ. of Bristol (BSc 1960, PhD 1964); Univ. of Wales (DSc 1975). Res. Fellow, Washington State Univ., 1964–65; Lectr in Zool., Univ. of Leeds, 1965–69; Lectr, subseq. Reader and Prof. of Zool., University Coll. of N Wales, Bangor, 1969–78. Mem., AFRC, 1984–. Scientific Medal, Zool Soc. of London, 1976. *Publications:* papers in physiol, endocrinol, and zool jls. *Address:* Department of Zoology, The University, Bristol.

FOLLETT, Samuel Frank, CMG 1959; BSc, CEng, FIEE, FRAeS; *b* 21 March 1904; *o s* of Samuel Charles Follett and Kate Bell; *m* 1932, Kathleen Matilda Tupper. *Educ:* Farnham Gram. Sch.; Univ. of London. Electrical Research Assoc., 1924–27; Electrical Engineering Dept, RAE Farnborough, 1927–45; Asst Dir of Instrument R&D (Electrics), Min. of Supply, 1946–50; Dir of Instrument R&D, 1950–54; Dep. Dir-Gen. Aircraft, Equipment, R&D, 1954–56; Dir.-Gen., Min. of Supply Staff, Brit. Jt Services Mission, Washington, DC, 1956–59; Dep. Dir, RAE Farnborough, 1959–63; Dep. Controller of Guided Weapons, Min. of Aviation, 1963–66; Scientific Adviser to BoT, 1966–69. *Address:* Darby Cottage, St Johns Road, Farnham, Surrey. *T:* Farnham 716610.

FONTAINE, André Lucien Georges; Editor-in-Chief, le Monde, since 1985; *b* 30 March 1921; *s* of Georges Fontaine and Blanche Rochon Duvigneaud; *m* 1943, Belita Cavaillé; two *s* one *d*. *Educ:* Paris Univ. (diplomes études supérieures droit public et économie politique, lic.lettres). Joined Temps Présent, 1946; with le Monde from 1947; Foreign Editor, 1951; Chief Editor, 1969. Editorialist, Radio Luxemburg, 1980–. Chm. Adv. Gp, Internat. Strategy for the 9th Plan, 1982–84; Mem. Bd, Institut Français des Relations Internationales, 1980–85. Mem. Bd, Bank Indosuez, 1983–85. Comdr, Italian Merit; Officer, Orders of Vasa (Sweden), Leopold (Belgium) and Lion (Finland); Kt, Danebrog (Denmark) and Crown of Belgium; Order of Tudor Vladimirescu (Romania). Atlas' Internat. Editor of the Year, 1976. *Publications:* L'Alliance atlantique à l'heure du dégel, 1960; Histoire de la guerre froide, vol. 1 1965, vol. 2 1966 (English trans., History of the Cold War, 1966 and 1967); La Guerre civile froide, 1969; Le dernier quart du siècle, 1976; La France au bois dormant, 1978; Un seul lit pour deux rêves, 1981; (with Pierre Li) Sortir de l'Hexagonie, 1984; contrib. Foreign Affairs, Affari Esteri, Europa Archiv, BBC, etc. *Address:* 5 rue des Italiens, 75009 Paris, France. *T:* 42 47 97 27.

FONTEYN, Dame Margot; *see* Arias, Dame Margot Fonteyn de.

FOOKES, Janet Evelyn; MP (C) Plymouth, Drake, since 1974 (Merton and Morden, 1970–74); *b* 21 Feb. 1936; *d* of late Lewis Aylmer Fookes and of Evelyn Margery Fookes (*née* Holmes). *Educ:* Hastings and St Leonards Ladies' Coll.; High Sch. for Girls, Hastings; Royal Holloway Coll., Univ. of London (BA Hons). Teacher, 1958–70. Councillor for County Borough of Hastings, 1960–61 and 1963–70 (Chm. Educn Cttee, 1967–70). Mem., Speaker's Panel of Chairmen, 1976–. Sec., Cons. Parly Educn Cttee, 1971–75; Chairman: Educn, Arts and Home Affairs Sub-Cttee of the Expenditure Cttee, 1975–79; Parly Gp for Animal Welfare, 1985– (Sec., 1974–82); Member: Unopposed Bills Cttee,

1973–75; Services Cttee, 1974–76; Select Cttee on Home Affairs, 1984–. Chm., Cons. West Country Mems Cttee, 1976–77, Vice-Chm., 1977. Mem. Council, RSPCA, 1975– (Chm., 1979–81); Member: Nat. Art Collections Fund; Council, SSAFA, 1980–; Council, Stonham Housing Assoc., 1980–. *Recreations:* gardening, gymnasium exercises. *Address:* House of Commons, SW1A 0AA. *Club:* Royal Over-Seas League.

FOOT, family name of **Baron Caradon** and **Baron Foot.**

FOOT, Baron *cr* 1967 (Life Peer), of Buckland Monachorum; **John Mackintosh Foot;** Senior Partner, Foot & Bowden, Solicitors, Plymouth; Chairman, United Kingdom Immigrants Advisory Service, 1970–78; *b* 17 Feb. 1909; 3rd *s* of late Rt Hon. Isaac Foot, PC and Eva Mackintosh; *m* 1936, Anne, *d* of Dr Clifford Bailey Farr, Bryn Mawr, Pa; one *s* one *d*. *Educ:* Forres Sch., Swanage; Bembridge Sch., IoW; Balliol Coll., Oxford. Pres., Oxford Union, 1931; Pres., OU Liberal Club, 1931; BA Oxon (2nd cl. hons Jurisprudence), 1931. Admitted Solicitor, 1934. Served in Army, 1939–45 (Hon. Major); jsc 1944. Contested (L); Basingstoke, 1934 and 1935; Bodmin, 1945 and 1950. Member: Dartmoor National Park Cttee, 1963–74; Commn on the Constitution, 1969–73; President: Dartmoor Preservation Assoc., 1976–; Commons, Open Spaces and Footpaths Preservation Soc., 1976–82; UK Immigrants Adv. Service, 1978–84. *Recreations:* chess, crosswords, defending Dartmoor. *Address:* Yew Tree, Crapstone, Yelverton, Devon. *T:* Yelverton 853417. *Club:* Royal Western Yacht.

See also Baron Caradon, Rt Hon. Michael Foot.

FOOT, Sir Geoffrey (James), Kt 1984; Chairman: Tasmania Permanent Building Society, 1982–85; Launceston Gas Co., since 1982; *b* 20 July 1915; *s* of James P. Foot and Susan J. Foot; *m* 1940, Mollie W. Snooks; two *s* one *d*. *Educ:* Launceston High Sch. AASA; ACIS. MLC, Tasmania, 1961–72 (Leader for Govt, 1969–72). Mem., Lilydale Commn—Local Govt, 1983–85; Associate Comr, Hydro Electric Commn of Tas, 1984–. Mem. Council, Univ. of Tas, 1970–85. *Recreations:* reading, music. *Address:* 85 Arthur Street, Launceston, Tas 7250, Australia. *T:* 003–340573. *Clubs:* Tasmanian (Hobart); Launceston (Launceston).

FOOT, Rt. Hon. Michael, PC 1974; MP (Lab) Blaenau Gwent, since 1983 (Ebbw Vale, Nov. 1960–1983); *b* 23 July 1913; *s* of late Rt Hon. Isaac Foot, PC; *m* 1949, Jill Craigie. *Educ:* Forres Sch., Swanage; Leighton Park Sch., Reading; Wadham Coll., Oxford (Exhibitioner). Pres. Oxford Union, 1933; contested (Lab) Mon, 1935; MP (Lab) Devonport Div. of Plymouth, 1945–55. Sec. of State for Employment, 1974–76; Lord President of the Council and Leader of the House of Commons, 1976–79; Leader of the Opposition, 1980–83. Mem., Labour Party Nat. Exec. Cttee, 1971–83; Deputy Leader of the Labour Party, 1976–80, Leader of the Labour Party 1980–83. Asst Editor, Tribune, 1937–38; Acting Editor, Evening Standard, 1942; Man. Dir, Tribune, 1945–74, Editor, 1948–52, 1955–60; political columnist on the Daily Herald, 1944–64; former Book Critic, Evening Standard. Hon. Fellow, Wadham Coll. 1969. *Publications:* Guilty Men (with Frank Owen and Peter Howard), 1940; Armistice 1918–39, 1940; Trial of Mussolini, 1943; Brendan and Beverley, 1944; Still at Large, 1950; Full Speed Ahead, 1950; Guilty Men (with Mervyn Jones), 1957; The Pen and the Sword, 1957; Parliament in Danger, 1959; Aneurin Bevan: Vol. I, 1897–1945, 1962; Vol. II, 1945–60, 1973; Debts of Honour, 1980; Another Heart and Other Pulses, 1984; Loyalists and Loners, 1986. *Recreations:* Plymouth Argyle supporter, chess, reading, walking. *Address:* House of Commons, SW1.

See also Baron Caradon, Baron Foot.

FOOT, Michael Richard Daniell; historian; *b* 14 Dec. 1919; *s* of late R. C. Foot and Nina (*née* Raymond); *m* twice; one *s* one *d*; 3rd, 1972, Mirjam Michaela, DLitt, *y d* of late Prof. C. P. M. Romme, Oisterwijk. *Educ:* Winchester (scholar); New Coll., Oxford (scholar). Served in Army, 1939–45 (Major RA, parachutist, wounded). Taught at Oxford, 1947–59; research, 1959–67; Prof of Modern Hist., Manchester, 1967–73; Dir of Studies, European Discussion Centre, 1973–75. French Croix de Guerre, 1945. *Publications:* Gladstone and Liberalism (with J. L. Hammond), 1952; British Foreign Policy since 1898, 1956; Men in Uniform, 1961; SOE in France, 1966; (ed) The Gladstone Diaries: vols I and II, 1825–1839, 1968; (ed) War and Society, 1973; (ed with Dr H. C. G. Matthew) The Gladstone Diaries: vols III and IV, 1840–1854, 1974; Resistance, 1976; Six Faces of Courage, 1978; (with J. M. Langley) MI9, 1979; SOE: an outline history, 1984. *Recreations:* reading, talking. *Address:* 45 Countess Road, NW5 2XH. *Clubs:* Savile, Special Forces.

FOOT, Paul Mackintosh; writer; journalist; with The Daily Mirror, since 1979; *b* 8 Nov. 1937; *m*; three *s*. Editor of Isis, 1961; President of the Oxford Union, 1961. TUC delegate from Nat. Union of Journalists, 1967 and 1971. Contested (Socialist Workers Party) Birmingham, Stechford, March 1977. Editor, Socialist Worker, 1974–75. Journalist of the Year, Granada, 1972; Campaigning Journalist of the Year, British Press Awards, 1980. *Publications:* Immigration and Race in British Politics, 1965; The Politics of Harold Wilson, 1968; The Rise of Enoch Powell, 1969; Who Killed Hanratty?, 1971; Why You Should Be a Socialist, 1977; Red Shelley, 1981; The Helen Smith Story, 1983; Murder at the Farm, 1986. *Address:* c/o The Daily Mirror, Holborn Circus, EC1.

FOOT, Mrs Philippa Ruth, FBA 1976; Senior Research Fellow, Somerville College, Oxford, since 1970; Professor of Philosophy, University of California at Los Angeles, since 1974; *b* 3 Oct. 1920; *d* of William Sydney Bence Bosanquet, DSO, and Esther Cleveland Bosanquet, *d* of Grover Cleveland, Pres. of USA; *m* 1945, M. R. D. Foot (marr. diss. 1960), *qv*; no *c*. *Educ:* St George's Sch., Ascot; privately; Somerville Coll., Oxford (BA 1942, MA 1946). Somerville Coll., Oxford: Lectr in philosophy, 1947; Fellow and Tutor, 1950–69; Vice-Principal, 1967–69. Formerly Vis. Prof., Cornell Univ., MIT, Univ. of California at Berkeley, Princeton Univ., City Univ. of NY; Fellow, Center for Advanced Studies in Behavioral Scis, Stanford, 1981–82. Pres., Pacific Div., Amer. Philos. Assoc., 1982–83. Fellow, Amer. Acad. of Arts and Scis, 1983. *Publications:* Theories of Ethics (ed), 1967; Virtues and Vices, 1978; articles in Mind, Aristotelian Soc. Proc., Philos. Rev., New York Rev., Philosophy and Public Affairs. *Address:* 15 Walton Street, Oxford OX1 2HG. *T:* Oxford 57130.

FOOTE, Maj.-Gen. Henry Robert Bowreman, VC 1944; CB 1952; DSO 1942; *b* 5 Dec. 1904; *s* of Lieut-Col H. B. Foote, late RA; *m* 1st, 1944, Anita Flint Howard (*d* 1970); 2nd, 1981, Mrs Audrey Mary Ashwell. *Educ:* Bedford Sch. Royal Tank Corps; 2nd Lieut, 1925; Lieut, 1927; Capt., 1936; Staff Coll., 1939; GSO3, WO, 1939; GSO2, WO, 1940; GSO2, Staff Coll., 1940–41; GSO1, 10th Armd Div., 1941–42; OC 7th Royal Tank Regt, 1942; Subst. Major, 1942; GSO1, AFHQ, Italy, 1944; 2i/c, 9th Armd Bde, 1945; Brig. RAC, MELF, 1945–47; Subst. Lieut-Col, 1946; Subst. Col, 1948; OC 2nd Royal Tank Regt, 1947–48; OC Automotive Wing, Fighting Vehicles Proving Establishment, Ministry of Supply, 1948–49; Comd 7th Armd Bde, 1949–50; Maj.-Gen. 1951; Comd 11th Armoured Div., 1950–53; Dir-Gen. of Fighting Vehicles, Min. of Supply, 1953–55; Dir, Royal Armoured Corps, at the War Office, 1955–58; retd. *Address:* Furzefield, West Chiltington Common, Pulborough, West Sussex. *Club:* Army and Navy.

FOOTE, Rev. John Weir, VC 1946; DD, LLD University of Western Ontario, 1947; Minister of Reform Institutions, Government of Ontario, 1950–57; *b* 5 May 1904; *s* of Gordon Foote, Madoc, Ontario; *m* 1929. *Educ:* University of Western Ontario, London, Ont; Presbyterian Coll. (McGill). Served War of 1939–45; Regimental Chaplain with Royal Hamilton Light Infantry (VC). Minister St Paul's Presbyterian Church, Port Hope, Ont. Canadian Army from 1939, Asst Principal Chaplain (P). *Recreations:* golf, fishing. *Address:* Front Road East, Coburg, Ontario, Canada.

FOOTE, Prof. Peter Godfrey; Emeritus Professor of Scandinavian Studies, University of London; *b* 26 May 1924; 4th *s* of late T. Foote and Ellen Foote, Swanage, Dorset; *m* 1951, Eleanor Jessie McCaig, *d* of late J. M. McCaig and Margaret H. McCaig; one *s* two *d*. *Educ:* Grammar Sch., Swanage; University Coll., Exeter; Univ. of Oslo; University Coll., London. BA London 1948; MA London 1951; Fil. dr *hc* Uppsala, 1972. Served with RNVR, 1943–46. University College London: Asst Lectr, Lectr and Reader in Old Scandinavian, 1950–63; Prof. of Scandinavian Studies, 1963–83. Jt Sec., Viking Soc., 1956–83, Pres., 1974–76, Hon. Life Mem., 1983. Member: Royal Gustav Adolfs Academy, Uppsala, 1967; Kungl. Humanistiska Vetenskapssamfundet, Uppsala, 1968; Vísindafélag Islands, 1969; Vetenskapssocieteten, Lund, 1973; Kungl. Vetenskaps-samhället, Göteborg; Det kongelige Norske Videnskabers Selskab, 1977; Societas Scientiarum Fennica, 1979; Det norske Videnskapsakademi, 1986; Hon. Member: Isl. Bókmenntafélag, 1965; Thjóðvinafélag Ísl. í Vesturheimi, 1975; Corresp. Mem., Kungl. Vitterhets Hist. och Antikvitets Akad., Stockholm, 1971. Crabtree Orator, 1968. Commander with star, Icelandic Order of the Falcon, 1984 (Comdr, 1973); Knight, Order of Dannebrog (Denmark); Comdr, Royal Order of North Star (Sweden), 1977. *Publications:* Gunnlaugs saga ormstungu, 1957; Pseudo-Turpin Chronicle in Iceland, 1959; Laing's Heimskringla, 1961; Lives of Saints: Icelandic manuscripts in fascimile IV, 1962; (with G. Johnston) The Saga of Gisli, 1963; (with D. M. Wilson) The Viking Achievement, 1970, 2nd edn 1980; Aurvandilstá (selected papers), 1984; Jt Editor, Mediæval Scandinavia; Mem. of Ed. Board, Arv, Scandinavica; papers in Saga-Book, Arv, Studia Islandica, Islenzk Tunga, etc. *Recreations:* bell-ringing, walking. *Address:* 18 Talbot Road, N6. *T:* 01–340 1860.

FOOTMAN, Charles Worthington Fowden, CMG 1952; *b* 3 Sept. 1905; *s* of Rev. William Llewellyn and Mary Elizabeth Footman; *m* 1947, Joyce Marcelle Law; one *s* two *d*. *Educ:* Rossall Sch.; Keble Coll., Oxford. Colonial Administrative Service, Zanzibar, 1930; seconded to East African Governors' Conference, 1942; seconded to Colonial Office, 1943–46; Financial Sec., Nyasaland, 1947; Chief Sec., Nyasaland, 1951–60. Retired from HM Overseas Civil Service, 1960. Chm., Public Service Commissions, Tanganyika and Zanzibar, 1960–61; Commonwealth Relations Office, 1962–64; Min. of Overseas Development, 1964–70. *Recreations:* golf and tennis. *Address:* c/o National Westminster Bank, Worthing, West Sussex.

FOOTS, Sir James (William), Kt 1975; mining engineer; Chairman, Westpac Banking Corporation, since 1987 (Director, since 1971); Deputy Chairman, MIM Holdings Ltd, Queensland, since 1983 (Chairman, 1970–83); Director, Asarco Inc., New York, since 1985; *b* 1916; *m* 1939, Thora H.Thomas; one *s* two *d*. *Educ:* Melbourne Univ. (BME). President: Austr. Inst. Mining and Metallurgy, 1974; Austr. Mining Industry Council, 1974 and 1975; 13th Congress, Council of Mining and Metallurgical Institns, 1986. Fellow, Australian Acad. of Technol Scis. University of Queensland: Mem. Senate, 1970–; Chancellor, 1985–. Hon. DEng Univ. of Qld, 1982. *Address:* GPO Box 2236, Brisbane, Qld 4001, Australia.

FORBES, family name of **Lord Forbes** and of **Earl of Granard.**

FORBES, 22nd Lord *cr* 1442 or before; **Nigel Ivan Forbes,** KBE 1960; JP, DL; Premier Lord of Scotland; Representative Peer of Scotland, 1955–63; Major (retired) Grenadier Guards; Director: Grampian Television PLC; Blenheim Travel Ltd; Chairman, Rolawn Ltd; President, Scottish Scout Association, since 1970; *b* 19 Feb. 1918; *o s* of 21st Lord and Lady Mabel Anson (*d* 1972), *d* of 3rd Earl of Lichfield; *S* father, 1953; *m* 1942, Hon. Rosemary Katharine Hamilton-Russell, *o d* of 9th Viscount Boyne; two *s* one *d*. *Educ:* Harrow; RMC Sandhurst. Served War of 1939–45 (wounded); Adjt, Grenadier Guards, Staff Coll. Military Asst to High Comr for Palestine, 1947–48. Minister of State, Scottish Office, 1958–59. Member: Inter-Parly Union Delegn to Denmark, 1956; Commonwealth Parly Assoc. Delegn to Canada, 1961; Parly Delegn to Pakistan, 1962; Inter-Parly Union Delegn to Hungary, 1965; Inter-Parly Union Delegn to Ethiopia, 1971. Mem., Aberdeen and District Milk Marketing Bd, 1962–72; Mem. Alford District Council, 1955–58; Chm., River Don District Bd, 1962–73. Pres., Royal Highland and Agricultural Society of Scotland, 1958–59; Member: Sports Council for Scotland, 1966–71; Scottish Cttee, Nature Conservancy, 1961–67; Chm., Scottish Br., Nat. Playing Fields Assoc., 1965–80. Dep. Chm., Tennant Caledonian Breweries Ltd, 1964–74. JP 1955, DL 1958, Aberdeenshire. *Recreations:* wildlife, travel. *Heir:* *s* Master of Forbes, *qv*. *Address:* Balforbes, Alford, Aberdeenshire. *T:* Alford (Aberdeen) 2516. *Club:* Army and Navy.

FORBES, Master of; Hon. Malcolm Nigel Forbes; Financial Director; *b* 6 May 1946; *s* and *heir* of 22nd Lord Forbes, *qv*; *m* 1969, Carole Jennifer Andrée (marr. diss. 1982), *d* of N. S. Whitehead, Aberdeen; one *s* one *d*. *Educ:* Eton; Aberdeen Univ. Director, Instock Disposables Ltd, 1974–. *Address:* Finzeauch, Forbes Estate, Alford, Aberdeenshire. *T:* Alford 2574. *Club:* Royal Northern and University (Aberdeen).

FORBES, Hon. Sir Alastair (Granville), Kt 1960; President, Courts of Appeal for St Helena, Falkland Islands and British Antarctic Territories, since 1965, and British Indian Ocean Territory, since 1986; *b* 3 Jan. 1908; *s* of Granville Forbes and Constance Margaret (*née* Davis); *m* 1936, Constance Irene Mary Hughes-White; two *d*. *Educ:* Blundell's Sch.; Clare Coll., Cambridge. Called to the Bar, Gray's Inn, 1932; Magistrate and Govt Officer, Dominica, BWI, 1936; Crown Attorney, Dominica, 1939; Resident Magistrate, Fiji, 1940; Crown Counsel, Fiji, 1942; Solicitor-Gen., Fiji, and Asst Legal Adviser, Western Pacific High Commission, 1945; Legal Draftsman, Federation of Malaya, 1947; Solicitor-Gen., Northern Rhodesia, 1950; Permanent Sec., Ministry of Justice, and Solicitor-Gen., Gold Coast, 1951; Puisne Judge, Kenya, 1956; Justice of Appeal, Court of Appeal for Eastern Africa, 1957; Vice-Pres., Court of Appeal for Eastern Africa, 1958; Federal Justice, Federal Supreme Court of Rhodesia and Nyasaland, 1963–64; Pres., Ct of Appeal: for Seychelles, 1965–76; for Gibraltar, 1970–83. Mem., Panel of Chairmen of Industrial Tribunals (England and Wales), 1965–73; Pres., Pensions Appeal Tribunals for England and Wales, 1973–80 (Chm., 1965–73); Chairman: Constituencies Delimitation Commissions, N Rhodesia, 1962 and 1963, and Bechuanaland, 1964; Gibraltar Riot Inquiry, 1968. *Publications:* Index of the Laws, Dominica, 1940; Revised Edition of Laws of Fiji, 1944. *Recreations:* fishing, shooting. *Address:* Badgers Holt, Church Lane, Sturminster Newton, Dorset DT10 1DH. *T:* Sturminster Newton 73268. *Club:* Royal Commonwealth Society.

FORBES, Anthony David Arnold William; Joint Senior Partner, Cazenove & Co., since 1980; *b* 15 Jan. 1938; *s* of late Lt-Col D. W. A. W. Forbes, MC, and Diana Mary (*née* Henderson), later Marchioness of Exeter; *m* 1st, 1962, Virginia June Ropner; one *s* one *d*; 2nd, 1973, Belinda Mary Drury-Lowe. *Educ:* Eton. Served Coldstream Guards,

1956–59. Joined Cazenove & Co., 1960; Member of Stock Exchange, 1965–. Chairman: Hospital and Homes of St Giles, 1975–; Wellesley House Educnl Trust, 1983–; Governor: Cobham Hall, 1975–; Royal Choral Soc., 1979–. *Recreations*: music, shooting, gardening. *Address*: 16 Halsey Street, SW3 2QH. *T*: 01–584 4749.

FORBES, Sir Archibald (Finlayson), GBE 1957; Kt 1943; Chartered Accountant; President, Midland Bank Ltd, 1975–83 (Director, 1959; Deputy Chairman, 1962–64; Chairman, 1964–75); *b* 6 March 1903; *s* of late Charles Forbes, Johnstone, Renfrewshire; *m* 1943, Angela Gertrude (*d* 1969), *o d* of late Horace Ely, Arlington House, SW1; one *s* two *d*. *Educ*: Paisley; Glasgow Univ. Formerly Mem. of firm of Thomson McLintock & Co., Chartered Accountants. Joined Spillers Ltd as Executive Dir, 1935: Dep. Chm., 1960; Chm., 1965–68; Pres., 1969–80. Mem. of various Reorganisation Commns and Cttees appointed by Minister of Agriculture, 1932–39; Chm., Nat. Mark Trade Cttees for Eggs and Poultry, 1936–39; Dir of Capital Finance, Air Min., 1940; Deputy Sec., Min. of Aircraft Production, 1940–43; Controller of Repair, Equipment and Overseas Supplies, 1943–45 (incl. Operational Control, nos 41 and 43 Gps, RAF and Dir, Gen. Repair and Maintenance, RAF); Mem. of Aircraft Supply Council, 1942–45; Chairman: First Iron and Steel Board from its formation, 1946, to dissolution 1949; Iron and Steel Board from its inception under the Iron and Steel Act, 1953, until 1959; British Millers' Mutual Pool Ltd, 1952–62 (Dep. Chm. 1940–52); Central Mining and Investment Corp., 1959–64; Debenture Corp. Ltd, 1949–79; Midland and International Banks Ltd, 1964–76; Director: Shell Transport & Trading Co. Ltd, 1954–73; English Electric Co. Ltd, 1958–76; Dunlop Holdings Ltd, 1958–76; Rand Mines Ltd, S Africa, 1959–64; Bank of Bermuda Ltd, 1966–75. Pres., FBI, 1951–53; Chm., Cttee of London Clearing Bankers, 1970–72 (Dep. Chm., 1968–70); Pres., British Bankers' Assoc., 1970–71, 1971–72 (Vice-Pres. 1969–70); Dir, 1950–53, Dep. Chm., 1961–64, Finance Corp. for Industry. Member: Cttee to enquire into Financial Structure of Colonial Develt Corp., 1959; Review Body on Doctors' and Dentists' Remuneration, 1962–65; Governing Body, Imp. Coll. of Science and Technology, 1959–75. Councillor for life, The Conference Board Inc., NY. Pres., Epsom Coll., 1964–. Hon. JDipMA. *Recreations*: golf and fishing. *Address*: 40 Orchard Court, Portman Square, W1. *T*: 01–935 9304. *Clubs*: Brooks's, Pratt's, Beefsteak.

FORBES, Bryan; *b* 22 July 1926; *m* 1958, Nanette Newman, *qv*; two *d*. *Educ*: West Ham Secondary Sch. Studied at RADA, 1941; entered acting profession, 1942, and (apart from war service) was on West End stage, then in films here and in Hollywood, 1948–60. Formed Beaver Films with Sir Richard Attenborough, 1959; wrote and co-produced The Angry Silence, 1960. Subseq. wrote, dir. and prod. numerous films; *films include*: The League of Gentlemen, Only Two Can Play, Whistle Down the Wind, 1961; The L-Shaped Room, 1962; Séance on a Wet Afternoon, 1963; King Rat (in Hollywood), 1964; The Wrong Box, 1965; The Whisperers, 1966; Deadfall, 1967; The Madwoman of Chaillot, 1968; The Raging Moon, 1970; The Tales of Beatrix Potter, 1971; The Stepford Wives, 1974 (USA); The Slipper and the Rose, 1975 (Royal Film Perf., 1976); International Velvet, 1978; (British segment) The Sunday Lovers, 1980; Better Late Than Never, 1981; The Naked Face, 1983; (narrator) I am a Dancer, 1971. *Stage*: Directed Macbeth, Old Vic, 1980; directed and acted in Star Quality, Th. Royal, Bath, 1983. *Television*: produced and directed: Edith Evans, I Caught Acting Like the Measles, Yorkshire TV, 1973; Elton John, Goodbye Norma Jean and Other Things, ATV 1973; Jessie, BBC, 1980; acted in December Flower, Granada, 1984. Man. Dir and Head of Production, ABPC Studios, 1969–71; Man. Dir and Chief Exec., EMI-MGM, Elstree Studios, 1970–71; Dir, Capital Radio Ltd, 1973–. Member: BBC Gen. Adv. Council, 1966–69; BBC Schs Council, 1971–73; Trustee, Writers' Guild of GB; President: Beatrix Potter Soc., 1982–; Nat. Youth Theatre, 1984–. Won British Acad. Award, 1960; Writers' Guild Award (twice); numerous internat. awards. *Publications*: Truth Lies Sleeping, 1950; The Distant Laughter, 1972; Notes for a Life, 1974; The Slipper and the Rose, 1976; Ned's Girl: biography of Dame Edith Evans, 1977; International Velvet, 1978; Familiar Strangers, 1979; That Despicable Race, 1980; The Rewrite Man, 1983; The Endless Game, 1986; contribs to: The Spectator, New Statesman, Queen, and other periodicals. *Recreations*: running a bookshop, reading, landscape gardening, photography. *Address*: The Bookshop, Virginia Water, Surrey.

See also Sir John Leon, Bt.

FORBES of Pitsligo, Sir Charles Edward Stuart-, 12th Bt *cr* 1626; Building contractor, retired; *b* 6 Aug. 1903; *s* of Sir Charles Hay Hepburn Stuart-Forbes, 10th Bt, and Ellen, *d* of Capt. Huntley; *S* brother, 1937; *m* 1966, Ijah Leah MacCabe (*d* 1974), Wellington, NZ. *Educ*: Ocean Bay Coll. *Recreations*: motoring, football, cricket, hockey, swimming, deep sea fishing, hunting, rowing, launching, tennis. *Heir*: *n* William Daniel Stuart-Forbes [*b* 21 Aug. 1935; *m* 1956, Jannette MacDonald; three *s* two *d*]. *Address*: 2/40 Stuart Street, Blenheim, New Zealand.

FORBES, Colin, RDI 1974; Partner, Pentagram Design, since 1972; *b* 6 March 1928; *s* of Kathleen and John Forbes; *m* 1961, Wendy Schneider; one *s* two *d*. *Educ*: Sir Anthony Browne's, Brentwood; LCC Central Sch. of Arts and Crafts. Design Asst, Herbert Spencer, 1952; freelance practice and Lectr, LCC Central Sch. of Arts and Crafts, 1953–57; Art Dir, Stuart Advertising, London, 1957–58; Head of Graphic Design Dept, LCC Central Sch. of Arts and Crafts, 1958–61; freelance practice, London, 1961–62; Partner: Fletcher/Forbes/Gill, 1962–65; Crosby/Fletcher/Forbes, 1965–72. Mem., Alliance Graphique Internationale, 1965– (Internat. Pres. 1976–79); Pres., Amer. Inst. Graphic Arts, 1984–. *Publications*: Graphic Design: visual comparisons, 1963; A Sign Systems Manual, 1970; Creativity and Communication, 1971; New Alphabets A to Z, 1973; Living by Design, 1978. *Address*: 40 Fifth Avenue, Apartment 14E, New York, NY 10011, USA. *T*: 212 460 5146.

FORBES, Donald James, MA; Headmaster, Merchiston Castle School, 1969–81; *b* 6 Feb. 1921; *s* of Andrew Forbes; *m* 1945, Patricia Muriel Yeo; two *s* one *d*. *Educ*: Oundle; Clare Coll., Cambridge (Mod. Lang. Tripos). Capt. Scots Guards, 1941–46; 1st Bn Scots Guards, 1942–46, N Africa, Italy. Asst Master, Dulwich Coll., 1946–55; Master i/c cricket, 1951–55; Headmaster, Dauntsey's Sch., 1956–69. Diploma in Spanish, Univ. of Santander, 1954; Lectr in Spanish, West Norwood Tech. Coll., 1954–55. *Recreations*: cricket, Rugby football, tennis, Rugby fives; history, literature; instrumental and choral music. *Address*: 33 Coates Gardens, Edinburgh EH12 5LG; Breachacha Castle, Isle of Coll. *Clubs*: Hawks (Cambridge); HCEG (Muirfield).

FORBES of Brux, Hon. Sir Ewan, 11th Bt *cr* 1630, of Craigievar; JP; landowner and farmer; *b* 6 Sept. 1912; 2nd *s* of Sir John Forbes-Sempill, 9th Bt (Forbes) of Craigievar, 18th Lord Sempill; *S* (to Btcy) brother, 1965; *m* 1952, Isabella, *d* of A. Mitchell, Glenrinnes, Banffshire. *Educ*: Dresden; Univ. of Munich; Univ. of Aberdeen. MB, ChB 1944. Senior Casualty Officer, Aberdeen Royal Infirmary, 1944–45; Medical Practitioner, Alford, Aberdeenshire, 1945–55. JP Aberdeenshire, 1969. *Recreations*: shooting, fishing, ski-ing and skating. *Heir*: *kinsman* John Alexander Cumnock Forbes-Sempill [*b* 29 Aug. 1927; *m* 1st, 1958, Penelope Margaret Ann (marr. diss. 1964), *d* of A. G. Grey-Pennington; 2nd, 1966, Jane Carolyn, *o d* of C. Gordon Evans]. *Address*: Brux, Alford, Aberdeenshire. *T*. Kildrummy 223.

See also Lady Sempill.

FORBES, Very Rev. Graham John Thomson; Provost, St Ninian's Cathedral, Perth, since 1982; *b* 10 June 1951; *s* of J. T. and D. D. Forbes; *m* 1973, Jane T. Miller; three *s*. *Educ*: George Heriot's School, Edinburgh; Univ. of Aberdeen (MA); Univ. of Edinburgh (BD). Curate, Old St Paul's Church, Edinburgh, 1976–82. *Recreations*: climbing, running, dry rot. *Address*: St Ninian's House, 40 Hay Street, Perth PH1 5HS. *T*: Perth 26874/27982.

FORBES, Major Sir Hamish (Stewart), 7th Bt *cr* 1823, of Newe; MBE 1945; MC 1945; Welsh Guards, retired; *b* 15 Feb. 1916; *s* of Lt-Col James Stewart Forbes (*d* 1957) (*g s* of 3rd Bt) and Feridah Frances Forbes (*d* 1953), *d* of Hugh Lewis Taylor; *S* cousin, 1984; *m* 1st, 1945, Jacynthe Elizabeth Mary, *d* of late Eric Gordon Underwood; one *s* three *d*; 2nd, 1981, Mary Christine, MBE, *d* of late Ernest William Rigby. *Educ*: Eton College; Lawrenceville, USA. Served Welsh Guards, France, Germany, Turkey, 1939–58. KJStJ 1984. *Recreation*: shooting. *Heir*: *s* James Thomas Stewart Forbes, *b* 28 May 1957. *Address*: 36 Wharton Street, WC1X 9PG. *T*: 01–833 1235. *Clubs*: Turf, Chelsea Arts.

FORBES, Ian, QPM 1966; retired 1979; Deputy Assistant Commissioner, Metropolitan Police and National Co-ordinator, Regional Crime Squads (England and Wales), 1970–72; *b* 30 March 1914; *y s* of John and Betsy Forbes, Auchlossan, Lumphanan, Aberdeenshire; *m* 1941, Lilian Edith Miller, Edgware, Mddx; two *s*. *Educ*: Lumphanan School, Aberdeenshire. Joined Metropolitan Police, 1939; served in East End, Central London Flying Squad, New Scotland Yard; Detective Superintendent, 1964; served on New Scotland Yard Murder Squad, 1966–69; Commander, No 9 Regional Crime Squad (London area), 1969. *Publication*: Squadman (autobiog.), 1973. *Recreations*: gardening, motoring, reading. *Address*: 13 Richmond Avenue, Compton, Wolverhampton WV3 9JB.

FORBES, Ian Alexander, PhD; *b* 27 Oct. 1915; *s* of Robert Douglas Forbes and Amy Forbes; *m* 1945, Rosemary Blair, DA; one *s* one *d*. *Educ*: Alloa Acad.; Edinburgh Univ. (BSc 1937, PhD 1939). ICI (Explosives) Ltd, 1939–48 (also seconded to M.A.P. Explosives); Distillers Co. Ltd, 1948–80: Man. Dir, Scottish Grain Distillers Ltd, 1972–80; Man Dir, D.C. (Malt Products) Ltd, 1966–80; Chm., John Watney & Co. Ltd, 1952–80; Dir, Thos Borthwick (Glasgow) Ltd, 1953–80; retd 1980. *Recreation*: golf. *Address*: Blackness, King's Road, Longniddry, East Lothian EH32 0NN. *T*: Longniddry 53136. *Clubs*: Muirfield Golf, Longniddry Golf.

FORBES, James, FCA; Forestry Commissioner, since 1982; *b* 2 Jan. 1923; *s* of Donald Forbes and Rona Ritchie Forbes (*née* Yeats); *m* 1948, Alison Mary Fletcher Moffat; two *s*. *Educ*: Christ's Hospital; Officers' Training School, Bangalore. Chartered Accountant. Commissioned 15th Punjab Regt, Indian Army, 1942; transf. IAOC, released 1947 (hon. Major); Peat Marwick Mitchell Co., 1952–58; Chief Accountant, L. Rose, 1958; Group Operational Research Manager, Schweppes, 1960, Group Chief Accountant, 1963 (Dir, subsid. cos); Sec. and Financial Adviser, Cadbury Schweppes (on formation), 1969, Main Board Dir, 1971, Group Finance Dir to April 1978; Senior Exec. Dir, Tate & Lyle, 1978, Vice-Chm., 1980–84; Chm., Tate & Lyle Gp Pension Fund, 1978–85. Non-exec. Director: British Rail Investments, 1980–84; Steetley plc, 1984–; Compass Hotels, 1984–; DRI Holdings, 1984–; Lavtro Ltd, 1986–. Mem. Council, Inst. of Chartered Accountants, 1971– (Treasurer, 1984–86); Treasurer and Chm. Council, Christ's Hospital, 1987– (Chm., Finance Cttee). Mem., Highland Society. *Recreation*: golf. *Clubs*: Caledonian, Royal Commonwealth Society; Porters Park Golf.

FORBES, Vice-Adm. Sir John Morrison, KCB 1978; a Chairman, Civil Service Commissioners interview panel, since 1980; Governor of various naval charities; *b* 16 Aug. 1925; *s* of late Lt-Col R. H. Forbes, OBE, and late Gladys M. Forbes (*née* Pollock); *m* 1950, Joyce Newenham Hadden; two *s* two *d*. *Educ*: RNC, Dartmouth. Served War: HMS Mauritius, Verulam and Nelson, 1943–46. HMS Aisne, 1946–49; Gunnery course and staff of HMS Excellent, 1950–51; served in RAN, 1952–54; Staff of HMS Excellent, 1954–56; HMS Ceylon, 1956–58; Staff of Dir of Naval Ordnance, 1958–60; Comdr (G) HMS Excellent, 1960–61; Staff of Dir of Seaman Officers' Appts, 1962–64; Exec. Officer, Britannia RN Coll., 1964–66; Operational Comdr and 2nd in Comd, Royal Malaysian Navy, 1966–68; Asst Dir, Naval Plans, 1969–70; comd HMS Triumph, 1971–72; comd Britannia RN Coll., Dartmouth, 1972–74; Naval Secretary, 1974–76; Flag Officer, Plymouth, Port Adm., Devonport, Comdr, Central Sub Area, Eastern Atlantic, and Comdr, Plymouth Sub Area, Channel, 1977–79. Naval ADC to the Queen, 1974. Kesatria Manku Negara (Malaysia), 1968. *Recreations*: country pursuits. *Address*: c/o National Westminster Bank, Waterlooville, Portsmouth, Hants. *Clubs*: Army and Navy, RN Sailing Association.

FORBES, John Stuart; Sheriff of Tayside, Central and Fife at Dunfermline, since 1980; *b* 31 Jan. 1936; *s* of late John Forbes and Dr A. R. S. Forbes; *m* 1963, Marion Alcock; one *s* two *d*. *Educ*: Glasgow High Sch.; Glasgow Univ. (MA, LLB). Solicitor, 1959–61; Advocate, Scottish Bar, 1962–76; Sheriff of Lothian and Borders, 1976–80. Life Trustee, Carnegie, Dunfermline and Hero Fund Trusts, 1985–. *Recreations*: squash, tennis, golf. *Address*: 8 Park Avenue, Dunfermline KY12 7HX. *T*: Dunfermline 722206. *Club*: Edinburgh Sports.

FORBES, Mrs Muriel Rose, CBE 1963; JP; Alderman, London Borough of Brent, 1972–74; *b* 20 April 1894; *yr d* of John Henry Cheeseright; *m* 1923, Charles Gilbert Forbes (*d* 1957); two *d*. *Educ*: Gateshead Grammar Sch.; Southlands Teacher Training Coll. Member: Willesden Borough Council, 1936–47; Middlesex CC, 1934–65 (Chm., 1960–61); GLC, 1964–67 (Vice-Chm., 1964–66). Chairman: St Charles's Gp Hosp. Management Cttee, 1968–69; Paddington Gp Hosp. Management Cttee, 1963–68; Mem., Central Middx Hosp. Management Cttee, 1948–63 (Vice-Chm., 1952–63). JP County of Middx, 1946. Hon. DTech Brunel Univ., 1966. *Address*: 9 Rosemary Road, Halesowen, West Midlands B63 1BN.

FORBES, Nanette; *see* Newman, N.

FORBES, Robert Brown; Director of Education, Edinburgh, 1972–75; *b* 14 Oct. 1912; *s* of Robert James Forbes and Elizabeth Jane Brown; *m* 1939, Nellie Shepley; one *s* one *d*. *Educ*: Edinburgh Univ. (MA, MEd). Asst Dir of Educn, Edinburgh, 1946, Depute Dir, 1952. Chm., Scottish Council for Research in Educn, 1972. *Address*: 7 Wilton Road, Edinburgh EH16 5NX. *T*: 031–667 1323.

FORBES, Thayne John; QC 1984; a Recorder, since 1986; *b* 28 June 1938; *s* of John Thompson Forbes and Jessie Kay Robertson Stewart; *m* 1960, Celia Joan; two *s* one *d*. *Educ*: Winchester College (Quirister); Wolverton Grammar Sch.; University College London (LLB, LLM). Served Royal Navy (Instructor Lieutenant), 1963–66. Called to Bar, Inner Temple, 1966. *Recreations*: music, reading, sailing, bird watching, astronomy. *Address*: 3 Paper Buildings, Temple, EC4Y 7EU. *T*: 01–353 1182. *Club*: Bar Yacht.

FORBES, Captain William Frederick Eustace; Vice Lord-Lieutenant of Stirling and Falkirk, since 1984; Forestry Commissioner, since 1982; *b* 6 July 1932; *er s* of late Lt-Col W. H. D. C. Forbes of Callendar, CBE and of Elizabeth Forbes; *m* 1956, Pamela Susan, *er d* of Lord McCorquodale of Newton, KCVO, PC; two *d*. *Educ*: Eton. Regular soldier, Coldstream Guards, 1950–59; farmer and company director, 1959–. Chairman: Scottish

Woodland Owners' Assoc., 1974–77; Nat. Playing Fields Assoc., Scottish Branch, 1980–. *Recreations:* country pastimes, golf, cricket, travel. *Address:* Dinning House, Gargunnock, Stirling FK8 3BQ. *T:* Gargunnock 289. *Clubs:* MCC; New (Edinburgh); Royal and Ancient Golf.

FORBES–LEITH of Fyvie, Sir Andrew (George), 3rd Bt *cr* 1923; landed proprietor; *b* 20 Oct. 1929; *s* of Sir R. Ian A. Forbes-Leith of Fyvie, 2nd Bt, KT, MBE, and Ruth Avis (*d* 1973), *d* of Edward George Barnett; *S* father, 1973; *m* 1962, Jane Kate (*d* 1969), *d* of late David McCall-McCowan; two *s* two *d. Heir: s* George Ian David Forbes-Leith, *b* 26 May 1967. *Address:* Dunachton, Kingussie, Inverness-shire. *T:* Kincraig 226. *Clubs:* Royal Northern (Aberdeen); Highland (Inverness).

FORBES–SEMPILL; *see* Sempill.

FORD; *see* St Clair-Ford.

FORD, Rev. Adam; Chaplain, St Paul's Girls' School, London, since 1976; *b* 15 Sept. 1940; *s* of John Ford and Jean Beattie Ford (*née* Winstanley); *m* 1969, Veronica Rosemary Lucia Verey; two *s* two *d. Educ:* Minehead Grammar Sch.; King's Coll., Univ. of London (BD Hons, AKC 1964); Lancaster Univ. (MA Indian Religion 1972). Asst, Ecumenical Inst. of World Council of Churches, Geneva, 1964; Curate, Cirencester Parish Church, Glos, 1965–69; Vicar of Hebden Bridge, W Yorkshire, 1969–76; Priest-in-Ordinary to the Queen, 1984–. Regular contributor to Prayer for the Day, Radio 4, 1978–. Hon. FRAS 1960. *Publications:* Spaceship Earth, 1981; Weather Watch, 1982; Star Gazers Guide to the Night Sky (audio guide to astronomy), 1982; Universe: God, Man and Science, 1986; articles in The Times and science jls on relationship between science and religion, also on dialogue between religions. *Recreations:* dry stone walling, astronomy, searching for neolithic flints. *Address:* 55 Bolingbroke Road, Hammersmith, W14 0AH. *T:* 01–602 5902.

FORD, Antony; HM Diplomatic Service; Counsellor, British Embassy, East Berlin, since 1984; *b* Bexley, 1 Oct. 1944; *s* of late William Ford and Grace Ford (*née* Smith); *m* 1970, Linda Gordon Joy; one *s* one *d. Educ:* St Dunstan's Coll., Catford; UCW, Aberystwyth (BA). Joined HM Diplomatic Service, 1967; Third, later Second, Sec., Bonn, 1968–71; Second Sec., Kuala Lumpur, 1971–73; First Secretary: FCO, 1973–77; Washington, 1977–81; FCO, 1981–84. *Recreations:* reading, gardening, cricket, the Weald of Kent. *Address:* c/o Foreign and Commonwealth Office, King Charles Street, SW1.

FORD, Benjamin Thomas; DL; *b* 1 April 1925; *s* of Benjamin Charles Ford and May Ethel (*née* Moorton); *m* 1950, Vera Ada (*née* Fawcett-Fancet); two *s* one *d. Educ:* Rowan Road Central Sch., Surrey. Apprenticed as compositor, 1941. War Service, 1943–47, Fleet Air Arm (Petty Officer). Electronic Fitter/Wireman, 1951–64; Convener of Shop Stewards, 1955–64. Pres., Harwich Constituency Labour Party, 1955–63; Mem., Clacton UDC, 1959–62; Alderman Essex CC, 1959–65; JP Essex, 1962–67. MP (Lab) Bradford N, 1964–83; contested (Lab Ind.) Bradford N, 1983. Mem., H of C Select Cttee (Services), 1970–83 (Chm., Accom. and Admin Sub-Cttee, 1979–83); Chairman: British-Portuguese Parly Gp, 1965–83; British-Argentinian Parly Gp, 1974–81; British-Brazilian Parly Gp, 1974–79; British-Malaysian Parly Gp, 1975–83; British-Venezuelan Parly Gp, 1977–83; All-Party Wool Textile Parly Gp, 1974–83; Vice-Chairman: British-Latin American Parly Gp, 1974–79; PLP Defence Cttee, 1979–82; Mem. Exec. Cttee, IPU British Gp (Chm., 1977–79); Sec., British-Namibian Parly Gp, 1980–83. Chm., Jt Select Cttee on Sound Broadcasting, 1976–77. Chm., English Shooting Council, 1982–; Mem. Council, Nat. Rifle Assoc., 1970–. DL W Yorks, 1982. *Publication:* Piecework, 1960. *Recreations:* music, shooting, family. *Address:* 9 Wynmore Crescent, Bramhope, Leeds LS16 9DH. *Club:* Idle Working Men's.

FORD, Prof. Boris, MA; Emeritus Professor, University of Bristol; freelance editor and writer; educational consultant; *b* 1 July 1917; *s* of late Brig. G. N. Ford, CB, DSO; *m* 1st, 1950, Noreen; one *s* three *d*; 2nd, 1977, Inge. *Educ:* Gresham's Sch., Holt, Norfolk; Downing Coll., Cambridge. Army Education, finally OC Middle East School of Artistic Studies, 1940–46. Chief Ed. and finally Dir, Bureau of Current Affairs, 1946–51; Information Officer, Technical Assistance Bd, UN (NY and Geneva), 1951–53; Sec., Nat. Enquiry into Liberalising Technical Educn, 1953–55; Editor, Journal of Education, 1955–58; first Head of Sch. Broadcasting, Associated-Rediffusion, 1957–58; Educn Sec., Cambridge Univ. Press, 1958–60; Prof. of Education and Dir of the Inst. of Education, Univ. of Sheffield, 1960–63; Prof. of Education, Univ. of Sussex, 1963–73, Dean, Sch. of Cultural and Community Studies (Educnl Studies), 1963–71, Chm., Educn Area, and Dir, Sch. of Educn, 1971–73; Prof. of Educn, Univ. of Bristol, 1973–82. Chm., Nat. Assoc. for the Teaching of English, 1963–65; Educational Dir, Pictorial Knowledge, 1968–71. Gen. Editor: Pelican Guide to English Literature, 1954–66; New Pelican Guide to English Literature, 1982–84; Editor, Universities Qly, Culture, Education & Society, 1955–86. *Publications:* Discussion Method, 1949; Teachers' Handbook to Human Rights, 1950; Liberal Education in a Technical Age, 1955; Young Readers: Young Writers, 1960; Changing Relationships between Universities and Teachers' Colleges, 1975; Collaboration and Commitment, 1984. *Recreation:* music. *Address:* 35 Alma Vale Road, Clifton, Bristol BS8 2HL.
See also R. H. Vignoles.

FORD, Sir Brinsley; *see* Ford, Sir R. B.

FORD, Charles Edmund, FRS 1965; DSc London, FLS, FZS, FIBiol; Member of Medical Research Council's External Staff, Sir William Dunn School of Pathology, Oxford, 1971–78, retired; *b* 24 Oct. 1912; *s* of late Charles Ford and late Ethel Eubornia Ford (*née* Fawcett); *m* 1940, Jean Ella Dowling; four *s. Educ:* Slough Grammar Sch.; King's Coll., University of London. Demonstrator, Dept of Botany, King's Coll., University of London, 1936–38; Geneticist, Rubber Research Scheme, Ceylon, 1938–41 and 1944–45. Lieut Royal Artillery, 1942–43. PSO Dept of Atomic Energy, Min. of Supply, at Chalk River Laboratories, Ont, Canada, 1946–49. Head of Cytogenetics Section, MRC, Radiobiology Unit, Harwell, 1949–71. *Publications:* papers on cytogenetics in scientific journals. *Recreations:* travel, friends. *Address:* 156 Oxford Road, Abingdon, Oxon. *T:* Abingdon 20001.

FORD, Colin John; Keeper, National Museum of Photography, Film and Television, since 1982; lecturer, writer and broadcaster on films, theatre and photography; exhibition organiser; *b* 13 May 1934; *s* of John William and Hélène Martha Ford; *m* 1st, 1961, Margaret Elizabeth Cordwell (marr. diss.); one *s* one *d*; 2nd, 1984, Susan Joan Frances Grayson; one *s. Educ:* Enfield Grammar Sch.; University Coll., Oxford (MA). Manager and Producer, Kidderminster Playhouse, 1958–60; Gen. Man., Western Theatre Ballet, 1960–62; Vis. Lectr in English and Drama, California State Univ. at Long Beach and UCLA (Univ. Extension), 1962–64; Dep. Curator, Nat. Film Archive, 1965–72. Organiser, 30th Anniv. Congress of Internat. Fedn of Film Archives, London, 1968; Dir, Cinema City Exhibn, 1970; Programme Dir, London Shakespeare Film Festival, 1972; Keeper of Film and Photography, Nat. Portrait Gall., 1972–81. *Film:* Masks and Faces, 1966 (BBC TV version, Omnibus, 1968). *Publications:* (with Roy Strong) An Early Victorian Album, 1974, 2nd edn 1977; The Cameron Collection, 1975; (ed) Happy and

Glorious: Six Reigns of Royal Photography, 1977; Rediscovering Mrs Cameron, 1979; People in Camera, 1979; (with Brian Harrison) A Hundred Years Ago (Britain in the 1880s), 1983; Portraits (Gallery of World Photography), 1983; (principal contrib.) Oxford Companion to Film; articles in many jls. *Recreations:* travel, music, small boats. *Address:* National Museum of Photography, Film and Television, Prince's View, Bradford, Yorkshire. *T:* Bradford 727488.

FORD, David Robert, LVO 1975; OBE 1976; Secretary for the Civil Service, Hong Kong Government, since 1985; *b* 22 Feb. 1935; *s* of William Ewart and Edna Ford; *m* 1958, Elspeth Anne (*née* Muckart); two *s* two *d. Educ:* Tauntons School. National Service, 1953–55; regular commn, RA, 1955; regimental duty, Malta, 1953–58; Lieut, UK, 1958–62; Captain, Commando Regt, 1962–66; active service: Borneo, 1964; Aden, 1966; Staff Coll., Quetta, 1967; seconded to Hong Kong Govt, 1967; retired from Army (Major), 1972. Dep. Dir, Hong Kong Govt Information Service, 1972–74, Dir, 1974–76; Dep. Sec., Govt Secretariat, Hong Kong, 1976; Under Sec., NI Office, 1977–79; Sec. for Information, Hong Kong Govt, 1979–80; Hong Kong Commissioner in London, 1980–81; RCDS, 1982; Dir of Housing, Hong Kong Govt, 1983–84, Sec. for Housing, 1985. *Recreations:* tennis, fishing, photography, theatre. *Address:* c/o Government Secretariat, Hong Kong; The Old Malthouse, Marnhull, Dorset.

FORD, Rt. Rev. Douglas Albert; Assistant Bishop of Calgary, since 1981; *b* 16 July 1917; *s* of Thomas George Ford and Elizabeth Eleanor (Taylor), both English; *m* 1944, Doris Ada (Elborne); two *s* one *d. Educ:* primary and secondary schs, Vancouver; Univ. of British Columbia (BA); Anglican Theological Coll. of BC (LTh); General Synod (BD). Deacon, 1941; Priest, 1942; Curate, St Mary's, Kerrisdale, 1941–42; St George's, Vancouver, 1942–44; Vicar of Strathmore, 1944–49; Rector of: Okotoks, 1949–52; Vermilion, 1952–55; St Michael and All Angels, Calgary, 1955–62; St Augustine, Lethbridge, 1962–66; Dean and Rector, St John's Cath., Saskatoon, 1966–70; Bishop of Saskatoon, 1970–81; Incumbent of All Saints', Cochrane, dio. Calgary, 1981–85. Hon. DD: Coll. of Emmanuel and St Chad, Saskatoon, 1970; Anglican Theological Coll. of BC, Vancouver, 1971. *Address:* 2212–142 Silvergrove Drive NW, Calgary, Alberta T3B 5H4, Canada.

FORD, Rev. Preb. Douglas William C.; *see* Cleverley Ford.

FORD, Edmund Brisco, FRS 1946; MA, DSc Oxon, Hon. DSc Liverpool; Senior Dean, and Fellow, 1958–71, Fellow Emeritus, 1976–77, and Distinguished Fellow and Senior Dean, since 1977, All Souls College, Oxford; Professor of Ecological Genetics, 1963–69, and Director of Genetics Laboratory, Zoology Department, 1952–69, Oxford; Emeritus Professor, since 1969; *b* 23 April 1901; unmarried; *s* of Harold Dodsworth Ford and Gertrude Emma Bennett. *Educ:* Wadham Coll., Oxford (Hon. Fellow, 1974). Research worker, Univ. Lectr and Demonstrator in Zoology and Comparative Anatomy, Univ. Reader in Genetics, Oxford; Pres., Genetical Soc. of Great Britain, 1946–49; Mem. of Nature Conservancy, 1949–59; Mem. various scientific (chiefly zoological) societies. Wild Life Conservation Cttee of Ministry of Town and Country Planning, 1945–47 (Cmd Rept 7122). Formerly represented British Empire on Permanent Internat. Cttee of Genetics. Has travelled in USA, NZ, Australia, Near and Far East. Initiated Science of Ecological Genetics. Darwin Medallist, Royal Society, 1954. Delivered Galton Lecture of London Univ., 1939; Woodhall Lectr of the Royal Institution, 1957; Woodward Lectr, Yale Univ., 1959 and 1973. Hon. FRCP 1974; Hon. FRES. Weldon Memorial Prize, Oxford Univ., 1959. Medallist of Helsinki Univ., 1967. Foreign Mem., Finnish Acad. Pres. Somerset Archæological Soc., 1960–61. *Publications:* Mendelism and Evolution, 1931, 8th edn 1965; (with G. D. Hale Carpenter) Mimicry, 1933; The Study of Heredity (Home University Library), 1938, 2nd edn 1950; Genetics for Medical Students, 1942, 7th edn 1973; Butterflies (Vol. I of New Naturalist Series), 1945, 2nd repr. of 4th edn, 1972, pbk 1975, rev. edn 1977; British Butterflies (King Penguin Series), 1951; Moths (New Naturalist Series), 1955, 4th edn 1976; Ecological Genetics, 1964, 4th edn 1975 (trans: Polish 1967, French 1972, Italian 1978); Genetic Polymorphism (All Souls Monographs), 1965; Evolution Studied by Observation and Experiment, 1973; Genetics and Adaptation, 1976; Understanding Genetics, 1979; Taking Genetics into the Countryside, 1981; (with J. S. Haywood) Church Treasures in the Oxford District, 1984; numerous contribs to scientific jls, on genetical and zoological subjects. Festschrift: Ecological Genetics and Evolution, ed E. R. Creed, 1971. *Recreations:* archæology, literature, travel. *Address:* 5 Apsley Road, Oxford; All Souls College, Oxford. *TA:* and *T:* Oxford 722251; Zoology Department, South Parks Road, Oxford. *Club:* Travellers'.

FORD, Sir Edward (William Spencer), KCB 1967 (CB 1952); KCVO 1957 (MVO 1949); OStJ 1976; MA; FRSA; DL; Secretary and Registrar of the Order of Merit, since 1975; Secretary to the Pilgrim Trust, 1967–75; *b* 24 July 1910; 4th (twin) *s* of late Very Rev. Lionel G. B. J. Ford, Headmaster of Repton and Harrow and Dean of York, and of Mary Catherine, *d* of Rt Rev. E. S. Talbot, Bishop of Winchester and Hon. Mrs Talbot; *m* 1949, Virginia, *er d* of 1st and last Baron Brand, CMG, and *widow* of John Metcalfe Polk, NY; two *s. Educ:* Eton (King's Schol.); New Coll., Oxford (Open Scholar; Hon. Fellow, 1982). 1st Class Hon. Mods; 2nd Class Lit. Hum. (Greats). Law Student (Harmsworth Scholar) Middle Temple, 1934–35; Tutor to King Farouk of Egypt, 1936–37; called to Bar, Middle Temple, 1937 and practised 1937–39; 2nd Lieut (Supplementary Reserve of Officers) Grenadier Guards, 1936; Lieut 1939; served in France and Belgium, 1939–40 (despatches), and in Tunisia and Italy, 1943–44 (despatches), Brigade Major 10th Infantry and 24th Guards Brigades; Instructor at Staff Coll., Haifa, 1944–45. psc†. Asst Private Secretary to King George VI, 1946–52, and to the Queen, 1952–67; Extra Equerry to the Queen, 1955. Dir, London Life Assoc., 1970–83. Member: Central Appeals Adv. Cttee, BBC and IBA, 1969–72, 1976–78; York Glaziers' Trust; Chairman: UK/USA Bicentennial Fellowships Cttee, 1975–80; St John Council for Northamptonshire, 1976–82; Grants Cttee, Historic Churches Preservation Trust, 1977–; Mem. Ct of Assts, Goldsmiths' Co., 1970–, Prime Warden, 1979. High Sheriff Northants 1970, DL 1972. *Address:* Canal House, 23 Blomfield Road, W9 1AD. *T:* 01–286 0028. *Clubs:* White's, Beefsteak, MCC.

FORD, Elbur; *see* Hibbert, Eleanor.

FORD, Air Marshal Sir Geoffrey (Harold), KBE 1979; CB 1974; Secretary, The Institute of Metals, since 1985; *b* 6 Aug. 1923; *s* of late Harold Alfred Ford, Lewes, Sussex; *m* 1951, Valerie, *d* of late Douglas Hart Finn, Salisbury; two *s. Educ:* Lewes Grammar Sch.; Bristol Univ. (BSc). Served War of 1939–45: commissioned, 1942; 60 Gp, 1943; Italy and Middle East, 1944–46. 90 (Signals) Gp, 1946–49; Bomber Development, 1954–57; Air Ministry, 1958–61; RAF Technical Coll., 1961–62; Min. of Aviation, 1963–64; Chief Signals Officer, RAF Germany, 1965–68; MoD, 1968–72; RCDS, 1972; AO Engineering, Strike Command, 1973–76; Dir-Gen. Engineering and Supply Management, RAF, 1976–78; Chief Engr (RAF), 1978–81. Dir, The Metals Soc., 1981–84. CEng, FIEE (Council, 1977–82). *Address:* c/o Barclays Bank, Lewes, East Sussex. *Club:* Royal Air Force.

FORD, George Johnson, DL; Member, Cheshire County Council, since 1962 (Chairman, 1976–82); *b* 13 March 1916; *s* of James and Esther Ford; *m* 1941, Nora Helen

Brocklehurst; three s one d. Educ: Chester Coll. Qualified estate agent, 1938. FAI 1938. Member, Runcorn RDC, 1953 (Chm., 1962); Mem. Bd, Warrington and Runcorn Develt Corp., 1981– (Runcorn Develt Corp., 1964–81). Mem., West Mercia Cttee, Nat. Trust, 1982. Pres., Frodsham Conservative Assoc., 1962–; Vice Pres., Eddisbury Parly Div., 1984. DL Cheshire, 1979. Recreations: horse racing, music and drama. Address: Manley Old Hall, Manley, via Warrington, Cheshire WA6 9EA. T: Manley 254. Club: City (Chester).

FORD, Gerald Rudolph; President of the United States of America, Aug. 1974–Jan. 1977; Director: Shearson Loeb Rhodes; Santa Fe International; lawyer; b Omaha, Nebraska, 14 July 1913; (adopted) s of Gerald R. Ford and Dorothy Gardner; m 1948, Elizabeth (née Bloomer); three s one d. Educ: South High Sch., Grand Rapids; Univ. of Michigan (BA); Law Sch., Yale Univ. (LLB). Served War: US Navy (Carriers), 1942–46. Partner in law firm of Ford and Buchen, 1941–42; Member, law firm of Butterfield, Keeney and Amberg, 1947–49; subseq. with Amberg, Law and Buchen. Member US House of Representatives for Michigan 5th District, 1948–73; Member: Appropriations Cttee, 1951; Dept of Defense Sub-Cttee, etc; House Minority Leader, Republican Party, 1965–73; Vice President of the United States, Dec. 1973–Aug. 1974. Attended Interparly Union meetings in Europe; Mem. US-Canadian Interparly Gp. Pres., Eisenhower Exchange Fellowship, 1977–; Chm., Acad. of Educational Develt, 1977–. Holds Amer. Pol. Sci. Assoc.'s Distinguished Congressional Service Award, 1961; several hon. degrees. Delta Kappa Epsilon, Phi Delta Phi. Publication: (with John R. Stiles) Portrait of an Assassin, 1965. Recreations: outdoor sports (formerly football), ski-ing, tennis, golf. Address: PO Box 927, Rancho Mirage, Calif 92270, USA.

FORD, Dr Gillian Rachel, CB 1981; FRCP, FFCM; Director of Studies, St Christopher's Hospice, Sydenham, on secondment from Department of Health and Social Security; b 18 March 1934; d of Cecil Ford and Grace Ford. Educ: Clarendon Sch., Abergele; St Hugh's Coll., Oxford; St Thomas' Hosp., London. MA, BM, BCh; FFCM 1976; FRCP 1985. Junior hospital posts, St Thomas', Oxford, Reading, 1959–64; Medical Officer, Min. of Health, 1965, Sen. Med. Officer, 1968; SPMO, 1974–77, Dep. Chief MO (Dep. Sec.), 1977–, DHSS. Publications: papers on health services research, terminal care and other health subjects in Portfolio for Health, Vol. 1 (Nuffield Provincial Hospitals Trust) and other med. jls. Recreations: music, ski-ing, tennis, children's literature. Address: 9 Ryecotes Mead, Dulwich Common, SE21. T: 01–693 6576.

FORD, Glyn; see Ford, J. G.

FORD, Harold Frank; Sheriff at Perth, 1971–80 (Sheriff Substitute at Forfar and Arbroath, 1951–71); b 17 May 1915; s of Sir Patrick Ford, 1st Bt, and b of Sir Henry Ford, qv; m 1948, Lucy Mary, d of late Sheriff J. R. Wardlaw Burnet, KC; one s three d. Educ: Winchester Coll.; University Coll., Oxford (BA); Edinburgh Univ. (LLB). War service with Lothians and Border Yeomanry (Prisoner of War, 1940–45): Hon. Capt. Scottish Bar, 1945; Legal Adviser to UNRRA and IRO in British Zone of Germany, 1947. Recreations: golf, gardening, shooting. Address: Millhill, Meikleour, Perthshire PH2 6EF. T: Caputh 311. Clubs: New (Edinburgh); Honourable Company of Edinburgh Golfers, Royal Perth Golfing Society.

FORD, Henry, II; Member of the Board and Chairman, Finance Committee, Ford Motor Company, Dearborn, Michigan; b Detroit, 4 Sept. 1917; s of Edsel B. and Eleanor (Clay) Ford; m 1st, 1940, Anne McDonnell (marr. diss.); one s two d; 2nd, 1965, Maria Cristina Vettore Austin (marr. diss. 1980); 3rd, 1980, Kathleen DuRoss. Educ: Hotchkiss Sch., Lakeville, Conn; Yale Univ. Dir, Ford Motor Co., 1938–; became employee, 1940; Vice-Pres., 1943; Executive Vice-Pres., 1944; Pres., 1945; Chief Executive Officer, 1945–79, and Chm., 1960–80; retd as officer and employee, 1982. Director: Sotheby's Holdings, Inc., 1983– (Vice-Chm., 1983–86); Manufacturers Trust Co. of Florida, NA, 1983–85. Graduate Mem., Business Council (Mem. 1947–). Trustee, The Ford Foundn, 1943–76; Chm. Trustees, Henry Ford Health Care Corp., 1982–; Mem., St Mary's Hosp. Adv. Bd of Trustees, 1984–. Address: (home) Palm Beach, Fla, USA; (office) Dearborn, Michigan, USA.

FORD, Sir Henry Russell, 2nd Bt cr 1929; TD; JP; b 30 April 1911; s of Sir Patrick Ford, 1st Bt, and Jessie Hamilton (d 1962), d of Henry Field, WS, Moreland, Kinross-shire, and Middlebluf, Manitoba; S father, 1945; m 1936, Mary Elizabeth, y d of late Godfrey F. Wright, Whiddon, Bovey Tracy; one s three d. Educ: Winchester; New Coll., Oxford. War of 1939–45 served in UK, North Africa and Italy (despatches). Chm., Berwick and E Lothian Unionist Assoc., 1948–50, 1958–60. JP 1951. TD 1960. Recreations: golf, gardening. Heir: s Andrew Russell Ford [b 29 June 1943; m 1968, Penelope Anne, d of Harry Relph; two s one d]. Address: Seaforth, Gullane, East Lothian. T: Gullane 842214. Club: Hon. Company of Edinburgh Golfers (Muirfield).
  See also Harold Frank Ford.

FORD, Prof. Sir Hugh, Kt 1975; FRS 1967; FEng 1977; Professor of Mechanical Engineering, since 1969, Pro-Rector, 1978–80, University of London (Imperial College of Science and Technology); Chairman: Sir Hugh Ford & Associates Ltd, since 1982; Advisory Board, Prudential Portfolio Managers; Director: Ricardo Consulting Engineers Ltd, since 1980; Air Liquide UK Ltd, since 1979; RD Projects Ltd, since 1982; Ford & Dain Research Ltd, since 1972; b 16 July 1913; s of Arthur and Constance Ford; m 1942, Wynyard, d of Major F. B. Scholfield; two d. Educ: Northampton Sch.; City and Guilds Coll., Univ. of London. DSc (Eng); PhD. Practical trng at GWR Locomotive Works, 1931–36; researches into heat transfer, 1936–39; R&D Engrg, Imperial Chemical Industries, Northwich, 1939–42; Chief Engr, Technical Dept, British Iron and Steel Fedn, 1942–45, then Head of Mechanical Working Div., British Iron and Steel Research Assoc., 1945–47; Reader in Applied Mechanics, Univ. of London (Imp. Coll. of Science and Technology), 1948–51, Prof., 1951–69; Head of Dept of Mech. Engineering, 1965–78. Mem. Bd of Governors, Imperial Coll., 1982–. Technical Dir, Davy-Ashmore Group, 1968–71; Dir, Herbert Ltd, 1972–79. John Player Lectr, IMechE, 1973. First Pres., Inst. of Metals, 1985– (merger of Inst. of Metallurgists and Metals Soc.); President: Section 6, British Assoc., 1975–76; Welding Inst., 1983–85; Fellow, 1977, Vice-Pres., 1981–84, Fellowship of Engineering; Member: Council, IMechE (Vice-Pres., 1972, 1975, Sen. Vice Pres., 1976, Pres., 1977–78); SRC, 1968–72 (Chm. Engineering Bd); Council, Royal Soc., 1973–74; ARC, 1976–81. FICE; Whitworth Schol.; FCGI. Hon. MASME, 1980; Hon. FIMechE 1984. Hon. DSc: Salford, 1976; QUB, 1977; Aston, 1978; Bath, 1978; Sheffield, 1984. Thomas Hawksley Gold Medallist, IMechE, 1948, for researches into rolling of metals; Robertson Medal, Inst. of Metals, 1954; James Alfred Ewing Gold Medal, ICE, 1982; James Watt Internat. Gold Medal, 1985. Publications: Advanced Mechanics of Materials, 1963; papers to Royal Soc., IMechE, Iron and Steel Inst., Inst. of Metals, foreign societies, etc. Recreations: gardening, music. Address: 18 Shrewsbury House, Cheyne Walk, SW3; Shamley Cottage, Stroud Lane, Shamley Green, Surrey. Club: Athenæum.

FORD, James Allan, CB 1978; MC 1946; b 10 June 1920; 2nd s of Douglas Ford and Margaret Duncan (née Allan); m 1948, Isobel Dunnett; one s one d. Educ: Royal High School, Edinburgh; University of Edinburgh. Served 1940–46, Capt. Royal Scots. Entered Civil Service, 1938; Asst Sec., Dept of Agriculture and Fisheries for Scotland, 1958;

Registrar Gen. for Scotland, 1966–69; Principal Establishment Officer, Scottish Office, 1969–79. A Trustee, Nat. Lib. of Scotland, 1981–. Publications: The Brave White Flag, 1961; Season of Escape, 1963; A Statue for a Public Place, 1965; A Judge of Men, 1968; The Mouth of Truth, 1972. Address: 29 Lady Road, Edinburgh EH16 5PA. T: 031–667 4489. Clubs: Royal Scots, Scottish Arts (Edinburgh).

FORD, (James) Glyn; Member (Lab) Greater Manchester East, European Parliament, since 1984; b 28 Jan. 1950; s of Ernest Benjamin Ford and Matilda Alberta Ford (née James); m 1973, Hazel Nancy Mahy; one d. Educ: Marling; Reading Univ. (BSc Geol. with Soil Sci.); UCL (MSc Marine Earth Sci.); Manchester Univ. Undergraduate Apprentice, BAC, 1967–68; Course Tutor in Oceanography, Open Univ., 1976–78; Teaching Asst, UMIST, 1977–78; Res. Fellow, Sussex Univ., 1978–79; Manchester University: Res. Asst, 1976–77; Res. Fellow, 1979; Lectr, 1979–80; Sen. Res. Fellow, Prog. of Policy Res. in Engrg Sci. and Technol., 1980–84; Hon. Vis. Res. Fellow, 1984–. Vis. Prof., Tokyo Univ., 1983. Tameside Borough Council: Mem., 1978–86; Chairman: Environmental Health and Control Cttee, 1979–80; Educn Services Cttee, 1980–85. Mem., Sci. and Technol. Policy Sub-Cttee, Lab Party NEC, 1981–83; Chm., Cttee of Inquiry into Growth of Racism and Fascism in Europe, Euro. Parlt, 1984–86. Prospective Parly Cand. (Lab), Hazel Grove, 1985–. Publications: contribs to learned jls on sci. and technol. policy. Recreations: Japan, travel, writing. Address: 149 Old Road, Ashton-under-Lyne, Lancs OL6 9DA. T: 061-330 9299; (office) 3 Market Place, Ashton-under-Lyne, Lancs OL6 7JD. T: 061–344 3000. Clubs: Park Bridge Working Mens Institute (Ashton-under-Lyne); Cheadle Labour.

FORD, Sir John (Archibald), KCMG 1977 (CMG 1967); MC 1945; HM Diplomatic Service, retired; b 19 Feb. 1922; s of Ronald Mylne Ford and Margaret Jesse Coghill, Newcastle-under-Lyme, Staffs; m 1956, Emaline Burnette, Leesville, Virginia; two d. Educ: St Michael's Coll., Tenbury; Sedbergh Sch., Yorks; Oriel Coll., Oxford. Served in Royal Artillery, 1942–46 (temp. Major); demobilised, 1947. Joined Foreign (subseq. Diplomatic) Service, 1947. Third Sec., British Legation, Budapest, 1947–49; Third Sec. and a Resident Clerk, FO, 1949–52; Private Sec. to Permanent Under-Sec. of State, FO, 1952–54; HM Consul, San Francisco, 1954–56; seconded to HM Treasury, 1956–59; attended Course at Administrative Staff Coll., 1959; First Sec. and Head of Chancery, British Residency, Bahrain, 1959–61; Asst, FO Personnel Dept, 1961–63; Asst, FO Establishment and Organisation Dept, 1963; Head of Diplomatic Service Establishment and Organisation Dept, 1964–66; Counsellor (Commercial), Rome, 1966–70; Asst Under-Sec., FCO, 1970–71; Consul-Gen., New York, and Dir-Gen., British Trade Develt in USA, 1971–75; Ambassador to Indonesia, 1975–78; British High Comr in Canada, 1978–81. Lay Administrator, Guildford Cathedral, 1982–84. Mem., Exec. Cttee, VSO, 1982–, Dep. Chm., 1983–. Chm. Trustees, Voluntary and Christian Service, 1985–. Recreations: walking, gardening, sailing. Address: Loquats, Guildown, Guildford, Surrey. Clubs: Farmers'; Yvonne Arnaud Theatre (Guildford).

FORD, (John) Peter, CBE 1969; Chairman and Managing Director, International Joint Ventures Ltd; b 20 Feb. 1912; s of Ernest and Muriel Ford; m 1939, Phoebe Seys, d of Herbert McGregor Wood, FRIBA; one s two d. Educ: Wrekin Coll.; Gonville and Caius Coll., Cambridge. BA (Hons Nat. Sci. Tripos) 1934; MA Cantab 1937. Cambridge Univ. Air Sqdn, 1932–35 (Pilot's A Licence, 1933–). Air Ministry (subsequently FO, RAFVR), 1939–40; Coventry Gauge and Tool Co. Ltd (Asst to Chm.), 1941–45; Gen. Man., Brit. Engineers Small Tools and Equipment Co. Ltd, and Gen. Man. Scientific Exports (Gt Brit.) Ltd, 1945–48; Man. Dir, Brush Export Ltd, Associated British Oil Engines (Export) Ltd and National Oil Engines (Export) Ltd, and Dir of other associated cos of The Brush Group, 1949–55; Dir, Associated British Engineering Ltd and subsidiaries, 1957–58; Man. Dir, Coventry Climax International Ltd, 1958–63; Director: Plessey Overseas Ltd, 1963–70; Bryant & May (Latin America) Ltd, 1970–73. Chm. Institute of Export, 1954–56, 1965–67; President: Soc. of Commercial Accountants, 1970–74 (Vice-Pres., 1956–70); Soc. of Company and Commercial Accountants, 1974–75; Member: Council, London Chamber of Commerce, 1951–72 (Dep. Chm., 1970–72; Vice-Pres., 1972–); London Ct of Arbitration, 1970–73; FBI, Overseas Trade Policy Cttee, 1952–63; Council, British Internal Combustion Engine Manufacturers Assoc., 1953–55; BNEC Cttee for Exports to Latin America, 1964–71 (Chm. 1968–71); NEDO Cttee for Movement of Exports, 1972–75; British Overseas Trade Adv. Council, 1975–82. Chm., British Shippers' Council, 1972–75 (Dep. Chm., 1971–72). Chm., British Mexican Soc., 1973–77; Vice-Pres., Hispanic and Luso Brazilian Council, 1980–. Freeman of City of London, 1945; Mem. Ct of Assistants, Ironmongers' Co. (Master, 1981); Governor: Wrekin Coll., 1953–57; Oversea Service Coll., 1966–86. CEng, CIMechE, CIMarE, MIEE, FIPE. Order of Rio Branco (Brazil), 1977. Publications: contributor to technical press and broadcaster on international trade subjects. Recreations: Athletics (Cambridge Univ. and Internat. Teams, 1932–35; held various county championships, 1932–37; Hon. Treas. Achilles Club, 1947–58; Pres., London Athletic Club, 1964–66). Address: 40 Fairacres, Roehampton Lane, SW15. T: 01–876 2146. Clubs: United Oxford & Cambridge University, City Livery, MCC; Hawks (Cambridge); Royal Wimbledon Golf.

FORD, Joseph Francis, CMG 1960; OBE 1949; HM Diplomatic Service, retired 1970; b 11 Oct. 1912; s of J. W. Ford, Chesterfield, Derbs; m 1938, Mary Margaret Ford (née Taylor); two s. Educ: Chesterfield Grammar Sch.; Emmanuel Coll., Cambridge (BA). BA (Hons) Modern Chinese, London, 1958. Appointed probationer Vice-Consul to Peking, Nov. 1935; served at Shanghai, Chungking, Washington, Peking, Hanoi, New Orleans and Saigon; Dir, Res. Dept, FCO (formerly Jt Res. Dept, FO/CO), 1967–70; Director: Univs Service Centre, Hong Kong, 1970–72; Great Britain-China Centre, London, 1974–78; Chm., China Soc., 1982–85. Address: 10 Raymond Road, Wimbledon, SW19. Club: Royal Automobile.

FORD, Peter; see Ford, J. P.

FORD, Peter George Tipping; Secretary, Medical Protection Society, since 1983; b 18 Sept. 1931; s of Raymond Eustace Ford, qv; m 1958, Nancy Elizabeth Procter; four d. Educ: Epsom College; St Bartholomew's Hosp. Med. Coll., Univ. of London (MB, BS); MRCGP, DObst RCOG, Nat. Service, RAMC, 1957–59. Gen. practice, Hythe, 1960–68; Asst Sec., Med. Protection Soc., 1968–72, Dep. Sec., 1972–83. Sec., Jt Co ordinating Cttee, UK Defence Organizations, 1985–. Mem., Soc. of Apothecaries. FRSM. Medal of Honour, Med. Defence Soc. of Queensland, 1984. Publications: contribs to medico-legal periodicals. Recreations: baroque choral music, gardening, bridge. Address: Braeside Cottage, Cannongate Road, Hythe, Kent CT21 5PT. T: Hythe (Kent) 67896. Club: Carlton.

FORD, Raymond Eustace, CBE 1963; MD, MRCP; retired as Principal Medical Officer i/c Regional Medical Service, Ministry of Health (1946–63); b 24 April 1898; s of Rev. George Ford; m 1924, Elsie (née Tipping); two s one d. Educ: Sheffield Univ. Recreations: crosswords and the garden. Address: St John's Road, Hythe, Kent.
  See also P. G. T. Ford.

FORD, Sir (Richard) Brinsley, Kt 1984; CBE 1978; FSA; Member of National Art-Collections Fund since 1927, and of Executive Committee since 1960; Vice-Chairman, 1974–75, Chairman 1975–80; Secretary, Society of Dilettanti, since 1972; b 10 June

1908; *e s* of late Capt. Richard Ford, Rifle Brigade, and Rosamund, *d* of Sir John Ramsden, 5th Bt; *m* 1937, Joan, *d* of late Capt. Geoffrey Vyvyan; two *s* one *d*. *Educ:* Eton; Trinity Coll., Oxford. Joined TA 1939; served for one year as Troop Sergeant Major, RA; commissioned 1941, and transferred to Intelligence Corps (Major 1945). Selected works for Arts Council Festival of Britain and Coronation Exhibitions; a Trustee of the National Gallery, 1954–61; Trustee, Watts Gall., Compton, 1955– (Chm., 1974–84); great-grandson of Richard Ford (1796–1858) who wrote the Handbook for Spain; owner of the Ford Collection of Richard Wilsons. Dir, Burlington Magazine, 1952–. Member: Council, Byam Shaw Sch., 1957–73; Exec. Cttee, City and Guilds of London Art Sch., 1976–. Pres., St Marylebone Soc., 1974–77. Hon. Adviser on Paintings to Nat. Trust, 1980; Hon. Fellow, Royal Acad., 1981. Corres. Mem., Royal Acad. of San Fernando, Madrid. Officer, Belgian Order of Leopold II; US Bronze Star; Médaille d'Argent de la Reconnaissance Française. *Publications:* The Drawings of Richard Wilson, 1951; contributor to the Burlington Magazine and Apollo. *Address:* 14 Wyndham Place, Bryanston Square, W1. *T:* 01–723 0826. *Club:* Brooks's.

FORD, Gen. Sir Robert (Cyril), GCB 1981 (KCB 1977; CB 1973); CBE 1971 (MBE 1958); Governor, Royal Hospital, Chelsea, since 1981; *b* 29 Dec. 1923; *s* of late John Stranger Ford and Gladys Ford, Yealmpton, Devon; *m* 1949, Jean Claudia Pendlebury, *d* of late Gp Capt. Claude Pendlebury, MC, TD, FLAS, FRICS, and late Muriel Pendlebury, Yelverton, Devon; one *s*. *Educ:* Musgrave's. War of 1939–45: commissioned into 4th/7th Royal Dragoon Guards, from Sandhurst, 1943; served with Regt throughout NW European campaign, 1944–45 (despatches) and in Egypt and Palestine, 1947–48 (despatches). Instructor, Mons OCS, 1949–50; Training Officer, Scottish Horse (TA), 1952–54; Staff Coll., Camberley, 1955; GSO 2 Mil. Ops, War Office, 1956–57; Sqdn Ldr 4/7 RDG, 1958–59; Bde Major, 20th Armoured Bde, 1960–61; Brevet Lt-Col, 1962; Sqdn Ldr, 4/7 RDG, 1962–63; GSO1 to Chief of Defence Staff, 1964–65; commanded 4/7 RDG in S Arabia and N Ireland, 1966–67; Comdr, 7th Armd Bde, 1968–69; Principal Staff Officer to Chief of Defence Staff, 1970–71; Cmdr Land Forces, N Ireland, 1971–73; Comdt, RMA Sandhurst, 1973–76; Military Secretary, 1976–78; Adjutant-General, 1978–81; ADC General to the Queen, 1980–81. Colonel Commandant: RAC, 1980–82; SAS Regt, 1980–85; Col 4th/7th Royal Dragoon Gds, 1984–. President: Services Kinema Corp., 1978–81; Army Boxing Assoc., 1978–81. Mem., Commonwealth War Graves Commn, 1981–; Chm., 1981–, and Pres., 1986–, Army Benevolent Fund; Chm., Royal Cambridge Home for Soldiers' Widows, 1981–; Nat. Pres., Forces Help Soc. and Lord Roberts Workshops, 1981–. Governor, Corps of Commissionaires, 1981–. Freeman, City of London, 1981. CBIM. *Recreations:* cricket, tennis, war studies. *Address:* Royal Hospital, Chelsea, SW3 4SR. *Clubs:* Cavalry and Guards, MCC.

FORD, Robert Stanley; HM Diplomatic Service, retired; *b* 30 Nov. 1929; *s* of late Robert Hempstead Ford and of Janet Mabel Elliot; *m* 1957, Cynthia Valerie Arscott, *d* of late Ronald Prowse Arscott, Bexhill-on-Sea, Sussex; one *s* two *d*. *Educ:* Daniel Stewart's Coll., Edinburgh; Univ. of Edinburgh (MA). Joined HM Diplomatic Service, 1949; HM Forces, 1949; FCO, 1951; Third Sec., Moscow, 1955; Consul, Dakar, 1958; FCO, 1959; Information Officer, NY, 1963; First Sec., Managua, 1965; Consul, Naples, 1968; FCO, 1972; Consul-Gen., Madrid, 1978; FCO, 1982; Counsellor (Admin), Paris, 1984–86. *Recreations:* music, photography, gardening, travel. *Address:* 20 Heatherbank, Haywards Heath, W Sussex RH16 1HY. *T:* Haywards Heath 455321.

FORD, Robert Webster, CBE 1982; HM Diplomatic Service, retired; *b* 27 March 1923; *s* of late Robert Ford; *m* 1956, Monica Florence Tebbett; two *s*. *Educ:* Alleyne's Sch. Served RAF, 1939–45. Served with British Mission, Lhasa, Tibet and Political Agency in Sikkim and Bhutan, 1945–47; joined Tibetan Govt Service, 1947; advised on and installed Tibet's first radio communication system and broadcasting stn; travelled extensively in Northern and Eastern Tibet, 1947–50; taken prisoner during Chinese Occupation of Tibet, 1950; imprisoned in China, 1950–55; free-lance writer and broadcaster on Chinese and Tibetan affairs, 1955; entered Foreign Service, 1956; 2nd Sec., Saigon, 1957–58; 1st Sec. (Information), Djakarta, 1959; Washington, 1960–62; FO, 1962–67; Consul-Gen., Tangier, 1967–70; Counsellor, 1970; Consul-General; Luanda, 1970–74; Bordeaux, 1974–78; Gothenburg, 1978–80; Geneva, 1980–83. *Publications:* Captured in Tibet, 1956. *Recreations:* ski-ing on snow and water, gardening, travelling. *Address:* Cedar Garth, Latimer Road, Monken Hadley, Barnet, Herts EN5 5NU. *Clubs:* Royal Commonwealth Society, Royal Geographical Society.

FORD, Roy Arthur, MA; Director of Visits, Canterbury Cathedral, since 1986; *b* 10 May 1925; *s* of Arthur Ford and Minnie Elizabeth Ford; *m* 1965, Christine Margaret Moore; two *s*. *Educ:* Collyer's Sch., Horsham; Corpus Christi Coll., Cambridge (Scholar; 1st Cl. Pts I and II, History Tripos; BA 1949, MA 1971). Asst Master: Uppingham Sch., 1951–54; Tonbridge Sch., 1954–66; Uppingham Sch., (also Head of History and Sixth Form Master), 1966–71; Headmaster: Southwell Minster Grammar Sch., 1971–75; King's Sch., Rochester, 1975–86. *Recreations:* walking, travel, music. *Address:* 28 West Street, Faversham, Kent. *T:* Faversham 537614.

FORD, Rev. Wilfred Franklin, CMG 1974; *b* 9 Jan. 1920; *s* of Harold Franklin Ford and Sarah Elizabeth Ford; *m* 1st, 1942, Joan Mary Holland (*d* 1981); three *d*; 2nd, 1982, Hilda Mary Astley. *Educ:* Auckland Univ., NZ (BA); Trinity Theological Coll., NZ. Served War, NZ Army, 1942–44. Entered Methodist Ministry, 1945; Dir, Christian Educn, Methodist Church of NZ, 1956–68; President: Methodist Church of NZ, 1971; NZ Marriage Guidance Council, 1981–84; Life Mem., Wellington Marriage Guidance Council. *Publications:* contribs to NZ and internat. jls, on Christian educn. *Recreations:* gardening, reading, bowls. *Address:* 122 Totara Drive, Hamilton, New Zealand.

FORD ROBERTSON, Francis Calder, OBE 1959; *b* 19 March 1901; 3rd *s* of Dr W. Ford Robertson, MD, and Marion Elam; *m* 1928, Cynthia Mary de Courcy Ireland (*d* 1977); two *s*; *m* 1977, Nora Aline de Courcy Chapman (*née* Ireland). *Educ:* Edinburgh Academy; Edinburgh Univ. Appointed to Indian Forest Service as probationer, 1923; IFS, 1924–47; Director: Commonwealth Forestry Bureau, Oxford, 1947–64; Dir-Editor, Multilingual Forestry Terminology Project, at Commonwealth Forestry Inst., Oxford and Washington, DC, USA, 1964–70. Hon. Mem., Soc. of American Foresters, 1970. Hon. MA Oxford, 1952. *Publications:* Our Forests, 1934; (ed) The Terminology of Forest Science, Technology, Practice and Products (English lang. version), 1971; also sundry scientific, mainly bibliographical, articles. *Recreations:* choral singing, gardening, local history and archaeology, Oxford guiding. *Address:* 54 Staunton Road, Headington, Oxford. *T:* Oxford 62073.

FORDE, Hon. Harold McDonald, MD; High Commissioner for Barbados in UK, 1984–86; *b* 10 Jan. 1916; *s* of Gertrude and William McDonald Forde; *m* 1949, Alice Leslie; one *s* two *d*. *Educ:* Harrison College, Barbados; University College London; University College Hospital (MB BS 1942; MD); DPH, DTM&H. MO, Colonial Med. Service, Belize, 1947–52; First Lectr, Dept. of Medicine, Univ. of West Indies, Jamaica, 1952–57; Consultant Physician, Barbados, 1957–78; Med. Supt, Barbados Gen. Hosp., 1961–64; Senior Lectr, Dept of Medicine, Univ. of West Indies, 1967–78 (Associate Dean, 1967–73); Mem. Senate, Univ. of W Indies, 1973–75; Chief Med. Officer, Commonwealth of Bahamas, 1978–79; Consultant Physician, Barbados, 1980–84; Chief Med. Officer, Life of Barbados, 1973–84. Mem. Privy Council, Barbados, 1980–; Senior Fellow, Commonwealth Fund, 1976; Tech. Expert, Commonwealth Fund for Tech Co-Opn, 1978–79; Governor, Commonwealth Foundn, 1984. Hon. Vice-President: West India Cttee; Commonwealth Inst. Hon. FRCPE 1972; Hon. FACP 1975. *Publications:* articles in WI med. jls. *Recreations:* cricket, soccer, bridge, chess, athletics, music. *Address:* c/o Barbados High Commission, 6 Upper Belgrave Street, SW1X 8AZ. *Club:* Royal Commonwealth Society.

FORDER, Ven. Charles Robert; Archdeacon Emeritus, Diocese of York, since 1974; *b* 6 Jan. 1907; *s* of late Henry Forder, Worstead, Norfolk; *m* 1933, Myra, *d* of late Harry Peat, Leeds; no *c*. *Educ:* Paston Sch., North Walsham; Christ's Coll. and Ridley Hall, Cambridge. Exhibitioner of Christ's Coll. and Prizeman, 1926; 1st Cl. Math. Trip. Part I, 1926, BA (Sen. Opt. Part II) 1928, MA 1932; Ridley Hall, 1928. Curate: St Peter's, Hunslet Moor, 1930–33; Burley, 1933–34; Vicar: Holy Trinity, Wibsey, 1934–40; St Clement's, Bradford, 1940–47; Organising Sec., Bradford Church Forward Movement Appeal, 1945–47; Vicar of Drypool, 1947–55; Rector of Routh and Vicar of Wawne, 1955–57; Canon, and Prebendary of Fenton, York Minster, 1957–76; Rector of Sutton-on-Derwent, 1957–63; Rector of Holy Trinity, Micklegate, York, 1963–66; Archdeacon of York, 1957–72. Chaplain to HM Prison, Hull, 1950–53; Proctor in Convocation, 1954–72; Organising Sec., Diocesan Appeal, 1955–76; Church Comr, 1958–73. *Publications:* A History of the Paston Grammar School, 1934, 2nd edn 1975; The Parish Priest at Work, 1947; Synods in Action, 1970; Churchwardens in Church and Parish, 1976; contrib. to Encyclopædia Britannica. *Recreations:* reading and writing. *Address:* Dulverton Hall, St Martin's Square, Scarborough YO11 2DQ. *T:* Scarborough 373082.

FORDER, Kenneth John; Registrar of the Architects Registration Council of the United Kingdom, since 1977; *b* 11 June 1925; *s* of late James A. Forder and Elizabeth Forder (*née* Hammond); *m* 1948, Dorothy Margôt Burles; two *d*. *Educ:* Westcliff Sch.; Hertford Coll., Oxford (MA); Queen's Coll., Cambridge. Called to Bar, Gray's Inn, 1963. RAF, Flt Lieut, Aircrew Navigator, 1943–47. District Officer, N Rhodesia, 1951–61; District Commissioner, N Rhodesia, 1962–64; General Secretary, National Federation of Meat Traders, 1964–73; Bar Practice, 1973–77; Registrar, Architects Registration Council of UK (established under Architects Registration Acts 1931 to 1969), 1977–. Freeman of the City of London, 1966. *Recreations:* tennis, bridge, chess. *Address:* Steeple Close, Church Gate, SW6. *T:* 01–736 3958. *Club:* Hurlingham.

FORDHAM, John Jeremy; His Honour Judge Fordham; a Circuit Judge, since 1986; *b* 18 April 1933; *s* of John Hampden Fordham, CBE and Rowena Langran; *m* 1962, Rose Anita (*née* Brandon), *d* of Philip Brandon, Wellington, New Zealand; one *s* one *d*. *Educ:* Gresham's Sch.; Univ. of New Zealand. LLB (NZ). Merchant Navy, 1950–55 (2nd Mate (Foreign Going) Cert.); labourer, fireman etc, 1955–60; Barrister and Solicitor, New Zealand, 1960–64; called to Bar, Inner Temple, 1965; practised 1965–71, 1976–78; Sen. Magistrate, Gilbert and Ellice Islands, 1971–75; a Metropolitan Stipendiary Magistrate, 1978–86; a Recorder, 1986. *Recreations:* boats, games. *Address:* 9 King's Bench Walk, Temple, EC4. *T:* 01–353 5638. *Club:* Garrick.

FORDHAM, Wilfrid Gurney; QC 1967; *s* of Edward Wilfrid Fordham and Sybil Harriet (*née* Langdon-Davies); *m* 1930, Peta Marshall Freeman; one *s*. *Educ:* St George's, Harpenden; Magdalene Coll., Cambridge. Called to Bar, Inner Temple, 1929 (Bencher 1981); retired from practice, 1986. Dep. Circuit Judge, 1972–74; a Recorder of the Crown Court, 1974–76. Contested: (L) Bromley, Kent, 1929, 1930; (Lab) Wycombe, Bucks, 1959. *Publications:* various legal books. *Recreation:* travel. *Address:* 4 Paper Buildings, Temple, EC4. *T:* 01–353 2739.

FORECAST, Kenneth George, CB 1985; Under Secretary, Central Statistical Office, Cabinet Office, 1979–85; *b* 21 Aug. 1925; *s* of late George Albert Forecast and late Alice Matilda Forecast (*née* Davies); unmarried. *Educ:* William Morris Sch., Walthamstow; SW Essex Tech. Coll. BSc (Econ) London. Statistical Officer, MAP, 1945–48; Economist/Statistician with de Zoete & Gorton, Stock Exchange, London, 1948–51; Statistician: Central Statistics Office, Dublin, 1951–58; BoT, London, 1958–66; Chief Statistician, MoT, 1966–70; Dir of Statistics, DES, 1970–79. *Publications:* contribs to Review of Internat. Statistical Inst. and to Jl of Statistical and Social Inquiry Soc. of Ireland. *Address:* 9 Mathart Court, The Avenue, Highams Park, E4 9QQ. *T:* 01–527 3023. *Club:* Civil Service.

FOREMAN, Michael; RDI 1985; AGI; FSIAD; writer and illustrator; *b* 21 March 1938; *s* of Walter and Gladys Mary Foreman; *m* 1st, 1959, Janet Charters (marr. diss. 1966); one *s*; 2nd, 1980, Louise Phillips; one *s*. *Educ:* Notley Road Secondary Modern Sch., Lowestoft; Royal College of Art, London (ARCA 1st Cl. Hons and Silver Medal). Freelance, 1963–; six animated films produced, 1967–68. Awarded Aigle d'Argent, Festival International du Livre, Nice, 1972; (jtly) Kurt Maschler Award, 1982; Graphics Prize, Bologna, 1982; Kate Greenaway Medal, Library Assoc., 1983. *Publications:* author and illustrator: The Perfect Present, 1966; The Two Giants, 1966; The Great Sleigh Robbery, 1968; Horatio, 1969; Moose, 1971; Dinosaurs and all that Rubbish, 1972 (Francis Williams Prize, 1972); War and Peas, 1974; All The King's Horses, 1976; Panda and his Voyage of Discovery, 1977 (Francis Williams Prize, 1977); Trick a Tracker, 1980; Panda and the Odd Lion, 1981; Land of Dreams, 1982; Panda and the Bunyips, 1984; Cat and Canary, 1984; Panda and the Bushfire, 1986; illustrator of many books by other authors. *Recreations:* football, travelling. *Address:* 5 Church Gate, SW6. *Club:* Zanzibar.

FOREMAN, Sir Philip (Frank), Kt 1981; CBE 1972; DLC; FEng, FIMechE, FIProdE, CBIM; DL; Managing Director, since 1967, Chairman, since 1983, Short Bros PLC; *b* 16 March 1923; *s* of late Frank and Mary Foreman; *m* 1971, Margaret Cooke; one *s*. *Educ:* Soham Grammar Sch., Cambs; Loughborough Coll., Leics. Royal Naval Scientific Service, 1943–58. Short Bros, 1958–. Pres., IMechE, 1985–86. Hon. FRAeS. Hon. DSc QUB, 1976; Hon. DTech Loughborough, 1983; DUniv Open, 1985. DL Belfast, 1975. *Publications:* papers to: Royal Aeronautical Soc.; Instn of Mechanical Engineers. *Recreations:* golf, gardening.

FORESTER; *see* Weld Forester, family name of Baron Forester.

FORESTER, 8th Baron *cr* 1821; **George Cecil Brooke Weld Forester;** *b* 20 Feb. 1938; *s* of 7th Baron Forester and of Marie Louise Priscilla, *d* of Col Sir Herbert Perrott, 6th Bt, CH, CB; *S* father, 1977; *m* 1967, Hon. Elizabeth Catherine Lyttelton, 2nd *d* of 10th Viscount Cobham, KG, PC, GCMG, GCVO, TD; one *s* three *d*. *Educ:* Eton; Royal Agricultural College, Cirencester (MRAC). *Heir:* *s* Hon. Charles Richard George Weld Forester, *b* 8 July 1975. *Address:* Willey Park, Broseley, Salop TF12 5JJ. *T:* Telford 882146.

FORESTIER-WALKER, Sir Michael (Leolin), 6th Bt *cr* 1835; Teacher, Feltonfleet School, since 1975; *b* 24 April 1949; *s* of Lt-Col Alan Ivor Forestier-Walker, MBE (*d* 1954) (*g s* of 2nd Bt), and of Margaret Joan Forestier-Walker (*née* Marcoolyn); *S* cousin, 1983. *Educ:* Wellington College, Crowthorne; Royal Holloway College, London Univ. (BA Hons). *Recreations:* sailing, electronics. *Heir:* *cousin* Alan David Forestier-Walker [*b*

29 Aug. 1944; *m* 1969, Adela Judith, *d* of late S. P. Davis; one *s* two *d*]. *Address:* 91 Tartar Road, Cobham, Surrey KT11 2AS. *T:* Cobham 4954.

FORFAR, Prof. John Oldroyd, MC; Professor of Child Life and Health, University of Edinburgh, 1964–82, now Professor Emeritus; *b* 16 Nov. 1916; *s* of Rev. David Forfar, MA and Elizabeth Edith Campbell; *m* 1942, Isobel Mary Langlands Fernback, MB, ChB, DPH, AFOM; two *s* one *d*. *Educ:* Perth Acad.; St Andrews Univ. BSc 1938, MB, ChB 1941, St Andrews; MRCP 1947; MRCPE 1948; DCH (London) 1948; FRCPE 1953; MD (Commendation) St Andrews, 1958; FRCP 1964; FRSE 1975. House Officer, Perth Royal Infirmary, 1941; RAMC, 1942–46: Med. Off., 47 Royal Marine Commando, 1943–45 (MC 1944; despatches, 1945); Registrar and Sen. Registrar, Dundee Royal Infirmary, 1946–48; Sen. Lectr in Child Health, St Andrews Univ., 1948–50; Sen. Paediatric Phys., Edinburgh Northern Gp of Hosps, and Sen. Lectr in Child Life and Health, Edinburgh Univ., 1950–64. Chairman: Medical Gp, Assoc. of British Adoption Agencies, 1966–76; Jt Paediatric Cttee of Royal Colls of Physicians and British Paediatric Assoc., 1979–85; President: Scottish Paediatric Soc., 1972–74; Assoc. of Clinical Professors and Heads of Departments of Paediatrics, 1980–83; Pres., BPA, 1985–. Fellow, Amer. Coll. of Nutrition, 1977. James Spence Medallist, BPA, 1983. *Publications:* (ed) Textbook of Paediatrics, 1973, 3rd edn 1984; contribs to general medical and to paediatric jls and books. *Recreations:* walking, travelling, gardening. *Address:* 110 Ravelston Dykes, Edinburgh EH12 6HB. *T:* 031–337 7081.

FORGAN, Elizabeth Anne Lucy; Deputy Controller of Programmes, Channel Four Television, since 1986; *b* 31 Aug. 1944; *d* of Thomas Moinet Forgan and Jean Margaret Muriel. *Educ:* Benenden Sch.; St Hugh's Coll., Oxford (BA). Journalist: Teheran Journal, 1967–68; Hampstead and Highgate Express, 1969–74; Chief Leader Writer, Evening Standard, 1974–78; Woman's Editor, Asst Features Editor, The Guardian, 1978–81; Sen. Commissioning Editor, 1981–86, Asst Controller of Progs, 1984–86, Channel Four TV. *Recreations:* church music, cheap novels, Scottish Islands. *Address:* 6 Quadrant Grove, NW5 4JN. *T:* 01–267 0818.

FORGE, Andrew Murray; artist, writer; Dean of School of Art, University of Yale, Conn, USA; *b* Hastingleigh, Kent, 10 Nov. 1923; *s* of Sidney Wallace Forge and Joanna Ruth Forge (*née* Bliss); *m* 1950, Sheila Deane (marr. diss.); three *d*; *m* 1974, Ruth Miller. *Educ:* Downs Sch.; Leighton Park; Camberwell Sch. of Art (NDD). Sen. Lectr, Slade Sch., UCL, 1950–64; Head of Dept of Fine Art, Goldsmith's Coll., 1964–70. Trustee: Tate Gallery, 1964–71 and 1972–74; National Gallery, 1966–72; Member: Nat. Council for Diplomas in Art and Design, 1964–72; Jt NCDAD/NACEA Cttee, 1968–70; Calouste Gulbenkian Foundn Cttee to report on future of conservation studies in UK, 1970–72; Pres., London Group, 1964–71. *Publications:* Klee, 1953; Vermeer, 1954; Soutine, 1965; Rauschenberg, 1972; (with C. Joyes) Monet at Giverny, 1975; (ed) The Townsend Journals, 1976. *Recreation:* travel. *Address:* Malthouse, Elmsted, near Ashford, Kent.

FORMAN, Sir Denis, Kt 1976; OBE 1956; Chairman: Granada Television Ltd, since 1974 (Joint Managing Director, 1965–81); Novello & Co., since 1971; Director, since 1964, Deputy Chairman, since 1984, Granada Group; *b* 13 Oct. 1917; *s* of late Rev. Adam Forman, CBE, and Flora Smith; *m* 1948, Helen de Mouilpied; two *s*. *Educ:* at home; Loretto; Pembroke Coll., Cambridge. Served War, 1940–45: Argyll and Sutherland Highlanders; Commandant, Orkney and Shetland Defences Battle Sch., 1942 (wounded, Cassino, 1944). Chief Production Officer, Central Office of Information Films, 1947; Dir, British Film Inst., 1948–55; Chm., Bd of Governors, British Film Inst., 1971–73. Fellow, British Acad. of Film and Television Arts, 1977; Dep. Chm., Royal Opera Hse, Covent Gdn, 1983– (Dir, 1981–); Mem. Council, RNCM, 1975–84 (Hon. Mem., RNCM, 1981). DUniv Stirling, 1982; Hon. LLD Manchester, 1983. Ufficiale dell'ordine Al Merito della Repubblica Italiana. *Publications:* Mozart's Piano Concertos, 1971; contrib. The Listener. *Recreation:* music. *Address:* Granada Group, 36 Golden Square, W1R 4AH. *Club:* Garrick.
See also M. B. Forman.

FORMAN, (Francis) Nigel; MP (C) Carshalton and Wallington, since 1983 (Carshalton, March 1976–1983); *b* 25 March 1943; *s* of late Brig. J. F. R. Forman and of Mrs P. J. M. Forman; *m*. *Educ:* Dragon Sch., Oxford; Shrewsbury Sch.; New Coll., Oxford; College of Europe, Bruges; Kennedy Sch. of Govt, Harvard; Sussex Univ. Information Officer, CBI, 1970–71; Conservative Research Dept, 1971–76. Secretary: Cons. Education Cttee, 1976–79; Cons. Energy Cttee, 1977–79; Mem., Select Cttee on Science and Technology, 1976–79; Vice-Chairman: Cons. Finance Cttee, 1983–; All Party Social Sci. and Policy Cttee, 1984–. PPS to Lord Privy Seal, 1979–81 and to Minister of State, FCO, 1979–83. *Publications:* Towards a More Conservative Energy Policy, 1977; Another Britain, 1979; Mastering British Politics, 1985; (with John Maples) Work to be Done, 1985. *Address:* House of Commons, SW1.

FORMAN, Air Vice-Marshal Graham Neil; Director of Legal Services, Royal Air Force, since 1982; *b* 29 Nov. 1930; *s* of late Stanley M. Forman and Eva Forman (*née* Barrett); *m* 1957, Valerie Fay (*née* Shaw); one *s* two *d*. *Educ:* Boston Grammar School; Nottingham Univ. Law School; Law Society's School of Law; admitted solicitor 1953. Commissioned RAF Legal Branch, 1957; served HQ Far East Air Force, Singapore, 1960–63 and 1965–68; Dep. Dir, RAF Legal Services, HQ Near East Air Force, Cyprus, 1971–72 and 1973–76; Dep. Dir, RAF Legal Services, HQ RAF Germany, 1978; Dep. Dir, Legal Services (RAF), 1978–82. *Recreations:* cricket, tennis, reading, traditional jazz music. *Address:* c/o Lloyds Bank, High Street, Berkhamsted, Herts. *Clubs:* Royal Air Force; MCC.

FORMAN, Sir John Denis; *see* Forman, Sir Denis.

FORMAN, Louis, MD London; FRCP; Consultant Dermatologist Emeritus, Guy's Hospital and St John's Hospital for Diseases of the Skin. *Educ:* Guy's Hosp., Univ. of London. MRCS, LRCP 1923; MB, BS 1924; MRCP 1925; FRCP 1939. Formerly Dermatologist SE Group, London CC; Medical Registrar, Guy's Hosp. Past President: British Assoc. Dermatology; Section of Dermatology, RSM. Hon. FRSM 1985. *Publications:* various articles in med. jls. *Address:* 22 Harley House, Regent's Park, NW1 5HE. *T:* 01–487 3834.

FORMAN, Michael Bertram, TD 1945; Chairman, Civil Service Appeal Board, since 1984; *b* 28 March 1921; *s* of late Rev. A. Forman, CBE, and Flora Smith; *m* 1947, Mary Railston-Brown, *d* of Rev. W. R. Railston-Brown; four *d*. *Educ:* Loretto Sch., Musselburgh; Manchester Coll. of Technology. TA commn, 7th KOSB, 1939. War Service in Inf. and Airborne Forces, 1939–46: UK, Holland, Germany (POW), India. Labour Management, Courtaulds Ltd, 1946–53; Dir, Inst. of Personnel Management, 1953–56; Head of Staff Planning, NCB, 1956–59; Chief Staff Officer, SW Div., NCB, 1959–62; TI Group plc (formerly Tube Investments Ltd): Personnel Relations Adviser and Dep. Dir of Personnel, 1962–68; Personnel Dir, Steel Tube Div., 1968–73; Dir of Personnel and Organisation, 1973–84, retired. Mem. NBPI, 1968–70. CIPM. FRSA. *Recreations:* reading, gardening, fishing, shooting. *Address:* The Priory, Stoke Prior, Bromsgrove, Worcs B60 4LY. *T:* Bromsgrove 32196. *Club:* Savile.
See also Sir D. Forman.

FORMAN, Miloš; film director; *b* Čáslav, 18 Feb. 1932. *Educ:* Acad. of Music and Dramatic Art, Prague. Director: Film Presentations, Czechoslovak Television, 1954–56; Laterna Magika, Prague, 1958–62. Co-chm. and Prof., Film Div., Columbia Univ. Sch. of Arts, 1978–. Films directed include: Talent Competition; Peter and Pavla, 1963 (Czech. Film Critics' Award; Grand Prix, Locarno, 1964; Prize, Venice Festival, 1965); A Blonde in Love (Grand Prix, French Film Acad., 1966); The Fireman's Ball, 1967; Taking Off, 1971; (co-dir) Visions of Eight, 1973; One Flew Over the Cuckoo's Nest, 1975 (Academy Award, 1976; BAFTA Award, 1977); Hair, 1979; Ragtime, 1982; Amadeus, 1985 (Oscar Award, 1985). *Address:* c/o Robert Lantz, The Lantz Office Inc., 888 Seventh Avenue, New York, NY 10106, USA.

FORMAN, Nigel; *see* Forman, F. N.

FORMAN, Roy; Managing Director, Private Patients Plan Ltd, since 1985; *b* 28 Dec. 1931; *s* of Leslie and Ena Forman; *m* 1954, Mary (*née* Nelson); three *s* one *d*. *Educ:* Nunthorpe Grammar Sch., York; Nottingham Univ. (BA Hons). RAF, 1953–56. Business economist, 1956–61; electricity supply industry, 1961–80: Chief Commercial Officer, S Wales Elec. Bd, 1972–76; Commercial Adviser, Electricity Council, 1976–80; Gen. Manager, Marketing and Sales, 1980–81, Marketing Dir, 1981–85, PPP. *Recreations:* music, walking, reading. *Address:* Private Patients Plan, PPP House, Crescent Road, Tunbridge Wells, Kent TN1 2PL. *Club:* Royal Air Force.

FORMARTINE, Viscount; George Ian Alastair Gordon; *b* 4 May 1983; *s* and *heir* of Earl of Haddo, *qv*.

FORMBY, Myles Landseer, CBE 1962; TD 1946; Consulting Otolaryngologist, retired: Consultant Emeritus to the Army, since 1971; University College Hospital, 1933–66, now Hon. Consulting Surgeon; Royal Masonic Hospital, 1948–66; *b* 13 March 1901; *s* of Arthur Formby, South Australia; *m* 1st, 1931, Dorothy Hussey Essex (marr. diss. 1952); one *s* one *d*; 2nd, 1974, Phyllis Mary Helps (*d* 1986), *d* of late Engr-Comdr G. S. Holgate, RN. *Educ:* St Peter's Coll., Adelaide, South Australia; Univ. of Adelaide; Magdalen Coll., Oxford. Elder Scholarship, Univ. of Adelaide, 1920 and 1921, Everard Scholarship, 1924; MB, BS, Adelaide, 1924; Rhodes Scholar for S Australia, 1925; BA Oxford, 1927; BSc Oxford, 1928; FRCS 1930; MA Oxford, 1953. Hon. Asst Surg., Ear, Nose and Throat Hosp., Golden Square, 1931; Hon. Surg., Ear, Nose and Throat, Miller Gen. Hosp., 1932; Hon. Asst Surg., Ear, Nose and Throat Dept, University Coll. Hosp., 1933; Hon. Surg., 1940; Hon. Surg., Ear, Nose and Throat Dept, Royal Masonic Hosp., 1948. RAMC TA, Lieut, 1932; Capt., 1933; Major, 1939; Lieut-Col, 1941; Brig. Consulting Oto-Rhino-Laryngologist to the Army, 1943; served in the Middle East, Italy, North West Europe and India, in War of 1939–45. Hon. Civilian Consultant to War Office, 1946. Mem. Court of Examiners, Royal College of Surgeons, 1947–53, Mem. Council, 1952–57; Royal Society of Medicine: Hon. Dir of Photography, 1958–61; Pres., Section of Laryngology, 1959–60; Hon. Treas., 1962–68; Hon. Fellow, 1970; Hon. Laryngologist to Royal Academy of Music; Pres., British Assoc. of Otolaryngologists. Bronze Star, USA, 1945. *Publications:* Dental Infection in the Aetiology of Maxillary Sinusitis, 1934; Treatment of Otitis Media, 1938; Nasal Allergy, 1943; chapters in Diseases of the Ear, Nose and Throat, 1952; The Maxillary Sinus, 1960; Ultrasonic Destruction of the Labyrinth, 1963. *Recreations:* rowing, lacrosse, golf. *Address:* Thorndene, Kithurst Lane, Storrington, West Sussex RH20 4LP. *T:* Storrington 2564. *Clubs:* Royal Automobile; Leander.

FORMSTON, Prof. Clifford; Professor of Veterinary Surgery in the University of London, 1943–74, now Emeritus; former Vice-Principal, Royal Veterinary College (1963); *b* 15 Jan. 1907; *s* of Alfred and Annie Formston; *m* 1934, Irene Pembleton (*d* 1973), *d* of Capt. Roland Wood; one *s* one *d*. *Educ:* Chester City Grammar Sch.; Royal Veterinary College, London. MRCVS 1928; FRCVS 1944. Mem. of Royal Veterinary Coll. staff, 1928–74, Fellow, 1974. Member of Council: BVA, 1949–55; RCVS, 1954–62. John Jeyes' Travel Scholarship, 1937; Visiting Professor: Univ. of Cairo, 1960; Univ. of Thessaloniki, 1966; Pahlavi Univ., Iran, 1975; Alfateh Univ., Libya, 1977, 1981; Sir Frederick Hobday Meml Lectr, 1971. Examiner in Veterinary Surgery, Nairobi Univ., 1977. Past President: Royal Counties Veterinary Assoc.; Central Veterinary Soc.; British Equine Veterinary Assoc. Examiner in veterinary surgery to Univs of Bristol, Cambridge, Dublin, Glasgow, Liverpool, London, Edinburgh and Khartoum; Hon. Res. Fellow, Inst. of Ophthalmology; Hon. Cons. Veterinary Surg. to Childe-Beale Trust. Pres., Vet. Benevolent Fund; Life Vice-Pres., Riding for the Disabled Assoc.; Veterinary Patron, Diamond Riding Centre for the Handicapped. Hon. Fellow, Farriers' Co., 1984. Blaine Award, 1971; John Henry Steel Meml Medallist, 1973; Simon Award, 1974; Victory Medal, Central Vet. Soc., 1975. *Publications:* contrib. scientific jls on general surgery and ophthalmology. *Recreations:* golf, gardening, reading. *Address:* 4 Marlow Court, Chase Side, Southgate, N14 5HR.

FORRES, 4th Baron *cr* 1922; **Alastair Stephen Grant Williamson;** Bt 1909; Director: Agriscot Pty Ltd; Jaga Trading Pty Ltd; *b* 16 May 1946; *s* of 3rd Baron Forres and of Gillian Ann Maclean, *d* of Major John Maclean Grant, RA; *S* father, 1978; *m* 1969, Margaret, *d* of late G. J. Mallam, Mullumbimby, NSW; two *s*. *Educ:* Eton. Patron, Sydney Scottish Week. *Heir:* *s* Hon. George Archibald Mallam Williamson, *b* 16 Aug. 1972. *Address:* Cotehele House, 177 Anson Street, Orange, NSW 2800, Australia. *Clubs:* Union, Australian Jockey, Sydney Turf (Sydney).

FORREST, Prof. Sir (Andrew) Patrick (McEwen), Kt 1986; Regius Professor of Clinical Surgery, University of Edinburgh, since 1970; part-time Chief Scientist, Scottish Home and Health Department, since 1981; Honorary Consultant Surgeon: Royal Infirmary of Edinburgh; Royal Prince Alfred Hospital, Sydney; Civilian Consultant to the Royal Navy; *b* 25 March 1923; *s* of Rev. Andrew James Forrest, BD, and Isabella Pearson; *m* 1955, Margaret Beryl Hall (*d* 1961); one *s* one *d*; *m* 1964, Margaret Anne Steward; one *d*. *Educ:* Dundee High Sch.; Univ. of St Andrews. BSc 1942; MB, ChB 1945; ChM hons, University Gold Medal, 1954; MD hons, Rutherford Gold Medal, 1958; FRCSE 1950; FRCS 1952; FRCSGlas 1962; FRSE 1976. Surg.-Lt RNVR, 1946–48. Mayo Foundation Fellow, 1952–53, Lectr and Sen. Lectr, Univ. of Glasgow, 1955–62; Prof. of Surgery, Welsh Nat. Sch. of Medicine, 1962–70. McIlrath Vis. Prof., Royal Prince Alfred Hosp., Sydney, 1969; Nimmo Vis. Prof., Royal Adelaide Hosp., 1973; McLauchlin-Gallie Prof., RCP of Canada, 1974; numerous other visiting professorships; Eponymous lectures include: Lister Meml, Canadian Med. Assoc., 1970; Inaugural Bruce Wellesley Hosp., Toronto, 1970; Inaugural Peter Lowe, RCP Glas., 1980. Member: Medical sub-cttee, UGC, 1967–76; MRC, 1974–79; Scientific Adv. Cttee, Cancer Res. Campaign, 1974–83; ABRC, 1982–85. Asst Editor and Editor, Scottish Med. Jl, 1957–61; Hon. Secretary: Scottish Soc. for Experimental Medicine, 1959–62; Surgical Research Soc., 1963–66, Pres., 1974–76; Chm., British Breast Gp, 1974–77. Member Council: Assoc. of Surgeons of GB and Ireland, 1971–74; RCSE, 1976–84; Member: Internat. Surgical Gp, 1963–; James IV Assoc. of Surgeons Inc., 1981–. Hon. Fellow, Amer. Surgical Assoc., 1981; Hon. FACS, 1978. Hon. DSc: Wales, 1981; Chinese Univ. of Hong Kong, 1986; Hon. LLD Dundee, 1986. *Publications:* (ed jtly) Prognostic Factors in Breast Cancer, 1968; (jtly) Principles and Practice of Surgery, 1985; various papers in surgical jls, mainly on gastro-intestinal disease and breast cancer. *Address:* Department of Clinical Surgery, University of Edinburgh, Royal Infirmary, Edinburgh EH3 9YW. *T:* 031–229 2477.

FORREST, Geoffrey; Consultant Chartered Surveyor; *b* 31 Oct. 1909; *er s* of late George Forrest, CA, Rossie Lodge, Inverness; *m* 1st, 1951, Marjorie Ridehalgh; two *s*; 2nd, 1974, Joyce Grey. *Educ:* Marlborough Coll. Chartered Surveyor. Served War of 1939–45, in Lovat Scouts. Joined Forestry Commn, 1946; Chief Land Agent for Forestry Commn in Wales, 1958–64; Chief Land Agent for Forestry Commn in Scotland, 1964–65; Sen. Officer of Forestry Commn in Scotland, 1965–69. Scottish Partner, Knight, Frank & Rutley, 1973–76. *Publications:* papers on land use and estate management in professional jls. *Recreations:* fishing, shooting, lawn tennis. *Address:* Leadervale House, Earlston, Berwickshire TD4 6AJ. *Club:* New (Edinburgh).

FORREST, Cdre (Retd) Geoffrey Cornish; Master of P & O vessel Arcadia from her completion in Jan. 1954 until Oct. 1956; Commodore P & O Fleet, 1955–56; *b* 1898. *Educ:* Thames Nautical Training Coll. (the Worcester). *Recreations:* photography, chess, bridge. *Address:* 44 Shirlow Avenue, Faulconbridge, NSW 2776, Australia.

FORREST, Sir James (Alexander), Kt 1967; FAA; Chairman: Chase NBA Group Ltd, 1969–80; Alcoa of Australia Ltd, 1970–78; Director, National Bank of Australasia Ltd, 1950–78 (Chairman, 1959–78); Director, Australian Consolidated Industries Ltd, 1950–77 (Chairman, 1953–77); *b* 10 March 1905; *s* of John and Mary Gray Forrest; *m* 1939, Mary Christina Forrest (*née* Armit); three *s*. *Educ:* Caulfield Grammar Sch.; Melbourne Univ. RAAF and Dept Aircraft Production, 1942–45. Partner, Hedderwick Fookes & Alston, Solicitors, 1933–70, Consultant, 1970–73; Dir, Australian Mutual Provident Society, 1961–77 (Dir, 1945–, Chm., 1955–77, Victoria Branch Bd); Dir, Western Mining Corp. Ltd, 1970–77. Member: Victoria Law Foundn, 1969–75; Council, Royal Children's Hosp. Research Foundn, 1960–78; Scotch Coll. Council, 1959–71; Council, Monash Univ., 1961–71; Council, Boy Scouts Assoc. of Aust., 1949–73; Aust. Scout Educn and Trng Foundn, 1976–; Board, Art Foundn of Victoria, 1977–. FAA (by Special Election) 1977. Hon. LLD Monash, 1979. *Recreations:* golf, fishing. *Address:* 11 Russell Street, Toorak, Victoria 3142, Australia. *T:* 20–5227. *Clubs:* Melbourne, Australian (Melbourne); Union (Sydney).

FORREST, John Richard, DPhil; FEng 1985, FIEE; Director of Engineering, Independent Broadcasting Authority, since 1986; *b* 21 April 1943; *s* of John Samuel Forrest, *qv*; *m* 1973, Jane Patricia Robey Leech; two *s* one *d*. *Educ:* Sidney Sussex Coll., Cambridge (MA); Keble Coll., Oxford (DPhil). Research Associate and Lectr, Stanford Univ., Calif, 1967–70; Lectr, later Prof., Electronic and Elect. Engrg Dept, University Coll. London, 1970–84; Technical Dir, Marconi Defence Systems Ltd, 1984–86. *Publications:* papers and contribs to books on phased array radar, satellite communications and optoelectronics. *Recreations:* travel, literature, study of mankind. *Address:* Hilfield Farm House, Hilfield Lane, Aldenham, Herts WD2 8DD. *T:* 01–950 1820.

FORREST, John Samuel, MA, DSc; FRS 1966; FInstP, FEng; Visiting Professor of Electrical Engineering, University of Strathclyde, since 1964; *b* 20 Aug. 1907; *m* 1st, 1940, Ivy May Olding (*d* 1976); one *s*; 2nd, 1985, Joan Mary Downie. *Educ:* Hamilton Acad.; Glasgow Univ. Physicist, Central Electricity Board: Glasgow, 1930; London, 1931; i/c of CEB Research Lab., 1934–40; Founder, 1940, Central Electricity Research Labs, Leatherhead, Dir, 1940–73; Sec., Electricity Supply Research Council, 1949–72. Hunter Memorial Lectr, 1961; Baird Memorial Lectr, 1963, 1975, 1979; Faraday Lectures, 1963–64; Kelvin Lecture, Royal Philosophical Soc. of Glasgow, 1971; Maurice Lubbock Meml Lecture, 1975. Mem. Bd, Inst. of Physics, 1945–49; Chm., London Br. Inst. of Physics, 1954–58; Chm., Supply Sect. of IEE, 1961–62; Chm., British Nat. Cttee, Conference Internationale des Grands Réseaux Electriques, 1972–76; Pres., Sect. A, Brit. Assoc., 1963; Member Council: IEE; Royal Meteorological Society, 1945–47; Research Associations; Vice-Pres., Royal Soc., 1972–75. Hon. FIEE. Foreign Associate, Nat. Acad. of Engrg of USA, 1979. Hon. DSc: Strathclyde, 1969; Heriot-Watt, 1972. Coopers Hill War Memorial Prize and Medal, 1941; Willans Medal, 1958. *Publications:* papers on electrical power transmission and insulation. *Address:* Arbores, Portsmouth Road, Thames Ditton, Surrey KT7 0EG. *T:* 01–398 4389.

See also J. R. Forrest.

FORREST, Prof. Sir Patrick; *see* Forrest, Prof. Sir A. P. M.

FORREST, Rear-Adm. Sir Ronald (Stephen), KCVO 1975; JP; DL; Commander, St John Ambulance, Devon, since 1981; *b* 11 Jan. 1923; *s* of late Stephen Forrest, MD, and Maud M. McKinstry; *m* 1st, 1947, Patricia (*d* 1966), *e d* of Dr and Mrs E. N. Russell; two *s* one *d*; 2nd, 1967, June (*née* Weaver), *widow* of late Lieut G. Perks, RN; one step *s* one step *d*. *Educ:* Belhaven Hill; RNC, Dartmouth. War Service at Sea, Lieut 1943 (despatches 1944); Comdr 1955; CO HMS Teazer, 1956; on loan to Pakistan Navy, 1958–60; Captain 1963; jssc 1963; Chief Staff Officer to Adm. Comdg Reserves, 1964; comd Dartmouth Trng Sqdn, 1966; Dir, Seaman Officers Appointments, 1968; CO, HMS London, 1970; Rear-Adm. 1972; Defence Services Secretary, 1972–75. County Comr, St John Amb. Bde, Devon, 1976–81. Naval Gen. Service Medal, 1949. CStJ 1983. JP Honiton, 1978; DL Devon, 1985. *Recreation:* gardening. *Address:* Higher Seavington, Millhayes, Stockland, near Honiton, Devon. *Clubs:* Naval, Army and Navy.

FORREST, Prof. William George Grieve; Wykeham Professor of Ancient History, Oxford University, since 1977; Fellow of New College, Oxford, since 1977; *b* 24 Sept. 1925; *s* of William and Ina Forrest; *m* 1956, Margaret Elizabeth Mary Hall; two *d*. *Educ:* University College Sch., Hampstead; New Coll., Oxford (MA). Served RAF, 1943–47; New Coll., Oxford, 1947–51; Fellow, Wadham Coll., Oxford, 1951–76. Visiting Professor: Trinity and University Colls, Toronto, 1961; Yale, 1968; Vis. Fellow, British Sch. at Athens, 1986. *Publications:* Emergence of Greek Democracy, 1966; History of Sparta, 1968, 2nd edn 1980; articles in classical and archaeological periodicals. *Address:* 9 Fyfield Road, Oxford. *T:* Oxford 56187; New College, Oxford. *T:* Oxford 248451.

FORREST, Surgeon Rear-Adm. (D) William Ivon Norman, CB 1970; Director of Naval Dental Services, Ministry of Defence, 1968–71; *b* 8 June 1914; *s* of late Eng. Lt James Forrest; *m* 1942, Mary Margaret McMordie Black; three *s*. *Educ:* Christ's Hospital. Guy's Hospital, 1931–36. LDS, RCS. Dental House Surgeon, Guy's Hosp., 1936–37. Royal Navy: Surg. Lieut (D), 1937; Surg. Lt-Comdr (D), 1943; Surg. Comdr (D), 1950; Surg. Capt. (D), 1960; Surg. Rear-Adm. (D), 1968. Consultant in Dental Surgery, 1963. *Recreations:* golf, gardening, photography. *Address:* 16 Queen's Road, Waterlooville, Hants PO7 7SB. *T:* Waterlooville 263139.

FORRESTER, John Stuart; MP (Lab) Stoke-on-Trent, North, since 1966; *b* 17 June 1924; *s* of Harry and Nellie Forrester; *m* 1945, Gertrude H. Weaver. *Educ:* Eastwood Council Sch.; City Sch. of Commerce, Stoke-on-Trent; Alsager Teachers' Training Coll. Teacher, 1946–66. Sec., Constituency Labour Party, 1961–84. Mem., Speaker's Panel of Chairmen, 1982–; Member: NUT, 1949–; APEX, 1942–43, 1946–49, 1984–. Councillor, Stoke-on-Trent, 1970–. *Address:* House of Commons, SW1A 0AA.

FORRESTER, Maj.-Gen. Michael, CB 1969; CBE 1963 (OBE 1960); DSO 1943 and Bar, 1944; MC 1939 and Bar, 1941; retired 1970; *b* 31 Aug. 1917; 2nd *s* of late James Forrester, Chilworth, Hants, and Elsie (*née* Mathwin); *m* 1947, Pauline Margaret Clara (marr. diss. 1960), *d* of late James Fisher, Crossmichael; two *s*. *Educ:* Haileybury. 2nd Lieut, Queen's Royal Regt, 1938; served in Palestine (Arab Rebellion), 1938–39; served War of 1939–45 in Palestine, Egypt, Greece, Crete, Western Desert, Syria, N Africa, Italy and France; GSO3 (Ops) British Military Mission, Greece, 1940–41; GSO3 (Ops), HQ Western Desert Force and HQ 13 Corps, 1941–42; Staff Coll., Haifa, 1942; Bde Major, 132 Inf. Bde, 1942 (despatches); GSO2 (Ops), HQ 13 Corps and HQ 18 Army Gp, 1943; Comdr, 1st/6th Bn, Queen's Royal Regt, 1943–44; wounded, Normandy; GSO1 (Ops), HQ 13 Corps, 1945–46; Mil. Asst to Supreme Allied Comdr Mediterranean, 1947; Mil. Asst to Comdr Brit. Army Staff and Army Mem., Brit. Jt Services Mission, Washington, DC, 1947–50; Co. Comdr, 2nd Bn Parachute Regt, Cyprus and Canal Zone, 1951–52; Dirg Staff, Staff Coll., Camberley, 1953–55; GSO1 (Ops), GHQ East Africa, 1955–57; transf. to Parachute Regt, 1957; Comdr, 3rd Bn Parachute Regt, 1957–60; Col., Military Operations (4), War Office, 1960–61; Comdr, 16 Parachute Bde Gp, 1961–63; Imp. Def. Coll., 1964; GOC 4th Div., BAOR, 1965–67; Dir of Infantry, MoD, 1968–70. Col Comdt, The Queen's Division, 1968–70. *Address:* Hammonds, West Worldham, near Alton, Hants. *T:* Alton 84470.

FORRESTER, Prof. Peter Garnett, CBE 1981; Chairman, Faculties Partnership, since 1983; Director, Jackson Taylor International Associates Ltd, since 1985; Professor Emeritus, Cranfield Institute of Technology; *b* 7 June 1917; *s* of Arthur Forrester and Emma (*née* Garnett); *m* 1942, Marjorie Hewitt, Berks; two *d*. *Educ:* Manchester Grammar Sch.; Manchester Univ. (BSc, MSc). Metallurgist, Thomas Bolton & Son Ltd, 1938–40; Research Officer, later Chief Metallurgist, Tin Research Inst., 1940–48; Chief Metallurgist and Research Man., Glacier Metal Co. Ltd, 1948–63; Dep. Principal, Glacier Inst. of Management, 1963–64; Consultant, John Tyzack & Partners, 1964–66; Prof. of Industrial Management, Coll. of Aeronautics, Cranfield, 1966; Dir, Cranfield Sch. of Management, 1967–82, Dean of Faculty, 1972; Pro-Vice-Chancellor, Cranfield Inst. of Technol., 1976–82. Chm., Conf. of Univ. Management Schs, 1976–77. Mem., Bd of Trustees, European Foundation for Management Develt, 1976–82. FIM, CBIM, FRSA. Hon. DSc Cranfield Inst. of Technol., 1983. Burnham Medal, BIM, 1979. *Publications:* papers and reports on management educn; numerous scientific and technological papers on metallurgy, bearing materials, tribology. *Recreations:* sailing, walking. *Address:* Strawberry Hole Cottage, Ewhurst Lane, Northiam, near Rye, Sussex. *T:* Northiam 2255.

FORRESTER-PATON, Douglas Shaw, QC 1965; **His Honour Judge Forrester-Paton;** a Circuit Judge (formerly a Judge of County Courts), since 1970; *b* 1921; 3rd *s* of late Alexander Forrester-Paton, JP; *m* 1948, Agnete, *d* of Holger Tuxen; one *s* two *d*. *Educ:* Gresham's Sch., Holt; Queen's Coll., Oxford (BA). Called to Bar, Middle Temple, 1947; North East Circuit. Served RAF, 1941–45. Recorder: Middlesbrough, 1963–68; Teesside, 1968–70. *Address:* 24 Kirkby Lane, Great Broughton, Middlesbrough, Cleveland TS9 7HG. *T:* Stokesley 712301; 5 King's Bench Walk, Temple, EC4.

FORSBERG, (Charles) Gerald, OBE 1955; Comdr RN (Retd); author; Assistant Director of Marine Services, Ministry of Defence (Navy Department), 1972–75 (Deputy Director, 1958–72); *b* Vancouver, 18 June 1912; *s* of Charles G. Forsberg and Nellie (*née* Wallman); *m* 1952, Joyce Whewell Hogarth, *d* of Dr F. W. Hogarth; one *s* one *d*. *Educ:* Polytechnic School; Training Ship Mercury; Sir John Cass Coll. Merchant Navy: Cadet to Chief Officer, 1928–38; qual. Master Mariner; transf. RN, 1938. Norwegian campaign, 1940; Malta Convoys, Matapan, Tobruk, Crete, etc, 1940–42; comd HMS Vega as Convoy Escort Comdr, 1943–45 (despatches). Comd HMS Mameluke and HMS Chaplet, 1945–49; comd Salvage Sqdn off Elba in recovery of crashed Comet aircraft in 100 fathoms, 1954. Swam Channel (England-France) in record time, 1957; first person to swim Lough Neagh and Loch Lomond, 1959; British long-distance champion, 1957–58–59; swam Bristol Channel in record time, 1964; many long-distance championships and records, 1951–. Younger Brother of Trinity House, 1958; Civil Service, 1962. President: Channel Swimming Assoc., 1963–; British Long Distance Swimming Assoc., 1982–83. Master of Navy Lodge, 1966; Liveryman, Hon. Co. of Master Mariners. Freeman, City of London, 1968. Elected to Internat. Marathon Swimming Hall of Fame, 1971; The Observer newspaper's Sports Nut of the Year, 1982. *Publications:* Long Distance Swimming, 1957; First Strokes in Swimming, 1961; Modern Long Distance Swimming, 1963; Salvage from the Sea, 1977; Pocket Book for Seamen, 1981; many short stories, articles, papers, and book reviews for general periodicals, technical jls and encyclopædia; regular monthly contribs to Swimming Times. *Recreations:* motoring, Association football affairs, books. *Address:* c/o Barclays Bank PLC, 13 Marine Road West, Morecambe, Lancs LA3 1BX. *Clubs:* Victory Services; Otter Swimming.

FORSTER, Archibald William, FEng, FIChemE, FInstPet; Chairman and Chief Executive: Esso UK plc, since 1983; Esso Petroleum Co. Ltd, since 1980; Esso Exploration & Production UK Ltd, since 1983; *b* 11 Feb. 1928; *s* of William Henry and Matilda Forster; *m* 1954, Betty Margaret Channing; three *d*. *Educ:* Tottenham Grammar Sch.; Univ. of Birmingham (BSc (Hons) ChemEng 1949, Cadman Medallist). Served Royal Air Force, Pilot (FO), 1949–51. Joined Esso Petroleum Co. Ltd, 1951; Refinery Manager, Milford Haven, 1962–63; Supply Manager, London, 1963–64; Refinery Manager, Fawley, 1964–69; Manager, Refining Dept, Esso Europe Inc., 1969–71; Exec. Dir, Esso Petroleum Co. Ltd, 1971–73; Exec. Asst to Chm., Exxon Corp., 1973–74; Manager, Corporate Planning Co-ordination, Exxon Corp., 1974–75; Vice-Pres., Esso Europe Inc., 1975–78; Dir, Exxon Research & Engineering Co., 1975–78; Man. Dir, Esso Petroleum Co. Ltd, 1979–80; Chairman: Exxon Ltd, 1980; Esso Pension Trust, 1980– (Dir, 1979–80); Director: Esso Europe Inc., 1980–; Esso Africa Inc., 1980–. Exec. Bd Mem., Lloyd's Register of Shipping, 1981–. President: Oil Industries Club, 1982–83; IChemE, 1985. Governor, E-SU, 1981–. Hon. DSc Birmingham, 1981. *Recreation:* sailing. *Address:* Esso House, Victoria Street, SW1E 5JW. *T:* 01–834 6677. *Club:* Royal Southampton Yacht.

FORSTER, Charles Ian Kennerley, CBE 1964; Consultant; *b* 18 July 1911; *s* of Douglas Wakefield Forster; *m* 1942, Thelma Primrose Horton (marr. diss. 1974); one *s* one *d*; *m* 1975, Mrs Loraine Huxtable. *Educ:* Rossall Sch. FIA 1936. With Sun Life Assurance Soc., 1928–39, and 1946. Served RA, 1939–45. Statistics Branch, Admty, 1946–54; Ministry of Power, 1954 (Chief Statistician, 1955–65, Dir of Statistics, 1965–69); Min. of Technology, 1969; Under-Sec., Dept of Trade and Industry, 1970–72, retd. Energy consultant to NCB, 1972–81. *Publications:* contribs to Jls of Inst. of Actuaries and Inst. of Actuaries Students Soc., Trans VII World Power Conf., Trans Manchester Statistical Soc., Statistical News. *Recreations:* bridge, stamps. *Address:* 140 Watchfield Court, Chiswick, W4. *T:* 01–994 3128.

FORSTER, Donald; Chairman, Merseyside Development Corporation, since 1984; Managing Director, 1945–81, and Chairman, 1981–86, B. Forster & Co. Ltd, Leigh (textile manufacturing company); *b* 18 Dec. 1920; *s* of Bernard and Rose Forster; *m* 1942, Muriel Steinman; one *s* two *d*. *Educ:* N Manchester Grammar School. Served War, RAF pilot (Flt Lieut), 1940–45. Mem., Skelmersdale Develt Corp., 1980–82; Chm.,

Warrington/Runcorn Develt Corp., 1982–86. *Recreations:* golf, music, paintings. *Address:* Melilia, Mereside Road, Mere, ·Knutsford, Cheshire WA16 6QW. *T:* Bucklow Hill 830374. *Clubs:* Whitefield Golf; Dunham Forst Country.

FORSTER, Donald Murray; His Honour Judge Forster; a Circuit Judge, since 1984; *b* 18 June 1929; *s* of John Cameron Forster and Maisie Constance Forster. *Educ:* Hollylea Sch., Liverpool; Merton House Sch., Penmaenmawr; Wrekin Coll., Wellington, Shropshire; St Edmund Hall, Oxford. Honour Sch. of Jurisprudence (2nd Cl. Hons). Called to Bar, Gray's Inn, 1953; Head of Chambers, 1968; a Recorder of the Crown Court, 1978–83. *Recreation:* sport. *Address:* 54 Castle Street, Liverpool L2 7LQ. *T:* 051–236 4421. *Clubs:* Liverpool Ramblers Association Football (Vice-Pres.); Liverpool Racquet; Mersey Bowmen Lawn Tennis (Liverpool).

FORSTER, Brig. Eric Brown, MBE 1952; General Manager, Potato Marketing Board, 1970–82; *b* 19 May 1917; *s* of late Frank and Agnes Forster; *m* 1943, Margaret Bessie Letitia, *d* of late Lt-Col Arthur Wood, MBE and late Edith Wood; one *s* two *d. Educ:* Queen Elizabeth Grammar Sch., Hexham. Commnd from RASC ranks into RAPC, 1941. Dir of Cost and Management Accounting (Army Dept), 1967–68. *Recreations:* golf, gardening. *Address:* Littledene, Guildown Avenue, Guildford, Surrey GU2 5HB. *T:* Guildford 62313. *Clubs:* MCC; Worplesdon Golf.

FORSTER, Prof. Leonard Wilson, FBA 1976; Schröder Professor of German, University of Cambridge, 1961–79; Fellow of Selwyn College, Cambridge, 1937–50 and since 1961; *b* 30 March 1913; *o s* of Edward James Forster, merchant, and Linda Charlotte (*née* Rogers), St John's Wood, NW8; *m* 1939, Jeanne Marie Louise, *e d* of Dr Charles Otto Billeter, Basel; one *s* two *d. Educ:* Marlborough Coll.; Trinity Hall, Cambridge (Thomas Carlyle Student, 1934–35; MA 1938; LittD 1976); Bonn Univ.; Basel Univ. (Dr phil. 1938). English Lektor: Univ. of Leipzig, 1934; Univ. of Königsberg, 1935–36; Univ. of Basel, 1936–38. Naval Staff Admiralty, 1939–41; Foreign Office, 1941–45; Lt-Comdr RNVR (Sp.), 1945–46. Faculty Asst Lectr, 1937, Univ. Lectr in German, 1947–50, Cambridge; Lectr, 1937, Dean and Asst Tutor, 1946–50, Selwyn Coll., Cambridge; Prof. of German, UCL, 1950–61. Pres., Internat. Assoc. for Germanic Studies (IVG), 1970–75. Corresponding Member: Deutsche Akademie für Sprache und Dichtung, 1957; Royal Belgian Academy of Dutch Language and Literature, 1973; Member: Maatschappij der Nederlandse Letterkunde, Leiden, 1966; Royal Netherlands Acad. of Sciences and Letters, 1968. Visiting Professor: Univ. of Toronto, 1957; Univ. of Heidelberg, 1964, 1980; McGill Univ., 1967–68; Univ. of Otago, 1968; Univ. of Utrecht, 1976; Univ. of Kiel, 1980–81; Univ. of Basel, 1985–86. Sen. Consultant: Folger Shakespeare Lib., Washington, 1975; Herzog August Bibliothek, Wolfenbüttel, 1976–83. Hon. DLitt: Leiden, 1975; Bath, 1979; Strasbourg, 1980; Heidelberg, 1986. Gold Medal, Goethe-Institut, Munich, 1966; Friedrich Gundolf-Preis für Germanistik im Ausland, 1981. Grosses Verdienstkreuz (Germany), 1976. *Publications:* G. R. Weckherlin, zur Kenntnis seines Lebens in England, 1944; Conrad Celtis, 1948; German Poetry, 1944–48, 1949; The Temper of Seventeenth Century German Literature, 1952; Penguin Book of German Verse, 1957; Poetry of Significant Nonsense, 1962; Lipsius, Von der Bestendigkeit, 1965; Die Niederlande und die Anfänge der deutschen Barocklyrik, 1967; Janus Gruter's English Years, 1967; The Icy Fire, 1969; The Poet's Tongues: Multilingualism in Literature, 1971; Kleine Schriften zur deutschen Literatur im 17 Jahrhundert, 1977; Literaturwissenschaft als Flucht vor der Literatur?, 1978; Iter Bohemicum, 1980; The Man Who Wanted to Know Everything, 1981; Christian Morgenstern, Sämtliche Galgenlieder, 1985; Christoffel van Sichem, in, Basel und der frühe deutsche Alexandriner, 1986; German Life and Letters (co-ed); articles in British and foreign jls. *Recreation:* foreign travel. *Address:* 49 Maids Causeway, Cambridge CB5 8DE. *T:* 357513; Selwyn College, Cambridge. *Club:* Athenæum.

FORSTER, Margaret; author; *b* 25 May 1938; *d* of Arthur Gordon Forster and Lilian (*née* Hind); *m* 1960, Edward Hunter Davies, *qv;* one *s* two *d. Educ:* Carlisle and County High Sch. for Girls; Somerville Coll., Oxford (BA). FRSL. Teacher, Barnsbury Girls' Sch., Islington, 1961–63. Member: BBC Adv. Cttee on Social Effects of Television, 1975–77; Arts Council Literary Panel, 1978–81. Chief non-fiction reviewer, Evening Standard, 1977–80. *Publications: non-fiction:* The Rash Adventurer: the rise and fall of Charles Edward Stuart, 1973; William Makepeace Thackeray: memoirs of a Victorian gentleman, 1978; Significant Sisters: grassroots of active feminism 1839–1939, 1984; *novels:* Dame's Delight, 1964; Georgy Girl, 1965 (filmscript with Peter Nichols, 1966); The Bogeyman, 1965; The Travels of Maudie Tipstaff, 1967; The Park, 1968; Miss Owen-Owen is At Home, 1969; Fenella Phizackerley, 1970; Mr Bone's Retreat, 1971; The Seduction of Mrs Pendlebury, 1974; Mother, can you hear me?, 1979; The Bride of Lowther Fell, 1980; Marital Rites, 1981; Private Papers, 1986. *Recreations:* walking on Hampstead Heath, reading contemporary fiction. *Address:* 11 Boscastle Road, NW5. *T:* 01–485 3785.

FORSTER, Neil Milward; Group Managing Director, British and Commonwealth Shipping Co. plc, since 1982 (Director since 1974); *b* 29 May 1927; *s* of Norman Milward Forster and Olive Christina Forster (*née* Cockrell); *m* 1954, Barbara Elizabeth Smith; one *s* two *d. Educ:* Hurstpierpoint College, Sussex; Pembroke College, Cambridge. BA Law and Economics; Fellow Inst. of Transport. Joined Clan Line Steamers, 1952; Chm., Calcutta Liners Conf., 1962–66; Director: Clan Line, 1967; Group and Associated cos, British & Commonwealth Shipping Co., 1974–. Chairman: Europe/SA Shipping Confs, 1977–; UK S Africa Trade Assoc., 1985–86. *Recreations:* golf and gardening. *Address:* 18 Carlton Road, Ealing, W5. *T:* 01–997 4913. *Clubs:* Oriental, MCC.
  See also Sir O. G. Forster.

FORSTER, Norvela; Founder Chairman and Managing Director of consultancy company researching into marketing and management problems in Europe and overseas; *b* 1931; *m* 1981, Michael, *s* of Norman and Margaret Jones. *Educ:* South Wilts Grammar School, Salisbury; London Univ. BSc Hons. Pres., Bedford Coll. Union Soc. Mem. (C) Birmingham South, European Parlt, 1979–84; contested (C) Birmingham East, European Parly elecn, 1984. Past Member: Hampstead Borough Council; Council, Bow Group. Mem. Council, Management Consultants Assoc. *Publication:* Chambers of Commerce: a comparative study of their role in the UK and in other EEC countries, 1983. *Address:* IAL Consultants Ltd, 14 Buckingham Palace Road, SW1W 0QP. *T:* 01–828 5036; 6 Regency House, Regency Street, SW1. *T:* 01–821 5749. *Clubs:* Royal Ocean Racing; Royal Mid Surrey Golf.

FORSTER, Sir Oliver (Grantham), KCMG 1983 (CMG 1976); LVO 1961; HM Diplomatic Service, retired; *b* 2 Sept. 1925; 2nd *s* of Norman Milward Forster and Olive Christina Forster (*née* Cockrell); *m* 1953, Beryl Myfanwy Evans; two *d. Educ:* Hurstpierpoint; King's Coll., Cambridge. Served in RAF, 1944–48. Joined Commonwealth Relations Office, 1951. Private Sec. to Parly Under-Sec., 1953–54; Second Sec., Karachi, 1954–56; Principal, CRO, 1956–59; First Sec., Madras, 1959–62; First Sec., Washington, 1962–65; Private Sec. to Sec. of State for Commonwealth Relations, 1965–67; Counsellor, Manila, 1967–70; Counsellor, New Delhi, 1970–75; Minister, 1975; Asst Under-Sec. of State and Dep. Chief Clerk, FCO, 1975–79; Ambassador to Pakistan, 1979–84. HQA 1984. *Address:* 71 Raglan Road, Reigate, Surrey.

Clubs: United Oxford & Cambridge University, Royal Commonwealth Society.
  See also N. M. Forster.

FORSTER, Sir William (Edward Stanley), Kt 1982; **Hon. Mr Justice Forster;** Chief Justice, Supreme Court of the Northern Territory, since 1979 (Senior Judge 1971, Chief Judge 1977); Judge of the Federal Court of Australia, since 1977; Chancellor, Diocese of the Northern Territory, since 1975; *b* 15 June 1921; *s* of F. B. Forster; *m* 1950, Johanna B., *d* of Brig. A. M. Forbes; one *s* two *d. Educ:* St Peter's Coll., Adelaide; Adelaide Univ. (Stowe Prize; David Murray Scholar; LLB). Served RAAF, 1940–46. Private legal practice, 1950–59; Magistrate, Adelaide Police Court, 1959–61; Master, Supreme Court of SA, and Dist Registrar, High Court of Aust., 1966–71 (Dep. Master, and Dep. Dist Registrar, 1961–66). Adelaide University: Lectr in Criminal Law, 1957–58; Lectr in Law of Procedure, 1967–71; Mem., Standing Cttee of Senate, 1967–71. President: NT Div., Australian Red Cross, 1973–; Aboriginal Theatre Foundn, 1972–75; Chairman: Museum and Art Galls Bd, NT, 1974–; NT Parole Bd, 1976–. Air Efficiency Award, 1953. *Address:* Judges' Chambers, Supreme Court, Darwin, NT 5790, Australia. *Clubs:* Adelaide (Adelaide); Darwin Golf.

FORSYTH OF THAT ILK, Alistair Charles William, JP; FSCA, FSAScot; FInstPet; Baron of Ethie; Chief of the Name and Clan of Forsyth; chairman and director of companies; *b* 7 Dec. 1929; *s* of Charles Forsyth of Strathendry, FCA, and Ella Millicent Hopkins; *m* 1958, Ann, *d* of Col P. A. Hughes, IA; four *s. Educ:* St Paul's Sch.; Queen Mary Coll., London. FInstPet 1973; FSCA 1976; FSAScot 1979. National Service, 2nd Lieut The Queen's Bays, 1948–50; Lieut The Parachute Regt, TA, 1950–54. Chairman, Caledonian Produce Holdings Ltd and subsidiaries, 1984–; Director: Carritt Moran & Co. Ltd, Calcutta, 1961–63; Caledonian Produce (Holdings) Ltd, 1969–84; Tuckfield Teas Ltd, Melbourne, 1978–85; Strathendry Investments Ltd, 1983–; Caledonian Investment and Finance Co. Ltd, 1985–. Member: Standing Council of Scottish Chiefs, 1978–; Council, 1977–81, Chapter, 1982–, Priory of Scotland of Most Ven. Order of St John of Jerusalem. CStJ 1982 (OStJ 1974). JP NSW, 1965. *Recreations:* hill walking, Scottish antiquities. *Address:* Ethie Castle, by Arbroath, Angus DD11 5SP. *Clubs:* Cavalry and Guards; New (Edinburgh).

FORSYTH, Bruce; see Forsyth-Johnson, B. J.

FORSYTH, Jennifer Mary; Under-Secretary, HM Treasury and Department of Transport, 1975–83, retired; *b* 7 Oct. 1924; *o d* of late Matthew Forsyth, theatrical director, and late Marjorie Forsyth. *Educ:* Frensham Heights; London Sch. of Economics and Political Science (Pres. of Students' Union, 1944–45) (BScEcon). Joined Home Finance Div., HM Treasury, 1945; UN Economic Commn for Europe, 1949–51; Information Div., HM Treasury, 1951–53; Principal, Estabts, Overseas Finance and Planning Divs, 1954–62; UK Treasury Delegn, Washington, 1962–64; Assistant Secretary: DEA, 1965–69; Social Services Div., HM Treasury, 1969–75; Under Secretary: Home, Transport and Education Gp, HM Treasury, 1975–80; Dept of Transport (Roads), 1980–83. Councillor (Lab) Borough of Kensington and Chelsea, 1986–. Governor, Frensham Heights, 1965–76. *Recreations:* going to the theatre and to the Mediterranean. *Address:* 51 Abingdon Road, W8 6AN.

FORSYTH, Michael Bruce; MP (C) Stirling, since 1983; *b* 16 Oct. 1954; *s* of John T. Forsyth and Mary Watson; *m* 1977, Susan Jane Clough; one *s* two *d. Educ:* Arbroath High School; St Andrews University. MA. Pres., St Andrews Univ. Cons. Assoc., 1972–75; Nat. Chm., Fedn of Cons. Students, 1976–77. Mem., Westminster City Council, 1978–83. Dir, Michael Forsyth Ltd, 1981–. *Publications:* The Scottish Conservative Party: the way ahead, 1975; Reservicing Britain, 1980; Reservicing Health, 1981; Down With the Rates, 1982; The Myths of Privatisation, 1983; Politics on the Rates, 1984; The Case for a Poll Tax, 1985. *Recreations:* photography, mountaineering, amateur astronomy. *Address:* House of Commons, SW1A 0AA. *Club:* Reform.

FORSYTH, William Douglass, OBE 1955; Australian Ambassador, retired 1969; *b* Casterton, Australia, 5 Jan. 1909; of Australian parents; *m* 1935, Thelma Joyce (*née* Sherry); one *s* two *d. Educ:* Ballarat High Sch.; Melbourne Univ. (MA, DipEd); Balliol Coll., Oxford (BLitt). Teacher of History, 1931–35; Rockefeller Fellow, Social Studies, Europe, 1936–37 and 1939; Research Fellow, Melbourne Univ., 1940; Editor Austral-Asiatic Bulletin, Melbourne, 1940; Research Sec., Aust. Inst. International Affairs, 1940–41; Australian Dept of Information, 1941–42; Australian Dept of External Affairs, 1942–69: First Sec., 1946; Counsellor, Aust. Embassy, Washington, 1947–48; Aust. rep. Trusteeship Council, 1948 and 1952–55; Sec.-Gen., South Pacific Commission, 1948–51. Australian Member UN Population Commission, 1946–47; Mem., Australian Delegns to UN General Assembly, 1946–48 and 1951–58; San Francisco UN Confs, 1945 and 1955; Minister, Australian Mission to UN, 1951–55; Asst-Sec., Dept of External Affairs, Canberra, 1956–59, 1961–63; Australian Minister to Laos, 1959–60; Australian Ambassador to Viet-Nam, 1959–61; Sec.-Gen., South Pacific Commn, Nouméa, 1963–66; Australian Ambassador to Lebanon, 1967–68. South Pacific Consultant, Dept of Foreign Affairs, 1973–74. Vis. Fellow, ANU, 1975. *Publications:* Governor Arthur's Convict System, 1935, reprinted 1970; The Myth of Open Spaces, 1942; Captain Cook's Australian Landfalls, 1970; articles in Economic Record, etc. *Address:* 88 Banks Street, Yarralumla, Canberra, ACT 2600, Australia.

FORSYTH-JOHNSON, Bruce Joseph, (Bruce Forsyth); entertainer and comedian; *b* 22 Feb. 1928; *m* 1st, 1953, Penny Calvert; three *d;* 2nd, 1973, Anthea Redfern (marr. diss. 1982); two *d;* 3rd, 1983, Wilnelia Merced. *Educ:* Higher Latimer Sch., Edmonton. Started stage career as Boy Bruce—The Mighty Atom, 1942; after the war, appeared in various double acts and did a 2 yr spell at Windmill Theatre; first television appearance, Music Hall, 1954; resident compère, Sunday Night at the London Palladium, 1958–60; own revue, London Palladium, 1962; leading role, Little Me, Cambridge Theatre, 1964; début at Talk of the Town (played there 7 times); compèred Royal Variety Show, 1971, and on subseq. occasions; London Palladium Show, 1973 (also Ottawa and Toronto) and 1980; commenced Generation Game, BBC TV series, 1971 (completed 7 series); compèred Royal Windsor to mark BBC Jubilee Celebrations, 1977; One Man Show, Theatre Royal, Windsor, and Lakeside, 1977; Bruce Forsyth's Big Night, ITV, 1978; Play Your Cards Right, ITV, 1980–. Films include. Star; Can Hieronymous Merkin Ever Forget Mary Humppe and Find True Happiness?; Bedknobs and Broomsticks; The Magnificent 7 Deadly Sins; Pavlova. Numerous records. Show Business Personality of the Year, Variety Club of GB, 1975; TV Personality of the Year, Sun Newspaper, 1976 and 1977; Male TV Personality of the Year, TV Times, 1975, 1976, 1977 and 1978; Favourite Game Show Host, TV Times, 1984. *Recreation:* golf (handicap 10, Wentworth Golf Club). *Address:* Straidarran, Wentworth Drive, Virginia Water, Surrey. *Clubs:* White Elephant, Crockfords, Empress, Tramp.

FORSYTHE, Clifford; MP (UU) Antrim South, since 1983, resigned seat Dec. 1985 in protest against Anglo-Irish Agreement; re-elected Jan. 1986; Member, Antrim South, Northern Ireland Assembly, 1982–86; plumbing and heating contractor; *b* 1929. *Educ:* Glengormley public elementary sch. Formerly professional football player, Linfield and Derry City. Mem., Newtownabbey Borough Council, 1981–85; Mayor, 1983. Dep.

Chm., DHSS Cttee, NI Assembly, 1982–86; UU Parly spokesman on transport and communications. Exec. Mem., Ulster Unionist Council, 1980–83; Chm., S Antrim Official Unionist Assoc., 1981–83. *Recreations:* church choir, football, running. *Address:* House of Commons, SW1A 0AA.

FORSYTHE, Air Cdre James Roy, CBE 1966; DFC; Director of Development, Look Ahead Housing Association Ltd; *b* 10 July 1920; *s* of W. R. and A. M. Forsythe; *m* 1946, Barbara Mary Churchman; two *s* two *d*. *Educ:* Methodist Coll., Belfast; Queen's Univ., Belfast. Bomber Comd, 1944–45; OC, Aberdeen Univ. Air Sqdn, 1952–54; psa 1955; Principal Staff Officer to Dir-Gen. Orgn (RAF), 1956–58; OC, 16 Sqdn, 1958–60; Dirg Staff, Coll. of Air Warfare, Manby, 1960–62; Head of RAF Aid Mission to India, 1963; Stn Comdr, RAF Acklington, 1963–65; Dep. Dir Air Staff Policy, MoD, 1965–68; Dir Public Relations, Far East, 1968–70; Dir Recruiting, RAF, 1971–73; Dir, Public Relations, RAF, 1973–75. Mem., Inst. of Public Relations. *Recreations:* Rugby (Chm., RAF RU, 1972, 1973, 1974; Chm., Combined Services RU, 1974; Vice-Pres., London Irish RFC, 1979), golf. *Address:* 104 Earls Court Road, W8 6EG. *T:* 01-937 5291. *Club:* Royal Air Force.

FORSYTHE, Dr (John) Malcolm; Regional Medical Officer, South East Thames Regional Health Authority, since 1978; *b* 11 July 1936; *s* of Dr John Walter Joseph Forsythe and late Dr Charlotte Constance Forsythe (*née* Beatty); *m* 1961, Delia Kathleen Moore (marr. diss. 1983); one *s* three *d*; *m* 1984, Patricia Mary Barnes. *Educ:* Repton Sch., Derby; Guy's Hosp. Med. Sch., London Univ. BSc(Hons), MB, BS, MSc; DObstRCOG, FRCP; FFCM. Area Medical Officer, Kent AHA, 1974–78. Hon. Consultant, Univ. of Kent Health Services Res. Unit, 1977–. Jack Masur Fellow, Amer. Hosp. Assoc., 1976. Head, UK Deleg., Hospital Cttee, EEC, 1980–85; Consultant, Urwick Orr Ltd; Member: Resource Allocation Wkg Pty and Adv. Gp on Resource Allocation, 1975–78; Technical Sub Gp, Review of Resource Allocation Working Party Formula, 1986; DHSS Med. Manpower Planning Review, 1986; NHS Computer Policy Cttee, 1981–85; Standing Med. Adv. Cttee to Sec. of State, 1982–86; Bd of Governors, United Med. Sch. of Guy's and St Thomas', 1982–; Delegacy, King's Coll. Hosp. Med. and Dental Schs, 1978–. FRSA 1985. Silver Core Award, IFIP, 1977. *Publications:* (ed jtly) Information Processing of Medical Records, 1969; Proceedings of First World Conference on Medical Informatics, 1975. *Recreations:* squash, music. *Address:* Harewood, Withyham Road, Cooden, Bexhill-on-Sea, East Sussex TN39 3BA. *T:* Cooden 5008; (office) Thrift House, Collington Avenue, Bexhill-on-Sea, East Sussex TN39 3NQ. *T:* Bexhill-on-Sea 222 555. *Clubs:* Royal Society of Medicine; Chasers.

FORT, Mrs Jean; Headmistress of Roedean School, Brighton, 1961–70; *b* 1915; *d* of G. B. Rae; *m* 1943, Richard Fort (*d* 1959), MP Clitheroe Division of Lancs; four *s* one *d*. *Educ:* Benenden Sch.; Lady Margaret Hall, Oxford (MA, DipEd). Asst Mistress, Dartford County Sch. for Girls, 1937–39; WVS Headquarters staff, 1939–40; Junior Civil Asst, War Office, 1940–41; Personal Asst to Sir Ernest Gowers, Sen. Regional Comr for Civil Def., London, 1941–44. *Address:* 6 King's Close, Henley-on-Thames, Oxon.

FORT, Maeve Geraldine; Head of West African Department, Foreign and Commonwealth Office, since 1986; *b* 19 Nov. 1940; *d* of late F. L. Fort. *Educ:* Trinity College, Dublin (MA); Sorbonne, Paris. Joined Foreign Service, 1963; UKMIS, NY, 1964; CRO, 1965; seconded to SEATO, Bangkok, 1966; Bonn, 1968; Lagos, 1971; Second, later First Sec., FCO, 1973; UKMIS, NY, 1978; Counsellor, FCO, 1982; RCDS, 1983; Counsellor, Hd of Chancery and Consul-Gen., Santiago, 1984–86. *Recreations:* talking, eating, reading, sleeping. *Address:* c/o Foreign and Commonwealth Office, King Charles Street, SW1A 2AH.

FORTE, family name of **Baron Forte.**

FORTE, Baron *cr* 1982 (Life Peer), of Ripley in the county of Surrey; **Charles Forte;** Kt 1970; FRSA; Chairman, Trusthouse Forte PLC, since 1982 (Executive Chairman, 1978–81, Deputy Chairman, 1970–78, and Chief Executive, 1971–78); *b* 26 Nov. 1908; *m* 1943, Irene Mary Chierico; one *s* five *d*. *Educ:* Alloa Academy; Dumfries Coll.; Mamiani, Rome. Fellow and Mem. Exec. Cttee, Catering Inst., 1949; Member, Small Consultative Advisory Cttee to Min. of Food, 1946; London Tourist Board. Hon. Consul Gen. for Republic of San Marino. FBIM 1971. Mem. AA. Grand Officier, Ordine al Merito della Repubblica Italiana; Cavaliere di Gran Croce della Repubblica Italiana. *Publications:* articles for catering trade papers. *Recreations:* golf, fishing, shooting, fencing, music. *Address:* 86 Park Lane, W1. *Clubs:* Carlton, Caledonian, Royal Thames Yacht.

FORTESCUE, family name of **Earl Fortescue.**

FORTESCUE, 7th Earl *cr* 1789; **Richard Archibald Fortescue,** JP; Baron Fortescue 1746; Viscount Ebrington 1789; *b* 14 April 1922; *s* of 6th Earl Fortescue, MC, TD, and Marjorie (*d* 1964), OBE, *d* of late Col C. W. Trotter, CB, TD; *S* father, 1977; *m* 1st, 1949, Penelope Jane (*d* 1959), *d* of late Robert Evelyn Henderson; one *s* one *d*; 2nd, 1961, Margaret Anne, *d* of Michael Stratton; two *d*. *Educ:* Eton; Christ Church, Oxford. Captain Coldstream Guards (Reserve). JP Oxon, 1964. *Heir:* *s* Viscount Ebrington, *qv*. *Address:* House of Lords, SW1. *Club:* White's.

FORTESCUE, John Adrian, LVO 1972; HM Diplomatic Service; on secondment as Chef de Cabinet to Lord Cockfield, Vice-President of the Commission of the European Communities, Brussels, since 1985; *b* 16 June 1941; *s* of T. V. N. Fortescue, *qv*. MECAS, 1964; served Amman, FCO and Paris, 1966–72; First Sec., UKDEL Brussels, 1972–73; on loan to EEC, 1973–76; FCO, 1976–79; Washington, 1979–81; Head of Presidency Unit, ECD, FCO, 1981–82; EC Brussels, 1982; Counsellor, Budapest, 1983–84. *Address:* c/o Foreign and Commonwealth Office, SW1; 1 Launceston Place, W8.

FORTESCUE, Trevor Victor Norman, (Tim), CBE 1984; Secretary-General, Food and Drink Industries Council, 1973–83; *b* 28 Aug. 1916; *s* of Frank Fortescue; *m* 1st, 1939, Margery Stratford (marr. diss. 1975), *d* of Dr G. H. Hunt; two *s* one *d*; 2nd, 1975, Anthea Maureen, *d* of Robert M. Higgins. *Educ:* Uppingham Sch.; King's Coll., Cambridge. BA 1938; MA 1945. Colonial Administrative Service, Hong Kong, 1939–47 and Kenya, 1949–51 (interned, 1941–45); FAO, UN, Washington, DC, 1947–49 and Rome, 1951–54; Chief Marketing Officer, Milk Marketing Bd of England and Wales, 1954–59; Manager, Nestlé Gp of Cos, Vevey, Switz., 1959–63 and London, 1963–66. MP (C) Liverpool, Garston, 1966–Feb. 1974; an Asst Govt Whip, 1970–71; a Lord Comr of HM Treasury, 1971–73. Chairman: Conference Associates Ltd, 1978–; Standing Cttee, Confedn of Food and Drink Industries of European Community (CIAA), 1982–84; Pres., British Food Manufg Industries Res. Assoc., 1984–; Member: Meat Promotion Rev. Body, 1984; Council, British Industrial Biol. Res. Assoc., 1980–83. Trustee, Uppingham Sch., 1957–63; Patron and Trustee, The Quest Community, Birmingham, 1971–85. *Recreations:* marriage to Anthea; Napoleon. *Address:* 34 Stanford Road, W8 5PZ. *T:* 01-937 2125.

See also J.A. Fortescue.

FORTEVIOT, 3rd Baron *cr* 1916; **Henry Evelyn Alexander Dewar,** Bt, *cr* 1907; MBE 1943; DL; Chairman, John Dewar & Sons Ltd, 1954–76; former Director, Distillers Co. Ltd; *b* 23 Feb. 1906; 2nd *s* of 1st Baron Forteviot and Margaret Elizabeth, *d* of late Henry Holland; *S* half-brother 1947; *m* 1933, Cynthia Monica (*d* 1986), *e d* of late Cecil Starkie, Hethe Place, Cowden, Kent; two *s* two *d*. *Educ:* Eton; St John's Coll., Oxford (BA). Served War of 1939–45, with Black Watch (RHR) (MBE). DL Perth, 1961. *Heir:* *s* Hon. John James Evelyn Dewar [*b* 5 April 1938; *m* 1963, Lady Elisabeth Waldegrave, 3rd *d* of 12th Earl Waldegrave, *qv*; one *s* three *d*]. *Address:* Dupplin Castle, Perth, Perthshire. *Club:* Brooks's; Royal (Perth).

See also Duke of Fife, Gen. Sir Richard Worsley.

FORTH, Eric; MP (C) Mid Worcestershire, since 1983; *b* 9 Sept. 1944; *s* of William and Aileen Forth; *m* 1967, Linda St Clair; two *d*. *Educ:* Jordanhill Coll. Sch., Glasgow; Glasgow Univ. (MA Hons Politics and Econs). Chm., Young Conservatives', Constituency CPC, 1970–73; Member: Glasgow Univ. Cons. Club, 1962–66; Brentwood UDC, 1968–72. Contested (C) Barking, Feb. and Oct. 1974. Member (C), North Birmingham, European Parlt, 1979–84; Chm., Backbench Cttee, European Democ. Gp, European Parlt, 1979–84. Vice-Chm., Cons. Backbench European Affairs Cttee, 1983–. *Publication:* Regional Policy—A Fringe Benefit?, 1983. *Recreation:* discussion and argument. *Address:* House of Commons, SW1A 0AA. *Club:* Carlton.

FORTIER, Most Rev. Jean-Marie; *see* Sherbrooke, Archbishop of, (RC).

FORTY, Prof. Arthur John, PhD, DSc; Principal and Vice-Chancellor, Stirling University, since 1986; *b* 4 Nov. 1928; *s* of Alfred Louis Forty and Elisabeth Forty; *m* 1950, Alicia Blanche Hart Gough; one *s*. *Educ:* Headlands Grammar Sch.; Bristol Univ. (BSc; PhD 1953; DSc 1967). Served RAF, 1953–56. Sen. Res. Scientist, Tube Investments Ltd, 1956–58; Lectr, Univ. of Bristol, 1958–64; University of Warwick: Foundn Prof. of Physics, 1964–86; Pro-Vice-Chancellor, 1970–86. Member: SRC Physics Cttee, 1969–73; SRC Materials Cttee, 1970–73; Computer Bd, 1982–85; University Grants Committee: Mem., 1982–86, Vice-Chm., 1985–86; Chairman: Physical Sciences Sub-cttee, 1985–86; Equipment Sub-cttee, 1985–86; Chairman: Jt ABRC, Computer Bd and UGC Working Party on Future Facilities for Advanced Res. Computing (author, Forty Report), 1985; Management Cttee for Res. Councils' Super computer Facility, 1986–. *Publications:* papers in Proc. Royal Soc., Phil Magazine and other learned jls. *Recreations:* dinghy sailing, gardening, the ancient metallurgy of gold. *Address:* Principal's House, University of Stirling, Stirling FK9 4LA.

FORTY, Francis John, OBE 1952; BSc, FICE, FSA, FRSH, FIMunE; City Engineer, Corporation of London, 1938–64; *b* Hull, Yorks, 11 Feb. 1900; *s* of J. E. Forty, MA Oxon, headmaster, Hull Grammar Sch., and Maud C. Forty; *m* 1st, 1926, Doris Marcon Francis (*d* 1958), *d* of Dr A. G. Francis, BA Cantab, FRCS; one *s* two *d*; 2nd, 1965, Elizabeth Joyce Tofield. *Educ:* Hymers Coll., Hull; Glasgow Univ. (BSc 1923). RNAS, RAF, 1918–19 (Commnd Pilot). Engineering Asst, Hull; Engineering Asst, York; Chief Engineering Asst, Willesden. Deputy Borough Surveyor, Ealing; Borough Engineer and Surveyor, Ealing, 1934–38. War duties, 1939–45, included i/c City of London Heavy Rescue Service (Civil Defence Long Service Medal). Works include: (with Sir Albert Richardson) St Paul's Garden, 1951; (in consultation with Prof. W. F. Grimes) exposure and preservation of section of Town Wall of London, 1951–53; London Wall new route between Moorgate and Aldersgate Street, with car park underneath, 1959; Blackfriars Bridgehead Improvement with underpass, 1962–; multi-storey car park, Upper Thames Street, 1962; Walbrook Wharf Public Cleansing Depot and Wharf (consultant architect, Sir Hugh Casson), 1963. Formerly Member: London Regional Bldg Cttee; Nat. Soc. for Clean Air; Roman and Mediaeval London Excavation Council; Festival of Britain Council for Architecture, Town Planning and Bldg Research; Minister of Transport's Parking Survey Cttee for Inner London; Minister of Housing and Local Govt's Thames Flooding Technical Panel; Sussex Archaeological Trust. Liveryman of the Worshipful Company of Painter-Stainers, of the City of London. *Publications:* Bituminous Emulsions for Use in Road Works (with F. Wilkinson), 1932; Swimming Bath Water Purification from a Public Health Point of View (with F. W. Wilkinson), various contribs technical and other jls; notably contrib. on exposure and preservation of Roman and Mediæval work in the Town Wall of London. *Address:* Flat 8, Emanuel House, 18 Rochester Row, SW1P 1BS. *T:* 01-834 4376. *Clubs:* Athenæum, Royal Air Force.

FORWELL, Dr George Dick, PhD; FRCP; Chief Administrative Officer, Greater Glasgow Health Board, and Hon. Lecturer, Department of Administrative Medicine, Glasgow University, since 1973; *b* 6 July 1928; *s* of Harold C. Forwell and Isabella L. Christie; *m* 1957, Catherine F. C. Cousland; two *d*. *Educ:* George Watson's Coll., Edinburgh; Edinburgh Univ. (MB, ChB 1950; PhD 1955). MRCPE 1957, DIH 1957, DPH 1959, FRCPE 1967, FFCM 1972, FRCPGlas 1974, FRCP 1985. House Officer and Univ. Clin. Asst, Edinburgh Royal Infirm., 1950–52; RAF Inst. of Aviation Med., 1952–54; MRC and RCPE grants, 1954–56; pneumoconiosis field res., 1956–57; Grad. Res. Fellow and Lectr, Edinburgh Univ. Dept of Public Health and Social Med., 1957–60; Asst Dean, Faculty of Med., Edinburgh Univ., 1960–63; Dep. Sen. and Sen. Admin. MO, Eastern Reg. Hosp. Bd, Dundee, 1963–67; PMO, Scottish Home and Health Dept, 1967–73; QHP, 1980–83. Mem., GMC, 1984–. *Publications:* papers on clin. res. and on health planning and services, in med. and other jls. *Address:* 60 Whittingehame Drive, Glasgow G12 0YQ. *T:* 041-334 7122. *Club:* Royal Air Force.

FORWOOD, Sir Dudley (Richard), 3rd Bt *cr* 1895; Member of Lloyd's; *b* 6 June 1912; *s* of Sir Dudley Baines Forwood, 2nd Bt, CMG, and Norah Isabella (*née* Lockett) (*d* 1962); *S* father, 1961; *m* 1952, Mary Gwendoline (who *m* 1st, Viscount Ratendone, later 2nd Marquis of Willingdon; 2nd, Robert Cullingford), *d* of Basil S. Foster. *Educ:* Stowe Sch. Attaché, British Legation, Vienna, 1934–37; Equerry to the Duke of Windsor, 1937–39. Served War of 1939–45, Scots Guards (Major). Master, New Forest Buckhounds, 1956–65; Official Verderer of the New Forest, 1974–82; Chairman: New Forest Consultative Panel, 1970–82; Crufts, 1973–. Hon. Dir, RASE, 1973–78. *Recreation:* hunting. *Heir:* *cousin* Peter Noel Forwood [*b* 1925; *m* 1950, Roy Murphy; six *d*]. *Address:* 43 Addison Road, W14. *T:* 01-603 3620; The Old House, Burley, near Ringwood, Hants. *T:* Burley 2345.

FOSKETT, Douglas John, OBE 1978; FLA; Director of Central Library Services and Goldsmiths' Librarian, University of London, 1978–83; *b* 27 June 1918; *s* of John Henry Foskett and Amy Florence Foskett; *m* 1948, Joy Ada (*née* McCann); one *s* two *d*. *Educ:* Bancroft's Sch.; Queen Mary Coll., Univ. of London (BA 1939); Birkbeck Coll., Univ. of London (MA 1954). Ilford Municipal Libraries, 1940–48; RAMC and Intell. Corps, 1940–46; Metal Box Co. Ltd, 1948–57; Librarian, Univ. of London Inst. of Educn, 1957–78. Chairman of Council, Library Assoc., 1962–63, Vice-Pres., 1966–73, Pres., 1976; Hon. Library Adviser, RNID, 1965–; Mem., Adv. Cttee on Sci. and Techn. Information, 1969–73; Mem. and Rapporteur, Internat. Adv. Cttee on Documentation, Libraries and Archives, UNESCO, 1968–73; Cons. on Documentation to ILO and to European Packaging Fedn; Cttee Mem., UNISIST/UNESCO and EUDISED/Council of Europe Projects; Member: Army Educn Adv. Bd, 1968–73; Library Adv. Council, 1975–77. Visiting Professor: Univ. of Michigan, 1964; Univ. of Ghana, 1967; Univ. of Ibadan, 1967; Brazilian Inst. for Bibliography and Documentation, 1971; Univ. of

Iceland, 1974. FLA 1949, Hon. FLA, 1975; Hon. Fellow, Polytechnic of North London, 1981. *Publications:* Assistance to Readers in Lending Libraries, 1952; (with E. A. Baker) Bibliography of Food, 1958; Information Service in Libraries, 1958, 2nd edn 1967; Classification and Indexing in the Social Sciences, 1963, 2nd edn 1974; Science, Humanism and Libraries, 1964; Reader in Comparative Librarianship, 1977; Pathways for Communication, 1984; contrib. to many professional jls. *Recreations:* books, travel, writing, cricket. *Address:* 1 Daleside, Gerrard's Cross, Bucks SL9 7JF. *T:* Gerrard's Cross 882835. *Clubs:* MCC; Sussex CCC.

FOSS, Kathleen, (Kate); Member, Direct Mail Services Standards Board, since 1983; *b* 17 May 1925; *d* of George Arden and May Elizabeth Arden; *m* 1951, Robert Foss; one *s.* *Educ:* Northampton High Sch.; Whitelands Coll. (Teaching Dip.). Teacher: Northants, 1945–47; Mddx, 1947–53 (Dep. Head); Westmorland, 1953–60 (History specialist). Chairman: Consumers in European Community Gp (UK), 1979–82; Insurance Ombudsman Bureau, 1985– (Mem. Council, 1984–); Member: Nat. Consumer Council, 1980–83; Consumers' Consultative Cttee, Brussels, 1981–; Standing Cttee of Law Commn on Conveyancing, 1985–; Data Protection Tribunal Panel, 1986–; Council for Licensed Conveyancers, 1986–. Vice Pres., Keep Britain Tidy Gp, 1982– (Vice-Chm., 1979–82); Mem. Exec., National Fedn of Women's Insts, 1969–81 (National Treasurer, 1974–78); Chm., Bd of Dirs, WI Books Ltd, 1981–. *Recreations:* golf, bridge. *Address:* Merston, Natland, Kendal, Cumbria LA9 7QH. *T:* Kendal 20855. *Club:* Ebury Court.

FOSTER; *see* Hylton-Foster.

FOSTER, Prof. Allan (Bentham); Professor of Chemistry, University of London, 1966–86, now Emeritus; Head, Drug Metabolism Team, Drug Development Section, Institute of Cancer Research, 1982–86; *b* 21 July 1926; *s* of late Herbert and Martha Alice Foster; *m* 1949, Monica Binns; two *s.* *Educ:* Nelson Grammar Sch., Lancs; University of Birmingham. Frankland Medal and Prize, 1947; PhD, 1950; DSc, 1957. University Res. Fellow, University of Birmingham, 1950–53; Fellow of Rockefeller Foundn, Ohio State Univ., 1953–54; University of Birmingham: ICI Res. Fellow, 1954–55; Lectr, 1955–62; Sen. Lectr, 1962–64; Reader in Organic Chemistry, 1964–66; Head of Chemistry Div., Chester Beatty Res. Inst., Inst. of Cancer Res., 1966–82. Sec., British Technology Gp, New Cancer Product Develt Adv. Bd, 1986. FChemSoc (Mem. Coun., 1962–65, 1967–70), Corresp. Mem., Argentinian Chem. Soc. Regional Editor, Carbohydrate Research. *Publications:* numerous scientific papers mainly in Jl Chem. Soc. and Carbohydrate Research. *Recreations:* golf, gardening. *Address:* 1 Pine Walk, Carshalton Beeches, Surrey SM5 4ES. *T:* 01-642 4102. *Clubs:* Athenæum; Banstead Downs.

FOSTER, Brendan, MBE 1976; UK Managing Director, Nike International, since 1981; Chairman, Nike (UK) Ltd, since 1985; Managing Director, Nike Europe, since 1985; *b* 12 Jan. 1948; *s* of Francis and Margaret Foster; *m* 1972; one *s* one *d.* *Educ:* St Joseph's Grammar Sch., Hebburn, Co. Durham; Sussex Univ. (BSc); Carnegie Coll., Leeds (DipEd). School Teacher, St Joseph's Grammar Sch., Hebburn, 1970–74; Sports and Recreation Manager, Gateshead Metropolitan Bor. Council, 1974–81. Commonwealth Games: Bronze medal: 1500 metres, 1970; 5000 m, 1978; Silver medal, 5000 m, 1974; Gold medal, 10,000 m, 1978; European Games: Bronze medal, 1500 m, 1971; Gold medal, 5000 m, 1974; Olympic Games: Bronze medal, 10,000 m, 1976; World Records: 2 miles, 1973; 3000 metres, 1974. Hon. Fellow, Sunderland Polytechnic, 1977; Hon. MEd, Newcastle, 1978; Hon. DLitt, Sussex, 1982. *Publications:* Brendan Foster, 1978; Olympic Heroes 1896–1984, 1984. *Recreations:* running (now only a recreation), sport (as spectator). *Address:* 3 Ivy Lane, Low Fell, Gateshead, Tyne and Wear NE9 6QD.

FOSTER, Sir Christopher David, Kt 1986; MA; Commercial Policy Adviser to British Telecom, since 1986; Visiting Professor, London School of Economics, since 1978; *b* 30 Oct. 1930; *s* of George Cecil Foster; *m* 1958, Kay Sheridan Bullock; two *s* three *d.* *Educ:* Merchant Taylors' Sch.; King's Coll., Cambridge (Scholar). Economics Tripos 1954; MA 1959. Hallsworth Research Fellow, Manchester Univ., 1957–59; Senior Research Fellow, Jesus Coll., Oxford, 1959–64; Official Fellow and Tutor, Jesus Coll., 1964–66; Dir-Gen. of Economic Planning, MoT, 1966–70; Head of Unit for Res. in Urban Economics, LSE, 1970–76; Prof. of Urban Studies and Economics, LSE, 1976–78. Governor, 1967–70, Dir, 1976–78, Centre for Environmental Studies. Vis. Prof. of Economics, MIT, 1970. A Dir and Head of Econ. and Public Policy Div., Coopers & Lybrand Associates, 1978–84; a Dir, Public Sector Practice Leader and Economic Advr, Coopers & Lybrand, 1984–86. Special Economic Adviser (part time), DoE, 1974–77; Member: (part time), PO Bd, 1975–77; Audit Commn, 1983–; ESRC, 1985–. Chm., Cttee of Inquiry into Road Haulage Licensing, 1977–78; Mem., Cttee of Inquiry into Civil Service Pay, 1981–82; Economic Assessor, Sizewell B Inquiry, 1982–86. *Publications:* The Transport Problem, 1963; Politics, Finance and the Role of Economics: an essay on the control of public enterprise, 1972; (with R. Jackman and M. Perlman) Local Government Finance, 1980; papers in various economic and other journals. *Address:* 6 Holland Park Avenue, W11. *T:* 01–727 4757. *Club:* Reform.

FOSTER, Christopher Norman; with Weatherbys, since 1973; Secretary to the Jockey Club, since 1983; *b* 30 Dec. 1946; *s* of Maj.-Gen. Norman Leslie Foster, *qv;* *m* 1981, Anthea Jane Sammons; two *s.* *Educ:* Westminster Sch. ACA 1969, FCA 1979. Cooper Brothers & Co., Chartered Accountants, 1965–73. Mem. Council, Westminster Sch. Soc., 1972–. *Recreations:* racing, shooting, fishing, gardening. *Address:* 29 Homefield Road, Chiswick, W4 2LW. *T:* 01–995 9309. *Club:* MCC.

FOSTER, Hon. Dennis (Haley), CVO 1983; CBE 1981; Chief Secretary, Cayman Islands, since 1976; *b* 26 March 1931; *s* of late Arnold and Agatha Foster; *m* 1955, Reba Raphael Grant; one *d.* *Educ:* Munro Coll., Kingston, Jamaica. Joined Cayman Is Civil Service, 1950; seconded as Asst Administrator, Turks and Caicos Is, 1959; Dist Comr, Lesser Is, 1960; Asst Administrator, Cayman Is, 1968. *Recreation:* gardening. *Address:* PO Box 860, George Town, Grand Cayman, Cayman Islands, WI. *T:* 9–2236.

FOSTER, Derek; MP (Lab) Bishop Auckland, since 1979; *b* 25 June 1937; *s* of Joseph and Ethel Maud Foster; *m* 1972, Florence Anne Bulmer. *Educ:* Bede Grammar Sch., Sunderland; Oxford Univ. (BA Hons PPE). In industry and commerce, 1960–70; Youth and Community Worker, 1970–73; Further Educn Organiser, Durham, 1973–74; Asst Dir of Educn, Sunderland Borough Council, 1974–79. Councillor: Sunderland Co. Borough, 1972–74; Tyne and Wear County Council, 1973–77 (Chm. Econ. Develt Cttee, 1973–76). Chm., North of England Develt Council, 1974–76. PPS to Leader of Opposition, 1983–85; Opposition Chief Whip, 1985–. Mem., Select Cttee on Trade and Industry, 1980–82; opposition front bench spokesman on social security, 1982–84. Vice Chm., Youthaid, 1979–. *Recreations:* brass bands, choirs, uniformed member Salvation Army. *Address:* 3 Linburn, Rickleton, Washington, Tyne and Wear. *T:* Washington 4171580.

FOSTER, George Arthur C.; *see* Carey-Foster.

FOSTER, Joan Mary; Under Secretary, Department of Transport, Highways Planning and Management, 1978–80, retired; *b* 20 January 1923; *d* of John Whitfield Foster and Edith Foster (*née* Levett). *Educ:* Northampton School for Girls. Entered Civil Service (HM Office of Works), Oct. 1939; Ministry of Transport, 1955; Asst Secretary, 1970. *Recreations:* gardening, cooking, good wine. *Address:* Saddlers, Water End, Hemel Hempstead, Herts HP1 3BH. *T:* Hemel Hempstead 47374.

FOSTER, Sir John (Gregory), 3rd Bt *cr* 1930; Consultant Physician, George, Cape Province; *b* 26 Feb. 1927; *s* of Sir Thomas Saxby Gregory Foster, 2nd Bt, and Beryl, *d* of late Dr Alfred Ireland; *S* father, 1957; *m* 1956, Jean Millicent Watts; one *s* three *d.* *Educ:* Michaelhouse Coll., Natal. South African Artillery, 1944–46; Witwatersrand Univ., 1946–51; MB, BCh 1951; Post-graduate course, MRCPE 1955; Medical Registrar, 1955–56; Medical Officer, Cape Town, 1957. DIH London, 1962; FRCPE 1981. *Recreation:* outdoor sport. *Heir:* *s* Saxby Gregory Foster, *b* 3 Sept. 1957. *Address:* 7 Caledon Street, PO Box 1325, George, Cape Province, South Africa. *T:* George 3251. *Club:* Johannesburg Country (S Africa).

FOSTER, (John) Peter; Surveyor of the Fabric of Westminster Abbey since 1973; *b* 2 May 1919; *s* of Francis Edward Foster and Evelyn Marjorie, *e d* of Sir Charles Stewart Forbes, 5th Bt of Newe; *m* 1944, Margaret Elizabeth Skipper; one *s* one *d.* *Educ:* Eton; Trinity Hall, Cambridge. BA 1940, MA 1946; ARIBA 1949. Commnd RE 1941; served Norfolk Div.; joined Guards Armd Div. 1943, served France and Germany; Captain SORE(2) 30 Corps 1945; discharged 1946. Marshall Sisson, Architect: Asst 1948, later Partner; Sole Principal 1971. Surveyor of Royal Academy of Arts, 1965; Partner with John Peters of Vine Press, Hemingford Grey, 1957–63. Art Workers' Guild: Mem., 1971; Master, 1980; Trustee, 1985. Pres., Surveyors Club, 1980. Member: Churches Cttee for Historic Building Council for England, 1977–84; Adv. Bd for Redundant Churches, 1979–; Exec. Cttee, Georgian Gp, 1983–. Governor, Suttons Hosp., Charterhouse, 1982–. FSA 1973. *Recreations:* painting, books, travel, shooting. *Address:* Harcourt, Hemingford Grey, Huntingdon, Cambs PE18 9BJ. *T:* St Ives 62200; 2a Little Cloister, Westminster Abbey, SW1P 3PA. *Club:* Athenæum.

FOSTER, John Robert; National Organiser, Amalgamated Union of Engineering Workers, 1962–81, retired; *b* 30 Jan. 1916; *s* of George Foster and Amelia Ann (*née* Elkington); *m* 1938, Catherine Georgina (*née* Webb); one *s* one *d.* *Educ:* London County Council. Apprentice toolmaker, 1931–36; toolmaker, 1936–47; Amalgamated Engineering Union: Kingston District Sec. (full-time official), 1947–62. In Guyana for ILO, 1982. Lectr on industrial relns and trade union educn, WEA, 1981–. Mem., Industrial Tribunals (England and Wales), 1984–86. Mem., Engrg Industry Trng Bd, 1974–80; Vice-Chm., Electricity Supply Industry Trng Cttee, 1967–81; Mem., Adv. Council on Energy Conservation, 1978–82. Mem., Soc. of Industrial Tutors, 1981–. MRI 1978. *Recreations:* music, photography, angling, 17th Century English Revolution. *Address:* 10 Grosvenor Gardens, Kingston-upon-Thames KT2 5BE.

FOSTER, Very Rev. John William, BEM 1946; Dean of Guernsey, since 1978; Rector of St Peter Port, Guernsey, since 1978; *b* 5 Aug. 1921; *m* 1943, Nancy Margaret Allen; one *s.* *Educ:* St Aidan's Coll., Birkenhead. Served Leicestershire Yeomanry, 1939–46; Chaplain, Hong Kong Defence Force, 1958–. Reserve of Officers, Hong Kong Defence Force, 1967–73. Priest 1955; Curate of Loughborough, 1954–57; Chaplain, St John's Cathedral, Hong Kong, 1957–60, Precentor, 1960–63; Dean of Hong Kong, 1963–73; Hon. Canon, St John's Cathedral, Hong Kong, 1973; Vicar of Lythe, dio. York, 1973–78; Hon. Canon of Winchester, 1979. *Address:* The Deanery, Guernsey.

FOSTER, Lawrence; conductor; Chief Conductor, Orchestre National of Monte Carlo, since 1978; General Music Director, Duisburg concert series and Principal Guest Conductor, Düsseldorf Opera, since 1982; Music Director, Lausanne Chamber Orchestra, since 1985; *b* Los Angeles, 23 Oct. 1941; *s* of Thomas Foster and Martha Wurmbrandt. *Educ:* Univ. of California, LA; studied under Fritz Zweig, Bruno Walter and Karl Böhm. Asst Conductor, Los Angeles Philharmonic, 1965–68; British début, Royal Festival Hall, 1968; Covent Garden début, Troilus and Cressida, 1976; Chief Guest Conductor, Royal Philharmonic Orchestra, 1969–74; Music Dir and Chief Conductor, Houston Symphony Orchestra, 1971–78. *Recreations:* water skiing, table tennis. *Address:* c/o Harrison/Parrott Ltd, 12 Penzance Place, W11 4PE.

FOSTER, Maj.-Gen. Norman Leslie, CB 1961; DSO 1945; *b* 26 Aug. 1909; *s* of late Col A. L. Foster, Wimbledon; *m* 1937, Joan Constance, *d* of late Canon T. W. E. Drury; two *s.* *Educ:* Westminster; RMA Woolwich. 2nd Lieut, RA, 1929; Served War of 1939–45 in Egypt and Italy; CRA 11th Armoured Division, 1955–56; Deputy Military Sec., War Office, 1958–59; Maj.-Gen., 1959; GOC Royal Nigerian Army, 1959–62; Pres., Regular Commissions Board, 1962–65; retired, 1965. Dir of Security (Army), MoD, 1965–73. Security Advr, CSD, 1974–79. Col Comdt, Royal Regt of Artillery, 1966–74. Pres., Truman and Knightley Educnl Trust Ltd, 1982– (Chm., 1976–80). *Address:* Besborough, Heath End, Farnham, Surrey. *Club:* Army and Navy.

See also C. N. Foster.

FOSTER, Norman Robert, ARA 1983; RIBA, FSIAD, FAIA; architect; Director: Foster Associates Ltd, London; Foster Associates Hong Kong; *b* 1 June 1935; *s* of late Robert Foster and Lilian Smith; *m* 1964, Wendy Ann Cheesman; two *s.* *Educ:* Burnage Grammar Sch., Manchester; Manchester Coll. of Commerce; Univ. of Manchester Sch. of Architecture (RIBA Silver Medal, Heywood Medal, Builders' Assoc. Travelling Schol., MSA Bronze Medal, DipArch 1961, CertTP); Yale Univ. Sch. of Architecture (Henry Fellow, Jonathan Edwards Coll., MArch 1962). Manchester City Treasurer's Dept, 1951–53; worked in offices of Casson & Conder, 1960 and Paul Rudolph, 1962; consultancy works on city planning and urban renewal, USA, 1962–63; private practice in London, 1963–67; in collab. with Dr Buckminster Fuller, 1968–83; Cons. Architect to Univ. of E Anglia, 1978–. Mem. Council: AA, 1969–70, 1970–71 (Vice Pres., 1974); RCA, 1982–. Taught at: Univ. of Pennsylvania; AA, London; Bath Acad. of Arts; London Polytechnic. External Examr and Mem. Visiting Bd of Educn, RIBA. Projects include: Fred. Olsen Centre and Terminal, Port of London, 1968; IBM Pilot Head Office, Hampshire, 1970; Central redevelopment, Oslo and Offices in Forest Vestby for Fred. Olsen A/S, 1974; Head Office for Willis Faber & Dumas, Ipswich, 1975; Sainsbury Centre for Visual Arts, Univ. of E Anglia, Norwich, 1977; Technical Park for IBM, Greenford, Mddx, Stage one, 1977; Hammersmith Centre, London, 1977; UK headquarters for Renault, 1977; New Generation Furniture System, 1977; Open House Community Centre, 1978; Experimental Dwelling System, 1978; Whitney Gallery develt, NY, 1979; winning design, internat. competition for new headquarters, Hongkong and Shanghai Banking Corp., Hong Kong, 1979 (IStructE Special Award, 1985); feasibility studies, Third London Airport, for British Airports Authority, 1981–; winning design, internat. competition for Nat. German Indoor Athletic Stadium, Frankfurt, 1981; limited competition headquarters for Humana, Kentucky, USA, 1981; winner: BBC new Radio Broadcasting Centre, 1983; international competition for Arts Centre, Nimes, France, 1984. Work exhibited: Mus. of Mod. Art, New York, 1979 and Permanent Exhibn, 1982; Parma, 1979; Copenhagen, 1979; Singapore, 1971; Three New Skyscrapers, Museum of Modern Art, NY, 1983; Britain Salutes New York, Drawing Centre NY, 1983; Summer Exhibn RA; Centro-Edile, Milan, 1983; ICA Gall., London, 1983. Exhibitions: Foster Associates, Barcelona, 1976; Foster Associates—Original Drawings,

RIBA, 1979; Norman Foster—Architect, Whitworth Gall., Manchester, 1984; Berlin, 1984; Paris, 1985. BBC TV Documentary for Omnibus by John Read, 1981; Anglia TV Documentary, Norman Foster, 1982. Guest Editor Special Issues Architectural Review, 1968. IBM Fellow, Aspen Conference, 1980; Hon. FAIA; Hon. Mem., Bund deutscher Architekten, 1983. Hon. LittD East Anglia, 1980. Awards include: R. S. Reynolds Internat. Awards, USA, 1976, 1979; RIBA Awards and Commendations, 1969, 1972, 1977, 1978, 1981; Royal Gold Medal for Architecture, 1983; Financial Times Awards for outstanding Industrial Architecture and Commendations, 1967, 1970, 1971, 1974, 1984; Structural Steel Awards, 1972, 1978, 1984; Internat. Design Award, 1976, 1980; RSA Award, 1976; Ambrose Congreve Award, 1980; Premier Architectural Award (Architects' Jl and Towco Gp), RA, 1983; Hon. Mention, Auguste Perret Awards, 1984. *Publications:* contribs to various books and technical publications. *Recreations:* flying sailplanes, helicopters and light aircraft; running. *Address:* (office) 172–182 Great Portland Street, W1N 5TB. *T:* 01–637 5431. *Club:* Royal Automobile.

FOSTER, Peter; *see* Foster, J. P.

FOSTER, Maj.-Gen. Peter Beaufoy, MC 1944; Major-General Royal Artillery, British Army of the Rhine, 1973–76; retired June 1976; *b* 1 Sept. 1921; *s* of F. K. Foster, OBE, JP, Allt Dinas, Cheltenham; *m* 1947, Margaret Geraldine, *d* of W. F. Henn, sometime Chief Constable of Glos; two *s* one *d* (and one *s* decd). *Educ:* Uppingham School. Commnd RA, 1941; psc 1950; jssc 1958; OC Para. Light Battery, 1958–60; DAMS MS5, WO, 1960–63; Mil. Assistant to C-in-C BAOR, 1963–64; CO 34 Light Air Defence Regt RA, 1964–66; GSO1, ASD5, MoD, 1966–68; BRA Northern Comd, 1968–71; Comdt Royal Sch. of Artillery, 1971–73. Col Comdt, RA, 1977–82; Regimental Comptroller, RA, 1985–86. Chapter Clerk, Salisbury Cathedral, 1978–85. *Recreations:* shooting, gardening. *Address:* 13B Bower Gardens, Salisbury, Wilts.

FOSTER, Peter Martin, CMG 1975; HM Diplomatic Service, retired; Chairman, International Social Service of Great Britain, since 1985; *b* 25 May 1924; *s* of Frederick Arthur Peace Foster and Marjorie Kathleen Sandford; *m* 1947, Angela Hope Cross; one *s* one *d*. *Educ:* Sherborne; Corpus Christi Coll., Cambridge. Army (Horse Guards), 1943–47; joined Foreign (now Diplomatic) Service, 1948; served in Vienna, Warsaw, Pretoria/Cape Town, Bonn, Kampala, Tel Aviv; Head of Central and Southern Africa Dept, FCO, 1972–74; Ambassador and UK Rep. to Council of Europe, 1974–78; Ambassador to German Democratic Republic, 1978–81. Dir, Council for Arms Control, 1984–86. *Address:* Rew Cottage, Abinger Lane, Abinger Common, Surrey. *T:* Dorking 730114. *Club:* Athenæum.

FOSTER, Robert, CBE 1963 (OBE 1955; MBE 1949); FCIS; FIB; President, Savings Banks Institute, 1970–75; *b* 4 March 1898; *s* of Robert Foster; *m* 1927, Edith Kathleen (*née* Blackburn); two *d*. *Educ:* Rutherford Coll., Newcastle upon Tyne. RNVR, 1915–19. London Trustee Savings Banks, 1924–63 (Gen. Manager, 1943–63), retired. Mem. Nat. Savings Cttee, 1957–62. Dir, City & Metropolitan Building Soc. Mem. Court, Worshipful Company of Plumbers, 1959– (Master, 1965). *Recreations:* golf, gardening. *Address:* Larchfield, Highercombe Road, Haslemere, Surrey. *T:* Haslemere 4353. *Club:* City Livery.

FOSTER, Sir Robert (Sidney), GCMG 1970 (KCMG 1964; CMG 1961); KCVO 1970; Governor-General and Commander-in-Chief of Fiji, 1970–73 (Governor and C-in-C, 1968–70); retired 1973; *b* 11 Aug. 1913; *s* of late Sidney Charles Foster and late Jessie Edith (*née* Fry); *m* 1947, Margaret (*née* Walker); no *c*. *Educ:* Eastbourne Coll.; Peterhouse, Cambridge. MA. Appointed Cadet, Administrative Service, Northern Rhodesia, 1936; District Officer, N Rhodesia, 1938. War Service, 2nd Bn Northern Rhodesia Regt, 1940–43, Major. Provincial Commissioner, N Rhodesia, 1957; Sec., Ministry of Native Affairs, N Rhodesia, 1960; Chief Sec., Nyasaland, 1961–63; Dep. Governor, Nyasaland, 1963–64; High Comr for W Pacific, 1964–68. Trustee: Beit Trust; Cambridge-Livingstone Trust. KStJ 1968. Officer of the Legion of Honour, 1966. *Recreation:* self-help. *Address:* Kenwood, 16 Ardnave Crescent, Southampton SO1 7FJ. *Clubs:* Royal Over-Seas League; Leander (Henley).

FOSTER-BROWN, Rear-Adm. Roy Stephenson, CB 1958; RN Retired; *b* 16 Jan. 1904; *s* of Robert Allen Brown and Agnes Wilfreda Stephenson; *m* 1933, Joan Wentworth Foster; two *s*. *Educ:* RNC, Osborne and Dartmouth. Specialised in Submarines, 1924–28; specialised in Signals, 1930. Fleet Signal Officer, Home Fleet, 1939–40; Staff Signal Officer, Western Approaches, 1940–44; Comdr HMS Ajax, 1944–46; Capt., 1946; Capt. Sixth Frigate Sqdn, 1951; Dir Signal Div., Admiralty, 1952–53; Capt. HMS Ceylon, 1954; Rear-Adm. 1955; Flag Officer, Gibraltar, 1956–59; retd 1959. Hon. Comdt, Girls Nautical Trng Corps, 1961–. Master, Armourers and Braziers Co., 1964–65, 1974–75. *Recreations:* sailing, shooting, golf, tennis. *Address:* 13 Ravenscroft Road, Henley on Thames, Oxon RG9 2DH. *Club:* Army and Navy.

FOSTER-SUTTON, Sir Stafford William Powell, KBE 1957 (OBE (mil.) 1945); Kt 1951; CMG 1948; QC (Jamaica, 1938, Fedn Malaya, 1948); *b* 24 Dec. 1898; *s* of late G. Foster Sutton and Mrs Foster Sutton; *m* 1919, Linda Dorothy, *d* of late John Humber Allwood, OBE, and of Mrs Allwood, Enfield, St Ann, Jamaica; one *d* (one *s* decd). *Educ:* St Mary Magdalen Sch.; private tutor. HM Army, 1914–26; served European War, 1914–18, Infantry, RFC and RAF, active service. Called to the Bar, Gray's Inn, 1926; private practice, 1926–36; Solicitor Gen., Jamaica, 1936; Attorney-Gen., Cyprus, 1940; Col Comdg Cyprus Volunteer Force and Inspector Cyprus Forces, 1941–44; Mem. for Law and Order and Attorney-Gen., Kenya, 1944–48; actg Governor, Aug. and Sept. 1947; Attorney-Gen., Malaya, 1948–50; Officer Administering Govt, Malaya, Sept., Dec. 1950; Chief Justice, Fedn of Malaya, 1950–51; Dir of Man-Power, Kenya, 1944–45; Chm. Labour Advisory Board, Kenya, and Kenya European Service Advisory Board, 1944–48; Pres. of the West African Court of Appeal, 1951–55; Chief Justice, Fedn of Nigeria, 1955–58; Actg Governor-Gen., Nigeria, May-June 1957. Pres., Pensions Appeal Tribunals for England and Wales, 1958–73. Chairman: Zanzibar Commn of Inquiry, 1961; Kenya Regional and Electorial Commns, 1962–; Referendum Observers, Malta, 1964; Vice Pres., Britain-Nigeria Assoc., 1982–. Mem. Court, Tallow Chandlers' Co. (Master, 1981). *Address:* 7 London Road, Saffron Walden, Essex.

FOTHERGILL, Dorothy Joan; Director, Postal Pay and Grading, 1974–83, retired; *b* 31 Dec. 1923; *d* of Samuel John Rimington Fothergill and Dorothy May Patterson. *Educ:* Haberdashers' Aske's Sch., Acton; University Coll. London. BA (Hons) History. Entered Civil Service as Asst Principal, 1948; Principal, Overseas Mails branch, GPO, 1953; UPU Congress, Ottawa, 1957; Establishments work, 1958–62; HM Treasury, 1963–65; Asst Sec., Pay and Organisation, GPO, 1965; Director: Postal Personnel, 1970; London Postal Region, 1971. *Recreations:* gardening, walking, theatre. *Address:* 38 Andrewes House, Barbican, EC2Y 8AX.

FOTHERGILL, Richard Humphrey Maclean; Director, Council for Educational Technology, since 1986; *b* 21 March 1937; *s* of late Col C. G. Fothergill, RM, and of Mrs E. G. Fothergill; *m* 1962, Angela Cheshire Martin; three *d*. *Educ:* Sandle Manor, Fordingbridge; Clifton Coll., Bristol; Emmanuel Coll., Cambridge (BA Hons Nat. Sci. Tripos, 1958). Commnd RASC, National Service, 1959–61. Contemporary Films Ltd, 1961; Head of Biology, SW Ham Technical Sch., 1961–69; Res. Fellow, Nat. Council for Educnl Technol., 1970–72; Founder and Head of PETRAS (Educnl Develt Unit), Newcastle upon Tyne Polytechnic, 1972–80; Dir, Microelectronics Educn Prog., DES, 1980–86. Co-founder, Sec. and Treasurer, Standing Conf. on Educnl Develt Services in Polytechnics, 1974–80; Member: London GCE Bd and Schools Council Science Cttee, 1968–72; Standards and Specifications Cttee, CET, 1972–80. *Publications:* A Challenge for Librarians, 1971; Resource Centres in Colleges of Education, 1973; (with B. Williams) Microforms in Education, 1977; Child Abuse: a teaching package, 1978; (with I. Butchart) Non-book Materials in Libraries: a practical guide, 1978, 2nd edn 1983; (with J. S. A. Anderson) Microelectronics Education Programme: policy and guidelines, 1983; articles in Visual Educn, Educn Libraries Bull., Educnl Media Internat., and Educnl Broadcasting Internat. *Recreations:* reading, television, films, walking. *Address:* 17 Grenville Drive, Brunton Park, Newcastle upon Tyne NE3 5PA. *T:* Tyneside 2363380. *Club:* National Film Theatre.

FOU TS'ONG; concert pianist; *b* 10 March 1934; *m* 1st, 1960, Zamira Menuhin (marr. diss. 1970); one *s*; 2nd, 1973, Hijong Hyun. *Educ:* Shanghai and Warsaw. Debut, Shanghai, 1953. Concerts all over Eastern Europe including USSR up to 1958. Arrived in Great Britain, Dec. 1958; London debut, Feb. 1959, followed by concerts in England, Scotland and Ireland; subsequently has toured all five Continents. *Recreations:* many different ones. *Address:* c/o Intermusica Artists' Management, Grafton House, 2/3 Golden Square, W1R 3AD. *T:* 01–434 1836.

FOULDS, Hugh Jon; Director, since 1976, and Chief Executive, Investors in Industry Group plc (formerly Finance for Industry Ltd) and subsidiaries; *b* 2 May 1932; *s* of Dr E. J. Foulds and Helen Shirley (*née* Smith); *m* 1st, 1960, Berry Cusack-Smith (marr. diss. 1970); two *s*; 2nd, 1977, Hélène Senn, *d* of Edouard Senn, Paris. *Educ:* Bootham Sch., York. Joined ICFC, 1959, Dir 1974; Dir, London Atlantic Investment Trust, 1983–; Dep. Chm., Brammer PLC, 1980–. Mem. Council, RHBNC (formerly of Bedford Coll.), 1981–. *Recreations:* tennis, ski-ing, pictures, occasionally gardening. *Address:* 72 Loudoun Road, St John's Wood, NW8 0NA. *T:* 01–722 4464. *Clubs:* Garrick, Hurlingham; Cercle Interallié (Paris).

FOULGER, Keith, BSc(Eng); CEng, MIMechE; FRINA, RCNC; Chief Naval Architect, Ministry of Defence, 1983–85, retired; *b* 14 May 1925; *s* of Percy and Kate Foulger; *m* 1951, Joyce Mary Hart; one *s* one *d*. *Educ:* Southgate County Sch., London; Univ. of London (Mech. Eng.); Royal Naval Coll., Greenwich. Asst Constructor, 1950; Constructor, 1955; Constructor Commander: Dreadnought Project, 1959; C-in-C Western Fleet, 1965; Chief Constructor, 1967; Asst Director, Submarines, 1973; Deputy Director: Naval Construction, 1979; Naval Ship Production, 1979–81; Submarines, Ship Dept, 1981–83; Asst Under-Sec. of State, 1983. *Recreations:* travel, cars, gardening. *Address:* Masons, Grittleton, Chippenham, Wilts SN14 6AP. *T:* Castle Combe 782308. *Club:* Civil Service.

FOULIS, Sir Ian P. L.; *see* Liston Foulis.

FOULKES, George, JP; MP (Lab Co-op) Carrick, Cumnock and Doon Valley, since 1983 (South Ayrshire, 1979–83); *b* 21 Jan. 1942; *s* of George and Jessie M. A. W. Foulkes; *m* 1970, Elizabeth Anna Hope; two *s* one *d*. *Educ:* Keith Grammar Sch., Keith, Banffshire; Haberdashers' Aske's Sch.; Edinburgh Univ. (BSc 1964). President: Edinburgh Univ. SRC, 1963–64; Scottish Union of Students, 1965–67; Manager, Fund for Internat. Student Cooperation, 1967–68. Scottish Organiser, European Movement, 1968–69; Director: European League for Econ. Cooperation, 1969–70; Enterprise Youth, 1970–73; Age Concern, Scotland, 1973–79. Councillor: Edinburgh Corp., 1970–75; Lothian Regional Council, 1974–79; Chairman: Lothian Region Educn Cttee, 1974–79; Educn Cttee, Convention of Scottish Local Authorities, 1975–78; Jt Chm., All Party Pensioners Cttee, 1983– (Sec./Treasurer 1979–83); Mem., H of C Select Cttee on Foreign Affairs, 1981–83; Opposition spokesman on European and Community Affairs, 1984–85, on Foreign Affairs, 1985–. UK Delegate to Parly Assembly of Council of Europe, 1979–81. Mem., Scottish Exec. Cttee, Labour Party, 1981–. Rector's Assessor, Edinburgh Univ. Court, 1968–70, Local Authority Assessor, 1971–79. Chm., Scottish Adult Literacy Agency, 1976–79. Dir, St Cuthbert's Co-op. Assoc., 1975–79. JP Edinburgh, 1975. *Publication:* Eighty Years On: history of Edinburgh University SRC, 1964. *Recreations:* boating, fishing. *Address:* 8 Southpark Road, Ayr. *T:* Ayr 265776. *Clubs:* Traverse Theatre, Edinburgh University Staff (Edinburgh).

FOULKES, Sir Nigel (Gordon), Kt 1980; Chairman: ECI Management (Jersey) Ltd, since 1986; Equity Capital Trustee Ltd, since 1983; *b* 29 Aug. 1919; *s* of Louis Augustine and Winifred Foulkes; *m* 1948, Elisabeth Walker, *d* of Ewart B. Walker, Toronto; one *s* one *d* of former marr. *Educ:* Gresham's Sch., Holt; Balliol Coll., Oxford (Schol., MA). RAF, 1940–45. Subsequently executive, consulting and boardroom posts with: H. P. Bulmer; P. E. Consulting Gp; Birfield; Greaves & Thomas; International Nickel; Rank Xerox (Asst Man. Dir 1964–67, Man. Dir 1967–70); Charterhouse Group Ltd (Dir, 1972–83); Dir, Charterhouse J. Rothschild plc, 1984–85; Chm., Equity Capital for Industry, 1983–86 (Vice-Chm., 1982); Dir, Bekaert Gp (Belgium), 1973–85. Chairman: British Airports Authority, 1972–77; Civil Aviation Authority, 1977–82. CBIM; FRSA. *Address:* c/o ECI Ventures, Leith House, 47/57 Gresham Street, EC2V 7EH. *Club:* Royal Air Force.

FOULKES, Maj.-Gen. Thomas Herbert Fischer, CB 1962; OBE 1945; *b* 29 May 1908; *e s* of late Maj.-Gen. C. H. Foulkes, CB, CMG, DSO; *m* 1947, Delphine Elizabeth Smith; two *s*. *Educ:* Clifton Coll., Bristol (Pres., Old Cliftonian Soc., 1963–65); RMA Woolwich; St Catharine's Coll., Cambridge. BA 1930, MA Cantab 1954. Commissioned into RE, 1928; served in India and Burma, 1931–46 (CRE 39 Indian Div., also CRE 17 Indian Div. during Burma campaign); Comdr Corps RE (Brig.) 1 Br. Corps in BAOR, 1956–57; Chief Engr (Brig.) Middle East, 1957–58; Chief Engr (Brig.) Southern Command, UK, 1958–60; Engineer-in-Chief (Maj.-Gen.), War Office, 1960–63. Col Comdt, Royal Engineers, 1963–73. Hon. Col, RE Resources Units, AER, 1964–67; Hon. Col, RE Volunteers (Sponsored Units), T&AVR, 1967–72. President: Instn of Royal Engrs, 1965–70; Royal Bombay Sappers and Miners Officers Assoc., 1982–. Governor: Clifton Coll., 1964; Handcross Park Sch., 1968–. Pres., Aldershot and N Hants Cons. Assoc., 1978–83. Liveryman, Worshipful Co. of Plumbers of City of London, 1960, Master, 1973. CEng, FICE. *Recreations:* travel, fishing, photography. *Address:* Caton, 32 Fitzroy Road, Fleet, Aldershot, Hants GU13 8JW. *T:* Fleet 616650. *Club:* Army and Navy.

FOURCADE, Jean-Pierre; Officier de l'ordre national du Mérite; Senator, French Republic, from Hauts-de-Seine, since 1977; *b* 18 Oct. 1929; *s* of Raymond Fourcade (Médecin) and Mme Fourcade (*née* Germaine Raynal); *m* 1958, Odile Mion; one *s* two *d*. *Educ:* Collège de Sorèze; Bordeaux Univ. Faculté de Droit, Institut des Etudes politiques (Dip.); Ecole nationale d'administration; higher studies in Law (Dip.). Inspecteur des Finances, 1954–73. Cabinet of M. Valéry Giscard d'Estaing: Chargé de Mission, 1959–61; Conseiller technique, 1962, then Dir Adjoint to chef de service, Inspection gén. des

Finances, 1962; Chef de service du commerce, at Direction-Gén. du Commerce intérieur et des Prix, 1968–70; Dir-gén. adjoint du Crédit industriel et commercial, 1970; Dir-gén., 1972, and Administrateur Dir-gén., 1973; Ministre de l'Economie et des Finances, 1974–76; Ministre de l'Equipement et de l'Aménagement du Territoire, 1976–77. Mayor of Saint-Cloud, 1971–; Conseiller général of canton of Saint-Cloud, 1973–; Conseiller régional d'Ile de France, 1976– (Vice-Président, 1982). Président: Clubs Perspectives et Realités, 1975–82; Comité des Finances Locales, 1980; Commn des Affaires Sociales du Sénat, 1983–; Vice-Pres., Union pour la Démocratie Française, 1978–. *Address:* Palais du Luxembourg, 75006 Paris, France; 8 Parc de Béarn, 92210 Saint-Cloud, France.

FOURNIER, Jean, CD 1972; Director: Royal Trustco Ltd, Toronto, since 1984; The Royal Trust Company, since 1979; The Royal Trust Company Mortgage Corporation, since 1981; Chairman, Board of Canadian Human Rights Foundation, since 1982; Commissioner of the Metric Commission, Canada, since 1981; *b* Montreal, 18 July 1914; *s* of Arthur Fournier and Emilie Roy; *m* 1942, May Coote; five *s*. *Educ:* High Sch. of Québec; Laval Univ. (BA 1935, LLB 1938). Admitted to Bar of Province of Quebec, 1939. Royal Canadian Artillery (NPAM) (Lieut), 1935; Canadian Active Service Force Sept. 1939; served in Canada and overseas; discharged 1944, Actg Lt-Col. Joined Canadian Foreign Service, 1944; Third Sec., Canadian Dept of External Affairs, 1944; Second Sec., Canadian Embassy, Buenos Aires, 1945; Nat. Defence Coll., Kingston, 1948 (ndc); Seconded: to Privy Council Office, 1948–50; to Prime Minister's Office, Oct. 1950–Feb. 1951; First Sec., Canadian Embassy, Paris, 1951; Counsellor, 1953; Consul Gen., Boston, 1954; Privy Council Office (Asst Sec. to Cabinet), 1957–61; Head of European Division (Political Affairs), Dept of External Affairs, 1961–64; Chm., Quebec Civil Service Commn, 1964–71; Agent Gen. for the Province of Quebec in London, 1971–78. Pres., Inst. of Public Administration of Canada, 1966–67; Member: Canadian Inst. of Strategic Studies; Canadian Inst. of Internat. Affairs. Freedom, City of London, 1976. Pres., Canadian Veterans Assoc. of the UK, 1976–77. *Address:* 201 Metcalfe Avenue, Apt 903, Westmount, Québec, Canada H3Z 2H7. *T:* 932–8633. *Clubs:* Oriental, Canada; St James's, Montreal (Montreal)

FOUYAS, Archbishop Methodios; Archbishop of Thyateira and Great Britain; Greek Orthodox Archbishop of Great Britain, since 1979; *b* 14 Sept. 1925. BD (Athens); PhD (Manchester), 1962. Vicar of Greek Church in Munich, 1951–54; Secretary-General, Greek Patriarchate of Alexandria, 1954–56; Vicar of Greek Church in Manchester, 1960–66; Secretary, Holy Synod of Church of Greece, 1966–68; Archbishop of Aksum (Ethiopia), 1968–79. Member, Academy of Religious Sciences, Brussels, 1974–. Estabd Foundn for Hellenism in GB, 1982; Editor, Texts and Studies: a review of the Foundn for Hellenism in GB, Vols I, II, III, IV, 1982–85; Founder-Editor, Abba Salama Review of Ethio-Hellenic Studies, 10 Volumes; Editor: Ekklesiastikos Pharos (Prize of Academy of Athens), 11 Volumes; Ecclesia and Theologia, vols I-IV, 1980–85. Hon. DD: Edinburgh, 1970; Gr. Th. School of Holy Cross, Boston, 1984. Grand Cordon: Order of Phoenix (Greece); of Sellassie (Ethiopia). *Publications:* Orthodoxy, Roman Catholicism and Anglicanism, 1972; The Person of Jesus Christ in the Decisions of the Ecumenical Councils, 1976; History of the Church in Corinth, 1968; Christianity and Judaism in Ethiopia, Nubia and Meroe, 1st Vol., 1979, 2nd Vol., 1982; Theological and Historical Studies, Vols 1–9, 1979–86; contrib. to many other books and treatises. *Recreation:* gardening. *Address:* Thyateira House, 5 Craven Hill, W2. *T:* (office) 01–723 4787 and 01–402 7444.

FOWDEN, Sir Leslie, Kt 1982; FRS 1964; Director of Arable Crops Research, Agricultural and Food Research Council, since 1986; *b* Rochdale, Lancs, 13 Oct. 1925; *s* of Herbert and Amy D. Fowden; *m* 1949, Margaret Oakes; one *s* one *d*. *Educ:* University Coll., London. PhD Univ. of London, 1948. Scientific Staff of Human Nutrition Research Unit of the MRC, 1947–50; Lecturer in Plant Chemistry, University Coll. London, 1950–55, Reader, 1956–64, Prof. of Plant Chemistry, 1964–73; Dean of Faculty of Science, UCL, 1970–73; Dir, Rothamsted Exptl Station, 1973–86. Rockefeller Fellow at Cornell Univ., 1955; Visiting Prof. at Univ. of California, 1963; Royal Society Visiting Prof., Univ. of Hong Kong, 1967. Consultant Dir, Commonwealth Bureau of Soils, 1973–. Member: Advisory Board, Tropical Product Inst., 1966–70; Council, Royal Society, 1970–72; Scientific Adv. Panel, Royal Botanic Gardens, 1977– (Trustee, 1983–); Radioactive Waste Management Adv. Cttee, 1983–. Foreign Member: Deutsche Akademie der Naturforscher Leopoldina, 1971; Lenin All-Union Acad. of Agricultural Sciences of USSR, 1978; Corresponding Mem., Amer. Soc. Plant Physiologists, 1981; Hon. Mem., Phytochemical Soc. of Europe, 1985. *Publications:* contribs to scientific journals on topics in plant biochemistry. *Address:* 1 West Common, Harpenden, Herts AL5 2JQ. *T:* Harpenden 64628.

FOWELLS, Joseph Dunthorne Briggs, CMG 1975; DSC 1940; Deputy Director General, British Council, 1976–77, retired; *b* 17 Feb. 1916; *s* of late Joseph Fowells and Maud Dunthorne, Middlesbrough; *m* 1st, 1940, Edith Agnes McKerracher (marr. diss. 1966); two *s* one *d*; 2nd, 1969, Thelma Howes (*d* 1974). *Educ:* Sedbergh Sch.; Clare Coll., Cambridge (MA). School teaching, 1938; service with Royal Navy (Lt-Comdr), 1939–46; Blackie & Son Ltd, Educnl Publishers, 1946; British Council, 1947: Argentina, 1954; Representative Sierra Leone, 1956; Scotland, 1957; Dir Latin America and Africa (Foreign) Dept, 1958; Controller Overseas B Division (foreign countries excluding Europe), 1966; Controller Planning, 1968; Controller European Div., 1970; Asst Dir Gen. (Functional), 1972; Asst Dir Gen. (Regional), 1973–76. *Recreations:* golf, sailing. *Address:* 5/57 Palmeira Avenue, Hove, East Sussex. *T:* Brighton 70349.

FOWKE, Sir Frederick (Woollaston Rawdon), 4th Bt *cr* 1814; *b* 14 Dec. 1910; *e s* of Sir Frederick Ferrers Conant Fowke, 3rd Bt, and Edith Frances Daubeney (*d* 1958), *d* of late Canon J. H. Rawdon; *S* father, 1948; *m* 1948, Barbara (*d* 1982), *d* of late E. Townsend; two *d*. *Educ:* Uppingham. Served War of 1939–45, in Derbys Yeomanry, 1939–43 (wounded). *Recreation:* shooting. *Heir:* *n* David Frederick Gustavus Fowke, *b* 28 Aug. 1950. *Address:* Lower Woolstone Farm, Bishops Tawton, Barnstaple, N Devon.

FOWLER, Prof. Alastair David Shaw, FBA 1974; University Fellow, University of Edinburgh, since 1985; *b* 17 Aug. 1930; *s* of David Fowler and Maggie Shaw; *m* 1950, Jenny Catherine Simpson; one *s* one *d*. *Educ:* Queen's Park Sch., Glasgow; Univ. of Glasgow; Univ. of Edinburgh; Pembroke Coll., Oxford. MA Edin. 1952 and Oxon 1955; DPhil Oxon 1957; DLitt Oxon 1972. Junior Res. Fellow, Queen's Coll., Oxford, 1955–59; Instructor, Indiana Univ., 1957; Lectr, UC Swansea, 1959; Fellow and Tutor in English Lit., Brasenose Coll., Oxford, 1962–71; Regius Prof. of Rhetoric and English Lit., Univ. of Edinburgh, 1972–84; Visiting Professor: Columbia Univ., 1964; Univ. of Virginia, 1969, 1979, 1985–; Mem. Inst. for Advanced Study, Princeton, 1966, 1980; Visiting Fellow: Council of the Humanities, Princeton Univ., 1974; Humanities Research Centre, Canberra, 1980; All Souls Coll., Oxford, 1984. Mem., Scottish Arts Council, 1976–77. Adv. Editor, New Literary History, 1972–; Gen. Editor, Longman Annotated Anthologies of English Verse, 1977–; Mem. Editorial Board: English Literary Renaissance, 1978–; Word and Image, 1984–. *Publications:* (trans. and ed) Richard Wills, De re poetica, 1958; Spenser and the Numbers of Time, 1964; (ed) C. S. Lewis, Spenser's Images of Life, 1967; (ed with John Carey) The Poems of John Milton, 1968; Triumphal Forms, 1970; (ed) Silent Poetry, 1970; (ed with Christopher Butler) Topics in Criticism, 1971; Seventeen, 1971; Conceitful Thought, 1975; Catacomb Suburb, 1976; Edmund Spenser, 1977; From the Domain of Arnheim, 1982; Kinds of Literature, 1982; contribs to jls and books. *Address:* Department of English, David Hume Tower, George Square, Edinburgh EH8 9JX.

FOWLER, Christopher B.; *see* Brocklebank-Fowler.

FOWLER, Dennis Houston, OBE 1979 (MBE 1963); HM Diplomatic Service, retired; *b* 15 March 1924; *s* of Joseph Fowler and Daisy Lilian Wraith Fowler (*née* Houston); *m* 1944, Lilias Wright Nairn Burnett; two *s* one *d*. *Educ:* Alleyn's Sch., Dulwich. Colonial Office, 1940; RAF, 1942–46; India Office (subseq. CRO), 1947; Colombo, 1951; Second Secretary, Karachi, 1955; CRO, 1959; First Secretary, Dar es Salaam, 1961; Diplomatic Service Administration (subseq. FCO), 1965; First Sec. and Head of Chancery, Reykjavik, 1969; FCO, 1973; First Sec., Head of Chancery and Consul, Kathmandu, 1977; Counsellor and Hd of Claims Dept, FCO, 1980–83. *Recreations:* golf, music, do-it-yourself. *Address:* 25 Dartnell Park Road, West Byfleet, Surrey KT14 6PN. *T:* Byfleet 41583. *Clubs:* West Byfleet Golf; Royal Nepal Golf (Kathmandu).

FOWLER, Derek, CBE 1979; a Vice-Chairman, since 1981, and Member for Finance and Planning, since 1978, British Railways Board (Finance Member, 1975–78); *b* 26 Feb. 1929; *s* of late George Edward Fowler and of Kathleen Fowler; *m* 1953, Ruth Fox; one *d*. *Educ:* Grantham, Lincs. Financial appointments with: Grantham Borough Council, 1944–50; Spalding UDC, 1950–52; Nairobi City Council, 1952–62; Southend-on-Sea CBC, 1962–64. British Railways Board: Internal Audit Manager, 1964–67, and Management Acct, 1967–69, W Region; Sen. Finance Officer, 1969–71; Corporate Budgets Manager, 1971–73; Controller of Corporate Finance, 1973–75; Chm., BR Pension Trustees Ltd, 1986–. Mem., UK Accounting Standards Cttee, 1982–84. Freeman, City of London, 1981; Liveryman, Worshipful Co. of Loriners, 1981. FCCA; IPFA (Mem. Council, 1974–83); JDipMA. *Recreation:* cartophily. *Address:* 30 Sutton Avenue, Slough, Berks SL3 7AW. *T:* Slough 34200.

FOWLER, Sir (Edward) Michael (Coulson), Kt 1981; FNZIA; Mayor of Wellington, New Zealand, 1974–83; Partner, Calder Fowler Styles and Turner, since 1960; Chairman, Queen Elizabeth II Arts Council, since 1983; company chairman and director; *b* 19 Dec. 1929; *s* of William Coulson Fowler and Faith Agnes Netherclift; *m* 1953, Barbara Hamilton Hall; two *s* one *d*. *Educ:* Christ's Coll., Christchurch, NZ; Auckland Univ. (MArch). ARIBA 1953; FNZIA 1970. Architect, London office, Ove Arup & Partners, 1954–56; own practice, Wellington, 1957–59. Chairman: Southern Cross Television Ltd, 1985–; FIN Export Ltd, 1985–; Director: Robt Jones Investments Ltd, 1983–; New Zealand Sugar Co., 1983–; AGC(NZ) Ltd, 1984–; Municipal Co-operative Insurance Co., 1977–; Cigna Insurance New Zealand Ltd, 1985–. Wellington City Councillor, 1968–74. Nat. Pres., YHA of NZ, 1984–. Medal of Honour, NZIA, 1983; Alfred O. Glasse Award, NZ Inst. of Planning, 1984. *Publications:* Wellington Sketches: Folio I, 1971, Folio II, 1974; Country Houses of New Zealand, 1972, 2nd edn 1977; The Architecture and Planning of Moscow, 1980; Eating Houses in Wellington, 1980; Wellington Wellington, 1981; Eating Houses of Canterbury, 1982; Wellington—A Celebration, 1983; The New Zealand House, 1983; Buildings of New Zealanders, 1984. *Recreations:* sketching, reading, writing, history, politics. *Address:* 31 Hobson Crescent, Thorndon, Wellington, New Zealand. *T:* Wellington 721.117. *Club:* Wellington (Wellington, NZ).

FOWLER, Prof. Gerald Teasdale; Director, North East London Polytechnic, since 1982; *b* 1 Jan. 1935; *s* of James A. Fowler, Long Buckby, Northants, and Alfreda (*née* Teasdale); *m* 1982, Lorna, *d* of William Lloyd, Preston. *Educ:* Northampton Grammar Sch.; Lincoln Coll., Oxford; University of Frankfurt-am-Main. Craven Fellowship, Oxford Univ., 1957–59; part-time Lectr, Pembroke Coll., Oxford, 1958–59; Lectr, Hertford and Lincoln Colls, Oxford, 1959–65; Lectr, Univ. of Lancaster, 1965–66; Asst Dir, The Polytechnic, Huddersfield, 1970–72; Prof. of Educnl Studies, Open Univ., 1972–74; Prof. Associate, Dept of Government, Brunel Univ., 1977–80; Dep. Dir, Preston Polytechnic, 1980–81. Vis. Prof., Dept of Admin, Strathclyde Univ., 1970–74. Oxford City Councillor, 1960–64; Councillor, The Wrekin DC, 1973–76, Leader, 1973–74; Councillor, Shropshire CC, 1979–85. Contested (Lab) Banbury, 1964; MP (Lab) The Wrekin, 1966–70, Feb. 1974–1979; Jt Parly Sec., Min. of Technology, 1967–69; Minister of State: Dept of Educn and Science, Oct. 1969–June 1970, March-Oct. 1974 and Jan.-Sept. 1976; Privy Council Office, 1974–76. President: Assoc. for Teaching of Social Science, 1976–79; Assoc. for Recurrent Educn, 1976–78, 1981–85; Assoc. for Liberal Educn, 1977–79; Comparative Educn in Europe Soc. (British Section), 1980; Vice-Pres., Soc. for Research into Higher Educn, 1983–. Chm., Youthaid, 1977–80; Vice Chm., Nat. Parly Youth Lobby, 1978–79. Trustee, Community Projects Foundn, 1978–80. Vice-Chm., Assoc. of Business Executives, 1982– (Pres., 1979–81; Hon. Fellow 1983). FBIM 1984; FRSA 1985. *Address:* North East London Polytechnic, Romford Road, Stratford, E15 4LZ. *T:* 01–590 7722; 4 Princess Road, NW1. *Club:* Reform.

FOWLER, Henry Hamill; investment banker; Limited Partner, Goldman Sachs & Co., New York; *b* 5 Sept. 1908; *s* of Mack Johnson Fowler and Bertha Browning Fowler; *m* 1938, Trudye Pamela Hathcote; two *d* (one *s* decd). *Educ:* Roanoke Coll., Salem, Va; Yale Law Sch. Counsel, Tennessee Valley Authority, 1934–38, Asst Gen. Counsel, 1939; Special Asst to Attorney-Gen. as Chief Counsel to Sub-Cttee, Senate Cttee, Educn and Labor, 1939–40; Special Counsel, Fed. Power Commn, 1941; Asst Gen. Counsel, Office of Production Management, 1941, War Production Board, 1942–44; Econ. Adviser, US Mission Econ. Affairs, London, 1944; Special Asst to Administrator, For. Econ. Administration, 1945; Dep. Administrator, National Production Authority, 1951, Administrator, 1952; Administrator, Defense Prodn Administration, 1952–53; Dir Office of Defense Mobilization, Mem. Nat. Security Coun., 1952–53; Under-Sec. of the Treasury, 1961–64; Secretary of the US Treasury, 1965–68. Sen. Mem. of Fowler, Leva, Hawes & Symington, Washington, 1946–51, 1953–61, 1964–65; Gen. Partner, Goldman Sachs & Co., 1969–80; Chm., Goldman Sachs Internat. Corp., 1969–84. Chairman: Roanoke Coll.; Atlantic Council of the US, 1972–77; Inst. of Internat. Educn, 1973–78; US Treasury Adv. Cttee on Reform of Internat. Monetary System, 1973–84; Co-Chm., Cttee on Present Danger, 1976–; Cttee to Fight Inflation, 1981–; Bretton Woods Cttee, 1985–; Dir, Atlantic Inst. Trustee: Lyndon B. Johnson Foundn; Franklin D. Roosevelt Four Freedoms Foundn. Hon. Degrees: Roanoke Coll., 1961; Wesleyan Univ., 1966; Univ. of William and Mary, 1966. *Recreation:* tennis. *Address:* 85 Broad Street, New York, NY 10004, USA. *Clubs:* Links, River (NYC); Metropolitan (Washington).

FOWLER, Ian; Principal Chief Clerk and Clerk to the Committee of Magistrates for the Inner London area, since 1979; *b* 20 Sept. 1932; *s* of Norman William Frederick Fowler, OBE, QPM, and late Alice May (*née* Wakelin); *m* 1961, Gillian Cecily Allchin, JP; two *s* one *d*. *Educ:* Maidstone Grammar Sch.; Skinners Sch., Tunbridge Wells; King's Sch., Canterbury; St Edmund Hall, Oxford (MA). National Service, commnd 2nd Bn The Green Howards, 1951–53. Called to Bar, Gray's Inn, 1957; entered Inner London Magistrates Courts Service, 1959. Councillor: Herne Bay UDC and Canterbury CC,

1961–83 (Mayor, 1976–77). Mem. Court, Univ. of Kent at Canterbury, 1976–. *Recreation:* reading. *Address:* 3rd Floor, North West Wing, Bush House, Aldwych, WC2B 4PJ. *T:* 01-836 9331; 6 Dence Park, Herne Bay, Kent.

FOWLER, John Francis, DSc, PhD; FInstP; Director of Cancer Research Campaign's Gray Laboratory, at Mount Vernon Hospital, Northwood, since 1970; *b* 3 Feb. 1925; *er s* of Norman V. Fowler, Bridport, Dorset; *m* 1953, Kathleen Hardcastle Sutton, MB, BS (marr. diss. 1984); two *s* five *d*. *Educ:* Bridport Grammar Sch.; University Coll. of the South-West, Exeter. BSc 1st class Hons (London) 1944; MSc (London) 1946; PhD (London) 1955; DSc (London) 1974; FInstP 1957. Research Physicist: Newalls Insulation Co. Ltd, 1944; Metropolitan Vickers Electrical Co. Ltd, 1947; Newcastle upon Tyne Regional Hosp. Board (Radiotherapy service), 1950; Principal Physicist at King's Coll. Hosp., SE5, 1956; Head of Physics Section in Medical Research Council Radiotherapeutic Res. Unit, Hammersmith Hosp., 1959 (later the Cyclotron Unit); Reader in Physics, London Univ. at Med. Coll. of St Bartholomew's Hosp., 1962; Prof. of Med. Physics, Royal Postgraduate Med. Sch., London Univ., Hammersmith Hosp., 1963–70, Vice-Dean, 1967–70. Vis. Prof. in Oncology, Mddx Hosp. Med. Sch., 1977–. President: Hosp. Physicists Assoc., 1966–67; Europ. Soc. Radiat. Biol., 1974–76; British Inst. Radiol., 1977–78. Hon. Fellow, Amer. Coll. of Radiology, 1981. Hon. MD Helsinki, 1981. Roentgen Award, BIR, 1965; Röntgen Plakette, Deutsches Röntgen Museum, 1978; Heath Meml Award, Univ. of Texas, Houston, 1981; Breur Medal, European Soc. Therapeutic Radiology and Oncology, 1983; Barclay Medal, BIR, 1985; Marie Sklodowska-Curie Medal, Polish Radiation Res. Soc., 1986. *Publications:* Nuclear Particles in Cancer Treatment, 1981; papers on radiation dosimetry, radio-biology, radioisotopes, in Brit. Jl Radiology, Brit. Jl Cancer, Radiotherapy and Oncology, etc. *Recreations:* theatre (Stage Dir, Theatre Workshop, Manchester, 1949); getting into the countryside. *Address:* Gray Laboratory, Mount Vernon Hospital, Northwood, Mddx HA6 2RN. *T:* Northwood 28611.

FOWLER, Sir Michael; *see* Fowler, Sir E. M. C.

FOWLER, Rt. Hon. Norman; *see* Fowler, Rt Hon. P. N.

FOWLER, Prof. Peter Howard, FRS 1964; DSc; Royal Society Research Professor, Physics Department, University of Bristol, since 1964; *b* 27 Feb. 1923; *s* of Sir Ralph Howard Fowler, FRS, and Eileen, *o c* of 1st and last Baron Rutherford; *m* 1949, Rosemary Hempson (*née* Brown); three *d*. *Educ:* Winchester Coll.; Bristol Univ. BSc 1948, DSc 1958. Flying Officer in RAF, 1942–46 as a Radar Technical Officer. Asst Lectr in Physics, 1948, Lectr, 1951, Reader, 1961, Bristol Univ. Visiting Prof., Univ. of Minnesota, 1956–57. Hughes Medal, Royal Soc., 1974. *Publication:* (with Prof. C. F. Powell and Dr D. H. Perkins) The Study of Elementary Particles by the Photographic Method, 1959. *Recreations:* gardening, meteorology. *Address:* 320 Canford Lane, Westbury on Trym, Bristol.

FOWLER, Peter James; HM Diplomatic Service; Head of North America Department, Foreign and Commonwealth Office, since 1985; *b* 26 Aug. 1936; *s* of James and Gladys Fowler; *m* 1962, Audrey June Smith; one *s* three *d*. *Educ:* Nunthorpe Grammar Sch., York; Trinity Coll., Oxford (BA). FCO, 1962–64; Budapest, 1964–65; Lisbon, 1965–67; Calcutta, 1968–71; FCO, 1971–75; East Berlin, 1975–77; Counsellor, Cabinet Office, 1977–80; Comprehensive Test Ban Delegn, Geneva, 1980; Counsellor, Bonn, 1981–85. *Recreations:* reading, opera. *Address:* c/o Foreign and Commonwealth Office, King Charles Street, SW1. *Club:* Royal Commonwealth Society.

FOWLER, Peter Jon, PhD; Professor of Archaeology, University of Newcastle upon Tyne, since 1985; *b* 14 June 1936; *s* of W. J. Fowler and P. A. Fowler; *m* 1959, Elizabeth (*née* Burley); three *d*. *Educ:* King Edward VI Grammar Sch., Morpeth, Northumberland; Lincoln Coll., Oxford (MA 1961); Univ. of Bristol (PhD 1977). Investigator on staff of RCHM (England), Salisbury office, 1959–65; Staff Tutor in Archaeology, Dept of Extra-Mural Studies, 1965–79, and Reader in Arch., 1972–79, Univ. of Bristol; Sec., Royal Commn on Historical Monuments (England), 1979–85. Member: Historic Bldgs and Ancient Monuments Adv. Cttees, Historic Buildings and Monuments Commn, 1983–86 (Ancient Monuments Bd, 1979–83); Council, National Trust, 1983–; Pres., Council for British Archaeol., 1981–83 (Vice-Pres., 1979–81). *Publications:* Regional Archaeologies: Wessex, 1967; (ed) Archaeology and the Landscape, 1972; (ed) Recent Work in Rural Archaeology, 1975; (ed with K. Branigan) The Roman West Country, 1976; Approaches to Archaeology, 1977; (ed with H. C. Bowen) Early Land Allotment in the British Isles, 1978; (with S. Piggott and M. L. Ryder) Agrarian History of England and Wales, I, pt 1, 1981; The Farming of Prehistoric Britain, 1983; contrib. to Antiquity, and Antiquaries Jl. *Recreations:* reading, writing, sport (esp. cricket). *Address:* Department of Archaeology, The University, Newcastle upon Tyne.

FOWLER, Rt. Hon. (Peter) Norman, PC 1979; MP (C) Sutton Coldfield, since Feb. 1974 (Nottingham South, 1970–74); Secretary of State for Social Services, since 1981; *b* 2 Feb. 1938; *s* of late N. F. Fowler and Katherine Fowler; *m* 1979, Fiona Poole, *d* of John Donald; two *d*. *Educ:* King Edward VI Sch., Chelmsford; Trinity Hall, Cambridge (MA). Nat. Service commn, Essex Regt, 1956–58; Cambridge, 1958–61; Chm., Cambridge Univ. Conservative Assoc., 1960. Joined staff of The Times, 1961; Special Corresp., 1962–66; Home Affairs Corresp., 1966–70; reported Middle East War, 1967. Mem. Council, Bow Group, 1967–69; Editorial Board, Crossbow, 1962–69; Vice-Chm., North Kensington Cons. Assoc., 1967–68; Chm., E Midlands Area, Cons. Political Centre, 1970–73. Mem., Parly Select Cttee on Race Relations and Immigration, 1970–74; Jt Sec., Cons. Parly Home Affairs Cttee, 1971–72, 1974 (Vice-Chm., 1974); Chief Opposition spokesman: Social Services, 1975–76; Transport, 1976–79; Opposition spokesman, Home Affairs, 1974–75; PPS, NI Office, 1972–74; Sec. of State for Transport, 1981 (Minister of Transport, 1979–81). *Publications:* After the Riots: the police in Europe, 1979; political pamphlets including: The Cost of Crime, 1973; The Right Track, 1977. *Address:* House of Commons, SW1A 0AA.

FOWLER, Robert Asa; Chairman, Fowler International; *b* 5 Aug. 1928; *s* of Mr and Mrs William Henry Fowler; *m* 1951, Grace Ohmer Grasselli; three *s* one *d*. *Educ:* Princeton Univ. (BA Econs); Harvard Business Sch. (MBA). Lieut USNR, 1950–53. Various appts with Continental Oil, 1955–75; Area Manager, Northwest Europe, Continental Oil Co., 1975–78; Chm. and Man. Dir, Conoco Ltd, 1979–81; Vice-Pres., Internat. Marketing, Conoco Inc. *Recreations:* tennis, skiing. *Address:* 154 Glynn Way, Houston, Texas 77056, USA. *T:* 713–965 1523. *Clubs:* Hurlingham; River, Knickerbocker (NY); Allegheny Country (Pa); Chagrin Valley Hunt (Ohio).

FOWLER, Ronald Frederick, CBE 1950; *b* 21 April 1910; *e s* of late Charles Frederick Fowler; *m* 1937, Brenda Kathleen Smith. *Educ:* Bancroft's Sch.; LSE, University of London; Universities of Lille and Brussels. BCom (hons) London, 1931. Sir Ernest Cassel Travelling Scholar, 1929–30; Asst, later Lectr in Commerce, LSE, 1932–40; Central Statistical Office, 1940–50; Dir of Statistics, Min. of Labour, 1950–68; Dir of Statistical Res., Dept of Employment, 1968–72. Consultant, Prices Div., Statistics Canada, Ottawa, 1971–72; Statistical Consultant, Prices Commn, 1973–77. *Publications:* The Depreciation of Capital, 1934; The Duration of Unemployment, 1968; Some Problems of Index Number Construction, 1970; Further Problems of Index Number Construction, 1973; articles in British and US economic and statistical jls. *Address:* 10 Silverdale Road, Petts Wood, Kent. *Club:* Reform.

FOWLER, Prof. William Alfred, PhD; Institute Professor Emeritus of Physics, California Institute of Technology, since 1982 (Institute Professor of Physics, 1970–82); *b* Pittsburgh, Pa, 9 Aug. 1911; *s* of late John McLeod Fowler and Jennie Summers (*née* Watson); *m* 1940, Ardiane Foy Olmsted, Pasadena, Calif.; two *d*. *Educ:* Ohio State Univ. (B.Eng. Phys); California Inst. of Technology (PhD Phys). Member: Tau Kappa Epsilon; Tau Beta Pi; Sigma Xi. California Inst. of Technology: Research Fellow in Nuclear Physics, 1936–39; Asst Prof. of Physics, 1939–42; Associate Prof. of Physics, 1942–46; Prof. of Physics, 1946–70. Defense record: Research and develt proximity fuses, rocket ordnance, and atomic weapons; Research staff mem.: Sect. T, NDRC, and Div. 4, NDRC, 1941; Asst Dir of Research, Sect. L. Div. 3, NDRC, 1941–45; Techn. Observer, Office of Field Services and New Develts Div., War Dept, in South and Southwestern Pacific Theatres, 1944; Actg Supervisor, Ord. Div., R&D, NOTS, 1945; Sci. Dir, Project VISTA, Dept Defense, 1951–52. Guggenheim Fellow and Fulbright Lectr, Cavendish Laboratory, Univ. of Cambridge, Eng., 1954–55; Guggenheim Fellow, St John's Coll., and Dept Applied Math. and Theor. Phys., Univ. of Cambridge, Eng., 1961–62; Walker-Ames Prof. of Physics, Univ. of Washington, 1963; Visitor, The Observatories, Univ. of Cambridge, Summer 1964; Vis. Prof. of Physics, Mass. Inst. of Technology, 1966; Vis. Fellow, Inst. of Theoretical Astronomy, Univ. of Cambridge, Summers 1967–72. Numerous lectureships in USA, 1957–; those given abroad include: Lectr, Internat. Sch. of Physics "Enrico Fermi", Varenna, 1965. Lectr, Advanced Sch. on Cosmic Physics, Erice, Italy, 1969, in addition to past lectures at Cavendish Laboratory, Cambridge; also Lectr at Research Sch. of Physical Sciences, Australian National Univ., Canberra, 1965; Jubilee Lectr, 50th Anniversary, Niels Bohr Inst., Copenhagen, 1970; Scott Lectr, Cavendish Laboratory, Cambridge Univ., Eng., 1971; George Darwin Lectr, RAS, 1973; E. A. Milne Lectr, Milne Soc., 1986; 22nd Liège Internat. Astrophysical Symposium, 1978; Vis. Scholar, Phi Beta Kappa, 1980–81. Member: Nat. Science Bd, Nat. Science Foundation, USA, 1968–74; Space Science Bd, Nat. Academy of Sciences, 1970–73 and 1977–80; Space Program Adv. Council, NASA, 1971–74; Bd of Directors, American Friends of Cambridge Univ., 1970–78; Governing Bd, Amer. Inst. of Physics, 1974–80; Cttee Chm., Nuclear Science Adv. Cttee, Nat. Science Foundn/Dept of Energy, USA, 1977–79; Chm., Off. Phys. Sci., Nat. Acad. Sci., 1981–82; Mem. Review Cttee APS Study: Radionuclide Release in Severe Accidents of Nuclear Power Reactors, 1984. Has attended numerous conferences, congresses and assemblies. Member: Internat. Astro. Union; Amer. Assoc. for Advancement of Science; Amer. Assoc. of Univ. Professors; Nat. Acad. of Sciences; Mem. corres., Soc. Royale des Sciences de Liège; Fellow: Amer. Physical Soc. (Pres., 1976); Amer. Acad. of Arts and Sciences; British Assoc. for Advancement of Science; Benjamin Franklin Fellow, RSA; ARAS. Hon. Member: Mark Twain Soc.; Naturvetenskapliga Foreningen, 1984. Hon. DSc: Chicago, 1976; Ohio State, 1978; Denison, 1982; Arizona State, 1985; Georgetown, 1986; Dr *hc*: Liège, 1981; Observatory of Paris, 1981. Various awards and medals for science etc, both at home and abroad, including Medal for Merit, USA, 1948; Vetlesen Prize, 1973; Nat. Medal of Sci., 1974; Eddington Medal, RAS, 1978; Bruce Gold Medal, Astron. Soc. Pacific, 1979; (jtly) Nobel Prize for Physics, 1983; Sullivandt Medal, Ohio State Univ., 1985; first William A. Fowler Award for Excellence in Physics, Ohio section, APS, 1986. *Publications:* contributor to: Physical Review, Astrophysical Jl, Proc. Nat. Acad. of Sciences, Amer. Jl of Physics, Geophysical Jl, Nature, Royal Astronomical Soc., etc. *Address:* Kellogg Radiation Laboratory 106–38, California Institute of Technology, Pasadena, California 91125, USA. *Clubs:* Cosmos (Washington, DC); Athenæum (Pasadena, Calif); Cambridge and District Model Engineering Society.

FOWLER HOWITT, William; *see* Howitt, W. F.

FOWLES, John; writer; *b* 31 March 1926; *s* of Robert John Fowles and Gladys May Richards; *m* 1956, Elizabeth Whitton. *Educ:* Bedford Sch.; New Coll., Oxford. English Centre PEN Silver Pen Award, 1969; W. H. Smith Award, 1970. *Publications:* The Collector, 1963; The Aristos, 1965; The Magus, 1966, rev. edn 1977; The French Lieutenant's Woman, 1969; Poems, 1973; The Ebony Tower, 1974 (televised, 1984); Shipwreck, 1975; Daniel Martin, 1977; Islands, 1978; (with Frank Horvat) The Tree, 1979; (ed) John Aubrey's Monumenta Britannica, parts 1 and 2, 1980, part 3 and Index, 1982; The Enigma of Stonehenge, 1980; Mantissa, 1982; Thomas Hardy's England, 1984; Land, 1985; A Maggot, 1985. *Recreations:* mainly Sabine. *Address:* c/o Anthony Sheil Associates, 43 Doughty Street, WC1N 2LF.

FOX; *see* Lane Fox.

FOX, Edward; actor; *b* 13 April 1937; *s* of Robin and Angela Muriel Darita Fox; *m* Tracy (*née* Pelissier); one *d*; and one *d* by Joanna Fox. *Educ:* Ashfold Sch.; Harrow Sch. RADA training, following National Service, 1956–58; entry into provincial repertory theatre, 1958, since when, films, TV films and plays, and plays in the theatre, have made up the sum of his working life. *Plays include:* Knuckle, Comedy, 1973; The Family Reunion, Vaudeville, 1979; Anyone for Denis, Whitehall, 1981; Quartermaine's Terms, Queen's, 1981; Hamlet, Young Vic, 1982; Interpreters, Queen's, 1985. *Films include:* The Go-Between, 1971 (Soc. of Film and Television Arts Award for Best Supporting Actor, 1971); The Day of the Jackal, A Doll's House, 1973; Galileo, 1976; The Squeeze, A Bridge Too Far (BAFTA Award for Best Supporting Actor, 1977), The Duellists, The Cat and the Canary, 1977; Force Ten from Navarone, 1978; The Mirror Crack'd, 1980; Gandhi, 1982; Never Say Never Again, The Dresser, 1983; The Bounty, 1984; The Shooting Party, 1985. *Television Series include:* Hard Times, 1977; Edward and Mrs Simpson, 1978 (BAFTA Award for Best Actor, 1978; TV Times Top Ten Award for Best Actor, 1978–79; British Broadcasting Press Guild TV Award for Best Actor, 1978; Royal TV Soc. Performance Award, 1978–79). *Recreations:* music, reading, walking. *Clubs:* Garrick, Savile.

FOX, Hazel Mary, (Lady Fox); Director, British Institute of International and Comparative Law, since 1982; *b* 22 Oct. 1928; *d* of J. M. B. Stuart, CIE; *m* 1954, Rt Hon. Sir Michael Fox, *qv*; three *s* one *d*. *Educ:* Roedean Sch.; Somerville Coll., Oxford (1st Cl. Jurisprudence, 1949; MA). Called to the Bar, Lincoln's Inn, 1950 (Buchanan Prize); practised at the Bar, 1950–54; Lectr in Jurisprudence, Somerville Coll., Oxford, 1951–58; Lectr, Council of Legal Educn, 1962–76; Fellow of Somerville Coll., 1976–81. Chairman: London Rent Assessment Panel, 1977–; London Leasehold Valuation Tribunal, 1981–; Mem., Home Office Deptl Cttee on Jury Service, 1963–65. JP London, 1959–77; Chm., Tower Hamlets Juvenile Court, 1968–76. Mem., Editorial Bd, Internat. and Comparative Law Qly, 1986–. *Publication:* (with J. L. Simpson) International Arbitration, 1959. *Address:* c/o British Institute of International and Comparative Law, 17 Russell Square, WC1B 5DR. *T:* 01-636 5802.

FOX, Sir (Henry) Murray, GBE 1974; MA, FRICS; *b* 7 June 1912; *s* of late S. J. Fox and Molly Button; *m* 1941, Helen Isabella Margaret (*d* 1986), *d* of late J. B. Crichton; one *s* two *d*. *Educ:* Malvern; Emmanuel Coll., Cambridge. Chairman: Trehaven Trust Group, 1963–; City of London Sinfonia, 1983–; Pres., City & Metropolitan Building Society, 1985– (Dir, 1972–; Chm., 1976–85); Managing Trustee, Municipal Mutual Insurance Ltd, 1977–. Dir, Toye, Kenning & Spencer Ltd, 1976–. Governor: Christ's Hosp., 1966–82; Bridewell Royal Hosp., 1966 (Vice-Pres. 1976–82); Trustee, Morden Coll., 1976–. Court of Common Council, 1963–82; Past Master: Wheelwrights' Co.; Coopers' Co.; Alderman, Ward of Bread Street, 1966–82; Sheriff, City of London, 1971–72; Lord Mayor of London, 1974–75; one of HM Lieutenants, City of London, 1976–83. Order of Rising Sun and Sacred Treasure (Japan), 1971; Order of Stor (Afghanistan), 1971; Order of Orange Nassau (Netherlands), 1972. *Recreations:* golf, reading. *Address:* 80 Defoe House, Barbican, EC2. *T:* 01–588 8306; (office) 20–24 Kirby Street, Hatton Garden, EC1N 8TU. *T:* 01–242 5205. *Clubs:* City of London, City Livery (Pres. 1966–67).

FOX, Sir (John) Marcus, Kt 1986; MBE 1963; MP (C) Shipley, since 1970; Parliamentary Under Secretary of State, Department of the Environment, 1979–81; *b* 11 June 1927; *s* of late Alfred Hirst Fox; *m* 1954, Ann, *d* of F. W. J. Tindall; one *s* one *d*. *Educ:* Wheelright Grammar Sch., Dewsbury. Mem. Dewsbury County Borough Council, 1957–65; contested (C): Dewsbury, 1959; Huddersfield West, 1966. An Asst Govt Whip, 1972–73; a Lord Comr, HM Treasury, 1973–74; Opposition Spokesman on Transport, 1975–76; Mem., Parly Select Cttee on Race Relations and Immigration, 1970–72; Sec., Cons. Party's Transport Industries Cttee, 1970–72; a Vice-Chairman: Cons. Party Orgn, 1976–79; 1922 Cttee, 1984–; Chm., Cttee of Selection, 1984–. *Recreations:* reading, tennis, squash. *Address:* House of Commons, SW1.

FOX, Kenneth Lambert; Public Sector Consultant, National Utility Services, since 1986; *b* 8 Nov. 1927; *s* of J. H. Fox, Grimsby, Lincolnshire; *m* 1959, P. E. Byrne; one *d*. *Educ:* City of London Coll.; Univ. of London. BSc (Hons); FInstPS, MIIM. Plant Man., Rowntree Gp, 1950–63; Supply Man., Ford Motor Co. (UK), 1963–67; Sen. Management Conslt, Cooper & Lybrand Ltd, 1967–70; Man. of Conslts (Europe), US Science Management Corp., 1971–72; Supply Management, British Gas Corp., 1972–75; Dir of Supplies, GLC, 1975–86. *Recreations:* tennis, painting, bird watching, DIY. *Address:* 39 Parkland Avenue, Upminster. *T:* Upminster 28927.

FOX, Rt. Rev. Langton Douglas, DD; retired Bishop of Menevia; *b* 21 Feb. 1917; *s* of Claude Douglas Fox and Ethel Helen (*née* Cox). *Educ:* Mark Cross, Wonersh and Maynooth. BA 1938; DD 1945. Priest 1942. Lectr, St John's Seminary, Wonersh, 1942–55; Mem., Catholic Missionary Soc., 1955–59; Parish Priest, Chichester, 1959–65; Auxiliary Bishop of Menevia, 1965–72; Bishop of Menevia, 1972–81. *Address:* Bishop's House, Pantasaph, Holywell, Clwyd CH8 8PB.

FOX, Prof. Leslie, DSc Oxon; Professor of Numerical Analysis, Oxford University, and Professorial Fellow, Balliol College, 1963–83, now Emeritus Fellow; Director, Oxford University Computing Laboratory, 1957–82; *b* 30 Sept. 1918; *m* 1st, 1943, Paulene Dennis; 2nd, 1973, Mrs Clemency Clements, *er d* of Thomas Fox. *Educ:* Wheelwright Grammar Sch., Dewsbury; Christ Church, Oxford. Admiralty Computing Service, 1943–45; Mathematics Div., Nat. Physical Laboratory, 1945–56; Associate Prof., Univ. of California, Berkeley, 1956–57; Research Prof., Univ. of Illinois, 1961–62; Vis. Prof., Open Univ., 1970–71. Pres., Math./Phys. Section, BAAS, 1975. Hon. Chm., 10th Canadian Conf. on Applied Mechanics, Univ. of Western Ontario, 1985. *Publications:* Numerical Solution of Boundary-value Problems in Ordinary Differential Equations, 1957; (ed) Numerical Solution of Ordinary and Partial Differential Equations, 1962; An Introduction to Numerical Linear Algebra, 1964; (ed) Advances in Programming and Non-Numerical Computation, 1966; Chebyshev Polynomials in Numerical Analysis (with I. J. Parker), 1968; Computing Methods for Scientists and Engineers (with D. F. Mayers), 1968; numerous papers in learned journals. *Recreations:* sport, music, literature. *Address:* 2 Elsfield Road, Marston, Oxford. *T:* Oxford 722668.

FOX, Sir Marcus; *see* Fox, Sir J. M.

FOX, Rt. Hon. Sir Michael John, Kt 1975; PC 1981; **Rt. Hon. Lord Justice Fox;** a Lord Justice of Appeal, since 1981; *b* 8 Oct. 1921; *s* of late Michael Fox; *m* 1954, Hazel Mary Stuart (*see* Hazel Mary Fox); three *s* one *d*. *Educ:* Drayton Manor Sch., Hanwell; Magdalen Coll., Oxford (BCL, MA). Admiralty, 1942–45. Called to the Bar, Lincoln's Inn, 1949, Bencher, 1975; QC 1968. Judge of the High Court of Justice, Chancery Div., 1975–81. *Address:* Royal Courts of Justice, Strand, WC2. *T:* 01–405 7641.

FOX, Sir Murray; *see* Fox, Sir H. M.

FOX, Paul Leonard, CBE 1985; Managing Director, Yorkshire Television, since 1977 (Director of Programmes, 1973–84); Chairman, Independent Television News, since 1986 (Director, 1977–86); Director: Channel Four, since 1985; World Television News, since 1986; *b* 27 Oct. 1925; *m* 1948, Betty Ruth (*née* Nathan); two *s*. *Educ:* Bournemouth Grammar Sch. Parachute Regt, 1943. Reporter: Kentish Times, 1946; The People, 1947; Scriptwriter, Pathé News, 1947; BBC Television: Scriptwriter, 1950; Editor, Sportsview, 1953, Panorama, 1961; Head, Public Affairs Dept, 1963; Head, Current Affairs Group, 1965; Controller, BBC1, 1967–73. Chairman: ITV Network Programme Cttee, 1978–80; Council, ITCA, 1982–84. Mem., Royal Commn on Criminal Procedure, 1978–80. Pres., RTS, 1985– (Vice-Pres., 1983–85); Nat. Mus. of Photography, Film and TV, 1985–. Hon. LLD Leeds, 1984. *Recreations:* television, attending race meetings. *Address:* Yorkshire Television, The Television Centre, Leeds LS3 1JS. *T:* Leeds 438283. *Club:* Garrick.

FOX, Roy, CMG 1980; OBE 1967; HM Diplomatic Service, retired; consultant with various companies; *b* 1 Sept. 1920; *s* of J. S. and A. Fox; *m* 1st, 1943, Sybil Verity; two *s* one *d*; 2nd, 1975, Susan Rogers Turner. *Educ:* Wheelwright Grammar Sch., Dewsbury; Bradford Technical Coll. Served in RNVR, 1940–46. Bd of Trade, 1947–58; British Trade Commissioner: Nairobi, 1958–60; Montreal, 1960–62; Winnipeg, 1962–64; Dep. Controller, Bd of Trade Office for Scotland, 1964–65. First Sec. Commercial, Karachi, 1965–68; Deputy High Comr, E Pakistan, 1968–70; Consul-Gen. and Comm. Counsellor, Helsinki, 1970–74; promoted to Minister, 1977; Consul-Gen., Houston, 1974–80. *Recreations:* golf, reading, tennis. *Address:* Beechcroft, Forest Drive, Kingswood, Surrey. *Club:* Royal Automobile.

FOX, Ruth W.; *see* Winston-Fox.

FOX, Sir Theodore, Kt 1962; MA, MD Cambridge, LLD Glasgow, DLitt Birmingham; FRCP; *b* 1899; 3rd *s* of late R. Fortescue Fox; *m* Margaret (*d* 1970), *e d* of late W. S. McDougall, Wallington, Surrey; four *s*. *Educ:* Leighton Park Sch.; Pembroke Coll., Cambridge (scholar); London Hosp. (house physician). Mem. of Friends' Ambulance Unit, BEF, 1918; Ship Surg., 1925; joined staff of The Lancet, 1925; served in RAMC, 1939–42 (late temp. Major); Ed., The Lancet, 1944–64. Dir, Family Planning Assoc., 1965–67. Croonian Lectr, RCP, 1951; Heath Clark Lectr, Univ. of London, 1963; Harveian Orator, RCP, 1965; Maurice Bloch Lectr, Univ. of Glasgow, 1966. Hon. Fellow: Royal Australian Coll. of Gen. Practitioners, 1962; NY Acad. of Medicine, 1984. *Publication:* Crisis in Communication, 1965. *Address:* Green House, Rotherfield, East Sussex. *T:* Rotherfield 2870. *Club:* Athenæum.

FOX, Prof. Wallace, CMG 1973; MD, FRCP, FFCM; Professor of Community Therapeutics, Cardiothoracic Institute, Brompton Hospital, 1979–86, now Emeritus; Director, Medical Research Council Tuberculosis and Chest Diseases Unit, Brompton Hospital, 1965–86; Hon. Consultant Physician, Brompton Hospital, since 1969; WHO Consultant, since 1961; Member of WHO Expert Advisory Panel on Tuberculosis, since 1965; *b* 7 Nov. 1920; *s* of Samuel and Esther Fox; *m* 1956, Gaye Judith Akker; three *s*. *Educ:* Cotham Grammar Sch., Bristol; Guy's Hosp. MB, BS (London) 1943; MRCS, LRCP, 1943; MRCP 1950; MD (Dist.) (London) 1951; FRCP 1962; FFCM 1976. Ho. Phys., Guy's USA Hosp., 1945–46; Resident Phys., Preston Hall Sanatorium, 1946–50; Registrar, Guy's Hosp., 1950–51; Asst Chest Physician, Hammersmith Chest Clinic, 1951–52; Mem. Scientific Staff of MRC Tuberculosis and Chest Diseases Unit, 1952–56, 1961–65; seconded to WHO, to establish and direct Tuberculosis Chemotherapy Centre, Madras, 1956–61; Dir, WHO Collaborating Centre for Tuberculosis Chemotherapy and its Application, 1976–. Lectures: Marc Daniels, RCP, 1962; First John Barnwell Meml, US Veterans Admin, 1968; Philip Ellman, RSocMed, 1976; Martyrs Meml, Bangladesh Med. Assoc., 1977; first Quezon Meml, Philippine Coll. of Chest Physicians, 1977; Morriston Davies Meml, BTA, 1981; Mitchell, RCP, 1982; E. Merck Oration, Indian Chest Soc., 1983; A. J. S. McFadzean, Univ. of Hong Kong, 1986. Waring Vis. Prof. in Medicine, Univ. of Colorado and Stanford Univ., 1974. Mem. Tropical Med. Research Bd, 1968–72; Mem., several MRC Cttees; Mem., BCG Vaccination Sub-Cttee, Min. of Health, 1968–; Mem. Council, Chest, Heart & Stroke Assoc., 1974–; International Union Against Tuberculosis: Mem., later Chm., Cttee of Therapy, 1964–71; Associate Mem., Scientific Cttees, 1973; Mem., Exec. Cttee, 1973– (Chm., 1973–77). Chm., Acid Fast Club, 1971–72. Editor, Advances in Tuberculosis Research. Elected Corresp. Mem., Amer. Thoracic Soc., 1962; Mem., Mexican Acad. of Medicine, 1976; Hon. Life Mem., Canadian Thoracic Soc., 1976; Corresp. Mem., Argentine Nat. Acad. of Medicine, 1977; Corresp. For. Member: Argentine Soc. of Phtisiol. and Thoracic Pathol., 1977; Coll. of Univ. Med. Phtisiologists of Argentine, 1978; Hon. Member: Argentine Med. Assoc., 1977; Singapore Thoracic Soc., 1978. Sir Robert Philip Medal, Chest and Heart Assoc., 1969; Weber Parkes Prize, RCP, 1973; Carlo Forlanini Gold Medal, Fedn Ital. contra la Tuberculosi e le Malattie Polmonari Sociali, 1976; Hon. Medal, Czech. Med. Soc., 1980; Robert Koch Centenary Medal, Internat. Union against Tuberculosis, 1982; Presidential Citation Award, Amer. Coll. of Chest Physicians, 1982. *Publications:* Reports on tuberculosis services in Hong Kong to Hong Kong Government: Heaf/Fox, 1962; Scadding/Fox, 1975; contribs to med. jls: on methodology of controlled clinical trials, on epidemiology and on chemotherapy, particularly in tuberculosis, asthma and carcinoma of the bronchus and other respiratory diseases. *Address:* 2 The Orchard, Bedford Park, W4 1JX. *T:* 01–994 0974.

FOX, Winifred Marjorie, (Mrs E. Gray Debros); Under-Secretary, Department of the Environment, 1970–76; *d* of Frederick Charles Fox and Charlotte Marion Ogborn; *m* 1953, Eustachy Gray Debros (*d* 1954); one *d*. *Educ:* Streatham County Sch.; St Hugh's Coll., Oxford. Unemployment Assistance Board, 1937; Cabinet Office, 1942; Ministry of Town and Country Planning, 1944; Ministry of Housing and Local Govt, 1952 (Under-Sec., 1963); Dept of the Environment, 1970; seconded to CSD as Chm., CS Selection Bd, 1971–72. *Address:* The Coach House, Hinton in the Hedges, S Northants. *T:* Brackley 702100.

FOX-ANDREWS, James Roland Blake; QC 1968; **His Honour Judge James Fox-Andrews;** a Circuit Judge (Official Referee), since 1985; *b* 24 March 1922; step *s* of late Norman Roy Fox-Andrews, QC; *m* 1950, Angela Bridget Swift; two *s*. *Educ:* Stowe; Pembroke Coll., Cambridge. Called to the Bar, Gray's Inn, 1949, Bencher, 1974. Dep. Chm., Devon QS, 1970–71; Recorder of Winchester, 1971, Hon. Recorder, 1972; a Recorder of Crown Court, 1972–85. Leader, Western Circuit, 1982–84. Member: Gen. Council of the Bar, 1968–72; Senate of Inns of Court and the Bar, 1976–79. *Publications:* (jtly) Leasehold Property (Temporary Provisions) Act, 1951; contrib. Halsbury's Laws of England, 3rd edn, building contracts, architects and engineers; (jtly) Landlord and Tenant Act, 1954; Business Tenancies, 1970, 3rd edn 1978. *Address:* 20 Cheyne Gardens, SW3. *T:* 01–352 9484; Lepe House, Exbury, Hants. *Club:* Hampshire (Winchester).

FOX-PITT, Maj.-Gen. William Augustus Fitzgerald Lane, CVO 1966 (MVO 1936); DSO 1940; MC 1916; retired; DL; Member of HM Bodyguard of Hon. Corps of Gentlemen-at-Arms, 1947–66; Lieutenant, 1963–66; (Standard Bearer, 1961–63); *b* 28 Jan. 1896; *s* of late Lieut-Col W. A. Fox-Pitt, Presaddfed, Anglesey; *m* 1931, Mary Stewart, *d* of A. H. H. Sinclair, MD, FRCSE; two *s* one *d*. *Educ:* Charterhouse. ADC to the King, 1945–47; joined Cheshire Regt 1914; served with Welsh Gds, 1915–39; Comd, 1st Bn, 1934–37; OC Welsh Guards Regt, 1937–40; Comd Gds Bde BEF, 1940, Armd Bde, 1941–43; Comdr, East Kent Dist as Maj.-Gen., 1943; retired with hon. rank of Maj.-Gen. 1947. Mem. Dorset CC 1952; DL Dorset, 1957. *Recreations:* shooting, golf. *Address:* Marsh Court, Sherborne, Dorset. *T:* Bishops Caundle 230. *Clubs:* Pratt's, Cavalry and Guards.

FOX-STRANGWAYS, family name of **Earl of Ilchester.**

FOXALL, Colin; Under Secretary, and Director of the Comprehensive Group, Export Credits Guarantee Department, since 1986; *b* 6 Feb. 1947; *s* of Alfred George Foxall and Ethel Margaret Foxall; *m* 1980, Diana Gail Bewick; two *s*. *Educ:* Gillingham Grammar Sch., Kent. Joined ECGD, 1966; Dept of Trade, 1974; ECGD, 1975–. *Recreation:* woodturning. *Address:* The Spinney, Colwinston, Cowbridge, S Glamorgan. *T:* Bridgend 57819.

FOXELL, Clive Arthur Peirson, FEng 1985; Managing Director, Engineering and Procurement, and Board Member, British Telecom, since 1986; *b* 27 Feb. 1930; *s* of Arthur Turner Foxell and Lillian Ellerman; *m* 1956, Shirley Ann Patey Morris; one *d*. *Educ:* Harrow High Sch.; Univ. of London. BSc; FIEE, FInstP, FInstPS. GEC Res. Labs, 1947; Man., GEC Semiconductor Labs, 1968; Man. Dir, GEC Semiconductors Ltd, 1971; Dep. Dir of Research, PO, 1975; Dep. Dir, PO Procurement Exec., 1978–79; Dir of Purchasing, PO, 1980; British Telecom: Dir of Procurement, 1981, Senior Dir, 1984, Chief Exec., Procurement, 1984; Dir, British Telecommunications Systems Ltd, 1982–. Chm., Fulcrum Communications Ltd, 1985–; Dir, BT&D Technologies Ltd, 1986–. Member: Council, IEE, 1975–78 and 1982– (Vice-Chm., Electronics Div., 1980–81, Dep. Chm., 1982–83, Chm., 1983–84); SERC (formerly SRC) Engrg Bd, 1977–80 (Chm., Silicon Working Party, 1980–81; Chm., Microelectronics, 1982–86); ACARD Working Party on Inf. Tech., 1981. Bulgin Premium, IERE, 1964. Liveryman, Engineers' Co. *Publications:* Low Noise Microwave Amplifiers, 1968; articles and papers on electronics. *Recreations:* photography, railways. *Address:* 4 Meades Lane, Chesham, Bucks. *T:* Chesham 785737.

FOXLEE, James Brazier; Under Secretary, Ministry of Agriculture, Fisheries and Food, 1971–81, retired; *b* 20 Nov. 1921; *s* of late Arthur Brazier Foxlee and late Mary Foxlee (*née* Fisher); *m* 1952, Vera June (*née* Guiver); one *s* two *d*. *Educ:* Brentwood Sch. Entered

Min. of Agric. and Fisheries (later MAFF) as Clerical Officer, 1938. Served War, RNVR, Ordinary Seaman, 1941; commissioned, 1942; Lieut, in comd Light Coastal Forces craft and mine-sweepers. MAFF: Exec. Officer, 1946; HEO, 1948; SEO, 1950; Principal, 1955 (Welsh Dept, 1955–57; Treas., 1961–62); Asst Sec., 1965 (Regional Controller, Leeds, 1965–69). Mem., Bristol Univ. Agricl Cttee, 1985–. Governor, Long Ashton Res. Station, 1984– (Vice-Chm., 1985–). Hon. Fellow, NIAB, 1982. *Recreations:* watching cricket, camping, oenology. *Address:* Arran, 43 Foxley Lane, Purley, Surrey CR2 3EH. *T:* 01–660 1085. *Club:* Farmers'.

FOXLEY-NORRIS, Air Chief Marshal Sir Christopher (Neil), GCB 1973 (KCB 1969; CB 1966); DSO 1945; OBE 1956; FRSA; Chairman: Cheshire Foundation, 1974–82, now Chairman Emeritus (Vice-Chairman, 1972–74); Battle of Britain Fighter Association, since 1978; Director, Brookdale Hutton & Associates, since 1974; Chairman, General Portfolio Life Assurance, since 1974; *b* 16 March 1917; *s* of Major J. P. Foxley-Norris and Dorothy Brabant Smith; *m* 1948, Joan Lovell Hughes; no *c. Educ:* Winchester; Trinity Coll., Oxford (Hon. Fellow, 1973); Middle Temple. Commissioned RAFO, 1936; France, 1940; Battle of Britain, 1940; various operational tours of duty in wartime. MA 1946. ACDS, 1963; AOC No 224 Gp, FEAF, 1964–67; Dir-Gen., RAF Organization, MoD, 1967–68; C-in-C, RAF Germany and Comdr, NATO 2nd Tactical Air Force, 1968–70; Chief of Personnel and Logistics, MoD, 1971–74; retd. Vice Pres., RUSI, 1979. Chairman: Gardening for the Disabled, 1980–; Freedom Orgn for Right to Enjoy Smoking Tobacco, 1979–; Trinity Coll. Oxford Soc., 1984–86; Ex RAF and Dependants Severely Disabled Holiday Trust, 1984. Chm., Air Costa del Sol, 1986–. CBIM. *Publications:* A Lighter Shade of Blue, 1978; various in RUSI and other service jls. *Recreations:* golf, philately. *Address:* Tumble Wood, Northend Common, Henley-on-Thames. *T:* Turville Heath 457. *Clubs:* Royal Air Force; Huntercombe (Oxon).

FOXON, David Fairweather, FBA 1978; Reader in Textual Criticism and Fellow of Wadham College, Oxford, 1968–82, now Emeritus Fellow; *b* 9 Jan. 1923; *s* of late Rev. Walter Foxon and Susan Mary (*née* Fairweather); *m* 1947, Dorothy June (marr. diss. 1963), *d* of late Sir Arthur Jarratt, KCVO; one *d. Educ:* Kingswood Sch., Bath; Magdalen Coll., Oxford. BA 1948, MA 1953. Foreign Office, 1942–45; Asst Keeper, Dept of Printed Books, British Museum, 1950–65; Harkness Fellow, 1959–61; Professor of English, Queen's Univ., Kingston, Ontario, 1965–67; Guggenheim Fellow, 1967–68. Sen. Res. Fellow, Clark Library, UCLA, 1974–75; Lyell Reader in Bibliography, Oxford, 1975–76; Sandars Reader in Bibliography, Cambridge, 1977–78. Pres., Bibliographical Soc., 1980–81 (Gold Medal, 1985). Hon. Mem., Bibliographical Soc. of America, 1986. John H. Jenkins Award for Bibliography, 1977. *Publications:* T. J. Wise and the Pre-Restoration Drama, 1959; Libertine Literature in England, 1660–1745, 1964; (ed) English Bibliographical Sources, 1964–67; English Verse 1701–1750: a catalogue, 1975; contribs to bibliographical jls. *Recreation:* music. *Address:* 7 Fane Road, Marston, Oxford OX3 0RZ. *T:* Oxford 248350.

FOXON, Harold Peter, OBE 1976; Group Managing Director, Inchcape plc, 1981–84 (Director, since 1971; a Managing Director, 1978); *b* 7 April 1919; *s* of William Henry Foxon and Kathleen Avis (*née* Perry); *m* 1948, Elizabeth Mary Butterfield; one *s* three *d. Educ:* Bancroft's. Served War, 1939–46, Royal Signals, Captain. Insurance, 1935–39; Smith Mackenzie & Co. Ltd (East Africa), 1946–69; Chm., Mackenzie Dalgety Ltd, 1966–69; Man. Dir, Gilman & Co. Ltd, Hong Kong, and Chm., Inchcape Hong Kong Ltd, 1969–77. Director: Dodwell & Co., Ltd, 1978–81; Anglo-Thai Corpn, 1978–82; Berry Trust Ltd, 1977–; Member: Hong Kong Trade Adv. Gp, 1978–84; South East Asia Trade Adv. Gp, 1978–82. *Recreation:* golf. *Address:* 48 Abingdon Court, Abingdon Villas, W8 6BT. *T:* 01–937 8713; Tanglin, Second Avenue, Frinton-on-Sea, Essex. *T:* Frinton 2208. *Clubs:* City of London, Oriental; Muthaiga (Kenya); Hong Kong (Hong Kong).

FOXTON, Maj.-Gen. Edwin Frederick, CB 1969; OBE 1959; MA; Fellow and Domestic Bursar, Emmanuel College, Cambridge, 1969–79; *b* 28 Feb. 1914; *y s* of F. Foxton and T. Wilson; unmarried. *Educ:* Worksop Coll.; St Edmund Hall, Oxford. Commissioned from General List TA, 1937; served: India, 1939–42; Middle East, 1942–45; India, 1945–47 (Chief Educn Officer, Southern Comd, India); War Office, 1948–52; Chief Instructor, Army Sch. of Educn, 1952–55; Dist Educn Officer, HQ Northumbrian District, 1955–57; War Office, 1957–60; Commandant, Army Sch. of Educn, 1961–63; War Office, 1963–65; Chief Educn Officer, FARELF, 1965; Dir of Army Educn, 1965–69. *Address:* 7 Tamar House, Kennington Lane, SE11. *Club:* United Oxford & Cambridge University.

FOYLE, Christina Agnes Lilian, (Mrs Ronald Batty); Managing Director, W. & G. Foyle Ltd; *d* of late William Alfred Foyle; *m* 1938, Ronald Batty. *Educ:* Aux Villas Unspunnen, Wilderswil, Switzerland. Began Foyle's Literary Luncheons, 1930, where book lovers have been able to see and hear great personalities. Member: Ct, Univ. of Essex; Council, RSA, 1963–69; Chm. East Anglian Region, RSA, 1978; Pres. Chelmsford District, Nat. Trust, 1979. DUniv Essex, 1975. *Publications:* So Much Wisdom, 1984; articles in various books and journals. *Recreations:* bird-watching, gardening, playing the piano. *Address:* Beeleigh Abbey, Maldon, Essex.

FOZARD, Dr John William, OBE 1981; FEng, FIMechE; FRAeS, FAIAA; Divisional Director, Special Projects, Military Aircraft Division, British Aerospace PLC, since 1984; *b* 16 Jan. 1928; *s* of John Fozard and Eleanor Paulkit; *m* 1st, 1951, Mary (marr. diss. 1985), *d* of Regtl Sgt-Major C. B. Ward, VC, KOYLI; two *s*; 2nd, 1985, Gloria Ditmars Stanchfield Roberts, *widow* of Alan Roberts, Alexandria, Va, USA. *Educ:* Univ. of London (1st Cl. Hons BScEng 1948); Coll. of Aeronautics, Cranfield (DCAe with distinction 1950). FIMechE 1971; FRAeS 1964; FAIAA 1981; FEng 1984. Hawker Aircraft Ltd: Design Engr, 1950; Head of Proj. Office, 1960; Hawker Siddeley Aviation: Chief Designer, Harrier, 1963–78; Exec. Dir, 1971; Marketing Dir, Kingston Brough Div., BAe, 1978–84. Vis. Prof., Sch. of Mechanical, Aeronautical and Production Engrg, Kingston Polytech., 1982–. Lectures: 1st J. D. North Meml, RAeS Wolverhampton Br., 1969, and 16th, 1985; 23rd R. J. Mitchell Meml, RAeS Southampton Br., 1976; 32nd Barnwell Meml, RAeS Bristol Br., 1982; 2nd Lindberg Meml, Nat. Air & Space Museum, Smithsonian Instn, Washington DC, 1978; Sir Izaac Newton series to young people around UK, IMechE, 1979–80; over 100 learned soc. lectures in UK, USA, Europe, Australia, China, 1965–. Vice Pres., 1980–85, Pres.-elect, 1985–86, Pres., 1986–87, RAeS. FRSA 1986. Hon. DSc Strathclyde, 1983. Simms Gold Medal, Soc. of Engrs, 1971; British Silver Medal for Aeronautics, 1977; James Clayton Prize, IMechE, 1983; Mullard Award (with R. S. Hooper), Royal Soc., 1983. *Publications:* papers in aeronautical jls and in specialist press, 1954–. *Recreations:* music, engineering history. *Address:* Wychbury Cottage, Warreners Lane, St George's Hill, Weybridge, Surrey KT13 0LH. *T:* Weybridge 45204.

FRAENKEL, Peter Maurice, FEng, FICE, FIStructE; Founder and Senior Partner, Peter Fraenkel & Partners, since 1972; Chairman, Peter Fraenkel International Ltd, since 1983; *b* 5 July 1915; *s* of Ernest Fraenkel and Luise (*née* Tessmann); *m* 1946, Hilda Muriel, *d* of William Norman; two *d. Educ:* Battersea Polytechnic; Imperial Coll., London. BSc(Eng). FICE 1954, FIStructE 1954, MConsE 1962; FEng 1984. Asst Engr with London firm of contractors, engaged on design and construction of marine and industrial structures, 1937–40; served in Army, 1941–42; Works Services Br., War Dept, 1942–45; Rendel, Palmer & Tritton, Cons. Engineers: Civil Engr, 1945; Sen. Engr, 1953; Partner, 1961–72. Has been responsible for, or closely associated with, technical and management aspects of many feasibility and planning studies, and planning, design and supervision of construction of large civil engrg projects, incl. ports, docks, offshore terminals, inland waterways, highways, power stations and tunnels in Gt Britain, Middle East, India, Far East and Australia, including: new Oil port at Sullom Voe, Shetland; new Naval Dockyard, Bangkok; Shatin to Tai Po coastal Trunk Road, Hong Kong; comprehensive study for DoE, of maintenance and operational needs of canals controlled by Brit. Waterways Bd (Fraenkel Report); new ore port at Port Talbot, UK, and new commercial port at Limassol, Cyprus; off-shore coal loading terminal at MacKay, Qld, and power stations at Aberthaw, Eggborough and Ironbridge, UK. James Watt Medal, 1963, Telford Gold Medal, 1971, ICE. *Publications:* (jtly) papers to Instn of Civil Engrs: Special Features of the Civil Engineering Works at Aberthaw Power Station, 1962; Planning and Design of Port Talbot Harbour, 1970. *Address:* Little Paddock, Oxted, Surrey RH8 0EL. *T:* Oxted 2927. *Club:* Athenæum.

FRAGA-IRIBARNE, Manuel; Founder-Member, Popular Alliance, Spain, 1976, Leader, since 1979; Member of the Cortes, since 1977; Leader of the Opposition, since 1982; *b* 23 Nov. 1922; *m* 1948, María del Carmen Estévez; two *s* three *d. Educ:* Insts of Coruña, Villalba and Lugo; Univs of Santiago de Compostela and Madrid. Prof. of Polit. Law, Univ. of Valencia, 1945; Prof. of Polit. Sci. and Constit. Law, Univ. of Madrid, 1953; Legal Adviser to the Cortes, 1945; entered Diplomatic Service, 1945; Sec.-Gen., Instituto de Cultura Hispánica, 1951; Sec.-Gen. in Min. of Educn, 1953; Head, Inst. of Polit. Studies, 1961; Minister of Information and Tourism, 1961–69; Ambassador to UK, 1973–75; Interior Minister, Spain, 1975–76. Holds numerous foreign orders. *Publications:* various books on law, polit. sci., history and sociology, incl. one on British Parlt. *Recreations:* shooting, fishing. *Address:* Joaquín María López 72, Madrid (15), Spain. *T:* 244 4980. *Clubs:* Athenæum, Travellers'.

FRAME, Sir Alistair (Gilchrist), Kt 1981; MA, BSc, FEng; Chairman, Rio Tinto-Zinc Corporation Ltd, since 1985; Director: Plessey Company Ltd, since 1978; Toronto Dominion Bank, since 1981; Glaxo, since 1985; *b* Dalmuir, Dunbartonshire, 3 April 1929; *s* of Alexander Frame and Mary (*née* Fraser); *m* 1953, Sheila (*née* Mathieson); one *d. Educ:* Glasgow and Cambridge Univs (Hon. Fellow, Fitzwilliam Coll., Cambridge, 1985). Director, Reactor and Research Groups, UK Atomic Energy Authority, 1964–68; joined Rio Tinto-Zinc Corp., 1968; appointed to main Board, 1973, Chief Exec. and Dep. Chm., 1978–85. Dir, Britoil, 1983–84. Member: NEB, 1978–79; Engineering Council, 1982–; Chm., Council of Mining and Metall. Instns, 1983–. *Recreations:* tennis, gardening, walking. *Address:* Pine Cottage, Holmbury St Mary, Dorking, Surrey.

FRAME, Rt. Rev. John Timothy, DD; Dean of Columbia and Rector of Christ Church Cathedral, Victoria, BC, since 1980; *b* 8 Dec. 1930; *m*; three *d. Educ:* Univ. of Toronto. Burns Lake Mission, Dio. Caledonia, 1957; Hon. Canon of Caledonia, 1965; Bishop of Yukon, 1968–80. *Address:* c/o Christ Church Cathedral, 912 Vancouver Street, Victoria, BC V8V 3V7, Canada.

FRANCE, Sir Arnold William, GCB 1972 (KCB 1965; CB 1957); retired; *b* 20 April 1911; *s* of late W. E. France; *m* 1940, Frances Margaret Linton, *d* of late Dr C. J. L. Palmer; four *d. Educ:* Bishop's Stortford Coll. District Bank, Ltd, 1929–40. Served War of 1939–45, Army, 1940–43; Deputy Economic and Financial Adviser to Minister of State in Middle East, 1943; HM Treasury, 1945; Asst Sec., 1948; Under Sec., 1952; Third Sec., 1960; Ministry of Health: Dep. Sec., 1963–64; Permanent Sec., 1964–68; Chm., Bd of Inland Revenue, 1968–73. Director: Pilkington Bros, 1973–81; Tube Investments, 1973–81; Rank Organisation, 1973–83. Chm., Central Bd of Finance, C of E, 1973–78. Chm., Bd of Management, Lingfield Hosp. Sch., 1973–81. *Address:* Thornton Cottage, Lingfield, Surrey. *T:* Lingfield 832278. *Club:* Reform.

See also J. N. B. Penny.

FRANCE, Christopher Walter, CB 1984; Second Permanent Secretary, Department of Health and Social Security, since 1986; *b* 2 April 1934; *s* of W. J. and E. M. France; *m* 1961, Valerie (*née* Larman); one *s* one *d. Educ:* East Ham Grammar Sch.; New College, Oxford (BA (PPE), DipEd). CDipAF. HM Treasury, 1959–84: Assistant Secretary, 1971; Principal Private Secretary to the Chancellor of the Exchequer, 1973–76; Under Secretary, 1976; Principal Establishment Officer, 1977–80; on secondment to Electricity Council, 1980–81; Dep. Sec., 1981; on secondment to MoD, 1981–84; Dep. Sec., DHSS, 1984–86. *Recreations:* keeping the house up and the garden down. *Address:* Brooks Grove, Halstead, Sevenoaks, Kent TN14 7EU.

FRANCIS, (Alan) David, CBE 1959; LVO 1957; *b* 2 Dec. 1900; *m* 1932, Norah Turpin; two *s. Educ:* Winchester; Magdalen Coll., Oxford (MA); Corpus Christi Coll., Cambridge (BA). Passed into General Consular Service, 1923; after course in Economics at Cambridge, appointed Vice-Consul, Antwerp, 1925; served as Vice-Consul at Rotterdam, Panama, Bogota and Prague; was also Lloyds Agent at Prague; served in FO, 1936, appointed Vice-Consul, Brussels, and Consul there, 1937. Attached to Costarican Delegation to Coronation of King George VI. Seconded as Principal in Aliens Dept, Home Office, 1940; Consul at Lisbon, 1941; Barcelona, 1942; First Sec. and Consul, Caracas, 1944; Chargé d'Affaires there, 1946; served in FO, 1947; Consul-Gen. at Danzig, 1949, New Orleans, 1951; Consul-Gen., Oporto, 1955–58; retired, 1958. Mem., Lord Chancellor's Advisory Council on Public Records, 1962–67. FRHistS. *Publications:* The Methuens and Portugal, 1966; The Wine Trade, 1972; The First Peninsular War, 1975; Portugal 1715–1808, 1985; articles in learned periodicals. *Recreation:* walking. *Address:* 21 Cadogan Street, SW3 2PP. *Club:* Travellers'.

FRANCIS, Clare Mary, MBE 1978; *b* 17 April 1946; *d* of Owen Francis, *qv*; *m* 1977, Jacques Robert Redon (marr. diss. 1985); one *s. Educ:* Royal Ballet Sch.; University Coll. London (BScEcon; Hon. Fellow, 1979). Crossed Atlantic singlehanded, Falmouth to Newport, in 37 days, 1973; placed 3rd in Round Britain Race with Eve Bonham, 1974; Azores and back, Singlehanded Race, 1975; L'Aurore Singlehanded Race, 1975; Observer Transatlantic Singlehanded Race: placed 14th, women's transatlantic singlehanded record (29 days), 1976; L'Aurore Singlehanded Race, 1976; Whitbread Round the World Race, first woman skipper, placed 5th, 1977–78. Hon. Fellow, UMIST, 1981. *Television series:* The Commanding Sea (BBC), 1981 (co-writer and presenter). *Publications:* Come Hell or High Water, 1977; Come Wind or Weather, 1978; The Commanding Sea, 1981; Night Sky (novel), 1983; Red Crystal (novel), 1985. *Recreations:* reading, music, opera. *Address:* c/o Wm Heinemann, 10 Upper Grosvenor Street, W1.

FRANCIS, David; *see* Francis, A. D.

FRANCIS, Dick, (Richard Stanley), OBE 1984; author; Racing Correspondent, Sunday Express, 1957–73; *b* 31 Oct. 1920; *s* of George Vincent Francis and Catherine Mary Francis; *m* 1947, Mary Margaret Brenchley; two *s. Educ:* Maidenhead County Boys' School. Pilot, RAF, 1940–45 (Flying Officer). Amateur National Hunt jockey, 1946–48,

Professional, 1948–57; Champion Jockey, season 1953–54. *Publications:* Sport of Queens (autobiog.), 1957, 3rd updated edn, 1982; Dead Cert, 1962; Nerve, 1964; For Kicks, 1965; Odds Against, 1965; Flying Finish, 1966; Blood Sport, 1967; Forfeit, 1968 (Edgar Allan Poe Award, 1970); Enquiry, 1969; Rat Race, 1970; Bonecrack, 1971; Smoke Screen, 1972; Slay-Ride, 1973; Knock Down, 1974; High Stakes, 1975; In the Frame, 1976; Risk, 1977; Trial Run, 1978; Whip Hand, 1979 (Golden Dagger Award, Crime Writers' Assoc., 1980); Reflex, 1980; Twice Shy, 1981; Banker, 1982; The Danger, 1983; Proof, 1984; Break In, 1985; Lester, the official biography, 1986; Bolt, 1986. *Recreations:* boating, tennis. *Address:* 5100 N Ocean Boulevard, #609, Fort Lauderdale, Florida 33308, USA. *T:* (305) 786 0838. *Clubs:* Detection, Crime Writers Association, Sportsman's, Press.

FRANCIS, Prof. Edward Howel, DSc; FRSE, FGS; Professor of Earth Sciences, University of Leeds, since 1977; *b* 31 May 1924; *s* of Thomas Howel Francis and Gwendoline Amelia (*née* Richards); *m* 1952, Cynthia Mary (*née* Williams); one *d. Educ:* Port Talbot County Sch.; Univ. of Wales, Swansea (BSc, DSc). FGS 1948; FRSE 1962. Served Army, 1944–47. Geological Survey of Great Britain (now incorporated in British Geol Survey): Field Geologist, Scotland, 1949–62; Dist Geologist, NE England, 1962–67, N Wales, 1967–70; Asst Dir, Northern England and Wales, 1971–77. Geological Society of London: Murchison Fund, 1963; Mem. Council, 1972–74; Pres., 1980–82; Pres., Section C (Geol.), BAAS, 1976; Mem., Inst. of Geol., 1978. Clough Medal, Edinburgh Geol Soc., 1983; Sorby Medal, Yorks Geol Soc., 1983. *Publications:* memoirs, book chapters and papers on coalfields, palaeovolcanic rocks and general stratigraphy, mainly of Britain. *Recreations:* opera, golf. *Address:* Michaelston, 11 Millbeck Green, Collingham, near Wetherby, W Yorks LS22 5AJ. *Club:* Sand Moor Golf.

FRANCIS, Ven. Edward Reginald; Archdeacon of Bromley, since 1979; *b* 31 Jan. 1929; *s* of Alfred John and Elsie Hilda Francis; *m* 1950, Joyce Noreen Atkins; three *s. Educ:* Maidstone and Dover Grammar Schools; Rochester Theological College. National Service, RAF, 1947–49. Insurance, including period at Chartered Insurance Inst. (ACII), 1950–59. Ordained, 1961; Chaplain, Training Ship Arethusa, and Curate of All Saints, Frindsbury, 1961–64; Vicar of St William's, Chatham, 1964–73; Vicar and Rural Dean of Rochester, 1973–78. Mem., General Synod of C of E, 1981–. Mem., Kent Industrial Mission; Jt Chm., Council for Social Responsibility, Dioceses of Canterbury and Rochester, 1983. *Recreations:* ornithology, walking, music. *Address:* 6 Horton Way, Farningham, Kent DA4 0DQ. *T:* Farningham 864522.

FRANCIS, Sir Frank (Chalton), KCB 1960 (CB 1958); FSA; FMA; Director and Principal Librarian, British Museum, 1959–68; *b* Liverpool, 5 Oct. 1901; *o s* of late F. W. Francis and Elizabeth Chalton; *m* 1927, Katrina McClennon, Liverpool; two *s* one *d. Educ:* Liverpool Inst.; Liverpool Univ.; Emmanuel Coll., Cambridge. Asst Master, Holyhead Co. Sch., 1925–26; British Museum: entered Library, 1926; Sec., 1946–47; Keeper, Dept of Printed Books, 1948–59. Lectr in Bibliography, Sch. of Librarianship and Archives, University Coll., London, 1945–59. David Murray Lectr, Univ. of Glasgow, 1957. Editor, The Library, 1936–53; Jt Editor, Jl of Documentation, 1947–68. Museums Association: Mem. Council, 1960–; Vice-Pres., 1964–65; Pres., 1965–66. Bibliographical Society: Jt Hon. Sec. (with late R. B. McKerrow), 1938–40; Hon. Sec. 1940–64; Pres., 1964–66. Library Association: Council, 1948–59; Chm. Exec. Cttee, 1954–57; Pres., 1965. President: ASLIB, 1957–58; Internat. Fedn of Library Assocs, 1963–69; Chm. Trustees, Nat. Central Library. Vice-Pres., Unesco Internat. Adv. Cttee on Bibliography, 1954–60. Chairman: Circle of State Librarians, 1947–50; Internat. Cttee of Library Experts, UN, 1948; Council, British Nat. Bibliography, 1949–59; Unesco Provisional Internat. Cttee on Bibliography, 1952; Academic Libraries Section, Internat. Fedn of Library Assocs; Anglo-Swedish Soc., 1964–68. Consultant, Council on Library Resources, Washington, DC, 1959–. Trustee, Imp. War Museum; Governor, Birkbeck Coll. Correspondant, Institut de France; Mem., Bibliographical Soc. of America, and other bibliographical socs; Corresp. Mem., Massachusetts Historical Soc.; Hon. Mem., Kungl. Gustav Adolfs Akademien; Foreign Hon. Mem., Amer. Acad. of Arts and Sciences. Master, Clockmakers' Co., 1974. Hon. Fellow: Emmanuel Coll., Cambridge; Pierpont Morgan Library, NY; Hon. FLA. Hon. LittD: Liverpool; TCD; Cambridge; Hon. DLitt: British Columbia; Exeter; Leeds; Oxford; New Brunswick; Wales. *Publications:* Historical Bibliography in Year's Work in Librarianship, 1929–38; (ed) The Bibliographical Society, 1892–1942: Studies in Retrospect, 1945; (ed) Facsimile of The Compleat Catalogue 1680, 1956; Robert Copland: Sixteenth Century Printer and Translator, 1961; (ed) Treasures of the British Museum, 1971; translations from German, including W. Cohn, Chinese Art, 1930; articles and reviews in The Library, TLS, etc. *Recreations:* golf, walking, bibliography. *Address:* The Vine, Nether Winchendon, Aylesbury, Bucks. *Clubs:* Athenæum, Royal Commonwealth Society; Grolier (New York).

FRANCIS, Gwyn Jones; Director-General and Deputy Chairman, Forestry Commission, since 1986; *b* 17 Sept. 1930; *s* of Daniel Brynmor Francis and Margaret Jane Francis; *m* 1st, 1954, Margaretta Meryl Jeremy (*d* 1985); two *s* one *d*; 2nd, 1986, Audrey Gertrude (*née* Gill). *Educ:* Llanelli Grammar Sch.; University Coll. of N Wales, Bangor (BSc Hons 1952); Univ. of Toronto (MSc 1965). Served RE, 1952–54. Forestry Commission: Dist Officer, 1954; Principal, Forester Training Sch., 1962; Asst Conservator, 1969; Head, Harvesting and Marketing Div., 1976; Comr, 1983–86. FICFor 1982; FIWSc 1984. *Recreations:* ornithology, gardening, walking. *Address:* 21 Campbell Road, Edinburgh EH12 6DT. *T:* 031–337 5037.

FRANCIS, Horace William Alexander, CBE 1976; FEng 1977; Consultant to Trafalgar Group, since 1985; Director: Trafalgar House Oil & Gas Ltd, since 1982; Census Computer Services Ltd, since 1982; Peakbeam Ltd, since 1985; *b* 31 Aug. 1926; *s* of Horace Fairie Francis and Jane McMinn Murray; *m* 1949, Gwendoline Maud Dorricott; two *s* two *d. Educ:* Royal Technical Coll., Glasgow. FICE. Dir, Tarmac Civil Engineering Ltd, 1960; Man. Dir, Tarmac Construction Ltd, 1963; Dir, Tarmac Ltd, 1964, Vice-Chm., 1974–77; Director: Trafalgar House Ltd, 1978–84; Trafalgar House Construction Hldgs, 1979–84, Dep. Chm., 1982–84; Cementation Civil and International Construction Hldgs, 1982–; Cementation Specialist Hldgs, 1982–; Cleveland Redpath Engineering Hldgs, 1982–; Trollope & Colls Hldgs, 1982–. Member: Export Guarantees Adv. Council, 1974–80; British Overseas Trade Bd, 1977–80; Chm., Overseas Projects Bd, 1977–80. Vice Pres., ICE, 1984–. *Recreations:* golf, shooting, fishing, construction. *Address:* The Firs, Cruckton, near Shrewsbury, Shropshire SY5 8PW. *T:* Shrewsbury 860796. *Clubs:* Livery, Royal Automobile.

FRANCIS, Dr John Michael; Director Scotland, Nature Conservancy Council, since 1984; *b* 1 May 1939; *s* of late William Winston Francis and of Beryl Margaret Francis (*née* Savage); *m* 1963, Eileen Sykes, Cyncoed, Cardiff; two *d. Educ:* Gowerton County Grammar Sch. for Boys; Royal Coll. of Sci., Imperial Coll. of Sci. and Tech., Univ. of London (BSc, ARCS, PhD, DIC); FRIC 1969. Res. Officer, CEGB, R&D Dept, Berkeley Nuclear Labs, 1963–70; First Dir, Society, Religion and Tech. Project, Church of Scotland, 1970–74; Sen. Res. Fellow in Energy Studies, Heriot-Watt Univ., 1974–76; Scottish Office, Edinburgh, 1976–84. Member: Oil Devlt Council for Scotland, 1973–76; Adv. Cttee for Scotland, Nature Conservancy Council, 1974–76; Indep. Commn on Transport, 1974. Consultant on Sci., Tech. and Social Ethics, WCC, Geneva, 1971–83; Chm., Sub-Cttee on Society, Religion and Tech., Church of Scotland, 1980–. *Publications:* Scotland in Turmoil, 1973; (jtly) Changing Directions, 1974; (jtly) The Future as an Academic Discipline, 1975; Facing up to Nuclear Power, 1976; (jtly) The Future of Scotland, 1977; contribs to scientific and professional jls and periodicals. *Recreations:* ecumenical travels, hill walking, theatre. *Address:* 49 Gilmour Road, Newington, Edinburgh EH16 5NU. *T:* 031–667 3996.

FRANCIS, Sir Laurie (Justice), Kt 1982; New Zealand High Commissioner to Australia, 1976–85; barrister and solicitor, High Court of New Zealand, as Consultant to Farry & Co., Commissioner of Oaths for Australian States, including Northern Territory; *b* 30 Aug. 1918; *m* 1952, Heather Margaret McFarlane; three *d. Educ:* Otago Boys High Sch.; Victoria University of Wellington; Univ. of Otago (LLB). Practised law as Barrister and Solicitor, Winton, Southland, until 1964. Hon. Life Mem., RSL. *Recreations:* golf occasionally, follower of Rugby and cricket, lover of jazz. *Address:* 42 Glengyle Street, Dunedin, New Zealand. *Club:* Dunedin (Fernhill).

FRANCIS, Norman; *see* Francis, W. N.

FRANCIS, Owen, CB 1960; Chairman, London Electricity Board, 1972–76; *b* 4 Oct. 1912; *yr s* of Sidney and Margaret Francis, The White House, Austwick, Yorks; *m* 1938, Joan St Leger (*née* Norman); two *d. Educ:* Giggleswick Sch., Yorks. Joined Govt Actuary's Dept, 1931. *Address:* Meadow Cottage, Stanford Dingley, Berks RG7 6LT. *T:* Bradfield 744394. *Clubs:* Royal Yacht Squadron; Seaview Yacht; St Moritz Tobogganing.
See also C. M. Francis.

FRANCIS, Richard Stanley; *see* Francis, Dick.

FRANCIS, Richard Trevor Langford; Director-General, British Council, from July 1987; *b* 10 March 1934; *s* of Eric Roland Francis and Esther Joy (*née* Todd); *m* 1st, 1958, Beate Ohlhagen (marr. diss.); two *s*; 2nd, 1974, Elizabeth Penelope Anne Fairfax Crone; two *s. Educ:* Uppingham Sch.; University Coll., Oxford. BA 1956, MA 1960. Commissioned in RA, 1957. BBC Trainee, 1958–60; TV: Prodn Asst, 1960–62; Producer: Afternoon Programmes, 1962–63; Panorama, 1963–65; Asst Editor: Panorama, 1965–66; 24 Hours, 1966–67; Projects Editor, Current Affairs, TV, 1967–70; Head, EBU Operations for US Elections and Apollo, 1968–69; Head of Special Projects, Current Affairs, TV, 1970–71; Asst Head, Current Affairs Group, TV 1971–73; Head, EBU Operations for US Elections, 1972; Controller, BBC NI, 1973–77; Dir, News and Current Affairs, BBC, 1977–82; Man. Dir, BBC Radio, 1982–86. Visnews: Dir, 1978; Dep. Chm., 1979–82. Mem. British Exec., IPI, 1978–, Dep. Chm., 1982–; Hon. Pres., Radio Acad., 1986–. CBIM 1984. *Recreations:* offshore sailing, photography, the children. *Address:* c/o British Council, 10 Spring Gardens, SW1A 2BN.

FRANCIS, William Lancelot, CBE 1961; *b* 16 Sept. 1906; *s* of G. J. Francis and Ethel, *d* of L. G. Reed, Durham; *m* 1st, 1937, Ursula Mary Matthew (*d* 1966); two *s* three *d*; 2nd, 1968, Margaret Morris (*d* 1978). *Educ:* Latymer Upper Sch., Hammersmith; King's Coll., Cambridge. MA, PhD. DSIR Sen. Research Award, Cambridge, 1931–33; Rockefeller Foundn Fellowship in Experimental Zoology, Rockefeller Institute, New York, 1933–34; Science Master, Repton Sch., 1935–40; Radar research and administration in Ministries of Supply and Aircraft Production (TRE Malvern), 1940–45; Dept of Scientific and Industrial Res. Headquarters, 1945–65; Secretary, Science Research Council, 1965–72; Consultant, Civil Service Dept, 1972–75. Member: Nat. Electronics Council, 1965–72; CERN, 1966–70; Advisory Councils: R&D, Fuel and Power, 1966–72; Iron and Steel, 1966–72. Mem. Council, Oxfam, 1975–83. *Publications:* papers on physical chemistry and experimental zoology in scientific jls, 1931–37. *Recreations:* gardening, travel. *Address:* 269 Sheen Lane, SW14. *T:* 01–876 3029. *Club:* Athenæum.

FRANCIS, (William) Norman; His Honour Judge Francis; a Circuit Judge (formerly Judge of County Courts), since 1969; *b* 19 March 1921; *s* of Llewellyn Francis; *m* 1951, Anthea Constance (*née* Kerry); one *s* one *d. Educ:* Bradfield; Lincoln Coll., Oxford (BCL, MA). Served War of 1939–45, RA. Called to Bar, Gray's Inn, 1946. Dep. Chm., Brecknock QS, 1962–71. Member: Criminal Law Revision Cttee, 1977–; Policy Adv. Cttee on Sexual Offences, 1977–85; County Court Rule Cttee, 1983–. Trustee, Cardiff Athletic Club. Chancellor, dio. of Llandaff, 1979–. Mem. Representative Body and Governing Body, Church in Wales. Fellow, Woodard Corp. (Western Div.), 1985–. *Recreations:* hockey, walking, golf. *Address:* 2 The Woodlands, Lisvane, near Cardiff. *T:* Cardiff 753070.

FRANCKENSTEIN, Baroness Joseph von; *see* Boyle, Kay.

FRANCKLIN, Comdr (Mavourn Baldwin) Philip, DSC 1940; RN; JP; Lord-Lieutenant of Nottinghamshire, 1972–83 (Vice-Lieutenant, 1968–72); *b* 15 Jan. 1913; *s* of Captain Philip Francklin, MVO, RN (killed in action, 1914); *m* 1949, Xenia Alexandra, *d* of Alexander Davidson, Kilpedder, Co. Wicklow; two *s* one *d* (and one *s* decd). *Educ:* RNC Dartmouth. Joined RN, 1926. Served War of 1939–45: Norway, N and S Atlantic, Indian Ocean (despatches twice); Asst to 5th Sea Lord, 1947–49; Comdr 1950; Korean War, 1950–51; Asst Naval Attaché, Paris, 1952–53. DL, 1963, JP 1958, Notts; High Sheriff of Notts, 1965. KStJ 1973. Croix de Guerre (France). *Address:* Gonalston Hall, Nottingham. *T:* Nottingham 3635. *Club:* Boodle's.

FRANÇOIS-PONCET, Jean André; Member of the French Senate, since 1983; Director, FMC Corporation, since 1982; *b* 8 Dec. 1928; *s* of André François-Poncet, Grand'Croix de la Légion d'Honneur, and Jacqueline (*née* Dillais); *m* 1959, Marie-Thérèse de Mitry; two *s* one *d. Educ:* Paris Law Sch.; Ecole Nationale d'Administration; Wesleyan Univ.; Fletcher Sch. of Law and Diplomacy. Joined Ministry of Foreign Affairs, 1955; Office of Sec. of State, 1956–58; Sec. Gen. of French delegn to Treaty negotiations for EEC and Euratom, 1956–58; Dep. Head, European Orgns, Ministry of Foreign Affairs, 1958–60; Head of Assistance Mission, Morocco, 1961–63; Dep. Head, African Affairs, 1963–65; Counsellor, Tehran, 1969–71. Professor, Institut d'Etudes Politiques, Paris, 1960–. Chm. 1971, Vice-Pres. 1972, Pres. and Chief Exec. 1973–75, Carnaud SA. Sec. of State for Foreign Affairs, Jan.-July 1976; Sec.-Gen. to Presidency of France, 1976–78; Minister for Foreign Affairs, 1978–81. President: Conseil Général of Lot-et-Garonne, 1978– (Member, from Laplume, 1967–); Comité du bassin Adour-Garonne, 1980–; Centre for Eur. Policy Studies, Brussels, 1983–. *Publication:* The Economic Policy of Western Germany, 1970. *Address:* 6 boulevard Suchet, 75116 Paris, France.

FRANCOME, John, MBE 1986; first jockey to F. T. Winter, 1975–85; *b* 13 Dec. 1952; *s* of Norman and Lillian Francome; *m* 1976, Miriam Stringer. *Educ:* Park Senior High School, Swindon. First ride, Dec. 1970; Champion Jockey (National Hunt), 1975–76, 1978–79, 1980–81, 1981–82, 1982–83, 1983–84, 1984–85; record number of jumping winners (1,036), May 1984; retired March 1985 (1138 winners). *Publication:* Born Lucky, 1985. *Recreations:* tennis, music. *Address:* Windy Hollow Stud, Lambourn, Berks. *T:* Lambourn 71058.

FRANK, Air Vice-Marshal Alan Donald, CB 1967; CBE 1962; DSO 1943; DFC 1941; Bursar, St Antony's College, Oxford, 1970–74; *b* 27 July 1917; *s* of late Major N. G. Frank and late M. H. Frank (*née* Donald); *m* 1941, Jessica Ann Tyrrell; two *s* two *d*. *Educ:* Eton; Magdalen Coll., Oxford. Commanded 51 Squadron Bomber Command, 1943; RAF Staff Coll., 1944; OC 83 Sqdn, 1957; OC RAF Honington, 1958–60; Group Captain Ops, Bomber Comd, 1960–62; Dir Operational Requirements, MoD, 1962–65; Air Attaché and OC, RAF Staff, Washington, 1965–68; SASO, RAF Air Support Command, 1968–70. *Recreations:* ski-ing, squash, tennis. *Address:* Roundway House, Devizes, Wilts.

FRANK, Sir Charles; *see* Frank, Sir F. C.

FRANK, Sir Douglas (George Horace), Kt 1976; QC 1964; President of the Lands Tribunal, since 1974; Deputy Judge of the High Court, since 1975; *b* 16 April 1916; *s* of late George Maurice Frank and late Agnes Winifred Frank; *m* 1979, Audrey, BA (Cantab), *yr d* of Charles Leslie Thomas, Neath, Glam; one *s* four *d* by a former marriage. War service in Royal Artillery. Called to the Bar, Gray's Inn, 1946 (Master of the Bench, 1970). One time Asst Commissioner, Boundary Commission for England. Mem., Cttee Public Participation in Planning (Min. Housing and Local Govt), 1968. Mem., Senate of Inns of Court and Bar, 1984–85. Chm., Planning and Local Govt Cttee of the Bar, 1966–73. Hon. Pres., Anglo-American Real Property Inst., 1980–. *Publications:* various legal. *Recreations:* theatre, music, walking. *Address:* 1 Verulam Buildings, WC1. *T:* 01–242 5949; Lands Tribunal, 48/49 Chancery Lane, WC2. *T:* 01–936 7185; La-Mayne-Longue-Haute, Sauveterre-La-Lémance, 47500 Fumel, France. *T:* (53)–71–68–98.

FRANK, Sir (Frederick) Charles, Kt 1977; OBE 1946; FRS 1954; DPhil; Henry Overton Wills Professor of Physics and Director of the H. H. Wills Physics Laboratory, University of Bristol, 1969–76 (Professor in Physics, 1954–69); now Emeritus Professor; *b* 6 March 1911; *e s* of Frederick and Medora Frank; *m* 1940, Maia Maita Asché, *y d* of late Prof. B. M. Asché; no *c*. *Educ:* Thetford Grammar Sch.; Ipswich Sch.; Lincoln Coll., Oxford. BA, BSc, Oxon. 1933; DPhil Oxon. 1937; Hon. Fellow, Lincoln Coll., 1968. Research: Dyson Perrins Laboratory and Engineering Laboratory, Oxford, 1933–36; Kaiser Wilhelm Institut für Physik, Berlin, 1936–38; Colloid Science Laboratory, Cambridge, 1939–40; Scientific Civil Service (temp.), 1940–46; Chemical Defence Research Establishment, 1940, Air Ministry, 1940–46; Research, H. H. Wills Physical Laboratory, Bristol Univ., 1946–; Research Fellow in Theoretical Physics, 1948; Reader in Physics, 1951–54; Vis. Prof., Univ. of California, San Diego, Inst. of Geophysics and Planetary Physics, and Dept of Physics, 1964–65; Raman Prof., Raman Res. Inst., Bangalore, 1979–80. A Vice-Pres., Royal Society, 1967–69. Foreign Associate, US Nat. Acad. of Engineering, 1980. Hon. FIP 1978; Hon. FIASc 1984. Hon. DSc: Ghent, 1955; Bath, 1974; TCD, 1978; Warwick, 1981; DUniv Surrey, 1977. Royal Medal, Royal Soc., 1979; Grigori Aminoff Gold Medal, Royal Swedish Acad. of Sciences, 1981; Guthrie Medal and Prize, Inst. of Physics, 1982. *Publications:* articles in various learned journals, mostly dealing either with dielectrics or the physics of solids, in particular crystal dislocations, crystal growth, mechanical properties of polymers and mechanics of the earth's crust. *Address:* Orchard Cottage, Grove Road, Coombe Dingle, Bristol BS9 2RL. *T:* Bristol 68–1708. *Club:* Athenæum.

FRANK, Ilya Mikhailovich; Professor, Moscow University, since 1940; Director, Laboratory of Neutron Physics, Joint Institute for Nuclear Research, Dubna, since 1957; *b* Leningrad, 23 Oct. 1908; *yr s* of Mikhail Lyudvigovich Frank, Prof. of Mathematics, and Dr Yelizaveta Mikhailovna Gratsianova; *m* 1937, Ella Abramovna Beilikhis, historian; one *s*. *Educ:* Moscow University (under S. I. Vavilov's guidance). Engaged by State Optical Inst. in Leningrad after graduation, 1931–34 (DSc 1935), and by P. N. Lebedev Physical Inst., USSR Acad. of Scis, Moscow, 1934, Head of Laboratory of Atomic Nucleus (from 1971 part of Inst. for Nuclear Res.), 1947–. Elected Corr. Mem. USSR Acad. of Sciences, 1946, Mem., 1968. Main works in field of optics and nuclear physics. Has participated from beginning in investigations dealing with Vavilov-Cerenkov radiation; carried out many theoretical investigations into Vavilov-Cerenkov effects and in related problems (The Doppler effect in a refractive medium, transition, radiation, etc.) and continues this research. Under his leadership research pulsed reactors of IBR type, IBR-30 with injector and IBR-2 are being developed as well as res. programmes for these pulsed neutron sources, 1957–. Awarded Nobel Prize for Physics (jointly with P. A. Cerenkov and I. E. Tamm) for discovery and interpretation of Cerenkov effect, 1958. USSR State Prize, 1946, 1954, 1971. Decorated with 3 orders of Lenin and 3 other orders. *Address:* Joint Institute for Nuclear Research, Dubna, near Moscow, USSR.

FRANK, Phyllis Margaret Duncan, (Mrs Alan Frank); *see* Tate, P. M. D.

FRANK, Sir Robert John, 3rd Bt, *cr* 1920; FRICS; late Flying Officer, RAFVR; Director, Ashdale Land and Property Co. Ltd, since 1963; *b* 16 March 1925; *s* of Sir Howard Frank, 1st Bt, GBE, KCB, and Nancy Muriel (she *m* 2nd, 1932, Air-Marshal Sir Arthur Coningham, KCB, KBE, DSO), *e d* of John Brooks; *S* brother, killed in action, 1944; *m* 1st, 1950, Angela Elizabeth (marr. diss. 1959), *e d* of Sir Kenelm Cayley, 10th Bt; two *d*; 2nd, 1960, Margaret Joyce Truesdale; one *s*. *Educ:* Shawnigan Lake, Vancouver Island; Harrow. FRICS 1951. *Heir: s* Robert Andrew Frank, *b* 16 May 1964. *Address:* Ruscombe End, Waltham St Lawrence, near Reading, Berks.

FRANKEL, Dan; *b* 18 Aug. 1900; *s* of Harris Frankel, Mile End; *m* 1921, Lily, *d* of Joseph Marks, Stepney; one *s*. Mem. LCC for Mile End Division of Stepney, 1931–46; MP (Lab) Mile End Division of Stepney, 1935–45.

FRANKEL, Prof. Herbert; *see* Frankel, Prof. S. H.

FRANKEL, Prof. Joseph; Professor of Politics, University of Southampton, 1963–78, now Emeritus; *b* 30 May 1913; *s* of Dr I. and Mrs R. Frankel; *m* 1944, Elizabeth A. Kyle (*d* 1985); one *d*. *Educ:* Univ. of Lwow, Poland (Master of Laws, 1935); Univ. of Western Australia (LLM 1948); Univ. of London (PhD Econ (Internat. Rel.) 1950). Legal Practice, Solicitor, in Poland, 1935–38. Farming in Western Australia, 1938–47; Temp. Asst Lectr, University Coll. London, 1950–51; Lectr and Sen. Lectr, Univ. of Aberdeen, 1951–62. Head of Dept of Politics, 1963–73, Dean, Faculty of Social Sciences, 1964–67, Univ. of Southampton. Res. Associate, RIAA, 1972–73. Vis. Prof., International Christian Univ., Tokyo, 1977; Vis. Fellow, Centre for Internat. Studies, Southampton, 1985–; Sen. Res. Associate, St Antony's Coll., Oxford, 1985–86. Hon. Professorial Fellow, Univ. of Wales, 1980–85. Hon. Pres., British Internat. Studies Assoc., 1973–. *Publications:* The Making of Foreign Policy, 1962, 2nd edn 1967; International Relations, 1963, 2nd edn 1969; International Politics: conflict and harmony, 1969; National Interest, 1970; Contemporary International Theory and the Behaviour of States, 1973; British Foreign Policy 1945–1973, 1975; International Relations in a Changing World, 1979; contribs to International Affairs, Brit. Jl Internat. Studies, etc. *Recreations:* gardening, literature, art and music. *Address:* Well Cottage, Lockinge, Wantage, Oxon OX12 8QD. *T:* Didcot 833114. *Club:* Athenæum.

FRANKEL, Sir Otto (Herzberg), Kt 1966; DSc; DAgr; FRS 1953; FRSNZ; FAA; Honorary Research Fellow, Division of Plant Industry, CSIRO, Canberra, Australia, since 1966; *b* 4 Nov. 1900; *m* 1939, Margaret Anderson. *Educ:* Vienna; Berlin; Cambridge. Plant Geneticist, 1929–42, and Chief Executive Officer, 1942–49, Wheat Research Institute, NZ; Dir, Crop Research Division, Dept of Scientific and Industrial Research, New Zealand, 1949–51; Chief, Division of Plant Industry, CSIRO, Australia, 1951–62; Member of Executive, Commonwealth Scientific and Industrial Research Organization, Melbourne, Aust, 1962–66. Hon. Mem., Japan Academy, 1983. *Publications:* (ed jtly) Genetic Resources in Plants: their exploration and conservation, 1970; (ed jtly) Crop Genetic Resources for Today and Tomorrow, 1975; (with M. E. Soulé) Conservation and Evolution, 1981; numerous articles in British, NZ and Australian scientific journals. *Recreations:* ski-ing, gardening, angling. *Address:* 4 Cobby Street, Campbell, Canberra, ACT 2601, Australia. *T:* 479460.

See also P. H. Frankel.

FRANKEL, Dr Paul Herzberg, CBE 1981; FInstPet; President, Petroleum Economics Ltd, since 1980 (Chairman, 1955–80); *b* 1 Nov. 1903; *s* of Ludwig and Teresa Herzberg-Frankel; *m* 1931, Helen Spitzer; one *s* four *d*. *Educ:* Vienna Univ. (Dr of Polit. Econ.). FInstPet 1941. Actively engaged in oil industry, mainly in oil refining and marketing, first on Continent and then in UK, mid 1930s-; Dir of Manchester Oil Refinery Ltd and associated cos in UK and on Continent until 1955; founded Petroleum Economics Ltd, the London internat. consulting firm, 1955. Chevalier de la Légion d'Honneur, 1976; Grosses Verdienstkreuz des Verdienstordens, Bundesrepublik Deutschland, 1977; Grosses Ehrenzeichen für Verdienste, Republik Osterreich, 1978. Cadman Medal, Inst. of Petroleum, 1973; Award for outstanding contributions to profession of energy economics and its literature, Internat. Assoc. of Energy Economists, 1985. *Publications:* Essentials of Petroleum, 1946; Oil: the facts of life, 1962; Mattei: oil and power politics, 1966. *Recreations:* walking, music. *Address:* 30 Dunstall Road, SW20 0HR. *T:* 01–946 5805. *Club:* Reform.

See also Sir O. H. Frankel.

FRANKEL, Prof. (Sally) Herbert, MA Rand, PhD London, DScEcon London, MA Oxon; Emeritus Professor in the Economics of Underdeveloped Countries, University of Oxford, and Emeritus Fellow, Nuffield College, Oxford (Professor, and Professorial Fellow, 1946–71); *b* 22 Nov. 1903; *e s* of Jacob Frankel; *m* 1928, Ilse Jeanette Frankel; one *s* one *d*. *Educ:* St John's Coll., Johannesburg; University of the Witwatersrand; London Sch. of Economics. Prof. of Economics, University of Witwatersrand, Johannesburg, 1931–46; responsible for calculations of National Income of S Africa for the Treasury, 1941–48; Jt Editor of South African Journal of Economics from its inception to 1946; Mem. of Union of South Africa Treasury Advisory Council on Economic and Financial Policy, 1941–45; Mem. of Union of South Africa Miners' Phthisis Commission, 1941–42; Commissioner appointed by Govts of Southern and Northern Rhodesia and the Bechuanaland Protectorate to report upon Rhodesia Railways Ltd, 1942–43; Chm. Commission of Enquiry into Mining Industry of Southern Rhodesia, 1945; Mem. East Africa Royal Commission, 1953–55; Consultant Adviser, Urban African Affairs Commn, Govt of S Rhodesia, 1957–58. Vis. Prof. of Econs, Univ. of Virginia, until 1974. Mem., Mont Pellerin Soc., 1950–. Chm., Bd of Governors, Oxford Centre for Postgrad. Hebrew Studies, 1983–. Hon. DSc Econ Rhodes Univ., 1969; Hon. DLitt Rand Univ., 1970. *Publications:* Co-operation and Competition in the Marketing of Maize in South Africa, 1926; The Railway Policy of South Africa, 1928; Coming of Age: Studies in South African Citizenship and Politics (with Mr J. H. Hofmeyr and others), 1930; Capital Investment in Africa: Its Course and Effects, 1938; The Economic Impact on Underdeveloped Societies: Essays on International Investment and Social Change, 1953; Investment and the Return to Equity Capital in the South African Gold Mining Industry 1887–1965: An International Comparison, 1967; Gold and International Equity Investment (Hobart Paper 45), 1969; Money: two philosophies, the conflict of trust and authority, 1977; Money and Liberty, 1980. *Recreation:* gardening. *Address:* 62 Cutteslowe House, Park Close, Oxford OX2 8NP. *T:* Oxford 514748. *Club:* Reform.

FRANKEL, William, CBE 1970; Editor, Jewish Chronicle, 1958–77; *b* 3 Feb. 1917; *s* of Isaac and Anna Frankel, London; *m* 1st, 1939, Gertrude Freda Reed (marr. diss.); one *s* one *d*; 2nd, 1973, Mrs Claire Neuman. *Educ:* elementary and secondary schs in London; London Univ. (LLB Hons). Called to Bar, Middle Temple, 1944; practised on South-Eastern circuit, 1944–55. General Manager, Jewish Chronicle, 1955–58. Special Adviser to The Times, 1977–81. Dir, Jewish Chronicle Ltd. Chairman: Mental Health Review Appeal Tribunal, 1978–; Social Security Appeal Tribunal, 1979–. Vis. Prof., Jewish Theological Seminary of America, 1968–69. JP Co. of London, 1963–69. *Publications:* (ed) Friday Nights, 1973; Israel Observed, 1980; (ed) Survey of Jewish Affairs (annual), 1982–. *Address:* 131–135 Temple Chambers, Temple Avenue, EC4Y 0DT. *T:* 01–353 0646. *Clubs:* Athenæum, MCC.

FRANKEN, Rose (Dorothy); Novelist; Playwright; *b* Texas, 28 Dec. 1895; *d* of Michael Lewin and Hannah (*née* Younker); *m* 1st, 1914, Dr S. W. A. Franken (*d* 1932); three *s*; 2nd, 1937, William Brown Melony (*d* 1970). *Educ:* Ethical Culture Sch., NYC. *Publications: novels:* Pattern, 1925; Twice Born, 1935, new edn 1970; Call Back Love, 1937; Of Great Riches, 1937 (as Gold Pennies, UK, 1938); Strange Victory, 1939; Claudia: the story of a marriage, 1939; Claudia and David, 1940; American Bred, 1941; Another Claudia, 1943; Women in White, 1945; Young Claudia, 1946; The Marriage of Claudia, 1948; From Claudia to David, 1949; The Fragile Years, The Antic Years (as The Return of Claudia, UK), 1952; Rendezvous (as The Quiet Heart, UK), 1954; (autobiography) When All is Said and Done, 1963; You're Well Out of Hospital, 1966; Swan Song, 1976; *plays:* Another Language, 1932; Mr Dooley, Jr: a comedy for children, 1932; Claudia, 1941; Outrageous Fortune, 1944; When Doctors Disagree, 1944; Soldier's Wife, 1945; Hallams, 1948; The Wing, 1971; also short stories in Colliers, Liberty, Cosmopolitan, Harper's Bazaar and anthologies.

FRANKHAM, Very Rev. Harold Edward; Provost of Southwark, 1970–82, now Provost Emeritus; *b* 6 April 1911; *s* of Edward and Minnie Frankham; *m* 1942, Margaret Jean Annear; one *s* two *d* (and one *s* decd). *Educ:* London Coll. of Divinity (LCD). Ordained, 1941; Curate: Luton, 1941–44; Holy Trinity, Brompton, 1944–46; Vicar of Addiscombe, 1946–52; Rector of Middleton, Lancs, 1952–61; Vicar of Luton, 1961–70. Hon. Canon of St Albans, 1967–70. Exec. Sec., Archbishops' Council on Evangelism, 1965–73. *Recreations:* music, travel. *Address:* Montague House, Lambridge, Bath, Avon BA1 6RX.

FRANKL, Peter; pianist; *b* 2 Oct 1935; *s* of Laura and Tibor Frankl; *m* 1958, Annie Feiner; one *s* one *d*. *Educ:* Liszt Ferenc Acad. of Music, Budapest. Regular concert tours with leading orchestras and conductors throughout the world; numerous festival appearances, including Edinburgh, Cheltenham, Lucerne, Flanders, Aldeburgh, Adelaide, Windsor. Winner of internat. competitions: Paris, 1957; Munich, 1957; Rio de Janeiro, 1959. Franz Liszt Award, Budapest, 1958. Hon. Citizen, Rio de Janeiro, 1960. Numerous recordings include: complete works for piano by Schumann and Debussy; orchestral and chamber pieces. *Recreations:* football, opera, theatre. *Address:* 5 Gresham Gardens, NW11 8NX. *T:* 01–455 5228.

FRANKLAND, family name of **Baron Zouche.**

FRANKLAND, (Anthony) Noble, CB 1983; CBE 1976; DFC 1944; MA, DPhil; historian and biographer; *b* 4 July 1922; *s* of late Edward Frankland, Ravenstonedale, Westmorland; *m* 1st, 1944, Diana Madeline Fovargue (*d* 1981), *d* of late G. V. Tavernor, of Madras and Southern Mahratta Rly, India; one *s* one *d*; 2nd, 1982, Sarah Katharine, *d* of His Honour the late Sir David Davies, QC and the late Lady Davies (Margaret Kennedy). *Educ:* Sedbergh; Trinity Coll., Oxford. Served Royal Air Force, 1941–45 (Bomber Command, 1943–45). Air Historical Branch Air Ministry, 1948–51; Official Military Historian, Cabinet Office, 1951–58. Rockefeller Fellow, 1953. Deputy Dir of Studies, Royal Institute of International Affairs, 1956–60; Dir, Imperial War Museum (at Southwark, 1960–82, Duxford Airfield, 1976–82, and HMS Belfast, 1978–82). Lees Knowles Lecturer, Trinity Coll., Cambridge, 1963. Historical advisor, Thames Television series, The World At War, 1971–74. Vice-Chm., British Nat. Cttee, Internat. Cttee for Study of Second World War, 1976–82. Biographer of His late Royal Highness The Duke of Gloucester. Mem., Council, Morley Coll., 1962–66; Trustee: Military Archives Centre, KCL, 1963–82; HMS Belfast Trust, 1971–78 (Vice-Chm., 1972–78); HMS Belfast Bd, 1978–82. *Publications:* Documents on International Affairs: for 1955, 1958; for 1956, 1959; for 1957, 1960; Crown of Tragedy, Nicholas II, 1960; The Strategic Air Offensive Against Germany, 1939–1945 (4 vols) jointly with Sir Charles Webster, 1961; The Bombing Offensive against Germany, Outlines and Perspectives, 1965; Bomber Offensive: the Devastation of Europe, 1970; (ed jtly) The Politics and Strategy of the Second World War (series), 1974–; (ed jtly) Decisive Battles of the Twentieth Century: Land, Sea, Air, 1976; Prince Henry, Duke of Gloucester, 1980; Historical Chapter in Manual of Air Force Law, 1956; other articles and reviews; broadcasts on radio and TV. *Address:* Thames House, Eynsham, Oxford. *T:* Oxford 881327.

FRANKLAND, Noble; *see* Frankland, A. N.

FRANKLIN, Albert Andrew Ernst, CVO 1965; CBE 1961 (OBE 1950); HM Diplomatic Service, retired; *b* 28 Nov. 1914; *s* of Albert John Henry Franklin; *m* 1944, Henrietta Irene Barry; two *d*. *Educ:* Merchant Taylors' Sch.; St John's Coll., Oxford. Joined HM Consular Service, 1937; served in Peking, Kunming, Chungking, Calcutta, Algiers, Marseilles, Kabul, Basle, Tientsin, Formosa, Düsseldorf and in the FO; HM Consul-General, Los Angeles, USA, 1966–74. Member of Kitchener Association. FRSA 1971. *Recreation:* chinese ceramics and paintings. *Address:* 5 Dulwich Wood Avenue, SE19. *T:* 01–670 2769.

FRANKLIN, Sir Eric (Alexander), Kt 1954; CBE 1952; *b* 3 July 1910; *s* of late William John Franklin; *m* 1936, Joy Stella, *d* of late George Oakes Lucas, Cambridge. *Educ:* The English Sch., Maymyo; Emmanuel Coll., Cambridge. Appointed to ICS in 1935 and posted to Burma; Subdivisional Officer, 1936–39. Deputy Registrar, High Court of Judicature at Rangoon, 1939–40; District and Sessions Judge, Arakan, 1941–42; Deputy Sec. to Government of Burma at Simla, 1942–45; Registrar, High Court of Judicature at Rangoon, 1946–47; retired prematurely from ICS, 1948. Appointed on contract as Deputy Sec. to Government of Pakistan. Cabinet Secretariat, 1949; Joint Sec., Cabinet Secretariat, 1952; Establishment Officer and Head of Central Organisation and Methods Office, 1953; Establishment Sec. to Government of Pakistan, 1956–58; Chm. Sudan Government Commission on terms of service, 1958–59; Civil Service Adviser to Government of Hashemite Kingdom of Jordan, 1960–63; acting Resident Representative, UN Technical Assistance Board, Jordan, 1961; Senior UN Administrative Adviser to Government of Nepal, 1964–66. Chm., Cambridgeshire Soc. for the Blind, 1969–74, Vice-Pres., 1974. FRSA 1971. El Kawkab el Urdoni (Star of Jordan), 1963. *Recreations:* walking, gardening, music. *Address:* The Birches, 16 Cavendish Avenue, Cambridge.

FRANKLIN, George Frederic; formerly Headmaster, Lincoln School, retired Dec. 1957; *b* Greenwich, 28 Dec. 1897; *s* of John and Alice Franklin; *m* 1926, Edith Kate Young; one *s* one *d*. *Educ:* Roan Sch.; King's Coll., Cambridge. Asst Master, Merchant Taylors' Sch., Crosby; Senior Mod. Langs Master, Christ's Hosp. *Publications:* French and German school texts. *Address:* Swan Hill House, Shrewsbury, Salop SY1 1NQ.

FRANKLIN, George Henry, RIBA, FRTPI; Consultant, Third World planning and development; *b* 15 June 1923; *s* of late George Edward Franklin, RN, and Annie Franklin; *m* 1950, Sylvia D. Franklin; three *s* one *d*. *Educ:* Hastings Grammar Sch.; Hastings Sch. of Art; Architectural Assoc. Sch. of Arch. (AADipl); Sch. of Planning and Research for Regional Develt, London (SPDip). Served War of 1939–45: Parachute Sqdn; RE, Europe; Bengal Sappers and Miners, SE Asia. Finchley Bor. Council, 1952–54; Architect, Christian Med. Coll., Ludhiana, Punjab, India, 1954–57; Physical Planning Adviser (Colombo Plan) to Republic of Indonesia, 1958–62, and Govt of Malaysia, 1963–64; Physical Planning Adviser, Min. of Overseas Develt, later Overseas Develt Admin, FCO, 1966–83 (Overseas Div., Building Research Station, 1966–73, ODM, later ODA, 1973–83). Hon. Prof., Dept of Town Planning, UWIST, 1982–. Commonwealth Assoc. of Planners: Mem. Exec. Cttee, 1970–; Pres., 1980–84; Hon. Sec., 1984–; Member: Exec. Cttee, Commonwealth Human Ecology Council, 1970–; Internat. Adv. Bd, Centre for Develt and Environmental Planning, Oxford Polytechnic; Bible Soc. and environmental interests and activities. Sen. Advr, Develt Planning Unit, UCL. *Publications:* papers to internat. confs and professional jls concerning planning, building and housing in the Third World. *Recreations:* work, promotion of physical planning in countries of the Third World; fly-fishing. *Address:* 24 Oakleigh Park North, N20 9AR. *T:* 01–445 0336. *Club:* Royal Commonwealth Society.

FRANKLIN, John; *see* Franklin, W. J.

FRANKLIN, Sir Michael (David Milroy), KCB 1983 (CB 1979); CMG 1972; Permanent Secretary, Ministry of Agriculture, Fisheries and Food, since 1983; *b* 24 Aug. 1927; *o s* of late Milroy Franklin; *m* 1951, Dorothy Joan Fraser; two *s* one *d*. *Educ:* Taunton Sch.; Peterhouse, Cambridge (1st cl. hons Economics). Served with 4th RHA, BAOR. Asst Principal, Min. of Agric. and Fisheries, 1950; Economic Section, Cabinet Office (subseq. Treasury), 1952–55; Principal, Min. of Agric., Fisheries and Food, 1956; UK Delegn to OEEC (subseq. OECD), 1959–61; Private Sec. to Minister of Agric., Fisheries and Food, 1961–64; Asst Sec., Head of Sugar and Tropical Foodstuffs Div., 1965–68; Under-Sec. (EEC Gp), MAFF, 1968–73; a Dep. Dir Gen., Directorate Gen. for Agric., EC, Brussels, 1973–77; Dep. Sec., Head of the European Secretariat, Cabinet Office, 1977–81; Permanent Sec., Dept of Trade, 1982–83. Governor, Henley Admin. Staff Coll., 1983. *Club:* United Oxford & Cambridge University.

FRANKLIN, Prof. Norman Laurence, CBE 1975 (OBE 1963); MSc, PhD; FRS 1981; FEng; Professor of Nuclear Engineering, Department of Chemical Engineering, Imperial College of Science and Technology, University of London, since 1984; part-time Member, UKAEA, since 1971; Director, AMEC plc, since 1985 (Chairman, AMEC Projects and Worley-Santa Fe); *b* 1 Sept. 1924; *s* of William Alexander and Beatrice Franklin; *m* 1949, Bessie Coupland; one *s* one *d*. *Educ:* Batley Grammar School; University of Leeds. British Coke Res. Assoc., 1945–48; Lecturer in Chemical Engineering, Univ. of Leeds, 1948–55; joined UKAEA, 1955; Mem. for Production, 1969–71. Man. Dir, Chief Executive and Dir, 1971–75, part-time Dir, 1975–85, British Nuclear Fuels Ltd; Chm. and Man. Dir, Nuclear Power Co. Ltd, 1975–80; Man. Dir, National Nuclear Corporation, 1980–84 (Dir, 1974–84). FEng, FIChemE (Pres. 1979). Hon. DSc Leeds, 1976. Chevalier de la Légion d'Honneur, 1984. *Publications:* Statistical Analysis in Chemistry and the Chemical Industry, 1954; The Transport Properties of Fluids, Vol. 4, Chemical Engineering Practice, 1957; Heat Transfer by Conduction, Vol. 7, Chemical Engineering Practice, 1963; papers in Trans Instn of Chemical Engineers, 1953–66. *Recreation:* walking. *Address:* Imperial College of Science and Technology, Exhibition Road, SW7; The Evergreens, Greenacre Close, Knutsford, Cheshire WA16 8NL. *T:* Knutsford 3045. *Club:* East India, Devonshire, Sports and Public Schools.

FRANKLIN, Olga Heather, CBE 1950 (MBE 1919); RRC 1946 (ARRC 1942); *b* 20 Sept. 1895; *e c* of late Robert Francis Franklin, OBE. *Educ:* St Michael's Lodge, Stoke, Devonport, VAD, 1915–17; WRNS, 1917–19; King's Coll. Hosp., 1923; Queen Alexandra's Royal Naval Nursing Service, 1927–50; Matron-in-Chief, 1947–50; King's Hon. Nursing Sister (the first appointed), 1947–50; retired, 1950. Prisoner of war, Hongkong, 1941–45. *Address:* 57 Dean Court Road, Rottingdean, Brighton BN2 7DL. *T:* Brighton 32202.

FRANKLIN, Prof. Raoul Norman, FInstP, FIMA; FIEE; CBIM; Vice Chancellor, since 1978, and Professor of Plasma Physics, since 1986, The City University, London; Fellow, Keble College, Oxford, since 1963; *b* 3 June 1935; *s* of Norman George Franklin and Thelma Brinley Davis; *m* 1961, Faith, *d* of Lt-Col H. T. C. Ivens and Eva Gray; two *s*. *Educ:* Howick District High Sch.; Auckland Grammar Sch., NZ; Univ. of Auckland (ME, DSc); Christ Church, Oxford (MA, DPhil, DSc). FInstP 1968; FIMA 1970. Officer, NZ Defence Scientific Corps, 1957–75. Sen. Res. Fellow, RMCS, Shrivenham, 1961–63; Univ. of Oxford: Tutorial Fellow, 1963–78, Dean, 1966–71, Hon. Fellow, 1980, Keble Coll.; Univ. Lectr in Engrg Science, 1966–78; Mem., Gen. Bd, 1967–74 (Vice Chm., 1971–74); Mem., Hebdomadal Council, 1971–74, 1976–78. Consultant, UKAEA Culham, 1968–. Member: UGC Equipment Sub Cttee, 1975–78; Plasma Physics Commn, IUPAP, 1971–; Science Bd, SERC, 1982–85; Exec. Council, Business in the Community, 1982–; Management Cttee, Spallation Neutron Source, 1983–86; Chairman: Internat. Science Cttee, Phenomena in Ionized Gases, 1976–77; City Techology Ltd, 1978–. Trustee, Ruskin School of Drawing, 1975–78; Mem. Council, Gresham Coll., 1981–. Liveryman, Curriers' Co., 1984–. FRSA. Freeman, City of London, 1981. Mem. Editorial Bd, Jl of Physics D, 1986–. *Publications:* Plasma Phenomena in Ionized Gases, 1976; papers on plasmas, gas discharges and granular materials. *Recreations:* tennis, walking, gardening. *Address:* The City University, Northampton Square, EC1V 0HB. *T:* 01–253 4399. *Club:* Athenæum.

FRANKLIN, Richard Harrington, CBE 1973; Consultant Emeritus to the Royal Navy (Consulting Surgeon, 1961–81); Hon. Visiting Surgeon, Royal Postgraduate Medical School (Surgeon, 1945–71); Emeritus Consultant Surgeon to Kingston and Long Grove Group of Hospitals (Surgeon, Kingston, 1946–71); *b* 3 April 1906; *s* of late P. C. Franklin; *m* 1933, Helen Margaret Kimber, *d* of Sir Henry D. Kimber, Bt; one *s* (and one *s* decd). *Educ:* Merchant Taylors' Sch.; St Thomas's Hosp., London Univ. MRCS, LRCP 1930; MB, BS 1930; FRCS 1934. First Asst, Brit. Postgrad. Med. Sch., 1936; Surgeon EMS, 1940–45; Hunterian Prof., RCS, 1947; Bradshaw Lectr, 1973; Grey-Turner Lectr, Internat. Soc. Surg., 1973; Hunterian Orator, RCS, 1977. Vis. Prof., Univ. of California, 1972. Mem. Ct of Examrs, RCS, 1956–66; Examr in Surgery, Cambridge Univ., 1958–69. Vice-Pres. 1960, Pres. 1969–70, Sect. of Surgery, RSM; Mem. Coun., RCS, 1965–77, Vice-Pres., 1974–76; Mem. Coun., Imperial Cancer Research Fund, 1967–82 (Vice-Chm., 1975–79), Life Governor, 1975. Hon. Consulting Surgeon, Star and Garter Home, Richmond, 1957–85, Governor, 1969–85. Hon. Mem., Hellenic Surgical Soc. *Publications:* Surgery of the Oesophagus, 1952; articles in various med. jls and text books. *Recreation:* sailing. *Address:* The Stern Walk, Crespigny Road, Aldeburgh, Suffolk IP15 5EZ. *T:* Aldeburgh 2600. *Clubs:* Ranelagh Sailing, Aldeburgh Yacht.

FRANKLIN, Rt. Rev. William Alfred, OBE 1964; Assistant Bishop (full time), Diocese of Peterborough, and Hon. Canon of the Cathedral, 1978–86, Canon Emeritus since 1986; *b* 16 July 1916; *s* of George Amos and Mary Anne Catherine Franklin; *m* 1945, Winifred Agnes Franklin (*née* Jarvis); one *s* one *d*. *Educ:* schools in London; Kelham Theol Coll. Deacon 1940, priest 1941, London; Curate, St John on Bethnal Green, Chaplain ATC and Univ. Settlements, 1941–43; Curate of St John's, Palmers Green, and Chm. for area Interdenominational Youth Activities, 1943–45; Asst Chaplain, St Saviour's, Belgrano, Buenos Aires, Argentina and teaching duties at Green's School, Buenos Aires, 1945–48; Rector of Holy Trinity, Lomas de Zamora, Buenos Aires, Domestic Chaplain to Bishop in Argentina, Sec. Dio. Bd of Missions, and Chaplain St Alban's Coll., Lomas, 1948–58; Rector, Canon and Sub-Dean of Anglican Cathedral, Santiago, Chaplain Grange School and Founder and Chm. Ecumenical Gp in Chile, 1958–65; Rector of St Alban's, Bogotá, Colombia, 1965–71; Archdeacon of Diocese, 1966–71; consecrated Bishop of Diocese, 1972; resigned, 1978, allowing a national to be elected. Founder and Editor of Revista Anglicana, official magazine of Arensa (Assoc. of Anglican Dioceses in North of S America). *Recreations:* fishing, tennis and cricket. *Address:* 26c The Beach, Walmer, near Deal, Kent. *T:* Deal 361807. *Clubs:* Royal Commonwealth Society; Anglo-American (Bogotá, Colombia).

FRANKLIN, (William) John, FCA; Deputy Chairman, Chartered Trust plc, since 1986 (Director, since 1982); Chairman, Howells Garages Ltd, since 1986; *b* 8 March 1927; *s* of late William Thomas Franklin and Edith Hannah Franklin; *m* 1951, Sally (*née* Davies); one *d*. *Educ:* Monkton House Sch., Cardiff. W. R. Gresty, Chartered Accountants, 1947–50; Peat Marwick Mitchell, Chartered Accountants, 1950–55; Powell Duffryn, 1956–86: Director, Cory Brothers, 1964; Man. Dir, Powell Duffryn Timber, 1967–70; Dir, 1970–86; Man. Dir and Chief Exec., 1976–85; Dep. Chm., Jan.–July 1986. *Recreation:* golf. *Address:* 80 South Road, Porthcawl, Mid Glamorgan CF36 3DA. *Club:* English-Speaking Union.

FRANKS, family name of **Baron Franks.**

FRANKS, Baron *cr* 1962, of Headington (Life Peer); **Oliver Shewell Franks,** OM 1977; GCMG 1952; KCB 1946; KCVO 1985; CBE 1942; PC 1949; DL; FBA 1960; Provost of Worcester College, Oxford, 1962–76; Chancellor of East Anglia University, 1965–84; Lord Warden of the Stannaries and Keeper of the Privy Seal of the Duke of Cornwall, 1983–85; *b* 16 Feb. 1905; *s* of late Rev. R. S. Franks; *m* 1931, Barbara Mary Tanner; two *d*. *Educ:* Bristol Grammar Sch.; Queen's Coll., Oxford (MA). Fellow and Praelector in Philosophy, Queen's College, Oxford, 1927–37; University Lecturer in Philosophy, 1935–37; Visiting Prof., Univ. of Chicago, 1935; Prof. of Moral Philosophy, University of Glasgow, 1937–45; temp. Civil Servant, Ministry of Supply, 1939–46; Permanent Sec. Ministry of Supply, 1945–46; Provost of Queen's Coll., Oxford, 1946–48; British Ambassador at Washington, 1948–52; Director: Lloyds Bank Ltd, 1953–75 (Chm., 1954–62); Schroders, 1969–84; Chm., Friends' Provident & Century Life Office, 1955–62; Cttee of London Clearing Bankers, 1960–62. Mem. of Rhodes Trust 1957–73; Chairman: Bd of Governors, United Oxford Hosps, 1958–64; Wellcome Trust, 1965–82 (Trustee, 1963–65); Commission of Inquiry into Oxford Univ., 1964–66; Cttee on Official Secrets

Act, Section 2, 1971–72; Cttee on Ministerial Memoirs, 1976; Political Honours Scrutiny Cttee, 1976–; Falkland Is Review Cttee, 1982. Mem., National Economic Development Council, 1962–64. Mem. Council, Duchy of Cornwall, 1966–85. Pres., Kennedy Memorial Cttee, 1963; Trustee: Pilgrim Trust, 1947–79; Rockefeller Foundn, 1961–70. Hon. Fellow: Queen's Coll., Oxford, 1948; St Catharine's Coll., Cambridge, 1966; Wolfson Coll., Oxford, 1967; Worcester Coll., Oxford, 1976; Lady Margaret Hall, Oxford, 1978; Visiting Fellow, Nuffield Coll., 1959. Hon. DCL, Oxford, and other Honorary Doctorates. DL Oxfordshire, 1978. *Address:* Blackhall Farm, Garford Road, Oxford OX2 6UY. *T:* Oxford 511286. *Club:* Athenæum.
See also Hon. A. E. Wright.

FRANKS, Sir Arthur Temple, (Sir Dick Franks), KCMG 1979 (CMG 1967); HM Diplomatic Service, retired; *b* 13 July 1920; *s* of late Arthur Franks, Hove; *m* 1945, Rachel Marianne, *d* of late Rev. A. E. S. Ward, DD; one *s* two *d*. *Educ:* Rugby; Queen's Coll., Oxford. HM Forces, 1940–46 (despatches). Entered Foreign Service, 1949; British Middle East Office, 1952; Tehran, 1953; Bonn, 1962; FCO, 1966–81. *Address:* Roefield, Alde Lane, Aldeburgh, Suffolk. *Clubs:* Travellers'; Aldeburgh Golf, Sunningdale Golf.

FRANKS, Cecil Simon; MP (C) Barrow and Furness, since 1983; solicitor; *b* 1 July 1935. *Educ:* Manchester Grammar Sch.; Manchester Univ. (LLB). Admitted solicitor, 1958; consultant, Cecil Franks & Co. Member: Salford City Council, 1960–74 (Leader, Cons. Gp); Manchester City Council, 1975–84 (Leader, Cons. Gp). Mem., North West RHA, 1973–75. *Address:* House of Commons, SW1A 0AA; Ivy Cottage, Satterthwaite, Cumbria.

FRANKS, Desmond Gerald Fergus; His Honour Judge Franks; a Circuit Judge, since 1972; *b* 24 Jan. 1928; *s* of F. Franks, MC, late Lancs Fus., and E. R. Franks; *m* 1952, Margaret Leigh (*née* Daniel); one *d*. *Educ:* Cathedral Choir Sch., Canterbury; Manchester Grammar Sch.; University Coll., London (LLB). Called to Bar, Middle Temple, 1952; Northern Circuit; Asst Recorder, Salford, 1966; Deputy Recorder, Salford, 1971; a Recorder of the Crown Court, 1972. Pres., SW Pennine Br., Magistrates' Assoc., 1977–. Chm., Selcare (Gtr Manchester) Trust, 1978–84, Vice-Pres., 1984–. *Recreations:* gardening, photography. *Address:* 4 Beathwaite Drive, Bramhall, Cheshire. *T:* 061–485 6065.

FRANKS, Sir Dick; *see* Franks, Sir A. T.

FRANKS, Air Vice-Marshal John Gerald, CB 1954; CBE 1949; RAF retired, 1960; *b* 23 May 1905; *e s* of late James Gordon Franks, and of Margaret, *y d* of Lord Chief Justice Gerald Fitz-Gibbon, Dublin; *m* 1936, Jessica Rae West; two *d*. *Educ:* Cheltenham Coll.; RAF Coll., Cranwell. RAF; commissioned from Cranwell, 1924; No 56 Fighter Sqdn, Biggin Hill, 1925–26; flying duties with FAA HMS Courageous, Mediterranean, 1928–29; India, 1930–35; Middle East, 1936; RAF Staff Coll., 1939; Air Armament Sch., Manby, 1941; Experimental Establishment, Boscombe Down, 1944; Dir Armament Research and Development, 1945–48; idc 1951; Comdt RAF Technical Coll., Henlow, 1952; Air Officer Commanding No 24 Group, Royal Air Force, 1952–55; Pres. of Ordnance Board, 1959–60. Comdr American Legion of Merit, 1948. *Recreations:* motoring and walking in the west of Ireland. *Address:* The Sextant, Schull, Co. Cork, Ireland.

FRASER, family name of **Barons Fraser of Kilmorack, Fraser of Tullybelton,** and **Lovat, Lady Saltoun,** and **Baron Strathalmond.**

FRASER OF ALLANDER; Barony of (*cr* 1964); title disclaimed by 2nd Baron; *see under* Fraser, Sir Hugh, 2nd Bt.

FRASER OF KILMORACK, Baron *cr* 1974 (Life Peer), of Rubislaw, Aberdeen; **Richard Michael Fraser,** Kt 1962; CBE 1955 (MBE 1945); Director: Glaxo Trustees Ltd, since 1975; Whiteaway Laidlaw Co. Ltd, since 1981; *b* 28 Oct. 1915; *yr s* of late Dr Thomas Fraser, CBE, DSO, TD, DL, LLD, Aberdeen and Maria-Theresia Kayser, Hanover; *m* 1944, Elizabeth Chloë, *er d* of late Brig. C. A. F. Drummond, OBE; one *s* (and one *s* decd). *Educ:* Aberdeen Grammar Sch.; Fettes; King's Coll., Cambridge. Begg Exhibition, 1934; James Essay Prize, 1935; BA Hons History, 1937; MA 1945. Served War of 1939–45 (RA); 2nd Lieut 1939; War Gunnery Staff Course, 1940; Capt. Feb. 1941; Major, June 1941; Lieut-Col (GSO1) 1945. Joined Conservative Research Dept, 1946; Head of Home Affairs Sect., 1950–51; Jt Dir, 1951–59, Dir, 1959–64, Chm., 1970–74; Dep. Chm., Cons. Party Orgn, 1964–75; Dep. Chm., Conservative Party's Adv. Cttee on Policy, 1970–75 (Sec., Aug. 1951–Oct. 1964); Sec. to the Conservative Leader's Consultative Cttee (Shadow Cabinet), Oct. 1964–June 1970 and March 1974–75. Director: Glaxo Holdings plc, 1975–85; Glaxo Gp Ltd, 1985; Glaxo Enterprises Inc., USA, 1983–85. Smith-Mundt Fellowship, USA, 1952. Mem. Council, Imperial Soc. of Knights Bachelor, 1971–. Pres., Old Fettesian Assoc., 1977–80. *Recreations:* reading, music, opera, ballet, travel; collecting and recollecting. *Address:* 18 Drayton Court, Drayton Gardens, SW10 9RH. *T:* 01–370 1543. *Clubs:* Brooks's, Carlton, St Stephen's Constitutional (Hon. Mem.); Coningsby (Hon. Mem.).

FRASER OF TULLYBELTON, Baron *cr* 1974 (Life Peer), of Bankfoot; **Walter Ian Reid Fraser,** PC 1974; a Lord of Appeal in Ordinary, 1975–85; Member of the Queen's Body Guard for Scotland (Royal Company of Archers); *b* 3 Feb. 1911; *o s* of late Alexander Reid Fraser, stockbroker, Glasgow; *m* 1943, (Mary Ursula) Cynthia (Gwendolen), *o d* of Col I. H. Macdonell, DSO (late HLI); one *s*. *Educ:* Repton; Balliol Coll., Oxford (scholar; Hon. Fellow, 1981). BA Oxon 1932; LLB Glasgow 1935; Advocate, 1936; QC Scotland 1953. Lecturer in Constitutional Law, Glasgow Univ., 1936; and at Edinburgh Univ., 1948. Served Army (RA and staff), 1939–45; UK; Burma. Contested (U) East Edinburgh constituency, Gen. Election, 1955. Mem. Royal Commission on Police, 1960. Dean of the Faculty of Advocates, 1959–64; a Senator of HM Coll. of Justice in Scotland, 1964–74. Hon. LLD: Glasgow, 1970; Edinburgh, 1978. Hon. Master of the Bench, Gray's Inn, 1975. *Publication:* Outline of Constitutional Law, 1938 (2nd edn, 1948). *Recreations:* shooting, walking. *Address:* Tullybelton House, Bankfoot, Perthshire. *T:* Bankfoot 312. *Clubs:* Garrick; New (Edinburgh).

FRASER, Alexander Macdonald, AO 1981; PhD; FAIM, FTS; Director, Queensland Institute of Technology, 1966–81, Life Fellow 1981; *b* 11 March 1921; *s* of late John Macdonald Fraser and of Esther Katie Fraser; *m* 1951, Rita Isabel Thomason; one *s*. *Educ:* Church of England Grammar Sch., Brisbane; Univ. of Queensland (BE); Imperial Coll. of Science and Technology, Univ. of London (DIC, PhD). MIE(Aust). Military service, 1942–45 (despatches, New Guinea, 1944). Engineer: British Malayan Petroleum Co., 1947–50; Irrigation and Water Supply Commission, Qld, 1951–54 and 1957–65; Research, Imperial Coll. of Science and Technology, 1954–57. *Recreation:* golf. *Address:* 3 Wynyard Street, Indooroopilly, Qld 4068, Australia. *T:* 370.7945. *Club:* Indooroopilly Golf (Brisbane).

FRASER, Sir Angus (McKay), KCB 1985 (CB 1981); TD 1965; Chairman, Board of Customs and Excise, since 1983; *b* 10 March 1928; *s* of late Thomas Douglas Fraser; *m* 1955, Margaret Neilson (marr. diss. 1968); one *s* one *d*. *Educ:* Falkirk High Sch.; Glasgow Univ.; Bordeaux Univ. Nat. Service in RA, 1950–52; 44 Parachute Bde (TA), 1953–66. Asst Principal, HM Customs and Excise, 1952; Principal, 1956; HM Treasury, 1961–64;

Asst Sec., HM Customs and Excise, 1965; Under-Sec. and Comr of Customs and Excise, 1972; Under-Sec., CSD, 1973; Comr of Customs and Excise, 1976; Dep. Chm., Bd of Customs and Excise, 1978; Dep. Sec., CSD, subseq. MPO, 1980–83; First CS Comr, 1981–83. Chm., Civil Service, PO and BT Lifeboat Fund, 1986–; Mem., Cttee of Management, RNLI, 1986–. FRSA 1985; FIPM 1986. Vice-Pres., RIPA, 1985–. *Publications:* (ed) A Journey to Eastern Europe in 1844, 1981; (ed) George Borrow's Letters to John Hasfeld 1835–1839, 1982, 1841–1846, 1984; (with M. Collie) George Borrow, a Bibliographical Study, 1984; articles and reviews in jls and encyclopedias, 1950–. *Recreations:* old inns, literary research, book collecting. *Address:* 84 Ennerdale Road, Kew, Richmond, Surrey TW9 2DL. *T:* 01–940 9913. *Clubs:* Reform, City Livery.

FRASER, Air Cdre Anthony Walkinshaw; Director, Society of Motor Manufacturers and Traders, since 1980; *b* 15 March 1934; *s* of late Robert Walkinshaw Fraser and Evelyn Elisabeth Fraser; *m* 1955, Angela Mary Graham Shaw; one *s* three *d*. *Educ:* Stowe Sch. FBIM, MIL. RAF Pilot and Flying Instructor, 1952–66; sc Camberley, 1967; MA/VCDS, MoD, 1968–70; Chief Instructor Buccaneer OCU, 1971–72; Air Warfare Course, 1973; Directing Staff, National Defence Coll., 1973; Dep. Dir, Operational Requirements, MoD, 1974–76; Comdt, Central Flying Sch., 1977–79. ADC to the Queen, 1977–79. President: Comité de Liaison de la Construction Automobile, 1980–83; Bureau Perm. Internat. des Constructeurs d'Automobiles, 1983– (Vice-Pres., 1981–83). FRSA. *Recreations:* shooting, golf, fishing, languages. *Address:* The Society of Motor Manufacturers and Traders Ltd, Forbes House, Halkin Street, SW1X 7DS. *T:* 01–235 7000. *Clubs:* Boodle's, Royal Air Force, Sunningdale.

FRASER, Lady Antonia, (Lady Antonia Pinter); FRSL 1983; writer; *b* 27 Aug. 1932; *d* of 7th Earl of Longford, *qv*, and Countess of Longford, *qv*; *m* 1st, 1956, Rt Hon. Sir Hugh Charles Patrick Joseph Fraser, MBE, MP (*d* 1984) (marr. diss. 1977); three *s* three *d*; 2nd, 1980, Harold Pinter, *qv*. *Educ:* Dragon School, Oxford; St Mary's Convent, Ascot; Lady Margaret Hall, Oxford. General Editor, Kings and Queens of England series. Member: Arts Council, 1970–72; Cttee, English PEN, 1979–; Chairman: Soc. of Authors, 1974–75; Crimewriters' Assoc., 1985–86. Hon. DLitt Hull, 1986. *Publications:* (as Antonia Pakenham): King Arthur and the Knights of the Round Table, 1954 (reissued, 1970); Robin Hood, 1955 (reissued, 1971); (as Antonia Fraser): Dolls, 1963; A History of Toys, 1966; Mary Queen of Scots (James Tait Black Memorial Prize, 1969), 1969 (reissued illus. edn, 1978); Cromwell Our Chief of Men, (in USA, Cromwell the Lord Protector), 1973; King James: VI of Scotland, I of England, 1974; (ed) Kings and Queens of England, 1975; (ed) Scottish Love Poems, a personal anthology, 1975; (ed) Love Letters: an anthology, 1976; Quiet as a Nun (mystery), 1977, adapted for TV series, 1978; The Wild Island (mystery), 1978; King Charles II, (in USA, Royal Charles), 1979; (ed) Heroes and Heroines, 1980; A Splash of Red (mystery), 1981 (basis for TV series Jemima Shore Investigates, 1983); (ed) Mary Queen of Scots: poetry anthology, 1981; (ed) Oxford and Oxfordshire in Verse: anthology, 1982; Cool Repentance (mystery), 1982; The Weaker Vessel: woman's lot in seventeenth century England, 1984 (Wolfson History Prize, 1984; Prix Caumont-La Force, 1985); Oxford Blood (mystery), 1985; Jemima Shore's First Case (mystery short stories), 1986; various mystery stories in anthols, incl. Have a Nice Death, 1983 (adapted for TV, 1984); TV plays: Charades, 1977; Mister Clay, Mister Clay (Time for Murder series), 1985. *Recreations:* swimming, life in the garden. *Address:* c/o Curtis Brown, 162–168 Regent Street, W1R 5TB. *Club:* PEN.

FRASER, Sir Basil (Malcolm), 2nd Bt, *cr* 1921; *b* 2 Jan. 1920; *s* of Sir (John) Malcolm Fraser, 1st Bt, GBE, and of Irene, *d* of C. E. Brightman of South Kensington; *S* father, 1949. *Educ:* Northaw, Pluckley, Kent; Eton Coll.; Queens' Coll., Cambridge (MA 1950). Served War of 1939–45, RE, 1940–42; Madras Sappers and Miners, 1942–46 (despatches). Mem. AA and RAC. *Recreations:* motoring, music, electronic reproduction of sound. *Heir:* none. *Address:* 175 Beach Street, Deal, Kent CT14 6LE. *Club:* Roadfarers'.

FRASER, Sir Bruce (Donald), KCB 1961 (CB 1956); *b* 18 Nov. 1910; *s* of late Maj.-Gen. Sir Theodore Fraser, KCB and late Constance Ruth Fraser (*née* Stevenson); *m* 1939, Audrey (*d* 1982), *d* of late Lieut-Col E. L. Croslegh; one *s* one *d* decd. *Educ:* Bedford Sch.; Trinity Coll., Cambridge (Scholar); First Class in Classical Tripos Part I, 1930 and in English Tripos Part II, 1932; BA 1932, MA 1964. Ed. the Granta, 1932. Entered Civil Service as Asst Principal, Scottish Office, 1933; transf. to HM Treasury, 1936; Private Sec. to Financial Sec., 1937, and to Permanent Sec., 1941; Asst Sec., 1945; Under Sec., 1951; Third Sec., 1956–60; Dep. Sec., Ministry of Aviation, Jan.-April 1960; Permanent Sec., Ministry of Health, 1960–64; Joint Permanent Under-Sec. of State, Dept of Education and Science, 1964–65; Permanent Sec., Ministry of Land and Natural Resources, 1965–66; Comptroller and Auditor-General, Exchequer and Audit Dept, 1966–71. *Publication:* Sir Ernest Gowers' The Complete Plain Words, rev. edn 1973. *Address:* Jonathan, St Dogmael's, Cardigan SA43 3LF. *T:* Cardigan 612387. *Club:* Athenæum.

FRASER, Sir Campbell; *see* Fraser, Sir J. C.

FRASER, Charles Annand, CVO 1985 (LVO 1968); DL; WS; Partner, W. & J. Burness, WS, Edinburgh; *b* 16 Oct. 1928; *o s* of late Very Rev. John Annand Fraser, MBE, TD; *m* 1957, Ann Scott-Kerr; four *s*. *Educ:* Hamilton Academy; Edinburgh Univ. (MA, LLB). Purse Bearer to Lord High Commissioner to General Assembly of Church of Scotland, 1969–. Chm., Morgan Grenfell (Scotland), 1985–86; Director: United Biscuits (Holdings) Ltd, 1978– (non-exec. Vice-Chm., 1986–); Scottish Widows' Fund, 1978–; British Assets Trust, 1969–; Scottish Television Ltd, 1979–, and other companies. Trustee, Scottish Civic Trust, 1978–; Mem. Council, Law Society of Scotland, 1966–72; Governor of Fettes, 1976–; Mem. Court, Heriot-Watt Univ., 1972–78. WS 1959; DL East Lothian, 1984–. *Recreations:* gardening, skiing, squash, piping. *Address:* Shepherd House, Inveresk, Midlothian. *T:* 031–665 2570. *Clubs:* New, Hon. Co. of Edinburgh Golfers (Edinburgh); Royal and Ancient (St Andrews).

FRASER, Maj.-Gen. Colin Angus Ewen, CB 1971; CBE 1968; General Officer Commanding, Southern Command, Australia, 1971–74; retired March 1974; *b* Nairobi, Kenya, 25 Sept. 1918; *s* of A. E. Fraser, Rutherglen, Vic.; *m* 1942, Dorothy, *d* of A. Champion; two *s* one *d*. *Educ:* Johannesburg; Adelaide High Sch.; RMC, Duntroon (grad. 1938); Melbourne Univ. (BA). Served War of 1939–45: UK, Middle East, Pacific. Staff Coll., Camberley, 1946; Dep. Comdr, Commonwealth Div., Korea, 1955–56; Dir, Military Trng, 1957–58; Services Attaché, Burma, 1960–62; Chief of Staff, Northern Command, Brisbane, 1964–68; Commandant, Royal Military Coll., Duntroon, 1968–69; Commander, Australian Force, Vietnam, 1970–71. *Address:* 107 Orana Road, Ocean Shores, Brunswick Heads, NSW 2483, Australia. *Clubs:* Tasmanian (Hobart); United Services (Qld).

FRASER, Gen. Sir David (William), GCB 1980 (KCB 1973); OBE 1962; DL; retired; *b* 30 Dec. 1920; *s* of Brig. Hon. William Fraser, DSO, MC, *y s* of 18th Lord Saltoun and Pamela, *d* of Cyril Maude and *widow* of Major W. La T. Congreve, VC, DSO, MC; *m* 1st, 1947, Anne Balfour; one *d*; 2nd, 1957, Julia de la Hey; two *s* two *d*. *Educ:* Eton; Christ Church, Oxford. Commnd into Grenadier Guards, 1941; served NW Europe; comd 1st Bn Grenadier Guards, 1960–62; comd 19th Inf. Bde, 1963–65; Dir, Defence Policy, MoD, 1966–69; GOC 4 Div., 1969–71; Asst Chief of Defence Staff (Policy), MoD,

1971–73; Vice-Chief of the General Staff, 1973–75; UK Mil. Rep. to NATO, 1975–77; Commandant, RCDS, 1978–80; ADC General to the Queen, 1977–80. Col, The Royal Hampshire Regt, 1981–. DL Hants, 1982. *Publications:* Alanbrooke, 1982; And We Shall Shock Them, 1983; The Christian Watt Papers, 1983; August 1988, 1983; A Kiss for the Enemy, 1985; The Killing Times, 1986. *Recreation:* shooting. *Address:* Vallenders, Isington, Alton, Hants. *T:* Bentley 23166. *Clubs:* Turf, Pratt's.

FRASER, Donald Blake, FRCS; FRCOG; Gynæcologist and Obstetrician, St Bartholomew's Hospital, 1946–75; retired 1978; *b* 9 June 1910; *o s* of Dr Thomas B. Fraser, Hatfield Point, NB, Canada; *m* 1939, Betsy, *d* of late Sir James Henderson, KBE; one *s* one *d. Educ:* University of New Brunswick; Christ Church, Oxford. Rhodes Scholar, 1930; BA 1st Cl. Hons, 1932, BM, BCh Oxon 1936; MRCS, LRCP, LMCC, 1936; FRCS, 1939; MRCOG, 1940, FRCOG, 1952. Former Examiner: Central Midwives Bd; Universities of Oxford and London; Conjoint Bd; Royal College of Obstetricians and Gynæcologists. *Publications:* (joint) Midwifery (textbook), 1956. Articles in medical journals. *Recreation:* philately. *Address:* Vine House, 6 Hampstead Square, NW3 1AB.

FRASER, Donald Hamilton, RA 1985 (ARA 1975); artist; Hon. Fellow, Royal College of Art, 1984; Member, Royal Fine Art Commission, since 1986; *b* 30 July 1929; *s* of Donald Fraser and Dorothy Christiana (*née* Lang); *m* 1954, Judith Wentworth-Sheilds; one *d. Educ:* Maidenhead Grammar Sch.; St Martin's Sch. of Art, London; Paris (French Govt Scholarship). Tutor, Royal Coll. of Art, 1958–83, Fellow 1970. Has held 40 one-man exhibitions in Britain, Europe and N America. Work in public collections includes: Museum of Fine Arts, Boston; Albright-Knox Gall., Buffalo; Carnegie Inst., Pittsburgh; City Art Museum, St Louis; Wadsworth Athenaeum, Hartford, Conn; Hirshhorn Museum, Washington, DC; Yale Univ. Art Museum; Palm Springs Desert Museum; Nat. Gall. of Canada, Ottawa; Nat. Gall. of Vic, Melbourne; many corporate collections and British provincial galleries; Arts Council, DoE, etc. Designed Commonwealth Day issue of postage stamps, 1983. Chm. and Vice-Pres. Artists Gen. Benevolent Inst., 1981–; Vice-Pres., Royal Over-Seas League, 1986–. *Publication:* Gauguin's 'Vision after the Sermon', 1969. *Address:* Bramham Cottage, Remenham Lane, Henley-on-Thames, Oxon RG9 2LR. *T:* Henley-on-Thames 574253.

FRASER, Sir Douglas (Were), Kt 1966; ISO 1962; Fellow, Royal Institute of Public Administration (Queensland); Honorary Fellow: Queensland Conservatorium of Music; Institute of Ambulance Officers (Australia); *b* 24 Oct. 1899; *s* of late Robert John Fraser and late Edith Harriet (*née* Shepherd); *m* 1927, Violet Pryke (*d* 1968); three *s. Educ:* State High Sch., Gympie, Qld. Entered Qld State Public Service, 1916; Public Service Board and Public Service Comr's Dept; Sec. to Public Service Comr, 1939; Sen. Public Service Inspector, 1947; Dep. Public Service Comr, 1952; Public Service Comr, 1956; retired 1965; War-time Asst Dir of Civil Defence, Sec., Public Safety Adv. Cttee. Mem. Senate, Univ. of Queensland, 1956–74; Chm. Council, Qld Conservatorium of Music, 1971–79; Pres., Qld Ambulance Transport Brigade Council, 1967–80. *Recreations:* gardening, fishing, music, reading. *Address:* 76 Prince Edward Parade, Redcliffe, Qld 4020, Australia. *T:* 203 4393.

FRASER, Edward; see Fraser, J. E.

FRASER, George MacDonald; author and journalist; *b* 2 April 1925; *s* of late William Fraser, MB, ChB and Anne Struth Donaldson; *m* 1949, Kathleen Margarette, *d* of late George Hetherington, Carlisle; two *s* one *d. Educ:* Carlisle Grammar Sch.; Glasgow Academy. Served in British Army, 1943–47: Infantryman XIVth Army, Lieut Gordon Highlanders. Newspaperman in England, Canada and Scotland from 1947; Dep. Editor, Glasgow Herald, 1964–69. *Publications:* Flashman, 1969; Royal Flash, 1970; The General Danced at Dawn, 1970; The Steel Bonnets, 1971; Flash for Freedom!, 1971; Flashman at the Charge, 1973; McAuslan in the Rough, 1974; Flashman in the Great Game, 1975; Flashman's Lady, 1977; Mr American, 1980; Flashman and the Redskins, 1982; The Pyrates, 1983; Flashman and the Dragon, 1985; *film screenplays:* The Three Musketeers, 1974; The Four Musketeers, 1975; Royal Flash, 1975; The Prince and the Pauper, 1977; Octopussy, 1983; Red Sonja, 1985. *Recreations:* snooker, talking to wife, history, singing. *Address:* Baldrine, Isle of Man.

FRASER, Air Marshal Rev. Sir (Henry) Paterson, KBE 1961 (CBE 1945); CB 1953; AFC 1937; RAF, retired; ordained 1977; Concrete Consultant; *b* 15 July 1907; *s* of late Harry Fraser, Johannesburg, South Africa; *m* 1933, Avis Gertrude Haswell; two *s. Educ:* St Andrews Coll., Grahamstown, South Africa; Pembroke Coll., Cambridge (MA), RAFO, and Pres. University Air Sqdn, Cambridge; joined RAF, 1929; served in India; RAF Engineering Course, Henlow, 1933–34; Aerodynamic Flight, RAE, Farnborough, 1934–38; RAF Staff Coll., 1938; Directorate of War Organization, Air Ministry, 1939–40; commanded Experimental Flying Section, RAE, Farnborough, 1941; Mem. RAF Element, Combined Chiefs of Staff, Washington DC, 1942; Dep. Dir of War Organization, Air Ministry, 1943; Senior Administrative Planner, 2nd Tactical Air Force, 1943–44, and Dep. Air Officer in Charge of Administration, 2nd TAF, 1944–45; commanded Aircraft and Armament Experimental Establishment, Boscombe Down, 1945–46; Dep. Dir (Air Staff) Policy, Air Ministry, 1947–48; Defence Research Policy Staff, Ministry of Defence, 1948–51; idc 1951; Senior Air Staff Officer, Headquarters Fighter Command, 1952–53; Chief of Staff, Headquarters Allied Air Forces, Central Europe, 1954–56; AOC No. 12 Group, Fighter Command, 1956–58; Dir, RAF Exercise Planning, 1959; UK Representative on Permanent Military Deputies Group of Cento, 1959–62; Inspector-Gen., RAF, 1962–64. Taylor Gold Medal of RAeS, 1937; FRAeS. *Address:* 803 King's Court, Ramsey, Isle of Man.

FRASER, Sir Hugh, 2nd Bt *cr* 1961, of Dineiddwg; Chairman, since 1982, and Joint Managing Director, since 1985, Sir Hugh & Sir Group; *b* 18 Dec. 1936; *s* of 1st Baron Fraser of Allander, DL, LLD, JP (Bt 1961) and of Kate Hutcheon, *d* of late Sir Andrew Lewis, LLD, JP; *S* to father's Btcy, and disclaimed Barony, 1966; *m* 1st, 1962, Patricia Mary (marr. diss. 1971), *e d* of John Bowie; three *d*; 2nd, 1973, Aileen Ross (marr. diss. 1982; she *d* 1984). *Educ:* St Mary's, Melrose; Kelvinside Academy. Director: Allander Hldgs Ltd; Ettinger Brothers (Tailoring) Ltd; Fras-air Ltd; Glen Gordon Knitwear Ltd; Internat. Caledonian Assets Ltd; Paisleys Ltd; North Cape Textiles Ltd; D & S Shirts Ltd; Black Bear Ltd; Twentieth Century Fashions Ltd; Zucker Textiles Ltd; Air Charter Scotland Ltd; Sir Shops Ltd; Hebridean Herbals Ltd, Caird Retail Ltd. Hon. Dr Stirling, 1985. *Recreations:* farming, show jumping. *Address:* Middleton of Mugdock, near Milngavie, Dunbartonshire.

FRASER, Col Hugh Vincent, CMG 1957; OBE 1946; TD 1947; retired 1960; *b* 20 Sept. 1908; *yr s* of William Neilson and Maude Fraser; *m* 1941, Noreen, *d* of Col M. O'C. Tandy; one *s* one *d. Educ:* Sherborne Sch. Commissioned into Royal Tank Regt; served War of 1939–45, India and Burma, with 14th Army. Military Attaché, Cairo, 1954–56; NATO, Washington DC, 1957–60. *Recreations:* hunting, shooting; Master Aldershot Command Beagles, 1939. *Address:* Cheyney Holt, Steeple Morden, Cambs.

FRASER, Sir Ian, Kt 1963; DSO 1943; OBE 1940; DL; FRSE, FRCS, FRCSI, FACS; Consulting Surgeon, Belfast; Senior Surgeon: Royal Victoria Hospital, Belfast, 1955–66;

Royal Belfast Hospital for Sick Children, 1955–66; Director: Provincial Bank of Ireland; Allied Irish Bank; *b* 9 Feb. 1901; *s* of Robert Moore Fraser, BA, MD, Belfast; *m* 1931, Eleanor Margaret Mitchell; one *s* one *d. Educ:* Royal Academical Institution, Belfast; Queen's Univ., Belfast. MB, BCh 1st Cl. Hons 1923; MD 1932; MCh 1927; FRCSI 1926; FRCS 1927; FRSE 1938; FACS 1945. Coulter Schol.; McQuitty Schol.; 1st place in Ire. as FRCSI. Resident Surgical Officer, St Helen's, Lancs; Surgeon: Royal Belfast Hosp. for Sick Children; Royal Victoria Hosp., Belfast, and former Asst Prof. of Surgery. Served War: (overseas) 1940–45 · in W Africa, N. Africa, Sicily, Italy (OBE, DSO, Salerno); invasion of France, India; Officer in charge of Penicillin in Research Team, N Africa; Brig. 1945. Hon. Col (TA): No 204 Gen. Hosp., 1961–71; No 4 Field Amb., 1948–71; Surgeon in Ordinary to the Governor of Northern Ireland; Hon. Cons. Surg. to the Army in NI; Chm., Police Authority, Royal Ulster Constabulary, 1970–76; Mem. Adv. Council, Ulster Defence Regt. Past President: RCSI (1956–57); Assoc. of Surgeons GB and Ireland (1957); BMA (1962–63); Irish Med. Graduates Assoc., London, Queen's Univ. Assoc., London; Services Club, QUB; Ulster Med. Soc. President: Ulster Surgical Club; Queen's Univ. Assoc., Belfast; Chm of Convocation and Mem. Senate QUB. Visiting Lecturer: Leicester, Birmingham, Edinburgh, Bradford, London, Sheffield, Dublin, Cheltenham, Rochester, New York, Copenhagen, Glasgow, Manchester, Middlesex Hosp., Bristol, Barnsley, etc; Delegate to various assocs abroad. John Snow Oration, 1967; Downpatrick Hosp. Bi-Centenary Oration, 1967; Bishop Jeremy Taylor Lecture, 1970; Maj.-Gen. Philip Mitchiner Lecture, 1971; Robert Campbell Orator, 1973; David Torrens Lectr, NUU, 1981; Thos Vicary Lecture, RCS, 1983. Visiting Examiner in Surgery: Liverpool, Cambridge, and Manchester Univs; NUI; Apothecaries' Hall, Dublin; TCD; RCS in Ire.; RCS of Glasgow, Councillor, RCSI; Mem. and Trustee, James IV Assoc. of Surgeons; Mem., Health Educn Cttee, Min. of Health, London; Fellow: BMA; Roy. Soc. Med. Lond.; Roy. Irish Acad. of Med.; Hon. FRCPGlas 1972; Hon. FRCSE; Hon. FRCPI 1977; Hon. Fellow: Brit. Assoc. of Paediatric Surgeons; Ulster Med. Soc., 1977; Foreign Mem., L'Académie de Chirurgie, Paris; Hon. Mem., Danish Assoc. of Surgery, Copenhagen; Mem., Internat. Soc. of Surgeons. Hon. Life Governor, Royal Victoria Hosp., Belfast; Governor for GB, Amer. Coll. Surgeons. Hon. DSc: Oxon, 1963; New Univ. of Ulster, 1977. GCStJ 1974 (KStJ 1940); Mem., Chapter General, London, and Knight Commander of Commandery of Ards, Ulster, Order of St John. DL Belfast, 1955. Gold Medal: Ulster Hosp. for Women and Children; Royal Belfast Hosp. for Sick Children. Commander: Ordre de la Couronne (Belgium) 1963; Order of Orange Nassau, 1969; Ordre des Palmes Académiques, 1970; Chevalier de la Legion d'Honneur, France, 1981. *Publications:* various monographs on surgical subjects. *Recreations:* golf, formerly hockey and rugby. *Address:* (residence) 19 Upper Malone Road, Belfast. *T:* Belfast 668235; (consulting rooms) 35 Wellington Park, Belfast BT9 6DN. *T:* Belfast 665543. *Clubs:* Ulster, Malone Golf (Belfast).

FRASER, Lt-Comdr Ian Edward, VC 1945; DSC 1943; RD and Bar 1948; JP; (former Managing Director, Universal Divers Ltd, 1947–65 and since 1983 Chairman); *b* 18 Dec. 1920; *s* of S. Fraser, Bourne End, Bucks; *m* 1943, Melba Estelle Hughes; four *s* two *d. Educ:* Royal Grammar Sch., High Wycombe; HMS Conway. Merchant Navy, 1937–39; Royal Navy, 1939–47; Lt-Comdr, RNR, 1951–65; Younger Brother of Trinity House, 1980. JP Wallasey, 1957. Officer, American Legion of Merit. *Publication:* Frogman VC, 1957. *Address:* Sigyn, 1 Lyndhurst Road, Wallasey, Merseyside L45 6AX. *T:* 051-639 3355. *Clubs:* Hoylake Sailing (life mem.); New Brighton Rugby (life mem.); Leasowe Golf (life mem.; Captain, 1975).

FRASER, Sir Ian (James), Kt 1986; CBE 1972; MC 1945; Chairman, Lazard Brothers, 1980–85; Deputy Chairman: Vickers Ltd, since 1980; TSB Group plc, since 1985; *b* 7 Aug. 1923; 2nd *s* of late Hon. Alastair Thomas Joseph Fraser and Lady Sibyl Fraser (*née* Grimston); *m* 1958, Evelyn Elizabeth Anne Grant (*d* 1984); two *s* two *d. Educ:* Ampleforth Coll.; Magdalen Coll., Oxford. Served War of 1939–45: Lieut, Scots Guards, 1942–45 (despatches, MC). Reuter Correspondent, 1946–56; S. G. Warburg & Co. Ltd, 1956–69; Dir-Gen., Panel on Take-overs and Mergers, 1969–72; Part-time Mem., CAA, 1972–74. Chairman, City Capital Markets Cttee, 1974–78; Accepting Houses Cttee, 1981–85; Member: Exec. Cttee, City Communications Centre, 1976–85; Cttee on Finance for Industry, NEDC, 1976–79; President's Cttee, CBI, 1979–81; Exec. Cttee, Jt Disciplinary Scheme of Accountancy Insts, 1979–81. Director: BOC International Ltd, 1972–85; Davy International Ltd, 1972–84; Chloride Gp Ltd, 1976–80; S. Pearson & Son Ltd, 1977–; EMI Ltd, 1977–80; Eurafrance SA, 1979–85; Pearson-Longman Ltd, 1980–83; Chairman: Rolls-Royce Motors, 1971–80; Datastream Ltd, 1976–77. Mem. Exec., Help the Hospices, 1985–; Vice-Pres., BBA, 1981–85. Trustee, Tablet Trust, 1976– (Chm., Finance Cttee, 1985–). Governor, More House Sch., 1970–75. FRSA 1970; CBIM (FBIM 1974). Kt of Honour and Devotion, SMO of Malta, 1971. *Recreations:* fishing, gardening, Scottish history. *Address:* 70 Limerston Street, SW10. *T:* 01–352 7092; South Haddon, Skilgate, Taunton, Somerset. *T:* Bampton (Devon) 31247. *Club:* White's.

FRASER, Ian Montagu, MC 1945; Secretary, The Buttle Trust, 1978–86 (Deputy Secretary, 1971–78); *b* 14 Oct. 1916; *e s* of Col Herbert Cecil Fraser, DSO, OBE, TD, and Sybil Mary Statter; *m* 1st, 1945, Mary Stanley (*d* 1964); one *s* one *d*; 2nd, 1967, Angela Meston; two *s. Educ:* Shrewsbury Sch.; Christ Church, Oxford. 1st Cl. Class. Hon. Mods, 1937; 1st Cl. Lit Hum 1939. Regular Commn in Frontier Force Rifles, IA, 1939, and served War of 1939–45, NW Frontier, Iraq, Syria and Western Desert (MC, despatches twice, POW); retired 1948. Executive, Guthrie and Co. Ltd, 1948; Gen. Sec., The John Lewis Partnership, 1956–59, Consultant, 1959–64. RARO, Rifle Bde, 1948– MP (C) Sutton Div. of Plymouth, 1959–66; PPS to Sec. of State for the Colonies, 1962; Asst Govt Whip, 1962–64; Opposition Whip, 1964–66; Conservative Research Dept, 1966–67. Exec. Dir, GUS Export Corp., 1967–70. *Recreations:* flyfishing, sailing. *Address:* How Hatch, Chipstead, Surrey CR3 3LN. *T:* Downland 51944. *Clubs:* Carlton; Royal Western Yacht (Plymouth).

FRASER, Very Rev. Dr Ian Watson, CMG 1973; Chairman, Nansen Home Committee, Presbyterian Support Services, since 1984 (Chairman NZ Refugee Homes Board, administering Nansen Home, 1962–84); retired as Minister of St Stephen's Presbyterian Church, Lower Hutt, Wellington, NZ (1961–73); *b* 23 Oct. 1907; *s* of Malcolm Fraser (*b* Inverness; 1st NZ Govt Statistician) and Caroline (*née* Watson; *b* Napier, NZ); *m* 1932, Alexa Church Stewart; one *s* two *d. Educ:* Scots Coll., Wellington, NZ; Victoria Univ. of Wellington (MA (Hons)); Theol Hall, Dunedin; BD (Melb.); Univ. of Edinburgh; Univ. of Bonn, Germany; Union Theol Seminary, NY (STM, ThD). Minister: St Andrew's Presbyterian Church, Levin, 1933–39; Presbyterian Ch., Wyndham, 1939–42; Chaplain, St Andrew's Coll., Christchurch, 1942–48; Minister, St John's Pres. Ch., Papatoetoe, Auckland, 1948–61. Moderator, Presbyterian Church of NZ, 1968–69. Refugee Award of Nat. Council of Churches, 1970. *Publications:* Understandest Thou? (Introd. to NT), 1946; Understanding the OT, 1958; The Story of Nansen Home, 1984; various booklets. *Recreations:* cabinet making, music, reading. *Address:* 19A Bloomfield Terrace, Lower Hutt, Wellington, New Zealand. *T:* Wellington 697–269.

See also T. R. C. Fraser.

FRASER, Sir (James) Campbell, Kt 1978; FRSE 1978; Chairman: Scottish Television plc, since 1975; Green Park Health Care plc, since 1985; *b* 2 May 1923; *s* of Alexander

Ross Fraser and Annie McGregor Fraser; *m* 1950, Maria Harvey (*née* McLaren); two *d*. *Educ:* Glasgow Univ.; McMaster Univ.; Dundee Sch. of Economics. BCom. Served RAF, 1941–45. Raw Cotton Commn, Liverpool, 1950–52; Economist Intelligence Unit, 1952–57; Dunlop Rubber Co. Ltd, 1957–: Public Relations Officer, 1958; Group Marketing Controller, 1962; Man. Dir, Dunlop New Zealand Ltd, 1967; Exec. Dir, 1969; Jt Man. Dir, 1971; Man. Dir, 1972; Chm., Dunlop Holdings, 1978–83; Chm. and Man. Dir, Dunlop Ltd, 1977–83; Chm., Dunlop Internat. AG, 1978–83; Director: British Petroleum, 1978–; BAT Industries, 1980–; Charterhouse J. Rothschild, 1982–84; Bridgewater Paper Co., 1984–; Tandem Computers Ltd, 1985–. Pres., CBI, 1982–84 (Dep. Pres., 1981–82). Founder Mem., Past Chm., and Pres., 1972–84, Soc. of Business Economists; Mem. Exec. Cttee, SMMT. Trustee, The Economist, 1978–. Vis. Professor: Strathclyde Univ., 1980–85; Stirling Univ., 1980–. FBIM 1971; FPRI 1978. Hon. LLD Strathclyde, 1979; DUniv Stirling, 1979. *Publications:* many articles and broadcasts. *Recreations:* reading, theatre, cinema, gardening, walking. *Address:* Silver Birches, 4 Silver Lane, Purley, Surrey. *T:* 01–660 1703. *Club:* Caledonian.

FRASER, Prof. Sir James (David), 2nd Bt, *cr* 1943; Postgraduate Dean, Faculty of Medicine, University of Edinburgh, since 1981; *b* 19 July 1924; *o s* of Sir John Fraser, 1st Bt, KCVO, MC, and Agnes Govane Herald (*d* 1983), The Manse, Duns, Berwickshire; *S* father 1947; *m* 1950, Maureen, *d* of Rev. John Reay, MC, Bingham Rectory, Nottingham; two *s. Educ:* Edinburgh Academy; Magdalen Coll., Oxford (BA); Edinburgh Univ. (MB, ChB); ChM 1961; FRCSE 1953; FRCS 1973; FRCPE 1980; FRCSI 1984; FRACS 1984. RAMC (Major), 1948–51; Senior Lectr in Clinical Surgery, Univ. of Edinburgh and Hon. Cons. Surgeon, Royal Infirmary, Edinburgh, 1951–70; Prof. of Surgery, Univ. of Southampton, 1970–80, and Hon. Cons. Surgeon, Southampton Univ. Hospital Gp, 1970–80. Pres., RCSEd, 1982–85. *Recreations:* golf, swimming. *Heir: s* Iain Michael Fraser [*b* 27 June 1951; *m* 1982, Sherylle, *d* of Keith Gillespie, New Zealand; one *s* one *d*]. *Address:* 2 Lennox Street, Edinburgh EH4 1QA.

FRASER, (James) Edward; Under Secretary, Scottish Home and Health Department, since 1981; *b* 16 Dec. 1931; *s* of late Dr James F. Fraser, TD, Aberdeen, and late Dr Kathleen Blomfield; *m* 1959, Patricia Louise Stewart; two *s. Educ:* Aberdeen Grammar Sch.; Univ. of Aberdeen (MA); Christ's Coll., Cambridge (BA). RA, 1953; Staff Captain 'Q', Tel-el-Kebir, 1954–55. Asst Principal, Scottish Home Dept, 1957–60; Private Sec. to Permanent Under Sec. of State, 1960–62, and to Parly Under-Sec. of State, 1962; Principal: SHHD, 1962–64; Cabinet Office, 1964–66; HM Treasury, 1966–68; SHHD, 1968–69; Asst Sec., SHHD, 1970–76; Asst Sec., 1976, Under Sec., 1976–81, Local Govt Finance Gp, Scottish Office. *Recreations:* reading, music, walking, Greece ancient and modern. *Address:* 59 Murrayfield Gardens, Edinburgh EH12 6DH. *T:* 031–337 2274. *Clubs:* Royal Commonwealth Society; Scottish Arts (Edinburgh).

FRASER, James Owen Arthur; a Sheriff of Grampian, Highland and Islands, since 1984; *b* 9 May 1937; *s* of James and Effie Fraser; *m* 1961, Flora Shaw MacKenzie; two *s. Educ:* Glasgow High Sch. (Classical Dux 1954); Glasgow Univ. (MA 1958; LlB 1961). Qualified as Solicitor, 1961; employed as solicitor, Edinburgh, 1961–65, Glasgow, 1965–66; Partner, Bird Son & Semple, later Bird Semple & Crawford Herron, Solicitors, Glasgow, 1967–84. Part-time Lectr in Evidence and Procedure, Glasgow Univ., 1976–83. Temp. Sheriff, 1983–84. *Recreation:* golf. *Address:* Averon Lodge, School Road, Conon Bridge, Ross-shire. *T:* Dingwall 61556.

FRASER, John Denis; MP (Lab) Norwood, since 1966; *b* 30 June 1934; *s* of Archibald and Frances Fraser; *m* 1960, Ann Hathaway; two *s* one *d. Educ:* Sloane Grammar Sch., Chelsea; Co-operative Coll., Loughborough; Law Soc. Sch. of Law (John Mackrell Prize). Entered Australia & New Zealand Bank Ltd, 1950; Army service, 1952–54, as Sergt, RAEC (educnl and resettlement work). Solicitor, 1960; practised with Lewis Silkin and Partners. Mem. Lambeth Borough Coun., 1962–68 (Chm. Town Planning Cttee; Chm. Labour Gp). PPS to Rt Hon. Barbara Castle, 1968–70; Opposition front bench spokesman on Home Affairs, 1972–74; Parly Under-Sec. of State, Dept of Employment, 1974–76; Minister of State, Dept of Prices and Consumer Protection, 1976–79; opposition spokesman on trade, 1979–83, on housing and construction, 1983–. *Recreations:* walking, music. *Address:* House of Commons, SW1.

FRASER, Rt. Hon. (John) Malcolm, CH 1977; PC 1976; MA Oxon; Prime Minister of Australia, 1975–83; Chairman and Chief Executive Officer, Asia-International Counselling Services; *b* 21 May 1930; *s* of late J. Neville Fraser, Nareen, Vic, Australia; *m* 1956, Tamara, *d* of S. R. Beggs; two *s* two *d. Educ:* Melbourne C of E Grammar Sch.; Magdalen Coll., Oxford (MA 1952; Hon. Fellow, 1982). MHR (L) for Wannon, Vic, 1955–83; Mem. Jt Party Cttee on Foreign Affairs, 1962–66; Minister: for the Army, 1966–68; for Educn and Science, 1968–69, 1971–72; for Defence, 1969–71; Leader of Parly Liberal Party, 1975–83; Leader of the Opposition, 1975. Sen. Adjunct Fellow, Center for Strategic and Internat. Studies, Georgetown Univ., Washington, 1983–. Distinguished Internat. Fellow, Amer. Enterprise Inst. for Public Policy Res., 1984; Fellow, Center for Internat. Affairs, Harvard Univ. Mem. Council, Aust. Nat. Univ., 1964–66. Hon. Vice President: Oxford Soc., 1983; Royal Commonwealth Soc., 1983. Hon. LLD Univ. of SC, 1981. *Recreations:* fishing, photography, vintage cars. *Address:* ANZ Tower, 55 Collins Street, Melbourne, Vic 3000, Australia. *Club:* Melbourne.

FRASER, Kenneth John Alexander; Head of Marketing Division, 1976–79 and since 1981, and of International Affairs, since 1985, Unilever; *b* 22 Sept. 1929; *s* of Jack Sears Fraser and Marjorie Winifred (*née* Savery); *m* 1953, Kathleen Grace Booth; two *s* one *d. Educ:* Thames Valley Grammar Sch., Twickenham; London School of Economics (BScEcon Hons). Joined Erwin Wasey & Co. Ltd, 1953, then Lintas Ltd, 1958; Managing Director, Research Bureau Ltd, 1962; Head of Marketing Analysis and Evaluation Group, Unilever, 1965; Head of Marketing Division, Unilever, 1976; seconded to NEDO as Industrial Dir, 1979–81. Member: Consumer Protection Adv. Cttee, Dept of Prices and Consumer Protection, 1975; Management Bd, ADAS, MAFF, 1986–; Chairman: CBI Marketing and Consumer Affairs Cttee, 1977; Internat. Chamber of Commerce Marketing Commn, 1978; Vice Chm., Advertising Assoc., 1981–. *Recreations:* canoeing, walking, music, reading. *Address:* 14 Coombe Lane West, Kingston, Surrey KT2 7BX. *T:* 01–949 3760. *Clubs:* Royal Commonwealth Society, Wig and Pen.

FRASER, Louis Nathaniel B.; *see* Blache-Fraser.

FRASER, Rt. Hon. Malcolm; *see* Fraser, Rt Hon. J. M.

FRASER, Air Marshal Rev. Sir Paterson; *see* Fraser, Air Marshal Rev. Sir H. P.

FRASER, Peter Lovat, QC (Scot.) 1982; MP (C) Angus East, since 1983 (South Angus, 1979–83); Solicitor General for Scotland, since 1982; advocate; *b* 29 May 1945; *s* of Rev. George Robson Fraser and Helen Jean Meiklejohn or Fraser; *m* 1969, Fiona Macdonald Mair; one *s* two *d. Educ:* St Andrews Prep. Sch., Grahamstown, S Africa; Loretto Sch., Musselburgh; Gonville and Caius Coll., Cambridge (BA Hons; LLB Hons); Edinburgh Univ. Legal apprenticeship, Edinburgh, 1968; called to Scottish Bar, 1969. Lectr in Constitutional Law, Heriot-Watt Univ., 1972–74; Standing Jun. Counsel in Scotland to FCO, 1979. Chm., Scottish Conservative Lawyers Law Reform Group, 1976. Contested

N Aberdeen, Oct. 1974; adopted Prospective Parly Candidate, S Angus, 1975. PPS to Sec. of State for Scotland, 1981–82. *Recreations:* skiing, golf, wind-surfing. *Address:* Slade House, Carmyllie, by Arbroath, Angus. *T:* Carmyllie 215.

FRASER, Peter Marshall, MC 1944; MA; FBA 1960; Fellow of All Souls College, Oxford, since 1954, Acting Warden, since 1985 (Sub-Warden, 1980–82); Lecturer in Hellenistic History, 1948–64, Reader 1964–85; *b* 6 April 1918; *y s* of late Archibald Fraser; *m* 1st, 1940, Catharine, *d* of late Prebendary Heaton-Renshaw (marr. diss.); one *s* three *d*; 2nd, 1955, Ruth Elsbeth, *d* of late F. Renfer, Bern, Switzerland; two *s*; 3rd, 1973, Barbara Ann Stewart, *d* of late L. E. C. Norbury, FRCS. *Educ:* City of London Sch.; Brasenose Coll., Oxford (Hon. Fellow 1977). Seaforth Highlanders, 1941–45; Military Mission to Greece, 1943–45. Sen. Scholar, Christ Church, Oxford, 1946–47; Junior Proctor, Oxford Univ., 1960–61; Domestic Bursar, All Souls Coll., 1962–65. Dir, British Sch. at Athens, 1968–71. Vis. Prof. of Classical Studies, Indiana Univ., 1973–74. Chm., Managing Cttee, Soc. of Afghan Studies, 1972–82 (Vice Pres., 1985–). Ordinary Mem., German Archaeol. Soc., 1979; Corresp. Fellow, Archaeolog. Soc. of Athens, 1971. Gen. Editor and Chm., British Acad. Cttee, Lexicon of Greek Personal Names, 1973–. Hon. Dr. phil Trier, 1984. *Publications:* (with G. E. Bean) The Rhodian Peraea and Islands, 1954; (with T. Rönne) Boeotian and West Greek Tombstones, 1957; Rostovtzeff, Social and Economic History of the Roman Empire, 2nd edn, revised, 1957; Samothrace, The Inscriptions, (Vol. ii, Excavations of Samothrace), 1960; E. Löfstedt, Roman Literary Portraits, trans. from the Swedish (Romare), 1958; The Wares of Autolycus; Selected Literary Essays of Alice Meynell (ed.), 1965; E. Kjellberg and G. Säflund, Greek and Roman Art, trans. from the Swedish (Grekisk och romersk konst), 1968; Ptolemaic Alexandria, 1972; Rhodian Funerary Monuments, 1977; A. J. Butler, Arab Conquest of Egypt, 2nd edn, revised, 1978; articles in learned journals. *Address:* All Souls College, Oxford.

FRASER, Ronald Petrie, CB 1972; Secretary, Scottish Home and Health Department, 1972–77; *b* 2 June 1917; *yr s* of late T. Petrie Fraser, Elgin; *m* 1962, Ruth Wright Anderson, Edinburgh; one *d. Educ:* Daniel Stewart's Coll., Edinburgh; University of Edinburgh; The Queen's Coll., Oxford. Joined Dept of Health for Scotland for work on emergency hosp. service, 1940; Asst Private Sec. to Sec. of State for Scotland, 1944; Cabinet Office, 1947; Sec., Scottish Hosp. Endowments Commn, 1950; Asst Sec., Dept of Health for Scotland, 1954; Asst Sec., Scottish Education Dept, 1961; Under-Sec., 1963; Under-Sec., 1968–71, Dep. Sec., 1971, Min. of Agriculture, Fisheries and Food. Chief Counting Officer for Scotland Act Referendum, 1979. *Recreations:* walking, music. *Address:* 40A Lygon Road, Edinburgh EH16 5QA. *T:* 031–667 8298. *Club:* New (Edinburgh).

FRASER, Russell; *see* Fraser, T. R. C.

FRASER, Rt. Hon. Thomas, PC 1964; retired; *b* 18 Feb. 1911; *s* of Thomas and Mary Fraser, Kirkmuirhill, Lanarks; *m* 1935, Janet M. Scanlon, Lesmahagow, Lanarks; one *s* one *d. Educ:* Lesmahagow Higher Grade Sch. Left school 1925 and started work in a coalmine (underground); worked underground, 1925–43; Miners' Union Branch Official, 1938–43; Sec., Lanark Constituency Labour Party, 1939–43; MP (Lab) Hamilton Div. of Lanarks, 1943–67; Joint Parliamentary Under-Sec. of State, Scottish Office, 1945–51; Minister of Transport, 1964–65. Member: Royal Commn on Local Govt in Scotland, 1966–69; Highlands and Islands Develt Bd, 1967–70; Chm., N of Scotland Hydro-Electric Bd, 1967–73; Mem., S of Scotland Electricity Bd, 1967–73; Chairman: Scottish Local Govt Staff Commn, 1973–77; Scottish Local Govt Property Commn, 1976–77; Commn for Local Authority Accounts in Scotland, 1974–79. Freeman of Hamilton, 1964. *Address:* 15 Broompark Drive, Lesmahagow, Lanarks.

FRASER, Prof. (Thomas) Russell (Cumming), MD, FRCP; Deputy Director, Medical Research Council, New Zealand, 1975–81; *s* of Malcolm Fraser and Caroline (*née* Watson). *Educ:* Otago Univ. Medical School. MB, ChB (distinction) 1932; MRCP 1936; DPM (Eng.) 1937; MD (NZ) 1945; FRCP 1948. Hallett Prize, 1935; NZ University Travel Fellowship, 1935; Rockefeller Travel Fellowship, 1938. Formerly Asst Med. Officer, Maudsley Hosp.; Research Fellow in Medicine, Harvard Univ.; Reader in Medicine, Postgrad. Med. Sch., London; Prof. of Clinical Endocrinology in Univ. of London, RPMS, 1957–74. Member: Assoc. Physicians of Gt Brit.; Med. Research Soc. Hon. DSc, NZ. *Publications:* contribs to medical journals. *Address:* 19B Long Drive, St Heliers, Auckland 5, New Zealand.

See also Very Rev. Dr I. W. Fraser.

FRASER, Veronica Mary; Diocesan Director of Education, Diocese of Worcester, since 1985; *b* 19 April 1933; *o d* of late Archibald Fraser. *Educ:* Richmond County Sch. for Girls; St Hugh's Coll., Oxford. Head of English Department: The Alice Ottley Sch., Worcester, 1962–65; Guildford County Sch. for Girls, 1965–67 (also Librarian); Headmistress, Godolphin Sch., Salisbury, 1968–80; Adviser on Schools to Bishop of Winchester, 1981–85. *Address:* The Old Palace, Deansway, Worcester.

FRASER, William, CBE 1969; CEng, FIEE; Chairman, BICC Ltd, 1973–76; *b* 15 July 1911; *e s* of late Alexander Fraser and Elizabeth Williamson Fraser; *m* 1938, Kathleen Mary Moore (*d* 1971), 3rd *d* of late Alderman and Mrs J. W. Moore; two *s* two *d. Educ:* Glasgow High Sch.; University Coll. London (BSc Hons). Production Engr, Joseph Lucas Ltd, 1935–37; joined Scottish Cables Ltd, 1937; Dir, 1938; Managing Dir, 1948–62; Chm., 1958–76; Chm., Scottish Cables (S Africa) Ltd, 1950–76; Dir, British Insulated Callender's Cables Ltd, 1959, on entry of Scottish Cables into BICC Group; Exec. Dir (Overseas Cos), 1962–64; Managing Dir (Overseas), 1964–68; Managing Dir (Overseas & Construction Gp), 1968–70; Dep. Chm. and Chief Exec., 1971–73. Vice-Chm., Phillips Cables Ltd (of Canada), 1961–70; Dir and Dep. Chm., Metal Manufactures Ltd (of Australia) and Subsidiaries, 1962–70; Chm., Balfour, Beatty & Co. Ltd, 1969–70; Director: Anglesey Aluminium Ltd, 1971–75; Clydesdale Bank Ltd, 1974–84. Chm., Scottish Council of FBI, 1959–61. Pres., Electrical and Electronics Industries Benevolent Assoc., 1974–75. *Recreations:* fishing, shooting, golf. *Address:* Fenwick Lodge, Ewenfield Road, Ayr. *T:* Ayr 265547.

FRASER, William James; JP; Lord Provost of Aberdeen, 1977–80; Member, City of Aberdeen District Council; *b* 31 Dec. 1921; *s* of late William and Jessie Fraser; *m* 1961, Mary Ann; three *s* one *d. Educ:* York Street Sch., Aberdeen; Frederick Street Sch., Aberdeen. Mem., Scottish Exec., Labour Party, 1949–74 (Chm., 1962–63). Pres., Aberdeen Trades Council, 1952. JP Aberdeen, 1950. *Address:* 79 Salisbury Place, Aberdeen AB1 6QU. *T:* Aberdeen 51040.

FRASER, Sir William (Kerr), GCB 1984 (KCB 1979; CB 1978); Permanent Under-Secretary of State, Scottish Office, since 1978; *b* 18 March 1929; *s* of A. M. Fraser and Rachel Kerr; *m* 1956, Marion Anne Forbes; three *s* one *d. Educ:* Eastwood Sch., Clarkston; Glasgow Univ. (MA, LLB). Joined Scottish Home Dept, 1955; Private Sec. to Parliamentary Under-Sec., 1959, and to Secretary of State for Scotland, 1966–67; Civil Service Fellow, Univ. of Glasgow, 1963–64; Asst Sec., Regional Development Div., 1967–71; Under Sec., Scottish Home and Health Dept, 1971–75; Dep. Sec., Scottish

Office, 1975–78. FRSE 1985. Hon. LLD Glasgow, 1982. *Address:* 14 Braid Avenue, Edinburgh EH10 6EE. *T:* 031–447 3751. *Club:* New (Edinburgh).

FRASER McLUSKEY, Rev. James; *see* McLuskey.

FRASER ROBERTS, John Alexander; *see* Roberts.

FRASER-TYTLER, Christian Helen, CBE (mil.) 1941; TD; Senior Controller ATS, retired; *b* 23 Aug. 1897; *d* of John Campbell Shairp, Houstoun; *m* 1919, Col Neil Fraser-Tytler, DSO, Croix de Guerre (*d* 1937); two *d. Educ:* Home. Foreign Office, 1917–19; War Office, 1939–43; AA Command until 1945 (TD). *Recreation:* fishing. *Address:* 116H Market Street, St Andrews. *T:* St Andrews 76826.
See also Sir Thomas David Erskine, Bt, Sir Patrick Morgan.

FRAYLING, Prof. Christopher John, MA, PhD; Professor and Head of Department of Cultural History, Royal College of Art, London, since 1979; *b* 25 Dec. 1946; *s* of Arthur Frederick Frayling and Barbara Kathleen (*née* Imhof); *m* 1981, Helen Snowdon. *Educ:* Repton Sch.; Churchill Coll., Cambridge (BA, MA, PhD). Churchill Research Studentship, 1968–71; Lectr in Modern History, Univ. of Exeter, 1971–72; Tutor, Dept of General Studies, Royal College of Art, 1972–73; Vis. Lectr, 1973–79; Research Asst, Dept of Information Retrieval, Imperial War Mus., 1973–74; Lectr in the History of Ideas and European Social History, Univ. of Bath, 1974–79; founded Dept of Cultural History (ex General Studies), RCA, 1979. Lectr, critic, regular contributor to radio and TV. Crafts Council: Mem., 1982–85; Mem., Educn Cttee, 1981–85; Chm., Pubns and Inf. Cttee, 1984–85. Arts Council of GB: Mem., Art Panel, 1983– (Dep. Chm., 1984–); Mem., Photography Adv. Panel, 1983–85; Chm., Projects Cttee. Chm. of Trustees, Crafts Study Centre, Bath, 1982–; Chm., Free Form Arts Trust, 1984–; Trustee, V&A Museum, 1984– (Mem., V&A Adv. Council, 1981–83). Governor, BFI, 1982– (Mem., 1982–86, Chm. 1984–86, Educn Cttee); Mem., Working Party on art and design advising NAB, 1985–. *Publications:* Napoleon Wrote Fiction, 1972; (ed) The Vampyre—Lord Ruthven to Count Dracula, 1978; Spaghetti Westerns: Cowboys and Europeans, from Karl May to Sergio Leone, 1981; contribs to: Reappraisals of Rousseau—studies in honour of R. A. Leigh, 1980; Cinema, Politics and Society in America, 1981; Rousseau et Voltaire en 1978, 1981; Rousseau After Two Hundred Years: Proc. of Cambridge Bicentennial Colloquium, 1982; articles on film, popular culture and the visual arts/crafts in Cambridge Rev., Cinema, Film, London Magazine, New Society, Crafts, Burlington Magazine, Design, TLS, Designer, Creative Review, Listener, and various learned jls. *Recreation:* finding time. *Address:* Department of Cultural History, Royal College of Art, Kensington Gore, SW7 2EU. *T:* 01–584 5020.

FRAYN, Michael; writer; *b* 8 Sept. 1933; *s* of late Thomas Allen Frayn and Violet Alice Lawson; *m* 1960, Gillian Palmer; three *d. Educ:* Kingston Gram. Sch.; Emmanuel Coll., Cambridge (Hon. Fellow, 1985). Reporter, Guardian, 1957–59; Columnist, Guardian, 1959–62; Columnist, Observer, 1962–68. TV: plays: Jamie, 1968; Birthday, 1969; documentaries: Imagine a City Called Berlin, 1975; Vienna—The Mask of Gold, 1977; Three Streets in the Country, 1979; The Long Straight, 1980; Jerusalem, 1984; stage plays: The Two of Us, 1970; The Sandboy, 1971; Alphabetical Order, 1975 (Evening Standard Drama Award for Best Comedy); Donkeys' Years, 1976 (SWET Best Comedy Award); Clouds, 1976; Liberty Hall, 1980; Make and Break, 1980 (New Standard Best Comedy Award); Noises Off, 1982 (Standard Best Comedy Award; SWET Best Comedy Award); Benefactors, 1984 (Standard Best Play Award; Laurence Olivier (formerly SWET) Award for Play of the Year; Plays and Players London Theatre Critics' Best New Play); filmscript: Clockwise, 1986. Nat. Press Award, 1970. *Publications:* collections of columns: The Day of the Dog, 1962; The Book of Fub, 1963; On the Outskirts, 1964; At Bay in Gear Street, 1967; The Original Michael Frayn, 1983; *non-fiction:* Constructions, 1974; *novels:* The Tin Men, 1965; The Russian Interpreter, 1966 (Somerset Maugham Award); Towards the End of the Morning, 1967 (Hawthornden Prize); A Very Private Life, 1968; Sweet Dreams, 1973; *translations:* The Cherry Orchard, 1978 (prod. 1978); The Fruits of Enlightenment, 1979 (prod. 1979); Three Sisters, 1983 (prod. 1985); Number One, 1984; Wild Honey, 1984 (prod. 1984); The Seagull, 1986. *Address:* c/o Elaine Greene Ltd, 31 Newington Green, N16.

FRAZER, Prof. Malcolm John, PhD, FRSC; Chief Officer, Council for National Academic Awards, since 1986; *b* 7 Feb. 1931; *m* 1957, Gwenyth Ida (*née* Biggs), JP, MA; three *s. Educ:* Univ. of London; BSc 1952, PhD 1955. Royal Military Coll. of Science, 1956–57; Lecturer and Head of Dept of Chemistry, Northern Polytechnic, London, 1965–72; Prof. of Chemical Educn, 1972–86, and Pro-Vice Chancellor, 1976–81, Univ. of East Anglia, Norwich. Mem., Soc. for Research into Higher Educn; Gen. Sec./Vice-Pres., Chm. Council, British Assoc. for the Advancement of Science. Hon. Dr Leuven, 1985. *Publications:* (jointly) Resource Book on Chemical Education in the UK, 1975; Problem Solving in Chemistry, 1982; contribs to Jl Chem. Soc., etc. *Address:* Council for National Academic Awards, 344–354 Gray's Inn Road, WC1X 8BP.

FREARS, Stephen Arthur; film director; *b* 20 June 1941; *s* of Dr Russell E. Frears and Ruth M. Frears; *m* 1968, Mary K. Wilmers (marr. diss. 1974); two *s;* lives with Anne Rothenstein; one *s* one *d. Educ:* Gresham's Sch., Holt; Trinity Coll., Cambridge (BA Law). Director: Gumshoe, 1971; Bloody Kids, 1980; Going Gently, 1981; Walter, 1982; Saigon, 1983; The Hit, 1984; My Beautiful Laundrette, 1985; Prick Up Your Ears, 1986. *Recreations:* reading, fell-walking. *Address:* Douglas Rae Management, 28 Charing Cross Road, WC1. *T:* 01–836 3903.

FREDERICK, Sir Charles Boscawen, 10th Bt *cr* 1723; *b* 11 April 1919; *s* of Sir Edward Boscawen Frederick, 9th Bt, CVO and Edith Katherine (Kathleen) Cortlandt (*d* 1970), *d* of late Col W. H. Mulloy, RE; *S* father, 1956; *m* 1949, Rosemary, *er d* of late Lt-Col R. J. H. Baddeley, MC; two *s* two *d. Educ:* Eton. 2nd Lieut Grenadier Guards, 1942; served N Africa and Italy, 1943–45 (despatches); Capt. 1945; Palestine, 1946–47 (despatches); Malaya, 1948–49; Egypt, 1952–53; Major, 1953. Member: London Stock Exchange, 1954–62; Provincial Brokers Stock Exchange, 1962 (Mem. Council, 1966; Dep. Chm. 1972); Stock Exchange Council, and Chm., Provincial Unit, 1973–75. JP 1960. General Commissioner of Income Tax, 1966. *Recreations:* sailing, fishing. *Heir: s* Christopher St John Frederick, *b* 28 June 1950. *Address:* The Granary, Lerryn, Lostwithiel, Cornwall PL22 0QQ.

FREDERICTON, Archbishop of, since 1980; **Most Rev. Harold Lee Nutter,** DD; Metropolitan of the Ecclesiastical Province of Canada; *b* 29 Dec. 1923; *s* of William L. Nutter and Lillian A. Joyce; *m* 1946, Edith M. Carew; one *s* one *d. Educ:* Mount Allison Univ. (BA 1944); Dalhousie Univ. (MA 1947); Univ. of King's College (MSLitt 1947). Rector: Simonds and Upham, 1947–51; Woodstock, 1951–57; St Mark, Saint John, NB, 1957–60; Dean of Fredericton, 1960–71; Bishop of Fredericton, 1971. Co-Chairman, NB Task Force on Social Development, 1970–71; Mem., Adv. Cttee to Sec. of State for Canada on Multi-culturalism, 1973. Member: Bd of Governors, St Thomas Univ., 1979–; Bd of Regents, Mount Allison Univ., 1978–; Vice-Chm., Bd of Governors, Univ. of King's Coll., 1971–. Pres., Atlantic Ecumenical Council, 1972–74, 1984–86. Hon. DD: Univ. of King's College, 1960; Montreal Diocesan Coll., 1982; Wycliffe Coll., 1983;

Trinity Coll., Toronto, 1985; Hon. LLD, Mount Allison Univ., 1972. *Publication:* (jointly) New Brunswick Task Force Report on Social Development, 1971. *Address:* 791 Brunswick Street, Fredericton, NB, Canada. *T:* 4558667.

FREEBODY, Air Vice-Marshal Wilfred Leslie, CB 1951; CBE 1943; AFC; retired. RAF Technical Branch; Director of Work Study, at Air Ministry. Squadron Leader, 1937; Acting Air Commodore commanding 226 Group, Air Cdre, 1949; Actg Air Vice-Marshal, 1956; Air Vice-Marshal, 1957. Has Order of Polonia Restituta 3rd class, of Poland. *Club:* Royal Air Force.

FREEDBERG, Prof. David Adrian; Professor of Art History, Barnard College and Columbia University, since 1984; *b* 1 June 1948; *s* of William Freedberg and Eleonore Kupfer; *m;* one *d. Educ:* S African Coll. High Sch., Cape Town; Yale Univ. (BA); Balliol Coll., Oxford (DPhil). Rhodes Scholar, Oxford, 1969–72; Lectr in History of Art: Westfield Coll., Univ. of London, 1973–76; Courtauld Inst. of Art, Univ. of London, 1976–84; Slade Prof. of Fine Art, Univ. of Oxford, 1983–84. Baldwin Prof., Oberlin Coll., Ohio, 1979; Vis. Mem., Inst. for Advanced Study, Princeton, NJ, 1980–81; Gerson Lectr, Univ. of Groningen, 1983. *Publications:* Dutch Landscape Prints of the Seventeenth Century, 1980; The Life of Christ after the Passion (Corpus Rubenianum Ludwig Burchard, VII), 1983; Iconoclasts and their Motives, 1985; articles in Burlington Magazine, Revue de l'Art, Gentse Bijdragen, Münchner Jahrbuch der Bildenden Kunst, Jl of Warburg and Courtauld Insts. *Address:* Department of Art History, Columbia University, Schermerhorn Hall, New York, NY 10027, USA.

FREEDMAN, Charles, CB 1983; Commissioner, Customs and Excise, 1972–84; *b* 15 Oct. 1925; *s* of late Solomon Freedman, OBE, and Lilian Freedman; *m* 1949, Sarah Sadie King; one *s* two *d. Educ:* Westcliff High Sch.; Cheltenham Grammar Sch.; Trinity Coll., Cambridge (Sen. Schol., BA). Entered HM Customs and Excise, 1947; Asst Sec., 1963. *Address:* 10 Cliff Avenue, Leigh-on-Sea, Essex SS9 1HF. *T:* Southend-on-Sea 73148. *Clubs:* Civil Service; Essex Yacht.

FREEDMAN, Dawn Angela, (Mrs N. J. Shestopal); barrister-at-law; Metropolitan Stipendiary Magistrate, since 1980; *b* 9 Dec. 1942; *d* of Julius and Celia Freedman; *m* 1970, Neil John Shestopal. *Educ:* Westcliff High Sch. for Girls; University Coll., London (LLB Hons). Called to the Bar, Gray's Inn, 1966. Mem., Bd of Deputies of British Jews. *Recreations:* theatre, television, cooking. *Address:* 3 Gray's Inn Square, Gray's Inn, WC1R 5AH. *T:* 01–242 0328.

FREEDMAN, Prof. Lawrence David, DPhil; Professor of War Studies, King's College, London, since 1982; *b* 7 Dec. 1948; *s* of Lt-Comdr Julius Freedman and Myra Freedman; *m* 1974, Judith Anne Hill; one *s* one *d. Educ:* Whitley Bay Grammar Sch. BAEcon Manchester; BPhil York; DPhil Oxford. Teaching Asst, York Univ., 1971–72; Research Fellow, Nuffield Coll., Oxford, 1974–75; Research Associate, International Inst. for Strategic Studies, 1975–76 (Mem. Council, 1984–); Research Fellow, Royal Inst. of International Affairs, 1976–78; Head of Policy Studies, RIIA, 1978–82. *Publications:* US Intelligence and the Soviet Strategic Threat, 1977, 2nd edn 1986; Britain and Nuclear Weapons, 1980; The Evolution of Nuclear Strategy, 1981; (jtly) Nuclear War & Nuclear Peace, 1983; (ed) The Troubled Alliance, 1983; The Atlas of Global Strategy, 1985; The Price of Peace, 1986. *Recreations:* tennis, political caricature. *Address:* c/o Department of War Studies, King's College, Strand, WC2R 2LS. *T:* 01–836 5454, ext. 2193.

FREEDMAN, Louis, CBE 1978; Proprietor, Cliveden Stud; *b* 5 Feb. 1917; 4th *s* of Sampson and Leah Freedman; *m* 1st, 1944, Cara Kathlyn Abrahamson (marr. diss.); one *s* one *d;* 2nd, 1960, Valerie Clarke; one *s. Educ:* University College School. FSVA. TA, RE, 1938; commnd RA, 1943; Devonshire Regt, 1944. Dir, Land Securities Investment Trust, 1958–77; Dir, GRA Gp, 1985–. Mem., Race Relations Bd, 1968–77. Chm., Nat. Assoc. Property Owners, 1971–72; Pres., Racehorse Owners Assoc., 1972–74. Vice-Chm., NE Thames RHA, 1975–79; Chairman: Camden and Islington AHA, 1979–82; City and Hackney DHA, 1982–84. Governor, Royal Hosp. of St Bartholomew the Great, 1971–74; Special Trustee, St Bartholomew's Hosp., 1974–. *Recreation:* gardening. *Address:* Cliveden Stud House, Taplow, Maidenhead, Berks SL6 0HL. *Clubs:* Garrick; Jockey (Newmarket) (Deputy Senior Steward, 1981–83).

FREEDMAN, Hon. Samuel; Chief Justice of Manitoba, 1971–83; Counsel to Aikins, MacAulay & Thorvaldson; *b* Russia, 1908; *s* of Nathan Freedman and Ada (*née* Foxman); came to Canada, 1911; *m* 1934, Claris Brownie Udow; one *s* two *d. Educ:* Winnipeg schs; Univ. of Manitoba. BA 1929, LLB 1933. Called to Manitoba Bar, 1933; KC (Canada) 1944; Judge, Court of Queen's Bench, Manitoba, 1952, Court of Appeal 1960. Chancellor, Univ. of Manitoba, 1959–68; Pres., Manitoba Bar Assoc., 1951–52; Mem. Bd of Governors, Hebrew Univ., Jerusalem, 1955–; Chm., Rhodes Scholarship Selection Cttee, Manitoba, 1956–66; Pres., Medico-Legal Soc. of Manitoba, 1954–55; Mem. Adv. Bd, Centre of Criminology, Univ. of Toronto; Mem. Bd of Dirs, Confedn Centre of the Arts in Charlottetown; one-man Industrial Inquiry Commn, CNR run-throughs, 1964–65. Holds numerous hon. degrees. *Publications:* Report of Industrial Inquiry Commission on Canadian National Railways Run-Throughs, 1965; (chapter) Admissions and Confessions, in, Studies in Canadian Criminal Evidence, ed Salhany and Carter, 1972; contrib. Canadian Bar Review. *Recreations:* walking, golf, reading. *Address:* 425 Cordova Street, Winnipeg, Manitoba R3N 1A5, Canada. *T:* 489–2922; (office) 30th Floor, Commodity Exchange Tower, Winnipeg, Manitoba R3L 4G1, Canada. *Club:* Glendale Country (Winnipeg).

FREELAND, Sir John Redvers, KCMG 1984 (CMG 1973); HM Diplomatic Service; Legal Adviser, Foreign and Commonwealth Office, since 1984; *b* 16 July 1927; *o s* of C. Redvers Freeland and Freda Freeland (*née* Walker); *m* 1952, Sarah Mary, *er d* of late S. Pascoe Hayward, QC; one *s* one *d. Educ:* Stowe; Corpus Christi Coll., Cambridge. Royal Navy, 1945 and 1948–51. Called to Bar, Lincoln's Inn, 1952, Bencher, 1985; Mem. *ad eundem,* Middle Temple. Asst Legal Adviser, FO, 1954–63, and 1965–67; Legal Adviser, HM Embassy, Bonn, 1963–65; Legal Counsellor, FCO (formerly FO), 1967–70; Counsellor (Legal Advr), UK Mission to UN, NY, 1970–73; Legal Counsellor, FCO, 1973–76; Second Legal Advr, FCO, 1976–84. Agent of UK govt, cases before European Commn of Human Rights, 1966–70. Member: Exec. Cttee, David Davies Meml Inst. of Internat. Studies, 1974–; Council of Management, British Inst. of Internat. and Comparative Law, 1984–; Cttee of Management, Inst. of Advanced Legal Studies, 1984–. *Address:* c/o Foreign and Commonwealth Office, SW1. *Club:* Travellers'.

FREELAND, Mary Graham; *see* McGeown, M. G.

FREELING, Nicolas; writer since 1960; *b* 1927, of English parents; *m* 1954, Cornelia Termes; four *s* one *d. Educ:* primary and secondary schs. Hotel-restaurant cook, throughout Europe, 1945–60; novelist, 1960–. *Publications:* (numerous trans.) Love in Amsterdam, 1961; Because of the Cats, 1962; Gun before Butter, 1962; Valparaiso, 1963; Double Barrel, 1963; Criminal Conversation, 1964; King of the Rainy Country, 1965; Dresden Green, 1966; Strike Out Where Not Applicable, 1967; This is the Castle, 1968; Tsing-Boum, 1969; Kitchen Book, 1970; Over the High Side, 1971; Cook Book, 1971; A Long Silence, 1972; Dressing of Diamond, 1974; What Are the Bugles Blowing For?, 1975;

Lake Isle, 1976; Gadget, 1977; The Night Lords, 1978; The Widow, 1979; Castang's City, 1980; One Damn Thing After Another, 1981; Wolfnight, 1982; Back of the North Wind, 1983; No Part in Your Death, 1984; A City Solitary, 1985; Cold Iron, 1986. *Address:* Grandfontaine, 67130 Schirmeck, France.

FREEMAN, Catherine; Controller, Documentaries and Features Department, Thames Television, since 1982; Director, Institute of Contemporary Arts, since 1983; *b* 10 Aug. 1931; *d* of Harold Dove and Eileen Carroll; *m* 1st, 1958, Charles Wheeler, *qv*; 2nd, 1962, John Freeman, *qv*; two *s* one *d*. *Educ:* Convent of the Assumption; St Anne's Coll., Oxford (MA Hons). Joined BBC as trainee producer, 1954; Producer/director: Panorama, Brains Trust, Monitor, Press Conference, 1954–58; joined Thames Television as Sen. Producer in Features Dept, 1976; Good Afternoon, A Plus and other programmes, 1976–82; originator and series producer: Citizen 2000, for Channel 4, 1982–. Member: Devlin Cttee on Identification Procedures, 1974–76; Literature Panel, Arts Council, 1981–84. *Address:* 2 Chalcot Crescent, NW1.

FREEMAN, David John; Senior Partner, and Founder, 1952, D. J. Freeman & Co., Solicitors; *b* 25 Feb. 1928; *s* of late Meyer Henry and Rebecca Freeman; *m* 1950, Iris Margaret Alberge; two *s* one *d*. *Educ:* Christ's Coll., Finchley. Lieut, Army, 1946–48. Admitted Solicitor, 1952. Dept of Trade Inspector into the affairs of AEG Telefunken (UK) Ltd, and Credit Collections Ltd, 1977. Governor, Royal Shakespeare Theatre, 1979–. *Recreations:* reading, theatre, gardening, golf. *Address:* 43 Fetter Lane, EC4. *T:* 01-583 4055. *Clubs:* Reform; Huntercombe Golf.

FREEMAN, (Edgar) James (Albert), MC 1945; Regional Chairman of Industrial Tribunals, Bury St Edmunds, since 1984; *b* 31 Dec. 1917; *yr s* of Horace Freeman and Beatrice Mary Freeman, Cricklewood; *m* 1948, Shirley Lake Whatmough, *d* of William Henry Whatmough, PhD, and Agnes Caroline Whatmough, Streatham; one *s* two *d*. *Educ:* Westminster Sch.; Trinity Coll., Cambridge (BA). Served in DLI, UK, India and Burma, 1940–46. Called to Bar, Lincoln's Inn, 1947; practised Chancery Bar, 1947–72; Vice-Pres., Value Added Tax Tribunals (England and Wales), 1972–; full-time Chm. of Industrial Tribunals, 1975–. *Recreations:* sailing, cycling. *Address:* 45 Nightingale Avenue, Cambridge CB1 4SG. *Clubs:* Royal Cruising, Bar Yacht.

FREEMAN, Dr Ernest Allan, CEng, FIEE, FIMA; Director, Trent Polytechnic, 1981–83; *b* 16 Jan. 1932; *s* of William Freeman and Margaret Sinclair; *m* 1954, Mary Jane Peterson; two *d*. *Educ:* Sunderland Technical Coll.; King's Coll., Univ. of Durham (Mather Scholarship, 1955–57). BSc, PhD, Durham; DSc Newcastle upon Tyne; MA (Oxon) 1972. Sunderland Forge & Engineering Co. Ltd. 1949–55; English Electric Co., 1957–58; Ferranti Ltd (Edinburgh), 1958–59; Sunderland Polytechnic: Dir of Research, 1959–65; Head of Control Engrg Dept, 1965–72; Rector, 1976–80; Tutor and Fellow in Engrg, St Edmund Hall, Oxford Univ., 1972–76. FRSA. *Publications:* contribs mainly in the fields of control engrg, systems theory and computing, to Wireless Engr, Proc. IEE (Heaviside Prize, 1974), Jl of Electronics and Control, Trans AIEE, Electronic Technol., Control, Jl of Optimisation Theory and Application, Trans Soc. of Instrument Technol., Proc. Internat. Fedn for Analogue Computation, Internat. Jl of Control. *Recreations:* swimming, browsing around antique shops. *Address:* 12 Rolfe Place, Headington, Oxford OX3 0DS.

FREEMAN, George Vincent; Under-Secretary (Legal), Treasury Solicitor's Department, 1973–76, retired; *b* 30 April 1911; *s* of Harold Vincent Freeman and Alice Freeman; *m* 1945, Margaret Nightingale; one *d*. *Educ:* Denstone Coll., Rocester. Admitted Solicitor, 1934; in private practice Birmingham until 1940. Served RN, 1940–46, Lieut RNVR. Legal Asst, Treasury Solicitor's Dept, 1946; Sen. Legal Asst 1950; Asst Treasury Solicitor 1964. *Recreations:* gardening, photography. *Address:* 8 Shelley Close, Ashley Heath, Ringwood, Hants. *T:* Ringwood 477102. *Clubs:* Civil Service; Conservative (Ringwood).

FREEMAN, Harold Webber; Author; *b* 1899; *s* of Charles Albert Freeman and Emma Mary Ann Mills; *m* Elizabeth Boedecker. *Educ:* City of London Sch.; Christ Church, Oxford (classical scholar). 1st class Hon. Mods, 2nd class Lit. Hum. Main background was work on the land, mostly organic gardening; travelled in Europe (foot and bicycle); casual work as linguist (translation, monitoring, travel trade). Has lived mostly in Suffolk, but also, for long periods, in Italy. *Publications:* Joseph and His Brethren, 1928; Down in the Valley, 1930; Fathers of Their People, 1932; Pond Hall's Progress, 1933; Hester and Her Family, 1936; Andrew to the Lions, 1938; Chaffinch's, 1941; Blenheim Orange, 1949; The Poor Scholar's Tale, 1954; Round the Island: Sardinia Re-explored, 1956. *Address:* c/o National Westminster Bank, 2 Tavern Street, Ipswich.

FREEMAN, Hugh Lionel, FRCPsych; Consultant Psychiatrist, Salford Health Authority, University of Manchester School of Medicine, since 1961; Senior Visiting Research Fellow, Green College, Oxford, 1986; *b* Salford, 4 Aug. 1929; *s* of late Bernard Freeman, FBOA and Dora Doris Freeman (*née* Kahn); *m* 1957, Sally Joan, MEd, PhD, FBPsS, *er d* of Philip and late Rebecca Casket; three *s* one *d*. *Educ:* Altrincham Grammar Sch.; St John's Coll., Oxford (open schol.; BM BCh 1954; MA); MSc Salford 1980. DPM 1958; FRCPsych 1971. Captain, RAMC, 1956–58. House Surg., Manchester Royal Inf., 1955; Registrar, Bethlem Royal and Maudsley Hosps, 1958–60; Sen. Registrar, Littlemore Hosp., Oxford, 1960–61; Consltnt Psychiatrist, Salford Royal Hosp., 1961–70; Hon. Consultant Psychiatrist: Salford Health Dept, 1961–74; Salford Social Services Dept, 1974–. Hon. Med. Consultant, and Mem., Public Inf. Cttee, NAMH, 1963–74. Consltnt Psychiatrist, NW Reg., DHSS, 1963–; Med. Advisor, NW Fellowship for Schizophrenia. Chairman: Psychiatric Sub-Cttee, NW Reg. Med. Adv. Cttee, 1978–83; Area Med. Cttee and Med. Exec. Cttee, Salford AHA, 1974–78. University of Manchester: pt-time Lectr, 1973–; Member: Deptl Bd, Psychiatry; Bd, Faculty of Medicine. Vis. Prof., Univ. of WI, 1970; Rockefeller Foundn Vis. Fellow, Italy, 1980. Examiner: Univ. of Manchester; RCPsych. Med. Mem., Mental Health Rev. Tribunal, 1982. Member: Sex Educn Panel, Health Educn Council, 1968–72; Working Party on Behaviour Control, Council for Sci. and Society, 1973–76; Minister of State's Panel on Private Practice, DHSS, 1974–75; UK Delgn to EC Conf. on Mental Health in Cities, Milan, 1980; Mental Health Act Commn, 1983–84; Historic Building Panel, City of Manchester. WHO Consultant: Grenada, 1970; Chile, 1978; Philippines, 1979; Bangladesh, 1981; Rapporteur: WHO Conf. on Mental Health Services in Pilot Study Areas, Trieste, 1984; WHO Workshop on Nat. Mental Health Progs, Ruanda, 1985; Council of Europe conf. on Health in Cities, 1985. Editor, British Jl of Clin. and Social Psych., 1982–84; Dep. Editor, Internat. Jl of Social Psych., 1980–83; Editor, British Jl of Psych., 1983– (Asst Editor, 1978–83); Co-Editor, Bull. of RCPsych, 1983; Associate Editor, Internat. Jl of Mental Health, 1981–. Mem. Internat. Res. Seminars, US National Inst. of Mental Health: Washington, 1966; Pisa, 1977; has lectured to and addressed univs, confs and hosps worldwide; advr on and participant in radio and TV progs. Member: Session Steering Cttee, BAAS, 1980; Exec. Cttees, Royal Medico-Psychol Assoc., 1965–69; Exec. Cttee, Soc. of Clin. Psychs. Royal College of Psychiatrists: Foundn Mem., 1971; Chm., Editorial Cttee; Vice-Chm., Social and Community Gp; External Assessor; FRSH (Hon. Sec., Mental Health Gp, 1973–76). Vice-Chm., MIND, 1983–. Corresp. Mem., US Assoc. for Behavioral Therapies; Hon. Member: Chilean Soc. of Psych., Neurol. and Neurosurgery; Egyptian Psychiatric Assoc.; Polish Psychiatric Assoc., 1986; Senior Common Room, Pembroke Coll., Oxford, 1981; Hon. Life Mem., Soc. of Clinical Psychiatrists. Vice-Chm., Manchester Heritage Trust; Mem., Mercian Regional Cttee, NT, 1986–. Hon. Professorial Fellow, Salford Univ., 1986. Freeman, City of London; Liveryman, Soc. of Apothecaries, 1984 (Yeoman, 1979–84). Distinguished Service Commendation, US Nat. Council of Community Mental Health Centers, 1982. *Publications:* (ed jtly) Trends in the Mental Health Services, 1963; (ed) Psychiatric Hospital Care, 1965; (ed jtly) New Aspects of the Mental Health Service, 1968; (ed) Progress in Behaviour Therapy, 1969; (ed) Progress in Mental Health, 1970; (ed) Pavlovian Approach to Psychopathology, 1971; (ed jtly) Dangerousness, 1982; Mental Health and the Environment, 1985; (jtly) Mental Health Services in Europe, 1985; (ed jtly) Mental Health Services in Britain: the way ahead, 1985; contribs to national press and learned jls. *Recreations:* architecture, travel, music. *Address:* Wykeham, Alan Drive, Hale, Cheshire WA15 0LR. *T:* 061–980 4597. *Clubs:* United Oxford & Cambridge University; Manchester Tennis and Racquet.

FREEMAN, Ifan Charles Harold, CMG 1964; TD 1961; Registrar, University of Malawi, 1965–72, retired; *b* 11 Sept. 1910; *s* of late C. E. D. W. Freeman; *m* 1937, Enid, *d* of late Edward Hallum; two *d*. *Educ:* Friars Sch., Bangor; Univ. of Wales (MA). Served with Royal Artillery, 1939–46 (Major; despatches). Colonial Service: Kenya, 1946–58; Nyasaland, 1958–65. *Recreation:* gardening. *Address:* Swn y Wylan, Marianglas, Gwynedd. *Club:* Mombasa (Kenya).

FREEMAN, James; *see* Freeman, E. J. A.

FREEMAN, His Eminence Sir James Darcy, Cardinal, KBE 1977; Knight of the Holy Sepulchre; *b* 19 Nov. 1907; *s* of Robert Freeman and Margaret Smith. *Educ:* Christian Brothers' High School, St Mary's Cathedral, Sydney; St Columba's Coll., Springwood, NSW; St Patrick's Coll., Manly, NSW. Priest, 1930; Private Secretary to HE Cardinal Gilroy, Archbishop of Sydney, 1941–46; Auxiliary Bishop to HE Cardinal Gilroy, 1957; Bishop of Armidale, 1968; Archbishop of Sydney, 1971–83. Cardinal, 1973. Hon. DD 1957. *Address:* PO Box 246, Randwick, NSW 2031, Australia. *T:* 3998564.

FREEMAN, Sir James Robin, 3rd Bt *cr* 1945; *S* father, 1981. *Heir:* none.

FREEMAN, Rt. Hon. John, PC 1966; MBE 1943; Visiting Professor of International Relations, University of California, Davis, since 1985. *Educ:* Westminster Sch.; Brasenose College, Oxford (Hon. Fellow, 1968). Active service, 1940–45. MP (Lab) Watford Div. of Herts, 1945–50; Borough of Watford, 1950–55; PPS to Sec. of State for War, 1945–46; Financial Sec., War Office, 1946; Parly Under Sec. of State for War, April 1947; Leader, UK Defence Mission to Burma, 1947; Parly Sec., Min. of Supply, 1947–51, resigned. Asst Editor, New Statesman, 1951–58; Deputy Editor, 1958–60; Editor, 1961–65. British High Commissioner in India, 1965–68; British Ambassador in Washington, 1969–71. Chairman: London Weekend Television Ltd, 1971–84; LWT (Holdings) plc, 1976–84; Page & Moy (Holdings) Ltd, 1976–84; Hutchinson Ltd, 1978–82 (Director till 1984); ITN, 1976–81. Governor, BFI, 1976–82. Vice-Pres., Royal Television Soc., 1975 (Gold Medal, 1981). *Address:* c/o Political Science Department, University of California, Davis, Calif 95616, USA.

FREEMAN, John Allen, OBE 1958; PhD; FRES, CBiol, FIBiol; Director, Ministry of Agriculture, Fisheries and Food's Pest Infestation Control Laboratory, 1977–79; *b* 30 Sept. 1912; *s* of Laurence Freeman and Maggie Rentoul Freeman; *m* 1945, Hilda Mary Jackson; one *s* one *d*. *Educ:* City of London Sch. (Jun. Corp. Scholar, Travers Scholar); Imperial Coll. of Science and Technol., London Univ. (BSc Special 1st Cl. Hons 1933, PhD 1938). ARCS; FRES 1943; FIBiol 1963. Min. of Agric. Scholar in Entomology, 1934–37: Hull University Coll., 1934–35; Rothamsted Exper. Stn, 1936; Cornell Univ., USA, 1936–37; Vineland Exper. Stn, Ont, Canadian Dept of Agric., 1937. Res. Asst, Imp. Coll., London, 1938–40; Jun. Scientific Officer, Dept of Science and Indust. Res. Pest Infestation Lab., 1940; seconded Min. of Food Infest. Control, 1940–47; Chief Entomologist, 1944; Sen. Sci. Officer, 1946; transf. Min. of Agric., 1947; Principal Sci. Off., 1947; seconded OECD, 1954–55, and CENTO, 1957–58; Sen. Principal Sci. Off., 1958; Dep. Chief Sci. Off., and Dep. Dir Pest Infest. Control Lab., 1971; Chief Sci. Off., 1977. Member: British Ecol Soc.; Assoc. of Applied Biol. Treasurer, Royal Entomol Soc. of London, 1977–84; Hon. Treas., Inst. of Biol, 1965–69. Pres., Royal Coll. of Science Union and Imp. Coll. Union, 1934. Has travelled professionally in N and S America, Europe, Africa, ME and Far East. Freeman of City of London, 1947. *Publications:* scientific articles, mainly on pests of stored foods. *Recreations:* gardening, photography, travel, DIY. *Address:* 5 Woodmere Way, Park Langley, Beckenham, Kent BR3 2SJ. *T:* 01–658 6970.

FREEMAN, Joseph William, OBE 1968; Director of Social Service, Leeds, 1970–78; *b* 8 April 1914; *s* of Thomas and Emma Freeman; *m* 1939, Louise King; one *s* one *d*. *Educ:* Liverpool Univ. (Dip. Soc. Sci.); Toynbee Hall; Open Univ. (BA 1983). CQSW 1970. Qual. social worker; Probation Service, Birmingham, 1938; served War of 1939–45: Army, 1940, commnd RA, 1941; Probation Service, Liverpool, 1946; Children's Officer: Warrington, 1948; Bolton, 1951; Sheffield, 1955. Church organist. *Publications:* papers in social work jls. *Recreations:* music, swimming. *Address:* 40 Forest Grove, Eccleston Park, Prescot, Merseyside L34 2RZ. *T:* 051–426 6928.

FREEMAN, Michael Alexander Reykers, MD; FRCS; Consultant Orthopaedic Surgeon, The London Hospital, since 1968; *b* 17 Nov. 1931; *s* of Donald George and Florence Julia Freeman; *m* 1st, 1951, Elisabeth Jean; one *s* one *d*; 2nd, 1959, Janet Edith; one *s* one *d*; 3rd, 1968, Patricia; one *d* (and one *s* decd). *Educ:* Stowe Sch.; Corpus Christi Coll., Cambridge (open scholarship and closed exhibn); London Hospital Med. Coll. BA (1st cl. hons), MB BCh, MD (Cantab). FRCS 1959. Trained in medicine and surgery, London Hosp., and in orthopaedic and traumatic surgery, London, Westminster and Middlesex Hosps; co-founder, Biomechanics Unit, Imperial Coll., London, 1964; Cons. Surg. in Orth. and Traum. Surgery, London Hosp., also Res. Fellow, Imperial Coll., 1968; resigned from Imperial Coll., to devote more time to clinical activities, 1979. Special surgical interest in field of reconstructive surgery in lower limb, concentrating on joint replacement; originator of new surgical procedures for reconstruction and replacement of arthritic hip, knee, ankle and joints of foot; has lectured and demonstrated surgery, Canada, USA, Brazil, Japan, China, Australia, S Africa, continental Europe; guest speaker at nat. and internat. profess. congresses. Member: BMA; Brit. Orth. Assoc.; Amer. Acad. Orth. Surgs; Orth. Res. Soc.; Soc. Internat. Chirurg. Orth. and Traum.; RSM; Past Member: MRC; Clin. Res. Bd, London Hosp. Bd of Governors; Brent and Harrow AHA; DHSS working parties. Pres., Internat. Hip Soc., 1982–85. Bacon and Cunning Prizes and Copeman Medal, CCC; Andrew Clark and T. A. M. Ross Prize in Clin. Med., London Hosp. Med. Coll.; Robert Jones Medal, Brit. Orth. Assoc. *Publications:* editor and part-author: Adult Articular Cartilage, 1973, 2nd edn 1979; Scientific Basis of Joint Replacement, 1977; Arthritis of the Knee, 1980; chapters in: Bailey and Love's Short Practice of Surgery; Mason and Currey's Textbook of Rheumatology; papers in Proc. Royal Soc., Jl Bone and Joint Surgery, and med. jls. *Recreations:* gardening, reading, surgery. *Address:* 79 Albert Street, NW1. *T:* 01–387 0817.

FREEMAN, Nicholas Hall, OBE 1985; barrister; a Recorder, since 1985; Leader, Kensington and Chelsea Borough Council, since 1977; *b* 25 July 1939; *s* of William Freeman and Grace Freeman, Leicester. *Educ:* Stoneygate Sch., Leicester; King's Sch., Canterbury. Admitted Solicitor, 1962; called to the Bar, Middle Temple, 1968. Chancellor, Diocese of Leicester, 1979–. Kensington and Chelsea Borough Council: Member, 1968; Vice-Chm., Town Planning Cttee, 1973, Chm., 1975. Vice-Chm., General Purposes Cttee, London Boroughs Assoc., 1978–. Mem., Conservative Central Office Policy Gp for London, 1981–. Contested (C) Hartlepool, Feb. and Oct. 1974. Governor, Emmanuel Sch., Clapham, 1974–78. Freeman, City of London, 1981. *Recreations:* reading, particularly biography, holidays in France, theatre. *Address:* 51 Harrington Gardens, SW7 4JU. *T:* 01–370 3197. *Clubs:* Carlton; Leicestershire (Leicester).

FREEMAN, Paul, ARCS, DSc (London), FRES; Keeper of Entomology, British Museum (Natural History), 1968–81; *b* 26 May 1916; *s* of Samuel Mellor Freeman and Kate Burgis; *m* 1942, Audrey Margaret Long; two *d. Educ:* Brentwood Sch., Essex; Imperial Coll., London. Demonstrator in Entomology, Imperial Coll., 1938. Captain, RA and Army Operational Research Group, 1940–45. Lecturer in Entomology, Imperial Coll., 1945–47. Asst Keeper, Dept of Entomology, British Museum (Nat. Hist.), 1947–64, Dep. Keeper, 1964–68, Keeper, 1968. Royal Entomological Soc. of London: Vice-Pres., 1956, 1957; Hon. Sec., 1958–62; Hon. Fellow, 1984. Sec., XIIth Internat. Congress of Entomology, London, 1964. *Publications:* Diptera of Patagonia and South Chile, Pt III-Mycetophilidae, 1951; Simuliidae of the Ethiopian Region (with Botha de Meillon), 1953; numerous papers in learned jls, on taxonomy of Hemiptera and Diptera. *Recreations:* gardening, natural history. *Address:* Briardene, 75 Towncourt Crescent, Petts Wood, Orpington, Kent BR5 1PH. *T:* Orpington 27296.

FREEMAN, Paul Illife, PhD; Director, Central Computer and Telecommunications Agency, HM Treasury, since 1983; *s* of late John Percy Freeman and of Hilda Freeman; *m* 1959, Enid Ivy May Freeman; one *s* one *d. Educ:* Victoria University of Manchester (BSc (Hons) Chemistry, PhD). Post Doctoral Fellow, Nat. Research Council of Canada, 1959–61; Research Scientist, Dupont De Nemours Co. Ltd, Wilmington, Del, USA, 1961–64; Nat. Physical Laboratory: Sen. Scientific Officer, 1964–70; Principal Scientific Officer, 1970–74; Exec. Officer, Research Requirements Bds, DoI, 1973–77; Director: Computer Aided Design Centre, 1977–83; National Engrg Lab., 1980–83. Member: CS Coll. Adv. Council, 1983–; Bd, NCC, 1983–. Vis. Prof. Univ. of Strathclyde, 1981. *Publications:* scientific papers. *Recreations:* reading, walking, gardening. *Address:* 12 Broadway, Wilburton, Ely, Cambridgeshire CB6 3RT. *T:* Ely 740576.

FREEMAN, Sir Ralph, Kt 1970; CVO 1964; CBE 1952 (MBE (mil.) 1945); FEng; Consultant, Freeman, Fox & Partners, Consulting Engineers, since 1979 (Senior Partner, 1963–79, Partner, 1947–79); *b* 3 Feb. 1911; *s* of late Sir Ralph Freeman and late Mary (*née* Lines); *m* 1939, Joan Elizabeth, *er d* of late Col J. G. Rose, DSO, VD, FRIC, Wynberg, Cape, S Africa; two *s* one *d. Educ:* Uppingham Sch.; Worcester Coll., Oxford (MA; Hon. Fellow, 1980). FICE, FCIT, FASCE. Construction Engineer: Dorman Long & Co., S Africa, Rhodesia and Denmark, 1932–36 and 1937–39; Braithwaite & Co., 1936–37; on staff of Freeman, Fox & Partners, 1939–46, Admty and other war work; served RE, 1943–45 (Temp. Major) at Exp. Bridging Estab. and later seconded as bridging adviser to CE 21 Army Gp HQ, NW Europe campaign. Consulting Engr to the Queen for Sandringham Estate, 1949–76. Past Pres., Instn of Civil Engrs (Mem. Council, 1951–55 and 1957–61, Vice-Pres., 1962–66; Pres., 1966–67); Member: Governing Body, SE London Techn. Coll., 1952–58; Nat. Cons. Council to Min. of Works, 1952–56; Bd of Governors, Westminster Hosp., 1963–69; Council, Worcester Coll. Soc., 1964–; Adv. Council on Scientific Res. and Develt (MoD), 1966–69; Defence Scientific Adv. Council, 1969–72; Royal Fine Art Commn, 1968–85; Council, Assoc. of Consulting Engrs, 1969–72, 1973–77, Chm., 1975–76; Governing Body, Imp. Coll. of Science and Technology, 1975–83; Chm., Limpsfield Common Local Management Cttee, Nat. Trust, 1972–82; Pres., Welding Inst., 1975–77. Col, Engr and Rly Staff Corps RE (T&AVR), 1963–76, Col comdg 1970–74. DUniv Surrey, 1978. Hon. Mem., Instn Royal Engrs, 1971; Hon. FIMechE, 1971; Hon. Fellow, Zimbabwe (formerly Rhodesian) Instn of Engrs, 1969; FRSA. Kt, Order of Orange Nassau (Netherlands), 1945. *Publications:* several papers in Proc. ICE. *Recreations:* wood and metal work, sailing. *Address:* Ballards Shaw, Ballards Lane, Limpsfield, Oxted, Surrey RH8 0SN. *T:* Oxted 723284. *Clubs:* Army and Navy; Leander (Henley-on-Thames).

See also D. L. Pearson.

FREEMAN, Raymond, MA, DPhil, DSc (Oxon); FRS 1979; Fellow of Magdalen College, Oxford, since 1973; Lecturer in Physical Chemistry, since 1973, Aldrichian Praelector in Chemistry, since 1982, Oxford University; *b* 6 Jan. 1932; *s* of late Albert and Hilda Frances Freeman; *m* 1958, Anne-Marie Périnet-Marquet; two *s* three *d. Educ:* Nottingham High Sch. (scholar); Lincoln Coll., Oxford (open scholar). Ingénieur, Centre d'Etudes Nucléaires de Saclay, Commissariat à l'Energie Atomique, France, 1957–59; Sen. Scientific Officer, Nat. Phys. Lab., Teddington, Mddx, 1959–63; Man., Nuclear Magnetic Resonance Research, Varian Associates, Palo Alto, Calif, 1963–73. Chem. Soc. Award in Theoretical Chem. and Spectroscopy, 1978. *Publications:* articles on nuclear magnetic resonance spectroscopy in various scientific journals. *Recreations:* swimming, traditional jazz. *Address:* 4 Rolfe Place, Harberton Mead, Headington, Oxford. *T:* Oxford 68362.

FREEMAN, His Honour Richard Gavin; a Circuit Judge (formerly County Court Judge), 1968–83; *b* 18 Oct. 1910; *s* of John Freeman, MD, and Violet Alice Leslie Hadden; *m* 1937, Marjorie Pear; one *s* two *d*; *m* 1961, Winifred Ann Bell. *Educ:* Charterhouse; Hertford Coll., Oxford. Called to Bar, Gray's Inn, 1947. Deputy Chairman, Warwicks Quarter Sessions, 1963–71. Hon. Major, RA. *Recreations:* cricket, gardening. *Address:* 10 Rees Street, N1. *Club:* Streatley Cricket.

FREEMAN, Roger Norman, MA; FCA; MP (C) Kettering, since 1983; Parliamentary Under-Secretary of State for Defence, since 1986; Executive Director, Lehman Brothers International Ltd, since 1972; *b* 27 May 1942; *s* of Norman and Marjorie Freeman; *m* 1969, Jennifer Margaret (*née* Watson); one *s* one *d. Educ:* Whitgift Sch., Croydon; Balliol Coll., Oxford (MA PPE). Chartered Accountant, 1969; FCA 1979. Articled with Binder Hamlyn & Co., 1964–69 (Hons Prize, 1968); Lehman Brothers (formerly Lehman Brothers Kuhn Loeb), 1969–. *Publication:* Professional Practice, 1968. *Recreation:* shooting. *Address:* House of Commons, SW1A 0AA. *Clubs:* Carlton, City of London, Kennel.

FREEMAN-GRENVILLE, family name of **Lady Kinloss.**

FREER, Charles Edward Jesse, DL; *b* 4 March 1901; *s* of late Canon S. Thorold Winckley, FSA and Elizabeth (*née* Freer); changed name to Freer by Deed Poll, 1922; *m* 1st, 1927, Violet Muriel (*d* 1944), *d* of H. P. Gee, CBE, Leicester; two *s* two *d*; 2nd, 1945, Cynthia Lilian, *d* of Leonard R. Braithwaite, FRCS, Leeds; two *d. Educ:* Radley Coll. Solicitor, 1924; served RA (TA) in France, 1940; DJAG in Iceland, 1941–42; at SHAEF, 1943–44, Lt-Col. Chm., Leicestershire QS, 1949–71. Chm. Leicester Diocesan Board of Finance, 1946–56; Chm. Mental Health Tribunal, Sheffield Regional Board, 1961–73. A Chm. of Industrial Tribunals, 1966–73. DL 1946, JP 1946–71, Leics. *Recreations:* reading, walking. *Address:* Shoal House, 48 Pearce Avenue, Parkstone, Dorset. *T:* Parkstone 748393. *Clubs:* East India, Devonshire, Sports and Public Schools; Parkstone Yacht.

FREER, Air Chief Marshal Sir Robert (William George), GBE 1981 (CBE 1966); KCB 1977; Commandant, Royal College of Defence Studies, 1980–82, retired; Director: Rediffusion PLC, since 1982; British Manufacturing & Research Co. Ltd, since 1984 (Consultant, 1982–84); Rediffusion Simulation Ltd, since 1985; *b* Darjeeling, 1 Sept. 1923; *s* of late William Freer, Stretton, Cirencester, Glos; *m* 1950, Margaret, 2nd *d* of late J. W. Elkington and Mrs M. Elkington, Ruskington Manor, near Sleaford, Lincs; one *s* one *d. Educ:* Gosport Grammar Sch. Flying Instructor, S Africa and UK, 1944–47; RAF Coll., Cranwell, 1947–50; served 54 and 614 Fighter Sqdns, 1950–52; Central Fighter Estabt, 1952–54; commanded 92 Fighter Sqdn, 1955–57 (Queen's Commendation, 1955); Directing Staff, USAF Acad., 1958–60; Staff of Chief of Defence Staff, 1961–63; Station Comdr, RAF Seletar, 1963–66; DD Defence Plans (Air), MoD, 1966–67. Air ADC to the Queen, 1969–71; Dep. Comdt, RAF Staff Coll., 1969–71; SASO, HQ Near East Air Force, 1971–72; AOC 11 Group, 1972–75; Dir-Gen., Organisation (RAF), April-Sept. 1975; AOC No 18 Group, RAF, 1975–78; Dep. C-in-C, Strike Command, 1978–79; psa, 1957; pfc, 1960; IDC, 1968. Pres., RAF LTA, 1975–81; Mem., Sports Council, 1980–82. CBIM (FBIM 1977). *Recreations:* golf, tennis. *Address:* c/o Lloyds Bank, 6 Pall Mall, SW1. *Clubs:* Royal Air Force; All England Lawn Tennis and Croquet; North Hants Golf.

FREESON, Rt. Hon. Reginald, PC 1976; MP (Lab) Brent East, since Feb. 1974 (Willesden East, 1964–74); *b* 24 Feb. 1926; *m*; one *s* one *d. Educ:* Jewish Orphanage, West Norwood. Served in Army, 1944–47. Middle East magazines and newspapers, 1946–48. Joined Labour Party on return to United Kingdom, 1948, Co-operative Party, 1958 and Poale Zion, 1964. Journalist, 1948–64: magazines, newspaper agencies and television; Everybody's Weekly, Tribune, News Chronicle, Daily Mirror. Asst Press Officer with Min. of Works, British Railways Board. Some short story writing, research and ghosting of books and pamphlets. Editor of Searchlight, against fascism and racialism, 1964–67. Radio and television: housing, urban planning, race relations and foreign affairs. Elected Willesden Borough Council, 1952; Alderman, 1955; Leader of Council, 1958–65; Chm. of new London Borough of Brent, 1964–65 (Alderman, 1964–68). PPS to Minister of Transport, 1964–67; Parly Secretary: Min. of Power, 1967–69; Min. of Housing and Local Govt, 1969–70; Labour Front-Bench spokesman on housing, 1970–74; Minister for Housing and Construction, DoE, 1974–79; Front-Bench spokesman on social security, 1979–81; Mem., Select Cttee on the Environment, 1982– (Chm., 1982–83). Member: Council of Europe Parly Assembly, 1984–; Western Eur. Assembly, 1984–. Mem., Internat. Voluntary Service and UNA International Service. Sponsor, three Willesden housing co-operatives, 1958–60. Founder-Chairman: Willesden (now Brent) Coun. of Social Service, 1960–62; Willesden Social Action, 1961–63; Willesden and Brent Friendship Council (now Brent Community Relns Council), 1959–63 (Vice-Pres., 1967); Chm., Warsaw Memorial Cttee, 1964–71; Mem., NCCL; Vice-Pres., Campaign for Democracy in Ulster; Mem., Jewish Welfare Bd, 1971–74 (Mem. Exec., 1973–74). *Recreations:* gardening, music, theatre, reading, country walking. *Address:* 159 Chevening Road, NW6.

FREETH, Denzil Kingson; Member of Stock Exchange; *b* 10 July 1924; *s* of late Walter Kingson and late Vera Freeth. *Educ:* Highfield Sch., Liphook, Hants; Sherborne Sch. (Scholar); Trinity Hall, Cambridge (Scholar). Served War, 1943–46: RAF (Flying Officer). Pres. Union Soc., Cambridge, 1949; Chm. Cambridge Univ. Conservative Assoc. 1949; debating tour of America, 1949, also debated in Ireland; Mem. Exec. Cttee Nat. Union, 1955. MP (C) Basingstoke Division of Hants, 1955–64. PPS to Minister of State, Bd of Trade, 1956, to Pres. of the Bd of Trade, 1957–59, to Minister of Educn, 1959–60; Parly Sec. for Science, 1961–63. Mem. Parliamentary Cttee of Trustee Savings Bank Assoc., 1956–61. Mem. Select Cttee on Procedure, 1958–59. Employed by and Partner in stockbroking firms, 1950–61 and 1964–; Mem. of Stock Exchange, 1959–61, 1965–. Churchwarden, All Saints' Church, Margaret St, W1, 1977–. *Recreations:* good food, wine and conversation. *Address:* 3 Brasenose House, 35 Kensington High Street, W8 5BA. *T:* 01–937 8685. *Clubs:* Carlton; Pitt (Cambridge).

FREETH, Hon. Sir Gordon, KBE 1978; Chairman, Australian Consolidated Minerals, since 1981; *b* 6 Aug. 1914; *s* of late Rt Rev. Robert Evelyn Freeth and Gladys Mary Snashall; *m* 1939, Joan Celia Carew Baker; one *s* two *d. Educ:* Sydney Church of England Grammar Sch.; Guildford Grammar Sch.; Univ. of Western Australia. Rowed for Australia in British Empire Games, Sydney, 1938. Admitted as Barrister and Solicitor, WA, 1938; practised Law at Katanning, WA, 1939–49. Served as Pilot, RAAF, 1942–45. Elected to House of Representatives as Member for Forrest, 1949; MP 1949–69; Minister: for Interior and Works, 1958–63; for Shipping and Transport, 1963–68; Assisting Attorney-Gen., 1962–64; for Air, and Minister Assisting the Treasurer, 1968; for External Affairs, 1969; Ambassador to Japan, 1970–73; practised law in Perth, WA, 1973–77; High Comr for Australia in UK, 1977–80. *Recreations:* gardening, golf. *Address:* Tingrith, 25 Owston Street, Mosman Park, WA 6012, Australia. *Club:* Weld (Perth).

FREMANTLE, family name of **Baron Cottesloe.**

FREMANTLE, Comdr Hon. John Tapling, RN (retired); JP; Lord-Lieutenant of Buckinghamshire, since 1984; *b* 22 Jan. 1927; *s* and *heir* of 4th Baron Cottesloe, *qv*, and late Lady Elizabeth Berwick; *m* 1958, Elizabeth Ann, *e d* of late Lt-Col H. S. Barker, DSO; one *s* two *d. Educ:* Summer Fields, Hastings; Eton College. Joined RN, 1945; CO HMS Palliser, 1959–61; retired at own request, 1966. High Sheriff, 1969–70, JP, 1984, Bucks. KStJ 1984. *Recreations:* shooting, stalking, crosswords. *Address:* The Old House, Swanbourne, Milton Keynes, Bucks MK17 0SH. *T:* (home) Mursley 263; (office) Mursley 256. *Clubs:* Travellers'; Royal Naval and Royal Albert Yacht (Portsmouth).

FRÉMAUX, Louis Joseph Felix; Principal Guest Conductor, Sydney Symphony Orchestra, since 1982 (Musical Director and Principal Conductor, 1979–81); *b* 13 Aug. 1921. *Educ:* Conservatoire National Supérieur de Musique de Paris. Chef d'orchestre permanent et directeur, l'Orchestre National de l'Opéra de Monte Carlo, 1956–66; Principal Conductor, Orchestre de Lyon, 1968–71; Musical Dir and Principal Conductor, City of Birmingham Symphony Orch., 1969–78. Hon. DMus Birmingham, 1978. Hon. Member, Royal Academy of Music, 1978. Légion d'Honneur; Croix de Guerre (twice). *Recreations:* walking, photography. *Address:* 25 Edencroft, Wheeley's Road, Birmingham B15 2LW.

FRENCH, family name of **Baron De Freyne** and **Earl of Ypres.**

FRENCH, Prof. Anthony Philip, PhD; Professor of Physics, Massachusetts Institute of Technology, since 1964; *b* 19 Nov. 1920; *s* of Sydney James French and Elizabeth Margaret (*née* Hart); *m* 1946, Naomi Mary Livesay; one *s* one *d. Educ:* Varndean Sch., Brighton; Sidney Sussex Coll., Cambridge (major schol.; BA Hons 1942, MA 1946, PhD 1948). British atomic bomb project, Tube Alloys, 1942–44; Manhattan Project, Los Alamos, USA, 1944–46; Scientific Officer, AERE, Harwell, 1946–48; Univ. Demonstrator in Physics, Cavendish Laboratory, Cambridge, 1948–51, Lectr 1951–55; Dir of Studies in Natural Sciences, Pembroke Coll., Cambridge, 1949–55, Fellow of Pembroke, 1950–55;

Visiting research scholar: California Inst. of Technology, 1951; Univ. of Michigan, 1954; Prof. of Physics, Univ. of S Carolina, 1955–62 (Head of Dept, 1956–62); Guignard Lectr, 1958; Vis. Prof., MIT, 1962–64; Vis. Fellow of Pembroke Coll., Cambridge, 1975. Member, Internat. Commn on Physics Educn, 1972–84 (Chm., 1975–81); Pres., Amer. Assoc. of Physics Teachers, 1985–86. *Publications:* Principles of Modern Physics, 1958; Special Relativity, 1968; Newtonian Mechanics, 1971; Vibrations and Waves, 1971; Introduction to Quantum Physics, 1978; Einstein: a centenary volume, 1979; Niels Bohr: a centenary volume, 1985; Introduction to Classical Mechanics, 1986. *Recreations:* music, squash, reading, writing. *Address:* c/o Physics Department, Massachusetts Institute of Technology, Cambridge, Mass 02139, USA.

FRENCH, Cecil Charles John, FEng 1982; Vice Chairman, Ricardo Consulting Engineers plc, since 1982; Chairman, G. Cussons Ltd, since 1984; *b* 16 April 1926; *s* of Ernest French and Edith Hannah French (*née* Norris); *m* 1st, 1956, Olive Joyce Edwards (*d* 1969); two *d*; 2nd, 1971, Shirley Frances Outten; one *s* one *d*. *Educ:* King's Coll., Univ. of London (MScEng); Columbia Univ., New York. FIMechE, FIMarE. Graduate apprentice, CAV Ltd, 1948–50; Marshall Aid scholar, MIT, USA (research into combustion in engines), 1950–52; Ricardo Consulting Engineers, 1952–, Director, 1969; Man. Dir, G. Cussons Ltd, 1979–83. Dep. President, Instn of Mechanical Engineers, 1986– (Vice-Pres., 1981–85). *Publications:* numerous articles on diesel engines in learned soc. jls world wide. *Recreations:* folk dancing, photography. *Address:* 303 Upper Shoreham Road, Shoreham-by-Sea, Sussex BN4 5QA. *T:* Shoreham-by-Sea 452050.

FRENCH, Hon. Sir Christopher James Saunders, Kt 1979; **Hon. Mr Justice French;** Judge of the High Court of Justice, Queen's Bench Division, since 1982 (Family Division, 1979–82); Judge of Employment Appeals Tribunal, since 1985; *b* 14 Oct. 1925; 2nd *s* of late Rev. Reginald French, MC, MA, Hon. Chaplain to the Queen, and Gertrude Emily Mary (*née* Haworth); *m* 1957, Philippa, *d* of Philip Godfrey Price, Abergavenny; one *s* one *d*. *Educ:* Denstone Coll. (scholar); Brasenose Coll., Oxford (scholar). Coldstream Guards, 1943–48 (Capt.). Called to the Bar, Inner Temple, 1950; QC 1966; Master of the Bench, 1975. Dep. Chm., Bucks QS, 1966–71. Recorder of Coventry, 1971–72; a Recorder, and Hon. Recorder of Coventry, 1972–79; Presiding Judge, SE Circuit, 1982–85. Member: Gen. Council of the Bar, 1963–67; Senate of Inns of Court and Bar, 1978–79; Lord Chancellor's Adv. Cttee on Trng Magistrates, 1974–80. *Publication:* (contrib.) Agency, in Halsbury's Laws of England, 4th edn. *Recreations:* walking, music, painting, fishing. *Address:* Royal Courts of Justice, Strand, WC2. *Club:* Garrick.

FRENCH, Henry William, CBE 1971; BSc (London); CEng, FIEE, FInstP; FCP; Senior Pro-Chancellor and Chairman of the Council, Loughborough University of Technology, 1981–86 (Pro-Chancellor since 1978); Member of Council, Brighton Polytechnic, since 1976; *b* 14 Feb. 1910; *s* of Henry Moxey French and Alice French (*née* Applegate); *m* 1936, Hazel Anne Mary Ainley; two *s*. *Educ:* Varndean School, Brighton; Woolwich Polytechnic. Engineering Technician, 1925–27; Armed Forces (Royal Corps of Signals, Army Educational Corps), 1927–38; Lecturer, Radar Engineering, Mil. Coll. of Science, 1938–46; Dep. Dir, Educn and Training, Electric and Musical Industries, 1946–48; HM Inspector of Schools (Further Education), 1948–56; Regional Staff Inspector (NW), 1956–59; Staff Inspector (Engineering), 1956–65; Chief Inspector for Further Educn for Industry and Commerce, DES, 1965–72; Sen. Chief Inspector, DES, 1972–74. Hon. DSc Loughborough Univ. of Technology, 1966. *Publications:* Technician Engineering Drawing 1, 1979; Engineering Technicians: some problems of nomenclature and classification, 1980. *Recreations:* polyphonic music, opera, physics of music, travel. *Address:* 26 Crossways, Sutton, Surrey. *T:* 01–642 5277.

FRENCH, Leslie Richard; actor; *b* Kent, 23 April 1904; *s* of Robert Gilbert French and Jetty Sands Leahy; unmarried. *Educ:* London Coll. of Choristers. Began stage work 1914; early Shakespearean training with Sir Philip Ben Greet; parts include Hansel in Hansel and Gretel, Bert in Derby Day; Shakespearean parts include Puck, Ariel, Feste, Costard, etc; The Spirit in Comus; played Feste in the ballet Twelfth Night with the International Ballet at His Majesty's Theatre. Joined the Royal Corps of Signals, 1942; Lord Fancourt Babberly in Charley's Aunt, Christmas 1943. Produced Much Ado About Nothing and The Tempest for OUDS; Everyman as a ballet for the International Ballet Co., Lyric Theatre, 1943; Comus for the International Ballet, London Coliseum, 1946. Productions include: Charles and Mary, Cheltenham Festival, 1948; The Servant of Two Masters; Aladdin (Widow Twanky); Mother Goose (Mother Goose); She Stoops to Conquer for Edinburgh Festival (Tony Lumpkin), 1949; pantomime, Cinderella, 1950; The Dish Ran Away, Whitehall, 1950; Midsummer Night's Dream (Puck), Open Air Theatre during Cheltenham Festival; Open Air Theatre, Regent's Park, 1951; pantomime, Nottingham, 1951–52; The Ghost Train, Huddersfield, 1952; Pisanio in Cymbeline, Attendant Spirit in Comus, Open Air Theatre, 1952; Dyrkin in Out of the Whirlwind, Westminster Abbey, 1953; Open Air Theatre, Cape Town: The Taming of the Shrew, 1956; Midsummer Night's Dream, 1957; As You Like It (Touchstone), 1958; Johannesburg: The Tempest, 1956; Hamlet, 1957; Shakespearean seasons in Cape Town, 1959, 1960, 1961, 1962, 1963, 1966, 1969; Tempest, E. Oppenheimer Theatre, OFS, 1968; The Tell Tale Heart, 1969; An Evening with Shakespeare (tour), 1969; Twelfth Night, Port Elizabeth, 1970; The Way of the World, S Africa, 1970; Co-dir, Open Air Theatre, Regent's Park, 1958. Prod., Twelfth Night (in Great Hall of Hampton Ct Palace), 1965; Le Streghe (for Visconti), 1966; toured USA, 1969–70 and 1970–71: One Man Shakespearean Recitals, and Shylock in Merchant of Venice; The Chaplain in The Lady's not for Burning, Chichester Festival, 1972; toured USA 1973; recitals and prod Twelfth Night; The Tempest, Cape Town, 1973; As You Like It, Port Elizabeth, 1973; Caroline, Yvonne Arnaud Theatre; Directed: Saturday Sunday Monday, Nat. Arts Council, S Africa, 1976; Romeo and Juliet, Cape Town, 1980; numerous appearances on TV. *Films:* Orders to Kill (M Lafitte), 1957; The Scapegoat (M Lacoste), 1958; The Singer not the Song (Father Gomez); The Leopard (Chevalley), 1963; The Witches, 1966; Happy Ever After, 1966; Joseph of Coppertino, 1966; Death in Venice (Visconti), 1970. Several TV appearances incl. Villette (serial), 1970. First Exhibition of Paintings—oil and water colour, Parsons Gall. Presented with Key to City of Cape Town, Jan. 1963. Gold Medals: Port Elizabeth Shakespeare Society, 1973; 1820 Settlers, 1978; Grahamstown Festival, 1977; Hon. Life Mem., Mark Twain Soc., USA, 1976 (all in recognition of his contribution to art and culture in the theatre in England and overseas). *Recreations:* gardening and painting. *Address:* Flat 2, 39 Lennox Gardens, SW1X 0DF. *T:* 01–584 4797; La Stalla, Dosso, Levanto, La Spezia, Italy. *T:* Levanto 800–172. *Club:* Garrick.

FRENCH, Neville Arthur Irwin, CMG 1976; LVO 1968; HM Diplomatic Service, retired; *b* Kenya, 28 April 1920; *s* of late Major Ernest French and Alice Irwin (*née* Powell); *m* 1945, Joyce Ethel, *d* of late Henry Robert Greene, Buenos Aires and Montevideo; one *s* two *d*. *Educ:* London Sch. of Economics (BSc (Econ)). Fleet Auxiliary and Special Duties, Min. of War Transport, 1939–45. Colonial Admin. Service, Tanganyika, 1948, later HMOCS; District Comr, 1949–61; Principal Asst Sec., (External Affairs), Prime Minister's Office, Dar es Salaam, 1961; retd from HMOCS, 1962; Central African Office, 1963–64; 1st Sec., British High Commn, Salisbury, 1964–66; Head of Chancery, British Embassy, Rio de Janeiro, 1966–69; Asst Head of Western Organisations Dept, FCO, 1970–72; Counsellor, and Chargé d'Affaires, Havana, 1972–75; Governor and C-in-C, Falkland Islands, and High Comr, British Antarctic Territory, 1975–77; Dep. High Comr, Madras, 1977–80. Comdr, Order of Rio Branco (Brazil), 1968. *Recreations:* sailing, books. *Address:* c/o Barclays Bank, 84 High Street, Bideford, Devon. *Clubs:* Royal Commonwealth Society, Naval; Madras.

FREND, Rev. Prof. William Hugh Clifford, TD 1959 (Clasp, 1966); DD, FRSE, FSA; FBA 1983; Priest-in-Charge of Barnwell with Thurning and Luddington, since 1984; Professor of Ecclesiastical History, 1969–84, now Professor Emeritus, and Dean of Divinity Faculty, 1972–75, Glasgow University; *b* 11 Jan. 1916; 2nd *s* of late Rev. E. G. C. Frend, Shottermill, Surrey and late Edith (*née* Bacon); *m* 1951, Mary Grace, *d* of late E. A. Crook, FRCS; one *s* one *d*. *Educ:* Fernden Sch.; Haileybury Coll. (Schol.); Keble Coll., Oxford (Schol.). 1st cl. hons Mod. Hist., 1937; Craven Fellow, 1937; DPhil 1940; BD Cantab 1964; DD Oxon 1966. Asst Princ., War Office, 1940; seconded Cabinet Office, 1941; FO, 1942; service in N Africa, Italy and Austria, 1943–46; Ed. Bd, German Foreign Min. Documents, 1947–51; Res. Fellow, Nottingham Univ., 1951; S. A. Cook Bye-Fellow, 1952, Fellow, 1956–69, Dir Studies, Archaeology, 1961–69, Gonville and Caius Coll.; University Asst Lectr, 1953, Lectr in Divinity, 1958–69; Birkbeck Lectr in Ecclesiastical History, 1967–68. Chm., AUT (Scotland), 1976–78. Vice-Pres., Assoc. internat. d'Etudes patristiques, 1983–; Président d'Honneur, Internat. Commn for Comparative Study of Ecclesiastical History (CIHEC), 1983 (Vice-Pres. 1975–80, Pres. 1980–83). Assoc. Dir, Egypt Exploration Soc. excavations at Q'asr Ibrim, Nubia, 1963–64; Guest Scholar at Rhodes Univ., 1964 and Peter Ainslie Meml Lecturer; Guest Prof., Univ. of S Africa, 1976; Vis. Prof. of Inter-religious Studies (Walter and Mary Tuohy Chair), John Carroll Univ., Cleveland, 1981; Vis. Fellow, Harvard Univ. Center for Byzantine Studies, Dumbarton Oaks, 1984. Licensed Lay Reader, 1956, Deacon, 1982, Priest, 1983; serving in Aberfoyle parish. Editor, Modern Churchman, 1963–82. Commission Queen's Royal Regt (TA), 1947–67. FSA 1952; FRHistS 1954; FRSE 1979. Hon. DD Edinburgh, 1974. *Publications:* The Donatist Church, 1952; Martyrdom and Persecution in the Early Church, 1965; The Early Church, 1965; (contrib.) Religion in the Middle East, 1968; The Rise of the Monophysite Movement, 1972; Religion Popular and Unpopular in the Early Christian Centuries, 1976; (contrib.) Cambridge History of Africa, vol. ii, 1978; Town and Country in the Early Christian Centuries, 1980; The Rise of Christianity, 1984; Saints and Sinners in the Early Church, 1985; articles in Jl Theol Studies, Jl Roman Studies, Jl Eccles. History, etc. *Recreations:* archæology, occasional golf and tennis, writing, collecting old coins and stamps. *Address:* The Rectory, Barnwell, Peterborough PE8 5PG. *Club:* Authors'.

FRERE, James Arnold, FSA, FRGS; *b* 20 April 1920; *e s* of late John Geoffrey Frere. *Educ:* Eton Coll.; Trinity Coll., Cambridge. Lieut Intelligence Corps, 1944–47. Regular Army R of O, 1949–67. Bluemantle Pursuivant of Arms, 1948–56; Chester Herald of Arms, 1956–60; an Officer of Supreme Court of Judicature, 1966–70. Member: Surrey Archæological Soc. (Council, 1949–53, 1954–58 and 1959–63); American Soc. of Authors; Council of the Harleian Soc., 1951–66; Hon. Mem. Heraldry Soc. of Southern Africa, 1953–; a Vice-Pres. of Museum of Costume, 1952–60. Press Sec., New Gallery Clinic, 1967–70. Liveryman, Worshipful Co. of Scriveners, 1950 (now Sen. Liveryman). Mountjoy King of Arms and Judge-at-Arms, Internat. Coll. of Arms of Noblesse, 1982–; Grand Master of Ceremonies, Supreme Military Order of Temple of Jerusalem; KM 1959; Knight Grand Cross, and Clairvaux King of Arms, SMO of Temple of Jerusalem, 1981; Kt of Justice and Devotion, Mil. Order of the Collar of St Agatha of Paterno', 1985; Rey de Armas y Cronista de Perpiñan, 1986. Hon. Consul for Poland (in exile), Powys, 1984–. Commander's Cross, Polonia Restituta, 1983; Polish Gold Cross of Merit, 1983. *Publications:* The British Monarchy at Home, 1963; (jointly with the Duchess of Bedford) Now . . . The Duchesses, 1964. *Recreations:* walking, painting, archæology. *Address:* c/o Society of Antiquaries, Burlington House, Piccadilly, W1.

FRERE, Prof. Sheppard Sunderland, CBE 1976; FSA 1944; FBA 1971; Professor of the Archæology of the Roman Empire, and Fellow of All Souls College, Oxford University, 1966–83, now professor Emeritus and Emeritus Fellow; *b* 23 Aug. 1916; *e s* of late N. G. Frere, CMG; *m* 1961, Janet Cecily Hoare; one *s* one *d*. *Educ:* Lancing Coll.; Magdalene Coll., Cambridge. BA 1938, MA 1944, LittD 1976, DLitt 1977. Master, Epsom Coll., 1938–40. National Fire Service, 1940–45. Master, Lancing Coll., 1945–54; Lecturer in Archæology, Manchester Univ., 1954–55; Reader in Archæology of Roman Provinces, London Univ. Inst. of Archæology, 1955–62; Prof. of the Archæology of the Roman Provinces, London Univ., 1963–66. Dir, Canterbury Excavations, 1946–60; Dir, Verulamium Excavations, 1955–61. Vice-Pres., Soc. of Antiquaries, 1962–66; President: Oxford Architectural and Historical Soc., 1972–80; Royal Archæological Inst., 1978–81; Soc. for Promotion of Roman Studies, 1983–86. Hon. Corr. Mem. German Archæological Inst., 1964, Fellow, 1967; Member: Royal Commn on Hist. Monuments (England), 1966–83; Ancient Monuments Board (England), 1966–82. Hon. LittD: Leeds, 1977; Leicester, 1983; Kent, 1985. Editor, Britannia, 1969–79. *Publications:* (ed) Problems of the Iron Age in Southern Britain, 1961; Britannia, a history of Roman Britain, 1967 (rev. edn 1974); Verulamium Excavations, vol. I, 1972, vol. II, 1983, vol. III, 1984; Excavations on the Roman and Medieval Defences of Canterbury, 1982; Excavations at Canterbury, vol. VII, 1983; (with J. K. St Joseph) Roman Britain from the Air, 1983; papers in learned jls. *Recreation:* gardening. *Address:* Netherfield House, Marcham, Abingdon, Oxon.

FRESHWATER, Prof. Donald Cole, FEng 1986; Head of Department of Chemical Engineering, since 1957, and Dean of Pure and Applied Science, 1982–85, University of Technology, Loughborough; *b* 21 April 1924; *s* of Thomas and Ethel May Freshwater; *m* 1948, Margaret D. Worrall (marr. diss. 1977); one *s* three *d*; *m* 1980, Eleanor M. Lancashire (*née* Tether). *Educ:* Brewood Grammar Sch.; Birmingham Univ. (BSc, PhD); Sheffield Univ.; Loughborough Coll. (DLC). Fuel Engineer, Min. of Fuel and Power, 1944; Chemical Engr: APV Co. Ltd, 1948; Midland Tar Distillers Co. Ltd, 1950; Lectr, Dept of Chem. Engrg, Univ. of Birmingham, 1952. Visiting Professor: Univ. of Delaware, USA, 1962; Georgia Inst. of Technology, 1980–81. Chm., Chem. Engrg Gp, Soc. of Chemical Industry, 1973–75; Mem. Council, IChemE, 1982– (Vice Pres., 1985–). *Publications:* Chemical Engineering Data Book, 1959; numerous papers on mass transfer and particle technology in chem. engrg jls. *Recreations:* sailing, collecting watercolours. *Address:* Head of Department of Chemical Engineering, Loughborough University of Technology, Ashby Road, Loughborough, Leics LE11 3TU. *T:* Loughborough 263171. *Club:* Athenæum.

FRETWELL, Elizabeth, OBE 1977; operatic and dramatic soprano; *b* Melbourne, Australia; *m* Robert Simmons; one *s* one *d*. *Educ:* privately. Joined National Theatre, Melbourne, 1950; came to Britain, 1955; joined Sadler's Wells, 1956; Australia, Elizabethan Opera Co., 1963; tour of W Germany, 1963; USA, Canada and Covent Garden, 1964; tour of Europe, 1965; guest soprano with Cape Town and Durban Opera Cos, South Africa, 1970; joined Australian Opera, 1970. Rôles include Violetta in La Traviata, Leonora in Fidelio, Ariadne in Ariadne auf Naxos, Senta in The Flying Dutchman, Minnie in The Girl of the Golden West, Leonora in Il Trovatore, Aida, Ellen Orford in Peter Grimes, Leonora in Forza del Destino, Alice Ford in Falstaff, Amelia in

Masked Ball, Georgetta in Il Tabarro, opening season of Sydney Opera Hse, 1973. Has sung in BBC Promenade Concerts and on TV. Mem., music bd, Opera Foundn Australia, 1982–. *Recreation:* rose-growing. *Address:* c/o Australian Opera, PO Box 291, Strawberry Hills, NSW 2012, Australia.

FRETWELL, Sir George (Herbert), KBE 1953; CB 1950; Director General of Works, Air Ministry, 1947–59, retired; *b* 21 March 1900; *s* of late Herbert Fretwell, Ripley, Derbyshire; *m* 1930, Constance Mabel, *d* of late George Ratcliffe, Woodford Green, Essex; no *c. Educ:* Heanor Grammar Sch., Derbs. Entered Air Ministry as Asst Civil Engineer, 1928; service in Inland area RAF, Aden, South Arabia and Air Defence Gp; Civil Engineer, 1934; Superintending Engineer, RAF Malaya, 1937; Chief Engineer, Far East Command, 1940; Chief Supt of Design (Works), 1941; Chief Engr ADGB/Fighter Command, 1944; Dep. Dir of Works, 1945, Dir, 1946. *Address:* North Lodge, 2 North Street, Sheringham, Norfolk. *T:* Sheringham 822336.

FRETWELL, Sir (Major) John (Emsley), KCMG 1982 (CMG 1975); HM Diplomatic Service; Ambassador to France, since 1982; *b* 15 June 1930; *s* of F. T. Fretwell; *m* 1959, Mary Ellen Eugenie Dubois; one *s* one *d. Educ:* Chesterfield Grammar Sch.; Lausanne Univ.; King's Coll., Cambridge (MA). HM Forces, 1948–50. Diplomatic Service, 1953; 3rd Sec., Hong Kong, 1954–55; 2nd Sec., Peking, 1955–57; FO, 1957–59; 1st Sec., Moscow, 1959–62; FO, 1962–67; 1st Sec. (Commercial), Washington, 1967–70; Commercial Counsellor, Warsaw, 1971–73; Head of European Integration Dept (Internal), FCO, 1973–76; Asst Under-Sec. of State, FCO, 1976–79; Minister, Washington, 1980–81. *Recreations:* skiing, walking. *Address:* c/o Foreign and Commonwealth Office, SW1A 2AH.

FREUD, Clement Raphael; MP (L) Cambridgeshire North-East, since 1983 (Isle of Ely, July 1973–1983); writer, broadcaster, caterer; *b* 24 April 1924; *s* of late Ernst and Lucie Freud; *m* 1950, Jill, 2nd *d* of H. W. Flewett, MA; three *s* two *d.* Apprenticed, Dorchester Hotel, London. Served War, Royal Ulster Rifles; Liaison Officer, Nuremberg war crimes trials, 1946. Trained, Martinez Hotel, Cannes. Proprietor, Royal Court Theatre Club, 1952–62. Sports writer, Observer, 1956–64; Cookery Editor: Time and Tide, 1961–63; Observer Magazine, 1964–68; Daily Telegraph Magazine, 1968–. Sports Columnist, Sun, 1964–69; Columnist: Sunday Telegraph, 1963–65; News of the World, 1965; Financial Times, 1964–; Daily Express, 1973–75. Liberal spokesman on education, the arts and broadcasting; sponsor, Official Information Bill. Chm., Standing Cttee, Liberal Party, 1982–. Rector, Univ. of Dundee, 1974–80. Patron, Down's Children Assoc. £5,000 class winner, Daily Mail London-NY air race, 1969. Award winning petfood commercial: San Francisco, Tokyo, Berlin, 1967. BBC (sound) Just a Minute, 1968–. *Publications:* Grimble, 1968; Grimble at Christmas, 1973; Freud on Food, 1978; Clicking Vicky, 1980; The Book of Hangovers, 1981; Below the Belt, 1983; contributor to: Punch, Queen, Town, Which, New Yorker, etc. *Recreations:* racing, backgammon. *Address:* 22 Wimpole Street, W1. *T:* 01–580 2222; 15 High Street, Mepal, Ely. *T:* Ely 778888. *Clubs:* MCC, Lord's Taverners'; British Rail Staff Assoc. (March).

See also Lucian Freud.

FREUD, Lucian, CH 1983; painter; *b* 8 Dec. 1922; *s* of late Ernst and Lucie Freud; *m* 1st, 1948, Kathleen Garman Epstein (marr. diss. 1952), *d* of Jacob Epstein; two *d*; 2nd, 1953, Lady Caroline Maureen Blackwood (marr. diss. 1957), *d* of 4th Marquess of Dufferin and Ava. *Educ:* Central Sch. of Art; East Anglian Sch. of Painting and Drawing. Worked on merchant ship SS Baltrover as ordinary seaman, 1942. Teacher, Slade Sch. of Art, 1948–58; Vis. Asst, Norwich Sch. of Art, 1964–65. Painted mostly in France and Greece, 1946–48. Exhibitions: Lefevre Gall., 1944, 1946; London Gall., 1947, 1948; British Council and Galérie René Drouin, Paris, 1948; Hanover Gall., 1950, 1952; British Council and Vancouver Art Gall., 1951; British Council, Venice Biennale, 1954; Marlborough Fine Art, 1958, 1963, 1968; Anthony d'Offay, 1972, 1978 (subseq. Davis & Long, NY), 1982; 1st retrospective, Hayward Gall., 1974 (subseq. Bristol, Birmingham and Leeds); Nishimura Gall., Tokyo, 1979; Thos Agnew & Sons, 1983. Works included in public collections: London: Tate Gall.; Nat. Portrait Gall.; V & A Museum; Arts Council of GB; British Council; British Mus.; DoE; provinces: Cecil Higgins Museum, Bedford; Fitzwilliam Mus., Cambridge; Nat. Mus. of Wales, Cardiff; Scottish Nat. Gall. of Mod. Art, Edinburgh; Hartlepool Art Gall.; Walker Art Gall., Liverpool; Liverpool Univ.; City Art Gall. and Whitworth Gall., Manchester; Ashmolean Mus. of Art, Oxford; Harris Mus. and Art Gall., Preston; Rochdale Art Gall.; Southampton Art Gall.; Australia: Queensland Art Gall., Brisbane; Art Gall. of S Australia, Adelaide; Art Gall. of WA, Perth; France: Musée National d'Art Moderne, Centre Georges Pompidou, Paris; USA: Beaverbrook Foundn, Fredericton, New Brunswick; Mus. of Mod. Art, NY; Cleveland Mus. of Art, Ohio; Mus. of Art, Carnegie Inst., Pittsburgh; Achenbaach Foundn for Graphic Arts and Fine Arts Mus. of San Francisco. *Relevant publication:* Lucian Freud, by Lawrence Gowing, 1982. *Address:* c/o James Kirkman, 46 Brompton Square, SW3 2AF.

See also C. R. Freud.

FREYBERG, family name of **Baron Freyberg.**

FREYBERG, 2nd Baron, *cr* 1951, of Wellington, New Zealand, and of Munstead in the Co. of Surrey; **Paul Richard Freyberg,** OBE 1965; MC 1945; *b* 27 May 1923; *s* of 1st Baron Freyberg, VC, GCMG, KCB, KBE, DSO (and 3 bars), and Barbara, GBE (*d* 1973), *d* of Sir Herbert Jekyll, KCMG, and Lady Jekyll, DBE; *S* father, 1963; *m* 1960, Ivry Perronelle Katharine Guild, Aspall Hall, Debenham, Suffolk; one *s* three *d. Educ:* Eton Coll. Joined NZ Army, 1940; served with 2nd NZEF: Greece, 1941; Western Desert, 1941–42; transferred to British Army, 1942; Grenadier Guards; North Africa, 1943; Italy, 1943–45 (MC); Palestine, 1947–48; Cyprus, 1956–58; British Cameroons, 1961; Comd HAC Infantry Battalion, 1965–68; Defence Policy Staff, MoD, 1968–71; Dir Volunteers, Territorials and Cadets, 1971–75; Col, Gen. Staff, 1975–78, retired. Staff Coll., 1952; jssc 1958; sowc 1971. *Heir: s* Hon. Valerian Bernard Freyberg, *b* 15 Dec. 1970. *Address:* Munstead House, Godalming, Surrey. *T:* Godalming 6004. *Clubs:* Boodle's, Royal Automobile.

FRICKER, (Anthony) Nigel; QC 1977; **His Honour Judge Fricker;** a Circuit Judge, since 1984; *b* 7 July 1937; *s* of late Dr William Shapland Fricker and of Margaret Fricker; *m* 1960, Marilyn Ann, *d* of A. L. Martin, Pa, USA; one *s* two *d. Educ:* King's School, Chester; Liverpool Univ. (LLB 1958). President of Guild of Undergraduates, Liverpool Univ., 1958–59. Called to Bar, Gray's Inn, 1960. Conf. Leader, Ford Motor Co. of Australia, Melbourne, 1960–61. Recorder, Crown Court, 1975–84; Prosecuting Counsel to DHSS, Wales and Chester Circuit, 1975–77; an asst comr, Boundary Commn for Wales, 1981–84. Member: Bar Council, 1966–70; Senate and Bar Council, 1975–78. Fellow, Internat. Acad. of Trial Lawyers, 1979–. Mem. Court: Liverpool Univ., 1977–; York Univ., 1984–. *Address:* 6 Park Square, Leeds LS1 2LW. *T:* Leeds (0532) 459763; Farrar's Building, Temple, EC4Y 7BD. *T:* 01–583 9241. *Club:* Yorkshire (York).

FRICKER, Prof. Peter Racine, FRCO, ARCM; Professor of Music, Music Department, University of California, Santa Barbara, since 1964; Director of Music, Morley College, 1952–64; *b* 5 Sept. 1920; *s* of late Edward Racine Fricker; *m* 1943, Audrey Helen Clench. *Educ:* St Paul's Sch. Royal College of Music, 1937–40. Served War, 1940–46, in Royal Air Force, working in Signals and Intelligence. Has worked as Composer, Conductor, and Music Administrator since 1946. Hon. Professorial Fellow, Univ. of Wales, Cardiff, 1971. Hon. RAM, 1966. Hon. DMus (Leeds), 1958. Order of Merit, West Germany, 1965. *Publications:* Four Fughettas for Two Pianos, 1946; Wind Quintet, 1947; Three Sonnets of Cecco Angiolieri da Siena, for Tenor and Seven Instruments, 1947; String Quartet in One Movement, 1948; Symphony No 1, 1948–49; Prelude, Elegy and Finale for String Orchestra, 1949; Concerto for Violin and Orchestra, 1949–50; Sonata for Violin and Piano, 1950; Concertante for Cor Anglais and String Orchestra, 1950; Symphony No 2, 1950; Concertante for Three Pianos, Strings and Timpani, 1951; Four Impromptus for Piano; Concerto for Viola and Orchestra, 1951–53; Concerto for Piano and Orchestra, 1952–54; String Quartet No 2, 1952–53; Rapsodia Concertante for Violin and Orchestra, 1953–54; Dance Scene for Orchestra, 1954; Musick's Empire for Chorus and Small Orchestra, 1955; Litany for Double String Orchestra, 1955; 'Cello Sonata, 1956; Oratorio, The Vision of Judgement, 1956–58; Octet, 1958; Toccata for Piano and Orchestra, 1958–59; Serenade No 1, 1959; Serenade No 2, 1959; Symphony No 3, 1960; Studies for Piano, 1961; Cantata for Tenor and Chamber Ensemble, 1962; O Longs Désirs: Song-cycle for Soprano and Orchestra, 1963; Ricercare for Organ, 1965; Four Dialogues for Oboe and Piano, 1965; Four Songs for High Voice and Orchestra, 1965; Fourth Symphony, 1966; Fantasy for Viola and Piano, 1966; Three Scenes for Orchestra, 1966; The Day and the Spirits for Soprano and Harp, 1967; Seven Counterpoints for Orchestra, 1967; Magnificat, 1968; Episodes for Piano, 1968; Concertante No 4, 1968; Toccata for Organ, 1968; Saxophone Quartet, 1969; Praeludium for Organ, 1969; Paseo for Guitar, 1970; The Roofs for coloratura soprano and percussion, 1970; Sarabande In Memoriam Igor Stravinsky, 1971; Nocturne for chamber orchestra, 1971; Intrada for organ, 1971; A Bourrée for Sir Arthur Bliss for cello, 1971; Concertante no 5 for piano and string quartet, 1971; Introitus for orchestra, 1972; Come Sleep for contralto, alto flute and bass clarinet, 1972; Fanfare for Europe for trumpet, 1972; Ballade for flute and piano, 1972; Seven Little Songs for chorus, 1972; Gigue for cello, 1973; The Groves of Dodona for six flutes, 1973; Spirit Puck, for clarinet and percussion, 1974; Two Petrarch Madrigals, 1974; Trio-Sonata for Organ, 1974; Third String Quartet, 1975; Fifth Symphony, 1975; Seachant for flute and double bass, 1976; Sinfonia for 17 wind instruments, 1976; Anniversary for piano, 1977; Sonata for two pianos, 1977; Serenade for four clarinets, 1977; Laudi Concertati for organ and orchestra, 1979; Serenade No 5, 1979; In Commendation of Music, 1980; Five Short Pieces for organ, 1980; Six Mélodies de Francis Jammes for tenor, violin, cello and piano, 1980; Spells for solo flute, 1980; Bagatelles for clarinet and piano, 1981; For Three, for oboes, 1981; Two Expressions for Piano, 1981; Rondeaux for horn and orchestra, 1982; Whispers at these Curtains (oratorio), 1984; Madrigals for Brass Quintet, 1984; Aspects of Evening for cello and piano, 1985; Concertino for St Paul's (orch.), 1985; Recitative, Impromptu, and Procession for organ, 1985; Concerto for orch., 1986; also music for film, stage and radio. *Recreation:* travel. *Address:* Department of Music, University of California, Santa Barbara, Calif 93106, USA. *Club:* East India, Devonshire, Sports and Public Schools.

FRIEDLANDER, Frederick Gerard, (Friedrich Gerhart), PhD; FRS 1980; Reader Emeritus, University of Cambridge, since 1982; Hon. Research Fellow, Department of Mathematics, University College London; *b* Vienna, 25 Dec. 1917. *Educ:* Univ. of Cambridge (BA, PhD). Fellow of Trinity Coll., Cambridge, 1940; Temporary Experimental Officer, Admiralty, 1943; Faculty Asst Lectr, Cambridge, 1945; Lecturer: Univ. of Manchester, 1946; Univ. of Cambridge, 1954; Fellow of St John's Coll., Cambridge, 1961; Fellow of Wolfson Coll., Cambridge, 1968; Reader in Partial Differential Equations, Univ. of Cambridge, 1979. *Publications:* Sound Pulses, 1958; The Wave Equation on a Curved Space-Time, 1975; Introduction to the Theory of Distributions, 1982; papers in mathematical jls. *Address:* 43 Narcissus Road, NW6 1TL. *T:* 01–794 8665.

FRIEDMAN, Prof. Milton, PhD; Economist, USA; Senior Research Fellow, Hoover Institution, Stanford University, since 1976; Professor Emeritus of Economics, University of Chicago, since 1982 (Professor of Economics, 1948–82); Member of Research Staff, National Bureau of Economic Research, 1948–81; Economic Columnist, Newsweek, 1966–84; *b* New York, 31 July 1912; *s* of Jeno Saul and Sarah E. Friedman; *m* 1938, Rose Director; one *s* one *d. Educ:* Rutgers (AB), Chicago (AM), and Columbia (PhD) Univs. Associate Economist, Natural Resources Cttee, Washington, 1935–37; Nat. Bureau of Economic Research, New York, 1937–45 (on leave 1940–45). During 1941–45: Principal Economist, Tax Research Div., US Treasury Dept, 1941–43; Associate Dir, Statistical Research Gp, Div. of War Research, Columbia Univ., 1943–45. Fulbright Lecturer, Cambridge Univ., 1953–54; Vis. Prof., Econs, Columbia Univ., 1964–65, etc. Member: President's Commn on an All-Volunteer Armed Force, 1969–70; Commn on White House Fellows, 1971–73. Mem. Bd of Editors, Econometrica, 1957–65; Pres., Amer. Economic Assoc., 1967; Pres., Mont Pelerin Soc., 1970–72. John Bates Clark Medal, Amer. Econ. Assoc., 1951; Fellowships and awards, in USA. Nobel Memorial Prize for Economics, 1976. Member various societies, etc., incl. Royal Economic Soc. (GB). Holds several Hon. doctorates. *Publications:* Income from Independent Professional Practice (with Simon Kuznets), 1946; Sampling Inspection (with others), 1948; Essays in Positive Economics, 1953; (ed) Studies in the Quantity Theory of Money, 1956; A Theory of the Consumption Function, 1957; A Program for Monetary Stability, 1960; Capitalism and Freedom, 1962; Price Theory: a Provisional Text, 1962; A Monetary History of the United States 1867–1960 (with Anna J. Schwartz), 1963; Inflation: Causes and Consequences, 1963; The Balance of Payments: Free versus Flexible Exchange Rates (with Robert V. Roosa), 1967; Dollars and Deficits, 1968; Optimum Quantity of Money and Other Essays, 1969; Monetary vs Fiscal Policy (with Walter W. Heller), 1969; Monetary Statistics of the United States (with Anna J. Schwartz), 1970; A Theoretical Framework for Monetary Analysis, 1971; Social Security: Universal or Selective? (with Wilbur J. Cohen), 1972; An Economist's Protest, 1972; Money and Economic Development, 1973; There's No Such Thing as a Free Lunch, 1975; Price Theory, 1976; Free to Choose (with Rose Friedman), 1980; Monetary Trends in the United States and the United Kingdom (with Anna J. Schwahtz), 1982; Bright Promises, Dismal Performance, 1983; (with Rose Friedman) Tyranny of the Status Quo, 1984. *Recreations:* tennis, carpentry. *Address:* Hoover Institution, Stanford, Calif 94305, USA. *Club:* Quadrangle (Chicago).

FRIEL, Brian; writer; *b* 9 Jan. 1929; *s* of Patrick Friel and Christina Friel (*née* MacLoone); *m* 1954, Anne Morrison; one *s* four *d. Educ:* St Columb's Coll., Derry; St Patrick's Coll., Maynooth; St Joseph's Trng Coll., Belfast. Taught in various schools, 1950–60; writing full-time from 1960. Lived in Minnesota during first season of Tyrone Guthrie Theater, Minneapolis. Member: Irish Acad. of Letters, 1972; Aosdana, 1983–. Hon. DLitt NUI, 1983. *Publications: collected stories:* The Saucer of Larks, 1962; The Gold in the Sea, 1966; *plays:* Philadelphia, Here I Come!, 1965; The Loves of Cass McGuire, 1967; Lovers, 1968; The Mundy Scheme, 1969; Crystal and Fox, 1970; The Gentle Island, 1971; The Freedom of the City, 1973; Volunteers, 1975; Living Quarters, 1976; Aristocrats, 1979; Faith Healer, 1979; Translations, 1981 (Ewart-Biggs Meml Prize, British Theatre Assoc. Award); (trans.) Three Sisters, 1981; The Communication Cord, 1983. *Recreations:* reading, trout-fishing, slow tennis. *Address:* Drumaweir House, Greencastle, Co. Donegal, Ireland.

FRIEND, His Honour Archibald Gordon; a Circuit Judge, 1972–84, retired; *b* 6 July 1912; *m* 1940, Patricia Margaret Smith; no *c*. *Educ:* Dulwich Coll.; Keble Coll., Oxford (MA). Called to the Bar, Inner Temple, 1933. Served War: enlisted RA, Feb. 1940, commnd Nov. 1940; on staff of JAG MEF and PAIFORCE, 1941–44 (Major); released 1945. Dep. Chairman: Herts Quarter Sessions, 1963–71; Inner London, later Mddx QS, 1965–71. *Recreation:* gardening. *Address:* 16 Ladbroke Grove, W11 3BQ.

FRIEND, Bernard Ernest, CBE 1986; Finance Director, British Aerospace, since 1977; *b* 18 May 1924; *s* of Richard Friend and Ada Florence Friend; *m* 1951, Pamela Florence Amor; one *s* two *d*. *Educ:* Dover Grammar Sch. Chartered Accountant. Flying Officer, RAF, 1943–47. Arthur Young & Co., Chartered Accountants, 1948–55; Comptroller, Esso Petroleum Co. Ltd, 1961–66; Dep. Controller, Esso Europe, 1967–68; Man. Dir, Essoheat, 1968–69; Vice-Pres., Esso Chemicals, Brussels, 1970–73; Chm. and Man. Dir, Esso Chemicals Ltd, 1974–76. Non-Exec. Dir, Iron Trades Insurance Gp, 1980–. *Address:* British Aerospace, Brooklands Road, Weybridge, Surrey KT13 0SJ. *Club:* Royal Air Force.

FRIEND, Dame Phyllis (Muriel), DBE 1980 (CBE 1972); Chief Nursing Officer, Department of Health and Social Security, 1972–82; *b* 28 Sept. 1922; *d* of Richard Edward Friend. *Educ:* Herts and Essex High Sch., Bishop's Stortford; The London Hospital (SRN); Royal College of Nursing (RNT). Dep. Matron, St George's Hospital, 1956–59; Dep. Matron, 1959–61, Matron, 1961–68, Chief Nursing Officer 1969–72, The London Hospital. *Address:* Barnmead, Start Hill, Bishop's Stortford, Herts. *T:* Bishop's Stortford 54873.

FRINK, Dame Elisabeth, DBE 1982 (CBE 1969); RA 1977 (ARA 1971); sculptor; *b* 14 Nov. 1930; British; *m* 1st, 1955, Michel Jammet (marr. diss. 1963); one *s*; 2nd, Edward Pool, MC (marr. diss. 1974); 3rd, Alexander Csáky. *Educ:* Convent of The Holy Family, Exmouth. Guildford Sch. of Art, 1947–49; Chelsea Sch. of Art, 1949–53. Exhibitions: Beaux Arts Gallery, 1952; St George's Gallery, 1955; Royal Academy, 1985; exhibits regularly at Waddington Gallery, later Waddington and Tooth Galleries, now Waddington Galleries, London. Represented in collections in USA, Australia, Holland, Sweden, Germany and Tate Gallery, London. Member: Bd Trustees, British Museum, 1975–; Royal Fine Art Commn, 1976–81. Hon. Fellow: St Hilda's Coll., Oxford, 1986; Newnham Coll., Cambridge, 1986. *Address:* c/o Waddington Galleries, 2 Cork Street, W1.

FRIPP, Alfred Thomas, BM; FRCS; *b* 3 July 1899; *s* of late Sir Alfred Fripp, KCVO, and late Lady M. S. Fripp, *d* of late T. B. Haywood; *m* 1931, Kathleen Kimpton, (Jennie) (*d* 1986); one *s* two *d*. *Educ:* Winchester; Christ Church, Oxford. 2nd Lieut 1st Life Guards, 1917–18. Christ Church, Oxford, 1919–21; Guy's Hospital, 1921; Surg., Royal National Orthopædic Hospital, 1934–64. Mem., Pensions Appeal Tribunal, 1966–74. FRCS 1927. Pres. Orthopædic Section, RSocMed, 1950–51. *Recreations:* gardening, rowing. *Address:* Shalesbrook, Forest Row, Sussex RH18 5LS. *Club:* Leander (Henley-on-Thames).

FRISBY, Audrey Mary; *see* Jennings, A. M.

FRISBY, Roger Harry Kilbourne; QC 1969; a Recorder, 1972–78 and since 1986; *b* 11 Dec. 1921; 2nd *s* of late Herbert Frisby and Hylda Mary Frisby; *m* 1961, Audrey Mary (*née* Jennings), *qv* (marr. diss. 1980); two *s* one *d* (and one *s* one *d* by previous marriage). *Educ:* Bablake Sch.; Christ Church, Oxford; King's Coll., Univ. of London. Called to the Bar, Lincoln's Inn, 1950. *Address:* Queen Elizabeth Building, Temple, EC4Y 9BS. *T:* 01–583 5766. *Clubs:* United Oxford & Cambridge University; Hurlingham.

FRISBY, Terence; playwright, actor, producer; *b* 28 Nov. 1932; *s* of William and Kathleen Frisby; *m* 1963, Christine Vecchione (marr. diss.); one *s*. *Educ:* Dobwalls Village Sch.; Dartford Grammar Sch.; Central Sch. of Speech Training and Dramatic Art. Substantial repertory acting experience, also TV, films and musicals, 1957–63; appeared in A Sense of Detachment, Royal Court, 1972–73 and X, Royal Court, 1974. Productions: Once a Catholic (tour), 1980–81; There's a Girl in My Soup (tour), 1982; Woza Albert!, 1983; The Real Inspector Hound/Seaside Postcard (double bill), 1983–84; Comic Cuts, 1984. Has written many TV scripts, incl. series Lucky Feller, 1976; film, There's A Girl in My Soup, 1970 (Writers Guild Award, Best British Comedy Screenplay). *Publications: plays:* The Subtopians, 1964; There's a Girl in My Soup, 1966; The Bandwagon, 1970; It's All Right if I Do It, 1977; Seaside Postcard, 1978. *Address:* c/o Harvey Unna and Stephen Durbridge Ltd, 24 Pottery Lane, Holland Park, W11. *T:* 01–727 1346. *Club:* Wentworth Golf.

FRISCHMANN, Wilem William, PhD; FEng 1985; FIStructE; Senior Partner, Pell Frischmann & Partners and Conseco International, Consulting Engineers, since 1968; *b* 27 Jan. 1931; *s* of Lajos Frischmann and Nelly Frischmann; *m* 1957, Sylvia Elvey; one *s* one *d*. *Educ:* Hungary; Hammersmith College of Art and Building; Imperial Coll. of Science and Technology (DIC); City University (PhD). MASCE, MSocIS, MConsE. Engineering training with F. J. Samuely and Partners and W. S. Atkins and Partners; joined C. J. Pell and Partners, 1958, Partner, 1961. Structural Engineer for Nat. Westminster Tower (ICE Telford Premium Award), Centre Point, Drapers Gardens tower (IStructE Oscar Faber Prize) and similar high buildings, leisure buildings, hotels and hospitals; Engineer for works at Bank of England, Mansion House and Alexandra Palace; particular interest and involvement in tall economic buildings, shear walls and diaphragm floors, large bored piles in London clay, deep basements, lightweight materials for large span bridges, monitoring and quality assurance procedures for offshore structures; advisory appts include: Hong Kong and Shanghai Bank HQ, Malayan Banking Berhad, Kuala Lumpur. *Publications:* The use and behaviour of large diameter piles in London clay (IStructE paper), 1962; papers to learned socs and instns, originator of concepts: English Channel free-trade port; industrial complex based on Varne and Colbart sandbanks; two-mile high vertical city. *Recreations:* ski-ing, tennis, swimming, architecture, work. *Address:* (office) 5 Manchester Square, W1A 1AU; Haversham Grange, Haversham Close, Twickenham, Middx TW1 2JP. *T:* 01–892 8829. *Club:* Arts.

FRITH, Anthony Ian Donald; Chairman, South Western Region, British Gas Corporation, since 1973; *b* 11 March 1929; *s* of Ernest and Elizabeth Frith; *m* 1952, Joyce Marcelle Boyce; one *s* one *d*. *Educ:* various grammar schs and techn. colls. CEng, FIGasE, MInstM. Various appts in North Thames Gas Bd and Gas Light & Coke Co., 1945–65; Sales Man. 1965–67, Dep. Commercial Man. 1967–68, North Thames Gas Bd; Marketing Man., Domestic and Commercial Gas, Gas Council, 1968–72; Sales Dir, British Gas Corp., 1972–73. CBIM 1983. *Publications:* various techn. and prof. in Gas Engineering and other jls. *Recreations:* fishing, golf. *Address:* Firbank, 32 High Street, Saltford, Avon.

FRITH, Donald Alfred, OBE 1980; MA; Chairman, North Yorkshire Forum for Voluntary Organisations, since 1983; Assistant Director, Centre for Study of Comprehensive Schools, since 1983; *b* 13 May 1918; *yr s* of late Charles Henry Frith and Mabel (*née* Whiting); *m* 1941, Mary Webster Tyler, *yr d* of late Raymond Tyler and Rosina Mary (*née* Wiles); four *s* one *d*. *Educ:* Whitgift Sch. (schol.); Christ's Coll., Cambridge (schol.). MA Cantab 1944. Served War, 1940–46; commnd RASC; served in Middle East, Italy and at WO. Deme Warden, University College Sch., 1946–52; Headmaster, Richmond Sch., Yorks, 1953–59; Headmaster, Archbishop Holgate's Grammar Sch., York, 1959–78. Sec., HMC, and Gen. Sec., SHA, 1979–83. Chm., School Curriculum (formerly Schools Council) Industry Project, 1979–86. Additional Mem., N Yorks CC Educn Cttee, 1973–77. Chm., York Community Council, 1971–79. JP York, 1966–79. *Publication:* (gen. ed.) School Management in Practice, 1985. *Recreations:* music, gardening, walking. *Address:* Kilburn, York YO6 4AQ. *Clubs:* Athenæum; Yorkshire (York).

FRITH, Air Vice-Marshal Edward Leslie, CB 1973; *b* 18 March 1919; *s* of late Charles Edward Frith, ISO. *Educ:* Haberdashers' Askes School. Gp Captain, 1961; Air Cdre, 1968; Dir of Personal Services (2) RAF, MoD, 1969–71; Air Vice-Marshal, 1971; Air Officer Administration, Maintenance Comd, later Support Comd, 1971–74. *Recreations:* lawn tennis, bridge. *Address:* 27 Chartwell, 80 Parkside, Wimbledon, SW19 5LN. *T:* 01–789 2979. *Clubs:* All England Lawn Tennis and Croquet, International Lawn Tennis of GB.

FRITSCH, Elizabeth; potter; *b* Wales, 1940. *Educ:* Royal College of Art, London. Established workshop at Welwyn Garden City. Won Herbert Read Memorial Prize; Royal Copenhagen Jubilee competition, 1972. Member, Crafts Council (Bursary awarded, 1980). Has exhibited: Crafts Advisory Cttee Exhibition, 1972; Copenhagen, 1974; Waterloo Place Gallery, London, 1976; Warwick Gallery, Modern Master Works, 1979. One-woman show, Victoria and Albert Museum, 1979. Work in museums, including Kunst-Industrie Museum, Copenhagen; Leeds Museum and Art Gallery.

FRIZZELL, Edward, CBE 1981; QPM 1978; HM Chief Inspector of Constabulary for Scotland, 1979–83; *b* 6 Dec. 1918; *s* of late Edward Frizzell and Mary (*née* Cox); *m* 1945, May Russell; one *s* one *d*. *Educ:* Greenhill Primary Sch.; Coatbridge High Sch. Served War, RAF, 1943–45 (Flying Officer). Det. Sgt, 1953, Det. Chief Inspector, 1961, Paisley Burgh Police; Det. Chief Supt, 1968, Asst Chief Constable, 1968, Renfrew and Bute Constab.; Chief Constable: Stirling and Clackmannan Police, 1970; Central Scotland Police, 1975. OStJ 1971. *Recreations:* shooting, golf. *Address:* 24 Alexander Drive, Bridge of Allan, Stirling FK9 4QB. *T:* Bridge of Allan 3846. *Club:* Stirling and County (Stirling).

FRODSHAM, Anthony Freer, CBE 1978; company director and management consultant; President, Institute of Linguists, since 1986; *b* Peking, China, 8 Sept. 1919; *er s* of late George William Frodsham and Constance Violet Frodsham (*née* Neild); *m* 1953, Patricia Myfanwy, *o c* of late Cmdr A. H. Wynne-Edwards, DSC, RN; two *s*. *Educ:* Ecole Lacordaire, Paris; Faraday House Engineering Coll., London. DFH, CEng, FIMechE, FIMC, CBIM. Served War, 1940–46: Engineer Officer, RN, Asst Fleet Engr Officer on staff of C-in-C Mediterranean, 1944–46 (despatches, 1945). P-E Consulting Group Ltd, 1947–73: Man. Dir and Gp Chief Exec., 1963–72; Group Specialist Adviser, United Dominions Trust Ltd, 1973–74; Dir-Gen., EEF, 1975–82; Director: Arthur Young Management Services, 1973–79; F. Pratt Engrg Corp. Ltd, 1982–85; Dep. Chm., Greyfriars Ltd (Dir, 1984–). Chairman: Management Consultants Assoc., 1968–70; Machine Tools EDC, 1973–79; Independent Chm., Compressed Air and Allied Machinery Cttee, 1976–; Chm., European Business Institute Adv. Cttee, 1982–; Vice-Chm., British Export Finance Adv. Council, 1982–; Pres., Inst. of Management Consultants, 1967–68; Member: CBI Grand Council, 1975–82; CBI President's Cttee, 1979–82; Engineering Industry Training Bd, 1975–79; W European Metal Working Employers' Assoc., 1975–82; Council, Eur. Business Sch., 1983–; a General Commissioner of Tax, 1975–. Conducted MoD Study into Provision of Engineer Officers for Armed Services, 1983. Hon. FIL. *Publications:* contrib. to technical jls; lectures and broadcasts on management subjects. *Address:* 36 Fairacres, Roehampton Lane, SW15 5LX. *T:* 01–878 9551. *Club:* Carlton.

FROGGATT, Sir Leslie (Trevor), Kt 1981; Director, Shell Australia Ltd, since 1969; Chairman and Chief Executive Officer, Shell Group in Australia, 1969–80; *b* 8 April 1920; *s* of Leslie and Mary Helena Froggatt (*née* Brassey); *m* 1945, Jessie Elizabeth Grant; three *s*. *Educ:* Birkenhead Park Sch., Cheshire. Joined Asiatic Petroleum Co. Ltd, 1937; Shell Singapore, Shell Thailand, Shell Malaya, 1947–54; Shell Egypt, 1955–56; Dir of Finance, Gen. Manager, Kalimantan, Borneo, and Dep. Chief Rep., PT Shell Indonesia, 1958–62; Shell International Petroleum Co. Ltd: Area Co-ordinator, S Asia and Australasia, 1962–63; assignment in various Shell cos in Europe, 1964–66; Shell Oil Co., Atlanta, 1967–69. Chm., Ashton Mining Ltd, 1981–; Director: Pacific Dunlop Ltd, 1978– (Vice-Chm., 1981); Australian Industry Develt Corp., 1978–; Australian Inst. of Petroleum Ltd, 1983–84. Member: Australian Nat. Airlines Commn (Trans Australia Airlines), 1981–; (Vice-Chm., 1984); Dir, Moonee Valley Racing Club Nominees Pty, 1977–. *Recreations:* reading, music, racing, golf. *Address:* 20 Albany Road, Toorak, Vic 3142, Australia. *T:* (03) 20.1357. *Clubs:* Melbourne, Australian, Victoria Racing, Victoria Amateur Turf, Moonee Valley Racing, Commonwealth Golf (all Melbourne).

FROGGATT, Sir Peter, Kt 1985; MD, FRCPI; President and Vice-Chancellor, Queen's University of Belfast, 1976–86. MB BCh, BAO 1952; DPH Belfast 1956; MD Dublin 1958; PhD Belfast 1967; FFCM 1972; FRCPI 1973; MRCP 1974; FFOM 1976; FFCMI 1977. Formerly Consultant, Eastern Area, Health and Social Services Board; Dean of Faculty of Medicine (Social and Preventive Medicine), and Prof. of Epidemiology, Queen's Univ., Belfast. Mem. Soc. Social Med.; FSS. *Publications:* (jtly) Causation of Bus-driver Accidents: Epidemiological Study, 1963; contribs to jls. *Address:* c/o Queen's University of Belfast, Belfast, Northern Ireland BT7 1NN.

FRÖHLICH, Prof. Albrecht, PhD; FRS 1976; Professor of Pure Mathematics, King's College, University of London, 1962–81, now Emeritus Professor; Senior Research Fellow, Imperial College, University of London, since 1982; Emeritus Fellow, Robinson College, Cambridge, (Fellow 1982–84); *b* 22 May 1916; *s* of Julius Fröhlich and Frida Fröhlich; *m* 1950, Dr Evelyn Ruth Brooks; one *s* one *d*. *Educ:* Realgymnasium, Munich; Bristol Univ. (BSc 1948, PhD 1951). Asst Lectr in Maths, University Coll., Leicester, 1950–52; Lectr in Maths, University Coll. of N Staffs, 1952–55; King's College, London: Reader in Pure Maths, 1955–62; Hd, Dept of Maths, 1971–81. Vis. Royal Soc.-Israeli Acad. Research Prof., 1978; George A. Miller Prof., Univ. of Illinois, 1981–82; Gauss Prof., Göttingen Acad. of Scis, 1983. Corres. Mem., Heidelberg Acad. of Scis, 1982. FKC 1977. Hon. DSc Bordeaux, 1986. Senior Berwick Prize, London Math. Soc., 1976. *Publications:* Formal Groups, 1968; Module Structure of Algebraic Integers, 1983; Class Groups and Hermitian Modules, 1984; papers in math. jls. *Recreations:* cooking, eating, walking, music. *Address:* Robinson College, Cambridge.

FRÖHLICH, Herbert, FRS 1951; DPhil; Professor of Theoretical Physics, The University of Liverpool, 1948–73, Professor Emeritus, since 1973; *b* 9 Dec. 1905; *m* 1950, Fanchon Aungst. *Educ:* Munich. Studied Theoretical Physics at University of Munich; DPhil 1930; Subsequently Privatdozent at Freiburg Univ. Left Germany in 1933. Research Physicist, Lecturer, and Reader in Theoretical Physics, University of Bristol, 1935–48; Prof. of Solid State Electronics, Univ. of Salford, 1973–76, Vis. Fellow, 1976–81; For. Mem., Max-Planck-Inst., Stuttgart, 1980–. Hon. Dr of Science, Rennes, 1955; Hon. LLD Alberta, 1968; Hon. ScD Dublin, 1969; Dr rer. nat. *hc* Stuttgart, 1980; Hon. DSc Purdue, 1981. Max Planck Medal, 1972. *Publications:* various scientific papers and books. *Address:*

Department of Physics, Oliver Lodge Laboratory, The University, Oxford Street, PO Box 147, Liverpool L69 3BX.

FROOD, Alan Campbell; Managing Director, since 1978, Crown Agent, since 1980, Crown Agents for Oversea Governments and Administrations; *b* 15 May 1926; *s* of James Campbell Frood, MC and Margaret Helena Frood; *m* 1960, Patricia Ann Cotterell; two *s* two *d*. *Educ:* Cranleigh Sch.; Peterhouse, Cambridge. Royal Navy, 1944–47 (Sub-Lt RNVR). Bank of England, 1949; Colonial Admin. Service, 1952; Bankers Trust Co., 1962; Dir., Bankers Trust Internat. Ltd, 1967; Gen. Man., Banking Dept, Crown Agents, 1975; Dir of Financial Services, Crown Agents, 1976–78. *Recreations:* sailing, gardening. *Address:* West Orchard, Holmbush Lane, Henfield, West Sussex. *T:* Poynings 257.

FROSSARD, Sir Charles (Keith), Kt 1983; Bailiff of Guernsey, since 1982; Judge of the Court of Appeal, Jersey, since 1983; *b* 18 Feb. 1922; *s* of late Edward Louis Frossard, CBE, MA, Hon. CF, Dean of Guernsey, 1947–67, and Margery Smith Latta; *m* 1950, Elizabeth Marguerite, *d* of late J. E. L. Martel, OBE; two *d*. *Educ:* Elizabeth Coll., Guernsey; Univ. de Caen (Bachelier en Droit). Enlisted Gordon Highlanders, 1940; commnd 1941, 17 Dogra Regt, Indian Army; seconded to Tochi Scouts and Chitral Scouts; served India and NW Frontier, 1941–46. Called to Bar, Gray's Inn, 1949; Advocate of Royal Court of Guernsey, 1949; People's Deputy, States of Guernsey, 1958–67; Conseiller, States of Guernsey, 1967–69; HM Solicitor General, Guernsey, 1969–73; HM Attorney General, Guernsey, 1973–76; Dep. Bailiff of Guernsey, 1977–82. Member, Church Assembly and General Synod, Church of England, 1960–82. KStJ 1985. Médaille de Vermeil, Paris, 1984. *Recreations:* hill walking, fishing. *Address:* Les Lierres, Rohais, St Peter Port, Guernsey. *T:* 22076. *Clubs:* Army and Navy, Naval and Military.

FROST, Abraham Edward Hardy, CBE 1972; Counsellor, Foreign and Commonwealth Office, 1972–78; *b* 4 July 1918; *s* of Abraham William Frost and Margaret Anna Frost; *m* 1972, Gillian (*née* Crossley); two *d*. *Educ:* Royal Grammar Sch., Colchester King's Coll., Cambridge (MA); London Univ. (BScEcon). FCIS. RNVR, 1940–46 (Lieut). ILO, Geneva, 1947–48; HM Treasury, 1948–49; Manchester Guardian, City Staff, 1949–51; FO (later FCO), 1951–78. *Publication:* In Dorset Of Course (poems), 1976. *Address:* Hill View, Buckland Newton, Dorset. *T:* Buckland Newton 415.

FROST, Albert Edward, CBE 1983; Director, Marks & Spencer Ltd, since 1976; Chairman, Remploy, since 1983; *b* 7 March 1914; *s* of Charles Albert Frost and Minnie Frost; *m* 1942, Eugénie Maud Barlow. *Educ:* Oulton Sch., Liverpool; London Univ. Called to the Bar, Middle Temple (1st Cl. Hons). HM Inspector of Taxes, Inland Revenue, 1937; Imperial Chemical Industries Ltd: Dep. Head, Taxation Dept, 1949; Dep. Treasurer, 1957; Treasurer, 1960; Finance Dir, 1968; retd 1976. Director: British Airways Corp., 1976–80; BL Ltd, 1977–80; S. G. Warburg & Co., 1976–83; British Steel, 1980–83 (Chm., Audit and Salaries Cttees); Guinness Peat Gp, 1983–84; Chairman: Guinness Mahon Hldgs Ltd, 1983–84; Guinness Mahon & Co., 1983–84; Mem. Council, St Thomas's Med. Sch., London, 1974– (Chm., Finance Cttee, 1978–85); Governor, United Med. Schs of Guy's and St Thomas's Hosps, 1982– (Chm., Finance and Investment Cttees, 1982–85); Member: Council and Finance Cttee, Morley Coll., London, 1975–85; Adv. Council, Assoc. for Business Sponsorship of the Arts (Jt Dep. Chm.); Exec. Cttee for Develt Appeal, Royal Opera House, Covent Garden; Arts Council of GB, 1982–84; Chairman: Robert Mayer Trust for Youth and Music, 1981– (Dir, 1977–); Jury, and of Org. Cttee, Carl Flesch Internat. Violin Competition, London. Trustee, Monteverdi Trust; Treas., Loan Fund for Mus. Instruments; Dir, City Arts Trust, 1982–. FRSA. *Publications:* (contrib.) Simon's Income Tax, 1952; (contrib.) Gunns Australian Income Tax Law and Practice, 1960; articles on financial matters affecting industry and on arts sponsorship. *Recreations:* violinist (chamber music); swimming (silver medallist, Royal Life Saving Assoc.); athletics (county colours, track and cross country); walking; arts generally. *Address:* Michael House, Baker Street, W1A 1DN. *T:* 01–935 4422. *Club:* Royal Automobile.

FROST, David (Paradine), OBE 1970; author, producer, columnist; star of "The Frost Report", "The Frost Programme", "Frost on Friday", "The David Frost Show", "The Frost Interview", etc; Joint Founder, London Weekend Television; Chairman and Chief Executive, David Paradine Ltd, since 1966; Joint Founder and Director, TV-am; *b* 7 April 1939; *s* of late Rev. W. J. Paradine Frost, Tenterden, Kent; *m* 1983, Lady Carina Fitzalan-Howard, 2nd *d* of Duke of Norfolk, *qv*; two *s*. *Educ:* Gillingham Grammar Sch.; Wellingborough Grammar Sch.; Gonville and Caius Coll., Cambridge (MA). Sec., The Footlights; Editor, Granta. LLD, Emerson Coll., USA. BBC Television series: That Was the Week That Was, 1962–63 (in USA, 1963–64); A Degree of Frost, 1963, 1973; Not So Much a Programme, More a Way of Life, 1964–65; The Frost Report, 1966–67; Frost Over England, 1967; Frost Over America, 1970; Frost's Weekly, 1973; The Frost Interview, 1974; We British, 1975–76; Forty Years of Television, 1976; The Frost Programme, 1977. David Frost at the Phonograph (BBC Sound), 1966, 1972. Frost on Thursday (LBC), 1974. ITV series and programmes: The Frost Programme, 1966–67, 1967–68; Frost on Friday, 1968–69, 1969–70; The Frost Programme, 1972, 1973; The Sir Harold Wilson Interviews, 1976; A Prime Minister on Prime Ministers, 1977–78; Are We Really Going to be Rich?, 1978; David Frost's Global Village, 1979, 1980, 1982; The 25th Anniversary of ITV, The Begin Interview, and Elvis—He Touched Their Lives, 1980; The BAFTA Awards, and Onward Christian Soldiers, 1981; A Night of Knights: a Royal Gala, 1982; The End of the Year Show, 1982, 1983; TV-am, 1983–; David Frost Presents Ultra Quiz, 1984; Twenty Years On, 1985. Other programmes include: David Frost's Night Out in London, (USA), 1966–67; The Next President, (USA), 1968; Robert Kennedy the Man, (USA), 1968; The David Frost Show, (USA), 1969–70, 1970–71, 1971–72; The David Frost Revue (USA), 1971–72, 1972–73; That Was the Year That Was, (USA), 1973; David Frost Presents the Guinness Book of Records (USA), 1973, 1974, 1975, 1976; Frost over Australia, 1972, 1973, 1974, 1977; Frost over New Zealand, 1973, 1974; The Unspeakable Crime (USA), 1975; Abortion—Merciful or Murder? (USA), 1975; The Beatles—Once Upon a Time (USA), 1975; David Frost Presents the Best (USA), 1975; The Nixon Interviews with David Frost, 1976–77; The Crossroads of Civilization, 1977–78; Headliners with David Frost, 1978; A Gift of Song—MUSIC FOR UNICEF Concert, The Bee Gees Special, and The Kissinger Interview, 1979; The Shah Speaks, and The American Movie Awards, 1980; Show Business, This Is Your Life 30th Anniversary Special, The Royal Wedding (CBS), 1981; David Frost Presents The Internat. Guinness Book of World Records, annually 1981–; The American Movie Awards, Rubinstein at 95, and Pierre Elliott Trudeau, 1982; Frost over Canada, 1982, 1983; David Frost Live by Satellite from London, 1983. Produced films: The Rise and Rise of Michael Rimmer, 1970; Charley One-Eye, 1972; Leadbelly, 1974; The Slipper and the Rose, 1975; James A. Michener's Dynasty, 1975; The Ordeal of Patty Hearst, 1978; The Remarkable Mrs Sanger, 1979. Mem., British/USA Bicentennial Liaison Cttee, 1973–76. Golden Rose, Montreux, for Frost Over England, 1967; Royal Television Society's Silver Medal, 1967; Richard Dimbleby Award, 1967; Emmy Award (USA), 1970, 1971; Religious Heritage of America Award, 1970; Albert Einstein Award, Communication Arts, 1971. *Stage:* An Evening with David Frost (Edinburgh Fest.), 1966. *Publications:* That Was the Week That Was, 1963; How to Live under Labour, 1964;

Talking with Frost, 1967; To England With Love, 1967; The Presidential Debate 1968, 1968; The Americans, 1970; Whitlam and Frost, 1974; I Gave Them a Sword, 1978; I Could Have Kicked Myself, (David Frost's Book of the World's Worst Decisions), 1982; Who Wants to be a Millionaire?, 1983. *Address:* David Paradine Ltd, Breakfast Television Centre, Hawley Crescent, NW1.

FROST, Jeffrey Michael Torbet; Executive Director, London & Continental Bankers, since 1983 (Associate Director, 1982 83); *b* 11 June 1938, *s* of late Basil Frost and Dorothy Frost. *Educ:* Diocesan Coll., Cape, South Africa; Radley Coll.; Oriel Coll., Oxford; Harvard Univ. Exec. Dir, Cttee on Invisible Exports, 1976–81. Hon. Sec., Anglo-Brazilian Soc., 1977–84. Liveryman, Worshipful Co. of Clockmakers. *Address:* 34 Paradise Walk, SW3. *T:* 01–352 8642; The Parish Room, Kintbury, near Newbury, Berks.

FROST, Maj.-Gen. John Dutton, CB 1964; DSO 1943 and Bar, 1945; MC 1942; DL; farmer; *b* 31 Dec. 1912; *s* of late Brig.-Gen. F. D. Frost, CBE, MC; *m* 1947, Jean MacGregor Lyle; one *s* one *d*. *Educ:* Wellington Coll.; RMC Sandhurst. Commissioned The Cameronians, Sept. 1932; Capt., Iraq Levies, 1938–41; Major and Lt-Col, Parachute Regt, 1941–45 (Bruneval raid 1942, Oudna 1942, Tunisian campaign, 1942–43, Primosole Bridge, 1943, Italian campaign, 1943, Arnhem Bridge, 1944)); Staff Coll., Camberley, 1946; GSO2, HQ Lowland Dist, 1948–49; GSO2, Senior Officers' Sch., 1949–52; AA and QMG, 17 Gurkha Div., 1952–53; GSO1, 17 Gurkha Div., 1953–55; Comd, Netheravon, 1955–57; Comd, 44 Parachute Bde, 1958–61; Comdr 52nd Lowland Div./District, 1961–64; GOC Troops in Malta and Libya, 1964–66; Comdr Malta Land Force, 1965; retired, 1967. DL West Sussex, 1982. Cross of Grand Officer, SMO, Malta, 1966. *Publications:* A Drop Too Many, 1980; Two Para-Falklands, 1983. *Recreations:* field sports, polo, golf. *Address:* Northend Farm, Milland, Liphook, Hants. *Club:* Army and Navy.

FROST, Dame Phyllis Irene, DBE 1974 (CBE 1963); JP; Vice-Chairman, Clean World International, since 1980; Chairman: Keep Australia Beautiful Council, Victoria, since 1968; State Relief Committee, Victoria, since 1975 (Member since 1964); Member, Victorian State Council, Australian Bicentennial Authority, since 1980; *b* 14 Sept. 1917; *née* Turner; *m* 1941, Glenn Neville Frost, LDS, BDSc, JP; three *d*. *Educ:* Croydon Coll., Vic.; St Duthus Coll.; Presbyterian Ladies' Coll.; Univ. of Melbourne. Dip. of Physiotherapy, 1938; studied Criminology, 1955. Chairman: Fairlea Women's Prison Council, Vic, 1953–; Aust. Contact Emergency Service, 1984–; Vice-Chairman: Victorians Citizens Council for 150th Anniversary Celebrations, 1984–85; Victorian Assoc. for Care and Resettlement of Offenders, 1977–; Member: Internat. Fedn of Abolitionists, 1960–; Aust. Inst. of Multicultural Affairs, 1981–; Aust. Olympic Games Fund; Waste Recycling Adv. Cttee, Environment Protection Authority, Vic, 1981–; State Disaster Welfare Cttees, Vic, 1983–; Aust. Convener, Migration Standing Cttee, Internat. Council of Women. Trustee, patron, hon. life mem., hon. convener, and life governor of many community service orgns. Has attended several internat. confs as Aust. delegate or representative, including: Internat. Council of Women; FAO; FFHC (Chm., 4th Session in Rome, 1969; Chm., 3rd Regional Congress for Asia and the Far East, at Canberra, 1970, and Rome, 1971). JP Croydon, Vic, 1957. Woman of the Year, Sun News Pictorial, 1970; Humanitarian Award, Rosicrucian Order, USA, 1971; Community Service Award, Victorian Employers' Fedn, 1978; Distinguished Service to Children Award, Aust. Parents without Partners, Vic, 1984. *Address:* 4 Jackson Street, Croydon, Victoria 3136, Australia. *T:* (03) 723 2382. *Club:* Royal Automobile (Vic.).

FROST, Hon. Sir Sydney; *see* Frost, Hon. Sir T. S.

FROST, Terence, (Terry Frost); artist; Professor of Painting, University of Reading, 1977–81 (formerly Reader in Fine Art), Professor Emeritus 1981; *b* Oct. 1915; *m* 1945; five *s* one *d*. *Educ:* Leamington Spa Central Sch. Exhibitions: Leicester Galls, 1952–58; Waddington Galls, 1958–; B. Schaeffer Gallery, New York, 1960–62; Plymouth 1976; Bristol 1976; Serpentine Gall., 1977; Paris, 1978; Norway, 1979. Oil paintings acquired by Tate Gallery, National Gallery of Canada, National Gallery of NSW; also drawing acquired by Victoria and Albert Museum. Other work in public collections; Canada, USA, Germany, Australia, and in Edinburgh, Dublin, Leeds, Hull, Manchester, Birmingham, Liverpool, Bristol, etc. Gregory Fellow in Painting, Univ. of Leeds, 1954–56. Hon. LLD CNAA, 1978. *Address:* Gernick Field Studio, Tredavoe Lane, Newlyn, Penzance. *T:* Penzance 65902.

FROST, Thomas Pearson, FIB; Director since 1984, and Deputy Group Chief Executive since 1985, National Westminster Bank; *b* 1 July 1933; *s* of James Watterson Frost and Enid Ella Crawte (*née* Pearson); *m* 1958, Elizabeth (*née* Morton); one *s* two *d*. *Educ:* Ormskirk Grammar Sch. FIB 1976. Joined Westminster Bank, 1950; Chief Exec. Officer and Vice Chm., NBNA (now National Westminster Bank USA), 1980; Gen. Man., Business Develt Div., National Westminster Bank, 1982. Fellow, World Scout Foundn, 1984. Freeman, City of London, 1978. *Recreations:* golf, greenhouse, theatre. *Address:* National Westminster Bank, 41 Lothbury, EC2P 2BP. *T:* 01–726 1266.

FROST, Hon. Sir (Thomas) Sydney, Kt 1975; Chief Justice of Papua New Guinea, 1975–78, retired; *b* 13 Feb. 1916; *s* of late Thomas Frost, Redfern, NSW; *m* 1943, Dorothy Gertrude (*née* Kelly); two *s* one *d*. *Educ:* Univ. of Melbourne (Alexander Rushall Meml Scholarship; LLM). Served 2nd AIF, 1941–45. Barrister, Victoria, 1945–64; QC 1961; Judge of the County Court of Victoria, 1964; Judge of Supreme Court of Papua New Guinea, 1964–75. Chairman: Aust. Govt Inquiry into Whales and Whaling, 1978; Royal Commn of Inquiry into Housing Commn Land Purchases and Valuation Matters, Vic., 1979–81; Bd of Accident Inquiry into causes of crash of Beechcraft Super King Air, Sydney, 21 Feb. 1980, 1982. Pres., Medical Services Review Tribunal, 1979–84. *Recreation:* golf. *Address:* Park Tower, 201 Spring Street, Melbourne, Victoria, Australia. *T:* 662 3239. *Clubs:* Australian, Royal Melbourne Golf (Melbourne).

FROY, Prof. Martin; Professor of Fine Art, University of Reading, since 1972; *b* 9 Feb. 1926; *s* of late William Alan Froy and Helen Elizabeth Spencer. *Educ:* St Paul's Sch.; Magdalene Coll., Cambridge (one year); Slade Sch. of Fine Art. Dipl. in Fine Art (London). Visiting Teacher of Engraving, Slade Sch. of Fine Art, 1952–55; taught at Bath Acad. of Art, latterly as Head of Fine Art, 1954–65; Head of Painting Sch., Chelsea Sch. of Art, 1965–72. Gregory Fellow in Painting, Univ. of Leeds, 1951–54; Leverhulme Research Award, six months study in Italy, 1963; Sabbatical Award, Arts Council, 1965. Mem., Fine Art Panel, 1962–71, Mem. Council, 1969–71, Nat. Council for Diplomas in Art and Design; Trustee: National Gall., 1972–79; Tate Gall., 1975–79. Fellow, UCL, 1978. One-Artist Exhibitions: Hanover Gall., London, 1952; Wakefield City Art Gall., 1953; Belgrade Theatre, Coventry, 1958; Leicester Galls, London, 1961; Royal West of England Acad., Bristol, 1964; Univ. of Sussex, 1968; Hanover Gall., London, 1969; Park Square Gall., Leeds, 1970; Arnolfini Gall., Bristol, 1970; City Art Gall., Bristol (seven paintings), 1972; Univ. of Reading, 1979; New Ashgate Gall., Surrey, 1979; Serpentine Gall., 1983 *Other Exhibitions:* Internat. Abstract Artists, Riverside Mus., NY, 1950; ICA, London, 1950; Ten English Painters, Brit. Council touring exhibn in Scandinavia, 1952; Drawings from Twelve Countries, Art Inst. of Chicago, 1952; Figures in their Setting, Contemp. Art Soc. Exhibn, Tate Gall., 1953; Beaux Arts Gall., London, 1953; British Painting and Sculpture,

Whitechapel Art Gall., London, 1954; Le Congrès pour la Liberté de la Culture Exhibn, Rome, Paris, Brussels, 1955; Pittsburgh Internat., 1955; Six Young Painters, Arts Council touring Exhibn, 1956; ICA Gregory Meml Exhibn, Bradford City Art Gall., Leeds, 1958; City Art Gall., Bristol, 1960; Malerei der Gegenwart ans Sudwestengland, Kunstverein, Hanover, 1962; Corsham Painters and Sculptors, Arts Council Touring Exhibn, 1965; Three Painters, Bath Fest. Exhibn, 1970; Park Square Gall., Leeds, 1978; Ruskin Sch., Univ. of Oxford, 1978; Newcastle Connection, Newcastle, 1980; Homage to Herbert Read, Canterbury, 1984. *Commissions, etc:* Artist Consultant for Arts Council to City Architect, Coventry, 1953–58; mosaic decoration, Belgrade Th., Coventry, 1957–58; two mural panels, Concert Hall, Morley Coll., London, 1958–59. *Works in Public Collections:* Tate Gall.; Mus. of Mod. Art, NY; Chicago Art Inst.; Arts Council; Contemp. Art Soc.; Royal W of England Acad.; Leeds Univ.; City Art Galls of Bristol, Carlisle, Leeds, Southampton and Wakefield; Reading Mus. and Art Gall. *Address:* Department of Fine Art, University of Reading, London Road, Reading, Berks RG1 5AQ.

FRY, Christopher; dramatist; *b* 18 Dec. 1907; *s* of Charles John Harris and Emma Marguerite Hammond, *d* of Emma Louisa Fry; *m* 1936, Phyllis Marjorie Hart; one *s*. *Educ:* Bedford Modern Sch. Actor at Citizen House, Bath, 1927; Schoolmaster at Hazlewood Preparatory Sch., Limpsfield, Surrey, 1928–31; Dir of Tunbridge Wells Repertory Players, 1932–35; life too complicated for tabulation, 1935–39; The Tower, a pageant-play produced at Tewkesbury Fest., 1939; Dir of Oxford Repertory Players, 1940 and 1944–46, directing at Arts Theatre, London, 1945; Staff dramatist, Arts, 1947. FRSL. Queen's Gold Medal (for Poetry), 1962. *Plays:* A Phoenix Too Frequent, Mercury, 1946, St George's Theatre, 1983; The Lady's Not for Burning, Arts, 1948, Globe, 1949, Chichester, 1972; The Firstborn, Edinburgh Festival, 1948; Thor, with Angels, Canterbury Festival, 1949; Venus Observed, St James's, 1950; The Boy with a Cart, Lyric, Hammersmith, 1950; Ring Round the Moon (translated from French of Jean Anouilh), Globe, 1950; A Sleep of Prisoners, produced St Thomas' Church, Regent Street, W1, 1951; The Dark is Light Enough, Aldwych, 1954; The Lark (trans. from French of Jean Anouilh), Lyric, Hammersmith, 1955; Tiger at the Gates (trans. from French of Jean Giraudoux), Apollo, 1955; Duel of Angels (trans. from Pour Lucrèce, of Jean Giraudoux), Apollo, 1958; Curtmantle, Edinburgh Festival, 1962; Judith (trans. from Giraudoux), Her Majesty's, 1962; A Yard of Sun, National, 1970; Peer Gynt (trans.), Chichester, 1970; Cyrano de Bergerac (trans.), Chichester, 1975. *TV:* The Brontës of Haworth, four plays, 1973 (also performed on stage, 1985); Sister Dora, 1977; The Best of Enemies, 1977. *Film Commentary* for The Queen is Crowned (Coronation film, 1953); *Film scripts:* (participation) Ben Hur; Barabbas; The Bible; The Beggar's Opera. *Publications:* The Boy with a Cart, 1939; The Firstborn, 1946; A Phoenix Too Frequent, 1946; The Lady's Not for Burning, 1949; Thor, with Angels, 1949; Venus Observed, 1950; (trans.) Ring Round the Moon, 1950; A Sleep of Prisoners, 1951; The Dark is Light Enough, 1954; (trans.) The Lark, 1955; (trans.) Tiger at The Gates, 1955; (trans.) Duel of Angels, 1958; Curtmantle, 1961 (Heinemann Award of RSL); (trans.) Judith, 1962; A Yard of Sun, 1970; (trans.) Peer Gynt, 1970 (this trans. included in The Oxford Ibsen, vol. III, Brand and Peer Gynt, 1972); Four television plays: The Brontës at Haworth, 1954; (trans.) Cyrano de Bergerac, 1975; Can You Find Me: a family history, 1978; (ed and introd) Charlie Hammond's Sketch Book, 1980; Selected Plays, 1985. *Address:* The Toft, East Dean, Chichester, West Sussex.

FRY, Donald William, CBE 1970; Director, Atomic Energy Establishment, Winfrith, 1959–73; *b* 30 Nov. 1910; *m* 1934, Jessie Florence (*née* Wright); three *s*. *Educ:* Weymouth Gram. Sch.; King's Coll., London. Research Physicist, GEC Laboratories, 1932; RAE Farnborough (Radio Dept), 1936; Air Min. Research Establishment (later the Telecommunications Research Establishment, TRE) Swanage, 1940; moved with the Estab. to Malvern, 1942; joined staff of AERE (still at Malvern), 1946; demonstrated with other mems of group a new Principle for accelerating particles: the travelling wave linear accelerator, 1947. Awarded Duddell Medal of Physical Soc., 1950; Head of Gen. Physics Div. at AERE Harwell, 1950; Chief Physicist, 1954, Dep. Dir, 1958, AERE Harwell. CEng, FIEE 1946; FIEEE 1960; FInstP 1970; Hon. Freeman of Weymouth, 1958. FKC London, 1959. *Publications:* papers in learned journals. *Address:* Coveway Lodge, Overcombe, near Weymouth, Dorset. *T:* Preston (Weymouth) 833276.

FRY, E. Maxwell, CBE 1953; RA 1972 (ARA 1966); BArch; FRIBA, FRTPI; Dist Town Planning; consultant architect and town planner in retirement; active painter; *b* 2 Aug. 1899; *s* of Ambrose Fry and Lydia Thompson; *m* 1927, Ethel Speakman (marr. diss.); one *d*; *m* 1942, Jane B. Drew, *qv*. *Educ:* Liverpool Inst.; Liverpool Univ. Sch. of Architecture. Practised with Walter Gropius as Gropius and Fry, 1934–36; as Maxwell Fry and Jane Drew, 1945–50, as Fry, Drew, Drake, & Lasdun, 1951–58; now as Fry, Drew, Knight & Creamer. Work includes schools, hospitals, working-class and other flats, houses in England and educational buildings in Ghana and Nigeria. Served with Royal Engineers, 1939–44. Town Planning Adviser to Resident Minister for West Africa, 1943–45; Senior Architect to New Capital Chandigarh, Punjab, 1951–54. One-man show, Drian Gall., 1974. Ex-Mem. Royal Fine Art Commission; Corr. Mem. Académie Flamande, 1956; Hon. FAIA 1963; Council Mem. RIBA (Vice-Pres. 1961–62) and RSA; Royal Gold Medal for Architecture, 1964. Hon. LLD Ibadan Univ., 1966. *Publications:* Fine Building, 1944; (jointly with Jane B. Drew) Architecture for Children, 1944; Tropical Architecture, 1964; Art in a Machine Age, 1969; Maxwell Fry: autobiographical sketches, 1975; contribs to architectural and other papers. *Address:* West Lodge, Cotherstone, Barnard Castle, Co. Durham DL12 9PF. *T:* Teesdale 50217.

FRY, Sir (Francis) Wilfrid, 5th Bt *cr* 1894; OBE 1967; CEng; MIME; Mining Engineer, retired; *b* 2 May 1904; *s* of Sir John Pease Fry, 2nd Bt and Margaret Theodora (*d* 1941), *d* of Francis Edward Fox; *S* brother, 1985; *m* 1943, Anne Pease, JP, *e d* of Kenneth Henry Wilson, OBE, JP. *Educ:* Clifton; Trinity Coll., Cambridge (BA). Served 1940–42 as Lieut RE, bomb disposal. Area General Manager for NCB, 1947–67; formerly Mining Agent and director of two companies. JP Co. Durham, 1949–67, N Yorks, 1968–74 (Chm. of Bench, 1971–74). *Recreations:* formerly hunting, fishing, bee-keeping; now light gardening. *Heir:* none. *Address:* Cleveland Lodge, Great Ayton, Middlesbrough, Cleveland TS9 6BT. *T:* Great Ayton 722215.

FRY, Dr Ian Kelsey, DM, FRCP, FRCR; Dean, Medical College of St Bartholomew's Hospital, since 1981; Consultant Radiologist, St Bartholomew's Hospital, since 1966; *b* 25 Oct. 1923; *s* of Sir William and Lady Kelsey Fry; *m* 1951, Mary Josephine Casey; three *s* (one *d* decd). *Educ:* Radley Coll.; New Coll., Oxford; Guy's Hosp. Medical Sch. BM BCh 1948, DM Oxon 1961; MRCP 1956, FRCP 1972; DMRD 1961; FFR 1963; FRCR 1975. RAF Medical Services, 1949–50 (Sqdn Ldr). Research Fellow, Guy's Hosp., 1956–59; Director, Dept of Radiology, BUPA Medical Centre, 1973–; Mem. Council, Royal College of Radiologists, 1979–82; President, British Institute of Radiology, 1982–83. *Publications:* chapters and articles in books and jls. *Recreations:* golf, walking. *Address:* The Pines, Woodlands Road, Bickley, Bromley, Kent. *T:* 01–467 4150.

FRY, John, OBE 1975; MD, FRCS, FRCGP; general practitioner, since 1947; *b* 16 June 1922; *s* of Ansel and Barbara Fry; *m* 1944, Joan, *d* of James and Catherine Sabel; one *s* one *d*. *Educ:* Whitgift Middle Sch., Croydon; Guy's Hosp., Univ. of London (MD). FRCS 1947, FRCGP 1967. Hon. Consultant in Gen. Practice to the Army, 1968–; Consultant to WHO, 1965–83; Trustee, Nuffield Provincial Hosps Trust, 1956–. Mem., GMC, 1970– (Sen. Treasurer, 1975–); Councillor, RCGP, 1960–. *Publications:* The Catarrhal Child, 1961; Profiles of Disease, 1966; Medicine in Three Societies, 1969; Common Diseases, 1974, 3rd edn 1983; Textbook of Medical Practice, 1976; Scientific Foundations of Family Medicine, 1978; A New Approach to Medicine, 1978; Primary Care, 1980; Family Good Health Guide, 1982; The Health Care Manual, 1983; Common Dilemmas in Family Medicine, 1983; A History of the Royal College of General Practitioners, 1983; NHS Data Book, 1984; Early Diagnosis, 1985; Disease Data Book, 1985; Primary Health Care: 2000, 1986. *Recreations:* reading, writing, researching, running. *Address:* 138 Croydon Road, Beckenham, Kent BR3 4DG. *T:* 01–650 0568.

FRY, Maxwell; *see* Fry, E. Maxwell.

FRY, Peter Derek; MP (C) Wellingborough since Dec. 1969; Insurance Broker since 1963; Chairman, PR&CI Ltd (Public Affairs consultants); *b* 26 May 1931; *s* of Harry Walter Fry and late Edith Fry; *m* 1st, 1958, Edna Roberts (marr. diss. 1982); one *s* one *d*; 2nd, 1982, Helen Claire Mitchell. *Educ:* Royal Grammar School, High Wycombe; Worcester College, Oxford (MA). Tillotsons (Liverpool) Ltd, 1954–56; Northern Assurance Co., 1956–61; Political Education Officer, Conservative Central Office, 1961–63. Member Bucks County Council, 1961–67. Contested (C) North Nottingham, 1964, East Willesden, 1966. Jt Chm., All Party Roads Study Gp; Chairman: All Party Footwear and Leather Gp; Anglo-Bahamian Parly Gp; British Yugoslav Parly Gp; Mem., Select Cttee on Transport. Played Rugby for Bucks County, 1956–58, Hon. Secretary, 1958–61. *Recreations:* watching Rugby football; reading history and biographies. *Address:* Glebe Farmhouse, 24 Church Lane, Cranford, Kettering, Northants. *Club:* Royal Automobile.

FRY, Peter George Robin Plantagenet S.; *see* Somerset Fry.

FRY, Richard Henry, CBE 1965; Financial Editor of The Guardian, 1939–65; *b* 23 Sept. 1900; *m* 1929, Katherine (*née* Maritz); no *c*. *Educ:* Berlin and Heidelberg Univs. *Publications:* Zero Hour, 1936; A Banker's World: the revival of the City, 1957–70, 1970; Bankers in West Africa, 1976. *Address:* 8 Montagu Mews West, W1. *T:* 01–262 0817. *Club:* Reform.

FRY, Ronald Ernest, FSS; Director of Economics and Statistics, Departments of the Environment and Transport, 1975–80, retired; *b* 21 May 1925; *s* of Ernest Fry and Lilian (*née* Eveling); *m* 1954, Jeanne Ivy Dawson; one *s* one *d*. *Educ:* Wilson's Grammar Sch., Camberwell; Birkbeck Coll., Univ. of London (BSc (Special)). MIS. Telecommunications Technician, Royal Signals, 1944–47; Scientific Asst, CEGB (London Region), 1948–52; Statistician: Glacier Metal Co., London, 1952–54; CEGB HQ, London, 1954–64; Gen. Register Office, 1965–66; Asst Dir of Research and Intelligence, GLC, 1966–69; Chief Statistician: (Social Statistics) Cabinet Office, 1969–74; (Manpower Statistics) Dept of Employment, 1974–75. *Publications:* various technical publns in statistical and other professional jls. *Recreations:* photography, reading, motoring. *Address:* 39 Claremont Road, Hadley Wood, Barnet, Herts EN4 0HR. *T:* 01–440 1393.

FRY, Sir Wilfrid; *see* Fry, Sir F. W.

FRY, Hon. Sir William Gordon, Kt 1980; President, Legislative Council of Victoria, Australia, 1976–79; *b* 12 June 1909; *s* of A. G. Fry, Ballarat; *m* 1936, Lilian G., *d* of A. W. Macrae; four *s*. *Educ:* Ballarat High School; Melbourne Univ. Served War of 1939–45, 2nd AIF (Lt-Col, despatches). Education Dept of Victoria for 40 years; Headmaster of various schools, including Cheltenham East, Windsor, Cheltenham Heights. Councillor, City of Moorabbin; Mayor, 1968; MLC (Lib) for Higinbotham, Vic, 1967–79. Past Chm., Parly Select Cttee, Road Safety. Vice-Pres., Victoria League; Mem., RSL. Formerly Dep. Chm., World Bowls. Life Governor: Melbourne and Dist Ambulance Soc.; Royal Women's Hosp.; Royal Melbourne Hosp.; Gen. Management Cttee, Royal Victoria Eye and Ear Hosp.; Management Bd, Cheltenham-Mordialloc Hosp.; Committee Member: Melbourne Family Care Orgn; Richmond Foundn; Legacy Australia; Brighton Tech. Coll. *Recreations:* lawn bowls, golf, swimming. *Address:* 16 Mariemont Avenue, Beaumaris, Victoria 3193, Australia. *Clubs:* West Brighton; Royal Commonwealth Society (Victoria); Returned Services League (Cheltenham-Moorabbin).

FRY, William Norman H.; *see* Hillier-Fry.

FRYBERG, Sir Abraham, Kt 1968; MBE 1941; retired; *b* 26 May 1901; *s* of Henry and Rose Fryberg; *m* 1939, Vivian Greensil Barnard; one *s*. *Educ:* Wesley Coll., Melbourne; Queen's Coll., University of Melbourne. MB, BS (Melbourne) 1928; DPH, DTM (Sydney) 1936; Hon. MD (Qld); Hon. FACMA. Served with 9 Australian Div. (Tobruk, Alamein), 1940–45. Resident Med. Officer, then Registrar, Brisbane Hosp. and Brisbane Children's Hosp., 1929–33; GP, Hughenden, 1934; Health Officer, Qld Health Dept, 1936–46 (except for war service); Dep. Dir-Gen., 1946, Dir-Gen. of Health and Medical Services, Qld, 1947–67, retired. Hon. Col, RAAMC Northern Comd, 1962–67. SBStJ 1958. *Recreation:* racing. *Address:* 19 Dublin Street, Clayfield, Qld 4011, Australia. *T:* Brisbane 2622549. *Club:* United Service (Brisbane).

FRYER, David Richard; Secretary-General, Royal Town Planning Institute, since 1976; *b* 16 May 1936; *s* of Ernest William Fryer and Gladys Edith Battey; *m* 1961, Carole Elizabeth Hayes; one *s* two *d*. *Educ:* Chesterfield Sch.; New Coll., Oxford (MA, BCL). LMRTPI. Admitted solicitor, 1961. Articled Clerk and Asst Solicitor, Chesterfield Bor. Council, 1958–61; Associate Lawyer, Messrs Jones, Day, Cockley & Reavis, Cleveland, Ohio, 1961–63; Asst Solicitor, N Riding CC, 1963–65; Sen. Asst Solicitor, Bucks CC, 1966–69; Dep. Sec., RICS, 1970–75. Sec., Brit. Chapter, Internat. Real Estate Fedn, 1970–75; Dep. Pres., Internat. Fedn for Housing and Planning, 1984– (Mem., Bureau and Council, 1976–); Member: Exec. Cttee and Council, Public Works Congress and Exhibn Council Ltd, 1976–; Exec. Cttee, Nat. Council for Social Service, 1976–79 (Chm., Planning and Environment Gp); Council and Standards Cttee, Nat. House-Bldg Council, 1976–; Jt Land Requirements Cttee, 1980–; Exec. Cttee, Commonwealth Assoc. of Planners, 1984–; UK Council, Internat Year for the Shelter of the Homeless, 1985–. FRSA 1981. *Recreations:* international affairs, architecture, the countryside. *Address:* Stairways, Portway Road, Hartwell, Aylesbury, Bucks. *T:* Aylesbury 748538. *Club:* East India.

FRYER, Dr Geoffrey, FRS 1972; Deputy Chief Scientific Officer, Windermere Laboratory, Freshwater Biological Association, since 1981; *b* 6 Aug. 1927; *s* of W. and M. Fryer; *m* 1953, Vivien Griffiths Hodgson; one *s* one *d*. *Educ:* Huddersfield College. DSc, PhD London. Royal Navy, 1946–48. Colonial Research Student, 1952–53; HM Overseas Research Service, 1953–60: Malawi, 1953–55; Zambia, 1955–57; Uganda, 1957–60; Sen., then Principal, then Sen. Principal Scientific Officer, Freshwater Biological Assoc., 1960–81. H. R. Macmillan Lectr, Univ. of British Columbia, 1963; Distinguished Vis. Schol., Univ. of Adelaide, 1985. Mem. Council, Royal Soc., 1978–80. Frink Medal, Zool Soc. of London, 1983. *Publications:* (with T. D. Iles) The Cichlid Fishes of the Great Lakes of Africa: their biology and evolution, 1972; numerous articles in scientific jls. *Recreations:*

natural history, walking, books, photography. *Address:* Elleray Cottage, Windermere, Cumbria LA23 1AW.

FRYER, Maj.-Gen. (retd) Wilfred George, CB 1956; CBE 1951 (OBE 1941); *b* 1 May 1900; *s* of James and Marion Fryer, Kington, Herefordshire; *m* 1931, Jean Eleanore Graham, *d* of Graham Binny, RSW, Edinburgh; two *s* (and one *s* decd). *Educ:* Christ Coll., Brecon; RMA Woolwich. Commissioned 2nd Lieut RE, 1919, Regular Army; served in India, Royal Bombay Sappers and Miners, 1933–38; Major RE, Instructor, Sch. of Mil. Engineering, Chatham, 1938. Served War of 1939–45: Lt-Col RE, ADWE & M, GHQ, Middle East, 1941; SO1 to Chief Engineer, Eighth Army, Western Desert Campaign (OBE), 1941; Col DDWE & M, GHQ, Middle East, 1942; GSO1 to Scientific Adviser to Army Council, 1944; ADWE & M, GHQ and Dep. Chief Engineer, 8 Corps, NW Europe Campaign (despatches), 1944–45; Brig.-Chief Engr, Brit. Army Staff, Washington, DC, 1945; Col E (Equipment), War Office, 1946–48; Brig.-Chief Engr, Singapore Dist, 1948–51; Brig.-Chief Engr, Southern Comd, UK, 1951–53; Maj.-Gen. 1954; Chief Engineer, Middle East Land Forces, 1954–57. "A" Licence air pilot, 1942. MIEE 1952. Chm., Warminster Press Ltd. Nat. Champion, Wayfarer Dinghy, 1960. *Recreations:* ocean racing (Transatlantic Race, 1931), ski-ing (Lauberhorn Cup, 1928), tennis. *Address:* 47 Belmore Lane, Lymington, Hants SO4 9NR. *Clubs:* Army and Navy, Royal Ocean Racing, Hurlingham.

FUAD, Kutlu Tekin; Hon. Mr Justice Fuad; Justice of Appeal, Court of Appeal, Hong Kong, since 1982; *b* 23 April 1926; *s* of Mustafa Fuad Bey, CMG, and Belkis Hilmi; *m* 1952, Inci Izzet; two *s* one *d*. *Educ:* Temple Grove; Marlborough Coll.; St John's Coll., Cambridge (MA). Called to the Bar, Inner Temple, 1952. Mil. Service, Lieut KRRC, 1944–48. Colonial Legal Service, 1953–62: Magistrate, Cyprus; Resident Magistrate, Sen. Crown Counsel, Legal Draftsman, and Dir of Public Prosecutions, Uganda; Judge of the High Court, Uganda, 1963–72 (Pres., Industrial Court; Chm., Law Reform Cttee); Dir, Legal Div., Commonwealth Secretariat, 1972–80; Judge, High Court of Hong Kong, 1980–82; Mem., Law Reform Commn, Hong Kong, 1983–. Formerly Chm., Visitation Cttee, Makerere University Coll. *Recreations:* music, Rugby football, tennis. *Address:* Supreme Court, Hong Kong; 51 Earl's Court Road, Kensington, W8 6EE. *T:* 01-937 9209. *Club:* Army and Navy.

FUCHS, Sir Vivian (Ernest), Kt 1958; MA, PhD; FRS 1974; Director of the British Antarctic Survey, 1958–73; Leader Commonwealth Trans-Antarctic Expedition, 1955–58; *b* 11 Feb. 1908; *s* of late E. Fuchs, Farnham, Surrey, and late Violet Anne Fuchs (*née* Watson); *m* 1933, Joyce, 2nd *d* of late John Connell; one *s* one *d* (and one *d* decd). *Educ:* Brighton Coll.; St John's Coll., Cambridge (Hon. Fellow, 1983). Geologist with: Cambridge East Greenland Expedn, 1929; Cambridge Expdn to E African Lakes, 1930–31; E African Archæological Expdn, 1931–32; Leader Lake Rudolf Rift Valley Expedn, 1933–34; Royal Geog. Society Cuthbert Peek Grant, 1936; Leader Lake Rukwa Expedn, 1937–38. 2nd Lieut Cambs Regt, TA, 1939; served in W Africa, 1942–43; Staff Coll., Camberley, 1943; served NW Europe (despatches), 1944–46; demobilized (Major), 1946. Leader Falkland Islands Dependencies Survey (Antarctica), 1947–50; Dir FIDSc Bureau, 1950–55. President: Internat. Glaciological Soc., 1963–66; British Assoc. for Advancement of Science, 1972; Mem. Council, RGS, 1958–61, Vice-Pres. 1961–64, Pres., 1982–84. Founder's Gold Medal, Royal Geog. Soc., 1951; Silver Medal RSA, 1952; Polar Medal, 1953, and Clasp, 1958; Special Gold Medal, Royal Geog. Soc., 1958; Gold Medal Royal Scottish Geog. Society 1958; Gold Medal Geog. Society (Paris), 1958; Richthofen Medal (Berlin), 1958; Kirchenpauer Medal (Hamburg), 1958; Plancius Medal (Amsterdam), 1959; Egede Medal (Copenhagen), 1959; Hubbard Medal, Nat. Geog. Soc. (Washington), 1959; Explorers Club Medal (New York), 1959; Geog. Soc. (Chicago) Gold Medal, 1959; Geol. Soc. of London Prestwich Medal, 1960. Hon. Fellow, Wolfson (formerly University Coll.), Cambridge, 1970. Hon. LLD Edinburgh 1958; Hon. DSc: Durham 1958; Cantab 1959; Leicester 1972; Hon. ScD Swansea, 1971; Hon. LLD Birmingham, 1974. *Publications:* The Crossing of Antarctica (Fuchs and Hillary), 1958; Antarctic Adventure, 1959; (ed) Forces of Nature, 1977; Of Ice and Men, 1982; (ed) The Physical World (Oxford Illustrated Encyclopedia), 1985; geographical and geological reports and papers in scientific jls. *Recreations:* gardening, swimming. *Address:* 78 Barton Road, Cambridge CB3 9LH. *T:* Cambridge 359238. *Club:* Athenæum.

FUGARD, Athol; playwright, director, actor; *b* 11 June 1932; *s* of Harold David Fugard and Elizabeth Magdalene Potgieter; *m* 1956, Sheila Meiring; one *d*. *Educ:* Univ. of Cape Town. Directed earliest plays, Nongogo, No Good Friday, Johannesburg, 1960; acted in The Blood Knot, touring S Africa, 1961; Hello and Goodbye, 1965; directed and acted in The Blood Knot, London, 1966; Boesman and Lena, S Africa, 1969; directed Boesman and Lena, London, 1971; directed Serpent Players in various prodns, Port Elizabeth, from 1963, directed co-authors John Kani and Winston Ntshona in Sizwe Bansi is Dead, SA, 1972, The Island, 1973, and London, 1973–74; acted in film, Boesman and Lena, 1972; directed and acted in Statements after an Arrest under the Immorality Act, in SA, 1972, directed in London, 1973; wrote Dimetos for Edinburgh Fest., 1975; directed and acted in, A Lesson from Aloes, SA, 1978, London, 1980 (directed, NY 1981, winning NY Critics Circle Award for Best Play); directed: Master Harold and the Boys, NY, 1982 (Drama Desk Award), Johannesburg, 1983, Nat. Theatre, 1983 (Standard award for Best Play); The Road to Mecca, Yale Repertory Theatre 1984. Hon. DLitt: Natal, 1981; Rhodes,1983; Cape Town, 1984; Hon. DFA Yale, 1983; Hon. DHL Georgetown, 1984. *Films:* Boesman and Lena, 1973; The Guest, 1977; (acted in) Meetings with Remarkable Men (dir, Peter Brook), 1979; (wrote and acted in) Marigolds in August (Silver Bear Award, Berlin), 1980; (acted in) Gandhi, 1982. *Publications:* The Blood Knot, 1962; People Are Living There, Hello and Goodbye, 1973; Boesman and Lena, 1973; (jtly) Three Port Elizabeth Plays: Sizwe Bansi is Dead, The Island, Statements after an Arrest under the Immorality Act, 1974; Tsotsi (novel), 1980 (also USA); A Lesson from Aloes, 1981 (also USA); Master Harold and the Boys, US 1982, UK 1983; Notebooks 1960–1977, 1983 (also USA). *Recreations:* angling, skin-diving, bird-watching. *Address:* PO Box 5090, Walmer, Port Elizabeth, South Africa.

FUJIYAMA, Naraichi; Senior Consultant to Scottish Development Agency, in Japan, since 1982; *b* 17 Sept. 1915; *m* 1946, Shizuko Takagi. *Educ:* Faculty of Law, Tokyo Univ., Univ. of NC, USA. Consul, New York, 1953–54; Counsellor, Austria, 1959, Indonesia, 1963, Chief of Protocol, Min. of Foreign Affairs, Tokyo, 1965; Dir-Gen., Public Inf. Bureau, Min. of For. Affairs, 1968; Ambassador to: Austria, 1971–75; Italy, 1975–79, Great Britain, 1979–82. Chm., Bd of Governors, IAEA, Vienna, 1973–74; Press Sec. to the Emperor of Japan for State Visit to USA, 1975. Grand Cross, Order Al Merito, Peru; Kt Grand Cross, Order Al Merito, Italy; Grand Decoration of Honour for Merit in Gold with Sash, Austria. *Recreation:* golf. *Address:* 7–7–19, Koyama, Shinagawa-ku, Tokyo, Japan.

FUKUI, Prof. Dr Kenichi; Order of Culture, Person of Cultural Merits (Japan), 1981; President, Kyoto Institute of Technology (formerly Kyoto University of Industrial Arts and Textile Fibers), since 1982; *b* 4 Oct. 1918; *s* of Ryokichi Fukui and Chie Fukui (*née* Sugizawa); *m* 1947, Tomoe Horie; one *s* one *d*. *Educ:* Kyoto Imperial Univ. (AB Engrg, PhD Engrg). Lecturer, 1943–45, Asst Professor, 1945–51, Professor, 1951–82, Kyoto Imperial University. Member: European Acad. of Arts, Sciences and Humanities, 1981–; Japan Acad., 1983–; Pontifical Acad. of Sciences, 1986–. Foreign Associate, Nat. Acad. of Sciences, 1981–; Foreign Hon. Mem., Amer. Acad. of Arts and Sciences, 1983–. Nobel Prize in Chemistry (jtly), 1981. *Address:* 23 Kitashirakawahirai-cho, Sakyo-ku, Kyoto-city, Kyoto 606, Japan. *T:* 075–781–5785.

FULBRIGHT, J. William, Hon. KBE 1975; US Senator (Democrat) for Arkansas, 1945–74; *b* Sumner, Mo, 9 April 1905; *s* of Jay Fulbright and Roberta (*née* Waugh); *m* 1932, Elizabeth Kremer Williams; two *d*. *Educ:* public schools of Fayetteville, Arkansas; University of Arkansas (AB); (Rhodes Scholar) Pembroke Coll., Oxford Univ. (BA, MA); George Washington Univ. Sch. of Law (LLB). Special Attorney, Dept. of Justice, 1934–35; Lectr in Law, George Washington Univ., 1935–36; Mem. Law Sch. Faculty, University of Arkansas, 1936–39, and Pres. of University, 1939–41. Elected to Congress for 3rd Dist of Arkansas, 1942; Mem. Foreign Affairs Cttee. Elected to Senate, 1945, and subsequently; Mem. US Delegn to Gen. Assembly, UN, 1954; Chm. Banking and Currency Cttee of Senate, 1955–59, resigning to become Chm. Senate Cttee on Foreign Relations, also Mem. Finance Cttee and Jt Economic Cttee. First McCallum Meml Lectr, Oxford, 1975. Hon. Fellow, Pembroke Coll., Oxford, 1949; Fellow, Amer. Acad. of Arts and Sciences (Boston), 1950; Award by Nat. Inst. of Arts and Letters, 1954. Holds several hon. degrees, including DCL Oxford, 1953, and LLD Cantab, 1971. *Publications:* Old Myths and New Realities, 1964; Prospects for the West, 1965; The Arrogance of Power, 1967. *Address:* 815 Connecticut Avenue, Washington, DC 20006, USA.

FULCHER, Derick Harold, DSC 1944; Interviewer for Civil Service Commission; *b* 4 Nov. 1917; *s* of late Percy Frederick Fulcher and Gertrude Lilian Fulcher; *m* 1943, Florence Ellen May Anderson; one *s* one *d*. *Educ:* St Olave's Grammar School. Served in Royal Navy, 1940–46 (Lieut, RNVR). Entered Civil Service (War Office), 1936; Asst Principal, Ministry of National Insurance, 1947; Principal, 1950; Admin. Staff Coll., Henley, 1952; Asst Sec. 1959. Seconded to HM Treasury, 1957–59; served on an ILO mission in Trinidad and Tobago, 1967–69; Asst Under-Sec. of State, Dept of Health and Social Security, 1969–70. UK Delegate to and Chairman: NATO Management Survey Cttee, 1970–71; Council of Europe Management Survey Cttee, 1971–72. Chm., Supplementary Benefit Appeal Tribunals, 1971–75; Head of UK res. project in W Europe into social security provision for disablement, 1971–72; Res. Consultant, Office of Manpower Econs, 1972–73; Served on technical aid mission to Indonesia, 1973; ILO Res. Consultant on Social Security, 1973–80; Consultant to: EEC Statistical Office, 1974; Govt of Thailand on Social Security, 1978–79 and 1981. Fellow, Inst. for European Health Services Research, Leuven Univ., Belgium, 1974–. *Publications:* Medical Care Systems, 1974; Social Security for the Unemployed, 1976. *Recreations:* walking, photography, travel. *Address:* 100 Downs Road, Coulsdon, Surrey CR3 1AF. *T:* Downland 54231. *Club:* Civil Service.

FULFORD, Robert John; Keeper, Department of Printed Books, British Library (formerly British Museum), 1967–85; *b* 16 Aug. 1923; *s* of John Fulford, Southampton; *m* 1950, Alison Margaret Rees; one *s* one *d*. *Educ:* King Edward VI Sch., Southampton; King's Coll., Cambridge; Charles Univ., Prague. Asst Keeper, Dept of Printed Books, British Museum, 1945–65; Dep. Keeper, 1965–67 (Head of Slavonic Div., 1961–67); Keeper, 1967–85. *Address:* 7 Tulip Tree Close, Tonbridge, Kent TN9 2SH. *T:* Tonbridge 350356; Maumont, 24390 Hautefort, France. *T:* 53–50–50–07.

FULHAM, Bishop Suffragan of, since 1985; **Rt Rev. Charles John Klyberg;** *b* 29 July 1931; *s* of Captain Charles Augustine Klyberg, MN and late Ivy Lilian Waddington, LRAM; unmarried. *Educ:* Eastbourne College. ARICS. Asst Estates Manager, Cluttons, 1952–57. Lincoln Theological Coll., 1957–60. Curate, S John's, East Dulwich, 1960–63; Rector of Fort Jameson, Zambia, 1963–67; Vicar, Christ Church and S Stephen, Battersea, 1967–77; Dean of Lusaka Cathedral, Zambia, and Rector of the parish, 1977–85, Dean Emeritus, 1985; Vicar General, 1978–85. UK Commissary for Anglican Church in Zambia, 1985–. Chm., Church Property Development Gp, 1978–85. *Recreations:* reading, music, travel. *Address:* 4 Cambridge Place, W8 5PB. *T:* 01-937 2560. *Club:* Athenæum.

FULLER, Geoffrey Herbert, CEng, FRINA, FIMarE; RCNC; Deputy Chairman, British Maritime Technology Ltd, Feltham, since 1985; *b* 16 Jan. 1927; *s* of late Major Herbert Thomas Fuller and Clarice Christine Fuller; *m* 1952, Pamela-Maria Quarrell; one *d*. *Educ:* Merchant Taylors', Northwood, Mddx; Royal Naval Engrg Coll., Keyham; Royal Naval Coll., Greenwich. FRINA 1965; FIMarE 1974. Constructor Commander: Staff of Flag Officer (Submarines), 1958; British Navy Staff, Washington, 1960; Chief Constructor, 1967; Sen. Officers War Course, 1969; RCDS, 1973; Head of Ship Material Engrg, 1974; Support Manager Submarines, 1976; Dep. Dir, Submarines/Polaris, Ship Dept, MoD, 1979; Dir of Naval Ship Production, 1981–82; Mem. Bd, and Man. Dir, Warship Div., British Shipbuilders, 1983–84; Exec. Chm., 1984–86, Technical Adviser, 1986–, Vickers Shipbuilding and Engrg Ltd, Barrow. *Address:* Foxhill Grove Farm, Fox Hill, Bath BA2 5AT. *T:* Combe Down 837546.

FULLER, Hon. Sir John (Bryan Munro), Kt 1974; President: Arthritis Foundation of Australia, since 1980; Barnardo's Australia, since 1985 (Member, Management Committee, 1980–85); *b* 22 Sept. 1917; *s* of late Bryan Fuller, QC; *m* 1940, Eileen, *d* of O. S. Webb; one *s* one *d*. *Educ:* Knox Grammar Sch., Wahroonga. Chm., Australian Country Party (NSW), 1959–64; MLC, NSW, 1961–78; Minister for Decentralisation and Development, 1965–73; NSW Minister for Planning and Environment, 1973–76; Vice-Pres. of Exec. Council and Leader of Govt in Legis. Council, 1968–76; Leader of Opposition, 1976–78. Vice-Pres., Graziers Assoc. of NSW, 1965; Member: Council, Univ. of NSW, 1967–78; Cttee, United World Colls Trust, NSW, 1978–; Bd, Foundn for Res. and Treatment Alcohol and Drug Dependence, 1980–85; Council, Nat. Heart Foundn, NSW, 1980–; Pres., Aust. Inst. of Export (NSW), 1985–; Leader of various NSW Govt trade missions to various parts of the world. Fellow Australian Inst. of Export 1969. *Recreations:* tennis, bowls. *Address:* 54/8 Fullerton Street, Woollahra, NSW 2025, Australia. *Clubs:* Australian (Sydney); Coolah Bowling, Royal Sydney Golf.

FULLER, Major Sir John (William Fleetwood), 3rd Bt *cr* 1910; Major, The Life Guards, retired; *b* 18 Dec. 1936; *s* of Major Sir John Gerard Henry Fleetwood Fuller, 2nd Bt, and Fiona, Countess of Normanton, (*d* 1985), *d* of 4th Marquess Camden, GCVO; *S* father, 1981; *m* 1968, Lorna Marian, *o d* of F. R. Kemp-Potter, Findon, Sussex; three *s*. *Heir:* *s* James Henry Fleetwood Fuller, *b* 1 Nov. 1970. *Address:* Neston Park, Corsham, Wilts.

FULLER, Roy Broadbent, CBE 1970; MA Oxon (by Decree); FRSL; poet and author; solicitor; Professor of Poetry, University of Oxford, 1968–73; *b* 11 Feb. 1912; *e s* of late Leopold Charles Fuller, Oldham; *m* 1936, Kathleen Smith; one *s*. *Educ:* Blackpool High Sch. Admitted a solicitor, 1934; served Royal Navy, 1941–46; Lieut, RNVR, 1944; Asst Solicitor to Woolwich Equitable Building Soc., 1938–58, Solicitor, 1958–69, Director, 1969–. Vice-Pres., Bldg Socs Assoc., 1969– (Chm. Legal Adv. Panel, 1958–69). A Governor of the BBC, 1972–79; Mem., Arts Council, 1976–77 (Chm., Literature Panel, 1976–77); Mem., Library Adv. Council for England, 1977–79. Hon. DLitt Kent, 1986. Queen's Gold Medal for Poetry, 1970. Cholmondeley Award, Soc. of Authors, 1980.

Publications: Poems, 1939; The Middle of a War, 1942; A Lost Season, 1944; Savage Gold, 1946; With My Little Eye; Byron for Today, 1948; Questions and Answers in Building Soc. Law and Practice; Epitaphs and Occasions, 1949; The Second Curtain, 1953; Counterparts; Fantasy and Fugue, 1954; Image of a Society, 1956; Brutus's Orchard, 1957; The Ruined Boys, 1959; The Father's Comedy, 1961; Collected Poems, 1962; The Perfect Fool, 1963; Buff, 1965; My Child, My Sister, 1965; Catspaw, 1966; New Poems, 1968 (Duff Cooper Memorial Prize 1968); Off Course, 1969; The Carnal Island, 1970; Owls and Artificers: Oxford lectures on poetry, 1971; Seen Grandpa Lately?, 1972; Tiny Tears, 1973; Professors and Gods: last Oxford lectures on poetry, 1973; From the Joke Shop, 1975; An Ill-Governed Coast, 1976; Poor Roy, 1977; The Other Planet, 1979; The Reign of Sparrows, 1980; Fellow Mortals: An Anthology of Animal Verse, 1981; The Individual and His Times (selected poems), 1982; (with Barbara Giles and Adrian Rumble) Upright Downfall, 1983; New and Collected Poems 1934–84, 1985; (ed with John Lehmann) The Penguin New Writing, 1985; Subsequent to Summer, 1985; Consolations, 1987; (ed) The Building Societies Acts, various dates; *autobiography:* Souvenirs, 1980; Vamp Till Ready, 1982; Home and Dry, 1984. *Address:* 37 Langton Way, Blackheath, SE3. *T:* 01–858 2334. *Club:* Athenæum.

FULLER, Simon William John; HM Diplomatic Service; Counsellor and Head of Chancery, British Embassy, Tel Aviv, since 1986; *b* 27 Nov. 1943; *s* of Rowland William Bevis Fuller and late Madeline Fuller (*née* Bailey); *m* 1984, Eleanor Mary Breedon; two *s*. *Educ:* Wellington College; Emmanuel College, Cambridge (BA Hist.). Served Singapore and Kinshasa, 1969–73; First Sec., Cabinet Office, 1973–75; FCO, 1975–77; UK Mission to UN, New York, 1977–80; FCO, 1980–86 (Counsellor, 1984). *Recreations:* cooking and cricket. *Address:* c/o Foreign and Commonwealth Office, SW1; 27 Carlisle Mansions, Carlisle Place, SW1P 1EZ. *T:* 01-828 6494.

FULLER-ACLAND-HOOD, Sir (Alexander) William; *see* Hood, Sir William Acland.

FULLERTON, Peter George Patrick Downing; Director, Domestic Programme, Energy Efficiency Office, Department of Energy, since 1985; *b* 17 Jan. 1930; *s* of late Major R. A. D. Fullerton and Janet Mary Fullerton (*née* Baird); *m* 1962, Elizabeth Evelyn Newman Stevens, *d* of late George Stevens; two *s* two *d*. *Educ:* Radley Coll.; Magdalen Coll., Oxford (MA). HMOCS, Kenya, 1953–63, retd as Dist Comr; joined CRO (later FCO), 1963; Private Sec. to Minister of State, 1963–64; Dar-es-Salaam, 1964–65; Lusaka, 1966–69; seconded to British Leyland Motor Corp., 1970; FCO, 1971; Northern Ireland Office, 1972; FCO, 1973; Canberra, 1974–77; Dept of Energy, 1977. *Address:* Hydon Heath Corner, Godalming, Surrey GU8 4BB. *T:* Hascombe 326. *Club:* United Oxford & Cambridge University.

FULLERTON, William Hugh; HM Diplomatic Service; Ambassador to Somalia, since 1983; *b* 11 Feb. 1939; *s* of late Major Arthur Hugh Theodore Francis Fullerton, RAMC, and of Mary (*née* Parker); *m* 1968, Arlene Jacobowitz; one *d*. *Educ:* Cheltenham Coll.; Queens' Coll., Cambridge (MA Oriental Langs). Shell Internat. Petroleum Co., Uganda, 1963–65; FO, 1965; MECAS, Shemlan, Lebanon, 1965–66; Information Officer, Jedda, 1966–67; UK Mission to UN, New York, 1967; FCO, 1968–70; Head of Chancery, Kingston, Jamaica, 1970–73, and Ankara, 1973–77; FCO, 1977–80; Counsellor (Economic and Commercial), 1980–83 and Consul-Gen., 1981–83, Islamabad. *Recreations:* travelling in remote areas, sailing, reading, walking. *Address:* c/o Foreign and Commonwealth Office, King Charles Street, SW1. *Club:* Travellers'.

FULTHORPE, Henry Joseph, FRINA; General Manager, HM Dockyard, Portsmouth (Deputy Director of Naval Construction), 1967–75; *b* Portsmouth, 2 July 1916; *s* of Joseph Henry and Clarissa Fulthorpe; *m* 1939, Bette May Forshew; two *s* one *d*. *Educ:* Royal Naval Coll., Greenwich. Principal (Ship) Overseer, Vickers, Barrow-in-Furness, 1943–46; Dep. Manager, HM Dockyard, Malta, 1946–49; Sec., Radiological Defence Panel, 1949–52; Staff Constr, first British atom bomb, Montebello Is, 1952–53; Constr i/c Minesweeper Design, Admty, Bath, 1953–54; Chief Constr, Maintenance, Bath, 1954–56; Dep. Manager, HM Dockyard, Portsmouth, 1956–58; Chief Constructor: HM Dockyard, Singapore, 1958–61; Dockyard Dept, Bath, 1961–63; Asst Dir of Naval Construction, Bath, 1963–64; Production Manager, HM Dockyard, Chatham, 1964–67; Manager, Constructive Dept, HM Dockyard, Portsmouth, 1967. *Recreations:* travel, winemaking, cooking. *Address:* Gerard House, 60 Granada Road, Southsea. *T:* Portsmouth 734876.

FULTON, Hon. Edmund Davie, PC (Canada) 1957; QC (BC) 1957; Barrister and Solicitor; Associate Counsel, Swinton & Company, Vancouver, since 1983; a Commissioner, Canadian Section, International Joint Commission, Ottawa, since 1986; *b* 10 March 1916; *s* of Frederick John Fulton, KC, and Winifred M. Davie; *m* 1946, Patricia Mary, *d* of J. M. Macrae and Christine Macrae (*née* Carmichael), Winnipeg; three *d*. *Educ:* St Michael's Sch., Victoria, BC; Kamloops High Sch.; University of British Columbia; St John's Coll., Oxford. BA (BC), BA Oxon (Rhodes Scholar, elected 1936). Admitted to Bar of British Columbia, 1940. Served in Canadian Army Overseas as Company Comdr with Seaforth Highlanders of Canada and as DAAG 1st Canadian Inf. Div., 1940–45, including both Italian and Northwest Europe campaigns (despatches); transferred to R of O with rank of Major, 1945. Practised law with Fulton, Verchere & Rogers, Kamloops, BC, 1945–68, and with Fulton, Cumming, Richards & Co., Vancouver, 1968–73; Judge, Supreme Court of Columbia, 1973–81. Elected to House of Commons of Canada, 1945; re-elected in 1949, 1953, 1957, 1958, 1962, 1965. Mem. Senate, University of British Columbia, 1948–57, 1969–75. Acting Minister of Citizenship and Immigration, June 1957–May 1958; Minister of Justice and Attorney Gen., Canada, June 1957–Aug. 1962; Minister of Public Works, Aug. 1962–April, 1963. Mem., Vancouver Adv. Cttee, Guaranty Trust Co. of Canada, 1984–. Member: Law Soc. of BC, 1940–; Law Soc. of Upper Canada, 1957–; Canadian Bar Assoc., 1940–; Arbitrators' Assoc. of BC, 1984–; Arbitrators Inst. of Canada Inc., 1984–. Hon. Col, Rocky Mountain Rangers, 1959. Hon. LLD: Ottawa, 1960; Queen's, 1963. Human Relns Award, Canadian Council of Christians and Jews, 1985; Citation for meritorious service to country and profession, Trial Lawyers Assoc. of BC, 1986. *Address:* (business) 1300–1090 West Georgia Street, Vancouver, BC V6E 3X9, Canada; (home) 1632 West 40th Avenue, Vancouver, BC V6M 1V9. *Clubs:* Vancouver, Shaughnessy Golf and Country (Vancouver); Rideau (Ottawa).

FULTON, Robert Andrew; HM Diplomatic Service; Counsellor, Oslo, since 1984; *b* 6 Feb. 1944; *s* of Rev. Robert M. Fulton and Janet W. Fulton (*née* Mackenzie); *m* 1970, Patricia Mary Crowley; two *s* one *d*. *Educ:* Rothesay Academy; Glasgow University (MA, LLB). Foreign and Commonwealth Office, 1968; Third later Second Secretary, Saigon, 1969; FCO, 1972; First Sec., Rome, 1973; FCO, 1977; First Sec., E Berlin, 1978; FCO, 1981. *Recreations:* golf, tennis, racing, reading, cinema. *Address:* c/o Foreign and Commonwealth Office, SW1A 2AH. *Club:* Oslo Golf.

FUNG, Hon. Sir Kenneth Ping-Fan, Kt 1971; CBE 1965 (OBE 1958); JP; Chairman, Fung Ping Fan & Co. Ltd, and Chairman or Director of other companies; Senior Consultant for External Economy of People's Government of Chongqing, since 1985; Director (and Chief Manager, retd), of The Bank of East Asia Ltd, Hong Kong; Chairman,

Thomas Cook Travel Services (Hong Kong) Ltd; Director, Hong Kong Macau International Investment Co. Ltd; *b* 28 May 1911; *yr s* of late Fung Ping Shan, JP; *m* 1933, Ivy (*née* Kan) Shiu-Han, OBE, JP, *d* of late Kan Tong-Po, JP; four *s* one *d*. *Educ:* Government Vernacular Sch.; Sch. of Chinese Studies, Univ. of Hong Kong. Unofficial Mem., Urban Council, 1951–60; Unofficial MLC, 1959–65, MEC, 1962–72; Life Mem., Court of Univ. of Hong Kong; Council of Chinese Univ. of Hong Kong; Fourth Pan-Pacific Rehabilitation Conf.; Pres., Chm., etc. of numerous social organisations, both present and past. Chm., Hong Kong Nat. Cttee, United World Colleges; Member: Program for Harvard and East Asia (Mem. Internat. Org. Cttee); Rotary Internat. (Paul Harris Fellow; 50-Year Membership Award, 1985); Bd of Overseers, Univ. of California Med. Sch., San Francisco; The 1001: a Nature Trust. Comr St John Ambulance Bde (first Chinese to serve), 1953–58; first Chinese Hon. ADC to 4 successive Governors and Officers Admin. Govt (rep. StJAB). JP Hong Kong, 1952; KStJ 1958. Hon. degrees: LLD, Chinese Univ. of Hong Kong, 1968; DSocSc, Univ. of Hong Kong, 1969. Founder Mem., Royal Asiatic Soc.; Mem. other Socs and Assocs. Silver Acorn, Commonwealth Scout Council (UK), 1976; Gold Dragon, Scout Assoc. of Hong Kong. Order of the Sacred Treasure (Japan), 1969; Knight Grand Officer, 1984 (Knight Commander, 1979), Internat. Order of St Hubert (Austria). *Recreations:* racing, golf, swimming. *Address:* (home) 14 South Bay Road, Hong Kong. *T:* 5–8122514; (office) Fung Ping Fan & Co. Ltd, 2705–2715 Connaught Centre, Hong Kong. *T:* 220311. *Clubs:* Royal Hongkong Jockey (Hon. Steward), Royal Hongkong Golf, Royal Hongkong Yacht, Hongkong Polo Assoc., Sports, Hongkong Country, Hongkong, Shek O Country, Hongkong Squash (Life Mem.), Chinese Recreation (Hon. Pres.), American, Japanese (Pres.), CASAM, Hongkong Automobile Assoc., Rotary (all in Hong Kong); Knickerbocker, Sky, Explorers', Amer. Photographic Soc., Bohemian (all in New York, USA); Hakone Country, Toride Internat. Golf, Hodogaya (Japan).

FUNSTON, G(eorge) Keith; *b* Waterloo, Iowa, USA, 12 Oct. 1910; *s* of George Edwin and Genevieve (Keith) Funston; *m* 1939, Elizabeth Kennedy; one *s* two *d*. *Educ:* Trinity Coll., Hartford, Conn; Harvard. AB, Trinity Coll., 1932; MBA (*cum laude*), Harvard, 1934. Mem. Research Staff, Harvard Business Sch., 1934–35; Asst to VP Sales, then Asst to Treas., American Radiator & Standard Sanitary, 1935–40; Dir, Purchases & Supplies, Sylvania Electronics, 1940–44; Special Asst to Chm., War Production Bd, 1941–44; Lt-Comdr, US Navy, 1944–46; Pres., Trinity Coll., Hartford, 1944–51; Pres. and Governor, New York Stock Exchange, 1951–67. Chm., Olin Corp., 1967–72; formerly Director: IBM; Metropolitan Life; Republic Steel; AVCO Corp.; Illinois Central Industries; Chemical Bank; Putnam Trust; Hartford Steam Boiler & Insurance Co.; Winn-Dixie Stores; Paul Revere Investors. Holds numerous hon. doctorates. *Recreations:* riding, reading, ski-ing, tennis. *Address:* (home) 74 Vineyard Lane, Greenwich, Conn 06830, USA. *T:* Townsend 9–5524. *Clubs:* Round Hill (Greenwich, Conn.); University, The Century Assoc., The Links (New York).

FURBER, Frank Robert; retired solicitor; *b* 28 March 1921; *s* of late Percy John Furber and Edith Furber; *m* 1948, Anne Wilson McArthur; three *s* one *d*. *Educ:* Willaston Sch.; Berkhamsted Sch.; University College London. LLB. Articled with Slaughter and May; solicitor 1945; Partner, Clifford-Turner, 1952–86; Mem., Planning Law Cttee, Law Society, 1964–69; Chairman: Blackheath Soc., 1968–; Blackheath Preservation Trust, 1972–; Film Industry Defence Organization, 1968–; Governor: Yehudi Menuhin Sch., 1964–; Live Music Now!, 1977–; Berkhamsted Sch., and Berkhamsted Sch. for Girls, 1976– (Chm., 1986–); Board Member: Trinity Coll. of Music, 1974–; Nat. Jazz Centre, 1982–; Common Law Inst. of Intellectual Property, 1982–; Chm., Rules of Golf Cttee, Royal and Ancient Golf Club, 1976–80; Trustee, Robert T. Jones Meml Trust, 1982–; Mem. and Hon. Sec., R & A Golf Amateurism Commn of Inquiry, 1984–85. Hon. Fellow, Trinity College, London. *Recreations:* golf, music, books, writing a history of The Moles Golfing Society. *Address:* 8 Pond Road, Blackheath, SE3 9JL. *T:* 01–852 8065. *Clubs:* Buck's; Royal Blackheath Golf, Royal St George's Golf (Captain, 1980–81), Royal and Ancient, Honourable Company of Edinburgh Golfers, Royal Worlington and Newmarket; Pine Valley (USA).

See also Ven. R. S. Brown.

FÜRER-HAIMENDORF, Prof. Christoph von, DPhil Vienna; Emeritus Professor and Hon. Fellow, School of Oriental and African Studies, University of London, since 1976; *b* 27 July 1909; *s* of Rudolf Fürer von Haimendorf und Wolkersdorf; *m* 1938, Elizabeth Barnardo; one *s*. *Educ:* Theresianische Akademie, Vienna. Asst Lecturer, Vienna Univ., 1931–34; Rockefeller Foundation Fellowship, 1935–37; Lecturer, Vienna University, 1938; Anthropological Fieldwork in Hyderabad and Orissa, 1939–43; Special Officer Subansiri, External Affairs Dept, Govt of India, 1944–45; Adviser to HEH the Nizam's Govt and Prof. of Anthropology in the Osmania Univ., 1945–49; Reader in Anthropology with special reference to India, University of London, 1949–51; Prof. of Asian Anthropology, School of Oriental and African Studies, 1951–76 (Dean of Sch., 1969–74, acting Director, 1974–75). Anthropological Research: in India and Nepal, 1953; in Nepal, 1957, 1962, 1966, 1972, 1976, 1981, 1983; in the Philippines, 1968; in India, 1970, 1976–. Munro Lectr, Edinburgh Univ., 1959; Visiting Prof., Colegio de Mexico, 1964, 1966. Pres., Royal Anthropological Inst., 1975–77. Corresponding Member: Austrian Academy of Science, 1964; Anthropological Soc. of Vienna, 1970. Rivers Memorial Medal of Royal Anthropological Institute, 1949; S. C. Roy Gold Medal, Asiatic Soc., Calcutta, 1964; Sir Percy Sykes Memorial Medal, Royal Central Asian Soc., 1965; King Birendra Prize, Royal Nepal Acad., 1976; Annandale Medal, Asiatic Soc. of Bengal, 1979. Austrian Order of Merit for Art and Science, 1982. *Publications:* The Naked Nagas, 1939; The Chenchus, 1943; The Reddis of the Bison Hills, 1945; The Raj Gonds of Adilabad, 1948; Himalayan Barbary, 1955; The Apa Tanis, 1962; (joint author) Mount Everest, 1963; The Sherpas of Nepal, 1964; (ed and jt author) Caste and Kin in Nepal, India and Ceylon, 1966; Morals and Merit, 1967; The Konyak Nagas, 1969; (ed and jt author) Peoples of the Earth, vol. 12: The Indian Sub-continent, 1973; (ed and jt author) Contributions to the Anthropology of Nepal, 1974; Himalayan Traders, 1975; Return to the Naked Nagas, 1976; The Gonds of Andhra Pradesh, 1979; A Himalayan Tribe, 1980; (ed and jt author) Asian Highland Societies, 1981; Highlanders of Arunachal Pradesh, 1982; Tribes of India, 1982; Himalayan Adventure, 1983; The Sherpas Transformed, 1984; Tribal Populations and Cultures of the Indian Subcontinent, 1985; articles in Journal of Royal Anthropological Inst., Man, Anthropos, Geographical Jl, Man in India. *Recreation:* music. *Address:* 32 Clarendon Road, W11. *T:* 01–727 4520, 01–637 2388.

FURLONG, Mrs Monica; writer; *b* 17 Jan. 1930; *d* of Alfred Gordon Furlong and Freda Simpson; *m* 1953, William John Knights (marr. diss. 1977); one *s* one *d*. *Educ:* Harrow County Girls' Sch.; University College London. Truth, Spectator, Guardian, 1956–61; Daily Mail, 1961–68; Producer, BBC, 1974–78. Moderator, Movement for the Ordination of Women, 1982–85. Hon. DD Gen. Theol Seminary, NY, 1986. *Publications:* Travelling In, 1971; Contemplating Now, 1971; God's A Good Man (poems), 1974; Puritan's Progress, 1975; Christian Uncertainties, 1975; The Cat's Eye (novel), 1976; Merton (biography), 1980; Cousins (novel), 1983; (ed) Feminine in the Church, 1984; Genuine Fake: a biography of Alan Watts, 1986. *Address:* c/o Anthony Sheil Associates, 43 Doughty Street, WC1. *T:* 01–405 9351. *Club:* Society of Authors.

FURLONG, Hon. Robert Stafford, MBE (mil.) 1945; Chief Justice of Newfoundland, 1959–79; *b* 9 Dec. 1904; *o s* of Martin Williams Furlong, KC, and Mary Furlong (*née* McGrath). *Educ:* St Bonaventure's Coll., St John's, Newfoundland. Called to the Bar, 1926, appointed KC 1944. Temp. Actg Lt-Comdr (S) RNVR. OStJ 1937; Knight of St Gregory 1958. *Recreations:* golf and motoring. *Address:* 8 Winter Avenue, St John's, Newfoundland. *T:* (709) 726–7228. *Clubs:* Naval (London); Bally Haly Golf and Country, Crow's Nest (all in St John's).

FURLONG, Ronald (John), FRCS; Hon. Consulting Orthopædic Surgeon: St Thomas' Hospital; King Edward VII Hospital for Officers; Queen Victoria Hospital, East Grinstead; and lately to the Army; *b* 3 March 1909; *s* of Frank Owen Furlong and Elsie Muriel Taffs, Woolwich; *m* 1st, 1936, Elva Mary Ruth Lefeaux (marr. diss., 1947); one *s* three *d*; 2nd, 1948, Nora Christine Pattinson (marr. diss. 1969); one *d*; 3rd, 1970, Eileen Mary Watford. *Educ:* Eltham Coll.; St Thomas's Hosp. MB, BS London 1931; MRCS, LRCP, 1931; FRCS 1934. Served with Royal Army Medical Corps, 1941–46. Home Commands, North Africa and Italy; Brigadier, Consulting Orthopædic Surgeon to the Army, 1946, Hon. Consulting Orthopædic Surgeon 1951; Orthopædic Surgeon, St Thomas' Hosp., 1946. *Publications:* Injuries of the Hand, 1957; (trans.) Pauwel's Atlas of the Biomechanics of the Normal and Diseased Hip, 1978; (trans.) Pauwel's Biomechanics of the Locomotor Apparatus, 1980. *Recreations:* reading, history and archæology. *Address:* 149 Harley Street, W1. *T:* 01–935 4444. *Club:* Athenæum.

FURLONGER, Robert William, CB 1981; retired public servant, Australia; *b* 29 April 1921; *s* of George William Furlonger and Germaine Rose Furlonger; *m* 1944, Verna Hope Lewis; three *s* one *d*. *Educ:* Sydney High Sch.; Sydney Univ. (BA). Served War, AMF, 1941–45. Australian Dept of External (later Foreign) Affairs, 1945–69 and 1972–77 (IDC, 1960; Dir, Jt Intell. Org., Dept of Def., 1960–72); appointments included: High Comr, Nigeria, 1961; Aust. Perm. Rep. to the European Office of the UN, 1961–64; Minister, Aust. Embassy, Washington, 1965–69; Ambassador to Indonesia, 1972–74, and to Austria, Hungary and Czechoslovakia, 1975–77; Dir-Gen., Office of National Assessments, Canberra, 1977–81. *Recreations:* golf, cricket, music. *Address:* 12 Norman Street, Deakin, ACT 2600, Australia. *T:* 813656. *Clubs:* Canberra; Royal Canberra Golf.

FURMSTON, Bentley Edwin, FRICS; Director of Overseas Surveys, Ordnance Survey, since 1984; *b* 7 Oct. 1931; *s* of Rev. Edward Bentley Furmston and Mary Furmston (*née* Bennett); *m* 1957, Margaret (*née* Jackson); two *s* one *d*. *Educ:* The Nelson Sch., Wigton, Cumbria; Victoria Univ., Manchester (BSc Mathematics). Entered Civil Service as Surveyor, Directorate of Overseas Surveys, 1953, with service in Gambia, Swaziland, Basutoland, N Rhodesia; Sen. Surveyor, N Rhodesia, 1960; Sen. Computer, DOS, 1963; seconded to Govt of Malawi as Dep. Commissioner of Surveys, 1965, Principal Survey Officer, DOS, 1968: Overseas Supervisor, Sch. of Military Survey; Regional Survey Officer, W Africa; Asst Director (Survey), 1971; Asst Dir (Cartography), Ordnance Survey, 1973; Dep. Dir, Field Survey, Ordnance Survey, 1974; Dep. Dir (Survey), DOS, 1977; Dir, Overseas Surveys and Survey Advr, Min. of Overseas Develt, 1980. *Publications:* contribs to technical jls. *Recreations:* reading, gardening, hill walking, climbing. *Address:* The Orchard, Carters Clay Road, Newtown, Romsey, Hants. *T:* Lockerly 41105.

FURNELL, Very Rev. Raymond; Provost, St Edmundsbury Cathedral, since 1981; *b* 18 May 1935; *s* of Albert George Edward and Hetty Violet Jane Furnell; *m* 1967, Sherril Whitcomb; one *s* three *d*. *Educ:* Hinchley Wood School, Surrey; Brasted Place Theological Coll.; Lincoln Theol Coll. Thomas Meadows & Co. Ltd, 1951; RAF, 1953; Lummus Co. Ltd, 1955; Geo. Wimpey & Co. Ltd, 1960; Brasted Place, 1961; Lincoln Theol Coll., 1963; Curate, St Luke's, Cannock, 1965; Vicar, St James the Great, Clayton, 1969; Rector, Hanley Team Ministry and RD, Stoke North, 1975. *Recreations:* music, drama. *Address:* Provost's House, Bury St Edmunds, Suffolk IP33 1RS.

FURNER, Air Vice-Marshal Derek Jack, CBE 1973 (OBE 1963); DFC 1943; AFC 1954; *b* 14 Nov. 1921; *s* of Vivian J. Furner; *m* 1948, Patricia Donnelly; three *s*. *Educ:* Westcliff High Sch., Essex. Joined RAF, 1941; commnd as navigator, 1942; Bomber Comd (2 tours), 1942–44; Transport Comd, Far East, 1945–47; Navigation Instructor, 1948–50; trials flying, Boscombe Down, 1951–53 and Wright-Patterson, Ohio, 1953–56; Air Min., 1957; OC Ops Wing, RAF Waddington, 1958–60; Planning Staff, HQ Bomber Comd, 1961–63 and SHAPE, Paris, 1964–65; Dep. Dir Manning, MoD (Air), 1966–67; OC RAF Scampton, 1968; AOC Central Reconnaissance Estab., 1969–70; Sec., Internat. Mil. Staff, NATO, Brussels, 1970–73; Asst Air Secretary, 1973–75. Gen. Manager, 1976–81, Dir, 1977–81, Harlequin Wallcoverings. FIPM 1975; FBIM 1975. *Recreations:* mathematical problems, music. *Address:* Greensleeves, Norwich Road, Saxlingham Nethergate, Norwich, Norfolk NR15 1TP. *T:* Hempnall 351. *Club:* Royal Air Force.

FURNESS, family name of **Viscount Furness.**

FURNESS, 2nd Viscount, *cr* 1918; **William Anthony Furness;** Baron Furness, *cr* 1910, of Grantley; *b* 31 March 1929; *s* of 1st Viscount and Thelma (*d* 1970), *d* of late Harry Hays Morgan, American Consul-Gen. at Buenos Aires; *S* father, 1940. *Educ:* Downside; USA. Served as Guardsman, Welsh Guards (invalided, 1947). Delegate to Inter-Parliamentary Union Conferences, Washington, 1953, Vienna, 1954, Helsinki, 1955, Warsaw, 1959, Brussels, 1961, Belgrade, 1963. Mem. Council, Hansard Soc. for Parliamentary Govt, 1955–67. Founder Chm., Anglo-Mongolian Soc., 1963; Vice-President: Tibet Soc. of the UK; Catholic Stage Guild. Sovereign Military Order of Malta: joined 1954; Sec., Assoc. of Brit. Members, 1956–65, Sec.-Gen. 1965–78; Regent, Brit. Sub-Priory of Bl. Adrian Fortescue, 1982–; Mem. Sovereign Council, 1960–62; Mem. Board of Auditors, 1979–80; Grand Cross, Order of Merit, 1984, Kt of Justice, 1977 (Solemn Vows, 1982). Grand Officer, Order of Merit, Italy, 1961; KStJ 1971 (CStJ 1964); KCSG 1966. *Heir:* none. *Address:* c/o Midland Bank, 69 Pall Mall, SW1. *Clubs:* Boodle's, Carlton; Travellers' (Paris).

FURNESS, Alan Edwin; HM Diplomatic Service; Head of South Pacific Department, Foreign and Commonwealth Office, since 1985; *b* 6 June 1937; *s* of Edwin Furness and Marion Furness (*née* Senton); *m* 1971, Aline Elizabeth Janine Barrett; two *s*. *Educ:* Eltham Coll.; Jesus Coll., Cambridge (BA, MA). Commonwealth Relations Office, 1961; Private Sec. to Parliamentary Under-Secretary of State, 1961–62; Third, later Second Secretary, British High Commn, New Delhi, 1962–66; First Secretary, DSAO (later FCO), 1966–69; First Sec., UK Delegn to European Communities, Brussels, 1969–72; First Sec. and Head of Chancery, Dakar, 1972–75; First Sec., FCO, 1975–78; Counsellor and Head of Chancery, Jakarta, 1978–81; Counsellor and Head of Chancery, Warsaw, 1982–85. *Recreations:* music, literature, gardening. *Address:* c/o Foreign and Commonwealth Office, SW1. *T:* 01–233 3000. *Club:* United Oxford & Cambridge University.

FURNESS, Robin; *see* Furness, Sir S. R.

FURNESS, Sir Stephen (Roberts), 3rd Bt *cr* 1913; farmer and sporting/landscape artist (as Robin Furness); *b* 10 Oct. 1933; *e s* of Sir Christopher Furness, 2nd Bt, and of Flower, Lady Furness, OBE, *d* of late Col G. C. Roberts; *S* father, 1974; *m* 1961, Mary, *e d* of J. F. Cann, Cullompton, Devon; one *s* one *d*. *Educ:* Charterhouse. Entered RN, 1952; Observer, Fleet Air Arm, 1957; retired list, 1962. NCA, Newton Rigg Farm Inst., 1964. Member: Armed Forces Art Soc.; Darlington Art Soc. Jt MFH, Bedale Hunt, 1979–. *Recreations:* looking at paintings, foxhunting, racing. *Heir:* *s* Michael Fitzroy Roberts Furness, *b* 12 Oct. 1962. *Address:* Stanhow Farm, Great Langton, near Northallerton, Yorks DL7 0TJ. *T:* Northallerton 748614.

FURNISS, Air Vice-Marshal Peter, DFC 1944; TD 1964; Director of Legal Services, RAF, 1978–82; *b* 16 July 1919; *s* of John and Mary Furniss; *m* 1954, Denise Cotet; one *s* two *d*. *Educ:* Sedbergh School. Commissioned 1st Bn The Liverpool Scottish TA, Queen's Own Cameron Highlanders, 1939; seconded to RAF, 1942; Comd No 73 Fighter Sqdn, 1945–46; demobilised 1946; admitted as Solicitor, 1948; commissioned in Legal Branch, RAF, 1950; Director of Legal Services: HQ Air Forces Middle East, Aden, 1961–63; HQ Far East Air Force, Singapore, 1969–71; HQ RAF Germany, 1973–74; Dep. Dir of Legal Services (RAF), 1975–78. *Recreations:* shooting, gardening, fishing. *Address:* 18 Sevington Park, Loose, Maidstone, Kent ME15 9SB. *T:* Maidstone 44620. *Club:* Royal Air Force.

FURNIVAL JONES, Sir (Edward) Martin, Kt 1967; CBE 1957; *b* 7 May 1912; *s* of Edward Furnival Jones, FCA; *m* 1955, Elizabeth Margaret, *d* of Bartholomew Snowball, BSc, AMIEE; one *d*. *Educ:* Highgate Sch.; Gonville and Caius Coll., Cambridge (exhibitioner). MA 1938. Admitted a Solicitor, 1937. Served War of 1939–45: General Staff Officer at Supreme Headquarters, Allied Expeditionary Force, and War Office (despatches, American Bronze Star Medal). Chm. of Bd, Frensham Heights, 1973–76 (Pres. 1977). *Recreation:* birdwatching. *Address:* Lindum, First Drift, Wothorpe, Stamford, Lincs. *T:* Stamford 63085.

FURNIVALL, Barony *cr* 1295; in abeyance. *Co-heiresses:* Hon. Rosamond Mary Dent (Sister Ancilla, OSB); *b* 3 June 1933; Hon. Patricia Mary Dent [*b* 4 April 1935; *m* 1st, 1956, Captain Thomas Hornsby (marr. diss., 1963; he *d* 1967); one *s* one *d*; 2nd, 1970, Roger Thomas John Bence; one *s* one *d*].

FURSDON, Maj.-Gen. Francis William Edward, CB 1980; MBE (Gallantry) 1958; KStJ 1980; defence consultant and correspondent; Director of Ceremonies, Order of St John, since 1980; *b* 10 May 1925; *s* of late G. E. S. Fursdon and Mrs Fursdon; *m* 1950, Joan Rosemary (*née* Worssam); one *s* one *d*. *Educ:* Westminster Sch. MLitt (Aberdeen) 1978; DLitt (Leiden) 1979. Passed AMIMechE; FBIM. Enlisted RE, 1942; RE Course, Birmingham Univ., 1943; in ranks until commnd, 1945; 1945–67: Royal W Afr. Frontier Force, India, Burma and Gold Coast; Student RMCS; staff and regtl duty, UK, Singapore, Canal Zone and Cyprus; Staff Coll.; DAA&QMG 19 Inf. Bde, UK and Port Said; GSO2 RE Sch. of Inf.; JSSC; OC 34 Indep. Fd Sqdn, E Africa and Kuwait; Instr, Staff Coll., Camberley; 2 i/c 38 Engr Regt; Admin. Staff Coll., Henley; CO 25 Engr Regt, BAOR, 1967–69; AA&QMG HQ Land Forces, Gulf, 1970–71; Dep. Comd and COS Land Forces, Gulf, 1971; Col Q (Qtg) HQ BAOR, 1972–73; Service Fellow, Aberdeen Univ., 1974; Dir of Def. Policy (Europe and NATO), MoD, 1974–77; Dir, Military Assistance Office, MoD, 1977–80; Mil. Adv. to Governor of Rhodesia, and later Senior British Officer, Zimbabwe, 1980, retired 1980. Defence and Military Correspondent, The Daily Telegraph, 1980–86. *Publications:* Grains of Sand, 1971; There are no Frontiers, 1973; The European Defence Community: a History, 1980. *Recreations:* photography (IAC Internat. Award, 1967), gardening, travel. *Address:* c/o National Westminster Bank, 1 St James's Square, SW1Y 4JX. *Clubs:* Army and Navy, St John House, Special Forces.

FURTADO, Robert Audley, CB 1970; Special Commissioner, 1946–77, Presiding Commissioner, 1963–77; *b* 20 August 1912; *yr s* of Montague C. Furtado; *m* 1945, Marcelle Elizabeth, *d* of W. Randall Whitteridge; one *s* one *d*. *Educ:* Whitgift Sch.; University Coll., London. LLB London Univ., 1933; called to Bar, Gray's Inn, 1934. Served War of 1939–45, in Army in India and Burma (Despatches); demobilised rank of Lieut-Col, 1945. *Recreation:* bricolage. *Address:* Hillfold, Langton Herring, Dorset. *T:* Abbotsbury 871502.

See also J. E. Pater, Prof. David Whitteridge and Sir Gordon Whitteridge.

FYFE, Prof. William Sefton, FRS 1969; Chairman, Department of Geology, and Professor of Geology, University of Western Ontario, since 1972; *b* 4 June 1927; *s* of Colin and Isabella Fyfe; *m* 1968; two *s* one *d*. *Educ:* Otago Univ., New Zealand. BSc 1948, MSc 1949, PhD 1952; FRSC 1980. Univ. of California, Berkeley, Calif: Lecturer in Chemistry, 1952, Reader, 1958; Prof. of Geology, 1959; Royal Soc. Res. Prof. (Geochemistry), Univ. of Manchester, 1967–72. Guggenheim Fellow, 1983. Hon. Fellow, Geological Soc. Amer.; Corresp. Mem., Brazilian Acad. of Science. Mineralogical Soc. of Amer. Award, 1964; Logan Medal, Geolog. Assoc. of Canada, 1982; Willet G. Miller Medal, Royal Soc. of Canada, 1985. *Publications:* Metamorphic Reactions and Metamorphic Facies, 1958; The Geochemistry of Solids, 1964; Fluids in the Earth's Crust, 1978; also numerous scientific papers. *Address:* Department of Geology, University of Western Ontario, London, Ontario N6A 5B7, Canada.

FYJIS-WALKER, Richard Alwyne, CMG 1980; CVO 1976; HM Diplomatic Service; Ambassador to Pakistan, since 1984; *b* 19 June 1927; *s* of Harold and Marion Fyjis-Walker; *m* 1st, 1951, Barbara Graham-Watson (marr. diss.); one *s*; 2nd, 1972, Gabrielle Josefi; one *s*. *Educ:* Bradfield Coll.; Magdalene Coll., Cambridge (BA). Army (KRRC), 1945–48. Joined Foreign (subseq. Diplomatic) Service, 1955; served: Amman, 1956; FO, 1957–61; Paris, 1961–63; Cairo, 1963–65; FCO, 1966–71; Counsellor, 1970; Ankara, 1971–74; Counsellor (Information), Washington, 1974–78; Counsellor, UK Mission to UN, NY, 1978–79; Ambassador to the Sudan, 1979–84. *Address:* c/o Foreign and Commonwealth Office, SW1.

FYNN, Sir Basil Mortimer L.; *see* Lindsay-Fynn.

G

GABB, (William) Harry, CVO 1974 (MVO 1961); DMus (Lambeth), 1974; Organist, Choirmaster and Composer at HM Chapels Royal, 1953–Easter 1974; Sub-Organist, St Paul's Cathedral, London, 1946–Easter 1974; Professor and Examiner of Organ Playing at The Trinity College of Music, London; Special Commissioner for Royal School of Church Music; Member, Council of the Royal College of Organists; Adjudicator and Recitalist; *b* 5 April 1909; *m* 1936, Helen Burnaford Mutton; one *s*. *Educ:* Scholarship at Royal Coll. of Music for Organ and Composition, ARCO 1928; FRCO 1930; ARCM Solo Organ, 1931; Organist, St Jude's, West Norwood, 1925; Organist and Choirmaster, Christ Church, Gypsy Hill, 1928; Sub-Organist, Exeter Cathedral, also Organist, Church of St Leonard's, Exeter and Heavitree Parish Church, 1929–37; Organist and Master of the Choristers, Llandaff Cathedral, 1937; Lectr, St Michael's Theological Coll., Llandaff; Royal Armoured Corps, War of 1939–45. Returned from Army to Llandaff, Jan. 1946. Played organ at the Coronation of Elizabeth II and at many Royal Weddings and Baptisms. Hon. FTCL, 1954. *Address:* St Lawrence Cottage, Bagshot Road, Chobham, Woking, Surrey GU24 8BY. *T:* Chobham 7879.

GADD, John; Chairman, North Thames Gas, since 1977; *b* 9 June 1925; *s* of late George Gadd and of Winifred Gadd (*née* Bowyer), Dunstable, Bedfordshire; *m* 1959, Nancy Jean, *d* of late Pryce Davies, Henley-on-Thames. *Educ:* Cedars Sch., Leighton Buzzard; Cambridgeshire Technical Coll. FIGasE 1967; MIPM 1975; CBIM 1979. Joined Gas Industry, 1941. Served War, RNVR, 1943–46. Southern Gas Bd, 1946–69: various engineering appts; Personnel Manager, 1962; Dep. Chm., 1969; Chm., Eastern Gas, 1973–77. Administrative Staff Coll., Henley-on-Thames, 1961. FRSA 1985. *Recreations:* gardening, walking. *Address:* c/o North Thames House, London Road, Staines, Middlesex TW18 4AE. *Clubs:* City Livery; Leander, Phyllis Court (Henley-on-Thames).

GADD, (John) Staffan; Chairman, Saga Securities Ltd, since 1985; Senior International Adviser, Yamaichi International Ltd, since 1986; *b* 30 Sept. 1934; *s* of John Gadd and Ulla Olivecrona; *m* 1958, Margaretha Löfborg; one *s* one *d*. *Educ:* Stockholm Sch. of Econs. MBA. Sec., Confedn of Swedish Industries, 1958–61; Skandinaviska Banken, Stockholm, 1961–69 (London Rep., 1964–67); Dep. Man. Dir, Scandinavian Bank Ltd, London, 1969–71, Chief Exec. and Man. Dir, 1971–80; Chief Exec., 1980–84, Chm., 1982–84, Samuel Montagu & Co. Ltd; Chm., Montagu and Co. AB, Sweden, 1982–86; Dir, Guyerzeller Zurmont Bank AG, Switzerland, 1983–84. *Recreations:* shooting, ski-ing, the arts, walking, travel. *Address:* Locks Manor, Hurstpierpoint, West Sussex BN6 9JZ.

GADDES, (John) Gordon; Director General, Federation of British Electrotechnical and Allied Manufacturers' Associations (formerly British Electrical and Allied Manufacturers' Association), since 1982; *b* 22 May 1936; *s* of late James Graham Moscrop Gaddes and of Irene Gaddes (*née* Murray; who married E. O. Kine); *m* 1958, Pamela Jean (*née* Marchbank); one *s* one *d*. *Educ:* Carres Grammar Sch., Sleaford; Selwyn Coll., Cambridge (MA Hons Geography); London Univ. (BScEcon Hons). Joint Services Sch. of Languages, Russian Translator in RAF, 1955–57. Asst Lectr in Business Studies, Peterborough Technical Coll., 1960–64; Lectr in Business Studies, later Head of Business Studies, then Vice-Principal, Dacorum Coll. of Further Educn, Hemel Hempstead, 1964–69; Head of Export Services: British Standards Instn, 1969–72; Quality Assurance Dept, 1972–73; Dir, BSI Hemel Hempstead Centre, 1973–77; Director: BASEC, 1974–80; BEAB, 1976–82; Commercial Dir, BSI, 1977–81; Dir, Information, Marketing and Resources, BSI, 1981–82. Secretary, BSI Quality Assurance Council, 1976–80; Treas., Nat. Council for Quality and Reliability, 1977–80; Member: Council, 1982–, President's Cttee, 1984–, Production Cttee, 1984–, CBI; Elec Engrg EDC, 1982–; Electrical Equipment Certification Management Bd, HSE, 1984–; Council, Elec. Res. Assoc. Ltd, 1982–; Council, British Elec. Approvals Bd, 1976–; Nat. Accreditation Council for Certification Bodies, 1984– (Chm., Assessment Panel, 1985–); Adv. Council for Calibration and Measurement, 1978–86; Project Leader for BNEC project in Hong Kong, 1970; BSI Assessor on Council of Agrément Bd, 1972–80; (first) Chm., British Approvals Service for Electric Cables (BASEC), 1973–74; Project Leader for ISO/UNESCO inf. network study, 1974–75; UK Rep., ORGALIME, 1982– (Chm., Electrical and Electronic Inds Liaison Cttee, 1982–). Former Mem., ISO Cttees. *Publications:* papers in range of jls and proc., *eg* Amer. Soc. for Quality Control, Instn of Gas Engrs, BSI News, Business Weekly, Business Educn, Europe Select Rev. *Recreations:* squash, running. *Address:* Federation of British Electrical and Allied Manufacturers' Associations, Leicester House, 8 Leicester Street, WC2H 7BN. *T:* 01–437 0678. *Club:* Athenæum.

GADSBY, Gordon Neville, CB 1972; *b* 29 Jan. 1914; *s* of William George and Margaret Sarah Gadsby; *m* 1938, Jeanne (*née* Harris); two *s* one *d*. *Educ:* King Edward VI Sch., Stratford-upon-Avon; University of Birmingham. BSc 1935, DipEd 1937, Cadbury Prizeman 1937, Birmingham; FRSC, CChem. Princ. Lectr, RMCS, 1946–51; Supt, Army Operational Research Gp, 1951–55; Dep. Sci. Adviser to Army Coun., 1955–59; idc 1960; Dir of Army Operational Science and Research, 1961; Dir, Army Operational Res. Estab., 1961–64; Dir of Biol. and Chem. Defence, MoD, 1965–67; Dep. Chief Scientist (Army), MoD, 1967–68; Dir, Chemical Defence Estabt, Porton, Wilts, 1968–72; Minister, Defence R&D, British Embassy, Washington, 1972–75, retired. *Publications:* Lubrication, 1949; An Introduction to Plastics, 1950. *Recreations:* oil painting, photography. *Address:* Ruan House, Cliff Road, Sidmouth, Devon EX10 8JN. *T:* Sidmouth 77842.

GADSDEN, Sir Peter (Drury Haggerston), GBE 1979; MA; FEng; Lord Mayor of London for 1979–80; Company Director; Underwriting Member of Lloyd's; Mineral Marketing Consultant since 1969; *b* Canada, 28 June 1929; *er s* of late Basil Claude Gadsden, ACT, ThL, and late Mabel Florence Gadsden (*née* Drury); *m* 1955, Belinda Ann, *e d* of late Captain Sir (Hugh) Carnaby de Marie Haggerston, 11th Bt; four *d*. *Educ:* Rockport, Northern Ireland; The Elms, Colwall; Wrekin Coll., Wellington; Jesus Coll., Cambridge (MA). 2nd Lieut King's Shropshire LI, attached Oxf. and Bucks LI and Durham LI, Germany, 1948–49; Man. Dir, London subsid. of Australian Mineral Sands Producer, 1964–70; Marketing Economist (Mineral Sands) to UN Industrial Development Organisation, 1969; pt-time Mem., Crown Agents for Oversea Govts and Admins, and Crown Agents Hldg and Realisation Bd, 1981–. Director: City of London (Arizona) Corp., 1970– (Chm., 1985–); Ellingham Estate Ltd (Chm., 1974–); Private Patients Plan Ltd (Chm., 1984–); Beam Components, 1981–; Ginsbury Electronics, 1981–; Wm Jacks PLC, 1984–; World Trade Centre in London Ltd, 1985–; Bann Systems Ltd, 1985–. Dir, Clothworkers' Foundn, 1978–; Hon. Mem. London Metal Exchange. President: Nat. Assoc. of Charcoal Manufacturers, 1970–; Embankment Rifle Club, 1975–; Leukaemia Res. Fund, City of London Br., 1975–; Metropolitan Soc. for the Blind; Publicity Club of London, 1983–; Council, London World Trade Centre Assoc., 1980–; St John Ambulance (Eastern Area). Sheriff London, 1970–71; Common Councilman (Cripplegate Within and Without), 1969–71; Alderman, City of London (Ward of Farringdon Without), 1971–; HM Lieutenant, City of London, 1979–; Founder Master, Engineers' Co., 1983–85; Liveryman: Clothworkers' Co. (Court), 1965– (Warden 1981–83); Plaisterers' Co. (Hon.), 1975–; Marketors Co. (Hon.), 1978–; Hon. Freeman, Actuaries' Co., 1981–; Master, Cripplegate Ward Club, 1982–83; Member: Guild of Freemen (Master 1984–85); Royal Soc. of St George (City of London Br.); Council, City Univ., 1985– (Chancellor, 1979–80). Member Council: Britain Australia Soc. (Vice-Chm.); Trinity Hospice, 1983–; Chm. Britain Australia Bicentennial Cttee. Hon. Freeman, Borough of Islwyn, S Wales, 1983. Vice-Pres., Sir Robert Menzies Meml Trust; Pres., Shropshire Soc. in London, 1986–. Governor: Voluntary Hosp. of St Bartholomew, 1983–; Hon. Irish Soc., 1984–. Fellowship of Engrg Distinction Lectr, 1980; Wm Menelaus Meml Lectr, SW Inst. of Engrs, 1983; paper to MANTECH Symposium, 1983. Trustee: Chichester Festival Theatre, 1978–; Mary Rose Develt Trust, 1980–; Pres., Ironbridge Gorge Museum Develt Trust, 1981–; Mem., Management Council, Shakespeare Theatre Trust, 1979–; Chm. and Mem. Council, Royal Commonwealth Soc., 1984–. JP, City of London, 1971 (Inner London Area of Greater London, 1969–71). Hon. FInstM, 1976; FIMM 1979; CEng 1979, FEng 1980. Mem. and Hon. Mem. Court, HAC. KStJ 1980 (OStJ 1977). Officier de l'Etoile Equatoriale de la République Gabonaise, 1970. Hon. DSc 1979. *Publications:* articles in: InstMM Transactions, 1971; RSM Jl, 1979; Textile Institute and Industry, 1980; articles on titanium, zirconium, and hafnium in Mining Jl Annual Reviews. *Recreations:* ski-ing, sailing, walking, photography, farming, forestry. *Address:* Harelaw House, Chathill, Northumberland NE67 5HE. *T:* Chathill 224, 333. *Clubs:* City of London (Mem. Cttee), City Livery (Mem. Council), United Wards, Farringdon Ward (patron), Pilgrims, British Malaysian Soc., Light Infantry (Hon.), Mining (Hon.); Presscala (Hon.), Canada; Alnmouth Golf, Royal London Yacht (Hon.); Birdham Yacht (Hon.).

GAEKWAD, Lt-Col Fatesinghrao P.; *b* 2 April 1930; *s* of HH Sir Pratapsingh Gaekwar, GCIE, Maharaja of Baroda; *S* father, 1968; title abolished, 1971. *Educ:* privately, under English tutor; passed Senior Cambridge Examination, 1947. Entered politics, 1956; elected to Lok Sabha 1957, 1962, 1971, 1977; Parly Sec. to Defence Minister, 1957–62, Mem. Public Accounts Cttee, 1963–64. MP (Congress), Gujarat, 1967–71; Minister for Health, Gujarat Govt, 1967–71. Chancellor, Maharaja Sayajirao Univ., Baroda, 1951–. Chairman: Baroda Rayon Corp. Chm., Bd of Governors, Nat. Inst. of Sports, Patiala, 1962–63; well-known cricketer and sportsman; Manager, Indian Cricket Team to England, 1959 and to Pakistan, 1978, 1982–83; Pres., Bd of Control for Cricket in India, 1963–66; expert commentator for cricket matches both in India and UK, summarises for BBC. Member: CCI, Bombay; MCC, London. FZS London. Internat. Trustee, World Wildlife Fund, for 6 years (Founder Pres., Indian Nat. Appeal); Pres., Indian Soc. of Naturalists; Member: IUCN; Fauna Preservation Soc.; RSPB; Indian Bd for Wildlife; World Poultry Science Assoc. Cultural Dr, World Univ. of USA, 1983; Hon. DHum World Acad. of Arts and Culture of Taipeh, Taiwan Rep. of China, 1984; Baden-Powell World Fellow, 1982. Travelled with four friends by car, India to Europe through Middle East, 1955; also two months safari in Belgian Congo and E Africa, 1955; has visited most countries around Globe. *Publication:* Palaces of India, 1980. *Recreations:* photography, cooking, reading, poetry. *Address:* Laxmi Vilas Palace, Baroda 390 001, (Gujarat), India.

GAFFNEY; *see* Burke-Gaffney.

GAFFNEY, James Anthony, CBE 1984; FEng; FICE; consulting engineer; *b* Bargoed, Glam, 9 Aug. 1928; *s* of James Francis and Violet Mary Gaffney; *m* 1953, Margaret Mary, 2nd *d* of E. and G. J. Evans, Pontypridd; one *s* two *d*. *Educ:* De La Salle Coll.; St Illtyd's Coll., Cardiff; UWIST; UC, Cardiff (Fellow, 1984). BSc (Eng) London. FEng 1979; FICE 1968; FInstHE 1970. Highway Engr, Glam CC, 1948–60; Asst County Surveyor, Somerset CC, 1960–64; Deputy County Surveyor, Notts CC, 1964–69; County Engr and Surveyor, WR Yorks, 1969–74; Dir Engrg Services, W Yorks MCC, 1974–86. President: County Surveyors' Soc., 1977–78; Instn of Highway Engrs, 1978–79; ICE, 1983–84. Hon. DSc: Wales, 1982; Bradford, 1984. *Recreations:* golf, travel, supporting Rugby. *Address:* Drovers Cottage, 3 Boston Road, Wetherby, W Yorks LS22 5HA. *Clubs:* Royal Automobile; Alwoodley Golf (Leeds).

GAGE, family name of **Viscount Gage.**

GAGE, 7th Viscount *cr* 1720; **George John St Clere Gage;** Bt 1622; Baron Gage (Ire.) 1720; Baron Gage (GB), 1790; *b* 8 July 1932; *s* of 6th Viscount Gage, KCVO, and Hon. Alexandra Imogen Clare Grenfell (*d* 1969), *yr d* of 1st Baron Desborough, KG, GCVO; *S* father, 1982; *m* 1971. *Educ:* Eton. *Heir:* *b* Hon. Henry Nicolas Gage [*b* 9 April 1934; *m*

1974, Lady Diana Adrienne Beatty, *d* of 2nd Earl Beatty; two *s*]. *Address:* Whitefriars, Alciston, Polegate, East Sussex.

GAGE, Sir Berkeley (Everard Foley), KCMG 1955 (CMG 1949); Retired; *b* 27 Feb. 1904; *s* of late Brig.-Gen. M. F. Gage, DSO; *m* 1931, Maria von Chapuis (marr. diss. 1954), Liegnitz, Silesia; two *s*; *m* 1954, Mrs Lillian Riggs Miller. *Educ:* Eton Coll.; Trinity Coll., Cambridge. 3rd Sec. Foreign Office or Diplomatic Service, 1928; appointed to Rome, 1928; transferred to Foreign Office, 1931; 2nd Sec., 1933; Private Sec. to Parl. Under-Sec. of State, 1934; served Peking, 1935; FO 1938; China, 1941; FO 1944; UK Deleg. Dumbarton Oaks Conf., 1944; UK Deleg., San Francisco Conf., April-June 1945; Foreign Service Officer, Grade 5, 1950; Counsellor, British Embassy, The Hague, 1947–50; Chargé d'Affaires, The Hague, in 1947 and 1948; Consul-Gen., Chicago, 1950–54; Ambassador to Thailand, 1954–57; Ambassador to Peru, 1958–63. Chairman: Latin America Cttee, BNEC, 1964–66; Anglo-Peruvian Soc., 1969–71; Member: Council for Volunteers Overseas, 1964–66; Council of Fauna Preservation Soc., 1969–73. Grand Cross, Order of the Sun (Peru), 1964. *Recreation:* swimming. *Address:* 24 Ovington Gardens, SW3 1LE. *T:* 01–589 0361. *Clubs:* Beefsteak (Life Hon. Mem.), Buck's, Saints and Sinners; Tavern (Chicago).

GAGE, William Marcus; QC 1982; a Recorder, since 1985; *b* 22 April 1938; *s* of His Honour Conolly Gage; *m* 1962, Penelope Mary Groves; three *s*. *Educ:* Repton; Sidney Sussex Coll., Cambridge. MA. National Service, Irish Guards, 1956–58. Called to the Bar, Inner Temple, 1963. Chancellor, diocese of Coventry, 1980–. *Recreations:* shooting, fishing, smallholding. *Address:* Evershaw House, Biddlesden, Brackley, Northants NN13 5TT.

GAINFORD, 3rd Baron *cr* 1917; **Joseph Edward Pease;** *b* 25 Dec. 1921; *s* of 2nd Baron Gainford, TD, and of Veronica Margaret, *d* of Sir George Noble, 2nd Bt; *S* father, 1971; *m* 1953, Margaret Theophila Radcliffe, *d* of late Henry Edmund Guise Tyndale; two *d*. *Educ:* Eton and Gordonstoun. FRGS; Member, Society of Surveying Technicians. RAFVR, 1941–46. Hunting Aerosurveys Ltd, 1947–49; Directorate of Colonial Surveys, 1951–53; Soil Mechanics Ltd, 1953–58; London County Council, 1958–65; Greater London Council, 1965–78. UK Delegate to UN, 1973. Mem., Coll. of Guardians, Nat. Shrine of Our Lady of Walsingham, 1979–. Mem., Plaisterers' Co., 1976. *Recreations:* golf, music, veteran and vintage aviation. *Heir:* *b* Hon. George Pease [*b* 20 April 1926; *m* 1958, Flora Daphne, *d* of late Dr N. A. Dyce Sharp; two *s* two *d*]. *Address:* 1 Dedmere Court, Marlow, Bucks SL7 1PL. *T:* Marlow 4679. *Clubs:* MCC, Pathfinder.

GAINHAM, Sarah Rachel, (Mrs Kenneth Ames), FRSL 1984; author; *b* 1 Oct. 1922; *d* of Tom Stainer and May Genevieve Gainham; *m* 1964, Kenneth Ames (*d* 1975). *Educ:* Newbury High Sch. for Girls; afterwards largely self educated. From 1947 onwards, travelled extensively in Central and E Europe; Central Europe Correspondent of The Spectator, 1956–66. *Publications:* Time Right Deadly, 1956; Cold Dark Night, 1957; The Mythmaker, 1957; Stone Roses, 1959; Silent Hostage, 1960; Night Falls on the City, 1967 (Book Soc. Choice and US Book of Month Club); A Place in the Country, 1968; Takeover Bid, 1970; Private Worlds, 1971; Maculan's Daughter, 1973; To the Opera Ball, 1975; The Habsburg Twilight, 1979; The Tiger, Life, 1983; contrib. to Encounter, Atlantic Monthly, BBC, etc. *Recreations:* theatre, opera, European history. *Address:* altes Forsthaus, Schlosspark, A2404 Petronell, Austria.

GAINSBOROUGH, 5th Earl of, (2nd) *cr* 1841; **Anthony Gerard Edward Noel,** Bt 1781; Baron Barham, 1805; Viscount Campden, Baron Noel, 1841; JP; *b* 24 Oct. 1923; *s* of 4th Earl and Alice Mary (*d* 1970), *e d* of Edward Eyre, Gloucester House, Park Lane, W1; *S* father 1927; *m* 1947, Mary, *er d* of Hon. J. J. Stourton (and of Mrs Kathleen Stourton, Withington, Glos), *qv*; four *s* three *d*. *Educ:* Georgetown, Garrett Park, Maryland, USA. Chairman: Oakham RDC, 1952–67; Executive Council RDC's Association of England and Wales, 1963 (Vice-Chairman 1962, Pres., 1965); Pres., Assoc. of District Councils, 1974–80; Vice-Chm. Rutland CC, 1958–70, Chm., 1970–73; Chm., Rutland Dist Council, 1973–76. Chm., Bd of Management, Hosp. of St John and St Elizabeth, NW8, 1970–80. Mem. Court of Assistants, Worshipful Co. of Gardeners of London, 1960 (Upper Warden, 1966; Master, 1967). Hon. FIMunE 1969. JP Rutland, 1957, Leics 1974. Knight of Malta, 1948; Bailiff Grand Cross Order of Malta, 1958; Pres. Br. Assoc., SMO, Malta, 1968–74. KStJ 1970. *Recreations:* shooting, sailing. *Heir:* *s* Viscount Campden, *qv*. *Address:* Exton Park, Oakham, Leics LE15 8AN. *T:* Oakham 812209. *Clubs:* Boodle's, Brooks's, Bembridge Sailing.

See also Earl of Liverpool, Hon. G. E. W. Noel.

GAINSBOROUGH, George Fotheringham, CBE 1973; PhD, FIEE; Barrister-at-law; Secretary, Institution of Electrical Engineers, 1962–80; *b* 28 May 1915; *o s* of late Rev. William Anthony Gainsborough and of Alice Edith (*née* Fennell); *m* 1937, Gwendoline (*d* 1976), *e d* of John and Anne Berry; two *s*. *Educ:* Christ's Hospital; King's Coll., London; Gray's Inn. Scientific Staff, Nat. Physical Laboratory, 1938–46; Radio Physicist, British Commonwealth Scientific Office, Washington, DC, USA, 1944–45; Administrative Civil Service (Ministries of Supply and Aviation), 1946–62. Imperial Defence College, 1960. Secretary, Commonwealth Engineering Conf., 1962–69; Sec.-General, World Fedn of Engineering Organizations, 1968–76. *Publications:* papers in Proc. Instn of Electrical Engineers. *Address:* 19 Glenmore House, Richmond Hill, Richmond, Surrey. *T:* 01–940 8515. *Club:* Athenæum.

See also Michael Gainsborough.

GAINSBOROUGH, Michael; Center for International Affairs, Harvard University, 1986–87; *b* 13 March 1938; *s* of George Fotheringham Gainsborough, *qv*; *m* 1962, Sally (*née* Hunter); one *s* two *d*. *Educ:* St Paul's Sch.; Trinity Coll., Oxford (MA). Air Ministry, 1959–64; Ministry of Defence, 1964–78; Defence Counsellor, UK Delegn to NATO, Brussels, FCO, 1978–81; Dir, Resources and Programmes (Strategic Systems), MoD, 1981–83; Asst Under-Sec. of State (Naval Staff), 1984, (Programmes), 1985, MoD. *Recreations:* listening to music, gardening, birds. *Address:* c/o Ministry of Defence, SW1.

GAINSFORD, Ian Derek, FDSRCS; Dean of the Faculty of Clinical Dentistry, King's College London, since 1983, and Director of Clinical Dental Services, King's College Hospital, since 1977 (Dean of Dental Studies, KCH, 1977–83); *b* 24 June 1930; *s* of late Rabbi Morris Ginsberg, MA, PhD, AKC, and Anne Freda; *m* 1957, Carmel Liebster; one *s* two *d*. *Educ:* Thames Valley Grammar Sch., Twickenham; King's Coll. and King's College Hosp. Med. Sch., London (BDS; FKC 1984); Toronto Univ., Canada (DDS Hons). Junior Staff, King's College Hosp., 1955–57; Member staff, Dept of Conservative Dentistry, London Hosp. Med. Sch., 1957–70; Sen. Lectr/Consultant, Dept of Conservative Dentistry, King's College Hosp., 1970–; Dep. Dean of Dental Studies, 1973–77. President, British Soc. for Restorative Dentistry, 1973–74; Member: Internat. Dental Fedn, 1966–; American Dental Soc. of London, 1960– (Pres., 1982); Amer. Dental Soc. of Europe, 1965– (Hon. Treas. 1971–77; Pres., 1982); Examiner for Membership in General Dental Surgery, RCS, 1979–84 (Chm., 1982–84); Fellow, and Mem. Odontological Sect., RSM, 1967–. Hon. Mem., Amer. Dental Assoc., 1983. Hon. Scientific Advr, British Dental Jl, 1982. FICD 1975; MGDS RCS 1979. *Publication:* Silver Amalgam in Clinical Practice, 1965, 2nd edn 1976. *Recreations:* theatre, canal cruising. *Address:* 31 York Terrace East, NW1 4PT. *T:* 01–935 8659. *Clubs:* Athenæum, Carlton.

GAIRY, Rt. Hon. Sir Eric Matthew, PC 1977; Kt 1977; Prime Minister of Grenada, 1974–79; also Minister of External Affairs, Planning and Development Lands and Tourism, Information Service, Public Relations and Natural Resources, 1974–79; *b* 18 Feb. 1922; *m* Cynthia Gairy; two *d*. Member of Legislative Council, 1951–52 and 1954–55; Minister of Trade and Production, 1956–57; Chief Minister and Minister of Finance until 1962; Premier, 1967–74; independence of Grenada, 1974.

GAISFORD, Ven. John Scott; Archdeacon of Macclesfield, since 1986; *b* 7 Oct. 1934; *s* of Joseph and Margaret Thompson Gaisford; *m* 1962, Gillian Maclean; one *s* one *d*. *Educ:* Univ. of Durham (BA Hons Theol. 1959, DipTh with Distinction 1960, MA 1976). Deacon 1960, priest 1961, Manchester; Assistant Curate: S Hilda, Audenshaw, 1960–62; S Michael, Bramhall, 1962–65; Vicar, S Andrew, Crewe, 1965–86; RD of Nantwich, 1974–85; Hon. Canon of Chester Cathedral, 1980–86. Proctor in Convocation, Mem. Gen. Synod, 1975–; Church Commissioner, 1986–. *Recreations:* Scout movement, fell walking, caravanning. *Address:* 2 Lovat Drive, Knutsford, Cheshire WA16 8NS. *T:* Knutsford 4456. *Club:* Victory Services.

GAISFORD, Prof. Wilfrid Fletcher, MD London, MSc Manchester, FRCP; Czechoslovak Military Medal of Merit, 1st class, 1945; First Professor of Child Health and Pædiatrics and Director of the Department of Child Health, University of Manchester, 1947–67, now Emeritus; *b* 6 April 1902; *s* of Captain Harold Gaisford, RN, and Annie, *d* of Captain Wm Fletcher, RIN; *m* 1933, Mary, *d* of Captain Wm Guppy; one *s* four *d*. *Educ:* Bristol Grammar Sch.; St Bartholomew's Hosp., London, MB London, 1925; MD London, 1928; Post-graduate study in St Louis Children's Hosp., University of Washington, USA, 1928–29; FRCP, 1940; MSc Manchester, 1951. Hon. Asst Physician, East London Children's Hosp., 1932; Mem., British Pædiatric Assoc., 1933. Physn, Dudley Road Hosp., Birmingham, 1935–42; Cons. Pædiatrician, Warwicks CC, 1942–47; Leonard Parsons Memorial Lecturer, University of Birmingham, 1954–55; Catherine Chisholm Memorial Lecturer, 1965. Hon. Physician, Royal Manchester Children's Hosp. and St Mary's Hosp., Manchester; Hon. Cons. Pædiatrician, United Manchester Hosp., 1967. Regional Adviser in Child Health, 1948. Hon. Member: Canadian Pædiatric Association, 1949; Swedish Pædiatric Association, 1960; Finnish Pædiatric Association, 1965; Hon. Fellow, American Acad. of Pediatrics, 1962; Pres., British Paediatric Assoc., 1964–65. Extraord. Mem., Swiss Paediatric Soc., 1965; Pres., Paediatric Section, Manchester Med. Soc., 1966–67. *Publications:* contrib. to the Encyclopædia of British Medical Practice, Lancet, BMJ, Practitioner, Archives of Disease in Childhood, Jl Pediatrics, etc. Joint Editor, Pædiatrics for the Practitioner (Gaisford and Lightwood). *Recreation:* gardening. *Address:* Treloyhan, Church Road, Perran-ar-Worthal, Truro TR3 7QE. *T:* Truro 864664.

GAITSKELL, Baroness, *cr* 1963, of Egremont (Life Peer); **Anna Dora Gaitskell;** *d* of Leon Creditor; *m* 1937, Rt Hon. Hugh Todd Naylor Gaitskell, PC, CBE, MP (*d* 1963), *s* of late Arthur Gaitskell, Indian Civil Service; two *d* (and one *s* by a former marriage). Trustee, Anglo-German Foundn, 1974–83. Mem., House of Lords All Party Cttee on Bill of Human Rights, 1977–. *Address:* 18 Frognal Gardens, NW3.

See also G. J. Wasserman.

GAJDUSEK, Daniel Carleton, MD; Director of Program for Study of Child Growth and Development and Disease Patterns in Primitive Cultures, and Laboratory of Slow Latent and Temperate Virus Infections, National Institute of Neurological and Communicative Disorders and Stroke, National Institutes of Health, Bethesda, Md, since 1958; Chief, Central Nervous System Studies Laboratory, NINCDS, since 1970; *b* Yonkers, NY, 9 Sept. 1923; *s* of Karol Gajdusek and Ottilia Dobroczki; thirty adopted *s* and *d* (all from New Guinea and Micronesia). *Educ:* Marine Biological Lab., Woods Hole, Mass; Univ. of Rochester (BS *summa cum laude*); Harvard Medical Sch. (MD); California Inst. of Technology (Post-Doctoral Fellow). Residencies: Babies Hosp., NY, 1946–47; Children's Hosp., Cincinatti, Ohio, 1947–48; Children's Hosp., Boston, Mass, 1949–51; Sen. Fellow, Nat. Research Council, Calif Inst. of Tech., 1948–49; Children's Hosp., Boston, Mass, 1949–51; Research Fellow, Harvard Univ. and Sen. Fellow, Nat. Foundn for Infantile Paralysis, 1949–52; Walter Reed Army Medical Center, 1952–53; Institut Pasteur, Tehran, Iran and Univ. of Maryland, 1954–55; Vis. Investigator, Nat. Foundn for Infantile Paralysis and Walter and Eliza Hall Inst., Australia, 1955–57. Member: Nat. Acad. of Sciences, 1974; Amer. Philos. Soc., 1978; Amer. Acad. of Arts and Scis, 1978; Amer. Acad. of Neurol.; Infectious Dis. Soc. of America; Amer. Pediatric Soc.; Amer. Epidemiological Soc.; Amer. Soc. for Virology; Deutsche Akademie der Naturforscher Leopoldina, 1982, and many others. Member, Scientific Council: Sino-Amer. Center for Internat. Scientific Studies (Dir, Bd of Dirs); Fondn pour l'Etude du Système Nerveux, Geneva. Studied unique forms of virus, brain diseases and human genetics. E. Meade Johnson Award, Amer. Acad. Pediatrics, 1963; DHEW Superior Service Award, 1970; DHEW Distinguished Service Award, 1975; Lucien Dautrebande Prize, Belgium, 1976; shared with Dr Baruch Blumberg Nobel Prize in Physiology or Medicine, for discoveries concerning new mechanisms for the origin and dissemination of infectious diseases, 1976; George Cotzias Meml Prize, Amer. Acad. of Neurol., 1978. Hon. Curator, Melanesian Ethnography, Peabody Mus., Salem, Mass. Hon. DSc: Univ. of Rochester, 1977; Med. Coll. of Ohio, 1977; Washington and Jefferson Coll., 1980; Harvard Med. Sch. (Bicentennial), 1982; Hahnemann Univ., 1983; Hon. LHD Hamilton Coll., 1977; Docteur *hc* Univ. of Marseille, 1977; Hon. LLD Aberdeen, 1980. *Publications:* Acute Infectious Hemorrhagic Fevers and Mycotoxicoses in the USSR, 1953; ed, with C. J. Gibbs, Jr and M. P. Alpers, Slow, Latent and Temperate Virus Infections, 1965; Journals 1954–84, 38 vols, 1963–84; Smadel-Gajdusek Correspondence 1955–1958; (ed with J. Farquhar) Kuru, 1981; over 750 papers in major jls of medicine, microbiology, immunology, pediatrics, developmental biology, neurobiology, genetics, evolution and anthropology. *Recreations:* mountaineering, linguistics. *Address:* Laboratory of Central Nervous System Studies, NINCDS, National Institutes of Health, Bethesda, Md 20892, USA. *T:* 301–496–3281.

GAJE GHALE, VC 1943; Subedar 2/5 Royal Gurkha Rifles FF; *b* 1 July 1922; *s* of Bikram Ghale; *m* 1939, Dhansuba; no *c*. *Educ.* IA 2nd class certificate of education. Enlisted as a Recruit Boy 2nd Bn 5th Royal Gurkha Rifles FF, Feb. 1935; transferred to the ranks, Aug. 1935; Naik, 1941; Acting Havildar, May 1942; War Subst. Havildar, Nov. 1942; Bn Havildar Major June 1943; Jemadar, Aug. 1943. Waziristan operations, 1936–37 (medal with clasp); Burma, 1942–43 (1939–45 Star, VC). *Recreations:* football, basketball, badminton and draughts.

GALBRAITH, family name of **Baron Strathclyde.**

GALBRAITH, James Hunter, CB 1985; Under Secretary, Department of Employment Industrial Relations Division, 1975–85; *b* 16 July 1925; *o s* of late Prof. V. H. Galbraith, FBA, and Dr G. R. Galbraith; *m* 1954, Isobel Gibson Graham; two *s*. *Educ:* Dragon Sch.; Edinburgh Academy; Balliol Coll., Oxford. 1st Cl. Litt Hum. Fleet Air Arm (pilot), 1944–46. Entered Ministry of Labour, 1950; Private Sec. to Permanent Sec., 1953–55; Jun. Civilian Instructor, IDC, 1958–61; Private Sec. to Minister of Labour, 1962–64;

Chm. Central Youth Employment Exec., 1964–67; Sen. Simon Research Fellow, Manchester Univ., 1967–68; Asst Under-Sec. of State, Dept of Employment and Productivity (Research and Planning Div.), 1968–71; Dir, Office of Manpower Economics, 1971–73; Under-Sec., Manpower Gen. Div., Dept of Employment, 1973–74; Sec., Manpower Services Commn, 1974–75. *Recreations:* rugby (Oxford Blue), golf, fishing. *Address:* 27 Sandy Lodge Lane, Moor Park, Mddx. *T:* Northwood 22458.

See also G. M. Moore.

GALBRAITH, Prof. John Kenneth; Paul M. Warburg Professor of Economics, Harvard University, 1949–75, now Emeritus Professor; *b* Ontario, Canada, 15 Oct. 1908; *s* of William Archibald and Catherine Galbraith; *m* 1937, Catherine M. Atwater; three *s*. *Educ:* Univ. of Guelph; California Univ. BS, MS, PhD. Tutor, Harvard Univ., 1934–39; Social Science Research Fellow, Cambridge Univ., 1937; Asst Prof. of Economics, Princeton Univ., 1939; Asst Administrator, Office of Price Administration, 1941; Deputy Administrator, 1942–43; Dir, State Dept Office of Economic Security Policy, 1945; Mem. Bd of Editors, Fortune Magazine, 1943–48. United States Ambassador to India, 1961–63 (on leave from Professorship). Reith Lecturer, 1966; Vis. Fellow, Trinity Coll., Cambridge, 1970–71. TV series, The Age of Uncertainty, 1977. Chm., Americans for Democratic Action, 1967–69; President: Amer. Econ. Assoc., 1972; Amer. Acad. of Arts and Letters, 1984– (Mem., 1982–). LLD Bard, 1958; Miami Univ., 1959; University of Toronto, 1961; Brandeis Univ., 1963; University of Mass, 1963; University of Saskatchewan, 1965; Rhode Island Coll., 1966; Boston Coll., 1967; Hobart and William Smith Colls, 1967; Univ. of Paris, 1975; and others. President's Certificate of Merit; Medal of Freedom. *Publications:* American Capitalism, the Concept of Countervailing Power, 1952; The Great Crash, 1929, 1955, new edn 1979; The Affluent Society, 1958, 4th edn, 1985; Journey to Poland and Yugoslavia, 1958; The Liberal Hour, 1960; Made to Last, 1964; The New Industrial State, 1967, rev. edn, 1978; Indian Painting, 1968; Ambassador's Journal, 1969; Economics, Peace and Laughter, 1971; A China Passage, 1973; Economics and the Public Purpose, 1974; Money: whence it came, where it went, 1975; The Age of Uncertainty, 1977; Almost Everyone's Guide to Economics, 1978; Annals of an Abiding Liberal, 1979; The Nature of Mass Poverty, 1979; A Life in Our Times, 1981; The Anatomy of Power, 1983; China Passage, 1983; contribs to learned jls. *Address:* 207 Littauer Center, Harvard University, Cambridge, Mass 02138, USA; 30 Francis Avenue, Cambridge, Mass 02138, USA. *Clubs:* Century (NY); Federal City (Washington).

GALBRAITH, Neil, CBE 1975; QPM 1959; DL; HM Inspector of Constabulary, 1964–76, retired; *b* 25 May 1911; *s* of late Peter and Isabella Galbraith; *m* 1942, Catherine Margaret Thornton; one *s* one *d*. *Educ:* Kilmarnock Academy. Constable to Inspector, Lancs Constabulary, 1931–46. Chief Supt, Herts Constabulary, 1946–51; Asst Chief Constable, Monmouthshire Constabulary, 1951–55; Chief Constable, Leicester City Police, 1956; Chief Constable, Monmouthshire Constabulary, 1957–64. DL Gwent (formerly Monmouth), 1973. *Recreation:* reading. *Address:* Neath House, Trostrey, Usk, Gwent. *T:* Usk 2779.

GALBRAITH, William Campbell, QC 1977; *b* 25 Feb. 1935; *s* of William Campbell Galbraith and Margaret Watson or Galbraith; *m* 1959, Mary Janet Waller; three *s* (and one *s* decd). *Educ:* Merchiston Castle Sch.; Pembroke Coll., Cambridge (BA); Edinburgh Univ. (LLB). Teacher, Turkey, 1959–61; Lectr, Meshed Univ., Iran, 1961–62; admitted to Faculty of Advocates, 1962; in practice at Scottish Bar, 1962–67; Sen. State Counsel, Malaŵi, 1967–70; Parly Draftsman, London, 1970–74; Parly Counsel, Canberra, 1974; returned to practice, 1975. *Recreations:* fishing, music, travel.

GALE, Prof. Ernest Frederick, FRS 1953; BSc London; BA, PhD, ScD Cantab; Professor of Chemical Microbiology, University of Cambridge, 1960–81, now Emeritus; Fellow of St John's College, Cambridge, since 1949; *b* 15 July 1914; *s* of Nellie Annie and Ernest Francis Edward Gale; *m* 1937, Eiry Mair Jones; one *s*. *Educ:* St John's Coll. Cambridge (Scholar). Research in biochemistry, Cambridge, 1936–83; Senior Student, Royal Commn for Exhibition of 1851, 1939; Beit Memorial Fellow, 1941; Scientific Staff of Med. Research Council, 1943; Reader in Chemical Microbiology, University of Cambridge, 1948–60; Dir, Medical Research Council Unit for Chemical Microbiology, 1948–62. Herter Lecturer, Johns Hopkins Hosp., Baltimore, USA, 1948; Commonwealth Travelling Fellow, Hanna Lecturer, Western Reserve Univ., 1951; Harvey Lectr, New York, 1955; Leeuwenhoek Lectr, Royal Society, London, 1956; Malcolm Lectr, Syracuse Univ., 1967; M. Stephenson Meml Lectr, 1971; Linacre Lectr, St John's Coll., Cambridge, 1973. Visiting Fellow, ANU, 1964–65. Hon. Mem., Society for General Microbiology, 1978– (Meetings Sec., 1954–58; International Representative, 1963–67; Pres., 1967–69); Mem. Food Investigation Board, 1954–58; Mem. International Union of Biochemistry Commission on Enzymes, 1957–61. *Publications:* Chemical Activities of Bacteria, 1947; The Molecular Basis of Antibiotic Action, 1972, 2nd edn 1981; scientific papers in Biochem. Journal, Journal of General Microbiology, Biochimica et Biophysica Acta, etc. *Recreation:* photography. *Address:* 25 Luard Road, Cambridge. *T:* Cambridge 247585.

GALE, Hon. George Alexander, CC 1977; Chief Justice of Ontario, 1967–76; Vice-Chairman, Ontario Law Reform Commission, 1977–81; *b* 24 June 1906; *s* of late Robert Henry and Elma Gertrude Gale; *m* 1934, Hilda Georgina Daly; three *s*. *Educ:* Prince of Wales High Sch., Vancouver; Toronto Univ. (BA); Osgoode Hall Law Sch., Toronto. Called to Ontario Bar, 1932; Partner, Mason, Foulds, Davidson & Gale, 1944; KC (Can.) 1945; Justice, Supreme Court of Ontario, 1946; Justice, Court of Appeal, Ontario, 1963; Chief Justice of High Court of Justice for Ontario, 1964. Formerly Chm. Judicial Council for Provincial Judges; Chm., Cttee on Rules of Practice for Ontario (Mem. 1941–76); former Mem. Canadian Bar Assoc. (formerly Mem. Council); Hon. Mem., Georgia Bar Assoc.; formerly Hon. Lectr, Osgoode Law Sch.; formerly Mem. Exec. Cttee, Canadian Judicial Council. Mem., Ontario Adv. Cttee on Confederation; formerly Chm., Ontario Rhodes Scholarship Selection Cttee; Hon. Mem., Canadian Corps of Commissionaires, 1977. Mem. Bd of Governors: Wycliffe Coll., Toronto Univ.; Ecumenical Foundn of Canada; formerly, Upper Canada Coll., Toronto; Mem. Delta Kappa Epsilon, Phi Delta Phi (Hon.). Anglican; Warden, St John's, York Mills, for 5 years. Hon. Pres., Ontario Curling Assoc. Hon. LLD: McMaster, 1968; York (Toronto), 1969; Windsor, 1980. *Publication:* (ed with Holmested) Practice and Procedure in Ontario, 6th edn. *Recreations:* golf, photography. *Address:* 2 Brookfield Road, Willowdale, Ontario M2P 1A9, Canada. *Clubs:* Lawyers, (Hon. Mem.) York (Toronto); Toronto Curling, Chippewa Golf.

GALE, George Stafford; journalist, author, broadcaster; *b* 22 Oct. 1927; *e s* of George Pyatt Gale and Anne Watson Gale (*née* Wood); *m* 1st, 1951, Patricia Marina Holley (marr, diss. 1983); four *s*; 2nd, 1983, Mary Kiernan Malone, *o d* of late Dr Louis Dillon Malone and late Dr Eileen Malone, Cannock, Staffs, and Dublin. *Educ:* Royal Grammar Sch., Newcastle upon Tyne; Peterhouse, Cambridge; Göttingen University. 1st cl. hons Historical Tripos, Cantab, 1948 and 1949. Leader writer, reporter, Labour Corresp., Manchester Guardian, 1951–55; Special and Foreign Corresp., Daily Express, 1955–67; Columnist, Daily Mirror, 1967–69; freelance journalist, 1969–70; Editor, The Spectator, 1970–73; columnist, Daily Express, 1976–86, Associate Editor, 1981–86, chief leader writer, 1981–82; freelance, 1986–; columnist, Daily Mirror and Sunday Mirror, 1986–. Presenter, phone-in programmes, London Broadcasting, 1973–80, 1984–85; commentator, Thames Television, 1977–79; panellist, What's My Line, 1984–. *Publications:* No Flies in China, 1955; (with P. Johnson) The Highland Jaunt, 1973; (contrib.) Conservative Essays, 1979; countless articles. *Recreations:* looking, brooding, disputing, writing poetry, and roasting beef. *Address:* Tattingstone Place, Tattingstone, Suffolk. *T:* Holbrook 327287, 327301. *Clubs:* Garrick, Wig and Pen, Scribes.

GALE, John; Director: Chichester Festival Theatre, since 1984; Lisden Productions Ltd, since 1975; John Gale Productions Ltd, since 1960; Gale Enterprises Ltd, since 1960; West End Managers Ltd, since 1972; Theatres Mutual Ltd, since 1977; *b* 2 Aug. 1929; *s* of Frank Haith Gale and Martha Edith Gale (*née* Evans); *m* 1950, Liselotte Ann (*née* Wratten); two *s*. *Educ:* Christ's Hospital; Webber Douglas Academy of Dramatic Art. Formerly an actor; presented his first production, Inherit the Wind, London, 1960; has since produced or co-produced, in London, British provinces, USA, Australia, New Zealand and S Africa, over 80 plays, including: Candida, 1960; On the Brighter Side, 1961; Boeing-Boeing, 1962; Devil May Care, 1963; Windfall, 1963; Where Angels Fear to Tread, 1963; The Wings of the Dove, 1963; Amber for Anna, 1964; Present Laughter, 1964, 1981; Maigret and the Lady, 1965; The Platinum Cat, 1965; The Sacred Flame, 1966; An Evening with G. B. S., 1966; A Woman of No Importance, 1967; The Secretary Bird, 1968; Dear Charles, 1968; Highly Confidential, 1969; The Young Churchill, 1969; The Lionel Touch, 1969; Abelard and Héloïse, 1970; No Sex, Please—We're British, 1971; Lloyd George Knew My Father, 1972; The Mating Game, 1972; Parents' Day, 1972; At the End of the Day, 1973; Birds of Paradise, 1974; A Touch of Spring, 1975; Separate Tables, 1977; The Kingfisher, 1977; Sextet, 1977; Cause Célèbre, 1977; Shut Your Eyes and Think of England, 1977; Can You Hear Me at the Back?, 1979; Middle Age Spread, 1979; Private Lives, 1980; A Personal Affair, 1982. The Secretary Bird and No Sex, Please—We're British set records for the longest run at the Savoy and Strand Theatres respectively; No Sex, Please—We're British is the longest running comedy in the history of World Theatre and passed 6,000 performances at the Garrick Theatre in Nov. 1985. Exec. Producer, Chichester Fest. Th., 1983–84. President, Soc. of West End Theatre Managers, 1972–75; Chm.. Theatres National Cttee, 1979–85. Governor and Almoner, Christ's Hospital, 1976–; Member, Amicable Soc. of Blues, 1981–. Liveryman, Gold and Silver Wyredrawers Company, 1974. *Recreations:* travel, Rugby. *Address:* Strand Theatre, Aldwych, WC2B 5LD. *T:* 01–240 1656. *Clubs:* Garrick, Green Room; London Welsh Rugby Football (Richmond) (Chairman, 1979–81).

GALE, Malcolm, CBE 1964 (MBE 1948); HM Diplomatic Service, retired; financial, portfolio and export consultant, since 1970; *b* 31 Aug. 1909; *s* of late George Alfred Gale and late Agnes Logan Gale (*née* Ruthven); *m* 1st, 1932, Doris Frances Wells; 2nd, 1936, Ilse Strauss; one *s* one *d*. *Educ:* Sedbergh; Madrid Univ. Market Officer, Santiago, 1945; Third Sec., Dec. 1947; Second Sec. (Commercial), Caracas, 1948; First Sec. (Commercial), 1952 (negotiated armament contracts with Venezuelan Govt); First Sec. (Commercial), Ankara, 1953; Actg Counsellor (Commercial), 1954; First Sec. (Commercial), Bahrein, 1955; Consul (Commercial), Milan, 1958; Acting Consul-Gen., Milan, 1958 and 1959; Counsellor, 1959; Counsellor (Commercial): Washington, 1960–64 (in charge of British export promotion and British store promotions in entire US market); Lisbon, 1964–67; Minister (Commercial) Buenos Aires, 1967–69. *Recreations:* cars, photography. *Address:* Apartado 32, Colares, 2710 Sintra, Portugal. *T:* Lisbon 929.0575.

GALE, Michael, QC 1979; a Recorder of the Crown Court, since 1977; *b* 12 Aug. 1932; *s* of Joseph Gale and Blossom Gale; *m* 1963, Joanna Stephanie Bloom; one *s* two *d*. *Educ:* Cheltenham Grammar Sch.; Grocers' Sch.; King's Coll., Cambridge (Exhibnr; BA History and Law, 1954, MA 1958). National Service, Royal Fusiliers and Jt Services Sch. for Linguists, 1956–58. Called to the Bar, Middle Temple, 1957; Harmsworth Law Scholar, 1958. *Recreations:* the arts and country pursuits. *Address:* 6 Pump Court, Temple, EC4Y 7AR. *T:* 01–353 7242. *Clubs:* United Oxford & Cambridge University, MCC.

GALE, Michael Sadler, MC 1945; Assistant Under-Secretary of State, Prison Department, Home Office, 1972–79; *b* 5 Feb. 1919; *s* of Rev. John Sadler and Ethel Gale; *m* 1950, Philippa, *d* of Terence and Betty Ennion; two *s* one *d* (and one *s* decd). *Educ:* Tonbridge Sch.; Oriel Coll., Oxford (Scholar, MA). Served War of 1939–45: enlisted 1939, Royal Fusiliers; commnd 1940, Queen's Own Royal W Kent Regt, Major 1944; served N Africa and NW Europe. Housemaster, HM Borstal, Rochester, 1946–48; Dep. Governor, HM Prison, Durham, 1948–49; Staff Course Tutor, Imperial Trng Sch., Wakefield, 1949–50; Principal, 1950–52; Governor, HM Prison: The Verne, 1952–57; Camp Hill, 1957–62; Wandsworth, 1962–66; Asst Dir, Prison Dept, Home Office, 1966–69; Controller, Planning and Develt, 1969–75; Controller, Operational Administration, 1975–79; Mem. Prisons Board, 1969–79. *Recreations:* walking, reading, gardening. *Address:* 21 Christchurch Road, Winchester, Hants. *T:* Winchester 53836.

GALE, Roger James; MP (C) North Thanet, since 1983; *b* Poole, Dorset, 20 Aug. 1943; *s* of Richard Byrne Gale and Phyllis Mary (*née* Rowell); *m* 1st, 1964, Wendy Dawn Bowman (marr. diss. 1967); 2nd, 1971, Susan Sampson (marr. diss.); one *d*; 3rd, 1980, Susan Gabrielle Marks; two *s*. *Educ:* Southbourne Prep. Sch.; Hardye's Sch., Dorchester; Guildhall Sch. of Music and Drama (LGSM). Freelance broadcaster, 1963–72; freelance reporter, BBC Radio, London, 1972–73; Producer, Current Affairs Gp, BBC Radio (progs included Newsbeat and Today), 1973–76; Producer/Dir, BBC Children's Television (progs included Blue Peter and Swap Shop), 1976–79; Producer/Dir, Thames TV, and Editor, teenage unit (progs included White Light, Smith & Goody, CBTV and Crying Out Loud), 1979–83. Joined Conservative Party, 1964; Mem. Cttee, Greater London Young Conservatives, 1964–65; Mem. National Cttee, Conservative Trade Unionists; Chm., All Party Parly Gp, Fund for Replacement of Animals in Med. Experiments; Secretary: Backbench Tourism Cttee; Backbench Media Cttee; contested Birmingham, Northfield, Oct. 1982 (Lab. majority, 289). Founder Mem., East Kent Development Assoc., 1984–. *Recreations:* swimming, sailing, canoeing. *Address:* House of Commons, Westminster, SW1A 0AA. *Club:* Parkstone Yacht.

GALES, Kathleen Emily, (Mrs Heinz Spitz); Senior Lecturer in Statistics, London School of Economics, since 1966; *b* 1927; *d* of Albert Henry and Sarah Thomson Gales; *m* 1970, Heinz Spitz. *Educ:* Gateshead Grammar Sch.; Newnham Coll., Cambridge (Exhibr); Ohio Univ. (Schol.). BA Cantab 1950, MA Ohio, 1951. Asst Statistician, Foster Wheeler Ltd, 1951–53; Statistician, Municipal Statistical Office, Birmingham, 1953–55; Res. Asst and part-time Lectr, LSE, 1955–58; Asst Lectr in Statistics, LSE, 1958–60, Lectr, 1960–66. Vis. Assoc. Prof. in Statistics, Univ. of California, 1964–65. Statistical Consultant: Royal Commn on Doctors' and Dentists' Remuneration, 1959; WHO, 1960; Turkish Min. of Health, 1963. Mem. Performing Rights Tribunal, 1974–80. *Publications:* (with C. A. Moser and P. Morpurgo) Dental Health and the Dental Services, 1962; (with B. Abel-Smith) British Doctors at Home and Abroad, 1964; (with T. Blackstone et al.) Students in Conflict: LSE in 1967, 1970; articles in Jl RSS. *Recreations:* badminton, theatre, travel. *Address:* 65 Knighton Drive, Woodford Green, Essex IG8 0NZ.

GALL, Henderson Alexander, (Sandy); Foreign Correspondent, since 1963, Newscaster, since 1968; Independent Television News; *b* 1 Oct. 1927; *s* of Henderson Gall and Jean Begg; *m* 1958, Eleanor Mary Patricia Ann Smyth; one *s* three *d*. *Educ:* Glenalmond;

Aberdeen Univ. (MA). Foreign Correspondent, Reuters, 1953–63, Germany, E Africa, Hungary, S Africa, Congo; joined ITN, 1963, working in Middle East, Africa, Vietnam, Far East, China, Afghanistan; Newscaster on News at Ten, 1970–; Producer/Presenter/Writer, documentaries on: King Hussein, 1972; Afghanistan, 1982, 1984; Cresta Run, 1984. Rector, Aberdeen Univ., 1978–81 (Hon. LLD, 1981). Sitara-i-Pakistan, 1986. *Publications:* Gold Scoop, 1977; Chasing the Dragon, 1981; Don't Worry About the Money Now, 1983; Behind Russian Lines, 1983. *Recreations:* golf, gardening, swimming. *Address:* Doubleton Oast House, Penshurst, Kent TN11 8JA. *T:* (office) 01–637 2424. *Clubs:* Turf, Special Forces.

GALL, Sandy; *see* Gall, H. A.

GALLACHER, family name of **Baron Gallacher.**

GALLACHER, Baron *cr* 1982 (Life Peer), of Enfield in Greater London; **John Gallacher;** retired; *b* 7 May 1920; *s* of William Gallacher and Janet Stewart; *m* 1947, Freda Vivian Chittenden; one *s. Educ:* St Patrick's High School, Dumbarton; Co-operative College, Loughborough. Chartered Secretary. President: Enfield Highway Co-operative Soc., 1954–68; Inst. of Meat, 1983–86; Secretary, International Co-operative Alliance, 1963–67; Parliamentary Sec., Co-operative Union, 1974–83; Mem., Select Cttee on the European Communities, 1983–. *Publication:* Service on the Board (a handbook for directors of retail co-operatives), 1974, 2nd edn 1976. *Recreation:* gardening. *Address:* House of Lords, SW1A 0PW. *T:* 01–219 3000.

GALLACHER, John; HM Diplomatic Service, retired; Group Security Adviser, Gallaher Ltd, since 1985; *b* 16 July 1931; *s* of John Gallacher and Catherine Gallacher (*née* Crilly); *m* 1956, Eileen Agnes (*née* McGuire); one *s. Educ:* Our Lady's High School, Motherwell. Nat. Service, RAF, 1950–52. Kenya Police, 1953–65 (retired as Supt of Police, 1965); Libyan Govt (attached to Min. of Interior), 1965–67; FCO, 1967–70; Lagos, 1970–73; FCO, 1973–74; Kuwait, 1974–77; FCO 1977; Counsellor, FCO, 1983–84. *Recreations:* reading, golf, travel, gardening. *Address:* 1 Clive Road, Strawberry Vale, Twickenham, Mddx TW1 4SQ. *Club:* Royal Over-Seas League.

GALLAGHER, (Francis George) Kenna, CMG 1963; HM Diplomatic Service, retired; *b* 25 May 1917; *er s* of late George and Johanna Gallagher. *Educ:* St Joseph's Coll.; King's Coll., University of London (LLB (Hons)). Clerical officer, Min. of Agric., 1935–38; Asst Examr, Estate Duty Office, 1938–44; served in HM Forces, 1941–45; Examr, Estate Duty Office, 1944–45; apptd a Mem., HM Foreign (subseq. Diplomatic) Service, 1945; Vice-Consul Marseilles, 1946–48; Acting Consul-Gen., there, in 1947; HM Embassy, Paris, 1948–50; FO, 1950–53; First Sec., HM Embassy, Damascus, 1953–55; acted as Chargé d'Affaires, 1953, 1954 and 1955; FO, 1955; appointed Counsellor and Head of European Economic Organisations Dept, 1960; Counsellor (Commercial), HM Embassy, Berne, 1963–65; acted as Chargé d'Affaires (Berne) in 1963 and 1964; Head of Western Economic Dept, CO, 1965–67, of Common Market Dept, 1967–68; Asst Under-Sec. of State, FCO, 1968–71; Ambassador and Head of UK Delegn to OECD, 1971–77. Consultant on Internat. Trade Policy, CBI, 1978–80. *Recreations:* music, chess. *Address:* 29A Lexham Gardens, W8 5JR. *T:* 01–373 5808; The Old Courthouse, Kirkwhelpington, Northumberland NE19 2RS. *T:* Otterburn 40373.

GALLAGHER, Francis Heath, CMG 1957; **Hon. Mr Justice Gallagher;** Coal Industry Tribunal (Australia), since 1947; *b* 10 Feb. 1905; *s* of James Gallagher; *m* 1938, Heather Elizabeth Clark; no *c. Educ:* Sydney Grammar Sch.; University of Sydney. BA 1929, LLB 1933, University of Sydney. Admitted as solicitor, Supreme Court of NSW, 1933. Mem. of Industrial Commn of NSW, 1955–57; Presidential Mem., Commonwealth Arbitration Commn, 1957–71. *Recreations:* reading, gardening, sailing, surfing. *Address:* 2 Foam Crest Avenue, Newport Beach, NSW 2106, Australia. *T:* 99–1724. *Clubs:* Australian Jockey, Turf (Sydney).

GALLAGHER, Kenna; *see* Gallagher, F. G. K.

GALLAGHER, Michael; *b* 1 July 1934; *s* of Michael and Annie Gallagher; *m* 1959, Kathleen Mary Gallagher; two *s* three *d. Educ:* Univ. of Nottingham; Univ. of Wales. Dip. General Studies. Branch Official, NUM, 1967–70; day release, Univ. of Nottingham, 1967–69; TUC scholarship, Univ. of Wales, 1970–72; Univ. of Nottingham, 1972–74. Councillor: Mansfield Borough Council, 1970–74; Nottinghamshire CC, 1973–. Contested (Lab) Rushcliffe, general election, Feb. 1974; Member (Lab) Nottingham, European Parlt, 1979–83, (SDP) 1983–84; contested (SDP) Lancs Central, European elecn, 1984. *Recreations:* leisure, sports. *Address:* The Cliff, 31 Woodhouse Road, Mansfield, Notts. *T:* Mansfield 31659.

GALLAGHER, Dame Monica (Josephine), DBE 1976; Chairman, YWCA Appeal Committee, Sydney; *m* 1946, Dr John Paul Gallagher, KCSG, KM; two *s* two *d.* Has been and remains active member: Adv. Bd, Festival of Light; Australian Church Women, NSW Div.; Inst. of Public Affairs (NSW); Dr Horace Nowland Travelling Scholarship Selection Cttee; Queen Elizabeth II Silver Jubilee Cttee; Exec. Cttee, Order of British Empire (Vice-Pres., 1985–). State Pres., NSW, and Gen. Pres., Sydney Archdiocese, Catholic Women's League, Aust., 1972–80 (Nat. Pres., 1972–74); Mem., Nursing Adv. Cttee, Catholic Coll. of Educn, Sydney; Past President: Catholic Central Cttee for Care of Aged; Catholic Women's Club, Sydney; Associated Catholic Cttee; Austcare. Former Member: NSW Div., UNA; UN Status of Women Cttee; Exec. Bd, Mater Misericordiae Hosp., N Sydney; Bd Mem., Gertrude Abbott Nursing Home. Tour Guide, St Mary's Cathedral, 1970–83, now Chm. of Friends of St Mary's. Augustae Crucis Insigne pro Ecclesia et Pontifice, 1980. *Address:* 1 Robert Street, Willoughby, NSW 2068, Australia.

GALLAGHER, Patrick Joseph, DFC 1943; Managing Director, Patrick Gallagher Associates, since 1979; Chairman, Company Solutions Ltd, since 1983; *b* 15 April 1921; *s* of Patrick Gallagher and Mary Bernadine Donnellan; *m* 1950, Veronica Frances Bateman (*d* 1981); one *s. Educ:* Prior Park, Bath. Served War, 1941–46: Flt Lieut; Pilot, RAFVR. Principal, HM Treasury, 1948–58: ASC, 1956; Adviser, Raisman Commn, Nigeria, 1957–58; Consultant, Urwick, Orr & Partners Ltd, 1958–60; Dir, Ogilvy, Benson & Mather, 1960–65, Man. Dir, Glendinning Internat. Ltd, 1965–69; Pres., Glendinning Cos Inc., 1970–74; Managing Director: London Broadcasting Co. Ltd, 1975–79, Independent Radio News Ltd, 1975–79; Chm., Radio Sales & Marketing Ltd, 1976–79. *Recreations:* music, travel. *Address:* 29 Gloucester Place, W1H 3PB. *T:* 01–935 2429. *Club:* Royal Air Force.

GALLAHER, Patrick Edmund, CBE 1975; Chairman, North West Gas, 1974–82; Part-time Member, British Gas Corporation, 1973–81; *b* 17 June 1917; *s* of late Cormac and Agnes Gallaher; *m* 1947, Louise Hatfield (*d* 1965); one *s* two *d. Educ:* St Philip's Grammar School and College of Technology, Birmingham. Chemist and Engineer, City of Birmingham Gas Dept, 1934–46; Asst Engineer, Redditch Gas Co., 1946–49. With West Midlands Gas Board: Engineer and Manager, Redditch, 1949–53; Divisional Engineer, 1953–62; Regional Distribution Engineer, 1962–64; Distribution Controller, 1964–66; Area Construction Engineer, 1966–67; Area Distribution Engineer, 1967–68. Wales Gas Board (later Wales Gas Region): Dep Chm., 1968–70; Chm., 1970–74. Pres., IGasE, 1977–78. *Recreations:* sailing, gardening, travel. *Address:* March, Warrington Road, Mere, Knutsford, Cheshire.

GALLEY, Robert Albert Ernest, PhD; FRSC; Director, Shell Research Ltd, Woodstock Agricultural Research Centre, Sittingbourne, Kent, 1960–69; *b* 23 Oct. 1909; *s* of John and Jane A. Galley; *m* 1933, Elsie Marjorie Walton; one *s* two *d. Educ:* Colfe's Gram. Sch.; Imperial Coll., London. BSc 1930, PhD 1932, FRIC 1944. Research Chemist, Wool Industries Research Assoc., 1932–34, Chemist, Dept of War Department Chemist, 1934–37; Lectr, Sir John Cass Coll., 1937–39; Prin. Exper. Officer, Min. of Supply, Chemical Inspectorate, 1939–45, Flax Establishment, 1945–46; Sen. Prin. Scientific Officer, Agric. Research Council (Sec. Interdepartmental Insecticides Cttees), 1946–50; seconded to Scientific Secretariat, Office of Lord Pres. of Council, 1950–52; Dir, Tropical Products Institute, Dept of Scientific and Industrial Research (formerly Colonial Products Laboratory), 1953–60. *Publications:* papers in Journal of Chem. Soc., Chemistry and Industry, World Crops, etc. *Recreations:* tennis, gardening, sailing. *Address:* 3 Jackson Close, Elmbridge, Cranleigh, Surrey. *Club:* Farmers'.

GALLEY, Roy; MP (C) Halifax, since 1983; *b* 8 Dec. 1947; *s* of Kenneth Haslam Galley and late Letitia Mary Chapman; *m* 1976, Helen Margaret Butcher; one *s* one *d. Educ:* King Edward VII Grammar Sch., Sheffield; Worcester Coll., Oxford. North-East Postal Bd, 1969–83: started as management trainee; Asst Controller, Projects (regional manager), 1980–83. Councillor, Calderdale Metropolitan Bor. Council, 1980–83. Chm., Yorks Young Conservatives, 1974–76; contested (C) Dewsbury, 1979. *Recreations:* history, European literature, theatre, music, gardening, wine-making. *Address:* Bank House, 23 Quarry Hill, Sowerby Bridge, West Yorks HX6 3BQ. *T:* Halifax 832846.

GALLIE, Prof. Walter Bryce; Professor of Political Science, and Fellow of Peterhouse, Cambridge University, 1967–78, Professor Emeritus, 1978, Emeritus Fellow 1982; *b* 5 Oct. 1912; 3rd *s* of Walter S. Gallie, structural engineer; *m* 1940, Menna Humphreys; one *s* one *d. Educ:* Sedbergh Sch.; Balliol Coll., Oxford (Classical Exhibitioner). BA (1st Cl. PPE), 1934, BLitt 1937, MA Oxon, 1947. University Coll. of Swansea; Asst Lectr, Philosophy, 1935; Lectr, 1938; Sen. Lectr, 1948; Prof. of Philosophy, University Coll. of North Staffordshire 1950; Prof. of Logic and Metaphysics, Queen's Univ., Belfast, 1954–67. Visiting Prof., New York Univ., 1962–63; Lectures: Lewis Fry Meml, Bristol Univ., 1964; Wiles, QUB, 1976; J.R. Jones Meml, UC Swansea, 1983. Pres., Aristotelian Soc., 1970–71. Hon. Professorial Fellow, Univ. of Wales, 1980. Served War, 1940–45, ending with rank of Major, Croix de Guerre, 1945. *Publications:* An English School, 1949; Peirce and Pragmatism, 1952; Free Will and Determinism Yet Again (Inaugural Lecture), 1957; A New University: A. D. Lindsay and the Keele Experiment, 1960; Philosophy and the Historical Understanding, 1964; Philosophers of Peace and War, 1978; articles in Mind, Aristotelian Soc. Proc., Philosophy, Political Studies, etc. *Recreations:* travelling and reading. *Address:* Cilhendre, Upper Saint Mary Street, Newport, Dyfed, Wales. *T:* Newport (Dyfed) 820574.

GALLIERS-PRATT, Anthony Malcolm, CBE 1977; President, F. Pratt Engineering Corporation Ltd, 1981 (Chairman, 1974–81); *b* 31 Jan. 1926; *s* of George Kenneth and Phyllis Galliers-Pratt; *m* 1950, Angela, *d* of Sir Charles Cayzer, 3rd Bt, and of Lady Cayzer, OBE; three *s. Educ:* Eton. Entered F. Pratt Engineering Corp. Ltd, as trainee, 1949; Director, 1951; subseq. Dep. Man. Dir, Man. Dir, Vice-Chm. Underwriting Member of Lloyd's. *Recreations:* yachting, shooting. *Address:* Résidence Europa, Place des Moulins, Monte Carlo. *Clubs:* Brooks's, Buck's.

GALLIFORD, Rt. Rev. David George; *see* Bolton, Bishop Suffragan of.

GALLINER, Peter; Director, International Press Institute, since 1975; Chairman, Peter Galliner Associates, since 1970; *b* 19 Sept. 1920; *s* of Dr Moritz and Hedwig Galliner; *m* 1948, Edith Marguerite Goldschmidt; one *d. Educ:* Berlin and London. Reuters, 1944–47; Foreign Manager, Financial Times, 1947–60; Chm. and Man. Dir, Ullstein Publishing Co., Berlin, 1960–64; Vice-Chm. and Man. Dir, British Printing Corporation Publishing Gp, 1965–70. Order of Merit, 1st cl. (German Federal Republic); Ecomienda, Orden de Isabel la Católica (Spain). *Recreations:* reading, music. *Address:* 27 Walsingham, St John's Wood Park, NW8 6RH. *T:* 01–722 5502; 8142 Uitikon-Waldegg, Mangoldweg 2, Switzerland. *Club:* Reform.

GALLOWAY, 13th Earl of, *cr* 1623; **Randolph Keith Reginald Stewart;** Lord Garlies, 1607; Bt 1627, 1687; Baron Stewart of Garlies (GB), 1796; *b* 14 Oct. 1928; *s* of 12th Earl of Galloway, and Philippa Fendall (*d* 1974), *d* of late Jacob Wendell, New York; *S* father, 1978; *m* 1975, Mrs Lily May Budge, DLJ, *y d* of late Andrew Miller, Duns, Berwickshire. *Educ:* Harrow. KLJ. *Heir: cousin* Andrew Clyde Stewart [*b* 13 March 1949; *m* 1977, Sara, *o d* of Brig. Patrick Pollock; one *s* two *d*]. *Address:* 4 Bernard Terrace, Edinburgh EH8 9NX.

GALLOWAY, Bishop of, (RC), since 1981; **Rt. Rev. Maurice Taylor,** DD; *b* 5 May 1926; *s* of Maurice Taylor and Lucy Taylor (*née* McLaughlin). *Educ:* St Aloysius Coll., Glasgow; Our Lady's High School, Motherwell; Pontifical Gregorian Univ., Rome (DD). Served RAMC in UK, India, Egypt, 1944–47. Ordained to priesthood, Rome, 1950; lectured in Philosophy, 1955–60, in Theology 1960–65, St Peter's Coll., Cardross; Rector, Royal Scots Coll., Valladolid, Spain, 1965–74; Parish Priest, Our Lady of Lourdes, East Kilbride, 1974–81. *Publication:* The Scots College in Spain, 1971. *Address:* Candida Casa, 8 Corsehill Road, Ayr KA7 2ST. *T:* Ayr 266750.

GALLOWAY, Rev. Prof. Allan Douglas; Professor of Divinity, University of Glasgow, 1968–82, now Emeritus Professor; Principal of Trinity College, Glasgow, 1972–82; *b* 30 July 1920; *s* of late William Galloway and Mary Wallace Galloway (*née* Junor); *m* 1948, Sara Louise Phillipp; two *s. Educ:* Stirling High Sch.; Univ. of Glasgow; Christ's Coll., Cambridge; Union Theol Seminary, New York. MA, BD, STM, PhD. Ordained, Asst Minister, Clune Park Parish, Port Glasgow, 1948–50; Minister of Auchterhouse, 1950–54; Prof. of Religious Studies, Univ. of Ibadan, Nigeria, 1954–60; Sen. Lectr, Univ. of Glasgow, 1960–66, Reader in Divinity, 1966–68. Hensley Henson Lectr in Theology, Oxford Univ., 1978; Cunningham Lectr, Edinburgh, 1979; Gifford Lectr, Glasgow, 1984. FRSE 1985. *Publications:* The Cosmic Christ, 1951; Basic Readings in Theology, 1964; Faith in a Changing Culture, 1966; Wolfhart Pannenberg, 1973. *Recreation:* sailing. *Address:* 5 Straid Bheag, Clynder, Helensburgh, Dunbartonshire G84 0QX.

GALLOWAY, Lt-Col Arnold Crawshaw, CIE 1946; OBE 1941; *b* 1901; *o s* of late Percy Christopher Galloway; *m* 1946, Mary, *d* of Arthur William Odgers, Oxford; three *s. Educ:* City of London Sch.; RMC. 2/10 Gurkha Rifles, 1921–28. Member, Middle Temple. Entered Indian Political Service, 1928; Under-Sec. Rajputana, 1929–30; Vice-Consul, Ahwaz, Persia, 1930–31; Vice-Consul, Zahidan, Persia, 1932–33; Under-Sec. to Resident, Persian Gulf, 1934; Sec., British Legation, Kabul, Afghanistan, 1935–36; Sec. to Polit. Resident, Persian Gulf, 1937–38; Polit. Agent, Kuwait, Persian Gulf, 1939–41; Polit. Advr to British Forces in Iraq and Persia, 1941–43 (despatches); Consul-Gen., Ahwaz, 1943–44; Polit. Agent, Muscat, 1944–45; Polit. Resident, Persian Gulf, 1945; Polit. Agent, Bahrein, 1945–47; Consul-Gen., Bushire, 1947; Polit. Agent, Kuwait, 1948–49; UK Repres. of Bahrain Petroleum Company Ltd, 1950–68; Chm., Middle East

Navigation Aids Service, 1958–68. *Address:* Yeo House, Long Load, near Langport, Somerset TA10 9JX. *T:* Long Sutton 329. *Club:* Flyfishers'.

GALLOWAY, Maj.-Gen. Kenneth Gardiner, CB 1978; OBE 1960; Director Army Dental Service, 1974–March 1978; *b* 3 Nov. 1917; *s* of David and Helen Galloway, Dundee and Oban; *m* 1949, Sheila Frances (*née* Dunsmor); two *d* (one *s* decd). *Educ:* Oban High Sch.; St Andrews Univ. LDS 1939, BDS 1940. Lieut Army Dental Corps, 1940; Captain 1941; Major 1948; Lt-Col 1955; Col 1963; Brig. 1972; Maj.-Gen. 1974. Served in Egypt, Palestine, Syria and Iraq, 1942–46; Chief Instructor and 2nd in comd, Depot and Training Establishment, RADC, 1956–60; Asst Dir Dental Service, MoD, 1967–71; Dep. Dir Dental Service: Southern Comd, 1971–72; BAOR, 1972–74. QHDS 1971–78. Col Comdt, RADC, 1980–83. OStJ 1960. *Recreations:* tennis, golf, gardening. *Address:* Berwyn Court, Avenue Road, Farnborough, Hants. *T:* Farnborough 544948.

GALLWEY, Sir Philip Frankland P.; *see* Payne-Gallwey.

GALPERN, family name of **Baron Galpern.**

GALPERN, Baron *cr* 1979 (Life Peer), of Shettleston in the District of the City of Glasgow; **Myer Galpern,** Kt 1960; DL; JP; *b* 1903. *Educ:* Glasgow Univ. Lord Provost of Glasgow and Lord Lieut for the County of the City of Glasgow, 1958–60. MP (Lab) Glasgow, Shettleston, 1959–79; Second Dep. Chm. of Ways and Means, 1974–76, First Dep. Chm., 1976–79. Mem. of the Court of Glasgow Univ.; Mem., Advisory Cttee on Education in Scotland. Hon. LLD Glasgow, 1961; Hon. FEIS, 1960. DL, Co. of City of Glasgow, 1962; JP Glasgow. *Address:* 42 Kelvin Court, Glasgow.

GALPIN, Brian John Francis; His Honour Judge Galpin; a Circuit Judge, since 1978; an Official Referee, Western Circuit, since 1986; *b* 21 March 1921; *s* of late Christopher John Galpin, DSO and late Gladys Elizabeth Galpin (*née* Souhami); *m* 1st, 1947, Ailsa McConnel (*d* 1959); one *d* decd; 2nd, 1961, Nancy Cecilia Nichols; two adopted *s. Educ:* Merchant Taylors' Sch.; Hertford Coll., Oxford. MA 1947. RAF Officer, 1941–45. Editor, Isis, 1946. Called to Bar, 1948; a Recorder of the Crown Court, 1972–78. Councillor, Metropolitan Borough of Fulham, 1950–59; Chm., Galpin Soc. for Study of Musical Instruments, 1954–72, Vice-Pres., 1974–; Mem. Cttee, Bach Choir, 1954–61. *Publications:* A Manual of International Law, 1950; Maxwell's Interpretation of Statutes, 10th edn 1953 and 11th edn 1962; Every Man's Own Lawyer, 69th edn 1962, 70th edn 1971, 71st edn 1981; contrib. Halsbury's Laws of England, 3rd and 4th edns, Encycl. of Forms and Precedents, Galpin Soc. Jl. *Recreations:* cricket (retired), music, chess. *Clubs:* Travellers', Pratt's; Hampshire (Winchester).

GALPIN, Rodney Desmond; Executive Director, Bank of England, since 1984; *b* 5 Feb. 1932; *s* of Sir Albert James Galpin, KCVO, CBE; *m* 1956, Sylvia Craven; one *s* one *d. Educ:* Haileybury and Imperial Service Coll. Joined Bank of England, 1952; Sec. to Governor (Lord Cromer), 1962–66; Dep. Principal, Discount Office, 1970–74; Dep. Chief Cashier, Banking and Money Markets Supervision, 1974–78; Chief of Establishments, 1978–80; Chief of Corporate Services, 1980–82; Associate Dir, 1982–84. Mem. Council, Foundn for Management Educn, 1984–86; Life Governor and Council Mem., Haileybury, 1973–; Mem. Council, Scout Assoc., 1972–. CBIM 1986 (FBIM 1979). Freeman, City of London, 1981. OStJ. *Recreations:* tennis, gardening, music. *Address:* Bank of England, Threadneedle Street, EC2R 8AH. *T:* 01–601 4444.

GALSWORTHY, Anthony Charles, CMG 1985; HM Diplomatic Service; Principal Private Secretary to Secretary of State for Foreign and Commonwealth Affairs, since 1986; *b* 20 Dec. 1944; *s* of Sir Arthur Norman Galsworthy, KCMG, and Margaret Agnes Galsworthy (*née* Hiscocks); *m* 1970, Jan Dawson-Grove; one *s* one *d. Educ:* St Paul's Sch.; Corpus Christi Coll., Cambridge (MA). FCO, 1966–67; Hong Kong (language training), 1967–69; Peking, 1970–72; FCO, 1972–77; Rome, 1977–81; Counsellor, Peking, 1981–84; Head of Hong Kong Dept, FCO, 1984–86. *Recreations:* bird-watching, wildlife. *Address:* c/o Foreign and Commonwealth Office, King Charles Street, SW1A 2AH. *Club:* United Oxford & Cambridge University.

GALSWORTHY, Sir John (Edgar), KCVO 1975; CMG 1968; HM Diplomatic Service, retired; *b* 19 June 1919; *s* of Arthur Galsworthy; *m* 1942, Jennifer Ruth Johnstone; one *s* three *d. Educ:* Emanuel Sch.; Corpus Christi Coll., Cambridge. HM Forces 1939–41; Foreign Office, 1941–46; Third Sec., Madrid, 1946; Second Sec., Vienna, 1949; First Sec., Athens, 1951; Foreign Office, 1954; Bangkok, 1958; Counsellor, Brussels (UK Delegation to EEC) 1962; Counsellor (Economic), Bonn, 1964–67; Counsellor and subsequently Minister (European Econ. Affairs), Paris, 1967–71; Ambassador to Mexico, 1972–77. *Recreation:* fishing. *Address:* Lanzeague, St Just in Roseland, Truro, Cornwall.

GALTON, Raymond Percy; author and scriptwriter since 1951; *b* 17 July 1930; *s* of Herbert and Christina Galton; *m* 1956, Tonia Phillips; one *s* two *d. Educ:* Garth Sch., Morden. *Television:* with Alan Simpson: Hancock's Half Hour, 1954–61 (adaptation and translation, Fleksnes, Scandinavian TV, film and stage); Comedy Playhouse, 1962–63; Steptoe and Son, 1962–74 (adaptations and translations: Sanford and Son, US TV; Stiefbeen and Zoon, Dutch TV; Albert och Herbert, Scandinavian TV, film and stage); Galton-Simpson Comedy, 1969; Clochemerle, 1971; Casanova '74, 1974; Dawson's Weekly, 1975; The Galton and Simpson Playhouse, 1976–77; with Johnny Speight: Tea Ladies, 1979; Spooner's Patch, 1979–80; with John Antrobus: Room at the Bottom, 1986; *films* with Alan Simpson: The Rebel, 1960; The Bargee, 1963; The Wrong Arm of the Law, 1963; The Spy with a Cold Nose, 1966; Loot, 1969; Steptoe and Son, 1971; Steptoe and Son Ride Again, 1973; Den Siste Fleksnes (Scandinavia), 1974; Die Skraphandlerne (Scandinavia), 1975; *theatre:* with Alan Simpson: Way Out in Piccadilly, 1966; The Wind in the Sassafras Trees, 1968; Albert och Herbert (Sweden), 1981; Fleksnes (Norway), 1983; Mordet pa Skolgatan 15 (Sweden), 1984; with John Antrobus: When Did You Last See Your Trousers?, 1986. Awards, with Alan Simpson: Scriptwriters of the Year, 1959 (Guild of TV Producers and Directors); Best TV Comedy Series, Steptoe and Son, 1962/3/4/5 (Screenwriters Guild); John Logie Baird Award (for outstanding contribution to Television), 1964; Best Comedy Series (Steptoe and Son, Dutch TV), 1966; Best comedy screenplay, Steptoe and Son, 1972 (Screenwriters Guild). *Publications:* (with Alan Simpson): Hancock, 1961; Steptoe and Son, 1963; The Reunion and Other Plays, 1966; Hancock Scripts, 1974; The Best of Hancock, 1986. *Recreations:* reading, worrying. *Address:* The Ivy House, Hampton Court, Mddx. *T:* 01–977 1236.

GALWAY, 12th Viscount *cr* 1727; **George Rupert Monckton-Arundell;** Baron Killard, 1727; Lieut Comdr RCN, retired; *b* 13 Oct. 1922; *s* of Philip Marmaduke Monckton (*d* 1965) (*g g s* of 5th Viscount) and of Lavender, *d* of W. J. O'Hara; *S* cousin, 1980; *m* 1944, Fiona Margaret, *d* of late Captain P. W. de P. Taylor; one *s* three *d. Heir: s* Hon. John Philip Monckton [*b* 8 April 1952; *m* 1980, Deborah Holmes]. *Address:* 583 Berkshire Drive, London, Ontario N6J 3S3, Canada.

GALWAY AND KILMACDUAGH, Bishop of, (RC), since 1976; **Most Rev. Eamonn Casey,** DD; also Apostolic Administrator of Kilfenora, since 1976; *b* Firies, Co. Kerry, 23 April 1927; *s* of John Casey and late Helena (*née* Shanahan). *Educ:* St Munchin's Coll., Limerick; St Patrick's Coll., Maynooth. LPh 1946; BA 1947. Priest, 1951. Curate, St John's Cath., Limerick, 1951–60; Chaplain to Irish in Slough; set up social framework to re-establish people into new environment; started social welfare scheme; set up lodgings bureau; savings scheme, 1960–63; invited by Cardinal Heenan to place Catholic Housing Aid Soc. on national basis; founded Family Housing Assoc.; Dir, British Council of Churches; Trustee, Housing the Homeless Central Fund; Founder-Trustee of Shelter (Chm. 1968); Mem. Council, Nat. Fedn of Housing Socs; Mem., Commn for Social Welfare; Founder Mem., Marian Employment Agency; Founder Trustee, Shelter Housing Aid Soc., 1963–69; Bishop of Kerry, 1969–76. Exec. Chm., Trocaire, 1973–; Sec., Irish Episcopal Commn for Emigrants. Mem. Bd, Siamsa Tire, Nat. Folk Th. of Ireland; Mem. Governing Body, University Coll., Galway, 1976–. *Publication:* (with Adam Ferguson) A Home of Your Own. *Recreations:* music, theatre, concerts, films when time, conversation, motoring. *Address:* Mount St Mary's, Galway, Ireland; (office) The Diocesan Office, The Cathedral, Galway. *T:* Galway 63566, 62255, 66553.

GALWAY, James, OBE 1977; FRCM 1983; fluteplayer; *b* 8 Dec. 1939; *s* of James Galway and Ethel Stewart Clarke; *m* 1965; one *s*; *m* 1972; one *s* two *d*; *m* 1984, Jeanne Cinnante. *Educ:* St Paul's Sch., and Mountcollyer Secondary Modern Sch., Belfast; RCM, and Guildhall Sch. of Music, London; Conservatoire National Supérieur de Musique, Paris. Principal Flute, London Symphony Orch., 1966, Royal Philharmonic Orch., 1967–69; Principal Solo Flute, Berlin Philharmonic Orch., 1969–75; international soloist, 1975–; soloist/conductor, 1984–. Recordings of works by C. P. E. Bach, J. S. Bach, Beethoven, Corigliano, Debussy, Franck, Handel, Khachaturian, Mancini, Mozart, Nielsen, Prokoviev, Reicha, Reincke, Rodrigo, Schubert, Stamitz, Telemann and Vivaldi; also albums of flute showpieces, Australian, Irish and Japanese collections. Hon. MA Open, 1979; Hon. DMus: QUB, 1979; New England Conservatory of Music, 1980. *Publications:* James Galway: an autobiography, 1978; Flute (Menuhin Music Guide), 1982; James Galway's Music in Time, 1983 (TV series, 1983). *Recreations:* music, walking, swimming, films, theatre, TV, chess, backgammon, talking to people. *Address:* c/o London Artists, 73 Baker Street, W1M 1AH.

GAMBLE, Sir David (Hugh Norman), 6th Bt *cr* 1897; *b* 1 July 1966; *s* of Sir David Gamble, 5th Bt and of Dawn Adrienne, *d* of late David Hugh Gittins; *S* father, 1984. *Educ:* Shiplake College, Henley-on-Thames. *Heir: uncle* Robert Meredith Gamble [*b* 31 Jan. 1909; *m* 1st, 1931, Phyllis Mary (marr. diss. 1940), *d* of C. E. Bradbury; 2nd, 1940, Diana Burnaby (*d* 1977), *d* of Walter F. Drayson; one *s* three *d* (and one *s* decd)]. *Address:* Keinton House, Keinton Mandeville, Somerton, Somerset. *T:* Charlton Mackrell 3964.

GAMBLING, Prof. William Alexander, PhD, DSc; FRS 1983; FEng, FIEE, Hon. FIERE; British Telecom Professor of Optical Communication, University of Southampton, since 1980; industrial consultant and company director; *b* 11 Oct. 1926; *s* of George Alexander Gambling and Muriel Clara Gambling; *m* 1952, Margaret Pooley; one *s* two *d. Educ:* Univ. of Bristol (BSc, DSc); Univ. of Liverpool (PhD). FIERE 1964; CEng, FIEE 1967; FEng 1979. Lectr in Electric Power Engrg, Univ. of Liverpool, 1950–55; National Res. Council Fellow, Univ. of BC, 1955–57; Univ. of Southampton: Lectr, Sen. Lectr, and Reader, 1957–64; Dean of Engrg and Applied Science, 1972–75; Prof. of Electronics, 1964–80, Hd of Dept, 1974–79. Vis. Professor: Univ. of Colo, USA, 1966–67; Bhabha Atomic Res. Centre, India, 1970; Osaka Univ., Japan, 1977; Selby Fellow, Australian Acad. of Science, 1982. Pres., IERE, 1977–78 (Hon. Fellow 1983). Member: Electronics Res. Council, 1977–80 (Mem., Optics and Infra-Red Cttee, 1965–69 and 1974–80); Board, Council of Engrg Instns, 1974–79; National Electronics Council, 1977–78; 1984–; Technol. Sub-Cttee of UGC, 1973–83; Adv. Bds, Optical and Quantum Electronics, Materials Letters and Internat. Jl of Optical Fibre Sensors; British Nat. Cttee for Radio Science, 1978–; Nat. Adv. Bd for Local Authority Higher Educn, Engrg Working Gp, 1982–84; Engineering Council, 1983–; British Nat. Cttee for Internat. Engineering Affairs, 1984–; Chm., Commn D, Internat. Union of Radio Science, 1984 - (Vice-Chm., 1981–84). FRSA. For. Mem., Polish Acad. of Scis, 1985; Hon. Prof. Huazhung Univ. of Sci. and Technol., Wuhan, China, 1986–. Bulgin Premium, IERE, 1961, Rutherford Premium, IERE, 1964, Electronics Div. Premium, IEE, 1976 and 1978, Oliver Lodge Premium, IEE, 1981, Heinrich Hertz Premium, IERE, 1981, for research papers, J. J. Thomson Medal, IEE, 1982, Faraday Medal, IEE, 1983 and Churchill Medal, Soc. of Engineers, 1984, for research papers. Academic Enterprise Award, 1982. *Publications:* papers on electronics and optical fibre communications. *Recreations:* music, reading, walking. *Address:* Department of Electronics, Information Engineering and Computer Science, University of Southampton, Southampton SO9 5NH. *T:* Southampton 559122.

GAMBON, Michael John; actor; *b* 19 Oct. 1940; *s* of Edward and Mary Gambon; *m* 1962, Anne Miller; one *s. Educ:* St Aloysius School for Boys, Somers Town, London. Served 7 year apprenticeship in engineering; first appeared on stage with Edwards/MácLiammoir Co., Dublin, 1962; Nat. Theatre, Old Vic, 1963–67; Birmingham Rep. and other provincial theatres, 1967–69 (title rôles incl. Othello, Macbeth, Coriolanus); RSC Aldwych, 1970–71; Norman Conquests, Globe, 1974; Otherwise Engaged, Queen's, 1976; Just Between Ourselves, Queen's 1977; Alice's Boys, Savoy, 1978; Galileo, NT, 1980 (London Theatre Critics' Award, Best Actor); Betrayal, NT, 1980; Tales From Hollywood, NT, 1980; King Lear and Antony and Cleopatra (title rôles), RSC Stratford and Barbican, 1982–83; Old Times, Haymarket, 1985; Chorus of Disapproval, NT, 1985 (Olivier Award, Best Comedy Performance); numerous TV and film appearances. *Recreations:* flying, gun collecting, clock making. *Address:* c/o Larry Dalzell Associates, 126 Kennington Park Road, SE11 4DJ.

GAMES, Abram, OBE 1958; RDI 1959; graphic designer; *b* 29 July 1914; *s* of Joseph and Sarah Games; *m* 1945, Marianne Salfeld; one *s* two *d. Educ:* Grocers' Company Sch., Hackney Downs. Studio, 1932–36; freelance designer, 1936–40. Infantry, 1940–41; War Office Poster Designer, 1941–46. Freelance, 1946–; Lecturer Royal College of Art, 1947–53. Postage Stamps for Great Britain and Israel, Festival of Britain, BBC Television, Queen's Award to Industry Emblems. One-man shows of graphic design: London, New York, Chicago, Brussels, Stockholm, Jerusalem, Tel Aviv, São Paulo. Rep. Gt Brit. at Museum of Modern Art, New York; first prizes, Poster Competitions: Helsinki, 1957; Lisbon, 1959; New York, 1960; Stockholm, 1962; Barcelona, 1964; Internat. Philatelic Competition, Italy, 1976; Design Medal, Soc. of Industrial Artists, 1960. Silver Medal, Royal Society of Arts, 1962. Inventor of Imagic Copying Processes. *Publication:* Over my Shoulder, 1960. *Recreations:* painting, carpentry. *Address:* 41 The Vale, NW11 8SE. *T:* 01–458 2811.

GAMINARA, Albert William, CMG 1963; HMOCS (retired); *b* 1 Dec. 1913; *s* of late Albert Sidney Gaminara and late Katherine Helen Copeman; *m* 1947, Monica (*née* Watson); one *s* three *d. Educ:* City of London Sch.; St John's Coll., Cambridge; Oriel Coll., Oxford. MA Cantab 1943. Appointed to Sierra Leone as Administrative Cadet, 1936; seconded to Colonial Office as Principal, 1947–50; Transferred as Administrative Officer to N Rhodesia, 1950; Mem. of Legislative Council, 1963; Admin. Sec. to Govt of Northern Rhodesia (now Zambia), 1961–63; Sec. to the Cabinet, 1964, Adviser, Cabinet Office, Zambia, 1965. *Recreation:* sailing. *Address:* Stratton House, Over Stratton, South Petherton, Somerset. *Club:* Hawks (Cambridge).

GAMMANS, Lady, (Ann Muriel); FRSA; *d* of late Frank Paul, Warblington, Hants; *m* 1917, David Gammans, 1st and last Bt, *cr* 1955, MP (*d* 1957). *Educ:* Portsmouth High Sch. Travelled widely in the Far East, Europe and North America. Spent many years of her married life in Malaya and Japan. MP (C) Hornsey, 1957–66. Retired March 1966. Order of the Sacred Treasure, 2nd class (Japan), 1971. *Recreation:* travel. *Address:* 34 Ashley Gardens, Ambrosden Avenue, SW1. *T:* 01–834 4558. *Club:* (Assoc. Lady Member) Naval and Military.

GAMMELL, James Gilbert Sydney, MBE 1944; CA; Chairman, Ivory & Sime plc, 1975–85; Director: Bank of Scotland, since 1969; Standard Life Assurance Company, since 1954; *b* 4 March 1920; *e s* of Lt-Gen. Sir James A. H. Gammell, KCB, DSO, MC; *m* 1944, Susan Patricia Bowring Toms, *d* of late Edward Bowring Toms; five *s* one *d. Educ:* Winchester Coll. Chartered Accountant, 1949. Served War, Major Grenadier Guards, 1939–46: France, 1940 and 1944, Russia, 1945. *Recreation:* farming. *Address:* Foxhall, Kirkliston, West Lothian EH29 9ER. *T:* 031–333 3275. *Club:* New (Edinburgh).
See also J. F. Gammell.

GAMMELL, John Frederick, MC 1943; MA; *b* 31 Dec. 1921; 2nd *s* of Lieut-Gen. Sir James A. H. Gammell, KCB, DSO, MC; *m* 1947, Margaret Anne, *d* of Ralph Juckes, Fiddington Manor, Tewkesbury; two *s* one *d. Educ:* Winchester Coll.; Trinity Coll., Cambridge. MA 1953. Asst Master, Horris Hill, Newbury, 1940–41. War Service with KRRC, 1941–44; wounded, 1943; invalided out, 1944. Trinity Coll., Cambridge, 1946–47 (BA); Asst Master, Winchester Coll., 1944–45 and 1947–68; Exchange with Sen. Classics Master, Geelong Grammar Sch., Australia, 1949–50; Housemaster of Turner's, Winchester Coll., 1958–68; Headmaster, Repton Sch., 1968–78; Asst Sec., Cambridge Univ. Careers Service, 1978–83. *Recreation:* friends. *Address:* The Old School House, Seaton, Uppingham LE15 9HR. *T:* Morcott 835.
See also J. G. S. Gammell.

GAMMIE, Gordon Edward, CB 1981; Counsel to the Speaker (European Legislation etc), House of Commons, since 1983; *b* 9 Feb. 1922; *e s* of Dr Alexander Edward Gammie and Ethel Mary Gammie (*née* Miller); *m* 1949, Joyce Rust; two *s. Educ:* St Paul's Sch.; The Queen's Coll., Oxford (MA). War service, 1941–45; Captain, 1st Bn Argyll and Sutherland Highlanders. Called to Bar, Middle Temple, 1948. Entered Govt Legal Service, 1949; Asst Solicitor, Mins of Health and of Housing and Local Govt, 1967; Under-Sec. (Principal Asst Solicitor), Min. of Housing and Local Govt, later DoE, 1969–74; Under-Sec., Cabinet Office, 1975–77; Dep. Treasury Solicitor, 1977–79; Legal Advr and Solicitor to MAFF, 1979–83. *Recreations:* tennis, listening to music. *Address:* Ty Gwyn, 52 Sutton Lane, Banstead, Surrey. *T:* Burgh Heath 55287. *Club:* Athenæum.

GAMON, Hugh Wynell, CBE 1979; MC 1944; Senior Partner, Sherwood & Co., since 1972; HM Government Agent, since 1970; *b* 31 March 1921; *s* of Judge Hugh R. P. Gamon and E. Margaret Gamon; *m* 1949, June Elizabeth, *d* of William and Florence Temple; one *s* three *d. Educ:* St Edward's Sch., Oxford; Exeter Coll., Oxford, 1946–48. MA 1st Cl. Hons Jurisprudence; Law Society Hons; Edmund Thomas Childe Prize. Served War, 1940–46: Royal Corps of Signals, N Africa, Italy and Palestine, with 1st Division. Articled to Clerk of Cumberland CC, 1949–51; Asst Solicitor, Sherwood & Co., 1951; Parly Agent, 1954; Partner, Sherwood & Co., 1955. *Recreations:* gardening, walking. *Address:* Black Charles, Underriver, Sevenoaks, Kent TN15 0RY. *T:* Hildenborough 833036. *Club:* St Stephen's Constitutional.

GANDAR, Hon. Leslie Walter; JP; Chairman: New Zealand Social Advisory Council, since 1982; Social Science Research Council, since 1984; *b* 26 Jan. 1919; *s* of Max Gandar and Doris Harper; *m* 1945, M. Justine, *d* of T. A. Smith and Florence Smith; four *s* one *d* (and one *d* decd). *Educ:* Wellington College; Victoria Univ., Wellington (BSc 1940). FNZIAS, FInstP. Served RNZAF and RAF, 1940–44. Farming, 1945–. MP, Ruahine, 1966–78; Minister of Science, Energy Resources, Mines, Electricity, 1972; Minister of Education, Science and Technology, 1975–78; High Comr for NZ in UK, 1979–82. Chairman, Pohangina County Council, 1954–69. Chancellor, Massey Univ., 1970–76. Chairman: Queen Elizabeth II Nat. Trust of NZ, 1983–; NZ Royal Society Prince and Princess of Wales Science Award Liaison Cttee. Hon. DSc Massey, 1977. JP 1958. *Recreations:* music—when not watching cricket; wood-carving; work. *Address:* 34 Palliser Road, Wellington, New Zealand. *Clubs:* Feilding, Rangitikei (NZ).

GANDAR DOWER, Eric Leslie, MA (Law); founder of Aberdeen Airport, Allied Airways (Gandar Dower) Ltd, Aberdeen Flying School Ltd, Aberdeen Flying Club Ltd, and Aberdeen Aerodrome Fuel Supplies Ltd; 3rd *s* of late Joseph Wilson Gandar-Dower and late Amelia Frances Germaine. *Educ:* Brighton Coll.; Jesus Coll., Cambridge. Trained for stage at RADA. Toured with Alan Stevenson, Cecil Barth and Harold V. Neilson's Companies in Kick In, Betty at Bay, The Witness for the Defence, and The Marriage of Kitty. Played wide range of parts on tour with Sir Philip Ben Greet's Shakespeare Company, including Horatio in Hamlet, Antonio in Merchant of Venice, Sicinius Velutus in Coriolanus, Don Pedro in Much Ado About Nothing and Oliver in As You Like It, also in London Shakespeare for Schools LCC Educational Scheme. Wrote and produced The Silent Husband. Toured under own management as Lord Stevenage in Young Person in Pink. Competed King's Cup Air Race 5 years. Holder of FAI Aviators Certificate. Built Dyce (Aberdeen) Airport. Founded Allied Airways (Gandar Dower) Ltd, 1934; Mem. Exec. Council Aerodrome Owners Assoc., 1934–45; Founder Mem. Air Registration Bd; Pioneered Scottish Air Lines Aberdeen/Edinburgh, Aberdeen/Glasgow, Aberdeen/Wick/Thurso/Kirkwall/Stromness and Shetland, which operated throughout 1939–45 War. Pioneered first British/Norwegian Air Line, 1937, Newcastle to Stavanger. Founded, May 1939, 102nd Aberdeen Airport Air Training Corps. Served as Flight Lieut RAFVR, 1940–43. First Chm. and Founder, Assoc. of Brit. Aircraft Operators, 1944. MP (C) Caithness and Sutherland, 1945–50. Attached Mau Mau Campaign, Kenya, 1952–53. *Recreations:* ski-ing, squash, tennis, lawn tennis, swimming, poetry, flying, motoring. *Address:* Westerings, Clos des Fosses, St Martin, Guernsey, Channel Islands. *T:* Guernsey 38637. *Clubs:* Royal Automobile; Hawks, Amateur Dramatic, Footlights (Cambridge); Automobile de France (Paris).

GANDEE, John Stephen, CMG 1967; OBE 1958; HM Diplomatic Service, retired; British High Commissioner in Botswana, 1966–69; *b* 8 Dec. 1909; *s* of John Stephen and Constance Garfield Gandee; *m* 1st, May Degenhardt (*d* 1954); one *s* two *d*; 2nd, Junia Henman (*née* Devine); two *d* (and one step *s* one step *d*). *Educ:* Dorking High Sch. Post Office, Dorking, 1923–30; India Office, 1930–47; Private Sec. to Parly Under-Sec. of State, 1946–47; and 1947–49; Asst Private Sec. to Sec. of State, 1947; First Sec., Ottawa, 1952–54; seconded to Bechuanaland Protectorate, 1958–60 and 1961; seconded to Office of High Comr for Basutoland, Bechuanaland Protectorate and Swaziland, 1960–61; Head of Administration Dept, CRO, 1961–64; Head of Office Services and Supply Dept, Diplomatic Service Administration, 1965–66. *Recreations:* walking, gardening. *Address:* South View, Holmwood, Dorking, Surrey RH5 4LT. *T:* Dorking 888713.

GANDELL, Sir Alan (Thomas), Kt 1978; CBE 1959; FCIT; FIPENZ; Member, National Ports Authority, New Zealand, 1969–81; Chancellor, Order of St John, New Zealand, 1972–81; *b* 8 Oct. 1904; *s* of William Gandell and Emma Gandell; *m* 1933, Edna Marion (*née* Wallis); one *s. Educ:* Greymouth Dist High Sch. Mem., Inst. of Engineers, NZ, 1940, now FIPENZ (1982); FCIT 1959. NZ Govt Railways: civil engrg appts, 1920–52; Mem., Bd of Management, 1953–57; Gen. Man., 1955–66, retd. GCStJ 1983 (KStJ 1971). *Recreations:* bowling, gardening. *Address:* 43 Donald Street, Karori, Wellington 5, New Zealand. *T:* Wellington 767–313.

GANDHI, Manmohan Purushottam, MA, FREconS, FSS; Editor, Major Industries of India Annual and Textile Industry Annual; Member, All India Board of Management Studies; Director: Indian Link Chain Manufacturers Ltd; Zenith Steel Pipes and Industries Ltd; Hon. Metropolitan Magistrate, Bombay; *b* 5 Nov. 1901; *s* of late Purushottam Kahanji Gandhi, of Limbdi (Kathiawad); *m* 1926, Rambhagauri, BA (Indian Women's Univ.), *d* of Sukhlal Chhaganlal Shah of Wadhwan. *Educ:* Bahauddin Coll., Junagad; Gujerat Coll., Ahmedabad; Hindu Univ., Benares. BA (History and Econs), Bombay Univ., 1923; MA (Political Econ. and Political Philosophy), Benares Hindu Univ., 1925; Ashburner Prize of Bombay Univ., 1925. Statistical Asst, Govt of Bombay, Labour Office, 1926; Asst Sec., Indian Currency League, Bombay, 1926; Sec., Indian Chamber of Commerce, Calcutta, 1926–36; Sec., Indian Sugar Mills Assoc., 1932–36; Officer-in-Charge, Credit Dept, National City Bank of New York, Calcutta, 1936–37; Chief Commercial Manager, Rohtas Industries Ltd; Dalmia Cement Ltd, 1937–39; Dir, Indian Sugar Syndicate Ltd, 1937–39; Controller of Supplies, Bengal and Bombay, 1941–43; Sec., Indian Nat. Cttee, Internat. Chamber of Commerce, Calcutta, 1929–31; Sec., Fedn of Indian Chambers of Commerce and Industry, 1928–29. Member: East Indian Railway Adv. Cttee, 1939–40; Bihar Labour Enquiry Cttee, 1937–39; UP and Bihar Power Alcohol Cttee, 1938; UP and Bihar Sugar Control Board, 1938; Western Railway Adv. Cttee, Bombay, 1950–52; Small Scale Industries Export Prom. Adv. Cttee; Technical Adviser, Indian Tariff Board, 1947. Hon. Prof., Sydenham Coll. of Commerce, 1943–49. Member: All India Council of Tech. Educn, 1948–73; All India Bd of Studies in Commerce, 1948–70; Senate and Syndicate, Bombay Univ., 1957–69; Dean, Commerce Faculty, Bombay Univ., 1966–67. Director: E India Cotton Assoc., 1953–73; Bombay Oils & Oilseeds Exchange, 1972–74. *Publications:* How to Compete with Foreign Cloth, 1931; The Indian Sugar Industry: Its Past, Present and Future, 1934; The Indian Cotton Textile Industry-Its Past, Present and Future, 1937; The Indian Sugar Industry (annually, 1935–64); The Indian Cotton Textile Industry, (annually, 1936–60); Centenary Volume of the Indian Cotton Textile Industry, 1851–1950; Major Industries of India (Annually, 1951–); Problems of Sugar Industry in India, 1946; Monograph on Handloom Weaving in India, 1953; Some Impressions of Japan, 1955. *Recreations:* tennis, badminton, billiards, bridge, swimming. *Address:* Nanabhay Mansions, Pherozeshah Mehta Road, Fort, Bombay 400001, India. *T:* (home) 828405, (office) 256033 and 250647. *TA:* Gandhi care Keen, Bombay. *Clubs:* Radio, National Sports, Rotary, Fifty-Five Tennis (Bombay).

GANDHI, Rajiv; Prime Minister of India, since 1984, and Minister of Atomic Energy, Defence, Electronics, Environment and Forests, Ocean Development, Personnel, Public Grievances, Pension, Planning, Science and Technology, and Space; *b* 20 Aug. 1944; *er s* of Feroze and Indira Gandhi; *m* 1968, Sonia Maino; one *s* one *d. Educ:* Shiv Niketan School, New Delhi; Imperial College of Science and Technology, Univ. of London; Trinity College, Cambridge (BScEng; MA 1962). Pilot with Indian Airlines, 1972–81; Member (Indian National Congress–I Party) for Amethi, UP, Lok Sabha, 1981–; Gen. Sec., 1983–84, Pres., 1984–, Indian Nat. Congress. Mem. Nat. Exec., Indian Youth Congress, 1981–83. *Address:* Office of the Prime Minister, South Block, New Delhi 110011, India; (home) 5 Race Course Road, New Delhi 110011, India.

GANDY, Christopher Thomas; HM Diplomatic Service, retired; *b* 21 April 1917; *s* of late Dr Thomas H. Gandy and late Mrs Ida Gandy (authoress of A Wiltshire Childhood, Around the Little Steeple, etc); unmarried. *Educ:* Marlborough; King's Coll., Cambridge. On active service with Army and RAF, 1939–45. Entered Foreign Office, Nov. 1945; Tehran, 1948–51; Cairo, 1951–52; FO, 1952–54; Lisbon, 1954–56; Libya, 1956–59; FO, 1960–62; apptd HM Minister to The Yemen, 1962, subsequently Counsellor, Kuwait; Minister (Commercial) Rio de Janeiro, 1966–68. *Publications:* articles in Asian Affairs, Middle East International, The New Middle East, The Annual Register of World Events, Art International and Arts of Asia. *Recreations:* music, photography, gardening. *Address:* 60 Ambleside Drive, Headington, Oxford. *Club:* Travellers'.

GANDY, David Stewart, OBE 1981; Head of Field Management, Crown Prosecution Service, since 1985; *b* 19 Sept. 1932; *s* of Percy Gandy and Elizabeth Mary (*née* Fox); *m* 1956, Mabel Sheldon; one *s* one *d. Educ:* Manchester Grammar Sch.; Manchester Univ. Nat. Service, Intell. Corps (Germany and Austria), 1954–56. Admitted Solicitor, 1954; Asst Solicitor, Town Clerk, Manchester, 1956–59; Chief Prosecuting Solicitor: Manchester, 1959–68; Manchester and Salford, 1968–74; Gtr Manchester, 1974–85. Lect. tour on English Criminal Justice System, for Amer. Bar Assoc., USA and Canada, 1976. Law Society: Mem., Criminal Law Standing Cttee, 1969–; Mem., Council, 1984–; Prosecuting Solicitors' Society of England and Wales: Mem., Exec. Council, 1966–85; Pres., 1976–78; Chm., Heads of Office, 1982–83; President: Manchester Law Soc., 1980–81; Manchester and Dist Medico-Legal Soc., 1982–84; Manchester Trainee Lawyers Gp, 1982–84. Mem. Council, Order of St John, 1978–85. *Recreations:* cricket, theatre, bridge, walking. *Address:* (office) 4–12 Queen Anne's Gate, SW1H 9AZ.

GANDY, Ronald Herbert; Treasurer to the Greater London Council, 1972–77, retired; *b* 22 Nov. 1917; *s* of Frederick C. H. Gandy and Olive (*née* Wilson) *m* 1942, Patricia M. Turney; two *s* one *d. Educ:* Banister Court Sch. and Taunton's Sch. (now Richard Taunton Coll.), Southampton. Town Clerk's Dept, Civic Centre, Southampton County Borough Council, 1936; LCC: Admin. Officer, Comptroller's (i.e. Treasurer's) Dept, 1937; Asst Comptroller, 1957; Dep. Comptroller, 1964; Dep. Treasurer, GLC, 1965; Dep. Chief Financial Officer, Inner London Educn Authority, 1967. Hon. Treas., Notting Hill Housing Trust, 1979–84. Mem. CIPFA. *Address:* Braemar, 4 Roughwood Close, Watford, Herts WD1 3HN. *T:* Watford 24215.

GANE, Barrie Charles, OBE 1978; HM Diplomatic Service; Counsellor, Foreign and Commonwealth Office, since 1982; *b* 19 Sept. 1935; *s* of Charles Ernest Gane and Margaret Gane; *m* 1974, Jennifer Anne Pitt; two *d* of former marriage. *Educ:* King Edward's School, Birmingham; Corpus Christi College, Cambridge. MA. Foreign Office, 1960; served Vientiane, Sarawak, Kuching and Warsaw; First Sec., Kampala, 1967; FCO, 1970; First Sec., later Counsellor, seconded to HQ British Forces, Hong Kong, 1977. *Recreations:* walking, reading. *Address:* c/o Foreign and Commonwealth Office, SW1A 2AH. *T:* 01–233 3000. *Club:* Brooks's.

GANE, Michael, DPhil, MA; economic and environmental consultant; *b* 29 July 1927; *s* of late Rudolf E. Gane and Helen Gane; *m* 1954, Madge Stewart Taylor; one *d. Educ:* Colyton Grammar Sch., Devon; Edinburgh Univ. (BSc Forestry 1948); London Univ. (BSc Econ 1963); Oxford Univ. (DPhil, MA 1967). Asst Conservator of Forests, Tanganyika, 1948–62; Sen. Research Officer, Commonwealth Forestry Inst., Oxford, 1963–69; Dir, Project Planning Centre for Developing Countries, Bradford Univ., 1969–74; Dir, England, Nature Conservancy Council, 1974–81. *Publications:* various contribs to scientific and technical jls. *Recreations:* natural history, gardening. *Address:* 1 Ridgeway Close, Sidbury, near Sidmouth, Devon EX10 0SW.

GANE, Richard Howard; Chairman of the Board of Directors, George Wimpey & Co. Ltd, 1973–76; *b* 5 Nov. 1912; *s* of Richard Howard Gane and Ada (*née* Alford); *m* 1st, 1939, Betty Rosemary Franklin (*d* 1976); two *s* one *d*; 2nd, 1977, Elizabeth Gaymer. *Educ:* Kingston Grammar School. Joined George Wimpey & Co. Ltd, 1934; also Chm. of George Wimpey Canada Ltd, and Dir, Markborough Properties Ltd, Toronto, 1965–73. *Recreations:* golf, shooting. *Address:* Woodlands, Cranley Road, Burwood Park, Walton-on-Thames, Surrey.

GANELLIN, Charon Robin, PhD, DSc, FRS 1986; CChem, FRSC; Smith Kline and French Professor of Medicinal Chemistry, University College London, since 1986; *b* 25 Jan. 1934; *s* of Leon Ganellin and Beila Cluer; *m* 1956, Tamara Greene; one *s* one *d*. *Educ:* Harrow County Grammar School for Boys; Queen Mary Coll., London Univ. (BSc, PhD, DSc). Res. Associate, MIT, 1960; Res. Chemist, then Dept Hd in Medicinal Chem., Smith Kline & French Labs Ltd, 1958–59, 1961–75; Smith Kline & French Research Ltd: Dir, Histamine Res., 1975–80; Vice-President: Research, 1980–84; Chem. Res., 1984–86. Hon. Lectr, Dept of Pharmacol., UCL, 1975–; Hon. Prof. of Medicinal Chem., Univ. of Kent at Canterbury, 1979–. Tilden Lectr, RSC, 1982. Chm., Soc. for Drug Res., 1985–; Hon. Mem., Soc. Española de Quimica Terapeutica, 1982. Medicinal Chem. Award, RSC, 1977; Prix Charles Mentzer, Soc. de Chimie Therap., 1978; Div. of Medicinal Chem. Award, ACS, 1980. *Publications:* Pharmacology of Histamine Receptors, 1982; Frontiers in Histamine Research, 1985; res. papers and reviews in various jls, incl. Jl Med. Chem., Jl Chem. Soc., Brit. Jl Pharmacol. *Recreations:* music, sailing, walking. *Address:* University College London, Gower Street, WC1.

GANILAU, Ratu Sir Penaia Kanatabatu, GCMG 1983 (CMG 1968); KCVO 1982 (CVO 1970); KBE 1974 (OBE 1960); DSO 1956; ED 1974; Governor-General of Fiji, since 1983; *b* 28 July 1918; Fijian; *m* 1949, Adi Laisa Delaisomosomo Yavaca (decd); five *s* two *d*; *m* 1975, Adi Davila Ganilau (decd); *m* 1985, Veniana Bale Cagilaba. *Educ:* Provincial Sch. Northern; Queen Victoria Meml Sch., Fiji. Devonshire Course for Admin. Officers, Wadham Coll., Oxford Univ., 1947. Served with FIR, 1940; demobilised, retained rank of Captain, 1946. Colonial Admin. Service, 1947; District Officer, 1948–53; Mem. Commn on Fijian Post Primary Educn in the Colony, 1953. Service with Fiji Mil. Forces, 1953–56; demobilised, retained rank of Temp. Lt-Col, 1956; Hon. Col, 2nd Bn (Territorial), FIR, 1973. Seconded to post of Fijian Econ. Develt Officer and Roko Tui Cakaudrove conjoint, 1956; Tour Manager and Govt Rep., Fiji Rugby football tour of NZ, 1957; Dep. Sec. for Fijian Affairs, 1961; Minister for Fijian Affairs and Local Govt, 1965; Leader of Govt Business and Minister for Home Affairs, Lands and Mineral Resources, 1970; Minister for Communications, Works and Tourism, 1972; Dep. Prime Minister, 1973–83; Minister for: Home Affairs, 1975–83; Fijian Affairs and Rural Develt, 1977–83. Member: House of Representatives; Council of Ministers; Official Mem., Legislative Council; Chairman: Fijian Affairs Bd; Fijian Develt Fund Bd; Native Land Trust Bd; Great Council of Chiefs. KStJ 1983. *Recreation:* Rugby football (rep. Fiji against Maori All Black, 1938 and during Rugby tour of NZ, 1939). *Address:* Government House, Suva, Fiji. *Clubs:* Fiji, Defence (Suva, Fiji).

GANZ, Prof. Peter Felix; Resident Fellow, Herzog August Bibliothek, Wolfenbüttel, West Germany, since 1985; *b* 3 Nov. 1920; *s* of Dr Hermann and Dr Charlotte Ganz; *m* 1949, Rosemary (*née* Allen); two *s* two *d*. *Educ:* Realgymnasium, Mainz; King's Coll., London. MA 1950; PhD 1954; MA Oxon 1960. Buchenwald, 1938; Internment Camp, IoM, 1940; Army service, 1940–45. Asst Lectr, Royal Holloway Coll., London Univ., 1948–49; Lectr, Westfield Coll., London Univ., 1949–60; Reader in German, 1960–72; Fellow of Hertford Coll., Oxford University: 1963–72 (Hon. Fellow, 1977); Prof. of German, 1972–85, now Emeritus; Fellow of St Edmund Hall, 1972–85, now Emeritus Fellow. Vis. Professor: Erlangen-Nürnberg Univ., 1964–65 and 1971; Munich Univ., 1970 and 1974. Comdr, Order of Merit, Germany, 1973. Jt Editor: Beiträge zur Geschichte der deutschen Sprache und Literatur, 1976–; Oxford German Studies, 1978–. *Publications:* Der Einfluss des Englischen auf den deutschen Wortschatz 1740–1815, 1957; Geistliche Dichtung des 12. Jahrhunderts, 1960; Graf Rudolf, 1964; (with F. Norman and W. Schwarz) Dukus Horant, 1964; (with W. Schröder) Probleme mittelalterlicher Überlieferung und Textkritik, 1967; Jacob Grimm's Conception of German Studies, 1973; Gottfried von Strassburgs 'Tristan', 1978; Jacob Burckhardt, Über das Studium der Geschichte, 1981; articles on German medieval literature and language in jls. *Recreations:* music, walking, travel. *Address:* Neuer Weg 17, 3340 Wolfenbüttel, West Germany. *T:* 05331–3 19 56.

GANZONI, family name of **Baron Belstead.**

GAON, Dr Solomon; Haham (Chief Rabbi) of the Communities affiliated to the World Sephardi Federation in the Diaspora, since 1978; *b* 15 Dec. 1912; *s* of Isaac and Rachael Gaon; *m* 1944, Regina Hassan; one *s* one *d*. *Educ:* Jesuit Secondary Sch., Travnik, Yugoslavia; Jewish Teachers Seminary, Sarajevo, Yugoslavia; Jews' Coll., London Univ. (BA 1941, PhD 1943; Rabbinic Dip. 1948). Spanish and Portuguese Jews Congregation: Student Minister, 1934–41; Asst Minister, 1941–44; Minister, 1944–46; Sen. Minister, 1946–49; Haham of Spanish and Portuguese Jews Congregation and Associated Sephardi Congregations, 1949–77; Haham (Chief Rabbi), Assoc. of Sephardi Congregations, 1977–80. Pres., Union of Sephardi Communities of England, N America and Canada, 1969–; Vice-Pres., World Sephardi Fedn, 1965–. Prof. of Sephardi Studies, Yeshiva Univ., New York, 1970–, Head of Sephardi Dept, 1977–. Hon. DD Yeshiva Univ., 1974. Alfonso el Sabio (for Cultural Work with and on Spanish Jewry), Spain, 1964. *Publications:* Influence of Alfonso Tostado on Isaac Abravanel, 1944; The Development of Jewish Prayer, 1949; Relations between the Spanish & Portuguese Synagogue in London and its Sister Congregation in New York, 1964; (ed) Book of Prayer of the Spanish & Portuguese Jews' Congregation, London, 1965; Edgar Joshua Nathan, Jr (1891–1965), 1965; Abravanel and the Renaissance, 1974; The Contribution of the English Sephardim to Anglo-Jewry, 1975. *Recreations:* walking, tennis, music. *Address:* Barclays Bank, 53 Maida Vale, W9.

GARBO, Greta, (Greta Lovisa Gustafsson); film actress; *b* Stockholm, 18 Sept. 1905; *d* of Sven and Louvisa Gustafsson. *Educ:* Dramatic Sch. attached to Royal Theatre, Stockholm. Began stage career as dancer in Sweden. First film appearance in The Atonement of Gosta Berling, 1924; went to US, 1925; became an American Citizen, 1951. Films include: The Torrent, 1926; The Temptress, 1926; Flesh and the Devil, 1927; Love, 1927; The Divine Woman, 1928; The Mysterious Lady, 1928; A Woman of Affairs, 1929; Wild Orchids, 1929; The Single Standard, 1929; The Kiss, 1929; Anna Christie, 1930 (first talking rôle); Susan Lenox, Her Fall and Rise, 1931; Mata Hari, 1931; Grand Hotel, 1932; As You Desire Me, 1932; Queen Christina, 1933; Anna Karenina, 1935; Camille, 1936; Conquest, 1937; Ninotchka, 1939; Two-Faced Woman, 1941.

GARCIA, Arthur; Hon. Mr Justice Garcia; Judge of the High Court, Hong Kong, since 1979; *b* 3 July 1924; *s* of late F. M. Garcia and of Maria Fung; *m* 1948, Hilda May; two *s*. *Educ:* La Salle Coll., Hong Kong; Inns of Court Sch. of Law. Called to the Bar, Middle Temple, 1957. Jun. Clerk, Hong Kong Govt, 1939–41; Staff Mem., British Consulate, Macao, 1942–45; Clerk to Attorney Gen., Hong Kong, 1946–47; Asst Registrar, 1951–54; Colonial Develt and Welfare Scholarship, Inns of Court Sch. of Law, 1954–57; Legal Asst, Hong Kong, 1957–59; Magistrate, 1959; Sen. Magistrate, 1968; Principal Magistrate, 1968; Dist Judge, 1971. *Recreations:* photography, swimming. *Address:* Supreme Court, Hong Kong. *Club:* Royal Hong Kong Jockey (Hong Kong).

GARCÍA MÁRQUEZ, Gabriel; *see* Márquez.

GARCIA-PARRA, Jaime; Gran Cruz, Orden de San Carlos, Colombia, 1977; Gran Cruz de Boyaca, Colombia, 1981; Senator, Colombia, since 1982; *b* 19 Dec. 1931; *s* of Alfredo Garcia-Cadena and Elvira Parra; *m* 1955, Lillian Duperly; three *s*. *Educ:* Gimnasio Moderno, Bogotá, Colombia; Univ. Javeriana, Bogotá; Univ. la Gran Colombia, Bogotá; Syracuse Univ., USA (MA); LSE, London (MSc). Lawyer. Minister (Colombian Delegn) to Internat. Coffee Org., 1963–66; Finance Vice-Pres., Colombian Nat. Airlines AVIANCA, 1966–69; Consultant in private practice, 1969–74; Actg Labour and Social Security Minister and Minister of Communications, 1974–75; Minister of Mines and Energy, 1975–77; Ambassador of Colombia to UK, 1977–78; Minister of Finance, Colombia, 1978–81; Exec. Dir, World Bank, 1981–82. Mem., several delegns to UNCTAD and FAO Confs at Geneva, 1964, New Delhi, 1968, Rome, 1970, 1971. Hon. Fellow, LSE, 1980. Gran Cruz, Orden del Baron de Rio Branco, Brasil, 1977. *Publications: essays:* La Inflación y el Desarrollo de América Latina (Inflation and Development in Latin America), 1968; La Estrategia del Desarrollo Colombiano (The Strategy of Colombian Development), 1971; El Problema Inflacionario Colombiano (Colombia's Inflationary Problem), 1972; Petróleo un Problema y una Política (Oil—a Problem and a Policy), 1975; El Sector Eléctrico en la Encrucijada (The Electrical Sector at the Cross-Roads), 1975; Una Política para el Carbón (A Policy for Coal), 1976; La Cuestión Cafetera (The Coffee Dilemma), 1977; Política Agraria (Agrarian Policy), 1977. *Recreations:* walking, reading, poetry, tennis, cooking. *Address:* Calle 111, No 2–10, Apt 201, Bogotá, Colombia. *Clubs:* Jockey, Country (Bogotá).

GARCÍA ROBLES, Alfonso, LLD; Permanent Representative of Mexico to Disarmament Conference, Geneva, since 1977; *b* 20 March 1911; *s* of Quirino and Teresa Robles de García; *m* 1950, Juana Maria de Szyslo; two *s*. *Educ:* Univ. Nacional Autónoma de México (LLB); Univ. of Paris (LLD 1937); Acad. of International Law, The Hague. Foreign Service, 1939; Sweden, 1939–41; Head, Dept. of Internat. Organisations, later Dir-Gen., Political Affairs and Diplomatic Service, 1941–46; Dir, Div. of Political Affairs, UN Secretariat, 1946–57; Head, Dept. for Europe, Asia and Africa, Mexican Min. of Foreign Affairs, 1957–61; Ambassador to Brazil, 1961–64; Under-Sec. for Foreign Affairs, 1964–70; Perm. Rep. to UN, 1971–75; Sec. for Foreign Affairs, 1975–76. Pres., Preparatory Commn for Denuclearization of Latin America, 1964–67; Chm., Mexican Delegn to UN Gen. Assembly special session on disarmament, NY 1978; Mem., Colegio Nacional, México. Nobel Peace Prize (jointly), 1982. *Publications:* Le Panaméricanisme et la Politique de Bon Voisinage, 1938; La Question du Pétrole au Mexique et le Droit International, 1939; La Sorbona Ayer y Hoy, 1943; México en la Postguerra, 1944; La Conferencia de San Francisco y su Obra, 1946; Política Internacional de México, 1946; Ecos del Viejo Mundo, 1946; El Mundo de la Postguerra, 2 vols, 1946; La Conferencia de Ginebra y la Anchura del Mar Territorial, 1959; La Anchura del Mar Territorial, 1966; The Denuclearization of Latin America, 1967; El Tratado de Tlatelolco: génesis, alcance y propósitos de la proscripción de las armas nucleares en la América Latina, 1967; México en las Naciones Unidas, 2 vols, 1970; Mesures de Désarmement dans des Zones Particulières: le traité visant l'interdiction des armes nucleaires en Amérique Latine, 1971; La Proscripción de las Armas Nucleares en la América Latina, 1975; Seis Años de la Política Exterior de México 1970–1976, 1976; La Conferencia de Revisión del Tratado sobre la no Proliferación de las Armas Nucleares, 1977; 338 Días de Tlatelolco, 1977; La Asamblea General del Desarme, 1979; El Comité de Desarme, 1980. *Address:* 13 Avenue de Budé, Geneva, Switzerland. *T:* 34–57–40.

GARDAM, David Hill, QC 1968; *b* 14 Aug. 1922; *s* of late Harry H. Gardam, Hove, Sussex; *m* 1954, Jane Mary Gardam, *qv*; two *s* one *d*. *Educ:* Oundle Sch.; Christ Church, Oxford. MA 1948. War Service, RNVR, 1941–46 (Temp. Lieut). Called to the Bar, Inner Temple, 1949; Bencher 1977. *Recreation:* painting. *Address:* 22 Old Buildings, Lincoln's Inn, WC2A 3UJ. *T:* 01–405 2072; 53 Ridgway Place, SW19.

GARDAM, Jane Mary; novelist; *d* of William Pearson, Coatham Sch., Redcar and Kathleen Mary Pearson (*née* Helm); *m* 1954, David Hill Gardam, *qv*; two *s* one *d*. *Educ:* Saltburn High Sch. for Girls; Bedford Coll., London Univ. Red Cross Travelling Librarian, Hospital Libraries, 1951; Sub-Editor, Weldon's Ladies Jl, 1952; Asst Literary Editor, Time and Tide, 1952–54. FRSL 1976. *Publications:* A Long Way From Verona, 1971; The Summer After The Funeral, 1973; Bilgewater, 1977; God on the Rocks, 1978; The Hollow Land (Whitbread Literary Award), 1981; Bridget and William, 1981; Horse, 1982; Kit, 1983; Crusoe's Daughter, 1985; Kit in Boots, 1986; *short stories:* A Few Fair Days, 1971; Black Faces, White Faces (David Highams Award, Winifred Holtby Award), 1975; The Sidmouth Letters, 1980; The Pangs of Love, 1983 (Katherine Mansfield Award, 1984). *Recreations:* walking, gardening. *Address:* 53 Ridgway Place, SW19 4SP. *Clubs:* University Women's, Arts.

GARDHAM, Air Vice-Marshal Marcus Maxwell, CB 1972; CBE 1965; *b* 5 Nov. 1916; *s* of late Arthur Gardham, High Wycombe; *m* 1954, Rosemary Hilda (*née* Wilkins); one *s*. *Educ:* Royal Grammar Sch., High Wycombe. Commissioned RAF (Accountant Br), 1939; RAF Ferry Command, 1941; HQ AEAF, 1944. BJSM, Washington, 1946 (SOA); RAPO, 1949; psc 1952; No 16 MU, 1953; 2nd TAF (Org. Staff), 1955; Air Ministry (Personnel Staff), 1957; jssc 1957; Technical Trng Command (Org. Staff), 1959; FEAF (Command Accountant), 1965; Dir of Personal Services, MoD (Air), 1966; Head of RAF Secretarial Br., 1971–72; AOA, RAF Trng Comd, 1969–72. Registrar, Ashridge Management Coll., 1972–82. *Recreations:* gardening, golf. *Address:* Four Winds, The Hamlet, Potten End, Berkhamsted, Herts HP4 2RD. *T:* Berkhamsted 2456. *Club:* Royal Air Force.

GARDINER, family name of **Baron Gardiner.**

GARDINER, Baron *cr* 1963, of Kittisford (Life Peer); **Gerald Austin Gardiner,** PC 1964; CH 1975; Chancellor, The Open University, 1973–78; *b* 30 May 1900; *s* of late Sir Robert Gardiner; *m* 1st, 1925, Lesly (*d* 1966), *o d* of Edwin Trounson, JP; one *d*; 2nd, 1970, Mrs Muriel Box. *Educ:* Harrow Sch.; Magdalen Coll., Oxford (MA; Hon. Fellow, 1983). 2nd Lieut Coldstream Guards, 1918; Pres. Oxford Union and OUDS, 1924; called to the Bar, 1925; KC 1948. Friends Ambulance Unit, 1943–45. Mem. Cttee on Supreme Court Practice and Procedure, 1947–53; Mem. of Lord Chancellor's Law Reform Cttee, 1952–63. A Master of the Bench of the Inner Temple, 1955; Chm. Gen. Council of the Bar, 1958 and 1959; former Chm., Council of Justice; Mem., Internat. Cttee of Jurists, 1971–. Chm (Jt), National Campaign for Abolition of Capital Punishment. Alderman, London County Council, 1961–63. Lord High Chancellor of Great Britain, 1964–70. BA Open Univ., 1977. Hon. LLD: Southampton, 1965; London, 1969; Manitoba, 1969; Law Soc. of Upper Canada, 1969; Birmingham, 1971; Melbourne, 1973; DUniv York, 1966.

Publications: Capital Punishment as a Deterrent, 1956; (ed jtly) Law Reform Now, 1963. *Recreations:* law reform and the theatre. *Address:* Mote End, Nan Clark's Lane, Mill Hill, NW7 4HH. *Club:* Garrick.

GARDINER, Duncan; *see* Gardiner, J. D. B.

GARDINER, Ernest David, CMG 1968; CBE 1967; Head of Science Department, Melbourne Grammar School, 1948–74; Chairman, Commonwealth Government's Advisory Committee on Standards for Science Facilities in Independent Secondary Schools, 1964–76; *b* 14 July 1909; 2nd *s* of Ernest Edward Gardiner and Isabella Gardiner (*née* Notman), Gisborne, Vic.; *m* 1940, Minnie Amanda Neill (*d* 1983); one *s* one *d*. *Educ:* Kyneton High Sch.; Melbourne Univ. BSc 1931, BEd 1936, Melbourne; FACE 1968. Secondary Teacher with Educn Dept of Vic., 1932–45; Melbourne Grammar Sch., 1946–74. *Publications:* Practical Physics (2 vols), 1948; Practical Problems in Physics, 1959; Problems in Physics, 1969, rex. and enl. edn (with B. L. McKittrick), 1985; Practical Physics, 1972. *Recreations:* music, theatre, swimming, Scottish country dancing. *Address:* 122 Ferguson Street, Williamstown, Vic 3016, Australia. *T:* 397 6132.

GARDINER, Frederick Keith, JP; Past President, Neepsend Steel and Tool Corporation, Ltd; *b* Plumstead, Kent; *s* of Frederick Gardiner and Edith Mann; *m* 1929, Ruth Dixon (*d* 1985); two *s*. Various editorial positions with newspaper companies in the South of England and at Darlington, York, Oxford and Sheffield; formerly Ed. and Dir, The Sheffield Telegraph; President: Inst. of Journalists, 1950; Hallam Cons. Assoc. Former Vice-Chm., Sheffield Wednesday FC. FJI. JP Sheffield; Chm., Magistrates' Courts Cttee; former Vice-Chm., Sheffield Bench. *Recreation:* golf. *Address:* 5 Chorley Road, Fulwood, Sheffield S10 3RJ. *Club:* Hallamshire Golf (Past Pres.) (Sheffield).
See also J. D. B. Gardiner.

GARDINER, George Arthur; MP (C) Reigate, since Feb. 1974; *b* 3 March 1935; *s* of Stanley and Emma Gardiner; *m* 1st, 1961, Juliet Wells (marr. diss. 1980); two *s* one *d*; 2nd, 1980, Helen Hackett. *Educ:* Harvey Grammar Sch., Folkestone; Balliol Coll., Oxford. 1st cl. hons PPE. Sec., Oxford Univ. Conservative Assoc., 1957. Chief Political Corresp., Thomson Regional Newspapers, 1964–74. Mem., Select Cttee on Home Affairs and its Sub-Cttee on Race Relations and Immigration, 1979–82; Sec., Cons. European Affairs Cttee, 1976–79, Vice-Chm., 1979–80, Chm., 1980–. Editor, Conservative News, 1972–79. Contested (C) Coventry South, 1970. *Publications:* The Changing Life of London, 1973; Margaret Thatcher: from childhood to leadership, 1975. *Address:* House of Commons, SW1.

GARDINER, Dame Helen (Louisa), DBE 1961 (CBE 1952); MVO 1937; *b* 24 April 1901; *y d* of late Henry Gardiner, Bristol. *Educ:* Clifton High School. Formerly in Private Secretary's Office, Buckingham Palace; Chief Clerk, 1946–61. *Recreations:* reading, gardening. *Address:* Higher Courlands, Lostwithiel, Cornwall.

GARDINER, (John) Duncan (Broderick); author and broadcaster; Editor, Western Mail, 1974–81; *b* 12 Jan. 1937; *s* of Frederick Keith Gardiner, *qv*; *m* 1965, Geraldine Mallen; one *s* one *d*. *Educ:* St Edward's School, Oxford. Various editorial positions in Sheffield, Newcastle, Sunday Times, London (1963–64, 1966–73) and Cardiff. *Recreations:* travel, all sport, wine and food, crosswords. *Address:* 145 Pencisely Road, Llandaff, Cardiff. *T:* 33022.

GARDINER, John Eliot; conductor; Musical Director, Lyons Opera, since 1983; Founder and Artistic Director, English Baroque Soloists, Monteverdi Choir and Monteverdi Orchestra; Artistic Director, Göttingen Handel Festival, since 1981; *b* 20 April 1943; *s* of Rolf Gardiner and Marabel Gardiner (*née* Hodgkin); *m* 1981, Elizabeth Suzanne Wilcock; one *d*. *Educ:* Bryanston Sch.; King's Coll., Cambridge (MA History); King's Coll., London (Certif. of Advanced Studies in Music, 1966). French Govt Scholarship to study in Paris and Fontainebleau with Nadia Boulanger, 1966–68. Founded: Monteverdi Choir, following performance of Monteverdi's Vespers of 1610, King's Coll. Chapel, Cambridge, 1964; Monteverdi Orchestra, 1968; English Baroque Soloists (period instruments), 1978. Youngest conductor of Henry Wood Promenade Concert, Royal Albert Hall, 1968; Début with: Sadler's Wells Opera, Coliseum, 1969; Royal Opera House, Covent Garden, 1973; Royal Festival Hall, 1972; Guest engagements conducting major European orchestras in Paris, Brussels, Frankfurt, Dresden, Leipzig and London; US débuts: Dallas Symphony, 1981; San Francisco Symphony, 1982; European Music Festivals: Aix-en-Provence, Aldeburgh, Bath, Berlin, Edinburgh, Flanders, City of London, etc.; concert revivals in London of major dramatic works of Purcell, Handel and Rameau, culminating in world première (staged) of Rameau's opera Les Boréades, Aix-en-Provence, 1982. Principal Conductor, CBC Vancouver Orchestra, 1980–83. Has made over 80 records ranging from Monteverdi and Mozart to Massenet, Rodrigo and Central American Percussion Music; Grand Prix du Disque, 1978, 1979, 1982; Gramophone Awards for early music and choral music records, 1978, 1980; Internat. Record Critics Award, 1983. *Publications:* (ed) Monteverdi L'Orfeo; (ed) Gay The Beggar's Opera; (ed) Claude le Jeune Hélas! Mon Dieu, 1971; contrib. to opera handbook on Gluck's Orfeo, 1980. *Recreations:* sheep-breeding, organic corn-growing (in Dorset). *Address:* Gore Farm, Ashmore, Salisbury, Wilts. *T:* Fontmell Magna 811295; 7 Pleydell Avenue, W6. *T:* 01-741 0987.

GARDINER, John Ralph, QC 1982; *b* 28 Feb. 1946; *s* of late Cyril Ralph Gardiner and of Mary Gardiner; *m* 1976, Pascal Mary Issard-Davies; one *d*. *Educ:* Bancroft's Sch., Woodford; Fitzwilliam Coll., Cambridge (BA (Law Tripos), LLB, MA). Called to the Bar, Middle Temple, 1968 (Harmsworth Entrance Scholar and Harmsworth Law Scholar); practice at the Bar, 1970–; Mem., Senate of Inns of Court and Bar, 1982–, Treas., 1985–. *Publications:* contributor to Pinson on Revenue Law, 6th to 15th (1982) edns. *Recreations:* tennis, cricket, squash. *Address:* 11 New Square, Lincoln's Inn, WC2. *T:* 01-242 3981; 21 Palace Gardens Terrace, W8. *T:* 01-229 2226. *Club:* Cumberland Lawn Tennis.

GARDINER, Patrick Lancaster, FBA 1985; Fellow and Tutor in Philosophy, Magdalen College, Oxford, since 1958; *b* 17 March 1922; *s* of Clive and Lilian Gardiner; *m* 1955, Kathleen Susan Booth; two *d*. *Educ:* Westminster School; Christ Church, Oxford (MA). Army service (Captain), 1942–45. Lectr, Wadham College, Oxford, 1949–52; Fellow, St Antony's College, Oxford, 1952–58. Vis. Prof., Columbia Univ., NY, 1955. *Publications:* The Nature of Historical Explanation, 1952; (ed) Theories of History, 1959; Schopenhauer, 1963, 2nd edn 1972; (ed) Nineteenth Century Philosophy, 1969; (ed) The Philosophy of History, 1974; articles in philosophical and literary jls, anthologies. *Address:* The Dower House, Wytham, Oxford. *T:* Oxford 242205.

GARDINER, Peter Dod Robin; First Deputy Head, Stanborough School, Hertfordshire, since 1979; *b* 23 Dec. 1927; *s* of Brig. R. Gardiner, *qv*; *m* 1959, Juliet Wright; one *s* one *d*. *Educ:* Radley College; Trinity Coll., Cambridge. Asst Master, Charterhouse, 1952–67, and Housemaster, Charterhouse, 1965–67; Headmaster, St Peter's School, York, 1967–79. *Publications:* (ed) Twentieth-Century Travel, 1963; (with B. W. M. Young) Intelligent Reading, 1964; (with W. A. Gibson) The Design of Prose, 1971. *Recreations:* reading, music, walking, acting. *Address:* Stanborough School, Lemsford Lane, Welwyn Garden City, Herts AL8 6YR.

GARDINER, Brig. Richard, CB 1954; CBE 1946 (OBE 1944); *b* 28 Oct. 1900; *s* of Major Alec Gardiner, RE; *m* 1st, 1924, Catherine Dod (*née* Oliver); two *s*; 2nd, 1982, Barbara Mary (*née* Whatmore). *Educ:* Uppingham Sch.; Royal Military Academy. Commissioned into RFA, 1920; transferred to RE, 1924; Asst Executive Engineer, E Indian Rly, 1927; Sec. to Agent, E Indian Rly, 1930; Exec. Engineer, 1934; Govt Inspector of Rlys, Burma, 1938; reverted to military duty, 1940; Dir of Transportation, India, 1942; reverted to Home Establishment, 1945; Dir of Transportation, War Office, 1948; Dir of Engineer Stores, War Office, 1950; retired Dec. 1953; Man. Dir, Peruvian Corp., Lima, 1954–63. Surrey CC, 1970–77. ADC to King George VI, 1951–52, to the Queen, 1952–53. FCIT. *Recreations:* music, gardening. *Address:* Botolph House, Botesdale, Diss, Norfolk IP22 1BX. *T:* Diss 898413.
See also P. D. R. Gardiner.

GARDINER, Robert (Kweku Atta); Commissioner for Economic Planning, Ghana, 1975–78; *b* Kumasi, Ghana, 29 Sept. 1914; *s* of Philip H. D. Gardiner and Nancy Torraine Ferguson; *m* 1943, Linda Charlotte Edwards; one *s* two *d*. *Educ:* Adisadel Coll., Cape Coast, Ghana; Fourah Bay Coll., Sierra Leone; Selwyn Coll., Cambridge (BA); New Coll., Oxford. Lectr in Economics at Fourah Bay Coll., 1943–46; UN Trusteeship Dept, 1947–49; Dir, Extra-Mural Studies, University Coll., Ibadan, 1949–53; Dir, Dept of Social Welfare and Community Development, Gold Coast, 1953–55; Perm. Sec., Min. of Housing, 1955–57; Head of Ghana Civil Service, 1957–59; Dep. Exec. Sec., Economic Commn for Africa, 1959–60; Mem. Mission to the Congo, 1961; Dir Public Admin. Div., UN Dept of Economic and Social Affairs, 1961–62; Officer-in-Charge, UN Operation in the Congo, 1962–63; Exec. Sec., UN Economic Commn for Africa, Addis Ababa, 1962–75. Chm., Commonwealth Foundation, 1970–73. Reith Lectures, 1965; David Livingstone Vis. Prof. of Economics, Strathclyde, 1970–75; Vis. Prof. of Economics, 1974–75, and Consultant, Centre for Development Studies, 1974–77, Univ. of Cape Coast. Lectures: Gilbert Murray Meml, 1969; J. B. Danquah Meml, 1970; Aggrey-Fraser-Guggisberg Meml, 1972. Mem Professional Socs, and activities in internat. affairs. Hon. Fellow: Univ. of Ibadan; Selwyn Coll., Cambridge. Hon. DCL: East Anglia, 1966; Sierra Leone, 1969; Tuskegee Inst., 1969; Liberia, 1972; Hon. LLD: Bristol, 1966; Ibadan, 1967; E Africa, 1968; Haile Sellassie I Univ., 1972; Strathclyde, 1973; Hon. PhD Uppsala, 1966; Hon. DSc: Kumasi, 1968; Bradford, 1969. *Publications:* (with Helen Judd) The Development of Social Administration, 1951, 2nd edn 1959; A World of Peoples (BBC Reith Lectures), 1965. *Recreations:* golf, music, reading, walking.

GARDINER, Victor Alec, OBE 1977; Director and General Manager, London Weekend Television, since 1971; Director: London Weekend Television (Holdings) Ltd, since 1976; London Weekend Services Ltd, since 1976; Richard Price Television Associates, since 1981; Chairman: Dynamic Technology Ltd, since 1972; Standard Music Ltd, since 1972; London Weekend Television International, since 1981; *b* 9 Aug. 1929; *m*; one *s* two *d*. *Educ:* Whitgift Middle Sch., Croydon; City and Guilds (radio and telecommunications). Techn. Asst, GPO Engrg, 1947–49; RAF Nat. Service, 1949–51; BBC Sound Radio Engr, 1951–53; BBC TV Cameraman, 1953–55; Rediffusion TV Sen. Cameraman, 1955–61; Malta TV Trng Man., 1961–62; Head of Studio Prodn, Rediffusion TV, 1962–67; Man. Dir, GPA Productions, 1967–69; Production Controller, London Weekend Television, 1969–71. Mem., Royal Television Soc., 1970– (Vice-Chm. Council, 1974–75; Chm. Papers Cttee, 1975; Chm. Council, 1976–77; Fellow, 1977). *Recreations:* music, building, gardening. *Address:* c/o London Weekend Television Ltd, Kent House, Upper Ground, SE1 9LT.

GARDINER-SCOTT, Rev. William, OBE 1974; MA; Emeritus Minister of Scots Memorial Church and Hospice, Jerusalem; *b* 23 February 1906; *o s* of late William Gardiner Scott, Portsoy, Banffshire; *m* 1953, Darinka Milo, *d* of late Milo Glogovac, Oakland, Calif; one *d*. *Educ:* Grange School, Bo'ness, West Lothian; Edinburgh University and New College, Edinburgh. In catering business, 1926–30; graduated in Arts, Edin., 1934; Theological Travel Scholarship to Palestine, 1936; travelled as ship's steward to America and India, 1936; ordained to Ministry of Church of Scotland, 1939; Sub-Warden 1939, Deputy Warden 1940, New College Settlement, Edinburgh; enlisted as Army Chaplain, 1941; served in Egypt, 1942–44 and developed community centre at RA Depot, Cairo and initiated publication of weekly Scots newspaper, The Clachan Crack; founded Montgomery House, Alexandria, as community centre for all ranks of allied troops, 1943; served in Palestine as Church of Scotland Chaplain for Galilee and district, 1944–46; Senior Chaplain at Scottish Command, 1946–47; Warden of Student Movement House, London, 1947–49; Chaplain at Victoria Univ. Coll., Wellington, NZ, 1950–54; locum tenens St John's West Church, Leith, 1955; Minister of Church of Scotland, Jerusalem, 1955–60 and 1966–73; Parish of Abernethy, 1960–66. ChStJ. Distinguished Citizen of Jerusalem. *Recreations:* travel, gardening, cooking, walking. *Address:* Scots Memorial Church and Hospice, PO Box 14216, Jerusalem, Israel.

GARDNER, family name of **Baroness Gardner of Parkes.**

GARDNER OF PARKES, Baroness *cr* 1981 (Life Peer), of Southgate, Greater London, and of Parkes, NSW; **(Rachel) Trixie (Anne) Gardner;** JP; dental surgeon; UK Representative, United Nations Status of Women Commission, since 1982; Member, London Electricity Board, since 1984; *b* Parkes, NSW, 17 July 1927; eighth *c* of late Hon. J. J. Gregory McGirr and late Rachel McGirr, OBE, LC; *m* 1956, Kevin Anthony Gardner, *o s* of George Waldron and Rita Gardner, Sydney, Australia; three *d*. *Educ:* Monte Sant Angelo Coll., N Sydney; East Sydney Technical Coll.; Univ. of Sydney (BDS 1954). Cordon Bleu de Paris, Diplôme 1956. Came to UK, 1955. Member: Westminster City Council, 1968–78; GLC, for Havering, 1970–73, for Enfield-Southgate, 1977–86. Contested (C) Blackburn, 1970; N Cornwall, Feb. 1974. Member: Inner London Exec. Council, NHS, 1966–71; Standing Dental Adv. Cttee for England and Wales, 1968–76; Westminster, Kensington and Chelsea Area Health Authority, 1974–82; Industrial Tribunal Panel for London, 1974–; N Thames Gas Consumer Council, 1980–82; Dept of Employment's Adv. Cttee on Women's Employment. British Chm., European Union of Women, 1978–82. Governor: Eastman Dental Hosp., 1971–80; Nat. Heart Hosp., 1974–. Hon. Pres., War Widows Assoc. of GB, 1984–. JP North Westminster, 1971. *Recreations:* gardening, reading, travel, needlework. *Address:* House of Lords, SW1A 0PW.

GARDNER, Antony John; Principal Registration Officer, Central Council for Education and Training in Social Work, since 1970; *b* 27 Dec. 1927; *s* of David Gardner, head gardener, and Lillian Gardner; *m* 1956, Eveline A. Burden. *Educ:* Elem. school; Co-operative Coll.; Southampton Univ. Pres. Union, Southampton, 1958–59; BSc (Econ) 1959. Apprentice toolmaker, 1941–45; National Service, RASC, 1946–48; building trade, 1948–53. Tutor Organiser, Co-operative Union, 1959–60; Member and Education Officer, Co-operative Union, 1961–66. Contested (Lab): SW Wolverhampton, 1964; Beeston, Feb. and Oct. 1974; MP (Lab) Rushcliffe, 1966–70. *Recreations:* angling, gardening and the countryside generally. *Address:* 118 Ringwood Road, Parkstone, Poole, Dorset. *T:* Poole 676683. *Club:* Parkstone Trades and Labour (Poole).

GARDNER, Prof. David Pierpont, PhD; President, University of California System, since 1983; Professor of Education, University of California at Berkeley, since 1983; *b* 24 March 1933; *s* of Reed S. Gardner and Margaret (*née* Pierpont); *m* 1958, Elizabeth Fuhriman; four *d*. *Educ:* Brigham Young Univ. (BS 1955); Univ. of Calif, Berkeley (MA 1959, PhD 1966). Dir, Calif Alumni Foundn and Calif Alumni Assoc., Univ. of Calif, Berkeley, 1962–64. University of California, Santa Barbara: Asst Prof. of Higher Educn, 1964–69; Associate Prof. of Higher Educn, 1969–70; Prof. of Higher Educn (on leave), 1971–73; Asst to the Chancellor, 1964–67; Asst Chancellor, 1967–69; Vice Chancellor and Exec. Asst, 1969–70; Vice Pres., Univ. of Calif System, 1971–73; Pres., and Prof. of Higher Educn, Univ. of Utah, 1973–83, Pres. Emeritus, 1985. Vis. Fellow, Clare Hall, Univ. of Cambridge, 1979 (Associate 1979). Mem., Nat. Acad. of Public Administration, 1984. Fulbright 40th Anniversary Distinguished Fellow, Japan, 1986; Fellow, Amer. Acad. of Arts and Scis, 1986. Hon. LLD: Univ. of The Pacific, 1983; Univ. of Nevada, Las Vegas, 1984; Hon. DH Brigham Young Univ., 1981; Hon. DLitt Univ. of Utah, 1983. Benjamin P. Cheney Medal, Eastern Washington Univ., 1984; James Bryant Conant Award, Educn Commn of the States, 1985. Chevalier, Légion d'Honneur (France), 1985. *Publications:* The California Oath Controversy, 1967; contrib. articles to professional jls. *Address:* (home) 70 Rincon Road, Kensington, Calif 94707, USA; (office) Office of the President, 714 University Hall, University of California, Berkeley, Calif 94720.

GARDNER, Sir Douglas Bruce B.; *see* Bruce-Gardner.

GARDNER, Sir Edward (Lucas), Kt 1983; QC 1960; MP (C) Fylde, since 1983 (South Fylde, 1970–83); a Recorder of the Crown Court, 1972–85; *b* 10 May 1912; *s* of late Edward Walker Gardner, Fulwood, Preston, Lancs; *m* 1st, 1950, Noreen Margaret (marr. diss. 1962), *d* of late John Collins, Moseley, Birmingham; one *s* one *d*; 2nd, 1963, Joan Elizabeth, *d* of late B. B. Belcher, Bedford; one *s* one *d*. *Educ:* Hutton Grammar Sch. Served War of 1939–45: joined RNVR as ordinary seaman, 1940; served in cruisers, Mediterranean; commnd RNVR; Chief of Naval Information, E Indies, 1945. Journalist (free-lance; Lancashire Daily Post, then Daily Mail) prior to 1940; broadcasting and free-lance journalism, 1946–49; called to Bar, Gray's Inn, 1947; Master of the Bench of Gray's Inn, 1968; admitted to Nigerian and British Guianan Bars, 1962; has also appeared in Courts of Goa, High Court of Singapore, and Supreme Court of India. Deputy Chairman of Quarter Sessions: East Kent, 1961–71; County of Kent, 1962–71; Essex, 1968–71. Contested (C) Erith and Crayford, April 1955; MP (C) Billericay Div. of Essex, 1959–66; PPS to Attorney-General, 1962–63. Chm., Select Cttee on Home Affairs, 1984–. Chairman: Justice Working Party on Bail and Remands in Custody, 1966; Bar Council Cttee on Parly Privilege, 1967; Chm., Soc. of Cons. Lawyers, 1975–85 (Chm. Exec. Cttee, 1969–75; Chm., Cttee responsible for pamphlets, Rough Justice, on future of the Law, 1968, Crisis in Crime and Punishment, 1971, The Proper Use of Prisons, 1978, Who Do We Think We Are?, 1980, on need for new nationality law); Exec. Cttee, Justice, 1968. Member: Departmental Cttee on Jury Service, 1963; Cttee on Appeals in Criminal Cases, 1964; Commonwealth War Graves Commn, 1971–. A Governor: Thomas Coram Foundn for Children, 1962–; Queenswood Sch., 1975. Steward, British Boxing Bd of Control, 1975–84. *Publication:* (part author) A Case for Trial (pamphlet recommending procedural reforms for committal proceedings implemented by Criminal Justice Act, 1967). *Recreation:* walking. *Address:* 4 Raymond Buildings, Gray's Inn, WC1. *T:* 01–242 4719; Outlane Head, Chipping, Lancs. *Clubs:* Garrick, Pratt's, United and Cecil (Chm. 1970).

GARDNER, Dame Frances, DBE 1975; FRCP; FRCS; Consulting Physician, Royal Free Hospital, London, since 1978; *b* 28 Feb. 1913; *d* of late Sir Ernest and Lady Gardner; *m* 1958, George Qvist, FRCS (*d* 1981). *Educ:* Headington Sch., Oxford; Westfield Coll., Univ. of London; Royal Free Hospital School of Medicine. BSc London, 1935; MB, BS London, 1940; MD London, 1943; MRCP 1943, FRCP 1952; FRCS 1983. Medical Registrar, Royal Free Hosp., 1943; Clinical Asst, Nuffield Dept of Medicine, Oxford, 1945; Fellow in Medicine, Harvard Univ., USA, 1946; Consultant Physician, Royal Free Hosp., 1946–78; Chief Asst, National Hosp. for Diseases of the Heart, 1947; late Physician: Royal National Throat, Nose and Ear Hosp., London; Hosp. for Women, Soho Sq., London; The Mothers' Hosp., London; former Dean, Royal Free Hosp. Sch. of Medicine; Visitor, Med. Faculty, Khartoum, 1981. Commonwealth Travelling Fellow, 1962; late Examnr, MB, BS, Univ. of London; Rep. Gen. Med. Schools on Senate of Univ. of London, 1967; Mem., Gen. Med. Council, 1971; Pres., Royal Free Hosp. Sch. of Medicine, 1979. Formerly Chm., London/Riyadh Univs Med. Faculty Cttee. *Publications:* papers on cardiovascular and other medical subjects in BMJ, Lancet, and British Heart Jl. *Address:* 72 Harley Street, W1. *T:* 01–580 9944; Fitzroy Lodge, Fitzroy Park, Highgate N6 6JA. *T:* 01–340 5873; Consulting Suite, Wellington Hospital, NW8 9LE.

GARDNER, Rear-Adm. Herbert, CB 1976; Chartered Engineer; *b* 23 Oct. 1921; *s* of Herbert and Constance Gladys Gardner; *m* 1946, Catherine Mary Roe, Perth, WA. *Educ:* Taunton Sch.; Weymouth Coll. War of 1939–45; joined Dartmouth, 1940; RN Engineering Coll., Keyham, 1940; HMS Nigeria, Cumberland, Adamant, and 4th Submarine Sqdn, 1944; HM S/M Totem, 1945. Dept of Engr-in-Chief, 1947; HM S/M Telemachus, 1949; Admty Develt Establishment, Barrow-in-Furness, 1952; HMS Eagle, 1954; Comdr, 1956; HMS Caledonia, 1956; HMS Blackpool, 1958; Asst to Manager Engrg Dept, Rosyth Dockyard, 1960; HMS Maidstone, 1963; Capt., 1963; Dep. Manager, Engrg Dept, Devonport Dockyard, 1964; Chief Engr and Production Manager, Singapore Dockyard, 1967; Chief Staff Officer (Technical) to Comdr Far East Fleet, 1968; course at Imperial Defence Coll., 1970; Chief of Staff to C-in-C Naval Home Comd, 1971–73; Vice Pres., Ordnance Bd, 1974–76, Pres., 1976–77. *Recreations:* sailing, golf. *Address:* 41 Mayfair Street, Mount Claremont, Perth, WA 6010, Australia. *Club:* Royal Freshwater Bay Yacht (Perth).

GARDNER, James, CBE 1959; RDI 1947; Major RE; industrial designer and consultant; *b* 29 Dec. 1907; *s* of Frederic James Gardner; *m* 1935, Mary Williams; two *s*. *Educ:* Chiswick and Westminster Schools of Art. Jewellery Designer, Cartier Ltd, 1924–31. Served War of 1939–45, Chief Development Officer, Army Camouflage, 1941–46. Designer, Britain Can Make It Exhibition, 1946; Chief Designer, Festival Gardens, Battersea, 1950; British Pavilion, Brussels, 1958; British Pavilion, Expo '67, Montreal; currently designer to Evoluon Museum, Eindhoven, Netherlands, and St Helens Glass Museum, Lancs; responsible for main display Geological Museum, London, 1972; responsible for visual design of QE2 and sternwheeler Riverboat Mississippi Queen, Heritage Centre, York and Mus. of Diaspora, Tel Aviv. *Publication:* Elephants in the Attic, 1983. *Address:* The Studio, 144 Haverstock Hill, Hampstead, NW3.

GARDNER, James Jesse, CBE 1986; DL; consultant; Chief Executive, Tyne and Wear County Council, 1973–86; Chairman, Tyne and Wear Passenger Transport Executive, 1983–86; *b* 7 April 1932; *s* of James and Elizabeth Rubina Gardner; *m* 1955, Diana Sotheran; three *s* one *d*. *Educ:* Kirkham Grammar Sch.; Victoria Univ., Manchester (LLB). Nat. Service, 1955–57. Articled to Town Clerk, Preston, 1952–55; Legal Asst, Preston Co. Borough Council, 1955; Crosby Borough Council: Asst Solicitor, 1957–59; Chief Asst Solicitor, 1959–61; Chief Asst Solicitor, Warrington Co. Borough Council, 1961–65; Stockton-on-Tees Borough Council: Dep. Town Clerk, 1966; Town Clerk, 1966–68; Asst Town Clerk, Teesside Co. Borough Council, 1968; Associate Town Clerk and Solicitor, London Borough of Greenwich, 1968–69; Town Clerk and Chief Exec. Officer, Co. Borough of Sunderland, 1970–73; Clerk to Lieutenancy, Tyne and Wear, 1974–. Chm., Prince's Trust, 1986– (former Chm., Northumbria Cttee, Royal Jubilee and Prince's Trusts). DL Tyne and Wear, 1976. FRSA 1976. *Recreations:* golf, music, theatre, food and drink. *Address:* Wayside, 121 Queen Alexandra Road, Sunderland, Tyne and Wear. *T:* Sunderland 282525.

GARDNER, John Linton, CBE 1976; composer; *b* 2 March 1917; *s* of late Dr Alfred Gardner, Ilfracombe, and Muriel (*née* Pullein-Thompson); *m* 1955, Jane, *d* of late N. J. Abercrombie; one *s* two *d*. *Educ:* Eagle House, Sandhurst; Wellington Coll.; Exeter Coll., Oxford (BMus). Served War of 1939–45: RAF, 1940–46. Chief Music Master, Repton Sch., 1939–40. Staff, Covent Garden Opera, 1946–52; Tutor: Morley Coll., 1952–76 (Dir of Music, 1965–69); Bagot Stack Coll., 1955–62; London Univ. (extra-mural) 1959–60; Dir of Music, St Paul's Girls' Sch., 1962–75; Prof. of Harmony and Composition, Royal Acad. of Music, 1956–. Conductor: Haslemere Musical Soc., 1953–62; Dorian Singers, 1961–62; European Summer Sch. for Young Musicians, 1966–; Bromley YSO, 1970–76. Brit. Council Lecturer: Levant, 1954; Belgium, 1960; Iberia, 1963; Yugoslavia, 1967. Adjudicator, Canadian Festivals, 1974, 1980. Member: Arts Council Music Panel, 1958–62; Council, Composers' Guild, 1961– (Chm., 1963; Delegate to USSR, 1964); Cttee of Management, Royal Philharmonic Soc., 1965–72, 1977–; Brit. Council Music Cttee, 1968. Dir, Performing Right Soc., 1965– (Dep. Chm., 1983–). Worshipful Co. of Musicians: Collard Fellow, 1962–64; elected to Freedom and Livery, 1965. Hon. RAM 1959. Bax Society's Prize, 1958. *Works include: orchestral:* Symphony no 1, 1947; Variations on a Waltz of Carl Nielsen, 1952; Piano Concerto no 1, 1957; Sinfonia Piccola (strings), 1960; Occasional Suite, Aldeburgh Festival, 1968; An English Ballad, 1969; Three Ridings, 1970; Sonatina for Strings, 1974; Divertimento, 1977; Symphony no 2, 1984; *chamber:* Concerto da Camera (4 insts), 1968; Partita (solo 'cello), 1968; Chamber Concerto (organ and 11 insts), 1969; English Suite (harpsichord), 1971; Sonata Secolare for organ and brass, 1973; Sonata da Chiesa for two trumpets and organ; String Quartet, 1979; Hebdomade, 1980; Sonatina Lirica for brass, 1983; Triad, 1984; Quartet for Saxes, 1985; *ballet:* Reflection, 1952; *opera:* A Nativity Opera, 1950; The Moon and Sixpence, 1957; The Visitors, 1972; Bel and the Dragon, 1973; The Entertainment of the Senses, 1974; Tobermory, 1976; *musical:* Vile Bodies, 1961; *choral:* Cantiones Sacrae 1973; (sop., chor. and orch.), 1952; Jubilate Deo (unacc. chor.), 1957; The Ballad of the White Horse (bar., chor. and orch.), 1959; Herrick Cantata (ten. solo, chor. and orch.), 1961; A Latter-Day Athenian Speaks, 1962; The Noble Heart (sop., bass, chor, and orch.), Shakespeare Quatercentenary Festival, 1964; Cantor popularis vocis, 18th Schütz Festival Berlin, 1964; Mass in C (unacc. chor.), 1965; Cantata for Christmas (chor. and chamb. orch.), 1966; Proverbs of Hell (unacc. chor.), 1967; Cantata for Easter (soli, chor., organ and percussion), 1970; Open Air (chor. and brass band), 1976; Te Deum for Pigotts, 1981; Mass in D, 1983. Many smaller pieces and music for films, Old Vic and Royal Shakespeare Theatres, BBC. Contributor to: Dublin Review, Musical Times, Tempo, Composer, Listener, Music in Education. *Recreations:* jazz, bore-watching. *Address:* 20 Firswood Avenue, Ewell, Epsom, Surrey KT19 0PR. *T:* 01–393 7181.

GARDNER, John William; writer; consultant; *b* 8 Oct. 1912; *s* of William Frederick and Marie (Flora) Gardner; *m* 1934, Aida Marroquin; two *d*. *Educ:* Stanford Univ. (AB 1935, AM 1936); Univ. of Calif. (PhD 1938). 1st Lt-Captain, US Marine Corps, 1943–46. Teaching Asst in Psychology, Univ. of Calif., 1936–38; Instructor in Psychology, Connecticut Coll., 1938–40; Asst Prof. in Psychology, Mt Holyoke Coll., 1940–42; Head of Latin Amer. Section, Federal Communications Commn, 1942–43. Carnegie Corporation of New York: Staff Mem., 1946–47; Exec. Associate, 1947–49; Vice-Pres., 1949–55; Pres., 1955–67; Pres., Carnegie Foundn for Advancement of Teaching, 1955–67; Sec. of Health, Education and Welfare, 1965–68; Chairman: Urban Coalition, 1968–70; Common Cause, 1970–77; Independent Sector, 1980–83; US Adv. Commn on Internat. Educational and Cultural Affairs, 1962–64; Pres. Johnson's Task Force on Educn, 1964; White House Conf. on Educn, 1965; President's Commn on White House Fellowships, 1977–81. Senior Fellow, Aspen Inst., 1981–. Dir, Amer. Assoc. for Advancement of Science, 1963–65. Director: New York Telephone Co., 1962–65; Shell Oil Co., 1962–65; Time Inc., 1968–71; American Airlines, 1968–71; Rockefeller Brothers Fund, 1968–77; New York Foundn, 1970–76. Trustee: Metropolitan Museum of Art, 1957–65; Stanford Univ., 1968–82. Benjamin Franklin Fellow, RSA, 1964. Holds hon. degrees from various colleges and univs. USAF Exceptional Service Award, 1956; Presidential Medal of Freedom, 1964; Public Welfare Medal, Nat. Acad. of Science, 1967. *Publications:* Excellence, 1961, rev. edn 1984; (ed) Pres. John F. Kennedy's book, To Turn the Tide, 1961; Self-Renewal, 1964, rev. edn 1980; No Easy Victories, 1968; The Recovery of Confidence, 1970; In Common Cause, 1972; Know or Listen to Those who Know, 1975; Morale, 1978; Quotations of Wit and Wisdom, 1980. *Address:* 1828 L Street NW, Suite 1200, Washington, DC 20036, USA.

GARDNER, Kenneth Burslam; Deputy Keeper of Oriental MSS and Printed Books, The British Library, 1974–86; *b* 5 June 1924; *s* of D. V. Gardner; *m* 1949, Cleone Winifred Adams; two *s* two *d*. *Educ:* Alleyne's Grammar Sch., Stevenage; University College, London; School of Oriental and African Studies, Univ. of London (BA Hons Japanese). War service, Intelligence Corps (Captain), 1943–47. Assistant Librarian, School of Oriental and African Studies, 1949–54; Assistant Keeper, Department of Oriental Printed Books and MSS, British Museum, 1955–57, Keeper, 1957–70; Principal Keeper of Printed Books, British Museum (later The British Library), 1970–74. Order of the Sacred Treasure (3rd class), Japan, 1979. *Publications:* Edo jidai no sashie hangaka-tachi (in Japanese, on book illustration in Japan and related topics), 1977; contrib. to jls of oriental studies, art and librarianship. *Address:* The Old Stables, 15 Farquhar Street, Bengeo, Hertford SG14 3BN. *T:* Hertford 53591.

GARDNER, Norman Keith Ayliffe; Under Secretary, Department of Trade and Industry, 1984–85; *b* 2 July 1925; *s* of late Charles Ayliffe Gardner and Winifred Gardner; *m* 1951, Margaret Patricia Vinson; one *s* one *d*. *Educ:* Cardiff High Sch.; University Coll., Cardiff (BScEng); College of Aeronautics, Cranfield; Univ. of London Commerce Degree Bureau (BScEcon Hons). CEng. Flight Test Observer, RAE, 1944; Test Observer, Westland Aircraft Ltd, 1946; Development Engr, Handley Page Ltd, 1950; Engr, Min. of Aviation, 1964; Economic Adviser, Min. of Technology, 1970; Asst Dir (Engrg), DTI, 1973; Sen. Economic Adviser, 1974, Under Secretary: DoI, 1977; Dept of Employment, 1979. *Publications:* The Economics of Launching Aid, in The Economics of Industrial Subsidies (HMSO), 1976; papers in Jl Instn Prodn Engrs and other engrg jls. *Recreation:* music. *Address:* 15 Chanctonbury Way, N12 7JB. *T:* 01–445 4162.

GARDNER, Ralph Bennett, MM 1944; Under Secretary (Legal), Treasury Solicitor's Department, 1976–82, retired; *b* 7 May 1919; *s* of late Ralph Wilson Gardner and Elizabeth Emma (*née* Nevitt-Bennett); *m* 1950, Patricia Joan Ward (*née* Bartlett); one *s* one *d*. *Educ:* Worksop Coll. Served War, 1939–46, RA. Admitted a solicitor, 1947; Solicitor, private practice, Chester, 1947–48; Legal Asst, Treasury Solicitor's Dept, 1948; Sen. Legal Asst, 1957; Asst Treas. Solicitor, 1972. Lord of the Manor of Shotwick, County of Chester (by inheritance, 1964). *Recreations:* gardening and local history. *Address:* Wychen, St Mary's Road, Leatherhead, Surrey. *T:* Leatherhead 373161. *Club:* East India, Devonshire, Sports and Public Schools.

GARDNER, Prof. Richard Lavenham, PhD; FRS 1979; Hon. Director, Imperial Cancer Research Fund's Developmental Biology Unit, since 1986; Royal Society Henry Dale Research Professor, since 1978; Student of Christ Church, Oxford, since 1974; *b* 10 June 1943; *s* of late Allan Constant and Eileen May Gardner; *m* 1968, Wendy Joy Cresswell; one *s*. *Educ:* St John's Sch., Leatherhead; North East Surrey Coll. of Technology; St Catharine's Coll., Cambridge (BA 1st Cl. Hons Physiol., 1966; MA; PhD 1971). Res. Asst, Physiological Lab., Cambridge, 1970–73; Lectr in Developmental and Reproductive Biology, Dept of Zoology, Oxford Univ., 1973–77; Res. Student, Christ Church, Oxford, 1974–77. Scientific Medal, Zoological Soc. of London, 1977. *Publications:* contribs to Jl of Embryology and Experimental Morphology, Nature, Jl of Cell Science, and various other jls and symposia. *Recreations:* ornithology, music, sailing, painting, gardening. *Address:* Christ Church, Oxford OX1 1DP.

GARDNER, Robert Dickson Robertson, CBE 1978; Secretary, Greater Glasgow Health Board, 1974–85, retired; *b* 9 May 1924; *s* of Robert Gardner and Isabella McAlonan; *m* 1950, Ada Stewart; two *s* one *d*. Dep. Sec., 1962–66, Sec., 1966–74, Western Regional Hospital Board, Scotland. *Recreations:* swimming, Scottish country dancing, reading. *Address:* 5 Linn Drive, Muirend, Glasgow G44 3PT. *T:* 041–637 8070.

GARDNER, William Maving; designer and craftsman in private practice; *b* 25 May 1914; *s* of Robert Haswell Gardner, MIMarE and Lucy (*née* Maving); *m* 1940, Joan Margaret Pollard (*d* 1982); two *s* one *d*. Trained at Royal College of Art, 1935–39 (ARCA 1938, Design Sch. Trav. Schol., Scandinavia, 1939). Mem., Royal Mint Panel of Artists, 1938–. Vis. lectr, Central Sch. of Arts and Crafts, 1959–62, Cambridgeshire Coll. of Art and Technology, 1959–62, Hampstead Garden Suburb Inst., 1959–73; Examr in craft subjects AEB City and Guilds of London Inst., 1957–60; served Typography Jury of RSA, Ind. Design Bursary Scheme. FRSA 1955, FSIA 1964, Leverhulme Res. Fellow, 1969–70. Vis. Prof. and Fine Art Program Lectr, Colorado State Univ., 1963; Churchill Meml Trav. Fellow, 1966–67 (USA, Polynesia, NZ, Australia, Nepal); Hon. Mem., RNS, NZ, 1966. Work exhib. Fort Collins and Denver, Colo, 1963, Monotype House, London, 1965, Portsmouth Coll. of Art, 1965, Hammond Mus., NY, 1970; (with family) Rye Art Gall., 1977. Awarded the Queen's Silver Jubilee Medal, 1977. *Works include:* HM Privy Council Seal 1955, HM Greater and Lesser Royal Signets 1955, Seal of HM Dependencies, 1955; seals for BMA, 1957, RSA, 1966, Univ. of Aston, Birmingham, 1966; *coinage models:* for Jordan 1950, UK 1953, Cyprus 1955 and 1963, Algeria 1964, New Zealand 1967, Guyana 1967, Dominican Republic 1969, UNFAO (Ceylon 1968, Cyprus 1970, Guyana 1970), Falkland Islands 1974, UK 20p coin 1982; *medallic work:* includes Britannia Commemorative Soc. Shakespeare Medal 1967, Churchill Meml Trust's Foundn Medal 1969, Nat. Commemorative Soc. Audubon Medal 1970, Internat. Iron and Steel Inst. Medal 1971, Inst. of Metals Kroll medal 1972, and thirty-six medallic engravings depicting the history of the Royal Arms, completed 1974; participant in series of Commonwealth Silver Jubilee crown pieces, 1977; *calligraphy:* includes Rolls of Honour for House of Commons 1949, LTE 1954, Household Cavalry and the five regiments of Foot Guards, completed 1956, Warrants of Appointment by Queen Elizabeth the Queen Mother as Lord Warden of the Cinque Ports, 1979, Royal Marines Corps Book of Remembrance, MSS for Canterbury Cath. and elsewhere; *work in other media* for Postmaster Gen. (Jersey definitive stamp 1958), Royal Soc. (Tercentenary stained glass window, 1960), King's College, London, 1971, City of London, 1972—and for Univs, schools, presses, libraries, banks, industrial and other authorities, also privately. *Publications:* Chapter VIII of The Calligrapher's Handbook, 1956; Calligraphy for A Wordsworth Treasury, 1978; Alphabet at Work, 1982; New Calligraphy on an Old Theme, 1984. *Address:* Alberta Lodge, Ide Hill, Sevenoaks, Kent TN14 6JA.

GARDNER-MEDWIN, Prof. Robert Joseph, RIBA, FRTPI; architect and town planning consultant; Professor Emeritus, Liverpool University, since 1973; *b* 10 April 1907; *s* of late Dr and Mrs F. M. Gardner-Medwin; *m* 1935, Margaret, *d* of late Mr Justice and Mrs Kilgour, Winnipeg; four *s*. *Educ:* Rossall Sch., Lancashire; School of Architecture, Liverpool Univ. (BArch, Dipl Civ Des). Commonwealth Fund Fellowship in City Planning and Landscape Design, Harvard Univ., 1933–35; private practice, and architectural teaching at Architectural Association and Regent Street Polytechnic, 1936–40. Served War of 1939–45, with Royal Engineers (Major, RE), 1940–43. Adviser in Town Planning and Housing to Comptroller of Development and Welfare in the British West Indies, 1944–47; Chief Architect and Planning Officer to Department of Health for Scotland, 1947–52; Roscoe Prof. of Architecture, Liverpool Univ., 1952–73. President, Liverpool Architectural Society, 1966; Chm., Merseyside Civic Soc., 1972–76, 1979–80. FRSA. Golden Order of Merit, Poland, 1976. *Publications:* (with H. Myles Wright, MA, FRIBA) Design of Nursery and Elementary Schools, 1938; contributions to Town Planning Review, Architects' Journal, Journals of the RIBA and the RTPI, etc. *Address:* 6 Kirby Mount, West Kirby, Wirral, Merseyside.

GARDNER-THORPE, Col and Alderman Sir Ronald (Laurence), GBE 1980; TD 1948 (3 bars); JP; company director; *b* 13 May 1917; *s* of Joseph Gardner and Hannah Coulthurst Thorpe; *m* 1938, Hazel Mary (*née* Dees); one *s*. *Educ:* De la Salle Coll. Commnd Hants Heavy Regt, 1938; served War, 1939–45: France, Germany, Italy, British Army Staff Washington; 1945–47: AA&QMG 56 London Div., and XIII Corps; Grade 1 SO XIII Corps; GSO 1 GHQ CMF; comd 5th Bn The Buffs, 1956–60; Col 1960. City of London: Alderman, Ward of Bishopsgate, 1972 (Pres., Bishopsgate Ward Club, 1975); Sheriff, 1978–79; Lord Mayor, 1980–81; HM Lieut, 1980–. Vice-Pres., City of London Red Cross, 1977–. Underwriting Mem. of Lloyd's, 1977–. Member: Lord Lieuts Cttee, 1955–; Council, Magistrates' Assoc., 1972–; London Court of Arbitration, 1975–85; Public Sch. Governing Body, 1963–; Governor: St John's Coll., Southsea, 1963– (Vice-Chm. Governors, 1976–); St Joseph's, Beulah Hill, 1966–; Christ's Hosp., 1972–; Trustee: United Westminster Schs, 1974–; The Buffs (Royal East Kent Regt) Museum, 1976–; Morden Coll., 1979–; Rowland Hill Benevolent Fund, 1979–85; Mental Health Foundn, 1981–; Royal Foundn of Greycoat Hosp., 1981–, Duke of Edinburgh's Award, 1982–; President: 25th Anniv. Appeal Fund, The Duke of Edinburgh's Award, 1980–; David Isaacs Fund, 1982–86 (Vice-Pres., 1973–82); Central London Br., SSAFA, 1983; League of Friends, Hosp. of St John and St Elizabeth, 1983–; Vice-Pres., Variety Club of GB, 1982–; Chm. Council, Distressed Gentlefolks' Aid Assoc., 1984–. Chancellor, City Univ., 1980–81; Adm., Port of London, 1980–81. Member: Kent Territorial Assoc., 1954–62 (Mem., Finance Cttee, 1954); City of London T & AVR Assoc., 1977–; Hon. Col, Kansas Cavalry, 1981–. Hon. Citizen: Baltimore; Kansas City; Arizona; Norfolk, Va; Cuzco, Peru. JP Inner London, 1964 (Dep. Chm. 1968); JP City of London, 1969 (Dep. Chm. 1970); Hon. Treas., Inner London Magistrates, 1972– (Vice Chm., 1977). Freeman, City of London, 1971; Liveryman and Member of Court: Worshipful Co. of Painter Stainers, 1972–; Worshipful Co. of Builders Merchants, 1979–; Mem. Court, Hon. Artillery Co., 1972; Hon. Freeman and Liveryman, Leathersellers' Co., 1986. Hon. FRCP 1986. KStJ 1980; Kt of Magistral Grace, SMO, 1982. Kt Comdr, Royal Order of the Dannebrog, 1960; Kt Comdr, Order of Infant Henri, Portugal, 1979; Kt Comdr, Right Hand of the Ghurka, Nepal, 1980; Kt Comdr, Royal Order of King Abdul Aziz, Saudi Arabia, 1981; Kt Grand Cordon of the Swan, USA, 1984; Kt Grand Cross, Holy Order of the Cross of Jerusalem, USA, 1985; Grand Officer of Merit, Il Melito Melitensi, Italy, 1986. Hon. DCL City, 1980; Hon. DH Lewis, Chicago, 1981. *Publication:* The City and the Buffs, 1985. *Recreations:* interest in Fine Arts and in City of London tradition. *Address:* 8 Cadogan Square, SW1X 0JU. *Clubs:* Belfry, City Livery, United Wards, Bishopsgate Ward.

GARDYNE; *see* Bruce-Gardyne.

GAREL-JONES, (William Armand Thomas) Tristan; MP (C) Watford, since 1979; Vice-Chamberlain of HM Household, since 1986; *b* 28 Feb. 1941; *s* of Bernard Garel-Jones and Meriel Garel-Jones (*née* Williams); *m* 1966, Catalina (*née* Garrigues); four *s* one *d*. *Educ:* The King's Sch., Canterbury. Principal, Language Sch., Madrid, Spain, 1960–70; Merchant Banker, 1970–74; worked for Cons. Party, 1974–79 (Personal Asst to Party Chm., 1978–79). Contested (C): Caernarvon, Feb. 1974; Watford, Oct. 1974. PPS to Minister of State, CSD, 1981; Asst Govt Whip, 1982–83; a Lord Comr of HM Treasury, 1983–86. *Recreation:* collecting books. *Address:* 12 Catherine Place, SW1E 6HF. *T:* 01–828 3348. *Clubs:* Carlton, Beefsteak; Watford Football; Club de Campo (Madrid).

GARFIELD, Leon, FRSL; author; *b* 14 July 1921; *s* of David Garfield and Rose Garfield; *m* 1949, Vivien Dolores Alcock; one *d*. *Educ:* Brighton Grammar Sch. Served War, RAMC, 1941–46: attained and held rank of Private. Worked in NHS (biochemistry), until 1969; full-time author, 1969–. FRSL 1985. Prix de la Fondation de France, 1984; Swedish Golden Cat, 1985. *Publications:* Jack Holborn, 1964; Devil-in-the-Fog, 1966; Smith, 1967; Black Jack, 1968 (filmed 1979); Mister Corbett's Ghost and Other Stories, 1969; The Boy and the Monkey, 1969; The Drummer Boy, 1970; The Strange Affair of Adelaide Harris, 1971; The Ghost Downstairs, 1972; The Captain's Watch, 1972; Lucifer Wilkins, 1973; Baker's Dozen, 1973; The Sound of Coaches, 1974; The Prisoners of September, 1975; The Pleasure Garden, 1976; The Booklovers, 1976; The House of Hanover, 1976; The Lamplighter's Funeral, 1976; Mirror, Mirror, 1976; Moss and Blister, 1976; The Cloak, 1976; The Valentine, 1977; Labour in Vain, 1977; The Fool, 1977; Rosy Starling, 1977; The Dumb Cake, 1977; Tom Titmarsh's Devil, 1977; The Filthy Beast, 1977; The Enemy, 1977; The Confidence Man, 1978; Bostock & Harris, 1978; John Diamond, 1980 (Whitbread Book of the Year Award, 1980); Mystery of Edwin Drood (completion), 1980; Fair's Fair, 1981; The House of Cards, 1982; King Nimrod's Tower, 1982; The Apprentices, 1982; The Writing on the Wall, 1983; The King in the Garden, 1984; The Wedding Ghost, 1984; Guilt and Gingerbread, 1984; Shakespeare Stories, 1985; The December Rose, 1986; with Edward Blishen: The God Beneath the Sea, 1970; The Golden Shadow, 1973; with David Proctor: Child O'War, 1972. *Recreations:* snooker, collecting pictures and china; also wine, women and song. *Address:* c/o John Johnson (Author's Agent) Ltd, Clerkenwell House, 45/47 Clerkenwell Green, EC1R 0HT. *T:* 01–251 0125. *Clubs:* PEN, Puffin.

GARFITT, Alan; His Honour Judge Garfitt; a Circuit Judge, since 1977, and Judge, Cambridge County Court and Wisbech Crown Court, since 1978; *b* 20 Dec. 1920; *s* of Rush and Florence Garfitt; *m* 1st, 1941, Muriel Ada Jaggers; one *s* one *d*; 2nd, 1973, Ivie Maud Hudson; 3rd, 1978, Rosemary Lazell; one *s* one *d*. *Educ:* King Edward VII Grammar Sch., King's Lynn; Metropolitan Coll. and Inns of Court Sch. of Law. Served War of 1939–45, RAF, 1941–46. LLB London 1947; called to the Bar, Lincoln's Inn, 1948; practising barrister. Hon. Fellow, Faculty of Law, Cambridge, 1978. *Publications:* Law of Contracts in a Nutshell, 4 edns 1949–56; The Book for Police, 5 vols, 1958; jt ed, Roscoe's Criminal Evidence, Practice and Procedure, 16th edn, 1952; contribs to Jl of Planning Law, Solicitors' Jl and other legal pubns. *Recreations:* farming, gardening, DIY activities, horse riding and, as a member since 1961 and President since 1978 of the Association of British Riding Schools, the provision of good teaching and riding facilities for non-horse owners. *Address:* Leap House, Barcham Road, Soham, Ely, Cambs CB7 5TU. *Club:* Wig and Pen.

GARING, Air Commodore William Henry, CBE 1943; DFC 1940; Director, Bryn Mawr Chianina Stud Cattle Company, since 1975; *b* Corryong, Victoria, 26 July 1910; *s* of late George Garing, retired grazier, and late Amy Evelyn Garing; *m* 1st, 1940 (marr. diss. 1951); one *s* one *d*; 2nd, 1954, Marjorie Irene Smith, Preston, England; two *d*. *Educ:* Corryong Higher Elementary School; Melbourne Technical Coll.; Royal Military Coll., Duntroon, ACT. Began career as Electrical and Mechanical Engineer, 1928; entered RMC, Duntroon, 1929, as specially selected RAAF Cadet; Flying Training in Australia, 1931–32, in UK 1934–35; Seaplane Flying Instructor and Chief Navigation Instructor, Point Cook, Victoria, 1936; commanded Seaplane Squadron, Point Cook; conducted first Specialist Air Navigation Course in Australia, 1938; posted to United Kingdom in 1939; served with No 10 Squadron, RAAF, as Flt Commander in Coastal Command, RAF, 1939; operations in N Atlantic, France and Mediterranean (DFC); flew Lord Lloyd to France for discussions with Pétain Government prior to collapse of France, 1940, and subsequently was pilot to the late Duke of Kent and to Mr Eden (later Viscount Avon), and others (despatches). Arrived Australia, 1941; Senior Air Staff Officer, HQ Northern Area (extended from Neth. Indies through New Guinea, British Solomons to New Caledonia), 1941; commanded No 9 (Ops) Group RAAF, New Guinea, 1942; Milne Bay Campaign, 1942; Buna Campaign, 1942–43 (American DSC); 1943 (CBE); commanded No 1 Operational Training Unit, 1943 (1939–43 star); Director Operational Requirements, 1944; SASO to RAAF Rep., Washington, 1945–46; OC Western Area, 1947; Joint Services Staff Coll., 1948; Commandant School Land/Air Warfare, NSW, 1950; OC Amberley, Qld, 1951; Imperial Defence Coll., London, 1952. AOC Overseas HQ, London, 1953; AOC RAAF, Richmond, NSW, 1953–55; AOC RAAF and Commandant RAAF Staff Coll., Point Cook, Victoria, 1955–60; Air Officer, South Australia, and OC, RAAF, Edinburgh Field, Salisbury, SA, 1960–64, retired. Exec. Dir, Rothmans Nat. Sport Foundn, Sydney, Australia, 1964; Commercial Relations Manager, Alfred Dunhill Ltd, 1971–75. Holds No 1 Air Navigators' Certificate (Australia); Air Master Navigator (RAF); Freeman, GAPAN, FAIM 1961. *Recreations:* Alpine ski-ing, water ski-ing, yachting, golf, shooting, flying (holds commercial pilot's licence). *Address:* 3 Womerah Street, Turramurra, NSW 2074, Australia. *Clubs:* Imperial Service, Royal Commonwealth (Sydney).

GARLAND, Basil; Registrar, Family Division of High Court of Justice (formerly Probate, Divorce and Admiralty Division), 1969–85; *b* 30 May 1920; *o c* of late Herbert George Garland and Grace Alice Mary Martha Garland; *m* 1942, Dora Mary Sudell Hope; one *s*. *Educ:* Dulwich Coll.; Pembroke Coll., Oxford (MA). Served in Royal Artillery, 1940–46: commnd 1941; Staff Officer, HQ RA, Gibraltar, 1943–45; Hon. Major 1946. Called to Bar, Middle Temple, 1948; Treasury Junior Counsel (Probate), 1965; Registrar, Principal Probate Registry, 1969. *Publications:* articles in Law Jl. *Recreations:* sailing, drama. *Address:* Dalethorpe End, Dedham, Essex. *T:* Colchester 322263. *Clubs:* Bar Yacht, Royal Harwich Yacht.

GARLAND, (Frederick) Peter (Collison), CVO 1969; QPM 1965; *b* 4 Sept. 1912; *s* of late Percy Frederick Garland, Southsea, Hants; *m* 1945, Gwendolen Mary, *d* of late Henry

James Powell, Putney; three *d*. *Educ:* Bradfield Coll. Joined Metropolitan Police, 1934. Served in RAF (Air Crew), 1941–45. Asst Chief Constable of Norfolk, 1952–56, Chief Constable, 1956–75. CStJ 1961. *Address:* 2 Eaton Road, Norwich. *T:* Norwich 53043. *Club:* Royal Air Force.

GARLAND, Patrick Ewart; director of plays, films, television; writer; *b* 10 April 1935; *s* of late Ewart Garland and Rosalind, *d* of Herbert Granville Fell, editor of The Connoisseur; *m* 1980, Alexandra Bastedo. *Educ:* St Mary's Coll., Southampton; St Edmund Hall, Oxford (BA). Actor, Bristol Old Vic, 1959; Age of Kings, BBC TV, 1961; lived in Montparnasse, 1961–62; writing—two plays for ITV, 1962; Research Asst, Monitor, BBC, 1963; Television interviews with: Stevie Smith, Philip Larkin, Sir Noel Coward, Sir John Gielgud, Sir Ralph Richardson, Dame Ninette de Valois, Claire Bloom, Tito Gobbi, Marcel Marceau, 1964–78. Director and Producer, BBC Arts Dept, 1962–74; Stage Director: 40 Years On, 1968, 1984; Brief Lives, 1968; Getting On, 1970; Cyrano, 1971; Hair (Israel), 1972; The Doll's House (New York and London), 1975; Under the Greenwood Tree, 1978; Look After Lulu, 1978; Beecham, 1980 (all West End); York Mystery Plays, 1980; My Fair Lady (US), 1980; Kipling (Mermaid and New York), 1984; co-author, Underneath the Arches, Chichester, and Prince of Wales, 1982–83; Artistic Director, Chichester Festival Theatre, 1980–84: The Cherry Orchard, 1981; The Mitford Girls, 1981 (also London, 1981); On the Rocks, 1982; Cavell, 1982; Goodbye, Mr Chips, 1982; As You Like It, 1983; Forty Years On, Merchant of Venice, 1984; prod., Fanfare for Elizabeth, the Queen's 60th birthday gala, Covent Garden, 1986. *Films:* The Snow Goose, 1974; The Doll's House, 1976. Creative Writing Fellowship, Bishop Otter Coll., Chichester, 1984–85. *Publications:* Brief Lives, 1967; poetry in: London Magazine, 1954; New Poems, 1956; Poetry West; Encounter; short stories in: Transatlantic Review, 1976; England Erzählt, Gemini, Light Blue Dark Blue. *Recreations:* reading Victorian novels, walking in Corsica. *Club:* Garrick.

GARLAND, Hon. Sir Patrick Neville, Kt 1985; **Hon. Mr Justice Garland;** a Judge of the High Court, Queen's Bench Division, since 1985; a Judge of the Employment Appeal Tribunal, since 1986; *b* 22 July 1929; *s* of Frank Neville Garland and Marjorie Garland; *m* 1955, Jane Elizabeth Bird; two *s* one *d*. *Educ:* Uppingham Sch. (Scholar); Sidney Sussex Coll., Cambridge (Exhibnr and Prizeman; MA, LLM). Called to Bar, Middle Temple, 1953, Bencher, 1979. Asst Recorder, Norwich, 1971; a Recorder, 1972–85; QC 1972; Dep. High Court Judge, 1981–85. Chairman: Official Referees Bar Assoc.; SE Circuit Area Liaison Cttee. Mem., Lloyd's, 1983–. *Publications:* articles in legal and technical jls. *Recreations:* shooting, gardening, industrial archaeology. *Address:* 9 Ranulf Road, NW2; c/o Royal Courts of Justice, Strand, WC2. *Clubs:* Norfolk (Norwich); Cumberland Lawn Tennis.

GARLAND, Peter; *see* Garland, F. P. C.

GARLAND, Peter Bryan, PhD; FRSE; Principal Scientist, Biosciences Division, Unilever Research, since 1984; *Educ:* Univ. of Cambridge (BChir 1958, MB 1959, PhD 1964). Formerly Reader in Biochem., Bristol Univ.; Prof. of Biochem., Med. Scis Inst., Dundee Univ., 1970–84. Mem., MRC, 1980–84. Mem., CRC Scientific Cttee, 1983–. *Publications:* numerous articles in scientific journals. *Address:* Biosciences Division, Unilever Research, Colworth Laboratory, Sharnbrook, Bedford MK44 1LQ.

GARLAND, Hon. Sir (Ransley) Victor, KBE 1982; Chairman, Stewart Nairn Group plc, since 1985; Company Director: Prudential Corporation plc, since 1984; Mitchell Cotts plc, since 1984; TR Australia Investment Trust, since 1984; Throgmorton Trust plc, since 1985; *b* Perth, 5 May 1934; *m* Lynette May Jamieson, Musc Bach (Melb.); two *s* one *d*. *Educ:* Univ. of Western Australia. BA(Econ); FCA. Practised as Chartered Accountant, 1958–70. MP for Curtin, Australian Federal Parliament, 1969–81; High Comr of Australia in UK, 1981–83. Minister for Supply, 1971–72; Executive Councillor, 1971–; Minister Asstg Treasurer, 1972 and 1975–76; Minister for Special Trade Representations, also Minister Asstg Minister for Trade and Resources, 1977–79; Minister for Business and Consumer Affairs, 1979–80. Govt Representative Minister: at Commonwealth Ministerial Meeting for Common Fund, London, 1978; at Ministerial Meetings of: ESCAP, New Delhi, 1978; SPEC, Tonga, 1979; Minister representing Treas., at Ministerial Meeting of OECD, Paris, 1978; Leader, Aust. Delegn to UNCTAD V and Chm. Commonwealth Delegns to UNCTAD V, Manila, 1979; attended, with Premier, Commonwealth Heads of Govt meeting, Lusaka, 1979. Parly Adviser, Aust. Mission to UN Gen. Assembly, New York, 1973; Chief Opposition Whip, 1974–75; Chairman: House of Reps Expenditure Cttee, 1976–77; Govt Members' Treasury Cttee, 1977. Dep. Chm., South Bank Bd, 1985–. Freeman, City of London, 1982. *Address:* Wilton Place, Knightsbridge, SW1X 8RL. *T:* 01–235 2729. *Clubs:* White's; Weld (Perth).

GARLICK, Prof. George Frederick John, BSc, PhD, DSc, FInstP; *b* 21 Feb. 1919; *s* of George Robert Henry Garlick and Martha Elizabeth (*née* Davies); *m* 1943, Dorothy Mabel Bowsher; one *d*; *m* 1977, Harriet Herta Forster. *Educ:* Wednesbury High Sch.; Univ. of Birmingham (BSc 1940, PhD 1943, DSc 1955). War service: Scientific Officer (Radar Research). In Charge Luminescence Laboratory, Birmingham Univ., 1946–56 (Research Physicist, 1946–49, Lecturer in Physics, 1949–56); Prof. of Physics, Univ. of Hull, 1956–78; Research Prof., Univ. of Southern California, LA, 1978–79; private scientific consultant, 1979–86. FInstP 1949. Jubilee Medal, 1977. *Publications:* Luminescent Materials, 1949; numerous papers in learned scientific journals. *Recreation:* music (organ). *Address:* 267 South Beloit Avenue, Los Angeles, California 90049, USA.

GARLICK, Sir John, KCB 1976 (CB 1973); Permanent Secretary, Department of the Environment, 1978–81; *b* 17 May 1921; *m* 1945, Frances Esther Munday; three *d*. *Educ:* Westcliff High Sch., Essex; University of London. Entered Post Office Engineering Dept, 1937; Ministry of Transport, 1948; Private Secretary to Rt Hon. Ernest Marples, 1959–60; Assistant Secretary, 1960; National Economic Development Office, 1962–64; Under-Sec., Min. of Transport, 1966, later DoE; Dep. Sec., DoE, 1972–73; Dir-Gen., Highways, DoE, 1973–74; Second Permanent Sec., Cabinet Office, 1974–77. Mem., London Docklands Develt Corp., 1981–. Dir, Abbey National Bldg Soc., 1981–. *Address:* 16 Astons Road, Moor Park, Northwood, Mddx. *T:* Northwood 24628.

GARLICK, Kenneth John; Keeper of Western Art, Ashmolean Museum, Oxford, 1968–84; Fellow of Balliol College, Oxford, 1968–84, now Emeritus; *b* 1 Oct. 1916; *s* of late D. E. Garlick and Annie Hallifax. *Educ:* Elmhurst Sch., Street; Balliol Coll., Oxford; Courtauld Inst. of Art, London. MA Oxon, PhD Birmingham; FSA, FMA. RAF Signals, 1939–46. Lectr, Bath Academy of Art, 1946–48; Asst Keeper, Dept of Art, City of Birmingham Museum and Art Gallery, 1948–50; Lectr (Sen. Lectr 1960), Barber Inst. of Fine Arts, Univ. of Birmingham, 1951–68. Governor, Royal Shakespeare Theatre, 1978–. *Publications:* Sir Thomas Lawrence, 1954; Walpole Society Vol. XXXIX (Lawrence Catalogue Raisonné), 1964; Walpole Society Vol. XLV (Catalogue of Pictures at Althorp), 1976; (ed with Angus Macintyre) The Diary of Joseph Farington, Vols I-II, 1978, III-VI, 1979; numerous articles and reviews. *Recreations:* travel, music. *Address:* 39 Hawkswell House, Hawkswell Gardens, Oxford OX2 7EX. *Club:* Reform.

GARMOYLE, Viscount; Simon Dallas Cairns; a Vice-Chairman: S. G. Warburg & Co., since 1985 (Managing Director, 1979–85); Mercury Securities Ltd, since 1984 (Man. Dir 1981–84); Chairman, Voluntary Service Overseas, since 1981 (Treasurer, 1974–81); *b* 27 May 1939; *er s* and *heir* of 5th Earl Cairns, *qv*; *m* 1964, Amanda Mary, *d* of late Major E. F. Heathcoat Amory, and of Mrs Roderick Heathcoat Amory, Oswaldkirk Hall, York; three *s*. *Educ:* Eton; Trinity Coll., Cambridge. *Heir:* *s* Hon. Hugh Sebastian Cairns, *b* 26 March 1965. *Address:* Bolehyde Manor, Allington, near Chippenham, Wilts SN14 6LW. *T:* Chippenham 652105. *Club:* Turf.

GARNER, Alan; author; *b* 17 Oct. 1934; *s* of Colin and Marjorie Garner; *m* 1st, 1956, Ann Cook; one *s* two *d*; 2nd, 1972, Griselda Greaves; one *s* one *d*. *Educ:* Alderley Edge Council Sch.; Manchester Grammar Sch.; Magdalen Coll., Oxford. Writer and presenter, documentary films: Places and Things, 1978; Images, 1981 (First Prize, Chicago Internat. Film Fest.). *Publications:* The Weirdstone of Brisingamen, 1960; The Moon of Gomrath, 1963; Elidor, 1965; Holly from the Bongs, 1966; The Old Man of Mow, 1967; The Owl Service, 1967 (Library Assoc. Carnegie Medal 1967, Guardian Award 1968); The Hamish Hamilton Book of Goblins, 1969; Red Shift, 1973 (with John Mackenzie, filmed 1978); (with Albin Trowski) The Breadhorse, 1975; The Guizer, 1975; The Stone Book, 1976; Tom Fobble's Day, 1977; Granny Reardun, 1977; The Aimer Gate, 1978; Fairy Tales of Gold, 1979; The Lad of the Gad, 1980; Alan Garner's Book of British Fairy Tales, 1984; A Bag of Moonshine, 1986; *plays:* Lamaload, 1978; Lurga Lom, 1980; To Kill a King, 1980; Sally Water, 1982; The Keeper, 1983; *dance drama:* The Green Mist, 1970; *libretti:* The Bellybag, 1971 (music by Richard Morris); Potter Thompson, 1972 (music by Gordon Crosse). *Recreation:* work. *Address:* Blackden, Cheshire CW4 8BY.

GARNER, Sir Anthony (Stuart), Kt 1984; Director of Organisation, Conservative Central Office, since 1976; *b* 28 Jan. 1927; *s* of Edward Henry Garner, MC, FIAS, and Dorothy May Garner; *m* 1967, Shirley Doris Taylor; two *s*. *Educ:* Liverpool Coll. Young Conservative Organiser, 1948–51; Conservative Agent, Halifax, 1951–56; Nat. Organising Sec., Young Conservative Org., 1956–61; Conservative Central Office Agent for: London Area, 1961–64; Western Area, 1964–66; North West Area, 1966–76. Chm., Conservative Agents' Examination Bd, 1976–. Pres., Conservative Agents' Benevolent Assoc., 1976–. Life Governor, Liverpool Coll., 1980–. *Recreations:* sailing, theatre. *Address:* 1 Blomfield Road, W9. *Clubs:* Carlton, St Stephen's Constitutional.

GARNER, Frank Harold; farmer since 1971; *b* 4 Dec. 1904; *m* 1929, Hilda May Sheppard; one *d*. *Educ:* Swindon Technical Sch.; Universities of Cambridge, Oxford, Reading and Minnesota, USA. MA (Cantab), MA (Oxon), MSc (Minnesota, USA); FRAgSs. Assistant to Director of Cambridge University Farm, 1924; University Demonstrator in Agriculture at Cambridge, 1927; University Lecturer (Animal Husbandry) at Cambridge, 1929; Assistant to Executive Officer, Cambridgeshire War Agriculture Executive Cttee, 1939; County Agricultural Organiser, East Suffolk, 1940; General Manager of Frederick Hiam Ltd, 1944–58; Principal, RAC, Cirencester, Glos, 1958–71. Chairman: Cambridgeshire NFU, 1956–57; Bucks NFU, 1978. Liveryman, Farmers' Livery Co., Master, 1971–72. *Publications:* Cattle of Britain, 1943; The Farmers Animals, 1943; British Dairy Farming, 1946; (with E. T. Halnan and A. Eden) Principles and Practice of Feeding Farm Animals, 1940, 5th edn 1966; (ed) Modern British Farming Systems, 1975. *Recreation:* swimming. *Address:* Brooklyn, Park Street, Princes Risborough, Bucks HP20 1BX. *Club:* Farmers'.

GARNER, Frederic Francis, CMG 1959; Ambassador to Costa Rica, 1961–67; retired; *b* 9 July 1910; *m* 1946, Muriel (*née* Merrick). *Educ:* Rugby Sch.; Worcester Coll., Oxford. Joined HM Consular Service in China, 1932; served at Peking, Canton, Shanghai, POW in Japan, 1942–45. Consul, Tangier, 1947–50; First Secretary, Bogota, 1950–54; Consul-General, Shanghai, 1954–56; Head of Consular Department, Foreign Office, 1956–58; Ambassador at Phnom Penh, 1958–61. *Address:* c/o National Westminster Bank, 111 Western Road, Brighton, E Sussex BN1 2AF.

GARNER, Frederick Leonard; Chairman, Pearl Assurance Company Ltd, 1977–83, now President; *b* 7 April 1920; *s* of Leonard Frank Garner and Florence Emily Garner; *m* 1953, Giovanna Maria Anzani, Italy. *Educ:* Sutton County Sch., Surrey. Served War, RA, 1940–46. Joined Pearl Assurance Co., 1936; rejoined, 1946; sole employment, 1946–83. Dir of cos. *Address:* 98 Tudor Avenue, Worcester Park, Surrey. *T:* 01–337 3313, (office) 01–405 8441. *Club:* Royal Automobile.

GARNER, John Donald, LVO 1979; HM Diplomatic Service; High Commissioner in The Gambia, since 1984; *b* 15 April 1931; *s* of Ronald Garner and Doris Ethel Garner (*née* Norton); *m* Karen Maria Conway; two *d*. *Educ:* Trinity Grammar Sch., N22. Royal Navy, National Service, 1949–51. Foreign Office, 1952–55; Third Secretary: Seoul, 1955; Bangkok, 1957; Foreign Office, 1959–63; Second Secretary: Benghazi and Tripoli, 1963–67; Sydney, 1967–69; First Sec., Tel Aviv, 1969–73; FCO, 1973–76; NDC 1976; Dep. High Commissioner, Lilongwe, 1977–80; Chargé d'affaires, Kabul, 1981–84. *Recreation:* golf. *Address:* c/o Foreign and Commonwealth Office, SW1A 2AH; 30 The Green, N14. *T:* 01–882 6808. *Club:* South Herts Golf.

GARNER, Maurice Richard; specialist in the structure and governmental control of public enterprises; *b* 31 May 1915; *o s* of Jesse H. Garner; *m* 1943, Joyce W. Chapman; one *s* one *d*. *Educ:* Glendale County Sch.; London Sch. of Economics and Political Science. Royal Armoured Corps, 1942–45 (despatches). Inland Revenue (Tax Inspectorate), 1938–46; BoT, Asst Principal and Principal, 1947; Commercial Sec. and UK Trade Comr in Ottawa, 1948–55; transf. to Min. of Power, 1957; Asst Sec. 1960; Under-Sec., Electricity Div., Min. of Technology, 1969, later DTI, retired 1973. Vis. Prof., Dept of Govt, LSE, 1981–85. *Recreations:* sailing, reading, oenology. *Address:* Albany Lodge, Staple, Canterbury, Kent CT3 1JX. *T:* Ash 812011.

GARNER, Michael Scott; a Recorder, since 1985; *b* 10 April 1939; *s* of William Garner and Doris Mary (*née* Scott); *m* 1st, 1964, Sheila Margaret (*d* 1981) (*née* Garland); one *s* one *d*; 2nd, 1982, Margaret Anne (*née* Senior). *Educ:* Huddersfield Coll.; Manchester Univ. (LLB). Admitted Solicitor, 1965. Asst Recorder, 1978–85. *Recreations:* motoring, photography. *Address:* Ramsden Street, Huddersfield HD1 2TH. *T:* Huddersfield 45311.

GARNETT, John; *see* Garnett, W. J. P. M.

GARNETT, Thomas Ronald, MA; Headmaster of Geelong Church of England Grammar School, Australia, 1961–73; *b* 1 Jan. 1915; *s* of E. N. Garnett; *m* 1946, Penelope, *d* of Philip Frere; three *s* two *d*. *Educ:* Charterhouse (Scholar); Magdalene Coll., Cambridge (Scholar). BA 1936, MA 1946. Assistant master: Westminster School, 1936–38; Charterhouse, 1938–52; Master of Marlborough College, 1952–61. Served War of 1939–45, RAF, India and Burma, 1941–46, Squadron Leader (despatches). Cricket for Somerset, 1939. *Publications:* Stumbling on Melons, 1984; (ed) A Gardener's Potpourri, 1986. *Recreations:* gardening, ornithology. *Address:* Simmons Reef, Blackwood, via Trentham, Victoria, Australia. *T:* 053 686514. *Club:* Melbourne (Melbourne).

GARNETT, (William) John (Poulton Maxwell), CBE 1970; MA; Chairman, West Lambeth Health Authority, since 1986; *b* 6 Aug. 1921; *s* of Dr Maxwell Garnett, CBE, and Margaret Lucy Poulton; *m* 1st, 1943, Barbara Rutherford-Smith (marr. diss.); two *s* two *d*; 2nd, 1986, Julia Cleverdon; two *d*. *Educ*: Rugby Sch.; Kent Sch., USA; Trinity Coll., Cambridge. Royal Navy, 1941–46 (commnd. 1942). ICI Ltd, 1947–62; Dir, Industrial Soc., 1962–86; Dir, 1975–85, Chm., 1979–81, Spencer Stuart & Associates, Management Consultants. Dep. Chm. UNA, 1954–56. Mem., Ct of inquiry into miners' strike, 1972; Arbitrator, Lorry Drivers' Strike, 1979. Mem., Royal Dockyard Policy Bd. Chm., Churches Council on Gambling, 1965–71. DUniv Essex, 1977; Hon. DTech Loughborough, 1978; Hon. LLD, CNAA, 1980. *Publications*: The Manager's Responsibility for Communication, 1964, The Work Challenge, 1973, 1985. *Recreation*: timber construction. *Address*: 8 Alwyne Road, Canonbury, N1. *Clubs*: Athenæum; Leander (Henley).

See also V. H. B. M. Bottomley.

GARNETT-ORME, Ion, CBE 1983; Vice-President, St Dunstan's, since 1983 (Member of Council, 1958–83); Chairman, 1975–83); Director: Brown Shipley Holdings Limited, 1960–81 (Chairman, 1963–75), retired; *b* 23 Jan. 1910; *er s* of George Hunter Garnett-Orme and Alice Richmond (*née* Brown); *m* 1946, Katharine Clifton, *d* of Brig.-Gen. Howard Clifton Brown. *Educ*: Eton; Magdalene Coll., Cambridge. Served War, Welsh Guards, 1939–45. Dir, 1951, Chm., 1958–78, United States Debenture Corp. Ltd. Joined: Brown, Shipley & Co., Merchant Bankers, 1945; Bd of London Scottish American Trust Ltd and United States Debenture Corp. Ltd, 1951; Bd of Avon Rubber Co. Ltd, 1956–66; Dir, Ellerman Lines Ltd, 1971–75. *Address*: Cheriton Cottage, Cheriton, near Alresford, Hants SO24 0PR. *Club*: Carlton.

GARNHAM, Prof. Percy Cyril Claude, CMG 1964; FRS 1964; MD; Professor of Medical Protozoology (now Emeritus Professor), London University, and Head of Department of Parasitology, London School of Hygiene and Tropical Medicine, 1952–68, Hon. Fellow, 1976; Senior Research Fellow, Imperial College of Science and Technology, 1968–79, Hon. Fellow, 1979; Visiting Professor, Department of Biology, University of Strathclyde, since 1970; *b* 15 Jan. 1901; *s* of late Lieut P. C. Garnham, RN Division, and late Edith Masham; *m* 1924, Esther Long Price, Talley, Carms; two *s* four *d*. *Educ*: privately; St Bartholomew's Hospital. MRCS, LRCP, 1923, MB, BS London, 1923, DPH Eng. 1924, MD London, 1928 (University Gold Medal); Dipl. de Méd. Malariol., University of Paris, 1931. Colonial Medical Service, 1925–47; on staff of London School of Hygiene and Tropical Medicine, first as Reader, then as Professor, 1947–68. Heath Clark Lectr, Univ. of London, 1968; Fogarty Internat. Scholar, Nat. Insts of Health, Maryland, 1970, 1972; Manson Orator, 1969, Theobald Smith Orator, 1970; Ross Orator, 1980; Swellengoebel Orator, 1986. Member, Expert Panel of Parasitic Diseases, of WHO; Hon. Pres., European Fedn of Parasitologists; Past President: British Soc. of Parasitologists; Royal Society of Tropical Medicine and Hygiene; Vice-President: World Federation of Parasitologists; International Association against Filariasis; Corresponding Member: Académie Royale des Sciences d'Outre Mer, Belgium; Accad. Lancisiana, Rome; Soc. de Geografia da Lisboa; Hon. Member: Amer. Soc. Tropical Medicine; Société Belge de Médecine Tropicale; Brazilian Soc. Tropical Medicine; Soc. Ital. Medicina Tropicale; Soc. of Protozoologists; Société de Pathologie Exotique (Médaille d'Or, 1971); Acad. Nationale de Médecine, France (Médaille en Vermeil, 1972); Amer. Soc. of Parasitology; Mexican Soc. of Parasitologists; Polish Soc. of Parasitologists; British Soc. of Parasitologists; Groupement des Protistologues de la Langue Française; Foreign Member: Danish Royal Acad. of Sciences and Letters, 1976; Acad. Royale de Médecine, Belgium, 1979; Royal Entomolog. Soc. of London, 1979. Hon. FRCP Edinburgh, 1966; FRCP 1967; FIBiol, 1962. Freedom, City of London in Farriers Co., 1964. DSc London, 1952; Hon. Dr: Univ. of Bordeaux, 1965; Univ. of Montpellier, 1980; Academician of Pontifical Acad. of Sciences, 1970. KLJ 1979. Darling Medal and Prize, 1951; Bernhard Nocht Medal, 1957; Gaspar Vianna Medal, 1962; Manson Medal, 1965; Emile Brumpt Prize, 1970; Laveran Medal, 1971; Mary Kingsley Medal, 1973; Rudolf Leuckart Medal, 1974; Frink Medal, 1985; Linnean Medal, 1986. *Publications*: Malaria Parasites, 1966; Progress in Parasitology, 1970; numerous papers on parasitology in medical journals. *Recreations*: chamber music and European travel. *Address*: Southernwood, Farnham Common, Bucks. *T*: 3863. *Club*: Nairobi (Kenya).

GARNIER, Rear-Adm. John, CBE 1982; LVO 1965; Flag Officer Royal Yachts, since 1985; *b* 10 March 1934; *s* of Rev. Thomas Vernon Garnier; *m* 1966, Joanna Jane Cadbury; two *s* one *d*. *Educ*: Berkhamsted School; Britannia Royal Naval College. FIL 1964. Joined RN 1950; served HM Yacht Britannia, 1956–57; HMS Tyne (Suez Operation, 1956); qualified navigation specialist, 1959; Naval Equerry to HM Queen, 1962–65; Comd HMS Dundas, 1968–69; Directorate of Naval Ops and Trade, 1969–71; Comd HMS Minerva, 1972–73; Defence Policy Staff, 1973–75; HMS Intrepid, 1976; Asst Dir, Naval Manpower Planning, 1976–78; RCDS 1979; Comd HMS London, 1980–81; Dir, Naval Ops and Trade, 1982–84; Commodore Amphibious Warfare, 1985. Younger Brother of Trinity House, 1974. Freeman of City of London, 1982. Order of St Olav (Norway), 1962; Ordre de Léopold (Belgium), 1963; Royal Order of George I (Greece), 1963; Order of the Two Niles, Class IV (Sudan), 1964. *Recreations*: sailing, golf, gardening, opera. *Address*: Flag Officer Royal Yachts, BFPO Ships.

GARNOCK, Viscount; James Randolph Lindesay-Bethune; landscape designer and consultant; *b* 19 Nov. 1955; *s* and *heir* of 15th Earl of Lindsay, *qv*; *m* 1982, Diana, *er d* of Major Nigel Chamberlayne-Macdonald, Cranbury Park, Winchester; one *d*. *Educ*: Eton; Univ. of Edinburgh (MA Hons); Univ. of Calif, Davis. Trustee, Gardens for the Disabled Trust; Mem. Council, London Gardens Soc. *Address*: 12 Pencombe Mews, Denbigh Road, W11.

GARNONS WILLIAMS, Basil Hugh; Headmaster of Berkhamsted School, 1953–72; *b* 1 July 1906; 5th *s* of Rev. A. Garnons Williams, Rector of New Radnor; *m* 1943, Margaret Olive Shearme (*d* 1981); one *s* two *d*. *Educ*: Winchester Coll. (Scholar); Hertford Coll., Oxford (Scholar). 1st Hon. Classical Moderations 1927; 2nd Lit Hum 1929; BA 1929; BLitt 1933; MA 1938; Classical VI Form Master, Sedbergh Sch., 1930–35; Marlborough Coll., 1935–45; Headmaster of Plymouth Coll., 1945–53. *Publications*: A History of Berkhamsted School, 1541–1972, 1980; articles in Classical Quarterly and Greece and Rome; contributor to History of the World (ed by W. N. Weech), 1944. *Address*: 26 Bridge Street, Berkhamsted, Herts HP4 2EB. *T*: Berkhamsted 5431.

GARNSEY, Rt. Rev. David Arthur; *b* 31 July 1909; *s* of Canon Arthur Henry Garnsey and Bertha Edith Frances Garnsey (*née* Benn); *m* 1934, Evangeline Eleanor Wood; two *s* two *d*. *Educ*: Trinity and Sydney Grammar Schs; St Paul's Coll., University of Sydney; New Coll., Oxford. University of Sydney, BA (1st cl. Latin and Greek) 1930; Travelling Sec. Australian SCM, 1930–31; NSW Rhodes Scholar, 1931, New Coll. Oxford, BA (2nd cl. Lit. Hum.) 1933, 2nd cl. Theol. 1934, MA 1937; Ripon Hall, Oxford, 1933. Deacon, 1934; Priest, 1935; Curate, St Mary the Virgin (University Church), and Inter-Collegiate Sec. of SCM, Oxford, 1934–38; St Saviour's Cathedral, Goulburn, NSW, 1938–41; Rector of Young, NSW, 1941–45; Gen. Sec. Australian SCM, 1945–48; Exam. Chap. to Bp of Goulburn, 1939–45, 1948–58; Head Master Canberra Grammar Sch., 1948–58; Canon of St Saviour's Cathedral, Goulburn, 1949–58; Bishop of Gippsland,

1959–74. Pres., Australian Council of Churches, 1970–73. Chm., Bd of Delegates, Aust. Coll. of Theology, 1971–77; Hon. ThD, Australian Coll. of Theology, 1955. Coronation Medal, 1953. *Publications*: A. H. Garnsey: a man for truth and freedom, 1985; booklets for study. *Recreation*: walking. *Address*: 33 Dutton Street, Dickson, Canberra, ACT 2602, Australia. *T*: 062–474786.

GARNSWORTHY, Most Rev. Lewis Samuel; *see* Toronto, Archbishop of.

GARRAN, Sir (Isham) Peter, KCMG 1961 (CMG 1954); HM Diplomatic Service, retired; Chairman, Quality Assurance Council, British Standards Institution, 1971–82; *b* 15 Jan. 1910; *s* of late Sir Robert Randolph Garran, GCMG, QC; *m* 1935, Mary Elisabeth, *d* of late Sir Richard Rawdon Stawell, KBE, MD; two *s* one *d*. *Educ*: Melbourne Grammar Sch.; Trinity Coll., Melbourne Univ. (BA 1st cl. Hons). Joined Foreign Office, 1934; Foreign posts: Belgrade, 1937–41; Lisbon, 1941–44; Berlin (seconded to CCG as Chief of Political Div.), 1947–50; The Hague, 1950–52; Inspector in HM Foreign Service, 1952–54; Minister (Commercial), Washington, 1955–60; Ambassador to Mexico, 1960–64; Ambassador to the Netherlands, 1964–70. Director: Lend-Lease Corp., NSW, 1970–78; UK Br., Australian Mutual Provident Soc., 1970–82; Chm., Securicor Nederland BV, 1976–82. *Recreation*: gardening. *Address*: The Coach House, Collingbeams, Donhead St Mary, Shaftesbury, Dorset. *T*: Donhead 8108. *Club*: Boodle's.

See also A. L. Coleby.

GARRARD, His Honour Henry John; a Circuit Judge (formerly a County Court Judge), 1965–84; *b* 15 Jan. 1912; *s* of late C. G. Garrard; *m* 1945, Muriel, *d* of late A. H. S. Draycott, Stratford-on-Avon; one *s* one *d*. *Educ*: Framlingham Coll., Suffolk. Called to the Bar, Middle Temple, Nov. 1937; Mem. of Oxford Circuit. Served 1939–45, Staffs Yeomanry (QORR) and Worcestershire Regt, East and North Africa, rank of Lieut; prisoner-of-war, 1942–45. Mem. of Mental Health Review Tribunal for Birmingham Area, 1963–65; Recorder of Burton-on-Trent, 1964–65. *Recreations*: family, dogs, country life. *Address*: Birtsmorton, Stowe Lane, Stowe-by-Chartley, Stafford ST18 0NA. *T*: Weston 270674.

GARRARD, Rev. Lancelot Austin, LLD; BD, MA; Professor of Philosophy and Religion, Emerson College, Boston, USA, 1965–71, now Emeritus; *b* 31 May 1904; *s* of late Rev. W. A. Garrard; *m* 1932, Muriel Walsh (*d* 1984); two *s*. *Educ*: Felsted (Scholar); Wadham Coll., Oxford (exhibitioner); Manchester Coll., Oxford; Marburg (Hibbert scholar). 2nd Class, Classical Mods; 2nd Class Lit Hum; Abbot Scholar; BD, MA (Oxon). Asst Master: Edinburgh Acad., 1927; St Paul's Sch., 1928; Unitarian Minister, Dover, 1932–33; Tutor and Bursar, Manchester Coll., Oxford, 1933–43; Minister, Lewins Mead Meeting, Bristol, 1941–43; Liverpool, Ancient Chapel of Toxteth, 1943–52; Tutor, Unitarian Coll., Manchester, 1945–51; Manchester Coll., Oxford, 1952–56; Principal of Manchester Coll., Oxford, 1956–65, Pres., 1980–; Editor of The Hibbert Journal, 1951–62. Hon. Chief, Chickasaw Nation. Hon. LLD (Emerson Coll, Boston). *Publications*: Duty and the Will of God, 1935; The Interpreted Bible, 1946; The Gospels To-day, 1953; The Historical Jesus: Schweitzer's Quest and Ours, 1956; Athens or Jerusalem?, 1965; Aide-de-Camp to Sir Stamford Raffles: Lt-Col R. C. Garnham, 1985; Index to The Hibbert Journal, 1986. *Address*: 7 Bancroft Court, Reigate, Surrey RH2 7RW. *T*: Reigate 49672. *Club*: Athenæum.

GARRATT, Gerald Reginald Mansel, MA, CEng, FIEE, FRAeS; retired; Keeper, Department of Aeronautics and Marine Transport, Science Museum, South Kensington, 1966–71; *b* 10 Dec. 1906; *s* of Reginald R. and Florence Garratt; *m* 1931, Ellen Georgina Brooks, Antwerp, Belgium; two *d*. *Educ*: Marlborough Coll.; Caius Coll., Cambridge. International Telephone & Telegraph Laboratories, 1929–30; RAE, Farnborough, 1930–34; Asst Keeper: Dept of Textiles and Printing, Science Museum, 1934; Dept of Telecommunications, 1936; Dep. Keeper 1949. Served RAF 1939–46 (Wing Comdr). Founder Mem., Cambridge Univ. Air Squadron, 1926. Commissioned RAF Reserve of Officers, 1928; retired 1966 (Wing Comdr). *Publications*: One Hundred Years of Submarine Cables, 1950; The Origins of Maritime Radio, 1972; numerous articles on history of telecommunications. *Recreations*: sailing, amateur radio. *Address*: Littlefield, 28 Parkwood Avenue, Esher, Surrey KT10 8DG. *T*: 01–398 1582. *Club*: Royal Automobile.

GARRELS, John Carlyle; retired; Chairman: Monsanto Chemicals Ltd, 1965–71; Monsanto Textiles Ltd, 1970–71; formerly Director: Forth Chemicals Ltd; Monsanto Australia Ltd; Monsanto Oil Co. of UK, Inc.; British Saccharin Sales Ltd; *b* 5 March 1914; *s* of John C. and Margaret Ann Garrels; *m* 1st, 1938, Valerie Smith; one *s* two *d*; 2nd, 1980, Isabelle Rogers Kehoe. *Educ*: Univ. of Michigan (BS (Chem. Eng.)); Harvard (Advanced Management Programme). Pennsylvania Salt Mfg Co., Production Supervisor, 1936–42; Monsanto Co.: various appts, 1942–54; Asst Gen. Manager, 1955; Monsanto Chemicals Ltd: Dep. Man. Dir, 1960; Man. Dir, 1961; Chm. and Man. Dir, 1965. Pres., British Plastics Fedn, 1970, 1971. Member: National Economic Development Cttee for Chemical Industry, 1971; Council, Chemical Industries Assoc. *Recreations*: golf, shooting, fishing. *Address*: 3111 SE Fairway West, Stuart, Fla 33494, USA. *T*: 305–283–6132. *Clubs*: American; Sunningdale Golf; Yacht and Country (Stuart, Fla).

GARRETT, Anthony David; Board Member, since 1983, and Managing Director of Parcels, since 1986, The Post Office; *b* 26 Aug. 1928; *s* of Sir William Garrett, MBE and Lady Garrett; *m* 1952, Monica Blanche Harris; three *s* one *d*. *Educ*: Ellesmere College; Clare College, Cambridge. MA. National Service, Subaltern IVth QO Hussars, 1946–48; Procter & Gamble Co., 1953–82, Vice-Pres., 1975–82. *Recreations*: sailing, golf, bridge, chess, walking. *Address*: Cammock House, Goldsmith Avenue, Crowborough, East Sussex TN6 1RH. *T*: Crowborough 4557. *Club*: United Oxford & Cambridge University.

GARRETT, Godfrey John, OBE 1982; HM Diplomatic Service; Counsellor, Bonn, since 1983; *b* 24 July 1937; *s* of Thomas and May Garrett; *m* 1963, Elisabeth Margaret Hall; four *s* one *d*. *Educ*: Dulwich Coll.; Cambridge Univ. (MA). Joined FO, 1961; Third Sec., Leopoldville (later Kinshasa), 1963; Second Sec. (Commercial), Prague, 1965; FCO, 1968; First Sec., Buenos Aires, 1971; FCO, 1973; First Sec., later Counsellor, Stockholm, 1981. Order of the Northern Star, Sweden, 1983. *Recreations*: all outdoor activities, especially skiing; squash, languages. *Address*: c/o Foreign and Commonwealth Office, SW1A 2AH; White Cottage, Henley, Haslemere, Surrey GU27 3HQ. *T*: Haslemere 52172.

GARRETT, Maj.-Gen. Henry Edmund Melvill Lennox, CBE 1975; Director of Security (Army), Ministry of Defence, since 1978; *b* 31 Jan. 1924; *s* of John Edmund Garrett and Mary Garrett; *m* 1973, Rachel Ann Beadon; one step *s* one step *d*. *Educ*: Wellington Coll.; Clare Coll., Cambridge (MA). Commnd 1944; psc 1956; DAAG, HQ BAOR, 1957–60; US Armed Forces Staff Coll., 1960; OC 7 Field Sqdn RE, 1961–63; GSO2 WO, 1963–65; CO 35 Engr Regt, 1965–68; Col GS MoD, 1968–69; Comdr 12 Engr Bde, 1969–71; RCDS, 1972; Chief of Staff HQ N Ireland, 1972–75; Maj.-Gen. i/c Administration, HQ UKLF, 1975–76; Vice Adjutant General, MoD, 1976–78. Col Comdt RE, 1982–. Mem., Nat. Exec. Cttee, Forces Help Soc., 1980–. Chm. Governors, Royal Soldiers' Daughters Sch., 1983–86. *Recreations*: riding, walking. *Address*: c/o National Westminster Bank, 1 Market Street, Bradford, Yorkshire BD1 1EQ. *Club*: Army and Navy.

GARRETT, John Laurence; Associate Director, Inbucon Ltd, since 1983; Director: West Midlands Enterprise Board; Statesman and Nation Publishing Co.; *b* 8 Sept. 1931; *s* of Laurence and Rosina Garrett; *m* 1959, Wendy Ady; two *d*. *Educ:* Selwyn Avenue Primary Sch., London; Sir George Monoux Sch., London; University Coll., Oxford (MA, BLitt); Grad. Business Sch. of Univ. of California at Los Angeles (King George VI Fellow). Labour Officer, chemical industry, 1958–59; Head of Market Research, motor industry, 1959–63; Management Consultant, Dir of Public Services, Inbucon Ltd, 1963–74. MP (Lab) Norwich South, Feb. 1974–1983; PPS to Minister for Civil Service, 1974, to Minister for Social Security, 1977–79; Opposition Treasury spokesman, 1979–80; spokesman on Industry, 1980–83. Contested (Lab) Norwich South, 1983. *Publications:* Visual Economics, 1966; (with S. D. Walker) Management by Objectives in the Civil Service, 1969; The Management of Government, 1972; Administrative Reform, 1973; Policies Towards People, 1973 (Sir Frederic Hooper Award); Managing the Civil Service, 1980; articles and papers on industry, management and govt. *Recreations:* theatre, dabbling, arguing. *Address:* c/o Inbucon, 197 Knightsbridge, SW7 1RN.

GARRETT, Hon. Sir Raymond (William), Kt 1973; AFC, AEA; JP; President, Legislative Council of Victoria, Australia, 1968–76 (Chairman of Committees, 1964–68); Chairman, Parliamentary Library Committee and Vice-Chairman, House Committee, 1968–76; *b* 19 Oct. 1900; *s* of J. J. P. Garrett, Kew, Australia; *m* 1934, Vera H., *d* of C. E. Lugton; one *s* two *d*. *Educ:* Royal Melbourne Technical Coll.; Univ. of Melbourne. Grad. RAAF Flying Sch., Point Cook, 1926; Citizen Air Force, 1927–37; Commercial Air Pilot, 1927–46. Founded Gliding Club of Vic., and Vic. Gliding Assoc., 1928; British Empire Glider Duration Record, 1931. Served War of 1939–45, RAAF; retd as Gp Captain, 1945 (AFC, AEA). Pres., No 2 Squadron RAAF Assoc. Councillor, Shire of Doncaster and Templestone, 1954–60; Pres. and Chief Magistrate, 1955–56. Member Legislative Council: for Southern Province, Vic., 1958–70; for Templestowe Province, 1970–76. Member, Statute Law Revision Cttee, 1963–64; Govt Rep. on Council of Monash Univ., 1967–71. Knighted for services in politics, civic affairs and defence, Victoria; Life Governor, Lady Nell Seeing Eye Dog School. Chairman of Directors: Ilford (Aust.) Pty Ltd, 1965–75; Cine Service Pty Ltd. Pres., Victorian Parly Former Members' Assoc; Pres., Baden Powell Guild, Victoria. FInstD. *Recreations:* photography, sports cars. *Address:* 22/330 Springvale Road, Donvale, Victoria 3111, Australia. *Clubs:* Royal Automobile, No 10 (London); Air Force (Vic.).

GARRETT, Richard Anthony, CBIM; Chairman, National Association of Boys' Clubs, since 1980; *b* 4 July 1918; 3rd *s* of Charles Victor Garrett and Blanche Michell; *m* 1946, Marie Louise Dalglish; one *s* two *d* (and one *d* decd). *Educ:* King's Sch., Worcester. MInstD; CBIM 1979. Served War, 1939–45 (despatches, 1945). Joined W.D. & H.O. Wills, 1936; Chm., ITL, retd 1979; Chm. and Man. Dir, John Player & Sons, 1968–71; Chm., Dataday Ltd, 1978–83; Director: HTV Gp plc (Vice-Chm., 1978–83); HTV Ltd; HTV West; Standard Commercial Tobacco Co. Inc., 1980–. Member: (Founder), Assoc. of Business Sponsorship of the Arts (Dep. Chm., Adv. Council); National Cttee for Electoral Reform. Chm., Bath Festival, 1986–; Trustee, Glyndebourne Arts Trust. Liveryman, Worshipful Co. of Tobacco Pipe Makers and Tobacco Blenders. *Recreations:* golf, gardening, music, opera, reading. *Address:* Marlwood Grange, Thornbury, Bristol BS12 2JB. *T:* Thornbury 412630. *Clubs:* Naval and Military, MCC, XL; Bristol and Clifton Golf; Clifton Rugby (Pres.); Clifton Cricket (Vice-Pres.).

GARRETT, Prof. Stephen Denis, FRS 1967; Professor of Mycology, 1971–73, now Professor Emeritus (Reader 1961–71), and Director of Sub-department of Mycology, 1952–73, University of Cambridge; Fellow of Magdalene College, Cambridge, since 1963; *b* 1 Nov. 1906; *s* of Stephen and Mary Garrett, Leiston, Suffolk; *m* 1934, Ruth Jane Perkins; three *d*. *Educ:* Eastbourne Coll.; Cambridge Univ.; Imperial Coll., London. Asst Plant Pathologist, Waite Agric. Res. Inst., Univ. of Adelaide, 1929–33; Research Student, Imperial Coll., 1934–35; Mycologist, Rothamsted Experimental Stn, 1936–48; Lectr, later Reader, Botany Sch., University of Cambridge, 1949–71. Hon. Member: British Mycological Soc., 1975; British Soc. for Plant Pathology, 1984. Hon. Fellow, Indian Acad. of Sciences, 1973. *Publications:* Root Disease Fungi, 1944; Biology of Root-infecting Fungi, 1956; Soil Fungi and Soil Fertility, 1963, 2nd edn 1981; Pathogenic Root-infecting Fungi, 1970. *Address:* 179 Hills Road, Cambridge CB2 2RN. *T:* Cambridge 247865.

GARRETT, Terence, CBE 1967; Deputy Chief Scientific Officer, Research and Technology Policy Division, Department of Trade and Industry, since 1982; *b* 27 Sept. 1929; *e s* of late Percy Herbert Garrett and Gladys Annie Garrett (*née* Budd); *m* 1960, Grace Elizabeth Bridgeman Braund, *yr d* of Rev. Basil Kelly Braund; two *s* three *d*. *Educ:* Alleyn's Sch.; Gonville and Caius Coll., Cambridge (Scholar; 1st Cl. Hons, Mathematics). DipMathStat. Instructor Lieut RN, 1952–55. Lecturer, Ewell County Technical Coll., 1955–56; Sen. Lectr, RMCS, Shrivenham, 1957–62; Counsellor (Scientific), British Embassy, Moscow, 1962–66 and 1970–74; Programmes Analysis Unit, Min. of Technology, 1967–70; Internat. Technological Collaboration Unit, Dept of Trade, 1974–76; Sec. to Bd of Governors and to Gen. Conf. of Internat. Atomic Energy Agency, Vienna, 1976–78; Counsellor (Science and Technology), Bonn, 1978–82. *Recreations:* squash, travel. *Address:* Lime Tree Farmhouse, Chilton, Didcot, Oxon OX11 0SW. *T:* Abingdon 834521.

GARRETT, Thomas John; Principal, Royal Belfast Academical Institution, since 1978; *b* 13 Sept. 1927; *s* of late Thomas John Garrett and of Violet Garrett; *m* 1958, Sheenah Agnew, *o d* of late Mr and Mrs G. Marshall, Drymen, Stirlingshire; one *d*. *Educ:* Royal Belfast Acad. Instn; QUB (BA); Heidelberg Univ. Asst Master: Royal Belfast Acad. Instn, 1951–54; Nottingham High Sch. for Boys, 1954–56; Sen. German Master, Campbell Coll., Belfast, 1956–73, Housemaster, 1968–73; Headmaster, Portora Royal Sch., Enniskillen, 1973–78. Mem., Broadcasting Council for N Ireland, 1982–84. *Publications:* Modern German Humour, 1969; Two Hundred Years at the Top—a dramatised history of Portora Royal School, 1977. *Recreations:* writing, hill-walking, ornithology. *Address:* Fairy Hill, 6 Osborne Gardens, Belfast BT9 6LE. *T:* Belfast 665635. *Club:* East India.

GARRETT, William Edward; MP (Lab) Wallsend since 1964; *b* 21 March 1920; *s* of John Garrett, coal miner, and Frances (*née* Barwise); *m* 1st, 1946, Beatrice Kelly (*d* 1978); one *s*; 2nd, 1980, Noel Stephanie Ann Johnson. *Educ:* Prudhoe Elementary Sch.; London Sch. of Economics. Commenced work in coal mines, 1934; served engineering apprenticeship, 1936–40; employed by ICI, 1946–64; Union Organiser at ICI, 1946–64; Mem. of AEU. Member: Prudhoe UDC, 1946–64; Northumberland County Council, 1955–64. Mem. of Labour Party, 1939–; Labour Candidate for Hexham 1953–55, Doncaster 1957–64. Member: Select Cttee on Agriculture, 1966–69; Expenditure Cttee, 1971–79; Council of Europe, 1979–; Sec., All-Party Group for Chem. Industry. Parliamentary Adviser, Machine Tools Trades Assoc. *Recreations:* gardening, walking, reading. *Address:* 84 Broomhill Road, Prudhoe-on-Tyne, Northumberland. *T:* Prudhoe 32580. *Club:* Prudhoe Working Men's.

GARRICK, Ronald, CBE 1986; FEng 1984; Managing Director and Chief Executive, Weir Group, since 1982; *b* 21 Aug. 1940; *s* of Thomas Garrick and Anne (*née* McKay); *m* 1965, Janet Elizabeth Taylor Lind; two *s* one *d*. *Educ:* Royal College of Science and Technology, Glasgow; Glasgow University (BSc MechEng, 1st cl. hons). FIMechE. Joined G. & J. Weir Ltd, 1962; Weir Pumps: Dir, Industrial Div., 1973; Dir Production Div., 1976; Managing Dir, 1981; Dir, Weir Group, 1981. Member: Scottish Council, CBI, 1982–; Gen. Convocation, Univ. of Strathclyde, 1985–; Restrictive Practices Court, 1986–. *Recreations:* golf, reading. *Address:* 3 Duart Drive, Newton Mearns, Glasgow G77 5DS. *T:* 041–639 3088. *Club:* Caledonian.

GARRINGTON, Rev. Elsie Dorothea C.; *see* Chamberlain-Garrington.

GARRIOCH, Sir (William) Henry, Kt 1978; Chief Justice, Mauritius, 1977–78, retired; *b* 4 May 1916; *s* of Alfred Garrioch and Jeanne Marie Madeleine Colin; *m* 1964, Jeanne Louise Marie-Thérèse Desvaux de Marigny. *Educ:* Royal Coll., Mauritius. Called to the Bar, Gray's Inn, 1952. Civil Service (clerical), Mauritius, 1936–48; law student, London, 1949–52; Dist Magistrate, Mauritius, 1955; Crown Counsel, 1958; Sen. Crown Counsel, 1960; Solicitor-Gen., 1964; Dir of Public Prosecutions, 1966; Puisne Judge, 1967; Sen. Puisne Judge, 1970; Actg Governor-Gen., 1977–78. *Recreations:* reading, chess, badminton. *Address:* Lees Street, Curepipe, Mauritius. *T:* 862708.

GARROD, Maj-Gen. John Martin Carruthers, OBE 1980; Chief of Staff to Commandant General Royal Marines, 1984–87; *b* 29 May 1935; *s* of Rev. William Francis Garrod and Isobel Agnes (*née* Carruthers); *m* 1963, Gillian Mary, *d* of late Lt-Col R. G. Parks-Smith, RM; two *d*. *Educ:* Sherborne School. Joined Royal Marines, 1953; served Malta, Cyprus, DS Officers' Training Wing, RM School of Music, Malaya, Borneo, 1955–66; Staff Coll., Camberley, 1967; HQ 17 Div., Malaya, 1968–69; HQ Farelf, Singapore, 1970–71; 40 Commando RM (Co. Comdr, Plymouth and N Ireland), 1972–73 (despatches); GSO2 Plans, Dept of CGRM, 1973–76; GSO1, HQ Commando Forces RM, 1976–78; CO 40 Commando RM, 1978–79 (OBE operational, NI); Col Ops/Plans, Dept of CGRM, 1980–82; Comdr 3 Commando Bde RM, 1983–84; ADC to the Queen, 1983–84. *Recreation:* portrait photography. *Address:* c/o Lloyds Bank, 5 The Square, Petersfield, Hants. *Club:* East India.

GARRY, Robert Campbell, OBE 1976; Regius Professor of Physiology, University of Glasgow, 1947–70, retired; *b* April 1900; *s* of Robert Garry and Mary Campbell; *m* 1928, Flora Macdonald, *d* of Archibald and Helen Campbell; one *s*. *Educ:* Glasgow Univ. MB, ChB with Hons, Glasgow Univ., 1922; Brunton Memorial Prize; DSc, Glasgow Univ., 1933; continued studies in Freiburg im B, Germany; University Coll., London; Medical Sch., Leeds; Asst and then Lectr, Institute of Physiology, Glasgow Univ.; Head of Physiology Dept, Rowett Research Institute, Aberdeen, 1933–35; Lectr on the Physiology of Nutrition, University of Aberdeen, 1933–35; Prof. of Physiology, University Coll., Dundee, The University of St Andrews, 1935–47; Member: MRC, 1955–59; Sci. Adv. Cttee on Med. Res. in Scotland, 1948–52, 1955–59; Physiol. Sub-Cttee of Flying Personnel Res. Cttee, 1951–75 (Chm., 1967–75); Bd of Management, Hill Farming Res. Orgn, 1963–72. Hon. Mem. Physiol. Soc., 1925; foundn Mem., Nutrition Soc., 1941, Pres., 1950–53, Hon. Mem., 1981. FRSE 1937; FRCPGlas 1948. *Publications:* Papers in scientific periodicals, dealing especially with gastrointestinal physiology and nutrition. *Recreations:* gardening, reading. *Address:* Laich Dyke, Dalginross, Comrie, Crieff, Perthshire PH6 2HB. *T:* Comrie 70474.

GARSIDE, Roger Ramsay; HM Diplomatic Service; Financial and Commercial Counsellor, Paris, since 1982; *b* 29 March 1938; *s* of Captain F. R. Garside and Mrs Peggie Garside; *m* 1969, Evelyne Madeleine Pierrette Guérin; three *d*. *Educ:* Eton; Clare Coll., Cambridge (BA EngLit, MA); Sloane Fellow in Management, Massachusetts Inst. of Technology. 2nd Lieut, 1/6 QEO Gurkha Rifles, 1958–59; entered HM Foreign Service, 1962; served, Rangoon, 1964–65; Mandarin Chinese Lang. Student, Hong Kong, 1965–67; Second Secretary, Peking, 1968–70; FCO, 1970–71, resigned 1971; World Bank, 1972–74; rejoined Foreign Service, 1975; served FCO, 1975; First Sec., Peking, 1976–79; on leave of absence, as Vis. Professor of East Asian Studies, US Naval Postgrad. Sch., Monterey, Calif, 1979–80; Dep. Head, Planning Staff, FCO, 1980–81; seconded, HM Treasury, 1981–82. *Publication:* Coming Alive: China after Mao, 1981. *Recreations:* writing, riding, offspring. *Address:* c/o Foreign and Commonwealth Office, SW1; c/o British Embassy, Paris. *T:* 266.91.42. *Club:* Cercle de l'Union Interalliée (Paris).

GARSON, Greer; Actress; *b* Northern Ireland, 29 Sept. 1908; *d* of George Garson and Nina Sophia Greer; *m* 1st, Edward A. Shelson (marr. diss.); 2nd, 1943, Richard Ney (marr. diss.); 3rd, 1949, Col E. E. Fogelson, Texas. *Educ:* London and Grenoble Univs. BA Hons London. Birmingham Repertory Theatre, 1932 and 1933; London Theatre debut, Whitehall, 1935; lead roles in 13 London plays; entered films in 1939; *films include:* Goodbye Mr Chips, Pride and Prejudice, When Ladies Meet, Blossoms in the Dust, Mrs Miniver (Academy Award), Random Harvest, Madame Curie, Mrs Parkington, Valley of Decision, That Forsyte Woman, Julius Caesar, The Law and the Lady, Her Twelve Men, Sunrise at Campobello (Golden Globe award), Strange Lady in Town, The Singing Nun, The Happiest Millionaire; *stage appearances include:* Auntie Mame, Tonight at 8.30, Captain Brassbound's Conversion. Appeared in pioneer British TV, on American TV. Hon. DHum, Rollins Coll., Florida, 1950; Hon. Dr in Communication Arts, Coll. of Santa Fe, 1970; Hon. DLitt Ulster, 1977; winner of many awards and medals; current interests include The Greer Garson Theater and Fogelson Library Center, Coll. of Santa Fe; Mem. Bd, Dallas Theater Center; adjunct prof. in drama, S.M.U. Univ., Dallas; Mem., State Commn on the arts in Texas and New Mexico; Mem. Nat. Cttee, St John's Coll., Santa Fe. With husband operates Forked Lightning Ranch, Pecos, New Mexico, also breeding and racing thoroughbred horses (stable includes Ack Ack, horse of the year, 1971). *Recreations:* nature study, music, golf, primitive art. *Address:* Republic Bank Building, Dallas, Texas 75201, USA.

GARSON, Cdre Robin William, CBE 1978; RN retd; Director of Leisure Services, London Borough of Hillingdon, since 1975; *b* 13 Nov. 1921; *s* of late Peter Garson and Ada Frances (*née* Newton); *m* 1946, Joy Ligertwood Taylor (*née* Hickman); one *s* one *d*. *Educ:* School of Oriental and African Studies. Japanese Interpreter. MBIM, AMINucE. Entered Royal Navy, 1937; served War of 1939–45, HM Ships: Resolution, Nigeria, Cyclops, and HM Submarines: Seawolf, H.33, Spark; subsequent principal appointments: In Command HM Submarines: Universal, Uther, Seraph, Saga, Sanguine, Springer, Thule, Astute, 1945–54; Chief Staff Officer Intelligence, Far East, 1966–68; Sen. Polaris UK Rep., Washington, 1969–71; Captain 1st Submarine Sqdn, 1971–73; Commodore, HMS Drake, 1973–75; ADC to the Queen, 1974. Adviser to AMA on Arts and Recreation, 1976; Adviser to Sports Council, 1985–; Mem., Library Adv. Council (England), 1977. *Recreations:* golf, ski-ing, tennis. *Address:* Ringwood, 44 Linksway, Northwood, Mddx HA6 2XB. *T:* Northwood 24380. *Clubs:* Army and Navy; Moor Park (Rickmansworth).

GARSTANG, Walter Lucian, BSc, MA; Headmaster of the Roan School, Greenwich, 1959–68, retired 1968; *b* 2 Sept. 1908; *o s* of late Walter Garstang, MA, DSc; *m* 1933, Barbara Mary, *d* of late Dr S. E. Denyer, CMG, MD; one *s* two *d*. (and one *s* decd). *Educ:* Oundle Sch.; Oxford (Scholar of Trinity Coll., 1927–31). Research chemist, The Gas Light and Coke Co., 1931–37; asst master, Oundle Sch., 1937–44; asst master, Merchant Taylors' Sch., 1944–46; senior science master, Maidstone Grammar Sch., 1946–48;

Headmaster, Owen's Sch., 1949–54; Headmaster, Loughborough Grammar Sch., 1955–58. *Address:* 21 Wells Close, Cheltenham GL51 5BX.

GARTHWAITE, Sir William, 2nd Bt, *cr* 1919; DSC 1941 and Bar, 1942; former Chairman, Sir William Garthwaite (Holdings) Ltd; *b* 3 Jan. 1906; *o s* of Sir William Garthwaite, 1st Bt and Francesca Margherita, *d* of James Parfett; *S* father 1956; *m* 1st, 1931, Hon. Dorothy Duveen (marr. diss. 1937) (*d* 1985), *d* of 1st Baron Duveen; 2nd, 1945, Patricia Leonard (marr. diss. 1952); one *s*; 3rd, 1957, Patricia Merriel, *d* of Sir Philip d'Ambrumenil; three *s* (one *d* decd). *Educ:* Bradfield Coll., Berks; Hertford Coll., Oxford. Lloyd's Underwriter and Insur. Broker at Lloyd's, 1926–. Farmer. Contested (C): Hemsworth Div. of W Riding of Yorks, 1931; Isle of Ely, 1935; E Div. of Wolverhampton, 1945; Pres., Royal Tunbridge Wells Cons. Assoc. Served War of 1939–45 as pilot, Fleet Air Arm (DSC and bar, despatches thrice, Air Crew Europe Star, Atlantic Star, Africa Star, 1939–45 Star, Defence Medal). Coronation Medal, 1953. *Recreations:* flying, ski-ing, golf and sailing. *Heir:* *s* William Mark Charles Garthwaite [*b* 4 Nov. 1946; *m* 1979, Mrs Victoria Lisette Hohler, *e d* of Gen. Sir Harry Tuzo, *qv*; one *s* two *d*]. *Address:* Matfield House, Matfield, Kent TN12 7JT. *T:* Brenchley 2454. *Clubs:* Portland, Naval, Royal Automobile, Royal Thames; Jockey (Paris).

GARTON, George Alan, PhD, DSc; FRSE 1966; FRS 1978; Hon. Research Associate, Rowett Research Institute, Bucksburn, Aberdeen, since 1983; *b* 4 June 1922; *o s* of late William Edgar Garton, DCM, and late Frances Mary Elizabeth Garton (*née* Atkinson), Scarborough, N Yorks; *m* 1951, Gladys Frances Davison; two *d*. *Educ:* Scarborough High Sch.; Univ. of Liverpool (BSc: (War Service) 1944, (Hons Biochem.) 1946; PhD 1949, DSc 1959). Experimental Asst, Chemical Inspection Dept, Min. of Supply, 1942–45; Johnston Research and Teaching Fellow, Dept of Biochem., Univ. of Liverpool, 1949–50; Biochemist, Rowett Research Inst., Bucksburn, 1950, Dep. Dir 1968–83, Head of Lipid Biochem. Dept, 1963–83. Hon. Research Associate, Univ. of Aberdeen, 1966–; Sen. Foreign Fellow of Nat. Science Foundn (USA), and Vis. Prof. of Biochem., Univ. of N Carolina, 1967. Chm., British Nat. Cttee for Nutritional and Food Sciences, 1982–; Pres., Internat. Confs on Biochem. Lipids, 1982–. SBStJ 1985. *Publications:* papers, mostly on aspects of lipid biochemistry, in scientific jls. *Recreations:* gardening, golf, foreign travel. *Address:* Ellerburn, 1 St Devenick Crescent, Cults, Aberdeen AB1 9LL. *T:* Aberdeen 867012. *Clubs:* Farmers'; Deeside Golf (Aberdeen).

GARTON, Rev. John Henry; Principal of Ripon College, Cuddesdon, since 1986; *b* 3 Oct. 1941; *s* of Henry and Dorothy Garton; *m* 1969, Pauline (*née* George); two *s*. *Educ:* RMA Sandhurst; Worcester Coll., Oxford (MA, DipTh); Cuddesdon Coll., Oxford. Commissioned in Royal Tank Regt, 1962. Ordained, 1969; CF, 1969–73; Lectr, Lincoln Theol Coll., 1973–78; Rector of Coventry East Team Ministry, 1978–86. *Address:* The Old Vicarage, High Street, Cuddesdon, Oxford OX9 9HP. *T:* Wheatley 4368.

GARTON, John Leslie, CBE 1974 (MBE (mil.) 1946); President, Henley Royal Regatta, since 1978; *b* 1 April 1916; *er s* of late C. Leslie Garton and Madeline Laurence; *m* 1939, Elizabeth Frances, *d* of late Sir Walter Erskine Crum, OBE; one *s* (and two *s* decd). *Educ:* Eton; Magdalen Coll., Oxford (MA). Commissioned TA, Royal Berkshire Regt, 1938. Served War, in France, 1940; psc 1943; Gen. Staff Ops Br., First Canadian Army HQ, in Europe, 1944–46; transf. to RARO, Scots Guards, 1951. Chm., Coca-Cola Bottling Co. (Oxford) Ltd, 1951–65, Coca-Cola Western Bottlers Ltd, 1966–71. Henley Royal Regatta: Steward, 1960; Mem. Cttee of Management, 1961–77; Chm., 1966–77. Amateur Rowing Association: Exec. Cttee and Council, 1948–77; Pres., 1969–77; Hon. Life Vice-Pres., 1978. Hon. Sec. and Treas., OUBC Trust Fund, 1959–69; Mem., Finance and Gen. Purposes Cttee, British Olympic Assoc., 1969–77; Thames Conservator, 1970–74; Chm., World Rowing Championships, 1975; Pres., Leander Club, 1980–83. Liveryman, Grocers' Company, 1947–. High Sheriff, Bucks, 1977. *Recreations:* supporting the sport of rowing (rowed in Eton VIII, 1934, 1935, Captain of the Boats, 1935; rowed in the Boat Race for Oxford, 1938, 1939, Pres. OUBC, 1939), shooting (particularly deer-stalking), fishing. *Address:* Mill Green House, Church Street, Wargrave, Berkshire RG10 8EP. *T:* Wargrave 2944. *Club:* Leander (elected 1936, Life Mem., 1953, Cttee, 1956, Chm. Executive, 1958–59).

GARTON, Prof. William Reginald Stephen, FRS 1969; Professor of Spectroscopy, University of London, Imperial College, 1964–79, now Professor Emeritus; Associate Head, 1970–79, and Senior Research Fellow, since 1979, Department of Physics, Imperial College; *b* Chelsea, SW3, 7 March 1912; *s* of William and Gertrude Emma Caroline Garton; *m* 1st, 1940, Margarita Fraser Callingham (marr. diss. 1976); four *d*; 2nd, 1976, Barbara Lloyd (*née* Jones). *Educ:* Sloane Sch., SW10; Chelsea Polytechnic, SW3; Imperial Coll., (Hon. Fellow 1983). BSc, ARCS 1936; DSc 1958. Demonstrator in Physics, Imperial Coll., 1936–39. Served in RAF, 1939–45. Imperial Coll.: Lectr in Physics, 1946–54; Sen. Lectr, 1954–57; Reader, 1957–64. Associate, Harvard Coll. Observatory, 1963–. W. F. Meggers Award, 1976, Fellow, 1979, Optical Soc. of America. Hon. DSc York Univ., Toronto, 1972. *Publications:* contrib. on Spectroscopy in Advances in Atomic and Molecular Physics (ed D. R. Bates), 1966 (New York); numerous papers on Spectroscopy and Atomic Physics. *Recreations:* speliology, Oriental history. *Address:* Blackett Laboratory, Imperial College, SW7. *T:* 01–589 5111; Chart House, Great Chart, Ashford, Kent TN23 3AP. *T:* Ashford 21657; 9 callé Tico Medina, Mojacar (Almeria), Spain.

GARTRELL, Rt. Rev. Frederick Roy; *b* 27 March 1914; *s* of William Frederick Gartrell and Lily Martha Keeble; *m* 1940, Grace Elizabeth Wood; three *s* one *d*. *Educ:* McMaster Univ. (BA); Wycliffe Coll. (LTh, BD). Deacon, 1938; Priest, 1939. Curate, St James the Apostle, Montreal, 1938; Rector, All Saints', Noranda, PQ, 1940; Senior Asst, St Paul's, Bloor Street, Toronto, 1944; Rector, St George's, Winnipeg, Manitoba, 1945; Archdeacon of Winnipeg, 1957; Rector, Christ Church Cathedral, Ottawa, and Dean of Ottawa, 1962–70; Bishop of British Columbia, 1970–80. DD (*hc*): Wycliffe Coll., Toronto, 1962; St John's Coll., Winnipeg, 1965. *Recreation:* golf. *Address:* 1794 Barrie, Victoria, BC V8N 2W7, Canada.

GARVAGH, 5th Baron *cr* 1818; **Alexander Leopold Ivor George Canning;** Accredited Representative, Trade and Industry, The Cayman Islands, 1981; *b* 6 Oct. 1920; *s* of 4th Baron and Gladys Dora May (*d* 1982), *d* of William Bayley Parker; *S* father 1956; *m* 1st, 1947, Christine Edith (marr. diss. 1974), *d* of Jack Cooper; one *s* two *d*; 2nd, 1974, Cynthia Valerie Mary, *d* of Eric E. F. Pretty, CMG, Kingswood, Surrey. *Educ:* Eton; Christ Church, Oxford. Commissioned Corps of Guides Cavalry, Indian Army, 1940; served Burma (despatches). Chm., Kennedy Trust Homes; Pres., Disaster Relief Assoc. Mem. Court, Painter Stainers Co. *Publications:* contrib. to The Manufacturing Optician, 1949. *Recreations:* travel, motoring, and motor sport; writing articles, short stories, etc. *Heir:* *s* Hon. Spencer George Stratford de Redcliffe Canning [*b* 12 Feb. 1953; *m* 1979, Julia Margery Morison Bye, *er d* of Col F. C. E. Bye, Twickenham; one *d*]. *Address:* Casa Canning, Costera del Mar, Moraira, Alicante, Spain. *Clubs:* Royal Over-Seas League, Steering Wheel.

GARVEY, Sir Ronald Herbert, KCMG 1950 (CMG 1947); KCVO 1953; MBE 1941; *b* 4 July 1903; *s* of Rev. H. R. Garvey, MA, and Alice M. Lofthouse; *m* 1934, Patricia Dorothy Edge, *d* of late Dr V. W. T. McGusty, CMG, OBE; one *s* three *d*. *Educ:* Trent Coll.; Emmanuel Coll., Cambridge. MA 1930; appointed to Colonial Service, 1926, and attached to Western Pacific High Commission, Suva, Fiji; District Officer British Solomon Islands, 1927–32; Asst Sec. Western Pacific High Commission, 1932–40; acted on various occasions as Res. Comr, Gilbert and Ellice Islands Colony; Asst to Res. Comr New Hebrides Condominium, 1940–41; acted as British Res. Comr, New Hebrides, on various occasions; Nyasaland Protectorate, District Officer, 1942–44; Administrator, St Vincent, Windward Islands, BWI, 1944–48; acted as Governor of Windward Is, 1946, 1948; Governor and C-in-C, British Honduras, 1948–52; Governor and C-in-C, Fiji, Governor, Pitcairn Is, Consul-Gen. for Western Pacific, and Senior Commissioner for UK on South Pacific Commission, 1952–58; Ambassador Plenipotentiary for Tonga, 1958; Lieutenant-Governor of the Isle of Man, 1959–66; Sec., Soil Assoc., 1967–71. Dir, Garvey (London) SA Ltd, 1966. Hon. Mem., E Anglia Tourist Bd. KStJ. *Publication:* Gentleman Pauper, 1984. *Recreations:* golf, deep-sea fishing, gardening. *Address:* The Priory, Wrentham, Beccles, Suffolk NR34 7LR.

GARVEY, Sir Terence Willcocks, KCMG 1969 (CMG 1955); HM Diplomatic Service, retired; *b* Dublin, 7 Dec. 1915; *s* of Francis Willcocks Garvey and Ethel Margaret Ray; *m* 1st, 1941, Barbara Hales Tomlinson (marr. diss.); two *s* one *d*; 2nd, 1957, Rosemary, *d* of late Dr Harold Pritchard. *Educ:* Felsted; University Coll., Oxford (Scholar). BA Oxon (1st Class Philosophy, Politics and Economics), 1938; Laming Fellow of The Queen's Coll., Oxford, 1938. Entered Foreign (subsequently Diplomatic) Service, 1938; has served in USA, Chile, Germany, Egypt and at Foreign Office; Counsellor, HM Embassy, Belgrade, 1958–62; HM Chargé d'Affaires, Peking, 1962–65 and Ambassador to Mongolia, 1963–65; Asst Under-Sec. of State, Foreign Office, 1965–68; Ambassador to Yugoslavia, 1968–71; High Comr in India, 1971–73; Ambassador to the USSR, 1973–75. Senior Associate Mem., St Antony's Coll., Oxford, 1976–. *Publication:* Bones of Contention, 1978. *Recreation:* fishing. *Address:* 11A Stonefield Street, N1 0HW. *Club:* Travellers'.

GARVEY, Thomas, (Tom); Director, Industrial Affairs Directorate, European Commission, since 1984; *b* 27 May 1936; *s* of Thomas and Brigid Garvey; *m* 1961, Ellen Devine; two *s* two *d*. *Educ:* University Coll., Dublin (MA Econ). Fellow, Management Inst. Ireland. Various marketing and internal trade appts, 1958–69; Chief Exec., Irish Export Bd, 1969–76; EEC Delegate, Nigeria, 1977–80; Chief Exec., Air Post (Irish Postal Service), 1980–84; Dir, Internal Market and Ind. Affairs, EEC Commn, Brussels, 1984–. *Publications:* various, in industrial, trade and academic jls. *Recreations:* golf, music. *Address:* 20 Rue de la Cambre, Bte 23, 1200 Brussels, Belgium. *Club:* United Services (Dublin).

GARVIN, Clifton Canter, Jr; Chairman of the Board and Chief Executive Officer, Exxon Corporation, 1975–86; *b* 22 Dec. 1921; *s* of Clifton C. Garvin, Sr, and Esther Ames; *m* 1943, Thelma Volland; one *s* three *d*. *Educ:* Virginia Polytechnic Inst. and State Univ. MS (ChemEng) 1947. Exxon: Process Engr, subseq. Refining Operating Supt, Baton Rouge, Louisiana Refinery, 1947–59; Asst Gen. Manager, Supply Dept, Exxon Corp., 1959–60; Gen. Manager, Supply Dept, Esso Eastern, 1960–61; Manager, Production, Supply & Distribution Dept, Exxon Co., USA, 1961–62, subseq. Vice-Pres., Central Region, 1963–64; Exec. Asst to Pres. and Chm., Exxon Corp., NY, 1964–65; Pres., Exxon Chemical (US), subseq. Pres. Exxon Chemical (Internat.), 1965–68; Dir, subseq. Exec. Vice-Pres., subseq. Pres., Exxon Corp., 1968–75. Mem., American Petroleum Inst.; Director: Citicorp and Citibank, PepsiCo, Inc.; Johnson & Johnson; J. C. Penney Co., Inc.; TRW Inc.; Director: Council for Financial Aid to Educn, Inc.; United Way of Tri-State; Member: ACS, Amer. Inst. of Chem. Engrs; Business Cttee for the Arts, Inc.; Business Roundtable; Council on Foreign Relns; Nat. Petroleum Council; Soc. of Chem. Ind.; Business Council; Vice-Chm., Bd of Managers, Sloan Kettering Inst. for Cancer Res.; Vice-Pres., Vanderbilt Univ. Bd of Trust; Sen. Mem., The Conference Bd; Trustee, Cttee for Econ. Develt; Vice-Chm., Bd of Governors, United Way of America; Nat. Associate, White Burkett Miller Center of Public Affairs, Univ. of Virginia. *Recreations:* golf, bird watching. *Address:* 1251 Avenue of the Americas, New York, NY 10020–1198, USA. *T:* 333–1000.

GARY, Lesley; *see* Blanch, L.

GASCH, Pauline Diana, (Mrs F. O. Gasch); *see* Baynes, P. D.

GASCOIGNE, Bamber, FRSL; author, broadcaster and publisher; *b* 24 Jan. 1935; *s* of Derick Gascoigne and Midi (*née* O'Neill); *m* 1965, Christina Ditchburn. *Educ:* Eton (Scholar); Magdalene Coll., Cambridge (Scholar). Commonwealth Fund Fellow, Yale, 1958–59. Theatre Critic, Spectator, 1961–63, and Observer, 1963–64; Co-editor, Theatre Notebook, 1968–74. Founded Saint Helena Press, 1977; Chm., Ackermann Publishing, 1981–85. Theatre: Share My Lettuce, London, 1957–58; Leda Had a Little Swan, New York, 1968; The Feydeau Farce Festival of Nineteen Nine, Greenwich, 1972; Big in Brazil, Old Vic, 1984. Television: presenter of: University Challenge, (weekly) 1962–; Cinema, 1964; (also author) The Christians, 1977; author of: The Four Freedoms, 1962; Dig This Rhubarb, 1963; The Auction Game, 1968. FRSL 1976. *Publications:* Twentieth Century Drama, 1962; World Theatre, 1968; The Great Moghuls (with photographs by Christina Gascoigne) 1971; Murgatreud's Empire, 1972; The Heyday, 1973; The Treasures and Dynasties of China (with photographs by Christina Gascoigne) 1973; Ticker Khan, 1974; The Christians (with photographs by Christina Gascoigne) 1977; Images of Richmond, 1978; Images of Twickenham, 1981; (illus. by Christina Gascoigne): Why the Rope went Tight, 1981; Fearless Freddy's Magic Wish, 1982; Fearless Freddy's Sunken Treasure, 1982; Quest for the Golden Hare, 1983; Cod Streuth, 1986; How to Identify Prints, 1986. *Address:* Saint Helena Terrace, Richmond, Surrey TW9 1NR.

GASCOIGNE, Maj.-Gen. Sir Julian (Alvery), KCMG 1962; KCVO 1953; CB 1949; DSO 1943; DL; *b* 25 Oct. 1903; *e s* of late Brig.-Gen. Sir Frederick Gascoigne, KCVO, CMG, DSO, and Lady Gascoigne, Ashtead Lodge, Ashtead, Surrey; *m* 1928, Joyce Alfreda (*d* 1981), *d* of late Robert Lydston Newman and Mrs Newman; one *s* one *d*. *Educ:* Eton; Sandhurst. 2nd Lieut Grenadier Guards, 1923; Staff Coll., Camberley, 1938–39; served War of 1939–45, commanding 1st Bn Grenadier Guards, 1941–42; commanding 201 Guards Brigade, 1942–43; North Africa and Italy, 1943 (wounded). Imperial Defence Coll., 1946; Dep. Comdr British Jt Services Mission (Army Staff), Washington, 1947–49. GOC London District and Maj.-Gen. commanding Household Brigade, 1950–53; retired pay, 1953; Mem. of Stock Exchange and Partner in Grieveson Grant & Co., 1955–59; Governor and C-in-C Bermuda, 1959–64; Col Commandant, Hon. Artillery Co., 1954–59. Patron, Union Jack Services Clubs, 1977 (Vice-Pres., 1955–64; Pres., 1964–76); a Comr of the Royal Hospital, Chelsea, 1958–59; Chm. Devon and Cornwall Cttee, The National Trust, 1965–75. JP 1966, DL Devon, 1966. KStJ, 1959. *Address:* Sanders, Stoke Fleming, Dartmouth, S Devon. *Club:* Royal Bermuda Yacht.

GASCOIGNE, Hon. Stanley, CMG 1976; OBE 1972; Secretary to the Cabinet, Bermuda, 1972–76; Member, Senate, 1976–85; *b* 11 Dec. 1914; *s* of George William Gascoigne and Hilda Elizabeth Gascoigne; *m* 1st, 1941, Sybil Wellspring Outerbridge (*d* 1980); 2nd, 1980, Sandra Alison Lee; two *s*. *Educ:* Mt Allison Univ., Canada (BA 1937): London Univ., England (DipEd 1938): Boston Univ., USA (MEd 1951). Teacher, 1939–51; Inspector of Schools, 1951–59; Director, Marine and Ports Authority, 1959–69;

Permanent Sec., Education, 1969–72. Exec. Dir, Inst. of Chartered Accountants of Bermuda, 1976–. *Recreation*: ornithology. *Address*: Alcyone, Shelly Bay, Hamilton Parish, Bermuda. *T*: 3–1304. *Clubs*: Royal Bermuda Yacht, Royal Hamilton Amateur Dinghy (Bermuda).

GASH, Prof. Norman, FBA 1963; FRSL 1973; FRSE 1977; FRHistS; Professor of History, St Salvator's College, University of St Andrews, 1955–80, now Emeritus; *b* 16 Jan. 1912; *s* of Frederick and Kate Gash; *m* 1935, Ivy Dorothy Whitehorn; two *d*. *Educ*: Reading Sch.; St John's Coll., Oxford. Scholar, St John's Coll.; 1st cl. Hons Mod. Hist., 1933; BLitt, 1934; MA 1938. FRHistS 1953. Temp. Lectr in Modern European History, Edinburgh, 1935–36; Asst Lectr in Modern History, University Coll., London, 1936–40. Served War, 1940–46: Intelligence Corps; Capt. 1942; Major (Gen. Staff), 1945. Lectr in Modern British and American History, St Salvator's Coll., University of St Andrews, 1946–53; Prof. of Modern History, University of Leeds, 1953–55; Vice-Principal, 1967–71, Dean of Faculty of Arts, 1978–80, St Andrews Univ. Hinkley Prof. of English History, Johns Hopkins Univ., 1962; Ford's Lectr in English History, Oxford Univ., 1963–64; Sir John Neale Lectr in English Hist., UCL, 1981. Vice-Pres., Hist. Assoc. of Scotland, 1963–64. Hon. DLitt: Strathclyde, 1984; St Andrews, 1985. *Publications*: Politics in the Age of Peel, 1953; Mr Secretary Peel, 1961; The Age of Peel, 1968; Reaction and Reconstruction in English Politics, 1832–1852, 1966; Sir Robert Peel, 1972; Peel, 1976; (jtly) The Conservatives: a history from their origins to 1965, 1978; Aristocracy and People: England 1815–1865, 1979; Lord Liverpool, 1984; Pillars of Government, 1986; articles and reviews in Eng. Hist. Review, Trans. Royal Historical Society, and other learned jls. *Recreations*: gardening, swimming. *Address*: Old Gatehouse, Portway, Langport, Som. *T*: Langport 250334.

GASK, Daphne Irvine Prideaux, (Mrs John Gask), OBE 1976; JP; Member, Inner London Commission of the Peace, since 1982; *b* 25 July 1920; *d* of Roger Prideaux Selby and Elizabeth May (*née* Stirling); *m* 1945, John Gask, MA, BM, BCh; one *s* one *d*. *Educ*: St Trinnean's, Edinburgh; Tolmers Park, Herts; Collège Brillantmont, Lausanne, Switzerland. BA Open Univ., 1979. Member: Shropshire Probation and After-Care Cttee, 1960–80 (Chm., 1978–80); Exec. Cttee, Central Council of Probation and After-Care Cttees, 1964–80 (Vice-Chm., 1977–80); Royal Commn on Criminal Procedure, 1978–80; Council, Magistrates Assoc., 1968–80 (Mem. Exec. Cttee, 1976–80); Sports Council Adv. Gp, 1978–80; NACRO, 1982–; Asst Sec., L'Association Internationale des Magistrats de la Jeunesse et de la Famille, 1979– (Mem. Exec. Bd). Served on Salop CC, 1965–77; Chm., Leisure Activities Cttee, 1974–77. Mem., W Midland Reg. Sports Council (Vice-Chm., 1970–77). JP Salop, 1952. *Recreations*: tennis, skiing, photography. *Address*: 5 The Old School House, Garrett Street, Cawsand, near Torpoint, Cornwall PL10 1PD. *T*: Plymouth 822136; Flat 5, 92 Westbourne Terrace, W2.

GASKELL, (John) Philip (Wellesley), MA, PhD, LittD; Fellow of Trinity College, Cambridge, since 1967 (Librarian, 1967–86; Tutor, 1973–83); Part-time Professor of Literature, California Institute of Technology, since 1983; *b* 6 Jan. 1926; *s* of John Wellesley Gaskell and Olive Elizabeth, *d* of Philip B. Baker; *m* 1st, 1948, Margaret (marr. diss.), *d* of late H. S. Bennett, FBA, and Joan Bennett; two *s* one *d*; 2nd, 1984, Annette Ursula Beighton. *Educ*: Dragon Sch., Oxford; Oundle Sch.; King's Coll., Cambridge. MA, PhD 1956, LittD, 1980. Served War, 1943–47, Lance-Bdr RA: BLA, 1944–45; Radio SEAC, 1946–47. Fellow of King's Coll., Cambridge, 1953–60, Dean, 1954–56, Tutor, 1956–58; Head of English Dept, and Librarian, Oundle Sch., 1960–62; Keeper of Special Collections, Glasgow Univ. Library, 1962–66; Warden of Maclay Hall, 1962–64, of Wolfson Hall, 1964–66, Glasgow Univ.; Sandars Reader in Bibliography, Cambridge Univ., 1978–79. Editor, The Book Collector, 1952–54. *Publications*: The First Editions of William Mason, 1951; John Baskerville, a bibliography, 1959, rev. edn 1973; Caught!, 1960; A Bibliography of the Foulis Press, 1964, rev. edn 1986; Morvern Transformed, 1968, rev. edn 1980; (with R. Robson) The Library of Trinity College, Cambridge, 1971; A New Introduction to Bibliography, 1972, rev. edns 1974, 1979, 1985; From Writer to Reader, 1978; Trinity College Library, the first 150 years, 1980; ed and trans (with P. Bradford) The Orthotypographia of Hieronymus Hornschuch, 1972; contrib. The Library, Jl Printing Historical Soc., etc. *Address*: Trinity College, Cambridge CB2 1TQ.

GASKILL, William; freelance stage director; *b* 24 June 1930; *s* of Joseph Linnaeus Gaskill and Maggie Simpson. *Educ*: Salt High Sch., Shipley; Hertford Coll., Oxford. Asst Artistic Dir, English Stage Co., 1957–59; freelance Dir with Royal Shakespeare Co., 1961–62; Assoc. Dir, National Theatre, 1963–65, and 1979; Artistic Director, English Stage Company, 1965–72, Mem. Council, 1978–; Dir, Joint Stock Theatre Gp, 1973. *Address*: 124A Leighton Road, NW5.

GASKIN, Catherine; author; *b* Co. Louth, Eire, 2 April 1929; *m* 1955, Sol Cornberg. *Educ*: Holy Cross Coll., Sydney, Australia. Brought up in Australia; lived in London, 1948–55, New York, 1955–65, Virgin Islands, 1965–67, Ireland, 1967–81. *Publications*: This Other Eden, 1946; With Every Year, 1947; Dust In Sunlight, 1950; All Else Is Folly, 1951; Daughter of the House, 1952; Sara Dane, 1955; Blake's Reach, 1958; Corporation Wife, 1960; I Know My Love, 1962; The Tilsit Inheritance, 1963; The File on Devlin, 1965; Edge of Glass, 1967; Fiona, 1970; A Falcon for a Queen, 1972; The Property of a Gentleman, 1974; The Lynmara Legacy, 1975; The Summer of the Spanish Woman, 1977; Family Affairs, 1980; Promises, 1982; The Ambassador's Women, 1985. *Recreations*: music, reading. *Address*: White Rigg, East Ballaterson, Maughold, Isle of Man.

GASKIN, Prof. Maxwell, DFC 1944 (and Bar 1945); Jaffrey Professor of Political Economy, Aberdeen University, 1965–85, now Professor Emeritus; *b* 18 Nov. 1921; *s* of late Albert and Beatrice Gaskin; *m* 1952, Brenda Patricia, *yr d* of late Rev. William D. Stewart; one *s* three *d*. *Educ*: Quarry Bank Sch., Liverpool; Liverpool Univ. (MA). Lever Bros Ltd, 1939–41. Served War, RAF Bomber Comd, 1941–46. Economist, Raw Cotton Commn, 1949–50; Asst Lectr, Liverpool Univ., 1950–51; Lectr and Sen. Lectr, Glasgow Univ., 1951–65; Visiting Sen. Lectr, Nairobi Univ., 1964–65. Member, Committee of Inquiry: into Bank Interest Rates (N Ire.), 1965–66; into Trawler Safety, 1967–68; Mem. and Chm., Bd of Management for Foresterhill and Associated Hosps, 1971–74; Independent Member: Scottish Agricl Wages Bd, 1972–; EDC for Civil Engineering, 1978–84; Chm., Industry Strategy Cttee for Scotland (Building and Civil Engrg EDCs), 1974–76. Director: Offshore Med. Support Ltd, 1978–85; Aberdeen Univ. Research & Industrial Services, 1981–85. President: Section F, British Assoc., 1978–79; Scottish Economic Soc., 1981–84. *Publications*: The Scottish Banks, 1965; (co-author and ed) North East Scotland: a survey of its development potential, 1969; (jtly) The Economic Impact of North Sea oil on Scotland, 1978; (ed) The Political Economy of Tolerable Survival, 1981; articles in economic and banking jls; reports on the international coal trade. *Recreations*: music and country life. *Address*: Westfield, Ancrum, Roxburghshire TD8 6XA. *T*: Ancrum 237. *Club*: Royal Commonwealth Society.

GASS, Prof. Ian Graham, PhD, DSc; FRS 1983; Professor of Earth Sciences and Head of Discipline, Open University, 1969–82, Personal Chair since 1982; *b* 20 March 1926; *s* of John George and Lillian Robinson Gass; *m* 1955, Florence Mary Pearce; one *s* one *d*. *Educ*: Royal Grammar Sch., Newcastle upon Tyne; Almondbury Grammar Sch.; Leeds Univ.

(BSc 1952, MSc 1955, PhD 1960, DSc 1972). Armed Forces, 1944–48. Undergrad., 1948–52; Geologist: Sudan Geol Survey, 1952–55; Cyprus Geol Survey, 1955–60; Asst Lectr, Leicester Univ., 1960–61; Lectr, then Sen. Lectr, Leeds Univ., 1961–69. Mem., NERC, 1985–. A Vice-Pres., Royal Soc., 1985–. Led Royal Soc. Expedn to Tristan da Cunha, 1962. Prestwich Medal, Geol Soc., 1979. *Publications*: (ed with T. N. Clifford) African Magmatism and Tectonics, 1970; (ed with P. J. Smith and R. C. L. Wilson) Understanding the Earth, 1971, 2nd edn 1972; articles in scientific jls. *Recreations*: bridge, hill-walking, geology. *Address*: 12 Greenacres, Bedford MK41 9AJ. *T*: Bedford 52712.

GASSMAN, Lewis, JP; a Recorder of the Crown Court, 1972–83; *b* 28 Oct. 1910; 2nd *s* of late Isaac Gassman and Dora Gassman; *m* 1940, Betty Henrietta, *o c* of late H. Jerrold and Mrs A. F. Annenberg; one *d*. Admitted Solicitor, 1933. Borough of Barnes: Councillor and Chm. of Cttees, 1933–41. Contested (Lab): Richmond, Surrey, 1935; Hastings, 1945. War of 1939–45: Army service, Capt. RAOC. JP Surrey, 1948, also SW London; Chm., Mortlake Magistrates, 1953–56 and 1961–71. Consultant in law firm of Kershaw, Gassman & Matthews. A Dep. Chm. of Surrey Quarter Sessions, 1968–71; Chm. of Magistrates, Richmond-upon-Thames, 1971–74. *Recreations*: music, painting, walking. *Address*: 21 Castelnau, Barnes, SW13 9RP. *T*: 01–748 7172. *Club*: Reform.

GASSON, John Gustav Haycraft; Secretary of the Law Commission, since 1982; *b* 2 Aug. 1931; *s* of late Dr S. G. H. Gasson and of Mrs S. G. H. Gasson; *m* 1964, Lesley, *d* of L. L. Thomas, Nyamandhlovu, Zimbabwe; two *s* one *d*. *Educ*: Diocesan Coll., Rondebosch, Cape Town; Cape Town Univ. (BA); Pembroke Coll., Oxford (Rhodes Schol. Rhodesia 1953; MA, BCL). Called to the Bar, Gray's Inn, 1957; Advocate of High Court of S Rhodesia, 1959; Lord Chancellor's Dept, 1964. *Recreations*: cycling, gardening. *Address*: 39 Lawn Crescent, Kew, Surrey TW9 3NS. *Club*: Bulawayo (Zimbabwe).

GASTON, John, CBE 1984; FIEE; Chairman, Northern Ireland Electricity Service, 1980–85; *b* 18 July 1925; *s* of Hill Gaston and Elizabeth (*née* McConnell); *m* 1951, Elizabeth Gordon; two *s*. *Educ*: Ballymena Acad.; QUB (BSc Elec. Eng, BScEcon). FIEE 1970. BICC Ltd, 1946–48; Anglo-Portuguese Telephone Co., 1948–49; Electricity Board, Northern Ireland: various positions, 1949–64; Distribution Engr, 1964–68; Asst Chief Engr, 1968–73; NI Electricity Service: Commercial Dir, 1973–77; Dep. Chm., 1977–80. FRSA. *Recreations*: gardening, walking, music. *Address*: 11 Larch Hill Avenue, Craigavad, Holywood, Co. Down BT18 0JW. *T*: Holywood 6453.

GATEHOUSE, Graham Gould; Director of Social Services, Surrey County Council, since 1981; *b* 17 July 1935; *s* of G. and G. M. Gatehouse; *m* 1960, Gillian M. Newell; two *s* one *d*. *Educ*: Crewkerne Sch., Somerset; Exeter Univ., Devon (DSA); London School of Economics (Dip. Mental Health). Served Royal Artillery, 1954–56. Somerset County Council, 1957–67; Worcestershire CC, 1967–70; Norfolk CC, 1970–73; West Sussex CC, 1973–81. *Recreations*: Rugby football, cricket, theatre. *Address*: Flat 1, 28 St Mary's Road, Long Ditton, Surrey. *Club*: Royal Automobile.

GATEHOUSE, Hon. Sir Robert Alexander, Kt 1985; **Hon. Mr Justice Gatehouse;** a Judge of the High Court, Queen's Bench Division, since 1985; *b* 30 Jan. 1924; *s* of late Major-Gen. A. H. Gatehouse, DSO, MC; *m* 1st, 1951, Henrietta Swann; 2nd, 1966, Pamela Fawcett. *Educ*: Wellington Coll.; Trinity Hall, Cambridge. Served War of 1939–45: commissioned into Royal Dragoons; NW Europe. Called to the Bar, Lincoln's Inn, 1950; Bencher, 1977; QC 1969. Governor, Wellington Coll., 1970–. *Recreation*: golf. *Address*: Royal Courts of Justice, Strand, WC2.

GATES, Emeritus Prof. Ronald Cecil, AO 1978; FASSA; Vice-Chancellor, University of New England, 1977–85; *b* 8 Jan. 1923; *s* of Earle Nelson Gates and Elsie Edith (*née* Tucker); *m* 1953, Barbara Mann; one *s* two *d* (and one *s* decd). *Educ*: East Launceston State Sch., Tas; Launceston C of E Grammar Sch., Tas; Univ. of Tas (BCom Econs and Commercial Law); Oxford Univ. (MA PPE). FASSA 1968. Served War, 1942–45: Private, AIF. Clerk, Aust. Taxation Office, Hobart, 1941–42; Rhodes Scholar (Tas), Oxford, 1946–48; Historian, Aust. Taxation Office, Canberra, 1949–52; Univ. of Sydney: Sen. Lectr in Econs, 1952–64; Associate Prof., 1964–65; Rockefeller Fellow in Social Sciences, 1955; Carnegie Travel Grant, 1960; Prof. of Econs, Univ. of Qld, 1966–77 (Pres., Professorial Bd, 1975–77). Pres., Econ. Soc. of Australia and NZ, 1969–72. Chairman: statutory Consumer Affairs Council of Qld, 1971–73; Aust. Inst. of Urban Studies, 1975–77. Comr, Commonwealth Commn of Inquiry into Poverty, 1973–77. Chairman: Aust. Nat. Commn for Unesco, 1981–83 (Vice-Chm., 1979); Adv. Council for Inter-govt Relations, 1979–85; Internat. Relations Cttee, Cttee of Australian Vice-Chancellors, 1981–84; Nat. Local Govt Industry Trng Cttee, 1983–. Hon. FRAPI 1976; Hon. Fellow, Aust. Inst. of Urban Studies, 1979. Hon. DEcon Qld, 1978. *Publications*: (with H. R. Edwards and N. T. Drane) Survey of Consumer Finances, Sydney 1963–65: Vol. 2, 1965; Vols 1, 3 and 4, 1966; Vols 5, 6 and 7, 1967; (jtly) The Price of Land, 1971; (jtly) New Cities for Australia, 1972; (jtly) Land for the Cities, 1973; (with P. A. Cassidy) Simulation, Uncertainty and Public Investment Analysis, 1977; chapters in books and articles in learned jls. *Recreations*: music, beef cattle. *Address*: Wangarang, Kelly's Plains Road, Armidale, NSW 2350, Australia.

GATES, William Thomas George, CBE 1967; Chairman, West Africa Committee, London, 1961–76; *b* 21 Jan. 1908; *s* of Thomas George and Katherine Gates; *m* 1938, Rhoda (*née* Sellars), *d* of Mrs W. E. Loveless; two *s*. *Educ*: Ilford County High Sch., London Univ. National Bank of New Zealand, London, 1925–30; John Holt & Co. (Liverpool) Ltd, resident Nigeria, 1930–46; Gen. Manager: Nigeria, 1940; Gold Coast, 1947; Liverpool, 1947; Man. Dir, 1956; Dep. Chm., 1964; retired, 1967. MLC, Nigeria, 1940–46; Director: W African Airways Corp, 1941–46; Campbell Co., Louisville, Ky, 1954–67; Edward Bates & Sons (Holdings) Ltd, 1964–70; Edinburgh & Overseas Investment Trust Ltd, Edinburgh, 1964–71. Dist Scout Comr, Northern Nigeria 1940–42; Mem. Liverpool Dist Cttee, Royal National Life-Boat Instn, 1956–73; Mem. Bd of Govs, United Liverpool Hosps, 1958–70; Gen. Comr of Income Tax, 1967–73; Chm., Liverpool Porterage Rates Panel, 1969–74. Chm., Royal African Soc., 1975–77, Vice-Pres., 1978–. *Recreations*: golf, fishing, cricket, gardening. *Address*: Masongill, Long Street, Sherborne, Dorset. *T*: Sherborne 814214. *Clubs*: MCC; Royal Liverpool Golf (Hoylake).

GATHORNE-HARDY, family name of **Earl of Cranbrook.**

GATTY, Trevor Thomas, OBE 1974; HM Diplomatic Service, retired; Consultant: KPG Inc., since 1985; Ernst and Whinney Inc., since 1985; MSL International; *b* 8 June 1930; *s* of Thomas Alfred Gatty and Lillian Gatty (*née* Wood); *m* 1956, Jemima Bowman (marr. diss. 1983); two *s* one *d*. *Educ*: King Edward's Sch., Birmingham. Served Army, 1948–50, 2/Lieut Royal Warwickshire Regt, later Lieut Royal Fusiliers (TA), 1950–53. Foreign Office, 1950; Vice-Consul, Leopoldville, 1954; FO, 1958–61; Second (later First) Sec., Bangkok, 1961–64; Consul, San Francisco, 1965–66; Commercial Consul, San Francisco, 1967–68; FCO, 1968–73; Commercial Consul, Zürich, 1973–75; FCO, 1975–76; Counsellor (Diplomatic Service Inspector), 1977–80; Head, Migration and Visa Dept, FCO, 1980–81; Consul-General, Atlanta, 1981–85. *Recreations*: reading, physical fitness, English Springer spaniels. *Address*: 4026 Land O'Lakes Drive, Atlanta, Georgia

30342, USA. *T:* 404 264 9033; Little Orchard, St Tudy, Bodmin, Cornwall PL30 3PJ. *T:* Bodmin 850348. *Club:* Travellers'.

GATWARD, (Anthony) James; Group Chief Executive, Television South plc, since 1984 (Managing Director, 1979–84); *b* 4 March 1938; *s* of George James Gatward and Lillian Georgina (*née* Strutton); *m* 1969, Isobel Anne Stuart Black, actress; three *d. Educ:* George Gascoigne Sch., Walthamstow; South West Essex Technical Coll. and Sch. of Art (drama course). Entered TV industry, 1957; freelance drama producer/director: Canada and USA, 1959–65; BBC and most ITV cos, 1966–70, partner in prodn co., acting as Exec. Prod. and often Dir of many internat. co-prodns in UK, Ceylon, Australia and Germany, 1970–78; Director: Southstar, Scottish and Global TV, 1971–78; Indep. TV Publications Ltd, 1982–; Oracle Teletext Ltd, 1982–; Solent Cablevision Ltd, 1983–; Channel 4 TV Co., 1984–; Indep. TV News Ltd, 1986–; ITV Superchannel Ltd, 1986–; Chm. and Chief Exec., TVS Television, 1984–; Chm., TVS Productions, 1984–. Instigated and led preparation of application for South and SE England television franchise, 1979–80 (awarded Dec. 1980). Member: Court of the Mary Rose; Council, Operation Raleigh; Governor, S of England Agricl Soc. *Recreations:* farming, sailing, music. *Address:* TVS, Television Centre, Southampton SO9 5HZ. *Clubs:* Reform, Royal Thames Yacht.

GAU, John Glen Mackay; independent television producer; Director, John Gau Productions, since 1981; *b* 25 March 1940; *s* of Cullis William Gau and Nan Munro; *m* 1966, Susan Tebbs; two *s. Educ:* Haileybury and ISC; Trinity Hall, Cambridge; Univ. of Wisconsin. BBC TV: Assistant Film Editor, 1963; Current Affairs Producer, 1965–74; Editor, Nationwide, 1975; Head of Current Affairs Programmes, 1978–81. Dir, Channel 4, 1984–. Chm., Indep. Programme Producers' Assoc., 1983–. Chm. Council, RTS, 1986–. FRTS 1986. *Publication:* (jtly) Soldiers, 1985. *Address:* 4 Queensmere Road, SW19 5NY. *T:* 01–946 4686.

GAUDRY, Roger, CC (Canada) 1968; DSc, FRSC; Chairman: Nordic Laboratories, since 1975; Bio-Research Laboratories, since 1984; *b* 15 Dec. 1913; *m* 1941, Madeleine Vallée; two *s* three *d. Educ:* Laval Univ. (BA 1933; BSc 1937; DSc 1940); Rhodes Scholar, Oxford Univ., 1937–39. Organic Chemistry, Laval Univ.: Lectr, 1940; Prof., 1945; Full Prof., 1950. Ayerst Laboratories: Asst Dir of Research, 1954; Dir of Research, 1957; Vice-Pres. and Dir of Research, 1963–65. Director: Corby Distilleries, 1975–; Hoechst Canada, 1977–; SKW Canada, 1978–; St Lawrence Starch, 1983–. Chm., Science Council of Canada, 1972–75; Rector, Univ. of Montreal, 1965–75; Pres., Internat. Assoc. of Univs, 1975–80. Chm. Bd, UN Univ., 1974–76; Dir, Inst. de recherches cliniques, Montreal, 1975–. Parizeau Medal from Assoc. Canadienne Française pour l'Avancement des Sciences, 1958. Hon. doctorates: (Laws) Univ. of Toronto, 1966; (Science) RMC of Kingston, 1966; (Science) Univ. of BC, 1967; (Laws) McGill Univ., 1967; Univ. of Clermont-Ferrand, France, 1967; (Laws) St Thomas Univ., 1968; (Laws) Brock Univ., 1969; (Civil Laws) Bishop's Univ., 1969; (Science) Univ. of Saskatchewan, 1970; (Science) Univ. of Western Ontario, 1976; (Laws) Concordia Univ., 1980; Hon. Fellow, RCPS (Can.) 1971. *Publications:* author and co-author of numerous scientific papers in organic and biological chemistry. *Address:* 445 Beverley Avenue, Town of Mount Royal, Montreal, PQ H3P 1L4, Canada.

GAULD, William Wallace; Under-Secretary, Department of Agriculture and Fisheries for Scotland, 1972–79; *b* 12 Oct. 1919; *e s* of late Rev. W. W. Gauld, DD, of Aberdeen, and Charlotte Jane Gauld (*née* Reid); *m* 1943, Jean Inglis Gray; three *d. Educ:* Fettes; Aberdeen Univ. MA (1st Cl. Hons Classics). Served Pioneer Corps, 1940–46 (Major 1945). Entered Dept of Agriculture for Scotland, 1947; Private Sec. to Secretary of State for Scotland, 1955–57; Asst Sec., 1958; Scottish Development Dept, 1968–72; Mem. Agricultural Research Council, 1972–79. Pres., Botanical Soc., Edinburgh, 1978–80. *Recreations:* natural history, hill walking. *Address:* 1 Banks Crescent, Crieff, Perthshire PH7 3SR.

GAULT, Charles Alexander, CBE 1959 (OBE 1947); retired from HM Foreign Service, 1959; *b* 15 June 1908; *o s* of Robert Gault, Belfast, and Sophia Ranken Clark; *m* 1947, Madge, *d* of late William Walter Adams, Blundellsands; no *c. Educ:* Harrow; Magdalene Coll., Cambridge. Entered Levant Consular Service, 1931; served in Egypt, Persia, Saudi Arabia, at Foreign Office, India (on secondment to Commonwealth Relations Office), Libya, Israel, Bahrain (HM Political Agent, 1954–59). *Address:* 22 Lansdown Parade, Cheltenham, Glos. *Club:* Oriental.

GAULT, David Hamilton; Executive Chairman, Gallic Management Co. Ltd, since 1974; *b* 9 April 1928; *s* of Leslie Hamilton Gault and Iris Hilda Gordon Young; *m* 1950, Felicity Jane Gribble; three *s* two *d. Educ:* Fettes Coll., Edinburgh. Nat. Service, commnd in RA, 1946–48; Clerk, C. H. Rugg & Co. Ltd, Shipbrokers, 1948–52; H. Clarkson & Co. Ltd, Shipbrokers: Man. 1952–56; Dir 1956–62; Jt Man. Dir 1962–72; Gp Man. Dir, Shipping Industrial Holdings Ltd, 1972–74; Chm., Jebsen (UK) Ltd, 1962–81; Chm., Seabridge Shipping Ltd, 1965–73. *Recreations:* gardening, walking. *Address:* Telegraph House, North Marden, Chichester, West Sussex. *T:* Harting 206. *Clubs:* Boodle's, City; India House (New York).

GAUNT SUDDARDS, Henry; *see* Suddards.

GAUSDEN, Ronald, CB 1982; nuclear consultant; *b* 15 June 1921; *s* of Jesse Charles William Gausden and Annie Gausden (*née* Durrant); *m* 1943, Florence May (*née* Ayres); two *s* two *d. Educ:* Varndean Grammar Sch., Brighton; Brighton Techn. Coll. and Borough Polytechnic. CEng, FIEE. RN Sci. Service, 1943–47; AERE, Harwell, 1947–50; UKAEA Windscale Works, Cumbria: Instrument Engr, 1950–53; Asst Gp Man., 1953–55; Gp Man., 1955–60; Nuclear Installations Inspectorate: Principal Inspector, 1960–63; Asst Chief Inspector, 1963–73; Dep. Chief Inspector, 1973–75; Chief Inspector, 1976–81; Dir, Hazardous Installations Gp, HSE, 1978–81. *Publications:* contrib. Brit. Nuclear Energy Soc. and Inst. Nuclear Engrs. *Recreations:* golf, shooting, fishing. *Address:* Granary Cottage, Itchingfield, near Horsham, Sussex. *T:* Slinfold 790646.

GAUTIER-SMITH, Peter Claudius, FRCP; Physician, National Hospitals for Nervous Diseases, Queen Square and Maida Vale, since 1962; *b* 1 March 1929; *s* of late Claudius Gautier-Smith and Madeleine (*née* Ferguson); *m* 1960, Nesta Mary Wroth; two *d. Educ:* Cheltenham Coll. (Exhibnr); King's Coll., Cambridge; St Thomas's Hosp. Med. Sch. MA, MD. Casualty Officer, House Physician, St Thomas' Hosp., 1955–56; Medical Registrar, University Coll. Hosp., 1958; Registrar, National Hosp., Queen Square, 1960–62; Consultant Neurologist, St George's Hosp., 1962–75; Dean, Inst. of Neurology, 1975–82. Mem., Bd of Governors, Nat. Hosps for Nervous Diseases, 1975–. *Publications:* Parasagittal and Falx Meningiomas, 1970; papers in learned jls on neurology. *Recreations:* literary (twenty-one novels published under a pseudonym); squash (played for Cambridge v Oxford, 1951; Captain, London Univ., 1954); tennis. *Address:* Institute of Neurology, Queen Square, WC1N 3BG. *T:* 01–837 3611. *Clubs:* MCC; Hawks (Cambridge); Jesters.

GAUTREY, Peter, CMG 1972; CVO 1961; DK (Brunei) 1972; HM Diplomatic Service, retired; High Commissioner in Guyana, 1975–78, concurrently Ambassador (non-resident) to Surinam, 1976–78; *b* 17 Sept. 1918; *s* of late Robert Harry Gautrey, Hindhead, Surrey, and Hilda Morris; *m* 1947, Marguerite Etta Uncles; one *s* one *d. Educ:* Abbotsholme Sch., Derbys. Joined Home Office, 1936. Served in Royal Artillery, (Capt.), Sept. 1939–March 1946. Re-joined Home Office; Commonwealth Relations Office, 1948; served in British Embassy, Dublin, 1950–53; UK High Commission, New Delhi, 1955–57 and 1960–63; British Deputy High Commissioner, Bombay, 1963–65; Corps of Diplomatic Service Inspectors, 1965–68; High Commissioner: Swaziland, 1968–71; Brunei, 1972–75. FRSA 1972. *Recreations:* golf, music, art. *Address:* 24 Fort Road, Guildford, Surrey.

GAVASKAR, Sunil Manohar; Padma Bhushan; cricketer; business executive; *b* 10 July 1949; *s* of Manohar Keshav Gavaskar and Meenal Manohar Gavaskar; *m* 1974, Marshniel Mehrotra; one *s. Educ:* St Xavier's High Sch.; St Xavier's Coll.; Bombay Univ. (BA). Represented India in cricket, 1971–; Captain, Indian Team, 1978, 1979–80, 1980–82 and 1984–85; passed previous world records: no of runs in Test Matches, 1983; no of Test centuries, 1984. *Publications:* Sunny Days, 1976; Idols, 1983; Runs 'n Ruins, 1984. *Address:* 40-A Sir Bhalchandra Road, Dadar, Bombay 400014, India. *T:* (office) 4931611. *Clubs:* Cricket Club of India, Bombay Gymkhana.

GAVIN, Maj.-Gen. James Merricks Lewis, CB 1967; CBE 1963 (OBE 1953); *b* Antofagasta, Chile, 28 July 1911; *s* of Joseph Merricks Gavin; *m* 1942, Barbara Anne Elizabeth, *d* of Group Capt. C. G. Murray, CBE; one *s* two *d. Educ:* Uppingham Sch.; Royal Military Academy; Trinity Coll., Cambridge. 2nd Lieut Royal Engineers, 1931. Mem. Mt Everest Expedn, 1936. Instructor, Royal Military Academy, 1938; Capt. 1939; served War of 1939–45 in Far East, Middle East, Italy, France, including special operations; Brit. Jt Services Mission, Washington, 1948–51; Commanding Officer, 1951–53; Col Staff Coll., Camberley, 1953–55; BAOR, 1956–58; Comdt (Brig.) Intelligence Centre, Maresfield, 1958–61; Maj.-Gen. 1964; Asst Chief of Staff (Intelligence), SHAPE, 1964–67. Technical Dir, BSI, 1967–76. Col Comdt, RE, 1968–73. *Recreations:* mountaineering, sailing, ski-ing. *Address:* Slathurst Farm, Milland, near Liphook, Hants GU30 7ND. *Clubs:* Royal Cruising, Royal Ocean Racing, Alpine; Royal Yacht Squadron (Cowes).

GAVIN, Malcolm Ross, CBE 1966 (MBE 1945); MA, DSc, CEng, FIEE, FInstP; Chairman of Council, Royal Dental Hospital School of Dental Surgery, University of London, 1974–81; *b* 27 April 1908; 3rd *s* of James Gavin; *m* 1935, Jessie Isobel Hutchinson; one *s* one *d. Educ:* Hamilton Acad.; Glasgow Univ. Mathematics Teacher, Dalziel High Sch., Motherwell, 1931–36; Physicist, GEC Res. Labs, Wembley, 1936–47; HMI, Scottish Education Dept, 1947–50; Head of Dept of Physics and Mathematics and Vice-Principal, College of Technology, Birmingham, 1950–55; Prof. of Electronic Engrg and Head of Sch. of Engrg Sci, University Coll. of N Wales, 1955–65; Principal, Chelsea Coll., Univ. of London, 1966–73; Dir, Fulmer Res. Inst., 1968–73. Member: Electronics Res. Coun., Min. of Aviation, 1960–64; Res. Grants Cttee of DSIR (Chm., Electrical and Systems Sub-Cttee, 1964–65); SRC (Mem. Univ. Sci. and Tech. Bd and Chm. Electrical Sub-Cttee, 1965–69, Chm. Control Engineering Cttee, 1969–73; Mem. Engineering Bd, 1969–73); Inter-Univ. Council for Higher Education Overseas, 1967–74; UGC, Hong Kong, 1966–76; Council, European Physical Soc., 1968–70; Murray Cttee, Univ. of London, 1970–72; Council, N Wales Naturalist Trust, 1973–77; Council, University Coll. of North Wales, 1974–77; Visitor, Nat. Inst. Industrial Psychology, 1970–74; Pres. Inst. of Physics and Physical Soc., 1968–70 (Vice-Pres., 1964–67). Hon. ACT, Birmingham, 1956; Hon. DSc (Ife), 1970. Hon. Fellow, Chelsea Coll. *Publications:* Principles of Electronics (with Dr J. E. Houldin), 1959. Numerous in Jl of IEE, Brit. Jl of Applied Physics, Wireless Engineer, Jl of Electronics, etc. *Recreations:* gardening, grandchildren. *Address:* Mill Cottage, Pluscarden, Elgin, Morayshire. *T:* Dallas 281.

GAVRON, Robert; Chairman, St Ives Group, since 1964; Chairman and Proprietor: Folio Society Ltd, since 1982; Carcanet Press Ltd, since 1983; *b* 13 Sept. 1930; *s* of Nathaniel and Leah Gavron. *Educ:* Leighton Park Sch., Reading; Oxford Univ. (MA). Called to the Bar, Middle Temple, 1955. Entered printing industry, 1955; founded St Ives Gp, 1964 (public co., 1985; acquired Richard Clay plc, 1985 and Chase Printers Ltd, 1986). Director: Octopus Publishing Gp, 1975–; Electra Management Plc, 1981–. Member: Literature Panel, Arts Council, 1979–83; Council, NBL, 1982–; Council, Poetry Soc., 1983–; Council, Morley Coll., 1975–85. *Address:* 47–58 Bastwick Street, EC1V 3PS. *T:* 01–251 1525. *Clubs:* Reform, Groucho.

GAY, Geoffrey Charles Lytton; Consultant, Knight, Frank & Rutley, since 1973; World President, International Real Estate Federation (FIABCI), 1973–75; a General Commissioner for Inland Revenue since 1953; *b* 14 March 1914; *s* of late Charles Gay and Ida, *d* of Sir Henry A. Lytton (famous Savoyard); *m* 1947, Dorothy Ann, *d* of Major Eric Rickman; one *s* two *d. Educ:* St Paul's School. FRICS. Joined Knight, Frank & Rutley, 1929. Served War of 1939–45: Durham LI, BEF, 1940; psc; Lt-Col; Chief of Staff, Sind District, India, 1943. Mem. Westminster City Council, 1962–71. Governor: Benenden Sch.; Council, Clayesmore Sch.; Mem. Council of St John, London, 1971–84; Liveryman, Broderers' Co. Licentiate, RPS, 1983; FRSA 1983. Chevalier de l'Ordre de l'Economie Nationale, 1960. OStJ 1961; KStJ 1979. *Recreations:* photography, fishing, music, theatre. *Address:* Brookmans Old Farm, Iwerne Minster, Blandford Forum, Dorset DT11 8NG. *T:* Fontmell Magna 811020. *Clubs:* Carlton, MCC, Flyfishers'.

GAY, Rear-Adm. George Wilsmore, CB 1969; MBE 1946; DSC 1943; JP; Director-General of Naval Training, 1967–69; retired; *b* 1913; *s* of late Engr Comdr G. M. Gay and Mrs O. T. Gay (*née* Allen); *m* 1941, Nancy Agnes Clark; two *s* one *d. Educ:* Eastman's Sch., Southsea; Nautical Coll., Pangbourne. Entered RN, 1930; Cadet Trng, 1930–32; RNEC, Keyham, 1932–35; HMS Glorious, 1935–37; Engr. Off., HMS Porpoise, 1939–41, HMS Clyde, 1941–43; HMS Dolphin, 1938 and 1943–46; HM Dockyard, Portsmouth, 1946–47; HMS Euryalus, 1947–49; Sqdn Engr Off., 1st Submarine Sqdn, HMS Forth, 1949–50; Trng Comdr, HMS Raleigh, 1951–53; Admiralty Engr Overseer, Vickers Armstrong Ltd, 1953–55; HMS Dolphin, 1956–58; Senior Officer, War Course, Royal Naval Coll., Greenwich, 1958; HM Dockyard, Malta, 1959–60; CO, HMS Sultan, Gosport, 1960–63; Chief Staff Off. Material to Flag Off. Submarines, 1963–66; Admty Interview Bd, 1966. Comdr 1947; Capt. 1958; Rear-Adm. 1967. FIMechE (MIMechE 1958). JP Plymouth 1970. *Recreations:* fishing, sailing, gardening. *Address:* 29 Whiteford Road, Mannamead, Plymouth, Devon. *T:* Plymouth 664486. *Club:* Army and Navy.

GAYDON, Prof. Alfred Gordon, FRS 1953; Warren Research Fellow of Royal Society, 1945–74; Professor of Molecular Spectroscopy, 1961–73, now Emeritus, and Fellow, since 1980, Imperial College of Science and Technology, London; *b* 26 Sept. 1911; *s* of Alfred Bert Gaydon and Rosetta Juliet Gordon; *m* 1940, Phyllis Maude Gaze (*d* 1981); one *s* one *d. Educ:* Kingston Grammar Sch., Kingston-on-Thames; Imperial Coll., London. BSc (Physics) Imperial Coll., 1932; worked on molecular spectra, and on measurement of high temperatures, on spectra and structure of flames, and shock waves; DSc (London) 1942; Hon. Dr (University of Dijon), 1957. Rumford Medal, Royal Society, 1960; Bernard Lewis Gold Medal, Combustion Inst., 1960. *Publications:* Identification of Molecular Spectra (with Dr R. W. B. Pearse), 1941, 1950, 1963, 1965, 1976; Spectroscopy and Combustion Theory, 1942, 1948; Dissociation Energies and Spectra of Diatomic Molecules, 1947, 1953, 1968; Flames, their Structure, Radiation and Temperature (with Dr H. G. Wolfhard), 1953, 1960, 1970, 1979; The Spectroscopy of Flames, 1957, 1974;

The Shock Tube in High-temperature Chemical Physics (with Dr I. Hurle), 1963. *Recreations:* wild-life photography; formerly rowing. *Address:* Dale Cottage, Shellbridge Road, Slindon Common, Sussex. *T:* Slindon 277.

GAYRE of Gayre and Nigg, Robert, ERD; Lieutenant-Colonel (late Reserve of Officers); ethnologist and armorist; Editor: The Armorial, since 1959; The Mankind Quarterly, 1960–78 (Hon. Editor in Chief, since 1979), etc; Director of several companies; *s* of Robert Gayre of Gayre and Nigg, and Clara Hull; *m* 1933, Nina Mary (*d* 1983), *d* of Rev. Louis Thomas Terry, MA and Margaret Nina Hill; one *s*. *Educ:* University of Edinburgh (MA); Exeter Coll., Oxford. BEF France, 1939; Staff Officer Airborne HQ, 1942; Educnl Adviser, Allied Mil. Govt, Italy, 1943–44; Dir of Educn, Allied Control Commn for Italy, 1944; Chief of Educn and Religious Affairs, German Planning Unit, SHAEF, 1944; Prof. of Anthropology and head of Dept of Anthropo-geography, University of Saugor, India, 1954–56; Falkland Pursuivant Extraord., 1958; Consultore pro lingua Anglica, Coll. of Heralds, Rome, 1954–; Chamberlain to the Prince of Lippe, 1958–; Grand Bailiff and Comr-Gen. of the English Tongue, Order of St Lazarus of Jerusalem, 1961–69; Grand Referendary, 1969–73; Grand Comdr and Grand Almoner, 1973–; Vicar-Gen., 1985–; Sec.-Gen., VIth Internat. Congress of Genealogy, Edinburgh, 1962. Chm., The Seventeen Forty-Five Association, 1964–80. President: Scottish Rhodesia Soc., to 1968; Aberdeenshire and Banffshire Friends of Rhodesia Assoc., 1969; St Andrew Soc. of Malta, 1968; Ethnological Soc. of Malta; Life Pres., Heraldic Soc. of Malta, 1970–; Hon. Pres., Sicilian Anthropological Soc. Sec.-Gen., Internat. Orders' Commn (Chm., 1978–); Mem. Coun. Internat. Inst. of Ethnology and Eugenics, New York. Mem. Cttee of Honour: Inst. Politicos, Madrid; Cercle Internat. Généalogique, Paris, Mem. Nat. Acad. Sci. of India; Fellow: Collegio Araldico, Rome; Nat. Soc., Naples; Peloritana Acad., Messina; Pontaniana Acad., Naples; Royal Academy, Palermo; F Ist Ital di Geneal. e Arald., Rome; FRSH; MInstBE. Hon. or corr. mem. of heraldic and other socs of many countries. Grand Cross of Merit, SMO Malta, 1963 (Kt Comdr, 1957). Holds knighthoods in international and foreign orders, hon. Doctorates from Italian Univs, and heraldic societies' medals, etc. Hon. Lt-Col, ADC to Governor, Georgia, USA, 1969–; Hon. Lt-Col, ADC, State Militia, Alabama; Hon. Lt-Col, Canadian Arctic Air Force. Hon. Citizen, Commune of Gurro, Italy. *Publications:* Teuton and Slav on the Polish Frontier, 1944; Italy in Transition, 1946; Wassail! In Mazers of Mead, 1948, new edn, USA, 1986; The Heraldry of the Knights of St John, 1956; Heraldic Standards and other Ensigns, 1959; The Nature of Arms, 1961; Heraldic Cadency, 1961, Gayre's Booke, 4 vols 1948–59; Who is Who in Clan Gayre, 1962; A Case for Monarchy, 1962; The Armorial Who is Who, 1961–62, 1963–65, 1966–68, 1969–75, 1976–79; Roll of Scottish Arms (Pt I Vol. I, 1964, Pt I Vol. II, 1969, Vol. III, 1980); Ethnological Elements of Africa, 1966; More Ethnological Elements of Africa, 1972; The Zimbabwean Culture of Rhodesia, 1972; Miscellaneous Racial Studies, 2 vols, 1972; The Knightly Twilight, 1974; Aspects of British and Continental Heraldry, 1974; The Lost Clan, 1974; Syro-Mesopotamian Ethnology, 1974; The Mackay of the Rhinns of Islay, 1979; Minard Castle, 1980; Minard Castle Collection of Pipe Music, 1986; contribs Mankind Quarterly, contrib. Encyc. Brit., etc. *Recreations:* yachting, ocean cruising. *Address:* c/o 1–3 Gloucester Lane, Edinburgh EH3 6ED. *T:* 031–225 1896; Lezayre Mount, Ramsey, Isle of Man. *T:* 813854; (owns as feudal baron of Lochoreshyre) Lochore Castle, Fife. *Clubs:* Army and Navy, United Oxford & Cambridge University, Royal Thames Yacht; Caledonian (Edinburgh); Pretoria (Pretoria, SA); Casino Maltese (Valletta); Raven (Ramsey, IoM); Royal Forth Yacht, Royal Highland Yacht, Royal Malta Yacht, etc.

GAZE, Dr Raymond Michael, FRS 1972; FRSE 1964; Head, Medical Research Council Neural Development and Regeneration Group, Edinburgh University, since 1984, Hon. Professor, since 1986; *b* 22 June 1927; *s* of late William Mercer Gaze and Kathleen Grace Gaze (*née* Bowhill); *m* 1957, Robinetta Mary Armfelt; one *s* two *d*. *Educ:* at home; Sch. of Medicine, Royal Colleges, Edinburgh. LRCPE, LRCSE, LRFPSG; MA, DPhil. House Physician, Chelmsford and Essex Hosp., 1949; National Service, RAMC, 1953–55; Lectr, later Reader, Dept of Physiology, Edinburgh Univ., 1955–70; Alan Johnston, Lawrence and Moseley Research Fellow, Royal Soc., 1962–66; Head, Div. of Developmental Biol., 1970–83, Dep. Dir 1977–83, Nat. Inst. for Med. Research. Visiting Professor: of Theoretical Biology, Univ. of Chicago, 1972; of Biology, Middlesex Hosp. Med. Sch., 1972–74. Mem. Physiological Soc. *Publications:* The Formation of Nerve Connections, 1970; Editor, 1975–, and contrib., Jl Embryology and Exper. Morphology, various papers on neurobiology in Jl Physiology, Qly Jl Exper. Physiology, Proc. Royal Soc., etc. *Recreations:* drawing, hill-walking, music. *Address:* c/o Dept of Zoology, University of Edinburgh, King's Buildings, West Mains Road, Edinburgh EH9 3JT. *T:* 031–667 1081; 37 Sciennes Road, Edinburgh EH9 1NS. *T:* 031–667 6915.

GAZZARD, Roy James Albert (Hon. Major); FRIBA; FRTPI; Director, Centre for Middle Eastern and Islamic Studies, Durham University, since 1984 (Pro-Director, 1982–84); *b* 19 July 1923; *s* of James Henry Gazzard, MBE, and Ada Gwendoline Gazzard (*née* Willis); *m* 1947, Muriel Joy Morgan; one *s* two *d* (and one *s* decd). *Educ:* Stationers' Company's Sch.; Architectural Assoc. Sch. of Architecture (Dip.); School of Planning and Research for Reg. Develt (Dip.). Commissioned, Mddx Regt, 1943; service Palestine and ME. Acting Govt Town Planner, Uganda, 1950; Staff Architect, Barclays Bank Ltd, 1954; Chief Architect, Peterlee Develt Corp., 1960; Dir of Develt, Northumberland CC, 1962; Lectr in Geography, Univ. of Durham, 1970; Chief Professional Adviser to Sec. of State's Environmental Bd, 1976; Under Sec., DoE, 1976–79. Prepared: Jinja (Uganda) Outline Scheme, 1954; Municipality of Sur (Oman) Develt Plan, 1975. Govt medals for Good Design in Housing; Civic Trust awards for Townscape and Conservation. *Publications:* (with Douglas Pocock) Durham: portrait of a cathedral city, 1983; contribs to HMSO pubns on built environment. *Recreations:* travel, writing, broadcasting. *Address:* 51 South Street, Durham DH1 4QP. *T:* Durham 64067. *Club:* City Livery.

GEACH, Gertrude Elizabeth Margaret; *see* Anscombe, G. E. M.

GEACH, Prof. Peter Thomas, FBA 1965; Professor of Logic, University of Leeds, 1966–81; *b* 29 March 1916; *o s* of Prof. George Hender Geach, IES, and Eleonora Frederyka Adolfina Sgonina; *m* 1941, Gertrude Elizabeth Margaret Anscombe, *qv*; three *s* four *d*. *Educ:* Balliol Coll., Oxford (Domus Schol.; Hon. Fellow, 1979). 2nd cl. Class, Hon. Mods, 1936; 1st cl. Lit. Hum., 1938. Gladstone Research Student, St Deiniol's Library, Hawarden, 1938–39; philosophical research, Cambridge, 1945–51; University of Birmingham: Asst Lectr in Philosophy, 1951; Lectr, 1952; Sen. Lectr, 1959; Reader in Logic, 1961. Vis. Prof., Univ. of Warsaw, 1985. Lectures: Stanton, in the Philosophy of Religion, Cambridge, 1971–74; Hägerström, Univ. of Uppsala, 1975; O'Hara, Univ. of Notre Dame, 1978. Forschungspreis, A. Von Humboldt Stiftung, 1983. *Publications:* Mental Acts, 1957; Reference and Generality, 1962, 3rd rev. edn 1980; (with G. E. M. Anscombe) Three Philosophers, 1961; God and the Soul, 1969; Logic Matters, 1972; Reason and Argument, 1976; Providence and Evil, 1977; The Virtues, 1977; Truth, Love, and Immortality: an introduction to McTaggart's philosophy, 1979; articles in Mind, Philosophical Review, Analysis, Ratio, etc. *Recreation:* reading stories of detection, mystery and horror. *Address:* 3 Richmond Road, Cambridge. *T:* 353950. *Club:* Union Society (Oxford).

GEAR, William, DA (Edinburgh) 1936; RBSA 1966; Painter; Head of Department of Fine Art, Birmingham Polytechnic (formerly Birmingham College of Art and Design), 1964–75; Member London Group, 1953; *b* Methil, Fife, 2 Aug. 1915; *s* of Porteous Gordon Gear; *m* 1949, Charlotte Chertok; two *s*. *Educ:* Buckhaven High Sch.; Edinburgh Coll. of Art; Edinburgh Univ.; Moray House Training Coll.; Edinburgh Coll. of Art: Post-grad. schol., 1936–37; Travelling schol., 1937–38; Académie Fernand Leger, Paris, 1937; study in France, Italy, Balkans; Moray House Trg Coll., 1938–39. War Service with Royal Corps of Signals, 1940–46, in Middle East, Italy and Germany. Staff Officer, Monuments, Fine Arts and Archives Br., CCG, 1946–47; worked in Paris, 1947–50; Curator, Towner Art Gallery, Eastbourne, 1958–64. Guest lecturer, Nat. Gall. of Victoria, Melbourne, and University of Western Australia, 1966. Chairman: Fine Art Panel, Nat. Council for Diplomas in Art and Design, 1972; Fine Art Bd, CNAA, 1974; Council Mem., Midlands Arts Centre, 1978. One-man exhibitions since 1944 in various European cities, N and S America, Japan, etc.; London; Gimpel Fils Gall., 1948–; S London Art Gall. (retrospective), 1954; Edinburgh Fest., 1966; (retrospective) Arts Council, N Ireland, 1969; (retrospective) Scottish Arts Council, 1969; Univ. of Sussex, 1964–75; RBSA Birmingham, 1976 (retrospective); Talbot Rice Art Centre, Univ. of Edinburgh, and Ikon Gall., Birmingham (retrospective), 1982; Spacex Gall., Exeter, 1983; Kirkcaldy Art Gall., 1985; Netherbow Art Centre, Edinburgh, 1985. Works shown in many exhibitions of contemporary art, also at Royal Acad., 1960, 1961, 1967, 1968, and RSA 1986. Awarded £500 Purchase prize, Fest. of Britain, 1951; David Cargill Award, Royal Glasgow Inst., 1967; Lorne Fellowship, 1976. FIAL, 1960; FRSA 1971. *Works in permanent collections:* Tate Gall.; Arts Council; Brit. Council; Contemp. Art Soc.; Scottish National Gall. of Modern Art; Scottish Arts Council; Victoria & Albert Museum; Laing Art Gall., Newcastle; Nat. Gall. of Canada; Bishop Suter Art Gall., NZ; Art Gall., Toronto; City Art Gall., Toledo, Ohio; Museum of Art, Tel Aviv; New Coll., Oxford; Cincinnati Art Gall., Ohio; Nat. Gall. of NSW; Bishop Otter Coll., Chichester; City Art Gall., Manchester; Albright Art Gall., Buffalo, NY; Musée des Beaux Arts, Liège; Inst. of Contemp. Art, Lima, Peru; Towner Art Gall., Eastbourne; Brighton Art Gall.; Pembroke Coll., Cambridge; Chelsea Coll. of Physical Educn; Southampton Art Gall.; Univ. of Glasgow; Arts Council of Northern Ireland; Whitworth Art Gall., Manchester; Univ. of Birmingham; City Museum and Art Gall., Birmingham; Museum of Art, Fort Lauderdale, Fla; Nat. Gall. of Aust.; Birmingham Polytech.; City Art Centre, Edinburgh; Kirkcaldy Art Gall.; Strathclyde Regl Council; Hereford Liby & Mus.; Dept of Educn, Manchester; Rye Art Gall.; Peir Gall., Orkney; Aberdeen, Dundee and Glasgow Art Galleries, and in numerous private collections in GB, USA, Canada, Italy, France, etc. Furnishing textiles designed for various firms. *Recreations:* cricket, music, gardening. *Address:* 46 George Road, Edgbaston, Birmingham B15 1PL.

GEDDES, family name of **Baron Geddes.**

GEDDES, 3rd Baron *cr* 1942; **Euan Michael Ross Geddes;** Company Director since 1964; *b* 3 Sept. 1937; *s* of 2nd Baron Geddes, KBE, and of Enid Mary, Lady Geddes, *d* of late Clarance H. Butler; *S* father, 1975; *m* 1966, Gillian, *d* of William Arthur Butler; one *s* one *d*. *Educ:* Rugby; Gonville and Caius Coll., Cambridge (MA 1964); Harvard Business School. *Recreations:* golf, bridge, music, gardening. *Heir: s* Hon. James George Neil Geddes, *b* 10 Sept. 1969. *Address:* House of Lords, SW1A 0PW. *T:* Basingstoke 862105. *Club:* Brooks's.

GEDDES, Air Cdre Andrew James Wray, CBE 1946 (OBE 1941); DSO 1943; *b* 31 July 1906; *s* of late Major Malcolm Henry Burdett Geddes, Indian Army, and late Mrs Geddes, Seaford, Sussex; *m* 1929, Anstice Wynter, *d* of late Rev. A. W. Leach, Rector of Leasingham, Lincs; one *s* one *d*. *Educ:* Oakley Hall, Cirencester, Glos; Wellington Coll., Berks; Royal Military Academy Woolwich. 2nd Lt Royal Artillery, 1926; seconded Flying Officer RAF 1928–32; Lieut RA 1929; seconded Flight Lieut RAF 1935–38; Capt. RA 1939; served War of 1939–45 (despatches twice, OBE, DSO, CBE, Commander Legion of Merit, USA); seconded Squadron Leader RAF 1939; Acting Wing Commander RAF 1940; Acting Group Capt., 1942; Acting Air Commodore, 1943; War Subst. Group Capt., 1943; Major RA 1943; Air Commodore Operations and Plans, HQ 2nd TAF for the Invasion. Prepared and signed Treaty for Operation Manna/Chowhound (dropping of food to 3,500,000 Dutch people and allied PoWs), 1945 (nicknamed Man Van Manna and presented with Dutch Erasmus Medal, 1985). Transferred from RA to RAF, 1945; Air Cdre Dir of Organisation (Establishments), Air Ministry, 1945–47 (the 'Geddes Axe'); Group Capt. (subst.), 1947; graduated Imperial Defence Coll., London, 1948; Commanding No. 4 Flying Training Sch. and RAF Station, Heany, S Rhodesia, 1949–51; Dep. Dir of Organisation, Plans, Air Ministry, 1951–54, retd with rank of Air Cdre, 1954; Asst County Civil Defence Officer (Plans), East Sussex County Council, 1957–65; Deputy Civil Defence Officer, Brighton County Borough, 1965–66. Mem., British Hang-gliding Assoc., 1975 (believed to be oldest living person who has flown a hang-glider; first solo when aged 68 years 9 months); qualified instructor/examiner, Nat. Cycling Proficiency Scheme, RoSPA, 1977; Founder Mem., Cuckmere Valley Canoeing Club. Pres., Manna Assoc., 1986. *Address:* c/o Midland Bank, 33 The Borough, Farnham, Surrey GU9 7NJ.

GEDDES, Sir (Anthony) Reay (Mackay), KBE 1968 (OBE 1943); President, Abbeyfield Society, since 1986; Chairman, Charities Aid Foundation, since 1985; Chairman of Council, Overseas Development Institute, since 1984; *b* 7 May 1912; *s* of late Rt Hon. Sir Eric Geddes, PC, GCB, GBE; *m* 1938, Imogen, *d* of late Captain Hay Matthey, Brixham; two *s* three *d*. *Educ:* Rugby; Cambridge. Bank of England, 1932–35; Dunlop Rubber Company Ltd, 1935, Dir 1947, Chm. 1968–78; Dep. Chm., Midland Bank, 1978–84 (Dir, 1967–84). Director: Shell Transport and Trading Co., 1968–82; Rank Orgn, 1975–84. Pres., Soc. of Motor Manufacturers and Traders, 1958–59; Part-time Mem., UKAEA, 1960–65; Mem. Nat. Economic Develt. Council, 1962–65; Chm., Shipbuilding Inquiry Cttee, 1965–66. Pres., Internat. Chamber of Commerce, 1980. Hon. DSc Aston, 1967; Hon LLD Leicester, 1969; Hon. DTech Loughborough, 1970. *Address:* 49 Eaton Place, SW1X 8DE.

GEDDES, Ford Irvine, MBE 1943; *b* 17 Jan. 1913; *e s* of Irvine Campbell Geddes and Dorothy Jefford Geddes (*née* Fowler); *m* 1945, Barbara Gertrude Vere Parry-Okeden; one *s* four *d*. *Educ:* Loretto Sch.; Gonville and Caius Coll., Cambridge (BA). Joined Anderson Green & Co. Ltd, London, 1934. Served War RE, 1939–45 (Major). Director: Bank of NSW (London Adv. Bd), 1950–81; Equitable Life Assce Soc., 1955–76 (Pres. 1963–71); British United Turkeys Ltd, 1962–78 (Chm., 1976–78); Chairman: P&O Steam Navigation Co., 1971–72 (a Dep. Chm., 1968–71; Dir, 1960–72); British Shipping Federation, 1965–68; Pres., Internat. Shipping Fedn, 1967–69. *Address:* 18 Gordon Place, W8 4JD. *Clubs:* City of London; Union (Sydney).

GEDDES, Sir Reay; *see* Geddes, Sir A. R. M.

GEDDES, William George Nicholson, CBE 1979; FRSE; FEng, FICE, FIStructE; Senior Partner, Babtie Shaw and Morton, Consulting Engineers, 1976–79, retired (Partner, 1950–76); *b* 29 July 1913; *s* of William Brydon Geddes and Ina (*née* Nicholson); *m* 1942, Margaret Gilchrist Wilson; one *s* one *d*. *Educ:* Dunbar High Sch.; Univ. of Edinburgh

(BSc, 1st Cl. Hons). Engineer: Sir William Arrol & Co., F. A. Macdonald & Partners, Shell Oil Co., ICI, Babtie Shaw and Morton, 1935–49. President: Instn of Structural Engrs, 1971–72; Instn of Engrs and Shipbuilders in Scotland, 1977–79; Instn of Civil Engrs, 1979–80. Visiting Professor, Univ. of Strathclyde, 1978. Hon. DSc Edinburgh, 1980. *Publications:* numerous papers to engrg instns and learned socs both at home and abroad. *Recreations:* fly-fishing, golf, hill-walking. *Address:* 17 Beechlands Avenue, Netherlee, Glasgow G44 3YT. *T:* 041–644 3216. *Clubs:* Caledonian; Royal Scottish Automobile (Glasgow).

GEDLING, Raymond, CB 1969; Deputy Secretary, Department of Health and Social Security, 1971–77; *b* 3 Sept. 1917; *s* of late John and late Mary Gedling; *m* 1956, Joan Evelyn Chapple; one *s*. *Educ:* Grangefield Grammar Sch., Stockton-on-Tees. Entered Civil Service as Executive Officer, Min. of Health, 1936; Asst Principal, 1942, Principal, 1947. Cabinet Office, 1951–52; Principal Private Sec. to Minister of Health, 1952–55; Asst Sec., 1955; Under-Sec., 1961; Asst Under-Sec. of State, Dept of Educn and Science, 1966–68; Dep. Sec., Treasury, 1968–71. *Recreations:* walking, chess. *Address:* 27 Wallace Fields, Epsom, Surrey. *T:* 01–393 9060.

GEE, Prof. Geoffrey, CBE 1958; FRS 1951; Sir Samuel Hall Professor of Chemistry, University of Manchester, 1955–76, now Emeritus Professor; *b* 6 June 1910; *s* of Thomas and Mary Ann Gee; *m* 1934, Marion (*née* Bowden); one *s* two *d*. *Educ:* New Mills Grammar Sch.; Universities of Manchester and Cambridge, BSc 1931, MSc 1932, Manchester; PhD 1936, ScD 1947, Cambridge. ICI (Dyestuffs Group) Research Chemist, 1933–38; British Rubber Producers' Research Association: Research Chemist, 1938–47; Dir, 1947–53. Prof. of Physical Chemistry, 1953–55, and Pro-Vice Chancellor, 1966–68, 1972–77, Univ. of Manchester. Pres., Faraday Soc., 1969 and 1970. Hon. Fellow, Manchester Polytechnic, 1979. Hon. DSc Manchester, 1983. *Publications:* numerous scientific papers in Transactions of the Faraday Soc., and other journals. *Recreation:* gardening. *Address:* 8 Holmfield Drive, Cheadle Hulme, Cheshire. *T:* 061–485 3713.

GEE, Timothy Hugh; HM Diplomatic Service; Head of Cultural Relations Department, Foreign and Commonwealth Office, since 1985; *b* 12 Nov. 1936; *s* of Arthur William Gee and Edith (*née* Ingham); *m* 1964, Gillian Eve St Johnston; two *s* one *d*. *Educ:* Berkhamsted; Trinity Coll., Oxford. 2 Lieut 3rd Regt RHA, 1959–61. Joined British Council, 1961; New Delhi, 1962–66; entered HM Diplomatic Service, 1966; FO, 1966–68; Brussels, 1968–72; FCO, 1972–74; Kuala Lumpur, 1974–79; Counsellor, on secondment to NI Office, 1979–81; Consul-General, Istanbul, 1981–85. *Address:* c/o Foreign and Commonwealth Office, King Charles Street, SW1. *Club:* Travellers'.

GEFFEN, Dr Terence John; Specialist in Community Medicine, NW Thames Regional Health Authority, since 1982; *b* 17 Sept. 1921; *s* of late Maximilian W. Geffen and Maia Geffen (later Reid); *m* 1965, Judith Anne Steward; two *s*. *Educ:* St Paul's Sch.; University Coll., London; UCH. MD, FRCP. House Phys., UCH, 1943; RAMC, 1944–47; hosp. posts, Edgware Gen. Hosp., Hampstead Gen. Hosp., UCH, 1947–55; Min. of Health (later DHSS), 1956–82, SPMO, 1972–82. *Publications:* various in BMJ, Lancet, Clinical Science, etc. *Recreations:* music, reading, bridge. *Address:* 2 Stonehill Close, SW14 8RP. *T:* 01–878 0516.

GELDER, Prof. Michael Graham; W. A. Handley Professor of Psychiatry, University of Oxford, since 1969; Fellow of Merton College, Oxford; *b* 2 July 1929; *s* of Philip Graham Gelder and Margaret Gelder (*née* Graham); *m* 1954, Margaret (*née* Anderson); one *s* two *d*. *Educ:* Bradford Grammar Sch.; Queen's Coll., Oxford. Scholar, Theodore Williams Prize 1949 and first class Hons, Physiology finals, 1950; MA, DM Oxon, FRCP, FRCPsych; DPM London (with distinction) 1961. Goldsmit Schol., UCH London, 1951. House Physician, Sen. House Physician, UCH, 1955–57; Registrar, Maudsley Hosp., 1958–61; MRC Fellow in Clinical Research, 1962–63; Sen. Lectr, Inst. of Psychiatry, 1965–67 (Vice-Dean, 1967–68); Physician, Bethlem Royal and Maudsley Hosps, 1967–68. Hon. Consultant Psychiatrist, Oxford RHA, later DHA, 1969–; Mem., Oxford DHA, 1985–. Mem., MRC (Chm., Neurosciences Bd), 1978–79. Mem., Wellcome Trust Neuroscience Panel, 1984–. Chairman: Assoc. of Univ. Teachers of Psychiatry, 1979–82; Jt Cttee on Higher Psychiatric Trng, 1981–85. Europ. Vice-Pres., Soc. for Psychotherapy Research, 1977–82. Mem., Assoc. of Physicians, 1983–. Mem. Council, RCPsych, 1981– (Vice Pres. 1982–83; Sen. Vice-Pres., 1983–84). Gold Medal, Royal Medico-Psychol Assoc., 1962. *Publications:* (jtly) Agoraphobia: nature and treatment, 1981; (jtly) The Oxford Textbook of Psychiatry, 1983; chapters in books and articles in medical jls. *Recreations:* photography, gardening, real-tennis. *Address:* St Mary's, Jack Straw's Lane, Oxford OX3 0DN.

GELDOF, Bob, Hon. KBE 1986; singer; songwriter; initiator and organiser, Band Aid, Live Aid and Sport Aid fund-raising events; *b* Dublin, 5 Oct. 1954; *m* 1986, Paula Yates; one *d*. *Educ:* Black Rock Coll. Sometime journalist: Georgia Straight, Vancouver; New Musical Express; Melody Maker. Jt Founder, Boomtown Rats, rock band, 1975. Acted in films: Pink Floyd—The Wall, 1982; Number One, 1985. Organised Band Aid, 1984, to record Do They Know It's Christmas, sales from which raised £8 million for famine relief in Ethiopia; organised simultaneous Live Aid concerts in London and Philadelphia to raise £50 million, 1985; organised Sport Aid to raise further £50 million, 1986. Chm., Band Aid Trust, 1985–; Founder, Live Aid Foundn, USA, 1985–. Freeman, Borough of Swale, 1985. Hon. MA Kent, 1985. *Publication:* Is That It? (autobiog.), 1986. *Address:* c/o Band Aid Trust, PO Box 4TX, W1; Davington Priory, near Faversham, Kent.

GELL, Prof. Philip George Houtham, FRS 1969; Professor and Head of Department of Experimental Pathology, Birmingham University, 1968–78; retired; *b* 20 Oct. 1914; *s* of late Major P. F. Gell, DSO, and Mrs E. Lewis Hall; *m* 1941, Albinia Susan Roope Gordon; one *s* one *d*. *Educ:* Stowe Sch.; Trinity Coll., Cambridge; University Coll. Hosp. MRCS, LRCP, 1939; MB, BCh, 1940; FRCPath, 1969. Ho. Phys. to Med. Unit, UCH, 1939; Emergency Public Health Laboratory Service, 1940–43. On staff of Nat. Inst. for Med. Research, 1943–48; Reader in Dept of Exptl Pathology, Birmingham Univ., 1948–60; Prof. (Personal) of Immunological Pathology, Dept of Exptl Pathology, 1960–68. *Publications:* (ed with R. R. A. Coombs and P. J. Lachmann) Clinical Aspects of Immunology, 3rd edn, 1974; contribs to Jl of Experimental Med., Immunology, 1960–. *Recreations:* gardening, painting, philosophy of science. *Address:* Wychwood, Cranes Lane, Kingston, Cambridge. *T:* Comberton 2714.

GELL-MANN, Murray; Robert Andrews Millikan Professor of Theoretical Physics at the California Institute of Technology since 1967; *b* 15 Sept. 1929; *s* of Arthur and Pauline Gell-Mann; *m* 1955, J. Margaret Dow (*d* 1981); one *s* one *d*. *Educ:* Yale Univ.; Massachusetts Inst. of Technology. Mem., Inst. for Advanced Study, Princeton, 1951; Instructor, Asst Prof., and Assoc. Prof., Univ. of Chicago, 1952–55; Assoc. Prof. 1955–56, Prof. 1956–66, California Inst. of Technology. Vis. Prof., Collège de France and Univ. of Paris, 1959–60. Overseas Fellow, Churchill Coll., Cambridge, 1966. Mem., President's Science Adv. Cttee, 1969–72. Regent, Smithsonian Instn, 1974–; Chm. of Bd, Aspen Center for Physics, 1973–79; Dir, J. D. and C. T. MacArthur Foundn, 1979–; Vice-Pres. and Chm. of Western Center, Amer. Acad. of Arts and Sciences, 1970–76; Mem., Nat. Acad. of Sciences, 1960–. Mem. Bd, California Nature Conservancy, 1984–. Foreign Mem., Royal Society, 1978. Dannie Heineman Prize (Amer. Phys. Soc.), 1959; Ernest O. Lawrence Award, 1966; Franklin Medal (Franklin Inst., Philadelphia), 1967; John J. Carty Medal (Nat. Acad. Scis), 1968; Research Corp. Award, 1969; Nobel Prize in Physics, 1969. Hon. ScD: Yale, 1959; Chicago, 1967; Illinois, 1968; Wesleyan, 1968; Utah, 1970; Columbia, 1977; Hon. DSc Cantab, 1980; Hon. Dr, Turin, 1969. *Publications:* (with Yuval Ne'eman) The Eightfold Way, 1964; various articles in learned jls on topics referring to classification and description of elementary particles of physics and their interactions. *Recreations:* walking in wild country, study of natural history, languages. *Address:* 1024 Armada Drive, Pasadena, Calif 91103, USA. *T:* 818–792–4740. *Clubs:* Cosmos (Washington) Explorers', Century (New York); Athenæum (Pasadena).

GELLHORN, Peter; Conductor and Chorus Master, Glyndebourne Festival Opera, 1954–61, rejoined Glyndebourne Music Staff, 1974 and 1975; Professor, Guildhall School of Music and Drama, since 1981; *b* 24 Oct. 1912; *s* of late Dr Alfred Gellhorn, and late Mrs Else Gellhorn; *m* 1943, Olive Shirley (*née* Layton), 3rd *d* of 1st Baron Layton, CH, CBE; two *s* two *d*. *Educ:* Schiller Realgymnasium, Charlottenburg; University of Berlin; Berlin Music Acad. After passing final exams (with dist.) as pianist and conductor, left Germany 1935. Musical Dir, Toynbee Hall, London, E1, 1935–39; Asst Conductor, Sadler's Wells Opera, 1941–43. On industrial war service, 1943–45. Conductor, Royal Carl Rosa Opera (115 perfs), 1945–46; Conductor and Head of Music Staff, Royal Opera House, Covent Garden (over 260 perfs), 1946–53; Dir, BBC Chorus, 1961–72; Conductor, Elizabethan Singers, 1976–80. Has also been working at National Sch. of Opera, annually at Summer Sch. of Music at Dartington Hall; broadcasting frequently as conductor or pianist; composes; wrote and arranged music for silhouette and puppet films of Lotte Reiniger (at intervals, 1933–57). Mem., Music Staff, London Opera Centre, 1973–78; Conductor: Morley Coll. Opera Gp, 1974–79; Barnes Choir; Associate Conductor, London Chamber Opera, 1982–; Music Dir, Opera Players Ltd; Mem. Staff, Opera Sch., RCM, 1980–, conducting its opera perfs, 1981. Lectures on Courses arranged by various County Councils and adult colleges; frequently adjudicates at music fests in UK and overseas. Musical Dir, Opera Barga, Italy, from foundn, 1967–69. *Recreations:* reading, walking and going to plays. *Address:* 33 Leinster Avenue, East Sheen, SW14 7JW. *T:* 01–876 3949. *Club:* BBC.

GELLNER, Prof. Ernest André, FBA 1974; William Wyse Professor of Social Anthropology, Cambridge University, since 1984; Professorial Fellow, King's College, Cambridge, since 1984; *b* Paris, 9 Dec. 1925; *s* of Rudolf Gellner and Anna (*née* Fantl), Prague; *m* 1954, Susan Ryan; two *s* two *d*. *Educ:* Prague English Grammar Sch.; St Albans County Sch.; Balliol Coll., Oxford. MA (Oxon), PhD (Lond). Pte, Czech. Armoured Brig., BLA, 1944–45. On staff of London School of Economics, 1949–84, Prof. of Philosophy, 1962–84. Visiting Fellow: Harvard, 1952–53; Univ. of California, Berkeley, 1968; Centre de Recherches et d'Études sur les Sociétés Méditerranéens, Aix-en-Provence, 1978–79. Member: Council, SSRC (later ESRC), 1980–86 (Chm., Internat. Activities Cttee, 1982–84); Council, British Acad., 1981–84. Lectures: Frazer Meml; Radcliffe-Brown Meml; Marett Meml; Myers Meml. Hon. DSc Bristol, 1981. Mem., Editorial or Adv. Boards: British Jl of Sociol.; Amer. Jl of Sociol.; Inquiry; Middle Eastern Studies; Jl of Peasant Studies; Society and Theory; Govt and Opposition; Co-Editor: Europ. Jl of Sociol., 1966–84; Govt and Opposition, 1980–. *Publications:* Words and Things, 1959; Thought and Change, 1964; Saints of the Atlas, 1969; (ed with G. Ionescu) Populism, 1969; Cause and Meaning in the Social Sciences, 1973; (ed with C. Micaud) Arabs and Berbers, 1973; Contemporary Thought and Politics, 1974; The Devil in Modern Philosophy, 1974; Legitimation of Belief, 1975; (ed with J. Waterbury) Patrons and Clients, 1977; Spectacles and Predicaments, 1979; (ed) Soviet and Western Anthropology, 1980; Muslim Society, 1981; Nations and Nationalism, 1983; (ed) Islamic Dilemmas: reformers, nationalists and industrialisation, 1985; The Psychoanalytic Movement, 1985; numerous contributions to learned jls. *Address:* King's College, Cambridge CB2 1ST. *Club:* Reform.

GENDERS, Rt. Rev. Roger Alban Marson, (Father Anselm, CR); *b* 15 Aug. 1919; *yr s* of John Boulton Genders and Florence Alice (*née* Thomas). *Educ:* King Edward VI School, Birmingham; Brasenose College, Oxford (Sen. Scholar 1938, BA Lit. Hum. 1946, MA 1946). Served War, Lieut RNVR, 1940–46. Joined Community of the Resurrection, Mirfield, 1948; professed, 1952; ordained, 1952; Tutor, College of the Resurrection, 1952–55; Vice-Principal 1955, and Principal 1957–65, Codrington Coll., Barbados; Exam. Chaplain to Bishop of Barbados, 1957–65; Treasurer of St Augustine's Mission, Rhodesia, 1966–75; Archdeacon of Manicaland, 1970–75; Asst Bursar, Community of the Resurrection, Mirfield, 1975–77; Bishop of Bermuda, 1977–82; Assistant Bishop of Wakefield, 1983–. *Publications:* contribs to Theology. *Address:* Community of the Resurrection, House of the Resurrection, Mirfield, W Yorks WF14 0BN.

GENGE, Rt. Rev. Mark; *see* Newfoundland, Central, Bishop of.

GENSCHER, Hans-Dietrich; Federal Minister for Foreign Affairs and Deputy Chancellor, Federal Republic of Germany, since May 1974 (in government of Helmut Schmidt, to Oct. 1982, then in government of Helmut Kohl); Chairman of the Free Democratic Party, 1974–85; *b* Reideburg/Saalkreis, 21 March 1927; *m* Barbara; one *d*. *Educ:* Higher Sch. Certif. (Abitur); studied law and economics in Halle/Saale and Leipzig Univs, 1946–49. Served War, 1943–45. Mem., state-level org. of LDP, 1946. Re-settled in W Germany, 1952: practical legal training in Bremen and Mem. Free Democratic Party (FDP); FDP Asst in Parly Group, 1956; Gen. Sec.: FDP Parly Group, 1959–65; FDP at nat. level, 1962–64. Elected Mem., Bundestag, 1965; a Parly Sec., FDP Parly Group, 1965–69; Dep. Chm., FDP, 1969–74; Federal Minister of the Interior, Oct. 1969 (Brandt-Scheel Cabinet); re-apptd Federal Minister of the Interior, Dec. 1972. He was instrumental in maintaining pure air and water; gave a modern structure to the Federal Police Authority; Federal Border Guard Act passed; revised weapons laws, etc. Mem. Delegn of FDP politicians who met Premier Kosygin in the Kremlin, 1969; campaigned for exchange of declarations of renunciation of force, with all Warsaw Pact countries. *Publications:* Umweltschutz: Das Umweltschutzprogramm der Bundesregierung, 1972; Bundestagsreden, 1972; Aussenpolitik im Dienste von Sicherheit und Freiheit, 1976; Deutsche Aussenpolitik, 1977, 3rd edn 1985; Bundestagsreden und Zeitdokumente, 1979. *Recreations:* reading, walking, swimming. *Address:* Auswärtiges Amt, Bonn, Federal Republic of Germany.

GENTLEMAN, David, RDI 1970; painter and designer; *b* 11 March 1930; *s* of late Tom and Winifred Gentleman; *m* 1st, 1953, Rosalind Dease (marr. diss. 1966); one *d*; 2nd, 1968, Susan, *d* of George Ewart Evans, *qv*; two *d* one *s*. *Educ:* Hertford Grammar Sch.; St Albans Sch. of Art; Royal College of Art. Work includes: watercolour painting, graphic design, lithography, book illustration and wood engraving; commissions include mural design for Charing Cross underground station, 1979; drawings, engravings and designs for many publishers, and for textiles and ceramics; postage stamps for the Post Office; posters for London Transport and the National Trust; symbols and devices for British Steel, Bodleian Library, etc. One-man exhibitions at Mercury Gallery: watercolours of: India, 1970; Carolina, 1973; East Africa, 1976; Pacific, 1981; Britain, 1982; London, 1985. Work in public collections incl. British Museum and Nat. Maritime Museum;

many works in private collections. Member: Alliance Graphique Internat.; Council, Artists' Gen. Benevolent Instn; Design Council, 1974–80. Hon. Fellow, RCA, 1981. Phillips Gold Medal for Stamp Design, 1969, 1979. *Publications include:* Fenella in Ireland, in Greece, in Spain, in France, 1967; Design in Miniature, 1972; Everyday Architecture in Towns, in Countryside, at the Seaside, Industrial, 1975 (RIBA wall-charts); David Gentleman's Britain, 1982; David Gentleman's London, 1985; (contrib.) Art and Graphics, 1983; *book illustrations include:* Plats du Jour, 1957; The Shepherd's Calendar, 1964; Pattern under the Plough, 1966; covers for New Penguin Shakespeare, 1968–78; Where Beards Wag All, 1970; The Dancing Tigers, 1979; Shakespeare and his Theatre, 1982; The Strength of the Hills, 1983; limited editions: Bridges on the Backs, 1961; Swiss Family Robinson, 1963 (USA); Poems of John Keats, 1966 (USA); The Jungle Book, 1968 (USA); King Solomon's Mines, 1970 (USA); Robin Hood, 1977 (USA); edns of lithographs of landscape and buildings, 1967–85; screenprints, 1970. *Address:* 25 Gloucester Crescent, NW1 7DL. *T:* 01–485 8824.

GENTRY, Maj.-Gen. (retd) Sir William George, KBE 1958 (CBE 1950); CB 1954; DSO 1942, and Bar 1945; *b* 20 Feb. 1899; *e s* of late Major F. C. Gentry, MBE and late Mrs F. C. Gentry; *m* 1926, Alexandra Nina Caverhill; one *s* one *d. Educ:* Wellington Coll., NZ; RMC of Australia. Commissioned NZ Army, Dec. 1919; attached Indian Army and served in Waziristan, 1921, and Malabar, 1921. Served War of 1939–45 with 2nd NZ Div. (Middle East and Italy): GSO 2 and AA and QMG, 1940; GSO 1, 1941–42; Comd 6 NZ Inf. Bde, 1942–43; DCGS, Army HQ, NZ, 1943–44; Comd 9 NZ Inf. Bde (Italy), 1945. Adjutant Gen., NZ Army, 1949–52; Chief of the Gen. Staff, NZ Army, 1952; retired, 1955. Mem. Licensing Control Commn, 1957–67. Hon. Pres. NZ Boy Scouts Assoc., 1957–67. Greek Military Cross, 1941; United States Bronze Star, 1945. *Address:* 52 Kings Crescent, Lower Hutt, New Zealand. *T:* 660208. *Clubs:* Wellington, United Services (Wellington, NZ).

GEORGALA, Douglas Lindley, CBE 1986; PhD; Head of Laboratory, Unilever Colworth Laboratory, since 1977; Member, Unilever Research Division Executive, since 1979; *b* 2 Feb. 1934; *s* of late John Michael Georgala and of Izetta Iris Georgala; *m* 1959, Eulalia Catherina Lochner; one *s* one *d. Educ:* South African College Sch., Cape Town; Univ. of Stellenbosch (BScAgric); Univ. of Aberdeen (PhD). Research Officer, Fishing Research Inst., Univ. of Cape Town, 1957–60; Research Microbiologist, 1960–69, Division Manager, 1969–72, Unilever Colworth Laboratory; Technical Member, Unilever Meat Products Co-ordination, 1973–77. Chairman: Fisheries Res. Bd, 1980–84; Adv. Cttee of Food Science Dept, Leeds Univ., 1984–; Member: Adv. Council of Applied Research & Development (ACARD), 1980–83; Food Cttee, AFRC, 1984–. FRSA 1984. *Publications:* papers in jls of general microbiology, applied bacteriology, hygiene, etc. *Recreations:* gardening, cycling, recorded music. *Address:* Unilever Colworth Laboratory, Sharnbrook, Bedford.

GEORGE; *see* Lloyd George and Lloyd-George.

GEORGE, Rev. (Alfred) Raymond, MA, BD; Warden, John Wesley's Chapel, Bristol, since 1982; *b* 26 Nov. 1912; *s* of A. H. and G. M. George. *Educ:* Crypt Sch., Gloucester; Balliol Coll., Oxford (1st cl. Hon. Classical Mods, 1st cl. Lit. Hum., BA 1935, MA 1938, BD 1955); Wesley House, Cambridge (1st cl. Theol Tripos, Pt I Sect. B, BA 1937, MA 1962); Marburg University. Asst Tutor, Handsworth Coll., Birmingham, 1938–40; ordained as Methodist minister, 1940; Asst Tutor, Hartley-Victoria Coll., Manchester, 1940–42; Circuit Minister, Manchester, 1942–46; Tutor, Wesley Coll., Headingley, Leeds, 1946–67, Principal, 1961–67; Associate Lectr, Leeds Univ., 1946–67; Actg Head, Theol. Dept, 1967–68; Principal, Richmond Coll., London Univ., 1968–72; Tutor, Wesley College, Bristol, 1972–81. Select Preacher, Cambridge, 1963; Member, World Council of Churches Commn on Faith and Order, 1961–75; Pres. of Methodist Conf., 1975–76; Moderator, Free Church Federal Council, 1979–80; Chm., Jt Liturgical Group, 1984–. *Publications:* Communion with God in the New Testament, 1953; chapter in vol. I, A History of the Methodist Church in Great Britain, 1965, ed (jtly), vol. II, 1978, and contrib. chapter, ed (jtly), vol. III, 1983; jt Editor of series: Ecumenical Studies in Worship; also articles in jls. *Address:* 40 Knole Lane, Bristol BS10 6SS. *T:* Bristol 503698.

GEORGE, Rear Adm. Anthony Sanderson, CB 1983; FBIM, CEng, FIIM; Chief Executive, World Energy Business, since 1986; *b* 8 Nov. 1928; *s* of Sandys Parker George and Winifred Marie George; *m* 1953, Mary Veronica Frances Bell; two *d. Educ:* Royal Naval Coll., Dartmouth; Royal Naval Engrg Coll., Manadon. MIMechE 1957; FBIM 1977; FIIM 1979. Sea-going appts, 1950–62; warship design, Ship Dept of MoD, 1962–64; RN Staff Coll., 1965; British High Commn, Canberra, 1966–67; MEO, HMS Hampshire, 1968–69; Staff of Flag Officer Sea Trng, 1970–71; Dep. Prodn Manager, HM Dockyard, Portsmouth, 1972–75; RCDS, 1976; CSO (Trng) to C-in-C Naval Home Comd, 1977–78; Prodn Manager, HM Dockyard, Portsmouth, 1979–81; Dir, Dockyard Prodn and Support, 1981–82; Chief Exec., Royal Dockyards, 1983–86. Comdr 1965, Captain 1972, Rear Adm. 1981. *Recreations:* sailing, swimming, walking. *Address:* c/o National Westminster Bank, 5 East Street, Chichester, West Sussex PO19 1HH.

GEORGE, Sir Arthur (Thomas), Kt 1972; solicitor and company director; Chairman and Managing Director, George Investment Pty Ltd Group, since 1943; Chairman, Australia Solenoid Holdings Ltd, since 1967; *b* 17 Jan. 1915; *s* of late Thomas George; *m* 1939, Renee, *d* of Anthony Freeleagus; one *d. Educ:* Sydney High Sch., NSW. Director: Thomas Nationwide Transport Ltd, 1973–; Ansett Transport Industries, 1981–; Bliss Welded Products, 1981–; Wyndham Estate Wines, 1985–. Chm., Assoc. for Classical Archæology, of Sydney Univ., 1966–. Chm., Australian Soccer Fedn., 1969–; Comr, Australian Sports Commn, 1986–; Member: Exec., FIFA, 1981–; Organising Cttee, 1983 World Youth Championship. Chm. and Founder, The Arthur T. George Foundation Ltd, 1972. Fellow, Confedn of Australian Sport, 1985; Hon. Fellow, Univ. of Sydney, 1985. Coronation Medal; Silver Jubilee Medal. Grand Commander (Keeper of the Laws), Cross of St Marks, and Gold Cross of Mount Athos, Greek Orthodox Church; Order of Phoenix (Greece). *Recreations:* interested in sport, especially Association football, etc. *Address:* 1 Little Queen's Lane, Vaucluse, NSW 2030, Australia.

GEORGE, Bruce Thomas; MP (Lab) Walsall South since Feb. 1974; *b* 1 June 1942. *Educ:* Mountain Ash Grammar Sch.; UCW Swansea; Univ. of Warwick. BA Politics Wales 1964, MA Warwick 1968. Asst Lectr in Social Studies, Glamorgan Polytechnic, 1964–66; Lectr in Politics, Manchester Polytechnic, 1968–70; Senior Lectr, Birmingham Polytechnic, 1970–74. Vis. Lectr, Univ. of Essex, 1985–86. Member: former Select Cttee on Violence in the Family; Select Cttee on Defence; North Atlantic Assembly, 1982– (Rapporteur Gen., Political Cttee); RIIA; IISS; RUSI. Patron, Nat. Assoc. of Widows; Co-founder, Sec., House of Commons FC; Hon. Consultant, Confed. of Long Distance Pigeon Racing Assocs; Vice-Pres., Psoriasis Assoc. Pres., Walsall and District Gilbert and Sullivan Soc. Fellow, Parliament and Industry Trust, 1977–78. *Publications:* numerous articles on defence and foreign affairs. *Recreations:* Association football, snooker, student of American Indians, eating Indian food. *Address:* 42 Wood End Road, Walsall, West Midlands WS5 3BG. *T:* Walsall 27898. *Clubs:* Darlaston Labour, Caldmore Liberal; North Walsall, Pleck and Station Street Working Men's Clubs.

GEORGE, Prof. Donald William, AO 1979; Vice-Chancellor and Principal, University of Newcastle, New South Wales, 1975–86; *b* 22 Nov. 1926; *s* of late H. W. George, Sydney; *m* 1950, Lorna M. Davey, Parkes, NSW; one *s* one *d. Educ:* Univ. of Sydney. BSc, BE, PhD, FTS, FIEE, FIMechE, FIEAust, FAIP. Lectr, Elec. Engrg, NSW Univ. of Technology, 1949–53; Exper. Officer, UKAEA, Harwell, 1954–55; Res. Officer, Sen. Res. Officer, AAEC, Harwell and Lucas Heights, 1956–59; Sen. Lectr, Elec. Engrg, Univ. of Sydney, 1960–66; Associate Prof., Elec. Engrg, Univ. of Sydney, 1967–68; P. N. Russell Prof. of Mech. Engrg, Univ. of Sydney, 1969–74. Chairman: Australian-American Educational Foundn, 1977–84; Australian Atomic Energy Commn, 1976–83. Trustee, Asian Inst. of Technology, 1978–. *Publications:* numerous sci. papers and techn. reports. *Address:* Shamley Green, Glenning Road, Berkeley Vale, NSW 2259, Australia. *T:* (043) 883056.

GEORGE, Edward Alan John; Executive Director, Bank of England, since 1982; *b* 11 Sept. 1938; *s* of Alan George and Olive Elizabeth George; *m* 1962, Clarice Vanessa Williams; one *s* two *d. Educ:* Dulwich Coll.; Emmanuel Coll., Cambridge (BAEcon 2nd Cl. (i); MA). Joined Bank of England, 1962; worked initially on East European affairs; seconded to Bank for International Settlements, 1966–69, and to International Monetary Fund as Asst to Chairman of Deputies of Committee of Twenty on Internat. Monetary Reform, 1972–74; Adviser on internat. monetary questions, 1974–77; Dep. Chief Cashier, 1977–80; Asst Dir (Gilt Edged Div.), 1980–82. *Recreations:* family, sailing, bridge. *Address:* Bank of England, EC2R 8AH. *T:* 01–601 4444.

GEORGE, Griffith Owen, TD; DL; a Recorder of the Crown Court, 1972–74; *b* 5 Dec. 1902; *s* of late John and Emiah Owen George, Hirwaun, Glam; *m* 1937, Anne Elinor, *e d* of late Charles and Anne Edwards, Llandaff; one *s. Educ:* Westminster Sch.; Christ Church, Oxford (MA). Beit Prize Essay, 1923; Barrister, Gray's Inn, 1927, Wales and Chester Circuit. Served War of 1939–45, 2nd Lieut RA, 1939; Capt. 1941; Major 1943; on JAG's staff, N Africa, Italy, Middle East, 1943–45. Contested Llanelly (Nat. Con.), 1945. Commissioner in Wales under the National Insurance Acts, 1950–67. Dep. Chm., Glamorgan Quarter Sessions, 1956–66, Chm., 1966–71. JP Glamorgan, 1952–72; DL Glamorgan, 1970. *Address:* Glanyrafon, Ponterwyd, Aberystwyth SY23 3JS. *T:* Ponterwyd 661.

GEORGE, Henry Ridyard, CBE 1979; FInstPet; oil and gas exploration and production consultant; *b* 14 May 1921; *s* of Charles Herbert George and Mary Ridyard; *m* 1st, 1948, Irene May Myers (*d* 1981); one *s*; 2nd, 1985, Gwen (*née* Gudrum), *widow* of Prof. E. O'Farrel Walsh. *Educ:* George Dixon's Secondary Sch., Birmingham; Univ. of Birmingham (1st Cl. Hons degree, Oil Engrg and Refining and Petroleum Technol., 1941). Served War, REME/IEME, 1941–46 (2nd Lieut, later Captain). Pet. Engr with Royal Dutch/Shell Gp, 1947–68: service in USA, Holland, Brunei, Nigeria and Venezuela in a variety of positions, incl. Chief Pet. Engr in last 3 countries; Dept of Energy, 1968–81, Dir of Pet. Engrg, 1973–81. FRSA 1979. *Recreations:* gardening, golf. *Address:* 39 Lodge Close, Stoke D'Abernon, Cobham, Surrey KT11 2SG. *T:* Cobham 63878.

GEORGE, Hywel, CMG 1968; OBE 1963; Bursar, Churchill College, Cambridge, since 1972; *b* 10 May 1924; *s* of Rev. W. M. George and Catherine M. George; *m* 1955, Edith Pirchl; three *d. Educ:* Llanelli Gram. Sch.; UCW Aberystwyth; Pembroke Coll., Cambridge. RAF, 1943–46. Cadet, Colonial Admin. Service, N Borneo, 1949–52; District Officer, 1952–58; Secretariat, 1959–62; Resident, Sabah, Malaysia, 1963–66; Administrator, 1967–69, Governor, 1969–70, St Vincent; Administrator, British Virgin Is, 1971. Panglima Darjah Kinabalu (with title of Dato), Sabah, 1964; JMN, Malaysia, 1966. CStJ 1969. *Recreations:* tennis, walking. *Address:* Churchill College, Cambridge. *T:* (home) Cambridge 336121.

GEORGE, Prof. Kenneth Desmond; Professor and Head of Department of Economics, University College, Cardiff, since 1973 (Deputy Principal, 1980–83); *b* 11 Jan. 1937; *s* of Horace Avory George and Dorothy Margaret (*née* Hughes); *m* 1959, Elizabeth Vida (*née* Harries); two *s* one *d. Educ:* Ystalyfera Grammar Sch.; University Coll. of Wales, Aberstwyth (MA). Res. Asst, then Lectr in Econs, Univ. of Western Australia, 1959–63; Lectr in Econs, University Coll. of N Wales, Bangor, 1963–64; Univ. Asst Lectr, Univ. of Cambridge, 1964–66, Univ. Lectr, 1966–73; Fellow and Dir of Studies in Econs, Sidney Sussex Coll., Cambridge, 1965–73. Vis. Prof., McMaster Univ., 1970–71. Part-time Mem., Monopolies and Mergers Commn, 1978–86. Editor, Jl of Industrial Economics, 1970–83. *Publications:* Productivity in Distribution, 1966; Productivity and Capital Expenditure in Retailing, 1968; Industrial Organisation, 1971, 3rd edn (with C. Joll), 1981; (with T. S. Ward) The Structure of Industry in the EEC, 1975; (ed with C. Joll) Competition Policy in the UK and EEC, 1975; (with J. Shorey) The Allocation of Resources, 1978; articles in Econ. Jl, Oxford Econ. Papers, Aust. Econ. Papers, Jl Indust. Econs, Rev. of Econs and Stats, Oxford Bull., Scottish Jl Polit. Econ., and British Jl Indust. Relations. *Recreations:* walking, music, cricket. *Address:* Ein-Tŷ-Ni, 39 St Fagans Drive, St Fagans, Cardiff. *T:* Cardiff 562801.

GEORGE, Llewellyn Norman Havard; a Recorder of the Crown Court, since 1980; *b* 13 Nov. 1925; *s* of Benjamin William George, DSO, RNR, and Annie Jane George; *m* 1950, Mary Patricia Morgan (*née* Davies); one *d. Educ:* Cardiff High Sch.; Fishguard Grammar Sch. HM Coroner, 1965–80; Recorder, Wales and Chester Circuit, 1980–. President: West Wales Law Society, 1973–74; Pembrokeshire Law Society, 1981–83; Chairman, (No 5) South Wales Law Society Legal Aid Cttee, 1979; Dep. Chm., Agricl Land Tribunal (Wales), 1985–. Mem., Farrand Cttee, 1984–85. *Recreations:* golf, reading, chess. *Address:* Four Winds, Tower Hill, Fishguard, Dyfed SA65 9LA. *T:* Fishguard 873894. *Clubs:* Pembrokeshire County; Newport (Pembs) Golf.

GEORGE, Peter John, OBE 1974; HM Diplomatic Service, retired; Counsellor and Consul General, British Embassy, Manila, 1976–79; Chargé d'Affaires *ai*, 1978; *b* 12 Dec. 1919; *s* of late Cecil John George and Mabel George; *m* 1946, Andrée Louise Pernon; one *d. Educ:* Sutton Grammar Sch., Plymouth. Served War, 1939–46: Captain. Home Civil Service, 1936; HM Diplomatic Service, 1966; First Secretary, Commercial: Colombo, 1967–70; Seoul, 1971–73 (Chargé d'Affaires *ai*, 1971 and 1972); Prague, 1973–76. *Recreations:* golf, tennis, ski-ing, bridge. *Address:* St Just, Walton Park, Walton-on-Thames, Surrey.

GEORGE, Rev. Raymond; *see* George, Rev. A. R.

GEORGE, Timothy John Burr; HM Diplomatic Service; Head of Republic of Ireland Department, Foreign and Commonwealth Office, since 1986; *b* 14 July 1937; *s* of Brig. J. B. George, late RAMC, retd; *m* 1962, Richenda Mary, *d* of Alan Reed, architect; one *s* two *d. Educ:* Aldenham Sch.; Christ's Coll., Cambridge (BA). National Service, 2nd Lieut RA, 1956–58; Cambridge Univ., 1958. FCO, 1961; 3rd Secretary: Hong Kong, 1962; Peking, 1963; 2nd, later 1st Sec., FCO, 1966; 1st Sec. (Economic), New Delhi, 1969; Asst Political Adviser, Hong Kong, 1972; Asst European Integration Dept (Internal), FCO, 1974; Counsellor and Head of Chancery, Peking, 1978–80; Res. Associate, IISS, 1980–81; Counsellor and Hd of Chancery, UK Perm. Delegn to OECD, 1982–86. *Publication:* (jtly) Security in Southern Asia, 1984. *Address:* c/o Foreign and Commonwealth Office, SW1.

GEORGE, Prof. William David, FRCS; Professor of Surgery, University of Glasgow, since 1981; *b* 22 March 1943; *s* of William Abel George and Peggy Eileen George; *m* 1967, Helen Marie (*née* Moran); one *s* three *d.* *Educ:* Reading Bluecoat Sch.; Henley Grammar Sch.; Univ. of London (MB, BS 1966; MS 1977). FRCS 1970. Jun. surgical jobs, 1966–71; Registrar in Surgery, Royal Postgrad. Med. Sch., 1971–73; Lectr in Surg., Univ. of Manchester, 1973–77; Sen. Lectr in Surg., Univ. of Liverpool, 1977–81. *Publications:* articles in BMJ, Lancet, British Jl of Surg. *Recreations:* veteran rowing, fishing, squash. *Address:* 21 Kingsborough Gardens, Glasgow G12 9NH. *T:* 041–339 9546. *Club:* Clyde Amateur Rowing (Glasgow).

GEORGES, Rt. Hon. (Philip) Telford; PC 1986; Chief Justice of the Bahamas, since 1984; Judge, Court of Appeal, Cayman Islands, since 1984; *b* Dominica, 5 Jan. 1923; *s* of John Georges and Milutine Cox; *m* 1954, Grace Glasgow (marr. diss.); *m* 1981, Joyce Cole. *Educ:* Dominica Grammar Sch.; Toronto Univ. (BA). Called to the Bar, 1949; in private practice, Trinidad and Tobago, 1949–62; Judge of the High Court, Trinidad and Tobago, 1962–74; on secondment as Chief Justice of Tanzania, 1965–71; acting Justice of Appeal, Trinidad and Tobago, 1972; Judge of the Courts of Appeal, Belize, Bahamas, Bermuda, Turks and Caicos Is, 1975–81; Judge of the Supreme Court, 1981–83, Chief Justice, 1983, Zimbabwe. Prof. of Law, 1974–81, and Dean of the Faculty of Law, 1977–79, Univ. of WI at Cave Hill. Vice-Chm., Trinidad and Tobago Constitutional Reform Commn, 1971–74; Chm., Crime Commn, Bermuda, 1977–78. Hon. LLD: Toronto; Dar-es-Salaam; West Indies, 1985. *Recreation:* walking. *Address:* Supreme Court, PO Box N8167, Nassau, Bahamas. *T:* 2–3315.

GEORGES-PICOT, Jacques Marie Charles, KBE (Hon.) 1963; Commandeur, Légion d'Honneur; Hon. Chairman of the Board, Suez Finance Company (Chairman, 1957–70); *b* 16 Dec. 1900; *s* of Charles Georges-Picot and Marthe Fouquet; *m* 1925, Angéline Pelle; five *s.* *Educ:* Lycée Janson de Sailly, Paris. Inspector of Finance, 1925; Chef de Cabinet, Minister of Budget, 1931; Dir Min. of Finance, 1934; Agent Supérieur in Egypt, of Suez Canal Co., 1937; Asst Dir-Gen. of Suez Canal Co., 1946; Dir-Gen., 1953; Pres., 1957. Dir, Fondation des Sciences Politiques, Paris. *Publication:* La véritable crise de Suez, 1975. *Recreation:* tennis. *Address:* 2 Square Mignot, 75016 Paris, France. *T:* 727–7968. *Club:* Circle Interallié (Paris).

GERARD, family name of **Baron Gerard.**

GERARD, 4th Baron, *cr* 1876, Bt 1611; **Robert William Frederick Alwyn Gerard;** *b* 23 May 1918; *o s* of 3rd Baron Gerard, MC, and late Mary Frances Emma, *d* of Sir Martin Le Marchant Hadsley Gosselin, GCVO, KCMG, CB; *S* father, 1953. *Heir: cousin* Anthony Robert Hugo Gerard [*b* 3 Dec. 1949; *m* Kathleen, *e d* of Dr Bernard Ryan, New York, USA; one *s*]. *Address:* Blakesware, Ware, Herts. *T:* 3665.

GERARD, Geoffrey; *see* Gerard, W. G.

GERARD, Ronald; Joint Managing Director, since 1959, Chairman, since 1982, London & Provincial Shop Centres (Holdings) plc; *b* 30 Oct. 1925; *s* of Samuel and Caroline Gerard; *m* 1952, Patricia Krieger; one *s* one *d.* *Educ:* Regent Street Polytechnic; College of Estate Management. FSVA; FRSA; FRSH. Royal Engineers, 1943–47, Italy and Egypt; articled to Bryan Anstey, FRICS, 1947–50; Principal, R. P. Gerard & Co., Surveyors and Valuers, 1952–59; Underwriting Mem. of Lloyd's, 1976–. Chm., Ronald Gerard Charitable Trust, 1983–; Vice-President: English Schools Cricket Assoc., 1981–; Middlesex Colts Assoc., 1986; Mem., Middlesex CCC Cttee, 1972– (Chm., Membership Cttee, 1985–); Trustee, Middlesex CCC Centenary Youth Trust; Mem. Council, Lord's Taverners, 1984–. *Recreations:* all the arts, all the sports. *Address:* 28 South Street, Park Lane, W1Y 5PJ. *T:* 01–629 6514. *Clubs:* Carlton, Guards' Polo, MCC, Lord's Taverners.

GERARD, (William) Geoffrey, CMG 1963; Chairman of Directors, Gerard Industries Pty Ltd, S Australia, 1950–80 (Managing Director, 1930–76); *b* 16 June 1907; *s* of late A. E. Gerard; *m* 1932, Elsie Lesetta, *d* of late A. Lowe; one *s* one *d.* *Educ:* Adelaide Technical High Sch. President: Electrical Manufrs' Assoc. of SA, 1949–52; Electrical Develt Assoc. of SA, 1952; SA Chamber of Manufactures, 1953–54; Associated Chambers of Manufactures of Aust., 1955; SA Metal Industries Assoc., 1952 and 1957; Aust.-Amer. Assoc. in SA Incorp., 1961–63; Aust. Metal Industries Assoc., 1962–64; Vice-Chm., Standards Assoc. of Aust., 1956–79; Chm., Nat. Employers' Assoc., 1964–66; Member: SA Industries Adv. Cttee, 1952–53; Commonwealth Immigration Planning Council, 1956–74; Commonwealth Manufg Industries Advisory Coun., 1958–62; Nat. Employers' Policy Cttee, 1964–66; Commonwealth Electrical Industries Adv. Council, 1977–80. Pres., Prince Alfred Coll. Foundn, 1975–80. Pres., Liberal and Country League, SA Div., 1961–64. Rotary Governor's representative in founding Barossa Valley Club, 1956. FAIM. *Recreations:* golf, tennis. *Address:* 9 Robe Terrace, Medindie, SA 5081, Australia. *T:* 44 2560. *Clubs:* Adelaide, Commonwealth (Adelaide), Kooyonga Golf (SA) (Captain, 1953–55, Pres., 1976–78), Rotary (Prospect) (Pres., 1954).

GERARD-PEARSE, Rear-Adm. John Roger Southey, CB 1979; Group Personnel Manager, Jardine Matheson Co. Ltd, Hong Kong, 1980–84; *b* 10 May 1924; *s* of Dr Gerard-Pearse; *m* 1955, Barbara Jean Mercer; two *s* two *d.* *Educ:* Clifton College. Joined RN, 1943; comd HM Ships Tumult, Grafton, Defender, Fearless and Ark Royal; Flag Officer, Sea Training, 1975–76; Asst Chief, Naval Staff (Ops), 1977–79. *Recreations:* sailing, carpentry. *Address:* Enbrook, 170 Offham Road, West Malling, Kent. *T:* West Malling 842375.

GERE, John Arthur Giles, FSA; FBA 1979; Keeper, Department of Prints and Drawings, British Museum, 1973–81; *b* 7 Oct. 1921; *o s* of Arnold Gere and Carol Giles; *m* 1958, Charlotte Douie; one *s* one *d.* *Educ:* Winchester; Balliol College, Oxford. Assistant Keeper, British Museum, 1946; Deputy Keeper, 1966. *Publications:* (with Robin Ironside) Pre-Raphaelite Painters, 1948; (with Philip Pouncey) Italian Drawings in the British Museum, vol. iii: Raphael and his Circle, 1962; Taddeo Zuccaro: his development studied in his drawings, 1969; I disegni dei maestri: il manierismo a Roma, 1971; (ed with John Sparrow) Geoffrey Madan's Notebooks, 1981; (with Philip Pouncey) Italian Drawings in the British Museum, vol. v: Artists Working in Rome c 1550–c 1640, 1983; (with Nicholas Turner) Drawings by Raphael in English Collections, 1983; various exhibition catalogues; contribs to Burlington Magazine, Master Drawings, etc. *Address:* 21 Lamont Road, SW10. *T:* 01–352 5107.

GERHARD, Dr Derek James (known as **Jeremy**), CB 1986; Deputy Master and Comptroller, Royal Mint, since 1977; *b* 16 Dec. 1927; *s* of late F. J. Gerhard, Banstead; *m* 1952, Dr Sheila Cooper, *d* of late Dr G. K. Cooper; three *s* two *d.* *Educ:* Highgate Sch.; Fitzwilliam Coll., Cambridge (MA); Reading Univ. (PhD). Served 3rd Carabiniers (Prince of Wales DG), 1945–48. Dept of Scientific Adviser, Air Ministry, 1952–57; transf. to DSIR, 1957; Sec., British Commonwealth Scientific Cttee, 1959–60; Asst Sci. Attaché, British Embassy, Washington, 1961–64; transf. to Admin. CS, 1964; Board of Trade, latterly leader UK Delgn to Internat. Consultative Shipping Gp, 1964–69; Head of Management Services, BoT, 1969–71; loaned to CSD (Personnel Management), 1971–73; Dept of Industry, leader UK Delgn to Internat. Tin Council, 1973–75; Air Div., DoI, 1975–77. Pres., Mint Dir's Conf., 1982–84. Mem., Welsh Council, CBI, 1984–. *Publications:* various scientific papers. *Recreation:* woodwork. *Address:* Royal Mint, 7 Grosvenor Gardens, SW1W 0BH.

GERKEN, Vice-Adm. Sir Robert William Frank, KCB 1986; CBE 1975; Flag Officer Plymouth, Port Admiral Devonport, Commander Central Sub Area Eastern Atlantic, Commander Plymouth Sub Area Channel, 1985–March 1987; *b* 11 June 1932; *s* of Francis Sydney and Gladys Gerken; *m* 1st, 1966, Christine Stephenson (*d* 1981); two *d*; 2nd, 1983, Mrs Ann Fermor. *Educ:* Chigwell Sch.; Royal Naval Coll., Dartmouth. Sea service as Lieut and Lt-Comdr, 1953–66; RN Staff Course, 1967; in command HMS Yarmouth, 1968–69; Commander Sea Training, 1970–71; Naval Staff, 1972–73; in command: Sixth Frigate Sqdn, 1974–75; HMS Raleigh, 1976–77; Captain of the Fleet, 1978–81; Flag Officer Second Flotilla, 1981–83; Dir Gen., Naval Manpower and Trng, 1983–85. *Recreations:* hearth and home maintenance. *Address:* c/o Midland Bank plc, 92 Kensington High Street, W8 4SH. *T:* 01–821 1344. *Club:* Army and Navy.

GERNSHEIM, Helmut Erich Robert; photo-historian and author; *b* Munich, 1 March 1913; 3rd *s* of Karl Gernsheim, historian of literature at Munich Univ., and Hermine Gernsheim (*née* Scholz); *m* 1942, Alison Eames, London (*d* 1969); no *c*; *m* 1971, Irène Guénin, Geneva. *Educ:* St Anne's Coll., Augsburg; State Sch. of Photography, Munich. Settled in England as free-lance photographer, 1937; became British subject, 1946; during War of 1939–45 made photogr. surveys of historic bldgs and monuments for Warburg Inst. (London Univ.); exhibns of these at Churchill Club and Courtauld Inst., 1945 and 1946, Nat. Gall., 1944; one-man show at Royal Photogr. Society 1948; since 1945 has built up Gernsheim photo-historical collection, since 1964 at University of Texas, Austin; selections were shown at art museums, Europe and America; retrospective exhibn of own photographs 1935–82, Hamburg, 1983, Hanover and Munich, 1984, Freiburg/Breisgau, 1986. Re-discovered world's first photograph (taken in 1826), 1952 and Lewis Carroll's chief hobby, 1948. Co-ed. Photography Yearbook, 1953–55; British Representative World Exhibition of Photography, Lucerne, 1952, Biennale and Unesco Conference on Photography, Paris, 1955, etc. Photographic adviser to Granada TV on first British action still films, 1958–62. Editorial Adviser, Encyclopædia Britannica and several Museums and Universities. Chm., History of Photo. Seminar, Rencontres Internat. de la Photo.: Arles, 1978, Venice, 1979; Frankfurt, 1981. Distinguished Visiting Professor: Univ. of Texas at Austin, 1979; Arizona State Univ., 1981; Regents Prof., Univ. of California, at Riverside, 1984, and at Santa Barbara, 1985. Dir, Photo-Graphic Editions. Trustee, Swiss Foundn for Photography, 1975–81. Hon. MSc, Brooks Inst., Santa Barbara, Calif., 1984; Hon. Fellow: Club Daguerre, Frankfurt, 1981; Amer. Photohist. Soc., 1979; Europ. Soc. for History of Photography, 1985. First German cultural prize for photography, 1959; Gold Medal, Accademia Italia, Parma, 1980; Hill Medal, German Soc. of Photography, 1983. Cross of Merit, Germany, 1970. *Publications include:* New Photo Vision, 1942; Julia Margaret Cameron, 1948, revd and enlarged edn, 1975; Lewis Carroll-Photographer, 1949, new edn 1969; Beautiful London, 1950; Masterpieces of Victorian Photography, 1951; Those Impossible English, 1952; Churchill, His Life in Photographs, 1955; Creative Photography, 1962, new edn 1986; (with Alison Gernsheim): Roger Fenton, 1954, new edn 1973; The History of Photography, 1955, new and enlarged edns, 1969, 1983 (Berlin), 1985 (Milan, NY); L. J. M. Daguerre, 1956, new edn 1968; Queen Victoria, a Biography in Word and Picture, 1959; Historic Events, 1960; Edward VII and Queen Alexandra, 1962; Fashion and Reality, 1963, new edn 1981; Concise History of Photography, 1965, new edn 1986; Alvin Langdon Coburn, photographer, 1966, new edn 1978; The Origins of Photography, 1982; Incunabula of British Photographic Literature, 1984; The Rise of Photography, 1986; contrib. Oxford History of Technology, 19th and 20th century; numerous articles in art and photographic journals in many countries. *Recreations:* travelling, classic music, opera. *Address:* Residenza Tamporiva, Via Tamporiva 28, 6976 Castagnola, Ticino, Switzerland. *T:* Lugano 091 515904.

GEROSA, Peter Norman; Secretary, The Tree Council, since 1983; *b* 1 Nov. 1928; *s* of late Enrico Cecil and Olive Doris Gerosa; *m* 1955, Dorothy Eleanor Griffin; two *d.* *Educ:* Whitgift Sch.; London Univ. (Birkbeck). BA (Hons) 1st Cl., Classics. Civil Service, 1945–82; Foreign Office, 1945; Home Office, 1949; HM Customs and Excise, 1953; Min. of Transport, 1966; DoE, 1970; Under Secretary: DoE, 1972; Dept of Transport, 1977; Directorate of Rural Affairs, DoE, 1981–82. *Recreations:* singing, gardening, walking. *Address:* 1 Wray Mill House, Reigate, Surrey. *T:* Redhill 64470.

GERRARD, Prof. Alfred Horace; Professor of Sculpture in University of London at University College Slade School of Fine Art, 1948–68, now Emeritus; *b* 7 May 1899; *m* 1933, Katherine Leigh-Pemberton (*d* 1970); *m* 1972, Nancy Sinclair. *Educ:* Hartford County Council Sch.; Manchester Sch. of Art; Slade Sch. of Fine Art, University Coll., London. Head of Dept of Sculpture, Slade Sch., UCL, 1925–48. Served European War, 1914–18, Cameron Highlanders, 1916–17; RFC, 1917–19; War of 1939–45, Staff Captain, War Office, attached Royal Engineers, 1939–43; war artist, 1944–45; temp. Head, Slade Sch. of Fine Art, 1948–49. RBS Silver Medal, 1960. Fellow, University Coll. London, 1969. *Recreation:* gardening. *Address:* Dairy House, Leyswood, Groombridge, Tunbridge Wells, Kent. *T:* Groombridge 268.

GERRARD, His Honour Basil Harding; a Circuit Judge (formerly a Judge of County Courts), 1970–82; *b* 10 July 1919; *s* of late Lawrence Allen Gerrard and Mary (*née* Harding); *m* Sheila Mary Patricia (*née* Coggins), *widow* of Walter Dring, DSO, DFC (killed in action, 1945); one *s* two *d* and one step *d.* *Educ:* Bryanston Sch.; Caius Coll., Cambridge (BA). Royal Navy, 1940–46. Called to Bar, Gray's Inn, 1947; Recorder of Barrow-in-Furness, 1969–70. Mem., Parole Bd for England and Wales, 1974–76. Chm., Selcare Trust, 1971–78, Vice Pres., 1978–; a Chm., Residential Home Tribunal, 1985–. *Recreation:* gardening. *Address:* Northwood, Toft Road, Knutsford, Cheshire. *Clubs:* Knutsford Golf; Bowdon Croquet.

See also J. J. Rowe.

GERRARD, John Henry, CBE 1981 (OBE 1972); MC 1944; QPM 1975; Assistant Commissioner, Metropolitan Police, 1978–81; *b* 25 Nov. 1920; *s* of Archie Reginald and Evelyn Gerrard; *m* 1943, Gladys Hefford; two *s.* *Educ:* Cordwainers Technical Coll. Served War, Army, 1939–46: Iceland, 1940–42; commissioned 1st Mddx Regt, 1943; NW Europe, 1944–46 (Captain). Constable to Commander, 1946–65; Comdr, West End Central, 1965–68; Comdr 'A' Dept (Public Order/Operations), 1968–70; Deputy Assistant Commissioner: 'A' (Operations), 1970–74; No 1 Area, 1974–78. KStJ 1986; Comr, London Dist, SJAB, 1983–. *Recreations:* philately, history. *Address:* c/o Edwina Mountbatten House, 63 York Street, W1H 1PS.

GERRARD, Ronald Tilbrook, FEng, FICE, FIWES; Consultant, Binnie & Partners, Consulting Engineers, since 1983 (Senior Partner, 1974–83); *b* 23 April 1918; *s* of Henry Thomas Gerrard and Edith Elizabeth Tilbrook; *m* 1950, Cecilia Margaret Bremner; three *s* one *d.* *Educ:* Imperial Coll. of Science and Technology, Univ. of London. BSc(Eng). FCGI; FEng 1979; FICE 1957; FIWE 1965; MEIC. Served War, RE, 1939–45. Resident Engr, sea defence and hydro-electric works, 1947–50; Asst Engr, design of hydro-power schemes in Scotland and Canada, 1951–54; Binnie & Partners: Sen. Engr, 1954; Partner, 1959; resp. for hydro-power, water supply, river engrg, coast protection and indust.

works in UK and overseas. Chm., Assoc. of Cons. Engrs, 1969–70; Mem. Council, ICE, 1974–77. Telford Silver Medal, ICE, 1968. *Publications:* (jtly) 4 papers to ICE. *Address:* 6 Ashdown Road, Epsom, Surrey. *T:* Epsom 24834. *Club:* Athenæum.

GERRARD-WRIGHT, Maj.-Gen. Richard Eustace John, CB 1985; CBE 1977 (OBE 1971; MBE 1963); Chief Executive and Secretary, Hurlingham Club, since 1985; *b* 9 May 1930; *s* of Rev. R. L. Gerrard-Wright; *m* 1960, Susan Kathleen Young; two *s* two *d.* *Educ:* Christ's Hospital; RMA, Sandhurst. Commnd Royal Lincolnshire Regt, 1949; served Egypt, Germany and UK, 1950–55; Malaya, 1955–58 (despatches, 1958); Instructor, RMA, Sandhurst, 1958–62 (2nd E Anglian Regt, 1960); Staff Coll., India, 1962–63; served Kenya, Aden, Malta, Malaya, 1963–70 (Royal Anglian Regt, 1964); Bn Comdr, UK, Germany, NI, 1970–73 (despatches 1973); Comdr, 39 Inf. Bde, Belfast, 1975–77; Nat. Defence Coll., Canada, 1977–78; Chief of Staff, 1 (Br) Corps, 1978–79; GOC Eastern District, 1980–82; Dir, TA and Cadets, 1982–84; retd 1985. Dep. Col, Royal Anglian Regt, 1975–80; Col Comdt, Queen's Div., 1981–84. *Address:* c/o Lloyds Bank, Cox's and King's Branch, 6 Pall Mall, SW1Y 5NH. *Clubs:* MCC; Free Foresters.

GERSHEVITCH, Dr Ilya, FBA 1967; Fellow of Jesus College, Cambridge, since 1962; Reader in Iranian Studies, University of Cambridge, 1965–82, now Emeritus; *b* Zürich, 24 Oct. 1914; *o s* of Arkadi and Mila Gershevitch, Smolensk, Russia; *m* 1951, Lisbeth, *d* of Josef Syfrig, Lucerne; one *d.* *Educ:* Swiss schools at Locarno and Lugano; Univ. of Rome (classics); Univ. of London (Oriental studies). Dottore in Lettere, Univ. of Rome, 1937; PhD, Univ. of London, 1943; MA Cantab 1948. Monitored foreign broadcasts, London, 1942–47; Lecturer in Iranian Studies, Univ. of Cambridge, 1948–65. First European to penetrate into certain areas of Western Makran (dialect field-work), 1956; Vis. Prof. at Columbia Univ., New York, 1960–61 and 1965–66; Univ. Exchange Visitor, USSR, 1965; Ratanbai Katrak Lecturer, Univ. of Oxford, 1968. Pres., Philological Soc., 1980–84. Mem., Danish Acad., 1982. Hon. PhD Berne, 1971. *Publications:* A Grammar of Manichean Sogdian, 1954; The Avestan Hymn to Mithra, 1959; Philologia Iranica, 1985; articles in specialist jls, encyclopaedias and collective books. *Recreation:* music. *Address:* 54 Owlstone Road, Cambridge CB3 9JH. *T:* Cambridge 357996.

GERSTENBERG, Frank Eric, MA; Principal, George Watson's College, Edinburgh, since 1985; *b* 23 Feb. 1941; *s* of Eric Gustav Gerstenberg and Janie Willis Gerstenberg; *m* 1966, Valerie Myra (*née* MacLellan); one *s* twin *d.* *Educ:* Trinity College, Glenalmond; Clare College, Cambridge (MA); Inst. of Education, Univ. of London (PGCE). Asst History Teacher, Kelly Coll., Tavistock, 1963–67; Housemaster and Head of History, Millfield School, 1967–74; Headmaster, Oswestry School, 1974–85. *Recreations:* skiing, golf. *Address:* 27 Merchiston Gardens, Edinburgh EH10 5DD. *T:* 031–447 7931. *Clubs:* Public Schools; New (Edinburgh).

GERSTENBERG, Richard Charles; *b* Little Falls, NY, 24 Nov. 1909; *s* of Richard Paul Gerstenberg and Mary Julia Booth; *m* 1934, Evelyn Josephine Hitchingham; one *s* one *d.* *Educ:* Univ. of Michigan (AB). General Motors Corporation: Asst Comptroller, 1949–55; Treasurer, 1956–60; Vice-Pres., in charge of financial staff, 1960–67; Exec. Vice-Pres. in charge of Finance, 1967–70; Vice-Chm. Bd and Chm. Finance Cttee, 1970–72; Chm., 1972–74; a Director, 1967–79. *Address:* 235 Barden Road, Bloomfield Hills, Michigan, USA. *Clubs:* Recess (Detroit); Bloomfield Hills Country; Paradise Valley Country (Scottsdale, Arizona).

GERVIS-MEYRICK, Sir George David Eliott Tapps-; *see* Meyrick.

GERY, Sir Robert Lucian W.; *see* Wade-Gery.

GESTETNER, David; Managing Director since 1982, and Joint Chairman, since 1972, Gestetner Holdings PLC; *b* 1 June 1937; *s* of Sigmund and Henny Gestetner; *m* 1961, Alice Floretta Sebag-Montefiore; one *s* three *d.* *Educ:* Midhurst Grammar Sch.; Bryanston Sch.; University Coll., Oxford (MA). *Recreation:* sailing.
See also J. Gestetner.

GESTETNER, Jonathan; Joint Chairman, Gestetner Holdings Ltd, since 1972; *b* 11 March 1940; *s* of Sigmund and Henny Gestetner; *m* 1965, Jacqueline Margaret Strasmore; two *s* one *d.* *Educ:* Bryanston Sch.; Massachusetts Institute of Technology (BScMechEngrg). Joined Gestetner Ltd, 1962. Member: Executive Council, Engineering Employers' London Assoc., 1972–77 (Vice-Pres., 1975–77); Maplin Development Authority, 1973–74; SSRC, 1979–82; Dir, Centre for Policy Studies. Mem., Educnl Council, MIT, 1973–. *Recreation:* the visual arts. *Address:* 7 Oakhill Avenue, NW3 7RD. *T:* 01–435 0905. *Clubs:* Brooks's, MCC.
See also David Gestetner.

GETHIN, Lt-Col (Retd) Sir Richard Patrick St Lawrence, 9th Bt, *cr* 1665; late REME; *b* 15 May 1911; *s* of Col Sir Richard Walter St Lawrence Gethin, 8th Bt, and Helen (*d* 1957), *d* of W. B. Thornhill; *S* father 1946; *m* 1946, Fara, *y d* of late J. H. Bartlett; one *s* four *d.* *Educ:* Oundle Sch. Lieut RAOC, 1935; Lieut-Col REME, 1943; Officer Commanding No 11 Vehicle Depot Workshops, until 1957, retired. Restorer of antique furniture. Hon. Research Fellow (Physics), Aston Univ., Birmingham, 1977–81. *Publication:* Restoring Antique Furniture, 1974. *Heir:* *s* Richard Joseph St Lawrence Gethin [*b* 29 Sept. 1949; *m* 1974, Jacqueline, *d* of Comdr David Cox; three *d*]. *Address:* Easter Cottage, Bredon, near Tewkesbury, Glos. *T:* Bredon 72354.

GETHING, Air Commodore Richard Templeton, CB 1960; OBE 1945; AFC 1939; *b* 11 Aug. 1911; *s* of George A. Gething, Wilmslow, Cheshire; *m* 1940, Margaret Helen, *d* of late Sir Herbert Gepp, Melbourne, Australia; one *s* one *d.* *Educ:* Malvern; Sydney Sussex Coll., Cambridge. Joined RAF, 1933. Served War of 1939–45: Canada; UK; India; Burma. Actg Group Capt., 1943; Group Capt., 1950; Actg Air Commodore, 1956; Dir Operations, Maritime Navigation and Air Traffic, Air Ministry, 1956–60, retired. FIN 1956. *Recreation:* gliding. *Address:* Garden Hill, Kangaroo Ground, Victoria 3097, Australia. *Club:* Royal Air Force.

GETTY, Hon. Donald Ross; MLA Edmonton Whitemud, 1967–79 and since 1985; Premier of Alberta, since 1985; *b* 30 Aug. 1933; *s* of Charles Ross Getty and Beatrice Lillian Getty; *m* 1955, Margaret Inez Mitchell; four *s.* *Educ:* Univ. of Western Ontario (Business Administration). MLA Alberta 1967; Minister of Federal and Intergovernmental Affairs, 1971; Minister of Energy and Natural Resources, 1975; resigned 1979; re-elected MLA, 1985. Joined Imperial Oil, 1955; Midwestern Industrial Gas, 1961; formed Baldonnel Oil & Gas, 1964 (Pres. and Man. Dir); Partner, Doherty Roadhouse & McCuaig, 1967; Pres., D. Getty Investments, 1979; Chm., Ipsco, 1981–85; former Chm. and Chief Exec., Nortek Energy Corp.; director of other cos. Played quarterback for Edmonton Eskimos Canadian Football team for 10 years. *Recreations:* horse racing, golf, hunting. *Address:* Legislature Building, Edmonton, Alberta T5K 2B6, Canada.

GHALE, Subedar Gaje; *see* Gaje Ghale.

GHURBURRUN, Sir Rabindrah, Kt 1981; Minister of Economic Planning and Development, Mauritius, 1976–82; *b* 27 Sept. 1929; *s* of Mrs Sookmeen Ghurburrun; *m* 1959; one *s* one *d.* *Educ:* Keble Coll., Oxford. Called to the Bar, Middle Temple; practised as Lawyer, 1959–68; High Comr for Mauritius in India, 1968–76; MLA 1976; Minister of Justice, 1976. Member: Central Board; Bar Council. Former President: Mauritius Arya Sabha; Mauritius Sugar Cane Planters' Assoc.; Hindu Educn Authority; Nat. Congress of Young Socialists. *Address:* 18 Dr Lesur Street, Cascadelle, Beau Bassin, Mauritius. *T:* 54–6421.

GIAEVER, Dr Ivar; Staff Member, General Electric Research and Development Center, since 1958; *b* 5 April 1929; *s* of John A. Giaever and Gudrun (*née* Skaarud); *m* 1952, Inger Skramstad; one *s* three *d.* *Educ:* Norwegian Inst. of Tech.; Rensselear Polytechnical Inst. ME 1952; PhD 1964. Norwegian Army, 1952–53; Norwegian Patent Office, 1953–54; Canadian General Electric, 1954–56; General Electric, 1956–58. Fellow, Amer. Phys. Soc.; Member: Nat. Acad. of Sciences; Nat. Acad. of Engineering; Amer. Acad. of Arts and Scis; Norwegian Acad. of Scis; Norwegian Acad. of Technology; Norwegian Profl Engrs. Oliver E. Buckley Prize, 1964; Nobel Prize for Physics, 1973; Zworykin Award, 1974. Hon. DSc: RPI, 1974; Union Coll., 1974; Hon. DEng, Michigan Tech. Univ., 1976; Hon. DPhys, Oslo, 1976. *Publications:* contrib. Physical Review, Jl Immunology. *Recreations:* ski-ing, tennis, camping, hiking. *Address:* General Electric Research and Development Center, PO Box 8, Schenectady, New York 12301, USA. *T:* 518–385–8434.

GIAMATTI, (Angelo) Bartlett, PhD; President of Yale University, USA, since 1978; *b* Boston, Mass, 4 April 1938; *s* of Prof. Emeritus Valentine Giamatti and Mary Walton; *m* 1960, Toni Smith; two *s* one *d.* *Educ:* South Hadley High Sch.; Internat. Sch. of Rome; Phillips Acad., Andover Mass; Yale Univ. (BA *magna cum laude*); Yale Grad. Sch. (PhD). Instructor in Italian and Comparative Literature, Princeton Univ., 1964; Asst Prof., 1965; Asst Prof. of English, Yale Univ., 1966; Associate Professor of: English, 1968, English and Comparative Literature, 1969; Prof. of English and Comparative Literature, Yale Univ., 1971 (Ford chair, 1976–77, but he relinquished to assume newly founded chair); John Hay Whitney Prof. of English and Comparative Lit., Yale Univ., 1977, also (Spring, 1977) Dir of Div. of Humanities, Faculty of Arts and Scis. Master of Ezra Stiles Coll. (a residential coll. of Yale), 1970–72; Dir of Visiting Faculty Program of Yale, 1974–76; Associate Dir of Nat. Humanities Inst., Yale, 1977. Guggenheim Fellow, 1969–70. Mem., Council on For. Relations, 1978–. Member: Mediaeval Acad. of America, 1963–; MLA, 1964–; Council for Financial Aid to Educn, 1980–; Amer. Philosophical Soc., 1982–; Bd of Trustees, Ford Foundation, 1983–; Trustee, Mount Holyoke Coll., 1983–; Fellow: Amer. Acad. of Arts and Scis; AAAS, 1980. Hon. LLD: Princeton, 1978; Harvard, 1978; Notre Dame, 1982; Coll. of New Rochelle, 1982; Dartmouth Coll., 1982; Hon. LittD: Amer. Internat. Coll., 1979; Jewish Theol Seminary of Amer., 1980; Atlanta Univ., 1981. Career Achievement Award in Educn, Nat. Italian American Foundn, 1982; Award for outstanding contribution to Higher Educn, Brown Univ. 1985; Comdr, l'Ordre National des Arts et des Lettres, France, 1985; Comdr, Order of Merit (Italy), 1979; Comdr's Cross of Fed. Order of Merit, Germany, 1985. *Publications:* (ed jtly) The Songs of Bernart de Ventadorn, 1962; The Earthly Paradise and the Renaissance Epic, 1966; (ed jtly) Ludovico Ariosto's Orlando Furioso, 1968; (ed jtly) A Variorum Commentary on the Poems of John Milton, vol. 1, 1970; Play of Double Senses: Spenser's Faerie Queene, 1975; The University and the Public Interest, 1981; Exile and Change in Renaissance Literature, 1984; gen. editor, 3 vol. anthology Western Literature, 1971. *Recreations:* interested in sport and ballet. *Address:* Office of the President, Yale University, New Haven, Conn 06520, USA.

GIBB, Andrew (McArthur); barrister; *b* 8 Sept. 1927; *s* of late William and of Ruth Gibb; *m* 1956, Olga Mary (*née* Morris); three *d.* *Educ:* Sedbergh; Queens' Coll., Cambridge (MA). Called to the Bar, Middle Temple, 1952. A Recorder of the Crown Court, 1977–82. Chm., Cttee of Public Inquiry into fire at Wensley Lodge, Hessle, Humberside, 1977. *Recreations:* golf, reading, music. *Address:* 263 Colne Road, Sough, Earby, via Colne, Lancs BB8 6SY.

GIBB, Bill; *see* Gibb, W. E.

GIBB, Francis Ross, CBE 1982; FEng; FICE; Chairman and Chief Executive, Taylor Woodrow Group, since 1985 (Joint Managing Director, 1979–85, and a Joint Deputy Chairman, 1983–85); President, Taylor Woodrow Construction, since 1985 (Chairman, 1978–85, Joint Managing Director, 1978–84); Chairman, National Nuclear Corporation, since 1981; *b* 29 June 1927; *s* of Robert Gibb and Violet Mary Gibb; *m* 1950, Wendy Marjorie Fowler; one *s* two *d.* *Educ:* Loughborough Coll. BSc(Eng); CEng. Engineer, Handley Page, 1947–48; Engineer, 1948–57, Manager, 1957–63, Dir, 1963–70, Man. Dir, 1970, Taylor Woodrow Construction; Director: Taylor Woodrow Internat., 1969–85; Taylor Woodrow Ltd, 1972–; Chm., Taywood Santa Fe, 1975–85. Dep. Chm., Seaforth Holdings, 1978–. Member: Construction Industry Adv. Cttee, HSE, 1978–81; Gp of Eight, 1979–81; Board, British Nuclear Associates, 1980– (Chm., Agrément Bd, 1980–82). Member: Council, CBI, 1979–80, 1985–; Industrial Policy Cttee, CBI, 1980–85. Dir, Holiday Pay Scheme, 1980–84 and Trustee, Benefits Scheme, 1980–84, Building and Civil Engrg Trustees. Federation of Civil Engineering Contractors: Vice-Chm., 1978–79; Chm., 1979–80; Vice Pres., 1980–84; Pres., 1984–. FRSA; CBIM 1983; Hon. FINucE, 1984. *Recreations:* ornithology, gardening, walking, music. *Address:* 10 Park Street, W1. *Club:* Arts.

GIBB, Ian Pashley; Director of Public Services, Planning and Administration, British Library (Humanities and Social Sciences), since 1985; *b* 17 April 1926; *s* of John Pashley Gibb and Mary (*née* Owen); *m* 1953, Patricia Mary Butler; two *s.* *Educ:* Latymer Upper Sch.; UCL (BA). ALA. Sen. Library Asst, Univ. of London, 1951–52; Asst Librarian, UCL, 1952–58; Dep. Librarian, National Central Library, 1958–73; British Library: Dep. Dir, Science Reference Library, 1973–75; Head of Divl Office, Reference Div., 1975–77; Dir and Keeper, Reference Div., 1977–85. Part-time Lectr, UCL, 1967–77, Hon. Research Fellow, 1977–, Examiner, 1985–. Hon. Treasurer, Bibliographical Soc., 1961–67; Mem., Council, Library Assoc., 1980–82. *Publications:* various articles. *Recreations:* music, watching cricket, bridge, wine-tasting, travel especially to Austria. *Address:* The Old Cottage, 16 Tile Kiln Lane, Leverstock Green, Hemel Hempstead, Herts HP3 8ND. *T:* Hemel Hempstead 56352.

GIBB, Walter Frame, DSO 1945; DFC 1943; Chairman, 1980–85, and Managing Director, 1978–85, British Aerospace, Australia, Ltd; *b* 26 March 1919; British; *m* 1944, Pauline Sylvia Reed; three *d.* *Educ:* Clifton Coll. Apprentice, Bristol Aero Engines, 1937. RAF, 1940–46. Test Pilot, Bristol Aircraft Ltd, 1946; Asst Chief Test Pilot, 1953; Chief Test Pilot, Bristol Aeroplane Co. Ltd, 1956–60; Product Support Manager, BAC Filton, 1960–78. World Altitude Height Record 63,668 feet in Olympus-Canberra, 1953, and second record 65,890 ft in same machine, 1955. MRAeS. JP Bristol, 1974. *Recreation:* sailing. *Address:* Merlin Haven Lodge, Wotton-Under-Edge, Glos GL12 7BA. *Clubs:* Royal Air Force; Royal Sydney Yacht Squadron.

GIBB, William Elphinstone, (Bill Gibb); Company Director, Bill Gibb Ltd, since 1972; Chairman, Bill Gibb Fashion Group Ltd, since 1982; *b* 23 Jan. 1943; *s* of George and Jessie Gibb. *Educ:* Fraserburgh Acad.; St Martin's Sch. of Art (DipAD); Royal Coll. of Art (DesRCA). Fellow, Indust. Arts Soc., 1976. First shop, Alice Paul, 1967; Designer at Baccarat, 1967–79; founded Bill Gibb Ltd, 1972. Created first ballet costumes for Remy

Charlip's Mad River, 1972; designed costume for Lynn Seymour as Salomé, 1981. Dress in Cecil Beaton Exhibn, V&A, 1971; 10 yrs Retrospective Fashion show for 7,000 people, Royal Albert Hall, 1977. Nominated for Yardley Award, New York, 1967; Vogue Designer of the Year, 1970 (outfit now in Bath Museum); Silver Heart, Variety Club of GB (for fashion spectacular at London Convention), 1975; award from Today programme (ITV) for best fashion show of 1979. *Recreations:* historical reading, travelling to regenerate inspiration. *Address:* 38 Drayton Court, Drayton Gardens, SW10. *Clubs:* Embassy, Legends, The Gardens, Ritz Casino, Chelsea Arts, Hippodrome.

GIBB, William Eric, MA, DM Oxon; FRCP; Consulting Physician, St Bartholomew's Hospital, since 1976; *b* 30 April 1911; *s* of late James Glenny Gibb, MD, FRCS, and Georgina Henman; *m* 1952, Mary Edith Gertrude Feetham; three *s. Educ:* Rugby Sch.; Oriel Coll., Oxford; St Bartholomew's Hosp. BA Oxon 1st Cl. Hons Final Sch. of Nat. Science; BM, BCh Oxon 1936; MRCP 1940; DM Oxon 1947; FRCP 1949; George Herbert Hunt Travelling Schol. (University of Oxford), 1938. War service with RAFVR Med. Br., 1941–46; Actg Wing-Comdr i/c a Med. Div. Res. House appts, St Bart's Hosp. and Brompton Chest Hosp.; Cattlin Research Scholar, 1947; Physician: St Bart's Hosp., 1947–76; The Metropolitan Hosp., 1952–76. Mem., Pensions Appeal Tribunal, 1976–85. Examiner in Medicine: University of Oxford, 1952–59; Examg Bd of England; RCP; Soc. of Apothecaries. Fellow, Royal Soc. Med. *Publications:* various articles in medical journals. *Recreation:* gardening. *Address:* 1 Bacon's Lane, Highgate, N6.

GIBBENS, Frank Edward Hilary George; His Honour Judge Frank Gibbens; a Circuit Judge, since 1973; *b* 23 April 1913; *s* of Frank Edward George and Geraldine Edel Gibbens; *m* 1940, Margaret Gertrude Wren; three *d. Educ:* Malvern; Peterhouse, Cambridge (BA). Called to Bar, Inner Temple, 1938. Served War, commission in RAF, 1940–46. Sqdn Leader, rank on demobilisation. On appt as Judge, retired from Bar, 1973. *Recreation:* golf. *Address:* Warren Close, Coombe Hill Road, Kingston-upon-Thames.

GIBBINGS, Peter Walter; Chairman, Guardian and Manchester Evening News plc, since 1973; Deputy Chairman, since 1986, and Director, since 1981, Anglia Television Group plc; *b* 25 March 1929; *s* of late Walter White Gibbings and Margaret Russell Gibbings (née Torrance); *m* 1st, Elspeth Felicia Macintosh; two *d;* 2nd, Hon. Louise Barbara, *d* of Viscount Lambert, *qv;* one *s. Educ:* Rugby; Wadham Coll., Oxford (Scholar). Called to Bar, Middle Temple, 1953 (Garraway Rice Pupillage Prize; Harmsworth Schol.). Served in 9th Queen's Royal Lancers, 1951–52; Dep. Legal Adviser, Trinidad Oil Co. Ltd, 1955–56; Associated Newspapers Ltd, 1956–60; The Observer, 1960–67 (Deputy Manager and Dir, 1965–67); Man. Dir, Guardian Newspapers Ltd, 1967–73; Dir, Manchester Guardian and Evening News Ltd, 1967–73. Director: Press Assoc. Ltd, 1982–; Reuters Holdings PLC, 1984–. Mem., Press Council, 1970–74. *Recreations:* lawn mowing, tennis. *Address:* c/o Guardian and Manchester Evening News plc, 119 Farringdon Road, EC1R 3ER.

GIBBINS, Elizabeth Mary, BA; Headmistress, St Mary's School, Calne, Wilts, 1946–72; *b* 2 May 1911; *d* of late Kenneth Mayoh Gibbins, MB, BS. *Educ:* Sandecotes Sch., Parkstone; Westfield Coll., University of London; Cambridge Univ. Training Coll. for Women (Postgraduate). History Mistress, St Brandons Clergy Daughters' Sch., Bristol, 1935–38; Headmistress, Diocesan Girls' Sch., Hongkong, 1939–45, Acting Headmistress, Oct. 1972–May 1973. Hon. Sec., Hong Kong Diocesan Assoc., 1974–80. *Address:* 8 Moreton Road, Old Bosham, Chichester, West Sussex. *T:* Bosham 573038.

GIBBINS, Rev. Dr Ronald Charles; Superintendent Minister, Wesley's Chapel, London, since 1978; *s* of Charles and Anne Gibbins; *m* 1949, Olive Ruth (née Patchett); one *s* two *d. Educ:* London Univ. (BScSociol); Wesley Theological Coll., Bristol; Eden Theological Seminary, US (DMin). Methodist Minister: Bradford, 1948–49; Spennymoor, 1949–50; Middlesbrough, 1950–57; Basildon, 1957–64; East End Mission, London, 1964–78. *Publications:* Mission for the Secular City, 1976; The Lumpen Proletariat, 1979; The Stations of the Resurrection, 1987. *Recreations:* travel, journalism. *Address:* 49 City Road, EC1Y 1AU. *T:* 01–253 2262.

GIBBON, Gen. Sir John (Houghton), GCB 1977 (KCB 1972; CB 1970); OBE 1945 (MBE 1944); Master-General of the Ordnance, 1974–77; ADC (General) to the Queen, 1976–77; *b* 21 Sept. 1917; *er s* of Brigadier J. H. Gibbon, DSO, The Manor House, Little Stretton, Salop; *m* 1951, Brigid Rosamund, *d* of late Dr D. A. Bannerman, OBE, ScD, FRSE, and Muriel, *d* of T. R. Morgan; one *s. Educ:* Eton; Trinity Coll., Cambridge. Commissioned into Royal Artillery, 1939. Served with 2nd Regt RHA: France, 1939–40; Western Desert, 1940–41; Greece, 1941; on staff of HQ 30 Corps; Western Desert, 1941–43; Sicily, 1943; GSO 1, RA, HQ 21 Army Gp, 1944–45; 6 Airborne Div., Palestine, 1946–47; Instructor and Chief Instructor, RMA Sandhurst, 1947–51; GSO 2, War Office, 1951–53; Battery Comdr, 1953–54; AQMG, War Office, 1955–58; CO Field Regt, BAOR, 1959–60; Bde Comdr, Cyprus, 1962; Dir of Defence Plans, Min. of Def., 1962–64; Sec., Chiefs of Staff Cttee, and Dir, Defence Operations Staff, 1966–69; Dir, Army Staff Duties, MoD, 1969–71; Vice-Chief of the Defence Staff, 1972–74. Col Comdt, RA, 1972–82. Chm., Regular Forces Employment Assoc., 1982–85 (Vice-Chm., 1977–82). *Recreations:* rowing, shooting, fishing. *Address:* Beech House, Northbrook Close, Winchester, Hants SO23 8JR. *T:* Winchester 66155.

GIBBON, Michael, QC 1974; **His Honour Judge Gibbon;** a Circuit Judge, since 1979; *b* 15 Sept. 1930; 2nd *s* of late F. O. Gibbon; *m* 1956, Malveen Elliot Seager; two *s* one *d. Educ:* Brightlands; Charterhouse; Pembroke Coll., Oxford (MA). Commnd in Royal Artillery, 1949. Called to Bar, Lincoln's Inn, 1954. A Recorder of the Crown Court, 1972–79; Hon. Recorder, City of Cardiff, 1986. Chm., Electoral Adv. Cttee to Home Sec., 1972. Chm., Local Govt Boundary Commn for Wales, 1978–79 (Dep. Chm., 1974–78); Mem., Parole Bd, 1986–. *Recreations:* music, golf. *Address:* Gellihirion, 3 Cefn-Coed Road, Cardiff CF2 6AN. *T:* Cardiff 751852. *Clubs:* Cardiff and County (Cardiff); Royal Porthcawl Golf, Cardiff Golf.

GIBBON, Monk; see Gibbon, W. M.

GIBBON, (William) Monk, PhD (Dublin); FRSL; poet and writer; *b* Dublin, 15 Dec. 1896; *o s* of late Canon William Monk Gibbon, MA, Rural Dean, Taney, Dundrum, Co. Dublin, and Isabel Agnes Pollock (née Meredith); *m* 1928, Mabel Winifred, *d* of Rev. Walter Molyneux Dingwall, MA, and Mabel Sophia Spender; two *s* four *d. Educ:* St Columba's Coll., Rathfarnham; Keble Coll., Oxford (Open History Exhibn). Served European War, 1914–18, as Officer, RASC; France, 1916–17; Invalided out, 1918. Taught in Switzerland; master at Oldfeld Sch., Swanage (12 yrs). Silver Medal for Poetry, Tailteann Games, 1928. Tredegar Memorial Lecture, Royal Society of Literature, 1952; Tagore Centenary Lecture, Abbey Theatre, Dublin, 1961. Mem. Irish Acad. of Letters, 1960 (Vice-Pres., 1967). *Publications: poetry:* The Tremulous String, 1926; The Branch of Hawthorn Tree, 1927; For Daws to Peck At, 1929; Seventeen Sonnets, 1932; This Insubstantial Pageant (collected poems), 1951; The Velvet Bow and other poems, 1972; *autobiography:* The Seals, 1935; Mount Ida, 1948; Inglorious Soldier, 1968; The Brahms Waltz, 1970; The Pupil, 1981; *biography:* Netta (Hon. Mrs Franklin), 1960; *novel:* The Climate of Love, 1961; *ballet and film criticism:* The Red Shoes Ballet, 1948; The Tales of

Hoffmann, 1951; An Intruder at The Ballet, 1952; *travel:* Swiss Enchantment, 1950; Austria, 1953; In Search of Winter Sport, 1953; Western Germany, 1955; The Rhine and its Castles, 1957; Great Houses of Europe, 1962; Great Palaces of Europe, 1964; *literary criticism:* The Masterpiece and the Man, 1959. The Living Torch (an Æ anthology), 1937. *Recreations:* watching ballet and good films. *Address:* 67 Springhill Park, Killiney, Co. Dublin, Eire. *T:* Dublin 853362.

GIBBONS, Hon. Sir David; see Gibbons, Hon. Sir J. D.

GIBBONS, Brig. Edward John, CMG 1956; CBE 1947 (MBE 1939); *b* 30 Aug. 1906; *s* of Edward Gibbons, Coventry; *m* 1946, Gabrielle Maria (*d* 1982), *widow* of Capt. P. A. Strakosh; one step *d. Educ:* King Henry VIII Sch., Coventry; Gonville and Caius Coll., Cambridge. Nigerian Administrative Service, 1929. Army Service, 1941–46: Dir of Civil Affairs, South East Asia Command; Brig. Sec. Eastern Provinces, Nigeria, 1948; Commissioner of the Cameroons (under UK Trusteeship), 1949–56; Dept of Technical Cooperation, 1962–64; Min. of Overseas Develt, 1964–68. *Recreation:* wood engraving. *Address:* 6 Grove House, The Grove, Epsom, Surrey. *T:* Epsom 26657. *Club:* Royal Automobile.

GIBBONS, Prof. Ian Read, FRS 1983; Professor of Biophysics in the University of Hawaii, since 1967; *b* 30 Oct. 1931; *s* of Arthur Alwyn Gibbons and Hilda Read Cake; *m* 1961, Barbara Ruth Hollingworth; one *s* one *d. Educ:* Faversham Grammar School; Cambridge Univ. (BA, PhD). Research Fellow, 1958–63, Asst Prof., 1963–67, Harvard Univ.; Associate Prof., 1967–69, Prof., 1969, Univ. of Hawaii. *Publications:* contribs to learned jls. *Recreations:* gardening, computer programming, music. *Address:* 41 Ahui Street, Honolulu, Hawaii 96813, USA. *T:* (808)-531–3538.

GIBBONS, Hon. Sir (John) David, KBE 1985; JP; Chairman: Bermuda Monetary Authority, 1984–86; Economic Council, Bermuda, since 1984; *b* 15 June 1927; *s* of late Edmund G. Gibbons, CBE, and Winifred G. Gibbons, MBE; *m* 1958, Lully Lorentzen; three *s* (and one *d* by former *m*). *Educ:* Saltus Grammar Sch., Bermuda; Hotchkiss Sch., Lakeville, Conn; Harvard Univ., Cambridge, Mass (BA). FBIM. Mem. Govt Boards: Social Welfare Bd, 1949–58; Bd of Civil Aviation, 1958–60; Bd of Educn, 1956–59 (Chm., 1973–74); Trade Develt Bd, 1960–74. MP Bermuda, 1972–84; Minister of Health and Welfare, 1974–75, of Finance, 1975–84; Premier of Bermuda, 1977–82. Mem., Law Reform Cttee, 1969–72. Mem. Governing Body, subseq. Chm., Bermuda Technical Inst., 1956–70. Mem., Bermuda Athletic Assoc. JP Bermuda, 1974. *Recreations:* tennis, golf, skiing, swimming. *Address:* Leeward, Point Shares, Pembroke, Bermuda. *T:* 809–29 52396. *Clubs:* Phoenix (Cambridge, Mass); Harvard (New York); Royal Bermuda Yacht, Royal Hamilton Amateur Dinghy, Mid-Ocean, Riddells Bay Golf, Spanish Point Boat (Bermuda).

GIBBONS, Ven. Kenneth Harry; Archdeacon of Lancaster, since 1981; Vicar of St Michael's-on-Wyre, since 1985; *b* 24 Dec. 1931; *s* of Harry and Phyllis Gibbons; *m* 1962, Margaret Ann Tomlinson; two *s. Educ:* Blackpool and Chesterfield Grammar Schools; Manchester Univ. (BSc); Cuddesdon Coll., Oxford. RAF, 1952–54. Ordained, 1956; Assistant Curate of Fleetwood, 1956–60; Secretary for Student Christian Movement in Schools, 1960–62; Senior Curate, St Martin-in-the-Fields, Westminster, 1962–65; Vicar of St Edward, New Addington, 1965–70; Vicar of Portsea, 1970–81; RD of Portsmouth, 1973–79; Hon. Canon of Portsmouth, 1974–81; Priest-in-charge of Weeton, 1981–85. *Recreations:* gardening, cinema. *Address:* The Vicarage, St Michael's-on-Wyre, Preston, Lancs PR3 0TQ.

GIBBONS, Stella Dorothea, (Mrs A. B. Webb), FRSL; Poet and Novelist; *b* London, 5 Jan. 1902; *d* of C. J. P. T. Gibbons, MD; *m* 1933, Allan Bourne Webb (*d* 1959), actor and singer; one *d. Educ:* N London Collegiate Sch.; University Coll., London. Journalist, 1923–33; BUP, Evening Standard, The Lady. *Publications:* The Mountain Beast (Poems), 1930; Cold Comfort Farm, 1932 (Femina Vie Heureuse Prize, 1933); Bassett, 1934; The Priestess (Poems), 1934; Enbury Heath, 1935; The Untidy Gnome, 1935; Miss Linsey and Pa, 1936; Roaring Tower (Short Stories), 1937; Nightingale Wood, 1938; The Lowland Venus (Poems), 1938; My American, 1939; Christmas at Cold Comfort Farm (Short Stories), 1940; The Rich House, 1941; Ticky, 1943; The Bachelor, 1944; Westwood, 1946; The Matchmaker, 1949; Conference at Cold Comfort Farm, 1949; Collected Poems, 1950; The Swiss Summer, 1951; Fort of the Bear, 1953; Beside the Pearly Water (short stories), 1954; The Shadow of a Sorcerer, 1955; Here Be Dragons, 1956; White Sand and Grey Sand, 1958; A Pink Front Door, 1959; The Weather at Tregulla, 1962; The Wolves were in the Sledge, 1964; The Charmers, 1965; Starlight, 1967; The Snow Woman, 1969; The Woods in Winter, 1970; *unpublished works:* Verses for Friends; The Yellow Houses; An Alpha. *Recreations:* reading, listening to music.

GIBBONS, Sir William Edward Doran, 9th Bt *cr* 1752; Ferry Line Manager (Harwich–Hook), Sealink British Ferries, since 1985; *b* 13 Jan. 1948; *s* of Sir John Edward Gibbons, 8th Bt, and of Mersa Wentworth, *y d* of late Major Edward Baynton Grove Foster; *S* father, 1982; *m* 1972, Patricia Geraldine Archer, *d* of Roland Archer Howse; one *s* one *d. Educ:* Pangbourne; RNC Dartmouth; Bristol Univ. (BSc). MCIT. Asst Shipping and Port Manager, Sealink UK, Parkeston Quay, 1979–82; Service Manager (Anglo-Dutch), Sealink UK Ltd, 1982–85. Chm., Manningtree Parish Council, 1985– (Mem., 1981–). *Heir: s* Charles William Edwin Gibbons, *b* 28 Jan. 1983. *Address:* Oxford House, Mistley, Manningtree, Essex.

GIBBS, family name of **Barons Aldenham** and **Wraxall.**

GIBBS, Air Vice-Marshal Charles Melvin, CB 1976; CBE 1966; DFC 1943; RAF retd; Recruiting Consultant with Selleck Associates, Colchester, 1977–86; *b* 11 June 1921; American father, New Zealand mother; *m* 1947, Emma Pamela Pollard; one *d. Educ:* Taumarunui, New Zealand. MECI 1980. Joined RNZAF, 1941; service in Western Desert and Mediterranean, 1942–44; Coastal Comd, 1945; India, 1946–47; commanded Tropical Experimental Unit, 1950–52; RAF Staff Coll., 1953; commanded No 118 Squadron, 1954–55; Directing Staff, RAF Staff Coll., 1956–58; Pakistan, 1958–61; Chief Instructor, RAF Chivenor, 1961–63; CO, Wattisham, 1963–66; idc 1967; Defence Policy Staff, 1968–69; Dir of Quartering, 1970–72; AOA, Germany, 1972–74; Dir-Gen. Personal Services, RAF, 1974–76. *Recreations:* fishing, golf. *Address:* c/o National Bank of New Zealand, Jean Batten Place, Auckland, New Zealand. *Clubs:* Royal Air Force; Nayland Golf (Nayland).

GIBBS, Hon. Sir Eustace Hubert Beilby, KCVO 1986; CMG 1982; HM Diplomatic Service, retired; Vice Marshal of the Diplomatic Corps, 1982–86; *b* 3 July 1929; 2nd *surv. s* of 1st Baron Wraxall, PC; *b* and *heir-pres.* of 2nd Baron Wraxall, *qv; m* 1957, Evelyn Veronica Scott; three *s* two *d. Educ:* Eton College; Christ Church, Oxford (MA). ARCM 1953. Entered HM Diplomatic Service, 1954; served in Bangkok, Rio de Janeiro, Berlin and Vienna; Counsellor, Caracas, 1971–73; Royal College of Defence Studies, 1974; Inspector, 1975–77; Consul-Gen., Paris, 1977–82. *Recreations:* music, golf. *Address:* Coddenham House, Coddenham, Ipswich, Suffolk. *Clubs:* Brooks's, Pratt's, Beefsteak.

GIBBS, Air Marshal Sir Gerald Ernest, KBE 1954 (CBE 1945); CIE 1946; MC; *b* 3 Sept. 1896; *s* of Ernest William Cecil and Fanny Wilmina Gibbs; *m* 1938, Margaret Jean Bradshaw; one *s* one *d*. Served European War, 1914–18; transferred from Army to RFC 1916, and RAF 1918 (MC and 2 bars, Légion d'Honneur, Croix de Guerre). ADC to Marshal of the Royal Air Force Sir Hugh Trenchard (later 1st Viscount Trenchard), 1927–28; served in Air Staff Plans, Air Ministry, under Gp Capt. C. F. A. Portal (later 1st Viscount Portal of Hungerford), and then Gp Capt. A. T. Harris (later Marshal of the Royal Air Force Sir Arthur Harris, Bt), 1930–34; served various overseas periods with RAF in Iraq, Palestine, Sudan and Kenya between the two wars; commanded No 47 Sqdn RAF Sudan and RAF Kenya. Senior Air Staff Officer of No 11 Group, Fighter Command, 1940–41 during Battle of Britain; Dir of Overseas Operations, Air Ministry, 1942–43; Senior Air Staff Officer, HQ 3rd Tactical Air Force, South-East Asia, 1943–44; Chief Air Staff Officer to Admiral Mountbatten (later Earl Mountbatten of Burma), Supreme HQ, SEAC, 1945–46; Senior Air Staff Officer, HQ, RAF Transport Command, 1946–48; Head of Service Advisers to UK Delegation and Chm. UK Members of Military Staff Cttee, UN, 1948–51; Chief of Air Staff and Commander-in-Chief, Indian Air Force, 1951–54, retired 1954. *Publication:* Survivor's Story, 1956. *Recreations:* golf, ski-ing, sailing. *Address:* Lone Oak, 170 Coombe Lane West, Kingston-upon-Thames, Surrey. *Clubs:* Royal Air Force; Royal Wimbledon Golf (Wimbledon); Seaford Golf (East Blatchington); Trevose Golf (Cornwall).

GIBBS, Rt. Hon. Sir Harry (Talbot), GCMG 1981; KBE 1970; PC 1972; **Rt. Hon. Mr Justice Gibbs**; Chief Justice of Australia, since 1981; *b* 7 Feb. 1917; *s* of late H. V. Gibbs, formerly of Ipswich, Qld; *m* 1944, Muriel Ruth (*née* Dunn); one *s* three *d*. *Educ:* Ipswich Grammar Sch., Qld; Univ. of Queensland (BA, LLM). Served War, Australia and New Guinea, 1939–45, Major (despatches). Admitted as Barrister, Qld, 1939; QC 1957; Judge of Supreme Court of Qld, 1961; Judge of Federal Court of Bankruptcy and of Supreme Court of Australian Capital Territory, 1967; Justice of High Court of Australia, 1970. Hon. Bencher, Lincoln's Inn, 1981. Hon. LLD Queensland, 1980. *Address:* 27 Stanhope Road, Killara, NSW 2071, Australia. *T:* 498–6924. *Clubs:* Australian (Sydney); Queensland (Brisbane); Commonwealth (Canberra).

GIBBS, Rt. Hon. Sir Humphrey Vicary, PC 1969; GCVO 1969 (KCVO 1965); KCMG 1960; OBE 1959; Governor of Rhodesia (lately S Rhodesia), 1959–69; *b* 22 Nov. 1902; 3rd *s* of 1st Baron Hunsdon; *m* 1934, Molly Peel Nelson (*see* Molly Peel Gibbs); five *s*. *Educ:* Eton; Trinity Coll., Cambridge. Started farming near Bulawayo, 1928; ceased farming operations, 1983. Hon. LLD Birmingham, 1969; Hon. DCL East Anglia, 1969. *Address:* 22 Dornie Road, Pomona, PO Borrowdale, Harare, Zimbabwe. *T:* Harare 883281. *Clubs:* Bulawayo (Bulawayo, Zimbabwe); Harare (Harare, Zimbabwe).

GIBBS, Rt. Rev. John; *b* 15 March 1917; *s* of late A. E. Gibbs, Bournemouth; *m* 1943, G. Marion, *d* of late W. J. Bishop, Poole, Dorset; one *s* one *d*. *Educ:* Univ. of Bristol; Western Coll., Bristol; Lincoln Theological Coll. BA (Bristol); BD (London). In the ministry of the Congregational Church, 1943–49. Student Christian Movement: Inter-Collegiate Sec., 1949–51; Study Sec. and Editor of Student Movement, 1951–55. Curate of St Luke's, Brislington, Bristol, 1955–57; Chaplain and Head of Divinity Dept, Coll. of St Matthias, Bristol, 1957–64, Vice-Principal, 1962–64; Principal, Keswick Hall Coll. of Education, Norwich, 1964–73; Examining Chaplain to Bishop of Norwich, Hon. Canon of Norwich Cathedral, 1968–73; Bishop Suffragan of Bradwell, Dio. Chelmsford, 1973–76; Bishop of Coventry, 1976–85. Member, Durham Commn on Religious Education, 1967–70; Chairman: C of E Children's Council, 1968–71; C of E Bd of Educn Publications Cttee, 1971–79, Education and Community Cttee, 1974–76; BCC Wkg Parties: The Child in the Church, 1973–76; Understanding Christian Nurture, 1979–81; Anglican–Lutheran European Reg. Commn, 1980–82 (Anglican Chm.); Assoc. of Voluntary Colls, 1985–; Further and Higher Educn Cttee, General Synod Bd of Educn, 1986–. Introduced H of L, 1982. *Recreations:* music, sailing, bird watching. *Address:* Farthingloe, Southfield, Minchinhampton, Stroud, Glos GL6 9DY.

GIBBS, Martin St John Valentine, CB 1958; DSO 1942; TD; JP; Lord-Lieutenant of Gloucestershire, since 1978; *b* 14 Feb. 1917; *er s* of late Major G. M. Gibbs, Parkleaze, Ewen, Cirencester; *m* 1947, Mary Margaret (*widow* of late Captain M. D. H. Wills, MC), *er d* of late Col Philip Mitford; two *d*. *Educ:* Eton. 2nd Lieut, Royal Wilts Yeomanry, 1937; served War of 1939–45 with Royal Wilts Yeo., Major 1942, Lieut-Col 1951, Brevet-Col 1955, Col 1958; Hon. Col: Royal Wilts Yeomanry Sqdn, T&AVR, 1972–82; The Royal Yeomanry, RAC, T&AVR, 1975–82; Col Comdt Yeomanry, RAC, 1975–82. Gloucestershire: JP 1965; High Sheriff, 1958; DL Wilts 1972. *Recreations:* country pursuits. *Address:* Ewen Manor, Ewen, Cirencester, Glos. *T:* Kemble 206. *Clubs:* Cavalry and Guards, MCC.

See also Field Marshal Sir R. C. Gibbs, Sir G. R. Newman, Bt.

GIBBS, Dame Molly (Peel), DBE 1969; (Hon. Lady Gibbs); *b* 13 July 1912; 2nd *d* of John Peel Nelson; *m* 1934, Rt hon. Sir Humphrey Vicary Gibbs, *qv*; five *s*. *Educ:* Girls' High School, Barnato Park, Johannesburg. *Address:* 22 Dornie Road, Pomona, PO Borrowdale, Harare, Zimbabwe. *T:* Harare 883281.

GIBBS, Prof. Norman Henry, MA, DPhil; Emeritus Fellow, All Souls College, Oxford, since 1977; Chichele Professor of the History of War in the University of Oxford, 1953–77; *b* 17 April 1910; *m* 1941, Joan Frances Leslie-Melville; two *d*; *m* 1955, Kathleen Phebe Emmett. Open Exhibitioner, Magdalen Coll., Oxford, 1928; Senior Demy, 1931; Asst Lecturer, University Coll., London, 1934–36; Fellow and Tutor in Modern History, Merton Coll., Oxford, 1936. 1st King's Dragoon Guards, 1939; Historical Section, War Cabinet Office, 1943. Former Chm., Naval Education Advisory Cttee; former Member: Internat. Council of Institute for Strategic Studies; Council, Royal United Service Institution; Research Associate, Center for Internat. Studies, Princeton, 1965–66. Visiting Professor: Univ. of New Brunswick, 1975–76; US Military Academy, West Point, 1978–79. US Outstanding Civilian Service Medal, 1979. *Publications:* 2nd edition, Keith, British Cabinet System, 1952; The Origins of the Committee of Imperial Defence, 1955; contribs to: Cambridge Modern History (new edn); L'Europe du XIXme et du XXme siècles, (Milan) 1966; (ed) The Soviet System and Democratic Society, 1967; History of the Second World War, Grand Strategy, Vol. 1, 1976. *Address:* All Souls College, Oxford; Flat No 1, Grange Court, Shore Road, Bonchurch, Isle of Wight.

GIBBS, Oswald Moxley, CMG 1976; High Commissioner for Grenada in London, 1974–78 and since 1984; Ambassador for Grenada to the European Economic Community, 1985; *b* St George's, Grenada, 15 Oct. 1927; *s* of Michael Gibbs and Emelda Mary (*née* Cobb); *m* 1955, Dearest Agatha Mitchell; two *s* two *d*. *Educ:* Happy Hill RC Sch.; St George's RC Sen. Boys' Sch.; Grenada Boys' Secondary Sch.; Christy Trades Sch., Chicago (Technical Drafting Dip.); City of London Coll. BScEcon London. Solicitors' Clerk, Grenada, 1948–51; petroleum refining, Royal Dutch Shell Co., Curaçao, Netherlands Antilles, 1951–55; Civil Servant, Agricl Rehabilitation Dept, Grenada, 1955–57; Transport Worker, London Transport, and Postman, London, 1957–60; Civil Servant, WI Federal Commn, London, 1961–62; Consular Officer, Commn for Eastern Caribbean Govts, London, 1965–75; Welfare Officer, 1965–67; Trade Sec., 1967–72; Dep. Comr,

1972–73; Actg Comr, 1973–75. Consultant, Centre for Industrial Develt, Lomé Convention, Brussels, 1979–80 (signed Lomé III Convention for Grenada, 1984); Admin. Dir, N Kensington Family Centre and Unity Assoc., 1980–83; Business Develt Manager, UK Caribbean Chamber of Commerce, 1983–84. Rep. Govt of St Kitts-Nevis-Anguilla on London Cttee of Commonwealth Sugar Producing Countries, 1971–75. Chairman: Civil Service Salaries Revision Commn, Grenada, 1970; Notting Hill Carnival and Arts Cttee, 1981–84. Mem. Governing Council, IFAD (Rome), 1986. Mem., delegns to constitutional, Commonwealth and ACP/EEC meetings and confs. Silver Jubilee Medal, 1977. *Recreations:* development economics, politics, photography. *Address:* Grenada High Commission, 1 Collingham Gardens, SW5; Woodside Green, SE25.

GIBBS, Dr Richard John; Under Secretary, and Director of Statistics and Management Information, Department of Health and Social Security, since 1986; *b* 15 May 1943; *s* of Leslie and Mary Gibbs; *m* 1968, Laura Wanda Olasmi; one *d*. *Educ:* Merchant Taylors' Sch., Northwood; Pembroke Coll., Cambridge (BA 1965); Warwick Univ. (PhD 1974). Teacher, City of London Sch. for Boys, 1965; Scientific Officer, Home Office, 1968; Sen. Scientific Officer, 1970, PSO, 1972, DHSS; Res. Schol., Internat. Inst. for Applied Systems Analysis, Austria, 1977; SPSO, DHSS, 1978; Central Policy Review Staff, 1980; Dir of Operational Res. (DCSO), 1982, CSO, 1985, DHSS. Vis. Prof., UCL, 1985. *Publications:* contribs to Jl of ORS. *Recreations:* windsurfing, cooking. *Address:* 84 Farquhar Road, SE19 1LT. *T:* 01–761 0819.

GIBBS, Richard John Hedley, QC 1984; barrister; a Recorder of the Crown Court, since 1981; *b* 2 Sept. 1941; *s* of Brian Conaway Gibbs and Mabel Joan Gibbs; *m* 1965, Janet (*née* Whittall); one *s* three *d*. *Educ:* Oundle Sch.; Trinity Hall, Cambridge (MA). Called to the Bar, Inner Temple, 1965. *Address:* 4 King's Bench Walk, Temple, EC4Y 7DL. *T:* 01–353 3581; 1 Fountain Court, Steelhouse Lane, Birmingham B4 6DR. *T:* 021–236 5721.

GIBBS, Roger Geoffrey; Chairman, Gerrard & National PLC, since 1975; *b* 13 Oct. 1934; 4th *s* of Hon. Sir Geoffrey Gibbs, KCMG, and late Hon. Lady Gibbs, CBE. *Educ:* Eton; Millfield. Jessel Toynbee & Co. Ltd, 1954, Dir 1960; de Zoete & Gorton, Stockbrokers, 1964, Partner 1966; Gerrard & National PLC, 1971–; Chm., London Discount Market Assoc., 1984–86. Mem. Council, Royal Nat. Pension Fund for Nurses, 1975–; Governor, London Clinic, 1983–; Trustee, Wellcome Trust, 1982–; Special Trustee, Guy's Hosp., 1985–. *Address:* 23 Tregunter Road, SW10 9LS. *T:* 01–370 3465. *Clubs:* Brooks's, Pratt's.

GIBBS, Field Marshal Sir Roland (Christopher), GCB 1976 (KCB 1972); CBE 1968; DSO 1945; MC 1943; Vice Lord-Lieutenant for Wiltshire, since 1982; Chief of the General Staff, 1976–79; ADC General to the Queen, 1976–79; Constable, HM Tower of London, since 1985; *b* 22 June 1921; *yr s* of late Maj. G. M. Gibbs, Parkleaze, Ewen, Cirencester; *m* 1955, Davina Jean Merry; two *s* one *d*. *Educ:* Eton Coll.; RMC Sandhurst. Commnd into 60th Rifles, 1940; served War of 1939–45 in N Africa, Italy and NW Europe. Comd 3rd Bn Parachute Regt, 1960–62; GSO1, Brit. Army Staff, Washington, 1962–63; Comdr 16 Para. Bde, 1963–66; Chief of Staff, HQ Middle East, 1966–67; IDC 1968; Commander, British Forces, Gulf, 1969–71; GOC 1 (British) Corps, 1972–74; C-in-C, UKLF, 1974–76. Colonel Commandant: 2nd Bn The Royal Green Jackets, 1971–78; Parachute Regt, 1972–77. Salisbury Regional Dir, Lloyds Bank, 1979–. Chm., Nat. Rifle Assoc., 1984–. DL Wilts, 1980. *Recreation:* out-of-door sports. *Address:* Patney Rectory, Devizes, Wilts. *Club:* Turf.

See also M. St J. V. Gibbs.

GIBBS, Stephen, CBE 1981; Chairman: Turner & Newall Ltd, 1979–82; Gascoigne Moody Associates, since 1984; Gibbs Littlewood Associates Ltd, since 1984; *b* 12 Feb. 1920; *s* of Arthur Edwin Gibbs and Anne Gibbs; *m* 1941, Louise Pattison; one *s* one *d*. *Educ:* Oldbury Grammar Sch.; Birmingham Univ. (part-time). FPRI. British Industrial Plastics Ltd, Oldbury, Warley, W Midlands, 1936–39. Served RASC, 1939–46. British Industrial Plastics Ltd: Technical Dept, 1946–52; General Sales Manager, 1952–56; Director, and Chm. of subsidiary cos, 1956–68; Turner & Newall Ltd, Manchester: Director, 1968–72; Man. Dir, 1972–76; Dep. Chm., 1976–79. Chm., Energy Policy Cttee, CBI, 1981–83. *Address:* Nicholas Green, Pumphouse Lane, Hanbury, near Droitwich, Worcs WR9 7EB. *T:* Hanbury 423.

GIBRALTAR IN EUROPE, Bishop of, since 1980; **Rt. Rev. John Richard Satterthwaite;** *b* 17 Nov. 1925; *s* of William and Clara Elisabeth Satterthwaite. *Educ:* Millom Grammar Sch.; Leeds Univ. (BA); Coll. of the Resurrection, Mirfield. History Master, St Luke's Sch., Haifa, 1946–48; Curate: St Barnabas, Carlisle, 1950–53; St Aidan, Carlisle, 1953–54; St Michael Paternoster Royal, London, 1955–59, Curate-in-Charge, 1959–65; Guild Vicar, St Dunstan-in-the-West, City of London, 1959–70. Gen. Sec., Church of England Council on Foreign Relations, 1959–70 (Asst Gen. Sec., 1955–59); Gen. Sec., Archbp's Commn on Roman Catholic Relations, 1965–70; Bishop Suffragan of Fulham, 1970; Bishop of Gibraltar, 1970; known as Bishop of Fulham and Gibraltar until creation of new diocese, 1980. Hon. Canon of Canterbury, 1963–; ChStJ 1972 (Asst ChStJ 1963); Hon. Canon of Utrecht, Old Catholic Church of the Netherlands, 1969. Holds decoration from various foreign churches. *Recreations:* fell walking, music. *Address:* 5A Gregory Place, W8 4NG. *T:* 01–937 2796. *Club:* Athenæum.

GIBRALTAR IN EUROPE, Suffragan Bishop of, since 1986; **Rt. Rev. Edward Holland;** *b* 28 June 1936; *s* of Reginald Dick Holland and Olive Holland (*née* Yeoman). *Educ:* New College School; Dauntsey's School; King's College London (AKC). National Service, Worcestershire Regt, 1955–57; worked for Importers, 1957–61; KCL, 1961–65. Deacon 1965, priest 1966, Rochester; Curate, Holy Trinity, Dartford, 1965–69; Curate, John Keble, Mill Hill, 1969–72; Precentor, Gibraltar Cathedral, and Missioner for Seamen, 1972–74; Chaplain at Naples, Italy, 1974–79; Vicar of S Mark's, Bromley, 1979–86. *Recreations:* travel, being entertained and entertaining. *Address:* 11 Lanark Road, W9 1DD. *T:* 01–286 3335.

GIBRALTAR IN EUROPE (Diocese), Auxiliary Bishops of; *see* Capper, Rt Rev. E. M. H.; Isherwood, Rt Rev. H.; Pina-Cabral, Rt Rev. D. P. dos S. de.

GIBSON, family name of **Barons Ashbourne** and **Gibson**.

GIBSON, Baron *cr* 1975 (Life Peer), of Penn's Rocks; **Richard Patrick Tallentyre Gibson;** Chairman, National Trust, 1977–86; *b* 5 Feb. 1916; *s* of Thornely Carbutt Gibson and Elizabeth Anne Augusta Gibson; *m* 1945, Elisabeth Dione Pearson; four *s*. *Educ:* Eton Coll.; Magdalen Coll., Oxford (Hon. Fellow, 1977). London Stock Exchange, 1937. Served with Mddx Yeo, 1939–46; N Africa, 1940–41; POW, 1941–43; Special Ops Exec., 1943–45; Political Intell. Dept, FO, 1945–46. Westminster Press Ltd, 1947–78 (Dir, 1948); Director: Whitehall Securities Corp. Ltd, 1948–60, 1973–; Financial Times Ltd, 1957–78 (Chm., 1975–77); Economist Newspaper Ltd, 1957–78; S. Pearson & Son Ltd, 1960–83 (Dep. Chm., 1969; Exec. Dep. Chm., 1975; Chm., 1978); Royal Exchange Assce, 1961–69; Chm., Pearson Longman Ltd, 1967–79. Hon. Treas. Commonwealth Press Union, 1957–67. Chm., Arts Council, 1972–77. Trustee, Historic Churches Preservation Trust, 1958; Member: Exec. Cttee, National Trust, 1963–72; Council, Nat.

Trust, 1966; Adv. Council, V&A Museum, 1968–75 (Chm., 1970); UK Arts Adv. Commn, Calouste Gulbenkian Foundn, 1969–72; Redundant Churches Fund, 1970–71; Exec. Cttee, Nat. Art Collections Fund, 1970; Bd, Royal Opera House, 1977–; Treasurer, Sussex Univ., 1983–; Trustee, Glyndebourne Fest. Opera, 1965–72 and 1977–. Hon. DLitt Reading, 1980. *Recreations:* music, gardening, architecture. *Address:* Penn's Rocks, Groombridge, Sussex. *T:* Groombridge 244. *Clubs:* Garrick, Brooks's.

GIBSON, Dr Alan Frank, FRS 1978; FInstP; Head of Laser Division, Rutherford and Appleton Laboratories, 1977–83; Hon. Research Fellow, Clarendon Laboratory, Oxford; Visiting Professor, University of Essex; *b* 30 May 1923; *s* of Hezeltine Gibson and Margaret Wilson; *m* 1945, Judith Cresswell; one *s* two *d. Educ:* Rydal Sch., Colwyn Bay; Birmingham Univ. (BSc, PhD). FInstP 1965. Joined TRE, Malvern, 1944; conducted research and later lead res. groups on aspects of solid state physics and devices, notably semiconductor devices; Dep. Chief Scientific Officer (by individual merit), 1961; Univ. of Essex: first Prof. of Physics, 1963; res. on optical properties of semiconductors using lasers; Chm. of Physics Dept, 1963–69 and 1971–76; Dean of Phys. Sciences, 1964–68; Pro-Vice-Chancellor, 1968–69 and 1974–75. FRSA. Glazebrook Medal and Prize, Inst. of Physics, 1983. *Publications:* (General Editor) Progress in Semiconductors: Vol. 1, 1956 to Vol. 9, 1965; An Introduction to Solid State Physics and its Applications, 1974 (repr. with corrections 1976); over 70 res. pubns in learned jls. *Address:* Dunstan Lodge, Letcombe Regis, Wantage, Oxon OX12 9JY. *T:* Wantage 66531.

GIBSON, Sir Alexander (Drummond), Kt 1977; CBE 1967; FRSE 1978; Founder, 1962 and Music Director, 1985–June 1987, Scottish Opera Company (Artistic Director, 1962–85), Conductor Laureate, since 1987; *b* 11 Feb. 1926; *s* of late James McClure Gibson and of Wilhelmina Gibson (*née* Williams); *m* 1959, Ann Veronica Waggett; three *s* one *d. Educ:* Dalziel; Glasgow Univ.; Royal College of Music; Mozarteum, Salzburg, Austria; Accademia Chigiano, Siena, Italy. Served with Royal Signals, 1944–48. Repetiteur and Asst Conductor, Sadler's Wells Opera, 1951–52; Asst Conductor, BBC Scottish Orchestra, Glasgow, 1952–54; Staff Conductor, Sadler's Wells Opera, 1954–57; Musical Dir, Sadler's Wells Opera, 1957–59; Principal Conductor and Musical Dir, Scottish Nat. Orch., 1959–84 (Hon. Pres., 1985–). Principal Guest Conductor, Houston Symphony Orch., 1981–83. FRSA 1980. Hon. RAM 1969; Hon. FRCM, 1973; Hon. FRSAMD, 1973; Hon. RSA, 1975. Hon. LLD Aberdeen, 1968; Hon. DMus Glasgow, 1972; DUniv: Stirling, 1972; Open, 1978. St Mungo Prize, 1970; ISM Distinguished Musician Award, 1976; Sibelius Medal, 1978. *Recreations:* motoring, tennis, reading. *Address:* 15 Cleveden Gardens, Glasgow G12 0PU. *T:* 041–339 6668. *Clubs:* Garrick, Oriental.

GIBSON, Sir Christopher (Herbert), 3rd Bt *cr* 1931; Sales Representative, National Homes Ltd, Abbotsford, BC, Canada; *b* 2 Feb. 1921; *s* of Sir Christopher H. Gibson, 2nd Bt, and Lady Dorothy E. O. Gibson (*née* Bruce); *S* father, 1962; *m* 1941, Lilian Lake Young, *d* of Dr George Byron Young, Colchester; one *s* three *d. Educ:* St Cyprian's, Eastbourne; St George's Coll., Argentina. Served, 1941–45 (5 war medals and stars): 28th Canadian Armd Regt (BCR), Lieut. Sugar Cane Plantation Manager, Leach's Argentine Estates, 1946–51; Manager, Encyclopædia Britannica, 1952–55; Design Draughtsman, Babcock & Wilcox, USA, 1956–57; Tea Plantation Manager, Liebig's, 1958–60; Ranch Manager, Liebig's Extract of Meat Co., 1961–64; Building Inspector, Industrias Kaiser, Argentina, 1964–68; Manager and part-owner, Lakanto Poultry Farms, 1969–76. *Recreations:* shooting, fishing, tennis, cricket. *Heir:* *s* Rev. Christopher Herbert Gibson, CP, *b* Argentina, 17 July 1948.

GIBSON, Rev. Sir David, 4th Bt *cr* 1926; Catholic Priest; *b* 18 July 1922; *s* of Sir Ackroyd Herbert Gibson, 3rd Bt; *S* father, 1975. Founder of Societas Navigatorum Catholica, 1954. *Address:* The Presbytery, Our Lady and St Neot, West Street, Liskeard, Cornwall PL14 6BW.

GIBSON, Vice-Adm. Sir Donald Cameron Ernest Forbes, KCB 1968 (CB 1965); DSC 1941; JP; *b* 17 March 1916; *s* of late Capt. W. L. D. Gibson, Queen's Own Cameron Highlanders, and of Elizabeth Gibson; *m* 1939, Marjorie Alice, *d* of H. C. Harding, Horley, Surrey; one *s. Educ:* Woodbridge Sch., Suffolk. Cadet, Brit. India SN Co. and Midshipman, Royal Naval Reserve, 1933–37; transf. to Royal Navy, 1937; specialised as Pilot, 1938. Served War of 1939–45: HMS Glorious, Ark Royal, Formidable, Audacity; trng Pilots in USA; Empire Central Flying Sch., 1942; Chief Flying Instr, Advanced Flying Sch., 1946–47; HMS Illustrious, 1947–48; Air Gp Comdr, HMS Theseus, 1948–49; Comdr (Air), RNAS Culdrose, 1950–52; RN Staff Course, 1952–53; Comdr (Air) HMS Indomitable and Glory, 1953–54; Capt. RNAS Brawdy, 1954–56, HMS Dainty, 1956–58; Dep. Dir Air Warfare, 1958–60; Canadian Nat. Defence Coll., 1960–61; Capt., HMS Ark Royal, 1961–63; Rear-Adm. 1963; Flag Officer: Aircraft Carriers, 1963–64; Naval Flying Trg, 1964–65; Naval Air Comd, 1965–68; Vice-Adm. 1967. Dir, HMS Belfast Trust, 1971–72; Mem., Gen. Cttee, Devon Community Housing Soc. Ltd, 1983–. JP Barnstaple 1973. *Recreation:* painting. *Address:* Lower Bealy Court, Chulmleigh, North Devon. *T:* Chulmleigh 80264.

GIBSON, Sir Donald (Evelyn Edward), Kt 1962; CBE 1951; DCL; MA, FRIBA (Distinction Town Planning), FRTPI; Controller General, Ministry of Public Building and Works, 1967–69, now Consultant; *b* 11 Oct. 1908; *s* of late Prof. Arnold Hartley Gibson; *m* 1st, 1936, Winifred Mary (*née* McGowan) (decd); three *s* one *d*; 2nd, 1978, Grace Haines. *Educ:* Manchester Gram. Sch.; Manchester Univ. BA Hons Architecture; MA. Work in USA, 1931; private practice, 1933; professional Civil Service (Building Research), 1935; Dep. County Architect, Isle of Ely, 1937; City Architect and Town Planning Officer, County and City of Coventry, 1939; County Architect, Notts, 1955; Dir-Gen. of Works, War Office, 1958–62; Dir-Gen., R&D, MPBW, 1962–67; Hoffmann Wood Prof. of Architecture, University of Leeds, 1967–68. Mem. Central Housing Advisory Cttee, 1951, 1953 and 1954. President: RIBA, 1964–65; Dist Heating Assoc., 1971–. Hon. FLI 1968. *Publications:* various publications dealing with housing, planning and architecture in RIBA and RTPI Journals. *Recreation:* model railways. *Address:* Bryn Castell, Llanddona, Beaumaris, Gwynedd LL58 8TR. *T:* Beaumaris 810399.

GIBSON, Prof. Frank William Ernest, FRS 1976; FAA; Professor of Biochemistry, Australian National University, since 1967; *b* 22 July 1923; *s* of John William and Alice Ruby Gibson; *m* 1st, 1949, Margaret Isabel Nancy (marr. diss. 1979); two *d*; 2nd, 1980, Robin Margaret; one *s. Educ:* Queensland, Melbourne, and Oxford Univs. BSc, DSc (Melb.), DPhil (Oxon). Research Asst, Melbourne and Queensland Univs, 1938–47; Sen. Demonstrator, Melbourne Univ., 1948–49; ANU Scholar, Oxford, 1950–52. Melbourne University: Sen. Lectr, 1953–58; Reader in Chem. Microbiology, 1959–65; Prof. of Chem. Microbiology, 1965–66; Prof. of Biochem. and Head of Biochem. Dept, John Curtin Sch. of Medical Res., ANU, 1967–76; Howard Florey Prof. of Medical Res., and Dir, John Curtin Sch. of Med. Res., ANU, 1977–79. Newton-Abraham Vis. Prof. and Fellow of Lincoln Coll., Oxford Univ., 1982–83. David Syme Research Prize, Univ. of Melb., 1963. FAA 1971. *Publications:* scientific papers on the biochemistry of bacteria, particularly the biosynthesis of aromatic compounds, energy metabolism. *Recreations:* tennis, skiing. *Address:* Biochemistry Department, John Curtin School of Medical Research, PO Box 334, Canberra City, ACT 2601, Australia.

GIBSON, Harold Leslie George, OBE 1978 (MBE 1971); General President, National Union of Hosiery and Knitwear Workers, 1975–82; *b* 15 July 1917; *s* of George Robert and Ellen Millicent Gibson; *m* 1941, Edith Lunt (decd); one *s* one *d. Educ:* elementary and grammar schools, Liverpool. Officer of National Union of Hosiery and Knitwear Workers, 1949; General Secretary, 1962–75. Member: Monopolies and Mergers Commn, 1978–; Management Cttee, Gen. Fedn of Trade Unions; TUC Textile Cttee; Exec. Cttee, British Textile Confdn; Knitting, Lace & Net Industry Training Board; Strategy Working Party for the Hosiery Industry. Pres., Internat. Textile, Garment and Leather Workers' Fedn, Brussels. Hon. LLM Leicester, 1982. JP 1949–77. *Recreations:* photography, golf, music. *Address:* 15 Links Road, Kibworth Beauchamp, Leics. *T:* (private) Kibworth 2149; (business) Leicester 556703.

GIBSON, John Peter; Director, Taylor Woodrow Energy Ltd, since 1982; Chief Executive, Seaforth Maritime, since 1986 (Deputy Chairman, 1978–83; Chairman, 1983–86); *b* 21 Aug. 1929; *s* of John Leighton Gibson and Norah Gibson; *m* 1954, Patricia Anne Thomas; two *s* three *d. Educ:* Caterham Sch.; Imperial Coll., London (BSc (Hons Mech. Engrg), ACGI). Post-grad. apprenticeship Rolls Royce Derby, 1953–55; ICI (Billingham and Petrochemicals Div.), 1955–69; Man. Dir, Lummus Co., 1969–73; Dir Gen. Offshore Supplies Office, Dept of Energy, 1973–76. *Recreations:* work, gardening, handyman. *Address:* The Old Manse, Leochel-Cushnie, by Alford, Aberdeenshire AB3 8LJ. *T:* Muir of Foulis 379.

GIBSON, John Sibbald; Under Secretary, Scottish Office, 1973–83, retired; historian; *b* 1 May 1923; *s* of John McDonald Frame Gibson and Marion Watson Sibbald; *m* 1948, Moira Helen Gillespie; one *s* one *d. Educ:* Paisley Grammar Sch.; Glasgow Univ. Army, 1942–46, Lieut in No 1 Commando from 1943; Far East. Joined Admin. Grade Home Civil Service, 1947; Asst Principal, Scottish Home Dept, 1947–50; Private Sec. to Parly Under-Sec., 1950–51; Private Sec. to Perm. Under-Sec. of State, Scottish Office, 1952; Principal, Scottish Home Dept, 1953; Asst Sec., Dept of Agriculture and Fisheries for Scotland, 1962; Under Secretary: Scottish Office, 1973; Dept of Agriculture and Fisheries for Scotland, 1980. Mem., Agricl Res. Council, 1979–83. Organiser, Scottish Office Centenary Exhibn, 1985. *Publications:* Ships of the '45: the rescue of the Young Pretender, 1967; Deacon Brodie: Father to Jekyll and Hyde, 1977; The Thistle and the Crown, 1985. *Recreation:* writing. *Address:* 28 Cramond Gardens, Edinburgh EH4 6PU. *T:* 031–336 2931. *Club:* Scottish Arts (Edinburgh).

GIBSON, John Walter; Chief of Operational Research, SHAPE Technical Centre, 1977–84; *b* 15 Jan. 1922; *s* of late Thomas John Gibson and Catherine Gibson (*née* Gregory), Bamburgh, Northumberland; *m* 1951, Julia, *d* of George Leslie Butler, Buxton, Derbyshire; two *s* one *d. Educ:* A. J. Dawson Sch., Durham; Sheffield Univ.; University Coll., London. RNVR, 1942–46. Sheffield Univ., 1940–42, 1946–47 (BSc); University Coll., London, 1947–48; Safety-in-Mines Research Estabt, 1948–53; BJSM, Washington, DC, 1953–56; Royal Armament Research and Develt Estabt, 1957–60; Head of Statistics Div., Ordnance Bd, 1961–64; Supt, Assessment Br., Royal Armament Research and Develt Estabt, 1964–66, Prin. Supt, Systems Div., 1966–69; Asst Chief Scientific Adviser (Studies), MoD, 1969–74; Under-Secretary: Cabinet Office, 1974–76; MoD, 1976–77. FSS 1953. *Address:* 17 Lyndhurst Drive, Sevenoaks, Kent. *T:* Sevenoaks 54589.

GIBSON, Joseph, CBE 1980; PhD; CChem, FRSC; FEng, FInstE; consultant; Coal Science Adviser, National Coal Board, 1981–83 (Member for Science, 1977–81); *b* 10 May 1916; *m* 1944, Lily McFarlane Brown; one *s* one *d. Educ:* King's Coll. (now Univ. of Newcastle upon Tyne; MSc, PhD). Res., Northern Coke Res. Lab. 1938; Head of Chemistry Dept, Sunderland Technical Coll., and Lectr, Durham Univ., 1946; Chief Scientist, Northern Div., 1958, and Yorks Div., 1964, NCB; Director: Coal Res. Estab., 1968; Coal Utilisation Res., 1975. President: Inst. of Fuel, 1975–76; BCURA, 1977–81 (Chm. 1972–77). Lectures: Cadman Meml, 1980, 1983; Prof. Moore Meml, 1981; Brian H. Morgans Meml, 1983. Coal Science Lecture Medal, 1977; Carbonisation Sci. Medal, 1979. Hon. FIChemE. Hon. DCL Newcastle, 1981. *Publications:* Carbonisation of Coal, 1971; Coal and Modern Coal Processing, 1979; Coal Utilisation: technology, economics and policy, 1981; papers on coal conversion and utilisation. *Recreations:* bridge, gardening, golf. *Address:* 31 Charlton Close, Charlton Kings, Cheltenham, Glos. *T:* Cheltenham 517832.

GIBSON, Joseph David, CBE 1979; Ambassador of Fiji to Japan, since 1984; *b* 26 Jan. 1928; *s* of late Charles Ivan Gibson and Mamao Lavenia Gibson; *m* Emily Susan Bentley; three *s* two *d. Educ:* Levuka Public Sch., Suva; Marist Brothers Secondary Sch.; Auckland Univ., NZ (BA); Auckland Teachers' Coll. (Teachers' Cert.). Asst Teacher, Suva Boys' Grammar Sch., 1952–57; Principal, Suva Educnl Inst., 1957; Principal, Queen Victoria School, Fiji, 1961–62 (Asst Teacher, 1958–59; Sen. Master, 1959; 1st Asst, 1960); Sec. Sch. Inspector, Fiji Educn Dept, 1964–65; Asst Dir of Educn, 1966–69; Dep. Dir of Educn, 1970; Dir of Educn and Permanent Sec. for Educn, 1971–74; Dep. High Comr, London, 1974–76, High Comr, 1976–81; High Comr, New Zealand, 1981–83. Represented Fiji at: Dirs of Educn Conferences, Western Samoa and Pago Pago, 1968, Honolulu, 1970; Commonwealth Ministers of Educn Meeting, Canberra, 1971; Head of Fiji Delegn, Commonwealth Ministers of Educn Meeting, Jamaica, 1974. Member: Fiji Broadcasting Commn, 1971–73; Univ. Council, Univ. of South Pacific, 1971–74. *Recreations:* golf, fishing, represented Auckland and Suva, Fiji, in hockey. *Address:* Embassy of Fiji, Noa Building (10th Floor), 3–5, 2–chome Azabudai, Minato-ku, Tokyo 106, Japan.

GIBSON, Col Leonard Young, CBE 1961 (MBE 1940); TD 1947; DL; Master of Newcastle and District Beagles, 1946–83; *b* 4 Dec. 1911; *s* of late William McLure Gibson and Wilhelmina Mitchell, Gosforth; *m* 1949, Pauline Mary Anthony; one *s* one *d. Educ:* Royal Grammar Sch., Newcastle upon Tyne; France and Germany. Service in TA, 1932–61: 72nd (N) Fd Regt RA TA, 1932–39; Staff Coll., Camberley, 1938–39; tsc; Bde Major RA: 50th (N) Div., rearguard Dunkirk, 1939–40 (MBE, despatches); 43rd (W) Div., 1941–42; GSO2, SE Army, 1942; GSO2 (Dirg Staff), Staff Coll., Camberley, 1942–43 (psc†); GSO1 Ops Eastern Comd, 1943–44; 2nd in Comd 107 Med. Regt S Notts Hussars, RHA TA, France, Belgium, Holland, Germany, 1944–45 (despatches; Croix de Guerre with Gold Star, France, 1944); GSO1 Mil. Govt Germany, 1945; Bty Comd, The Elswick Bty, 1947–51; OC 272 (N) Field Regt RA TA, 1956–58; Dep. Comdr RA 50th Inf. Div. TA, 1959–61; Colonel TA, retd. Mem., Northumberland T&AFA, 1958–68. Pres., Masters of Harriers and Beagles Assoc., 1968–69. DL Northumberland, 1971. *Recreations:* hunting, breeding horses and hounds. *Address:* Simonburn Cottage, Humshaugh, Northumberland. *T:* Humshaugh 402. *Clubs:* Army and Navy; Northern Counties (Newcastle upon Tyne).

GIBSON, Hon. Sir Marcus (George), Kt 1970; *b* 11 Jan. 1898; *e s* of late Clyde Gibson, Oatlands, Tasmania, and Lucy Isabel (*née* Stanfield); *m* 1929, Iris Lavinia, *d* of A. E. Shone, East Risdon, Tas; one *s* one *d. Educ:* Leslie House Sch., Hobart; Univ. of Tasmania. LLB (Tas) 1921; LLM (Tas) 1924. Served European War: Gunner, AIF, 1917–19. Admitted to bar of Supreme Court, Tasmania, 1921; private practice, 1921–29; Solicitor to the Public Trust Office, 1929–38; Police Magistrate, 1939–42; Asst Solicitor-General, 1942–46; KC 1946; Solicitor-General, 1946–51; Puisne Judge, Supreme Court of Tasmania, 1951–68; on several occasions Actg Chief Justice and Administrator, Govt of

Tasmania. President: Tasmanian Council on the Ageing, 1964–76; E-SU (Tasmanian Br.). *Recreations:* theatre, gardening. *Address:* 296 Sandy Bay Road, Hobart, Tas. 7005, Australia. *T:* Hobart 235624. *Club:* Tasmanian (Hobart).

GIBSON, Rt. Hon. Sir Maurice White, PC 1975; Kt 1975; **Rt. Hon. Lord Justice Gibson;** Lord Justice of Appeal, Supreme Court of Judicature, Northern Ireland, since 1975; Member, Restrictive Practices Court, since 1971; *b* 1 May 1913; 2nd *s* of late William James Gibson, Montpelier House, Belfast, and of Edith Mary Gibson; *m* 1945, Cecily Winifred, *e d* of late Mr and Mrs Dudley Roy Johnson, Cordova, Bexhill-on-Sea, Sussex; one *s* one *d*. *Educ:* Royal Belfast Academical Institution; Queen's Univ., Belfast (LLB, BA). English Bar Final Exam. First Cl. and Certif. of Honour, 1937; Called to Bar of NI with Special Prize awarded by Inn of Court of NI, 1938; called to Inner Bar, NI, 1956. Puisne Judge, NI High Court of Justice, 1968–75. Apptd Mem. several Govt Cttees on Law Reform in NI; Dep. Chm., Boundary Commn for NI, 1971–75; Chm., SLS Legal Publications (NI). Chm., NI Scout Council. *Address:* 29a Purdysburn Hill, Belfast BT8 8JY. *T:* Drumbo 762. *Club:* Royal Belfast Golf.

GIBSON, Captain Michael Bradford; Managing Director of Racquet Sports International Ltd, since 1975; *b* 20 March 1929; *s* of Lt-Col B. T. Gibson; *m* 1953, Mary Helen Elizabeth Legg; two *s*. *Educ:* Taunton Sch.; RMA Sandhurst; Sidney Sussex Coll., Cambridge (BA). Commnd into RE, 1948, retd 1961. Official Referee to Lawn Tennis Assoc. and All England Lawn Tennis Club, 1961–75. Mem., Inst. of Directors. *Recreations:* hunting, boating. *Address:* Olde Denne, Warnham, Horsham, Sussex. *T:* Horsham 65589. *Clubs:* All England Lawn Tennis and Croquet; Cottesmore Golf.

GIBSON, Rear-Adm. Peter Cecil, CB 1968; *b* 31 May 1913; 2nd *s* of Alexander Horace Cecil Gibson and Phyllis Zeline Cecil Gibson (*née* Baume); *m* 1938, Phyllis Anna Mary Hume, *d* of late Major N. H. Hume, IMS, Brecon; two *s* one *d*. *Educ:* Ealing Priory; RN Engrg Coll., Keyham. RN, 1931; HMS Norfolk, EI, 1936–38; maintenance test pilot, RN Aircraft Yard, Donibristle, 1940–41; Air Engr Officer, RNAS, St Merryn, 1941–42; Staff of RANAS, Indian Ocean, E Africa, 1942–43, Ceylon, 1943–44; Staff Air Engr. Off., British Pacific Fleet, 1945–46; Aircraft Maintenance and Repair Dept, 1946–49; loan service RAN, 1950–52; Trng Off., RNAS, Arbroath, 1952–54; Engr Off., HMS Gambia, 1954–56 and as Fleet Engr. Off, E Indies, 1955–56; Staff Engr. Off., Flag Off. Flying Trng, 1957–60; Dep. Dir Service Conditions, 1960–61; Dir Engr Officers' Appts, 1961–63; Supt RN Aircraft Yard, Fleetlands, 1963–65; Dep. Controller Aircraft (RN), Min. of Aviation, 1966–67, Min. of Technology, 1967–69, retired, 1969. ADC, 1965–66. Comdr 1946; Capt. 1957; Rear-Adm. 1966. Chm. United Services Catholic Assoc., 1966–69. *Recreations:* vintage cars, bridge. *Address:* Pangmere, Hampstead Norreys, Newbury, Berks. *Club:* Army and Navy.

GIBSON, Hon. Sir Peter (Leslie), Kt 1981; **Hon. Mr Justice Peter Gibson;** Judge of the High Court of Justice, Chancery Division, since 1981; *b* 10 June 1934; *s* of late Harold Leslie Gibson and Martha Lucy (*née* Diercking); *m* 1968, Katharine Mary Beatrice Hadow; two *s* one *d*. *Educ:* Malvern Coll.; Worcester Coll., Oxford (Scholar). 2nd Lieut RA, 1953–55 (National Service). Called to the Bar, Inner Temple, 1960; Bencher, Lincoln's Inn, 1975. 2nd Jun. Counsel to Inland Revenue (Chancery), 1970–72; Jun. Counsel to the Treasury (Chancery), 1972–81. A Judge of the Employment Appeal Tribunal, 1984–. *Address:* Royal Courts of Justice, Strand, WC2A 2LL.

GIBSON, Prof. Quentin Howieson, FRS 1969; Professor of Biochemistry and Molecular Biology, Cornell University, Ithaca, NY, since 1966; *b* 9 Dec. 1918; *s* of William Howieson Gibson, OBE, DSc; *m* 1951, Audrey Jane, *yr d* of G. H. S. Pinsent, CB, CMG, and Katharine Kentisbeare, *d* of Sir George Radford, MP; one *s* three *d*. *Educ:* Repton. MB, ChB, BAO, Belfast, 1941, MD 1944, PhD 1946, DSc 1951. Demonstrator in Physiology, Belfast, 1941–44; Lecturer in Physiology: Belfast, 1944–46; Sheffield Univ., 1946–55; Professor of Biochem., Sheffield Univ., 1955–63; Prof. of Biophys. Chem., Johnson Research Foundn, University of Pennsylvania, 1963–66. Fellow, Amer. Acad. of Arts and Sciences, 1971; MNAS 1982. *Recreation:* sailing. *Address:* 98 Dodge Road, Ithaca, NY 14850, USA.

GIBSON, Rt. Hon. Sir Ralph (Brian), PC 1985; Kt 1977; **Rt. Hon. Lord Justice Gibson;** a Lord Justice of Appeal, since 1985; *b* 17 Oct. 1922; 2nd *s* of Roy and Emily Gibson; *m* 1949, Ann Chapman Ruether, Chicago; one *s* two *d*. *Educ:* Charterhouse; Brasenose Coll., Oxford (Hon. Fellow 1986). MA Oxon 1948. Army Service, 1941–45: Lieut, 1st KDG; Captain, TJFF. Called to Bar, Middle Temple, 1948, Bencher 1974; QC 1968. A Recorder of the Crown Court, 1972–77; Judge of the High Court of Justice, Queen's Bench Div., 1977–85. Chm., Law Commn, 1981–85. Bigelow Teaching Fellow, University of Chicago, 1948–49. Member: Council of Legal Educn, 1971–; Parole Bd, 1979–81; Pres., Central Council of Probation Cttees, 1982–86. Hon. LLD Dalhousie, 1983. *Address:* 8 Ashley Gardens, SW1. *T:* 01–828 9670.

GIBSON, Prof. Robert Donald Davidson, PhD; Professor of French, since 1965, and Master of Rutherford College, since 1985, University of Kent at Canterbury; *b* Hackney, London, 21 Aug. 1927; *o s* of Nicol and Ann Gibson, Leyton, London; *m* 1953, Sheila Elaine, *o d* of Bertie and Ada Goldsworthy, Exeter, Devon; three *s*. *Educ:* Leyton County High Sch. for Boys; King's Coll., London; Magdalene Coll., Cambridge; Ecole Normale Supérieure, Paris. BA (First Class Hons. French) London, 1948; PhD Cantab. 1953. Asst Lecturer, St Salvator's Coll., University of St Andrews, 1954–55; Lecturer, Queen's Coll., Dundee, 1955–58; Lecturer, Aberdeen Univ., 1958–61; Prof., Queen's Univ. of Belfast, 1961–65. *Publications:* The Quest of Alain-Fournier, 1953; Modern French Poets on Poetry, 1961; (ed) Le Bestiaire Inattendu, 1961; Roger Martin du Gard, 1961; La Mésentente Cordiale, 1963; (ed) Brouart et le Désordre, 1964; (ed) Provinciales, 1965; (ed) Le Grand Meaulnes, 1968; The Land Without a Name, 1975; Alain-Fournier and Le Grand Meaulnes, 1986; reviews and articles in: French Studies, The London Magazine, Times Literary Supplement, Encyclopædia Britannica, Collier's Encyclopædia. *Recreations:* reading, writing, talking. *Address:* 7 Sunnymead, Tyler Hill, Canterbury, Kent CT2 9NW.

GIBSON, Sir Ronald (George), Kt 1975; CBE 1970 (OBE 1961); DL; MA Cantab; FRCS, FRCGP; Chairman of Council, British Medical Association, 1966–71; *b* 28 Nov. 1909; *s* of George Edward Gibson and Gladys Muriel, *d* of William George Prince, JP, CC, Romsey, Hants; *m* 1934, Dorothy Elisabeth Alberta, *d* of Thomas Alfred Rainey, Southampton; two *d*. *Educ:* Mill Hill Sch., St John's Coll., Cambridge; St Bartholomew's Hosp., London. Gen. Practitioner, retired 1977. MO, Winchester Coll. and St Swithun's Sch., Winchester, 1950–77. Lieut-Col RAMC (Emergency Reserve), PMO Italian Somaliland, 1944–45. Mem. Council: BMA, 1950–72 (Chm., Representative Body, 1963–66; Chm. Council, 1966–71); RCS, 1962–67 (FRCS 1968); Mem., GMC, 1974–79. First Provost, SE Eng. Faculty, Royal College of General Practitioners, 1954 (James Mackenzie Lectr, 1967; FRCGP 1967). Member: Central Health Services Council, 1966–76 (Vice-Chm., 1972–76); Personal Social Services Council, DHSS, 1973–76; Standing Med. Adv. Cttee, 1966–76 (Chm., 1972–76); Adv. Council on Misuse of Drugs; Steering Cttee on Barbiturates (Chm.); Adv. Cttee, Drug Surveillance Res. Unit, Southampton Univ. (Chm.); Council, Med. Insurance Agency (Chm. 1977–82); Medical Information Rev. Panel, British Library, 1978– (Chm.); Tribunal on Alleged Atrocities, NI, 1971; Dir, Brendoncare Foundn, 1983– (Pres.). FRSA 1983. Governor, Eastleigh Coll. of Further Educn, 1977–85. Mem. Ct, Univ. of Southampton, 1979–. High Steward, Winchester Cathedral, 1985–. Mem., Ct of Assts, Worshipful Soc. of Apothecaries of London, 1971 (Liveryman, 1964; Master, 1980). Gold Medallist, BMA, 1970; BMA Winchester Address, 1979 (And Is There Honey Still For Tea). DL Hants 1983. Hon. LLD Wales, 1965; Hon. DM Southampton, 1980. *Publications:* Care of the Elderly in General Practice (Butterworth Gold Medal), 1956; The Satchel and the Shining Morning Face, 1971; The One with the Elephant, 1976; Adolescence, 1978; The Family Doctor, His Life and History, 1981; contrib. Lancet, BMJ, etc. *Recreations:* medicine, music, cricket, gardening. *Address:* 21 St Thomas' Street, Winchester, Hants SO23 9HJ. *T:* Winchester 54582. *Clubs:* Athenæum, MCC.

GIBSON, Roy; Director General, British National Space Centre, since 1985; *b* 4 July 1924; *s* of Fred and Jessie Gibson; *m* 1st, 1946, Jean Fallowes (marr. diss. 1971); one *s* one *d*; 2nd, 1971, Inga Elgerus. *Educ:* Chorlton Grammar Sch.; Wadham College, Oxford; SOAS. Malayan Civil Service, 1948–58; Health and Safety Br., UKAEA, 1958–66; European Satellite Research Orgn, 1967–75 (Dir of Admin, 1970–75); Dir Gen., European Space Agency, 1975–80; aerospace consultant, 1980–85. DSC (Kedah, Malaysia), 1953; Das Grosse Silberne Ehrenzeichen mit Stern (Austria), 1977. *Publications:* numerous articles in aerospace technical jls. *Recreations:* music, chess, walking. *Address:* 47 rue des Ecoles, La Boissière Ecole, 78120 France. *T:* 33 1 34 85 02 76. *Club:* Naval and Military.

GIBSON, Ven. Terence Allen; Archdeacon of Suffolk since 1984; *b* 23 Oct. 1937; *s* of Fred William Allen and Joan Hazel Gibson. *Educ:* Jesus Coll., Cambridge (MA); Cuddesdon Coll., Oxford. Curate of St Chad, Kirkby, 1963–66; Warden of Centre 63, Kirkby C of E Youth Centre, 1966–75; Rector of Kirkby, Liverpool, 1975–84; RD of Walton, Liverpool, 1979–84. *Address:* Starlings, Yoxford, Saxmundham, Suffolk IP17 3HP. *T:* Yoxford 387.

GIBSON, Thomas, FRCSE, FRCSGlas, FRSE; Director, Glasgow and West of Scotland Regional Plastic and Maxillofacial Surgery Service, 1970–80; Consultant Plastic Surgeon to Greater Glasgow Health Board (formerly Western Regional Hospital Board), 1947–80; *b* 24 Nov. 1915; *s* of late Thomas Gibson and Mary Munn; *m* 1944, Patricia Muriel McFeat; two *s* two *d*. *Educ:* Paisley Grammar Sch.; Glasgow Univ. (MB, ChB 1938). FRCSE 1941, FRFPSG 1955, FRCSGlas 1962; FRSE 1974. House Surg. and Phys., Western Infirmary, Glasgow, 1939–40; Asst Lectr in Surg., Glasgow Univ., and Extra Dispensary Surg., Western Infirm., Glasgow, 1941–42; full-time appt with MRC, Burns Unit, Glasgow Royal Infirm., 1942–44; RAMC, 1944–47: Lieut, rank of Major 1945; OC No 1 Indian Maxillofacial Unit, 1945–47. Vis. Prof., Bioengrg Unit, Univ. of Strathclyde, 1966–85, Emeritus Prof., 1985–. Royal Coll. of Physicians and Surgeons of Glasgow: Hon. Librarian, 1963–73; Visitor, 1975–76; Pres., 1977–78. Hon. FRACS 1977. Hon. DSc Strathclyde, 1972. Editor, British Jl of Plastic Surgery, 1968–79. *Publications:* Modern Trends in Plastic Surgery: vol. 1, 1964; vol. 2, 1966; The Royal College of Physicians and Surgeons of Glasgow, 1983; contrib. med. and surg. jls. *Recreations:* history, horticulture, handicrafts. *Address:* Eastbrae, 26 Potterhill Avenue, Paisley PA2 8BA. *T:* 041–884 2181.

GIBSON, Wilford Henry, CBE 1980; QPM 1976; Assistant Commissioner (Administration and Operations), Metropolitan Police, 1977–84, retired; *b* 12 Oct. 1924; *s* of late Ernest Gibson and Frances Mary (*née* Kitching); *m* 1949, Betty Ann Bland; two *d*. Served War, Signaller, RAF, 1943–47. Joined Metropolitan Police as Constable, 1947; Inspector 1960; Supt 1965; Comdr 1971; Dep. Asst Comr, A Dept (Operations), 1974. Chm., Met. Police Flying Club and Met. Police Modern Pentathlon Club, 1976–84. OStJ 1977. *Recreations:* riding, boxing, swimming, flying. *Club:* Special Forces.

GIBSON, Major William David; Chairman, W. J. Tatem Ltd, since 1974 (Director, since 1957); *b* 26 Feb. 1925; *s* of G. C. Gibson, OBE, Landwade Hall, Exning, Newmarket, Suffolk; *m* 1st, 1959, Charlotte Henrietta (*d* 1973), *d* of N. S. Pryor; three *s* one *d*; 2nd, 1975, Jane Marion, *d* of late Col L. L. Hassell, DSO, MC. *Educ:* St Peter's Court; Harrow; Trinity Coll., Cambridge. Commissioned into Welsh Guards, July 1945; retired as Major, 1957. Dir, West of England Ship Owners Mutual Protection & Indemnity Assoc., 1959–86; Chm., Internat. Shipowners Investment Co., SA Luxembourg, 1978–83. National Hunt Cttee, Oct. 1959– (Sen. Steward, 1966); Jockey Club, 1966– (Dep. Sen. Steward, 1969–71); Tattersalls Cttee, 1963–69 (Chm., 1967–69). Master, Worshipful Co. of Farriers, 1979. *Recreations:* racing (won 4 Grand Military Gold Cups, 1950–52 and 1956); shooting, sailing. *Address:* Bishopswood Grange, Bishopswood, near Ross-on-Wye, Herefordshire HR9 5QX. *T:* Dean 60444. *Clubs:* Royal Thames Yacht, Royal Yacht Squadron.

GIBSON-BARBOZA, Mario, GCMG 1968; Brazilian Ambassador to the Court of St James's, 1982–86; *b* Olinda, Pernambuco, 13 March 1918; *s* of Oscar Bartholomeu Alves Barboza and Evangelina Gibson Barboza; *m* 1975, Julia Blacker Baldassarri Gibson-Barboza. *Educ:* Law School of Recife, Pernambuco (graduated in Law, 1937); Superior War College, 1951. Entered Brazilian Foreign Service, 1940; served: Houston, Washington and Brussels, 1943–54; Minister-Counsellor: Buenos Aires, 1956–59; Brazilian Mission to United Nations, New York, 1959–60; Ambassador: to Vienna, 1962–66; to Asunción, 1967–68; Secretary General for Foreign Affairs, 1968–69; Ambassador to Washington, 1969; Minister of State for External Relations, 1969–74; Ambassador: to Athens, 1974–77; to Rome, 1977–82. Several Grand Crosses of Orders of Brazil and other countries. *Recreations:* riding, reading, theatre. *Address:* c/o Brazilian Embassy, 32 Green Street, W1Y 3FD. *Clubs:* Athenæum, Travellers', White's; Jockey Clube Brasileiro (Rio de Janeiro).

GIBSON-CRAIG-CARMICHAEL, Sir David Peter William, 15th Bt *cr* 1702 (Gibson Carmichael) and 8th Bt *cr* 1831; *b* 21 July 1946; *s* of Sir Archibald Henry William Gibson-Craig-Carmichael, 14th Bt and Rosemary Anita (*d* 1979), *d* of George Duncan Crew, Santiago, Chile; *S* father, 1969; *m* 1973, Patricia, *d* of Marcos Skarnic, Santiago, Chile; one *s* one *d*. *Educ:* Queen's Univ., Canada (BSc, Hons Geology, 1971). *Heir: s* Peter William Gibson-Craig-Carmichael, *b* 29 Dec. 1975.

GIBSON-WATT, Baron *cr* 1979 (Life Peer), of the Wye in the District of Radnor; **James David Gibson-Watt,** MC 1943 and 2 Bars; PC 1974; DL; a Forestry Commissioner, 1976–86; *b* 11 Sept. 1918; *er s* of late Major James Miller Gibson-Watt, DL, JP; *m* 1942, Diana, 2nd *d* of Sir Charles Hambro; two *s* two *d* (and one *s* decd). *Educ:* Eton; Trinity Coll (BA). Welsh Guards, 1939–46; N African and Italian campaigns. Contested (C) Brecon and Radnor constituency, 1950 and 1951; MP (C) Hereford, Feb. 1956–Sept. 1974; a Lord Commissioner of the Treasury, 1959–61; Minister of State, Welsh Office, 1970–74. FRAgS; Pres., Royal Welsh Agric. Soc., 1976 (Chm. Council, 1976–). Chm., Council on Tribunals, 1980–86. Mem., Historic Buildings Council, Wales, 1975–79. DL Powys, 1968. *Address:* Doldowlod, Llandrindod Wells, Powys. *T:* Newbridge-on-Wye 208. *Club:* Boodle's.

GICK, Rear-Adm. Philip David, CB 1963; OBE 1946; DSC and Bar, 1942; Chairman, Emsworth Shipyard Group; *b* 22 Feb. 1913; *s* of late Sir William John Gick, CB, CBE; *m* 1938, Aylmer Rowntree; one *s* three *d*. *Educ:* St Lawrence Coll., Ramsgate. Joined RN, 1931; qualified as Pilot, 1936. Capt. 1952; Comd HMS Daring, RNAS, Lossiemouth, HMS Bulwark, 1952–58; Pres., Second Admiralty Interview Board; Rear-Adm. 1961; Flag Officer, Naval Flying Training, 1961–64, retd. *Recreation:* sailing. *Address:* Furzefield, Bosham Hoe, Sussex. *T:* Bosham 572219. *Clubs:* Royal Yacht Squadron, Royal Ocean Racing; Royal Naval Sailing Association; Bosham Sailing.

GIDDEN, Barry Owen Barton, CMG 1962; *b* Southampton, 4 July 1915; *s* of late Harry William Gidden, MA, PhD. *Educ:* King Edward VI Sch., Southampton; Jesus Coll., Cambridge (Scholar; Class. Tripos Pts 1 and 2; BA). Apptd Asst Principal, HM Office of Works, 1939. Served War of 1939–45: BEF, 1939–40, Major 1943. Principal, Min. of Works, 1946; Private Sec. to Minister of Works, 1946–48; Principal, Colonial Office, 1949, Asst Sec 1951; Counsellor, UK Mission to UN, New York, 1954–58; Establishment Officer, Colonial Office, 1958–65; Asst Sec., DHSS, 1965–75. *Recreation:* golf. *Address:* 15 Chesham Street, SW1. *T:* 01-235 4185. *Club:* Walton Heath.

GIDDINGS, Air Marshal Sir (Kenneth Charles) Michael, KCB 1975; OBE 1953; DFC 1945; AFC 1950 and Bar 1955; Independent Panel Inspector, Department of the Environment, since 1979; *b* 27 Aug. 1920; *s* of Charles Giddings and Grace Giddings (*née* Gregory); *m* 1946, Elizabeth McConnell; two *s* two *d*. *Educ:* Ealing Grammar Sch. Conscripted, RAF, 1940; Comd, 129 Sqdn, 1944; Empire Test Pilots Sch., 1946; Test pilot, RAE, 1947–50; HQ Fighter Command, 1950–52; RAF Staff Coll., 1953; OC, Flying Wing, Waterbeach, 1954–56; CFE, 1956–58; OC, 57 Sqdn, 1958–60; Group Captain Ops, Bomber Command, 1960–62; Supt of Flying, A&AEE, 1962–64; Dir Aircraft Projects, MoD, 1964–66; AOC, Central Reconnaissance Estabt, 1967–68; ACAS (Operational Requirements), 1968–71; Chief of Staff No 18 (M) Group, Strike Command, RAF, 1971–73; Dep. Chief of Defence Staff, Op. Requirements, 1973–76. *Recreations:* golf, gardening, music. *Address:* 159 Long Lane, Tilehurst, Reading, Berks. *T:* Reading 423012.

GIELGUD, Sir (Arthur) John, CH 1977; Kt 1953; Hon. LLD St Andrews 1950; Hon. DLitt Oxon 1953; Hon. DLitt London 1977; Actor; *b* 14 April 1904; *s* of late Frank Gielgud and Kate Terry Lewis; unmarried. *Educ:* Westminster. First appearance on stage at Old Vic, 1921; among parts played are Lewis Dodd in Constant Nymph, Inigo Jollifant in The Good Companions, Richard II in Richard of Bordeaux, Hamlet, and Romeo; Valentine in Love for Love, Ernest Worthing in The Importance of Being Earnest, Macbeth and King Lear. Directed Macbeth, Piccadilly, 1942. Raskolnikoff in Crime and Punishment, Jason in The Medea, New York, 1947. Eustace in The Return of the Prodigal, Globe, 1948; directed The Heiress, Haymarket, 1949; directed and played Thomas Mendip, The Lady's not for Burning, Globe, 1949; Shakespeare Festival, Stratford-on-Avon, 1950; Angelo in Measure for Measure, Cassius in Julius Caesar, Benedick in Much Ado About Nothing, the name part in King Lear; directed Much Ado About Nothing and King Lear; Shakespeare season at Phoenix, 1951–52; Leontes in The Winter's Tale, Phoenix, 1951, directed Much Ado About Nothing and played Benedick, 1952. Season at Lyric, Hammersmith, 1953; directed Richard II and The Way of the World (played Mirabel); played Jaffeir in Venice Preserved; directed A Day by the Sea, and played Julian Anson, Haymarket, Nov. 1953–54; also directed Charley's Aunt, New Theatre, Dec. 1953, and directed The Cherry Orchard, Lyric, May, 1954, and Twelfth Night, Stratford, 1955; played in King Lear and Much Ado About Nothing (also produced Much Ado), for Shakespeare Memorial Theatre Company (London, provinces and continental tour), 1955; directed The Chalk Garden, Haymarket, 1956; produced (with Noel Coward) Nude with Violin, and played Sebastien, Globe, 1956–57; produced The Trojans, Covent Garden, 1957; played Prospero, Stratford, and Drury Lane, 1957; played James Callifer in The Potting Shed, Globe, 1958 and Wolsey in Henry VIII, Old Vic, 1958; directed Variation on A Theme, 1958; produced The Complaisant Lover, Globe, 1959; (Shakespeare's) Ages of Man, Queen's, 1959 (recital, based on Shakespeare anthology of G. Rylands); previous recitals at Edinburgh Fest. and in US, also subseq. in US, at Haymarket, 1960 and tour of Australia and NZ, 1963–64; Gothenburg, Copenhagen, Warsaw, Helsinki, Leningrad, Moscow and Dublin, 1964; produced Much Ado About Nothing, at Cambridge, Mass, Festival, and subseq. in New York, 1959; prod. Five Finger Exercise, Comedy, 1958, NY, 1959; acted in The Last Joke, Phœnix, 1960; prod. Britten's A Midsummer Night's Dream, Royal Opera House, 1961; prod Big Fish Little Fish, New York, 1961; prod Dazzling Prospect, Globe, 1961. Stratford-on-Avon Season, 1961: took part of Othello, also of Gaieff in The Cherry Orchard, Aldwych, 1962; produced The School for Scandal, Haymarket, 1962; prod The School for Scandal, and played Joseph Surface, USA tour, and New York, 1962–63; dir. The Ides of March, and played Julius Caesar, Haymarket, 1963; dir. Hamlet, Canada and USA, 1964; Julian in Tiny Alice, New York, 1965; played Ivanov and directed Ivanov, Phœnix, 1965, United States and Canada, 1966; played Orgon in Tartuffe, Nat. Theatre, 1967; directed Halfway up the Tree, Queen's, 1967; played Oedipus in Oedipus, Nat. Theatre, 1968; produced Don Giovanni, Coliseum, 1968; played Headmaster in 40 Years On, Apollo, 1968; played Sir Gideon in The Battle of Shrivings, Lyric, 1970; Home, Royal Court, 1970, NY 1971 (Evening Standard Best Actor award and Tony award, NY, 1971); dir, All Over, NY, 1971; Caesar and Cleopatra, Chichester Festival, 1971; Veterans, Royal Ct, 1972; dir, Private Lives, Queen's, 1972; dir, The Constant Wife, Albery, 1973; played Prospero, Nat. Theatre, 1974; Bingo, Royal Court, 1974; dir, The Gay Lord Quex, Albery, 1975; No Man's Land, Nat. Theatre, 1975, Toronto, Washington, NY, 1977; Julius Caesar, Volpone, Nat. Theatre, 1977; Half-Life, NT and Duke of York's, 1977; *films include:* (GB and US) The Good Companions, 1932; The Secret Agent, 1937; The Prime Minister (Disraeli), 1940; Julius Caesar (Cassius), 1952; Richard III (Duke of Clarence), 1955; The Barretts of Wimpole Street (Mr Moulton Barrett), 1957; St Joan (Warwick), 1957; Becket (Louis VII), 1964; The Loved One, 1965; Chimes at Midnight, 1966; Mister Sebastian, 1967; The Charge of the Light Brigade, 1968; Shoes of the Fisherman, 1968; Oh What a Lovely War!, 1968; Julius Caesar, 1970; Eagle in a Cage, Lost Horizon, 1973; 11 Harrowhouse, 1974; Gold, 1974; Murder on the Orient Express, 1974; Aces High, 1976; Providence, Joseph Andrews, Portrait of a Young Man, Caligula, 1977; The Human Factor, The Elephant Man, 1979; The Conductor, Murder by Decree, Sphinx, Chariots of Fire, The Formula, Arthur (Oscar, 1982), 1980; Lion of the Desert, 1981; Priest of Love, 1982; Wagner, Invitation to the Wedding, Scandalous, The Wicked Lady, 1983; Camille, 1984; The Shooting Party, 1985; Plenty, 1985; Leave All Fair. President: Shakespeare Reading Soc., 1958–; RADA, 1977–. Has appeared on television, including Great Acting, 1967, The Mayfly and the Frog, Dorian Gray, In Good King Charles's Golden Days, Parson's Pleasure, Inside the Third Reich, Richard Wagner, Marco Polo, and Edward Ryder in Brideshead Revisited, 1981; Neck, 1983; The Scarlet and the Black, 1983; presenter of Six Centuries of Verse, 1984; Time After Time, 1985. Special award for services to theatre, Laurence Olivier Awards, 1985. Hon. degree Brandeis Univ. Companion, Legion of Honour, 1960. *Publications:* Early Stages, 1938; Stage Directions, 1963; Distinguished Company, 1972; (jtly) An Actor and His Time (autobiog.), 1979. *Recreations:* music, painting. *Address:* South Pavilion, Wotton Underwood, Aylesbury, Bucks. *Clubs:* Garrick, Arts; Players' (New York).

GIELGUD, Maina; free-lance ballerina; Artistic Director, Australian Ballet, since 1983; *b* 14 Jan. 1945; *d* of Lewis Gielgud and Elisabeth Grussner. *Educ:* BEPC (French). Ballet du Marquis de Cuevas, 1962–63; Ballet Classique de France, 1965–67; Ballet du XXème Siècle, Maurice Béjart, 1967–72; London Festival Ballet, 1972–77; Royal Ballet, 1977–78; free-lance, 1978–; rehearsal director, London City Ballet, 1981–82. *Address:* c/o Australian Ballet, PO Box 75, Flemington, Vic 3031, Australia; Stirling Court, 3 Marshall Street, W1. *T:* 01-734 6612.

GIFFARD, family name of **Earl of Halsbury.**

GIFFARD, Adam Edward; *b* 3 June 1934; *o s* of 3rd Earl of Halsbury, *qv* (but does not use courtesy title Viscount Tiverton); *m* 1st, 1963, Ellen, *d* of late Brynjolf Hovde; 2nd, 1976, Joanna Elizabeth, *d* of Frederick Harry Cole; two *d*. *Address:* PO Box 13, North Branch, NY 12766, USA.

GIFFARD, Sir (Charles) Sydney (Rycroft), KCMG 1984 (CMG 1976); HM Diplomatic Service, retired; *b* 30 Oct. 1926; *m* 1st, 1951, Wendy Patricia Vidal (marr. diss. 1976); one *s* one *d*; 2nd, 1976, Hazel Beatrice Coleby Roberts, OBE. Served in Japan, 1952; Foreign Office, 1957; Berne, 1961; Tokyo, 1964; Counsellor, FCO, 1968; Royal Coll. of Defence Studies, 1971; Counsellor, Tel Aviv, 1972; Minister in Tokyo, 1975–80; Ambassador to Switzerland, 1980–82; Dep. Under-Sec. of State, FCO, 1982–84; Ambassador to Japan, 1984–86. *Address:* Winkelbury House, Berwick St John, Wilts, near Shaftesbury, Dorset.

GIFFORD, family name of **Baron Gifford.**

GIFFORD, 6th Baron, *cr* 1824; **Anthony Maurice Gifford;** QC 1982; Barrister at Law, practising since 1966; *b* 1 May 1940; *s* of 5th Baron Gifford and Lady Gifford (*née* Margaret Allen), Sydney, NSW; *S* father 1961; *m* 1965, Katherine Ann, *o d* of Dr Mundy; one *s* one *d*. *Educ:* Winchester Coll. (scholar); King's Coll., Cambridge (scholar; BA 1961). Student at Middle Temple, 1959–62, called to the Bar, 1962. Chairman: Cttee for Freedom in Mozambique, Angola and Guiné, 1968–75; Mozambique Angola Cttee, 1982–. Chairman: N Kensington Neighbourhood Law Centre, 1974–77 (Hon. Sec., 1970–74); Legal Action Gp, 1978–83; Vice-Chm., Defence and Aid Fund (UK), 1983–. *Publication:* Where's the Justice?, 1986. *Heir: s* Hon. Thomas Adam Gifford, *b* 1 Dec. 1967. *Address:* 35 Wellington Street, WC2. *T:* 01-836 5917.

GIFFORD, Prof. Charles Henry, FBA 1983; Winterstoke Professor of English, University of Bristol, 1967–75, Professor of English and Comparative Literature, Jan.–July 1976, retired; *b* 17 June 1913; *s* of Walter Stanley Gifford and Constance Lena Gifford (*née* Henry); *m* 1938, Mary Rosamond van Ingen; one *s* one *d*. *Educ:* Harrow Sch.; Christ Church, Oxford. BA 1936, MA 1946. War Service, 1940–46, Royal Armoured Corps; Univ. of Bristol: Asst Lectr, 1946; Sen. Lectr, 1955; Prof. of Modern English Literature, 1963. Clark Lectr, Trinity Coll., Cambridge, 1985. Gen. Editor, Cambridge Studies in Russian Literature, 1980–84. *Publications:* The Hero of his Time, 1950; (with Charles Tomlinson) Castilian Ilexes: versions from Antonio Machado, 1963; The Novel in Russia, 1964; Comparative Literature, 1969; Tolstoy: a critical anthology, 1971; Pasternak: a critical study, 1977; Tolstoy, 1982; Poetry in a Divided World (1985 Clark Lectures), 1986; articles and reviews on English and comparative literature. *Address:* 10 Hyland Grove, Bristol BS9 3NR. *T:* Bristol 502504.

GIFFORD, (James) Morris, CBE 1973; FCIT; Director-General, National Ports Council, 1963–78 (Member of Council, 1964–78); *b* 25 March 1922; *y s* of Frederick W. Gifford, Dunfermline; *m* 1943, Margaret Lowe Shaw, MA, Dunfermline; two *s* one *d*. *Educ:* Dunfermline High Sch. (Dux 1939); Edinburgh Univ. (First Bursar). MA Hons Classics, 1946. Lieut RA, 1942–45. Called to Bar, Middle Temple, 1951. Shipping Fedn, 1946–55: Asst Sec., Mersey, 1948–50 and Thames, 1950–53; Sec., Clyde, 1954–55; Gen. Man., Nat. Assoc. of Port Employers, and Mem. Nat. Dock Labour Bd, 1955–63. Vice-Pres., CIT, 1975, Pres., 1976. *Recreations:* crosswords, reading, gardening. *Address:* 15 Bourne Avenue, Southgate, N14 6PB. *T:* 01-886 1757. *Club:* Oriental (Chm., 1978–79).

GIGGALL, Rt. Rev. George Kenneth, OBE 1961; Assistant Bishop, Diocese of Blackburn, since 1982; *b* 15 April 1914; *s* of Arthur William and Matilda Hannah Giggall; unmarried. *Educ:* Manchester Central High Sch.; Univ. of Manchester; St Chad's Coll., Univ. of Durham. BA, DipTheol. Deacon, 1939; Priest, 1940. Curate of St Alban's Cheetwood, Dio. Manchester, 1939–41, St Elisabeth's Reddish, 1941–45; Chaplain, RN, 1945; HMS Braganza, 1945; 34th Amphibious Support Regt, RM, 1945–46; Chaplain, Sch. of Combined Ops, 1946–47; HMS: Norfolk, 1947–49; Ocean, 1949–50; Flotilla Comd Mediterranean and HMS Phoenicia, 1950–52; HMS Campania for Operation Hurricane, 1952; RNC Dartmouth, 1952–53; HMS: Centaur, 1953–56; Ceylon, 1956–58; Fisgard, 1958–60; Royal Arthur and Lectr RAF Chaplains' Sch., 1960–63; HMS: Eagle, 1963–65; Drake, 1965–69; QHC, 1967–69; Dean of Gibraltar and Officiating Chaplain, HMS Rooke and Flag Officer, Gibraltar, 1969–73; Bishop of St Helena, 1973–79; Chaplain of San Remo with Bordighera, Italy, and Auxiliary Bishop, dio. of Gibraltar, 1979–81. *Recreation:* music. *Address:* Fosbrooke House, 8 Clifton Drive, Lytham, Lancs FY8 5RQ. *T:* Lytham 735683. *Clubs:* Royal Commonwealth Society, Sion College; Exiles (Ascension Island).

GILBERD, Rt. Rev. Bruce Carlyle; *see* Auckland (NZ), Bishop of.

GILBERT, Frederick; retired as Special Commissioner of Income Tax; *b* North Cornwall, 15 Nov. 1899; *s* of William Gilbert, farmer, and Jessie Cleave; *m* 1st, Ethel (decd), *d* of William Baily, Launceston; three *d*; 2nd, Blanche, *d* of William Banyard, Cambridge. *Recreations:* bowls, painting. *Address:* 2 Grinley Court, Cranfield Road, Bexhill-on-Sea, East Sussex TN40 1QD. *T:* Bexhill 211793.

GILBERT, Prof. Geoffrey Alan, FRS 1973; Professor of Biochemistry, University of Birmingham, 1969–85, now Emeritus; *b* 3 Dec. 1917; *s* of A. C. Gilbert and M. M. Gilbert (*née* Cull); *m* 1948, Lilo M. Gilbert (*née* Czigler de Egerszalok); two *s*. *Educ:* Kingsbury County Sch., Mddx; Emmanuel Coll., Cambridge; Dept of Colloid Science, Cambridge. MA, PhD, ScD (Cantab). Lectr, Chemistry Dept, Univ. of Birmingham, 1943–46. Research Fellow, Medical Sch., Harvard Univ., 1946–47. Univ. of Birmingham: Sen. Lectr, Chemistry Dept, 1947–61, Reader, 1961–69. Chm., British Biophysical Soc., 1974. Mem., Editorial Bd, Jl of Molecular Biol., 1972–. *Publications:* articles and papers in scientific jls. *Recreations:* photography, gardening, fox-watching. *Address:* 194 Selly Park Road, Birmingham B29 7HY. *T:* 021-472 0755.

GILBERT, Maj.-Gen. Glyn Charles Anglim, CB 1974; MC 1944; Vice Chairman, Fitness for Industry Ltd, since 1986; *b* 15 Aug. 1920; *s* of C. G. G. Gilbert, OBE, MC, and H. M. Gilbert, MBE; *m* 1943, Heather Mary Jackson; three *s* one *d*. *Educ:* Eastbourne Coll.; RMC Sandhurst. Commnd 1939; served with 2nd Lincolns, 1940–47, NW Europe and Palestine; Instructor, Sch. of Infantry, 1948–50; 3rd Bn Para. Regt, 1951; Staff Coll., 1952; staff and regimental appts in MoD, Airborne Forces, Royal Lincolns and Para. Regt, 1952–66, Cyprus, Egypt and Malaya; idc 1966; comd Sch. of Infantry, 1967–70; GOC 3rd Div., 1970–72; Comdt, Joint Warfare Estab., 1972–74, retired. *Recreation:* following the sun. *Address:* c/o Lloyds Bank, Warminster, Wilts. *Clubs:* Army and Navy; Royal Bermuda Yacht.

GILBERT, Hugh Campbell; Chairman and Chief Executive Officer, Price & Pierce Group Limited (USA), since 1983; *b* 25 March 1926; *s* of Hugh Gilbert and Nessie Campbell; *m* 1956, Beti Gwenllian, *d* of Prof. Henry Lewis, CBE. *Educ:* John Neilson High Sch.; Univ. of Glasgow (MA 1st Cl. Hons Pol. Econ.). Mil. Service in Scots Gds, then in Argyll and Sutherland Highlanders, Europe and ME, 1944–48; Territorial Service with 5/6 Argyll and Sutherland Highlanders (Captain), 1948–53. Imperial Chemical Industries, 1951–53; PA Management Consultants Ltd, 1953–62; Dir, Blyth, Greene, Jourdain & Co. Ltd, 1962–81; Dir, Tozer, Kemsley & Millbourn (Holdings) Ltd, 1971–83; Man. Dir, Price & Pierce (Holding Co.) Ltd, 1969, Chm. and Chief Exec. Officer, 1972–83. Hon. Professorial Fellow, UCNW, Bangor, 1975–79. *Recreations:* racing, opera, travel. *Address:* 59 Wynnstay Gardens, W8 6UU. *T:* 01-937 3134. *Clubs:* Caledonian, MCC.

GILBERT, Ian Grant; Under Secretary, International Relations Division, Department of Health and Social Security, 1979–85, retired; *b* Kikuyu, Kenya, 18 June 1925; *s* of Captain Alexander Grant Gilbert, DCM, indust. missionary, Lossiemouth and Kenya, and Marion Patrick Cruickshank; *m* 1960, Heather Margaret Donald, PhD (biographer of Lord Mount Stephen), *y d* of Rev. Francis Cantlie and Mary Donald, Lumphanan, Aberdeenshire. *Educ:* Fordyce Acad., Banffshire; Royal High Sch. of Edinburgh; Univ. of Edinburgh (MA 1950). Served HM Forces (Captain Indian Artillery), 1943–47. Entered Home Civil Service as Asst Principal and joined Min. of National Insurance, 1950; Private Sec. to Perm. Sec., 1953, and to Parly Sec., 1955; Principal, Min. of Pensions and Nat. Ins., 1956; seconded to HM Treasury, 1962–66; Asst Sec., Min. of Social Security (later DHSS), 1967; Head of War and Civilian Disabled Branches, DHSS, 1974–79. UK Member: Social Security, Health and Social Affairs Cttees, Council of Europe, Strasbourg, 1979–85; EEC Adv. Cttee on Social Security for Migrant Workers, Brussels, 1979–85; UK Delegate, Governing Body, Internat. Soc. Security Assoc., Geneva, 1979–85; Mem., UK Delegn to World Health Assembly, Geneva, 1979–84. Hon. Treasurer, Presbytery of England (Church of Scotland), 1965–77; Session Clerk, Crown Court Ch. of Scotland, Covent Garden, 1975–80. Chm., Caledonian Christian Club, 1984–86. *Recreations:* keeping half-an-acre in good heart, local and natural history, choral singing, France. *Address:* Wellpark, Moorside, Sturminster Newton, Dorset DT10 1HJ. *T:* Marnhull 820306. *Club:* Royal Commonwealth Society.

See also C. R. C. Donald.

GILBERT, Prof. John Cannon; Professor of Economics in the University of Sheffield, 1957–73, now Emeritus; Dean of Faculty of Economic and Social Studies, 1959–62; *b* 28 Sept. 1908; *s* of James and Elizabeth Louisa Gilbert; *m* 1938, Elizabeth Hadley Crook; two *s. Educ:* Bancroft's Sch.; The London Sch. of Economics and Political Science, University of London. Student of the Handels-Hochschule, Berlin (Sir Ernest Cassel Travelling Schol.), 1927–28; BCom Hons London, 1929. Asst on teaching staff, LSE, 1929–31; Lecturer in Economics, Sch. of Economics, Dundee, 1931–41. Ministry of Supply, 1941–45. Lecturer in Economics, University of Manchester, 1945–48; Senior Lecturer in Economics, University of Sheffield, 1948–56, Reader, 1956–57. Mem. Editorial Bd Bulletin of Economic Research, 1949–73. *Publications:* A History of Investment Trusts in Dundee, 1873–1938, 1939; Keynes's Impact on Monetary Economics, 1982; articles in Economica, Review of Economic Studies, etc. *Recreations:* walking, hill climbing. *Address:* 81 High Storrs Drive, Ecclesall, Sheffield S11 7LN. *T:* Sheffield 663544.

GILBERT, John Orman, CMG 1958; retired; *b* London, 21 Oct. 1907; *s* of Rev. T. H. Gilbert, late of Chedgrave Manor, Norfolk; *m* 1935, Winifred Mary Harris, Dublin; two *s* two *d. Educ:* Felsted Sch., Essex; Pembroke Coll., Oxford. Joined Sarawak Civil Service, 1928; various posts, from Cadet, to District Officer in 1940. During War of 1939–45 served in Bengal Sappers and Miners stationed in India and attained rank of Major. Came back to Sarawak with BM Administration, 1946; Resident, 4th Div., Sarawak, 1946–53; British Resident, Brunei, 1953–58; retd 1959. Coronation Medal, 1953. *Recreations:* conservation of wild life, animal welfare. *Address:* PO Box 100, Somerset West, Cape, South Africa.

GILBERT, Rt. Hon. Dr John (William); PC 1978; MP (Lab) Dudley East, since Feb. 1974 (Dudley, 1970–74); *b* April 1927; *m* 1963, Jean Olive Ross Skinner; two *d* of previous marriage. *Educ:* Merchant Taylors' Sch.; St John's Coll., Oxford; New York Univ. (PhD in Internat. Economics, Graduate Sch. of Business Administration). Chartered Accountant, Canada. Contested (Lab): Ludlow, 1966; Dudley, March 1968. Opposition front-bench spokesman on Treasury affairs, 1972–74; Financial Secretary to the Treasury, 1974–75; Minister for Transport, DoE, 1975–76; Minister of State, MoD, 1976–79. Mem., Select Cttee on Defence; Chm., PLP Defence Gp, 1981–83; Vice-Chm., Lab. Finance and Industry Group, 1983–. Member: Fabian Soc.; RIIA; NCCL; IISS; Council for Arms Control; Amnesty Internat.; GMBATU; WWF. Hon. LLD Wake Forest, N Carolina, 1983. *Address:* House of Commons, SW1. *Club:* Reform.

GILBERT, Air Chief Marshal Sir Joseph (Alfred), KCB 1985 (CB 1983); CBE 1974; Deputy Commander-in-Chief, Allied Forces Central Europe, since 1986; *b* 15 June 1931; *s* of Ernest and Mildred Gilbert; *m* 1955, Betty, *yr d* of late William and Eva Lishman; two *d. Educ:* William Hulme's Sch., Manchester; Univ. of Leeds (BA, Hons Econ. and Pol Science). Commnd into RAF, 1952; Fighter Sqdns, 1953–61; Air Secretary's Dept, 1961–63; RAF Staff Coll., 1964; CO 92 (Lightning) Sqdn, 1965–67; jssc 1968; Sec., Defence Policy Staff, and Asst Dir of Defence Policy, 1968–71; CO, RAF Coltishall, 1971–73; RCDS, 1974; Dir of Forward Policy (RAF), 1975; ACAS (Policy), MoD, 1975–77; AOC 38 Group, 1977–80; ACDS (Policy), 1980–82; Asst Chief of Staff (Policy), SHAPE, 1983–84; Dep. C-in-C, RAF Strike Command, 1984–86. CBIM. *Publications:* articles in defence jls. *Recreations:* hockey, tennis, South of France, strategic affairs. *Club:* Royal Air Force.

GILBERT, Martin (John), MA; FRSL; historian; Fellow of Merton College, Oxford, since 1962; Official Biographer of Sir Winston Churchill since 1968; *b* 25 Oct. 1936; *s* of Peter and Miriam Gilbert; *m* 1st, 1963, Helen Constance, *yr d* of late Joseph Robinson, CBE; one *d*; 2nd, Susan, *d* of late Michael Sacher; two *s. Educ:* Highgate Sch.; Magdalen Coll., Oxford. Nat. Service (Army), 1955–57; Sen. Research Scholar, St Antony's Coll., Oxford, 1960–62; Vis. Lectr, Budapest Univ., 1961; Res. Asst (sometime Sen. Res. Asst) to Hon. Randolph S. Churchill, 1962–67; Vis. Prof., Univ. of S Carolina, 1965; Recent Hist. Correspt for Sunday Times, 1967; Res. Asst (Brit. Empire) for BBC, 1968; Historical Adviser (Palestine) for Thames Television, 1977–78. Visiting Professor: Tel-Aviv Univ., 1979; Hebrew Univ. of Jerusalem, 1980– (Vis. Lectr 1975); Vis. Lectr, Univ. of Cape Town (Caplan Centre), 1984; has lectured on historical subjects at Univs throughout Europe and USA. Script designer and co-author, Genocide (Acad. Award winner, best doc. feature film), 1981; Historical Consultant to Southern Pictures TV series, Winston Churchill: The Wilderness Years, 1980–81; Historical Adviser, BBC TV, for Auschwitz and the Allies, 1981–82; historical consultant, Yalta 1945, for BBC TV, 1982–83. Governor, Hebrew Univ. of Jerusalem, 1978–. Hon. DLitt Westminster Coll., Fulton, 1981. *Publications:* The Appeasers, 1963 (with Richard Gott) (trans. German, Polish, Rumanian); Britain and Germany Between the Wars, 1964; The European Powers, 1900–1945, 1965 (trans. Italian, Spanish); Plough My Own Furrow: The Life of Lord Allen of Hurtwood, 1965; Servant of India: A Study of Imperial Rule 1905–1910, 1966; The Roots of Appeasement, 1966; Recent History Atlas 1860–1960, 1966; Winston Churchill (Clarendon Biogs for young people), 1966; British History Atlas, 1968; American History Atlas, 1968; Jewish History Atlas, 1969, 3rd edn 1985 (trans. Spanish, Dutch, Hebrew); First World War Atlas, 1970; Winston S. Churchill, vol. iii, 1914–1916, 1971, companion volume (in two parts) 1973; Russian History Atlas, 1972; Sir Horace Rumbold: portrait of a diplomat, 1973; Churchill: a photographic portrait, 1974; The Arab-Israeli Conflict: its history in maps, 1974, 4th edn 1985 (trans. Spanish, Hebrew); Churchill and Zionism (pamphlet), 1974; Winston S. Churchill, vol. iv, 1917–1922, 1975, companion volume (in three parts), 1977; The Jews in Arab Lands: their history in maps, 1975, illustr. edn, 1976 (trans. Hebrew, Arabic, French, German); Winston S. Churchill, vol. v, 1922–1939, 1976, companion volume, part one, The Exchequer Years 1922–1929, 1980, part two, The Wilderness Years 1929–1935, 1981, part three, The Coming of War 1936–1939, 1982; The Jews of Russia: Illustrated History Atlas, 1976 (trans. Spanish); Jerusalem Illustrated History Atlas, 1977 (trans. Hebrew, Spanish); Exile and Return: The Emergence of Jewish Statehood, 1978; Children's Illustrated Bible Atlas, 1979; Final Journey, the Fate of the Jews of Nazi Europe, 1979 (trans. Dutch, Hebrew); Auschwitz and the Allies, 1981 (trans. German, Hebrew); Churchill's Political Philosophy, 1981; The Origin of the 'Iron Curtain' speech, 1981 (pamphlet); Atlas of the Holocaust (Macmillan Atlas of the Holocaust, in USA), 1982 (trans. German, Hebrew); Winston S. Churchill, vol. vi, Finest Hour, 1939–41, 1983 (Wolfson Award, 1983); The Jews of Hope: the plight of Soviet Jewry today, 1984 (trans. Hebrew); Jerusalem: rebirth of a city, 1985; The Holocaust: the Jewish tragedy, 1986; Winston S. Churchill, vol vii, Road to Victory, 1986; Shcharansky: hero of our time, 1986 (trans. Dutch, Hebrew); Editor: A Century of Conflict: Essays Presented to A. J. P. Taylor, 1966; Churchill, 1967, and Lloyd George, 1968 (Spectrum Books); compiled Jackdaws: Winston Churchill, 1970; The Coming of War in 1939, 1973; contribs historical articles and reviews to jls (incl. Purnell's History of the Twentieth Century). *Recreation:* drawing maps. *Address:* Merton College, Oxford. *T:* Oxford 49651. *Club:* Athenæum.

GILBERT, Michael Francis, CBE 1980; TD 1950; crime writer; *b* 17 July 1912; *s* of Bernard Samuel Gilbert and Berwyn Minna Cuthbert; *m* 1947, Roberta Mary, *d* of Col R. M. W. Marsden; two *s* five *d. Educ:* Blundell's Sch.; London University. LLB 1937. Served War of 1939–45, Hon. Artillery Co., 12th Regt RHA, N Africa and Italy (despatches 1943). Joined Trower Still & Keeling, 1947 (Partner, 1952–83). Legal Adviser to Govt of Bahrain, 1960. Member: Arts Council Cttee on Public Lending Right, 1968; Royal Literary Fund, 1969; Council of Soc. of Authors, 1975; (Founder) Crime Writers' Assoc.; Mystery Writers of America. *Publications: novels:* Close Quarters, 1947; They Never Looked Inside, 1948; The Doors Open, 1949; Smallbone Deceased, 1950; Death has Deep Roots, 1951; Death in Captivity, 1952; Fear to Tread, 1953; Sky High, 1955; Be Shot for Sixpence, 1956; The Tichborne Claimant, 1957; Blood and Judgement, 1958; After the Fine Weather, 1963; The Crack in the Tea Cup, 1965; The Dust and the Heat, 1967; The Etruscan Net, 1969; The Body of a Girl, 1972; The Ninety Second Tiger, 1973; Flash Point, 1974; The Night of the Twelfth, 1976; The Empty House, 1978; Death of a Favourite Girl, 1980; The Final Throw, 1983; The Black Seraphim, 1983; The Long Journey Home, 1985; *short stories:* Games Without Rules; Stay of Execution; Petrella at Q, 1977; Mr Calder and Mr Behrens, 1982; *plays:* A Clean Kill; The Bargain; Windfall; The Shot in Question; *edited:* Crime in Good Company, 1959; The Oxford Book of Legal Anecdotes, 1986; has also written radio and TV scripts. *Recreations:* walking, croquet, contract bridge. *Address:* Luddesdown Old Rectory, Cobham, Kent. *T:* Meopham 814272. *Club:* Garrick.

GILBERT, Patrick Nigel Geoffrey; General Secretary of the Society for Promoting Christian Knowledge, since 1971; *b* 12 May 1934; adopted *s* of late Geoffrey Gilbert and Evelyn (*née* Miller), Devon. *Educ:* Cranleigh Sch.; Merton Coll., Oxford. OUP, 1964–69; Linguaphone Group (Westinghouse), 1969–71 (Man. Dir in Group, 1970). World Assoc. for Christian Communication: Trustee, 1975–; European Vice-Chm., 1975–82; representative to EEC, 1975–82, to Conf. of Eur. Churches, 1976–82, to Council of Europe, 1976–82, and to Central Cttee, 1979–84. Member: Bd for Mission and Unity of Gen. Synod, 1971–78; Archbishops' Cttee on RC Relations, 1971–81; Church Inf. Cttee, 1978–81; Church Publishing Cttee, 1980–84; Council, Conf. of British Missionary Socs, 1971–78; Council, Christians Abroad, 1974–79; Exec., Anglican Centre, Rome, 1981– (Vice Chm. of Friends, 1984–); British National Cttee, UNESCO World Bank Congress, 1982. Greater London Arts Association: Mem. Exec., 1968–78; Hon. Life Mem., 1978; Chm., 1980–84 (Dep. Chm., 1979–80); Initiator, 1972 Festivals of London. Art Workers' Guild: Hon. Brother, 1971; Chm. Trustees and Hon. Treas., 1976–86 (Trustee, 1975). Chairman: Standing Conf. of London Arts Councils, 1975–78; Embroiderers' Guild, 1977–78 (Hon. Treas., 1974–77); Concord Multicultural Arts Trust, 1980–; Harold Buxton Trust, 1983–; Nikaean Club, 1984–; Vice-President: Camden Arts Council, 1974– (Chm., 1970–74); Nat. Assoc. of Local Arts Councils, 1980– (Founder Chm., 1976–80); Mem., Arts Adv. Cttee, CRE, 1979; Steward, Artists' Gen. Benevolent Instn, 1971–. Trustee: Overseas Bishoprics Fund, 1973–; All Saints Trust, 1978– (Chm., Investment Cttee); Schulze Trust, 1980–83; Dancers' Resettlement Fund, 1982– (Chm., Finance Cttee); Richards Trust; ACC Res. Fund, 1982–84; Vis. Trustee, Seabury Press, NY, 1978–80. Mem. Executive: GBGSA, 1981–84; Assoc. of Vol. Colls, 1980–; Mem. Governing Body: SPCK Australia, 1977–; SPCK (USA), 1984–; Partners for World Mission, 1979–; Governor: Contemp. Dance Trust, 1981–; All Saints Coll., Tottenham, 1971–78; St Martin's Sch. for Girls, 1971– (Vice Chm., 1978–; Rep. to Tertiary Educn Council); Ellesmere Coll., 1978– (Rep. to ISCO; Mem. Exec., 1984–); St Michael's Sch., Petworth, 1978– (rep. to GBGSA; Mem. Exec., 1981–84); Roehampton Inst., 1978– (rep. to Assoc. of Vol. Colls); Pusey House, 1985–; Patron, Pusey House Appeal, 1984–; Fellow, Corp. of SS Mary and Nicholas (Woodard Schs), 1972– (Mem. Exec., 1981–; Chm., S Div. Res. Cttee, 1972–84; Trustee, Endowment Fund; Dir, Corp. Trustee Co.). Development Cttee, SPAB, 1985–; London Symphony Chorus, 1985–. Freeman, City of London, 1966; Liveryman, Worshipful Co. of Woolmen (Master, 1985–86); Parish Clerk, All Hallows, Bread Street; Member: Worshipful Co. of Parish Clerks; Guild of Freemen. Lord of the Manor of Cantley Netherhall, Norfolk. FRSA 1978; FBIM 1982; FInstD 1982. Hon. DLitt Columbia Pacific, 1982. Order of St Vladimir, 1977. *Publications:* articles in various jls. *Recreations:* walking, reading, travel, enjoying the Arts, golf. *Address:* 3 The Mount Square, NW3 6SU. *T:* 01-794 8807. *Clubs:* Athenæum, City Livery; Walton Heath Golf.

GILBERT, Ronald Stuart J.; *see* Johnson-Gilbert.

GILBERT, Stuart William, CB 1983; Director, Department for National Savings, 1981–86 (Deputy Secretary); *b* 2 Aug. 1926; *s* of Rodney Stuart Gilbert and Ella Edith (*née* Esgate); *m* 1955, Marjorie Laws Vallance; one *s* one *d. Educ:* Maidstone Grammar Sch.; Emmanuel Coll., Cambridge (Open Exhibnr and State Scholar; MA). Served RAF,

1944–47. Asst Principal, Min. of Health, 1949; Asst Private Sec.: to Minister of Housing and Local Govt, 1952; to Parly Sec., 1954; Principal, 1955; Sec., Parker Morris Cttee on Housing Standards, 1958–61, Rapporteur to ECE Housing Cttee, 1959–61; Reporter to ILO Conf. on Workers' Housing, 1960; Asst Sec., Local Govt Finance Div., 1964; Under-Sec., DoE, 1970–80 (for New Towns, 1970, Business Rents, 1973, Construction Industries, 1974, Housing, 1974, Planning Land Use, 1977); Dep. Dir, Dept for Nat. Savings, 1980–81. *Recreations:* sailing, music, woodwork. *Address:* 3 Westmoat Close, Beckenham, Kent. *T:* 01–650 7213. *Club:* United Oxford & Cambridge University.

GILBERT, Prof. Walter; Professor of Biology, since 1985, and Timken Professor of Science, Department of Cellular and Developmental Biology, Harvard University; Founder, 1978, and Director, Biogen NV (Chairman and Principal Executive Officer, 1981–84); *b* Boston, 21 March 1932; *s* of Richard V. Gilbert and Emma (*née* Cohen); *m* 1953, Celia Stone; one *s* one *d. Educ:* Harvard Coll. (AB *summa cum laude* Chem. and Phys., 1953); Harvard Univ. (AM Phys., 1954); Cambridge Univ. (DPhil Maths, 1957). National Science Foundn pre-doctoral Fellow, Harvard Univ. and Cambridge Univ., 1953–57, post-doctoral Fellow in Phys., Harvard, 1957–58; Harvard University: Lectr in Phys., 1958–59; Asst Prof. in Phys., 1959–64; Associate Prof. of Biophys., 1964–68; Prof. of Biochem., 1968–72; Amer. Cancer Soc. Prof. of Molecular Biology, 1972–81; Guggenheim Fellow, Paris, 1968–69. Member: Amer. Acad. of Arts and Sciences, 1968; National Acad. of Sciences, 1976; Amer. Phys. Soc.; Amer. Soc. of Biol Chemists. Lectures: V. D. Mattia, Roche Inst. of Molecular Biol., 1976; Smith, Kline and French, Univ. of Calif, Berkeley, 1977. Hon. DSc: Chicago, 1978; Columbia, 1978; Rochester, 1979. Many prizes and awards, incl. (jtly) Nobel Prize for Chemistry, 1980. *Publications:* chapters, articles and papers on theoretical physics and molecular biology. *Address:* Biological Laboratories, 16 Divinity Avenue, Cambridge, Mass 02138, USA. *T:* (017) 495–0760; 107 Upland Road, Cambridge, Mass 02140. *T:* (617) 864–8778.

GILBERT, Brig. Sir William (Herbert Ellery), KBE 1976 (OBE 1945); DSO 1944; Director, New Zealand Security Intelligence Service, 1956–76, retired; *b* 20 July 1916; *s* of Ellery George Gilbert and Nellie (*née* Hall); *m* 1944, Patricia Caroline Anson Farrer; two *s* one *d. Educ:* Wanganui Collegiate Sch., NZ; RMC, Duntroon, Australia. NZ Regular Army, 1937–56; War Service with 2NZEF, ME and Italy, 1940–45; retd, Brig. Bronze Star, USA, 1945. *Recreations:* golf, fishing, gardening. *Address:* 38 Chatsworth Road, Silverstream, New Zealand. *T:* Wellington 286570. *Clubs:* Wellington, Wellington Golf (NZ).

GILBERTSON, Sir Geoffrey, Kt 1981; CBE 1972; *b* 29 May 1918; *s* of A. J. Gilbertson and M. O. Gilbertson; *m* 1940, Dorothy Ness Barkes; four *c. Educ:* Durham Sch.; Jesus Coll., Cambridge. Served War, 4th/7th Royal Dragoon Guards, 1940–45, Captain. Imperial Chemical Industries, 1946–74: Director, Agricl Div., 1960–67; Plant Protection Ltd, 1964–67; Group General Manager, 1967–74. Dir, Guildway Ltd, 1979–83. Member, Pay Board, 1973–74. Chairman: NEDC (Ship building), 1974–77; Nat. Adv. Cttee, Employment of Disabled People, 1975–81; Fit for Work Award Scheme, 1980–84. FRSA; FIPM. Croix de Guerre (Gold Star), 1944. *Recreation:* fishing. *Address:* Greta Bridge, Barnard Castle, County Durham DL12 9SD. *T:* Teesdale 27276. *Clubs:* Flyfishers'; Leander (Henley-on-Thames); Hawks (Cambridge).

GILBEY, family name of **Baron Vaux of Harrowden.**

GILBEY, Sir (Walter) Derek, 3rd Bt, *cr* 1893; Lieut 2nd Bn Black Watch; *b* 11 March 1913; *s* of Walter Ewart Gilbey and Dorothy Coysgarne Sim; *S* grandfather, 1945; *m* 1948, Elizabeth Mary, *d* of Col Keith Campbell and Marjorie Syfret; one *s* one *d. Educ:* Eton. Served War of 1939–45 (prisoner). *Heir: s* Walter Gavin Gilbey [*b* 14 April 1949; *m* 1980, Mary Pacetti, *d* of late William E. E. Pacetti and of Mrs Mary Greer]. *Address:* Grovelands, Wineham, near Henfield, Sussex. *T:* Bolney 311. *Club:* Portland.

GILCHRIST, Sir Andrew (Graham), KCMG 1964 (CMG 1956); HM Diplomatic Service, retired; formerly Ambassador and administrator; *b* 19 April 1910; *e s* of late James Graham Gilchrist, Kerse, Lesmahagow; *m* 1946, Freda Grace, *d* of late Alfred Slack; two *s* one *d. Educ:* Edinburgh Acad.; Exeter Coll., Oxford. Diplomatic career, 1933–70, included junior posts in Bangkok, Paris, Marseilles, Rabat, Stuttgart, Singapore, Chicago, also in FO; subseq. Ambassador at Reykjavik, Djakarta and Dublin, retired. Chm., Highlands and Islands Develt Bd, 1970–76. War Service as Major, Force 136 in SE Asia (despatches). *Publications: memoirs:* Bangkok Top Secret, 1970; Cod Wars and How to Lose Them, 1978 (Icelandic edn 1977); *novels:* The Russian Professor, 1984; The Watercress File, 1985; The Ultimate Hostage, 1986. *Address:* Arthur's Crag, Hazelbank, by Lanark ML11 9XL. *T:* Crossford 263. *Clubs:* Special Forces; New (Edinburgh).

GILCHRIST, (Andrew) Rae, CBE 1961; MD Edinburgh, FRCPE, FRCP, Hon. FRACP, Hon. FRFPS Glasgow; Consulting Physician Royal Infirmary, Edinburgh; *b* 7 July 1899; *o s* of late Rev. Andrew Gilchrist, BA, Edinburgh; *m* 1st, 1931, Emily Faulds (*d* 1967), *yr d* of late W. Work Slater, Edinburgh and Innerleithen, Peeblesshire; one *s* one *d*; 2nd, 1975, Elspeth, *widow* of Dr Arthur Wightman. *Educ:* Belfast, Edinburgh, New York. RFA 1917–18; MB, ChB Edinburgh, 1921; Lauder-Brunton Prizeman, Milner-Fothergill Medallist, McCunn Medical Res. Scholar, Edinburgh Univ., 1924; MD (gold medal) 1933; resident hospital appointments at Addenbrooke's Hosp., Cambridge, Princess Elizabeth Hosp. for Children, London, E1, and at Royal Infirmary, Edinburgh, 1922–24; Resident Asst Physician Rockefeller Hosp. for Medical Research, New York, USA, 1926–27; Asst Physician, 1930; Physician, Royal Infirmary, Edinburgh, 1939–64; Gibson Lecturer RCP Edinburgh, 1944; Lecturer: Canadian Heart Assoc., 1955; Litchfield Lecture, Oxford Univ., 1956; Californian Heart Assoc., 1957; St Cyres Lecturer, National Heart Hosp., London, 1957; Hall Overseas Lecturer, Australia and NZ, 1959; Carey Coombs Memorial Lecture, Bristol Univ., 1960; Gwladys and Olwen Williams Lecture in Medicine, Liverpool Univ., 1961; Orford Lectr, College of Physicians of S Africa, 1962. William Cullen Prize, 1962 (shared). Pres. of the Royal College of Physicians of Edinburgh, 1957–60. Examr in Med. in Univs of Edinburgh, Glasgow, Aberdeen, St Andrews, East Africa (Makerere Coll.), and Baghdad. Mem. Assoc. of Physicians of Gt Brit., of Brit. Cardiac Soc. Hon. Mem. Cardiac Soc. of Australia and NZ. *Publications:* numerous contributions on disorders of heart and circulation, in British and American medical journals. *Recreation:* fishing. *Address:* 16 Winton Terrace, Edinburgh EH10 7AP. *T:* 031–445 1119. *Clubs:* Flyfishers'; New (Edinburgh).

GILCHRIST, Archibald; Managing Director, Vosper Private, Singapore, since 1980; Director, Vosper PLC, since 1983; *b* 17 Dec. 1929; *m* 1958, Elizabeth Jean Greenlees; two *s* one *d. Educ:* Loretto; Pembroke Coll., Cambridge (MA). Barclay Curle & Co. Ltd, Glasgow, 1954–64, various managerial posts; ultimately Dir, Swan Hunter Group; Brown Bros & Co. Ltd, Edinburgh, 1964–72: Dep. Man. Dir, 1964; Man. Dir, 1969; Man. Dir, Govan Shipbuilders, 1971–79, Chm., 1978–79. *Recreations:* golf, shooting, fishing, music. *Address:* 19 Victoria Park Road, Singapore 1026. *Clubs:* Western (Glasgow); Hon. Company of Edinburgh Golfers.

GILCHRIST, Sir (James) Finlay (Elder), Kt 1978; OBE 1946; Life President and Director, Harrisons & Crosfield PLC (Chairman, 1962–77); *b* 13 Aug. 1903; *s* of late Thomas Dunlop Gilchrist and Agnes Crawford Elder; *m* 1933, Dorothy Joan Narizzano; two *s* one *d. Educ:* Glasgow Academy. *Address:* South Cottage, Hapstead Farm, Ardingly, Sussex. *T:* Ardingly 892368. *Club:* East India.

GILCHRIST, Rae; *see* Gilchrist, A. R.

GILDER, Robert Charles, FIA; Directing Actuary, Government Actuary's Department, 1979–83; *b* 22 April 1923; *s* of Charles Henry Gilder and Elsie May (*née* Sayer); *m* 1954, Norah Mary Hallas; two *s. Educ:* Brentwood School. Liverpool Victoria Friendly Soc., 1940–41 and 1946–48. Served War, RAF, 1941–46. Government Actuary's Dept, 1948–83; Actuary, 1959; Principal Actuary, 1973. FIA 1951. *Recreations:* cricket, playing the clarinet, hill-walking, golf.

'GILES'; *see* Giles, Carl Ronald.

GILES, Sir Alexander (Falconer), KBE 1965 (MBE 1946); CMG 1960; HM Colonial Service retired; *b* 1915; *o s* of late A. F. Giles, MA, LLD; *m* 1953, Mrs M. E. Watson, *d* of late Lieut-Col R. F. D. Burnett, MC, and *widow* of Lieut-Col J. L. Watson; two *step s* one *step d. Educ:* The Edinburgh Academy; Edinburgh Univ.; Balliol Coll., Oxford (BA). Pres. Oxford Union Soc., 1939. 2nd Lieut the Royal Scots, 1940; attached RWAFF, 1941; 81 (WA) Div., 1943; Lieut-Col comdg 5 GCR, 1945 (MBE, despatches). Cadet Colonial Service, Tanganyika, 1947; Administrator, St Vincent, 1955–62; Resident Commissioner, Basutoland, 1962–65; British Govt Representative, Basutoland, 1965–66. Chairman: Victoria League in Scotland, 1968–70; Scottish Council, Royal Over-Seas League, 1969–70, Central Council, 1972–75. Dir, Toc H, 1968–74. Gen. Sec., Scotland, Royal Over-Seas League, 1976–78. *Publications:* articles in service jls. *Recreation:* the printed word. *Address:* 4 Royal Crescent, Edinburgh EH3 6PZ.

GILES, Carl Ronald, OBE 1959; Cartoonist, Daily and Sunday Express, since 1943; *b* 29 Sept. 1916; *m* 1942, Sylvia Joan Clarke. Trained as animated cartoonist; Animator for Alexander Korda, 1935; Cartoonist, Reynolds News, 1937–43. Cartoons extensively reproduced in US and syndicated throughout world. Produced and animated Documentary Films for Min. of Information, also War Correspondent-cartoonist in France, Belgium, Holland and Germany, War of 1939–45. *Publications:* "Giles" Annual, 1945–; various overseas collections. *Recreations:* sailing, workshops, farming. *Address:* Express Newspapers, Fleet Street, EC4P 4JK. *Clubs:* Press, Saints & Sinners, Lord's Taverners; British Racing Drivers', Royal Harwich Yacht.

GILES, Frank Thomas Robertson; Editor, The Sunday Times, 1981–83 (Deputy Editor, 1967–81); *b* 31 July 1919; *s* of late Col F. L. N. Giles, DSO, OBE, and Mrs Giles; *m* 1946, Lady Katharine Pamela Sackville, *o d* of 9th Earl De La Warr and Countess De La Warr; one *s* two *d. Educ:* Wellington Coll.; Brasenose Coll., Oxford (Open Scholarship in History; MA 1946). ADC to Governor of Bermuda, 1939–42; Directorate of Mil. Ops, WO, 1942–45; temp. mem. of HM Foreign Service, 1945–46 (Private Sec. to Ernest Bevin; Mem. of Sir Archibald Clark Kerr's mission to Java); joined editorial staff of The Times, 1946; Asst Correspondent, Paris, 1947; Chief Corresp., Rome, 1950–53, Paris, 1953–60; Foreign Editor, Sunday Times, 1961–77; Dir, Times Newspapers Ltd, 1981–85. Mem., Exec. Cttee, GB-USSR Assoc. Chm., Painshill Park Trust; Mem., Governing Body, British Inst. of Florence; Governor: Wellington Coll.; Sevenoaks Sch. *Publications:* A Prince of Journalists: the life and times of de Blowitz, 1962; Sundry Times (autobiog.), 1986. *Recreations:* going to the opera; collecting, talking about, consuming the vintage wines of Bordeaux and Burgundy. *Address:* 42 Blomfield Road, W9 1AH; Bunns Cottage, Lye Green, Crowborough, East Sussex TN6 1UY. *Clubs:* Brooks's, Beefsteak.

GILES, Rear-Adm. Sir Morgan Charles M.; *see* Morgan-Giles.

GILES, Air Commandant Dame Pauline, DBE 1967; RRC; Matron-in-Chief, Princess Mary's Royal Air Force Nursing Service, 1966–70, retired; *b* 17 Sept. 1912. *Educ:* Sheffield. Joined PMRAFNS, Nov. 1937; later appointments included Principal Matron for Royal Air Force Command in Britain and Western Europe; became Matron-in-Chief, PMRAFNS, Sept. 1966. *Address:* 7 Hever Crescent, Bexhill-on-Sea, East Sussex TN39 4HQ. *Club:* Royal Air Force.

GILES, Robert Frederick; Senior Clerk, House of Commons, 1979–83; *b* 27 Dec. 1918; *s* of Robert and Edith Giles; *m* 1948, Mabel Florence Gentry; two *d. Educ:* Drayton Manor Sch., Hanwell. Min. of Agriculture, 1936–39. Royal Navy, 1939–45: CO, HMS Tango, 1942–44. Various assignments, MAF, from 1945; Regional Controller, Northern Region MAFF, 1963–68; Head, Food Standards/Food Science Div., 1968–74; Under Sec., MAFF, 1975–78; Food Standards and Food Subsidies Gp, 1975; Food Feedingstuffs and Fertilizer Standards Gp, 1977. *Recreations:* walking, theatre. *Address:* 8 The Ridings, Copthill Lane, Kingswood, Surrey KT20 6HJ. *Club:* Civil Service.

GILES, Roy Curtis, MA; Head Master, Highgate School, since 1974; *b* 6 Dec. 1932; *s* of Herbert Henry Giles and Dorothy Alexandra Potter; *m* 1963, Christine von Alten; two *s* one *d. Educ:* Queen Elizabeth's Sch., Barnet; Jesus Coll., Cambridge (Open Scholar). Asst Master, Dean Close Sch., 1956–60; Lektor, Hamburg Univ., 1960–63; Asst Master, Eton Coll., 1963–74, Head of Modern Languages, 1970–74. Educnl Selector, ACCM, 1981–; Mem., House of Bishops' Panel on Marriage Educn, 1983–. Mem., Council of Management, Davies's Educn Services, 1975–; Governor: The Hall, Hampstead, 1976–; Channing Sch., 1977–. *Recreations:* music, theatre. *Address:* Head Master's House, 12 Bishopswood Road, N6 4NY. *T:* 01–340 7626.

GILKISON, Sir Alan (Fleming), Kt 1980; CBE 1972; Chairman: J. E. Watson & Co. Ltd, Invercargill, New Zealand, 1958–81; Southland Frozen Meat & P.E. Co. Ltd, 1959–82; *b* 4 Nov. 1909; *s* of John Gilkison and Margaret Gilkison (*née* Thomson); *m* 1950, Noeline Cramond; two *s. Educ:* Southland Boys' High School; Timaru Boys' High School. Started work with J. E. Watson & Co. Ltd, 1930; became General Manager, 1958. Director and Deputy Chairman, Air New Zealand, 1961–75; Chairman, NZ National Airways Corp., 1967–75. *Address:* PO Box 208, Wanaka, New Zealand. *T:* Wanaka 597. *Clubs:* Invercargill, Wellington (NZ).

GILL, Anthony Keith, FEng 1983; FIMechE, FIProdE; Group Managing Director, since 1984, and Deputy Chairman, since 1986; Lucas Industries plc; *b* 1 April 1930; *s* of Frederick William and Ellen Gill; *m* 1953, Phyllis Cook; one *s* two *d. Educ:* High Sch., Colchester; Imperial Coll., London (BScEng Hons). National Service officer, REME, 1954–56. Joined Bryce Berger Ltd, 1956, subseq. Director and Gen. Manager until 1972; Lucas CAV Ltd, 1972, subseq. Director and Gen. Manager until 1978; Divisional Managing Director, Joseph Lucas Ltd, 1978; Jt Gp Man. Dir, Lucas Industries, 1980. Member: Adv. Council for Applied R&D, 1985; DTI Technology Requirements Bd, 1986. Pres., IProdE, 1986. Mem. Court, Univ. of Warwick, 1986. FCGI 1979. *Recreation:* music. *Address:* Mockley Close, Gentleman's Lane, Ullenhall, near Henley in Arden, Warwickshire. *T:* Tanworth in Arden 2337.

GILL, Austin, CBE 1955; MA, Licencié-ès-lettres; Marshall Professor of French, University of Glasgow, 1966–71, retired; *b* 3 Sept. 1906; *m* 1939, Madeleine Monier. *Educ:* Bury Municipal Secondary Sch.; Universities of Manchester, Grenoble, Paris. Research Fellow,

1929–30, Faulkner Fellow, 1930–31, and Langton Fellow, 1931–33, Manchester Univ. Asst Lecturer in French, Edinburgh Univ., 1933–34; Lecturer in French, Edinburgh Univ., 1934–43; British Council Representative in French North Africa, 1943–44; British Council Actg Rep. in France, 1944–45; Official Fellow, Tutor in Modern Langs, Magdalen Coll., Oxford, 1945–50 and 1954–66. Dir of Brit. Inst. in Paris, 1950–54. *Publications:* (ed) Les Ramonneurs, 1957; (ed) Life and Letters in France, 1970; The Early Mallarmé, vol. I, 1980, vol. II, 1986; articles and reviews in literary and philological journals. *Address:* 15 Beaumont Gate, Glasgow G12 9ED.

GILL, Brian; QC (Scot.) 1981; *b* 25 Feb. 1942; *s* of Thomas and Mary Gill, Glasgow; *m* 1969, Catherine Fox; five *s* one *d*. *Educ:* St Aloysius' Coll., Glasgow; Glasgow Univ. (MA 1962, LLB 1964); Edinburgh Univ. (PhD 1975). Lectr, Faculty of Law, Edinburgh Univ., 1964–69 and 1972–77; Advocate, 1967; Advocate Depute, 1977–79; Standing Junior Counsel: Foreign and Commonwealth Office (Scotland), 1974–77; Home Office (Scotland), 1979–81; Scottish Education Dept, 1979–81; Chm., Industrial Tribunals, 1981–. Chm., Cttee of Investigation for Scotland (Agricl Marketing), 1985–. *Publications:* The Law of Agricultural Holdings in Scotland, 1982; articles in legal jls. *Recreation:* church music. *Address:* 13 Lauder Road, Edinburgh EH9 2EN. *T:* 031–667 1888. *Club:* Western (Glasgow).

GILL, Cyril James, CB 1965; Senior Lecturer in Education, University of Keele, 1968–71, retired (Gulbenkian Lecturer in Education, 1965–68); *b* 29 March 1904; *s* of William Gill, Carnforth, Lancs; *m* 1939, Phyllis Mary, *d* of Joseph Windsor, Ramsey, Isle of Man. *Educ:* Ulverston Grammar Sch.; Liverpool Univ. Sch. Master, Ramsey, IOM and Archbishop Tenison's, London, 1926–42; Head Master, Salford Grammar Sch., 1942–45. HM Inspectorate of Schools, 1945–65; Midland Divisional Inspector, 1954–61; Chief Inspector (Teacher Training), 1961–65. *Publications:* articles on counselling and guidance. *Recreations:* gardening, walking, photography, theatre. *Address:* Grosvenor House, Ballure Road, Ramsey, Isle of Man.

GILL, Cyril James; Telecommunications Management Consultant, 1972–77; *b* 24 Dec. 1907; *s* of William and Alice Gill; *m* 1931, Dae M. (*née* Bingley); one *s* one *d*. *Educ:* Mundella Gram. Sch., Nottingham. Served Army, Royal Signals, 1942–46, to Col GHQI. Engrg Dept, GPO, 1929–48; Telephone Man., Sheffield, 1949; Princ., Post Office HQ, 1950; Princ. Private Sec. to PMG, 1957; Dep. Dir, External Telecommunications Exec., 1958; Controller of Supplies, 1959; Vice-Dir, ETE, 1964; Dir, External Telecomm. Exec., GPO, 1967–69; Dir, Cable and Wireless Ltd, 1967–69; Chm. Commonwealth Telecomm. Council, 1968–69; Chm. Grading Commn, Nigerian Min. of Communications, 1970–71. *Recreations:* gardening, golf, travel. *Address:* 65 Longton Avenue, Upper Sydenham, SE26 6RF. *T:* 01–699 2745.

GILL, David, FRSA; television producer; *b* 9 June 1928; *s* of Cecil and Iona Gill; *m* 1953, Pauline Wadsworth; two *d*. *Educ:* Belmont Abbey, Hereford. Dancer with Sadler's Wells Theatre Ballet, 1948–55; joined film-cutting rooms, Associated-Rediffusion TV, 1955; produced Stations of the Cross (mime), BBC, 1957; Film Editor, This Week, Rediffusion TV, 1957–68 (also documentaries); Technical Advisor and Editor, Dave Clark Special, 1968; directed for Thames Television: This Week, 1969–73; Till I End My Song (documentary), 1970; Destination America (documentary series), 1975; with Kevin Brownlow: co-wrote and produced: Hollywood, 1980; Unknown Chaplin, 1983; co-produced Abel Gance's Napoleon (TV version) 1983; British Cinema—Personal View, 1986; co-produces Thames Silents (also TV versions for Channel 4). *Recreations:* cinema, theatre, music, skiing, planting trees. *Address:* c/o Thames Television, Euston Road, NW1.

GILL, Evan W. T.; Director, Atlantic Salmon Federation (Canada), 1983–86; Canadian Ambassador to Ireland, 1965–68; *b* 2 Nov. 1902; *s* of Robert Gill; *m* 1930, Dorothy Laurie; two *s* one *d*. *Educ:* RMC, Kingston, Ont.; McGill Univ., Montreal, PQ. Began career with industrial and commercial organs; served Canadian Army, 1940–46; Cabinet Secretariat, 1946–50; External Affairs, 1950; Canada House, 1950–51; High Comr for Canada to Union of S Africa, 1954–57; High Comr for Canada to Ghana, 1957–59; Asst Under-Sec. of State for External Affairs, 1959–62; High Commissioner for Canada in Australia, 1962–64. *Address:* St Andrews, New Brunswick E0G 2X0, Canada. *Clubs:* Rideau (Ottawa); University (Toronto).

GILL, Frank Maxey; Director, Gill & Duffus Group Ltd, 1957–80; *b* 25 Sept. 1919; fifth *s* of Frederick Gordon Gill, DSO, and Mary Gill; *m* 1st, 1942, Sheila Rosemary Gordon (decd); three *d*; 2nd, 1952, Erica Margaret Fulcher; one *s*. *Educ:* Kingsmead Prep. Sch., Seaford; Marlborough Coll.; De Havilland Aeronautical Technical Sch. Joined Gill & Duffus Ltd, 1940; served RAF (Flt/Lt), 1940–46; rejoined Gill & Duffus Ltd, 1946; Joint Managing Director, 1959; Chm., 1976–79. Hon. Trustee, Confectioners' Benevolent Fund, 1981– (Pres., 1970). Mem., Surrey Soc. of Model Engineers. *Recreation:* model engineering. *Address:* Tile House, Reigate Heath, Reigate, Surrey.

GILL, (George) Malcolm; Head of Foreign Exchange Division, Bank of England, since 1982; *b* 23 May 1934; *s* of Thomas Woodman Gill and late Alice Muriel Gill (*née* Le Grice); *m* 1966, Monica Kennedy Brooks; one *s* one *d*. *Educ:* Cambridgeshire High Sch.; Sidney Sussex Coll., Cambridge (MA). Entered Bank of England, 1957; seconded to UK Treasury Delegation, Washington DC, 1966–68; Private Sec. to Governor of Bank of England, 1970–72; Asst Chief Cashier, 1975; seconded to HM Treasury, 1977–80; Chief Manager, Banking and Credit Markets, Bank of England, 1980–82. *Recreations:* family, music, gardening. *Address:* Bank of England, EC2R 8AH. *T:* 01–601 4444.

GILL, Air Vice-Marshal Harry, CB 1979; OBE 1968; Director-General of Supply, Royal Air Force, 1976–79; *b* 30 Oct. 1922; *s* of John William Gill and Lucy Gill, Newark, Notts; *m* 1951, Diana Patricia, *d* of Colin Wood, Glossop; one *d*. *Educ:* Barnby Road Sch.; Newark Technical Coll. Entered RAF, 1941; pilot trng, 1942; commnd 1943; flying duties, 1943–49; transf. to Equipment Br., 1949; Officer Commanding: Supply Sqdns, RAF Spitalgate and RAF North Coates, 1949–52; HQ Staff No 93 Maintenance Unit Explosives and Fuels Supply Ops, 1952–55; Explosives and Fuels Sch., 1955–58; Staff Officer Logistics Div., HQ Allied Forces Northern Europe, 1958–61; Head of Provision Br., Air Min., 1961–64; Chief Equipment Officer, No 25 Maintenance Unit, RAF Hartlebury, 1964–66; Equipment Staff Officer, HQ Air Forces Middle East, 1966–67; Dep. Dir Supply Systems, MoD Air, 1968–70; RCDS, 1971; Comdt, RAF Supply Control Centre, 1972–73; Dir, Supply Management, MoD Air, 1973–76. *Recreations:* shooting, fishing, squash, tennis, cricket. *Address:* Gretton Brook, South Collingham, Newark, Notts. *T:* Newark 892142. *Club:* Royal Air Force.

GILL, Maj.-Gen. Ian Gordon, CB 1972; OBE 1959 (MBE 1949); MC 1940, Bar 1945; idc, psc; Colonel, 4/7 Royal Dragoon Guards, 1973–78; *b* Rochester, 9 Nov. 1919; *s* of late Brig. Gordon Harry Gill, CMG, DSO and Mrs Doris Gill, Rochester, Kent; *m* 1963, Elizabeth Vivian Rohr, MD, MRCP, *o d* of late A. F. Rohr; no *c*. *Educ:* Edinburgh House, Hants; Repton School. Commnd from SRO into 4th/7th Roy. Dragoon Guards, 1938; served with Regt in: BEF, France, 1939–40; BLA, NW Europe, 1944–45 (despatches, 1945); Palestine, 1946–48; Tripolitania, 1951–52; Instructor, Armoured Sch., 1948–50; Staff Coll., Camberley, 1952; Bde Maj., HQ Inf. Bde, 1953–55; comdg 4th/7th RDG, 1957–59; Asst Mil. Sec., HQ, BAOR, 1959–61; Coll. Comdt RMA Sandhurst, 1961–62; Imp. Def. Coll., 1963; Comdr, 7th Armoured Bde, 1964–66; Dep. Mil. Sec. 1, MoD (Army), 1966–68; Head, British Defence Liaison Staff, Dept of Defence, Canberra, 1968–70; Asst Chief of Gen. Staff (Op. Requirements), 1970–72, retired. Hon. Liveryman, Coachmakers' Co., 1974. *Recreations:* equitation, ski-ing, cricket, squash rackets. *Address:* Cheriton House, Thorney, Peterborough PE6 0QD. *Clubs:* Cavalry and Guards, MCC.

GILL, Jack, CB 1984; Chief Executive (formerly Secretary), Export Credits Guarantee Department, 1983–87; *b* 20 Feb. 1930; *s* of Jack and Elizabeth Gill; *m* 1954, Alma Dorothy; three *d*. *Educ:* Bolton Sch. Export Credits Guarantee Department: Clerical Officer, 1946; Principal, 1962; Asst Sec., 1970; Asst Sec., DTI, 1972–75; Export Credits Guarantee Department: Under Sec., 1975–79; Principal Finance Officer, 1978–79; Sec., Monopolies and Mergers Commn, 1979–81; Dep. Sec., and Dir of Industrial Develt Unit, DoI, 1981–83. Mem., BOTB, 1981–87. National Service, REME, 1948–50. *Recreations:* music, chess. *Address:* 9 Ridley Road, Warlingham, Surrey CR3 9LR. *T:* Upper Warlingham 2688.

GILL, James Kenneth; President, Saatchi and Saatchi Company PLC, since 1985 (Chairman, 1976–85); *b* 27 Sept. 1920; *s* of late Alfred Charles and Isabel Gill; *m* 1948, Anne Bridgewater; one *s*. *Educ:* Highgate Sch. Served RAC, 24th Lancers and Intelligence Corps, GSO II, 1939–45. Copywriter, S. T. Garland Advertising Service, 1938–39; Chm., Garland-Compton Ltd, 1970–76. FIPA. *Recreations:* the theatre, the cinema, cricket. *Address:* Davenport House, Duntisbourne Abbots, Cirencester, Glos GL7 7JN. *T:* Miserden 468; 80 Charlotte Street, W1. *T:* 01–636 5060. *Clubs:* Royal Automobile, MCC.

GILL, Kenneth; General Secretary, Amalgamated Union of Engineering Workers (Technical, Administrative and Supervisory Section) and Member of General Council of TUC, since 1974 (President, TUC, 1985–86); *b* 30 Aug. 1927; *s* of Ernest Frank Gill and Mary Ethel Gill; *m* 1967, Sara Teresa Paterson; two *s* one *d*. *Educ:* Chippenham Secondary School. Engrg apprentice, 1943–48; Draughtsman Designer, Project Engr, Sales Engr in various cos, 1948–62; District Organiser, Liverpool and Ireland TASS, 1962–68; Editor, TASS Union Jl, 1968–72; Dep. Gen. Sec., 1972–74. Mem., Commn for Racial Equality, 1981–. *Recreations:* sketching, political caricaturing. *Address:* 164 Ramsden Road, Balham, SW12. *T:* 01–675 1489.

GILL, Air Vice-Marshal Leonard William George, DSO 1945; Consultant in personnel planning, since 1973; Chairman, since 1985, and Director, since 1979, Merton Associates (Consultants) Ltd; *b* 31 March 1918; *s* of L. W. Gill, Hornchurch, Essex, and Marguerite Gill; *m* 1st, 1943, Joan Favill Appleyard (marr. diss.); two *s* two *d*; 2nd, Mrs Constance Mary Cull. *Educ:* University Coll. Sch., London. Joined RAF, 1937; served in Far East until 1942; then UK as night fighter pilot; comd No 68 Sqdn for last 6 months of war; subseq. served in various appts incl. comd of Nos 85 and 87 night fighter Sqdns and tour on directing staff at RAF Staff Coll.; Stn Comdr No 1 Flying Trng Sch., Linton-on-Ouse, 1957–60; Dir of Overseas Ops, 1960–62; Nat. Def. Coll. of Canada, 1962–63; Dir of Organisation (Estabs), 1963–66; SASO, RAF Germany, 1966–68; Dir-Gen., Manning (RAF), MoD, 1968–73, retired. Manpower and Planning Advr, P&O Steam Navigation Co., 1973–79. Vice-Pres., RAF Assoc., 1973– (Pres. E Area, 1974–81; Vice-Chm., Central Council, 1984). FIPM; FBIM. *Recreations:* shooting, cricket, boats, amateur woodwork. *Address:* 101 Admirals Walk, West Cliff, Bournemouth, Hants BH2 5HF. *T:* Bournemouth 24722; 4 Boston House, 31 Collingham Road, Kensington, SW5 0NU. *T:* 01–370 2716. *Club:* Royal Air Force.

GILL, Malcolm; *see* Gill, G. M.

GILL, Peter, OBE 1980; Associate Director, National Theatre, since 1980; Director, National Theatre Studio, since 1984; *b* Cardiff, 7 Sept. 1939; *s* of George John Gill and Margaret Mary Browne. *Educ:* St Illtyd's Coll., Cardiff. Associate Dir, Royal Court Theatre, 1970–72; Dir, 1976–80, Associate Dir, 1980, Riverside Studios, Hammersmith. Productions include: Royal Court: A Collier's Friday Night, 1965; The Local Stigmatic, The Ruffian on the Stair, A Provincial Life, 1966; A Soldier's Fortune, The Daughter-in-law, 1967; The Widowing of Mrs Holroyd, 1968; Life Price, Over Gardens Out, The Sleepers' Den, 1969; The Duchess of Malfi, 1971; Crete & Sergeant Pepper, Crimes of Passion, 1972; The Merry-go-round, 1973; Small Change, 1976; Riverside Studios: As You Like It, 1976; Small Change, 1977; The Cherry Orchard, The Changeling, 1978; Measure for Measure, 1979; Julius Caesar, 1980; Scrape off the Black, 1980; National Theatre: A Month in the Country, Don Juan, Scrape off the Black, Much Ado about Nothing, 1981; Danton's Death, Major Barbara, 1982; Kick for Touch, Tales from Hollywood, 1983; Venice Preserv'd, Fool for Love, 1984; (also adapted) As I Lay Dying, 1985; other London theatres: O'Flaherty VC, Mermaid, 1966; has also produced plays by Shakespeare and modern writers at Stratford-upon-Avon, Nottingham, Edinburgh and in Canada, Germany, Switzerland and USA. Television productions include: Grace, 1972; Girl, 1973; A Matter of Taste, Fugitive, 1974; Hitting Town, 1976. *Publications:* plays: The Sleepers' Den, 1965; Over Gardens Out, 1969; Small Change, 1976; Small Change and Kick for Touch, 1985. *Address:* c/o Margaret Ramsay, 14a Goodwin's Court, St Martin's Lane, WC2N 4LL.

GILL, Stanley Sanderson; His Honour Judge Gill; a Circuit Judge, since 1972; *b* Wakefield, 3 Dec. 1923; *s* of Sanderson Henry Briggs Gill, OBE and Dorothy Margaret Gill (*née* Bennett); *m* 1954, Margaret Mary Patricia Grady; one *s* two *d*. *Educ:* Queen Elizabeth Grammar Sch., Wakefield; Magdalene Coll., Cambridge (MA). Served in RAF, 1942–46: 514 and 7 (Pathfinder) Sqdns, Flt Lt 1945. Called to Bar, Middle Temple, 1950; Asst Recorder of Bradford, 1966; Dep. Chm., WR Yorks QS, 1968; County Court Judge, 1971. Mem., County Court Rule Cttee, 1980–84. Chm., Rent Assessment Cttee, 1966–71. *Recreations:* walking, reading. *Address:* Downe, Baldersby, Thirsk, North Yorks. *T:* Melmerby 283.

GILLAM, Group Captain Denys Edgar, DSO (and 2 bars); DFC (and bar), 1940; AFC 1938; DL; Director, Homfray & Co. Ltd, 1950–81 (Chairman, 1971–81); *b* 18 Nov. 1915; *s* of Maj. T. H. J. and D. Gillam; *m* 1st, 1945, Nancye Joan Short (*d* 1982); one *s* two *d*; 2nd, 1983, Irene Scott. *Educ:* Bramcote, Scarborough; Wrekin Coll., Salop. Joined RAF, 1935; trained No 1 FTS Netheravon; served 29 Fighter Sqdn, Middle East, 1937–39, Meteorological Flight Aldergrove. Award Air Force Cross, 1938. 616 Sqdn (Fighter), 1939–40 (DFC, after Battle of Britain); 312 Sqdn (F), 1940–41; HQ 9 Group till March 1941, rank Sqdn Ldr; commanded 306 Sqdn (Polish), then 615 Sqdn (F) (bar DFC and DSO for shipping attacks in Channel); RAF Staff Coll.; then commanded first Typhoon Wing (despatches); graduated US Command and Gen. Staff Coll.; commanded Tangmere Wing (Typhoons), Jan.–March 1944 (bar, DSO for attacks on V-weapon sites); promoted Group Capt., commanded 20 Sector 2nd TAF, then 146 Wing 2 TAF (Typhoon) till March 1945 (2nd bar DSO); then Group Capt. Ops 84 Group (Main) 2nd TAF. DL for West Riding of Yorks and the City and County of York, 1959. *Recreations:* fishing, shooting, sailing. *Address:* The Glebe, Brawby, Malton, North Yorks. *T:* Kirbymoorside 31530. *Club:* Royal Ocean Racing.

GILLAM, Patrick John; Managing Director, British Petroleum Company plc, since 1981; Chairman: BP Shipping Ltd, since 1981; BP Minerals International Ltd/Selection Trust Ltd, since 1982; BP Coal Ltd, since 1986; *b* 15 April 1933; *s* of late Cyril B. Gillam and of Mary J. Gillam; *m* 1963, Diana Echlin; one *s* one *d*. *Educ:* London School of Economics (BA Hons History). Foreign Office, 1956–57; British Petroleum Co. Ltd, 1957–: Vice-Pres., BP North America Inc., 1971–74; General Manager, Supply Dept, 1974–78; Director, BP International Ltd (formerly BP Trading Ltd), 1978–. *Recreation:* gardening. *Address:* British Petroleum Company plc, Britannic House, Moor Lane, EC2Y 9BU. *T:* 01–920 6615.

GILLAM, Stanley George, MA, MLitt; Librarian, The London Library, 1956–80; *b* 11 Aug. 1915; *s* of Harry Cosier Gillam, Oxford; *m* 1950, Pauline, *d* of Henry G. Bennett, Oxford; one *s*. *Educ:* Southfield Sch.; Saint Catherine's Coll., Oxford. Bodleian Library, Oxford, 1931–40 and 1946–54. Oxfordshire and Bucks Light Infantry (1st Bucks Bn), 1940–46. Asst Sec. and Sub-Librarian, The London Library, 1954–56. *Publications:* The Building Accounts of the Radcliffe Camera, 1958; articles in The Bodleian Library Record and other periodicals. *Address:* 18 Forest Side, Kennington, Oxford OX1 5LQ. *T:* Oxford 730832.

GILLANDERS, Prof. Lewis Alexander; Clinical Professor in Radiology, University of Aberdeen, and Consultant in Charge, Radiology Services (Grampian Health Board), since 1964; *b* 7 Feb. 1925; *s* of Kenneth John Alexander Gillanders and Nellie May Sherris; *m* 1960, Nora Ellen Wild; one *s* one *d*. *Educ:* Dingwall Academy; Univ. of Glasgow (graduated in medicine, 1947). Commissioned, RAMC, 1948–50; general medical practice, Scottish Highlands, 1950–52; trained in Diagnostic Radiology, Glasgow Royal Infirmary and United Birmingham Hosps, 1953–58; Consultant Radiologist, Aberdeen Teaching Hosps, 1958. Examiner in Radiology for: RCR, 1969–79, and DMRD, 1983–; Faculty of Radiologists, RCSI, 1975–77; Univ. of Nairobi, 1978–80; Univ. of Wales, 1981–83. Member, GMC, 1979–84; Vice-Pres., RCR, 1981–83. *Publications:* chapter in Pye's Surgical Handicraft (1st edn 1884), 19th edn 1969, 20th edn 1977; papers in general medical and radiological literature, students' magazines, etc. *Recreations:* derivations and meanings; golf, do-it-yourself. *Address:* Lyndhurst, 41 Deeview Road South, Cults, Aberdeen AB1 9NA. *Clubs:* Victory Services; Royal Northern & University (Aberdeen).

GILLARD, Francis George, CBE 1961 (OBE 1946); public broadcasting interests in USA, since 1970; *b* 1 Dec. 1908; *s* of late Francis Henry Gillard and of late Emily Jane Gillard, Stockleigh Lodge, Exford; unmarried. *Educ:* Wellington Sch., Som.; St Luke's Coll., Exeter (BSc London). Schoolmaster, 1932–41; Freelance broadcaster, 1936–; joined BBC as Talks Producer, 1941; BBC War Correspondent, 1941. BBC Head of West Regional Programmes, 1945–55; Chief Asst to Dir of Sound Broadcasting with Controller rank, 1955–56; Controller, West Region, BBC, 1956–63; Dir of Sound Broadcasting, 1963–68; Man. Dir, Radio, BBC, 1969–70, retired. Distinguished Fellow, Corp. for Public Broadcasting, Washington, 1970–73. Chm., Council, Educational Foundn for Visual Aids, 1977–86. Mem. Finance Cttee, Exeter Univ., 1968–; Chm. of Governors, Wellington Sch., 1974–80. FRSA 1971. *Address:* Trevor House, Poole, Wellington, Somerset. *T:* Wellington 2890.

GILLES, Prof. Dennis Cyril; Professor of Computing Science, University of Glasgow, since 1966; *b* 7 April 1925; *s* of George Cyril Gilles and Gladys Alice Gilles (*née* Batchelor); *m* 1955, Valerie Mary Gilles; two *s* two *d*. *Educ:* Sidcup Gram. Sch.; Imperial Coll., University of London. Demonstrator, Asst Lectr, Imperial Coll., 1945–47; Asst Lectr, University of Liverpool, 1947–49; Mathematician, Scientific Computing Service, 1949–55; Research Asst, University of Manchester, 1955–57; Dir of Computing Lab., University of Glasgow, 1957–66. *Publications:* contribs to Proc. Royal Society and other scientific jls. *Address:* 21 Bruce Road, Glasgow G41 5EE. *T:* 041–429 2473.

GILLES, Prof. Chevalier Herbert Michael Joseph, MD; FRCP, FFCM; Alfred Jones and Warrington Yorke Professor of Tropical Medicine, University of Liverpool, since 1972; *b* 10 Sept. 1921; *s* of Joseph and Clementine Gilles; *m* 1955, Wilhelmina Caruana (*d* 1972); three *s* one *d*; *m* 1979, Dr Mejra Kačić-Dimitri. *Educ:* St Edward's Coll., Malta; Royal Univ. of Malta (MD). Rhodes Schol. 1942. MSc Oxon; FMCPH (Nig.), DTM&H. Served War of 1939–45 (1939–45 Star, Africa Star, VM). Mem., Scientific Staff, MRC Lab., Gambia, 1954–58; University of Ibadan: Lectr, Tropical Med., 1958–63; Prof. of Preventive and Social Med., 1963–65; Liverpool University: Sen. Lectr, Tropical Med., 1965–70; Prof. of Tropical Med. (Personal Chair), 1970; Dean, Liverpool Sch. of Tropical Medicine, 1978–83. Vis. Prof., Tropical Medicine, Univ. of Lagos, 1965–68; Royal Society Overseas Vis. Prof., Univ. of Khartoum, Sudan, 1979–80. Consultant Physician in Tropical Medicine, Liverpool AHA(T) and Mersey RHA, 1965–; Consultant in Malariology to the Army, 1974; Consultant in Tropical Medicine to the RAF, 1978, to the DHSS, 1980. Pres., RSTM & H, 1985–87. Hon. Prof. of Tropical Medicine, Zhongshan Med. Coll., Guangzhou, People's Republic of China, 1984. KStJ 1972. Title of Chevalier awarded for medical work in the tropics. Hon. MD Karolinska Inst., 1979; Hon. DSc Malta, 1984. *Publications:* Tropical Medicine for Nurses, 1955, 4th edn 1975; Pathology in the Tropics, 1969, 2nd edn 1976; Management and Treatment of Tropical Diseases, 1971; A Short Textbook of Preventive Medicine for the Tropics, 1973, 2nd edn 1984; Atlas of Tropical Medicine and Parasitology, 1976, 2nd edn 1981; Recent Advances in Tropical Medicine, 1984; Human Antiparasitic Drugs, Pharmacology and Usage, 1985. *Recreations:* swimming, music. *Address:* 3 Conyers Avenue, Birkdale, Southport PR8 4SZ. *T:* Southport 66664.

GILLESPIE, Prof. Iain Erskine, MD, MSc, FRCS; Professor of Surgery, since 1970 and Dean of the Faculty of Medicine, since 1983, University of Manchester; *b* 4 Sept. 1931; *s* of John Gillespie and Flora McQuarie; *m* 1957, Mary Muriel McIntyre; one *s* one *d*. *Educ:* Hillhead High Sch., Glasgow; Univ. of Glasgow. MB, ChB, 1953; MD (Hons) 1963; MSc Manchester 1974; FRCSE 1959; FRCS 1963; FRCSGlas 1970. Series of progressive surgical appts in Univs of Glasgow, Sheffield, Glasgow (again), 1953–70. Nat. service, RAMC, 1954–56; MRC grantee, 1956–58; US Postdoctoral Research Fellow, Los Angeles, 1961–; Titular Prof. of Surgery, Univ. of Glasgow, 1969. Vis. Prof. in USA, Canada, S America, Kenya, S Africa, Australia and New Zealand. Member: Cttee of Surgical Res. Soc. of GB and Ireland, 1975–; Univ. Grants Cttee, Medical Sub-Cttee, 1975–, Univs and Polytechnics Grants Cttee, Hong Kong, 1984–. *Publications:* jt editor and contributor to several surgical and gastroenterological books; numerous articles in various med. jls of GB, USA, Europe. *Recreations:* none. *Address:* 27 Athol Road, Bramhall, Cheshire SK7 1BR. *T:* 061–439 2811.

GILLESPIE, Prof. John Spence; Head of Department of Pharmacology, Glasgow University, since 1968; *b* 5 Sept. 1926; *s* of Matthew Forsyth Gillespie and Myrtle Murie Spence; *m* 1956, Jemima Simpson Ross; four *s* one *d*. *Educ:* Dumbarton Academy; Glasgow Univ. MB ChB (Commendation), PhD. FRCP; FRSE. Hosp. Residency (Surgery), 1949–50; Nat. Service as RMO, 1950–52; hosp. appts, 1952–53; McCunn Res. Schol. in Physiology, Glasgow Univ., 1953–55; Faulds Fellow then Sharpey Schol. in Physiology Dept, University Coll. London, 1955–57; Glasgow University: Lectr in Physiol., 1957–59; Sophie Fricke Res. Fellow, Royal Soc., in Rockefeller Inst., 1959–60; Sen. Lectr in Physiol., 1961–63; Henry Head Res. Fellow, Royal Soc., 1963–68; Vice-Principal, 1983–87. *Publications:* articles in Jls of Physiol. and Pharmacol. *Recreations:* gardening, painting. *Address:* 5 Boclair Road, Bearsden, Glasgow G61 2AE. *T:* 041–942 0318.

GILLESPIE, Robert, CBE 1951; *b* 24 Nov. 1897; *s* of late James Gillespie and Ann Wilson Gillespie; *m* 1928, Isabella Brown (*d* 1980), *d* of late Dr Donald Murray, MP; one *s* one *d*. *Educ:* Queen's Park Sch., Glasgow. Joined Brit. Tanker Co. Ltd, 1922; Asst Manager, 1936; Gen. Manager, 1944; Dir and Gen. Manager, 1946; Managing Dir, 1950–56; a Dir, 1956–67; a Managing Dir of The British Petroleum Co. Ltd, 1956–58, retired; Mem., Council, Chamber of Shipping of UK, 1943–70. Served European War in Army, 1914–19; in ranks with Cameronians (Scottish Rifles) TF in UK; commnd KOSB, served UK, Palestine and France. War of 1939–45, served as Asst Dir, Tanker Div. of Ministry of War Transport, 1942–43. *Recreation:* contract bridge. *Address:* Craigrathan, Kippford, Dalbeattie, Kirkcudbrightshire. *T:* Kippford 653.

GILLESPIE, Prof. Ronald James, PhD, DSc; FRS 1977; FRSC; FRSC (UK); FCIC; Professor of Chemistry, McMaster University, Hamilton, Ont, since 1960; *b* London, England, 21 Aug. 1924; Canadian citizen; *s* of James A. Gillespie and Miriam G. (*née* Kirk); *m* 1950, Madge Ena Garner; two *d*. *Educ:* London Univ. (BSc 1945, PhD 1949, DSc 1957). FRSC 1965; FCIC 1960; FRIC; Mem., Amer. Chem. Soc. Asst Lectr, Dept of Chemistry, 1948–50, Lectr, 1950–58, UCL; Commonwealth Fund Fellow, Brown Univ., RI, USA, 1953–54; McMaster University: Associate Prof., Dept of Chem., 1958–60; Prof., 1960–62; Chm., Dept of Chem., 1962–65. Professeur Associé, l'Univ. des Sciences et Techniques de Languedoc, Montpellier, 1972–73; Visiting Professor: Univ. of Geneva, 1976; Univ. of Göttingen, 1978. Member: Chem. Soc. (Nyholm Lectr 1979); Faraday Soc. Medals: Ramsay, UCL, 1949; Harrison Meml, Chem. Soc., 1954; Canadian Centennial, 1967; Chem. Inst. of Canada, 1977; Silver Jubilee, 1978. Awards: Noranda, Chem. Inst. of Canada, 1966 (for inorganic chem.); Amer. Chem. Soc. N-Eastern Reg., 1971 (in phys. chem.); Manufg Chemists Assoc. Coll. Chem. Teacher, 1972; Amer. Chem. Soc., 1973 (for distinguished service in advancement of inorganic chem.), 1980 (for creative work in fluorine chem.); Chem. Inst. of Canada/Union Carbide, 1976 (for chemical educn); Henry Marshall Tory Medal, Royal Soc. of Canada, 1983. *Publications:* Molecular Geometry, 1972 (London; German and Russian trans, 1975); (jtly) Chemistry, 1986; papers in Jl Amer. Chem. Soc., Canadian Jl of Chem., and Inorganic Chem. *Recreations:* skiing, sailing, Scottish country dancing. *Address:* Department of Chemistry, McMaster University, Hamilton, Ont L8S 4M1, Canada. *T:* (416) 525–9140, ext. 3304.

GILLESPIE, William Hewitt, MD, FRCP; FRCPsych; Emeritus Physician, Maudsley Hospital (Physician, 1936–70); Hon. Member, British Psychoanalytical Society, 1975; *b* 6 Aug. 1905; *s* of Rev. W. H. Gillespie, Manchuria and Co. Down, and of Isabella B. Gillespie (*née* Grills), Co. Down, N Ireland; *m* 1st, 1932, Dr Helen Turover (*d* 1975); one *s* one *d*; 2nd, 1975, Sadie Mervis. *Educ:* George Watson's Coll.; Universities of Edinburgh and Vienna. University of Edinburgh: 1st pl. Open Bursary Exam., 1924, MB, ChB (hons), 1929, Dip. in Psychiatry, 1931, MD 1934; MRCP 1936; FRCP 1962; McCosh Travelling Scholarship, in Vienna, 1930–31. LCC Mental Hosps Service, 1931–36; Lecturer, Inst. of Psychiatry, 1944–70; Dir, London Clinic of Psychoanalysis, 1944–47. Freud Meml Vis. Prof. of Psychoanalysis, Univ. Coll. London, 1976–77. Trng Sec., Inst. of Psychoanalysis, 1947–50; Chm., Inst of Psychoanalysis, 1954–56; President: British Psychoanalytical Soc., 1950–53 and 1971–72; Internat. Psychoanalytic Assoc., 1957–61. FRSocMed. *Publications:* contrib to: Recent Advances in Psychiatry, 1944; Psychiatrie sociale de l'enfant, 1951; Psychoanalysis and the Occult, 1953; The Sexual Perversions, 1956; The Pathology and Treatment of Sexual Deviation, 1964; Foundations of Child Psychiatry, 1968. Various articles in medical, psychiatric and psychoanalytic jls. *Recreations:* music, reading, walking. *Address:* 4 Eton Villas, NW3 4SX.

GILLETT, Eric; Vice-Chairman, Scottish Wildlife Trust, since 1982; *b* 22 July 1920; *m* 1945, Dorothy; one *s*. *Educ:* public primary and secondary schs; Downing Coll., Cambridge. Royal Artillery, 1942; Dept of Health for Scotland, 1946; Under-Sec., Scottish Home and Health Dept, 1969–71; Fisheries Sec., Dept of Agric. and Fisheries for Scotland, 1971–76; Sec., Scottish Develt Dept, 1976–80. Comr (Ombudsman) for Local Authority Services in Scotland, 1982–86. Chm., Scottish Assoc. of CAB, 1982–86. *Publication:* Investment in the Environment: a study of environmental policies in Scotland, 1983. *Recreations:* amateur chamber and orchestral music, hill walking, ancient buildings and the modern environment, Citizens' Advice Bureaux. *Address:* 66 Caiystane Terrace, Edinburgh EH10 6SW. *T:* 031–445 1184.

GILLETT, Maj.-Gen. Sir Peter (Bernard), KCVO 1979 (CVO 1973); CB 1966; OBE 1955; Governor, Military Knights of Windsor, since 1980; *b* 8 Dec. 1913; *s* of Bernard George Gillett, OBE, Milford on Sea, Hants; *m* 1952, Pamela Graham, *widow* of Col R. J. Lloyd Price and *d* of Col Spencer Graham Walker, Winsley, Wilts. *Educ:* Marlborough Coll.; RMA, Woolwich. Commissioned RA, 1934; apptd to RHA, 1945; service in UK and India to 1944; War Office, 1944; BAOR, 1944–45; Instructor, Staff Coll., 1947–49; staff appts in UK and E Africa to 1955; Comd 5 RHA, 1955; SHAPE, 1958; CRA 3 Inf. Div., 1959; IDC, 1962; Chief of Staff, HQ Eastern Comd, 1962–65; GOC, 48th Div. TA, W Midland District, 1965–68. Sec., Central Chancery of the Orders of Knighthood, 1968–79. Col Comdt, Royal Regt of Artillery, 1968–78. *Recreations:* sailing, shooting and travel. *Address:* Mary Tudor Tower, Windsor Castle, Windsor, Berks. *T:* Windsor 868286. *Clubs:* Army and Navy, MCC, Royal Ocean Racing.

GILLETT, Sir Robin (Danvers Penrose), 2nd Bt *cr* 1959; GBE 1976; RD 1965; Consultant, Sedgwick Ltd; Underwriting Member of Lloyd's; Lord Mayor of London for 1976–77; *b* 9 Nov. 1925; *o s* of Sir (Sydney) Harold Gillett, 1st Bt, MC, and Audrey Isabel Penrose Wardlaw (*d* 1962); *S* father, 1976; *m* 1950, Elizabeth Marion Grace, *e d* of late John Findlay, JP, Busby, Lanarks; two *s*. *Educ:* Nautical Coll., Pangbourne. Served Canadian Pacific Steamships, 1943–60; Master Mariner 1951; Staff Comdr 1957; Hon. Comdr RNR 1971. Elder Brother of Trinity House; Fellow and Founder Mem., Nautical Inst. City of London (Ward of Bassishaw): Common Councilman 1965–69; Alderman 1969; Sheriff 1973; one of HM Lieuts for City of London, 1975; Chm. Civil Defence Cttee, 1967–68; Pres., City of London Civil Defence Instructors Assoc., 1967–78, Chm., City of London Centre, St John Ambulance Assoc.; Pres., Nat. Waterways Transport Assoc., 1979–83; Dep. Commonwealth Pres., Royal Life Saving Soc. Vice-Chm., PLA, 1979–84. Master, Hon. Co. of Master Mariners, 1979–80. Trustee, Nat. Maritime Mus., 1982–. Chm. of Governors, Pangbourne Coll.; Governor, King Edward's Sch., Witley. Chancellor, City Univ., 1976–77. FIAM (Pres., 1980–84; Gold Medal, 1982). Hon. DSc City, 1976. Gentleman Usher of the Purple Rod, Order of the British Empire, 1985–. KStJ 1977 (OStJ 1974). Gold Medal, Administrative Management Soc., USA, 1983. Officer, Order of Leopard, Zaire, 1973; Comdr, Order of Dannebrog, 1974; Order of Johan Sedia Mahkota (Malaysia), 1974; Grand Cross of Municipal Merit (Lima), 1977. *Recreation:* sailing. *Heir: s* Nicholas Danvers Penrose Gillett, BSc, ARCS, *b* 24 Sept. 1955. *Address:* 4 Fairholt Street, Knightsbridge, SW7 1EQ. *T:* 01–589 9860. *Clubs:* City Livery, City Livery Yacht (Admiral), Guildhall, Royal Yacht Squadron, Royal London Yacht (Cdre, 1984–85).

GILLIAT, Lt-Col Sir Martin (John), GCVO 1981 (KCVO 1962; CVO 1954); MBE 1946; DL; Private Secretary to Queen Elizabeth the Queen Mother since 1956; formerly Vice-Lieutenant of Hertfordshire; *b* 8 Feb. 1913; *s* of late Lieut-Col John Babington Gilliat and Muriel Helen Lycette Gilliat; unmarried. *Educ:* Eton; RMC, Sandhurst. Joined KRRC, 1933. Served War of 1939–45 (despatches, Prisoner of War). Dep. Military Sec. to Viceroy and Governor-Gen. of India, 1947–48; Comptroller to Commissioner-Gen. for UK in South-East Asia, 1948–51; Mil. Sec. to Governor-Gen. of Australia, 1953–55. Hon. Bencher, Middle Temple, 1977. Hon. LLD London, 1977. DL Herts, 1963. *Address:* Appletrees, Welwyn, Herts. *T:* Welwyn 4675; 31A St James's Palace, SW1. *T:* 01–930 1440. *Clubs:* Travellers', Buck's, Brooks's.

GILLIATT, Penelope Ann Douglass Conner, FRSL; fiction writer for the New Yorker, since 1967; also employed by The Sunday Times and The Observer; freelance fiction writer of books, plays and films; *b* London, 25 March 1932; UK citizen; *d* of late Cyril Conner, and Mary Stephanie Douglass; *m* 1st, 1954, Prof. R. W. Gilliatt, *qv* (marr. diss.); 2nd, 1963, John Osborne, *qv* (marr. diss.); one *d. Educ:* Queen's Coll., Harley St, London; Bennington Coll., Vermont. FRSL 1978. Formerly, contributor to New Statesman, Spectator, Guardian, Sight and Sound, Encore, Grand Street, Encounter, London Magazine, London Review of Books, etc; film critic, Observer, 1961–65 and 1966–67, theatre critic, 1965–66; film critic, New Yorker, 1967–79 (six months of each yr). Mem., Bd of Adv. Sponsors, Symphony of UN, 1985–. Mem., Labour Party. Property, and Nobody's Business (plays), perf. Amer. Place Theatre, New York, 1980; But When All's Said and Done (play), Actor's Studio, 1981; BBC plays incl. Living on the Box, The Flight Fund, 1978, and In the Unlikely Event of an Emergency, 1979; Beach of Aurora (original libretto, with music by Tom Eastwood), ENO, 1982. Oscar nomination for best original screenplay, 1971; awards for best original screenplay, New York Film Critics Circle, National Soc. of Film Critics, USA, and British Soc. of Film Critics, 1971; Grant for creative achievement in fiction, National Inst. of Arts and Letters, 1972. *Publications: novels:* One by One, 1965; A State of Change, 1967; The Cutting Edge, 1979; Mortal Matters, 1983; *short story collections:* What's It Like Out?, 1968 (Come Back If It Doesn't Get Better, NY 1967); Nobody's Business, 1972; Splendid Lives, 1978; Quotations from Other Lives, 1982; They Sleep Without Dreaming, 1985; 22 stories, 1986; (contrib.) Penguin Modern Stories, 1970; *non-fiction:* Unholy Fools: film and theatre, 1975; Jean Renoir: essays, conversations, reviews, 1975; Jacques Tati, 1977; Three-Quarter Face: profiles and reflections (with much additional material), 1980; *screenplay:* Sunday, Bloody Sunday, 1971, repr. with new essay by author as Making Sunday Bloody Sunday, 1986; profiles: in New Yorker on Jean Renoir, Woody Allen, Jean-Luc Godard, Jacques Tati, Henri Langlois of the French Cinemathèque, Jeanne Moreau, Diane Keaton, Graham Greene, and Luis Buñuel; in Sunday Telegraph Magazine on John Huston; in Observer on Fred Astaire, Fellini, Whoopi Goldberg, Woody Allen. *Address:* c/o New Yorker Magazine, 25 West 43rd Street, New York, NY 10036, USA; 31 Chester Square, SW1W 9HT.

GILLIATT, Prof. Roger William, MC; DM; FRCP; Professor of Clinical Neurology, University of London, 1962–Sept. 1987; Physician, National Hospital, Queen Square, and Hammersmith Hospital; only *s* of late Sir William Gilliatt, KCVO; *m* 1963, Mary Elizabeth, *er d* of A. J. W. Green; one *s* two *d. Educ:* Rugby; Magdalen Coll., Oxford (BA 1st Cl. Hons Nat. Sci. (MA), BM, BCh Oxon 1949); MRCP 1951, FRCP 1961; DM 1955. Served in KRRC, 1942–45 (MC, despatches). Mem., Association of British Neurologists (Pres., 1984–85); Corr. Mem., Amer. Neurological Assoc.; Hon. Member: Amer. Acad. of Neurology; Amer. Assoc. of Electromyography and Electrodiagnosis; Société Française de Neurologie; Australian Assoc. of Neurologists; Soc. Suisse de Neurologie; Acad. Royale de Médecine, Belgium. *Publications:* contribs on neurological topics to medical and scientific jls. *Address:* Institute of Neurology, Queen Square, WC1N 3BG. *T:* 01–837 3611.

GILLICK, Rev. John, SJ, MA Oxon; Spiritual Director, St Peter's National Seminary, Hammanskraal, S Africa; *b* Wallasey, 27 March 1916; 2nd *s* of Laurence Gillick and Catherine Devine. *Educ:* St Francis Xavier's Coll., Liverpool; Heythrop and Campion Hall, Oxford (1st Cl. Hons Mod. History). Asst Master at Mount St Mary's and Beaumont. Two years writing and photography in Italy and Africa. Headmaster, Beaumont Coll., 1964–67; studied psychology at Loyola Univ., Chicago, 1967–68 (MA); Dir, Laboratories for the Training of Religious Superiors in S Africa, 1969; Dir, Fons Vitae (Pastoral Institute for Religious), 1970–84. *Publications:* Teaching the Mass, 1961; Baptism, 1962; followed by Teaching the Mass: African, 1963; Teaching the Sacraments: African, 1964; Teaching Confirmation: African, 1964, etc; *illustrations for:* The Breaking of Bread, 1950; The Pilgrim Years, 1956; Our Faith, 1956; The Holy Mass, 1958; Christ Our Life, 1960. *Address:* 493 Marshall Street, Belgravia, Johannesburg, 2094, South Africa; c/o 114 Mount Street, W1Y 6AH.

GILLIES, Gordon; *see* Gillies, Maurice G.

GILLIES, (Maurice) Gordon, TD and Bar 1948; QC (Scotland) 1958; Sheriff Principal of South Strathclyde, Dumfries and Galloway, since 1982; *b* 17 Oct. 1916; *s* of James Brown Gillies, Advocate in Aberdeen, and Rhoda Ledingham; *m* 1954, Anne Bethea McCall-Smith. *Educ:* Aberdeen Grammar Sch.; Merchiston Castle; Edinburgh Univ. Advocate, 1946; Advocate Depute, 1953–58; Sheriff of Lanarkshire, later S Strathclyde, Dumfries and Galloway, 1958–82. *Recreation:* golf. *Address:* Redwalls, Biggar, Lanarkshire. *T:* Biggar 20281. *Clubs:* New (Edinburgh); Hon. Company of Edinburgh Golfers.

GILLILAND, David; *see* Gilliland, J. A. D.

GILLILAND, David Jervois Thetford; practising solicitor and farmer; *b* 14 July 1932; *s* of late Major W. H. Gilliland and of Mrs N. H. Gilliland; *m* 1st, 1958, Patricia, *o d* of late J. S. Wilson and late Mrs Wilson (marr. diss. 1976); two *s* three *d*; 2nd, 1976, Jennifer Johnston, *qv. Educ:* Rockport Prep. Sch.; Wrekin Coll.; Trinity Coll., Dublin. BA 1954, LLB 1955. Qualified as solicitor, 1957, own practice. Mem. ITA, 1965–70; Chm., N Ireland Adv. Cttee of ITA, 1965–70. Mem. Council, Internat. Dendrology Soc., 1966–75; etc. *Recreations:* gardening, sailing, fishing. *Address:* Brook Hall, 65 Culmore Road, Londonderry, Northern Ireland. *T:* Londonderry 51297.

GILLILAND, (James Andrew) David; QC 1984; *b* 29 Dec. 1937; *s* of James Albin Gilliland and Mary Gilliland (*née* Gray); *m* 1961, Elsie McCully; two *s. Educ:* Campbell College; Queen's University Belfast. LLB (1st Class Hons) 1960. Called to the Bar, Gray's Inn, 1964 (Holt Scholar, Atkin Scholar, Macaskie Scholar); Lectr in Law, Manchester University, 1960–72. *Recreations:* music, opera, stamp collecting, wind surfing, skiing. *Address:* The Shieling, Highfield, Prestbury, Cheshire SK10 4DA. *T:* Prestbury 828029; (chambers) 7 New Square, Lincoln's Inn, WC2A 3QS. *T:* 01–405 1266; 20 North John Street, Liverpool L2 9RL. *T:* 051–236 6757. *Club:* Athenæum (Liverpool).

GILLILAND, Jennifer, (Mrs David Gilliland); *see* Johnston, J.

GILLING, Lancelot Cyril Gilbert, OBE 1985; CBiol, FIBiol; FRAgS; Member, Royal Commission on Environmental Pollution, since 1984; *b* 7 March 1920; *s* of Gilbert Joseph Gilling and Esther Marianne Gilling (*née* Clapp); *m* 1951, Brenda Copp; two *d. Educ:* Shebbear Coll., N Devon; Reading Univ. (BSc Agr). Pres. Union, Reading Univ., 1948–49. Lectr, Dorset Coll. of Agric., 1949–51; Head of Agric. Dept, Writtle Coll. of Agric., Essex, 1951–57; Principal, Askham Bryan Coll. of Agric. & Hortic., 1957–84. Member: Technical Develt Cttee and Educn and Gen. Purposes Cttee, Royal Agricl Soc., 1970–85; Northern Regional Panel, MAFF, 1982–; Adv. Cttee on Agric. and Vet. Sci., British Council, 1972–86; Chm., York Agricl Soc., 1983– (Pres., 1981–82); Vice-Chm., Sub-Cttee, Yorkshire Museum, 1985–; Chm. and Life Vice-Pres., Yorks Philosophical Soc., 1982–. Gov., Diocesan Coll. of Ripon and York St John, 1976–. Hon. Mem., CGLI. *Publications:* contribs to Agricultural Progress, Jl of Agricl Educn Assoc. and Jl of Royal Agricl Soc. *Recreations:* tennis, badminton, choral music. *Address:* The Spinney, Brandsby, York YO6 4RQ.

GILLINGHAM, (Francis) John, CBE 1982 (MBE 1944); FRSE 1970; Professor of Neurological Surgery, University of Edinburgh, 1963–80, now Emeritus; at Royal Infirmary of Edinburgh and Western General Hospital, Edinburgh, 1963–80; Consultant Neuro-Surgeon to the Army in Scotland, 1966–80; *b* 15 March 1916; *s* of John H. Gillingham, Upwey, Dorset; *m* 1945, Irene Judy Jude; four *s. Educ:* Hardye's Sch., Dorset; St Bartholomew's Hosp. Medical Coll., London. Matthews Duncan Gold Medal, 1939, MRCS, LRCP Oct. 1939; MB, BS (London) Nov. 1939; FRCS 1947; FRCSE 1955; FRCPE 1967; FRCPGlas 1982. Prof. of Surgical Neurol., King Saud Univ., Saudi Arabia, 1983–85, now Emeritus. Hunterian Prof., RCS, 1957; Morison Lectr, RCP of Edinburgh, 1960; Colles Lectr, College of Surgeons of Ireland, 1962; Elsberg Lectr, College of Physicians and Surgeons, NY, 1967; Penfield Lectr, Middle East Med. Assembly, 1970. Hon. Mem., Soc. de Neurochirurgie de Langue Française, 1964; Hon. Mem., Soc. of Neurol. Surgeons (USA), 1965; Hon. Mem., Royal Academy of Medicine of Valencia, 1967; Hon. and Corresp. Mem. of a number of foreign neuro-surgical societies; Hon. Pres., World Fedn of Neurosurgical Socs. President: Medico-Chirurgical Soc. of Edinburgh, 1965–67; European Soc. of Stereostatic and Functional Neurosurgery, 1972–76; Vice-Pres., RCSE, 1974–77, Pres., 1979–82. Hon. MD Thessaloniki, 1973. Jim Clark Foundn Award, 1979. *Publications:* Clinical Surgery: Neurological Surgery, 1969; papers on surgical management of cerebral vascular disease, head and spinal injuries, Parkinsonism and the dyskinesias, epilepsy and other neurosurgical subjects. *Recreations:* sailing, travel, photography. *Address:* Easter Park House, Barnton Avenue, Edinburgh EH4 6JR. *T:* 031–336 3528. *Clubs:* English-Speaking Union; New (Edinburgh); Nautico (Javea, Alicante).

GILLINGHAM, Rev. Canon Peter Llewellyn, LVO 1955; MA 1940; Chaplain to the Queen, 1952–84; Hon. Canon of Chichester Cathedral (Wisborough Prebendary), 1969–77, Canon Emeritus since 1977; *b* 3 May 1914; *s* of late Rev. Canon Frank Hay Gillingham; *m* 1947, Diana, *d* of Lieut-Gen. Sir Alexander Hood; two *s* two *d. Educ:* Cheam; Marlborough; Oriel Coll., Oxford. Curate, Tonbridge Parish Church, 1937–40; Curate-in-Charge, St George's Church, Oakdale, Poole, 1940–43. Served War of 1939–45, Chaplain, RNVR, 1943–46; Chaplain, Blundell's Sch., Tiverton, 1946–49; Hon. Chaplain to King George VI, 1949–52; Chaplain to Royal Chapel of All Saints, Windsor Great Park, 1949–55; Vicar of St Mildred's, Addiscombe, 1955; Vicar of St Mary the Virgin, Horsham, 1960–77; Rural Dean of Horsham, 1974–77; Asst Chaplain, Sherborne Girls' Sch., 1977–79, Chaplain and Librarian, 1979–82. *Recreations:* golf, sailing. *Address:* Maplestead Cottage, Leiston Road, Aldeburgh, Suffolk. *T:* 2739.

GILLIS, His Honour Bernard Benjamin, QC 1954; MA Cantab; a Circuit Judge (Additional Judge, Central Criminal Court), 1964–80; *m*; one *s. Educ:* Downing Coll., Cambridge, Hon. Fellow, 1976. Squadron Leader, RAF, 1940–45. Called to the Bar, Lincoln's Inn, 1927, Bencher 1960, Treasurer 1976; North Eastern Circuit and Central Criminal Court. Commr, Central Criminal Court, 1959; Commissioner of Assize: Lancaster, 1960; Chelmsford, 1961; Bodmin, 1963. Recorder of Bradford, 1958–64. *Address:* 3 Adelaide Crescent, Hove, E Sussex. *Club:* Royal Air Force.

GILLMAN, Bernard Arthur, (Gerry Gillman); General Secretary, Society of Civil and Public Servants, 1973–85; *b* 14 April 1927; *s* of Elias Gillman and Gladys Gillman; *m* 1951, Catherine Mary Antonia Harvey. *Educ:* Archbishop Tenison's Grammar Sch. Civil Service, 1946–53; Society of Civil Servants, 1953–85. Mem., Police Complaints Authy, 1986–. *Recreations:* watching London Welsh Rugby, theatre, music. *Address:* 2 Burnham Street, Kingston-upon-Thames, Surrey KT2 6QR. *T:* 01–546 6905. *Club:* MCC.

GILLMORE, Air Vice-Marshal Alan David, CB 1955; CBE 1944; RAF (retired); *b* 17 Oct. 1905; *s* of late Rev. David Sandeman Gillmore and Allis Emily Widmer; *m* 1931, Kathleen Victoria Morris; three *s. Educ:* St Dunstan's Sch., Burnham-on-Sea; King's Sch., Ely. RAF Cadet Coll., Cranwell, Lincs, 1923–25; Commission in RAF, 1925; 13 Sqdn, 1925–27; 208 Sqdn (Egypt), 1927–29; Instr, Sch. of Air Pilotage, 1931–33; O i/c Navigation Flight, 1934–35; 202 Flying Boat Sqdn (Malta), 1935–36; HQ no 6 (Aux.) Gp, 1936–39; RN Staff Coll., 1939; Future Ops Planning Staff, 1940–41; Dep. Dir, Overseas Orgn (Air Min.), 1940–41; Instr, RAF Staff Coll., 1942; OC RAF Station Wick, 1943–44; Dir, Maritime Ops (Air Min.), 1944–45; AOC RAF W Africa, 1945–46; Dir of Postings (Air Min.), 1946–47; IDC, 1948; AOC 64 Gp, 1949–51; Commandant RAF Staff Coll., Bracknell, 1951–53; SASO, FEAF, 1953–56; SASO, Home Command, 1956–59; retired 1959. *Address:* Southpen, 17 Naish Road, Burnham-on-Sea, Som. *Club:* Royal Air Force.

See also D. H. Gillmore.

GILLMORE, David Howe, CMG 1982; HM Diplomatic Service; Deputy Under-Secretary of State, Foreign and Commonwealth Office, since 1986; *b* 16 Aug. 1934; *s* of Air Vice-Marshal A. D. Gillmore, *qv*; *m* 1964, Lucile Morin; two *s. Educ:* Trent Coll.; King's Coll., Cambridge (MA). Reuters Ltd, 1958–60; Asst to Dir-Gen., Polypapier, SA, Paris, 1960–65; Teacher, ILEA, 1965–69; HM Diplomatic Service, 1970; Foreign and Commonwealth Office, 1970–72; First Sec., Moscow, 1972–75; Counsellor, UK Delegn, Vienna, 1975–78; Head of Defence Dept, FCO, 1979–81; Asst Under Sec. of State, FCO, 1981–83; High Comr in Malaysia, 1983–86. *Publication: novel* A Way From Exile, 1967. *Recreations:* books, music, exercise. *Address:* Foreign and Commonwealth Office, Downing Street, SW1.

GILMARTIN, Hugh, OBE 1981; HM Diplomatic Service, retired; *b* 20 Nov. 1923; *s* of late Edward Gilmartin and Catherine Gilmartin (*née* McFadyen); *m* 1962, Olga, *d* of late Nicholas Alexander Plotnikoff; two *s* one *d. Educ:* Holy Cross Academy; Edinburgh Univ. Entered HM Diplomatic Service, 1945; Rome, 1945; Vienna, 1945–47; FO, 1947; UN Special Cttee on the Balkans, 1948; Bahrain, 1949–50; FO, 1951–53; Jakarta, 1953–55; Buenos Aires, 1955–57; Second Secretary, Asuncion, 1957–58; Bahrain, 1959–60; Panama, 1961–63; FO, 1963–65; First Sec. and Head of Chancery, Tegucigalpa, 1965–67; Zürich, 1968–73; First Sec., Office of UK Permanent Representative to the European Communities, Brussels, 1973–75; Asst Head of Training Dept, FO, 1975–79; Basle, 1979–80; Consul-Gen., Brisbane, 1980–83; retired 1983; assigned to Falkland Is Dept, FCO, 1984–85, Governor, Rye St Antony Sch., Oxford. *Recreations:* walking, swimming, gardening. *Address:* 19 Phillimore Road, Emmer Green, Reading, Berks RG4 8UR. *T:* Reading 476902. *Club:* Royal Commonwealth Society (Queensland).

GILMORE, Brian Terence; Under Secretary, HM Treasury, since 1981; *b* 25 May 1937; *s* of John Henry Gilmore and Edith Alice Gilmore; *m* 1962, Rosalind Edith Jean Fraser. *Educ:* Wolverhampton Grammar Sch.; Christ Church, Oxford (Passmore-Edwards Prize, 1956; BA Lit. Hum.; MA 1961). CRO and Diplomatic Service Admin Office, 1958–65: Private Sec. to Perm. Sec., 1960–61, to Parly Under Sec., 1961–62; Asst Private Sec. to Sec. of State, 1962–64; British Embassy, Washington, 1965–68; Min. of Technology and DTI, 1968–72: Private Sec. to Minister of State, Industry, 1969–70, and to Lord Privy Seal and Leader of the House of Lords, 1971–72; CSD, 1972–81; Under Sec., 1979; Principal, CS Coll., 1979–81, HM Treasury, 1981–; Principal Estab. Officer and Principal Finance Officer, 1982–84. *Recreations:* reading, music, Greece. *Address:* 3 Clarendon Mews, W2 2NR. *T:* 01-262 4459. *Club:* Athenæum.

GILMORE, Carol Jacqueline; *see* Ellis, C. J.

GILMOUR, Dr Alan Breck, CBE 1984; FRCGP; Director, National Society for the Prevention of Cruelty to Children, since 1979; *b* 30 Aug. 1928; *er* surv. *s* of Andrew Gilmour, *qv; m* 1957, Elizabeth, *d* of late H. and of L. Heath; two *d. Educ:* Clayesmore Sch.; King's Coll., London; King's Coll. Hosp. (Raymond Gooch Schol.). MB BS, LMSSA 1956; FRCGP 1974 (MRCGP 1965). General medical practitioner, 1958–67; during this period served as Member: Standing Med. Adv. Cttee, Min. of Health; Working Party on General Practice; Educn Cttee, RCGP; BMA Council, and others. British Medical Association Secretariat, 1967–79: Asst Sec., 1967; Under Sec., 1972; Dep. Sec., 1977; appts included: Overseas Sec. and Med. Dir, Commonwealth Med. Adv. Bureau, 1967–72; Med. Dir, Career Service, 1967–76; Sec., Bd of Sci. and Educn, 1972–76 (Commonwealth Med. Assoc. meetings, Singapore/Malaysia, Jamaica, Ghana; Observer, Commonwealth Med. Conf., Mauritius, 1971); Jt Sec., Med. Sci. meetings, Vancouver, Jamaica, Dublin; Dep. Sec., Jt Consultants Cttee, 1976–79. Chm., Internat. Alliance on Child Abuse and Neglect, 1983–. Hon. Treas., Assoc. for Study of Med. Educn, 1975–80; Vice-Pres., Sect. Med. Educn, RSM, 1979–82. Liveryman, Worshipful Soc. of Apothecaries of London, 1973–. *Publications:* various articles on child abuse and on med. educn, careers in medicine, gen. practice; ed or ed jtly, Care of the Elderly, Primary Health Care Teams, Competence to Practise, and other reports. *Recreations:* gardening, homecare, walking, music. *Address:* NSPCC, 67 Saffron Hill, EC1N 8RS. *T:* 01-242 1626.

GILMOUR, Alexander Clement; Director, Tide (UK) Ltd, since 1986; *b* 23 Aug. 1931; *s* of Sir John Little Gilmour, 2nd Bt, and of Lady Mary Gilmour; *m* 1954, Barbara M. L. Constance Berry; two *s* one *d*; *m* 1983, Susan Lady Chetwode. *Educ:* Eton. National Service, commn in Black Watch, 1950–52. With Joseph Sebag & Co. (subseq. Carr, Sebag), 1954–82; Dir, Safeguard Industrial Investments, 1974–84; Exec. Dir, Equity Finance Trust Ltd, 1984–86. Chm., Gilmour & Associates Ltd, 1983–84; Consultant, Grieveson Grant, 1982. Chm., Nat. Playing Fields Assoc., 1976– (Past-Chm. Appeals Cttee, 10 yrs). Governor, LSE, 1969–. *Recreations:* tennis, skiing, fishing, gardening, golf. *Address:* Knighton Farm House, Ramsbury, Wilts SN8 2QB. *Clubs:* White's; Hon. Company of Edinburgh Golfers.

See also Rt Hon. Sir Ian Gilmour, Bt.

GILMOUR, Colonel Allan Macdonald, OBE 1961; MC 1942, and Bar 1943; Lord-Lieutenant of Sutherland, since 1972; Member: Sutherland District Council, since 1975; Highland Regional Council, since 1977; *b* 23 Nov. 1916; *o s* of late Captain Allan Gilmour, of Rosehall, Sutherland, and late Mary H. M. Macdonald, of Viewfield, Portree, Skye; *m* 1941, Jean Wood; three *s* one *d. Educ:* Winchester Coll. Gazetted, The Seaforth Highlanders, Jan. 1939. Served War, in Middle East, France and Germany (despatches, 1945); DSC (USA) 1945. Staff Coll., 1946; Regimental and Staff Service in: Germany, Middle East, UK, Pakistan and Africa, 1946–67, incl. Instructor, Staff Coll., Quetta, on loan to Pakistan Army, 1952–54. Chief of Gen. Staff, Ghana Armed Forces, 1959–62; service in Congo, 1961–62; retired from Army, 1967. Chairman: Sutherland Council of Social Service, 1973–77; Highland Health Bd, 1981–83 (Mem., 1973–83). Chm., Sutherland District Council, 1975–77. Mem., Sutherland CC, 1970. DL Sutherland, 1971. *Recreations:* fishing, local government. *Address:* Invernauld, Rosehall, Lairg, Sutherland. *T:* Rosehall 204.

GILMOUR, Andrew, CMG 1949; Malayan Civil Service, retired; *b* 18 July 1898; *s* of late James Parlane Gilmour, Solicitor, Burntisland, and late Mima Simpson; *m* Nelle Twigg (*d* 1983); two *s* three *d* (and one *s* killed in action). *Educ:* Royal High Sch., Edinburgh; Edinburgh Univ. (MA Hons Classics, 1920). Served European War, Argyll and Sutherland Highlanders, 1915–17. Appointed to Malayan Civil Service, 1921; Asst Controller of Labour, 1923–26; Head of Preventive Service, Singapore, 1927; Resident, Labuan, 1928–29; District Officer, Jasin, 1929–30, Ulu Kelantan, 1930–36; Asst Colonial Sec., SS, 1936–38; Registrar-Gen. of Statistics, SS and FMS, 1938–39; Shipping Controller, Singapore, 1939–41; Defence Intelligence Officer, Hong Kong, Dec. 1941; interned Hong Kong 1942–45; Sec. for Economic Affairs, Singapore, 1946–52; Staff Grade, MCS, 1947; Chm. N Borneo Rubber Commn, 1949; MEC and MLC Singapore (nominated official); acted as Colonial Sec., Singapore, June-Aug. 1948 and March-April 1952; ret. from Colonial Service, 1953; Planning Economist, UN Technical Assistance Mission, Cambodia, 1953–55; Economic Survey Commissioner, British Honduras, 1956. Secretary: British European Assoc., Singapore, 1956–75; Tanglin Trust Ltd, 1961–75; Raeburn Park School Ltd, 1961–75; Editor, BEAM, 1959–75. *Publications:* My Role in the Rehabilitation of Singapore 1946–53, 1973; An Eastern Cadet's Anecdotage, 1974. *Recreations:* cricket (Hon. Life Pres., Singapore Cricket Club); philately (Patron, Singapore Stamp Club). *Address:* Garden Cottage, Gifford, East Lothian EH41 4JE. *T:* Gifford 604. *Clubs:* Royal Over-Seas League; Singapore Cricket (Hon. Life Pres.).

See also A. B. Gilmour.

GILMOUR, Rt. Hon. Sir Ian (Hedworth John Little), 3rd Bt *cr* 1926, of Liberton and Craigmillar; PC 1973; MP (C) Chesham and Amersham, since 1974 (Norfolk Central, Nov. 1962–1974); *b* 8 July 1926; *er s* of Lt-Col Sir John Little Gilmour, 2nd Bt, and of Hon. Victoria Laura, OBE, TD, *d* of late Viscount Chelsea (*e s* of 5th Earl Cadogan); *S* father, 1977; *m* 1951, Lady Caroline Margaret Montagu-Douglas-Scott, *yr d* of 8th Duke of Buccleuch and Queensberry, KT, GCVO, PC; four *s* one *d. Educ:* Eton; Balliol Coll., Oxford. Served with Grenadier Guards, 1944–47; 2nd Lieut 1945. Called to the Bar, Inner Temple, 1952. Editor, The Spectator, 1954–59. Parly Under-Sec. of State, MoD, 1970–71; Minister of State: for Defence Procurement, MoD, 1971–72; for Defence, 1972–74; Sec. of State for Defence, 1974; Lord Privy Seal, 1979–81. Chm., Cons. Res. Dept, 1974–75. *Publications:* The Body Politic, 1969; Inside Right: a study of Conservatism, 1977; Britain Can Work, 1983. *Heir: s* David Robert Gilmour [*b* 14 Nov. 1952; *m* 1975, Sarah Anne, *d* of M. H. G. Bradstock; one *s* three *d*]. *Address:* The Ferry House, Old Isleworth, Mddx. *T:* 01-560 6769. *Clubs:* Pratt's, White's.

See also A. C. Gilmour.

GILMOUR, Col Sir John (Edward), 3rd Bt, *cr* 1897; DSO 1945; TD; JP; Lord-Lieutenant of Fife, since 1980 (Vice Lord-Lieutenant, 1979–80); Lord High Commissioner, General Assembly of the Church of Scotland, 1982 and 1983; *b* 24 Oct. 1912; *o s* of Col Rt Hon. Sir John Gilmour, 2nd Bt, GCVO, DSO, MP, and Mary Louise (*d* 1919), *e d* of late E. T. Lambert, Telham Court, Battle, Sussex; *S* father, 1940; *m* 1941, Ursula Mabyn, *yr d* of late F. O. Wills; two *s. Educ:* Eton; Trinity Hall, Cambridge. Served War of 1939–45 (DSO). Bt Col 1950; Captain, Royal Company of Archers (Queen's Body Guard for Scotland); Hon. Col, The Highland Yeomanry, RAC, T&AVR, 1971–75. MP (C) East Fife, 1961–79. Chm., Cons. and Unionist Party in Scotland, 1965–67. DL Fife, 1953. *Heir: s* John Gilmour [*b* 15 July 1944; *m* 1967, Valerie, *yr d* of late G. W. Russell, and of Mrs William Wilson; two *s* two *d*]. *Address:* Montrave, Leven, Fife. *TA:* Leven. *T:* Leven 26159. *Clubs:* Cavalry and Guards, Royal and Ancient Golf (St Andrews).

See also Dame Anne Bryans, Viscount Younger.

GILPIN, Rt. Rev. William Percy; *b* 26 July 1902; *e s* of late Percy William and Ethel Annie Gilpin. *Educ:* King Edward's, Birmingham; Keble Coll., Oxford. BA 1st class, Theology, 1925; MA 1928. Curate of Solihull, Warwicks, 1925–28; Vice-Principal of St Paul's Coll., Burgh, 1928–30; Chaplain of Chichester Theological Coll., 1930–33; Vicar of Manaccan with St Anthony, 1933–36; Vicar of St Mary, Penzance, 1936–44; Dir of Religious Education, Gloucester, 1944–51; Canon Missioner of Gloucester, 1946–52; Archdeacon of Southwark, 1952–55; Bishop Suffragan of Kingston-upon-Thames, 1952–70. Examining Chaplain to: Bishop of Truro, 1934–44, Bishop of Gloucester, 1945–52. *Recreation:* general railway matters. *Address:* 50 Lower Broad Street, Ludlow, Shropshire SY8 1PH. *T:* Ludlow 3376.

GILROY BEVAN, David; *see* Bevan, A. D. G.

GILSENAN, Prof. Michael Dermot Cole; Khalid bin Abdullah al Saud Professor for the study of the contemporary Arab world, Oxford, since 1984; *b* 6 Feb. 1940; *s* of Michael Eugene Cole Gilsenan and Joyce Russell Horn. *Educ:* Eastbourne Grammar Sch.; Oxford Univ. BA (Oriental Studies), Dip. Anth., MA, DPhil (Soc. Anthropology). Research Fellow, Amer. Univ. in Cairo, 1964–66; Research studentship, St Antony's Coll., Oxford, 1966–67; Research Fellow, Harvard Middle East Center, 1967–68; Asst Prof., Dept of Anthropology, UCLA, 1968–70; Research Lectr, Univ. of Manchester, 1970–73; Associate Fellow, St Antony's Coll., Oxford, 1970–73; Lectr, 1973–78, Reader, 1978–83, Dept of Anthropology, University College London; Mem., Sch. of Social Sci., Inst. for Advanced Study, Princeton, 1979–80. Anthrop. field work, Egypt, 1964–66, Lebanon, 1971–72. Mem. Edtl Bds, Past and Present, and formerly of Man, and Internat. Jl of Middle Eastern Studies. *Publications:* Saint and Sufi in Modern Egypt, 1973; Recognizing Islam, 1982. *Recreations:* music, theatre, being elsewhere. *Address:* Magdalen College, Oxford. *T:* Oxford 241781.

GILSON, John Cary, CBE 1967 (OBE 1945); Director, Medical Research Council's Pneumoconiosis Research Unit, 1952–76; *b* 9 Aug. 1912; 2nd *s* of late Robert Cary Gilson, MA and late Marianne C. Gilson, MA (*née* Dunstall); *m* 1945, Margaret Evelyn Worthington, MA, *d* of late Robert A. Worthington, OBE, FRCS; two *s* one *d. Educ:* Haileybury Sch.; Gonville and Caius Coll., Cambridge. MB, BChir Cantab 1937; MRCP 1940; FRCP 1956; FFOM 1979. 1st Asst, London Hosp.; Staff of RAF Inst. of Aviation Medicine, 1940–46; Mem. Scientific Staff of MRC, 1946–76, at Pneumoconiosis Research Unit, Asst Ed., Brit. Jl Industr. Med., 1955–64, and on Ed. Bd of various other jls; Mem., Govt and internat. cttees on Pneumoconiosis and health hazards of asbestos; Pres., British Occupational Hygiene Soc., 1960–61; Pres., Occupational Medicine Section, RSM, 1968–69; Hon. Life Mem., NY Acad. of Sciences, 1966. *Publications:* papers on pulmonary physiology and industrial medicine in scientific jls. *Recreations:* domestic engineering; clouds. *Address:* Hembury Hill Farm, Honiton, Devon EX14 0LA. *T:* Broadhembury 203.

GILSON, Rev. Nigel Langley, DFC 1944; Chairman, Wolverhampton and Shrewsbury District, Methodist Church, since 1975; President of the Methodist Conference, June 1986–June 1987; *b* 11 April 1922; *s* of Clifford Edric and Cassandra Jeanette Gilson; *m* 1951, Mary Doreen (*née* Brown); four *d. Educ:* Holcombe Methodist Elementary; Midsomer Norton Co. Secondary; St Catherine's Soc., Oxford Univ. (MA Hons); Wesley House and Fitzwilliam House, Cambridge Univ. (BA Hons). Served RAF, 1941–45 (Navigator (Wireless) 107 Sqdn, 1944–45), Flying Officer. Methodist Minister: Tintagel, Cornwall, 1950–52; Newark-upon-Trent, 1952–58; Rhodesia Dist, 1958–67; Chaplain, Hunmanby Hall Sch., Filey, Yorks, 1967–71; Superintendent Minister, Oxford Circuit, 1971–75. *Recreations:* gardening, theatre, family, community and multi-cultural activities. *Address:* 53 York Avenue, Wolverhampton, West Midlands WV3 9BX. *T:* Wolverhampton 24430. *Club:* Royal Commonwealth Society.

GIMINGHAM, Prof. Charles Henry; FRSE 1961; Regius Professor of Botany, University of Aberdeen, since 1981 (Professor of Botany, since 1969); *b* 28 April 1923; *s* of late Conrad Theodore Gimingham and Muriel Elizabeth (*née* Blake), Harpenden; *m* 1948, Elizabeth Caroline, *o d* of late Rev. J. Wilson Baird, DD, Minister of St Machar's Cathedral, Aberdeen; three *d. Educ:* Gresham's Sch., Holt, Norfolk; Emmanuel Coll., Cambridge (Open scholarship; BA 1944; ScD 1977); PhD Aberdeen 1948. FIBiol 1967. Research Asst, Imperial Coll., Univ. of London, 1944–45; University of Aberdeen: Asst, 1946–48, Lectr, 1948–61, Sen. Lectr, 1961–64, Reader, 1964–69, Dept of Botany. Pres., British Ecological Soc., 1986–. Member: Countryside Commn for Scotland, 1980–; Bd of Management, Hill Farming Res. Organisation, 1981–; Council of Management, Macaulay Inst. for Soil Research, 1983–. Mem. Governing Body, Aberdeen Coll. of Educn, 1979–. *Publications:* Ecology of Heathlands, 1972; An Introduction to Heathland Ecology, 1975; papers, mainly in botanical and ecological jls. *Recreations:* hill walking, photography, foreign travel, history and culture of Japan. *Address:* 2 Carden Terrace, Aberdeen AB1 1US.

GIMSON, George Stanley, QC (Scotland) 1961; Sheriff Principal of Grampian, Highland and Islands, 1975–82; Chairman: Pensions Appeals Tribunals, Scotland, since 1971 (President, 1971–75); Medical Appeal Tribunals, since 1985; *b* 1915. *Educ:* High School of Glasgow; Glasgow Univ. Advocate, 1949; Standing Junior Counsel, Department of Agriculture for Scotland and Forestry Commission, 1956–61; Sheriff Principal of Aberdeen, Kincardine and Banff, 1972–74. Mem., Board of Management: Edinburgh Central Hosps, 1960–70 (Chm., 1964–70); Edinburgh Royal Victoria Hosps, 1970–74 (Vice-Chm.); Dir, Scottish Nat. Orchestra Soc. Ltd, 1962–80; Trustee, Nat. Library of Scotland, 1963–76; Chm., RSSPCC, Edinburgh, 1972–76. Hon. LLD Aberdeen, 1981. *Address:* 11 Royal Circus, Edinburgh EH3 6TL. *T:* 031-225 8055. *Clubs:* University Staff (Edinburgh); Royal Northern and University (Aberdeen).

GINGELL, Air Chief Marshal Sir John, GBE 1984 (CBE 1973; MBE 1962); KCB 1978; RAF, retired; Gentleman Usher of the Black Rod, Serjeant-at-Arms, House of Lords, and Secretary to the Lord Great Chamberlain, since 1985; *b* 3 Feb. 1925; *e s* of late E. J. Gingell; *m* 1949, Prudence, *d* of late Brig. R. F. Johnson; two *s* one *d. Educ:* St Boniface Coll., Plymouth. Entered RAF, 1943; Fleet Air Arm, 1945–46 as Sub-Lt (A) RNVR; returned to RAF, 1951; served with Nos 58 and 542 Sqdns; CFS 1954; psc 1959; jssc 1965; comd No 27 Sqdn, 1963–65; Staff of Chief of Defence Staff, 1966; Dep. Dir Defence Ops Staff (Central Staff), 1966–67; Mil. Asst to Chm. NATO Mil. Cttee, Brussels, 1968–70; AOA, RAF Germany, 1971–72; AOC 23 Group, RAF Trng Comd, 1973–75; Asst Chief of Defence Staff (Policy), 1975–78; Air Member for Personnel, 1978–80;

AOC-in-C, RAF Support Comd, 1980–81; Dep. C-in-C, Allied Forces Central Europe, 1981–84. Mem., Commonwealth War Graves Commn, 1986–. *Recreations:* ornithology, walking, music. *Address:* House of Lords, SW1A 0PW. *Club:* Royal Air Force.

GINGELL, Maj.-Gen. Laurie William Albert, CB 1980; OBE 1966; General Secretary, Officers' Pensions Society, since 1979; *b* 29 Oct. 1925; *s* of late William George Gingell and of Elsie Grace Gingell; *m* 1949, Nancy Margaret Wadsworth; one *s* one *d. Educ:* Farnborough Grammar Sch.; Oriel Coll., Oxford. Commissioned into Royal Gloucestershire Hussars, 1945; transf. Royal Tank Regt, 1947; psc 1956; jssc 1961; Commanded: 1st Royal Tank Regt, 1966–67; 7th Armoured Bde, 1970–71; DQMG, HQ BAOR, 1973–76; Maj.-Gen. Admin, HQ UKLF, 1976–79. ADC to the Queen, 1974–76. FBIM 1979. *Recreations:* golf, tennis, swimming, reading. *Address:* 54 Station Road, Thames Ditton, Surrey KT7 0NS. *T:* 01–398 4521. *Club:* Army and Navy.

GINGER, Phyllis Ethel, (Mrs Leslie Durbin), RWS 1958 (ARWS 1952); freelance artist since 1940; *b* 19 Oct. 1907; *m* 1940, Leslie Durbin, *qv*; one *s* one *d. Educ:* Tiffin's Girls' Sch., Kingston on Thames. LCC three years' scholarship at Central School of Arts and Crafts, 1937–39. Water colours for Pilgrim Trust Recording Britain Scheme, 1941–42; Royal Academy Exhibitor; Drawings and Lithographs purchased by: Washington State Library, 1941; Victoria and Albert Museum, 1952; London Museum, 1954; South London Art Gallery, 1960. *Publications:* Alexander the Circus Pony, 1941; book jacket designs; book illustrations include: London by Mrs Robert Henrey, 1948; The Virgin of Aldemanbury, by Mrs Robert Henrey, 1960. *Address:* 298 Kew Road, Kew, Richmond, Surrey. *T:* 01–940 2221.

GINGOLD, Hermione Ferdinanda; Actress; *b* 9 Dec.; *d* of James and Kate Gingold; *m* 1st, Michael Joseph (marr. diss.); one *s* (and one *s* decd); 2nd, Eric Maschwitz (marr. diss.). *Educ:* privately. Started as child actress at His Majesty's Theatre with Sir Herbert Tree in Pinkie and the Fairies. Played in Shakespeare at Old Vic and Stratford on Avon. Five years in intimate revue. O Dad, Poor Dad, Piccadilly, 1965; Highly Confidential, Cambridge, 1965; A Little Night Music, Majestic, New York, 1973, Adelphi, London, 1975; Side by Side by Sondheim, 1977–78. *Films:* Bell, Book and Candle, 1958; Gigi, 1959; Jules Verne's Rocket to the Moon, 1967; A Little Night Music. Many US television appearances. Has recorded Façade and Lysistrata. *Publications:* The World is Square: my own unaided work, 1945; Sirens should be Seen and Not Heard, 1963; articles and short stories. *Address:* 405 East 54th Street, New York, NY 10022, USA.

GINSBURG, David; company director; economic, marketing and market research consultant; broadcaster; *b* 18 March 1921; *o s* of late N. Ginsburg; *m* 1954, Louise, *er d* of late S. P. Cassy. *Educ:* University Coll. Sch.; Balliol Coll., Oxford. Chm. OU Democratic Socialist Club, 1941; 2nd Cl, Hons Sch. of Politics, Philosophy and Economics, 1941. Commissioned Oxford and Bucks LI, 1942; Capt. Intelligence duties, 1944–45. Senior Research Officer, Govt Social Survey, 1946–52; Sec. of Research Dept of Labour Party and Sec. of Home Policy Sub-Cttee of National Executive Cttee, 1952–59. MP Dewsbury, 1959–83 (Lab, 1959–81, SDP, 1981–83). Chm., Parly and Scientific Cttee, 1968–71 (Life Mem., 1984); Mem., Select Cttee, Parly Comr for Admin, 1982–83. Contested (SDP) Dewsbury, 1983. FRSM 1986. *Publications:* miscellaneous articles and book reviews in contemporary publications. *Recreations:* walking, swimming, opera. *Address:* 3 Bell Moor, East Heath Road, NW3. *Club:* Reform.

GINSBURY, Norman; playwright; *b* Nov. 1902; *s* of late J. S. and Rachel Cecily Ginsbury; *m* 1945, Dorothy Jennings. *Educ:* Grocers' Co. Sch.; London University (BSc (Hons)). Plays produced: Viceroy Sarah, Arts Theatre, 1934, Whitehall Theatre, 1935; Walk in the Sun, "Q", and Embassy, 1939; Take Back Your Freedom (with late Winifred Holtby), Neighbourhood, 1940; The Firstcomers, Bradford Civic Playhouse, 1944; The First Gentleman (written, 1935), New and Savoy, 1945; Belasco, New York, 1956; The Gambler (from the story of Dostoievsky), Embassy, 1946; The Happy Man, New, 1948; Portrait by Lawrence (with M. Moiseiwitsch), Theatre Royal, Stratford, 1949; School for Rivals, Bath Assembly and Old Vic, Bristol, 1949. Also following adaptations of plays by Henrik Ibsen: Ghosts, Vaudeville, 1937; Enemy of the People, Old Vic, 1939; Peer Gynt, Old Vic Season at New Theatre, 1944; A Doll's House, Winter Garden, 1946; John Gabriel Borkman, Mermaid, 1961. A new version of Strindberg's Dance of Death at Tyrone Guthrie Theatre, Minneapolis; and at Yvonne Arnaud Theatre, Guildford, 1966; for the Mayflower 350th anniv., The Forefathers, Athenaeum Theatre, Plymouth, 1970; The Wisest Fool, Yvonne Arnaud, 1974. *Publications:* Viceroy Sarah, 1934; Take Back Your Freedom (collab.), 1939; The First Gentleman, 1946; and the following versions of plays by Ibsen: Ghosts, 1938; Enemy of the People, 1939; Peer Gynt, 1945; A Doll's House, 1950; John Gabriel Borkman, 1960; Rosmersholm, 1961; Pillars of Society, 1962. The Old Lags' League (from a story by W. Pett Ridge), in The Best One-Act Plays of 1960–61; version of Dance of Death by Strindberg in Plays of the Year, 1966; The Shoemaker And The Devil (from a story by Tchehov), in The Best Short Plays of 1968 (NY); The Safety Match (from a story by Tchehov), in Best Short Plays of the World Theatre 1968–73 (NY). *Address:* 10 Bramber House, Michel Grove, Eastbourne, East Sussex BN21 1LA. *T:* Eastbourne 29603. *Club:* Dramatists'.

GIOLITTI, Dr Antonio; Member, Commission of the European Communities, 1977–84; *b* 12 Feb. 1915; *s* of Giuseppe and Maria Giolitti; *m* 1939, Elena d'Amico; one *s* two *d. Educ:* Rome Univ. (Dr Law); Oxford; München. Mem. Italian Parlt, 1946–77; Minister of Budget and Economic Planning, 1964, 1970–72, 1973–74. Member: Italian Communist Party, 1943–57; Italian Socialist Party, 1958–; Exec., Italian Socialist Party, 1958–. *Publications:* Riforme e rivoluzione, 1957; Il comunismo in Europa, 1960; Un socialismo possibile, 1967. *Recreations:* music, walking. *Address:* Camera dei Deputati, Rome, Italy.

GIORDANO, Richard Vincent; Chairman, since 1985, and Chief Executive Officer, since 1979, The BOC Group; *b* March 1934; *s* of late Vincent Giordano and of Cynthia Giordano; *m* 1956, Barbara Claire Beckett; one *s* two *d. Educ:* Harvard Coll., Cambridge, Mass, USA (BA); Columbia Univ. Law Sch. (LLB). Shearman & Sterling, 1959; Airco, Inc., 1964–78: Gp Vice Pres., 1967; Gp Pres., Chief Operating Officer and Mem. Bd, 1971; Dir, BOC Internat. Ltd, 1974; Chief Exec. Officer, Airco, Inc., 1978; Gp Man. Dir, BOC, 1979–85. Mem., CEGB, 1982–; part-time Mem. Bd, Georgia Pacific Corp., Atlanta, Ga, 1984–; Bd Mem., Grand Metropolitan plc, 1985–. Hon. Dr of Commercial Science, St John's Univ., 1975. *Recreations:* ocean sailing, tennis. *Address:* c/o The BOC Group plc, Chertsey Road, Windlesham, Surrey GU20 6HJ. *T:* Bagshot 77222. *Clubs:* The Links, New York Yacht (New York), Edgartown Yacht (Mass); Duquesne (Pittsburgh, Pa).

GIPPSLAND, Bishop of, since 1980; **Rt. Rev. Neville James Chynoweth,** ED 1966; *b* 3 Oct. 1922; *s* of Percy James and Lilian Chynoweth; *m* 1951, Joan Laurice Wilson; two *s* two *d. Educ:* Manly High School; Sydney Univ. (MA); Melbourne Coll. of Divinity (BD); Moore Theological Coll. (ThL). Assistant, St Michael's, Sydney, 1950; Rector, Kangaroo Valley, 1951–52; Chaplain, Royal Prince Alfred Hospital, 1952–54; Rector: St John's, Deewhy, 1954–63; St Anne's, Strathfield, 1963–66; All Saints, Canberra, 1966–71; St Paul's, Canberra, 1971–74; Archdeacon of Canberra, 1973–74; Assistant Bishop of Canberra and Goulburn, 1974–80. *Recreations:* music, biography. *Address:* Bishopscourt, Sale, Victoria 3850, Australia. *T:* 051–44:2046. *Clubs:* Royal Commonwealth Society; Sale (Sale, Vic.), Savage (Melbourne).

GIRDWOOD, Ronald Haxton, CBE 1984; MD, PhD, FRCP, FRCPE, FRCPI, FRCPath; FRSE 1978; President, Royal College of Physicians of Edinburgh, 1982–85; *b* 19 March 1917; *s* of late Thomas Girdwood; *m* 1945, Mary Elizabeth, *d* of late Reginald Williams, Calstock, Cornwall; one *s* one *d. Educ:* Daniel Stewart's Coll., Edinburgh; University of Edinburgh; University of Michigan. MB, ChB (Hons) Edinburgh 1939; Ettles Schol., Leslie Gold Medallist, Royal Victoria Hosp.; Tuberculosis Trust Gold Medallist, Wightman, Beaney and Keith Memorial Prize Winner, 1939; MD (Gold Medal for thesis), 1954. Pres. Edinburgh Univ. Church of Scotland Soc., 1938–39. Served RAMC, 1942–46 (mentioned in Orders); Nutrition Research Officer and Officer i/c Med. Div. in India and Burma. Lectr in Medicine, University of Edinburgh, 1946; Rockefeller Research Fellow, University of Michigan, 1948–49; Cons. Phys., Chalmers Hosp., Edinburgh, 1950–51; Sen. Lectr in Med. and Cons. Phys., Royal Infirmary, 1951; Vis. Lectr, Dept of Pharmacology, Yale Univ., 1956; Reader in Med., University of Edinburgh, 1958; Dean of Faculty of Medicine, Edinburgh Univ., 1975–79; Prof. of Therapeutics and Clinical Pharmacology, Univ. of Edinburgh, 1962–82, Emeritus 1982; Consultant Physician, Royal Infirmary of Edinburgh, 1951–82. Examiner for RCPE; sometime External Examiner for Universities of London, Sheffield, St Andrews, Dundee, Dublin, Glasgow and Hong Kong, and for Med. Colls in Singapore, Dhaka and Karachi; Chm., Scottish National Blood Transfusion Assoc.; Mem. Council, RCPE, 1966–70, 1978–80, Vice-Pres., 1981–82, Pres. 1982–85; Member: South-Eastern Reg. Hosp. Board (Scotland), 1965–69; Board of Management, Royal Infirmary, Edinburgh, 1958–64; Cttee on Safety of Medicines, 1972–83; Exec., Medico-Pharmaceutical Forum, 1972–74 (Vice-Chm., 1983–85; Chm., 1985–); Chairman: Scottish Group of Hæmophilia Soc., 1954–60; Non-Professional Medical Teachers and Research Workers Gp Cttee (Scot.) of BMA, 1956–62; Scottish Gp of Nutrition Soc., 1961–62; Consultative Council, Edinburgh Medical Gp, 1977–82; Pres. Brit. Soc. for Hæmatology, 1963–64; Member: Coun. Brit. Soc. of Gastroenterology, 1964–68; Council of Nutrition Soc., 1957–60 and 1961–64; numerous Med. Socs; former Chm., Bd of Management, Scottish Med. Jl and Mem. of Editorial Bds of Blood and of Brit. Jl of Haematology; Mem. Editorial Bd, Brit. Jl of Nutrition, 1960–65; British Council visitor to W African Hosps, 1963, to Middle East, 1977, to India, 1980; Visiting Prof. and WHO Consultant, India, 1965, Pakistan, 1985. Gov., St Columba's Hospice, 1985–. Awarded Freedom of the township of Sirajgunj, Bangladesh, 1984. Hon. FACP 1983; Hon. FRACP 1985. Cullen Prize, 1970, Lilly Lectr, 1979, RCPE; Suniti Panja gold medal, Calcutta Sch. Trop. Med., 1980. *Publications:* about 300, particularly in relation to nutrition, hæmatology, gastroenterology and medical history; (ed with A. N. Smith) Malabsorption, 1969; (ed) Blood Disorders due to Drugs and Other Agents, 1973; contrib. Davidson's Principles and Practice of Medicine, all edns 1952–81; (ed with S. Alstead) Textbook of Medical Treatment, 12th edn 1971 to 14th edn 1978; (ed) Clinical Pharmacology, 23rd edn 1976, 25th edn 1984. *Recreations:* photography, painting. *Address:* 2 Hermitage Drive, Edinburgh EH10 6DD. *T:* (home) 031–447 5137. *Clubs:* East India, Devonshire, Sports and Public Schools; University Staff (Edinburgh).

GIRLING, Maj.-Gen. Peter Howard, CB 1972; OBE 1961; CEng, FIMechE, FIEE, FIERE; Director of Operations, Open University, 1972–80; *b* 18 May 1915; *m* 1942, Stella Muriel (*née* Hope); two *d.* Commissioned, RAOC, 1939; transferred to REME, 1942; served War of 1939–45; India, 1945–47; Staff Coll., Camberley, 1948; Egypt, 1949–52; JSSC, Latimer, 1953; BAOR, 1953–55; Col, 1961; WO, 1961–65; HQ FARELF 1965–67; Brig., 1965; Comd Berkshire Sub-District, 1967–68; Comdt, REME Training Centre, 1967–69; Maj.-Gen., 1969; Dir of Electrical and Mechanical Engineering (Army), 1969–72; Col Comdt, REME, 1972–77. Freeman of City of London, 1973; Liveryman, Turners' Co., 1973–. Hon. MA Open Univ., 1982. *Address:* The Folly, Wicken, Northants. *T:* Wicken 204. *Club:* Army and Navy.

GIROLAMI, Paul, FCA; Chairman, Glaxo Holdings, since 1985 (Chief Executive, 1980–86); *b* 25 Jan. 1926; *m* 1952, Christabel Mary Gwynne Lewis; two *s* one *d. Educ:* London School of Economics. Chantrey & Button, Chartered Accountants, 1950–54; Coopers & Lybrand, Chartered Accountants, 1954–65; Glaxo Holdings: Financial Controller, 1965; Finance Director, 1968; Chief Exec., 1980. Director, Inner London Board of National Westminster Bank, 1974–. Liveryman and Mem., Ct of Assistants, Goldsmiths' Co., 1980–. *Recreations:* reading, golf.

GIROUARD, Mark, PhD; writer and architectural historian; Slade Professor of Fine Art, University of Oxford, 1975–76; *b* 7 Oct. 1931; *s* of Richard D. Girouard and Lady Blanche Girouard; *m* 1970, Dorothy N. Dorf; one *d. Educ:* Ampleforth; Christ Church, Oxford (MA); Courtauld Inst. of Art (PhD); Bartlett Sch., UCL (BSc, Dip. Arc). Staff of Country Life, 1958–66; studied architecture, Bartlett Sch., UCL, 1966–71; staff of Architectural Review, 1971–75. Member: Council, Victorian Soc., 1979– (Founder Mem. 1958; Mem. Cttee, 1958–66); Royal Fine Art Commn, 1972–; Royal Commn on Historical Monuments (England), 1976–81; Historic Buildings Council (England), 1978–84; Commn for Historic Buildings and Monuments, 1984– (Mem., Buildings Adv. Cttee, 1984; Mem., Historic Area Grants Cttee, 1986); Chm., Spitalfields Historic Buildings Trust, 1977–83. Hon. FRIBA, 1980. Hon. DLitt Leicester, 1982. *Publications:* Robert Smythson and the Architecture of the Elizabethan Era, 1966, 2nd edn, Robert Smythson and the Elizabethan Country House, 1983; The Victorian Country House, 1971, 2nd edn 1979; Victorian Pubs, 1975, 2nd edn 1984; (jtly) Spirit of the Age, 1975 (based on BBC TV series); Sweetness and Light: the 'Queen Anne' movement 1860–1900, 1977; Life in the English Country House, 1978 (Duff Cooper Meml Prize; W. H. Smith Award, 1979); Historic Houses of Britain, 1979; Alfred Waterhouse and the Natural History Museum, 1981; The Return to Camelot: chivalry and the English gentleman, 1981; Cities and People, 1985; articles in Country Life, Architect. Rev., Listener. *Address:* 35 Colville Road, W11. *Club:* Beefsteak.

GISBOROUGH, 3rd Baron, *cr* 1917; **Thomas Richard John Long Chaloner,** JP; Lord-Lieutenant of Cleveland, since 1981; *b* 1 July 1927; *s* of 2nd Baron and Esther Isabella Madeleine (*d* 1970), *yr d* of late Charles O. Hall, Eddlethorpe; *S* father 1951; *m* 1960, Shane, *e d* of late Sidney Newton, London, and *g d* of Sir Louis Newton, 1st Bt; two *s. Educ:* Eton. 16th/5th Lancers, 1948–52; Captain Northumberland Hussars, 1955–61; Lt-Col Green Howards (Territorials), 1967–69. Mem., Develt Commn, 1985–. CC NR Yorks, 1964–74, Cleveland, 1974–77. Hon. Col, Cleveland County Army Cadet Force, 1981. DL N Riding of Yorks and Cleveland, 1973; JP Langbaurgh East, 1981–. KStJ 1981. *Heir: s* Hon. Thomas Peregrine Long Chaloner, *b* 17 Jan. 1961. *Address:* Gisborough House, Guisborough, Cleveland. *T:* Guisborough 32002. *Club:* Northern Counties (Newcastle upon Tyne).

GISCARD d'ESTAING, Valéry; Grand Croix de la Légion d'Honneur; Croix de Guerre (1939–45); President of the French Republic, 1974–81; Deputy for Clermont, French National Assembly, since 1986; Member from Chamalières, Conseil Général of Puy-de-Dôme, since 1982, re-elected 1984; *b* Coblence, 2 Feb. 1926; *s* of late Edmond Giscard d'Estaing and May Bardoux; *m* 1952, Anne-Aymone de Brantes; two *s* two *d. Educ:* Lycée Janson-de-Sailly, Paris; Ecole Polytechnique; Ecole Nationale d'Administration. Inspection of Finances: Deputy, 1952; Inspector, 1954; Dep. Dir, Cabinet of Président du Conseil, June-Dec. 1954. Elected Deputy for Puy-de-Dôme, 1956; re-elected for Clermont N and SW, Nov. 1958, Nov-Dec. 1962, March 1967, June 1968 and March 1973; Sec. of State for Finance, 1959; Minister of Finance, Jan.-April 1962; Minister of Finance and Economic Affairs, April-Nov. 1962 and Dec. 1962–Jan. 1966; Minister of Economy and Finance, 1969–74. Pres., Nat. Fedn of Indep. Republicans, 1966–73 (also a Founder); Pres., comm. des finances de l'économie générale et du plan de l'Assemblée nationale, 1967–68. Mayor of Chamalières, 1967–74. Deleg. to Assembly of UN, 1956, 1957, 1958. Nansen Medal, 1979. *Publication*. Démocratie Française, 1976 (Towards a New Democracy, 1977); 2 Français sur 3, 1984. *Address:* 11 rue Bénouville, 75116 Paris, France. *Club:* Polo (Paris).

GISH, Lillian Diana; Actress; *b* 14 Oct. 1899. *Educ:* privately. Began acting in theatre at five years of age and at twelve entered motion pictures. Katrina in Crime and Punishment (with John Gielgud), 1948, Ophelia in Hamlet (with John Gielgud), The Curious Savage, 1950, Miss Mabel, 1951 (USA). Acting mainly on television, 1952; in play, The Trip to Bountiful (for the Theatre Guild), 1953–54; The Chalk Garden, 1957; The Family Reunion, 1958; directed, The Beggar's Opera, 1958; All the Way House, 1960–61 (won Drama Critics and Pulitzer prize as best play); A Passage to India, play (Chicago), 1962–63; Too True to be Good (G. B. Shaw's play) (New York), 1963; Romeo and Juliet (Stratford Festival Theatre), 1965; Anya (musical), 1967; I Never Sang for my Father, 1968; Uncle Vanya, NY, 1973; A Musical Jubilee (musical), NY, 1975. Lillian Gish and the Movies: the art of film, 1900–28 (concert programmes), Moscow, Paris, London and USA, 1969–73, QE2 World tour, 1975; lecturing and performing for The Theatre Guild at Sea on the Rotterdam, 1975; Celebration, Metropolitan Opera 100th Gala Benefit (Spectre de la Rose, with Patrick DuPond), 1984. *Early films include:* Birth of a Nation; Intolerance; Souls Triumphant; Hearts of the World; The Great Love; Broken Blossoms; Way Down East; The Orphans of the Storm; The White Sister; Romola; The Wind; *later films include:* The Night of the Hunter, 1954; The Cobweb, 1955; Orders to Kill, 1957; The Unforgiven, 1959; Follow Me Boys, 1966; Warning Shot, 1966; The Comedians, 1967; A Wedding, 1978; Hambone and Hillie, 1984; Sweet Liberty, 1985. *Television:* frequent appearances include three plays, 1962; plays, 1963; Arsenic and Old Lace, 1969; Sparrow, CBS, 1978; Love Boat, and Thin Ice, CBS, 1980. Film Life, documentary by Jeanne Moreau; Hommage à Lillian Gish (ballet by Catherine Berge), France, 1984. Hon. AFD, Rollins Coll., Fla; Hon. HHD, Holyoke Coll.; Hon. Dr of Performing Arts, Bowling Green State Univ., Ohio, 1976. Hon. Oscar, Acad. Motion Picture Arts and Scis, 1971; Life Achievement Award, AFI, 1984; Handel Medallion, NYC, 1973; Medal of Arts and Letters (France), 1983. *Publications:* Lillian Gish: an autobiography, 1968; Lillian Gish, The Movies, Mr Griffith and Me, 1969; Dorothy and Lillian Gish, 1973. *Recreation:* travel. *Address:* 430 East 57th Street, New York, NY 10022, USA.

GITTINGS, Robert (William Victor), CBE 1970; LittD Cantab, 1970; poet; biographer; playwright; *b* 1 Feb. 1911; *s* of late Surg.-Capt. Fred Claude Bromley Gittings, RN (retd) and late Dora Mary Brayshaw; *m* 1st, 1934, Katherine Edith Cambell (marr. diss.); two *s*; 2nd, 1949, Joan Grenville Manton; one *d*. *Educ:* St Edward's Sch., Oxford; Jesus Coll., Cambridge (Scholar). 1st Cl. Historical Tripos, 1933. Research Student, and Research Fellow, 1933–38, Supervisor in History, 1938–40, Hon. Fellow, 1979, Jesus Coll., Cambridge, Leslie Stephen Lectr, 1980; writer and producer for broadcasting, 1940–63; Professor: Vanderbilt University, Tennessee, 1966; Boston Univ., 1970; Univ. of Washington, 1972, 1974 and 1977 (Danz Lectr); Meiji Univ., Tokyo, 1985. Hon. LittD Leeds, 1981. *Publications: poetry and verse-plays:* The Roman Road, 1932; The Story of Psyche, 1936; Wentworth Place, 1950; The Makers of Violence (Canterbury Festival), 1951; Through a Glass Lightly, 1952; Famous Meeting, 1953; Out of This Wood (sequence of plays), 1955; This Tower My Prison, 1961; Matters of Love and Death, 1968; Conflict at Canterbury, 1970; American Journey, 1972; Collected Poems, 1976; People, Places, Personal, 1985; *biography and criticism:* John Keats: The Living Year, 1954; The Mask of Keats, 1956; Shakespeare's Rival, 1960; (ed) The Living Shakespeare, 1960; (ed with E. Hardy) Some Recollections by Emma Hardy, 1961; (with Jo Manton) The Story of John Keats, 1962; The Keats Inheritance, 1964; (ed) Selected Poems and Letters of John Keats, 1966; John Keats, 1968 (W. H. Smith Literary Award, 1969); John Keats: Selected Letters, 1970; The Odes of Keats, 1970; Young Thomas Hardy, 1975 (Christian Gauss Award, Phi Beta Kappa, 1975); The Older Hardy, 1978 (RSL Heinemann Award, 1979, James Tait Black Meml Prize, 1979); The Nature of Biography, 1978; (with Jo Manton) The Second Mrs Hardy, 1979; (ed with J. Reeves) Selected Poems of Thomas Hardy, 1981; (with Jo Manton) Dorothy Wordsworth, 1985; contrib. to Keats-Shelley Memorial Bulletin, Keats-Shelley Journal, Harvard Library Bulletin, etc. *Recreations:* outdoor pursuits except blood-sports. *Address:* The Stables, East Dean, Chichester, West Sussex. *T:* Singleton 328.

GIULINI, Carlo Maria; conductor; Music Director, Los Angeles Philharmonic Orchestra, 1978–84; *b* 9 May 1914; *m*; three *s*. *Educ:* Accademia Santa Cecilia, Rome. Début as conductor, Rome, 1944; formed Orchestra of Milan Radio, 1950; Principal Conductor, La Scala, Milan, 1953–55; début in Great Britain, conducting Verdi's Falstaff, Edinburgh Festival, 1955; closely associated with Philharmonia Orchestra, 1955–; début at Royal Opera House, Covent Garden, Don Carlos, 1958; Principal Guest Conductor, Chicago Symphony Orch., 1969–78; Music Dir, Vienna Symphony Orch., 1973–76; Music Dir, Los Angeles Philharmonic Orch., 1978–84; conducted new prodn of Falstaff in Los Angeles and at Covent Garden, 1982, after 14 year absence from opera (co-prodn by LA Philharmonic, Covent Garden and Teatro Comunale). Hon. Mem., Gesell. der Musikfreunde, Vienna, 1978; Hon. DHL DePaul Univ., Chicago, 1979. Gold Medal: Bruckner Soc., 1978; International Mahler Society; Una Vita Nella Musica. *Recreation:* sailing. *Address:* c/o Robert Leslie, 53 Bedford Road, SW4.

GIVEN, Edward Ferguson, CMG 1968; CVO 1979; HM Diplomatic Service, retired; *b* 13 April 1919; *s* of James K. Given, West Kilbride, Ayrshire; *m* 1st, 1946, Philida Naomi Bullwinkle; one *s*; 2nd, 1954, Kathleen Margaret Helena Kelly. *Educ:* Sutton County Sch.; University Coll., London. Served RA, 1939–46. Entered HM Foreign Service, 1946; served at Paris, Rangoon, Bahrain, Bordeaux, Office of Political Adviser to C-in-C Far East, Singapore, Moscow, Beirut; Ambassador: United Republic of Cameroon and Republic of Equatorial Guinea, 1972–75; Bahrain, 1975–79, retired, 1979. Dir-Gen., Middle East Assoc., 1979–83. *Recreation:* sailing. *Address:* 10 Clarendon Park, Lymington, Hants SO41 8AX. *Club:* Army and Navy.

GIVEN, Rear-Adm. John Garnett Cranston, CB 1955; CBE 1945 (OBE 1943); MIMechE, MIMarE; retired from Royal Navy, June 1955; *b* 21 Sept. 1902; *s* of late J. C. M. Given, MD, FRCP, and Mrs May Given, Liverpool; *m* 1931, Elizabeth Joyce (*née* Payne) (*d* 1985), Brenchley, Kent, and Durban, Natal; one *s* two *d*. *Educ:* King William's Coll., IOM; Charterhouse, Godalming. RNEC Keyham, 1922–25; HMS Hood, 1926; RNC Greenwich, 1928; Admiralty, 1930; HMS Berwick, China Station, 1933; HMS Neptune, 1940; Admiralty, 1942; HMS Howe, East Indies, 1944; Fleet Train, British Pacific Fleet, 1945; Asst Engineer-in-Chief, Admiralty, 1947; Commanding Officer Royal Naval Engineering Coll., Plymouth, 1948–51; idc 1952; Staff of Comdr-in-Chief, The Nore, 1953–55; Managing Dir, Parsons Marine Turbine Co., Wallsend, 1955–62. *Recreations:* fishing and walking. *Address:* c/o National Westminster Bank, 26 The Haymarket, SW1.

GIVENS, Willie Alan; Liberian Ambassador to the Court of St James's, since 1985; *b* 27 Aug. 1938; *s* of Isaac and Frances Givens; *m* 1963, Marion Cooper; one *s* three *d*. *Educ:* Regent Street Polytechnic (journalism); Morgan State University, USA (sociology, anthropology). Ministry of Information, Liberia, 1964–67; Afro-American newspapers, Baltimore, USA, 1968–73; Dir, Culture Center, Cape Mount, Liberia, 1974–76; Press Sec. to President of Liberia, 1977–80; Dep. Minister of State for Public Affairs, Exec. Mansion, 1980–85. Grand Band, Order of Star of Africa (Liberia), 1985; Order of the Republic (Sudan), 1982; Diplomatic Service Merit (Republic of Korea), 1983. *Recreation:* listening to music. *Address:* 176 Coombe Lane West, Kingston-upon-Thames, Surrey. *T:* 01–589 9405.

GLADSTONE, David Arthur Steuart; HM Diplomatic Service; Consul-General, Marseilles, since 1983; *b* 1 April 1935; *s* of Thomas Steuart Gladstone and Muriel Irene Heron Gladstone; *m* 1961, April (*née* Brunner); one *s* one *d*. *Educ:* Eton; Christ Church, Oxford (MA History). National Service, 1954–56; Oxford Univ., 1956–59. Annan, Dexter & Co. (Chartered Accountants), 1959–60; FO, 1960; MECAS, Lebanon, 1960–62; Bahrain, 1962–63; FO, 1963–65; Bonn, 1965–69; FCO, 1969–72; Cairo, 1972–75; British Mil. Govt, Berlin, 1976–79; Head of Western European Dept, FCO, 1979–82. *Recreations:* squash, tennis, music, theatre, cinema, dreaming, carpentry, gardening. *Address:* 2 Mountfort Terrace, N1 1JJ. *T:* 01–607 8200.

GLADSTONE, Sir (Erskine) William, 7th Bt *cr* 1846; JP; Lord-Lieutenant of Clwyd, since 1985; *b* 29 Oct. 1925; *s* of Charles Andrew Gladstone, (6th Bt), and Isla Margaret, *d* of late Sir Walter Erskine Crum; *S* father, 1968; *m* 1962, Rosamund Anne, *yr d* of late Major A. Hambro; two *s* one *d*. *Educ:* Eton; Christ Church, Oxford. Served RNVR, 1943–46. Asst Master at Shrewsbury, 1949–50, and at Eton, 1951–61; Head Master of Lancing Coll., 1961–69. Chief Scout of UK and Overseas Branches, 1972–82; Mem., World Scout Cttee, 1977–83 (Chm., 1979–81). DL Flintshire, 1969, Clwyd, 1974, Vice Lord-Lieut, 1984; Alderman, Flintshire CC, 1970–74. Chm., Rep. Body of Church in Wales 1977–; Chm., Council of Glenalmond Coll. (formerly Trinity Coll., Glenalmond), 1982–86. JP Clwyd 1982. *Publications:* various school textbooks. *Recreations:* reading history, watercolours, shooting, gardening. *Heir:* *s* Charles Angus Gladstone, *b* 11 April 1964. *Address:* Hawarden Castle, Clwyd CH5 3PB. *T:* Hawarden 532210; Fasque, Laurencekirk, Kincardineshire AB3 1DJ. *T:* Fettercairn 341.

GLADSTONE, Sir William; *see* Gladstone, Sir E. W.

GLADWIN, Derek Oliver, CBE 1979 (OBE 1977); JP; Regional Secretary (Southern Region), General and Municipal Workers' Union, since 1970; Member: Post Office Board (formerly Post Office Corporation), since 1972; British Aerospace, since 1977; *b* 6 June 1930; *s* of Albert Victor Gladwin and Ethel Gladwin (*née* Oliver); *m* 1956, Ruth Ann Pinion; one *s*. *Educ:* Carr Lane Junior Sch., Grimsby; Wintringham Grammar Sch.; Ruskin Coll., Oxford; London Sch. of Economics. British Railways, Grimsby, 1946–52; fishing industry, Grimsby, 1952–56; Regional Officer 1956–63, Nat. Industrial Officer 1963–70, Gen. and Municipal Workers' Union. Chm., Labour Party's Conf. Arrangements Cttee. Trustee, Duke of Edinburgh's Commonwealth Study Conf. (UK Fund); Chm., Governing Council, Ruskin Coll., Oxford, 1979–. Vis. Fellow, Nuffield Coll., Oxford, 1978–86. JP Surrey, 1969. *Address:* 2 Friars Rise, Ashwood Road, Woking, Surrey; (office) Cooper House, 205 Hook Road, Chessington, Surrey KT9 1EP. *T:* 01–397 8881.

GLADWYN, 1st Baron *cr* 1960; **Hubert Miles Gladwyn Jebb,** GCMG 1954 (KCMG 1949; CMG 1942); GCVO 1957; CB 1947; Grand Croix de la Légion d'Honneur, 1957; Deputy Leader of Liberal Party in House of Lords, and Liberal Spokesman on foreign affairs and defence, since 1965; *b* 25 April 1900; *s* of late Sydney Jebb, Firbeck Hall, Yorks; *m* 1929, Cynthia, *d* of Sir Saxton Noble, 3rd Bart; one *s* two *d*. *Educ:* Eton; Magdalen Coll., Oxon. 1st in History, Oxford, 1922. Entered Diplomatic Service, 1924; served in Tehran, Rome, and Foreign Office; Private Sec. to Parliamentary Under-Sec. of State, 1929–31; Private Sec. to Permanent Under-Sec. of State, 1937–40; appointed to Ministry of Economic Warfare with temp. rank of Asst Under-Sec., Aug. 1940; Acting Counsellor in Foreign Office, 1941; Head of Reconstruction Dept, 1942; Counsellor, 1943, in that capacity attended the Conferences of Quebec, Cairo, Tehran, Dunbarton Oaks, Yalta, San Francisco and Potsdam. Executive Sec. of Preparatory Commission of the United Nations (Aug. 1945) with temp. rank of Minister; Acting Sec.-Gen. of UN, Feb. 1946; Deputy to Foreign Sec. on Conference of Foreign Ministers, March 1946; Assistant Under-Sec. of State and United Nations Adviser, 1946–47; UK rep. on Brussels Treaty Permanent Commission with personal rank of Ambassador, April 1948; Dep. Under-Sec., 1949–50; Permanent Representative of the UK to the United Nations, 1950–54; British Ambassador to France, 1954–60, retired. Mem., European Parlt, 1973–76 (Vice Pres., Political Cttee); contested (L) Suffolk, European Parlt, 1979. Pres., European Movement; former Pres., Atlantic Treaty Assoc.; Chm., Campaign for European Political Community; Mem., Parly Delegns to Council of Europe and WEU Assemblies, 1966–73. Governor, Atlantic Institute. Hon. DCL: Oxford; Syracuse, NY 1954; Essex 1974; Hon. Fellow Magdalen Coll. *Publications:* Is Tension Necessary?, 1959; Peaceful Co-existence, 1962; The European Idea, 1966; Half-way to 1984, 1967; De Gaulle's Europe, or, Why the General says No, 1969; Europe after de Gaulle, 1970; The Memoirs of Lord Gladwyn, 1972. *Recreations:* gardening, broadcasting, cooking, shooting and most other forms of sport. *Heir:* *s* Hon. Miles Alvery Gladwyn Jebb [*b* 3 March 1930. *Educ:* Eton and Oxford]. *Address:* Bramfield Hall, Halesworth, Suffolk. *T:* Bramfield 241; 62 Whitehall Court, SW1A 2EL. *T:* 01–930 3160. *Club:* Garrick.

See also Baron Thomas of Swynnerton.

GLAMANN, Prof. Kristof, OBE 1985; Hon. FBA 1985; President, Carlsberg Foundation, since 1976 (Director, since 1969); Chairman, United Breweries Ltd, since 1977 (Director, since 1970); *b* 26 Aug. 1923; *s* of Kai Kristof Glamann, bank manager, and Ebba Henriette Louise (*née* Madsen); *m* 1954, Kirsten Lise (*née* Jantzen), MA, lecturer; two *s*. *Educ:* Odense Katedral-skole; Univ. of Copenhagen (MA Hist. 1948, PhD Econ. Hist., 1958). Univ. of Copenhagen: Research Fellow, 1948–56; Associated Prof., 1956–60; Prof. of History, 1960–80. Visiting Professor: Pennsylvania, 1960; Wisconsin, 1961; LSE 1964; Vis. Overseas Fellow, Churchill Coll., Cambridge, 1971–72; Toho Gakkai, Japan, 1977; Master, 4th May and Hassager Coll., Copenhagen, 1961–81. Chm., Scand. Inst. of Asian Studies, 1967–71; Hon. Pres., Internat. Econ. Hist. Assoc., 1974 (Pres., 1970–74; Vice-Pres., 1968–70). Director: Carlsberg Brewery Ltd, UK, 1977; Fredericia Brewery Ltd, 1975; Royal Copenhagen (Holmegaard) Ltd, 1975; Politiken Ltd, 1975; InvestorReinvest (Cttee Chm.), 1986. Chm., Danish State Research Council of Humanities, 1968–70; Mem. Bd, HM Queen Ingrid's Roman Foundn, 1980; Vice-Pres., Scandinavia-Japan Sasakawa Foundn, 1985–; Member: Royal Danish Acad. of Science and Letters, 1969; Royal Danish Hist. Soc., 1961; Swedish Acad., Lund, 1963; Hist. Soc. of Calcutta, 1962; Corresp. FRHistS 1972. Editor, Scand. Econ. History Review, 1961–70. Hon. LittD Gothenburg, 1974, Festschrift 1983. Knight of Dannebrog, 1984; Comdr, Northern Star of Sweden, 1984; Order of Orange-Nassau, Netherlands, 1984. *Publications:* History of Tobacco

Industry in Denmark 1875–1950, 1950; Dutch-Asiatic Trade 1620–1740, 1958, 2nd edn 1981; (with Astrid Friis) A History of Prices and Wages in Denmark 1660–1800, vol. I, 1958; A History of Brewing in Denmark, 1962; Studies in Mercantilism, 1966, 2nd edn 1984; European Trade 1500–1750, 1971; The Carlsberg Foundation, 1976; Cambridge Econ. Hist. of Europe, vol. V, 1977. *Recreation:* painting. *Address:* The Carlsberg Foundation, 35 H. C. Andersen's Boulevard, DK-1553 Copenhagen V, Denmark. *T:* 01–14 21 28.

GLAMIS, Lord; Michael Fergus Bowes Lyon; Captain, Scots Guards; *b* 7 June 1957; *s* and *heir* of 17th Earl of Strathmore and Kinghorne, *qv*; *m* 1984, Isobel, *yr d* of Capt. A. E. Weatherall, Cowhill, Dumfries; one *s*. *Educ:* Univ. of Aberdeen (BLE 1979). Page of Honour to HM Queen Elizabeth The Queen Mother, 1971–73; commissioned, Scots Guards, 1980. *Heir: s* Master of Glamis, *qv*. *Address:* Glamis Castle, Forfar, Angus. *Clubs:* Turf, Buck's, Pratt's; Third Guards'.

GLAMIS, Master of; Hon. Simon Patrick Bowes Lyon; *b* 18 June 1986; *s* and *heir* of Lord Glamis, *qv*.

GLANCY, Dr James Edward McAlinney; Senior Principal Medical Officer, Department of Health and Social Security, 1972–76; *b* 9 Feb. 1914; *s* of Dr Michael James Glancy and Anne Teresa McAlinney; *m* 1945, Margaret Mary Redgrove; one *s* one *d*. *Educ:* Blackrock Coll., Dublin; National Univ. of Ireland (MD). FRCP, FRCPsych. Consultant Psychiatrist: Goodmayes Hosp., 1948–; King George Hosp., Ilford, and Barking Hosp., 1970–; Whipps Cross Hosp., 1948–72; Consultant in Clinical Neurophysiology, Oldchurch Hosp., Romford, 1950–60; Physician Supt, Goodmayes Hosp., 1960–72. *Recreations:* painting, photography, gardening. *Address:* 129 Goddard Way, Saffron Walden, Essex CB10 2DQ.

GLANDINE, Viscount; Richard James Graham-Toler; *b* 5 March 1967; *s* and *heir* of 6th Earl of Norbury, *qv*.

GLANUSK, 4th Baron, *cr* 1899; **David Russell Bailey;** Bt, *cr* 1852; Lieutenant-Commander RN (retired); *b* 19 Nov. 1917; *o s* of late Hon. Herbert Crawshay Bailey, 4th *s* of 1st Baron Glanusk and late Kathleen Mary, *d* of Sir Shirley Harris Salt, 3rd Bt; *S* cousin 1948; *m* 1941, Lorna Dorothy, *o d* of late Capt. E. C. H. N. Andrews, MBE, RA; one *s* one *d*. *Educ:* Orley Farm Sch., Harrow; Eton. RN, 1935–51. Managing Dir, Wandel & Goltermann (UK) Ltd, 1966–81; Chm., W&G Instruments Ltd, 1981–. *Heir: s* Hon. Christopher Russell Bailey [*b* 18 March 1942; *m* 1974, Frances, *d* of Air Chief Marshal Sir Douglas Lowe, *qv*; one *s* one *d*]. *Address:* 16 Clarendon Gardens, W9 1AY.

GLANVILLE, Alec William; Assistant Under-Secretary of State, Home Office, 1975–81, retired; *b* 20 Jan. 1921; *y s* of Frank Foster and Alice Glanville; *m* 1941, Lilian Kathleen Hetherton; one *s* one *d*. *Educ:* Portsmouth Northern Secondary Sch.; Portsmouth Municipal Coll. War service, RAMC, 1939–46. Exchequer and Audit Dept, 1939–47; General, Criminal, Police and Probation and After-care Depts, Home Office, 1947–81 (seconded to Cabinet Office, 1956–58); Private Sec. to Permanent Under Sec. of State, 1949–50; Principal Private Sec. to Sec. of State, 1960–63; Sec., Interdepartmental Cttee on Mentally Abnormal Offenders, 1972–75.

GLANVILLE, Brian Lester; author and journalist since 1949; *b* 24 Sept. 1931; *s* of James Arthur Glanville and Florence Glanville (*née* Manches); *m* 1959, Elizabeth Pamela de Boer (*née* Manasse), *d* of Fritz Manasse and Grace Manasse (*née* Howden); two *s* two *d*. *Educ:* Newlands Sch.; Charterhouse. Joined Sunday Times (football correspondent), 1958. *Publications:* The Reluctant Dictator, 1952; Henry Sows the Wind, 1954; Along the Arno, 1956; The Bankrupts, 1958; After Rome, Africa, 1959; A Bad Streak, 1961; Diamond, 1962; The Director's Wife, 1963; The King of Hackney Marshes, 1965; A Second Home, 1965; A Roman Marriage, 1966; The Artist Type, 1967; The Olympian, 1969; A Cry of Crickets, 1970; The Financiers, 1972; The History of the World Cup, 1973; The Thing He Loves, 1973; The Comic, 1974; The Dying of the Light, 1976; Never Look Back, 1980; (jtly) Underneath The Arches (musical), 1981; A Visit to the Villa (play), 1981; Kissing America, 1985; Love is Not Love, 1985; *juvenile:* Goalkeepers are Different (novel), 1971; Target Man (novel), 1978; The Puffin Book of Football, 1978; The Puffin Book of Tennis, 1981. *Recreation:* playing football. *Address:* 160 Holland Park Avenue, W11. *T:* 01–603 6908. *Club:* Chelsea Casuals.

GLANVILLE BROWN, William; *see* Brown, W. G.

GLANVILLE-JONES, Thomas; *see* Jones, T. G.

GLASER, Prof. Donald Arthur; Professor of Physics and Molecular Biology, University of California, since 1960; *b* 21 Sept. 1926; *s* of William Joseph and Lena Glaser. *Educ:* Case Institute of Technology; California Inst. of Technology. Prof., University of Michigan, 1949–59; National Science Foundation Fellow, 1961; Guggenheim Fellow, 1961–62; Research Biophysicist (Miller Research Professorship, University of Calif, 1962–64). Member: National Academy of Sciences (USA), 1962; NY Acad. of Science; Fellow Amer. Physical Soc.; FAAAS. Henry Russel Award, 1955; Charles Vernon Boys Prize, 1958; Amer. Phys. Soc. Prize, 1959; Nobel Prize, 1960. Hon. ScD Case Inst., 1959. *Publications:* chapters in: Topics in the Biology of Aging, 1965; Biology and the Exploration of Mars, 1966; Frontiers of Pattern Recognition, 1972; New Approaches to the Identification of Microorganisms, 1975; contrib. to Yearbook of the Physical Soc., London, 1958; articles in Physical Review, Bulletin of Amer. Phys. Soc., Nuovo Cimento, Handbuch der Physik, Jl Molecular Biol., Jl of Bacteriol., Cell, Applied and Environmental Microbiol., Annual of NY Acad. of Scis, Pattern Recognition and Image Processing, Somatic Cell Genetics, Cell Tissue Kinetics, Computers and Biomed. Res., Proc. Nat. Acad. of Scis (USA), Cold Spring Harbor Symposium Quant. Biol. 1968, etc. *Address:* 229 Molecular Biology-Virus Laboratory, University of California, Berkeley, Calif 94720, USA.

GLASGOW, 10th Earl of, *cr* 1703; **Patrick Robin Archibald Boyle;** Lord Boyle, 1699; Viscount of Kelburn, 1703; Baron Fairlie (UK), 1897; television director/producer; *b* 30 July 1939; *s* of 9th Earl of Glasgow, CB, DSC, and of Dorothea, *o d* of Sir Archibald Lyle, 2nd Bt; *S* father, 1984; *m* 1975, Isabel Mary James; one *s* one *d*. *Educ:* Eton; Paris Univ. National Service in Navy; Sub-Lt, RNR, 1959–60. Worked in Associated Rediffusion Television, 1961; worked at various times for Woodfall Film Productions; Asst on Film Productions, 1962–64; Asst Dir in film industry, 1962–67; producer/director of documentary films, Yorkshire TV, 1968–70; freelance film producer, 1971–, making network television documentaries for BBC Yorkshire Television, ATV and Scottish Television. Formed Kelburn Country Centre, May 1977, opening Kelburn estate and gardens in Aryshire to the public. *Recreations:* ski-ing, theatre. *Heir: s* Viscount of Kelburn, *qv*. *Address:* Kelburn, Fairlie, Ayrshire. *T:* Fairlie 204; (office) South Offices, Kelburn Estate, Fairlie, Aryshire. *T:* Fairlie 685.

GLASGOW, Archbishop of, (RC), since 1974; **Most Rev. Thomas J. Winning,** DCL, STL, DD. Formerly parish priest, St Luke, Braidhurst, Motherwell; Auxiliary Bishop of Glasgow, 1971–74; parish priest, Our Holy Redeemer's, Clydebank, 1972–74. Mem., Sacred Congregation for the Doctrine of the Faith, 1978–83. Pres., Bishops' Conf. of Scotland, 1985. FEIS 1986. Hon. DD Glasgow, 1983. *Address:* 40 Newlands Road, Glasgow G43 2JD.

GLASGOW, Auxiliary Bishops of, (RC); *see* Mone, Rt Rev. J. A.; Renfrew, Rt Rev. C. McD.

GLASGOW, Provost of (St Mary's Cathedral); *see* Grant, Very Rev. M. E.

GLASGOW AND GALLOWAY, Bishop of, since 1981; **Rt. Rev. Derek Alec Rawcliffe,** OBE 1971; *b* 8 July 1921; *s* of James Alec and Gwendoline Rawcliffe; *m* 1977, Susan Kathryn Speight. *Educ:* Sir Thomas Rich's School, Gloucester; Univ. of Leeds (BA, 1st cl. Hons English); College of the Resurrection, Mirfield. Deacon 1944, priest 1945, Worcester; Assistant Priest, Claines St George, Worcester, 1944–47; Asst Master, All Hallows School, Pawa, Solomon Islands, 1947–53; Headmaster, 1953–56; Headmaster, S Mary's School, Maravovo, Solomon Is, 1956–58; Archdeacon of Southern Melanesia, New Hebrides, 1959–74; Assistant Bishop, Diocese of Melanesia, 1974–75; First Bishop of the New Hebrides, 1975–80. New Hebrides Medal, 1980; Vanuatu Independence Medal, 1980. *Recreation:* music. *Address:* 48 Drymen Road, Bearsden, Glasgow G61 2RH. *T:* 041–943 0612.

GLASGOW AND GALLOWAY, Dean of; *see* Singer, Very Rev. S. S.

GLASHOW, Prof. Sheldon Lee, PhD; Higgins Professor of Physics, Harvard University, since 1979 (Professor of Physics, since 1966); *b* 5 Dec. 1932; *s* of Lewis and Bella Glashow; *m* 1972, Joan (*née* Alexander); three *s* one *d*. *Educ:* Cornell Univ. (AB); Harvard Univ. (AM, PhD). National Science Foundn Fellow, Copenhagen and Geneva, 1958–60; Res. Fellow, Calif Inst. of Technol., 1960–61; Asst Prof., Stanford Univ., 1961–62; Associate Prof., Univ. of Calif at Berkeley, 1962–66. Vis. Professor: CERN, 1968; Marseille, 1971; MIT, 1974 and 1980; Boston Univ., 1983; Univ. Schol., Texas A&M Univ., 1983–. Consultant, Brookhaven Nat. Lab., 1966–; Affiliated Senior Scientist, Univ. of Houston, 1983–. Pres., Sakharov Internat. Cttee, Washington, 1980–. Hon. DSc: Yeshiva, 1978; Aix-Marseille, 1982. Nobel Prize for Physics (jtly), 1979. *Publications:* articles in learned jls. *Recreations:* scuba diving, tennis. *Address:* 30 Prescott Street, Brookline, Mass 02146, USA. *T:* 617–277–5446.

GLASS, Anthony Trevor; QC 1986; a Recorder of the Crown Court, since 1985; *b* 6 June 1940. *Educ:* Royal Masonic School; Lincoln College, Oxford (BA Hons). Called to the Bar, Inner Temple, 1965. *Address:* Queen Elizabeth Building, Temple, EC4. *T:* 01–583 5766.

GLASS, Ven. Edward Brown; Archdeacon of Man, 1964–78, now Emeritus; Rector of Kirk Andreas, Isle of Man, 1964–78; *b* 1 July 1913; *s* of William and Phoebe Harriet Glass; *m* 1940, Frances Katharine Calvert; one *s* two *d*. *Educ:* King William's Coll., IoM; Durham Univ. (MA). Deacon 1937, priest 1938, dio. Manchester; Curate: St Mary's, Wardleworth, Rochdale, 1937; Gorton Parish Church, Manchester, 1937–42; Vicar: St John's, Hopwood, Heywood, Manchester, 1942–51; St Olave's, Ramsey, IoM, 1951–55; Castletown, IoM, 1955–64. Sec., Diocesan Convocation, 1958–64; Proctor for Clergy, Convocation of York, 1959–64; Member, Church Assembly and General Synod, 1959–78; Warden of Diocesan Readers, 1969–78; Chm., Diocesan Advisory Cttee, 1975–78. *Recreations:* gardening, ornithology, touring in Norway. *Address:* Balholm, Lhen Bridge, Kirk Andreas, Isle of Man. *T:* Kirk Andreas 568.

GLASS, Sir Leslie (Charles), KCMG 1967 (CMG 1958); HM Diplomatic Service, retired; Chairman, Anglo-Romanian Bank, 1973–81; *b* 28 May 1911; *s* of Ernest Leslie and Kate Glass; *m* 1st, 1942, Pamela Mary Gage; two *s* (one *d* decd); 2nd, 1957, Betty Lindsay Hoyer-Millar (*née* Macpherson); two step *d*. *Educ:* Bradfield Coll.; Trinity Coll., Oxford (Hon. Fellow, 1982); Sch. of Oriental Studies, London Univ. Indian Civil Service, 1934; Asst Warden, Burma Oilfields, 1937; Settlement Officer, Mandalay, 1939; Far Eastern Bureau Min. of Inf., 1942; Lt-Col Head of Burma Section, Psychological Warfare Div., SEAC; Head of Information Div., Burma Mil. Admin, 1943; Sec. Information Dept, Govt of Burma, 1945; Comr of Settlements and Land Records, Govt of Burma, 1946; joined Foreign Office as 1st Sec. (Oriental Sec.), HM Embassy, Rangoon, 1947; Foreign Office, 1949–50; Head of Chancery, HM Legation Budapest (Chargé d'Affaires, 1951–52), 1950–53; Head of Information Div., British Middle East Office, 1953; seconded to Staff of Governor of Cyprus, 1955–56; Counsellor and Consul-Gen., British Embassy, Washington, 1957–58; Dir-Gen. of British Information Services in the US and Information Minister, British Embassy, Washington 1959–61; Minister employed in the Foreign Office, 1961; Asst Under-Sec. of State, Foreign Office, 1962–65; Ambassador to Romania, 1965–67; Ambassador and Dep. Permanent UK Representative to UN, 1967–69; High Comr in Nigeria, 1969–71, retired; re-employed FCO, 1971–72; Mem., Panel of Chairmen, CSSB, 1973–81. Governing Council, Bradfield Coll., 1973–81. Trustee, Thomson Foundn, 1974–86; Dir, Irvin Great Britain, 1981–. *Publication:* The Changing of Kings: memories of Burma 1934–1949, 1985. *Recreation:* fishing. *Address:* Stone House, Ivington, Leominster, Herefordshire. *T:* Ivington 204. *Club:* East India, Devonshire, Sports and Public Schools.

GLASS, Ruth, MA; Director, Centre for Urban Studies, University College London, since 1958; *d* of Eli and Lilly Lazarus; *m* 1st, 1935, Henry Durant (marr. diss. 1941); 2nd, 1942, David V. Glass, FRS, FBA (*d* 1978); one *s* one *d*. *Educ:* Geneva and Berlin Univs; London Sch. of Economics; Columbia Univ., NY. Sen. Research Officer, Bureau of Applied Social Research, Columbia Univ., 1940–42; Res. Off., Min. of Town and Country Planning, 1948–50; University College London: Dir, Soc. Res. Unit, Dept of Town Planning, 1951–58; Hon. Res. Associate, 1951–71; Vis. Prof., 1972–86; Hon. Res. Fellow, 1985–. Visiting Professor: Essex Univ., 1980–86; London Univ. Inst. of Educn, 1984–86. Chm., Urban Sociol. Res. Cttee, Internat. Sociol Assoc., 1958–75. Editorial Adviser: London Jl; Internat. Jl of Urban and Regional Res.; Sage Urban Studies Abstracts. Hon. FRIBA, 1972. Hon. LittD Sheffield, 1982. *Publications:* Watling, A Social Survey, 1939; (ed) The Social Background of a Plan, 1948; Urban Sociology in Great Britain, 1955; Newcomers, The West Indians in London, 1960; London's Housing Needs, 1965; Housing in Camden, 1969; contributor to: Town Planning Review; Architectural Review; Population Studies; Internat. Social Science Jl; Monthly Review; Trans. World Congresses of Sociology, New Society, etc. *Address:* 10 Palace Gardens Terrace, W8; Eastway Cottage, Walberswick, Suffolk.

GLASSCOCK, John Lewis, FCIS; Commercial Director, British Aerospace PLC, since 1986 (Director, since 1982); *b* 12 July 1928; *s* of Edgar Henry and Maude Allison Glasscock; *m* 1959, Anne Doreen Baker; two *s*. *Educ:* Tiffin Sch.; University Coll. London (BA Hons). Served Royal Air Force, 1950–53. Joined Hawker Aircraft Ltd, 1953, Asst Sec., 1956, Commercial Man., 1961; Hawker Siddeley Aviation Ltd: Divl Commercial Man., 1964; Dir and Gen. Man. (Kingston), 1965; Dir and Gen. Man., 1977; British Aerospace Aircraft Group: Admin. Dir, 1978; Commercial Dir, 1979; Man. Dir (Military), 1981; Dep. Chief Exec. and Man. Dir, Civil Aircraft Div., 1983. Mem. Supervisory Bd, Airbus Industrie, 1983–85. Mem. Council, SBAC, 1979–. *Recreations:* golf, tennis. *Address:* British Aerospace PLC, 11 Strand, WC2. *T:* 01–930 1020. *Clubs:* Royal Air Force, Royal Automobile.

GLASSE, Thomas Henry, CMG 1961; MVO 1955; MBE 1946; retired as Counsellor in HM Diplomatic Service, and Head of Protocol Department, Foreign Office (1957–61); *b* 14 July 1898; *s* of late Thomas and Harriette Glasse; *m* 1935, Elsie May Dyter (*d* 1965); no *c*; *m* 1966, Ethel Alice Needham (*d* 1985). *Educ:* Latymer Foundation Upper Sch., Hammersmith. Entered Civil Service as a Boy Clerk, 1914. Army Service, 1/10th Bn Mx Regt, 1917–19. Joined the Foreign Office, 1921. Delegate of United Kingdom to Vienna Conference on Diplomatic Relations, 1961. *Recreations:* books, music, garden, travel. *Address.* 72 Lynch Road, Farnham, Surrey. *T:* Farnham 716662. *Club:* Travellers'.

GLASSPOLE, Most Hon. Sir Florizel (Augustus), ON 1973; GCMG 1981; GCVO 1983; CD 1970; Governor-General of Jamaica, since 1973; *b* Kingston, Jamaica, 25 Sept. 1909; *s* of late Rev. Theophilus A. Glasspole (Methodist Minister) and Florence (*née* Baxter); *m* 1934, Ina Josephine Kinlocke; one *d*. *Educ:* Central British Elementary Sch.; Wolmer's Sch.; Ruskin Coll., Oxford. British TUC Schol., 1946–47. Accountant (practising), 1932–44. Gen. Sec: Jamaica United Clerks Assoc., 1937–48; Jamaica TUC, 1939–52, resigned; Water Commn and Allied Workers Assoc., 1941–48; Municipal and Parochial Gen. Workers Union, 1945–47; First Gen. Sec., Nat. Workers Union, 1952–55; President: Jamaica Printers & Allied Workers Union, 1942–48; Gen. Hosp. and Allied Workers Union, 1944–47; Mental Hosp. Workers Union, 1944–47; Machado Employees Union, 1945–52; etc. Workers rep. on Govt Bds, etc, 1942–. Mem. Bd of Governors Inst. of Jamaica, 1944–57; Mem., Kingston Sch. Bd, 1944–. Founding Mem., PNP, 1938; MHR (PNP) for Kingston Eastern and Port Royal, 1944; Sec., PNP Parly Gp, 1944–73, resigned; Vice-Pres., People's National Party; Minister of Labour, Jamaica, 1955–57; Leader, House of Representatives, 1957–62, 1972–73; Minister of Educn, 1957–62, 1972–73; A Rep. for Jamaica, on Standing Fedn Cttee, West Indies Federation, 1953–58; Mem. House of Reps Cttee which prepared Independence of Jamaica Constitution, 1961; Mem. Delegn to London which completed Constitution document, 1962. Hon. LLD Univ. of the West Indies, 1982. Order of Andres Bello (1st cl.), Venezuela, 1973; Order of the Liberator, Venezuela, 1978. *Recreations:* gardening, sports, reading. *Address:* Kings House, Kingston 10, Jamaica.

GLAUERT, Audrey Marion, JP, ScD; Head of Electron Microscopy Department, since 1956, and Associate Director, since 1979, Strangeways Research Laboratory, Cambridge; Fellow of Clare Hall, Cambridge, since 1966; *b* 21 Dec. 1925; *d* of late Hermann Glauert, FRS and Muriel Glauert (*née* Barker). *Educ:* Perse Sch. for Girls, Cambridge; Bedford Coll., Univ. of London. BSc 1946, MSc 1947, London; MA Cantab 1967, ScD Cantab 1970. Asst Lectr in Physics, Royal Holloway Coll., Univ. of London, 1947–50; Mem. Scientific Staff, Strangeways Res. Lab., Cambridge, Sir Halley Stewart Research Fellow, 1950–. Chairman: British Joint Cttee for Electron Microscopy, 1968–72; Fifth European Congress on Electron Microscopy, 1972; Pres., Royal Microscopical Soc., 1970–72, Hon. Fellow, 1973. JP Cambridge, 1975. Editor: Practical Methods in Electron Microscopy, 1972–; Jl of Microscopy, Royal Microscopial Soc., 1986–. *Publications:* Fixation Dehydration and Embedding of Biological Specimens, 1974; papers on cell and molecular biology in scientific jls. *Recreations:* sailing, gardening. *Address:* 29 Cow Lane, Fulbourn, Cambridge. *T:* Cambridge 880463; Strangeways Research Laboratory, Worts' Causeway, Cambridge. *T:* Cambridge 243231.

GLAVES-SMITH, Frank William, CB 1975; Deputy Director-General of Fair Trading, 1973–79, retired; *b* 27 Sept. 1919; *m* 1941, Audrey Glaves; one *s* one *d*. *Educ:* Malet Lambert High Sch., Hull. War Service, 1940–46 (Captain, Royal Signals). Called to Bar, Middle Temple, 1947. Board of Trade, 1947; Princ. Private Sec. to Pres. of Bd of Trade, 1952–57; Asst Secretary: HM Treasury, 1957–60; Cabinet Office, 1960–62; Bd of Trade, 1962–65; Under-Sec., BoT, 1965–69, Dept of Employment and Productivity, 1969–70, DTI, 1970–73; Dep. Sec., 1975. Mem., Export Guarantees Adv. Council, 1971–73. *Recreations:* rock-climbing, fell-walking. *Address:* 8 Grange Park, Keswick, Cumbria.

GLAVIN, William Francis; Vice Chairman, since 1985, and President, Business Equipment Groups, since 1983, Xerox Corporation; *b* 29 March 1932; *m* 1955, Cecily McClatchy; three *s* four *d*. *Educ:* College of the Holy Cross, Worcester, Mass (BS); Wharton Graduate Sch. (MBA). Vice-Pres., Operations, Service Bureau Corp. (subsid. of IBM), 1968–70; Exec. Vice-Pres., Xerox Data Services, 1970; Pres., Xerox Data Systems, 1970–72; Gp Vice-Pres., Xerox Corp., and Pres., Business Development Gp, 1972–74; Rank Xerox Ltd: Man. Dir, 1974–80; Chief Operating Officer, 1974–77; Chief Exec. Officer, 1977–80; Xerox Corp.: Exec. Vice-Pres. Chief Staff Officer, 1980–82; Pres., Reprographics and Ops, 1982–83. *Recreations:* golf, music, tennis. *Address:* 3 Alden Terrace, Greenwich, Conn 06830, USA.

GLAZE, Michael John Carlisle, (James); HM Diplomatic Service; Ambassador to the Republic of Cameroon, since 1984; concurrently Ambassador (non-resident) to the Central African Republic and to Equatorial Guinea; *b* 15 Jan. 1935; *s* of late Derek Glaze and of Shirley Gardner (formerly Glaze, *née* Ramsay); *m* 1965, Rosemary Duff; two step-*d*. *Educ:* Repton; St Catharine's Coll., Cambridge (open Exhibitioner, BA 1958); Worcester Coll., Oxford. Colonial Service, Basutoland, 1959–65; HMOCS, Dep. Permanent Sec., Finance, Lesotho, 1966–70; Dept of Trade (ECGD), 1971–73; FCO, 1973–75; Abu Dhabi, 1975–78; Rabat, 1978–80; Consul-Gen., Bordeaux, 1980–84. *Recreations:* golf, grand opera, the garden. *Address:* c/o Foreign and Commonwealth Office, SW1.

GLAZEBROOK, His Honour Francis Kirkland; a Circuit Judge (formerly a Judge of County Courts), 1950–72; *b* 18 Feb. 1903; 3rd *s* of late William Rimington Glazebrook; *m* 1930, Winifred Mary Elizabeth Davison (*d* 1984); one *s* two *d*. *Educ:* Marlborough Coll.; Trinity Coll., Cambridge; Harvard Univ., USA. Called to the Bar, Inner Temple, 1928; Practised in the Common Law. Served War in Army, 1939–45. Croix de Guerre (France); Bronze Star (USA). *Recreations:* fishing, gardening, golf. *Address:* Rectory Park, Horsmonden, Kent.

GLAZEBROOK, Mark; *see* Glazebrook, R. M.

GLAZEBROOK, (Reginald) Mark; writer and art dealer; Director, Albemarle Gallery, London, since 1986; *b* 25 June 1936; *s* of late Reginald Field Glazebrook; *m* 1st, 1965, Elizabeth Lea Claridge (marr. diss. 1969); one *d*; 2nd, 1974, Wanda Barbara O'Neill (*née* Osińska); one *d*. *Educ:* Eton; Pembroke Coll., Cambridge (MA); Slade School of Fine Art. Worked at Arts Council, 1961–64; Lectr at Maidstone Coll. of Art, 1965–67; Art Critic, London Magazine, 1967–68; Dir, Whitechapel Art Gall., 1969–71; Head of Modern English Paintings and Drawings, P. and D. Colnaghi & Co. Ltd, 1973–75; Gallery Director and Art History Lectr, San José State Univ., 1977–79. FRSA 1971. *Publications:* (comp.) Artists and Architecture of Bedford Park 1875–1900 (catalogue), 1967; (comp.) David Hockney: paintings, prints and drawings 1960–1970 (catalogue), 1970; Edward Wadsworth 1889–1949: paintings, prints and drawings (catalogue), 1974; (introduction) John Armstrong 1893–1973 (catalogue), 1975; (introduction) John Tunnard (catalogue), 1976; articles in: Studio International, London Magazine. *Recreations:* travelling, theatre, tennis, swimming. *Address:* 5 Priory Gardens, Bedford Park, W4 1TT. *Clubs:* Beefsteak, Ognisko Polski.

GLEADELL, Maj.-Gen. Paul, CB 1959; CBE 1951; DSO 1945; *b* 23 Feb. 1910; *s* of late Captain William Henry and Katherine Gleadell; *m* 1937, Mary Montgomerie Lind, *d* of late Col Alexander Gordon Lind, DSO, and Mrs Lind; two *s* two *d*. *Educ:* Downside Sch.; Sandhurst. Commissioned in The Devonshire Regt, 1930 (Adjutant 1936–39); DAAG, Rawalpindi Dist, 1940; Staff Coll. (Quetta), 1941; Brigade Major 80th Indian Bde, 1942; Commanded 12th Bn The Devonshire Regt (6th Airborne Div.), 1944–45; Secretariat, Offices of the Cabinet and Ministry of Defence, 1945–48; Joint Services Staff Coll., 1948; Col (G S Intelligence), GHQ Far East Land Forces, 1949–51; comd 1st Bn The Devonshire Regt (3rd Inf. Div.), 1951–53; Senior Army Instructor, Joint Services Staff Coll., 1953–55; Brigade Comdr, 24th Independent Infantry Brigade, 1955–56; Imperial Defence Coll., 1957; Chief of Staff to Dir of Operations, Cyprus, 1958–59; in command 44th Div. (TA) and Home Counties District, and Dep. Constable of Dover Castle, 1959–62; Dir of Infantry, 1962–65. Clerk to Governors, Rookesbury Park School, 1966–72, Governor, 1973–80. French Croix de Guerre with Palm, 1944. *Address:* Down Wood Lodge, Came, Dorchester, Dorset DT2 8NR. *Clubs:* Naval and Military, Challoner.

GLEAVE, Ruth Marjory; Headmistress, Bradford Girls' Grammar School, since 1976; *b* 29 May 1926; *d* of Harold Gleave and Alice Lillian Dean. *Educ:* Birkenhead High Sch., GPDST; Univ. of Liverpool (BA Hons Geography, DipEd). Head of Geography Dept, Wade Deacon Girls' Grammar Sch., Widnes, 1947–54; Head of Geography Dept and Deputy Head, Withington Girls' Sch., Manchester, 1954–60; Head, Fairfield High Sch., Droylsden, Manchester, 1960–75. *Recreations:* travel, natural history, outdoor activities, the arts—literature and art. *Address:* Bradford Girls' Grammar School, Squire Lane, Bradford BD9 6RB.

GLEDHILL, Anthony John, GC 1967; Detective Sergeant, Metropolitan Police, since 1976; *b* 10 March 1938; *s* of Harold Victor and Marjorie Edith Gledhill; *m* 1958, Marie Lilian Hughes; one *s* one *d*. *Educ:* Doncaster Technical High Sch., Yorks. Accounts Clerk, Officers' Mess, RAF Bruggen, Germany, 1953–56. Metropolitan Police Cadet, 1956–57; Police Constable, Metropolitan Police, 1957–75. *Recreations:* football, carpentry. *Address:* 98 Pickhurst Lane, Hayes, Bromley, Kent. *T:* 01–462 4033. *Club:* No 4 District Metropolitan Police (Hayes, Kent).

GLEESON, Most Rev. James William, AO 1979; CMG 1958; DD 1957; FACE 1967; Archbishop Emeritus of Adelaide, (RC), since 1985; *b* 24 Dec. 1920; *s* of John Joseph and Margaret Mary Gleeson. *Educ:* St Joseph's Sch., Balaklava, SA; Sacred Heart Coll., Glenelg, SA. Priest, 1945; Inspector of Catholic Schs, 1947–52; Dir of Catholic Education for South Australia, 1952–58; Auxiliary Bishop to the Archbishop of Adelaide and Titular Bishop of Sesta, 1957–64; Coadjutor Archbishop of Adelaide and Titular Archbishop of Aurusuliana, 1964–71; Archbishop of Adelaide, 1971–85. Episcopal Chm., Young Catholic Students Movement of Australia, 1958–65. *Address:* Archbishop's House, 91 West Terrace, Adelaide, SA 5000, Australia. *T:* 51.3551.

GLEISSNER, Dr Heinrich; at Federal Ministry for Foreign Affairs, Vienna, since 1982; *b* Linz, Upper Austria, 12 Dec. 1927; *s* of Heinrich and Maria Gleissner. *Educ:* Univ. of Vienna (Dr jur 1950); Univ. of Innsbruck; Bowdoin Coll., Brunswick, Maine, USA; Coll. of Europe, Bruges. Entered Austrian Foreign Service, 1951; Austrian Embassy, Paris, and Office of Austrian Observer at Council of Europe, Strasbourg, 1952–53; Min. for Foreign Affairs, Vienna, 1953–55; Austrian Embassy, London, 1955–57; sabbatical, Univ. of Vienna, 1957–59; Min. for For. Affairs, 1959–61; Austrian National Bank, 1961; Min. for For. Affairs, 1961–62; Mission to Office of UN, Geneva, 1962–65; Consulate-General, New York, 1965–66, Consul-Gen., 1966–73; Min. for For. Affairs, 1973–75 (Head, Western Dept, 1974–75); Dir, Security Council and Polit. Cttees Div., UN, New York, 1975–79; Austrian Ambassador to the Court of St James's, 1979–81. *Recreation:* music. *Address:* Federal Ministry for Foreign Affairs, Ballhausplatz 2, 1010 Vienna, Austria. *Club:* St Johann's (Wien).

GLEN, Sir Alexander (Richard), KBE 1967 (CBE 1964); DSC 1942 (and Bar, 1945); Chairman, British Tourist Authority, 1969–77; *b* 18 April 1912; *s* of late R. Bartlett Glen, Glasgow; *m* 1947, Baroness Zora de Collaert. *Educ:* Fettes Coll.; Balliol Coll., Oxford. BA, Hons Geography. Travelled on Arctic Expeditions, 1932–36; Leader, Oxford Univ. Arctic Expedition, 1935–36; Banking, New York and London, 1936–39. RNVR, 1939–59, Capt. 1955. Export Council for Europe: Dep. Chm., 1960–64; Chm., 1964–66; Chairman: H. Clarkson & Co., 1965–73; Anglo World Travel, 1978–81; Dep. Chm., British Transport Hotels, 1978–83; Director: BICC, 1964–70; Gleneagles Hotels, 1980–83. Member: BNEC, 1966–72; Board of BEA, 1964–70; Nat. Ports Council, 1966–70; Horserace Totalisator Bd, 1976–84. Chm., Adv. Council, V&A Museum, 1978–84; Mem., Historic Buildings Council, 1976–80. Pres., BALPA, 1982–. Awarded Cuthbert Peek Grant by RGS, 1933; Bruce Medal by RSE, 1938; Andrée Plaque by Royal Swedish Soc. for Anthropology and Geography, 1939; Patron's Gold Medal by RGS, 1940. Polar Medal (clasp Arctic 1935–36), 1942; Norwegian War Cross, 1943; Chevalier (1st Class), Order of St Olav, 1944; Czechoslovak War Cross, 1946. *Publications:* Young Men in the Arctic, 1935; Under the Pole Star, 1937; Footholds Against a Whirlwind (autobiog.), 1975. *Recreations:* travel, ski-ing, sailing. *Address:* Stanton Court, Stanton, Worcs WR12 7NE. *Clubs:* City of London; Explorers (NY).

GLEN, Archibald; Solicitor; *b* 3 July 1909; *m* 1938, Phyllis Mary; one *s* two *d*. *Educ:* Melville Coll., Edinburgh. Admitted Solicitor, 1932. Town Clerk: Burnley, Lancs, 1940–45; Southend-on-Sea, 1945–71. President: Soc. of City and Borough Clerks of the Peace, 1960; Soc. of Town Clerks, 1963–64; Assoc. of Town Clerks of British Commonwealth, 1963–64, etc. Lay Member, Press Council, 1969–75; Mem., Local Govt Staff Commn for England, 1972–76. Hon. Freeman, Southend-on-Sea, 1971. *Recreations:* golf, swimming. *Address:* Harbour House, 2 Drummochy, Lower Largo, Fife. *T:* Lundin Links 320724.

GLEN HAIG, Mrs Mary Alison, CBE 1977 (MBE 1971); *b* 12 July 1918; *e d* of late Captain William James and Mary (*née* Bannochie); *m* 1943, Andrew Glen Haig (decd). *Educ:* Dame Alice Owen's Girls' School. Mem., Sports Council, 1966–82; Vice Pres., CCPR, 1982– (Chm., 1974–80); Mem., Internat. Olympic Cttee, 1982–; Pres., British Sports Assoc. for the Disabled, 1981–. Hon. Pres., Amateur Fencing Assoc., 1986– (Hon. Sec., 1956–64; Pres., 1974–86); Pres., Ladies' Amateur Fencing Union, 1964–74. British Ladies' Foil Champion, 1948–50. Olympic Games, 1948, 1952, 1956, 1960; Commonwealth Games Gold Medal, 1950, 1954, Bronze Medal, 1958; Captain, Ladies' Foil Team, 1950–57. Asst Dist Administrator, S Hammersmith Health District, 1975–82. Chm. of Trustees, HRH The Princess Christian Hosp., Windsor, 1981–. *Recreations:* fencing, gardening. *Address:* 66 North End House, Fitzjames Avenue, W14 0RX. *T:* 01–602 2504; 2 Old Cottages, Holyport Street, Holyport, near Maidenhead, Berks. *T:* Maidenhead 33421. *Club:* Lansdowne.

GLENAMARA, Baron *cr* 1977 (Life Peer), of Glenridding, Cumbria; **Edward Watson Short,** PC 1964; CH 1976; Chairman, Cable and Wireless Ltd, 1976–80; *b* 17 Dec. 1912; *s* of Charles and Mary Short, Warcop, Westmorland; *m* 1941, Jennie, *d* of Thomas Sewell, Newcastle upon Tyne; one *s* one *d*. *Educ:* Bede College, Durham. LLB London. Served War of 1939–45 and became Capt. in DLI. Headmaster of Princess Louise County

Secondary School, Blyth, Northumberland, 1947; Leader of Labour Group on Newcastle City Council, 1950; MP (Lab) Newcastle upon Tyne Central, 1951–76; Opposition Whip (Northern Area), 1955–62; Dep. Chief Opposition Whip, 1962–64; Parly Sec. to the Treasury and Govt Chief Whip, 1964–66; Postmaster General, 1966–68; Sec. of State for Educn and Science, 1968–70; Lord Pres. of the Council and Leader, House of Commons, 1974–76. Dep. Leader, Labour Party, 1972–76. Mem. Council, WWF, 1983–. Pres., Finchale Abbey Training Coll. for the Disabled (Durham). Chancellor, Polytechnic of Newcastle upon Tyne. Hon. FCP, 1965. *Publications:* The Story of The Durham Light Infantry, 1944; The Infantry Instructor, 1946; Education in a Changing World, 1971; Birth to Five, 1974; I Knew My Place, 1983. *Recreation:* painting. *Address:* 21 Priory Gardens, Corbridge, Northumberland. *T:* Corbridge 2880; Glenridding, Cumbria. *T:* Glenridding 273.

GLENAPP, Viscount; (Kenneth) Peter (Lyle) Mackay, AIB; Director, Duncan Macneill & Co. Ltd, London; *b* 23 Jan. 1943; *er s* and *heir* of 3rd Earl of Inchcape, *qv; m* 1966, Georgina, *d* of S. C. Nisbet and of Mrs G. R. Sutton; one *s* two *d. Educ:* Eton. Late 2nd Lieut 9/12th Royal Lancers. *Recreations:* shooting, fishing, golf, farming. *Heir: s* Hon. Fergus James Kenneth Mackay, *b* 9 July 1979. *Address:* Manor Farm, Clyffe Pypard, near Swindon, Wilts SN4 7PY; 63E Pont Street, SW1. *Clubs:* White's, Oriental, City of London.

GLENARTHUR, 4th Baron *cr* 1918; **Simon Mark Arthur;** Bt 1903; Minister of State, Scottish Office, since 1986; *b* 7 Oct. 1944; *s* of 3rd Baron Glenarthur, OBE, and of Margaret, *d* of late Captain H. J. J. Howie; *S* father, 1976; *m* 1969, Susan, *yr d* of Comdr Hubert Wyndham Barry, RN; one *s* one *d. Educ:* Eton. Commissioned 10th Royal Hussars (PWO), 1963; ADC to High Comr, Aden, 1964–65; Captain 1970; Major 1973; retired 1975; Royal Hussars (PWO), TA, 1976–80. British Airways Helicopters Captain, 1976–82; Dir, Aberdeen and Texas Corporate Finance Ltd, 1977–82. A Lord in Waiting (Govt Whip), 1982–83; Parly Under Sec. of State, DHSS, 1983–85, Home Office, 1985–86. Mem., Queen's Body Guard for Scotland (Royal Co. of Archers). MCIT 1979. *Recreations:* field sports, flying, gardening, choral singing. *Heir: s* Hon. Edward Alexander Arthur, *b* 9 April 1973. *Address:* Birch Hill, Torphins, Banchory, Kincardineshire. *T:* Torphins 287. *Club:* Cavalry and Guards.

GLENCONNER, 3rd Baron *cr* 1911; **Colin Christopher Paget Tennant;** Bt 1885; Governing Director, Tennants Estate Ltd, since 1967; Chairman, Mustique Co. Ltd, since 1969; *b* 1 Dec. 1926; *s* of 2nd Baron Glenconner, and of Pamela Winefred, 2nd *d* of Sir Richard Paget, 2nd Bt; *S* father, 1983; *m* 1956, Lady Anne Coke, *e d* of 5th Earl of Leicester, MVO; three *s* twin *d. Educ:* Eton; New College, Oxford. Director, C. Tennant Sons & Co. Ltd, 1953; Deputy Chairman, 1960–67, resigned 1967. *Heir: s* Hon. Charles Edward Pevensey Tennant, *b* 15 Feb. 1957. *Address:* Hill Lodge, Hillsleigh Road, W8. *T:* 01–221 6826.

GLENCROSS, David; Director of Television, Independent Broadcasting Authority, since 1983; *b* 3 March 1936; *s* of John William and Elsie May Glencross; *m* 1965, Elizabeth Louise, *d* of John and Edith Richardson; one *d. Educ:* Salford Grammar School; Trinity College, Cambridge (BA Hons). BBC: general trainee, 1958; talks producer, Midlands, 1959; TV Midlands at Six, 1962; Staff Training section, 1964; Senior Producer, External Services, 1966; Asst Head of Programmes, N Region, 1968; Senior Programme Officer, ITA, 1970; Head of Programme Services, IBA, 1976; Dep. Dir, Television, IBA, 1977. FRTS 1981; FRSA 1985. *Publications:* articles on broadcasting in newspapers and jls. *Recreations:* music, reading, listening to radio, walking. *Address:* IBA, 70 Brompton Road, SW3. *T:* 01–584 7011.

GLENDEVON, 1st Baron, *cr* 1964; **John Adrian Hope;** PC 1959; Director and Deputy Chairman, Ciba-Geigy (UK) Ltd (formerly Geigy (UK) Ltd), 1971–78 (Chairman, 1967–71); Director: ITT (UK) Ltd; Colonial Mutual Life Assurance Society Ltd, 1952–54, 1962–82; British Electric Traction Omnibus Services Ltd, 1947–52, 1962–82; *b* 7 April 1912; *yr* twin *s* of 2nd Marquess of Linlithgow, KG, KT, PC; *m* 1948, Elizabeth Mary, *d* of late (William) Somerset Maugham, CH; two *s. Educ:* Eton; Christ Church, Oxford (MA 1936). Served War of 1939–45 (Scots Guards) at Narvik, Salerno and Anzio (despatches twice); psc†. MP (C) Northern Midlothian and Peebles, 1945–50, Pentlands Div. of Edinburgh, 1950–64; (Joint) Parliamentary Under-Sec. of State for Foreign Affairs, Oct. 1954–Nov. 1956; Parliamentary Under-Sec. of State for Commonwealth Relations, Nov. 1956–Jan. 1957; Jt Parly Under-Sec. of State for Scotland, 1957–Oct. 1959; Minister of Works, Oct. 1959–July 1962. Mem., Departmental Cttee to examine operation of Section 2 of Official Secrets Act, 1971. Chairman: Royal Commonwealth Society, 1963–66; Historic Buildings Council for England, 1973–75. Fellow of Eton, 1956–67. FRSA 1962. *Publication:* The Viceroy at Bay, 1971. *Heir: s* Hon. Julian John Somerset Hope, *b* 6 March 1950. *Address:* Mount Lodge, Mount Row, St Peter Port, Guernsey.

GLENDINING, Rev. Canon Alan, LVO 1979; Vicar of Ranworth with Panxworth with Woodbastwick, Bishop's Chaplain for the Broads and Senior Chaplain for Holidaymakers, since 1985; Chaplain to the Queen, since 1979; Hon. Canon of Norwich Cathedral, since 1977; *b* 17 March 1924; *s* of late Vincent Glendining, MS, FRCS and Freda Alice; *m* 1948, Margaret Locke, *d* of Lt-Col C. M. Hawes, DSO and Frances Cooper Richmond; one *s* one *d* (and one *d* decd). *Educ:* Radley; Westcott House, Cambridge. Newspaper publishing, 1945–58. Deacon, 1960; Priest, 1961. Asst Curate, South Ormsby Group of Parishes, 1960–63; Rector of Raveningham Group of Parishes, 1963–70; Rector, Sandringham Group of Parishes, and Domestic Chaplain to the Queen, 1970–79; Rural Dean of Heacham and Rising, 1972–76; Rector of St Margaret's, Lowestoft, and Team Leader of Lowestoft Group, 1979–85. *Recreation:* writing. *Address:* Ranworth Vicarage, Norwich NR13 6HT.

GLENDINNING, James Garland, OBE 1973; Chairman: Masterpack Ltd, since 1982; Investment Committee, Guinness Mahon Venture Founders Fund, since 1984; Director: The Fine Art Society plc, since 1972; L. E. Vincent & Partners Ltd, since 1984; *b* 27 April 1919; *er s* of late George M. Glendinning and Isabella Green; *m* 1st, 1943, Margaret Donald (*d* 1980); one *d*; 2nd, Mrs Anne Ruth Law. *Educ:* Boroughmuir Sch., Edinburgh; Military Coll. of Science. Mil. Service, 1939–46: 2nd Bn London Scottish and REME in UK and NW Europe. HM Inspector of Taxes, 1946–50; various appts with Shell Petroleum Co. Ltd, 1950–58; Dir Anglo Egyptian Oilfields Ltd in Egypt, 1959–61; Gen. Manager in Borneo and East Java for Shell Indonesia, 1961–64; Head of Industrial Studies (Diversification) in Shell Internat. Petroleum Co. Ltd, London, 1964–67; various Shell appts in Japan, 1967–72, incl.: Vice-President: Shell Sekiyu KK; Shell Kosan KK; Dir, various Shell/Showa and Shell/Mitsubishi jt venture cos. Chm., British Chamber of Commerce in Japan, 1970–72; Mem., London Transport Exec., 1972–80; Chairman: London Transport Pension Fund Trustees Ltd, 1974–80; North American Property Unit Trust, 1975–80; Dir, Industrial and Commercial Property Unit Trust, 1977–81; Man. Dir, Gestam International Realty Ltd, 1981–83. Mem. Council, Japan Soc., London, 1974–78 and 1981–. FCIT 1973; FRSA 1977. *Address:* 20 Albion Street, W2 2AS. *Clubs:* Caledonian, Oriental.

GLENDINNING, Hon. Victoria, (Hon. Mrs de Vere White), FRSL; author and journalist, since 1969; *b* 23 April 1937; *d* of Baron Seebohm, *qv; m* 1st, 1958, Prof. (Oliver) Nigel (Valentine) Glendinning (marr. diss. 1981); four *s*; 2nd, 1982, Terence de Vere White, *qv. Educ:* St Mary's Sch., Wantage; Millfield Sch.; Somerville Coll., Oxford (MA Mod. Langs); Southampton Univ. (Dip. in Social Admin). FRSL 1982. Part-time teaching, 1960–69; part-time psychiatric social work, 1970–73; Editorial Asst, TLS, 1974–78. *Publications:* A Suppressed Cry, 1969; Elizabeth Bowen: portrait of a writer, 1977; Edith Sitwell: a unicorn among lions, 1981; Vita: a biography of V. Sackville-West, 1983; articles in TLS, TES, New Statesman, Irish Times, Observer, Washington Post, New York Times, Listener, Sunday Times, etc. *Recreation:* gardening. *Address:* c/o David Higham Associates, 5–8 Lower John Street, Golden Square, W1R 4HA. *Club:* Groucho.

GLENDYNE, 3rd Baron, *cr* 1922; **Robert Nivison,** Bt 1914; Senior Partner in the firm of R. Nivison & Co., Stockbrokers; *b* 27 Oct. 1926; *o s* of 2nd Baron and late Ivy May Rose; *S* father, 1967; *m* 1953, Elizabeth, *y d* of late Sir Cecil Armitage, CBE; one *s* two *d. Educ:* Harrow. Grenadier Guards, 1944–47. *Heir: s* Hon. John Nivison, *b* 18 Aug. 1960. *Address:* Hurdcott, Barford St Martin, near Salisbury, Wilts. *Club:* City of London.

See also Maj.-Gen. P. R. Leuchars, Maj.-Gen. D. J. St M. Tabor.

GLENISTER, Prof. Tony William, CBE (mil.) 1979; TD; Professor of Anatomy, University of London, at Charing Cross and Westminster Medical School, since 1984 (at Charing Cross Hospital Medical School, 1970–84); Dean, Charing Cross and Westminster Medical School, since 1984; *b* 19 Dec. 1923; *o s* of late Dudley Stuart Glenister and Maria (*née* Leytens); *m* 1948, Monique Marguerite, *o d* of Emile and Marguerite de Wilde; four *s. Educ:* Eastbourne Coll.; St Bartholomew's Hosp. Med. Coll. MRCS, LRCP 1947; MB, BS 1948, PhD 1955, DSc 1963, London. House appts, St Bartholomew's Hosp. and St Andrew's Hosp., Dollis Hill, 1947–48; served in RAMC, 1948–50; Lectr and Reader in Anatomy, Charing Cross Hosp. Med. Sch., 1950–57; Internat. Project Embryological Res., Hubrecht Lab., Utrecht, 1954; Prof. of Embryology, Univ. of London, 1967–70; Dean, Charing Cross Hosp. Med. Sch., 1976–84 (Vice-Dean, 1966–69, 1971–76); Hon. Cons. in Clin. Anatomy and Genetics to Charing Cross Gp of Hosps, 1972–; Hon. Brig. late RAMC, TA (TD, TA 1963 and TAVR 1978). Apothecaries' Soc. Lectr in History of Medicine, 1971–; Arnott Demonstrator, RCS, 1972, 1986; Pres., Anatomical Soc. GB and Ireland, 1979–81 (Sec., 1974–76). ADMS 44 (Home Counties) Div. TA, 1964–67; CO 217 (London) Gen. Hosp. RAMC(V), 1968–72; QHP 1971–73; Hon. Col 220 (1st Home Counties) Field Amb. RAMC(V), 1973–78; TAVR Advr to DGAMS, 1976–79; Hon. Col 217 (London) Gen. Hosp. RAMC, TAVR, 1981–86. Member: Ealing, Hammersmith and Hounslow AHA(T), 1976–82; Hammersmith and Fulham DHA, 1982–83; North West Thames RHA, 1983–; GMC, 1979–; sometime examiner: Univs of Cambridge, Liverpool, London, St Andrews, Singapore, NUI, Chinese Univ., Hong Kong; RCS; RCSE; RCPGlas. Special Trustee, Charing Cross Hosp.; Trustee, Tablet Trust; Mem. Governing Body, Soc. for Study of Med. Ethics. Mem., Ct of Assts, Soc. of Apothecaries of London; Freeman, City of London. OStJ 1967. *Publications:* (with J. R. W. Ross) Anatomy and Physiology for Nurses, 1965, 3rd edn 1980; (contrib.) A Companion to Medical Studies, ed Passmore, 1963, 2nd edn 1976; (contrib.) Methods in Mammalian Embryology, ed Daniel, 1971; (contrib.) Textbook of Human Anatomy, ed Hamilton, 1976; papers and articles mainly on prenatal development. *Recreations:* the countryside, history. *Club:* Army and Navy.

GLENN, Sir Archibald; *see* Glenn, Sir J. R. A.

GLENN, Senator John H(erschel), Jr; US Senator from Ohio (Democrat), since 1975; *b* Cambridge, Ohio, 18 July 1921; *s* of John H. and Clara Glenn; *m* 1943, Anna Castor; one *s* one *d. Educ:* Muskingum Coll., New Concord, Ohio. Joined US Marine Corps, 1943; Served War (2 DFC's, 10 Air Medals); Pacific Theater, 1944; home-based, Capt., 1945–46; Far East, 1947–49; Major, 1952; served Korea (5 DFC's, Air Medal with 18 clusters), 1953. First non-stop supersonic flight, Los Angeles-New York (DFC), 1957; Lieut-Col, 1959. In Jan. 1964, declared candidacy for US Senate from Ohio, but withdrew owing to an injury; recovered and promoted Col USMC, Oct. 1964; retired from USMC, Dec. 1964. Became one of 7 volunteer Astronauts, man-in-space program, 1959; made 3-orbit flight in Mercury capsule, Friendship 7, 20 Feb. 1962 (boosted by rocket; time 4 hrs 56 mins; distance 81,000 miles; altitude 160 miles; recovered by destroyer off Puerto Rico in Atlantic). Vice-Pres. (corporate develt), Royal Crown Cola Co., 1966–68; Pres., Royal Crown Internat., 1967–69. Holds hon. doctorates, US and foreign. Awarded DSM (Nat. Aeronautics and Space Admin.), Astronaut Wings (Navy), Astronaut Medal (Marine Corps), etc, 1962; Galabert Internat. Astronautical Prize (jointly with Lieut-Col Yuri Gagarin), 1963; also many other awards and citations from various countries and organizations. *Address:* SH-503 Hart Senate Office Building, Washington, DC 20510, USA.

GLENN, Sir (Joseph Robert) Archibald, Kt 1966; OBE 1965; BCE; FIChemE, FIE (Aust.); Chairman: Collins Wales Pty Ltd, 1973–84; I.C. Insurance Australia Ltd, 1973–85; Director: Tioxide Australia Ltd, since 1973; Westpac Banking Corporation (formerly Bank of New South Wales), 1967–84; Newmont Pty Ltd, since 1977; *b* 24 May 1911; *s* of late J. R. Glenn, Sale, Vic., Aust.; *m* 1939, Elizabeth M. M., *d* of late J. S. Balderstone; one *s* three *d. Educ:* Scotch Coll. (Melbourne); University of Melbourne; Harvard (USA). Joined ICI Australia Ltd, 1935; Design and Construction Engr, 1935–44; Explosives Dept, ICI (UK), 1945–46; Chief Engineer, ICI Australia Ltd, 1947–48; Controller, Nobel Group, 1948–50; ICI Australia Ltd: General Manager, 1950–52; Managing Director, 1953–73; Chm., 1963–73; Director: ICI, London, 1970–75; Hill Samuel Australia Ltd, 1973–83; Westralian Sands Ltd, 1977–85; Alcoa of Australia Ltd, 1973–86; Chairman: Fibremakers Ltd, 1963–73; IMI Australia Ltd, 1970–78. Chancellor, La Trobe Univ., 1967–72 (Hon. DUniv 1981); Chairman: Council of Scotch Coll., 1960–81. Ormond Coll. Council, 1976–81; Member: Manufacturing Industry Advisory Council, 1960–77; Industrial Design Council, 1958–70; Australia/Japan Business Co-operation Cttee, 1965–75; Royal Melbourne Hospital Bd of Management, 1960–70; Melbourne Univ. Appointments Bd; Bd of Management, Melbourne Univ. Engrg Sch. Foundn, 1982–; Council, Inst. of Pacific Affairs, 1976–; Governor, Atlantic Inst. of Internat. Affairs. J. N. Kirby Medal, 1970. *Recreations:* golf, tennis, collecting rare books. *Address:* 1A Woorigoleen Road, Toorak, Vic 3142, Australia. *T:* 241 6367. *Clubs:* Australian, Melbourne, Frankston Golf, Melbourne Univ. Boat (all in Melbourne); Australian (Sydney).

GLENNIE, Charles Milne, PhD; Registrar General for Scotland, since 1982; *b* 29 Oct. 1934; *s* of Herbert Charles Glennie and Jane Anderson (*née* Todd); *m* 1960, Eileen Margaret Mason; one *d* (and one *d* decd). *Educ:* Fettes Coll.; Edinburgh Univ. (MA 1956); Peterhouse, Cambridge (MA 1963); Yale Univ. (PhD 1963). Lectr in Mathematics: Univ. of Western Ont, 1960–63; Univ. of St Andrews, 1963–64; Univ. of Edinburgh, 1964–68; Statistician, Home Office, 1968–72, Chief Statistician, 1972–76; Dir of Statistics, Scottish Office, 1976–82. *Publications:* papers on Jordon algebras. *Address:* 106 Ravelston Dykes, Edinburgh EH12 6HB. *T:* 031–337 6878. *Club:* Royal Commonwealth Society.

GLENNY, Dr Robert Joseph Ervine, CEng, FIM; Consultant to UK Government and industry, since 1983; *b* 14 May 1923; *s* of late Robert and Elizabeth Rachel Glenny; *m* 1947, Joan Phillips Reid; one *s* one *d. Educ:* Methodist Coll., Belfast; QUB (BSc Chemistry); London Univ. (BSc Metallurgy, PhD). CEng, 1979; FIM 1958. Res. Metallurgist, English Electric Co. Ltd, Stafford, 1943–47; National Gas Turbine Establishment, 1947–70; Materials Dept, 1947–66; Head of Materials Dept, 1966–70; Supt, Div. of Materials Applications, National Physical Lab., 1970–73; Head of Materials Dept, RAE, 1973–79; Group Head of Aerodynamics, Structures and Materials Depts, RAE, 1979–83. *Publications:* research and review papers on materials science and technology, mainly related to gas turbines, in ARC (R&M series) and in Internat. Metallurgical Rev. *Recreations:* reading, gardening. *Address:* 77 Gally Hill Road, Church Crookham, Aldershot, Hants GU13 0RU. *T:* Fleet 615877.

GLENTORAN, 2nd Baron, *cr* 1939, of Ballyalloly; **Daniel Stewart Thomas Bingham Dixon,** 4th Bt, *cr* 1903; PC (Northern Ireland) 1953; KBE 1973; Lord-Lieutenant, City of Belfast, 1976–85 (HM Lieutenant, 1950–76); *b* 19 Jan. 1912; *s* of 1st Baron, PC, OBE and Hon. Emily Ina Florence Bingham (*d* 1957), *d* of 5th Baron Clanmorris; *S* father 1950; *m* 1933, Lady Diana Mary Wellesley, (*d* 1984), *d* of 3rd Earl Cowley; two *s* one *d. Educ:* Eton; RMC Sandhurst. Reg. Army, Grenadier Guards; served War of 1939–45 (despatches); retired 1946 (with hon. rank of Lieut-Col); psc. MP (U) Bloomfield Division of Belfast, NI Parliament, Oct. 1950–Feb. 1961; Parliamentary Sec., Ministry of Commerce, NI, 1952–53; Minister of Commerce, 1953–61; Minister in Senate, NI, 1961–72, Speaker of Senate, 1964–72. Hon. Col 6th Battalion Royal Ulster Rifles, 1956–61, retd rank of Hon. Col. *Heir: s* Hon. Thomas Robin Valerian Dixon, MBE [*b* 21 April 1935; *m* 1st, 1959, Rona, *d* of Capt. G. C. Colville, Mill House, Bishop's Waltham, Hants; three *s*; 2nd, 1979, Alwyn Mason]. *Address:* Drumadarragh House, Doagh, Co. Antrim, Northern Ireland. *T:* Doagh 222. *Club:* Ulster (Belfast).

GLENTWORTH, Viscount; Edmund Christopher Pery; *b* 10 Feb. 1963; *s* and *heir* of 6th Earl of Limerick, *qv. Educ:* Eton; New Coll., Oxford; Pushkin Inst., Moscow. *Recreations:* skiing, travelling. *Address:* 30 Victoria Road, W8 5RG. *T:* 01–937 0573; Chiddinglye, West Hoathly, East Grinstead, West Sussex RH19 4QT. *T:* Sharpthorne 810214.

GLIDEWELL, Rt. Hon. Sir Iain (Derek Laing), Kt 1980; PC 1985; **Rt. Hon. Lord Justice Glidewell;** a Lord Justice of Appeal, since 1985; Presiding Judge, North Eastern Circuit, since 1982; *b* 8 June 1924; *s* of late Charles Norman and Nora Glidewell; *m* 1950, Hilary, *d* of late Clinton D. Winant; one *s* two *d. Educ:* Bromsgrove Sch.; Worcester Coll., Oxford (Hon. Fellow 1986). Served RAFVR, 1942–46. Called to the Bar, Gray's Inn, 1949, Bencher 1977. QC 1969; a Recorder of the Crown Court, 1976–80; a Judge of Appeal, Isle of Man, 1979–80; a Judge of the High Court of Justice, Queen's Bench Division, 1980–85; Presiding Judge, NE Circuit, 1982–85; Member: Senate of Inns of Court and the Bar, 1976–79; Supreme Court Rule Cttee, 1980–84. Chm., Panels for Examination of Structure Plans: Worcestershire, 1974; W Midlands, 1975; conducted Heathrow Fourth Terminal Inquiry, 1978. Associate, RICS, 1982. *Recreations:* beagling, walking, theatre. *Address:* Royal Courts of Justice, Strand, WC2A 2LL. *Clubs:* Garrick; Manchester (Manchester).

GLIN, Knight of; see Fitz-Gerald, D. J. V.

GLOAK, Graeme Frank, CB 1980; Solicitor for the Customs and Excise, 1978–82; *b* 9 Nov. 1921; *s* of late Frank and of Lilian Gloak; *m* 1944, Mary, *d* of Stanley and Jane Thorne; one *s* one *d* (and one *s* decd). *Educ:* Brentwood School. Royal Navy, 1941–46; Solicitor, 1947; Customs and Excise: Legal Asst, 1947; Sen. Legal Asst, 1953; Asst Solicitor, 1967; Principal Asst Solicitor, 1971. Sec., Civil Service Legal Soc., 1954–62. Member: Dairy Produce Quota Tribunal, 1984–85; Agricl Wages Cttee for Essex and Herts, 1984–; Chm., Agricl Dwelling House Adv. Cttee, Essex and Herts, 1984–. *Publication:* (with G. Krikorian and R. K. F. Hutchings) Customs and Excise, in Halsbury's Laws of England, 4th edn, 1973. *Recreations:* badminton, walking, watching cricket. *Address:* Northwold, 123 Priests Lane, Shenfield, Essex. *T:* Brentwood 212748. *Clubs:* MCC; Essex County Cricket (Chelmsford).

GLOCK, Sir William (Frederick), Kt 1970; CBE 1964; Chairman, London Orchestral Concerts Board, 1975–86; Artistic Director, Bath Festival, 1975–84; *b* London, 3 May 1908. *Educ:* Christ's Hospital; Caius Coll., Cambridge. Studied pianoforte under Artur Schnabel. Joined The Observer, 1934; chief music critic, 1939–45. Served in RAF, 1941–46. Dir, Summer Sch. of Music, Bryanston, 1948–52, Dartington Hall, 1953–79. Editor of music magazine The Score, 1949–61; adjudicated at Canadian music festivals, 1951; has lectured on music throughout England and Canada. Music Critic, New Statesman, 1958–59; Controller of Music, BBC, 1959–72. Editor, Eulenburg books on music, 1973–. Member: Bd of Dirs, Royal Opera House, 1968–73; Arts Council, 1972–75. Hon. Mem., Royal Philharmonic Soc., 1971. Hon. DMus Nottingham Univ., 1968; DUniv York, 1972; Hon. DLitt Bath, 1984. Albert Medal, RSA, 1971. *Address:* Vine House, Brightwell cum Sotwell, Wallingford, Oxon. *T:* Wallingford 37144.

GLOSSOP, Peter; Principal Baritone, Royal Opera House, Covent Garden, until 1967, now Guest Artist; *b* 6 July 1928; *s* of Cyril and Violet Elizabeth Glossop; *m* 1st, 1955, Joyce Elizabeth Blackham (marr. diss. 1977); no *c*; 2nd, 1977, Michèle Yvonne Amos; two *d. Educ:* High Storrs Grammar Sch., Sheffield. Began singing professionally in chorus of Sadler's Wells Opera, 1952, previously a bank clerk; promoted to principal after one season; Covent Garden Opera, 1962–67. Début in Italy, 1964; La Scala, Milan, début, Rigoletto, 1965. Sang Otello and Rigoletto with Metropolitan Opera Company at Newport USA Festival, Aug. 1967; Rigoletto and Nabucco with Mexican National Opera Company, Sept. 1967. Guest Artist (Falstaff, Rigoletto, Tosca) with American National Opera Company, Oct. 1967. Has sung in opera houses of Bologna, Parma Catania, Vienna, 1967–68, and Berlin and Buenos Aires. Is a recording artist. Hon. DMus, Sheffield, 1970. Winner of 1st Prize and Gold Medal in First International Competition for Young Opera Singers, Sofia, Bulgaria, 1961; Gold Medal for finest performance (in Macbeth) of 1968–69 season, Barcelona. *Films:* Pagliacci, Otello. *Recreations:* New Orleans jazz music, golf. *Address:* Elmcroft, 91 Cambridge Road, Teddington, Mddx. *Club:* Green Room.

GLOSTER, Prof. John, MD; Hon. Consulting Ophthalmologist, Moorfields Eye Hospital; Emeritus Professor of Experimental Opthalmology, University of London; *b* 23 March 1922; *m* 1947, Margery (*née* Williams); two *s. Educ:* Jesus Coll., Cambridge; St Bartholomew's Hosp. MB, BChir 1946; MRCS, LRCP 1946; DOMS 1950; MD Cantab 1953; PhD London 1959. Registrar, Research Dept, Birmingham and Midland Eye Hosp., 1950–54; Mem. Staff, Ophth. Research Unit, MRC, 1954–63; Prof. of Experimental Ophthalmology, Inst. of Ophth., Univ. of London, 1975–82; Dean of the Inst. of Ophthalmology, 1975–80. FRSocMed; Mem. Ophth. Soc. UK. *Publications:* Tonometry and Tonography, 1966; (jtly) Physiology of the Eye, System of Ophthalmology IV, ed Duke-Elder, 1968; contribs to jls. *Address:* Oversley, 24C Ickenham Road, Ruislip, Middlesex.

GLOUCESTER, Bishop of, since 1975; **Rt. Rev. John Yates;** *b* 17 April 1925; *s* of late Frank and late Edith Ethel Yates; *m* 1954, Jean Kathleen Dover; one *s* two *d. Educ:* Battersea Grammar School; Blackpool Grammar School; Jesus College, Cambridge (MA). RAFVR (Aircrew), 1943–47; University of Cambridge, 1947–49; Lincoln Theological College, 1949–51. Curate, Christ Church, Southgate, 1951–54; Tutor and Chaplain, Lincoln Theological College, 1954–59; Vicar, Bottesford-with-Ashby, 1959–65; Principal, Lichfield Theological College, 1966–72; Bishop Suffragan of Whitby, 1972–75. *Address:* Bishopscourt, Pitt Street, Gloucester GL1 2BQ.

GLOUCESTER, Dean of; see Jennings, Very Rev. K. N.

GLOUCESTER, Archdeacon of; see Wagstaff, Ven. C. J. H.

GLOVER, Anthony Richard Haysom; Chief Executive Officer, City Council of Norwich, since 1980; *b* 29 May 1934; 2nd *s* of late Arthur Herbert Glover and late Marjorie Florence Glover; *m* 1960, Ann Penelope Scupham, *d* of John Scupham, *qv;* two *s* one *d. Educ:* Culford Sch., Bury St Edmunds; Emmanuel Coll., Cambridge (BA). HM Customs and Excise: Asst Principal, 1957; Principal, 1961; on secondment to HM Treasury, 1965–68; Asst Sec., 1969; Asst Sec., HM Treasury, 1972–76; Dep. Controller, HM Stationery Office, 1976–80. MBIM 1978. Mem. Council, UEA Norwich, 1984–. FRSA 1985. *Recreations:* music, reading, writing, alpine gardening. *Address:* 7 Hillside Road, Thorpe St Andrew, Norwich. *T:* Norwich 33508.

GLOVER, Eric; Secretary-General, Institute of Bankers, since 1982; *b* 28 June 1935; *s* of William and Margaret Glover; *m* 1960, Adele Diane Hilliard; three *s. Educ:* Liverpool Institute High Sch.; Oriel Coll., Oxford (MA). Shell International Petroleum (Borneo and Uganda), 1957–63; Institute of Bankers, 1963–; Asst Sec., 1964–69; Dir of Studies, 1969–82. Member: Regional Adv. Council for Further Educn, London and SE Region, 1977–; Council for Accreditation of Correspondence Colls, 1983–; British Accreditation Council for Indep. Further and Higher Educn, 1985–.. *Publications:* articles on banking education. *Recreations:* mainly sport-golf, squash, tennis. *Address:* 12 Manor Park, Tunbridge Wells, Kent TN4 8XP. *T:* Tunbridge Wells 31221; (business) 01–623 3531. *Club:* Overseas Bankers'.

GLOVER, Sir Gerald (Alfred), Kt 1971; Consultant, Glover & Co.; President, Edger Investments Ltd, since 1980; *b* 5 June 1908; *m* 1933, Susan Drage (OBE 1982; Chm., Nat. Adoption Soc. for England); two *d. Educ:* City of London School. Solicitor, 1932. King's Messenger, 1938–40; served War of 1939–45, Mil. Intell., at home and abroad; Major. Conservative Party: Mem. 1935–; Chm. 1963–71, Vice-Pres. 1972–74, Patron 1978–, E Midland Area Exec.; Treas. Kettering Div., 1953–67; President: Kettering Cons. Club, 1970–; Kettering Cons. Assoc., 1971–. Patron, London Branch, Red Cross; Trustee: National Adoption Soc. for England; Bankside Arts Centre; Founder: South Bank Arts Centre and Gallery, Southwark; East Kent Arts Centre and Gallery, Folkestone; Pres., Kettering and District Scouts; Past Pres., Northants Agricultural Soc. (Pres., 1970). CC Northants (Vice-Chm., 1972–74; Chm., Police Authority, 1978–81). Liveryman, Basketmakers' Co. Freeman, City of London. *Recreations:* bloodstock breeding and racing (bred, raced and owns Privy Councillor, winner of 2000 Guineas, 1962), landscape gardening, visual art. *Address:* Pytchley House, Northants. *T:* Kettering 790258. *Clubs:* White's, Boodle's.
See also Sir James Spooner.

GLOVER, Harold, CB 1977; coinage consultant; *b* 29 Jan. 1917; 4th *s* of late George Glover, Wallasey, Ches; *m* 1949, Olive, *d* of late E. B. Robotham, Sawbridgeworth, Herts; two *s. Educ:* Wallasey Gram. Sch. Joined Customs and Excise, 1933; joined Min. of Works, 1949 (now DoE); Controller of Supplies, 1957; Under-Secretary, 1967–70; Dep. Master, Royal Mint, 1970–74; Controller, HMSO, 1974–77. Served RAF, 1940–46 (Flt Lieut Signals). FRSA 1963 (Mem Council, 1974–79; Bicentenary Medal, 1967); Hon. FSIAD 1975. *Recreation:* music. *Address:* 23 Walnut Tree Crescent, Sawbridgeworth, Herts. *T:* Bishops Stortford 723256. *Clubs:* Reform, Royal Air Force.

GLOVER, Gen. Sir James (Malcolm), KCB 1981; MBE 1964; Commander-in-Chief, United Kingdom Land Forces, since 1985; *b* 25 March 1929; *s* of Maj.-Gen. Malcolm Glover, CB, OBE; *m* 1958, Janet Diones De Pree; one *s* one *d. Educ:* Wellington College; RMA, Sandhurst. Commissioned, RA, 1949; RHA, 1950–54; Instructor RMA Sandhurst, 1955–56; transferred to Rifle Brigade, 1956; Brigade Major, 48 Gurkha Bde, 1960–62; Directing Staff, Staff Coll., 1966–68; CO, 3rd Bn Royal Green Jackets, 1970–71; Col General Staff, Min. of Defence, 1972–73; Comdr 19 Airportable Bde, 1974–75; Brigadier General Staff, Min. of Defence, 1977–78; Commander Land Forces N Ireland, 1979–80; Dep. Chief of Defence Staff (Intell.), 1981–83; Vice Chief of General Staff, and Mem., Army Bd, 1983–85. Has served in W Germany, Malaya, Singapore, Hong Kong, Cyprus and N Ireland. Col Commandant: RMP, 1983–; 3rd Bn, Royal Green Jackets, 1984–. *Recreations:* travel, gardening, shooting, hill walking military history. *Address:* c/o Lloyds Bank, Cox's & King's Branch, 6 Pall Mall, SW1Y 5NH. *Club:* Boodle's.

GLOVER, Jane Alison, DPhil; conductor; Artistic Director, London Mozart Players, since 1984; Musical Director, London Choral Society, since 1983; Senior Research Fellow, St Hugh's College, Oxford, since 1982; *b* 13 May 1949; *d* of Robert Finlay Glover, *qv. Educ:* Monmouth School for Girls; St Hugh's Coll., Oxford (BA, MA, DPhil). Junior Research Fellow, St Hugh's Coll., 1973–75; Lecturer in Music: St Hugh's Coll., 1976–84; St Anne's Coll., 1976–80; Pembroke Coll., 1979–84; elected to OU Faculty of Music, 1979. Professional conducting début at Wexford Festival, 1975; thereafter, operas and concerts for BBC; Musica nel Chiostro; English Bach Fest.; Camden Fest.; Glyndebourne Festival Opera: joined Music Staff, 1979; Chorus Dir, 1980; Fest. conductor, 1982–; Musical Dir, Touring Opera, 1982–85; Teatro la Fenice, Venice; London Symphony Orch.; London Philharmonic Orch.; Philharmonia Orch.; Royal Philharmonic Orch.; English Chamber Orch.; BBC Welsh Symphony Orch.; Bournemouth Sinfonietta; RTE Symphony Orch., etc. Member: BBC Central Music Adv. Cttee, 1981–85; Music Adv. Panel, Arts Council, 1986–. Television documentaries and series, and presentation for BBC and LWT, esp. Orchestra, 1983, Mozart, 1985, and South Bank Show. Governor, RAM, 1985–. Hon. DMus Exeter, 1986. *Publications:* Cavalli, 1978; contribs to: The New Monteverdi Companion, 1986; Monteverdi 'Orfeo' handbook, 1986; articles in Music and Letters, Proc. of Royal Musical Assoc., Musical Times, The Listener, TLS, Early Music, and others. *Recreations:* The Times crossword puzzle, theatre. *Address:* c/o Ibbs and Tillett, 450–452 Edgware Road, W2 1EG. *T:* 01–262 2864.

GLOVER, John Neville, CMG 1963; *b* 12 July 1913; *s* of John Robert Glover and Sybil Glover (*née* Cureton); *m* 1st, 1940, Margot Burdick; one *s*; 2nd, 1956, June Patricia Bruce Gaskell. *Educ:* Tonbridge Sch. Commissioned 6th Bn Devonshire Regt (TA), 1933; RAF (Gen. Duties Branch), 1934. Served RAF, 1934–46; RAFRO, 1946–59 (retained rank of Group Capt.). Called to Bar, Gray's Inn, 1949. Appointed to Colonial Legal Service, 1951; served: Ghana (Crown Counsel and Senior Crown Counsel), 1951–57; Western Pacific High Commission (Legal Adviser and Attorney-General, British Solomon Islands Protectorate), 1957–63. QC (Western Pacific), 1962. Retired from HM Overseas Civil Service, 1963. Comr to examine Human Rights Laws in the Bahamas, 1964–65. Legal

Draftsman in the Bahamas, 1965–66. Law Revision Comr for certain overseas territories, 1967–. *Recreation:* fishing. *Address:* Clam End, Trebullett, near Launceston, Cornwall. *T:* Coad's Green 82347. *Club:* Royal Air Force.

GLOVER, Kenneth Frank; Assistant Under-Secretary of State (Statistics), Ministry of Defence, 1974–81, retired; *b* 16 Dec. 1920; *s* of Frank Glover and Mabel Glover; *m* 1951, Iris Clare Holmes. *Educ:* Bideford Grammar Sch.; UC of South West, Exeter; LSE (MScEcon). Joined Statistics Div., MoT, 1946; Statistician, 1950; Statistical adviser to Cttee of Inquiry on Major Ports (Rochdale Cttee), 1961–62; Dir of Econs and Statistics at Nat. Ports Council, 1964–68; Chief Statistician, MoT and DoE, 1968–74. *Publications:* various papers; articles in JRSS, Dock and Harbour Authority. *Recreations:* boating, idleness. *Address:* Riverdown, 11 Platway Lane, Shaldon, Teignmouth, South Devon TQ14 0AR. *T:* Shaldon 872700.

GLOVER, Myles Howard; Clerk of the Skinners' Company since 1959; Hon. Secretary, Governing Bodies' Association since 1967; *b* 18 Dec. 1928; *yr s* of Cedric Howard Glover and Winifred Mary (*née* Crewdson); *m* 1969, Wendy Gillian, *er d* of C. M. Coleman; one *s* two *d*. *Educ:* Rugby; Balliol Coll., Oxford (MA). Called to the Bar, Lincoln's Inn, 1954. Chm., Cttee of Clerks to Twelve Chief Livery Cos of City of London, 1975–81; Member: City & Guilds Art Sch. Cttee, 1960–71; City Univ. Adv. Cttee on the Arts, 1975–; Adv. Cttee, Gresham Coll., 1985–; Council, St Paul's Cathedral Choir Sch., 1986–. *Recreation:* music. *Address:* Buckhall Farm, Bull Lane, Bethersden, near Ashford, Kent TN26 3HB. *T:* Bethersden 634.

GLOVER, Maj.-Gen. Peter James, CB 1966; OBE 1948; *b* 16 Jan. 1913; *s* of late G. H. Glover, CBE, Sheephatch House, Tilford, Surrey, and late Mrs G. H. Glover; *m* 1946, Wendy Archer; one *s* two *d*. *Educ:* Uppingham; Cambridge (MA). 2nd Lieut RA, 1934; served War of 1939–45, BEF France and Far East; Lieut-Col 1956; Brig. 1961; Comdt, Sch. of Artillery, Larkhill, 1960–62; Maj.-Gen. 1962; GOC 49 Infantry Division TA and North Midland District, 1962–63; Head of British Defence Supplies Liaison Staff, Delhi, 1963–66; Director, Royal Artillery, 1966–69, retd. Col Comdt, RA, 1970–78. *Address:* Lukesland, Diptford, Totnes, Devon.

GLOVER, Robert Finlay, TD 1954; Headmaster, Monmouth School, 1959–76; *b* 28 June 1917; *yr s* of T. R. Glover, Public Orator in University of Cambridge, and Alice, *d* of H. G. Few; *m* 1941, Jean, *d* of late N. G. Muir, Lincoln; one *s* two *d*. *Educ:* The Leys Sch.; Corpus Christi Coll., Oxford. Served in Royal Artillery (TA), 1939–46; Staff Coll., Camberley, 1944; Major, 1944. Asst Master, Ampleforth Coll., 1946–50; Head of Classics Dept, King's Sch., Canterbury, 1950–53; Headmaster, Adams' Grammar Sch., Newport, Salop, 1953–59; Dep. Sec., Headmasters' Conference and Assoc., 1977–82. Fellow, Woodard Corp., 1982. *Publications:* Notes on Latin, 1954; (with R. W. Harris) Latin for Historians, 1954. *Recreations:* normal. *Address:* Brockhill Lodge, West Malvern Road, The Wyche, Malvern, Worcs WR14 4EJ. *T:* Malvern 64247. *Club:* East India, Devonshire, Sports and Public Schools.
See also J. A. Glover.

GLOVER, William James, QC 1969; a Recorder of the Crown Court, since 1975; *b* 8 May 1924; *s* of late H. P. Glover, KC and Martha Glover; *m* 1956, Rosemary D. Long; two *s*. *Educ:* Harrow; Pembroke Coll., Cambridge. Served with Royal West African Frontier Force in West Africa and Burma, 1944–47. Called to Bar, Inner Temple, 1950, Bencher, 1977. Second Junior Counsel to Inland Revenue (Rating Valuation), 1963–69. *Recreation:* golf. *Address:* 1 Mitre Court Buildings, Temple, EC4Y 7BX.

GLUE, George Thomas; Director-General of Supplies and Transport (Naval), Ministry of Defence, 1973–77; *b* 3 May 1917; *s* of Percy Albert Glue and Alice Harriet Glue (*née* Stoner); *m* 1947, Eileen Marion Hitchcock; one *d*. *Educ:* Portsmouth Southern Secondary School. Admiralty: Asst Naval Store Officer, 1937; Dep. Naval Store Officer, Mediterranean, 1940; Naval Store Officer, Mediterranean, 1943; Asst Dir of Stores, 1955; Suptg Naval Store Officer, Devonport, 1960; Dep. Dir of Stores, 1963; Dir of Stores, 1970; Dir, Supplies and Transport (Naval), 1971. *Recreations:* gardening, bridge. *Address:* 18 Late Broads, Winsley, near Bradford-on-Avon, Wilts BA15 2NW. *T:* Limpley Stoke 2717.

GLYN, family name of **Baron Wolverton.**

GLYN, Dr Alan, ERD; MP (C) Windsor and Maidenhead, since 1974 (Windsor, 1970–74); *b* 26 Sept. 1918; *s* of John Paul Glyn, late Royal Horse Guards (Blues), Barrister-at-Law, Middle Temple, and late Margaret Johnston, Edinburgh; *m* 1962, Lady Rosula Caroline Windsor Clive, OStJ, *y d* of 2nd Earl of Plymouth, PC, GCStJ (*d* 1943), St Fagan's, Cardiff, S Wales; two *d*. *Educ:* Westminster; Caius Coll., Cambridge; St Bartholomew's and St George's Hosps. BA (Hons) Cantab 1939. Qualified medical practitioner, 1948. Served War of 1939–45; Far East, 1942–46; psc 1945; Bde Major, 1946; re-employed Captain (Hon. Major) Royal Horse Guards (ER) until 1967; att. French Foreign Legion, 1960. Called to Bar, Middle Temple, 1955. Co-opted Mem. LCC Education Cttee, 1956–58. MP (C) Clapham Div. of Wandsworth, 1959–64. Member: Chelsea Borough Council, 1959–62; No 1 Divisional Health Cttee (London), 1959–61; Inner London Local Med. Cttee, 1967–; Governing Body, Brit. Postgrad. Med. Fedn, 1967–82; Greater London Cent. Valuation Panel, 1967–; Bd of Governors, Nat. Heart and Chest Hosps Special Health Auth., 1982–. Former Governor, Henry Thornton and Aristotle Schs; Manager, Macaulay C. of E. Sch., Richard Atkins, Henry Cavendish, Telfescot, Glenbrook and Boneville Primary Schs in Clapham. One of Earl Marshal's Green Staff Officers at Investiture of HRH Prince of Wales, Caernarvon, 1969. Freeman, Worshipful Soc. of the Art and Mystery of Apothecaries of the City of London, 1961. Pro-Hungaria Medal of SMO Malta, 1959. *Publication:* Witness to Viet Nam (the containment of communism in South East Asia), 1968. *Address:* 17 Cadogan Place, Belgrave Square, SW1. *T:* 01–235 2957. *Clubs:* Carlton, Pratt's, Special Services.

GLYN, Sir Anthony (Geoffrey Leo Simon), 2nd Bt, *cr* 1927; author; *b* 13 March 1922; *s* of Sir Edward Davson, 1st Bt, and Margot, OBE (*d* 1966), *er d* of late Clayton Glyn and late Mrs Elinor Glyn; *S* father, Sir Edward Rae Davson, KCMG, 1937; assumed by deed poll, 1957, the surname of Glyn in lieu of his patronymic, and the additional forename of Anthony; *m* 1946, Susan Eleanor, barrister-at-law, 1950, *er d* of Sir Rhys Rhys-Williams, 1st Bt, DSO, QC, and Dame Juliet Rhys-Williams, DBE; one *d* (and one *d* decd). *Educ:* Eton. Jnd Welsh Guards, 1941; served Guards Armoured Div., 1942–45; Staff Captain, 1945. Vermeil Medal, City of Paris, 1985. *Publications:* Romanza, 1953; The Jungle of Eden, 1954; Elinor Glyn, a biography, 1955 (Book Society Non-Fiction Choice); The Ram in the Thicket, 1957 (Dollar Book Club Choice); I Can Take it All, 1959 (Book Society Choice); Kick Turn, 1963; The Terminal, 1965; The Seine, 1966; The Dragon Variation, 1969; The Blood of a Britishman, 1970 (US edn, The British; trans. French, Spanish, Japanese); The Companion Guide to Paris, 1985. *Recreations:* ski-ing, Aubusson tapestry designing. *Heir:* *b* Christopher Michael Edward Davson, ACA, late Capt. Welsh Guards [*b* 26 May 1927; *m* 1962, Evelyn Mary (marr. diss. 1971), *o d* of late James Wardrop; one *s*; 2nd, 1975, Kate, *d* of Ludovic Foster, Greatham Manor, Pulborough]. *Address:* 13 Rue le Regrattier, Ile Saint-Louis, 75004 Paris, France. *T:* 4633:3475; Friedegg, Westendorf, Tyrol, Austria. *Clubs:* Savile, Pratt's.

GLYN, Hilary B.; *b* 12 Jan. 1916; *s* of Maurice Glyn and Hon. Maud Grosvenor; *m* 1938, Caroline Bull; one *s* two *d*. *Educ:* Eton; New Coll., Oxford. DipEconPolSc. Joined Gallaher Ltd, 1937. Served, RASC Supp. Reserve, 1939–46 (A/Major). Director, Gallaher Ltd, 1962; Asst. Man. Dir, 1975; retd, 1976. *Recreations:* shooting, horse trials. *Address:* Castle Hill Cottage, Boothby Graffoe, Lincoln LN5 0LF. *T:* Lincoln 810885.
See also Baron Wolverton.

GLYN, Sir Richard (Lindsay), 10th Bt *cr* 1759, and 6th Bt *cr* 1800; *b* 3 Aug. 1943; *s* of Sir Richard Hamilton Glyn, 9th and 5th Bt, OBE, TD, and Lyndsay Mary (*d* 1971), *d* of T. H. Baker; *S* father, 1980; *m* 1970, Carolyn Ann Williams (marr. diss. 1979); one *s* one *d*. *Educ:* Eton. *Recreation:* tennis. *Heir:* *s* Richard Rufus Francis Glyn, *b* 8 Jan. 1971. *Address:* Ashton Farmhouse, Wimborne, Dorset. *T:* Witchampton 840585.

GLYNN, Prof. Alan Anthony, MD; FRCP, FRCPath; Director, Central Public Health Laboratory, Colindale, London, since 1980; Visiting Professor of Bacteriology, London School of Hygiene and Tropical Medicine, since 1983; *b* 29 May 1923; *s* of Hyman and Charlotte Glynn; *m* 1962, Nicole Benhamou; two *d*. *Educ:* City of London Sch.; University Coll. London (Fellow, 1982) and UCH Med. Sch., London (MB, BS 1946, MD 1959). MRCP 1954, FRCP 1974; MRCPath 1963, FRCPath 1973. House Physician, UCH, 1946; Asst Lectr in Physiol., Sheffield Univ., 1947–49; National Service, RAMC, 1950–51; Registrar, Canadian Red Cross Meml Hosp., Taplow, 1955–57; St Mary's Hospital Medical School: Lectr in Bacteriology, 1958–61; Sen. Lectr, 1961–67; Reader, 1967–71; Prof., 1971–80; Hon. Consultant Bacteriologist, 1961–83; Visiting Prof. of Bacteriology, St. Mary's Hosp., 1980–83. Examr in Pathol., Univs of Edinburgh, 1974–76, 1983–85, Glasgow, 1975–78, and London, 1979–80. Member: DHSS Jt Cttee on Vaccination and Immunization, 1979–85; Adv. Gp, ARC Inst. for Res. in Animal Diseases. Almroth Wright Lectr, Wright-Fleming Inst., 1972; Erasmus Wilson Demonstrator, RCS, 1973. Mem. Editorial Board: Immunology, 1969–79; Parasite Immunity, 1979–. *Publications:* papers on bacterial infection and immunity in jls. *Recreations:* theatre, walking, carpentry. *Club:* Athenæum.
See also Prof. I. M. Glynn.

GLYNN, Prof. Ian Michael, MD, PhD, FRS 1970; Professor of Physiology, University of Cambridge, since 1986; Fellow, Trinity College, since 1955 (Vice-Master, 1980–86); *b* 3 June 1928; 2nd *s* of Hyman and Charlotte Glynn; *m* 1959, Jenifer Muriel, 2nd *d* of Ellis and Muriel Franklin; one *s* two *d*. *Educ:* City of London Sch.; Trinity Coll., Cambridge; University Coll. Hosp. 1st cl. in Pts I and II of Nat. Sci. Tripos; BA (Cantab) 1949; MB, BChir, 1952; MD 1970. House Phys., Central Mddx Hosp., 1952–53; MRC Scholar at Physiol. Lab., Cambridge; PhD 1956. Nat. Service in RAF Med. Br., 1956–57. Cambridge University: Res. Fellow, 1955–59, Staff Fellow and Dir of Med. Studies, 1961–73, Trinity Coll.; Univ. Demonstrator in Physiology, 1958–63; Lecturer, 1963–70; Reader, 1970–75; Prof. Membrane Physiology, 1975–86. Vis. Prof., Yale Univ., 1969. Member: MRC, 1976–80 (Chm., Physiological Systems and Disorders Bd, 1976–78); Council, Royal Soc., 1979–81; AFRC (formerly ARC), 1981–86. Chm., Editorial Bd, Jl of Physiology, 1968–70. *Publications:* scientific papers dealing with transport of ions across living membranes, mostly in Jl of Physiology. *Address:* Physiological Laboratory, Cambridge; Daylesford, Conduit Head Road, Cambridge. *T:* Cambridge 353079.
See also Prof. A. A. Glynn.

GLYNN GRYLLS, Rosalie; *see* Mander, Lady (Rosalie).

GOAD, Sir (Edward) Colin (Viner), KCMG 1974; Secretary-General, Inter-Governmental Maritime Consultative Organization, 1968–73 (Deputy Secretary-General, 1963–68); Member, Advisory Board, International Bank, Washington DC, since 1974; *b* 21 Dec. 1914; *s* of Maurice George Viner Goad and Caroline (*née* Masters); *m* 1939, Joan Olive Bradley (*d* 1980); one *s*. *Educ:* Cirencester Grammar Sch.; Gonville and Caius Coll., Cambridge (Scholar, BA). Ministry of Transport: Asst Principal, 1937; Principal, 1942; Asst Sec., 1948; Imperial Defence Coll., 1953; Under-Sec., 1963. *Address:* The Paddock, Ampney Crucis, Glos. *T:* Poulton 353.

GOADBY, Hector Kenneth, FRCP; retired; Hon. Consulting Physician, St Thomas' Hospital, London; *b* 16 May 1902; *s* of late Sir Kenneth Goadby, KBE; *m* 1937, Margaret Evelyn (*née* Boggon); one *s* two *d*. *Educ:* Winchester; Trinity Coll., Cambridge (MA, MD). MRCS, LRCP 1926; FRCP 1936. Physician, St Thomas's Hosp., 1934–67; Cons. Physician, Southern Army and Eastern Comd, India, 1945; Physician, St Peter's Hosp., Chertsey, 1948. *Publications:* contribs to Jl of Physiology, Lancet, Acta Medica Scandinavica. *Recreations:* sailing, golf. *Address:* Dolphin Cottage, Iden Rye, East Sussex TN31 7PT. *T:* Iden 355. *Club:* Rye Golf.

GOBBO, Hon. Sir James (Augustine), Kt 1982; **Hon. Mr Justice Gobbo;** Judge of the Supreme Court of Victoria, Australia, since 1978; *b* 22 March 1931; *s* of Antonio Gobbo and Regina Gobbo (*née* Tosetto); *m* 1957, Shirley Lewis; two *s* three *d*. *Educ:* Xavier Coll., Kew, Victoria; Melbourne Univ. (BA Hons); Magdalen Coll., Oxford Univ. (MA). Called to Bar, Gray's Inn, London, 1956; Barrister and Solicitor, Victoria, Aust., 1956; signed Roll of Counsel, Victorian Bar, 1957; QC 1971. Comr, Victorian Law Reform Commn. Chairman: Aust. Refugee Council, 1977; Mercy Private Hosp., Melbourne (Mem. Bd, Mercy Maternity Hosp.); Member: Nat. Population Council, 1983–; Newman Coll. Council, 1970–; Bd, Pres., CO-AS-IT, 1979–84. Trustee, Victorian Opera Foundn, 1983–. Vice-Pres., Aust. Assoc. of SMO Malta, 1984–. Commendatore all'Ordine di Merito, Republic of Italy, 1971. Kt Grand Cross SMO Malta, 1982. *Publications:* (ed) Cross on Evidence (Australian edn), 1970–1978. *Address:* 6 Florence Avenue, Kew, Victoria 3101, Australia. *T:* (03) 817–1669.

GOBLE, John Frederick; Solicitor; Senior Partner, Herbert Smith, since 1983 (partner since 1953; Hong Kong office, 1982–83); *b* 1 April 1925; *o s* of late John and Evileen Goble; *m* 1953, Moira Murphy O'Connor; one *s* three *d*. *Educ:* Highgate Sch.; Brasenose Coll., Oxford. Sub-Lieut, RNVR, 1944–46. Admitted solicitor, 1951. A Crown Agent, 1974–79 (Dep. Chm., 1975–79); Mem. and Dep. Chm., Crown Agents for Oversea Govts and Admins, and Crown Agents Holding and Realisation Bd, 1980–82. Director: Holt Lloyd International plc, 1970–; British Telecommunications plc, 1984–; pt-time Mem., British Telecom Corp., 1983–. Governor, Highgate Sch., 1976. Chm., The Friends of Highgate Sch. Soc., 1978–; Pres., Old Cholmeleian Soc., 1983–84. *Recreations:* music, golf. *Address:* 52 Chelsea Park Gardens, SW3 6AD; Watling House, 35 Cannon Street, EC4M 5SD. *T:* 01-489 8000. *Clubs:* Garrick, MCC, Hurlingham; New Zealand Golf (West Byfleet).

GODBER, Geoffrey Chapham, CBE 1961; DL; Chief Executive, West Sussex County Council, 1974–75, retired (Clerk of the Peace and Clerk to the Council, 1966–74); Clerk to the Lieutenancy of West Sussex, 1974–76 (Sussex, 1968–74); *b* 22 Sept. 1912; *s* of late Isaac Godber, Willington Manor, near Bedford; *m* 1937, Norah Enid (*née* Finney); three *s*. *Educ:* Bedford Sch. LLB (London) 1935; Solicitor, 1936. Deputy Clerk of the Peace, Northants, 1938–44; Clerk of the Peace, Clerk of the County Council and Clerk of the

Lieutenancy, Salop, 1944–66; Hon. Sec., Soc. of Clerks of the Peace of Counties, 1953–61 (Chm., 1961–64); Chm., Assoc. of County Chief Executives, 1974–75. Member: Probation Adv. and Trg Bd, 1949–55; Child Care Adv. Council, 1953–56; Cttee of Inquiry into Inland Waterways, 1956–58; Redevelopment Adv. Cttee, Inland Waterways, 1959–62; Waterways Sub-Commn, Brit. Transport, 1959–62; Central Adv. Water Cttee, 1961–70; Minister of Health's Long Term Study Group, 1965–69; W Midlands Economic Planning Council, 1965–66; S-E Economic Planning Council, 1969–75; CS Adv. Council, 1971–78; British Waterways Bd, 1975–81; Chichester Harbour Conservancy, 1975–78; Shoreham Port Authority, 1976–82 (Dep. Chm., 1978–82); Chm., Open Air Museum, Weald and Downland, 1975–82. DL W Sussex 1975. *Recreations:* sailing, shooting. *Address:* Pricklows, Singleton, Chichester, West Sussex. *T:* Singleton 238. *Club:* Naval and Military.

See also Sir G. E. Godber.

GODBER, Sir George (Edward), GCB 1971 (KCB 1962; CB 1958); *b* 4 Aug. 1908; *s* of late I. Godber, Willington Manor, Bedford; *m* 1935, Norma Hathorne Rainey; two *s* one *d* (and two *s* two *d* decd). *Educ:* Bedford Sch.; New Coll., Oxford (Hon. Fellow, 1973); London Hospital; London Sch. of Hygiene. BA Oxon 1933; DM Oxon 1939; FRCP 1947; DPH London 1936. Medical Officer, Min. of Health, 1939; Dep. Chief Medical Officer, Min. of Health, 1950–60; Chief Medical Officer, DHSS, DES and Home Office, 1960–73. Chm., Health Educn Council, 1977–78 (Mem., 1976–78). QHP, 1953–56. Scholar in Residence, NIH Bethesda, 1975. Vice-Pres., RCN, 1973. Fellow: American Hospital Assoc., and American Public Health Assoc., 1961; British Orthopaedic Assoc.; Mem. Dietetic Assoc., 1961; Hon. Member: Faculty of Radiologists, 1958; British Pædiatric Assoc.; Pharmaceut. Soc., 1973. FRCOG *ad eundem*, 1966; FRCPsych 1973; FFCM 1974; Hon. FRCS, 1973; Hon. FRSM, 1973. Hon. LLD: Manchester, 1964; Hull, 1970; Nottingham, 1973; Hon. DCL: Newcastle 1972; Oxford 1973; Hon. DSc Bath, 1979. Hon. Fellow, London Sch. of Hygiene and Tropical Medicine, 1976. Bisset Hawkins Medal, RCP, 1965; 150th Anniversary Medal, Swedish Med. Soc., 1966; Leon Bernard Foundn Medal, 1972; Ciba Foundn Gold Medal, 1970; Therapeutics Gold Medal, Soc. of Apothecaries, 1973. Lectures: Thomas and Edith Dixon Belfast, 1962; Bartholomew, Rotunda, Dublin, 1963; Woolmer, Bio-Engineering Soc., 1964; Monkton Copeman, Soc. of Apothecaries, 1968; Michael M. Davis, Chicago, 1969; Harold Diehl, Amer. Public Health Assoc., 1969; Rhys Williams, 1969; W. M. Fletcher Shaw, RCOG, 1970; Henry Floyd, Inst. of Orthopaedics, 1970; First Elizabeth Casson Meml, Assoc. of Occ. Therapists, 1973; Cavendish, W London Med.-Chir. Soc., 1973; Heath Clark, London Univ., 1973; Rock Carling, Nuffield Provincial Hosps Trust, 1975; Thom Bequest, RCSE, 1975; Maurice Bloch, Glasgow, 1975; Ira Hiscock, Yale, 1975; John Sullivan, St Louis, 1975; Fordham, Sheffield, 1976; Lloyd Hughes, Liverpool, 1977; Gale Meml, SW England Faculty RCGP, 1978; Gordon, Birmingham, 1979; Samson Gamgee, Birm. Med. Inst., 1979; W. H. Duncan, Liverpool, 1984; W. Pickles, RCGP, 1985. *Publications:* (with Sir L. Parsons and Clayton Fryers) Survey of Hospitals in the Sheffield Region, 1944; The Health Service: past, present and future (Heath Clark Lectures), 1974; Change in Medicine (Rock Carling monograph), 1975; British National Health Service: Conversations, 1977; papers in Lancet, BMJ, Public Health. *Recreation:* golf. *Address:* 21 Almoners' Avenue, Cambridge CB1 4NZ. *T:* Cambridge 247491.

See also G. C. Godber.

GODDARD, Ann Felicity, QC 1982; a Recorder of the Crown Court, since 1979; *b* 22 Jan. 1936; *o c* of late Graham Elliott Goddard and Margaret Louise Hambrook Goddard (*née* Clark). *Educ:* Grey Coat Hosp., Westminster; Birmingham Univ. (LLB); Newnham Coll., Cambridge (LLB and Dip. in Comparative Legal Studies). Called to the Bar, Gray's Inn, 1960. *Recreation:* travel. *Address:* 3 Temple Gardens, Temple, EC4Y 9AU. *T:* 01–353 3102.

GODDARD, David Rodney, MBE 1985; Director, Exeter Maritime Museum, since 1968; *b* 16 March 1927; *s* of Air Marshal Sir Victor Goddard, *qv*; *m* 1952, Susan Ashton; two *s* one *d. Educ:* Bryanston School; Wanganui Collegiate Sch., New Zealand; Peterhouse, Cambridge. MA Hons Geography. Joined Royal Marines, 1944, hostilities only commn, 1946, demob. 1948. Whaling, United Whalers, 1949; Schoolmaster, 1950–52. Joined Somerset Light Infantry, 1952; active service, Malaya (mentioned in despatches, 1954); served: Germany, Kenya (King's African Rifles), Bahrein, N Ireland; retired at own request, as Major, 1968; to found and direct Internat. Sailing Craft Assoc. and Exeter Maritime Museum. *Recreations:* shooting, fishing, sailing, bird watching, photography. *Address:* The Mill, Lympstone, Exmouth, Devon. *T:* Exmouth 265575.

GODDARD, Lt.-Gen. Eric Norman, CB 1947; CIE 1944; CBE 1942 (OBE 1919); MVO 1936; MC; IA, retired; *b* 6 July 1897; 3rd *s* of late Arthur Goddard, Chartered Acct, London; *m* 1939, Elizabeth Lynch, *d* of late Major Lynch Hamilton, and late Frances Prioleau; one *s. Educ:* Dulwich Coll. Commissioned Indian Army, 1915; service in Mesopotamia, Persia and Kurdistan, 1916–19 (despatches twice, OBE, MC); GSO3 AHQ India, 1923–25; 12th Frontier Force Regt, 1928; Staff Coll., Quetta, 1928–29; Bde Major, Nowshera Bde, 1932–34; Chitral relief, 1932 (despatches, bar to MC); Mohmand operations, 1933 (despatches); Bt Major, 1933; GSO2 Eastern Comd, 1934–36; Officer i/c King's Indian Orderly Officers, 1936 (MVO 4th class); Comdt 4th Bn 15 Punjab Regt, 1936; Bt Col 1939 and Col i/c Administration, Burma Army; Brigade Commander, Oct. 1940; Maj.-Gen. i/c Administration Army in Burma, Dec. 1941; served in Burma and on Eastern front, Dec. 1941–Dec. 1944, including Maj.-Gen. i/c Admin 11th Army Group and Allied Land Forces SE Asia, 1943–44 (despatches four times, CIE, CBE); GOC-in-C Southern Comd, India, 1947–48; Subst. Maj.-Gen. 1944; Actg Lieut-Gen. 1947; retired Nov. 1948 with hon. rank of Lieut-Gen. Special appointment CC Germany, 1949–53; Dir of Civil Defence, North-Western Region (Manchester), 1955–63; Pres., East Lancs Br., British Red Cross, 1964–66. *Address:* Muddles Cottage, Sparrows Green, Wadhurst, East Sussex TN5 6TW. *T:* Wadhurst 2364.

GODDARD, Harold Keith; QC 1979; barrister-at-law; a Recorder of the Crown Court, since 1978; *b* 9 July 1936; *s* of late Harold Goddard and Edith Goddard, Stockport, Cheshire; *m* 1st, 1963, Susan Elizabeth (marr. diss.), *yr d* of late Ronald Stansfield and of Evelyn Stansfield, Wilmslow, Cheshire; two *s*; 2nd, 1983, Alicja Maria, *d* of late Czeslaw Lazuchiewicz and of Eleonora Lazuchiewicz, Lodz, Poland. *Educ:* Manchester Grammar Sch.; Corpus Christi Coll., Cambridge (Scholar; 1st Cl. Law Tripos 1957, MA, LLM). Bacon Scholar, Gray's Inn; called to the Bar, Gray's Inn, 1959. Practised on Northern Circuit, 1959–. Chm., Disciplinary Appeals Cttee, 1974–80, Mem. Council, 1980–, Mem. Ct of Governors, 1981, UMIST. *Recreation:* golf. *Address:* Deans Court Chambers, Cumberland House, Crown Square, Manchester M3 3HA. *T:* 061–834 4097. *Clubs:* Manchester Tennis and Racquet; Wilmslow Golf.

GODDARD, Maj.-Gen. John Desmond, MC 1944; *b* 13 Jan. 1919; *s* of late Major J. Goddard, HAC, Bombay and Gerrards Cross, Bucks; *m* 1948, Sheila Noel Vera, *d* of late C. W. H. P. Waud, Bombay and St John, Jersey; three *s* one *d. Educ:* Sherborne; RMA Woolwich. 2 Lieut, RA, 1939. Served War of 1939–45: France, 1939–40; N Africa, 1943; Italy, 1943–45. Brevet Lt-Col 1957; JSSC 1957; CO, 2 Fd Regt, RA, 1960–62; IDC 1964; CRA, 3 Div., 1965–66; BGS, Directorate Mil. Ops, MoD, 1966–69; Dir, Mil.

Assistance Office, MoD, 1969–72, retired. Staff Dir, British Leyland Internat., 1972–78. *Recreations:* yachting, riding, shooting, golf, carpentry, gardening. *Address:* Cranford, Pinewood Hill, Fleet, Hants. *T:* Fleet 614825. *Clubs:* Army and Navy; Royal Lymington Yacht.

GODDARD, Air Marshal (retired) Sir (Robert) Victor, KCB 1947 (CB 1943); CBE 1940; MA Cantab; *b* 1897; *s* of late Charles Ernest Goddard, OBE, TD, MD; *m* 1924, Mildred Catherine Jane (*d* 1979), *d* of Alfred Markham Inglis; two *s* one *d. Educ:* RN Colls Osborne and Dartmouth; Jesus Coll., Cambridge; Imperial Coll. of Science, London. Served European War, 1914–19, with RN, RNAS, RFC and RAF; War of 1939–45 (despatches, American DSM); Dep. Dir of Intelligence, Air Min., 1938–39; AOA, GHQ, BEF, France, 1939, SASO 1940; Dir of Military Co-operation, Air Ministy, 1940–41; Chief of the Air Staff, New Zealand, and Commander Royal NZ Air Forces, South Pacific, 1941–43; AOA, Air Command, South-East Asia, 1943–46; RAF Representative at Washington, USA, 1946–48; Mem. of Air Council for Technical Services, 1948–51; retd 1951. Principal of the Coll. of Aeronautics, 1951–54. Vice-Pres., Airship Assoc., 1984– (Pres., 1975–84). Governor (Chm. 1948–57), St George's Sch., Harpenden, 1948–64; Governor, Bryanston Sch., 1957–78. Occasional broadcaster, 1934–. *Publications:* The Enigma of Menace, 1959; Flight towards Reality, 1975; Skies to Dunkirk, 1982. *Address:* Meadowgate Lodge, Brasted, Westerham, Kent TN16 1LN.

See also D. R. Goddard.

GODDEN, Charles Henry, CBE 1982; HM Diplomatic Service, retired; Governor (formerly HM Commissioner), Anguilla, 1978–83; *b* 19 Nov. 1922; *s* of late Charles Edward Godden and Catherine Alice Godden (*née* Roe); *m* 1943, Florence Louise Williams; two *d. Educ:* Tweeddale Sch., Carshalton; Morley Coll., Westminster. Served Army, 1941–46. Colonial Office, 1950–66 (seconded British Honduras, 1961–64: Perm. Sec., External Affairs; Dep. Chief Sec.; Clerk of Executive Council); FCO, 1966–: First Sec., 1968; Asst Private Sec. to Sec. of State for Colonies; Private Secretary: to Minister of State, FCO, 1967–70; to Parly Under Sec. of State, 1970; First Sec. (Commercial), Helsinki, 1971–75; First Sec., Belize, 1975–76; Dep. High Comr and Head of Chancery, Kingston, 1976–78. *Recreations:* cricket, walking, reading. *Address:* Stoneleigh, Blackboys, Sussex. *T:* Framfield 410. *Clubs:* MCC, Royal Commonwealth Society.

GODDEN, Ven. Max Leon, Archdeacon of Lewes and Hastings, since 1975 (of Lewes, 1972–75); *b* 25 Nov. 1923; *s* of Richard George Nobel and Lucy Godden; *m* 1945, Anne, *d* of Kenneth and Edith Hucklebridge; four *d. Educ:* Sir Andrew Judd Sch., Tonbridge; Worcester Coll., Oxford (MA 1950). Served RAFVR, 1940–47 (despatches). Deacon, 1952; priest, 1953; Assistant Curate: Cuckfield, 1952–53; Brighton, 1953–57; Vicar of Hangleton, 1957–62; Vicar of Glynde, Firle and Beddingham, 1962–82. *Recreations:* life in a country parish, the garden. *Address:* Glynde Vicarage, Lewes, East Sussex. *T:* Glynde 234.

GODDEN, Rumer, (Margaret Rumer Haynes-Dixon); writer, playwright, poet; *b* 10 Dec. 1907; *d* of late Arthur Leigh Godden, Lydd House, Aldington, Kent, and Katherine Norah Hingley; *m* 1934, Laurence Sinclair Foster, Calcutta; two *d*; *m* 1949, James Haynes Dixon, OBE (*d* 1973). *Educ:* abroad and Moira House, Eastbourne. *Publications:* Chinese Puzzle, 1935; Lady and Unicorn, 1937; Black Narcissus (novel and play), 1938; Gypsy Gypsy, 1940; Breakfast with the Nikolides, 1941; Fugue in Time (novel and play), 1945; The River, 1946 (filmed, 1950); Rungli-Rungliot (biography), 1943; Candle for St Jude, 1948; In Noah's Ark (poetry), 1949; A Breath of Air, 1950; Kingfishers Catch Fire, 1953; Hans Christian Andersen (biography), 1955; An Episode of Sparrows, 1955 (filmed 1957); Mooltiki, 1957; The Greengage Summer, 1958 (filmed, 1961); China Court, 1961; The Battle of the Villa Florita, 1963 (filmed 1964); (with Jon Godden) Two Under the Indian Sun, 1966; The Kitchen Madonna, 1967; Swans and Turtles, 1968; In This House of Brede, 1969; (comp.) The Raphael Bible, 1970; The Tale of the Tales, 1971; The Old Woman Who Lived in a Vinegar Bottle, 1972; (with Jon Godden) Shiva's Pigeons, 1972; The Peacock Spring, 1975; Five for Sorrow, Ten for Joy, 1979; Gulbadan Begum: portrait of a Rose Princess at the Mughal Court (biography), 1980; The Dark Horse, 1981; The Dragon of Og, 1981; Four Dolls, 1983; Thursday's Children, 1984; children's books, incl. The Diddakoi, 1972 (Whitbread Award); published internationally (11 languages). *Address:* Macmillan & Co., 4 Little Essex Street, WC2R 3LF.

GODDEN, Tony Richard Hillier, CB 1975; Secretary, Scottish Development Department, since 1980; *b* 13 Nov. 1927; *o s* of late Richard Godden and of Gladys Eleanor Godden; *m* 1953, Marjorie Florence Snell; one *s* two *d. Educ:* Barnstaple Grammar Sch.; London Sch. of Economics (BSc (Econ.) 1st cl.). Commissioned, RAF Education Branch, 1950. Entered Colonial Office as Asst Principal, 1951; Private Sec. to Parly Under-Sec. of State, 1954–55; Principal, 1956; Cabinet Office, 1957–59; transferred to Scottish Home Dept, 1961; Asst Sec., Scottish Development Dept, 1964; Under-Sec., 1969; Sec., Scottish Economic Planning Dept, 1973–80. *Address:* New St Andrew's House, Edinburgh EH1 3SZ. *Club:* New (Edinburgh).

GODFREY, Derrick Edward Reid, MSc, PhD; Director, Thames Polytechnic, 1970–78; *b* 3 May 1918; *s* of Edward Godfrey; *m* 1944, Jessie Mary Richards; three *s* one *d. Educ:* Shooters Hill Grammar Sch.; King's Coll., London. Design and development of aero-engines, with D. Napier & Sons, 1940–45; Lectr and Reader in Applied Mathematics, Battersea Polytechnic, 1945–58; Head of Dept of Mathematics and later Principal, Woolwich Polytechnic, 1958–70. Mem. Council for Nat. Academic Awards, 1964–67. *Publications:* Elasticity and Plasticity for Engineers, 1959; contribs to learned jls, etc, on mathematics and on educational matters. *Recreations:* music, gardening. *Address:* Higher Pitt, Coombelake, Ottery St Mary, Devon. *T:* Ottery St Mary 2551.

GODFREY, Gerald Michael, QC 1971; *b* 30 July 1933; *s* of late Sidney Godfrey and late Esther (*née* Lewin); *m* 1960, Anne Sheila, *er d* of David Goldstein; three *s* two *d. Educ:* Lower Sch. of John Lyon, Harrow; King's Coll., London Univ. LLB 1952, LLM 1954. Called to the Bar: Lincoln's Inn, 1954 (Bencher 1978); Bahamas, 1972; Hong Kong, 1974; Kenya, 1978; Singapore, 1978; Malaysia, 1979; Brunei, 1979; National Service as 2nd Lt, RASC, 1955; Temp. Captain, 1956. In practice at the Chancery Bar, 1957–. Chm., Justice Cttee on Parental Rights and Duties and Custody Suits (Report, 1975); DoT Inspector into Affairs of Saint Piran Ltd (Report, 1981). Member: Senate of Inns of Court and the Bar, 1974–77, 1981–84 (Chm., Law Reform Cttee, 1981–83, 1986–); Council of Justice, 1976–81. *Publication:* Editor, Business Law Review, 1958. *Recreations:* cricket, travel. *Address:* The Garden Flat, 76 Hamilton Terrace, NW8 9UL; 9 Old Square, Lincoln's Inn, WC2A 3SR. *Club:* MCC.

GODFREY, Dr Malcolm Paul Weston, CBE 1986; JP; Second Secretary, Medical Research Council, since 1983; *b* 11 Aug. 1926; *s* of late Harry Godfrey and of Rose Godfrey; *m* 1955, Barbara Goldstein; one *s* two *d. Educ:* Hertford Grammar Sch.; King's Coll., London Univ.; KCH Med. Sch. MB, BS (Hons and Univ. Medal) 1950; MRCP 1955, FRCP 1972. Hosp. posts at KCH, Nat. Heart and Brompton Hosps; RAF Med. Br., 1952–54; Fellow in Med. and Asst Physician, Johns Hopkins Hosp., USA, 1957–58; MRC Headquarters Staff, 1960–74: MO, 1960; Sen. MO, 1964; Principal MO, 1970; Sen. Principal MO, 1974; Dean, Royal Postgrad. Med. Sch., 1974–83 (Hon. Fellow,

1985). University of London: Member: Senate, 1980–83; Court, 1981–83; Chairman: Jt Med. Adv. Cttee, 1979–82; Brit. Council Med. Adv. Cttee, 1985–; Member: Sci. Adv. Panel CIBA Foundn, 1974–; Ealing, Hammersmith and Hounslow AHA(T), 1975–80; NW Thames RHA, 1980–83, 1985–; Hammersmith SHA, 1982–83; Sec. of States Adv. Gp on London Health Services, 1980–81; GMC, 1979–81. Consultant Advr, WHO Human Reproduction Programme, 1979–. Member, Council: Charing Cross Hosp. Med. Sch., 1975–80; St Mary's Hosp. Med. Sch., 1983–; Governing Body, British Postgrad. Med. Fedn, 1974–. Mem. Court of Assts, Worshipful Soc. of Apothecaries, 1979–. JP Wimbledon, 1972 (Chm., Juvenile Panel, 1983–). *Publications:* contrib. med. jls on cardiac and respiratory disorders. *Recreations:* theatre, planning holidays (sometimes taking them), walking. *Address:* 17 Clifton Hill, St John's Wood, NW8 0QE. *T:* 01–624 6335; Medical Research Council, 20 Park Crescent, W1N 4AL. *T:* 01–636 5422.

GODFREY, Norman Eric; consultant on international trade procedures; *b* 16 Aug. 1927; *s* of Cecil and Beatrice Godfrey. *Educ:* Northampton Grammar Sch.; London Sch. of Econs (BScEcon). Career mainly in HM Customs but also served in Min. of Transport/DoE, 1968–71, and Price Commn, 1976–79; Comr, HM Customs and Excise, 1979–86. *Address:* 2 Belsize Avenue, NW3 4AU. *T:* 01–435 6085.

GODFREY, Peter, FCA; Senior Partner, Ernst & Whinney, Chartered Accountants, 1980–86; Chairman, Accounting Standards Committee, 1984–Sept. 1986 (Member, 1983–86); *b* 23 March 1924; *m* 1951, Heather Taplin; two *s* one *d*. *Educ:* West Kensington Central Sch.; City of London Coll. Served War, Army, 1942, until released, rank Captain, 1947. Qual. as an Incorporated Accountant, 1949; joined Whinney Smith & Whinney, 1949; admitted to partnership, 1959; Chm., Ernst & Whinney Internat., 1981–83, 1985–86. Appointed: BoT Inspector into Affairs of Pinnock Finance Co. (GB) Ltd, Aug. 1967; DTI Inspector into Affairs of Rolls-Royce Ltd, April 1971; Mem., ODM Cttee of Inquiry on Crown Agents, April 1975. Institute of Chartered Accountants: Mem., Inflation Accounting Sub-Cttee, 1982–84; Mem., Council, 1984–86. *Recreation:* family. *Address:* 2N Maple Lodge, Lythe Hill Park, Haslemere, Surrey. *T:* Haslemere 56729. *Clubs:* Army and Navy, City of London.

GODLEY, family name of **Baron Kilbracken.**

GODLEY, Prof. Hon. Wynne Alexander Hugh; Director of Department of Applied Economics, since 1970, Professor of Applied Economics, since 1980, University of Cambridge; Fellow of King's College, Cambridge, since 1970; *b* 2 Sept. 1926; *yr s* of Hugh John, 2nd Baron Kilbracken, CB, KC and Elizabeth Helen Monteith, *d* of Vereker Monteith Hamilton; *m* 1955, Kathleen Eleonora, *d* of Sir Jacob Epstein, KBE; one *d*. *Educ:* Rugby; New Coll., Oxford; Conservatoire de Musique, Paris. Professional oboist, 1950. Joined Economic Section, HM Treasury, 1956; Dep. Dir, Economic Sect., HM Treasury, 1967–70. Dir, Investing in Success Equities Ltd, 1970–85; a Dir, Royal Opera House, Covent Garden, 1976–. An Economic Consultant, HM Treasury, 1975; Official Advr, Select Cttee on Public Expenditure. *Publications:* (with T. F. Cripps) Local Government Finance and its Reform, 1976; The Planning of Telecommunications in the United Kingdom, 1978; (with K. J. Coutts and W. D. Nordhaus) Pricing in the Trade Cycle, 1978; (with T. F. Cripps) Macroeconomics, 1983; articles, in National Institute Review, Economic Jl, London and Cambridge Economic Bulletin, Cambridge Economic Policy Review, Economica. *Address:* 16 Eltisley Avenue, Cambridge.

GODMAN, Norman Anthony, PhD; MP (Lab) Greenock and Port Glasgow, since 1983; *b* 19 April 1938; *m* Patricia. *Educ:* Westbourne Street Boys' Sch., Hessle Road, Hull; Hull Univ. (BA); Heriot-Watt Univ. (PhD 1982). Nat. Service, Royal Mil. Police, 1958–60. Shipwright to trade teacher in Scottish further and higher educn. Contested (Lab) Aberdeen South, 1979. *Address:* House of Commons, SW1.

GODMAN IRVINE, Rt. Hon. Sir Bryant; *see* Irvine, Rt. Hon. Sir B. G.

GODSELL, Stanley Harry; Regional Director (South West), Departments of Environment and Transport, 1978–80; retired; *b* 19 March 1920; *s* of Thomas Harry Godsell and Gladys Godsell; *m* 1946, Rosemary Blackburn; one *s* (and one *s* decd). *Educ:* Alsop High Sch., Liverpool. Civil Service: PO, 1937–48; Min. of Town and Country Planning, 1948; Asst Sec., Min. of Housing and Local Govt, 1965. *Recreations:* swimming, photography. *Address:* 6 Pitch and Pay Park, Sneyd Park, Bristol BS9 1NJ. *T:* Bristol 683791.

GODWIN, Dame (Beatrice) Anne, DBE 1962 (OBE 1952); a Governor of the BBC, 1962–68; a full-time Member of the Industrial Court, 1963–69; *b* 1897. Gen. Sec., Clerical and Administrative Workers' Union, 1956–62. Chm. of the TUC, 1961–62. *Recreations:* talking, gardening, reading. *Address:* 25 Fullbrooks Avenue, Worcester Park, Surrey KT4 7PE.

GODWIN, William Henry; *b* 29 Nov. 1923; *s* of George Godwin and Dorothy (*née* Purdon); *m* 1961, Lela Milosevic; one *s* one *d*. *Educ:* Colet Court; Lycée Français de Londres; St John's Coll., Cambridge. Called to the Bar, Middle Temple, 1948. Treasury Solicitor's Office, 1948–85; Under Sec., 1977; Head of Europ. Div., and Legal Advr to Europ. Secretariat, Cabinet Office, 1982–85. Chm. of Industrial Tribunals, 1985; Senior Legal Asst, Registry of Friendly Societies, 1985–. *Address:* 54 Gerard Road, SW13 3QQ.

GOEHR, Prof. Alexander; composer; Professor of Music, and Fellow of Trinity Hall, University of Cambridge, since 1976; *b* 10 Aug. 1932; *s* of Walter and Laelia Goehr. *Educ:* Berkhamsted; Royal Manchester Coll. of Music; Paris Conservatoire. Lectr, Morley Coll., 1955–57; Music Asst, BBC, 1960–67; Winston Churchill Trust Fellowship, 1968; Composer-in-residence, New England Conservatory, Boston, Mass, 1968–69; Associate Professor of Music, Yale University, 1969–70; West Riding Prof. of Music, Leeds Univ., 1971–76. Artistic Dir, Leeds Festival, 1975; Vis. Prof., Peking Conservatoire of Music, 1980. Mem., Bd of Dirs, Royal Opera House, 1982–. Hon. Vice-Pres., SPNM, 1983–. Hon. FRMCM; Hon. FRAM 1975; Hon. FRNCM 1980; Hon. FRCM 1981. Hon. DMus Southampton, 1973. *Compositions include:* Fantasia Op. 4; Violin Concerto; Little Symphony; Pastorals; Romanza for 'cello; Symphony in one Movement, Op. 29; Piano Concerto, 1970; Concerto for Eleven, 1972; Metamorphosis/Dance, 1973; Lyric Pieces, 1974; Konzertstück, 1974; Kafka Fragments, 1979; Sinfonia, 1980; Deux Etudes, 1981; chamber music; *operas:* Arden must die, 1967; Behold the Sun, 1985; *cantatas:* Sutter's Gold; The Deluge; Triptych (Naboth's Vineyard; Shadowplay; Sonata about Jerusalem); Babylon the Great is Fallen. *Address:* Trinity Hall, Cambridge; University Music School, West Road, Cambridge; c/o Schott & Co Ltd, 48 Great Marlborough Street, W1.

GOFF, family name of **Baron Goff of Chieveley.**

GOFF OF CHIEVELEY, Baron *cr* 1986 (Life Peer), of Chieveley in the Royal County of Berkshire; **Robert Lionel Archibald Goff;** Kt 1975; PC 1982; DCL; a Lord of Appeal in Ordinary, since 1986; *b* 12 Nov. 1926; *s* of Lt-Col L. T. Goff and Mrs Goff (*née* Denroche-Smith); *m* 1953, Sarah, *er d* of Capt. G. R. Cousins, DSC, RN; one *s* two *d* (and one *s* decd). *Educ:* Eton Coll.; New Coll., Oxford (MA 1953, DCL 1972; Hon. Fellow, 1986). Served in Scots Guards, 1945–48 (commnd 1945). 1st cl hons Jurisprudence, Oxon, 1950. Called to the Bar, Inner Temple, 1951; Bencher, 1975; QC 1967. Fellow and Tutor, Lincoln Coll., Oxford, 1951–55; in practice at the Bar, 1956–75; a Recorder, 1974–75; Judge of the High Ct, QBD, 1975–82; Judge i/c Commercial List, and Chm. Commercial Court Cttee, 1979–81; a Lord Justice of Appeal, 1982–86. Chairman: Council of Legal Educn, 1976–82 (Vice-Chm., 1972–76; Chm., Bd of Studies, 1970–76); Common Professional Examination Bd, 1976–78. Hon. Prof. of Legal Ethics, Univ. of Birmingham, 1980–81; Maccabean Lectr, British Acad., 1983. Member: Gen. Council of the Bar, 1971–74; Senate of Inns of Court and Bar, 1974–82 (Chm., Law Reform and Procedure Cttee, 1974–76). Chm., British Inst. of Internat. and Comparative Law, 1986–. President: CIArb, 1986–; Bentham Club, 1986. Hon. Fellow, Lincoln Coll., Oxford, 1985. Hon. DLitt City, 1977. *Publications:* (with Prof. Gareth Jones) The Law of Restitution, 1966. *Address:* Royal Courts of Justice, Strand, WC2.

GOFF, Martyn, OBE 1977; Chief Executive, Book Trust (formerly Director of the National Book League), since 1970; *b* 7 June 1923; *s* of Jacob and Janey Goff. *Educ:* Clifton College. Served in Royal Air Force, 1941–46. Film business, 1946–48; Bookseller, 1948–70. Has lectured on: music; English fiction; teenager morality; the book trade, 1946–70; Fiction reviewer, Daily Telegraph, 1975–. Founder and Chm., Bedford Square Bookbang, 1971. Member: Arts Council Literature Panel, 1970–78; Arts Council Trng Cttee, 1973–78; Greater London Arts Assoc. Literature Panel, 1973–81; British Nat. Bibliography Res. Fund, 1976–; British Library Adv. Council, 1977–82; PEN Exec. Cttee, 1978–; Exec. Cttee, Gtr London Arts Council, 1982–; Library and Information Services Council, 1984–; Bd Mem., British Theatre Assoc., 1983–85; Chairman: Paternosters '73 Library Adv. Council, 1972–74; New Fiction Soc., 1975–; School Bookshop Assoc., 1977–; Soc. of Bookmen, 1982–84; Trustee: Cadmean Trust, 1981–; Battersea Arts Centre, 1981–85. FIAL 1958, FRSA 1979. *Publications:* The Plaster Fabric, 1957; A Short Guide to Long Play, 1957; A Season with Mammon, 1958; A Further Guide to Long Play, 1958; A Sort of Peace, 1960; LP Collecting, 1960; The Youngest Director, 1961; Red on the Door, 1962; The Flint Inheritance, 1965; Indecent Assault, 1967; Why Conform?, 1968; Victorian and Edwardian Surrey, 1972; Record Choice, 1974; Royal Pavilion, 1976; The Liberation of Rupert Bannister, 1978; Organising Book Exhibitions, 1982. *Recreations:* travel, collecting paintings and sculptures, music. *Address:* Book House, 45 East Hill, Wandsworth, SW18 2QZ. *T:* 01–870 9055/8. *Clubs:* Athenæum, Savile, Groucho.

GOFF, Sir Robert (William Davis-), 4th Bt *cr* 1905; Director, Cynthia O'Connor & Co. Ltd, Art Dealers, Dublin; *b* 12 Sept. 1955; *s* of Sir Ernest William Davis-Goff, 3rd Bt, and of Alice Cynthia Davis-Goff (*née* Woodhouse); *S* father, 1980; *m* 1978, Nathalie Sheelagh, *d* of Terence Chadwick; one *s* one *d*. *Educ:* Cheltenham College, Glos. *Recreation:* shooting. *Heir:* *s* William Nathaniel Davis-Goff, *b* 20 April 1980. *Address:* Seafield, Donabate, Co. Dublin. *Club:* Kildare Street and University (Dublin).

GOHEEN, Robert Francis; educator; President Emeritus, Princeton University; *b* Venguria, India, 15 Aug. 1919; *s* of Dr Robert H. H. Goheen and Anne Ewing; *m* 1941, Margaret M. Skelly; two *s* four *d*. *Educ:* Princeton Univ. AB 1940; PhD 1948. Princeton University: Instructor, Dept of Classics, 1948–50; Asst Prof., 1950–57; Prof., 1957–72; President, 1957–72; Sen. Fellow, Woodrow Wilson Sch., 1981–. Chm., Council on Foundns, 1972–77; US Ambassador to India, 1977–80. Dir, Mellon Fellowships in the Humanities, 1982–. Sen. Fellow in Classics, Amer. Academy in Rome, 1952–53; Dir Nat. Woodrow Wilson Fellowship Program, 1953–56. Member: Internat. Adv. Bd, Chemical Bank; Adv. Commn on Oceans and Internat. Scientific and Environmental Affairs, US State Dept; Adv. Council, Woodrow Wilson Sch., Princeton Univ.; American Philosophical Soc.; American Philological Soc.; American Academy of Arts and Sciences; Phi Beta Kappa; Trustee: Midlantic Banks Inc.; Thomson Newspapers Inc.; American Univ. in Beirut; Carnegie Endowment for Internat. Peace; Inst. of Internat. Educn; United Bd of Christian Higher Educn in Asia; Fund for New Jersey; Bharatiya Vidya Bhavan (USA). Former Member of Board: Carnegie Foundn for Advancement of Teaching; Rockefeller Foundn; Amer. Acad. in Rome; Equitable Life Assce Soc.; Dreyfus Third Century Fund; Reza Shah Kabir Univ., Iran. Hon. degrees: Harvard, Rutgers, Yale, Temple, Brown, Columbia, New York, Madras, Pennsylvania, Hamilton, Middlebury, Saint Mary's (Calif), State of New York, Denver, Notre Dame, N Carolina, Hofstra, Nebraska, Dropsie, Princeton; Tusculum Coll.; Trinity Coll., USA; Coll. of Wooster; Jewish Theological Seminary of America; Ripon Coll.; Rider Coll. *Publications:* The Imagery of Sophocles' Antigone, 1951; The Human Nature of a University, 1969; articles. *Recreations:* tennis and golf. *Address:* 1 Orchard Circle, Princeton, New Jersey 08540, USA. *T:* 452–3000. *Clubs:* Princeton, University, Century Association (New York); Cosmos (Washington); Nassau (Princeton); Gymkhana, Delhi Golf (Delhi).

GOLD, Sir Arthur (Abraham), Kt 1984; CBE 1974; President, European Athletic Association, since 1976; Chairman, Commonwealth Games Council for England, since 1979; Honorary Secretary, British Amateur Athletic Board, 1965–77 (Life Vice President, 1977); President, Counties Athletic Union, since 1978; Member, Sports Council, since 1980; *b* 10 Jan. 1917; *s* of late Mark and Leah Gold; *m* 1942, Marion Godfrey, *d* of late N. Godfrey; one *s*. *Educ:* Grocers' Company's Sch. Inst. of Motor Industry Wakefield Gold Medallist, 1945. Internat. high jumper, 1937; Past President: London AC; Middlesex County AAA; Athletics Team Leader Olympic Games: Mexico, 1968; Munich, 1972; Montreal, 1976. Council Mem., European Athletic Assoc., 1966–76; Vice-Chm., British Olympic Assoc.; Mem. Exec. Cttee, CCPR. *Publications:* Ballet Training Exercises for Athletes, 1960; various contribs to technical books on athletics. *Recreations:* walking, talking, reading, weeding. *Address:* 49 Friern Mount Drive, Whetstone, N20 9DJ. *T:* 01–445 2848. *Clubs:* City Livery, MCC; London Athletic.

GOLD, Jack; film director; *b* 28 June 1930; British; *m* 1957, Denyse (*née* Macpherson); two *s* one *d*. *Educ:* London Univ. (BSc (Econs), LLB). Asst Studio Manager, BBC radio, 1954–55; Editor, Film Dept, BBC, 1955–60; Dir, TV and film documentaries and fiction, 1960–. Desmond Davies Award for services to television, BAFTA, 1976. *TV films:* Tonight; Death in the Morning (BAFTA Award, 1964); Modern Millionairess; Famine; Dispute; 90 Days; Dowager in Hot Pants; World of Coppard (BAFTA Award, 1968); Mad Jack (Grand Prix, Monte Carlo, 1971); Stocker's Copper (BAFTA Award, 1972); Arturo Ui; The Lump; Catholics (Peabody Award, 1974); The Naked Civil Servant (Italia Prize, 1976, Internat. Emmy, and Critics Award, 1976); Thank You Comrades; Marya; Charlie Muffin; A Walk in the Forest; Merchant of Venice; Bavarian Night; A Lot of Happiness (Kenneth Macmillan), 1981 (Internat. Emmy Award); Praying Mantis, Macbeth, L'Elegance, 1982; The Red Monarch, 1983; Good and Bad at Games, 1983; Sakharov, 1984; Murrow, 1986; Me and the Girls, 1985; *cinema:* The Bofors Gun, 1968; The Reckoning, 1969; The National Health, 1973 (Evening News Best Comedy Award); Who?, 1974; Man Friday, 1974; Aces High, 1976 (Evening News Best Film Award); The Medusa Touch, 1977; The Sailor's Return, 1978 (jt winner, Martin Luther King Meml Prize, 1980; Monte Carlo Catholic Award, 1981; Monte Carlo Critics Award, 1981); Little Lord Fauntleroy, 1981 (Christopher Award); The Chain, 1985; *stage play:* The Devil's Disciple, Aldwych, 1976. *Recreations:* music, reading. *Address:* 18 Avenue Road, N6 5DW.

GOLD, John (Joseph Manson); Public Relations Consultant, since 1979; Manager of Public Relations, Hong Kong Mass Transit Railway, 1975–79; *b* 2 Aug. 1925; *m* 1953, Berta Cordeiro; one *d. Educ:* Clayesmore Sch., Dorset. Yorkshire Evening News, 1944–47; London Evening News, 1947–52; Australian Associated Press (New York), 1952–55; New York Corresp., London Evening News, 1955–66; Editor, London Evening News, 1967–72; Dir, Harmsworth Publications Ltd, 1967–73. Free-lance writer and lectr, Far East, 1973–75. *Address:* 21 Brookside, Cambridge CB2 1JQ.

GOLD, Sir Joseph, Kt 1980; Senior Consultant, International Monetary Fund, since 1979; *b* 12 July 1912; *m* 1939, Ruth Schechter; one *s* two *d. Educ:* Univ. of London (LLB 1935, LLM 1936); Harvard Univ. (SJD). Asst Lectr, University Coll., London, 1937–39; British Mission, Washington, DC, 1942–46; joined IMF, 1946; General Counsel and Dir, Legal Dept, 1960–79. Hon. LLD Southern Methodist Univ., 1985. *Publications:* The Fund Agreement in the Courts, vol. I, 1962, vol. II, 1982; The Stand-by Arrangements of the IMF, 1970; Voting and Decisions in the IMF, 1972; Membership and Nonmembership in the IMF, 1974; Los Acuerdos de Derechos de Giro del Fondo Monetario Internacional, 1976; Legal and Institutional Aspects of the International Monetary System, vol I, 1979, vol II, 1984; Aspectos Legales de La Reforma Monetario Internacional, 1979; numerous pamphlets and articles on internat. and nat. monetary law in many countries. *Recreations:* collecting first editions 20th century English and American poetry, assemblages of found objects, gardening, defence of English language. *Address:* 7020 Braeburn Place, Bethesda, Maryland 20817, USA. *T:* 301–229–3278.

GOLD, Stephen Charles, MA, MD, FRCP; Consulting Physician to: the Skin Department, St George's Hospital; St John's Hospital for Diseases of the Skin; King Edward VII Hospital for Officers; Former Hon. Consultant in Dermatology: to the Army; to Royal Hospital, Chelsea; *b* Bishops Stortford, Herts, 10 Aug. 1915; *yr s* of late Philip Gold, Stansted, Essex, and late Amy Frances, *er d* of James and Mary Perry; *m* 1941, Betty Margaret, *o d* of late Dr T. P. Sheedy, OBE; three *s* one *d. Educ:* Radley Coll.; Gonville and Caius Coll., Cambridge; St George's Hosp. (Entrance Exhibnr); Zürich and Philadelphia. BA 1937; MRCS, LRCP 1940; MA, MB, BChir 1941; MRCP 1947; MD 1952; FRCP 1958. Served RAMC, 1941–46. Late Med. First Asst to Out-Patients, St George's Hosp., Senior Registrar, Skin Dept, St George's Hosp., Sen. Registrar, St John's Hosp. for Diseases of the Skin; Lectr in Dermatology, Royal Postgraduate Med. Sch., 1949–69. Sec., Brit. Assoc. of Dermatology, 1965–70 (Pres., 1979). FRSM (late Sec. Dermatological Section, Pres., 1972–73); Fellow St John's Hosp. Dermatological Soc. (Pres., 1965–66). *Address:* 149 Harley Street, W1N 2DE. *T:* 01–935 4444.

GOLD, Prof. Thomas, FRS 1964; John L. Wetherill Professor of Astronomy, Cornell University, since 1971; *b* 22 May 1920; *s* of Max and Josefine Gold; *m* 1st, 1947, Merle E. Gold (*née* Tuberg); three *d*; 2nd, 1972, Carvel B. Gold (*née* Beyer); one *d. Educ:* Zuoz Coll., Switzerland; Trinity Coll., Cambridge (Hon. Fellow, 1986). BA Mechanical Sciences (Cambridge), 1942; MA Mechanical Sciences, Cambridge, 1946; ScD, Cambridge, 1969. Fellow Trinity Coll., Cambridge, 1947. British Admiralty, 1942–46; Cavendish Laboratory, Cambridge, 1946–47 and 1949–52; Med. Research Council, Zoological Lab., Cambridge, 1947–49; Sen. Principal Scientific Officer (Chief Asst), Royal Greenwich Observatory, 1952–56; Prof. of Astronomy, 1957–58, Robert Wheeler Willson Prof. of Applied Astronomy, 1958–59, Harvard Univ. Dir, Center for Radio-Physics and Space Research, Cornell Univ., 1959–81. Hon. MA (Harvard), 1957. Member: Amer. Philosophical Soc.; Nat. Acad. of Sciences; Fellow, Amer. Acad. of Arts and Sciences. Gold Medal, RAS, 1985. *Publications:* contribs to learned journals on astronomy, physics, biophysics, geophysics. *Recreations:* ski-ing, travelling. *Address:* Center for Radiophysics and Space Research, Space Sciences Building, Cornell University, Ithaca, NY 14853, USA.

GOLDBERG, Prof. Sir Abraham, Kt 1983; Regius Professor of the Practice of Medicine, University of Glasgow, since 1978 (Regius Professor of Materia Medica, 1970–78); Consultant Physician, Western Infirmary, Glasgow; *b* 7 Dec. 1923; *s* of late Julius Goldberg and Rachel Goldberg (*née* Varinofsky); *m* 1957, Clarice Cussin; two *s* one *d. Educ:* George Heriot's Sch., Edinburgh; Edinburgh University. MB, ChB 1946, MD (Gold Medal for thesis) 1956, Edinburgh; DSc Glasgow 1966; FRCP, FRCPE, FRCPGlas, FRSE. Nuffield Research Fellow, UCH Med. Sch., London, 1952–54; Eli Lilly Trav. Fellow in Medicine (MRC) in Dept of Medicine, Univ. of Utah; Lectr in Medicine 1956, Titular Prof. 1967, Univ. of Glasgow. Mem., Grants Cttee, Clinical Res. Bd, MRC, 1971–77, Chm., Grants Cttee I, Clinical Res. Bd, MRC, 1973–77. Mem., Chief Scientist Cttee, SHHD, 1977–83; Chm., Biomed. Res. Cttee, SHHD Chief Scientist Orgn, 1977–83; Chm., Cttee on Safety of Medicines, 1980–86. Mem., Editorial Bd, Jt Formulary Cttee, British Nat. Formulary, 1972–78. Editor, Scottish Medical Jl, 1962–63. Lectures: Sydney Watson Smith, RCPE, 1964; Henry Cohen, Hebrew Univ., Jerusalem, 1973. Watson Prize, RCPGlas, 1959; Alexander Fleck Award, Univ. of Glasgow, 1967. *Publications:* (jtly) Diseases of Porphyrin Metabolism, 1962; (ed jtly) Recent Advances in Haematology, 1971; papers on clinical and investigative medicine. *Recreations:* swimming, writing. *Address:* 16 Birnam Crescent, Bearsden, Glasgow G61 2AU.

GOLDBERG, Arthur J(oseph), DJur; lawyer, USA; Ambassador-at-Large, 1977–78; private practice, Washington DC, since 1971; *b* Chicago, Ill, 8 Aug. 1908; *s* of Joseph Goldberg and Rebecca (*née* Perlstein); *m* 1931, Dorothy Kurgans; one *s* one *d. Educ:* City Coll., Chicago; North-western Univ. (JD). Admitted to Bar of Ill., 1929, US Supreme Ct Bar, 1937. Private practice, 1929–48. Gen. Counsel: Congress of Industrial Workers, 1948–55; United Steel workers, 1948–61; Industrial Union Dept, AFL-CIO, 1955–61; Special Counsel, AFL-CIO, 1955–61. Member firm: Goldberg, Devoe, Shadur & Mikva, Chicago, 1945–61; Goldberg, Feller & Bredhoff, Washington, 1952–61; Paul, Weiss, Goldberg, Rifkind, Wharton & Garrison, NY, 1968–71. Sec. of Labor, 1961–62. Associate Judge, US Supreme Court, Washington, 1962–65; US Ambassador to UN, 1965–68; Chm., UNA of USA, 1968–70, Hon. Chm., 1970–; Chm., US Delegn to Conf. on Security and Co-operation in Europe, Belgrade, 1977–78. Is a Democrat. Charles Evans Hughes Prof., Woodrow Wilson Sch. of Diplomacy, Princeton Univ., 1968–69; Distinguished Prof., Sch. of Internat. Relations, Columbia Univ., 1969–70; Univ. Prof. of Law and Diplomacy, Amer. Univ., 1971–73; Distinguished Prof., Univ. of Calif, SF, 1974–. Assoc. Fellow, Morse Coll., Yale Univ. Member: Chicago Bar Assoc.; Ill. Bar Assoc.; Amer. Bar Assoc.; DC Bar Assoc.; Assoc. Bar City of NY; Amer. Acad. Arts and Scis. Holds numerous awards and Hon. degrees. *Publications:* Civil Rights in Labor-Management Relations: a Labor Viewpoint, 1951; AFL-CIO-Labor United, 1956; Unions and the Anti-Trust Laws, 1956; Management's Reserved Rights, 1956; Ethical Practices, 1958; A Trade Union Point of View, 1959; Suggestions for a New Labor Policy, 1960; The Role of the Labor Union in an Age of Bigness, 1960; The Defenses of Freedom: The Public Papers of Arthur J. Goldberg, 1966; Equal Justice: the Warren era of the Supreme Court, 1972. *Address:* 2801 New Mexico Avenue NW, Washington, DC 20007, USA.

GOLDBLATT, Simon, QC 1972. Called to the Bar, Gray's Inn, 1953 (Bencher, 1982). *Address:* 2 Garden Court, Temple, EC4Y 9BL.

GOLDBY, Prof. Frank; Professor of Anatomy, London University, St Mary's Hospital Medical School, 1945–70, now Emeritus; *b* Enfield, Middlesex, 25 May 1903; *s* of Frank and Ellen Maud Goldby; *m* 1932, Helen Rosa Tomlin; five *s* one *d. Educ:* Mercers' School, Holborn; Gonville and Caius College, Cambridge; King's College Hospital; MRCS, LRCP 1926; MRCP 1928; MD (Cambridge), 1936; FRCP, 1963; Resident appointments King's Coll. Hospital, 1926–28; Asst Clinical Pathologist, King's College Hospital, 1929–30; Senior Demonstrator in Anatomy, University College, London, 1931; Lecturer in charge of Anatomy Dept, Hong Kong, 1932–33; Lecturer in Anatomy, University of Cambridge and Fellow of Queens' College, 1934–37; Prof. of Anatomy, Univ. of Adelaide, 1937–45. *Publications:* papers on Embryology and on the Pathology and Comparative Anatomy of the Nervous System. *Address:* 1 St Mark's Court, Barton Road, Cambridge CB3 9LE.

GOLDEN, Grace Lydia, ARCA (London); *b* 2 April 1904; *d* of H. F. Golden. *Educ:* City of London Sch. for Girls. Art Training at Chelsea Art Sch. and Royal College of Art; further studies at Regent Street Polytechnic; Black and White Illustrator, Posters, Panoramas, watercolour artist and wood-engraver; Exhibitor at Royal Academy, 1936, 1937, 1938 and 1940; watercolour, Summer Evening, Embankment Gardens, and oil-painting, Free Speech, purchased by Chantry Trustees; work also purchased by V&A Mus., Imp. War Mus., Mus. of London, and S London Art Gall. Retrospective exhibn, South London Art Gall., 1979. *Publication:* Old Bankside, 1951. *Recreation:* theatre. *Address:* 21 Douglas Waite House, 73–75 Priory Road, NW6 3NJ. *T:* 01–624 3204.

GOLDFINGER, Ernő, RA 1975; FRIBA 1963; private architect; *b* Budapest, 11 Sept. 1902; *s* of late Dr Oscar Goldfinger and Regine (*née* Haiman); *m* 1931, Ursula Ruth Blackwell; two *s* one *d. Educ:* Gymnasium Budapest; Le Rosay Rolle, Gstad, Switzerland; Ecole des Beaux Arts, Paris; Inst. d'Urbanisme, Sorbonne, 1927–28. DPLG 1932; RIBA 1946. Main Buildings: Shop, Helena Rubinstein, London, 1926; Monument, Algiers, 1928; House, Broxted, Essex, 1935; Terraced Houses, Willow Road, Hampstead, 1937 (scheduled as bldg of Architect. Interest, 1974); Houses, Bruxelles, 1951; (competition winner) Alex. Fleming House, Min. of Health, 1960 (Civic Trust Award, 1964); French govt's Tourist Offices, London and Paris; houses, flats, schs, neighbourhood units, newspaper bldg offices, warehouse, factories, farm, shops, old people's home, cinema; also Sunlight Studies, 1931 (designed Heliometer Machine). Exhibitions: Sect. of British Pavilion, Internat. Exhibn, Paris, 1937; ICI, Olympia BIF, 1938; MARS Gp, 1938; Grille CIAM, Aix en Provence, 1955; This is Tomorrow, London, 1956; Architectural Assoc., and Royal Acad. of Arts, 1983; Les Premiers Elévès d'Auguste Perret, Institut Français d'Architecture, Paris, 1985. Drawing and models at RIBA Heinz Gall. collection and RA. Lecture tours: English and Amer. univs; France, Spain, Hungary. Hon. Sec., Brit. Sect., Internat. Reunion of Architects, parent body of Internat. Union of Archs (UIA), 1936; 1st Org. Sec., UIA, 1946 (drafted Statutes); RIBA Deleg., UIA Council, Cuba and Mexico, 1963; Deleg., UIA Sports Bldgs Commission: Oslo, 1964; Krakow, 1967; Mexico City, 1968; Moscow, 1970. Member: French Sect., CIAM, 1928 (deleg. Congress, Athens, 1933); MARS Gp, 1934; Architect. Assoc., 1935 (Mem. Council, 1960–63, 1965–68); For. Relns Cttee, RIBA, 1937–45; Council, ARCUK, 1941–49; Bldg Req. Sub-cttee, Sci. Adv. Cttee to MPBW, 1943–45; Council of Industrial Design, 1961–65; Cercle d'Etudes Architecturals, Paris, 1975. Hon. Member: AASTA (now ABT), 1937; Assoc. of Hungarian Architects, 1963. FRSA. British Corresp., Architecture d'Aujourd'hui, 1934–74. *Publications:* County of London Plan Explained (jtly), 1945; British Furniture Today, 1951; contrib. Arch. Rev., RIBA Jl, Jl Inst. Amer. Architects, Architect. Year Book; *relevant publications:* Goldfinger Ernő, by Prof. M. Major, 1973 (Bupapest); Catalogue, 1920–1983, by James Dunnett and Gavin Stamp (Architectural Assoc. exhibn catalogue), 1983; special number Architect. Design (Jan. 1963); articles in Architect. Rev., Archs Jl, Architecture d'Aujourd'hui, Arch. & Urbanism, Tokyo, New Yorker 1957, Contemporary Architects, 1980. *Recreations:* travel, architecture. *Address:* 2 Willow Road, Hampstead, NW3 1TH. *T:* 01–435 6166.

GOLDING, Dame (Cecilie) Monica, DBE 1958; RRC 1950 (ARRC 1940); *b* 6 Aug. 1902; *o d* of Ben Johnson and Clara (*née* Beames); *m* 1961, Brig. the Rev. Harry Golding, CBE (*d* 1969). *Educ:* Croydon Secondary Sch. Professional training: Royal Surrey County Hospital, Guildford, 1922–25; Louise Margaret Hosp., Aldershot and Queen Victoria's Institute of District Nursing. Joined Army Nursing Services, 1925; India, 1929–34; France, 1939–40; Middle East, 1940–43 and 1948–49; Southern Comd, 1943–44 and 1950–52; WO, 1945–46; India and SE Asia, 1946–48; Far East, 1952–55; Eastern Comd, 1955–56; Matron-in-Chief and Dir of Army Nursing Services, 1956–60, retired (with rank of Brig.), 1960. QHNS 1956–60; Col Commandant, Queen Alexandra's Royal Army Nursing Corps, 1961–66. OStJ 1955. *Recreations:* motoring; amateur bird watching and nature study. *Address:* 9 Sandford Court, 32 Belle Vue Road, Southbourne, Bournemouth, Dorset BH6 3DR. *T:* 431608. *Club:* United Nursing Services.

GOLDING, John; General Secretary, National Communications Union, since 1986; *b* Birmingham, 9 March 1931; *m* 1958, Thelma Gwillym; one *s*; *m* 1980, Llinos Lewis (*see* Llinos Golding). *Educ:* Chester Grammar Sch.; London Univ.; Keele Univ. BA History, Politics, Economics, 1956. Asst Res. Officer, 1960–64, Education Officer, 1964–69, Political and Parly Officer, 1969, Post Office Engineering Union. MP (Lab) Newcastle-under-Lyme, 1969–86; PPS to Minister of State, Min. of Technology, Feb.-June 1970; Opposition Whip, July 1970–74; a Lord Comr, HM Treasury, Feb.-Oct. 1974; Parly Under-Sec. of State, Dept of Employment, 1976–79. Chm., Select Cttee on Employment, 1979–82; Former Mem. Select Cttee on Nationalised Industries; Chm., Lab. Party Home Policy Cttee, 1982–83. Mem., NEC, Lab. Party, 1978–83. Governor: University Coll. Hosp., 1970–74; Ruskin Coll., 1970–. *Publications:* co-author Fabian Pamphlets: Productivity Bargaining; Trade Unions—on to 1980. *Address:* NCU, Greystoke House, Brunswick Road, Ealing, W5.

GOLDING, John, PhD; painter; Senior Tutor in the School of Painting, Royal College of Art, 1981–86 (Tutor, 1973); *b* 10 Sept. 1929; *s* of Harold S. Golding and Dorothy Hamer. *Educ:* Ridley Coll. (St Catherine's, Ontario); Univ. of Toronto; Univ. of London. BA; MA; PhD. Lectr, 1962–77, and Reader in History of Art, 1977–81, Courtauld Inst., Univ. of London; Slade Prof. of Fine Art, Cambridge Univ., 1976–77. Trustee, Tate Gallery, 1984–. *Publications:* Cubism 1907–14, 1959, rev. edn, 1968; (with Christopher Green) Leger & Purist Paris, 1970; Duchamp: The Bride Stripped Bare by her Bachelors, Even, 1972; (ed with Roland Penrose) Picasso, 1881–1973, 1973. *Address:* 24 Ashchurch Park Villas, W12. *T:* 01–749 5221.

GOLDING, John Anthony, CVO 1966; Queen's Messenger, 1967–80; *b* 25 July 1920; *s* of George Golding, Plaxtol, Kent; *m* 1950, Patricia May, *d* of Thomas Archibald Bickel; two *s. Educ:* Bedford Sch.; King's Coll., Auckland. Served with King's African Rifles and Military Administration, Somalia, 1939–46 (Captain). Entered Colonial Service, 1946; Dep. Provincial Comr, Tanganyika, 1961; Administrator, Turks and Caicos Is, 1965–67. *Recreations:* gardening, fishing. *Address:* Flat 40, Regency Court, Bartholomew Street, Hythe, Kent CT21 5BY.

GOLDING, Hon. Sir John (Simon Rawson), Kt 1986; OJ 1980; CD 1974; OBE 1959; Princess Alice Professor of Orthopaedic Surgery, University of the West Indies, since

1965; *b* 15 April 1921; *s* of Mark Golding and Louise Golding; *m* 1961, Alice Patricia Levy; one *s* one *d*. *Educ:* Marlborough College; Cambridge Univ. MA, MB BChir. Middlesex Hosp., 1941–46 and 1948–52; RAMC, 1946–48; Royal Nat. Orthop. Hosp., 1952–53; Univ. of the West Indies, 1953–. ABC Travelling Fellow, Amer., British and Canadian Orthopaedic Assoc., 1956; Hunterian Prof., RCS, 1956; Nuffield Fellow, 1961–62. Hon. LLD Univ. of Toronto, 1984. *Publications:* papers in Jl of Bone and Joint Surgery, West Indian Med. Jl, etc. *Recreations:* sailing, walking, bridge. *Address:* 2A Bamboo Avenue, Kingston 6, Jamaica, WI.

GOLDING, Llinos; MP (Lab) Newcastle-under-Lyme, since July 1986; *b* 21 March 1933; *d* of Rt Hon. Ness Edwards, MP and Elina Victoria Edwards; *m* 1st, 1957, Dr John Roland Lewis; one *s* two *d*; 2nd, 1980, John Golding, *qv*. *Educ:* Caerphilly Girls' Grammar Sch.; Cardiff Royal Infirmary Sch. of Radiography. Mem., Soc. of Radiographers. Worked as a radiographer at various times; Assistant to John Golding, MP, 1972–86. Former Mem., Dist Manpower Services Cttee; Mem., N Staffs DHA, 1983–. Sec., Newcastle (Dist) Trades Council, 1976–. *Address:* 6 Lancaster Avenue, Newcastle-under-Lyme, Staffs ST5 1DR. *T:* Newcastle (Staffs) 636200. *Club:* King Street Working Men's (Newcastle-under-Lyme).

GOLDING, Dame Monica; *see* Golding, Dame C. M.

GOLDING, Terence Edward, FCA; Chief Executive, National Exhibition Centre, Birmingham, since 1978; *b* 7 April 1932; *s* of Sydney Richard Golding and Elsie Golding; *m* 1955, Sheila Jean (*née* Francis); one *s* one *d*. *Educ:* Harrow County Grammar Sch. FCA 1967. Earls Court Ltd (Exhibition Hall Proprietors): Chief Accountant, 1960; Co. Sec., 1965; Financial Dir, 1972; Financial Dir, Olympia Ltd, and Earls Court & Olympia Ltd, 1973; Commercial Dir, Earls Court & Olympia Group of Cos, 1975; Dep. Chief Exec., National Exhibn Centre, 1978. Chm., Exhibition Liaison Cttee, 1979 and 1980. Director: British Exhibitions Promotion Council, 1981–83; Birmingham Convention and Visitor Bureau, 1981–; Heart of England Tourist Bd, 1984–; Birmingham Heartbeat 1986 Ltd, 1986–; Sport Aid Promotions Ltd, 1986–. *Recreation:* following sport. *Address:* Pinn Cottage, Pinner Hill, Pinner, Mddx. *T:* 01–866 2610.

GOLDING, William (Gerald), CBE 1966; CLit 1984; FRSL 1955; author; *b* 19 Sept. 1911; *s* of Alec A. and Mildred A. Golding; *m* 1939, Ann, *e d* of late E. W. Brookfield, The Homestead, Bedford Place, Maidstone; one *s* one *d*. *Educ:* Marlborough Grammar Sch.; Brasenose Coll., Oxford. MA Oxon 1961. Hon. Fellow, Brasenose Coll., Oxford, 1966. Hon. DLitt: Sussex, 1970; Kent, 1974; Warwick, 1981; Oxford, 1983; Sorbonne, 1983; Hon. LLD Bristol, 1984. Nobel Prize for Literature, 1983. *Publications:* Lord of the Flies, 1954 (filmed 1963); The Inheritors, 1955; Pincher Martin, 1956; Brass Butterfly (play), 1958; Free Fall, 1959; The Spire, 1964; The Hot Gates (essays), 1965; The Pyramid, 1967; The Scorpion God, 1971; Darkness Visible, 1979 (James Tait Black Memorial Prize, 1980); Rites of Passage, 1980 (Booker McConnell Prize); A Moving Target (essays), 1982; The Paper Men, 1984; An Egyptian Journal (travel), 1985. *Recreations:* music, Greek, riding. *Address:* c/o Faber & Faber, 3 Queen Square, WC1N 3AU. *Clubs:* Athenæum, Savile.

GOLDMAN, Antony John; Under Secretary, Public Transport London and Metropolitan Directorate, Department of Transport; *b* 28 Feb. 1940; *s* of Sir Samuel Goldman, *qv*; *m* 1964, Anne Rosemary Lane; three *s*. *Educ:* Marlborough College; Peterhouse, Cambridge (BA). International Computers Ltd, 1961–73; entered Civil Service, DoE, 1973; Private Sec. to Sec. of State for Transport, 1976–78; Asst Sec., 1977; seconded to HM Treasury, 1981–83; Under Sec., 1984. Non. exec. Dir, Hugh Baird & Sons, 1985–86. *Recreations:* music, sailing. *Address:* Maltings, 1 Knoll Wood, Godalming, Surrey GU7 2EW. *T:* Godalming 4950.

GOLDMAN, Peter, CBE 1959; Director of Consumers' Association, since 1964; Patron of International Organisation of Consumers Unions (President, 1970–75); President, Bureau Européen des Unions de Consommateurs, since 1983 (Vice-President, 1979–83); *b* 4 Jan. 1925; *o s* of late Captain Samuel Goldman and late Jessie Goldman (*née* Englander); *m* 1st, 1961, Cicely Ann Magnay (marr. diss. 1969; decd); 2nd, 1970, Stella Maris Joyce. *Educ:* Pembroke Coll., Cambridge; London Univ. BA 1st cl. hons History 1946, MA 1950, Cantab; Pres., Cambridge Union; Hadley Prize, Pembroke Coll., 1946; BA 1st cl. hons History, London, 1948. Smith-Mundt Fellowship, USA, 1955–56. Joined Conservative Research Dept, 1946; Head of Home Affairs Section, 1951–55; Dir of Conservative Political Centre, 1955–64; Mem., LCC Educn Cttee, 1958–59; contested (C) West Ham South, 1959, Orpington, 1962; Chm., Coningsby Club, 1958–59, Treas., 1953–58, 1963–83, Pres., 1983–; Sec., Research Inst. for Consumer Affairs, 1964–; Sec., Good Food Club, 1965–; Member: Post Office Users' Nat. Council, 1970–72; Community Relations Commn, 1973–75; Wine Standards Bd, 1973–81; Cttee of Inquiry into the Future of Broadcasting, 1974–77; Royal Commn on Legal Services, 1976–79; Council on Internat. Develt, 1977–79; Consumer Consultative Cttee, EEC, 1979–80; Monopolies and Mergers Commn, 1980–83. FRSA 1970 (Silver Medal, 1969). *Publications:* County and Borough, 1952; Some Principles of Conservatism, 1956; The Welfare State, 1964; Consumerism: art or science?, 1969; Multinationals and the Consumer Interest, 1974. *Address:* 34 Campbell Court, Queen's Gate Gardens, SW7. *T:* 01–589 9464. *Club:* Carlton.

GOLDMAN, Sir Samuel, KCB 1969 (CB 1964); *b* 10 March 1912; *y s* of late Philip and late Sarah Goldman; *m* 1st, 1933, Pearl Marre (*d* 1941); one *s*; 2nd, 1943, Patricia Rosemary Hodges. *Educ:* Davenant Foundation Sch.; Raine's Sch.; London Sch. of Economics, London Univ. Inter-Collegiate Scholar. BSc (Econ.), First Class Hons in Economics and Gladstone Memorial Prize, 1931; MSc (Econ.), 1933. Hutchinson Silver Medallist. Moody's Economist Services, 1934–38; Joseph Sebag & Co., 1938–39; Bank of England, 1940–47. Entered Civil Service, 1947, as Statistician in Central Statistical Office; transferred to Treasury, Sept. 1947; Chief Statistician, 1948; Asst Sec., 1952; Under-Sec., 1960–62; Third Sec., 1962–68; Second Perm. Sec., 1968–72. UK Alternate Executive Dir, International Bank, 1961–62. Exec. Dir, 1972–74, Man. Dir, 1974–76, Orion Bank Ltd. Chm., Henry Ansbacher Holdings Ltd and Henry Ansbacher Ltd, 1976–82. Chm., Covent Garden Market Authority, 1976–81. Hon. Fellow LSE. *Publication:* Public Expenditure Management and Control, 1973. *Recreation:* gardening. *Address:* White Gate, Church Lane, Haslemere, Surrey. *T:* Haslemere 4889.
See also A. J. Goldman.

GOLDREIN, Neville Clive; Consultant, Deacon, Goldrein Green, Solicitors, since 1985; Senior Partner, Goldrein & Co., 1953–85; *b* 28 Aug.; *s* of Saville and Nina Goldrein; *m* 1949, Dr Sonia Sumner, MB, BS Dunelm; one *s* one *d*. *Educ:* Hymers Coll., Hull; Pembroke Coll., Cambridge (MA). Served Army: commnd E Yorks Regt; served East Africa Comd. Admitted Solicitor of the Supreme Court, 1949. Mem., Crosby Bor. Council, 1957–71; Mayor of Crosby, 1966–67, Dep. Mayor, 1967–68; Mem., Lancs CC, 1965–74; Merseyside County Council: Mem., 1973–86; Dep. Leader, Cons. Gp, 1974–77; Vice-Chm. of Council, 1977–80; Leader, 1980–81; Leader, Cons. Gp, 1981–86. Chm., Crosby Constituency Cons. Assoc., 1986–. Chm., S Sefton Div., St John Ambulance, 1975–; Member: NW Econ. Planning Council, 1966–72; Bd of Deputies of British Jews, 1966–85; Council, Liverpool Univ., 1977–81; Council, Merseyside Chamber of Commerce. Director: Merseyside Economic Develt Co. Ltd, 1981–; Merseyside Waste Derived Fuels Ltd, 1983–. Governor, Merchant Taylors' Sch., Crosby, 1965–74. *Recreations:* swimming, cine and video photography, music, grandchildren. *Address:* Torreno, St Andrew's Road, Blundellsands, Merseyside L23 7UR. *T:* 051–924 2065; (office) 81 Dale Street, Liverpool L2 2JA. *T:* 051-227 4911. *Club:* Athenæum (Liverpool).

GOLDRING, Mary; freelance economist; Presenter, BBC 'Analysis' programme, since 1977. *Educ:* Our Lady's Priory, Sussex; Lady Margaret Hall, Oxford (PPE). Air and Science correspondent, 1949–74, Business editor, 1966–74, Economist Newspaper; economist and broadcaster, 1974–. Mem. Selection Cttee, Harkness Fellowships, 1980–86. Blue Circle Award for industrial journalism, 1979; Sony Radio Award for best current affairs programme (Analysis: Post-Recession Britain), 1985; Industrial Journalist Award, Industrial Soc., 1985; Outstanding Personal Contribution to Radio, Broadcasting Press Guild, 1986. *Publication:* Economics of Atomic Energy, 1957. *Recreation:* small-scale landscaping. *Address:* c/o BBC, Portland Place, W1.

GOLDS, Anthony Arthur, CMG 1971; LVO 1961; HM Diplomatic Service, retired; Director, British National Committee, International Chamber of Commerce, 1977–83; *b* 31 Oct. 1919; *s* of late Arthur Oswald Golds and Florence Golds (*née* Massey); *m* 1944, Suzanne Macdonald Young; one *s* one *d*. *Educ:* King's Sch., Macclesfield; New Coll., Oxford (Scholar). HM Forces (Royal Armoured Corps), 1939–46; CRO, 1948; 1st Sec., Calcutta and Delhi, 1951–53; Commonwealth Office, 1953–56; Head of Chancery, British Embassy, Ankara, 1957–59; Karachi, 1959–61; Counsellor in Commonwealth Office and Foreign Office, 1962–65; Head of Joint Malaysia/Indonesia Dept, 1964–65; Counsellor, HM Embassy, Rome, 1965–70; Ambassador to the Republic of Cameroon, the Republic of Gabon and the Republic of Equatorial Guinea, 1970–72; High Comr to Bangladesh, 1972–74; Senior Civilian Instructor, RCDS, 1975–76. *Recreations:* music, cricket, golf, literature. *Address:* 4 Oakfield Gardens, SE19 1HF. *T:* 01–670 7621. *Club:* United Oxford & Cambridge University.

GOLDSMID, Sir James Arthur d'A.; *see* d'Avigdor-Goldsmid.

GOLDSMITH, Alexander Kinglake, (Alick); HM Diplomatic Service; Consul-General, Hamburg, since 1986; *b* 16 Jan. 1938; *s* of Maj.-Gen. Robert Frederick Kinglake Goldsmith, *qv*; *m* 1971, Deirdre Stafford; one *s* one *d*. *Educ:* Sherborne; Trinity Coll., Oxford (MA Modern History). National Service, 1956–58 (DCLI and Queen's Own Nigeria Regt). Asst Principal, CRO, 1961; Hindi student, SOAS, 1962; Third Sec., New Delhi, 1963; FCO, 1967; First Sec. (Inf.), Wellington, NZ, 1971; FCO, 1975; Head of Chancery, E Berlin, 1978; FCO, 1980; Hd of Commonwealth Co-ordination Dept, FCO, 1982; seconded to Hong Kong Govt, 1984. *Recreations:* walking, swimming, tennis. *Address:* c/o Foreign and Commonwealth Office, SW1A 2AH. *Clubs:* Royal Automobile, Royal Commonwealth Society.

GOLDSMITH, Edward René David; author; Publisher and Editor, The Ecologist, since 1970; *b* 8 Nov. 1928; *s* of late Frank B. H. Goldsmith, OBE, TD, MP (C) for Stowmarket, Suffolk, 1910–18, and Marcelle (*née* Mouiller); *m* 1st, 1953, Gillian Marion Pretty; one *s* two *d*; 2nd, 1981, Katherine Victoria James; two *s*. *Educ:* Magdalen Coll., Oxford (MA Hons). Environmental Consultant: Environment Canada, 1975; Atlanta 2000, 1973–76. Adjunct Associate Prof., Univ. of Michigan, 1975; Vis. Prof., Sangamon State Univ., 1984. Contested (Ecology Party): Eye, Feb. 1974; Cornwall and Plymouth, European parly election, 1979. *Publications:* (ed) Can Britain Survive?, 1971; (with R. Allen) A Blueprint for Survival, 1972; The Future of an Affluent Society: the case of Canada (report for Env. Canada) 1976; The Stable Society, 1977; (ed with J. M. Brunetti) La Médecine à la Question, 1981; The Social and Environmental Effects of Large Dams, vol. I (with N. Hildyard), 1984, vol. II (ed with N. Hildyard), 1986; (ed with N. Hildyard) Green Britain or Industrial Wasteland?, 1986. *Address:* Whitehay, Withiel, Bodmin, Cornwall. *T:* Lanivet 831237. *Club:* Travellers' (Paris).
See also Sir James Goldsmith.

GOLDSMITH, Sir James (Michael), Kt 1976; Chairman: Générale Occidentale SA Paris; General Oriental, Cayman; Publisher, L'Express magazine, France; *b* 26 Feb. 1933; *s* of Frank Goldsmith, OBE and Marcelle Mouiller; *m* 1st, Maria Isabel Patino (*d* 1954); one *d*; 2nd, Ginette Lery; one *s* one *d*; 3rd, Lady Annabel Vane Tempest Stewart; two *s* one *d*. *Educ:* Eton College. Chevalier, Légion d'Honneur, 1978. *Address:* Cavenham House, Park Lane, Cranford, Middlesex TW5 9RW. *Clubs:* Buck's, Brooks's; Travellers' (Paris).
See also E. R. D. Goldsmith.

GOLDSMITH, John Herman Thorburn, CBE 1959; a Manager of the Royal Institution, 1964–67 and 1968–71, Vice President 1969; Part-time Member, NW Area Gas Board, 1955–64; *b* 30 May 1903; *m* 1932, Monica, *d* of late Capt. Harry Simon; one *d*. *Educ:* Marlborough; Magdalen Coll., Oxford. War of 1939–45, Fire Staff Officer, Grade I, National Fire Service. Dep. Chm., Civil Service Selection Bd, 1945; Chm., Civil Service Selection Board, and a Civil Service Commissioner, 1951–63. Haakon Cross, Norway, 1945; Order of Orange Nassau, Netherlands, 1945. *Publications:* Hildebrand (Children's Stories), 1931, 1949; Three's Company, 1932. *Recreation:* fly-fishing. *Address:* 46 Regency House, Newbold Terrace, Leamington Spa, Warwickshire CV32 4HD. *T:* Leamington Spa 39246.

GOLDSMITH, John Stuart, CB 1984; Director General Defence Accounts, Ministry of Defence, 1980–84; *b* 2 Nov. 1924; *o s* of R. W. and S. E. Goldsmith; *m* 1948, Brenda; two *s* one *d*. *Educ:* Whitgift Middle Sch.; St Catharine's Coll., Cambridge. Royal Signals, 1943–47 (Captain). War Office, 1948; Principal, 1952; Treasury, 1961–64; Asst Sec., MoD, 1964; RCDS 1971; Asst Under-Sec. of State, MoD, 1973; Chm. Civil Service Selection Bd, 1973. *Recreations:* gardening, jazz, travel. *Address:* Cobthorne House, Church Lane, Rode, Somerset. *T:* Frome 830681.

GOLDSMITH, Philip; Director (Earth Observation and Microgravity), European Space Agency, since 1985; *b* 16 April 1930; *s* of late Stanley Thomas Goldsmith and Ida Goldsmith (*née* Rawlinson); *m* 1952, Daphne (*d* 1983), *d* of William Webb; two *s* two *d*. *Educ:* Almondbury Grammar Sch.; Pembroke Coll., Oxford (MA). Meteorologist with the Meteorological Office, 1947–54, incl. National Service, RAF, 1948–50; Research Scientist, AERE Harwell, 1957–67; Meteorological Office: Asst Director (Cloud Physics Research), 1967–76; Dep. Director (Physical Research), 1976–82; Dir (Res.), 1982–84. President: Royal Meteorological Society, 1980–82; Internat. Commn on Atmospheric Chem. and Global Pollution, 1979–83. *Publications:* articles in scientific jls mainly on atmospheric physics and chemistry. *Recreations:* golf, gardening, antiques, old cars. *Address:* Hill House, Broad Lane, Bracknell, Berks RG12 3BY. *T:* Bracknell 54195. *Club:* East Berks Golf.

GOLDSMITH, Maj.-Gen. Robert Frederick Kinglake, CB 1955; CBE 1952; retired; *b* 21 June 1907; *s* of late Col Harry Dundas Goldsmith, CBE, DSO; *m* 1935, Brenda (*d* 1983), *d* of Frank Bartlett, late Ceylon Civil Service; one *s*. *Educ:* Wellington Coll., Berks. Commnd Duke of Cornwall's LI, 1927; served War of 1939–45, in N Africa, Italy, NW Europe; Dep. Chief of Staff, First Allied Airborne Army, 1944–45; comd 131 Inf. Bde

(TA), 1950–51; Chief of Staff, British Troops in Egypt, 1951–54, and of HQ Western Command, 1956–59; GOC Yorks District, 1959–62; Col, Duke of Cornwall's LI, 1958–59; Col Somerset and Cornwall LI, 1960–63. Editor, The Army Quarterly, 1966–73. Comdr, Legion of Merit (US) 1945. *Address:* 4 Paternoster House, Colebrook Street, Winchester, Hants SO23 9LG. *Club:* Army and Navy.
See also A. K. Goldsmith.

GOLDSMITH, Walter Kenneth, FCA; FRSA; CBIM; Group Planning and Marketing Director, Trusthouse Forte, since 1984; *b* 19 Jan. 1938; *s* of Lionel and Phoebe Goldsmith; *m* 1961, Rosemary Adele, *d* of Joseph and Hannah Salter; two *s* two *d. Educ:* Merchant Taylors' School. Admitted Inst. of Chartered Accountants, 1960; Manager, Mann Judd & Co., 1964; joined Black & Decker Ltd, 1966: Dir of Investment, Finance and Administration, Europe, 1967; Gen. Man., 1970; Man. Dir, 1974; Chief Executive and European Dir, 1975; Black & Decker USA, 1976–79: Corporate Vice-Pres. and Pres. Pacific Internat. Operations; Dir Gen., Inst. of Dirs, 1979–84. Korn/Ferry International Ltd: Chm., 1984–86; Chief Exec., 1984–85; Chm., Leisure Develt Ltd, 1984–85. Director: Bestobell PLC, 1980–85; BUPA Medical Centre, 1980–84; Director Publications Ltd, 1983–84; The Lesser Group, 1983–85; Bank Leumi (UK), 1984–. Member: Council, British Exec. Service Overseas, 1979–84; English Tourist Board, 1982–84; BTA, 1984–86; BOTB for Israel, 1984–. Mem., Policy Planning Gp, Inst. of Jewish Affairs, 1983–. Trustee, Israel Diaspora Trust, 1982–; Chm. of Trustees, Stress Foundation, 1984–. Pres., Inst. of Word Processing, 1983–. Liveryman, Worshipful Co. of Chartered Accountants in England and Wales, 1985. *Publications:* (with D. Clutterbuck) The Winning Streak, 1984; The Winning Streak Workout Book, 1985. *Recreations:* boating, music. *Address:* 86 Park Lane, W1A 4AA. *T:* 01-493 4090.*Clubs:* Carlton, Durbar (Vice-Pres., 1984–).

GOLDSTEIN, Alfred, CBE 1977; FEng; Chairman, Travers Morgan Group, since 1985 (Senior Partner, Travers Morgan & Partners, 1972–85); *b* 9 Oct. 1926; *s* of late Sigmund and Regina Goldstein; *m* 1959, Anne Milford, *d* of late Col R. A. M. Tweedy and of Maureen Evans, and step *d* of Hubert Evans; two *s. Educ:* Rotherham Grammar Sch.; Imperial Coll., Univ. of London. BSc (Eng); ACGI 1946; DIC. FICE 1959; FIStructE 1959; FIHE 1959; MConsE 1959; FEng 1979; FCIT. Partner, R. Travers Morgan & Partners, 1951; responsible for planning, design and supervision of construction of major road and bridge projects and for planning and transport studies, incl. M23, Belfast Transportation Plan, Clifton Bridge, Nottingham, Elizabeth Bridge, Cambridge, Itchen Bridge, Southampton. Transport Consultant to Govt SE Jt Planning Team for SE Regional Plan; in charge London Docklands Redevelopment Study; Cost Benefit Study for 2nd Sydney Airport for Govt of Australia; Mem. Cttee on Review of Railway Finances, 1982; UK full mem., EC Article 83 Cttee (Transport), 1982–; TRRL Visitor on Transport Res. and Develt, 1982–. Member: Building Research Bd, subseq. Adv. Cttee on Building Research, 1963–66; Civil Engrg EDC on Contracting in Civil Engrg since Banwell, 1965–67; Baroness Sharp's Adv. Cttee on Urban Transport Manpower Study, 1967–69; Commn of Inquiry on Third London Airport, 1968–70; Urban Motorways Cttee, 1969–72; Genesys Bd, 1969–74; Chairman: DoE and Dept of Transport Planning and Tnspt Res. Adv. Council, 1973–79; DoE Environmental Bd, 1975–78; Mem., TRRL Adv. Cttee on Transport, 1974–80; Mem. Bd, Coll. of Estate Management, Reading Univ., 1979–. *Publications:* papers and lectures (inc. Criteria for the Siting of Major Airports, 4th World Airports Conf., 1973; Highways and Community Response, 9th Rees Jeffreys Triennial Lecture, RTPI, 1975; Environment and the Economic Use of Energy, (Plenary Paper, Hong Kong Transport Conf., 1982); Decision-taking under Uncertainty in the Roads Sector, PIARC Sydney, 1983; Investment in Transport (Keynote address, CIT Conf., 1983); Buses: social enterprise and business (main paper, 9th annual conf., Bus and Coach Council, 1983); Public Road Transport: a time for change (Keynote address, 6th Aust. passenger trans. conf., 1985)). *Recreations:* carpentry, music, bridge. *Address:* 136 Long Acre, WC2E 9AE. *T:* 01–836 5474; Kent Edge, Crockham Hill, Edenbridge, Kent TN8 6TA. *T:* Edenbridge 866227. *Club:* Athenæum.

GOLDSTEIN, Joan Delano, (Mrs Julius Goldstein); see Aiken, J. D.

GOLDSTEIN, Simon Alfred; a Recorder of the Crown Court, since 1980; *b* 6 June 1935; *s* of Harry and Constance Goldstein; *m* 1973, Zoë Philippa, *yr d* of Basil Gerrard Smith, *qv. Educ:* East Ham Grammar Sch.; Fitzwilliam Coll., Cambridge (BA 1956). Educn Officer, RAF, 1957–60. Called to the Bar, Middle Temple, 1961; Dep. Circuit Judge, 1975. *Recreation:* bridge. *Address:* 13 King's Bench Walk, Temple, EC4. *Club:* London Duplicate Bridge.

GOLDSTEIN, Sydney, FRS 1937; MA; PhD; Gordon McKay Professor of Applied Mathematics, Harvard University, Emeritus; *b* 3 Dec. 1903; *o s* of Joseph and Hilda Goldstein, Hull; *m* 1926, Rosa R. Sass, Johannesburg; one *s* one *d. Educ:* Bede Collegiate Sch., Sunderland; University of Leeds; St John's Coll., Cambridge. Mathematical Tripos, 1925; Smith's Prize, 1927; PhD, 1928; Rockefeller Research Fellow, University of Göttingen, 1928–29; Lectr in Mathematics, Manchester Univ., 1929–31; Lectr in Mathematics in the Univ. of Cambridge, 1931–45; Fellow of St John's Coll., Cambridge, 1929–32, 1933–45; Leverhulme Research Fellow, Calif. Inst. of Technology, 1938–39; Beyer Prof. of Applied Mathematics, Manchester Univ., 1945–50; Prof. of Applied Mathematics, 1950–55; and Chm. Aeronautical Engineering Dept, 1950–54, Technion Institute of Technology, Haifa, Israel, and Vice-Pres. of the Institute, 1951–54. Worked at Aerodynamics Div., National Physical Laboratory, 1939–45; Adams Prize, 1935. Chm., Aeronautical Research Council, 1946–49. Foreign Member: Royal Netherlands Acad. of Sciences and Letters (Section for Sciences), 1950; Finnish Scientific Soc. (Section for maths and phys), 1975. Hon. Fellow: St John's Coll., Cambridge, 1965; Weizmann Inst. of Science, 1971; Hon. FRAeS, 1971; Hon. FIMA, 1972. Hon. DEng Purdue Univ., 1967; Hon. DSc: Case Inst. of Technology, 1967; The Technion, Israel Inst. of Technology, Haifa, Israel, 1969; Leeds Univ., 1973. Timoshenko Medal of Amer. Soc. of Mech. Engrs (for distinguished contribs to Applied Mechanics), 1965; Hon. Mem., ASME, 1981. *Publications:* (ed) Modern Developments in Fluid Dynamics, 1938; Lectures on Fluid Mechanics, 1960; papers on mathematics and mathematical physics, especially hydrodynamics and aerodynamics. *Address:* 28 Elizabeth Road, Belmont, Mass 02178, USA.

GOLDSTEIN-JACKSON, Kevin Grierson; writer; TV consultant/producer; *b* 2 Nov. 1946; *s* of H. G. and W. M. E. Jackson; *m* 1975, Jenny Mei Leng, *e d* of Ufong Ng, Malaysia; two *d. Educ:* Reading Univ. (BA Phil. and Sociol.); Southampton Univ. (MPhil Law). Staff Relations Dept, London Transport (Railways), 1966; Scottish Widows Pension & Life Assurance Soc., 1967; Prog. Organizer, Southern TV, 1970–73; Asst Prod., HK-TVB, Hong Kong, 1973; freelance writer/TV prod., 1973–75; Head of Film, Dhofar Region TV Service, Sultanate of Oman, 1975–76; Founder and Dir, Thames Valley Radio, 1974–77; Asst to Head of Drama, Anglia TV, 1977–81; Founder, TSW-Television South West: Programme Controller and Dir of Progs, 1981–85; Jt Man. Dir, 1981–82; Chief Exec., 1982–85. Writer of TV scripts. FRSA 1978, FBIM 1982, FInstD 1982. *Publications:* 12 published books incl.: The Right Joke for the Right Occasion, 1973; Experiments with Everyday Objects, 1976; Joke After Joke, 1977; Things to make with

Everyday Objects, 1978; Magic with Everyday Objects, 1979; Activities with Everyday Objects, 1980; Dictionary of Essential Quotations, 1983; Jokes for Telling, 1986; contrib. law, sociol, financial and gen. pubns. *Recreations:* writing, TV, films, theatre, travel, music, walking, philosophical and sociological investigation. *Address:* c/o Barclays Bank, 49 St Leonard's Road, Windsor, Berks SL4 3BP.

GOLDSTONE, David Israel, CBE 1971; JP; DL; Chairman, Sterling McGregor Ltd Group of Companies; *b* Aug. 1908; *s* of Philip and Bessie Goldstone; *m* 1931, Belle Franks; one *s* two *d.* Manchester Chamber of Commerce and Industry: Pres., 1970–72; Emeritus Dir, 1978; Chm., Pension Bd, 1968; Chm., NW Regions Chambers of Commerce Council, 1970–73; Exec. Mem., Association British Chambers of Commerce Nat. Council, 1970–73; Exec. Mem., British Nat. Council, Internat. Chambers of Commerce; Mem., NW Telecommunications Bd; Vice-Pres., Greater Manchester Youth Assoc.; Trustee and Exec. Mem., Greater Manchester Museum of Science and Industry; Mem. local tribunals, charitable organisations, etc. JP Manchester, 1958; DL Manchester, 1978; High Sheriff of Greater Manchester, 1980–81. Hon. MA Manchester, 1979. *Address:* Dellstar, Elm Road, Didsbury, Manchester M20 0XD. *T:* 061–445 1868.

GOLDSTONE, Prof. Jeffrey, PhD; FRS 1977; Cecil and Ida Green Professor in Physics, and Director, Center for Theoretical Physics, Massachusetts Institute of Technology, since 1983; *b* 3 Sept. 1933; *s* of Hyman Goldstone and Sophia Goldstone; *m* 1980, Roberta Gordon; one *s. Educ:* Manchester Grammar Sch.; Trinity Coll., Cambridge (MA 1956, PhD 1958). Trinity Coll., Cambridge: Entrance Scholar, 1951; Res. Fellow, 1956; Staff Fellow, 1962; Cambridge University: Lectr, 1961; Reader in Math. Physics, 1976; Prof. of Physics, MIT, 1977. Vis. appointments: Institut for Teoretisk Fysik, Copenhagen; CERN, Geneva; Harvard Univ.; MIT; Inst. for Theoretical Physics, Santa Barbara; Stanford Linear Accelerator Center; Lab. de Physique Théorique, L'Ecole Normale Supérieure, Paris. Smith's Prize, Cambridge Univ., 1955; Dannie Heineman Prize, Amer. Phys. Soc., 1981; Guthrie Medal, Inst. of Physics, 1983. *Publications:* articles in learned jls. *Address:* Department of Physics, (6–313) Massachusetts Institute of Technology, Cambridge, Mass 02139, USA. *T:* (office) 617–253–6263.

GOLDSTONE, Peter Walter; His Honour Judge Goldstone; a Circuit Judge, since 1978; *b* 1 Nov. 1926; *y s* of late Adolph Lionel Goldstone and Ivy Gwendoline Goldstone; *m* 1955, Patricia (née Alexander), JP; one *s* two *d. Educ:* Manchester Grammar Sch.; Manchester Univ. Solicitor, 1951. Fleet Air Arm, 1944–47. Partner in private practice with brother Julian S. Goldstone, 1951–71. Manchester City Councillor (L), 1963–66; Chm., Manchester Rent Assessment Panel, 1967–71; Reserve Chm., Manchester Rent Tribunal, 1969–71; Dep. Chm., Inner London QS, Nov. 1971; a Metropolitan Stipendiary Magistrate, 1971–78; a Recorder of the Crown Court, 1972–78. *Recreations:* walking, gardening, reading. *T:* 01–954 1901. *Club:* MCC.

GOLDSWORTHY, Rt. Rev. (Arthur) Stanley; *b* 18 Feb. 1926; *s* of Arthur and Doris Irene Goldsworthy; *m* 1952, Gwen Elizabeth Reeves; one *s* one *d. Educ:* Dandenong High School, Vic; St Columb's Theological Coll., Wangaratta. Deacon 1951, priest 1952; Curate of Wodonga, in charge of Bethanga, 1951–52; Priest of Chiltern, 1952; Kensington, Melbourne, 1955; Yarrawonga, Wangaratta, 1959; Shepparton (and Archdeacon), 1972; Parish Priest of Wodonga, and Archdeacon of Diocese of Wangaratta, 1977; Bishop of Bunbury, 1977–83; Parish Priest of St John, Hendra, Brisbane, 1983; an Assisting Bishop to Primate of Australia, 1983. Chaplain to Community of the Sisters of the Church, 1956–77. *Recreations:* music, bush walking.

GOLDTHORPE, John Harry, FBA 1984; Official Fellow, Nuffield College, Oxford, since 1969; *b* 27 May 1935; *s* of Harry Goldthorpe and Lilian Eliza Goldthorpe; *m* 1963, Rhiannon Esyllt (née Harry); one *s* one *d. Educ:* Wath-upon-Dearne Grammar School; University College London (BA Hons 1st Class Mod. Hist.); LSE. MA Cantab; MA Oxon. Asst Lectr, Dept of Sociology, Univ. of Leicester , 1957–60; Fellow of King's College, Cambridge, 1960–69; Asst Lectr and Lectr, Faculty of Economics and Politics, Cambridge, 1962–69. *Publications:* The Affluent Worker: industrial attitudes and behaviour (with David Lockwood and others), 1968; The Affluent Worker: political attitudes and behaviour (with David Lockwood and others), 1968; The Affluent Worker in the Class Structure (with David Lockwood and others), 1969; The Social Grading of Occupations (with Keith Hope), 1974; The Political Economy of Inflation (with Fred Hirsch), 1978; Social Mobility and Class Structure in Modern Britain, 1980; Order and Conflict in Contemporary Capitalism, 1984; Die Analyse Sozialer Ungleichheit (with Hermann Strasser), 1985; papers in British Jl of Sociology, Sociological Review, Sociology, European Jl of Sociology, Sociologie du Travail. *Recreations:* lawn tennis, bird watching, computer chess. *Address:* 32 Leckford Road, Oxford OX2 6HX. *T:* Oxford 56602.

GOLDWATER, Barry M(orris); US Senator from Arizona, 1953–64, and since 1969; *b* Phoenix, Arizona, 1 Jan. 1909; *s* of late Baron Goldwater and Josephine Williams; *m* 1934, Margaret Johnson; two *s* two *d. Educ:* Staunton Mil. Acad., Virginia; University of Arizona. 2nd Lieut, Army Reserve, 1930; transferred to USAAF, 1941; served as ferry-command and fighter pilot instructor, Asia, 1941–45 (Lieut-Col); Chief of Staff, Arizona Nat. Guard, 1945–52 (Col); Maj.-Gen., USAF Reserves. Joined Goldwater's Inc., 1929 (Pres., 1937–53). City Councilman, Phoenix, 1949–52; Republican Candidate for the Presidency of the USA, 1964. Chm., Senate Armed Services Cttee, 1985–; Member: Advisory Cttee on Indian Affairs, Dept of Interior, 1948–50; Commerce, Science and Transportation Cttee; Small Business Cttee; Heard Museum; Museum of Northern Arizona; St Joseph's Hosp.; Vice-Chairman: Amer. Graduate Sch. of Internat. Management; Bd of Regents, Smithsonian Institution; Member: Veterans of Foreign Wars; American Legion; Royal Photographic Society, etc. US Junior Chamber of Commerce Award, 1937; Man of the Year, Phoenix, 1949; Medal of Freedom, 1986. 33° Mason. *Publications:* Arizona Portraits (2 vols), 1940; Journey Down the River of Canyons, 1940; Speeches of Henry Ashurst: The Conscience of a Conservative, 1960; Why Not Victory?, 1962; Where I Stand, 1964; The Face of Arizona, 1964; People and Places, 1967; The Conscience of the Majority, 1970; Delightful Journey, 1970; The Coming Breakpoint, 1976; With No Apologies, 1979. *Address:* PO Box 1601, Scottsdale, Arizona 85252, USA.

GOLIGHER, Prof. John Cedric, ChM, FRCS; Professor and Chairman, Department of Surgery, Leeds University, 1954–77, now Emeritus; Consulting Surgeon, St Mark's Hospital for Diseases of Rectum and Colon, London, since 1954; *b* Londonderry, N Ireland, 13 March 1912; *s* of John Hunter Goligher; *m* 1952, Gwenllian Nancy, *d* of Norman R. Williams, Melbourne, Aust.; one *s* two *d. Educ:* Foyle Coll., Londonderry; Edinburgh Univ. MB, ChB 1934; ChM 1948, Edinburgh; FRCS, FRCSE 1938. Junior hosp. appts mainly in Edinburgh area; Res. Surg. Officer, St Mark's Hosp., London; served War 1940–46, RAMC, as Surgical Specialist; then Surgical Registrar, St Mary's Hosp., London; Surg., St Mary's Hosp., and St Mark's Hosp. for Diseases of the Rectum and Colon, 1947–54. Mem. Council, RCS, 1968–80. FRSocMed (Past Pres., Section of Proctology); Fellow, Assoc. Surgeons of Gt Brit. and Ire. (Past Pres.); Mem. Brit. Soc. of Gastroenterology (Past Pres.). Hon. FACS, 1974; Hon. FRCSI, 1977; Hon. FRACS, 1978; Hon. FRSM 1986; Hon. Fellow: Brasilian Coll. of Surgeons; Amer. Surg. Assoc.; Amer.

Soc. of Colon and Rectal Surgeons; Soc. for Surgery of the Alimentary Tract. Corresp. Mem., German Surgical Soc.; Hon. Mem., French, Swiss and Austrian Surg. Socs. Many vis. professorships and named lectures in UK, Europe and USA. Hon. MD: Göteborg, 1976; Belfast, 1981; Uruguay, 1983; Hon. DSc Leeds, 1980. Liston Award, RCSE, 1977; Lister Award, RCS, 1981. *Publications:* Surgery of the Anus, Rectum and Colon, 1961, 5th edn 1984; contribs to books and med. journals, dealing mainly with gastric and colorectal surgery. *Recreations:* reading, tennis, music, travel. *Address:* Ladywood, Linton, Wetherby, West Yorks LS22 4HP.

GOLLANCZ, Livia Ruth; Chairman, Victor Gollancz Ltd, since 1983, (Governing Director, Joint Managing Director, 1965–85); *b* 25 May 1920; *d* of Victor Gollancz and Ruth Lowy. *Educ:* St Paul's Girls' Sch.; Royal Coll. of Music (ARCM, solo horn). Horn player: LSO, 1940–43; Hallé Orch., 1943–45; Scottish Orch., 1945–46; BBC Scottish Orch., 1946–47; Covent Garden, 1947; Sadler's Wells, 1950–53. Joined Victor Gollancz Ltd as editorial asst and typographer, 1953; Dir, 1954. *Publication:* (ed and introd) Victor Gollancz, Reminiscences of Affection, 1968 (posthumous). *Recreations:* singing, hill walking, gardening. *Address:* 14 Henrietta Street, WC2E 8QJ. *T:* 01–836 2006. *Club:* Alpine.

GOLLIN, Prof. Alfred M., DLitt; Professor of History, University of California, Santa Barbara, since 1967 (Chairman, Department of History, 1976–77); *b* 6 Feb. 1926; 2nd *s* of Max and Sue Gollin; *m* 1st, 1951, Gurli Sørensen (marr. diss.); two *d;* 2nd, 1975, Valerie Watkins (*née* Kilner). *Educ:* New York City Public Schs; City College of New York; Harvard Univ.; New Coll., Oxford (BA); St Antony's Coll., Oxford (MA); DPhil Oxon 1957; DLitt Oxon 1968. Served US Army, 1943–46; taught history at New Coll., Oxford, 1951–54; official historian for The Observer, 1952–59; Lectr, City Coll. of New York, 1959; Univ. of California, Los Angeles: Acting Asst Prof., 1959–60; Research Associate, 1960–61; Associate Prof., Univ. of California, Santa Barbara, 1966–67. Dir, Study Center of Univ. of California, UK and Ire., 1971–73; Mem., US-UK Educnl Commn, 1971–72. Fellow, J. S. Guggenheim Foundn, 1962, 1964, 1971; Fellow, Amer. Council of Learned Socs, 1963, 1975. FRHistS 1976. *Publications:* The Observer and J. L. Garvin, 1960; Proconsul in Politics: a study of Lord Milner, 1964; From Omdurman to V. E. Day: the Life Span of Sir Winston Churchill, 1964; Balfour's Burden, 1965; Asquith, a New View, in A Century of Conflict, Essays for A. J. P. Taylor, 1966; Balfour, in The Conservative Leadership (ed D. Southgate), 1974; No Longer an Island, 1984; articles and reviews in various jls. *Recreation:* swimming. *Address:* Department of History, University of California, Santa Barbara, Calif 93106, USA. *Clubs:* Reform, United Oxford & Cambridge University.

GOLOMBEK, Harry, OBE 1966; Chess Correspondent, The Times, since 1945; writer on chess; *b* London, 1 March 1911; *s* of Barnet and Emma Golombek; unmarried. *Educ:* Wilson's Gram. Sch.; London Univ. Editor British Chess Magazine, 1938, 1939, 1940. Served in RA, 1940–42, Foreign Office, 1942–45. Joint Editor, British Chess Magazine, 1949–67; Chess corresp. for The Observer, 1955–79. British Chess Champion, 1947, 1949, and 1955 (prize-winner 14 times); Jt British Veteran Chess Champion, 1984; 1st prize in 4 international chess tournaments. Recognized as international master by Federation Internationale des Echecs, 1948; Internat. Grandmaster, World Chess Fedn, 1985. Represented Great Britain in 9 Chess Olympiads and capt. Brit. team, Helsinki, 1952, Amsterdam, 1954, Munich, 1958, Leipzig, 1960, Varna, 1962. Pres., Zone 1 World Chess Fedn, 1974–78. *Publications:* 50 Great Games of Modern Chess, 1942; Capablanca's 100 Best Games of Chess, 1947; World Chess Championship, 1948, 1949; Pocket Guide to Chess Openings, 1949; Hastings Tournament, 1948–49, 1949; Southsea Tournament, 1949, 1949; Prague, 1946, 1950, Budapest, 1952, 1952; Reti's Best Games of Chess, 1954; World Chess Championship, 1954, 1954; The Game of Chess (Penguin), 1954; 22nd USSR Chess Championship, 1956; World Chess Championship, 1957, 1957; Modern Opening Chess Strategy, 1959; Fischer *v* Spassky 1972, 1973; A History of Chess, 1976; (with W. Hartston) The Best Games of C. H. O'D. Alexander, 1976; Encyclopedia of Chess, 1977 (new edn 1981 as Penguin Handbook); Beginning Chess, 1981. *Recreations:* music, the Stock Exchange and the theatre. *Address:* Albury, 35 Albion Crescent, Chalfont St Giles, Bucks HP8 4ET. *T:* Chalfont 2808. *Clubs:* Athenæum; Surrey County Cricket.

GOLT, Sidney, CB 1964; Consultant; Adviser on International Trade, International Chamber of Commerce; Director: Malmgren Inc. (Washington DC); Malmgren, Golt, Kingston & Co. Ltd; *b* West Hartlepool, 31 March 1910; *s* of late Wolf and Fanny Golt; *m* 1947, Jean, *d* of Ralph Oliver; two *d. Educ:* Portsmouth Grammar Sch.; Christ Church, Oxford. PPE 1931; James Mew Scholar, Oxford, 1934; Statistician, Tin Producers' Assoc., 1936–40; joined Central Price Regulation Cttee, 1941; Asst Sec., Bd of Trade, 1945–60; Sec., Central Price Regulation Cttee, 1945–46; Under-Sec., Bd of Trade, 1960–68, Adviser on Commercial Policy, 1964–68, Deputy Secretary, 1968–70. UK Mem., Preparatory Cttee for European Free Trade Assoc., Geneva, 1960; Leader, UK Delegns to UN Conf. on Trade and Development, New Delhi, 1968, and to Trade and Development Bd, 1965–68; UK Mem., Commonwealth Gp of Experts on Internat. Economic Policy, 1975–77; Chm., Linked Life Assurance Gp, 1972–81. *Publications:* Ed., Tin, and Tin World Statistics, 1936–40; (jtly) Towards an Open World Economy, 1972; The GATT Negotiations, 1974, 1978; The New Mercantilism, 1974; The Developing Countries in the GATT System, 1978; (jtly) Western Economies in Transition, 1980; Trade Issues in the Mid 1980's, 1982. *Recreations:* travel, reading, bridge. *Address:* 37 Rowan Road, W6 7DT. *T:* 01–602 1410; The Gore Cottage, Burnham, Bucks. *T:* 4948. *Club:* Reform.

GOMBRICH, Sir Ernst (Hans Josef), Kt 1972; CBE 1966; FBA 1960; FSA 1961; PhD (Vienna); MA Oxon and Cantab; Director of the Warburg Institute and Professor of the History of the Classical Tradition in the University of London, 1959–76, now Emeritus Professor; *b* Vienna, 30 March 1909; *s* of Dr Karl B. Gombrich, Vice-Pres. of Disciplinary Council of Lawyer's Chamber, Vienna, and Prof. Leonie Gombrich (*née* Hock), pianist; *m* 1936, Ilse Heller; one *s. Educ:* Theresianum, Vienna; Vienna Univ. Research Asst, Warburg Inst., 1936–39. Served War of 1939–45 with BBC Monitoring Service. Senior Research Fellow, 1946–48, Lectr, 1948–54, Reader, 1954–56, Special Lectr, 1956–59, Warburg Inst., Univ. of London; Durning-Lawrence Prof. of the History of Art, London Univ., at University Coll., 1956–59; Slade Prof. of Fine Art in the University of Oxford, 1950–53; Visiting Prof. of Fine Art, Harvard Univ., 1959; Slade Prof. of Fine Art, Cambridge Univ., 1961–63; Lethaby Prof., RCA, 1967–68; Andrew D. White Prof.-at-Large, Cornell, 1970–77. A Trustee of the British Museum, 1974–79; Mem., Museums and Galleries Commn (formerly Standing Commn on Museums and Galleries), 1976–82. Hon. Fellow, Jesus Coll., Cambridge, 1963; FRSL 1969; Foreign Hon. Mem., American Academy of Arts and Sciences, 1964; For. Mem., Amer. Philosophical Soc., 1968; Hon. Member: American Acad. and Inst. of Arts and Letters, 1985; Akad. der Wissenschaften zu Göttingen, 1986; Corresponding Member: Accademia delle Scienze di Torino, 1962; Royal Acad. of Arts and Sciences, Uppsala, 1970; Koninklijke Nederlandse Akademie van Wetenschapen, 1973; Bayerische Akad. der Wissenschaften, 1979; Royal Swedish Acad. of Sciences, 1981; European Acad. of Arts, Scis and Humanities, 1980; Accademia Nazionale dei Lincei, 1986. Hon. FRIBA, 1971; Hon. Fellow: Royal Acad. of Arts, 1982; Bezalel Acad. of Arts and Design, 1983. Hon. DLit: Belfast, 1963; London, 1976; Hon. LLD St Andrews, 1965; Hon. LittD: Leeds, 1965; Cambridge, 1970; Manchester, 1974; Hon. DLitt: Oxford, 1969; Harvard, 1976; Hon. Dr Lit. Hum.: Chicago, 1975; Pennsylvania, 1977; DU Essex, 1977; Hon. DHL Brandeis, 1981; Hon. Dr RCA, 1984. W. H. Smith Literary Award, 1964; Erasmus Prize, 1975; Hegel Prize, 1976. Medal of New York Univ. for Distinguished Visitors, 1970; Ehrenkreuz für Wissenschaft und Kunst, 1st cl., Austria, 1975; Medal of Collège de France, 1977; Orden Pour le Mérite für Wissenschaften und Künste, 1977; Ehrenzeichen für Wissenschaft und Kunst, Austria 1984; Premio Rosina Viva of Anacapri, 1985; (jtly) Internat. Balzan Prize, 1985. *Publications:* Weltgeschichte für Kinder, 1936, 1985; (with E. Kris) Caricature, 1940; The Story of Art, 1950, 14th edn 1984; Art and Illusion (The A. W. Mellon Lectures in the Fine Arts, 1956), 1960; Meditations on a Hobby Horse, 1963; Norm and Form, 1966; Aby Warburg, an intellectual biography, 1970; Symbolic Images, 1972; In Search of Cultural History, 1972; (jtly) Art, Perception and Reality, 1973; (ed jtly) Illusion in Nature and Art, 1973; Art History and the Social Sciences (Romanes Lect.), 1975; The Heritage of Apelles, 1976; Means and Ends (W. Neurath Lect.), 1976; The Sense of Order (Wrightsman Lect.), 1979; Ideals and Idols, 1979; The Image and the Eye, 1982; Tributes, 1984; New Light on Old Masters, 1986; contributions to learned journals. *Address:* 19 Briardale Gardens, NW3 7PN. *T:* 01–435 6639.

See also R. F. Gombrich.

GOMBRICH, Prof. Richard Francis, DPhil; Boden Professor of Sanskrit, Oxford University, since 1976; Fellow of Balliol College, Oxford, since 1976; Emeritus Fellow of Wolfson, 1977; *b* 17 July 1937; *s* of Sir Ernst Gombrich, *qv; m* 1st, 1964, Dorothea Amanda Friedrich (marr. diss. 1984); one *s* one *d;* 2nd, 1985, Sanjukta Gupta. *Educ:* Magdalen Coll., Oxford (MA, DPhil); Harvard Univ. (AM). Univ. Lectr in Sanskrit and Pali, Oxford Univ., 1965–76; Fellow of Wolfson Coll., 1966–76. Hon. Sec., Pali Text Soc., 1982–. *Publications:* Precept and Practice: traditional Buddhism in the rural highlands of Ceylon, 1971; (with Margaret Cone) The Perfect Generosity of Prince Vessantara, 1977; On being Sanskritic, 1978; (ed with Heinz Bechert) The World of Buddhism, 1984; contribs to oriental and anthropological journals. *Recreations:* singing, walking, photography. *Address:* Balliol College, Oxford OX1 3BJ.

GOMEZ, Jill; singer; *b* Trinidad, of Spanish and English parents. *Educ:* Royal Academy of Music and Guildhall School of Music, London. Operatic début with Glyndebourne Festival Opera, 1969, where she won the John Christie Award and has subseq. sung leading roles, incl. Mélisande, Calisto, Anne Truelove in The Rake's Progress, Helena in A Midsummer Night's Dream; has appeared with The Royal Opera, English Opera Gp, ENO, WNO and Scottish Opera in roles including Pamina, Ilia, Fiordiligi, The Countess in Figaro, Elizabeth in Elegy for Young Lovers, Tytania, Lauretta in Gianni Schicchi, and the Governess in The Turn of the Screw, Jenifer in The Midsummer Marriage, Leila in Les Pêcheurs de Perles; with Kent Opera: Tatiana in Eugene Onegin, 1977; Violetta in La Traviata, 1979; created the role of Flora in Tippett's The Knot Garden, at Covent Garden, and of the Countess in Thea Musgrave's Voice of Ariadne, Aldeburgh, 1974; created title role in William Alwyn's Miss Julie for radio, 1977; title rôle BBC world première, Prokoviev's Maddalena, 1979; other rôles include Donna Elvira, Donna Anna, Cinna in Mozart's Lucio Silla, Cleopatra in Giulio Cesare, Teresa in Benvenuto Cellini, title rôle in Massenet's Thaïs, Desdemona in Otello, at Edinburgh, Wexford, and in Austria, France, Germany and Switzerland. Also recitalist; première of Eighth Book of Madrigals, Monteverdi Fest., Zürich, 1979; concert repertoire includes Rameau, Bach, Handel (Messiah and cantatas), Haydn's Creation and Seasons, Mozart's Requiem and concert arias, Beethoven's Ninth, Berlioz's Nuits d'Eté, Brahms's Requiem, Fauré's Requiem, Ravel's Shéhérazade, Mahler's Second, Fourth and Eighth Symphonies, Strauss's Four Last Songs, Britten's Les Illuminations, Spring Symphony and War Requiem, Tippett's A Child of Our Time, Messiaen's Poèmes pour Mi, Webern op. 13 and 14 songs, and Schubert songs orch. Webern. Regular engagements in France, Belgium, Holland, Germany, Scandinavia, Switzerland, Italy, Spain, Israel, America; festival appearances include Aix-en-Provence, Spoleto, Bergen, Versailles, Flanders, Holland, Prague, Edinburgh, Aldeburgh, and BBC Prom. concerts. Recent recordings include three solo recitals (French, Spanish, and songs by Mozart), Ravel's Poèmes de Mallarmé, Handel's Admeto, Acis and Galatea, Elvira in Don Giovanni, Fauré's Pelléas et Mélisande, Handel's Ode on St Cecilia's Day, Rameau's La Danse, Britten's Quatre Chansons Françaises, and Canteloube's Songs of the Auvergne. *Address:* 22 Edwin Road, Twickenham TW2 6SC.

GOMM, Richard Culling C.; *see* Carr-Gomm, R. C.

GOMME, Robert Anthony; Under Secretary, Department of the Environment, since 1981; *b* 19 Nov. 1930; *s* of Harold Kenelm Gomme and Alice Grace (*née* Jacques); *m* 1960, Helen Perris (*née* Moore); one *s* one *d. Educ:* Colfe's Grammar Sch., Lewisham; London School of Economics, Univ. of London (BScEcon 1955). National Service, Korea, with Royal Norfolk Regt, 1951–52; Pirelli Ltd, 1955–66; NEDO, 1966–68; Principal, Min. of Public Building and Works, 1968; Asst Sec., DoE, 1972; RCDS 1975; Cabinet Office, 1976–78; Director of Defence Services I, DoE/Property Services Agency, 1981–. Mem., Print Collectors Club, 1977–. *Recreations:* reading, listening to music, theatre, talking. *Address:* c/o Department of the Environment, Whitgift Centre, Wellesley Road, Croydon CR9 3LY. *T:* 01–686 8710.

GOOCH, Sir (Richard) John Sherlock, 12th Bt *cr* 1746; JP; *b* 22 March 1930; *s* of Sir Robert Eric Sherlock Gooch, 11th Bt, KCVO, DSO and Katharine Clervaux (*d* 1974), *d* of late Maj.-Gen. Sir Edward Walter Clervaux Chaytor, KCMG, KCVO, CB; *S* father, 1978. *Educ:* Eton. Captain, The Life Guards; retired, 1963. JP Suffolk, 1970. *Heir: b* Major Timothy Robert Sherlock Gooch, MBE [*b* 7 Dec. 1934; *m* 1963, Susan Barbara Christie, *o d* of late Maj.-Gen. Kenneth Christie Cooper, CB, DSO, OBE; two *d*]. *Address:* Benacre Hall, Beccles, Suffolk. *T:* Lowestoft 740333.

GOOCH, Sir Robert Douglas, 4th Bt *cr* 1866; *b* 19 Sept. 1905; *m;* one *d. Heir: kinsman,* Trevor Sherlock Gooch.

GOOD, Tan Sri Donal Bernard Waters, CMG 1962; JMN (Malaysia), 1965; PSM (Malaysia), 1970; Commissioner of Law Revision, Malaysia, 1963; *b* 13 April 1907; *er s* of William John and Kathleen Mary Good, Dublin; *m* 1930, Kathryn, *er d* of Frank Lucas Stanley and Helena Kathleen Stanley, Dublin; one *s* one *d. Educ:* The High Sch., and Trinity Coll., Dublin. Scholar and Moderator in Classics, TCD, 1927–29; MA 1932; LLB 1933; Barrister, King's Inns, Dublin (Benchers' Prizeman), 1935; Barrister, Gray's Inn, 1948. Resident Magistrate, Kenya, 1940–45; Malayan Planning Unit, 1945; Crown Counsel, Malayan Union, 1946–48; Legal Adviser: Negri Sembilan and Malacca, 1948–49; Johore, 1949–50; Legal Draftsman, Sierra Leone, 1951–52; Legal Adviser, Selangor, 1952; Senior Federal Counsel, Federation of Malaya, 1952–55; Actg Solicitor-Gen., 1953 and 1955; Actg Judge of Supreme Court, 1953; Judge of Supreme Court, 1955–59; Judge of the Court of Appeal, Federation of Malaya, 1959–62. Chm. Detainees Review Commn, 1955–60; Pres. Industrial Court, 1956–57; Chm. Detained Persons Advisory Board, 1960. Coronation Medal, 1953. *Recreations:* orchid-growing, bridge. *Address:* Attorney-General's Chambers, Kuala Lumpur, Malaysia. *T:* 83551. *Clubs:* Kildare Street and University (Dublin); Selangor, Lake and Ipoh (Malaysia).

GOOD, Sir John K.; *see* Kennedy-Good.

GOOD, Prof. Ronald D'Oyley, ScD; Head of Department of Botany, University of Hull, 1928–59, Professor Emeritus, 1959; *b* 5 March 1896; 2nd *s* of William Ernest and Mary Gray Good; *m* 1927, Patty Gwynneth Griffith (*d* 1975); one *d*. *Educ:* Weymouth Coll.; Downing Coll., Cambridge (Senior Scholar). MA, ScD Cantab. Served European War, 1914–18, 4th Bn Dorset Regt, and 2/5th Bn Lincolnshire Regt (France); Staff of Botany Department, British Museum (Nat. Hist.), 1922–28. *Publications:* Plants and Human Economics, 1933; The Old Roads of Dorset, 1940, 1966; Weyland, 1945; The Geography of the Flowering Plants, 1947, revd new edn, 1974; A Geographical Handbook of the Dorset Flora, 1948; Features of Evolution in the Flowering Plants, 1956, new edn USA, 1974; The Last Villages of Dorset, 1979; The Philosophy of Evolution, 1981; A Concise Flora of Dorset, 1984; contribs to scientific journals. *Address:* The Mansion, Albury Park, Albury, Guildford, Surrey GU5 9BB. *T:* Shere 3138.

GOODACRE, Kenneth, TD 1952; DL; Deputy Clerk to GLC, 1964–68; Clerk and Solicitor of Middlesex CC, 1955–65; Clerk of the Peace for Middlesex, 1959–65; practising under name of K. Goodacre & Co., Solicitors, since 1971; *b* 29 Oct. 1910; *s* of Clifford and Florence Goodacre; *m* 1936, Dorothy, *d* of Harold Kendall, Solicitor, Leeds; one *s*. *Educ:* Doncaster Grammar Sch. Admitted Solicitor, 1934; Asst Solicitor: Doncaster Corp., 1934–35; Barrow-in-Furness Corp., 1935–36; Sen. Solicitor, Blackburn Corp., 1936–39; served War of 1939–45, TA with E Lancs Regt and Staff 53 Div. (Major), and 2nd Army (Lieut-Col); released from Army Service, 1945, and granted hon. rank of Major; Dep. Town Clerk: Blackburn, 1945–49, Leicester, 1949–52; Town Clerk, Leicester, 1952–55. Partner, Gillhams, Solicitors, 1968–71. DL, Greater London (DL Middlesex, 1960–65), 1965. *Address:* 4 Chartfield Avenue, Putney, SW15. *T:* 01–789 0794. *Club:* Hurlingham.

GOODALE, Cecil Paul; *b* 29 Dec. 1918; *s* of Cecil Charles Wemyss Goodale and Annie Goodale; *m* 1st, 1946, Ethel Margaret (*née* Studer); 2nd, 1984, Margaret Beatrice (*née* Cook). *Educ:* East Sheen County Sch. War Office, 1936; Min. of Supply, 1939; Min. of Health, later DHSS, 1947–: Sen. Exec. Officer, 1950; Principal, 1953; Principal Regional Officer, 1962; Asst Sec., 1967; Under-Sec., 1976–78. *Recreations:* music, photography. *Address:* 37 Highfield Drive, Kingsbridge, Devon. *T:* Kingsbridge 3511.

GOODALL, His Honour Anthony Charles, MC 1942; a Circuit Judge (formerly a Judge of County Courts), 1968–86; *b* 23 July 1916; *er s* of late Charles Henry and Mary Helen Goodall, The Manor House, Sutton Veny, Wilts; *m* 1947, Anne Valerie, *yr d* of late John Reginald Chichester and of Audrey Geraldine Chichester, Lurley Manor, Tiverton, Devon; one *s* two *d*. *Educ:* Eton; King's Coll., Cambridge. Called to Bar, Inner Temple, 1939 (Certif. of Hon.). Served War of 1939–45, 1st Royal Dragoons; taken prisoner (twice), 1944. Practised at Bar, 1946–67. Pres., Plymouth Magistrates' Assoc., 1976–84; Mem., County Court Rule Cttee, 1978–83; Jt Pres., Council of HM Circuit Judges, 1986 (Jt Vice-Pres., 1985). *Publications:* (ed jtly) Faraday on Rating; contrib. to Encycl. Court Forms and Precedents. *Address:* Mardon, Moretonhampstead, Devon. *T:* Moretonhampstead 40239.

GOODALL, (Arthur) David (Saunders), CMG 1979; HM Diplomatic Service; Deputy Under-Secretary of State, Foreign and Commonwealth Office, since 1984; *b* 9 Oct. 1931; *o c* of late Arthur William and Maisie Josephine Goodall; *m* 1962, Morwenna, *y d* of late Percival George Beck Peecock; two *s* one *d*. *Educ:* Ampleforth; Trinity Coll., Oxford. 1st Cl. Hons Lit. Hum., 1954; MA. Served 1st Bn KOYLI (2nd Lieut), 1955–56. Entered HM Foreign (now Diplomatic) Service, 1956; served at: Nicosia, 1956; FO, 1957–58; Djakarta, 1958–60; Private Sec. to HM Ambassador, Bonn, 1961–63; FO, 1963–68; Head of Chancery, Nairobi, 1968–70; FCO, 1970; Dep. Head, Permanent Under-Secretary's Dept, FCO, 1971–73; UK Delegn, MBFR, Vienna, 1973–75; Head of Western European Dept, FCO, 1975–79; Minister, Bonn, 1979–82; Dep. Sec., Cabinet Office, 1982–84. *Publications:* contribs to: Ampleforth Jl; Tablet; Irish Genealogist; The Past. *Recreation:* painting in watercolours. *Address:* c/o Foreign and Commonwealth Office, SW1. *Club:* United Oxford & Cambridge University.

GOODALL, David William, PhD (London); DSc (Melbourne); ARCS, DIC, FLS; FIBiol; Senior Fellow, CSIRO Division of Wildlife and Rangelands Research, since 1983; *b* 4 April 1914; *s* of Henry William Goodall; *m* 1st, 1940, Audrey Veronica Kirwin (marr. diss. 1949); one *s*; 2nd, 1949, Muriel Grace King (marr. diss. 1974); two *s* one *d*; 3rd, 1976, Ivy Nelms (*née* Palmer). *Educ:* St Paul's Sch.; Imperial Coll. of Science and Technology (BSc). Research under Research Inst. of Plant Physiology, on secondment to Cheshunt and East Malling Research Stns, 1935–46; Plant Physiologist, W African Cacao Research Inst., 1946–48; Sen. Lectr in Botany, University of Melbourne, 1948–52; Reader in Botany, University Coll. of the Gold Coast, 1952–54; Prof. of Agricultural Botany, University of Reading, 1954–56; Dir, CSIRO Tobacco Research Institute, Mareeba, Qld, 1956–61; Senior Principal Research Officer, CSIRO Div. of Mathematical Statistics, Perth, Australia, 1961–67; Hon. Reader in Botany, Univ. of Western Australia, 1965–67; Prof. of Biological Science, Univ. of California Irvine, 1966–68; Dir, US/IBP Desert Biome, 1968–73; Prof. of Systems Ecology, Utah State Univ., 1969–74; Sen. Prin. Res. Scientist, 1974–79, Sen. Res. Fellow, 1979–83, Land Resources Management Div., CSIRO. *Publications:* Chemical Composition of Plants as an Index of their Nutritional Status (with F. G. Gregory), 1947; ed, Evolution of Desert Biota, 1976; editor-in-chief, Ecosystems of the World (series), 1977–; co-editor: Simulation Modelling of Environmental Problems, 1977; Arid-land Ecosystems: Structure, Functioning and Management, vol. 1 1979, vol. 2 1981; Mediterranean-type Shrublands, 1981; Hot Deserts, 1985; numerous papers in scientific journals. *Recreations:* acting, reading, walking. *Address:* CSIRO, Private Bag No 4, PO Midland, WA 6056, Australia.

GOODALL, Rt. Rev. Maurice John; *see* Christchurch, Bishop of.

GOODALL, Peter, CBE 1983; TD 1950; Executive Chairman and Chief Executive, 1977–86, and Director, since 1970, Hepworth Ceramic Holdings PLC; *b* 14 July 1920; *s* of Major Tom Goodall, DSO, MC and Alice (*née* Black); *m* 1948, Sonja Jeanne (*née* Burt); one *s* one *d*. *Educ:* Ashville Coll., Harrogate. Admitted Solicitor, 1948. Served War, Duke of Wellington's Regt and Parachute Regt, 1939–46 (Captain). Practised as Solicitor with family firm, Goodall & Son, and Whitfield Son & Hallam, 1948–67; Dir, Hepworth Iron Co. Ltd, 1967–70; company merged with General Refractories Group Ltd to form Hepworth Ceramic Holdings Ltd, 1970; Man. Dir, 1971–77. Member Council: CBI, 1981–; British United Industrialists, 1984–. *Recreations:* shooting, fishing. *Address:* Mill Bank House, High Flatts, near Huddersfield, West Yorks. *T:* Huddersfield 606227; 82 Whitehall Court, SW1. *T:* 01–930 8359.

GOODALL, Sir Reginald, Kt 1985; CBE 1975; Conductor, Royal Opera House, since 1947; *b* 13 July 1901; *m* 1932, Eleanor Gipps. RCM, RAM; Hon. DMus: Leeds Univ; Oxford, 1986; Hon. MusD Newcastle Univ. Hon. Freeman, Musicians' Co., 1986. *Address:* Barham Court, Barham, Canterbury, Kent. *T:* Barham 831392.

GOODCHILD, David Hicks, CBE 1973; Partner of Clifford-Turner, Solicitors, since 1962 (resident in Paris); *b* 3 Sept. 1926; *s* of Harold Hicks Goodchild and Agnes Joyce Wharton Goodchild (*née* Mowbray); *m* 1954, Nicole Marie Jeanne (*née* Delamotte); one *s* one *d*. *Educ:* Felsted School. Lieut, Royal Artillery, 1944–48; articled clerk, Longmores, Hertford; qual. Solicitor, 1952; HAC, 1952–56. *Recreations:* golf, cricket. *Address:* 53 Avenue Montaigne, 75008 Paris, France. *T:* 42–25–49–27. *Clubs:* MCC, HAC; Cercle Interallié, Polo (Paris).

GOODCHILD, David Lionel Napier, CMG 1986; a Director, Directorate-General of External Relations, Commission of the European Communities, 1985–86; *b* 20 July 1935; *s* of Hugh N. Goodchild and Beryl C. M. Goodchild. *Educ:* Eton College; King's College, Cambridge (MA). Joined Foreign Office, 1958; served Tehran, NATO (Paris), and FO, 1959–70; Dep. Political Adviser, British Mil. Govt, Berlin, 1970–72; transferred to EEC, Brussels, 1973; Head of Division, 1973, Principal Counsellor then Director, 1979–86. *Address:* Orchard House, Thorpe Morieux, Bury St Edmunds, Suffolk. *T:* Cockfield Green 828181.

GOODCHILD, Rt. Rev. Ronald Cedric Osbourne; an Assistant Bishop, Diocese of Exeter, since 1983; *b* 17 Oct. 1910; *s* of Sydney Osbourne and Dido May Goodchild; *m* 1947, Jean Helen Mary (*née* Ross); one *s* four *d*. *Educ:* St John's School, Leatherhead; Trinity Coll. (Monk Schol.), Cambridge; Bishops' Coll., Cheshunt. 2nd Cl. Hist. Tripos Parts I and II, 1931, Dealtry Exhibn. 1932, 3rd Class Theol. Tripos, 1932, Asst Master, Bickley Hall Sch., Kent, 1932–34; Curate, Ealing Parish Church, 1934–37; Chap. Oakham Sch., 1937–42. Chap. RAFVR, 1942–46 (despatches), Warden St Michael's House, Hamburg, 1946–49; Gen. Sec., SCM in Schools, 1949–53; Rector of St Helen's Bishopgate with St Martin Outwich, 1951–53; Vicar of Horsham, Sussex, 1953–59; Surrogate and Rural Dean of Horsham, 1954–59; Archdeacon of Northampton and Rector of Ecton, 1959–64; Bishop Suffragan of Kensington, 1964–80. Examiner, Religious Knowledge, Southern Univs Jt Bd, 1954–58; Examining Chaplain to Bishop of Peterborough, 1959. Chairman Christian Aid Dept, British Council of Churches, 1964–74. Mem. of General Synod of C of E, 1974–80. *Publication:* Daily Prayer at Oakham School, 1938. *Recreations:* tennis, golf, photography. *Address:* Mead, Welcombe, near Bideford, N Devon EX39 6HH. *Club:* Royal Air Force.

GOODCHILD, Lt-Col Sidney, MVO 1969; DL; retired; Vice-Lieutenant of Caernarvonshire, 1969–74; *b* 4 Jan. 1903; *s* of late Charles Goodchild; *m* 1934, Elizabeth G. P. Everett; two *s* one *d*. *Educ:* Friars Sch.; Staff Coll., Quetta. Commnd Royal Welch Fusiliers, 1923; 14th Punjab Regt, Indian Army, 1930; Staff Captain, 4th Inf. Bde, 1937; DAQMG (Movements), Army HQ India, 1939; AQMG (Movts), Iraq, 1940; comd 7/14 Punjab Regt, 1942; AQMG, Army HQ India, 1945; comd 1st Sikh LI and 5th Bde, 4th Indian Div., 1946; despatches thrice, 1940–44. Chm., NW Wales War Pensioners' Cttee; Pres., Gwynedd Br., SSAFA, 1969–. Alderman, Caernarvonshire CC, 1972–74. DL Caernarvonshire, 1964; DL Gwynedd, 1974. *Address:* Plas Oerddwr, Beddgelert, Gwynedd, N Wales. *T:* Beddgelert 237.

GOODDEN, Robert Yorke, CBE 1956; RDI 1947; Architect and Designer; Professor, School of Silversmithing and Jewellery, 1948–74, and Pro-Rector, 1967–74, Royal College of Art; *b* 7 May 1909; 2nd *s* of late Lieut-Col R. B. Goodden, OBE and Gwendolen Goodden; *m* 1st, 1936, Kathleen Teresa Burrow; 2nd, 1946, Lesley Macbeth Mitchell; two *s* two *d*. *Educ:* Harrow Sch. Trained AA Sch. of Architecture, 1926–31; AA Diploma 1932; ARIBA 1933; private practice as architect and designer, 1932–39; served RAFVR, 1940–41; RNVR, 1941–45; resumed private practice, 1946. Joint architect and designer: Lion and Unicorn Pavilion, South Bank Exhibition, 1951; Western Sculpture Rooms, Print Room Gall. and Gall. of Oriental Art, British Museum, 1969–71; designer of: domestic pressed glassware for Chance Brothers, 1934–48; Asterisk Wallpapers, 1934; sports section, Britain Can Make It Exhbn, 1946; Coronation hangings for Westminster Abbey, 1953; gold and silver plate in collections: Victoria and Albert Museum, Worshipful Co. of Goldsmiths, Royal Society of Arts, Downing Coll. and Sidney Sussex Coll., Cambridge, Royal Coll. of Art; glass for King's Coll., Cambridge, Grosvenor House, Min. of Works, and others; metal foil mural decorations in SS Canberra, 1961. Consulting Architect to Board of Trade for BIF, Olympia, 1947, Earls Ct, 1949, Olympia, 1950 and 1951. Member: Council of Industrial Design, 1955; National Council for Diplomas in Art and Design, 1961; Adv. Council, V&A Museum, 1977; Chm., Crafts Council, 1977–82. Mem. Council, Essex Univ., 1973. FSIA, 1947; Hon. Fellow, Sheffield Polytechnic, 1971. Hon. DesRCA, 1952; Hon. Dr RCA, 1974; Sen. Fellow, RCA, 1981. SIAD Design Medal, 1972. Master of Faculty, RDI, 1959–61. Liveryman, Worshipful Co. of Goldsmiths, Prime Warden 1976. *Publication:* (with P. Popham) Silversmithing, 1972. *Recreation:* daydreaming. *Address:* 16 Hatfield Buildings, Widcombe Hill, Bath, Avon BA2 6AF.

GOODE, Prof. Royston Miles, OBE 1972; Crowther Professor of Credit and Commercial Law, since 1973, and Director, Centre for Commercial Law Studies, since 1980, Queen Mary College, University of London; *b* 6 April 1933; *s* of Samuel and Bloom Goode; *m* 1964, Catherine Anne Rueff; one *d*. *Educ:* Highgate School. LLB London, 1954; LLD London, 1976. Admitted Solicitor, 1955. Partner, Victor Mishcon & Co., solicitors, 1966–71, Consultant 1971–; Mem. Cttee on Consumer Credit, 1968–71; Prof. of Law, Queen Mary Coll., London, 1971–73, Head of Dept and Dean of Faculty of Laws, 1976–80. Vis. Prof., Melbourne, 1975; Aust. Commonwealth Vis. Fellow, 1975. Chm., Advertising Adv. Cttee, IBA, 1976–80. Member: Monopolies and Mergers Commn, 1981–86; Departmental Cttee on Arbitration Law. Mem. Council, Justice. *Publications:* Hire-Purchase Law and Practice, 1962, 2nd edn 1970, with Supplement 1975; The Hire-Purchase Act 1964, 1964; (with J. S. Ziegel) Hire-Purchase and Conditional Sale: a Comparative Survey of Commonwealth and American Law, 1965; Introduction to the Consumer Credit Act, 1974; Consumer Credit Legislation, 1977; (ed) Consumer Credit, 1978; Commercial Law, 1982; Legal Problems of Credit and Security, 1982; Payment Obligations in Commercial and Financial Transactions, 1983; contrib. Halsbury's Laws of England, 4th edn. *Recreations:* chess, reading, walking, browsing in bookshops. *Address:* 20 Hocroft Road, NW2 2BL.

GOODENOUGH, Anthony Michael; HM Diplomatic Service; Head of Personnel Policy Department, Foreign and Commonwealth Office, since 1986; *b* 5 July 1941; *s* of late Rear-Adm. M. G. Goodenough, CMG, DSO, and of Nancy Waterfield (*née* Slater); *m* 1967, Veronica Mary, *d* of Col Peter Pender-Cudlip, MVO; two *s* one *d*. *Educ:* Wellington Coll.; New Coll., Oxford. MA 1980. Voluntary Service Overseas, Sarawak, 1963–64; Foreign Office, 1964; Athens, 1967; Private Secretary to Parliamentary Under Secretary, 1971, and Minister of State, FCO, 1972; Paris, 1974; Asst Hd of Maritime Aviation and Environment Dept, 1977 and of European Community Dept (Internal), 1978, FCO; Counsellor on secondment to Cabinet Office, 1980; Hd of Chancery, Islamabad, 1982. *Address:* c/o Foreign and Commonwealth Office, SW1.

GOODENOUGH, Cecilia Phyllis, MA; STh; DD; *b* 9 Sept. 1905; *d* of late Adm. Sir William Goodenough, GCB, MVO. *Educ:* Rochester Grammar Sch.; Liverpool Coll., Huyton; St Hugh's Coll., Oxford. LCC Care Cttee Sec., 1927–30; Sunday Sch. and Evangelistic work, Diocese of Caledonia, Fort St John, BC, Canada, 1931–36; Head of Talbot Settlement, 14 Bromley Hill, Bromley, Kent, 1937–45; Asst to Diocesan Missioner,

Diocese of Southwark, 1954–72. *Address:* 115 Camberwell Grove, Camberwell, SE5 8JH. *T:* 01–701 0093.

GOODENOUGH, Frederick Roger, FIB; Director: Barclays PLC, since 1985; Barclays Bank PLC, since 1979; Barclays Bank UK Ltd, since 1971; Barclays Bank International Ltd, since 1977; *b* 21 Dec. 1927; *s* of Sir William Macnamara Goodenough, 1st Bt, and Lady (Dorothea Louisa) Goodenough; *m* 1954, Marguerite June Mackintosh; one *s* two *d*. *Educ:* Eton; Magdalene Coll., Cambridge (MA). MA Oxon; FIB 1968. Joined Barclays Bank Ltd, 1950; Local Director: Birmingham, 1958; Reading, 1960; Oxford, 1969–; Mem., London Cttee, Barclays Bank DCO, 1966–71, Barclays Bank Internat. Ltd, 1971–80. Sen. Partner, Broadwell Manor Farm, 1968–; Curator, Oxford Univ. Chest, 1974–; Trustee: Nuffield Med. Trust, 1968–; Nuffield Dominions Trust, 1968–; Nuffield Orthopaedic Trust, 1978– (Chm., 1981–); Oxford and Dist Hosps Improvement and Develt Fund, 1968– (Chm., 1982–); Oxford Preservation Trust, 1980–; Governor: Shiplake Coll., 1963–74 (Chm., 1966–70); Wellington Coll., 1968–74. Fellow of Linnean Soc. (Mem. Council, 1968–75, Treasurer, 1970–75); FRSA. *Recreations:* shooting, fishing, photography, ornithology. *Address:* Broadwell Manor, Lechlade, Glos GL7 3QS. *T:* Filkins 326. *Club:* Brooks's.

GOODENOUGH, Prof. John Bannister; Professor and Head of the Department of Inorganic Chemistry, University of Oxford, since 1976; *b* 25 July 1922; *s* of Erwin Ramsdell Goodenough and Helen Lewis Goodenough; *m* 1951, Irene Johnston Wiseman. *Educ:* Yale Univ. (AB, Maths); Univ. of Chicago (MS, PhD, Physics). Meteorologist, US Army Air Force, 1942–48; Research Engr, Westinghouse Corp., 1951–52; Research Physicist (Leader, Electronic Materials Gp), Lincoln Laboratory, MIT, 1952–76. Raman Prof., Indian Acad. of Science, 1982–83 (Hon. Mem., 1980). Mem., Nat. Acad., of Engrg, 1976–. Dr *hc*, Bordeaux, 1967. Associate Editor: Materials Research Bulletin, 1966–; Jl Solid State Chemistry, 1969–; Structure and Bonding, 1978–; Solid State Ionics, 1980–; Co-editor, International Series of Monographs on Chemistry, 1979–. *Publications:* Magnetism and the Chemical Bond, 1963; Les oxydes des elements de transition, 1973; numerous research papers in learned jls. *Recreations:* walking, travel. *Address:* Inorganic Chemistry Laboratory, Oxford University, South Parks Road, Oxford OX1 3QR.

GOODENOUGH, Sir Richard (Edmund), 2nd Bt *cr* 1943; *b* 9 June 1925; *e s* of Sir William (Macnamara) Goodenough, 1st Bt, and of Dorothea (Louisa), *er d* of late Ven. and Hon. K. F. Gibbs, DD; *S* father 1951; *m* 1951, Jane, *d* of late H. S. P. McLernon and of Mrs McLernon, Gisborne, NZ; one *s* two *d*. *Educ:* Eton Coll.; Christ Church, Oxford. Military service, 1943–45, invalided. Christ Church, Oxford, 1945–47. *Heir: s* William McLernon Goodenough [*b* 5 Aug. 1954; *m* 1982, Louise Elizabeth, *d* of Captain Michael Ortmans, MVO, RN and Julia Ortmans; one *d*].

GOODFELLOW, Mark Aubrey; HM Diplomatic Service; Ambassador to Gabon, since 1986; *b* 7 April 1931; *y s* of Alfred Edward Goodfellow and Lucy Emily (*née* Potter); *m* 1964, Madelyn Susan Scammell; one *s* one *d*. *Educ:* Preston Manor County Grammar Sch. Served RAF, 1949–51. Joined HM Foreign (subseq. Diplomatic) Service, 1949; FO, 1951–54; British Mil. Govt, Berlin, 1954–56; Second Sec., Khartoum, 1956–59; FO, 1959–63; Second Sec., Yaoundé, 1963–66; Asst Comr, later Trade Comr, Hong Kong, 1966–71; FCO, 1971–74; First Sec., Ankara, 1974–78; Consul, Atlanta, 1978–82; Counsellor: Washington (Hong Kong Commercial Affairs), 1982–84; Lagos (Econ. and Comm.), 1984–86. *Recreations:* travelling, photography, visiting historic sites and buildings, gardening. *Address:* c/o Foreign and Commonwealth Office, Downing Street, SW1A 2AH. *Clubs:* Travellers', Civil Service; Hong Kong (Hong Kong); Ikoyi (Lagos).

GOODFELLOW, Mrs Rosalind Erica, JP; Moderator of the General Assembly of the United Reformed Church, 1982–83; *b* 3 April 1927; *d* of late Rev. William Griffith-Jones and Kathleen (*née* Speakman); *m* 1949, Keith Frank Goodfellow, QC (*d* 1977); two *s* one *d*. *Educ:* Milton Mount Coll. (now Wentworth Milton Mount); Royal Holloway Coll., London Univ. (BA Hons). Member: British Council of Churches Div. of Community Affairs Bd, 1980–83; Churches' Council for Covenanting, 1981–82; Chm., World Church and Mission Dept, URC, 1983. Chm., Surrey and W Sussex CAB, 1985. JP Surrey (Esher and Walton PSD), 1960. *Recreation:* attending committee meetings. *Address:* Kilverstone House, Gordon Road, Claygate, Surrey. *T:* Esher 67656.

GOODHART, Charles Albert Eric, PhD; Norman Sosnow Professor of Banking and Finance, London School of Economics and Political Science, since 1985; *b* 23 Oct. 1936; *s* of late Prof. Arthur Goodhart, Hon. KBE, QC, FBA, and Cecily (*née* Carter); *m* 1960, Margaret (Miffy) Ann Smith; one *s* three *d*. *Educ:* Eton; Trinity Coll., Cambridge (scholar; 1st Cl. Hons Econs Tripos); Harvard Grad. Sch. of Arts and Sciences (PhD 1963). National Service, 1955–57 (2nd Lieut KRRC). Prize Fellowship in Econs, Trinity Coll., Cambridge, 1963; Asst Lectr in Econs, Cambridge Univ., 1963–64; Econ. Adviser, DEA, 1965–67; Lectr in Monetary Econs, LSE, 1967–69; Bank of England: Adviser with particular reference to monetary policy, 1969–80; a Chief Adviser, 1980–85. *Publications:* The New York Money Market and the Finance of Trade, 1900–13, 1968; The Business of Banking, 1891–1914, 1972; Money, Information and Uncertainty, 1975; Monetary Theory and Practice: the UK experience, 1984; The Evolution of Central Banks, 1985; articles in econ. jls and papers contrib. to econ. books. *Recreations:* keeping sheep, gardening, tennis, skiing. *Address:* London School of Economics and Political Science, Houghton Street, WC2A 2AE. *T:* 01–405 7686 (ext. 2555).
See also Sir P. C. Goodhart, W. H. Goodhart.

GOODHART, Rear-Adm. (Hilary Charles) Nicholas, CB 1972; FRAeS; *b* 28 Sept. 1919; *s* of G. C. Goodhart; *m* 1975, Molly Copsey. *Educ:* RNC Dartmouth; RNEC Keyham. Joined RN, 1933; served in Mediterranean in HM Ships Formidable and Dido, 1941–43; trained as pilot, 1944; served as fighter pilot in Burma Campaign, 1945; trained as test pilot, 1946; served on British Naval Staff, Washington, 1953–55; idc 1965; Rear-Adm. 1970; Mil. Dep. to Head of Defence Sales, MoD, 1970–73, retired. Editor, Brasseys British Defence Directory, 1981–85. British Gliding Champion, 1962, 1967 and 1971. Holder of UK gliding distance record, 360 miles. Freedom of London, 1945; Mem. Ct of Grocers' Co., 1975, Master, 1981. US Legion of Merit, 1958. *Recreations:* computer programming, bee-keeping. *Address:* Lower Farm, Inkpen Common, Newbury, Berks. *T:* Inkpen 297. *Club:* Army and Navy.

GOODHART, Sir Philip (Carter), Kt 1981; MP (C) Beckenham, since March 1957; *b* 3 Nov. 1925; *s* of late Prof. Arthur Goodhart, Hon. KBE, QC, FBA, and Cecily (*née* Carter); *m* 1950, Valerie Winant; three *s* four *d*. *Educ:* Hotchkiss Sch., USA; Trinity Coll., Cambridge. Served KRRC and Parachute Regt, 1943–47. Editorial staff, Daily Telegraph, 1950–55; Editorial staff, Sunday Times, 1955–57. Contested (C) Consett, Co. Durham, Gen. Election, 1950; Member: LCC Educn Cttee, 1956–57; British Delegation to Council of Europe and WEU, 1961–63; British Delegation to UN Gen. Assembly, 1963; North Atlantic Assembly, 1964–79 (Chm. Arms Standardization Sub-Cttee, 1966–69, 1983–). Parly Under-Sec. of State, Northern Ireland Office, and Minister responsible for Dept of the Environment (NI), 1979–81; Parly Under Sec. of State, MoD, 1981. Joint Hon. Sec., 1922 Cttee, 1960–79. Sec., Cons. Parly Defence Cttee, 1967–72, Chm., 1972–74, Vice-Chm., 1974–79; Mem., Cons. Adv. Cttee on Policy, 1973–79; Chairman: Parly NI Cttee, 1976–79; Parly Select Cttee on Sound Broadcasting, 1983; All-Party Parly Gp on Road Safety, 1983–; Member: Council, Consumers' Assoc., 1959–68, 1970–79 (Vice-Pres., 1983–); Adv. Council on Public Records, 1970–79; Exec. Cttee, British Council, 1974–79; Council, RUSI, 1973–76. Chm., Bd of Sulgrave Manor, 1982–. *Publications:* The Hunt for Kimathi (with Ian Henderson, GM), 1958; In the Shadow of the Sword, 1964; Fifty Ships that Saved the World, 1965; (with Christopher Chataway) War without Weapons, 1968; Referendum, 1970; (with Ursula Branston) The 1922: the history of the 1922 Committee, 1973; Full-Hearted Consent, 1975; various pamphlets incl.: Stand on Your Own Four Feet: a study of work sharing and job splitting, 1982; Jobs Ahead, 1984; Skip Ahead, 1985. *Recreation:* skiing (Chm., Develt Cttee, Nat. Ski Fedn of GB, 1970–71; Chm., Lords and Commons Ski Club, 1971–73). *Address:* 27 Phillimore Gardens, W8. *T:* 01–937 0822; Whitebarn, Boars Hill, Oxford. *T:* Oxford 735294. *Clubs:* Beefsteak, Carlton, Garrick.
See also C. A. E. Goodhart, W. H. Goodhart.

GOODHART, Sir Robert (Anthony Gordon), 4th Bt *cr* 1911; Medical Practitioner, Beaminster, Dorset; *b* 15 Dec. 1948; *s* of Sir John Gordon Goodhart, 3rd Bt, FRCGP, and of Margaret Mary Eileen, *d* of late Morgan Morgan; *S* father, 1979; *m* 1972, Kathleen Ellen, *d* of late Rev. A. D. MacRae; two *s* one *d*. *Educ:* Rugby; Guy's Hospital Medical School, London Univ. MB BS (Lond.), MRCS, LRCP, MRCGP, DObstRCOG. Qualification, 1972; Junior Medical Registrar, Guy's Hosp., 1974; GP, Bromley, 1976–80. *Recreations:* cricket, music, sailing. *Heir: s* Martin Andrew Goodhart, *b* 9 Sept. 1974. *Address:* The Old Rectory, Netherbury, Dorset.

GOODHART, William Howard, QC 1979; *b* 18 Jan. 1933; *s* of late Prof. A. L. Goodhart, Hon. KBE, QC, FBA and Cecily (*née* Carter); *m* 1966, Hon. Celia McClare Herbert, *d* of 2nd Baron Hemingford; one *s* two *d*. *Educ:* Eton; Trinity Coll., Cambridge (Scholar, MA); Harvard Law Sch. (Commonwealth Fund Fellow, LLM). Nat. Service, 1951–53 (2nd Lt, Oxford and Bucks Light Infantry). Called to Bar, Lincoln's Inn, 1957, Bencher, 1986. Vice-Chm., Exec. Cttee, Justice (British Section, Internat. Commn of Jurists), 1978–. Contested (SDP) Kensington, 1983. Trustee, Campden Charities, 1975–. *Publications:* (with Prof. Gareth Jones) Specific Performance, 1986; contribs to Halsbury's Laws of England; articles in legal periodicals. *Recreations:* walking, skiing. *Address:* 43 Campden Hill Square, W8 7JR. *T:* 01–221 4830; Youlbury House, Boars Hill, Oxford. *T:* Oxford 735477. *Club:* Brooks's.
See also C. A. E. Goodhart, Sir P. C. Goodhart.

GOODHEW, Sir Victor (Henry), Kt 1982; *b* 30 Nov. 1919; *s* of late Rudolph Goodhew, Mannings Heath, Sussex; *m* 1st, 1940, Sylvia Johnson (marr. diss.); one *s* one *d*; 2nd, 1951, Suzanne Gordon-Burge (marr. diss. 1972); 3rd, 1972, Eva Rittinghausen (marr. diss. 1981). *Educ:* King's Coll. Sch. Served War of 1939–45: RAF, 1939–46; comd Airborne Radar Unit, attached 6th Airborne Div.; Sqdn Ldr 1945. Member: Westminster City Council, 1953–59; LCC, 1958–61. Contested (C) Paddington North, 1955; MP (C) St Albans Div., Herts, Oct. 1959–83. PPS to Mr C. I. Orr-Ewing, OBE, MP (when Civil Lord of the Admiralty), May 1962–63; PPS to Hon. Thomas Galbraith, MP (Jt Parly Sec., Min. of Transport), 1963–64; Asst Govt Whip, June-Oct. 1970; a Lord Comr, HM Treasury, 1970–73. Member: Speaker's Panel of Chairmen, 1975–83; Select Cttee, House of Commons Services, 1978–83; House of Commons Commn, 1979–83; Jt Sec. 1922 Cttee, 1979–83; Vice-Chm., Cons. Defence Cttee, 1974–83. *Recreations:* swimming, reading. *Address:* 71 Whitelands House, Cheltenham Terrace, SW3 4QZ. *T:* 01–235 4911. *Clubs:* Buck's, United and Cecil, 1900.

GOODING, Air Vice-Marshal Keith Horace, CB 1966; OBE 1951; *b* 2 Sept. 1913; *s* of Horace Milford Gooding, Romsey, Hants; *m* 1st, 1943, Peggy Eileen (*d* 1962), *d* of Albert William Gatfield, Guildford, Surrey; one *s*; 2nd, 1968, Jean, *d* of Maurice Stanley Underwood, Andover, Hants; two *s* one *d* (of whom one *s* one *d* are twins). *Educ:* King Edward VI Sch., Southampton. Joined RAF 1938; served Aden, Fighter Comd, 1939–45; Germany, 1945–47; NATO Defence Coll., 1953–54; NATO, Oslo, 1954–55; Bomber Comd, 1958–61; AOA Maintenance Comd, 1965–68; Dir-Gen. of Equipment, later Supply (RAF), 1968–71, retired. *Recreations:* tennis, bridge. *Address:* c/o Lloyds Bank, Guildford, Surrey. *Club:* Royal Air Force.

GOODINGS, Rt. Rev. Allen; *see* Quebec, Bishop of.

GOODISON, Sir Alan (Clowes), KCMG 1985 (CMG 1975); CVO 1980; HM Diplomatic Service, retired; Ambassador in Dublin, 1983–86; *b* 20 Nov. 1926; *o s* of Harold Clowes Goodison and late Winifred Goodison (*née* Ludlam); *m* 1956, Anne Rosemary Fitton; one *s* two *d*. *Educ:* Colfe's Grammar Sch.; Trinity Coll., Cambridge. Scholar, Mod. and Medieval Langs Tripos, first cl.; MA 1951. Army, Lieut, 1947–49. Foreign Office, Third Sec., 1949; Middle East Centre for Arab Studies, 1950; Cairo, 1950–51; Tripoli, 1951–53; Khartoum, 1953; FO, 1953–56; Second Sec., later First Sec. (Commercial), Lisbon, 1956–59; Amman, 1960–62; FO, 1962–66; Bonn, 1966–68; Counsellor, Kuwait, 1969–71; Head of Trg Dept and Dir, Diplomatic Service Lang. Centre, FCO, 1971–72; Head of S European Dept, FCO, 1973–76; Minister, Rome, 1976–80; Asst Under-Sec. of State, FCO, 1980–83. Pres., Beckenham Chorale, 1972–73. Licensed Lay Reader of Anglican Church, 1959–62 and 1966–82. Mem. Council: Jerusalem and the East Mission, 1964–65; Anglican Centre, Rome, 1977–80. Grande Ufficiale dell'Ordine al Merito della Repubblica Italiana (Hon.), 1980. *Publications:* trans. articles for Encyclopaedia of Islam, and on devotional subjects. *Recreations:* looking at pictures, music, reading. *Address:* 12 Gardnor Mansions, Churchrow, NW3 6UR. *Club:* Travellers'.

GOODISON, Sir Nicholas (Proctor), Kt 1982; stockbroker; Chairman, Quilter Goodison Co. Ltd, since 1975; Chairman of The Stock Exchange, since 1976; *b* 16 May 1934; *s* of Edmund Harold Goodison and Eileen Mary Carrington Proctor; *m* 1960, Judith Abel Smith; one *s* two *d*. *Educ:* Marlborough Coll.; King's Coll., Cambridge (Scholar; BA Classics 1958, MA; PhD Architecture and History of Art, 1981). H. E. Goodison & Co. (later Quilter Goodison & Co., now Quilter Goodison Co. Ltd), Members of the Stock Exchange, 1958; Partner, 1962; elected to Council of Stock Exchange, 1968. Hon. Treas., Furniture History Soc.; Hon. Keeper of Furniture, Fitzwilliam Museum, Cambridge; Mem., Exec. Cttee, Nat. Art-Collections Fund (Chm., 1986–); Chm., Management Cttee, Courtauld Inst. of Art; Vice-Chm., English Nat. Opera; Dir, City Arts Trust; Pres., Antiquarian Horological Soc. Editorial Dir, Burlington Magazine. Governor, Marlborough Coll. FSA, FRSA. *Publications:* English Barometers 1680–1860, 1968, 2nd edn 1977; Ormolu: The Work of Matthew Boulton, 1974; many papers and articles on history of furniture, clocks and barometers. *Recreations:* history of furniture and decorative arts, opera, walking, fishing. *Address:* Garrard House, Gresham Street, EC2V 7LH; Stock Exchange, EC2. *Club:* Beefsteak.

GOODISON, Robin Reynolds, CB 1964; consultant; Deputy Chairman, 1972–77, Acting Chairman, Jan.-March 1972, Civil Aviation Authority; *b* 13 Aug. 1912; *s* of Arthur Leathley Goodison; *m* 1936, Betty Lydia, *d* of Comdr L. Robinson, OBE, Royal Navy (retired); three *d*. *Educ:* Finchley Grammar Sch.; University Coll., London Univ. (MA). Joined Ministry of Labour, 1935, transferred to Ministry of Transport, 1936;

Principal, 1940; Asst Sec., 1946; Imperial Defence Coll., 1950; Under-Sec., Ministry of Transport and Civil Aviation, 1957, Ministry of Aviation, 1959, Board of Trade, 1966; Second Sec., BoT, 1969–70; Dep. Sec., DTI, 1970–72. Assessor, Heathrow Terminal Inquiry, 1978–79; Specialist Adviser, House of Lords Select Cttee, 1979–80, 1984–85. *Recreation:* sailing. *Address:* 37 Coldharbour Lane, Bushey, Herts. *T:* 01–950 1911.

GOODLAD, Alastair Robertson; MP (C) Eddisbury, since 1983 (Northwich, Feb. 1974–1983); Parliamentary Under-Secretary of State, Department of Energy, since 1984; *b* 4 July 1943; *y s* of late Dr John Goodlad and late Isabel (*née* Sinclair); *m* 1968, Cecilia Barbara, 2nd *d* of late Col Richard Hurst and Lady Barbara Hurst; two *s*. *Educ:* Marlborough Coll.; King's Coll., Cambridge (MA, LLB). Contested (C) Crewe Div., 1970. An Asst Govt Whip, 1981–82; a Lord Commissioner of HM Treasury, 1982–84. Jt Hon. Secretary: Cons. Party Trade Cttee, 1978– (Jt Vice-Chm., 1979–81); Cons. NI Cttee, 1979–81; Hon. Sec., All Party Heritage Gp, 1979–81; Mem., Select Cttee on Agriculture, 1979–81. *Address:* House of Commons, SW1A 0AA. *Club:* Brooks's.

GOODMAN, family name of **Baron Goodman.**

GOODMAN, Baron, *cr* 1965, of the City of Westminster (Life Peer); **Arnold Abraham Goodman,** CH 1972; MA, LLM; Master of University College, Oxford, 1976–86 (Hon. Fellow, 1986); Senior Partner, Goodman Derrick and Co., Solicitors; *b* 21 Aug. 1913; *s* of Joseph and Bertha Goodman; unmarried. *Educ:* University Coll., London; Downing Coll., Cambridge (Hon. Fellow, 1968). Enlisted Gunner, RA, TA, Sept. 1939, retd as Major, Nov. 1945. Mem., Royal Commn on Working of Tribunals of Enquiry (Evidence) Act, 1921, 1966–; Chm., Cttee of Inquiry on Charity Law, 1974. Chairman: Housing Corporation, 1973–77; Nat. Building Agency, 1973–78. Chairman: Cttee (on behalf of Arts Council) on London orchestras, 1964, reporting 1965; Arts Council of GB, 1965–72; Australian Musical Foundation, 1975–; Theatres' Trust, 1976–; Assoc. for Business Sponsorship of the Arts, 1976–; Motability, 1977–; Jewish Chronicle Trust; Pres., Theatre Investment Fund, 1985– (Chm., 1976–85); Member: British Council, 1967– (Dep. Chm., 1974–); South Bank Theatre Board, 1968–82; Life Mem., Royal Phil. Orch., 1976; Director: Royal Opera House, Covent Garden, 1972–83; English National Opera Ltd, 1973– (Chm., 1977–86); The Observer Ltd, 1976–81; Governor, Royal Shakespeare Theatre, 1972–; President: Nat. Book League, 1972–85; Theatres Adv. Council, 1972–; Inst. of Jewish Affairs, 1975–. Chairman: Observer Trust, 1967–76; Newspaper Publishers' Assoc., 1970–75; British Lion Films Ltd, 1965–72; Charter Film Productions, 1973–84; Dir of various companies. Mem., British/USA Bicentennial Liaison Cttee, 1973. Governor, College of Law, 1975–84. Fellow UCL; Hon. LLD London and other Univs; Hon. DLitt City, 1975. *Address:* 9–11 Fulwood Place, Gray's Inn, WC1V 6HQ. *T:* 01–404 0606.

GOODMAN, Maj.-Gen. David; *see* Goodman, Maj.-Gen. J. D. W.

GOODMAN, Geoffrey George; Assistant Editor, 1976–86, and Industrial Editor, 1969–86, The Daily Mirror; *b* 2 July 1921; *s* of Michael Goodman and Edythe (*née* Bowman); *m* 1947, Margit (*née* Freudenbergova); one *s* one *d*. *Educ:* elementary schs, Stockport and Manchester; grammar schs, London; LSE (BScEcon). RAF, 1940–46. Manchester Guardian, 1946–47; Daily Mirror, 1947–48; News Chronicle, 1949–59; Daily Herald, 1959–64; The Sun (IPC), 1964–69; Daily Mirror, 1969–. Fellow, Nuffield Coll., Oxford, 1974–76. Head of Govt's Counter-inflation Publicity Unit, 1975–76; Member: Labour Party Cttee on Industrial Democracy, 1966–67; Royal Commn on the Press, 1974–77; TGWU; NUJ. Hon. MA Oxon. *Publications:* General Strike of 1926, 1951; Brother Frank, 1969; The Awkward Warrior, 1979; The Miners' Strike, 1985; contrib. London Inst. of World Affairs, 1948. *Recreations:* pottering, poetry, supporting Tottenham Hotspur FC, and climbing—but not social. *Address:* 64 Flower Lane, Mill Hill, NW7. *Club:* Savile.

GOODMAN, Howard; *see* Goodman, R. H.

GOODMAN, Maj.-Gen. (John) David (Whitlock); Director, Army Air Corps, since 1983; *b* 20 May 1932; *s* of late Brig. Eric Whitlock Goodman, DSO, MC and Norah Dorothy Goodman (*née* Stacpoole); *m* 1957, Valerie-Ann McDonald; one *s* two *d*. *Educ:* Wellington Coll.; RMA Sandhurst. Commnd RA, 1952; served in UK and Northern Ireland, BAOR, Aden and Hong Kong; Staff Coll. 1962; Battery Comdr, 3rd Regt Royal Horse Artillery, 1966–69; Jt Services Staff Coll., Latimer, 1970; BMRA 2nd Div., 1970–72; Instr, Staff Coll. Camberley and Sudan, 1972–73; CO 26 Field Regt, RA, 1973–76; Comdt, Royal Sch. of Artillery, 1978–80; Royal Coll. of Defence Studies, 1980; Asst Military Secretary, MoD, 1981–82; No 282 Army Pilots Course, 1983. Pres., Army Flying Assoc. and Army Gliding Assoc., 1983–; Chm., Army Athletic Assoc., 1980–. FBIM 1980. *Recreations:* skiing, tennis, shooting. *Address:* c/o Lloyds Bank, 6 Pall Mall, SW1Y 5NH.

GOODMAN, Prof. John Francis Bradshaw, PhD; CIPM; Frank Thomas Professor of Industrial Relations, University of Manchester Institute of Science and Technology, since 1975 (Vice-Principal, 1979–81); *b* 2 Aug. 1940; *s* of Edwin and Amy Goodman; *m* 1967, Elizabeth Mary Towns; one *s* one *d*. *Educ:* Chesterfield Grammar Sch.; London Sch. of Economics (BSc Econ; PhD); MSc Manchester. FIPM. Personnel Officer, Ford Motor Co. Ltd, 1962–64; Lectr in Industrial Econs, Univ. of Nottingham, 1964–69; Industrial Relations Adviser, NBPI, 1969–70; Sen. Lectr in Industrial Relations, Univ. of Manchester, 1970–74; Chm., Dept of Management Scis, UMIST, 1977–79. Vis. Professor: Univ. of WA, 1981, 1984; McMaster Univ., 1985. Pres., British Univs Industrial Relations Assoc., 1983–. *Publications:* Shop Stewards in British Industry, 1969; Shop Stewards, 1973; Rulemaking and Industrial Peace, 1977; Ideology and Shop-floor Industrial Relations, 1981; Employment Relations in Industrial Society, 1984; Unfair Dismissal Law and Employment Practice, 1985; contribs to British Jl of Industrial Relations, ILR, Industrial Relations Jl, Monthly Labor Rev., Jl of Management Studies, Personnel Management, etc. *Recreations:* fell walking, ornithology, squash, football. *Address:* 24 Regent Close, Bramhall, Stockport, Cheshire. *T:* 061–439 7136.

GOODMAN, Michael Bradley; His Honour Judge Goodman; a Circuit Judge, since 1983; *b* 3 May 1930; *s* of Marcus Gordon Goodman and Eunice Irene May Goodman (*née* Bradley); *m* 1967, Patricia Mary Gorringe; two *d* (one *s* decd). *Educ:* Aldenham; Sidney Sussex Coll., Cambridge (MA). Called to Bar, Middle Temple, 1953; Western Circuit; a Recorder of the Crown Court, 1972–83. Prosecuting Counsel to DHSS, 1975–83; Pres., Wireless Telegraphy Appeals Tribunal, 1977–; Member: Commn on Deployment and Payment of the Clergy, 1965–67; C of E Legal Adv. Commn, 1973– (Chm., 1986–); General Synod, Church of England, 1977–83; Faculty Jurisdiction Commn, 1980–83; Chancellor: Dio. Guildford, 1968–; Dio. Lincoln, 1970–; Dio. Rochester, 1971–; Lay Chm., Dulwich Deanery Synod, 1970–73; Vicar-Gen., Province of Canterbury, 1977–83. Chm., William Temple Assoc., 1963–66; Governor: Liddon Hse, London, 1964–; Pusey Hse, Oxford, 1965–. *Address:* Parkside, Dulwich Common, SE21 7EU. *T:* 01–693 3564.

GOODMAN, Michael Jack, PhD; Social Security Commissioner (formerly National Insurance Commissioner), since 1979; *b* 3 Oct. 1931; *s* of Vivian Roy Goodman and Muriel Olive Goodman; *m* 1958, Susan Kerkham Wherry; two *s* one *d*. *Educ:* Sudbury Grammar Sch., Suffolk; Corpus Christi Coll., Oxford (MA). PhD Manchester. Solicitor. Lectr, Gibson & Weldon, 1957; solicitor, Lincoln, 1958–60; Lectr, Law Society's Sch., 1961–63; Lectr, then Sen. Lectr in Law, Manchester Univ., 1964–70; Prof. of Law, Durham Univ., 1971–76; Perm. Chm. of Indust. Tribunals, Newcastle upon Tyne, 1976–79. Gen. Editor, Encyclopedia of Health and Safety at Work, 1974–. *Publications:* Industrial Tribunals' Procedure, 1976, 3rd edn 1985; contrib. Mod. Law Rev., and Conveyancer. *Recreations:* amateur radio (licence holder), model railways, The Times crossword. *Address:* Office of the Social Security Commissioners, 6 Grosvenor Gardens, SW1W 0DH. *T:* 01–730 0344.

GOODMAN, Rt. Rev. Morse Lamb; *b* Rosedale, Ont, 27 May 1917; *s* of Frederick James Goodman and Mary Mathilda Arkwright; *m* 1943, Patricia May Cunningham; three *s* one *d*. *Educ:* Trinity Coll., Univ. of Toronto. BA Trin., 1940; LTh Trin., 1942. Deacon, 1942, Priest, 1943, Diocese of Algoma; Asst Curate, St Paul's, Ft William, 1942–43; Incumbent, Murillo, Algoma, 1943–46; Rector, St Thomas, Ft William, 1946–53; Rector, St James, Winnipeg, 1953–60; Dean of Brandon, 1960–65; Rector, Christ Church, Edmonton, 1965–67; Bishop of Calgary, 1968–83. Conductor of Canadian Broadcasting Corporation Programme, Family Worship, 1954–68. Hon. DD: Trinity, 1961; Emmanuel and St Chad's, 1968. Companion, Order of Coventry Cross of Nails, 1974; GCKLJ. Columnist, Country Guide, 1961–. *Publication:* Let's Think It Over (A Christian's Day Book), 1986. *Recreations:* fishing, walking, photography, enology. *Address:* Box 15, Blind Bay, BC V0E 1H0, Canada. *Club:* Ranchman's.

GOODMAN, Perry; Deputy Chief Scientific Officer, Department of Trade and Industry, since 1980; *b* 26 Nov. 1932; *s* of Cyril Goodman and Anne (*née* Rosen); *m* 1958, Marcia Ann (*née* Morris); one *s* one *d*. *Educ:* Haberdashers' Aske's Hampstead Sch.; University Coll., London. BSc, MICeram. 2nd Lieut, Royal Corps of Signals, 1955–57; Jt Head, Chemistry Res. Lab., then Project Leader, Morgan Crucible Co. Ltd, 1957–64; Sen. Scientific Officer, DSIR, 1964–65; Principal Scientific Officer, Process Plant Br., Min. of Technology, 1965–67; 1st Sec. (Scientific), 1968–70, Counsellor (Scientific), 1970–74, British Embassy, Paris; Research Gp, DoI, 1974–79; Hd, Policy and Perspectives Unit, DoI, 1980–81. FRSA 1986. *Recreations:* travel, walking, conversation. *Address:* 118 Westbourne Terrace Mews, W2 6QG. *T:* 01–262 0925.

GOODMAN, (Robert) Howard, ARIBA; DipArch (Hons); Director Health Building, Department of Health and Social Security, since 1986; *b* 29 March 1928; *s* of Robert Barnard Goodman and Phyllis Goodman; *m* 1955; two *s*. *Educ:* St George Grammar Sch., Bristol; Northern Polytechnic, London. Articled pupil, 1944–47; Arch. Asst to City of Bristol, 1947–49; Asst Architect to SW Regional Hosp. Bd, 1949–54. Design of various hosp. projects in SW England; with various private architects, 1954–60; design of several hosps in UK, Africa and India. MOH (now DHSS): Main Grade Arch., 1960; Sen. Grade, 1961; Principal Arch., 1963; Asst Chief Arch., 1966; Chief Arch., 1971–78; Dir of Develt, 1978–85. Member: Constr. and Housing Res. Adv. Council; Bldg Res. Estab. Adv. Council; Council of Centre on Environment for the Handicapped. Research and develt into health planning, systems building and computer aided design. Hon. FICW, 1984; Hon. FBID, 1985. *Publications:* contribs to: Hospitals Handbook, 1960; Hospital Design, 1963; Hospital Traffic and Supply Problems, 1968; Portfolio for Health, 1971; Technology of the Eighties, 1972; Industrialised Hospital Building, 1972; CAD Systems, 1976; various articles in architectural, medical and general press. *Recreations:* eating, drinking, talking. *Address:* Ion House, 44 Nutley Lane, Reigate, Surrey.

GOODPASTER, Gen. Andrew Jackson; United States Army, retired; US Medal of Freedom, 1984; DSC (US); DSM (Def.) (Oak Leaf Cluster); DSM (Army) (3 Oak Leaf Clusters); DSM (Navy); DSM (Air Force); Silver Star; Legion of Merit (Oak Leaf Cluster); Purple Heart (Oak Leaf Cluster); Superintendent, United States Military Academy, West Point, New York (in grade of Lt-Gen.), 1977–81; *b* 12 Feb. 1915; *s* of Andrew Jackson Goodpaster and Teresa Mary Goodpaster (*née* Mrovka); *m* 1939, Dorothy Anderson Goodpaster (*née* Anderson); two *d*. *Educ:* McKendree Coll., Lebanon, Ill; US Mil. Academy, 1935–39 (BS); Princeton Univ., 1947–50 (MSE, MA, PhD). 11th Eng. Panama, 1939–42; Ex O, 390th Eng. Gen. Svc Regt, Camp Claiborne, La, 1942–43; Comd and Gen. Staff Sch., Ft Leavenworth, Kansas, Feb.-April 1943; CO, 48th Eng. Combat Bn, II Corps, Fifth Army, 1943–44; Ops Div., Gen. Staff, War Dept (incl. Jt War Plans Cttee, JCS, 1945–46), 1944–47; Student, Civil Eng. Course and Polit. Sc. Grad. Sch., Princeton Univ., 1947–50; Army Mem., Jt Advanced Study Cttee, JCS, 1950–51; Special Asst to Chief of Staff, SHAPE, 1951–54; Dist Eng., San Francisco Dist, Calif, July-Oct. 1954; Def. Liaison Officer and Staff Sec. to President of US, 1954–61; Asst Div. Comdr, 3rd Inf. Div., April-Oct. 1961, and CG, 8th Inf. Div., Oct. 1961–Oct. 1962, USAREUR; Sp. Asst (Policy) to Chm., JCS, Washington, DC, Nov. 1962–Jan. 1964; Asst to Chm., JCS, Washington, DC, Jan. 1964–July 1966; Dir Joint Staff, JCS, Washington, DC, Aug. 1966–Mar. 1967; Dir of Sp. Studies, Office Chief of Staff, USA, Washington, DC, April 1967–July 1967; Senior US Army Mem., Mil. Staff UN, May 1967–July 1968; Comdt, Nat. War Coll., Washington, DC, Aug. 1967–July 1968; Mem. US Delegn for Negotiations with N Vietnam, Paris (addl duty), April 1968–July 1968; Dep. Comdr, US Mil. Assistance Comd, Vietnam, July 1968–April 1969; Supreme Allied Commander Europe, 1969–74; C-in-C, US European Command, 1969–74. Sen. Fellow, Woodrow Wilson Internat. Center for Scholars, Washington DC, 1975–76; Prof. of Govt and Internat. Studies, The Citadel, Charleston, SC, 1976–77. Pres., Inst. for Defence Analyses, Alexandria, Va, 1983–85; Chm., Atlantic Council of the US, 1985–. *Publication:* For the Common Defense, 1977. *Recreations:* golf, fishing, ski-ing, music. *Address:* 409 North Fairfax Street, Alexandria, Va 22314, USA.

GOODRICH, David, CEng, RCNC; Managing Director, British Maritime Technology Ltd, since 1985; *b* 15 April 1941; *s* of William B. Goodrich and Florence B Goodrich; *m* 1965, Margaret R. Riley; one *s* three *d*. MBA. Shipbuilding management apprentice, 1958–63; shipbuilding designer/estimator, 1963–65; Constructor, RCNC, 1965–77; Manager, Shipbuilding Technology, 1977–79, Man. Dir, 1979–85, BSRA. MRINA (Mem. Council). *Publication:* paper to Royal Soc. *Recreations:* squash, walking, family. *Address:* Whitecroft, Hatton Hill, Windlesham, Surrey.

GOODRICH, Rt. Rev. Philip Harold Ernest; *see* Worcester, Bishop of.

GOODSON, Alan, OBE 1978; QPM 1972; Chief Constable of Leicestershire (sometime Leicester and Rutland), 1972–86; *b* 2 June 1927; *m* 1954, Mary Anne Reilly; one *s* two *d*. *Educ:* Hitchin Grammar Sch.; King's Coll., London (LLB). Royal Navy, 1945–48. Metropolitan, Pembrokeshire, Dyfed-Powys, and Essex Police, 1951–72; idc 1970. Mem. Adv. Council on Penal System, 1975–78; UK Rep., Interpol, 1980–82. Assessor, Inquiry into Crowd Safety and Control at Sports Grounds, 1985. President: Assoc. of Chief Police Officers, 1979–80; Chief Constables Club, 1981–82; Vice-Pres., European Police Sports Union, 1982–86; Chm., Police Athletic Assoc., 1984–86 (Hon. Sec., 1975–84). *Address:* c/o 420 London Road, Leicester LE2 2PT. *T:* Leicester 700911.

GOODSON, Sir Mark (Weston Lassam), 3rd Bt *cr* 1922, of Waddeton Court, Co. Devon; *b* 12 Dec. 1925; *s* of Major Alan Richard Lassam Goodson (*d* 1941) (2nd *s* of 1st Bt) and Clarisse Muriel Weston (*d* 1982), *d* of John Weston Adamson; *S* uncle, 1986; *m*

1949, Barbara Mary Constantine, *d* of Surg.-Capt. Reginald Joseph McAuliffe Andrews, RN; one *s* three *d*. *Educ:* Radley; Jesus College, Cambridge. *Heir: s* Alan Reginald Goodson, *b* 15 May 1960. *Address:* Kilham, Mindrum, Northumberland TD12 4QS. *T:* Mindrum 217.

GOODSON, Michael John; Assistant Auditor General, National Audit Office, since 1984; *b* 4 Aug. 1937; *s* of late Herbert Edward William Goodson and Doris Maud Goodson; *m* 1958, Susan Elizabeth (*née* Higley); one *s* one *d*. *Educ:* King Henry VIII Sch., Coventry. Joined Exchequer and Audit Dept, 1955; Asst Auditor, 1955; Auditor, 1965; Private Sec. to Comptroller and Auditor Gen., 1967–70; Sen. Auditor, 1970; Health Service Ombudsman (on secondment), 1973–76; Chief Auditor, Exchequer and Audit Dept, 1976; Dep. Dir of Audit, 1978; Dir of Audit, 1981. *Recreations:* ornithology, model engineering. *Address:* 5 Alzey Gardens, Harpenden, Herts AL5 5SZ. *T:* Harpenden 62744.

GOODWIN, Prof. Albert, MA; Professor of Modern History in the University of Manchester, 1953–69 (Dean of the Faculty of Arts, 1966–68), now Emeritus Professor; *b* 2 Aug. 1906; 3rd *s* of Albert and Edith Ellen Goodwin; *m* 1st, 1935, Mary Ethelwyn (*d* 1981), *e d* of late Capt. W. Millner, Tettenhall, Staffs; two *s* one *d*; 2nd, 1985, Mrs Barbara Mallows. *Educ:* King Edward VII School, Sheffield; Jesus Coll., Oxford; Sorbonne. Scholar; Gladstone Memorial Prizeman (Oxford), 1926; 1st Cl. Mod. Hist., 1928; Laming Travelling Fellow, The Queen's Coll., Oxford, 1928–29. Asst Lectr in European History, Univ. of Liverpool, 1929–31; Lectr in Mod. Hist. and Economics, 1931, Fellow and Tutor, Jesus Coll., Oxford, 1933; Junior Dean, Librarian and Dean of Degrees, 1931–39; Univ. Lectr in Mod. French Hist., 1938. Staff Officer (Sqdn Ldr) in RAFVR in Air Ministry War Room, 1940–43; Historical Branch, Air Ministry, 1944–45. Senior Tutor, 1947–48, and Vice-Principal of Jesus Coll., Oxford, 1949–51. Examiner in Final Hon. Sch. of Mod. Hist. (Oxford) 1948–49, Chm., 1950; Senior Univ. Lectr in Revolutionary and Napoleonic Period, 1948–53; Vis. Fellow, All Souls Coll., Oxford, 1969–70. Member: Council of Royal Historical Soc. (Vice-Pres.); Royal Commn on Historical MSS, 1966–81; Governor of John Rylands Library, Manchester. Pres., Sherborne Hist. Soc.; Chm., Sherborne Museum Council, 1981–82. *Publications:* The Abbey of St Edmundsbury, 1931; The Battle of Britain (Air Ministry Pamphlet 156), 1943; The French Revolution, 1953; The European Nobility in the Eighteenth Century (contrib. and ed), 1953; A select list of works on Europe and Europe Overseas, 1715–1815 (co-editor contributor), 1956; The Friends of Liberty: the English democratic movement in the age of the French Revolution, 1979; (ed and contrib.) Vol. VIII New Cambridge Modern History; articles in Eng. Hist. Review, History, Encyclopædia Britannica, etc. *Recreations:* golf, antiques. *Address:* Newland Orchard, 2 The Avenue, Sherborne, Dorset DT9 3AH.

GOODWIN, Air Vice-Marshal Edwin Spencer, CB 1944; CBE 1941; AFC. Served European War, 1914–19; Flt Sub-Lieut RNAS, 1916; War of 1939–45 (CBE, CB). Group Capt. 1939; Air Commodore, 1941; Air Vice-Marshal, 1948. Air Officer i/c Administration, HQ Bomber Command, 1945; retired, 1948.

GOODWIN, Dr Eric Thomson, CBE 1975; retired; *b* 30 July 1913; *s* of John Edward Goodwin and Florence Goodwin; *m* 1st, 1940, Isobel Philip (*d* 1976); two *s*; 2nd, 1977, Avis Mary (*née* Thomson). *Educ:* King Edward VI Sch., Stafford; Harrow County Sch.; Peterhouse, Cambridge. BA 1934, Rayleigh Prize 1936, MA 1937, PhD 1938. Asst Lectr, Sheffield Univ., 1937–39; war service: Mathematical Lab., Cambridge, 1939–43; Admty Signal Estabt, Witley, 1943–44; Admty Computing Service, Bath, 1945; Maths Div., Nat. Physical Lab., 1945–71 (Supt 1951–71); Dep. Dir, Nat. Phys. Lab., 1971–74, retd. *Publications:* papers in learned jls on theoretical physics and numerical analysis. *Recreations:* music, reading, the countryside, philately. *Address:* 32 Castle Mount Crescent, Bakewell, Derbyshire DE4 1AT. *T:* Bakewell 3647.

GOODWIN, Prof. Geoffrey Lawrence, BSc (Econ.); Montague Burton Professor of International Relations in the University of London (tenable at London School of Economics), 1962–78, now Emeritus; *b* 14 June 1916; *s* of Rev. J. H. Goodwin and Mrs E. M. Goodwin; *m* 1951, Janet Audrey (*née* Sewell); one *s* two *d*. *Educ:* Marlborough Coll.; RMC, Sandhurst; London Sch. of Economics. Regular Army Officer, 1936–43 (The Suffolk Regt; Army Physical Training Staff; Combined Ops; Major, comdg Indep. Company, Gibraltar). Foreign Office, 1945–48; London Sch. of Economics, 1948–81. Principal, St Catharine's, Windsor Great Park, 1971–72. Comr on Internat. Affairs, World Council of Churches, 1968–76. Mem. Council, 1974–77, Sen. Advr, 1983–84, RIIA; Vis. Mem., Inst. for Advanced Study, Princeton 1959; Vis. Prof., Institut Universitaire des Hautes Etudes Internationales, Geneva, 1962; Vis. Fellow, ANU, Canberra, 1978. Hon. Pres., British Internat. Studies Assoc., 1977–80. FRSA 1975. *Publications:* (ed) The University Teaching of International Relations, 1951; Britain and the United Nations, 1958; (ed) New Dimensions of World Politics, 1975; (ed) A New International Commodity Regime, 1979; (ed) Ethics and Nuclear Deterrence, 1982; articles in International Affairs, International Organization, Political Studies, etc. *Recreations:* painting, sketching, singing. *Address:* Webbs Farm, Church Lane, Headley, Epsom, Surrey. *T:* Leatherhead 377354.

GOODWIN, Prof. John Forrest, MD, FRCP; Professor of Clinical Cardiology, Royal Postgraduate Medical School, London, 1963–84, now Emeritus; Consulting Physician, Hammersmith Hospital, since 1949; Hon. Consulting Cardiologist: St Mary's Hospital, Paddington, since 1982; St George's Hospital, 1986; *b* 1 Dec. 1918; *s* of late Col William Richard Power Goodwin, DSO, RAMC, and late Myrtle Dale Goodwin (*née* Forrest); *m* 1943, Barbara Cameron Robertson; one *s* one *d*. *Educ:* Cheltenham Coll.; St Mary's Hosp. Medical Sch. (Univ. of London). FRSocMed 1943; MD London 1946; FRCP 1957. Med. Registrar, St Mary's Hosp., 1943–44; Physician, Anglo-Iranian Oil Co., Abadan, 1944–45; Med. 1st Asst, Royal Infirmary, Sheffield, 1946–49; Lectr in Medicine and Cons. Physician, Postgraduate Med. Sch., London, 1949–59; Sen. Lecturer, 1959–63. Visiting Professor: Univ. of California at Los Angeles, 1966; Georgetown Univ. Sch. of Med., Washington, 1973; Mayo Clinic, 1985; Lumleian Lectr, RCP, 1980. Mem., Expert Cttee on Cardiovascular Diseases, WHO, 1979. Member: Brit. Cardiac Soc., 1950 (Pres., 1972–76); Med. Res. Soc., 1952; Assoc. of Physicians of Great Britain and Ireland, 1953; Council, Brit. Heart Foundation, 1964; Past Pres., Internat. Soc. and Fedn of Cardiology (Pres., 1977–81); 2nd Vice-Pres., RCP, 1979–80; Chm., Coronary Prevention Gp, 1985–. Member: Società Italiana di Cardiologia, 1964; Assoc. of European Pædiatric Cardiologists, 1967; Cardiac Soc. of Australia and NZ, 1974; Venezuelan Soc. of Cardiology, 1969; Hon. Member: Swiss Cardiol. Soc.; Cardiac Soc., Ecuador; Hellenic Cardiac Soc., 1974; Cardiac Soc. of Mexico, 1977; Fellow Amer. Coll. of Cardiology, 1967; Fellow, Council on Clinical Cardiology, Amer. Heart Assoc., 1970; Hon. FACP 1985. Dr *hc* Lisbon, 1985. Gifted Teacher Award, Amer. Coll. of Cardiol., 1984. SPk 1968. Commander, Order of Icelandic Falcon, 1972. *Publications:* (jt ed. with R. Daley and R. E. Steiner) Clinical Disorders of the Pulmonary Circulation, 1960; (with W. Cleland, L. McDonald, D. Ross) Medical and Surgical Cardiology, 1969; (ed with P. Yu) Progress in Cardiology, annually since 1973; papers on diagnosis and treatment of congenital and acquired heart disease in British and foreign cardiac and other journals. *Recreations:* photography, history, travel. *Address:* 2 Pine Grove, Lake Road, Wimbledon, SW19 7HE. *T:* 01–947 4851. *Clubs:* Athenæum, Royal Society of Medicine.

GOODWIN, Leonard George, CMG 1977; FRCP; FRS 1976; Director, Nuffield Laboratories of Comparative Medicine, Institute of Zoology, The Zoological Society of London, 1964–80; Director of Science, Zoological Society of London, 1966–80; Consultant, Wellcome Trust, since 1984; *b* 11 July 1915; *s* of Harry George and Lois Goodwin; *m* 1940, Marie Evelyn Coates; no *c*. *Educ:* William Ellis Sch., London; University Coll. London (Fellow, 1981); School of Pharmacy, London; University Coll. Hospital. BPharm 1935, BSc 1937, MB, BS 1950, (London). MRCP 1966, FRCP 1972. Demonstrator, Sch. of Pharmacy, London, 1935–39; Head of Wellcome Labs of Tropical Medicine, 1958–63 (Protozoologist, 1939–63). Jt Hon. Sec., Royal Soc. of Tropical Medicine and Hygiene, 1968–74, Pres., 1979–81. Chairman: Trypanosomiasis Panel, ODM, 1974–77; Filariasis Steering Cttee, WHO Special Programme, 1978–82. Hon. Dir, Wellcome Museum for Med. Sci., 1984–85. Hon. FPS, 1977; Hon. DSc Brunel, 1986. Soc. of Apothecaries Gold Medal, 1975; Harrison Meml Medal, 1978; Schofield Medal, Guelph Univ., 1979; Silver Medal, Zoological Soc., 1980. Chm. Editorial Bd, Parasitology, 1980–. *Publications:* (pt author) Biological Standardization, 1950; (contrib.) Biochemistry and Physiology of Protozoa, 1955; (jointly) A New Tropical Hygiene, 1960, 2nd edn 1972; (contrib.) Recent Advances in Pharmacology, 1962; many contribs to scientific jls, mainly on pharmacology and chemotherapy of tropical diseases, especially malaria, trypanosomiasis and helminth infections. *Recreations:* Dabbling in arts and crafts especially pottery (slipware), gardening and passive participation in music and opera. *Address:* Shepperlands Farm, Park Lane, Finchampstead, Berks RG11 4QF. *T:* Eversley 732153.

GOODWIN, Michael Felix James; Director, Institute for the Study of Conflict, since 1979 (Administrative Director, 1971–79); *b* 31 Jan. 1916; *e s* of late F. W. Goodwin; *m* 1944, Alison, *y d* of Capt. Lionel Trower and Ethel Matheson of Achany; one *s* one *d*. *Educ:* privately. Joined BBC, 1935; North Reg. Drama Dir, 1938; West Reg. Drama Dir, 1939. Served War of 1939–45, in Royal Artillery, 1939–43. Returned to BBC in Features Dept and Overseas News Service, 1943–47. Dramatic critic, The Weekly Review, 1945–46; succeeded Helen Waddell as Asst Editor, The Nineteenth Century and After, 1945–47; Editor, The Twentieth Century (formerly The Nineteenth Century and After), 1947–52; toured US at invitation of State Dept, 1952; Editor, Bellman Books, 1952–55; Dir, Contact Publications, 1955–60; Dir, Newman Neame Ltd, 1960–65. Financial Advr, Internat. Assoc. for Cultural Freedom, Paris, 1967–73. *Publications:* Nineteenth Century Opinion, 1949 (Penguin); Artist and Colourman, 1966; Concise Dictionary of Antique Terms, 1967. *Address:* 16 Cope Place, W8. *T:* 01–937 3802. *Club:* Travellers'.

GOODWIN, Noël; *see* Goodwin, T. N.

GOODWIN, Peter Austin, CBE 1986; Secretary, Public Works Loan Commission, since 1979; Comptroller General, National Debt Office, since 1980; Director, National Investment and Loans Office, since 1980; *b* 12 Feb. 1929; *s* of late Stanley Goodwin and of Louise Goodwin; *m* 1950, Audrey Vera Webb; one *d*. *Educ:* Harrow County School. Served Royal Air Force, 1947–49. Executive Officer, Public Works Loan Commn, 1950; Principal, Civil Aviation Authority, 1973–76; Asst Secretary and Establishment Officer, Public Works Loan Commn, 1976–79. UK Mem., Gp of Experts advising on management of Pension Reserve Fund, Europ. Patent Office, 1986–. *Recreations:* theatre, opera, ballet, country dancing, model railways. *Address:* 87 Woodmansterne Road, Carshalton Beeches, Surrey SM5 4JW. *T:* 01–643 3530.

GOODWIN, Lt-Gen. Sir Richard (Elton), KCB 1963 (CB 1959); CBE 1954; DSO 1944; DL; Vice Lord-Lieutenant, Suffolk, 1978–83; *b* 17 Aug. 1908; *s* of late Col W. R. P. Goodwin, DSO, and Mrs Goodwin; *m* 1940, Anthea Mary Sampson; three *s*. *Educ:* Cheltenham Coll.; Royal Military Coll., Sandhurst. Commissioned into Suffolk Regt, 1928; served in India, 1930–38; ADC to Governor of Madras, 1935; Adjutant 2nd Suffolk, 1935–38; 2nd i/c 9th Royal Warwickshire, 1941–42; CO 1st Suffolk, 1943–45; College Comdr, RMA Sandhurst, 1947–49; Comdt, Sch. of Infantry, 1951–54; Comdr, 6th Infty Bde, 1954–57; GOC 49th Infty Div. (TA) and N Midland Dist, 1957–60; GOC, E Africa Comd, 1960–63; Comdr 1st (British) Corps, 1963–66; Military Secretary, MoD (Army), 1966–69. Lieutenant, HM Tower of London, 1969–72. Col 1st E Anglian Regt (Royal Norfolk and Suffolk), 1962–64; Dep. Col The Royal Anglian Regt, 1964–66, Col, 1966–71. DL Suffolk 1973. *Recreations:* hunting and other field sports. *Address:* The Old Plough, Denham, Bury St Edmunds, Suffolk IP29 5EW. *Club:* Army and Navy.

GOODWIN, Prof. Richard Murphey; Professor of Economic Science, Siena University, since 1980; *b* 24 Feb. 1913; *s* of William Murphey Goodwin and Mary Florea Goodwin; *m* 1937, Jacqueline Wynmalen; no *c*. *Educ:* Harvard Univ. (AB, PhD); Oxford Univ. (BA, BLitt). Harvard Univ.: Instructor in Econs, 1939–42; Instructor in Physics, 1942–45; Asst Prof. of Econs, 1945–51; Lectr in Econs, 1951–69, Reader in Economics, 1969–80, and Fellow of Peterhouse, 1956–80 (Emeritus Fellow, 1982), Univ. of Cambridge. *Publications:* Elementary Economics from the Higher Standpoint, 1970; Essays in Economic Dynamics, 1982; Essays in Linear Economic Structures, 1983; contrib. Econ. Jl, Econometrica, Review of Econs and Statistics. *Recreations:* painting, walking. *Address:* Dorvis's, Ashdon, Saffron Walden, Essex. *T:* Ashdon 302.

GOODWIN, (Trevor) Noël; freelance critic, writer and broadcaster, specialising in music and dance; *b* 25 Dec. 1927; *s* of Arthur Daniel Goodwin and Blanche Goodwin (*née* Stephens); *m* 1st, 1954, Gladys Marshall Clapham (marr. diss. 1960); 2nd, Anne Myers (*née* Mason); one step *s*. *Educ:* mainly in France. BA (London). Assistant Music Critic: News Chronicle, 1952–54; Manchester Guardian, 1954–55; Music and Dance Critic, Daily Express, 1956–78; Exec. Editor, Music and Musicians, 1963–71; regular reviewer for: The Times, 1978–; Internat. Herald Tribune, 1978–84; Opera News, 1975–; Ballet News, 1979–86; Dance and Dancers, 1957– (Associate Editor, 1972–); Opera, 1984– (Overseas News Editor, 1985–). Member: Arts Council of GB, 1979–81 (Mem., 1973–81, Chm., 1979–81, Dance Adv. Panel; Mem., 1974–81, Dep. Chm., 1979–81, Music Adv. Panel; Council's rep. on Visiting Arts Unit of GB, 1979–81); Dance Adv. Panel, UK Branch, Calouste Gulbenkian Foundn, 1972–76; Nat. Enquiry into Dance Educn and Trng in Britain, 1975–80; Drama and Dance Adv. Cttee, British Council, 1973–; HRH The Duke of Kent's UK Cttee for European Music Year 1985, 1982–84 (Chm., sub-cttee for Writers and Critics); Trustee-dir, Internat. Dance Course for Professional Choreographers and Composers, 1975–. Pres., The Critics' Circle, 1977 (Jt Trustee, 1984–). Planned and presented numerous radio programmes of music and records for BBC Home and World Services during past 25 years, and contributes frequently to music and arts programmes on Radios 3 and 4. *Publications:* London Symphony: portrait of an orchestra, 1954; A Ballet for Scotland, 1979; (with Sir Geraint Evans) A Knight at the Opera, 1984; editor, Royal Opera and Royal Ballet Yearbooks, 1978, 1979, 1980; area editor and writer, New Grove Dictionary of Music and Musicians, 1981; contribs to: Encyclopaedia Britannica, 15th edn, 1974; Encyclopaedia of Opera, 1976; Britannica Books of the Year, annually 1980–; Cambridge Encyclopaedia of Russia and the Soviet Union, 1982; New Oxford Companion to Music, 1983. *Recreation:* travel. *Address:* 76 Skeena Hill, SW18 5PN. *T:* 01–788 8794.

GOODWIN, Prof. Trevor Walworth, CBE 1975; FRS 1968; Johnston Professor of Biochemistry, University of Liverpool, 1966–83; *b* 22 June 1916; British; *m* 1944, Kathleen Sarah Hill; three *d*. *Educ:* Birkenhead Inst.; Univ. of Liverpool. Lectr 1944, Sen. Lectr 1949, in Biochemistry, University of Liverpool; Prof. of Biochemistry and Agricultural Biochemistry, UCW, Aberystwyth, 1959. Chairman: Cttee, Biochem. Soc., 1970–73; Brit. Nat. Cttee for Biochem., 1976–82; Member: Council, Royal Society, 1972, 1974, 1985; UGC, 1974–81; SRC Science Bd, 1975–78; ARC Grants Bd, 1975–82; Wirral Educn Cttee, 1974–84; Lawes Agricl Trust Cttee, 1977–; Exec. Cttee, FEBS, 1975–83 (Chm., Publication Cttee, 1975–83); Mem. Court, Univ. of N Wales, Bangor, 1983–; Morton Lectr, Biochem. Soc., 1983. Corresp. Mem., Amer. Soc. Plant Physiologists, 1982; Hon. Member: Phytochemical Soc. of Europe, 1983; Biochem Soc., 1985. Diplôme d'honneur, FEBS, 1984. Ciba Medallist, Biochemical Soc., 1970; Prix Roussel, Societé Roussel Uclaf, 1982. *Publications:* Comparative Biochemistry of Carotenoids, 1952, 2nd edn, vol. 1 1980, vol. 2 1983; Recent Advances in Biochemistry, 1960; Biosynthesis of Vitamins, 1964; (ed) Chemistry and Biochemistry of Plant Pigments, 1965, 2nd edn, 2 vols, 1976; (with E. I. Mercer) Introduction to Plant Biochemistry, 1972, 2nd edn 1982; numerous articles in Biochem. Jl, Phytochemistry, etc. *Recreation:* gardening. *Address:* Monzar, 9 Woodlands Close, Parkgate, Wirral, Cheshire L64 6RU. *T:* 051–336 4494.

GOODY, Prof. John Rankine, FBA 1976; William Wyse Professor of Social Anthropology, University of Cambridge, 1973–84; Fellow, St John's College, Cambridge, since 1960; *b* 27 July 1919; *m* 1956, Esther Robinson Newcomb; one *s* four *d*. *Educ:* St Albans Sch.; St John's Coll., Cambridge; Balliol Coll., Oxford. BA 1946, Dip. Anthrop. 1947, PhD 1954, ScD 1969, Cantab; BLitt Oxon 1952. HM Forces, 1939–46. Educnl admin, 1947–49; Cambridge Univ.: Asst Lectr, 1954–59; Lectr, 1959–71; Dir, African Studies Centre, 1966–73; Smuts Reader in Commonwealth Studies, 1972. Foreign Hon. Mem., Amer. Acad. of Arts and Scis, 1980. *Publications:* The Social Organisation of the LoWiili, 1956; (ed) The Developmental Cycle in Domestic Groups, 1958; Death, Property and the Ancestors, 1962; (ed) Succession to High Office, 1966; (with J. A. Braimah) Salaga: the struggle for power, 1967; (ed) Literacy in Traditional Societies, 1968; Comparative Studies in Kinship, 1969; Technology, Tradition and the State in Africa, 1971; The Myth of the Bagre, 1972; (with S. J. Tambiah) Bridewealth and Dowry, 1973; (ed) The Character of Kinship, 1973; (ed) Changing Social Structure in Ghana, 1975; Production and Reproduction, 1977; The Domestication of the Savage Mind, 1977; (with J. W. D. K. Gandah) Une Recitation du Bagré, 1981; Cooking, Cuisine and Class, 1982; The Development of the Family and Marriage in Europe, 1983; The Logic of Writing and the Organization of Society, 1986; contrib. learned jls. *Address:* St John's College, Cambridge. *T:* Cambridge 61621.

GOODY, Most Rev. Launcelot John, KBE 1977; PhD, DD; Former Archbishop of Perth (RC); *b* 5 June 1908; *s* of late Ernest John Goody and of Agnes Goody. *Educ:* Christian Brothers' College, Perth, WA; Urban University, Rome. PhD 1927, DD 1931. Ordained priest at Rome, 1930; Asst Parish Priest, Perth Cathedral, 1932–35, Kalgoorlie, 1935–37; Parish Priest, Toodyay, 1937; Director of Seminary, Guildford, 1940–47; Domestic Prelate to the Pope, 1947; Parish Priest, Bedford Park, 1947–51; Auxiliary Bishop of Perth, 1951; first RC Bishop of Bunbury, 1954–68; Archbishop of Perth, 1968–83. *Address:* St Mary's Cathedral, Perth, WA 6000, Australia. *T:* 3259177.

GOODYEAR, Prof. Francis Richard David, FBA 1984; Visiting Professor and Chairman of Governing Committee, Department of Classics, University of the Witwatersrand, since 1984; *b* 2 Feb. 1936; *s* of Francis Goodyear and Gladys Ivy Goodman; *m* 1967, Cynthia Rosalie Attwood; one *s*. *Educ:* Luton Grammar Sch.; St John's Coll., Cambridge. MA, PhD (Cantab). Open schol., St John's Coll., Cambridge, 1953; Craven schol., Hallam Prize, 1956; Classical Tripos, Pts 1 and 2, cl. 1, 1956–57; Chancellor's Medal, H. A. Thomas Studentship, 1957. Cambridge University: Research Fellow, St John's Coll., 1959–60; Official Fellow, 1960–66, Librarian, 1960–64, Queens' Coll.; London University: Hildred Carlile Prof. of Latin, 1966–83; Hd of Dept of Latin, 1966–83, Dean of Faculty of Arts, 1971–73, Bedford Coll.; Chm., Bd of Studies in Classics, 1977–78. Mem., Accademia Nazionale Virgilian, 1975. Mem., Adv. Editorial Bd, Cambridge Classical Texts and Commentaries, 1974–. *Publications:* Incerti auctoris Aetna, 1965; Appendix Vergiliana (jt editor), 1966; Corippi Iohannidos libri viii (jt editor), 1970; Tacitus, a survey, 1970; The Annals of Tacitus, vol. i, 1972, vol. ii, 1981; papers and reviews in learned jls, contribs to works of reference. *Recreations:* light reading, travel. *Address:* 78 George V Avenue, Pinner, Mddx HA5 5SW; Department of Classics, University of the Witwatersrand, 1 Jan Smuts Avenue, Johannesburg, 2001, South Africa.

GOOLD, Sir George (Leonard), 7th Bt *cr* 1801; retired engineer; *b* 26 Aug. 1923; *s* of Sir George Ignatius Goold, 6th Bt, and Rhoda Goold; *S* father, 1967; *m* 1945, Joy Cecelia, *d* of William Cutler, Melbourne; one *s* four *d*. *Educ:* Port Pirie, S Australia. Mem., Standing Council of the Baronetage. *Heir:* *s* George William Goold [*b* 25 March 1950; *m* 1973, Julie Ann, *d* of Leonard Crack; two *s*]. *Address:* 60 Canterbury Road, Victor Harbour, SA 5211, Australia. *T:* (085) 522872.

GOOLD, Sir James (Duncan), Kt 1983; DL; CA; Director, Mactaggart & Mickel Ltd, since 1965; Chairman, Scottish Conservative Party, since 1983; *b* 28 May 1934; *s* of John Goold and Janet Agnes Kirkland; *m* 1959, Sheena Paton; two *s* one *d*. *Educ:* Belmont House; Glasgow Acad. Apprentice, Reid & Mair, CA, 1952–58 (CA 1958); W. E. C. Reid & Co., Accountants, NZ, 1958–60; Price Waterhouse & Co., Accountants, Australia, 1960; Sec., Mactaggart & Mickel Ltd, 1961–65. Director: Gibson & Goold Ltd, 1978–; Morgan Grenfell (Scotland) Ltd, 1983–; American Trust plc, 1984–. President: Scottish Bldg Contractors Assoc., 1971; Scottish Bldg Employers Fedn, 1977; Chm., CBI Scotland, 1981–83. Hon. Treasurer, Scottish Cons. Party, 1981–83; Hon. Pres., Eastwood Cons. Assoc., 1978–. Governor: Belmont House Sch., 1972–84; Glasgow Acad., 1982–; Paisley Coll. of Technol., 1981–. DL Renfrewshire, 1985. Hon. FCIOB 1979; Hon. FFB 1983. *Recreations:* gardening, the open air, hill walking, golf, tennis. *Address:* Sandyknowe, Waterfoot, Clarkston, Glasgow G76 8RN. *T:* 041–644 2764. *Clubs:* Carlton; The Western, Royal Scottish Automobile (Glasgow); Royal Troon Golf (Troon); Lamlash Golf; Arran Yacht.

GOOLD-ADAMS, Richard John Moreton, CBE 1974, MA; Vice-President, SS Great Britain Project, since 1982 (Chairman, 1968–82); *b* Brisbane, Australia, 24 Jan. 1916; *s* of Sir Hamilton Goold-Adams, Governor of Qld, and Elsie Riordon, Montreal; *m* 1939, Deenagh Blennerhassett. *Educ:* Winchester; New Coll., Oxford. Served 1939–46 in Army, Major, in Middle East and Italy. The Economist, latterly as an Asst Editor, 1947–55. Councillor: Internat. Inst. for Strategic Studies, 1958–76 (a Founder and Vice-Chm., 1958–62; Chm., 1963–73; Hon. Mem., 1985); National Inst. of Industrial Psychology, 1956–70; Royal Inst. of Internat. Affairs, 1957–81; Soc. for Nautical Research, 1970–73, 1975–78; Chm., British Atlantic Cttee, 1959–62, Vice-Pres., 1963–83. Governor: Atlantic Inst. in Paris, 1962–71; Academic Council, Wilton Park, 1963–83. Dep. Chm., Guthrie Estates Agency Ltd, 1962–63, resigned; re-elected to board, 1964; merged into The Guthrie Corp., 1965; Dir, 1965–69. Formerly broadcasting and television on current affairs, and lecturing. *Publications:* South Africa To-day and Tomorrow, 1936; Middle East Journey, 1947; The Time of Power: a reappraisal of John Foster Dulles, 1962; The Return of the Great Britain, 1976. *Recreation:* photography. *Address:* c/o National Westminster Bank, 116 Fenchurch Street, EC3M 5AN. *Club:* Travellers'.

GOOLDEN, Barbara; novelist; *b* 5 June 1900; *d* of Charles and Isabel Goolden (*née* Armit); one adopted *s* decd. *Educ:* Community of the Holy Family; two private schools. Has appeared on TV and spoken on radio. *Publications:* The Knot of Reluctance, 1926; The Sleeping Sword, 1928; Children of Peace, 1928; The Conquering Star, 1929; The Waking Bird, 1929; The Ancient Wheel, 1930; Toils of Law, 1931, Thin Ice, 1931; Sugared Grief, 1932; Eros, 1933; Separate Paths, 1933; Slings and Arrows, 1934; Victory to the Vanquished, 1935; Wise Generations, 1936; The Primrose Path, 1936; Morning Tells the Day, 1937; The Wind My Posthorse, 1937; Within a Dream, 1938; Young Ambition, 1938; Call the Tune, 1939; The Asses Bridge, 1940; The Best Laid Schemes, 1941; Crown of Life, 1941; Men as Trees, 1942; Swings and Roundabouts, 1943; Community Singing, 1944; Ichabod, 1945; Daughters of Earth, 1947; Jig Saw, 1948; From the Sublime to the Ridiculous, 1949; Strange Strife, 1952; Venetia, 1952; The China Pig, 1953; Truth is Fallen in the Street, 1953; Return Journey, 1954; Who is my Neighbour?, 1954; Bread to the Wise, 1955; The World His Oyster, 1955; At the Foot of the Hills, 1956; To Have and to Hold, 1956; The Singing and the Gold, 1956; The Nettle and the Flower, 1957; Through the Sword Gates, 1957; The Linnet in the Cage, 1958; The Ships of Youth, 1958; Sweet Fields, 1958; A Pilgrim and his Pack, 1959; For Richer, For Poorer, 1959; Falling in Love, 1960; New Wine, 1960; Where Love is, 1960; To Love and to Cherish, 1961; One Autumn Face, 1961; Against the Grain, 1961; The Little City, 1962; The Pebble in the Pond, 1962; Marriages are Made in Heaven, 1963; Love-in-a-Mist, 1963; Battledore and Shuttlecock, 1963; Fools' Paradise, 1964; The Gentle Heart, 1964; The Gift, 1964; Blight on the Blossom, 1965; A Finger in the Pie, 1965; The Lesser Love, 1965; Anvil of Youth, 1966; Nobody's Business, 1966; A Time to Love, 1966; Second Fiddle, 1967; A Time to Build, 1967; All to Love, 1968; The Eleventh Hour, 1968; The Reluctant Wife, 1968; A Marriage of Convenience, 1969; Today Belongs to Us, 1969; The Snare, 1970; A Question of Conscience, 1970; Fortune's Favourite, 1971; No Meeting Place, 1971; Before the Flame is Lit, 1971; A Leap in the Dark, 1972; A Law for Lovers, 1973; Time to Turn Back, 1973; The Broken Arc, 1974; Mirage, 1974; The Crystal and the Dew, 1975; Silver Fountains, 1975; Goodbye to Yesterday, 1976; In the Melting Pot, 1976; Unborn Tomorrow, 1977; The Rags of Time, 1978; *for children:* Minty, 1959; Five Pairs of Hands, 1961; Minty and the Missing Picture, 1963; Minty and the Secret Room, 1964; Trouble for the Tabors, 1966; Top Secret, 1969. *Recreation:* reading. *Address:* Stildon, London Road, East Grinstead, West Sussex.

GOONERATNE, Tilak Eranga; Ambassador of Sri Lanka to the Commission of the European Communities, and concurrently to Belgium, 1975–78; *b* 27 March 1919; *m* 1948, Pamela J. Rodrigo (*d* 1978); two *d*. *Educ:* BA (London Univ.); Ceylon Law Coll. Advocate, Supreme Ct of Ceylon. Joined Ceylon Civil Service, 1943; Asst Sec., Min. of External Affairs, 1947–51; Govt Agent: Trincomalee, 1951–54; Matara, 1954–56; Registrar Gen., Marriages, Births and Deaths, 1956–58; Dir-Gen. of Broadcasting and Dir of Information, Ceylon, 1958–60; Comr Co-operative Develt, 1960–63; Dir of Economic Affairs, 1963; Dep. Sec. to Treasury, 1963–65; Pres., Colombo Plan Council for Technical Co-operation in S and SE Asia, 1964–65; Ceylon deleg. to UN Gen. Assembly, 1964–65; Dep. Sec.-Gen., Commonwealth Secretariat, London, 1965–70; High Comr in UK, 1970–75. Commonwealth Fund for Technical Co-operation: Chm., Bd of Representatives, 1975–76; Chm., Review Gp of Experts. *Publications:* An Historical Outline of the Development of the Marriage and Divorce Laws of Ceylon; An Historical Outline of the Development of the Marriage and Divorce Laws Applicable to Muslims in Ceylon; Fifty Years of Co-operative Development in Ceylon. *Address:* 17B Warwick Avenue, W9. *T:* 01–286 4675.

GOOSSENS, Léon Jean, CBE 1950; FRCM; Hon. RAM; Solo Oboist; *b* Liverpool, 12 June 1897; *s* of late Eugène Goossens, musician and conductor; *m* 1st, 1926; one *d*; 2nd, 1933, Leslie (*d* 1985), *d* of Brig. A. Burrowes; two *d*. *Educ:* Christian Brothers Catholic Institute, Liverpool; Liverpool Coll. of Music. Started oboe studies at 10 yrs of age with Charles Reynolds; at 14 studied at RCM, London, and at 16 joined London Symphony Orchestra on tour with Nikisch; same year toured Wales with Sir Henry Wood and Queen's Hall Orchestra as principal oboist, the following year accepting post as permanency. Served in European War, 1915–18 (wounded). Principal oboe, London Philharmonic Orchestra, also at Covent Garden Opera House with Sir Thomas Beecham; Prof. at RCM and RAM; after recitals in London and other English cities, toured USA, 1927 and 1928; Rep. British Music in most European capitals, at NY World Fair, with Sir Adrian Boult; also in Washington with Dr Clarence Raybould; recitals for BBC and lectures in schools, music clubs, univs and on TV. Has produced in England a new school of oboe-playing and promoted the oboe to the ranks of other solo instruments, for which leading composers of the day have written and, in many cases, dedicated their works to this artist; *works include:* concerti by Malcolm Arnold, Arnold Cooke, Dr Vaughan Williams, Rutland Boughton, Cyril Scott, Gordon Jacob, Francesco Ticciati, Ralph Nicholson, Sir Eugène Goossens; solo or chamber works by Dr Walter Stanton, Gustav Holst, Sir Edward Elgar, Sir George Henschel, John Addison, Dame Ethel Smyth, Franz Reizenstein, Thomas Pitfield, Somers Cocks, Gerald Finzi, Sir Arthur Bliss, Sir Arnold Bax, William Wordsworth, Lord Britten, Sigtenhurst Meyer, Alec Templeton, Alec Rowley, Alan Richardson, Francis Poulenc, Morgan Nicholas, Thomas Dunhill and Edwin Roxburgh. Toured Australia and New Zealand, also played in Singapore, 1954; visited Persia and Turkey, also Austria, 1955; toured Jugoslavia, 1954; toured USSR with Music Delegation headed by Master of The Queen's Musick, 1956; Coast to Coast Tour Canada, 1957; toured Scandinavia and Portugal, 1959, USA 1965, Munich 1972, St Moritz and Aberdeen (with Internat. Youth Orch.), 1971–73. Recitals in Malta, 1962–77. Pres., Art Soc., Gordonstoun Sch., 1980–. Belgrade Jurist, Internat. Wind Competition, 1981. Cobbett Medal for services to Chamber Music, 1954. *Publication:* (jtly with Edwin Roxburgh) The Oboe, 1977. *Relevant publication:* Music in the Wind, by Barry Wynne, 1967. *Recreation:* sailing. *Address:* Dulas Court, Dulas, Hereford HR2 0HL. *T:* Golden Valley 240214. *Clubs:* Chelsea Arts, London Corinthian Sailing; Malta Union.

GOPAL, Dr Sarvepalli; Professor of Contemporary History, Jawaharlal Nehru University, New Delhi, 1972–83, now Emeritus; Fellow of St Antony's College, Oxford, since 1966; *b* 23 April 1923; *y c* and *o s* of Sir Sarvepalli Radhakrishnan, Hon. OM, Hon. FBA. *Educ:* Mill Hill School; Madras Univ.; Oxford Univ. MA (Madras and Oxon), BL (Madras), DPhil (Oxon), DLitt (Oxon). Lecturer and Reader in History, Andhra Univ., Waltair, 1948–52; Asst Dir, Nat. Archives of India, 1952–54; Dir, Historical Div., Min. of Extl Affairs, New Delhi, 1954–66; Commonwealth Fellow, Trin. Coll., Cambridge, 1963–64; Reader in S Asian History, Oxford Univ., 1966–71. Chm. Nat. Book Trust, India, 1973–76; Member: Indian UGC, 1973–79; UNESCO Exec. Bd, 1976–80; Vis. Prof., Leeds, 1977. Pres., Indian History Congress, 1978. Corresp. FRHistS. Hon. Prof., Tirupati; Hon. DLitt: Andhra Univ., 1975; Tirupati Univ., 1979; Banaras Univ., 1984. Sahitya Akademi award, 1976. *Publications:* The Permanent Settlement in Bengal, 1949; The Viceroyalty of Lord Ripon, 1953; The Viceroyalty of Lord Irwin, 1957; British Policy in India, 1965; Modern India, 1967; Jawaharlal Nehru, vol. 1, 1975, vol. 2, 1979, vol. 3, 1984; general editor, Selected Works of Jawaharlal Nehru; contribs articles to historical jls. *Recreations:* good food and travel. *Address:* St Antony's College, Oxford; 97 Radhakrishna Salai, Mylapore, Madras 4, India. *Club:* United Oxford & Cambridge University.

GORAI, Rt. Rev. Dinesh Chandra; *see* Calcutta, Bishop of.

GORARD, Anthony John; hotel proprietor; *b* 15 July 1927; *s* of William James and Rose Mary Gorard; *m* 1954, Barbara Kathleen Hampton; one *s* three *d.* *Educ:* Ealing Grammar School. Chartered Accountant, 1951; Manufacturing Industry, 1952–58; Anglia Television Ltd, 1959–67, Executive Director and Member of Management Cttee; Managing Director, HTV Ltd, 1967–78; Chief Exec., HTV Gp Ltd, 1976–78; Director: Independent Television Publications Ltd, 1967–78; Independent Television News Ltd, 1973–78; Chief Exec., Cardiff Broadcasting Co. Ltd, 1979–81; Consultant, Mitchell Beazley Television, 1982–83. Chm., British Regional Television Association, 1970–71. *Recreations:* tennis, rambling. *Address:* Ludgate House, Haytor, Ilsington, Devon. *T:* Haytor 353.

GORAY, Narayan Ganesh; High Commissioner for India in London, 1977–79; *b* 15 June 1907; *s* of Ganesh Govind Gore and Saraswati; *m* 1935, Sumati Kirtani (decd); one *d.* *Educ:* Fergusson Coll., Poona. BA, LLB. Mem., Congress Socialist Party, 1934; (Mem. Nat. Exec., 1934); Jt Sec., Socialist Party, 1948; Gen. Sec., Praja Socialist Party, 1953–65, Chm., 1965–69; Member: Lok Sabha, 1957–62; Rajya Sabha, 1970–76. Mayor of Pune, 1968. Editor, Janata Weekly, 1971–. *Publications include:* History of the United States of America, 1959. *Recreations:* music, painting, writing. *Address:* 1813 Sadashiv Peth, Poona 30, Maharashtra State, India.

GORBACHYOV, Mikhail Sergeyevich; General Secretary of Central Committee, Communist Party of the Soviet Union, since 1985 (Member, since 1971; Member, Political Bureau, since 1980); Member, Presidium of the Supreme Soviet of USSR, since 1985; Deputy to Supreme Soviet, since 1970; Chairman, Foreign Affairs Committee, since 1984; *b* 2 March 1931; *m* Raisa Gorbachyova; one *d.* *Educ:* Moscow State Univ. (law graduate); Stavropol Agric. Inst. Machine operator, 1946; joined CPSU 1952; First Sec., Stavropol Komsomol City Cttee, 1955–58, later Dep. Head of Propaganda; 2nd, later 1st Sec., Komsomol Territorial Cttee; Party Organizer, Stavropol Territorial Production Bd of Collective and State Farms, 1962–66; Head, Dept of party bodies, CPSU Territorial Cttee, 1962–66; 1st Sec., Stavropol City Party Cttee, 1966–68; 2nd Sec., 1968–70, 1st Sec., 1970–78, Stavropol Territorial CPSU Cttee; Sec., with responsibility for agric., Central Cttee of CPSU, 1978–85; Alternate Mem., Political Bureau, Central Cttee of CPSU, 1979–80; Deputy to Supreme Soviet, RSFSR, 1979–; Chm., Foreign Affairs Commn of the Soviet of the Union, 1984–85. Orders of Lenin, of Red Banner of Labour, Badge of Honour. *Address:* Central Committee of Communist Party of the Soviet Union, Staraya Place 4, Moscow, USSR.

GORDIMER, Nadine; Author; *b* 20 Nov. 1923; *d* of Isidore Gordimer; *m* Reinhold Cassirer; one *s* one *d.* *Educ:* Convent Sch.; Witwatersrand Univ. Neil Gunn Fellowship, Scottish Arts Council, 1981. Hon. Member: Amer. Acad. of Art and Literature, 1979; Amer. Acad. of Arts and Sciences, 1980. DLit *hc* Leuven, Belgium, 1980; DLitt *hc:* City Coll. of NY, 1985; Smith Coll., 1985. MLA Award, USA, 1981; Malaparte Prize, Italy, 1985; Nelly Sachs Prize, W Germany, 1985. *Publications:* The Soft Voice of the Serpent (stories), 1953; The Lying Days (novel), 1953; Six Feet of the Country (stories), 1956; A World of Strangers (novel), 1958; Friday's Footprint (stories), 1960 (W. H. Smith Lit. Award, 1961); Occasion for Loving (novel), 1963; Not for Publication (stories), 1965; The Late Bourgeois World (novel), 1966; South African Writing Today (jt editor), 1967; A Guest of Honour (novel), 1971 (James Tait Black Meml Prize, 1971); Livingstone's Companions (stories), 1972; The Conservationist (novel), 1974 (jtly, Booker Prize 1974; Grand Aigle d'Or, France, 1975); Selected Stories, 1975; Some Monday for Sure (stories), 1976; Burger's Daughter, 1979; A Soldier's Embrace (stories), 1980; July's People (novel), 1981; Something Out There (stories), 1984. *Address:* 7 Frere Road, Parktown West, Johannesburg, South Africa.

GORDINE, Dora, (Hon. Mrs Richard Hare); FRBS; FRSA; sculptor and painter; *b* 1906; *d* of late Mark Gordin, St Petersburg, Russia; *m* 1936, Hon. Richard Hare (*d* 1966). Studied sculpture, Paris. First exhibited in the Salon des Tuileries, Paris, 1932. One-man exhibitions: Leicester Galleries, London, 1928, 1933, 1938, 1945, 1949; Flechtheim Gallery, Berlin, 1929. Commissioned to decorate with bronzes new Town Hall in Singapore, 1930–35; built studio and sculpture gallery in London according to her own designs (1936). Spent a year in America, executing commissions in Hollywood and delivering lectures on art (1947). Also represented by Sculpture in American, Asiatic, African and Australian collections. In England 3 works are in Tate Gallery; other bronzes in: Senate House, London Univ.; RIBA; Westminster Infant Welfare Centre; Maternity Ward in Holloway Prison; Esso Petroleum Refinery, Milford Haven; Royal Marsden Hospital, Surrey; Herron Museum of Art, Indianapolis; schs, institutions and many private collections. *Publications:* articles in Journal of Royal Asiatic Society. *Address:* Dorich House, Kingston Vale, SW15.

GORDON, family name of **Marquess of Aberdeen and Temair** and **Marquess of Huntly.**

GORDON, (Alexander) Esmé, RSA, FRIBA, FRIAS; *b* 12 Sept. 1910; *s* of Alexander Shand Gordon, WS and Elizabeth Catherine (*née* Logan); *m* 1937, Betsy, *d* of James and Bessie McCurry, Belfast; two *s* one *d.* *Educ:* Edinburgh Acad.; School of Arch., Edinburgh Coll. of Art. RIBA. Owen Jones Schol., 1934. War Service with RE in Europe. RSA 1967 (ARSA 1956); Sec., RSA, 1973–78; Pres., Edinburgh AA, 1955–57; Mem. Scottish Cttee, Arts Council of Gt Brit., 1959–65. *Work in Edinburgh includes:* Third Extension and other work for Heriot-Watt Coll.; Head Office for Scottish Life Assce Co. Ltd; Head Office and Showroom for S of Scotland Elec. Bd; for the High Kirk of St Giles: East End treatment for National Service in Coronation year, War Memorial Chapel, and (in Chapel of Order of Thistle) Memorial to HM King George VI, and other work. *Publications:* A Short History of St Giles Cathedral, 1954; The Principles of Church Building, Furnishing, Equipment and Decoration, 1963; The Royal Scottish Academy 1826–1976, 1976. *Address:* 10a Greenhill Park, Edinburgh EH10 4DW. *T:* 031–447 7530.

GORDON, Alexander John, CBE 1974 (OBE 1967); RIBA; architect; Consultant, Alex Gordon Partnership, since 1983; *b* 25 Feb. 1917; *s* of John Tullis Gordon and Euphemia Baxter Simpson Gordon. *Educ:* Swansea Grammar Sch.; Welsh Sch. of Architecture (Diploma with Special Distinction). ARIBA 1949; FRIBA 1962; FSIAD 1975. Served RE, 1940–46. Partnership with T. Alwyn Lloyd, 1948–60; Sen. Partner, Alex Gordon and Partners, 1960–82. Member: Welsh Arts Council, 1959–73 (Vice-Chm. 1969–73); Central Housing Adv. Cttee, 1959–71; Exec. Bd, BSI, 1971–74 (Chm., Codes of Practice Cttee for Building, 1965–77); UGC Planning, Architecture and Building Studies Sub-Cttee, 1971–74; UGC Technology Sub-Cttee, 1974–79; NAB UGC Review Gp in Architecture, 1983–84; Construction and Housing Res. Adv. Council, 1971–79; ARCUK, 1968–71; Design Council, 1973–77; Council, Architectural Heritage Year (and Welsh Cttee), 1973–76; Royal Fine Art Commn, 1973–; RCA Visiting Cttee, 1973–82; Council for Sci. and Soc., 1973– (Vice-Chm., 1982–); Bldg Res. Estab. Adv. Council (Chm., 1975–83); Adv. Cttee, York Centre for Continuing Educn, 1975–80; Construction Industry Continuing Professional Develt Gp (Chm. 1981–); Standing Cttee on Structural Safety, 1976–; British Council Wales Cttee, 1976– (Chm., 1980–, and Mem. Bd British Council); Pres., Comité de Liaison des Architectes du Marché Commun, 1974–75. Trustee, Civic Trust Board for Wales, 1965–. Pres., Building Centre Trust, 1976–. Life Mem., Court, UWIST (Mem. Council, 1980–85, Vice-Pres., 1982–85); Vis. Prof., Sch. of Environmental Studies, UCL, 1969, Mem. Bd of Studies, 1970–83, Governor, Centre for Environmental Studies, 1974–77. Vis. Fellow, Clare Hall, Cambridge Univ., 1983. Associate, RICS, 1986. RIBA: Chm., Bd of Educn, 1968–70; Pres., 1971–73; Chm., European Affairs Cttee, 1973–80; Chm., Co-ordinating Cttee for Project Inf., 1979–. Reg. Dir, Nationwide Bldg Soc., 1972– (Chm., Welsh Bd, 1986–). Extraord. Hon. Mem., Bund Deutscher Architekten; Hon. Mem., Soc. Mexican Architects; Hon. Corresp. Mem., Fedn of Danish Architects, 1976; Hon. FRAIC; Hon. FAIA, 1974; Hon. FCIBSE 1975; Hon. FISE 1980. Hon. LLD Univ. of Wales, 1972. *Publications:* periodic contribs to professional jls. *Recreations:* skiing, the visual arts. *Address:* River Cottage, Llanblethian, near Cowbridge, S Glam CF7 7JL. *T:* Cowbridge 3672; 32 Grosvenor Street, W1. *T:* 01–629 7910. *Clubs:* Arts; Cardiff and County.

GORDON, Sir Andrew C. L. D.; *see* Duff Gordon.

GORDON, Rt. Rev. Archibald Ronald McDonald; head of the Archbishop of Canterbury's staff (with title of Bishop at Lambeth), since 1984; Bishop to the Forces, since 1985; an Assistant Bishop, Diocese of Southwark, since 1985; *b* 19 March 1927; *s* of late Sir Archibald Gordon, CMG, and late Dorothy Katharine Gordon, Bridge House, Gerrards Cross, Bucks. *Educ:* Rugby Sch.; Balliol Coll., Oxford (Organ Schol., MA 1950); Cuddesdon Theol. Coll. Deacon 1952; Priest 1953; Curate of Stepney, 1952–55; Chaplain, Cuddesdon Coll., 1955–59; Vicar of St Peter, Birmingham, 1959–67; Res. Canon, Birmingham Cathedral, 1967–71; Vicar of University Church of St Mary the Virgin with St Cross and St Peter in the East, Oxford, 1971–75; Bishop of Portsmouth, 1975–84. Fellow of St Cross Coll., Oxford, 1975; Select Preacher, Univ. of Oxford, 1985. Mem., Church Assembly and General Synod and Proctor in Convocation, 1965–71; Chm., ACCM, 1976–83. *Address:* Lambeth Palace, SE1 7JU.

GORDON, Aubrey Abraham; a Recorder of the Crown Court, since 1978; *b* 26 July 1925; *s* of Isaac and Fanny Gordon; *m* 1949, Reeva R. Cohen; one *s* twin *d.* *Educ:* Bede Collegiate Boys' Sch., Sunderland; King's Coll., Durham Univ., Newcastle upon Tyne (LLB 1945). Admitted solicitor, 1947. President: Houghton le Spring Chamber of Trade, 1955; Hetton le Hole Rotary Club, 1967; Sunderland Law Soc., 1976; Chairman: Houghton Round Table, 1959; Sunderland Victims Support Scheme, 1978–80; Sunderland Guild of Help, 1984–. *Recreations:* local communal and religious interests, photography. *Address:* 1 Acer Court, Sunderland SR2 7EJ. *T:* Sunderland 658993.

GORDON, Boyd; Fisheries Secretary, Department of Agriculture and Fisheries for Scotland, 1982–86; *b* 18 Sept. 1926; *er s* of David Gordon and Isabella (*née* Leishman); *m* 1951, Elizabeth Mabel (*née* Smith); two *d.* *Educ:* Musselburgh Grammar School. Following military service with the Royal Scots, joined the Civil Service, initially with Min. of Labour, then Inland Revenue; Department of Agriculture and Fisheries for Scotland: joined, 1953; Principal, Salmon and Freshwater Fisheries Administration and Fisheries R&D, 1962–73; Asst Secretary, Agriculture Economic Policy, EEC Co-ordination and Agriculture Marketing, 1973–82. *Recreations:* family and church affairs, gardening, sport of all kinds, though only golf as participant now, reading, music. *Address:* 87 Duddingston Road, Edinburgh EH15 1SP. *Club:* Civil Service.

GORDON, Brian William, OBE 1974; HM Diplomatic Service, 1949–81, retired; Commercial Counsellor, Caracas, 1980–81; *b* 24 Oct. 1926; *s* of William and Doris Margaret Gordon; *m* 1951, Sheila Graham Young; two *s* one *d.* *Educ:* Tynemouth Grammar School. HM Forces (Lieut in IA), 1944–47; joined HM Foreign Service (now Diplomatic Service), 1949; served in: Saigon; Libya; Second Sec. in Ethiopia, 1954–58 and in Peru, 1959–61; HM Consul: Leopoldville, Congo, 1962–64; New York, 1965–67; Puerto Rico, 1967–69; Consul-General, Bilbao, 1969–73; Asst Head, Trade Relations and Export Dept, FCO, 1974–77; Dep. Consul-Gen., Los Angeles, 1977–80. *Recreations:* golf, walking. *Address:* 16 Woodburn Drive, Whitley Bay, Tyne and Wear.

GORDON, Sir Charles (Addison Somerville Snowden), KCB 1981 (CB 1970); Clerk of the House of Commons, 1979–83; *b* 25 July 1918; *s* of late C. G. S. Gordon, TD, Liverpool, and of Mrs E. A. Gordon, Rydons, Wimbledon; *m* 1943, Janet Margaret Beattie; one *s* one *d.* *Educ:* Winchester; Balliol Coll., Oxford. Served in Fleet Air Arm throughout War of 1939–45. Apptd Asst Clerk in House of Commons, 1946; Senior Clerk, 1947; Fourth Clerk at the Table, 1962; Principal Clerk of the Table Office, 1967; Second Clerk Assistant, 1974; Clerk Asst, 1976. Sec., Soc. of Clerks-at-the-Table in Commonwealth Parliaments, and co-Editor of its journal, The Table, 1952–62. *Publications:* Parliament as an Export (jointly), 1966; Editor, Erskine May's Parliamentary Practice, 20th edn, 1983 (Asst Editor, 19th edn); contribs to: The Table; The Parliamentarian. *Recreation:* dolce far niente. *Address:* 279 Lonsdale Road, Barnes, SW13 9QB. *T:* 01–748 6735.

GORDON, Prof. Cyrus H.; Gottesman Professor of Hebrew, since 1973 and Director, Center for Ebla Research, since 1982, New York University; *b* 29 June 1908; *s* of Dr Benj. L. and Dorothy Cohen Gordon; *m* 1946, Joan Elizabeth Kendall (*d* 1985); two *s* three *d.* *Educ:* Univ. of Pennsylvania (AB, MA, PhD). Harrison Schol., Univ. of Pennsylvania 1928–29, and Harrison Fellow, 1929–30; US Army Officer on active duty, 1942–46 (Col, US Air Force Reserve, retired). Instructor of Hebrew and Assyrian, University of Penn., 1930–31; Fellow and Epigrapher, American Schs of Oriental Research in Jerusalem and Baghdad, 1931–35; Fellow, Amer. Coun. of Learned Socs, 1932–33; Teaching Fellow, Oriental Seminary, Johns Hopkins Univ., 1935–38; Lecturer in Hebrew and Ancient History, Smith Coll., 1938–39 and 1940–41; Fellow, Amer.-Scandinavian Foundn, 1939; Mem., Institute for Advanced Study, Princeton, NJ, 1939–40 and 1941–42; Professor of Assyriology and Egyptology, Dropsie Coll., 1946–56; Joseph Foster Prof. of Near Eastern Studies, and Chm., Dept of Mediterranean Studies, Brandeis Univ., 1956–73 (Dean of Graduate Sch. and Associate Dean of Faculty, 1957–58). Mem. Managing Cttee, Amer. Sch. of Classical Studies, Athens, 1958–73; Vis. Fellow in Humanities, Univ. of Colorado, March 1967; Vis. Prof., New York Univ., 1970–73; Vis. Prof. in History and Archaeology, Univ. of New Mexico, 1976; Distinguished Vis. Professor: in Humanities, SW Missouri State Univ., 1977–79; in Archaeology, New Mexico State Univ., 1979; Gay Lectr, Simmons Coll., 1970; Visitor's Fellowship, Japan Foundn, 1974. Fellow: Amer. Acad. of Arts and Sciences, 1968–; Explorers Club, 1968–; Amer. Acad. of Jewish Res., 1981–; Hon. Fellow, Royal Asiatic Soc., 1975–. Member: Amer. Oriental Soc.; Soc. of Biblical Literature; Archæological Inst. of America; Amer. Historical Assoc.; Amer. Philological Assoc.; Amer. Assoc. of Univ. Professors. Corresp. Mem., Inst. for Antiquity and Christianity, Claremont Graduate Sch. and University Center, 1967–. Trustee: Boston Hebrew Coll., 1965–; Internat. Council for Etruscan

Studies, Jerusalem, 1970–; Fenster Gallery of Jewish Art, Tulsa, Oklahoma, 1977–. Hon. Dr of Hebrew Letters, Baltimore Hebrew Coll., 1981; Hon.DHL, Hebrew Union Coll., 1985. Alumni Award, Gratz Coll., 1961; Directory of Educational Specialists Award, 1970. *Publications:* Nouns in the Nuzi Tablets, 1936; Lands of the Cross and Crescent, 1948; Ugaritic Literature, 1949; Smith College Tablets, 1952; Ugaritic Manual, 1955; Adventures in the Nearest East, 1957; Hammurapi's Code, 1957; World of the Old Testament, 1958 (rev. edn: The Ancient Near East, 1965); Before the Bible, 1962 (rev. edn: The Common Background of Greek and Hebrew Civilizations, 1965); Ugaritic Textbook, 1965, rev. edn 1967; Ugarit and Minoan Crete, 1966; Evidence for the Minoan Language, 1966; Forgotten Scripts: How they were deciphered and their Impact on Contemporary Culture, 1968, rev. edn, Forgotten Scripts: their ongoing discovery and decipherment, 1982; Poetic Legends and Myths from Ugarit, 1977; (ed and contrib.) Publications of the Center for Ebla Research, vol. I, Eblaitica: essays on the Elba archives and Eblaite Language, 1986; some works translated other languages; numerous articles in learned jls dealing with Near East, Mediterranean, OT and Egypto-Semitic philology; *relevant publications:* Orient and Occident: essays presented to Cyrus H. Gordon on the occasion of his Sixty-Fifth Birthday, 1973; The Bible World: essays in honor of Cyrus H. Gordon, 1980. *Address:* (home) 130 Dean Road, Brookline, Mass 02146, USA. *T:* 617–734–3046.

GORDON, David Sorrell; Group Managing Director, The Economist Newspaper Ltd, since 1981; *b* 11 Sept. 1941; *s* of Sholom and Tania Gordon; *m* 1st, 1963, Enid Albagli (marr. diss. 1969); 2nd, 1974, Maggi McCormick; two *s*. *Educ:* Clifton College; Balliol College, Oxford (PPE, BA 1963); LSE; Advanced Management Program, Harvard Business Sch. FCA. Articles with Thomson McLintock, 1965–68; The Economist: editorial staff, 1968–78; Production and Develt Dir, 1978–81. Dir, Financial Times, 1983–. Mem., South Bank Bd, 1986–; a Governor, BFI, 1983–; Member: British Screen Adv. Council (formerly Cinematograph Films Council), 1974–82. Interim Action Cttee on film industry, 1976–. *Publication:* (with Fred Hirsch) Newspaper Money, 1975. *Recreations:* movies, magic lanterns. *Address:* Rockwood, 36 Netheravon Road, Chiswick, W4 2NA. *T:* 01–994 3126. *Clubs:* Groucho; Harvard (New York).

GORDON, Maj.-Gen. Desmond Spencer, CB 1961; CBE 1952; DSO 1943; JP; DL; Commissioner-in-Chief, St John Ambulance Brigade, 1973–78; *b* 25 Dec. 1911; *s* of late Harold Easty Gordon and Gwendoline (*née* Blackett); *m* 1940, Sybil Mary Thompson; one *s* one *d*. *Educ:* Haileybury Coll.; RMC Sandhurst. Commissioned into Green Howards, 1932; India, 1933–38: Adjutant, Regimental Depot, 1938–40; War of 1939–45 (despatches 1944): Norway with Green Howards, 1940; Bde Major, 69 Inf. Bde, 1941–42; Student Staff Coll., Quetta, 1942; Comd 1/7 Queens, 1943; Comd 151 (Durham) Inf. Bde, 146 Inf. Bde, 131 Lorried Inf Bde, 1944–46; Col. GSHQ BAOR, 1946–49; Student Joint Service Staff Coll., 1949; GSO1 Inf. Directorate, War Office, 1950; Dep. Dir Inf., War Office, 1951–52; Comd 16 Indep. Para. Bde Gp, 1952–55; Asst Comd RMA Sandhurst, 1956–57; Student, Imperial Defence Coll., 1958; DA & QMG HQ I (BR) Corps, 1959; GOC 4th Division, 1959–61; Chief Army Instructor, Imperial Defence Coll., 1962–64; Asst Chief of Defence Staff (G), 1964–66: Col The Green Howards, 1965–74. JP Hants, 1966; DL Hants, 1980. KStJ 1973 (CStJ 1972). Knight Commander, Order of Orange Nassau with swords (Holland), 1947. *Recreations:* fishing, gardening. *Address:* Southfields, Greywell, Basingstoke, Hants. *Club:* Army and Navy.

GORDON, Rt. Rev. Eric; *see* Gordon, Rt Rev. G. E.

GORDON, Esmé; *see* Gordon, A. E.

GORDON, Rt. Rev. (George) Eric; *b* 29 July 1905; *s* of George Gordon, Dulwich; *m* 1938, Elizabeth St Charaine (*d* 1970), *d* of Lt-Comdr A. J. Parkes, OBE, RN, Squeen, Ballaugh, Isle of Man; one *d*; *m* 1971, Rose Gwynneth Huxley-Jones, FRBS, *d* of Benjamin Holt, Wednesbury, and *widow* of Thomas Bayliss Huxley-Jones, FRBS, Broomfield, Essex. *Educ:* St Olave's Sch., London; St Catharine's Coll., Cambridge (MA); Wycliffe Hall, Oxford. Deacon, Leicester, 1929; Priest, Peterborough for Leicester, 1930; Vice-Principal, Bishop Wilson Coll., Isle of Man, 1931, Principal, and Domestic Chaplain to Bishop of Sodor and Man, 1935; Rector of Kersal, and Examining Chaplain to Bishop of Manchester, 1942; Rector and Rural Dean of Middleton, Manchester, 1945; Proctor in Convocation, 1948; Provost of Chelmsford Cathedral and Rector of Chelmsford, 1951–66; Bishop of Sodor and Man, 1966–74. *Recreation:* local history. *Address:* Cobden, Queen Street, Eynsham, Oxford. *T:* Oxford 881378.

GORDON, Gerald Henry, QC (Scot.) 1972; LLD; Sheriff of Glasgow and Strathkelvin, since 1978; *b* 17 June 1929; *er s* of Simon Gordon and Rebecca Gordon (*née* Bulbin), Glasgow; *m* 1957, Marjorie Joseph, *yr d* of Isaac and Aimée Joseph (*née* Strump), Glasgow; one *s* two *d*. *Educ:* Queen's Park Senior Secondary Sch., Glasgow; Univ. of Glasgow (MA (1st cl. Hons Philosophy with English Literature) 1950; LLB (Distinction) 1953; PhD 1960); LLD Edinburgh 1968. National Service, RASC, 1953–55 (Staff-Sgt, Army Legal Aid, BAOR, 1955). Admitted Scottish Bar 1953; practice at Scottish Bar, 1953, 1956–59; Faulds Fellow, Univ. of Glasgow, 1956–59. Procurator Fiscal Depute, Edinburgh, 1960–65. University of Edinburgh: Sen. Lectr, 1965; Personal Prof. of Criminal Law, 1969–72; Head of Dept of Criminal Law and Criminology, 1965–72; Prof. of Scots Law, 1972–76; Dean of Faculty of Law, 1970–73; Sheriff of S Strathclyde, Dumfries and Galloway at Hamilton, 1976–77. Commonwealth Vis. Fellow and Vis. Res. Fellow, Centre of Criminology, Univ. of Toronto, 1974–75. Temporary Sheriff, 1973–76. Mem., Interdepartmental Cttee on Scottish Criminal Procedure, 1970–77. *Publications:* The Criminal Law of Scotland, 1967, 2nd edn 1978; (ed) Renton and Brown's Criminal Procedure, 4th edn 1972, 5th edn 1983); (ed) Scottish Criminal Case Reports, 1981–; various articles. *Recreations:* Jewish studies, coffee conversation, swimming. *Address:* 52 Eastwoodmains Road, Giffnock, Glasgow G46 6QD. *T:* 041–638 8614.

GORDON, Hannah Cambell Grant; actress; *b* 9 April 1941; *d* of William Munro Gordon and Hannah Grant Gordon; *m* 1970, Norman Warwick; one *s*. *Educ:* St Denis School for Girls, Edinburgh; Glasgow Univ. (Cert. Dramatic Studies); College of Dramatic Art, Glasgow (Dip. in speech and drama). FRSAMD 1980. Winner, James Bridie Gold Medal, Royal Coll. of Music and Dramatic Art, Glasgow, 1962. *Stage:* Dundee Rep., Glasgow Citizens Theatre, Belgrade Theatre, Coventry, Ipswich, Windsor; Can You Meet me at the Back, Piccadilly, 1979; The Killing Game, Apollo, 1980; The Jeweller's Shop, Westminster, 1982; The Country Girl, Apollo, 1983; Light Up the Sky, Old Vic, 1985; *television:* 1st TV appearance, Johnson Over Jordan, 1965; series: Great Expectations, 1969; Middlemarch, 1969; My Wife Next Door, 1972; Upstairs, Downstairs, 1976; Telford's Change, 1979; Goodbye Mr Kent, 1983; Gardener's Calendar, 1986; *films:* Spring and Port Wine, 1970; The Elephant Man, 1979; numerous radio plays. *Recreations:* tennis, gardening, cooking. *Address:* c/o David White Associates, 31 King's Road, SW3. *Club:* St James's.

GORDON, Dr Hugh Walker, MC 1917; MA; MB; FRCP; Consulting Physician to Department of Skin Diseases, St George's Hospital; Consulting Dermatologist to Royal Marsden Hospital and West London Hospital; Fellow Royal Society Medicine (Past President of Section of Dermatology); Hon. Member (Past President) British Association of Dermatology; Member of St John's Dermatological Society; *b* Maxwellton, Kircudbrightshire, 5 Aug. 1897; *er s* of late H. Sharpe Gordon, OBE, JP, Dumfries, Scotland and of late John Ann, *d* of Hugh Gilmour, London; *m* 1929, Jean Helen, *d* of late H. W. Robertson, Butterfield and Swire, London; one *s* one *d*. *Educ:* Marlborough Coll.; Pembroke Coll., Cambridge (History Exhibitioner); St George's Hospital (entrance scholar); Paris; Vienna, MB, BCh Cambridge, 1926; MRCS 1925; FRCP 1940. Late Vice-Dean, St George's Hosp. Med. Sch., 1946–51, Actg Dean, 1944–46; Dermatologist EMS Sector VII, 1939–46; Med. Officer i/c St George's Hosp., EMS, 1939–45; late Dermatologist to St John's Hosp., Lewisham, Shadwell Children's Hosp. and East Ham Memorial Hosp. Late Resident Med. Officer, St George's Hosp., and House Surg. and House Physician. Served European War, 1914–18, RFA, 1916–18, invalided out of Army with rank of Capt. *Publications:* chapters in Modern Practice of Dermatology, 1950; articles on dermatology in med. journals. *Recreations:* country pursuits. *Address:* 3 High Street, Kirkcudbright, SW Scotland. *T:* Kirkcudbright 30740. *Club:* Oriental.

GORDON, Prof. Ian Alistair, CBE 1971; MA, PhD; Professor of English Language and Literature, University of Wellington, NZ, 1936–74, now Emeritus; *b* Edinburgh, 1908; *e s* of Alexander and Ann Gordon; *m* 1936, Mary Ann McLean Fullarton, Ayr; one *s* three *d*. *Educ:* Royal High Sch., Edinburgh; University of Edinburgh. Bruce of Grangehill Bursar, Sloan Prizeman, Gray Prizeman, Scott Travelling Scholar (Italy), Dickson Travelling Scholar (Germany), Elliot Prizeman in English Literature, Pitt Scholar in Classical and English Literature; MA (Hons Classics) 1930, (Hons English) 1932; PhD 1936. Asst Lecturer in English language and lit., University of Edinburgh, 1932; Sub-Ed., Scot. Nat. Dictionary, 1930–36; Dean: Faculty of Arts, Victoria Univ. Coll., Wellington, 1944–47, 1952, 1957–61; Faculty of Languages, 1965–68; Vice-Chancellor Univ. of New Zealand, 1947–52; Chm., Academic Bd, 1954–61. Visiting Professor: KCL 1954; Univ. of Edinburgh, 1962; Univ. of South Pacific, Fiji, 1972; France and Belgium, 1976; Univ. of Waikato, 1980; Research Associate, UCL, 1969; Vis. Fellow, Edinburgh Univ., 1974–75; Vis. Fellow in Commonwealth Literature, Univ. of Leeds, 1975. Columnist, NZ Listener, 1977–. Member: Copyright Cttee and Tribunal, 1958; UGC, 1960–70; Chairman: English Language Institute,, 1961–72; NZ Literary Fund, 1951–73; Exec. Council, Assoc. of Univs of Br. Commonwealth, 1949–50. NZ representative at internat. confs: Utrecht, 1948; Bangkok, 1960; Kampala, 1961; Karachi, 1961. Army Educ. Service, 2 NZEF, Hon. Major. Hon. LLD Bristol, 1948; Hon. DLitt NZ, 1961; DUniv Stirling, 1975. *Publications:* John Skelton, Poet Laureate, 1943; New Zealand New Writing, 1943–45; The Teaching of English, a study in secondary education, 1947; English Prose Technique, 1948; Shenstone's Miscellany, 1759–1763, 1952; Katherine Mansfield, 1954; The Movement of English Prose, 1966; John Galt (biog.), 1972; Word (festschrift), 1974; Undiscovered Country, 1974; Katherine Mansfield's Urewera Notebook, 1979; Word Finder, 1979; A Word in Your Ear, 1980; (ed) Collins Concise English Dictionary, NZ edn, 1982; (ed) Collins Compact New Zealand Dictionary, 1985; edited the following works of John Galt: The Entail, 1970; The Provost, 1973; The Member, 1975; The Last of the Lairds, 1976; Short Stories, 1978; part-author: Edinburgh Essays in Scottish Literature, 1933; Essays in Literature, 1934; The University and the Community, 1946; John Galt (bicent. vol.), 1980; articles in research journals and other periodicals. *Address:* 91 Messines Road, Wellington, NZ. *Club:* Aorangi Ski, New Zealand (former Pres.).

GORDON, James Stuart, CBE 1984; Managing Director, Radio Clyde, since 1973; *b* 17 May 1936; *s* of James Gordon and Elsie (*née* Riach); *m* 1971, Margaret Anne Stevenson; two *s* one *d*. *Educ:* St Aloysius' Coll., Glasgow; Glasgow Univ. (MA Hons). Political Editor, STV, 1965–73. Chm., Scottish Exhibn Centre, 1983–; Mem., Scottish Develt Agency, 1981–. Mem. Court, Univ. of Glasgow, 1984–. *Recreations:* walking, genealogy, golf. *Address:* Deil's Craig, Strathblane, Glasgow G63 9ET. *T:* Blanefield 70604. *Clubs:* Buchanan Castle Golf, Prestwick Golf.

GORDON, Rt. Hon. John Bowie, (Peter), PC 1978; retired politician; company director (banking, insurance, tyres, transport); *b* 24 July 1921; *s* of Dr W. P. P. Gordon, CBE, and Dr Doris Gordon, OBE; *m* 1943, Dorothy Elizabeth (*née* Morton); two *s* one *d*. *Educ:* Stratford Primary Sch.; St Andrew's Coll., Christchurch; Lincoln Coll., Canterbury. Served War, RNZAF, 1941–45 (Flt Lt, pilot; mentioned in despatches, 1943). Farming cadet, 1936–39; road transp. industry, 1945–47; farming on own account, 1947–; Nuffield Scholarship, farming, 1954; co. dir, 1950–60; MP Clutha, 1960–78; Minister: Transport, Railways and Aviation, 1966–72; Marine and Fisheries, 1969–71; Labour and State Services, 1975–78; retd from politics on med. grounds, 1978. Past Pres., Returned Services, Federated Farmers, and A. & P. Show Assoc. USA Leadership Award, 1964. *Publication:* Some Aspects of Farming in Britain, 1955. *Recreations:* golf, gardening, cooking. *Address:* Tapanui, Otago, New Zealand. *T:* Tapanui 48 397. *Club:* Tapanui Services.

GORDON, John Gunn Drummond, CBE 1964; Director: Grindlays Bank Ltd, 1969–79; Steel Brothers Holdings Ltd, 1974–79; *b* 27 April 1909; *s* of late Rev. J. Drummond Gordon, MA, BD, BSc, and A. S. Gordon; *m* 1947, Mary Livingstone Paterson; two *s* one *d*. *Educ:* Edinburgh Academy. Served War, King's African Rifles, 1940–45. Career: spent 30 years out of 45, overseas, mainly in Eastern Africa, but also in India, with Grindlays Bank Ltd, finishing up as Group Managing Director; retired 1974. Mem., Bd of Crown Agents, 1974–77. *Address:* Threeways, Boneashe Lane, St Mary's Platt, near Sevenoaks, Kent TN15 8NW. *T:* Sevenoaks 884749. *Clubs:* Wilderness Golf (Sevenoaks); Nairobi (Nairobi).

GORDON, John Keith; HM Diplomatic Service; Head of Nuclear Energy Department, Foreign and Commonwealth Office, since 1986; *b* 6 July 1940; *s* of James Gordon and Theodora (*née* Sinker); *m* 1965, Elizabeth Shanks; two *s*. *Educ:* Marlborough Coll.; Cambridge Univ. (1st Cl. Hons History). Henry Fellow, Yale Univ., 1962–63; research in Russian history, LSE, 1963–66; entered FCO, 1966; Budapest, 1968–70; seconded to Civil Service Coll., 1970–72; FCO, 1972–73; UK Mission, Geneva, 1973–74; Head of Chancery and Consul, Yaoundé, 1975–77 (concurrently Chargé d'Affaires, Gabon and Central African Republic); FCO, 1977–80; Cultural Attaché, Moscow, 1980–81; Office of UK Rep. to European Community, Brussels, 1982–83; UK Perm. Deleg. to UNESCO, Paris, 1983–85. *Recreations:* jogging, sailing, reading. *Address:* c/o Foreign and Commonwealth Office, SW1. *Club:* Royal Commonwealth Society.

GORDON, Sir Keith (Lyndell), Kt 1979; CMG 1971; Chairman, Public Service Board of Appeal, St Lucia, since 1978; Justice of Appeal, West Indies Associated States Supreme Court, 1967–72, retired; *b* 8 April 1906; 3rd *s* of late George S. E. Gordon, Journalist, and Nancy Gordon; *m* 1947, Ethel King; one *d*. *Educ:* St Mary's Coll., St Lucia, WI; Middle Temple, London. Magistrate, Grenada, 1938; Crown Attorney, Dominica, 1942; Trinidad and Tobago: Magistrate, 1943–46 and 1949–53; Exec. Off., Black Market Board, 1946–48; Puisne Judge, Windward Islands and Leeward Islands, 1954–59, Puisne Judge, British Guiana, 1959–62; Chief Justice, West Cameroon, 1963–67. *Recreation:* gardening. *Address:* Vigie, Castries, St Lucia.

GORDON, Sir Lionel Eldred Peter S.; *see* Smith-Gordon.

GORDON, Nadia, (Mrs Charles Gordon); *see* Nerina, N.

GORDON, Patrick W.; *see* Wolrige-Gordon.

GORDON, Rt. Hon. Peter; *see* Gordon, Rt Hon. J. B.

GORDON, Peter Macie, CMG 1964; *b* 4 June 1919; *o s* of late Herbert and Gladys Gordon (*née* Simpson); *m* 1945, Marianne, *er d* of Dr Paul Meerwein, Basle; two *d. Educ:* Cotham Sch., Bristol; University Coll., Exeter; Merton Coll., Oxford. Served War, 1940–46; commissioned Argyll and Sutherland Highlanders, 1941; Campaign in North-West Europe, 1944–45 (despatches). Entered Colonial Administrative Service as District Officer, 1946; Senior District Commissioner, 1957; Asst Sec., Ministry of Agriculture, 1958; Under-Sec., 1960; Permanent Sec., Ministry of Agriculture and Animal Husbandry, Kenya, 1961; retired, 1964; Asst Sec., Univ. of Exeter, 1964–70. Supervisor, Zimbabwe-Rhodesia Elections, 1980; Mem., Commonwealth Observer Gp, Uganda Elections, 1980. *Address:* Old Poplars Farm House, Chipping Campden, Glos.

GORDON, Richard, (Dr Gordon Ostlere); formerly: anaesthetist at St Bartholomew's Hospital, and Oxford University; assistant editor, British Medical Jl; ship's surgeon. Mem., Punch Table. Author of the "Doctor" series, and other books, etc.

GORDON, Sir Robert James, 10th Bt *cr* 1706, of Afton and Earlston, Kirkcudbrightshire; farmer since 1958; *b* 17 Aug. 1932; *s* of Sir John Charles Gordon, 9th Bt and of Marion, *d* of late James B. Wright; *S* father, 1982; *m* 1976, Helen Julia Weston Perry. *Educ:* Barker College, Sydney; North Sydney Boys' High School; Wagga Agricultural Coll., Wagga Wagga, NSW (Wagga Dip. of Agric., Hons I and Dux). *Recreations:* tennis, ski-ing, swimming. *Heir:* none. *Address:* Earlstoun, Guyra, NSW 2365, Australia. *T:* (067) 79 1343.

GORDON, Robert Wilson, MC 1944; Deputy Chairman of the Stock Exchange, London, 1965–68; Partner, Pidgeon de Smitt (Stockbrokers), 1978–80; *b* 3 March 1915; *s* of late Malcolm Gordon and late Blanche Fayerweather Gordon; *m* 1st, 1946, Joan Alison (*d* 1965), *d* of late Brig. A. G. Kenchington, CBE, MC; one *d*; 2nd, 1967, Mrs Dianna E. V. Ansell (*née* Tyrwhitt-Drake) (*d* 1980). *Educ:* Harrow. Served War of 1939–45 (despatches); Royal Ulster Rifles, and Parachute Regt; Instructor, Staff Coll., 1943–44. Elected to the Council, Stock Exchange, London, 1956. Chm., Airborne Forces Security Fund, 1974–. *Recreation:* golf. *Address:* 41 Cadogan Square, SW1. *T:* 01–235 4496.

GORDON, Rt. Rev. Ronald; *see* Gordon, Rt Rev. A. R. McD.

GORDON, Sir Sidney, Kt 1972; CBE 1968 (OBE 1965); CA; JP; Chairman: Sir Elly Kadoorie Continuation Ltd, since 1971; Rediffusion (Hong Kong) Ltd; The Hong Kong Building & Loan Agency Ltd; Deputy Chairman: China Light & Power Co. Ltd; *b* 20 Aug. 1917; *s* of late P. S. Gordon and late Angusina Gordon; *m* 1950, Olive W. F. Eldon, *d* of late T. A. Eldon and late Hannah Eldon; two *d. Educ:* Hyndland Sch., Glasgow; Glasgow Univ. Sen. Partner, Lowe Bingham & Matthews, Chartered Accountants, Hong Kong, 1956–70. MLC, 1962–66, MEC, Hong Kong, 1965–80. Chm., Univ. and Polytechnic Grants Cttee, 1974–76. JP Hong Kong, 1961. Hon. LLD The Chinese University of Hong Kong, 1970. *Recreation:* golf. *Address:* 7 Headland Road, Hong Kong. *T:* 5–8122577. *Clubs:* Oriental; Hong Kong, Royal Hong Kong Jockey (Steward), Royal Hong Kong Golf (Pres.), Hong Kong Country, Hong Kong Cricket, Shek O Country, etc.

GORDON, Vera Kate, (Mrs E. W. Gordon); *see* Timms, V. K.

GORDON, Lt-Col William Howat Leslie, CBE 1957 (MBE 1941); MC 1944; Adviser on overseas business to firms, to Ministry of Overseas Development, 1971–75, and to International Finance Corporation; *b* 8 April 1914; *o s* of late Frank Leslie Gordon, ISE, FICE; *m* 1944, Margot Lumb; one *s* three *d. Educ:* Rugby; RMA Woolwich. Commnd Royal Signals, 1934; Palestine, Africa, Italy, NW Europe; 1 Armoured, 1 Airborne Divs (despatches); Instructor, Staff Coll., Camberley, 1947–49. Chief Executive, The Uganda Co. Ltd, 1949–60; John Holt & Co. (Liverpool) Ltd and Lonrho Exports Ltd, 1960–71; MLC Uganda, 1952–57; Chm., Rickmansworth Water Co. Chm., St John Council, Bucks, 1974–82; KStJ. *Recreations:* golf, fishing, shooting. *Address:* Acre End, Chalfont St Giles, Bucks. *T:* Little Chalfont 2047. *Clubs:* White's, Institute of Directors, MCC; Rye Golf.

GORDON-BROWN, Alexander Douglas, CB 1984; Receiver for the Metropolitan Police District, since 1980; *b* 5 Dec. 1927; *s* of late Captain and Mrs D. S. Gordon-Brown; *m* 1959, Mary Hilton; three *s. Educ:* Bryanston Sch.; New Coll., Oxford. MA; 1st cl. hons PPE. Entered Home Office, 1951; Asst Private Sec. to Home Sec., 1956; Sec., Franks Cttee on section 2 of Official Secrets Act 1911, 1971; Asst Under-Sec. of State, Home Office, 1972–75, 1978–80; Under Sec., Cabinet Office, 1975–78. *Recreations:* music, golf. *Address:* New Scotland Yard, 10 Broadway, SW1.

GORDON-CUMMING, Alexander Roualeyn, CMG 1978; CVO 1969; Director, Invest in Britain Bureau, Department of Industry, 1979–84; *b* 10 Sept. 1924; *s* of late Lt-Comdr R. G. Gordon-Cumming and Mrs M. V. K. Wilkinson; *m* 1st, 1965, Beryl Joyce Macnaughton Dunn (*d* 1973); one *d*; 2nd, 1974, Elizabeth Patricia Blackley (*d* 1983); one *d. Educ:* Eton Coll. RAF, 1943; retd with rank of Gp Captain, 1969. Board of Trade, 1969; Dept of Trade and Industry, 1973; seconded HM Diplomatic Service, 1974–78. *Recreations:* gardening, skiing, fell walking, ballet. *Address:* Woodstock, West Way, West Broyle, Chichester, Sussex. *T:* Chichester 776413. *Club:* Royal Air Force.

GORDON CUMMING, Sir William Gordon, 6th Bt, *cr* 1804; Royal Scots Greys; *b* 19 June 1928; *s* of Major Sir Alexander Penrose Gordon Cumming, 5th Bt, MC, and of Elizabeth Topham, *d* of J. Topham Richardson, Harps Oak, Merstham; *S* father, 1939; *m* 1953, Elisabeth (marr. diss. 1972), *d* of Maj.-Gen. Sir Robert Hinde, KBE, CB, DSO; one *s* three *d. Educ:* Eton; RMC, Sandhurst. Late Royal Scots Greys; retired 1952. *Heir: s* Alexander Penrose Gordon Cumming, *b* 15 April 1954. *Address:* Altyre, Forres, Morayshire.

GORDON DAVIES, Rev. John; *see* Davies, Rev. John G.

GORDON-DUFF, Col Thomas Robert, MC 1945; JP; Lord-Lieutenant of Banffshire since 1964; Convener of County Council, 1962–70; *b* 1911; *er s* of Lachlan Gordon-Duff (killed in action, 1914); *m* 1946, Jean (*d* 1981), *d* of late Leslie G. Moir, Bicester; one *s. Educ:* Eton; RMC, Sandhurst. Entered Army, 2nd Lieut, Rifle Brigade, 1932; served War of 1939–45 (MC); retired, 1947. Lt-Col 5/6 Bn Gordon Highlanders (TA), 1947, retiring as Col. DL 1948, JP 1959, Vice-Lieut 1961, Banffshire. *Address:* Drummuir, Keith, Banffshire. *T:* Drummuir 224. *Club:* Army and Navy.

GORDON-FINLAYSON, Air Vice-Marshal James Richmond, DSO 1941; DFC 1940; *b* 19 Aug. 1914; *s* of late Gen. Sir Robert Gordon-Finlayson, KCB, CMG, DSO, and late Lady (Mary) Gordon-Finlayson, OBE; *m* 1953, Margaret Ann (*d* 1965), *d* of Col G. C. Richardson, DSO, MC; one *s* one *d* by a former marriage. *Educ:* Winchester; Pembroke Coll., Cambridge (MA). Mem. Inner Temple, 1935; joined RAF, 1936; ADC to Gov. of Kenya, 1938–39; served in Libya, 1940 and 1941–42, Greece, 1940–41 (despatches), Syria, 1941; Sqdn Ldr 1940; OC 211 Sqdn, 1940–41; RAF Staff Coll., 1942; Air Staff, Air Min., 1942–45; RAF Liaison Offr to HQ, US Army Strategic Air Force, Guam, 1945; Air Staff, Air Comd, SEA, 1945–46; SASO, AHQ, Burma, 1946; OC 48 Sqdn, 1946–47; on directing staff, JSSC, Group Captain 1951; Air Staff, Air Min., 1951–54, OC, RAF Deversoir, 1954; OC, RAF Khormaksar, 1954–56; on staff of HQ Bomber Command, 1956, Asst Comdt, RAF Staff Coll., Bracknell; Air Cdre, 1958; Air Vice-Marshal, 1961; Dir-Gen. of Personal Services, Air Ministry, 1960–63; retired, June 1963. Greek DFC, 1941; Sheikh el Bilharith. *Publications:* Epitaph for a Squadron, 1965; Their Finest Hour, 1976; articles on strategic and air and military affairs in various jls; verse. *Recreations:* fishing, sailing, travel and literary interests. *Address:* Avenida del Cobre 9–11, Apartado 187, Algeciras (Prov. de Cadiz), Spain. *Clubs:* Naval and Military, MCC; RAF Yacht.

See also Maj.-Gen. R. Gordon-Finlayson.

GORDON-FINLAYSON, Maj.-Gen. Robert, OBE 1957 (MBE 1945); JP; DL; *b* 28 Oct. 1916; *yr s* of late Gen. Sir Robert Gordon-Finlayson, KCB, CMG, DSO, DL; *m* 1945, Alexandra, *d* of late John Bartholomew, Rowde Court, Rowde, Wilts; two *s. Educ:* Winchester Coll.; RMA, Woolwich. 2 Lt RA, 1936; Major, BEF, 1940; Staff Coll., 1941; Middle East, 1942–43; NW Europe, 1944–45; India and Burma, 1945–47; GSO 1 1945; RHA, 1952–53; JSSC, 1953; Bt Lieut-Col, 1955; AA and QMG, 3 Inf. Div., 1955–57; Near East (Suez Ops), 1956; Middle East, 1958; Lieut-Col 1958; Comdr, 26 Field Regt RA, 1958–59; Col 1959; GSO 1, Staff Coll., 1960–62; Brig. CRA, 49 Div. TA, 1962–64; Brig. DQMG, HQ, BAOR, 1964–66. GOC 49 Inf. Div., TA/N Midland Dist, 1966–67; GOC E Midland District, 1967–70; retd, 1970. Hon. Col, 3rd (Volunteer) Bn The Worcestershire and Sherwood Foresters Regt, TAVR, 1971–78; Chm., Notts Co. Army Benevolent Fund, 1970–85; Mem., Notts Co. and E Midlands TAVR Assocs, 1971–85. Pres., Notts Co. Royal British Legion, 1971–79; Vice-President: Notts Co. SSAFA and PDSA, 1970–; Central Notts Scout Assoc., 1971–80. JP 1972, High Sheriff 1974, DL 1974, Notts. *Recreations:* shooting, fishing, ski-ing, gardening, walking. *Address:* South Collingham Manor, near Newark, Notts. *T:* Newark 892204; c/o Lloyds Bank, Cox's & King's Branch, 6 Pall Mall, SW1.

See also Air Vice-Marshal J. R. Gordon-Finlayson.

GORDON-HALL, Maj.-Gen. Frederick William, CB 1958; CBE 1945; *b* 28 Dec. 1902; *s* of Col Frederick William George Gordon-Hall and Clare Frances (*née* Taylor); *m* 1930, Phyllis Dorothy Miller (*d* 1985); one *s* one *d. Educ:* Winchester Coll.; RMC Sandhurst. Gazetted Royal Tank Corps, 1923; Staff Capt., War Office, 1935–39; Ministry of Supply, 1939–43; HQ Allied Armies in Italy, 1943–45; Military Dir of Studies, Mil. Coll. of Science, 1946–49; Dir of Technical Services (Land), British Joint Staff Mission, Washington, 1950–52; Dir of Inspection of Fighting Vehicles, Ministry of Supply, Dec. 1952–June 1955. Dir-Gen. of Fighting Vehicles, Min. of Supply, 1955–58, retd. *Recreations:* domestic engineering, cabinet making. *Address:* Whitegates, Salisbury Road, Horsham, West Sussex. *T:* Horsham 3304.

See also Sir James Murray.

GORDON JONES, Air Marshal Sir Edward, KCB 1967 (CB 1960); CBE 1956 (OBE 1945); DSO 1941; DFC 1941; idc; jssc; qs; Air Officer Commanding-in-Chief, Near East Air Force, and Administrator, Sovereign Base Areas, 1966–69; Commander, British Forces Near East, 1967–69; retired 1969; *b* 31 Aug. 1914; *s* of late Lt-Col Dr A. Jones, DSO, MC, MD, DPh; *m* 1938, Margery Thurston Hatfield, BSc; two *s.* Served War of 1939–45 (despatches, DFC, DSO, OBE, Greek DFC). ACOS (Intelligence), Allied Air Forces Central Europe, 1960–61; Air Officer Commanding RAF Germany, 1961–63; Senior RAF Directing Staff, Imperial Defence Coll., 1963–65; AOC, RAF, Malta, and Dep. C-in-C (Air), Allied Forces, Mediterranean, 1965–66. Comdr Order of Orange Nassau. *Recreations:* sport, photography, travel, music. *Address:* 20 Marlborough Court, Grange Road, Cambridge CB3 9BQ. *T:* Cambridge 63029. *Club:* Royal Air Force.

GORDON-LENNOX, family name of **Duke of Richmond.**

GORDON LENNOX, Rear-Adm. Sir Alexander (Henry Charles), KCVO 1972; CB 1962; DSO 1942; Serjeant at Arms, House of Commons, 1962–76; *b* 9 April 1911; *s* of Lord Bernard Charles Gordon Lennox and Evelyn (*née* Loch); *m* 1936, Barbara, *d* of Maj.-Gen. Julian Steele; two *s. Educ:* Hetherdown, Ascot; RNC Dartmouth. Served as young officer in small ships in Far East and Home Fleet; communication specialist. Served War of 1939–45 (despatches 1943); in ME, East Coast Convoys, Russian Convoys; subsequently commanded HMS Surprise, HMS Mermaid and 2nd Frigate Sqdn, HMS Mercury and HMS Newcastle. Dep. Chief of Supplies and Transport, 1959–62; President, RNC Greenwich, 1961–62. Liberty Medal (Norway). *Recreations:* shooting, fishing and gardening. *Address:* Quags Corner, Minstead, Midhurst, West Sussex. *T:* Midhurst 3623. *Club:* Naval (Portsmouth).

GORDON LENNOX, Maj.-Gen. Bernard Charles, CB 1986; MBE 1968; Senior Army Member, Royal College of Defence Studies, since 1986; *b* 19 Sept. 1932; *s* of Lt-Gen. Sir George Gordon Lennox, *qv*; *m* 1958, Sally-Rose Warner; three *s. Educ:* Eton; Sandhurst. 2nd Lt, Grenadier Guards, 1953; Hong Kong, 1965; HQ Household Div., 1971; Commanding 1st Bn Grenadier Guards, 1974; Army Directing Staff, RAF Staff College, 1976–77; Command, Task Force H, 1978–79; RCDS, 1980; Dep. Commander and Chief of Staff, SE District, 1981–82; GOC Berlin (British Sector), 1983–85. *Recreations:* field sports, cricket, squash, music. *Address:* c/o Lloyds Bank, Cox's & King's Branch, 6 Pall Mall, SW1. *Clubs:* Army and Navy, MCC.

GORDON LENNOX, Lieut-Gen. Sir George (Charles), KBE 1964; CB 1959; CVO 1952; DSO 1943; King of Arms, Order of British Empire, 1968–83; *b* 29 May 1908; *s* of late Lord Bernard Charles Gordon Lennox, 3rd *s* of 7th Duke of Richmond and Gordon and late Evelyn Loch, *d* of 1st Baron Loch; *m* 1931, Nancy Brenda Darell; two *s. Educ:* Eton; Sandhurst. Served Grenadier Guards, 1928–52; served with Regt and on Staff, war of 1939–45, in Europe, Africa and Far East; Lieut-Col Commanding Grenadier Guards, Jan. 1951–July 1952; Comdr 1st Guards Brigade, 1952–54; IDC, 1955; BGS (SD and Trg), HQ, BAOR, 1956–57; GOC 3rd Div., 1957–59; Comdt, RMA Sandhurst, 1960–63; Dir-Gen. of Military Training, 1963–64; GOC-in-C Scottish Comd and Governor of Edinburgh Castle, 1964–66. Col, Gordon Highlanders, 1965–78. *Recreations:* field sports. *Address:* Gordon Castle, Fochabers, Morayshire. *T:* Fochabers 820275. *Club:* Cavalry and Guards.

See also B. C. Gordon Lennox.

GORDON LENNOX, Lord Nicholas Charles, KCMG 1986 (CMG 1978); LVO 1957; HM Diplomatic Service; Ambassador to Spain, since 1984; *b* 31 Jan. 1931; *yr s* of Duke of Richmond and Gordon, *qv*; *m* 1958, Mary, *d* of late Brig. H. N. H. Williamson, DSO, MC; one *s* three *d. Educ:* Eton; Worcester Coll., Oxford (Scholar). 2nd Lieut KRRC, 1950–51. Entered HM Foreign Service, 1954; FO, 1954–57; Private Sec. to HM Ambassador to USA, 1957–61; 2nd, later 1st Sec., HM Embassy, Santiago, 1961–63; Private Sec. to Perm. Under-Sec., FO, 1963–66; 1st Sec. and Head of Chancery, HM Embassy, Madrid, 1966–71; seconded to Cabinet Office, 1971–73; Head of News Dept,

FCO, 1973–74, Head of N America Dept, 1974–75; Counsellor and Head of Chancery, Paris, 1975–79; Asst Under-Sec. of State, FCO, 1979–84. *Address:* c/o Foreign and Commonwealth Office, SW1. *Clubs:* Boodle's, Beefsteak.
See also Earl of March and Kinrara.

GORDON-SMITH, David Gerard; CMG 1971; Director-General in Legal Service, Council of Ministers, European Communities, since 1976; *b* 6 Oct. 1925; *s* of late Frederic Gordon-Smith, QC, and Elsie Gordon-Smith (*née* Foster); *m* 1952, Angela Kirkpatrick Pile; one *d* (and one *s* decd). *Educ:* Rugby Sch.; Trinity Coll., Oxford. Served in RNVR, 1944–46. BA (Oxford) 1948; called to Bar, Inner Temple, 1949; Legal Asst, Colonial Office, 1950; Sen. Legal Asst, 1954; CRO, 1963–65; Asst Legal Adviser, CO, 1965–66; Legal Counsellor, CO, later FCO, 1966–72; Dep. Legal Advr, FCO, 1973–76. *Address:* Kingscote, Westcott, Surrey; 14 Avenue Ptolémée, 1180 Brussels, Belgium.

GORDON-SMITH, Ralph; President, since 1973 (Chairman, 1951–73), Smiths Industries Ltd (formerly Smith and Sons (England) Ltd); *b* 22 May 1905; *s* of late Sir Allan Gordon-Smith, KBE, DL and Hilda Beatrice Cave; *m* 1932, Beryl Mavis Cundy; no *c.* *Educ:* Bradfield Coll. Joined Smiths Industries, 1927; Dir, 1933. Dir of EMI Ltd, 1951–75. FBHI 1961. *Recreations:* shooting, fishing. *Address:* Brook House, Bosham, West Sussex. *T:* Bosham 573475; 23 Kingston House East, Princes Gate, SW7. *T:* 01–584 9428. *Club:* Bosham Sailing.

GORDON WATSON, Hugh; *see* Watson.

GORE, family name of **Earl of Arran.**

GORE; *see* Ormsby Gore.

GORE, Frederick John Pym, RA 1972 (ARA 1964); Painter; Head of Painting Department, St Martin's School of Art, WC2, 1951–79, and Vice-Principal, 1961–79; *b* 8 Nov. 1913; *s* of Spencer Frederick Gore and Mary Johanna Kerr. *Educ:* Lancing Coll.; Trinity Coll., Oxford; studied art at Ruskin, Westminster and Slade Schs. Taught at: Westminster Sch. of Art, 1937; Chelsea and Epsom, 1947; St Martin's, 1946–79. Chm., RA exhibitions cttee, 1976–. Trustee, Imperial War Mus., 1967–84 (Chm., Artistic Records Cttee). *One-man exhibitions:* Gall. Borghèse, Paris, 1938; Redfern Gall., 1937, 1949, 1950, 1953, 1956, 1962; Mayor Gall., 1958, 1960; Juster Gall., NY, 1963. *Paintings in public collections include:* Contemporary Art Soc., Leicester County Council, GLC, Southampton, Plymouth, Rutherston Collection and New Brunswick. Served War of 1939–45: Mx Regt and RA (SO Camouflage). *Publications:* Abstract Art, 1956; Painting, Some Principles, 1965; Piero della Francesca's 'The Baptism', 1969. *Recreation:* Russian folk dancing. *Address:* Flat 3, 35 Elm Park Gardens, SW10. *T:* 01–352 4940.

GORE, Paul Annesley, CMG 1964; CVO 1961; *b* 28 Feb. 1921; *o s* of late Charles Henry Gore, OBE and late Hon. Violet Kathleen (*née* Annesley); *m* 1946, Gillian Mary, *d* of T. E. Allen-Stevens; two *s* (and one *s* decd). *Educ:* Winchester Coll.; Christ Church, Oxford. Military Service, 1941–46: 16/5 Lancers. Colonial Service, 1948–65; Dep. Governor, The Gambia, 1962–65. JP City of Oxford, 1973–74; JP Suffolk, 1977–83. *Address:* 1 Burkitt Road, Woodbridge, Suffolk.

GORE, Sir Richard (Ralph St George), 13th Bt *cr* 1621; *b* 19 Nov. 1954; *s* of Sir (St George) Ralph Gore, 12th Bt, and of Shirley, *d* of Clement Tabor; *S* father, 1973. *Educ:* The King's Sch., Parramatta; Univ. of New England; Queensland Coll. of Art. *Heir: uncle* Nigel Hugh St George Gore [*b* 23 Dec. 1922; *m* 1952, Beth Allison (*d* 1976), *d* of R. W. Hooper; one *d*]. *Address:* 54 Mackenzie Street, Toowoomba, Queensland 4350, Australia.

GORE-BOOTH, Hon. David Alwyn; HM Diplomatic Service; Counsellor and Head of Chancery, UK Mission to UN, New York, since 1983; *b* 15 May 1943; twin *s* of late Baron Gore-Booth, GCMG, KCVO; *m* 1st, 1964, Jillian Sarah (*née* Valpy) (marr. diss. 1970); one *s*; 2nd, 1977, Mary Elisabeth Janet (*née* Muirhead). *Educ:* Eton Coll.; Christ Church, Oxford (MA Hons). Entered Foreign Office, 1964; Middle East Centre for Arabic Studies, 1964; Third Secretary, Baghdad, 1966; Third, later Second Sec., Lusaka, 1967; FCO, 1969; Second Sec., Tripoli, 1969; FCO, 1971; First Sec., UK Permanent Representation to European Communities, Brussels, 1974; Asst Head of Financial Relations Dept, FCO, 1978; Counsellor, Jedda, 1980. *Recreations:* tennis, squash, the island of Hydra (Greece). *Address:* c/o Foreign and Commonwealth Office, SW1A 2AH; 28 Chesilton Road, SW6 5AB. *T:* 01–736 8757. *Clubs:* MCC; Bill's Bar (Hydra).

GORE-BOOTH, Sir Michael Savile, 7th Bt, *cr* 1760; *b* 24 July 1908; *s* of 6th Bt and Mary (*d* 1968), *d* of Rev. S. L'Estrange-Malone; *S* father, 1944. *Educ:* Rugby; Trinity Coll., Cambridge. *Heir: b* Angus Josslyn Gore-Booth [*b* 25 June 1920; *m* 1948, Hon. Rosemary Vane (marr. diss., 1954), *o d* of 10th Baron Barnard; one *s* one *d*]. *Address:* Lissadell, Sligo.

GORE BROWNE, Sir Thomas (Anthony), Kt 1981; Senior Government Broker, 1973–81; Treasurer, Imperial Cancer Research Fund, since 1980; *b* 20 June 1918; 2nd *s* of Sir Eric Gore Browne, DSO; *m* 1946, Lavinia, *d* of Gen. Sir (Henry) Charles Loyd, GCVO, KCB, DSO, MC; three *s* one *d*. *Educ:* Eton Coll.; Trinity Coll., Cambridge. Served Grenadier Guards, 1938–48, France, N Africa, Italy. Joined Mullens & Co., 1948, Partner 1949–81. Dir, SW Regional Bd, Nat. Westminster Bank, 1981–84. *Address:* Flat 62, Melton Court, SW7 3JH. *T:* 01–589 0530. *Clubs:* Brooks's, White's, Pratt's.

GORE-LANGTON; *see* Temple-Gore-Langton, family name of Earl Temple of Stowe.

GORELL, 4th Baron *cr* 1909; **Timothy John Radcliffe Barnes;** *b* 2 Aug. 1927; *e s* of 3rd Baron Gorell and Elizabeth Gorell, *d* of Alexander Nelson Radcliffe; *S* father, 1963; *m* 1954, Joan Marion, *y d* of late John Edmund Collins, MC, Sway, Hants; two adopted *d*. *Educ:* Eton Coll.; New Coll., Oxford. Lieut, Rifle Brigade, 1946–48. Barrister, Inner Temple, 1951. Sen. Executive, Royal Dutch/Shell Group, 1959–84. *Heir: b* Hon. Ronald Alexander Henry Barnes [*b* 28 June 1931; *m* 1957, Gillian Picton Hughes-Jones; one *s* one *d*]. *Address:* 4 Roehampton Gate, SW15. *T:* 01–876 6042. *Club:* Roehampton Golf.

GORELL BARNES, Sir William (Lethbridge), KCMG 1961 (CMG 1949); CB 1956; Deputy Under-Secretary of State, Colonial Office, 1959–63; Deputy Chairman, Royal Group of Insurance Companies, 1972–80 (Director, 1963–80); *b* 23 Aug. 1909; *y s* of late Sir Frederic Gorell Barnes and Caroline Anne Roper Lethbridge; *m* 1935, Barbara Mary Louise, *e d* of late Brig. A. F. B. Cottrell, DSO, OBE; three *d* (one *s* decd). *Educ:* Marlborough Coll.; Pembroke Coll., Cambridge, 1st Cl. Classical Tripos Pt 1, 1st Cl. Mod. Langs Tripos Pt 2. Served in HM Diplomatic Service (Foreign Office, Baghdad and Lisbon), 1932–39; Offices of War Cabinet, 1939–45; Personal Asst to Lord Pres. of the Council, 1942–45; Asst Sec., HM Treasury, 1945–46; Personal Asst to Prime Minister, Oct. 1946–Feb. 1948; Seconded to Colonial Office, 1948; Asst Under-Sec. of State, 1948–59. Mem. UK delegn for negotiations with European Economic Community, 1962. Director: Doulton & Co., 1966–80 (Dep. Chm., 1969–80); Limmer Holdings Ltd, 1966–71 (Chm., 1971); Tarmac PLC, 1971–83; Tarmac Roadstone Hldgs Ltd, 1983–84; Donald Macpherson Gp, 1972–84; Vice-Chm. and Financial Dir, Harvey's of Bristol, 1963–66; Chm., James Templeton & Co., 1967–69. Chm., Cons. Commonwealth and Overseas Council, 1974–75. Mem. Council, Westfield Coll., London Univ., 1970–77 (Hon. Fellow, 1978). *Publication:* Europe and the Developing World, 1967. *Recreations:* gardening, walking, reading. *Address:* Mattishall Hall, Dereham, Norfolk. *T:* Dereham 858181. *Clubs:* Reform; Norfolk (Norwich).

GORING, Marius; Actor; *b* Newport, IOW, 23 May 1912; *s* of Dr Charles Buckman Goring, MD, BSc, and Katie Winifred Macdonald; *m* 1931, Mary Westwood Steel (marr. diss.); one *d*; *m* 1941, Lucie Mannheim (*d* 1976), *m* 1977, Prudence FitzGerald. *Educ:* Perse Sch., Cambridge; Universities of Frankfurt, Munich, Vienna, and Paris. Studied for stage under Harcourt Williams and at Old Vic dramatic school. First stage appearance in London in one of Jean Sterling Mackinlay's matinées, 1927; toured in France and Germany with English Classical Players, 1931; played two seasons at Old Vic and Sadler's Wells, 1932–34. First West End appearance as Hugh Voysey in The Voysey Inheritance, Shaftesbury, 1934; toured France, Belgium, and Holland with Compagnie des Quinze (acting in French), 1934–35; appeared London, 1935–39, in: Hamlet, Noah, The Hangman, Sowers of the Hills, Mary Tudor, The Happy Hypocrite, Girl Unknown, The Wild Duck, The Witch of Edmonton, Twelfth Night, Henry V, Hamlet, The Last Straw, Surprise Item, The White Guard; Satyr. In management at Duke of York's, 1939; produced Nora (A Doll's House); played Ariel in, and partly produced, The Tempest, Old Vic, 1940. Served War of 1939–45, Army, 1940–41; Foreign Office, 1941–45; supervisor of productions of BBC broadcasting to Germany, 1941. Toured British zone of Germany, 1947 (playing in German), 1948; Rosmersholm, Too True to be Good, Cherry Orchard, Marriage, The Third Man, at Arts Theatre; Daphne Laureola, Berlin (playing in German), 1949; The Madwoman of Chaillot, St James's, 1951; Richard III, Antony and Cleopatra, Taming of the Shrew, King Lear, Stratford-upon-Avon, 1953; Antony and Cleopatra, Princes, 1953; Marriage, Wuppertal, 1954; has toured France, Holland, Finland, 1957, and India, 1958, with own company of English comedians; Tonight at 8.30 (in German), Berlin Fest., 1960; Measure for Measure, Stratford-upon-Avon, 1962; A Penny for a Song, Aldwych, 1962; Ménage à Trois, Lyric, 1963; The Poker Session, Globe, 1964; The Apple Cart, Cambridge, 1965; The Bells, Vaudeville, 1968; The Demonstration, Nottingham, 1969; Sleuth, 1970–73; Zaïde, Old Vic, 1982; Peer Gynt, Nottingham, 1982; narrator and storyteller, Metamorphoses, RCM, 1983; Dame of Sark, nat. tour, 1983; The Winslow Boy, nat. tour, 1984. Co-founder, London Theatre Studio. *Films include:* The Case of the Frightened Lady, A Matter of Life and Death, Take my Life, The Red Shoes, Mr Perrin and Mr Traill, Odette, Circle of Danger, Highly Dangerous, So Little Time, Nachts auf den Strassen (Germany), The Man Who Watched the Trains Go By, Rough Shoot, The Barefoot Contessa, Family Doctor, Ill Met by Moonlight, The Inspector, The Crooked Road, Up from the Beach, 25th Hour, The Late Nancy Irvine. Broadcaster and writer of radio scripts. *Television:* co-prod. and played lead in The Scarlet Pimpernel (series), 1955; The Expert (series), 1968–70; The Old Men at the Zoo (serial), 1983; appears on TV in Germany and France. Vice-Pres. British Actors' Equity Assoc., 1963–65 and 1975–82. *Recreations:* skating and riding. *Address:* c/o Film Rights Ltd, 4 New Burlington Place, W1. *T:* 01–437 7151; Middle Court, The Green, Hampton Court, Surrey. *T:* 01–977 4030. *Club:* Garrick.

GORING, Sir William (Burton Nigel), 13th Bt, *cr* 1627; Member of London Stock Exchange since 1963; *b* 21 June 1933; *s* of Major Frederick Yelverton Goring (*d* 1938) (6th *s* of 11th Bt) and Freda Margaret, *o d* of N. V. Ainsworth, 2 Closewalks, Midhurst, Sussex; *S* uncle, Sir Forster Gurney Goring, 12th Bt, 1956; *m* 1960, Hon. Caroline Thellusson, *d* of 8th Baron Rendlesham, *qv*, and of Mrs Patrick Barthropp. *Educ:* Wellington; RMA Sandhurst, Lieut, The Royal Sussex Regt. *Recreation:* bridge. *Heir: b* Edward Yelverton Combe Goring [*b* 20 June 1936; *m* 1969, Daphne Christine Sellar; two *d*]. *Address:* 16 Linver Road, SW6 3RB. *T:* 01–736 6032. *Club:* Hurlingham.

GORING-MORRIS, Rex, OBE 1975; HM Diplomatic Service, retired; *b* 17 Oct. 1926; *s* of late Cecil Goring Morris and Doris Flora Edna (*née* Howell); *m* 1st, 1950, Constance Eularia Heather (*d* 1979), *d* of late Mr and Mrs Cecil Bartram, Oxford; two *s* three *d*; 2nd, 1979, Mrs Mary Poole (*née* King), Aldenham, Herts; one step *s* one step *d*. *Educ:* Chichester High Sch.; New Coll., Oxford; RAF Coll., Cranwell, 1945–46. No 66 (F) Sqdn, 1947–50; Central Flying Sch., 1950; No 6 FTS, 1950–51; French Air Force, Marrakech and Rabat, 1951–53; RAF Odiham, 1954–56; Flt Cdr No 66 (F) Sqdn, 1956–57; HQ Fighter Comd, 1957; HQ RAF Germany, 1957–59; RAF Staff Coll., 1959; Sqdn Cdr, Central Fighter Estabt, 1959–61; Military Agency for Standardisation, NATO, London, 1962–63; Wing Comdr 1963; Air Attaché, Tel Aviv, 1964–67; jssc 1968; Jt Warfare Estabt, 1969; retired from RAF and joined HM Diplomatic Service, 1969; 1st Sec., FCO, 1969–71; 1st Secretary and Head of Chancery: Tunis, 1971–75; Bangkok, 1975–77; Counsellor, Consul-Gen. and Hd of Chancery, Bangkok, 1978–79, Stockholm, 1979–82. *Recreations:* travel, photography; Oxford blue for Association Football, 1944–45. *Address:* Woodlands, High Coppice, Amersham, Bucks HP7 0AW. *T:* Amersham 6528. *Club:* Royal Air Force.

GORLEY PUTT, Samuel; *see* Putt.

GORMAN, John Peter, QC 1974; a Recorder of the Crown Court, since 1972; *b* 29 June 1927; *er s* of James S. Gorman, Edinburgh; *m* 1st, 1955; one *s* three *d*; 2nd, 1979, Patricia (*née* Myatt). *Educ:* Stonyhurst Coll.; Balliol Coll., Oxford (MA). Served with RA, 1945–48. Called to Bar, Inner Temple, 1953, Bencher 1983; Midland and Oxford Circuit. Dep. Chm. 1969, Chm. 1972–79, Agricultural Lands Tribunal (E Midlands); Dep. Chm., Northants QS, 1970–71. *Address:* 2 Dr Johnson's Buildings, Temple, EC4Y 7AY. *Club:* Reform.

GORMAN, John Reginald, CVO 1961; CBE 1974 (MBE 1959); MC 1944; DL; Vice-Chairman and Chief Executive, Northern Ireland Housing Executive, 1979–85; *b* 1 Feb. 1923; *s* of Major J. K. Gorman, MC; *m* 1948, Heather, *d* of George Caruth, solicitor, Ballymena; two *s* two *d*. *Educ:* Rockport, Haileybury and ISC Portora; Glasgow Univ.; Harvard Business Sch. FCIT, FIPM; MIH. Irish Guards, 1941–46, Normandy, France, Belgium, Holland, Germany (Captain, 1944–46). Royal Ulster Constabulary, 1946–60; Chief of Security, BOAC, 1960–63 (incl. Royal Tour of India, 1961); Personnel Dir and Mem. Bd of Management, BOAC, 1964–69; British Airways: Regional Man., Canada, 1969–75; Regional Man., India, Bangladesh, Sri Lanka, 1975–79. Mem., NI Bd, Nationwide Building Soc., 1986–. Pres., British Canadian Trade Assoc., 1972–74; Vice-Chm., Federated Appeal of Montreal, 1973–74. Chm., Bd of Airline Representatives, India, 1977–79; Chm., Inst. of Housing (NI), 1984; Dir, Industrial Devélt Authority of Ireland, 1986–. DL Co. Down, 1982. *Recreations:* gardening, bee keeping, country pursuits. *Address:* The Forge, Jericho Road, Killyleagh, Co. Down. *T:* Killyleagh 828400. *Clubs:* Cavalry and Guards; Ulster (Belfast); St James (Montreal); Gymkhana (Delhi).

GORMAN, William Moore, FBA 1978; Senior Research Fellow, Nuffield College, Oxford, since 1983 (Official Fellow, 1979–83); *b* 17 June 1923; *s* of late Richard Gorman, Lusaka, Northern Rhodesia, and Sarah Crawford Moore, Kesh, Northern Ireland; *m* 1950, Dorinda Scott. *Educ:* Foyle Coll., Derry; Trinity Coll., Dublin. Asst Lectr, 1949, Lectr, 1951, and Sen. Lectr, 1957, in Econometrics and Social Statistics, University of Birmingham; Prof. of Economics, University of Oxford, and Fellow of Nuffield Coll.,

Oxford, 1962–67; Prof. of Economics, London Univ., at LSE, 1967–79. Vice-Pres. 1970–71, Pres. 1972, Econometric Soc. Hon. DSocSc Birmingham,·1973; Hon. DSc(SocSc) Southampton, 1974; Hon. DEconSc NUI, 1986. *Publications:* articles in various economic journals. *Address:* Nuffield College, Oxford; Moorfield, Fountainstown, Myrtleville, Co. Cork, Ireland. *T:* Cork 831174.

GORMANSTON, 17th Viscount *cr* 1478; **Jenico Nicholas Dudley Preston;** Baron Gormanston (UK), 1868; Premier Viscount of Ireland; *b* 19 Nov. 1939; *s* of 16th Viscount and Pamela (who *m* 2nd, 1943, M. B. O'Connor, Irish Guards; he *d* 1961, she *d* 1975), *o d* of late Capt. Dudley Hanly, and Lady Marjorie Heath (by her 1st marriage); *S* father, who was officially presumed killed in action, France, 9 June 1940; *m* 1974, Eva Antoine Landzianowska (*d* 1984); two *s. Educ:* Downside. *Heir: s* Hon. Jenico Francis Tara Preston, *b* 30 April 1974. *Address:* 8 Dalmeny House, Thurloe Place, SW7.

GORMLEY, family name of **Baron Gormley.**

GORMLEY, Baron *cr* 1982 (Life Peer), of Ashton-in-Makerfield in Greater Manchester; **Joseph Gormley,** OBE 1969; President, National Union of Mineworkers, 1971–82; *b* 5 July 1917; *m* 1937, Sarah Ellen Mather; one *s* one *d. Educ:* St Oswald's Roman Catholic Sch., Ashton-in-Makerfield. Entered Mining Industry at age of 14 and was employed in practically every underground job in mining. Served as Councillor in Ashton-in-Makerfield. Elected to Nat. Exec. Cttee of Nat. Union of Mineworkers, 1957; Gen. Sec. of North Western Area, 1961, when he relinquished his appt as a JP, owing to other commitments. Mem., Nat. Exec. Cttee, Labour Party, 1963–73; former Chm., Internat. and Organisation Cttee, Labour Party. Member: TUC Gen. Council, 1973–80. Dir, United Racecourses Ltd, 1982–. *Publication:* Battered Cherub (autobiog.), 1982.

GORMLY, Allan Graham; Group Managing Director, John Brown PLC, since 1983; *b* 18 Dec. 1937; *s* of William Gormly and Christina Swinton Flockhart Arnot; *m* 1962, Vera Margaret Grant; one *s* one *d. Educ:* Paisley Grammar School. CA. Peat Marwick Mitchell & Co., 1955–61; Rootes Group, 1961–65; John Brown PLC, 1965–68; Brownlee & Co. Ltd, 1968–70; John Brown PLC, 1970: Finance Director, John Brown Engineering Ltd, 1970–77; Director, Planning and Control, John Brown PLC, 1977–80; Dep. Chairman, John Brown Engineers and Constructors Ltd, 1980–83; Chairman: Roxby Engineering International Ltd, 1980–83; UDI Group Ltd, 1980–83; CJB (Developments) Ltd, 1980–83. *Recreation:* golf. *Address:* 56 North Park, Gerrards Cross, Bucks SL9 8JR. *T:* Gerrards Cross 885079. *Club:* Caledonian.

GORRINGE, Christopher John; Chief Executive, All England Lawn Tennis and Croquet Club, Wimbledon, since 1983; *b* 13 Dec. 1945; *s* of Maurice Sydney William Gorringe and Hilda Joyce Gorringe; *m* 1976, Jennifer Mary Chamberlain; two *d. Educ:* Bradfield Coll., Berks; Royal Agricl Coll., Cirencester. ARICS. Asst Land Agent, Iveagh Trustees Ltd (Guinness family), 1968–73; Asst Sec., 1973–79, Sec., 1979–83, All England Lawn Tennis and Croquet Club. *Recreations:* lawn tennis, squash, soccer. *Address:* All England Lawn Tennis Club, Church Road, Wimbledon, SW19 5AE. *T:* 01–946 2244. *Clubs:* East India, Devonshire, Sports and Public Schools; All England Lawn Tennis and Croquet, International Lawn Tennis of GB, Queen's, St George's Hill Lawn Tennis, Jesters.

GORST, John Michael; MP (C) Hendon North, since 1970; *b* 28 June 1928; *s* of Derek Charles Gorst and Tatiana (*née* Kolotinsky); *m* 1954, Noël Harington Walker; five *s. Educ:* Ardingly Coll.; Corpus Christi Coll., Cambridge (MA). Advertising and Public Relations Manager, Pye Ltd, 1953–63; and Trade Union and Public Affairs Consultant, John Gorst & Associates, 1964–. Public relations adviser to: British Lion Films, 1964–65; Fedn of British Film Makers, 1964–67; Film Production Assoc. of GB, 1967–68; BALPA, 1967–69; Guy's Hosp., 1968–74. Founder: Telephone Users' Assoc., 1964–80 (Sec. 1964–70); Local Radio Assoc. 1964 (Sec., 1964–71). Contested (C) Chester-le-Street, 1964; Bodmin, 1966. Sec., Cons. Consumer Protection Cttee, 1973–74; Mem., Employment Select Cttee, 1980–; Vice-Chm., Cons. Media Cttee, 1983–. *Recreations:* gardening, photography and video recording, chess. *Address:* House of Commons, SW1A 0AA. *Club:* Garrick.

GORT, 8th Viscount (Ire.), *cr* 1816; **Colin Leopold Prendergast Vereker,** JP; Baron Kiltarton 1810; company director; *b* 21 June 1916; *s* of Commander Leopold George Prendergast Vereker, RD, RNR (*d* 1937) (*g s* of 4th Viscount) and Helen Marjorie Campbell (*d* 1958); *S* kinsman, 1975; *m* 1946, Bettine Mary Mackenzie, *d* of late Godfrey Greene; two *s* one *d. Educ:* Sevenoaks. Trained at Air Service Training, Hamble, in Aeronautical Engineering, etc., 1937–39; served Fleet Air Arm, 1939–45 (despatches). Member of House of Keys, IOM, 1966–71. JP IOM 1962. *Recreations:* golf, fishing, gardening. *Heir: er s* Hon. Foley Robert Standish Prendergast Vereker [*b* 24 Oct. 1951; *m* 1979, Julie Denise, *o d* of D. W. Jones, Ballasalla, IoM]. *Address:* Westwood, The Crofts, Castletown, Isle of Man. *T:* Castletown 822545.

GORTON, Rt. Hon. Sir John (Grey), PC 1968; GCMG 1977; CH 1971; MA; retired; *b* 1911; *m* 1935, Bettina, *d* of G. Brown, Bangor, Me, USA; two *s* one *d. Educ:* Geelong Gram. Sch.; Brasenose Coll., Oxford (MA, Hon. Fellow, 1968). Orchardist. Enlisted RAAF, Nov. 1940; served in UK, Singapore, Darwin, Milne Bay; severely wounded in air ops; discharged with rank of Flt-Lt, Dec. 1944. Councillor, Kerang Shire, 1947–52 (Pres. of Shire). Mem., Lodden Valley Regional Cttee. Senator for State of Victoria, Parlt of Commonwealth of Australia, 1949–68 (Govt Leader in Senate, 1967–68); Minister for Navy, 1958–63; Minister Assisting the Minister for External Affairs, 1960–63 (Actg Minister during periods of absence overseas of Minister); Minister in Charge of CSIRO, 1962–68; Minister for Works and, under Prime Minister, Minister in Charge of Commonwealth Activities in Educn and Research, 1963–66; Minister for Interior, 1963–64; Minister for Works, 1966–67; Minister for Educn and Science, 1966–68; MHR (L) for Higgins, Vic, 1968–75; Prime Minister of Australia, 1968–71; Minister for Defence, and Dep. Leader of Liberal Party, March-Aug. 1971; Mem. Parly Liberal Party Exec., and Liberal Party Spokesman on Environment and Conservation and Urban and Regional Develt, 1973–75; Dep. Chm., Jt Parly Cttee on Prices, 1973–75. Contested Senate election (Ind.), ACT, Dec. 1975. *Address:* Suite 3, 9th Floor, 197 London Circuit, Canberra City, ACT 2601, Australia.

GORTVAI, Rosalinde; *see* Hurley, R.

GOSCHEN, family name of **Viscount Goschen.**

GOSCHEN, 4th Viscount *cr* 1900; **Giles John Harry Goschen;** *b* 16 Nov. 1965; *s* of 3rd Viscount Goschen, KBE, and of Alvin Moyanna Lesley, *yr d* of late Harry England, Durban, Natal; *S* father, 1977. *Address:* Hilton House, Crowthorne, Berks.

GOSCHEN, Sir Edward (Christian), 3rd Bt, *cr* 1916; DSO 1944; Rifle Brigade; *b* 2 Sept. 1913; *er s* of Sir Edward Henry Goschen, 2nd Bt, and Countess Mary, 7th *d* of Count Danneskiold Samsoe, Denmark; *S* father, 1933; *m* 1946, Cynthia, *d* of late Rt Hon. Sir Alexander Cadogan, PC, OM, GCMG, KCB; one *s* one *d. Educ:* Eton; Trinity Coll., Oxford. Mem., Stock Exchange Council (Dep. Chm., 1968–71). Commonwealth War Graves Comr, 1977–86. *Heir: s* Edward Alexander Goschen [*b* 13 March 1949; *m* 1976,

Louise Annette, *d* of Lt-Col R. F. L. Chance, MC, and Lady Ava Chance; one *d*]. *Address:* Lower Farm House, Hampstead Norreys, Newbury, Berks RG16 0SG. *T:* Hermitage 201270.

GOSFORD, 7th Earl of, *cr* 1806; **Charles David Nicholas Alexander John Sparrow· Acheson;** Bt (NS) 1628; Baron Gosford 1776; Viscount Gosford 1785; Baron Worlingham (UK) 1835; Baron Acheson (UK) 1847; *b* 13 July 1942; *o s* of 6th Earl of Gosford, OBE, and Francesca Augusta, *er d* of Francesco Cagiati, New York; *S* father, 1966; *m* 1983, Lynnette Redmond. *Educ:* Harrow; Byam Shaw Sch. of drawing and painting; Royal Academy Schs. Chm., Artists Union, 1976–80; Mem. Visual Arts Panel, Greater London Arts Assoc., 1976–77; Council Member, British Copyright Council, 1977–80. Recent one-man shows: Barry Stern Exhibiting Gall., Sydney, Aust., 1983; Von Bertouch Galls, Newcastle, NSW, 1985. *Heir: u* Hon. Patrick Bernard Victor Montagu Acheson [*b* 4 Feb. 1915; *m* 1946, Judith, *d* of Mrs F. B. Bate, Virginia, USA; three *s* two *d*]. *Address:* c/o House of Lords, SW1.

GOSKIRK, (William) Ian (Macdonald), CBE 1986; Director, Coopers and Lybrand Associates, since 1986; *b* 2 March 1932; *s* of William Goskirk and Flora Macdonald; *m* 1969, Hope Ann Knaizuk; one *d. Educ:* Carlisle Grammar Sch.; Queen's Coll., Oxford (MA). Served REME, 1950–52. Shell Internat. Petroleum, 1956–74; Anschutz Corp., 1974–76; BNOC, 1976–85; Man. Dir, BNOC Trading, 1980–82; Chief Exec., BNOC, 1982–85. *Recreations:* gardening, philately. *Address:* c/o 94 Piccadilly, W1. *Club:* Naval and Military.

GOSLING, Allan Gladstone; Director, Scottish Services, Property Services Agency, Department of the Environment, since 1983; *b* 4 July 1933; *s* of late Gladstone Gosling and of Elizabeth Gosling (*née* Ward); *m* 1961, Janet Pamela (*née* Gosling); one *s* one *d. Educ:* Kirkham Grammar Sch.; Birmingham Sch. of Architecture. DipArch; RIBA 1961; RIAS 1984. Asst Architect, Lancs County Council, 1950–54; Birmingham Sch. of Architecture, 1954–57; Surman Kelly Surman, Architects, 1957–59; Royal Artillery, 1959–61; Army Works Organisation, 1961–63; Min. of Housing R&D Group, 1963–68; Suptg Architect, Birmingham Regional Office, Min. of Housing, 1968–72; Regional Works Officer, NW Region, PSA, 1972–76; Midland Regional Dir, PSA, 1976–83. *Recreations:* walking, gardening, DIY. *Address:* 8 Winton Terrace, Edinburgh EH10 7AP. *T:* 031–445 1519.

GOSLING, Sir Donald, Kt 1976; Joint Chairman, National Car Parks Ltd, since 1950; Chairman, Palmer & Harvey Ltd, since 1967; *b* 2 March 1929; *m* 1959, Elizabeth Shauna, *d* of Dr Peter Ingram and Lecky Ingram; three *s.* Joined RN, 1944; served Mediterranean, HMS Leander. Mem., Council of Management, White Ensign Assoc. Ltd, 1970– (Chm., 1978–83); Vice Pres., 1983–); Chm., Berkeley Square Ball Trust, 1982–; Trustee: Fleet Air Arm Museum, Yeovilton, 1974– (Chm., Mountbatten Meml Hall Appeals Cttee, 1980); RYA Seamanship Foundn, 1981–; Patron: Submarine Meml Appeal, 1978–; HMS Ark Royal Welfare Trust, 1986. *Recreations:* swimming, sailing, shooting. *Address:* National Car Parks Ltd, 21 Bryanston Street, Marble Arch, W1A 4NH. *T:* 01–499 7050. *Clubs:* Royal Thames Yacht, Royal London Yacht, Royal Naval Sailing Association, Thames Sailing; Saints and Sinners.

GOSLING, Justin Cyril Bertrand; Principal, St Edmund Hall, Oxford, since 1982; *b* 26 April 1930; *s* of Vincent and Dorothy Gosling; *m* 1958, Margaret Clayton; two *s* two *d. Educ:* Ampleforth Coll.; Wadham Coll., Oxford (BPhil, MA). Univ. of Oxford: Fereday Fellow, St John's Coll., 1955–58; Lectr in Philosophy, Pembroke Coll. and Wadham Coll., 1958–60; Fellow in Philosophy, St Edmund Hall, 1960–82; Sen. Proctor, 1977–78. Barclay Acheson Prof., Macalester Coll., Minnesota, 1964; Vis. Res. Fellow, ANU, Canberra, 1970. *Publications:* Pleasure and Desire, 1969; Plato, 1973; (ed) Plato, Philebus, 1975; (with C. C. W. Taylor) The Greeks on Pleasure, 1982; articles in Mind, Phil Rev. and Proc. Aristotelian Soc. *Recreations:* gardening, intaglio printing, recorder music. *Address:* St Edmund Hall, Oxford OX1 4AR. *T:* Oxford 245511.

GOSLING, Col Richard Bennett, OBE 1957; TD 1947; DL; *b* 4 Oct. 1914; 2nd *s* of late T. S. Gosling, Dynes Hall, Halstead; *m* 1st, 1950, Marie Terese Ronayne (*d* 1976), Castle Redmond, Co. Cork; one adopted *s* one adopted *d* (one *s* decd); 2nd, 1978, Sybilla Burgers van Oyen, *widow* of Bernard Burgers, 't Kasteel, Nijmegen. *Educ:* Eton; Magdalene Coll., Cambridge (MA). CEng, FIMechE, FIMC. Served with Essex Yeomanry, RHA, 1939–45; CO, 1953–56; Dep. CRA, East Anglian Div., 1956–58. Dir-Gen., British Agricl Export Council, 1971–73. Chairman: Constructors, 1965–68; Hearne & Co., 1971–82. Director: P-E International, 1956–76; Doulton & Co., 1962–72; Revertex Chemicals, 1974–81; Press Mouldings, 1977–. DL 1954, High Sheriff 1982, Essex. French Croix de Guerre, 1944. *Recreation:* country pursuits. *Address:* Canterburys Lodge, Margaretting, Essex. *T:* Ingatestone 353073. *Clubs:* Naval and Military, MCC; Beefsteak (Chelmsford).

GOSS, Brig. Leonard George, CB 1946; *b* 30 May 1895; *s* of Alfred Herbert Goss, Wellington, NZ; *m* 1920, Ella May, *d* of John Airth Mace, New Plymouth, NZ; one *d. Educ:* New Plymouth Boys' High Sch. (NZ); RMC of Australia. Commissioned in NZ Staff Corps, Lieut 1916; Captain 1919; Major, 1935; Lt-Col 1939; Temp. Brig. 1942. *Recreations:* Rugby, cricket, swimming, boxing. *Address:* 17 Waitui Crescent, Lower Hutt, NZ. *Club:* United Service (Wellington, NZ).

GOSS, Prof. Richard Oliver, PhD; Professor, Department of Maritime Studies, University of Wales Institute of Science and Technology, since 1980; *b* 4 Oct. 1929; *s* of late Leonard Arthur Goss and Hilda Nellie Goss (*née* Casson); *m* Lesley Elizabeth Thurbon (marr. diss. 1983); two *s* one *d. Educ:* Christ's Coll., Finchley; HMS Worcester; King's Coll., Cambridge. Master Mariner 1956; BA 1958; MA 1961; PhD 1979. FCIT 1970; MNI (Founder) 1972; FNI 1977. Merchant Navy (apprentice and executive officer), 1947–55; NZ Shipping Co. Ltd, 1958–63; Economic Consultant (Shipping, Shipbuilding and Ports), MoT, 1963–64; Econ. Adviser, BoT (Shipping), 1964–67; Sen. Econ. Adviser (Shipping, Civil Aviation, etc), 1967–74; Econ. Adviser to Cttee of Inquiry into Shipping (Rochdale Cttee), 1967–70; Under-Sec., Depts of Industry and Trade, 1974–80. Nuffield/Leverhulme Travelling Fellow, 1977–78. Governor, Plymouth Polytechnic, 1973–84; Mem. Council: RINA, 1969–; Nautical Inst. (from foundn until 1976); Member: CNAA Nautical Studies Bd, 1971–81; CNAA Transport Bd, 1976–78. *Publications:* Studies in Maritime Economics, 1968; (with C. D. Jones) The Economies of Size in Dry Bulk Carriers, 1971; (with M. C. Mann, et al) The Cost of Ships' Time, 1974; Advances in Maritime Economics, 1977; A Comparative Study of Seaport Management and Administration, 1979; Policies for Canadian Seaports, 1984; numerous papers in various jls, transactions and to conferences. *Recreations:* cruising inland waterways, travel. *Address:* 8 Dunraven House, Castle Court, Westgate Street, Cardiff CF1 1DL. *T:* Cardiff 44338.

GOSS, Very Rev. Thomas Ashworth; Dean of Jersey, 1971–85; *b* 27 July 1912; *s* of George Woolnough Goss and Maud M. (*née* Savage); *m* 1946, Frances Violet Patience Frampton; one *s* one *d. Educ:* Shardlow Hall; Aldenham Sch.; St Andrews Univ. (MA). Deacon, 1937; Priest, 1938; Curate of Frodingham, 1937–41. Chaplain, RAFVR, 1941–47 (PoW Japan, 1942–45). Vicar of Sutton-le-Marsh, 1947–51; Chaplain, RAF, 1951–67;

QHC, 1966–67. Rector of St Saviour, Jersey, 1967–71. *Recreations:* gardening, theatricals. *Address:* Les Pignons, Mont de la Rosière, St Saviour, Jersey, CI. *Clubs:* Royal Air Force; Victoria, Société Jersiaise (Jersey).

GOSTIN, Larry, DJur; Executive Director, American Society of Law and Medicine, since 1986; Instructor, School of Public Health, Harvard University, since 1986 (Senior Fellow of Health Law, 1985); *b* 19 Oct. 1949; *s* of Joseph and Sylvia Gostin; *m* 1977, Jean Catherine Allison; two *s. Educ:* State Univ. of New York, Brockport (BA Psychology); Duke Univ. (DJur 1974). Dir of Forensics and Debate, Duke Univ., 1973–74; Fulbright Fellow, Social Res. Unit, Univ. of London, 1974–75; Legal Dir, MIND (Nat. Assoc. for Mental Health), 1975–83; Gen. Sec., NCCL, 1983–85. Legal Counsel in series of cases before Eur. Commn and Eur. Court of Human Rights, 1974–. Vis. Prof., Sch. of Social Policy, McMaster Univ., 1978–79; Vis. Fellow in Law and Psychiatry, Centre for Criminological Res., Oxford Univ., 1982–83. Chm., Advocacy Alliance, 1981–83; Member: National Cttee, UN Internat. Year for Disabled People, 1981; Legal Affairs Cttee, Internat. League of Socs for Mentally Handicapped People, 1980–; Cttee of Experts, Internat. Commn of Jurists to draft UN Human Rights Declarations, 1982–; Adv. Council, Interights, 1984–; AE Trust, 1984–85; WHO Expert Cttee on Guidelines on the Treatment of Drug and Alcohol Dependent Persons, 1985. Western European and UK Editor, Internat. Jl of Law and Psychiatry, 1978–81; Executive Editor: Amer. Jl of Law and Medicine, 1986–; Jl of Law, Medicine and Health Care, 1986–. Rosemary Delbridge Meml Award for most outstanding contribution to social policy, 1983. *Publications:* A Human Condition: vol. 1, 1975; vol. 2, 1977; A Practical Guide to Mental Health Law, 1983; The Court of Protection, 1983; (ed) Secure Provision: a review of special services for mentally ill and handicapped people in England and Wales, 1985; Mental Health Services: law and practice, 1986; articles in learned jls. *Recreations:* family outings, walking on the mountains and fells of the Lake District. *Address:* American Society of Law and Medicine, 765 Commonwealth Avenue, 16th Floor, Boston, Mass 02215, USA. *T:* 617-2624990; Harvard School of Public Health, Department of Health Policy and Management, 677 Huntington Avenue, Boston, Mass 02115, USA. *T:* 617-7321090.

GOSTLING, Maj.-Gen. Philip le Marchant Stonhouse S.; *see* Stonhouse-Gostling.

GOTTLIEB, Bernard, CB 1970; industrial relations consultant; *b* 1913; *s* of late James Gottlieb and Pauline (*née* Littaur); *m* 1955, Sybil N. Epstein; one *s* one *d. Educ:* Haberdashers' Hampstead Sch.; Queen Mary Coll., London Univ. BSc First Class Maths, 1932. Entered Civil Service as an Executive Officer in Customs and Excise, 1932. Air Ministry, 1938; Asst Private Sec., 1941, and Private Sec., 1944, to Permanent Under-Sec. of State (late Sir Arthur Street), Control Office for Germany and Austria, 1945; Asst Sec., 1946. Seconded to National Coal Board, 1946; Min. of Power, 1950; Under-Sec., 1961, Dir of Establishments, 1965–69; Under-Sec., Min. of Posts and Telecommunications, 1969–73; Secretariat, Pay Board, 1973–74, Royal Commn for Distribution of Income and Wealth, 1974–78. Gwilym Gibbon Research Fellow, Nuffield Coll., Oxford, 1952–53. *Address:* 49 Gresham Gardens, NW11. *T:* 01–455 6172. *Club:* Reform.

GOTTMANN, Prof. Jean, FRGS; FBA 1977; Professor of Geography, University of Oxford, 1968–83, now Emeritus; Fellow of Hertford College, Oxford, 1968–83; now Emeritus; *b* 10 Oct. 1915; *s* of Elie Gottmann and Sonia-Fanny Ettinger Gottmann; *m* 1957, Bernice Adelson. *Educ:* Lycée Montaigne; Lycée St Louis; Sorbonne. Research Asst Human Geography, Sorbonne, 1937–40; Mem., Inst. for Advanced Study, Princeton, NJ, several times, 1942–65; Lectr, then Associate Prof. in Geography, Johns Hopkins Univ., Baltimore, 1943–48; Dir of Studies and Research, UN Secretariat, NY, 1946–47; Chargé de Recherches, CNRS, Paris, 1948–51; Lectr, then Prof., Institut d'Etudes Politiques, University of Paris, 1948–56; Research Dir, Twentieth Century Fund, NY, 1956–61; Prof. Ecole des Hautes Etudes, Sorbonne, 1960–. Pres., World Soc. for Ekistics, 1971–73; Governor, Univ. of Haifa, 1972–. Hon. Member: Amer. Geograph. Soc., 1961; Royal Netherlands Geog. Soc., 1963; Soc. Géographique de Liège, 1977; Società Geografica Italiana, 1981; Ateneo Veneto, 1986; For. Hon. Mem., Amer. Acad. of Arts and Sciences, 1972. Hon. LLD Wisconsin, 1968; Hon. DSc S Illinois, 1969; Hon. LittD Liverpool, 1986. Charles Daly Medal of Amer. Geograph. Soc., 1964; Prix Bonaparte-Wyse, 1962; Prix Sully-Olivier de Serre, Min. of Agriculture, France, 1964; Palmes Académiques, 1968; Victoria Medal, RGS, 1980; Grand Prix, Société de Géographie, Paris, 1984. Hon. Citizen: Yokohama, 1976; Guadalajara, 1978. Chevalier, Légion d'Honneur, 1974. *Publications:* Relations Commerciales de la France, 1942; L'Amérique, 1949 (3rd edn 1960); A Geography of Europe, 1950 (4th edn 1969); La politique des Etats et leur géographie, 1952; Virginia at Mid-century, 1955; Megalopolis, 1961; Essais sur l'Aménagement de l'Espace habité, 1966; The Significance of Territory, 1973; Centre and Periphery, 1980; The Coming of the Transactional City, 1983; La Citta invincibile, 1984; Orbits, 1984. *Address:* 19 Belsyre Court, Woodstock Road, Oxford OX2 6HU. *T:* Oxford 57076. *Club:* United Oxford & Cambridge University.

GOUDIE, Prof. Andrew Shaw; Professor of Geography and Head of Department, University of Oxford, since 1984; *b* 21 Aug. 1945; *s* of William and Mary Goudie. *Educ:* Dean Close Sch., Cheltenham; Trinity Hall, Cambridge. BA, PhD Cantab; MA Oxon. Departmental Demonstrator, Oxford, 1970–76; Univ. Lectr, 1976–84; Fellow of Hertford College, Oxford, 1976–. Hon. Secretary: British Geomorphological Res. Gp, 1977–80; RGS, 1981–; Member: Council, Inst. of British Geographers, 1980–83; British Nat. Cttee for Geography, 1982–; Dep. Leader: Internat. Karakoram Project, 1980; Kora Project, 1983. Cuthbert Peek award, RGS, 1975; Geographic Soc. of Chicago Publication award, 1982. *Publications:* Duricrusts of Tropical and Sub-tropical Landscapes, 1973; Environmental Change, 1976, 2nd edn, 1983; The Warm Desert Environment, 1977; The Prehistory and Palaeogeography of the Great Indian Desert, 1978; Desert Geomorphology, 1980; The Human Impact, 1981, 2nd edn 1986; Geomorphological Techniques, 1981; The Atlas of Swaziland, 1983; Chemical Sediments and Geomorphology, 1983; The Nature of the Environment, 1984; (jtly) Discovering Landscape in England and Wales, 1985; The Encyclopædic Dictionary of Physical Geography, 1985; contribs to learned jls. *Recreations:* bush life, old records, old books. *Address:* Hertford College, Oxford. *T:* Oxford 241791. *Clubs:* Geographical; Gilbert (Oxford).

GOUDIE, James; *see* Goudie, T. J. C.

GOUDIE, Rev. John Carrick, CBE 1972; Assistant Minister at St John's United Reformed Church, Northwood, since 1985; *b* 25 Dec. 1919; *s* of late Rev. John Goudie, MA and late Mrs Janet Goudie, step *s* of late Mrs Evelyn Goudie; unmarried. *Educ:* Glasgow Academy; Glasgow Univ. (MA); Trinity Coll., Glasgow. Served in RN: Hostilities Only Ordinary Seaman and later Lieut RNVR, 1941–45; returned to Trinity Coll., Glasgow to complete studies for the Ministry, 1945; Asst Minister at Crown Court Church of Scotland, London and ordained, 1947–50; Minister, The Union Church, Greenock, 1950–53; entered RN as Chaplain, 1953; Principal Chaplain, Church of Scotland and Free Churches (Naval), 1970–73; on staff of St Columba's Church of Scotland, Pont Street, 1973–77; Minister of Christ Church URC, Wallington, 1977–80; on staff of Royal Scottish Corp., London, 1980–84. QHC 1970–73. *Recreations:* tennis, the theatre.

Address: 501 Frobisher House, Dolphin Square, SW1V 3LL. *T:* 01–798 8537. *Club:* Army and Navy.

GOUDIE, (Thomas) James (Cooper), QC 1984; a Recorder, since 1986; *b* 2 June 1942; *s* of late William Cooper Goudie and Mary Isobel Goudie; *m* 1969, Mary Teresa Brick; two *s. Educ:* Dean Close Sch.; London School of Economics (LLB Hons). Solicitor, 1966–70; called to the Bar, Inner Temple, 1970. Contested (Lab) Brent North, General Elections, Feb and Oct. 1974; Leader of Brent Council, 1977–78. *Address:* 11 King's Bench Walk, Temple, EC4Y 7EQ. *T:* 01–583 0610.

GOUDIE, Hon. William Henry, MC 1944; Executive Director and Deputy Chairman, Law Reform Commission of Tasmania, 1974–81; *b* 21 Aug. 1916; *s* of Henry and Florence Goudie; *m* 1948, Mourilyan Isobel Munro (*d* 1981); two *s. Educ:* Bristol Grammar School. Solicitor (England), 1938; called to Bar, Gray's Inn, 1952. War service, 1939–45, London Scottish Regt and Som LI; JAG's Dept, 1945–48; Prosecutor, Dep. JA, Officer i/c branches Italy, Greece, Austria; Officer i/c Legal Section War Crimes Gp, SE Europe; Sen. Resident Magistrate, Acting Judge, Kenya, 1948–63; Puisne Judge, Aden, 1963–66; Puisne Judge, Uganda (Contract), 1967–71; Puisne Judge, Fiji (Contract), 1971–73. Editor, Kenya and Aden Law Reports. *Recreations:* golf, swimming. *Address:* 24 Nimala Street, Rosny, Hobart, Tasmania 7018, Australia. *Clubs:* Royal Commonwealth Society; Tasmanian (Hobart).

GOUGH, family name of Viscount Gough.

GOUGH, 5th Viscount (of Goojerat, of the Punjaub, and Limerick), *cr* 1849; **Shane Hugh Maryon Gough;** Irish Guards, 1961–67; *b* 26 Aug. 1941; *o s* of 4th Viscount Gough and Margaretta Elizabeth (*d* 1977), *o d* of Sir Spencer Maryon-Wilson, 11th Bt; S father 1951. *Educ:* Abberley Hall, Worcs; Winchester Coll. Mem. Queen's Bodyguard for Scotland, Royal Company of Archers. Heir: none. *Address:* Keppoch Estate Office, Strathpeffer, Ross-shire IV14 9AD. *T:* Strathpeffer 224; 17 Stanhope Gardens, SW7 5RQ. *Clubs:* Pratt's, White's; MCC.

GOUGH, Brandon; *see* Gough, C. B.

GOUGH, Cecil Ernest Freeman, CMG 1956; Director and Secretary, 1974–78, Assistant Director-General, 1978–80, acting Director-General, 1980–81, British Property Federation; *b* 29 Oct. 1911; *s* of Ernest John Gough; *m* 1938, Gwendolen Lily Miriam Longman; one *s* one *d. Educ:* Southend High Sch.; London Sch. of Economics (School of Economics Scholar in Law, 1932). LLB 1934. Asst Examiner Estate Duty Office, Board of Inland Revenue, 1930; Air Ministry, 1938; Principal, 1944; Ministry of Defence, 1947; Asst Sec., 1949; on loan to Foreign Office, as Counsellor, United Kingdom Delegation to NATO, Paris, 1952–56; Chairman: NATO Infrastructure Cttee, 1952–53; Standing Armaments Cttee Western European Union, 1956; returned Ministry of Defence, 1956; Under-Sec., 1958; Under-Sec. at the Admiralty, 1962–64; Asst Under-Sec. of State, Min. of Defence, 1964–68. Man. Dir, Airwork (Overseas) Ltd, 1968–71; Dir, Airwork Services Ltd and Air Holdings Ltd, 1968–73; Sec., Associated Owners of City Properties, 1975–77. Medal of Freedom (USA), 1946; Coronation Medal, 1953. *Recreations:* cookery, gardening, reading, travel. *Address:* 23 Howbridge Road, Witham, Essex CM8 1BY. *T:* Witham 518969. *Clubs:* Naval and Military, Civil Service.

GOUGH, (Charles) Brandon, FCA; Senior Partner, Coopers & Lybrand, Chartered Accountants, since 1983; *b* 8 Oct. 1937; *s* of Charles Richard Gough and Mary Evaline (*née* Goff); *m* 1961, Sarah Smith; one *s* two *d. Educ:* Douai Sch.; Jesus Coll., Cambridge (MA). FCA 1974. Joined Cooper Brothers & Co. (now Coopers & Lybrand), 1964, Partner 1968; Mem., Exec. Cttee, Coopers & Lybrand (Internat.), 1982– (Chm., 1985). Mem. Council, Inst. of Chartered Accountants in England and Wales, 1981–84; Chm., CCAB Auditing Practices Cttee, 1981–84 (Mem., 1976–84). Member: City Adv. Panel, City Univ. Business Sch., 1980–; Council of Lloyd's, 1982–; Cambridge Univ. Careers Service Syndicate, 1983–; Governing Council, Business in the Community, 1984–; Management Council, GB–Sasakawa Foundn, 1985–. *Recreations:* music, sailing. *Address:* 14 Calverley Park, Tunbridge Wells, Kent TN1 2SH. *T:* Tunbridge Wells 32982.

GOUGH, Brig. Guy Francis, DSO; MC; late Royal Irish Fusiliers; *b* 9 Aug. 1893; *e s* of late Hugh George Gough, Hyderabad, Deccan; *m* 1st, 1914, Dorothy (*d* 1953), *d* of late Edwin Paget Palmer, Patcham House, Sussex; one *s* one *d*; *m* 2nd, 1954, Elizabeth Treharn, *d* of Lewis David Thomas, Newton, near Porthcawl. *Educ:* The Oratory Sch.; RMC Sandhurst. 2nd Lieut, Royal Irish Fusiliers, Aug. 1914; European War, 1914–18. France and Belgium with 1st Royal Irish Fusiliers, and on the Staff (wounded, despatches, MC, 1915 Star); Staff Course, 1916. Commanded 1st Bn Nigeria Regt, 1936–37; War of 1939–45: Commanded ITC Royal Irish Fusiliers, 1st Battalion Royal Irish Fusiliers (in France and Belgium, May 1940), 202nd and 11th Infantry Brigades, Advanced Base I Army (N Africa), North Aldershot Sub-District. DSO, 1939–45 Star, Africa Star (with 1st Army clasp); retd pay, 1946. Control Commission, Germany as a Senior Control Officer, 1947–48. Coronation Medal, 1937. *Address:* Glyn Deri, Talybont-on-Usk, near Brecon, Powys LD3 7YP.

GOUGH, Rt. Rev. Hugh Rowlands, CMG 1965; OBE (mil.) 1945; TD 1950; DD Lambeth; *b* 19 Sept. 1905; *o s* of late Rev. Charles Massey Gough, Rector of St Ebbe's, Oxford; *m* 1929, Hon. Madeline Elizabeth, *d* of 12th Baron Kinnaird, KT, KBE; one *d. Educ:* Weymouth Coll.; Trinity Coll., Cambridge; London Coll. Divinity. BA 1927, MA Cantab 1931. Deacon, 1928; Priest, 1929; Curate of St Mary, Islington, 1928–31; Perpetual Curate of St Paul, Walcot, Bath, 1931–34; Vicar of St James, Carlisle, 1934–39; Chaplain to High Sheriff of Cumberland, 1937; CF (TA), 1937–45; Chaplain to 4th Bn The Border Regt, 1937–39; Vicar of St Matthew, Bayswater 1939–46; Chaplain to 1st Bn London Rifle Bde, 1939–43; served Western Desert and Tunisia (wounded); Senior Chap. to 1st Armd Div., Tunisia, 1943; DACG 10 Corps, Italy, 1943–45 (despatches); DACG, North Midland Dist, 1945. Hon. Chaplain to the Forces (2nd cl.) 1945. Vicar of Islington, Rural Dean of Islington, 1946–48. Preb. St Paul's Cathedral, 1948; Suffragan Bishop of Barking, 1948–59; Archdeacon of West Ham, 1948–58; Archbishop of Sydney and Primate of Australia, also Metropolitan of New South Wales, 1959–66, retired, 1966. Rector of Freshford, dio. of Bath and Wells, 1967–72; Vicar of Limpley Stoke, 1970–72. Chaplain and Sub-Prelate, Order of St John of Jerusalem, 1959–72. Formerly Member Council: London Coll. of Divinity, Clifton Theol. Coll. (Chm.), Haileybury Coll., Monkton Combe Sch., St Lawrence Coll. (Ramsgate), Chigwell Sch., Stowe Sch., Kingham Hill Trust. Golden Lectr Haberdashers' Co., 1953 and 1955. Pres. Conference, Educational Assoc., 1956. Mem., Essex County Education Cttee, 1949–59; DL Essex, 1952–59. Hon. DD Wycliffe Coll., Toronto; Hon. ThD, Aust. *Recreation:* birdwatching. *Address:* Forge House, Over Wallop, Stockbridge, Hants. *T:* Andover 781315. *Club:* National.

GOUGH, John, CBE 1972; Director of Administration, and Secretary, Confederation of British Industry, 1965–74; *b* 18 June 1910; *o s* of H. E. and M. Gough; *m* 1939, Joan Renee Cooper; one *s* one *d. Educ:* Repton Sch.; Keble Coll., Oxford. BA 1st cl. hons History. Senior History Tutor, Stowe Sch., 1933; Fedn of British Industries: Personal Asst to Dir, 1934; Asst Sec., 1940; Sec., 1959; Dir of Administration and Sec., CBI, 1965.

Recreations: walking, reading, music. *Address:* West Yard, North Bovey, Newton Abbot, Devon. *T:* Moretonhampstead 40395. *Club:* Reform.

GOUGH-CALTHORPE, family name of **Baron Calthorpe.**

GOULD, Bryan Charles; MP (Lab) Dagenham, since 1983; *b* 11 Feb. 1939; *s* of Charles Terence Gould and Elsie May Driller; *m* 1967, Gillian Anne Harrigan; one *s* one *d*. *Educ:* Auckland Univ. (BA, LLM); Balliol Coll., Oxford (MA, BCL). HM Diplomatic Service: FO, 1964–66; HM Embassy, Brussels, 1966–68; Fellow and Tutor in Law, Worcester Coll., Oxford, 1968–74. MP (Lab) Southampton Test, Oct. 1974–1979; an opposition spokesman on trade. Presenter/Reporter, TV Eye, Thames Television, 1979–83. *Publications:* Monetarism or Prosperity?, 1981; Socialism and Freedom, 1985. *Recreations:* gardening, food, wine. *Address:* Marymead, Russells Water, near Henley, Oxon; House of Commons, SW1. *T:* 01–219 3423.

GOULD, Cecil Hilton Monk; Keeper and Deputy Director of the National Gallery, 1973–78; *b* 24 May 1918; *s* of late Lieut Commander R. T. Gould and Muriel Hilda Estall. *Educ:* Westminster Sch. Served in Royal Air Force: France, 1940; Middle East, 1941–43; Italy, 1943–44; Normandy, Belgium and Germany, 1944–46. National Gallery: Asst Keeper, 1946; Dep. Keeper, 1962. Vis. Lectr, Melbourne Univ., 1978. FRSA 1968. *Publications:* An Introduction to Italian Renaissance Painting, 1957; Trophy of Conquest, 1965; Leonardo da Vinci, 1975; The Paintings of Correggio, 1976; Bernini in France, 1981; various publications for the National Gallery, including 16th-century Italian Schools catalogue; articles in Encyclopædia Britannica, Chambers's Encyclopedia, Dizionario Biografico degli Italiani, and specialist art journals of Europe and USA. *Recreations:* music, travel. *Address:* Jubilee House, Thorncombe, Dorset. *Club:* Reform.

GOULD, Donald (William), BSc (Physiol.), MRCS, DTM&H; writer and broadcaster on medical and scientific affairs; *b* 26 Jan. 1919; *s* of late Rev. Frank J. Gould; *m* 1st, 1940, Edna Forsyth; three *s* four *d*; 2nd, 1969, Jennifer Goodfellow; one *s* one *d*. *Educ:* Mill Hill Sch.; St Thomas's Hosp. Med. Sch., London. Orthopædic House Surg., Botley's Park Hosp., 1942; Surg. Lieut, RNVR, 1942–46; Med. Off., Hong Kong Govt Med. Dept, 1946–48; Lectr in Physiol., University of Hong Kong, 1948–51, Sen. Lectr, 1951–57; King Edward VII Prof. of Physiol., University of Malaya (Singapore), 1957–60; Lectr in Physiol., St Bartholomew's Hosp. Med. Coll., London, 1960–61, Sen. Lectr, 1961–63; External Examr in Physiol., University of Durham (Newcastle), 1961–63; Dep. Ed., Medical News, 1963–65; Editor: World Medicine, 1965–66; New Scientist, 1966–69; Med. Correspondent, New Statesman, 1966–78. Chm., Med. Journalists' Assoc., 1967–71; Vice-Chm., Assoc. of British Science Writers, 1970–71. *Publications:* The Black & White Medicine Show, 1985; contributions to: Experimentation with Human Subjects, 1972; Ecology, the Shaping Enquiry, 1972; Better Social Services, 1973; scientific papers in physiological jls; numerous articles on medical politics, ethics and science in lay and professional press. *Recreations:* writing poems nobody will publish, listening, talking, and walking. *Address:* 15 Waterbeach Road, Landbeach, Cambs CB4 4EA. *T:* Cambridge 861243.

GOULD, Edward John Humphrey, MA; FRGS; Headmaster, Felsted School, since 1983; *b* Lewes, Sussex, 31 Oct. 1943; *s* of Roland and Ruth Gould; *m* 1970, Jennifer Jane, *d* of I. H. Lamb; two *d*. *Educ:* St Edward's Sch., Oxford; St Edmund Hall, Oxford (BA 1966, MA 1970, DipEd 1967). FRGS 1974. Harrow School, 1967–83: Asst Master, 1967–83; Head, Geography Dept, 1974–79; Housemaster, 1979–83. Mem., Curriculum Cttee, HMC, GSA and IAPS, 1985–. *Recreations:* Rugby (Oxford Blue, 1963–66), swimming (Half Blue, 1965), rowing (rep. GB, 1967), music. *Address:* The Headmaster's House, Felsted School, Dunmow, Essex CM6 3LL. *T:* Great Dunmow 820258. *Clubs:* East India, Devonshire, Sports and Public Schools; Vincent's (Oxford).

GOULD, Maj.-Gen. John Charles, CB 1975; Paymaster-in-Chief and Inspector of Army Pay Services, 1972–75, retired; *b* 27 April 1915; *s* of late Alfred George Webb and Hilda Gould; *m* 1941, Mollie Bannister; one *s* one *d*. *Educ:* Brighton, Hove and Sussex Grammar School. Surrey and Sussex Yeomanry (TA), 1937; Royal Army Pay Corps, 1941; served: N Africa, Sicily, Italy (despatches), Austria, 1941–46; Egypt, Jordan, Eritrea, 1948–51; Singapore, 1957–59; Dep. Paymaster-in-Chief, 1967–72. *Recreations:* golf, bridge. *Address:* Squirrels Wood, Ringles Cross, near Uckfield, East Sussex TN22 1HB. *T:* Uckfield 4592. *Clubs:* Lansdowne; Piltdown Golf, Rye Golf.

GOULD, Joyce Brenda; Director of Organisation, Labour Party, since 1985; *b* 29 Oct. 1932; *d* of Sydney and Fanny Manson; *m* 1952, Kevin Gould (separated); one *d*. *Educ:* Cowper Street Primary Sch.; Roundhay High Sch. for Girls; Bradford Technical Coll. Dispenser, 1952–65; Asst Regional Organiser, 1969–75, Asst Nat. Agent and Chief Women's Officer, 1975–85, Labour Party. Sec., National Jt Cttee of Working Women's Orgns, 1975–; Vice-Pres., Socialist Internat. Women, 1978–. *Publications:* (ed) Women and Health, 1979; pamphlets on feminism, socialism and sexism, women's right to work, and on violence in society; articles and reports on women's rights and welfare. *Recreations:* relaxing, sport as a spectator, theatre, cinema, reading. *Address:* 5 Foulser Road, SW17.

GOULD, Patricia, CBE 1978; RRC 1972; Matron-in-Chief, Queen Alexandra's Royal Naval Nursing Service, 1976–80; *b* 27 May 1924; *d* of Arthur Wellesley Gould. *Educ:* Marist Convent, Paignton. Lewisham Gen. Hosp., SRN, 1945; Hackney Hosp., CMB Pt I, 1946; entered QARNNS, as Nursing Sister, 1948; accepted for permanent service, 1954; Matron, 1966; Principal Matron, 1970; Principal Matron Naval Hosps, 1975. QHNS 1976–80. OStJ (Comdr Sister), 1977. *Recreations:* gardening, photography. *Address:* 18 Park Road, Denmead, Portsmouth PO7 6NE. *T:* Waterlooville 255499.

GOULD, Thomas William, VC 1942; Lieutenant RNR retired; *b* 28 Dec. 1914; *s* of late Mrs C. E. Cheeseman and late Reuben Gould (killed in action, 1916); *m* 1941, Phyllis Eileen Eldridge (*d* 1985); one *s*. *Educ:* St James, Dover, Kent. Royal Navy, 1933–37; Submarines, 1937–45 (despatches); invalided Oct. 1945. Business Consultant, 1965–; company director. Pres., British Sect., Internat. Submariners' Assoc. *Address:* 6 Howlands, Orton Goldhay, Peterborough, Cambs. *T:* Peterborough 238918.

GOULDEN, (Peter) John; HM Diplomatic Service; Counsellor and Head of Chancery, Office of the UK Permanent Representative to the EEC, Brussels, since 1984; *b* 21 Feb. 1941; *s* of George Herbert Goulden and Doris Goulden; *m* 1962, Diana Margaret Elizabeth Waite; one *s* one *d*. *Educ:* King Edward VII Sch., Sheffield; Queen's Coll., Oxford (BA 1st Cl. Hons History, 1962). FCO (formerly FO), 1962–: Ankara, 1963–67; Manila, 1969–70; Dublin, 1976–79; Head of Personnel Services Dept, 1980–82; Head of News Dept, FCO, 1982–84. *Recreations:* early music, bookbinding, tennis, skiing. *Address:* c/o Foreign and Commonwealth Office, King Charles Street, SW1.

GOULDING, Sir (Ernest) Irvine, Kt 1971; Judge of the High Court of Justice, Chancery Division, 1971–85; *b* 1 May 1910; *s* of late Dr Ernest Goulding; *m* 1935, Gladys (*d* 1981), *d* of late Engineer Rear-Adm. Marrack Sennett; one *s* one *d*. *Educ:* Merchant Taylors' Sch., London; St Catharine's Coll., Cambridge, Hon. Fellow, 1971–. Served as Instructor Officer, Royal Navy, 1931–36 and 1939–45. Called to Bar, Inner Temple, 1936; QC 1961; Bencher, Lincoln's Inn, 1966, Treasurer, 1983. Pres., Internat. Law Assoc., British branch, 1972–81, Hon. Pres., 1983–. *Address:* Penshurst, Wych Hill Way, Woking, Surrey GU22 0AE. *T:* Woking 61012. *Club:* Travellers'.
See also M. I. Goulding.

GOULDING, Sir Lingard; *see* Goulding, Sir W. L. W.

GOULDING, Marrack Irvine, CMG 1983; Under Secretary-General, Special Political Affairs, United Nations, New York, since 1986; *b* 2 Sept. 1936; *s* of Sir Irvine Goulding, *qv*; *m* 1961, Susan Rhoda D'Albiac, *d* of Air Marshal Sir John D'Albiac, KCVO, KBE, CB, DSO, and of Lady D'Albiac; two *s* one *d*. *Educ:* St Paul's Sch.; Magdalen Coll., Oxford (1st cl. hons. Lit. Hum. 1959). Joined HM Foreign (later Diplomatic) Service, 1959; MECAS, 1959–61; Kuwait, 1961–64; Foreign Office, 1964–68; Tripoli (Libya), 1968–70; Cairo, 1970–72; Private Sec., Minister of State for Foreign and Commonwealth Affairs, 1972–75; seconded to Cabinet Office (CPRS), 1975–77; Counsellor, Lisbon, 1977–79; Counsellor and Head of Chancery, UK Mission to UN, NY, 1979–83; Ambassador to Angola, and concurrently to São Tomé e Principe, 1983–85. *Recreations:* travel, birdwatching. *Address:* 82 Claverton Street, SW1V 3AX. *T:* 01–834 3046; 40 E 61st Street, Apt 18, New York, NY 10021, USA. *T:* (212) 935 6157. *Club:* Royal Over-Seas League.

GOULDING, Lt-Col Terence Leslie Crawford P.; *see* Pierce-Goulding.

GOULDING, Sir (William) Lingard (Walter), 4th Bt *cr* 1904; Headmaster of Headfort School, since 1977; *b* 11 July 1940; *s* of Sir (William) Basil Goulding, 3rd Bt, and of Valerie Hamilton (Senator, Seanad Éireann), *o d* of 1st Viscount Monckton of Brenchley, PC, GCVO, KCMG, MC, QC; *S* father, 1982. *Educ:* Ludgrove; Winchester College; Trinity College, Dublin (BA, HDipEd). Computer studies for Zinc Corporation and Sulphide Corporation, Conzinc Rio Tinto of Australia, 1963–66; Systems Analyst, Goulding Fertilisers Ltd, 1966–67; Manager and European Sales Officer for Rionore, modern Irish jewellery company, 1968–69; Racing Driver, formulae 5000, 3 and 2, 1967–71; Assistant Master: Brook House School, 1970–74; Headfort School (IAPS prep. school), 1974–76. *Recreations:* squash, cricket, running, bicycling, tennis, music, reading, computers. *Heir:* *b* Timothy Adam Goulding, *b* 15 May 1945. *Address:* Headfort School, Kells, Co. Meath. *T:* Navan 40065; Dargle Cottage, Enniskerry, Co. Wicklow. *T:* Dublin 862315.

GOURLAY, Gen. Sir (Basil) Ian (Spencer), KCB 1973; OBE 1956 (MBE 1948); MC 1944; Director General, United World Colleges, since 1975; *b* 13 Nov. 1920; *er s* of late Brig. K. I. Gourlay, DSO, OBE, MC; *m* 1948, Natasha Zinovieff; one *s* one *d*. *Educ:* Eastbourne Coll. Commissioned, RM, 1940; HMS Formidable, 1941–44; 43 Commando, 1944–45; 45 Commando, 1946–48; Instructor, RNC Greenwich, 1948–50; Adjt RMFVR, City of London, 1950–52; Instructor, RM Officers' Sch., 1952–54; psc 1954; Bde Major, 3rd Commando Bde, 1955–57 (despatches); OC RM Officers' Trng Wing, Infantry Training Centre RM, 1957–59; 2nd in Comd, 42 Commando, 1959–61; GSO1, HQ Plymouth Gp, 1961–63; CO 42 Commando, 1963–65; Col GS, Dept of CGRM, Min. of Defence, 1965–66; Col 1965; Comdr, 3rd Commando Bde, 1966–68; Maj.-Gen. Royal Marines, Portsmouth, 1968–71; Commandant-General, Royal Marines, 1971–75; Lt-Gen., 1971; Gen., 1973. Admiral, Texas Navy. Vice Patron, RM Museum. *Recreations:* do-it-yourself, watching cricket, playing at golf. *Address:* c/o Lloyds Bank, 15 Blackheath Village, SE3. *Clubs:* Army and Navy, MCC; Royal Navy Cricket (Vice-Pres.).

GOURLAY, Harry Philp Heggie, JP; DL; MP (Lab) Kirkcaldy, since Feb. 1974 (Kirkcaldy Burghs, 1959–74); *b* 10 July 1916; *s* of William Gourlay; *m* 1942, Margaret McFarlane Ingram; no *c*. *Educ:* Kirkcaldy High Sch. Coachbuilder, 1932; Vehicle Examiner, 1947. Mem. Kirkcaldy Town Council, 1946, Hon. Treasurer, 1953–57; Magistrate, 1957–59; Vice-Chm. Fife Education Cttee, 1958; Mem. Hospital Management Cttee; Sec. Kirkcaldy Burghs Constituency Labour Party, 1945–59; Mem. Estimates Cttee, 1959–64; Chm. Scottish Parly Labour Group, 1963–64 and 1976–77; Government Whip, 1964–66; a Lord Comr of the Treasury, 1966–68; Dep. Speaker and Dep. Chm. of Ways and Means, 1968–70; Mem., Select Cttee on Procedure, 1974–79; Chm., Scottish Grand Cttee, 1979–. DL Fife, 1978. *Recreations:* chess, golf. *Address:* 34 Rosemount Avenue, Kirkcaldy, Fife. *T:* Kirkcaldy 261919.

GOURLAY, Gen. Sir Ian; *see* Gourlay, Gen. Sir B. I. S.

GOURLAY, Dame Janet; *see* Vaughan, Dame Janet.

GOVAN, Sir Lawrence (Herbert), Kt 1984; Deputy Chairman, Lichfield (NZ) Ltd, since 1979; *b* 13 Oct. 1919; *s* of Herbert Cyril Charles Govan and Janet Armour Govan (*née* Edmiston); *m* 1946, Clara Hiscock; one *s* three *d*. *Educ:* Christchurch Boys' High School. Started in garment industry with Lichfield (NZ) Ltd, 1935, Managing Director, 1950, retired 1979. Pres., NZ Textile and Garment Fedn, 1961–63, Life Mem., 1979. Director: United Building Soc.; Superannuation Investments Ltd; Lichfield (NZ) Ltd; Paynter Holdings Ltd; Allied Mortgage Guarantee Co. Ltd. Dir, Canterbury Regional Develt Council (Chm.). *Recreations:* golf, swimming, horticulture. *Address:* 11 Hamilton Avenue, Christchurch 4, New Zealand. *T:* 519–557. *Club:* Rotary (Christchurch) (Pres. 1963–64).

GOW, Ian, TD 1970; MP (C) Eastbourne since Feb. 1974; *b* 11 Feb. 1937; *yr s* of late Dr and Mrs A. E. Gow; *m* 1966, Jane Elizabeth Packe; two *s*. *Educ:* Winchester. Commnd 15th/19th Hussars, 1956. Solicitor 1962. Contested (C): Coventry East, 1964; Clapham, 1966. PPS to the Prime Minister, 1979–83; Minister for Housing and Construction, 1983–85; Minister of State, HM Treasury, 1985. *Recreations:* tennis, cricket, gardening. *Address:* The Dog House, Hankham, Pevensey, East Sussex. *T:* Eastbourne 763316; 25 Chester Way, Kennington, SE11. *T:* 01–582 6626. *Clubs:* Carlton, Pratt's, Cavalry and Guards, MCC.

GOW, Gen. Sir (James) Michael, GCB 1983 (KCB 1979); Commandant, Royal College of Defence Studies, 1984–86; *b* 3 June 1924; *s* of late J. C. Gow and Mrs Alastair Sanderson; *m* 1946, Jane Emily Scott, *e d* of late Capt. and Hon. Mrs Mason Scott; one *s* four *d*. *Educ:* Winchester College. Commnd Scots Guards, 1943; served NW Europe, 1944–45; Malayan Emergency, 1949; Equerry to HRH the Duke of Gloucester, 1952–53; psc 1954; Bde Major 1955–57; Regimental Adjt Scots Guards, 1957–60; Instructor Army Staff Coll., 1962–64; comd 2nd Bn Scots Guards, Kenya and England, 1964–66; GSO1, HQ London District, 1966–67; comd 4th Guards Bde, 1968–69; idc 1970; BGS (Int) HQ BAOR and ACOS G2 HQ Northag, 1971–73; GOC 4th Div. BAOR, 1973–75; Dir of Army Training, 1975–78; GOC Scotland and Governor of Edinburgh Castle, 1979–80; C-in-C BAOR and Comdr, Northern Army Gp, 1980–83 (awarded die Plakette des deutschen Heeres); ADC Gen. to the Queen, 1981–84. Colonel Commandant: Intelligence Corps, 1973–86; Scottish Division, 1979–80. Brig., Queen's Body Guard for Scotland, Royal Company of Archers. President: Royal British Legion, Scotland, 1986–; Earl Haig Fund, 1986–. Vice-Pres., Royal Patriotic Fund Corp., 1983–. Vice-President: Queen Victoria Sch., Dunblane, 1979–80; Royal Caledonian Schs, Bushey, 1980–. County Comr, British Scouts W Europe, 1980–83 (Silver Acorn). Freeman: City of London, 1980; State of Kansas, USA, 1984; Freeman and Liveryman, Painters' and Stainers' Co., 1980.

Publications: articles in mil. and hist. jls. *Recreations*: sailing, music, travel, reading. *Address*: c/o Lloyds Bank (Guards and Cavalry), Cox's & King's Branch, 6 Pall Mall, SW1Y 5NH. *Clubs*: Pratt's; New (Edinburgh).

GOW, John Stobie, PhD; CChem, FRSC; FRSE 1978; Secretary-General, Royal Society of Chemistry, since 1986; *b* 12 April 1933; *s* of David Gow and Anne Scott; *m* 1955, Elizabeth Henderson; three *s*. *Educ*: Alloa Acad.; Univ. of St Andrews (BSc, PhD). Res. Chemist, ICI, Billingham, 1958; Prodn Man., Chem. Co. of Malaysia, 1966–68; ICI: Res. Man., Agric. Div., 1968–72; Gen. Man. (Catalysts), Agric. Div., 1972–74; Res. Dir, Organics, 1974–79; Dep. Chm., Organics, 1979–84; Man. Dir, Speciality Chemicals, 1984–86. FRSA 1980. *Publications*: papers and patents in Fertilizer Technology and Biotechnology. *Recreations*: choral music, Rugby. *Address*: 19 Longcroft Avenue, Harpenden, Herts AL5 2RD. *T*: Harpenden 64889.

GOW, Brig. John Wesley Harper, CBE 1958 (OBE 1945); DL; JP; retired Shipowner; *b* 8 April 1898; *s* of late Leonard Gow, DL, LLD, Glasgow, and Mabel A. Harper, *d* of John W. Harper, publisher, Cedar Knoll, Long Island, NY; *m* 1925, Frances Jean, JP (*d* 1975), *d* of James Begg, Westlands, Paisley; three *s*. *Educ*: Cargilfield; Sedbergh; RMC Sandhurst; Trinity Coll., Oxford. Entered Scots Guards, 1917; severely wounded, France. Late partner, Gow Harrison & Co. Mem. Queen's Body Guard for Scotland (Royal Company of Archers), 1941. MFH, Lanarkshire and Renfrewshire, 1949–54; Pres. Royal Caledonian Curling Club, 1958–60; Chm. West Renfrewshire Unionist Assoc., 1947–60, Pres. 1960–68; Life Vice-Pres., RNLI, 1978 (Chm. Glasgow Branch, 1937–73); Mem. Council, SS&AFA, 1961–73, Hon. Life Mem. 1983 (Pres., West of Scotland Br., 1969–85; Pres., Glasgow Branch, 1955–73); Member Council: Erskine Hosp., 1946–78 (Hon. Pres., 1978); Earl Haig Fund Officers Assoc. (Scotland), 1946–75; Mem. Glasgow TA & AFA, 1947–56. Served War of 1939–45: Scots Guards, RARO; Lt-Col attached RA (LAA), NW Europe; commanded 77 AA Bde, RA (TA), 1947–48; Brig. 1948. Hon. Col 483 HAA (Blythswood) Regt RA, TA, 1951–56; Hon. Col 445 LAA Regt RA (Cameronians) TA, 1959–67, later 445 (Lowland) Regt RA (TA). DL Renfrewshire (formerly City of Glasgow), 1948; JP Renfrewshire, 1952. Lord Dean of Guild, Glasgow, 1965–67. OStJ 1969. Chevalier Order of Crown of Belgium and Croix de Guerre (Belgian), 1945. *Recreations*: curling, hunting, shooting. *Address*: The Old School House, Beith Road, Howwood, Renfrewshire PA9 1AW. *T*: Kilbarchan 2503. *Clubs*: Army and Navy; Western (Glasgow); Prestwick Golf.

GOW, Sir Leonard Maxwell H.; *see* Harper Gow.

GOW, Gen. Sir Michael; *see* Gow, Gen. Sir J. M.

GOW, Neil, QC (Scot.) 1970; Sheriff of South Strathclyde, at Ayr, since 1976; *b* 24 April 1932; *s* of Donald Gow, oil merchant, Glasgow; *m* 1959, Joanna, *d* of Comdr S. D. Sutherland, Edinburgh; one *s*. *Educ*: Merchiston Castle Sch., Edinburgh; Glasgow and Edinburgh Univs. MA, LLB. Formerly Captain, Intelligence Corps (BAOR). Carnegie Scholar in History of Scots Law, 1956. Advocate, 1957–76. Standing Counsel to Min. of Social Security (Scot.), 1964–70. Contested (C): Kirkcaldy Burghs, Gen. Elections of 1964 and 1966; Edinburgh East, 1970; Mem. Regional Council, Scottish Conservative Assoc. An Hon. Sheriff of Lanarkshire, 1971. Pres., Auchinleck Boswell Soc. FSA (Scot.). *Publications*: A History of Scottish Statutes, 1959; Jt Editor, An Outline of Estate Duty in Scotland, 1970; A History of Belmont House School, 1979; numerous articles and broadcasts on legal topics and Scottish affairs. *Recreations*: golf, books, antiquities. *Address*: Old Auchenfail Hall, by Mauchline, Ayrshire. *T*: Mauchline 50822. *Clubs*: Western (Glasgow); Prestwick Golf.

GOW, Dame Wendy; *see* Hiller, Dame Wendy.

GOW, Very Rev. William Connell; Dean of Moray, Ross and Caithness, 1960–77, retired; Canon of St Andrew's Cathedral, Inverness, 1953–77, Hon. Canon, since 1977; Rector of St James', Dingwall, 1940–77; *b* 6 Jan. 1909; *s* of Alexander Gow, Errol, Perthshire; *m* 1938, Edith Mary, *d* of John William Jarvis, Scarborough; two *s*. *Educ*: Edinburgh Theological Coll.; Durham Univ. (LTh). Deacon, 1936; Priest, 1937; Curate St Mary Magdalene's, Dundee, 1936–39. Awarded Frihetsmedalje (by King Haakon), Norway, 1947. *Recreations*: fishing, bridge. *Address*: 14 Mackenzie Place, Maryburgh, Ross-shire.

GOWANS, Sir Gregory; *see* Gowans, Sir U. G.

GOWANS, Sir James (Learmonth), Kt 1982; CBE 1971; FRCP 1975; FRS 1963; Deputy Chairman, Medical Research Council, 1978–Autumn 1987 (Secretary, 1977–Autumn 1987); *b* 7 May 1924; *s* of John Gowans and Selma Josefina Ljung; *m* 1956, Moyra Leatham; one *s* two *d*. *Educ*: Trinity Sch., Croydon; King's Coll. Hosp. Med. Sch. (MB BS (Hons) 1947; Fellow, 1979); Lincoln Coll., Oxford (BA (1st cl. Hons Physiology) 1948; MA; DPhil 1953; Hon. Fellow, 1984). MRC Exchange Scholar, Pasteur Institute, Paris, 1952–53; Research Fellow, Exeter Coll., Oxford, 1955–60 (Hon. Fellow, 1983–); Fellow, St Catherine's Coll., Oxford, 1961–; Henry Dale Res. Prof. of Royal Society, 1962–77; Hon. Dir, MRC Cellular Immunology Unit, 1963–77; Dir, Celltech Ltd, 1980–. Member: MRC, 1965–69; Adv. Bd for Res. Councils, 1977–. Royal Society: Mem. Council and a Vice-Pres., 1973–75; Assessor to MRC, 1973–75. Vis. Prof., NY Univ. Sch. of Med., 1967; Lectures: Harvey, NY, 1968; Dunham, Harvard, 1971; Bayne-Jones, Johns Hopkins, 1973. Foreign Associate, Nat. Acad. of Scis, USA, 1985. Hon. Member: Amer. Assoc. of Immunologists; Amer. Soc. of Anatomists. Hon. ScD Yale, 1966; Hon. DSc: Chicago, 1971; Birmingham, 1978; Hon. MD Edinburgh, 1979. Gairdner Foundn Award, 1968; Paul Ehrlich Award, 1974; Royal Medal, Royal Society, 1976; Feldberg Foundn Award, 1979; Wolf Prize in Medicine, 1980. *Publications*: articles in scientific journals. *Address*: (until Autumn 1987) Medical Research Council, 20 Park Crescent, W1N 4AL; 75 Cumnor Hill, Oxford OX2 9HX.

GOWANS, James Palmer, JP; DL; Lord Provost of Dundee and Lord-Lieutenant of the City of Dundee, 1980–84; *b* 15 Sept. 1930; *s* of Charles Gowans and Sarah Gowans (*née* Palmer); *m* 1950, Davina Barnett; one *s* four *d* (and one *s* decd). *Educ*: Rockwell Secondary School, Dundee. Joined National Cash Register Co., Dundee, 1956; now employed testing electronic modules. Elected to Dundee DC, May 1974. JP 1977; DL Dundee 1984. *Recreations*: golf, motoring. *Address*: 41 Dalmahoy Drive, Dundee DD2 3UT. *T*: Dundee 84918.

GOWANS, Hon. Sir (Urban) Gregory, Kt 1974; Judge of Supreme Court of Victoria, Australia, 1961–76; *b* 9 Sept. 1904; *s* of late James and Hannah Theresa Gowans; *m* 1937, Mona Ann Freeman; one *s* four *d*. *Educ*: Christian Brothers Coll., Kalgoorlie, WA; Univs of Western Australia and Melbourne. BA (WA) 1924; LLB (Melb.) 1926. Admitted Victorian Bar, 1928; QC 1949; Mem., Overseas Telecommunications Commn (Aust.), 1947–61; Lectr in Industrial Law, Melb. Univ., 1948–56. Constituted Bd of Inquiry into Housing Commn Land Deals, 1977–78. *Publication*: The Victorian Bar: professional conduct practice and etiquette, 1979. *Recreation*: bush walking. *Address*: 3 Stanley Grove, Canterbury, Melbourne, Vic. 3126, Australia. *T*: 813–2992. *Club*: Melbourne (Melbourne).

GOWDA, Prof. Deve Javare, (De-Ja-Gou); Vice-Chancellor, University of Mysore, 1969–76; Senior Fellow, International School of Dravidian Linguistics, Trivandrum, Kerala; *b* Chakkare, Bangalore, 6 July 1918; *s* of Deve Gowda; *m* 1943, Savithramma Javare Gowda; one *s* one *d*. *Educ*: Univ. of Mysore. MA Kannada, 1943. Mysore University: Lectr in Kannada, 1946; Asst Prof. of Kannada and Sec., Univ. Publications, 1955; Controller of Examinations, 1957; Principal, Sahyadri Coll., Shimoga, Mysore Univ., 1960; Prof. of Kannada Studies, 1966. Hon. Dir of Researches, Kuvempu Vidyavardhaka Trust, Mysore. DLit Karnataka, 1975. Soviet Land Award, 1967. *Publications*: (as De-Ja-Gou) numerous books in Kannada; has also edited many works. *Recreations*: writing, gardening. *Address*: Kalanilaya, J. L. Puram, Mysore-12, India. *T*: 21920.

GOWENLOCK, Prof. Brian Glover, CBE 1986; PhD, DSc; FRSE; FRSC; Professor of Chemistry, Heriot-Watt University, since 1966; *b* 9 Feb. 1926; *s* of Harry Hadfield Gowenlock and Hilda (*née* Glover); *m* 1953, Margaret L. Davies; one *s* two *d*. *Educ*: Hulme Grammar Sch., Oldham; Univ. of Manchester (BSc, MSc, PhD). DSc Birmingham. FRIC 1966; FRSE 1969. Asst Lectr in Chemistry 1948, Lectr 1951, University Coll. of Swansea; Lectr 1955, Sen. Lectr 1964, Univ. of Birmingham; Dean, Faculty of Science, Heriot-Watt Univ., 1969–72. Vis. Scientist, National Res. Council, Ottawa, 1963; Erskine Vis. Fellow, Univ. of Canterbury, NZ, 1976. Mem., UGC, 1976–85, Vice-Chm., 1983–85 (Chm., Physical Scis and Equipment Sub-cttees, 1982–85). *Publications*: Experimental Methods in Gas Reactions (with Sir Harry Melville), 1964; First Year at the University (with James C. Blackie), 1964; contribs to scientific jls. *Recreations*: genealogy, foreign travel. *Address*: 49 Lygon Road, Edinburgh EH16 5QA. *T*: 031–667 8506.

GOWER; *see* Leveson Gower.

GOWER, Most Rev. Godfrey Philip, DD; *b* 5 Dec. 1899; *s* of William and Sarah Ann Gower; *m* 1932, Margaret Ethel Tanton; two *s* one *d*. *Educ*: Imperial College, University of London; St John's College, Winnipeg, University of Manitoba. Served RAF, 1918–19. Deacon 1930; Priest 1931; Rector and Rural Dean of Camrose, Alta, 1932–35; Rector of Christ Church, Edmonton, Alta, 1935–41; Exam. Chaplain to Bishop of Edmonton, 1938–41; Canon of All Saints' Cathedral, 1940–44. Chaplain, RCAF, 1941–44. Rector of St Paul's, Vancouver, 1944–51; Bishop of New Westminster, 1951–71; Archbishop of New Westminster, and Metropolitan of British Columbia, 1968–71. Holds Hon. doctorates in Divinity. *Address*: 305–1520 Vidal Street, White Rock, BC V4B 3T7, Canada. *T*: 531–7254.

GOWER, Sir (Herbert) Raymond, Kt 1974; MP (C) Vale of Glamorgan, since 1983 (Barry Division of Glamorganshire, 1951–83); journalist and broadcaster; *b* 15 Aug. 1916; *s* of late Lawford R. Gower, FRIBA, County Architect for Glamorgan, and Mrs Gower; *m* 1973, Cynthia, *d* of Mr and Mrs James Hobbs. *Educ*: Cardiff High Sch.; Univ. of Wales; Cardiff Sch. of Law. Solicitor, admitted 1944; practised Cardiff, 1948–63; Partner, S. R. Freed & Co., Harewood Place, W1, 1964–. Contested (C) Ogmore Division of Glamorgan, general election, 1950. Political Columnist for Western Mail for Cardiff, 1951–64. Parliamentary Private Secretary: to Mr Gurney Braithwaite, 1951–54, to Mr R. Maudling, 1951–52, to Mr J. Profumo, 1952–57, to Mr Hugh Molson, 1954–57, Min. of Transport and Civil Aviation, and to Minister of Works, 1957–60. Member: Speaker's Conf. on Electoral Law, 1967–69, 1971–74; Select Cttee on Expenditure, 1970–73; Select Cttee on Welsh Affairs, 1979–83; Treasurer, Welsh Parly Party, 1966–; Chm., Welsh Cons. Members, 1970–74, 1979–. Jt Founder and Dir, first Welsh Unit Trust. Governor, University Coll., Cardiff, 1951–; Member Court of Governors: National Museum of Wales, 1952–; National Library of Wales, 1951–; University Coll., Aberystwyth, 1953–; Vice-President: National Chamber of Trade, 1956–; Cardiff Business Club, 1952; South Wales Ramblers, 1958–; Sec., Friends of Wales Soc. (Cultural); Mem., Welsh Advisory Council for Civil Aviation, 1959–62; President: Wales Area Conservative Teachers' Assoc., 1962–; Glamorgan (London) Soc., 1967–69. FInstD 1958. *Recreations*: tennis, squash rackets, and travelling in Italy. *Address*: House of Commons, SW1; 45 Winsford Road, Sully, South Glam. *Clubs*: Carlton, Royal Over-Seas League.

GOWER, Jim; *see* Gower, L. C. B.

GOWER, John Hugh, QC 1967; **His Honour Judge Gower**; a Circuit Judge, since 1972; *b* 6 Nov. 1925; *s* of Henry John Gower, JP and Edith (*née* Brooks); *m* 1960, Shirley Mameena Darbourne; one *s* one *d*. *Educ*: Skinners' Sch., Tunbridge Wells. RASC, 1945–48 (Staff Sgt). Called to Bar, Inner Temple, 1948. Dep. Chm., Kent QS, 1968–71; Resident and Liaison Judge of Crown Courts in E Sussex, 1986–. Pres., Tunbridge Wells Council of Voluntary Service, 1974–. Hon. Vice-Pres., Kent Council of Voluntary Service, 1971–. Freeman, City of London (by purchase), 1960. *Recreations*: fishing, foxhunting, gardening. *Address*: The Coppice, Lye Green, Crowborough, East Sussex. *T*: Crowborough 4395.

GOWER, Laurence Cecil Bartlett, (Jim), FBA 1965; Solicitor; Professor Emeritus, Southampton University; *b* 29 Dec. 1913; *s* of Henry Lawrence Gower; *m* 1939, Helen Margaret Shepperson, *d* of George Francis Birch; two *s* one *d*. *Educ*: Lindisfarne Coll.; University Coll., London. LLB 1933; LLM 1934. Admitted Solicitor, 1937. Served War of 1939–45, with RA and RAOC. Sir Ernest Cassel Prof. of Commercial Law in University of London, 1948–62, Visiting Prof., Law Sch. of Harvard Univ., 1954–55; Adviser on Legal Educn in Africa to Brit. Inst. of Internat. and Comparative Law and Adviser to Nigerian Council of Legal Educn, 1962–65; Prof. and Dean of Faculty of Law of Univ. of Lagos, 1962–65; Law Comr, 1965–71; Vice-Chancellor, Univ. of Southampton, 1971–79. Holmes Lectr, Harvard Univ., 1966. Fellow of University Coll., London; Comr on Company Law Amendment in Ghana, 1958; Member: Jenkins Cttee on Company Law Amendment, 1959–62; Denning Cttee on Legal Education for Students from Africa, 1960; Ormrod Cttee on Legal Education, 1967–71; Royal Commn on the Press, 1975–77. Trustee, British Museum, 1968–83. Hon. Fellow: LSE, 1970; Portsmouth Polytech., 1981; Hon. LLD: York Univ., Ont; Edinburgh Univ.; Dalhousie Univ.; Warwick Univ.; QUB; Southampton Univ.; Bristol Univ.; London Univ.; Hon. DLitt Hong Kong. *Publications*: Principles of Modern Company Law, 1954, 4th edn 1979; Independent Africa: The Challenge to the Legal Profession, 1967; Review of Investor Protection, Part 1, 1984, Part 2, 1985; numerous articles in legal periodicals. *Recreation*: travel. *Address*: 26 Willow Road, Hampstead, NW3. *T*: 01–435 2507. *Club*: Athenæum.

GOWER, Sir Raymond; *see* Gower, Sir H. R.

GOWER ISAAC, Anthony John; *see* Isaac.

GOWING, Sir Lawrence (Burnett), Kt 1982; CBE 1952; MA Dunelm 1952; ARA 1978; painter and writer on painting; Samuel H. Kress Professor, Centre for Advanced Study in the Visual Arts, National Gallery of Art, Washington, 1986–87; Hon. Curator, Royal Academy collections, since 1985; *b* 21 April 1918; *s* of late Horace Burnett and Louise Gowing; *m* Jennifer Akam Wallis; three *d*. *Educ*: Leighton Park Sch., and as a pupil of William Coldstream. Exhibitions: 1942, 1946, 1948, 1955, (Leicester Gall.), 1965 (Marlborough), 1982 (Waddington); retrospective, Serpentine Gall., 1983; Hatton Gall., Newcastle, Ferens Gall., Hull, Plymouth City Art Gall., 1983; works in collections of Contemp. Art Soc., Tate Gallery, National Portrait Gallery, National Gallery of Canada,

National Gallery of South Australia, British Council, Arts Council, Ashmolean and Fitzwilliam Museums, and galleries of Brighton, Bristol, Exeter, Manchester, Middlesbrough, Newcastle, Nottingham, Swindon, Wolverhampton, etc. Prof. of Fine Art, Univ. of Durham, and Principal of King Edward VII Sch. of Art, Newcastle upon Tyne, 1948–58; Principal, Chelsea Sch. of Art, 1958–65; Keeper of the British Collection, and Dep. Dir of the Tate Gallery, 1965–67; Prof. of Fine Art, Leeds Univ., 1967–75; Slade Prof. of Fine Art, UCL, 1975–85. Adjunct Prof. of History of Art, Univ. of Pa, 1977–. Mem. Arts Council, 1970–72, and 1977–81, Art Panel, 1953–58, 1959–65, 1969–72, 1976–81, Dep. Chm., 1970–72, 1977–81, Chm. Art Films Cttee, 1970–72; a Trustee of Tate Gallery, 1953–60 and 1961–64; a Trustee of National Portrait Gallery, 1960–; Trustee, British Museum, 1976–81; a Member of National Council for Diplomas in Art and Design, 1961–65; Chairman: Adv. Cttee on Painting, Gulbenkian Foundation, 1958–64. Hon. DLitt: Heriot-Watt, 1980; Leicester, 1983. *Television:* Three Painters, BBC2, 1984, second series, 1986. *Publications:* Renoir, 1947; Vermeer, 1952; Cézanne (catalogue of Edinburgh and London exhibns), 1954; Constable, 1960; Vermeer, 1961; Goya, 1965; Turner: Imagination and Reality, 1966; Matisse: 64 paintings (Museum of Modern Art, New York), 1966, (Hayward Gallery), 1968; Hogarth (Tate Gallery exhibition), 1971; Watercolours by Cézanne (Newcastle and London exhibn), 1973; Matisse, 1979; Lucian Freud, 1982; The Originality of Thomas Jones, 1986; many exhibition catalogues and writings in periodicals. *Address:* 49 Walham Grove, SW6. *T:* 01–385 5941.

GOWING, Prof. Margaret Mary, CBE 1981; FBA 1975; FRHistS; Professor of the History of Science, University of Oxford, and Fellow of Linacre College, 1973–86; *b* 26 April 1921; *d* of Ronald and Mabel Elliott; *m* 1944, Donald J. G. Gowing (*d* 1969); two *s*. *Educ:* Christ's Hospital; London Sch. of Economics (BSc(Econ)). Bd of Trade, 1941–45; Historical Section, Cabinet Office, 1945–59; Historian and Archivist, UK Atomic Energy Authority, 1959–66; Reader in Contemporary History, Univ. of Kent, 1966–72. Member: Cttee on Deptl Records (Grigg Cttee), 1952–54; Adv. Council on Public Records, 1974–82; BBC Archives Adv. Cttee, 1976–79; Public Records Inquiry (Wilson Cttee), 1978–80; Trustee: Nat. Portrait Gall., 1978–; Imperial War Mus., 1986–. Hon. Dir, Contemporary Scientific Archives Centre, 1973–86. Royal Society Wilkins Lectr, 1976; Enid Muir Lectr, Newcastle, 1976; Bernal Lectr, Birkbeck, 1977; Rede Lectr, Cambridge, 1978; Herbert Spencer Lectr, Oxford, 1982. Hon. DLitt: Leeds, 1976; Leicester, 1982; Hon. DSc Manchester, 1985. *Publications:* (with Sir K. Hancock) British War Economy, 1949; (with E. L. Hargreaves) Civil Industry and Trade, 1952; Britain and Atomic Energy, 1964; Dossier Secret des Relations Atomiques, 1965; Independence and Deterrence: vol. I, Policy Making, vol. II, Policy Execution, 1974; Reflections on Atomic Energy History, 1978; (with Lorna Arnold) The Atomic Bomb, 1979; various articles and reviews. *Address:* Linacre College, Oxford.

GOWING, Prof. Noel Frank Collett; Emeritus Professor of Pathology, University of London; Consultant Pathologist and Director of the Department of Histopathology, The Royal Marsden Hospital, SW3, 1957–82; Professor of Tumour Pathology (formerly Senior Lecturer), Institute of Cancer Research: The Royal Cancer Hospital, 1971–82; *b* 3 Jan. 1917; *s* of Edward Charles Gowing and Annie Elizabeth Gowing; *m* 1942, Rela Griffel; one *d*. *Educ:* Ardingly Coll., Sussex; London Univ. MRCS, LRCP 1941; MB, BS, London, 1947; MD London, 1948. Served RAMC (Capt.), 1942–46, 52nd (Lowland) Div. Lectr in Pathology, St George's Hosp. Med. Sch., 1947–52; Sen. Lectr in Pathology and Hon. Cons. Pathologist, St George's Hosp., 1952–57. Sometime Examiner in Pathology to: Univ. of London; RCPath; Univ. of Newcastle-upon-Tyne; Univ. of Malta; Nat. Univ. of Malaysia. Lectures: Kettle Meml, RCPath, 1968; Whittick Meml, Saskatchewan Cancer Soc., 1974; Symeonidis Meml, Thessaloniki Cancer Inst., Greece, 1977. Pres., Assoc. of Clinical Pathologists, 1982–83. FRCPath (Founder Fellow, Coll. of Pathologists, 1964). *Publications:* A Colour Atlas of Tumour Histopathology, 1980; articles on pathology in medical journals. *Recreations:* gardening, astronomy.

GOWLAND, Rev. William; Founder Principal, Luton Industrial College, 1957–85, Emeritus Principal, 1985; President of the Methodist Conference, 1979–80; *b* 3 Oct. 1911; *s* of George and Jane Gowland; *m* 1939, Helen Margaret Qualtrough; three *s* one *d*. *Educ:* Darlington Technical Coll.; Hartley Victoria Coll. Methodist Minister: Port Erin, IOM, 1935–39; Tilehurst, Reading, 1939–48; Albert Hall, Manchester, 1948–54; Luton, 1954–; founded Luton Industrial Mission and Community Centre, 1954, and Luton Indust. Coll., 1957. Mem., NUAAW. *Publications:* Militant and Triumphant, 1954 (Australia 1957, USA 1959); San Francisco, 1960 (Glide Lecture); Youth in Community, 1967 (King George VI Meml Lecture); Men, Machines and Ministry, 1971 (Beckley Lecture); contrib. to jls; research papers. *Recreations:* gardening, photography. *Address:* Luton Industrial College, Chapel Street, Luton, Beds LU1 2SE. *T:* Luton 29374.

GOWLLAND, (George) Mark, MVO 1979; HM Diplomatic Service; Overseas Inspectorate, Foreign and Commonwealth Office, since 1986; *b* 24 Feb. 1943; *s* of late Mr G. P. Gowlland and Mrs A. M. Gowlland; *m* 1967, Eleanor Julia Le Mesurier; two *s* one *d*. *Educ:* Tonbridge Sch.; Balliol Coll., Oxford. Entered Foreign Service, 1964; served Warsaw, Accra, Lomé, Kuala Lumpur, Dubai, Algiers. *Address:* c/o Foreign and Commonwealth Office, SW1A 2AH.

GOWON, Gen. Yakubu; PhD; jssc, psc; Head of the Federal Military Government and C-in-C of Armed Forces of the Federal Republic of Nigeria 1966–75; *b* Pankshin Div., Benue-Plateau State, Nigeria, 19 Oct. 1934; *s* of Yohanna Gowon (an Angas, a Christian evangelist of CMS) and Saraya Gowon; *m* 1969, Victoria Hansatu Zakari; one *s* two *d*. *Educ:* St Bartholomew's Schs (CMS), Wusasa, and Govt Coll., Zaria, Nigeria; Warwick Univ. (BA Hons 1978; PhD). Regular Officer, Special Trng Sch., Teshie, Ghana; Eaton Hall Officer Cadet Sch., Chester, RMA, Sandhurst, Staff Coll., Camberley and Joint Services Staff Coll., Latimer (all in England). Enlisted, 1954; Adjt, 4th Bn Nigerian Army, 1960 (Independence Oct. 1960); UN Peace-Keeping Forces, Congo, Nov. 1960–June 1961 and Jan.-June 1963 (Bde Major). Lt-Col and Adjt-Gen., Nigerian Army, 1963; Comd, 2nd Bn, Nigerian Army, Ikeja, 1966; Chief of Staff, 1966; Head of State and C-in-C after July 1966 coup; Maj.-Gen. 1967. Maintained territorial integrity of his country by fighting, 1967–70, to preserve unity of Nigeria (after failure of peaceful measures) following on Ojukwu rebellion, and declared secession of the Eastern region of Nigeria, July 1967; created 12 equal and autonomous states in Nigeria, 1967; Biafran surrender, 1970. Promoted Gen., 1971. Chm. Trustees, Commonwealth Human Ecology Council, 1986–. Is a Christian; works for internat. peace and security within the framework of OAU and UNO. Hon. LLD Cambridge, 1975; also hon. doctorates from Univs of Ibadan, Lagos, Abu-Zaria, Nigeria at Nsuka, Benin, Ife, and Shaw Univ., USA, 1973. Holds Grand Cross, etc, of several foreign orders. *Publication:* Faith in Unity, 1970. *Recreations:* squash, lawn tennis, pen-drawing, photography, cinephotography. *Address:* c/o Department of Politics, Warwick University, Coventry CV4 7AL.

GOWRIE, 2nd Earl of, *cr* 1945; **Alexander Patrick Greysteil Hore-Ruthven;** PC 1984; Baron Ruthven of Gowrie, 1919; Baron Gowrie, 1935; Viscount Ruthven of Canberra, 1945; Chairman, Sotheby's, since 1987 (Chairman, Sotheby's International, 1985–86); Provost, Royal College of Art, since 1986; *b* 26 Nov. 1939; *er s* of late Capt. Hon. Alexander Hardinge Patrick Hore-Ruthven, Rifle Bde, and Pamela Margaret (as Viscountess Ruthven of Canberra, she *m* 1952, Major Derek Cooper, MC, The Life Guards), 2nd *d* of late Rev. A. H. Fletcher; *S* grandfather, 1955; *m* 1st, 1962, Xandra (marr. diss. 1973), *yr d* of Col R. A. G. Bingley, CVO, DSO, OBE; one *s*; 2nd, 1974, Adelheid Gräfin von der Schulenburg, *y d* of late Fritz-Dietlof, Graf von der Schulenburg. *Educ:* Eton; Balliol Coll., Oxford. Visiting Lectr, State Univ. of New York at Buffalo, 1963–64; Tutor, Harvard Univ., 1965–68; Lectr in English and American Literature, UCL, 1969–72. Fine Art consultant, 1974–79. Chm., The Really Useful Gp, 1985–. A Conservative Whip, 1971–72; Parly Rep. to UN, 1971; a Lord in Waiting (Govt Whip), 1972–74; Opposition Spokesman on Economic Affairs, 1974–79; Minister of State: Dept of Employment, 1979–81; NI Office, 1981–83 (Dep. to Sec. of State); Privy Council Office (Management and Personnel), 1983–84; Minister for the Arts, 1983–85; Chancellor, Duchy of Lancaster, 1984–85. *Publications:* A Postcard from Don Giovanni, 1972; (jt) The Genius of British Painting, 1975; (jt) The Conservative Opportunity, 1976. *Recreation:* wine. *Heir: s* Viscount Ruthven of Canberra, *qv*. *Address:* House of Lords, SW1.

GOYDER, Daniel George; solicitor; Consultant to Birketts, Ipswich, since 1983 (Partner, 1968–83); *b* 26 Aug. 1938; *s* of George Armin Goyder, *qv*; *m* 1962, Jean Mary Dohoo; two *s* two *d*. *Educ:* Rugby Sch.; Trinity Coll., Cambridge (MA, LLB); Harvard Law Sch. (Harkness Commonwealth Fund Fellow, LLM). Admitted Solicitor, 1962; Asst Solicitor, Messrs Allen & Overy, 1964–67. Pt-time Lectr in Law, Univ. of Essex, 1981–. Chm., St Edmundsbury and Ipswich Diocesan Bd of Finance, 1977–85; Mem., Monopolies and Mergers Commn, 1980–. Leverhulme Trust Res. Grant, for research into EEC competition law, 1986. *Publication:* (with Sir Alan Neale) The Antitrust Laws of the USA, 3rd edn 1981. *Recreations:* choral singing, table tennis, sport. *Address:* Manor House, Old London Road, Capel St Mary, Ipswich, Suffolk IP9 2JU. *T:* Ipswich 310583. *Clubs:* Law Society; Ipswich and Suffolk (Ipswich).

GOYDER, George Armin, CBE 1976; Managing Director, British International Paper Ltd, 1935–71; *b* 22 June 1908; *s* of late William Goyder and Lili Julia Kellersberger, Baden, Switzerland; *m* 1937, Rosemary, 4th *d* of Prof. R. C. Bosanquet, Rock, Northumberland; five *s* three *d*. *Educ:* Mill Hill Sch.; London Sch. of Economics; abroad. Gen. Man., Newsprint Supply Co., 1940–47 (responsible for procurement supply and rationing of newsprint to British Press); The Geographical Magazine, 1935–58. Mem., Gen. Synod of C of E (formerly Church Assembly), 1948–75; Chm., Liberal Party Standing Cttee on Industrial Partnership, 1966. Vice-Pres., Centre for Internat. Briefing, Farnham Castle. Founder Trustee, William Blake Trust; Governor: Mill Hill Sch., 1943–69; Monkton Combe Sch.; Trustee and Hon. Fellow, St Peter's Coll., Oxford; Mem. Council, Wycliffe Hall; Founder Mem. and Sec., British-North American Cttee, 1969. Chm., Suffolk Preservation Soc., 1983–85. *Publications:* The Future of Private Enterprise, 1951, 1954; The Responsible Company, 1961; The People's Church, 1966; The Responsible Worker, 1975. *Recreations:* music, old books, theology. *Address:* Mansel Hall, Long Melford, Sudbury, Suffolk. *Club:* Reform.

See also D. G. Goyder.

GRAAFF, Sir de Villiers, 2nd Bt *cr* 1911; MBE 1946; BA Cape, MA, BCL Oxon; Barrister-at-Law, Inner Temple; Advocate of the Supreme Court of S Africa; MP for Hottentots Holland in Union Parliament 1948–58, for Rondebosch, Cape Town, 1958–77; *b* 8 Dec. 1913; *s* of 1st Bt and Eileen (*d* 1950), *d* of Rev. Dr J. P. Van Heerden, Cape Town; *S* father, 1931; *m* 1939, Helena Le Roux, *d* of F. C. M. Voigt, Provincial Sec. of Cape Province; two *s* one *d*. Served War of 1939–45 (prisoner, MBE). Leader, United Party, S Africa, 1956–77; formerly Leader of Official Opposition. Hon. LLD, Rhodes. Decoration for Meritorious Service (RSA), 1979. *Heir: s* David de Villiers Graaff [*b* 3 May 1940; *m* Sally Williams; three *s* one *d*]. *Address:* De Grendel, Private Bag, GPO, Capetown, South Africa. *Club:* Civil Service (Cape Town).

GRABHAM, Anthony Herbert, FRCS; Chairman of Council, British Medical Association, 1979–84; *b* 19 July 1930; *s* of John and Lily Grabham; *m* 1960, Eileen Pamela Rudd; two *s* two *d*. *Educ:* St Cuthbert's Grammar School, Newcastle upon Tyne. MB, BS Durham. RSO, Royal Victoria Infirmary, Newcastle upon Tyne; Consultant Surgeon, Kettering and District Gen. Hosp., 1965–. Chairman: Central Cttee for Hosp. Med. Services, BMA, 1975–79; Jt Consultants Cttee, 1984–; Member: GMC, 1979–; Council, World Med. Assoc., 1979–84; Hon. Sec. and Treasurer, Commonwealth Med. Assoc., 1982– (Vice-Pres., 1980–84). *Recreations:* collects committees, working parties and European porcelain. *Address:* (home) Rothesay House, 56 Headlands, Kettering, Northants. *T:* Kettering 513299; (business) British Medical Association, Tavistock Square, WC1H 9JP. *T:* 01–387 4499. *Club:* Army and Navy.

GRABINER, Anthony Stephen, QC 1981; *b* 21 March 1945; *e s* of late Ralph Grabiner and of Freda Grabiner (*née* Cohen); *m* 1983, Jane, *er d* of Dr Benjamin Portnoy, TD, JP, MD, PhD, FRCP, Hale, Cheshire; one *s*. *Educ:* Central Foundn Boys' Grammar Sch., London, EC2; LSE, Univ. of London (LLB 1st Cl. Hons 1966, LLM with Distinction 1967). Lincoln's Inn: Hardwicke Scholar, 1966; called to the Bar, 1968; Droop Scholar, 1968. Standing Jun. Counsel to Dept of Trade, Export Credits Guarantee Dept, 1976–81; Jun. Counsel to the Crown, 1978–81. *Publications:* (ed jtly) Sutton and Shannon on Contracts, 7th edn 1970; contrib. to Encyclopedia of Forms and Precedents, 5th edn, 1986. *Recreations:* theatre, swimming, tennis. *Address:* 1 Essex Court, Temple, EC4Y 9AR. *T:* 01–353 5362. *Clubs:* Garrick, MCC.

GRACE, David Mabe; QC 1985; *b* 23 May 1945; *s* of Edwin and Evelyn Grace; *m* 1975, Eileen Marian, 5th *d* of Patrick and Joanna Duffy; one *s* two *d*. *Educ:* Birkenhead Sch.; Exeter Coll., Univ. of Oxford (BA). Called to the Bar, Gray's Inn, 1967. *Address:* 3 Essex Court, Temple, EC4Y 9AL. *T:* 01–583 9294.

GRACE, Sir John (Te Herekiekie), KBE 1968; MVO 1953; AE (RNZAF) 1950; New Zealand High Commissioner in Fiji, 1970–73; sheep and cattle station owner since 1958; *b* 28 July 1905; *s* of John Edward Grace, JP and Rangiamohia Herekiekie; *m* 1st, 1940, Marion Linton McGregor (*d* 1962); no *c*; 2nd, 1968, Dorothy Kirkcaldie. *Educ:* Wanganui Boys' Coll.; Te Aute Coll., Hawkes Bay. Served War of 1939–45, Royal NZ Air Force (Sqdn-Ldr). NZ Public Service, 1926–58: Private Sec. to Ministers of the Crown incl. three Prime Ministers, 1947–58; Member: NZ Historic Places Trust, 1952–68; NZ Geographic Bd, 1952–68; Maori Purposes Fund Bd, 1961–68; Maori Educn Foundn, 1962–68; Nature Conservation Coun., 1963–68; Nat. Coun. of Adult Educn, 1964–68; Lake Taupo Forest Trust, 1968–; Fiji Leper Trust Bd, 1972; Rotoaira Forest Trust, 1974–; Tuwharetoa Trust Bd, 1974–; Lake Taupo Reserves Bd, 1975–; Vice-Pres. and Dominion Councillor, NZ Nat. Party, 1959–67. JP 1947. *Publication:* Tuwharetoa, a History of the Maori People of the Taupo District, NZ. *Recreations:* golf, trout fishing, gardening. *Address:* 84 Parkes Avenue, St Johns Hill, Wanganui, New Zealand. *T:* Wanganui 55.323. *Clubs:* Wellesley (Wellington); Wanganui (Wanganui).

GRACE, Dr Michael Anthony, FRS 1967; Reader in Nuclear Physics, Oxford University, 1972–Oct. 1987; Student and Tutor in Physics, Christ Church, 1959–Oct. 1987; *b* 13 May 1920; *er s* of late Claude Saville Grace, Haslemere, Surrey, and Evelyn Doris (*née* Adams); *m* 1948, Philippa Agnes Lois, *o d* of Sir (Vincent) Zachary Cope, MD, MS,

FRCS; one *s* three *d*. *Educ:* St Paul's; Christ Church, Oxford. MA 1948; DPhil 1950. Mine Design Dept, HMS Vernon, 1940–45. ICI Research Fellowship, Clarendon Laboratory, Oxford, 1951; University Sen. Res. Officer, Dept of Nuclear Physics, 1955–72; Lectr in Physics, Christ Church, 1958, Censor, 1964–69; Dr Lee's Reader in Physics, 1972. Governor: St Paul's Schools, 1959; Harrow School, 1969. *Publications:* papers in various jls including Phil. Mag., Proc. Royal Soc., Proc. Phys. Soc., Nuclear Physics. *Recreations:* lawn tennis, swimming. *Address:* 13 Blandford Avenue, Oxford, *T:* Oxford 58464. *Club:* Athenæum.

GRACEY, Howard, FIA, FIAA, FPMI; consulting actuary; Partner, R. Watson and Sons, since 1970; *b* 21 Feb. 1935; *s* of late Charles Douglas Gracey and of Margaret Gertrude (*née* Heggie); *m* 1960, Pamela Jean Bradshaw; one *s* two *d*. *Educ:* Birkenhead Sch. FIA 1959; FIAA 1982; FPMI 1977; ASA 1978. National Service, 1960–61 (2nd Lieut). Royal Insurance Co., 1953–69. Church Comr, 1978–; Member: Gen. Synod of CofE, 1970–; CofE Pensions Bd, 1970– (Chm., 1980–); Treasurer and Vice Chm., S Amer. Missionary Soc., 1975–; Pres., Pensions Management Inst., 1983–85. *Recreations:* fell-walking, tennis, photography. *Address:* Timbers, 18 Broadwater Rise, Guildford, Surrey GU1 2LA. *Club:* Army and Navy.

GRACEY, John Halliday, CB 1984; Director General (Management), Board of Inland Revenue, 1981–85; Commissioner of Inland Revenue 1973–85; *b* 20 May 1925; *s* of Halliday Gracey and Florence Jane (*née* Cudlipp); *m* 1950, Margaret Procter; three *s*. *Educ:* City of London Sch.; Brasenose Coll., Oxford. Army, 1943–47. Entered Inland Revenue, 1950; HM Treasury, 1970–73. *Address:* 3 Woodberry Down, Epping, Essex. *T:* Epping 72167. *Club:* Reform.
See also T. A. Lloyd Davies.

GRACIE, George H. H.; *see* Heath-Gracie.

GRADE, family name of **Baron Grade.**

GRADE, Baron *cr* 1976 (Life Peer), of Elstree, Herts; **Lew Grade,** Kt 1969; Chairman, The Grade Co., since 1985; Vice-Chairman, Loews, since 1985; *b* 25 Dec. 1906; *s* of late Isaac Winogradsky and Olga Winogradsky; *m* 1942, Kathleen Sheila Moody; one *s*. *Educ:* Rochelle Street Sch. Joint Managing Dir of Lew and Leslie Grade Ltd, until Sept. 1955; Chm. and Man. Dir, ITC Entertainment Ltd, 1958–82; Chm. and Chief Exec., Associated Communications Corp. Ltd, 1973–82; Pres., ATV Network Ltd, 1977–82; Chairman: Bentray Investments Ltd, 1979–82; ACC Enterprises Inc., 1973–82; Stoll Moss Theatres Ltd, 1969–82; Chm. and Chief Exec., Embassy Communications Internat. Ltd, 1982–85. Governor, Royal Shakespeare Theatre. Fellow, BAFTA, 1979. KCSS 1979. *Address:* Embassy House, 3 Audley Square, W1Y 5DR.
See also Baron Delfont.

GRADE, Michael Ian; Director of Programmes, BBC Television, since 1986; *b* 8 March 1943; *s* of Leslie Grade and *g s* of Olga Winogradski; *m* 1967, Penelope Jane (*née* Levinson) (marr. diss. 1981); one *s* one *d*; 2nd, 1982, Hon. Sarah Lawson, *y d* of Baron Burnham, *qv*. *Educ:* St Dunstan's Coll., London. Daily Mirror: Trainee Journalist, 1960; Sports Columnist, 1964–66; Theatrical Agent, Grade Organisation, 1966; joined London Management and Representation, 1969, Jt Man. Dir until 1973; London Weekend Television: Dep. Controller of Programmes (Entertainment), 1973; Dir of Programmes and Mem. Bd, 1977–81; Pres., Embassy Television, 1981–84; Controller, BBC1, 1984–86. Mem. Council, LAMDA, 1981–. *Recreation:* entertainment. *Address:* Wycombe End House, Wycombe End, Beaconsfield, Bucks HP9 1NE. *T:* 01-743 8000.

GRADY, Terence, MBE 1967; HM Diplomatic Service, retired; Ambassador at Libreville, 1980–82; *b* 23 March 1924; *s* of Patrick Grady and Catherine (*née* Fowles); *m* 1960, Jean Fischer; one *s* four *d*. *Educ:* St Michael's Coll., Leeds. HM Forces, 1942–47; Foreign Office, 1949; HM Embassy: Baghdad, 1950; Paris, 1951; Asst Private Secretary to Secretary of State for Foreign Affairs, 1952–55; HM Legation, Budapest, 1955–58; HM Embassy, Kabul, 1958–60; FO, 1960–63; Vice Consul, Elisabethville, 1963; Consul, Philadelphia, 1964–69; UK High Commission, Sydney, 1969–72; FCO, 1972–75; Head of Chancery, Dakar, 1975–77; Consul, Istanbul, 1977–80. *Recreations:* tennis, walking. *Address:* 2 Camberley Road, Norwich NR4 6SJ. *Club:* Royal Commonwealth Society.

GRAEF, Roger Arthur; writer, director and producer of films; *b* NYC, 18 April 1936; *m* 1971, Karen Bergemann (marr. diss. 1983); one *s* one *d*. *Educ:* Horace Mann Sch., NYC; Putney Sch., Vermont; Harvard Univ. (BA Hons). Directed, USA, 26 plays and operas, including: The Mother of Us All; Brother to Dragons; The Gamblers (off-off Broadway Obie Award); The Moon is Blue; Major Barbara; The Prodigal; Intimate Relations; also directed CBS drama, including: Mandy; Seven who were Hanged; Observer/Dir, Actors Studio, NYC, 1958–62; resident in England, 1962–; Director, London: Period of Adjustment; Afternoon Men; has written, produced and directed more than 50 films, usually documentary, for broadcasting cos mainly in England but also in other Eur. countries and N America; *films include:* The Life and Times of John Huston, Esq., 1965; (Exec. Producer) 13-part Who Is series, 1966–67 (wrote/dir. films on Pierre Boulez, Jacques Lipchitz, Walter Gropius, Maurice Béjart); Günter Grass' Berlin, 1965; Why Save Florence?, 1968; In the Name of Allah, 1970; The Space between Words (5 films on communication), 1971–72; State of the Nation: a Law in the Making, 1973, Inside the Brussels HQ, 1975; Is This the Way to Save our Cities?, 1975; Decision series: British Steel, Occidental Petroleum, and Hammersmith Council, 1976–77, British Communism Pts I, II and III, 1978 (Royal Television Soc. Award); (Producer/Dir, for Amnesty Internat.) Pleasure at Her Majesty's, The Mermaid Frolics, The Secret Policeman's Ball, 1977–78; (Producer) Inside Europe, 1977–78 (wrote/dir. Italy: chain reaction); (Exec. Producer/Co-Dir) Police series, 1980–82 (BAFTA, Television Critics, Eur. Television Mag. Awards); (Producer/Co-Dir) Police: Operation Carter, 1981–82. Dept of Environment: Mem., Control Review (Dobry Cttee), Chm., Study Gp on Public Participation in Planning, and Mem., Cttee on Control of Demolition, 1974–76. Member: Council, ICA, 1970–82; Council, BAFTA, 1976–77; Bd, Channel Four, 1980–; Governor, BFI, 1974–78. Adviser on broadcasting to Brandt Commn, 1979–80; Consultant on broadcasting and video to Collins Publishing, 1983–; Consultant to London Transport, 1980– (Mem. Bd, LTE, 1976–79; co designer, new London Bus Map). Founded ICA Archtl Forum and ALLCHANGE, ICA Transport Reform Gp, 1974–76; lectures and broadcasts on planning and communication. *Publications:* contrib. The Listener, Guardian, Sunday Times. *Recreations:* tennis, music, gardening. *Address:* 72 Westbourne Park Villas, W2. *T:* 01-727 7868.

GRÆME, Maj.-Gen. Ian Rollo, CB 1967; OBE 1955; Secretary, National Ski Federation of Great Britain, 1967–78; *b* 23 May 1913; *s* of late Col J. A. Græme, DSO, late RE; *m* 1941, Elizabeth Jean Dyas; two *d*. *Educ:* Boxgrove; Stowe; RMA Woolwich. King's Medal and Benson Memorial Prize, RMA, 1933. 2nd Lt RA 1933; pre-war service at regimental duty UK; War Service in Singapore, Java, India, Burma, Siam; psc 1942; Instructor Staff Coll., Quetta, 1944; CO 1st Burma Field Regt, 1945–46; OC, K Battery, RHA, 1949; jssc 1952; GSO1, HQ Northern Army Group, 1953–54; CO 27 Regt RA, 1955–57; Col GS Staff Coll., Camberley, 1957–59; idc 1960; Dep. Mil. Sec., WO, 1961–63; Dep. Dir Personnel Admin, WO, 1963–64; Dir Army Recruiting, 1964–67; Retd 1967. Mem. Royal Yachting Assoc., 1950–; Life Governor, Royal Life Saving Soc., 1956–; Life Mem., British Olympic Assoc., 1958–; Chm., Army Holiday Cttee for ski-ing, 1963–67; Council, Army Ski Assoc., 1958–; Member: Council, Nat. Ski Fedn of GB, 1964–67 (Life Mem. Fedn); Cttee, Sports Aid Foundn, 1976– (Governor, 1982); Trustee, Sports Aid Trust, 1983–; Vice-President: English Ski Council, 1979–82; British Ski Fedn, 1981–84. Chm., Hampshire Sch. Trust, 1980–. FBIM; MInstD. Gold Medal, Austrian Govt, 1972. *Recreations:* ski-ing, sailing, mountains. *Clubs:* Army and Navy, English-Speaking Union (Life Mem.); Ski Club of Great Britain, Army Ski Association, Alpbach Visitors Ski, Garvock Ski (Pres. 1969–), Kandahar Ski; Royal Artillery Yacht.

GRAESSER, Col Sir Alastair Stewart Durward, Kt 1973; DSO 1945; OBE 1963; MC 1944; TD; DL; President: National Union of Conservative and Unionist Associations, 1984–85 (Chairman, 1974–76; Hon. Vice President, 1976); Wales and Monmouth Conservative and Unionist Council, 1972–77; *b* 17 Nov. 1915; *s* of Norman Hugo Graesser and Annette Stewart Durward; *m* 1939, Diana Aline Elms Neale; one *s* three *d*. *Educ:* Oundle; Gonville and Caius Coll., Cambridge. Director: Municipal Life Assurance Ltd; Municipal General Assurance Ltd; Managing Trustee, Municipal Mutual Insurance Ltd; Trustee, TSB of Wales and Border Counties, 1970–86; Mem., CBI Regional Council for Wales (Past Chm.). Pres., Wales and Monmouth Conservative Clubs Council, 1972–76. Vice-Chm., Wales and Monmouth TA&VR Assoc.; Hon. Col, 3rd Bn Royal Welch Fusiliers (TA), 1972–80. High Sheriff of Flintshire, 1962; DL 1960, JP 1956–78, Vice Lord-Lieut, 1980–83, Clwyd (formerly Flints). CStJ 1980. *Recreation:* shooting. *Address:* Sweet Briar, Berghill Lane, Babbinswood, Whittington, Oswestry, Salop SY11 4PF. *T:* Oswestry 662395. *Clubs:* Naval and Military; Hawks (Cambridge); Leander (Henley-on-Thames); Grosvenor (Chester).

GRAFFTEY-SMITH, Sir Laurence Barton, KCMG 1951 (CMG 1944); KBE 1947 (OBE 1932); *b* 16 April 1892; *s* of late Rev. Arthur Grafftey-Smith and late Mabel, *d* of Rev. Charles Barton, Cheselbourne, Dorset; *m* 1930, Vivien (marr. diss., 1937), *d* of G. Alexander Alderson; two *s*; *m* 1946, Evgenia Owen, *d* of late P. H. Coolidge, Berkeley, Calif. *Educ:* Repton; Pembroke Coll., Cambridge. Student Interpreter, Levant Consular Service, 1914. HM Vice Consul, 1920; served at Alexandria, Cairo (Residency), Jeddah, Constantinople; Asst Oriental Sec. at the Residency, Cairo, 1925–35; HM Consul, Mosul, 1935–37; Baghdad, 1937–39; HM Consul-Gen. in Albania, 1939–40; attached British Embassy, Cairo, 1940; Chief Political Adviser, Diego Suarez, May 1942; Chief Political Officer, Madagascar, July 1942; Consul-Gen., Antananarivo, 1943; Minister to Saudi Arabia, 1945–47; High Comr for UK in Pakistan, 1947–51; retired from Govt service on 31 Dec. 1951; UK Rep. on Gov.-Gen.'s Commn, Khartoum, 1953–56. *Publications:* (with Godfrey Haggard) Visa Verses, 1915 (privately printed); Bright Levant, 1970; Hands to Play, 1975. *Address:* Broom Hill House, Coddenham, Suffolk.

GRAFTON, 11th Duke of, *cr* 1675; **Hugh Denis Charles FitzRoy;** KG 1976; DL; Earl of Euston, Viscount Ipswich; Captain Grenadier Guards; *b* 3 April 1919; *e s* of 10th Duke of Grafton, and Lady Doreen Maria Josepha Sydney Buxton (*d* 1923), *d* of 1st Earl Buxton; *S* father, 1970; *m* 1946, Fortune (*see* Duchess of Grafton); two *s* three *d*. *Educ:* Eton; Magdalene Coll., Cambridge. ADC to the Viceroy of India, 1943–46. Member: Historic Buildings Council for England, 1953–84; Historic Bldgs Adv. Cttee, 1984–; Chairman: Soc. for the Protection of Ancient Buildings; Jt Cttee, Soc. for Protection of Ancient Buildings, Georgian Gp, Victorian Soc., and Civic Trust; Architectural Heritage Fund; Mem., National Trust Properties Cttee; Nat. Pres., Council of British Soc. of Master Glass Painters; Pres., International Students Trust. Chm., Cathedrals Advisory Commn for England, 1981–; Chm. of Trustees, Historic Churches Preservation Trust; Mem., Royal Fine Art Commn, 1971–; Chm. Trustees, Sir John Soane's Museum; Vice-Chm. Trustees, Nat. Portrait Gallery; Patron, Hereford Herd Book Soc. Hon. Air Cdre, No 2623 RAuxAF Regt Sqdn, 1982–. DL Suffolk, 1973. *Heir: s* Earl of Euston, *qv*. *Address:* Euston Hall, Thetford, Norfolk IP24 2QW. *T:* Thetford 3282. *Club:* Boodle's.

GRAFTON, Duchess of; (Ann) Fortune FitzRoy, GCVO 1980 (DCVO 1970; CVO 1965); JP; Mistress of The Robes to The Queen since 1967; *o d* of Captain Eric Smith, MC, LLD, Lower Ashfold, Slaugham; *m* 1946, Duke of Grafton, *qv*; two *s* three *d*. Lady of the Bedchamber to the Queen, 1953–66. SRCN Great Ormond Street, 1945; Mem. Bd of Governors, The Hospital for Sick Children, Great Ormond Street, 1952–66. President: W Suffolk Mission to the Deaf; W Suffolk Decorative and Fine Arts Soc.; Vice-Pres., Suffolk Br., Royal British Legion Women's Section. Governor: Felixstowe Coll.; Riddlesworth Hall. JP County of London, 1949, W Suffolk, 1972. *Address:* Euston Hall, Thetford, Norfolk. *T:* Thetford 3282.

GRAFTON, NSW, Bishop of, since 1985; **Rt. Rev. Bruce Allan Schultz;** *b* 24 May 1932; *s* of Percival Ferdinand and Elsie Amelia Schultz; *m* 1962, Janet Margaret Gersbach; two *s* two *d* (and one *s* decd). *Educ:* Culcairn High School; St Columb's Hall and St John's Coll., Morpeth. ThL (ACT) 1960. Sheep and wheat property, Manager–Owner, 1950–57. Theolog. student, 1957–60; deacon 1959, priest 1960, dio. Riverina; Asst Priest, Broken Hill, 1961–63; Priest-in-charge, Ariah Park with Ardlethan and Barellan with Weethalle, 1964–67; Rector: Deniliquin, 1967–73; Gladstone, dio. Rockhampton, 1973–79; Archdeacon and Commissary of Rockhampton, 1975–79; Rector of Grafton and Dean of Christ Church Cathedral, 1979–83; Asst Bishop of Brisbane (Bishop for the Northern Region), 1983–85. *Recreations:* family, fishing, tennis, water skiing, gardening. *Address:* Bishopsholme, 35 Victoria Street, Grafton, NSW 2460, Australia. *T:* (home) (066) 42 2070, (office) (066) 42 4122. *Club:* Grafton (Grafton).

GRAFTON, Col Martin John, CBE 1976 (OBE 1964, MBE 1944); TD 1958; DL; Director-General, National Federation of Building Trades Employers, 1964–79, retired; *b* 28 June 1919; *o s* of Vincent Charles Grafton and Maud (*née* Brazier); *m* 1948, Jean Margaret, *d* of James Drummond-Smith, OBE, MA, and Edith M. Drummond-Smith, MBE, MA; two *d*. *Educ:* Bromsgrove Sch. FFB 1968–80. Served War, RE, 1940–46: Captain 1943; Normandy and NW Europe, 1944–46 (MBE 1944, Rhine Crossing); served TA RE, 1947–66 (TD 1958, Bar 1963): Major 1954, Lt-Col 1960, Col 1964; comd 101 Fd Engr Regt, 1960 64; Dep. Chief Engr, E Anglian Dist, 1964–66. Joined John Lewis Partnership, 1948: Gen. Man., Peter Jones, Sloane Square, 1951–52; Dir of Bldg, 1954–60; a Man. Dir, 1960–63. Dir, Alfred Booth & Co. Ltd, 1979–80. Member: Council, CBI, 1964–79; EDC for Building, 1964–75; Nat. Consult. Council for Building and Civil Engrg, 1964–79. Hon. FCIOB 1978; Mem., Co. of Builders, 1977–80. DL Greater London, 1967–83; Freeman, City of London, 1978. *Recreations:* travel, reading, music. *Address:* Urchfont House, Urchfont, Devizes, Wiltshire SN10 4RP. *T:* Chirton 404. *Club:* Army and Navy.

GRAFTON, Peter Witheridge, CBE 1972; Senior Partner, G. D. Walford & Partners, Chartered Quantity Surveyors, 1978–82 (Partner 1949–78); *b* 19 May 1916; *s* of James Hawkins Grafton and Ethel Marion (*née* Brannan); *m* 1st, 1939, Joan Bleackley (*d* 1969); two *d* (and one *s* one *d* decd); 2nd, 1971, Margaret Ruth Ward; two *s*. *Educ:* Westminster City Sch.; Sutton Valence Sch.; Coll. of Estate Management. FRICS, FCIArb. Served War of 1939–45, Queen's Westminster Rifles, Dorsetshire Regt and RE, UK and Far East

(Captain). Pres., RICS, 1978–79 (Vice-Pres., 1974–78); Mem. and Past Chm., Quantity Surveyors Council; Mem. Council, Construction Industries Research and Information Assoc., 1963–69; Member: Research Adv. Council to Minister of Housing and Construction, 1967–71; Nat. Cons. Council for Building and Civil Engrg Industries, 1968–76; British Bd of Agrément, 1973–; Chm., Nat. Jt Consultative Cttee for Building Industry, 1970–77. Master, Worshipful Co. of Chartered Surveyors, 1983–84. Trustee, United Westminster Schs; Chm. of Governors, Sutton Valence Sch.; Past Chm., Old Suttonians Assoc. Contested (L) Bromley, 1959. *Publications:* numerous articles on techn. and other professional subjects. *Recreations:* golf (founder and Chm., Public Schs Old Boys Golf Assoc., Co-donor Grafton Morrish Trophy); past Captain of Chartered Surveyors Golfing Soc.); writing. *Address:* Corner Cottage, 10 Stanhopes, Limpsfield, Oxted, Surrey RH8 0TY. *T:* Oxted 6685. *Clubs:* Reform; Rye Golf, W Sussex Golf, Tandridge Golf.

GRAHAM, family name of **Duke of Montrose** and **Baron Graham of Edmonton.**

GRAHAM, Marquis of; James Graham; *b* 6 April 1935; *s* of 7th Duke of Montrose, *qv*; *m* 1970, Catherine Elizabeth MacDonell, *d* of late Captain N. A. T. Young, and of Mrs Young, Ottawa; two *s* one *d*. *Educ:* Loretto. Brig. Royal Company of Archers (Queen's Body Guard for Scotland), 1986 (Mem., 1965–). Area Pres., Scottish NFU, 1986 (Mem. Council, 1982–86). OStJ 1978. *Heir:* *s* Lord Fintrie, *qv*. *Address:* Auchmar, Drymen, Glasgow. *T:* 221.

GRAHAM OF EDMONTON, Baron *cr* 1983 (Life Peer), of Edmonton in Greater London; **Thomas Edward Graham;** *b* 26 March 1925; *m* 1950; two *s*. *Educ:* elementary sch.; WEA Co-operative College. BA Open Univ., 1976. FBIM. Newcastle-on-Tyne Co-operative Soc., 1939–52; Organiser, British Fedn of Young Co-operators, 1952–53; Educn Sec., Enfield Highway Co-operative Soc., 1953–62; Sec., Co-operative Union Southern Section, 1962–67; Nat. Sec., Co-operative Party, 1967–74. MP (Lab and Co-op) Enfield, Edmonton, Feb. 1974–1983; PPS to Minister of State, Dept of Prices and Consumer Protection, 1974–76; A Lord Comr of HM Treasury, 1976–79; Opposition spokesman on the environment, 1980–83. Contested (Lab) Edmonton, 1983. Mem. and Leader, Enfield Council, 1961–68. *Address:* 17a Queen Annes Grove, Bush Hill Park, Enfield, Mddx EN1 2JR.

GRAHAM, Prof. Alastair, DSc, FRS 1979; Professor of Zoology, University of Reading, to 1972, now Emeritus Professor; *b* 6 Nov. 1906. *Educ:* Edinburgh Univ. (MA, BSc); London Univ. (DSc). Fellow, Zoological Soc., 1939 (Frink Medal, 1976). *Publications:* British Prosobranch Molluscs (jtly), 1962; Other Operculate Gastropod Molluscs, 1971. *Address:* 6 Belle Avenue, Reading, Berks. *T:* Reading 62276.

GRAHAM, Alastair Carew; FRSA; Head Master, Mill Hill School, since 1979; *b* 23 July 1932; *s* of Col J. A. Graham and Mrs Graham (*née* Carew-Hunt); *m* 1969, Penelope Rachel Beaumont; two *d*. *Educ:* Winchester Coll.; Gonville and Caius Coll., Cambridge (1st Cl. Mod. and Med. Langs). Served 1st Bn Argyll and Sutherland Highlanders, 1951–53. Foy, Morgan & Co. (City), 1956–58; Asst Master, Eton, 1958; House Master, 1970–79. *Recreations:* ball games, walking; theatre and opera; music listening, gardening, boys' club. *Address:* The Grove, Mill Hill, NW7. *T:* 01–959 1006. *Clubs:* Athenæum; Hawks (Cambridge).

See also Maj.-Gen. J. D. C. Graham.

GRAHAM, Alexander Michael, JP; FCII, FBIBA; Managing Director, Frizzell Group Ltd, since 1973; Sheriff of City of London, 1986–87; *b* 27 Sept. 1938; *s* of Dr Walter Graham and Suzanne Graham (*née* Simon); *m* 1964, Carolyn, *d* of Lt-Col Alan Wolryche Stansfeld, MBE; three *d*. *Educ:* Fyvie Village Sch.; Hall Sch., Hampstead; St Paul's Sch. MBIM. Joined Norman Frizzell & Partners Ltd, 1957; Underwriting Member of Lloyd's. National Service, 1957–59; commnd Gordon Highlanders; TA 1959–67. Mercers' Co.: Liveryman, 1971–; Mem., Ct of Assistants, 1980; Master, 1983–84; Mem., Ct of Common Council, City of London, 1978; Alderman for Ward of Queenhithe, 1979–; Pres., Queenhithe Ward Club, 1979–. Governor: Hall Sch., Hampstead, 1975–; St Paul's Sch., 1980–; St Paul's Girls' Sch., 1980–; City of London Boys' Sch., 1983–85; Mem. Council, Gresham Coll., 1983–. FRSA. JP City of London, 1979–. *Recreations:* wine, genealogy, music, reading, silver, bridge, golf, swimming, tennis, shooting. *Address:* Walden Abbotts, Whitwell, Hitchin, Herts SG4 8AJ. *T:* Whitwell (Herts) 223. *Clubs:* Carlton, City Livery; Highland Brigade.

GRAHAM, Alistair; *see* Graham, J. A.

GRAHAM, Rt. Rev. Andrew Alexander Kenny; *see* Newcastle, Bishop of.

GRAHAM, Andrew Winston Mawdsley; Fellow, and Tutor in Economics, Balliol College, Oxford, since 1969; *b* 20 June 1942; *s* of Winston Mawdsley Graham, *qv*; *m* 1970, Peggotty Fawssett. *Educ:* Charterhouse; St Edmund Hall, Oxford. MA (PPE). Economic Assistant: NEDO, 1964; Dept of Economic Affairs, 1964–66; Asst to Economic Adviser to the Cabinet, 1966–68; Economic Adviser to Prime Minister, 1968–69; Policy Adviser to Prime Minister (on leave of absence from Balliol), 1974–75. Tutor, Oxford Univ. Business Summer Sch., 1971, 1972, 1973 and 1976. Estates Bursar, Balliol Coll., 1978, Investment Bursar, 1979–83. Vis. Researcher, SE Asian Central Banks Res. and Trng Centre, Malaysia, 1984; Vis. Fellow, Griffith Univ., Brisbane, 1984. Member: Wilson Cttee to Review the Functioning of Financial Institutions, 1977–80; Economics Cttee, SSRC, 1978–80; British Transport Docks Bd, 1979–82; Chm., St James Gp (Economic Forecasting), 1982–84, 1985–. Mem., ILO/Jobs and Skills Prog. for Africa (JASPA) Mission to Ethiopia, 1982; Hd, Queen Elizabeth House/Food Studies Gp team assisting Govt of Republic of Zambia, 1984. Founder Mem. Editorial Bd, Library of Political Economy, 1982–. *Publications:* contribs to books on economics and philosophy. *Recreation:* sail-boarding on every possible occasion. *Address:* Balliol College, Oxford OX1 3BJ. *T:* Oxford 249601.

GRAHAM, Prof. Angus Charles, FBA 1981; Professor of Classical Chinese, School of Oriental and African Studies (SOAS), London University, 1971–84, retired; *b* 8 July 1919; *s* of Charles Harold and Mabelle Graham; *m* 1955, Der Pao (*née* Chang); one *d*. *Educ:* Ellesmere Coll., Salop; Corpus Christi Coll., Oxford (MA Theol.); SOAS, London (BA, PhD Chinese). Lectr in Chinese, SOAS, 1950–71. *Publications:* Two Chinese Philosophers: Ch'eng Ming-tao and Ch'eng Yi-ch'uan, 1958; The Book of Lieh Tzŭ, 1960; The Problem of Value, 1961; Poems of the Late T'ang, 1965; Later Mohist Logic, Ethics and Science, 1978; Chuang-tzŭ: the Seven Inner Chapters and other writings from the book Chuang-tzŭ, 1981; Reason and Spontaneity, 1985. *Address:* 33 Barham Avenue, Elstree, Herts. *T:* 01–207 1558.

GRAHAM, Mrs Anne Silvia; formerly Deputy Solicitor, Department of the Environment; *b* 1 Aug. 1934; *o d* of late Benjamin Arthur Garcia and Constance Rosa (*née* Journeaux); *m* Peter Graham, *qv*. *Educ:* Francis Holland Sch., SW1; LSE (LLB). Called to the Bar, Inner Temple, 1958; Yarborough-Anderson Scholar, 1959. Joined Min. of Housing and Local Govt, 1960. *Recreations:* gardening, cookery. *Address:* Stony Dale, Field Broughton, Grange over Sands, Cumbria LA11 6HN.

GRAHAM, Antony Richard Malise; management consultant; Director, Clive & Stokes International, since 1985; *b* 15 Oct. 1928; *s* of late Col Patrick Ludovic Graham, MC, and late Barbara Mary Graham (*née* Jury); *m* 1958, Gillian Margaret, *d* of late L. Bradford Cook and of Mrs W. V. Wrigley; two *s* one *d*. *Educ:* Abberley Hall; Nautical Coll., Pangbourne. Merchant Navy, 1945–55 (Master Mariner). Stewarts and Lloyds Ltd, 1955–60; PE Consulting Group Ltd, management consultants, 1960–72 (Regional Dir, 1970–72); Regional Industrial Dir (Under-Sec.), DTI, 1972–76; Dir, Barrow Hepburn Group Ltd, and Maroquinerie Le Tanneur et Tanneries du Bugey SA, 1976–81; Chm., Paton & Sons (Tillicoultry) Ltd, 1981–82. Contested (C) Leeds East, 1966. *Address:* 17 Waldemar Avenue, SW6 5LB. *T:* 01–731 3896.

GRAHAM, Billy; *see* Graham, William F.

GRAHAM, Sir Charles (Spencer Richard), 6th Bt *cr* 1783; Lord-Lieutenant of Cumbria, since 1983; *b* 16 July 1919; *s* of Sir (Frederick) Fergus Graham, 5th Bt, KBE, and of Mary Spencer Revell, CBE (*d* 1985), *d* of late Maj.-Gen. Raymond Reade, CB, CMG; *S* father, 1978; *m* 1944, Isabel Susan Anne, *d* of late Major R. L. Surtees, OBE; two *s* one *d*. *Educ:* Eton. Served with Scots Guards, 1940–50, NW Europe (despatches) and Malaya. President, Country Landowners' Assoc., 1971–73. Mem., Nat. Water Council, 1973–83. Master, Worshipful Co. of Farmers, 1982–83. High Sheriff 1955, DL 1971, Cumbria (formerly Cumberland). KStJ 1983. *Heir:* *s* James Fergus Surtees Graham [*b* 29 July 1946; *m* 1975, Serena Jane, *yr d* of Ronald Frank Kershaw; one *s* two *d*]. *Address:* Crofthead, Longtown, Cumbria CA6 5PA. *T:* Longtown 791231. *Clubs:* Brooks's, Pratt's.

GRAHAM, Dr Christopher Forbes, FRS 1981; Professor of Animal Development, and Professorial Fellow, St Catherine's College, University of Oxford, since 1985; *b* 23 Sept. 1940. *Educ:* Oxford Univ. (BA 1963, DPhil 1966). Formerly Junior Beit Memorial Fellow in Med. Research, Sir William Dunn Sch. of Pathology. Lectr, Zoology Dept, Oxford Univ., 1970–85. Member: Brit. Soc. Cell Biology; Brit. Soc. for Developmental Biology; Soc. for Experimental Biology; Genetical Soc. *Publication:* The Developmental Biology of Plants and Animals, 1976. *Address:* Department of Zoology, University of Oxford, South Parks Road, Oxford OX1 3PS.

GRAHAM, Clifford; Under Secretary, Department of Health and Social Security, since 1983; *b* 3 April 1937; *s* of late James Mackenzie and Monica Graham; *m* 1960, Audrey Edith Stubbington; two *s* one *d*. *Educ:* Alsop High Sch., Liverpool; London Univ. (LLB). Called to the Bar, Gray's Inn, 1969. Nat. Service, RAF, Aden, 1955–57. With Admiralty, 1954–59; Exec. Officer, Customs and Excise, 1959–65; Higher Exec. Officer, Min. of Health, 1965–68; Principal, 1969–74, Asst Sec., 1975–82, DHSS. *Publications:* contrib. to Oxford Textbook of Public Health, 1984; articles in journals and DHSS reports. *Recreations:* cycling, walking, reading, music. *Address:* 77 Westcombe Park Road, Blackheath, SE3. *T:* 01–858 0467. *Club:* Gray's Inn.

GRAHAM, Colin; Artistic Director: English Music Theatre, since 1975; Aldeburgh Festival, since 1969; Opera Theatre of St Louis, since 1984 (Associate Artistic Director, 1979–84); Director of Productions, English National Opera, 1977–82, Associate Artist, since 1982; stage director, designer, lighting designer, and author; *b* 22 Sept. 1931; *s* of Frederick Eaton Graham-Bonnalie and Alexandra Diana Vivian Findlay. *Educ:* Northaw Prep. Sch.; Stowe Sch.; RADA (Dip.). Dir of Productions, English Opera Gp, 1963–74; Associate Dir of Prodns, Sadler's Wells Opera/English National Opera, 1967–75. Principal productions for: English Music Theatre; Royal Opera, Covent Garden; Scottish Opera; New Opera Co.; Glyndebourne Opera; BBC TV; Brussels National Opera; St Louis Opera Theatre; Santa Fe Opera; Metropolitan Opera, New York; NYC Opera; dir. world premières: of all Benjamin Britten's operas since 1954; of other contemp. composers. Theatre productions for: Old Vic Co.; Bristol Old Vic; Royal Shakespeare Co. Hon. DA Webster Univ., 1985. Orpheus award (Germany) for best opera production, 1973 (War and Peace, ENO). *Publications:* A Penny for a Song (libretto for Richard Rodney Bennett), 1969; The Golden Vanity (libretto for opera by Britten), 1970; King Arthur (libretto for new version of Purcell opera), 1971; The Postman Always Rings Twice (libretto for opera by Stephen Paulus), 1981; Jōruri (libretto for opera by Minoru Miki), 1985; The Woodlanders (libretto for opera by Stephen Paulus), 1984; production scores for Britten's: Curlew River, 1969; The Burning Fiery Furnace, 1971; The Prodigal Son, 1973; contrib. Opera. *Recreations:* motor cycles, movies, weight lifting. *Address:* PO Box 13148, Saint Louis, Mo 63119, USA.

GRAHAM, David; *see* Graham, S. D.

GRAHAM, David Alec, CBE 1983; FCA, FCIT; Director General, Greater Manchester Passenger Transport Executive, since 1976; *b* 18 Jan. 1930; *s* of John Leonard Graham and May Susan (*née* Wymark); *m* 1956, Valerie Monica Dartnall. *Educ:* Sutton High Sch. FCA 1953; FCIT 1970; CIPFA. Accountant/Finance Dir, Threlfalls Chesters Ltd, 1959–69; Dir of Finance and Admin, Greater Manchester Passenger Transp. Exec., 1969–76. *Recreations:* sailing, gardening. *Address:* The Spinney, Rowanside, Castleford Park, Prestbury, Cheshire. *T:* Prestbury 829963.

GRAHAM, Douglas; *see* Graham, M. G. D.

GRAHAM, Rev. Douglas Leslie, MA (Dublin); retired; *b* 4 Oct. 1909; *s* of late Very Rev. G. F. Graham; *m* 1935, Gladys Winifred Ann, *y d* of J. W. Brittain, JP, Kilronan, Donnybrook, Co. Dublin; three *s*. *Educ:* Portora Royal Sch.; Dublin Univ. (BA); Munich Univ. Lectr in Classics, Dublin Univ., 1932–34; MA and Madden Prizeman, 1934; Asst Master, Eton Coll., 1934–41. Ordained, 1937. Served War as Temp. Chaplain, RNVR, 1941–45; HMS Trinidad, 1941; HMS King Alfred, 1942; HMS Daedalus, 1944; HMS Ferret, 1944; Headmaster, Portora Royal School, 1945–53; Headmaster, Dean Close Sch., 1954–68; Asst Master and Chaplain, Williston Acad., Easthampton, Mass, USA, 1968–72. Select Preacher to the Univs of Dublin, 1945, 1961 and 1965, and Oxford, 1956–57. FRSA. *Publications:* Bacchanalia (trans. from Greek Anthology), 1970; occasional articles on classical subjects. *Recreations:* books, birds and boxing. *Address:* Forest Cottage, West Woods, Lockeridge, near Marlborough, Wilts SN8 4EG. *T:* Lockeridge 432.

GRAHAM, Euan Douglas, CB 1985; Principal Clerk of Private Bills, House of Lords, 1961–84; *b* 29 July 1924; *yr s* of Brig. Lord D. M. Graham, CB, DSO, MC; RA. *Educ:* Eton; Christ Church, Oxford (MA). Served RAF, 1943–47. Joined Parliament Office, House of Lords, 1950; Clerk, Judicial Office, 1950–60; Principal Clerk of Private Bills, Examiner of Petitions for Private Bills, Taxing Officer, 1961–84. *Address:* 122 Beaufort Mansions, Beaufort Street, SW3. *Clubs:* Brooks's, Beefsteak, Pratt's.

GRAHAM, Maj.-Gen. Frederick Clarence Campbell, CB 1960; DSO 1945; Lord-Lieutenant of Stirling and Falkirk (Central Region), 1979–83; *b* Ardencaple Castle, Helensburgh, Scotland, 14 Dec. 1908; *s* of Sir Frederick Graham, 2nd Bt, and Lady Irene Graham (*née* Campbell); *m* 1936, Phyllis Mary, *d* of late Maj.-Gen. H. F. E. MacMahon, CB, CSI, CBE, MC; three *s*. *Educ:* Eton Coll.; RMC Sandhurst. Commissioned Argyll and Sutherland Highlanders, 1929; served 1st and 2nd Bn Argyll and Sutherland Highlanders in China, India, UK and Palestine, 1929–39; Adjutant 1st Bn, 1937; War of 1939–45, served Palestine, N Africa, Crete, Syria, India, Italy; commanded 1st Bn Argyll and Sutherland Highlanders, 1944–end of war in Europe. Since 1945: GSO1, Home Counties District and Home Counties Div.; Joint Services Staff Coll.; Staff Coll., Camberley (Col); Comdr 61 Lorried Infantry Brigade (Brig.); Asst Commandant, RMA Sandhurst; Dep. Comdr, Land Forces, Hong Kong and Comd (Brig.) 40 Inf. Div.; Adviser in recruiting, MoD; Comdr Highland District and 51st (Highland) Div., TA, 1959–62; retd from HM Forces, 1962. Col, The Argyll and Sutherland Highlanders, 1958–72. Col Comdt, The Scottish Div., 1968–69; Hon. Col, Argyll and Sutherland Highlanders of Canada, 1972–77. Mem. of Royal Company of Archers, The Queen's Body Guard for Scotland, 1958–. Member: Perth CC, 1973–75; Stirling DC, 1976–80 (Vice-Chm., 1977–80). DL Perthshire, 1966. *Address:* Mackeanston House, Doune, Perthshire.

GRAHAM, George Boughen, QC 1964; *b* 17 July 1920; *s* of Sydney Boughen and Hannah Graham, Keswick, Cumberland; *m* Mavis, *o d* of late Frederick Worthington, Blackpool. *Educ:* Keswick Sch. Royal Signals, 1940–46. Barrister, Lincoln's Inn, 1950, Bencher, 1972. Chancellor, Diocese of Wakefield, 1959, Dio. of Sheffield, 1971. Member of Lloyd's, 1968. Comdr, Order of Merit (W Germany); Order of Aztec Eagle (Mexico). *Publications:* Covenants, Settlements and Taxation, 1953; Estate Duty Handbook, 1954. *Recreations:* walking and dining. *Address:* Brocklehurst, Keswick, Cumbria. *T:* Keswick 72042. *Clubs:* Athenæum; Derwent (Keswick).

GRAHAM, George Ronald Gibson, CBE 1986; Partner, Maclay, Murray & Spens, Solicitors, Glasgow and Edinburgh, since 1968; Director, Scottish Widows' Fund and Life Assurance Society, since 1984; President, Law Society of Scotland, 1984–85, Member of Council, since 1977; *b* 15 Oct. 1939; *o s* of James Gibson Graham, MD, and Elizabeth Waddell; *m* 1965, Mirren Elizabeth Carnegie; three *s*. *Educ:* Glasgow Academy; Loretto Sch., Musselburgh; Oriel Coll., Oxford (MA); Glasgow Univ. (LLB). Co-ordinator of Diploma in Legal Practice, Glasgow Univ., 1979–83. *Recreations:* fishing, swimming, walking. *Address:* 44 Kingsborough Gardens, Glasgow G12 9NL. *T:* 041–334 2730. *Clubs:* The Western, Western Baths (Glasgow).

GRAHAM, Gerald Sandford, MA, PhD, FRHistS; Rhodes Professor of Imperial History, London University, 1949–70, now Emeritus; *b* Sudbury, Ontario, 27 April 1903; *s* of Rev. H. S. Graham and Florence Marian Chambers; *m* 1929, Winifred Emily Ware (marr. diss. 1950); one *s*; *m* 1950, Constance Mary Greey, Toronto; one *s* two *d*. *Educ:* Queen's Univ., Canada; Harvard, 1926–27; Cambridge, 1927–29; Berlin and Freiburg-im-Breisgau, 1929–30; Instructor in History, and Tutor, Harvard Univ., 1930–36; successively Asst, Associate, and Prof. of History, Queen's Univ., 1936–46; Guggenheim Fellowship to US, 1941; RCNVR, 1942–45; Reader in History, Birkbeck Coll., Univ. of London, 1946–48. Mem., Inst. for Advanced Study, Princeton, 1952. Kemper Knapp Vis. Prof., Univ. of Wisconsin, 1961, Univ. of Hong Kong, 1966; Vis. Prof. of Strategic Studies, Univ. of Western Ontario, 1970–72; Vis. Montague Burton Prof. of Internat. Relations, Univ. of Edinburgh, 1974. FKC 1981. Hon. DLitt Univ. of Waterloo, Ont, 1973; Hon. LLD Queen's Univ., Ont, 1976.; Hon. LitD Western Ontario, 1986. *Publications:* British Policy and Canada, 1774–1791, 1930; Sea Power and British North America, 1783–1820, 1941; Empire of the North Atlantic, 1950 (2nd edn 1958); Canada, A Short History, 1950; The Walker Expedition to Quebec, 1711 (Navy Records Soc., and Champlain Soc.), 1953; The Politics of Naval Supremacy, 1965; (with R. A. Humphreys) The Navy and South America, 1807–1823 (Navy Records Soc.), 1962; Britain in the Indian Ocean, 1810–1850, 1967; A Concise History of Canada, 1968; A Concise History of the British Empire, 1970; Tides of Empire, 1972; The Royal Navy in the American War of Independence, 1976; The China Station: War and Diplomacy 1830–60, 1978; contributor to: Newfoundland, Economic, Diplomatic and Strategic Studies, 1946; Cambridge History of the British Empire, vol. III, 1959; Regionalism in the Canadian Community 1867–1967, ed Mason Wade, 1969. *Recreation:* sawing wood. *Address:* Hobbs Cottage, Beckley, Rye, Sussex. *T:* Beckley 308. *Clubs:* Athenæum, Royal Commonwealth Society.

GRAHAM, Gordon; *see* Graham, W. G.

GRAHAM, Gordon, CBE 1980; PPRIBA; Director, Foster Associates Ltd, since 1984; *b* Carlisle, 4 June 1920; *s* of late Stanley Bouch Graham and Isabel Hetherington; *m* 1946, Enid Pennington; three *d*. *Educ:* Creighton Sch.; Nottingham Sch. of Architecture. DipArch, RIBA, 1949; RIBA Arthur Cates Prizeman, 1949; travelling schol., S and Central America, 1953. Served Royal Artillery, N Africa, Italy and NW Europe, 1940–46. Sen. Lectr, Nottingham Sch. of Architecture, 1949–61; Sen. Partner, Architects Design Gp, 1958–84. Pres., Nottingham, Derby and Lincoln Soc. of Architects, 1965–66; RIBA: Chm., E Midlands Region, 1967–69; Mem. Council, 1967–73 and 1974; Vice-Pres., 1969–71; Hon. Sec., 1971–72 and 1975–76; Sen. Vice-Pres., 1976; Pres., 1977–79. Mem., Building EDC, 1978–83. Hon. FRAIC 1978. Hon. MA Nottingham, 1979. *Recreations:* Rugby football, architecture. *Club:* Reform.

GRAHAM, Air Vice-Marshal Henry Rudolph, CB 1958; CBE 1955; DSO 1941; DFC 1942; *b* 28 March 1910; *s* of Major Campbell Frederick Graham, late Cape Mounted Rifles and South African Mounted Rifles, and Frances Elizabeth Cheeseman; *m* 1949, Maisie Frances Butler; two *s*. *Educ:* Rondebosch; SA Trng Ship General Botha, S Africa. Union Castle Line, 1926–31; RAF, 1931–62. National Trust, 1966–69. Military Cross (Czechoslovakia), 1940. *Recreation:* farming. *Address:* Majoro, PO Box 189, Magaliesburg, 2805, South Africa. *Clubs:* Wanderers', RAF Officers' (Johannesburg).

GRAHAM, Ian James Alastair, FSA; Assistant Curator, Peabody Museum of Archaeology, Harvard University; *b* 12 Nov. 1923; *s* of Captain Lord Alastair Graham, RN, *y s* of 5th Duke of Montrose, and Lady Meriel Olivia Bathurst (*d* 1936), *d* of 7th Earl Bathurst; unmarried. *Educ:* Winchester Coll.; Trinity Coll., Dublin. RNVR (A), 1942–47; TCD 1947–51; Nuffield Foundn Research Scholar at The National Gallery, 1951–54; independent archaeological explorer in Central America from 1959. Occasional photographer of architecture. MacArthur Foundn Prize Fellowship, 1981. *Publications:* Splendours of the East, 1965; Great Houses of the Western World, 1968; Archaeological Explorations in El Peten, Guatemala, 1967; Corpus of Maya Hieroglyphic Inscriptions, 11 parts, 1975–; other reports in learned jls. *Address:* Chantry Farm, Campsey Ash, Suffolk; c/o Peabody Museum, Harvard University, Cambridge, Mass, USA.

GRAHAM, Sir James Bellingham, 11th Bt *cr* 1662; Research Assistant, Cecil Higgins Museum and Art Gallery, Bedford; *b* 8 Oct. 1940; *e s* of Sir Richard Bellingham Graham, 10th Bt, OBE, and of Beatrice, *d* of late Michael Spencer-Smith, DSO, MC; *S* father, 1982; *m* 1986, Halina, *d* of Wiktor and Eleonora Grubert. *Educ:* Eton College; Christ Church, Oxford (MA). *Publication:* Guide to Norton Conyers, 1976. *Recreations:* reading, visiting historic houses and museums. *Heir:* *b* William Reginald Graham, *b* 7 July 1942. *Address:* Norton Conyers, Ripon, N Yorks. *T:* Melmerby 333; 1 Oberon Court, Shakespeare Road, Bedford.

GRAHAM, James Lowery; Managing Director, Border Television, Carlisle, since 1982; *b* 29 Oct. 1932; *s* of William and Elizabeth Graham; *m* 1984, Ann Graham; two *d* by previous marr. *Educ:* Whitehaven Grammar School. Journalist, North West Evening Mail, Barrow, 1955–62; News Editor, Border Television, 1962–67; Producer, BBC, Leeds, 1967–70; BBC: Regional News Editor, North, 1970–75; Regional Television Manager, North East, 1975–80; Head of Secretariat, Broadcasting House, 1980–82. Jt Sec., Broadcasters' Audience Res. Bd, 1980–82. Dir, Indep. Television Publications. Member: BAFTA; RTS; European movement. News Film Award, RTS, 1975; Beffroi d'Or, Lille (European regional broadcasting award), 1983. *Recreations:* hill walking, skiing. *Address:* Oak House, Great Corby, Carlisle, Cumbria.

GRAHAM, John, CB 1976; Fisheries Secretary, Ministry of Agriculture, Fisheries and Food, 1967–76; *b* 17 March 1918; *s* of late John Graham; *m* 1940, Betty Ramage Jarvie; two *s* three *d*. *Educ:* Fettes Coll., Edinburgh; Trinity Coll., Cambridge (Schol.). Classical Tripos, MA Cantab. Entered Post Office as Asst Principal, 1939; Min. of Food, 1940.

GRAHAM, Sir John (Alexander Noble), 4th Bt *cr* 1906, of Larbert; GCMG 1986 (KCMG 1979; CMG 1972); HM Diplomatic Service; Ambassador and UK Permanent Representative to NATO, Brussels, 1982–86; *b* 15 July 1926; *s* of Sir John Reginald Noble Graham, 3rd Bt, VC, OBE and Rachel Septima (*d* 1984), *d* of Col Sir Alexander Sprot, 1st and last Bt; *S* father, 1980; *m* 1956, Marygold Ellinor Gabrielle Austin; two *s* one *d*. *Educ:* Eton Coll.; Trinity Coll., Cambridge. Army, 1944–47; Cambridge, 1948–50; HM Foreign Service, 1950; Middle East Centre for Arab Studies, 1951; Third Secretary, Bahrain 1951, Kuwait 1952, Amman 1953; Asst Private Sec. to Sec. of State for Foreign Affairs, 1954–57; First Sec., Belgrade, 1957–60, Benghazi, 1960–61; FO 1961–66; Counsellor and Head of Chancery, Kuwait, 1966–69; Principal Private Sec. to Foreign and Commonwealth Sec., 1969–72; Cllr (later Minister) and Head of Chancery, Washington, 1972–74; Ambassador to Iraq, 1974–77; Dep. Under-Sec. of State, FCO, 1977–79; Ambassador to Iran, 1979–80; Deputy Under-Sec. of State, FCO, 1980–82. *Heir:* *s* Andrew John Noble Graham, Captain Argyll and Sutherland Highlanders [*b* 21 Oct. 1956; *m* 1984, Suzi M. B. O'Riordan, *er d* of Captain Paddy O'Riordan, RN, Chitterne, Wilts; one *d*]. *Address:* 8 St Maur Road, SW6 4DP. *Club:* Army and Navy.

GRAHAM, (John) Alistair; Director, Industrial Society, since 1986; *b* 6 Aug. 1942; *s* of late Robert Graham and of Dorothy Graham; *m* 1968, Dorothy Jean Wallace; one *s* one *d*. *Educ:* Royal Grammar Sch., Newcastle upon Tyne. Clerical Asst, St George's Hosp., Morpeth, 1961; Admin Trainee, Northern Regional Hosp. Bd, 1963; Higher Clerical Officer, Royal Sussex County Hosp., Brighton, 1964; Legal Dept, TGWU, 1965; The Civil and Public Services Association: Asst Sec., 1966; Asst Gen. Sec., 1975; Dep. Gen. Sec., 1976; Gen. Sec., 1982–86. Vis. Fellow, Nuffield Coll., Oxford, 1984–. Member: TUC Gen. Council, 1982–84, 1985–; Econ. and Internat. Cttees of TUC, 1983–. Parly Candidate (Lab), Brighton Pavilion, 1966. *Recreations:* music, theatre. *Address:* The Industrial Society, Peter Runge House, 3 Carlton House Terrace, SW1Y 5DG.

GRAHAM, Maj.-Gen. John David Carew, CB 1978; CBE 1973 (OBE 1966); Secretary to the Administrative Trustees of the Chevening Estate, 1978–86; *b* 18 Jan. 1923; *s* of late Col J. A. Graham, late RE, and of Constance Mary Graham (*née* Carew-Hunt); *m* 1956, Rosemary Elaine Adamson; one *s* one *d*. *Educ:* Cheltenham Coll. psc 1955; jssc 1962. Commissioned into Argyll and Sutherland Highlanders, 1942 (despatches, 1945); served with 5th (Scottish) Bn, The Parachute Regt, 1946–49; British Embassy, Prague, 1949–50; HQ Scottish Comd, 1956–58; Mil. Asst to CINCENT, Fontainebleau, 1960–62; comd 1st Bn, The Parachute Regt, 1964–66; Instr at Staff Coll., Camberley, 1967; Regtl Col, The Parachute Regt, 1968–69; Comdr, Sultan's Armed Forces, Oman, 1970–72; Indian Nat. Defence Coll., New Delhi, 1973; Asst Chief of Staff, HQ AFCENT, 1974–76; GOC Wales, 1976–78. Hon. Col, Kent ACF, 1981– (Chm. Kent ACF Cttee, 1979–86); Hon. Col, 203 (Welsh) Gen. Hosp., RAMC, TA, 1983–. OStJ 1978, and Chm., St John Council for Kent, 1978–86; CStJ 1983. Order of Oman, 1972. *Address:* RHQ The Parachute Regiment, Browning Barracks, Aldershot, Hants GU11 2BS.

See also A. C. Graham.

GRAHAM, Sir John (Moodie), 2nd Bt *cr* 1964; Director, Kinnegar Inns Ltd, since 1981; Chairman, John Graham (Dromore) Ltd, 1966–83; *b* 3 April 1938; *s* of Sir Clarence Graham, 1st Bt, MICE, and Margaret Christina Moodie (*d* 1954); *S* father, 1966; *m* 1970, Valerie Rosemary (marr. diss. 1983), *d* of Frank Gill, Belfast; three *d*. *Educ:* Trinity Coll., Glenalmond; Queen's Univ., Belfast. BSc, Civil Engineering, 1961. Joined family firm of John Graham (Dromore) Ltd, Building and Civil Engineering Contractors, on graduating from University. Director: Electrical Supplies Ltd, 1967–83; Concrete (NI) Ltd, 1967–83; Ulster Quarries Ltd; Graham (Contracts) Ltd, 1971–83; Fieldhouse Plant (NI) Ltd, 1976–83. Chm., Concrete Soc., NI, 1972–74; Senior Vice-Pres., Concrete Soc., 1980; Pres., Northern Ireland Leukaemia Research Fund, 1967. *Recreations:* sailing, squash, photography. *Address:* #19 Superservicio Jesus, Jesus, Ibiza.

GRAHAM, Sir (John) Patrick, Kt 1969; Judge of the High Court of Justice, Chancery Division, 1969–81; Senior Patent Judge; *b* 26 Nov. 1906; *s* of Alexander Graham and Mary Adeline Cock; *m* 1931, Annie Elizabeth Newport Willson; four *s*. *Educ:* Shrewsbury; Caius Coll., Cambridge. Called to Bar, Middle Temple, 1930; read with Sir Lionel Heald, QC, MP; QC 1953; Treasurer, Middle Temple, 1979. Served War of 1939–45: RAF (VR) and with SHAEF, demobilised, 1945, with rank of Group Capt. Dep.-Chm., Salop Quarter Sessions, 1961–69. Mem., Standing Cttee on Structural Safety, 1975–. *Publication:* Awards to Inventors, 1946. *Recreations:* golf, tennis, sailing. *Address:* Tall Elms, Radlett, Herts. *T:* Radlett 6307.

GRAHAM, Kathleen Mary, CBE 1958 (MBE 1945); *d* of late Col R. B. Graham, CBE, and Mrs M. G. Graham, London; unmarried. *Educ:* Cheltenham Ladies' Coll.; Univ. of London (Courtauld Inst. of Art). Courtauld Inst., Dept of Technology War-time Laboratory, 1940–41; Political Warfare Executive, 1942–45; entered HM Foreign Service, 1945; served in FO, 1946–49; Consul (Information) at San Francisco, Calif, 1949–53; served in FO, 1953–55; made Counsellor in HM Foreign Service in 1955 and appointed Dep. Consul-Gen. in New York, 1955–59; HM Consul-Gen. at Amsterdam, 1960–63; in FO, 1964–69, retired. Exec. Dir, 1970–73, a Governor, 1973–80, E-SU. *Recreations:* music, history of art. *Address:* 16 Graham Terrace, SW1W 8JH. *T:* 01–730 4611.

GRAHAM, Kenneth, OBE 1971; Deputy General Secretary, Trades Union Congress, since 1985; Member (part-time), Manpower Services Commission, since 1974; National Council for Vocational Qualifications, 1986; *b* 18 July 1922; *er s* of late Ernest Graham and of Ivy Hutchinson, Cleator, Cumbria; *m* 1945, Ann Winifred Muriel Taylor. *Educ:* Workington Techn. Sch.; Leyton Techn. Coll.; Univ. of London (external). Engrg apprentice, 1938–42; Wartime Radar Research Unit, 1942–45; Air Trng Sch., qual. licensed engr, Air Registration Bd, 1947; employed in private industry, Mins of Aircraft Prodn and Supply, BOAC, and RN Scientific Service. Joined AEU, 1938: Mem. Final Appeal Court, Nat. Cttee, Divisional Chm., District Pres., etc, 1947–61; Tutor (part-time) in Trade Union Studies, Univ. of Southampton and WEA, 1958–61; joined TUC Organisation Dept, 1961, Head of TUC Organisation and Industrial Relations Dept, 1966–77; Asst Gen. Sec., TUC, 1977–85. Member: Council, Inst. of Manpower Studies, 1975; Bd, European Foundn for Improvement of Living and Working Conditions, 1976; Adv. Cttee, European Social Fund, 1976; Council, Templeton Coll. (Oxford Centre for Management Studies), 1984. Special Award of Merit, AUEW, 1981. *Publications:* contrib.

Job Satisfaction: Challenge and Response in Modern Britain, 1976. *Recreations:* music, military history. *Address:* 90 Springfield Drive, Ilford, Essex. *T:* 01–554 0839.

GRAHAM, (Malcolm Gray) Douglas; Chairman, The Midland News Association Ltd, since 1984 (Deputy Chairman, 1978–84); *b* 18 Feb. 1930; *s* of Malcolm Graham and Annie Jeanette Robinson; *m* 1980, Sara Anne Elwell (*née* Anderson). *Educ:* Shrewsbury Sch. National Service, RM, 1948–50. Newspaper trng, UK and Australia, 1950–53; Dir, Express & Star (Wolverhampton) Ltd, 1957. President: Young Newspapermen's Assoc., 1969; W Midlands Newspaper Soc., 1973–74; Chm., Evening Newspaper Advertising Bureau, 1978–79. *Recreation:* shooting. *Address:* Roughton Manor, Bridgnorth, Shropshire. *T:* Worfield 209.

GRAHAM, Martha; dancer; choreographer; director and teacher of dancing at the Martha Graham School of Contemporary Dance in New York; *b* Pittsburgh, Pa; *d* of Dr and Mrs George Graham. *Educ:* privately, and with Ruth St Denis and Ted Shawn. First appeared in Xochitl, New York, 1920; first recital by pupils, 1926; danced lead in Stravinsky's La Sacre du Printemps, 1930; founded Dance Repertory Theatre, 1930; choreographer of 167 solo and ensemble productions inc. three films (A Dancer's World, 1957; Appalachian Spring, 1958; Night Journey, 1960). Foreign tours, 1954, 1955–56, 1958, 1962, 1963, 1967, 1968, 1979; US tours, 1966, 1970, 1978, 1979; performed and lectured in major cities of Europe, Middle East, Iron Curtain countries, and throughout the Orient; has given solo performances with leading orchestras of United States. Three by Martha Graham, TV, 1969. Teacher: Neighbourhood Playhouse; Juilliard Sch. of Music. In the last five years her sch. has taken students from over forty foreign countries. Guggenheim Fellow, 1932, 1939; holds many doctorates and awards, including the Capezio Award, 1959, Aspen Award in the Humanities, 1965, and Distinguished Service to Arts Award, Nat. Inst. of Arts and Letters, 1970; Medal of Freedom (USA), 1976. Chevalier, Légion d'Honneur, 1984. *Publication:* The Notebooks of Martha Graham, 1973; *relevant publication:* Martha Graham: Portrait of a Lady as an Artist, by LeRoy Leatherman, 1966. *Address:* Martha Graham School of Contemporary Dance, 316 East 63rd Street, New York, NY 10021, USA. *Club:* Cosmopolitan (New York).

GRAHAM, Martin, QC 1976; **His Honour Judge Graham;** a Circuit Judge, since 1986; *b* 10 Feb. 1929; *m* 1962, Jane Filby; one *d*. *Educ:* Emanuel School; Trinity College, Oxford (Scholar; MA, PPE). Called to Bar, Middle Temple, 1952; a Recorder, 1986. Nat. Service, Officer BAOR, 1953–55. *Recreations:* swimming, tennis. *Address:* 7 Oakeshott Avenue, N6; 1 Garden Court, Temple, EC4. *Clubs:* Reform, Royal Automobile, Hurlingham.

GRAHAM, Sir Norman (William), Kt 1971; CB 1961; FRSE; Secretary, Scottish Education Department, 1964–73, retired; *b* 11 Oct. 1913; *s* of William and Margaret Graham; *m* 1949, Catherine Mary Strathie; two *s* one *d*. *Educ:* High Sch. of Glasgow; Glasgow Univ. Dept of Health for Scotland, 1936; Private Sec. to Permanent Under-Sec. of State, 1939–40; Ministry of Aircraft Production, 1940; Principal Private Sec. to Minister, 1944–45; Asst Sec., Dept of Health for Scotland, 1945; Under-Sec., Scottish Home and Health Dept, 1956–63. Hon. DLitt Heriot-Watt, 1971; DUniv Stirling, 1974. *Recreations:* golf, gardening. *Address:* Suilven, Longniddry, East Lothian. *T:* Longniddry 52130. *Club:* New (Edinburgh).

GRAHAM, Hon. Sir Patrick; *see* Graham, Hon. Sir J. P.

GRAHAM, Peter, CB 1982; Second Parliamentary Counsel since 1987 (Parliamentary Counsel, 1972–86); *b* 7 Jan. 1934; *o s* of late Alderman Douglas Graham, CBE, Huddersfield, and Ena May (*née* Jackson); *m* 1st, Judith Mary Dunbar; two *s*; 2nd, Anne Silvia Garcia (*see* A. S. Graham). *Educ:* St Bees Sch., Cumberland (scholar); St John's Coll., Cambridge (scholar, 1st cl. Law Tripos, MA, LLM, McMahon Law Studentship). Served as pilot in Fleet Air Arm, 1952–55, Lieut, RNR. Called to Bar, Gray's Inn, 1958 (Holker Exhbn; H. C. Richards Prize, Ecclesiastical Law), Lincoln's Inn, 1982; joined Parliamentary Counsel Office, 1959. External Examr (Legislation), Univ. of Edinburgh, 1977–81; with Law Commn, 1979–81. Hon. Legal Adviser, Historic Vehicle Clubs Cttee, 1967–86. *Recreations:* village church organist, gardening, bridge. *Address:* Stony Dale, Field Broughton, Grange over Sands, Cumbria LA11 6HN. *Club:* Sette of Odd Volumes.

GRAHAM, Peter Alfred, OBE 1969; FIB, CBIM; Senior Deputy Chairman, since 1983, Group Managing Director, 1977–83, Standard Chartered Bank Limited; Chairman, Crown Agents for Oversea Governments and Administrations, since 1983; *b* 25 May 1922; *s* of Alfred Graham and Margaret (*née* Winder); *m* 1953, Luned Mary (*née* Kenealy-Jones); two *s* two *d*. *Educ:* St Joseph's Coll., Beulah Hill. FIB 1975; CBIM 1981. Served War, RNVR: Pilot, FAA. Joined The Chartered Bank of India, Australia and China, 1947; 24 yrs overseas banking career, incl. appts in Japan, India and Hong Kong; i/c The Chartered Bank, Hong Kong, 1962–70; Chm. (1st), Hong Kong Export Credit Insurance Corp., 1965–70; General Manager 1970, Dep. Man. Dir 1975, Standard Chartered Bank, London. Director: Standard Chartered Finance Ltd, Sydney (formerly Mutual Acceptance Corp.), 1974–; First Bank Nigeria, Lagos, 1976–; Union Bank Inc., Los Angeles, 1979–; Chairman: Standard Chartered Merchant Bank Ltd, 1977–83; Mocatta Commercial Ltd, 1983–; Mocatta & Goldsmid Ltd, 1983–; Deputy Chairman: Chartered Trust plc, 1983–85; Governing Body, ICC UK, 1985–; Mem., Bd of Banking Supervision, 1986–; Pres., Inst. of Bankers, 1981–83; Chm., Adv. Cttee, City University Business Sch., 1981–; formerly Chm., Exchange Banks' Assoc., Hong Kong; Mem., Govt cttees connected with trade and industry, Hong Kong. Hon. DSc City Univ., 1985. *Recreations:* golf, tennis, skiing. *Address:* 3 Somers Crescent, W2 2PN. *Clubs:* Naval; Hong Kong (Hong Kong); Rye Golf.

GRAHAM, Prof. Philip Jeremy; Professor of Child Psychiatry, since 1975, Dean, since 1985, Institute of Child Health, University of London; *b* 3 Sept. 1932; *s* of Jacob Rackham Graham and Pauline Graham; *m* 1960, Nori (*née* Burawoy); two *s* one *d*. *Educ:* Perse Sch., Cambridge; Cambridge Univ. (MA); University Coll. Hosp., London. FRCP 1973; FRCPsych 1972. Consultant Psychiatrist: Maudsley Hosp., London, 1966–68; Hosp. for Sick Children, Great Ormond Street, London, 1968–74. *Publications:* A Neuropsychiatric Study in Childhood (jtly), 1970; (ed) Epidemiological Approaches to Child Psychiatry, 1977; various publications on child and adolescent psychiatry. *Recreations:* reading, play-going, tennis. *Address:* 27 St Albans Road, NW5. *T:* 01–485 7937.

GRAHAM, Sir Ralph Wolfe, 13th Bt *cr* 1629; *b* 14 July 1908; *s* of Percival Harris Graham (2nd *s* of 10th Bt) (*d* 1954) and Louise (*d* 1934), *d* of John Wolfe, Brooklyn, USA; *S* cousin, 1975; *m* 1st, 1939, Gertrude (marr. diss. 1949), *d* of Charles Kaminski; 2nd, 1949, Geraldine, *d* of Austin Velour; two *s*. *Heir:* *s* Ralph Stuart Graham [*b* 5 Nov. 1950; *m* 1st, 1972, Roxanne (*d* 1978), *d* of Mrs Lovette Gurzan; 2nd, 1979, Deena Vandergrift]. *Address:* 134 Leisureville Boulevard, Boynton Beach, Fla 33435, USA.

GRAHAM, Robert Martin; Chief Executive, British United Provident Association, since 1984; *b* 20 Sept. 1930; *s* of Francis P. Graham and Margaret M. Graham (*née* Broderick); *m* 1959, Eileen (*née* Hoey); two *s* two *d*. *Educ:* Dublin; ACII. Hibernian Fire and General Insurance Co. Ltd, 1948–57; Voluntary Health Insurance Board, 1957–82 (to Chief Exec.); Dep. Chief Exec., BUPA 1982. Chm., Board of Management, Meath Hosp., 1972–82; Dep. Pres., Internat. Fedn of Voluntary Health Service Funds; Mem., Bd of Govs, Assoc. Internationale de la Mutualité; former Mem., Central Council, Federated Voluntary Hosps, Ireland. *Address:* BUPA, 24 Essex Street, WC2R 3AX. *T:* 01–353 5212. *Clubs:* Royal Automobile, Rotary Club of London.

GRAHAM, Dr Ronald Cairns; General Manager, Tayside Health Board, since 1985 (Chief Administrative Medical Officer, 1973–85); *b* 8 Oct. 1931; *s* of Thomas Graham and Helen Cairns; *m* 1959, Christine Fraser Osborne; two *s* one *d*. *Educ:* Airdrie Acad.; Glasgow Univ. MB, ChB Glasgow 1956; DipSocMed Edin. 1968; FFCM 1973; FRCPE 1983. West of Scotland; house jobs, gen. practice and geriatric med., 1956–62; Dep. Med. Supt, Edin. Royal Infirmary, 1962–65; Asst Sen. Admin. MO, SE Regional Hosp. Bd, 1965–69; Dep. and then Sen. Admin. MO, Eastern Regional Hosp. Bd, 1969–73. *Recreation:* fishing. *Address:* 34 Dalgleish Road, Dundee DD4 7JT. *T:* Dundee 43146.

GRAHAM, Samuel Horatio, CMG 1965; OBE 1962; Chairman: Grenada Development Bank, since 1985; Grenada Industrial Development Corporation, since 1985; *b* 3 May 1912; *o s* of late Rev. Benjamin Graham, Trinidad; *m* 1943, Oris Gloria (*née* Teka); two *s* four *d*. *Educ:* Barbados; External Student, London Univ. BA (London) 1945; LLB (London) 1949. Teacher and journalist until called to Bar, Gray's Inn, 1949. Private practice as Barrister in Grenada, 1949–53; Magistrate, St Lucia, 1953–57; Crown Attorney, St Kitts, 1957–59; Attorney-General, St Kitts, 1960–62; Administrator of St Vincent, 1962–66; Puisne Judge, British Honduras, 1966–69; Pres., Industrial Court of Antigua, 1969–70 (Associate Pres., 1981–84); Puisne Judge, Supreme Court of the Commonwealth of the Bahamas, 1973–78. Acted Chief Justice: British Honduras, Feb.-May 1968; Bahamas, Oct. 1977; Temp. Judge, Belize Court of Appeal, 1980. Judicial Mem., Bermuda Constituencies Boundaries Commn, 1979. Mem., Council of Legal Educn, WI, 1971–. Chairman Inquiries into: Income Tax Reliefs; Coconut Industry, St Lucia, 1955; Legislators' Salaries, St Kitts, 1962. Acted Administrator of St Lucia, St Kitts and Dominica on various occasions. CStJ 1964. *Recreations:* bridge, swimming. *Address:* PO Box 99, L'Anse-Aux-Epines, St George, Grenada, West Indies.

GRAHAM, (Stewart) David, QC 1977; Director, Cork Gully, since 1985; *b* 27 Feb. 1934; *s* of late Lewis Graham and of Gertrude Graham; *m* 1959, Corinne Carmona; two *d*. *Educ:* Leeds Grammar Sch.; St Edmund Hall, Oxford (MA, BCL). Called to the Bar, Middle Temple, 1957; Harmsworth Law Scholar, 1958. Member: Council of Justice, 1976–; Insolvency Rules Adv. Cttee, 1984–; Chm., Law, Parly and Gen. Purposes Cttee, Bd of Deputies of British Jews, 1983–. *Publications:* (ed jtly) Williams and Muir Hunter on Bankruptcy, 18th edn 1968, 19th edn 1979; (ed) legal textbooks. *Recreations:* biography, music, travel. *Address:* (office) Shelley House, 3 Noble Street, EC2V 7DQ. *T:* 01–606 7700; (home) 133 London Road, Stanmore, Mddx HA7 4PQ. *T:* 01–954 3783.

GRAHAM, Stuart Twentyman, CBE 1981; DFC 1943; FCIS, FIB; Chairman, International Commodities Clearing House Ltd, 1982–86; *b* 26 Aug. 1921; *s* of late Twentyman Graham; *m* 1948, Betty June Cox; one *s*. *Educ:* Kilburn Grammar Sch. Served War, 1940–46: commissioned, RAF, 1942. Entered Midland Bank, 1938; Jt Gen. Manager, 1966–70; Asst Chief Gen. Manager, 1970–74; Chief Gen. Manager, 1974–81; Gp Chief Exec., 1981–82; Dir, 1974–85. Chairman: Northern Bank Ltd, 1982–85; Director: Allied Lyons plc, 1981–; Sheffield Forgemasters Holdings, 1983–85; Aitken Hume International, 1985–; Efamol Hldgs, 1985–. *Recreations:* music, reading. *Address:* 30 City Road, EC1. *Club:* St James's.

GRAHAM, Walter Gerald Cloete, CBE 1952; retired 1975; *b* 13 May 1906; *s* of late Lance Graham Cloete Graham, of HBM Consular Service in China; *m* 1937, Nellor Alice Lee Swan; one *s*; *m* 1949, Cynthia Anne, *d* of late Sir George Clayton East, Bt; one *s* one *d*. *Educ:* Malvern Coll.; The Queen's Coll., Oxford. Laming Travelling Fellow of Queen's, 1927–29. Entered Consular Service in China, 1928; served in Peking, Nanking, Shanghai, Mukden Chefoo and Tientsin; Consul: Port Said, 1942–44, Chengtu, 1944–45, Urumchi (Chinese Turkestan), 1945–47; Consul-General, Mukden, 1947–49; Chinese Counsellor, Peking, 1949–50; Counsellor, Foreign Office, 1951–52; Minister to Republic of Korea, 1952–54; Ambassador to Libya, 1955–59; Asia Adviser to Defence Intelligence Staff (formerly Jt Intell. Bureau), Min. of Defence, 1959–67; Res. Adviser, FCO Res. Dept, 1967–75. *Recreations:* golf, watching cricket, gardening. *Address:* Knabb's Farmhouse, Fletching, Uckfield, Sussex. *T:* Newick 2198.

GRAHAM, Rear-Adm. Wilfred Jackson, CB 1979; Director and Secretary, Royal National Lifeboat Institution, since 1979; *b* 17 June 1925; *s* of William Bryce Graham and Jean Hill Graham (*née* Jackson); *m* 1951, Gillian Mary Finlayson; three *s* one *d*. *Educ:* Rossall Sch., Fleetwood, Lancs. Served War of 1939–45, Royal Navy: Cadet, 1943; specialised in gunnery, 1951; Comdr 1960; Captain 1967; IDC, 1970; Captain, HMS Ark Royal, 1975–76; Flag Officer, Portsmouth, 1976–79, retired. MNI. *Recreations:* sailing, walking, skiing. *Address:* Ackland Cottage, Shirley Holms, near Lymington, Hants; RNLI, West Quay Road, Poole, Dorset. *Clubs:* Army and Navy; Royal Naval Sailing Association, Royal Yacht Squadron, Royal Lymington Yacht.

GRAHAM, William Franklin, (Billy Graham); Evangelist; *b* Charlotte, NC, 7 Nov. 1918; *s* of William Franklin Graham and Morrow (*née* Coffey); *m* 1943, Ruth McCue Bell; two *s* three *d*. *Educ:* Florida Bible Institute, Tampa (ThB); Wheaton Coll., Ill (AB). Ordained to Baptist ministry, 1940; first Vice-Pres., Youth for Christ Internat., 1946–48; Pres., Northwestern Coll., Minneapolis, 1947–52; Evangelistic campaigns, 1946–; world-wide weekly broadcast, 1950–; many evangelistic tours of Great Britain, Europe, the Far East, South America, Australia and Russia. Chairman, Board of World Wide Pictures Inc. FRGS. Holds numerous honorary degrees in Divinity, Laws, Literature and the Humanities, from American universities and colleges; also varied awards from organisations, 1954–, inc. Templeton Foundn Prize, 1982; President's Medal of Freedom Award, 1983. *Publications include:* Peace with God, 1954; World Aflame, 1965; Jesus Generation, 1971; Angels—God's Secret Agents, 1975; How to be Born Again, 1977; The Holy Spirit, 1978; Till Armageddon, 1981. *Recreations:* golf, jogging. *Address:* (office) 1300 Harmon Place, Minneapolis, Minnesota 55403, USA. *T:* (612)338–0500.

GRAHAM, (William) Gordon, MC 1944 (Bar 1945); FRSA; Group Chairman and Chief Executive, Butterworth Publishers, since 1974; *b* 17 July 1920; *s* of Thomas Graham and Marion Hutcheson; *m* 1st, 1943, Margaret Milne, Bombay (*d* 1946); one *d*; 2nd, 1948, Friedel Gramm, Zürich; one *d*. *Educ:* Hutchesons' Grammar Sch.; Glasgow Univ. (MA 1940). Commissioned, Queen's Own Cameron Highlanders, 1941; served in India and Burma, 1942–46: Captain 1944, Major 1945; GSO II India Office, 1946. Newspaper correspondent and publishers' representative in India, 1946–55; Internat. Sales Manager, 1956–63, Vice-Pres., 1961, McGraw-Hill Book Co., New York; US citizen, 1963; Man. Dir, McGraw-Hill Publishing Co., UK, 1963–74; Director: W & R Chambers, Edinburgh, 1974–83; International Publishing Corp., 1975–82; Reed Publishing Gp, 1982–; Reed Holdings Inc., 1982–; Reed Telepublishing, 1983–; Chairman: Internat. Electronic Publishing Res. Centre Ltd, 1981–84; Publishers Database Ltd, 1982–84; R. R. Bowker Co., 1986–. Chm., Soc. of Bookmen, 1972–75; Publishers Association: Mem. Council, 1972–; Chm., Electronic Publishing Panel, 1980–83; Vice Pres., 1984–85; Pres., 1985–. Mem. Board, British Libr., 1980–86. Correspondent, Christian Science Monitor,

1946–56. FRSA 1978. *Publications:* articles in US and British trade press. *Recreations:* skiing, writing, fostering transatlantic understanding. *Address:* White Lodge, Beechwood Drive, Marlow, Bucks. *T:* Marlow 3371; Juniper Acres, East Hill, Keene, New York State, USA.

GRAHAM, Winston Mawdsley, OBE 1983; FRSL; *b* Victoria Park, Manchester; *m* 1939, Jean Mary Williamson; one *s* one *d.* Chm., Soc. of Authors, 1967–69. Books trans. into 17 languages. *Publications:* some early novels (designedly) out of print, and: Night Journey, 1941 (rev. edn 1966); The Merciless Ladies, 1944 (rev. edn 1979); The Forgotten Story, 1945 (ITV prodn, 1983); Ross Poldark, 1945; Demelza, 1946; Take My Life, 1947 (filmed 1947); Cordelia, 1949; Night Without Stars, 1950 (filmed 1950); Jeremy Poldark, 1950; Fortune is a Woman, 1953 (filmed 1956); Warleggan, 1953; The Little Walls, 1955; The Sleeping Partner, 1956 (filmed 1958; ITV prodn, 1967); Greek Fire, 1957; The Tumbled House, 1959; Marnie, 1961 (filmed 1963); The Grove of Eagles, 1963 (Book Society Choice); After the Act, 1965; The Walking Stick, 1967 (filmed 1970); Angell, Pearl and Little God, 1970; The Japanese Girl (short stories), 1971; The Spanish Armadas, 1972; The Black Moon, 1973; Woman in the Mirror, 1975; The Four Swans, 1976; The Angry Tide, 1977; The Stranger from the Sea, 1981; The Miller's Dance, 1982; Poldark's Cornwall, 1983; The Loving Cup, 1984; The Green Flash, 1986. BBC TV Series Poldark (the first four Poldark novels), 1975–76, second series (the next three Poldark novels), 1977; Circumstantial Evidence (play), 1979. *Recreations:* golf, gardening. *Address:* Abbotswood House, Buxted, East Sussex TN22 4PB. *Clubs:* Savile, Beefsteak.
See also A. W. M. Graham.

GRAHAM-BRYCE, Ian James, DPhil; Head of Environmental Affairs Division, Shell Internationale Petroleum Maatschappij BV, since 1986; *b* 20 March 1937; *s* of late Alexander Graham-Bryce, FRCS, and of Dame Isabel Graham Bryce, *qv*; *m* 1959, Anne Elisabeth Metcalf; one *s* three *d.* *Educ:* William Hulme's Grammar Sch., Manchester; University Coll., Oxford (Exhibnr). BA, MA, BSc, DPhil (Oxon); FRSC, CChem 1981. Research Asst, Univ. of Oxford, 1958–61; Lectr, Dept of Biochemistry and Soil Sci., UCNW, Bangor, 1961–64; Sen. Scientific Officer, Rothamsted Exper. Station, 1964–70; Sen. Res. Officer, ICI Plant Protection Div., Jealott's Hill Res. Station, Bracknell, Berks, 1970–72; Special Lectr in Pesticide Chemistry, Dept of Zoology and Applied Entomology, Imperial Coll. of Science and Technology, 1970–72 (Vis. Prof., 1976–79); Rothamsted Experimental Station: Head, Dept of Insecticides and Fungicides, 1972–79; Dep. Director, 1975–79; Dir, East Malling Res. Stn, Maidstone, Kent, 1979–86; Cons. Dir, Commonwealth Bureau of Horticulture and Plantation Crops, 1979–; Hon. Lectr, Dept of Biology, Univ. of Strathclyde, 1977–80. Society of Chemical Industry, London: Pres., 1982–85; Mem. Council, 1969–72 and 1974– ; Hon. Sec., Home Affairs, 1977–80; Chm., Pesticides Gp, 1978–80; Sec., Physico-Chemical and Biophysical Panel, 1968–70, Chm., 1973–75; Mem., British Nat. Cttee for Chemistry, 1982–84. Chm., Agrochemical Planning Gp, IOCD. Governor: Wye Coll., 1979–, Imperial Coll., 1985–, Univ. of London. Member, Editorial Board: Chemico-Biological Interactions, 1973–77; Pesticide Science, 1978–80; Agriculture, Ecosystems and Environment, 1978–. *Publications:* Physical Aspects of Pesticide Behaviour, 1980; papers on soil science, plant nutrition and crop protection in sci. jls. *Recreations:* music (espec. opera), squash racquets, fly fishing. *Address:* Shell International Petroleum Maatschappij BV, Postbus 162, 2501 An Den Haag, Netherlands. *Club:* Athenæum.

GRAHAM BRYCE, Dame Isabel, DBE 1968; Chairman: Oxford Regional Hospital Board, 1963–72; National Nursing Staff Committee, 1967–75; National Staff Committee, 1969–75; Consultant, British Transport Hotels, 1979–81 (Board Member, 1962–79); Vice-President, Princess Christian College, Manchester, since 1953; President, Goring and District Day Centre for the Elderly; *b* 30 April 1902; *d* of late Prof. James Lorrain Smith, FRS; *m* 1934, Alexander Graham Bryce, FRCS (*d* 1968); two *s.* *Educ:* St Leonards Sch., St Andrews; Edinburgh Univ. (MA). Investigator, Industrial Fatigue Research Board, 1926–27; HM Inspector of Factories, 1928–34; Centre Organiser, WVS, Manchester, 1938–39; Dir of Organization, Ontario Div., Canadian WVS, 1941–42; Tech. Adviser, American WVS, 1942–43; Res. Fellow Fatigue Lab. Harvard Univ., 1943–44; Nat. Council of Women: Chm., Manchester Br., 1947–50; Vice-Chm., Education Cttee, 1950–51. JP and Mem. Juvenile Court Panel, Manchester City, 1949–55; Vice-Chairman: Assoc. of HMC's, 1953–55; Bd of Visitors, Grendon Prison, 1962–67. Member: Nurses and Midwives Whitley Council, 1953–57; General Nursing Council, 1956–61; Bd of Governors, Eastman Dental Hosp., 1957–63; Maternity and Midwifery Standing Cttee, 1957–72; Public Health Insp., Education Bd, 1958–64; Independent Television Authority, 1960–65 (Chm., General Advisory Council, 1964–65); Bd, ATV Network Ltd, 1968–72; Ancillary Dental Workers Cttee, 1956–68; Experimental Scheme for Dental Auxiliaries, 1958–69; Council, Tyringham Foundn Ltd. Life Mem., British Fedn Univ. Women; Mem., Open Section, Royal Soc. of Medicine. Hon. Mem., Oxford Br., Zouta International. *Publications:* (joint) reports on research into industrial psychological problems. *Address:* Flat 32, Charles Ponsonby House, 21 Osberton Road, Oxford OX2 7PQ.
See also I. J. Graham-Bryce.

GRAHAM-CAMPBELL, David John, MA Cantab; Liaison Officer to Schools, Aberdeen University, 1972–76; *b* 18 Feb. 1912; *s* of late Sir R. F. Graham-Campbell; *m* 1940, Joan Sybil, *d* of late Major H. F. Maclean; three *s.* *Educ:* Eton Coll.; Trinity Coll., Cambridge (Exhibitioner). Assistant Master, Eton Coll., 1935–64; Warden, Trinity Coll., Glenalmond, 1964–72. Served with 2nd Bn KRRC and on the staff, 1939–45 (Lt-Col). *Publications:* Writing English, 1953; Portrait of Argyll and the Southern Hebrides, 1978; Portrait of Perth, Angus and Fife, 1979; Scotland's Story in her Monuments, 1982. *Recreations:* fishing, gardening, walking. *Address:* 17 Muirton Bank, Perth, Perthshire.
See also Baron Maclean.

GRAHAM-DIXON, Anthony Philip, QC 1973; *b* 5 Nov. 1929; *s* of late Leslie Charles Graham-Dixon, QC; *m* 1956, Margaret Suzanne Villar; one *s* one *d.* *Educ:* Westminster School; Christ Church, Oxford. MA (1st Cl. Hon. Mods, 1st Cl. Lit. Hum.). RNVR, 1953–55, Lieut (SP). Called to the Bar, Inner Temple, 1956, Bencher 1982; Member of Gray's Inn, 1965–. Mem. Council, Charing Cross Hosp. Medical School, 1976–83. Chm., London Concertino Ltd, 1982–. *Publication:* (mem. adv. bd) Competition Law in Western Europe and the USA, 1976. *Recreations:* music (especially opera), gardening, tennis. *Address:* 31 Hereford Square, SW7. *T:* 01–373 1461; Masketts Manor, Nutley, Uckfield, East Sussex. *T:* Nutley 2719.

GRAHAM DOW, Ronald; *see* Dow.

GRAHAM HALL, Jean; *see* Hall, J. G.

GRAHAM-HARRISON, Francis Laurence Theodore, CB 1962; Deputy Under-Secretary of State, Home Office, 1963–74; *b* 30 Oct. 1914; *s* of late Sir William Montagu Graham-Harrison, KCB, KC, and Lady Graham-Harrison, *d* of Sir Cyril Graham, 5th and last Bt, CMG; *m* 1941, Carol Mary St John, 3rd *d* of late Sir Francis Stewart, CIE; one *s* three *d.* *Educ:* Eton; Magdalen Coll., Oxford. Entered Home Office, 1938. Private Secretary to Parliamentary Under-Secretary of State, 1941–43; Asst Private Secretary to Prime Minister, 1946–49; Secretary, Royal Commission on Capital Punishment, 1949–53; Asst Secretary, Home Office, 1953–57; Asst Under-Secretary of State, Home Office, 1957–63. Trustee: Tate Gallery, 1975–82; Nat. Gallery, 1981–82. Chm., Exec. Finance Cttee, Dr Barnardo's, 1978–81. *Address:* 32 Parliament Hill, NW3. *T:* 01–435 6316.
See also R. M. Graham-Harrison.

GRAHAM-HARRISON, Robert Montagu; Head, British Development Division in Eastern Africa, Nairobi, since 1982; *b* 16 Feb. 1943; *s* of Francis Laurence Theodore Graham Harrison, *qv*; *m* 1977, Kathleen Patricia Maher; two *d.* *Educ:* Eton Coll.; Magdalen Coll., Oxford. VSO India, 1965; GLC, 1966; Min. of Overseas Development (later Overseas Development Administration), 1967; World Bank, Washington, 1971–73; Private Sec. to Minister for Overseas Development, 1978; Asst Sec., ODA, 1979. *Address:* c/o Foreign and Commonwealth Office, SW1.

GRAHAM-MOON, Sir Peter Wilfred Giles; *see* Moon.

GRAHAM-SMITH, Sir Francis; *see* Smith.

GRAHAM SMITH, Stanley, CBE 1949; *b* 18 Jan. 1896; *s* of late George and Minnie Elizabeth Graham Smith; *m* 1929, Mrs Blanche Violet Horne (*d* 1974), *widow* (*née* Venning); one *s.* *Educ:* Strand Sch., King's Coll., London. Entered Civil Service, 1914 (Admiralty). Served European War as pilot in Royal Naval Air Service, Dec. 1916–Jan. 1919. Rejoined Admiralty, 1919. Private Secretary to Accountant-General of the Navy, 1922–32; Private Secretary to Civil Lord of Admiralty, 1932–35; Head of Air Branch, Admiralty, 1941–49; Under Secretary (Naval Staff), Admiralty, 1950–56; retired from Civil Service, 1956.

GRAHAM-TOLER, family name of the **Earl of Norbury.**

GRAHAME-SMITH, Prof. David Grahame; Professor of Clinical Pharmacology, University of Oxford, since 1972; Hon. Director, Medical Research Council Unit of Clinical Pharmacology, Radcliffe Infirmary, Oxford; Fellow of Corpus Christi College, Oxford, since 1972; *b* 10 May 1933; *s* of George E. and C. A. Smith; *m* 1957, Kathryn Frances, *d* of Dr F. R. Beetham; two *s.* *Educ:* Wyggeston Grammar Sch., Leicester; St Mary's Hosp. Medical Sch., Univ. of London. MB, BS (London) 1956; MRCS, LRCP 1956; MRCP 1958; PhD (London) 1966; FRCP 1972. House Phys., Paddington Gen. Hosp., London, 1956; House Surg., Battle Hosp., Reading, 1956–57. Captain, RAMC, 1957–60. Registrar and Sen. Registrar in Medicine, St Mary's Hosp., Paddington, 1960–61; H. A. M. Thompson Research Scholar, RCP, 1961–62; Saltwell Research Scholar, RCP, 1962–65; Wellcome Trust Research Fellow, 1965–66; Hon. Med. Registrar to Med. Unit, St Mary's Hosp., 1961–66; MRC Travelling Fellow, Dept of Endocrinology, Vanderbilt Univ., Nashville, Tennessee, USA, 1966–67; Sen. Lectr in Clinical Pharmacology and Therapeutics, St Mary's Hosp. Med. Sch., Univ. of London, 1967–71; Hon. Cons. Physician, St Mary's Hosp., Paddington, 1967–71. Vis. Prof., Peking Union Medical Coll., Beijing, China, 1985–. Mem., Cttee on Safety of Medicines, 1975–. *Publications:* (with J. K. Aronson) Oxford Textbook of Clinical Pharmacology and Drug Therapy, 1984; papers on biochemical, therapeutic and med. matters in scientific jls. *Recreations:* horse riding, jazz. *Address:* Romney, Lincombe Lane, Boars Hill, Oxford. *T:* Oxford 735889.

GRAHAMSTOWN, Bishop of, since 1974; **Rt. Rev. Kenneth Cyril Oram;** *b* 3 March 1919; *s* of Alfred Charles Oram and Sophie Oram; *m* 1943, Kathleen Mary Malcolm; three *s* one *d.* *Educ:* Selhurst Grammar Sch., Croydon; King's Coll., London; Lincoln Theol Coll. BA Hons English, 1st Cl. AKC. Asst Curate: St Dunstan's, Cranbrook, 1942–45; St Mildred's, Croydon, 1945–46; Upington with Prieska, S Africa, 1946–48; Rector of Prieska and Dir of Prieska Mission District, 1949–51; Rector of Mafeking, 1952–59; Dir of Educn, dio. Kimberley and Kuruman, 1953–62; Archdeacon of Bechuanaland, 1953–59; Dean and Archdeacon: of Kimberley, 1960–64; of Grahamstown, 1964–74. *Recreations:* music, walking. *Address:* Bishopsbourne, PO Box 162, Grahamstown, South Africa. *T:* 2500. *Club:* Albany (Grahamstown).

GRAINGER, Leslie, CBE 1976; BSc; FEng; MInstF; Chairman, Mountain Petroleum Ltd, since 1984; *b* 8 August 1917. Mem. for Science, NCB, 1966–77; Chairman: NCB (Coal Products) Ltd, 1975–78; NCB (IEA Services) Ltd, 1975–79; Man. Dir, Branon PLC, 1981–83; Dir, Cavendish Petroleum Plc, 1982–85 (Chm., 1982–84). *Publication:* Coal Utilisation: Technology, Economics and Policy (with J. G. Gibson), 1981. *Address:* 100 Rochester Row, SW1. *T:* 01–828 4355.

GRANADO, Donald Casimir, TC 1970; *b* 4 March 1915; *m* 1959, Anne-Marie Faustin Lombard; one *s* two *d.* *Educ:* Trinidad. Gen. Sec., Union of Commercial and Industrial Workers, 1951–53; Sec./Treas., Fedn of Trade Unions, 1952–53; Elected MP for Laventille, Trinidad, 1956 and 1961; Minister of: Labour and Social Services, 1956–61; Health and Housing, and Dep. Leader House of Representatives, 1961–63. Ambassador to Venezuela, 1963–64; High Comr to Canada, 1964–69; Ambassador to Argentina and to Brazil, 1965–69; High Comr to London, 1969–71, and Ambassador to France, Germany, Belgium, Switzerland, Italy, Holland, Luxembourg and European Common Market, 1969–71. Led Trinidad and Tobago delegations to: India, 1958; CPA in Nigeria, Israel, Ceylon, Pakistan, 1962; UN, 1965; St Lucia, 1966; Chile, Brazil, Granada and Jamaica; attended Heads of Commonwealth Govts Conf., Singapore, 1971. First Gen. Sec., People's National Movement. President: Fidelis Youth Club; National Golf Club; Vice-Pres., Trinidad & Tobago Golf Assoc. National Father of the Year 1981. Speaks, reads and writes French and Spanish. *Recreations:* cricket, soccer, bridge and golf; music (tape-recording), writing. *Address:* 20 Grove Road, Valsayn Park, Trinidad.

GRANARD, 9th Earl of, *cr* 1684; **Arthur Patrick Hastings Forbes,** AFC, 1941; Bt 1628; Viscount Granard and Baron Clanehugh, 1675; Baron Granard (UK), 1806; Air Commodore late RAFVR; *b* 10 April 1915; *e s* of 8th Earl of Granard, KP, PC, GCVO, and Beatrice (*d* 1972), OBE, *d* of Ogden Mills, Staatsburg, Dutchess County, USA; *S* father, 1948; *m* 1949, Marie-Madeleine Eugènie, *y d* of Jean Maurel, Millau, Aveyron, formerly wife of late Prince Humbert de Faucigny Lucinge; two *d.* *Educ:* Eton; Trinity Coll., Cambridge. Served War of 1939–45 (despatches, AFC). Mem. Jockey Club of France. Commandeur Légion d'Honneur; Croix de Guerre with Palm; Officer Legion of Merit, USA; Croix des Vaillants of Poland; Order of George I of Greece. *Heir:* *nephew* Peter Arthur Edward Hastings Forbes, [*b* 15 March 1957; *m*; two *s*]. *Address:* 11 rue Louis de Savoie, 1110 Morges, Switzerland. *Clubs:* White's, Pratt's; Kildare Street and University (Dublin); Royal St George's Yacht.
See also Marquess of Bute.

GRANBY, Marquis of; David Charles Robert Manners; *b* 8 May 1959; *s* and *heir* of 10th Duke of Rutland, *qv.* Dealer in antique weapons. Mem. Civilian cttee, ATC Sqdn, Grantham; Governor, RNLI, 1985–. *Recreations:* shooting, fishing, gliding. *Address:* The Old Saddlery, Belvoir Castle, Grantham, Lincs NG32 1PD. *T:* Grantham 870789. *Clubs:* Turf; Annabel's.

GRANDI, Count (di Mordano) *cr* 1937, **Dino;** retired; President Chamber of Fasci and Corporazioni, Italy, 1939–43; late Member of the Chamber of Deputies and of the Fascist

Grand Council; *b* Mordano (Bologna), 4 June 1895; *m* 1924, Antonietta Brizzi; one *s* one *d*. Graduated in Law at the University of Bologna, 1919; volunteered for the war and was promoted to Captain for merit and decorated with silver medal, bronze medal, and three military crosses for valour; journalist and political organiser, after the war led the Fascist movement in the North of Italy and took part in the March on Rome as Chief of the General Staff of the Quadrunvirato; elected member of the Chamber of Deputies, 1921, 1924, 1929, 1934, and 1939; member of the General Direction of the Fascist Party Organisation, 1921–23–24; Deputy President of the Chamber of Deputies, 1924; Italian Delegate to the IV, V, International Labour Conference, 1922, 1923; Under-Secretary of State for the Interior, 1924; Under Secretary of State for Foreign Affairs, 1925–29; Italian Delegate, Locarno Conference, 1925; to Conferences for Settlement of War Debt, Washington, 1925 and London, 1926; and Hague Conference on War Debts, 1929; Head of Italian Delegation, London Naval Conference, 1930; Italian Delegate, Danubian Conference, London, 1932; Head of Italian Delegation, Geneva Disarmament Conference, 1932; Minister of Foreign Affairs, 1929–32; Permanent Italian Delegate to the Council of the League of Nations, 1925–32; Italian Ambassador in London, 1932–39; Keeper of the Seal and Minister of Justice, Italy, 1939–43; Head of Italian Delegation to London Naval Conference, 1936; Italian Representative to London Session of Council of League of Nations, 1936; at London Meeting of Locarno Powers, 1936; and on the London International Cttee for Non-Intervention in Spain, 1936, 1937, 1938, 1939. *Publications:* Origins of Fascism, 1929; Italian Foreign Policy, 1931; The Spanish War in the London Committee, 1939; The Frontiers of the Law, 1941, etc. *Recreations:* book collecting, riding, gardening, mountaineering. *Address:* I-41030 Albareto Di Modena, Italy.

GRANDY, Marshal of the Royal Air Force Sir John, GCB 1967 (KCB 1964; CB 1956); KBE 1961; DSO 1945; RAF; Constable and Governor of Windsor Castle, since 1978; *b* Northwood, Middlesex, 8 Feb. 1913; *s* of late Francis Grandy and Nellie Grandy (*née* Lines); *m* 1937, Cecile Elizabeth Florence Rankin, CStJ, *yr d* of Sir Robert Rankin, 1st and last Bt; two *s*. *Educ:* University College Sch., London. Joined RAF 1931. No 54 (Fighter) Sqdn, 1932–35; 604 (Middx) Sqdn., RAuxAF, 1935–36; Adjt and Flying Instructor, London Univ. Air Sqdn, 1937–39; Comd No 249 (Fighter) Sqdn during Battle of Britain; Staff Duties, HQ Fighter Comd, and Wing Comdr Flying RAF Coltishall, 1941; commanded: RAF Duxford, 1942 (First Typhoon Wing); HQ No 210 Group, No 73 Op Training Unit, and Fighter Conversion Unit at Abu Sueir, 1943–44; No 341 Wing (Dakotas), SE Asia Comd, 1944–45; DSO 1945, despatches 1943 and 1945. SASO No 232 Gp, 1945; *psc* 1946; Dep. Dir Operational Training, Air Min., 1946; Air Attaché, Brussels, 1949; Comd Northern Sector, Fighter Comd, 1950; Air Staff HQ Fighter Comd, 1952–54; Comdt, Central Fighter Estab., 1954–57; *idc* 1957; Comdr, Task Force Grapple (British Nuclear Weapon Test Force), Christmas Is., 1957–58; Assistant CAS (Ops), 1958–61; Commander-in-Chief, RAF, Germany and Comdr, Second Allied TAF, 1961–63; AOC-in-C, Bomber Command, 1963–65; C-in-C, British Forces, Far East, and UK Mil. Adviser to SEATO, 1965–67; Chief of the Air Staff, 1967–71; Governor and C-in-C, Gibraltar, 1973–78. Dir, Brixton Estate Ltd, 1971–73, 1978–83; Chm. Trustees, Imperial War Museum, 1978–; Dep. Chm. Council, RAF Benevolent Fund, 1980–; Trustee: Burma Star Assoc., 1979– (Vice-Pres.); Shuttleworth Remembrance Trust, 1978– (Chm., Aerodrome Cttee, 1980–); RAF Church, St Clement Danes, 1971–; Prince Philip Trust Fund, Windsor and Maidenhead, 1982–; past Pres., Officers' Assoc.; Vice-President: Officers' Pension Soc., 1971–; Nat. Assoc. of Boys' Clubs, 1971–; President: Disablement in the City, 1980–; Berks Br., BLESMA, 1981–; Air League, 1984–; Member: Management Cttee, RNLI, 1971–; Cttee, Royal Humane Soc., 1978–; Patron: King Edward VII League of Hosp. Friends, Windsor, 1979–; Polish Air Force Assoc. in GB, 1979–. PMN 1967. Hon. Liveryman, Haberdashers' Co., 1968. Freeman, City of London, 1968. KStJ 1974. *Address:* Norman Tower, Windsor Castle, Berks. *Clubs:* White's, Pratt's, Royal Air Force; Royal Yacht Squadron (Cowes); Swinley Forest Golf.

GRANGE, Kenneth Henry, CBE 1984; RDI, FSIAD; industrial designer; in private practice since 1958; Partner, Pentagram Design Partnership, since 1972; *b* 17 July 1929; *s* of Harry Alfred Grange and Hilda Gladys (*née* Long). *Educ:* London. Technical Illustrator, RE, 1948–50; Design Asst, Arcon Chartered Architects, 1948; Bronek Katz & Vaughn, 1950–51; Gordon Bowyer & Partners, 1951–54; Jack Howe & Partners, 1954–58. Pres., SIAD, 1987–88; Master of Faculty, RDI, 1985–87. RDI 1969; FSIAD 1959. Hon Dr: RCA, 1985; Heriot-Watt, 1986. 8 CoID Awards; Duke of Edinburgh Award for Elegant Design, 1963. *Recreations:* tennis, ski-ing. *Address:* 11 Needham Road, W11 2RP; Acrise Cottage, Christchurch Hill, NW3.

GRANGER, Stewart; (James Lablache Stewart); actor (stage and films); *b* London, 6 May 1913; *s* of late Major James Stewart, RE, and Frederica Lablache; *m* 1st, Elspeth March (marr. diss., 1948); two *c*; 2nd, 1950, Jean Simmons, *qv* (marr. diss. 1960); one *c*; 3rd, 1964, Viviane Lecerf (marr. diss. 1969). *Educ:* Epsom Coll. Began training as doctor but decided to become an actor. Studied at Webber-Douglas School of Dramatic Art; played at Little Theatre, Hull, and with Birmingham Repertory Company; appeared at Malvern Festivals, 1936–37; first London appearance as Captain Hamilton in The Sun Never Sets, Drury Lane, 1938; appeared on London stage, 1938–39; joined Old Vic Company, 1939; Dr Fleming in Tony Draws a Horse, Criterion, 1940; George Winthrop in A House in the Square, St Martin's, 1940; toured, 1940; served War of 1939–45, Army, 1940–42 (invalided). Toured, 1942; succeeded Owen Nares as Max de Winter in Rebecca, Lyric, 1942. Began film career in 1938, and has appeared in many films, including: The Man in Grey, The Lamp Still Burns, Fanny by Gaslight, Waterloo Road, Love Story, Madonna of the Seven Moons, Cæsar and Cleopatra, Caravan, The Magic Bow, Captain Boycott, Blanche Fury, Saraband for Dead Lovers, Woman Hater, Adam and Evelyne, King Solomon's Mines, Soldiers Three, Light Touch, Wild North, Scaramouche, Young Bess, Salome, Prisoner of Zenda, All the Brothers were Valiant, Beau Brummell, Footsteps in the Fog, Moonfleet, Green Fire, Bhowani Junction, Last Hunt, The Little Hut, Gun Glory, The Whole Truth, Harry Black and the Tiger, North to Alaska, Swordsman of Siena, The Secret Invasion, The Trygon Factor, The Wild Geese. *Publication:* Sparks Fly Upward (autobiog.), 1981. *Address:* c/o Michael Ladkin, 11 Garrick Street, WC2.

GRANIT, Prof. Ragnar Arthur, Commander, Order of Nordstjernan, Sweden, 1964; Professor Emeritus, since 1967, Karolinska Institutet, Stockholm; *b* 30 Oct. 1900; *s* of Arthur W. Granit and Albertina Helena Granit (*née* Malmberg); *m* 1929, Baroness Marguerite (Daisy) Bruun; one *s*. *Educ:* Swedish Normallyceum; Helsingfors University. MagPhil 1923, MD 1927. Prof. of Physiology, Helsingfors, 1937; Prof. of Neurophysiology, Stockholm, 1940; Dir of Dept of Neurophysiology, Medical Nobel Inst., 1945; retired, 1967. President, Royal Swedish Acad, Science, 1963–65. Lectures: Silliman, Yale, 1954; Sherrington, London, 1967; Liverpool, 1971; Murlin, Rochester, NY 1973; Hughlings Jackson, McGill, 1975. Visiting Professor: Rockefeller Univ., NY, 1956–66; St Catherine's Coll., Oxford, 1967; Pacific Medical Center, San Francisco, 1969; Fogarty Internat. Foundn, Nat. Inst. of Health, Bethesda, USA, 1971–72, 1975; Düsseldorf Univ., 1976; Max-Planck Inst., Bad Nauheim, 1977. Foreign Member: Royal Soc., 1960; Nat. Acad. Sci., Washington, 1968; Accad. Naz. dei Lincei, 1978; Acad of Finland, 1985; Hon. Member: Amer. Acad. of Arts and Sciences; Indian Acad of Sci., 1964. Mem. and Hon. Mem. of several learned societies. Hon. MD: Oslo, 1951; Loyola, 1969; Pisa, 1970; Hon. DSc: Oxford, 1956; Hong Kong, 1961; Hon. DPhil Helsingfors, 1982; Catedr. Hon., Lima, Santiago, Bogotá, 1958. Retzius Gold Medal, 1957; Donders Medal, 1957; Jahre Prize (Oslo), 1961; III Internat. St Vincent Prize, 1961; Nobel Prize for Medicine (jointly), 1967; Sherrington Medal, 1967; Purkinje Gold Medal, 1969. Cross of Freedom (Finland), 1918. *Publications:* Ung Mans Väg till Minerva, 1941; Sensory Mechanisms of the Retina, (UK) 1947 (US 1963); Receptors and Sensory Perception, (US) 1955; Charles Scott Sherrington: An Appraisal, (UK) 1966; Basis of Motor Control, (UK) 1970; Regulation of the Discharge of Motoneurons (UK), 1971; The Purposive Brain (US), 1977; Hur det kom sig (A Memoir), 1983. *Recreations:* island life, gardening. *Address:* 14 Eriksbergsgatan, S-114 30 Stockholm, Sweden. *T:* 08–21 37 28.

GRANT, family name of **Baron Strathspey.**

GRANT, Alec Alan; a Master of the Supreme Court, Queen's Bench Division, since 1982; *b* 27 July 1932; *s* of late Emil Grant, OBE and Elsie Louise (*née* Marks). *Educ:* Highgate Sch.; Merton Coll., Oxford (MA). National Service, RA, 1951–52. Pres., Oxford Union, 1956. Called to the Bar, Middle Temple, 1957; practised at the Bar, 1958–82. Member: Mddx CC, 1961–65; GLC, 1964–67 and 1970–73; Governing Body, SOAS, 1965– (Vice-Chm., 1978–); Court of Governors, Thames Polytechnic, 1972– (Chm., 1982–85). *Recreations:* hill-walking, watching cricket. *Address:* Royal Courts of Justice, Strand, WC2A 2LL. *Clubs:* MCC; Austrian Alpine.

GRANT, Alexander (Marshall), CBE 1965; Artistic Director, National Ballet of Canada, 1976–83; *b* Wellington, New Zealand, 22 Feb. 1925; *s* of Alexander and Eleather Grant. *Educ:* Wellington Coll., NZ. Arrived in London, Feb. 1946, to study with Sadler's Wells School on Scholarship given in New Zealand by Royal Academy of Dancing, London; joined Sadler's Wells Ballet (now Royal Ballet Company), Aug. 1946. Dir, Ballet for All (touring ballet company), 1971–76 (Co-director, 1970–71). Senior Principal, London Festival Ballet, 1985–; Guest Artist, Royal Ballet, 1985. Danced leading rôles in following: Mam'zelle Angot, Clock Symphony, Boutique Fantasque, Donald of the Burthens, Rake's Progress, Job, Three Cornered Hat, Ballabile, Cinderella, Sylvia, Madame Chrysanthème, Façade, Daphnis and Chloé, Coppélia, Petrushka, Ondine, La Fille Mal Gardée, Jabez and the Devil, Perséphone, The Dream, Jazz Calendar, Enigma Variations, Sleeping Beauty (Carabosse), A Month in the Country, La Sylphide, The Nutcracker; *films:* Tales of Beatrix Potter (Peter Rabbit and Pigling Bland); Steps of the Ballet. *Recreations:* gardening, cinema going, cuisine.

GRANT, Alexander Thomas Kingdom, CB 1965; CMG 1949; MA; Fellow of Pembroke College, Cambridge, 1966–73, now Fellow Emeritus; *b* 29 March 1906; *s* of late Harold Allan Grant and Marie F. C. Grant; *m* 1930, Helen Frances, *d* of late Dr and Mrs H. Newsome, Clifton, Bristol. *Educ:* St Olave's Sch.; University Coll., Oxford (Scholar in Modern History). Research on international financial problems at RIIA, 1932–35. Leverhulme Research Fellow, 1935–37. Lectr in Dept of Polit. Econ., UCL, 1938–39. Joined HM Treasury, 1939; Under-Sec., 1956; Under Sec., ECGD, 1958–66. UK member on Managing Board of European Payments Union, 1952–53; Secretary of Faculty of Economics, Cambridge, 1966–71; Senior Research Officer, Dept of Applied Economics, 1971–73. *Publications:* Society and Enterprise, 1934; A Study of the Capital Market in Post-War Britain, 1937; The Machinery of Finance and the Management of Sterling, 1967; The Strategy of Financial Pressure, 1972; Economic Uncertainty and Financial Structure, 1977; miscellaneous articles. *Address:* 11 Marlowe Road, Newnham, Cambridge CB3 9JW. *T:* Cambridge 63119.

GRANT, Alistair; *see* Grant, D. A. A.

GRANT, Allan Wallace, OBE 1974; MC 1941; TD 1947; President, Ecclesiastical Insurance Office Ltd, since 1981 (Managing Director, 1971–77; Chairman, 1975–81); *b* 2 Feb. 1911; *s* of late Henry Grant and late Rose Margaret Sheppard; *m* 1939, Kathleen Rachel Bamford; one *d*. *Educ:* Dulwich Coll. LLB Hons (London). FCII. Eccles. Insurance Office, 1929; Chief Officer, 1952; Dir, 1966. Served War of 1939–45: Major, 2 i/c, 3rd Co. of London Yeomanry (Sharpshooters), N Africa, Sicily, Italy, NW Europe. Pres., Sharpshooters Assoc. Called to Bar, Gray's Inn, 1948. President: Insurance Inst. of London, 1966–67; Chartered Insce Inst., 1970–71; Insce Charities, 1973–74; Insce Orchestral Soc., 1973–74; Chairman: Insce Industry Training Council, 1973–75; Clergy Orphan Corp., 1967–80 (Vice-Pres., 1980); Coll. of All Saints, Tottenham, 1967–76; Chm., Allchurches Trust Ltd, 1975–85; Governor: St Mary's Sch., Wantage, 1967–; St Edmund's Sch., Canterbury, 1967–; St Margaret's Sch., Bushey, 1967–; Mem., Policyholders Protection Bd, 1975–81; Treasurer: Historic Churches Preservation Trust, 1977–85; Soc. for Advancing Christian Faith, 1977–. Master, Coopers' Co., 1984–85; Asst, Insurers' Co., 1979–. Hon. DCanL Lexington, 1975. *Recreations:* golf, travel. *Address:* 24 Alexandra Lodge, Monument Hill, Weybridge, Surrey KT13 8RY. *T:* Weybridge 58178. *Clubs:* City Livery; Richmond Golf; Parkstone Golf.

GRANT, Andrew Francis Joseph, CB 1971; BSc, CEng, FICE; *b* 25 Feb. 1911; *er s* of Francis Herbert and Clare Grant; *m* 1934, Mary Harrison; two *s* two *d*. *Educ:* St Joseph's Coll., Beulah Hill; King's Coll., London. Asst Civil Engr with Contractors on London Underground Rlys, 1931; Port of London Authority, 1935; entered Civil Engineer-in-Chief's Dept, Admiralty, and posted to Singapore, 1937; Suptg Civil Engr, Durban, 1942; Civil Engr. Adviser, RN Home Air Comd, 1947; Suptg Civil Engr, Malta, 1951; Asst Dir, Navy Works, 1959; Fleet Navy Works Officer, Mediterranean, 1960; Director for Wales, MPBW, 1963; Regional Director, Far East, 1966; Dir, Home Regional Services, DoE, 1968–71. *Recreations:* painting, golf, travel. *Address:* 48 Cecil Road, Norwich, Norfolk NR1 2QN. *Club:* Civil Service.

GRANT, Sir Anthony, Kt 1983; MP (C) Cambridgeshire South-West, since 1983 (Harrow Central, 1964–83); Solicitor and Company Director; *b* May 1925; *m* Sonia Isobel; one *s* one *d*. *Educ:* St Paul's Sch.; Brasenose Coll., Oxford. Admitted a Solicitor, 1952; Liveryman, Worshipful Company of Solicitors; Freeman, City of London; Master, Guild of Freemen, 1979. Army 1943–48, Third Dragoon Guards (Capt.). Opposition Whip, 1966–70; Parly Sec., Board of Trade, June-Oct. 1970; Parliamentary Under-Secretary of State: Trade, DTI, 1970–72; Industrial Develt, DTI, 1972–74; Chm., Cons. back bench Trade Cttee, 1979–; Mem., Foreign Affairs Select Cttee, 1980–; a Vice-Chm., Conservative Party Organisation, 1974–76. Member: Council of Europe (Chm., Econ. Cttee, 1980–); WEU. *Recreations:* watching Rugby and cricket, playing golf; Napoleonic history. *Address:* House of Commons, SW1.

GRANT of Monymusk, Sir Archibald, 13th Bt, *cr* 1705; *b* 2 Sept. 1954; *e s* of Captain Sir Francis Cullen Grant, 12th Bt, and of Lady Grant (Jean Margherita, *d* of Captain Humphrey Douglas Tollemache, RN), who *m* 2nd, Baron Tweedsmuir, *qv*; *S* father, 1966; *m* 1982, Barbara Elizabeth, *e d* of A. G. D. Forbes, Drumminnor Castle, Rhynie, Aberdeenshire; one *d*. *Heir:* *b* Francis Tollemache Grant, *b* 18 Dec. 1955. *Address:* House of Monymusk, Aberdeenshire. *T:* Monymusk 220.

GRANT, His Honour Brian; *see* Grant, His Honour H. B.

GRANT, Cary; actor; Director: Fabergé Inc.; Metro Goldwyn Mayer Inc.; *b* Bristol, 18 Jan. 1904; *s* of Elias Leach and Elsie Kingdom; became US citizen, 1942; *m* 1st 1934, Virginia Cherill (marr. diss., 1934); 2nd, 1942, Barbara Hutton (marr. diss., 1945); 3rd, 1949, Betsy Drake; 4th, 1965, Dyan Cannon (marr. diss., 1968); one *d*; 5th, 1981, Barbara Harris. *Educ:* Fairfield Academy, Somerset. Dir Emeritus, Western Airlines. Mem., Board of Governors, United Services Orgn, 1976–. Started acting, New York, 1921; appeared in: Golden Dawn; Polly; Boom Boom; Wonderful Night; Street Singer; Nikki. *Films include:* Arsenic and Old Lace; None but the Lonely Heart; The Bishop's Wife; The Bachelor and the Bobby Soxer; Mr Blandings Builds His Dream House; To Catch a Thief; The Pride and the Passion; An Affair to Remember; Indiscreet; North by North-West; Operation Petticoat; A Touch of Mink; Charade; Father Goose; Walk, Don't Run. Special Academy Award for contributions to motion picture industry, 1969. *Recreation:* riding.

GRANT, Rt. Rev. Charles Alexander, MA; LCL; Bishop of Northampton, (RC), 1967–82, Apostolic Administrator 1982; *b* 25 Oct. 1906; *s* of Frank and Sibylla Christina Grant. *Educ:* Perse Sch., Cambridge; St Edmund's, Ware; Christ's Coll., Cambridge; Oscott Coll., Birmingham; Gregorian Univ., Rome. Curate, Cambridge, 1938; Parish Priest: Ely, 1943; Kettering, 1945. Bishop-Auxiliary of Northampton, 1961–67. *Address:* St John's Convent, Kiln Green, near Reading RG10 9XP.

GRANT, Sir Clifford (Harry), Kt 1977; Chief Stipendiary Magistrate, Western Australia, since 1982; *b* England, 12 April 1929; *m* 1962, Karen Ann Ferguson. *Educ:* Montclair, NJ, USA; Harrison Coll., Barbados; Liverpool Coll.; Liverpool Univ. (LLB (Hons) 1949). Solicitor, Supreme Court of Judicature, 1951; Comr for Oaths, 1958; in private practice, London; apptd to HM Overseas Judiciary, 1958; Magistrate, Kenya, 1958, Sen. Magistrate, 1962; transf. to Hong Kong, Crown Solicitor, 1963, Principal Magistrate, 1965; transf. to Fiji, Sen. Magistrate, 1967; admitted Barrister and Solicitor, Supreme Court of Fiji, 1969; Chief Magistrate, 1971; Judge of Supreme Court, 1972; Chief Justice of Fiji, 1974–80. Pres., Fiji Court of Appeal, and Chm., Judicial and Legal Services Commn, 1974–80; sole Comr, Royal Commn on Crime, 1975 (report published 1976). Sometime Actg Governor-General, 1973–79. Fiji Independence Medal, 1970. *Publications:* articles for legal jls. *Recreations:* sociobiology, photography, literature, music. *Address:* Central Law Courts, Perth, WA 6000, Australia.

GRANT, His Honour Derek Aldwin, DSO 1944; QC 1962; a Circuit Judge (formerly an Additional Judge of the Central Criminal Court), 1969–84; *b* 22 Jan. 1915; *s* of late Charles Frederick Grant, CSI, ICS; *m* 1954, Phoebe Louise Wavell-Paxton; one *s* three *d*. *Educ:* Winchester Coll.; Oriel Coll., Oxford. Called to Bar 1938. Served in RAF, 1940–46 (King's Commendation, DSO). Master of the Bench, Inner Temple, 1969. Deputy Chairman, East Sussex County Sessions, 1962–71; Recorder of Salisbury, 1962–67, of Portsmouth, 1967–69. *Address:* Carters Lodge, Handcross, West Sussex.

GRANT, Donald Blane, TD 1964; Partner, KMG Thomson McLintock, CA (formerly Moody Stuart & Robertson, then Thomson McLintock & Co.), since 1950; *b* 8 Oct. 1921; *s* of Quintin Blane Grant and Euphemia Phyllis Grant; *m* 1944, Lavinia Margaret Ruth Ritchie; three *d*. *Educ:* High Sch. of Dundee. CA 1948. Served War, RA, 1939–46: TA Officer, retd as Major. Director: Dundee & London Investment Trust PLC, 1969–; HAT Group PLC, 1969–; Don Brothers Buist PLC, 1984–. Inst. of Chartered Accountants of Scotland: Mem. Council, 1971–76; Vice Pres., 1977–79, Pres., 1979–80. Chm., Tayside Health Bd, 1984–. *Recreations:* shooting, fishing, golf, bridge, gardening. *Address:* Summerfield, 24 Albany Road, West Ferry, Dundee. *T:* Dundee 737804. *Clubs:* Institute of Directors; New (Edinburgh); Royal and Ancient Golf (St Andrews); Panmure Golf (Carnoustie); Blairgowrie Golf (Rosemount).

GRANT, Donald David, CB 1985; Director General, Central Office of Information, 1982–85; *b* 1 Aug. 1924; *s* of Donald Herbert Grant and Florence Emily Grant; *m* 1954, Beatrice Mary Varney; two *d*. *Educ:* Wandsworth Sch. Served War, RNVR, Sub-Lt (A), 1942–46. Journalist, Evening Standard, Reuters, 1946–51; Dir, Sidney Barton Ltd, PR Consultants, 1951–61; Chief Information Officer, Min. of Aviation and Technology, 1961–67; Dir, Public Relations, STC Ltd, 1967–70; Director of Information: GLC, 1971–72; DTI, 1972–74; Home Office, 1974–82. Vis. Prof., Graduate Centre for Journalism, City Univ., 1986–. *Recreation:* sailing. *Address:* Holly Lodge, 1 Calonne Road, Wimbledon, SW19. *T:* 01–947 2383. *Club:* Reform.

GRANT, Douglas Marr Kelso; Sheriff of South Strathclyde, Dumfries and Galloway (formerly of Ayr and Bute), since 1966; *b* 5 April 1917; *m* 1952, Audrey Stevenson Law; two *s* two *d*. *Educ:* Rugby; Peterhouse, Cambridge. Entered Colonial Admin. Service, Uganda Protectorate, 1939. Army Service, 1940–46. Called to Bar, Gray's Inn, 1945; Judicial and Legal Dept, Malaya, 1946–57. Admitted to Faculty of Advocates and Scottish Bar, 1959. *Address:* Drumellan House, Maybole, Ayrshire. *T:* Maybole 82279.

GRANT, Prof. (Duncan) Alistair (Antoine), RBA, ARCA; Professor of Printmaking, since 1984, Head of Printmaking Department, since 1970, Royal College of Art; Chairman, Faculty of Printmaking, British School at Rome, since 1978; *b* London, 3 June 1925; *s* of Duncan and Germaine Grant; *m* 1949, Phyllis Fricker; one *d*. *Educ:* Froebel, Whitehill, Glasgow; Birmingham Sch. of Art; Royal Coll. of Art. Joined staff of RCA, 1955. *One Man Shows* at the following galleries: Zwemmer; Piccadilly; AIA; Ashgate; Bear Lane, Oxford; Midland Group, Nottingham; Balclutha; Ware, London; 46, Edinburgh; Editions Alecto; Redfern. *Works in the collections of:* V&A Museum; Tate Gallery; Min. of Works; LCC (now GLC); Arts Council; Carlisle Art Gall.; Ferens Art Gall., Hull; The King of Sweden; Dallas Museum; Cincinnati; Boston; Museum of Modern Art, New York; Chicago Art Inst.; Lessing J. Rosenwald Collection; Beaverbrook Foundn, Fredericton, NB; Vancouver Art Gall.; Victoria Art Gall. *Group Exhibitions* in Bahamas, Canada, Europe, S America, USA and UK. Awarded Silver Medal, Internat. Festival of Youth, Moscow, 1957. *Address:* 13 Redcliffe Gardens, SW10 9BG. *T:* 01–352 4312.

GRANT, Edward; Lord Mayor, City of Manchester, May 1972–May 1973; *b* 10 Aug. 1915; *s* of Edward and Ada Grant; *m* 1942, Winifred Mitchell. *Educ:* Moston Lane Sch.; Manchester High Sch. of Commerce. City Councillor, Manchester, 1950–84 (Alderman, 1970–74); Hosp. Administrator, Manchester AHA (T) North Dist (formerly NE Manchester HMC), 1948–75, now retired. *Recreations:* swimming, reading, gardening. *Address:* 14 Rainton Walk, New Moston, Manchester M10 0FR. *T:* 061–681 4758.

GRANT, Brig. Eneas Henry George, CBE 1951; DSO 1944 and Bar, 1945; MC 1936; JP; Hon. DL; retired; *b* 14 Aug. 1901; *s* of late Col H. G. Grant, CB, late Seaforth Highlanders and late Mrs Grant, Balnespick, Inverness-shire; *m* 1926, Lilian Marion (*d* 1978), *d* of late S. O'Neill, Cumberstown House, Co. Westmeath; one *s* (and *er s*, Lieut Seaforth Highlanders, killed in action, Korea, 1951). *Educ:* Wellington Coll., Berks; RMC, Sandhurst. 2nd Lieut Seaforth Highlanders, 1920; Adjt Lovat Scouts, 1928–33; served in Palestine, 1936; War of 1939–45; France 1940; France and Germany, 1944–45. Lieut-Colonel 1942 (Subs. 1947); Colonel 1944 (Subs. 1948); Brigadier 1944 (Subs. 1952); Bde Commander, 1944–49; Comdr Gold Coast District, 1949–52. Col Comdt Gold Coast Regt, 1949–52; Deputy Commander, Northumbrian District, 1952–55; retired 1955. JP Inverness-shire, 1957. DL Inverness-shire, 1958–80. Chairman Inverness-shire TA and Air Force Association, 1961–65. *Recreations:* country pursuits. *Address:* Inverbrough Lodge, Tomatin, Inverness-shire. *Club:* Highland (Inverness).

GRANT, Maj.-Gen. Ferris Nelson, CB 1967; *b* 25 Dec. 1916; *s* of late Lieut-Gen. H. G. Grant and of Mrs N. L. B. Grant (*née* Barker); *m* 1940, Patricia Anne (*née* Jameson); one *s* one *d*. *Educ:* Cheltenham Coll. Joined Royal Marines, 1935. Capt., HMS Suffolk, 1940–42; US Marine Corps Staff Coll., Major, 1943; Staff of SACSEA, Lt-Col 1943; Army Staff Coll., Camberley, 1946; 45 Commando, 1947; Chief Instructor, Commando Sch., 1949; CO 41 Commando, Korea, 1950; jssc, 1951; Bde Major, Commando Bde, 1952; Instructor, USMC Staff Coll., 1958; CO Amphibious Trng Unit, 1960; CO Depot RM, 1961; CO Infantry Trng Centre, 1963; Comdr, Plymouth Group, Royal Marines, 1965–68, retired. Member, panel of independent inspectors for public inquiries, 1983–. Governor, Sch. for Visually Handicapped, 1974–82. Lay reader. Legion of Merit (US). *Recreations:* sailing, gardening, painting; Past Pres. RN Boxing Assoc. *Address:* Little Burrow Farmhouse, Broadclyst, Exeter, Devon. *Clubs:* Army and Navy; Royal Yacht Squadron, Royal Naval Sailing Association.

GRANT, George; *b* 11 Oct. 1924; *m* 1948, Adeline (*née* Conroy), Morpeth; one *s* four *d*. *Educ:* Netherton Council Sch. and WEA. Member Bedlingtonshire UDC, 1959–70 (Chm. for two years). Member: Labour Party, 1947–; NUM (Chm., 1963–70). MP (Lab) Morpeth, 1970–83; PPS to Minister of Agriculture, 1974–76. *Recreations:* sport, gardening. *Address:* 4 Ringway, Choppington, Northumberland. *Clubs:* Working Men's, in the Bedlington and Ashington area.

GRANT, His Honour (Hubert) Brian; a Circuit Judge of Sussex and Kent (formerly Judge of County Courts), 1965–82; *b* Berlin, 5 Aug. 1917; *m* 1946, Jeanette Mary Carroll; one *s* three *d*. *Educ:* Trinity Coll., Cambridge (Sen. Schol.). 1st cl. hons, Law Tripos, 1939; MA. War service, 1940–44: Commandos, 1942–44. Called to Bar, Gray's Inn, 1945 (Lord Justice Holker Senior Scholar). Mem., Law Reform Cttee, 1970–73. Vice-Chm., Nat. Marriage Guidance Council, 1970–72; Founder Pres., Parenthood, 1979. *Publications:* Marriage, Separation and Divorce, 1946; Family Law, 1970; Conciliation and Divorce, 1981; The Quiet Ear, 1987. *Address:* Eden Hill, Armathwaite, Carlisle CA4 9PQ. *Club:* Penrith Golf.

GRANT, Maj.-Gen. Ian Hallam L.; *see* Lyall Grant.

GRANT, Ian Nicholas, (Nick); Public Affairs Advisor, Mirror Group, since 1985; *b* 24 March 1948; *s* of Hugo and Cara Grant; *m* 1977, Rosalind Louise Pipe; one *s* one *d*. *Educ:* Univ. of London (external LLB); Univ. of Warwick (MA, Industrial Relns). Confederation of Health Service Employees: Research Officer, 1972–74; Head of Research and Public Relations, 1974–82; Dir of Publicity, Labour Party, 1982–85. Member: Council London Borough of Lambeth, 1978–84; Lambeth, Southwark and Lewisham AHA, 1978–82; W Lambeth DHA, 1982–83. Contested (Lab) Reigate, 1979. *Publications:* contrib. to: Economics of Prosperity, by David Blake and Paul Ormerod, 1980; Political Communications: the general election campaign of 1983, ed M. Harrop, 1985; many articles on politics, industrial relations and NHS policy in various jls. *Recreations:* walking, reading, photography, music, children. *Address:* 23 Orlando Road, Clapham, SW4 0LD. *T:* 01–720 1091.

GRANT, Rt. Rev. James Alexander; Bishop Coadjutor, Diocese of Melbourne, since 1970; Dean of St Paul's Cathedral, Melbourne, since 1985; *b* 30 Aug. 1931; *s* of late V. G. Grant, Geelong; *m* 1983, Rowena Margaret Armstrong. *Educ:* Trinity College, Univ. of Melbourne (BA Hons); Melbourne College of Divinity (BD). Deacon 1959 (Curate, St Peter's, Murrumbeena), Priest 1960; Curate, West Heidelberg 1960, Broadmeadows 1961; Leader Diocesan Task Force, Broadmeadows, 1962; Domestic and Examining Chaplain to Archbishop of Melbourne, 1966; Chairman, Brotherhood of St Laurence, 1971– (Director, 1969); Chaplain, Trinity Coll., Univ. of Melbourne, 1970–75, Fellow, 1975–. *Publications:* (with Geoffrey Serle) The Melbourne Scene, 1957; Perspective of a Century-Trinity College, 1872–1972, 1972. *Recreation:* historical research. *Address:* Cathedral Buildings, Flinders Lane, Melbourne, Vic 3000, Australia.

GRANT, James Currie, CBE 1975; Editor, The Press and Journal, Aberdeen, 1960–75, Associate Editor, 1975–76, retired; *b* 5 May 1914; *s* of Alexander Grant, Elgin; *m* 1940, Lillias Isabella Gordon; one *d*. *Educ:* Elgin Academy. With the Northern Scot, Elgin, 1930–36; joined The Press and Journal, as reporter, 1936; served with Royal Artillery, 1940–46; Sub-editor, The Press and Journal, 1946, Dep. Chief Sub-Editor, 1947–53, Asst Editor, 1953–56, Dep. Editor, 1956–60. Chm., Editorial Cttee, Scottish Daily Newspaper Soc., 1972–75. *Recreations:* voluntary social work, gardening, swimming. *Address:* 42 Fonthill Road, Aberdeen AB1 2UJ. *T:* 582090.

GRANT, James Pineo; Executive Director, United Nations Children's Fund (UNICEF), since 1980; *b* 12 May 1922; *s* of John B. and Charlotte Grant; *m* 1943, Ethel Henck; three *s*. *Educ:* Univ. of California, Berkeley (BA); Harvard Univ. (JD). US Army, 1943–45; UN Relief and Rehabilitation Admin, 1946–47; Acting Exec. Sec. to Sino-American Jt Cttee on Rural Reconstruction, 1948–50; Law Associate, Covington and Burling, Washington, DC, 1951–54; Regional Legal Counsel in New Delhi for US aid programs for S Asia, 1954–56; Dir, US aid mission to Ceylon, 1956–58; Dep. to Dir of Internat. Co-operation Admin, 1959–62; Dep. Asst Sec. of State for Near East and S Asian Affairs, 1962–64; Dir, AID program in Turkey, with rank of Minister, 1964–67; Asst Administrator, Agency for Internat. Develt (AID), 1967–69; Pres., Overseas Develt Council, 1969–80. Hon. Prof., Capital Medical Coll. of China, 1983. Hon. LLD: Notre Dame, 1980; Maryville Coll., 1981; Tufts, 1983; Denison, 1983. Hon. DrSci Hacettepe, Ankara, 1980. Rockefeller Public Service Award, 1980; Boyaca Award, Colombia, 1984; Gold Mercury Internat. Award, Internat. Orgn for Co-operation, 1984; Presidential Citation, APHA, 1985. *Publications:* The State of the World's Children Report, annually; articles in Foreign Affairs, Foreign Policy, Annals. *Address:* 866 United Nations Plaza, Room A-6004, New York, NY 10017, USA. *T:* (212) 415–8290. *Clubs:* Metropolitan, Cosmos (Washington, DC).

GRANT, James Shaw, CBE 1968 (OBE 1956); Member, Highlands and Islands Development Board, 1970–82; *b* 22 May 1910; *s* of William Grant and Johanna Morison Grant, Stornoway; *m* 1951, Catherine Mary Stewart; no *c*. *Educ:* Nicolson Inst.; Glasgow Univ. Editor, Stornoway Gazette, 1932–63; Mem., Crofters' Commn, 1955–63, Chm., 1963–78. Dir, Grampian Television, 1969–80. Mem. Scottish Adv. Cttee, British Council, 1972. Governor, Pitlochry Festival Theatre, 1954–84, Chairman, 1971–83; Chm., Harris Tweed Assoc. Ltd, 1972–84. Mem. Council, Nat. Trust for Scotland, 1979–84. FRAgS 1973; FRSE 1982. Hon. LLD Aberdeen, 1979. *Publications:* Highland Villages, 1977; Their Children Will See, 1979; The Hub of My Universe, 1983; Surprise Island, 1983; The Gaelic Vikings, 1984; Stornoway and the Lews, 1985; several plays. *Recreations:* golf, photography. *Address:* Ardgrianach, Inshes, Inverness. *T:* Inverness 231476. *Club:* Royal Over-Seas League.

GRANT, Joan, (Mrs Denys Kelsey); *b* 12 April 1907; *d* of John Frederick Marshall, CBE; *m* 1st, 1927, Arthur Leslie Grant; one *d*; 2nd, 1940, Charles Robert Longfield Beatty; 3rd, 1960, Denys Edward Reginald Kelsey, MB, MRCP. *Publications:* Winged Pharaoh, 1937; Life as Carola, 1939; Eyes of Horus, 1942; The Scarlet Fish and other Stories, 1942; Lord of the Horizon, 1943; Redskin Morning, 1944; Scarlet Feather, 1945; Vague Vacation, 1947; Return to Elysium, 1947; The Laird and the Lady, 1949 (US edn, Castle Cloud); So Moses Was Born, 1952; Time out of Mind (autobiography), 1956 (US edn, Far Memory); A Lot to Remember, 1962; (with Denys Kelsey) Many Lifetimes, 1969; The Collected Works of Joan Grant, 1979; The Blue Faience Hippopotamus, 1984; The Monster Who Grew Small, 1986; translations in Icelandic, Swedish, Finnish, Danish, Dutch, Polish, Hungarian, French, German, Italian. *Address:* c/o A. P. Watt Ltd, 26–28 Bedford Row, WC1R 4HL.

GRANT, Rear-Adm. John, CB 1960; DSO 1942; *b* 13 Oct. 1908; *s* of late Maj.-Gen. Sir Philip Grant, KCB, CMG, and Annette, *d* of John Coventry, Burgate, Fordingbridge; *m* 1935, Ruth Hayward Slade; two *s* two *d*. *Educ:* St Anthony's, Eastbourne; RN Colls, Dartmouth and Greenwich. Midshipman, HMS Queen Elizabeth, 1926; Sub-Lieut, HMS Revenge, 1930; Lieut, HMS Kent, China Station, 1932; specialised in anti-submarine warfare, 1933–39; Staff Officer Convoys, Rosyth, 1940; in comd HMS Beverley, 1941–42 (DSO); Trng Comdr, HMS Osprey, 1942, and subseq. in HMS Western Isles; in comd HMS Philante, 1943; Trng Comdr, HMS Osprey, 1944; in comd HMS Opportune, Fame and Crispin, 1945–47; Joint Staff Coll., 1947; Executive Officer, HMS Vernon; Capt. 1949; Dep. Dir Torpedo Anti-Submarine and Mine Warfare Div., Naval Staff, Admiralty, 1949–51; in comd HMS Cleopatra, 1952–53; Imperial Defence Coll., 1954; in comd HMS Vernon, 1955–57; on staff of Chief of Defence Staff, Min. of Defence, 1957–59; Rear-Adm., 1959; Flag Officer Commanding Reserve Fleet, 1959–60; retired list, 1961. Rank Organisation, 1961–65; Director, Conference of the Electronics Industry, 1965–71. *Address:* 9 Rivermead Court, Ranelagh Gardens, SW6 3RT.

GRANT, Sir (John) Anthony; *see* Grant, Sir A.

GRANT, John Douglas; Head of Communications, Electrical, Electronic, Telecommunication and Plumbing Union, since 1984; *b* 16 Oct. 1932; *m* 1955, Patricia Julia Ann; two *s* one *d*. *Educ:* Stationers' Company's Sch., Hornsey. Reporter on various provincial newspapers until 1955; Daily Express, 1955–70 (Chief Industrial Correspondent, 1967–70). Contested (Lab) Beckenham, 1966; Chm., Bromley Constituency Labour Party, 1966–70. Chm., Labour and Industrial Correspondents' Group, 1967. MP Islington East, 1970–74, Islington Central, 1974–83 (Lab, 1970–81, SDP, 1981–83). Opposition Front Bench Spokesman for policy on broadcasting and the press, 1973–74, on employment, 1979–81; Parly Sec., CSD, March-Oct. 1974; Parliamentary Under-Secretary of State: ODM, 1974–76; Dept of Employment, 1976–79; SDP employment spokesman, 1981–83; SDP industry spokesman, 1982–83. Contested (SDP) Islington North, 1983. *Publications:* Member of Parliament, 1974; articles in national newspapers and periodicals. *Recreations:* tennis, watching soccer. *Address:* 1 Betts Close, Beckenham, Kent. *T:* 01–650 8643.

GRANT, John James, CBE 1960; Director, University of Durham Institute of Education, 1963–77; *b* 19 Oct. 1914; *s* of John and Mary Grant; *m* 1945, Jean Graham Stewart; two *s*. *Educ:* Shawlands Academy, Glasgow; Univ. of Glasgow (MA, EdB). Supply teaching, Glasgow, 1939–40. Served War: UK, India, Burma, 1940–46. Mod. Lang. Master, High Sch. of Glasgow, 1946–48; Lectr in Educn, Univ. of Durham, 1948–52; Vice-Principal, Fourah Bay Coll., Sierra Leone, 1953–55, Principal, 1955–60; Principal, St Cuthbert's Soc., Univ. of Durham, 1960–63. Hon. DCL Durham, 1960. *Recreations:* golf, theatre, gardening. *Address:* Tithe Barn, Shincliffe, Durham. *T:* Durham 64728.

GRANT, Keith Wallace; Director, Design Council, since 1977; *b* 30 June 1934; *s* of Randolph and Sylvia Grant; *m* 1968, Deanne (*née* Bergsma); one *s* one *d*. *Educ:* Trinity Coll., Glenalmond; Clare Coll., Cambridge (MA). Account Exec., W. S. Crawford Ltd, 1958–62; General Manager: Covent Garden Opera Co., later Royal Opera, 1962–73; English Opera Group, 1962–73; Sec., Royal Soc. of Arts, 1973–77. Member: Adv. Council, V&A Mus., 1977–83; PO Stamp Adv. Cttee, 1978–; Exec. Bd, Internat. Council of Socs of Industrial Design, 1983–. Chm., English Music Theatre Co., 1979–; Governor: Central Sch. of Art and Design, 1974–77; Birmingham Polytechnic, 1981–; Edinburgh Coll. of Art, 1982–. Hon. FSIAD, 1983. *Address:* c/o Design Council, 28 Haymarket, SW1Y 4SU. *Clubs:* Garrick, Arts.

GRANT, Sir (Kenneth) Lindsay, CMT 1969; Kt 1963; OBE 1956; ED 1944; Director, T. Geddes Grant Ltd (Chairman, 1946–64); Chairman, Vice-Chairman, and Director of numerous other companies; *b* Trinidad, 10 Feb. 1899; *s* of T. Geddes Grant (Canadian); *m* 1923, (Edith) Grace Norman; no *c*. *Educ:* Queen's Royal College, Trinidad; Maritime Business Coll., Halifax, NS. Served European War: (3rd Trinidad Contingent, 1916–17, 5th BWI Regt, 1917, RFC, 1917) 2nd Lieut; (RAF 1917–19) Flying Officer; War of 1939–45: (Trinidad Volunteers) Major, 2nd in Comd, 1944–45. Joined T. Geddes Grant Ltd, 1919; Manager, Office Appliances Dept, 1921; Director, 1927; Chm. and Man. Dir, 1946 (retd as Man. Dir, Sept. 1962; Chm. until 1964; Pres., 1964–68 and 1979–). Pres., 1957–75, Hon. Life Pres., 1975–, Trinidad and Tobago Leprosy Relief Assoc. Past and present activities: Church (Elder, Greyfriars); Boy Scouts; Cadets; Social Service. Chaconia Gold Medal, 1969. *Recreations:* none now; played cricket, Association football, tennis, golf. *Address:* (office) T. Geddes Grant Ltd, Box 171, Port of Spain, Trinidad. *T:* 54805; (home) 50 Ellerslie Park, Maraval, Trinidad. *T:* 25202, Port of Spain. *Clubs:* Royal Commonwealth Society, Royal Over-Seas League, (Hon. Life) MCC (all London); Union, Country, Queen's Park Cricket, etc (Trinidad).

GRANT, Sir Lindsay; *see* Grant, Sir K. L.

GRANT, Very Rev. Malcolm Etheridge; Provost and Rector of St Mary's Cathedral, Glasgow, since 1981; *b* 6 Aug. 1944; *s* of Donald Etheridge Grant and Nellie Florence May Grant (*née* Tuffey); *m* 1984, Katrina Russell Nuttall (*née* Dunnett). *Educ:* Dunfermline High School; Univ. of Edinburgh (Bruce of Grangehill Bursar, 1962; BSc (Hons Chemistry); BD (Hons New Testament); Divinity Fellowship, 1969); Edinburgh Theological College. Deacon 1969, priest 1970; Assistant Curate: St Mary's Cathedral, Glasgow, 1969; St Wulfram's, Grantham (in charge of Church of the Epiphany, Earlesfield), 1972; Team Vicar of Earlesfield, Grantham, 1972; Priest-in-charge, St Ninian's, Invergordon, 1978; Examining Chaplain to Bishop of Moray, Ross and Caithness, 1979; Member, Highland Regional Council Education Cttee, 1979–81. *Address:* 45 Rowallan Gardens, Glasgow G11 7LH. *T:* 041–339 4956; (office) St Mary's Cathedral, 300 Great Western Road, Glasgow. G4 9JB. *T:* 041–339 6691.

GRANT, Michael, CBE 1958 (OBE 1946); MA, LittD (Cambridge); *b* 21 Nov. 1914; *s* of late Col Maurice Harold Grant and Muriel, *d* of C. Jörgensen; *m* 1944, Anne Sophie Beskow, Norrköping, Sweden; two *s*. *Educ:* Harrow Sch.; Trinity Coll., Cambridge. Porson Prizeman, First Chancellor's Classical Medallist, Craven Student; Fellow Trinity Coll., Cambridge, 1938–49. Served War of 1939–45, Army, War Office, 1939–40, Actg Capt.; first British Council Rep. in Turkey, 1940–45; Prof. of Humanity at Edinburgh Univ., 1948–59; first Vice-Chancellor, Univ. of Khartoum, 1956–58; Pres. and Vice-Chancellor of the Queen's Univ. of Belfast, 1959–66; Pres., 1953–56, Medallist, 1962, and Hon. Fellow, 1984, Royal Numismatic Soc.; Huntington Medalist, American Numismatic Soc., 1965. J. H. Gray Lectr, Cambridge, 1955; FSA. Chairman, National Council for the Supply of Teachers Overseas, 1963–66. President: Virgil Soc., 1963–66; Classical Assoc., 1977–78. Chm., Commonwealth Conf. on Teaching of English as 2nd Language at Makerere, Uganda, 1961. Hon. LittD Dublin, 1961; Hon. LLD QUB, 1967. Gold Medal for Educn, Sudan, 1977. *Publications:* From Imperium to Auctoritas, 1946; Aspects of the Principate of Tiberius, 1950; Roman Anniversary Issues, 1950; Ancient History, 1952; The Six Main Aes Coinages of Augustus, 1953; Roman Imperial Money, 1954; Roman Literature, 1954; translations of Tacitus and Cicero; Roman History from Coins, 1958; The World of Rome, 1960; Myths of the Greeks and Romans, 1962; Birth of Western Civilization (ed), 1964; The Civilizations of Europe, 1965; The Gladiators, 1967; The Climax of Rome, 1968; The Ancient Mediterranean, 1969 (Premio del Mediterraneo, Mazara del Vallo, 1983, for Italian edn); Julius Caesar, 1969; The Ancient Historians, 1970; The Roman Forum, 1970; Nero, 1970; Cities of Vesuvius, 1971; Herod the Great, 1971; Roman Myths, 1971; Cleopatra, 1972; The Jews in the Roman World, 1973; The Army of the Caesars, 1974; The Twelve Caesars, 1975; (ed) Greek Literature, 1976; The Fall of the Roman Empire, 1976; Saint Paul, 1976; Jesus, 1977; History of Rome, 1978; (ed) Latin Literature, 1978; The Etruscans, 1980; Greek and Latin Authors 800 BC-AD 1000, 1980; The Dawn of the Middle Ages, 1981; From Alexander to Cleopatra, 1982; History of Ancient Israel, 1984; The Roman Emperors, 1985. *Address:* Le Pitturacce, Gattaiola, Lucca, Italy. *Club:* Athenæum.

GRANT, Nick; *see* Grant, I. N.

GRANT of Dalvey, Sir Patrick Alexander Benedict, 14th Bt *cr* 1688 (NS); Chieftain of Clan Donnachy; (Donnachaidh); Managing Director, Grainger & Campbell Ltd, Glasgow, since 1980; Director, Duncan MacRae Ltd, Edinburgh, since 1982; *b* 5 Feb. 1953; *e s* of Sir Duncan Alexander Grant, 13th Bt, and of Joan Penelope, *o d* of Captain Sir Denzil Cope, 14th Bt; *S* father, 1961; *m* 1981, Dr Carolyn Elizabeth Highet, MB, ChB, DRCOG, MRCGP, *d* of Dr John Highet, Glasgow; two *s*. *Educ:* St Conleth's Coll., Dublin; The Abbey Sch., Fort Augustus; Univ of Glasgow (LLB 1981). FSAScot. Former deer-stalker, inshore fisherman. *Recreation:* professional competing piper. *Heir:* *s* Duncan Archibald Ludovic Grant, *b* 19 April 1982. *Address:* 2 The Crescent, Busby, Glasgow G76 8HT. *T:* 041–644 4121.

GRANT, Peter James; Chairman: Sun Life Assurance Society plc, since 1983 (Director, since 1973, Vice-Chairman, 1976); Deputy Chairman, Lazard Brothers & Co. Ltd, since 1985 (Vice-Chairman, 1983–85); *b* 5 Dec. 1929; 2nd *s* of late Lt-Col P. C. H. Grant, Scots Guards, and Mrs Grant (*née* Gooch); *m* 1st, Ann, *d* of late Christopher Pleydell-Bouverie; one *s* one *d*; 2nd, Paula, *d* of late E. J. P. Eugster; one *s* two *d*. *Educ:* Winchester; Magdalen Coll., Oxford. Lieut, Queen's Own Cameron Highlanders. Edward de Stein & Co., 1952, merged with Lazard Brothers & Co. Ltd, 1960; Director: Walter Runciman plc, 1973–; Standard Industrial Gp, 1966–72; Charrington, Gardner, Lockett & Co. Ltd, 1970–74. Mem., Industrial Develt Adv. Bd, 1985–. Mem. Council and Chm., Finance Cttee, British Red Cross Soc., 1972–85. *Recreations:* shooting, golf, gardening. *Address:* Vinehall Manor, Robertsbridge, Sussex. *T:* Sedlescombe 279; Letter Kilmuir, North Kessock, Inverness. *T:* Kessock 275. *Clubs:* Boodle's, Caledonian.

GRANT, Prof. Peter John, MA, PhD, MIMechE, FInstP; Professor of Nuclear Power, Imperial College of Science and Technology, since 1966, and Dean of Engineering, since 1984, London University; *b* London, 2 July 1926; *s* of Herbert James Grant; *m* Audrey, *d* of Joseph Whitham; one *s*. *Educ:* Merchant Taylors' Sch.; Sidney Sussex Coll., Cambridge. BA 1947, MA, PhD 1951. Research in Nuclear Physics at Cavendish Laboratory, 1947–50; Lectr in Natural Philosophy, Univ. of Glasgow, 1950–55; Chief Physicist, Atomic Energy Div., GEC Ltd, 1956–59; Reader in Engineering Science, Imperial Coll. of Science and Technology, 1959–66. *Publications:* Elementary Reactor Physics, 1966; Nuclear Science, 1971; papers on radioactivity, nuclear reactions, physics of nuclear reactors. *Address:* 49 Manor Road South, Esher, Surrey. *T:* 01–398 2001.

GRANT, Ronald Thomson, OBE; FRS 1934; MD, FRCP, DPH; formerly physician on staff of Medical Research Council; Consultant Physician Emeritus, Guy's Hospital; *b* 5 Nov. 1892. *Educ:* Glasgow Univ. *Publications:* articles in scientific journals. *Address:* Farley Green Cottage, Shophouse Lane, Albury, Guildford, Surrey GU5 9EQ. *T:* Shere 2164.

GRANT, Air Vice-Marshal Stanley Bernard, CB 1969; DFC 1942; bar to DFC 1943; RAF; *b* 31 May 1919; *s* of late Harry Alexander Gwatkin Grant and Marjorie Gladys Hoyle; *m* 1948, Barbara Jean Watts (*d* 1963); one *s* one *d*; *m* 1965, Christiane Marie Py (*née* Bech); one step *s* two step *d*. *Educ:* Charterhouse; RAF Coll., Cranwell. Joined RAF, 1937; War of 1939–45: service in UK, Malta, Egypt and Italy. Air Ministry, 1946–47; Flying Training Command, 1948–54; Fighter Command, 1955–56; SEATO, Bangkok, 1957–59; Fighter Command, 1960–61; idc course, 1962; NATO, Fontainebleau, 1963–64; Directing Staff, IDC, 1965–68; Comdr, British Forces, Gulf, 1968–69; retired 1970. *Address:* 14 rue des Cordeliers, 83170 Brignoles, France. *Club:* Royal Air Force.

GRANT-FERRIS, family name of **Baron Harvington.**

GRANT-SUTTIE, Sir (George) Philip; *see* Suttie, Sir G. P. G.

GRANTCHESTER, 2nd Baron *cr* 1953; **Kenneth Bent Suenson-Taylor,** CBE 1985; QC 1971; a Recorder of the Crown Court, since 1975; President, Value-added Tax Tribunals, since 1972; Chairman: Licensed Dealers' Tribunal, since 1976; Dairy Produce Quota Tribunal, since 1984; *b* 18 Aug. 1921; *s* of 1st Baron Grantchester, OBE, and of Mara Henriette (Mamie), *d* of late Albert Suenson, Copenhagen; *S* father, 1976; *m* 1947, Betty, *er d* of Sir John Moores, *qv*; three *s* three *d*. *Educ:* Westminster School; Christ's College, Cambridge (MA, LLM). Lieut RA, 1941–45. Called to the Bar, Middle Temple, 1946; admitted *ad eundem* by Lincoln's Inn, 1947. Lecturer in Company Law, Council of Legal Education, 1951–72. Pres., Aircraft and Shipbuilding Ind. Arbitration Tribunal, 1980–83. *Heir:* *e s* Hon. Christopher John Suenson-Taylor [*b* 8 April 1951; *m* 1972, Jacqueline, *d* of Dr Leo Jaffé; one *s* two *d*]. *Address:* The Gate House, Coombe Wood Road, Kingston Hill, Surrey. *T:* 01–546 9088.

GRANTHAM, Bishop Suffragan of, since 1972; **Rt. Rev. Dennis Gascoyne Hawker;** *b* 8 Feb. 1921; *o s* of late Robert Stephen and Amelia Caroline Hawker; *m* 1944, Margaret Hamilton, *d* of late Robert and Daisy Henderson; one *s* one *d*. *Educ:* Addey and Stanhope Grammar Sch.; Queens' Coll., Cambridge (MA); Cuddesdon Theological Coll., Oxford. Lloyds Bank, 1939–40. Served War, Commissioned Officer, Royal Marines, 1940–46 (War Substantive Major). Deacon, 1950; Priest, 1951; Asst. Curate, St Mary and St Eanswythe, Folkestone, 1950–55; Vicar, St Mark, South Norwood, 1955–60; St Hugh's Missioner, Dio. Lincoln, 1960–65; Vicar, St Mary and St James, Gt Grimsby, 1965–72; Canon and Prebendary of Clifton, in Lincoln Cath., 1964–; Proctor in Convocation, 1964–74. Hon. Chaplain, RNR, 1979–. *Address:* Fairacre, 243 Barrowby Road, Grantham, Lincs NG31 8NP. *T:* Grantham 64722. *Club:* Army and Navy.

GRANTHAM, Adm. Sir Guy, GCB 1956 (KCB 1952; CB 1942); CBE 1946; DSO 1941; retired; Governor and Commander-in-Chief of Malta, 1959–62; *b* 9 Jan. 1900; *s* of late C. F. Grantham, The Hall, Skegness, Lincs; *m* 1934, Beryl Marjorie, *d* of late T. C. B. Mackintosh-Walker, Geddes, Nairn; two *d.* Served War of 1939–45 (despatches, twice, DSO, CB, CBE); Chief of Staff to C-in-C, Mediterranean, 1946–48; Naval ADC to the King, 1947–48; Flag Officer (Submarines), 1948–50; Flag Officer, Second-in-Command, Mediterranean Fleet, 1950–51; Vice-Chief of Naval Staff, 1951–54; Comdr-in-Chief, Mediterranean Station, and Allied Forces, Mediterranean, 1954–57; Comdr in Chief, Portsmouth, Allied Comdr-in-Chief, Channel and Southern North Sea, 1957–59; First and Principal Naval ADC to the Queen, 1958–59. Retired list, 1959. Hon. Freeman of Haberdashers' Company. Mem., Commonwealth War Graves Commn 1962–70 (Vice-Chm. 1963–70). Governor, Corps of Commissionaires, 1964–. *Address:* Stanleys, Hatch Lane, Liss, Hants. *T:* Liss 892135.

GRANTHAM, Roy Aubrey; General Secretary, Association of Professional, Executive, Clerical & Computer Staff (APEX), since 1970; *b* 12 Dec. 1926; *m* 1964; two *d. Educ:* King Edward Grammar Sch., Aston, Birmingham. APEX: Midland area Organiser, 1949; Midland area Sec., 1959; Asst Sec., 1963. Mem., TUC Gen. Council, 1983–. Exec. Member: European Movement; Labour Cttee for Europe; Confedn of Shipbuilding and Engineering Unions. Member: Royal Commn on Environmental Pollution, 1976–79; CNAA, 1976–79; IBA, 1984–; MSC. A Dir, Chrysler UK Ltd, 1977–79, Talbot UK Ltd, 1979–81. Governor, Henley Management Coll., 1979–; Mem., Ditchley Foundn, 1982–. Vice-Chm., Inst. for Alcohol Studies. *Publication:* Guide to Grading of Clerical and Administrative Work, 1968. *Recreations:* walking, reading, chess. *Address:* 18 The Grange, Shirley, Croydon CR0 8AP.

GRANTLEY, 7th Baron, *cr* 1782; **John Richard Brinsley Norton,** MC 1944; Baron of Markenfield, 1782; a Member of Lloyd's; *b* 30 July 1923; *o s* of 6th Baron and Jean Mary (*d* 1945), *d* of Sir David Alexander Kinloch, CB, MVO, 11th Bt; *S* father 1954; *m* 1955, Deirdre Mary Freda, *e d* of 5th Earl of Listowel, *qv*; two *s. Educ:* Eton; New Coll., Oxford. Served War of 1939–45, 1942–45, in Italy as Capt. Grenadier Guards (MC). *Heir: s* Hon. Richard William Brinsley Norton, *b* 30 Jan. 1956. *Address:* 53 Lower Belgrave Street, SW1; Markenfield Hall, Ripon, North Yorks. *Clubs:* White's, Pratt's.

GRANVILLE, family name of **Baron Granville of Eye.**

GRANVILLE, 5th Earl, *cr* 1833; **Granville James Leveson Gower,** MC 1945; Viscount Granville, 1815; Baron Leveson, 1833; Major Coldstream Guards (Supplementary Reserve); Lord-Lieutenant, Islands Area of the Western Isles, since 1983 (Vice Lord-Lieutenant, 1976–83); *b* 6 Dec. 1918; *s* of 4th Earl Granville, KG, KCVO, CB, DSO, and Countess Granville, GCVO; *S* father, 1953; *m* 1958, Doon Aileen, *d* of late Hon. Brinsley Plunket and of Mrs V. Stux-Rybar, Luttrellstown Castle, Co. Dublin; two *s* one *d. Educ:* Eton. Served throughout War, 1939–45, Tunisia and Italy (twice wounded, despatches, MC). DL Inverness, 1974. *Heir: s* Lord Leveson, *qv. Address:* 49 Lyall Mews, SW1. *T:* 01–235 1026; Callernish, Sollas, North Uist, Outer Hebrides, Inverness-shire. *T:* Bayhead 213.

GRANVILLE OF EYE, Baron *cr* 1967, of Eye (Life Peer); **Edgar Louis Granville;** *s* of Reginald and Margaret Granville; *b* Reading, 12 Feb. 1899; *m* 1943, Elizabeth *d* of late Rev. W. C. Hunter; one *d. Educ:* High Wycombe, London and Australia. Served as officer in AIF, Gallipoli, Egypt and France. Capt. RA, 1939–40. MP (L) Eye Div. of Suffolk, 1929–51; Hon. Sec., Liberal Agricultural Group, House of Commons, 1929–31; Hon. Sec. Foreign Affairs Group, Vice-Pres. National League of Young Liberals; Chm., Young Liberals Manifesto Group; Parliamentary Private Sec. to Sir Herbert Samuel, first National Government, 1931; Parliamentary Private Sec. to Sir John Simon, National Government, 1931–36; Mem. of Inter-Departmental Cttee for the World Economic Conference, 1933. Sits in House of Lords as an Independent. *Recreations:* cricket, football, ski-ing. *Address:* 112 Charlton Lane, Cheltenham, Glos.

GRANVILLE, Sir Keith, Kt 1973; CBE 1958; FCIT; Hon. FRAeS; *b* 1 Nov. 1910; *m* 1st, 1933, Patricia Capstick; one *s* one *d*; 2nd, 1946, Truda Belliss; one *s* four *d. Educ:* Tonbridge Sch. Joined Imperial Airways as Trainee, 1929 and served Italy, Tanganyika, Southern and Northern Rhodesia, Egypt, India. BOAC: Manager African and Middle East Div., 1947; Commercial Dir, 1954; Dep. Managing Dir, 1958–60; Mem. Bd, 1959–72; Dep. Chm., 1964–70; Man. Dir, 1969–70; Chm. and Chief Exec., 1971–72; Mem. Bd, BEA, 1971–72; British Airways Board: Mem., 1971–74; Dep. Chm., 1972–74; Chairman: BOAC Associated Companies Ltd, 1960–64; BOAC Engine Overhaul Ltd, 1971–72; International Aeradio Ltd, 1965–71 (Dep.-Chm., 1962–65). Mem. Bd, Maplin Development Authority, 1973–74. President: Inst. of Transport, 1963–64; IATA, 1972–73. Chm., British Residents' Assoc. of Switzerland, 1979–81. Hon. FRAeS, 1977. *Address:* Speedbird, 1837 Château d'Oex, Switzerland. *T:* (029) 4 76 03.

GRANVILLE SLACK, George; *see* Slack, G. G.

GRASS, Günter Wilhelm; German writer and artist; *b* Danzig, 16 Oct. 1927; *m* 1st 1954, Anna Schwarz; three *s* (inc. twin *s*) one *d*; 2nd, 1979, Ute Grunert. *Educ:* Volksschule and Gymnasium, Danzig; Düsseldorf Kunstakademie; Hochschule für Bildende Künste. Lecture Tour of US, 1964, and many other foreign tours. Member: Akademie der Künste, Berlin; Deutscher PEN, Zentrum der Bundesrepublik; Verband Deutscher Schriftsteller; Amer. Academy of Arts and Sciences. Prizes: Lyric, Süddeutscher Rundfunk, 1955; Gruppe 47, 1959; Bremen Literary, 1959 (zurückgezogen); Literary, Assoc. of German Critics, 1960; Meilleur livre étranger, 1962; Georg-Büchner, 1965; Fontane, Berlin, 1968; Theodor-Heuss, 1969; Internat. Literatur, 1978; Antonio-Feltrinelli, 1982. *Publications: novels:* Die Blechtrommel, 1959 (The Tin Drum, 1962; filmed 1979); Katz und Maus, 1961 (Cat and Mouse, 1963); Hundejahre, 1963 (Dog Years, 1965); Örtlich Betäubt, 1969 (Local Anaesthetic, 1970); Der Butt, 1977 (The Flounder, 1978); Das Treffen in Telgte, 1979 (The Meeting at Telgte, 1981); Kopfgeburten, 1980 (Headbirths, 1982); *poetry:* Die Vorzüge der Windhühner, 1956; Gleisdreieck, 1960; Ausgefragt, 1967; Ach Butt, dein Märchen geht böse aus, 1983; *poetry in translation:* Selected Poems, 1966; Poems of Günter Grass, 1969; In the Egg and other poems, 1978, *drama:* Hochwasser, 1957 (Flood, 1968); Noch zehn Minuten bis Buffalo, 1958 (Only Ten Minutes to Buffalo, 1968); Onkel, Onkel, 1958 (Onkel, Onkel, 1968); Die bösen Köche, 1961 (The Wicked Cooks, 1968); Die Plebejer proben den Aufstand, 1966 (The Plebeians rehearse the Uprising, 1967); Davor, 1969; *prose:* Über das Selbsverständlische, 1968 (Speak Out!, 1969); Aus dem Tagebuch einer Schnecke, 1972 (From the Diary of a Snail, 1974); Dokumente zur politischen Wirkung, 1972; Der Bürger und seine Stimme, 1974; Denkzettel, 1978; Aufsätze zur Literatur, 1980; Zeichnen und Schreiben, Band I, 1982, Band II, 1984; Widerstand lernen, 1984; On Writing and Politics 1967–83, 1985. *Address:* Niedstrasse 13, 1 Berlin 41, Federal Republic of Germany.

GRATTAN, Donald Henry; Chairman, Adult Continuing Education Development Unit, since 1984; *b* St Osyth, Essex, 7 Aug. 1926; *s* of Arthur Henry Grattan and Edith Caroline Saltmarsh; *m* 1950, Valmai Dorothy Morgan; one *s* one *d. Educ:* Harrow Boys Grammar Sch.; King's Coll., Univ. of London. BSc 1st Cl. Hons, Mathematics Dip. in Radio-Physics. Jun. Scientific Officer, TRE, Gt Malvern, 1945–46; Mathematics Teacher, Chiswick Grammar Sch., 1946–50; Sen. Master, Downer Grammar Sch., Mddx, 1950–56. BBC: Sch. Television Producer, 1956–60; Asst Head, Sch. Television, 1960–64; Head of Further Educn, Television, 1964–70; Asst Controller, Educnl Broadcasting, 1970–72, Controller, 1972–84. Member: Open Univ. Council, 1972–84 and Univ. Delegacy for Continuing Educn, 1978–84; Adv. Council for Adult and Continuing Educn, 1978–83; European Broadcasting Union Working Party on Educn, 1972–84; Venables' Cttee on Continuing Educn, 1976–78. Chairman: Adult Literacy Support Services Fund, 1975–80; Council for Educnl Technology, 1985– (Mem., 1973–84). Mem., Royal TV Soc., 1982–. DUniv Open, 1985. Burnham Medal of BIM for services to Management Educn, 1969. *Publications:* Science and the Builder, 1963; Mathematics Miscellany (jt, BBC), 1966; numerous articles. *Recreations:* education (formal and informal), boating, planning and organizing, people. *Address:* Delabole, Gossmore Close, Marlow, Bucks. *T:* Marlow 73571.

GRATTAN-BELLEW, Sir Henry Charles, 5th Bt, *cr* 1838; *b* 12 May 1933; *s* of Lt-Col Sir Charles Christopher Grattan-Bellew, 4th Bt, MC, KRRC and Maureen Peyton, *niece* and adopted *d* of late Sir Thomas Segrave, Shenfield, Essex; *S* father, 1948; *m* 1st, 1956, Naomi Ellis (marr. diss. 1966); 2nd, 1967, Gillian Hulley (marr. diss. 1973); one *s* one *d*; 3rd, 1978, Elzabé Amy (*née* Body), *widow* of John Westerveld, Pretoria, Tvl, SA. *Educ:* St Gerard's, Bray, Co. Wicklow; Ampleforth Coll., York. Publisher: Horse and Hound, SA, and Sustagen Supersport, 1977. Sports administrator, leading radio and TV commentator, hotelier, thoroughbred breeder and owner. *Heir: s* Patrick Charles Grattan-Bellew, *b* 7 Dec. 1971. *Address:* Sandford Park, PO Box 7, Bergville, Natal, 3350, South Africa.

GRATTAN-COOPER, Rear Admiral Sidney, CB 1966; OBE 1946; *b* 3 Dec. 1911; *s* of Sidney Cooper; *m* 1940, Felicity Joan Pitt; two *s. Educ:* privately. Entered RN 1936; served in war of 1939–45; Chief of Staff Flag Officer (Air) Home, 1957–59; Staff of Supreme Allied Cdr Atlantic (NATO), 1961–63; Dep. Controller (Aircraft) RN, Min. of Aviation, 1964–66; retired 1966. *Recreations:* golf, swimming. *Address:* Hursley, St James, Cape 7951, S Africa. *Club:* Army and Navy.

GRATWICK, John, OBE 1979; Chairman: Empire Stores (Bradford) Ltd, since 1978; Lovat Enterprise Fund Ltd, since 1980; Ladyline Ltd, since 1984; Director, Export Finance Co. Ltd (Exfinco), since 1982; *b* 23 April 1918; *s* of Percival John and Kathleen Mary Gratwick; *m* 1944, Ellen Violet Wright; two *s* two *d. Educ:* Cranbrook Sch., Kent; Imperial Coll., Univ. of London. Asst Production Manager, Armstrong Siddeley, 1941–45; Director, Urwick, Orr & Partners Ltd, 1959, Man. Dir, 1968, Vice-Chm., 1971. Chm., British Export Finance Council, 1985– (Mem., 1982–85); Member: Monopolies and Mergers Commn, 1969–76; CAA, 1972–74; EDC for the Clothing Industry, 1967–; Senate of Univ. of London, 1967–; Univ. of London Careers Adv. Bd, 1962–78; Chm., Management Consultants Assoc., 1971–72. Governor, Cranbrook Sch., Kent, 1972–85; Trustee, Foundn for Business Responsibilities. Liveryman: Worshipful Co. of Farriers; Glovers' Co. *Recreations:* golf, sailing, photography, philately. *Address:* Silver Howe, Nuns Walk, Virginia Water, Surrey. *T:* Wentworth 3121. *Clubs:* Royal Automobile, City Livery; Wentworth (Surrey).

See also Stephen Gratwick.

GRATWICK, Stephen, QC 1968; *b* 19 Aug. 1924; *s* of late Percival John Gratwick, Fawkham, Kent; *m* 1954, Jocelyn Chaplin, Horton Kirby, Kent; four *d. Educ:* Charterhouse, Balliol Coll., Oxford. Oxford 1942–44; Signals Research and Develt Estab., 1944–47. BA (Physics) 1946; MA 1950. Called to Bar, Lincoln's Inn, 1949, Bencher, 1976. *Recreations:* tennis, swimming, making and mending things. *Address:* 11 South Square, Gray's Inn, WC1R 5EU.

See also John Gratwick.

GRAVE, Walter Wyatt, CMG 1958; MA (Cambridge); Hon. LLD (Cambridge and McMaster); Hon. Fellow of Fitzwilliam College, Cambridge; *b* 16 Oct. 1901; *o s* of late Walter and Annie Grave; *m* 1932, Kathleen Margaret, *d* of late Stewart Macpherson; two *d. Educ:* King Edward VII Sch., King's Lynn; Emmanuel Coll., Cambridge (Scholar); Fellow of Emmanuel Coll., 1926–66, 1972–; Tutor, 1936–40; University Lecturer in Spanish, 1936–40; Registrary of Cambridge Univ., 1943–52; Principal of the University Coll., of the West Indies, Jamaica, 1953–58; Censor of Fitzwilliam House, Cambridge, 1959–66; Master of Fitzwilliam Coll., Cambridge, 1966–71. Temporary Administrative Officer, Ministry of Labour and National Service, 1940–43. *Publication:* Fitzwilliam College Cambridge 1869–1969, 1983. *Address:* 16 Kingsdale Court, Peacocks, Great Shelford, Cambridge CB2 5AT. *T:* Cambridge 840722.

GRAVES, family name of **Baron Graves.**

GRAVES, 8th Baron, *cr* 1794; **Peter George Wellesley Graves;** Actor; *b* 21 Oct. 1911; *o s* of 7th Baron Graves; *S* father, 1963; *m* 1960, Vanessa Lee. *Educ:* Harrow. First appeared on London stage in 1934, and has subsequently played many leading parts. Mem. Windsor repertory co., 1941. Has appeared in films since 1940. *Recreation:* lawn tennis. *Heir: kinsman,* Evelyn Paget Graves [*b* 17 May 1926; *m* 1957, Marjorie Ann, *d* of late Dr Sidney Ernest Holder; two *s* two *d*]. *Address:* c/o Messrs Coutts & Co., 440 Strand, WC2. *Club:* All England Lawn Tennis.

GRAVESON, Prof. Ronald Harry, CBE 1972; QC 1966; Barrister-at-Law; Professor Emeritus of Private International Law, King's College, University of London, 1978; *b* 2 Oct. 1911; *o s* of Harry Graveson, Sheffield; *m* 1937, Muriel, *o d* of John Saunders, Sheffield; one *s* two *d. Educ:* King Edward VII Sch., Sheffield. LLB 1932, LLM 1933, LLD 1955 Sheffield; SJD Harvard 1936; PhD London 1941; LLD London 1951; Gregory Scholar in International Law of Harvard Univ.; Solicitor (Hons), 1934. Army, 1940–46 (Driver, RE; Lieut-Col RASC, G5 Div. SHAEF; CCG). Called to Bar, Gray's Inn, 1945; Bencher, 1965; Treas., 1983. Reader in English Law, University Coll., Univ. of London, 1946–47; Prof. of Law, 1947–74, and of Private Internat. Law, 1974–78, KCL; Dean of the Faculty of Laws, Univ. of London, 1951–54, 1972–74, and KCL, 1951–58, 1959–63, 1966–70. Vis. Prof., Harvard Law Sch., 1958–59. Chm., UK, National Cttee of Comparative Law, 1955–57. Member: Review Body on pay of doctors and dentists, 1971–81; Cttees of Inquiry into Pay of Nurses and Midwives and of Professions supplementary to Medicine, 1974–75; Pres., Harvard Law Sch. Assoc. of the UK, 1959–61, 1977–81. Jt Editor, Internat. and Comparative Law Quarterly, 1955–61; Consultant Editor of the Law Reports and the Weekly Law Reports, 1970–75. Pres. International Association of Legal Science (UNESCO), 1960–62. Mem. Inst. of International Law; Pres., Soc. of Public Teachers of Law, 1972–73. Member: Polish Acad. of Sci., 1977; Council, Luxembourg Soc.; Institut Grand-Ducal, Luxembourg, 1985–; Chm., Anglo-Belgian Soc.; Member: Council, British Inst. of Internat. and Comparative Law; Council, Selden Soc.; Internat. Acad. of Comparative Law. Hon. Life Mem., Instn of RCT. Liveryman: Clockmakers' Co.; Carmens' Co. Pres., KCL Assoc., 1982–84; FKC 1962. LLD (*hc*) Ghent, 1964; Uppsala, 1977; Leuven, 1978; Dr Juris (*hc*) Freiburg, 1969. JP St Alban's City, 1961–66. Commandeur de l'Ordre de la Couronne de Chêne, 1964; Comdr, Order of Oranje Nassau, 1970; Order of National Merit, France, 1970; Grand

Cross of Order of Merit, German Federal Republic, 1975; Legion of Honour, 1977; Comdr, Order of the Crown (Belgium), 1977. *Publications:* English Legal System, 1939; Conflict of Laws, 1948 (7th edition 1974); Cases on the Conflict of Laws, 1949; The Comparative Evolution of Principles of the Conflict of Laws in England and the USA 1960; General Principles of Private International Law, 1964; (jtly) The Conflict of Laws and International Contracts, 1951; Status in the Common Law, 1953, reprinted 1983; (jtly) A Century of Family Law, 1957; Law: An Introduction, 1967; (jtly) Unification of the International Law of Sale, 1968; Problems of Private International Law in Non-unified Legal Systems, 1975; Comparative Conflict of Laws, 1976; One Law, 1976; Gen. Editor, Problems in Private International Law, 1977; various articles, notes or reviews since 1936 in English and foreign law reviews. Contributor to various collective volumes including essays in honour of British and foreign colleagues; Apollo; Connoisseur. *Recreations:* works of art, international friendship. *Address:* 2 Gray's Inn Square, Gray's Inn, WC1R 5AA. *T:* 01–242 8492; Castle Hill Farm House, Bakewell, Derbys. *Clubs:* Athenæum, Royal Commonwealth Society, Anglo-Belgian.

GRAY, family name of **Baron Gray of Contin.**

GRAY, 22nd Lord, *cr* 1445; **Angus Diarmid Ian Campbell-Gray;** *b* 3 July 1931; *s* of Major Hon. Lindsay Stuart Campbell-Gray, Master of Gray, MC (*d* 1945), and Doreen (*d* 1948), *d* of late Cyril Tubbs, Thedden Grange, Alton, Hants; *S* grandmother 1946; *m* 1959, Patricia Margaret, *o d* of late Capt. Philip Alexander, Kilmorna, Lismore, Co. Waterford; one *s* three *d.* *Heir: s* Master of Gray, *qv.* *Address:* Airds Bay House, Taynuilt, Argyll. *Clubs:* Carlton, MCC.

GRAY, Master of; Hon. Andrew Godfrey Diarmid Stuart Campbell-Gray; *b* 3 Sept. 1964; *s* and *heir* of 22nd Lord Gray, *qv.*

GRAY OF CONTIN, Baron *cr* 1983 (Life Peer), of Contin in the District of Ross and Cromarty; **James, (Hamish), Hector Northey Gray;** PC 1982; Government Spokesman on energy, House of Lords; *b* 28 June 1927; *s* of late J. Northey Gray, Inverness, and of Mrs E. M. Gray; *m* 1953, Judith Waite Brydon, BSc, Helenburgh; two *s* one *d.* *Educ:* Inverness Royal Academy. Served in Queen's Own Cameron Hldrs, 1945–48. MP (C) Ross and Cromarty, 1970–83; an Asst Govt Whip, 1971–73; a Lord Comr, HM Treasury, 1973–74; an Opposition Whip, 1974–Feb. 1975; Opposition spokesman on Energy, 1975–79; Minister of State: Dept of Energy, 1979–83; Scottish Office, 1983–86. Contested (C) Ross, Cromarty and Skye, 1983. Member, Inverness Town Council, 1965–70. *Recreations:* golf, walking, family life. *Address:* Achneim House, Flichity, Inverness-shire IV1 2XE.

GRAY, Alexander Stuart, FRIBA; Consultant to Watkins, Gray, Woodgate International, 1968–75, retired; *b* 15 July 1905; *s* of Alexander and Mary Gray; *m* 1932, Avis (*d* 1980), *d* of John Radmore, Truro; one *s* two *d.* *Educ:* Mill Hill Sch. Articled to R. S. Balgarnie Wyld, ARIBA; studied at Central Sch. of Arts and Crafts; Royal Academy Schools (Bronze Medal, 1928; Silver Medal and Travelling Studentship, 1932; Gold Medal and Edward Stott Trav. Studentship (Italy), 1933); Brit. Instn Schol., 1929. Lectr on Arch. subjects at Central Sch. of Arts and Crafts, Brixton Sch. of Bldg, and Hammersmith Sch. of Bldg, 1936–39; Lectr on Hosp. Planning at King Edward VII Hosp. Fund Colleges, 1950–. In partnership with W. H. Watkins won architectural comp. for new St George's Hosp., Hyde Park Corner, London (partnership 1939–68); before retirement Architect with partners to: Radcliffe Infirmary, Oxford, United Bristol Hospitals, Royal Free Hospital, Guy's Hospital, London Hospital, Eastman Dental Hospital, St Mary's, Manchester, and other hosps in London and the provinces; also in West Indies, where they were responsible for banks, and commercial buildings as well; hospitals for Comptroller of Development and Welfare in BWI, 1941–46; rebuilding of centre of Georgetown, British Guiana, after the fire of 1945, including new GPO, Telecommunications Building, etc. In Nigeria, University Coll. Hosp., Ibadan, and other works, also in Qatar (Persian Gulf), etc. *Publications:* Edwardian Architecture: a biographical dictionary, 1985; various papers read at confs on Hosp. Planning with special ref. to designing for the tropics, and contrib. Tech. Jls. *Address:* 1 Temple Fortune Hill, NW11. *T:* 01–458 5741. *Clubs:* Arts, Old Millhillians.

GRAY, Andrew Aitken, MC 1945; Chairman, Wellcome Foundation Ltd, 1971–77; *b* 11 Jan. 1912; *s* of John Gray and Margaret Eckford Gray (*née* Crozier); *m* 1st, 1939, Eileen Mary Haines (*d* 1980); three *s*; 2nd, 1984, Jess, *widow* of C. M. Carr. *Educ:* Wyggeston School, Leicester; Christ Church, Oxford. Served Royal Engineers, 1939–46 (MC, despatches). Unilever Ltd, 1935–52. Dir, Wellcome Foundation Ltd, 1954, Dep. Chm., 1967; Chm. and Man. Dir, Cooper, McDougall & Robertson, 1963–70. Chm., Herts AHA, 1974–77. Comdr, Orden del Mérito Agricola; Comdr, Order of Merit, Italy. *Recreations:* fishing, gardening, theatre. *Address:* Rainhill Spring, Stoney Lane, Bovingdon, Herts. *T:* Hemel Hempstead 833277. *Club:* East India, Devonshire, Sports and Public Schools.

GRAY, Sir Anthony; *see* Gray, Sir F. A.

GRAY, Anthony James; Chief Executive, Cogent (Holdings) Ltd, since 1982; *b* 12 Feb. 1937; *o s* of Sir James Gray, CBE, MC, FRS; *m* 1963, Lady Lana Mary Gabrielle Baring (*d* 1974), *d* of Earl of Cromer, *qv;* one *s* one *d;* *m* 1980, Mrs Maxine Redmayne, *er d* of Captain and Mrs George Brodrick. *Educ:* Marlborough Coll.; New Coll., Oxford. C. T. Bowring & Co. (Insurance) Ltd, 1959–64; Sen. Investment Analyst, de Zoete & Gorton, 1965–67; Head of Investment Research and Partner, James Capel & Co., 1967–73. Member, London Stock Exchange, 1971–73. Dep. Dir, Industrial Development Unit, Dept of Industry, 1973–75; Adviser, Special Industry Problems, Dept of Industry, 1975–76. Assoc., PA Management Consultants Ltd, 1977–81; Dir, PA Developments Ltd, 1980–81. Member: Foundries EDC (NEDO), 1977–79; Hammersmith and Fulham DHA, 1982–85. Member Council: Charing Cross Hosp. Med. Sch., 1982–84; ERA Technology Ltd (formerly Electrical Res. Assoc.), 1986–. Director: Apollo Soc., 1966–73; Nat. Trust Concert Soc., 1966–73; PEC Concerts, 1979–81. *Recreations:* golf, fishing, music. *Address:* 5 Ranelagh Avenue, SW6. *Club:* Garrick.

GRAY, Basil, CB 1969; CBE 1957; MA; FBA 1966; Keeper of Oriental Antiquities, British Museum, 1946–69, Acting Director and Principal Librarian, 1968; *b* 21 July 1904; *s* of late Surgeon-Major Charles Gray and Florence Elworthy, *d* of Rev. H. v. H. Cowell; *m* 1933, Nicolete, *d* of late Laurence Binyon, CH; two *s* two *d* (and one *d* decd). *Educ:* Bradfield; New Coll., Oxford. British Academy excavations in Constantinople, 1928; entered British Museum (Printed Books), 1928; transferred to sub-Dept of Oriental Prints and Drawings, 1930; in charge of Oriental Antiquities (including Oriental Prints and Drawings) from 1938; Dep. Keeper, 1940. Mem. of Art Panel of the Arts Council, 1952–57, and 1959–68; President: Oriental Ceramic Soc., 1962–65, 1971–74, 1977–78; 6th Internat. Congress of Iranian Art and Archaeology, Oxford, 1972. Mem., Reviewing Cttee on Export of Works of Art, 1971–79; Chm., Exhibn cttee, The Arts of Islam, Hayward Gallery, 1976. Pres., Soc. for S Asian Studies (formerly Soc. for Afghan Studies), 1979–. A Visitor of Ashmolean Museum, Oxford, 1969–79. Sir Percy Sykes Meml Medal, 1978. *Publications:* Persian Painting, 1930; Persian Miniature Painting (part author), 1933; Chinese Art (with Leigh Ashton), 1935; The English Print, 1937; Persian Painting, New York, 1940; Rajput Painting, 1948; (joint) Commemorative Catalogue of the Exhibition of the Art of India and Pakistan, 1947–48, 1950; Treasures of Indian Miniatures in the Bikanir Palace Collection, 1951; Early Chinese Pottery and Porcelain, 1953; Japanese Screen-paintings, 1955; Buddhist Cave paintings at Tun-huang, 1959; Treasures of Asia; Persian Painting, 1961; (with D. E. Barrett) Painting of India, 1963; An Album of Miniatures and Illuminations from the Bâysongnhori Manuscript of the Shāhnāmeh of Ferdowsi, 1971; The World History of Rashid al-Din, a study of the RAS manuscript, 1979; (ed, and jt author) The Arts of the Book in Central Asia 1370–1506, 1979; (ed, and jt author) The Arts of India, 1981; Sung Porcelain and Stoneware, 1984; Studies in Chinese and Islamic Art, 2 vols, 1985, 1986; (ed) Faber Gallery of Oriental Art and Arts of the East Series. *Address:* Dawber's House, Long Wittenham, Oxon OX14 4QQ. *Club:* Savile.

GRAY, Charles Antony St John, QC 1984; *b* 6 July 1942; *s* of late Charles Herbert Gray and Catherine Margaret Gray; *m* 1968, Rosalind Macleod Whinney; one *s* one *d.* *Educ:* Winchester; Trinity College, Oxford (scholar). Called to Bar, Lincoln's Inn, 1966. *Recreations:* skiing, fishing. *Address:* 79 Ravenscourt Road, W6 0UJ; Trinity Cottage, Loders, Dorset. *Club:* Brooks's.

GRAY, Charles Horace, MD (London), DSc, FRCP, FRSC, FRCPath; Emeritus Professor of Chemical Pathology in the University of London (Professor, at King's College Hospital Medical School, 1948–76); Consulting Chemical Pathologist, King's College Hospital District, 1976–81 (Consultant, 1938–76); *b* 30 June 1911; *s* of Charles H. Gray and Ethel Hider, Erith, Kent; *m* 1938, Florence Jessie Widdup, ARCA, *d* of Frank Widdup, JP, Barnoldswick, Yorks; two *s.* *Educ:* Imperial Coll. and University Coll., London (Fellow, UCL, 1979); University Coll. Hospital Medical Sch. Demonstrator in Biochemistry, University Coll., London, 1931–36; Bayliss-Starling Scholar in Physiology and Biochemistry, 1932–33; Visiting Teacher in Biochemistry, Chelsea Polytechnic, 1933–36; Demonstrator and Lecturer in Physiology, University Coll., 1935–36; Graham Scholar in Pathology, UCH Medical Sch., 1936–38; Pathologist in Charge Sector Biochemical Laboratory, Sector 9, Emergency Health Service, 1939–44; Hon. Consultant, Miles Laboratories Ltd, 1953–76. Acting Head, Dept of Chem. Pathol., Hosp. for Sick Children, Gt Ormond St, Jan.-Dec. 1979. Vis. Prof., Div. of Clinical Chem., MRC Clinical Res. Centre, Harrow, 1976–83. Member: Clinical Res. Bd of Med. Res. Council, 1964–68; Arthritis and Rheumatism Council Res. Cttee, 1960–68 (Chm., 1963–66); Chairman: MCB Exams Cttee, 1971–73; Steroid Reference Collection and Radioactive Steroid Synthesis Steering Cttee, MRC, 1973–76; Regional Scientific Cttee, SE Thames RHA, 1974–76 (Mem. Regional Research Cttee, 1974–82). Sec., Soc. for Endocrinology, 1950–53; Chm. Cttee of Management, Jl of Endocrinology Ltd, 1970–74; Member: Cttee of Management, Inst. of Psychiatry, 1966–73; Council and Chm., Specialist Adv. Cttee in Chemical Pathology, RCPath, 1972–75; Assoc. of Clinical Biochemists, 1961– (Pres. 1969–71, Emeritus Mem., 1980–). Mem. Livery, Worshipful Soc. of Apothecaries of London, 1951–. Mem., Editorial Bd, Biochemical Jl, 1955–60. *Publications:* The Bile Pigments, 1953; Clinical Chemical Pathology, 1953, 10th edn (jtly), 1985; The Bile Pigments in Health and Disease, 1961; (ed) Laboratory Handbook of Toxic Agents; (ed jtly) Hormones in Blood, 1961, 3rd edn vols 1–3, 1979, vols 4–5, 1983; (ed jtly) High Pressure Liquid Chromatography in Clinical Chemistry, 1976; contributions to medical and scientific journals. *Recreations:* music and travel. *Address:* Barn Cottage, Linden Road, Leatherhead, Surrey KT22 7JF. *T:* Leatherhead 372415; 34 Cleaver Square, SE11 4EA. *T:* 01–735 9652. *Clubs:* Athenæum, Royal Over-Seas League.

GRAY, David, CBE 1977 (OBE 1964); QPM 1960; HM Chief Inspector of Constabulary for Scotland, 1970–79; retired; *b* 18 Nov. 1914; *s* of William Gray and Janet Borland; *m* 1944, Mary Stewart Scott (*d* 1985); two *d.* *Educ:* Preston Grammar Sch. Chief Constable: Greenock, 1955–58; Stirling and Clackmannan, 1958–69. Hon. Sec., Chief Constables' (Scotland) Assoc., 1958–69. English-Speaking Union Thyne Scholar, 1969. *Recreations:* fishing, shooting, golf. *Address:* Kingarth, 42 East Barnton Avenue, Edinburgh EH4 6AQ. *T:* 031–336 6342. *Club:* Bruntsfield (Edinburgh).

GRAY, Dr Denis Everett, CBE 1983 (MBE 1972); JP; Resident Staff Tutor since 1957, and Senior Lecturer, 1967–84, Department of Extramural Studies, University of Birmingham; *b* 25 June 1926; *s* of Charles Norman Gray and Kathleen Alexandra (*née* Roberts); *m* 1949, Barbara Joyce, *d* of Edgar Kesterton. *Educ:* Bablake Sch., Coventry; Univ. of Birmingham (BA); Univ. of London; Univ. of Manchester (PhD). Tutor-organiser, WEA, S Staffs, 1953–57. Chairman: Jt Negotiating Cttees for Justices' Clerks and Justices' Clerks' Assts, 1978–; Central Council of Magistrates' Courts Cttees, 1980– (Dep. Chm., 1978–80); Member: Magistrates' Courts Rule Cttee, 1982–; Lord Chancellor's Adv. Cttee on Trng of Magistrates, 1974–84. JP Solihull, 1962; Dep. Chm., 1968–71 and 1978–82, Chm., 1971–75, Solihull Magistrates; Chm., Licensing Cttee, 1972–76. *Publication:* Spencer Perceval: the evangelical Prime Minister, 1963. *Recreations:* travel, church architecture, reading. *Address:* 11 Brueton Avenue, Solihull, West Midlands B91 3EN. *T:* 021–705 2935.

GRAY, Rev. Canon Dr Donald Clifford, TD 1970; Rector of Liverpool, since 1974; Canon Diocesan of Liverpool, since 1982; Chaplain to HM The Queen, since 1982; *b* 21 July 1930; *s* of Henry Hackett Gray and Constance Muriel Gray; *m* 1955, Joyce (*née* Jackson); one *s* two *d.* *Educ:* Newton Heath Technical High Sch.; King's Coll., London and Warminster (AKC); Univ. of Liverpool (MPhil); Univ. of Manchester (PhD). Curate, Leigh Parish Church, 1956–60; Vicar: St Peter's, Westleigh, 1960–67; All Saints', Elton Bury, 1967–74; Rural Dean of Liverpool, 1975–81. Proctor-in-Convocation for Manchester, 1964–74; Mem., Gen. Synod, 1980–. Chm., Soc. for Liturgical Study, 1978–84; Treasurer, Societas Liturgica, 1981–; Member: Liturgical Commn, 1968–; Jt Liturgical Gp, 1969– (Sec., 1980–). Chm., Alcuin Club, 1987–. CF (TA), 1958–67; CF (T&AVR), 1967–77; QHC, 1974–77; Sub Chaplain, Order of St John of Jerusalem, 1982. *Publications:* (contrib.) Worship and the Child, 1975; (contrib.) Getting the Liturgy Right, 1982; (contrib.) Liturgy Reshaped, 1982; (ed) Holy Week Services, 1983; Earth and Altar, 1986. *Recreations:* watching cricket, reading modern poetry. *Address:* Liverpool Parish Church, Old Churchyard, Liverpool L2 8TZ. *T:* 051–236 5287. *Clubs:* Army and Navy; Athenæum (Liverpool).

GRAY, Prof. Douglas; J. R. R. Tolkien Professor of English Literature and Language, University of Oxford, since 1980; *b* 17 Feb. 1930; *s* of Emmerson and Daisy Gray; *m* 1959, Judith Claire Campbell; one *s.* *Educ:* Wellington College, NZ; Victoria Univ. of Wellington (MA 1952); Merton Coll., Oxford (BA 1954, MA 1960). Asst Lecturer, Victoria Univ. of Wellington, 1952–54; Lectr, Pembroke and Lincoln Colls, Oxford, 1956–61; Fellow, Pembroke Coll., 1961–80, now Emeritus; University Lectr in English Language, 1976–80; Professorial Fellow, Lady Margaret Hall, Oxford, 1980–. Mem. Council, EETS, 1981–; Pres., Soc. for Study of Mediæval Langs and Lit., 1982–86. *Publications:* (ed) Spenser, The Faerie Queene, Book 1, 1969; Themes and Images in the Medieval English Religious Lyric, 1972; (ed) A Selection of Religious Lyrics, 1975; (part of) A Chaucer Glossary, 1979; Robert Henryson, 1979; (ed with E. G. Stanley): Middle English Studies presented to Norman Davies, 1983; Five Hundred Years of Words and

Sounds for E. J. Dobson, 1983; (ed) The Oxford Book of Late Medieval Verse and Prose, 1985; articles on medieval literature. *Address:* Lady Margaret Hall, Oxford.

GRAY, Dulcie; *see* Denison, D. W. C.

GRAY, Dr Edward George, FRS 1976; Head of the Laboratory of Ultrastructure, National Institute for Medical Research, Mill Hill, 1977–83; *b* 11 Jan. 1924; *s* of Will and Charlotte Gray; *m* 1953, May Eine Kyllikki Rautiainen; two *s*. *Educ:* University Coll. of Wales, Aberystwyth (BSc, PhD). Anatomy Dept, University Coll., London: Lectr, 1958; Reader, 1962; Prof. (Cytology), 1968–77. *Recreations:* violin playing, water colouring, gardening. *Address:* 58 New Park Road, Newgate Street, Hertford SG13 8RF. *T:* Cuffley 872891.

GRAY, Sir (Francis) Anthony, KCVO 1981; Secretary and Keeper of the Records of the Duchy of Cornwall, 1972–81; *b* 3 Aug. 1917; *s* of late Major F. C. Gray; *m* 1947, Marcia, *d* of late Major Hugh Wyld; one *s* two *d*. *Educ:* Marlborough; Magdalen Coll., Oxford. Treas., Christ Church, Oxford, 1952–72, Emeritus Student, 1972. Mem., Agricultural Adv. Council, 1963–68; Mem. Council, Royal Coll. of Art, 1967–73. *Address:* Temple House, Upton Scudamore, Warminster, Wilts. *Club:* Travellers'.

GRAY, Geoffrey Leicester, CMG 1958; OBE 1953; Secretary for Local Government, N Borneo (now Sabah), 1956–61, retired; *b* 26 Aug. 1905; *s* of late Leonard Swainson Gray, Resident Magistrate of Kingston, Jamaica, and of late Marion Scotland, Vale Royal, Kingston, Jamaica; *m* 1932, Penelope Milnes (*d* 1971), MBE 1962, *o c* of late Philip Henry Townsend, OBE and late Gwenyth Gwendoline Roberts. *Educ:* Latymer Upper Sch. Cadet, North Borneo Civil Service, under British North Borneo (Chartered) Co., 1925; after qualifying in Malay and Law, served in various admin. posts, 1925–30; studied Chinese in Canton, 1931; attached Secretariat for Chinese Affairs and Educ. Dept, Hong Kong, 1931; Dist Officer, Jesselton, Supt, Govt Printing Office, and Editor, British North Borneo Herald and Official Gazette, 1932–35; Dist Officer, Kudat, 1935; Under-Sec., 1935–38; Govt Sec. Class 1b and *ex-officio* MLC, 1938–46; Additional Sessions and High Court Judge, 1938–46; interned by Japanese, 1941–45; Class 1a, 1946; accredited to HQ Brit. Mil. Admin (Brit. Borneo) at Labuan, 1946; assimilated into HM Colonial Admin. Service (later HM Overseas Service) on cession of North Borneo to the Crown, 1946; Actg Dep. Chief Sec., 1946; Protector of Labour and Sec. for Chinese Affairs, 1947; Resident, E Coast, in addition, 1947; Mem. Advisory Council, 1947–50; Comr of Immigration and Labour, 1948–51: Official MLC and MEC, 1950–61; Actg Fin. Sec., 1951–52; Dep. Chief Sec., Staff Class, 1952–56; represented North Borneo at Coronation, 1953; Chm., Bd of Educn and Town and Country Planning Bd, 1956–61; Actg Chief Sec. (intermittently), 1952–60; administered Govt, 1958, 1959; acted as High Comr, Brunei, 1959; retd, 1961. Life Associate, N Borneo and UK Branches, CPA, 1961. Commissary for Bp of Jesselton (later Sabah), 1961. Incorporated Mem. of USPG (formerly SPG), 1964– (Mem. Council, and various Cttees and Gps, 1965–83); Cttee Mem., Borneo Mission Assoc., 1961– (Chm. 1961–76). *Address:* 36A Osborne Villas, Hove, East Sussex BN3 2RB. *T:* Brighton 203478. *Clubs:* Royal Commonwealth Society, Travellers'.

GRAY, Prof. George William, PhD; FRS 1983; CChem, FRSC; G. F. Grant Professor of Chemistry and Head of Department of Chemistry, University of Hull, since 1984 (Professor of Organic Chemistry, 1978–84); *b* 4 Sept. 1926; *s* of John William Gray and Jessie Colville (*née* Hunter); *m* 1953, Marjorie Mary (*née* Canavan); three *d*. *Educ:* Univ. of Glasgow (BSc); Univ. of London (PhD). CChem, FRSC 1972. Staff of Chem. Dept, Univ. of Hull, 1946–: Sen. Lectr, 1960; Reader, 1964. Clifford Paterson Prize Lectr, Royal Soc., 1985. Queen's Award for Technol Achievement, 1979; Rank Prize for Optoelectronics, 1980. *Publications:* Molecular Structure and the Properties of Liquid Crystals, 1962; (ed and jtly with P. A. Winsor) Liquid Crystals and Plastic Crystals, 1974; (ed. jtly with G. R. Luckhurst) The Molecular Physics of Liquid Crystals, 1979; (with J. W. Goodby) Smectic Liquid Crystals – textures and structures, 1984; 180 pubns on liquid crystals in Jl Chem. Soc., Trans Faraday Soc., Phys. Rev., Molecular Cryst. and Liquid Cryst., Jl Chem. Phys., and Proc. IEEE. *Recreations:* gardening, philately. *Address:* Department of Chemistry, University of Hull, Hull HU6 7RX. *T:* Hull 497485 and 497450; Glenwood, 33 Newgate, Cottingham, N Humberside HU16 4DY. *T:* Hull 844853.

GRAY, Gilbert, QC 1971; a Recorder of the Crown Court, since 1972; *b* 25 April 1928; *s* of late Robert Gray, JP, Scarborough, and of Mrs Elizabeth Gray; *m* 1954, Olga Dilys Gray (*née* Thomas), BA, JP; two *s* two *d*. *Educ:* Scarborough Boys' High Sch.; Leeds Univ. (LLB). Pres., Leeds Univ. Union. Called to the Bar, Gray's Inn, 1953; Bencher, 1979. Leader of NE Circuit, 1984–. *Recreation:* sailing. *Address:* Treasurer's House, York; 2 Park Square, Leeds LS1 2NE; 4 Paper Buildings, Temple, EC4Y 7EX; Lingholm Farm, Lebberston, Scarborough.

GRAY, His Eminence Cardinal Gordon Joseph, MA (Hon.) St Andrews; Hon. DD St Andrews, 1967; Retired Archbishop of St Andrews and Edinburgh; *b* 10 August 1910; 2nd *s* of Francis William and Angela Gray. *Educ:* Holy Cross Acad., Edinburgh; St John's Seminary, Wonersh. Assistant-Priest, St Andrews, 1935–41; Parish Priest, Hawick, 1941–47; Rector of Blairs College, Aberdeen (Scottish National Junior Seminary), 1947–51; Archbishop of St Andrews and Edinburgh, 1951–85. Cardinal, 1969. Member Pontifical Congregation: for Evangelization of Peoples; for Divine Worship; Mem., Pontifical Commn for Social Communications. Hon. FEIS, 1970. DUniv. Heriot-Watt, 1981. *Address:* St Margaret's Convent, The Hermitage, Whitehouse Loan, Edinburgh EH9 1BB.

GRAY, Rear-Adm. Gordon Thomas Seccombe, CB 1964; DSC 1940; *b* 20 Dec. 1911; *s* of late Rev. Thomas Seccombe Gray and Edith Gray; *m* 1939, Sonia Moore-Gwyn; one *s* one *d*. *Educ:* Nautical Coll., Pangbourne. Entered RN, 1929; Sub-Lieut and Lieut, Mediterranean Fleet, 1934–36, ashore Arab revolt in Palestine (despatches); 1st Lieut, HMS Stork, 1939, Norwegian campaign (despatches, DSC); Comd HMS Badsworth, 1942–43 (despatches); Comd HMS Lamerton, 1943–45 (despatches). After the War comd destroyers Consort, Contest and St Kitts; JSSC, 1948, Comdr 1949; Directing Staff, RN Staff Coll., Greenwich, 1950; Exec. Officer, cruiser HMS Glasgow, 1951–53; Capt. 1953; Naval Deputy to UK Nat. Military Representative, at SHAPE; Capt. of 5th Frigate Sqdn, and Comd HMS Wakeful and HMS Torquay, 1956–59; Asst Chief of Staff to C-in-C Eastern Atlantic Command, 1959–61; in comd of Naval Air Anti-Submarine Sch. at Portland and Chief Staff Officer to Flag Officer Sea Trng, 1961–62; Senior Naval Instructor, Imperial Defence Coll., 1963–65, retd. *Recreation:* yachting. *Address:* Hollies, Wispers, Midhurst, West Sussex.

GRAY, Hanna Holborn, PhD; President, University of Chicago, since 1978; *b* 25 Oct. 1930; *d* of Hajo and Annemarie Holborn; *m* 1954, Charles Montgomery Gray. *Educ:* Bryn Mawr Coll., Pa (BA); Univ. of Oxford (Fulbright Schol.); Univ. of Harvard (PhD). Instructor, Bryn Mawr Coll., 1953–54; Harvard University: Teaching Fellow, 1955–57, Instr, 1957–59, Asst Prof., 1959–60, Vis. Lectr, 1963–64; Asst Prof., Univ. of Chicago, 1961–64, Associate Prof., 1964–72; Dean and Prof., Northwestern, Evanston, Ill, 1972–74; Provost, and Prof. of History, Yale Univ., 1974–78, Acting Pres., 1977–78. Hon. degrees: MA Yale, 1971; LHD: Grinnell Coll. Lawrence, Dennison, 1974; Wheaton Coll., 1976; Marlboro', Rikkyo, 1979; Roosevelt, Knox, 1980; Thomas Jefferson, Coe Coll., 1981; Duke, Clark, New Sch. for Social Research, 1982; Brandeis, Colgate, 1983; Wayne State, Miami, Southern Methodist, 1984; City Univ. of New York, Denver, 1985; LittD St Lawrence, 1974; HHD St Mary's Coll., 1974; LLD: Union Coll., 1975; Regis Coll., 1976; Dartmouth Coll., Trinity Coll., Bridgeport, Yale, 1978; Dickenson Coll., Wittenberg, Brown, 1979; Rochester, Notre Dame, Southern California, 1980; Michigan, 1981; Princeton, 1982; Georgetown, 1983; Marquette, 1984; West Virginia Wesleyan Coll., Hamilton Coll., 1985; DLitt: Oxford, 1979; Washington, 1985. *Publications:* ed (with Charles M. Gray) Jl Modern History, 1965–70; articles in professional jls. *Address:* (office) 5801 South Ellis Avenue, Chicago, Illinois 60637, USA. *T:* (312) 962–8001. *Clubs:* Commercial, Mid-America, Economic, Fortnightly, Quadrangle, Women's Athletic, University, Chicago (Chicago); University, Cosmopolitan (New York City).

GRAY, Harold James, CMG 1956; retired, 1972; *b* 17 Oct. 1907; 2nd *s* of late John William Gray and of Amelia Frances (*née* Miller); *m* 1928, Katherine Gray (*née* Starling) (*d* 1985); one *d*. *Educ:* Alleyn's Sch.; Dover County Sch.; Queen Mary Coll., London Univ. (MSc, LLB); Gray's Inn; Harvard University, USA (MPA). MInstP, CPhys; FRSA. Customs and Excise Dept, 1927; Asst Examiner, Patent Office, 1930, Examiner, 1935; Industries and Manufactures Dept, Board of Trade, 1938; Ministry of Supply, 1939; Asst Sec., Min. of Supply, 1942. transf. to Bd of Trade, 1946; Commercial Relations and Exports Dept, Board of Trade, 1950; Under-Sec., 1954; UK Senior Trade Comr and Economic and Commercial Adviser to High Comr in Australia, 1954–58; UK Senior Trade Comr and Economic Adviser to the High Comr in Union of South Africa, 1958–60; Dir, Nat. Assoc. of British Manufacturers, 1961–65; Dir, Legal Affairs, CBI, 1965–72. Commonwealth Fund Fellowship, 1949–50. Chm., NUMAS (Management Services) Ltd. *Publications:* Electricity in the Service of Man, 1949; Economic Survey of Australia, 1955; Dictionary of Physics, 1958; (jtly) New Dictionary of Physics, 1975. *Recreations:* golf, swimming, riding. *Address:* 27 Byron Road, Penenden Heath, Maidstone, Kent ME14 2HA.

GRAY, Hugh, BSc(Soc), PhD; General Secretary, Theosophical Society in England, since 1982; *b* 19 April 1916; *s* of William Marshall Kemp Gray; *m* 1954, Edith Esther (*née* Rudinger); no *c*. *Educ:* Battersea Grammar Sch.; London Sch. of Economics. Army Service, Intelligence Corps. UNRRA and Internat. Refugee Organisation, 1945–52; Social Worker; Lectr at SOAS, University of London, 1962–66 and 1970–81; Chm., Centre for S Asian Studies, 1980–81. MP (Lab) Yarmouth, 1966–70. *Publications:* various articles on Indian politics and philosophy. *Address:* 22 Bridstow Place, W2; Castello 1852, Venice.

GRAY, Maj.-Gen. John; *see* Gray, Maj.-Gen. R. J.

GRAY, Rev. Prof. John; Professor of Hebrew, University of Aberdeen, 1961–80, now Professor Emeritus; *b* 9 June 1913; *s* of James Telfer Gray; *m* Janet J. Gibson; five *c*. *Educ:* Kelso High Sch.; Edinburgh Univ. (MA, BD, PhD). Colonial Chaplain and Chaplain to Palestine Police, 1939–41; Minister of the Church of Scotland, Kilmory, Isle of Arran, 1942–47; Lectr in Semitic Languages and Literatures, Manchester Univ., 1947–53; Lectr in Hebrew and Biblical Criticism, University of Aberdeen, 1953–61. Mem., Soc. for Old Testament Study. Hon. DD St Andrews, 1977. *Publications:* The Krt Text in the Literature of Ras Shamra, 1955 (2nd edn 1964); The Legacy of Canaan, 1957 (2nd edn 1965); Archæology and the Old Testament World, 1962; The Canaanites, 1964; Kings I and II: a Commentary, 1964, 3rd edn 1977; Joshua, Judges and Ruth, 1967; A History of Jerusalem, 1969; Near Eastern Mythology, 1969, 2nd edn 1982; The Biblical Doctrine of the Reign of God, 1979; contribs to various Bible Dictionaries, memorial volumes and learned journals. *Recreations:* beekeeping, gardening, trout-fishing. *Address:* Tanlaw Cottage, Hendersyde Park, Kelso, Roxburgh. *T:* Kelso 24374.

GRAY, Sir John (Archibald Browne), Kt 1973; MA, MB, ScD; FRS 1972; Member, External Scientific Staff, MRC, 1977–83; working at Marine Biological Association Laboratory, Plymouth, since 1977; *b* 30 March 1918; *s* of late Sir Archibald Gray, KCVO, CBE; *m* 1946, Vera Kathleen Mares; one *s* one *d*. *Educ:* Cheltenham Coll.; Clare Coll., Cambridge (Hon. Fellow, 1976); University Coll. Hospital. BA 1939; MA 1942; MB, BChir 1942; ScD 1962. Service Research for MRC, 1943–45; Surg. Lieut, RNVR, 1945–46; Scientific Staff of MRC at Nat. Inst. for Med. Research, 1946–52; Reader in Physiology, University Coll., London, 1952–58; Prof. of Physiology, University Coll., London, 1959–66; Medical Research Council: Second Sec., 1966–68; Sec., 1968–77; Dep. Chm., 1975–77. QHP 1968–71. FIBiol; FRCP 1974. Hon. DSc Exeter, 1985. *Publications:* papers, mostly on sensory receptors and sensory nervous system, in Jl of Physiology, Procs of Royal Soc. series B, Jl of Marine Biol Assoc., etc. *Recreations:* painting, sailing, tennis. *Address:* Seaways, North Rock, Kingsand, near Plymouth PL10 1NG. *T:* Plymouth 822745; Marine Biological Association Laboratory, Citadel Hill, Plymouth.

GRAY, Air Vice-Marshal John Astley, CB 1945; CBE 1943; DFC; GM; retired; *b* 1899. *Educ:* Framlingham Coll. Served European War, 1917–19; War of 1939–45. Air Vice-Marshal 1944; AOC 91 (B) Gp, 1944–46; AOC RAF Mission to Greece, 1947–48; SASO, HQ Transport Comd, 1949–51; AOA, HQ ME Air Force, 1951–54; retired, 1954. *Address:* Bittern, Thorpeness, Suffolk. *Club:* Royal Air Force.

GRAY, John Magnus, CBE 1971 (MBE 1945); ERD 1946; Chairman, Northern Ireland Electricity Service, 1974–80 (Deputy Chairman, 1973–74); *b* 15 Oct. 1915; *o s* of Lewis Campbell Gray, CA and Ingeborg Sanderson Gray (*née* Ross), Glasgow; *m* 1947, Patricia Mary, OBE 1976, *widow* of Major Aubrey D. P. Hodges and *d* of John Norman Eggar and Emma Frances Eggar (*née* Garrett), Epsom and Godalming; one *d*. *Educ:* Horris Hill, Newbury; Winchester College. Served RA, 1939–46 (Major). Joined Wm Ewart & Son Ltd, Linen Manufrs, Belfast, 1934; Dir 1950; Man. Dir 1958–72. Chairman: Irish Linen Guild, 1958–64; Central Council, Irish Linen Industry, 1968–74 (Mem., 1957; Vice-Chm., 1966–68); Linen Industry Standards Cttee of BSI, 1969–74; Belfast Br., RNLI, 1970–76; Member: Council of Belfast T&AFA, 1948–68; Council of Belfast Chamber of Commerce, 1955–59; Gen. Synod of Church of Ireland, 1955–84; Councils of FBI and CBI, 1956–74, 1979–80; NI Legal Aid Cttee, 1958–59; Export Council for Europe, 1964–70; Northern Ireland Adv. Council for BBC, 1968–72; Design Council, 1974–80; Asst Comr for Commn on Constitution, 1969–73. Captain, Royal Co. Down Golf Club, 1963. *Recreations:* golf, gardening. *Address:* Blairlodge, Dundrum, Newcastle, Co. Down BT33 0NF. *T:* Dundrum 271. *Club:* Army and Navy.

GRAY, Vice-Adm. Sir John (Michael Dudgeon), KBE 1967 (OBE 1950); CB 1964; *b* Dublin, 13 June 1913; British; *m* 1939, Margaret Helen Purvis; one *s* one *d*. *Educ:* RNC, Dartmouth. HMS Nelson, 1931; Midshipman, HMS Enterprise, 1932–33; Sub-Lieut, HMS Devonshire, 1934; specialised in Gunnery, 1938. Served War of 1939–45; HMS Hermes; HMS Spartan; with US in Anzio; 8th Army in Italy; French Army in France (despatches). HMS Duke of York, 1945, Comdr 1947; Naval Adviser, UK Mission, Japan, 1947–50 (OBE Korean War); HMS Swiftsure, 1950, Capt. 1952; HMS Lynx, 1956; HMS Victorious, 1961; Rear-Adm. 1962; Dir-Gen. of Naval Trng, Min. of Def., 1964–65 (Admiralty, 1962–64); Vice-Adm. 1965; C-in-C, S Atlantic and S America,

1965–67. Sec., Oriental Ceramic Soc., 1974–. *Recreations:* squash, tennis, athletics (represented RN in 220 and 440 yds). *Address:* 55 Elm Park Gardens, SW10. *T:* 01–352 1757. *Club:* Naval and Military.

GRAY, Prof. John Richard; Professor of African History, University of London, since 1972; *b* 7 July 1929; *s* of Captain Alfred William Gray, RN and of Christobel Margaret Gray (*née* Raikes); *m* 1957, Gabriella, *d* of Dr Camillo Cattaneo; one *s* one *d. Educ:* Charterhouse; Downing Coll., Cambridge (Richmond Scholar). BA Cantab 1951; PhD London 1957. Lectr, Univ. of Khartoum, 1959–61; Res. Fellow, Sch. of Oriental and African Studies, London, 1961–63, Reader, 1963–72. Vis. Prof., UCLA, 1967. Mem., NERC, 1986–. Editor, Jl African History, 1968–71; Chairman: Africa Centre, Covent Garden, 1967–72; Britain-Zimbabwe Soc., 1981–84. Mem., Pontifical Cttee of Historical Sciences, 1982–. Order of St Silvester, 1966. *Publications:* The Two Nations: aspects of the development of race relations in the Rhodesias and Nyasaland, 1960; A History of the Southern Sudan, 1839–1889, 1961; (with D. Chambers) Materials for West African History in Italian Archives, 1965; (ed, with D. Birmingham) Pre-Colonial African Trade, 1970; (ed) The Cambridge History of Africa, vol. 4, 1975; (ed, with E. Fasholé-Luke and others) Christianity in Independent Africa, 1978. *Recreation:* things Italian. *Address:* 39 Rotherwick Road, NW11 7DD. *T:* 01–458 3676.

GRAY, John Walton David, CMG 1986; HM Diplomatic Service; Ambassador to Lebanon, since 1985; *b* Burry Port, Carmarthenshire, 1 Oct. 1936; *s* of Myrddin Gray and Elsie Irene (*née* Jones), Llanelli, Carms; *m* 1957, Anthoula, *e d* of Nicolas Yerasimou, Nicosia, Cyprus; one *s* two *d. Educ:* Blundell's Sch.; Christ's Coll., Cambridge (MA; Scholar and Tancred Student); ME Centre, Oxford; Amer. Univ., Cairo. National Service, 1954–56. Joined Foreign Service, 1962; served: Mecas, 1962; Bahrain Agency, 1964; FO, 1967; Geneva, 1970; Sofia, 1974; Counsellor (Commercial), 1978, Counsellor and Hd of Chancery, 1980, Jedda; Hd of Maritime, Aviation and Environment Dept, FCO, 1982–85. *Recreations:* most spectator sports, amateur dramatics, light history, things Welsh. *Address:* c/o Foreign and Commonwealth Office, SW1A 2AH. *T:* 01–233 3000. *Club:* Royal Commonwealth Society.

GRAY, Rt. Rev. Joseph; *see* Shrewsbury, Bishop of, (RC).

GRAY, Kenneth Walter, PhD; Technical Director, THORN EMI plc, since 1986 (Director of Research, 1984–86); *b* 20 March 1939; *s* of Robert W. Gray and late Ruby M. Gray; *m* 1962, Jill Henderson; two *s* one *d. Educ:* Blue Coat Sch.; Univ. of Wales (BSc, PhD). Research on magnetic resonance, as Nat. Res. Council of Canada post-doctoral Fellow, Univ. of British Columbia, Vancouver, 1963–65; research on semiconductor devices and on radiometry, N American Rockwell Science Center, Thousand Oaks, Calif, 1965–70; research on devices and systems at Royal Signals and Radar Estabt, 1971; Supt Solid State Physics and Devices Div., 1976; Head of Physics Group, 1979; RCDS 1981. Royal Signals and Radar Establishment: CSO, MoD, Dep. Dir (Applied Physics), 1982–84; Under Sec., Dep. Dir (Information Systems), 1984. Visiting Research Fellow: Univ. of Newcastle, 1972–74; Univ. of Leeds, 1976–; Vis. Prof., Univ. of Nottingham, 1986–. *Publications:* over 30 scientific and technical papers in various learned jls. *Recreations:* squash, tennis, bridge. *Address:* Broadgates, Manor Road, Penn, Buckinghamshire HP10 8JA.

GRAY, Linda Esther, (Mrs Peter McCrorie); opera singer; *b* 29 May 1948; *d* of James and Esther Gray; *m* 1971, Peter McCrorie; one *d. Educ:* Greenock Academy; Royal Scottish Academy of Music and Drama. Cinzano Scholarship, 1969; Goldsmith Schol., 1970; James Caird Schol., 1971; Kathleen Ferrier Award, 1972; Christie Award, 1972. London Opera Centre, 1969–71; Glyndebourne Festival Opera, 1972–75; Scottish Opera, 1974–79; Welsh Opera, 1980–; English National Opera, 1979–; American début, 1981; Royal Opera House: Sieglinde, 1982; Fidelio, 1983. Record of Tristan und Isolde, 1981. Principal rôles: Isolde, Sieglinde, Kundry (Wagner); Tosca (Puccini); Fidelio (Beethoven). *Recreations:* cooking, swimming. *Address:* 171 Queens Road, SW19. *T:* 01–542 3053.

GRAY, Margaret Caroline, MA Cantab; Headmistress, Godolphin and Latymer School, 1963–Dec. 1973; *b* 25 June 1913; *d* of Rev. A. Herbert Gray, DD, and Mrs Gray (Mary C. Dods, *d* of Principal Marcus Dods of New Coll., Edinburgh). *Educ:* St Mary's Hall, Brighton; Newnham Coll., Cambridge. Post graduate fellowship to Smith Coll., Mass, USA, 1935–36. Asst History mistress, Westcliff High Sch. for Girls, 1937–38; Head of History Dept, Mary Datchelor Girls' Sch., Camberwell, 1939–52; Headmistress, Skinners' Company's Sch., Stamford Hill, 1952–63. Chm., Nat. Advisory Centre on Careers for Women, 1970–. Governor: Francis Holland Schs, 1974–; Hampton Sch., 1976–; West Heath Sch., Sevenoaks, 1974–; Unicorn Sch., Kew, 1974; Chm. of Trustees, Godolphin and Latymer Bursary Fund, 1976–. *Recreations:* gardening, motoring, walking. *Address:* 15 Fitzwilliam Avenue, Kew, Richmond, Surrey. *T:* 01–940 4439.

GRAY, Lt-Gen. Sir Michael Stuart, KCB 1986; OBE 1970; General Officer Commanding, South East District, and Commander Joint Force Headquarters, since 1985; *b* Beverley, E Yorkshire, 3 May 1932; *e s* of late Lieut Frank Gray, RNVR, and Joan Gray (*née* Gibson); *m* 1958, Juliette Antonia Noon, Northampton; two *s* one *d. Educ:* Christ's Hosp., Horsham; RMA, Sandhurst. FBIM. Enlisted RA, 1950; commissioned E Yorkshire Regt, 1952; served Malaya; transf. to Parachute Regt, 1955; served Cyprus, Suez, Jordan, Greece, Bahrein, Aden, N Ireland; sc Camberley, 1963; commanded 1st Bn Parachute Regt, 1969–71; DS Staff Coll., Camberley, 1971–73; Col GS 1 Div. BAOR, 1973–75; RCDS 1976; last Comdr 16 Para Bde, 1977; Comdr 6 Field Force and COMUKMF, 1977–79; Comdr British Army Staff and Mil. Attaché, Washington, 1979–81, and Head of British Def. Staff and Def. Attaché, Washington, 1981; GOC SW District, and Maj.-Gen., UKMF(L), 1981–83; COS, HQ BAOR, 1984–85. Actg Col Comdt, Parachute Regt, 1986–. Hon. Col, 10th (Volunteer) Bn, Parachute Regt (V), 1984–. Jt Chm. of Managing Trustees, Airborne Assault Normandy Trust (AAN), to preserve the history of 6 AB Division in Normandy, 1978–; Jt Chm., British American Forces Dining Club, 1982–. Pres., Army Parachute Assoc., 1981–. Freeman, City of London, 1983. *Recreations:* military history, travelling, DIY, photography, painting; sporting interests: Rugby, cricket, swimming, squash. *Address:* c/o National Westminster Bank, 60 Market Place, Beverley, North Humberside.

GRAY, Milner Connorton, CBE 1963; RDI 1938; FSIAD; AGI; FInstPack; Founder Partner and Senior Consultant, Design Research Unit; Past Master, Faculty of Royal Designers for Industry; Past President, Society of Industrial Artists and Designers; Past Master Art Workers' Guild; *b* 8 Oct. 1899; *s* of late Archibald Campbell Gray and Katherine May Hart, Eynsford, Kent; *m* 1934, Gnade Osborne-Pratt; no *c. Educ:* studied painting and design, London Univ., Goldsmiths' Coll. Sch. of Art. Head of Exhibitions Branch, Ministry of Information, 1940–41, and Adviser on Exhibitions, 1941–44; Senior Partner in Industrial Design Partnership, 1934–40; Principal, Sir John Cass Coll. of Art, 1937–40; on Visiting Staff: Goldsmiths' Coll. Sch. of Art, London Univ., 1930–40; Chelsea Sch. of Art, 1934–37; Royal Coll. of Art, 1940; Founder Mem., Soc. of Industrial Artists, 1930, Hon. Sec., 1932–40, Pres., 1943–48 and 1968; Member of Council: Design and Industries Assoc., 1935–38; RSA, 1959–65; Artists Gen. Benevolent Instn, 1959–; Adviser to BBC "Looking at Things" Schs Broadcasts, 1949–55. Member: Min. of Education Nat. Adv. Cttee on Art Examinations, 1949–52; Nat. Adv. Council on Art Education, 1959–69; Royal Mint Adv. Cttee, 1952–. Mem. Council, RCA, 1963–67, Mem. Court 1967–, Senior Fellow, 1971. British Pres., Alliance Graphique Internationale, 1963–71. Consultant Designer: BR Bd for BR Corporate Design Prog., 1963–67; (jointly) to Orient Line, SS Oriana, 1957–61; Ilford Ltd, 1946–66; Internat. Distillers and Vintners, 1954–; Watney Mann Group, 1956–; British Aluminium Co., 1965–; ICI, 1966–; Min. of Technology, 1970–. Governor: Central Sch. of Art and Design, 1944–46; Hornsey Coll. of Art and Design, 1959–65. Hon. Fellow, Soc. of Typographic Designers, 1979. Hon. Des. RCA, 1963, Hon. Dr RCA, 1979; Hon. DA Manchester, 1964. Served in 19th London Regt, and Royal Engineers, attached Camouflage Sch., 1917–19. Gold Medal, Soc. of Ind. Artists and Designers, 1955. *Publications:* The Practice of Design (jointly), 1946; Package Design, 1955; (jtly) Lettering for Architects and Designers, 1962; articles, lectures and broadcasts on various aspects of design. *Address:* 8 Holly Mount, Hampstead, NW3 6SG. *T:* 01–435 4238; Felix Hall, Kelvedon, Essex. *Club:* Arts.

GRAY, Monique Sylvaine, (Mrs P. F. Gray); *see* Viner, M. S.

GRAY, Nicol; *see* Gray, W. N.

GRAY, Paul Edward, ScD; President, Massachusetts Institute of Technology, since 1980; *b* 7 Feb. 1932; *s* of Kenneth Frank Gray and Florence (*née* Gilleo); *m* 1955, Priscilla Wilson King; one *s* three *d. Educ:* Massachusetts Inst. of Technol. (SB 1954, SM 1955, ScD 1960). Served Army, 1955–57 (1st Lieut). Massachusetts Inst. of Technology: Mem., Faculty of Engrg, 1960–71; Class of 1922 Prof. of Electrical Engrg, 1968–71; Dean, Sch. of Engrg, 1970–71; Chancellor, 1971–80, Mem. of Corp., 1971–. Mem., White House Science Council, 1982–. Director: Shawmut Bank, Boston; New England Mutual Life Insurance Co., Boston; A. D. Little Inc., Cambridge; Cabot Corp., Boston. Trustee and Mem. of Corporation: Museum of Science, Boston; Woods Hole Oceanographic Inst.; Chm., Bd of Trustees, Wheaton Coll., Mass. Trustee: Carroll Sch., Lincoln, Mass; (ex officio) WGBH Educational Foundation, Boston; Kennedy Meml Trust, London; Nat. Action Council for Minorities in Engrg; Cole Center for Dyslexia, Lincoln, Mass; Whitaker Health Scis Fund, Cambridge, Mass. Fellow, Amer. Acad. of Arts and Sciences; Member: National Acad. of Engrg; Mexican National Acad. of Engrg; AAAS; Fellow, IEEE. *Address:* Massachusetts Institute of Technology, 77 Massachusetts Avenue, Cambridge, Mass 02139, USA; 111 Memorial Drive, Cambridge, Mass 02142.

GRAY, Prof. Peter, MA, PhD, ScD (Cantab); FRS 1977; CChem, FRSC; Professor and Head of Department of Physical Chemistry, University of Leeds, since 1965; *b* Newport, 25 Aug. 1926; *er s* of late Ivor Hicks Gray and Rose Ethel Gray; *m* 1952, Barbara Joan Hume, PhD, 2nd *d* of J. B. Hume, London; two *s* two *d. Educ:* Newport, High Sch.; Gonville and Caius Coll., Cambridge. Major Schol., 1943; Prizeman, 1944, 1945 and 1946, Gonville and Caius Coll.; BA 1st cl hons Nat. Sci. Tripos, 1946; Dunlop Res. Student, 1946; Ramsay Mem. Fellow, 1949–51; PhD 1949; Fellow, Gonville and Caius Coll., 1949–53; ICI Fellow, 1951; ScD 1963. University Demonstrator in Chem. Engrg, University of Cambridge, 1951–55; Physical Chemistry Dept, University of Leeds: Lectr, 1955; Reader, 1959; Prof., 1962; Chm., Bd of Combined Faculties of Science and Applied Science, 1972–74. Visiting Professor: Univ. of BC, 1958–59; Univ. of W Ont., 1969; Univ. of Göttingen, 1979, 1986; Macquarie Univ., 1980; Univ. of Paris, 1986; Visitor, Fire Res. Organisation, 1984–. Mem. Council: Faraday Soc., 1965 (Vice-Pres., 1970; Treasurer, 1973; Pres., 1983–85); Chemical Soc., 1969. Meldola Medal, Royal Inst. Chem., 1956; Marlow Medal, Faraday Soc., 1959; Gold Medal, Combustion Inst., 1978. Associate Editor, Royal Society, 1983–. *Publications:* paper on phys. chem. subjects in scientific jls. *Recreation:* hill walking. *Address:* 4 Ancaster Road, Leeds LS16 5HH. *T:* Leeds 752826.

GRAY, Peter Francis; Managing Director, Touche Remnant Holdings Ltd, since 1983; Director, TR Industrial & General Trust, since 1984; *b* 7 Jan. 1937; *s* of Revd George Francis Selby Gray; *m* 1978, Fiona Elspeth Maud Lillias Bristol; two *s. Educ:* Marlborough; Trinity College, Cambridge. MA; FCA. Served Royal Fusiliers, attached 4th Kings African Rifles, Uganda, 1956–58. Coopers & Lybrand, 1967–69; Samuel Montagu & Co., 1970–77; Head of Investment Div., Crown Agents for Oversea Govts & Admins, 1977–83. Dep. Chm., Assoc. of Investment Trust Cos, 1985–. Trustee, John Hancock Global Trust, 1985–. *Address:* 1 Bradbourne Street, SW6 3TF. *Club:* Buck's.

GRAY, Maj.-Gen. (Reginald) John, CB 1973; Chairman, RAMC Association, since 1980; *b* 26 Nov. 1916; *s* of late Dr Cyril Gray and Frances Anne Higgins, Higginsbrook, Co. Meath; *m* 1943, Esme, *d* of late G. R. G. Shipp; one *s* one *d. Educ:* Rossall Sch.; Coll. of Medicine, Univ. of Durham. MB, BS. Commissioned into RAMC, 1939; served War of 1939–45 in India; later Burma, NW Europe, Egypt, Malta, BAOR. Comd of 9 (Br.) CCS, 1945; Medical Gold Staff Officer, 1953; Asst Dir-Gen., AMS, WO, AMD3, 1954–57; comd of David Bruce Mil. Hosp., Mtarfa, 1957–60; 14 Field Amb., 4 Guards Bde, 1960–63; Brit. Mil. Hosp., Rinteln, 1963–64; The Queen Alexandra Mil. Hosp., Millbank, 1964–67; Asst Dir-Gen., AMS, Min. of Defence AMD1, 1967–69; Dep. Dir-Gen., AMS, 1969–71. QHS 1970–73; DMS, UK Land Forces, 1972–73, retired. Col Comdt, RAMC, 1977–81. Chief MO, British Red Cross Soc., 1974–83; Chm., BMA Armed Forces Cttee, 1981–85. Dir, International Generics Ltd, 1974–83. Mem., Casualty Surgeons Assoc., 1976–; Hon. Mem., St Andrews Ambulance Assoc., 1982; Life Mem., BRCS, 1983; Hon. Mem., Inst. of Civil Defence, 1983. FRSM; FFCM 1972. CStJ 1971 (OStJ 1957). *Recreations:* gardening, wine making, d-i-y slowly. *Address:* 11 Hampton Close, Wimbledon, SW20 0RY. *T:* 01–946 7429.

GRAY, Robert; JP; Lord Provost and Lord-Lieutenant of Glasgow, since 1984; *b* 3 March 1928; *s* of John Gray and Mary (*née* McManus); *m* 1955, Mary (*née* McCartney); one *d. Educ:* St Mungo's Acad., Glasgow. LIOB 1970. Lecturer: Glasgow Coll. of Building, 1964–65; Anniesland Coll., 1965–70; Sen. Lectr, Cardonald Coll., 1970–84. Mem. (Lab) Glasgow Dist Council, 1974–. OStJ. *Recreations:* walking, reading, music. *Address:* 106 Churchill Drive, Glasgow G11 7EZ. *T:* 041–357 3328. *Clubs:* Royal Scottish Automobile, Art (Glasgow).

GRAY, Robert Michael Ker, QC 1983; QC (NI) 1984; a Recorder, since 1985; *b* 29 Aug. 1938; *y s* of late Brig. Walter Ker Gray, DSO and of Violet Lascelles, Checkendon, Oxfordshire. *Educ:* Radley (Scholar); Humboldt Gymnasium, Düsseldorf (Exchange Scholar); Balliol College, Oxford (Scholar) (MA 1963); St John's College, Cambridge (LLM (LLB 1967), Russian Tripos 1968). Called to the Bar, Lincoln's Inn and Gray's Inn, 1969; MacMahon Studentship, St John's College, Cambridge, 1969–73. European Office, UN, Geneva, 1962–64; Dept of Slavonic Studies, Cambridge, 1964, returned to University. Mem., Gen. Council of the Bar, 1972–74; Mem., Senate of the Bar, 1974–79, 1980– (Chm., Young Barristers, 1978–79). Chm., Harrison Homes (formerly Homes for the Aged Poor), 1980–; Sec., Friends of St George's Cathedral, Cape Town, 1983–. *Recreations:* walking, swimming. *Address:* 4–5 Gray's Inn Square, WC1R 5AY. *T:* 01–404 5252; Yew Tree Cottage, Whitchurch-on-Thames, Oxon RG8 7EX. *T:* Pangbourne 2802. *Clubs:* Garrick, Royal Automobile, Budleigh Salterton, Pangbourne Working Men's.

GRAY, Robin, (Robert Walker Gray), CB 1977; Deputy Secretary, Department of Trade, 1975–84; retired; *b* 29 July 1924; *s* of Robert Walker Gray and Dorothy (*née* Lane); *m* 1955, Shirley Matilda (*née* Taylor); two *s* one *d*. *Educ:* Headstone Council Sch.; Pinner Park Council Sch.; John Lyon Sch., Harrow; Birkbeck Coll., Univ. of London; London Sch. of Economics. BScEcons 1946; Farr Medal in Statistics. Air Warfare Analysis Section of Air Min., 1940–45; BoT, 1947; UK Delegn to OEEC, 1950–51; BoT, 1952–66; Commercial Counsellor, British High Commn, Ottawa, 1966–70; Under-Secretary: DTI, 1971–74; Dept of Prices and Consumer Protection, 1974–75; Dep. Sec., DoI, 1975. Vice-Pres., Guildford and Dist Rifle and Pistol Club, 1986. *Recreations:* fishing, growing rhododendrons. *Address:* Tansy, Brook Road, Wormley, Godalming, Surrey GU8 5UA. *T:* Wormley 2486.

GRAY, Hon. Robin (Trevor); MHA (L) for Lyons (formerly Wilmot), since 1976; Premier of Tasmania, Treasurer, Minister for Energy, since 1982, and for State Development, since 1984; *b* 1 March 1940; *s* of late Rev. W. J. Gray; *m* 1965, Judith Boyd; two *s* one *d*. *Educ:* Box Hill High Sch.; Dookie Agricl Coll., Melbourne Univ. Teacher, 1961–65 (in UK, 1964); agricl consultant, Colac, Vic, 1965, Launceston, Tas, 1965–76; pt-time Lectr in Agricl Econs, Univ. of Tasmania, 1970–76. Dep. Leader of the Opposition, 1979–81, Leader of the Opposition, 1981–82, Tasmania. *Address:* House of Assembly, Hobart, Tas 7000, Australia; 11 Beech Road, Launceston, Tas 7250, Australia.

GRAY, Roger Ibbotson, QC 1967; a Recorder of the Crown Court, since 1972; *b* 16 June 1921; *o s* of Arthur Gray and Mary Gray (*née* Ibbotson); *m* 1952, Anne Valerie, 2nd *d* of late Capt. G. G. P. Hewett, CBE, RN; one *s*. *Educ:* Wycliffe Coll.; Queen's Coll., Oxford. 1st cl. hons Jurisprudence, Oxon, 1941. Commissioned RA, 1942; served with Ayrshire Yeomanry, 1942–45; Normandy and NW Europe, 1944–45; GSO3 (Mil. Ops), GHQ, India, 1946. Pres. of Oxford Union, 1947. Called to Bar, Gray's Inn, 1947; South-Eastern Circuit. A Legal Assessor: GNC, 1976–83; UKCC, 1983–. Contested (C) Dagenham, 1955. *Publication:* (with Major I. A. Graham Young) A Short History of the Ayrshire Yeomanry (Earl of Carrick's Own) 151st Field Regiment, RA, 1939–46, 1947. *Recreations:* cricket, reading, talk. *Address:* Queen Elizabeth Building, Temple, EC4. *T:* 01–583 7837. *Clubs:* Carlton, Pratt's, MCC.

GRAY, Simon James Holliday; writer; *b* 21 Oct. 1936; *s* of Dr James Davidson Gray and Barbara Cecelia Mary Holliday; *m* 1965, Beryl Mary Kevern; one *s* one *d*. *Educ:* Westminster; Dalhousie Univ.; Trinity Coll., Cambridge (MA). Trinity Coll., Cambridge: Sen. Schol., Research Student and Harper-Wood Trav. Student, 1960; Supervisor in English, 1960–63; Sen. Instructor in English, Univ. of British Columbia, 1963–64; Lectr in English, QMC, London Univ., 1965–85 (Hon. Fellow, 1985). *Publications: novels:* Colmain, 1963; Simple People, 1965; Little Portia, 1967; (as Hamish Reade) A Comeback for Stark, 1968; *plays:* Wise Child, 1968; Sleeping Dog, 1968; Dutch Uncle, 1969; The Idiot, 1971; Spoiled, 1971; Butley, 1971; Otherwise Engaged, 1975 (voted Best Play, 1976–77, by NY Drama Critics Circle); Plaintiffs and Defendants, 1975; Two Sundays, 1975; Dog Days, 1976; Molly, 1977; The Rear Column, 1978; Close of Play, 1979; Stage Struck, 1979; Quartermaine's Terms, 1981; adap. Tartuffe (for Washington, DC; unpublished), 1982; The Common Pursuit, 1984; *non-fiction:* An Unnatural Pursuit and Other Pieces, 1985. *Recreations:* watching cricket and soccer, tennis, swimming. *Address:* c/o Judy Daish Associates, 83 Eastbourne Mews, W2 6LQ.

GRAY, Sylvia Mary, CBE 1975 (MBE 1952); *b* 10 July 1909; *d* of Henry Bunting and Mary Elizabeth Gray. *Educ:* Wroxall Abbey. Chm., Bay Tree Hotels Ltd, 1946–83. Mem., Witney RDC, 1943–54 (Vice-Chm. 1950–54); Chairman: Oxon Fedn Women's Insts, 1951–54; Nat. Fedn of Women's Insts, 1969–74 (Mem., Exec. Cttee, 1955; Hon. Treas., 1958). Member: Keep Britain Tidy Group Exec., 1967–78, Vice-Chm., 1974; Post Office Users' Nat. Council, 1969–78; National Trust, 1971–81, Chm., S Midlands Regional Cttee, 1975–81; IBA Advertising Standards Adv. Cttee, 1972; Council for European Architectural Heritage, 1972; Nat. Consumer Council, 1975–77; Redundant Churches Cttee, 1976–84. *Recreation:* reading. *Address:* St Winnow, Burford, Oxon. *T:* Burford 2210. *Club:* Naval and Military.

GRAY, Prof. Thomas Cecil, CBE 1976; KCSG 1982; JP; MD, FRCS, FRCP, FFARCS; FFARACS (Hon.); FFARCSI (Hon.); Professor of Anæsthesia, The University of Liverpool, 1959–76, now Emeritus; Dean of Postgraduate Medical Studies, 1966–70, of Faculty of Medicine, 1970–76; *b* 11 March 1913; *s* of Thomas and Ethel Gray; *m* 1st, 1937, Marjorie Kathleen (*née* Hely) (*d* 1978); one *s* one *d*; 2nd, 1979, Pamela Mary (*née* Corning); one *s*. *Educ:* Ampleforth Coll.; University of Liverpool. General Practice, 1937–39. Hon. Anaesthetist to various hospitals, 1940–47. Active Service, Royal Army Medical Corps, 1942–44. Demonstrator in Anæsthesia, University of Liverpool, 1942, 1944–46; Reader in Anæsthesia, University of Liverpool, 1947–59; Hon. Cons Anæsthetist: United Liverpool Hosps, Royal Infirmary Branch; Liverpool Thoracic Surgical Centre, Broadgreen Hosp.; Mem. Bd, Faculty of Anæsthetists, RCSEng, 1948–69 (Vice-Dean, 1952–54; Dean, 1964–67). Member Council: RCS, 1964–67; Assoc. of Anæsthetists of Great Brit. and Ire., 1948–67 (Hon. Treas. 1950–56; Pres. 1957–59); ASME, 1972–76; FRSocMed (Mem. Council, 1958–61; Pres. Anæsthetic Section, 1955–56; Mem. Council, Sect. of Med. Educn, 1969–72); Chm. BMA Anæsthetic Group, 1957–62; Mem., Liverpool Regional Hosp. Board, 1968–74 (Chm., Anæsthetic Adv. Cttee, 1948–70; Chm., Med. Adv. Council, 1970–74); Mem., Merseyside RHA, 1974–77; Mem., Bd of Governors, United Liverpool Hosps., 1969–74; Mem. Clinical Res. Bd, Med. Res. Council, 1965–69; Hon. Civilian Consultant in Anæsthetics to the Army at Home, 1964–78 (Guthrie Medal 1977), Emeritus Consultant to the Army, 1979. Hon. Consultant to St John's Ambulance; Member Council, Order of St John for Merseyside; Asst Dir-Gen., St John Ambulance, 1977–82; Vice-Pres., Med. Defence Union, 1956– (Treasurer, 1977–82); Chm., Bd of Governors, Linacre Center for Study of Ethics of Health Care, 1973–83. Examiner in FFARCS, 1953–70; FFARCSI 1967–70: Dip. Vet. Anæsth., RCVS, 1968–76. Hon. FRSocMed, 1979; Hon. Member: Sheffield and East Midlands Soc. of Anæsthetists; Yorks Soc. of Anæsthetists; Austrian Soc. of Anæesthetists; Soc. Belge d'Anesthesie et de Reanimation; Argentinian and Brazilian Socs of Anesthesiologists; Australian and Malaysian Socs of Anæsthetists; Assoc. of Veterinary Anæsthetists. Hon. Corresp. Member: Sociedade das Ciencias Medical di Lisboa; W African Assoc. of Surgeons. Clover Lectr and Medallist, RCS, 1953; Lectures: Simpson-Smith Meml, W London Sch. of Med., 1956; Jenny Hartmann Meml, Univ. of Basle, 1958; Eastman, Univ. of Rochester, NY, 1958; Sir James Young Simpson Meml, RCSE, 1967; Torsten Gordh, Swedish Soc. of Anaesthetists, 1978; Kirkpatrick, Faculty of Anaesthetists, RCSI, 1981; John Gillies, Scottish Soc. of Anaesthetists, 1982; Mitchiner Meml, RAMC, 1983; Florence Elliott, Royal Victoria Hosp., Belfast, 1984. Sims Commonwealth Travelling Prof., 1961. JP City of Liverpool, 1966 (retd list). Freeman, City of London, 1984; Liveryman, Soc. of Apothecaries, 1956. OStJ 1979. Medallist, Univ. of Liège, 1947; Henry Hill Hickman Medal, 1972; Hon. Gold Medal, RCS, 1978; Ralph M. Waters medal and award, Illinois Soc. of Anesthesiologists, 1978; Silver Medal, Assoc. of Anaesthetists, 1982. *Publications:* Modern Trends in Anæsthesia (ed jtly), 1958, 3rd edn 1967; (ed jtly) General Anæsthesia, 1959, 4th edn 1980 (Spanish edns, 1974, 1983);(ed jtly) Paediatric Anæsthesia, 1981; many contribs to gen. med. press and specialist jls. *Recreations:* music, golf, amateur dramatics. *Address:* 6 Raven Meols Lane, Formby, Liverpool L37 4DF.

GRAY, Sir William (Hume), 3rd Bt *cr* 1917; Director, Egglestone Estate Co.; *b* 26 July 1955; *s* of William Talbot Gray (*d* 1971) (*er s* of 2nd Bt), and of Rosemarie Hume Gray, *d* of Air Cdre Charles Hume Elliott-Smith; *S* grandfather, 1978; *m* 1984, Catherine Victoria Willoughby, *y d* of late John Naylor and of Mrs Naylor, Bramley, Hants; one *s*. *Educ:* Aysgarth School, Bedale, Yorks; Eton College; Polytechnic of Central London BA (Hons) Architecture; DipArch; RIBA. *Recreation:* sport. *Heir:* *s* William Willoughby Gray, *b* 24 Aug. 1986. *Address:* Eggleston Hall, Barnard Castle, Co. Durham. *T:* Teesdale 50403.

GRAY, (William) Nicol, CMG 1948; DSO 1944, Bar, 1945; KPM 1951; FRICS; *b* 1 May 1908; *e s* of late Dr W. Gray, Westfield, West Hartlepool; *m* 1st, 1953, Jean Marie Frances Backhouse (marr. diss. 1966), *o c* of Lieut-Col G. R. V. Hume-Gore, MC and Mrs W. Lyne-Stephens, and *widow* of Major Sir John Backhouse, Bt, MC; two *d*; 2nd, 1967, Margaret Clare Galpin, *widow* of Commander Walter Galpin, RN. *Educ:* Trinity Coll., Glenalmond. Royal Marines, 1939–46; GSO II RM Div., no I (Experimental) WOSB; Mil. Instructor, HMS Dorlin; CO 45 RM Commando; Comdt, RM Octu; Inspector-Gen., Palestine Police, 1946–48; Commissioner of Police, Federation of Malaya, 1948–52. Agent to the Jockey Club, Newmarket, 1953–64. Administrator, MacRobert Trusts, 1970–74. Trustee, Duke of Edinburgh's Award Scheme, 1973–78, Hon. Trustee, 1979–83. *Address:* The Bacchus House, Elsdon, Northumberland. *T:* Otterburn 20665.

GRAY, Sir William (Stevenson), Kt 1974; JP; DL; solicitor and notary public; Lord Provost, City of Glasgow and Lord Lieutenant, County of the City of Glasgow, 1972–75; *b* 3 May 1928; *o s* of William Stevenson Gray and Mary Johnstone Dickson; *m* 1958, Mary Rodger; one *s* one *d*. *Educ:* Hillhead High Sch.; Glasgow Univ. Admitted solicitor, 1958; notary public, 1960. Chm., Webtec Industrial Technology Ltd, 1984–. Chairman: Scottish Special Housing Assoc., 1966–72; World of Property Housing Trust Scottish Housing Assoc. Ltd, 1974–; Irvine New Town Develt Corp., 1974–76; Scotland W Industrial Promotion Gp, 1972–75; Scottish Develt Agency, 1975–79; Member: Exec., Scottish Council (Develt and Industry), 1971–75; Scottish Econ. Council, 1975–83; Lower Clyde Water Bd, 1971–72; Clyde Port Authority, 1972–75; Adv. Council for Energy Conservation, 1974–84; Convention of Royal Burghs, 1971–75; Central Adv. Cttee on JPs, 1975–. Chairman: Third Eye Centre Ltd, Glasgow, 1975–84; Glasgow Independent Hosp. Ltd (Ross Hall Hosp.), 1982–; Clyde Tourist Assoc., 1972–75; Member: Nat. Trust for Scotland, 1971–72; Scottish Opera Bd, 1971–72; Scottish Nat. Orch. Soc., 1972 75; Vice-President: Glasgow Citizens' Theatre, 1975– (Mem., Bd of Dirs, 1970–75); Strathclyde Theatre Gp, 1975–; Charles Rennie Mackintosh Soc., 1974–; Scottish Assoc. for Care and Resettlement of Offenders, 1982– (Chm., 1975–82); Governor, Glasgow Sch. of Art, 1961–75; Patron, Scottish Youth Theatre, 1978–; Chm., The Oil Club, 1975–. Member: Court, Glasgow Univ., 1972–75; Council, Strathclyde Univ. Business Sch., 1978–. Hon. LLD: Strathclyde, 1974; Glasgow, 1980. Mem., Glasgow Corp., 1958–75 (Chm., Property Management Cttee, 1964–67); Treasurer, City of Glasgow, 1971–72. JP City of Glasgow, 1961–64, Co. of City of Glasgow 1965; DL Co. of City of Glasgow, 1971, City of Glasgow 1976. *Recreations:* sailing, theatre. *Address:* 13 Royal Terrace, Glasgow G3 7NY. *T:* 041–332 8877.

GRAY DEBROS, Winifred Marjorie, (Mrs E. Gray Debros); *see* Fox, W. M.

GRAYSON, Prof. Cecil, MA; FBA 1979; Serena Professor of Italian Studies in the University of Oxford, and Fellow of Magdalen College, 1958–Oct. 1987; *b* 5 Feb. 1920; *s* of John M. Grayson and Dora Hartley; *m* 1947, Margaret Jordan; one *s* three *d*. *Educ:* Batley Grammar Sch.; St Edmund Hall, Oxford (Hon. Fellow, 1986). Army service (UK and India), 1940–46 (Major); First Class Hons (Mod. Langs), 1947; Univ. Lectr in Italian, Oxford, 1948; Lectr at St Edmund Hall, 1948; Lectr at New Coll., 1954. Corresp. Fellow, Commissione per i Testi di Lingua, Bologna, 1957; Mem., Accademia Letteraria Ital. dell' Arcadia, 1958; Corresp. Mem., Accademia della Crusca, 1960; Accademia delle Scienze, Bologna, 1964; Accademia dei Lincei, 1967; Istituto Veneto di Scienze, Lettere ed Arti, 1977; Barlow Lecturer, University Coll., London, 1963; Resident Fellow, Newberry Library, Chicago, 1965; Visiting Professor: Yale Univ., 1966; Berkeley, Calif, 1969, 1973; UCLA, 1980, 1984; Perth, WA, 1973, 1980; Cape Town, 1980, 1983. An editor of Italian Studies. Premio Internazionale Galileo (storia della lingua italiana), 1974; Serena Medal for Italian Studies, British Academy, 1976. Comdr, Order of Merit, Italy, 1975. *Publications:* Early Italian Texts (with Prof. C. Dionisotti), 1949; Opuscoli inediti di L. B. Alberti, 1954; Alberti and the Tempio Malatestiano, 1957; Vincenzo Calmeta, Prose e Lettere edite e inedite, 1959; A Renaissance Controversy: Latin or Italian?, 1960; L. B. Alberti, Opere volgari, I, 1960, II, 1966, III, 1973; L. B. Alberti e la prima grammatica volgare, 1964; Cinque saggi su Dante, 1972; (trans.) The Lives of Savonarola, Machiavelli and Guicciardini by Roberto Ridolfi, 1959, 1963, 1967; (ed) selected works of Guicciardini, 1964; (ed and trans.) L. B. Alberti, De pictura, De statua, 1972; (ed) The World of Dante, 1980; articles in Bibliofilia, Burlington Mag., English Misc., Giorn. Stor. d. Lett. Ital., Ital. Studies, Lettere Italiane, Lingua Nostra, Rassegna d. Lett. Ital., Rinascimento, The Year's Work in Mod. Languages. *Recreation:* music. *Address:* 11 Norham Road, Oxford. *T:* 57045.

GRAYSON, Sir Ronald Henry Rudyard, 3rd Bt of Ravens Point, *cr* 1922; *b* 15 Nov. 1916; *s* of Sir Denys Henry Harrington Grayson, 2nd Bt, and Elsie May (*d* 1973), *d* of Richard Davies Jones; *S* father 1955; *m* 1st, 1936; 2nd, 1946, Vicki Serell. *Educ:* Harrow Sch. Engineering apprenticeship Grayson, Rollo & Clover Docks Ltd, 1934. Dir, 1940–49; Emigrated to Australia, 1953. Served War of 1939–45, RAF. *Heir: uncle* Rupert Stanley Harrington Grayson, writer. *Recreation:* books. *Address:* 5 Cheero Point Road, Cheero Point, NSW 2254, Australia.

GRAYSTON, Rev. Prof. Kenneth, MA; Professor of Theology, Bristol University, 1965–79, now Emeritus Professor; Pro-Vice-Chancellor, Bristol University, 1976–July 1979; *b* Sheffield, 8 July 1914; *s* of Ernest Edward and Jessie Grayston; *m* 1942, Elizabeth Alison, *d* of Rev. Walter Mayo and Beatrice Aste, Elsfield, Oxon.; no *c*. *Educ:* Colfe's Grammar Sch., Lewisham; Universities of Oxford and Cambridge. Ordained Methodist Minister, 1942; Ordnance Factory Chaplain, 1942–44; Asst Head of Religious Broadcasting, BBC, 1944–49; Tutor in New Testament Language and Literature, Didsbury Coll., 1949–64; Special Lecturer in Hellenistic Greek, Bristol Univ., 1950–64; Dean, Faculty of Arts, Bristol Univ., 1972–74. Select Preacher to Univ. of Cambridge, 1952, 1962, to Univ. of Oxford, 1971; Sec. Studiorum Novi Testamenti Societas, 1955–65; Chairman: Theolog. Adv. Gp, British Council of Churches, 1969–72; Christian Aid Scholarships Cttee, 1973–78. *Publications:* The Epistles to the Galatians and to the Philippians, 1957; The Letters of Paul to the Philippians and the Thessalonians, 1967; The Johannine Epistles, 1984; (contrib. in): A Theological Word Book of the Bible, 1950; The Teacher's Commentary, 1955; The Interpreter's Dictionary of the Bible, 1962; A New Dictionary of Christian Theology, 1983, etc. (Contrib. to): Expository Times, New Testament Studies, Theology, Epworth Review, etc. *Recreation:* travel. *Address:* 11 Rockleaze Avenue, Bristol BS9 1NG. *T:* Bristol 683872.

GREATBATCH, Sir Bruce, KCVO 1972 (CVO 1956); Kt 1969; CMG 1961; MBE 1954; *b* 10 June 1917; *s* of W. T. Greatbatch; unmarried. *Educ:* Malvern Coll.; Brasenose Coll., Oxford. Appointed Colonial Service, 1940, Northern Nigeria. War Service with Royal W African Frontier Force, 1940–45, rank of Major, Burma Campaign (despatches). Resumed Colonial Service, Northern Nigeria, 1945; Resident, 1956; Sec. to Governor and Executive Council, 1957; Senior Resident, Kano, 1958; Sec. to the Premier of Northern Nigeria and Head of Regional Civil Service, 1959; Dep. High Comr, Nairobi, Kenya, 1963; Governor and C-in-C, Seychelles, and Comr for British Indian Ocean Territory, 1969–73; Head of British Development Div., Caribbean, 1974–78; freelance consultant, 1978–. KStJ 1969. *Recreations:* shooting, gardening. *Address:* Greenleaves, Painswick, near Stroud, Glos GL6 6TX. *T:* Painswick 813517. *Clubs:* East India, Devonshire, Sports and Public Schools, Royal Commonwealth Society.

GREAVES, Jeffrey; HM Diplomatic Service, retired; Consul General, Alexandria, 1978–81; *b* 10 Dec. 1926; *s* of Willie Greaves and Emily Verity; *m* 1949, Joyce Mary Farrer; one *s* one *d*. *Educ:* Pudsey Grammar Sch. Served RN, 1945–48. Joined HM Foreign Service, 1948; FO, 1948; Benghazi, 1951; Vice Consul, Tehran, 1953; ME Centre for Arab Studies, 1955; Second Sec. and Vice Consul, Paris, 1960; Vice Consul, Muscat, 1962; Second Sec. and Consul, Athens, 1965; Second Sec. (Commercial), Cairo, 1968; First Sec. and Consul, Muscat, 1970; First Sec. (Com.), Bangkok, 1972; FCO, 1976. *Recreations:* walking, flying. *Address:* 38 Alexandra Road, Pudsey, West Yorks LS28 8BY. *Club:* Yorks Aeroplane.

GREAVES, Prof. Ronald Ivan Norreys, MD, FRCP; Professor of Pathology, University of Cambridge, 1963–75, now Emeritus Professor; Fellow of Gonville and Caius College, since 1935; *b* 15 July 1908; *s* of late Rt Rev. Arthur I. Greaves, Bishop of Grimsby and Blanche, *d* of late Joseph Meadows; *m* 1936, Anne, *d* of late Philip Bedingfeld; one *d*. *Educ:* Uppingham Sch.; Clare Coll.; Cambridge (Nat. Scis Tripos, 1st Cl. Part I, 1930, 1st Cl Part II (Pathology), 1931, BA 1930, MA, MB, BCh 1935, MD 1946); Harmsworth Scholar, 1931, St Mary's Hosp., Paddington. Demonstrator in Pathology, Cambridge Univ., 1935; seconded to Med. Research Council, 1939–45 for res. and production of freeze-dried blood plasma for transfusion; Reader in Bacteriology, Cambridge, 1946; Head of Department of Pathology, 1963–75. Past Pres., Soc. for Cryobiology. *Publications:* chapters in books and articles in med. jls, principally on freeze-drying of blood plasma and its transfusion, and on preservation of micro-organisms by freeze-drying. *Recreations:* electronics and gardening. *Address:* 59 Barrow Road, Cambridge CB2 2AR. *T:* Cambridge 353548.

GREBENIK, Eugene, CB 1976; MSc (Economics); Editor, Population Studies; Consultant, Office of Population Censuses and Surveys, 1977–84; *b* 20 July 1919; *s* of S. Grebenik; *m* 1946, Virginia, *d* of James D. Barker; two *s* one *d*. *Educ:* abroad; London Sch. of Economics. Statistician, Dept of Economics, Univ. of Bristol, 1939–40; London Sch. of Economics: Asst. 1940–44 and Lecturer, 1944–49, in Statistics (on leave, 1944–46); served in RN, 1944; Temp. Statistical Officer, Admiralty, 1944–45; Secretariat, Royal Commn on Population, 1945–46); Reader in Demography, Univ. of London, 1949–54; Research Sec., Population Investigation Cttee, 1947–54; Prof. of Social Studies, Univ. of Leeds, 1954–69. Principal, Civil Service Coll., 1970–76 and Dep. Sec., Civil Service Dept, 1972–76. Mem., Impact of Rates Cttee, Ministry of Housing, 1963–64. Social Science Research Council: Statistics Cttee, 1966–69; Cttee on Social Science and Government, 1968–72; Population Panel, 1971–73; Member: Cttee on Governance of London Univ., 1970–72; Council, RHBNC (formerly RHC), Univ. of London, 1971–. Pres., British Soc. for Population Studies, 1979–81. Sec.-Treasurer, Internat. Union for Scientific Study of Population, 1963–73. Hon. Fellow, LSE, 1969; Vis. Fellow, ANU, 1982–83; Hon. Vis. Prof., City Univ., 1986–. *Publications:* (with H. A. Shannon) The Population of Bristol, 1943; (with D. V. Glass) The Trend and Pattern of Fertility in Great Britain; A Report on the Family Census of 1946, 1954; various articles in statistical and economic journals. *Address:* Little Mead, Tite Hill, Egham, Surrey TW20 0NH. *T:* Egham 32994.

GREEN, Alan, CBE 1974; Chairman: Walmsley (Bury) Group since 1970; Beloit Walmsley Ltd; Director: Scapa Group Ltd; Wolstenholme Bronze Powders Ltd (Vice-Chairman); Porritts & Spencer (Asia) Ltd, since 1969; Local Director, Barclays Bank, Manchester District, since 1969; *b* 29 Sept. 1911; *s* of Edward and Emily Green; *m* 1935, Hilda Mary Wolstenholme; three *d*. *Educ:* Brighton Coll. Schoolmaster, 1931–35; joined Scapa Dryers Ltd, Blackburn, 1935. Army Service, 1940–45. Formerly: Dir of Scapa Dryers Ltd, 1945; Vice-Chm. of Scapa Dryers Ltd, 1956; Dir of Scapa Dryers Inc., 1955; Dir of companies associated with Walmsley (Bury) Group, 1950; Chm. of Walmsley Operating Companies, 1954. Contested (C): Nelson and Colne, 1950 and 1951; MP (C) Preston S, 1955–64, 1970–Feb. 1974; Parly Sec., Min. of Labour, 1961–62; Minister of State, BoT, 1962–63; Financial Sec. to the Treasury, 1963–64. Mem., Australia Cttee, BNEC, 1968–72; frequent business visits to Northern and Western Europe, Australasia, Japan, India and North America. *Recreations:* cricket, golf, tennis, gardening, history. *Address:* The Stables, Sabden, near Blackburn, Lancs. *T:* Padiham 71528. *Clubs:* Reform, Royal Automobile.

See also D. C. Waddington.

GREEN, Prof. Albert Edward, FRS 1958; MA, PhD, ScD (Cambridge); Sedleian Professor of Natural Philosophy, University of Oxford, 1968–77, now Emeritus Professor; Supernumerary Fellow, The Queen's College, Oxford, since 1977 (Fellow, 1968–77); *m* 1939, Gwendoline May Rudston. *Educ:* Jesus Coll., Cambridge Univ. (Scholar). PhD 1937; MA 1938; ScD 1943. Fellow, Jesus Coll., Cambridge, 1936–39; Lecturer in Mathematics, Durham Colls, University of Durham, 1939–48; Prof. of Applied Mathematics, University of Newcastle upon Tyne, 1948–68. Hon. DSc: Durham, 1969; NUI, 1977; Hon. LLD Glasgow, 1975. Timoshenko Medal, ASME, 1974; Theodore von Karmen Medal, ASCE, 1983. *Address:* 20 Lakeside, Oxford.

GREEN, Allan David; First Senior Prosecuting Counsel to the Crown at the Central Criminal Court, since 1985; a Recorder of the Crown Court, since 1979; *b* 1 March 1935; *s* of Lionel and Irene Green; *m* 1967, Eva, *yr d* of Prof. Artur Attman and Elsa Attman, Gothenburg, Sweden; one *s* one *d*. *Educ:* Charterhouse; St Catharine's Coll., Cambridge (Open Exhibnr, MA). Served RN, 1953–55. Called to the Bar, Inner Temple, 1959, Bencher, 1985; Jun. Prosecuting Counsel to the Crown, Central Criminal Court, 1977, Sen. Prosecuting Counsel, 1979. *Publications:* trans. with wife several Swedish books. *Recreations:* music, squash. *Address:* 1 Hare Court, Temple, EC4Y 7BE. *T:* 01–353 5324.

GREEN, Andrew Curtis; farmer and horticulturist, since 1960; *b* 28 March 1936; *s* of Christopher Green and Marjorie (*née* Bennett); *m* 1966, Julia Margaret (*née* Davidson); two *s*. *Educ:* Charterhouse; Magdalene Coll., Cambridge. MA (Nat. Scis), Dip. of Agriculture. Commnd RNVR, 1954–56. Farm management, 1960–67; founded Greens of Soham farming and horticultural business, 1967; Dir, Elsoms Spalding Seed Co., 1982–; Chm., Hassy Ltd, 1983–. Mem., AFRC, 1984–. FLS 1978; Hon. Fellow, Inst. Hort. 1986. *Recreations:* sailing, fishing, shooting, skiing. *Address:* Kingfishers Bridge, Wicken, Ely,

Cambs CB7 5XL. *T:* Ely 721112. *Clubs:* Army and Navy, Farmers'; Hawks (Cambridge); Royal Thames Yacht.

GREEN, Andrew Fleming; HM Diplomatic Service; Counsellor, Head of Chancery and Consul General, Riyadh, since 1985; *b* 6 Aug. 1941; *s* of late Gp Captain J. H. Green, RAF, and Beatrice Mary (*née* Bowditch); *m* 1968, C. Jane Churchill; one *s* one *d*. *Educ:* Haileybury and ISC; Magdalene Coll., Cambridge (MA). Served Army, 1962–65; joined HM Diplomatic Service, 1965; Middle East Centre for Arab Studies, 1966–68; Aden, 1968–69; Asst Political Agent, Abu Dhabi, 1970–71; First Secretary, FCO, 1972–74; Private Sec. to Minister of State, FCO, 1975, and to Parliamentary Under Sec. of State, 1976; First Secretary, UK Delegn to OECD, Paris, 1977–79; Asst Head of Economic Relations Dept, FCO, 1980–81; Counsellor, Washington, 1982–85. *Recreations:* tennis, sailing, bridge. *Address:* c/o Foreign and Commonwealth Office, SW1.

GREEN, Anthony Eric Sandall, RA 1977 (ARA 1971); Member, London Group, 1964; Artist (Painter); *b* 30 Sept. 1939; *s* of late Frederick Sandall Green and Marie Madeleine (*née* Dupont); *m* 1961, Mary Louise Cozens-Walker; two *d*. *Educ:* Highgate Sch., London; Slade Sch. of Fine Art, University Coll. London. Henry Tonks Prize for drawing, Slade Sch., 1960; French Govt Schol., Paris, 1960; Gulbenkian Purchase Award, 1963; Harkness Fellowship, in USA, 1967–69. Has exhibited in: London, New York, Haarlem, Rotterdam, Stuttgart, Hanover, Helsingborg, Malmö, Tokyo and Brussels. Paintings in various public collections, including: Tate Gallery; Olinda Museum, Brazil; Baltimore Mus. of Art, USA; Nat. Mus. of Wales; Gulbenkian Foundn; Arts Council of Gt Brit.; British Council; Contemporary Art Soc.; Frans Hals Mus., Holland; Boymans-van Bevningen Mus., Holland; Ulster Mus., Belfast; Ikeda Mus., Tokyo. Exhibit of the Year award, RA, 1977. *Publication:* A Green Part of the World, 1984. *Recreations:* travelling, family life. *Address:* 17 Lissenden Mansions, Highgate Road, NW5. *T:* 01–485 1226.

GREEN, Arthur Edward Chase, MBE (mil.) 1955; TD (and Bar); DL; FRICS; Chartered Surveyor; Property Adviser, J. H. Schroder Wagg & Co., 1972–82; Director, Schroder Properties Ltd, 1974–82; *b* 5 Nov. 1911; *s* of Harry Catling and Sarah Jane Green, Winchmore Hill, London; *m* 1941, Margaret Grace, *yr d* of John Lancelot and Winifred Churchill, Wallington, Surrey; one *s* two *d*. *Educ:* Merchant Taylors' Sch.; Coll. of Estate Management. HAC, 1932–: King's Prize, 1938; commnd, 1939; Adjt 11 (HAC) Regt RHA, 1941–42; Western Desert, ME; PoW 1942; despatches 1945; Territorial Efficiency Medal and bar; Court of Assistants, HAC, 1946–76, Treasurer, 1966–69, Vice-Pres., 1970–72; Metropolitan Special Constabulary, HAC Div., 1937–39 and 1946–74 (Long Service Medal and bar); Hon. Mem., Transvaal Horse Artillery. Surveyor, Legal and General Assce Soc., 1934–46, Chief Estates Surveyor, 1946–71. Mem., Cttee of Management, Pension Fund Property Unit Trust, 1972–82; Advr on Policy, Post Office Staff Superannuation Fund, until 1977, Dir, Mereacre Ltd, and Mereacre Farms Ltd (PO Staff Superann. Fund), 1977–83; Member: Chancellor of the Exchequer's Property Adv. Panel, 1975–80; Govt Cttee of Inquiry into Agriculture in GB, 1977–79 (Northfield Cttee). Chm., Elecrent Properties Ltd (Electronic Rentals Gp), 1974–83; Director: Marlborough Property Hldgs plc; Studley Farms Ltd, 1980–82. Mem., TA&VR Assocs for City of London, to 1977, and for Greater London, to 1981. President: Camden and Islington Corps, St John Ambulance, 1974–75, No 7 Corps, City of London and Hackney, 1976–77, City of London, 1978–. Governor: Bridewell Royal Hosp.; City of London Sch., to 1981; Mem. Court and Governor, Corp. of Sons of the Clergy; former Governor, Queenswood Sch. Vice-Pres., Brunswick Boys' Club Trust, 1978– (formerly Founder-Trustee). City of London Court of Common Council (Bread Street Ward), 1971–81. Freedom of the City of London, 1939; Liveryman: Merchant Taylors' Co.; Gunmakers' Co. DL Greater London, 1967 (Representative DL for London Borough of Islington, 1967–81). OStJ 1984. *Recreations:* shooting, gardening, travel, photography. *Address:* Mariners, The Common, Southwold, Suffolk. *T:* Southwold 723410. *Clubs:* Guildhall, Sloane.

See also Very Rev. J. H. Churchill.

GREEN, Arthur Jackson; Under Secretary, Department of Education for Northern Ireland; *b* 12 Nov. 1928; *s* of F. Harvey Green and Sylvia Marsh Green, MB; *m* 1957, Rosemary Bradley, MA; two *s*. *Educ:* Friends Sch., Lisburn, Co. Antrim; Leighton Park Sch., Reading; Lincoln Coll., Oxford (BA Mod. Hist.); Haverford Coll., Philadelphia (MA Philosophy). Asst Principal, NICS, 1952; Secretary: Cameron Commn, 1969; Scarman Tribunal, 1969–72; Asst Sec., NI Dept of Finance, 1972–78; Under Sec., NI Office, 1978–79; Dir, NI Court Service (Lord Chancellor's Dept), 1979–82; Fellow, Center for Internat. Affairs, Harvard Univ., 1982–83. *Address:* 36 St Patrick's Road, Saul, Downpatrick, N Ireland. *T:* Downpatrick 4360. *Club:* Reform.

GREEN, Barry Spencer, QC 1981; a Recorder of the Crown Court, since 1979; *b* 16 March 1932; *s* of Lionel Maurice Green, FRCS and Juliette Green; *m* 1960, Marilyn Rebecca Braverman; two *s*. *Educ:* Westminster Sch.; Christ Church, Oxford (MA, BCL). Called to the Bar, Inner Temple, 1954. A Chm., Mental Health Review Tribunals, 1983–. *Recreation:* tennis. *Address:* 4 Paper Buildings, Temple, EC4Y 7EX. *T:* 01–353 1131. *Club:* Roehampton.

GREEN, Father Benedict; *see* Green, Rev. H. C.

GREEN, Benny; free-lance writer; *b* 9 Dec. 1927; *s* of David Green and Fanny Trayer; *m* 1962, Antoinette Kanal; three *s* one *d*. *Educ:* Clipstone Street Junior Mixed; subsequently uneducated at St Marylebone Grammar Sch. Mem., West Central Jewish Lads Club (now extinct). Saxophonist, 1947–60 (Most Promising New Jazz Musician, 1953); Jazz Critic, Observer, 1958–77; Literary Critic, Spectator, 1970–; Film Critic, Punch, 1972–77, TV Critic, 1977–; frequent radio and TV appearances, 1955–. Artistic Dir, New Shakespeare Co., 1973–; Mem., BBC Archives Cttee, 1976. Book and lyrics, Boots with Strawberry Jam, Nottingham Playhouse, 1968; revised libretto, Showboat, Adelphi Theatre, London, 1972; co-deviser: Cole, Mermaid, 1974; Oh, Mr Porter, Mermaid, 1977; D. D. Lambeth, 1985. *Publications:* The Reluctant Art, 1962; Blame it on my Youth, 1967; 58 Minutes to London, 1969; Drums in my Ears, 1973; I've Lost my little Willie, 1976; Swingtime in Tottenham, 1976; (ed) Cricket Addict's Archive, 1977; Shaw's Champions, 1978; Fred Astaire, 1979; (ed) Wisden Anthology, vol. I 1864–1900, 1979, vol. II 1900–1940, 1980, vol. III 1940–1963, 1982, vol. IV 1963–1982, 1983; P. G. Wodehouse: a literary biography, 1981; Wisden Book of Obituaries, 1986. *Recreation:* cricket. *Address:* c/o BBC, Broadcasting House, Portland Place, W1.

GREEN, Rev. Bernard; General Secretary, Baptist Union of Great Britain and Ireland, since 1982; *b* 11 Nov. 1925; *s* of George Samuel Green and Laura Annie Agnes (*née* Holliday); *m* 1952, Joan Viccars; two *s* one *d*. *Educ:* Wellingborough Sch.; Bristol Baptist Coll.; Bristol Univ. (BA); Regent's Park Coll., Oxford, and St Catherine's Coll., Oxford (MA); London Univ. BD taken externally. Served War as coal-miner, 1944–47. Ordained as Baptist Minister, 1952; pastorates at: Yardley, Birmingham, 1952–61; Mansfield Road, Nottingham, 1961–76; Horfield, Bristol, 1976–82. Regular broadcaster on BBC Radio Nottingham until 1976 and on BBC Radio Bristol until 1982. *Recreations:* reading, music (listening), gardening. *Address:* Baptist Church House, 4 Southampton Row, WC1B 4AB. *T:* 01–405 9803.

GREEN, Rev. Canon Bryan Stuart Westmacott, BD; DD (*hc*); Canon Emeritus of Birmingham Cathedral since 1970 (Hon. Canon, 1950–70); *b* 14 Jan. 1901; *s* of late Hubert Westmacott Green and late Sarah Kathleen Green (*née* Brockwell); *m* 1926, Winifred Annie Bevan; one *s* one *d*. *Educ:* Merchant Taylors' Sch.; London Univ. BD 1922; Curate, New Malden, 1924–28; Staff of Children's Special Service Mission, 1928–31; Chap., Oxford Pastorate, 1931–34; Vicar of Christ Church, Crouch End, 1934–38; Vicar of Holy Trinity, Brompton, 1938–48; Rector of Birmingham, 1948–70. Conducted evangelistic campaigns: Canada and America, 1936, 1944, and annually, 1947–; Australia and New Zealand, 1951, 1953, 1958, 1974; West Africa, 1953; S Africa, 1953, 1955, 1956, 1957, 1959 and 1960; Ceylon, 1954, 1959. DD Hon. St John's Coll. Winnipeg, 1961; DD Lambeth, 1985. *Publications:* The Practice of Evangelism, 1951; Being and Believing, 1956; Saints Alive, 1959. *Recreation:* golf. *Address:* West Field, Southern Road, Thame, Oxon OX9 2EP. *T:* Thame 2026. *Club:* National.

GREEN, Christopher Edward Wastie, MA, FCIT; Director, Network SouthEast, British Rail, since 1986; *b* 7 Sept. 1943; *s* of James Wastie Green and Margarita Mensing; *m* 1966, Mitzie Petzold; one *s* one *d*. *Educ:* St Paul's School, London; Oriel College, Oxford. MA Mod. Hist. Management Trainee, British Rail, 1965–67; served Birmingham, Nottingham, Hull, Wimbledon; Passenger Operating Manager, BR HQ, 1979–80; Chief Operating Manager, Scotland, 1980–83; Dep. Gen. Manager, Scotland, 1983–84; Gen. Manager, Scottish Region, BR, 1984–86. *Recreations:* music, reading, walking, architecture. *Address:* Berkhamsted, Herts.

GREEN, Prof. Dennis Howard; Schröder Professor of German, University of Cambridge, since 1979; Fellow of Trinity College, Cambridge, since 1949; *b* 26 June 1922; *s* of Herbert Maurice Green and Agnes Edith Green (*née* Fleming); *m* 1972, Margaret Parry. *Educ:* Latymer Upper Sch., London; Trinity Coll., Cambridge; Univ. of Basle. Univ. of Cambridge, 1940–41 and 1945–47; Univ. of Basle (Dr Phil.), 1947–49; Military service (RAC), 1941–45; Univ. Lecturer in German, St Andrews, 1949–50; Research Fellowship, Trinity Coll., Cambridge (first year held *in absentia*), 1949–52; Univ. Asst Lectr in German, Cambridge, 1950–54; Teaching Fellowship, Trinity Coll., Cambridge, 1952–66; Head of Dept of Other Languages, 1956–79, and Prof. of Modern Languages, Cambridge, 1966–79; Visiting Professor: Cornell Univ., 1965–66; Auckland Univ., 1966; Yale Univ., 1969; ANU, Canberra, 1971; UCLA, 1975; Univ. of Pennsylvania, 1975; Univ. of WA, 1976; Vis. Fellow, Humanities Res. Centre, Canberra, 1978. *Publications:* The Carolingian Lord, 1965; The Millstätter Exodus: a crusading epic, 1966; (with Dr L. P. Johnson) Approaches to Wolfram von Eschenbach, 1978; Irony in the Medieval Romance, 1979; The Art of Recognition in Wolfram's Parzival, 1982; reviews and articles in learned journals. *Recreations:* walking and foreign travel. *Address:* Trinity College, Cambridge; 7 Archway Court, Barton Road, Cambridge. *T:* Cambridge 358070.

GREEN, Rev. Canon (Edward) Michael (Bankes); Professor of Evangelism at Regent College, Vancouver, University of British Columbia, since 1987; *b* 20 Aug. 1930; British; *m* 1957, Rosemary Wake (*née* Storr); two *s* two *d*. *Educ:* Clifton Coll.; Oxford and Cambridge Univs. BD Cantab 1966. Exeter Coll., Oxford, 1949–53 (1st cl. Lit. Hum.); Royal Artillery (Lieut, A/Adjt), 1953–55; Queens' Coll., Cambridge, 1955–57 (1st cl. Theol. Tripos Pt III; Carus Greek Testament Prize; Fencing Blue), and Ridley Hall Theol Coll., 1955–57; Curate, Holy Trinity, Eastbourne, 1957–60; Lectr, London Coll. of Divinity, 1960–69; Principal, St John's Coll., Nottingham (until July 1970, London Coll. of Divinity), 1969–75; Canon Theologian of Coventry, 1970–76, Canon Theologian Emeritus, 1978–; Rector of St Aldate's, Oxford, 1975–87 (with Holy Trinity, Oxford, 1975–82 and with St Matthew, 1982–87). Member: Doctrine Commission of the Church, 1968–77; Church Unity Commn, 1974–. Leader of missions, overseas and in UK. *Publications:* Called to Serve, 1964; Choose Freedom, 1965; The Meaning of Salvation, 1965; Man Alive, 1967; Runaway World, 1968; Commentary on 2 Peter and Jude, 1968; Evangelism in the Early Church, 1970; Jesus Spells Freedom, 1972; New Life, New Lifestyle, 1973; I Believe in the Holy Spirit, 1975, new edn 1985; You Must Be Joking, 1976; (ed) The Truth of God Incarnate, 1977; Why Bother With Jesus?, 1979; Evangelism—Now and Then, 1979; What is Christianity?, 1981; I Believe in Satan's Downfall, 1981; The Day Death Died, 1982; To Corinth with Love, 1982; World on the Run, 1983; Freed to Serve, 1983; The Empty Cross of Jesus, 1984; Come Follow Me, 1984; Lift Off to Faith, 1985; contribs to various jls. *Recreations:* family, countryside pursuits, cricket, squash, fly fishing. *Address:* Regent College, 2130 Westbrook Mall, Vancouver, BC V6T 1W6, Canada. *T:* (604) 224 3245.

GREEN, Sir (Edward) Stephen (Lycett), 4th Bt, *cr* 1886; CBE 1964; DL, JP; Chairman, East Anglian Regional Hospital Board, 1959–74; *b* 18 April 1910; *s* of Sir E. A. Lycett Green, 3rd Bt, and Elizabeth Williams; *S* father, 1941; *m* 1935, Constance Mary, *d* of late Ven. H. S. Radcliffe; one *d*. *Educ:* Eton; Magdalene Coll., Cambridge. Called to Bar, Lincoln's Inn, 1933. Served War of 1939–45 (Major, RA). CC 1946–49, JP 1946, DL 1961, High Sheriff 1973, Norfolk; Dep. Chairman Norfolk QS, 1948–71. Chairman: King's Lynn Hospital Management Cttee, 1948–59; Assoc. of Hosp. Management Cttees, 1956–58; Cttee of Inquiry into Recruitment, Training and Promotion of Administrative and Clerical Staff in Hospital Service, 1962–63; Docking RDC, 1950–57. *Recreations:* shooting, reading. *Heir: b* Lt-Col Simon Lycett Green, TD, Yorks Dragoons Yeomanry [*b* 11 July 1912; *m* 1st, 1935, Gladys (marr. diss. 1971; she *d* 1980), *d* of late Arthur Ranicar, JP, Springfield, Wigan; one *d*; 2nd, 1971, Mary, *d* of late George Ramsden]. *Address:* Ken Hill, Snettisham, King's Lynn. *TA:* Snettisham, Norfolk. *T:* Heacham 70001. *Clubs:* White's, Pratt's; Norfolk (Norwich); Allsorts (Norfolk).

GREEN, Dr Frank Alan, CEng; FIM, FBIM; Senior Consultant, General Technology Systems Ltd, Brentford, since 1984; Principal, Charing Green Associates, Kent, since 1983; *b* 29 Oct. 1931; *s* of Frank Green and Winifred Hilda (*née* Payne); *m* 1957, Pauline Eleanor Tayler; one *s* two *d*. *Educ:* Mercers Sch., London; Univ. of London (BScEng, PhD). CEng 1980; FIM 1978; FBIM 1979. UKAEA, 1956–57; various appts, Glacier Metal Co. Ltd (Associated Engrg Gp), 1957–65; Technical Dir, Alta Friccion SA, Mexico City, 1965–68; Manufg Dir, Stewart Warner Corp., 1968–72; Marketing Develt Manager, Calor Gp, 1972–74; Manufg Dir, 1974–77, Man. Dir, 1977–81, British Twin Disc Ltd, Rochester; Industrial Advr (Under-Sec.), DTI, 1981–84. Dir, Anglo-Mexican Chamber of Commerce, Mexico City, 1966–68. Chm., Gen. Educn Cttee, Inst. of Metals. *Publications:* contrib. technical, historical and managerial jls in UK and Mexico. *Recreations:* photography, military history, rough walking, wine. *Address:* Courtwood, Burleigh Road, Charing, Kent TN27 0JB. *T:* Charing 3152. *Club:* Old Mercers.

GREEN, Geoffrey Hugh, CB 1977; Deputy Under-Secretary of State (Policy), Procurement Executive, Ministry of Defence, 1975–80; *b* 24 Sept. 1920; *o s* of late Duncan M. and Kate Green, Bristol; *m* 1948, Ruth Hazel Mercy; two *d*. *Educ:* Bristol Grammar Sch.; Worcester Coll., Oxford (Exhibr), 1939–41, 1945–47 (MA). Served with Royal Artillery (Ayrshire Yeomanry): N Africa and Italy, 1942–45 (Captain). Entered Min. of Defence, Oct. 1947; Principal, 1949; Asst Sec., 1960; Asst Under-Sec. of State, 1969; Dep. Under-Sec. of State, 1974. *Recreations:* travel, music, walking. *Address:* 47 Kent Avenue, Ealing, W13 8BE.

GREEN, Sir George (Ernest), Kt 1963; Past Chairman of Eagers Holdings Ltd; *b* 1892; *s* of Jabez Green, Brisbane, and Catherine Genevieve, *d* of T. Cronin; *m* Ailsa Beatrice, *d* of Charles George Rools Crane. *Educ:* Maryborough Grammar Sch. Pres., Royal National Agricultural and Industrial Assoc. of Qld, 1955–61. *Address:* 35 Markwell Street, Hamilton, Brisbane, Qld 4007, Australia.

GREEN, Major George Hugh, MBE; MC 1945; TD and 3 bars; Vice-Lieutenant of Caithness, since 1973; retired; *b* 21 Oct. 1911; *s* of George Green, The Breck, John O'Groats; *m* 1936, Isobel Elizabeth Myron; two *s*. *Educ:* Wick High Sch.; Edinburgh Univ. (MA). Retired as schoolmaster, 1977. Commnd into Seaforth Highlanders, TA, 1935; served War of 1939–45 with 5th Seaforths in 51st (H) Div., N Africa and NW Europe; retd from TA, 1963. DL Caithness 1965. *Recreations:* gardening, bee-keeping. *Address:* Tjaldur, Halkirk, Caithness. *T:* Halkirk 639. *Club:* Highland Brigade (Inverness).

GREEN, Hon. Sir Guy (Stephen Montague), KBE 1982; Chief Justice of Tasmania, since 1973; Lieutenant-Governor of Tasmania, since 1982; Chancellor, University of Tasmania, since 1985; *b* 26 July 1937; *s* of Clement Francis Montague Green and Beryl Margaret Jenour Green; *m* 1963, Rosslyn Mary Marshall; two *s* two *d*. *Educ:* Launceston Church Grammar Sch.; Univ. of Tasmania. Alfred Houston Schol. (Philosophy) 1958; LLB (Hons) 1960. Admitted to Bar of Tasmania, 1960; Partner, Ritchie & Parker Alfred Green & Co. (Launceston), 1963–71; Mem., Faculty of Law, Univ. of Tas, 1974–85. Pres., Tasmanian Bar Assoc., 1968–70 (Vice-Pres., 1966–68); Magistrate 1971–73. Chm., Council of Law Reporting, 1978–85. Chairman: Tasmanian Cttee, Duke of Edinburgh's Award Scheme in Australia, 1975–80; Sir Henry Baker Meml Fellowship Cttee, 1973–; Dir, Winston Churchill Meml Trust, 1975–85 (Dep. Nat. Chm., 1980–85; Chm. Tasmanian Regional Cttee, 1975–80); Mem., Tasmanian Cttee, United World Colls, 1981–. Priory Exec. Officer, Order of St John in Australia, 1984–; Pres., St John Council for Tasmania, 1984–. KStJ 1984. *Address:* Judges' Chambers, Supreme Court, Salamanca Place, Hobart, Tasmania 7000. *Clubs:* Launceston (Launceston, Tas.); Tasmanian, Athenæum (Hobart).

GREEN, Henry Rupert, CBE 1960; MA; Legal Senior Commissioner of Board of Control, 1953–60, later Ministry of Health; retired 1977; *b* 29 Dec. 1900; *o s* of late Henry Green, JP, solicitor, and Margaret Helen Green, Stockport, Cheshire; *m* 1937, Marie Elizabeth Patricia Bailey; three *s* one *d*. *Educ:* Charterhouse; Hertford Coll., Oxford (Exhibitioner). Barrister, Lincoln's Inn, 1926; practised on Northern Circuit, 1926–36; Commissioner of Board of Control, 1936. War of 1939–45: commissioned RAF, 1940; served as Operations Staff Officer, Malta, 1941–43; released, 1944. Pres. Governors, St Mary's Sch. for Girls, Gerrards Cross. *Publications:* title: Persons Mentally Disordered (Pts 2 and 3), Halsbury's Laws of England, 3rd Edn, 1960; title: Persons of Unsound Mind, Halsbury's Statutes (Burrows Edn), 1950 and similar title: Encyclopædia of Court Forms, 1949. *Recreation:* carpentry. *Address:* The Square House, Latchmoor Grove, Gerrards Cross, Bucks. *T:* Gerrards Cross 882316.

GREEN, Hon. Howard Charles, PC (Canada); QC (BC); LLD (University of British Columbia); *b* Kaslo, BC, 5 Nov. 1895; *s* of Samuel Howard and Flora Isabel Green; *m* 1st, 1923, Marion Jean (decd), *d* of Lewis Mounce, Vancouver; two *s*; 2nd, 1956, Donna Enid (decd), *d* of Dr D. E. Kerr, Duncan, BC. *Educ:* High Sch., Kaslo; University of Toronto (BA); Osgoode Hall Law Sch. Served European War, 1915–19. Called to Bar of British Columbia, 1922; elected to Federal Parliament, 1935; Minister of Public Works and Govt House Leader, 1957–59; Acting Minister of Defence Production, 1957–58; Dep. Prime Minister, 1957–63; Canadian Sec. of State for External Affairs, 1959–63. Is a Progressive Conservative. *Address:* 4160 W 8th Avenue, Vancouver, British Columbia, Canada. *Club:* Terminal City (Vancouver, BC).

GREEN, Rev. Humphrey Christian, (Father Benedict Green, CR); formerly Principal, College of the Resurrection, Mirfield; *b* 9 Jan. 1924; *s* of late Rev. Canon Frederick Wastie Green and Marjorie Susan Beltt Green (*née* Gosling). *Educ:* Dragon Sch., Oxford; Eton (King's Scholar); Merton Coll., Oxford (Postmaster). BA 1949, MA 1952. Served War, RNVR, 1943–46. Deacon 1951, priest 1952; Asst Curate of Northolt, 1951–56; Lectr in Theology, King's Coll., London, 1956–60. Professed in Community of the Resurrection (taking additional name of Benedict), 1962; Vice-Principal, Coll. of the Resurrection, 1965–75; Principal, 1975–84. Associate Lectr in Dept of Theology and Religious Studies, Univ. of Leeds, 1967–. *Publications:* The Gospel according to Matthew (New Clarendon Bible), 1975; contrib.: Towards a Church Architecture (ed P. Hammond), 1962; The Anglican Synthesis (ed W. R. F. Browning), 1964; Synoptic Studies (ed C. M. Tuckett), 1984; theological jls. *Recreations:* walking, synoptic criticism. *Address:* House of the Resurrection, Mirfield, W Yorks WF14 0BN. *T:* Mirfield 494318.

GREEN, (James) Maurice (Spurgeon), MBE, TD, MA; Editor, The Daily Telegraph, 1964–74 (Deputy Editor, 1961–64); *b* 8 Dec. 1906; *s* of Lieut-Col James Edward Green, DSO; *m* 1st 1929, Pearl (*d* 1934), *d* of A. S. Oko, Cincinnati, USA; 2nd, 1936, Janet Grace, *d* of Maj.-Gen. C. E. M. Norie, CB, CMG, DSO; two *s*. *Educ:* Rugby Sch. (scholar); University Coll., Oxford (scholar, 1st Class, Honour Mods and Lit. Hum.). Editor of The Financial News, 1934–38; Financial and Industrial Editor of The Times, 1938–39 and 1944–53 (served in Royal Artillery, 1939–44); Asst Editor, 1953–61. Pres., Inst. of Journalists, 1976–77. *Recreations:* books, music, fishing. *Address:* The Hermitage, Twyford, near Winchester, Hants. *T:* Twyford 713980. *Club:* Reform.

GREEN, John Dennis Fowler; *b* 9 May 1909; *s* of late Capt. Henry and Amy Gertrude Green, Chedworth, Glos; *m* 1946, Diana Judith, JP, *y d* of late Lt-Col H. C. Elwes, DSO, MVO, Colesbourne, Glos. *Educ:* Cheltenham Coll.; Peterhouse, Cambridge. President of the Union. Called to the Bar, Inner Temple, 1933; BBC, 1934–62 (Controller, Talks Div., 1956–61); established agricultural broadcasting, 1935. Special Agric. Mission to Aust. and NZ (MAFF), 1945–47; Pres. National Pig Breeders Assoc., 1955–56; Chm., Agricultural Adv. Council, 1963–68; Exec. Mem., Land Settlement Assoc., 1965–80; Trustee, RASE, 1984– (Dep. Pres., 1983–84); Chm., Glos Br., CPRE, 1964–85, Mem., National Exec., 1967–80. Chm., Cirencester and Tewkesbury Conservative Assoc., 1964–78. *Publications:* Mr Baldwin: A Study in Post War Conservatism, 1933; articles and broadcasts on historical and agricultural subjects. *Recreations:* livestock breeding, forestry, shooting. *Address:* The Manor, Chedworth, Cheltenham GL54 4AA. *T:* Fossebridge 233. *Clubs:* Oriental, Naval and Military, Buck's, Farmers'.

GREEN, John Edward, PhD, CEng, FRAeS; Deputy Director (Aircraft), Royal Aircraft Establishment, since 1985; *b* 26 Aug. 1937; *s* of John Green and Ellen O'Dowd; *m* 1959, Gillian (*née* Jackson); one *s* one *d*. *Educ:* Birkenhead Inst. Grammar Sch.; St John's Coll., Cambridge (Scholar). BA 1959; MA 1963; PhD 1966. Student Apprentice, Bristol Aircraft Ltd, 1956; De Havilland Engine Co., 1959–61; Royal Aircraft Establishment, 1964–81: Head of Transonic/Supersonic Wind Tunnel Div., 1971; Head of Propulsion Div., 1973; Head of Noise Div., 1974; Head of Aerodynamics Dept., 1978–81; Dir, Project Time and Cost Analysis, MoD (PE), 1981–84; Minister–Counsellor Defence Equipment, and Dep. Head of British Defence Staff, Washington, 1984–85. Mem. Council, RAeS, 1986–. *Publications:* contribs to books and learned jls, chiefly on fluid mechanics and aerodynamics. *Recreations:* music, mountain walking. *Address:* Royal Aircraft Establishment, Farnborough, Hants.

GREEN, John Michael, CB 1976; Commissioner, 1971–85, Deputy Chairman, 1973–85, Board of Inland Revenue; *b* 5 Dec. 1924; *s* of late George Green and of Faith Green; *m* 1951, Sylvia (*née* Crabb); one *s* one *d*. *Educ:* Merchant Taylors' Sch., Rickmansworth; Jesus Coll., Oxford (MA (Hons)). Served War, Army, RAC, 1943–46. Entered Inland Revenue as Asst Principal, 1948; served in HM Treasury, as Principal, 1956–57; Asst Sec., 1962; Under Sec., Bd of Inland Revenue, 1971. *Recreation:* gardening. *Address:* 5 Bylands, White Rose Lane, Woking, Surrey GU22 7LA. *T:* Woking 72599. *Club:* Reform.

GREEN, Julian Hartridge; American and French writer; Member of Académie Française, 1971; *b* Paris, France, 6 Sept. 1900. *Educ:* Lycée Janson, Paris; Univ. of Virginia. Member: Acad. de Bavière, 1950; Royal Acad. of Belgium, 1951; Ravenclub, 1922; Acad. de Mannheim, 1952; Phi Beta Kappa, 1948; Amer. Acad. of Arts and Sciences. Prix Harper, Prix Bookman, Prix de Monaco, 1951; Grand Prix National des Lettres, 1966; Grand Prix, Académie Française, 1970; Grand Prix Littérature de Pologne, 1985. *Publications: fiction:* The Apprentice Psychiatrist, 1920; Le voyageur sur la terre, 1924; Mont-Cinère, 1926; Adrienne Mesurat, 1927; Les clés de la mort, 1928; Léviathan, 1929; L'autre sommeil, 1930; Epaves, 1932; Le visionnaire, 1934; Minuit, 1936; Varouna, 1940; Si j'étais vous ...., 1947; Moira, 1950; Le malfaiteur, 1956, new enl. edn 1974; Chaque homme dans sa nuit, 1960; L'autre, 1971; La nuit des fantômes, 1976; Le Mauvais Lieu, 1977; Histoires de Vertige, 1984; *plays:* Sud, 1953; L'ennemi, 1954; L'ombre, 1956; Demain n'existe pas, 1979; L'automate, 1980; *autobiography and journals:* Memories of Happy Days, 1942; Jeunes Années: i, Partir avant le jour, 1963; ii, Mille chemins ouverts, 1964; iii, Terre lointaine, 1966; iv, Jeunesse, 1974; Liberté, 1974; Ce qu'il faut d'amour a l'homme, 1978; Journal: i, Les années faciles, 1928–34, 1938; ii, Derniers beaux jours, 1935–39, 1939; iii, Devant la porte sombre, 1940–43, 1946; iv, L'œil de l'houragan, 1943–45, 1949; v, Le revenant, 1946–50, 1952; vi, Le miroir intérieur, 1950–54, 1955; vii, Le bel aujourd'hui, 1955–58, 1958; viii, Vers l'invisible, 1958–66, 1967; ix, Ce qui reste de jour, 1967–72, 1972; x, La bouteille à la mer, 1972–76, 1976; xi, La Terre est si belle, 1976–78, 1982; xii, La lumière du monde, 1978–81, 1983; Dans la gueule du temps (illust. jl), 1979–; Œuvres complètes (La Pleïade), vol. I, 1972; vols II and III, 1973; vols IV and V, 1974; *history:* Frère François, 1983; *essays:* Suite Anglaise, 1925; Paris, 1983; Villes, 1985; Le Langage et son double, 1985. *Address:* Editions de la Pleïade, 5 rue Sébastien-Bottin, 75007 Paris, France.

GREEN, Kenneth, MA; Director, Manchester Polytechnic, since 1981; *b* 7 March 1934; *s* of James William and Elsie May Green; *m* 1961, Glenda (*née* Williams); one *d*. *Educ:* Helsby Grammar Sch.; Univ. of Wales, Bangor (BA 1st Cl. Hons); Univ. of London (MA). 2nd Lieut, S Wales Borderers, 1955–57. Management Trainee, Dunlop Rubber Co., 1957–58; Teacher, Liverpool, 1958–60; Lecturer: Widnes Technical Coll., 1961–62; Stockport College of Technology, 1962–64; Sen. Lectr, Bolton College of Education, 1964–68; Head of Educn, City of Birmingham College of Education, 1968–72; Dean of Faculty, Manchester Polytechnic, 1973–81. *Recreations:* Rugby football, beer tasting. *Address:* 40 Royden Avenue, Runcorn, Cheshire WA7 4SP. *T:* Runcorn 75201.

GREEN, Maj.-Gen. Kenneth David, CB 1982; OBE; ED; FICE; Secretary, Premier's Department, Government of Victoria, 1972–82; *b* 20 Nov. 1917; *s* of D. W. Green; *m* 1945, Phyl, *d* of J. Roohan; one *s*. *Educ:* Williamstown High Sch.; Melbourne High Sch.; Melbourne Univ. (BCE). Served 2nd AIF. Joined State Rivers and Water Supply Commn, Vic, 1939; design and exec. engrg appts, 1958–65; Commissioner: State Rivers and Water Supply Commn, Vic, 1965–72; Australian Cities Commn, 1972–75. Fourth Task Force, CMF, 1966–69; Southern Comd Trng Gp, 1969–70; Comdr 3rd Div., CMF, 1970–73; Col Comdt, RAE, Vic, 1976–82. Chairman: State Recreation Council (formerly Nat. Fitness Council), Vic; Duke of Edinburgh's Award Scheme Cttee, Vic, 1971–81; Nat. Water Research Council, 1982–83; Member: Council, Order of Australia, 1974–82; Australia Day Cttee (Vic), 1982–; Film Victoria Bd, 1982. Pres. Council, Chisholm Inst. of Technology, 1982–85; Vice-Pres., Victoria Br., Scout Assoc. of Aust., 1982–. FTS; FASCE; Hon. FIE (Aust). *Publications:* technical papers. *Recreations:* golf, swimming, listening to classical music. *Address:* 226 Were Street, East Brighton, Vic 3187, Australia. *Clubs:* Melbourne, Athenæum, Naval and Military (Melbourne); Melbourne Cricket, Huntingdale Golf, Frankston Golf.

GREEN, Prof. Leslie Leonard, PhD; FInstP; Professor of Experimental Physics, University of Liverpool, 1964–86; Director, Daresbury Laboratory, since 1981; *b* 30 March 1925; *s* of Leonard and Victoria Green; *m* 1952, Dr Helen Therese Morgan; one *s* one *d*. *Educ:* Alderman Newton's Sch., Leicester; King's Coll., Cambridge (MA, PhD). FInstP 1966. British Atomic Energy Proj., 1944–46; Univ. of Liverpool: Lectr, 1948–57; Sen. Lectr, 1957–62; Reader, 1962–64; Dean, Faculty of Sciences, 1969–72; Pro-Vice-Chancellor, 1978–81. Mem., SRC Nuclear Physics Bd, 1972–75 and 1979–82. *Publications:* articles on nuclear physics in scientific jls. *Address:* Seafield Cottage, De Grouchy Street, West Kirby, Merseyside L48 5DX. *Club:* South Caernarvonshire Yacht.

GREEN, Lucinda Jane, MBE 1978; three-day event rider; *b* 7 Nov. 1953; *d* of late Maj.-Gen. George Erroll Prior-Palmer, CB, DSO, and of Lady Doreen Hersey Winifred Prior-Palmer; *m* 1981, David, *s* of Burrington Green, Brisbane; one *s*. *Educ:* St Mary's, Wantage; Idbury Manor, Oxon. Member of winning Junior European Team, 1971; Winner, 3 Day Events: Badminton Horse Trials Championships, 1973, 1976, 1977, 1979, 1983, 1984; Burghley, 1977, 1981; Individual European Championships, 1975, 1977; World Championship, 1982; Member: Olympic Team, Montreal, 1976, Los Angeles, 1984; European Championship Team, Burghley, 1977 (team Silver Medallist); European Team, 1979, 1983 (team Silver Medallist); Alternative Olympic Team, 1980; World Championship Team: Kentucky, 1978; Luhmühlen, W Germany, 1982 (1st place). *Publications:* Up, Up and Away, 1978; Four Square, 1980; Regal Realm, 1983. *Recreations:* driving, skiing, scuba diving, travelling abroad. *Address:* Appleshaw House, Andover, Hants. *T:* Weyhill 2333.

GREEN, Malcolm Leslie Hodder, PhD; FRS 1985; CChem, FRSC; Septcentenary Fellow and Tutor in Inorganic Chemistry, Balliol College, Oxford, since 1963; Lecturer, University of Oxford, since 1965; *b* 16 April 1936; *s* of late Leslie Ernest Green, MD and Sheila Ethel (*née* Hodder); *m* 1965, Jennifer Clare Bilham; two *s* one *d*. *Educ:* Denstone Coll.; Acton Technical Coll. (BSc); Imperial Coll. of Science and Technol., London Univ. (DIC, PhD 1958); MA Cantab. CChem, FRSC 1981. Asst Lectr in Inorganic Chem., Univ. of Cambridge, 1960–63; Fellow of Corpus Christi Coll., Cambridge, 1961–63; Deptl Demonstrator, 1963, British Gas Royal Soc. Sen Res. Fellow, 1979–86, Univ. of Oxford. A. P. Sloan Vis. Prof., Harvard Univ., 1973; Sherman Fairchild Vis. Scholar, CIT, 1981. Tilden Lectr and Prize, RSC, 1982; Debye Lectr, Cornell Univ., 1985. Corday–Morgan Medal and Prize in Inorganic Chem., Chemical Soc., 1974; Medal for Transition Metal Chem., Chemical Soc., 1978; Award for Inorganic Chem., Amer. Chemical Soc., 1984; Royal Soc. Award for Organometallic Chem., 1986. *Publications:* Organometallic Compounds: Vol. II, The Transition Elements, 1968; (with G. E. Coates, P. Powell and K. Wade) Principles of Organometallic Chemistry, 1968. *Address:* Balliol College, Oxford OX1 3BJ. *T:* Oxford 53424.

GREEN, Malcolm Robert, DPhil; Lecturer, University of Glasgow, since 1967; Chairman, Strathclyde Region Education Committee, since 1982; *b* 4 Jan. 1943; *m* 1971; one *s* two *d*. *Educ:* Wyggeston Boys' School, Leicester; Magdalen College, Oxford. MA, DPhil. Member: Glasgow Corp., 1973–75; Strathclyde Regional Council, 1975–; Chairman: Management Side, Scottish Teachers and Lecturers Negotiating Bodies, 1977–; Nat. Cttee for In-Service Training of Teachers, 1977–; Educn Cttee, Convention of Scottish Local Authorities, 1978–; Commissioner, Manpower Services Commn, 1983–85. *Recreation:* talking politics. *Address:* 46 Victoria Crescent Road, Glasgow G12 9DE. *T:* 041–339 2007.

GREEN, Rt. Rev. Mark, MC 1945; Hon. Assistant, Christ Church, St Leonards-on-Sea, since 1982; an Assistant Bishop, Diocese of Chichester, since 1982; *b* 28 March 1917; *s* of late Rev. Ernest William Green, OBE, and Miranda Mary Green; unmarried. *Educ:* Rossall Sch.; Lincoln Coll., Oxford (MA). Curate, St Catherine's Gloucester, 1940; Royal Army Chaplains' Dept, 1943–46 (despatches, 1945); Dir of Service Ordination Candidates, 1947–48; Vicar of St John, Newland, Hull, 1948–53; Short Service Commn, Royal Army Chaplains' Dept, 1953–56; Vicar of South Bank, Teesside, 1956–58; Rector of Cottingham, Yorks, 1958–64; Vicar of Bishopthorpe and Acaster Malbis, York, 1964–72; Hon. Chaplain to Archbp of York, 1964–72; Rural Dean of Ainsty, 1964–68; Canon and Prebendary of York Minster, 1963–72; Bishop Suffragan of Aston, 1972–82; Chm. of Governing Body, Aston Training Scheme, 1977–83; Provost, Woodard Schs Southern Div., 1982–. Hon. DSc Aston, 1980. *Publication:* Diary of Doubt and Faith, 1974. *Recreations:* Aston Villa, ballet. *Address:* 13 Archery Court, Archery Road, St Leonards-on-Sea, E Sussex TN38 0HZ. *T:* Hastings 444649.

GREEN, Dame Mary Georgina, DBE 1968; BA; Head Mistress, Kidbrooke School, SE3, 1954–73; Chairman, BBC London Local Radio Council, 1973–78; Chairman, General Optical Council, 1979–85 (Member, 1977–79); *b* 27 July 1913; *er d* of late Edwin George Green and Rose Margaret Green (*née* Gibbs). *Educ:* Wellingborough High Sch.; Westfield Coll., University of London (Hon. Fellow, 1976). Assistant Mistress: Clapham High Sch., 1936–38; Streatham Hill and Clapham High Sch., 1938–40; William Hulme's Sch., Manchester, 1940–45; Head Mistress, Colston's Girls' Sch., Bristol, 1946–53. Member: Central Advisory Council for Education (Eng.), 1956–63; Church of England Board of Education, 1958–65; Council King George's Jubilee Trust, 1963–68; Court of Governors, London Sch. of Economics and Political Science, 1964–83; Royal Commission on Trade Unions and Employers' Assocs, 1965–68; Council, City University, 1969–78; Cttee of Inquiry into Nurses' Pay, 1974; Press Council, 1976–79; Review Body on Doctors' and Dentists' Remuneration, 1976–79. Dep. Chm., E-SU, 1976–82 (Governor, 1974–82); a Governor: BBC, 1968–73; Royal Ballet Sch., 1969–72; Centre for Educnl Develt Overseas, 1970–74; Rachel McMillan Coll. of Educn, 1970–73; Ditchley Foundn, 1978–. Hon. DSc: City, 1981; Bradford, 1986. Hon. MADO 1985; Hon. FBCO 1985. *Address:* 45 Winn Road, SE12 9EX. *T:* 01–857 1514.

GREEN, Maurice; *see* Green, J. M. S.

GREEN, Rev. Canon Michael; *see* Green, Rev. Canon E. M. B.

GREEN, Dr Michael Frederick; Consultant Physician, Department of Geriatric Medicine, Royal Free Hospital, London, since 1971; Editor, Geriatric Medicine, since 1972; *b* 29 Aug. 1939; *s* of Frederick and Kathleen Green; *m* 1977, Janet Mary; seven *s* one *d*. *Educ:* Dulwich Coll.; Jesus Coll., Cambridge (MA); St Thomas' Hosp. (MB, BChir). FRCP 1980. Consultant, N Middlesex and St Ann's Hosps, 1969–71. Mem., GMC, 1973–79. Medical Adviser, Royal Life Saving Soc., 1970–. Member various bodies mainly involved with the elderly, including: British Geriatrics Soc.; Age Concern; Cruse (Nat. Assoc. for Widows); London Medical Gp; British Soc. for Research on Ageing. Governor: Queen Elizabeth Schs, Barnet, 1973–79; Christchurch Sch., Hampstead, 1980–83. Mem. Bd, Jl of Medical Ethics. *Publications:* Health in Middle Age, 1978; co-author books on medical admin; articles on geriatric medicine, heating, lifesaving, hypothermia, endocrinology, medical records, psychiatry in old age, pressure sores. *Recreations:* family, decorating, swimming and lifesaving, writing, lecturing and teaching. *Address:* 1 Binfield Road, Wokingham, Berkshire.

GREEN, Michael John; Controller, BBC Radio 4, since 1986; *b* 28 May 1941; *s* of David Green and Kathleen (*née* Swann); *m* 1965, Christine Margaret Constance Gibson; one *s* one *d*. *Educ:* Repton Sch.; Barnsley Grammar Sch.; New Coll., Oxford (BA Modern Langs). Swiss Broadcasting Corp., 1964–65; Sheffield Star, 1965–67; Producer, BBC Radio Sheffield, 1967–70; Documentary Producer, BBC Manchester, 1970–77; Editor, File on Four, 1977; Head of Network Radio, Manchester, 1978–86. *Recreations:* France, canals, cinema, collecting glass. *Address:* 6 Lees Road, Bramhall, Stockport, Cheshire. *T:* 061–439 4341. *Club:* Rugby.

GREEN, Dr Norman Michael, FRS 1981; Research Staff, Division of Biochemistry, National Institute for Medical Research, since 1964; *b* 6 April 1926; *s* of Ernest Green and Hilda Margaret Carter; *m* 1953, Iro Paulina Moschouti; two *s* one *d*. *Educ:* Dragon Sch., Oxford; Clifton Coll., Bristol; Magdalen Coll., Oxford (BA; Athletics Blue, Cross Country Blue); UCH Med. Sch., London (PhD). Res. Student, Univ. of Washington, Seattle, 1951–53; Lectr in Biochemistry, Univ. of Sheffield, 1953–55; Res. Fellow and Lectr in Chem. Pathol., St Mary's Hosp. Med. Sch., London, 1956–62; Vis. Scientist, NIH, Maryland, 1962–64. *Publications:* research papers on the structure of proteins and of membranes, in scientific jls. *Recreations:* mountain climbing, pyrotechnics. *Address:* 57 Hale Lane, Mill Hill, NW7 3PS.

GREEN, Sir Owen (Whitley), Kt 1984; Chairman and Chief Executive, BTR plc, since 1984; *b* Stockton-on-Tees, 14 May 1925; *m* Doreen Margaret Green; one *s* two *d*. FCA 1950. Served RN, 1942–46. With Charles Wakeling & Co., accountants, 1947–56; Oil Feed Engineering, later BTR: Financial Dir, 1956; Asst Man. Dir, 1966; Man. Dir, 1967. *Recreation:* golf. *Address:* (office) Silvertown House, Vincent Square, SW1P 2PL. *T:* 01–834 3848.

GREEN, Brig. Percy William Powlett, CBE 1960 (OBE 1956); DSO 1946; *b* 10 Sept. 1912; *er s* of late Brig.-Gen. W. G. K. Green, CB, CMG, DSO, Indian Army; *m* 1943, Phyllis Margery Fitz Gerald May, *d* of late Lieut-Col A. H. May, OBE; one *s* one *d*. *Educ:* Wellington Coll.; RMC. Commnd Northamptonshire Regt, 1932; Op. NW Frontier, India, 1936–37; BEF 1939–40; Lt-Col Comdg 2nd W Yorks Regt, 1945–46; Burma, 1944–45; Lt-Col Comdg 1 Malay Regt, 1946–47; Comd 4th King's African Rifles, 1954–56; Op. against Mau Mau; Col, Gen. Staff, War Office, 1956–57; Chief of Staff (Brig.) E Africa Comd, 1957–60; DDMI, War Office, 1961–63; Chief of Staff, N Ireland Command, 1963–65; Dep. Comdr, Aldershot District, 1965–67; retired, 1967. ADC to the Queen, 1965–67. Dep. Colonel, Royal Anglian Regt, 1966–76. *Recreations:* field sports. *Address:* Grudds, South Warnborough, Basingstoke, Hants. *T:* Basingstoke 862472. *Club:* Army and Navy.

GREEN, Sir Peter (James Frederick), Kt 1982; Chairman, Janson Green Ltd, since 1966; Chairman, Lloyd's, 1980, 1981, 1982, 1983; *b* 28 July 1924; *s* of J. E. Green and M. B. Holford; *m* 1950, A. P. Ryan (*d* 1985); *m* 1986, Jennifer Whitehead. *Educ:* Harrow Sch.; Christ Church, Oxford. Lloyd's: Underwriter, 1947; Mem. Cttee, 1974–77; Dep. Chm., 1979; Gold Medal, 1983. *Recreations:* shooting, fishing, sailing, working. *Address:* Janson Green Ltd, 10 Crescent, EC3. *T:* 01–480 6440. *Clubs:* City of London, Royal Ocean Racing, Pratt's; Royal Yacht Squadron (Cowes); Cruising of America (New York).

GREEN, Prof. Peter Morris; author and translator since 1953; Professor of Classics, University of Texas at Austin, since 1972 (James R. Dougherty Jr Centennial Professor of Classics, 1982–84 and since 1985); *b* 22 Dec. 1924; *o c* of late Arthur Green, CBE, MC, LLB, and Olive Slaughter; *m* 1st, 1951, Lalage Isobel Pulvertaft (marr. diss.); two *s* one *d*; 2nd, 1975, Carin Margreta, *y d* of G. N. Christensen, Saratoga, USA. *Educ:* Charterhouse; Trinity Coll., Cambridge. Served in RAFVR, 1943–47: overseas tour in Burma Comd, 1944–46. 1st Cl. Hons, Pts I and II, Classical Tripos, 1949–50; MA and PhD Cantab 1954; Craven Schol. and Student, 1950; Dir of Studies in Classics, 1951–52; Fiction Critic, London Daily Telegraph, 1953–63; Literary Adviser, The Bodley Head, 1957–58; Cons. Editor, Hodder and Stoughton, 1960–63; Television Critic, The Listener, 1961–63; Film Critic, John o'London's, 1961–63; Mem. Book Soc. Cttee, 1959–63. Former Mem. of selection cttees for literary prizes: Heinemann Award, John Llewellyn Rhys, W. H. Smith £1000 Award for Literature. Translator of numerous works from French and Italian, including books by Simone de Beauvoir, Fosco Maraini, Joseph Kessel. FRSL 1956; Mem. Council, Royal Society of Literature, 1958–63 (resigned on emigration). In 1963 resigned all positions and emigrated to Greece as full-time writer (1963–71). Vis. Prof. of Classics: Univ. of Texas, 1971–72; UCLA, 1976; Mellon Prof. of Humanities, Tulane Univ., 1986; Sen. Fellow for independent study and res., National Endowment for the Humanities, 1983–84. *Publications:* The Expanding Eye, 1953; Achilles His Armour, 1955; Cat in Gloves (pseud. Denis Delaney), 1956; The Sword of Pleasure (W. H. Heinemann Award for Literature), 1957; Kenneth Grahame, 1859–1932: A Study of his Life, Work and Times, 1959; Essays in Antiquity, 1960; Habeas Corpus and other stories, 1962; Look at the Romans, 1963; The Laughter of Aphrodite, 1965; Juvenal: The Sixteen Satires (trans.), 1967; Armada from Athens: The Failure of the Sicilian Expedition, 415–413 BC, 1970; Alexander the Great: a biography, 1970; The Year of Salamis, 480–479 BC, 1971; The Shadow of the Parthenon, 1972; The Parthenon, 1973; A Concise History of Ancient Greece, 1973; Alexander of Macedon 356–323 BC: a historical biography, 1974; Ovid: The Erotic Poems (trans.), 1982; Beyond the Wild Wood: the world of Kenneth Grahame, 1982. *Recreations:* travel, swimming, spear-fishing, lawn tennis, table-tennis, squash racquets, amateur archæology, avoiding urban life. *Address:* c/o Department of Classics, University of Texas, Waggener Hall 123, Austin, Texas 78712, USA. *T:* 512 471–5742. *Club:* Savile.

GREEN, Robert James; Under Secretary, Departments of the Environment and Transport, since 1982; *b* 27 Jan. 1937; *er s* of Ronald Percy Green and Doris Rose (*née* Warman); *m* 1960, Jill Marianne Small; one *d* (one *s* decd). *Educ:* Kent College, Canterbury. Executive Officer, Board of Trade, 1957; Asst Principal, 1963, Principal, 1967, Min. of Housing and Local Govt; Secretary, Water Resources Board, 1972–74; Asst Secretary: Dept of the Environment, 1974; Dept of Transport, 1980; Regl Dir, Northern Reg., 1982–83, and Yorks and Humberside Reg., 1982–86, Depts of the Environment and Transport. *Recreations:* amateur dramatics, horses. *Address:* Runge's Cottage, St Andrews Road, Caversham, Reading RG4 7PH. *T:* Reading 477372.

GREEN, Maj.-Gen. Robert Leslie Stuart; Executive Governor, Care for the Mentally Handicapped, since 1980; *b* 1 July 1925; *s* of Leslie Stuart Green and Eliza Dorothea Andrew; *m* 1952, Nancy Isobel Collier; two *d*. *Educ:* Chorlton Sch. 2nd Bn Black Watch, India, 1944–46; 6 Airborne Div., Palestine, 1946; 2 Parachute Bde, UK and Germany, 1946–47; 1st Bn HLI, UK, ME and Cyprus, 1947–56; ptsc 1959; jssc 1962; 1st Bn Royal Highland Fusiliers, UK, Germany and Gibraltar, 1959–69, Comd 1967–69; staff apptmt 1970; Military Dir of Studies, RMCS, 1970–72; Sen. Military Officer, Royal Armament Res. and Develt Estabt, 1973–75; Vice-Pres., Ordnance Bd, 1976–78, Pres., March-June 1978. Col, The Royal Highland Fusiliers, 1979–. Freeman, City of London, 1983. FBIM. *Recreations:* rough shooting, painting, music and sailing. *Address:* Royal Bank of Scotland, 43 Curzon Street, Mayfair, W1. *Club:* Naval and Military.

GREEN, Roger (Gilbert) Lancelyn; author; *b* 2 Nov. 1918; *s* of Major G. A. L. Green, MC, RFA, and H. M. P. Sealy; *m* 1948, June, *d* of S. H. Burdett, Northampton; two *s* one *d*. *Educ:* Dane Court Sch., Surrey; Liverpool Coll.; privately; Merton Coll., Oxford (MA, BLitt). Part-time professional actor, 1942–45; Dep. Librarian, Merton Coll., Oxford, 1945–50; William Nobel Research Fellow in Eng. Lit., Liverpool Univ., 1950–52; Mem. Council, Univ. of Liverpool, 1964–70; Andrew Lang Lectr, Univ. of St Andrews, 1968. Editor, Kipling Journal, 1957–79. Mythopoeic Schol. Award (USA), 1975. Hon. DLitt Liverpool, 1981. *Publications:* The Lost July, and other poems, 1945; Tellers of Tales, 1946, rev. edn 1965; The Searching Satyrs, 1946; Andrew Lang: a critical biography, 1946; The Sleeping Beauty, and other tales, 1947; The Singing Rose, and other poems, 1947; From the World's End: a fantasy, 1948, repr. USA 1971; Beauty and the Beast, and other tales, 1948; Poulton-Lancelyn: the story of an ancestral home, 1948; The Story of Lewis Carroll, 1949; The Wonderful Stranger, 1950; The Luck of the Lynns, 1952; A. E. W. Mason: a biography, 1952; The Secret of Rusticoker, 1953; King Arthur and his Knights of the Round Table, 1953, 8th edn 1967; The Diaries of Lewis Carroll, 1953; Fifty Years of Peter Pan, 1954; The Theft of the Golden Cat, 1955; The Adventures of Robin Hood, 1956, 6th edn 1966; Mystery at Mycenae, 1957; Two Satyr Plays (Penguin Classics), 1957; Into Other Worlds: space flight in fiction from Lucian to Lewis, 1957; Old Greek Fairy Tales, 1958; The Land Beyond the North, 1958; The Land of the Lord High Tiger, 1958; Tales of the Greek Heroes, 1958, 8th edn 1973; The Tale of Troy, 1958, 10th edn 1973; Lewis Carroll, 1960; The Saga of Asgard, 1960, 3rd edn as Myths of the Norsemen, 1970; J. M. Barrie, 1960; The True Book About Ancient Greece, 1960; The Luck of Troy, 1961, 4th edn 1973; Mrs Molesworth, 1961; Ancient Greece, 1962; Andrew Lang, 1962; The Lewis Carroll Handbook, 1962; Once, Long Ago, 1962; C. S. Lewis, 1963; Authors and Places, 1963; Ancient Egypt, 1963; Tales of the Greeks and Trojans, 1964; Tales from Shakespeare, 2 vols, 1964–65; A Book of Myths, 1965; Tales the Muses Told, 1965; Myths from Many Lands, 1965; Kipling and the Children, 1965; Andrew Lang: the greatest bookman of his age (Indiana Bookman), 1965; Folk Tales of the World, 1966; Sir Lancelot of the Lake, 1966; Tales of Ancient Egypt, 1967; Stories of Ancient Greece, 1968; Jason and the Golden Fleece, 1968; The Tale of Ancient Israel, 1969; St Andrew's Church, Bebington: a short history, 1969; The Book of Dragons, 1970; Kipling: the critical heritage, 1971; The Book of Magicians, 1973; (with Walter Hooper) C. S. Lewis: a biography, 1974; Holmes, this is Amazing: essays in unorthodox research, 1975; The Book of Other Worlds, 1976; The Tale of Thebes, 1977; (with M. N. Cohen) The Letters of Lewis Carroll, 2 vols, 1979. *Recreations:* book collecting, Greece Ancient and Modern, Greek and Roman theatre. *Address:* Poulton Hall, Poulton-Lancelyn, Bebington, Wirral, Merseyside L63 9LN. *T:* 051–334 2057. *Clubs:* Arts, National Book League.

GREEN, Roger James N.; *see* Northcote-Green.

GREEN, Sam, CBE 1960; Chairman: Dula (ISMA) Ltd, since 1969; Green & Associates Ltd, since 1970; Spear Bros Ltd, since 1970; Vice Chairman, Royal British Legion Poppy Factory, Richmond (Director since 1964); Director, Royal British Legion Industries, since 1967; *b* Oldham, Lancs, 6 Feb. 1907; *s* of Fred Green; *m* 1942, Dr Lilly (*née* Pollak); one *d*. *Educ:* Manchester Coll. of Technology. Apprentice, Platt Bros, Oldham, 1920–34; Designer and Development Engr, British Northrop Automatic Loom Co., Blackburn, 1934–39 (invented 4-colour loom); Chief Engr, Betts & Co., London, 1939–42; Works Manager, Morphy-Richards Ltd, St Mary Cray, Kent, 1942–44; General Works Manager, Holoplast Ltd, New Hythe, near Maidstone, 1944–47; Industrial Adviser, Industrial and Commercial Finance Corp., London, 1947–52; Managing Dir of Remploy Ltd, 1952–64; Chm. and Man. Dir, Ralli Bros (Industries) Ltd, 1964–69; Chm., Industrial Advisers to the Blind, 1964–74; Director: J. E. Lesser Group Ltd, 1969–74; New Day Holdings Ltd, 1972–74. Chm., Inst. of Patentees and Inventors, 1975 (Vice-Chm., 1961); Vice Pres., Internat. Fed. of Inventors' Assocs, 1984–. FRSA 1962. CEng; FIEE; FIProdE. Gold Medal, World Intellectual Property Orgn, 1984. *Recreations:* reading, gardening, cycling, walking, golf. *Address:* Holly Lodge, 39 Westmoreland Road, Bromley, Kent BR2 0TF. *T:* 01–460 3306. *Clubs:* Reform, Directors', Pickwick (oldest Bicycle Club).

GREEN, Sir Stephen; *see* Green, Sir E. S. L.

GREEN, Thomas Charles, CB 1971; Chief Charity Commissioner, 1966–75; *b* 13 Oct. 1915; *s* of late Charles Harold Green and late Hilda Emma Green (*née* Thomas); *m* 1945, Beryl Eva Barber, *widow* of Lieut N. Barber; one *d* (and one step *d*). *Educ:* Eltham Coll.; Oriel Coll., Oxford. Entered Home Office, 1938. Served with RAF, 1940–45. Asst Secretary: Home Office, 1950–64; Charity Commn, 1964–65. UK representative on UN Commn on Narcotic Drugs, 1957–64. Nuffield Travelling Fellowship, 1959–60. *Recreations:* gardening, photography. *Address:* Silver Birch Cottage, Burntwood Road, Sevenoaks, Kent.

GREEN, Rev. Vivian Hubert Howard, DD, FRHistS; Fellow and Tutor in History, Lincoln College, Oxford, since 1951, and Rector, 1983–Aug. 1987 (Senior Tutor 1953–62, 1974–77; Chaplain, 1951–69; Sub-Rector, 1970–83; acting Rector, 1972–73); *b* 18 Nov. 1915; *s* of Hubert James and Edith Eleanor Playle Green; unmarried. *Educ:* Bradfield Coll., Berks; Trinity Hall, Cambridge (Scholar). Goldsmiths' Exhibnr; 1st Cl. Hist. Tripos, Parts I and II; Lightfoot Schol. in Ecclesiastical Hist.; Thirlwall Medal and Prize, 1941; MA 1941; MA Oxon by incorp., 1951; DD Cambridge, 1958; DD Oxon by incorp., 1958. Gladstone Research Studentship, St Deiniol's Library, Hawarden, 1937–38; Fellow of St Augustine's Coll., Canterbury, 1939–48; Chaplain, Exeter Sch. and St Luke's Training Coll., Exeter, 1940–42; Chaplain and Asst Master, Sherborne Sch., Dorset, 1942–51. Deacon, 1939; Priest, 1940. Select Preacher, Oxford, 1959–60. Vis. Prof. of History, Univ. of S Carolina, 1982. *Publications:* Bishop Reginald Pecock, 1945; The Hanoverians, 1948; From St Augustine to William Temple, 1948; Renaissance and Reformation, 1952; The Later Plantagenets, 1955; Oxford Common Room, 1957; The Young Mr Wesley, 1961; The Swiss Alps, 1961; Martin Luther and the Reformation, 1964; John Wesley, 1964; Religion at Oxford and Cambridge (historical survey), 1964; The Universities, 1969; Medieval Civilization in Western Europe, 1971; A History of Oxford University, 1974; The Commonwealth of Lincoln College 1427–1977, 1979; Love in a Cool Climate: the letters of Mark Pattison and Meta Bradley 1879–1884, 1985; contributor to: Dictionary of English Church History (ed Ollard, Crosse and Bond); The Oxford Dictionary of the Christian Church (ed Cross); European Writers, The Middle Ages and Renaissance (ed W. T. H. Jackson and G. Stade), vols I and II, 1983. *Address:* Lincoln College, Oxford; Calendars, Burford, Oxford. *T:* Burford 3214.

GREEN-PRICE, Sir Robert (John), 5th Bt, *cr* 1874; Lecturer in English, Chiba University of Commerce, since 1982; *b* 22 Oct. 1940; *o s* of Sir John Green-Price, 4th Bt, and Irene Marion (*d* 1954), *d* of Major Sir (Ernest) Guy Lloyd, 1st Bt, *qv*; *S* father, 1964. *Educ:* Shrewsbury. Army Officer, 1961–69; Captain, RCT, retd. ADC to Governor of Bermuda, 1969–72. Lectr in English, Teikyo Univ., 1975–82. Part-time Lecturer: Keio Univ., 1977–; Waseda Univ., 1986–; Guest Lectr, NHK Radio, 1978–83. *Heir:* uncle Powell Norman Dansey Green-Price [*b* 22 July 1926; *m* 1963, Ann Stella, *d* of late Brig. Harold George Howson, CBE, MC, TD; one *s* one *d*]. *Address:* Ichikawa Apts 603, 2–8–9 Takadanobaba, Shinjuku-ku, Tokyo 160, Japan. *T:* 03–209–6378.

GREENALL, family name of **Baron Daresbury.**

GREENAWAY, Alan Pearce, JP; Vice-President, Daniel Greenaway & Sons Ltd, 1978–82 (Joint Managing Director, 1951–78; Vice-Chairman, 1965–76; Chairman, 1976–78); *b* 25 Nov. 1913; *yr s* of Sir Percy Walter Greenaway, 1st Bt, and Lydie Amy (*d* 1962), *er d* of James Burdick; *m* 1948, Patricia Frances (*d* 1982), *yr d* of Ald. Sir Frederick Wells, 1st Bt; one *s* one *d*. *Educ:* Canford. Served in King's Liverpool Regt during War of 1939–45, reaching rank of Captain. Liveryman: Worshipful Co. of Merchant Taylors; Worshipful Co. of Stationers and Newspaper Makers (Under-Warden 1971–72, Upper Warden, 1972–73, Master 1973–74). Mem. Court of Common Council for Ward of Bishopsgate, 1952–65; Sheriff for the City of London, 1962–63; JP, Co. London, 1964; Alderman, Lime Street Ward, City of London, 1965–72; Chm. and Treasurer, City of London Sheriffs' Soc., 1979–82. Officer, l'Ordre de la Valeur Camerounaise, 1963; Commandeur, l'Ordre de Leopold Class III, 1963; Commander, Royal Order of the Phoenix, 1964. *Recreations:* golf, fishing, swimming, bowls. *Address:* Hove, East Sussex. *Clubs:* City Livery (Vice-Pres. 1971–72, Pres., 1972–73), Royal Automobile, Unites Wards; St George's Hill Golf.

GREENAWAY, Sir Derek (Burdick), 2nd Bt *cr* 1933; CBE 1974; TD; JP; DL; First Life President, Daniel Greenaway & Sons Ltd, 132 Commercial Street, E1, since 1976 (Chairman, 1956–76); *b* 27 May 1910; *er s* of Sir Percy Walter Greenaway, 1st Bt and Lydie Amy (*d* 1962), *er d* of James Burdick; *S* father 1956; *m* 1937, Sheila Beatrice, *d* of late Richard Cyril Lockett, 58 Cadogan Place, SW1; one *s* one *d*. *Educ:* Marlborough. Served in Field Artillery during War of 1939–45; Hon. Col: 44 (HC) Signal Regt (Cinque Ports) TA, 1966; 36th (Eastern) Signal Regt (V), 1967–74. Joint Master, Old Surrey and Burstow Foxhounds, 1958–66. Chm. Sevenoaks Constituency C & U Assoc., 1960–63; Pres. 1963–66; Vice Pres., 1966–. Asst Area Treasurer, SE Area Nat. Union of Cons. Assocs, 1966–69, Area Treasurer, 1969–75, Chm. 1975–79. Master, Stationers' and Newspapermakers Co., 1974–75 (Silver Medal, 1984). JP County of Kent, 1962–; High Sheriff, 1971, DL 1973, Kent. FRSA. Life Mem., Assoc. of Men of Kent and Kentish Men. *Recreations:* hunting, shooting. *Heir:* *s* John Michael Burdick Greenaway [*b* 9 Aug. 1944; *m* 1982, Susan M., *d* of Henry Birch, Tattenhall, Cheshire; one *s* one *d*. Late Lieut, The Life Guards]. *Address:* Dunmore, Four Elms, Edenbridge, Kent. *T:* Four Elms 275. *Clubs:* Charlton, City of London, MCC.

See also A. P. Greenaway, H. F. R. Sturge.

GREENAWAY, Frank, MA, PhD; CChem, FRSC, FSA, FMA; Keeper, Department of Chemistry, The Science Museum, 1967–80; Reader in the History of Science, Davy-Faraday Research Laboratory of the Royal Institution, 1970–85; *b* 9 July 1917; 3rd *s* of late Henry James Greenaway; *m* 1942, Margaret (Miranda), 2nd *d* of late R. G. Heegaard Warner and *widow* of John Raymond Brumfit; two *s* three *d*. *Educ:* Cardiff High Sch.;

Jesus Coll., Oxford (Meyricke Exhibitioner); University Coll. London. MA Oxon, PhD London. Served War of 1939–45, RAOC, as Inspecting Ordnance Officer, 1940–41 (invalided). Science Master: Bournemouth Sch., 1941–42; Epsom Gram. Sch., 1942–43; Research Labs, Kodak Ltd, 1944–49; Asst Keeper, Science Museum, 1949; Dep. Keeper, 1959; Keeper, 1967. Regent Fellow, Smithsonian Instn, Washington, DC, 1985. Mem. Council: Brit. Soc. for the Hist. of Science, 1958–68, 1974–78 (Vice-Pres. 1962–65); Museums Assoc., 1961–70, 1973–76 (Hon. Editor, 1965–70). Chm., Cttee of Visitors, Royal Instn, 1964–65; Mem. Brit. Nat. Cttee of Internat. Council of Museums, 1956–58, 1962–71, 1977–83; Membre Correspondant de l'Académie Internationale d'Histoire des Sciences, 1963. Member: Council, Soc. for History of Alchemy and Chemistry, 1967– (Sec., 1967–74); History of Medicine Adv. Panel, The Wellcome Trust, 1968–74; Higher Educn Adv. Cttee, The Open Univ., 1970–73; British Nat. Cttee for Hist. of Sci., 1972–81; British Nat. Cttee, ICSU, 1972–77; Council, Internat. Union of the Hist. and Philos. of Science, 1972–81 (Sec., 1972–77); Council of Management, Royal Philharmonic Soc., 1980–84; Pres., Commonwealth Assoc. of Museums, 1979–83. Boerhaave Medal, Leyden Univ., 1968. *Publications:* Science Museums in Developing Countries, 1962; John Dalton and the Atom, 1966; (ed) Lavoisier's Essays Physical and Chemical, 1971; Editor, Royal Institution Archives, 1971–; Official Publications of the Science Museum; Papers on history of chemistry and on museology. *Recreations:* music, travel. *Address:* 135 London Road, Ewell, Epsom, Surrey. *T:* 01–393 1330. *Club:* Athenæum.

GREENBAUM, Prof. Sidney; Quain Professor of English Language and Literature, and Director of the Survey of English Usage, University College, London, since 1983; *b* 31 Dec. 1929; *s* of Lewis and Nelly Greenbaum. *Educ:* Univ. of London (BA Hons and MA Hebrew and Aramaic; Postgrad. Cert. in Educn; BA Hons English; PhD Mod. English Grammar). Teacher at London primary sch., 1954–57; Head of English Dept at London grammar sch., 1957–64; Research asst, Survey of English Usage, UCL, 1965–68; Vis. Asst Prof., English Dept, Univ. of Oregon, 1968–69; Associate Prof., English Dept, Univ. of Wisconsin-Milwaukee, 1969–72; Vis. Prof., English Dept, Hebrew Univ., Jerusalem, 1972–73; Prof., English Dept, Univ. of Wisconsin-Milwaukee, 1972–83. *Publications:* Studies in English Adverbial Usage, 1969; Verb-Intensifier Collocations in English: an experimental approach, 1970; (with R. Quirk) Elicitation Experiments in English: linguistic studies in use and attitude, 1970; (jtly) A Grammar of Contemporary English, 1972; (with R. Quirk) A University Grammar of English (Amer. edn A Concise Grammar of Contemporary English), 1973; Acceptability in Language, 1977; (jtly) Studies in English Linguistics: for Randolph Quirk, 1980; The English Language Today, 1985; (jtly) A Comprehensive Grammar of the English Language, 1985; (with C. Cooper) Studying Writing: linguistic approaches, 1986; (with J. Whitcut) rev. edn of Gower's Complete Plain Words, 1986; numerous articles in learned jls. *Address:* Department of English, University College London, Gower Street, WC1E 6BT. *T:* 01–387 7050. *Club:* Reform.

GREENBOROUGH, Sir John Hedley, KBE 1979 (CBE 1975); Chairman, Newarthill, since 1980; Deputy Chairman: Bowater Industries (formerly Bowater Corporation), since 1984 (Director, since 1979); Lloyds Bank, since 1985 (Director, since 1980); Director, Hogg Robinson Group, since 1980; Chairman, Review Body for Nursing and Midwifery Staff and the Professions Allied to Medicine, since 1983; *b* 7 July 1922; *s* of William Greenborough and Elizabeth Marie Greenborough (*née* Wilson); *m* 1951, Gerta Ebel; one step *s. Educ:* Wandsworth School. War service: Pilot, RAF, later Fleet Air Arm, 1942–45; graduated Pensacola; Naval Aviator, USN, 1944. Joined Asiatic Petroleum Co., London, 1939; served with Shell Oil, Calif, 1946–47; Shell Brazil Ltd, 1948–57; Commercial Dir, later Exec. Vice-Pres., Shell Argentina Ltd, Buenos Aires, 1960–66; Area Coordinator, East and Australasia, Shell Internat., London, 1967–68; Man. Dir (Marketing), Shell-Mex and BP Ltd, 1969–71; Man. Dir and Chief Exec., 1971–75; Chm., UK Oil Pipelines Ltd, 1971–77; Dep. Chm., 1976–80, Man. Dir, 1976–78, Shell UK Ltd. Dir, Laporte Industries (Hldgs), 1983–86. President of Confederation of British Industry, 1978–80 (Mem. Council, 1971–). Chairman: UK Oil Ind. Emergency Cttee, 1971–80; UK Petroleum Ind. Adv. Cttee, 1971–77; Member: British Productivity Council, 1969–72; Clean Air Council, 1971–75; Bd of Fellows, BIM, 1973–78 (Chm., 1976–78); NEDC, 1977–80; Vice-Chairman: British Chamber of Commerce in Argentina, 1962–66; British Road Fedn, 1969–75. President: Nat. Soc. for Clean Air, 1973–75; Incorporated Soc. of British Advertisers (ISBA), 1976–78; Inst. of Petroleum, 1976–78; Nat. Council for Voluntary Orgns, 1980–86; Strategic Planning Soc., 1986–. Fellow, Inst. Petroleum; CBIM. Governor, Ashridge Management Coll., 1972– (Chm., 1977–); Chm. Governing Council, UMDS of Guy's and St Thomas' Hosps, 1982–. Liveryman, Co. of Distillers, 1975–. Freeman, City of London. Hon. LLD Birmingham, 1983. *Recreations:* golf, travel, music. *Address:* 30 Burghley House, Oakfield, Somerset Road, Wimbledon Common, SW19. *Clubs:* Carlton, MCC; Royal and Ancient Golf; Royal Wimbledon Golf.

GREENBURY, Richard; Chief Operating Officer, Marks & Spencer plc, since 1986 (Joint Managing Director, 1978–86); *b* 31 July 1936; *s* of Richard Oswald Greenbury and Dorothy (*née* Lewis); *m* 1st, 1959, Sian Eames Hughes; two *s* two *d*; 2nd, 1985, Gabrielle Mary McManus. *Educ:* Ealing County Grammar Sch. Joined Marks & Spencer Ltd as Jun. Management Trainee, 1953; Alternate Dir, 1970; Full Dir, 1972. Part-time Dir, British Gas Corp., 1976–; Dir, Metal Box, 1985–. *Recreation:* tennis (Member Mddx County Team for 12 years, has also played for International Tennis Club of GB). *Address:* Tarbay Farm, Tarbay Lane, Oakley Green, Windsor, Berks. *T:* Windsor 55497. *Club:* International Tennis Club of GB.

GREENE, family name of **Baron Greene of Harrow Weald.**

GREENE OF HARROW WEALD, Baron *cr* 1974 (Life Peer), of Harrow; **Sidney Francis Greene,** Kt 1970; CBE 1966; Director: Trades Union Unit Trust, since 1970; RTZ Corporation, 1975–80; Times Newspapers Holdings Ltd, 1980–82 (Times Newspapers Ltd, 1975–80); *b* 12 Feb. 1910; *s* of Frank James Greene and Alice (*née* Kerrod); *m* 1936, Masel Elizabeth Carter; three *d. Educ:* elementary. Joined Railway Service, 1924; appointed Union Organiser, 1944, Asst Gen. Sec., 1954, Gen. Sec., Nat. Union of Railwaymen, 1957–74. Mem., TUC Gen. Council, 1957–75 (Chm., 1969–70); Chm., TUC Economic Cttee, 1968–75. Member: National Economic Development Council, 1962–75; Advisory Council, ECGD, 1967–70; part-time Member: Southern Electricity Board, 1964–77; Nat. Freight Corp., 1973–77; a Dir, Bank of England, 1970–78. JP London, 1941–65. FCIT. *Recreations:* reading, gardening. *Address:* 26 Kynaston Wood, Boxtree Road, Harrow Weald, Mddx HA3 6UA.

GREENE, Edward Reginald, CMG 1953; FRSA; *b* Santos, Brazil, 26 Nov. 1904; *s* of late Edward Greene and of Eva Greene; *m* Irmingard Fischges. *Educ:* Bedales Sch.; St John's Coll., Cambridge (BA 1926). After Continental banking experience joined coffee merchant firm E. Johnston & Co. Ltd, 1927; has since travelled and traded in coffee, Brazil, USA, East Africa, Continent; Dir of Coffee, Ministry of Food, 1943, subsequently Dir of Raw Cocoa; resigned 1952; resp. for establishment of London Robusta Coffee Exchange, 1953. Chm., Coffee Fedn, 1952–53; Mem., Commn of Inquiry into Coffee Industry, Uganda Protectorate, 1957. Hon. Vice-Pres., Brazilian Chamber of Commerce,

1968–. Mem., The Cambridge Soc. FRSA 1971. *Recreations:* walking and above all keeping fit. *Address:* Orbell House, Castle Hedingham, Essex. *T:* Hedingham 60298. *Clubs:* City of London (Hon. Mem.), Garrick.

GREENE, Graham, OM 1986; CH 1966; CLit 1984; Hon. LittD, Cambridge, 1962; Hon. Fellow of Balliol, 1963; Hon. DLitt: Edinburgh, 1967; Oxford, 1979; Chevalier de la Légion d'Honneur, 1967; *b* 2 Oct. 1904; *s* of late Charles Henry Greene; *m* 1927, Vivien Dayrell-Browning; one *s* one *d. Educ:* Berkhamsted; Balliol Coll., Oxford. On staff of The Times, 1926–30; Literary Editor, The Spectator, 1940–41; department of Foreign Office, 1941–44. Director: Eyre & Spottiswoode Ltd, 1944–48; Bodley Head, 1958–68. Mem., Panamanian delegn to Washington for signing of Canal Treaty, 1977. Grand Cross, Order of Vasco Nuñez de Balboa, Panama, 1983. Shakespeare Prize, Hamburg, 1968; John Dos Passos Prize, 1980; Medal, City of Madrid, 1980; Jerusalem Prize, 1981. Hon. Citizen, Anacapri, 1978; Commandeur des Arts et des Lettres, France, 1984. *Publications:* Babbling April, 1925; The Man Within, 1929; The Name of Action, 1930; Rumour at Nightfall, 1931; Stamboul Train, 1932; It's a Battlefield, 1934; The Old School (Editor), 1934; The Bear Fell Free (limited edn), 1935; England Made Me, 1935; The Basement Room (short stories), 1935; Journey without Maps (account of a journey through Liberia), 1936; A Gun for Sale, 1936; Brighton Rock, 1938; The Lawless Roads, 1939; The Confidential Agent, 1939; The Power and the Glory, 1940 (Hawthornden Prize for 1940); British Dramatists, 1942; The Ministry of Fear, 1943; Nineteen Stories, 1947; The Heart of the Matter, 1948; The Third Man, 1950; The End of the Affair, 1951; The Lost Childhood and other essays, 1951; Essais Catholiques, 1953; Twenty one Stories, 1954; Loser Takes All, 1955; The Quiet American, 1955; Our Man in Havana, 1958; A Burnt-Out Case, 1961; In Search of a Character, Two African Journals, 1961; A Sense of Reality, 1963; The Comedians, 1966; May we borrow your Husband? And other Comedies of the Sexual Life (short stories), 1967; Collected Essays, 1969; Travels with my Aunt, 1969; A Sort of Life (autobiog.), 1971; The Pleasure-Dome: the collected film criticism 1935–40, ed John Russell Taylor, 1972; Collected Stories, 1972; The Honorary Consul 1973; Lord Rochester's Monkey, 1974; An Impossible Woman: the Memories of Dottoressa Moor of Capri, 1975; The Human Factor, 1978; Dr Fischer of Geneva, 1980 (filmed for TV, 1984); Ways of Escape (autobiog.), 1980; J'Accuse: the dark side of Nice, 1982; Monsignor Quixote, 1982 (filmed for TV, 1985); Getting to Know the General, 1984; The Tenth Man, 1985; *plays:* The Living Room, 1953; The Potting Shed, 1957 (filmed for TV, 1981); The Complaisant Lover, 1959; Carving a Statue, 1964; The Return of A. J. Raffles, 1975; Yes and No, 1980; For Whom the Bell Chimes, 1980; The Great Jowett, 1981; *for children:* The Little Train, 1947; The Little Fire Engine, 1950; The Little Horse Bus, 1952; The Little Steamroller, 1953; *film plays:* Brighton Rock, 1948; The Fallen Idol, 1948; The Third Man, 1949; Our Man in Havana, 1960; The Comedians, 1967. *Address:* c/o The Bodley Head, 30 Bedford Square, WC1B 3RP.

See also R. O. Dennys, Sir Hugh Greene.

GREENE, Graham Carleton, CBE 1986; Managing Director, Jonathan Cape Ltd, since 1966, and Joint Chairman, Chatto, Virago, Bodley Head & Jonathan Cape Ltd, since 1970; *b* 10 June 1936; *s* of Sir Hugh Carleton Greene, *qv*, and Helga Mary Connolly; *m* 1957, Judith Margaret (marr. diss.), *d* of Rt Hon. Lord Gordon-Walker, CH, PC; *m* 1976, Sally Georgina Horton, *d* of Sidney Wilfred Eaton; one *s. Educ:* Eton; University Coll., Oxford (MA). Merchant Banking, Dublin, New York and London, 1957–58; Publishing: Secker & Warburg Ltd, 1958–62; Jonathan Cape, 1962– (Dir, 1962). Director: Chatto, Virago, Bodley Head & Jonathan Cape Ltd, 1969–; Jackdaw Publications Ltd (Chm. 1964–); Cape Goliard Press Ltd, 1967–; Guinness Mahon Holdings Ltd, 1968–79; Australasian Publishing Co. Pty Ltd, 1969– (Chm., 1978–); Sprint Productions Ltd, 1971–80; Book Reps (New Zealand) Ltd, 1971– (Chm., 1984); CVBC Services Ltd (Chm. 1972–); Guinness Peat Group PLC, 1973–; Grantham Book Storage Ltd (Chm. 1974–); Triad Paperbacks Ltd, 1975–; Chatto, Virago, Bodley Head & Jonathan Cape Australia Pty Ltd (Chm., 1977–); Greene, King & Sons PLC, 1979–; Statesman & Nation Publishing Co. Ltd, 1980–85 (Chm., 1981–85); Statesman Publishing Co. Ltd, 1980–85 (Chm., 1981–85); Nation Pty Co. Ltd (Chm., 1981–); New Society (Chm., 1984–86). Pres., Publishers Assoc., 1977–79 (Mem. Council, 1969–); Member: Book Develt Council, 1970–79 (Dep. Chm., 1972–73); Internat. Cttee, Internat. Publishers Assoc., 1977– (Exec. Cttee, 1981–); Groupe des Editeurs de Livres de la CEE, 1977–86 (Pres., 1984–86); Arts Council Working Party Sub-Cttee on Public Lending Right, 1970; Paymaster General's Working Party on Public Lending Right, 1970–72; Board, British Council, 1977–; Chm., Nat. Book League, 1974–76 (Dep. Chm., 1971–74); Mem. Gen. Cttee, Royal Literary Fund, 1975. Trustee, British Museum, 1978–. Leader, 1st deleg. British publishers to China, 1978, etc.; Chm., GB-China Centre, 1986–. Chevalier de l'Ordre des Arts et des Lettres, France, 1985. *Address:* 32 Bedford Square, WC1B 3EL. *T:* 01–636 3344.

GREENE, Sir Hugh (Carleton), KCMG 1964; OBE 1950; Hon. President, The Bodley Head, since 1981 (Chairman, 1969–81); Chairman, Greene, King & Sons Ltd, Westgate Brewery, Bury St Edmunds, 1971–78; Member, Observer Editorial Trust, 1969–76; *b* Nov. 1910; *s* of late Charles Henry Greene; *m* 1934, Helga Guinness (marr. diss.); two *s*; *m* 1951, Elaine Shaplen (marr. diss.); two *s*; *m* 1970, Tatjana Sais (*d* 1981); *m* 1984, Sarah Grahame. *Educ:* Berkhamsted; Merton Coll., Oxford (MA). Daily Telegraph Berlin staff, 1934; Chief Correspondent, 1938; expelled from Germany as reprisal, May 1939; Warsaw correspondent, 1939; after the outbreak of war reported events in Poland, Rumania, Bulgaria, Turkey, Holland, Belgium, and France. Joined BBC as head of German Service, 1940, after service in RAF; Controller of Broadcasting in British Zone of Germany, 1946–48; BBC East European Service, 1949–50; Head of Emergency Information Services, Federation of Malaya, 1950–51; Asst Controller, BBC Overseas Services, 1952–55; Controller, Overseas Services, 1955–56; Chm. Federal Commn of Inquiry into Organisation of Broadcasting in Fed. of Rhodesia and Nyasaland, 1955; Dir of Administration, BBC, 1956–58; Dir, News and Current Affairs, BBC, 1958–59; Director-General, 1960–69; a Governor, BBC, 1969–71. Vice Pres., European Broadcasting Union, 1963–69; Chm., European-Atlantic Action Cttee on Greece, 1971–74. Reported for Govt of Israel on Israel Broadcasting Authority, 1973; reported for Greek Govt on constitution of Greek broadcasting, 1975. CBIM, 1966. Fellow, BAFTA, 1984. Hon. DCL E Anglia, 1969; DUniv Open Univ., 1973; DUniv York, 1973. Grand Cross, Order of Merit (Germany), 1977. *Publications:* The Spy's Bedside Book (with Graham Greene), 1957; The Third Floor Front, 1969; (ed) The Rivals of Sherlock Holmes, 1970; (ed) More Rivals of Sherlock Holmes: cosmopolitan crimes, 1971; The Future of Broadcasting in Britain, 1972; (ed) The Crooked Counties, 1973; (ed) The American Rivals of Sherlock Holmes, 1976; (ed) The Pirate of the Round Pond and Other Strange Adventure Stories, 1977; (ed) The Complete Rivals of Sherlock Holmes, 1983; (with Graham Greene) Victorian Villainies, 1984. *Address:* Earl's Hall, Cockfield, near Bury St Edmunds, Suffolk.

See also R. O. Dennys, Graham Greene, Graham C. Greene.

GREENE, Ian Rawdon; *b* 3 March 1909; *o s* of Rawdon Greene and Marie Louise, Rahan, Bray, County Wicklow, Ireland; *m* 1937, Eileen Theodora Stack; one *d. Educ:*

Cheltenham Coll.; Trinity Coll., Dublin (BA, LLB). Crown Counsel, Tanganyika, 1935; Resident Magistrate, Zanzibar, 1937. Military Service, Kenya, 1940–41. Sen. Resident Magistrate, Zanzibar, 1950; Actg Asst Judge, Zanzibar, on numerous occasions; Actg Chief Justice, Zanzibar, June 1954, and May-Oct. 1955; Judge-in-charge, Somaliland Protectorate, 1955; Chief Justice, Somaliland Protectorate, 1958–60, retired; Stipendiary Magistrate, North Borneo, 1961–64. Registrar to Dean and Chapter, St Patrick's Cathedral, Dublin, 1973–82. Order of Brilliant Star of Zanzibar (4th Cl.), 1953. *Publications:* Jt Ed., Vols VI and VII, Zanzibar Law Reports. *Recreations:* cricket, golf, bridge, chess. *Address:* Malindi, Kilmacanogue, Co. Wicklow, Ireland. *T:* Dublin 867322. *Clubs:* The Victory (Services) Association; English (Zanzibar); Hargeisa (Somaliland).

GREENE, Jenny; Editor, Country Life, since 1986; food columnist for Today, since 1985; *b* 9 Feb. 1937; *d* of James Wilson Greene and Mary Emily Greene; *m* 1971, John Gilbert (marr. diss. 1986). *Educ:* Rochelle Sch., Cork; Trinity Coll., Dublin (BA); Univ. of Montpellier, France (Dip. d'Etudes Françaises). Researcher, Campbell-Johnson Ltd, 1963–64; Account-Exec., Central News, 1964–65; Account-Exec., Pemberton Advertising, 1965–66; Publicity Exec., Revlon, 1966–71; Beauty Editor, Woman's Own, 1971–75; Features Writer and Theatre Critic, Manchester Evening News, 1975–77; Asst Editor, Woman's Own, 1977–78; Editor: Homes and Gardens, 1978–86; A La Carte, 1984–85. *Publications:* contrib. The Times, Daily Mail, BBC. *Recreations:* gardening, cooking, moving house. *Address:* Michaelmas House, Church Yard, Kimbolton, Cambs PE18 0HH.

GREENE, Sir (John) Brian M.; *see* Massy-Green.

GREENE, Dame Judith; *see* Anderson, Dame Judith.

GREENEWALT, Crawford Hallock; Director and Member of the Finance Committee, E. I. du Pont de Nemours & Co., Inc. (Chairman, 1967–74); *b* Cummington, Mass, 16 Aug. 1902; *s* of Frank Lindsay and Mary Hallock Greenewalt; *m* 1926, Margaretta Lammot du Pont; two *s* one *d*. *Educ:* William Penn Charter Sch.; Mass. Institute of Technology (BS). With E. I. du Pont de Nemours & Co., Inc. from 1922; Asst Dir Exptl Station, Central Research Dept, 1939; Dir Chem. Div., Industrial and Biochemicals Dept, 1942; Technical Dir, Explosives Department, 1943; Asst Dir, Development Dept, 1945; Asst Gen. Man. Pigments Dept, 1945–46; Vice-Pres., 1946; Vice-Pres. and Vice-Chm. Exec. Cttee, 1947; Pres., Chm. Exec. Cttee and Mem. Finance Cttee, 1948–62; Chm. Board, 1962–67; Chm. Finance Cttee, 1967–74; Member Board of Directors of various other organisations. Member: Amer. Acad. of Arts and Sciences, National Academy of Sciences, Amer. Philos. Soc.; Carnegie Inst. of Washington; Trustee Emeritus, Nat. Geographic Soc. Holds hon. degrees in Science, Engineering and Laws, and has various scientific awards and medals. *Publications:* The Uncommon Man, 1959; Hummingbirds, 1960; Bird Song: acoustics and physiology, 1969. *Recreation:* photography. *Address:* Greenville, Delaware 19807, USA; (office) Du Pont Building, Wilmington, Delaware 19898, USA. *Clubs:* Wilmington, Wilmington Country, Du Pont Country, Greenville Country (USA).

GREENFIELD, Prof. (Archibald) David (Mant), CBE 1977; FRCP; Foundation Dean of the Medical School, 1966–81 and Professor of Physiology, 1966–82 in the University of Nottingham; now Professor Emeritus; *b* 31 May 1917; *s* of late A. W. M. Greenfield, MA, and Winifred (*née* Peck), Parkstone, Dorset; *m* 1943, Margaret (*née* Duane); one *s* one *d*. *Educ:* Poole Grammar Sch.; St Mary's Hospital Medical Sch. BSc London, 1st class hons Physiology, 1937; MB, BS, 1940, MSc 1947, DSc 1953, London; FRCP, 1973. Dunville Prof. of Physiology in the Queen's Univ. of Belfast, 1948–64; Prof. of Physiology in the Univ. of London, at St Mary's Hosp. Med. Sch., 1964–67. WHO Visiting Prof., India, 1960; Visiting Prof., Univ. of California, San Francisco Medical Centre, 1962–63. Sometime Examr, Oxford, Cambridge and 21 other Univs, RCS and RCSI; Chm., Special Trustees, Nottingham Univs Hosps, 1984–. Member: Physiol. Systems Bd, MRC, 1976–77; UGC, 1977–82 (Chm. Med. and Dental Sub-Cttees, Assessor to MRC); UPGC, Hong Kong, 1984– (Mem. 1981– and Chm. 1985–, Med. Sub-Cttee); GMC and GMC Educn Cttee, 1979–82; Med. Acad. Adv. Cttee, Chinese Univ., Hong Kong, 1976–80; Foundn Cttee, Sultan Qaboos Univ., Oman, 1981–86; Councils for Postgrad. Med. Educn, for England and Wales, and Scottish Council, 1977–82; DHSS Adv. Cttee on Artificial Limbs, 1971–75; DHSS Med. Manpower and Educn Liaison Cttee, 1974–78; DHSS Academic Forum, 1980–82; Sheffield RHB, 1968–74; Nottingham Univ. HMC, 1969–74; Notts AHA(T), 1974–79. Pres., Sect. of Biomed. Scis, British Assoc. for Advancement of Sci., 1972; Mem., Physiological, Biochemical and Medical Research Societies. Chm., Editorial Bd, Monographs of the Physiological Soc., 1975–79; Member, Editorial Board: Amer. Heart Jl, 1959–66; Clinical Science, 1960–65; Cardiovascular Research, 1966–79; Circulation Res., 1967–73. OStJ 1978. Hon. LLD Nottingham, 1977; Hon DSc QUB, 1978. *Publications:* papers on control of circulation of the blood, mainly in Lancet, Journal of Physiology, Clinical Science, and Journal of Applied Physiology. *Recreations:* sketching, bird watching, travel. *Address:* 25 Sutton Passeys Crescent, Nottingham NG8 1BX. *T:* Nottingham 782424.

GREENFIELD, Edward Harry; Chief Music Critic, The Guardian, since 1977; *b* 30 July 1928; *s* of Percy Greenfield and Mabel (*née* Hall). *Educ:* Westcliff High Sch.; Trinity Hall, Univ. of Cambridge (MA). Joined staff of Manchester Guardian, 1953: Record Critic, 1955; Music Critic, 1964; succeeded Sir Neville Cardus as Chief Music Critic, 1977. Broadcaster on music and records for BBC radio, 1957–. Mem., critics' panel, Gramophone, 1960–. Goldener Verdienstzeichen, Salzburg, 1980. *Publications:* Puccini: keeper of the seal, 1958; monographs on Joan Sutherland, 1972, and André Previn, 1973; (with Robert Layton, Ivan March and initially Denis Stevens) Stereo Record Guide, 9 vols, 1960–74; Penguin Stereo Record Guide, 5th edn 1986. *Recreations:* work, living in Spitalfields. *Address:* 16 Folgate Street, E1. *T:* 01–377 7555. *Club:* Critics' Circle.

GREENFIELD, Howard; *see* Greenfield, R. H.

GREENFIELD, Hon. Julius MacDonald, CMG 1954; Judge of the High Court of Rhodesia, 1968–74; *b* Boksburg, Transvaal, 13 July 1907; *s* of late Rev. C. E. Greenfield; *m* 1935, Florence Margaret Couper; two *s* one *d*. *Educ:* Milton Sch., Bulawayo; Universities of Capetown and Oxford. BA, LLB Cape; Rhodes Scholar, 1929; BA, BCL Oxon. Called to the Bar at Gray's Inn, 1933. QC 1948; practised at Bar in S Rhodesia, 1933–50; elected MP for Hillside, S Rhodesia, 1948, and appointed Minister of Internal Affairs and Justice, 1950; participated in London Conferences on Federation in Central Africa. MP Federal Parliament, in Umguza Constituency, 1953–63; Minister of Law, Federation of Rhodesia and Nyasaland, 1954–63; Minister for Home Affairs, 1962–63. *Publications:* Instant Crime, 1975; Instant Statute Case Law, 1977; Testimony of a Rhodesian Federal, 1978. *Address:* 17 Alder Way, West Cross, Swansea. *Clubs:* Bulawayo, Harare (Zimbabwe); City and Civil Service (Cape Town).

GREENFIELD, Dr Peter Rex; Senior Principal Medical Officer, Department of Health and Social Security, since 1983; *b* 1 Dec. 1931; *s* of late Rex Youhill Greenfield and of Elsie Mary Greenfield (*née* Douthwaite); *m* 1954, Faith Stella, *d* of George and Stella Gigg; eight *s* two *d*. *Educ:* Cheltenham College; Pembroke College, Cambridge (BA 1954; MB, BChir 1957; MA 1985); St George's Hosp. Med. Sch., London. DObst RCOG 1960. 2nd Lieut, R Signals, 1950–51; House appts, St George's Hosp., 1958; Gen. Med. Pract., Robertsbridge, Sussex, 1959–69; MO, Vinehall Sch., Robertsbridge, 1964–69; MO, Battle Hosp., 1964–69; joined DHSS, 1969; Chief Med. Advr (Social Security), with rank of SPMO, 1983–86. Mem., Jt Formulary Cttee, British Nat. Formulary, 1978–82; Chm., Informal Working Gp on Effective Prescribing, 1981–82; Divl Surgeon, Robertsbridge Div., St John Ambulance Brigade, 1965–. *Publications:* contribs to med. jls on geriatric day care, hypothermia and DHSS Regional Med. Service. *Recreations:* golf, swimming, walking, music, pinball. *Address:* Lorne House, Robertsbridge, East Sussex TN32 5DW. *T:* Robertsbridge 880209.

GREENFIELD, (Robert) Howard, FCA; CBIM; IGasE; Chairman, British Gas North Western (formerly North Western Region, British Gas Corporation), since 1985; *b* 4 Feb. 1927; *s* of James Oswald Greenfield and Doris Burt Greenfield; *m* 1951, Joyce Hedley Wells; one *s* one *d*. *Educ:* Rutherford Coll., Newcastle upon Tyne. FCA 1953; Companion IGasE 1982. Northern Gas Board: Chief Accountancy Asst, 1956; Dep. Divl Manager, Tees Area, 1961; Divl Manager, Cumberland Div., 1963; Regional Service Manager, 1968; Northern Gas: Dir of Customer Service, 1974; Dir of Marketing, 1976; Dep. Chm., 1977; Chm., N Eastern Reg., 1982–85. *Recreations:* salmon fishing, photography. *Address:* British Gas North Western, Welman House, Altrincham, Cheshire WA15 8AE. *T:* 061–928 6311.

GREENGROSS, Sir Alan (David), Kt 1986; Managing Director, Indusmond (Diamond Tools) Ltd; Director, Blazy & Clement Ltd and associated companies; *b* 1929; *m*; one *s* three *d*. *Educ:* University Coll. Sch.; Trinity Coll., Cambridge (MA). Member Council, London Borough of Camden (past Alderman). GLC: Member, 1977–84; Leader, Planning and Communications Policy, 1979–81; Leader of the Opposition, 1983–84. Mem., Port of London Authority, 1979–83. Mem. Governing Council, Univ. Coll. Sch. *Address:* 9 Dawson Place, W2 4TD. *Club:* Hurlingham.

GREENHALGH, Jack; Vice-Chairman, Cavenham Ltd, 1974–81; retired; *b* 25 July 1926; *s* of Herbert Greenhalgh and Alice May (*née* Clayton); *m* 1951, Kathleen Mary Hammond; two *s* two *d*. *Educ:* Manchester Grammar Sch.; Trinity Coll., Cambridge (MA Hons). FBIM. Marketing Dept, Procter & Gamble Ltd, Newcastle upon Tyne, 1950–59; Marketing Dir, Eskimo Foods Ltd, Cleethorpes, 1959–64; Dir of Continental Ops, Compton Advertising Inc., NY, 1964–65; Cavenham Ltd, 1965–81: Man. Dir, 1968–79. *Recreations:* golf, sailing.

GREENHALGH, Prof. Roger Malcolm, FRCS; Professor of Surgery, Charing Cross and Westminster Medical School (formerly Charing Cross Hospital Medical School), London, since 1982; *b* 6 Feb. 1941; *s* of John Greenhalgh and Phyllis Poynton; *m* 1964, Karin Maria Gross; one *s* one *d*. *Educ:* Clare Coll., Cambridge; St Thomas' Hosp., London. BA 1963, BChir 1966, MB, MA 1967, MChir 1974, MD 1983 (Cantab); FRCS 1971. Ho. Surg., 1967, Casualty Officer, 1968, St Thomas' Hosp.; Sen. Ho. Officer, Hammersmith Hosp., 1969; Registrar in Surgery, Essex County Hosp., Colchester, 1970–72; Lectr and Sen. Registrar in Surgery, St Bartholomew's Hosp., 1972–76; Sen. Lectr in Surgery and Hon. Cons. Surg., Charing Cross Hosp., 1976–81; Head of Dept of Surgery, Charing Cross Hosp. Med. Sch., 1981. Chm., Liaison Cttee, Bioengrg Centre, Roehampton, London; Mem., Ind. Scientific Enquiry into Smoking and Health. Sec. Gen. and Chm. Exec. Cttee, Assoc. of Internat. Vascular Surgeons; Vice Pres., Section of Surgery, RSM. Moynihan Fellow of Assoc. of Surgeons, 1974; Hunterian Prof., RCS, 1980. Chm. Editl Bd, European Jl of Vascular Surgery, 1987–. *Publications:* Progress in Stroke Research, 1, 1979; Smoking and Arterial Disease, 1981; Hormones and Vascular Disease, 1981; Femoro-distal bypass, 1981; Extra-Anatomic and Secondary Arterial Reconstruction, 1982; Progress in Stroke Research, 2, 1983; Vascular Surgical Techniques, 1984; Diagnostic Techniques and Assessment Procedures in Vascular Surgery, 1985. *Recreations:* tennis, skiing, swimming, music. *Address:* 271 Sheen Lane, East Sheen, SW14 8RN. *T:* 01–878 1110. *Club:* Roehampton.

GREENHAM, Peter George, CBE 1978; RA 1960 (ARA, 1951); PPRBA; RP; NEAC; Keeper of the Royal Academy Schools, 1964–85; *b* 9 Sept. 1909; *s* of George Frederick Greenham, MBE, civil servant; *m* 1964, Jane, *d* of late Dr G. B. Dowling, FRCP, and Mary Elizabeth Kelly; one *s* one *d*. *Educ:* Dulwich Coll.; Magdalen Coll., Oxford (Hist. Demy, BA); Byam Shaw Sch. of Art. Pres., RBA, to 1982. Paintings in permanent collections: Tate Gall.; Arts Council; Contemp. Art Soc.; Carlisle Gall.; Plymouth Gall. *Publication:* Velasquez, 1969. *Address:* c/o Royal Academy, Piccadilly, W1.

GREENHILL, family name of **Barons Greenhill** and **Greenhill of Harrow.**

GREENHILL, 2nd Baron, *cr* 1950, of Townhead; **Stanley E. Greenhill,** MD, DPH; FRCP(C), FACP, FFCM; Professor Emeritus, Department of Medicine and Community Medicine, University of Alberta, Edmonton, Alberta, 1982; *b* 17 July 1917; *s* of 1st Baron Greenhill and Ida Goodman; *S* father, 1967; *m* 1946, Margaret Jean, *d* of Thomas Newlands Hamilton, Ontario, Canada; two *d*. *Educ:* Kelvinside Academy, Glasgow; California and Toronto Univs. MD Toronto, DPH Toronto, FRSM. British Information Services, 1941; RAF, 1944. Prof., Dept of Medicine, University of Alberta, 1952–82. WHO Consultant, 1973–74. *Publications:* contrib. medical journals. *Recreations:* photography, travel. *Heir:* *b* Hon. Malcolm Greenhill, *b* 5 May 1924. *Address:* 10223, 137th Street, Edmonton, Alta T5N 2G8, Canada. *T:* 403–452–4650; c/o 28 Gorselands, Newbury, Berks. *Club:* Faculty (Edmonton, Alta).

GREENHILL OF HARROW, Baron *cr* 1974 (Life Peer), of the Royal Borough of Kensington and Chelsea; **Denis Arthur Greenhill,** GCMG 1972 (KCMG 1967; CMG 1960); OBE 1941; HM Government Director, British Petroleum Co. Ltd, 1973–78; Member, Security Commission, 1973–82; *b* 7 Nov. 1913; *s* of James and Susie Greenhill, Loughton; *m* 1941, Angela McCulloch; one *s* (and one *s* decd). *Educ:* Bishop's Stortford Coll.; Christ Church, Oxford (Hon. Student 1977). Served War of 1939–45 (despatches twice): Royal Engineers; in Egypt, N Africa, Italy, India and SE Asia; demobilised with rank of Col. Entered Foreign Service, 1946; served: Sofia, 1947–49; Washington, 1949–52; Foreign Office, 1952–54. Imperial Defence Coll., 1954; UK Delegation to NATO, Paris, 1955–57; Singapore, 1957–59; Counsellor, 1959–62; Minister, 1962–64, Washington DC; Asst Under-Sec. of State, FO, 1964–66; Dep. Under-Sec. of State, FO, 1966–69; Perm. Under-Sec. of State, FCO, and Head of the Diplomatic Service, 1969–73. Director: S. G. Warburg & Co., 1974–; Clerical Medical and General Assce Soc., 1974–86; Wellcome Foundn Ltd, 1974–85; BAT Industries Ltd, 1974–83; Hawker Siddeley Group, 1974–84; Leyland International, 1977–82; Mem., Internat. Adv. Cttee, First Chicago Ltd, 1976–81. A Governor of the BBC, 1973–78. Governor, BUPA, 1978–84, Dep. Chm., 1979–84. President: Royal Soc. for Asian Affairs, 1976–84; Anglo-Finnish Soc., 1981–84. Chm., KCH Med. Sch. Council, 1977–83; Fellow, King's Coll., London, 1984. Trustee, Rayne Foundn, 1974; Governor, Wellington Coll., 1974–83; Chm. of Governors, SOAS, 1978–85. Grand Cross, Order of the Finnish Lion, 1984. *Address:* 25 Hamilton House, Vicarage Gate, W8. *T:* 01–937 8362. *Club:* Travellers'.

GREENHILL, Dr Basil Jack, CB 1981; CMG 1967; FRHistS; FSA; Chairman, SS Great Britain Project, since 1982; author; *b* 26 Feb. 1920; *o c* of B. J. and Edith Greenhill; *m* 1st, 1950, Gillian (*d* 1959), *e d* of Capt. Ralph Tyacke Stratton, MC; one *s*; 2nd, 1961, Ann, *d* of Walter Ernest Giffard; one *s*. *Educ:* Bristol Grammar Sch.; Bristol Univ. (T. H. Green Scholar; PhD 1980). Served War of 1939–45: Lieut RNVR (Air Br.). Diplomatic Service, 1946–66; served: Pakistan; UK Delegn, New York; Tokyo; UK Delegate to Conf. on Law of the Sea, Geneva; British Dep. High Comr in E Pakistan; Ottawa. Dir, Nat. Maritime Mus., Greenwich, 1967–83, Caird Res. Fellow, 1983–. Member: Ancient Monuments Bd for England, 1972–84; Council, Maritime Trust, 1977–83 (Hon. Vice-Pres., 1984–); Finnish Exhibn 1985 Cttee, 1983–85; Vice Chm. Bd, Trustees of the Royal Armouries, 1984–; Vice Pres., Soc. for Nautical Res., 1975–; First Pres., Internat. Congress of Maritime Museums, 1975–81 (Hon. Life Mem., 1981); Pres., Devonshire Assoc., 1984; Trustee: Royal Naval Museum, Portsmouth, 1973–83; Mary Rose Trust, 1979–83. Governor, Dulwich Coll., 1974–; Chairman: Dulwich Picture Gall., 1977–; Nat. Museums' Directors' Conf., 1980–83; Govt Adv. Cttee on Historic Wreck Sites, 1986–. Principal Advisor: BBC TV series: The Commanding Sea, 1980–82; Trade Winds, 1984–85; BBC Radio series, The British Seafarer, 1980–82. Hon. Fellow, Univ. of Exeter, 1985. Kt Comdr, Order of White Rose, Finland, 1980. *Publications:* The Merchant Schooners, Vol. I, 1951, Vol. II, 1957, rev. edns 1968, 1978; (ed and prefaced) W. J. Slade's Out of Appledore, 1959, rev. edns 1972, 1974, 1980; Sailing For A Living, 1962; (with Ann Giffard) Westcountrymen in Prince Edward's Isle, 1967 (Amer. Assoc. Award) (filmed 1975); (with Ann Giffard) The Merchant Sailing Ship: A Photographic History, 1970; (with Ann Giffard) Women under Sail, 1970; Captain Cook, 1970; Boats and Boatmen of Pakistan, 1971; (with Ann Giffard) Travelling by Sea in the Nineteenth Century, 1972; (with Rear-Adm. P. W. Brock) Sail and Steam, 1973; (with W. J. Slade) West Country Coasting Ketches, 1974; A Victorian Maritime Album, 1974; A Quayside Camera, 1975; (with L. Willis) The Coastal Trade: Sailing Craft of British Waters 900–1900, 1975; Archaeology of the Boat, 1976; (with Ann Giffard) Victorian and Edwardian Sailing Ships, 1976; (with Ann Giffard) Victorian and Edwardian Ships and Harbours, 1978; (ed and prefaced) Georg Kåhrés The Last Tall Ships, 1978; (with Ann Giffard) Victorian and Edwardian Merchant Steamships, 1979; Schooners, 1980; The Life and Death of the Sailing Ship, 1980; (with Michael Mason) The British Seafarer, 1980; (with Denis Stonham) Seafaring Under Sail, 1981; Karlsson, 1982; The Woodshipbuilders, 1986; The Grain Races, 1986; numerous articles, reviews and broadcasts. *Recreations:* boating, travel, coarse gardening. *Address:* West Boetheric Farm, St Dominic, Saltash, Cornwall. *Clubs:* Arts; Royal Western Yacht (Plymouth); Karachi Yacht (Karachi); Åland Nautical (Mariehamn).

See also Sir C. S. R. Giffard.

GREENING, Rear-Adm. Sir Paul (Woollven), KCVO 1985; Master of HM's Household, since 1986; an Extra Equerry to the Queen, since 1983; *b* 4 June 1928; *s* of late Captain Charles W. Greening, DSO, DSC, RN, and Mrs Molly K. Greening (*née* Flowers); *m* 1951, Monica, *d* of late Mr and Mrs W. E. West, East Farndon, Market Harborough; one *s* one *d*. *Educ:* Mowden Sch., Brighton; Nautical Coll., Pangbourne. Entered RN, 1946; Midshipman, HMS Theseus, 1947–48; Sub-Lt and Lieut, HM Ships Zodiac, Neptune, Rifleman, Asheldham (CO), and Gamecock, 1950–58; Lt-Comdr, HM Ships Messina (CO), Loch Killisport, Urchin, and Collingwood, 1958–63; Comdr 1963; CO HMS Lewiston, and SO 2nd Minesweeping Sqdn, 1963–64; jssc 1964; Naval Plans, MoD (Navy), 1965–67; CO HMS Jaguar, 1967–68; Fleet Plans Officer, Far East Fleet, 1969; Captain 1969; CO HMS Aurora, 1970–71; Captain Naval Drafting, 1971–74; Sen. Officers War Course, 1974; Dir of Officers Appts (Seamen), MoD (Navy), 1974–76; Captain BRNC Dartmouth, 1976–78; Naval Sec., 1978–80; Flag Officer, Royal Yachts, 1981–85; retired 1985. ADC to the Queen, 1978. Younger Brother of Trinity House, 1984. *Recreations:* cricket, tennis, gardening. *Address:* Kingsmead Cottage, Kingsmead, Wickham, Hants. *Club:* Army and Navy.

GREENING, Wilfrid Peter, FRCS; Consultant Surgeon to Royal Marsden Hospital, 1952–79; Consulting Surgeon, Charing Cross Hospital since 1975; Lecturer in Surgery to Charing Cross Hospital Medical School; *s* of Rev. W. Greening and M. M. Waller, Saxlingham, Norfolk; *m* 1st, 1939, Hilary Berryman (marr. diss., 1961); one *d*; 2nd, 1962, Susan Ann Clair Huber (marr. diss. 1977); 3rd, 1978, Touba Ghazinoor. *Educ:* St Edmund's Sch., Canterbury; King's Coll.; Charing Cross Hospital Medical Sch. MRCS 1937; LRCP 1937; FRCS 1939. Houseman and Surgical Registrar, Charing Cross Hosp., 1938. Served War of 1939–45 (despatches); Wing Comdr i/c Surgical Div., RAFVR, 1943. Surgical Registrar, Gordon Hospital, 1946; Consultant Surgeon: Woolwich Hospital, 1948; Bromley and District Hospital, 1947–66. *Publications:* contributions to medical literature. *Recreations:* fishing, golf. *Address:* Flat 5, 125 Harley Street, W1. *Club:* Garrick.

GREENLAND, Dennis James, DPhil; FIBiol; Deputy Director General, International Rice Research Institute, Los Baños, Philippines, since 1979; *b* 13 June 1930; *s* of James John and Lily Florence Greenland; *m* 1955, Edith Mary Johnston; one *s* two *d*. *Educ:* Portsmouth Grammar Sch.; Christ Church, Oxford (MA, DPhil). Lecturer: Univ. of Ghana, 1955–59; Waite Agric Res. Inst., Adelaide, 1959–63; Reader and Head of Soil Science, Waite Agricl Res. Inst., 1963–70; Professor and Head of Dept of Soil Science, Univ. of Reading, 1970–79. Director of Research, Internat. Inst. of Tropical Agriculture, Nigeria, 1974–76 (on secondment from Univ. of Reading). FInstBiol 1974. Hon. DrAgSci Ghent, 1982. *Publications:* contributions: (jtly) The Soil Under Shifting Cultivation, 1960; (ed jtly) Soil Conservation and Management in the Humid Tropics, 1977; (ed jtly) Chemistry of Soil Constituents, 1978; (ed jtly) Soil Physical Properties and Crop Production in the Tropics, 1979; (ed) Characterisation of Soils in Relation to Their Classification and Management for Crop Production: some examples from the humid tropics, 1981; (ed jtly) The Chemistry of Soil Processes, 1981; numerous scientific articles in learned jls. *Recreations:* golf, bridge, watching cricket. *Address:* International Rice Research Institute, Box 933, Manila, Philippines. *T:* 742–0595.

GREENLEES, Ian Gordon, OBE 1963; MA; *b* 10 July 1913; *s* of Samuel Greenlees and Rosalie Stewart. *Educ:* Ampleforth Coll.; Magdalen Coll., Oxford. Reader in English Literature at University of Rome, 1934–36; supervisor of cultural centres of English for the British Council and Acting British Council Representative in Italy, 1939–40; Dir, British Institute, Rome, 1940; commissioned in Army, 1940; served in North African and Italian Campaigns, 1942–45, with rank of Major (despatches). Second Sec. (Asst Press Attaché) at British Embassy, Rome, Jan.-Dec. 1946; Asst British Council Representative, Italy, May 1947–Sept. 1948; Deputy British Council Representative, Italy, 1948–54; Dir, British Inst. of Florence, 1958–81. Medaglia d'Argento ai Benemeriti della Cultura (Italy), 1959; Cavaliere Ufficiale, 1963; Hon. Citizen, Bagni di Lucca, 1972; Commendatore dell' Ordine del Merito della Repubblica Italiana, 1975. *Publication:* Norman Douglas, 1957. *Recreations:* swimming, walking, and talking. *Address:* Casa Mansi, Via del Bagno 20, Bagni di Lucca, Prov. di Lucca, Italy. *T:* 0583 87522. *Club:* Athenæum.

GREENOCK, Lord; Charles Alan Andrew Cathcart; *b* 30 Nov. 1952; *s* and *heir* of 6th Earl Cathcart, *qv*; *m* 1981, Vivien Clare, *o d* of F. D. McInnes Skinner; one *s* one *d*. *Educ:* Eton. Commnd Scots Guards, 1972–75. *Heir:* *s* Hon. Alan George Cathcart, *b* 16 March 1986. *Address:* 18 Smith Terrace, SW3. *Club:* Cavalry and Guards.

GREENOUGH, Beverly, (Mrs P. B. Greenough); *see* Sills, B.

GREENSHIELDS, Robert McLaren; HM Diplomatic Service; Counsellor, Foreign and Commonwealth Office, since 1985; *b* 27 July 1933; *s* of late Brig. James Greenshields, MC, TD, and of Mrs J. J. Greenshields; *m* 1960, Jean Alison Anderson; one *s* two *d*. *Educ:* Edinburgh Academy; Lincoln Coll., Oxford (MA Hons). National Service, 2nd Lieut Highland Light Infantry, 1952–54. District Officer, Tanganyika, HMOCS, 1958–61; Asst Master and Housemaster, Gordonstoun Sch., 1962–68; HM Diplomatic Service, 1969–. *Recreations:* ornithology, golf. *Address:* c/o Foreign and Commonwealth Office, SW1A 2AH. *Club:* Royal Commonwealth Society.

GREENSMITH, Edward William, OBE 1972; BScEng; FCGI; Deputy President, Executive Board of the British Standards Institution, 1973–79 (Chairman, 1970–73); *b* 20 April 1909; *m* 1937, Edna Marjorie Miskin (*d* 1971); three *s*; *m* 1972, Margaret Boaden Miles. ICI, Engrg Adviser, 1964–71. Dir (non-executive), Peter Brotherhood Ltd, 1970–78. *Publications:* contribs: Chemistry Ind., 1957, 1959. *Recreations:* walking, gardening. *Address:* Pound Cottage, Graffham, near Petworth, W Sussex GU28 0QA. *T:* Graffham 374.

GREENSMITH, Edwin Lloydd, CMG 1962; *b* 23 Jan. 1900; *s* of Edwin Greensmith; *m* 1932, Winifred Bryce; two *s* two *d*. *Educ:* Victoria Univ., Wellington, NZ. MCom (Hons), 1930. Accountant; Solicitor. Chief Accountant, Ministry of Works, New Zealand, to 1935; then Treasury (Secretary, 1955–65). Chm., NZ Wool Commn, 1965–72. *Recreation:* gardening. *Address:* Lowry Bay, Wellington, NZ. *T:* 683240. *Club:* Wellington (Wellington NZ).

GREENSTOCK, Jeremy Quentin; HM Diplomatic Service; Counsellor (Commercial), Jedda, 1983–85 and Riyadh, since 1985; *b* 27 July 1943; *s* of John Wilfrid Greenstock and late Ruth Margaret Logan; *m* 1969, Anne Derryn Ashford Hodges; one *s* two *d*. *Educ:* Harrow Sch.; Worcester Coll., Oxford (MA Lit. Hum.). Asst Master, Eton Coll., 1966–69; entered HM Diplomatic Service, 1969; MECAS, 1970–72; Dubai, 1972–74; Private Sec. to the Ambassador, Washington, 1974–78; FCO, 1978–83 (Planning Staff, Personnel Ops Dept, N East and N African Dept). *Recreations:* travel, photography, court games. *Address:* c/o Foreign and Commonwealth Office, Whitehall, SW1A 2AH.

GREENWAY, family name of **Baron Greenway.**

GREENWAY, 4th Baron *cr* 1927; **Ambrose Charles Drexel Greenway;** Bt 1919; photographer and author; *b* 21 May 1941; *s* of 3rd Baron Greenway and of Cordelia Mary, *d* of late Major Humfrey Campbell Stephen; *S* father, 1975; *m* 1985, Mrs Rosalynne Schenk. *Educ:* Winchester. *Publications:* Soviet Merchant Ships, 1976; Comecon Merchant Ships, 1978; A Century of Cross Channel Passenger Steamers, 1980. *Recreations:* ocean racing and cruising, swimming. *Heir:* *b* Hon. Mervyn Stephen Kelvynge Greenway, *b* 19 Aug. 1942. *Address:* c/o House of Lords, SW1. *Clubs:* House of Lords Yacht; Royal London Yacht (Cowes).

GREENWAY, Harry; MP (C) Ealing North, since 1979; *b* 4 Oct. 1934; *s* of John Kenneth Greenway and Violet Adelaide (*née* Bell); *m* 1969, Carol Elizabeth Helena, *e d* of late John Robert Thomas Hooper, barrister at law and Metropolitan Stipendiary Magistrate; one *s* two *d*. *Educ:* Warwick Sch.; College of St Mark and St John, London; Univ. of Caen, Normandy. Assistant Master, Millbank Sch., 1957–60; successively, Head of English Dept, Sen. Housemaster, Sen. Master, Acting Dep. Head, Sir William Collins Sch., 1960–72; Dep. Headmaster, Sedgehill Sch. (Comprehensive for 2,000 plus pupils), 1972–79. Vice-Chm., Greater London Cons. Members, 1981–; Chm., All Party Adult Educn Cttee, 1979–; Mem., Parly Select Cttee on Educn, Science and the Arts, 1979–; Vice-Chm., Cons. Parly Educn Cttee, 1983– (Sec., 1981); Parly Sec., Cons. National Adv. Cttee on Educn, 1981–. Led All Party Parly Delegn to Sri Lanka, 1985. Pres., Cons. Trade Unionist Teachers, 1982–83; Chm., Atlantic Educn Cttee, 1981–; Member: Educn Cttee, NACRO, 1985–; Council, Open Univ., 1982–; Trustee, St Clare's Coll., Oxford, 1982–. British Horse Soc. Award of Merit, 1980. *Publications:* Adventure in the Saddle, 1971; regular contributor to educnl and equestrian jls. *Recreations:* riding, ski-ing, choral music, hockey (Vice-Pres., England Schoolboys' Hockey Assoc.; Founder, Lords and Commons Hockey Club), cricket, parliamentary parachutist. *Address:* House of Commons, SW1. *Clubs:* St Stephen's Constitutional, Ski Club of Gt Britain.

GREENWELL, Sir Edward (Bernard), 4th Bt *cr* 1906; farmer, since 1975; *b* 10 June 1948; *s* of Sir Peter McClintock Greenwell, 3rd Bt, TD, and of Henrietta (who *m* 1985, Hugh Kenneth Haig), 2nd *d* of late Peter and Lady Alexandra Haig-Thomas; *S* father, 1978; *m* 1974, Sarah Louise Gore-Anley; three *d*. *Educ:* Eton; Nottingham University (BSc); Cranfield Institute of Technology (MBA). *Heir:* *b* Captain James Peter Greenwell [*b* 27 May 1950; *m* 1979, Serena Jane, *yr d* of Major Hon. Colin James Dalrymple; one *s* one *d*]. *Address:* Gedgrave Hall, Woodbridge, Suffolk. *T:* Orford 450440. *Club:* Turf.

GREENWOOD, family name of **Viscount Greenwood.**

GREENWOOD, 2nd Viscount, *cr* 1937; **David Henry Hamar Greenwood;** Baron, *cr* 1929; Bt, *cr* 1915; *b* 30 Oct. 1914; *e s* of 1st Viscount Greenwood, PC, KC, LLD, BA, and Margery (*d* 1968), 2nd *d* of Rev. Walter Spencer, BA; *S* father 1948; unmarried. *Educ:* privately and at Bowers Gifford. Agriculture and Farming. *Heir:* *b* Hon. Michael George Hamar Greenwood, *b* 5 May 1923. *Recreations:* shooting and reading.

GREENWOOD, Allen Harold Claude, CBE 1974; JP; Deputy Chairman, British Aerospace, 1977–83 (Member, Organizing Committee, 1976–77); Chairman, British Aircraft Corporation, 1976 (Deputy Chairman, 1972–75); *b* 4 June 1917; *s* of Lt-Col Thomas Claude Greenwood and Hilda Letitia Greenwood (*née* Knight). *Educ:* Cheltenham Coll. Coll. of Aeronautical Engineering. Pilot's Licence, 1939. Joined Vickers-Armstrongs Ltd, 1940; served RNVR (Fleet Air Arm), 1942–52 (Lt-Cmdr); rejoined Vickers-Armstrongs Ltd, 1946, Dir, 1960; British Aircraft Corp., 1962, Dep. Man. Dir, 1969; Director: British Aircraft Corp. (Holdings), 1972; BAe Australia Ltd, 1977–83; Chm., BAe Inc., 1977–80. Director: SEPECAT SA, 1964; Europlane Ltd, 1974–83; Chairman: Panavia GmbH, 1969–72; Remploy Ltd, 1976–79 (Vice-Chm., 1973). Pres., Assoc. Européenne des Constructeurs de Material Aerospatial, 1974–76; Pres., 1970–72, Dep. Pres., 1981–82, SBAC; Vice-Pres., Engineering Employers' Fedn, 1982–83; Mem., National Def. Industry Council, 1970–72. Pres., Cheltenham Coll. Council, 1980–85; Member: Council, Cranfield Inst. of Technology, 1970–79; Council, CBI, 1970–77; Assoc. of Governing Bodies of Public Schools, 1982–85; Council, St John's Sch., Leatherhead, 1970–85 (Chm., 1979–85). JP Surrey 1962, Hampshire, 1975. Freeman, City of London. Liveryman, Company of Coachmakers, Guild of Air Pilots. General Comr for Income Tax, 1970–74. *Address:* 2 Rookcliff, Park Lane, Milford-on-Sea, Hants. *T:* Lymington 42893. *Clubs:* White's, Royal Automobile; Royal Lymington Yacht.

GREENWOOD, Duncan Joseph, PhD, DSc; FRS 1985; CChem, FRSC; Head of Soil Science, National Vegetable Research Station, Wellesbourne, Warwick, since 1966;

Visiting Professor of Plant Sciences, Leeds University, since 1985; Hon. Professor of Agricultural Chemistry, Birmingham University, since 1986; *b* 16 Oct. 1932; *s* of Herbert James Greenwood and Alison Fairgrieve Greenwood; unmarried. *Educ:* Hutton Grammar Sch., near Preston; Liverpool Univ. (BSc 1954); Aberdeen Univ. (PhD 1957; DSc 1972). CChem, FRSC 1977. Res. Fellow, Aberdeen Univ., 1957–59; Res. Leader, National Vegetable Res. Station, 1959–66. Chm., Agriculture Gp, Soc. of Chemical Industry, 1975–77; Pres., Internat. Cttee of Plant Nutrition, 1978–82. Lectures: Blackman, Univ. of Oxford, 1982; Distinguished Scholars, QUB, 1982; Hannaford, Univ. of Adelaide, 1985. Sir Gilbert Morgan Medal, Soc. of Chemical Industry, 1962; Res. Medal, RASE, 1979. *Publications:* over 90 scientific papers on soil science, crop nutrition and fertilizers. *Address:* 23 Shelley Road, Stratford-upon-Avon, Warwicks CV37 7JR. *T:* Stratford-upon-Avon 204735.

GREENWOOD, Jack Neville; General Manager, Stevenage Development Corporation, 1976–80, retired; *b* 17 March 1922; *s* of Daniel Greenwood and Elvina Stanworth; *m* 1947, Margaret Jane Fincher; two *s* two *d*. *Educ:* Harrow County Sch. Mem., Chartered Inst. of Public Finance and Accountancy. RAF, 1941–46. Ruislip Northwood UDC, 1938–49; Southall Borough Council, 1949–50; Stevenage Develt Corp., 1950–, Chief Finance Officer, 1967–76. *Recreation:* gardening. *Address:* 70 Churchill Road, Chipping Norton, Oxon OX7 5HP. *T:* Chipping Norton 3157.

GREENWOOD, James Russell, MVO 1975; HM Diplomatic Service, retired; Professor of Asian Studies, Matsusaka University, Japan, since 1983; *b* 30 April 1924; *s* of late J. Greenwood and L. Greenwood (*née* Moffat), Padiham; *m* 1957, Mary Veronica, *d* of late Dr D. W. Griffith and Dr Grace Griffith, Bures; one *s*. *Educ:* RGS, Clitheroe; Queen's Coll., Oxford. Army Service, 1943–47. BA, MA (Oxon) 1949; Foreign Office, 1949; subseq. service in Bangkok, 1950–52; Tokyo and Osaka, 1952–54; London, 1955–58; Rangoon, 1958–61; Rome, 1961–63; Bangkok, 1964–68; Counsellor (Information), Tokyo, 1968–73; Consul-General, Osaka, 1973–77. PRO, The APV Company and APV International, 1980–82. Order of Sacred Treasure (3rd cl.) Japan, 1975. *Recreations:* travel, golf, cricket. *Address:* Faculty of Political Science and Economics, Matsusaka University, 1846 Kubo-Cho, Matsusaka, Mie 515, Japan. *Clubs:* United Oxford & Cambridge University, MCC.

GREENWOOD, Joan; Actress; Theatre, Films, Radio, Television; *b* 4 March 1921; *d* of late Earnshaw Greenwood, Artist; *m* 1960, André Morell (*d* 1978); one *s*. *Educ:* St Catherine's Sch., Bramley, Surrey. First professional stage appearance in Le Malade Imaginaire, 1938; since then has appeared in: Little Ladyship; The Women; Striplings; Damaged Goods; Heartbreak House; Hamlet; Volpone; A Doll's House; Frenzy; Young Wives' Tale; The Confidential Clerk (New York); Peter Pan 1951; The Moon and the Chimney, 1955; Bell, Book and Candle, 1955; Cards of Identity, 1956; Lysistrata, 1957–58; The Grass is Greener, 1959; Hedda Gabler, 1960, 1964; The Irregular Verb to Love, 1961; Oblomov (later Son of Oblomov), 1964; Fallen Angels, 1967; The Au Pair Man, 1969; The Chalk Garden, 1971; Eden End, 1972; In Praise of Love, 1973; The Understanding, 1982. Acted at Chichester Festival, 1962. *Television includes:* Country, 1981; Ellis Island, USA, 1984; Caring, 1985. *Films include:* They Knew Mr Knight, Latin Quarter, Girl in a Million, Bad Sister, The October Man, Tight Little Island, Bad Lord Byron, Train of Events, Flesh and Blood, Kind Hearts and Coronets, The Man in the White Suit, Young Wives Tale, Mr Peek-a-Boo, The Importance of Being Earnest, Monsieur Ripois, Father Brown, Moonfleet, Stage Struck, Tom Jones, The Moonspinners, The Water Babies, Hound of the Baskervilles, Wagner, Little Dorrit, Caring. *Recreations:* reading, ballet, music, painting. *Address:* c/o National Westminster Bank, 352A King's Road, SW3.

GREENWOOD, John Arnold Charles, OBE 1943; Chief General Manager, Sun Alliance & London Insurance Group, 1971–77; *b* 23 Jan. 1914; *o s* of late Augustus George Greenwood and Adele Ellen O'Neill Arnold; *m* 1940, Dorothy Frederica Pestell; two *d*. *Educ:* King's College Sch., Wimbledon. FCII; FRES. Joined Sun Insce Office Ltd, 1932; posted India, 1937–47; served War of 1939–45, TA, 36th Sikh Regt and AA&QMG 4th Indian Div. (Lt-Col, OBE, despatches); subseq. various appts; a Gen. Man., Sun Alliance & London, 1965; Dep. Chief Gen. Man., 1969. Morgan Owen Medal, 1939. *Publications:* papers on insurance, entomology. *Recreations:* entomology, writing, gardening. *Address:* Hambledon House, Rogate, Petersfield, Hants. *T:* Rogate 744.

GREENWOOD, Prof. Norman Neill, DSc Melbourne; PhD; ScD Cambridge; CChem, FRSC; Professor and Head of Department of Inorganic and Structural Chemistry, University of Leeds, since 1971; *b* Melbourne, Vic., 19 Jan. 1925; *er s* of Prof. J. Neill Greenwood, DSc and Gladys, *d* of late Moritz and Bertha Uhland; *m* 1951, Kirsten Marie Rydland, Bergen, Norway; three *d*. *Educ:* University High School, Melbourne; University of Melbourne; Sidney Sussex Coll., Cambridge. Laboratory Cadet, CSIRO Div. of Tribophysics, Melbourne, 1942–44; BSc Melbourne 1945, MSc Melbourne 1948; DSc Melbourne 1966. Masson Memorial Medal, Royal Australian Chem. Institute, 1945. Resident Tutor and Lecturer in Chemistry, Trinity Coll., Melbourne, 1946–48. Exhibn of 1851, Overseas Student, 1948–51; PhD Cambridge 1951; ScD Cambridge 1961. Senior Harwell Research Fellow, 1951–53; Lectr, 1953–60 Senior Lectr, 1960–61, in Inorganic Chemistry, Univ. of Nottingham; Prof. of Inorganic Chemistry, Univ. of Newcastle upon Tyne, 1961–71. Vis. Professor: Univ. of Melbourne, 1966; Univ. of Western Australia, 1969; Univ. of Western Ontario, 1973; Univ. of Copenhagen, 1979; La Trobe Univ., Melbourne, 1985; National Science Foundation Distinguished Vis. Prof., Michigan State Univ., USA, 1967. International Union of Pure and Applied Chemistry: Mem., 1963–83; Vice-Pres., 1975–77, Pres., 1977–81, Inorganic Chemistry Div.; Chm., Internat. Commn on Atomic Weights, 1969–75; Chemical Society: Tilden Lectr, 1966–67; Vice Pres., 1979–80; Pres., Dalton Div., 1979–81; Award in Main Group Chemistry, 1975. Gesellschaft Deutscher Chemiker Hofmann Lectr, 1983; RSC Liversidge Lectr, 1983. Dr *hc* de l'Université de Nancy I, 1977. *Publications:* Principles of Atomic Orbitals, 1964 (rev. edns 1968, 1973, 1980); Ionic Crystals, Lattice Defects, and Nonstoichiometry, 1968; (jointly) Spectroscopic Properties of Inorganic and Organometallic Compounds, vols I-IX, 1968–76; (with W. A. Campbell) Contemporary British Chemists, 1971, (with T. C. Gibb) Mössbauer Spectroscopy, 1971; Periodicity and Atomic Structure, 1971; (with B. P. Straughan and E. J. F. Ross) Index of Vibrational Spectra, vol. I, 1972, (with E. J. F. Ross) vol. II, 1975, vol. III, 1977; The Chemistry of Boron, 1973 (rev. edn 1975); (with A. Earnshaw) Chemistry of the Elements, 1984; numerous original papers and reviews in chemical jls and chapters in scientific monographs. *Recreations:* ski-ing, music. *Address:* Department of Inorganic and Structural Chemistry, The University, Leeds LS2 9JT.

GREENWOOD, Peter Bryan; His Honour Judge Greenwood; a Circuit Judge, since 1972. Called to the Bar, Gray's Inn, 1955. Dep. Chm., Essex QS, 1968–71.

GREENWOOD, Peter Humphry, DSc; FRS 1985; FIBiol; Deputy Chief Scientific Officer, Ichthyologist, British Museum (Natural History), since 1985 (Senior Principal Scientific Officer, 1967–85); *b* 21 April 1927; *s* of Percy Ashworth Greenwood and Joyce May Wilton; *m* 1950, Marjorie George; four *d*. *Educ:* St John's Coll., Johannesburg; Krugersdorp High Sch.; Univ. of Witwatersrand. BSc (Hons), DSc. S African Naval forces, seconded to RN, 1944–46. Colonial Office Fishery Res. Student, 1950–51; Res. Officer, E African Fisheries Res. Orgn, Jinja, Uganda, 1951–58; British Museum (Natural History): Sen. Res. Fellow, 1958–59; Sen., later Principal, Scientific Officer and Curator of Fishes, 1959–67. Res. Associate, Amer. Mus. of Natural Hist., 1965; H. B. Bigelow Vis. Prof. of Ichthyology, Harvard Univ., 1979. Mem., British subcttee on productivity of freshwaters, Internat. Biol Prog., 1964–75; Chm., Royal Soc./Internat. Biol Prog. subcttee on res. in Lake George, 1967–74. Pres., Linnean Soc. of London, 1976–79. Hon. For. Mem., Amer. Soc. of Ichthyologists and Herpetologists, 1972; For. Mem., Swedish Royal Acad. of Science, 1984. Scientific Medal, Zoological Soc. of London, 1963; Medal for Zoology, Linnean Soc., 1982. *Publications:* Fishes of Uganda, 1958, 2nd edn 1966; The Cichlid Fishes of Lake Victoria: the biology and evolution of a species flock, 1974; (ed) J. R. Norman, A History of Fishes, 1st revd edn 1963, 2nd revd edn 1975; (ed with C. Patterson) Fossil Vertebrates, 1967; (ed with C. Patterson and R. Miles) Interrelationships of Fishes, 1973; The Haplochromine Fishes of the East African Lakes, 1981; numerous papers on taxonomy, anatomy, biology and evolution of fishes. *Recreations:* ballet, art, reading, thinking, model building. *Address:* 20 Cromer Villas Road, SW18 1PN. *T:* 01–874 9588.

GREENWOOD, Ronald, CBE 1981; Manager, England Association Football Team, 1977–82; *b* 11 Nov. 1921; *s* of Sam and Margaret Greenwood; *m* Lucy Joan Greenwood; one *s* one *d*. *Educ:* Alperton School. Apprenticed signwriter, 1937; joined Chelsea FC, 1940; served RAF, 1940–45; Bradford Park Avenue FC, 1945 (Captain); Brentford FC, 1949 (over 300 matches); rejoined Chelsea FC, 1952 (League Champions, 1954–55); Fulham FC, Feb. 1955; coached Oxford Univ. team, 3 years, Walthamstow Avenue FC, 2 years; Manager, Eastbourne United FC and England Youth team; Asst Manager, Arsenal FC, 1958; Team Manager, England Under-23, 1958–61; Manager and Coach, later Gen. Manager, West Ham United FC, 1961–77 (FA Cup, 1964 and 1975; European Cup Winners' Cup, 1965); a FIFA technical advisor, World Cup series, 1966 and 1970. *Publication:* Yours Sincerely, 1984. *Address:* 8 Kestrel Close, Upper Drive, Hove, Sussex.

GREENWOOD WILSON, J.; *see* Wilson, John G.

GREER, Prof. David Clive; Professor of Music and Chairman of Music Board of Study, University of Durham, since 1986; *b* 8 May 1937; *s* of William Mackay Greer and Barbara (*née* Avery); *m* 1961, Patricia Margaret Regan; two *s* one *d*. *Educ:* Dulwich Coll.; Queen's Coll., Oxford (MA). Lectr in Music, Birmingham Univ., 1963–72; Hamilton Harty Prof. of Music, QUB, 1972–84; Prof. of Music, Univ. of Newcastle upon Tyne, 1984–86. *Publications:* (ed) English Madrigal Verse, 1967; Hamilton Harty: his life and music, 1979, 2nd edn 1980; Hamilton Harty: early memories, 1979; editions of 16th and 17th century music; articles in Music and Letters, Musical Times, Shakespeare Qly, Notes & Queries, Lute Soc. Jl. *Recreations:* reading, walking, squash. *Address:* The Music School, Palace Green, Durham DH1 3RL. *T:* Durham 3742000. *Club:* Athenæum.

GREER, Germaine, PhD; author and lecturer; Founder Director, The Tulsa Centre for the Study of Women's Literature, 1979–82; *b* 29 Jan. 1939. *Educ:* Melbourne Univ.; Sydney Univ.; Cambridge Univ. (BA, PhD). Lecturer in English, Warwick Univ., 1968–73. *Publications:* The Female Eunuch, 1970; The Obstacle Race, 1979; Sex and Destiny: the politics of human fertility, 1984; (contrib.) Women: a world report, 1985; Shakespeare, 1986; contribs: articles to Listener, Spectator, Esquire, Harpers Magazine, Playboy, Private Eye (as Rose Blight). *Address:* c/o Aitken W. Stone, 29 Fernshaw Road, SW10 0TG.

GREET, Rev. Dr Kenneth Gerald; Secretary of the Methodist Conference, 1971–84; President of the Methodist Conference, July 1980–81; Moderator, Free Church Federal Council, 1982–83; Co-Chairman, World Disarmament Campaign, since 1984; *b* 17 Nov. 1918; *e s* of Walter and Renée Greet, Bristol; *m* 1947, Mary Eileen Edbrooke; one *s* two *d*. *Educ:* Cotham Grammar Sch., Bristol; Handsworth Coll., Birmingham. Minister: Cwm and Kingstone Methodist Church, 1940–42; Ogmore Vale Methodist Church, 1942–45; Tonypandy Central Hall, 1947–54; Sec. Dept of Christian Citizenship of Methodist Church, 1954–71; Member: Brit. Council of Churches, 1955– (Chm. of Exec., 1977–81); World Methodist Council, 1957– (Chm., Exec. Cttee, 1976–81); Chairman: Exec., Temperance Council of Christian Churches, 1961–71; World Christian Temperance Fedn, 1962–72. Rep. to Central Cttee, World Council of Churches, Addis Ababa, 1971, Nairobi, 1975; Beckly Lectr, 1962; Willson Lectr, Kansas City, 1966; Cato Lectr, Sydney, 1975. Hon. DD Ohio, USA. *Publications:* The Mutual Society, 1962; Man and Wife Together, 1962; Large Petitions, 1964; Guide to Loving, 1965; The Debate about Drink, 1969; The Sunday Question, 1970; The Art of Moral Judgement, 1970; When the Spirit Moves, 1975; A Lion from a Thicket, 1978; The Big Sin: Christianity and the arms race, 1983; What Shall I Cry?, 1986. *Recreations:* tennis, photography. *Address:* 89 Broadmark Lane, Rustington, Sussex BN16 2JA. *T:* Rustington 773326.

GREETHAM, (George) Colin; Headmaster, Bishop's Stortford College, 1971–84; *b* 22 April 1929; *s* of late George Cecil Greetham and of Gertrude Greetham (*née* Heavyside); *m* 1963, Rosemary (*née* Gardner); two *s* one *d*. *Educ:* York Minster Song Sch.; St Peter's Sch., York; (Choral Scholar) King's Coll., Cambridge. BA (Hons) History Tripos Cantab, Class II, Div. I, 1952; Certif. of Educn (Cantab), 1953. *Recreations:* hockey, cricket, music, choral training. *Address:* Chapelhead Farm, Crossroads, Keith, Banffshire AB5 3LQ.

GREEVES, Rev. Derrick Amphlet; Methodist Minister; *b* 29 June 1913; *s* of Edward Greeves, Methodist Minister; *m* 1942, Nancy (*née* Morgans); one *s* three *d*. *Educ:* Bolton Sch.; Preston Gram. Sch.; Manchester Univ. 1931–34 (BA); Cambridge Univ. (Wesley Hse), 1934–37 (MA). Entered Methodist Ministry, 1935; Barnet, 1937; Bristol, 1939; RAF Chaplain, 1943; S Norwood, 1947; Bowes Park, 1952; Westminster Central Hall, 1955; Guildford, 1964; Worcester, 1969; Salisbury, 1974; Langwathby, Cumbria, 1978. *Publications:* Christ in Me, a study of the Mind of Christ in Paul, 1962; A Word in Your Ear (broadcast talks), 1970; Preaching through St Paul, 1980. *Address:* Red Barn, Langwathby, Penrith, Cumbria CA10 1LW. *T:* Langwathby 707.

GREEVES, John Ernest, CB 1966; Permanent Secretary, Ministry of Home Affairs for Northern Ireland, 1964–70, retired; *b* 9 Oct. 1910; *s* of late R. D. Greeves, Grange, Dungannon, Co. Tyrone; *m* 1942, Hilde Alexandra, *d* of E. Hülbig, Coburg, Bavaria; one *s* one *d*. *Educ:* Royal School, Dungannon. Entered Min. of Labour, NI, 1928; Asst Sec., 1956–62; Permanent Sec., 1962–64; subseq. Min. of Home Affairs. *Address:* 22 Downshire Road, Belfast BT6 9JL. *T:* 648380.

GREEVES, Maj.-Gen. Sir Stuart, KBE 1955 (CBE 1945; OBE 1940); CB 1948; DSO 1944; MC 1917; (ex-Indian Army) Deputy Adjutant General, India, until 1957, retired; *b* 2 April 1897; *s* of late J. S. Greeves; unmarried. *Educ:* Northampton Sch. Served European War, 1914–18 (MC and Bar); War of 1939–45 (DSO and Bar, CBE). *Address:* c/o Lloyds Bank, 6 Pall Mall, SW1; Flat 601, Grosvenor Square, College Road, Rondebosch, Cape Town, S Africa. *Club:* Naval and Military.

GREGG, Hubert Robert Harry; actor, composer, lyricist, author, playwright and director; *b* London, 19 July 1914; *s* of Robert Joseph Gregg and Alice Maud (*née* Bessant);

m 1st, 1943, Zoe Gail (marr. diss. 1950); one *d*; 2nd, 1956, Pat Kirkwood (marr. diss. 1979); 3rd, 1980, Carmel Lytton; one *s* one *d*. *Educ*: St Dunstan's Coll.; Webber-Douglas Sch. of Singing and Dramatic Art. Served War, 1939–44: private, Lincs Regt, 1939; commnd 60th Rifles, 1940; transf. Intell.; with Polit. Warfare Exec., 1942 (duties included broadcasting in German). *Stage*: 1st London appearance, Julien in Martine, Ambassadors', 1933; Birmingham Rep., 1933–34; Shakespearean roles, Open Air Theatre, Regent's Park and at Old Vic, 1934, 1935; 1st New York appearance, Kit Neilan in French without Tears, 1937 (and London, 1938–39); London appearances include: Pip in The Convict, 1935; roles in classics (Orlando, Henry V, Hamlet), 1935–36; Frederick Hackett in Great Possessions, 1937; Peter Scott-Fowler in After the Dance, 1939; Polly in Men in Shadow, 1942; Michael Caraway in Acacia Avenue, 1944; Earl of Harpenden in While the Sun Shines, 1945, 1946; Tom D'Arcy in Off the Record, 1947; Gabriel Hathaway in Western Wind, 1949; (1st musical), John Blessington-Briggs in Chrysanthemum, 1958; Lionel Toope in Pools Paradise, 1961. *Chichester Festival Theatre*: Alexander MacColgie Gibbs in The Cocktail Party, Antonio in The Tempest, and Announcer in The Skin of our Teeth, 1968; Sir Lucius O'Trigger in The Rivals, Britannus in Caesar and Cleopatra, and Marcellin in Dear Antoine (also London), 1971. *Directed, London*: The Hollow (Agatha Christie's 1st stage success), 1951; re-staged To Dorothy - a Son, 1952 (subseq. toured in play, 1952–53); The Mousetrap (for 7 yrs from 1953); Speaking of Murder, 1958; The Unexpected Guest, 1958; From the French, 1959; Go Back for Murder, 1960; Rule of Three, 1962; re-staged The Secretary Bird, 1969 (subseq. toured in play, 1969–70). 1st solo performance, Leicester, 1970; subseq. performances in Britain and America (subjects include Shakespeare, Shaw, Jerome K. Jerome, the London Theatre, and the 20s, 30s and 40s); solo perf., Words by Elgar, Music by Shaw, Malvern Fest., 1978, Edinburgh Fest., 1979. *Films include*: In Which We Serve; Flying Fortress; Acacia Avenue (USA as The Facts of Love); The Root of all Evil; Vote for Huggett; Once upon a Dream; Robin Hood (Walt Disney); The Maggie (USA as High and Dry); Svengali; Doctor at Sea (also wrote music and lyrics); Simon and Laura; Speaking of Murder; Final Appointment; Room in the House; Stars in Your Eyes (also co-dir. and wrote music and lyrics). *Author of plays*: We Have Company (played in tour, 1953); Cheque Mate (dir. and appeared in); Villa Sleep Four (played in tour, 1965); From the French (written under pseudonym of Jean-Paul Marotte); Who's Been Sleeping . . . ? (also appeared in); The Rumpus (played in tour, 1967); Dear Somebody (perf. Germany as Geliebtes Traumbild, 1984); (screenplay) After the Ball (adapted from own television biog. of Vesta Tilley). *Songs*: Author of over 100, including: I'm going to get lit up; Maybe it's because I'm a Londoner. BBC broadcasts in drama, revue, poetry, etc, 1933–; announcer, BBC Empire Service, 1934–35; weekly radio progs with accent on nostalgia, 1965– (A Square Deal, I Remember it Well, Now and Then, Thanks for the Memory); Chairman: BBC TV Brains Trust, 1955; Youth Wants to Know, ITV, 1957; 40 week radio series on London theatres, 1974–75; biog. series: I Call it Genius, 1980–81; I Call it Style, 1981–; Hubert Gregg Remembers, ITV solo series, 1982–; 50 Years of Broadcasting, BBC celebration prog. (Hubert Gregg says Maybe It's Because . . .), 1984 (Sony Radio Award, 1985); Hubert Gregg Remembers (series for BBC World Service), 1985–; (wrote book, music and lyrics, and appeared in) Sweet Liza (radio musical play), 1985. Has dir., lectured and adjudicated at Webber-Douglas Sch., Central Sch. of Speech Trng and RADA. Patron, Cinema Theatre Assoc., 1973–; President: Northern Boys' Book Club, 1975– (succeeded P. G. Wodehouse); Concert Artists Assoc., 1979–80. Freedom of City of London, 1981. Gold Badge of Merit, British Acad. of Composers, Authors and Song Writers, 1982. *Publications*: April Gentleman (novel), 1951; We Have Company (play), 1953; A Day's Loving (novel), 1974; Agatha Christie and all that Mousetrap, 1980; Thanks for the Memory (biographies collected from radio series I Call it Genius and I Call it Style), 1983; Geliebtes Traumbild (play), 1984; music and lyrics. *Recreation*: cinematography. *Address*: c/o Broadcasting House, W1A 1AA. *Club*: Garrick.

GREGOIRE, Most Rev. Paul; *see* Montreal, Archbishop of, (RC).

GREGORY, Alan Thomas, CBE 1984; Director: Stewart Wrightson Holdings plc, since 1985; National Home Loans Corporation, since 1985; *b* 13 Oct. 1925; *s* of Lloyd Thomas Gregory and Florence Abbott; *m* 1952, Pamela Douglas Scott (*d* 1986); one *s* two *d*. *Educ*: Dulwich Coll.; St John's Coll., Cambridge (Classics). Directed into coal mining, coal face worker, 1944; Min. of Power, 1948; JSSC 1957; Chm., NATO Petroleum Planning Cttee, 1967–70; joined British Petroleum, 1971; Gen. Manager, BP Italiana, 1972–73; Dir, Govt and Public Affairs, 1975–85, and Dir, UK and Ireland Region, 1980–85, British Petroleum Co.; Chm., BP Oil Ltd, 1981–85; Dir, BP Chemicals International Ltd, 1981–85. Governor, Queen Mary Coll., London Univ., 1981–. President, Inst. of Petroleum, 1982–84. *Recreations*: books, gardening, theatre. *Address*: 14 Courtleas, Fairmile Park Road, Cobham, Surrey KT11 2PW. *T*: Cobham 64457. *Club*: Travellers'.

GREGORY, Clifford; Chief Scientific Officer, Department of Health and Social Security, 1979–84, retired; *b* 16 Dec. 1924; *s* of Norman and Grace Gregory; *m* 1948, Wyn Aveyard; one *d* (one *s* decd). *Educ*: Royal Coll. of Science, London Univ. (2nd Cl. Hons Physics; ARCS). Served War, RN, 1943–46. Lectr, Mddx Hosp. Med. Sch., 1949; Sen. Physicist, Mount Vernon Hosp., 1954; Dep. Reg. Physicist, Sheffield, 1960; Sen. Principal Scientific Officer, Min. of Health, 1966; Dep. Chief Scientific Officer, DHSS, 1972. *Publications*: scientific papers in med. and scientific jls. *Recreations*: outdoor pursuits, natural history, squash. *Address*: 53 Roundwood Park, Harpenden, Herts AL5 3AG. *T*: Harpenden 2047.

GREGORY, Conal Robert; MP (C) York, since 1983; international wine consultant and lecturer, since 1977; *b* 11 March 1947; *s* of Patrick George Murray Gregory and Marjorie Rose Gregory; *m* 1971, Helen Jennifer Craggs; one *s* one *d*. *Educ*: King's College Sch., Wimbledon; Univ. of Sheffield (BA Hons Mod. Hist. and Pol Theory and Instns, 1968). Master of Wine by examination, Vintners' Co., 1979. Manager, Saccone & Speed Vintage Cellar Club, 1971–73; Wine Buyer, Reckitt & Colman, 1973–77; Editor, Internat. Wine and Food Soc.'s Jl, 1980–83. Contested Lakenham, Norwich City election, 1976; Norfolk County Councillor, Thorpe Div., 1977–81 (Vice-Chm., Schools Cttee 1977–78); Mem., Educn Cttee 1977–81); Vice-Pres., Norwich Jun. Chamber of Commerce, 1975–76; Mem., E Anglia Tourist Bd, 1979–81. Chairman: Norwich N Cons. Assoc., 1980–82; Norwich CPC, 1978–81; Vice-Chm., Eastern Area CPC, 1980–83; Member: Cons. Eastern Area Agric. Cttee, 1975–79; Norfolk Cons. Eur. Constituency Council, 1981–82; Cons. Provincial Council, Eastern Area, 1978–82; Chm. and Founder, Bow Gp of E Anglia, 1975–82; Nat. Vice-Chm., Bow Gp, 1976–77. Secretary: Cons. Parly Transport Cttee, 1983–; All Party Parly Tourism Cttee, 1983–; Vice Chairman: Cons. Parly Food and Drinks Industries Cttee, 1985–; Cons. Parly Tourism Cttee, 1985–; Member: All Party Parly Arts and Heritage and Disablement Gps, 1983–; Nat. Adv. Cttee, Cons. Political Centre, 1984–; CPA, 1983–; British Gp, IPU, 1983–; Cttee, British Atlantic Gp of Young Politicians, 1983–; Pres., York Young Conservatives, 1982–; Vice-President: Nat. Soc. of Cons. and Unionist Agents, Yorks Br., 1983–; York Br., UNA, 1983–. Parly Consultant: The Market Res. Soc., 1984–; Consort Hotels Ltd, 1984–. Fellow Elect, Industry and Parlt Trust, 1984–. Private Member's Bill on consumer safety, 1985. Patron, Nat. Trust for Welfare of the Elderly, 1983–; Founder Mem., Wymondham Br., CEMS, 1979; Member: Wymondham Abbey PCC, 1982–83; Humbleyard Deanery Synod,

1982–83; High Steward's Cttee, York Minster Fund, 1983–; York Archaeol Trust, 1983–; York Georgian Soc., 1982–; York Civic Trust, 1982–. A Friend of York Festival. Governor, Heartsease Sch., Norwich, 1977–83; Mem., Court of Governors: Univ. of Sheffield, 1980–; Univ. of York, 1983–; Univ. of Hull, 1983–. Wine Corresp., Catering Times, 1979–83. *Publications*: (with W. Knock) Beers of Britain, 1975; (with R. A. Adley) A Policy for Tourism?, 1977; A Caterer's Guide to Drinks, 1979; contribs to The Times, Wine and Spirit, Wines and Vines, Survey, Money Magazine, Travel GBI, Conference Britain, etc. *Address*: House of Commons, SW1A 0AA. *T*: 01–219 4603. *Clubs*: Acomb and District Conservative, Conservative Central (York).

GREGORY, John Peter, JP; CEng, FIMechE; Chairman, Data Recording Instruments Ltd, 1982–84; *b* 5 June 1925; *s* of Mr and Mrs P. Gregory; *m* 1949, Lilian Mary (*née* Jarvis); one *s* one *d*. *Educ*: Ernest Bailey Sch., Matlock; Trinity Hall, Cambridge (MA). CEng, FIMechE 1970. Served War, RAF Pilot, 1943–47. Joined Cadbury Bros Ltd, 1949, Dir 1962; Vice Chm., Cadbury Ltd, 1969–70, Dir, Cadbury Schweppes, 1971–82 (Chm., Overseas Gp and Internat. Tech. Dir, 1973–80); Director: National Vulcan Engrg Ins. Group Ltd, 1970–79; Amalgamated Power Engrg Ltd, 1973–81. Gen. Comr of Income Tax, 1978–82. Chm. Trustees, Middlemore Homes, 1970–82. Liveryman, Worshipful Co. of Needlemakers. JP Birmingham, 1979. *Recreations*: music, bridge, country pursuits, sailing. *Address*: Moorgreen Hall, Weatheroak, Alvechurch, Worcs. *T*: Wythall 822303. *Club*: Carlton.

GREGORY, Leslie Howard James; former National Officer of EETPU; *b* 18 Jan. 1915; *s* of J. F. and R. E. Gregory; *m* 1949, D. M. Reynolds; one *s* one *d*. *Educ*: Junior Section, Ealing College (formerly Acton Coll.) and state schools. Mem. Exec. Council, ETU, 1938–54; full-time Nat. Officer, 1954–79, retired. Member: CSEU Nat. Sub-Cttees, for Shipbuilding, 1966–79, for Railway Workshops, 1968–78; Craft Training Cttees of Shipbuilding ITB, 1965–77, and Engineering ITB, 1965–68; EDC for Elec. Engrg, 1967–74; EDC for Shipbuilding, 1974–76; Org. Cttee, British Shipbuilders, 1976–77; Bd, British Shipbuilders (part-time), 1977–80. *Address*: 1 St Margarets, Exeter Road, Honiton, Devon. *T*: Honiton 3594.

GREGORY, Michael Anthony; Chief Legal Adviser, Country Landowners' Association, since 1977; *b* 8 June 1925; *s* of late Wallace James Ignatius Gregory, FRIBA, FRICS, AMIMechE, and Dorothy Gregory; *m* 1951, Patricia Ann, *d* of late Frank Hodges and late Gwendoline Hodges; three *s* four *d* (and one *d* decd). *Educ*: Douai Sch.; University Coll. London (LLB). Served RAF, Air Navigator, 1943–47; called to the Bar, Middle Temple, 1952; practised at Bar, 1952–60; Legal Dept, Country Landowners' Assoc., 1960–. Hon. Sec., Soc. of Our Lady of Good Counsel, 1953–58; Mem., Management Cttee, Catholic Social Service for Prisoners, 1952– (Chm., 1960–71 and 1974–85; Hon. Sec., 1953–60); Pres., Douai Soc., 1984–86; Chm., Internat. Help for Children, Fleet and Dist Br., 1967–77. Mem., BSI Cttee on Installation of Pipelines in Land, 1965–83; Hon. Legal Advr, Nat. Anglers' Council, 1968–; Mem., Thames Water Authority Reg. Fisheries Adv. Cttee, 1974–; Founder Mem., Agricl Law Assoc., 1975; Mem. Council: Salmon and Trout Assoc., 1980–; Anglers' Coop. Assoc., 1980– (Mem. Legal Cttee, 1981–); Trustee, CLA Charitable Trust, 1980–; Member: Cttee, Fedn for Promotion of Horticulture for the Disabled, 1981–; Inland Waterways Amenity Adv. Council, 1982–; Council, John Eastwood Water Protection Trust, 1984–. *Publications*: Organisational Possibilities in Farming, 1968; (with C. Townsend) Joint Enterprises in Farming, 1968, 2nd edn 1973; Angling and the Law, 1967, 2nd edn 1974, supp. 1976; Title, Pipelines, for Encycl. of Forms and Precedents, 1970; (with Richard Seymour) All for Fishing, 1970; contributor to Walmsley's Rural Estate Management, 6th edn, 1978; (with G. R. Williams) Farm Partnerships, 1979; (with Margaret Parrish) Essential Law for Landowners and Farmers, 1980, 2nd edn 1987; (with Richard Stratton and G. R. Williams) Share Farming, 1983, 2nd edn 1985; numerous articles, booklets, short stories. *Recreations*: fishing, ball and saloon games, music, playing saxophones. *Address*: 63 Gally Hill Road, Church Crookham, Aldershot, Hants GU13 0RU.

GREGORY, Prof. Richard Langton, DSc; FRSE 1969; Professor of Neuropsychology and Director of Brain and Perception Laboratory, University of Bristol, since 1970; *b* 24 July 1923; *s* of C. C. L. Gregory, astronomer, and Patricia (*née* Gibson); *m* 1st, 1953, Margaret Hope Pattison Muir (marr. diss. 1966); one *s* one *d*.; 2nd, 1967, Freja Mary Balchin (marr. diss. 1976). *Educ*: King Alfred Sch., Hampstead; Downing Coll., Cambridge, 1947–50. DSc Bristol, 1983. Served in RAF (Signals), 1941–46; Research, MRC Applied Psychology Research Unit, Cambridge, 1950–53; Univ. Demonstrator, then Lecturer, Dept of Psychology, Cambridge, 1953–67; Fellow, Corpus Christi Coll., Cambridge, 1962–67; Professor of Bionics, Dept of Machine Intelligence and Perception, Univ. of Edinburgh, 1967–70 (Chm. of Dept, 1968–70). Visiting Prof.: UCLA, 1963; MIT, 1964; New York Univ., 1966. Founder and Chm. Trustees, The Exploratory ("hands-on" science centre), 1983–. President: Section J, British Assoc. for Advancement of Science, 1975, and Section X, 1986; Experimental Psychol. Soc., 1981–82. Royal Instn Christmas Lectr, 1967–68. CIBA Foundn Research Prize, 1956; Craik Prize for Physiological Psychology, St John's Coll., Cambridge, 1958; Waverley Gold Medal, 1960. FRMS 1961; FZS 1972; FRSA 1973. Manager of Royal Instn, 1971–74. Founder Editor, Perception, 1972. *Publications*: Recovery from Early Blindness (with Jean Wallace), 1963; Eye and Brain, 1966, 3rd edn 1977; The Intelligent Eye, 1970; Concepts and Mechanisms of Perception, 1974; (ed jtly) Illusion in Nature and Art, 1973; Mind in Science, 1981; Odd Perceptions (essays), 1986; articles in various scientific jls and patents for optical and recording instruments and a hearing aid; radio and television appearances. *Recreations*: punning and pondering. *Address*: Brain and Perception Laboratory, Department of Anatomy, The Medical School, University Walk, Bristol BS8 1TD. *Club*: Savile.

GREGORY, Roderic Alfred, CBE 1971; FRS 1965; George Holt Professor of Physiology, University of Liverpool, 1948–81, now Emeritus Professor; *b* 29 Dec. 1913; *o c* of Alfred and Alice Gregory, West Ham, London; *m* 1939, Alice, *o c* of J. D. Watts, London; one *d*. *Educ*: George Green's Sch., London; University Coll. and Hospital, London. BSc Hons Physiology, 1934; MSc Biochemistry, 1938; MRCS, LRCP, 1939, FRCP 1977; PhD Physiology, 1942; DSc Physiology, 1949; Paul Philip Reitlinger Prize, 1938; Schafer Prize, 1939; Bayliss-Starling Scholar, 1935; Sharpey Scholar, 1936–39 and 1941–42; Rockefeller Fellow, 1939–41; Lecturer in Physiology, University Coll., London (Leatherhead), 1942–45; Senior Lecturer in Experimental Physiology, University of Liverpool, 1945–48; Mem. Biolog. Res. Bd, MRC, 1965–71, Chm. 1969; Mem., MRC, 1967–71; a Vice-Pres., Royal Soc., 1971–73. Hon. Member: Amer. Gastroenterological Assoc., 1967; British Soc. of Gastroenterology, 1974; Physiol. Soc., 1982; Amer. Physiol. Soc., 1982; For. Mem., Amer. Acad. of Arts and Sciences, 1980. Inaugural Bengt Ihre Lecture and Anniversary Medal, Swedish Med. Soc., 1963; Lectures: Purser, TCD, 1964; Waller, Univ. of London, 1966; Meml Lecture, Amer. Gastroenterolog. Assoc., 1966; Ravdin, Amer. Coll. of Surgeons, 1967; Harvey, 1968; William Mitchell Banks, Liverpool Univ., 1970; Finlayson, RCPGlas, 1970; Bayliss-Starling, Physiological Soc. of GB, 1973. Baly Medal, RCP, 1965; John Hunter Medal, RCS, 1969; Beaumont Triennial Prize, Amer. Gastroenterological Assoc., 1976; Royal Medal, Royal Soc., 1978. Fellow, University Coll., London, 1965; Feldberg Foundn Prize, 1966; Feltrinelli Internat. Prize for Medicine, Accademia Nazionale dei Lincei, Rome, 1979. Hon. DSc, Univ. of Chicago, 1966. *Publications:* Secretory Mechanisms of the Gastro-intestinal Tract, 1962; various papers in Jl Physiol., Qly Jl exp. Physiol. and elsewhere since 1935. *Recreation:* music. *Address:* University of Liverpool, PO Box 147, Liverpool L69 3BX.

GREGORY, Roland Charles Leslie; *see* Gregory, Roy.

GREGORY, Ronald, CBE 1980; QPM 1971; DL; Chief Constable of West Yorkshire Metropolitan Police, 1974–83, retired; *b* 23 Oct. 1921; *s* of Charles Henry Gregory and Mary Gregory; *m* 1942, Grace Miller Ellison; two *s*. *Educ:* Harris College. Joined Police Service, Preston, 1941. RAF (Pilot), 1942–44; RN (Pilot), 1944–46. Dep. Chief Constable, Blackpool, 1962–65; Chief Constable, Plymouth, 1965–68; Dep. Chief Constable, Devon and Cornwall, 1968–69; Chief Constable, West Yorkshire Constabulary, 1969–74. DL West Yorks, 1977. *Recreations:* golf, sailing.

GREGORY, Roy, (Roland Charles Leslie Gregory), CBE 1973; QC 1982; *b* 16 Jan. 1916; *s* of Charles James Alfred and Lilian Eugenie Gregory; *m* 1st, 1949, Olive Elizabeth (*d* 1973), *d* of late Andrew Gay; one *s*; 2nd, 1974, Charlotte, *d* of Lt-Col Peter Goddard, MBE. *Educ:* Strand Sch.; London Univ (LLB Hons). Served in Army, 1941–42. Called to Bar, Gray's Inn, 1950. First entered Civil Service, 1933; Head of Civil Procedure Br., Lord Chancellor's Office, 1966–79, retired; Consultant, 1979–82. Secretary: Austin Jones Cttee on County Court Procedure, 1947–49; Evershed Cttee on Supreme Court Practice and Procedure, 1949–53; County Court Rule Cttee, 1962–79; Matrimonial Causes Rule Cttee, 1967–79; Asst Sec., Supreme Court Rule Cttee, 1968–79; Chm., Working Party on Revision of County Court Rules, 1979–81; Mem., Expert Cttees of Council of Europe, 1978–82. *Publications:* County Court Manual, 1st edn 1946 to 4th edn 1962; editor, County Court Practice, 1950–; contribs to legal publications on civil procedure. *Recreations:* music, travel. *Address:* 36 Howard Avenue, Ewell, Surrey KT17 2QJ. *T:* 01–393 8933; 16 Ratton Garden, Ratton Drive, Eastbourne, E Sussex. *T:* Eastbourne 509716. *Club:* Royal Over-Seas League.

GREGSON, family name of **Baron Gregson.**

GREGSON, Baron *cr* 1975 (Life Peer), of Stockport in Greater Manchester; **John Gregson,** AMCT, CBIM; DL; Chairman, Fairey Nuclear Ltd, since 1983; Executive Director, Fairey Holdings Ltd, since 1978; Director: Fairey Engineering Ltd, since 1970; Fairey Hydraulics Ltd, since 1977; Manchester Industrial Centre Ltd, since 1982; Part-time Member, British Steel Corporation, since 1976; *b* 29 Jan. 1924. Joined Stockport Base Subsidiary, 1939; Fairey R&D team working on science of nuclear power, 1946; held overall responsibility for company's work on Trawsfynydd nuclear power station; appointed to Board, 1966. Mem., Hse of Lords Select Cttee on Sci. & Technol., 1980–; Pres., Parly and Scientific Cttee, 1986–; Mem., Sub-Cttee F, House of Lords Eur. Communities Cttee; Chm., Finance and Industry Gp of Labour Party, 1978–; Vice Pres., Assoc. of Metropolitan Authorities, 1984–. Pres., Defence Manufacturers Assoc., 1984– (Chm., 1980–84); Chairman: Chemical Industries EDC, 1983–; Manufg Technol. Cttee, DTI, 1983; Mem., Mech. and Elec. Engrg Requirements Bd, DTI, 1982–. Mem. Council, Univ. of Manchester Inst. of Science and Technology, 1976–. Hon. Fellow, Manchester Polytechnic, 1983; Hon. FIProdE 1982. Pres., Stockport Youth Orch.; Vice-Pres., Fedn of British Police Motor Clubs. DL Greater Manchester, 1979. *Recreations:* mountaineering, skiing. *Address:* Fairey Holdings Limited, Cranford Lane, Heston, Hounslow, Middlesex TW5 9NQ; The Hollow, Offerton Road, Stockport, Cheshire SK2 5HL; 407 Hawkins House, Dolphin Square, SW1V 3XL.

GREGSON, Maj.-Gen. Guy Patrick, CB 1958; CBE 1953; DSO 1943 and Bar 1944; MC 1942; retired as General Officer Commanding 1st Division, Salisbury Plain District (1956–59); *b* 8 April 1906; *m* 1st, Oriel Lucas Scudamore; one *s*; 2nd, Iris Crookenden; one *d*. *Educ:* Gresham's Sch., Holt; RMA. 2nd Lieut RA, 1925. Served War of 1939–45 (despatches twice, MC, DSO and Bar, Croix de Guerre); Lt-Col 1942; Brig. 1950. Korea, 1953 (CBE). Regional Dir of Civil Defence, Eastern Region, 1960–68. *Address:* Bear's Farm, Hundon, Sudbury, Suffolk. *T:* Hundon 205.

GREGSON, Peter Lewis, CB 1983; Permanent Under-Secretary of State, Department of Energy, since 1985; *b* 28 June 1936; *s* of late Walter Henry Gregson and of Lillian Margaret Gregson. *Educ:* Nottingham High Sch.; Balliol Coll., Oxford. Classical Hon. Mods, class I; Lit. Hum. class I; BA 1959, MA 1962. Nat Service, 1959–61; 2nd Lieut RAEC, attached to Sherwood Foresters. Board of Trade: Asst Principal, 1961; Private Sec. to Minister of State, 1963–65; Principal, 1965; Resident Observer, CS Selection Bd, 1966; London Business Sch., 1967; Private Sec. to the Prime Minister, 1968–72 (Parly Affairs, 1968–70; Econ. and Home Affairs, 1970–72); Asst Sec., DTI, and Sec., Industrial Development Adv. Bd, 1972–74; Under Sec., DoI, and Sec., NEB, 1975–77; Under Sec., Dept of Trade, 1977–80, Dep. Sec. (Civil Aviation and Shipping), 1980–81; Dep. Sec., Cabinet Office, 1981–85. *Recreations:* gardening, listening to music. *Address:* Department of Energy, Thames House South, Millbank, SW1P 4QJ. *T:* 01–211 4391.

GREGSON, William Derek Hadfield, CBE 1970; DL; Deputy Chairman, British Airports Authority, 1975–85; *b* 27 Jan. 1920; *s* of William Gregson; *m* 1944, Rosalind Helen Reeves; three *s* one *d*. *Educ:* King William's Coll., IoM; Alpine Coll., Villars; Faraday House Engrg College. DFH, CEng, FIEE, CBIM, FIIM. Served with RAF, NW Europe, 1941–45 (Sqdn Ldr); Techn. Sales Man., Ferranti Ltd, Edinburgh, 1946–51, London Man., 1951–59; Asst Gen. Man., Ferranti (Scotland) Ltd, 1959–83; Director: Ferranti El, New York, 1969–83; Ferranti Hldgs, 1983–85. Director: British Telecom Scotland (formerly Scottish Telecommunications Bd), 1977–85; Anderson Strathclyde plc, 1978–; Brammer plc, 1983–; East of Scotland Industrial Investments plc, 1980–; Consultant to ICI, 1984–. Chm., Scottish Gen. Practitioners Res. Support Unit, 1971–79; Dep. Chm., Scottish Council (Develt and Industry), 1982– (Dir, 1974–); Mem. Council: Electronic Engrg Assoc. 1959–83 (Pres. 1963–64); Soc. of British Aerospace Companies, 1966–83 (Chm. Equipment Gp Cttee 1967); BIM, 1975–80. BEAMA: Chm. Industrial Control and Electronics Bd 1964; Mem. Council, 1970–; Chm., Measurement, Control and Automation Conference Bd, 1973; Dep. Pres., 1982–83; Pres., 1983–85. Member: BIM Adv. Bd for Scotland, 1969–85 (Chm., 1970–75); Electronics EDC, 1965–75; Bd of Livingston New Town, 1968–76; Jt BIM/NEDO Prof. Management Adv. Cttee on Indust. Strategy, 1976–78; Management Assoc. of SE Scotland, 1977– (Chm., 1980–81); Scottish Econ. Planning Council, 1965–71; Machine Tool Expert Cttee, 1969–70; Scottish Design Council, 1974–81; Design Council, 1980–85; CBI (Mem., Scottish Council, 1977–81); Bd, BSI, 1985; Edinburgh Chamber of Commerce, 1975–83. Commissioner, Northern Lighthouse Bd, 1975– (Chm., 1979). Dir, Scottish Nat. Orch., 1977–85 (Vice-Chm., 1981–84; Chm., 1984–85). DL City of Edinburgh, 1984–. FRSA. *Recreations:* reading, cabinet-making, automation in the home. *Address:* 15 Barnton Avenue, Edinburgh EH4 6AJ. *T:* 031–336 3896. *Clubs:* Royal Air Force; New (Edinburgh).

GREIG, (Henry Louis) Carron, CVO 1973; CBE 1986; Chairman, H. Clarkson (Holdings) plc, since 1976; Director: James Purdey & Sons Ltd, since 1972; Royal Bank of Scotland, since 1985; Gentleman Usher to the Queen, since 1961; *b* 21 Feb. 1925; *s* of late Group Captain Sir Louis Greig, KBE, CVO, DL; *m* 1955, Monica Kathleen, *d* of Hon. J. J. Stourton, *qv*; three *s* one *d*. *Educ:* Eton. Scots Guards, 1943–47, Captain. Joined H. Clarkson & Co. Ltd, 1948; Dir, 1954; Man. Dir, 1962; Chairman: H. Clarkson & Co. Ltd, 1973–85; Baltic Exchange (formerly Baltic Mercantile and Shipping Exchange), 1983–85 (Dir, 1978–85); Dir, Williams & Glyn's Bank, 1983–85. Vice-Chm., Not Forgotten Assoc., 1979–. *Address:* Brook House, Fleet, Hants; Binsness, Forres, Moray. *Clubs:* White's; Royal Findhorn Yacht.

GREIG, Prof. James, MSc (London), PhD (Birmingham), William Siemens Professor of Electrical Engineering, University of London, King's College, 1945–70, now Emeritus Professor; *b* 24 April 1903; *s* of James Alexander Greig and Helen Bruce Meldrum, Edinburgh; *m* 1931, Ethel May, *d* of William Archibald, Edinburgh; one *d*. *Educ:* George Watson's Coll. and Heriot-Watt Coll., Edinburgh; University Coll., University of London. Experience in telephone engineering with Bell Telephone Company, Montreal, 1924–26; Mem. research staff, General Electric Company, London, 1928–33; Asst lectr, University Coll., London, 1933–36; Lectr, Univ. of Birmingham, 1936–39; Head of Dept of Electrical Engineering, Northampton Polytechnic, 1939–45. FIEE (Chm. Measurement Section, 1949–50; Mem. Council, 1955–58); Dean of the Faculty of Engineering, Univ. of London, 1958–62, and Mem. Senate, 1958–70; Mem. Court, Univ. of London, 1967–70. MRI; Fellow Heriot-Watt Coll., 1951; FRSE 1956; FKC 1963. Mem., British Assoc. for the Advancement of Science. Chm., Crail Preservation Soc., 1959–74. *Publications:* papers (dealing mainly with subject of electrical and magnetic measurements) to: Jl Inst. Electrical Engineers, The Wireless Engineer, and Engineering. *Address:* Inch of Kinnordy, Kirriemuir, Angus. *T:* Kirriemuir 72350. *Club:* Athenæum.

GREIG of Eccles, James Dennis, CMG 1967; commodity and financial futures trader and company director; *b* 1926; *o s* of late Dennis George Greig of Eccles and Florence Aileen Marjoribanks; *m* 1st, 1952, Pamela Marguerite Stock (marr. diss., 1960); one *s* one *d*; 2nd, 1960 (marr. diss., 1967); one *s*; 3rd, 1968, Paula Mary Sterling. *Educ:* Winchester Coll.; Clare Coll., Cambridge; London Sch. of Economics. Military Service (Lieut, The Black Watch, seconded to Nigeria Regt), 1944–47. HMOCS: Administrative Officer, Northern Nigeria, 1949–55; Fedn of Nigeria, 1955–59; Dep. Financial Sec. (Economics), Mauritius, 1960–64; Financial Secretary, Mauritius, 1964–67; retired voluntarily on Mauritius achieving internal self-government, 1967. With Booker Bros. (Liverpool) Ltd, 1967–68; Head of Africa and Middle East Bureau, IPPF, 1968–76; Dir, Population Bureau, ODA, 1976–80. *Recreations:* rough shooting, bowls, gardening, bridge. *Address:* 6 Beverley Close, Barnes, SW13. *T:* 01–876 5354; The Braw Bothy, Eccles, Kelso, Roxburghshire. *Club:* Hurlingham.

GRENFELL, family name of **Baron Grenfell.**

GRENFELL, 3rd Baron *cr* 1902; **Julian Pascoe Francis St Leger Grenfell;** Special Adviser, World Bank, since 1983; *b* 23 May 1935; *o s* of 2nd Baron Grenfell, CBE, TD, and of Elizabeth Sarah Polk, *o d* of late Captain Hon. Alfred Shaughnessy, Montreal, Canada; *S* father, 1976; *m* 1st, 1961, Loretta Maria (marr. diss. 1970), *e d* of Alfredo Reali, Florence, Italy; one *d*; 2nd, 1970, Gabrielle Katharina, *o d* of late Dr Ernst Raab, Berlin, Germany; two *d*. *Educ:* Eton; King's Coll., Cambridge. BA (Hons), President of the Union, Cambridge, 1959. 2 Lieut, KRRC (60th Rifles), 1954–56; Captain, Queen's Royal Rifles, TA, 1963; Programme Asst, ATV Ltd, 1960–61; frequent appearances and occasional scripts, for ATV religious broadcasting and current affairs series, 1960–64. Film and TV adviser, Encyclopaedia Britannica Ltd, 1961–64. Joined World Bank, Washington, DC, 1965; Chief of Information and Public Affairs for World Bank Group in Europe, 1970; Dep. Dir, European Office of the World Bank, 1973; Special rep. of World Bank to UN, 1974–81. *Publication:* (novel) Margot, 1984. *Recreations:* walking, diplomatic history, wine tasting. *Heir: cousin* Francis Pascoe John Grenfell [*b* 28 Feb. 1938; *m* 1977, Elizabeth Katharine, *d* of Hugh Kenyon]. *Address:* c/o World Bank, 1818 H Street NW, Washington, DC 20433, USA. *T:* (202) 477 8843. *Clubs:* Travellers', Royal Green Jackets.

GRENFELL, Andrée, (Mrs Roy Warden); President, Glemby International, UK and Europe, 1976–80; Senior Vice President, Glemby International, USA, 1976–80; Non-Executive Director, NAAFI, since 1981; *b* 14 Jan. 1940; *d* of Stephen Grenfell (writer) and Sybil Grenfell; *m* 1972, Roy Warden; two step *s*. *Educ:* privately. Man. Dir, Elizabeth Arden Ltd, UK, 1974–76; Director: Harvey Nichols Knightsbridge, 1972–74; Peter Robinson Ltd, 1968–72. Mem. Council, Inst. of Dirs, 1976; FBIM 1977. *Recreations:* riding, dressage, swimming, yoga. *Address:* Crown Cottage, Little Missenden, Amersham, Bucks.

GRENFELL, Simon Pascoe; a Recorder of the Crown Court, since 1985; *b* 10 July 1942; *s* of Osborne Pascoe Grenfell and Margaret Grenfell; *m* 1974, Ruth De Jersey Harvard; one *s* three *d*. *Educ:* Fettes College; Emmanuel College, Cambridge (MA). Called to the Bar, Gray's Inn, 1965; practice on NE Circuit. *Recreations:* music, sailing, coarse gardening. *Address:* St John's House, Sharow, Ripon, North Yorks HG4 5BN. *T:* Ripon 5771. *Clubs:* Special Forces; Ripon.

GRENFELL-BAINES, Prof. Sir George, Kt 1978; OBE 1960; DL; FRIBA; FRTPI; consultant architect-planner; consultant to Building Design Partnership; *b* Preston, 30 April 1908; *s* of Ernest Charles Baines and Sarah Elizabeth (*née* Grenfell); *m* 1st, 1939, Dorothy Hodson (marr. diss. 1952); two *d*; 2nd, 1954, Milena Ruth Fleischmann; one *s* one *d*. *Educ:* Roebuck Street Council Sch.; Harris Coll., Preston; Manchester Univ. (DipTP). RIBA Dist Town Planning, 1963. Commenced architectural practice, 1937; founded: Grenfell Baines Gp, 1940; Building Design Partnership, a multi-disciplinary practice covering all aspects of built environment, 1959 (Partner/Chm.), retired 1974; The Design Teaching Practice, 1974, retired 1979. Prof. and Head of Dept of Architecture, Univ. of Sheffield, 1972–75, Emeritus, 1976. Lectr/Critic, 14 USA and Canadian univs, 1966; initiated own lecture tour USSR, visiting 19 cities, 1971; expert adviser: UNESCO Conf. Bldgs; Higher Educn, Chile, 1968; Conescal, Mexico City, 1973. RIBA: Mem. Council (nationally elected), 1952–70; Vice-Pres., 1967–69; Ext. Examr, 12 Schs of Architecture, 1953–70. Chm. of Cttees on Professional Practice, Town Planning, Gp Practice and Consortia; Architectural Competition Assessor 8 times; competition entrant, several awards: first place in 7 (one internat.); 18 premiums (four internat.). Hon. Fellow: Manchester Polytechnic, 1974; Lancashire Polytechnic, 1985; Hon. Vice-Pres., N Lancs Soc. Architects, 1977. Hon. Fellow, Amer. Inst. of Architects, 1982. Broadcaster, UK and Canada. Hon. DLitt Sheffield, 1981. DL Lancs, 1982. *Publications:* contribs to tech. jls. *Recreations:* brooding: on economics and alternative medicine; walking: on hills and by sea-shore. *Address:* 56 & 60 West Cliff, Preston, Lancs PR1 8HU. *T:* Preston 55824, 555824.

GRENIER, Rear-Adm. Peter Francis, (Frank); Chief of Staff to C-in-C Naval Home Command, since 1985; *b* 27 Aug. 1934; *s* of late Dr F. W. H. Grenier and Mrs M. Grenier; *m* 1957, Jane Susan Bradshaw; two *s* one *d* (and one *s* decd). *Educ:* Montpelier School, Paignton; Blundell's School, Tiverton. Entered RN (Special Entry), 1952; Midshipman, Mediterranean Fleet, 1953; commissioned, 1955; joined Submarine service, 1956; 1st command (HMS Ambush), 1965; final command (HMS Liverpool), 1982. Chairman: Royal Naval FA, 1987–; Combined Services FA, 1987–. Liveryman, Painter-

Stainers' Co., 1984. *Recreations:* family, sketching and painting, glass engraving, golf. *Address:* Keyford, Upton Scudamore, near Warminster, Wilts BA12 0AQ. *T:* Warminster 215401. *Clubs:* Army and Navy; West Wilts Golf.

GRENSIDE, Sir John (Peter), Kt 1983; CBE 1974; Senior Partner, Peat, Marwick, Mitchell & Co., Chartered Accountants, 1977–Sept. 1986; *b* 23 Jan. 1921; *s* of late Harold Cutcliffe Grenside and late Muriel Grenside; *m* 1946, Yvonne Thérèse Grau; one *s* one *d*. *Educ:* Rugby School. ACA 1948, FCA 1960. War Service, Royal Artillery, 1941–46 (Captain). Joined Peat, Marwick, Mitchell & Co., 1948, Partner, 1960, Senior Partner, 1977. Inst. Chartered Accountants: Mem. Council, 1966–83; Chm. of Parliamentary and Law Cttee, 1972–73; Vice-Pres., 1973–74; Dep. Pres., 1974–75; Pres., 1975–76; Chm., Overseas Relations Cttee, 1976–78; UK Rep. on Internat. Accounting Standards Cttee, 1976–80. Jt Vice-Pres., Groupe d'Etudes des Experts Comptables de la CEE, 1972–75; Chm., Review Bd for Govt Contracts, 1983–86; Mem. Panel of Judges for Accountants' Award for Company Accounts, 1973–77. *Publications:* various articles for UK and US accountancy jls. *Recreations:* tennis, bridge, travel. *Address:* 51 Cadogan Lane, SW1. *T:* 01–235 3372. *Clubs:* Athenæum, MCC, All England Lawn Tennis, Queens', Hurlingham.

GRENVILLE; see Freeman-Grenville.

GRENVILLE, Prof. John Ashley Soames; Professor of Modern History, University of Birmingham, since 1969; *b* Berlin, 11 Jan. 1928; *m* 1st, 1960, Betty Anne Rosenberg (*d* 1974), New York; three *s*; 2nd, 1975, Patricia Carnie; one *d* one step *d*. *Educ:* Mistley Place and Orwell Park Prep. Sch.; Cambridge Techn. Sch.; corresp. courses; Birkbeck Coll.; LSE; Yale Univ. BA, PhD London; FRHistS. Postgrad. Schol., London Univ., 1951–53; Asst Lectr, subseq. Lectr, Nottingham Univ., 1953–64; Commonwealth Fund Fellow, 1958–59; Postdoctoral Fellow, Yale Univ., 1960–63; Reader in Modern History, Nottingham Univ., 1964–65; Prof. of Internat. History, Leeds Univ., 1965–69. Vis. Prof., Queen's Coll., NY City Univ., 1964, etc; Guest Professor, Univ. of Hamburg, 1980. Chm., British Univs History Film Consortium, 1968–71; Mem. Council: RHistS, 1971–73; List and Index Soc., 1966–71; Baeck Inst., London, 1981–. Consultant, American and European Bibliographical Centre, Oxford and California and Clio Press, 1960–; Dir of Film for the Historical Assoc., 1975–78; Historical Adviser, The World of the Thirties, German Television (channel ZDF), 1982–86. Editor, Fontana History of War and Society, 1969–78. *Publications:* (with J. G. Fuller) The Coming of the Europeans, 1962; Lord Salisbury and Foreign Policy, 1964 (2nd edn 1970); (with G. B. Young) Politics, Strategy and American Diplomacy: studies in foreign policy 1873–1917, 1966 (2nd edn 1971); Documentary Films (with N. Pronay), The Munich Crisis, 1968; The End of Illusions: from Munich to Dunkirk, 1970; The Major International Treaties 1914–1973: a history and guide, 1974; Europe Reshaped 1848–78, 1975; Nazi Germany, 1976; World History of the Twentieth Century I, 1900–1945, 1980; contrib. various learned jls. *Recreation:* listening to music. *Address:* University of Birmingham, PO Box 363, Birmingham B15 2TT. *Club:* Athenæum.

GRENVILLE-GREY, Wilfrid Ernest; Secretary for Public Affairs to Archbishop of Canterbury, since 1984; *b* 27 May 1930; *s* of late Col Cecil Grenville-Grey, CBE and of Monica Grenville-Grey (*née* Morrison-Bell); *m* 1963, Edith Sibongile Dlamini, *d* of Rev. Jonathan Dlamini, Johannesburg; two *s* one *d*. *Educ:* Eton; Worcester College, Oxford (scholar; MA); Yale University (Henry Fellow, 1953–54). 2nd Lieut, KRRC, 1949–50. Overseas Civil Service, Nyasaland, 1956–59; Booker McConnell Ltd, 1960–63; Mindolo Ecumenical Foundn, Zambia, 1963–71 (Dir, 1966–71); Sec., Univ. Study Project on Foreign Investments in S Africa, 1971–72; Dir, Centre for Internat. Briefing, Farnham Castle, 1973–77; Internat. Defence and Aid Fund for Southern Africa, London and UN, 1978–83. *Publication:* All in an African Lifetime, 1969. *Recreations:* golf, gardening. *Address:* Losehyll House, Dippenhall, Farnham, Surrey. *T:* Farnham 713482. *Club:* Travellers'.

GRENYER, Herbert Charles, FRICS; Vice-President, London Rent Assessment Panel, 1973–79; Deputy Chief Valuer, Board of Inland Revenue, 1968–73; *b* 22 Jan. 1913; *s* of Harry John and Daisy Elizabeth Grenyer (*née* De Maid); *m* 1940, Jean Gladwell Francis; one *s* one *d*. *Recreations:* golf, gardening, listening to music. *Address:* Old Rickford, Worplesdon, Surrey. *T:* Worplesdon 232173.

GRESWELL, Air Cdre Jeaffreson Herbert, CB 1967; CBE 1962 (OBE 1946); DSO 1944; DFC 1942; RAF, retired; *b* 28 July 1916; *s* of William Territt Greswell; *m* 1939, Gwyneth Alice Hayes; one *s* three *d*. *Educ:* Repton. Joined RAF, 1935, Pilot. Served War of 1939–45, in Coastal Command, Anti-Submarine No. 217 Sqdn, 1937–41; No. 172 Sqdn, 1942; OC No. 179 Sqdn, Gibraltar, 1943–44. Air Liaison Officer, Pacific Fleet, 1946–47; Staff of Joint Anti-Submarine Sch., 1949–52; Staff of Flying Coll., Manby, 1952–54; Planning Staff, Min. of Defence, 1954–57; OC, RAF Station Kinloss, 1957–59; Plans HQ, Coastal Comd, 1959–61; Standing Group Rep. to NATO Council, Paris, 1961–64; Commandant, Royal Observer Corps, 1964–68. Sqdn Ldr 1941; Wing Comdr 1942; Gp Capt. 1955; Air Cdre 1961. *Recreation:* croquet. *Address:* Picket Lodge, Ringwood, Hants.

GRETTON, family name of **Baron Gretton.**

GRETTON, 3rd Baron *cr* 1944, of Stapleford; **John Henrik Gretton;** farmer; *b* 9 Feb. 1941; *s* of 2nd Baron Gretton and of Margaret, *e d* of Captain Henrik Loeffler; *S* father, 1982; *m* 1970, Jennifer Ann, *o d* of Edmund Moore, York; one *s* one *d*. *Educ:* Shrewsbury. Career in malting and brewing, 1961–74. *Recreations:* travel, miniature railways, reading, music. *Heir:* *s* Hon. John Lysander Gretton, *b* 17 April 1975. *Address:* Holygate Farm, Stapleford, Melton Mowbray, Leics. *T:* Wymondham 540.

GRETTON, Vice-Adm. Sir Peter (William), KCB 1963 (CB 1960); DSO 1942; OBE 1941; DSC 1936; MA; *b* 27 Aug. 1912; *s* of Major G. F. Gretton; *m* 1943, D. N. G. Du Vivier; three *s* one *d*. *Educ:* Roper's Preparatory Sch.; RNC, Dartmouth. Prize for Five First Class Certificates as Sub.-Lieut; Comdr 1942; Capt. 1948; Rear-Adm. 1958; Vice-Adm. 1961. Served War of 1939–45 (despatches, OBE, DSO and two Bars). Senior Naval Mem. of Directing Staff of Imperial Defence Coll., April 1958–60; Flag Officer, Sea Training, 1960–61; a Lord Commissioner of the Admiralty, Dep. Chief of Naval Staff and Fifth Sea Lord, 1962–63, retd. Domestic Bursar, University Coll., Oxford, 1965–71, Senior Research Fellow, 1971–79. Vice-Pres., Royal Humane Soc. (Testimonial of Royal Humane Society, 1940). *Publications:* Convoy Escort Commander, 1964; Maritime Strategy: A Study of British Defence Problems, 1965; Former Naval Person: Churchill and the Navy, 1968; Crisis Convoy, 1974. *Address:* 29 Northmoor Road, Oxford. *Club:* Army and Navy.

GREVE, Prof. John; Professor of Social Policy and Administration, University of Leeds, since 1974; *b* 23 Nov. 1927; *s* of Steffen A. and Ellen C. Greve; *m* Stella (*née* Honeywood); one *s* one *d*. *Educ:* elementary and secondary Schs in Cardiff; London Sch. of Economics (BSc(Econ)). Various jobs, incl. Merchant Navy, Youth Employment Service, and insurance, 1946–55; student, 1955–58; research work, then Univ. teaching, 1958–. Has worked in Norway at research institutes. Community Programmes Dept, Home Office, 1969–74; Prof. of Social Admin, Univ. of Southampton, 1969–74. Mem., Royal Commn

on Distribution of Income and Wealth, 1974–79. *Publications:* The Housing Problem, 1961 (and 1969); London's Homeless, 1964; Private Landlords in England, 1965; (with others) Comparative Social Administration, 1969, 2nd edn 1972; Housing, Planning and Change in Norway, 1970; Voluntary Housing in Scandinavia, 1971; (with others) Homelessness in London, 1971; Low Incomes in Sweden, 1978; (jtly) Sheltered Housing for the Elderly, 1983; various articles and papers, mainly on social problems, policies and administration, a few short stories. *Recreations:* walking, painting, listening to music, writing, good company. *Address:* c/o Department of Social Policy and Health Services Studies, University of Leeds, Leeds LS2 9JT.

GREVILLE, family name of **Baron Greville,** and of **Earl of Warwick.**

GREVILLE, 4th Baron, *cr* 1869; **Ronald Charles Fulke Greville;** *b* 11 April 1912; *s* of 3rd Baron and Olive Grace (*d* 1959), *d* of J. W. Grace, Leybourne Grange, Kent, and widow of Henry Kerr; *S* father 1952. *Educ:* Eton; Magdalen Coll., Oxford Univ. *Recreations:* music, travel, tennis, gardening, swimming. *Heir:* none. *Address:* 75 Swan Court, Chelsea Manor Street, SW3. *T:* 01–352 3444; Lionsmead House, Shalbourne, near Marlborough, Wilts. *T:* Marlborough 870440. *Club:* Hurlingham.

GREVILLE, Brig. Phillip Jamieson, CBE 1972; Defence Writer for Adelaide Advertiser, since 1980; Director, Dominant Australia Pty, since 1982; *b* 12 Sept. 1925; *s* of Col S. J. Greville, OBE and Mrs D. M. Greville; *m* 1948, June Patricia Anne Martin; two *s* one *d* (and one *s* one *d* decd). *Educ:* RMC Duntroon; Sydney Univ. (BEng). 2/8 Field Co., 2nd AIF, New Guinea, 1945; 1 RAR Korea (POW), 1951–53; Senior Instructor SME Casula, 1953–55; CRE, RMC Duntroon, 1955–58; Staff Coll., Camberley and Transportation Trng UK, 1959–61; Dir of Transportation AHQ, 1962–65; GSO1 1st Div., 1966; CE Eastern Comd, 1969–71; Comdr 1st Australian Logistic Support Group, Vietnam, 1971; Actg Comdr 1st Australian Task Force, Vietnam, 1971–72 (CBE); Dir of Transport, 1973–74; Dir Gen., Logistics, 1975–76; Comdr, Fourth Mil. District, 1977–80, retired. Nat. Pres., RUSI of Aust., 1983–. FIE Aust, FCIT. *Publications:* A Short History of Victoria Barracks Paddington, 1969; The Central Organisation for War and its Application to Movements, 1975, Sapper series (RE Officers in Australia); The Army Portion of the National Estate, 1977. *Recreation:* golf. *Address:* 68 Fourth Avenue, St Peters, SA 5069, Australia. *Clubs:* Adelaide; Naval, Military and Air Force (Adelaide); Royal Sydney Golf; Royal Adelaide Golf.

GREY, family name of **Earl Grey,** and of **Baron Grey of Naunton.**

GREY; see De Grey.

GREY, 6th Earl, *cr* 1806; **Richard Fleming George Charles Grey;** Bt 1746; Baron Grey, 1801; Viscount Howick, 1806; *b* 5 March 1939; *s* of late Albert Harry George Campbell Grey (Trooper, Canadian Army Tanks, who *d* on active service, 1942) and Vera Helen Louise Harding; *S* cousin, 1963; *m* 1st, 1966, Margaret Ann (marr. diss. 1974), *e d* of Henry Bradford, Ashburton; 2nd, 1974, Stephanie Caroline, *o d* of Donald Gaskell-Brown and formerly wife of Surg.-Comdr Neil Leicester Denham, RN. *Educ:* Hounslow Coll.; Hammersmith Coll. of Bldg (Quantity Surveying). Pres., Assoc. of Cost and Executive Accountants, 1978. Mem., Liberal Party. *Recreations:* golf, sailing. *Heir:* *b* Philip Kent Grey [*b* 11 May 1940; *m* 1968, Ann Catherine, *y d* of Cecil Applegate, Kingsbridge, Devon; one *s* one *d*]. *Address:* House of Lords, SW1.

GREY OF NAUNTON, Baron, *cr* 1968 (Life Peer); **Ralph Francis Alnwick Grey,** GCMG 1964 (KCMG 1959, CMG 1955); GCVO 1973 (KCVO 1956); OBE 1951; Chancellor, University of Ulster, since 1984 (New University of Ulster, 1980–84); *b* 15 April 1910; *o s* of late Francis Arthur Grey and Mary Wilkie Grey (*née* Spence); *m* 1944, Esmé, CStJ, widow of Pilot Officer Kenneth Kirkcaldie, RAFVR, and *d* of late A. V. Burcher and Florence Burcher, Remuera, Auckland, New Zealand; two *s* one *d*. *Educ:* Wellington Coll., NZ; Auckland Univ. Coll.; Pembroke Coll., Cambridge. LLB (NZ). Barrister and Solicitor of Supreme Court of New Zealand, 1932; Associate to Hon. Mr Justice Smith, 1932–36; Probationer, Colonial Administrative Service, 1936; Administrative Service, Nigeria: Cadet, 1937; Asst Financial Sec., 1949; Administrative Officer, Class I, 1951; Development Sec., 1952; Sec. to Governor-Gen. and Council of Ministers, 1954; Chief Sec. of the Federation, 1955–57; Dep. Gov.-Gen., 1957–59; Gov. and C-in-C, British Guiana, 1959–64; Governor and C-in-C of The Bahamas, 1964–68, and of the Turks and Caicos Islands, 1965–68; Governor of N Ireland, 1968–73. Dep. Chm., Commonwealth Development Corp., 1973–79, Chm. 1979–80. Pres., Chartered Inst. of Secretaries, NI, 1970–; Hon. Life Mem., NI Chamber of Commerce and Industry, 1970; Hon. Pres., Lisburn Chamber of Commerce, 1972. Mem., Bristol Regional Bd, Lloyds Bank Ltd, 1973–81; Chm., Central Council, Royal Over-Seas League, 1976–81, Pres., 1981–. President: Scout Council, NI, 1968–; Britain–Nigeria Assoc., 1983–; Overseas Service Pensioners' Assoc., 1983–. Mem. Council, Cheltenham Ladies' College, 1975–86. Hon. Bencher, Inn of Court of N Ireland. Hon. Freeman: City of Belfast, 1972; Lisburn, 1975; Freeman, City of London, 1980. Hon. LLD: QUB, 1971; NUI, 1985; Hon. DLitt NUU, 1980; Hon. DSc Ulster, 1985. GCStJ. Kt Comdr, Commandery of Ards, 1968–76. Bailiff of Egle. *Recreation:* golf. *Address:* Overbrook, Naunton, near Cheltenham, Glos. *T:* Guiting Power 263. *Club:* Travellers'.

GREY, Alan Hartley; HM Diplomatic Service, retired; re-employed in Foreign and Commonwealth Office (as Staff Assessor), since 1985; *b* 26 June 1925; *s* of William Hartley Grey and Gladys Grey; *m* 1950, Joan Robinson (*d* 1985); one *s* one *d*. *Educ:* Bootle Secondary Sch. for Boys. RAF, 1943–48; Foreign Service (Br. B), 1948; Tel Aviv, 1949; Tabriz and Khorramshahr, 1950–52; 3rd Sec., Belgrade, 1952–54; Vice-Consul, Dakar, 1954–57; Second Sec. (Commercial), Helsinki, 1958–61; FO, 1961–64; Second Sec. (Econ.), Paris, 1964–66; FO (later FCO), 1966–70; Consul (Commercial), Lille, 1970–74; FCO, 1974–82; Ambassador at Libreville, 1982–84. *Recreations:* gardening, Civil Service trade unionism. *Address:* c/o Foreign and Commonwealth Office, SW1A 2AH.

GREY, Sir Anthony (Dysart), 7th Bt *cr* 1814; Inspector, Department of Industrial Affairs, Government of Western Australia; *b* 19 Oct. 1949; *s* of Edward Elton Grey (*d* 1962) (*o s* of 6th Bt) and of Nancy, *d* of late Francis John Meagher, Perth, WA; *S* grandfather, 1974; *m* 1970. *Educ:* Guildford Grammar School, WA. *Recreations:* fishing, painting. *Address:* 41A View Street, Peppermint Grove, WA 6011, Australia.

GREY, Beryl, (Mrs S. G. Svenson), CBE 1973; Prima Ballerina, Sadler's Wells Ballet, now Royal Ballet, 1942–57; Artistic Director, London Festival Ballet, 1968–79; *b* London, 11 June 1927; *d* of late Arthur Ernest Groom; *m* 1950, Dr Sven Gustav Svenson; one *s*. *Educ:* Dame Alice Owens Girls' Sch., London. Professional training: Madeline Sharp Sch., Sadler's Wells Sch. (Schol.), de Vos Sch. Début Sadler's Wells Co., 1941, with Ballerina rôles following same year in Les Sylphides, The Gods Go A'Begging, Le Lac des Cygnes, Act II, Comus. First full-length ballet, Le Lac des Cygnes on 15th birthday, 1942. Has appeared since in leading rôles of many ballets including: Sleeping Beauty, Giselle, Sylvia, Checkmate, Ballet Imperial, Donald of the Burthens, Homage, Birthday Offering, The Lady and the Fool. Film: The Black Swan (3 Dimensional Ballet Film), 1952. Left Royal Ballet, Covent Garden, Spring 1957, to become free-lance ballerina. Regular guest appearances with Royal Ballet at Covent Garden and on European, African, American and Far Eastern Tours. Guest Artist, London's Festival Ballet in London and abroad, 1958–64. First Western ballerina to appear with Bolshoi Ballet: Moscow, Leningrad, Kiev, Tiflis, 1957–58; First Western ballerina to dance with Chinese Ballet Co. in Peking and Shanghai, 1964. Engagements and tours abroad include: Central and S America, Mexico, Rhodesia and S Africa, Canada, NZ, Lebanon, Germany, Norway, Sweden, Denmark, Finland, Belgium, Holland, France, Switzerland, Italy, Portugal, Austria, Czechoslovakia, Poland, Rumania: Producer: Giselle, Western Australia Ballet, 1984; Sleeping Beauty, Royal Swedish Co., Stockholm, 1985. Regular television and broadcasts in England and abroad; concert narrator. Dir-Gen., Arts Educational Trust, 1966–68. Pres., Dance Council of Wales, 1981–; Vice-Pres., Royal Acad. of Dancing, 1980– (Exec. Mem., 1982–); Chm., Imperial Soc. of Teachers of Dancing, 1984– (Mem. Council, 1966); Trustee: London City Ballet, 1978–; Adeline Genée Theatre, 1982–; Royal Ballet Benevolent Fund, 1982–; Dance Teachers Benevolent Fund, 1981–; Vice-President: Keep Fit Assoc., 1968–; British Fedn of Music Festivals, 1985. Governor: Dame Alice Owens Girls' Sch., London, 1960–77; Frances Mary Buss Foundn, 1963–72. Hon. DMus Leicester, 1970; Hon. DLitt City Univ., 1974. Publications: Red Curtain Up, 1958; Through the Bamboo Curtain, 1965; My Favourite Ballet Stories, 1981. Relevant publications: biographical studies (by Gordon Anthony), 1952, (by Pigeon Crowle), 1952; Beryl Grey, Dancers of Today (by Hugh Fisher), 1955; Beryl Grey, a biography (by David Gillard), 1977. Recreations: music, painting, reading, swimming. Address: Fernhill, Priory Road, Forest Row, Sussex. T: Forest Row 2539.

GREY, Charles Frederick, CBE 1966; miner; Independent Methodist Minister; b 25 March 1903; m 1925, Margaret, d of James Aspey. Mem. of Divisional Labour Exec. MP (Lab) Durham, 1945–70; Opposition Whip (Northern), 1962–64; Comptroller of HM Household, 1964–66, Treasurer, 1966–69. President: Independent Methodist Connexion, 1971; Sunderland and District Free Church Council; Mem., Univ. of Durham Council. Freeman of Durham City, 1971. Hon. DCL Durham, 1976. Address: 38 Gelt Crescent, Lyons Avenue, Hetton-le-Hole, Tyne and Wear DH5 0HX. T: Hetton-le-Hole 2292.

GREY, John Egerton, CB 1980; Clerk Assistant and Clerk of Public Bills, House of Lords, since 1974; b 8 Feb. 1929; s of late John and Nancy Grey; m 1961, Patricia Hanna; two adopted s. Educ: Dragon Sch., Oxford; Blundell's; Brasenose Coll., Oxford. MA, BCL. Called to Bar, Inner Temple, 1954; practised at Chancery Bar, 1954–59. Clerk in Parliament Office, House of Lords, 1959–. Recreation: gardening. Address: 8 Baird Gardens, Dulwich Wood Park, SE19 1HJ. T: 01–670 7819. Club: Arts.

GREY, Maj.-Gen. John St John; Royal Marines Chief of Staff, since 1987; b 6 June 1934; s of late Major Donald John Grey, RM and Doris Mary Grey (née Beavan); m 1958, Elisabeth Ann (née Langley); one s one d. Educ: Christ's Hospital. rcds, ndc, psc(M), osc(US). FBIM. Commissioned 2/Lt 1952; Commando service, Malta, Egypt, Cyprus, 1955–58; Support Co. Comdr, 43 Cdo RM, 1962–64; Cruiser HMS Lion as OC RM, 1964–65; Instructor, Army Sch. of Infantry, 1967–69; Rifle Co. Comdr, 41 Cdo RM (incl. 1st emergency tour in W Belfast), 1969–70; with US Marine Corps, 1970–71; Commanded 45 Cdo Gp (incl. tours in N Ireland and Arctic Norway), 1976–78; Mil. Sec. and Col Ops/Plans, MoD, 1979–84; Maj.-Gen. RM Commando Forces, 1984–87. Recreation: sailing. Address: c/o Lloyds Bank, 4 Regent Street, Teignmouth, S Devon TQ14 8SL. Clubs: Army and Navy; Hurlingham; Royal Naval Sailing Association (Portsmouth); Royal Western Yacht (Plymouth); Royal Marines Sailing (Cdre, 1986–).

GREY, Sir Paul (Francis), KCMG 1963 (CMG 1951); b 2 Dec. 1908; s of Lt-Col Arthur Grey, CIE, and Teresa (née Alleyne); m 1936, Agnes Mary, d of late Richard Weld-Blundell, Ince-Blundell Hall, Lancs; three s. Educ: Charterhouse; Christ Church, Oxford. Entered Diplomatic Service, 1933; served in Rome, 1935; Foreign Office, 1939; Rio de Janeiro, 1944; The Hague, 1945; Counsellor, Lisbon, 1949; Minister, British Embassy, Moscow, 1951–54; Assistant Under Sec., Foreign Office, Sept. 1954–57; HM Ambassador to Czechoslovakia, 1957–60; HM Ambassador to Switzerland, 1960–64. Recreations: shooting and fishing. Address: Holm Wood, Elstead, Godalming, Surrey.

GREY, Robin Douglas, QC 1979; a Recorder of the Crown Court, since 1979; b 23 May 1931; s of Dr Francis Temple Grey, MA, MB, and Eglantine Grey; m 1972, Berenice Anna Wheatley; one s one d. Educ: Summer Fields Prep. Sch., Oxford; Eastbourne Coll.; London Univ. (LLB Hons). Called to the Bar, Gray's Inn, 1957. Crown Counsel, Colonial Legal Service, Aden, 1959–63 (Actg Registrar Gen. and Actg Attorney Gen. for short periods); practising barrister, 1963–; Dep. Circuit Judge, 1977. Mem., British Acad. of Forensic Sciences. Recreations: tennis, golf, fishing, conversation. Address: Queen Elizabeth Building, Temple EC4Y 9BS. T: 01–583 5766; Court Farm, Worminghall, Bucks HP18 9LD. T: Ickford 694. Club: Hurlingham.

GREY, Wilfrid Ernest G.; see Grenville-Grey.

GREY EGERTON, Sir (Philip) John (Caledon), 15th Bt, cr 1617; b 19 Oct. 1920; er s of Sir Philip Grey Egerton, 14th Bt; S father, 1962; m 1952, Margaret Voase (d 1971) (who m 1941, Sqdn Ldr Robert A. Ullman, d 1943), er d of late Rowland Rank. Educ: Eton. Served Welsh Guards, 1939–45. Recreation: fishing. Heir: b Brian Balguy Le Belward Egerton, b 5 Feb. 1925. Address: Home Cottage, Orford Street, Puddletown, Dorchester, Dorset. Club: Marylebone Cricket (MCC).

GRIBBLE, Rev. Canon Arthur Stanley, MA; Canon Residentiary and Chancellor of Peterborough Cathedral, 1967–79; Canon Emeritus since 1979; b 18 Aug. 1904; er s of J. B. Gribble; m 1938, Edith Anne, er d of late Laurence Bailey; one s. Educ: Queens' Coll. and Westcott House, Cambridge (Burney Student, Univ. of Cambridge); Univ. of Heidelberg. Curate: St Mary, Windermere, 1930–33, Almondbury, 1933–36; Chaplain Sarum Theological Coll., 1936–38; Rector of Shepton Mallet, 1938–54. Examining Chaplain to Bp of Bath and Wells, 1947–54; Proctor in Convocation, diocese Bath and Wells, 1947–54; Rural Dean of Shepton Mallet, 1949–54; Prebendary of Wiveliscombe in Wells Cathedral, 1949–54; Principal, Queen's Coll., Birmingham, 1954–67; Recognised Lectr, Univ. of Birmingham, 1954–67. Hon. Canon, Birmingham Cathedral, 1954–67. Commissary for the Bishop of Kimberley and Kuruman, 1964–66. Examng Chaplain to Bishop of Peterborough, 1968–84. Visiting Lectr, Graduate Theological Union, Berkeley, USA, 1970. Recreation: mountaineering. Address: 2 Princes Road, Stamford, Lincs. T: Stamford 55838.

GRIBBON, Maj.-Gen. Nigel St George, OBE 1960; Deputy Chairman, Sallingbury Casey Ltd, since 1986; Director, Chancellor Insurance Co. Ltd, since 1986; b Feb. 1917; s of late Brig. W. H. Gribbon, CMG, CBE; m 1943, Rowan Mary MacLeish; two s one d. Educ: Rugby Sch.; Sandhurst. King's Own, 1937–42; GSO3 10th Indian Div., 1942; Staff Coll. Quetta, 1943; Bde Major, 1st Parachute Bde, 1946; RAF Staff Coll., 1947; OC 5 King's Own, 1958–60; AMS WO, 1960–62; Comdr 161 Bde, 1963–65; Canadian Nat. Defence Coll., 1965–66; DMC MoD, 1966–67; ACOS NORTHAG, 1967–69; ACOS (Intelligence), SHAPE, 1970–72. Managing Director: Partnerplan Public Affairs Ltd, 1973–75; Sallingbury Ltd, 1977–83 (Chm., 1975–77 and 1984–85); Dir, Gatewood Engineers Ltd, 1976–83. Canada-UK Chamber of Commerce: Mem. Council, 1979–; Chm., Trade Cttee, 1980; Pres., 1981; Chm., Jt Cttee, 1982–. Chairman: European

Channel Tunnel Gp Public Affairs Cttee, 1980–85; UK Falkland Islands Trust, 1982–; Forces Financial Services, 1983–85; SHAPE Assoc. (UK Chapter), 1984–. Member: Council, British Atlantic Cttee, 1975– (Mem. Exec. Cttee, 1983–); Cttee, Amer. European Atlantic Cttee, 1985–; Eur. Atlantic Gp, 1974–; Council, Mouvement Européen Français (Londres), 1979–; Council, Wyndham Place Trust, 1979–82. Radio commentator and lectr on public affairs. Freeman, City of London; Liveryman, Worshipful Co. of Shipwrights. Recreations: sailing, ski-ing. Address: 99 Pump Street, Orford, Woodbridge, Suffolk IP12 2LX. T: Orford 413. Clubs: Army and Navy, Canada; Little Ship (Rear Commodore Training, 1978–80); Royal Yachting Association; Army Sailing Association.

GRIDLEY, family name of **Baron Gridley.**

GRIDLEY, 2nd Baron, cr 1955; **Arnold Hudson Gridley;** b 26 May 1906; er surv. s of 1st Baron Gridley, KBE, Culwood, Lye Green, Chesham, Bucks; S father, 1965; m 1948, Edna Lesley, d of late Richard Wheen of Shanghai, China; one s three d. Educ: Oundle. Overseas Civil Service, Malaya, 1928–41; served in various Govt appts; interned during Japanese occupation in Changi Gaol, Singapore, 1941–45; returned to duty, 1945; Dep.-Comptroller of Customs and Excise, Malaya, 1956, retired 1957. Mem. Exec. Cttee, Overseas Service Pensioners Assoc., 1957–; Govt Trustee, Far East (POW and Internee) Fund, 1973–; with Parly Delegn to BAOR, 1976; visited and toured Rhodesia during Lancaster House Conf. on Public Service Pensions, 1979. Chm., Centralised Audio Systems Ltd, 1970–85, Life Pres., 1985; Chm. and Dir, Family Insurance Advisory Services, 1981–. Mem., Somerset CC Rating Appeals Tribunal, 1970–73; Adviser to Peoples' Trust for Endangered Species, 1979–; Chm., Board of Governors, Hall Sch., Bratton Seymour, Som, 1970–76. Heir: s Hon. Richard David Arnold Gridley [b 22 Aug. 1956; m 1983, Suzanne Elizabeth Ripper; one s one d]. Address: Coneygore, Stoke Trister, Wincanton, Somerset. T: Wincanton 32209. Club: Royal Over-Seas League.

GRIER, Anthony MacGregor, CMG 1963; General Manager, Redditch Development Corporation, 1964–76; Member (C), Hereford and Worcester County Council, 1977–85; b 12 April 1911; e s of late Very Rev. R. M. Grier, St Ninian's House, Perth, Scotland, and late Mrs E. M. Grier; m 1946, Hon. Patricia Mary Spens, er d of 1st Baron Spens, PC, KBE, QC; two s one d. Educ: St Edward's Sch.; Exeter Coll., Oxford. Colonial Administrative Service, Sierra Leone, 1935; attached to Colonial Office in London and Delhi, 1943–47; North Borneo, now Sabah, Malaysia, 1947–64; Chm., Sabah Electricity Board, 1956–64. Chm. of Governors, King's School, Worcester, 1976–86. Recreations: golf, shooting. Address: Mulberry House, Abbots Morton, Worcester WR7 4NA. T: Inkberrow 792422. Club: East India.

See also P. A. Grier.

GRIER, Patrick Arthur, OBE 1963; HM Diplomatic Service, retired; b 2 Dec. 1918; s of late Very Rev. R. M. Grier, Provost of St Ninian's Cath., Perth, and Mrs E. M. Grier; m 1946, Anna Fraembs, y d of Hüttendirektor H. Fraembs, Rasselstein, Neuwied, Germany; one d. Educ: Lancing; King's Coll., Cambridge (MA 1946). Served War of 1939–45 with RA and Indian Mountain Artillery, NW Frontier of India and Burma (Major). Kreis Resident Officer of Mönchen-Gladbach, 1946–47; Colonial Administrative Service, N Nigeria, 1947, later HMOCS; Clerk to Exec. Council, Kaduna, 1953–55; W African Inter-territorial Secretariat, Accra, 1955–57; Principal Asst Sec. to Governor of N Nigeria, 1957–59; Dep. Sec. to Premier, 1959–63; retired from HMOCS, 1963. CRO, 1963–64; First Sec., Canberra, 1964–66; Head of Chancery, Port of Spain, 1966–69; Dep. UK Permanent Rep. to Council of Europe, Strasbourg, 1969–74; Counsellor and Head of Chancery, Berne, 1974–78. Recreations: tennis, ski-ing. Address: Buffalo Cottage, Wootton, New Milton, Hants. T: New Milton 618398. Club: Royal Commonwealth Society.

See also A. M. Grier.

GRIERSON, Prof. Philip, MA, LittD; FBA 1958; FSA; Fellow, since 1935, Librarian, 1944–69, and President, 1966–76, Gonville and Caius College, Cambridge; Professor of Numismatics, University of Cambridge, 1971–78, now Emeritus; Professor of Numismatics and the History of Coinage, University of Brussels, 1948–81; Hon. Keeper of the Coins, Fitzwilliam Museum, Cambridge, since 1949; Adviser in Byzantine Numismatics to the Dumbarton Oaks Library and Collections, Harvard University, at Washington, USA, since 1955; b 15 Nov. 1910; s of Philip Henry Grierson and Roberta Ellen Jane Pope. Educ: Marlborough Coll.; Gonville and Caius Coll., Cambridge (MA 1936, LittD 1971). University Lectr in History, Cambridge, 1945–59; Reader in Medieval Numismatics, Cambridge, 1959–71. Literary Dir of Royal Historical Society, 1945–55; Ford's Lectr in History, University of Oxford, 1956–57. Pres. Royal Numismatic Society, 1961–66. Corresp. Fellow, Mediaeval Acad. of America, 1972; Corresp. Mem., Koninklijke Vlaamse Acad., 1955; Assoc. Mem., Acad. Royale de Belgique, 1968. Hon. LittD: Ghent, 1958; Leeds, 1978. Publications: Les Annales de Saint-Pierre de Gand, 1937; Books on Soviet Russia, 1917–42, 1943; Sylloge of Coins of the British Isles, Vol. I (Fitzwilliam Museum: Early British and Anglo-Saxon Coins), 1958; Bibliographie numismatique, 1966, 2nd edn 1979; English Linear Measures: a study in origins, 1973; (with A. R. Bellinger) Catalogue of the Byzantine Coins in the Dumbarton Oaks Collection and in the Whittemore Collection, vols 1, 2, 3, 1966–73; Numismatics, 1975; Monnaies du Moyen Age, 1976; The Origins of Money, 1977; Les monnaies, 1977; Dark Age Numismatics, 1979; Later Medieval Numismatics, 1979; Byzantine Coins, 1982; (with M. Blackburn) Medieval European Coinage, vol. 1 The Early Middle Ages, 1986; trans. F. L. Ganshof, Feudalism, 1952; editor: C. W. Previté-Orton, The Shorter Cambridge Medieval History, 1952; H. E. Ives, The Venetian Gold Ducat and its Imitations, 1954; Studies in Italian History presented to Miss E. M. Jamison, 1956; Studies in Numismatic Method, presented to Philip Grierson (Festschrift), 1983. Recreations: squash racquets, science fiction. Address: Gonville and Caius College, Cambridge CB2 1TA. T: Cambridge 332450.

GRIERSON, Sir Richard Douglas, 11th Bt cr 1685; b 25 June 1912; o s of Sir Robert Gilbert White Grierson, 10th Bt, and Hilda (d 1962), d of James Stewart, Surbiton, Surrey; S father 1957; unmarried. Educ: Imperial Service Coll., Windsor. Journalist. Heir: cousin Michael John Bewes Grierson [b 24 July 1921; m 1971, Valerie Anne, d of Russell Wright]. Address: 4 Modena Road, Hove BN3 5QG. T: Brighton 736355.

GRIERSON, Ronald Hugh; Vice-Chairman, General Electric Co. since 1983 (Director, since 1968); Executive Chairman, South Bank Board, since 1985; Director: RJR Nabisco Inc., since 1977; Chrysler Corporation, since 1982, and other cos; b Nürnberg, Bavaria, 1921; s of Mr and Mrs E. J. Griessmann (name changed by Deed Poll in 1943); m 1966, Elizabeth Heather, Viscountess Bearsted, er d of Mr and Mrs G. Firmston-Williams; one s. Educ: Realgymnasium, Nürnberg; Lycée Pasteur, Paris; Highgate Sch., London; Balliol Coll., Oxford. Served War 1939–45 (despatches). Staff Mem., The Economist, 1947–48; S. G. Warburg & Co., 1948–68 (Dir, 1958–68 and 1980–86); Dep. Chm. and Man. Dir, IRC, 1966–67; Chm., Orion Bank, 1971–73; Dir-Gen., Industrial and Technological Affairs, EEC, 1973–74. Board Member: BAC, 1970–71; Internat. Computers, 1974–76; Davy Internat., 1969–73; Nat. Bus Co., 1984–86. Mem., Adv. Council, Phillips Collection, Washington, 1980–. Chm., EORTC Foundation, 1975–; Member: Arts Council of GB, 1984–; Ernst von Siemens Music Foundn, 1977–; Bd of Visitors, N Carolina Sch. of the

Arts, 1984–. Hon. Mem., Philharmonia Orch. Hon. Dr Grove City Coll., USA, 1986. Comdr, Order of Merit of the Republic of Italy, 1980. *Address:* General Electric Company, 1 Stanhope Gate, W1A 1EH.

GRIEVE, Hon. Lord; William Robertson Grieve, VRD 1958; a Senator of the College of Justice in Scotland, since 1972; *b* 21 Oct. 1917; *o s* of late William Robertson Grieve (killed in action 1917) and late Mrs Grieve; *m* 1947, Lorna St John, *y d* of late Engineer Rear-Adm. E. P. St J. Benn, CB; one *s* one *d. Educ:* Glasgow Academy; Sedbergh; Glasgow Univ. MA 1939, LLB 1946 (Glasgow); Pres. Glasgow Univ. Union, 1938–39. John Clark (Mile-end) Scholar, 1939. RNVR: Sub-Lt 1939; Lieut 1942; Lt-Comdr 1950; served with RN, 1939–46. Admitted Mem. of Faculty of Advocates, 1947; QC (Scot.) 1957. Junior Counsel in Scotland to Bd of Inland Revenue, 1952–57. Advocate-Depute (Home), 1962–64; Sheriff-Principal of Renfrew and Argyll, 1964–72; Procurator of the Church of Scotland, 1969–72; a Judge of the Courts of Appeal of Jersey and Guernsey, 1971. Chm. of Governors, Fettes Trust, 1978–86. *Recreations:* golf, painting. *Address:* 20 Belgrave Crescent, Edinburgh EH4 3AJ. *T:* 031–332 7500. *Clubs:* New (Edinburgh); Hon. Company of Edinburgh Golfers.

GRIEVE, Percy; *see* Grieve, W. P.

GRIEVE, Prof. Sir Robert, Kt 1969; MA, FRSE, FRTPI, MICE; Professor Emeritus, University of Glasgow; Hon. Professor, Heriot-Watt University, since 1986; *b* 11 Dec. 1910; *s* of Peter Grieve and Catherine Boyle; *m* 1933, Mary Lavinia Broughton Blackburn; two *s* two *d. Educ:* N. Kelvinside Sch., Glasgow; Royal Coll. of Science and Technology (now Univ. of Strathclyde), Glasgow. Trng and qual. as Civil Engr, eventually Planner. Local Govt posts, 1927–44; preparation of Clyde Valley Regional Plan, 1944–46; Civil Service, 1946–54; Chief Planner, Scottish Office, 1960–64. Prof. of Town and Regional Planning, Glasgow Univ., 1964–74; retired from Chair, 1974. Chairman: Highlands and Islands Develt Bd, 1965–70; Highlands and Islands Development Consultative Council, 1978–; Royal Fine Art Commn for Scotland, 1978–83; Pres., Scottish Countryside Rangers Assoc.; Hon. President: Scottish Rights of Way Soc.; New Glasgow Soc.; Inverness Civic Trust; Stewartry Mountaineering Club; Scottish Branch, RTPI; Friends of Loch Lomond. Former President: Scottish Mountaineering Council; Scottish Mountaineering Club; Former Vice-Pres., Internat. Soc. of Town and Regional Planners. Hon. Vice-Pres., Scottish Youth Hostels Assoc. Gold Medal, RTPI, 1974. Hon. DLitt Heriot-Watt; Hon. LLD Strathclyde, 1984; Dr *hc* Edinburgh, 1985. Hon. FRIAS. *Publications:* part-author and collaborator in several major professional reports and books; many papers and articles in professional and technical jls. *Recreations:* mountains, poetry. *Address:* 5 Rothesay Terrace, Edinburgh EH3 7RY. *Club:* Scottish Arts (Edinburgh).

GRIEVE, Thomas Robert, CBE 1968; MC 1944; Deputy Chairman, Hunterston Development Company Ltd, since 1973; *b* 11 Sept. 1909; *s* of Robert Grieve and Annie Craig (*née* Stark); *m* 1st, 1946, Doreen Bramley Whitehead; two *d*; 2nd, 1978, Mrs R. K. Dimoline (*d* 1985); 3rd, 1986, Mrs M. A. McNeil. *Educ:* Cargilfield and Fettes Coll., Edinburgh. Joined Anglo-Saxon Petroleum Co. Ltd, 1930; served in London, 1930–40. Commissioned 9th Highland Lt Inf. (TA), 1928, seconded Movement Control, Royal Engineers, 1943–45; served NW Europe, rank of Major. Vice-Pres. in charge of Operations, Shell Oil Co. of Canada, 1945; Exec. Asst to Regional Vice-Pres. of Shell Oil Co., Houston, Texas, 1949; Manager of Distribution and Supply Dept, Shell Petroleum Co. Ltd, London, 1951; Director: Shell-Mex and BP Ltd, Shell Refining Co. Ltd, Shell Co. UK Ltd, 1959–65; Shell International Petroleum Co. Ltd, 1963–65; Vice-Chm. and Man. Dir, Shell-Mex and BP Ltd, 1965–71; Chm., United Kingdom Oil Pipelines Ltd, 1965–71; Director: London and Provincial Trust Ltd, 1970–80; Oil and Associated Investment Trust, 1971–84; Viking Resources Trust, 1972–85; Chairman: Hogg Robinson (Scotland) Ltd, 1975–78; Newarthill Ltd, 1977–80. Chm., London Exec. Cttee, Scottish Council, 1971–77. Mem., Management Cttee, AA, 1971–80. Governor, Shiplake Coll., Henley-on-Thames, 1980–. *Recreations:* bridge, travel. *Address:* Gearholm, 84 Bell Street, Henley, Oxon RG9 2BD. *T:* Henley 577901. *Clubs:* Caledonian, MCC.

GRIEVE, William Percival, (W. Percy Grieve), QC 1962; a Recorder, since 1972 (Recorder of Northampton, 1965–71); *b* 25 March 1915; *o s* of 2nd Lieut W. P. Grieve, the Middlesex Regt (killed in action, Ypres, Feb. 1915), Rockcliffe, Dalbeattie; *m* 1949, Evelyn Raymonde Louise, *y d* of late Comdt Hubert Mijouain, Paris, and of Liliane, *e d* of late Sir George Roberts, 1st and last Bt; one *s* one *d* (and one *s* decd). *Educ:* privately; Trinity Hall, Cambridge. Exhibitioner, Trinity Hall, 1933; Lord Kitchener Nat. Memorial Schol., 1934; BA 1937, MA 1940. Harmsworth Law Schol., 1937, called to Bar, 1938, Middle Temple; Bencher, 1969. Joined Midland Circuit, 1939. Called to the Hong Kong Bar, 1960. Commissioned the Middlesex Regt, 1939; Liaison Officer, French Mil. Censorship, Paris, 1939–40; Min. of Information, 1940–41; HQ Fighting France, 1941–43; Staff Capt. and Exec. Officer, SHAEF Mission to Luxembourg, 1944; Major and GSO2 Brit. Mil. Mission to Luxembourg, 1945; DAAG, BAOR, 1946. Asst Recorder of Leicester, 1956–65; Dep. Chm., Co. of Lincoln (Parts of Holland) QS, 1962–71. Mem. Mental Health Review Tribunal, Sheffield Region, 1960–64. Has served on Gen. Council of the Bar. Contested (C) Lincoln By-election, 1962; MP (C) Solihull Div., Warks, 1964–83. Member: House of Commons Select Cttees on Race Relations and Immigration, 1968–70, on Members' Interests, 1979–83; UK Delegn, Council of Europe (Chm., Legal Affairs Cttee) and WEU (Chm. Procedure Cttee), 1969–83; Hon. Vice-Pres., Franco-British Parly Relations Cttee, 1975–83 (Chm., 1970–75); Chm., Luxembourg Soc., 1975; Chm., Parly Anglo Benelux Group, 1979–83. Pres., Fulham Cons. Assoc., 1982–. Member: Council, Officers' Assoc., 1969–; Council of Justice, 1971–; Council, Franco-British Soc., 1970; Council, Alliance Française, 1974. Officier avec Couronne, Order of Adolphe of Nassau; Chevalier, Order of Couronne de Chêne and Croix de Guerre avec Palmes (Luxembourg), 1945–46; Bronze Star (USA), 1945; Chevalier de la Légion d'Honneur, 1974; Commandeur de l'Ordre de Mérite (Luxembourg), 1976; Officer de l'ordre de la Couronne (Belgium), 1980. *Recreations:* swimming, travel, the theatre. *Address:* 1 King's Bench Walk, Temple, EC4. *T:* 01–353 8436. *Clubs:* Carlton, Hurlingham, Royal Automobile, Special Forces.

GRIEVE, William Robertson; *see* Grieve, Hon. Lord.

GRIEVES, David; Board Member, British Steel Corporation, since 1983; *b* 10 Jan. 1933; *s* of Joseph and Isabel Grieves; *m* 1960, Evelyn Muriel Attwater; two *s. Educ:* Durham Univ. BSc. PhD. Graduate apprentice, United Steel cos, 1957; Labour Manager, Appleby Frodingham Steel Co., 1962; British Steel Corporation: Manager, Industrial Relations, S Wales Group, 1967; Gen. Man., Stocksbridge and Tinsley Park Works, 1971; Personnel Dir, Special Steels Div., 1973; Dir, Indust. Relations, 1975; Man. Dir, Personnel and Social Policy, 1977; Dep. Chm. BSC Industry plc, 1980. Mem., Employment Appeal Tribunal, 1983. *Address:* 4 Oak Way, West Common, Harpenden, Herts. *T:* Harpenden 67425.

GRIEW, Prof. Stephen, PhD; University Professor, Athabasca University, since 1986 (President, 1980–85); *b* 13 Sept. 1928; *e s* of late Harry and Sylvia Griew, London, England; *m* 1st, 1955, Jane le Geyt Johnson (marr. diss.); one *s* two *d* (and one *s* decd); 2nd, 1977, Eva Margareta Ursula, *d* of late Dr Johannes Ramberg and of Fru Betty Ramberg, Stockholm, Sweden; one *d* and one step *s. Educ:* Univ. of London (BSc, Dip

Psych); Univ. of Bristol (PhD). Vocational Officer, Min. of Labour, 1951–55; Univ. of Bristol: Research Worker, 1955–59; Lectr, 1959–63; Kenneth Craik Research Award, St John's Coll., Cambridge, 1960; Prof. of Psychology: Univ. of Otago, Dunedin, NZ, 1964–68 (Dean, Faculty of Science, 1967–68); Univ. of Dundee, 1968–72; Vice-Chancellor, Murdoch Univ., Perth, WA, 1972–77; Chm., Dept of Behavioural Science, Faculty of Medicine, Univ. of Toronto, 1977–80. Consultant, OECD, Paris, 1963–64; Expert, ILO, 1966–67; Mem., Social Commn of Rehabilitation Internat., 1967–75; Consultant, Dept of Employment, 1970–72; Vis. Prof., Univ. of Western Ont., London, Canada, 1970 and 1971; Vis. Fellow, Wolfson Coll., Cambridge, 1985–86. Vice-Pres., Australian Council on the Ageing, 1975–76. FBPsS 1960; Fellow, Gerontological Soc. (USA), 1969. *Publications:* handbooks and monographs on ageing and vocational rehabilitation, and articles in Jl of Gerontology and various psychological jls. *Recreations:* music, travel. *Address:* Athabasca University, 10324–82 Avenue, Edmonton, Alberta T6E 1Z8, Canada.

GRIFFIN, Adm. Sir Anthony (Templer Frederick Griffith), GCB 1975 (KCB 1971; CB 1967); President, Royal Institution of Naval Architects, 1981–84; Chairman, British Shipbuilders, 1977–80 (Chairman-designate, Dec. 1975); *b* Peshawar, 24 Nov. 1920; *s* of late Col F. M. G. Griffin, MC, and B. A. B. Griffin (*née* Down); *m* 1943, Rosemary Ann Hickling; two *s* one *d. Educ:* RN Coll., Dartmouth. Joined RN, 1934; to sea as Midshipman, 1939; War Service in E Indies, Mediterranean, Atlantic, N Russia and Far East; specialised in navigation, 1944; Staff Coll., 1952; Imp. Defence Coll., 1963; comd HMS Ark Royal, 1964–65; Naval Secretary, 1966; Asst Chief of Naval Staff (Warfare), 1966–68; Flag Officer, Second-in-Command, Far East Fleet, 1968–69; Flag Officer, Plymouth, Comdr Central Sub Area, Eastern Atlantic, and Comdr Plymouth Sub Area, Channel, 1969–71; Adm. Supt Devonport, 1970–71; Controller of the Navy, 1971–75. Comdr 1951; Capt. 1956; Rear-Adm. 1966; Vice-Adm. 1968; Adm., 1971. Vice-Pres., Wellington College, 1980–; Chm., British Maritime League, 1982–. Hon. FRINA 1984. *Recreation:* sailing. *Address:* Moat Cottage, The Drive, Bosham, West Sussex PO18 8JG. *T:* Bosham 573373. *Club:* Army and Navy, Pratt's.

GRIFFIN, Sir (Charles) David, Kt 1974; CBE 1972; Chairman: Australian Petroleum Co. Pty Ltd, since 1961; Atlas Copco Australia Pty Ltd, since 1986; Robert Bosch (Australia) Pty Ltd, since 1972; Icle Finance Corporation Ltd, since 1986; Mirvac Funds Ltd, since 1983; Vanguard Insurance Co. Ltd, since 1973; *b* 8 July 1915; *s* of Eric Furnival Griffin and Nellie Clarendon Griffin (*née* Devenish-Meares); *m* 1941, Jean Falconer Whyte; two *s. Educ:* Cranbrook Sch., Sydney; Univ. of Sydney (LLB and Golf Blue). 8th Aust. Div. 2nd AIF, 1940–45; POW Changi, Singapore, 1942–45. Associate to Sir Dudley Williams and Mem. Bar NSW, 1946–49; Solicitor, Sydney, 1949–64. Alderman, Sydney City Council, 1962–74, Chm. Finance Cttee, 1969–72; Lord Mayor of Sydney, 1972–73. Hon. Chm., Nabalco Pty Ltd, 1980–; Director: John Fairfax Ltd; Oil Search Ltd. Mem. Council, Royal Agricl Soc.; Dir, Australian Elizabethan Theatre Trust; Mem. Nat. Council, Scout Assoc. of Australia (Life Councillor, NSW Br). *Publications:* The Happiness Box (for children); The Will of the People; sundry speeches and short stories. *Recreations:* golf, fly-fishing. *Address:* 2A Kent Road, Rose Bay, NSW 2029, Australia. *Clubs:* Union (Sydney); Royal Sydney Golf, Pine Valley Golf (NJ, USA).

GRIFFIN, Sir David; *see* Griffin, Sir C. D.

GRIFFIN, Col Edgar Allen, CMG 1965; OBE (mil.) 1943; ED 1945; Regional Director, Northern Region (Arras, France), Commonwealth War Graves Commission, 1969–72; *b* 18 Jan. 1907; 3rd *s* of Gerald Francis and Isabella Margaret Griffin; *m* 1936, Alethea Mary Byrne; two *s* two *d.* Retired from AMF, 1947; Australian Govt Nominee to Staff of War Graves Commn, 1947; Chief Admin. Officer, Eastern Dist (Cairo), 1947–54; UK Dist (London), 1954–58; Regional Dir, Southern Region (Rome), 1958–69. *Address:* 9 Arley Close, Plas Newton, Chester CH2 1NW.

GRIFFIN, Mrs Francis D.; *see* Dunne, Irene.

GRIFFIN, Jasper, FBA 1986; Fellow and Tutor in Classics, Balliol College, Oxford, since 1963; *b* 29 May 1937; *s* of Frederick William Griffin and Constance Irene Griffin (*née* Cordwell); *m* 1960, Miriam Tamara Dressler; three *d. Educ:* Christ's Hospital; Balliol College, Oxford (1st Cl. Hon. Mods 1958; 1st Cl. Lit. Hum. 1960; Hertford Scholar 1958; Ireland Scholar 1958). Jackson Fellow, Harvard Univ., 1960–61; Dyson Research Fellow, Balliol Coll., Oxford, 1961–63. T. S. Eliot Meml Lectr, Univ. of Kent at Canterbury, 1984. *Publications:* Homer on Life and Death, 1980; Homer, 1980; Snobs, 1982; Latin Poets and Roman Life, 1985; The Mirror of Myth, 1986; (ed with J. Boardman and O. Murray) The Oxford History of the Classical World, 1986; Virgil, 1986. *Address:* Balliol College, Oxford. *T:* Oxford 249601.

GRIFFIN, Sir John Bowes, Kt 1955; QC 1938; *b* 19 April 1903; *o s* of late Sir Charles Griffin; *m* 1st, Eva Orrell (*d* 1977), 2nd *d* of late John Mellifont Walsh, Wexford; two *d*; 2nd, 1984, Margaret Guthrie (*née* Sinclair), *widow* of H. F. Lever. *Educ:* Clongowes; Dublin Univ. (MA, LLD, First Cl. Moderatorship, Gold Medallist); Cambridge. Barrister-at-Law, Inner Temple, 1926. Administrative Officer, Uganda, 1927; Asst District Officer, 1929; Registrar, High Court, 1929; Crown Counsel, 1933; Actg Solicitor-Gen. and Attorney-Gen., various periods; Attorney-Gen., Bahamas, 1936 (Acting Governor and Acting Chief Justice, various periods); Solicitor-Gen., Palestine, 1939, Acting Attorney-Gen., various periods; Attorney-Gen., Hong Kong, 1946; Chief Justice of Uganda, 1952–56. Secretary: East Africa Law Officers Conference, 1933; Commission of Enquiry Admin. of Justice, East Africa, 1933; Chm. Prisons Enquiry, Bahamas, 1936; miscellaneous Bds and Cttees; Chairman: Tel Aviv Municipal Commn of Enquiry, Palestine, 1942; Review Cttees, Detainees (Defence and Emergency Regulations), Palestine, 1940–46. Retired, Dec. 1956; Actg Chief Justice, N Rhodesia, 1957; Chm. Commn of Enquiry Gwenbe Valley Disturbances, N Rhodesia, 1958; Speaker, Legislative Council, Uganda, 1958–62; Speaker, Uganda National Assembly, 1962–63, retd. Chairman: Public Service Commissions, 1963 and Constitutional Council, 1964, N Rhodesia; retd 1965. CStJ 1960. *Publications:* Revised Edn of Laws (Uganda), 1935; (joint) Hong Kong, 1950. *Address:* c/o Royal Bank of Scotland, Holt's Branch, Kirkland House, Whitehall, SW1. *Clubs:* East India; Union (Malta).

See also M. H. M. Reid.

GRIFFIN, Dr John Parry, BSc, PhD, MB, BS; MRCP, FRCPath; Director, Association of the British Pharmaceutical Industry, since 1984; Hon. Consultant, Lister Hospital, Stevenage; *b* 21 May 1938; *o s* of David J. Griffin and Phyllis M. Griffin; *m* 1962, Margaret, *o d* of late Frank Cooper and of Catherine Cooper; one *s* two *d. Educ:* Howardian High Sch., Cardiff; London Hosp. Medical Coll. Lethby and Buxton Prizes, 1958; BSc (1st Cl. Hons) 1959; PhD 1961; George Riddoch Prize in Neurology, 1962; MB, BS 1964; LRCP, MRCS 1964; MRCP 1980; FRCPath 1986 (MRCPath 1982). Ho. Phys., London Hosp. Med. Unit, and Ho. Surg., London Hosp. Accident and Orthopaedic Dept, 1964–65; Lectr in Physiology, King's Coll., London, 1965–67; Head of Clinical Research, Riker Laboratories, 1967–71; SMO, Medicines Div., 1971–76; PMO, Medicines Div., and Medical Assessor, Cttee on Safety of Medicines, 1976–77; SPMO and Professional Head of Medicines Div., DHSS, 1977–84; Med. Assessor, Medicines Commn, 1977–84.

Mem., Jt Formulary Cttee for British Nat. Formulary, 1978–84; UK Rep., EEC Cttee on Proprietary Med. Products; Chm., Cttee on Prop. Med. Products Working Party on Safety Requirements, 1977–84. FRSM. *Publications:* (jtly) Iatrogenic Diseases, 1972, 3rd edn 1985; (jtly) Manual of Adverse Drug Interactions, 1975, 3rd edn 1984; (jtly) Drug Induced Emergencies, 1980; numerous articles in sci. and med. jls, mainly on aspects of neurophysiology and clinical pharmacology and toxicology. *Recreations:* gardening, local history. *Address:* 20 Mornington, Digswell, Herts AL6 0AJ. *T:* Welwyn 4592. *Club:* Athenæum.

GRIFFIN, Keith Broadwell, DPhil; President, Magdalen College, Oxford, since 1979; Senior Adviser, OECD Development Centre, Paris, Jan–July 1987; *b* 6 Nov. 1938; *s* of Marcus Samuel Griffin and Elaine Ann Broadwell; *m* 1956, Dixie Beth Griffin; two *d. Educ:* Williams Coll., Williamstown, Mass (BA; Hon DLitt, 1980); Balliol Coll., Oxford (BPhil, DPhil). Fellow and Tutor in Econs, Magdalen Coll., Oxford, 1965–76, Fellow by special election, 1977–79; Warden, Queen Elizabeth House, Oxford, 1978–79 (Actg Warden, 1973 and 1977–78); Dir, Inst. of Commonwealth Studies, Oxford, 1978–79 (Actg Dir, 1973 and 1977–78). Chief, Rural and Urban Employment Policies Br., ILO, 1975–76; Vis. Prof., Inst. of Econs and Planning, Univ. of Chile, 1962–63 and 1964–65. Consultant: ILO, 1974, 1982; Internat. Bank for Reconstruction and Develt, 1973; UN Res. Inst. for Social Develt, 1971–72; FAO, 1963–64, 1967, 1978; Inter-Amer. Cttee for Alliance for Progress, 1968; US Agency for Internat. Develt, 1966. Res. Adviser, Pakistan Inst. of Develt Econs, 1965, 1970; Pres., Develt Studies Assoc., 1978–80. Mem. Council, UN Univ., 1986–. Exec. Editor, World Development, 1978–79; Editor, Oxford Economic Papers, 1979–. *Publications:* (with Ricardo ffrench-Davis) Comercio Internacional y Politicas de Desarrollo Economico, 1967; Underdevelopment in Spanish America, 1969; (with John Enos) Planning Development, 1970; (ed) Financing Development in Latin America, 1971; (ed with Azizur Rahman Khan) Growth and Inequality in Pakistan, 1972; The Political Economy of Agrarian Change, 1974, 2nd edn 1979; (ed with E. A. G. Robinson) The Economic Development of Bangladesh, 1974; Land Concentration and Rural Poverty, 1976, 2nd edn 1981; International Inequality and National Poverty, 1978; (with Ashwani Saith) Growth and Equality in Rural China, 1981; (with Jeffrey James) The Transition to Egalitarian Development, 1981; (ed) Institutional Reform and Economic Development in the Chinese Countryside, 1984; World Hunger and the World Economy, 1987. *Recreation:* travel. *Address:* Magdalen College, Oxford. *T:* Oxford 241781. *Clubs:* Athenæum, United Oxford & Cambridge University.

GRIFFIN, Kenneth James, OBE 1970; Deputy Chairman, Instant Muscle; a Deputy Chairman, British Shipbuilders, 1977–83; *b* 1 Aug. 1928; *s* of late Albert Griffin and late Catherine (*née* Sullivan); *m* 1951, Doreen Cicely Simon; one *s* one *d* (and one *s* decd). *Educ:* Dynevor Grammar Sch., Swansea; Swansea Technical College. Area Sec., ETU, 1960; Dist Sec., Confedn of Ship Building Engrg Unions, 1961; Sec., Craftsmen Cttee (Steel), 1961; Mem., Welsh Council, 1968; Mem., Crowther Commn on Constitution (Wales), 1969; Joint Sec., No 8 Joint Industrial Council Electrical Supply Industry, 1969; Industrial Adviser, DTI, 1971–72; Co-ordinator of Industrial Advisers, DTI, 1972–74; Special Adviser, Sec. of State for Industry, 1974; part-time Mem., NCB, 1973–82; Chm., Blackwall Engrg, 1983–85; Member: Suppl. Benefits Commn, 1968–80; Solicitors Disciplinary Tribunal, 1982–. *Recreations:* golf, music, reading. *Address:* 214 Cyncoed Road, Cyncoed, Cardiff CF2 6RS. *T:* Cardiff 752184. *Club:* Reform.

GRIFFIN, Rear-Adm. Michael Harold, CB 1973; antiquarian horologist; *b* 28 Jan. 1921; *s* of late Henry William Griffin and Blanche Celia Griffin (*née* Michael); *m* 1947, Barbara Mary Brewer; two *d. Educ:* Plymouth Junior Techn. Coll. CEng, FIMechE, FIMarE. MBHI. Commnd, 1941; HMS Kent, 1942; HM Submarines Trusty, Tactician, Tally Ho, Alderney, 1944–50; Admty, 1950–52; HMS Eagle, 1952–54; staff C-in-C Portsmouth, 1954–57; HM Dockyard, Rosyth, 1957–60; Third Submarine Sqdn, 1960–62; Captain, 1962; HM Dockyard, Chatham, 1963–65; HMS St Vincent, 1966–69; Cdre Supt, Singapore, 1969–71; Dir of Dockyard Production and Support, MoD, 1972–77, retired. Naval Adviser to Vosper Shiprepairers Ltd, 1977–81. *Recreations:* yachting, cruising and racing; tennis, badminton; horology. *Address:* 48 Little Green, Alverstoke, Gosport, Hants. *T:* Gosport 83348.

GRIFFIN, Paul, MBE 1961; MA Cantab; Treasurer, Corporation of Sons of the Clergy, 1978–86; *b* 2 March 1922; *s* of late John Edwin Herman Griffin; *m* 1946, Felicity Grace, *d* of late Canon Howard Dobson; one *s* one *d. Educ:* Framlingham Coll.; St Catharine's Coll., Cambridge. Served War in Gurkhas, India, Burma, Malaya, 1940–46; North-West Frontier, 1941–43; Chindits, 1943–44. Asst Master and Senior English Master, Uppingham Sch., 1949–55; Principal, English Sch. in Cyprus, 1956–60; Headmaster, Aldenham Sch., 1962–74; Principal, Anglo-World Language Centre, Cambridge, 1976–82. *Publications:* (contrib.) Peacocks and Commas, 1983; (contrib.) How to become Ridiculously Well-Read in One Evening, 1985; poems, humour, articles, broadcasts. *Recreations:* sea angling, bridge, literary competitions. *Address:* 1 Strickland Place, Southwold, Suffolk IP18 6HN. *T:* Southwold 723709. *Club:* Army and Navy.

GRIFFIN, Very Rev. Victor Gilbert Benjamin; Dean of St Patrick's Cathedral, Dublin, since 1969; *b* 24 May 1924; *s* of Gilbert B. and Violet M. Griffin, Carnew, Co. Wicklow; *m* 1958, Daphne E. Mitchell; two *s. Educ:* Kilkenny Coll.; Mountjoy Sch., and Trinity Coll., Dublin. MA, 1st class Hons in Philosophy. Ordained, 1947; Curacy, St Augustine's, Londonderry, 1947–51; Curacy, Christ Church, Londonderry, 1951–57; Rector of Christ Church, Londonderry, 1957–69. Lecturer in Philosophy, Magee Univ. Coll., Londonderry, 1950–69. *Publications:* Trends in Theology, 1870–1970, 1970; Anglican and Irish, 1976; (contrib.) Pluralism and Ecumenism, 1983; contrib. to New Divinity. *Recreations:* music, golf. *Address:* The Deanery, St Patrick's Cathedral, Dublin 8. *T:* Dublin 752451. *Club:* Friendly Brothers of St Patrick (Dublin).

GRIFFITH, Rev. (Arthur) Leonard; Lecturer in Homiletics, Wycliffe College, Toronto; *b* 20 March 1920; *s* of Thomas Griffiths and Sarah Jane Taylor; *m* 1947, Anne Merelie Cayford; two *d. Educ:* Public and High Schs, Brockville, Ont; McGill Univ., Montreal (BA, McGill, 1942); United Theological Coll., Montreal (BD 1945; Hon. DD 1962); Mansfield Coll., Oxford, England, 1957–58. Ordained in The United Church of Canada, 1945, Minister: United Church, Arden, Ont, 1945–47; Trinity United Church, Grimsby, Ont, 1947–50; Chalmers United Church, Ottawa, Ont, 1950–60; The City Temple, London, 1960–66; Deer Park United Church, Toronto, 1966–75; ordained in Anglican Church 1976; Minister, St Paul's Church, Bloor St, Toronto, 1975–85. Hon. DD Wycliffe Coll., Toronto, 1985. *Publications:* The Roman Letter Today, 1959; God and His People, 1960; Beneath The Cross of Jesus, 1961; What is a Christian?, 1962; Barriers to Christian Belief, 1962; A Pilgrimage to the Holy Land, 1962; The Eternal Legacy, 1963; Pathways to Happiness, 1964; God's Time and Ours, 1964; The Crucial Encounter, 1965; This is Living!, 1966; God in Man's Experience, 1968; Illusions of our Culture, 1969; The Need to Preach, 1971; Hang on to the Lord's Prayer, 1973; We Have This Ministry, 1973; Ephesians: a positive affirmation, 1975; Gospel Characters, 1976; Reactions to God, 1979; Take Hold of the Treasure, 1980. *Recreations:* music, drama, golf, fishing. *Address:* 102 Arjay Crescent, Willowdale, Ontario M2L 1C7, Canada.

GRIFFITH, Edward Michael Wynne, CBE 1986; Vice Lord-Lieutenant for the County of Clwyd, since 1986; Chairman, Clwyd Health Authority, since 1980; *b* 29 Aug. 1933; *e s* of Major H. W. Griffith, MBE; *m* Jill Grange, *d* of Major D. P. G. Moseley, Dorfold Cottage, Nantwich; two *s* (and one *s* decd). *Educ:* Eton; Royal Agricultural College. Regional Dir, National Westminster Bank Ltd, 1974–. High Sheriff of Denbighshire, 1969. Chm., National Trust Cttee for Wales, 1984–; Member: Countryside Commn Cttee for Wales, 1972–78; Min. of Agriculture Regional Panel, 1972–77; ARC, 1973–82. DL Clwyd, 1985. *Address:* Greenfield, Trefnant, Clwyd. *T:* Trefnant 633. *Club:* Boodle's.

GRIFFITH, Prof. John Aneurin Grey, LLB London, LLM London; Hon. LLD Edinburgh 1982, York, Toronto, 1982; FBA 1977; Barrister-at-law; Chancellor of Manchester University, since 1986; Emeritus Professor of Public Law, University of London; *b* 14 Oct. 1918; *s* of Rev. B. Grey Griffith and Bertha Griffith; *m* 1941, Barbara Eirene Garnet, *d* of W. Garnet Williams; two *s* one *d. Educ:* Taunton Sch.; LSE. British and Indian armies, 1940–46. Lectr in Law, UCW, Aberystwyth, 1946–48; Lectr in Law and Reader, LSE, 1948–59, Prof. of English Law, 1959–70, Prof. of Public Law, 1970–84. Vis. Professor of Law: Univ. of California at Berkeley, 1966; York Univ., 1985. Mem., Marlow UDC, 1950–55, and Bucks CC, 1955–61. Editor, Public Law, 1956–81. *Publications:* (with H. Street) A Casebook of Administrative Law, 1964; Central Departments and Local Authorities, 1966; (with H. Street) Principles of Administrative Law, 5th edn, 1973; Parliamentary Scrutiny of Government Bills, 1974; (with T. C. Hartley) Government and Law, 1975, 2nd edn 1981; (ed) From Policy to Administration, 1976; The Politics of the Judiciary, 1977, 3rd edn 1985; Public Rights and Private Interests, 1981; articles in English, Commonwealth and American jls of law, public administration and politics. *Recreations:* drinking beer and writing bad verse. *Address:* The Close, Spinfield Lane, Marlow, Bucks.

GRIFFITH, Kenneth; actor, writer and documentary film-maker; formed own film company, Breakaway Productions Ltd, 1982; *b* 12 Oct. 1921; *g s* of Ernest and Emily Griffith; three marriages dissolved; three *s* two *d. Educ:* council and grammar schs, Tenby, Pembrokeshire, SW Wales. Became a professional actor at Festival Theatre, Cambridge, 1937; films and television; served War, RAF; post war, associated with Tyrone Guthrie at Old Vic; unknown number of films, partic. for Boulting brothers; unknown number of television plays; rarely theatre, though much under influence of Bernard Miles and Robin Midgley; made first documentary film at invitation of David Attenborough and Huw Wheldon, 1964; best documentaries include: Life of Cecil Rhodes; Hang Out Your Brightest Colours (life of Michael Collins; suppressed by Lew Grade at behest of IBA); The Public's Right to Know; The Sun's Bright Child (life of Edmund Kean); Black as Hell, Thick as Grass (the 24th Regt in Zulu War); The Most Valuable Englishman Ever (life of Thomas Paine for BBC TV); Clive of India (Channel Four); The Light (life of David Ben Gurion for Channel Four). *Publications:* Thank God we kept the Flag Flying, 1974; (with Timothy O'Grady) Curious Journey, 1981 (based on unshown TV documentary). *Recreations:* talking; collecting British Empire military postal history (envelopes, post-cards), also ephemera connected with southern Africa. *Address:* 110 Englefield Road, Islington, N1 3LQ. *T:* 01–226 9013.

GRIFFITH, Rev. Leonard; *see* Griffith, Rev. A. L.

GRIFFITH, Owen Glyn, CBE 1980 (OBE 1969); MVO 1954; HM Diplomatic Service, retired; High Commissioner in Lesotho, 1978–81; *b* 19 Jan. 1922; *s* of late William Glyn Griffith and Gladys Glyn Griffith (*née* Picton Davies); *m* 1949, Rosemary Elizabeth Cecil Earl; two *s. Educ:* Oundle Sch.; Trinity Hall, Cambridge. Commnd in Welsh Guards (twice wounded in N Africa), 1941–43; Colonial Service (later HMOCS), Uganda, 1944–63: District Officer, 1944–51; Private Sec. to Governor, 1952–54; Dist Comr, 1954–61; Perm. Sec., Min. of Commerce and Industry, 1961–63; Principal, CRO, 1963; 1st Sec. and Head of Chancery, British Embassy, Khartoum, 1965; 1st Sec. (Commercial), British Embassy, Stockholm, 1969; Dep. British High Comr, Malaŵi, 1973; Inspector, 1976–78. *Recreations:* golf, fishing. *Address:* The Sundial, Marsham Way, Gerrards Cross, Bucks SL9 8AD. *Club:* Denham Golf.

GRIFFITH, Stewart Cathie, CBE 1975; DFC 1944; TD 1954; Secretary, MCC, 1962–74; *b* 16 June 1914; *yr s* of H. L. A. Griffith, Middleton, Sussex; *m* 1939, Barbara Reynolds; one *s* one *d. Educ:* Dulwich Coll.; Pembroke Coll., Cambridge (MA). Asst Master, Dulwich Coll., 1937–39. Army, 1939–46. Glider Pilot Regt, Lieut-Col. Sec., Sussex County Cricket Club, 1946–50; Cricket Correspondent, Sunday Times, 1950–52; Asst Sec., MCC, 1952–62; Secretary: Internat. Cricket Conference, 1962–74; Cricket Council, 1969–74; Test and County Cricket Bd, 1969–73; President: Sussex CCC, 1975–77; MCC, 1979–80. *Recreations:* cricket, golf, real tennis, walking. *Address:* 7 Sea Way, Middleton, Sussex PO22 7RZ. *T:* Middleton-on-Sea 3000. *Clubs:* East India, Devonshire, Sports and Public Schools, MCC; Hawks (Cambridge), etc.

GRIFFITH EDWARDS, James; *see* Edwards, J. G.

GRIFFITH-WILLIAMS, Brig. Eric Llewellyn Griffith, CBE 1945; DSO 1918; MC and Bar; DL; psc; late RA; 5th *s* of late A. L. G. Griffith-Williams, Highfields, Marlow, Bucks; *b* 2 May 1894; *m* 1938, Delia (*d* 1964), *o c* of late Lt-Col H. S. Follett, CBE, Rockbeare Manor, Devon; one *d. Educ:* Tonbridge Sch.; RMA, Woolwich. Served European War, 1914–19; Bt. Lt-Col, 1937; War of 1939–45; Col 1940; Brig. 1940; retired pay, 1946. High Sheriff of Devonshire, 1966; DL Devon 1966. *Address:* Westcott House, Rockbeare, near Exeter, Devon EX5 2LU. *Club:* Army and Navy.

GRIFFITHS, family name of **Baron Griffiths.**

GRIFFITHS, Baron *cr* 1985 (Life Peer), of Govilon in the County of Gwent; **William Hugh Griffiths;** Kt 1971; MC 1944; PC 1980; a Lord of Appeal in Ordinary, since 1985; Chairman, Security Commission, since 1985; *b* 26 Sept. 1923; *s* of late Sir Hugh Griffiths, CBE, MS, FRCS; *m* 1949, Evelyn, *d* of Col K. A. Krefting; one *s* three *d. Educ:* Charterhouse; St John's Coll., Cambridge (Hon. Fellow, 1985). Commissioned in Welsh Guards, 1942; demobilised after war service, 1946. Cambridge, 1946–48. BA 1948. Called to the Bar, Inner Temple, 1949, Bencher, 1971; QC 1964; Treasurer of the Bar Council, 1968–69. Recorder of Margate, 1962–64, of Cambridge, 1964–70; a Judge of the High Court of Justice, Queen's Bench Division, 1971–80; a Lord Justice of Appeal, 1980–85. A Judge, National Industrial Relations Court, 1973–74. Mem., Adv. Council on Penal Reform, 1967–70; Chm., Tribunal of Inquiry on Ronan Point, 1968; Vice-Chm., Parole Bd, 1976–77; Mem., Chancellor's Law Reform Cttee, 1976–; Pres., Senate of the Inns of Court and the Bar, 1982–84. *Recreations:* golf, fishing. *Address:* c/o The Royal Courts of Justice, WC2. *Clubs:* Garrick, MCC; Hawks (Cambridge); Royal and Ancient (St Andrews); Sunningdale Golf.

GRIFFITHS, Prof. Allen Phillips; Professor of Philosophy, University of Warwick, since 1964; Director, Royal Institute of Philosophy, since 1979; *b* 11 June 1927; *s* of John Phillips Griffiths and Elsie Maud (*née* Jones); *m* 1st, 1948, Margaret Lock (*d* 1974); one *s* one *d*; 2nd, 1984, Vera Clare. *Educ:* University Coll., Cardiff (BA; Hon. Fellow 1984); University Coll., Oxford (BPhil). Sgt, Intell. Corps, 1945–48 (despatches). Asst Lectr, Univ. of Wales, 1955–57; Lectr, Birkbeck Coll., Univ. of London, 1957–64. Pro-Vice-

Chancellor, Univ. of Warwick, 1970–77. Vis. Professor: Swarthmore Coll., Pa, 1963; Univ. of Calif, 1967; Univ. of Wisconsin, 1965 and 1970; Carleton Coll., Minnesota, 1985. Silver Jubilee Medal, 1977. *Publications:* (ed) Knowledge & Belief, 1967; (ed) Of Liberty, 1983; (ed) Philosophy and Literature, 1984; Philosophy and Practice, 1985; articles in learned philosophical jls. *Recreations:* handwriting, poker, clocks. *Address:* Department of Philosophy, University of Warwick, Coventry CV4 7AL. *T:* Coventry 523320. *Club:* Conservative (Kenilworth).

GRIFFITHS, Rt. Rev. Ambrose; *see* Griffiths, Rt. Rev. M. A.

GRIFFITHS, Air Vice-Marshal Arthur, CB 1972; AFC 1964; Director, Trident Safeguards Ltd; *b* 22 Aug. 1922; *s* of late Edward and Elizabeth Griffiths; *m* 1950, Nancy Maud Sumpter; one *d. Educ:* Hawarden Grammar School. Joined RAF, 1940; war service with No 26 Fighter Reconnaissance Sqdn; post-war years as Flying Instructor mainly at CFS and Empire Flying Sch.; pfc 1954; comd No 94 Fighter Sqdn Germany, 1955–56; Dirg Staff, RCAF Staff Coll., Toronto, 1956–59; HQ Bomber Comd, 1959–61; comd No 101 Bomber Sqdn, 1962–64; Gp Captain Ops, Bomber Comd, 1964–67; comd RAF Waddington, 1967–69; AOA and later Chief of Staff, Far East Air Force, 1969–71; Head of British Defence Liaison Staff, Canberra, 1972–74; Dir Gen., Security (RAF), 1976–77, and Comdt-Gen. RAF Regt, 1975–77. *Address:* Water Lane House, Marholm Road, Castor, Peterborough PE5 7BJ. *T:* Castor 742. *Club:* Royal Air Force.

GRIFFITHS, Brian; Head of Prime Minister's Policy Unit, since 1985; *b* 27 Dec. 1941; *s* of Ivor Winston Griffiths and Phyllis Mary Griffiths (*née* Morgan); *m* 1965, Rachel Jane Jones; one *s* two *d. Educ:* Dynevor Grammar School; London School of Economics, Univ. of London. BSc (Econ), MSc (Econ). Assistant Lecturer in Economics, LSE, 1965–68, Lecturer in Economics, 1968–76; City University: Prof. of Banking and Internat. Finance, 1977–85; Dir, Centre for Banking and Internat. Finance, 1977–82; Dean, Business Sch., 1982–85. Vis. Prof., Univ. of Rochester, USA, 1972–73; Prof. of Ethics, Gresham Coll., 1984–. Dir, Bank of England, 1984–86 (Mem., Panel of Academic Consultants, 1977–86). *Publications:* Is Revolution Change? (ed and contrib.), 1972; Mexican Monetary Policy and Economic Development, 1972; Invisible Barriers to Invisible Trade, 1975; Inflation: The Price of Prosperity, 1976; (ed with G. E. Wood) Monetary Targets, 1980; The Creation of Wealth, 1984; (ed with G. E. Wood) Monetarism in the United Kingdom, 1984. *Recreations:* the family and reading. *Address:* c/o 10 Downing Street, SW1. *Club:* Athenæum.

GRIFFITHS, His Honour Bruce (Fletcher); QC 1970; a Circuit Judge, 1972–86; *b* 28 April 1924; *s* of Edward Griffiths and Nancy Olga (*née* Fuell); *m* 1952, Mary Kirkhouse Jenkins, *y d* of late Judge George Kirkhouse Jenkins, QC; two *s* one *d. Educ:* Whitchurch Grammar Sch., Cardiff; King's Coll., London. RAF, 1942–47. LLB (Hons) London, 1951 (Jelf Medallist). Chm., Local Appeals Tribunal (Cardiff), Min. of Social Security, 1964–70; an Asst Recorder of Cardiff, Swansea and Merthyr Tydfil, 1966–71; Vice-Chm., Mental Health Review Tribunal for Wales, 1968–72; Dep. Chm., Glamorgan QS, 1971; Comr of Assize, Royal Cts of Justice, London, 1971; Mem., Parole Bd, 1983–85; Chancellor, Dio. of Monmouth, 1977–; President of Provincial Court, and Mem. Governing Body (Panel of Chairmen), Church in Wales. Chm., Welsh Sculpture Trust; former Mem., Welsh Arts Council, and Chm., Art Cttee; Purchaser, Contemp. Art Soc. for Wales, 1975–76 (Vice-Chm., 1977–). *Address:* 15 Heol Don, Whitchurch, Cardiff CF4 2AR. *T:* Cardiff 625001. *Clubs:* Carlton, Naval and Military; Cardiff and County (Cardiff).

GRIFFITHS, David Howard, OBE 1982; Chairman, Eastern Region, British Gas Corporation, since 1981; *b* 30 Oct. 1922; *s* of David Griffiths and Margaret (*née* Jones); *m* 1949, Dilys Watford John; two *d. Educ:* Monmouth Sch.; Sidney Sussex Coll., Cambridge (Exhibnr; BA 1941, MA 1946, LLB 1946). Admitted Solicitor of the Supreme Court, 1948. Asst Solicitor, Newport Corp., 1948; Wales Gas Board: Solicitor, 1949; Management Develt Officer, 1965; Dir of Develt, 1967; Wales Gas: Dir of Conversion, 1970; Sec., 1973; Dep. Chm., Eastern Gas, 1977. Vice Pres., Contemporary Arts Soc., Wales, 1977. *Recreations:* reading, golf, music. *Address:* Star House, Potters Bar, Herts EN6 2PD. *T:* Potters Bar 51151. *Club:* United Oxford & Cambridge University.

GRIFFITHS, David Hubert; Fisheries Secretary, Ministry of Agriculture, Fisheries and Food, since 1983; *b* 24 Dec. 1940; *s* of Hubert Griffiths and Margaret Joan Waldron. *Educ:* Kingswood School, Bath; St Catharine's College, Cambridge (MA). Joined Ministry of Agriculture, Fisheries and Food as Asst Principal, 1963; Principal, 1968; Asst Secretary, 1975; Under Secretary, 1982. *Recreations:* golf, cooking, music. *Address:* 4 Marlborough House, Somerset Road, SW19 5HZ. *T:* 01–946 1948. *Club:* Richmond Golf.

GRIFFITHS, David John; His Honour Judge David Griffiths; a Circuit Judge, since 1984; *b* 18 Feb. 1931; *m* Anita; three *s* one *d. Educ:* St Dunstan's Coll., Catford, SE6. Admitted to Roll of Solicitors, 1957; apptd Notary Public, 1969; Principal: D. J. Griffiths & Co., Bromley, 1960–84; Harveys, Lewisham, 1970–84. A Recorder, 1980–84. Mem., Scriveners Co., 1983. *Recreations:* riding, squash, music (male voice choir). *Address:* Moat Farm, Crockenhill, Kent BR8 8JG.

GRIFFITHS, Rev. Canon David Nigel, FSA; Rector of Windsor, since 1973; Chaplain to The Queen, since 1977; Hon. Canon of Christ Church, Oxford, since 1983; Rural Dean of Maidenhead, since 1985; *b* 29 Oct. 1927; *o s* of late William Cross Griffiths, LDS, and Doris May (*née* Rhodes); *m* 1953, Joan Fillingham; two *s* one *d. Educ:* King Edward's Sch., Bath; Cranbrook; Worcester Coll., Oxford (MA; Gladstone Meml Prize, Arnold Historical Essay Prize); Lincoln Theol Coll. An economist before ordination; Consultant at FAO, Rome, 1952–53. Curate, St Matthew, Northampton, 1958–61; Headquarters Staff, SPCK, 1961–67; Rector of St Mary Magdalene with St Paul and Vicar of St Michael-on-the-Mount, Lincoln, 1967–73; Vice-Chancellor and Librarian, Lincoln Cathedral, 1967–73; Rural Dean of Maidenhead, 1977–82. Served TARO and RMFVR, 1946–50; Chaplain, RNR, 1963–77 (Reserve Decoration, 1977); OCF: Household Cavalry, 1973–; 1st Bn Irish Guards, 1977–80. FSA 1973. *Publications:* articles on bibliography and church history. *Recreations:* walking, bibliomania. *Address:* The Rectory, Park Street, Windsor, Berks SL4 1LU. *T:* Windsor 864572.

GRIFFITHS, Edward; *b* 7 March 1929; Welsh; *m* 1954, Ella Constance Griffiths; one *s* one *d. Educ:* University Coll. of N Wales, Bangor. Industrial Chemist, 1951. Mem., Flintshire CC, 1964. MP (Lab) Brightside Div. of Sheffield, June 1968–Sept. 1974; contested (Ind Lab) Sheffield Brightside, Oct. 1974. *Recreation:* sport.

GRIFFITHS, Sir Eldon (Wylie), Kt 1985; MA Cantab, MA Yale; MP (C) Bury St Edmunds, since May 1964; *b* 25 May 1925; *s* of Thomas H. W. Griffiths and Edith May; *m*; one *s* one *d. Educ:* Ashton Grammar Sch.; Emmanuel Coll., Cambridge. Fellow, Saybrook Coll., Yale, 1948–49; Correspondent, Time and Life magazines, 1949–55; Foreign Editor, Newsweek, 1956–63; Columnist, Washington Post, 1962–63; Conservative Research Department, 1963–64. Parly Sec., Min. of Housing and Local Govt, June-Oct. 1970; Parly Under-Sec. of State, DoE, and Minister for Sport, 1970–74; opposition spokesman on Europe, 1975–76. Chairman: Anglo-Iranian Parly Gp; Anglo-Polish Parly Gp. Chm., Special Olympics (UK). Consultant/Adviser, Nat. Police Federation; Consultant, National Caravan Council; Pres., Assoc. of Public Health Inspectors, 1969–70. Director: Barber Greene Ltd; Caparo Gp Ltd; Support Systems Associates. *Recreations:* reading, swimming, cricket. *Address:* The Wallow, East Barton, Bury St Edmunds, Suffolk.

GRIFFITHS, Sir (Ernest) Roy, Kt 1985; Deputy Chairman since 1975, and Managing Director since 1979, J. Sainsbury plc; Deputy Chief Executive, National Health Service Management Board, since 1986; *b* 8 July 1926; *s* of Ernest and Florence Griffiths; *m* 1952, Winifred Mary Rigby; one *s* two *d. Educ:* Wolstanton Grammar Sch., N Staffs; Keble Coll., Oxford (Open Scholar; MA, BCL); Columbia Business Sch., New York. Solicitor; FCIS 1959; FIGD 1975 (Pres., 1985–); CBIM 1980. Monsanto Cos, 1956–68: Legal Adviser, 1956; Dir, Monsanto Europe, 1964–68; J. Sainsbury plc, 1968–: Dir, Personnel, 1969. Chm., Management Enquiry, NHS, 1983 (report publd 1983); Mem., Health Services Supervisory Bd, 1983–. *Recreations:* cricket, gardening. *Address:* Little Earlylands, Crockham Hill, Edenbridge, Kent TN8 6SN. *T:* Edenbridge 866362.

GRIFFITHS, Harold Morris; Assistant Secretary, HM Treasury, 1978–86; *b* 17 March 1926; *s* of Rt Hon. James Griffiths, CH; *m* 1st, 1951, Gwyneth Lethby (*d* 1966); three *s* one *d*; 2nd, 1966, Elaine Burge (*née* Walsh); two *s. Educ:* Llanelly Grammar Sch.; London Sch. of Economics. Editorial Staff: Glasgow Herald, 1949–55; Guardian, 1955–67; Information Division, HM Treasury: Deputy Head, 1967–68, Head, 1968–72; Asst Sec., HM Treasury, 1972–75; Counsellor (Economic), Washington, 1975–78. *Address:* 32 Teddington Park, Teddington, Mddx. *T:* 01–977 2464.

GRIFFITHS, Howard; Assistant Secretary, Defence Arms Control Unit, Ministry of Defence, since 1986; *b* 20 Sept. 1938; *s* of Bernard and Olive Griffiths; *m* 1963, Dorothy Foster (*née* Todd); one *s* one *d. Educ:* London School of Economics (BScEcon, MScEcon). Ministry of Defence: Research Officer, 1963–69; Principal, Army Dept, 1970–72; Central Staffs, 1972–76; Asst Secretary, Head of Civilian Faculty, National Defence Coll., 1976–78; Procurement Executive, 1978–80; Deputy and Counsellor (Defence), UK Delegn, Mutual and Balanced Force Reductions (Negotiations), Vienna, 1980–84; Asst Sec., Office of Management and Budget, MoD, 1984–86. *Address:* c/o Ministry of Defence, Whitehall, SW1A 2HB.

See also L. Griffiths.

GRIFFITHS, Islwyn Owen, QC 1973; a Recorder of the Crown Court, since 1972; *b* 24 Jan. 1924; *m* 1951, Pamela Norah Blizard. *Educ:* Swansea Grammar Sch.; Christ Church, Oxford (MA, BCL). Army (Royal Artillery), 1942–47; TA (RA), 1947–51; TARO, 1951. Called to Bar, Lincoln's Inn, 1953; Dep. Chm., Bucks QS, 1967–71. Comr, 1979–84, Chief Comr, 1981–84, National Insurance, later Social Security, Commn. *Recreation:* sailing. *Address:* Kings Farm House, Wimland Road, Faygate, near Horsham, Sussex RH12 4SS. *Club:* Garrick.

GRIFFITHS, John Calvert, CMG 1983; QC 1972; a Recorder of the Crown Court, since 1972; *b* 16 Jan. 1931; *s* of Oswald Hardy Griffiths and Christina Flora Griffiths; *m* 1958, Jessamy, *er d* of Prof. G. P. Crowden and Jean Crowden; three *d. Educ:* St Peter's Sch., York (scholar); Emmanuel Coll., Cambridge (sen. exhibnr) (BA 1st Cl. Hons 1955; MA 1960). Called to Bar, Middle Temple, 1956 (Bencher, 1983). Attorney-General of Hong Kong, Mem. Exec. and Legislative Councils, and Chm. Hong Kong Law Reform Commn, 1979–83. Member: Exec. Cttee, General Council of the Bar, 1967–71; Senate of Inns of Court and the Bar, 1983– (Mem., Exec. Cttee, 1973–77); Council of Legal Educn, 1983–; Nat. Council of Social Service, 1974–; Greater London CAB Exec. Cttee, 1978–79; (co-opted) Develt and Special Projects Cttee, 1977–79; Court, Hong Kong Univ., 1980–; Exec. Cttee, Prince Philip Cambridge Scholarships, 1980–. Lieutenant, RE, 1949–50 (Nat. Service). *Recreations:* fishing reading, gardening. *Address:* 1 Brick Court, Temple, EC4. *T:* 01–583 0777. *Clubs:* Flyfishers', Hurlingham; Hong Kong, Royal Hong Kong Jockey (Hong Kong).

GRIFFITHS, John Charles, JP; Chairman: (and founder) The Arts Channel (formerly British Cable Programmes), since 1983; Rodhales Ltd, since 1978; *b* 19 April 1934; *s* of Sir Percival Griffiths, *qv*; *m* 1st, 1956, Ann Timms (marr. diss.); four *s*; 2nd, 1983, Carole Jane Mellor; one *d. Educ:* Uppingham; Peterhouse, Cambridge (MA). Dep. General Manager, Press Association, 1968–70; PR adviser, British Gas, 1970–74; Chm., MSG Public Relations, 1974–78. Chairman: National League of Young Liberals, 1962–64 (Mem., Nat. Exec., 1964–66); Assoc. of Liberals in Small Business and Self Employed, 1980; Pres., Liberal Party, 1982–83. Contested (L): Ludlow, 1964; Wanstead and Woodford, 1966; Bedford, Feb. 1974, Oct. 1974. JP Cardiff, 1960. *Publications:* The Survivors, 1964; Afghanistan, 1967; Modern Iceland, 1969; Three Tomorrows, 1980; The Science of Winning Squash, 1981; Afghanistan: key to a Continent, 1981; The Queen of Spades, 1983; The Forgotten War, 1986. *Recreations:* squash, conversation, reading, music. *Address:* Llethrgneuen, Pontfaen, Brecon, Powys LD3 9RP, Wales. *T:* Brecon 89306. *Club:* Royal Automobile.

GRIFFITHS, John Edward Seaton, CMG 1959; MBE 1934; retired; *b* 27 Sept. 1908; *s* of A. E. Griffiths, MA, Cape Town; *m* 1937, Helen Parker, *d* of C. C. Wiles, MA, Grahamstown, SA; two *s* one *d. Educ:* South African Coll. Sch.; Cape Town Univ.; Selwyn Coll., Cambridge. Colonial Service (later HM Oversea Civil Service), Tanganyika, 1931–59; Asst Comr, East African Office, 1960–63; Director of Studies, Royal Inst. Public Administration, 1963–67; Administrative Training Officer, Govt of Botswana, 1967–73. *Publications:* articles in Tanganyika Notes and Records, Botswana Notes and Records and in Journal of Administration Overseas. *Address:* c/o National Westminster Bank, 249 Banbury Road, Summertown, Oxford. *Clubs:* Royal Commonwealth Society; Mountain Club of South Africa (Cape Town).

GRIFFITHS, Sir John N.; *see* Norton-Griffiths.

GRIFFITHS, John Pankhurst, RIBA; Director, Building Conservation Trust, since 1979; *b* 27 Sept. 1930; *s* of late William Bramwell Griffiths and Ethel Doris Griffiths (*née* Pankhurst); *m* 1959, Helen Elizabeth (*née* Tasker); two *s* one *d. Educ:* Torquay Grammar School; King George V School, Southport; School of Architecture, Manchester Univ. Dip Arch. Resident architect, Northern Nigeria, for Maxwell Fry, 1956–58; staff architect, Granada Television, 1959; Founder and first Dir, Manchester Building Centre, 1959–65; Head of Tech. Inf., Min. of Public Buildings and Works, later DoE, 1965–77; formed Building Conservation Assoc. (now Building Conservation Trust), 1977. *Publications:* articles in tech. and prof. jls. *Recreations:* designing odd things, examining buildings, cooking on solid fuel Aga. *Address:* The Building Conservation Trust, Apartment 39, Hampton Court Palace, East Molesey, Surrey KT8 9BS. *T:* 01–943 2277.

GRIFFITHS, Prof. John William Roger; Professor of Electronics, Department of Electronic and Electrical Engineering, Loughborough University of Technology, since 1967; *b* 27 Nov. 1921; *s* of Samuel William Henry Griffiths and Alice Griffiths; *m* 1945, Pauline Edyth Griffiths (*née* Marston); one *s. Educ:* Waterloo Grammar Sch.; Bristol Univ. BSc 1949, PhD 1958. CEng, FIEE; FIERE; FIOA. Served War, HM Forces, 1939–46. Scientific Civil Service, 1949–55; Lectr, then Sen. Lectr, Birmingham Univ., 1955–67; Loughborough Univ. of Technology: Head of Dept, 1968–80; Dean of Engineering, 1972–75; Sen. Pro-Vice-Chancellor, 1978–80. Vis. Prof., Inst. of Radio

Physics, Calcutta, 1963–65. Mem., Govt Adv. Panel on Satellite TV Standards, 1983. *Publications:* Signal Processing in Underwater Acoustics, 1972; many papers in learned jls. *Recreations:* sport, gardening. *Address:* 80 Rectory Road, Wanlip, Leicestershire. *T:* Leicester 676336.

GRIFFITHS, Lawrence; a Recorder of the Crown Court, since 1972; *b* 16 Aug. 1933; *s* of Bernard Griffiths and Olive Emily Griffiths (*née* Stokes); *m* 1959, Josephine Ann (*née* Cook); one *s* two *d*. *Educ:* Gowerton Grammar Sch.; Christ's Coll., Cambridge (MA). Called to Bar, Inner Temple, 1957; practised Swansea, 1958–; Mem. Wales and Chester Circuit; Prosecuting Counsel to Inland Revenue for Wales and Chester Circuit, 1969. Mem., Mental Health Review Tribunal for Wales, 1970. *Address:* 26 Hillside Crescent, Uplands, Swansea. *T:* Swansea 473513; (chambers) Iscoed Chambers, 86 St Helens Road, Swansea. *T:* Swansea 52988. *Clubs:* Cardiff and County (Cardiff); Bristol Channel Yacht (Swansea).

See also H. Griffiths.

GRIFFITHS, Rt. Rev. (Michael) Ambrose, OSB; Parish Priest, St. Mary's, Leyland, Preston, since 1984; *b* 4 Dec. 1928; *s* of Henry and Hilda Griffiths. *Educ:* Ampleforth Coll.; Balliol Coll., Oxford (MA, BSc Chemistry). Entered monastery at Ampleforth, 1950; theological studies at S Anselmo, Rome, 1953–56; ordained priest, 1957; Prof. of Theology at Ampleforth, 1963; Sen. Science Master, Ampleforth Coll., 1967; Inspector of Accounts for English Benedictine Congregation, 1971 and 1985–; Procurator (Bursar) at Ampleforth, 1972; Abbot of Ampleforth, 1976–84. Mem. Public School Bursars' Assoc. Cttee, 1975. *Recreation:* walking. *Address:* St Mary's, Leyland, Preston PR5 1PD.

GRIFFITHS, Paul Anthony; Music Critic of The Times, since 1982; *b* 24 Nov. 1947; *s* of Fred Griffiths and Jeanne Veronica (*née* George); *m* 1977, Rachel Isabel Reader (*née* Cullen); two *s*. *Educ:* King Edward's Sch., Birmingham; Lincoln Coll., Oxford (BA, MSc). Area Editor for Grove's Dictionary of Music and Musicians, 6th edn, 1973–76; Asst Music Critic of The Times, 1979–82. *Publications:* A Concise History of Modern Music, 1978; Boulez, 1978; A Guide to Electronic Music, 1979; Modern Music, 1980; Cage, 1981; Igor Stravinsky: The Rake's Progress, 1982; Peter Maxwell Davies, 1982; The String Quartet, 1983; György Ligeti, 1983; Bartók, 1984; Olivier Messiaen, 1985; New Sounds, New Personalities, 1985; The Thames & Hudson Encyclopaedia of 20th-Century Music, 1986. *Recreations:* swimming in natural waters, mushrooms. *Address:* The Old Bakery, Lower Heyford, Oxford OX5 3NS. *T:* Steeple Aston 40584.

GRIFFITHS, Sir Percival Joseph, KBE 1963; Kt 1947; CIE 1943; ICS (retired); formerly President, India, Pakistan and Burma Association; Director of various companies; *b* 15 Jan. 1899; *s* of late J. T. Griffiths, Ashford, Middx; *m* 1st, Kathleen Mary (*d* 1979), *d* of late T. R. Wilkes, Kettering; two *s* (and one *s* decd); 2nd, 1985, Marie, *widow* of Sir Hubert Shirley Smith. *Educ:* Peterhouse, Cambridge (MA). BSc London; entered Indian Civil Service, 1922; retired, 1937. Leader, European Group, Indian Central Legislature, 1946; Central Organiser, National War Front, India, and Publicity Adviser to Government of India; Mem. Indian Legislative Assembly, 1937. Hon. Fellow, SOAS, 1971. *Publications:* The British in India, 1947; The British Impact on India, 1952; Modern India, 1957; The Changing Face of Communism, 1961; The Road to Freedom, 1964; History of the Indian Tea Industry, 1967; Empire into Commonwealth, 1969; To Guard My People: the history of the Indian Police, 1971; A Licence to Trade: the History of English Chartered Companies, 1975; A History of the Inchcape Group, 1977; A History of the Joint Steamer Companies, 1979; Vignettes of India, 1986. *Address:* St Christopher, Abbotts Drive, Wentworth, Virginia Water, Surrey. *Club:* Oriental.

See also J. C. Griffiths.

GRIFFITHS, Prof. Peter Denham, MD, FRCPath; Professor of Biochemical Medicine since 1968, and Dean, Faculty of Medicine and Dentistry, since 1985, University of Dundee (Vice-Principal, 1979–85); Hon. Consultant Clinical Chemist, Tayside Health Board, since 1966; *b* 16 June 1927; *s* of Bernard Millar Griffiths and Florence Marion Fletcher; *m* 1949, Joy Burgess; three *s* one *d*. *Educ:* King Edward VI Sch., Southampton; Guy's Hosp. Med. Sch., Univ. of London (BSc 1st Cl. Hons, MD). LRCP, MRCS; MBCS; FRCPath 1978. Served RN, 1946–49. Jun. Lectr in Physiol., Guy's Hosp. Med. Sch., 1957–58; Registrar, then Sen. Registrar in Clin. Path., Guy's and Lewisham Hosps, London, 1958–64; Consultant Pathologist, Harlow Gp of Hosps, Essex, 1964–66; Sen. Lectr in Clin. Chemistry, Univ. of St Andrews and subseq. Univ. of Dundee, 1966–68. Chm., Council of Assoc. of Clin. Biochemists, UK, 1973–76; Member: Tayside Health Bd, 1977–85; various cttees of SHHD and DHSS, 1969–. Dir, Drug Development (Scotland), 1982–. Dir, Dundee Rep. Theatre, 1977–. Consulting Editor, Clinica Chimica Acta, 1986– (Mem. Editl Bd, 1976; Jt Editor-in-Chief, 1979–85). *Publications:* contrib. scientific and med. jls (pathology, clin. chemistry, computing). *Recreations:* music, gardening, decorating, walking. *Address:* 52 Albany Road, West Ferry, Dundee, Scotland DD5 1NW. *T:* Dundee 76772. *Club:* Royal Commonwealth Society.

GRIFFITHS, Peter Harry Steve; MP (C) Portsmouth North, since 1979; *b* 24 May 1928; *s* of W. L. Griffiths, West Bromwich; *m* 1962, Jeannette Christine (*née* Rubery); one *s* one *d*. *Educ:* City of Leeds Training Coll. BSc (Econ.) Hons London, 1956; MEd Birmingham, 1963. Headmaster, Hall Green Road Sch., West Bromwich, 1962–64. Senior Lectr in Economic Hist., The Polytechnic, Portsmouth (formerly Portsmouth Coll. of Technology), 1967–79. Fulbright Exchange Prof. of Economics, Pierce Coll., Los Angeles, Calif, 1968–69. Chm., Smethwick Education Cttee; Leader, Conservative Group of Councillors in Smethwick, 1960–64. MP (C) Smethwick, 1964–66; Contested (C) Portsmouth N, Feb. 1974. *Publication:* A Question of Colour?, 1966. *Recreations:* motoring, writing, camping. *Address:* c/o House of Commons, SW1A 0AA. *Clubs:* Sloane; Conservative (Smethwick and Portsmouth).

GRIFFITHS, Sir Reginald (Ernest), Kt 1973; CBE 1965; Secretary, Local Authorities' Advisory Board, 1957–73; *b* 4 April 1910; *s* of Arthur Griffiths; *m* 1935, Jessica Lilian Broad; two *s*. *Educ:* St Marylebone Grammar Sch.; London Univ. (external). Asst Clerk, LCC, 1948–52; Dir of Estabs, LCC, 1952–57. Jt Sec., Police Council, 1957–72; Jt Sec., Nat. Jt Industrial Councils (Local Authorities), 1957–72; Mem., Nat. Industrial Relations Court, 1972–74. *Recreations:* gardening, golf. *Address:* 10 Woolbrook Park, Sidmouth, Devon. *T:* Sidmouth 4884.

GRIFFITHS, Roger Noel Price, MA Cantab; JP; Deputy Secretary, Headmasters' Conference and Secondary Heads' Association, since 1986; *b* 25 Dec. 1931; *er s* of late William Thomas and of Annie Evelyn Griffiths; *m* 1966, Diana, *y d* of late Capt. J. F. B. Brown, RN; three *d*. *Educ:* Lancing Coll.; King's Coll., Cambridge. Asst Master at Charterhouse, 1956–64; Headmaster, Hurstpierpoint Coll., 1964–86. Asst to Court of Worshipful Co. of Wax Chandlers, 1985. MA Oxon, by incorporation, 1960. JP Mid Sussex, 1976. *Recreations:* music, theatre, bowls. *Address:* Hanbury Cottage, Cocking, near Midhurst, West Sussex GU29 0HF. *T:* Midhurst 3503. *Clubs:* East India, Devonshire, Sports and Public Schools; Sussex.

GRIFFITHS, Sir Roy; *see* Griffiths, Sir (Ernest) Roy.

GRIFFITHS, Trevor, BScEng, CEng, FIMechE, FIEE; registered professional engineer, State of California; Engineer Specialist (retired), Bechtel Power Corporation, Norwalk, California; *b* 17 April 1913; *m* 1939, Evelyn Mary Colborn; one *d*. *Educ:* Bishop Gore Gram. Sch., Swansea; University Coll., London. Metropolitan Vickers Electrical Co. Ltd, 1934; Air Min., 1938; UKAEA, 1955; Min. of Power, 1960; Min. of Technology, 1969 (Chief Inspector of Nuclear Installations, 1964–71); Dep. Chief Inspector of Nuclear Installations, DTI, 1971–73. *Address:* 4240 SE Knapp Street, Portland, Oregon 97206, USA.

GRIFFITHS, Trevor; playwright; *b* 4 April 1935; *s* of Ernest Griffiths and Anne Connor. *Educ:* Manchester Univ. BA (Hons) Eng. Lang. and Lit. Teaching, 1957–65; Educn Officer, BBC, 1965–72. Writer's Award, BAFTA, 1981. *Publications:* Occupations, 1972, 3rd edn 1980; Sam Sam, 1972; The Party, 1974, 2nd edn 1978; Comedians, 1976, 2nd edn 1979; All Good Men, and Absolute Beginners, 1977; Through the Night, and Such Impossibilities, 1977; Thermidor and Apricots, 1977; (jtly) Deeds, 1978; (trans.) The Cherry Orchard, 1978; Country, 1981; Oi for England, 1982; Sons and Lovers (television version), 1982; Judgement Over the Dead (television screenplays of The Last Place on Earth), 1986. *Address:* c/o A. D. Peters, 10 Buckingham Street, WC2.

GRIFFITHS, Ward David; Part-time Member Board, British Steel Corporation, 1970–79; *b* 9 Oct. 1915; *s* of David and Maud Griffiths; *m* 1940, Maisie Edith Williams; three *s* two *d*. *Educ:* elementary and technical schools. Steelworker, 1936–70. Br. Sec. and subseq. Exec. Mem., Iron and Steel Trades Assoc., 1960–68. Deleg., Tinplate Jt Industrial Council, 1965–68; Employee Dir, S Wales Gp and subseq. Strip Mills Div., British Steel Corp., 1968–70; Director: Grundy Auto Products Ltd, 1975–79; Ruthner Continuous Crop Systems Ltd, 1976–78. *Recreations:* motoring, Rugby football. *Address:* 18 Cambridge Gardens, Ebbw Vale, Gwent NP3 5HG. *T:* Ebbw Vale 303716. *Club:* Ernest Lever Works (Ebbw Vale).

GRIFFITHS, William Arthur; Director, National Council for Voluntary Organisations, 1985; *b* 25 May 1940; *s* of Glyndwr and Alice Rose Griffiths; *m* 1963, Margaret Joan Dodd; two *s* one *d*. *Educ:* Owen's Sch., London; Queens' Coll., Cambridge; Univ. of Manchester. Probation Officer, Southampton, 1965–71; Home Office, 1971–76; Chief Probation Officer, N Ireland, 1977–84. Member Executive Committee: NI Council for Voluntary Action, 1985; Wales Council for Voluntary Action, 1985; Scottish Council for Community and Voluntary Organisations, 1985; Trustee, Charities Aid Foundn, 1985. *Recreation:* literature.

GRIFFITHS, Winston James; Member (Lab) South Wales, European Parliament, since 1979; a Vice President of the European Parliament, since 1984; *b* 11 Feb. 1943; *s* of (Rachel) Elizabeth Griffiths and (Evan) George Griffiths; *m* 1966, (Elizabeth) Ceri Griffiths; one *s* one *d*. *Educ:* State schools in Brecon; University College of South Wales and Monmouthshire, Cardiff. BA, DipEd. Taught in Tanzania, Birmingham, Barry, Cowbridge. Member: World Development Movement; Christian Socialist Movement; Amnesty International; Campaign for Nuclear Disarmament; Fabian Society; Anti-Apartheid Movement; VSO; Socialist Educn Assoc., 1986–. Chm., Parliamentarians Global Action for Disarmament, Develt and World Reform (formerly Parliamentarians for World Order), Eur. Parlt; Mem., Eur. Parlt delegn to S Asia. Pres., Kenfig Hill and Dist Male Voice Choir, 1986. Methodist local preacher, 1966–. *Address:* Tŷ Llon, John Street, Y Graig, Cefn Cribwr, Mid Glamorgan CF32 0AB. *T:* Kenfig Hill 740526.

GRIGG, John (Edward Poynder); writer; *b* 15 April 1924; *s* of late 1st Baron Altrincham and Joan Dickson-Poynder; *m* 1958, Patricia, *d* of late H. E. Campbell and of Marion Wheeler; two *s*. *Educ:* Eton; New Coll., Oxford (Exhibitioner). MA, Modern History; Gladstone Memorial Prize. Grenadier Guards, 1943–45. Editor, National and English Review, 1954–60; Columnist for The Guardian, 1960–70. Chm., The London Library, 1985–. Pres., Blackheath Soc.; Vice-Chm., Greenwich Festival Trustees. Contested (C) Oldham West, 1951 and 1955. Pres., Greenwich Cons. Assoc., 1979–82. Joined SDP, 1982. FRSL. *Publications:* Two Anglican Essays, 1958; The Young Lloyd George, 1973; Lloyd George: the People's Champion, 1978 (Whitbread Award); 1943: The Victory That Never Was, 1980; Nancy Astor: Portrait of a Pioneer, 1980; Lloyd George: From Peace to War 1912–1916, 1985 (Wolfson Literary Prize); contribs to other books; articles and reviews. *Address:* 32 Dartmouth Row, SE10. *T:* 01–692 4973. *Clubs:* Garrick, Beefsteak.

See also W. A. Campbell.

GRIGGS, Ven. Ian Macdonald; Archdeacon of Ludlow, since 1984; Priest-in-Charge, St Michael, Tenbury, since 1984; *b* 17 May 1928; *s* of late Donald Nicholson Griggs and of Agnes Elizabeth Griggs; *m* 1953, Patricia Margaret Vernon-Browne; two *s* three *d* (and one *s* decd). *Educ:* Brentwood School; Trinity Hall, Cambridge (MA); Westcott House, Cambridge. Curate, St Cuthbert, Copnor, dio. Portsmouth, 1954–59; Domestic Chaplain to Bishop of Sheffield, 1959–62; Diocesan Youth Chaplain (part-time), 1959–64; Vicar of St Cuthbert, Fir Vale, dio. Sheffield, 1964–71; Vicar of Kidderminster, 1971–83; Hon. Canon of Worcester Cathedral, 1977–83. *Recreations:* mountaineering and hill-walking. *Address:* Archdeacon's House, Clee Hill, near Ludlow SY8 3JG. *T:* Ludlow 890223.

GRIGGS, Norman Edward, CBE 1976; Vice-President: The Building Societies Association, since 1981 (Secretary-General, 1963–81); Metropolitan Association of Building Societies, since 1981; *b* 27 May 1916; *s* of late Archibald Griggs and late Maud Griggs (*née* Hewing); *m* 1947, Livia Lavinia Jandolo; one *s* one step *s*. *Educ:* Newport Grammar Sch.; London Sch. of Econs and Polit. Science (BScEcon). FCIS. Accountancy Dept, County of London Electric Supply Co. Ltd, 1933–40; service in RE and RAPC, Middle East, 1940–46; Asst Sec., Glass Manufrs' Fedn, 1946–52; Sec., Plastics Inst., 1952–56; Asst Sec., Building Socs Assoc., 1956–61, Dep. Sec. 1961–63; Sec.-Gen., Internat. Union of Building Socs and Savings Assocs, 1972–77; Vice-Pres., Chartered Building Socs Inst., 1981–. *Recreation:* print addict. *Address:* 5 Gledhow Gardens, SW5 0BL. *T:* 01–373 5128.

GRIGOROV, Mitko; Hero of Socialist Labour, 1980; Order of Georgi Dimitrov, 1959, 1970, 1980; Member since 1971, Vice-President, since 1974, State Council of People's Republic of Bulgaria; *b* 9 Sept. 1920; *m* 1956, Stanka Stanoeva; one *d*. *Educ:* Sofia University. Mem. of Parliament from 1953, Minister without Portfolio, 1962–66; Sec., Central Cttee, Bulgarian Communist Party, 1958–66 (Mem., Politbureau, Central Cttee, 1961–66). Bulgarian Ambassador to the Court of St James's, 1969–71. Mem., Editorial Board of magazine Problems of Peace and Socialism, 1966–69. *Recreation:* mountaineering. *Address:* c/o Durzhaven Suvet (State Council of Bulgaria), Dondoukov 2, Sofia, Bulgaria.

GRIGSON, Jane; Cookery Correspondent, Observer Colour Magazine, since 1968; *b* 13 March 1928; *d* of George Shipley McIntire, CBE, and Doris Berkley; *m* Geoffrey Grigson (*d* 1985); one *d*. *Educ:* Casterton Sch., Westmorland; Newnham Coll., Cambridge. Editorial Assistant, Rainbird McLean Ltd, and Thames and Hudson Ltd, 1953–55; translator from Italian, 1956–67; cookery writer, 1967–. *Publications:* Charcuterie and French Pork Cookery, 1967; Good Things, 1971; Fish Cookery, 1973; English Food, 1974 (rev. edn 1979); The Mushroom Feast, 1975; Jane Grigson's Vegetable Book, 1978

(Glenfiddich Writer of the Year; André Simon Meml Prize); Food with the Famous, 1979; Jane Grigson's Fruit Book, 1982 (Glenfiddich Writer of the Year; André Simon Meml Prize); The Observer Guide to European Cookery, 1983; The Observer Guide to British Cookery, 1984; Exotic Fruit and Vegetables (with paintings by Charlotte Knox), 1986; *translation:* Of Crimes and Punishments, by Cesare Beccaria, 1964 (John Florio prize). *Address:* Broad Town Farmhouse, Broad Town, Swindon, Wiltshire. *T:* Broad Hinton 259.

GRILLER, Sidney Aaron, CBE 1951; Leader of Griller String Quartet since 1928; *b* London, 10 Jan. 1911; *s* of Salter Griller and Hannah (*née* Green); *m* 1932, Elizabeth Honor, *y d* of James Linton, JP, Co. Down, N Ireland; one *s* one *d*. *Educ:* Royal Academy of Music. Toured British Isles, Holland, Germany, Switzerland, France, Italy, 1928–38; first concert tour in USA, 1939. Served RAF, 1940–45. Lecturer in Music, University of California, 1949; world tours, 1951, 1953. Prof. of Music: Royal Irish Acad. of Music, 1963; Royal Academy of Music, 1964 (Dir of Chamber Music, 1983–86). Worshipful Company of Musicians Medal for Chamber Music, 1944; FRAM, 1945. DUniv York, 1981. *Address:* 63 Marloes Road, W8. *T:* 01–937 7067.

GRILLET, Alain R.; *see* Robbe-Grillet.

GRILLS, Michael Geoffrey; a Recorder of the Crown Court, since 1982; County Court and District Registrar, since 1973; *b* 23 Feb. 1937; *s* of Frank and Bessie Grills; *m* 1969, Ann Margaret Irene (*née* Pyle); two *d*. *Educ:* Lancaster Royal Grammar Sch.; Merton Coll., Oxford (MA). Admitted Solicitor, 1961; Partner with Crombie Wilkinson & Robinson, York, 1965; County Court and Dist Registrar, York and Harrogate District Registries, 1973; a Recorder on NE Circuit, 1982. *Recreations:* music, tennis. *Address:* Cobblestones, Skelton, York YO3 6XX. *T:* York 470 246. *Club:* Yorkshire (York).

GRIMA, Andrew Peter; Jeweller by appointment to HM the Queen; Managing Director: H. J. Co. Ltd, since 1951; Andrew Grima Ltd, since 1966; *b* 31 May 1921; *s* of late John Grima and Leopolda Farnese; *m* 1st, 1947, Helène Marianne Haller (marr. diss. 1977); one *s* two *d*; 2nd, 1977, Joanne Jill Maughan-Brown, *d* of late Captain Nigel Maughan-Brown, MC and of Mrs G. Rawdon; one *d*. *Educ:* St Joseph's Coll., Beulah Hill; Nottingham Univ. Served War of 1939–45, REME, India and Burma, 1942–46 (despatches, 1945); commanded div. workshop. Director and jewellery designer, H. J. Co., 1947–. Exhibitions in numerous cities all over the world; designed and made prestige collection of watches, "About Time", 1970; exhibited at Goldsmiths' Hall. Opened shops in Sydney and New York, 1970; Zürich, 1971; Tokyo, 1973. Has donated annual Andrew Grima award to Sir John Cass Coll. of Art, 1963–. Duke of Edinburgh Prize for Elegant Design, 1966; 11 Diamond Internat. New York Awards, 1963–67. Freeman, City of London, 1964; Liveryman, Worshipful Co. of Goldsmiths, 1968. *Publications:* contribs to: International Diamond Annual, S Africa, 1970; 6 Meister Juweliere unserer Zeit, 1971. *Recreations:* paintings, sculpture, food and wine, campaign to rule out red tape. *Address:* Albany, Piccadilly, W1V 9RR. *Clubs:* Royal Automobile, Institute of Directors.

GRIMES, Prof. William Francis, CBE 1955; DLitt, FSA; FMA; Director of the Institute of Archæology, and Professor of Archæology, University of London, 1956–73; *b* 31 Oct. 1905; *e s* of Thomas George Grimes, Pembroke; *m* 1st, 1928, Barbara Lilian Morgan (marr. diss. 1959); one *s* one *d*; 2nd, 1959, Audrey Williams (*née* Davies) (*d* 1978); 3rd, 1980, Molly Waverley Sholto Douglas (*née* Penn). *Educ:* University of Wales (MA); DLitt Wales, 1961. Asst Keeper of Archæology, National Museum of Wales, Cardiff, 1926–38; Asst Archæology Officer, Ordnance Survey, 1938–45; seconded to Min. of Works to record historic monuments on defence sites, 1939–45; Dir London Museum, 1945–56. Mem. Royal Commn on Ancient Monuments in Wales, 1948–78 (Chm., 1967–78), and of Ancient Monuments Boards, England, 1954–77, Wales, 1959–78; Mem. Royal Commn on Historical Monuments (England), 1964–78. Sec. to Coun. for British Archæology, 1949–54, Pres. 1954–59, Vice-Pres., 1961–65, Treas., 1964–74; Pres. London and Middlesex Archæological Soc., 1950–59, Hon. Vice-Pres., 1976–; Pres. Royal Archæological Institute, 1957–60 (Vice-Pres. 1951–57); Vice-President: Soc. of Antiquaries, 1953–57; Soc. for Medieval Archæology; Prehistoric Soc., 1958–61; Soc. for Roman Studies, 1973–; Hon. Dir of Excavations for the Roman and Mediæval London Excavation Council, 1946–; Chm., London Topographical Soc., 1961–73. Pres., Cambrian Archæological Assoc., 1963–64 (G. T. Clark Prize, 1946); Chm., Faculty of Archæology, History and Letters, British Sch. at Rome, 1963–66; President: Stanmore Archæological Soc., 1962–; Tenby Museum, 1969–; Field Studies Council, 1975– (Chm., 1966–75). Hon. Professorial Fellow, Univ. of Wales, 1961 (University Coll. Swansea); Fellow, University Coll. Cardiff, 1974. *Publications:* Holt, Denbighshire, Legionary Works Depôt (Y Cymmrodor), 1930; Pre-history of Wales, 1951; (ed) Aspects of Archæology in Britain and Beyond, 1951; (with M. D. Knowles) Charterhouse, 1954; (with others) Brooke House, Hackney (London Survey, Vol. XXVIII), 1960; Excavations in Defence Sites, 1939–1945, I, 1960; The Excavation of Roman and Mediæval London, 1968; many papers in learned jls. *Address:* 29 Bryn Road, Swansea, West Glamorgan SA2 0AP.

GRIMLEY EVANS, Prof. John, FRCP; Professor of Geriatric Medicine, University of Oxford, since 1985; Fellow of Green College, Oxford, since 1985; *b* 17 Sept. 1936; *s* of Harry Walter Grimley Evans and Violet Prenter Walker; *m* 1966, Corinne Jane Cavender; two *s* one *d*. *Educ:* King Edward's Sch., Birmingham; St John's Coll., Cambridge (MA, MD); Balliol Coll., Oxford (DM); FFCM. Res. Asst, Nuffield Dept of Clin. Med., Oxford, 1963–65; Res. Fellow, Med. Unit, Wellington Hosp., NZ, 1966–69; Lectr in Epidemiology, LSHTM, 1970–71; Prof. of Medicine (Geriatrics), Univ. of Newcastle upon Tyne, 1973–84. *Publications:* Care of the Elderly, 1977; (jtly) Advanced Geriatric Medicine (series), 1981–; papers on geriatric medicine and epidemiology of chronic disease. *Recreations:* photography, fly-fishing, literature. *Address:* Donnington Farmhouse, Meadow Lane, Iffley, Oxford OX4 4ED. *Club:* Royal Society of Medicine.

GRIMOND, family name of **Baron Grimond.**

GRIMOND, Baron *cr* 1983 (Life Peer), of Firth in the County of Orkney; **Joseph Grimond,** TD; PC 1961; Leader of the Parliamentary Liberal Party, 1956–67, and May-July 1976; Trustee, The Manchester Guardian and Evening News Ltd, 1967–83; Chancellor of University of Kent at Canterbury, since 1970; *b* 29 July 1913; *s* of Joseph Bowman Grimond and Helen Lydia Richardson; *m* 1938, Hon. Laura Miranda, *d* of late Sir Maurice Bonham Carter, KCB, KCVO, and Baroness Asquith of Yarnbury, DBE; two *s* one *d* (and one *s* decd). *Educ:* Eton; Balliol Coll., Oxford (Brackenbury Scholar; 1st Class Hons (Politics, Philosophy, and Economics); Hon. Fellow 1984). Called to the Bar, Middle Temple (Harmsworth Scholar), 1937. Served War of 1939–45, Fife and Forfar Yeomanry and Staff 53 Div. (Major). Contested Orkney and Shetland (L), 1945; MP (L) Orkney and Shetland, 1950–83. Dir of Personnel, European Office, UNRRA, 1945–47; Sec. of the National Trust for Scotland, 1947–49. Rector: Edinburgh Univ., 1960–63; Aberdeen Univ., 1969–72. Chubb Fellow, Yale; Romanes Lectr, 1980. Hon. LLD: Edinburgh, 1960; Aberdeen, 1972; Birmingham, 1974; Buckingham, 1983; Hon. DCL Kent, 1970; DUniv Stirling, 1984. *Publications:* The Liberal Future, 1959; The Liberal Challenge, 1963; (with B. Neve) The Referendum, 1975; The Common Welfare, 1978; Memoirs, 1979; A Personal Manifesto, 1983; contributor: The Prime Ministers, 1976; My Oxford, 1977; Britain—a view from Westminster, 1986. *Address:* Old Manse of Firth, Kirkwall, Orkney.

GRIMSBY, Bishop Suffragan of, since 1979; **Rt. Rev. David Tustin;** *b* 12 Jan. 1935; *s* of John Trevelyan Tustin and Janet Reynolds; *m* 1964, Mary Elizabeth (*née* Glover); one *s* one *d*. *Educ:* Solihull School; Magdalene Coll., Cambridge (MA Hons); Geneva Univ. (Cert. in Ecumenical Studies); Cuddesdon Coll., Oxford. Philip Usher Memorial Scholar (in Greece), 1957–58; Deacon 1960, priest 1961; Curate of Stafford, 1960–63; Asst Gen. Sec., C of E Council on Foreign Relations and Curate of St Dunstan-in-the-West, Fleet St, 1963–67; Vicar of S Paul's, Wednesbury, 1967–71; Vicar of Tettenhall Regis, 1971–79; RD of Trysull, 1977–79. Canon and Prebendary of Lincoln Cathedral, 1979–. *Recreations:* music, family life, languages, travel. *Address:* 43 Abbey Park Road, Grimsby, South Humberside DN32 0HS. *T:* Grimsby 58223.

GRIMSHAW, Maj.-Gen. Ewing Henry Wrigley, CB 1965; CBE 1957 (OBE 1954); DSO 1945; *b* 30 June 1911; *s* of Col E. W. Grimshaw; *m* 1943, Hilda Florence Agnes Allison; two *s* one *d*. *Educ:* Brighton Coll. Joined Indian Army, 1931. Served War of 1939–45, Western Desert and Burma (despatches twice). Transferred to Royal Inniskilling Fusiliers, 1947; Active Service in Malaya, Kenya and Suez, 1956 and Cyprus, 1958. GOC 44th Div. (TA) and Home Counties Dist, 1962–65. Col, The Royal Inniskilling Fusiliers, 1966–68; Dep. Col, The Royal Irish Rangers, 1968–73. *Address:* The Trellis House, Copford Green, near Colchester, Essex.

GRIMSTON, family name of **Baron Grimston of Westbury** and of **Earl of Verulam.**

GRIMSTON, Viscount; James Walter Grimston; *b* 6 Jan. 1978; *s* and *heir* of Earl of Verulam, *qv*.

GRIMSTON OF WESTBURY, 2nd Baron *cr* 1964; **Robert Walter Sigismund Grimston;** Bt 1952; Chairman, Gray's Inn (Underwriting Agency) Ltd, since 1970; Director, Stewart & Hughman Ltd, since 1983; *b* 14 June 1925; *s* of 1st Baron Grimston of Westbury and Sybil Edith Muriel Rose (*d* 1977), *d* of Sir Sigismund Neumann, 1st Bt; *S* father, 1979; *m* 1949, Hon. June Mary Ponsonby, *d* of 5th Baron de Mauley; two *s* one *d*. *Educ:* Eton. Served as Lt Scots Guards, 1943–47; NW Europe, 1944–45. Oil Industry, 1948–53; Sales Director, Ditchling Press, 1953–61; Dir, Hinton Hill & Coles Ltd, 1962–83. Freeman, City of London, 1981; Liveryman, Worshipful Co. of Gold and Silver Wyre Drawers, 1981. *Recreations:* tennis and shooting. *Heir:* *s* Hon. Robert John Sylvester Grimston [*b* 30 April 1951; *m* 1984, Emily Margaret, *d* of Major John Shirley. *Educ:* Eton; Reading Univ. (BSc). Chartered Accountant. Commnd The Royal Hussars (PWO), 1970–81, Captain 1976]. *Address:* The Old Rectory, Westwell, near Burford, Oxon. *Clubs:* Boodle's, City of London.

GRIMTHORPE, 4th Baron, *cr* 1886; **Christopher John Beckett,** Bt 1813; OBE 1958; DL; Deputy Commander, Malta and Libya, 1964–67; *b* 16 Sept. 1915; *e s* of 3rd Baron Grimthorpe, TD, and Mary Lady Grimthorpe (*d* 1962); *S* father, 1963; *m* 1954, Lady Elizabeth Lumley, (*see* Lady Grimthorpe); two *s* one *d*. *Educ:* Eton. 2nd Lieut, 9 Lancers, 1936; Lt-Col, 9 Lancers, 1955–58; AAG, War Office, 1958–61; Brigadier, Royal Armoured Corps, HQ, Western Command, 1961–64. Col, 9/12 Royal Lancers, 1973–77. ADC to the Queen, 1964–67. Director: Standard Broadcasting Corp. of Canada (UK), 1972–86; Thirsk Racecourse Ltd, 1972–; Yorkshire Post Newspapers, 1973–86; Pres., London Metropolitan Region YMCA, 1972–86. Mem., Jockey Club. DL North Yorkshire, 1969. *Recreations:* travel, horse sports. *Heir:* *s* Hon. Edward John Beckett, *b* 20 Nov. 1954. *Address:* 87 Dorset House, Gloucester Place, NW1. *T:* 01–486 4374; Westow Hall, York. *T:* Whitwell-on-the-Hill 225. *Club:* Cavalry and Guards.

GRIMTHORPE, Lady; Elizabeth Beckett, CVO 1983; Lady of the Bedchamber to HM Queen Elizabeth The Queen Mother, since 1973; *b* 22 July 1925; 2nd *d* of 11th Earl of Scarbrough, KG, GCVO, PC and Katharine Isobel, Countess of Scarbrough, DCVO, K-i-H Gold Medal; *m* 1954, 4th Baron Grimthorpe, *qv*; two *s* one *d*. *Address:* Westow Hall, York. *T:* Whitwell-on-the-Hill 225.

GRIMWADE, Sir Andrew (Sheppard), Kt 1980; CBE 1977; Australian industrialist; *b* 26 Nov. 1930; *s* of late Frederick and Gwendolen Grimwade; *m* 1959, Barbara, *d* of J. B. D. Kater; one *s*. *Educ:* Melbourne C of E Grammar Sch.; Trinity Coll., Melbourne Univ. (Exhib. Eng., BSc); Oriel Coll., Oxford (swimming blue; MA). FRACI, FAIM, FInstD. Chairman: Australian Consolidated Industries Ltd, 1977–; Kemtron Ltd Gp, 1964–; Director: National Bank of Australasia; Commonwealth Ind. Gases; National Mutual Life Assoc.; IBM (Aust.); Sony (Aust.); AHI (NZ); Pilkington ACI Ltd. Mem., Australian Govt Remuneration Tribunal, 1976–. Pres., Walter and Eliza Hall Inst. of Med. Research, 1978–. Dep. Pres., Australiana Fund, 1978–. Chairman: Australian Arts Exhibn Corp., 1976–77; Australian Govt Official Estabts Trust, 1979–83; Pres., Nat. Gallery of Vic., 1976–; Trustee, Victorian Arts Centre, 1980–. Member: Council for Order of Australia, 1974–; Felton Bequests' Cttee, 1973–. *Publication:* Involvement: The Portraits of Clifton Pugh and Mark Strizic, 1969. *Recreations:* skiing, Santa Gertrudis cattle breeding, Australiana art and books. *Address:* 320 St Kilda Road, Melbourne, Vic. 3004, Australia. *T:* (03)-699–1433. *Clubs:* Melbourne, Australian (Melbourne).

GRIMWADE, Rev. Canon John Girling; Priest-in-Charge of Stonesfield, Oxford Diocesan Press Officer and Agenda Secretary of Oxford Diocesan Synod, since 1983; Chaplain to the Queen, since 1980; *b* 13 March 1920; *s* of Herbert Alfred and Edith Grimwade; *m* 1951, Adini Anne Carus-Wilson; one *s* one *d*. *Educ:* Colet Court; St Paul's Sch.; Keble Coll., Oxford; Cuddesdon Coll. MA Oxon. Friends' Ambulance Unit, 1940–45. Curate of Kingston-upon-Thames, 1950–53; Curate, University Church of St Mary-the-Virgin, Oxford, and Secretary of Oxford Univ. Student Christian Movement, 1953–56; Vicar of St Mark's, Smethwick, 1956–62; Rector of Caversham, 1962–81, and Priest-in-Charge of Mapledurham, 1968–81; Rector of Caversham and Mapledurham, 1981–83. Chm., House of Clergy, Oxford Diocesan Synod, 1976–82. Hon. Canon of Christ Church, Oxford, 1974–. *Recreations:* gardening, walking, swimming in the Evenlode. *Address:* The Rectory, Stonesfield, Oxford OX7 2PB. *T:* Stonesfield 664.

GRIMWOOD, Frank Southgate, BA; DPhil; ABPsS; *b* 14 July 1904; *s* of late Frank Grimwood, Ipswich and Newbury, and Rose Grimwood (*née* Lake), Bucklebury, Berks; *m* 1935, Mary Habberley Price, MA Oxon; one *s* one *d*. *Educ:* Isleworth County High Sch.; Reading Univ. (Wantage Hall); The Queen's Coll., Oxford. DPhil Oxon; BA Hons University of Reading. Sub-Warden and Foreign Student Sec., SCM, 1929–30; Lecturer in Philosophy and Psychology, City Literary Institute, 1930–40; training in Deep Analysis under Drs J. A. Hadfield and R. G. Hargreaves of Tavistock Clinic, London; Welfare Officer (Oxon, Bucks, and Berks), Min. of Labour and Nat. Service, 1940–48. Advanced Student, The Queen's Coll., Oxford, 1948–56, including one year (1951) at Cuddesdon Theological Coll. (thesis on psychotherapy and religion). Lecturer and Tutor, Oxford Univ. Extra-Mural Delegacy, 1956–61; Warden and Director of Studies, Moor Park College, 1961–72; lecturing and tutoring groups for Nat. Marriage Guidance Council, 1965–70; Exec. Sec., Keble Coll., Oxford, Centenary Appeal, 1972–74. Private Consulting Psychotherapist. *Publication:* Journey towards Belief in God, 1986. *Recreations:* painting, walking, biography. *Address:* 69A Jack Straw's Lane, Oxford OX3 0DW. *T:* Oxford 68535.

GRINDEA, Miron, OBE 1986 (MBE 1977); Editor, ADAM International Review (Anglo-French literary magazine), since 1941; *b* 31 Jan. 1909; *m* 1936, Carola Rabinovici, concert pianist; one *d. Educ:* Bucharest Univ.; Sorbonne. Literary and music critic, 1928–39; settled in England, Sept. 1939; together with Benjamin Britten and Henry Moore founded the International Arts Guild, 1943; war-time work with BBC European Service and Min. of Information; coast to coast lecture tours, USA. Visiting Lecturer: Univs of Paris, Aix-en-Provence, Athens, Karachi, Kyoto, Montreal, Toronto, Rejkiavik, Jerusalem, etc. Hon. DLitt Kent, 1983. Prix de l'Académie Française, 1955; Lundquist Literary Prize, Sweden, 1965. Chevalier de la Légion d'Honneur, 1974; Comdr, Order of Arts and Letters, France, 1985. *Publications:* Malta Calling, 1943; Henry Wood (a symposium), 1944; Jerusalem, a literary chronicle of 3000 years, 1968, 2nd edn, Jerusalem, the Holy City in literature, preface by Graham Greene, 1982; Natalie Clifford Barney, 1963; The London Library (a symposium), 1978; contrib. The Listener, TLS, Figaro, Les Nouvelles Littéraires, New Statesman, The Times, Books and Bookmen. *Recreations:* Mozart, lazing in the sun. *Address:* 28 Emperor's Gate, SW7. *T:* 01–373 7307.

GRINDLE, Captain John Annesley, CBE 1943; RN; JP; *b* 17 Sept. 1900; *s* of late George Annesley Grindle and late Eveleen Grindle; *m* 1925, Joyce Lilian Alton, *d* of J. W. A. Batchelor, Blackheath; two *s. Educ:* Pembroke Lodge, Southbourne; RN Colleges, Osborne and Dartmouth; Pembroke Coll., Cambridge; Midshipman, 1917; Comdr 1934; Captain 1941; Commanded HMS Apollo, 1944–55, Glenearn, 1946, Victorious 1949–50; Dep. Chief of Combined Ops (Naval), 1946–48. Retired list, 1950. JP (Hants) 1952. *Recreation:* gardening. *Address:* Anchor House, Wicor Path, Castle Street, Portchester, Hants. *T:* Cosham 376067.

GRINDON, John Evelyn, CVO 1957; DSO 1945; AFC 1948; Group Captain, RAF retired; *b* 30 Sept. 1917; *s* of Thomas Edward Grindon (killed in action, Ypres, Oct. 1917), and Dora (*née* Eastlake), Corisande, East Pentire, Cornwall. *Educ:* Dulwich College. Flight Cadet at RAF College, Cranwell, 1935–37; served in Advanced Air Striking Force, BEF, France, 1939–40 (No 150 Sqdn) and in No 5 Group Bomber Command (Nos 106, 630 and 617 Sqdns) during War of 1939–45, as Flight and Sqdn Comdr; Chief Instructor, Long Range Transport Force, 1946–49; Commanded The Queen's Flight, 1953–56; V-bomber captain and Station Comdr, 1956–57; retired at own request 1959. Dir/Gen. Manager in printing/publishing, 1961–71; Metropolitan Police, New Scotland Yard, 1976–81. *Recreations:* music, ocean surf, racing. *Address:* 1 Ovington Gardens, SW3. *T:* 01–589 1594. *Club:* Royal Air Force.

GRINDROD, Helen Marjorie, QC 1982; a Recorder of the Crown Court, since 1981; *b* 28 Feb. 1936; *d* of late Joseph and Marjorie Pritchard; *m* 1958, Robert Michael Grindrod; one *s. Educ:* Liverpool Inst. High Sch. for Girls; St Hilda's Coll., Oxford. MA. Teacher, 1957–59. Called to the Bar, Lincoln's Inn, 1966; Northern Circuit, 1966–. *Address:* Cerin Amroth, Beechfield Road, Alderley Edge, Cheshire SK9 7AU. *T:* Alderley Edge 585464.

GRINDROD, Most Rev. John Basil Rowland; *see* Brisbane, Archbishop of.

GRINKE, Frederick, CBE 1979; FRAM; Solo Violinist; Professor of Violin, Royal Academy of Music, London, retired; *b* Winnipeg, Canada, 8 Aug. 1911; *s* of Arthur Grinke, Winnipeg; *m* 1942, Dorothy Ethel Sirr Sheldon; one *s. Educ:* Winnipeg; Royal Academy of Music, London (all prizes for solo and chamber music playing). Studied with Adolf Busch in Switzerland, with Carl Flesch in London and Belgium. Was leader and soloist with the Boyd Neel Orchestra for 10 years. Appeared regularly as Soloist with leading orchestras; has played in many countries in Europe also in America, Australia and New Zealand. Has appeared at Festivals: Edinburgh, Bath, Cheltenham, Three Choirs, Salzburg. Has taken part in many Promenade Concerts. A sonata was dedicated to him by Vaughan Williams; has made numerous recordings, including many works with the composers as pianists (such as Rubbra, Ireland, Berkeley, Benjamin). Has acted as mem. of the Jury for several international violin competitions. FRSA 1979. *Recreations:* music, cooking, wine, reading, the theatre. *Address:* Albion House, 14 Lambeth Street, Eye, Suffolk IP23 7AG. *T:* Eye 870483.

GRINLING, Jasper Gibbons, CBE 1978; CBIM; Chairman, Apple and Pear Development Council, since 1986; *b* 29 Jan. 1924; *s* of late Lt-Col Antony Gibbons Grinling, MBE, MC, and Jean Dorothy Turing Grinling; *m* 1950, Jane Moulsdale; one *s* two *d. Educ:* Harrow (Scholar); King's Coll., Cambridge (Exhibnr, BA). FBIM 1969. Served War, 12th Lancers, 1942–46 (Captain). Joined W. & A. Gilbey Ltd, 1947, Dir 1952; Man. Dir, Gilbeys Ltd, 1964; Man. Dir, International Distillers & Vintners Ltd, 1967; Dir, North British Distillery Co. Ltd, 1968–86; Dir of Corporate Affairs, Grand Metropolitan, 1981–85, Dir of Trade Relations, 1985–86, retd. Pres., EEC Confedn des Industries Agricoles et Alimentaires, 1976–80; Mem. Council, Scotch Whisky Assoc., 1968–86. FRSA. Chevalier, Ordre National du Mérite, France, 1983. *Publication:* The Annual Report, 1986. *Recreations:* gardening, jazz drumming, painting, vineyard proprietor. *Address:* The Old Vicarage, Helions Bumpstead, near Haverhill, Suffolk CB9 7AS. *T:* Steeple Bumpstead 316. *Club:* Oriental.

GRINSTEAD, Sir Stanley Gordon, Kt 1986; FCA; CBIM; Chairman, Grand Metropolitan PLC, since 1982 (Group Chief Executive, 1982–86); *b* 17 June 1924; *s* of Ephraim Grinstead and Lucy Grinstead (*née* Taylor); *m* 1955, Joyce Preston; two *d. Educ:* Strodes, Egham. Served Royal Navy, 1943–46 (Pilot, FAA). Franklin, Wild & Co., Chartered Accountants, 1946–56; Hotel York Ltd, 1957; Grand Metropolitan Ltd, 1957–62; Union Properties (London) Ltd, 1958–66; Grand Metropolitan Ltd, 1964– (Dep. Chm. and Group Man. Dir, 1980–82); Dir, Reed International PLC, 1981–. Trustee, FAA Museum. Master, Brewers' Co., 1983–84. *Recreations:* gardening, cricket, racing, breeding of thoroughbred horses. *Address:* 11/12 Hanover Square, W1A 1DP. *T:* 01–629 7488. *Clubs:* MCC; Surrey County Cricket.

GRINT, Edmund Thomas Charles, CBE 1960; *b* 14 Feb. 1904; *e s* of Edmund Albert Grint; *m* 1930, Olive Maria, *d* of Albert Cheyne Sherras; one *s* two *d. Educ:* London Univ. (Dip. Econs). Joined ICI 1929; Commercial Dir, Nobel Div., 1946; Director: Billingham Div., 1952–61; Alkali Div., 1961–63; Mond Div., 1964. Dep. Chief Labour Officer, 1951; Chief Labour Officer, 1952–63; Gen. Manager Personnel, 1963–65. Chm., Nat. Dock Labour Board, 1966–69; Pres., Midland Iron and Steel Wages Bd, 1971–79. *Recreations:* golf, gardening. *Address:* Old Walls, Seal, Sevenoaks, Kent. *T:* Sevenoaks 61364.

GRINYER, Prof. Peter Hugh; Esmée Fairbairn Professor of Economics (Finance and Investment), since 1979, Vice-Principal, since 1985, University of St Andrews; *b* 3 March 1935; *s* of Sidney George and Grace Elizabeth Grinyer; *m* 1958, Sylvia Joyce Boraston; two *s. Educ:* Balliol Coll., Oxford (BA, subseq. MA, PPE); LSE (PhD in Applied Economics). Unilever Sen. Managerial Trainee, 1957–59; PA to Man. Dir, E. R. Holloway Ltd, 1959–61; Lectr and Sen. Lectr, Hendon Coll. of Tech., 1961–64; Lectr, City Univ., 1965–69; Reader, 1972–74, Prof. of Business Strategy, 1974–79, City Univ. Business School. Mem., Business and Management Studies Sub-Cttee, UGC, 1979–85. Director: John Brown PLC, 1984–; Don Bros Buist PLC, 1985–. *Publications:* Corporate Models Today (with J. Wooller), 1975, 2nd edn 1979; (with G. D. Vaughan and S. Birley) From Private to Public, 1977; (with J.-C. Spender) Turnaround: the fall and rise of Newton Chambers, 1979; over 40 papers in academic jls. *Recreations:* hill walking, golf. *Address:* 60 Buchanan Gardens, St Andrews, Fife KY16 9LX. *Club:* Royal & Ancient Golf (House Mem.) (St Andrews).

GRISEWOOD, Harman Joseph Gerard, CBE 1960; Chief Assistant to the Director-General, BBC, 1955–64, retired; *b* 8 Feb. 1906; *e s* of late Lieut-Col Harman Grisewood and Lucille Cardozo; *m* 1940, Clotilde Margaret Bailey; one *d. Educ:* Ampleforth Coll., York; Worcester Coll., Oxford. BBC Repertory Co., 1929–33; Announcer, 1933–36; Asst to Programme Organiser, 1936–39; Asst Dir Programme Planning, 1939–41; Asst Controller, European Div., 1941–45; Actg Controller, European Div., 1945–46; Dir of Talks, 1946–47; Planner, Third Programme, 1947–48; Controller of the Third Programme, BBC, 1948–52; Dir of the Spoken Word, BBC, 1952–55. Member: Younger Cttee on Privacy, 1970–72; Lord Chancellor's Cttee on Defamation, 1971; Res. Officer, Royal Commn on Civil Liberty, 1973–75. Vice-President: European Broadcasting Union, 1953–54; Royal Literary Fund. Chm., The Latin Mass Soc., 1969. King Christian X Freedom Medal, 1946. Mem. Hon. Soc. of Cymmrodorion, 1956. Knight of Grace and Devotion, SMO Malta, 1960. *Publications:* Broadcasting and Society, 1949; The Recess, 1963 (novel); The Last Cab on the Rank, 1964 (novel); David Jones: Welsh National Lecture, 1966; One Thing at a Time (autobiography), 1968; The Painted Kipper, 1970. *Address:* The Old School House, Castle Hill, Eye, Suffolk IP23 7AP.

GRIST, Ian; MP (C) Cardiff Central, since 1983 (Cardiff North, Feb. 1974–1983); *b* 5 Dec. 1938; *s* of Basil William Grist, MBE and late Leila Helen Grist; *m* 1966, Wendy Anne (*née* White), JP, BSc; two *s. Educ:* Repton Sch.; Jesus Coll., Oxford (Schol.). Plebiscite Officer, Southern Cameroons, 1960–61; Stores Manager, United Africa Co., Nigeria, 1961–63; Wales Information Officer, Conservative Central Office, 1963–74; Conservative Research Dept, 1970–74. Chm., Cons. W African Cttee, 1977–. Vice-Chm., Assoc. of Conservative Clubs, 1978–82. PPS to Secretary of State for Wales, 1979–81; Mem., Select Cttee on: Violence in the Family, 1977–79; Welsh Affairs, 1981–83 and 1986–; Register of Members' Interests, 1983–. Mem. Court of Governors: Univ. of Wales, 1983–; UWIST, 1983–. *Recreations:* reading, listening to music, politics. *Address:* House of Commons, SW1A 0AA; 126 Penylan Road, Cardiff.

GRIST, John Frank; Managing Director, Services Sound and Vision Corporation, since 1982; *b* 10 May 1924; *s* of Austin Grist, OBE, MC, and Ada Mary Grist (*née* Ball); *m* Gilian, *d* of late Roger Cranage and Helen Marjorie Rollett; one *s* two *d. Educ:* Ryde Sch., IoW; London Sch. of Economics and Political Science (BSc Econ); Univ. of Chicago. RAF Pilot, 1942–46. BBC External Services, 1951–53; Talks Producer, Programme Organiser, Northern Region; Controller, Nat. Programmes, Nigerian Broadcasting Service, 1953–56; BBC TV Talks and Current Affairs at Lime Grove, 1957–72, producer of political programmes and Editor of Gallery and of Panorama; Hd of Current Affairs Gp, 1967–72; Controller, English Regions BBC, 1972–77; US Rep., BBC, 1978–81; Founder and first Man. Dir, NY World Television Fest., 1978. Chm., Howard Steele Foundn for Training in Television, Film and Video, 1985–; Mem. Council, RTS, 1984–. Gov., Royal Star and Garter Home, 1986–. FRTS 1986. *Address:* Chalfont Grove, Gerrard's Cross, Bucks SL9 8TN. *T:* Chalfont St Giles 4461. *Club:* Reform.

GRIST, Prof. Norman Roy, FRCPEd; Professor of Infectious Diseases, University of Glasgow, 1965–83, now Emeritus; *b* 9 March 1918; *s* of Walter Reginald Grist and Florence Goodwin Grist (*née* Nadin); *m* 1943, Mary Stewart McAlister. *Educ:* Shawlands Acad., Glasgow; University of Glasgow. Postgrad. studies at Dept of Bacteriology, University of Liverpool, 1948–49; Virus Reference Lab., Colindale, London, 1951–52; Dept of Epidemiology, University of Michigan, 1956–57. BSc 1939; MB, ChB (Commendation), 1942; Mem. 1950, Fellow 1958, RCP, Edinburgh; Founder Mem., 1963, FRCPath 1967; Mem. 1980, Fellow 1983, RCPGlas. Ho. Phys. Gartloch Hosp., 1942–43; RAMC, GDO 223 Fd Amb. and RMO 2/KSLI, 1943–46; Ho. Surg. Victoria Inf., Glasgow, 1946–47; Res. Phys, Ruchill Hosp., Glasgow, 1947–48; Research Asst, Glasgow Univ. Dept of Infectious Diseases, 1948–52; Lectr in Virus Disease, Glasgow Univ., 1952–62, and Regional Adviser in Virology to Scottish Western Reg. Hosp. Bd, 1960–74; Reader in Viral Epidemiology, Glasgow Univ., 1962–65. Mem., Expert Adv. Panel on Virus Diseases to WHO, 1967–. Bronze Medal, Helsinki Univ., 1973; Orden Civil de Sanidad, cat. Encomienda, Spain, 1974. *Publications:* Diagnostic Methods in Clinical Virology, 1966, 3rd edn, 1979; (with D. Reid and I. W. Pinkerton) Infections in Current Medical Practice, 1986; numerous contribs. to British and international med. jls. *Recreations:* gardener's mate, travelling, bird-watching. *Address:* 6A Sydenham Road, Glasgow G12 9NR. *T:* 041–339 5242. *Clubs:* Royal Automobile; Royal Scottish Automobile (Glasgow).

GROBECKER, Ven. Geoffrey Frank, MBE 1959; Archdeacon of Lynn, since 1980; *b* 1922; *s* of Archibald Douglas and Ethel May Grobecker; *m* 1949, Audrey Kathleen Bessell; two *d. Educ:* St Paul's School; Queens' Coll., Cambridge (BA 1949, MA 1953); Ridley Hall, Cambridge. Deacon 1950, priest 1951, dio. Southwark; Curate of Morden, 1950–52; CF, 1952; Senior Chaplain, RMA, Sandhurst, 1966–69; DACG, 1969–72; ACG, 1972–77; Hon. Chaplain to the Queen, 1973–77; Vicar of Swaffham, 1977–80. *Recreations:* family, walking, gardening, bird-watching. *Address:* Lynn House, Scarning, Dereham, Norfolk NR19 2PF.

GROBLER, Richard Victor; Deputy Secretary of Commissions, since 1984; *b* Umtali, S Rhodesia, 27 May 1936; *m* 1961, Julienne Nora de la Cour (*née* Sheath); one *s* three *d. Educ:* Bishop's, Capetown; Univ. of Cape Town (BA). Called to the Bar, Gray's Inn, 1961; joined staff of Clerk of the Court, Central Criminal Court, 1961; Dep. Clerk of the Court, 1970; Dep. Courts Administrator, 1972; Courts Administrator, Inner London Crown Court, 1974; Sec., Lord Chancellor's Adv. Cttee on Justices of the Peace for Inner London and Jt Hon. Sec., Inner London Br. of Magistrates' Assoc., 1974–77; Courts Administrator, Central Criminal Court, and Co-ordinator, Crown Courts Taxations, SE Circuit, 1977–79; Dep. Circuit Administrator, S Eastern Circuit, 1979–83. Liveryman, Worshipful Company of Gold and Silver Wyre Drawers. *Recreations:* gardening, swimming, golf. *Address:* Commissions Office, 4th Floor, North Thames House, Millbank SW1P 4QE. *T:* 01–211 0183.

GROCOTT, Bruce Joseph; television journalist; *b* 1 Nov. 1940; *s* of Reginald Grocott and Helen Grocott (*née* Stewart); *m* 1965, Sally Barbara Kay Ridgway; two *s. Educ:* Hemel Hempstead Grammar Sch.; Leicester and Manchester Univs. BA(Pol), MA(Econ). Admin. Officer, LCC, 1963–64; Lectr in Politics, Manchester Univ., Birmingham Polytechnic, and N Staffs Polytechnic, 1964–74. Chm., Finance Cttee, Bromsgrove UDC, 1972–74. MP (Lab) Lichfield and Tamworth, Oct. 1974–1979; PPS to: Minister for Local Govt and Planning, 1975–76; Minister of Agriculture, 1976–78. Contested (Lab): Lichfield and Tamworth, 1979; The Wrekin, 1983. *Recreations:* cricket, snooker, fiction writing. *Address:* 1 Brookside House, Birch Cross, Uttoxeter, Staffs. *Club:* Trench Labour.

GROMYKO, Andrei Andreevich, Order of Lenin (four awards); President of the Presidium, Supreme Soviet of the USSR, since 1985; Member, Politburo, since 1973; Member, Central Committee, Communist Party of the Soviet Union; *b* 18 July 1909; *m* Lydia D. Grinevich; one *s* one *d*. *Educ:* Agricultural Institute and Institute of Economics, Moscow. Scientific worker (senior), Acad. of Sciences USSR, 1936–39, also lecturing in Moscow Universities. Chief of American Division National Council of Foreign Affairs, 1939; Counsellor, USSR Washington Embassy, 1939–43; Ambassador to USA and Minister to Cuba, 1943–46; Soviet Representative on UN Security Council, 1946–48; Deputy Foreign Minister, 1946–49, 1953–54; 1st Deputy Minister of Foreign Affairs, 1949–52; Soviet Ambassador in London, 1952–53; First Deputy Foreign Minister in Moscow, 1954–57; Minister of Foreign Affairs, USSR, 1957–85; First Dep. Prime Minister, 1983–85. Chm. of Delegates, Conference on Post-War Security, Dumbarton Oaks, USA, 1944. Holds many orders and awards of USSR and other countries. *Publication:* Only for Peace, 1979. *Address:* Central Committee, CPSU, Kremlin, Moscow, USSR.

GRONHAUG, Arnold Conrad; *b* 26 March 1921; *s* of James Gronhaug, MBE, and Beatrice May Gronhaug; *m* 1945, Patricia Grace Smith; two *d*. *Educ:* Barry Grammar Sch.; Cardiff Technical Coll. CEng, FIEE; Hon. FCIBSE. Electrical Officer, RNVR, 1941–46. Air Ministry Works Directorate, 1946–63: Area Mech. and Elec. Engr, AMWD Malaya, 1951–52; Air Min. Headquarters, 1952–60; Dep. Chief Engr, AMWD, RAF Germany, 1960–63; Sen. Mech. and Elec. Engr, Portsmouth Area MPBW, 1963–67; Jt Services Staff Coll., 1964–65; Suptg Engr, MPBW, 1967–71; Dir Defence Works (Overseas), MPBW, 1971–73; Dir of Social and Research Services, DoE, 1973–75; Dir of Engrng Services Develt, 1975–76; Dir of Mechanical and Electrical Engineering Services, 1976–81. Freeman, City of London, 1979; Liveryman, Engineers Co., 1984. *Recreations:* music, photography, do-it-yourself. *Address:* 6 Pine Hill, Epsom, Surrey KT18 7BG. *T:* Epsom 21888.

GRONOW, Alun Gwilym; Secretary, Association of Metropolitan Authorities, since 1985; *b* 22 Oct. 1931; *s* of Ivor Austin Gronow and Kate Evelyn Gronow; *m* 1977, Kathleen Margaret Hodge; two *s* one *d*. *Educ:* Dorking Grammar School; King's College London (BA Hons). Teacher, 1955–67; Education Administration, 1967–77; Asst Sec., Local Authorities' Conditions of Service Adv. Bd, 1978–81; Under Sec., 1981–83, Dep. Sec., 1983–85, AMA. *Recreations:* theatre, travel, bridge. *Address:* 7 Helford Walk, Woking, Surrey GU21 3PL. *T:* Woking 20953. *Club:* Reform.

GRONOW, David Gwilym Colin, PhD; Member, Electricity Council, since 1985; *b* Leigh-on-Sea, 13 Jan. 1929; *s* of David Morgan Gronow and Harriet Hannah Gronow; *m* 1st, 1953, Joan Andrew Bowen Jones (marr. diss. 1970); one *s* one *d*; 2nd, 1970, Rosemary Freda Iris Keys. *Educ:* North Street Elem. Sch., Leigh-on-Sea; Grammar Sch., Swansea; University Coll. London (MSc, PhD). Institute of Aviation Medicine, RAF Farnborough, Hants: Jun. Technician, 1951–53; Sci. Officer, then Sen. Sci. Officer, 1953–57; Sen. Sci. Officer, UKAEA, Capenhurst, Cheshire, 1957; Second Asst Engr, then Sen. Asst Engr, CEGB, HQ Operations Dept, London, 1957–64; Asst Commercial Officer/Asst Chief Commercial Officer/Chief Commercial Officer, SSEB, Glasgow, 1964–78; Marketing Advr, 1978–80, Commercial Advr, 1980–85, Electricity Council, London. *Recreations:* golf, walking, bird watching, theatre. *Address:* 6 Willow Lodge, River Gardens, Stevenage Road, Fulham SW6 6NW. *T:* 01–385 2142.

GROOM, Maj.-Gen. John Patrick, CB 1984; CBE 1975 (MBE 1963); Director General, Guide Dogs for the Blind Association, since 1983; *b* Hagley, Worcs, 9 March 1929; *s* of Samuel Douglas Groom and Gertrude Groom (*née* Clinton); *m* 1951, Jane Mary Miskelly; three *d*. *Educ:* King Charles I Sch., Kidderminster; Royal Military Academy, Sandhurst. Enlisted as Sapper, Dec. 1946; commnd into RE, 1949; regimental service, N Africa, Egypt, Singapore, Malaya, UK, 1949–59; sc Camberley, 1960; War Office, 1961–63; regimental service, UK, Aden, 1963–65 (despatches); Directing Staff, Staff Coll., 1965–68; Regimental Comdr, BAOR, 1968–70; MoD, Military Operations, 1970–71; Dep. Sec., Chiefs of Staff Cttee, 1971–73; HQ Near East Land Forces, Cyprus, 1973–75; RCDS 1976; Comdr, Corps of Royal Engineers, BAOR (Brig.), 1976–79; Chief Engineer, HQ BAOR, 1979–82; Head of Army Trng Rev. Team, MoD (Army), 1982–83. Col Comdt, 1983–86, Rep. Col Comdt, 1986, RE. FBIM 1979; FIPlantE 1976. Liveryman, Worshipful Co. of Plumbers, 1978. *Recreations:* ocean racing, riding, painting, antiques, ornithology, the environment. *Address:* Withybed, All Saints Road, Lymington, Hants SO41 8FB. *Clubs:* Army and Navy, Royal Ocean Racing; Royal Engineer Yacht; Royal Lymington Yacht; British Kiel Yacht (W Germany) (Life Mem.); Kieler Yacht (W Germany) (Hon. Mem.).

GROOM, Sir (Thomas) Reginald, Kt 1961; Chartered Accountant; Partner, Peat, Marwick, Mitchell & Co, Brisbane, Qld, 1932–77; Commissioner, Australian National Airlines Commission, 1961–75; Director: Woodland Ltd (Chairman), 1969–80; Consolidated Rutile Ltd, 1964–78; Mount Isa Mines Holdings Ltd, 1962–77; P & O Australia Ltd, 1958–78; Elder Smith Goldsbrough Mort Ltd, 1966–78; Member of Commonwealth Banking Corporation Board, 1964–74, and of several private companies; *b* 30 Dec. 1906; *s* of Roy Graeme Groom and May Augusta Groom; *m* 1932, Jessie Mary Grace Butcher; two *s* one *d*. *Educ:* Brisbane Grammar Sch.; University of Qld (BA, BCom). Admitted to Institute of Chartered Accountants in Australia, 1932; in public practice, 1932–77. Alderman, Brisbane City Council, 1943–; Lord Mayor of Brisbane, 1955–61. Commissioner, Qld Local Govt Grants Commn, 1977–79. Dir, Australian Elizabethan Theatre Trust. *Recreations:* farming, fishing, golf. *Address:* 39 Ferguson Avenue, Buderim, Qld 4556, Australia. *T:* (office) 221–9411. *Clubs:* Queensland, Johnsonian (Brisbane).

GROOM, Air Marshal Sir Victor E., KCVO 1953; KBE 1952 (CBE 1945; OBE 1940); CB 1944; DFC 1918, and Bar, 1921; RAF retired; *b* 4 Aug. 1898; *e s* of late William E. Groom; *m* 1st, 1924, Maisie Monica Maule (*d* 1961); one *s* (and one *s* decd); 2nd, 1969, Mrs Muriel Constance Brown, *widow* of Captain G. S. Brown. *Educ:* Alleyns, Dulwich. Served European War, 1916–18 (DFC); Egypt, Turkey, Iraq, 1919–22 (bar to DFC); RAF Staff Coll. (psc 1928); India, 1929–34; Bomber Command, 1936–41 (OBE); Directorate of Plans, Air Min., 1941–42; Head of RAF Staff planning the invasion under Chief of Staff to the Supreme Allied Commander, 1942–43; SASO 2nd Tactical Air Force, 1943–45; AOA Flying Trg Command, 1945–46; Dir-Gen. of Manning, Air Ministry, 1947–49; AOC 205 Group RAF, MEAF, 1949–51; C-in-C, MEAF, 1952; AOC-in-C, Technical Training Command, 1952–55, retired 1955. Officer Legion of Honour (France). *Address:* 8 Somerville House, Manor Fields, SW15 3LX. *T:* 01–788 1290. *Club:* Royal Air Force.

GROOTENHUIS, Prof. Peter, FEng 1982, FIMechE; Professor of Mechanical Engineering Science, Imperial College of Science and Technology, since 1972; *b* 31 July 1924; *yr s* of Johannes C. Grootenhuis and Anna C. (*née* van den Bergh); *m* 1954, Sara J. Winchester, *o d* of late Major Charles C. Winchester, MC, The Royal Scots (The Royal Regt), and Margaret I. (*née* de Havilland); one *d* one *s*. *Educ:* Nederlands Lyceum, The Hague; City and Guilds College. BSc MechEng 1944, PhD, DIC, DSc London Univ.; FCGI 1976, Mem., Inst. of Acoustics; Fellow, Soc. of Environmental Engineers (Pres., 1964–67). Apprenticeship and Design Office, Bristol Aero Engine Co., 1944–46; Lectr 1949, Reader 1959, Mech. Eng. Dept, Imperial College, research in heat transfer and in dynamics; Dir, Derritron Electronics, 1969–82; Partner, Grootenhuis Allaway Associates, consultants in noise and vibration, 1970–; Associate Mem., Ordnance Board, 1965–70; Mem. Governing Body, Imperial College, 1974–79. *Publications:* technical papers to learned jls, and patents. *Recreations:* sailing, gardening.

GROSBERG, Prof. Percy, PhD; CEng, MIMechE, FTI; Research Professor of Textile Engineering, University of Leeds, since 1961; *b* 5 April 1925; *s* of late Rev. G. Grosberg and of Mrs P. Grosberg, Tel-Aviv; *m* 1951, Queenie Fisch; one *s* one *d* (and one *s* decd). *Educ:* Parktown Boys' High Sch., Johannesburg; Univ. of the Witwatersrand; Univ. of Leeds. BScEng, MScEng, PhD Witwatersrand; CEng, MIMechE 1965; FTI 1966. Sen. Res. Officer S African Wool Textile Res. Assoc., 1949–55; Univ. of Leeds: ICI Res. Fellow, 1955; Lectr in Textile Engrg, 1955–61; Head, Dept of Textile Industries, 1975–83. Warner Memorial Medal, 1968; Textile Inst. Medal, 1972; Distinguished Service Award, Indian Inst. of Technol., Delhi, 1985. *Publications:* An Introduction to Textile Mechanisms, 1968; Structural Mechanics of Fibres, Yarns and Fabrics, 1969; papers on rheology of fibrous assemblies, mechan. processing of fibres, and other res. topics in Jl of Textile Inst., Textile Res. Jl, and other sci. jls. *Recreations:* music, gardening, travel. *Address:* 2 Sandringham Crescent, Leeds LS17 8DF. *T:* Leeds 687478.

GROSE, Rear-Adm. Alan; Assistant Chief of Operational Requirements (Sea Systems), Ministry of Defence, since 1986; *b* 24 Sept. 1937; *s* of George William Stanley Grose and Ann May Grose (*née* Stanford); *m* 1961, Gillian Ann (*née* Dryden-Dymond); two *s* one *d*. *Educ:* Strodes School; Britannia Royal Naval College, Dartmouth. Mediterranean and S Atlantic, 1957–63; sub-specialised in Navigation, 1964; RAN, 1964–66; Home, W Indies, Med., 1966–72; Comd, HMS Eskimo, 1973–75; Staff of C-in-C, Naval Home Command, 1975–77; MoD, 1977–79; RCDS 1980; Comd, HMS Bristol, 1981–82; RN Presentation Team, 1983–84; Comd, HMS Illustrious, 1984–86; Flag Officer, Sept. 1986. *Recreations:* tennis, walking, reading. *Address:* c/o Barclays Bank, Plymouth. *Clubs:* Army and Navy, Royal Naval Reserve.

GROSS, John Jacob; writer and editor; on the staff of the New York Times, since 1983; *b* 12 March 1935; *s* of late Abraham Gross and Muriel Gross; *m* 1965, Miriam May; one *s* one *d*. *Educ:* City of London Sch.; Wadham Coll., Oxford. Editor, Victor Gollancz Ltd, 1956–58; Asst Lectr, Queen Mary Coll., Univ. of London, 1959–62; Fellow, King's Coll., Cambridge, 1962–65; Literary Editor, New Statesman, 1973; Editor, TLS, 1974–81; editorial consultant, Weidenfeld (Publishers) Ltd, 1982; Dir, Times Newspapers Holdings, 1982. A Trustee, National Portrait Gall., 1977–84. *Publications:* The Rise and Fall of the Man of Letters (1969 Duff Cooper Memorial Prize), 1969; Joyce, 1971; (ed) The Oxford Book of Aphorisms, 1983. *Address:* 24A St Petersburgh Place, W2. *Club:* Beefsteak.

GROSS, Solomon Joseph, CMG 1966; Board Member, British Steel Corporation, since 1978; Director: Barnes Court (New Barnet) Ltd, since 1984; Technical Audit Group, since 1986; *b* 3 Sept. 1920; *s* of late Abraham Gross; *m* 1948, Doris Evelyn (*née* Barker); two *d*. *Educ:* Hackney Downs Sch.; University Coll., London. RAF, Burma, India. Ministry of Supply, 1947; OEEC, Paris, 1948–51; British Embassy, Washington, 1951–53; Board of Trade, 1954–57; British Trade Commr, Pretoria, SA, 1958–62; Principal British Trade Commr, Ghana, 1963–66; British Deputy High Commr, Ghana, 1966–67; Board of Trade, 1967–69; Minister, British Embassy, Pretoria, 1969–73; Chargé d'Affaires at various times in Ghana and S Africa; Under-Sec., Dept of Industry, 1974–80; Dir for Regional Affairs, British Technology Gp, 1983–84. *Recreations:* gardening, history, do-it-yourself. *Address:* 38 Barnes Court, Station Road, New Barnet, Herts EN5 1QY. *T:* 01–449 2710. *Club:* Royal Automobile.

GROSSART, Angus McFarlane McLeod; Managing Director, Noble Grossart Ltd, Merchant Bankers, Edinburgh, since 1969; Chairman: Edinburgh Fund Managers PLC, since 1983; Scottish Investment Trust PLC, since 1975; director of companies; *b* 6 April 1937; 3rd *s* of William John White Grossart and Mary Hay Gardiner; *m* 1978, Mrs Gay Thomson; one *d*. *Educ:* Glasgow Acad.; Glasgow Univ. (MA 1958, LLB 1960). CA 1962; Mem., Faculty of Advocates, 1963. Practised at Scottish Bar, 1963–69. Director: American Trust PLC; Alexander and Alexander, USA; Goldcrest Films & Television Holdings Ltd; North Sea Assets PLC; Pict Petroleum PLC; Reed Stenhouse Cos Ltd, Canada; Royal Bank of Scotland plc. Mem., Scottish Develt Agency, 1974–78. Trustee, National Galleries of Scotland. Hon. LLD Glasgow, 1985. Formerly, Scottish Editor, British Tax Encyc., and British Tax Rev. *Recreations:* golfing (runner-up, British Youths' Golf Championship, 1957; Captain, Scottish Youths Internat., 1956 and 1957), the decorative arts, Scottish castle restoration. *Address:* 48 Queen Street, Edinburgh EH2 3NR. *T:* 031–226 7011. *Clubs:* New, Honourable Company of Edinburgh Golfers (Edinburgh); Royal and Ancient (St Andrews).

GROSSCHMID-ZSÖGÖD, Prof. Géza (Benjamin), LLD; Professor, since 1955, and Chairman, since 1978, Division of Economic Sciences, Duquesne University, Pittsburgh, USA; *b* Budapest, Hungary, 29 Oct. 1918; *o s* of late Prof. Lajos de Grosschmid and Jolán, *o d* of Géza de Szitányi; *m* 1946, Leonora Martha Nissler, 2nd *d* of Otto Nissler and Annemarie Dudt; one *d*. *Educ:* Piarist Fathers, Budapest; Royal Hungarian Pázmány Péter Univ., Budapest (LLD 1943). With private industry in Hungary, 1943–44; Royal Hungarian Army, 1944–45; UNRRA, 1946–47; Duquesne University: Asst Prof. of Econs, 1948–52; Associate Prof., 1952–55; Dir, Inst. of African Affairs, 1958–70; Dir, African Language and Area Center, 1960–74; Academic Vice Pres., 1970–75. Ford Foundn Fellow, 1958; Fulbright-Hays Fellow, S Africa, 1965; attended Cambridge Colonial Conf., King's Coll., 1961. Director: World Affairs Council of Pittsburgh, 1974–80; Afuture Fund of Philadelphia, 1976–84. Mem., Bd of Visitors, Coll. of Arts and Sciences, Univ. of Pittsburgh; Governor, Battle of Britain Museum Foundn, 1977–84. Consultore pro lingua hungarica, Collegio Araldico, Rome. Kt of Malta, 1955 (Comdr of Merit, 1956; Kt of Obedience, 1974; Grand Cross of Obedience, 1984); Kt, Sacred Mil. Constantinian Order of St George (Naples), 1959 (Kt of Justice, 1961; Comdr of Justice, 1984; Pres., Amer. Assoc., 1978); Kt Comdr of St Gregory, 1968. Order of: Valour, Cameroon, 1967; Zaire, 1970; Equatorial Star, Gabon, 1973; Lion, Senegal, 1977. *Publications:* (jtly) Principles of Economics, 1959; (trans. with P. Colombo) The Spiritual Heritage of the Sovereign Military Order of Malta, 1958; contrib. Encyc. Britannica; articles in learned jls. *Recreations:* walking, golf, heraldry, polo. *Address:* 3115 Ashlyn Street, Pittsburgh, Pa 15204, USA. *T:* (412) 331–7744. *Clubs:* Athenæum, MCC; Royal Forth Yacht (Edinburgh); Duquesne (Pittsburgh); Metropolitan, Army & Navy (Washington).

GROSVENOR, family name of **Baron Ebury,** and of **Duke of Westminster.**

GROTRIAN, Sir Philip Christian Brent, 3rd Bt *cr* 1934; *b* 26 March 1935; *s* of Robert Philip Brent Grotrian (*d* on active service, 1945) (*y s* of 1st Bt), and Elizabeth Mary, *d* of Major Herbert Hardy-Wrigley; *S* uncle, 1984; *m* 1st, 1960, Anne Isabel, *d* of Robert Sieger Whyte, Toronto; one *s*; 2nd, 1979, Sarah Frances, *d* of Reginald Harry Gale,

Montreal; one s one d. Educ: Eton; Trinity Coll., Toronto. Heir: s Philip Timothy Adam Brent Grotrian, b 9 April 1962. Address: RR3, Mansfield, Ontario LON 1MO.

GROUES, Henri Antoine; see Pierre, Abbé.

GROUND, (Reginald) Patrick, QC 1981; MP (C) Feltham and Heston, since 1983; b 9 Aug. 1932; s of late Reginald Ground and Ivy Elizabeth Grace (née Irving); m 1964, Caroline Dugdale; three s one d. Educ: Beckenham and Penge County Grammar Sch.; Lycée Gay Lussac, Limoges, France; Selwyn Coll., Cambridge (Open Exhibnr; MA Mod. Langs, French and Spanish); Magdalen Coll., Oxford (MLitt, Mod. History). Inner Temple Studentship and Foster Boulton Prize, 1958; called to the Bar, Inner Temple, 1960. National Service, RN, 1954–56: Sub-Lt RNVR; served in Mediterranean Fleet and on staff of C-in-C Mediterranean; rep. RN at hockey and lawn tennis; Lt-Comdr RNR. Worked for FO on staff of Wilton Park European Conf. Centre, 1958–60. Councillor, London Bor. of Hammersmith, 1968–71 (Chm., Cttees responsible for health and social services, 1969–71); contested (C), Hounslow, Feltham and Heston, Feb. and Oct. 1974, and 1979. Treasurer and Pres., Oxford Univ. Cons. Assoc., 1958; Chm., Fulham Soc., 1975–. Publications: articles on housing, security of tenure and the Rent Acts in jls and periodicals. Recreations: lawn tennis, sailing, travel. Address: 13 Ranelagh Avenue, SW6 3PJ. T: 01–736 0131. Clubs: Brooks's, Carlton.

GROUNDS, Stanley Paterson, CBE 1968; Charity Commissioner, 1960–69; b 25 Oct. 1904; 2nd s of late Thomas Grounds and Olivia Henrietta (née Anear), Melbourne, Australia; m 1932, Freda Mary Gale Ransford; twin s and d. Educ: Melbourne High Sch.; Queen's Coll., Melbourne Univ. (1st Cl. hons, MA). With Melbourne Herald, 1926–28; British Empire Producers' Organisation, London, 1928–33. Called to Bar, Middle Temple, 1933; at Chancery Bar, 1934–40. Served Royal Air Force, 1940–45 (Squadron Leader). Asst Charity Commissioner, 1946–58; Sec., Charity Commission, 1958–60. Publications: contrib. Encyclopædia of Forms and Precedents, Encyclopædia of Court Forms (on Charities), Halsbury's Laws of England, 3rd edn (on Charities). Articles in law jls. Recreation: other men's flowers. Address: St Helena, 19 Bell Road, Haslemere, Surrey GU27 3DQ. T: Haslemere 51230. Club: Army and Navy.

GROVE, Sir Charles Gerald, 5th Bt cr 1874; b 10 Dec. 1929; s of Walter Peel Grove (d 1944) (3rd s of 2nd Bt) and Elena Rebecca, d of late Felipe Crosthwaite; S brother, 1974. Heir: b Harold Thomas Grove, b 6 Dec. 1930.

GROVE, Sir Edmund (Frank), KCVO 1982 (MVO(V) 1953, MVO(IV) 1963, CVO 1974); Chief Accountant of the Privy Purse, 1967–82, and Serjeant-at-Arms, 1975–82, retired; b 20 July 1920; s of Edmund Grove and Sarah Caroline (née Hunt); m 1945, Grete Elisabet, d of Martinus Skou, Denmark; two d. Served War, RASC, ME, 1940–46. Entered the Household of King George VI, 1946 and of Queen Elizabeth II, 1952. Chevalier: Order of the Dannebrog, Denmark, 1974; Légion d'Honneur, France, 1976; Officer, Order of the Polar Star, Sweden, 1975. Recreations: gardening, fishing. Address: Chapel Cottage, West Newton, King's Lynn, Norfolk PE31 6AU.

GROVE, Rear-Adm. John Scott, CB 1984; OBE 1964; RN retired, 1985; Chief Strategic Systems Executive (formerly Chief Polaris Executive), 1980–85; Chief Naval Engineer Officer, 1983–85; b 7 July 1927; s of late William George Grove and Frances Margaret Scott Grove; m 1950, Betty Anne (née Robinson); one s (one d decd). Educ: Dundee High Sch.; St Andrews Univ. University Coll., 1944–47 (BScEng 1st Cl. Hons). National Service, Royal Engineers, 1947–48; Instructor Br., Royal Navy, 1948–50; Electrical Engrg Br., RN, 1950, qualified in Submarines, 1953; post graduate trng in Nuclear Engrg, Imperial Coll., London, 1958–59; sea service in HMS Forth and HM Submarines Tally-Ho, Turpin, Porpoise, Dreadnought; service in Ship Dept, 1964–67; staff of Flag Officer Submarines, 1967–70; Naval Asst to Controller of the Navy, 1970–73; staff of Flag Officer Submarines, 1975–77; commanded HMS Fisgard, 1977–79. Comdr 1963; Captain 1970; Rear-Adm. 1980. Recreations: walking, the garden. Address: Maryfield, South Close, Wade Court, Havant, Hants PO9 2TD. T: Havant 475116. Club: Royal Commonwealth Society.

GROVE-WHITE, Robin Bernard; Director, Council for the Protection of Rural England, since 1981; b 17 Feb. 1941; s of Charles William Grove-White and Cecile Mary Rabbidge; m 1st, 1970, Virginia Harriet Ironside (marr. diss.); one s; 2nd, 1979, Helen Elizabeth Smith; two s one d. Educ: Uppingham Sch.; Worcester Coll., Oxford (BA). Freelance writer for TV, radio, press and advertising in UK, Canada and US, 1963–70; McCann-Erickson Ltd, London, 1970; Asst Secretary, CPRE, 1972–80. Publications: (contrib.) Politics of Physical Resources, 1975; (contrib.) Future Landscapes, 1976; (with Michael Flood) Nuclear Prospects, 1976; contribs to New Scientist, Nature, Times, Vole, etc. Recreations: walking, cricket. Address: 77 Chevening Road, NW6 6DA. T: 01–969 7375.

GROVES, Sir Charles (Barnard), Kt 1973; CBE 1968 (OBE 1958); FRCM, Hon. RAM, CRNCM; conductor; Associate Conductor, Royal Philharmonic Orchestra, since 1967; b 10 March 1915; s of Frederick Groves and Annie (née Whitehead); m 1948, Hilary Hermione Barchard; one s two d. Educ: St Paul's Cathedral Choir Sch.; Sutton Valence Sch.; Royal College of Music. Free lance accompanist and organist. Joined BBC, Chorus-Master Music Productions Unit, 1938; Asst Conductor BBC Theatre Orchestra, 1942; Conductor BBC Revue Orchestra, 1943; Conductor BBC Northern Orchestra, 1944–51; Dir of Music, Bournemouth Corporation, and Conductor, Bournemouth Municipal Orchestra, 1951–54; Conductor of Bournemouth Symphony Orchestra, 1954–61; Resident Musical Dir, Welsh National Opera Company, 1961–63; Musical Dir and Resident Conductor, Royal Liverpool Philharmonic Orchestra, 1963–77; Music Dir, ENO, 1978–79. President: Nat. Youth Orchestra of GB, 1977–; Incorporated Soc. of Musicians, 1982–83; Life Mem., RPO, 1976. FRCM 1961; Hon. RAM 1967; Hon. FTCL 1974; Hon. GSM 1974; CRNCM 1983 (Hon. FRNCM 1974). Conductor of the Year Award, 1968, 1978. Has toured Australia, New Zealand, South Africa, N and S America, Japan and Europe. Hon. DMus Liverpool, 1970; DUniv. Open, 1978. Recreation: English literature. Address: 12 Camden Square, NW1 9UY. Club: Savage.

GROVES, John Dudley, CB 1981; OBE 1964; Director-General, Central Office of Information, 1979–82; Head of Profession for Government Information Officer Group, 1981–82; b 12 Aug. 1922; y s of late Walter Groves; m 1943, Pamela Joy Holliday; one s two d. Educ: St Paul's Sch. Reporter, Richmond Herald, 1940–41; Queen's Royal Regt, 1941–42; commnd in 43rd Reconnaissance Regt, 1942; served in NW Europe, 1944–45 (despatches); Observer Officer, Berlin, 1945; Press Association (Press Gallery), 1947–51; Times (Press Gallery and Lobby), 1951–58; Head of Press Sect., Treasury, 1958–62; Dep. Public Relations Adviser to Prime Minister, 1962–64 (Actg Adviser, 1964); Chief Information Officer, DEA, 1964–68; Chief of Public Relations, MoD, 1968–77; Dir of Information, DHSS, 1977–78. Mem., Working Party on Censorship, 1983. Publication: (with R. Gill) Club Route, 1945. Recreations: walking, painting. Address: Mortimers, Manningford Bohune, Pewsey, Wilts.

GROVES, Richard Bebb, TD 1966; RD 1979; His Honour Judge Groves; a Circuit Judge, since 1985; b 4 Oct. 1933; s of George Thomas Groves and Margaret Anne (née Bebb); m 1958, Eileen Patricia (née Farley); one s one d. Educ: Bancroft's Sch., Woodford Green, Essex. Admitted Solicitor of the Supreme Court, 1960. Partner, H. J. Smith & Co. and Richard Groves & Co., 1962–85. Dep. Circuit Judge, 1978–80; a Recorder, 1980–85. Nijmegen Medal, Royal Netherlands League for Physical Culture, 1965 and 1966. Recreations: Royal Naval Reserve, tennis, philately, walking, reading. Address: Pinemead, Wakes Colne, Colchester, Essex CO6 2BX. T: Earls Colne 2644. Clubs: Colchester Garrison Officers (Colchester); Chelmsford (Chelmsford).

GROVES, Ronald, MA, BSc Oxon; FRSC; FKC; Member of Council, Sir Richard Stapley Educational Trust, (Secretary, 1969–83); Fellow, King's College Hospital Medical School (Vice Chairman of Council, 1975–83); b 19 Aug. 1908; s of late John Ackroyd Groves and Annie Groves, Bradford; m 1939, Hilary Annot, yr d of late George Smith; two s. Educ: Bradford Grammar Sch.; Christ Church, Oxford. 1st Class Hons Nat. Sci. (Chemistry), 1931. Asst Master, Bradfield Coll., 1931–32; Worksop Coll., 1932–35; Senior Science Master and Housemaster, King's Sch., Canterbury, 1935–43; Bursar, 1937–43; Headmaster, Campbell Coll., Belfast, 1943–54; Master, Dulwich Coll., 1954–66. Adviser, Jt Working Party of Governing Bodies' Assoc. and Headmasters' Conf., 1966–73. Chm., Food Standards Cttee, 1959–62. Address: 83 Cumnor Hill, Oxford. Clubs: Athenæum, MCC.

GROVES, Ronald Edward, CBE 1972; CBIM; Chairman, Meyer International PLC, since 1982; Chairman, since 1976 and Chief Executive, since 1973, International Timber PLC; b 2 March 1920; s of Joseph Rupert and Eva Lilian Groves; m 1940, Beryl Doris Lydia Collins; two s one d. Educ: Watford Grammar School. Joined J. Gliksten & Son Ltd; served War of 1939–45, Flt-Lt RAF, subseq. Captain with BOAC; re-joined J. Gliksten & Son Ltd, 1946: Gen. Works Man. 1947; Dir 1954; Jt Man. Dir 1964; Vice-Chm. 1967; Dir, Gliksten (West Africa) Ltd, 1949; Vice-Chm., International Timber Corp. Ltd, 1970 (name of J. Gliksten & Son Ltd changed to International Timber Corp. Ltd, 1970 following merger with Horsley Smith & Jewson Ltd). Dir, Nat. Building Agency, 1978–82; Member: EDC for Building, 1982–; Cttee of Management, National Council of Building Material Producers, 1982–. President: Timber Trade Fedn of UK, 1969–71; London and District Sawmill Owners Assoc., 1954–56; Vice-Pres., Timber Res. and Develt Assoc., 1985–; Chm., Nat. Sawmilling Assoc., 1966–67; Mem., London and Regional Affairs Cttee, 1980–, and Mem. Council, 1982–, London Chamber of Commerce and Industry; Mem., London Regl Council, CBI, 1983–; Dir, Business in the Community, 1984–. Chairman: Rickmansworth UDC, 1957–58, 1964–65 and 1971–72; W Herts Main Drainage Authority, 1970–74; Three Rivers District Council, 1977–78. Chairman of Governors: Watford Grammar Sch. for Girls, 1980–; Watford Grammar Sch. for Boys, 1980–. Recreations: visiting theatre and opera; local community work. Address: 8 Pembroke Road, Moor Park, Northwood, Mddx. T: Northwood 23187.

GRUENBERG, Prof. Karl Walter; Professor of Pure Mathematics in the University of London, at Queen Mary College, since 1967; b 3 June 1928; s of late Paul Gruenberg and of Anna Gruenberg; m 1973, Margaret Semple; one s one d. Educ: Shaftesbury Grammar Sch.; Kilburn Grammar Sch.; Cambridge Univ. BA 1950, PhD 1954. Asst Lectr, Queen Mary Coll., 1953–55; Commonwealth Fund Fellowship, 1955–57 (at Harvard Univ., 1955–56; at Inst. for Advanced Studies, Princeton, 1956–57). Queen Mary College: Lectr, 1957–61; Reader, 1961–67; Prof., 1967–. Visiting Professor: Univ. of Michigan, 1961–62, 1978; Cornell Univ., 1966–67; Univ. of Illinois, 1972; Australian Nat. Univ., 1979. Publications: Cohomological Topics in Group Theory, 1970; Relation Modules of Finite Groups, 1976; Linear Geometry (jtly with A. J. Weir), 2nd edn 1977; articles on algebra in various learned jls. Address: Department of Pure Mathematics, Queen Mary College (University of London), Mile End Road, E1 4NS. T: 01–980 4811.

GRUFFYDD, Prof. (Robert) Geraint; Director, University of Wales Centre for Advanced Welsh and Celtic Studies, Aberystwyth, since 1985; b 9 June 1928; s of Moses and Ceridwen Griffith; m 1953, Elizabeth Eluned Roberts; two s one d. Educ: University Coll. of N Wales, Bangor (BA); Jesus Coll., Oxford (DPhil). Asst Editor, Geiriadur Prifysgol Cymru, 1953–55; Lectr, Dept of Welsh, UCNW, 1955–70; Prof. of Welsh Language and Literature, UCW, Aberystwyth, 1970–79; Librarian, Nat. Library of Wales, 1980–85. Publications: (ed) Meistri'r Canrifoedd, 1973; (ed) Cerddi '73, 1973; (ed) Bardos, 1982; articles, etc, on Welsh literary and religious history in various collaborative vols and learned jls. Recreations: reading (preferably theology), walking (preferably in Wales), learning to fly (in receding contemplation). Address: Eirianfa, Caradog Road, Aberystwyth, Dyfed. T: Aberystwyth 3396.

GRUFFYDD JONES, Daniel; see Jones, D. G.

GRUGEON, Sir John (Drury), Kt 1980; DL; Chairman, Tunbridge Wells Health Authority, since 1984; b 20 Sept. 1928; s of Drury Grugeon and Sophie (née Pratt); m 1955, Mary Patricia (née Rickards); one s one d. Educ: Epsom Grammar Sch.; RMA, Sandhurst. Commissioned, The Buffs, Dec. 1948; served 1st Bn in Middle and Far East and Germany; Regimental Adjt, 1953–55; Adjt 5th Bn, 1956–58; left Army, 1960. Joined Save and Prosper Group, 1960. Mem., Kent CC, 1967– (Leader, 1973–82). Chm., Policy Cttee, Assoc. of County Councils, 1978–81 (Chm., Finance Cttee, 1976–79). Dir, Internat. Garden Fest. '84, Liverpool, 1982–83. Member: SE Economic Planning Council, 1971–74; Cons. Council on Local Govt Finance, 1975–82; Medway Ports Authority, 1977–; Dep. Chm., Medway (Chatham) Dock Co., 1983–. DL Kent, 1986. Recreations: cricket, shooting, local govt. Address: Sand Pett, Charing, Ashford, Kent TN27 0AT. T: Charing 2322. Clubs: Carlton, MCC; Kent County CC.

GRUNDY, Air Marshal Sir Edouard (Michael FitzFrederick), KBE 1963 (OBE 1942); CB 1960; Chairman, Short Brothers and Harland, 1968–76; b 29 Sept. 1908; s of late Frederick Grundy and Osca Marah Ewart; m 1st, 1945, Lucia le Sueur (née Corder) (d 1973); three s (and one d decd); 2nd, 1975, Mrs Marie Louise Holder. Educ: St Paul's Sch.; RAF Coll., Cranwell. 56 (F) Sqdn 1928; 403 Flight FAA, 1929–31; Signals Specialist Course, 1932; RAF North Weald, 1933–36; RNZAF HQ, 1937–40; OC No 80 (S) Wing, 1941–42; CSO, NW African AF, 1942–43; CSO Mediterranean Allied Tactical Air Forces, 1943–44; CSO, RAF, Middle East, 1944–45; Commandant, Empire Radio Sch., 1945–46; Dep. Dir Air Staff Policy, Air Ministry, 1947–49; Air Adviser, Royal Norwegian AF, 1949–51; Dep. CSO, Supreme HQ Allied Powers Europe, 1951–52; idc 1953; Senior Air Staff Officer, Brit. Jt Services Mission in USA, 1954–55; Chm. NATO Military Agency for Standardisation, 1955–58; Air Officer i/c Administration, FEAF, 1958–61; Commandant-Gen. RAF Regt, 1961–62; Controller, Guided Weapons and Electronics, Ministry of Aviation, 1962–66; retired, 1966. Mem., Engineering Industries Council, 1975–. Pres., SBAC, 1975–76. FRAeS. Chevalier, Royal Norwegian Order of St Olaf, 1953. Recreations: usual. Address: c/o Lloyds Bank, 6 Pall Mall, SW1. Club: Royal Air Force.

GRUNDY, Fred, MD; MRCP; DPH; Barrister-at-law; Assistant Director General, World Health Organization, Geneva, 1961–66; retired; b 15 May 1905; s of Thomas Grundy, Manchester; m 1932, Ada Furnell Leppington, Hessle, Yorks; one s one d. Educ: Leeds and London Univs. MB, ChB (Hons), Leeds; MRCS, LRCP, 1927; DPH, RCPS, 1931; MD Leeds, 1933; MRCP, 1951. Called to the Bar, Inner Temple, 1934. Resident hospital appts and gen. practice, 1927–31; Asst County Medical Officer, E Suffolk, 1931–34; Asst MOH to Borough of Willesden, 1934–35; Deputy MOH to Borough of Luton, 1935–37; MOH to Borough of Luton, 1937–49; Mansel Talbot Prof. of Preventive Medicine, Welsh Nat. Sch. of Medicine, 1949–61. *Publications:* A Note on the Vital Statistics of Luton, 1944; (with R. M. Titmuss) Report on Luton, 1945; Handbook of Social Medicine, 1945; The New Public Health, 1949; Preventive Medicine and Public Health: An Introduction for Students and Practitioners, 1951; papers on public health and scientific subjects. *Recreations:* mountaineering, yachting, golf, etc. *Address:* Weir House, Radyr, near Cardiff.

GRUNDY, (James) Milton; Founder and Chairman of the Warwick Arts Trust, since 1978; *b* 13 June 1926. *Educ:* Sedbergh Sch.; Gonville and Caius Coll., Cambridge (MA). Called to the Bar, Inner Temple, 1954. Founder Mem. and Pres., Internat. Tax Planning Assoc., 1975–; Mem. Cttee, Revenue Bar Assoc., 1978–. Founder and Chm., Gemini Trust for the Arts, 1959 66; Charter Mem., Peggy Guggenheim Collection, 1980–. *Publications:* Tax and the Family Company, 1956, 3rd edn 1966; Tax Havens, 1968, 4th edn 1983; Venice, 1971, 4th edn 1985; The World of International Tax Planning, 1984; contrib. British Tax Rev. and Jl of Business Law. *Recreation:* conversation. *Address:* New House, Shipton-under-Wychwood, Oxon OX7 6DD. *T:* Shipton-under-Wychwood 830495.

GRUNDY, John Brownsdon Clowes, TD 1951; Officier d'Académie, 1937; MA, PhD, DLit; *b* 21 April 1902; *m* 1939, Dorothea, *d* of Enid Pennington; two *s* three *d*. *Educ:* Emanuel Sch.; Fitzwilliam Hall, Cambridge (Exhibitioner); University Coll., London (research). Asst Master, St Paul's Sch., 1923–27; English Lektor, University of Göttingen, 1928; "The Connoisseur", 1928–29; Sen. Mod. Langs Master, Shrewsbury Sch., 1929–39. Served War of 1939–45, The Rangers (KRRC); principally in Gen. Staff (Intell.); Normandy-Germany, 1944; rank at release, temp. Col. First Rep. of Brit. Council in Finland, 1945–49; Dir, Brit. Institute, Cairo, 1949–50; head of mod. langs, Harrow Sch., 1950–53; Headmaster of Emanuel Sch., 1953–63; Head of Dept of Modern Languages, University Coll. of Sierra Leone, 1964–66. *Publications:* Tieck and Runge, 1929; Brush Up Your German, series, 1931–61; French Style, 1937; Life's Five Windows, 1968; various edns and translations of foreign texts. *Recreations:* antiquities, hills, foreign parts. *Address:* Llyn Du, Llansantffraid, Powys.

GRUNDY, Milton; *see* Grundy, J. M.

GRUNDY, R(upert) F(rancis) Brooks; consultant engineer; General Manager, Corby Development Corporation, 1950–68, and Industrial Projects Consultant to the Corporation, 1968–70; *b* 6 Sept. 1903; *s* of J. F. E. Grundy, fine art publisher, London and Emily Grundy (*née* Brownsdon); *m* 1938, Heather Mary, *d* of William and Mabel Thomas, Swansea; one *s* one *d*. *Educ:* Emanuel Sch., London; University Coll., London (BSc (Eng.)); Open Univ. (BA 1975). FICE, FIMunE. Municipal Engrg, 1922–44, at Croydon, Bournemouth, Swansea, Carlisle and Harrow; Borough Engr and Surveyor: Mansfield, 1944–45; Wallasey, 1945–49; Wandsworth, 1949–50. Mem., BBC Midlands Region Adv. Coun., 1966–68. *Publications:* Builders' Materials, 1930; Essentials of Reinforced Concrete, 1939, 1948; papers presented to ICE and IMunE. *Recreations:* golf, walking, reading. *Address:* The Mill House, Brigstock, Kettering, Northants. *T:* Brigstock 218.

GRUNFELD, Prof. Cyril; Professor of Law, London School of Economics, 1966–82; *b* 26 Sept. 1922; *o s* of Samuel and Sarah Grunfeld; *m* 1945, Phyllis Levin; one *s* two *d*. *Educ:* Canton High Sch., Cardiff; Trinity Hall, Cambridge (MA, LLB). Called to Bar, Inner Temple. British Army, 1942–45; Trinity Hall (Studentship), 1946–48; LSE: Asst, 1946–47; Asst Lectr, 1947–49; Lectr, 1949–56; Reader in Law, 1956—66; Pro-Dir, 1973–76; Convener, Law Dept, 1976–79; Dean, Faculty of Law, Univ. of London, 1978–80. Vis. Research Fellow, ANU, 1970–71; Legal Adviser: to Commn on Industrial Relations, 1971–74; to Industrial Soc., 1982–. *Publications:* Modern Trade Union Law, 1966; The Law of Redundancy, 1971, 2nd edn, 1980; contrib. to books and learned jls. *Recreations:* reading, walking. *Address:* c/o London School of Economics and Political Science, Houghton Street, WC2A 2AE.

GRUNFELD, Henry; President, S. G. Warburg & Co. Ltd, since 1974 (Chairman 1969–74); *b* 1 June 1904; *m* 1931, Berta Lotte Oliven; one *s*. *Address:* 33 King William Street, EC4R 9AS. *T:* 01–280 2222.

GRUNSELL, Prof. Charles Stuart Grant, CBE 1976; PhD; Professor of Veterinary Medicine, University of Bristol, 1957–80, now Emeritus; *b* 6 Jan. 1915; *s* of Stuart and Edith Grunsell; *m* 1939, Marjorie Prunella Wright; one *s* two *d*. *Educ:* Shanghai Public Sch.; Bristol Grammar Sch. Qualified as MRCVS at The Royal (Dick) Veterinary Coll., Edinburgh, 1937; FRCVS 1971. In general practice at Glastonbury, Som., 1939–48. PhD Edinburgh, 1952. Senior Lecturer in Veterinary Hygiene and Preventive Medicine, University of Edinburgh, 1952. Pro-Vice-Chancellor, Univ. of Bristol, 1974–77. Chm., Veterinary Products Cttee, 1970–80. Mem., General Synod of C of E, 1980–85; a Diocesan Reader. Editor, Veterinary Annual. Defence Medal 1946. *Publications:* papers on the Erythron of Ruminants, on Vital Statistics in Veterinary Medicine, on Preventive Medicine, and on veterinary education. *Recreation:* gardening. *Address:* Towerhead House, Banwell, near Weston-super-Mare, Avon BS24 6PQ. *T:* Banwell 822461.

GRYLLS, Michael; *see* Grylls, W. M. J.

GRYLLS, Rosalie G.; *see* Mander, Lady (Rosalie).

GRYLLS, (William) Michael (John); MP (C) North West Surrey, since 1974 (Chertsey, 1970–74); *b* 21 Feb. 1934; *s* of Brig. W. E. H. Grylls, OBE; *m* 1965, Sarah Smiles Justice, *d* of Captain N. M. Ford and of Lady (Patricia) Fisher, *qv*; one *s* one *d*. *Educ:* RN College, Dartmouth; Univ. of Paris. Lieut, Royal Marines, 1952–55. Mem., St Pancras Borough Council, 1959–62. Contested (C) Fulham, Gen. Elecs, 1964 and 1966; Mem., Select Cttee on Overseas Develt, 1970–78; Chairman: Cons. Trade and Industry Cttee, 1981– (Vice-Chm., Cons. Industry Cttee, 1975–81); Small Business Bureau, 1979–; Parly Spokesman, Inst. of Directors, 1979–. Mem. GLC, 1967–70; Dep. Leader, Inner London Educn Authority, 1969–70; Chm., Further and Higher Educn, 1968–70. *Recreations:* sailing, riding, gardening. *Address:* c/o House of Commons, SW1. *Club:* Royal Yacht Squadron (Cowes).

GUAZZELLI, Rt. Rev. Victor; Auxiliary Bishop of Westminster (Bishop in East London) (RC), and Titular Bishop of Lindisfarne since 1970; *b* 19 March 1920; *s* of Cesare Guazzelli and Maria (*née* Frepoli). *Educ:* Parochial Schools, Tower Hamlets; English Coll., Lisbon. Priest, 1945. Asst, St Patrick's, Soho Square, 1945–48; Bursar and Prof. at English Coll., Lisbon, 1948–58; Westminster Cathedral: Chaplain, 1958–64; Hon. Canon, 1964; Sub-Administrator, 1964–67; Parish Priest of St Thomas', Fulham, 1967–70; Vicar General of Westminster, 1970. *Address:* The Lodge, Pope John House, Hale Street, E14. *T:* 01–987 4663.

GUDERLEY, Mrs C.; *see* Hyams, Daisy Deborah.

GUÐMUNDSSON, Guðmundur I., Comdr with Star, Order of the Falcon, 1957; Ambassador of Iceland to Belgium, 1977–79, and concurrently to Luxembourg, NATO and EEC; *b* 17 July 1909; *m* 1942, Rósa Ingólfsdóttir; four *s*. *Educ:* Reykjavík Grammar Sch.; Univ. of Iceland. Grad. in Law 1934. Practised as Solicitor and Barrister from 1934; Barrister to Supreme Court, 1939; Sheriff and Magistrate, 1945–56. Mem. Central Cttee, Social Democratic Party, 1940–65, Vice-Chm. of Party, 1954–65; Member of Althing (Parlt), 1942–65; Minister of Foreign Affairs, 1956–65; Minister of Finance, 1958–59; Chm., Icelandic Delegn to UN Conf. on Law of the Sea, Geneva, 1958 and 1960; Mem. and Chm. of Board of Dirs, Fishery Bank in Reykjavík, 1957–65; Ambassador of Iceland: to UK, 1965–71, and concurrently to the Netherlands, Portugal and Spain; to United States, 1971–73, and concurrently to Argentina, Brazil, Canada, Mexico and Cuba; to Sweden, 1973–77 and concurrently to Finland, Austria and Yugoslavia. Establishment of Republic Medal, 1944. Hon. KBE; Grand Cross, Order of: White Rose (Finland); North Star (Sweden); Orange-Nassau (Netherlands); Chêne (Luxembourg); Southern Cross (Brazil); St Olav (Norway); Phoenix (Greece). *Address:* Solvallagata 8, 101 Reykjavik, Iceland.

GUERISSE, Chevalier Albert Marie Edmond, GC 1946; Hon. KBE 1979; DSO 1942 (under name of Patrick Albert O'Leary); medical officer; Major-General in the Belgian Army; Director-General, Medical Service, Belgian Forces; retired 1970; *b* Brussels, 5 April 1911; *m* 1947, Sylvia Cooper Smith (*d* 1985); one *s*. *Educ:* in Belgium; Louvain; Brussels University. Medical Officer, Lieut, 1940; after Belgian capitulation embarked at Dunkirk and became, in Sept. 1940, Lieut-Comdr, RN; first officer of "Q" ship, HMS Fidelity (under name of P. A. O'Leary). Engaged on secret work in France from April 1941 until arrest by Gestapo in March 1943 (chief of an escape organisation). After 2 years in Concentration Camps returned to England. After demobilisation from RN rejoined Belgian Army (1st Lancers); joined Belgian Volunteer Bn, 1951, as Chief of Medical Service in Korea. Officier Légion d'Honneur, 1947; Medal of Freedom with golden palm, 1947; Officier Ordre Léopold, 1946, Grand Officier, 1970; French Croix de Guerre, 1945; Polish Croix de Guerre, 1944. Hereditary Nobility with personal title of Chevalier granted by King of the Belgians, 1981. *Address:* 15 Chaussée de Boitsfort, 1050 Brussels, Belgium.

GUERITZ, Rear-Adm. Edward Findlay, CB 1971; OBE 1957; DSC 1942, and Bar, 1944; defence consultant, writer and broadcaster; *b* 8 Sept. 1919; *s* of Elton and Valentine Gueritz; *m* 1947, Pamela Amanda Bernhardina Britton, *d* of Commander L. H. Jeans; one *s* one *d*. *Educ:* Cheltenham Coll. Entered Navy, 1937; Midshipman, 1938; served War of 1939–45 (wounded; DSC and Bar): HMS Jersey, 5th Flotilla, 1940–41; Combined Ops (Indian Ocean, Normandy), 1941–44; HMS Saumarez (Corfu Channel incident), 1946; Army Staff Coll., Camberley, 1948; Staff of C-in-C S Atlantic and Junior Naval Liaison Officer to UK High Comr, S Africa, 1954–56; Near East Operations, 1956 (OBE); Dep. Dir, RN Staff Coll., 1959–61; Naval Staff, Admty, 1961–63; idc 1964; Captain of Fleet, Far East Fleet, 1965–66; Dir of Defence Plans (Navy), 1967; Dir, Jt Warfare Staff, MoD, 1968; Admiral-President, Royal Naval Coll., 1968–70 (concurrently first Pres., RN Staff Coll.); Comdt, Jt Warfare Estabt, 1970–72. Lt-Comdr 1949; Comdr 1953; Captain 1959; Rear-Adm. 1969; retd 1973. Dep. Dir and Editor, 1976–79, Dir and Editor-in-Chief, 1979–81, RUSI. Specialist Adviser, House of Commons Select Cttee on Defence, 1975–. Chief Hon. Steward, Westminster Abbey, 1975–85. Pres., Soc. for Nautical Res., 1974–; Vice Chm., Victoria League, 1985–; Member Council: Marine Soc.; Operation Drake; British Atlantic Cttee; Mem., Bd of War Studies, Univ. of London, 1969–85. *Publications:* (jtly) The Third World War, 1978; (ed jtly) Ten Years of Terrorism, 1979; (ed jtly) Will the Wells Run Dry, 1979; (ed jtly) Nuclear Attack: Civil Defence, 1982; editor, RUSI Brassey's Defence Year Book, 1977–78, 1978–79, 1980, 1981. *Recreations:* history, reading. *Address:* 56 The Close, Salisbury, Wilts. *Club:* Army and Navy.

GUERNSEY, Lord; Charles Heneage Finch-Knightley; *b* 27 March 1947; *s* and *heir* of 11th Earl of Aylesford, *qv*; *m* 1971, Penelope Anstice, *y d* of Kenneth A. G. Crawley; one *s* four *d* (incl. twin *d*). *Educ:* Oundle, Trinity Coll., Cambridge. *Recreations:* shooting, fishing, Real tennis, cricket. *Heir:* *s* Hon. Heneage James Daniel Finch-Knightley, *b* 29 April 1985. *Address:* Packington Hall, Meriden, Coventry. *T:* Meriden 22274.

GUERNSEY, Dean of; *see* Foster, Very Rev. J. W.

GUEST, family name of **Viscount Wimborne.**

GUEST; *see* Haden-Guest.

GUEST, Prof. Anthony Gordon, FCIArb; Barrister-at-Law; Professor of English Law, King's College, University of London, since 1966; *b* 8 Feb. 1930; *o s* of late Gordon Walter Leslie Guest and of Marjorie (*née* Hooper), Maidencombe, Devon; unmarried. *Educ:* Colston's Sch., Bristol; St John's Coll., Oxford (MA). Exhibr and Casberd Schol., Oxford, 1950–54; 1st cl. Final Hon. Sch. of Jurisprudence, 1954. Bacon Schol., Gray's Inn, 1955; Barstow Law Schol., 1955; called to Bar, Gray's Inn, 1956, Bencher, 1978. University Coll., Oxford: Lectr, 1954–55; Fellow and Prælector in Jurisprudence, 1955–65; Dean, 1963–64; Reader in Common Law to Council of Legal Educn (Inns of Court), 1967–80. Travelling Fellowship to S Africa, 1957; Mem., Lord Chancellor's Law Reform Cttee, 1963–84; Mem., Adv. Cttee on establishment of Law Faculty in University of Hong Kong, 1965; UK Deleg. to UN Commn on Internat. Trade Law, NY, Geneva and Vienna, 1968–84 and 1986, to UN Conf. on Limitation of Actions, 1974; Mem., Board of Athlone Press, 1968–73; Mem. Governing Body, Rugby Sch., 1968–. FKC 1982; FCIArb 1984. Served Army and TA, 1948–50 (Lieut RA). *Publications:* (ed) Anson's Principles of the Law of Contract, 21st to 26th edns, 1959–84; Chitty on Contracts: (Asst Editor) 22nd edn, 1961, (Gen. Editor) 23rd to 25th edns, 1968–82; (ed) Oxford Essays in Jurisprudence, 1961; The Law of Hire-Purchase, 1966; (Gen. Editor) Benjamin's Sale of Goods, 1st to 3rd edns, 1974–87; (ed jtly) Encylopedia of Consumer Credit, 1975; (jtly) Introduction to the Law of Credit and Security, 1978; articles in legal jls. *Address:* 16 Trevor Place, SW7. *T:* 01–584 9260. *Club:* Garrick.

GUEST, Douglas Albert, CVO 1975; MA Cantab and Oxon; MusB Cantab; MusD Cantuar; FRCM, Hon. RAM, FRCO, FRSCM; Organist Emeritus, Westminster Abbey, since 1981; Examiner to Associated Board of Royal Schools of Music, since 1948; *b* 9 May 1916; 2nd *s* of late Harold Guest, Henley-on-Thames, Oxon; *m* 1941, Peggie Florentia, *d* of late Thomas Falconer, FRIBA, Amberley, Gloucestershire; two *d*. *Educ:* Reading Sch.; Royal College of Music, London; King's Coll., Cambridge. Organ Scholar, King's Coll., Cambridge, 1935–39; John Stewart of Rannoch Scholar in Sacred Music, Cambridge Univ., 1936–39. Served War of 1939–45, Major (Battery Comdr), Royal Artillery (HAC) (despatches 1944). Gazetted Hon. Major, RA, April 1945. Dir of Music, Uppingham Sch., 1945–50; Organist and Master of the Choristers, Salisbury Cathedral, 1950–57; Conductor of Salisbury Musical Soc., 1950–57; Dir of Music St Mary's Sch., Calne, 1950–57; Master of the Choristers and Organist, Worcester Cathedral, 1957–63; Conductor Worcester Festival Chorus and Three Choirs Festival, 1957–63; Organist and Master of the Choristers, Westminster Abbey, 1963–81. Prof., RCM, 1963–81. First Vice-Pres., National Youth Orchestra of Great Britain, 1984– (Chm. Council, 1953–84); Member Council: RCO, 1966–; Musicians' Benevolent Fund, 1968–. *Recreations:* fly fishing, golf. *Address:* The Gables, Minchinhampton, Glos GL6 9JE. *T:* Brimscombe 883191. *Club:* Flyfishers'.

GUEST, Eric Ronald; Metropolitan Magistrate (West London), 1946–68; Barrister-at-Law; *b* 7 June 1904; *s* of late William Guest; *m* 1932, Sybil Blakelock; one *d*. *Educ:* Berkhamsted Sch.; Oriel Coll., Oxford. BA 1925 (1st Class Hons Sch. of Jurisprudence); BCL 1926; called to Bar, 1927; practised in London and on Oxford Circuit. Recorder of Worcester, 1941–46; served as Sqdn Leader with RAFVR, 1940–45.

GUEST, George Howell, MA, MusB (Cantab); MusD (Lambeth), 1977; FRCO 1942; FRSCM 1973; Hon. RAM 1984; Organist of St John's College, Cambridge, since 1951 (Fellow, 1956); University Organist, Cambridge University, since 1974; Special Commissioner, Royal School of Church Music, since 1953; Examiner to Associated Board of Royal Schools of Music, since 1959; *b* 9 Feb. 1924; *s* of late Ernest Joseph Guest and late Gwendolen (*née* Brown); *m* 1959, Nancy Mary, *o d* of late W. P. Talbot; one *s* one *d*. *Educ:* Friars Sch., Bangor; King's Sch., Chester; St John's Coll., Cambridge. Chorister: Bangor Cath., 1933–35; Chester Cath., 1935–39. Served in RAF, 1942–46. Sub-Organist, Chester Cath., 1946–47; Organ Student, St John's Coll., Cambridge, 1947–51; John Stewart of Rannoch Scholar in Sacred Music, 1948; University Asst Lectr in Music, Cambridge, 1953–56, Univ. Lectr, 1956–82; Prof. of Harmony and Counterpoint, RAM, London, 1960–61. Director: Berkshire Boy Choir, USA, 1967, 1970; Arts Theatre, Cambridge, 1977. Concerts with St John's Coll. Choir in USA, Canada, Japan, Aust., most countries in W Europe; concerts and choral seminars in the Philippines and in S Africa. Mem. Council: RCO, 1964– (Pres., 1978–80); RSCM, 1983–. Aelod er Anrhydedd, Gorsedd y Beirdd, Eisteddfod Genedlaethol Cymru, 1977; Dir, Côr Cenedlaethol Ieuenctid Cymru, 1984–; Artistic Dir, Llandaff Festival, 1985–. Pres., Cathedral Organists' Assoc., 1980–82. *Recreation:* the Welsh language. *Address:* 9 Gurney Way, Cambridge. *T:* Cambridge 354932.

GUEST, Henry Alan; Chairman, Rhodes Foods Ltd, since 1980; *b* 29 Feb. 1920; *m* 1947, Helen Mary Price; one *s* one *d*. *Educ:* Lindisfarne College. FHCIMA. War Service, 1940–46, France, India, Malaya; Captain RA. Supplies Man., J. Lyons & Co. Ltd, Catering Div., 1955; Rank Organisation, Theatre Div.: Dep. Controller, Catering, 1963; Controller, 1965; Group Catering Adviser, Associated British Foods, 1966; Chief Exec., Civil Service Catering Organisation, 1972–80. Mem. Royal Instn of Great Britain. *Publications:* papers on marketing and organisation in techn. jls and financial press. *Recreation:* swimming. *Address:* 14 Pensford Avenue, Kew, Surrey TW9 4HP.

GUEST, Ivor Forbes, FRAD 1982; Chairman, since 1969, Member, since 1965, Executive Committee of the Royal Academy of Dancing; Solicitor; *b* 14 April 1920; *s* of Cecil Marmaduke Guest and Christian Forbes Guest (*née* Tweedie); *m* 1962, Ann Hutchinson; no *c*. *Educ:* Lancing Coll.; Trinity Coll., Cambridge (MA). Admitted a Solicitor, 1949; Partner, A. F. & R. W. Tweedie, 1951–83, Tweedie & Prideaux, 1983–85. Organised National Book League exhibn of books on ballet, 1957–58; Mem. Cttee, Soc. for Theatre Research, 1955–72; Chm., Exec. Cttee, Soc. for Dance Research, 1982–; British Theatre Museum: Mem. Exec. Cttee, 1957–77 (Vice-Chm., 1966–77); Mem., Adv. Council, 1974–83; Mem. Cttee, 1984–. Editorial Adviser to the Dancing Times, 1963–; Sec., Radcliffe Trust, 1966–; Trustee: Calvert Trust, 1976–; Cecchetti Soc. Trust, 1978–. *Publications:* Napoleon III in England, 1952; The Ballet of the Second Empire, 1953–55; The Romantic Ballet in England, 1954; Fanny Cerrito, 1956; Victorian Ballet Girl, 1957; Adeline Genée, 1958; The Alhambra Ballet, 1959; La Fille mal gardée, 1960; The Dancer's Heritage, 1960; The Empire Ballet, 1962; A Gallery of Romantic Ballet, 1963; The Romantic Ballet in Paris, 1966; Carlotta Zambelli, 1969; Dandies and Dancers, 1969; Two Coppélias, 1970; Fanny Elssler, 1970; The Pas de Quatre, 1970; Le Ballet de l'Opéra de Paris, 1976; The Divine Virginia, 1977; Adeline Genée: a pictorial record, 1978; Lettres d'un Maître de ballet, 1978; contrib. Costume and the 19th Century Dancer, in Designing for the Dancer, 1981; Adventures of a Ballet Historian, 1982; Jules Perrot, 1984; Gautier on Dance, 1986; Gautier on Spanish Dance, 1987. *Address:* 17 Holland Park, W11. *T:* 01–229 3780. *Clubs:* Garrick, MCC.

GUEST, Prof. John Rodney, FRS 1986; Professor of Microbiology, Sheffield University, since 1981; *b* 27 Dec. 1935; *s* of Sidney Ramsey Guest and Dorothy Kathleen Walker; *m* 1962, Barbara Margaret (*née* Dearsley); one *s* two *d*. *Educ:* Campbell College, Belfast; Leeds Univ. (BSc); Trinity Coll., Oxford Univ. (DPhil). Guinness Fellow, Oxford, 1960–62, 1965; Fulbright Scholar and Research Associate, Stanford, 1963, 1964; Sheffield University: Lectr, Sen. Lectr, Reader in Microbiology, 1965–81. EMBO Fellow, 1977; SERC Special Fellow, 1981–86. *Publications:* contribs to Jl of Gen. Microbiol., Biochem. Jl, European Jl of Biochem. *Recreations:* walking in the Peak district, squash, beekeeping, polyfilling. *Address:* Department of Microbiology, Sheffield University, Western Bank, Sheffield S10 2TN. *T:* Sheffield 78555.

GUEST, Trevor George; Registrar of the Principal Registry of the Family Division of the High Court of Justice, since 1972; Barrister-at-Law; *b* 30 Jan. 1928; *m* 1951, Patricia Mary (*née* Morrison); two *d*. *Educ:* Denstone Coll., Uttoxeter, Staffs; Birmingham Univ. (LLB (Hons)). Called to the Bar, Middle Temple, 1953. *Recreations:* dogs, Church affairs. *Address:* The Old Rectory, Purleigh, Essex. *T:* Maldon 828375.

GUILD, Ivor Reginald, CBE 1985; Partner in Shepherd and Wedderburn, WS, since 1951; *b* 2 April 1924; 2nd *s* of Col Arthur Marjoribanks Guild, DSO, TD, DL, and Phyllis Eliza Cox. *Educ:* Cargilfield; Rugby; New Coll., Oxford (MA); Edinburgh Univ. (LLB). WS 1950. Procurator Fiscal of the Lyon Court, 1960–; Bailie of Holyrood House, 1980–; Registrar, Episcopal Synod of Episc. Church in Scotland, 1967–; Chancellor, dioceses of Edinburgh and St Andrews, 1985–. Chairman: Edinburgh Investment Trust Ltd; First Scottish American Trust Co. Ltd; Northern American Trust Co. Ltd; Dir, Fleming Universal Investment Trust. Chm., Nat. Mus. of Antiquities of Scotland, 1981–85. Editor, Scottish Genealogist, 1959–. *Recreations:* genealogy, golf. *Club:* New (Edinburgh).

GUILDFORD, Bishop of, since 1983; **Rt. Rev. Michael Edgar Adie**; *b* 22 Nov. 1929; *s* of Walter Granville Adie and Kate Emily Adie (*née* Parish); *m* 1957, Anne Devonald Roynon; one *s* three *d*. *Educ:* Westminster School; St John's Coll., Oxford (MA). Assistant Curate, St Luke, Pallion, Sunderland, 1954–57; Resident Chaplain to the Archbishop of Canterbury, 1957–60; Vicar of St Mark, Sheffield, 1960–69; Rural Dean of Hallam, 1966–69; Rector of Louth, 1969–76; Vicar of Morton with Hacconby, 1976–83; Archdeacon of Lincoln, 1977–83. *Recreations:* gardening, walking, sneezing. *Address:* Willow Grange, Woking Road, Guildford GU4 7QS. *T:* Guildford 573922.

GUILFORD, 9th Earl of *cr* 1752; **Edward Francis North**; Baron Guilford, 1683; DL; *b* 22 Sept. 1933; *s* of Major Lord North (*d* 1940) and Joan Louise (she *m* 2nd, 1947, Charles Harman Hunt), *er d* of late Sir Merrik Burrell, 7th Bt, CBE; *S* grandfather, 1949; *m* 1956, Osyth Vere Napier, *d* of Cyril Napier Leeston Smith; one *s*. *Educ:* Eton. DL Kent 1976. *Heir:* *s* Lord North, *qv*. *Address:* Waldershare Park, Dover, Kent. *T:* Dover 820244.
See also Major Hon. Sir Clive Bossom, Bt, Sir Jonathan North, Bt.

GUILFOYLE, Dame Margaret (Georgina Constance), DBE 1980; Senator for Victoria, since 1971; *b* 15 May 1926; *d* of William and Elizabeth McCartney; *m* 1952, Stanley M. L. Guilfoyle; one *s* two *d*. Accountant, 1947–. Minister: for Education, Commonwealth of Australia, 1975; for Social Security, 1975–80; for Finance, 1980–83. ACIS; FASA. *Recreations:* reading, gardening. *Address:* Parliament House, Canberra, ACT 2600, Australia. *Club:* Lyceum (Melbourne).

GUILLEMIN, Roger Charles Louis, MD, PhD; Resident Fellow and Research Professor, Salk Institute for Biological Studies, La Jolla, California, since 1970; Adjunct Professor of Medicine, University of California, San Diego, since 1970; *b* Dijon, France, 11 Jan. 1924 (naturalized US Citizen, 1963); *s* of Raymond Guillemin and Blanche (*née* Rigollot); *m* 1951, Lucienne Jeanne Billard; one *s* five *d*. *Educ:* Univ. of Dijon (BA 1941, BSc 1942); Faculty of Medicine, Lyons (MD 1949); Univ. of Montreal (PhD 1953). Resident Intern, univ. hosps, Dijon, 1949–51; Associate Dir, then Asst Prof., Inst. of Exper. Medicine and Surgery, Univ. of Montreal, 1951–53; Associate Dir, Dept of Exper. Endocrinol., Coll. de France, Paris, 1960–63; Prof. of Physiol., Baylor Coll. of Med., Houston, 1953–70; Adjunct Prof. of Physiol., Baylor Coll. of Med., 1970–. Member: Nat. Acad. of Sciences, USA; Amer. Acad. Arts and Scis; Amer. Physiol Soc.; Endocrine Soc.; Soc. of Exptl Biol. and Medicine; Internat. Brain Res. Orgn; Internat. Soc. Res. Biol Reprodn. Foreign Associate: Acad. des Sciences, France; Acad. Nat. de Médecine, Paris; Hon Mem., Swedish Soc. of Med. Scis. Mem. Club of Rome. Hon. DSc: Rochester, NY, 1976; Chicago, 1977; Manitoba, 1984; Hon. MD: Ulm, 1978; Montreal, 1979; Univ. Libre de Bruxelles, Belgium, 1979; Turin, 1985; Hon. LMed Baylor Coll. of Med., 1978. Gairdner Internat. Award, 1974; Lasker Award, USA, 1975; Dickson Prize in Medicine, Univ. of Pittsburgh, 1976; Passano Award in Med. Sci., Passano Foundn, Inc., 1976; Schmitt Medal in Neuroscience, Neurosciences Res. Prog., MIT, 1977; National Medal of Science, USA, 1977; (jtly) Nobel Prize in Physiology or Medicine, 1977; Barren Gold Medal, USA, 1979; Dale Medal (Soc. for Endocrinology), UK, 1980. Légion d'Honneur, France, 1974. *Publications:* scientific pubns in learned jls. *Address:* Salk Institute, Box 85800, San Diego, Calif 92138.

GUILLERY, Prof. Rainer Walter, PhD; FRS 1983; Dr Lee's Professor of Anatomy, and Fellow of Hertford College, University of Oxford, since 1984; *b* 28 Aug. 1929; *s* of Hermann Guillery and Eva (*née* Hackel); *m* 1954, Margot Cunningham Pepper; three *s* one *d*. *Educ:* University Coll. London (BSc, PhD). Asst Lectr, subseq. Reader, Anatomy Dept, UCL, 1953–64; Associate Prof., subseq. Prof., Anatomy Dept, Univ. of Wisconsin, Madison, USA, 1964–77; Prof., Dept of Pharmacol and Physiol Sciences, Univ. of Chicago, 1977–84. *Publications:* contrib. Jl of Anat., Jl of Comp. Neurol., Jl of Neuroscience, and Brain Res. *Address:* Department of Human Anatomy, South Parks Road, Oxford OX1 3QX.

GUILLY, Rt. Rev. Richard Lester, SJ; OBE 1945; Parish Priest in Barbados, since 1981; *b* 6 July 1905; *s* of late Richard Guilly. *Educ:* Stonyhurst Coll.; Campion Hall, Oxford (Hons Mod. Hist.; BA, MA); Heythrop Coll. Entered Soc. of Jesus, 1924; Asst Master, Beaumont Coll., 1933–35; ordained 1938. Served War of 1939–45, Chaplain to the Forces: BEF (France), 1939–40; CF 3rd Cl. 1940; Senior RC Chaplain, N Ireland, 1 Corps District, AA Cmd, 2nd Army, 1940–45 (OBE, despatches). Superior of Soc. of Jesus in British Guiana and Barbados, 1946–54; Titular Bishop of Adraa and Vicar Apostolic of British Guiana and Barbados, 1954–56; Bishop of Georgetown, 1956–72; Parish Priest in Barbados, 1972–77; Apostolic Administrator, Archdiocese of Castries, 1977–81. *Publications:* various articles on Church History, Christian Social Doctrine and Church in Guyana. *Address:* Church of Our Lady of Sorrows, Ashton Hall, St Peter, Barbados, WI.

GUINNESS, family name of **Earl of Iveagh** and **Baron Moyne.**

GUINNESS, Sir Alec, Kt 1959; CBE 1955; Hon. DLitt, Hon. DFA; actor; *b* Marylebone, 2 April 1914; *m* 1938, Merula Salaman; one *s*. *Educ:* Pembroke Lodge, Southbourne; Roborough, Eastbourne. On leaving school went into Arks Publicity, Advertising Agents, as copywriter. First professional appearance walking on in Libel at King's Theatre, Hammersmith, 1933; played Hamlet in modern dress, Old Vic, 1938; toured the Continent, 1939. Served War of 1939–45; joined Royal Navy as a rating, 1941; commissioned 1942. Rejoined Old Vic, 1946–47. Hon. D Fine Arts Boston Coll., 1962; Hon. DLitt Oxon, 1977. Special Oscar, for contribution to film, 1979. *Films include:* Oliver Twist; Kind Hearts and Coronets; The Lavender Hill Mob; The Bridge on the River Kwai (Oscar for best actor of the year, 1957); The Horse's Mouth; Tunes of Glory; Lawrence of Arabia; Star Wars; Little Lord Fauntleroy; A Passage to India. *Plays include:* The Cocktail Party (New York); Hotel Paradiso, Ross, Dylan (New York); A Voyage Round My Father; Habeas Corpus; The Old Country, 1977; The Merchant of Venice, 1984; *television:* Tinker, Tailor, Soldier, Spy, 1979 (BAFTA Award, 1980); Smiley's People, 1981–82 (BAFTA Award, 1983); Edwin, 1984; Monsignor Quixote, 1985. *Publication:* Blessings in Disguise (autobiog.), 1985. *Address:* c/o London Management, 235/241 Regent Street, W1. *Club:* Athenæum.

GUINNESS, Bryan; *see* Moyne, 2nd Baron.

GUINNESS, Hon. Desmond (Walter); writer; President, Irish Georgian Society, since 1958; *b* 8 Sept. 1931; *yr s* of Baron Moyne, *qv*; *m* 1st, 1954, Marie-Gabrielle von Urach (marr. diss. 1981); one *s* one *d*; 2nd, Penelope, *d* of Graham and Teresa Cuthbertson. *Educ:* Gordonstoun; Christ Church, Oxford (MA). Founder, 1958, Irish Georgian Society to work for the study of, and protection of, buildings of architectural merit in Ireland, particularly of the Georgian period. Hon. LLD TCD, 1980. *Publications:* Portrait of Dublin, 1967; Irish Houses and Castles, 1971; Mr Jefferson, Architect, 1973; Palladio, 1976; Georgian Dublin, 1980; The White House: an architectural history, 1981; Newport Preserv'd, 1982. *Clubs:* Chelsea Arts; Kildare Street and University (Dublin).
See also Hon. J. B. Guinness.

GUINNESS, Sir Howard (Christian Sheldon), Kt 1981; VRD 1953; *b* 3 June 1932; *s* of late Edward Douglas Guinness, CBE and Martha Letière (*née* Sheldon); *m* 1958, Evadne Jane Gibbs; two *s* one *d*. *Educ:* King's Mead, Seaford, Sussex; Eton Coll. National Service, RN (midshipman); Lt-Comdr RNR. Union Discount Co. of London Ltd, 1953; Guinness Mahon & Co. Ltd, 1953–55; S. G. Warburg & Co. Ltd, 1955–85 (Exec. Dir, 1970–85). Dir, Harris & Sheldon Gp Ltd, 1960–81; Dir and Dep. Chm., Youghal Carpets (Holdings) Ltd, 1972–80. Chm., N Hampshire Conservative Assoc., 1971–74; Vice-Chm. 1974, Chm. 1975–78, and Treasurer 1978–81, Wessex Area, Cons. Assoc. Mem. Council, English Guernsey Cattle Soc., 1963–72. *Recreations:* skiing, tennis. *Address:* The Manor House, Glanvilles Wootton, Sherborne, Dorset DT9 5QF. *T:* Holnest 217. *Club:* White's.
See also J. R. S. Guinness.

GUINNESS, James Edward Alexander Rundell, CBE 1986; Director, Guinness Peat Group, since 1973 (Joint Chairman, 1973–77; Deputy Chairman, 1977–84); Deputy Chairman, Provident Mutual Life Assurance Association, since 1983; *b* 23 Sept. 1924; *s* of late Sir Arthur Guinness, KCMG and Frances Patience Guinness, MBE (*née* Wright); *m* 1953, Pauline Mander; one *s* four *d*. *Educ:* Eton; Oxford. Served in RNVR, 1943–46. Joined family banking firm of Guinness Mahon & Co., 1946, Partner 1953; Chm., Guinness Mahon Hldgs Ltd, 1968–72. Chm., Public Works Loan Bd, 1979– (Comr, 1960–). *Recreations:* shooting, fishing. *Address:* Coldpiece Farm, Mattingley, Basingstoke RG27 8LQ. *T:* Heckfield 292. *Clubs:* Brooks's, Pratt's; Royal Yacht Squadron (Cowes).

GUINNESS, John Ralph Sidney, CB 1985; Deputy Secretary, Department of Energy, since 1983; *b* 23 Dec. 1935; *s* of late Edward Douglas Guinness and Martha Letière (*née* Sheldon); *m* 1967, Valerie Susan North; one *s* one *d* (and one *s* decd). *Educ:* Rugby Sch.; Trinity Hall, Cambridge (BA Hons History, MA Hons). Union Discount Co. Ltd, 1960–61; Overseas Develt Inst., 1961–62; joined FO, 1962; Econ. Relations Dept, 1962–63; Third Sec., UK Mission to UN, New York, 1963–64; seconded to UN Secretariat as Special Asst to Dep. Under-Sec. and later Under-Sec. for Econ. and Social Affairs, 1964–66; FCO, 1967–69; First Sec. (Econ.), Brit. High Commn, Ottawa, 1969–72; seconded to Central Policy Rev. Staff, Cabinet Office, 1972–75; Counsellor, 1974; Alternate UK Rep. to Law of the Sea Conf., 1975–77; seconded to CPRS, 1977–79; transferred to Home Civil Service, 1980; Under-Sec., Dept of Energy, 1980–83. Governor, Oxford Energy Inst., 1984–. *Recreation:* iconography. *Address:* 9 Hereford Square, SW7 4TT. *T:* 01–373 8648. *Clubs:* Brooks's, Beefsteak.
See also Sir H. C. S. Guinness.

GUINNESS, Hon. Jonathan Bryan; Director: Arthur Guinness Son & Co. Ltd; The Red Bank Manufacturing Co. Ltd; *b* 16 March 1930; *s* and *heir* of Baron Moyne, *qv*, and of Diana (*née* Mitford, now Lady Mosley); *m* 1st, 1951, Ingrid Wyndham (marr. diss. 1962); two *s* one *d*; 2nd, 1964, Suzanne Phillips (*née* Lisney); one *s* one *d*. *Educ:* Eton; Oxford (MA, Mod. Langs). Journalist at Reuters, 1953–56. Merchant Banker: trainee at Erlangers Ltd, 1956–59, and at Philip Hill, 1959–62; Exec. Dir, 1962–64, non-exec. Dir, 1964–, Leopold Joseph. CC Leicestershire, 1970–74; Chairman, Monday Club, 1972–74. *Publication:* (with Catherine Guinness) The House of Mitford, 1984. *Address:* Osbaston Hall, Nuneaton, Warwickshire. *Clubs:* Carlton, Beefsteak; Ibstock Working Men's.
See also Hon. D. W. Guinness, Lord Neidpath.

GUINNESS, Sir Kenelm (Ernest Lee), 4th Bt, *cr* 1867; independent engineering consultant; *b* 13 Dec. 1928; *s* of late Kenelm Edward Lee Guinness and of Mrs Josephine Lee Guinness; *S* uncle 1954; *m* 1961, Mrs Jane Nevin Dickson; two *s*. *Educ:* Eton Coll.; Massachusetts Institute of Technology, USA. Late Lieut, Royal Horse Guards. With IBRD, Washington, 1954–75. *Heir:* *s* Kenelm Edward Lee Guinness, *b* 30 Jan. 1962. *Address:* (home) Rich Neck, Claiborne, Maryland 21624, USA. *T:* 301 745 5079. *Club:* Cavalry and Guards.

GUINNESS, Loel; *see* Guinness, T. L. E. B.

GUINNESS, Thomas Loel Evelyn Bulkeley, OBE 1942; late Irish Guards; *b* 9 June 1906; *s* of late Benjamin S. Guinness; *m* 1st, 1927, Hon. Joan Yarde-Buller (from whom he obtained a divorce, 1936); one *s* decd; 2nd, 1936, Lady Isabel Manners (marr. diss., 1951), *yr d* of 9th Duke of Rutland; one *s* one *d*; 3rd, 1951, Gloria (*d* 1980), *d* of Raphael Rubio, Mexico. *Educ:* Sandhurst. MP (U) City of Bath, 1931–45; Contested Whitechapel, 1929, and By-election, 1930; Group Captain Auxiliary Air Force Reserve. Served War of 1939–45: RAF (despatches five times). Comdr Order of Orange Nassau; Officer Legion of Honour, France; Croix de Guerre. *Address:* Villa Zanroc, Epalinges 1066, Vaud, Switzerland. *Clubs:* White's, Buck's, Turf, Beefsteak; Royal Yacht Squadron (Cowes).
See also Marquess of Dufferin and Ava.

GUISE, Sir John, GCMG 1975; KBE 1975 (CBE 1972); MP (Ind), Parliament of Papua New Guinea, since 1977; *b* Papua, 29 Aug. 1914; *m*; five *s* four *d*. Served War, Australian New Guinea Administrative Unit. Royal Papuan Constabulary, 1946, Mem. contingent attending Queen Elizabeth's Coronation, London, 1953, Sgt Major, later transferred to Dept of Native Affairs for local govt and welfare duties, Port Moresby. Mem., 1st Select Cttee Political Develt, 1961–63, which drew up 1st House of Assembly, 1964; Chm., House of Assembly Select Cttee on Political and Constitutional Develt which drew up 1st Ministerial Govt for 2nd House of Assembly, 1968. Mem. for E Papua, Legislative Council, 1961–63; MHA, Milne Bay District, 1964–67; Speaker, Papua New Guinea House of Assembly, Minister for Interior, and later Deputy Chief Minister and Minister for Agriculture, Papua New Guinea, to 1975; unofficial leader of elected Members, Papua New Guinea House of Assembly, 1964–68. Governor-General, Papua New Guinea, 1975–77. Delegate, S Pacific Conf., Pago Pago, 1962; Mem., Australian delegn to UN, 1962 and 1963; attended UNESCO Conf., Paris, Geneva, London, 1963. Prominent layman in Anglican Church affairs. Hon. LLD. KStJ 1976. *Address:* National Parliament, Port Moresby, Papua New Guinea; Lalaura Village, Cape Rodney, Central Province, Papua New Guinea.

GUISE, Sir John (Grant), 7th Bt *cr* 1783; Jockey Club Official since 1968; *b* 15 Dec. 1927; *s* of Sir Anselm William Edward Guise, 6th Bt and of Lady Guise (Nina Margaret Sophie, *d* of Sir James Augustus Grant, 1st Bt); *S* father, 1970. *Educ:* Winchester; RMA, Sandhurst. Regular officer, 3rd The King's Own Hussars, 1948–61. *Recreations:* hunting, shooting. *Heir:* *b* Christopher James Guise [*b* 10 July 1930; *m* 1969, Mrs Carole Hoskins Benson, *e d* of Jack Master; one *s* one *d*]. *Address:* Elmore Court, Gloucester. *T:* Gloucester 720293.

GUJADHUR, Hon. Sir Radhamohun, Kt 1976; CMG 1973; solicitor; Chairman, Consortium Cinematographique Maurice Ltée; Director, Trianon Estates Ltd; Managing Director of Companies; *b* Curepipe Road, Mauritius, 1909; *m*; eight *c*. *Educ:* Church of England Aided Sch., Curepipe; Curepipe De la Salle Sch., Port Louis; Royal Coll., Curepipe; St Xavier Coll., Calcutta. Mem. Municipal Council, 1943–47; Dep. Mayor, Port Louis, 1947; Mem. (nominated) Town Council, Curepipe, 1957–60 (Chm., 1963). MLA, Bon-Accord/Flacq, 1967–82; Dep. Speaker of Legislative Assembly, Mauritius, 1968–69, 1974–82. *Address:* Port Louis, Mauritius. *Club:* Mauritius Turf (Steward, 1970; Chm. 1974).

GULL, Sir Michael Swinnerton Cameron, 4th Bt, *cr* 1872; *b* 24 Jan. 1919; *o s* of 3rd Bt and Dona Eva Swinnerton (*d* 1973), *e d* of late Sir Thomas Swinnerton Dyer, 11th Bt; *S* father 1960; *m* 1st, 1950, Mrs Yvonne Bawtree (decd), *o d* of Dr Albert Oliver Macarius Heslop, Cape Town; one *s* one *d*; *m* 2nd. *Educ:* Eton. Late 2nd Lieut, Scots Guards (SRO). *Heir:* *s* Rupert William Cameron Gull [*b* 14 July 1954; *m* 1980, Gillian Lee, *d* of Robert MacFarlaine]. *Address:* Wedgeport, Bertha Avenue, Newlands, Cape Town, S Africa.

GULLAND, John Alan, PhD; FRS 1984; Senior Research Fellow, Centre for Environmental Technology, Imperial College, London, since 1984; *b* 16 Sept. 1926; *s* of late Alan Gulland; *m* 1951, Frances Audrey James; two *s* one *d*. *Educ:* Marlborough Coll.; Jesus Coll., Cambridge (BA 1950, PhD 1971). Scientist at Fisheries Laboratory, Lowestoft, Suffolk, 1951–66; Staff member, Fisheries Dept, FAO, Rome, 1966–84. Adviser to Internat. Whaling Commn, 1964–, Internat. Commn for Northwest Atlantic Fisheries, 1960–67, and other bodies. Hon. DSc: Rhode Island, 1979; Helsinki, 1984. *Publications:* The Fish Resources of the Ocean, 1972; The Management of Marine Fisheries, 1974; (ed) Fish Population Dynamics, 1977; Fish Stock Assessment, 1983; papers in scientific jls. *Recreations:* golf, gardening. *Address:* 41 Eden Street, Cambridge. *T:* Cambridge 322035.

GULLIVER, James Gerald; Chairman: Argyll Group PLC (formerly James Gulliver Associates Ltd), since 1977; Argyll Foods PLC, since 1980; Amalgamated Distilled Products PLC, since 1981; Country House Hotels Ltd, since 1983; Director, Manchester United Football Club PLC, since 1979; *b* 17 Aug. 1930; *s* of William Frederick and Mary Gulliver; *m* 1st, 1958, Margaret Joan (*née* Cormack) (marr. diss.) three *s* two *d*; 2nd, 1977, Joanne (*née* Sims) (marr. diss.); 3rd, 1985, Marjorie H. Moncrieff. *Educ:* Campbeltown Grammar Sch.; Univ of Glasgow; Georgia Inst. of Technol., USA. Royal Navy (Short Service Commn), 1956–59; Dir, Concrete (Scotland) Ltd, 1960–61; Management Consultant, Urwick, Orr & Partners Ltd, 1961–65; Man. Dir, 1965–72, Chm., 1967–72, Fine Fare (Holdings) Ltd; Dir, Associated British Foods Ltd, 1967–72. Vis. Prof., Glasgow Univ., 1985–. Mem. Council, Inst. of Directors; Vice-Pres., Marketing Soc. Mem., Prime Minister's Enquiry into Beef Prices, 1973; Mem., Governing Council, Scottish Business in the Community, 1983–. FInst D; FRSA; FBIM. Freedom and Livery, Worshipful Co. of Gardeners. Guardian Young Businessman of the Year, 1972. *Recreations:* ski-ing, sailing, music, motoring. *Address:* 8 Chesterfield Hill, W1X 7RG. *Clubs:* Carlton; Royal Thames Yacht.

GULLY, family name of **Viscount Selby.**

GUMLEY, Frances Jane, MA; Roman Catholic Assistant to Head of Religious Broadcasting, BBC, since 1981; *b* 28 Jan. 1955; *o d* of late Franc Stewart Gumley and of Helen Teresa (*née* McNicholas). *Educ:* St Augustine's Priory, Ealing; St Benedict's Sch., Ealing (Greek only); Newnham Coll., Cambridge (MA). Parly research, 1974; Braille transcriber, 1975; Catholic Herald: Editorial Assistant and Assistant Literary Editor, Dec. 1975; Literary Editor and Staff Reporter, 1976–79; Editor, 1979–81. Mistress of The Keys, Guild of Catholic Writers, 1983–. *Recreations:* disappearing, distaff throwing. *Address:* 2 Rathgar Avenue, Ealing, W13 9PL.

GUMMER, Ellis Norman, CBE 1974 (OBE 1960); Assistant Director-General (Administration), British Council, 1972–75; *b* 18 June 1915; *o s* of late Robert Henry Gummer, engr, and of Mabel Thorpe, Beckenham, Kent; *m* 1949, Dorothy Paton Shepherd; one *s* (and one *s* decd). *Educ:* St Dunstan's Coll.; St Catherine's Society, Oxford. BLitt, MA. Library service: Nottingham Univ., 1939; Queen's Coll., Oxford, 1940–42; served War of 1939–45, Admty, 1942–45; British Council: East Europe Dept, 1945–50; Personnel Dept, 1950–52; Student Welfare Dept, 1952–59; Literature Group, 1959–61; Controller, Arts and Science Div., 1961–66; Controller, Finance Div., 1966–71. *Publication:* Dickens' Works in Germany, 1940. *Recreations:* books, topography, archaeology. *Address:* 9 Campden Street, W8 7EP. *T:* 01–727 4823.

GUMMER, Rt. Hon. John Selwyn, PC 1985; MP (C) Suffolk Coastal, since 1983 (Eye, Suffolk, 1979–83); Minister of State, Ministry of Agriculture, Fisheries and Food, since 1985; *b* 26 Nov. 1939; *s* of Canon Selwyn Gummer and Sybille (*née* Mason); *m* 1977, Penelope Jane, *yr d* of John P. Gardner; two *s* two *d*. *Educ:* King's Sch., Rochester; Selwyn Coll., Cambridge (Exhibr). BA Hons History 1961; MA 1971; Chm., Cambridge Univ. Conservative Assoc., 1961; Pres., Cambridge Union, 1962; Chm., Fedn of Conservative Students, 1962. Editor, Business Publications, 1962–64; Editor-in-Chief, Max Parrish & Oldbourne Press, 1964–66; BPC Publishing: Special Asst to Chm., 1967; Publisher, Special Projects, 1967–69; Editorial Coordinator, 1969–70. Mem., ILEA Educn Cttee, 1967–70; Dir, Shandwick Publishing Co., 1966–81; Man. Dir, EP Gp of Cos, 1975–81; Chairman: Selwyn Shandwick Internat., 1976–81, Siemssen Hunter Ltd, 1979–80 (Dir, 1973–80). Contested (C) Greenwich, 1964 and 1966; MP (C) Lewisham W, 1970–Feb. 1974; PPS to Minister of Agriculture, 1972; an additional Vice-Chm., Conservative Party, 1972–74; an Asst Govt Whip, 1981; a Lord Comr of HM Treasury, 1981–83; Parly Under-Sec. of State for Employment, Jan.–Oct. 1983; Minister of State, Dept of Employment, 1983–84; Paymaster-Gen., 1984–85; Chm., Cons. Party, 1983–85. Mem., Gen. Synod of the Church of England, 1979–. *Publications:* (jtly) When the Coloured People Come, 1966; The Permissive Society, 1971; (with L. W. Cowie) The Christian Calendar, 1974; (contrib.) To Church with Enthusiasm, 1969. *Address:* House of Commons, SW1; Clarence House, Fressingfield, Eye, Suffolk. *T:* Fressingfield 347.

GÜMRÜKÇÜOGLU, Rahmi Kamil; Turkish Ambassador to the Court of St James's, since 1981; *b* 18 May 1927; *m*. Elçin; one *s* one *d*. *Educ:* Haydar Pasha Lycée, Istanbul; Faculty of Political Sciences, Ankara Univ. Master's degree in Pol. Economy and Govt, Harvard Univ. Second Secretary, 1952–55, First Sec., 1955, Turkish Embassy, London; Head of Section dealing with Internat. Economic Affairs, Min. of Foreign Affairs, Ankara, 1958–60; Counsellor, Turkish Embassy, Cairo, 1960–63; Dep. Director General, Dept of Internat. Economic Affairs, Ankara, 1963–65; Head of Special Bureau dealing with Economic Co-operation between Turkey and the Soviet Union, 1965–67; Dir Gen., Dept of Internat. Economic Affairs, 1967–71; Turkish Ambassador: to Council of Europe, Strasbourg, 1971–75; to Iran, 1975–78; Sen. Adviser to Min. of Foreign Affairs, and Pres., Defence Industry Co-ordination Board, Ankara, 1978–79; Dep. Sec. Gen. for Economic Affairs, Min. of Foreign Affairs, 1979–81. *Publications:* various articles and booklets on foreign investment, questions of economic develt, Soviet economic develt, economic integration amongst developing countries. *Address:* Turkish Embassy, 43 Belgrave Square, SW1. *T:* 01–235 5252.

GUN-MUNRO, Sir Sydney Douglas, GCMG 1979; Kt 1977; MBE 1957; FRCS; Governor-General of St Vincent and the Grenadines, 1979–85, retired (Governor, 1977–79); *b* 29 Nov. 1916; *s* of Barclay Justin Gun-Munro and Marie Josephine Gun-Munro; *m* 1943, Joan Estelle Benjamin; two *s* one *d*. *Educ:* Grenada Boys' Secondary Sch.; King's Coll. Hosp., London (MB, BS Hons 1943); Moorfields Hosp., London (DO 1952). MRCS, LRCP 1943; FRCS 1985. House Surg., EMS Hosp., Horton, 1943; MO, Lewisham Hosp., 1943–46; Dist MO, Grenada, 1946–49; Surg., Gen. Hosp., St Vincent, 1949–71; Dist MO, Bequia, St Vincent, 1972–76. *Recreations:* tennis, boating. *Address:* PO Box 51, Bequia, St Vincent and the Grenadines, West Indies. *T:* St Vincent 83261.

GUNDRY, Rev. Canon Dudley William, MTh; Canon Residentiary and Chancellor of Leicester since 1963; Church Affairs Consultant and Correspondent to the Daily Telegraph, 1978–86; *b* 4 June 1916; *e s* of late Cecil Wood Gundry and Lucy Gundry; unmarried. *Educ:* Sir Walter St John's Sch.; King's Coll., London. BD (1st cl. Hons) 1939, AKC (1st cl. Hons Theology) 1939, MTh 1941. Deacon, 1939; Priest 1940. Curate of St Matthew, Surbiton, 1939–44; Lectr in History of Religions, University Coll. of North Wales, Bangor, 1944–60; Mem. Senate and Warden of Neuadd Reichel, 1947–60; Dean of Faculty of Theology, 1956–60; Hon. Sec., British Section, Internat. Assoc. for History of Religions, 1954–60; Select Preacher, Trinity Coll., Dublin, 1957; Prof. and Head of Dept of Religious Studies, and Mem. of Senate, University Coll., Ibadan, 1960–63; Commissary to Bishop of Northern Nigeria, 1963–69; Rural Dean of Christianity, Leicester, 1966–74; Proctor in Convocation, 1970–80. Sometime Examining Chaplain to Bishops of Bangor, St Davids and Leicester; Examiner to Universities of Leeds, London, Keele, St David's Coll., Lampeter, Gen. Ordination Examination. Chm. of Governors, Newton's Educnl Foundn, 1977–. *Publications:* Religions: An Historical and Theological Study, 1958; Israel's Neighbours (in Neil's Bible Companion), 1959; The Teacher and the World Religions, 1968; contrib. to: Collins Dictionary of the English Language, 1979; The Synod of Westminster, 1986; many articles and signed reviews in theological and kindred journals; Editor, Leicester Cathedral Qly, 1963–79. *Recreation:* wandering about England and Wales. *Address:* 28 Stoneygate Court, London Road, Leicester LE2 2AH. *T:* Leicester 704133. *Clubs:* Athenæum; Leicestershire (Leicester).

GUNLAKE, John Henry, CBE 1946; FIA; FSS; FIS; consulting actuary; *b* 23 May 1905; *s* of late John Gunlake, MRCS, LRCP, and late Alice Emma Gunlake; unmarried. *Educ:* Epsom Coll. Institute of Actuaries: Fellow, 1933; Hon. Sec., 1952–54; Vice-Pres., 1956–59; Pres., 1960–62. A Statistical Adviser, Min. of Shipping, 1940–47. Member: Cttee on Econ. and Financial Problems of Provision for Old Age, 1953–54; Royal Commn on Doctors' and Dentists' Remuneration, 1957–60; Permanent Advisory Cttee on Doctors' and Dentists' Remuneration, 1962–70. *Publications:* Premiums for Life Assurances and Annuities, 1939. Contrib. to Jl of Inst. of Actuaries. *Recreations:* reading, music, working. *Address:* 120 Clapham Common North Side, SW4 9SP. *T:* 01–228 3008. *Club:* Reform.

GUNN, Mrs Bunty Moffat, OBE 1981; JP; Chairman, Lanarkshire Health Board, since 1981; *b* 4 Sept. 1923; *d* of William M. and Dolina Johnston; *m* 1946, Hugh McVane Houston Gunn; three *s* one *d*. *Educ:* Grange School for Girls; Grangemouth High School. DSCHE 1980. Councillor: Lanark CC, 1970–73; Strathclyde Regional Council, 1973–; Chairman, Scottish Council for Health Education, 1974–80; Member, Lanarkshire Health Board, 1973–81. Vice-Pres., Royal British Legion, CS&W Branch, 1978–. JP City of Glasgow 1972. *Recreations:* golf, theatre, music. *Address:* Kinnoul, 1 Beech Avenue, High Burnside, Rutherglen, Strathclyde. *T:* 041–634 4510. *Club:* Cathkin Braes Golf (Strathclyde).

GUNN, John Angus Livingston; Under-Secretary, Department of the Environment, since 1976; *b* 20 Nov. 1934; *s* of late Alistair L. Gunn, FRCOG, and Mrs Sybil Gunn, JP; *m* 1959, Jane, *d* of Robert Cameron; one *s* one *d*. *Educ:* Fettes Coll., Edinburgh (Foundationer); Christ Church, Oxford (Scholar). MA Oxford, 1st Cl. Hons in Classical Hon. Mod., 1955, and in final sch. of Psychology, Philosophy and Physiology, 1957; Passmore-Edwards Prizeman, 1956. National Service, commnd in S Wales Borderers (24th Regt), 1957–59. Entered Min. of Transport, 1959; Principal Private Sec. to Ministers of Transport, 1967–68; Asst Sec., MoT, DoE and Civil Service Dept, 1969–75. *Address:* Department of the Environment, Romney House, 43 Marsham Street, SW1P 3EB.

GUNN, Prof. Sir John (Currie), Kt 1982; CBE 1976; MA (Glasgow and Cambridge); FRSE, FIMA; FInstP; Cargill Professor of Natural Philosophy, 1949–82 and Head of Department, 1973–82, University of Glasgow; *b* 13 Sept. 1916; *s* of Richard Robertson Gunn and Jane Blair Currie; *m* 1944, Betty Russum (OBE 1984); one *s*. *Educ:* Glasgow Acad.; Glasgow Univ.; St John's Coll., Cambridge. Engaged in Admiralty scientific service, first at Admiralty Research Laboratory, later at Mine Design Dept, 1939–45; Research Fellow of St John's Coll., Cambridge, 1944; Lecturer in Applied Mathematics: Manchester Univ., 1945–46; University Coll., London, 1946–49. Member: SRC, 1968–72; UGC, 1974–81. Hon. DSc: Heriot-Watt, 1981; Loughborough, 1983. *Publications:* papers on mathematical physics in various scientific journals. *Recreations:* golf, music, chess. *Address:* 32 Beaconsfield Road, Glasgow G12 0NY. *T:* 041–357 2001.

GUNN, Peter Nicholson; author; *b* 15 Aug. 1914; 2nd *s* of Frank Lindsay Gunn, CBE, and Adèle Margaret (*née* Dunphy); *m* 1953, Diana Maureen James; one *s*. *Educ:* Melbourne; Trinity Coll., Cambridge (MA). Served War 1939–45: Rifle Bde; POW 1942. Sen. Lectr, RMA, Sandhurst, 1949–54. *Publications:* Naples: a Palimpsest, 1961 (German trans. 1964, Italian trans. 1971); Vernon Lee: a Study, 1964; The Companion Guide to Southern Italy, 1969; My Dearest Augusta: a Biography of Augusta Leigh, Byron's half-sister, 1969; A Concise History of Italy, 1971; (ed) Byron's Prose, 1972; Normandy: Landscape with figures, 1975; Burgundy: Landscape with figures, 1976; The Actons, 1978; Napoleon's Little Pest: The Duchess of Abrantès, 1979; (with R. Beny) Churches of Rome, 1981 (trans. German, Italian and Danish, 1982); Yorkshire Dales: Landscape with figures, 1984; (ed) Lord Byron: Selected Letters and Journals, 1984. *Address:* 8 Albion Street, Lewes, Sussex BN7 2ND. *T:* Lewes 471755. *Clubs:* Lansdowne; University Pitt (Cambridge).

GUNN, Robert Norman; Chairman, since 1985, Chief Executive, since 1983 and Director, since 1976, The Boots Company PLC; *b* 16 Dec. 1925; *s* of late Donald Macfie Gunn and Margaret (*née* Pallister); *m* 1956, Joan Parry; one *d*. *Educ:* Royal High Sch., Edinburgh; Worcester Coll., Oxford (MA). Served RAC, 1944–47 (Lieut). Joined Boots, 1951; Merchandise Buyer, 1962–70; Head of Warehousing and Distribn, 1971–73; Dir of Property, 1973–78; Dir, Industrial Div., 1979–83 (Man. Dir 1980–83); Vice-Chm., 1983–85. Dir, Foseco Minsep plc, 1984–. Member: Bd of Management, Assoc. of British Pharmaceutical Industry, 1981–84 (Vice-Pres., 1983–84); Council, CBI, 1985–. CBIM 1983; FInstD 1985. *Recreations:* gardening, theatre. *Address:* Tor House, Pinfold Lane, Elston, near Newark, Notts NG23 5PD.

GUNN, Thomson William, (Thom Gunn); poet; Visiting Lecturer, English Department, University of California (Berkeley), since 1975; *b* 29 Aug. 1929; *s* of Herbert Smith Gunn, and Ann Charlotte Gunn (*née* Thomson); unmarried. *Educ:* University Coll. Sch., Hampstead; Trinity Coll., Cambridge. British Army (National Service), 1948–50; lived in Paris six months, 1950; Cambridge, 1950–53; lived in Rome, 1953–54; has lived in California since 1954. Lectr, later Associate Prof., English Dept, University of Calif (Berkeley), 1958–66. *Publications:* Poetry from Cambridge, 1953; Fighting Terms, 1954; The Sense of Movement, 1957; My Sad Captains, 1961; Selected Poems (with Ted Hughes), 1962; Five American Poets (ed with Ted Hughes), 1962; Positives (with Ander Gunn), 1966; Touch, 1967; Poems 1950–1966: a selection, 1969; Moly, 1971; Jack Straw's Castle and other poems, 1976; Selected Poems, 1979; The Passages of Joy, 1982; The Occasions of Poetry (ed Clive Wilmer), 1982. *Recreations:* cheap thrills. *Address:* 1216 Cole Street, San Francisco, Calif 94117, USA.

GUNN, Sir William (Archer), KBE 1961; CMG 1955; JP; Australian grazier and company director; Chairman, International Wool Secretariat, 1961–73; *b* Goondiwindi, Qld, 1 Feb. 1914; *s* of late Walter and Doris Isabel Gunn, Goondiwindi; *m* 1939, Mary (Phillipa), *d* of F. B. Haydon, Murrurundi, NSW; one *s* two *d*. *Educ:* The King's Sch., Parramatta, NSW. Director: Rothmans of Pall Mall (Australia) Ltd; Grazcos Co-op. Ltd; Clausen Steamship Co. (Australia) Pty Ltd; Walter Reid and Co. Ltd; Gunn Rural Management Pty Ltd; Chairman and Managing Director: Moline Pastoral Co. Pty Ltd; Roper Valley Pty Ltd; Coolibah Pty Ltd; Mataranka Pty Ltd; Unibeef Australia Pty Ltd; Gunn Development Pty Ltd; Chairman: Australian Wool Bd, 1963–72; Qld Adv. Bd, Develt Finance Corp., 1962–72; Member: Commonwealth Bank Bd, 1952–59; Qld Bd, Nat. Mutual Life Assoc., 1955–67; Reserve Bank Bd, 1959–; Aust. Meat Bd, 1953–66; Aust. Wool Bureau, 1951–63 (Chm. 1958–63); Aust. Wool Growers Council, 1947–60 (Chm. 1955–58); Graziers Federal Council of Aust., 1950–60 (Pres. 1951–54); Aust. Wool Growers and Graziers Council, 1960–65; Export Develt Council, 1962–65; Australian Wool Corp., 1973; Faculty of Veterinary Science, University of Qld, 1953–; Exec. Council, United Graziers Assoc. of Qld, 1944–69 (Pres., 1951–59; Vice-Pres., 1947–51); Aust. Wool Testing Authority, 1958–63; Council, NFU of Aust., 1951–54; CSIRO State Cttee, 1951–68; Chairman: The Wool Bureau Inc., New York, 1962–69; Trustee: Qld Cancer Fund; Australian Pastoral Research Trust, 1959–71. Coronation Medal, 1953; Golden Fleece Achievement Award (Bd of Dirs of Nat. Assoc. of Wool Manufrs of America), 1962; Award of Golden Ram (Natal Woolgrowers Assoc. of SA), 1973. *Address:* (home) 98 Windermere Road, Ascot, Qld 4007, Australia. *T:* Brisbane 268 2688; (office) Wool Exchange, 69 Eagle Street, Brisbane, Qld 4000. *T:* Brisbane 21 4044. *Clubs:* Queensland, Tattersalls, Queensland Turf (Brisbane); Union (Sydney); Australian (Melbourne).

GUNNELL, (William) John; Chairman, West Yorkshire Enterprise Board, since 1982; *b* 1 Oct. 1933; *s* of late William Henry and Norah Gunnell; *m* 1955, Jean Louise, *d* of late Frank and of Harriet Louise Lacey; three *s* one *d*. *Educ:* King Edward's Sch., Birmingham; Univ. of Leeds (BSc Hons). Hospital porter, St Bartholomew's, London, 1955–57; Teacher, Leeds Modern Sch., 1959–62; Head of Science, United Nations International Sch., New York, 1962–70; Lectr, Centre for Studies in Science and Mathematics Education, Univ. of Leeds, 1970–. County Councillor for Hunslet, 1977–86; Leader of Opposition, 1979–81, Leader, 1981–86, W Yorks MCC; Mem. for Hunslet, Leeds MDC, 1986–. Chairman: Yorks and Humberside Develt Assoc., 1981–; Leeds/Bradford Airport jt cttee, 1981–83; N of England Regional Consortium, 1984–; Mem., Audit Commn, 1983–. Mem. Bureau, Conseil des Régions d'Europe, 1985–86. Hon. Pres., RETI. Spokesman for MCCs in their campaign against abolition, 1983–85. Mem., Fabian Soc., 1972–. *Publications:* Selected Experiments in Advanced Level Chemistry, 1975, and other texts (all with E. W. Jenkins). *Recreations:* music, opera, watching cricket and soccer. *Address:* 6 Arthington View, Leeds LS10 2ND. *T:* Leeds 770592. *Clubs:* East Hunslet Labour (Leeds); Warwickshire CC; Yorkshire CC.

GUNNING, Prof. Brian Edgar Scourse, FRS 1980; FAA 1979; Professor of Developmental Biology, Australian National University, since 1974; *b* 29 Nov. 1934; *s* of William Gunning and Margaret Gunning (*née* Scourse); *m* 1964, Marion Sylvia Forsyth; two *s*. *Educ:* Methodist Coll., Belfast; Queen's Univ., Belfast (BSc (Hons), MSc, PhD); DSc ANU. Lecturer in Botany, 1957, Reader in Botany, 1965, Queen's Univ., Belfast. *Publications:* Ultrastructure and the Biology of Plant Cells (with Dr M. Steer), 1975; Intercellular Communication in Plants: studies on plasmodesmata (with Dr A. Robards), 1976; contribs to research jls. *Recreations:* hill walking, photography. *Address:* 29 Millen Street, Hughes, ACT 2605, Australia. *T:* (062) 812879.

GUNNING, John Edward Maitland, CBE 1960 (OBE 1945); Barrister-at-law; *b* 22 Sept. 1904; *s* of late John Elgee Gunning, Manor House, Moneymore, Co. Derry, and late Edythe, *er d* of T. J. Reeves, London; *m* 1936, Enid Katherine, *o d* of George Menhinick; two *s*. *Educ:* Harrow; Magdalene Coll., Cambridge. Called to Bar, Gray's Inn, 1933. Practised South Eastern Circuit, Central Criminal Court, North London Sessions, Herts and Essex Sessions. Joined Judge Advocate General's office, Oct. 1939. War of 1939–45: served BEF, France, 1939–40; N Africa, 1942–43; Italy, 1943–45 (despatches, OBE). Middle East, 1945–50; Deputy Judge Advocate Gen. with rank of Col, CMF, 1945, Middle East, 1946; Deputy Judge Advocate Gen. (Army and RAF): Germany, 1951–53, 1960–63, 1968–70; Far East, 1957–59, 1965–67; Senior Asst Judge Advocate Gen., 1965–70. *Recreations:* bridge, watching cricket, reading. *Address:* 31 Brunswick Court, Regency Street, SW1. *Clubs:* Travellers', MCC.

GUNNING, Sir Robert Charles, 8th Bt, *cr* 1778; gold-mine owner and farmer; *b* 2 Dec. 1901; *o s* of late Charles Archibald John Gunning and Beatrice Constance Purvis; *S* cousin 1950; *m* 1934, Helen Nancy, *d* of late Vice-Adm. Sir T. J. Hallet, KBE, CB; eight *s* two *d*. *Educ:* St Paul's Sch.; Leeds Univ. Business in the Sudan and Nigeria, 1924–33; prospecting and gold-mining in Nigeria, 1933–38; pegged first Nigerian lode gold-mine of the least importance, this in 1935 at Bin Yauri; served AA Command, 1939–46, temp. Capt. Emigrated to Alberta, 1948. Chairman: Peace River Hosp. Bd; Peace Region Mental Health Council. *Recreations:* gardening, cricket, and almost any ball game. *Heir:* *s* Lt-Comdr Charles Theodore Gunning, CD; RCN retd; PEng [*b* 19 June 1935; *m* 1969, Sarah (marr. diss. 1982), *d* of Col Patrick Arthur Easton; one *d*]. *Address:* c/o Postmaster, Peace River, Alberta, Canada.

GUNSTON, Sir Richard (Wellesley), 2nd Bt *cr* 1938, of Wickwar, Co. Gloucester; *b* 15 March 1924; *s* of Sir Derrick Wellesley Gunston, 1st Bt, MC, and of Evelyn Bligh, OBE, *d* of late Howard Bligh St George; *S* father, 1985; *m* 1st, 1947, Elizabeth Mary (marr. diss. 1956), *e d* of late Sir Arthur Colegate; one *d*; 2nd, 1959, Mrs Joan Elizabeth Marie Coldicott (marr. diss.), *o d* of Reginald Forde, Johannesburg; one *s*; 3rd, 1976, Veronica Elizabeth (*née* Haines), *widow* of Captain V. G. Loyd. *Educ:* Harrow; Clare Coll., Cambridge. Served War in RAF (Aircrew), 1942–45. Entered Colonial Admin. Service, 1946; served N Nigeria, 1948–51; Nyasaland, 1951–63; Bechuanaland, 1964–65; Colonial Office, 1966. Asst Sec., Council for Care of Churches and Cathedrals Adv. Cttee, 1967. *Recreations:* hunting, big game shooting, sailing, gliding, painting, photography, architecture, gardening. *Heir:* *s* John Wellesley Gunston, *b* 25 July 1962. *Address:* 4 Little Manor, Coker House, East Coker, Yeovil, Somerset BA22 9HS. *Club:* East India.

GUNTER, John Forsyth; freelance designer; *b* 31 Oct. 1938; *s* of Herbert and Charlotte Gunter; *m* 1969, Micheline McKnight; two *d*. *Educ:* Bryanston Public Sch.; Central Sch. of Art and Design (Dip. with distinction). Started career in rep. theatre in GB; Resident Designer: English Stage Co., 1965–66 (subseq. designed 28 prodns for co.); Zürich Schauspielhaus, 1970–73 (also designed plays and operas throughout German-speaking theatre); freelance design work for West End, NT, RSC and for Broadway, New York, 1973–; designer of operas for cos in GB and Germany. Head, Theatre Dept, Central Sch. of Art and Design, 1974–82. FRSA 1982. Many awards for design of Guys and Dolls, NT, 1982, incl. SWET Award for Best Design 1982, Drama Magazine Best Design Award 1982, Plays and Players Award for Best Design 1983; Plays and Players and Olivier Awards for Best Design 1984, for design of Wild Honey, NT, 1984. *Recreation:* getting out into the countryside. *Address:* 25 Hillfield Park, Muswell Hill, N10 3QT. *T:* 01–444 0551.

GURD, Surg. Rear-Adm. Dudley Plunket, CB 1968; Medical Officer-in-Charge, Royal Naval Hospital, Malta, 1966–69; now in private practice; *b* 18 June 1910; *s* of Frederick Plunket Gurd and Annie Jane Glenn; *m* 1939, Thérèse Marie, *d* of John and Frances Delenda, Salonika, Greece; one *s* one *d*. *Educ:* Belfast Royal Academy; Queen's Univ., Belfast, MB, BCh, BAO (Hons) 1932; MD (High Commend) 1942; FRACS 1945; MCh 1959; FRCS (Eng.) 1964. Gilbert Blane Medal, 1943. Sen. Consultant and Adviser in Ophthalmology to the Navy, 1952–66; Hon. Lectr and Examiner in Ophthalmology, Univ. of Hong Kong, 1945–48; Warden, Ophthalmic Hosp. of St John, Jerusalem, Jordan, 1952–55. Joined RN as Surg. Lieut, 1934; Lieut-Comdr 1939; Comdr 1945; Capt. 1958; Rear-Adm. 1966; retired 1969; Served in Royal Naval Hosps at Malta, Barrow Gurney, Hong Kong, Plymouth and Haslar. QHS 1964. KStJ 1967 (CStJ 1954). Hon. DSc QUB, 1969. Chevalier de l'Ordre Nationale du Viet-Nam, 1949; Gold Cross, Order of Holy Sepulchre, 1955. *Publications:* various contribs to ophthalmic literature. *Recreations:* interested in all kinds of sport and athletics, also in languages, religion and medical education. *Address:* Shanklin Lodge, Eastern Villas Road, Southsea, Hants PO4 0SU. *T:* Portsmouth 731496. *Clubs:* Athenæum, Royal Naval and Royal Albert Yacht; Union (Malta).

GURDEN, Sir Harold Edward, Kt 1983; *s* of late Arthur William and late Ada Gurden; *m* 1st, Lucy Isabella Izon (*d* 1976); three *d*; 2nd, Elizabeth Joan, *widow* of Arthur Taylor.

Birmingham City Council, Selly Oak Ward, 1946–56; Pres. Birmingham and Dist Dairyman's Assoc., 1947–50; Chm. Soc. of Dairy Technology, Midland Div.; Pres.-Elect, Nat. Dairyman's Assoc., 1951; Chm., Northfield Div. Conservative Assoc., 1950–52. MP (C) Selly Oak Div. of Birmingham, 1955–Oct. 1974; Mem. of Speaker's Panel, House of Commons, 1966; Chm., Selection Cttee, House of Commons, 1970. Chm., Park Farm Preserves Ltd, 1954–84. Rector's Warden, St Margaret's Westminster, 1973–75, Dep. Rector's Warden, 1975–83, Rector's Warden Emeritus, 1983. Pres., Birmingham Branch RSPCA, 1966–79. *Recreations:* bridge, golf, numismatics. *Address:* 20 Portland Road, Oxford OX2 7EY.

GURDON, family name of **Baron Cranworth.**

GURDON, Prof. John Bertrand, DPhil; FRS 1971; John Humphrey Plummer Professor of Cell Biology, University of Cambridge, since 1983; Fellow of Churchill College, Cambridge, since 1973; Fellow of Eton College, since 1978; *b* 2 Oct. 1933; *s* of late W. N. Gurdon, DCM, formerly of Assington, Suffolk, and of late Elsie Marjorie (*née* Byass); *m* 1964, Jean Elizabeth Margaret Curtis; one *s* one *d. Educ:* Edgeborough; Eton; Christ Church, Oxford; BA 1956; DPhil 1960. Beit Memorial Fellow, 1958–61; Gosney Research Fellow, Calif. Inst. Technol., 1962; Departmental Demonstrator, Dept of Zool., Oxford, 1963–64; Vis. Research Fellow, Carnegie Instn, Baltimore, 1965; Lectr, Dept of Zoology, Oxford, 1965–72; Research Student, Christ Church, 1962–72; Mem. Staff, MRC Lab. of Molecular Biology, Cambridge, 1972–83 (Hd, Cell Biology Div., 1979–83). Fullerian Prof. of Physiology and Comparative Anatomy, Royal Instn, 1985–. Lectures: Harvey Soc., NY, 1973; Dunham, Harvard, 1974; Croonian, Royal Soc., 1976; Carter-Wallace, Princeton, 1978; Woodhull, Royal Instn, 1980. Hon. Foreign Mem., Amer. Acad. of Arts and Scis, 1978; Foreign Associate: Nat. Acad. of Sciences, USA, 1980; Belgian Royal Acad. of Scis, Letters and Fine Arts, 1984; Foreign Mem., Amer. Philos. Soc., 1983. Hon. Student, Christ Church, Oxford, 1985. Hon. DSc: Chicago, 1978; René Descartes, Paris, 1982. Albert Brachet Prize (Belgian Royal Academy), 1968; Scientific Medal of Zoological Soc., 1968; Feldberg Foundn Award, 1975; Paul Ehrlich Award, 1977; Nessim Habif Prize, Univ. of Geneva, 1979; CIBA Medal, Biochem. Soc., 1980; Comfort Crookshank Award for Cancer Research, 1983; William Bate Hardy Prize, Cambridge Philos. Soc., 1984; Prix Charles Léopold Mayer, Acad. des Scis, France, 1984; Ross Harrison Prize, Internat. Soc. Develt Biol., 1985; Royal Medal, Royal Soc., 1985. *Publications:* Control of Gene Expression in Animal Development, 1974; articles in scientific jls, especially on nuclear transplantation. *Recreations:* skiing, tennis, horticulture, Lepidoptera. *Address:* Whittlesford Grove, Whittlesford, Cambridge CB2 4NZ. *Club:* Eagle Ski.

GURNEY, Nicholas Bruce Jonathan; Grade 3, Cabinet Office and Civil Service Commissioner, since 1983; *b* 20 Jan. 1945; *s* of Bruce William George Gurney and Cynthia Joan Watkins Mason (*née* Winn); *m* 1970, Wendy Patricia (*née* Tulip); two *s* one *d. Educ:* Wimbledon College; Christ's College, Cambridge. BA 1966, MA 1969. Lectr in English, Belize Teachers' Training College, Belize, as part of British Volunteer Programme, 1966–67; MoD 1967; Asst Private Sec., Minister of State for Defence, 1970–72; Civil Service Dept, 1972–74; Private Sec. to Lord Privy Seal and Leader of House of Lords, 1974–77; Civil Service Dept and Management Personnel Office, 1978–83. *Address:* Civil Service Commission, Alencon Link, Basingstoke, Hants RG21 1JB. *T:* Basingstoke 29222.

GURNEY, Oliver Robert, MA, DPhil Oxon; FBA 1959; Shillito Reader in Assyriology, Oxford University, 1945–78; Professor, 1965; Fellow of Magdalen College, 1963–78, now Emeritus; *b* 28 Jan. 1911; *s* of Robert Gurney, DSc, and Sarah Gamzu, MBE, *d* of Walter Garstang, MD, MRCP; *m* 1957, Mrs Diane Hope Grazebrook (*née* Esencourt); no *c. Educ:* Eton Coll.; New Coll., Oxford. Served War of 1939–45, in Royal Artillery and Sudan Defence Force. Freeman of City of Norwich. For. Mem., Royal Danish Acad. of Sciences and Letters, 1976. Pres., British Institute of Archaeology at Ankara, 1983–. *Publications:* The Hittites (Penguin), 1952; (with J. J. Finkelstein and P. Hulin) The Sultantepe Tablets, 1957, 1964; (with John Garstang) The Geography of the Hittite Empire, 1959; Ur Excavations, Texts, VII, 1974; (with S. N. Kramer) Sumerian Literary Texts in the Ashmolean Museum, 1976; Some Aspects of Hittite Religion (Schweich Lectures, 1976), 1977; The Middle Babylonian Legal and Economic Texts from Ur, 1983; articles in Annals of Archæology and Anthropology (Liverpool), Anatolian Studies, etc. *Recreations:* lawn tennis, golf. *Address:* Bayworth Corner, Boars Hill, Oxford. *T:* Oxford 735322.

GUTCH, Sir John, KCMG 1957 (CMG 1952); OBE 1947; *b* 12 July 1905; *s* of late Clement Gutch, MA, King's Coll., Cambridge, and late Isabella Margaret Newton; *m* 1938, Diana Mary Worsley; three *s. Educ:* Aldenham Sch.; Gonville and Caius Coll., Cambridge. Classical scholar, 1924; 1st class Classical Tripos, Part I, 1926; 2nd class Classical Tripos, Part II, 1927; BA 1927; MA 1931. Cadet, Colonial Administrative Service, 1928; Asst District Commissioner, Gold Coast, 1928; Asst Colonial Secretary, Gold Coast, 1935; Asst Secretary, Palestine, 1936, Principal Asst Secretary, 1944, Under Sec., 1945; Asst Sec., Middle East Department, Colonial Office, 1947; Chief Secretary, British Administration, Cyrenaica, 1948; Adviser to the Prime Minister, Government of Cyrenaica, 1949; Chief Secretary, British Guiana, 1950–54; High Commissioner for Western Pacific, 1955–60. British Electric Traction Co. Ltd, 1961–69. Governor, Aldenham School, 1964–81; Mem., Cttee of Management, Institute of Opthalmology, 1965–80 (Fellow, 1968). *Publications:* Martyr of the Islands: the life and death of John Coleridge Patteson, 1971; Beyond the Reefs: the life of John Williams, missionary, 1974. *Address:* Meadow House, 45 Larkhill Road, Crondall Lane, Farnham, Surrey GU9 7DB. *T:* Farnham 721456.

GUTFREUND, Prof. Herbert, FRS 1981; Professor of Physical Biochemistry, University of Bristol, 1972–86, now Emeritus; part-time Scholar in Residence, National Institutes of Health, Bethesda, USA, since 1986; *b* 21 Oct. 1921; *s* of late Paul Peter Gutfreund and Clara Angela (*née* Pisko); *m* 1958, Mary Kathelen, *er d* of late Mr and Mrs L. J. Davies, Rugby; two *s* one *d. Educ:* Vienna; Univ. of Cambridge (PhD). Research appts at Cambridge Univ., 1947–57; Rockefeller Fellow, Yale Univ., 1951–52; part-time Research Associate, Yale Univ., 1953–58; Principal Scientific Officer, National Inst. for Research in Dairying, Univ. of Reading, 1957–65; Visiting Professor: Univ. of California, 1965; Max Planck Inst., Göttingen, 1966–67; Reader in Biochemistry and Director of Molecular Enzymology Laboratory, Univ. of Bristol, 1967–72. Visiting appointments: Univ. of Leuven, 1972; Univ. of Adelaide, 1979; Univ. of Alberta, 1983. *Publications:* An Introduction to the Study of Enzymes, 1966; Enzymes: Physical Principles, 1972; ed, Chemistry of Macromolecules, 1974; ed, Biochemical Evolution, 1981; Biothermodynamics, 1983; papers and reviews on many aspects of physical biochemistry. *Recreations:* mountain walking in Austria, gardening, reading general literature and philosophy of science, listening to music and all other good things in life. *Address:* University of Bristol Medical School, University Walk, Bristol BS8 1TD. *T:* Bristol 24161; 12a The Avenue, Bristol BS9 1PA. *T:* Bristol 684453. *Club:* United Oxford & Cambridge University.

GUTHRIE, Maj.-Gen. Charles Ronald Llewelyn, LVO 1977; OBE 1980; GOC North East District and Commander 2nd Infantry Division, since 1986; *b* 17 Nov. 1938; *s* of late Ronald Guthrie and of Nina (*née* Llewelyn); *m* 1971, Catherine, *er d* of late Lt Col Claude Worrall, MVO, OBE, Coldstream Guards; two *s. Educ:* Harrow; RMA Sandhurst. Commnd Welsh Guards, 1959; served: BAOR, Aden; 22 SAS Regt, 1965–69; psc 1972; MA (GSO2) to CGS, MoD, 1973–74; Brigade Major, Household Div., 1976–77; Comdg 1st Bn Welsh Guards, Berlin and N Ireland, 1977–80; Col GS Military Ops, MoD, 1980–82; Commander: British Forces New Hebrides, 1980; 4th Armoured Brigade, 1982–84; Chief of Staff 1st (BR) Corps, 1984–86. Col Comdt, Intelligence Corps, 1986–. *Recreations:* tennis, ski-ing, travel. *Address:* c/o Lloyds Bank, Knightsbridge Branch, 79 Brompton Road, SW3 1DD. *Club:* White's.

GUTHRIE, Rev. Donald Angus; Rector, Holy Spirit Episcopal Church, Missoula, Montana, since 1979; *b* 18 Jan. 1931; *s* of Frederick Charles and Alison Guthrie; *m* 1959, Joyce Adeline Blunsden (*d* 1976); two *s* one *d*; *m* 1977, Lesley Josephine Boardman (marr. diss. 1983); *m* 1984, Carolyn Wallop Alderson. *Educ:* Marlborough Coll.; Trinity Coll., Oxford (MA). Rector, St John's Church, Selkirk, 1963–69; Vice-Principal, Episcopal Theological Coll., Edinburgh, 1969–74; Priest-in-Charge, Whitburn Parish Church, Tyne and Wear, 1974–76; Provost, St Paul's Cathedral, Dundee, 1976–77; Episcopal Chaplain to Univ. of Montana, 1977–79. *Recreations:* walking, reading. *Address:* 655 West Mountain View Drive, Missoula, Montana 59802, USA.

GUTHRIE, Air Vice-Marshal Kenneth MacGregor, CB 1946; CBE 1944; CD 1948; retired; *b* 9 Aug. 1900; *s* of Rev. Donald and Jean Stirton Guthrie; *m* 1926, Catherine Mary Fidler; one *d. Educ:* Baltimore, USA; Montreal and Ottawa, Canada. RFC and RAF, 1917–19; RCAMC 1919–20; Canadian Air Board and RCAF since 1920. Asst Director of Military and Air Force Intelligence, General Staff, Ottawa, 1935–38; CO, RCAF Station, Rockcliffe, 1938–39; Senior Air Staff Officer, Eastern Air Command, 1939–41; CO, RCAF Station, Gander, Nfld, 1941; Air Officer i/c Administration, Western Air Command, 1942; Deputy Air Member Air Staff (Plans) AFHQ, Dec. 1942–44; AOC Northwest Air Command, RCAF, 1944–49. Retired, 1949. Legion of Merit (USA), 1946. *Recreations:* hunting, fishing, gardening. *Club:* United Services Institute (Edmonton and Victoria).

GUTHRIE, Sir Malcolm (Connop), 3rd Bt *cr* 1936; *b* 16 Dec. 1942; *s* of Sir Giles Connop McEacharn Guthrie, 2nd Bt, OBE, DSC, and of Rhona, *d* of late Frederic Stileman; *S* father, 1979; *m* 1967, Victoria, *o d* of late Brian Willcock; one *s* one *d. Educ:* Millfield. *Heir:* *s* Giles Malcolm Welcome Guthrie, *b* 16 Oct. 1972. *Address:* Brent Eleigh, Belbroughton, Stourbridge, Worcs.

GUTHRIE, Robert Isles Loftus; Director, Joseph Rowntree Memorial Trust, since 1979; *b* 27 June 1937; *s* of late Prof. W. K. C. Guthrie, FBA and of Adele Marion Ogilvy, MA; *m* 1963, Sarah Julia Weltman; two *s* one *d. Educ:* Clifton Coll.; Trinity Coll., Cambridge (MA); Liverpool Univ. (CertEd); LSE (MScEcon). Head of Cambridge House (Univ. settlement in S London), 1962–69; teacher, ILEA, 1964–66; Social Develt Officer, Peterborough Develt Corp., 1969–75; Asst Dir, Social Work Service, DHSS, 1975–79. Mem., expedns in Anatolia, British Inst. of Archaeol. at Ankara, 1958–62. Member: Arts Council of GB, 1979–81 (Regional Cttee, 1976–81); Council, Policy Studies Institute, 1979–; Council, York Univ., 1982–; Chairman: Yorkshire Arts Assoc., 1984–; Council of Regional Arts Assocs, 1985–. FRSA. *Publications:* (ed) Outlook, 1963; (ed) Outlook Two, 1965; articles, esp. in New Society. *Recreations:* music, mountains, travel, sheep. *Address:* Braeside, Acomb, York YO2 4EZ. *Club:* United Oxford & Cambridge University.

GUTHRIE, Roy David, (Gus), PhD, DSc; CChem, FRSC, FRACI; FAIM; President, New South Wales Institute of Technology, since 1986; *b* 29 March 1934; *s* of David Ephraim Guthrie and Ethel (*née* Kimmins); *m* 1st, 1956, Ann Hoad (marr. diss. 1981); three *s*; 2nd, 1982, Lyn Fielding. *Educ:* Dorking Grammar Sch.; King's Coll., Univ. of London (BSc, PhD, DSc). Shirley Inst., Manchester, 1958–60; Asst Lectr, then Lectr, Univ. of Leicester, 1960–63; Lectr, then Reader, Univ. of Sussex, 1963–73; Griffith Univ., Brisbane: Foundation Prof. of Chemistry, 1973–81; Inaugural Chm., School of Science, 1973–78; Pro-Vice-Chancellor, 1980–81; Professor Emeritus, 1982. Sec. Gen., Royal Soc. of Chemistry, 1982–85. Hon. DUniv. Griffith, 1981. *Publications:* An Introduction to the Chemistry of Carbohydrates (with J. Honeyman), 2nd edn 1964, 3rd edn 1968, 4th edn 1974; over 130 scientific papers. *Recreations:* theatre, music, antique maps. *Address:* NSWIT, Broadway, NSW 2007, Australia. *T:* 02.218.9101.

GUTHRIE, Hon. Sir Rutherford (Campbell), Kt 1968; CMG 1960; *b* 28 Nov. 1899; *s* of late Thomas O. Guthrie, Rich Avon, Donald; *m* 1927, Rhona Mary McKellar, *d* of late T. McKellar; one *s* (and one *s* decd). *Educ:* Melbourne Church of England Grammar Sch.; Jesus Coll., Cambridge (BA 1921). Farmer and grazier, Skipton, Victoria. Served European War of 1914–18 and War of 1939–45 (wounded, despatches): 9 Australian Div., El Alamein. MP Ripon, Victoria, 1947–50; Minister for Lands and for Soldier Settlement, 1948–50. *Recreations:* fishing and golf. *Address:* Jedburgh Cottage, Howey Street, Gisborne, Vic. 3437, Australia. *Clubs:* Melbourne, Naval and Military; Hawks, Pitt (Cambridge); Leander (Henley on Thames).

GUTHRIE-JAMES, David, MBE 1944; DSC 1944; author; *b* 25 Dec. 1919; *s* of Sir Archibald James, KBE, MC; *m* 1950, Hon. Jaquetta Digby, *y d* of 11th Baron Digby, KG, DSO, MC, TD; four *s* two *d. Educ:* Eton; Balliol. Served before the mast, Finnish 4–m. barque Viking, 1937–38; Balliol Coll., Oxford, 1938–39. Served War of 1939–45, RNVR, 1939–46; PoW 1943; escaped from Germany to Sweden, 1944. Mem. Antarctic Exped., 1945–46; Polar Adviser, Film Scott of the Antarctic, 1946–48. Joined Burns & Oates Ltd, Publishers, 1951. MP (C) Kemp Town Division of Brighton, 1959–64; MP (C) Dorset North, 1970–79. Council Mem., Outward Bound Trust, 1948–72; Trustee, National Maritime Museum, 1953–65. Knight of Malta, 1962. *Publications:* A Prisoner's Progress, 1946; Scott of the Antarctic: The Film, 1950; That Frozen Land, 1952; The Life of Lord Roberts, 1954; (ed) Wavy Navy, 1948; (ed) Outward Bound, 1957; (ed) In Praise of Hunting, 1960. *Recreations:* country pursuits. *Address:* Torosay Castle, Craignure, Isle of Mull, Scotland. *T:* Craignure 421.

GUTTERIDGE, Joyce Ada Cooke, CBE 1962; retired; *b* 10 July 1906; *d* of late Harold Cooke Gutteridge, QC, and late Mary Louisa Gutteridge (*née* Jackson). *Educ:* Roedean Sch.; Somerville Coll., Oxford. Called to the Bar, Middle Temple, Nov. 1938. Served in HM Forces (ATS), War of 1939–45. Foreign Office: Legal Assistant, 1947–50; Asst Legal Adviser, 1950–60; Legal Counsellor, 1960–61; Counsellor (Legal Adviser), UK Mission to the United Nations, 1961–64; Legal Counsellor, FO, 1964–66; re-employed on legal duties, FO, 1966–67. Hon. LLD, Western College for Women, Oxford, Ohio, 1963. *Publications:* The United Nations in a Changing World, 1970; articles in British Year Book of International Law and International and Comparative Law Quarterly. *Recreations:* reading, travel. *Address:* 1 Croftgate, Fulbrooke Road, Cambridge CB3 9EG. *Club:* University Women's.

GUY, Geoffrey Colin, CMG 1964; CVO 1966; OBE 1962 (MBE 1957); farmer; Governor and Commander in Chief, St Helena and its Dependencies, 1976–80, retired; *b* 4 Nov. 1921; *s* of late E. Guy, 14 Woodland Park Road, Headingley, Leeds, and of

Constance Reed Guy (*née* Taylor); *m* 1946, Joan Elfreda Smith; one *s*. *Educ:* Chatham House Sch., Ramsgate; Brasenose Coll., Oxford. Served as Pilot, RAF, 1941–46, Middle East and Burma (Flight Lieut). Colonial Administrative Service, Sierra Leone: Cadet, 1951; District Commissioner, 1955; seconded Administrator, Turks and Caicos Islands, 1958–65; Administrator, Dominica, 1965–67, Governor, March-Nov. 1967; Sec., Forces Help Soc. and Lord Roberts' Workshops, 1970–73; Administrator, Ascension Island, 1973–76. *Recreations:* swimming, riding. *Address:* Tamarisk Cottage, Kirk Hammerton, York; Farm Lodge, St Helena, South Atlantic. *Clubs:* Royal Commonwealth Society, Royal Air Force.

GUY, (Leslie) George; Assistant Secretary, Craft Sector, Amalgamated Union of Engineering Workers/Technical Administrative and Supervisory Section, since 1983; *b* 1 Sept. 1918; *s* of Albert and Annie Guy; *m* 1940, Audrey Doreen (*née* Symonds); two *d*. *Educ:* secondary modern school. National Union of Sheet Metal Workers: shop steward; Member: Branch and District Cttees; Nat. Executive Cttee; National President, June 1972–74; Asst General Secretary, 1974–77; Gen. Sec., Nat. Union of Sheet Metal Workers, Coppersmiths, Heating and Domestic Engrs, 1977–83, when Union transferred its engagements to AEUW/TASS. Member: General Council, TUC, 1977–83; Exec., CSEU, 1977–; Engrg Industry Trng Bd, 1979–. *Recreations:* work and politics. *Address:* TASS/AUEW, Onslow Hall, Little Green, Richmond, Surrey TW9 1QN.

GUY, Commander Robert Lincoln, LVO 1980; RN; *b* 4 Sept. 1947; *s* of late John Guy and Susan Guy; *m* 1981, Rosemary Ann Walker. *Educ:* Radley Coll. Entered BRNC Dartmouth, 1966; ADC to Governor and Commander-in-Chief, Gibraltar, 1973; commanded: HMS Ashton, 1974; HMS Kedleston, 1975; HMS Sirius, 1984–85. Equerry to the Queen, 1977–80; First Lieut, HMS Antelope, 1981–82. Lieut 1971; Lt-Comdr 1979; Comdr 1983. *Recreations:* polo, skiing, shooting. *Address:* Stable House, South Warnborough, Basingstoke, Hants. *T:* Basingstoke 862254. *Club:* Army and Navy.

GUY, Gen. Sir Roland (Kelvin), KCB 1981; CBE 1978 (MBE 1955); DSO 1972; Adjutant General, 1984–86; Aide-de-Camp General to the Queen, 1984–86; *b* 25 June 1928; *s* of Lt-Col Norman Greenwood Guy and Mrs Edna Guy; *m* 1957, Dierdre, *d* of Brig. P. H. Graves Morris, DSO, MC, and Mrs Auriol Graves-Morris; two *d*. *Educ:* Wellington Coll.; RMA Sandhurst. Commnd KRRC, 1948; 1950–71: Signals Officer, Germany; Adjt Kenya Regt, and 2 KRRC; Weapon Trng Officer 1 KRRC; Staff Coll., Camberley; MoD; Co. Comdr 2 RGJ; DS Staff Coll.; Bn 2 i/c; Mil. Asst to Adjt Gen.; CO 1 RGJ; Col GS HQ Near East Land Forces, 1971; Comd 24 Airportable Bde, 1972; RCDS, 1975; Principal SO to CDS, 1976–78; Chief of Staff, HQ BAOR, 1978–80; Mil. Sec., 1980–83; served in Kenya, Libya, British Guiana, Cyprus, Malaysia, W Germany and Berlin. Col Comdt: 1st Bn Royal Green Jackets, 1981–86 (Rep. Col Comdt, 1985–86); Small Arms School Corps, 1981–86. Governor, Centre for Internat. Briefing, Farnham Castle, 1984–. President: Army Boxing Assoc., 1981–86; Army Lawn Tennis Assoc., 1981–86. *Recreations:* music, skiing, golf, gardening. *Address:* c/o Grindlays Bank, 13 St James's Square, SW1. *Club:* Army and Navy.

GUYATT, Richard Gerald Talbot, CBE 1969; Rector, Royal College of Art, 1978–81 (Pro-Rector, 1974–78; Professor of Graphic Arts, 1948–78); *b* 8 May 1914; *s* of Thomas Guyatt, sometime HM Consul, Vigo, Spain and Cecil Guyatt; *m* 1941, Elizabeth Mary Corsellis; one step *d*. *Educ:* Charterhouse. Freelance designer: posters for Shell-Mex and BP, 1935. War Service: Regional Camouflage Officer for Scotland, Min. of Home Security. Dir and Chief Designer, Cockade Ltd, 1946–48; Co-designer of Lion and Unicorn Pavilion, Festival of Britain, 1951; Consultant Designer to: Josiah Wedgwood & Sons, 1952–55, 1967–70; Central Electricity Generating Bd, 1964–68; British Sugar Bureau, 1965–68; W. H. Smith, 1970–. Vis. Prof., Yale Univ., 1955 and 1962. Ceramic Designs for Min. of Works (for British Embassies), King's Coll. Cambridge, Goldsmiths' Co. and Wedgwood commem. mugs for Coronation, 1953, Investiture, 1969 and Royal Silver Wedding, 1973. Designed: silver medal for Royal Mint, Mint Dirs Conf., 1972; 700th Anniv. of Parlt stamp, 1965; Postal Order forms, 1964 for Post Office; Silver Jubilee stamps, 1977; commem. crown piece for 80th birthday of HM Queen Elizabeth The Queen Mother, 1980. Member: Stamp Adv. Cttee, 1963–74; Internat. Jury, Warsaw Poster Biennale, 1968; Bank of England Design Adv. Cttee, 1968–; Adv. Council, Victoria and Albert Mus., 1978–81. Chm., Guyatt/Jenkins Design Group. Governor, Imperial Coll. of Sci. and Technol., 1979–81. FSIA; Hon. ARCA. *Address:* Flat 1, 5 Onslow Square, SW7. *T:* 01–584 5398; Forge Cottage, Ham, Marlborough, Wilts. *T:* Inkpen 270.

GWANDU, Emir of; Alhaji Haruna, (Muhammadu Basharu), CFR 1965; CMG 1961; CBE 1955; 18th Emir of Gwandu, 1954; Member, North Western State House of Chiefs, and Council of Chiefs; Member, and Chairman, Executive Council, State Self-Development Funds Council; President, former Northern Nigeria House of Chiefs, since 1957 (Deputy President 1956); *b* Batoranke, 1913; *m* 1933; fifteen *c*. *Educ:* Birnin Kebbi Primary Sch.; Katsina Training Coll. Teacher: Katsina Teachers Coll., 1933–35; Sokoto Middle Sch., 1935–37; Gusau Local Authority Sub-Treasurer, 1937–43; Gwandu Local Authority Treasurer, 1943–45; District Head, Kalgo, 1945–54. Member former N Reg. Marketing Board. *Recreations:* hunting, shooting. *Address:* Emir's Palace, PO Box 1, Birnin Kebbi, North Western State, Nigeria.

GWILLIAM, John Albert, MA Cantab; Headmaster of Birkenhead School, since Sept. 1963; *b* 28 Feb. 1923; *s* of Thomas Albert and Adela Audrey Gwilliam; *m* 1949, Pegi Lloyd George; three *s* two *d*. *Educ:* Monmouth Sch.; Trinity Coll., Cambridge. Assistant Master: Trinity Coll., Glenalmond, 1949–52; Bromsgrove Sch., 1952–56; Head of Lower Sch., Dulwich Coll., 1956–63. *Address:* The Lodge, Beresford Road, Birkenhead, Merseyside.

GWILLIAM, Prof. Kenneth Mason, FCIT; Professor of Transport Economics, University of Leeds, since 1967; *b* 27 June 1937; *s* of John and Marjorie Gwilliam; *m* 1961, Jennifer Mary Bell; two *s*. *Educ:* Magdalen Coll., Oxford (BA 1st Cl. Hons PPE). Res. Asst, Fisons Ltd, 1960–61; Lecturer: Univ. of Nottingham, 1961–65; Univ. of E Anglia, 1965–67. Dir, Nat. Bus Co., 1978–82. Editor, Jl of Transport Economics and Policy. *Publications:* Transport and Public Policy, 1964; (jtly) Criteria for Investment in Transport Infrastructure, 1973; Economics and Transport Policy, 1975; (jtly) Deregulating the Bus Industry, 1984. *Recreations:* badminton, tennis. *Address:* 53 Primley Park Avenue, Alwoodley, Leeds LS17 7HX. *T:* Leeds 681183.

GWILT, George David, FFA; Managing Director and Actuary, since 1985, Director, since 1984, Standard Life Assurance Company; Deputy Chairman, Associated Scottish Life Offices, since 1986; *b* 11 Nov. 1927; *s* of Richard Lloyd Gwilt and Marjory Gwilt (*née* Mair); *m* 1956, Ann Dalton Sylvester; three *s*. *Educ:* Sedbergh Sch.; St John's Coll., Cambridge (MA). FFA 1952; FBCS. Joined Standard Life Assurance Co., 1949; Asst Official, 1956; Asst Actuary, 1957; Statistician, 1962; Mechanisation Manager, 1964; Systems Manager, 1969; Dep. Pensions Manager, 1972; Pensions Actuary, 1973; Asst General Manager and Pensions Manager, 1977; Asst Gen. Man. (Finance), 1978; Gen. Manager, 1979. Trustee, TSB of South of Scotland, 1966–83. Member: Younger Cttee on Privacy, 1970–72; Monopolies and Mergers Commn, 1983–. Pres., Faculty of Actuaries, 1981–83. *Recreation:* flute playing. *Address:* 39 Oxgangs Road, Edinburgh EH10 7BE. *T:* 031–445 1266. *Clubs:* Royal Air Force; New (Edinburgh).

GWYNEDD, Viscount; David Richard Owen Lloyd George; *b* 22 Jan. 1951; *s* and *heir* of 3rd Earl Lloyd George of Dwyfor, *qv*; *m* 1985, Pamela, *o d* of late Alexander Kleyff; one *s*. *Educ:* Eton. *Heir:* *s* Hon. William Alexander Lloyd George, *b* 16 May 1986. *Address:* 43 Cadogan Square, SW1; Brimpton Mill, near Reading, Berks.

GWYNN, Edward Harold, CB 1961; Deputy Under-Secretary of State, Ministry of Defence, 1966–72; retired 1972; *b* 23 Aug. 1912; *y s* of late Dr E. J. Gwynn, Provost of Trinity Coll., Dublin, and late Olive Ponsonby; *m* 1937, Dorothy, *d* of late Geoffrey S. Phillpotts, Foxrock, Co. Dublin; one *s* four *d*. *Educ:* Sedbergh School; TCD. Entered Home Office, 1936; Assistant Secretary, 1947; Assistant Under Secretary of State, 1956; Principal Finance Officer (Under-Secretary), Ministry of Agriculture, 1961–62; Deputy Under-Secretary of State, Home Office, 1963–66. *Recreations:* gardening, the countryside. *Address:* The Chestnuts, Minchinhampton, Glos. *T:* Nailsworth 2863.

GWYNN-JONES, Peter Llewellyn; Lancaster Herald of Arms, since 1982; *b* 12 March 1940; *s* of late Major Jack Llewellyn Gwynn-Jones, Cape Town, and late Mary Muriel Daphne, *d* of Col Arthur Patrick Bird Harrison, and step *s* of late Lt-Col Gavin David Young, Long Burton, Dorset. *Educ:* Wellington Coll.; Trinity Coll., Cambridge (MA). Assistant to Garter King of Arms, 1970; Bluemantle Pursuivant of Arms, 1973; Secretary, Harleian Society, 1981; House Comptroller of College of Arms, 1982. *Recreations:* tropical forests, wild life conservation, fishing. *Address:* College of Arms, Queen Victoria Street, EC4V 4BT. *T:* 01–248 0911; 79 Harcourt Terrace, SW10. *T:* 01–373 5859.

GWYNNE-EVANS, Sir Francis Loring, 4th Bt *cr* 1913, of Oaklands Park, Awre, Co. Gloucester; *b* 22 Feb. 1914; *s* of Sir Evan Gwynne Gwynne-Evans, 2nd Bt and Ada Jane (*d* 1977), *d* of Walter Scott Andrews, New York; *S* brother, 1985; *m* 1st, 1937, Elisabeth Fforde (marr. diss. 1958), *d* of J. Fforde Tipping; two *s* one *d*; 2nd, 1958, Gloria Marie Reynolds; two *s* three *d*. Career as professional singer under name of Francis Loring. *Heir:* *s* David Gwynne Gwynne-Evans, *b* 25 Nov. 1943.

GWYNNE JONES, family name of **Baron Chalfont.**

GWYTHER, (Arthur) David; Inspector General, Insolvency Service, Department of Trade, 1981–84; *b* 8 Dec. 1924; *s* of late Arthur James Gwyther and of Lily Elizabeth Gwyther; *m* 1949, Agnes, (Nan), Boyd; one *s* two *d*. *Educ:* Sutton High Sch. for Boys, Plymouth. Dept of Trade Insolvency Service: Asst Examiner, 1948; Examiner, 1951; Assistant Official Receiver: Brighton, 1955; Southampton, 1957; Official Receiver, Plymouth, 1959; Inspector of Official Receivers, 1961; Official Receiver, Birmingham, 1965; Dep. Inspector Gen., 1976. *Recreation:* gardening. *Address:* Tarnhow, 65 Abbots Lane, Kenley, Surrey CR2 5JG. *T:* 01–668 6145.

GYLLENHAMMAR, Dr Pehr Gustaf; Chairman and Chief Executive Officer, Volvo, since 1983; *b* 28 April 1935; *s* of Pehr Gustaf Victor Gyllenhammar and Aina Dagny Kaplan; *m* 1959, Eva Christina, *d* of Gunnar Ludvig Engellau; one *s* three *d*. *Educ:* University of Lund. LLB. Mannheimer & Zetterlöf, solicitors, 1959; Haight, Gardner, Poor & Havens, NY, 1960; Amphion Insurance Co., Gothenburg, 1961–64; Skandia Insurance Co., 1965, Exec. Vice-Pres., 1968, Pres. and Chief Exec. Officer, 1970; AB Volvo, Gothenburg, 1970, Man. Dir and Chief Exec. Officer, 1971; Dir of companies in Sweden, UK and USA. Vice-Chm., Bd of Trustees, Aspen Inst. for Humanistic Studies, Aspen, Colorado, 1980–; Member: Internat. Adv. Cttee, Chase Manhattan Bank, NA, NY, 1972–; Bd, Cttee of Common Market Automobile Constructors, 1977–; Bd, Swedish Employers' Confedn, 1979–; Bd, Fedn of Swedish Industries, 1979–. Lethaby Prof., Royal Coll. of Art, London, 1977; Mem., Royal Swedish Acad. of Engineering Scis, 1974. DM *hc* Gothenburg Univ., 1981; Golden Award, City of Gothenburg, 1981. Officer, Royal Order of Vasa, 1973; King's Medal, with Ribbon of Order of Seraphim, 1981; Comdr, Order of Lion of Finland, 1977; Comdr, Ordre National du Mérite, France, 1980; Comdr, St Olav's Order, Norway, 1984. *Publications:* Mot sekelskiftet på måfå (Toward the Turn of the Century, at Random), 1970; Jag tror på Sverige (I Believe in Sweden), 1973; People at Work (US), 1977; En industripolitik för människan (Industrial policy for human beings), 1979. *Recreations:* tennis, sailing, skiing, riding. *Address:* AB Volvo, S405 08, Gothenburg, Sweden.

GYÖRGYI, Albert S.; *see* Szent-Györgyi.

H

HABAKKUK, Sir John (Hrothgar), Kt 1976; FBA 1965; FRHistS; Principal of Jesus College, Oxford, 1967–84, Hon. Fellow, 1984; a Pro Vice-Chancellor, University of Oxford, 1977–83; President, University College, Swansea, 1975–84; *b* 13 May 1915; *s* of Evan Guest and Anne Habakkuk; *m* 1948, Mary Richards; one *s* three *d*. *Educ:* Barry County Sch.; St John's Coll., Cambridge (scholar and Strathcona student), Hon. Fellow 1971. Historical Tripos: Part I, First Class, 1935; Part II, First Class (with distinction), 1936; Fellow, Pembroke Coll., Cambridge, 1938–50, Hon. Fellow 1973; Director of Studies in History and Librarian, 1946–50. Temporary Civil Servant: Foreign Office, 1940–42, Board of Trade, 1942–46. University Lecturer in Faculty of Economics, Cambridge, 1946–50; Chichele Prof. of Economic History, Oxford, and Fellow of All Souls Coll., 1950–67; Vice-Chancellor, Oxford Univ., 1973–77. Visiting Lecturer, Harvard University, 1954–55; Ford Research Professor, University of California, Berkeley, 1962–63; Ford Lecturer, 1984–85. Member: Grigg Cttee on Departmental Records, 1952–54; Advisory Council on Public Records, 1958–70; SSRC, 1967–71; Nat. Libraries Cttee, 1968–69; Royal Commn on Historic Manuscripts, 1978–; Admin. Bd, Internat. Assoc. of Univs, 1975–85. Chairman: Cttee of Vice Chancellors and Principals of Univs of UK, 1976–77; Adv. Gp on London Health Servs, 1980–81; Oxfordshire DHA, 1981–84. Pres., RHistS, 1976–80. Foreign Member: Amer. Phil. Soc.; Amer. Acad. of Arts and Sciences. Hon. DLitt: Wales, 1971; Cambridge, 1973; Pennsylvania, 1975; Kent, 1978. *Publications:* American and British Technology in the Nineteenth Century, 1962; Population Growth and Economic Development since 1750, 1971; articles and reviews. *Address:* 28 Cunliffe Close, Oxford. *T:* Oxford 56583.

HABERFELD, Dame Gwyneth; *see* Jones, Dame Gwyneth.

HABGOOD, Most Rev. and Rt. Hon. John Stapylton; *see* York, Archbishop of.

HACAULT, Most Rev. Antoine; *see* St Boniface, Archbishop of, (RC).

HACKER, Alan Ray; clarinettist and conductor; Senior Lecturer in Music, York University, since 1984 (Lecturer, 1976–84); *b* 30 Sept. 1938; *s* of Kenneth and Sybil Hacker; *m* 1st, 1959, Anna Maria Sroka; two *d*; 2nd, 1977, Karen Evans; one *s*. *Educ:* Dulwich Coll.; Royal Academy of Music. FRAM. Joined LPO, 1958; Prof., RAM, 1960–76. Founded: Pierrot Players (with S. Pruslin and H. Birtwistle), 1965; Matrix, 1971; Music Party for authentic performance of classical music, 1972; Classical Orch., 1977; Guest Cond., Orchestra la Fenice, Venice, 1981–. First modern "authentic" perfs, 1977–, incl: Mozart's Symphonies 39, 40; Beethoven's Symphonies 2, 3, 7, 9 and Egmont; Haydn's Harmonie and Creation Masses, Symphony 104 and Trumpet Concerto. Revived basset clarinet and restored orig. text, Mozart's concerto and quintet, 1967; revived baroque clarinet (hitherto unplayed), 1975. Premieres of music by Birtwistle, Boulez, Feldman, Goehr, Maxwell Davies, Stockhausen, Blake, Mellers and Sciarrino; cond 5 staged perfs of Bach's St John Passion for European Music Year, 1984. Sir Robert Mayer Lectr, Leeds Univ., 1972–73. Mem. Fires of London, 1970–76; Dir, York Early Music Festival. Set up nat. video music teaching network with Gulbenkian assistance, 1982–83. Many recordings. *Publications:* Scores of Mozart Concerto and Quintet, 1972; 1st edn of reconstructed Mozart Concerto, 1973; Schumann's Soiréestucke, 1985. *Recreation:* cookery. *Address:* University of York, Heslington, York YO1 5DD.

HACKER, Rt. Rev. George Lanyon; *see* Penrith, Bishop Suffragan of.

HACKER, Prof. Louis M., MA (Columbia); Emeritus Professor of Economics, Columbia University, USA, 1967 (Economics Department, 1935; Dean of School of General Studies, 1952–58, Director, 1949–52; Professor of Economics, 1948–67); *b* 17 March 1899; *s* of Morris Hacker; *m* 1st, 1921, Lillian Lewis (*d* 1952); one *s* one *d*.; 2nd, 1953, Beatrice Larson Brennan (*d* 1977). *Educ:* Columbia Coll.; Columbia University. Assistant and contributing Editor of New International Encyclopædia, Social Science Encyclopædia, Columbia Encyclopædia; taught economics and history at University of Wisconsin, Ohio State University, Utah State Agricultural College, University of Hawaii, Yeshiva University, Penn State University, Univ. of Puget Sound, Army War College, National War College. Executive sec. American Academic Freedom Study; Editor, American Century Series; Chairman, Academic Freedom Cttee, American Civil Liberties Union, resigned 1968; Guggenheim Fellow, 1948, 1959; Relm Foundation Fellow, 1967. Harmsworth Professor of American History, Oxford Univ., 1948–49; Lecturer, Fulbright Conference on American Studies, Cambridge, 1952. Visiting Distinguished Professor of Economics, Fairleigh Dickinson, 1967–68. Fellow, Queen's Coll., Oxford, and MA (Oxon); Benjamin Franklin Fellow of RSA; Hon. LLD Hawaii; Hon. LHD Columbia. Students Army Training Corps, 1918. *Publications:* (with B. B. Kendrick) United States since 1865, 1932, 4th edn 1949; The Farmer is Doomed, 1933; Short History of the New Deal, 1934; The US: a Graphic History, 1937; American Problems of Today, 1939; Triumph of American Capitalism, 1940; (with Allan Nevins) The US and Its Place in World Affairs, 1943; The Shaping of the American Tradition, 1947; New Industrial Relations (jointly), 1948; Government Assistance and the British Universities (jointly), 1952; (with H. S. Zahler) The United States in the 20th Century, 1952; Capitalism and the Historians (jointly), 1954; Alexander Hamilton in the American Tradition, 1957; American Capitalism, 1957; Larger View of the University, 1961; Major Documents in American Economic History, 2 vols, 1961; The World of Andrew Carnegie, Part 1, 1861–1901, 1968; The Course of American Economic Growth and Development, 1970; (with M. D. Hirsch) Proskauer: his life and times, 1978; contributions to learned journals and reviews. *Recreations:* walking, bridge, travel. *Address:* 430 W 116th Street, New York, NY 10027, USA. *Clubs:* Athenæum (London); Faculty, Columbia University (New York); Pilgrims (USA).

HACKETT, Prof. Brian; Professor of Landscape Architecture, University of Newcastle upon Tyne, 1967–77, now Emeritus Professor; *b* 3 Nov. 1911; *s* of Henry and Ida Adeline Mary Hackett; *m* 1st, 1942, Frederica Claire Grundy (*d* 1979); one *s* two *d*; 2nd, 1980, Dr Elizabeth Ratcliff. *Educ:* Grammar Sch., Burton-on-Trent; Birmingham Sch. of Architecture; Sch. of Planning for Regional Development, London. MA Dunelm, PPILA, RIBA, MRTPI. Professional experience, 1930–40; Flt-Lt, RAFVR, 1941–45; Lectr, Sch. of Planning for Regional Develt, London, 1945–47; Univ. of Durham: Lectr in Town and Country Planning, 1947; Lectr in Landscape Architecture, 1948, Sen. Lectr, 1949–59; Vis. Prof. of Landscape Architecture, Univ. of Illinois, 1960–61; Reader in Landscape Arch., Univ. of Newcastle upon Tyne, 1962–66. Member: N England Regl Adv. Cttee, Forestry Commn, 1963–; Water Space Amenity Commn, 1973–80. Pres., Inst. of Landscape Architects, 1967–68; Hon. Corresp. Mem., Amer. Soc. of Landscape Architects, 1962. European Prize for Nature Conservation and Landscape Develt, 1975. *Publications:* Man, Society and Environment, 1950; (jtly) Landscape Techniques, 1967; Landscape Planning, 1971; Steep Slopes Landscape, 1971; (jtly) Landscape Reclamation, 1971–72; (jtly) Landscape Reclamation Practice, 1977; Planting Design, 1979; Landscape Conservation, 1980; numerous papers in internat. jls. *Recreation:* musical performance. *Address:* 27 Larkspur Terrace, Jesmond, Newcastle upon Tyne NE2 2DT. *T:* Newcastle upon Tyne 2810747. *Club:* Royal Commonwealth Society.

HACKETT, Prof. Cecil Arthur, MA Cantab, Docteur de l'Université de Paris; Professor of French, University of Southampton, 1952–70, now Professor Emeritus; *b* 19 Jan. 1908; *s* of Henry Hackett and Alice Setchell; *m* 1942, Mary Hazel Armstrong. *Educ:* King's Norton Grammar Sch., Birmingham; University of Birmingham; Emmanuel Coll., Cambridge (Scholar and Prizeman). Assistant d'Anglais, Lycée Louis-le-Grand, Paris, 1934–36; Lecturer in French and English, Borough Road Coll., Isleworth, 1936–39. Served War of 1939–45: enlisted 1/8th Bn Middlesex Regt, 1939. Education Representative, British Council, Paris, 1945–46; Lecturer in French, University of Glasgow, 1947–52. Hon. DLitt Southampton 1984. Chevalier de la Légion d'Honneur. *Publications:* Le Lyrisme de Rimbaud, 1938; Rimbaud l'Enfant, 1948; An Anthology of Modern French Poetry, 1952, 4th edn 1976; Rimbaud, 1957; Autour de Rimbaud, 1967; (ed and introd) New French Poetry: an anthology, 1973; Rimbaud, a critical introduction, 1981; Rimbaud, a critical edition, 1986; contributions to English and French Reviews. *Address:* Shawford Close, Shawford, Winchester, Hants. *T:* Twyford 713506.

HACKETT, Dennis William; journalist; publishing and communications consultant; Executive Editor, Today, since 1986; TV critic: New Scientist, since 1983; The Tablet, since 1984; *b* 5 Feb. 1929; *s* of James Joseph Hackett and Sarah Ellen Hackett (*née* Bedford); *m* 1st, 1953, Agnes Mary Collins; two *s* one *d*; 2nd, 1974, Jacqueline Margaret Totterdell; one *d*. *Educ:* De La Salle College, Sheffield. Served with RN, 1947–49. Sheffield Telegraph, 1945–47 and 1949–54; Daily Herald, 1954; Odhams Press, 1954; Deputy Editor, Illustrated, 1955–58; Daily Express, 1958–60; Daily Mail, 1960; Art Editor, Observer, 1961–62; Deputy Editor, 1962, Editor, 1964–65, Queen; Editor, Nova, 1965–69; Publisher, Twentieth Century Magazine, 1965–72; Editorial Dir, George Newnes Ltd, 1966–69; Dir, IPC Newspapers, 1969–71; Associate Editor, Daily Express, 1973–74; TV critic, The Times, 1981–85; Editorial Consultant, You, The Mail on Sunday magazine, 1982–86. Chm., Design and Art Directors' Assoc., 1967–68. *Publications:* The History of the Future: Bemrose Corporation 1826–1976, 1976; The Big Idea: the story of Ford in Europe, 1978. *Recreations:* reading, walking. *Address:* 4 East Heath Road, NW3 1BN. *Club:* Royal Automobile.

HACKETT, John Charles Thomas, FBIM; Director General, British Insurance Brokers' Association, since 1985; *b* 4 Feb. 1939; *s* of Thomas John Hackett and late Doris Hackett; *m* 1958, Patricia Margaret, *d* of Eric Ronald Clifford and Margaret Tubb. *Educ:* Glyn Grammar Sch., Epsom, Surrey; London Univ. (LLB Hons, external). FBIM 1981. Prodn Planning Manager, Rowntree Gp, 1960–64; Prodn Controller, Johnson's Wax, 1964; Commercial Sec., Heating and Ventilating Contractors' Assoc., 1964–70; Sec., Cttee of Assocs of Specialist Engrg Contractors, 1968–79; Dep. Dir, 1970–79, Dir, 1980–84, British Constructional Steelwork Assoc. Member: Council, CBI, 1980–; CBI Gp of Chief Execs of Major Sector Assocs, 1980–84; Constructional Steelwork EDC, NEDO, 1980–84. MInstD. *Publication:* BCSA Members' Contractual Handbook, 1972, 2nd edn 1979. *Recreations:* music, reading, walking, motoring. *Address:* 15 Downsway Close, Tadworth, Surrey KT20 5DR. *T:* Tadworth 3024.

HACKETT, John Wilkings; Director, Financial, Fiscal and Enterprise Affairs, Organisation for Economic Co-operation and Development, Paris, since 1979; *b* 21 Jan. 1924; *s* of Albert and Bertha Hackett; *m* 1952, Anne-Marie Le Brun. *Educ:* LSE (BSc(Econ) 1950); Institut d'Etudes Politiques, Paris (Diplôme 1952); Univ. of Paris (Dr d'état ès sciences economiques 1957). Served RN, 1942–46. Economic research, 1952–57; OECD, 1958–. FRSA. *Publications:* Economic Planning in France (with A.-M. Hackett), 1963; L'Economie Britannique—problèmes et perspectives, 1966; (with A.-M. Hackett) The British Economy, 1967; articles on economic subjects in British and French economic jls. *Recreations:* music, painting, reading. *Address:* 48 rue de la Bienfaisance, 75008 Paris, France.

HACKETT, Gen. Sir John Winthrop, GCB 1967 (KCB 1962; CB 1958); CBE 1953 (MBE 1938); DSO 1942 and Bar 1945; MC 1941; DL; BLitt, MA Oxon; FRSL 1982; Principal of King's College, London, 1968–July 1975; *b* 5 Nov. 1910; *s* of late Sir John Winthrop Hackett, KCMG, LLD, Perth, WA; *m* 1942, Margaret, *d* of Joseph Frena, Graz, Austria; one *d* (and two adopted *step d*). *Educ:* Geelong Grammar Sch., Australia; New

Coll., Oxford, Hon. Fellow 1972. Regular Army, commissioned 8th KRI Hussars, 1931; Palestine, 1936 (despatches); seconded to Transjordan Frontier Force, 1937–41 (despatches twice); Syria, 1941 (wounded); Sec. Commn of Control Syria and Lebanon; GSO2 9th Army; Western Desert, 1942 (wounded); GSO1 Raiding Forces GHQ, MELF; Comdr 4th Parachute Brigade, 1943; Italy, 1943 (despatches); Arnhem, 1944 (wounded); BGS (1) Austria, 1946–47; Comdr Transjordan Frontier Force, 1947; idc 1951; DQMG, BAOR, 1952; Comdr 20th Armoured Bde, 1954; GOC 7th Armoured Div., 1956–58; Comdt, Royal Mil. Coll. of Science, 1958–61; GOC-in-C, Northern Ireland Command, 1961–63; Dep. Chief of Imperial Gen. Staff, 1963–64; Dep. Chief of the Gen. Staff, Ministry of Defence, 1964–66. Comdr-in-Chief, British Army of the Rhine, and Comdr Northern Army Gp, 1966–68. ADC (Gen.), 1967–68. Col. Commandant, REME, 1961–66; Hon. Col: 10th Bn The Parachute Regt, TA, 1965–67; 10th Volunteer Bn, The Parachute Regt, 1967–73; Oxford Univ. Officers Training Corps, 1967–78; Col, Queen's Royal Irish Hussars, 1969–75. Mem., Lord Chancellor's Cttee on Reform of Law of Contempt, 1971–74; Mem., Disciplinary Tribunal, Inns of Court and Bar, 1972–83. Vis. Prof. in Classics, KCL, 1977–. Lectures: Lees Knowles, Cambridge, 1961; Basil Henriques Meml, 1970; Harmon Meml, USAF Acad., 1970; Jubilee, Imperial Coll., 1979. President: UK Classical Assoc., 1971; English Assoc., 1973–74. Hon. Liveryman, Worshipful Company of Dyers, 1975; Freeman of City of London, 1976. DL Glos 1982. Hon. LLD: Queen's Univ. Belfast; Perth, WA, 1963; Exeter, 1977. FKC, 1968; Hon. Fellow St George's Coll., University of Western Australia, 1965. Chesney Gold Medal, RUSI, 1985. Publications: I Was a Stranger, 1977; (jtly) The Third World War, 1978; (jtly) The Untold Story, 1982; The Profession of Arms, 1983; articles and reviews. Address: Coberley Mill, Cheltenham, Glos GL53 9NH. T: Coberley 207. Clubs: Cavalry and Guards, Carlton, United Oxford & Cambridge University, White's.

HACKETT, Peter, PhD; FEng 1983; Principal, Camborne School of Mines, since 1970; b 1 Nov. 1933; s of Christopher and Evelyn Hackett; m 1958, Esmé Doreen (née Lloyd); one s one d. Educ: Mundella Grammar Sch.; Nottingham Univ. (BSc 1st Cl. Hons Mining Engrg; PhD). FIMM. Lecturer, Nottingham Univ., 1958–70; Vis. Lectr, Univ. of Minnesota, 1969; Vis. Professor, Univ. of California at Berkeley, 1979. Publications: contribs to learned jls on geotechnical subjects and mining engrg educn. Recreations: sailing, vintage vehicles, shooting. Address: Camborne School of Mines, Redruth, Cornwall TR15 3SE. Club: Royal Cornwall Yacht (Falmouth).

HACKING, family name of Baron Hacking.

HACKING, 3rd Baron cr 1945, of Chorley; Douglas David Hacking; Bt 1938; Solicitor of Supreme Court of England and Wales; Attorney and Counselor-at-Law of State of New York; b 17 April 1938; er s of 2nd Baron Hacking, and of Daphne Violet, e d of late R. L. Finnis; S father, 1971; m 1982, Dr Tessa M. Hunt, MB, MRCP, FFARCS, er d of Roland C. C. Hunt, qv; one s (two s one d by former marriage). Educ: Aldro School, Shackleford; Charterhouse School; Clare College, Cambridge (BA 1961, MA 1968). Called to the Bar, Middle Temple, Nov. 1963 (Astbury and Harmsworth Scholarships). Served in RN, 1956–58; Ordinary Seaman, 1956; Midshipman, 1957; served in HMS Ark Royal (N Atlantic), 1957; HMS Hardy (Portland) and HMS Brocklesby (Portland and Gibraltar), 1958; transferred RNR as Sub-Lt, 1958, on completion of National Service; transf. List 3 RNR, HMS President, 1961; Lieut 1962; retired RNR, 1964. Barrister-at-Law, 1963–76; in practice, Midland and Oxford Circuits, 1964–75. Admitted to State and Federal Bar, New York State, 1975; admitted Solicitor of Supreme Court, 1977; with Simpson, Thacher and Bartlett, NYC, 1975–76; with Lovell, White and King, 1976–79. Member: Amer. Bar Assoc.; NY State Bar Assoc.; Bar Assoc. of City of New York. Pres., Assoc. of Lancastrians in London, 1971–72. Apprenticed to Merchant Taylors' Co., 1955, admitted to Freedom, 1962; Freedom, City of London, 1962. FCIArb 1979. Recreations: running, walking. Heir: s Hon. Douglas Francis Hacking, b 8 Aug. 1968. Address: 21 West Square, SE11 4SN; Richards Butler & Co., 5 Clifton Street, EC2A 4DQ. T: 01–247 6555. Clubs: MCC; Century (NY).

HACKING, Anthony Stephen; QC 1983; a Recorder, since 1985; b 12 Jan. 1941; s of John Kenneth and Joan Horton Hacking, Warwick; m 1969, Carin, d of Dr Svante and Brita Holmdahl, Gothenburg; one d three s. Educ: Warwick Sch.; Lincoln Coll., Oxford (MA). Called to the Bar, Inner Temple, 1965. Address: 1 King's Bench Walk, Temple, EC4. T: 01–583 6266.

HACKLAND, Sarah Ann; see Spencer, S. A.

HACKNEY, Archdeacon of; see Sharpley, Ven. R. E. D.

HACKNEY, Arthur, RWS 1957 (VPRWS 1974–77); RE 1960; ARCA 1949; artist; Deputy Head of Fine Art Department, West Surrey College of Art and Design (Farnham Centre) (formerly Farnham School of Art), 1979–85, retired; b 13 March 1925; s of late J. T. Hackney; m 1955, Mary Baker, ARCA; two d. Educ: Burslem Sch. of Art; Royal Coll. of Art, London. Served in Royal Navy, 1942–46. Travelling scholarship, Royal College of Art, 1949; part-time Painting Instructor, Farnham Sch. of Art, 1949, Lecturer, 1962; Head of Dept: Graphic, 1963–68; Printmaking, 1968–79. Work represented in Public Collections, including Bradford City Art Gallery, Victoria and Albert Museum, Ashmolean Museum, Wellington Art Gallery (NZ), Nottingham Art Gallery, Keighley Art Gallery (Yorks), Wakefield City Art Gallery, Graves Art Gallery, Sheffield, GLC, Preston Art Gallery, City of Stoke-on-Trent Art Gall., Kent Educn Cttee, Staffordshire Educn Cttee. Mem., Fine Art Bd, CNAA, 1975–78. Address: Woodhatches, Spoil Lane, Tongham, Farnham, Surrey. T: Aldershot 23919. Club: Chelsea Arts.

HADDEN-PATON, Major Adrian Gerard Nigel, DL, JP; b 3 Dec. 1918; s of late Nigel Fairholt Paton, Covehithe, Suffolk; m 1951, Mary-Rose, d of Col A. H. MacIlwaine, DSO, MC, Troutbeck, S Rhodesia; two s (and two step s). Educ: Rugby; Worcester Coll., Oxford. BA. 2nd Lt, 1st The Royal Dragoons, 1940; Adjutant, 1943–44; served 1940–45: Western Desert, Tunisia, Italy, France, Belgium, Holland, Germany and Denmark; (despatches); Maj. 1945. Instructor, RMA, Sandhurst, 1947–50; retired 1950. Mem. Estates Cttee of Nat. Trust, 1956, Properties Cttee, 1970, Finance Cttee, 1973–82; Mem. Exec. Cttee, 1959–73, and Finance Cttee, 1961–73 (Chm. 1962–68) of Country Landowners Association. Is an Underwriting Mem. of Lloyd's; Chm. Holland & Holland Ltd, 1962–82; Chm. Hertfordshire Agricultural Soc., 1961–69; Past Pres. Hertfordshire & Middlesex Trust for Nature Conservation; Vice-Pres., Royal Forestry Soc., 1980–82. Chm. of Governors, Berkhamsted Sch. and Berkhamsted Sch. for Girls, 1973–78 (Governor 1950–78). JP 1951, DL 1962, Herts; High Sheriff, 1961. Recreations: shooting, forestry. Address: Rossway, Berkhamsted, Herts. T: Berkhamsted 3264. Club: Cavalry and Guards.

HADDINGTON, 13th Earl of, cr 1619; John George Baillie-Hamilton; Lord Binning, 1613; Lord Binning and Byres, 1619; b 21 Dec. 1941; o s of 12th Earl of Haddington, KT, MC, TD, and of Sarah, y d of G. W. Cook, Montreal; S father, 1986; m 1st, 1975, Prudence Elizabeth (marr. diss. 1981), d of A. Rutherford Hayles; 2nd, 1984, Susan Jane Antonia, 2nd d of John Heyworth; one s. Educ: Ampleforth. Heir: s Lord Binning, qv.

Address: Mellerstain, Gordon, Berwickshire; Tyninghame, Dunbar, East Lothian. Clubs: Turf; New (Edinburgh).

HADDO, Earl of; Alexander George Gordon; ARICS; Development Manager with Speyhawk plc, since 1985; b 31 March 1955; s and heir of 6th Marquess of Aberdeen and Temair, qv; m 1981, Joanna Clodagh Houldsworth; two s. Educ: Cothill House, Abingdon; Harrow School; Polytechnic of Central London (DipBE). ARICS 1979. With Gardiner and Theobald, Chartered Quantity Surveyors, 1976–82; Speyhawk plc, Property Developers, 1982–. Recreations: Rugby, golf, cricket, music, theatre. Heir: s Viscount Formartine, qv. Address: 22 Beauclerc Road, W6 0NS. T: 01–748 4849. Clubs: Arts, MCC; London Scottish Rugby Football; Saint Saracens; Harrow Wanderers Cricket, Butterflies Cricket.

HADDON-CAVE, Sir (Charles) Philip, KBE 1980; CMG 1973; Chief Secretary, Hong Kong, 1981–85; b 6 July 1925; m 1948, Elizabeth Alice May Simpson; two s one d. Educ: Univ. Tasmania; King's Coll., Cambridge. Entered Colonial Administrative Service, 1952: East Africa High Commn, 1952; Kenya, 1953–62; Seychelles, 1961–62; Hong Kong, 1962–85; Financial Secretary, Hong Kong, 1971–81. Publication: (with D. M. Hocking) Air Transport in Australia, 1951. Address: The Old Farmhouse, Nethercote Road, Tackley, Oxon. Clubs: Oriental; Hong Kong, Royal Hong Kong Golf.

HADDOW, Sir (Thomas) Douglas, KCB 1966 (CB 1955); FRSE; Permanent Under-Secretary of State, Scottish Office, 1965–73; b 9 Feb. 1913; s of George Haddow, Crawford, Lanarkshire; m 1942, Margaret R. S. Rowat (d 1969); two s. Educ: George Watson's Coll., Edinburgh; Edinburgh Univ.; Trinity Coll., Cambridge. MA (Edinburgh) 1932; BA (Cambridge) 1934. Department of Health for Scotland, 1935; Private Sec. to Sec. of State for Scotland, 1941–44. Commonwealth Fund Fellow, 1948. Secretary: Dept of Health for Scot., 1959–62; Scottish Develt Dept, 1962–64; Chm., N of Scotland Hydro-Electric Bd, 1973–78; Mem. (pt-time), S of Scotland Electricity Bd, 1973–78; Dir, British Investment Trust, 1978–83. Chm. Court, Heriot-Watt Univ., 1978–84. Hon. LLD Strathclyde Univ., 1967; Hon. DLitt Heriot-Watt Univ., 1971. Recreation: golf. Address: The Coach House, Northumberland Street Lane SW, Edinburgh EH3 6JD. T: 031–556 3650; Castle View, Dirleton, East Lothian EH39 5EH. T: Dirleton 266. Club: Royal Commonwealth Society.

HADEN, William Demmery, TD, MA; Headmaster, Royal Grammar School, Newcastle upon Tyne, 1960–72, retired; b 14 March 1909; s of Reverend William Henry and Gertrude Haden, Little Aston; m 1939, Elizabeth Marjorie, d of R. S. Tewson, Chorley Wood; one s two d. Educ: Nottingham High Sch.; Wadham Coll., Oxford (2nd Class Lit. Hum.; MA 1934). English Master, Merchant Taylors' Sch., 1938–46; Headmaster, Mercers' Sch., 1946–59. War Service, 1940–45: served as Battery Comdr RA with Fourteenth Army in Burma Campaign (despatches twice); Administrative Commandant, Hmawbi Area, S Burma District, 1945. Recreations: games, gardening, listening to music. Address: 11 Pensham Hill, Pershore, Worcs WR10 3HA.

HADEN-GUEST, family name of Baron Haden-Guest.

HADEN-GUEST, 3rd Baron cr 1950, of Saling, Essex; Richard Haden Haden-Guest; b 1904; s of 1st Baron Haden-Guest, MC, and Edith (d 1944), d of Max Low; S brother, 1974; m 1st, 1926, Hilda (marr. diss. 1934), d of late Thomas Russell-Cruise; one d; 2nd, 1934, Olive Maria, d of late Anders Gotfrid Nilsson; one s decd; 3rd, 1949, Marjorie, d of late Dr Douglas F. Kennard. Educ: Bembridge. Heir: half-b Hon. Peter Haden Haden-Guest [b 1913; m 1945, Jean, d of late Dr Albert George Hindes; two s one d]. Address: 3 Chemin des Cret de Champel, 1206 Geneva, Switzerland. T: Geneva 476940.

HADFIELD, (Ellis) Charles (Raymond), CMG 1954; b 5 Aug. 1909; s of Alexander Charles Hadfield, South Africa Civil Service; m 1945, Alice Mary Miller, d of Lt-Col Henry Smyth, DSO; one s one d (and one s decd). Educ: Blundell's Sch.; St Edmund Hall, Oxford. Joined Oxford University Press, 1936; Dir of Publications, Central Office of Information, 1946–48; Controller (Overseas), 1948–62. Dir, David and Charles (Publishers) Ltd, 1960–64. Mem., British Waterways Bd, 1962–66. Publications: The Young Collector's Handbook (with C. Hamilton Ellis), 1940; Civilian Fire Fighter, 1941; (with Alexander d'Agapayeff) Maps, 1942; (with Frank Eyre) The Fire Service Today, 1944; (with Frank Eyre) English Rivers and Canals, 1945; (with J. E. MacColl) Pilot Guide to Political London, 1945; (with J. E. MacColl) British Local Government, 1948; (as Charles Alexander) The Church's Year, 1950; British Canals, 1950, 7th edn 1984; The Canals of Southern England, 1955; Introducing Canals, 1955; The Canals of South Wales and the Border, 1960; (with John Norris) Waterways to Stratford, 1962; Canals of the World, 1964; Canals and Waterways, 1966; (with Alice Mary Hadfield) The Cotswolds, 1966; The Canals of the East Midlands, 1966; The Canals of the West Midlands, 1966; The Canals of South West England, 1967; Atmospheric Railways, 1967; (with Michael Streat) Holiday Cruising on Inland Waterways, 1968; The Canal Age, 1968; The Canals of South and South East England, 1969; (with Gordon Biddle) The Canals of North West England, 1970; The Canals of Yorkshire and North East England, 1972; Introducing Inland Waterways, 1973; (with Alice Mary Hadfield) Introducing the Cotswolds, 1976; Waterways Sights to See, 1976; Inland Waterways, 1978; (with A. W. Skempton) William Jessop, Engineer, 1979; (with Alice Mary Hadfield) Afloat in America, 1979; World Canals, 1986; Canals: a new look; studies in honour of Charles Hadfield, 1984 (Festschrift ed M. Baldwin and A. Burton). Recreations: writing; exploring canals. Address: 13 Meadow Way, South Cerney, Cirencester, Glos GL7 6HY. T: Cirencester 860422. Club: United Oxford & Cambridge University.

HADFIELD, Esmé Havelock, FRCS; Consultant Ear, Nose and Throat Surgeon, High Wycombe, Amersham and Chalfont Hospitals; Associate Surgeon (Hon.), Ear, Nose and Throat Department, Radcliffe Infirmary, Oxford; b 1921; o d of late Geoffrey Hadfield, MD. Educ: Clifton High Sch.; St Hugh's Coll., Oxford; Radcliffe Infirmary Oxford. BA (Oxon) 1942; BM, BCh Oxon 1945; FRCS 1951; MA Oxon 1952. House Officer appts, Radcliffe Infirmary, Oxford, 1945; Registrar to ENT Dept, Radcliffe Infirmary, Oxford, 1948, Asst Ohren, Nase, Hals Klinik, Kantonspital, University of Zurich, 1949. First Asst ENT Dept, Radcliffe Infirmary, Oxford, 1950. Mem. Court of Examrs, RCS, 1978–84. Pres., Sect. of Laryngology, RSocMed, 1983–84. British Empire Cancer Campaign Travelling Fellow in Canada, 1953; Hunterian Prof., RCS, 1969–70. Hon. Mem., Assoc. of Surgeons of Pakistan, 1982. Publications: articles on ENT surgery in medical journals. Recreation: travel. Address: Linaver, Lane End, High Wycombe, Bucks. T: High Wycombe 881473.

See also G. J. Hadfield, J. I. H. Hadfield.

HADFIELD, Geoffrey John, CBE 1980; TD 1963; MS, FRCS; Surgeon, Stoke Mandeville Hospital, since 1960; b 19 April 1923; s of late Prof. Geoffrey Hadfield, MD, and Eileen Irvine; m 1960, Beryl, d of late Hubert Sleigh, Manchester; three d. Educ: Merchant Taylors' Sch.; St Bartholomew's Hosp., London Univ. MB BS 1947, MS 1954, London; MRCS LRCP 1946, FRCS 1948. Ho. Officer Appts, Demonstr. of Anatomy, Registrar and Sen. Lectr in Surgery, St Bart's Hosp.; Fellow in Surgery, Memorial Hosp., New York; served RAMC, Far East, 1948–50; TAVR, 1950–73; Bt-Col, RAMC RARO,

Hon. Col 219 Gen. Hosp., TAVR. Royal College of Surgeons of England: Arris and Gale Lectr, 1954; Hunterian Prof., 1959; Erasmus Wilson Demonstr., 1969; Arnott Demonstr., 1972; Stamford Cade Meml Lectr, 1978; Mem., Council, 1971–83, Vice-Pres., 1982–83; Mem., Court of Examiners, Final FRCS, 1972–78 (Chm., 1977–78); Mem., Ct of Examiners, Primary FRCS, 1982–. Examiner in Surgery for Univs of Liverpool, Bristol and Leeds, and Vis. Examiner to univs in Middle and Far East. Fellow, Assoc. of Surgs of Gt Britain and Ireland, 1955–; Associate Fellow and Council Mem., Brit. Assoc. of Urol Surgs, 1960–; Mem., Brit. Assoc. of Surg. Oncology, 1973–; Mem. Council, Brit. Assoc. of Clin. Anatamists, 1976–. *Publications:* Current Surgical Practice (with M. Hobsley), vol. 1, 1976, vol. 2, 1978, vol. 3, 1981, vol. 4, 1986; (with M. Hobsley and B. C. Morsan) Pathology in Surgical Practice, 1985; articles in jls and chapters in books on diseases of the breast, cancer, urology, trauma, varicose veins and med. educn. *Recreations:* dinghy sailing, travel, walking, golf. *Address:* Milverton House, 3 Spenser Road, Aylesbury, Bucks HP21 7LR. *T:* Aylesbury 5343.

See also E. H. Hadfield, J. I. H. Hadfield.

HADFIELD, James Irvine Havelock, FRCS, FRCSE; Consultant Surgeon (Urologist), Bedford General Hospital, since 1965; *b* 12 July 1930; *s* of Prof. G. Hadfield and S. V. E. Hadfield (*née* Irvine); *m* 1957, Ann Pickernell Milner; one *s* two *d. Educ:* Radley College; Brasenose College, Oxford (MA, BM, BCh 1955, MCh Pt I 1960); St Thomas's Hosp. Med. Sch. FRCS 1960, FRCSE 1960. House Surgeon, St Thomas' Hosp., 1955; Lectr in Anatomy, St Thomas's Hosp. Med. Sch., 1956–57; RSO, Leicester Royal Inf., 1960–62; Surgical Tutor, Oxford Univ., 1962–66; Arris and Gale Lectr, RCS, 1967; Examnr in Surgery, Univ. of Cambridge, 1976–82; Examnr in MRCS, LRCP, 1974–80. *Publications:* articles in surgical jls on Metabolic Response to Trauma, Urology, and Surgical Anatomy of the Veins of the Legs. *Recreations:* watching rowing, shooting, unwilling gardener, trying to catch unwilling salmon in South West Wales. *Address:* Baker's Barn, Stagsden West End, near Bedford MK43 8SZ. *T:* Oakley 4514. *Clubs:* Leander, London Rowing.

See also E. H. Hadfield, G. J. Hadfield.

HADFIELD, John Charles Heywood; author; Proprietor, The Cupid Press, since 1949; Director, Rainbird Publishing Group, 1965–82; *b* 16 June 1907; 2nd *s* of H. G. Hadfield, Birmingham; *m* 1st, 1931, Phyllis Anna McMullen (*d* 1973); one *s*; 2nd, 1975, Joy Westendarp. *Educ:* Bradfield. Editor, J. M. Dent & Sons, Ltd, 1935–42; Books Officer for British Council in the Middle East, 1942–44; Dir of the National Book League, 1944–50; Organiser, Festival of Britain Exhibition of Books, 1951; Editor, The Saturday Book, 1952–73. *Publications:* The Christmas Companion, 1939; Georgian Love Songs, 1949; Restoration Love Songs, 1950; A Book of Beauty, 1952, rev. edn 1976; A Book of Delights, 1954, rev. edn 1977; Elizabethan Love Songs, 1955; A Book of Britain, 1956; A Book of Love, 1958, revd edn 1978; Love on a Branch Line, 1959; A Book of Pleasures, 1960; A Book of Joy, 1962; A Chamber of Horrors, 1965; (ed) The Shell Guide to England, 1970, rev. edn 1981; (ed) Cowardy Custard, 1973; (ed) The Shell Book of English Villages, 1980; (ed) Everyman's Book of English Love Poems, 1980; The Best of The Saturday Book, 1981; Every Picture Tells a Story, 1985; (with Miles Hadfield): The Twelve Days of Christmas, 1961; Gardens of Delight, 1964. *Recreations:* books, pictures, gardens. *Address:* 2 Quay Street, Woodbridge, Suffolk. *T:* Woodbridge 7414. *Club:* Savile.

HADFIELD, Ven. John Collingwood; Archdeacon of Caithness, Rector of St John the Evangelist, Wick, and Priest-in-Charge of St Peter and The Holy Rood, Thurso, Caithness, since 1977; *b* 2 June 1912; *s* of Reginald Hadfield and Annie Best Hadfield (*née* Gribbin); *m* 1939, Margretta Mainwaring Lewis Matthews; three *s* three *d. Educ:* Manchester Grammar School; Jesus Coll., Cambridge (Exhibnr, BA 1st cl. Hons, Classical Tripos Pt 2 1934, MA 1938); Wells Theological College. Deacon 1935, priest 1936, Manchester; Curate of S Chad, Ladybarn, Manchester, 1935–44 (in charge from 1940); Vicar of S Mark, Bolton-le-Moors, Lancs, 1944–50; Vicar of S Ann, Belfield, Rochdale, Lancs, 1950–62; Surrogate, 1944–62; Proctor in Convocation for Dio. Manchester, 1950–62. Diocese of Argyll and The Isles: Rector of S Paul, Rothesay, Bute, 1962–64; Itinerant Priest, 1964–77; Canon of S John's Cathedral, Oban, 1965–77; Inspector of Schools, 1966–77; Synod Clerk, 1973–77. *Recreation:* music. *Address:* 4 Sir Archibald Road, Thurso, Caithness KW14 8HN. *T:* Thurso 62047.

HADINGHAM, Reginald Edward Hawke, OBE 1971; MC 1943 and Bar 1943; TD 1946; Chairman, All England Lawn Tennis Club, Wimbledon, since 1984; *b* 6 Dec. 1915; *s* of Edward Wallace Hadingham and Ethel Irene Penelope Gwynne-Evans; *m* 1940, Lois Pope, *d* of Edward and Nora Pope; two *d. Educ:* Rokeby Preparatory, Wimbledon; St Paul's. Joined Slazengers, 1933, European Sales Manager, 1936. Joined TA, 57th Anti-Tank Regt, 1938, commnd into 67th Anti-Tank Regt 1938; served War of 1939–45 with 67th Anti-Tank Regt, RA; commanded 302 Battery, 1942–45 (MC Salerno 1943 and Bar, Garigliano 1943); CO 67 Regt, 1945 until disbanded, Oct. 1945. Returned to Slazengers as Asst Export Manager, Jan. 1946; Export Manager, 1949; Gen. Sales Manager, 1951; Sales Dir, 1952; Man. Dir, 1969; Chm. and Man. Dir, 1973; Chm. (Non-Exec.), 1976–83. Dep. Chm., Action Research for the Crippled Child, 1976–; Chm., Sparks, the sportsman's charity, 1968–; Vice-Pres., PHAB, 1978–; Twice Pres., Sette of Odd Volumes, Treasurer, 1953–. *Recreations:* lawn tennis and writing verse. *Address:* The Hill Farm House, 118 Wimbledon Hill Road, Wimbledon, SW19 5QU. *T:* 01–946 9611. *Clubs:* Eccentric, Queen's, All England Lawn Tennis.

HADLEY, David Allen; Under Secretary, Ministry of Agriculture, Fisheries and Food, since 1981; *b* 18 Feb. 1936; *s* of Sydney and Gwendoline Hadley; *m* 1965, Veronica Ann Hopkins; one *s. Educ:* Wyggeston Grammar Sch., Leicester; Merton Coll., Oxford. MA. Joined MAFF, 1959; Asst Sec., 1971; HM Treas., 1975–78. *Recreations:* gardening, music. *Address:* Old Mousers, Dormansland, Lingfield, Surrey. *T:* Lingfield 832259.

HADLEY, Graham Hunter; FRSA; Secretary, Central Electricity Generating Board, since 1983; *b* 12 April 1944; *s* of Dr A. L. Hadley and Mrs L.E. Hadley; *m* 1971, Lesley Ann Smith; one *s. Educ:* Eltham Coll., London; Jesus Coll., Cambridge (BA Hons Mod. Hist.). Entered Civil Service (Min. of Aviation), 1966; Dept of Energy, 1974; seconded to: Civil Service Commn, 1976–77; British Aerospace, 1980–81; Under-Sec., Dept of Energy, 1983. *Recreations:* include cricket, running, golf, theatre, architecture, aviation. *Address:* The Coach House, 14 Genoa Avenue, SW15. *T:* 01–788 2698.

HADLEY, Sir Leonard Albert, Kt 1975; JP; Union Secretary, Wellington, NZ; *b* Wellington, 8 Sept. 1911; *s* of Albert A. Hadley, JP; *m* 1st, 1939, Jean Lyell (*d* 1965), *d* of E. S. Innes; one *s* one *d*; 2nd, 1978, Amelia Townsend. Mem., Nat. Exec., NZ Fedn of Labour, 1946–76; Dir, Reserve Bank of NZ, 1959–; Mem., Bd of Trustees since formation, 1964, Pres., 1976–79, Wellington Trustee Savings Bank. Relieving Mem., Industrial Commn and Industrial Court, since 1974 (and its predecessor, Arbitration Court, 1960); Mem., Waterfront Industry Tribunal, 1981. Member: NZ Immigration Adv. Council, 1964–; Periodic Detention Work Centre Adv. Cttee (Juvenile), 1964–, and Adult Centre, 1967– (both since formation); Absolute Liability Enquiry Cttee, 1963–, and Govt Cttees to review Exempted Goods, 1959 and 1962. Rep., NZ Fedn of Labour Delegns to ILO, Geneva, 1949 and 1966; Internat. Confedn of Free Trade Unions Inaugural Conf., 1949; Social Security Conf., Moscow, 1971; SE Asian Trade Union Conf., Tokyo, 1973; OECD Conf., Paris, 1974. Mem., Terawhiti Licensing Trust, 1975–80. Life Mem., Wellington Working Men's Club and Literary Inst., 1979. Awarded Smith-Mundt Ldr Study Grant in USA, 1953. JP 1967. *Recreations:* reading, music, outdoor bowls, Rugby, tennis, and sport generally. *Address:* (private) 3 Cheesman Street, Brooklyn, Wellington, New Zealand.

HADOW, Sir Gordon, Kt 1956; CMG 1953; OBE 1945; Deputy Governor of the Gold Coast (now Ghana), 1954–57; *b* 23 Sept. 1908; *e s* of late Rev. F. B. Hadow and Una Ethelwyn Durrant; *m* 1946, Marie (*d* 1985), *er d* of late Dr L. H. Moiser; two *s. Educ:* Marlborough; Trinity Coll., Oxford. Administrative Service, Gold Coast, 1932; Dep. Financial Sec., Tanganyika, 1946; Under-Sec. Gold Coast, 1948; Sec. for the Civil Service, 1949; Sec. to Governor and to Exec. Council, 1950–54. *Address:* Little Manor, Coat, Martock, Somerset. *Club:* Athenæum.

HADOW, Sir (Reginald) Michael, KCMG 1971 (CMG 1962); HM Diplomatic Service, retired; *b* 17 Aug. 1915; *s* of Malcolm McGregor Hadow and Constance Mary Lund; *m* 1976, Hon. Mrs Daphne Sieff. *Educ:* Berkhamsted Sch.; King's Coll., Cambridge. Selected for ICS, 1937; Private Sec. to HM Ambassador, Moscow, 1942; Under-Sec., External Affairs Dept, Delhi, 1946–47; transferred to Foreign Office, 1948; FO, 1948–52; Private Sec. to Minister of State, 1949–52; Head of Chancery, Mexico City, 1952–54; FO, 1955; Head of Levant Dept and promoted Counsellor, 1958; Counsellor, Brit. Embassy, Paris, 1959–62; Head of News Dept, FO, 1962–65; Ambassador to Israel, 1965–69; Ambassador to Argentina, 1969–72. *Recreations:* all field sports. *Address:* Old Farm, Ashford Hill, near Newbury, Berks.

HAENDEL, Ida; violinist; *b* Poland, 15 Dec. 1928; Polish parentage. Began to play at age of 3½; amazing gift discovered when she picked up her sister's violin and started to play. Her father, a great connoisseur of music, recognised her unusual talent and abandoned his own career as an artist (painter) to devote himself to his daughter; studied at Warsaw Conservatorium and gained gold medal at age of seven; also studied with such masters as Carl Flesch and Georges Enesco. British début, Queen's Hall, with Sir Henry Wood, playing Brahms' Concerto. Gave concerts for British and US troops and in factories, War of 1939–45; after War, career developed to take in North and South America, USSR and Far East, as well as Europe; has accompanied British orchestras such as London Philharmonic, BBC Symphony, Bournemouth Symphony and English Chamber on foreign tours including Hong Kong, China, Australia and Mexico. Has performed with conductors such as Beecham, Klemperer, Szell, Barenboim, Mata, Pritchard and Rattle. Sibelius Medal, Finland, 1982. *Publication:* Woman with Violin (autobiog.), 1970. *Address:* c/o Harold Holt, 31 Sinclair Road, W14.

HAFERKAMP, Wilhelm; a Vice-President, Commission of the European Communities, 1970–84; *b* Duisburg, 1 July 1923. *Educ:* Universität zu Köln. German Trade Union Federation: Head of Division for Social Questions, 1950–63, Dep. Chm. 1953, Chm. 1957, N Rhine—Westphalia Area; Mem. Fed. Exec., 1962–67. Socialist Mem., Landtag of North Rhine—Westphalia, 1958–67; Mem., Commn of European Communities, 1967–84, responsible for Energy policy, Euratom Supply Agency and Euratom Safeguards; Vice-Pres., 1970, resp. for internal market and legal harmonisation; 1973, resp. for economic and financial affairs; 1977, resp. for external relations. *Address:* Rodenwaldstrasse 14, 4033 Hösel bei Düsseldorf, W Germany.

HAFFNER, Albert Edward, PhD; Chairman, North Eastern Gas Board, 1971–72 (Deputy Chairman, 1966–71); *b* 17 Feb. 1907; 4th *s* of late George Christian and late Caroline Haffner, Holme, near Burnley, Lancs; *m* 1934, Elizabeth Ellen Crossley, Cheadle Heath, Stockport; one *s* one *d. Educ:* Burnley Grammar Sch.; Royal College of Science; Imperial Coll., London; Technische Hochschule, Karlsruhe. BSc (1st Cl. Hons), ARCS, PhD, DIC, London. Burnley Gas Works, 1924–26; Gas Light & Coke Co, 1932–56; Research Chemist and North Thames Gas Bd; Gp Engr, Chief Engineer and later Bd Member, Southern Gas Bd, 1956–66. Past Pres., Instn Gas Engineers (Centenary Pres., 1962–63); Past Vice-Pres., Internat. Gas Union. CEng, MIChemE. *Publications:* Contributor to: Proc. Roy. Soc., Jl Instn Gas Engrs, Instn Chem. Engrs, Inst. of Fuel, New Scientist; papers presented to Canadian Gas Assoc., French Chem. Soc., Japanese Gas Industry and at IGU Confs in USA, USSR and Germany, etc. *Recreations:* photography, travel, gardening, cabinetmaking. *Address:* Burnthwaite, Iwerne Courtney, near Blandford Forum, Dorset DT11 8QL. *T:* Child Okeford 860749.

HAGART-ALEXANDER, Sir Claud; *see* Alexander.

HAGEN, Dr John P(eter), Presidential Certificate of Merit (US), 1947; DSM (US), 1959; Professor of Astronomy and Head of Department of Astronomy, Pennsylvania State University, 1967–75, now Emeritus; Director, Office of United Nations Conference, National Aeronautics and Space Administration, 1960–62 (Director, Vanguard Division, 1958–60); *b* 31 July 1908; *s* of John T. and Ella Bertha Hagen (*née* Fisher); *m* 1935, Edith W. Soderling; two *s. Educ:* Boston, Wesleyan, Yale and Georgetown Univs. Res. Associate, Wesleyan Univ., 1931–35; Supt Atmosphere and Astrophysics Div., US Naval Res. Lab., 1935–58; Dir, Project Vanguard, 1955–58. Lecturer, Georgetown Univ., 1949–52. FRAS 1969; FIEEE; Fellow: Amer. Acad. of Arts and Sciences; Amer. Assoc. for Advancement of Science; Amer. Astronomical Soc. Chairman: Study Gp 2 (Radioastronomy and Space Res.), Comité Consultative Internat. Radio; IUCAF Cttee of ISCU. Hon. ScD: Boston, 1958; Adelphi, Loyola, Fairfield, 1959; Mt Allison, 1960. Phi Beta Kappa. *Publications:* contrib. to Astrophysical Journal and to Proc. Inst. Radio Engrg; contributor to Encyclopædia Britannica. *Address:* 613 W Park Avenue, State College, Pa 16803, USA. *T:* 237–3031. *Club:* Cosmos (Washington, DC).

HAGEN, Victor W. Von; *see* Von Hagen.

HAGESTADT, John Valentine; Director, Invest in Britain Bureau, New York, since 1984; *b* 11 Oct. 1938; *s* of late Leonard and Constance Hagestadt; *m* 1963, Betty Tebbs; three *d. Educ:* Dulwich Coll.; Worcester Coll., Oxford (BA). Asst Principal, Min. of Aviation, 1963; Principal, BoT, 1967; Nuffield Travelling Fellow, 1973–74; Asst Sec., Vehicles Div., Dept of Industry, 1976; Asst Sec., Overseas Trade Div. (Middle East and Latin America), Dept of Trade, 1980; Dir, British Trade Develt Office, NY 1982. *Address:* Invest in Britain Bureau, 845 Third Avenue, New York, NY 10022, USA. *T:* 212–593 2258.

HAGGARD, William; *see* Clayton, Richard Henry Michael.

HAGGART, Most Rev. Alastair Iain Macdonald; *b* 10 Oct. 1915; *s* of Alexander Macdonald Haggart and Jessie Mackay; *m* 1st, 1945, Margaret Agnes Trundle (*d* 1979); two *d*; 2nd, 1983, Mary Elizabeth Scholes, *qv. Educ:* Hatfield Coll. (Exhibnr); Durham Univ. (Exhibnr); Edinburgh Theol College. LTh 1941; BA 1942; MA 1945. Deacon, 1941, Priest 1942. Curate: St Mary's Cath., Glasgow, 1941–45; St Mary's, Hendon, 1945–48; Precentor, St Ninian's Cath., Perth, 1948–51; Rector, St Oswald's, King's Park, Glasgow, 1951, and Acting Priest-in-Charge, St Martin's, Glasgow, 1953–58; Synod Clerk of Glasgow Dio. and Canon of St Mary's Cath., Glasgow, 1958–59; Provost, St

Paul's Cathedral, Dundee, 1959–71; Principal and Pantonian Prof., Episcopal Theological Coll., Edinburgh, 1971–75; Canon, St Mary's Cathedral, Edinburgh, 1971–75; Bishop of Edinburgh, 1975–85; Primus of the Episcopal Church in Scotland, 1977–85. Exam. Chap. to Bp of Brechin, 1964. Hon. LLD Dundee, 1970. *Recreations:* walking, reading, listening to music, asking questions. *Address:* 19 Eglinton Crescent, Edinburgh EH12 5BY. *T:* 031–337 8948.

HAGGART, Mary Elizabeth; *see* Scholes, M. E.

HAGGERSTON GADSDEN, Sir Peter Drury; *see* Gadsden.

HAGGETT, Prof. Peter; Professor of Urban and Regional Geography, University of Bristol, since 1966, Vice-Chancellor (Acting), 1984–85; *b* 24 Jan. 1933; *s* of Charles and Elizabeth Haggett, Pawlett, Somerset; *m* 1956, Brenda Woodley; two *s* two *d. Educ:* Dr Morgan's Sch., Bridgwater; St Catharine's Coll., Cambridge (Exhib. and Scholar; MA, PhD). Asst Lectr, University Coll. London, 1955; Demonstrator and University Lectr, Cambridge, 1957; Fellow, Fitzwilliam Coll., 1964, Visiting Fellow, 1983; Leverhulme Research Fellow (Brazil), 1959; Canada Council Fellow, 1977; Erskine Fellow (NZ), 1979; Res. Fellow, Res. Sch. of Pacific Studies, ANU, 1983. Visiting Professor: Berkeley; Monash; Pennsylvania State; Toronto; Western Ontario; Wisconsin. Member, SW Economic Planning Council, 1967–72. Governor, Centre for Environmental Studies, 1975–78; Member: Council, RGS, 1972–73, 1977–80; UGC, 1985–; Nat. Radiological Protection Bd, 1986–. Hon. DSc York, Canada, 1983; Hon LLD Bristol, 1986. Cullum Medal of American Geographical Soc., 1969; Meritorious Contribution Award, Assoc. of American Geographers, 1973; Patron's Medal, RGS, 1986. *Publications:* Locational Analysis in Human Geography, 1965; (ed jtly) Frontiers in Geographical Teaching, 1965; Models in Geography, 1967; (with R. J. Chorley) Network Analysis in Geography, 1969; Progress in Geography, vols 1–9, 1969–77; Regional Forecasting, 1971; Geography: a modern synthesis, 1972, 4th edn, 1983; (with A. D. Cliff and others) Elements of Spatial Structure, 1975; Processes in Physical and Human Geography: Bristol Essays, 1975; Spatial Diffusion, 1981; Epidemics as a Spatial Process, 1987; research papers. *Recreations:* natural history, cricket. *Address:* 5 Tun Bridge Close, Chew Magna, Somerset.

HÄGGLÖF, Gunnar, GCVO (Hon.), 1954; Swedish Diplomat; *b* 15 Dec. 1904; *s* of Richard Hägglöf and Sigrid Ryding, Stockholm, Sweden; *m* Anna, *d* of Count Folchi-Vici, Rome. *Educ:* Upsala Univ., Sweden. Entered Swedish Diplomatic Service, 1926; Minister without Portfolio, 1939. During War of 1939–45, led various Swedish delegns to Berlin, London, and Washington; Envoy to Belgian and Dutch Govts, 1944; Envoy in Moscow, 1946; permanent delegate to UN, 1947; Ambassador to Court of St James's, 1948–67; Ambassador to France, 1967–71. Delegate to Conf. for Constitution, European Council, 1949; delegate to Suez Confs, 1956; Mem. of Menzies Cttee to Cairo, 1956. Hon. DCL Birmingham, 1960. *Publications:* Diplomat, 1972; several books and essays in economics, politics and history. *Recreations:* ski-ing, swimming, reading and writing. *Address:* Les Hauts de Vaugrenier, 06270 Villeneuve-Loubet, France.

HAGUE, Prof. Sir Douglas (Chalmers), Kt 1982; CBE 1978; Chairman: Economic and Social Research Council, since 1983; Oxford Strategy Network, since 1984; Metapraxis Ltd, since 1984; Associated Fellow, Templeton College, Oxford, since 1983; *b* Leeds, 20 Oct. 1926; *s* of Laurence and Marion Hague; *m* 1947, Brenda Elizabeth Fereday (marr. diss. 1986); two *d. Educ:* Moseley Grammar Sch.; King Edward VI High Sch., Birmingham; University of Birmingham. Assistant Tutor, Faculty of Commerce, Birmingham Univ., 1946; Assistant Lecturer, University College, London, 1947, Lecturer, 1950; Reader in Political Economy in University of London, 1957; Newton Chambers Professor of Economics, University of Sheffield, 1957–63. Visiting Professor of Economics, Duke Univ., USA, 1960–61; Head of Department of Business Studies, University of Sheffield, 1962–63; Professor of Applied Economics, University of Manchester, 1963–65; Prof. of Managerial Economics, Manchester Business Sch., 1965–81, Dep. Dir, 1978–81, Vis. Prof., 1981–. Director: Economic Models Ltd, 1970–78; The Laird Gp, 1976–79. Rapporteur to International Economic Association, 1953–78, Editor General, 1981–86; Member Working Party of National Advisory Council on Education for Industry and Commerce, 1962–63; Consultant to Secretariat of NEDC, 1962–63; Member: Treasury Working Party on Management Training in the Civil Service, 1965–67; EDC for Paper and Board, 1967–70; (part-time) N Western Gas Board, 1966–72; Working Party, Local Govt Training Bd, 1969–70; Price Commn, 1973–78 (Dep. Chm., 1977); Director: Manchester School of Management and Administration, 1964–65; Centre for Business Research, Manchester, 1964–66. Member Council, Manchester Business School, 1964–81; Chairman, Manchester Industrial Relations Society, 1964–66; President, NW Operational Research Group, 1967–69; British Chm., Carnegie Project on Accountability, 1968–72; Jt Chm., Conf. of Univ. Management Schools, 1971–73; Chm., DoI Working Party, Kirkby Manufacturing and Engineering Co., 1978. Economic adviser to Mrs Thatcher, Gen. Election campaign, 1979; Adviser to PM's Policy Unit, 10 Downing St, 1979–83. Industrial Consultant. *Publications:* Costs in Alternative Locations: The Clothing Industry (with P. K. Newman), 1952; (with A. W. Stonier) A Textbook of Economic Theory, 1953, 4th edn 1973; (with A. W. Stonier) The Essentials of Economics, 1955; The Economics of Man-Made Fibres, 1957; (ed) Stability and Progress in the World Economy, 1958; (ed) The Theory of Capital, 1961; (ed) Inflation, 1962; (ed with Sir Roy Harrod) International Trade Theory in a Developing World, 1965; (ed) Price Formation in Various Economies, 1967; Managerial Economics, 1969; (ed with Bruce L. R. Smith) The Dilemma of Accountability in Modern Government, 1970; Pricing in Business, 1971; (with M. E. Beesley) Britain in the Common Market: a new business opportunity, 1973; (with W. E. F. Oakeshott and A. A. Strain) Devaluation and Pricing Decisions: a case study approach, 1974; (with W. J. M. Mackenzie and A. Barker) Public Policy and Private Interests: the institutions of compromise, 1975; (with Geoffrey Wilkinson) The IRC: an experiment in industrial intervention, 1983; (with Peter Hennessy) How Adolf Hitler reformed Whitehall, 1985; articles in economic, financial and management journals. *Recreations:* church organs, watching Manchester United. *Address:* Economic and Social Research Council, 160 Great Portland Street, W1N 6BA. *Club:* Athenæum.

HAGUE, Harry; a Recorder of the Crown Court, 1972–79; *b* 9 April 1922; *o c* of Harry Hague and Lilian (*née* Hindle), Stalybridge and Blackpool; *m* 1967, Vera, *d* of Arthur Frederick and Sarah Ann Smith, Manchester; two step *d. Educ:* Arnold Sch., Blackpool; Manchester and London Univs. LLB London. Army, 1941–44. Called to Bar, Middle Temple, 1946; Northern Circuit. Asst Recorder, Burnley, 1969–71. Contested (L): Blackburn East, 1950; Blackpool North, 1959, 1962 (bye-election) and 1964; Mem. Nat. Exec., Liberal Party, 1956–59 and 1962–64. *Recreations:* activities concerning animals, motoring, historical buildings.

HAHN, Dr Carl Horst; *b* 1 July 1926. Chairman, Board of Management, Volkswagen AG, Wolfsburg; Chairman, Supervisory Board: Audi AG, Ingolstadt; Gerling-Konzern Speziale Kreditversicherungs-AG, Cologne; Deputy Chairman, Supervisory Board: Aktiengesellschaft für Industrie und Verkehrswesen, Frankfurt (Main); Gerling-Konzern Zentrale Vertriebs-AG, Cologne; Member, Supervisory Board: Gerling-Konzern Allgemeine Versicherungs-AG, Cologne; Wilhelm Karmann GmbH, Osnabrück; Deutsche Messe- und Ausstellungs-AG, Hanover; Deutsche BP AG; Erste Allgemeine Versicherung, Vienna. Member: Foreign Trade Adv. Cttee, Fed. Economics Min.; Internat. Adv. Cttee, Salk Inst., La Jolla, Calif; Bd of Management Founders' Assoc. of German Science; Consultants' Group, Deutsche Bank AG; Exec. Cttee, VDA; Exec. Cttee, BDI; Bd of Dirs, Deutsche Automobilgesellschaft mbH, Hanover. *Address:* Volkswagen AG, Postfach, 3180 Wolfsburg 1, West Germany.

HAHN, Prof. Frank Horace, FBA 1975; Professor of Economics, University of Cambridge, since 1972; Fellow of Churchill College, Cambridge, since 1960; *b* 26 April 1925; *s* of Dr Arnold Hahn and Maria Hahn; *m* 1946, Dorothy Salter; no *c. Educ:* Bournemouth Grammar School; London School of Economics. PhD London, MA Cantab. Univ. of Birmingham, 1948–60, Reader in Mathematical Economics, 1958–60; Univ. Lectr in Econs, Cambridge, 1960–67; Prof. of Economics, LSE, 1967–72; Frank W. Taussig Res. Prof., Harvard, 1975–76. Visiting Professor: MIT, 1956–57; Univ. of California, Berkeley, 1959–60. Fellow, Inst. of Advanced Studies in Behavioural Sciences, Stanford, 1966–67. Mem. Council for Scientific Policy, later Adv. Bd of Res. Councils, 1972–75. Fellow, Econometric Soc., 1962; Vice-Pres., 1967–68; Pres., 1968–69; Pres., Royal Economic Soc., 1986–. Managing Editor, Review of Economic Studies, 1965–68. Foreign Hon. Mem., Amer. Acad. of Arts and Sciences, 1974; Hon. Mem., Amer. Economic Assoc., 1986. Hon. DSocSci Birmingham, 1981; Hon DLitt East Anglia, 1984; Dr Econ *hc* Strasbourg, 1984; Hon. DSc(Econ) London, 1985. *Publications:* (with K. J. Arrow) General Competitive Analysis, 1971; The Share of Wages in the National Income, 1972; Money and Inflation, 1982; Equilibrium and Macro-Economics, 1985; Money, Growth and Stability, 1986; articles in learned journals. *Address:* 16 Adams Road, Cambridge. *T:* Cambridge 352560; 30 Tavistock Court, Tavistock Square, WC1. *T:* 01–387 4293.

HAIDER, Michael Lawrence; Chairman of the Board, Chief Executive Officer, and Chairman of Executive Committee, Standard Oil Co. (NJ), 1965–69, retired; *b* 1 Oct. 1904; *s* of Michael Haider and Elizabeth (*née* Milner). *Educ:* Stanford Univ. BS 1927. Chemical Engineer, Richfield Oil Co., 1927–29; Carter Oil Co., Tulsa, Okla., 1929–38 (Chief Engineer, 1935–38); Manager, Research and Engineering Dept, Standard Oil Development Co., 1938–45; Standard Oil Co. (NJ): Executive, Producing Dept, 1945–46; Deputy Co-ordinator of Producing Activities, 1952–54; Vice-President, 1960–61; Executive Vice-President, 1961–63; President and Vice-Chairman, Executive Cttee, 1963–65. Was with: Imperial Oil Ltd, Toronto, 1946–52 (Vice-President and Director, 1948–52); International Petroleum Co. Ltd (President and Director), 1954–59. President, American Institute of Mining and Metallurgical Engineers, 1952. *Publications:* (ed) Petroleum Reservoir Efficiency and Well Spacing, 1943; articles in technical journals. *Address:* (office) Room 1250, 1 Rockefeller Plaza, New York, NY 10020, USA; (home) 35 Adam Way, Atherton, Calif 94025, USA.

HAIG, family name of **Earl Haig.**

HAIG, 2nd Earl, *cr* 1919; **George Alexander Eugene Douglas Haig,** OBE 1966; DL; Viscount Dawick, *cr* 1919; Baron Haig and 30th Laird of Bemersyde; is a painter; Member, Queen's Body Guard for Scotland; *b* March 1918; *o s* of 1st Earl and Hon. Dorothy Vivian (*d* 1939) (Author of A Scottish Tour, 1935), *d* of 3rd Lord Vivian; *S* father, 1928; *m* 1st, 1956, Adrienne Thérèse, *d* of Derrick Morley; one *s* two *d*; 2nd, 1981, Donna Geroloma Lopez y Royo di Taurisano. *Educ:* Stowe; Christ Church, Oxford. MA Oxon. 2nd Lieut Royal Scots Greys, 1938; retired on account of disability, 1951, rank of Captain; Hon. Major on disbandment of HG 1958; studied painting Camberwell School of Art; paintings in collections of Arts Council and Scottish Nat. Gallery of Modern Art. War of 1939–45 (prisoner). Member: Royal Fine Art Commission for Scotland, 1958–61; Council and Executive Cttee, Earl Haig Fund, Scotland, 1950–65 and 1966– (Pres., 1980–86); Scottish Arts Council, 1969–75; President, Scottish Craft Centre, 1950–75. Member Council, Commonwealth Ex-Services League; Chairman, Officers' Association (Scottish Branch), 1977; Vice-President: Scottish National Institution for War Blinded; Royal Blind Asylum and School; President Border Area British Legion, 1955–61; Chairman SE Scotland Disablement Advisory Cttee, 1960–73; Vice-Chairman, British Legion, Scotland, 1960, Chairman, 1962–65, Pres., 1980–86; Chm., Bd of Trustees, Scottish National War Memorial, 1983– (Trustee, 1961–); Trustee, National Gallery of Scotland, 1962–72; Chairman: Berwickshire Civic Soc., 1971–73; Friends of DeMarco Gall., 1968–71. Berwickshire: DL 1953; Vice-Lieutenant, 1967–70; DL Ettrick and Lauderdale (and Roxburghshire), 1977–. KStJ 1977. FRSA 1951. *Heir: s* Viscount Dawick, *qv. Address:* Bemersyde, Melrose, Scotland. *T:* St Boswells 22762. *Clubs:* Cavalry and Guards; New (Edinburgh).

See also Baron Astor of Hever, Baron Dacre of Glanton.

HAIG, General Alexander Meigs, Jr; President, Worldwide Associates, Inc., since 1984; Chairman, Atlantic and Pacific Advisory Councils, United Technologies, since 1982; *b* 2 Dec. 1924; *m* 1950, Patricia Fox; two *s* one *d. Educ:* schs in Pennsylvania; Univ. of Notre Dame; US Mil. Acad., West Point (BS); Univs of Columbia and Georgetown (MA); Ground Gen. Sch., Fort Riley; Armor Sch., Fort Knox; Naval and Army War Colls. 2nd Lieut 1947; Far East and Korea, 1948–51; Europe, 1956–59; Vietnam, 1966–67; CO 3rd Regt, subseq. Dep. Comdt, West Point, 1967–69; Sen. Mil. Adviser to Asst to Pres. for Nat. Security Affairs, 1969–70; Dep. Asst to Pres. for Nat. Security Affairs, 1970–73; Vice-Chief of Staff, US Army, Jan.-July 1973, retd; Chief of White House Staff, 1973–74 when recalled to active duty; Supreme Allied Commander Europe, 1974–79, and Commander-in-Chief, US European Command, 1974–79. President and Chief Operating Officer, United Technologies, 1979–81. Secretary of State, USA, 1981–82. Sen. Fellow, Hudson Inst. for Policy Research, 1982–84. Director: Carteret Savings Bank; Allegheny Internat. Inc.; Commodore Internat. Ltd; Leisure Technol. Inc.; Murray Industries/Chris Craft. Member: Presidential Cttee on Strategic Forces, 1983–; Presidential Commn on Chemical Warfare Review, 1985. Hon. LLD: Niagara; Utah; hon. degrees: Syracuse, Fairfield, Hillsdale Coll., 1981. Awarded numerous US medals, badges and decorations; also Vietnamese orders and Cross of Gallantry; Medal of King Abd el-Aziz (Saudi Arabia). *Publication:* Caveat: realism, Reagan and foreign policy, 1984. *Recreations:* tennis, golf, squash, equitation. *Address:* 1155 15th Street, NW (Suite 800), Washington, DC 20005, USA.

HAIG, Ian Maurice; Director, Scan Pacific Investments Ltd, since 1985; *b* 13 Dec. 1936; *s* of P. K. Haig; *m* 1959, Beverley, *d* of J. A. Dunning, OBE; two *s* one *d. Educ:* Pulteney Grammar School, Adelaide; University of Adelaide. Private Sec. to Pres. of Senate, Canberra, 1958–59; Asst Sec., Commonwealth Parly Conf., London, 1960; Public Relations Officer, Shell Co. of Australia, 1962; British Foreign Office School of Middle East Studies, 1963; Asst Trade Comr and Trade Comr, Los Angeles, 1966–68; Trade Comr, Beirut, 1969–73; Ambassador at large, Middle East, 1973; Ambassador to Saudi Arabia, Kuwait and United Arab Emirates, 1974–76; Australian Comr, Hong Kong, 1976–79; Dir of Administration, A.C.I. Ltd, 1979–81; Man. Dir, A.C.I. Fibreglass (Aust.), 1982; Agent Gen. for Victoria in London, 1983–85. *Publications:* Arab Oil Politics, 1978; Oil and Alternative Sources of Energy, 1978; Australia and the Middle East, 1983.

Recreations: cricket, golf. *Address:* 3 Chasteleton Avenue, Toorak, Vic 3142, Australia. *Clubs:* MCC; Australian (Melbourne); Royal Canberra Golf.

HAIG, Mrs Mary Alison G.; *see* Glen Haig.

HAIGH, (Austin) Anthony (Francis), CMG 1954; retired as Director of Education and of Cultural and Scientific Affairs, Council of Europe, 1962–68; *b* 29 Aug. 1907; *s* of late P. B. Haigh, ICS, and Eliza (*d* 1963), *d* of George Moxon; *m* 1st, 1935, Gertrude (marr. diss. 1971), 2nd *d* of late Frank Dodd; two *s* two *d*; 2nd, 1971, Eleanore Margaret, *d* of late T. H. Bullimore and *widow* of J. S. Herbert. *Educ:* Eton; King's Coll., Cambridge. Entered Diplomatic Service, 1932; served in Foreign Office and at HM Embassies at Rio de Janeiro, Tokyo, Lisbon, Ankara, Cairo and Brussels; Head of Cultural Relations Department, Foreign Office, 1952–62. Chairman Cttee of Cultural Experts, Council of Europe, 1960–61; Chairman, Admin. Board, Cultural Fund of Council of Europe, 1961–62. *Publications:* A Ministry of Education for Europe, 1970; Congress of Vienna to Common Market, 1973; Cultural Diplomacy in Europe, 1974. *Address:* The Furnace, Crowhurst, near Battle, East Sussex. *Club:* Leander.

HAIGH, Brian Roger; Contracts Consultant and Director of Professional Education and Training, Lion International Division, Kaiser Associates Inc., since 1986; *b* 19 Feb. 1931; *s* of Herbert Haigh and Ruth Haigh (*née* Lockwood); *m* 1953, Sheila Carter; one *s* one *d*. *Educ:* Hillhouse Central School, Huddersfield. Min. of Supply, 1949; National Service, RAF, 1949–51. Min. of Supply/Min. of Aviation, 1951–62; NATO Bullpup Production Orgn, 1962–67 (Head of Contracts, Finance and Admin, 1965–67); Min. of Technology, Aviation Supply, Defence (Defence Sales Orgn), 1968–73 (Asst Dir, Sales, 1971–73); Nat. Defence Coll., 1973–74; Ministry of Defence: Asst Dir, Contracts, 1974; Dir of Contracts (Weapons), Dec. 1974; Principal Dir of Navy Contracts, 1978; Under Secretary, 1980; Dir-Gen., Defence Contracts, 1980–86. *Recreations:* family, music, opera, bridge. *Address:* 150 Southampton Row, WC1B 5AL. *T:* 01–833 2705.

HAIGH, Clement Percy, PhD; CPhys, FInstP; scientific and engineering consultant; *b* 11 Jan. 1920; *m* 1945, Ruby Patricia Hobdey; three *s*. *Educ:* Univ. of Leeds (BSc); King's Coll., London (PhD). Radiochemical Centre, Thorium Ltd, 1943–49; Medical Physicist, Barrow Hosp., Bristol, 1949–56; joined CEGB, 1956: Director, Berkeley Nuclear Laboratories, 1959–73; Dep. Director-General, Design and Construction Div., Gloucester, 1973–78; Dir of Research, BNOC, 1978–81. Dir, South Western Industrial Res., 1981–86. Distinguished Lectr, American Nuclear Soc., San Francisco, 1965; Assessor, Nuclear Safety Adv. Cttee, 1972–76; Member: BBC West Adv. Council, 1972–76; Mechanical Engrg and Machine Tools Requirements Bd, 1973–76; Off-Shore Energy Technology Bd, 1978–81; Board, National Maritime Inst., 1981–82; UK Chm., Joint UK/USSR Working Gp on Problems of Electricity Supply, 1974–78; Chm., Programme Steering Cttee, UK Offshore Steels Res. Project, 1981–. FRSA. *Publications:* various papers on applied nuclear physics and on nuclear energy. *Recreations:* music; study of magnificent failures in technology. *Address:* Painswick, Old Sneed Park, Bristol, Avon BS9 1RG. *T:* Bristol 68 2065. *Clubs:* Savile, Royal Automobile.

HAIGH, Clifford; Editor, The Friend, 1966–73; *b* 5 Feb. 1906; *yr s* of Leonard and Isabel Haigh, Bradford, Yorks; *m* 1st, 1934, Dora Winifred Fowler (*d* 1959); one *s* one *d*; 2nd, 1970, Grace Elizabeth Cross. Editorial Staff: Yorkshire Observer, 1924–27; Birmingham Post, 1928–46; The Times, 1947–61; Assistant Editor, The Friend, 1961–65. *Recreation:* walking. *Address:* 4 Chichester Road, Sandgate, Kent. *T:* Folkestone 38212.

HAIGH, Maurice Francis; Barrister; a Recorder of the Crown Court, since 1981; a Chairman, Medical Appeal Tribunals, since 1984; *b* 6 Sept. 1929; *s* of William and Ceridwen Francis Haigh. *Educ:* Repton. Asst cameraman in film production; worked for Leslie Laurence Productions Ltd, London, Manchester Film Studios, and finally for Anglo-Scottish Pictures Ltd at London Film Studios, Shepperton, 1946–49; in commerce, 1950–52. Called to the Bar, Gray's Inn, 1955. *Recreations:* reading, cycling, fell and mountain walking. *Address:* 26 Cross Street, Manchester M2 7AN. *T:* 061–832 4036. *Club:* English-Speaking Union.

HAILEY, Arthur; author; *b* 5 April 1920; *s* of George Wellington Hailey and Elsie Mary Wright; *m* 1st, 1944, Joan Fishwick (marr. diss. 1950); three *s*; 2nd, 1951, Sheila Dunlop; one *s* two *d*. *Educ:* English elem. schs. Pilot, RAF, 1939–47 (Flt-Lt). Emigrated to Canada, 1947; various positions in industry and sales until becoming free-lance writer, 1956. *Publications:* (in 35 languages): Flight Into Danger (with John Castle), 1958; Close-Up (Collected Plays), 1960; The Final Diagnosis, 1959; In High Places, 1962; Hotel, 1965; Airport, 1968; Wheels, 1971; The Moneychangers, 1975; Overload, 1979; Strong Medicine, 1985. *Films:* Zero Hour, 1956; Time Lock, 1957; The Young Doctors, 1961; Hotel, 1966; Airport, 1970; The Moneychangers, 1976; Wheels, 1978; Strong Medicine, 1986. *Address:* (home) Lyford Cay, PO Box N7776, Nassau, Bahamas; (office) Seaway Authors Ltd, First Canadian Place-6000, PO 130, Toronto, Ont M5X 1A4, Canada. *Clubs:* River (New York); Lyford Cay (Bahamas).

HAILSHAM, 2nd Viscount, *cr* 1929, of Hailsham; Baron, *cr* 1928 [disclaimed his peerages for life, 20 Nov. 1963]; *see under* Baron Hailsham of St Marylebone.

HAILSHAM OF SAINT MARYLEBONE, Baron *cr* 1970 (Life Peer), of Herstmonceux; **Quintin McGarel Hogg,** PC 1956; CH 1974; FRS 1973; Lord High Chancellor of Great Britain, 1970–74 and since 1979; Editor, Halsbury's Laws of England, 4th edition, since 1972; Chancellor, University of Buckingham, since 1983; *b* 9 Oct. 1907; *er s* of 1st Viscount Hailsham, PC, KC, and Elizabeth (*d* 1925), *d* of Judge Trimble Brown, Nashville, Tennessee, USA, and *widow* of Hon. A. J. Marjoribanks; *S* father, 1950, as 2nd Viscount Hailsham, but disclaimed his peerages for life, 20 Nov. 1963 (Baron *cr* 1928, Viscount *cr* 1929); *m* 1st, 1944, Mary Evelyn (*d* 1978), *d* of late Richard Martin of Ross; two *s* three *d*; 2nd, 1986, Deirdre Shannon. *Educ:* Eton (Schol., Newcastle Schol.); Christ Church, Oxford (Scholar). First Class Hon. Mods, 1928; First Class Lit. Hum., 1930; Pres., Oxford Union Soc., 1929. Served War of 1939–45: commissioned Rifle Bde Sept. 1939; served Middle East Forces, Western Desert, 1941 (wounded); Egypt, Palestine, Syria, 1942; Temp. Major, 1942. Fellow of All Souls Coll., Oxford, 1931–38, 1961–; Barrister, Lincoln's Inn, 1932; a Bencher of Lincoln's Inn, 1956, Treasurer, 1975; QC 1953. MP (C) Oxford City, 1938–50, St Marylebone, (Dec.) 1963–70; Jt Parly Under-Sec. of State for Air, 1945; First Lord of the Admiralty, 1956–57; Minister of Education, 1957; Dep. Leader of the House of Lords, 1957–60; Leader of the House of Lords, 1960–63; Lord Privy Seal, 1959–60; Lord Pres. of the Council, 1957–59 and 1960–64; Minister for Science and Technology, 1959–64; Minister with special responsibility for: Sport, 1962–64; dealing with unemployment in the North-East, 1963–64; higher education, Dec. 1963–Feb. 1964; Sec. of State for Education and Science, April-Oct. 1964. Chm. of the Conservative Party Organization, Sept. 1957–Oct. 1959. Rector of Glasgow Univ., 1959–62. Pres. Classical Assoc., 1960–61. John Findley Green Foundation Lecture, 1960; Richard Dimbleby Lecture, 1976; Hamlyn Lectures, 1983. Hon. Student of Christ Church, Oxford, 1962; Hon. Bencher, Inn of Court of NI, 1981; Hon. FICE 1963; Hon. FIEE 1972; Hon. FIStructE 1960. Hon. Freeman, Merchant Taylors' Co., 1971. Hon. DCL: Westminster Coll., Fulton, Missouri, USA, 1960; Newcastle, 1964; Oxon, 1974; Hon. LLD: Cambridge, 1963; Delhi, 1972; St Andrews, 1979; Leeds, 1982. *Publications:* The Law of Arbitration, 1935; One Year's Work, 1944; The Law and Employers' Liability, 1944; The Times We Live In, 1944; Making Peace, 1945; The Left was never Right, 1945; The Purpose of Parliament, 1946; Case for Conservatism, 1947; The Law of Monopolies, Restrictive Practices and Resale Price Maintenance, 1956; The Conservative Case, 1959; Interdependence, 1961; Science and Politics, 1963; The Devil's Own Song, 1968; The Door Wherein I Went, 1975; Elective Dictatorship, 1976; The Dilemma of Democracy, 1978; Hamlyn Revisited: the British legal system (Hamlyn Lectures), 1983. *Heir:* (*to disclaimed viscountcy*): *s* Hon. Douglas Martin Hogg, *qv*. *Recreations:* walking, climbing, shooting, etc. *Address:* House of Lords, SW1. *Clubs:* Carlton, Alpine, MCC.

HAILSTONE, Bernard, RP; painter; *b* 6 Oct. 1910; *s* of William Edward Hailstone; *m* 1934, Joan Mercia Kenet Hastings; one *s*. *Educ:* Sir Andrew Judd's Sch., Tonbridge. Trained at Goldsmiths' Coll. and Royal Academy Schs; Practising Artist, 1934–39; NFS, London (Fireman Artist), 1939–42; Official War Artist to Ministry of Transport, 1942–44; Official War Artist to SEAC, 1944–45. Recent portraits include: HM Queen; Prince Charles and Princess Anne; Mrs Anne Armstrong, US Ambassador to UK; Pres. of USA, Jimmy Carter, 1977; HM Queen Elizabeth The Queen Mother, 1980; Prince Andrew, 1981. *Recreation:* tennis. *Address:* 43a Glebe Place, Chelsea, SW3. *T:* 01–352 1309; 49 Roland Gardens, SW7. *T:* 01–373 2970. *Club:* Chelsea Arts.

HAIMENDORF, Christoph von F.; *see* Fürer-Haimendorf.

HAINES, Sir Cyril (Henry), KBE 1962 (CBE 1953; MBE 1930); Chairman, South West London Rent Tribunal, 1962–66; *b* 2 March 1895; *s* of late Walter John Haines, OBE, formerly Deputy Chief Inspector of Customs and Excise; *m* 1934, Mary Theodora, *d* of late Rev. J. W. P. Silvester, BD, Hon. CF, Vicar of Wembley; two *d*. *Educ:* Hele's Sch., Exeter. Apptd to Scottish Education Dept, 1914. On active service with Army, 1915–19. Appt to Foreign Office, Dec. 1919. Called to Bar, Middle Temple, 1926. Asst Brit. Agent to Anglo-Mexican Revolutionary Claims Commn, 1928; Registrar, HM Supreme Court, for China, 1930 (acted as Asst Judge during absences from China of one of Judges); Asst Judge, HM Consular Court in Egypt, and, for Naval Courts, HM Consul at Alexandria, Egypt, 1943; Judge of HM Consular Court in Egypt, 1946. Indep. Referee for War Pension Appeals in Egypt, 1946; Asst Judge of HM Chief Court for the Persian Gulf, 1949–59, and Head of Claims Dept, Foreign Office, 1949–54; Judge of HM Chief Court for the Persian Gulf, 1959–61. Vice Pres., Abbeyfield Orpington Soc., 1985– (Chm., 1962–75; Pres., 1975–85). *Address:* Wood Lea, 6 The Glen, Farnborough Park, Orpington, Kent. *T:* Farnborough, Kent, 54507.

HAINES, Joseph Thomas William; Assistant Editor, The Daily Mirror, since 1984; Group Political Editor, Mirror Group Newspapers, since 1984; *b* 29 Jan. 1928; *s* of Joseph and Elizabeth Haines; *m* 1955, Irene Betty Lambert; no *c*. *Educ:* Elementary Schools, Rotherhithe, SE16. Parly Correspondent, The Bulletin (Glasgow) 1954–58, Political Correspondent, 1958–60; Political Correspondent: Scottish Daily Mail, 1960–64; The Sun, 1964–68; Dep. Press Sec. to Prime Minister, Jan.-June 1969; Chief Press Sec. to Prime Minister, 1969–70 and 1974–76, and to Leader of the Opposition, 1970–74; Feature Writer, 1977–78, Chief Leader Writer, 1978–, The Daily Mirror. Director: Mirror Gp Newspapers Ltd, 1986–; Scottish Daily Record & Sunday Mail Ltd, 1986–. Mem. Tonbridge UDC, 1963–69, 1971–74. Mem., Royal Commn on Legal Services, 1976–79. *Publication:* The Politics of Power, 1977. *Recreations:* heresy and watching football. *Address:* 7 Hazel Shaw, Tonbridge, Kent. *T:* Tonbridge 365919.

HAINING, Thomas Nivison, CMG 1983; HM Diplomatic Service, retired; independent consultant and writer on international affairs and personnel selection; *b* 15 March 1927; *m* 1955, Dorothy Patricia Robson; one *s*. Foreign Office, 1952; served Vienna, Moscow, Rome and New York; Counsellor, FCO, 1972–79; Ambassador and Consul-Gen. to Mongolia, 1979–82. FRGS 1980. *Address:* 14 Stompond Lane, Walton-on-Thames, Surrey KT12 1HB. *Club:* Royal Automobile.

HAINSWORTH, Gordon, MA; Chief Education Officer, Manchester, since 1983; *b* 4 Nov. 1934; *s* of Harry and Constance Hainsworth; *m* 1962, Diane (*née* Thubron); one *s* one *d*. *Educ:* Leeds Modern Sch.; Trinity Coll., Cambridge (MA). Teaching, Leeds, Birmingham and West Riding, 1958–65; Admin. Assistant, Leeds, 1965–69; Asst Education Officer, Manchester, 1969–74; Under-Secretary (Education), Assoc. of Metropolitan Authorities, 1974–76; Dep. Educn Officer, Manchester, 1976–80; Director of Education, Gateshead, 1980–83. *Recreations:* family, books, golf, bridge, walking. *Address:* 161 Burnage Lane, Manchester M19 1EE. *T:* 061–224 9571.

HAINSWORTH, Col John Raymond, CMG 1953; CBE 1945; retired; *b* 14 March 1900; *s* of William Henry Hainsworth, Keighley, Yorks; *m* 1925, Dora Marguerite Skiller, Rochester, Kent; one *s* one *d*. *Educ:* Taunton Sch.; RMA, Woolwich. Commissioned in Royal Engineers, 1919; posted to India, 1922. Served War of 1939–45 (despatches twice, CBE): Burma Campaign, 1942–45; apptd Dir of Works, GHQ, India, March 1945; seconded to Civil Employment in PWD, NWFP, India, 1946; Chief Engineer and Secretary to Government, PWD, NWFP, Pakistan, 1948–52; retired with rank of Col, 1952. *Recreations:* shooting, fishing. *Address:* 12A Horace Brightman Close, Leamington Road, Luton, Beds LU3 3UR. *T:* Luton 584359.

HAINWORTH, Henry Charles, CMG 1961; HM Diplomatic Service, retired; *b* 12 Sept. 1914; *o s* of late Charles S. and Emily G. I. Hainworth; *m* 1944, Mary, *yr d* of late Felix B. and Lilian Ady; two *d*. *Educ:* Blundell's Sch.; Sidney Sussex Coll., Cambridge. Entered HM Consular Service, 1939; HM Embassy, Tokyo, 1940–42; seconded to Ministry of Information (Far Eastern Bureau, New Delhi), 1942–46; HM Embassy, Tokyo, 1946–51; Foreign Office, 1951–53; HM Legation, Bucharest, 1953–55; NATO Defence Coll., Paris, 1956; Political Office, Middle East Forces (Nicosia), 1956; Foreign Office, 1957–61 (Head of Atomic Energy and Disarmament Dept, 1958–61); Counsellor, United Kingdom Delegation to the Brussels Conference, 1961–63; HM Minister and Consul-Gen. at British Embassy, Vienna, 1963–68; Ambassador to Indonesia, 1968–70; Ambassador and Perm. UK Rep. to Disarm. Conf., Geneva, 1971–74. *Publication:* A Collector's Dictionary, 1980. *Recreations:* reading, fishing. *Address:* c/o Barclays Bank, 50 Jewry Street, Winchester, Hants SO23 8RG.

HAITINK, Bernard, Hon. KBE 1977; Artistic Director and Permanent Conductor, Concertgebouw Orchestra, Amsterdam, since 1964; Musical Director, Glyndebourne Opera, since 1978; Music Director, Royal Opera House, Covent Garden, from Sept. 1987; *b* Amsterdam, 4 March 1929. *Educ:* Amsterdam Conservatory. Studied conducting under Felix Hupke, but started his career as a violinist with the Netherlands Radio Philharmonic; in 1954 and 1955 attended annual conductors' course (org. by Netherlands Radio Union) under Ferdinand Leitner; became 2nd Conductor with Radio Union at Hilversum with co-responsibility for 4 radio orchs and conducted the Radio Philharmonic in public during the Holland Fest., in The Hague, 1956; conducted the Concertgebouw Orch. (as a subst. for Giulini), Oct. 1956; then followed guest engagements with this and other orchs in the Netherlands and elsewhere. Debut in USA, with Los Angeles Symph. Orch., 1958; 5 week season with Concertgebouw Orch., 1958–59, and toured Britain with it, 1959;

apptd (with Eugen Jochum) as the Orchestra's permanent conductor, Sept. 1961; became sole artistic dir and permanent conductor of the orch., 1964; toured Japan and USSR, 1974; Japan, 1977; début at Royal Opera House, Covent Garden, 1977. London Philharmonic Orchestra: Principal Conductor, Artistic Dir, 1967–79; toured: Japan, 1969; USA, 1970, 1971, 1976; Berlin, 1972; Holland, Germany, Austria, 1973; USSR, 1975. Hon. RAM 1973; Hon. FRCM 1984. Bruckner Medal of Honour, 1970; Gold Medal, Internat. Gustav Mahler Soc., 1971. Chevalier de L'Ordre des Arts et des Lettres, 1972; Order of Orange Nassau, 1969; Officer, Order of the Crown (Belgium), 1977. *Address:* c/o Harold Holt Ltd, 31 Sinclair Road, W14.

HAJNAL, John, FBA 1966; Professor of Statistics, London School of Economics, 1975–86 (Reader, 1966–75); *b* 26 Nov. 1924; *s* of late Kálmán and Eva Hajnal-Kónyi; *m* 1950, Nina Lande; one *s* three *d*. *Educ:* University Coll. Sch., London; Balliol Coll., Oxford. Employed by: Royal Commission on Population, 1944–48; UN, New York, 1948–51; Office of Population Research, Princeton Univ., 1951–53; Manchester Univ., 1953–57; London Sch. of Economics, 1957–. Vis. Fellow Commoner, Trinity Coll., Cambridge, 1974–75; Vis. Prof., Rockefeller Univ., NY, 1981. Mem. Internat. Statistical Institute. *Publications:* The Student Trap, 1972; papers on demography, statistics, mathematics, etc. *Address:* 95 Hodford Road, NW11 8EH. *T:* 01–455 7044.

HALABY, Najeeb Elias; President, Halaby International Corporation; Chairman: Dulles Access Rapid Transit Inc.; Janelle Aviation Inc.; *b* 19 Nov. 1915; *s* of late Najeeb Elias Halaby and of Laura Wilkins Halaby; *m* 1st, 1946, Doris Carlquist (marr. diss. 1976); one *s* two *d*; 2nd, 1980, Jane Allison Coates. *Educ:* Stanford Univ. (AB); Yale Univ. (LLB); Bonar Law Coll., Ashridge, (Summer) 1939. Called to the Bar: California, 1940; District of Columbia, 1948; NY, 1973. Practised law in Los Angeles, Calif, 1940–42, 1958–61; Air Corps Flight Instructor, 1940; Test pilot for Lockheed Aircraft Corp., 1942–43; Naval aviator, established Navy Test Pilot Sch., 1943; formerly Chief of Intelligence Coordination Div., State Dept; Foreign Affairs Advisor to Sec. of Defense; Chm., NATO Military Production and Supply Board, 1950; Asst Administrator, Mutual Security Economic Cooperation Administration, 1950–51; Asst Sec. of Defense for Internat. Security, 1952–54; Vice-Chm., White House Advisory Group whose report led to formation of Federal Aviation Agency, 1955–56, Administrator of the Agency, 1961–65; Pan American World Airways: Director, 1965–73; Member, Executive Committee of Board, 1965–68; Senior Vice-President, 1965–68, President, 1968–71; Chief Executive, 1969–72; Chairman, 1970–72; Associate of Laurance and Nelson Rockefeller, 1954–57; Past Exec. Vice-Pres. and Dir, Servomechanisms Inc.; Sec.-Treas., Aerospace Corp., 1959–61; Pres., American Technology Corp. Member of Board: Mem. Exec. Cttee, (Founder-Chm., 1971–73), US-Japan Econ. Council; Trustee: Aspen Inst., Aspen, Colo.; Eisenhower Exchange Fellowships, Inc.; Amer. Univ. of Beirut. Monsanto Safety Award; FAA Exceptional Service Medal. Fellow, Amer. Inst. of Aeronautics and Astronautics. Hon. LLB: Allegheny Coll., Pa, 1967; Loyola Coll., LA, 1968. *Publication:* Crosswinds (memoir), 1979. *Recreations:* golf, skiing. *Address:* (office) PO Drawer Y, McLean, Va 22101, USA; (residence) 175 Chain Bridge Road, McLean, Va 22101, USA. *Clubs:* F Street, Metropolitan, Chevy Chase (Washington); Bohemian Grove (California).

HALAS, John, OBE 1972; FSIAD; Chairman, Educational Film Centre, since 1960; President: British Federation of Film Societies, since 1980; International Animated Film Association, 1975–85, now Hon. President; *b* 16 April 1912; *s* of Victor and Bertha Halas; *m* 1940, Joy Batchelor; one *s* one *d*. *Educ:* Académie des Beaux-Arts, Paris; Mühely, Budapest. Founded: (with Joy Batchelor) Halas and Batchelor Animation Ltd, 1940; (with Lord Snow, Morris Goldsmith, Joy Batchelor and Roger Manvell) Educational Film Centre, 1960; ASIFA (International Animated Film Assoc.), 1960. Produced 2,000 animated films, 1940–80, incl. first feature-length animated film in GB, Animal Farm; latest productions incl: Autobahn, 1979; First Steps, 1981; Dilemma, 1982 (world's first fully digitized film); Players, 1983; A New Vision: the life and work of Botticelli, 1984. Past President, Internat. Council of Graphic Design Assocs; Hon. Fellow, BKSTS, 1972. *Publications:* How to Cartoon, 1959; The Technique of Film Animation, 1961; Film and TV Graphics, 1967; Computer Animation, 1974; Visual Scripting, 1977; Film Animation, a Simplified Approach, 1978; Timing for Animation, 1981; Graphics in Motion, 1981; Masters of Animation, 1986. *Recreations:* painting, music. *Address:* 6 Holford Road, Hampstead, NW3 1AD. *T:* 01–435 8674.

HALE, John Hampton; Director: Pearson plc (Managing Director, 1983–86); Pearson Inc. (USA) (Chairman, 1983–86); Chairman, Fairey Holdings, since 1983; *b* 8 July 1924; *s* of Dr John Hale and Elsie (Coles) Hale; *m* 2nd, 1980, Nancy Ryrie Birks; one *s* two *d* by former marriage. *Educ:* Eton College (King's Scholar); Magdalene Coll., Cambridge (Mech. Scis Tripos, BA, MA); Harvard Grad. Sch. of Business Admin (Henry Fellow, 1948). RAF and Fleet Air Arm Pilot, 1943–46. Alcan Aluminium Ltd, Montreal, NY and London, 1949–83; Man. Dir, Alcan Booth Industries, 1964–70; Exec. Vice-Pres., Finance, 1970–82, Dir, Alcan Aluminium, 1970–85; Dir, Aluminium Co. of Canada, 1970–85 (Chm., 1979–83). Director: Nippon Light Metal Co., Japan, Indian Aluminium Co. and Alcan Australia, 1970–83; Canadian Adv. Bd, Allendale Mutual Insurance Co., 1977–83; Scovill Inc. (USA), 1978–85; Ritz-Carlton Hotel, Montreal, 1981–83; Concordia Univ. Business Sch., 1981–83; Bank of Montreal, 1985– (Mem., Internat Adv. Council, 1986–); The Economist Newspaper, 1984–. Member: Lloyds, 1960–; Exec. Cttee, British-North American Cttee, 1980–; Council, Industry for Management Educn, 1983–. Chairman: Chambly County Protestant Central Sch. Bd, 1957–60; Business Graduates Assoc., 1967–70; Mem., Accounting Research Adv. Bd, Canadian Inst. of Chartered Accountants, 1975–81 (Chm., 1978–81). Dir, Mont St Hilaire Nature Conservation Assoc., 1977–83 (Pres., 1980–83); Governor, Stratford Festival, Ontario, 1981–83. CBIM. *Recreations:* ski-ing, sailing, fishing, shooting, old Canadian books. *Address:* 71 Eaton Terrace, SW1W 8TN. *T:* 01–730 2929. *Clubs:* Royal Thames Yacht; Mount Royal (Montreal).

HALE, Prof. Sir John (Rigby), Kt 1984; FBA 1977; Professor of Italian History, University College London, since 1985 (Professor of Italian, 1970–85); Public Orator, University of London, 1981–83; *b* 17 Sept. 1923; *s* of E. R. S. Hale, FRCP, MD, and Hilda Birks; *m* 1st, 1952, Rosalind Williams; one *s* two *d*; 2nd, 1965, Sheila Haynes MacIvor; one *s*. *Educ:* Neville Holt Preparatory Sch.; Eastbourne Coll.; Jesus Coll., Oxford. BA first cl. hons Mod. Hist., 1948; MA (Oxon) 1950; DLitt (Oxon) 1986. Served War, Radio Operator in Merchant Service, 1942–45. Commonwealth Fellow, Johns Hopkins and Harvard Univs, 1948–49; Fellow and Tutor in Modern History, Jesus Coll., Oxford, 1949–64, Hon. Fellow, 1986; Prof. of History, Univ. of Warwick, 1964–69. Editor, Oxford Magazine, 1958–59; Visiting Prof., Cornell Univ., 1959–60; Vis. Fellow, Harvard Centre for Renaissance Studies, I Tatti, 1963; Vis. Prof., Univ. of California, Berkeley, 1969–70; Folger Library Washington, Fellowship, 1970. Fellow, Davis Center, Univ. of Princeton, 1982; Mem., Princeton Inst. for Adv. Study, 1984–85. Chm. of Trustees, Nat. Gallery, 1974–80 (Trustee, 1973–80); Trustee: V&A Museum, 1984– (Chm., Theatre Museum Cttee, 1984–); BM, 1985–; Member: Royal Mint Adv. Cttee, 1979–; Museums and Galleries Commn, 1983–; Royal Commn for Exhibn of 1851, 1983–. Chm., British Soc. for Renaissance Studies, 1973–76. Chm. Advisory Cttee, Govt Art Collection, 1983–. FSA 1962; FRHistS 1968; FRSA 1974. Socio Straniero, Accademia Arcadia, 1972. Academicus ex Classe (Bronze Plaque Award), Academia Medicea, 1980; Commendatore, Ordine al Merito della Repubblica Italiana, 1981; Premio Bolla (services to Venice), 1982; Serena Medal, British Acad., 1986. *Publications:* England and the Italian Renaissance, 1954; The Italian Journal of Samuel Rogers, 1956; Machiavelli and Renaissance Italy, 1961; (trans. and ed) The Literary Works of Machiavelli, 1961; (ed) Certain Discourses Military by Sir John Smythe, 1964; The Evolution of British Historiography, 1964; (co-ed) Europe in the Late Middle Ages, 1965; Renaissance Exploration, 1968; Renaissance Europe 1480–1520, 1971; (ed) Renaissance Venice, 1973; Italian Renaissance Painting, 1977; Renaissance Fortification: art or engineering?, 1978; Florence and the Medici: the pattern of control, 1977; The Travel Journal of Antonio de Beatis, 1979; (ed) A Concise Encyclopaedia of the Italian Renaissance, 1981; Renaissance War Studies, 1983; (with M.E. Mallett) The Military Organisation of a Renaissance State: Venice *c* 1400–1617, 1984; War and Society in Renaissance Europe 1450–1620, 1985; contributor: New Cambridge Modern History, vols 1, 2, 3; The History of the King's Works vol. 4; Past and Present; Studi Veneziani, Italian Studies, etc. *Recreation:* Venice. *Address:* Department of History, University College, Gower Street, WC1E 6BT. *T:* 01–387 7050; 26 Montpelier Row, Twickenham, Mddx TW1 2NQ. *T:* 01–892 9636. *Club:* Beefsteak.

HALE, Kathleen, (Mrs Douglas McClean), OBE 1976; artist; illustrator and author of books for children; *b* 24 May 1898; *d* of Charles Edward Hale and Ethel Alice Aylmer Hughes; *m* 1926, Dr Douglas McClean (*d* 1967); two *s*. *Educ:* Manchester High Sch. for Girls; Manchester Sch. of Art; Art Dept (scholar) of University Coll., Reading; Central Sch. of Art; East Anglian Sch. of Painting and Drawing. Has exhibited paintings at: New English Art Club, Whitechapel Art Gallery, London Group, Grosvenor Galleries, Vermont Gallery, Warwick Public Library Gallery; Gallery Edward Harvane, New Grafton Gallery, Parkin Gallery; metal groups and pictures at: Lefèvre Galleries; Leicester Galleries; Oxford Arts Council, Arts Centre; Mural for South Bank (Festival) Schs Section, 1951; Orlando Ballet for Festival Gardens, 1951; contrib. ballet exhibn and exhibited Orlando Ballet costume and scenery designs, V & A Museum. *Publications:* The Orlando The Marmalade Cat Series, since 1938: Camping Holiday; Trip Abroad; Buys a Farm; Becomes a Doctor; Silver Wedding; Keeps a Dog; A Seaside Holiday; The Frisky Housewife; Evening Out; Home Life; Invisible Pyjamas; The Judge; Zoo; Magic Carpet; Country Peep-Show; Buys a Cottage; and The Three Graces; Goes to the Moon; and the Water Cats; Henrietta, the Faithful Hen, 1946; Puss-in-Boots Peep-Show, 1950; Manda, 1952; Henrietta's Magic Egg, 1973. TV and radio programmes. *Recreation:* painting. *Address:* Tod House, Forest Hill, near Oxford. *T:* Stanton St John 390.

HALE, Norman Morgan; Under Secretary, Department of Health and Social Security, since 1975; *b* 28 June 1933; *s* of late T. N. Hale and Mrs A. E. Hale, Evesham, Worcs; *m* 1965, Sybil Jean (*née* Maton); one *s* one *d*. *Educ:* Prince Henry's Grammar Sch., Evesham; St John's Coll., Oxford (MA). Min. of Pensions and National Insurance, 1955; Asst Sec., Nat. Assistance Bd, 1966; Min. of Social Security, 1966; CSD, 1970–72. *Address:* 64 Castle Avenue, Ewell, Epsom, Surrey. *T:* 01–393 3507.

HALE, Raymond, IPFA; FCCA; County Treasurer, Leicestershire County Council, since 1977; *b* 4 July 1936; *s* of Tom Raymond Hale and Mary Jane (*née* Higgin); *m* 1959, Ann Elvidge; one *s*. *Educ:* Baines Grammar Sch., Poulton-le-Fylde. Lancashire CC, 1952–54; served Royal Air Force, 1954–56; Lancashire CC, 1956–61; Nottinghamshire CC, 1961–65; Leicestershire CC, 1965–. *Recreations:* Rugby, cricket, gardening. *Address:* Windycroft, 19 Swithland Lane, Rothley, Leics LE7 7SG. *T:* Leicester 302230.

HALES, Prof. (Charles) Nicholas, PhD, MD; FRCPath; FRCP; Professor of Clinical Biochemistry, University of Cambridge, since 1977; *b* 25 April 1935; *s* of late Walter Bryan Hales and Phyllis Marjory Hales; *m* 1st, 1959, Janet May Moss; two *s*; 2nd, 1978, Margaret Griffiths; one *d*. *Educ:* King Edward VI Grammar Sch., Stafford; Univ. of Cambridge (BA 1956, MB, BChir, MA 1959, PhD 1964, MD 1971). MRCPath 1971, FRCPath 1980; MRCP 1971, FRCP 1976. House Surgeon, UCH, 1959, House Physician, 1960; Stothert Res. Fellow, Royal Soc., 1963–64; Lectr, Dept of Biochem., Univ. of Cambridge, 1964–70; Clinical Asst, Addenbrooke's Hosp., Cambridge, 1961–68, Hon. Consultant in Clin. Biochem, 1968–70; Prof. of Med. Biochem., Welsh National Sch. of Medicine, Cardiff, and Hon. Consultant in Med. Biochem., University Hosp. of Wales, Cardiff, 1970–77. Consultant in Med. Biochem., South Glam Health Authority (T). *Recreations:* music, fishing. *Address:* Department of Clinical Biochemistry, Addenbrooke's Hospital, Hills Road, Cambridge CB2 2QR. *T:* Cambridge 336787.

HALES, Prof. Frederick David, FIMechE, FIMA; Head of Department of Transport Technology, since 1982, Loughborough University of Technology, and Senior Pro-Vice-Chancellor, 1985–87; *b* 19 Dec. 1930; *s* of Christina Frances and Frederick David Hales; *m* 1955, Pamela Hilary Warner; one *s* one *d* (and one *d* decd). *Educ:* Kingswood Grammar Sch.; Bristol Univ. (BSc Hons Maths, PhD). MBCS, Sigma Xi. Asst Chief Aerodynamicist, Bristol Aircraft, 1953–60; Group Research Head, MIRA, 1960–67; Vis. Scientist, Stevens Inst., Hoboken, 1967–68; Prof. of Surface Transport, Loughborough, 1968–, Pro-Vice-Chancellor, 1984–85. Mem., Tech. Adv. Council to Ford Motor Co., 1985–; Scientific Visitor to Dept of Transport, 1986–. *Publications:* papers on dynamics and vehicle control and stability. *Recreations:* sailing, bridge, wine. *Address:* 14 Kenilworth Avenue, Loughborough, Leics LE11 0SL. *T:* Loughborough 261767. *Clubs:* Rutland Sailing, Clyde Cruising.

HALES, Prof. Nicholas; *see* Hales, Prof. C. N.

HALEY, Prof. Keith Brian, PhD; FIMA, CEng, FIProdE, FOR; Professor of Operational Research since 1968, and Head of Department of Engineering Production since 1981, Birmingham University; *b* 17 Nov. 1933; *s* of Arthur Leslie Haley and Gladys Mary Haley; *m* 1960, Diana Elizabeth Mason; one *s*. *Educ:* King Edward VI, Five Ways, Birmingham; Birmingham Univ. (BSc, PhD). FIMA 1970; FOR 1976. OR Scientist, NCB, 1957–59; Lectr, 1959–63, Sen. Lectr, 1963–68, Birmingham Univ. Pres., ORS, 1982–83; Vice Pres., IFORS, 1983–; Editor, Jl of ORS, 1972–80. Governor, Bromsgrove Sch., 1968–. *Publications:* Mathematical Programming for Business and Industry, 1966; Operational Research '75, 1976; Operational Research '78, 1979; Search Theory and Applications, 1980; Applied Operations Research in Fishing, 1981; many articles. *Recreations:* squash, bridge. *Address:* 22 Eymore Close, Selly Oak, Birmingham B29 4LB. *T:* 021–475 3331. *Club:* Royal Over-Seas League.

HALEY, Philip William Raymond Chatterton, MBE 1956; HM Diplomatic Service, retired 1976; *b* 18 June 1917; 2nd *s* of late Joseph Bertram Haley and late Lilian Anne Chatterton Haley; *m* 1941, Catherine Skene Stewart, LRAM, LRCM; two *d*. *Educ:* Perse Sch.; London University. HM Services, 1940–47 in KOSB and on Gen. Staff; 2nd Lieut 1941, Lieut 1942, Captain 1943, Major 1945, Lt-Col 1946; Control Commn for Germany, 1947–56, serving also with Internat. Commn for the Saar. HM Diplomatic Service, 1956: Consul, Düsseldorf; Hamburg, 1959; 1st Sec. and Embassy spokesman, Bonn, 1960; Dep. Consul-General, Chicago, 1964; Johannesburg, 1968; Consul-Gen., Hanover, 1973. Hon. PhD Chicago, 1967. Croix de la Libération, 1946. *Recreations:* gardening, painting, senile delinquency (*eg* bird watching), collecting gasteropod molluscs. *Address:* Casa Iris, 6 Calle el Tulipan, San Patricio, Santa Ursula, Tenerife, Canary Isles. *T:* 300814.

HALEY, Sir William (John), KCMG, 1946; Hon. LLD Cambridge 1951, Dartmouth, New Hampshire, 1957, London, 1963, St Andrews, 1965; Hon. Fellow Jesus College, Cambridge 1956; FRSL; Commissioner of Appeal for Income Tax, Jersey, 1971–83; *b* Jersey, CI, 24 May 1901; *s* of Frank Haley, Bramley, Leeds, and Marie Sangan; *m* 1921, Edith Susie Gibbons; two *s* two *d*. *Educ:* Victoria Coll., Jersey. Joined Manchester Evening News, 1922; Chief Sub-Editor, 1925; Managing Editor, 1930; Dir Manchester Guardian and Evening News, Ltd, 1930; Jt Managing Dir, 1939–43; Dir Press Association, 1939–43; Dir Reuters, 1939–43; Editor-in-Chief, BBC, 1943–44; Dir-Gen., BBC, 1944–52; Editor of the Times, 1952–66; Dir and Chief Executive, The Times Publishing Co. Ltd, 1965–66; Chm., Times Newspapers Ltd, 1967; Editor-in-Chief, Encyclopædia Britannica, 1968–69. Pres., Nat. Book League, 1955–62; Chm., Jersey Arts Council, 1976–77. Chevalier Legion of Honour, 1948; Grand Officer, Order of Orange Nassau, 1950. *Address:* Beau Site, Gorey, Jersey, Channel Islands. *T:* Jersey 51068.

HALFORD, Maj.-Gen. Michael Charles Kirkpatrick, DSO 1946; OBE 1957; DL; *b* 28 Oct. 1914; *s* of Lieut-Col M. F. Halford, OBE, and Violet Halford (*née* Kirkpatrick); *m* 1945, Pamela Joy (*née* Wright); three *s*. *Educ:* Wellington Coll.; Trinity Coll., Cambridge. Commissioned Royal Guernsey Militia, 1932; 2nd Lieut York and Lancaster Regt, 1935; served Egypt and Palestine, 1936; France 1940; N Africa, Italy, France and Germany; comd Hallamshire Bn, York and Lancaster Regt, 1945, 1st Bn, 1954; Asst Army Instr, Imperial Defence Coll., 1957; comd 147 Inf. Bde (TA), 1960; GOC 43 (Wessex) Div./District, 1964–67; retd, 1967. Representative Col The York and Lancaster Regt, 1966–79. DL Hants 1975. *Recreations:* fishing, golf. *Address:* Fairfields, Poulner Hill, Ringwood, Hants. *Club:* Army and Navy.

HALFORD-MacLEOD, Aubrey Seymour, CMG 1958; CVO 1965; HM Diplomatic Service, retired; *b* 15 Dec. 1914; *o s* of late Joseph and Clara Halford; changed name by deed poll from Halford to Halford-MacLeod, 1964; *m* 1939, Giovanna Mary, *o d* of late W. H. Durst; three *s* one *d*. *Educ:* King Edward's Sch., Birmingham; Magdalen Coll., Oxford. Entered HM Diplomatic (subseq. Foreign, now again Diplomatic) Service as Third Sec., 1937; Bagdad, 1939; Second Sec., 1942; transferred to Office of Minister Resident in N Africa, 1943; First Sec., 1943; British mem. of Secretariat of Advisory Council for Italy, 1944; British High Commission in Italy, 1944; Asst Political Adviser to Allied Commission in Italy, Sept, 1944, Political Adviser, 1945; transferred to HM Foreign Office, 1946, Principal Private Sec. to Permanent Under-Sec.; Dep. Exec. Sec. to Preparatory Commission for Council of Europe, May 1949, and promoted Counsellor; Dep. Sec. Gen. of the Council of Europe, 1949–52; Counsellor, HM Embassy, Tokyo, 1953–55; in charge of HM Legation, Seoul, 1954; Counsellor at HM Embassy in Libya, 1955–57; HM Political Agent at Kuwait, 1957–59; HM Consul-Gen., Munich, 1959–65; HM Ambassador to Iceland, 1966–70. Foreign Affairs Adviser, Scottish Council (Develt and Ind.), 1971–78. Dir, Scottish Opera, 1971–78. Pres., Scottish Soc. for Northern Studies, 1973–76. Vice-Pres., Clan MacLeod Soc. of Scotland, 1976–79. *Publication:* (with G. M. Halford) The Kabuki Handbook, 1956. *Recreations:* fishing, shooting, ornithology. *Address:* Mulag House, Ardvourlie, N Harris PA85 3AB. *T:* Harris 2054.

HALIFAX, 3rd Earl of, *cr* 1944; **Charles Edward Peter Neil Wood;** Bt 1784; Viscount Halifax, 1866; Baron Irwin, 1925; DL; *b* 14 March 1944; *s* of 2nd Earl of Halifax, and of Ruth, *d* of late Captain Rt Hon. Neil James Archibald Primrose, MC, sometime MP; *S* father, 1980; *m* 1976, Camilla, *d* of C. F. J. Younger, *qv*; one *s* one *d*. *Educ:* Eton; Christ Church, Oxford. Contested (C) Dearne Valley, Feb. and Oct. 1974. Director: Hambros Bank, 1978–; Yorkshire Post Newspapers, 1985–. DL Humberside, 1983. *Heir:* *s* Lord Irwin, *qv*. *Address:* Garrowby, York. *Clubs:* White's, Pratt's.

HALIFAX (NS), Archbishop of, (RC), since 1967; **Most Rev. James Martin Hayes;** *b* 27 May 1924; *s* of late L. J. Hayes. *Educ:* St Mary's Univ., Halifax; Holy Heart Seminary, Halifax; Angelicum Univ., Rome. Asst, St Mary's Basilica, 1947–54; Chancellor and Sec. of Archdiocese of Halifax, 1957–65; Rector, St Mary's Basilica, 1963–65; Auxil. Bp of Halifax, 1965–66; Apostolic Administrator of Archdiocese of Halifax, 1966–67. Vice-Pres., Canadian Conf. of Catholic Bishops, 1985–87. Hon. Dr of Letters, St Anne's Coll., Church Point, NS; Hon. Dr of Sacred Theology, King's Coll., Halifax, NS; Hon. Dr Humane Letters Mount St Vincent Univ., Halifax; Hon. Dr Laws St Mary's Univ., Halifax; Hon. Dr Divinity Atlantic Sch. of Theology, Halifax. *Address:* 6541 Coburg Road, PO Box 1527, Halifax, Nova Scotia B3J 2Y3, Canada. *T:* 902–429–9388.

HALIFAX, Archdeacon of; *see* Chesters, Ven. A. D.

HALL, Adam; *see* Trevor, Elleston.

HALL, Rt. Rev. Albert Peter; *see* Woolwich, Bishop Suffragan of.

HALL, Alfred Charles, CBE 1977 (OBE 1966); HM Diplomatic Service, retired; *b* 2 Aug. 1917; *s* of Alfred Hall and Florence Mary Hall; *m* 1945, Clara Georgievna Strunina, Moscow; five *s* one *d*. *Educ:* Oratory Sch.; Polytechnic of Central London (Rothschild Prize; Local Govt Dip.); Open Univ. Served War, RA and Intell. Corps, 1939–43. LCC, 1934–39 and 1946–49; FO, with service in Saudi Arabia, Algeria, Egypt, Iran and USSR, 1943–46; FCO (formerly CRO and CO), with service in Pakistan, India, Nigeria, Canada and Australia, 1949–75; Dep. High Comr in Southern India, 1975–77. Grants Officer, SCF, 1979–82. *Publications:* freelance journalism and technical papers. *Recreations:* music, reading, gardening, linguistics. *Address:* White Cliff, St Margaret's Bay, Kent CT15 6HR. *T:* Dover 852230. *Club:* Royal Commonwealth Society.

HALL, Prof. Alfred Rupert, LittD; FBA 1978; Professor of the History of Science and Technology, Imperial College of Science and Technology, University of London, 1963–80; *b* 26 July 1920; *s* of Alfred Dawson Hall and Margaret Ritchie; *m* 1st, 1942, Annie Shore Hughes; two *d*; 2nd, 1959, Marie Boas. *Educ:* Alderman Newton's Boy's Sch., Leicester; Christ's Coll., Cambridge (scholar). LittD Cantab 1975. Served in Royal Corps of Signals, 1940–45. 1st cl. Historical Tripos Part II, 1946; Allen Scholar, 1948; Fellow, Christ's Coll., 1949–59, Steward, 1955–59; Curator, Whipple Science Mus., Cambridge and University Lectr, 1950–59. Medical Research Historian, University of Calif, Los Angeles, 1959–60, Prof. of Philosophy, 1960–61; Prof. of History and Logic of Science, Indiana Univ., 1961–63. Wilkins Lectr, Royal Soc., 1973. FRHistS. Pres., British Soc. for History of Science, 1966–68; Pres., Internat. Acad. of the History of Science, 1977–81. Co-editor, A History of Technology, 1951–58. Corresp. Mem., Soc. for the History of Technology, 1970. Silver Medal, RSA, 1974; (jtly) Sarton Medal, History of Science Soc., 1981. *Publications:* Ballistics in the Seventeenth Century, 1952; The Scientific Revolution, 1954; From Galileo to Newton, 1963; The Cambridge Philosophical Society: a history, 1819–1969, 1969; Philosophers at War, 1980; Short History of the Imperial College, 1982; The Revolution in Science 1500–1750, 1983. With Marie Boas Hall: Unpublished Scientific Papers of Isaac Newton, 1962; Correspondence of Henry Oldenburg, 1965–86; (with Laura Tilling) Correspondence of Isaac Newton, vols 5–7, 1974–77; (ed with Norman Smith) History of Technology, 1976–83; (with B. A. Bembridge) Physic and Philanthropy: a history of the Wellcome Trust, 1986. Contributor to Isis, Annals of Science, etc. *Address:* 14 Ball Lane, Tackley, Oxford OX5 3AG. *T:* Tackley 257.

HALL, Sir Arnold (Alexander), Kt 1954; FRS 1953; MA; FEng; Chairman, Hawker Siddeley Group plc, 1967–86 (Director, 1955, Vice-Chairman, 1963–67, Managing Director, 1963–81; Executive Chairman, 1967–84); former Chairman: Hawker Siddeley Diesels Ltd; Hawker Siddeley Electric Ltd; Hawker Siddeley Canada Inc.; Hawker Siddeley Rail Ltd; Director: Rolls-Royce Ltd, since 1983; Royal Ordnance, since 1984; Chancellor, Loughborough University of Technology, since 1980; *b* 23 April 1915. *Educ:* Clare Coll., Cambridge (Rex Moir Prize in Engineering, John Bernard Seely Prize in Aeronautics, Ricardo Prize in Thermodynamics). Res. Fellow in Aeronautics of the Company of Armourers and Brasiers (held at University of Cambridge), 1936–38; Principal Scientific Officer, Royal Aircraft Establishment, Farnborough, Hants, 1938–45; Zaharoff Prof. of Aviation, University of London, and Head of Dept of Aeronautics, Imperial Coll. of Science and Technology, 1945–51; Dir of the Royal Aircraft Establishment, Farnborough, 1951–55. Chm., Fasco Industries Inc., 1980–81. Pres., Royal Aeronautical Society, 1958–59, Hon. Fellow, 1965; Dep. Pres., BEAMA, 1966–67, Pres., 1967–68; Vice-Pres., Engineering Employers' Fedn, 1968–80, 1984–; President: Locomotive and Allied Manufacturers Assoc. of GB, 1968–69, 1969–70; SBAC, 1972–73. Member: Advisory Council on Scientific Policy, 1962–64; Air Registration Board, 1963–73; Electricity Supply Research Council, 1963–72; Advisory Council on Technology (Min. of Technology), 1964–67; Defence Industries Council, 1969–77; Industrial Develt Adv. Bd, 1973–75; Dep. Chm., Engineering Industries Council, 1975–. Director: Lloyds Bank, 1966–85; Lloyds Bank UK Management Ltd, 1979–84; Phoenix Assurance, 1969–85; ICI, 1970–85; Onan Corp., 1976–80. Pro-Chancellor, Warwick Univ., 1965–70; Chm. Bd of Trustees, Science Museum, 1983–85. Fellow, Imperial Coll. of Science and Technology, 1963–; Founder Fellow, Fellowship of Engineering, 1976 (Vice-Pres., 1977); For. Associate, US Nat. Acad. of Engrg, 1976–; Hon. Fellow, Clare Coll., Cambridge, 1966; Hon. ACGI; Hon. FRAeS; Hon. FAIAA; Hon. MIMechE, 1968; Hon. FIEE, 1975; Hon. DTech Loughborough 1976. Gold Medal, RAeS, 1962; Hambro Award (Business Man of the Year), 1975; Gold Medal, BIM, 1981; Albert Medal, RSA, 1983. *Address:* Wakehams, Dorney, near Windsor, Berks SL4 6QD. *Club:* Athenæum.

HALL, Arthur Herbert; Librarian and Curator, Guildhall Library and Museum, and Director of Guildhall Art Gallery, 1956–66; retired; *b* 30 Aug. 1901; *y s* of Henry and Eliza Jane Hall, Islington, London; *m* 1927, Dorothy Maud (*née* Barton); two *s* one *d*. *Educ:* Mercers' Sch., Holborn, London. Entered Guildhall Library as junior asst, 1918; Dep. Librarian, 1943–56. Hon. Librarian, Clockmakers' and Gardeners' Companies, 1956–66. Served with RAOC, 1942–46. Chm. Council, London and Middlesex Archæological Soc., 1957–64, Vice-Pres., 1962–; Member: Council of London Topographical Soc., 1960–67; Exec. Cttee, Friends of Nat. Libraries, 1965–69. Hon. Sec., Middlesex Victoria County History Council, 1966–78; Enfield Archaeological Soc. (Hon. Sec., 1966–71); Master, 1974–75, Hon. Clerk, 1965–74, Asst Hon. Clerk, 1975–86, Civic Guild of Old Mercers. Liveryman of the Clockmakers Co.; FLA 1930; FSA 1963. *Address:* 23 Uvedale Road, Enfield, Mddx. *T:* 01–363 2526.

HALL, Sir Basil (Brodribb), KCB 1977 (CB 1974); MC 1945; TD 1952; Member, European Commission of Human Rights, since 1985; Legal Adviser, Broadcasting Complaints Commission, since 1981; *b* 2 Jan. 1918; *s* of late Alfred Brodribb Hall and of Elsie Hilda Hall, Woking, Surrey; *m* 1955, Jean Stafford Gowland; two *s* one *d*. *Educ:* Merchant Taylors' Sch. Articled Clerk with Gibson & Weldon, Solicitors, 1935–39; admitted Solicitor, 1942. Served War of 1939–45: Trooper, Inns of Court Regt, 1939; 2nd Lieut, 12th Royal Lancers, 1940; Captain, 27th Lancers, 1941; Major, 27th Lancers, 1942. Legal Asst, Treasury Solicitor's Dept, 1946; Sen. Legal Asst, 1951; Asst Treasury Solicitor, 1958; Principal Asst Solicitor, 1968; Dep. Treasury Solicitor, 1972; HM Procurator Gen. and Treasury Solicitor, 1975–80. Chm., Civil Service Appeal Bd, 1981–84 (Dep. Chm., 1980–81). Mem. Council, Nat. Army Museum, 1981–. *Recreations:* military history, travel. *Address:* Woodlands, Danes Way, Oxshott, Surrey. *T:* Oxshott 2032. *Club:* Athenæum.

HALL, Very Rev. Bernard, SJ; English Assistant to Father General, Society of Jesus, Rome, since 1982; *b* 17 Oct. 1921. *Educ:* St Michael's Coll., Leeds; Heythrop Coll., Oxford. LicPhil, STL. Captain RA, 1941–46. Entered Society of Jesus, 1946; ordained priest, 1955; Provincial of the English Province, Society of Jesus, 1970–76; Rector, Collegio San Roberto Bellarmino, Rome, 1976–82. *Address:* Borgo Santo Spirito 5, 00193 Rome, Italy.

HALL, Betty, CBE 1977; Regional Nursing Officer, West Midlands Regional Health Authority, 1974–81; *b* 6 June 1921; *d* of John Hall and Jane (*née* Massey), Eagley, Lancs. *Educ:* Bolton Sch.; Royal Infirm., Edinburgh (RGN); Radcliffe Infirm., Oxford and St Mary's Hosp., Manchester (SCM); Royal Coll. of Nursing (RNT). Nursed tuberculous patients from concentration camps, Rollier Clinic, Leysin, 1948–49; Ward Sister, Salford Royal Hosp., 1949–51; Sister Tutor, Royal Masonic Hosp., London, 1952–54; Principal Tutor, St Luke's Hosp., Bradford, 1954–61 (Mem. Leeds Area Nurse Trng Cttee); King Edward's Hosp. Fund Admin. Staff Coll., 1961–62; Work Study Officer to United Bristol Hosps, 1961–64; Asst Nursing Officer to Birmingham Regional Hosp. Bd, 1964–65, Regional Nursing Officer, 1966–74. Member: W Mids Regional Nurse Trng Cttee; Exec. Cttee, Grange-over-Sands Abbeyfield Soc., 1982–. *Recreations:* reading, tapestry making, cricket. *Address:* Chailey, Ash Mount Road, Grange-over-Sands, Cumbria LA11 6BX. *Club:* Naval and Military.

HALL, Dame Catherine (Mary), DBE 1982 (CBE 1967); FRCN; General Secretary, Royal College of Nursing of the United Kingdom, 1957–82; *b* 19 Dec. 1922; *d* of late Robert Hall, OBE and late Florence Irene Hall (*née* Turner). *Educ:* Hunmanby Hall Sch. for Girls, Filey, Yorks. Gen. Infirmary, Leeds: nursing trng, 1941–44 (SRN); Ward Sister, 1945–47; sen. nursing appts, 1949–53; midwifery trng, Leeds and Rotherham, 1948 (SCM); travelling fellowship, US and Canada, 1950–51; student in nursing administration, Royal College of Nursing, 1953–54; Asst Matron, Middlesex Hosp., London, 1954–56. Part-time Member: CIR, 1971–74; British Railways Regional Bd for London and the South East, 1975–77; Mem. GMC, 1979–; Chm., UK Central Council for Nursing, Midwifery and Health Visiting, 1980–85. Hon. Mem., Florida Nurses Assoc., 1973. FRCN 1976. OStJ 1977. Hon. DLitt City, 1975. *Address:* Barnsfield, Barnsfield Lane, Buckfastleigh, Devon TQ11 0NP. *T:* Buckfastleigh 42504.

HALL, Dr Cecil Charles, CB 1968; retired; Director, Warren Spring Laboratory, Ministry of Technology, 1964–68; *b* 10 May 1907; *s* of Frederick Harrington and Alice Hall; *m* 1950, Margaret Rose Nicoll; no *c*. *Educ:* Beckenham Gram. Sch.; London Univ. Jun. Chemist, S Metropolitan Gas Co., 1925–30; BSc 1st Hons Chem. (London), 1929; MSc (London), 1931. Jun. Asst, Fuel Research Stn, DSIR, 1930: PhD (London), 1934. Research in high pressure hydrogenation of coal tar and synthesis of oils and chemicals from coal by catalytic processes. Special Merit Promotion to Sen. Princ. Scientific Off., 1952; Dep. Chief Chemist, Fuel Res. Stn, DSIR, 1953; Dep. Dir, Warren Spring Lab.,

1959. Chm. Governors, N Herts Coll., 1978–83. FRSC (FRIC 1944); FInstE (FInstF 1954). *Publications:* (with T. P. Hilditch) Catalytic Processes in Industrial Chemistry, 1937; numerous research and review papers in scientific and techn. jls dealing with chemistry of high pressure hydrogenation processes and with Fischer Tropsch synthesis. *Recreation:* gardening, specialising in iris growing and hybridising (Pres., British Iris Soc., 1967–70). *Address:* Tanglewood, Sollershott West, Letchworth, Herts. *T:* Letchworth 4339. *Clubs:* Civil Service; Rotary (Stevenage).

HALL, Christopher Myles; Editor of The Countryman, since 1981; *b* 21 July 1932; *s* of Gilbert and Muriel Hall; *m* 1957, Jennifer Bevan Keech (marr. diss. 1980); one *s* one *d*. *Educ:* New Coll., Oxford. 2nd cl. Hons PPE. Reporter and Feature-writer, Daily Express, 1955–58; Sub-editor and Leader-writer, Daily Mirror, 1958–61; Feature-writer and Leader-writer, Daily Herald/Sun, 1961–65; Special Asst (Information): to Minister of Overseas Develt, 1965–66; to Minister of Transport, 1966–68; Chief Information Officer, MoT, 1968; Ramblers' Association: Sec., 1969–74; Mem. Exec. Cttee, 1982–84; Vice-Chm., 1984–; Chm., Oxfordshire Area, 1984–; Dir, Council for Protection of Rural England, 1974–80. Pres., The Holiday Fellowship, 1974–77; Vice-Chm., S Reg. Council of Sport and Recreation, 1976–82; Member: DoT Cttee of Inquiry into Operators' Licensing, 1977–79; Common Land Forum, 1984–86; Hon. Sec., Chiltern Soc., 1965–68. *Publications:* (contrib.) Motorways in London, 1969; How to Run a Pressure Group, 1974; (contrib.) No Through Road, 1975; (contrib.) The Countryman's Britain, 1976; (contrib.) Book of British Villages, 1980; (contrib.) Sunday Times Book of the Countryside, 1981; (contrib.) Walker's Britain, 1982; (contrib.) Britain on Backroads, 1985; pamphlets; contrib. to Vole, The Countryman, New Statesman, New Scientist, The Geographical Magazine, The Guardian and various jls. *Recreation:* walking in the countryside. *Address:* c/o The Countryman, Sheep Street, Burford, Oxon OX8 4LH.

HALL, David, CBE 1983; QPM 1977; Chief Constable of Humberside Police, since 1976; *b* 29 Dec. 1930; *s* of Arthur Thomas Hall and Dorothy May Charman; *m* 1952, Molly Patricia Knight; two *s*. *Educ:* Richmond and East Sheen Grammar School for Boys. Joined Metropolitan Police and rose through ranks from PC to Chief Supt, 1950–68; Staff Officer to Chief Inspector of Constabulary, Col Sir Eric St Johnson, 1968; Asst Chief Constable, 1970, Dep. Chief Constable, 1976, Staffordshire Police. Vice-Pres., Assoc. of Chief Police Officers of England, Wales and NI, 1982–83, Pres. 1983–84. OStJ 1980. *Recreations:* gardening, walking, playing the piano. *Address:* Humberside Police, Police Headquarters, Queens Gardens, Hull HU1 3DJ. *T:* Hull 220113.

HALL, Denis C.; *see* Clarke Hall.

HALL, Denis Whitfield, CMG 1962; late Provincial Commissioner, Kenya; *b* 26 Aug. 1913; *s* of late H. R. Hall, Haslemere, Surrey; *m* 1940, Barbara Carman; two *s*. *Educ:* Dover College; Wadham Coll., Oxford. Dist Officer, Kenya, 1936; Personal Asst to Chief Native Comr, 1948; Senior Dist Comr, 1955; Provincial Comr, Coast Province, 1959. *Recreations:* sailing, tennis, walking, motoring. *Address:* Martins, Priory Close, Boxgrove, West Sussex. *Club:* Oxford University Yacht.

HALL, Air Marshal Sir Donald (Percy), KCB 1984 (CB 1981); CBE 1975; AFC 1963; Deputy Chief of the Defence Staff (Systems), 1985–86; *b* 11 Nov. 1930; *s* of William Reckerby Hall and Elsie Hall; *m* 1953, Joyce (*née* Warburton); two *d*. *Educ:* Hull Grammar Sch. Royal Air Force Coll., 1949; flying appts until 1963; Staff, Germany, 1964–66; OC, No 111 Sqdn, 1966–68; Staff, IDC, 1968–70; OC, Empire Test Pilots Sch., 1970–73; OC, RAF Akrotiri, 1974–75; SASO, No 11 Gp, 1975–77; AOC No 11 Gp, 1977; ACAS (Operational Requirements), 1977–80; AOC No 38 Gp, 1980–83; Dep. Chief, Defence Staff, 1983–84. *Recreations:* shooting, walking, swimming. *Address:* c/o Lloyds Bank, Cox's and King's Branch, 6 Pall Mall, SW1. *Club:* Royal Air Force.

HALL, Sir Douglas (Basil), 14th Bt *cr* 1687; KCMG 1959 (CMG 1958); *b* 1 Feb. 1909; *s* of late Capt. Lionel Erskine Hall and late Jane Augusta Hall (*née* Reynolds); *S* brother, Sir Neville Hall, 13th Bt, 1978; *m* 1933, Rachel Marion Gartside-Tippinge; one *s* two *d* (and one *s* decd). *Educ:* Radley Coll.; Keble Coll., Oxford (MA). Joined Colonial Admin. Service, 1930; posted to N Rhodesia as Cadet; District Officer, 1932; Senior District Officer, 1950; Provincial Commr, 1953; Administrative Sec., 1954; Sec. for Native Affairs to Government of Northern Rhodesia, 1956–59, Acting Chief Sec. for a period during 1958; Governor and C-in-C, Somaliland Protectorate, 1959–60. JP Co. Devon, 1964, Chm., Kingsbridge Petty Sessional Div., 1971–79. *Publications:* various technical articles. *Recreation:* vintage cars. *Heir:* *s* John Douglas Hoste Hall [*b* 7 Jan. 1945; *m* 1972, Angela Margaret, *d* of George Keys; two *s*]. *Address:* Barnford, Ringmore, near Kingsbridge, Devon. *T:* Bigbury-on-Sea 810401.

HALL, Ven. Edgar Francis, MA; Archdeacon of Totnes, 1948–62, Archdeacon Emeritus, 1962; Canon Residentiary of Exeter, 1934–62; Treasurer, Exeter Cathedral, 1951–62; *b* 14 Aug. 1888; *s* of Francis R. Hall, Oxford; *m* 1915, Anstice (*d* 1982) *d* of Dr Louis Tosswill, Exeter; three *d*. *Educ:* Oxford High Sch.; Jesus Coll., Oxford (Scholar). Asst Master, Exeter Sch., 1911; Deacon 1914; Priest 1915; Curate of St James', Exeter, 1914; Chaplain of Exeter Sch., 1917; Vicar of Leusden, Devon, 1921; Diocesan Dir of Relig. Education, Exeter, 1934; Proctor in Convocation, 1944; Gen. Sec. Nat. Soc., 1943–47; Chm. Church of England Council for Education, 1949–58 (Sec. 1948–49). Retired, 1962. *Address:* The Old Parsonage, Leusdon, Poundsgate, Newton Abbot, Devon. *T:* Poundsgate 329.

HALL, Edward, RP 1958; *b* 5 Feb. 1922; *s* of James and Elizabeth Hall; *m* 1946, Daphne Cynthia, (*née* Grogan); two *s* one *d*. *Educ:* Wyggeston Sch., Leicester. Leicester Coll. of Art, 1939–41; Royal Air Force, 1941–46; Wimbledon Sch. of Art, 1946–48; Slade Sch. of Fine Art, 1949–52. Since 1952, portrait painting; exhibits annually at Royal Academy; part-time teaching and lecturing in various London and provincial art schools, including Sir John Cass School of Art, Chelsea School of Art, Medway Coll. of Design. Hon. Treasurer, Royal Soc. of Portrait Painters, 1977–. *Recreations:* music, playing the piano. *Address:* 51 St George's Drive, SW1. *T:* 01–834 5366.

HALL, Maj.-Gen. Edward Michael, CB 1970; MBE 1943; DL; *b* 16 July 1915; *s* of late Brig. E. G. Hall, CB, CIE; *m* 1948, Nina Diana (*née* McArthur); three *s*. *Educ:* Sherborne; RMA; Peterhouse, Cambridge. Commissioned RE, 1935; BA (Cantab) 1937. Served 1939–46, with Royal Bombay Sappers and Miners; Western Desert, India, Burma. CRE, 10th Armd and 3rd Inf. Div., 1957–59; Comd Training Bde, RE, 1962–63; Chief of Staff, Western Command, 1965–66; Military Deputy to Head of Defence Sales, 1966–70. Col Comdt, RE, 1973–76. Comdr and Comr, St John Ambulance, Cornwall, 1971–80. DL Cornwall, 1971, High Sheriff of Cornwall, 1985–86. KStJ 1981. *Recreation:* country pursuits. *Address:* Treworgey Manor, Liskeard, Cornwall.

HALL, Dr Edward Thomas; Professor, Research Laboratory for Archaeology and the History of Art, Oxford University, since 1975 (Director since 1954); Fellow of Worcester College, Oxford, since 1969; *b* 10 May 1924; *s* of late Lt-Col Walter D'Arcy Hall, MC, and of Ann Madelaine Hall; *m* 1957, Jennifer (Jeffie) Louise de la Harpe; two *s*. *Educ:* Eton; Oxford Univ. BA 1948, MA 1953, DPhil 1953, Oxon; FPhysS. Chm., Hon. Scientific Cttee, National Gallery, 1971–; Trustee: British Museum, 1973–; National Gallery, 1977–84; Science Mus., 1984–. Member: Science Mus. Adv. Council, 1979–84; Ancient Monuments Adv. Cttee, 1984–. Mem. Court, Goldsmiths' Co., 1976, Prime Warden, 1985–86. FSA. Hon. FBA 1984. *Publications:* contrib. Archaeometry, various jls concerning science applied to archaeology. *Recreations:* the sea, hot-air ballooning, collecting. *Address:* Beenhams, Littlemore, Oxford OX4 4PZ. *T:* Oxford 777800; 11A Elm Park Lane, SW3 6DD. *T:* 01–352 5847.

HALL, Francis Woodall; HM Diplomatic Service, retired 1970, *b* 10 May 1918; *s* of Francis Hall and Florence Adelaide Woodall; *m* 1951, Phyllis Anne Amelia Andrews; one *s* one *d*. *Educ:* Taunton School. Inland Revenue, 1936–40; Admty (Alexandria, Port Said, Haifa, Freetown), 1940–46; FO, 1946; Bahrain and Baghdad, 1949; Vice-Consul, Malaga, 1950; FO, 1952; 2nd Sec., Cairo, 1955; Consul: Madrid, 1957; Zagreb, 1960; FO 1962; Consul, Stockholm, 1964; Head of Mombasa Office of British High Commn to Kenya, 1969; Consul-Gen., Alexandria, 1971–78; Hon. Consul, Seville, 1979–83. *Recreations:* music, walking. *Address:* Burton Cottage, Burton Lane, East Coker, Somerset.

HALL, Sir (Frederick) John (Frank), 3rd Bt, *cr* 1923; *b* 14 Aug. 1931; *er s* of Sir Frederick Henry Hall, 2nd Bt, and Olwen Irene, *yr d* of late Alderman Frank Collis, Stokeville, Stoke-on-Trent, and Deganwy, Llandudno; *S* father, 1949; *m* 1st, 1956, Felicity Anne (marr. diss. 1960), *d* of late Edward Rivers-Fletcher, Norwich, and of Mrs L. R. Galloway; 2nd, 1961, Patricia Ann Atkinson (marr. diss. 1967); two *d*; re-married, 1967, 1st wife, Felicity Anne Hall; two *d*. *Heir:* *b* David Christopher Hall [*b* 30 Dec. 1937; *m* 1962, Irene, *d* of William Duncan, Aberdeen; one *s* one *d*]. *Address:* Carradale, 29 Embercourt Road, Thames Ditton, Surrey. *T:* 01–398 2801.

HALL, Frederick Thomas Duncan; Chairman, West Midlands County Council, 1977–78 (Member, 1974–82); Lord Mayor of Birmingham, May 1972–May 1973; *b* 12 Jan. 1902; *s* of Frederick James and Catherine Harriett Hall; *m* 1925, Irene Margaret Lawley; one *s*. *Educ:* Bourne Coll., Quinton, Birmingham. Chairman, Hall & Rice Ltd and associated cos. Member: West Bromwich Educn Cttee, 1933–46 (co-opted); Birmingham City Council, 1949–73 (Alderman, 1961); served Cttees: Educn, 1949–73 (Chm., 1966–69); Finance, 1966–73; Gen. Purposes, 1956–74; Jt Consultative, 1969–72 (Chm.); Allotments, 1949–66. Governor: Birmingham Univ., 1967–73; Aston Univ., 1957–80; Handsworth Grammar Sch., 1960–. Member: AMC (Educn) Cttee, 1967–72 (Vice-Chm., 1971–72); Assoc. of Educn Cttees Exec., 1968–72; Chm., Sandwell Ward Conservative Assoc., 1947–65; Pres., Handsworth Div. Conservative Assoc., 1973; Dir, Birmingham Repertory Theatre, 1970–73; formed Handsworth Historical Soc., 1951 (Chm., 1951–65). Vice-Pres., West Bromwich Albion FC, 1979–. *Recreations:* hockey, golf, historical research. *Address:* 32 Englestede Close, Birmingham B20 1BJ. *T:* 021–554 6060. *Clubs:* Aberdovey Golf (Pres., 1967–79); Sandwell Park Golf (Captain, 1948–49).

HALL, Maj.-Gen. Frederick William G.; *see* Gordon-Hall.

HALL, Rear-Adm. Geoffrey Penrose Dickinson, CB 1973; DSC 1943; DL; Hydrographer of the Navy 1971–75; retired; *b* 19 July 1916; *er s* of late Major A. K. D. Hall and late Mrs P. M. Hall; *m* 1945, Mary Ogilvie Carlisle; two *s* one *d*. *Educ:* Haileybury. Served in American waters, 1935–37 and on Nyon Patrol during Spanish Civil War; joined surveying service, 1938, served in Indian Ocean until 1939 when transf. to minesweeping in Far East; hydrographic duties, home waters, Iceland, W Africa; navigational and minesweeping duties, Icelandic waters; transf. to Combined Ops, SE Asia; subseq. comd frigate, British Pacific Fleet; from 1947, hydrographic work: with RNZN, 1949–51; subseq. five comds i/c surveys at home and abroad; served ashore and in Atlantic, Indian Ocean, Antarctic waters (Cuthbert Peek Grant, RGS, for work in furtherance of oceanographical exploration); twice Asst Hydrographer; surveyed between S Africa and Iceland, 1965–67; Asst Dir (Naval), Hydrographic Dept, Taunton, 1970. Cadet 1934; Midshipman 1935; Sub-Lt 1938; Lieut 1939; Lt-Comdr 1945; Comdr 1953; Captain 1961; Rear-Adm. 1971. Pres., Hydrographic Soc., 1975. FRGS; FRICS. DL Lincs, 1982. *Publications:* contribs to Nature, Deep Sea Research, Internat. Hydrographic Review, Navy International. *Recreation:* country pursuits. *Address:* Manby House, Manby, Louth, Lincs LN11 8UF. *T:* South Cockerington 777. *Clubs:* Naval and Military, Royal Navy; Lincolnshire; Louth (Louth).

HALL, Geoffrey Ronald, CBE 1985; FEng, CChem, FRSC, SFInstE; Director, Brighton Polytechnic, since 1970; *b* 18 May 1928; *er s* of late Thomas Harold Hall, JP, and late Muriel Frances Hall, Douglas, IoM; *m* 1950, Elizabeth Day Sheldon; two *s* one *d*. *Educ:* Douglas High Sch., IoM; Univ. of Manchester (BSc). Research in Nuclear Science and Engineering at AERE, Harwell, 1949–56; sabbatical at Oxford Univ., 1955; Colombo Plan Expert to Indian Atomic Energy Commn, 1956–58; Reader in Nuclear Technology, Imperial Coll., London, 1958–63; Prof. of Nuclear Technology, Imperial Coll., 1963–70. Member: CNAA, 1977–82; Engineering Council, 1981–86 (Vice-Chm., 1984–85); SERC, 1982–86 (Mem., Engrg Bd, SRC, later SERC, 1978–83); Chm., Engrg Working Gp, Nat. Adv. Body for Local Authority Higher Educn, 1982–84. President: British Nuclear Energy Soc., 1970–71; Inst. of Fuel, 1976–77; Founder Fellow, Fellowship of Engineering, 1976. *Publications:* papers related to nuclear science, fuels and engineering. *Recreations:* travel, caravanning. *Address:* 1 Great Wilkins, Brighton BN1 9QW.

HALL, Harold George; His Honour Judge Hall; a Circuit Judge, since 1975; *b* 20 Sept. 1920; *s* of late Albert Hall and Violet Maud Hall (*née* Etherington); *m* 1950, Patricia Delaney; four *s* one *d*. *Educ:* Archbishop Holgate's Grammar Sch., York. RAF, 1940–46 (Flt-Lt). Called to Bar, Middle Temple, 1958; practised NE Circuit; Dep. Chm., WR Yorks QS, 1970; a Recorder, 1972–75.

HALL, Harold Percival, CMG 1963; MBE 1947; Director of Studies, Royal Institute of Public Administration, since 1974; *b* 9 Sept. 1913; *s* of late Major George Charles Hall; *m* 1939, Margery Hall, *d* of late Joseph Dickson; three *s* (including twin *s*). *Educ:* Portsmouth Grammar Sch.; Royal Military College, Sandhurst. Commissioned Indian Army, 1933. Indian Political Service, 1937–47. Private Sec. to Resident, Central India States, 1937; Magistrate and Collector, Meerut, 1938–39. Military Service, 1938–43 (Major). Staff Coll., Quetta, 1941. Asst Political Agent, Loralai, 1943, Nasirabad, 1944; Dir, Food and Civil Supplies, and Dep. Sec., Revenue, Baluchistan, 1945–46; Principal, Colonial Office, 1947; Asst Sec. (Head of Pacific and Indian Ocean Dept), Colonial Office, 1955–62; Seconded to Office of UK Comr-Gen. for SE Asia, 1962–63; British Dep. High Comr for Eastern Malaysia, Kuching, Sarawak, 1963–64; Asst Sec., Colonial Office, 1965–66; Assistant Under-Secretary of State: Commonwealth Office, 1966–68; MoD, 1968–73. Mem. Governing Body, Sch. of Oriental and African Studies, 1971–74. *Recreation:* gardening. *Address:* Robina, The Chase, Ringwood, Dorset BH24 2AN. *T:* Ringwood 479880.

HALL, (Harold) Peter; Legal Adviser and Solicitor, Crown Estate Commissioners, 1976–80; Solicitor of Supreme Court; *b* 10 Dec. 1916; *s* of Arthur William Henry and Ethel Amelia Hall; *m* 1946, Tessibel Mary Mitchell (*née* Phillips); one *s* one *d*. *Educ:* Bristol Grammar Sch.; Bristol Univ. (LLB Hons). Articled to, and Asst Solicitor with, Burges Salmon & Co., Solicitors, Bristol, 1934–39. Served War of 1939–45: enlisted Somerset Light Inf., Dec. 1939; commnd in E Yorkshire Regt, 1940; service Home and

Far East, 1940–45. Asst Provost Marshal (Major), Southern Army, India Command, 1945. Legal Branch, Min. of Agric., Fisheries and Food, 1946–66; Asst Legal Adviser, Land Commn, 1967–71; Asst Solicitor, Dept of the Environment, 1971–76. *Recreations:* reading, photography, walking. *Address:* The Ridings, 9 Steep Hill Court Road, Ventnor, Isle of Wight PO38 1UH. *Club:* Royal Solent Yacht (Yarmouth, IoW).

HALL, Prof. Henry Edgar, FRS 1982; Professor of Physics, University of Manchester, since 1961; *b* 1928; *s* of John Ainger Hall; *m* 1962, Patricia Anne Broadbent; two *s* one *d*. *Educ:* Latymer Upper Sch., Hammersmith; Emmanuel Coll., Cambridge. BA 1952; PhD 1956. At Royal Society Mond Laboratory, Cambridge, 1952–58; Senior Student, Royal Commission for the Exhibition of 1851, 1955–57; Research Fellow of Emmanuel Coll., 1955–58; Lecturer in Physics, Univ. of Manchester, 1958–61. Simon Memorial Prize (with W. F. Vinen), 1963. Visiting Professor: Univ. of Western Australia, 1964; Univ. of Oregon, 1967–68; Cornell Univ., 1974, 1982–83; Univ. of Tokyo, 1985. *Publications:* Solid State Physics, 1974; papers in scientific journals. *Recreation:* mountain walking. *Address:* The Schuster Laboratory, The University, Manchester M13 9PL.

HALL, Air Vice-Marshal Hubert Desmond, CB 1979; CBE 1972; AFC 1963; RAF retd; Director: RO&K Australia, since 1983; MRS Australia, since 1983; *b* 3 June 1925; *s* of Charles William and Violet Victoria Kate Hall; *m* 1951, Mavis Dorothea (*née* Hopkins). *Educ:* Portsmouth Municipal Coll. FBIM. Commissioned RAF, 1945; RAF Coll., Cranwell QFI, 1951–55; Flt Comdr, 9 Sqdn, 1955–56; 232 OCU Gaydon, Sqdn Ldr, Medium Bomber Force; Instructor, Wing Comdr 1962; 3 Group Headquarters (Training), 1963–65; Air Warfare Coll., 1965; commanded No 57 Sqdn (Victors), 1966–68; Gp Captain Nuclear Operations SHAPE HQ, 1968–71; comd RAF Waddington, 1971–73; Overseas Coll. of Defence Studies India, 1974; MoD: Director (Air Cdre) of Establishments, RAF, 1975–77; Air Comdr Malta, 1977–79; Air Vice-Marshal 1979; Defence Advr, Canberra, 1980–82. Queen's Commendation, 1957. CStJ 1983. *Recreations:* shooting, gardening, reading. *Address:* 7 Richardson Street, Garran, ACT 2605, Australia; c/o Lloyds Bank, 115 Commercial Road, Portsmouth, Hants PO1 1BY. *Clubs:* Royal Air Force, Royal Commonwealth Society; Commonwealth (Canberra).

HALL, Prof. James Snowdon, CBE 1976; Professor of Agriculture, Glasgow University, and Principal, West of Scotland Agricultural College, 1966–80; *b* 28 Jan. 1919; *s* of Thomas Blackburn Hall and Mary Milburn Hall; *m* 1942, Mary Smith; one *s* one *d*. *Educ:* Univ. of Durham (BSc Hons). FRAgS, FIBiol. Asst Technical Adviser, Northumberland War Agric. Exec. Commn, 1941–44; Lectr in Agriculture, Univ. of Newcastle upon Tyne, 1944–54; Principal, Cumbria Coll. of Agriculture and Forestry, 1954–66. *Address:* 26 Earls Way, Doonfoot, Ayr. *T:* Alloway 41162. *Club:* Farmers'.

HALL, Jean Graham, LLM (London); **Her Honour Judge Graham Hall;** a Circuit Judge (formerly Deputy Chairman, South-East London Quarter Sessions), since 1971; *b* 26 March 1917; *d* of Robert Hall and Alison (*née* Graham). *Educ:* Inverkeithing Sch., Fife; St Anne's Coll., Sanderstead; London Sch. of Economics. Gold Medal (Elocution and Dramatic Art), Incorporated London Acad. of Music, 1935; Teacher's Dipl., Guildhall Sch. of Music, 1937; Social Science Cert., London Sch. of Economics, 1937; LLB (Hons), London, 1950. Club Leader and subseq. Sub-Warden, Birmingham Univ. Settlement, 1937–41; Sec., Eighteen Plus (an experiment in youth work), 1941–44; Probation Officer, Hants, subseq. Croydon, 1945–51. Called to Bar, Gray's Inn, 1951. Metropolitan Stipendiary Magistrate, 1965–71. Pres., Gray's Inn Debating Soc., 1953; Hon. Sec., Soc. of Labour Lawyers, 1954–64; Pres., British Soc. of Criminology, 1971–74. Chm. Departmental Cttee on Statutory Maintenance Limits, 1966–68. Contested (Lab) East Surrey, 1955. Pres., Edridge Benevolent Trust, 1984. Hon. LLD Lincoln, USA, 1979. *Publications:* Towards a Family Court, 1971; (jtly) Child Abuse: procedure and evidence in juvenile courts, 1978. *Recreations:* travel, congenial debate. *Address:* 2 Dr Johnson's Buildings, Temple, EC4. *Club:* University Women's.

HALL, Joan Valerie; Member, Central Transport Consultative Committee, since 1981; *b* 31 Aug. 1935; *d* of late Robert Percy Hall and of Winifred Emily Umbers. *Educ:* Queen Margaret's Sch., Escrick, York; Ashridge House of Citizenship. Contested (C) Barnsley, 1964 and 1966. MP (C) Keighley, 1970–Feb. 1974; PPS to Minister of State for Agriculture, Fisheries and Food, 1972–74. Vice-Chm., Greater London Young Conservatives, 1964. Mem. Council, University Coll. Buckingham, 1977–. *Address:* Mayfields, Darton Road, Cawthorne, Barnsley, South Yorks S75 4HY. *T:* Barnsley 790230.

HALL, Sir John; *see* Hall, Sir F. J. F.

HALL, John; *see* Hall, W. J.

HALL, John Anthony Sanderson, DFC 1943; QC 1967; FCIArb 1982; *b* 25 Dec. 1921; *s* of late Rt Hon. W. Glenvil Hall, PC, MP, and late Rachel Ida Hall (*née* Sanderson); *m* 1st, Nora Ella Hall (*née* Crowe) (marr. diss. 1974); one *s* two *d*; 2nd, Elizabeth Mary, widow of Alan Riley Maynard. *Educ:* Leighton Park Sch.; Trinity Hall, Cambridge (MA). Served RAF, 1940–46, 85 Squadron and 488 (NZ) Squadron (Squadron Leader; DFC and Bar). Called to Bar, Inner Temple, 1948, Master of the Bench, 1975; Western Circuit; Dep. Chm., Hants Quarter Sessions, 1967; Recorder of Swindon, 1971; a Recorder of the Crown Court, 1972–78. Member: Gen. Council of the Bar, 1964–68, 1970–74; Senate of the Four Inns of Court, 1966–68, 1970–74; Council of Legal Educn, 1970–74. Mem., 1972–79, Chm., 1978–79, UK Deleg. to Consultative Cttee, Bars and Law Socs of EEC; Mem., Foreign Compensation Commn, 1983–. Dir Gen., Internat. Fedn of Producers of Phonograms and Videograms, 1979–81. Governor: St Catherine's Sch., Bramley (Chm.); Cranleigh Sch., 1972–. *Recreations:* walking, sailing, fishing. *Address:* 2 Dr Johnson's Buildings, Temple, EC4; Swallows, Blewbury, Oxon. *Club:* Garrick.

HALL, Sir John (Bernard), 3rd Bt *cr* 1919; Managing Director, European Brazilian Bank Ltd, since 1983 (Director, since 1976); *b* 20 March 1932; *s* of Lieut-Col Sir Douglas Hall, DSO, 2nd Bt, and Ina Nancie Walton, *d* of late Col John Edward Mellor, CB (she *m* 2nd, 1962, Col Peter J. Bradford, DSO, OBE, TD); *S* father, 1962; *m* 1957, Delia Mary, *d* of late Lieut-Col J. A. Innes, DSO; one *s* two *d*. *Educ:* Eton; Trinity Coll., Oxford (MA). FIB 1976. Lieut, Royal Fusiliers (RARO). J. Henry Schroder Wagg & Co. Ltd, formerly J. Henry Schroder & Co, 1955–73 (Dir, 1967–73); Director: The Antofagasta (Chili) and Bolivia Rly Co. Ltd, 1967–73; Bank of America International, 1974–82; a Vice Pres., Bank of America NT and SA, 1982–; Chm., Assoc. of British Consortium Banks, 1985–86. Chm., Anglo-Colombian Soc., 1978–81. *Recreations:* travel, fishing. *Heir:* *s* David Bernard Hall, *b* 12 May 1961. *Address:* Penrose House, Patmore Heath, Albury, Ware, Herts SG11 2LT. *T:* Albury 255. *Clubs:* Boodle's, Lansdowne, Overseas Bankers'.

HALL, John Edward Beauchamp, CMG 1959; *b* 9 Dec. 1905; *s* of Henry William Hall, MA, and Emily (*née* Odam); *m* 1936, Jane Gordon (*née* Forbes); two *d*. *Educ:* Bradfield Coll., Berks; Worcester Coll., Oxford. Foundation Scholar, Bradfield Coll., 1919–24; Exhibitioner, Worcester Coll., Oxford, 1924–28. Appointed to Colonial Administrative Service, Nigeria, 1930; Permanent Sec., Federal Government of Nigeria, 1958–60; retired, 1961. *Recreation:* gardening. *Address:* The Croft, Church Road, Sandhurst, Hawkhurst, Kent TN18 5NS. *T:* Sandhurst 302.

HALL, Julian; His Honour Judge Julian Hall; a Circuit Judge, since 1986; *b* 13 Jan. 1939; *s* of Dr Stephen Hall, FRCP and late Dr Mary Hall, Boarstall Tower, Bucks; *m* 1968, M. Rosalind, *d* of John and Natalie Perry, Hale Barns, Cheshire; one *s* one *d*. *Educ:* Eton (Scholar); Christ Church, Oxford (Scholar; MA); Trinity Coll., Dublin (LLB). ARCM (flute). Industrial Chemist, Shell Internat. Chemical Co., 1961–63. Called to the Bar, Gray's Inn, 1966; in practice in Common Law Chambers on Northern Circuit, Manchester, 1966–86; Standing Prosecuting Counsel to Inland Revenue, Northern Circuit, 1985–86; a Recorder, 1982–86. *Recreation:* making music, in orchestras, choirs and at home. *Address:* c/o Courts of Justice, Crown Square, Manchester 3. *T:* 061–832 8393.

HALL, Maj.-Gen. Kenneth, CB 1976; OBE 1962 (MBE 1958); Director of Army Education, 1972–76; *b* 29 July 1916; *s* of Frank Hall and Hannah Hall (*née* Clayton); *m* 1945, Celia Adelaide Elizabeth Francis; two *s*. *Educ:* Worksop Coll.; St John's Coll., Cambridge (MA). Served War of 1939–45: commissioned in Royal Tank Regt, 1940–49; transf. to Royal Army Educational Corps, 1949; War Office, 1945–52; HQ Malta Garrison, 1953–57; War Office, 1958–62; HQ Aldershot District, 1962–64; Chief Educn Officer, GHQ, MELF, 1965; Comdt Army Sch. of Educn, 1965–66; MoD, 1966–69; Chief Educn Officer, HQ Southern Comd, 1969–71; Comdt RAEC Centre, 1971–72. Col Comdt, RAEC, 1978–82. *Recreations:* boxing (Cambridge Univ. Blue, 1937–38–39), reading, golf. *Address:* 42 Exeter House, Putney Heath, SW15. *T:* 01–788 4794. *Clubs:* Roehampton; Hawks (Cambridge).

HALL, (Laura) Margaret; *see* MacDougall, Laura Margaret.

HALL, Prof. Laurance David, PhD; FRS(Can) 1982; CChem; FCIC, FRSC; Herchel Smith Professor of Medicinal Chemistry, University of Cambridge, since 1984; *b* 18 March 1938; *s* of Daniel William Hall and Elsie Ivy Hall; *m* 1962, Winifred Margaret (*née* Golding); two *s* two *d*. *Educ:* Leyton County High Sch.; Bristol Univ. (BSc 1959; PhD 1962). FCIC 1973; FRSC 1985. Post-doctoral Fellow, Ottawa Univ., 1962–63; Dept of Chemistry, Univ. of British Columbia: Instr II, 1963–64; Asst Prof., 1964–69; Associate Prof., 1969–73; Prof., 1973–84. Alfred P. Sloan Foundn Res. Fellow, 1971–73; Canada Council Killam Res. Fellow, 1982–84. Lederle Prof., RSM, 1984; Vis. Professor: Univ. of NSW, 1967; Univ. of Cape Town, 1974; Northwestern Univ., Evanston, Ill, 1982. Lectures: Van Cleave, Univ. of Saskatchewan, Regina, 1983; Cecil Green, Galveston Univ., Texas, 1983; Brotherton, Leeds Univ., 1985; Philip Morris, Richmond Univ., Va, 1985. Fellow, Cambridge Philosophical Soc. Jacob Bielly Faculty Res. Prize, Univ. of BC, 1974; Tate and Lyle Award for Carbohydrate Chemistry, Chemical Soc., 1974; Merck, Sharpe and Dohme Lecture Award, Chemical Inst. of Canada, 1975; Corday Morgan Medal and Prize, Chemical Soc., 1976; Barringer Award, Spectroscopy Soc. of Canada, 1981. *Publications:* over 200 research pubns. *Recreations:* sailing, skiing, wine-making, music, travel, research. *Address:* 22 Long Road, Cambridge CB2 2QS. *T:* Cambridge 211999.

HALL, Sir Laurence Charles B.; *see* Brodie-Hall.

HALL, Margaret Dorothy, OBE 1973; RDI 1974; FSIAD; Head of Design, British Museum, since 1964; *b* 22 Jan. 1936; *d* of Thomas Robson Hall and Millicent (*née* Britton). *Educ:* Bromley County Grammar Sch.; Bromley College of Art; Royal College of Art (DesRCA). Design Assistant: Casson, Condor & Partners, 1960–61; Westwood Piet & Partners, 1961–63; Dennis Lennon & Partners, 1963–64; British Museum, 1964–: exhibitions designed include: Masterpieces of Glass, 1968; Museum of Mankind, 1970; Treasures of Tutankhamun, 1972; Nomad and City, 1976; Captain Cook in the South Seas, 1979. Designer, Manuscripts and Men, National Portrait Gallery, 1969. Chm., Gp of Designers/Interpreters in Museums, 1978–81. FSIAD 1975 (MSIAD 1968) (Chm., SIAD Salaried Designers Cttee, 1979–81). Chm., Wynkyn de Worde Soc., 1982. Governor, Ravensbourne College of Art, 1973–78. FRSA 1974; FMA 1983. *Publication:* On Display: a grammar of museum exhibition design, 1986. *Address:* The British Museum, WC1B 3DG. *T:* 01–636 1555. *Clubs:* Arts; Double Crown.

HALL, Michael Kilgour H.; *see* Harrison-Hall.

HALL, Prof. Michael Robert Pritchard, FRCP, FRCPE; Professor of Geriatric Medicine, University of Southampton, since 1970; Hon. Consultant Physician, Southampton University Hospitals, since 1970; *b* 13 May 1922; *s* of Augustus Henry Hall, MC and Elizabeth Jane Lord; *m* 1947, Joan Jardine, (Eileen), *d* of Dr John McCartney; two *d*. *Educ:* Shrewsbury Sch.; Worcester Coll., Oxford (MA, BM, BCh). FRCP 1970; FRCPE 1971. Served War, Indian Army, 1941–46 (Temp. Captain). Consultant Physician, Newcastle-upon-Tyne Gen. Hosp., 1962–70; Hon. Lecturer in Medicine: Univ. of Durham, 1962–63; Univ. of Newcastle upon Tyne, 1963–70. Auckland Savings Bank Vis. Prof., Univ. of Auckland, NZ, 1974; Vis. Lecturer: Dalhousie Univ., NS, 1979; (Tayside Health Bd), Univ. of Dundee, 1981; Examr, Dip. of Geriatric Medicine, RCP, 1985–. Chairman: British Soc. for Res. on Ageing, 1976–79; Assoc. of Professors of Geriatric Medicine, 1985–86; Member: DHSS Cttee for Review of Medicines, 1976–82; Fitness and Health Adv. Gp to Sports Council, 1977–; Governing Body and Exec. Cttee, Age Concern (England), 1975–77 and 1980–83; Council, Internat. Assoc. of Gerontology, 1981–85; Pres., Tissue Viability Soc., 1983–84. Life Vice-Pres., Northumberland Cheshire Home, 1970; Trustee and Governor, British Foundn for Age Res., 1979–. *Publications:* Medical Care of the Elderly, 1978, 2nd edn 1986; chapters and contribs to various books on aspects of ageing and geriatric medicine; articles and papers in med. jls. *Recreations:* fly-fishing, golf, gardening. *Address:* Peartree Cottage, Emery Down, Lyndhurst, Hants SO4 7FH. *T:* Lyndhurst 2541. *Club:* MCC.

HALL, Peter; *see* Hall, H. P.

HALL, Peter Dalton, CB 1986; Under Secretary, Solicitor's Office, Board of Inland Revenue, since 1979; *b* 1 Aug. 1924; *s* of Edward and Kathleen Hall; *m* 1952, Stella Iris Breen; four *s* two *d*. *Educ:* Rishworth Sch.; St Catharine's Coll., Cambridge (exhibnr; MA, LLB). Served War of 1939–45, Intelligence Corps; seconded to AIF and served with US Forces in New Guinea and Philippines; Major. Called to the Bar, Middle Temple, 1951; entered Inland Revenue Solicitor's Office, 1952. Mem., Bar Council 1967–70. *Publications:* contrib.: Simon's Taxes; Foster's Capital Taxes Encyclopaedia. *Recreations:* cricket, gardening, music, conservation. *Address:* Apple Tree Cottage, Woughton-on-the-Green, Bucks MK6 3BE.

HALL, Peter Edward; HM Diplomatic Service; Under Secretary, Cabinet Office, since 1986; *b* 26 July 1938; *s* of Bernard Hall and late Monica Hall (*née* Blackbourn); *m* 1972, Marnie Kay; one *s* one *d*. *Educ:* Portsmouth Grammar Sch.; HM Services (Jt Services Sch. for Linguists); Pembroke Coll., Cambridge (Scholar; 1st Cl. parts I and II, Mediaeval and Modern Langs Tripos). Foreign Office, 1961–63; 3rd Sec., Warsaw, 1963–66; 2nd Sec., New Delhi, 1966–69; FCO (European Integration Dept), 1969–72; 1st Sec., UK Permanent Representation to EEC, 1972–76; Asst Head, Financial Relations Dept, FCO,

1976–77; Counsellor, Caracas, 1977–78; Hd of British Information Services, NY, 1978–83 and Counsellor, British Embassy, Washington, 1981–83; Dir of Res., FCO, 1983–86. *Recreations:* reading (A. Powell, Byron), music (Rolling Stones, Mozart). *Address:* c/o Foreign and Commonwealth Office, King Charles Street, SW1.

HALL, Prof. Peter Geoffrey, FBA 1983; Professor, since 1968 and Head of Department of Geography, 1968–80, Chairman, School of Planning Studies, 1971–77 and since 1983, Dean of Urban and Regional Studies, 1975–78, University of Reading; *b* 19 March 1932; *s* of Arthur Vickers Hall and Bertha Hall (*née* Keefe); *m* 1st, 1962, Carla Maria Wartenberg (marr. diss. 1966); 2nd, 1967, Magdalena Mróz; no *c*. *Educ:* Blackpool Grammar Sch.; St Catharine's Coll., Cambridge Univ. (MA, PhD). Asst Lectr, 1957, Lectr, 1960, Birkbeck Coll., Univ. of London; Reader in Geography with ref. to Regional Planning, London Sch. of Economics and Political Science, 1966. Prof., City and Regional Planning, Associate Dir, Inst. of Urban and Regional Develt, 1980–, Univ. of Calif, Berkeley. Member: SE Regional Planning Council, 1966–79; Nature Conservancy, 1968–72; Transport and Road Research Laboratory Adv. Cttee on Transport, 1973–; Environmental Bd, 1975–79; SSRC, 1975–80 (Chm., Planning Cttee); EEC Expert Gp on New Tendencies of Social and Economic Develt, 1975–77; Standing Adv. Cttee on Trunk Road Assessment, 1978–80; Exec. Cttee, Regional Studies Assoc., 1967– (Hon. Jl Editor, 1967–78); Exec. Cttee, Fabian Soc., 1964–80 (Chm. 1971–72); Governor, Centre for Environmental Studies, 1975–80. Chm., Tawney Soc., 1983–85 (Vice-Chm., 1982–83). FRGS; Hon. RTPI, 1975. Editor, Built Environment, 1977–. *Publications:* The Industries of London, 1962; London 2000, 1963 (reprint, 1969); Labour's New Frontiers, 1964; (ed) Land Values, 1965; The World Cities, 1966, 3rd edn 1984; Containment of Urban England, 1973; Urban and Regional Planning, 1974, 2nd edn 1982; Europe 2000, 1977; Great Planning Disasters, 1980; Growth Centres in the European Urban System, 1980; The Inner City in Context, 1981; Silicon Landscapes, 1985; Can Rail Save the City?, 1985; High Tech America, 1986. *Recreations:* writing, reading, talking. *Address:* Department of Geography, University of Reading, Whiteknights, Reading RG6 2AB. *Club:* Athenæum.

HALL, Peter George; President, Esso Norge, since 1984; *b* 10 Dec. 1924; *s* of Charles and Rosina Hall; *m* 1949, Margaret Gladys (*née* Adams); two *s* two *d*. *Educ:* Sandown, IoW, Grammar Sch.; Southampton Univ. (BScEng). FInstPet. Anglo-Iranian Oil Co., 1946–51; Esso Petroleum Co. Ltd: various positions at Fawley Refinery, 1951–63; Manager, Milford Haven Refinery, 1963–66; Employee Relations Manager, 1966–70; Vice-Pres., General Sekiyu Seisei, Tokyo, 1971–74; Asst Gen. Man., Refining, Imperial Oil Ltd, Toronto, 1974–76; Refining Man., Exxon Corp., New York, 1976–77; Director, Esso Petroleum Co. Ltd, London, 1977–78; Vice-Pres., Esso Europe Inc. London, 1979–81; Man. Dir, Esso Petroleum Co., 1982–84. *Recreations:* opera, classical music, walking, gardening. *Address:* PO Box 1369, Vika 0114, Oslo, Norway.

HALL, Sir Peter (Reginald Frederick), Kt 1977; CBE 1963; director of plays, films and operas; Director, National Theatre, since 1973; Artistic Director, Glyndebourne Festival, since 1984; *b* Bury St Edmunds, Suffolk, 22 Nov. 1930; *s* of Reginald Edward Arthur Hall and Grace Pamment; *m* 1956, Leslie Caron (marr. diss. 1965); one *s* one *d*; *m* 1965, Jacqueline Taylor (marr. diss. 1981); one *s* one *d*; *m* 1982, Maria Ewing; one *d*. *Educ:* Perse Sch., Cambridge; St Catharine's Coll., Cambridge (MA Hons; Hon. Fellow, 1964). Dir, Arts Theatre, London, 1955–56 (directed several plays incl. first productions of Waiting for Godot, South, Waltz of the Toreadors); formed own producing company, International Playwrights' Theatre, 1957, and directed their first production, Camino Real; at Sadler's Wells, directed his first opera, The Moon and Sixpence, 1957. First productions at Stratford: Love's Labour's Lost, 1956; Cymbeline, 1957; first prod. on Broadway, The Rope Dancers, Nov. 1957. Plays in London, 1956–58: Summertime, Gigi, Cat on a Hot Tin Roof, Brouhaha, Shadow of Heroes; Madame de . . ., Traveller Without Luggage, A Midsummer Night's Dream and Coriolanus (Stratford), The Wrong Side of the Park, 1959; apptd Dir of Royal Shakespeare Theatre, Jan. 1960, responsible for creation of RSC as a permanent ensemble, and its move to Aldwych Theatre, 1960; Man. Dir at Stratford-on-Avon and Aldwych Theatre, London, 1960–68; Co-Dir, RSC, 1968–73; plays produced/directed for *Royal Shakespeare Company:* Two Gentlemen of Verona, Twelfth Night, Troilus and Cressida, 1960; Ondine, Becket, Romeo and Juliet, 1961; The Collection, Troilus and Cressida, A Midsummer Night's Dream, 1962; The Wars of the Roses (adaptation of Henry VI Parts 1, 2 and 3, and Richard III), 1963 (televised for BBC, 1965); Sequence of Shakespeare's histories for Shakespeare's 400th anniversary at Stratford: Richard II, Henry IV Parts 1 & 2, Henry V, Henry VI, Edward IV, Richard III, 1964; The Homecoming, Hamlet, 1965; The Government Inspector, Staircase, 1966; The Homecoming (NY), Macbeth, 1967; A Delicate Balance, Silence and Landscape, 1969; The Battle of the Shrivings, 1970; Old Times, 1971 (NY, 1971, Vienna, 1972); All Over, Via Galactica (NY), 1972; plays produced/directed for *National Theatre:* The Tempest, 1974; John Gabriel Borkman, 1975; No Man's Land, Happy Days, Hamlet, 1975; Tamburlaine the Great, 1976; No Man's Land (NY), Volpone, Bedroom Farce, The Country Wife, 1977; The Cherry Orchard, Macbeth, Betrayal, 1978; Amadeus, 1979, NY 1981 (Tony Award for Best Director); Othello, 1980; Family Voices, The Oresteia, 1981; Importance of Being Earnest, 1982; Other Places, 1982; Jean Seberg, 1983; Animal Farm, Coriolanus, 1984; Martine, Yonadab, 1985; The Petition, 1986. *Films:* Work is a Four Letter Word, 1968; A Midsummer Night's Dream, Three into Two Won't Go, 1969; Perfect Friday, 1971; The Homecoming, 1973; Akenfield, 1974. *Opera:* at Covent Garden: Moses and Aaron, 1965; The Magic Flute, 1966; The Knot Garden, 1970; Eugene Onegin, Tristan and Isolde, 1971; at Glyndebourne: La Calisto, 1970; Il Ritorno d'Ulisse in Patria, 1972; The Marriage of Figaro, 1973; Don Giovanni, Così Fan Tutte, 1978, 1984; Fidelio, 1979; A Midsummer Night's Dream, 1981; Orfeo ed Euridice, 1982; L'Incoronazione di Poppea, 1984, 1986; Carmen, 1985; Albert Herring, 1985, 1986; Simon Boccanegra, 1986; at Metropolitan Opera, NY: Macbeth, 1982; at Bayreuth: The Ring, 1983. *Television:* Presenter, Aquarius (LWT), 1975–77; Oresteia (C4), 1986. Associate Prof. of Drama, Warwick Univ., 1966–. Mem., Arts Council, 1969–73; Founder Mem., Theatre Dirs' Guild of GB, 1983–. DUniv York, 1966; Hon. DLitt Reading, 1973; Hon. LittD: Liverpool, 1974; Leicester, 1977. Tony Award (NY) for best director, 1966; Hamburg Univ. Shakespeare Prize, 1967; Standard Special Award, 1979; Standard Award Best Director, 1981; Standard Award for outstanding achievement in Opera, 1981. Chevalier de l'Ordre des Arts et des Lettres, 1965. *Publication:* Peter Hall's Diaries (ed John Goodwin), 1983. *Recreation:* music. *Address:* The National Theatre, Upper Ground, SE1. *Club:* Athenæum.

HALL, Prof. Reginald, FRCP; Professor of Medicine, University of Wales College of Medicine (formerly Welsh National School of Medicine), since 1980; *b* 1 Oct. 1931; *s* of Reginald P. Hall and Maggie W. Hall; *m* 1960, Dr Molly Hill; two *s* three *d*. *Educ:* Univ. of Durham (BSc, MB BS, MD). Harkness Fellow of Commonwealth Fund, Clinical and Research Fellow in Medicine, Harvard, 1960–61; Wellcome Sen. Research Fellow in Clinical Science, 1964–67; Cons. Physician, Royal Victoria Infirmary, Newcastle upon Tyne, 1967–79; Prof. of Medicine, Univ. of Newcastle upon Tyne, 1970–79. *Publications:* Fundamentals of Clinical Endocrinology, 1969, 3rd edn 1980; Atlas of Endocrinology, 1980. *Recreations:* bryology, literature. *Address:* 37 Palace Road, Llandaff, Cardiff CF5 2AG. *T:* Cardiff 567689; (office) Cardiff 755944, ext. 2307.

HALL, Sir Robert de Zouche, KCMG 1953 (CMG 1952); MA; FSA; *b* 27 April 1904; *s* of late Arthur William Hall, Liverpool; *m* 1932, Lorna Dorothy (*née* Markham); one *s* one *d*. *Educ:* Willaston Sch.; Gonville and Caius Coll., Cambridge. MA, 1932. Colonial Administrative Service, Tanganyika, 1926; Provincial Comr, 1947; Senior Provincial Comr, 1950; Mem. for Local Government, Tanganyika, 1950–53. Governor, Comdr-in-Chief, and Vice-Adm., Sierra Leone, 1953–56. Hon. Sec. Vernacular Architecture Group, 1959–72, Pres., 1972–73; Chm. Governing Body, Somerset County Museum, 1961–73; Mem. Gisborne Museum Staff, NZ, 1974–80. *Publication:* (ed) A Bibliography on Vernacular Architecture, 1973. *Address:* 1 Lewis Street, Gisborne, New Zealand.

HALL, Robert King, PhD; international consultant, educator and executive; *b* Kewanee, Ill, 13 March 1912; *s* of Dr Nelson Hall and Nellie Jean Hyer; *m* 1938, Margaret Wheeler, Belmont, Mass; one *s* two *d*. *Educ:* Lake Forest Univ. (AB); Harvard Univ. (AM); Univ. of Chicago (AMEduc); Columbia Univ. (AM); Sch. of Asiatic Studies, NY (AM); Univ. of Michigan (PhD). Master: Cranbrook Sch. (Mich), 1936–40; Dir Research Milwaukee Country Day Schs, 1940–41; Asst Dir, Commn on Eng. Lang. Studies, Harvard Univ., 1941–43; Lt-Comdr, USNR, 1943–46; Assoc. Prof. Teachers Coll., Columbia Univ., 1947–50, Prof. of Comparative Education, 1950–55; Dir of Trng, Arabian Amer. Oil Co., Saudi Arabia, 1955–60. Hon. Lectr, Teachers Coll., Columbia Univ., 1955–57; Internat. Consultant, 1960–64; Sen. Advisor, Univ. of Petroleum and Minerals, Dhahran, 1964. Vis. Prof. and Lectr, English, American and foreign Univs; special assignments in connection with education, in Japan, South America, Iran, Arabia; Jt Editor, Year Book of Education (London), 1952–57. Vice-Pres. and Treasurer, Coll. of Petroleum and Minerals Foundn, 1977–. Deleg. to numerous internat. educnl congresses. Holder of hon. degrees. *Publications:* Federal Control of Education in ABC Republics, 1942; The Teaching of English, 1942; Report of Latin-American Workshop, 1941; A Basic English for South America, 1943; Ingles Basico Para Brasil, 1943; Education for a New Japan, 1949; Kokutai no Hongi (with J. O. Gauntlett), 1949; Shūshin: The Ethics of a Defeated Nation, 1949; Educación en Crisis, 1950; Problemas de Educação Rural, 1950; Report of a Study of YMCA World Services Policy and Practices, 1962; A Strategy for the Inner City, 1963. Articles in English and foreign educnl jls; numerous monographs and consulting reports. *Recreation:* travel. *Club:* Explorers' (New York).

HALL, Prof. the Rev. Stuart George; Professor of Ecclesiastical History, King's College, University of London, since 1978; *b* 7 June 1928; *s* of George Edward Hall and May Catherine Hall; *m* 1953, Brenda Mary Henderson; two *s* two *d*. *Educ:* University Coll. Sch., Hampstead; New Coll., and Ripon Hall, Oxford (BA 1952, MA 1955, BD 1973). National Service, Army, 1947–48. Deacon 1954, priest 1955; Asst Curate, Newark-on-Trent Parish Church, 1954–58; Tutor, Queen's Coll., Birmingham, 1958–62; Lectr in Theology, Univ. of Nottingham, 1962–73, Sen. Lectr, 1973–78. Editor for early church material, Theologische Realenzyklopädie. *Publications:* Melito of Sardis On Pascha and fragments: (ed) texts and translations, 1979; contrib. to Heythrop Jl, Jl of Eccles. History, Jl of Theol Studies, Religious Studies, Studia Evangelica, Studia Patristica, Theology and Theologische Realenzyklopädie. *Recreations:* gardening, choral music. *Address:* 15 High Street, Elie, Leven, Fife KY9 1BY. *T:* Elie 330216.

HALL, Prof. Stuart McPhail; Professor of Sociology, The Open University, since 1979; *b* 3 Feb. 1932; *s* of Herman and Jessie Hall; *m* 1964, Catherine Mary Barrett; one *s* one *d*. *Educ:* Jamaica Coll.; Merton Coll., Oxford (MA; Rhodes Scholar, 1951). Editor, New Left Review, 1957–61; Lectr, Film and Mass Media Studies, Chelsea Coll., London Univ., 1961–64; Centre for Cultural Studies, Univ. of Birmingham: Res. Fellow, 1964–68; Actg Dir, 1968–72; Dir, 1972–79. *Publications:* The Popular Arts, 1964; Resistance Through Rituals, 1974; Policing The Crisis, 1978; Culture, Media, Language, 1980. *Address:* 5 Mowbray Road, Kilburn, NW6.

HALL, Thomas William; Under-Secretary, Department of Transport, 1976–79 and since 1981; *b* 8 April 1931; *s* of Thomas William and Euphemia Jane Hall; *m* 1961, Anne Rosemary Hellier Davis; two *d*. *Educ:* Hitchin Grammar Sch.; St John's Coll., Oxford (MA). Asst Principal, Min. of Supply, 1954; Principal: War Office, Min. of Public Building and Works, Cabinet Office, 1958–68; Asst Sec., Min. of Public Building and Works, later DoE, 1968–76; Under Sec., Depts of Environment and Transport, 1979–81. *Recreations:* music, literature, gardening, walking. *Address:* Department of Transport, 2 Marsham Street, SW1. *T:* 01–212 3164.

HALL, Dr Trevor Henry, JP; MA; PhD; FSA; FRICS; writer, historian, lecturer; *b* 28 May 1910; *o s* of H. Roxby Hall, Wakefield; received grant of arms, 1974; *m* 1st, 1937, Dorothy (*d* 1973), *d* of late A. H. Keningley, Nostell; one *s* one *d*; 2nd, 1977, Marguerite, widow of Dr R. L. McMorris, Selby; one step *s* one step *d*. *Educ:* Wakefield Sch.; Trinity Coll., Cambridge (Perrott Student; MA); London Coll. of Estate Management (first place in final prof. exams, 1932). FSA 1978. Served War of 1939–45, Army. Sen. Partner, with Richard Gamble Walker, V. Stanley Walker & Son, chartered surveyors, Leeds, Wakefield, Rothwell and Woodlesford, 1945–82; Pres., Huddersfield & Bradford (now Yorkshire) Building Soc., 1972–74; Chm., Legal & General Assce Soc. (North Regional and Scottish Bds), 1978–80. Cecil Oldman Meml Lectr in bibliography and textual criticism, Univ. of Leeds, 1972–73. One of 300 invited Founder Life Mems, Cambridge Soc., 1977; Mem., Oxford Univ. Soc. of Bibliophiles, 1981 (Lectr, 1980, 1983). Chm., Leeds Cttee, Nat. Trust, 1968–70. Pres., Leeds Library (founded 1768), 1969–85. JP City of Leeds, 1959. *Publications:* The Testament of R. W. Hull, 1945; (with E. J. Dingwall and K. M. Goldney) The Haunting of Borley Rectory: A Critical Survey of the Evidence, 1956; A Bibliography of Books on Conjuring in English from 1580 to 1850, 1957; (with E. J. Dingwall) Four Modern Ghosts, 1958; The Spiritualists: The Story of William Crookes and Florence Cook, 1962; The Strange Case of Edmund Gurney, 1964; The Mystery of the Leeds Library, 1965; New Light on Old Ghosts, 1965; (with J. L. Campbell) Strange Things, 1968; Sherlock Holmes: Ten Literary Studies, 1969; Mathematical Recreations, 1633: An Exercise in 17th Century Bibliography, 1970; The Late Mr Sherlock Holmes, 1971; Old Conjuring Books: a bibliographical and historical study, 1972; The Card Magic of Edward G. Brown, 1973; The Early Years of the Huddersfield Building Society, 1974; A New Era, 1974; The Winder Sale of Old Conjuring Books, 1975; (with Percy H. Muir) Some Printers and Publishers of Conjuring Books and Other Ephemera, 1800–1850, 1976; The Leeds Library, 1977; Sherlock Holmes and his Creator, 1978; Search for Harry Price, 1978; The Strange Story of Ada Goodrich Freer, 1979; Dorothy L. Sayers: Nine Literary Studies, 1980; Twelve Friends, 1981; The Leeds Library: a checklist of publications relating to its history from 1768 to 1977, 1983; Daniel Home: a Victorian Enigma, 1984. *Recreations:* walking, gardening, book collecting, writing. *Address:* The Lodge, Selby, N Yorks YO8 0PW. *T:* Selby 703372. *Club:* Leeds (Leeds).

HALL, Vernon F., CVO 1960; Anæsthetist, King's College Hospital, 1931–69, retired; *b* 25 Aug. 1904; *s* of Cecil S. and M. M. Hall; *m* 1935, C. Marcia Cavell; one *s* two *d*. *Educ:* Haberdashers' Sch.; King's Coll. Hosp., London. MRCS, LRCP, 1927; DA, 1938; FFARCS, 1948. Served War of 1939–45 in Army (Emergency Commission), 1942–46; Consultant Anæsthetist, India Command (Local Brig.), 1945; Dean, King's Coll. Hosp. Medical Sch., 1951–65. FKC 1958; Hon. FFARCS 1975. *Publications:* History of King's College Hospital Dental School, 1973; A Scrapbook of Snowdonia, 1982; chapters on

Anaesthesia in Rose & Carless, Surgery, etc. *Recreations:* riding, walking, reading and music. *Address:* Deercombe, Brendon, N Devon. *T:* Brendon 281.

HALL, (Wallace) John; Assistant Secretary, Overseas Trade, Department of Trade and Industry, since 1985; *b* 5 Oct. 1934; *s* of Claude Corbett Hall and Dulcie Hall (*née* Brinkworth); *m* 1962, Janet Bowen; three *d. Educ:* Crypt Sch., Gloucester; Hertford Grammar Sch.; Downing Coll., Cambridge (MA Classics). National Service, RAF, 1953–55. Pirelli-General Cable Works Ltd, 1958–62; Sales Manager, D. Meredew Ltd, 1962–67; Principal, Min. of Technology, 1967–70; Dept of Trade and Industry, Civil Aviation Policy, 1970–72; Consul (Commercial), São Paulo, Brazil, 1972–76; Asst Secretary, Dept of Trade, Shipping Policy, 1976–79; Counsellor (Economic), Brasilia, 1979–81; Consul-Gen., São Paulo, 1981–83; Asst Sec., Internat. Trade Policy, DTI, 1983–85. *Recreations:* bridge, tennis and other sports, daughters. *Address:* 27 Wilbury Road, Letchworth, Herts.

HALL, William, DFC 1944, FRICS; Member of the Lands Tribunal for Scotland, since 1971, and for England and Wales, since 1979; *b* 25 July 1919; *s* of Archibald and Helen Hall; *m* 1945, Margaret Semple (*née* Gibson); one *s* three *d. Educ:* Paisley Grammar Sch. FRICS 1948. Served War, RAF (pilot) 1939–45 (despatches, 1944). Sen. Partner, R. & W. Hall, Chartered Surveyors, 1949–79. Chm., Scottish Br., RICS, 1971; Member: Valuation Adv. Council, 1970–80; Erskine Hosp. Exec., 1976–. Hon. Sheriff, Paisley, 1974–. *Recreation:* golf. *Address:* Windyridge, Brediland Road, Paisley, Renfrewshire PA2 9HF. *T:* Brediland 3614. *Club:* Royal Air Force.

HALL, Prof. William Bateman, FEng 1986; Professor of Nuclear Engineering, University of Manchester, 1959–86, now Emeritus; *b* 28 May 1923; *s* of Sidney Bateman Hall and Doris Hall; *m* 1950, Helen Mary Dennis; four *d. Educ:* Urmston Grammar Sch.; College of Technology, Manchester. Engineering apprenticeship, 1939–44; Royal Aircraft Establishment, 1944–46; United Kingdom Atomic Energy Authority (formerly Dept of Atomic Energy, Min. of Supply), 1946–59: Technical Engineer, 1946–52; Principal Scientific Officer, 1952–56; Senior Principal Scientific Officer, 1956–58; Dep. Chief Scientific Officer, 1958. Mem., Adv. Cttee on Safety of Nuclear Installations, 1972–83. Pro-Vice-Chancellor, Univ. of Manchester, 1979–82. *Publications:* Reactor Heat Transfer, 1958; papers to scientific and professional institutions. *Recreations:* music, fell walking. *Address:* High Raise, Eskdale, Holmrook, Cumbria CA19 1UA. *T:* Eskdale 275.

HALL, Brig. Sir William (Henry), KBE 1979 (CBE 1962); Kt 1968; DSO 1942; ED; Comptroller of Stores, State Electricity Commission of Victoria, 1956–70; Colonel Commandant, RAA Southern Command, since 1967; *b* 5 Jan. 1906; *s* of William Henry Hall, Edinburgh, Scotland; *m* 1930, Irene Mary, *d* of William Hayes; one *s* four *d. Educ:* Morgan Acad., Dundee; Melbourne Univ. Joined Staff of State Electricity Commn of Vic, 1924. Enlisted AIF, 1939: Capt. Royal Aust. Artillery, Palestine, Egypt; Syria, Papua, New Guinea, 1941 (Major); Aust. Dir of Armaments at AHQ, 1942 (Lt-Col); Dir of Armament at AHQ, 1945 (Col); CRA 3 Div. Artillery CMF, 1955–59 (Brig.). Director: Royal Humane Society of Vic.; Multiple Sclerosis Soc.; Chairman: War Widows and Widowed Mothers' Trust; RSL War Veterans' Trust; State Pres. Victorian Br., RSL, 1964–74 (now Chm. Trustees); Nat. Pres., Aust. RSL, 1974–78; Aust. Councillor, World Veterans' Foundn; Patron: Aust.-Free China Economic Assoc.; Royal Artillery Assoc. (Vic.); Carry On, Vic.; Trustee, Victorian Overseas Foundn. Associate Fellow, Aust. Inst. Management; Mem., Inst. of Purchasing and Supply (London). *Recreation:* golf. *Address:* Rosemont, 112 Kooyong Road, Caulfield, Vic. 3162, Australia; Montrose, Flinders, Victoria 3929. *Clubs:* Naval and Military (Melbourne); Melbourne Cricket, Peninsula Country Golf, Flinders Golf.

HALL, Willis; writer; *b* 6 April 1929; *s* of Walter and Gladys Hall; *m* 1973, Valerie Shute; one *s* (and three *s* by previous marriages). *Educ:* Cockburn High Sch., Leeds. TV plays include: The Villa Maroc; They Don't all Open Men's Boutiques; Song at Twilight; The Road to 1984; TV series: The Fuzz, 1977; The Danedyke Mystery, 1979; Stan's Last Game, 1983; The Bright Side, 1985; The Return of the Antelope, 1986; (with Keith Waterhouse): The Upper Crusts, 1973; Billy Liar, 1974; Worzel Gummidge, 1979 (adapted as stage musical, 1981). *Publications:* (with Michael Parkinson) The A-Z of Soccer, 1970; Football Report, 1973; Football Classified, 1974; My Sporting Life, Football Final, 1975; *children's books:* The Royal Astrologer, 1960; The Gentle Knight, 1967; The Incredible Kidnapping, 1975; The Summer of the Dinosaur, 1977; The Last Vampire, 1982; The Inflatable Shop, 1984; The Return of the Antelope, 1985; *plays:* The Long and the Short and the Tall, 1959; A Glimpse of the Sea, 1969; Kidnapped at Christmas, 1975; Walk on, Walk on, 1975; Stag Night, 1976; Christmas Crackers, 1976; A Right Christmas Caper, 1977; (with Keith Waterhouse): Billy Liar, 1960; Celebration, 1961; All Things Bright and Beautiful, 1962; England Our England, 1962; Squat Betty and The Sponge Room, 1963; Say Who You Are, 1965; Whoops-a-Daisy, 1968; Children's Day, 1969; Who's Who, 1972; Saturday, Sunday, Monday (adaptation from de Filippo), 1973; Filumena (adaptation from de Filippo), 1977; *musicals:* (with Keith Waterhouse) The Card, 1973; (with Denis King): Treasure Island, 1985; The Wind in the Willows (adaptation from A. A. Milne), 1985. *Address:* c/o London Management, 235–241 Regent Street, W1A 2JT. *Clubs:* Garrick, Savage, Lansdowne.

HALL-MATTHEWS, Rt. Rev. Anthony Francis; *see* Carpentaria, Bishop of.

HALL-THOMPSON, Major (Robert) Lloyd, ERD; TD; JP; *b* 9 April 1920; *s* of Lt-Col Rt Hon. S. H. Hall-Thompson, PC (NI), DL, JP, MP; *m* 1948, Alison F. Leitch, MSR; one *s* one *d. Educ:* Campbell Coll. Prep. Sch.; Campbell Coll. Royal School. Major, Royal Artillery, 1939–46; TA, 1946–56. Joined Unionist Party, 1938; Vice-Pres., Clifton Unionist Assoc. (Chm. 1954–57); MP (U) Clifton, 1969–73; Mem (U), N Belfast, NI Assembly, 1973–75 (Leader of the House, 1973–74); Chief Whip, NI Executive, 1973–74; Mem. (UPNI) for N Belfast, NI Constitutional Convention, 1975–76. Director of several companies. Formerly Mem. NI Hosps Authority (Past Vice-Chm. Finance and Gen. Purposes Cttee); Past Vice-Chm., Samaritan Hosp. Management Cttee; Life Governor, Samaritan Hosp.; Pres. and Trustee, North Belfast Working Men's Club; Trustee and Hon. Sec., Belfast Newsboys' Club and W. S. Armour Girls' Club; Vice-Pres., Cliftonville Football and Athletic Club; Founder, Trustee & Pres., Duncairn Friendship Assoc.; Life Mem., (Past Hon. Sec. and Hon. Treas.), Not Forgotten Assoc.; Life Mem., Royal Ulster Agric. Soc.; Freeman and Steward, Down Royal Corp. of Horse Breeders; Chm., Irish Draught Horse Soc.; Hon. Sec., Half-Bred Horse Breeders' Soc.; Mem. Cttee, NI Nurses Housing Assoc. *Recreations:* horse riding, hunting, racing, eventing, show jumping, horse breeding; golf, reading. *Address:* Maymount, Ballylesson, Belfast BT8 8JY, Northern Ireland. *T:* Drumbo 327. *Club:* Ulster (Belfast).

HALLADAY, Eric, MA; Master, Grey College, University of Durham, since 1980; *b* 9 July 1930; *s* of Rev. A. R. Halladay and Helena Renton; *m* 1956, Margaret Baister; one *s* two *d. Educ:* Durham Sch.; St John's Coll., Cambridge (MA History Tripos Pts I and II, Cl. II Div. I); Ripon Hall, Oxford. National Service, commnd 5th Regt, RHA, 1948–50. Exeter Sch., 1954–60, Sen. History Master, 1956–60; Sen. Lectr in History, RMA, Sandhurst, 1960–64; Sen. Tutor, Grey Coll., Univ. of Durham, and part-time Lectr in History, 1964–80; Vice-Master, Grey Coll., 1967–80. Chm., Northumbrian Univs

Military Educn Cttee, 1981–; Mem. Exec. Cttee, Council of Military Educn Cttees of Univs of UK, 1982–. Mem., TA&VRA, N of England, 1980–; Sec., Durham Br., SSAFA, 1977–. Chm., Durham Regatta, 1982–. *Publications:* The Building of Modern Africa (with D. D. Rooney), 1966, 2nd edn 1968; The Emergent Continent: Africa in the Nineteenth Century, 1972. *Recreations:* gardening, rowing. *Address:* The Master's House, Hollingside Lane, Durham. *T:* Durham 40049; Haven Cottage, Over Norton, Chipping Norton, Oxon. *T:* Chipping Norton 2995. *Club:* Leander (Henley-on-Thames).

HALLAM, Bishop of, (RC), since 1980; **Rt. Rev. Gerald Moverley,** JCD; *b* 9 April 1922; *s* of William Joseph Moverley and Irene Mary Moverley (*née* Dewhirst). *Educ:* St Bede's Grammar Sch., Bradford; Ushaw Coll., Durham; Angelicum Univ., Rome. Priest, 1946; Sec. to Bishop Poskitt, Leeds, 1946–51; Angelicum Univ., 1951–54; Chancellor, Dio. Leeds, 1958–68; Domestic Prelate to HH Pope Paul VI, 1965; apptd Bishop, Dec. 1967; Titular Bishop of Tinisa in Proconsulari and Bishop Auxiliary of Leeds, 1968–80; translated to new diocese of Hallam, established May 1980. *Address:* Quarters, Carsick Hill Way, Sheffield S10 3LT. *T:* Sheffield 309101.

HALLAM HIPWELL, H.; *see* Vivenot, Baroness Raoul de.

HALLCHURCH, David Thomas, TD 1965; barrister-at-law; a Recorder of the Crown Court, since 1980; *b* 4 April 1929; *s* of Walter William Hallchurch and Marjorie Pretoria Mary Hallchurch (*née* Cooper); *m* 1st, 1954, Gillian Mary Jagger (marr. diss. 1972); three *s*; 2nd, 1972, Susan Kathryn Mavor Brennan; one step *s* one step *d. Educ:* Bromsgrove Sch.; Trinity Coll., Oxford (MA Hons). Called to the Bar, Gray's Inn, 1953; Whitehead Travelling Scholarship, Canada and USA, 1953–54; practised as barrister-at-law on Midland and Oxford Circuit, 1954–60 and 1964–. Major, Staffs Yeomanry (Queen's Own Royal Regiment), TA, 1953–66. Legal Mem., Mental Health Review Tribunal for the West Midlands, 1979–. *Recreations:* cricket, drawing (cartoons). *Address:* Neachley House, Tong, near Shifnal, Shropshire TF11 8PH. *T:* Albrighton 3542. *Clubs:* Vincent's (Oxford); Greenflies Cricket (Brewood, Staffs).

HALLETT, Cecil Walter; retired as General Secretary, Amalgamated Engineering Union, 1957–64; *b* 10 Dec. 1899; *m* 1923, Edith Nellie Hallett (*née* Smith); two *s* two *d. Educ:* New City Road Elementary Sch., London. Messenger, Commercial Cable Co., 1913–15; apprentice fitter and turner, Gas Light and Coke Co., Becton, N Woolwich, 1916–18. HM Forces, 10th London Regt, 1918–19; journeyman fitter and turner, various firms, 1923–48; Asst Gen. Sec. AEU, 1948–57. Former Editor, AEU Monthly Jl and The Way. *Address:* 317 High Street South, Carterton, North Island, New Zealand. *T:* Carterton 8565.

HALLETT, Prof. George Edward Maurice, MDS; Child Dental Health Professor, University of Newcastle upon Tyne (formerly King's College, University of Durham), 1951–77, now Emeritus; Dean, Sutherland Dental School, 1960–77, and Hospital, 1970–77; retired; *b* 30 July 1912; *s* of Edward Henry and Berthe Hallett; *m* 1936, Annetta Eva Grant Napier; three *d. Educ:* Birkenhead Institute; Liverpool Univ. (LDS, Gilmour Medal and other prizes). HDD RCSE 1939; FDS RCS 1948; MDS Durham, 1952; DOrth RCS, 1954; FDS RCSE 1960; FFD RCSI 1964. House Surgeon, Liverpool Dental Hosp., 1934–35; School Dental Officer, Doncaster CB, 1935–36, Notts, 1936–40; served War, 1940–46: Army Dental Corps, Major, despatches. University of Durham: Lecturer in Children's Dentistry, 1946, Reader, 1948; Lectr in Orthodontics, 1946. Examiner in Dental subjects, Universities of Dundee, Durham, Edinburgh and Glasgow; RCS of Eng., 1954–77; Consultant, United Teaching Hosps, Newcastle upon Tyne; Head of Dept of Child Dental Health, Dental Hosp., Newcastle upon Tyne, 1948. Mem. Dental Council, RCSE; Past President: Société Française d'Orthopedie Dento-Faciale; European Orthodontic Soc. (also former Editor; Hon. Life Mem.); North of England Odontological Soc.; Brit. Soc. for the study of Orthodontics (Hon. Life Mem.); Newcastle Medico-Legal Soc.; former Mem., Newcastle RHB; former Mem., Newcastle AHA (T). Hon. Life Mem., British Dental Assoc. Past Pres., British Med. Pilots' Assoc. Hon. FDSRCPS Glas 1979. Silver Medal, Ville de Paris, 1980. *Publications:* contribs to scientific and dental jls. *Recreations:* dilettantism in the glyptic arts, flying. *Address:* 63 Runnymede Road, Darras Hall, Ponteland, Newcastle upon Tyne NE20 9HJ. *T:* Ponteland 22646. *Club:* Newcastle Aero.

HALLETT, Victor George Henry; Social Security (formerly National Insurance) Commissioner, since 1976; *b* 11 Feb. 1921; *s* of Dr Denys Bouhier Imbert Hallett; *m* 1947, Margaret Hamlyn. *Educ:* Westminster; Queen's Coll., Oxford (MA). Served War, 1939–45 (despatches 1946). Called to Bar, Inner Temple, 1949. Mem., Land Registration Rules Cttee, 1971–76; Conveyancing Counsel of the Court, 1971–76. *Publications:* Key and Elphinstone's Conveyancing Precedents (ed jtly), 15th edn, 1952; Prideaux's Precedents in Conveyancing (ed jtly), 25th edn, 1953; Hallett's Conveyancing Precedents, 1965; (with Nicholas Warren) Settlements, Wills and Capital Transfer Tax, 1979. *Address:* Office of the Social Security Commissioners, 6 Grosvenor Gardens, SW1W 0DH.

HALLEY, Laurence; *see* O'Keeffe, P. L.

HALLGARTEN, Anthony Bernard Richard, QC 1978; *b* 16 June 1937; *s* of Fritz and late Friedel Hallgarten; *m* 1962, Katherine Borchard; one *s* three *d. Educ:* Merchant Taylors' Sch., Northwood; Downing Coll., Cambridge (BA). Called to the Bar, Middle Temple, 1961; Barstow Scholar, Inns of Court, 1961. *Recreations:* cricket, canals, cycling. *Address:* 3 Essex Court, Temple, EC4Y 9AL. *T:* 01–583 9294. *Clubs:* Garrick, MCC.

HALLIBURTON, Rev. Canon Robert John; Priest in Charge, All Souls, St Margaret's-on-Thames, since 1982; *b* 23 March 1935; *s* of Robert Halliburton and Katherine Margery Halliburton (*née* Robinson); *m* 1968, Jennifer Ormsby Turner; one *s* three *d* (and one *s* decd). *Educ:* Tonbridge Sch.; Selwyn Coll., Cambridge (MA), Keble Coll., Oxford (DPhil); St Stephen's House, Oxford. Curate, St Dunstan and All Saints, Stepney, 1961; Tutor, St Stephen's House, Oxford, 1967; Vice-Principal, St Stephen's House, 1971; Lectr, Lincoln Coll., Oxford, 1973; Principal of Chichester Theol Coll., 1975–82, Canon and Prebend of Chichester Cathedral, 1976–82, Canon Emeritus, 1982–. Lecturer: Southwark Ordination Course, 1984–; Missionary Inst., Mill Hill, 1984–. Select Preacher, Oxford Univ., 1976–77. Consultant, Anglican-Roman Catholic Internat. Commn, 1971–81; Mem., Doctrinal Commn of C of E, 1978–86. Examining Chaplain to Bishop of Kensington, 1983–. *Publications:* contribs to: The Eucharist Today, ed. R. C. D. Jasper, 1974; The Study of Liturgy, ed C. P. M. Jones, 1978; Believing in the Church: report of C of E Doctrinal Commission, 1982; The Authority of a Bishop, 1986; (contrib.) We Believe in God: report of C of E Doctrinal Commission, 1986; articles in Studia Patristica, La Revue des Etudes Augustiniennes, Faith and Unity. *Recreations:* music, gardening. *Address:* 30 Ailsa Road, St Margaret's-on-Thames, Twickenham, Middlesex TW1 1QW. *Club:* Athenæum.

HALLIDAY, Sir George Clifton, Kt 1967; Consultant Otolaryngologist, Royal Prince Alfred Hospital and Prince Henry Hospital (Consultant Surgeon, since 1960); *b* 22 April 1901; *s* of late Edward James Halliday, NSW; *m* 1927, Hester Judith Macansh; two *s* one *d. Educ:* The King's Sch., Parramatta; St Paul's Coll., Univ. of Sydney. MB, ChM Sydney Univ., 1925; FRCSE 1934; FRACS 1954. Surg., St George Hosp., 1935; Surg., Royal

Prince Alfred Hosp., 1936; Lectr in Otolaryngology, Sydney Univ., 1948–61. Served in AAMC, Middle East, 1940–43 (Lt-Col). Patron, Australian Assoc. for Better Hearing. Hon. Mem., RSM, 1970; Corresp. Fellow, Amer. Laryngological Assoc., 1970; Hon. Fellow, Aust. Med. Assoc., 1971. Hon. Fellow, Sydney Univ., 1985. *Recreations:* tennis, cricket, golf. *Address:* 67 Cranbrook Road, Rose Bay, NSW 2029, Australia. *T:* FM 2280. *Clubs:* Union, Royal Sydney Golf (Sydney).

HALLIDAY, Ian Francis, FCA; Finance Director, Lowndes Lambert Group Ltd, since 1981; *b* 16 Nov. 1927; *s* of Michael and Jean Halliday; *m* 1952, Mary Busfield; one *s* two *d. Educ:* Wintringham Grammar Sch., Grimsby; Lincoln Coll., Oxford (MA Mathematics). Armitage & Norton, Chartered Accountants, 1951–69; qual. as Chartered Accountant, 1954; Partner, 1957; Finance Dir, Allied Textile Co. Ltd, 1970–74; on secondment as Dep. Director of Industrial Development Unit, Dept of Industry, 1974–77; Finance Dir, Leslie & Godwin (Holdings) Ltd, internat. insce and re-insce Lloyd's Brokers, 1977–80; Chief Exec., NEB, 1980. Mem., PLA, 1984–. *Recreation:* gardening. *Address:* 40 Finthorpe Lane, Huddersfield HD5 8TU.

HALLIDAY, John Frederick; Assistant Under Secretary of State, Home Office, since 1983; *b* 19 Sept. 1942; *s* of E. Halliday; *m* 1970, Alison Burgess; four *s. Educ:* Whitgift School, Croydon; St John's College, Cambridge (MA). Teacher, under VSO, Aitchison College, Lahore, 1964–66; Home Office, 1966; Principal Private Sec. to Home Sec., 1980. *Recreations:* music, squash, theatre.

HALLIDAY, Prof. Michael Alexander Kirkwood; Professor of Linguistics in the University of Sydney, since 1976; *b* 13 April 1925; *s* of late Wilfrid J. Halliday and of Winifred Halliday (*née* Kirkwood). *Educ:* Rugby School; University of London. BA London; MA, PhD, Cambridge. Served Army, 1944–47. Asst Lectr in Chinese, Cambridge Univ., 1954–58; Lectr in General Linguistics, Edinburgh Univ., 1958–60; Reader in General Linguistics, Edinburgh Univ., 1960–63; Dir, Communication Res. Centre, UCL, 1963–65; Linguistic Soc. of America Prof., Indiana Univ., 1964; Prof. of General Linguistics, UCL, 1965–71; Fellow, Center for Advanced Study in the Behavioral Sciences, Stanford, Calif., 1972–73; Prof. of Linguistics, Univ. of Illinois, 1973–74; Prof. of Language and Linguistics, Essex Univ., 1974–75. Visiting Professor of Linguistics: Yale, 1967; Brown, 1971; Nairobi, 1972. FAHA 1979. Dr *hc* Nancy. *Publications:* The Language of the Chinese 'Secret History of the Mongols', 1959; (with A. McIntosh and P. Strevens) The Linguistic Sciences and Language Teaching, 1964; (with A. McIntosh) Patterns of Language, 1966; Intonation and Grammar in British English, 1967; A Course in Spoken English: Intonation, 1970; Explorations in the Functions of Language, 1973; Learning How To Mean, 1975; (with R. Hasan) Cohesion in English, 1976; System and Function in Language, ed G. Kress, 1976; Language as Social Semiotic, 1978; An Introduction to Functional Grammar, 1985; Spoken and Written Language, 1985; articles in Jl of Linguistics, Word, Trans of Philological Soc., etc. *Address:* Department of Linguistics, University of Sydney, NSW 2006, Australia.

HALLIDAY, Norman Pryde; Senior Principal Medical Officer (Under Secretary), Department of Health and Social Security, since 1977; *b* 28 March 1932; *s* of late James and Jessie Thomson Hunter Halliday; *m* 1953, Eleanor Smith; three *s* one *d. Educ:* Woodside, Glasgow; King's Coll., London; King's Coll. Hosp. Med. Sch. SRN 1955; MB, BS, MRCS, LRCP 1964; DCH RCPGlas 1969. Various posts in clinical medicine, incl. Registrar (Paediatrics), KCH, London; SMO, DHSS, 1972. *Publications:* articles on medical subjects in professional journals. *Recreations:* photography, sub aqua diving, fashion, DIY, cross-bow shooting. *Address:* 12 Regalfield Close, Guildford, Surrey GU2 6YG. *T:* Worplesdon 233577.

HALLIDAY, Vice-Adm. Sir Roy (William), KBE 1980; DSC 1944; Director General of Intelligence, Ministry of Defence, 1981–84; *b* 27 June 1923; *m* 1945, Dorothy Joan Meech. *Educ:* William Ellis Sch.; University College Sch. Joined Royal Navy, 1941; served in Fleet Air Arm (fighter pilot) in World War II, in HMS Chaser, HMSs Victorious and Illustrious; test pilot, Boscombe Down, 1947–48; Comdg Officer 813 Sqdn (Wyverns, HMS Eagle), 1954; Army Staff Coll., Camberley; Comdr, 1958; Exec. Officer Coastal Forces Base (HMS Diligence), 1959; Sen. Officer 104th Minesweeping Sqdn, Far East Flt, in comd (HMS Houghton), 1961–62; Naval Asst to Chief of Naval Information, 1962–64; comdr (Air) HMS Albion, 1964–66; Captain, 1966; Dep. Dir Naval Air Warfare, 1966–70; HMS Euryalus in comd and as Captain D3 Far East Fleet and D6 Western Fleet, 1970–71; Commodore, 1971; Cdre Amphibious Warfare, 1971–73; Cdre Intelligence, Defence Intelligence Staff, 1973–75; Comdr British Navy Staff, Washington, Naval Attaché, and UK Nat. Liaison Rep. to SACLANT, 1975–78; Dep. Chief of Defence Staff (Intelligence), 1978–81. ADC to the Queen, 1975. *Recreations:* gardening, walking. *Address:* c/o Barclays Bank, Lyndhurst, Hants. *Club:* Naval.

HALLIFAX, Adm. Sir David (John), KCB 1983; KBE 1982; Commandant, Royal College of Defence Studies, since 1986; *b* 3 Sept. 1927; *s* of Ronald H. C. Hallifax and Joanne M. Hallifax; *m* 1962, Anne Blakiston Houston; two *s* one *d. Educ:* Winchester. Joined RN 1945; minesweeping, Gulf of Salonika, 1949–51; CO MTB 5008, 1953; Long TAS Course, 1954; HMS Salerno, Suez, 1956; Staff Coll., Camberley, 1959; CO HMS Agincourt, 1964–65; RCDS 1972; CO HMS Fife, 1973–75; Flag Officer, First Flotilla, 1978–80; Chief of Staff to C-in-C Fleet, 1980–82; Dep. Supreme Allied Comdr, Atlantic, 1982–84. *Recreations:* sailing, conchology. *Clubs:* Pratt's, Farmers', Royal Yacht Squadron.

HALLINAN, Sir (Adrian) Lincoln, Kt 1971; DL; Barrister-at-law; Stipendiary Magistrate, South Glamorgan (Cardiff), since 1976; a Recorder of the Crown Court, 1972–82; *b* 13 Nov. 1922; *e s* of late Sir Charles Hallinan, CBE and late Theresa Doris Hallinan, JP (*née* Holman); *m* 1955, Mary Parry Evans, *qv*; two *s* two *d. Educ:* Downside. Lieut, Rifle Bde, 1942–47; TA, 1950–52 (Captain). Called to Bar, Lincoln's Inn, 1950; Wales and Chester Circuit. A Legal Mem., Mental Health Review Tribunal for Wales, 1966–76; Chm., Med. Appeals Tribunal, 1970–76. Cardiff CC, 1949–74 (serving on several educational and cultural cttees); Alderman, 1961–74; Lord Mayor of Cardiff, 1969–70. Contested (C), Aberdare, 1946, Cardiff West, 1951, 1959. Chm., Cardiff Educn Cttee, 1961–63 and 1965–70; Chm., Governing Body, Cardiff Coll. of Art, and Cardiff Coll. of Music and Drama, 1961–73; First Chm., Nat. Court of Governors, Welsh Coll. of Music and Drama, 1970; Chairman: Commemorative Collectors Soc.; S Wales Gp, Victorian Soc.; Founder and Chm., Cardiff 2000–Cardiff Civic Trust, 1964–73, 1st Pres. 1973; Chm., Cardiff-Nantes Fellowship, 1961–68. Chevalier, Ordre des Palmes Académiques, 1965; Chevalier de la Légion d'Honneur, 1973. OStJ 1969. DL Glamorgan, 1969. *Recreations:* music, the arts.

HALLINAN, Sir Lincoln; *see* Hallinan, Sir A. L.

HALLINAN, Mary Alethea, (Lady Hallinan); *see* Parry Evans, M.A.

HALLIWELL, Brian; Value Added Tax Consultant, Peat, Marwick, Mitchell & Co., since 1985; *b* 17 Dec. 1930; *s* of late Norman and Emma Halliwell; *m* 1957, Agnes Lee. *Educ:* Preston Grammar Sch. DMS 1968. Joined HM Customs and Excise as Clerical Officer, 1947; Principal, 1969; Asst Sec., 1973; Dep. Accountant General, 1976; Accountant and Comptroller Gen., 1980–85. FBIM. *Recreations:* chess, reading, sport. *Address:* 3 Knollcroft, Ulster Avenue, Shoeburyness, Southend-on-Sea SS3 9JY. *T:* Shoeburyness 7570.

HALLIWELL, Leslie; Programme Buyer: ITV since 1968; Granada Television, since 1960; Channel Four, since 1981; *b* 23 Feb. 1929; *s* of James and Lily Halliwell; *m* 1958, Ruth (*née* Turner); one *s* (and one step *s* one step *d*). *Educ:* Bolton Sch.; St Catharine's Coll., Cambridge (MA). Journalist, Picturegoer, 1952; Prog. Manager, specialised cinemas in Cambridge, 1953–55; Exec. Trainee, 1956, Administrator of Publicity Div., 1957, Rank Org.; Prog. Buyer, Southern Television, 1958; Film Researcher, Granada Television, 1959. TV: devised and presented: Home Front, (series), 1982; What the Censor Saw, 1983; Looks Familiar, 1984; The British at War (series), 1984; Americans at War, 1985; Yesterday's Britain, 1985. Author of plays professionally performed (Harrogate, Bristol, Blackpool, Bolton, Hastings, Leeds etc): Make your own Bed, 1957; A Night on the Island, 1960. *Publications:* The Filmgoer's Companion, 1965 (8th edn 1984); The Filmgoer's Book of Quotes, 1973 (2nd edn 1978); (with Graham Murray) The Clapperboard Book of the Cinema, 1975; Halliwell's Movie Quiz, 1977; Halliwell's Film Guide, 1977, 5th edn 1985; Mountain of Dreams, 1977; Halliwell's Teleguide, 1979, revd edn (with Philip Purser) as Halliwell's Television Companion, 1982; Halliwell's Hundred, 1982; The Ghost of Sherlock Holmes (short stories), 1983; Seats in All Parts (autobiog.), 1985; Halliwell's Harvest, 1986; The Dead that Walk, 1986; Return to Shangri-La (novel), 1986; A Demon Close Behind (short stories), 1987; Double Take and Fade Away, 1987; contrib. Spectator, New Statesman, TLS, Sight and Sound, Photoplay, Variety, Television Radio Age, Television Today. *Recreations:* country driving, travel, chess, collecting, walking. *Address:* Clovelly, 26 Atwood Avenue, Richmond, Surrey.

HALLOWES, Odette Marie Celine, GC 1946; MBE 1945; Légion d'Honneur, 1950; Vice-President, Women's Transport Services (FANY); Member Royal Society of St George; housewife; *b* 28 April 1912; *d* of Gaston Brailly, Croix-de-Guerre, Médaille Militaire; *m* 1931, Roy Sansom (decd); three *d*; *m* 1947, late Captain Peter Churchill, DSO; *m* 1956, Geoffrey Macleod Hallowes. *Educ:* The Convent of Ste Therèse, Amiens (France) and privately. Entered Special Forces and landed in France, 1942; worked as British agent until capture by Gestapo, 1943; sentenced to death June 1943; endured imprisonment and torture until 28 April 1945, when left Ravensbrück Concentration Camp (MBE, GC). Member: Military Medallists League (Vice-Pres.); Cttee, Victoria Cross and George Cross Assoc. Pres., 282 (East Ham) Air Cadet Sqdn. Founder Vice-Pres., Women of the Year Luncheon. *Recreations:* reading, travelling, cooking, trying to learn patience. *Address:* Rosedale, Eriswell Road, Burwood Park, Walton-on-Thames, Surrey. *Clubs:* Naval and Military, FANY, Special Forces.

HALLOWS, Ralph Ingham, CMG 1973; MBE 1947; retired from Bank of England, 1973; *b* 4 May 1913; *s* of Ralph Watson Hallows, MA Cantab, TD, and Muriel Milnes-Smith; *m* 1939, Anne Lorna Bond; one *s* one *d. Educ:* Berkhamsted Sch. Indian Police Service, 1932; Indian Political Service, 1937; India Office/Commonwealth Relations Office, 1947; Kuwait Oil Co., 1948; Bank of England, 1954. Specialist Advr to Select Cttee on Overseas Develt, 1974. *Recreations:* golf, fishing, sailing. *Address:* Apple Tree Cottage, Thursley Road, Elstead, Surrey. *T:* Elstead 702284.

HALLSWORTH, Prof. Ernest Gordon, DSc, FRSC, FTS; Science Policy Research Unit, University of Sussex, since 1979; *b* 1913; *s* of Ernest and Beatrice Hallsworth, Ashton-under-Lyne, Lancs; *m* 1st, 1943, Elaine Gertrude Seddon (*d* 1970), *d* of R. C. Weatherill, Waverley, NSW; two *s* one *d* and one step *s*; 2nd, 1976, Merrily Ramly; one step *d. Educ:* Ashton Grammar Sch., Ashton-under-Lyne, Lancs; Univ. of Leeds. University of Leeds: First Cl. Hons in Agric. Chem., Sir Swire Smith Fellow, 1936; Asst Lectr in Agric. Chem., 1936; PhD 1939; DSc 1964. Lectr in Agric. Chem., Univ. of Sydney, 1940–51; Prof. of Soil Science, Univ. of West Australia, 1960–61; Prof. of Agric. Chem. and Head Dept Agric. Sci., Univ. Nottingham, 1951–64 (Dean, Faculty of Agric. and Hort., 1951–60); Chief of Div. of Soils, CSIRO, 1964–73; Chm., Land Resources Labs, CSIRO, 1973–78. Pres. Lecturers' Assoc., Sydney Univ., 1946–49. Treas., Aust. Assoc. of Scientific Workers, 1943; Member: Science Advisory Panel, Australian Broadcasting Commn, 1949–51; Pasture Improvement Cttee, Australian Dairy Produce Bd (NSW), 1948–51; Chm. Insecticides and Fungicides Cttee, Australian Standards Inst., 1949–51. President: Internat. Soc. of Soil Science, 1964–68; Sect. 13, Aust. and NZ Assoc. for the Advancement of Science, 1976. Mem. Council, Flinders Univ., 1967–79; Chief Scientific Liaison Officer (Aust.), London, 1971. Fellow, Aust. Acad. of Technol Scis, 1976. Mem., Académie d'Agriculture de France, 1983–. Prescott Medal, Aust. Soc. Soil Science, 1984. *Publications:* (Ed) Nutrition of the Legumes, 1958; (ed with D. V. Crawford) Experimental Pedology, 1964; (with others) Handbook of Australian Soils, 1968; (with others) Principles of a Balanced Land Use Policy for Australia, 1976; Where Shall We Build Our New Cities?, 1978; Land and Water Resources of Australia, 1979; Socio-economic Restraints in Tropical Forest Management, 1982; The Anatomy, Physiology and Psychology of Erosion, 1986; contributions to: Aust. Jl Science, Jl Soc. Chem. Indust., Empire Jl Experimental Agric., Jl Agric. Science, Aust. Medical Jl, Jl Soil Science. *Recreations:* talking, pedology. *Address:* 30 Fowlers Road, Glen Osmond, SA 5064, Australia. *T:* 08–338 1094; 1 Bellevue Cottages, Blackboys, near Uckfield, Sussex. *T:* Framfield 606. *Club:* Farmers'.

HALLWARD, Bertrand Leslie, MA; *b* 24 May 1901; *er s* of late N. L. Hallward, Indian Educational Service, and Evelyn A. Gurdon; *m* 1926, Catherine Margaret, 2nd *d* of late Canon A. J. Tait, DD; four *d. Educ:* Haileybury Coll. (Scholar); King's Coll., Cambridge (Scholar). Fellow of Peterhouse, 1923–39. Hon. Fellow 1956. Headmaster of Clifton Coll., 1939–48; Vice-Chancellor, Nottingham Univ., 1948–65. Hon. LLD: Sheffield, 1964; Nottingham, 1965. *Publications:* Chapters II, III, IV, and part of VII (the Second and Third Punic Wars) in Cambridge Ancient History, Vol. VIII, 1930; Editor of the Classical Quarterly, 1935–39. *Address:* Flat 4, Gretton Court, Girton, Cambridge. *T:* Cambridge 277327.

See also W. O. Chadwick, G. C. H. Spafford.

HALNAN, Patrick John; His Honour Judge Halnan; a Circuit Judge, since 1986; *b* 7 March 1925; *s* of E. T. and A. B. Halnan; *m* 1955, Judith Mary (*née* Humberstone); four *c. Educ:* Perse Sch., Cambridge; Trinity Coll., Cambridge (MA). Army, 1943–47. Solicitor. Asst Solicitor, Hants CC, 1954–58; Clerk to the Justices, Cambs, 1958–78; Metropolitan Stipendiary Magistrate, 1978–86; a Recorder, 1983–86; SE Circuit. Sec., Justices' Clerks' Soc., 1972–76, Pres., 1978. Chm., Road Traffic Cttee, Magistrates' Assoc., 1981–. *Publications:* (ed with Prof. R. M. Jackson) Leo Page, Justice of the Peace, 3rd edn 1967; (ed) Wilkinson's Road Traffic Offences, 12th edn, 1985 (also ed 7th, 8th, 9th, 10th, 11th edns); (with David Latham) Drink/Driving Offences, 1979; Road Traffic, 1981; Drink/Drive: the new law, 1984. *Recreations:* village bridge, stamp collecting. *Address:* Snaresbrook Crown Court, The Court House, Hollybush Hill, Snaresbrook, E11 1QW.

HALPERN, Prof. Jack, FRS 1974; Louis Block Distinguished Service Professor of Chemistry, University of Chicago, since 1984; *b* Poland, 19 Jan. 1925 (moved to Canada, 1929; USA 1962); *s* of Philip Halpern and Anna Sass; *m* 1949, Helen Peritz; two *d. Educ:* McGill Univ., Montreal. BSc 1946, PhD 1949. NRC Postdoc. Fellow, Univ. of

Manchester, 1949–50; Prof. of Chem., Univ. of Brit. Columbia, 1950–62 (Nuffield Foundn Travelling Fellow, Cambridge Univ., 1959–60); Prof. of Chem., Univ. of Chicago, 1962–71, Louis Block Prof., 1971–84. Visiting Prof.: Univ. of Minnesota, 1962; Harvard Univ., 1966–67; California Inst. of Techn., 1969; Princeton Univ., 1970–71; Copenhagen Univ., 1978; Firth Vis. Prof., Sheffield, 1982; Sherman Fairchild Dist. Scholar, California Inst. of Technology, 1979; Guest Scholar, Kyoto Univ., 1981; External Sci. Mem., Max Planck Institut für Kohlenforschung, Mulheim, 1983; Lectureships: 3M, Univ. of Minnesota, 1968; FMC, Princeton Univ., 1969; Du Pont, Univ. of Calif., Berkeley, 1970; Frontier of Chemistry, Case Western Reserve Univ., 1971; Venable, Univ. of N Carolina, 1973; Ritter Meml, Miami Univ., 1980; University, Univ. of Western Ontario, 1981; F. J. Toole, Univ. of New Brunswick, 1981; Werner, Univ. of Kansas, 1982; Lansdowne, Univ. of Victoria, 1982; Welch, Univ. of Texas, 1983; Kilpatrick, Illinois Inst. of Tech., 1984; Dow, Univ. of Ottawa, 1985; Boomer, Univ. of Alberta, 1985; Bailar, Univ. of Illinois, 1986. Associate Editor: Jl of Amer. Chem. Soc.; Inorganica Chimica Acta; Mem. Editorial Bds: Accounts of Chemical Research; Jl of Catalysis; Catalysis Reviews; Jl of Coordination Chem.; Inorganic Syntheses; Jl of Molecular Catalysis; Jl of Organometallic Chemistry; Amer. Chem. Soc. Advances in Chemistry series; Gazzetta Chimica Italiana; Organometallics; Co-editor, OUP International Series of Monographs in Chemistry. Member: Nat. Sci. Foundn Chemistry Adv. Panel, 1967–70; MIT Chemistry Vis. Cttee, 1968–70; Argonne Nat. Lab. Chemistry Vis. Cttee, 1970–73; Amer. Chem. Soc. Petroleum Res. Fund Adv. Bd, 1972–74; NIH Medicinal Chem. Study Sect., 1975–78 (Chm., 1976–78); Princeton Univ. Chem. Adv. Council, 1982–; Encyclopaedia Britannica Univ. Adv. Cttee, 1985–. Mem., Bd of Trustees and Council, Gordon Research Confs, 1968–70; Chm., Gordon Conf. on Inorganic Chem., 1969; Chm., Amer. Chemical Soc. Div. of Inorganic Chem., 1971; Mem. Bd of Dirs, Renaissance Soc., 1984–. Fellow, Amer. Acad. of Arts and Sciences, 1967; Sci. Mem., Max Planck Soc., 1983; For. Mem., Nat. Acad. of Scis, 1984–85, Mem., 1985–. Hon. DSc Univ. of British Columbia, 1986. Holds several honours and awards, including: Amer. Chem. Soc. Award in Inorganic Chem., 1968; Chem. Soc. Award, 1976; Humboldt Award, 1977; Kokes Award, Johns Hopkins Univ., 1978; Amer. Chem. Soc. Award for Distinguished Service in the Advancement of Inorganic Chemistry, 1985; Willard Gibbs Medal, 1986. *Publications:* Editor (with F. Basolo and J. Bunnett) Collected Accounts of Transition Metal Chemistry, vol. I, 1973, vol. II, 1977; contrib. articles on Catalysis and on Coordination Compounds to Encyclopaedia Britannica; numerous articles to Jl of Amer. Chemical Soc. and other scientific jls. *Recreations:* art, music. *Address:* Department of Chemistry, University of Chicago, 5735 South Ellis Avenue, Chicago, Illinois 60637, USA. *T:* (312) 962–7095. *Clubs:* Quadrangle (Chicago); Chemists (New York).

HALPIN, Most Rev. Charles A.; *see* Regina, Archbishop of, (RC).

HALPIN, Miss Kathleen Mary, CBE 1953 (OBE 1941); Chief Administrator, Regions, WRVS (formerly WVS), 1945–73; *b* 19 Nov. 1903; unmarried. *Educ:* Sydenham High Sch. (GPDST). Organising Sec., Women's Gas Council, 1935, and represented Gas Industry at International Management Congress, Washington, USA, 1936, Sweden, 1947. Appointed Chief of Metropolitan Dept, WVS, 1939; lent to Min. of Health and went to Washington as UK representative on Standing Technical Cttee on Welfare, UNRRA; Comr, Trainer, and Camp Adviser, Girl Guides Assoc., 1924–48; Comdt, BRCS, 1937–39; Mem. Council London Hostels Assoc., 1941–; Chm. Women's Gas Fedn, 1945–49, Pres., 1949–60. A Governor of St Bartholomew's Hospital, 1948–74. Chm., Soroptomist (London) Housing Assoc., 1963–; President Fedn of Soroptomist Clubs of Gt Britain and Ireland, 1959–60; Vice-Pres., Fawcett Soc., 1978– (Chm., 1967–71); Trustee, Women's Service Trust, 1964–. OStJ. *Recreations:* motoring, reading, theatre. *Address:* 7 Chagford House, Chagford Street, NW1 6EG. *T:* 01–262 6226.

HALSBURY, 3rd Earl of, *cr* 1898; **John Anthony Hardinge Giffard,** FRS 1969; FEng 1976; Baron Halsbury, 1885; Viscount Tiverton, 1898; Chancellor of Brunel University, since 1966; *b* 4 June 1908; *o s* of 2nd Earl and Esmé Stewart (*d* 1973), *d* of late James Stewart Wallace; *S* father, 1943; *m* 1st, 1930, Ismay Catherine, *er d* of late Lord Ninian Crichton-Stuart and Hon. Mrs Archibald Maule Ramsay; one *s*; 2nd, 1936, Elizabeth Adeline Faith (*d* 1983), *o d* of late Major Harry Crewe Godley, DSO, Northamptonshire Regt and of late Mrs Godley, of Claremont Lodge, Cheltenham; two *d*. *Educ:* Eton. BSc (1st Cl. Hons Chem. and Maths) London (External), 1935; FRIC 1947, Hon. FRSC 1983; FInstP 1946; CEng, FIProdE 1956, Hon. FIProdE 1979. Employed by Lever Bros, 1935–42; Brown-Firth Res. Labs, 1942–47; Dir of Res., Decca Record Co., 1947–49; Man. Dir, Nat. Research Development Corporation, 1949–59; Consultant and Director: Joseph Lucas Industries, 1959–74; Distillers Co. Ltd, 1959–78; Head-Wrightson Ltd, 1959–78. External Examiner, OECD, on mission to Japan, 1965. Chairman: Science Museum Advisory Council, 1951–65; Cttee on Decimal Currency, 1961–63; Cttee of Management, Inst. of Cancer Research, Royal Marsden Hosp., 1962–77; Review Body on Doctors' and Dentists' Pay, 1971–74; Deptl Cttee of Enquiry into pay of Nurses, Midwives, Speech Therapists and Professions Supplementary to Medicine, 1974–75; Meteorological Cttee, 1970–82; President: Institution of Production Engineers, 1957–59; Instn of Nuclear Engineers, 1963–65; Nat. Inst. of Industrial Psychol., 1963–75; Machine Tool Industry Res. Assoc., 1964–77; Coll. of Speech Therapists, 1983–; Nat. Council for Christian Standards in Society, 1986–; Member: Adv. Council to Cttee of Privy Council for Scientific and Industrial Research, 1949–54; SRC, 1965–69; Computer Bd for Univs and Research Councils, 1966–69; Decimal Currency Bd, 1966–71; Nationalised Transport Advisory Council, 1963–67; Standing Commn on Museums and Galleries, 1960–76; MRC, 1973–77; Cttee of Managers, Royal Institution, 1976–79. A Governor: BBC, 1960–62; LSE, 1959–; UMIST, 1966– (formerly Mem. Council, Manchester Coll. of Sci. and Technol., 1956–65). Hon. FICE 1975; Hon. ARCVS, 1984. Hon. DTech Brunel Univ., 1966; Hon. DUniv Essex, 1968. *Heir: s* Adam Edward Giffard, *qv*. *Address:* 4 Campden House, 29 Sheffield Terrace, W8. *T:* 01–727 3125.

HALSEY, Prof. Albert Henry; Professor of Social and Administrative Studies, University of Oxford, since 1978; Professorial Fellow of Nuffield College, Oxford, since 1962; *b* 13 April 1923; *m* 1949, Gertrude Margaret Littler; three *s* two *d*. *Educ:* Kettering Grammar Sch.; London Sch. of Econs. BSc (Econ), PhD London, MA Oxon. RAF, 1942–47; student LSE, 1947–52; Research Worker, Liverpool Univ., 1952–54; Lectr in Sociology, Birmingham Univ., 1954–62; Dir, Dept of Social and Admin. Studies, Oxford Univ., 1962–78. Fellow, Center for Advanced Study of Behavioral Sciences, Palo Alto, Calif, 1956–57; Vis. Prof. of Sociology, Univ. of Chicago, 1959–60. Adviser to Sec. of State for Educn, 1965–68; Chm. of CERI at OECD, Paris, 1968–70. Reith Lectr, 1977. Foreign Associate, Amer. Acad. of Educn. *Publications:* (jtly) Social Class and Educational Opportunity, 1956; (jtly) Technical Change and Industrial Relations, 1956; (with J. E. Floud) The Sociology of Education, Current Sociology VII, 1958; (jtly) Education, Economy and Society, 1961; Ability and Educational Opportunity, 1962; (with G. N. Ostergaard) Power in Co-operatives, 1965; (with Ivor Crewe) Social Survey of the Civil Service, 1969; (with Martin Trow) The British Academics, 1971; (ed) Trends in British Society since 1900, 1972; (ed) Educational Priority, 1972; Traditions of Social Policy, 1976; Heredity and Environment, 1977; Change in British Society, 1978, 3rd edn 1986; (jtly) Origins and Destinations, 1980; numerous articles and reviews. *Address:* 28 Upland Park Road, Oxford. *T:* Oxford 58625.

HALSEY, Rt. Rev. Henry David; *see* Carlisle, Bishop of.

HALSEY, Rev. John Walter Brooke, 4th Bt *cr* 1920 (but uses designation Brother John Halsey); *b* 26 Dec. 1933; *s* of Sir Thomas Edgar Halsey, 3rd Bt, DSO, and of Jean Margaret Palmer, *d* of late Bertram Willes Dayrell Brooke; *S* father, 1970. *Educ:* Eton; Magdalene College, Cambridge (BA 1957). Deacon, 1961, priest, 1962, Diocese of York; Curate of Stocksbridge, 1961–65; Brother in Community of the Transfiguration, 1965–. *Heir: cousin* Patrick Johnston Halsey, *b* 17 Feb. 1905. *Address:* Community of the Transfiguration, 23 Manse Road, Roslin, Midlothian.

HALSEY, Philip Hugh, CB 1986; LVO 1972; Deputy Secretary, Department of Education and Science, since 1982; *b* 9 May 1928; *s* of Sidney Robert Halsey and Edith Mary Halsey; *m* 1956, Hilda Mary Biggerstaff; two *s*. *Educ:* University Coll. London (BSc). Headmaster, Hampstead Sch., 1961; Principal, DES, 1966; Under-Sec., 1977.

HALSTEAD, Sir Ronald, Kt 1985; CBE 1976; Deputy Chairman, British Steel Corporation, since 1986; *b* 17 May 1927; *s* of Richard and Bessie Harrison Halstead; *m* 1968, Yvonne Cecile de Monchaux (*d* 1978); two *s*. *Educ:* Lancaster Royal Grammar Sch.; Queens' Coll., Cambridge (Hon. Fellow, 1986). MA, FRSC. Research Chemist, H. P. Bulmer & Co, 1948–53; Manufg Manager, Macleans Ltd, 1954–55; Factory Manager, Beecham Products Inc. (USA), 1955–60; Asst Managing Dir, Beecham Research Labs, 1960–62; Vice-Pres. (Marketing), Beecham Products Inc. (USA), 1962–64; Pres., Beecham Research Labs Inc. (USA), 1962–64; Chairman: Food and Drink Div., Beecham Group Ltd, 1964–67; Beecham Products, 1967–84; Man. Dir (Consumer Products) Beecham Gp, 1973–84; Chm. and Chief Exec., Beecham Gp, 1984–85. Dir, Otis Elevator Co. Ltd (UK), 1978–83; Non-Exec. Director: BSC, 1979–; The Burmah Oil PLC, 1983–; Amer. Cyanamid Co. (USA), 1986–; Davy Corp. plc, 1986–. Mem. Egg Re-organisation Commn, 1967–68; Pres., Incorp. Soc. of Brit. Advertisers, 1971–73; Chairman: British Nutrition Foundn, 1970–73; Knitting EDC (formerly Knitting Sector Working Party), NEDO, 1978–; Bd for Food Studies, Reading Univ., 1983–86; Vice-Chairman: Proprietary Assoc. of GB, 1968–77; Advertising Assoc., 1973–81; Food and Drink Industries Council, 1973–76; Member: Council and Exec. Cttee, Food Manufrs' Fedn Inc., 1966–85 (Pres., 1974–76); Council, British Nutrition Foundn, 1967–79; Cambridge Univ. Appts Bd, 1969–73; Council, CBI, 1970–86; Council, BIM, 1972–77; Council, Univ. of Buckingham (formerly University Coll. at Buckingham), 1973–; Council, Nat. Coll. of Food Technol., 1977–78 (Chm. Bd, 1978–83); Council, Univ. of Reading, 1978–; AFRC, 1978–84; Newspaper Panel, Monopolies and Mergers Commn, 1980–; Industrial Develt Adv. Bd, 1984– (Chm., 1985–). Dir and Hon. Treas., Centre for Policy Studies, 1984–. Trustee, Inst. of Economic Affairs, 1980–. Governor, Ashridge Management Coll., 1970– (Vice-Chm., 1977–); President: Nat. Advertising Benevolent Soc., 1978–80; Inst. of Packaging, 1981–82 (a Vice-Pres., 1979–81). Fellow, Marketing Soc., 1981; FBIM; FInstM; FIGD; FRSA; FRSC. Hon. Fellow, Inst. of Food Sci. and Technol., 1983–84. Hon. DSc Reading, 1982. *Recreations:* sailing, squash racquets, ski-ing. *Address:* 37 Edwardes Square, W8 6HH. *T:* 01–603 9010. *Clubs:* Hurlingham, Carlton, Lansdowne, Royal Thames Yacht.

HAM, David Kenneth R.; *see* Rowe-Ham.

HAM, Prof. James Milton, OC 1980; ScD; FIEEE; Professor of Science, Technology and Public Policy, University of Toronto, since 1983 (President, 1978–83); *b* 21 Sept. 1920; *s* of James Arthur Ham and Harriet Boomer Gandier; *m* Mary Caroline, *d* of Albert William Augustine; one *s* two *d*. *Educ:* Runnymede Coll. Inst., Toronto, 1936–39; Univ. of Toronto (BASc 1943); MIT (SM, ScD). Served with RCNVR as Elect. Lt, 1944–45. Lectr and Housemaster, Univ. of Toronto, 1945–46; Mass Inst. of Technology: Res. Associate, 1949–51; Res. Fellow in Electronics, 1950; Asst Prof. of Elect. Engrg, 1951–52; Univ. of Toronto: Associate Prof., 1952–59; Prof., 1959–; Fellow, New Coll., 1963; Head, Dept of Elect. Engrg, 1964–66; Dean, Fac. of Applied Science and Engrg, 1966–73; Chm., Research Bd, 1974–76; Dean, Sch. of Graduate Studies, 1976–78. Vis. Scientist, Cambridge Univ. and USSR, 1960–61. Dir, Shell Canada, 1981. Mem., Nat. Res. Council, 1969–74 (Chm., Associate Cttee on Automatic Control, 1959–65); Governor, Ont. Res. Foundn, 1971–86; Chairman: Cttee on Engrg Educn of World Fed. of Engrg Orgs, 1970; Res. and Technol. Review Bd, Noranda Inc., 1985; Industrial Disease Standards Panel, Ont., 1986. Member: Assoc. Prof. Engrs, Ont., 1943; Internat. Fed. Automatic Control (Exec. Council), 1966–72; Fellow, Engrg Inst. Canada. British Assoc. for Advancement of Science Medal, 1943; McNaughton Medal, IEEE, 1977; Centennial Medal, 1967, Engrg Medal, 1974, Gold Medal, 1984, Assoc. Professional Engrs, Ontario; Queens' Jubilee Medal, 1977; Engrg Alumni Medal, 1973; Sir John Kennedy Medal, Engrg Inst. Canada, 1983. Hon. DèsScA Montreal, 1973; Hon. DSc: Queen's, 1974; New Brunswick, 1979; McGill, 1979; McMaster, 1980; Hon. LLD: Manitoba, 1980; Hanyang (Korea), 1981; Hon. DEng: Tech. Univ. of Nova Scotia, 1980; Memorial Univ., 1981; Concordia Univ., 1983; Hon. DSacLet Wycliffe Coll., 1983. *Publications:* Scientific Basis of Electrical Engineering (with G. R. Slemon), 1961; Report of Royal Commission on Health and Safety of Workers in Mines; papers for scientific jls on automatic control. *Recreations:* sailing, skiing, photography. *Address:* 135 Glencairn Avenue, Toronto, Ontario M4R 1N1, Canada.

HAM, Rear-Adm. John Dudley Nelson, CB 1955; RN retired; *b* 7 Sept. 1902; *s* of Eng. Rear-Adm. John William Ham and Lily Florence Nelson; *m* 1927, Margery Lyne Sandercock; no *c*. *Educ:* Edinburgh House, Lee-on-Solent; RN Colleges, Osborne and Dartmouth. Junior Service, 1920–37; HMS Ramillies, HMS Ceres; staff of RN Engineering College; Destroyers; Commander, 1937; Engineer Officer, Yangtse, China, 1938–40; served War of 1939–45: Chief Engineer, HMS Danae, 1940–41; Asst Dir Combined Operations Material, 1942; Chief Engineer, HMS Indomitable, 1945; Capt., 1946; Fleet Engineer Officer, Home Fleet, 1949; Staff Air Engineer Officer, 1951; Rear-Admiral, 1953; Dir of Aircraft Maintenance and Repair, 1953–55; Flag Officer Reserve Aircraft, 1955–57, retired. *Recreations:* golf, cabinet-making. *Address:* Green Lane Cottage, Lee-on-Solent, Hants. *T:* Lee-on-Solent 550660.

HAMBIDGE, Most Rev. Douglas Walter; *see* New Westminster, Archbishop of.

HAMBLEDEN, 4th Viscount, *cr* 1891; **William Herbert Smith;** *b* 2 April 1930; *e s* of 3rd Viscount and Lady Patricia Herbert, DCVO 1953, *o d* of 15th Earl of Pembroke, MVO; *S* father 1948; *m* 1955, Donna Maria Carmela Attolico di Adelfia, *d* of late Count Bernardo Attolico and of Contessa Eleonora Attolico di Adelfia, Via Porta Latina, Rome; five *s*. *Educ:* Eton. *Heir: s* Hon. William Henry Bernard Smith [*b* 18 Nov. 1955; *m* 1983, Sarah Suzanne, *d* of Joseph F. Anlauf and Mrs Suzanne K. Anlauf]. *Address:* The Manor House, Hambleden, Henley-on-Thames, Oxon. *TA:* Hambleden. *T:* Hambleden 335.

See also Baron Margadale.

HAMBLEN, Derek Ivens Archibald, CB 1978; OBE 1956; *b* 28 Oct. 1917; *s* of Leonard Tom Hamblen and late Ruth Mary Hamblen, *d* of Sir William Frederick Alphonse Archibald; *m* 1950, Pauline Alison, *d* of late Gen. Sir William Morgan, GCB, DSO, MC; one *s* one *d*. *Educ:* St Lawrence Coll., Ramsgate; St John's Coll., Oxford (Casberd Exhibn); Portuguese Essay Prize, 1938; BA Hons (Mod. Langs) 1940, MA 1949. Served War,

1940–46: 1st Army, N Africa, 1942–43; Major, GS, AFHQ, N Africa and Italy, and Adv. Mission to British Mil. HQ, Greece, 1944–45; GSO1, Allied Commn for Austria, 1945–46; Lt-Col, 1946. War Office, later Ministry of Defence, 1946–77: seconded HQ British Troops, Egypt, 1946–47; Asst Sec., Office of UK High Commn in Australia, 1951–55; seconded Foreign Office, 1957–60; Asst Sec., 1964–68; a Special Advr to NATO and SHAPE, 1968–74; Under Sec., 1974–77, retired. Mem. Bd of Governors, St Lawrence Coll., 1977–. Medal of Merit, 1st cl. (Czechoslovakia), 1946. *Recreations:* cricket, hockey (represented Oxford v Cambridge, 1940), golf, music, reading. *Address:* c/o Lloyds Bank, East Grinstead, West Sussex. *Clubs:* MCC; Vincent's (Oxford).

HAMBLETON, Kenneth George; Director General, Air Weapons and Electronic Systems, Ministry of Defence, since 1986; *b* 15 Jan. 1937; *s* of George William Hambleton and Gertrude Nellie Hambleton (*née* Brighouse); *m* 1959, Glenys Patricia Smith; one *s* one *d. Educ:* Chesterfield Grammar Sch.; Queens' Coll., Cambridge (MA). CEng, FIEE. Services Electronics Res. Lab., Baldock, 1958–73; ASWE, Portsdown, 1973–81; a Dep. Dir, ASWE, 1981–82; Dir, Strategic Electronics-RADAR, MoD PE, 1982–85; Asst Chief Scientific Advr (Projects and Res.), MoD, 1985–86. *Publications:* numerous articles and letters in nat. and internat. physics and electronic jls. *Recreations:* chess, bridge, golf, music—especially jazz. *Address:* c/o Ministry of Defence, Prospect House, 100 New Oxford Street, WC1A 1HE. *Clubs:* does not admit to clubs (or diamonds)—prefers the major suits or no trumps.

HAMBLING, Sir (Herbert) Hugh, 3rd Bt, *cr* 1924; *b* 3 Aug. 1919; *s* of Sir (Herbert) Guy (Musgrave) Hambling, 2nd Bt; *S* father 1966; *m* 1950, Anne Page Oswald, Spokane, Washington, USA; one *s. Educ:* Wixenford Preparatory Sch.; Eton Coll. British Airways Ltd, 1937–39. RAF Training and Atlantic Ferry Command, 1939–46. British Overseas Airways: Montreal, 1948; Seattle, 1950; Manager, Sir Guy Hambling & Son, 1956; BOAC Representative, Douglas, Los Angeles, and Boeing Co., Seattle, 1957–75; Royal Brunei Airlines Rep., Boeing Co., Seattle, 1975. *Heir: s* (Herbert) Peter Hugh Hambling [*b* 6 Sept. 1953; *m* 1982, Jan Elizabeth Frederick, *d* of Stanton Willard Frederick, jr, and Mrs Frederick, Seattle, Washington]. *Address:* 1219 Evergreen Point Road, Bellevue, Washington 98004, USA. *T:* 206–454–0905 (USA); Rookery Park, Yoxford, Suffolk, England. *T:* Yoxford 310.

HAMBRO, Charles Eric Alexander; Chairman, Hambros PLC, since 1983; *b* 24 July 1930; *s* of late Sir Charles Hambro, KBE, MC, and Pamela Cobbold; *m* 1st, 1954, Rose Evelyn (marr. diss. 1976), *d* of Sir Richard Cotterell, 5th Bt, CBE; two *s* one *d*; 2nd, 1976, Cherry Felicity Twiss, *d* of Sir John Huggins, GCMG, MC. *Educ:* Eton. Served Coldstream Guards, 1949–51; joined Hambros Bank Ltd, 1952: Man. Dir, 1957; Dep. Chm., 1965; Chm., 1972–83; Dep. Chm., Guardian Royal Exchange Assurance, 1974. Chm., Royal National Pension Fund for Nurses, 1968. Trustee, British Museum, 1984–. *Recreations:* shooting, cricket, flying. *Address:* Dixton Manor, Gotherington, Cheltenham, Glos GL52 4RB. *T:* Bishops Cleeve 2011. *Clubs:* White's, MCC.

HAMBRO, Jocelyn Olaf, MC 1944; Chairman: Charter Consolidated, since 1982 (Director, since 1965); Waverton Property Co. Ltd; Wiltons (St James's) Ltd; *b* 7 March 1919; *s* of late Ronald Olaf Hambro and late Winifred Martin-Smith; *m* 1st, 1942, Ann Silvia (*d* 1972), *d* of R. H. Muir; three *s*; 2nd, 1976, Margaret Elisabeth (*d* 1983), *d* of late Frederick Bradshaw McConnel and *widow* of 9th Duke of Roxburghe. *Educ:* Eton; Trinity Coll., Cambridge. Coldstream Guards, 1939–45. Joined Hambros Bank Ltd, 1945; Man. Dir, 1947–72; Chm., 1965–72; Chm., Hambros Ltd, 1970–83, Pres. 1983–. Formerly Chairman: The Hambro Trust Ltd; Hambros Investment Trust Ltd; HIT Securities Ltd. Chm., Phœnix Assurance Co. Ltd, 1978–85 (Dir, 1952–). Member, Jockey Club. *Recreations:* racing, shooting. *Address:* 101 Eaton Place, SW1. *T:* 01–235 7210; Waverton House, Moreton in Marsh, Glos GL56 9PB. *T:* Blockley 700700. *Clubs:* Pratt's, White's.

See also R. N. Hambro.

HAMBRO, Rupert Nicholas; Chairman, Hambros Bank Ltd, since 1983; a Deputy Chairman, Hambros PLC, since 1985 (Director, since 1981); *b* 27 June 1943; *s* of Jocelyn Olaf Hambro, *qv*; *m* 1970, Mary Robinson Boyer; one *s* one *d. Educ:* Eton; Aix-en-Provence. Joined Hambros Bank, 1964, Director, 1969. Director: Anglo American Corporation of South Africa, 1981–; Diners Club Ltd, 1980–85; Racecourse Hldgs Trust Ltd, 1985–. Chairman, Assoc. of International Bond Dealers, 1979–82. *Recreations:* racing, shooting. *Address:* 42 Eaton Place, SW1. *T:* 01–235 5656; Chalk House, Chalkhouse Green, Kidmore End, Oxon. *T:* Kidmore End 723544.

HAMBURGER, Michael Peter Leopold, MA (Oxon); *b* Berlin, 22 March 1924; *e s* of late Prof. Richard Hamburger and Mrs L. Hamburger (*née* Hamburg); *m* 1951, Anne Ellen File; one *s* two *d. Educ:* Westminster Sch.; Christ Church, Oxford. Army Service, 1943–47; Freelance Writer, 1948–52; Asst Lectr in German, UCL, 1952–55; Lectr, then Reader in German, Univ. of Reading, 1955–64. Florence Purington Lectr, Mount Holyoke Coll., Mass, 1966–67; Visiting Professor, State Univ. of NY: at Buffalo, 1969; at Stony Brook, 1971; Vis. Fellow, Center for Humanities, Wesleyan Univ., Conn, 1970; Vis. Prof. Univ. of S Carolina, 1973; Regent's Lectr, Univ. of California, San Diego, 1973; Vis. Prof., Boston Univ., 1975–77; part-time Prof., Univ. of Essex, 1978. Bollingen Foundn Fellow, 1959–61, 1965–66. FRSL 1972. Corresp. Mem., Deutsche Akademie für Sprache und Dichtung, Darmstadt, 1973; Akademie der Künste, Berlin; Akad. der Schönen Künste, Munich. Translation Prizes: Deutsche Akademie für Sprache und Dichtung, Darmstadt, 1964; Arts Council, 1969; Arts Prize, Inter Nationes, Bonn, 1976; Medal, Inst. of Linguists, 1977; Schlegel-Tieck Prize, London, 1978, 1981; Wilhelm-Heinse Prize (medallion), Mainz, 1978; Goethe Medal, 1986. *Publications: poetry:* Flowering Cactus, 1950; Poems 1950–1951, 1952; The Dual Site, 1958; Weather and Season, 1963; Feeding the Chickadees, 1968; Penguin Modern Poets (with A. Brownjohn and C. Tomlinson), 1969; Travelling, 1969; Travelling, I-V, 1973; Ownerless Earth, 1973; Travelling VI, 1975; Real Estate, 1977; Moralities, 1977; Variations, 1981; Collected Poems, 1984; *translations:* Poems of Hölderlin, 1943, rev. edn as Hölderlin: Poems, 1952; C. Baudelaire, Twenty Prose Poems, 1946, repr. 1968; L. van Beethoven, Letters, Journals and Conversations, 1951, repr. 1967, 1978; J. C. F. Hölderlin, Selected Verse, 1961, repr. 1986; G. Trakl, Decline, 1952; A. Goes, The Burnt Offering, 1956; (with others) H. von Hofmannsthal, Poems and Verse Plays, 1961; B. Brecht, Tales from the Calendar, 1961; (with C. Middleton) Modern German Poetry 1910–1960, 1962; (with others) H. von Hofmannsthal, Selected Plays and Libretti, 1964; G. Büchner, Lenz, 1966; H. M. Enzensberger, Poems, 1966; (with C. Middleton) G. Grass, Selected Poems, 1966; J. C. F. Hölderlin, Poems and Fragments, 1967, new enlarged edn 1980; (with J. Rothenberg and the author) H. M. Enzensberger, The Poems of Hans Magnus Enzensberger, 1968; H. M. Enzensberger, Poems For People Who Don't Read Poems, 1968; (with C. Middleton), G. Grass, The Poems of Günter Grass, 1969; P. Bichsel, And Really Frau Blum Would Very Much Like To Meet The Milkman, 1968; G. Eich, Journeys, 1968; N. Sachs, Selected Poems, 1968; Peter Bichsel, Stories for Children, 1971; Paul Celan, Selected Poems, 1972, new enlarged edn 1980; (ed) East German Poetry, 1972; Peter Huchel, Selected Poems, 1974; German Poetry 1910–1975, 1977; Helmut Heissenbüttel, Texts, 1977; Franco Fortini, Poems, 1978; An Unofficial Rilke, 1981; Peter Huchel, The Garden of Theophrastus, 1983; Goethe, Poems and Epigrams, 1983; *criticism:* Reason and Energy, 1957; From Prophecy to Exorcism, 1965; The Truth of Poetry, 1970, new edn 1982; Hugo von Hofmannsthal, 1973; Art as Second Nature, 1975; A Proliferation of Prophets, 1983; *autobiography:* A Mug's Game, 1973. *Recreations:* gardening, walking. *Address:* c/o Royal Bank of Scotland, Kirkland House, Whitehall, SW1.

See also P. B. Hamlyn.

HAMBURGER, Sir Sidney (Cyril), Kt 1981; CBE 1966; JP; DL; Chairman, North Western Regional Health Authority, 1973–82; *b* 14 July 1914; *s* of Isidore and Hedwig Hamburger; *m* 1940; three *s. Educ:* Salford Grammar Sch. Served in Army, 1940–46, Capt. Salford City Council: Mem., 1946–70; Alderman, 1961–70; Mayor of Salford, 1968–69. Chairman: NE Manchester Hosp. Management Cttee, 1970–74; NW ASH, 1977–; Age Concern, Salford, 1984–; Manchester Cttee for Soviet Jewry, 1984–; Gtr Manchester Area CAB, 1985–; Member: Manchester Regional Hosp. Bd, 1966–74 (Chm. Finance Cttee); Supplementary Benefits Commn, 1967–77; BBC NW Adv. Cttee, 1970–73. Pres. Council, Manchester-Salford Jews, 1962–65; Life-President: Manchester Jewish Homes for the Aged, 1965–; Zionist Central Council of Greater Manchester; Nat. Pres., Trades Advisory Council, 1984–. Governor, Ben Gurion Univ., Israel, 1979–. Hon. Fellow, Bar-Ilan Univ., Israel, 1979; Hon. MA Salford, 1979; Hon. LLD Manchester, 1983. Pro Ecclesia, Papal Award, 1982. JP Salford, 1957; DL Greater Manchester, 1981. *Recreation:* football. *Address:* 26 New Hall Road, Salford M7 0JU.

HAMEED, A. C. Shahul; Minister of Foreign Affairs, Sri Lanka, since 1977; *b* 10 April 1929. Mem., United National Party; Mem. for Harispattuwa, Nat. Parliament, 1960–; former Dep. Chm., Public Accounts Cttee; has been concerned with foreign affairs, public finance and higher education. Leader of delegns to internat. confs, incl. UN; Chm., Ministerial Conf. of Non-Aligned Countries; Mem., Conf. of UN Cttee on Disarmament. Governor, Univ. of Sri Lanka. *Publications:* In Pursuit of Peace: on non-alignment and regional cooperation, 1983; short stories and poems. *Address:* Ministry of Foreign Affairs, Republic Building, Colombo 1, Sri Lanka.

HAMER, John, MBE 1944; VMH 1975; Secretary, Royal Horticultural Society, 1962–75; *b* 14 June 1910; 2nd *s* of late John and Katherine Hamer; *m* 1st, 1940, Marjorie Agnes (*d* 1970), *e d* of late Major A. H. Martin, RE and E. Martin; one *s* one *d*; 2nd, 1980, Joan Edith MacKinlay (*née* Prior). *Educ:* University of Leeds (BA, DipEd). Commnd, The Loyal Regt, 1930. Educn Service, 1933–38. Attached S Lancs Regt, 1938–39; War Service, 1939–46 (despatches, MBE): The Loyal Regt, Hertfordshire Regt, Royal Tank Regt; SO2, 20 British Mil. Mission (Free French), DAQMG 36 Brick (18 DLI) Combined Ops, ME, Italy, NW Europe, 1943–45; Lieut-Col, Comd 36 Brick (18 DLI), AAQMG Lille Area, 1945; Food Controller, Price Controller, Controller of Supplies, Singapore, 1945. Joined Malayan Civil Service, 1946: District Officer, Jasin, Malacca, 1948, Klang, Selangor, 1952; British Adviser, Perlis, 1955; Deputy Chm., Rural Industrial Development Authority, Federation of Malaya, 1957; Ministry of Agriculture, 1958; State Sec., Penang, 1958–61. Joined Royal Horticultural Soc., 1961. *Recreation:* gardening. *Address:* Wildacres, Itchingfield, West Sussex RH13 7NZ. *T:* Slinfold 790467.

HAMER, Hon. Sir Rupert (James), KCMG 1982; ED; LLM (Melb.); Premier of Victoria, Australia, and Treasurer, 1972–81; *b* 29 July 1916; *s* of H. R. Hamer; *m* 1944, April F., *d* of N. R. Mackintosh; two *s* two *d. Educ:* Melbourne Grammar and Geelong Grammar Schs; Trinity Coll., Univ. of Melbourne (LLM). Solicitor, admitted 1940. Served War of 1939–45: 5½ years, AIF, Tobruk, Alamein, NG, Normandy. MLA (Lib.) E Yarra, 1958–71, Kew, Vic., 1971–81; Minister for: Immigration, 1962–64; Local Govt, 1964–71; Chief Sec. and Dep. Premier, Victoria, 1971–72; Minister for: the Arts, 1972–79; State Develt, Decentralization and Tourism, 1979–81. Chm., Vic. State Opera; Vice-Chm., Cttee of Management, Werribee Park; Pres., Vic. Coll. of the Arts; Mem., Melbourne Scots Council; Trustee, Yarra Bend Park. CO, Vic. Scottish Regt, CMF, 1954–58. Hon. LLD Univ. of Melbourne, 1982. *Recreations:* tennis, Australian Rules football, walking, music. *Address:* 39 Monomeath Avenue, Canterbury, Victoria 3126, Australia. *Club:* Naval and Military.

HAMES, Jack Hamawi, QC 1972; a Recorder of the Crown Court, since 1977; *b* 15 June 1920; *s* of Elie and Edmee Hamawi; *m* 1949, Beryl Julia Cooper; two *s. Educ:* English School, Cairo; Queens' Coll., Cambridge (MA, LLM). Called to Bar, Inner Temple, 1948, Bencher, 1979, Master of the Archives. Vice-Chm. of Governors, John Ruskin Sch., Croydon. *Publication:* contrib. to Solicitors' Jl. *Recreations:* squash, tennis, gardening, painting, music, poetry, history, literature. *Address:* 18 Castlemaine Avenue, South Croydon CR2 7HQ. *T:* 01–688 6326; 10 Old Square, Lincoln's Inn, WC2A 3SO. *T:* 01–405 0758. *Clubs:* Warlingham Sports (Chm.), Warlingham Squash (Vice-Chm.).

HAMILL, Sir Patrick, Kt 1984; QPM 1979; Chief Constable, Strathclyde Police, 1977–85; *b* 29 April 1930; *s* of Hugh Hamill and Elizabeth McGowan; *m* 1954, Nell Gillespie; four *s* one *d. Educ:* St Patrick's High Sch., Dumbarton. Joined Dunbartonshire Constabulary, 1950; transf. to City of Glasgow Police, 1972; apptd Assistant Chief Constable: Glasgow, 1974; Strathclyde Police, 1975; attended Royal Coll. of Defence Studies Course, 1976. Assoc. of Chief Police Officers (Scotland): Rep. to Interpol, 1977–81; Pres., 1982–83; Hon. Sec., 1983–85. Chm., Management Bd, St Margaret's Hospice, Clydebank; Member Board of Governors: Scottish Police Coll., 1977–85; St Aloysius' Coll., Glasgow, 1983– (Vice-Chm.); Mem., Gen. Convocation, Univ. of Strathclyde, 1984–. OStJ 1978. *Recreations:* walking, gardening, golf.

HAMILTON, family name of **Duke of Abercorn,** of **Lord Belhaven,** and of **Barons Hamilton of Dalzell** and **HolmPatrick.**

HAMILTON; *see* Baillie-Hamilton, family name of Earl of Haddington.

HAMILTON; *see* Cole-Hamilton.

HAMILTON; *see* Douglas-Hamilton.

HAMILTON, 15th Duke of, *cr* 1643, Scotland, **AND BRANDON,** 12th Duke of, *cr* 1711, Great Britain; **Angus Alan Douglas Douglas-Hamilton;** Premier Peer of Scotland; Hereditary Keeper of Palace of Holyroodhouse; *b* 13 Sept. 1938; *e s* of 14th Duke of Hamilton and Brandon, PC, KT, GCVO, AFC, and of Lady Elizabeth Percy, DL, *er d* of 8th Duke of Northumberland, KG; *S* father, 1973; *m* 1972, Sarah, *d* of Sir Walter Scott, Bt, *qv*; two *s* two *d. Educ:* Eton; Balliol Coll., Oxford (BAEngrg). Flt Lieut RAF; retired, 1967. Flying Instructor, 1965; Sen. Commercial Pilot's Licence, 1967; Test Pilot, Scottish Aviation, 1971–72. Mem. Council, CRC, 1978–. Mem., Queen's Body Guard for Scotland, 1975–. Hon. Mem., Royal Scottish Pipers Soc., 1977; Patron, British Airways Pipe Band, 1977–. Hon. Air Cdre, No 2 (City of Edinburgh) Maritime HQ Unit, RAuxAF, 1982–. KStJ 1975 (Prior, Order of St John in Scotland, 1975–82). *Heir: s* Marquess of Douglas and Clydesdale, *qv*. *Address:* 8 Eccleston Mews, SW1. *T:* 01–235 7213; Lennoxlove, Haddington, E Lothian. *Clubs:* Royal Air Force; New (Edinburgh).

See also Lord James Douglas-Hamilton.

HAMILTON, Marquess of; James Harold Charles Hamilton; *b* 19 Aug. 1969; *s* and *heir* of Duke of Abercorn, *qv*. A Page of Honour to the Queen, 1982–84.

HAMILTON OF DALZELL, 3rd Baron, *cr* 1886; **John d'Henin Hamilton,** KCVO 1981; MC 1945; JP; Lord Lieutenant of Surrey, 1973–86 (Vice-Lieutenant, 1957–73); President, National Association of Probation Officers, 1964–74; a Lord-in-Waiting to the Queen, 1968–81; *b* 1 May 1911; *s* of late Major Hon. Leslie d'Henin Hamilton, MVO, and Amy Cecile, *e d* of late Col Horace Ricardo, CVO; *S* uncle, 1952; *m* 1935, Rosemary Olive, *d* of late Major Hon. Sir John Coke, KCVO; two *s* one *d*. *Educ:* Eton; RMC, Sandhurst. Coldstream Guards, 1931–37 and 1939–45 (Major). Min. of Agriculture's Liaison Officer in South-East, 1960–64. Mem., Council on Tribunals, 1964–72; Chm., Lord Chancellor's Adv. Cttee on Legal Aid, 1972–79. Chairman: Surrey Agricultural Exec. Cttee, 1958–68; Surrey Council of Social Service, 1960–73; Guildford Bench, 1968–78; Guildford Cathedral Council, 1958–69. DL Surrey, 1957; JP Guildford, 1957. KStJ 1973. *Heir: s* Hon. James Leslie Hamilton [*b* 11 Feb. 1938; *m* 1967, Corinna, *yr d* of late Sir Pierson Dixon, GCMG, CB and of Lady Dixon; four *s*]. *Address:* Snowdenham House, Bramley, Guildford, Surrey GU5 0DB. *T:* Guildford 892002.
See also Hon. A. G. Hamilton.

HAMILTON, Adrian Walter, QC 1973; a Recorder of the Crown Court, since 1974; *b* 11 March 1923; *er s* of late W. G. M. Hamilton, banker, Fletching, Sussex and of late Mrs S. E. Hamilton; *m* 1966, Jill, *d* of S. R. Brimblecombe, Eastbourne; two *d*. *Educ:* Highgate Sch.; Balliol Coll., Oxford. BA 1st cl. Jurisprudence 1948, MA 1954. Served with RN, 1942–46: Ord. Seaman, 1942; Sub-Lt RNVR, 1943, Lieut 1946. Balliol Coll., 1946–48: Jenkyns Law Prize; Paton Mem. Student, 1948–49; Cassel Scholar, Lincoln's Inn, 1949; called to Bar, Lincoln's Inn, 1949 (Bencher 1979), Middle Temple and Inner Temple; Mem., Senate of Inns of Court and the Bar, 1976–82, Treas., 1979–82. Mem., Council of Legal Educn, 1977–. Inspector, Peek Foods Ltd, 1977. *Recreations:* family, golf, sailing, gardening. *Address:* 7 King's Bench Walk, Temple, EC4. *T:* 01–583 0404. *Clubs:* Garrick, Roehampton; Piltdown Golf.

HAMILTON, Adrianne Pauline U.; *see* Uziell-Hamilton.

HAMILTON, Rt. Rev. Alexander Kenneth, MA; *b* 11 May 1915; *s* of Cuthbert Arthur Hamilton and Agnes Maud Hamilton; unmarried. *Educ:* Malvern Coll.; Trinity Hall, Cambridge; Westcott House, Cambridge. MA 1941. Asst Curate of Birstall, Leicester, 1939–41; Asst Curate of Whitworth with Spennymoor, 1941–45. Chaplain, RNVR, 1945–47. Vicar of S Francis, Ashton Gate, Bristol, 1947–58; Vicar of S John the Baptist, Newcastle upon Tyne, 1958–65; Rural Dean of Central Newcastle, 1962–65; Bishop Suffragan of Jarrow, 1965–80. *Publication:* Personal Prayers, 1963. *Recreations:* golf, trout fishing. *Address:* 3 Ash Tree Road, Burnham-on-Sea, Somerset TA8 2LB. *Clubs:* Naval; Burnham and Berrow Golf.

HAMILTON, Alexander Macdonald, CBE 1979; Senior Partner, McGrigor, Donald & Moncrieffs, Solicitors, Glasgow, since 1977; *b* 11 May 1925; *s* of John Archibald Hamilton and Thomasina Macdonald or Hamilton; *m* 1953, Catherine Gray; two *s* one *d*. *Educ:* Hamilton Acad. (Dux, 1943); Glasgow Univ. (MA 1948, LLB 1951). Solicitor. Served War, RNVR, 1943–46. Dir, Royal Bank of Scotland, 1978–. Law Soc. of Scotland: Mem. Council, 1970–82; Vice-Pres., 1975–76; Pres., 1977–78. Pres., Glasgow Juridical Soc., 1955–56; Vice-Pres. and Chm., Greater Glasgow Scout Council, 1978–85; Session Clerk, Cambuslang Old Parish Church, 1969–; Vice-Chm., Cambuslang Community Council, 1978–. *Recreations:* golf, sailing, swimming. *Address:* 30 Wellshot Drive, Cambuslang, Glasgow G72 8BT. *T:* 041–641 1445. *Clubs:* Royal Scottish Automobile (Glasgow); Royal Northern & Clyde Yacht.

HAMILTON, Anthony Norris; *b* 19 July 1913; 3rd *s* of Capt. Claude Hamilton, RD, RNR, and Kathleen Sophia Hamilton (*née* Mack); *m* 1942, Jean Philippa, 3rd *d* of Rev. David Railton, MC; one *s* three *d*. *Educ:* Kelly Coll.; Exeter Coll., Oxford. Asst Master Clifton Coll., 1935–40. Served War of 1939–45: commnd 6 Bn Argyll and Sutherland Highlanders, 1940; Gen. Staff, V Corps HQ, 1942, X Corps HQ 1943, VIII Army HQ, 1944. Ops Editor of VIII Army History of Italian Campaign, 1945. House Master, Clifton Coll., 1946–48; Headmaster, Strathallan Sch., 1948–51; Headmaster, Queen Mary's Grammar Sch., Walsall, 1951–55; Headmaster, Hardye's Sch., Dorchester, 1955–74. *Recreation:* painting. *Address:* Primrose Cottage, Staunton-on-Wye, Hereford.

HAMILTON, Hon. Archibald Gavin; MP (C) Epsom and Ewell, since April 1978; Parliamentary Under-Secretary of State for Defence Procurement, Ministry of Defence, since 1986; *b* 30 Dec. 1941; *yr s* of Baron Hamilton of Dalzell, *qv*; *m* 1968, Anne Catharine Napier; three *d*. *Educ:* Eton Coll. Borough Councillor, Kensington and Chelsea, 1968–71. Contested (C) Dagenham, Feb. and Oct., 1974. PPS to Sec. of State for Energy, 1979–81, to Sec. of State for Transport, 1981–82; an Asst Govt Whip, 1982–84; a Lord Comr of HM Treasury (Govt Whip), 1984–86. *Address:* House of Commons, SW1A 0AA.

HAMILTON, Arthur Campbell; QC (Scot.) 1982; *b* 10 June 1942; *s* of James Whitehead Hamilton and Isobel Walker Hamilton (*née* McConnell); *m* 1970, Christine Ann Croll; one *d*. *Educ:* The High School of Glasgow; Glasgow Univ.; Worcester Coll., Oxford (BA); Edinburgh Univ. (LLB). Admitted member, Faculty of Advocates, 1968; Standing Junior Counsel: to Scottish Development Dept, 1975–78; to Board of Inland Revenue (Scotland), 1978–82; Advocate Depute, 1982–85. *Recreations:* hill walking, fishing. *Address:* 8 Heriot Row, Edinburgh. *T:* 031–556 4663. *Club:* New (Edinburgh).

HAMILTON, Sir Bruce S.; *see* Stirling-Hamilton.

HAMILTON, Sir (Charles) Denis, Kt 1976; DSO 1944; TD 1975; Editor-in-Chief, Times Newspapers Ltd, 1967–81 (Chief Executive, 1967–70, Chairman, 1971–80); Chairman, Reuters Ltd, 1979–85; Director, Standard Chartered Bank, since 1982; *b* 6 Dec. 1918; *er s* of Charles and Helena Hamilton; *m* 1939, Olive, author, *yr d* of Thomas Hedley Wanless and Mary Anne Wanless; four *s*. *Educ:* Middlesbrough High Sch. Editorial Staff: Evening Gazette, Middlesbrough, 1937–38; Evening Chronicle, Newcastle, 1938–39; Editorial Asst to Viscount Kemsley, 1946–50; Editorial Dir, Kemsley (now Thomson) Newspapers, 1950–67; Editor of the Sunday Times, 1961–67; Chm., Times Newspapers Hldgs, 1980–81. Director: Evening Gazette Ltd, 1960–82; Newcastle Chronicle and Journal Ltd, 1960–82; Internat. Thomson Orgn Plc (formerly Kemsley Newspapers, Thomson Newspapers, Thomson British Holdings), 1950–83. Chm., British Cttee, 1972–78, first Pres., 1978–83, Internat. Press Inst.; Pres., Commonwealth Press Union, 1981–83. Member: Council, Newspaper Publishers' Association, 1950–80; Press Council, 1959–81; National Council for the Training of Journalists (Chm., 1957); BOTB, 1976–79; British Library Bd, 1975–; IBA, 1981–84; Chm., British Museum Publications Ltd; Trustee: British Museum, 1969–; Henry Moore Foundn, 1980–; Visnews, 1981–85; Vice-Pres., Exec. Cttee, GB-China Centre, 1986– (Vice Chm., 1981–84; Chm., 1984–86); Governor, British Inst. Florence, 1974–. Joint Sponsor of exhibitions: Tutankhamun, BM, 1972; China, RA, 1973; 1776–US Bicentennial, Nat. Maritime Mus., 1976; Gold of Eldorado, RA, 1978; Vikings, BM, 1980. Served War of 1939–45, TA, Durham Light Infantry; Lt-Col comdg 11th Bn Durham LI and 7th Bn Duke of Wellington's Regt. Hon. DLitt: Southampton, 1975; City, 1977; Hon. DCL Newcastle upon Tyne 1979. Grande Officiale, Order of Merit (Italy), 1976. *Publications:* Jt Editor, Kemsley Manual of Journalism, 1952; Who is to own the British Press (Haldane Meml Lecture), 1976. *Recreation:* military history. *Address:* 78A Ashley Gardens, Thirleby Road, SW1P 1HG. *T:* 01–828 0410. *Clubs:* Garrick, Royal Automobile, Grillions.

HAMILTON, Cyril Robert Parke, CMG 1972; Director: Rank Organisation and subsidiary companies, 1963–77; A. Kershaw & Sons Ltd, 1966–77; Rank Xerox Ltd, 1967–77; *b* 4 Aug. 1903; *s* of Alfred Parke and Annie Hamilton; *m* 1st, 1929, Cecily May Stearn (*d* 1966); one *s* one *d*; 2nd, 1971, Betty Emily Brand. *Educ:* High Sch., Ilford; King's Coll., London Univ. Entered Bank of England, 1923, and retired as Deputy Chief Cashier, 1963, after career mainly concerned with internat. financial negotiations and Exchange Control. Vice-Chm., Standard and Chartered Banking Gp Ltd, 1969–74; Dep. Chm., Standard Bank, 1963–74; Director: Standard Bank of SA, 1963–74; Midland and International Banks, 1964–74; Banque Belge d'Afrique, 1969–74; Chairman: Malta International Banking Corp, 1969–74; Tozer Standard and Chartered Ltd, 1973–74. *Recreations:* golf, gardening. *Address:* Peat Moor, Harborough Hill, Pulborough, West Sussex RH20 2PR. *T:* West Chiltington 2171. *Clubs:* Brooks's, MCC.

HAMILTON, Sir Denis; *see* Hamilton, Sir C. D.

HAMILTON, Dundas; *see* Hamilton, J. D.

HAMILTON, Eben William; QC 1981; *b* 12 June 1937; *s* of Rev. John Edmund Hamilton, MC and Hon. Lilias Maclay; *m* 1st, 1973, Catherine Harvey (marr. diss. 1977); 2nd, 1985, Themy Rusi Bilimoria, *y d* of late Brig. Rusi Bilimoria. *Educ:* Winchester; Trinity Coll., Cambridge. Nat. Service: 4/7 Royal Dragoon Guards, 1955–57; Fife and Forfar Yeomanry/Scottish Horse, TA, 1958–66. Called to the Bar, Inner Temple, 1962, Bencher, 1985. *Address:* 1 New Square, Lincoln's Inn, WC2. *T:* 01–405 0884. *Club:* Garrick.
See also Martha Hamilton, P. J. S. Hamilton.

HAMILTON, Sir Edward (Sydney), 7th and 5th Bt, *cr* 1776 and 1819; *b* 14 April 1925; *s* of Sir (Thomas) Sydney (Percival) Hamilton, 6th and 4th Bt, and Bertha Muriel, *d* of James Russell King, Singleton Park, Kendal; *S* father, 1966. *Educ:* Canford Sch. Served Royal Engineers, 1943–47; 1st Royal Sussex Home Guard, 1953–56. *Recreations:* Spiritual matters, music. *Address:* The Cottage, East Lavant, near Chichester, West Sussex PO18 0AL. *T:* Chichester 527414.

HAMILTON, Francis Hugh; Sheriff of North Strathclyde, since 1984; *b* 3 Dec. 1927; *s* of late Hugh Hamilton and Mary Catherine (*née* Gallagher); *m* 1968, Angela Haffey; one *d*. *Educ:* Notre Dame Convent, Glasgow; St Aloysius' Coll., Glasgow; Univ. of Glasgow (BL 1948). Nat. Service, 1948–50; commnd RASC. Admitted Solicitor, 1951; Town Clerk's Office, Glasgow, 1952–53; in private practice, 1953–84; Sen. Partner, Hamilton & Co., Solicitors, Glasgow, 1967–84; Temp. Sheriff, 1980; Floating Sheriff, 1984–. Pres., Glasgow Bar Assoc., 1963–64; Mem. Council, Law Soc. of Scotland, 1975–84. *Recreations:* music, playing the piano rather badly and bridge very badly. *Address:* 4 Park Quadrant, Glasgow G3 6BS. *T:* 041–332 2265.

HAMILTON, Prof. George Heard; Director, Sterling and Francine Clark Art Institute, 1966–77, now Emeritus; Professor of Art, Williams College, Williamstown, Massachusetts, 1966–75, now Emeritus; Director of Graduate Studies in Art History, Williams College, 1971–75; *b* 23 June 1910; *s* of Frank A. Hamilton and Georgia Neale Heard; *m* 1945, Polly Wiggin; one *s* one *d*. *Educ:* Yale Univ. BA 1932; MA 1934; PhD 1942. Research Asst, Walters Art Gallery, Baltimore, 1934–36; Mem. Art History Faculty, Yale Univ., 1936–66 (Prof., 1956–66); Robert Sterling Clark Prof. of Art, Williams Coll., 1963–64. Slade Prof. of Fine Art, Cambridge Univ., 1971–72; Kress Prof. in Residence, Nat. Gall of Art, Washington, DC, 1978–79. FRSA 1973; Fellow, Amer. Acad. of Arts and Science, 1979. Hon. LittD Williams Coll., 1977; Wilbur Lucius Cross Medal, Yale Grad. Sch., 1977; Amer. Art Dealers' Assoc. award for excellence in art hist., 1978. *Publications:* (with D. V. Thompson, Jr) De Arte Illuminandi, 1933; Manet and His Critics, 1954; The Art and Architecture of Russia, 1954; Monet's Paintings of Rouen Cathedral, 1960; European Painting and Sculpture, 1880–1940, 1967; (with W. C. Agee) Raymond Duchamp-Villon, 1967; 19th and 20th Century Art: Painting, Sculpture, Architecture, 1970; Articles in Burlington Magazine, Gazette des Beaux-Arts, Art Bulletin, etc. *Recreations:* music, gardening. *Address:* Williamstown, Mass 01267, USA. *T:* (413) 458–8626. *Clubs:* Century Association (New York); Elizabethan (New Haven); Edgartown Yacht (Mass).

HAMILTON, Graeme Montagu, TD; QC 1978; a Recorder of the Crown Court, since 1974; *b* 1 June 1934; *s* of late Leslie Montagu Hamilton and of Joan Lady Burbidge (Joan Elizabeth Burbidge, *née* Moxey); *m* 1978, Mrs Deirdre Lynn. *Educ:* Eton; Magdalene Coll., Cambridge (MA). National Service, 4/7 Royal Dragoon Guards, 1953–55. Called to Bar, Gray's Inn, 1959; Mem., Senate of Inns of Court and Bar, 1975–78. TA City of London Yeomanry, Inns of Court and City Yeomanry, 1955–70. *Recreations:* sailing, shooting, gardening. *Address:* 2 Crown Office Row, Temple, EC4Y 7HJ. *Clubs:* Cavalry and Guards, Royal Thames Yacht, Royal Automobile.

HAMILTON, Hamish; Founder and President, Hamish Hamilton Ltd, Publishers (Chairman, 1931–81, and Managing Director, 1931–72); *b* Indianapolis, 15 Nov. 1900; *o s* of James Neilson Hamilton, and Alice van Valkenburg; *m* 1st, 1929, Jean Forbes-Robertson (marr. diss. 1933), *d* of Sir Johnston and Lady Forbes-Robertson; 2nd, 1940, Countess Yvonne Pallavicino, of Rome; one *s*. *Educ:* Rugby; Caius Coll., Cambridge (Medical Student, 1919). MA (Hons Mod. Langs), LLB. Travelled in USA, 1922–23; called to Bar (Inner Temple), 1925; London Manager Harper and Brothers, Publishers, 1926; founded Hamish Hamilton Ltd, 1931; served in Army, 1939–41 (Holland and France, 1940); seconded to American Division, Ministry of Information, 1941–45; Hon. Sec. Kinsmen Trust, 1942–56; founded Kathleen Ferrier Meml Scholarships, 1954; a Governor, the Old Vic, 1945–75; Member Council, English-Speaking Union; a Governor, British Institute, Florence. Chevalier de la Légion d'Honneur, 1953; Grande Ufficiale, Order of Merit (Italy), 1976. *Publications:* articles on publishing, Anglo-American relations and sport. Commemorative Anthologies: Decade, 1941, Majority, 1952. *Recreations:* music, the theatre, travel; formerly rowing (spare stroke Cambridge Eight, 1921; stroked Winning Crews Grand Challenge Cup, Henley, 1927 and 1928, and Olympic Eight, Amsterdam, 1928 (silver medal)), ski-ing, flying, squash. *Address:* Palazzo Guicciardini, 15 Via Guicciardini, Florence, Italy. *T:* 294 330. *Clubs:* Garrick; Leander.

HAMILTON, Brig. Hugh Gray Wybrants, CBE 1964 (MBE 1945); DL; Chairman, Forces Help Society and Lord Roberts Workshops (in an honorary capacity), since 1974; *b* 16 May 1918; *s* of Lt-Col H. W. Hamilton, late 5th Dragoon Guards; *m* 1944, Claire Buxton; two *d*. *Educ:* Wellington Coll., Berks; Peterhouse, Cambridge; Royal Mil. Academy. Commissioned with Royal Engineers, 1938. War Service in BEF, BNAF, BLA, 1939–45. Post War Service in Australia, BAOR, France and UK. Instructor, Army Staff Coll., Camberley, 1954–56; Student, IDC, 1965; retired, 1968. Gen. Manager, Corby Develt Corp., 1968–80. DL Northants, 1977. *Recreations:* riding, sailing, farming. *Address:*

Covert House, East Haddon, Northants. *T:* Northampton 770488. *Club:* Army and Navy.

HAMILTON, Iain Ellis, BMus, FRAM; composer; pianist; Mary Duke Biddle Professor of Music, Duke University, North Carolina, USA, 1962–78 (Chairman of the Department, 1966); *b* Glasgow, 6 June 1922; *s* of James and Catherine Hamilton. *Educ:* Mill Hill; Royal Academy of Music. Engineer (Handley Page Ltd), 1939–46; RAM (Scholar) 1947–51; BMus (London University), 1951. Lecturer at Morley Coll., 1952–58; Lecturer, London Univ., 1956–60. Prizes and awards include: Prize of Royal Philharmonic Society, 1951; Prize of Koussevitsky Foundation (America), 1951; Butterworth Award, 1954; Arnold Bax Gold Medal, 1956; Ralph Vaughan Williams Award, Composers' Guild of GB, 1975. FRAM, 1960. Chm. Composers' Guild, 1958; Chm. ICA Music Cttee, 1958–60. *Works: orchestral works:* Symphonies; Sinfonia for two orchestras (Edinburgh Festival Commission); Concertos, for piano, clarinet, organ and violin; The Bermudas, for baritone, chorus and orchestra (BBC Commission); Symphonic Variations for string orchestra; Overture, Bartholomew Fair; Overture, 1912; Ecossaise; Concerto for jazz trumpet and orchestra (BBC Commn); Scottish Dances; 5 Love Songs for tenor and orchestra; (BBC Commission) Cantos; Jubilee; Arias for small orchestra; Circus (BBC Commn); Epitaph for this World and Time: 3 choruses and 2 organs; Vespers, for chorus, 2 pianos, harp and percussion; Voyage for horn and orchestra; Alastor; Amphion for violin and orchestra; Commedia; Threnos for solo organ; Aubade and Paraphrase for solo organ; Clerk Saunders, a ballet; *chamber works include:* four String Quartets; String Octet; Sonatas for piano, viola, clarinet and flute; Sonata for chamber orchestra; Flute Quartet; Clarinet Quintet; 3 Nocturnes for clarinet and piano; 5 Scenes for trumpet and piano; Sextet; Sonatas and Variants for 10 winds; Dialogues for soprano and 5 instruments; Nocturnes with Cadenzas for solo piano; 4 Border Songs, The Fray of Suport, a Requiem and a Mass for unaccompanied voices; St Mark Passion for 4 soloists, chorus and orchestra; Cleopatra for soprano and orchestra; *Opera:* Agamemnon; Royal Hunt of the Sun; Pharsalia; The Catiline Conspiracy; Tamburlaine; Anna Karenina; Dick Whittington; Lancelot; Raleigh's Dream. Music for theatre and films. Hon. DMus Glasgow, 1970. *Publications:* articles for many journals. *Address:* 1 King Street, WC2.

HAMILTON, Ian; poet; *b* 24 March 1938; *s* of Robert Tough Hamilton and Daisy McKay; *m* 1st, 1963, Gisela Dietzel; one *s*; 2nd, 1981, Ahdaf Soueif; one *s*. *Educ:* Darlington Grammar Sch.; Keble Coll., Oxford (BA Hons). Editor, Review, 1962–72; Poetry and Fiction Editor, Times Literary Supplement, 1965–73; Lectr in Poetry, Univ. of Hull, 1972–73; Editor, The New Review, 1974–79. Presenter, Bookmark (BBC TV series), 1984–. E. C. Gregory Award, 1963; Malta Cultural Award, 1974. *Publications:* (ed) The Poetry of War 1939–45, 1965; (ed) Alun Lewis: poetry and prose, 1966; (ed) The Modern Poet, 1968; The Visit (poems), 1970; A Poetry Chronicle, 1973; (ed) Robert Frost: selected poems, 1973; The Little Magazines, 1976; Returning (poems), 1976; Robert Lowell: a biography, 1983; (ed) Yorkshire in Verse, 1984; (ed) The New Review Anthology, 1985; J. D. Salinger: a writing life, 1986. *Address:* 18 Dorset Square, NW1. *T:* 01–262 0517.

HAMILTON, Ian Robertson; QC (Scot.) 1980; *b* Paisley, Scotland, 13 Sept. 1925; *s* of John Harris Hamilton and Martha Robertson; *m* 1974, Jeannette Patricia Mari Stewart, Connel, Argyll; one *s* (one *s* two *d* by former *m*). *Educ:* John Neilson Sch., Paisley; Allan Glens Sch., Glasgow; Glasgow and Edinburgh Univs (BL). Served RAFVR, 1944–48. Called to the Scottish Bar, 1954 and to the Albertan Bar, 1982. Advocate Depute, 1962; Dir of Civil Litigation, Republic of Zambia, 1964–66; Hon. Sheriff of Lanarks, 1967; retd from practice to work for National Trust for Scotland and later to farm in Argyll, 1969; returned to practice, 1974; Sheriff of Glasgow and Strathkelvin, May-Dec. 1984; resigned commn Dec. 1984, and apptd Temp. Sheriff, 1984–; returned to practice. *Publications:* No Stone Unturned, 1952 (also New York); The Tinkers of the World, 1957 (Foyle award-winning play); contrib. various jls. *Recreation:* sailing. *Address:* Advocates' Library, Parliament House, Edinburgh.

HAMILTON, James, CBE 1979; MP (Lab) Motherwell North, since 1983 (Bothwell, 1964–83); *b* 11 March 1918; *s* of George Hamilton and Margaret Carey; *m* 1945, Agnes McGhee; one *s* three *d* (and one *s* decd). *Educ:* St Bridget's, Baillieston; St Mary's, High Whifflet. District Councillor, 6th Lanarks, 1955–58; Lanarks County Council, 1958–64. National Executive Mem., Constructional Engrg Union, 1958–71, Pres., 1968–69; Chm., Trade Union Group, Parly Labour Party, 1969–70. Asst Govt Whip, 1969–70; an Opposition Whip, 1970–74; a Lord Comr of the Treasury and Vice-Chamberlain of the Household, 1974–78; Comptroller of HM Household, 1978–79. *Recreations:* tennis, badminton, golf. *Address:* 12 Rosegreen Crescent, North Road, Bellshill, Lanarks.

HAMILTON, Prof. James; Professor of Physics, Nordic Institute for Theoretical Atomic Physics, 1964–85; *b* 29 Jan. 1918; *s* of Joseph Hamilton, Killybegs, Co. Donegal and Jessie Mackay, Keiss, Caithness; *m* 1945, Glen, *d* of Charles Dobbs, Verwood, Dorset; two *s* one *d*. *Educ:* Royal Academical Institution, Belfast; Queen's Univ., Belfast; Institute for Advanced Study, Dublin; Manchester Univ. Scientific Officer (Ops Research), Admiralty, London, and South East Asia Command, 1943–45; ICI Fellow, Manchester Univ., 1945–48; Lectr in Theoretical Physics, Manchester Univ., 1948–49; University Lectr in Mathematics, Cambridge Univ., 1950–60. Fellow of Christ's Coll., Cambridge, 1953–60; Research Associate in Nuclear Physics, Cornell Univ., NY, 1957–58; Prof. of Physics, University Coll., London, 1960–64. Donegall Lectr, TCD, 1969. Dir, Nordita, 1985–. Foreign Mem., Royal Danish Acad., 1967. Dr *hc* Trondheim, 1982; DrPhil *hc* Lund, 1986. *Publications:* The Theory of Elementary Particles, 1959; (with B. Tromborg) Partial Wave Amplitudes and Resonance Poles, 1972; papers and articles on interaction of radiation with atoms, elementary particle physics, causality, and related topics. *Address:* Nordita, Blegdamsvej 17, 2100 Copenhagen Ø, Denmark; 4 Almoners Avenue, Cambridge CB1 4PA. *T:* Cambridge 244175.

HAMILTON, Sir James (Arnot), KCB 1978 (CB 1972); MBE 1952; FRSE; FEng 1981; Permanent Under-Secretary of State, Department of Education and Science, 1976–83; *b* 2 May 1923; *m* 1947, Christine Mary McKean (marr. diss.); three *s*. *Educ:* University of Edinburgh (BSc). Marine Aircraft Experimental Estab., 1943: Head of Flight Research, 1948; Royal Aircraft Estab., 1952; Head of Projects Div., 1964; Dir, Anglo-French Combat Aircraft, Min. of Aviation, 1965; Dir Gen. Concorde, Min. of Technology, 1966–70; Deputy Secretary: (Aerospace), DTI, 1971–73; Cabinet Office, 1973–76. Dir, Hawker Siddeley Gp, 1983–; Mem. Adv. Bd, Brown and Root (UK) Ltd, 1983–. Trustee, British Museum (Natural Hist.), 1984–. President: Assoc. for Science Educn, 1984–85; NFER in England and Wales, 1984–. Mem. Council, Reading Univ., 1983–; Vice-Chm. Council, UCL, 1985–. DUniv Heriot-Watt, 1983; Hon. LLD CNAA, 1983. *Publications:* papers in Reports and Memoranda series of Aeronautical Research Council, Jl RAeS, and technical press. *Address:* Pentlands, 9 Cedar Road, Farnborough, Hants. *T:* Farnborough 543254. *Club:* Athenæum.

HAMILTON, (James) Dundas, CBE 1985; Chairman: UDT Holdings Ltd, since 1985 (Director, since 1983); United Dominions Trust Ltd, since 1985; Wates City of London Properties plc, since 1984; *b* 11 June 1919; *o s* of late Arthur Douglas Hamilton and Jean Scott Hamilton; *m* 1954, Linda Jean, *d* of late Sinclair Frank Ditcham and Helen Fraser Ditcham; two *d*. *Educ:* Rugby; Clare Coll., Cambridge. Served War, Army (Lt-Col RA), 1939–46. Member, Stock Exchange, 1948, Mem. Council, 1972–78 (Dep. Chm., 1973–76). Partner, 1951–86, Sen. Partner, 1977–85, Fielding, Newson-Smith & Co. Director: Richard Clay plc, 1971–84 (Vice-Chm., 1981–84); LWT (Holdings) plc, 1981–; Datastream Hldgs Ltd, 1982–; TSB Gp, 1985–; TSB Investment Management Ltd, 1986–. Chm., City and Industry Liaison Council, 1970–73; Dep. Chm., British Invisible Exports Council, 1976–; Mem. Exec. Cttee, City Communications Centre, 1976–. Governor, Pasold Res. Fund, 1976– (Chm., 1978–86). Member: Council of Industrial Soc., 1959– (Exec. Cttee, 1963–68; Life Mem., 1978); Adv. Bd, RCDS, 1980–. Contested (C) East Ham North, 1951. *Publications:* The Erl King (radio play), 1949; Lorenzo Smiles on Fortune (novel), 1953; Three on a Honeymoon (TV series), 1956; Six Months Grace (play, jointly with Robert Morley), 1957; Stockbroking Today, 1968, 2nd edn 1979; Stockbroking Tomorrow, 1986. *Recreations:* writing, swimming, golf, watching tennis. *Address:* 45 Melbury Court, W8 6NH. *T:* 01–602 3157. *Clubs:* City of London; All England Lawn Tennis and Croquet, Hurlingham; Worplesdon Golf (Life Mem.).

HAMILTON, Adm. Sir John (Graham), GBE 1966 (KBE 1963; CBE 1958); CB 1960; National President, Institute of Marketing, 1972–75 (Director-General, 1968–72); *b* 12 July 1910; *s* of late Col E. G. Hamilton, CMG, DSO, MC, and Ethel Marie (*née* Frith); *m* 1938, Dorothy Nina Turner, 2nd *d* of late Col J. E. Turner, CMG, DSO; no *c*. *Educ:* RN Coll., Dartmouth. Joined RN 1924; specialised in Gunnery, 1936. Served War of 1939–45: destroyers; on staff of Adm. Cunningham, Mediterranean; Gunnery Officer, HMS Warspite; Admiralty; SE Asia; Comdr, 1943 (despatches). In command, HMS Alacrity, Far East, 1946–48; Capt., 1949; Dep. Dir, Radio Equipment, 1950–51; in command, 5th Destroyer Squadron, 1952–53; Dir of Naval Ordnance, Admiralty, 1954–56; in command HMS Newfoundland, Far East, 1956–58; despatches, 1957; Rear-Adm., 1958; Naval Sec. to First Lord of the Admiralty, 1958–60; Vice-Adm., 1961; Flag Officer: Flotillas, Home Fleet, 1960–62; Naval Air Command, 1962–64; C-in-C Mediterranean, and C-in-C Allied Forces, Mediterranean, 1964–67; Adm. 1965. *Recreations:* walking, climbing, photography. *Address:* Chapel Barn, Abbotsbury, Dorset DT3 4LF. *T:* Abbotsbury 871507.

HAMILTON, Loudon Pearson; Secretary, Department of Agriculture and Fisheries for Scotland, since 1984; *b* 12 Jan. 1932; *s* of Vernon Hamilton and Jean Mair Hood; *m* 1956, Anna Mackinnon Young; two *s*. *Educ:* Hutchesons' Grammar Sch., Glasgow; Glasgow Univ. (MA Hons Hist.). National Service, 2nd Lieut RA, 1953–55. Inspector of Taxes, Inland Revenue, 1956–60; Asst Principal, Dept of Agriculture and Fisheries for Scotland, 1960; Private Sec. to Parly Under-Secretary of State for Scotland, 1963–64; First Secretary, Agriculture, British Embassy, Copenhagen and The Hague, 1966–70; Asst Secretary, Dept of Agriculture and Fisheries for Scotland, 1973–79; Principal Estabt Officer, Scottish Office, 1979–84. Mem., AFRC, 1984–. *Address:* 5 Belgrave Road, Edinburgh EH12 6NG. *T:* 031–334 5398. *Club:* Royal Commonwealth Society.

HAMILTON, Martha, (Mrs R. R. Steedman); Headmistress, St Leonards School, St Andrews, since 1970; *d* of Rev. John Edmund Hamilton and Hon. Lilias Maclay; *m* 1977, Robert Russell Steedman, *qv*. *Educ:* Roedean Sch.; St Andrews Univ. (MA Hons Hist.); Cambridge Univ. (DipEd); Edinburgh Univ. (Dip. Adult Educn). Principal, Paljor Namgyal Girls' High School, Gangtok, Sikkim, 1959–66. Awarded Pema Dorji (for services to education), Sikkim, 1966. *Recreations:* ski-ing, photography. *Address:* St Leonards School, St Andrews, Fife. *T:* St Andrews 72126.

See also E. W. Hamilton, P. J. S. Hamilton.

HAMILTON, Mary Margaret; *see* Kaye, M. M.

HAMILTON, Sir Michael Aubrey, Kt 1983; *b* 5 July 1918; *s* of late Rt Rev. E. K. C. Hamilton, KCVO; *m* 1947, Lavinia, 3rd *d* of late Col Sir Charles Ponsonby, 1st Bt, TD; one *s* three *d*. *Educ:* Radley; Oxford. Served War of 1939–45, with 1st Bn, Coldstream Guards. MP (C): Wellingborough Div. Northants, 1959–64; Salisbury, Feb. 1965–1983; Asst Govt Whip, 1961–62; a Lord Comr of the Treasury, 1962–64; PPS to Sec. of State for Foreign and Commonwealth Affairs, 1982–83. UK Representative: UN Gen. Assembly, 1970; US Bicentennial Celebrations, 1976. *Address:* Lordington House, Chichester, Sussex. *T:* Emsworth 371717.

HAMILTON, (Mostyn) Neil; MP (C) Tatton, since 1983; *b* 9 March 1949; *s* of Ronald and Norma Hamilton; *m* 1983, (Mary) Christine Holman. *Educ:* Amman Valley Grammar School; University College of Wales, Aberystwyth (BSc Econ, MSc Econ); Corpus Christi College, Cambridge (LLB). Called to the Bar, Middle Temple, 1979. Secretary: Conservative backbench Trade and Industry Cttee, 1983, Vice-Chm., 1984–; UK–ANZAC Parly Gp, 1984–; Vice-Chm., Small Business Bureau, 1985–. Vice Pres., League for Introduction of Canine Controls, 1984–. *Publications:* The Facts on State Industry, 1971; UK/US Double Taxation, 1980; The European Community—a Policy for Reform, 1983; (ed) Land Development Encyclopaedia, 1981–; (jtly) No Turning Back, 1985. *Recreations:* gardening, book collecting, the arts, architecture and conservation, country pursuits, silence. *Address:* House of Commons, SW1A 0AA. *T:* 01–219 4157.

HAMILTON, Myer Alan Barry K.; *see* King-Hamilton.

HAMILTON, Neil; *see* Hamilton, M. N.

HAMILTON, Nigel John Mawdesley, QC 1981; *b* 13 Jan. 1938; *s* of Archibald Dearman Hamilton and Joan Worsley Mawdesley; *m* 1963; Leone Morag Elizabeth Gordon; two *s*. *Educ:* St Edward's Sch., Oxford; Queens' Coll., Cambridge. Nat. Service, 2nd Lieut, RE, Survey Dept, 1956–58. Assistant Master: St Edward's Sch., Oxford, 1962–63; King's Sch., Canterbury, 1963–65. Called to the Bar, Inner Temple, 1965. *Recreation:* fishing. *Address:* Moonrakers, Compton Martin, Somerset BS18 6JP. *T:* West Harptree 221421.

HAMILTON, North Edward Frederick D.; *see* Dalrymple Hamilton.

HAMILTON, Sir Patrick George, 2nd Bt, *cr* 1937; Chairman, Possum Controls Ltd; Trustee: Eleanor Hamilton Trust; Sidbury Trust; Disabled Living Foundation Trust; *b* 17 Nov. 1908; *o s* of Sir George Clements Hamilton, 1st Bt, and Eleanor (*d* 1958), *d* of late Henry Simon and *sister* of 1st Baron Simon of Wythenshawe; *S* father, 1947; *m* 1941, Winifred Mary Stone (CBE, MA), *o c* of Hammond Jenkins, Maddings, Hadstock, Cambs. *Educ:* Eton; Trinity Coll., Oxford (MA). First Managing Director and later Chairman of Tyresoles Ltd, 1934–53 (Dir, Propeller Production, MAP, 1943–44); Director: Simon Engineering Ltd and other Simon cos, 1937–78; Renold Ltd, 1952–78; Lloyds Bank Ltd, 1953–79; Chm., Expanded Metal Co. Ltd, 1955–78. Chm., Advisory Cttee on Commercial Information Overseas, 1957–59. Dep. Chm., Export Publicity Council, 1960–63. Chm., Transport Users Consultative Cttee, NW Area, 1957–64; Mem., Central Transport Consultative Cttee, 1963–64. Treas., Fedn of Commonwealth Chambers of Commerce, 1962–64. Mem., ITA, 1964–69. Chm., Central Mddx Gp Hosp. Management

Cttee, 1964–70. *Recreations:* gardening, travel. *Heir:* none. *Address:* 21 Madingley Road, Cambridge CB3 0EG *T:* Cambridge 351577.

HAMILTON, Prof. Patrick John Sinclair; Professor of Community Health, University of London, since 1982; *b* 28 July 1934; *s* of Rev. John Edmund Hamilton, MC, BA, and Hon. Lilias Hamilton (*née* Maclay); *m* 1972, Fiona Elizabeth Hunter; one *s* one *d. Educ:* Winchester Coll.; Christ's Coll., Cambridge; Edinburgh Univ.; London Univ. BA Cantab; MB, ChB Edinburgh; DPH, DTM&H London. FFCM; FRCP. National Service, RAMC Bde of Gurkhas, 1960–62. Lecturer, Makerere University Coll. Med. Sch., Uganda, 1963–65; Lectr/Sen. Lectr, Dept of Medical Statistics and Epidemiology, London School of Hygiene and Tropical Medicine, 1967–74; Dir, Pan American Health Organization/WHO Caribbean Epidemiology Centre, Port of Spain, Trinidad, 1975–82. Member, Director General WHO Independent Commn on Onchocerciasis Control Programme, 1979–81. *Publications:* on epidemiology and control of infectious and non-infectious disease and tropical medicine. *Recreations:* riding, walking, collecting medical history. *Address:* 6 Redburn Street, SW3. *T:* 01–351 3988.

See also E. W. Hamilton, Martha Hamilton.

HAMILTON, Richard; painter; *b* 24 Feb. 1922; *s* of Peter and Constance Hamilton; *m* 1947, Terry O'Reilly (*d* 1962); one *s* one *d. Educ:* elementary; Royal Academy Schs; Slade Sch. of Art. Jig and Tool draughtsman, 1940–45. Lectr, Fine Art Dept, King's Coll., Univ. of Durham (later Univ. of Newcastle upon Tyne), 1953–66. Devised exhibitions: Growth and Form, 1951; Man, Machine and Motion, 1955. Collaborated on: This is Tomorrow, 1956; 'an Exhibit', 1957; exhibn with D. Roth, ICA New Gall., 1977. One man art exhibitions: Gimpel Fils, 1951; Hanover Gall., 1955, 1964; Robert Fraser Gall., 1966, 1967, 1969; Whitworth Gall, 1972; Nigel Greenwood Inc., 1972; Serpentine Gall., 1975; Stedelijk Mus., Amsterdam, 1976; Waddington Gall., 1980, 1982, 1984; Anthony d'Offay Gall., 1980; Charles Cowles Gall., NY, 1980; Galérie Maeght, Paris, 1981; Tate Gall., 1983–84; Thorden and Wetterling, Stockholm, 1984; DAAD Gall., Berlin, 1985. Retrospective exhibitions: Tate Gallery, 1970 (also shown in Eindhoven and Bern); Guggenheim Museum, New York, 1973 (also shown in Cincinnati, Munich, Tübingen, Berlin); Musée Grenoble, 1977; Kunsthalle Bielefeld, 1978; other exhibitions abroad include: Kassel, 1967, New York, 1967; Milan, 1968, 1969, 1971, 1972; Hamburg, 1969; Berlin, 1970, 1971, 1973. William and Noma Copley award, 1960; John Moores prize, 1969; Talens Prize International, 1970. *Publication:* Collected Words 1953–1982, 1982. *Address:* c/o Tate Gallery, Millbank, SW1P 4RG.

HAMILTON, Sir Richard Caradoc; *see* Hamilton, Sir Robert C. R. C.

HAMILTON, Richard Graham; a Recorder of the Crown Court, since 1974; Chancellor, Diocese of Liverpool, since 1976; *b* 26 Aug. 1932; *s* of Henry Augustus Rupert Hamilton and Frances Mary Graham Hamilton; *m* 1960, Patricia Craghill Hamilton (*née* Ashburner); one *s* one *d. Educ:* Charterhouse; University Coll., Oxford (MA). Called to Bar, Middle Temple, 1956. Regular broadcasting work for Radio Merseyside, inc. scripts: Van Gogh in England, 1981; Voices from Babylon, 1983; A Longing for Dynamite, 1984. *Publications:* Foul Bills and Dagger Money, 1979; All Jangle and Riot, 1986. *Recreations:* reading, walking, films. *Address:* 15 Gwydrin Road, Liverpool L18 3HA. *T:* 051–722 5806. *Club:* Athenæum (Liverpool).

HAMILTON, Sir (Robert Charles) Richard (Caradoc), 9th Bt, *cr* 1647; *b* 8 Sept. 1911; *s* of Sir Robert Caradoc Hamilton, 8th Bt, and Irene Lady Hamilton (*née* Mordaunt) (*d* 1969); *S* father, 1959; *m* 1952, Elizabeth Vidal Barton; one *s* three *d. Educ:* Charterhouse; St Peter's Coll., Oxford (MA). Served in the Intelligence Corps, 1940–45. Schoolmaster at Ardingly Coll., Sussex, 1946–60. Owner, Walton Estate, Warwick; Chm., Warwickshire Br., CLA, 1980–84. *Publication:* (trans.) A History of the Royal Game of Tennis, 1979. *Recreations:* dramatist; Real tennis. *Heir:* *s* Andrew Caradoc Hamilton, *b* 23 Sept. 1953. *Address:* Walton, Warwick. *T:* Stratford-on-Avon 840460.

HAMILTON, Robert William, FBA 1960; *b* 26 Nov. 1905; *s* of William Stirling Hamilton and Kathleen Hamilton (*née* Elsmie); *m* 1935, Eileen Hetty Lowick; three *s* two *d. Educ:* Winchester Coll.; Magdalen Coll., Oxford. Chief Insp. of Antiquities, Palestine, 1931–38; Dir of Antiquities, Palestine, 1938–48; Sec.-Librarian, British Sch. of Archæology, Iraq, 1948–49; Senior Lecturer in Near Eastern Archæology, Oxford, 1949–56; Keeper of Dept of Antiquities, 1956–72, Keeper, 1962–72, Ashmolean Museum, Oxford. Fellow Magdalen Coll., Oxford, 1959–72. *Publications:* The Church of the Nativity, Bethlehem, 1947; Structural History of the Aqsa Mosque, 1949; Khirbat al Mafjar, 1959; (with others) Oxford Bible Atlas, 1974. *Address:* The Haskers, Westleton, Suffolk.

HAMILTON, Walter, MA; Hon. DLitt Durham; FRSL; Master of Magdalene College, Cambridge, 1967–78, Hon. Fellow, since 1978; *b* 10 Feb. 1908; *s* of late Walter George Hamilton and Caroline Mary Stiff; *m* 1951, Jane Elizabeth, *o d* of Sir John Burrows, *qv*, Ridlands Cottage, Limpsfield Chart, Surrey; three *s* one *d. Educ:* St Dunstan's Coll.; Trinity Coll., Cambridge (Scholar). 1st Class Classical Tripos, Part I, 1927; Part II, 1929; Craven Scholar, 1927; Chancellor's Classical Medallist, 1928; Porson Prizeman and Craven Student, 1929. Fellow of Trinity Coll., 1931–35; Asst Lecturer, University of Manchester, 1931–32; Asst Master, Eton Coll., 1933–46, Master in Coll., 1937–46, Fellow, 1972–81; Fellow and Classical Lecturer, Trinity Coll., 1946–50; Tutor, 1947–50; University Lectr in Classics, 1947–50; Head Master: of Westminster Sch., 1950–57; of Rugby Sch., 1957–66. Editor, Classical Quarterly, 1946–47. Chairman: Scholarship Cttee, Lord Kitchener Nat. Meml Fund, 1953–59, Exec. Cttee, 1967–77; Headmasters' Conference, 1955, 1956, 1965, 1966; Governing Body, Shrewsbury Sch., 1968–81; Governing Bodies Assoc., 1969–74. Member: Exec. Cttee, British Council, 1958–70; Council of Senate of Cambridge Univ., 1969–74. *Publications:* A new translation of Plato's Symposium, 1951; Plato's Gorgias, 1960; Plato's Phaedrus and Letters VII and VIII, 1973; (with A. F. Wallace-Hadrill) Ammianus Marcellinus, the later Roman Empire, 1986; contributions to Classical Quarterly, Classical Review, etc. *Address:* 6 Hedgerley Close, Cambridge. *T:* Cambridge 63202.

HAMILTON, Prof. William Donald, FRS 1980; Royal Society Research Professor, Department of Zoology, and Fellow of New College, Oxford University, since 1984; *b* 1 Aug. 1936; *s* of Archibald Milne Hamilton and Bettina Matraves Hamilton (*née* Collier); *m* 1967, Christine Ann Friess; three *d. Educ:* Tonbridge Sch.; Cambridge Univ. (BA); London Univ. (PhD). Lecturer in Genetics, Imperial Coll., London Univ., 1964–77; Prof. of Evolutionary Biology, Mus. of Zoology and Div. of Biol Scis, Michigan Univ., 1978–84. For. Member, American Acad. of Arts and Sciences, 1978. *Publications:* contribs to Jl of Theoretical Biology, Science, Nature, Amer. Naturalist. *Address:* Department of Zoology, South Parks Road, Oxford OX1 3PS.

HAMILTON, William Winter; MP (Lab) Fife Central, since 1974 (Fife West, 1950–74); *b* 26 June 1917; *m* (wife died 1968); one *s* one *d*; *m* 1982, Mrs Margaret Cogle. *Educ:* Washington Grammar Sch., Co. Durham; Sheffield Univ. (BA, DipEd). Joined Lab. Party, 1936; contested W Fife, 1945; Chairman, H of C Estimates Cttee, 1964–70; Vice-Chm., Parly Labour Party, 1966–70; Mem., European Parlt, 1975–79, Vice-Chm., Rules and Procedure Cttee, 1976–79 (Chm., 1975–76). School teacher; Mem. COHSE. Served War of 1939–45, Middle East, Capt. *Publication:* My Queen and I, 1975. *Address:* House of Commons, SW1.

HAMILTON-DALRYMPLE, Sir Hew; *see* Dalrymple.

HAMILTON FRASER, Donald; *see* Fraser.

HAMILTON-JONES, Maj.-Gen. (retd) John, CBE 1977; Director of International Marketing, General Defense Corporation of Pennsylvania, since 1984; Chairman, Richmond Enterprises Ltd, since 1984; President: Ordnance Board, 1980–81; Army Advance Class, 1981–83; *b* 6 May 1926; *s* of late George and of Lillian Hamilton-Jones; *m* 1952, Penelope Ann Marion Derry; three *d. Educ:* Cranbrook Sch.; Edinburgh Univ.; Technical Staff Coll. US Army Guided Missile Grad., 1957. Commnd RA, 1945; Indian Artillery, 1945–47; Regtl Service, Far East/ME, 1947–60; Jt Services Staff Coll., 1966; comd a regt, 1966–69; DS RMCS, 1970–72; MoD Dir, 1975–78 (Brig.). CEng; FRAeS; FInstD; MIERE; FBIM (MBIM 1979). Commandeur, Assoc. Franco-Britannique, 1979. *Recreations:* rowing, Rugby, squash, music, hi-fi. *Address:* c/o Lloyds Bank, Cox's & King's Branch, 6 Pall Mall, SW1Y 5NH.

HAMILTON-RUSSELL, family name of **Viscount Boyne.**

HAMILTON-SMITH, family name of **Baron Colwyn.**

HAMILTON-SPENCER-SMITH, Sir John; *see* Spencer-Smith.

HAMLEY, Donald Alfred, CBE 1985; HM Diplomatic Service, retired; *b* 19 Aug. 1931; *s* of Alfred Hamley and Amy (*née* Brimacombe) *m* 1958, Daphne Griffith; two *d. Educ:* Devonport High Sch., Plymouth. Joined HM Foreign (subseq. Diplomatic) Service, 1949; Nat. Service, 1950–52; returned to FO; served in: Kuwait, 1955–57; Libya, 1958–61; FO, 1961–63; Jedda, 1963–65 and 1969–72; Rome, 1965–69; seconded to DTI, 1972–73; Commercial Counsellor, Caracas, 1973–77; seconded to Dept of Trade, 1977–80; Consul-Gen., Jerusalem, 1980–84; retired prematurely, 1984. *Recreations:* anything outdoors; music, reading. *Address:* 1 Forge Close, Hayes, Bromley BR2 7LP. *T:* 01–462 6696. *Club:* Royal Automobile.

HAMLIN, Prof. Michael John, FICE, FIWES, FEng 1985; Professor of Water Engineering since 1970, Head of Department of Civil Engineering since 1980, Pro-Vice-Chancellor since 1985, and Vice-Principal from Oct. 1987, University of Birmingham; *b* 11 May 1930; *s* of late Dr Ernest John Hamlin and of Dorothy Janet Hamlin; *m* 1951, Augusta Louise, *d* of late William Thomas Tippins and of Rose Louise Tippins; three *s. Educ:* St John's Coll., Johannesburg; Dauntsey's Sch.; Bristol Univ. (BSc); Imperial Coll. of Science and Technol., London (DIC). FIWES 1973; FICE 1981; Asst Engineer, Lemon & Blizard, Southampton, 1951–53; Engineer: Anglo-American Corp., Johannesburg, 1954–55; Stewart, Sviridov & Oliver, Johannesburg, 1955; Partner, Rowe & Hamlin, Johannesburg, 1956–58; Univ. of Witwatersrand, 1959–60; Univ. of Birmingham, 1961–. Chm., Aquatic and Atmospheric Phys. Scis Grants Cttee, NERC, 1975–79; Member: Severn Trent Water Authority, 1974–79; British National Cttee for Geodesy and Geophysics, 1979–84 (Chm., Hydrology Sub-Cttee, 1979–84). Pres., Internat. Commn on Water Resource Systems of the Internat. Assoc. of Hydrological Scis (IAHS), 1983–87. President's Premium, IWES, 1972. *Publications:* contribs on public health engrg and water resources engrg in learned jls. *Recreations:* walking, gardening. *Address:* 70 Oakfield Road, Selly Park, Birmingham B29 7EG.

HAMLYN, Prof. David Walter; Professor of Philosophy and Head of Philosophy Department, Birkbeck College, University of London, since 1964, and Head of Classics Department, 1981–86; Vice-Master, Birkbeck College, since 1983; *b* 1 Oct. 1924; *s* of late Hugh Parker Hamlyn and late Gertrude Isabel Hamlyn; *m* 1949, Eileen Carlyle Litt; one *s* one *d. Educ:* Plymouth Coll.; Exeter Coll., Oxford. BA (Oxon) 1948, MA 1949 (1st cl. Lit. Hum., 1st cl. Philosophy and Psychology, 1950). War Service, RAC and IAC, Hodson's Horse (Lieutenant), 1943–46. Research Fellow, Corpus Christi Coll., Oxford, 1950–53; Lecturer: Jesus Coll., Oxford, 1953–54; Birkbeck Coll., London, 1954–63, Reader, 1963–64. Pres., Aristotelian Soc., 1977–78. Mem. Council, Royal Inst. of Philosophy, 1968– (Exec., 1971–). Mem., London Univ. Senate, 1981– (Mem. several cttees; Chm., Academic Council Standing Sub-cttee in Theology, Arts and Music, 1984–); Governor: Birkbeck Coll., 1965–69; City Lit., 1982–86 (Vice-Chm., 1985–86); Chm. Governors, Heythrop Coll., 1971–78, Mem., 1984–, Fellow, 1978. Editor of Mind, 1972–84; Consulting Editor, Jl of Medical Ethics, 1981–. *Publications:* The Psychology of Perception, 1957 (repr. with additional material, 1969); Sensation and Perception, 1961; Aristotle's *De Anima*, Books II and III, 1968; The Theory of Knowledge, 1970 (USA), 1971 (GB); Experience and the Growth of Understanding, 1978 (Spanish trans., 1981); Schopenhauer, 1980; Perception, Learning and the Self, 1983; Metaphysics, 1984; Penguin History of Western Philosophy, 1987; contrib. to several other books and to many philosophical, psychological and classical jls. *Recreations:* playing and listening to music. *Address:* 7 Burland Road, Brentwood, Essex CM15 9BH. *T:* Brentwood 214842; Department of Philosophy, Birkbeck College, Malet Street, WC1E 7HX. *T:* 01–580 6622.

HAMLYN, Paul (Bertrand); Founder and Chairman: Octopus Publishing Group (London, New York and Sydney), since 1971; Mandarin Publishers (Hong Kong), since 1971; Chairman: Heinemann Group of Publishers Ltd, since 1985; Octopus Books, since 1971; Hamlyn Publishing Group, since 1986; Co-founder (with David Frost) and Director, Sundial Publications, since 1973; Co-founder (with Doubleday & Co., New York) and Director, Octopus Books International BV (Holland), since 1973; Co-founder (with Sir Terence Conran) and Co-chairman, Conran Octopus, since 1983; Director: News America, since 1980; Tigerprint, since 1980; Brimax Books Ltd, since 1983; *b* 12 Feb. 1926; 2nd *s* of late Prof. Richard Hamburger and Mrs L. Hamburger (*née* Hamburg); *m* 1st, 1952, Eileen Margaret (Bobbie) (marr. diss. 1969), *d* of Col Richard Watson; one *s* one *d*; 2nd, 1970, Mrs Helen Guest. *Educ:* St Christopher's Sch., Letchworth, Herts. Founder of Hamlyn Publishing Gp, which he re-purchased from Reed International, 1986; Formed: Books for Pleasure, 1949; Prints for Pleasure, 1960; Records for Pleasure, Marketing long-playing classical records, and Golden Pleasure Books (jt co. with Golden Press Inc., NY), 1961; Music for Pleasure (with EMI), 1965. Paul Hamlyn Gp acquired by Internat. Publishing Corp, 1964; joined IPC Bd with special responsibility for all Corporation's book publishing activities; Butterworth & Co. acquired 1968; Director, IPC, 1965–70; Chm., IPC Books, controlling Hamlyn Publishing Gp, 1965–70 (formerly Chm., Paul Hamlyn Holdings Ltd, and associated Cos); Jt Man. Dir, News International Ltd, 1970–71; Dir, News International, 1971–86; Dir, TV am, 1981–83. Chm. Trustees, Public Policy Centre, 1985–. *Address:* 59 Grosvenor Street, W1. *T:* 01–493 5841.

See also M. P. L. Hamburger.

HAMMARSKJÖLD, Knut (Olof Hjalmar Åkesson); Working Vice Chairman and Chairman of the Board, AB C. F. Berling Malmö, since 1986; Director: Sydsvenska Dagbladet AB Malmö, since 1948; No 48 Cronholm AB Malmö, since 1974; Institute of Air Transport, Paris, since 1968; Minister Plenipotentiary, 1966; *b* Geneva, 16 Jan. 1922;

Swedish; *m*; four *s*. *Educ*: Sigtunaskolan; Stockholm Univ. Swedish Foreign Service, 1946; Attaché, Swedish Embassy, Paris, 1947–49; Foreign Office, Stockholm, 1949–51; Attaché, Swedish Embassy, Vienna, 1951–52; 2nd Sec., Moscow, 1952–54, 1st Sec, 1954–55; 1st Sec., Foreign Office, 1955–57; Head of Foreign Relations Dept, Swedish Civil Aero. Bd, 1957–59; Counsellor, Paris, also Dep. Head of Swedish Delegn to OEEC, 1959–60; Dep. Sec.-Gen., EFTA, Geneva, 1960–66; International Air Transport Association: Dir Gen., 1966–84; Chm. Exec. Cttee, 1981–84; Internat. Affairs Counsel, 1985–87. Hon. Fellow, Canadian Aeronautics and Space Inst.; Hon. Academician, Mexican Acad. of Internat. Law; Hon. FCIT (London). Governor, Atlantic Inst. for Internat. Affairs, 1983–. Edward Warner Award, ICAO, 1983. Comdr (1st cl.), Order of North Star (Sweden); NOR (Sweden); Grand Cross Order of Civil Merit (Spain); Grand Officer, Order of Al-Istiqlal (Jordan); Commander: Order of Lion (Finland); Oranje Nassau (Netherlands); Order of Falcon (1st cl.) (Iceland); Order of Black Star (Benin); Légion d'Honneur (France). *Publications*: articles on political, economic and aviation topics. *Recreations*: music, painting, ski-ing. *Address*: c/o IATA, 26 Chemin de Joinville, PO Box 160, 1216 Cointrin-Geneva, Switzerland. *T*: 983366; c/o IATA, 2000 Peel Street, Montreal, PQ H3A 2R4, Canada.

HAMMER, Armand, MD; Chairman of Board and Chief Executive Officer, Occidental Petroleum Corp., Los Angeles, since 1957; *b* 21 May 1898; *s* of Dr Julius Hammer and Rose Robinson; *m* 1956, Frances Barrett; two *s*. *Educ*: Columbia University (BS 1919; MD 1921, Coll. of Physicians and Surgeons). President: Allied Amer. Corp., 1923–25; A. Hammer Pencil Co., 1925–30; Hammer Galleries Inc., 1930–; J. W. Dant Distilling Co., 1943–54; Pres. and Chm. Board, Mutual Broadcasting System, NY, 1957–58; Chm., M. Knoedler & Co. Inc., 1972–; Mem., Nat. Petroleum Council, 1968–; Member, Board of Directors: Canadian Occidental Petroleum Ltd, 1964–; Cities Service Co., 1982–; Southland Corp., 1983–; Amer. Petroleum Inst., 1975; Founder and Hon. Chm., Armand Hammer Coll. of American West, New Mexico, 1981–; Mem. Court, Mary Rose Trust, 1981–; Chm., Internat. Council, Shakespeare Globe Centre (and Chm., N Amer. Div.), 1982–. Hon. Corresp. Mem., RA, 1975–; Hon. Mem., Royal Scottish Acad. Hon LLD: Pepperdine, 1978; Southeastern, 1978; Columbia, 1978; Aix-en-Provence, 1981; Hon. LHD Colorado, 1979; Hon. DPS Salem, 1979; Hon. DSc S Carolina, 1983. Comdr, Order of Crown, Belgium, 1969; Comdr, Order of Andres Bellos, Venezuela, 1975; Order of Aztec Eagle, Mexico, 1977; Royal Order of Polar Star, Sweden, 1979; Grand Officer, Order of Merit, Italy, 1981; Kt Comdr's Cross, Austria, 1982; Comdr, French Legion of Honour, 1983 (Officer, 1978); numerous awards and distinctions from USA bodies. *Publication*: Quest of the Romanoff Treasure, 1932; *relevant publications*: The Remarkable Life of Dr Armand Hammer, by Robert Considine, 1975, UK edn, Larger than Life, 1976, numerous foreign edns; The World of Armand Hammer, by John Bryson, 1985. *Address*: Occidental Petroleum Corporation, 10889 Wilshire Boulevard, Los Angeles, Calif 90024, USA. *T*: (office) (213) 879 1700. *Clubs*: Los Angeles Petroleum; Jockey (New York).

HAMMER, James Dominic George, CB 1983; Deputy Director General, Health and Safety Executive, since 1985; *b* 21 April 1929; *s* of E. A. G. and E. L. G. Hammer; *m* 1955, Margaret Eileen Halse; two *s* one *d*. *Educ*: Dulwich Coll.; Corpus Christi Coll., Cambridge. BA Hons Mod. Langs. Joined HM Factory Inspectorate, 1953; Chief Inspector of Factories, 1975–84. Vice Chm., Camberwell HA. Pres., Internat. Assoc. of Labour Inspectors, 1984–. FRSA 1984. *Address*: Health and Safety Executive, Regina House, 259 Old Marylebone Road, NW1 5RR. *T*: 01–723 1262.

HAMMER, Rev. Canon Raymond Jack, PhD; Director, Bible Reading Fellowship, 1977–85; *b* 4 July 1920; *s* of Paul and Lily Hammer; *m* 1949, Vera Winifred (*née* Reed); two *d*. *Educ*: St Peter's Coll., Oxford (MA, Dip.Theol.); Univ. of London (BD, MTh, PhD). Asst Curate, St Mark's, St Helens, 1943–46; Sen. Tutor, St John's Coll., Durham, 1946–49; Lectr in Theol., Univ. of Durham, 1946–49; Prof., Central Theol Coll., Tokyo, 1950–64; Prof. in Doctrine, St Paul's Univ., Tokyo, 1958–64; Chaplain at British Embassy, Tokyo, 1954–64; Hon. Canon, St Michael's Cathedral, Kobe, Japan, 1964–; Lectr, Queen's Coll., Birmingham, and Lectr in Theol., Univ. of Birmingham, 1965–77. Examining Chaplain to: Bishop of Liverpool, 1965–78; Bishop of Birmingham, 1973–78. Archbishops' Consultant on Relations with Other Faiths, 1978–; Sec., Anglican Inter-Faith Consultants, 1983–. Treasurer, Studiorum Novi Testamenti Societas, 1970–82. *Publications*: Japan's Religious Ferment, 1961 (US 1962); The Book of Daniel (commentary), 1976; contrib: Theological Word Book of the Bible, 1950; Oxford Dictionary of the Christian Church, 1957, 2nd edn 1975; Concise Dictionary of the Bible, 1966; Concise Dictionary of the Christian World Mission, 1970; Man and his Gods, 1971; Shorter Books of the Apocrypha, 1972; Perspectives on World Religions, 1978; The World's Religions, 1982; World Religions, 1982. *Recreations*: travel, literature. *Address*: 22 Midsummer Meadow, Inkberrow, Worcs WR7 4HD. *T*: Inkberrow 792883. *Clubs*: Athenæum; Sion College.

HAMMERSLEY, Dr John Michael, FRS 1976; Reader in Mathematical Statistics, University of Oxford, and Professorial Fellow, Trinity College, Oxford, 1969–Oct. 1987; *b* 21 March 1920; *s* of late Guy Hugh Hammersley and Marguerite (*née* Whitehead); *m* 1951, Shirley Gwendolene (*née* Bakewell); two *s*. *Educ*: Sedbergh Sch.; Emmanuel Coll., Cambridge. MA, ScD (Cantab); MA, DSc (Oxon). War service in Royal Artillery, Major, 1940–45. Graduate Asst, Design and Analysis of Scientific Experiment, Univ. of Oxford, 1948–55; Principal Scientific Officer, AERE, Harwell, 1955–59; Sen. Research Officer, Inst. of Economics and Statistics, Univ. of Oxford, 1959–69; Sen. Research Fellow, Trinity Coll., Oxford, 1961–69. FIMS 1959; FIMA 1964; Fulbright Fellow, 1955; Erskine Fellow, 1978; Rouse Ball lectr, Univ. of Cambridge, 1980. Mem., ISI, 1961. Von Neumann Medal for Applied Maths, Brussels, 1966; IMA Gold Medal, 1984. *Publications*: (with D. C. Hanscomb) Monte Carlo Methods, 1964, rev. edn 1966, 5th edn 1984, trans. as Les Méthodes de Monte Carlo, 1967; papers in scientific jls. *Address*: Trinity College, Oxford. *T*: Oxford 249631; (from Oct. 1987) 11 Eynsham Road, Oxford OX2 9BS. *T*: Oxford 862181.

HAMMERSLEY, Rear-Adm. Peter Gerald, CB 1982; OBE 1965; Director, British Marine Equipment Council, since 1985; *b* 18 May 1928; *s* of Robert Stevens Hammersley and Norah Hammersley (*née* Kirkham); *m* 1959, Audrey Cynthia Henderson Bolton; one *s* one *d*. *Educ*: Denstone Coll.; RNEC Manadon; Imperial Coll., London (DIC). Served RN, 1946–82; Long Engrg Course, RNEC Manadon, 1946–50; HMS Liverpool, 1950–51; Advanced Marine Engrg Course, RNC Greenwich, 1951–53; HMS Ocean, 1953–54; joined Submarine Service, 1954; HMS Alaric, HMS Tiptoe, 1954–58; Nuclear Engrg Course, Imperial Coll., 1958–59; First Marine Engineer Officer, first RN Nuclear Submarine, HMS Dreadnought, 1960–64; DG Ships Staff, 1965–68; Base Engineer Officer, Clyde Submarine Base, 1968–70; Naval Staff, 1970–72; Asst Director, S/M Project Team, DG Ships, 1973–76; CO, HMS Defiance, 1976–78; Captain, RNEC Manadon, 1978–80; CSO (engrg) to C-in-C Fleet, 1980–82. Comdr 1964; Captain 1971; Rear-Adm. 1980; Chief Exec., British Internal Combustion Engine Manufacturers' Assoc., 1982–85. Junior Warden, Engineers' Co., 1986. *Recreations*: walking, gardening. *Address*: Wistaria Cottage, Linersh Wood, Bramley, near Guildford GU5 0EE. *Club*: Army and Navy.

HAMMERTON, Rolf Eric; His Honour Judge Hammerton; a Circuit Judge, since 1972; *b* 18 June 1926; *s* of Eric Maurice Hammerton and Dora Alice Hammerton (*née* Zander); *m* 1953, Thelma Celestine Hammerton (*née* Appleyard); one *s* three *d*. *Educ*: Brighton, Hove and Sussex Grammar Sch.; Peterhouse, Cambridge (MA, LLB). Philip Teichman Prize, 1952; called to Bar, Inner Temple, 1952. *Recreation*: cooking. *Address*: The Old Rectory, Falmer, near Brighton BN1 9PG.

HAMMETT, Sir Clifford (James), Kt 1969; Chief Justice, Fiji, 1967–72; Acting Governor General of Fiji, 1971; Regional Legal Adviser with British Development Division in the Caribbean, 1975; *b* 8 June 1917; *s* of late Frederick John and Louisa Maria Hammett; *m* 1946, Olive Beryl Applebee; four *s* one *d*. *Educ*: Woodbridge. Admitted Solicitor, 1939. Indian Army, 1st Punjab Regt, 1940, North Africa, 1941; captured at Singapore, 1942 (despatches); POW on Siam Railway, 1942–45. Magistrate, Nigeria, 1946–52. Called to the Bar, Middle Temple, 1948. Transferred to Fiji, 1952; Senior Magistrate, Fiji, 1954, Puisne Judge, 1955; conjointly Chief Justice, Tonga, 1956–68. *Recreation*: gardening. *Address*: c/o Lloyds Bank, 6 Pall Mall, SW1. *Club*: Naval and Military.

HAMMETT, Harold George; British Deputy High Commissioner, Peshawar, 1964–66; *b* 2 Aug. 1906; 2nd *s* of Arthur Henry Hammett; *m* 1st, 1936, Daphne Margaret Vowler; one *s*; 2nd, 1947, Natalie Moira Sherratt; one *s* one *d*. *Educ*: St Olave's; Clare Coll., Cambridge. Malayan Civil Service, 1928–57; retired from post of Resident Commissioner, Malacca, on Malayan Independence, 1957; Commonwealth Office (formerly CRO), 1958–66. *Recreations*: woodwork, gardening. *Address*: Hole Head, Holcombe, Dawlish, Devon EX7 0JW. *T*: Dawlish 862114. *Clubs*: East India, Devonshire, Sports and Public Schools, Royal Commonwealth Society.

HAMMICK, Sir Stephen (George), 5th Bt, *cr* 1834; *b* 27 Dec. 1926; *s* of Sir George Hammick, 4th Bt; *S* father, 1964; *m* 1953, Gillian Elizabeth Inchbald; two *s* one *d*. *Educ*: Stowe. Royal Navy as Rating (hostilities only), 1944–48; RAC Coll., Cirencester, 1949–50; MFH Cattistock Hunt, 1961 and 1962. Vice-Chm., Dorset CC, 1985– (County Councillor, 1958–). High Sheriff, Dorset, 1981–82. Farmer, with 450 acres. *Recreations*: hunting, fishing, sailing. *Heir*: *s* Paul St Vincent Hammick, *b* 1 Jan. 1955. *Address*: Badgers, Wraxall, Dorchester. *T*: Evershot 343.

HAMMOND, Anthony Hilgrove; Principal Assistant Legal Adviser to Home Office and Northern Ireland Office, since 1980; *b* 27 July 1940; *s* of late Colonel Charles William Hilgrove Hammond and Jessie Eugenia Hammond (*née* Francis). *Educ*: Malvern Coll.; Emmanuel Coll., Cambridge (BA, LLB). Admitted Solicitor of Supreme Court, 1965. Articled with LCC, 1962; Solicitor, GLC, 1965–68; Home Office: Legal Assistant, 1968; Sen. Legal Assistant, 1970; Asst Legal Advr, 1974. *Recreations*: bridge, music, opera, walking, birdwatching. *Address*: 48 Rosebank, Holyport Road, Fulham, SW6. *T*: 01–385 7966. *Club*: Athenæum.

HAMMOND, Catherine Elizabeth, CBE 1950; Colonel, WRAC (retired); *b* 22 Dec. 1909; *d* of late Frank Ernest Rauleigh Eddolls and late Elsie Eddolls (*née* Cooper); *m*; one *s* one *d*. *Educ*: Lassington House, Highworth, Wilts; Chesterville Sch., Cirencester, Glos. Joined ATS (TA) (FANY), 1938; Private, 7th Wilts MT Co. 1939; 2nd Subaltern 1940; Capt., 1942; Major, Commanding Devon Bn, 1942; Lieut-Col, Asst Dir ATS Oxford, 1943; Col, Dep. Dir ATS (later WRAC), Eastern Command 1947–50; Hon. Col 54 (East Anglia) Div./Dist WRAC/TA, 1964–67. Chm., WRAC Assoc., 1966–70, Life Vice-Pres., 1971. Chm., Highworth and District Br., RNLI, 1970–; President: Royal British Legion, Highworth (Women's Section), 1977–84; Highworth Amateur Dramatic Soc., 1982–86. Deputy Mayor, Highworth Town Council, 1978, Mayor, 1979–81, 1984–85. *Recreations*: hockey—Army (women), 1947–48; all games; racing. *Address*: Red Down, Highworth, Wilts SN6 7SH. *T*: Swindon 762331.

HAMMOND, Eric Albert Barratt, OBE 1977; General Secretary, Electrical, Electronic, Telecommunication and Plumbing Union, since 1984; Member, General Council, TUC, since 1983; *b* 17 July 1929; *s* of Arthur Edgar Hammond and Gertrude May Hammond; *m* 1953, Brenda Mary Edgeler; two *s*. *Educ*: Corner Brook Public Sch. Shop Steward, 1953–63; Branch Sec., 1958–63, Exec. Councillor, 1963–, EETPU. Borough and Urban District Councillor, 1958–63. Member: Electronics EDC, 1967–; Industrial Development Adv. Bd, 1977–; Adv. Council on Energy Conservation, 1974–77; (part-time) Monopolies and Mergers Commn, 1978–84; Engrg Council, 1984–; ACARD, 1985–; Chm., Electronic Components Sector Working Party, 1975–. *Recreations*: gardening, photography. *Address*: 9 Dene Holm Road, Northfleet, Kent DA11 8LF. *T*: Gravesend 63856. *Clubs*: Northfleet Traders'; Gravesend Rugby.

HAMMOND, James Anthony; His Honour Judge Hammond; a Circuit Judge, since 1986; *b* 25 July 1936; *s* of James Hammond and Phyllis Eileen Hammond; *m* 1963, Sheila Mary Hammond, JP (*née* Stafford); three *d*. *Educ*: Wigan Grammar Sch.; St Catherine's Coll., Oxford (BA). Called to Bar, Lincoln's Inn, 1959; National Service, 1959–61; a Recorder, 1980–86. Councillor: Up Holland UDC, 1962–66; Skelmersdale and Holland UDC, 1970–72. Chairman: NW Branch, Society of Labour Lawyers, 1975–86; W Lancs CAB, 1982–86. *Recreations*: hockey, walking, sailing, pub quizzes. *Clubs*: Wigan Hockey (Vice Pres., 1983–); Orrell Rugby Union Football.

HAMMOND, Dame Joan (Hood), DBE 1974 (CBE 1963; OBE 1953); CMG 1972; Australian operatic, concert, oratorio, and recital singer; *b* 24 May 1912; *d* of late Samuel Hood Hammond and Hilda May Blandford. *Educ*: Presbyterian Ladies Coll., Pymble, Sydney, Australia. Student of violin and singing at Sydney Conservatorium of Music; played with Sydney Philharmonic Orchestra for three years. Sports writer, Daily Telegraph, Sydney. Commenced public appearances (singing) in Sydney, 1929; studied in Europe from 1936; made operatic debut, Vienna, 1939; London debut in Messiah, 1938. World Tours: British Isles, USA, Canada, Australasia, Malaya, India, E and S Africa, Europe, Scandinavia, Russia, etc. Guest Artist: Royal Opera House, Covent Garden; Carl Rosa; Sadler's Wells; Vienna Staatsoper; Bolshoi, Moscow; Marinsky, Leningrad; Riga, Latvia; New York City Centre; Australian Elizabethan Theatre Trust; Netherlands Opera, Barcelona Liceo. Operatic roles: Aida, Madame Butterfly, Tosca, Salome, Otello, Thaïs, Faust, Don Carlos, Eugene Onegin, Invisible City of Kitej, La Traviata, Il Trovatore, La Bohème, Pique Dame, Manon, Manon Lescaut, La Forza del Destino, Fidelio, Simone Boccanegra, Turandot, Tannhauser, Lohengrin, Damnation of Faust, Martha, Pagliacci, Der Freischutz, Oberon, Magic Flute, Dido and Aeneas; World Premieres: Trojan Women, Wat Tyler, Yerma; British Premiere, Rusalka. HMV Recording artist. Head of Vocal Studies, Victorian College of the Arts. Volunteer Ambulance Driver, London, War of 1939–45. Sir Charles Santley Award, Worshipful Co. of Musicians, 1970. Hon. Life Member: Australian Opera; Victoria State Opera. Hon. MusD Western Australia, 1979. Coronation Medal 1953. *Publication*: A Voice, A Life, 1970. *Recreations*: golf (won first junior Golf Championship of NSW, 1930 and 1931; NSW LGU State Title, 1932, 1934, 1935; runner-up Australian Open Championship, 1933; Mem. first LGU team of Australia to compete against Gt Brit., 1935) (runner-up NSW State Squash Championship, 1934), yachting, swimming, tennis, writing, reading. *Address*: 46 Lansell Road, Toorak,

Victoria 3142, Australia. *Clubs:* New Century (London); Royal Sydney Golf; Royal Motor Yacht (Dorset, England).

HAMMOND, (John) Martin; Headmaster, City of London School, since 1984; *b* 15 Nov. 1944; *s* of Thomas Chatterton Hammond and Joan Cruse; *m* 1974, Meredith Jane Shier; one *s* one *d.* *Educ:* Winchester Coll. (Scholar); Balliol Coll., Oxford (Domus Scholar). Oxford University: Hertford Scholar and (1st) de Paravicini Scholar, (2nd) Craven Scholar, 1st Cl. Hons Mods, 1963; Chancellor's Latin Prose Prize, Chancellor's Latin Verse Prize, Ireland Scholar, 1964; Gaisford Greek Prose Prize, Gaisford Greek Verse Prize (jtly), 1965; 2nd Cl. Lit. Hum. 1966. Asst Master, St Paul's Sch., 1966–71; Teacher, Anargyrios Sch., Spetsai, Greece, 1972–73; Asst Master, Harrow Sch., 1973–74; Head of Classics, 1974–80, and Master in College, 1980–84, Eton Coll. *Address:* City of London School, Queen Victoria Street, EC4V 3AL. *T:* 01–489 0291.

HAMMOND, Michael Harry Frank; Chief Executive and Town Clerk, Nottingham City Council, since 1974; *b* 5 June 1933; *s* of late Edward Cecil Hammond and Kate Hammond; *m* 1965, Jenny Campbell; two *s* one *d.* *Educ:* Leatherhead; Law Society Sch. of Law. Admitted solicitor, 1958; Asst Sol. in Town Clerk's office, Nottingham, 1961–63; Prosecuting Sol., 1963–66; Asst Town Clerk, 1966–69; Dep. Town Clerk, Newport, Mon, 1969–71; Dep. Town Clerk, Nottingham, 1971–74. Hon. Sec., Major City Councils Gp, and Notts County Br., Assoc. of District Councils. An Elections Supervisor, Rhodesia/Zimbabwe Independence Elections, 1980. Rhodesia Medal, 1980; Zimbabwe Independence Medal, 1980. *Recreations:* gardening, walking. *Address:* 41 Burlington Road, Sherwood, Nottingham NG5 2GR. *T:* Nottingham 602000.

HAMMOND, Prof. Nicholas Geoffrey Lemprière, CBE 1974; DSO 1944; FBA 1968; DL; Henry Overton Wills Professor of Greek, University of Bristol, 1962–73; a Pro-Vice-Chancellor, 1964–66; *b* 15 Nov. 1907; *s* of late Rev. James Vavasour Hammond, Rector of St Just-in-Roseland, Cornwall, and Dorothy May; *m* 1938, Margaret Campbell, *d* of James W. J. Townley, CBE, MIEE; two *s* three *d.* *Educ:* Fettes Coll. (schol.); Caius Coll., Cambridge (schol.). 1st Cl. Classical Tripos Pts I and II, dist. in Hist., Pt II; Montagu Butler Prize; Sandys Student; Pres. CU Hockey Club; Treas. Union Soc. Fellow Clare Coll., Cambridge, 1930; University Lectr in Classics, 1936; Junior Proctor, 1939; Sen. Tutor, Clare Coll., 1947–54 (Hon. Fellow, 1974); Headmaster, Clifton Coll., 1954–62. Johnson Prof., Wisconsin Univ., 1973–74; Mellon Prof., Reed Coll., Oregon, 1975–76; Brittingham Prof., Wisconsin Univ., 1977; Leverhulme Prof., Univ. of Ioannina, 1978; Visiting Professor: Haverford Coll., 1978; Univ. of Auckland, 1980; St Olaf Coll., Minnesota, 1981; Pennsylvania Univ., 1982; Cornell Prof., Swarthmore Coll., Pennsylvania, 1983; Trinity Coll., Hartford, 1984; Adelaide Univ., 1984; Nat. Hellenic Res. Foundn, 1985; Nat. Humanities Center, N Carolina, 1986. Chm., Managing Cttee, British Sch. at Athens, 1972–75. Served War of 1939–45, as Lt-Col, campaigns in Greece, Crete, Syria, and Mem. Allied Mil. Mission, Greece, 1943–44 (despatches twice, DSO). Pres., Hellenic Soc., 1965–68. DL: Bristol, 1965; Cambridge, 1974. Hon. DLett: Wisconsin, 1981; St Olaf Coll., 1982. Officer, Order of the Phœnix, Greece, 1946. *Publications:* Memoir of Sir John Edwin Sandys, 1933; History of Greece, 1959, 2nd edn, 1967; Epirus, 1967; A History of Macedonia, Vol. 1, 1972, Vol. 2, 1979; Studies in Greek History, 1973; The Classical Age of Greece, 1976; Migrations and Invasions in Greece, 1976; Alexander the Great: King Commander and Statesman, 1981; Venture into Greece: with the guerillas, 1943–44, 1983; Three Historians of Alexander the Great, 1983; Editor: Clifton Coll. Centenary Essays, 1962; Cambridge Ancient History, 3rd edn, vols I, II and III; Oxford Classical Dictionary, 2nd edn, 1970; Atlas of the Greek and Roman World in Antiquity, 1981; articles and reviews in learned jls. *Address:* 3 Belvoir Terrace, Trumpington Road, Cambridge. *T:* Cambridge 357151.

HAMMOND, Roy John William; Director, City of Birmingham Polytechnic, 1979–84; *b* 3 Oct. 1928; *s* of John James Hammond and Edith May Hammond; *m* 1949, Audrey Cecilia Dagmar Avello; three *d.* *Educ:* East Ham Grammar Sch.; University College of the South West, Exeter; Sorbonne, Paris. BA Hons, 1st Cl. French and Latin, London. Royal Air Force Education Branch, 1952–56; Asst Lectr, Blackburn Municipal Technical Coll. and School of Art, 1956–59; Head of Department: Herefordshire Technical Coll., 1960–66; Leeds Polytechnic, 1966–71; Asst Dir, City of Birmingham Polytechnic, 1971–79. *Recreations:* cricket, theatre, music, walking.

HAMMOND INNES, Ralph, CBE 1978; DLitt; author and traveller; *b* 15 July 1913; *s* of late William Hammond and Dora Beatrice Innes; *m* 1937, Dorothy Mary Lang. Staff of Financial News, 1934–40. Served Artillery, 1940–46. Member: various cttees, Soc. of Authors, sailing foundns, Timber Growers' Orgn; Vice President: Assoc. of Sea Training Orgns; World Ship Trust. Works regularly translated into numerous languages; many book club and paperback edns throughout the world. *Publications include:* Wreckers Must Breathe, 1940; The Trojan Horse, 1940; Attack Alarm, 1941; Dead and Alive, 1946; The Lonely Skier, 1947; The Killer Mine, 1947; Maddon's Rock, 1948; The Blue Ice, 1948; The White South (Book Society Choice), 1949; The Angry Mountain, 1950; Air Bridge, 1951; Campbell's Kingdom (Book Society Choice), 1952; The Strange Land, 1954; The Mary Deare (chosen by Literary Guild of America, Book Soc. Choice), 1956; The Land God Gave to Cain, 1958; Harvest of Journeys (Book Soc. Choice), 1959; The Doomed Oasis (chosen by Literary Guild of America, Book Soc. Choice), 1960; Atlantic Fury (Book Society Choice), 1962; Scandinavia, 1963; The Strode Venturer, 1965; Sea and Islands (Book Society Choice), 1967; The Conquistadors (Book of the Month and Literary Guild), 1969; Levkas Man, 1971; Golden Soak, 1973; North Star, 1974; The Big Footprints, 1977; The Last Voyage (Cook), 1978; Solomons Seal, 1980; The Black Tide, 1982; High Stand, 1985; Hammond Innes' East Anglia, 1986; *films:* Snowbound, Hell Below Zero, Campbell's Kingdom, The Wreck of the Mary Deare; *TV:* Explorers (Cook), 1975; Golden Soak, 1979; Levkas Man, 1981. *Recreations:* cruising and ocean racing, forestry. *Address:* Ayres End, Kersey, Suffolk IP7 6EB. *T:* Hadleigh 823294. *Clubs:* Royal Ocean Racing, Royal Cruising; Royal Yacht Squadron.

HAMMOND-STROUD, Derek; concert and opera baritone; *b* 10 Jan. 1926; *s* of Herbert William Stroud and Ethel Louise Elliott. *Educ:* Salvatorian Coll., Harrow, Mddx; Trinity Coll. of Music, London; in Vienna and Munich with Elena Gerhardt and Gerhard Hüsch. Glyndebourne Festival Opera, 1959; Sadler's Wells Opera (later ENO), 1961; Houston Grand Opera, USA, 1975; Royal Opera, Covent Garden, 1975; Netherlands Opera, 1976; Metropolitan Opera, NY, 1977; Teatro Colón, Buenos Aires, 1981. Concerts and Lieder recitals at Edinburgh, Aldeburgh, Munich and Vienna Festivals, and in Spain, Iceland and Denmark. Pres., Univ. of London Opera Gp, 1971. Freeman, City of London, 1952; Hon. RAM 1976; Hon. FTCL, 1982. Recordings include: The Ring (Goodall); Der Rosenkavalier (de Waart). *Recreations:* chess, study of philosophy. *Address:* 18 Sutton Road, Muswell Hill, N10 1HE.

HAMNETT, Thomas Orlando; Chairman, Greater Manchester Council, 1975–1976, Vice-Chairman, 1976; *b* 28 Sept. 1930; *s* of John and Elizabeth Hamnett; *m* 1954, Kathleen Ridgway; one *s* five *d.* *Educ:* Stockport Jun. Techn. Sch. Sheetmetal craftsman, 1946–. Member, Manchester City Council, 1963 until re-organisation (Vice-Chm., Health Cttee, Chm. sub cttee on Staff on Cleansing Cttee, Mem. Policy and Finance Cttees), and 1978– (Member Direct works, Markets, and Personnel Cttees); Mem. Transportation, Education, and Recreation and Arts Cttees, Greater Manchester Council; Chm., Environmental Services Cttee, City of Manchester, 1982–. *Recreations:* football, cricket, table tennis. *Address:* 199 Chapman Street, Gorton, Manchester M18 8WP. *T:* 061–223 3098. *Club:* Gorton Trades and Labour (Chm.).

HAMPDEN; *see* Hobart-Hampden.

HAMPDEN, 6th Viscount *cr* 1884; **Anthony David Brand;** land agent; *b* 7 May 1937; *s* of 5th Viscount Hampden and of Imogen Alice Rhys, *d* of 7th Baron Dynevor; *S* father, 1975; *m* 1969, Cara Fiona, *e d* of Claud Proby; two *s* one *d.* *Educ:* Eton. Chairman: Sussex CLA, 1985–; Governing Body, Emanuel Sch., 1985–. *Publication:* Henry and Eliza, 1980. *Heir:* *s* Hon. Francis Anthony Brand, *b* 17 Sept. 1970. *Address:* Glynde Place, Glynde, Lewes, Sussex. *Club:* White's.

HAMPSHIRE, Margaret Grace, MA; JP; Principal of Cheltenham Ladies' College, 1964–79; *b* 7 Sept. 1918; *o d* of Dr C. H. Hampshire, CMG, MB, BS, BSc, sometime Sec. of British Pharmacopœia Commission, and Grace Mary Hampshire. *Educ:* Malvern Girls' Coll.; Girton Coll., Cambridge. BA 1941; MA 1945. Entered Civil Service, Board of Trade, 1941. Joined Staff of Courtaulds, 1951. Head of Government Relations Department, 1959–64. Member: Board of Governors, University Coll. Hosp., 1961–64; Marylebone Borough Council, 1962–64; SW Regional Hosp. Board, 1967–70; Midlands Electricity Consultative Council, 1973–80; Vice-Pres., Intensive Care Trust, Cheltenham Hosp., 1985– (Chm., 1982–85). County Sec., Gloucestershire Girl Guides, 1980–85; Governor, Alice Ottley Sch., Worcester, 1979–. JP Cheltenham, 1970. *Recreations:* music, reading, foreign travel. *Address:* Ringwood, 9 The Croft, Painswick, Glos GL6 6QP.

HAMPSHIRE, Sir Stuart (Newton), Kt 1979; FBA 1960; Warden of Wadham College, Oxford University, 1970–84; *b* 1 Oct. 1914; *s* of G. N. Hampshire and Marie West; *m* 1st, 1961, Renee Ayer (*d* 1980); 2nd, 1985, Nancy Cartwright; two *d.* *Educ:* Repton; Balliol Coll., Oxford. 1st Cl. Lit Hum, Oxford, 1936. Fellow of All Souls Coll., and Lectr in Philosophy, Oxford, 1936–40. Service in Army, 1940–45. Personal Asst to Minister of State, Foreign Office, 1945; Lectr in Philosophy, University Coll., London, 1947–50; Fellow of New Coll., Oxford, 1950–55; Domestic Bursar and Research Fellow, All Souls Coll., 1955–60; Grote Prof. of Philosophy of Mind and Logic, Univ. of London, 1960–63; Prof. of Philosophy, Princeton Univ., 1963–70. Fellow, Amer. Acad. of Arts and Sciences, 1968. Hon. DLitt Glasgow, 1973. *Publications:* Spinoza, 1951; Thought and Action, 1959; Freedom of the Individual, 1965; Modern Writers and other essays, 1969; Freedom of Mind and other essays, 1971; (ed jtly) The Socialist Idea, 1975; Two Theories of Morality, 1977; (ed) Public and Private Morality, 1978; Morality and Conflict, 1983; articles in philosophical journals. *Address:* 79 Old High Street, Headington, Oxford. *T:* Oxford 750977; 334 Laurel Avenue, Menlo Park, Calif 94025, USA.

HAMPSHIRE, Susan; actress; *b* 12 May 1942; *d* of George Kenneth Hampshire and June Hampshire; *m* 1st, 1967, Pierre Granier-Deferre (marr. diss. 1974); one *s* (one *d* decd); 2nd, 1981, Eddie Kulukundis, *qv.* *Educ:* Hampshire Sch., Knightsbridge. *Stage:* Expresso Bongo, 1958; 'that girl' in Follow That Girl, 1960; Fairy Tales of New York, 1961; Marion Dangerfield in Ginger Man, 1963; Kate Hardcastle in She Stoops to Conquer, 1966; On Approval, 1966; Mary in The Sleeping Prince, 1968; Nora in A Doll's House, 1972; Katharina in The Taming of the Shrew, 1974; Peter in Peter Pan, 1974; Jeannette in Romeo and Jeannette, 1975; Rosalind in As You Like It, 1975; title rôle in Miss Julie, 1975; Elizabeth in The Circle, 1976; Ann Whitefield in Man and Superman, 1978; Siri Von Essen in Tribades, 1978; Victorine in An Audience Called Edouard, 1978; Irene in The Crucifer of Blood, 1979; Ruth Carson in Night and Day, 1979; Elizabeth in The Revolt, 1980; Stella Drury in House Guest, 1981; *TV Serials:* Andromeda (title rôle), Fleur Forsyte in The Forsyte Saga (Emmy Award for Best Actress, 1970), Becky Sharp in Vanity Fair (Emmy Award for Best Actress, 1973), Sarah Churchill, Duchess of Marlborough, in The First Churchills (Emmy Award for Best Actress, 1971), Glencora Palliser in The Pallisers; Lady Melfont in Dick Turpin; Signora Neroni in The Barchester Chronicles; Martha in Leaving, 1 and 2; Katy in What Katy Did; Going to Pot, 1, 2 and 3. *Films include:* During One Night, The Three Lives of Thomasina, Night Must Fall, Wonderful Life, Paris in August, The Fighting Prince of Donegal, Monte Carlo or Bust, Rogan, David Copperfield, Living Free, A Time for Loving, Malpertius (E. Poe Prizes du Film Fantastique, Best Actress, 1972), Neither the Sea Nor the Sand, Roses and Green Peppers, Bang. Dir, Conservation Foundn; Mem. Exec. Cttee, Population Concern. Hon. DLitt: City, 1984; St Andrews, 1986. *Publications:* Susan's Story, 1981; The Maternal Instinct, 1984; Lucy Jane at the Ballet, 1985; Lucy Jane Makes a Film, 1986. *Recreations:* gardening, music, the study of antique furniture. *Address:* c/o Midland Bank, 92 Kensington High Street, W8 4SH. *T:* 01–937 0962.

HAMPSON, Prof. Elwyn Lloyd, MDS, FDSRCS; HDD RCSE; Professor of Restorative Dentistry, University of Sheffield, 1960–81, now Emeritus; Hon. Consultant Dental Surgeon to Sheffield Area Health Authority; *b* 31 Jan. 1916; *s* of John and Mary Hampson; *m* 1940, Anne Cottrell; one *s* one *d.* *Educ:* Calday Grange Grammar Sch., W Kirby, Cheshire; Univ. of Liverpool. BDS with 1st Class Hons 1939; HDD RCSE 1944; FDSRCS 1949; MDS 1954; FDSE 1964. House surg., Liverpool Dental Hosp., 1939; Royal Army Dental Corps, 1941–45; Lecturer in Operative Dental Surgery, Edinburgh Dental Sch., 1945–47; Lecturer and later Senior Lecturer in Operative Dental Surgery, Univ. of Sheffield, 1947–60, Dean of Sch. of Clinical Dentistry, 1968–72. Mem., GDC, 1968–73. *Publications:* Hampson's Textbook of Operative Dental Surgery, 1961, 4th edn 1980; many papers in scientific jls. *Recreations:* water colour painting, golf. *Address:* 8 Milborne Close, Chester CH2 1HH.

HAMPSON, Dr Keith; MP (C) Leeds North-West, since 1983 (Ripon, Feb. 1974–1983); *b* 14 Aug. 1943; *s* of Bertie Hampson and Mary Elizabeth Noble; *m* 1st, 1975, Frances Pauline (*d* 1975), *d* of Mr and Mrs Mathieu Donald Einhorn; 2nd, 1979, Susan, *d* of Mr and Mrs John Wilkie Cameron. *Educ:* King James I Grammar Sch., Bishop Auckland, Co. Durham; Univ. of Bristol; Harvard Univ. BA, CertEd, PhD. Personal Asst to Edward Heath, 1966 and 1970 Gen. Elections and in his House of Commons office, 1968; Lectr in American History, Edinburgh Univ., 1968–74. PPS: to Minister for Local Govt, 1979–83; to Sec. of State for Environment, 1983; to Sec. of State for Defence, 1983–84. Vice Chm., Cons. Parly Educn Cttee, 1975–79; Mem., Educn Adv. Cttee of UK Commn for UNESCO, 1980–. Vice President: WEA, 1978–; Assoc. of Business Executives, 1979–; Vice-Chm., Youthaid, 1979–. *Recreations:* tennis, DIY, music. *Address:* House of Commons, SW1A 0AA. *T:* 01–219 4463. *Club:* Carlton.

HAMPSON, Prof. Norman, FBA 1980; Professor of History, University of York, since 1974; *b* 8 April 1922; *s* of Frank Hampson and Elizabeth Jane Fazackerley; *m* 1948, Jacqueline Gardin; two *d.* *Educ:* Manchester Grammar Sch.; University Coll., Oxford (MA); Dr de l'Univ. Paris. Service in Royal Navy, 1941–45. Manchester Univ., 1948–67: Lectr and Sen. Lectr; Prof. of Modern History, Univ. of Newcastle, 1967–74. *Publications:* La Marine de l'an II, 1959; A Social History of the French Revolution, 1963; The Enlightenment, 1968; The First European Revolution, 1969; The Life and Opinions of Maximilien Robespierre, 1974; A Concise History of the French Revolution, 1975;

Danton, 1978; Will and Circumstance: Montesquieu, Rousseau and the French Revolution, 1983. *Address:* 305 Hull Road, York YO1 3LB. *T:* York 412661.

HAMPSTEAD, Archdeacon of; *see* Coogan, Ven. R. A. W.

HAMPTON, 6th Baron *cr* 1874; **Richard Humphrey Russell Pakington;** Bt 1846; *b* 25 May 1925; *s* of 5th Baron Hampton, OBE, and Grace Dykes (*d* 1959), 3rd *d* of Rt Hon. Sir Albert Spicer, 1st Bt; *S* father, 1974; *m* 1958, Jane Elizabeth Farquharson, *d* of late T. F. Arnott, OBE, TD, MB, ChB; one *s* two *d. Educ:* Eton; Balliol Coll., Oxford. Observer in Fleet Air Arm, RNVR, 1944–47. Varied employment, mainly with advertising agencies, 1949–58; Worcestershire Branch Council for the Protection of Rural England, 1958–71; Tansley Witt & Co., Chartered Accts, Birmingham, 1971–73. *Publication:* (written with his father, Humphrey Pakington) The Pakingtons of Westwood, 1975. *Heir: s* Hon. John Humphrey Arnott Pakington, *b* 24 Dec. 1964. *Address:* Palace Farmhouse, Upton-on-Severn, Worcester WR8 0SN. *T:* Upton-on-Severn 2512.

HAMPTON, Antony Barmore, TD 1954; DL; President, Record Marples Tools Ltd (formerly Bahco Record Tools), since 1981 (Chairman, 1958–81); Chairman, Hamptons Wholefoods Ltd, since 1985; President, Engineering Employers Federation, 1980–82; *b* 6 March 1919; *s* of Charles William Hampton and Winifred Elizabeth Hampton; *m* 1948, Helen Patricia Lockwood; five *s. Educ:* Rydal Sch.; Christ's Coll., Cambridge, 1938–40 (MA). Indian Army 1941–46 (despatches). C. and J. Hampton Ltd, 1947, until merger with Ridgway, 1972 (Chm. of both, 1958–81); Lloyds Bank Ltd: Chm., Yorkshire Board, 1972–84 (Mem., 1961–85); Director, UK Board, 1972–85. Dir, Black Horse Agencies Ltd, 1983–85; Mem., Engrg Industry Trng Bd, 1979–82; Master Cutler of Hallamshire, 1966–67. Chm., Crucible Theatre Trust, Sheffield, 1970–82. DL S Yorkshire (previously W Riding) 1972. *Recreations:* sailing, fishing. *Address:* Tideway, 20 Wittering Road, Hayling Island, Hants PO11 9SP. *T:* Hayling Island 4361. *Club:* Little Ship.

HAMPTON, Bryan; Head, Branch 1, Atomic Energy Division, Department of Energy, since 1986; *b* 4 Dec. 1938; *s* of William Douglas Hampton and Elizabeth Cardwell; *m* 1964, Marilyn Joseph; five *d. Educ:* Harrow County Grammar Sch. for Boys. Board of Trade: Exec. Officer, 1957; Asst Private Sec. to Parly Sec., 1961; Private Sec. to Minister of State (Lords), 1963; Asst Principal, 1965; Second Sec., UK Delegn to EFTA/GATT, Geneva, 1966; Principal, DTI, 1969; Asst Sec., Dept of Energy, 1974; Counsellor (Energy), Washington, 1981–86. *Recreations:* music, cricket, golf. *Address:* Orchard House, Berks Hill, Chorleywood, Herts WD3 5AG. *T:* Chorleywood 2311. *Club:* International (Washington).

HAMPTON, Christopher James, FRSL 1976; playwright; *b* 26 Jan. 1946; *s* of Bernard Patrick Hampton and Dorothy Patience Hampton (*née* Herrington); *m* 1971, Laura Margaret de Holesch; two *d. Educ:* Lancing Coll.; New Coll., Oxford (MA). First play: When Did You Last See My Mother?, 1964 (perf. Royal Court Theatre, 1966; transf. Comedy Theatre; prod. at Sheridan Square Playhouse, New York, 1967). Resident Dramatist, Royal Court Theatre, Aug. 1968–70. Mem. Council, RSL, 1984–. *Plays:* Total Eclipse, Prod. Royal Court, 1968; The Philanthropist, Royal Court and Mayfair, 1970 (Evening Standard Best Comedy Award, 1970; Plays & Players London Theatre Critics Best Play, 1970), Ethel Barrymore Theatre, New York, 1971, Chichester, 1985; Savages, Royal Court, 1973, Comedy, 1973, Mark Taper Forum Theatre, Los Angeles, 1974 (Plays & Players London Theatre Critics Best Play, Jt Winner, 1973; Los Angeles Drama Critics Circle Award for Distinguished Playwriting, 1974); Treats, Royal Court, 1976, Mayfair, 1976; Able's Will, BBC TV, 1977; After Mercer, Nat. Theatre, 1980; The History Man (from Malcolm Bradbury) BBC TV, 1981; Total Eclipse (rev. version) Lyric, Hammersmith, 1981; The Portage to San Cristobal of A. H. (from George Steiner), Mermaid, 1982; Tales from Hollywood, Mark Taper Forum Theatre, Los Angeles, 1982, NT 1983 (Standard Best Comedy Award, 1983); Les Liaisons Dangereuses (from Laclos), RSC, 1985 (Plays & Players London Theatre Critics Best Play, Jt Winner, 1985); Hotel du Lac (from Anita Brookner), BBC TV, 1986; *translations:* Marya, by Isaac Babel, Royal Court, 1967; Uncle Vanya, by Chekhov, Royal Court, 1970; Hedda Gabler, by Ibsen, Fest. Theatre, Stratford, Ont, 1970, Almeida, Islington, 1984; A Doll's House, by Ibsen, Playhouse Theatre, New York, 1971, Criterion, London, 1973, Vivian Beaumont Theatre, New York, 1975; Don Juan, by Molière, Bristol Old Vic, 1972; Tales from the Vienna Woods, by Horváth, National Theatre, 1977; Don Juan Comes Back from the War, by Horváth, Nat. Theatre, 1978; Ghosts, by Ibsen, Actors' Co., 1978; The Wild Duck, by Ibsen, Nat. Theatre, 1979; The Prague Trial, by Chereau and Mnouchkine, Paris Studio, 1980; Tartuffe, by Molière, RSC, 1983; *films:* A Doll's House, 1973; Tales From the Vienna Woods, 1979; The Honorary Consul, 1983; The Good Father, 1986. *Publications:* When Did You Last See My Mother?, 1967; Total Eclipse, 1969, rev. version, 1981; The Philanthropist, 1970, 2nd edn 1985; Savages, 1974; Treats, 1976; Able's Will, 1979; Tales from Hollywood, 1983; The Portage to San Cristobal of A. H. (George Steiner), 1983; Les Liaisons Dangereuses, 1985; *translations:* Isaac Babel, Marya, 1969; Chekhov, Uncle Vanya, 1971; Ibsen, Hedda Gabler, 1972; Ibsen, A Doll's House, 1972; Molière, Don Juan, 1972; Horváth, Tales from the Vienna Woods, 1977; Horváth, Don Juan Comes Back from the War, 1978; Ibsen: The Wild Duck, 1980; Ghosts, 1983; Molière, Tartuffe, 1984. *Recreations:* travel, cinema. *Address:* 2 Kensington Park Gardens, W11. *Club:* Dramatists'.

HAMPTON, John; a Recorder of the Crown Court, since 1983; *b* 13 Nov. 1926; *e s* of late Thomas Victor Hampton and Alice Maud (*née* Sturgeon), Oulton Broad; *m* 1954, Laura Jessie, *d* of Ronald Mylne Ford and Margaret Jessie Ford (*née* Coghill), Newcastle-under-Lyme; three *d. Educ:* Bradford Grammar School; University College London (LLB). Served Royal Navy, 1945–47. Called to the Bar, Inner Temple, 1952; NE Circuit; Solicitor General and Attorney General; Dep. Circuit Judge, 1975–82. Dep. Chm., Agricultural Land Tribunal, Yorks and Lancs Area, 1980–82, Yorks and Humberside Area, 1982–. *Recreations:* mountaineering, sailing. *Address:* 38 Park Square, Leeds LS1 2PA. *T:* Leeds 439422. *Club:* Leeds (Leeds).

HAMPTON, Surgeon Rear-Adm. Trevor Richard Walker, QHP 1983; FRCPE; Surgeon Rear-Admiral (Operational Medical Services), since 1987; *b* 6 June 1930; *s* of Violet and Percy Hampton; *m* 1st, 1952, Rosemary (*née* Day); three *d*; 2nd, 1976, Jennifer (*née* Bootle). *Educ:* King Edward VII Grammar School, King's Lynn; Edinburgh University. MB, ChB 1954; MRCPE 1964. Resident House Officer, Edinburgh Royal Infirmary, 1954–55; joined RN as Surgeon Lieut, 1955; served in HM Ships Ganges, Harrier and Victorious, 1955–62; Clinical Asst, Dept of Medicine, Edinburgh Univ., 1964; RN Hosp., Gibraltar, 1965–68; Consultant Physician, RN Hospitals, Plymouth, 1969–74, Haslar, 1975–79; MO i/c, RN Hosp., Gibraltar, 1980–82, RN Hosp., Plymouth, 1982–84; Surgeon Rear-Adm., Support Medical Services, 1984–87. OStJ 1983. *Publications:* contribs to Jl of RN Med. Service. *Recreations:* cricket, amateur theatre, resting. *Address:* c/o Lloyds Bank, Cosham, Hants.

HAMSON, Prof. Charles John, QC 1975; Professor of Comparative Law, University of Cambridge, 1953–73; Fellow of Trinity College, since 1934; Barrister-at-Law, Gray's Inn, Bencher, 1956, Treasurer, 1975; Correspondent, Institut de France (Acad. Sci. Mor. et Pol.), since 1961; Doctor *hc* Universities of Grenoble, Nancy, Poitiers, Bordeaux, Brussels, Montpellier, Strasbourg; Hon. Fellow, St Edmund's House, Cambridge, 1976; Chevalier de la Légion d'Honneur; *b* 23 Nov. 1905; *er s* of Charles Edward Hamson (formerly of Constantinople), and of Thérèse Boudon; *m* 1933, Isabella (*d* 1978), *y d* of Duncan Drummond and Grace Gardiner of Auchterarder; one *d. Educ:* Downside; Trinity Coll., Cambridge. Entrance and Sen. Scholar in Classics; Classical Tripos Part I 1925, Part II 1927 (distinction); Capt. CU Epée Team, 1928; Davison Scholar, Harvard Law Sch., 1928–29; Linthicum Foundation Prize (North-western Univ.) 1929; Yorke Prize, 1932; LLB 1934; LLM 1935. Asst Lecturer, 1932, Lecturer, 1934, Reader in Comparative Law, 1949; Chm. Faculty Board of Law, 1954–57. Editor, Cambridge Law Jl, 1955–74; Univ. Press Syndic, 1955–69; Library Syndic, 1966–73; Gen. Bd, 1966–69. President: Internat. Acad. of Comparative Law, 1966–79; CU Catholic Assoc., 1964–76; St Edmund's Assoc., 1977–81. Served War of 1939–45; commissioned in Army, 1940; detached for service with SOE; Battle of Crete, 1941; POW Germany, 1941–45. Hamlyn Lectures on Conseil d'Etat, 1954; Visiting Professor: University of Michigan Law Sch. (Ann Arbor), 1957; Paris Faculty of Law, 1959; Univ. of Pennsylvania, 1964; Auckland Univ., 1967; professeur associé, Paris II, 1973–74; Sherill Lectr, Yale Law Sch., 1960; Wiener-Anspach Inaugural Lectr, Univ. of Brussels, 1978. *Address:* Trinity College, Cambridge. *T:* Cambridge 338525.

See also J. R. Cann.

HAMYLTON JONES, Keith, CMG 1979; HM Diplomatic Service, retired; HM Ambassador, to Costa Rica, 1974–79, to Honduras, 1975–78, and to Nicaragua, 1976–79; *b* 12 Oct. 1924; *m* 1953, Eira Morgan; one *d. Educ:* St Paul's Sch.; Balliol Coll., Oxford (Domus Scholar in Classics, 1943); BA 1948; MA 1950. Welsh Guards, 1943; Italy, 1944 (Lieut); S France, 1946 (Staff Captain). HM Foreign Service, 1949; 3rd Sec., Warsaw, 1950; 2nd Sec., Lisbon, 1953; 1st Sec., Manila, 1957; Head of Chancery and HM Consul, Montevideo, 1962; Head of Chancery, Rangoon, 1967; Asst Head of SE Asia Dept, FCO, 1968; Consul-General, Lubumbashi, 1970–72; Counsellor, FCO, 1973–74. Operation Raleigh: Chm. for Devon and Cornwall, 1983–85; led internat. expedn to Costa Rica, Feb–May 1985. *Publication:* (as Peter Myllent) The Ideal World, 1972. *Recreations:* reading, writing, walking. *Address:* Morval House, Morval, near Looe, Cornwall.

HAN Suyin, (Dr Elizabeth Comber); doctor and author; (*née* Elizabeth Kuanghu Chow); *b* 12 Sept. 1917; *d* of Y. T. Chow (Chinese) and M. Denis (Belgian); *m* 1st, 1938, General P. H. Tang, (*d* 1947); 2nd, 1952, L. F. Comber (marr. diss. 1968). *Educ:* Yenching Univ., Peking, China; Brussels Univ., Brussels, Belgium; London Univ., London, England. Graduated MB, BS, London (Hons) in 1948, a practising doctor until 1964. *Publications: as Han Suyin:* Destination Chungking, 1942; A Many Splendoured Thing, 1952; And the Rain My Drink, 1956; The Mountain Is Young, 1958; Cast but One Shadow and Winter Love, 1962; The Four Faces, 1963; China in the Year 2001, 1967; The Morning Deluge, 1972; Wind in the Tower, 1976; Lhasa, the Open City, 1977; Les Cent Fleurs: La Peinture Chinoise, 1978; La Chine aux Mille Visages, 1980; Chine: Terre Eau et Hommes, 1981; Till Morning Comes, 1982; The Enchantress, 1985; *autobiography:* China: autobiography, history (4 vols): The Crippled Tree, 1965; A Mortal Flower, 1966; Birdless Summer, 1968; My House Has Two Doors, 1980. *Recreations:* botany, riding, swimming, lecturing. *Address:* c/o Sidgwick & Jackson, 1 Tavistock Chambers, Bloomsbury Way, WC1.

HANANIYA, Maj.-Gen. Haldu A., OFR 1986; Nigerian Ambassador to Ethiopia since 1984; *b* 2 Feb. 1942; *m* Rhoda A. Hananiya; one *s* five *d. Educ:* Boys Secondary School, Gindiri; Nigerian Military Training Centre; Officer Cadet School, UK (commissioned 1963); RSME course, 1963; Plant Engr Officers' Course, 1965–66, Engr Advance Officers' Course, 1971–72, Fort Belvoir, USA. Nigerian Army Engineers: Comdr 1 and 2 Field Engr Sqdns, 1966; Cmdr 1 Field Regt, 1966–70; Comdr 2 Field Engr Regt, 1970–71, 1972–73; Inspector of Engrs, 1974–77; Command and Staff Coll., 1977; Comdr, 1 Inf. Bde, Nigerian Army, 1977–78; Defence Adviser, London, 1979–80; student, Nigerian Inst. for Policy and Strategic Studies, 1979–80; Director of Training, Army HQ, 1981; GOC 2 Mech. Inf. Div., Nigerian Army, 1981–83 (Defence Resources Management Course, 1982); GOC 1 Mech. Inf. Div., 1983–84; High Comr to UK, 1984. *Recreations:* squash, tennis, billiards, snooker. *Address:* Nigerian Embassy, PO Box 1019, Addis Ababa, Ethiopia.

HANBURY, Lt-Col Hanmer Cecil, LVO 1953; MC 1943; JP; HM Lord-Lieutenant of Bedfordshire, since 1978; *b* 5 Jan. 1916; *yr s* of late Sir Cecil Hanbury, MP, FLS, and late Mrs Hanbury-Forbes, OBE, of Kingston Maurward, Dorchester, Dorset, and La Mortola, Ventimiglia, Italy; *m* 1939, Prunella Kathleen Charlotte, *d* of late Air Cdre T. C. R. Higgins, CB, CMG, DL, JP, Turvey House, Beds; one *s* one *d. Educ:* Eton; RMC, Sandhurst. 2nd Lieut Grenadier Guards, 1936; served 1939–45 with Grenadier Guards, France, Belgium, N Africa, Italy; Capt. 1943; Temp. Major, 1944; Major 1948; Temp. Lt-Col, 1955–57; retired 1958. BRCS, Bedfordshire: Dir, 1959–71; Dep. Pres., 1972–78; Patron, 1978–; Pres., St John's Council for Bedfordshire, 1979–; Chm., Beds T&AVR Cttee, 1970–78, Pres., 1978; Vice-Pres., E Anglia T&AVRA, 1978–80, 1986 (Vice-Chm., 1970–78; Pres., 1980–86). DL 1958, Vice-Lieut, later Vice Lord-Lieut, 1970–78, JP 1959, Beds; High Sheriff, Beds, 1965. KStJ 1980. *Recreations:* shooting and country pursuits. *Address:* Turvey House, Turvey, Beds MK43 8EL. *T:* Turvey 227. *Clubs:* White's, Army and Navy, Pratt's.

HANBURY, Harold Greville, QC 1960; DCL; Vinerian Professor Emeritus of English Law, Oxford; Hon. Fellow, Lincoln College, Oxford; Hon. Master of the Bench, Inner Temple; *b* 19 June 1898; *s* of late Lt-Col Basil Hanbury and late Hon. Patience Verney; *m* 1927, Anna Margaret (*d* 1980), *d* of late Hannibal Dreyer, Copenhagen, Denmark. *Educ:* Charterhouse; Brasenose Coll., Oxford (Scholar). Vinerian Law Scholar, 1921; Fellow of Lincoln Coll., Oxford 1921–49; Fellow of All Souls Coll., 1949–64, Emeritus Fellow, 1980; Vinerian Prof. of English Law, Oxford, 1949–64. Visiting Prof., Univ. of Ife, 1962–63; Dean of Law Faculty, Univ. of Nigeria, 1964–66. Barrister-at-Law, Inner Temple, 1922; Rhodes Travelling Fellow, 1931–32; Senior Proctor, Oxford Univ., 1933–34 and 1944–45. President: Bentham Club, UCL, 1954–55; Soc. of Public Teachers of Law, 1958–59. Chairman: Court of Inquiry into Provincial Omnibus Industry, 1954; Board of Inquiry into West Indian Airways, Trinidad, 1958; Tribunal for Industrials, Gibraltar, 1960; Independent Mem. Commns of Inquiry on Retail Distributive Trades, 1946; Minimum Wage Arbitrator in Nigeria, 1955. Hon. Mem., Mark Twain Soc., 1977. *Publications:* Le Système Actuel de l'Equité dans le Système Juridique de l'Angleterre (trans. Robert Kiéfé), 1929; Essays in Equity, 1934, German edn 1977; Modern Equity, 1935 (12th edn *sub nom.* Hanbury and Maudsley, 1985); Traité Pratique des Divorces et des Successions en Droit Anglais (with R. Moureaux), 1939 (2nd edn 1952); English Courts of Law, 1944 (5th edn *sub nom.* Hanbury and Yardley, 1979); Principles of Agency, 1952 (2nd edn, 1960); The Vinerian Chair and Legal Education, 1958; Biafra: a challenge to the conscience of Britain, 1968; Shakespeare as Historian, 1985; articles in legal periodicals. *Recreations:* reading, aelurophily (Vice-Pres. Oxford and District Cat Club), formerly cricket, travelling. *Address:* 14 Dan Pienaar Road, Kloof, Natal, South Africa. *T:* 744617.

HANBURY, Sir John (Capel), Kt 1974; CBE 1969; Formerly Chairman, Allen and Hanburys Ltd, 1954–73 (Director, 1944); *b* 26 May 1908; *e s* of late Frederick Capel

Hanbury; *m* 1935, Joan Terry Fussell; two *s* one *d* (and one *s* decd). *Educ:* Downside; Trinity Coll., Cambridge. Mem., Pharmacopoeia Commn, 1948–73; Chm., Central Health Services Council, 1970–76; Pres. Assoc. of Brit. Pharmaceutical Industry, 1950–52; Chm., Assoc. of Brit. Chemical Manufacturers, 1961–63; Pres. Franco-British Pharmaceutical Commn, 1955. Mem., Thames Water Authority, 1974–79. FRSC (FRIC 1947); FPS 1955. Fellow, UCL, 1977. *Recreations:* horticulture, archæology. *Address:* Amwellbury House, Ware, Herts. *T:* Ware 2108. *Club:* United Oxford & Cambridge University.

HANBURY-TENISON, Airling Robin, OBE 1981; MA, FLS, FRGS; farmer; President, Survival International (Chairman since 1969); *b* 7 May 1936; *s* of late Major Gerald Evan Farquhar Tenison, Lough Bawn, Co. Monaghan, Ireland, and Ruth, *o surv. c* of late John Capel Hanbury, JP, DL, Pontypool Park, Monmouthshire; *m* 1st, 1959, Marika Hopkinson (*d* 1982); one *s* one *d*; 2nd, 1983, Mrs Louella Edwards, *d* of Lt Col G. T. G. Williams, DL, and Mrs Williams, Menkee, St Mabyn, Cornwall; one *s*. *Educ:* Eton; Magdalen Coll., Oxford (MA). Made first land crossing of South America at its widest point, 1958 (Mrs Patrick Ness Award, RGS, 1961); explored Tassili N'Ajjer, Tibesti and Aïr mountains in Southern Sahara, 1962–66; crossed S America in a small boat from the Orinoco to Buenos Aires, 1964–65; Geographical Magazine Amazonas Expedn, by Hovercraft, 1968; Trans-African Hovercraft Expedn (Dep. Leader), 1969; visited 33 Indian tribes as guest of Brazilian Govt, 1971; Winston Churchill Memorial Fellow, 1971; British Trans Americas Expedn, 1972; explored Outer Islands of Indonesia, 1973; Eastern Sulawesi, 1974; Sabah, Brunei, Sarawak, 1976; RGS Mulu (Sarawak) Expedn (Leader), 1977–78; expedns to Ecuador, Brazil and Venezuela, 1980–81. Comr of Income Tax, 1965–; Mem. of Lloyd's, 1976. Mem. Council, RGS, 1968–70, 1971–76, 1979–; Patron's Medal, RGS, 1979; Krug Award of Excellence, 1980. *Publications:* The Rough and the Smooth, 1969; Report of a Visit to the Indians of Brazil, 1971; A Question of Survival, 1973; A Pattern of Peoples, 1975; Mulu: the rain forest, 1980; Aborigines of the Amazon Rain Forest: the Yanomami, 1982; Worlds Apart (autobiog.), 1984; White Horses Over France, 1985; articles in: The Times, Spectator, Blackwood's Magazine, etc; articles and reviews in Geographical Magazine (numerous), Geographical Jl, Ecologist, Expedition, etc. *Recreations:* travelling, riding across France. *Address:* Maidenwell, Cardinham, Bodmin, Cornwall PL30 4DW. *T:* Cardinham 224. *Clubs:* Groucho; Kildare Street and University (Dublin).
See also R. Hanbury-Tenison.

HANBURY-TENISON, Richard, JP; Lord-Lieutenant of Gwent, since 1979; *b* 3 Jan. 1925; *e s* of late Major G. E. F. Tenison, Lough Bawn, Co. Monaghan, Ireland, and Ruth, *o surv. c* of late J. C. Hanbury, JP, DL, Pontypool Park, Monmouthshire; *m* 1955, Euphan Mary, JP, *er d* of late Major A. B. Wardlaw-Ramsay, 21st of Whitehill, Midlothian; three *s* two *d*. *Educ:* Eton; Magdalen Coll., Oxford. Served Irish Guards, 1943–47 (Captain, wounded). Entered HM Foreign Service, 1949: 1st Sec., Vienna, 1956–58; 1st Sec. (and sometime Chargé d'Affaires), Phnom Penh, 1961–63, and Bucharest, 1966–68; Counsellor, Bonn, 1968–70; Head of Aviation and Telecommunications Dept, FCO, 1970–71; Counsellor, Brussels, 1971–75; retired from Diplomatic Service, 1975. South Wales Regional Dir, Lloyds Bank, 1980–. Mem. Council and Ct, Nat. Museum of Wales, 1980– (Chm., Art Cttee, 1986–). President: Monmouthshire Rural Community Council, 1959–75; Gwent Local Hist. Council; SE Wales Arts Assoc.; Gwent County Scout Council; Gwent Community Services Council, 1985– (Chm., 1975–85); TA & VRA for Wales, 1985–. Hon. Col, 3rd (V) Bn, The Royal Regt of Wales, 1982–. DL 1973, High Sheriff 1977, JP 1979, Gwent. CStJ 1980. *Recreations:* shooting, fishing, conservation. *Address:* Clytha Park, Abergavenny, Gwent. *T:* Abergavenny 840300; Lough Bawn, Co. Monaghan. *Clubs:* Boodle's; Kildare Street and University (Dublin).
See also A. R. Hanbury-Tenison.

HANBURY-TRACY, family name of **Baron Sudeley.**

HANCOCK, Lt-Col Sir Cyril (Percy), KCIE 1946 (CIE 1941); OBE 1930; MC; *b* 18 Sept. 1896; *m* Joyce (*d* 1982), *d* of F. R. Hemingway, ICS; three *s* one *d*. *Educ:* Wellington Coll.; RMC, Sandhurst. Commd Indian Army, 114th Mahrattas, 1914; ADC to GOC 1st Corps MEF (Gen. Sir Alexander Cobbe, VC), 1918; GSO 3 at GHQ Baghdad, 1919; transf. to Bombay Political Dept, 1920; Asst Pvte Sec. to Governor of Bombay (Lord Lloyd), 1921; Asst Pvte Sec. to Viceroy (Lord Reading), 1923; Sec., Rajkot Pol. Agency, 1925; Sec. to Resident for Rajputana, 1929; Prime Minister, Bharatpur State, Rajputana, 1932; Dep. Sec., Govt of India (Pol. Dept, i/c War Br.), 1939; Resident: Eastern States, Calcutta, 1941; Western India States and Baroda Rajkot, 1943. *Address:* Woodhayes, Firgrove Road, Yateley, Hants GU17 7NH. *T:* Yateley 873240. *Club:* Indian Cricket.
See also G. F. Hancock.

HANCOCK, Sir David (John Stowell), KCB 1985; Permanent Secretary, Department of Education and Science, since 1983; *b* 27 March 1934; *s* of late Alfred George Hancock and Florence Hancock (*née* Barrow); *m* 1966, Sheila Gillian Finlay; one *s* one *d*. *Educ:* Whitgift Sch.; Balliol Coll., Oxford. Asst Principal, Bd of Trade, 1957; transf. to HM Treasury, 1959; Principal, 1962; Harkness Fellow, 1965–66; Private Sec. to Chancellor of the Exchequer, 1968–70; Asst Sec., 1970; Financial and Economic Counsellor, Office of UK Permanent Rep. to European Communities, 1972–74; Under Sec., 1975–80; Dep. Sec., 1980–82; Dep. Sec., Cabinet Office, 1982–83. Dir, European Investment Bank, 1980–82. Mem., British Selection Cttee of Harkness Fellowships, 1984–. *Recreations:* gardening, theatre. *Address:* c/o Department of Education and Science, Elizabeth House, York Road, SE1 7PH. *Clubs:* Athenæum, Civil Service.

HANCOCK, Geoffrey Francis, CMG 1977; HM Diplomatic Service, retired; Foreign and Commonwealth Office, 1979–82; *b* 20 June 1926; *s* of Lt-Col Sir Cyril Hancock, *qv*; *m* 1960, Amelia Juana Aragon; one *s* one *d*. *Educ:* Wellington; Trinity Coll., Oxford. MA 1951. Third Sec., Mexico City, 1953; Second Sec., Montevideo, 1956; Foreign Office, 1958; Madrid, 1958; FO, 1960; MECAS, 1962; First Sec., Baghdad, 1964–67 and 1968–69; FCO, 1969–73; Counsellor, Beirut, 1973–78. Founder, Middle East Consultants, 1983. *Recreations:* music, sailing. *Address:* c/o Lloyds Bank, 6 Pall Mall, SW1Y 5NH. *Clubs:* Athenæum, Royal Air Force.

HANCOCK, Prof. Sir Keith; *see* Hancock, Prof. Sir W. K.

HANCOCK, Prof. Keith Jackson; Vice-Chancellor, since 1980, Professor of Economics, since 1964, The Flinders University of South Australia; *b* 4 Jan. 1935; *s* of late A. S. Hancock and Mrs R. D. Hancock; *m* 1958, Joan, *d* of W. Taggert; two *s* one *d*. *Educ:* Univ. of Melbourne (BA); Univ. of London (PhD). Tutor in Economic History, Univ. of Melbourne, 1956–57; Lectr in Economics, Univ. of Adelaide, 1959–63; Pro-Vice-Chancellor, Flinders Univ. of South Australia, 1975–79. Pres., Acad. of Social Sciences in Australia, 1981–84. FASSA 1968. Hon. Fellow, LSE, 1982. *Publications:* (with P. A. Samuelson and R. H. Wallace) Economics (Australian edn), 1969, 2nd edn 1975; articles in Economic Jl, Economica, Amer. Econ. Rev. and other jls. *Recreations:* bridge, sailing, music. *Address:* 34 Ramsgate Street, Glenelg, SA 5045, Australia. *T:* 08–2953475. *Clubs:* South Australian Bridge Association, Royal South Australian Yacht Squadron.

HANCOCK, Maj.-Gen. Michael Stephen, CB 1972; MBE 1953; retired 1972; Planning Inspector, Department of the Environment, since 1972; *b* 19 July 1917; *s* of late Rev. W. H. M. Hancock and late Mrs C. C. Hancock (*née* Sherbrooke); *m* 1941, Constance Geraldine Margaret Ovens, *y d* of late Brig.-Gen. R. M. Ovens, CMG; one *s* one *d*. *Educ:* Marlborough Coll.; RMA, Woolwich. Commnd into Royal Signals, 1937; Comdr, Corps Royal Signals, 1st British Corps, 1963–66; Sec., Mil. Cttee, NATO, 1967–68; Chief of Staff, FARELF, 1968–70; VQMG, MoD, 1970–72. Col Comdt, Royal Signals, 1970–77. Chm., CCF Assoc., 1972–82, Vice Pres., 1982–; Chm., NE Surrey Dist Scouts, 1979–82, Pres., 1982–. CEng; FIEE. *Recreation:* sailing. *Address:* Brakey Hill, Godstone, Surrey. *T:* Godstone 842273. *Club:* Army and Navy.

HANCOCK, Michael Thomas; MP (SDP) Portsmouth South, since June 1984; *b* 9 April 1946; *m* 1967; one *s* one *d*. *Educ:* well. Member: Portsmouth City Council, 1971–, for Fratton Ward, 1973–; Hampshire County Council, 1973– (Leader of the Opposition, 1977–81). Joined SDP, 1981 (Mem., Nat. Cttee, 1984); contested (SDP) Portsmouth S, 1983. Hon. award for contrib. to Anglo-German relations, Homborn, W Germany, 1981. *Publications:* contribs to various jls. *Recreations:* people, living life to the full. *Address:* 196 Fratton Road, Fratton, Portsmouth. *T:* Portsmouth 861055. *Clubs:* too many to mention.

HANCOCK, Norman, CB 1976; CEng, FRINA; RCNC; Director of Warship Design, and Project Director, Invincible and Broadsword, Ministry of Defence, 1969–76; *b* 6 March 1916; *o s* of Louis Everard Hancock, Plymouth; *m* 1940, Marie E., *d* of William E. Bow; two *s*. *Educ:* Plymouth Grammar Sch.; RNC Greenwich. Asst Constructor, AEW, Haslar, 1940; Constructor, Naval Construction Dept, 1944; British Services Observer (Constructor Comdr), Bikini, 1946. HM Dockyard, Singapore, 1949; Frigate design, Naval Construction Dept, 1952; Chief Constructor in charge of R&D, 1954; Prof. of Naval Architecture, RNC, Greenwich, 1957–62; Asst Dir of Naval Construction, in charge of Submarine Design and Construction, 1963–69. Liveryman, Worshipful Co. of Shipwrights; past Mem. Council, RINA. *Recreations:* organ music, cabinet making, travel. *Address:* 41 Cranwells Park, Bath, Avon. *T:* Bath 26045.

HANCOCK, P(ercy) E(llis) Thompson, FRCP; Hon. Consultant Physician: The Royal Free Hospital; The Royal Marsden Hospital; Potters Bar and District Hospital; *b* 4 Feb. 1904; *s* of Frank Hancock; *m* 1932, Dorothy Barnes (*d* 1953); two *d*; *m* 1955, Laurie Newton Sharp. *Educ:* Wellington Coll., Berks; Caius Coll., Cambridge; St Bartholomew's Hospital. MB 1937, BCh 1930, Cantab; FRCP 1944. Formerly: Senior Examiner in Medicine, Univ. of London; Dir of Dept of Clinical Res., Royal Marsden Hosp. and Inst. of Cancer Res. Member: Council, Imperial Cancer Res. Fund; Grand Council, Cancer Research Campaign; Mem. Exec. Cttee, Action on Smoking and Health. Hosp. Visitor, King Edward's Hosp. Fund for London. FRSocMed (Pres., Section of Oncology, 1974–75); Fellow, Assoc. Européene de Médecine Interne d'Ensemble. Corresp. Mem., Società Italiana de Cancerologia. Hon. Member: American Gastroscopic Soc., 1958; Sociedad Chilena de Cancerología; Sociedad Chilena de Hematología; Sociedad Médica de Valparaíso. *Publications:* (joint) Cancer in General Practice; The Use of Bone Marrow Transfusion with massive Chemotherapy, 1960; (joint) Treatment of Early Hodgkin's Disease, 1967. *Recreations:* dining and wining. *Address:* 23 Wigmore Place, W1H 9DD. *T:* 01–631 4679.

HANCOCK, Ronald John; Director, Chloride Group plc, since 1985; *b* 11 Feb. 1934; *s* of George and Elsie Hancock; *m* 1970, Valerie Hancock; two *d*. *Educ:* Dudley Grammar Sch., Dudley. FCMA. Served HM Forces, 1952–61. Schweppes Ltd, 1962–63; Mullard Ltd, 1963–66; Valor Group, 1966–68; BL Ltd, 1968–85. Chairman: Leyland Vehicles, 1981–85; Leyland Vehicles Exports Ltd, 1981–85; Bus Manufacturers Limited, 1981–85; Bus Manufacturers (Holdings) Ltd, 1981–85; Eastern Coachworks Ltd, 1981–85; Bristol Commercial Vehicles Ltd, 1981–85; Self-Changing Gears Ltd, 1981–85; Director: BL Staff Trustees Ltd, 1981–85; Leyland Nigeria Ltd, 1981–85; BL International Ltd, 1981–85; Land Rover-Leyland International Holdings Ltd (formerly BLIH), 1982–85; Land Rover-Leyland Ltd, 1983–85. *Recreations:* travel, reading. *Address:* (office) Chloride Group plc, 52 Grosvenor Gardens, SW1W 0AU.

HANCOCK, Sheila, OBE 1974; actress and director; *d* of late Enrico Hancock and late Ivy Woodward; *m* 1st, 1955, Alexander Ross (*d* 1971); one *d*; 2nd, 1973, John Thaw; one *d*. *Educ:* Dartford County Grammar Sch.; Royal Academy of Dramatic Art. Acted in Repertory, Theatre Workshop, Stratford East, for 8 years. Associate Dir, Cambridge Theatre Co., 1980–82; Artistic Dir, RSC Regional Tour, 1983–84; acted and directed, NT, 1985–86. Dir, The Actors Centre, 1978–. West End starring roles in: Rattle of a Simple Man, 1962; The Anniversary, 1966; A Delicate Balance (RSC), 1969; So What About Love?, 1969; Absurd Person Singular, 1973; Déjà Revue, 1974; The Bed Before Yesterday, 1976; Annie, 1978; Sweeney Todd, 1980; The Winter's Tale, RSC, Stratford 1981, Barbican 1982. Has starred in several successful revues; repeated stage role in film of The Anniversary. Appeared on Broadway in Entertaining Mr Sloane. Many Television successes, including her own colour spectacular for BBC2, and several comedy series. Dir, The Soldier's Fortune, Lyric, Hammersmith, 1981; Awards: Variety Club, London Critics, Whitbread Trophy (for best Actress on Broadway). *Recreations:* reading, music. *Address:* c/o Jeremy Conway Ltd, Eagle House, 109 Jermyn Street, SW1.

HANCOCK, Air Marshal Sir Valston Eldridge, KBE 1962 (CBE 1953); CB 1958; DFC 1945; retired; grazier; *b* 31 May 1907; *s* of R. J. Hancock, Perth, W Australia; *m* 1932, Joan E. G., *d* of Col A. G. Butler, DSO, VD; two *s* one *d*. *Educ:* Hale Sch., Perth; RMC, Duntroon; psa; idc. Joined Royal Military College, Duntroon, 1925; transferred RAAF, 1929; Dir of Plans, 1940–41; commanded 71 (Beaufort) Wing, New Guinea, 1945; Commandant RAAF Academy, 1947–49; Deputy Chief of Air Staff, 1951–53; Air Mem. for Personnel, Air Board, 1953–54; Head of Australian Joint Services Staff, UK, 1955–57; Extra Gentleman Usher to the Royal Household, 1955–57; AOC 224 Group, RAF, Malaya, 1957–59; Air Officer Commanding Operational Command, 1959–61; Chief of Air Staff, Royal Australian Air Force, 1961–65. Commissioner-Gen., Australian Exhibit Organization, Expo 1967. Foundation Chm., Australian Defence Assoc., 1975–81. *Recreations:* literature and sport. *Address:* 108a Victoria Avenue, Dalkeith, WA 6009, Australia. *Clubs:* Royal Commonwealth Society (WA) (Chm., 1976–81; Life Mem.); Weld (Perth).

HANCOCK, Prof. Sir (William) Keith, KBE 1965; Kt 1953; MA; FBA 1950; Emeritus Professor and Hon. Fellow; Professor of History, Australian National University, Canberra, 1957–65; *b* Melbourne, 26 June 1898; *s* of Archdeacon William Hancock, MA; *m* 1st, 1925, Theaden Brocklebank (*d* 1960); 2nd, 1961, Marjorie Eyre. Fellow of All Souls Coll., Oxford, 1924–30; Prof. of Modern History in the University of Adelaide, 1924–33; Prof. of History, Birmingham Univ., 1934–44; Chichele Prof. of Economic History, University of Oxford 1944–49; Dir, Institute of Commonwealth Studies, and Prof. of British Commonwealth Affairs in the University of London, 1949–56; Dir of the Research Sch. of Social Sciences, Australian National Univ., 1957–61; appointed to War Cabinet Offices as Supervisor of Civil Histories, 1941, thereafter editor of series. Fellow: Churchill Coll., Cambridge, 1964; St John's Coll., Cambridge, 1971–72. Hon. Fellow, Balliol Coll., Oxford; Corresp. Mem., Sch. of Oriental and African Studies. FAHA

(1st Pres.) 1969. Hon. DLitt (Rhodes, Cambridge, Birmingham, Oxford, Cape Town, Melbourne, ANU, Adelaide, WA). Foreign Hon. Member: American Historical Association; American Academy of Arts and Sciences. Order of Merit of Republic of Italy. *Publications:* Ricasoli, 1926; Australia, 1930; Survey of British Commonwealth Affairs, 1937, 1940, and 1942; Politics in Pitcairn, 1947; (with M. M. Gowing) British War Economy, 1949; Country and Calling, 1954; War and Peace in this Century, 1961; Smuts: The Sanguine Years, 1870–1919, Vol. I, 1962; The Fields of Force, 1919–1950, Vol. II, 1968; Discovering Monaro, 1972; Professing History, 1976; Perspective in History, 1982; Testimony, 1985. *Address:* 49 Gellibrand Street, Campbell, Canberra, ACT 2601, Australia. *Club:* Athenæum.

HAND, Rt. Rev. Geoffrey David, KBE 1984 (CBE 1975); *b* 11 May 1918; *s* of Rev. W. T. Hand. *Educ:* Oriel College, Oxford; Cuddesdon Theological Coll., BA 1941, MA 1946. Deacon, 1942; Priest, 1943. Curate of Heckmondwike, 1942–46; Missioner, Diocese of New Guinea, 1946–50; Priest in charge: Sefoa, 1947–48; Sangara, 1948–50; Archdeacon, North New Guinea, 1950–65; Bishop Coadjutor of New Guinea, 1950–63; Bishop of New Guinea (later Papua New Guinea), 1963–77; Archbishop of Papua New Guinea, 1977–83; Bishop of Port Moresby, 1977–83; Priest-in-charge, East with West Rudham, Houghton next Harpley, Syderstone, Tatterford and Tattersett, dio. Norwich, 1983–84. *Address:* PO Box 49, Gerehu, NCD, Papua New Guinea.

HAND, Prof. Geoffrey Joseph Philip, DPhil; Barber Professor of Jurisprudence in the University of Birmingham, since 1980; *b* 25 June 1931; *s* of Joseph and Mary Macaulay Hand. *Educ:* Blackrock Coll.; University Coll., Dublin (MA); New Coll., Oxford (DPhil); King's Inns, Dublin. Called to Irish Bar, 1961. Lecturer: Univ. of Edinburgh, 1960; Univ. of Southampton, 1961; University Coll., Dublin, 1965; Professor: University Coll., Dublin, 1972–76; European University Inst., Fiesole, 1976–80; Dean of Faculty of Law, University Coll., Dublin, 1970–75. Chairman, Arts Council of Ireland, 1974–75. *Publications:* English Law in Ireland 1290–1324, 1967; Report of the Irish Boundary Commission 1925, 1969; (with Lord Cross of Chelsea) Radcliffe and Cross's English Legal System, 5th edn 1971, 6th edn 1977; (with J. Georgel, C. Sasse) European Election Systems Handbook, 1979; Towards a Uniform System of Direct Elections, 1981; numerous periodicals. *Recreations:* listening to classical music, chess playing. *Address:* c/o Faculty of Law, University of Birmingham, PO Box 363, Birmingham B15 2TT. *T:* 021–472 1301. *Clubs:* United Oxford & Cambridge University; Royal Irish Yacht (Dun Laoghaire); Kildare Street and University (Dublin).

HANDCOCK, family name of **Baron Castlemaine.**

HANDFORD, Ven. (George) Clive; Archdeacon of Nottingham since 1984; *b* 17 April 1937; *s* of Cyril Percy Dawson Handford and Alice Ethel Handford; *m* 1962, Anne Elizabeth Jane Atherley; one *d*. *Educ:* Hatfield Coll., Durham (BA); Queen's Coll., Birmingham and Univ. of Birmingham (DipTh). Curate, Mansfield Parish Church, 1963–66; Chaplain: Baghdad, 1967; Beirut, 1967–73; Dean, St George's Cathedral, Jerusalem, 1974–78; Archdeacon in the Gulf and Chaplain in Abu Dhabi and Qatar, 1978–83; Vicar of Kneesall with Laxton, and Wellow and Rufford, 1983–84; RD of Tuxford and Norwell, 1983–84. ChStJ 1976. *Address:* 16 Woodthorpe Avenue, Woodthorpe, Nottingham NG5 4FD. *T:* Nottingham 267349.

HANDLEY, Ven. Anthony Michael; Archdeacon of Norwich, since 1981; *b* 3 June 1936; *s* of Eric Harvey Handley and Janet Handley; *m* 1962, Christine May Adlington; two *s* one *d*. *Educ:* Spalding Grammar School; Selwyn Coll., Cambridge (MA Hons); Chichester Theological Coll. Asst Curate, Thorpe St Andrew, 1962–66; Anglican Priest on Fairstead Estate, 1966–72; Vicar of Hellesdon, 1972–81; RD of Norwich North, 1979–81. Research Project, The Use of Colour, Shape, and Line Drawings as Experiential Training Resources, 1976. County Scout Chaplain for Norfolk. *Publication:* A Parish Prayer Card, 1980. *Recreations:* climbing mountains, painting, bird watching. *Address:* 40 Heigham Road, Norwich NR2 3AU. *T:* Norwich 611808.

HANDLEY, Mrs Carol Margaret; Headmistress, Camden School for Girls, 1971–85; *b* 17 Oct. 1929; *d* of Claude Hilary Taylor and Margaret Eleanor Taylor (*née* Peebles); *m* 1952, Eric Walter Handley, *qv*. *Educ:* St Paul's Girls' Sch.; University Coll., London (BA), Fellow 1977. Asst Classics Mistress: North Foreland Lodge Sch., 1952; Queen's Gate Sch., 1952; Head of Classics Dept, Camden Sch. for Girls, 1956; Deputy Headmistress, Camden Sch. for Girls, 1964. Member Council: Royal Holloway Coll., 1977–85; Mddx Hosp. Med. Sch., 1980–84; Royal Holloway and Bedford New Coll., 1985–; Mem. Governors and Council, Bedford Coll., 1981–85. *Publications:* articles and book reviews for classical jls. *Recreations:* walking, driving, travel. *Address:* Colt House, High Street, Little Eversden, Cambs.

HANDLEY, Sir David John D.; *see* Davenport-Handley.

HANDLEY, Prof. Eric Walter, CBE 1983; FBA 1969; Regius Professor of Greek, and Fellow of Trinity College, Cambridge, since 1984; *b* 12 Nov. 1926; *s* of late Alfred W. Handley and A. Doris Cox; *m* 1952, Carol Margaret Taylor (*see* C. M. Handley). *Educ:* King Edward's Sch., Birmingham; Trinity Coll., Cambridge. Stewart of Rannoch Schol. and Browne Medal, 1945. Asst Lectr in Latin and Greek, University Coll. London, 1946, Lectr, 1949, Reader, 1961, Prof. of Latin and Greek, 1967–68; Prof. and Head of Dept of Greek, UCL, 1968–84, and Dir, Inst. of Classical Studies, Univ. of London, 1967–84. Cromer Greek Prize (jtly), 1958; Vis. Lectr on the Classics, Harvard, 1966; Vis. Mem., Inst. for Advanced Study, Princeton, 1971; Visiting Professor: Stanford Univ., 1977; Melbourne Univ., 1978; Vis. Senior Fellow, Council of the Humanities, Princeton, 1981. Sec. Council Univ. Classical Depts, 1969–70, Chm., 1975–78. Pres., Classical Assoc., 1984–85; Member: Comité Scientifique, Fondation Hardt, Geneva, 1978–; Commn des Affaires Internes, Union Académique Internationale, 1984–; Foreign Sec., British Academy, 1979–; Foreign Mem., Societas Scientiarum Fennica, 1984–. *Publications:* (with John Rea) The Telephus of Euripides, 1957; The Dyskolos of Menander, 1965; (contrib.) Cambridge History of Classical Literature, 1985; Greek literary papyri, papers in class. jls, etc. *Recreations:* boating, hill-walking, travel. *Address:* Trinity College, Cambridge CB2 1TQ. *Club:* United Oxford & Cambridge University.

HANDLEY, Vernon George, FRCM 1972; Associate Conductor, London Philharmonic Orchestra, since 1983 (Guest Conductor, 1961–83); Principal Conductor: Ulster Orchestra, since 1985; Malmö Symphony Orchestra, since 1985; *b* 11 Nov. 1930; 2nd *s* of Vernon Douglas Handley and Claudia Lilian Handley, Enfield; *m* 1954, Barbara (marr. diss.), *e d* of Kilner Newman Black and Joan Elfriede Black, Stoke Gabriel, Devon; one *s* one *d* (and one *s* decd); *m* Victoria, *d* of Vaughan and Nona Parry-Jones, Guildford, Surrey; one *s* one *d*. *Educ:* Enfield Sch.; Balliol Coll., Oxford (BA); Guildhall Sch. of Music. Conductor: Oxford Univ. Musical Club and Union, 1953–54; OUDS, 1953–54; Tonbridge Philharmonic Soc., 1958–61; Hatfield Sch. of Music and Drama, 1959–61; Proteus Choir, 1962–81; Musical Dir and Conductor, Guildford Corp., and Conductor, Guildford Philharmonic Orch. and Choir, 1962–83; Prof. at RCM: for Orchestra and Conducting, 1966–72; for Choral Class, 1969–72. Guest Conductor from 1961: Bournemouth Symph. Orch.; Birmingham Symph. Orch.; Royal Philharmonic Orch.; BBC Welsh Orch.; BBC Northern Symph. Orch.; Royal Liverpool Philharmonic Orch.; Ulster Orch.; Scottish Nat. Orch.; Philharmonia Orch.; Strasbourg Philharmonic Orch., 1982–; Helsinki Philharmonic, 1984–; Amsterdam Philharmonic, 1985; Guest Conductor, 1961–83, Principal Guest Conductor, 1983–Sept. 1985, BBC Scottish Symphony Orch.; conducted London Symphony Orch. in internat. series, London, 1971; toured: Germany, 1966, 1980; S Africa, 1974; Holland, 1980; Sweden, 1980, 1981; Germany, Sweden, Holland and France, 1982–83; Musical Dir, Great British Music Festival, 1984–85; Artistic Dir, Norwich and Norfolk Triennial Fest., 1985. Regular broadcaster and has made many records. Pres., Nat. Federation of Gramophone Socs, 1984–; Vice-Pres., Elgar Soc., 1984–. Hon. RCM, 1970; FRCM 1972. Arnold Bax Meml Medal for Conducting, 1962; Conductor of the Year, British Composers' Guild, 1974; Hi-Fi News Audio Award, 1982. DUniv Surrey, 1980. *Recreations:* bird photography, old-fashioned roses. *Address:* Hen Gerrig, Pen-y-Fan, near Monmouth, Gwent. *T:* Trelleck 860318.

HANDLEY-TAYLOR, Geoffrey, FRSL 1950; author; *b* 25 April 1920; 2nd *s* of Walter Edward Taylor and Nellie Hadwin (*née* Taylor), Horsforth. *Educ:* widely. Served War of 1939–45: Duke of Wellington's Regt and War Office. Chairman, British Poetry-Drama Guild, 1948–52; Vice-Pres., Leeds Univ. Tudor Players, 1948–50; Publisher, Leeds University Poetry, 1949; featured in NBC-TV (USA) People series, 1955; Founder, Winifred Holtby Meml Collection, Fisk Univ., Nashville, 1955; Hon. Gen. Sec., Dumas Assoc., 1955–57; Founder, Sir Ralph Perring City of London Collection, Fisk Univ., 1962; Pres., St Paul's Literary Soc., Covent Garden, 1966–68; Chm., General Council, Poetry Society, 1967–68; served on PCC, St Paul's, Covent Garden, 1967–68; Mem. Gen. Council, National Book League, 1968; Dep. Pres., Lancashire Authors' Assoc., 1967–69 (Pres., 1969–72); a Trustee, Gladstone Meml Library, London, 1974–78; Jt Literary Executor, Estate of Vera Brittain, 1979–. Several Foreign decorations and awards. *Publications:* Mona Inglesby, Ballerina and Choreographer, 1947; Italian Ballet Today, 1949; New Hyperion, 1950; Literary, Debating and Dialect Societies of GB, Ireland and France, 5 pts, 1950–52; A Selected Bibliography of Literature Relating to Nursery Rhyme Reform, 1952; Winifred Holtby Bibliography and Letters, 1955; (with Frank Granville Barker) John Gay and the Ballad Opera, 1956; (with Thomas Rae) The Book of the Private Press, 1958; John Masefield, OM, The Queen's Poet Laureate, 1960; (with Vera Brittain) Selected Letters of Winifred Holtby and Vera Brittain 1920–1935, 1961, 2nd edn 1970; Bibliography of Monaco, 1961, 2nd edn 1968; Bibliography of Iran, 1964, 5th edn 1969; (with Timothy d'Arch Smith) C. Day Lewis, Poet Laureate, 1968; ed, County Authors Today Series, 9 vols, 1971–1973; Pogg (a satire), 1980; (with John Malcolm Dockeray) Vera Brittain, Occasional Papers, 1983–; also contribs to Encycl. Britannica, Hinrichsen Music Book, 1949–1958; Airs from The Beggar's Opera, arr. Edith Bathurst, 1953; The Beggar's Opera, ed Edward J. Dent, 1954; (foreword to) John Masefield Bibliography, ed Crocker Wright, 1986. *Address:* c/o Lloyds Bank, 185 Baker Street, NW1 6XB.

HANDLIN, Prof. Oscar; Carl M. Loeb University Professor, Harvard University, since 1984; Director, Harvard University Library, 1979–84; *b* 29 Sept. 1915; *m* 1st, 1937, Mary Flug; one *s* two *d*; 2nd, 1977, Lilian Bombach. *Educ:* Brooklyn Coll. (AB); Harvard (MA, PhD). Instructor, Brooklyn Coll., 1938–39; Harvard Univ.: Instructor, 1939–44; Asst Prof., 1944–48; Associate Prof., 1948–54; Prof. of History, 1954–65; Charles Warren Prof. of Amer. Hist., and Dir, Charles Warren Center for Studies in Amer. Hist., 1965–72; Carl H. Pforzheimer Univ. Prof., 1972–84; Harmsworth Prof. of Amer. History, Oxford Univ., 1972–73. Dir, Center for Study of History of Liberty in America, 1958–67; Chm., US Bd of Foreign Scholarships, 1965–66 (Vice-Chm. 1962–65). Hon. Fellow, Brandeis Univ., 1965. Hon. LLD Colby Coll., 1962; Hon. LHD: Hebrew Union Coll., 1967; Northern Michigan, 1969; Seton Hall Univ., 1972; Hon. HumD Oakland, 1968; Hon. LittD Brooklyn Coll., 1972; Hon. DHL: Boston Coll., 1975; Lowell, 1980; Cincinnati, 1981; Massachusetts, 1982. *Publications:* Boston's Immigrants, 1790–1865, 1941; (with M. F. Handlin) Commonwealth, 1947; Danger in Discord, 1948; (ed) This Was America, 1949; Uprooted, 1951, 2nd edn 1972; Adventure in Freedom, 1954; American People in the Twentieth Century, 1954 (rev. edn 1963); (ed jtly) Harvard Guide to American History, 1954; Chance or Destiny, 1955; (ed) Readings in American History, 1957; Race and Nationality in American Life, 1957; Al Smith and his America, 1958; (ed) Immigration as a Factor in American History, 1959; John Dewey's Challenge to Education, 1959; (ed) G. M. Capers, Stephen A. Douglas, Defender of the Union, 1959; Newcomers, 1960; (ed jtly) G. Mittleberger, Journey to Pennsylvania, 1960; (ed) American Principles and Issues, 1961; (with M. F. Handlin) The Dimensions of Liberty, 1961; The Americans, 1963; (with J. E. Burchard) The Historian and the City, 1963; Firebell in the Night, 1964; A Continuing Task, 1964; (ed) Children of the Uprooted, 1966; The History of the United States, vol. 1, 1967, vol. 2, 1968; America: a History, 1968; (with M. F. Handlin) The Popular Sources of Political Authority, 1967; The American College and American Culture, 1970; Facing Life: Youth and the Family in American History, 1971; A Pictorial History of Immigration, 1972; (with M. F. Handlin) The Wealth of the American People, 1975; Truth in History, 1979; (with L. Handlin) Abraham Lincoln and the Union, 1980; The Distortion of America, 1981; (with L. Handlin) A Restless People, 1982; (with L. Handlin) Liberty and Power, 1986. *Address:* 18 Agassiz Street, Cambridge, Mass 02140, USA. *Clubs:* St Botolph (Boston); Harvard (NY); Faculty (Cambridge, Mass).

HANDS, Terence David, (Terry Hands); Joint Artistic Director, Royal Shakespeare Company, since 1978 (Associate Director, 1967–77); *b* 9 Jan. 1941; *s* of Joseph Ronald Hands and Luise Berthe Kohler; *m* 1st, 1964, Josephine Barstow (marr. diss. 1967); 2nd, 1974, Ludmila Mikael (marr. diss. 1980); one *d*. *Educ:* Woking Grammar Sch.; Birmingham Univ. (BA Hons Eng. Lang. and Lit.); RADA (Hons Dip.). Founder-Artistic Dir, Liverpool Everyman Theatre, 1964–66; Artistic Dir, RSC Theatregoround, 1966–67; Consultant Dir, Comédie Française, 1975–77. Associate Mem., RADA; Trust Mem., Acacia Theatre Trust. Chevalier des Arts et des Lettres, 1973. *Director* (for Liverpool Everyman Theatre, 1964–66): The Importance of Being Earnest; Look Back in Anger; Richard III; The Four Seasons; Fando and Lis; *Artistic Director* (for RSC Theatregoround): The Proposal, 1966; The Second Shepherds' Play, 1966; The Dumb Waiter, 1967; Under Milk Wood, 1967; *directed for RSC:* The Criminals, 1967; Pleasure and Repentance, 1967; The Latent Heterosexual, 1968; The Merry Wives of Windsor, 1968, Japan tour, 1970; Bartholomew Fair, 1969; Pericles, 1969; Women Beware Women, 1969; Richard III, 1970, 1980; Balcony, 1971; Man of Mode, 1971; The Merchant of Venice, 1971; Murder in the Cathedral, 1972; Cries from Casement, 1973; Romeo and Juliet, 1973; The Bewitched, 1974; The Actor, 1974; Henry IV, Parts 1 and 2, 1975; Henry V, 1975, USA and European Tour, 1976; Old World, 1976; Henry VI parts 1, 2 and 3 (SWET Award, Dir of the Year, Plays and Players, Best Production, 1978), Coriolanus, 1977, European tour, 1979; The Changeling, 1978; Twelfth Night, The Children of the Sun, 1979; As You Like It, Richard II, 1980; Troilus and Cressida, 1981; Arden of Faversham, Much Ado About Nothing, 1982 (European tour and Broadway, 1984), Poppy, 1982; Cyrano de Bergerac, 1983 (SWET Best Dir award), Broadway, 1984 (televised, 1985); Red Noses, 1985; Othello, 1985; The Winter's Tale, 1986; *directed for Comédie Française:* Richard III, 1972 (Meilleur Spectacle de l'Année award); Pericles, 1974; Twelfth Night,

1976 (Meilleur Spectacle de l'Année award); Le Cid, 1977; Murder in the Cathedral, 1978; *directed for Paris Opéra:* Verdi's Otello, 1976 (televised 1978); *directed for Burg Theatre, Vienna:* Troilus and Cressida, 1977; As You Like It, 1979; *directed for Teatro Stabile di Genova, Italy:* Women Beware Women, 1981; *directed for Royal Opera:* Parsifal, 1979; *recording:* Murder in the Cathedral, 1976. *Publications:* trans. (with Barbara Wright) Genet, The Balcony, 1971; Pleasure and Repentance, 1976; (ed Sally Beauman) Henry V, 1976; contribs to Theatre 72, Playback. *Address:* c/o Royal Shakespeare Theatre, Stratford-upon-Avon, Warwicks CV37 6BB. *T:* Stratford-upon-Avon 296655.

HANES, Prof. Charles Samuel, FRS 1942; FRSC 1956; Professor of Biochemistry, University of Toronto, 1951–68, now Emeritus; Hon. Fellow of Downing College, Cambridge; *b* 1903; *m* 1931, Theodora Burleigh Auret, Johannesburg; one *d*. *Educ:* University of Toronto (BA 1925); University of Cambridge, PhD Cantab 1929; ScD Cantab 1952. Lately Reader in Plant Biochemistry, University of Cambridge, and Director, Agricultural Research Council Unit of Plant Biochemistry; previously Dir of Food Investigation, Dept of Scientific and Industrial Research. Flavelle Medal, Royal Society of Canada, 1958. *Address:* 9 Crescent Place, Apt 2414, Toronto, Ontario M4C 5L8, Canada. *T:* 416–699 0900.

HANHAM, Prof. Harold John; Vice-Chancellor, University of Lancaster, since 1985; *b* Auckland, New Zealand, 16 June 1928; *s* of John Newman Hanham and Ellie Malone; *m* 1973, Ruth Soule Arnon, *d* of Prof. Daniel I. Arnon, Univ. of Calif, Berkely. *Educ:* Mount Albert Grammar Sch.; Auckland UC (now Univ. of Auckland); Univ. of New Zealand (BA 1948, MA 1950); Selwyn Coll, Cambridge (PhD 1954). FRHistS 1960; FAAAS 1974. Asst Lectr to Sen. Lectr, in Govt, Univ. of Manchester, 1954–63; Prof. and Head of Dept of Politics, Univ. of Edinburgh, 1963–68; Prof. of History, 1968–73 and Fellow of Lowell House, 1970–73, Harvard Univ.; Prof. of History and Political Science, 1972–85 and Dean, Sch. of Humanities and Social Sci., 1973–84, MIT; Hon. Prof. of History, Univ. of Lancaster, 1985–. Guggenheim Fellow, 1972–73. Hon. AM Harvard, 1968. John H. Jenkins Prize for Bibliography, Union Coll., 1978. *Publications:* Elections and Party Management, 1969, 2nd edn 1978; The Nineteenth-Century Constitution, 1969; Scottish Nationalism, 1969; Bibliography of British History 1851–1914, 1976. *Recreations:* discovering Canada, squash. *Address:* The Croft, Bailrigg Lane, Bailrigg, Lancaster LA1 4XP. *T:* Lancaster 65201. *Clubs:* United Oxford & Cambridge University, Royal Commonwealth Society; Harvard (New York); St Botolph (Boston).

HANHAM, Leonard Edward; HM Diplomatic Service, retired; Consul-General, Amsterdam, 1978–80; *b* 23 April 1921; *m* 1945, Joyce Wrenn; two *s* two *d*. Served War, RN, 1939–48. Foreign Office, 1948; Vice-Consul: Rouen, 1949; Basra, 1950; Ponta Delgada, 1952; Foreign Office, 1955; 1st Sec. and Consul: Rangoon, 1957; Tegucigalpa, 1961; Foreign Office, 1963; Consul: Durban, 1965; Medan, 1969; FCO, 1972; Counsellor and Consul-Gen., Lisbon, 1975–78. *Address:* 26 First Avenue, Gillingham, Kent.

HANHAM, Sir Michael (William), 12th Bt *cr* 1667; DFC 1945; RAFVR; *b* 31 Oct. 1922; *s* of Patrick John Hanham (*d* 1965) and Dulcie (*d* 1979), *yr d* of William George Daffarn and *widow* of Lynn Hartley; *S* kinsman, Sir Henry Phelips Hanham, 11th Bt, 1973; *m* 1954, Margaret Jane, *d* of W/Cdr Harold Thomas, RAF retd, and Joy (*née* MacGeorge); one *s* one *d*. *Educ:* Winchester. Joined RAF 1942, as Aircrew Cadet; served No 8 (Pathfinder) Gp, Bomber Command, 1944–45; FO 1945. At end of war, retrained as Flying Control Officer; served UK and India, 1945–46; demobilised, 1946. Joined BOAC, 1947, Traffic Branch; qualified as Flight Operations Officer, 1954; served in Africa until 1961; resigned, 1961. Settled at Trillinghurst Farmhouse, Kent and started garden and cottage furniture making business, 1963; moved to Wimborne, 1974; now engaged with upkeep of family house and estate. Governor of Minster and of Dumpton School. *Recreations:* conservation (Vice-Chm. Weald of Kent Preservation Soc., 1972–74 and Wimborne Civic Soc., 1977–); preservation of steam railways; sailing, gardening. *Heir:* *s* William John Edward Hanham [*b* 4 Sept. 1957; *m* 1982, Elizabeth Anne Keyworth, *yr d* of Paul Keyworth, Farnham and Mrs Keith Thomas, Petersfield]. *Address:* Deans Court, Wimborne, Dorset. *Club:* Pathfinder.

HANKES-DRIELSMA, Claude Dunbar; Chairman, Management Committee, Price Waterhouse and Partners, since 1983; *b* 8 March 1949. *Educ:* Grey. With Manufacturers Hanover, 1968–72; Robert Fleming & Co. Ltd, 1972–77, Director 1974; Chairman: Export Finance Co. Ltd, 1982–; British Export-Finance Adv. Council, 1981–. Vice-Chm., Action Resource Centre, 1983–; delegate, speaker, Chm., internat confs. Mem., PCC and Deanery Synod. *Publications:* contribs to Euromoney. *Recreations:* gardening, polo, walking, ski-ing, reading. *Address:* Stanford Place, Faringdon, Oxon. *T:* Faringdon 20547. *Club:* Turf.

HANKEY, family name of **Baron Hankey.**

HANKEY, 2nd Baron *cr* 1939, of The Chart; **Robert Maurice Alers Hankey,** KCMG 1955 (CMG 1947); KCVO 1956; *b* 4 July 1905; *s* of 1st Baron Hankey, PC, GCB, GCMG, GCVO, FRS, and Adeline (*d* 1979), *d* of A. de Smidt; *S* father, 1963; *m* 1st, 1930, Frances Bevyl Stuart-Menteth (*d* 1957); two *s* two *d*; 2nd, 1962, Joanna Riddall Wright, *d* of late Rev. James Johnstone Wright. *Educ:* Rugby Sch.; New Coll., Oxford. Diplomatic Service, 1927; served Berlin, Paris, London, Warsaw, Bucharest, Cairo, Teheran, Madrid, Budapest. HM Ambassador at Stockholm, 1954–60. Permanent UK Delegate to OEEC and OECD, and Chm., Economic Policy Cttee, 1960–65; Vice-Pres., European Inst. of Business Administration, Fontainebleau, 1966–82. Dir, Alliance Bldg Soc., 1970–83. Member: Internat. Council of United World Colleges, 1966–78; Council, Internat. Baccalaureati Foundn, Geneva, 1967–76. Pres., Anglo-Swedish Soc., 1969–75. Grand Cross of Order of the North Star (Sweden), 1954. *Recreations:* reading, tennis, ski-ing, music. *Heir:* *er s* Hon. Donald Robin Alers Hankey [*b* 12 June 1938; *m* 1st, 1963, Margaretha, *yr d* of H. Thorndahl, Copenhagen; 2nd, 1974, Eileen Désirée, *yr d* of Maj.-Gen. Stuart Battye, *qv*; two *d*]. *Address:* Hethe House, Cowden, Edenbridge, Kent TN8 7DZ. *T:* Cowden 538.

See also Sir Jonathan Benn, Hon. H. A. A. Hankey.

HANKEY, Col George Trevor, OBE 1945; TD; late RAMC (TA); Consulting Oral Surgeon; *b* London, 15 March 1900; *er s* of J. Trevor Hankey, Lingfield, Surrey; *m* 1933, Norah (*d* 1939), *y d* of late R. H. G. Coulson, Tynemouth; (one *s* decd); *m* 1945, Mary Isobel, *d* of late R. H. G. Coulson, Tynemouth. *Educ:* Oakham Sch; Guy's Hosp. LDSEng, 1922; LRCP, MRCS 1925; elected FDS, RCS, 1948, FRCS 1977; Consultant Dental Surgeon, St Bartholomew's Hospital, 1928–65, retd; Consultant, The London Hosp. Dental Sch., 1928–66; Lectr in Oral Surg., University of London. Fellow, Royal Society of Medicine; Examr in Dental Surgery, RCS England, 1948–54; Examiner in Dental and Oral Surgery, University of London, 1948–56; Pres. Odontological Section, RSM 1957–58 (now Hon. Mem.); Charles Tomes Lecturer, RCS, 1953; Mem. Bd Dent. Faculty RCS, 1958–73; Vice-Dean, 1966–67. John Tomes Prize, RCS, 1960, Mem. Bd Govs, London Hosp., 1954–63, and NE Metrop. Reg. Hosp. Bd, 1959–62; Founder Fellow, Brit. Assoc. Oral Surgeons, Pres., 1963–64; Sprawson Lectr, 1967. Served War, 1917–19; 2nd Lt, RHA; Commissioned RAMC(TA), 1927; OC 141 Field Ambulance, 1939; OC 12 Gen. Hosp., 1952; Hon. Col 1957–62. Served War of 1939–45 (despatches, prisoner, OBE). Officer, Legion of Merit, USA, 1951. *Publications:* chapter on Mandibular Joint Disorders, in Surgical Progress, 1960; contrib. Brit. Dental Jl and British Jl of Oral Surgery; various communications on Oral Surgery and Pathology to Proc. Royal Society of Medicine. *Recreations:* golf, fishing. *Address:* 22 East Hill Road, Oxted, Surrey RH8 9HZ. *T:* Oxted 3553.

HANKEY, Hon. Henry Arthur Alers, CMG 1960; CVO 1959; HM Diplomatic Service, retired; *b* 1 Sept. 1914; *y s* of 1st Baron Hankey, PC, GCB, GCMG, GCVO, FRS; *m* 1941, Vronwy Mary Fisher; three *s* one *d*. *Educ:* Rugby Sch.; New Coll., Oxford. Entered HM Diplomatic Service, 1937; Third Sec., HM Embassy, Paris, 1939; Second Sec., Madrid, 1942; First Sec., Rome, 1946; Consul, San Francisco, 1950; First Sec., Santiago, 1953; promoted Counsellor and apptd Head of American Dept, Foreign Office, Sept. 1956; Counsellor, HM Embassy, Beirut, 1962–66; Ambassador, Panama, 1966–69; Asst Under-Sec. of State, FCO, 1969–74. Director: Lloyds Bank International, 1975–80; Antofagasta (Chile) & Bolivia Railway Co. Ltd, 1975–82. Sec., British North American Cttee, 1981–85. *Recreations:* ski-ing, tennis, music, painting. *Address:* Hosey Croft, Hosey Hill, Westerham, Kent. *T:* Westerham 62309. *Club:* United Oxford & Cambridge University.

HANKINS, (Frederick) Geoffrey; Chairman and Chief Executive, Fitch Lovell plc, since 1983; *b* 9 Dec. 1926; *s* of Frederick Aubrey Hankins and Elizabeth Stockton; *m* 1951, Iris Esther Perkins; two *d*. *Educ:* St Dunstan's College. Commissioned Army, 1946–48; J. Sainsbury management trainee, 1949–51, manufacturing management, 1951–55; Production/Gen. Manager, Allied Suppliers, 1955–62; Production Dir, Brains Food Products, 1962–69; Kraft Foods, 1966–69; Gen. Man., Millers, Poole, 1970–72, Man. Dir, 1972–82, Chm., 1975–86; Fitch Lovell: Dir, 1975–; Chief Exec., 1982; Chm., Manufacturing Div., 1975–84; Chairman: Robirch, 1975–84; Jus Rol, 1976–85; Blue Cap Frozen Food Services, 1975–84; Newforge Foods, 1979–84; Bells Bacon (Evesham), 1980–83; L. Noel, 1982–84; Dir, Salaison Le Vexin, 1980–. *Recreations:* genealogy, antiques, practical pursuits. *Address:* 51 Elms Avenue, Parkstone, Poole, Dorset BH14 8EE. *T:* Poole 745874.

HANKINS, Prof. Harold Charles Arthur, PhD; CEng, FIEE; Principal, University of Manchester Institute of Science and Technology, since 1984; *b* 18 Oct. 1930; *s* of Harold Arthur Hankins and Hilda Hankins; *m* 1955, Kathleen Higginbottom; three *s* one *d*. *Educ:* Crewe Grammar Sch.; Univ. of Manchester Inst. of Science and Technol. (BSc Tech, 1st Cl. Hons Elec. Engrg, 1955; PhD 1971). CEng, FIEE 1975; AMCT 1952. Engrg Apprentice, British Rail, 1947–52; Electronic Engr, subseq. Asst Chief Engr, Metropolitan Vickers Electrical Co. Ltd, 1955–68; Univ. of Manchester Inst. of Science and Technology: Lectr in Elec. Engrg, 1968–71; Sen. Lectr in Elec. Engrg, 1971–74; Prof. of Communication Engrg, and Dir of Med. Engrg Unit, 1974–84; Vice Principal, 1979–81; Dep. Principal, 1981–82; Actg Principal, 1982–84. Non-Exec. Dir, THORN EMI Lighting Ltd, 1979–85. Instn of Electrical Engineers: Mem., NW Centre Cttee, 1969–77, Chm. 1977–78; Chm., M2 Exec. Cttee, 1979–82; Mem., Management and Design Div. Bd, 1980–82. Chm., Chemical Engrg, Instrumentation, Systems Engrg Bd, CNAA, 1975–81; Member: Cttee for Science and Technol., CNAA, 1975–81; Cttee of Vice-Chancellors and Principals, 1984–; Parly Scientific Cttee, 1985–. Hon. Fellow, Manchester Polytechnic, 1984. *Publications:* 55 papers in learned jls; 10 patents for research into computer visual display systems. *Recreations:* hill walking, music, choral work. *Address:* Rosebank, Kidd Road, Glossop, Derbyshire SK13 9PN. *T:* Glossop 3895. *Club:* Athenæum.

HANLEY, Gerald Anthony; author; *b* 17 Feb. 1916; *s* of Edward Michael Hanly and Bridget Maria Roche. *Publications:* Monsoon Victory, 1946; The Consul at Sunset, 1951; The Year of the Lion, 1953; Drinkers of Darkness, 1955; Without Love (Book Society Choice), 1957; The Journey Homeward (Book Society Choice), 1961; Gilligan's Last Elephant, 1962; See You in Yasukuni, 1969; Warriors and Strangers, 1971; Noble Descents, 1982. *Recreations:* music, languages. *Address:* c/o Gillon Aitken, 17 South Eaton Place, SW1.

HANLEY, Howard Granville, CBE 1975; MD, FRCS; Consulting Urologist, King Edward VII's Hospital for Officers, London; Dean, 1968–72, Chairman, 1972–80, President, 1980–86, Institute of Urology, University of London; *b* 27 July 1909; *s* of F. T. Hanley; *m* 1939, Margaret Jeffrey; two *s*. *Educ:* St Bees Sch., Cumberland. MB 1932; MD 1934; FRCS 1937. Urologist: St Peter's Hosps Gp, 1947–75; Royal Masonic Hosp., London, 1960–77; Urol Consultant to Army, 1951–75; Hon. Consulting Urologist, Royal Hosp., Chelsea, 1951–75. Visiting Prof. of Urology: University of Calif, Los Angeles, 1958; Ohio State Univ., Columbus, 1961; University of Texas Southwestern Medical Sch., 1963; Tulane University, New Orleans, 1967. Royal College of Surgeons: Hunterian Prof., 1955; Dean, Inst. of Basic Med. Scis, 1972–76; Mem. Council, 1969–81; Vice-Pres., 1979–81; Royal Society of Medicine: Pres., Urol Sect., 1969–81; Hon. Librarian. Trustee, St Peter's Research Trust Kidney Disease, 1970–86. Fellow, Assoc. of Surgeons of GB and Ireland; Past Pres. (formerly Sec. and Treasurer), British Assoc. Urological Surgeons; Past Sec., Hunterian Soc.; Past Pres., Chelsea Clinical Soc. Member: Internat. Soc. Urology; German Urol. Soc.; Soc. Française d'Urologie; European Assoc. of Urology. Corresponding Member: Amer. Assoc. Genito-urinary Surgeons; Western Sect. Amer. Urological Assoc. Liveryman, Worshipful Soc. of Apothecaries of London. Hon. FACS. *Publications:* chapters in: British Surgical Practice, 1957; Recent Advances in Urology, 1960; contribs to: A Textbook of Urology, 1960; Modern Trends in Urology, 1960; contribs to jls on surgery and urology. *Recreation:* gardening. *Address:* Brandon House, North End Avenue, NW3 7HP. *T:* 01–458 2035. *Club:* Athenæum.

HANLEY, Jeremy James; MP (C) Richmond and Barnes, since 1983; chartered accountant, certified accountant, chartered secretary, lecturer and broadcaster; *b* 17 Nov. 1945; *s* of late Jimmy Hanley and of Dinah Sheridan; *m* 1973, Verna, Viscountess Villiers (*née* Stott); two *s* one *d*. *Educ:* Rugby. FCA 1969; FCCA 1980; FCIS 1980. Peat Marwick Mitchell & Co., 1963–66; Lectr in law, taxation and accountancy, Anderson Thomas Frankel, 1969, Dir 1969; Man. Dir, ATF (Jersey and Ireland), 1970–73; Dir, The Financial Training Co. Ltd, 1973–; Sec., Park Place PLC, 1977–; Chm., Fraser Green Ltd, 1986–. Contested (C) Lambeth Central, April 1978, 1979. Member: Soc. of Cons. Lawyers Company Law Reform Cttee, 1976–; H of C Select Cttee on Home Affairs; H of C Select Subcttee on Race Relns and Immigration; CPA; Inter-Parly Union; British-American Parly Gp; Anglo-French Parly Gp; Vice-Chm., Nat. Anglo-West Indian Cons. Soc., 1982–83; Chm., Cons Candidates Assoc., 1982–83. Jt Vice-Chm., Cons. Backbench Trade and Industry Cttee, 1983–. Member: Bow Gp, 1974– (Chm., Home Affairs Cttee); European Movt, 1974–; Mensa, 1968–. *Recreations:* cookery, chess, cricket, languages, theatre, cinema, music, golf. *Address:* House of Commons, SW1A 0AA. *T:* 01–219 4099.

HANLEY, Sir Michael (Bowen), KCB 1974; *b* 24 Feb. 1918; *s* of late Prof. J. A. Hanley, PhD, ARCS; *m* 1957, Hon. Lorna Margaret Dorothy, *d* of late Hon. Claude Hope-Morley. *Educ:* Sedbergh School; Queen's Coll., Oxford (MA). Served War of 1939–45. *Address:* c/o Ministry of Defence, SW1.

HANMER, Sir John (Wyndham Edward), 8th Bt *cr* 1774; JP; DL; *b* 27 Sept. 1928; *s* of Sir (Griffin Wyndham) Edward Hanmer, 7th Bt, and Aileen Mary (*d* 1967), *er d* of

Captain J. E. Rogerson; *S* father, 1977; *m* 1954, Audrey Melissa, *d* of Major A. C. J. Congreve; two *s*. *Educ:* Eton. Captain (retired), The Royal Dragoons. JP Flintshire, 1971; High Sheriff of Clwyd, 1977; DL Clwyd, 1978. *Recreations:* horseracing, shooting. *Heir:* *s* Wyndham Richard Guy Hanmer [*b* 27 Nov. 1955; *m* 1986, Elizabeth A., *yr d* of Neil Taylor]. *Address:* The Mere House, Hanmer, Whitchurch, Salop. *T:* Hanmer 383. *Club:* Army and Navy.

See also Sir James Wilson, Bt.

HANN, Air Vice-Marshal Derek William; Director General, RAF Personal Services, Ministry of Defence, since 1987; *b* 22 Aug. 1935; *s* of Claude and Ernestine Hann; *m* 1958, Jill Symonds (marr. diss. 1986); one *s* one *d*. *Educ:* Dauntsey's Sch., Devizes. Joined RAF, 1954; served in Fighter (65 Sqdn) and Coastal (201 and 203 Sqdns) Commands and at HQ Far East Air Force, 1956–68; MoD, 1969–72 and 1975–77; Comd No 42 Sqdn, RAF St Mawgan, 1972–74; Comd RAF St Mawgan, 1977–79; RCDS 1980; Dir of Operational Requirements 2, MoD, 1981–84; C of S, HQ No 18 Gp, RAF Strike Comd, 1984–87. *Recreations:* theatre, music, gardening, watching sport. *Address:* Adastral House, Theobalds Road, WC1X 8RU. *T:* 01–430 7239; 01–267 5429.

HANNAH, Prof. Leslie, Director, Business History Unit, London School of Economics, since 1978; *b* 15 June 1947; *s* of Arthur Hannah and Marie (*née* Lancashire); *m* 1984, Nuala Barbara Zahedieh (*née* Hockton), *e d* of Thomas and Deirdre Hockton; two step *d*. *Educ:* Manchester Grammar Sch.; St John's and Nuffield Colleges, Oxford. MA, PhD, DPhil. Research Fellow, St John's Coll., Oxford, 1969–73; Lectr in economics, Univ. of Essex, 1973–75; Lectr in recent British economic and social history, Univ. of Cambridge, and Fellow and Financial Tutor, Emmanuel Coll., Cambridge, 1976–78; LSE, 1978–, Professor, 1982–. Vis. Prof., Harvard Univ., 1984–85. *Publications:* Rise of the Corporate Economy, 1976, 2nd edn 1983; (ed) Management Strategy and Business Development, 1976; (with J. A. Kay) Concentration in Modern Industry, 1977; Electricity before Nationalisation, 1979; Engineers, Managers and Politicians, 1982; Entrepreneurs and the Social Sciences, 1983; Inventing Retirement, 1986; contribs to jls. *Recreations:* walking, lying on beaches, reading novels. *Address:* Lionel Robbins Building, 10 Portugal Street, WC2A 2HD. *T:* 01–405 7686.

HANNAM, John Gordon; MP (C) Exeter, since 1970; *b* 2 Aug. 1929; *s* of Thomas William and Selina Hannam; *m* 1st, 1956, Wendy Macartney; two *d*; 2nd, 1983, Mrs Vanessa Wauchope (*née* Anson). *Educ:* Yeovil Grammar Sch. Studied Agriculture, 1945–46. Served in: Royal Tank Regt (commissioned), 1947–48; Somerset LI (TA), 1949–51. Studied Hotel industry, 1950–52; Managing Dir, Hotels and Restaurant Co., 1952–61; Developed Motels, 1961–70; Chm., British Motels Fedn, 1967–74, Pres. 1974–80; Mem. Council, BTA, 1968–69; Mem. Economic Research Council, 1967–. PPS to: Minister for Industry, 1972–74; Chief Sec., Treasury, 1974. Secretary: Cons. Parly Trade Cttee, 1971–72; All-Party Disablement Gp, 1974–; Mem., Govt Adv. Cttee on Transport for Disabled, 1983–; Chairman: West Country Cons. Cttee, 1973–74, 1979–81; Cons. Party Energy Cttee, 1979–; Arts and Leisure Standing Cttee, Bow Group, 1975–84; Vice-Chairman: Arts and Heritage Cttee, 1974–79; British Cttee of Internat. Rehabilitation, 1979–. Captain: Lords and Commons Tennis Club, 1975–; Lords and Commons Ski Club, 1977–82; Cdre, House of Commons Yacht Club, 1975. Mem., Snowdon Working Party on the Disabled, 1975–76. Vice-President: Disablement Income Gp; Royal Assoc. for Disability and Rehabilitation; Council, Action Research for the Crippled Child; Disabled Motorists Gp; Altzheimer's Disease Soc.; Bd, Nat. Theatre. Mem., Glyndebourne Festival Soc. Pres., Exeter Chambers of Trade and Commerce. Hon. MA Open, 1986. *Recreations:* music (opera), theatre, sailing (anything), skiing (fast), Cresta toboganning (foolish); county tennis and hockey (Somerset tennis champion, 1953). *Address:* House of Commons, SW1A 0AA; Pightel Cottage, Plymtree, near Exeter, Devon. *Clubs:* Royal Yacht Squadron, All England Lawn Tennis, International Lawn Tennis.

HANNAM, Michael Patrick Vivian, CBE 1980; HM Diplomatic Service, retired; Consul General, Jerusalem, 1976–80; *b* 13 Feb. 1920; *s* of Rev. Wilfrid L. Hannam, BD, and Dorothy (*née* Parker); *m* 1947, Sybil Huggins; one *s* one *d*. *Educ:* Westminster Sch. LMS Railway, 1937–40. Served in Army, 1940–46 (Major, RE). LMS Railway, 1946–50; Malayan Railway, 1950–60. FO, 1960–62; First Sec., British Embassy, Cairo, 1962–65; Principal British Trade Comr, Hong Kong, 1965–69 (and Consul, Macao, 1968–69); Counsellor, Tripoli, 1969–72; Counsellor (Economic and Commercial), Nairobi, 1972–73, Dep. High Commissioner, Nairobi, 1973–76. Chm. Governors, Rose Hill Sch., Tunbridge Wells, 1980–85; Chm. Council, British Sch. of Archaeology in Jerusalem, 1983–. *Recreation:* music. *Address:* Little Oaklands, Langton Green, Kent TN3 0HP. *T:* Langton 2163. *Club:* Army and Navy.

HANNAN, William; insurance agent; *b* 30 Aug. 1906; *m*; one *d*. *Educ:* North Kelvinside Secondary Sch. MP (Lab) Maryhill, Glasgow, 1945–Feb. 1974; Lord Commissioner of HM Treasury, 1946–51; an Opposition Whip, Nov. 1951–53; PPS to Rt Hon. George Brown as First Sec. and Sec. of State for Economic Affairs, 1964–66, as Sec. of State for Foreign Affairs, 1966–68; retired from Parliament, General Election, Feb. 1974. Mem., British Delegation to Council of Europe. Town Councillor, Glasgow, 1941–45. Mem. SDP, 1981–. *Recreation:* music. *Address:* 24 Galbraith Drive, Milngavie, Dunbartonshire.

HANNAY, Sir David (Hugh Alexander), KCMG 1986 (CMG 1981); HM Diplomatic Service; Ambassador and UK Permanent Representative to the European Communities, Brussels, since 1985; *b* 28 Sept. 1935; *s* of Julian Hannay; *m* 1961, Gillian Rex; four *s*. *Educ:* Winchester; New Coll., Oxford. Foreign Office, 1959–60; Tehran, 1960–61; 3rd Sec., Kabul, 1961–63; 2nd Sec., FO, 1963–65; 2nd, later 1st Sec., UK Delegn to European Communities, Brussels, 1965–70; 1st Sec., UK Negotiating Team with European Communities, 1970–72; Chef de Cabinet to Sir Christopher Soames, Vice President of EEC, 1973–77; Head of Energy, Science and Space Dept, FCO, 1977–79; Head of Middle East Dept, FCO, 1979; Asst Under-Sec. of State (European Community), FCO, 1979–84; Minister, Washington, 1984–85. *Recreations:* travel, gardening, photography. *Address:* c/o Foreign and Commonwealth Office, SW1A 2AH. *Club:* Travellers'.

HANNAY, Elizabeth Anne Scott, MA; Head Mistress, Godolphin School, Salisbury, since 1980; *b* 28 Dec. 1942; *d* of Thomas Scott Hannay and Doreen Hewitt Hannay. *Educ:* Heathfield Sch., Ascot; St Hugh's Coll., Oxford (MA). Assistant Mistress: St Mary's Sch., Calne, 1966–70; Moreton Hall Sch., Shropshire, 1970–72; S Michael's, Burton Park, Petworth, 1973–75; Dep. Headmistress, St George's Sch., Ascot, 1975–80. *Address:* Downend Cottage, Tichborne, near Alresford, Hants SO24 0NA.

HANNEN, Rt. Rev. John Edward; *see* Caledonia, Bishop of.

HANNEN, Mrs Nicholas; *see* Seyler, Athene.

HANNIGAN, Rt. Rev. James; *see* Menevia, Bishop of, (RC).

HANNIGAN, James Edgar, CB 1981; Deputy Secretary, Department of Transport, since 1980; *b* 12 March 1928; *s* of late James Henry and of Kathleen Hannigan; *m* 1955, Shirley Jean Bell; two *d*. *Educ:* Eastbourne Grammar Sch.; Sidney Sussex Coll., Cambridge (BA). Civil Service, 1951; Asst Sec., Housing Div., Min. of Housing and Local Govt, 1966–70; Asst Sec., Local Govt Div., DoE, 1970–72. Under Sec. 1972; Regional Dir for West Midlands, DoE, 1972–75; Chm., West Midlands Economic Planning Bd, 1972–75; Dir of Housing 'B', DoE, 1975–78; Dep. Sec., NI Office, 1978–80. *Address:* 4 Pashley Road, Eastbourne, East Sussex.

HANNON, Rt. Rev. Brian Desmond Anthony; *see* Clogher, Bishop of.

HANON, Bernard; Officier, Ordre National du Mérite, 1980; Chairman and President, Régie Nationale des Usines Renault, 1981–85; *b* 7 Jan. 1932; *s* of Max Hanon and Anne Smulevicz; *m* 1965, Ghislaine de Bragelongne; two *s*. *Educ:* HEC 1955; Columbia Univ. (MBA 1956; PhD 1962). Dir of Marketing, Renault Inc., USA, 1959–63; Asst Prof. of Management Sci., Grad. Sch. of Business, NY Univ., 1963–66; Head, Dept of Economic Studies and Programming, 1966–69, Dir of Corporate Planning and Inf. Systems, 1970–75, Régie Nat. des Usines Renault; Dir, Renault Automotive Ops, 1976; Executive Vice President: i/c Automobile Div., 1976–81; Renault Gp, 1981. *Address:* 51–53 Champs-Elysées, 75008 Paris, France. *Clubs:* Racing Club de France (Paris); Golf de St Germain.

HANRAHAN, Brian; Moscow correspondent, BBC Television, since 1986; *b* 22 March 1949; *s* of Thomas Hanrahan and Kathleen McInerney; *m* 1986, Honor Wilson. *Educ:* Essex University (BA). BBC, 1971–. *Publication:* I Counted Them All Out and I Counted Them All Back, 1982. *Address:* c/o Foreign News Department, BBC TV Centre, Wood Lane, W12.

HANROTT, Francis George Vivian, CBE 1981; Chief Officer, Technician Education Council, 1973–82; *b* 1 July 1921; *s* of late Howard Granville Hanrott and Phyllis Sarah Hanrott; *m* 1953, Eileen Winifred Appleton; three *d*. *Educ:* Westminster Sch.; King's Coll., Univ. of London (BA Hons). Served War, RN (Air Br.), 1940–45; Lieut (A) RNVR. Asst Master, St Marylebone Grammar Sch., 1948–50; Lectr, E Berks Coll. of Further Educn, 1950–53; Asst Educn Officer, Wilts, 1953–56; Staff Manager, GEC Applied Electronics Labs, 1956–59; Asst Educn Officer, Herts, 1959–66; Registrar and Sec., CNAA, 1966–73. Governor, Millfield Sch., 1982–. Hon. MA Open Univ., 1977. *Recreations:* music, angling. *Address:* Coombe Down House, Salcombe Road, Malborough, Kingsbridge, Devon. *T:* Salcombe 2721.

HANSFORD, John Edgar, CB 1982; Under-Secretary, Defence Policy and Matériel Group, HM Treasury, 1976–82, retired; *b* 1 May 1922; *s* of Samuel George Hansford, ISO, MBE, and Winifred Louise Hansford; *m* 1947, Evelyn Agnes Whitehorn; one *s*. *Educ:* Whitgift Middle Sch., Croydon. Clerical Officer, Treasury, 1939. Served War of 1939–45: Private, Royal Sussex Regt, 1940; Lieutenant, Royal Fusiliers, 1943; served in: Africa, Mauritius, Ceylon, India, Burma, on secondment to King's African Rifles; demobilised, 1946. Exec. Officer, Treasury, 1946–50; Higher Exec. Officer, Regional Bd for Industry, Leeds, 1950–52; Exchange Control, Treasury, 1952–54; Agricultural Policy, Treasury, 1954–57; Sen. Exec. Officer, and Principal, Defence Div., Treasury, 1957–61; Principal, Social Security Div., Treasury, 1961–66; Public Enterprises Div., 1966–67; Overseas Develt Div., 1967–70; Asst Sec., Defence Policy and Matériel Div., Treasury, 1970–76; Under-Sec. in charge of Gp, 1976. *Recreations:* gardening, motoring.

HANSON, family name of **Baron Hanson.**

HANSON, Baron *cr* 1983 (Life Peer), of Edgerton in the County of West Yorkshire; **James Edward Hanson;** Kt 1976; Chairman: Hanson Trust PLC, since 1965; Hanson Transport Group Ltd, since 1965; Director, Lloyds Bank Plc, since 1984; *b* 20 Jan. 1922; *s* of late Robert Hanson, CBE and late Louisa Ann (Cis) (*née* Rodgers); *m* 1959, Geraldine (*née* Kaelin); two *s* one *d*. War Service 1939–46, 7th Bn Duke of Wellington's Regt, TA, etc. Trustee, Hanson Fellowship of Surgery, Oxford Univ.; Fellow, Cancer Res. Campaign. Freeman, City of London, 1964; Liveryman, Worshipful Co. of Saddlers, 1965. Hon. LLD Leeds, 1984. FRSA; CBIM. *Address:* 180 Brompton Road, SW3 1HF. *T:* 01–589 7070. *Clubs:* Brooks's; Huddersfield Borough; The Brook (NY); Toronto.

HANSON, Sir Anthony (Leslie Oswald), 4th Bt, *cr* 1887; *b* 27 Nov. 1934; *s* of Sir Gerald Stanhope Hanson, 2nd Bt, and Flora Liebe (*d* 1956), *e d* of late Lieut-Col W. A. R. Blennerhassett; *S* half-brother, 1951; *m* 1964, Denise Jane (Tuppence), *e d* of R. S. Rolph; one *d*. *Educ:* Hawtrey's, Savernake, Wilts; Gordonstoun, Elgin, Morayshire. Career in Royal Navy until 1955; farming, from 1956. Went into voluntary liquidation, 1967. In 1970, entered Exeter Univ. via St Luke's College (BEd Hons 1974). Teacher, Plymouth, 1974–83, resigned due to severe road accident. Conservation Officer, MSC, 1984. *Recreations:* drinking, talking; looking for a job, preferably remunerative. *Address:* Woodland Cottage, Woodland, Ashburton, Devon. *T:* Ashburton 52711.

HANSON, Dr Bertram Speakman, CMG 1963; DSO 1942; OBE 1941; ED; *b* 6 Jan. 1905; *s* of William Speakman Hanson and Maggie Aitken Hanson; *m* 1932, Mayne, *d* of T. J. Gilpin; three *s* one *d*. *Educ:* St Peter's Coll., Adelaide; University of Adelaide (MB, BS). War Service: Comd 2/8 Aust. Field Amb., 1940–43; ADMS, 9 Aust. Div., 1943–44. Pres., SA Branch of BMA, 1952–53; Pres. College of Radiologists of Australasia, 1961–62; Mem., Radiation Health Cttee of Nat. Health and Med. Research Coun., 1963–67; Hon. Radiotherapist, Royal Adelaide Hospital, 1952–64; Pres., The Australian Cancer Soc., 1964–67 (Gold Medal, 1979); Chairman: Exec. Board, Anti-Cancer Foundation, University of Adelaide, 1955–74; Anti-Cancer Foundation, Universities of South Aust., 1980–; Mem. Council, International Union Against Cancer, 1962–74. Pres., Nat. Trust of South Aust., 1979–82. FFR (Hon.) 1964; FAMA 1967; FRCR (Hon.) 1975. DUniv Adelaide, 1985. *Publications:* sundry addresses and papers in Med. Jl of Australia. *Recreation:* gardening. *Address:* Private Box, Longwood PO, Longwood, SA 5153, Australia. *Club:* Adelaide.

HANSON, Brian John Taylor; Registrar and Legal Adviser to General Synod of Church of England, since 1975; Joint Principal Registrar, Provinces of Canterbury and York, since 1980; Registrar, Convocation of Canterbury, since 1982; *b* 23 Jan. 1939; *o s* of Benjamin John Hanson and Gwendoline Ada Hanson (*née* Taylor); *m* 1972, Deborah Mary Hazel, *yr d* of Lt-Col R. S. P. Dawson, OBE; two *s* three *d*. *Educ:* Hounslow Coll.; Law Society's Coll. of Law. Solicitor (admitted 1963) and ecclesiastical notary; in private practice, Wilson Houlder & Co., 1963–65; Solicitor with Church Comrs, 1965–; Asst Legal Advr to General Synod, 1970–75. Mem., Legal Adv. Commn of General Synod, 1980– (Sec., 1970–86). Guardian, Nat. Shrine of Our Lady of Walsingham, 1984–; Mem. Council, St Luke's Hosp. for the Clergy, 1985–. *Publications:* (ed) The Canons of the Church of England, 2nd edn 1975, 4th edn 1986; (ed) The Opinions of the Advisory Commission, 6th edn 1985. *Recreations:* the family, gardening, genealogy. *Address:* Dalton's Farm, The Street, Bolney, West Sussex RH17 5PG. *T:* Bolney 890. *Club:* Royal Commonwealth Society.

HANSON, Sir (Charles) John, 3rd Bt *cr* 1918; *b* 28 Feb. 1919; *o s* of Major Sir Charles Edwin Bourne Hanson, 2nd Bt, and Violet Sybil (*d* 1966), 3rd *d* of late John B. Johnstone, Coombe Cottage, Kingston Hill, Surrey; *S* father 1958; *m* 1st, 1944, Patricia Helen (marr. diss. 1968), *o c* of late Adm. Sir (Eric James) Patrick Brind, GBE, KCB; one *s* one *d*; 2nd,

1968, Mrs Helen Yorke, *d* of late Charles Ormonde Trew. *Educ:* Eton; Clare Coll., Cambridge. Late Captain, The Duke of Cornwall's Light Infantry; served War of 1939–45. *Heir: s* Charles Rupert Patrick Hanson [*b* 25 June 1945; *m* 1977, Wanda, *d* of Don Arturo Larrain, Santiago, Chile; one *s*]. *Address:* Gunn House, Shelfanger, near Diss, Norfolk. *T:* Diss 3207. *Clubs:* Army and Navy, MCC.

HANSON, Derrick George; financial adviser; writer, director of companies; Chairman: Moneyguide Ltd, since 1978; City of London & European Property Company Ltd, since 1980; A. C. Morrell Ltd, since 1983; Key Fund Managers Ltd, since 1984; Director: Midshires Building Society, since 1982; Albany Investment Trust plc, since 1980; Toye & Co. plc, since 1981; British Leather Co. Ltd, since 1983; James Beattie PLC, since 1984; Barrister-at-Law; *b* 9 Feb. 1927; *s* of late John Henry Hanson and of Frances Elsie Hanson; *m* 1st, 1951, Daphne Elizabeth (*née* Marks) (decd); one *s* two *d*; 2nd, 1974, Hazel Mary (*née* Buckley) (*d* 1984); 3rd, 1986, Patricia (*née* Skillicorn). *Educ:* Waterloo Grammar Sch.; London Univ. (LLB (Hons)); Liverpool Univ. (LLM). Called to Bar, Lincoln's Inn, 1952. Joined Martins Bank Ltd, 1943; Chief Trustee Manager, Martins Bank Ltd, 1963; Dir and Gen. Manager, Martins Bank Trust Co. Ltd, 1968; Dir and Gen. Manager, Barclays Bank Trust Co. Ltd, 1969–76; Chairman: Barclays Unicorn Ltd, 1972–76; Barclays Life Assce Co. Ltd, 1972–76; Director: Barclaytrust Property Management Ltd, 1971–76; Barclays Bank plc, Manchester Bd, 1976–77; Sen. Adviser (UK), Manufacturers Hanover Trust Co., 1977–79; Adviser, Phillips Gp, Fine Art Auctioneers, 1977–82. Assessor, Cameron Tribunal, 1962; Dir, Oxford Univ. Business Summer Sch., 1971. Chm., Southport and Formby DHA, 1986–; Member: NW Industrialists' Council, 1977–83; South Sefton Health Authority, 1979–82; Mersey RHA, 1982–86. Pres., Assoc. of Banking Teachers, 1979–. Mem. Council, Liverpool Univ., 1980–84; Chm., Christian Arts Trust, 1980–86. George Rae Prize of Inst. of Bankers; FIB. Hon. Fellow, City Univ. *Publications:* Within These Walls: a century of Methodism in Formby, 1974; Service Banking, 1979; Moneyguide: The Handbook of Personal Finance, 1981; Dictionary of Banking and Finance, 1985. *Recreations:* golf, gardening, hill-walking. *Address:* Tower Grange, Grange Lane, Formby, Liverpool L37 7BR. *T:* Formby 74040; Deepdale Cottage, Deepdale, Cumbria. *Club:* Formby Golf (Formby, Lancs).

HANSON, James Donald; Senior Partner, Arthur Andersen & Co., since 1982; *b* 4 Jan. 1935; *s* of late Mary and Leslie Hanson; *m* 1st, 1959, Patricia Margaret Talent (marr. diss. 1977); two *s*; 2nd, 1978, Anne Barbara Asquith. *Educ:* Heath Grammar School, Halifax. ACA 1956, FCA 1966. Joined Arthur Andersen & Co., Chartered Accountants, 1958; established north west practice, 1966, Managing Partner, 1968–82. Member: Internat. Operating Cttee, 1982–; Internat. Board of Partners, 1985–; Manchester Soc. of Chartered Accountants, 1967–81 (Pres., 1979); Council, CBI, 1982–. Mem., Council and Court, Manchester Univ., 1982–. *Recreations:* ski-ing, tennis. *Address:* Arthur Andersen & Co., 1 Surrey Street, WC2R 2PS. *T:* 01–438 3693.

HANSON, Sir John; *see* Hanson, Sir Charles John.

HANSON, John Gilbert, CBE 1979; Head, British Council Division and Minister (Cultural Affairs), British High Commission, New Delhi, since 1984; *b* 16 Nov. 1938; *s* of Gilbert Fretwell Hanson and Gladys Margaret (*née* Kay); *m* 1962, Margaret Clark; three *s*. *Educ:* Manchester Grammar Sch.; Wadham Coll., Oxford (BA Lit. Hum. 1961, MA 1964). Asst Principal, WO, 1961–63; British Council: Madras, India, 1963–66; ME Centre for Arab Studies, Lebanon, 1966–68; Rep., Bahrain, 1968–72; Dep. Controller, Educn and Science Div., 1972–75; Representative, Iran, and Counsellor (Cultural) British Embassy, Tehran, 1975–79; Controller, Finance Div., 1979–82; RCDS, 1983. *Recreations:* books, music, sport, travel. *Address:* c/o The British Council, 10 Spring Gardens, SW1A 2BN. *T:* 01–930 8466. *Clubs:* Athenæum, MCC; Delhi Golf; Gymkhana (Madras).

HANSON, Neil; Under Secretary, and Controller, Newcastle upon Tyne Central Office, Department of Health and Social Security, 1981–83; *b* 21 March 1923; *s* of late Reginald William Hanson and Lillian Hanson (*née* Benson); *m* 1st, 1950, Eileen Ashworth (*d* 1976); two *s*; 2nd, 1977, Margaret Brown-Smelt. *Educ:* City of Leeds Sch. Served War, 1942–46, N Africa, Sicily, Italy. Jun. Clerk, Leeds Social Welfare Cttee, 1939; Clerical Officer, 1948–50, Exec. Officer, 1950–56, Nat. Assistance Bd; Manager, Suez and Hungarian Refugee Hostels, 1956–59; Higher Exec. Officer, 1959–62, Sen. Exec. Officer, 1963–66, Nat. Assistance Bd; Principal, Min. of Social Security, 1967–73; Sen. Principal, 1973–76, Asst Sec., 1976–80, DHSS. *Recreations:* cricket, music, walking. *Address:* 4 Woodbourne, Park Avenue, Leeds LS8 2JW. *T:* Leeds 653452.

HANSON, Rt. Rev. Richard Patrick Crosland, MA, DD; MRIA; Professor of Historical and Contemporary Theology, University of Manchester, 1973–82, now Emeritus; Assistant Bishop: Diocese of Manchester, 1973–83; Diocese of Chester, since 1983; *b* 24 Nov. 1916; *s* of late Sir Philip Hanson, CB, and late Lady Hanson; *m* 1950, Mary Dorothy, *d* of late Canon John Powell; two *s* two *d*. *Educ:* Cheltenham Coll.; Trinity Coll., Dublin. 1st Hons BA in Classics also in Ancient Hist., 1938; BD with Theol. Exhibn, 1941; DD 1950; MA 1961. Asst Curate, St Mary's, Donnybrook, Dublin, and later in Banbridge, Co. Down, 1941–45; Vice-Principal, Queen's Coll., Birmingham, 1946–50; Vicar of St John's, Shuttleworth, dio. Manchester, 1950–52; Dept of Theol., Univ. of Nottingham, Lectr, Sen. Lectr and Reader, 1952–62; Lightfoot Prof. of Divinity, Univ. of Durham, and Canon of Durham, 1962–64; Prof. of Christian Theology, Univ. of Nottingham, 1964–70; Hon. Canon of Southwell, 1964–70; Canon Theologian of Coventry Cathedral, 1967–70; Examining Chaplain to the Bishop of Southwell, 1968; Bishop of Clogher, 1970–73. *Publications:* Origen's Doctrine of Tradition, 1954; II Corinthians (commentary, Torch series), 1954; Allegory and Event, 1959; God: Creator, Saviour, Spirit, 1960; Tradition in the Early Church, 1962; New Clarendon Commentary on Acts, 1967; Saint Patrick: his origins and career, 1968; Groundwork for Unity, 1971; The Attractiveness of God, 1973; Mystery and Imagination: reflections upon Christianity, 1976; (ed, abridged and trans.), Justin Martyr's Dialogue with Trypho, 1963; Saint Patrick, Confession et Lettre à Coroticus, avec la collaboration de Cécile Blanc, 1978; Christian Priesthood Examined, 1979; Eucharistic Offering in the Early Church, 1979; (with A. T. Hanson) Reasonable Belief: a Survey of the Christian Faith, 1980; The Continuity of Christian Doctrine, 1981; The Life and Writings of the Historical St Patrick, 1982; Studies in Christian Antiquity, 1986; contribs to: Institutionalism and Church Unity, 1963; The Anglican Synthesis, 1964; Vindications, 1966; (ed) Difficulties for Christian Belief, 1966; (co-ed) Christianity in Britain 300–700, 1968; (ed) Pelican Guide to Modern Theology, 1969–70; contribs to: A Dictionary of Christian Theology, 1969; Lambeth Essays on Ministry, 1969; Le Traité sur le Saint-Esprit de Saint Basile, 1969; Cambridge History of The Bible, vol. 1, 1970; Dogma and Formula in the Fathers (Studia Patristica XIII 2 etc, 1975); The Christian Attitude to Pagan Religions (Aufstieg und Niedergang der römischen Welt II.23.2, 1980); articles in: Jl of Theol Studies, Vigiliae Christianae, Expository Times, Theology, Modern Churchman, The Times. *Recreations:* tennis, drama. *Address:* 24 Styal Road, Wilmslow, Cheshire SK9 4AG.

HANTON, Alastair Kydd, OBE 1986; Deputy Managing Director, National Girobank, Post Office, since 1982; *b* 10 Oct. 1926; *er s* of late Peter Hanton and Maude Hanton; *m* 1956, Margaret Mary (*née* Lumsden); two *s* one *d*. *Educ:* Mill Hill Sch.; Pembroke Coll., Cambridge. Commonwealth Develt Corp., 1948–54; ICFC, 1954–57; Unilever, 1957–66; Rio Tinto-Zinc, 1966–68; Post Office, 1968–. *Recreation:* forestry. *Address:* 8 Gilkes Crescent, Dulwich Village, SE21 7BS. *T:* 01–693 2618.

HANWORTH, 2nd Viscount, *cr* 1936, of Hanworth; **David Bertram Pollock,** CEng, MIMechE, FIEE, FRPS, FIQA; Baron, *cr* 1926; Bt, *cr* 1922; Lt-Col Royal Engineers, retired; Barrister-at-Law (Inner Temple), 1958; *b* 1 Aug. 1916; *s* of Charles Thomas Anderson Pollock and Alice Joyce Becher; *S* grandfather, 1936; *m* 1940, Isolda Rosamond, *yr d* of Geoffrey Parker, of Cairo; two *s* one *d*. *Educ:* Wellington Coll.; Trinity Coll., Cambridge. (Mechanical Science Tripos, 1939). Joined Social Democratic Alliance, 1981. *Publications:* Amateur Carbro Colour Prints, 1950; Amateur Dye Transfer Colour Prints, 1956. *Recreations:* ski-ing, photography, gardening, canal cruising. *Heir: s* Hon. David Stephen Geoffrey Pollock [*b* 16 Feb. 1946; *m* 1968, Elizabeth Liberty, *e d* of Lawrence Vambe; two *d*]. *Address:* Quoin Cottage, Shamley Green, Guildford, Surrey GU5 0UJ.

HAPPOLD, Prof. Edmund, RDI 1983, FEng 1983; Professor of Building Engineering, University of Bath, since 1976; Senior Partner, Buro Happold, consulting engineers, since 1976; *b* 8 Nov. 1930; *s* of Prof. Frank Charles Happold, *qv*; *m* 1967, Evelyn Claire Matthews; two *s*. *Educ:* Leeds Grammar Sch.; Bootham Sch., York; Leeds Univ. BSc, FICE, FIStructE, FCIOB. Site Engineer, Sir Robert McAlpine & Sons, 1952–54; Engineer, Ove Arup & Partners, 1956–58, Severud Elstad & Kruger, NY, 1958–60; Senior Engineer then Associate, later Exec. Partner, Ove Arup & Partners, 1960–76; assisted Tom Hancock in winning 2nd prize, Houses of Parlt competition, 1972; won jtly with 4 others Centre Pompidou, Plateau Beaubourg competition, 1971; won jtly with 2 others Vauxhall Cross competition, 1982; jtly with 3 others second in Leeds Playhouse competition, 1985. Institution of Structural Engineers: Mem. Council, 1974–77, 1979–; Chm., Educn Cttee, 1979–82; Vice-Pres., 1982–86; Pres., 1986–87; Guthrie Brown Medal, 1970; Oscar Faber Medal, 1974, 1977; Henry Adams Award, 1976; Mem., Standing Cttee on Structural Safety, 1976–86; International Association of Bridge and Structural Engineers: Mem., Nat. Council, 1977–; Mem., Internat. Tech. Cttee, 1978–83; Chm., Commn V, 1978–83. Mem. Board, Property Services Agency, 1979–81, Adv. Bd, 1981–86. Murray Leslie Medal, CIOB, 1982. Hon. FRIBA 1983. *Publications:* papers in learned journals. *Recreations:* engineering and family activities. *Address:* Flat 18, 32 Grosvenor Street, W1; 4 Widcombe Terrace, Bath, Avon. *T:* Bath 337510. *Club:* Athenæum.

HAPPOLD, Prof. Frank Charles, PhD, DSc (Manchester); Professor of Biochemistry, University of Leeds, 1946–67, Emeritus Professor, 1967; *b* Barrow-in-Furness, 23 Sept. 1902; *s* of Henry Happold and Emma Happold (*née* Ley); *m* 1926, A. Margaret M. Smith, MA, Brighton; one *s* one *d*. *Educ:* privately; Barrow Gram. Sch.; University of Manchester. PhD (Manchester) 1927; DSc (Manchester) 1934. University of Leeds: Department of Bacteriology, 1926–36; Dept of Physiology, 1936–46; Dept of Biochemistry, 1946–67; Research Prof., University of Florida, 1958–59. First Chm., Fedn of European Biochem. Socs, 1964. Leverhulme Fellowship to Harvard Univ. Post Graduate Medical Sch., 1939; Visiting Prof., University of Ghana, 1967–70; Royal Soc. Vis. Prof., Univ. of Science and Technology, Kumasi, 1972. Co-founder with wife of International Tramping Tours, 1929. Diplôme d'Honneur, Fedn European Biochem. Socs, 1974. Bronze Medal, Ville de Paris, 1964. *Publications:* numerous scientific publications, mainly in Microbiological Chemistry and Enzymology. *Recreations:* gardening and travel. *Address:* Three Roods, Arnside, Carnforth LA5 0BB.

See also E. Happold.

HARARE, Diocese; *see* Mashonaland.

HARARE (formerly **SALISBURY), Archbishop of,** (RC), since 1976; **Most Rev. Patrick Chakaipa;** *b* 25 June 1932; *s* of Chakaipa and Chokutaura. *Educ:* Chishawasha Minor and Regional Major Seminary, nr Harare; Kutama Teachers' Coll. Ecclesiastic qualifications in Philosophy and Theology; Teacher Training Cert. Asst priest, Makumbi Mission, 1967–69; Priest-in-Charge, All Souls Mission, Mutoko, 1969–73; Episcopal Vicar, Mutoko-Mrewa Area, 1970–73; Auxiliary Bishop of Salisbury, 1973–76. *Publications:* Karikoga, 1958; Pfumo reRopa, 1961; Rudo Ibofu, 1961; Garandichauya, 1963; Dzasukwa, 1967. *Recreation:* chess. *Address:* PO Box 8060, Causeway, Harare, Zimbabwe. *T:* 792125.

HARARE, Bishop of, since 1981; **Rt. Rev. Ralph Peter Hatendi;** *b* 9 April 1927; *s* of Fabian and Amelia Hatendi; *m* 1954, Jane Mary Chikumbu; two *s* three *d*. *Educ:* St Peter's Coll., Rosettenville, S Africa (LTh). AKC. School teacher, 1952–; clergyman, 1957–; Seminary Tutor, 1968–72; Executive Secretary, 1973–75; Distribution Consultant, 1976–78; Suffragan Bishop of Mashonaland, 1979–80. *Publications:* Sex and Society, 1971; Shona Marriage and the Christian Churches, in Christianity South of the Zambezi, 1973. *Recreation:* poultry. *Address:* PO UA7, Harare, Zimbabwe. *T:* 44113. *Club:* Harare (Zimbabwe).

HARBERTON, 10th Viscount *cr* 1791; **Thomas de Vautort Pomeroy;** Baron Harberton 1783; *b* 19 Oct. 1910; *s* of 8th Viscount Harberton, OBE, and Mary Katherine (*d* 1971), *d* of A. W. Leatham; *S* brother, 1980; *m* 1978, Vilma, *widow* of Sir Alfred Butt, 1st Bt. *Educ:* Eton. Joined Welsh Guards, 1932; transferred to RAOC, 1939; served BEF, then in India; retired, 1952. *Heir: b* Hon. Robert William Pomeroy [*b* 29 Feb. 1916; *m* 1953, Winifred Anne, *d* of late Sir Arthur Colegate, MP; two *s*]. *Address:* Residence Europa, Place des Moulins, Monte Carlo. *Club:* Cavalry and Guards.

HARBISON, Air Vice-Marshal William, CB 1977; CBE 1965; AFC 1956; RAF, retired; Vice-President, British Aerospace Inc., Washington, DC, since 1979; *b* 11 April 1922; *s* of W. Harbison; *m* 1950, Helen, *d* of late William B. Geneva, Bloomington, Illinois; two *s*. *Educ:* Ballymena Academy, N Ireland. Joined RAF, 1941; 118 Sqdn Fighter Comd, 1943–46; 263, 257 and 64 Sqdns, 1946–48; Exchange Officer with 1st Fighter Group USAF, 1948–50; Central Fighter Estabt, 1950–51; 4th Fighter Group USAF, Korea, 1952; 2nd ATAF Germany: comd No 67 Sqdn, 1952–55; HQ No 2 Group, 1955; psc 1956; Air Min. and All Weather OCU, 1957; comd No 29 All Weather Sqdn Fighter Comd, Acklington and Leuchars, 1958–59; British Defence Staffs, Washington, 1959–62; jssc 1962; comd RAF Leuchars Fighter Comd, 1963–65; ndc 1965–66; Gp Capt. Ops: HQ Fighter Comd, 1967–68; No 11 Group Strike Comd, 1968; Dir of Control (Ops), NATCS, 1968–72; Comdr RAF Staff, and Air Attaché, Washington, 1972–75; AOC 11 Group, RAF, 1975–77. *Recreations:* flying, motoring. *Address:* c/o Lloyds Bank, Cox's & King's Branch, 6 Pall Mall, SW1. *Club:* Royal Air Force.

HARBORD, Rev. and Hon. Derek; a Judge of the High Court of Tanganyika, and Member, Court of Appeal for East Africa, 1953–59, retired; Earl Marshal's warrant for grant of arms, 1966; *b* 25 July 1902; *yr s* of F. W. Harbord, Birkenhead, and Isabella (*née* Gardner), Sale; *m* Grace Rosalind (*d* 1969), *o d* of A. S. Fowles, Birmingham; two *s* one *d*. *Educ:* Mount Radford Sch., Exeter; Gray's Inn; St Michael's Theol Coll., Llandaff. Barrister-at-Law, 1925; Deacon, 1925; Priest, 1926; Curate, W Norwood, 1925–27; Streatham, 1927–29; Vicar, Stoke Lyne, 1929; Royal Army Chaplains Dept, 1929; Chaplain i/c Depot RAMC, Crookham, and V Lt Bde RA, Ewshott, 1929–30; Vicar, Hindolveston (where he built a new parish church, the ancient one having collapsed 40 years earlier), 1930–33; Vicar, Good Shepherd, W Bromwich, 1933–35; resigned to become a Roman Catholic, 1935. Practised at English Bar, 1935–40: Central Criminal Court, SE Circuit, Mddx and N London Sess; Sec., Bentham Cttee for Poor Litigants, 1937–40; Army Officers Emergency Reserve, 1938; HM Colonial Legal Service, 1940; Dist Magistrate and Coroner, Gold Coast, 1940–44; Registrar of High Court of N Rhodesia and High Sheriff of the Territory, 1944–46; Resident Magistrate and Coroner, N Rhodesia, 1946–53; Chm., Reinstatement in Civil Employment (Mining Industry) Cttee; Chm., Liquor Licensing Appeal Tribunal for N Rhodesia; admitted to Ghana Bar, 1959; Senior Lecturer, Ghana Sch. of Law, and Editor of Ghana Law Reports, 1959–61. Reconciled with Anglican Communion and licensed to offic. Accra dio., 1959–61; Rector of St Botolph-without-Aldgate (which, with its ancient peal of bells, he restored after extensive damage by fire) with Holy Trinity, Minories, 1962–74; Fellow of Sion College, 1962–74; permission to officiate, dio. Rochester, 1974–. *Publications:* Manual for Magistrates (N Rhodesia), 1951; Law Reports (N Rhodesia), 1952; Law Reports (Ghana), 1960. *Recreations:* keeping track of 26 grand and great grandchildren, reading modern theology and other whodunnits, pottering about. *Address:* College of St Barnabas, Lingfield, Surrey RH7 6NJ. *T:* Dormans Park 706. *Club:* Athenæum.

HARBORD-HAMOND, family name of **Baron Suffield.**

HARBOTTLE, Rev. Anthony Hall Harrison, LVO 1979; Rector of East Dean with Friston and Jevington, since 1981; Chaplain to the Queen, since 1968; *b* 3 Sept. 1925; *y s* of Alfred Charles Harbottle, ARIBA, and Ellen Muriel, *o d* of William Popham Harrison; *m* 1955, Gillian Mary, *o d* of Hugh Goodenough; three *s* one *d. Educ:* Sherborne Sch.; Christ's Coll., Cambridge (MA); Wycliffe Hall, Oxford. Served War in Royal Marines, 1944–46. Deacon 1952, priest 1953; Asst Curacies: Boxley, 1952–54; St Peter-in-Thanet, 1954–60; Rector of Sandhurst with Newenden, 1960–68; Chaplain of the Royal Chapel, Windsor Great Park, 1968–81. Founder Mem., Kent Trust for Nature Conservation, 1954; Mem., Green Alliance, 1984. County Chaplain, Royal British Legion (Sussex), 1982–. FRES 1971. *Publications:* contribs to entomological jls, on lepidoptera. *Recreations:* butterflies and moths, nature conservancy, entomology, ornithology, philately, coins, Treasury and bank notes, painting, cooking, lobstering. *Address:* East Dean Rectory, Eastbourne, East Sussex. *T:* East Dean 3266.

HARBOTTLE, (George) Laurence; Senior Partner, Harbottle & Lewis, Solicitors, since 1956; *b* 11 April 1924; *s* of George Harbottle and Winifred Ellen Benson Harbottle. *Educ:* The Leys Sch., Cambridge; Emmanuel Coll., Cambridge (MA). Solicitor 1952. Served War: commnd RA, 1942; Burma and India; Temp. Captain; Adjt 9th Fd Regt, 1945–47. Theatre Companies: Chairman: Theatre Centre, 1959–; Prospect, 1966–77; Royal Exchange (69), 1968–83; Cambridge, 1969–; Director: The Watermill, 1970–75; The Bush (Alternative), 1975–77. Arts Council: Mem., 1976–77–78; Mem., Drama Panel, 1974–78; Chairman: Housing the Arts, 1977–78; Trng Cttee, 1977–78; Chm., Central Sch. of Speech and Drama, 1982– (Vice Chm., 1977); Dep. Chm., ICA, 1977–. Pres., Theatrical Management Assoc., 1979–85; Vice-Chm., Theatres Adv. Council, 1986–. Member: Justice Cttee on Privacy, 1970; Theatres Trust, 1980–. *Recreations:* works of art, gardening, tennis. *Address:* 34 South Molton Street, W1Y 2BP. *T:* 01–629 7633. *Club:* Savile.

HARBOTTLE, Brig. Michael Neale, OBE 1959; Director, London Centre for International Peacebuilding, since 1983; *b* 7 Feb. 1917; *s* of Thomas Benfield Cecil and Kathleen Milicent Harbottle; *m* 1st, 1940, Alison Jean Humfress; one *s* one *d*; 2nd, 1972, Eirwen Helen Simonds. *Educ:* Marlborough Coll.; Royal Military Coll., Sandhurst. Commissioned Oxfordshire and Buckinghamshire Light Infantry, 1937 (despatches 1944); commanded 1st Royal Green Jackets, 1959–62; Chief of Staff, UN Peacekeeping Force Cyprus, 1966–68; retired, 1968. Vice-Pres., Internat. Peace Academy, 1971–73, Consultant, 1973–84; Vis. Sen. Lectr (Peace Studies), Bradford Univ., 1974–79; Vice-Pres., UN Assoc. (UK), 1974–84; Cons., United World College of Atlantic, 1974–81; Mem., Management Cttee, Council for Educn in World Citizenship, 1978–84; Educn Planning Dir, British Council for Aid to Refugees (Vietnamese Sec.), 1979–80; Gen. Sec., World Disarmament Campaign, 1980–82. *Publications:* The Impartial Soldier, 1970; The Blue Berets, 1971, 2nd edn 1975; (jtly) The Thin Blue Line: International Peacekeeping and its Future, 1974; The Knaves of Diamonds, 1976; (collator) Peacekeeper's Handbook, 1978; (jtly) 10 Questions Answered, 1983; contributor to: Unofficial Diplomats, 1977 (USA); The Arab-Israel Conflict, Readings and Documents, 1977 (USA). *Recreations:* cricket, golf, crossword puzzles. *Address:* 86d Hamilton Terrace, NW8 9UL. *T:* 01–289 0314.

HARCOURT, Geoffrey David, JP; RDI, DesRCA, FSIAD; freelance designer, since 1962; Consultant to Artifort, Dutch furniture manufacturer, since 1963; *b* 9 Aug. 1935; *s* of William and Barbara Harcourt; *m* 1965, Jean Mary Vaughan Pryce-Jones; one *s* one *d. Educ:* High Wycombe Sch. of Art; Royal Coll. of Art; DesRCA, Silver Medal 1960. FSIAD 1968; RDI 1978. Designer: Latham, Tyler, Jensen, Chicago, 1960–61; Jacob Jensen, Copenhagen, 1961; Andrew Pegram Ltd, London, 1961–62. Vis. Lecturer: High Wycombe Coll. of Art and Design, 1963–74; Leicester Polytechnic, 1982, 1983; Ext. Assessor for BA Hons degrees, Kingston Polytechnic, 1974–77, Loughborough Coll. of Art and Design, 1978–81, Belfast Polytechnic, 1977–81 and Buckinghamshire Coll. of Higher Educn, 1982–. Chair design for Artifort awarded first prize for creativity, Brussels, 1978; Mem., Design Awards Cttee, Design Council, 1979–80; Chm., RSA Bursaries Cttee, 1982– (Furniture Design Section, 1982–). Work exhibited: Steidlijk Mus., Amsterdam, 1967; Prague Mus. of Decorative Arts, 1972; Science Mus., London, 1972; Design Council, London and Glasgow, 1976 and 1981. FRSA 1979. Freeman, City of London; Liveryman, Worshipful Co. of Furniture Makers. JP Watlington, Oxon, 1981. *Recreations:* making things, cooking, golf. *Address:* The Old Vicarage, Benson, Oxfordshire. *Club:* Goring and Streatley Golf.

HARCOURT-SMITH, Air Marshal Sir David, KCB 1984; DFC 1957; Controller Aircraft, Ministry of Defence, Procurement Executive, since 1986; *b* 14 Oct. 1931; *s* of late Air Vice-Marshal G. Harcourt-Smith, CB, CBE, MVO, and of M. Harcourt-Smith; *m* 1957, Mary (*née* Entwistle); two *s* one *d. Educ:* Felsted Sch.; RAF College. Commnd 1952, flying appts with Nos 11, 8 and 54 Squadrons; Staff Coll., 1962; OC No 54 Squadron, 1963–65; PSO to AOC-in-C, Tech. Training Comd, 1965–67; Defence Planning Staff, 1967–68; OC No 6 Squadron, 1969–70; Central Tactics and Trials Organisation, 1970–72; OC RAF Brüggen, 1972–74; Dir of Op. Requirements, 1974–76; RCDS, 1977; Comdt, RAF Coll., Cranwell, 1978–80; Asst Chief of Air Staff (Op. Reqs), 1980–84; AOC-in-C, RAF Support Command, 1984–85. *Recreations:* tennis, walking, golf. *Address:* c/o Barclays Bank, PO Box 41, 16 High Street, High Wycombe, Bucks HP11 2BG. *Club:* Royal Air Force.

HARCUS, Rear-Adm. Ronald Albert, CB 1976; RN retired; *b* 25 Oct. 1921; *s* of Henry Alexander Harcus and Edith Maud (*née* Brough); *m* 1946, Jean Heckman; two *s* two *d. Educ:* St Olave's Grammar Sch.; RNC Greenwich. Entered Royal Navy, 1937; Comdr 1956; Captain 1964; Rear-Adm. 1974; served in HM Ships Nigeria, Jamaica, Ocean, Dainty (despatches, Korea, 1953); Fleet Marine Engr Officer Home Fleet, 1965–67; Dep. Dir Fleet Maintenance, 1968–69; Captain, HMS Sultan, 1971–72; attended Royal Coll. of Defence Studies, 1973; Asst Chief of Fleet Support, MoD (Navy), 1974–76. Managing Director: RWO (Marine Equipment) Ltd, 1976–79; R. W. Owen Ltd, 1976–79. Chairman: Management Cttee, British Seamen's Boys Home, 1981–84; NSPCC South Devon, 1981–. *Recreations:* fishing, sailing. *Address:* 2 Church Hill Close, Blackawton, Devon TQ9 7BQ.

HARDAKER, Rev. Canon Ian Alexander; Clergy Appointments Adviser, since 1985; *b* 14 May 1932; *s* of Joseph Alexander Hardaker and Edna Mary (*née* Theede); *m* 1963, Susan Mary Wade Bottom; two *s* two *d. Educ:* Kingston Grammar Sch.; Royal Military Acad., Sandhurst; King's Coll., London (BD, AKC). Commnd East Surrey Regt, 1952. Curate, Beckenham Parish Ch., 1960–65; Vicar of Eynsford and Rector of Lullingstone, 1965–70; Vicar of St Stephen's, Chatham, 1970–85; Rural Dean of Rochester, 1978–85. *Recreations:* walking, photography, family. *Address:* 29 Maidstone Road, Chatham, Kent ME4 6DP. *T:* Medway 811742.

HARDCASTLE, Alan John, FCA; Partner, Peat, Marwick, Mitchell & Co., since 1967; *b* 10 Aug. 1933; *s* of late William and of Catherine Hardcastle; *m* 1st, 1958, Dinah (*née* Beattie) (marr. diss. 1983); two *s*; 2nd, 1983, Ione Marguerite (*née* Cooney). *Educ:* Haileybury Coll. Articled to B. W. Brixey, 1951–56; qualified, 1956; Nat. Service as Sub-Lieut RNVR, 1956–58. Joined Peat, Marwick, Mitchell & Co., 1958; Partner 1967, Gen. Partner 1972; DoT Inspector into affairs of Saint Piran Ltd (reported 1981). Inst. of Chartered Accountants in England and Wales: Mem. Council, 1974–; Pres., 1983–85; Chairman: London and District Soc. of Chartered Accountants, 1973–74; Consultative Cttee of Accountancy Bodies, 1983–85; Pres., Chartered Accountants Students' Soc. of London, 1976–80. Mem., Bd of Banking Supervision, 1986–. Master, Co. of Chartered Accountants in England and Wales, 1978–79. Mem., Council of Management, The White Ensign Assoc.; Hon. Treas., Berkeley Square Ball. Mem. Court, Mary Rose Trust. Speaker and author of papers on accountancy topics. *Recreations:* music, theatre, fishing, the company of family and friends. *Clubs:* City Livery, Naval.

HARDCASTLE, Prof. Jack Donald, MChir (Cantab); FRCP, FRCS; Professor of Surgery, University of Nottingham, since 1970; *b* 3 April 1933; *s* of Albert Hardcastle and Bertha (*née* Ellison); *m* 1965, Rosemary Hay-Shunker; one *s* one *d. Educ:* St Bartholomew's Grammar Sch., Newbury; Emmanuel Coll., Cambridge (Senior Scholar 1954; BA, MA); Windsor Postgrad. Schol.); London Hospital (Open Scholarship 1955; MB, BChir, MChir (Distinction)). MRCP 1961; FRCS 1962; FRCP 1984. House Phys./Surg., Resident Accoucheur, London Hosp., 1959–60; Ho. Surg. to Prof. Aird, Hammersmith Postgraduate Hosp., 1961–62; London Hospital: Research Asst, 1962; Lectr in Surgery, 1963; Registrar in Surgery, 1964; Registrar in Surgery, Thoracic Unit, 1965; Sen. Registrar in Surgery, 1965; Sen. Registrar, St Mark's Hosp., London, 1968; Sen. Lectr in Surgery, London Hosp., 1968. Sir Arthur Sims Commonwealth Travelling Prof., RCS, 1985. *Publications:* Isolated Organ Perfusion (with H. D. Ritchie), 1973; various scientific papers. *Recreation:* field sports. *Address:* Wild Briars, Goverton, Bleasby, Nottingham. *T:* Newark 830316.

HARDEN, Donald Benjamin, CBE 1969 (OBE 1956); MA Cantab, MA Oxon, PhD Mich; FSA; Director of the London Museum, 1956–70; Acting Director of the Museum of London, 1965–70; *b* Dublin, 8 July 1901; *er s* of late John Mason Harden and Constance Caroline Sparrow; *m* 1st, 1934, Cecil Ursula (*d* 1963), *e d* of late James Adolphus Harriss; one *d*; 2nd, 1965, Dorothy May, *er d* of late Daniel Herbert McDonald. *Educ:* Kilkenny Coll.; Westminster Sch.; Trinity Coll., Cambridge; University of Michigan. Travelled in Italy and Tunisia, 1923–24; Senior Asst, Dept of Humanity, University of Aberdeen, 1924–26; Commonwealth Fund Fellow, University of Michigan, 1926–28; Asst, University of Michigan Archæol. Exped. to Egypt, 1928–29; Asst Keeper, Dept of Antiquities, Ashmolean Museum, Oxford, 1929–45; Keeper, Dept of Antiquities, and Sec., Griffith Institute, 1945–56. Temp. Civil Servant, Ministries of Supply and Production, 1940–45. Vice-Pres. Soc. of Antiquaries of London, 1949–53, 1964–67; President: Council for British Archæology, 1950–54; Oxford Architectural and Historical Soc., 1952–55; Section H, British Assoc., 1955; London and Middlesex Archæol. Soc., 1959–65; Royal Archæol. Inst., 1966–69; Internat. Assoc. for History of Glass, 1968–74; Chm., Directors' Conf. (Nat. Museums), 1968–70; Hon. Sec. Museums Assoc., 1949–54, Chm. Educ. Cttee 1954–59, Pres. 1960; Hon. Editor, Soc. for Medieval Archæology, 1957–73, Pres., 1975–77; Mem. of Council, British School of Archæology in Iraq, 1949–84; Member: Ancient Monuments Board for England, 1959–74; Royal Commission on Historical Monuments (England), 1963–71; Trustee, RAEC Museum, 1966–84. Mem., German Archaeol. Inst. Leverhulme Fellowship for research on ancient glass, 1953. Gold Medal, Soc. of Antiquaries, 1977; Hon. Fellow and Rakow Award, Corning Museum of Glass, NY, 1983. *Publications:* Roman Glass from Karanis, 1936; The Phoenicians, 1962, rev. edns 1971, 1980; Catalogue of Greek and Roman Glass in the British Museum, I, 1981; (with E. T. Leeds) The Anglo-Saxon Cemetery at Abingdon, Berks, 1936; (jointly) Masterpieces of Glass, British Museum, 1968; (ed) Dark-Age Britain, 1956; numerous articles on archæology and museums. *Address:* 12 St Andrew's Mansions, Dorset Street, W1H 3FD. *T:* 01–935 5121. *Club:* Athenæum.

HARDEN, Major James Richard Edwards, OBE 1983; DSO; MC; farmer; *b* 12 Dec. 1916; *s* of late Major J. E. Harden, DL, JP, Royal Irish Fusiliers, and L. G. C. Harden; *m* 1948, Ursula Joyce, *y d* of G. M. Strutt, Newhouse, Terling, Chelmsford, Essex; one *s* two *d. Educ:* Oriel House, St Asaph; Bedford Sch.; Sandhurst. Commissioned into Royal Tank Regt 1937; retired on agricultural release, 1947; MP (UU) for County Armagh, 1948–54. JP County Armagh, 1956, Cærnarvonshire, later Gwynedd, 1971–82; DL, Co. Armagh, 1946; High Sheriff, Cærnarvonshire, 1971–72. *Recreations:* shooting, fishing. *Address:* Nanhoran, Pwllheli, Gwynedd LL53 8DL. *T:* Botwnnog 610.

HARDERS, Sir Clarence Waldemar, Kt 1977; OBE 1969; Lawyer with Freehill, Hollingdale and Page, Canberra, ACT, since 1980; *b* Murtoa, 1 March 1915; *s* of E. W. Harders, Dimboola, Vic; *m* 1947, Gladys, *d* of E. Treasure; one *s* two *d. Educ:* Concordia Coll., Unley, S Australia; Adelaide Univ. (LLB). Joined Dept of the Attorney-General, 1947, Dep. Sec., 1965–70, Sec., 1970–79; Legal Adviser, Dept of Foreign Affairs, 1979–80. *Address:* c/o Freehill, Hollingdale and Page, 10th Floor, National Mutual Centre, Darwin Place, Canberra, ACT, Australia; 43 Stonehaven Crescent, Deakin, ACT 2600, Australia. *Clubs:* Commonwealth, National Press, Canberra Bowling (Canberra), Royal Canberra Golf, Royal Automobile of Victoria.

HARDIE, Ven. Archibald George; Archdeacon of West Cumberland and Hon. Canon of Carlisle Cathedral, 1971–79; also Vicar of Haile, 1970–79; *b* 19 Dec. 1908; *s* of late Archbishop Hardie and late Mrs Hardie; *m* 1936, Rosalie Sheelagh Hamilton (*née* Jacob); three *s* one *d. Educ:* St Lawrence Coll., Ramsgate; Trinity Coll., Cambridge (MA); Westcott House, Cambridge. Hockey Blue, Cambridge, 1931–32. Curate of All Hallows, Lombard St, EC, and London Sec. of Student Christian Movement, 1934–36; Chaplain, Repton Sch., 1936–38; Vicar of St Alban, Golders Green, London, NW11, 1938–44; OCF. Rector of Hexham Abbey, 1944–63; Vicar and Rural Dean of Halifax, 1963–71, and Hon. Canon of Wakefield Cathedral. *Recreations:* tilling the soil and chewing the cud. *Address:* Grasslees Cottage, Swindon, Sharperton, Morpeth, Northumberland.

HARDIE, Sir Charles (Edgar Mathewes), Kt 1970; CBE 1963 (OBE 1943); chartered accountant; Partner in Dixon, Wilson and Co., 1934–81, Senior Partner, 1975–81; *b* 10 March 1910; *s* of Dr C. F. and Mrs R. F. Hardie (*née* Moore), Barnet, Herts; *m* 1st, 1937, Dorothy Jean (*née* Hobson) (*d* 1965); one *s* three *d*; 2nd, 1966, Mrs Angela Richli, *widow* of Raymond Paul Richli; 3rd, 1975, Rosemary Margaret Harwood. *Educ:* Aldenham Sch. Qualified as Chartered Accountant, 1932; practised in London, 1934–81. War Service, 1939–44 (Col). Chairman: BOAC, 1969–70; Metropolitan Estate & Property Corp., 1964–71; White Fish Authority, 1967–73; Fitch Lovell plc, 1970–77; Director: British American and General Trust plc, 1961–85; British Printing Corp. plc, 1965–82 (Chm., 1969–76); Royal Bank of Canada, 1969–81; Mann Egerton & Co. Ltd, 1959–80; Trusthouse Forte plc, 1970– (Dep. Chm., 1983–); Hill Samuel Group plc, 1970–77. Dep. Chm., NAAFI, 1953–72; Member: BEA Board, 1968–70; Council, Inst. of Directors, 1966–80. Legion of Merit, USA, 1944. *Recreation:* bridge. *Address:* Pitt House, 25 New Street, Henley-on-Thames, Oxon RG9 2BP. *T:* Henley-on-Thames 577944.
See also C. J. M. Hardie.

HARDIE, (Charles) Jeremy (Mawdesley), CBE 1983; Chairman, National Provident Institution, since 1980 (Director, since 1972; Deputy Chairman, 1977); *b* 9 June 1938; *s* of Sir Charles Hardie, *qv*; *m* 1st, 1962, Susan Chamberlain (marr. diss. 1976); two *s* two *d*; 2nd, 1978, Xandra, Countess of Gowrie, *d* of late Col R. A. G. Bingley, CVO, DSO, OBE; one *d*. *Educ:* Winchester Coll.; New Coll., Oxford (2nd Cl. Hon. Mods, 1st Cl. Lit. Hum.); Nuffield Coll., Oxford (BPhil Econs). ACA 1965, Peat, Marwick, Mitchell & Co.; Nuffield Coll., Oxford, 1966–67; Jun. Res. Fellow, Trinity Coll., Oxford, 1967–68; Fellow and Tutor in Econs, Keble Coll., Oxford, 1968–75. Partner, Dixon Wilson & Co., 1975–82. Chairman: Alexander Syndicate Management Ltd, 1982–; Alexanders Discount Co. Ltd, 1984– (Dir, 1978, Dep. Chm., 1981); Alexanders Laing & Cruickshank Ltd, 1986–; Radio Broadland Ltd, 1983–85 (Dir, 1983–); David Mann Underwriting Agency Ltd, 1983–; Director: Stockholders Investment Trust Ltd, 1979–86; Unilever Pensions Investment Management Ltd, 1980–86; IBM UK Pensions Trust Ltd, 1981–83; NAAFI, 1981–; John Swire and Sons, 1982–; Amdahl (UK) Ltd, 1983–86; London Bd, Bank of Scotland, 1983–86; BAII Holdings Ltd, 1983–86; Mercantile House Holdings Ltd, 1984–; Additional Underwriting Agencies (No 3) Ltd, 1985–; Duke's Palace Hotel, 1986–. Chm., Centre for Economic Policy Res., 1984–; Dep. Chm., NAAFI, 1986–. Member: Monopolies and Mergers Commn, 1976–83 (Dep. Chm., 1980–83); Council, Oxford Centre for Management Studies, 1978–85; Hammersmith Health Authority, 1982–83; Arts Council of GB, 1984–86; Peacock Cttee on Financing of BBC, 1985–86. Contested (SDP) Norwich South, 1983. Trustee: Esmée Fairbairn Charitable Trust, 1972–; Bowthorpe Trust, 1983–; Butler Trust, 1985–. *Recreations:* sailing, skiing. *Address:* The Old Rectory, Metton, Norwich NR11 8QX. *T:* Cromer 761765. *Club:* Norfolk (Norwich).

HARDIE, Colin Graham; Official Fellow and Tutor in Classics, Magdalen College, Oxford, 1936–73; Public Orator of Oxford University, 1967–73; Hon. Professor of Ancient Literature, Royal Academy of Arts, since 1971; *b* 16 Feb. 1906; 3rd *s* of William Ross Hardie, Fellow of Balliol Coll. and Prof. of Humanity in Edinburgh Univ., and Isabella Watt Stevenson; *m* 1940, Christian Viola Mary Lucas; two *s*. *Educ:* Edinburgh Acad.; Balliol Coll., Oxford (Warner Exhibitioner and Hon. Scholar); 1st class Classical Moderations, 1926, and Lit Hum BA, 1928; MA, 1931; Craven Scholar, 1925; Ireland Scholar, 1925; Hertford Scholar, 1926; Gaisford Prize for Greek Prose, 1927; Junior Research Fellow of Balliol, 1928–29; Fellow and Classical Tutor, 1930–33; Dir of the British Sch. at Rome, 1933–36. *Publications:* Vitae Vergilianae antiquae, 1954; papers on Virgil and Dante. *Recreation:* gardening. *Address:* Rackham Cottage, Greatham, Pulborough, Sussex. *T:* Pulborough 3170.

HARDIE, Jeremy; *see* Hardie, C. J. M.

HARDIE, John William Somerville, MA Cantab; Hon. DLitt; Principal, Loughborough College of Education, 1963–73; *b* 21 Aug. 1912; 2nd *s* of late Most Rev. W. G. Hardie, CBE, DD; *m* 1938, Evelyn Chrystal, 5th *d* of J. C. Adkins, Uppingham, Rutland; one *s* two *d*. *Educ:* St Lawrence Coll., Ramsgate; Trinity Coll., Cambridge. Second Cl. Hon. (Div. I) Modern and Medieval Lang. Tripos. Asst Master St Lawrence Coll., 1933–35; Asst Master Uppingham Sch., 1935–40; Headmaster Cornwall Coll., Montego Bay, Jamaica 1940–42; Headmaster Jamaica Coll., Kingston, Jamaica, 1943–46; Asst Master Blundell's Sch., 1946–47; Headmaster, Canford Sch., 1947–60; Headmaster-Elect, Hesarack Sch., Iran, 1960–61; consultant Voluntary Service Overseas, 1961; Managing Dir, The Broadcasting Company of Northern Nigeria Ltd (seconded by Granada TV Ltd), 1961–62; Head of Information and Research, The Centre for Educational Television Overseas, Nuffield Lodge, 1962–63. Chm., HMC Overseas Cttee, 1958–60. Mem. Council Loughborough Univ. of Technology, 1968–76; a Governor, St Luke's Coll., Exeter, 1974–78. Hon. DLitt Loughborough, 1973. *Recreations:* hockey (Cambridge Univ. Hockey XI, 1931, 1932, Captain 1933; Welsh Hockey XI, 1931, 1932, Captain 1933–39), music, painting. *Address:* 15 Parc-an-Dillon, Portscatho, Truro, Cornwall TR2 5DU.

HARDIE, Miles Clayton; Director General, International Hospital Federation, since 1975; *b* 27 Feb. 1924; *s* of late Frederick Hardie and Estelle (*née* Clarke); *m* 1st, 1949, Pauline (marr. diss. 1974), *d* of late Sir Wilfrid Le Gros Clark, FRS; two *s*; 2nd, 1974, Melissa (marr. diss. 1984), *d* of late James Witcher, Houston, Texas; 3rd, 1985, Elizabeth, *d* of late Dudley Ash, *widow* of H. Spencer Smith. *Educ:* Charterhouse; Oriel Coll., Oxford (MA). Served War, RAF, 1943–46. Admin. Asst, Hosp. for Sick Children, London, 1949–51; Sec., Victoria Hosp. for Children, 1951–55; Sec., Bahrain Govt Med. Dept, 1956–58; joined staff of King Edward's Hosp. Fund for London, 1958, Dep. Dir, King's Fund Centre, 1963–66, Dir, 1966–75. Hon. Sec., British Hosps Export Council, 1964–67, Mem. Council, 1967–75; Mem. Council, Nat. Assoc. of Leagues of Hosp. Friends, 1970–75; Member: Adv. Council, Nat. Corp. Care of Old People, 1973–76; Council of Management, MIND/Nat. Assoc. for Mental Health, 1967–86; Man. Cttee of Spinal Injuries Assoc., 1975–79; Bd of Governors, Volunteer Centre, 1977–80; Court of Assistants, Salters' Co., 1969–79. Adviser to WHO, 1978–. Hon. Member: Amer. Hosp. Assoc., 1983–; Polish Hosp. Assoc., 1985–. *Recreations:* gardening, tennis, fell-walking. *Address:* 4 The Vineyard, Richmond, Surrey TW10 6AQ. *T:* 01–940 5530.

HARDIE, William Francis Ross; President, Corpus Christi College, Oxford, 1950–69; Hon. Fellow, 1969; *b* 25 April 1902; *s* of late W. R. Hardie, Professor of Humanity, University of Edinburgh; *m* 1938, Isobel St Maur Macaulay; two *s*. *Educ:* Edinburgh Academy; Balliol Coll., Oxford. Fellow by Examination, Magdalen Coll., 1925; Fellow and Tutor in Philosophy, Corpus Christi Coll., Oxford, 1926–50. *Publications:* A Study in Plato, 1936; Aristotle's Ethical Theory, 1968, 2nd edn 1980; articles in philosophical journals. *Address:* 28 Turnpike Road, Cumnor Hill, Oxford OX2 9JQ.

HARDING, family name of **Baron Harding of Petherton.**

HARDING OF PETHERTON, 1st Baron *cr* 1958, of Nether Compton; **Field-Marshal Allan Francis, (John), Harding,** GCB 1951 (KCB 1944); CBE 1940; DSO 1941; MC; *b* 1896; *s* of late Francis E. Harding, Compton Way, S Petherton, Somerset; *m* 1927, Mary G. M. (*d* 1983), *d* of late Wilson Rooke, JP, Knutsford, Cheshire; one *s*. *Educ:* Ilminster Grammar Sch. Served European War, 1914–19, with TA and Machine Gun Corps (MC); Lieut Somerset Light Infantry 1920; Capt. 1923; psc 1928; Brigade Major British Force, Saar Plebiscite; Bt Major, 1935; Bt Lieut-Col 1938; Lieut-Col 1939; Brig. 1942; Maj.-Gen. 1942; Lieut-Gen. 1943; General, 1949; Field-Marshal, 1953. Served War of 1939–45 (despatches, CBE, DSO and two Bars, KCB). GOC CMF, 1946–47; GOC-in-C Southern Command, 1947–49; C-in-C, Far East Land Forces, 1949–51; Comdr-in-Chief, British Army of the Rhine, 1951–52; Chief of the Imperial Gen. Staff, 1952–55. Governor and Comdr-in-Chief, Cyprus, 1955–Nov. 1957. Director: Nat. Provincial Bank, 1957–69; Standard Bank, 1965–71; Williams (Hounslow) Ltd, 1962–74 (Chm. 1962–71); Plessey Co. Ltd, 1967–70 (Dir, 1962–75; Dep. Chm., 1964–67; Chm., 1967–70). ADC Gen. to King George VI, 1950–52, to the Queen, 1952–53. Col 6th Gurkha Rifles, 1951–61; Col Somerset and Cornwall LI (Somerset LI, 1953–60); Col, The Life Guards, and Gold Stick to the Queen, 1957–64. KStJ. Hon. DCL (Durham). *Recreation:* gardening. *Heir:* *s* Major Hon. John Charles Harding [*b* 12 Feb. 1928; *m* 1966, Harriet, *yr d* of late Maj.-Gen. J. F. Hare and Mrs D. E. Hare; two *s* one *d*]. *Address:* The Barton, Nether Compton, Sherborne, Dorset. *Clubs:* Army and Navy, Cavalry and Guards, Naval and Military.

HARDING, Christopher George Francis; Chairman, British Nuclear Fuels, since 1986 (Director, since 1984); Managing Director, Hanson Transport Group, since 1974; *b* 17 Oct. 1939; *s* of Frank Harding and Phyllis Rachel Pledger (*née* Wise); *m* 1st, 1963, Susan Lilian Berry; one *s* one *d*; 2nd, 1978, Françoise Marie Baile de Laperrière (*née* Grouillé). *Educ:* Merchant Taylors' School; Corpus Christi College, Oxford (MA Hons). Imperial Chemical Industries, 1961–69; Hanson Trust, 1969–, Non-Exec. Dir, 1979–. *Recreations:* theatre, music, travel, tennis, pocillovy. *Address:* c/o Hanson Trust PLC, 180 Brompton Road, SW3 1HF. *T:* 01–589 7070. *Club:* Huddersfield Borough.

HARDING, Prof. Dennis William, MA, DPhil; FRSE; Abercromby Professor of Archaeology, University of Edinburgh, since 1977; Dean, Faculty of Arts, since 1983; *b* 11 April 1940; *s* of Charles Royston Harding and Marjorie Doris Harding. *Educ:* Keble Coll., Oxford (BA, MA, DPhil). Assistant Keeper, Dept of Antiquities, Ashmolean Museum, Oxford, 1965–66; Lecturer in Celtic Archaeology, 1966, Sen. Lectr, 1975–77, Univ. of Durham. Member: Board of Trustees, National Museum of Antiquities of Scotland, 1977–85; Ancient Monuments Board for Scotland, 1979–83. FRSE 1986. *Publications:* The Iron Age in the Upper Thames Basin, 1972; The Iron Age in Lowland Britain, 1974; (with A. J. Challis) Later Prehistory from the Trent to the Tyne, 1975; ed and contrib., Archaeology in the North: Report of the Northern Archaeological Survey, 1976; ed and contrib., Hillforts: later prehistoric earthworks in Britain and Ireland, 1976; Prehistoric Europe, 1978. *Recreation:* private flying. *Address:* Department of Archaeology, 16–20 George Square, Edinburgh EH8 9JZ. *T:* 031–667 1011. *Club:* Athenæum.

HARDING, Denys Wyatt, MA; Emeritus Professor of Psychology, University of London, since 1968; *b* 13 July 1906; *s* of Clement and Harriet Harding; *m* 1930, Jessie Muriel Ward; no *c*. *Educ:* Lowestoft Secondary Sch.; Emmanuel Coll., Cambridge. Investigator and Mem. of research staff, National Institute of Industrial Psychology, 1928–33; Asst (later Lecturer) in Social Psychology, London Sch. of Economics, 1933–38; Senior Lecturer in Psychology, University of Liverpool, 1938–45 (leave of absence for national service, 1941–44); part-time Lecturer in Psychology, University of Manchester, 1940–41 and 1944–45; Prof. of Psychology, Univ. of London, at Bedford Coll., 1945–68. Clark Lectr, Trinity Coll., Cambridge, 1971–72. Hon. Gen. Sec., British Psychological Soc., 1944–48. Mem. of editorial board of Scrutiny, a Quarterly Review, 1933–47. Editor, British Journal of Psychology (Gen. Section) 1948–54. *Publications:* The Impulse to Dominate, 1941; Social Psychology and Individual Values, 1953; Experience into Words: Essays on Poetry, 1963; Words into Rhythm, 1976; ed (with Gordon Bottomley) The Complete Works of Isaac Rosenberg, 1937; translated (with Erik Mesterton) Guest of Reality, by Pär Lagerkvist, 1936; various papers on psychology and literary criticism. *Address:* Ashbocking Old Vicarage, near Ipswich, IP6 9LG. *T:* Helmingham 347.

HARDING, Derek William; Executive Secretary, Royal Statistical Society, since 1986; *b* 16 Dec. 1930; *o s* of late William Arthur Harding; *m* 1954, Daphne Sheila, *yr d* of late Reginald Ernest Cooke; one *s* one *d*. *Educ:* Glendale Grammar Sch., London; Univ. of Bristol (BSc). FInstP, CPhys, FIM, CEng. Develt Engr, Pye Ltd, 1954–56; Sen. Physics Master, Thornbury Grammar Sch., Bristol, 1956–60; Sen. Lectr in Physical Science, St Paul's Coll., Cheltenham, 1960–64; Asst Organiser, Nuffield Foundn Science Teaching Project, 1964–67; joined staff of Instn Metallurgists, 1967, Registrar-Sec., 1969–76. Sec.-Gen., British Computer Soc., 1976–86. *Recreation:* off-shore sailing. *Address:* 16 Exeter Road, N14 5JY. *T:* 01–368 1463. *Clubs:* Athenæum, Cruising Association.

HARDING, Sir (George) William, KCMG 1983 (CMG 1977); CVO 1972; HM Diplomatic Service, retired; *b* 18 Jan. 1927; *s* of late Lt Col G. R. Harding, DSO, MBE, and of Grace Henley (*née* Darby); *m* 1955, Sheila Margaret Ormond Riddel; four *s*. *Educ:* Aldenham; St John's College, Cambridge. Royal Marines, 1945–48. Entered HM Foreign Service, 1950; served (other than in London) in Singapore, 1951–52; Burma, 1952–55; Paris, 1956–59; Santo Domingo, 1960–63; Mexico City, 1967–70; Paris, 1970–74; Ambassador to Peru, 1977–79; Asst Under-Sec. of State, FCO, 1979–81; Ambassador to Brazil, 1981–84. Dep. Under-Sec. of State, FCO, 1984–86. *Address:* c/o Lloyds Bank, 16 St James's Street, SW1A 1EY. *Clubs:* Garrick, Beefsteak; Leander.

HARDING, Hugh Alastair, CMG 1958; Under-Secretary, Department of Education and Science, 1967–77; *b* 4 May 1917; 2nd *s* of late Roland Charles Harding, Norton-le-Moors, Staffordshire; *m* 1943, Florence Esnouf; one *s* one *d*. *Educ:* Rugby; Trinity Coll., Cambridge. Colonial Office, 1939; Asst Sec., 1950; Asst Sec., Treasury, 1961; Under-Sec., Treasury, 1962–64; Minister, UK Delegation to OECD, 1964–67. Served War of 1939–45, Army (Captain RA). *Address:* c/o National Westminster Bank, Town Hall Buildings, Tunstall, Stoke-on-Trent, Staffs.

HARDING, John Philip, PhD; Keeper of Zoology, British Museum (Natural History), 1954–71, retired; *b* 12 Nov. 1911; *s* of Philip William and Eleanor Harding, Rondebosch, Cape Town; *m* 1937, Sidnie Manton, PhD, ScD, FRS (*d* 1979); one *s* one *d*. *Educ:* Torquay; University Coll., Exeter; University of Cincinnati; King's Coll., Cambridge. Ministry of Agriculture and Fisheries, 1936–37; British Museum (Natural History), 1937–71. Vis. Prof., Westfield Coll., Univ. of London, 1971–77. *Publications:* scientific papers on Crustacea. *Recreations:* photomicrography, bees and pollen, mechanical devices. *Address:* 7 Ashcroft Close, Ringmer, Lewes, East Sussex. *T:* Ringmer 812385.

HARDING, Air Chief Marshal Sir Peter (Robin), KCB 1983 (CB 1980); CBIM; FRAeS 1983; Air Officer Commanding-in-Chief, RAF Strike Command, and Commander-in-Chief, United Kingdom Air Forces, since 1985; *b* 2 Dec. 1933; *s* of Peter Harding and Elizabeth Kezia Clear; *m* 1955, Sheila Rosemary May; three *s* one *d*. *Educ:* Chingford High Sch. Joined RAF, 1952; Pilot, 12 Sqdn, 1954–57; QFI and Flt Comdr, RAF Coll., Cranwell, 1957–60; Pilot, 1 Sqdn, RAAF, 1960–62; sc 1963; Air Secretary's

Dept, MoD, 1964–66; OC, 18 Sqdn, Gutersloh and Acklington, 1966–69; jssc, Latimer, 1969–70; Sec. and 'C' Team Mem., Defence Policy Staff, MoD, 1970–71; Director, Air Staff, Briefing, MoD, 1971–74; Comdr, RAF Brüggen, 1974–76; Dir of Defence Policy, MoD, 1976–78; Asst Chief of Staff (Plans and Policy), SHAPE, 1978–80; AOC No 11 Group, 1981–82; VCAS, 1982–84; VCDS, 1985. ADC to the Queen, 1975. *Publications:* articles for professional jls and magazines. *Recreations:* music, pianoforte, bridge, birdwatching. *Address:* Headquarters Strike Command, RAF High Wycombe, Bucks. *Club:* Royal Air Force.

HARDING, Roger John, CMG 1986; Counsellor, Defence Supply, British Embassy, Washington DC, since 1982; *b* 7 April 1935; *s* of Charles William Harding and Lilian Mabel (*née* Trowbridge); *m* 1960, June Elizabeth Tidy; four *d*. *Educ:* Price's Sch., Fareham, Hants; Southern Grammar Sch., Portsmouth, Hants. Board of Trade, 1954–74; War Office, then Min. of Defence, 1974–: Head of Defence Secretariat 8, 1979–82. *Recreations:* soccer, cricket, golf, following fortunes of Portsmouth FC. *Club:* St John's Village (Woking).

HARDING, Air Vice-Marshal Ross Philip, CBE 1968; RAF retired; *b* 22 Jan. 1921; *s* of P. J. Harding, Salisbury; *m* 1948, Laurie Joy Gardner; three *s*. *Educ:* Bishop Wordsworth Sch., Salisbury; St Edmund Hall, Oxford (MA). No 41 Sqdn Fighter Comd and 2 TAF, 1943–45; RAF Staff Coll., Andover, 1951; Air Min. (ACAS Ops), 1952–54; CO No 96 Sqdn, Germany, 1955–58; Directing Staff, RAF Staff Coll., Andover, 1958–60; CO Oxford Univ. Air Sqdn, 1960–62; Dep. Chief, British Mil. Mission, Berlin, 1963–65; CO RAF Valley, 1965–68; Senior Directing Staff (Air), Jt Services Staff Coll., 1968–69; Defence and Air Attaché, Moscow, 1970–72; Dir of Personal Services 1, MoD (Air), 1973; Senior RAF Member, RCDS, 1974–76. Specialist Advr to H of C Defence Cttee, 1979–84. *Recreations:* ski-ing, shooting. *Address:* Tally-Ho, 8 Hadrian's Close, Lower Bemerton, Salisbury, Wilts. *Club:* Royal Air Force.

HARDING, His Honour Rowe, LLD; DL; a Circuit Judge (formerly County Court Judge), 1953–76; Chairman, Swansea Porcelain Ltd, since 1976; *b* 10 Sept. 1901; *s* of late Albert Harding, Swansea, and Elizabeth Harding; *m* 1933, Elizabeth Adeline, *d* of John Owen George, Hirwaun, S Wales; one *s* one *d* (and one *s* decd). *Educ:* Gowerton County Sch.; Pembroke Coll., Cambridge. Qualified as solicitor, 1924; called to Bar, Inner Temple, 1928. Captain, Wales, Cambridge and Swansea Rugby football, 1924–28. Home Guard, 1940–44. Contested (Nat. L and C): Swansea East, 1945; Gower, 1950 and 1951. Mem., Swansea Town Council, 1945–48. Deputy Chairman, Quarter Sessions: Haverfordwest, 1945 (Chm., 1948–49): Breconshire, 1953 (Chm., 1955–71); Pembrokeshire, 1953 (Chm., 1971); Carmarthenshire, 1956–65; Glamorganshire, 1959–71; Chm., Radnorshire, QS, 1953–59. Dep. Chm., Local Tribunal for Conscientious Objectors in Wales, 1956–; Pres., Royal Institution of S Wales, 1960–61; Mem., Nat. Adv. Council on the Training of Magistrates, 1964; Chancellor: Diocese of St David's, 1949–85; Diocese of Swansea and Brecon, 1974–82; former Mem., Governing and Rep. Bodies of Church in Wales; Judge of the Provincial Court of Church in Wales, 1966–; Member: Council, Lampeter Coll., 1945–80; Court of Governors, UC Swansea, 1956–81 (Council, 1957), Univ. of Wales, 1971–74; Chm., Welsh Regional Cttee, Cheshire Homes, 1961–63; Trustee, Cheshire Foundation, 1962–70. Vice-Pres., Welsh Rugby Union, 1953–56; Chm., Glamorgan County Cricket Club, 1959–76, Pres., 1977–; Pres., Crawshay's Welsh RFC, 1985–. Life Patron, Swansea Cricket and Football Club, 1978. DL Glamorgan, later West Glamorgan, 1970. Hon. LLD Wales, 1971. *Publications:* Rugby Reminiscences and Opinions, 1929; Rugby in Wales, 1970. *Recreations:* walking, gardening, watching Rugby football and cricket. *Address:* The Old Rectory, Ilston, Gower, near Swansea, West Glamorgan. *T:* Penmaen 243. *Clubs:* Swansea City and County; Hawks (Cambridge).

HARDING, Sir Roy (Pollard), Kt 1985; CBE 1978; education consultant; General Secretary, Society of Education Officers, since 1984; *b* 3 Jan. 1924; *s* of W. F. N. Harding, BEM and P. E. Harding; *m* 1948, Audrey Beryl Larkin, JP; two *s* one *d*. *Educ:* Liskeard Grammar Sch.; King's Coll., Univ. of London (BSc; AKC; DPA). FIMA, FZS. Ballistics research, schools and college teaching, to 1950; Educn Admin, Wilts, Bucks, Herts, Leics, to 1960; Dep. Chief Educn Officer, 1960–66, Chief Educn Officer, 1966–84, Bucks. Adviser: County Councils Assoc., 1972–74; Assoc. of County Councils, 1973–84 (incl. Finance, 1978–81, Policy, 1981–84); Council of Local Educn Authorities, 1975–84; Mem., County Educn Officers' Soc., 1966–84, Sec. 1973–76, Chm. 1978–79; Mem. Exec., Soc. of Educn Officers, 1974–79, Pres. 1977–78, Chm. Internat. Cttee, 1980–83. Member: Printing and Publishing Ind. Trng Bd, 1970–72; BBC Further Educn Adv. Council, 1970–75; Burnham Cttee, 1972–77; Sec. of State's Vis. Cttee, Cranfield Inst. of Technology, 1976–81; DES/Local Authority Expenditure Steering Gp, Educn, 1976–84; Councils and Educnl Press (Longmans) Editorial Adv. Panel, 1977–86; Teaching of Mathematics in Schools (Cockcroft) Cttee, 1978–82; Educn Management Inf. Exchange, 1981–; Board, Nat. Adv. Body for Higher Educn, 1982–84; various univ. cttees, incl. Open Univ. Council, 1985–; Chm. Open Univ. INSET Sector Programme Bd, 1983–. Chm., Educn Policy Interchange Cttee, 1979–. President: British Educnl Equipment Assoc., 1980–83; Educn Sect., BAAS, 1986–87; Vice-Chm., Secondary Exams Council, 1983–86. Mem. Council, Inst. of Maths and its Applications, 1983– (Vice-Pres., 1986–). DUniv Open, 1985. Wappenteller, Rheinland/Pfalz, Germany, 1978. Gold Cross of Merit, Polish Govt in Exile, 1984. *Publications:* chapters on educnl matters, miscellaneous contribs to learned jls. *Recreations:* travel, music, DIY. *Address:* 27 King Edward Avenue, Aylesbury, Bucks HP21 7JE. *T:* Aylesbury 23006. *Clubs:* Royal Over-Seas League; Rotary.

HARDING, Wilfrid Gerald, CBE 1978; FRCP, FFCM, DPH; Area Medical Officer, Camden and Islington Area Health Authority (Teaching), 1974–79; Hon. Consultant in Community Medicine, University College Hospital, London, 1971–79; *b* 17 March 1915; *s* of late Dr *hc* Ludwig Ernst Emil Hoffman and Marie Minna Eugenie (*née* Weisbach); *m* 1st, 1938, Britta Charlotta Haraldsdotter, Malmberg (marr. diss. 1970); three *s*; 2nd, 1973, Hilary Maxwell. *Educ:* Französisches Gymnasium, Berlin; Süddeutsches Landerziehungsheim, Schondorf, Bavaria; Woodbrooke Coll., Selly Oak, Birmingham; University Coll. London; University Coll. Hosp. Med. Sch. (interned twice in 1939 and 1940). MRCS, LRCP 1941; DPH London 1949; MRCP 1968; FFCM 1972; FRCP 1972. Ho. Phys. and Ho. Surg., UCH, 1941–42; Asst MOH, City of Oxford, 1942–43; RAMC, 1943–47, Field Units in NW Europe, 1 Corps Staff and Mil. Govt, Lt-Col (Hygiene Specialist). In charge of health services, Ruhr Dist of Germany, CCG, 1947–48; LSHTM, 1948–49; career posts in London public health service, 1949–64; MOH, London Bor. of Camden, and Principal Sch. MO, ILEA, 1965–74. Hon. Lectr, Dept of Sociol., Bedford Coll., London Univ., 1969–77; Civil Consultant in Community Medicine to RAF, 1974–78. Chm. of Council, Soc. of MOH, 1966–71 (Pres. 1971–72); Chm., Prov. Bd of FCM, Royal Colls of Physicians of UK, 1971–72 (Vice-Pres., 1972–75, Pres., 1975–78). Member: Central Health Services Council and Standing Med. Adv. Cttee, 1966–71 and 1975–78; Standing Mental Health Adv. Cttee, 1966–71; Bd of Studies in Preventive Med. and Public Health, Univ. of London, 1963–79; Council, UCH Med. Sch., 1965–78; Bd of Management, LSHTM, 1968–82; Council for Educn and Trng of Health Visitors, 1965–77; Council, ASH, 1970–73 and 1978–82; Public Health Laboratory Service Bd, 1972–83. Armed Services Med. Adv. Bd, 1975–78; GMC, 1979–84; Vice-Chm., Dartford and Gravesham CHC, 1984–. Chm., DHSS Working Gp on Primary Health Team, 1978–80 (reported 1981). Hon. Advr, Office of Health Econs, 1977–. Councillor, Sevenoaks DC, 1979–; Chm., Farningham Parish Council, 1983–. *Publications:* papers on public health and community med. in medical books and jls; Parkes Centenary Meml Lecture (Community, Health and Service), 1976. *Recreations:* watching river birds, music, wine. *Address:* Bridge Cottage, High Street, Farningham, Dartford DA4 0DW. *T:* Farningham 862733. *Club:* Athenæum.

HARDING, Sir William; *see* Harding, Sir G. W.

HARDINGE, family name of **Viscount Hardinge** and **Baron Hardinge of Penshurst.**

HARDINGE, 6th Viscount *cr* 1846, of Lahore and of King's Newton, Derbyshire; **Charles Henry Nicholas Hardinge;** *b* 25 Aug. 1956; *s* of 5th Viscount Hardinge and of Zoë Anne, *d* of Hon. Hartland de Montarville Molson, OBE, Montreal; *S* father, 1984. *Heir:* *b* Hon. Andrew Hartland Hardinge, *b* 7 Jan. 1960. *Address:* 74 Forthbridge Road, SW11.

HARDINGE OF PENSHURST, 3rd Baron *cr* 1910; **George Edward Charles Hardinge;** *b* 31 Oct. 1921; *o s* of 2nd Baron Hardinge of Penshurst, PC, GCB, GCVO, MC, and Helen Mary Cecil (*d* 1979); *S* father, 1960; *m* 1st, 1944, Janet Christine Goschen (marr. diss. 1962, she *d* 1970), *d* of late Lt-Col F. C. C. Balfour, CIE, CVO, CBE, MC; three *s*; 2nd, 1966, Margaret Trezise; one *s*, and one step-*s*, now adopted. *Educ:* Eton; Royal Naval College, Dartmouth. RN 1940–47; subsequently in publishing; Sen. Editor: Collins; Longmans; Macmillan (London) Ltd, 1968– (also dir); Founder and Editor, Winter's Crime series. *Publication:* An Incompleat Angler, 1976. *Recreations:* reading, fishing. *Heir:* *s* Hon. Julian Alexander Hardinge, *b* 23 Aug. 1945. *Address:* Bracken Hill, 10 Penland Road, Bexhill-on-Sea, East Sussex. *T:* Bexhill 211866. *Club:* Brooks's.
See also Lt-Col Sir J. F. D. Johnston.

HARDINGE, Sir Robert Arnold, 7th Bt *cr* 1801; *b* 19 Dec. 1914; *s* of Sir Robert Hardinge, 6th Bt and Emma Vera, *d* of Charles Arnold; *S* father, 1973. *Heir:* *kinsman* Viscount Hardinge, *qv*.

HARDINGHAM, Sir Robert (Ernest), Kt 1969; CMG 1953; OBE 1947; Chief Executive, Air Registration Board, 1947–68; *b* 16 Dec. 1903; *s* of late Robert Henry Hardingham and Florence Elizabeth Hardingham; *m* 1929, I. Everett; one *s* one *d*. *Educ:* Farnborough; de Havilland Technical Coll. RAE Farnborough, 1918–21; de Havilland Aircraft Co., 1921–34; Air Min., 1934–37; Air Registration Board, 1937–68. Pres., Soc. of Licenced Aircraft Engineers and Technologists, 1968–72. Liveryman, Guild of Air Pilots and Navigators, 1966. CEng; FRAeS 1949 (Empire and Commonwealth Lecturer, 1952). Wakefield Gold Medal, RAeS, 1965; Silver Medal, Royal Aero Club, 1965. Cavaliere Ordino Merito della Repubblica Italiana. *Publications:* many technical papers. *Recreation:* golf. *Address:* Wortheal House, Southam Lane, Cheltenham GL52 3NY. *T:* Cheltenham 36765. *Club:* Naval and Military.

HARDMAN, Amy Elizabeth; Matron, The Royal Free Hospital, London, 1953–70; *b* 23 Dec. 1909; *d* of late Charlton James Hardman and Elizabeth Clark. *Educ:* Godolphin and Latymer Sch., Hammersmith; Rosebery Sch. for Girls, Epsom. General Training, St Bartholomew's Hosp., London, 1930–34 (SRN); Midwifery Training, Kingston County Hosp., 1937 (SCM); Asst Matron, Sister Tutor, Metropolitan Hosp., E8, 1937–42; Matron, The Guest Hospital, Dudley, Worcs, 1942–49; Matron, St Margaret's Hospital, Epping, 1949–53. *Publication:* An Introduction to Ward Management, 1970. *Address:* Apple Tree Cottage, Main Street, Northiam, Rye, East Sussex. *T:* Northiam 2319.

HARDMAN, David Rennie, MA, LLB; JP; Secretary, Cassel Educational Trust; Secretary, Stafford Cripps Memorial Appeal and Trustees; *b* 1901; *s* of David Hardman, MSc, and Isobel Rennie, Mansfield House University Settlement; *m* 1928, Freda Mary Riley; one *d*; *m* 1946, Barbara, *er d* of late Herbert Lambert, Bath; one *s* one *d*. *Educ:* Coleraine Academical Instn; Christ's Coll., Cambridge. Mem. Railway Clerks' Assoc., 1919–21; Pres. Cambridge Union Soc., 1925; Contested (Lab) Cambridge Borough, 1929. Cambridge Borough Councillor and Cambridge County Councillor, 1937–46; late Chm. Cambs Education Cttee; JP Cambridge, 1941–47; MP (Lab) Darlington, 1945–51; Parl. Sec., Min. of Education, 1945–51; contested (Lab) Rushcliffe Div. of Notts, 1955; leader UK delegns UNESCO, Paris 1946, Mexico 1947, Beirut 1948, Paris 1949, Florence 1950, Paris 1951; Vice-Pres. Shaw Soc.; Pres., Holiday Fellowship, 1962–69. Visiting Prof. of English Literature, Elmira, New York, 1964–66. Barclay Acheson Prof. Internat. Studies, Macalester Coll., Minn, 1967. *Publications:* What about Shakespeare?, 1939; Poems of Love and Affairs, 1949; Telscombe: A Sussex Village, 1964; History of Holiday Fellowship 1913–1940, 1981; History of Sir E. Cassel Educational Trust 1919–1982, 1982. *Recreation:* gardening. *Address:* 21 Hassocks Road, Hurstpierpoint, West Sussex BN6 9QH. *T:* Brighton 833194. *Club:* Savile.

HARDMAN, Sir Fred, Kt 1982; MBE 1972; Board Member, Telford Development Corporation, since 1980; Chairman, Taws Printers Ltd, Telford, since 1983; *b* 26 Sept. 1914; *s* of Fred Hardman (killed in action, 1915, Hooge; KSLI) and Annie (*née* Walsh); *m* 1941, Ennis Lawson; one *s*. *Educ:* Basle, Switzerland. Served Royal Air Force, 1936–46. Conservative Political Agent, 1946–52; Senior Executive, Lectr and Public Relations, Rentokil, 1952–74; Industrial Relations Consultant, 1974–. Vice-Chm., Severn Navigation Restoration Trust Ltd, 1982–. President: Coalbrookdale, Royal British Legion, 1970–; S Telford RAFA, 1980–; W Midlands Cons. Trade Unionists, 1980–; Vice Pres., Nat. Union of Cons. Assocs, 1982– (Chm. 1980–81). Chairman: Conservative Trade Unionists, 1977–80; Conservative Party Conference, Blackpool, 1981. *Address:* Coppice House, Coalbrookdale, Telford, Shropshire TF8 7EZ. *T:* Ironbridge 3423. *Clubs:* St Stephen's Constitutional, Royal Over-Seas League.

HARDMAN, Sir Henry, KCB 1962 (CB 1956); *b* 15 Dec. 1905; *s* of late Harry Hardman and Bertha Hardman; *m* 1937, Helen Diana, *d* of late Robert Carr Bosanquet and Ellen Sophia Bosanquet; one *s* two *d*. *Educ.* Manchester Central High Sch.; University of Manchester. Lecturer for Workers' Educational Association, 1929–34; Economics Tutor, University of Leeds, 1934–45; joined Ministry of Food, 1940; Deputy Head, British Food Mission to N America, 1946–48; Under-Sec., Ministry of Food, 1948–53; Minister, UK Permanent Delegation, Paris, 1953–54; Dep. Sec., Ministry of Agriculture, Fisheries and Food, 1955–60; Dep. Sec., Ministry of Aviation, 1960; Permanent Sec., 1961–63: Permanent Sec., Ministry of Defence, 1963–64; Permanent Under Sec. of State, Min. of Defence, 1964–66. Mem., Monopolies Commn, 1967–70 (Dep. Chm., 1967–68); Chm., Cttee of enquiry into the Post Office pay dispute, 1971; Consultant to CSD on dispersal of govt work from London, 1971–73 (report published, 1973). Chairman: Covent Garden Mkt Authority, 1967–75; Home-Grown Cereals Authority, 1968–77. Governor and Trustee, Reserve Bank of Rhodesia, 1967–79. Hon. LLD Manchester, 1965. *Address:* 33 Durand Gardens, SW9 0PS. *T:* 01-582 1757; 9 Sussex Square, Brighton BN2 1FJ. *T:* Brighton 688904. *Club:* Reform.

HARDMAN, James Arthur, MBE 1968; HM Diplomatic Service; First Secretary (Commercial), Algiers, since 1985; *b* 12 Sept. 1929; *er s* of late James Sidney Hardman and Rachel Hardman; *m* 1953, Enid Mary Hunter; two *s. Educ*: Manchester Grammar Sch.; Manchester Univ. (BA Hons 1950). FCIS (FCCS 1964). Served in Intelligence Corps, 1951–53; Admiralty, 1953–54. HM Foreign Service, 1954; served: Tehran, 1955; FO, 2nd Sec., 1960; Bonn, 2nd, later 1st, Sec. (Comm.), 1962; Atlanta, Consul, 1967; New York, Consul (Comm.), 1970; FCO, Dep. Dir Diplomatic Service Language Centre, 1972; Consul-Gen., Strasbourg, 1975–79; Consul (Commercial), Düsseldorf, 1979–83; FCO, 1983–85. *Address*: c/o Foreign and Commonwealth Office, SW1. *Club*: Civil Service.

HARDWICK, Christopher, MD, FRCP; Physician Emeritus, Guy's Hospital, since 1976; *b* 13 Jan. 1911; *s* of Thomas Mold Hardwick and Harriet Taylor; *m* 1938, Joan Dorothy Plummer; two *s. Educ*: Berkhamsted Sch.; Trinity Hall, Cambridge; Middlesex Hospital. MRCS, LRCP 1935; MA (Cambridge) 1937; MD (Cambridge) 1940; FRCP 1947. House Physician, House Surgeon and Med. Registrar, Middlesex Hosp., 1935 and 1938–41; House physician and Registrar, Hosp. for Sick Children, Gt Ormond Street, 1936–38. Wing Comdr, Medical Specialist, RAF Med. Service, 1941–46. Physician, Guy's Hosp., 1946–76. Hon. Vis. Phys., Johns Hopkins Hosp., Baltimore, 1954. Mem. Council, RCP, 1965–68; Mem. Board of Governors, Guy's Hospital, 1967–74. Chm., British Diabetic Assoc., 1974–80. *Publications*: contribs to medical literature. *Recreations*: gardening, reading. *Address*: Blue Firs, Broomfield Park, Westcott, Dorking, Surrey RH4 3QQ.

HARDWICK, Donald, CBE 1980; PhD; Chairman, Steel Division, Johnson & Firth Brown plc, since 1975; *b* 1926; *m* 1950, Dorothy Mary Hardwick; two *s. Educ*: Tadcaster Grammar Sch.; Sheffield Univ. (BMet 1st Cl. Hons 1947, Mappin Medal; PhD 1954). FIM. After appointments with English Electric Co., BISRA, and BSA Gp Research Centre, became first C. H. Desch Res. Fellow, Sheffield Univ. Joined Brown Firth Res. Laboratories, 1959; Man. Dir, Firth Brown Ltd, 1974–78; Mem. Bd, Johnson & Firth Brown, on amalgamation with Richard Johnson & Nephew, 1973. Director, Mitchell Somers Gp, 1974–; Pres., BISPA, 1977–79. *Recreations*: fell walking, gardening. *Address*: Steel Division, Johnson & Firth Brown plc, PO Box 175, Smithfield House, Sheffield S1 2AS; 43 Dore Road, Dore, Sheffield.

HARDWICK, Prof. James Leslie, MSc, PhD, DDS; FDSRCS; Professor of Preventive Dentistry, University of Manchester, 1960–78, now Emeritus; *b* 27 March 1913; *o s* of George Hardwicke and Mary Ann Hardwick; *m* 1954, Eileen Margaret Isobel Gibson; two *s* two *d. Educ*: Rugby Sch.; Birmingham Univ. MDS 1948, PhD 1950, DDS 1984, Birmingham; FDSRCS 1954; MSc 1964. Private and hospital dental practice, 1935–39. Served War of 1939–45, Army Dental Corps. University of Birmingham: Lecturer, 1945–48, Sen. Lecturer in Operative Dental Surgery, 1948–52; Reader in Dental Surgery, 1952–60. *Publications*: editor of and contributor to dental and other scientific journals and textbooks. *Address*: 167 Stanley Road, Cheadle Hulme, Cheshire SK8 6RF. *T*: 061–437 3555.

HARDWICK, Michael John Drinkrow; author and dramatist; *b* 10 Sept. 1924; *s* of George Drinkrow Hardwick and Katharine Augusta Townend; *m* 1961, Mollie (*née* Greenhalgh), *qv*; one *s. Educ*: Leeds Grammar Sch. Morley Observer, 1942–43; Indian Army, 1943–47, served in India and Japan, Captain 1944. Dir, NZ Nat. Film Unit, 1948–53; Freedom Newspaper, NZ, 1953–54; Drama Dept, BBC (Radio), 1958–63; freelance, 1963–. FRSA 1966. *Publications*: The Royal Visit to New Zealand, 1954; Emigrant in Motley: letters of Charles Kean and Ellen Tree, 1954; Seeing New Zealand, 1955; Opportunity in New Zealand, 1955; (ed with Baron Birkett) The Verdict of the Court, 1960; Doctors on Trial, 1961; The Plague and Fire of London, 1966; The World's Greatest Air Mysteries, 1970; The Discovery of Japan, 1970; The Osprey Guide to Gilbert and Sullivan, 1972; The Osprey Guide to Jane Austen, 1973; A Literary Atlas and Gazetteer of the British Isles, 1973; The Osprey Guide to Oscar Wilde, 1973; Upstairs Downstairs: Mr Hudson's Diaries, 1973, Mr Bellamy's Story, 1974, On with the Dance, 1975, Endings and Beginnings, 1975; The Osprey Guide to Anthony Trollope, 1974; The Inheritors, 1974; (abridger) The Pallisers, 1974; The Four Musketeers, 1975; A Christmas Carol (play), 1975; The Man Who Would be King, 1976; The Cedar Tree, 1976; The Cedar Tree: Autumn of an Age, 1977, A Bough Breaks, 1978; Regency Royal, 1978; Prisoner of the Devil, 1979; Regency Rake, 1979; Regency Revenge, 1980; Bergerac, 1981; The Chinese Detective, 1981; Regency Revels, 1982; (abridger) The Barchester Chronicles, 1982; The Private Life of Dr Watson, 1983; Sherlock Holmes: my life and crimes, 1984; Last Tenko, 1984; Complete Guide to Sherlock Holmes, 1986; *as John Drinkrow*: The Vintage Operetta Book, 1972; The Vintage Musical Comedy Book, 1973; *with Mollie Hardwick*: The Jolly Toper, 1961; The Sherlock Holmes Companion, 1962; Sherlock Holmes Investigates, 1963; The Man Who Was Sherlock Holmes, 1964; Four Sherlock Holmes Plays, 1964; The Charles Dickens Companion, 1965; The World's Greatest Sea Mysteries, 1967; Writers' Houses: a literary journey in England, 1968; Alfred Deller: A Singularity of Voice, 1968, rev. edn 1980; Charles Dickens As They Saw Him, 1969; The Game's Afoot (Sherlock Holmes Plays), 1969; Plays from Dickens, 1970; Dickens's England, 1970; The Private Life of Sherlock Holmes (novel), 1970; Four More Sherlock Holmes Plays, 1973; The Bernard Shaw Companion, 1973; The Charles Dickens Encyclopedia, 1973; The Charles Dickens Quiz Book, 1974; The Upstairs Downstairs Omnibus, 1975; The Gaslight Boy, 1976; The Hound of the Baskervilles and Other Sherlock Holmes Plays, 1982; author of numerous plays and scripts for radio and TV; contribs to many publications. *Recreation*: watching cricket. *Address*: Barton House, The Street, Kennington, Ashford, Kent TN24 9HB. *T*: Ashford 23838.

HARDWICK, Mollie; author; *b* Manchester; *d* of Joseph Greenhalgh and Anne Frances Atkinson; *m* 1961, Michael Hardwick, *qv*; one *s. Educ*: Manchester High Sch. for Girls. Announcer, BBC (Radio) N Region, 1940–45; BBC (Radio) Drama Dept, 1946–62; freelance, 1963–. FRSA 1966. *Publications*: Stories from Dickens, 1968; Emma, Lady Hamilton, 1969; Mrs Dizzy, 1972; Upstairs Downstairs: Sarah's Story, 1973, The Years of Change, 1974, The War to end Wars, 1975, Mrs Bridges' Story, 1975, The World of Upstairs Downstairs, 1976; Alice in Wonderland (play), 1975; Beauty's Daughter, 1976 (Elizabeth Goudge Award for best historical romantic novel of year); The Duchess of Duke Street: The Way Up, 1976, The Golden Years, 1976, The World Keeps Turning, 1977; Charlie is my Darling, 1977; The Atkinson Heritage, 1978; Thomas and Sarah, 1978; Thomas and Sarah: Two for a Spin, 1979; Lovers Meeting, 1979; Sisters in Love, 1979; Dove's Nest, 1980; Willowwood, 1980; Juliet Bravo 1, 1980; Juliet Bravo 2, 1980; Monday's Child, 1981; Calling Juliet Bravo: New Arrivals, 1981; I Remember Love, 1982; The Shakespeare Girl, 1983; By the Sword Divided, 1983; The Merrymaid, 1984; Girl with a Crystal Dove, 1985; Malice Domestic, 1986; Parson's Pleasure, 1987; *with Michael Hardwick*: The Jolly Toper, 1961; The Sherlock Holmes Companion, 1962; Sherlock Holmes Investigates, 1963; The Man Who Was Sherlock Holmes, 1964; Four Sherlock Holmes Plays, 1964; The Charles Dickens Companion, 1965; The World's Greatest Sea Mysteries, 1967; Writers' Houses: a literary journey in England, 1968; Alfred Deller: A Singularity of Voice, 1968, rev. edn 1980; Charles Dickens As They Saw Him,

1969; The Game's Afoot (Sherlock Holmes Plays), 1969; Plays from Dickens, 1970; Dickens's England, 1970; The Private Life of Sherlock Holmes, 1970; Four More Sherlock Holmes Plays, 1973; The Charles Dickens Encyclopedia, 1973; The Bernard Shaw Companion, 1973; The Charles Dickens Quiz Book, 1974; The Upstairs Downstairs Omnibus, 1975; The Gaslight Boy, 1976; The Hound of the Baskervilles and Other Sherlock Holmes Plays, 1982; numerous plays and scripts for radio and TV; contribs to women's magazines. *Recreations*: reading, theatre, watching cricket. *Address*: Barton House, The Street, Kennington, Ashford, Kent TN24 9HB. *T*: Ashford 23838.

HARDWICKE, 10th Earl of, *cr* 1754; **Joseph Philip Sebastian Yorke**; Baron Hardwicke 1733; Viscount Royston 1754; *b* 3 Feb. 1971; *s* of Philip Simon Prospero Rupert Lindley, Viscount Royston (*d* 1973) and of Virginia Anne, *d* of Geoffrey Lyon; *S* grandfather, 1974. *Heir*: cousin Richard Charles John Yorke, *b* 25 July 1916. *Address*: The Mustique Company, St Vincent, West Indies.

HARDY; see Gathorne-Hardy.

HARDY, Alan; Member (C) for Brent North, Greater London Council, 1967–86 (Chairman, Finance and Establishment Committee, 1977–81); *b* 24 March 1932; *s* of late John Robert Hardy and of Emily Hardy; *m* 1972, Betty Howe, *d* of late Walter and Hilda Howe. *Educ*: Hookergate Grammar Sch.; Univ. of Manchester; Inst. of Historical Res., Univ. of London (MA). Res. Asst to Sir Lewis Namier, History of Parliament Trust, 1955–56; Res. Officer and Dep. Dir, London Municipal Soc., 1956–63; Mem. British Secretariat, Council of European Municipalities, 1963–64. Lectures on British Monarchy. Member: Local Authorities' Conditions of Service Adv. Bd, 1977–81; Nat. Jt Council for Local Authorities' Services (Manual Workers), 1977–81. Mem. Bd, Harlow Develt Corp., 1968–80. Hon. Life Pres., Brent North Conservative Assoc. Contested (C) Islington SW, 1966. *Publications*: Queen Victoria Was Amused, 1976; The Kings' Mistresses, 1980. *Recreation*: exercising wife's dog. *Address*: 20 Meadowside, Cambridge Park, Twickenham, Mddx. *T*: 01–892 7968. *Club*: Guards' Polo.

HARDY, Prof. Barbara Gladys; Professor of English Literature, Birkbeck College, University of London, since 1970; teacher and author; *d* of Maurice and Gladys Nathan; *m* Ernest Dawson Hardy (decd); two *d. Educ*: Swansea High Sch. for Girls; University Coll. London. BA, MA. Subsequently on staff of English Dept of Birkbeck Coll., London; Prof. of English, Royal Holloway Coll., Univ. of London, 1965–70. DUniv. Open, 1981. Hon. Mem., MLA. *Publications*: The Novels of George Eliot, 1959; The Appropriate Form, 1964; (ed) George Eliot: Daniel Deronda, 1967; (ed) Middlemarch: Critical Approaches to the Novel, 1967; The Moral Art of Dickens, 1970; (ed) Critical Essays on George Eliot, 1970; The Exposure of Luxury: radical themes in Thackeray, 1972; (ed) Thomas Hardy: The Trumpet-Major, 1974; Tellers and Listeners: the narrative imagination, 1975; (ed) Thomas Hardy: A Laodicean, 1975; A Reading of Jane Austen, 1975; The Advantage of Lyric, 1977; Particularities: readings in George Eliot, 1982; Forms of Feeling in Victorian Fiction, 1985. *Address*: Birkbeck College, Malet Street, WC1E 7HX.

HARDY, Very Rev. Brian Albert; Rector of St Columba's by the Castle Episcopal Church, Edinburgh, since 1982; Dean of the Diocese of Edinburgh, since 1986; *b* 3 July 1931; *s* of Albert Charles Hardy and Edith Maude Sarah Mabe. *Educ*: City Boys' School, Leicester; St John's Coll., Oxford (MA, DipTheol); Westcott House, Cambridge. Curate, Rugeley, Staffs, 1957–62; Chaplain, Downing Coll., Cambridge, 1962–66; Livingston (West Lothian) Ecumenical Team Ministry, 1966–74; Churches' Planning Officer for Telford, Salop, 1974–78; Chaplain, Coates Hall Theological Coll., Edinburgh, 1978–82; Episcopalian Chaplain, Royal Infirmary of Edinburgh and Royal Edinburgh Hosp., 1982–86. *Recreations*: music, especially choral and piano; cycling. *Address*: 2/2 Boswell's Court, 352 Castlehill, Edinburgh EH1 2NF. *T*: 031–225 1634.

HARDY, David William; Executive Chairman, Globe Investment Trust PLC, since 1983 (Director, since 1976); Chairman: London Park Hotels, since 1983; Docklands Light Railway, since 1984; Swan Hunter Ltd, since 1986; Deputy Chairman: London Regional Transport, since 1984; Agricultural Mortgage Corporation, since 1985 (Director, since 1973); MGM Assurance, since 1986 (Director, since 1985); Director: Sturge Holdings PLC, since 1985; Waterford Glass plc, since 1984; Aynsley China Ltd, since 1984; Paragon Group, since 1985; Aberfoyle Holdings, since 1986; Chelsea Harbour Ltd, since 1986; *b* 14 July 1930; 3rd *s* of late Brig. John H. Hardy, CBE, MC; *m* 1957, Rosemary, *d* of late Sir Godfrey F. S. Collins, KCIE, CSI, OBE; one *s* one *d. Educ*: Wellington Coll.; Harvard Business School (AMP). Chartered Accountant. Served 2nd RHA, 2/Lt, 1953–54. With Funch Edye Inc., and Imperial Tobacco, USA, 1954–70; HM Govt Co-ordinator of Industrial Advrs, 1970–72; Gp Finance Dir, Tate & Lyle Ltd, 1972–77; Dir, Ocean Transport & Trading PLC, 1977–83; Chm., Ocean Inchcape, 1980–83. Member: NEDC Cttee for Agriculture, 1970–72; Export Credit Guarantees Adv. Council, 1973–78; Co-opted Council of Inst. of Chartered Accountants, 1974–78; Cttee, 100 Group Chartered Accountants; Economic and Fiscal Policy Cttee, CBI; Council, BIM, 1974–78 (Mem. Economic and Social Affairs Cttee); CBIM 1975. Hon. British Consul, Norfolk, Va, 1960–62. *Address*: Electra House, Temple Place, Victoria Embankment, WC2R 3HP. *Clubs*: Brooks's, MCC.

HARDY, Brig. George Alfred, FRGS; FRICS; Deputy Director and Keeper of the Maproom, Royal Geographical Society, 1977–84; *b* 5 June 1923; *s* of Charles A. Hardy and Caroline A. Hodges; *m* 1946, Olive (*née* Tennant); one *d. Educ*: Duke of York's Royal Military School. 2nd Lieut, RE, 1944; served W African Frontier Force, 1945–46; Survey of India, 1946–47; Sch. of Military Engineering and Sch. of Military Survey, 1948–50; British Schools' Exploring Soc., Norway, 1949; Air Survey Officer, Ordnance Survey, 1953–56; Sen. Instr., Sch. of Mil. Survey, 1956–59; OC 19 Topog. Survey Sqdn, S Arabia, 1959–61; OC 13 Field Survey Sqdn, BAOR, 1961–63; Chief Geographic Officer, Allied Forces N Europe, Oslo, 1964–66; Staff Officer, MoD, 1966–68; Geographic Adviser to Supreme Allied Command, NATO, 1968–70; Dep. Dir, Cartography and Map Production, 1970–73, Dir, Field Survey, 1973–77, Ordnance Survey; ADC to the Queen, 1976–77. *Publications*: contribs to Geographical Jl, RGS. *Address*: c/o Lloyds Bank, Cox & King's Branch, 6 Pall Mall, SW1.

HARDY, Herbert Charles; Chief Executive, Evening Standard Co. Ltd, since 1980; Director, Associated Newspapers Holdings, since 1986; *b* 13 Dec. 1928; *s* of Charles John Hardy and Margaret Elizabeth (*née* Burniston); *m* 1959, Irene Burrows; one *d. Educ*: RMA, Sandhurst. *Recreations*: golf, horse racing. *Address*: Evening Standard Co. Ltd, Fleet Street, EC4. *T*: 01–353 8000. *Club*: Thirty.

HARDY, Sir James (Gilbert), Kt 1981; OBE 1975; Chairman of Directors, Thomas Hardy & Sons Pty Ltd, since 1981; *b* 20 Nov. 1932; *s* of Thomas Mayfield Hardy and Eileen C. Hardy; *m* 1956, Anne Christine Jackson; two *s. Educ*: St Peter's Coll., Adelaide, SA; S Australian Sch. of Mines; S Australian Inst. of Technol. (Dip. in Accountancy). AASA. National Service, 13th Field Artillery Regt, Adelaide, 1951. Elder Smith & Co. Ltd, 1951; J. C. Correll & Co., 1952; Thomas Hardy & Sons Pty Ltd, Winemakers, Adelaide, 1953–: Shipping Clerk, Sales Rep., Sales Supervisor and Lab. Asst, 1953–62; Dir and Manager, Sydney Br., 1962–77; Regional Dir, Eastern Australia, 1977–81. Director: S Australian Film Corp., 1981–; America's Cup Challenge 1983 Ltd, 1981–85; Advertiser Newspapers Ltd, 1983–; Dep. Chm., Racing Rules Cttee, Yachting Fedn, 1969–81; Dir of Sailing/Captain, S Australian Challenge for the Defence of America's Cup 1987–. Treasurer, Liquor Trade Supervisory Council of NSW, 1965–70; Fellow, Catering Inst. of Australia, 1972; Wine and Brandy Assoc. of NSW: Mem. Exec., 1963; Treas., 1965; Vice Pres., 1968; Pres., 1980–83. NSW Chm., Aust. National Travel Assoc., 1976; Vice Pres., Royal Blind Soc. of NSW, 1980– (Mem. Council, 1967–); Pres., NSW Aust. Football League and Sydney Football League, 1982–83; Pres., "One and All" Sailing Ship Assoc. of SA Inc., 1981–; Member: Bd of Advice, Rothmans Nat. Sport Foundn, 1985–; Brisbane Olympic Cttee, 1985–. Mem. Adv. Bd, John Curtin Sch. of Medical Res., ANU, Canberra, 1982–. Dep. Grand Master, United Grand Lodge of NSW, 1977–80. *Recreation:* yachting (skipper or helmsman in America's Cup and Admiral's Cup races). *Address:* Thomas Hardy & Sons Pty Ltd, 104 Bay Street, East Botany, NSW 2019, Australia. *T:* (02) 666–5855. *Clubs:* Australian, Tattersalls, Royal Sydney Yacht Squadron (Sydney); Cruising Yacht of Australia (NSW); Brighton and Seacliff Yacht (Cdre, 1957) (SA); Canberra Yacht (ACT); Southport Yacht (Qld); Fort Worth Boat (Texas, USA).

HARDY, Maj.-Gen. John Campbell, CB 1985; LVO 1978; Deputy Chief of Staff (Support) to C-in-C Allied Forces Northern Europe, since 1984; *b* 13 Oct. 1933; *s* of late General Sir Campbell Hardy, KCB, CBE, DSO; *m* 1961, Jennifer Mary Kempton; one *s* one *d*. *Educ:* Sherborne School. Joined Royal Marines, 1952; 45 Commando, 1954; HMS Superb, 1956; Instructor, NCOs' School, Plymouth, 1957; 42 Commando, 1959; 43 Commando, 1962; Adjt, Jt Service Amphibious Warfare Centre, 1964; Company Comdr, 45 Commando, 1965; sc Bracknell, 1966; Instr, RNC Greenwich, 1967; Extra Equerry to Prince Philip, 1968–69; SO, Dept of CGRM, 1969; Rifle Company Comdr, 41 Commando, 1971; ndc Latimer, 1972; Staff of Chief of Defence Staff, 1973; Staff Officer HQ Commando Forces, 1975; CO RM Poole, 1977; CofS and Asst Defence Attaché, British Defence Staff Washington, 1979; ADC to the Queen, 1981–82; Chief of Staff to Comdt Gen. RM, 1982–84. *Recreations:* dinghy sailing, shooting. *Address:* c/o National Westminster Bank plc, 51 The Strand, Walmer, Deal, Kent. *Club:* Army and Navy.

HARDY, Peter; MP (Lab) Wentworth, since 1983 (Rother Valley, 1970–83); *b* 17 July 1931; *s* of Lawrence Hardy and of Mrs I. Hardy, Wath upon Dearne; *m* 1954, Margaret Anne Brookes; one *s*. *Educ:* Wath upon Dearne Grammar Sch.; Westminster Coll., London; Sheffield Univ. Schoolmaster in S Yorkshire, 1953–70. Member: Wath upon Dearne UDC, 1960–70 (Chm. Council, 1968–69); Governing Body of Wath Grammar Sch. (Chm. of Governors, 1969–70). Pres., Wath upon Dearne Labour Party, 1960–68; contested (Lab): Scarborough and Whitby, 1964; Sheffield, Hallam, 1966. PPS to Sec. of State for the Environment, 1974–76; PPS to Foreign Sec., 1976–79. Mem., UK delegn to Council of Europe, 1976–; Leader, Lab. delegn to Council of Europe and WEU, 1983–; Chm., Cttee on Environment, Council of Europe; Chm., PLP Energy Cttee. Member: Council, RSPB, 1983–; Central Exec. Cttee, NSPCC; Patron, Yorkshire Wildlife Trust. *Publications:* A Lifetime of Badgers, 1975; various articles on educational and other subjects. *Recreation:* watching wild life, exhibiting son's Irish Wolfhound. *Address:* 53 Sandygate, Wath upon Dearne, Rotherham, South Yorkshire. *T:* Rotherham 874590. *Club:* Rawmarsh Trades and Labour.

HARDY, Robert; *see* Hardy, T. S. R.

HARDY, Robert James; His Honour Judge Hardy; a Circuit Judge, since 1979; *b* 12 July 1924; *s* of James Frederick and Ann Hardy; *m* 1951, Maureen Scott; one *s* one *d*. *Educ:* Mostyn House Sch.; Wrekin Coll.; University Coll., London (LLB). Served, 1942–46, Royal Navy, and Pilot, Fleet Air Arm. Called to Bar, 1950; a Recorder of the Crown Court, 1972–79. *Recreation:* sailing. *Address:* Smithy House, Sandlebridge, Little Warford, Cheshire SK9 7TY. *T:* Mobberley 2535; Betlem, Mallorca.

HARDY, Rt. Rev. Robert Maynard; *see* Lincoln, Bishop of.

HARDY, Sir Rupert (John), 4th Bt, *cr* 1876; Lieutenant-Colonel Life Guards, retired; *b* 24 Oct. 1902; *s* of 3rd Bt and Violet Agnes Evelyn (*d* 1972), *d* of Hon. Sir Edward Chandos Leigh, KCB, KC; *S* father 1953; *m* 1930, Hon. Diana Joan Allsopp, *er d* of 3rd Baron Hindlip; one *s* one *d*. *Educ:* Eton; Trinity Hall, Cambridge. BA 1925. Joined The Life Guards, 1925; Major, 1940; retired, 1948, and rejoined as RARO, 1952; Lieut-Col comdg Household Cavalry Regt, 1952–56; ceased to belong to R of O, Dec. 1956; granted hon. rank of Lieut-Col. *Recreations:* hunting and shooting. *Heir:* *s* Richard Charles Chandos Hardy [*b* 6 Feb. 1945; *m* 1972, Venetia, *d* of Simon Wingfield Digby, *qv*; four *d*]. *Address:* Gullivers Lodge, Guilsborough, Northampton. *Club:* Turf.

HARDY, (Timothy Sydney) Robert, CBE 1981; actor and writer; *b* 29 Oct. 1925; *s* of late Major Henry Harrison Hardy, CBE, and Edith Jocelyn Dugdale; *m* 1st, 1952, Elizabeth (marr. diss.), *d* of late Sir Lionel Fox and Lady Fox; one *s*; 2nd, 1961, Sally (marr. diss. 1986), *d* of Sir Neville Pearson, 2nd Bt, and Dame Gladys Cooper, DBE; two *d*. *Educ:* Rugby Sch.; Magdalen Coll., Oxford (Hons degree, Eng. Lit.). *Stage:* Shakespeare Meml Theatre, 1949–51; London, West End, 1951–53; Old Vic Theatre, 1953–54; USA, 1954 and 1956–58 (plays incl. Hamlet and Henry V); Shakespeare Meml 1959 Centenary Season; Rosmersholm, Comedy, 1960; The Rehearsal, Globe, 1961; A Severed Head, Criterion, 1963; The Constant Couple, New, 1967; I've Seen You Cut Lemons, Fortune, 1969; Habeas Corpus, Lyric, 1974; Dear Liar, Mermaid, 1982; *films and television:* David Copperfield; Age of Kings; Trouble-shooters; Elizabeth R; Manhunt; Edward VII; All Creatures Great and Small; Speed King; Fothergill; Winston Churchill—The Wilderness Years, 1981; The Far Pavilions, 1983; The Shooting Party, 1985; Jenny's War, 1985; Hot Metal, 1986; Paying Guests, 1986; Make and Break, 1986; Churchill in the USA, 1986. Author of TV documentaries: Picardy Affair, 1962; The Longbow, 1972; Horses in our Blood, 1977; Gordon of Khartoum, 1982. Consultant, Mary Rose Trust, 1979–; Trustee, WWF (UK), 1983–; Mem., Bd of Trustees of the Royal Armouries, 1984–; Chm., Berkshire, Buckinghamshire and Oxfordshire Naturalists' Trust Appeal, 1984–. Upper Warden, Court of Worshipful Co. of Bowyers, 1986–. *Publication:* Longbow, 1976. *Recreations:* archery, horsemanship, bowyery. *Address:* Upper Bolney House, Upper Bolney, near Henley-on-Thames, Oxon RG9 4AQ. *Clubs:* Buck's, Royal Toxophilite, British Longbow.

HARDY-ROBERTS, Brig. Sir Geoffrey (Paul), KCVO 1972; CB 1945; CBE 1944 (OBE 1941); JP; DL; Master of HM's Household, 1967–73; Extra Equerry to the Queen, since 1967; Secretary-Superintendent of Middlesex Hospital, 1946–67; *b* 1907; *s* of A. W. Roberts; *m* 1945, Eldred, *widow* of Col J. R. Macdonell, DSO. *Educ:* Eton; RMC Sandhurst. Regular Commission, 9th Lancers, 1926–37. Served War of 1939–45 (OBE, CBE, CB). Mem., West Sussex AHA, 1974–82; Dep. Chm., King Edward VII Hospital, Midhurst, 1972–82. JP 1960, DL 1964, West Sussex (formerly Sussex), High Sheriff, 1965, Sussex. Officer, Legion of Merit, 1945. *Address:* The Garden House, Coates, Pulborough, West Sussex RH20 1ES. *T:* Fittleworth 446.

HARDYMAN, Norman Trenchard, CB 1984; Secretary, University Grants Committee, since 1982; *b* 5 Jan. 1930; *s* of late Rev. Arnold Victor Hardyman and late Laura Hardyman; *m* 1961, Carol Rebecca Turner; one *s* one *d*. *Educ:* Clifton Coll.; Christ Church, Oxford. Asst Principal, Min. of Educn, 1955; Principal 1960; Private Sec. to Sec. of State for Educn and Science, 1966–68; Asst Sec. 1968–75, Under-Sec., 1975–79, DES; Under-Sec., DHSS, 1979–81. *Recreations:* walking, gardening, reading, photography. *Address:* 16 Rushington Avenue, Maidenhead, Berks. *T:* Maidenhead 24179.

HARE, family name of **Viscount Blakenham** and **Earl of Listowel.**

HARE, Hon. Alan Victor, MC 1942; Deputy Chairman, The Economist, since 1985; *b* 14 March 1919; 4th *s* of 4th Earl of Listowel and Hon. Freda, *d* of 2nd Baron Derwent; *m* 1945, Jill Pegotty (*née* North); one *s* one *d*. *Educ:* Eton Coll.; New Coll., Oxford (MA). Army, 1939–45. Foreign Office, 1947–61; Industrial and Trade Fairs, 1961–63; Financial Times, 1963–84; Man. Dir, 1971–78, Chm., 1978–84, and Chief Executive, 1975–83, Financial Times Ltd; Director: Pearson Longman Ltd, 1975–83; Economist Newspaper Ltd, 1975–; Chm., Industrial and Trade Fairs Holdings, 1979–83 (Dir, 1977–83); Dir, English National Opera, 1982–; Trustee, Reuters plc, 1985–. Pres., Société Civile du Vignoble de Château Latour, 1983–. Mem., Press Council, 1975–78. Comdr, Order of Merit (FDR), 1985. *Recreations:* walking, opera, swimming. *Address:* Flat 12, 53 Rutland Gate, SW7. *T:* 01–581 2184. *Club:* White's.
See also Viscount Blakenham.

HARE, David; playwright; Associate Director, National Theatre, since 1984; *b* 5 June 1947; *s* of Clifford Theodore Rippon Hare and Agnes Cockburn Hare; *m* 1970, Margaret Matheson (marr. diss. 1980); two *s* one *d*. *Educ:* Lancing Coll.; Jesus Coll., Cambridge (MA Hons). Founded Portable Theatre, 1968; Literary Manager and Resident Dramatist, Royal Court, 1969–71; Resident Dramatist, Nottingham Playhouse, 1973; founded Joint Stock Theatre Group, 1975; US/UK Bicentennial Fellowship, 1977; founded Greenpoint Films, 1982. Author of plays: Slag, Hampstead, 1970, Royal Court, 1971 (Evening Standard Drama Award, 1970); The Great Exhibition, Hampstead, 1972; Knuckle, Comedy, 1974 (John Llewellyn Rhys Award, 1974); Fanshen, Joint Stock, 1975; The Knife, opera libretto, NY Shakespeare Fest., 1987; author and director of plays: (with Howard Brenton) Brassneck, Nottingham Playhouse, 1973; Teeth 'n' Smiles, Royal Court, 1975, Wyndhams, 1976; Plenty, NT, 1978, NY, 1983 (NY Critics' Circle Award); A Map of the World, Adelaide Fest., 1982, NT, 1983, NY 1985; (with Howard Brenton) Pravda, NT, 1985 (London Standard Award; Plays and Players Award; City Limits Award); The Bay at Nice, and Wrecked Eggs, NT, 1986. *TV plays:* Man Above Men (Play for Today), 1973; Licking Hitler (Play for Today), 1978 (BAFTA award, 1978); Dreams of Leaving (Play for Today), 1980 (also directed); Saigon—Year of the Cat (Thames TV), 1983. *Directed:* The Party, NT, 1974; Weapons of Happiness, NT, 1976; Total Eclipse, Lyric, Hammersmith, 1981; King Lear, NT, 1986. *Films:* (wrote and directed) Wetherby, 1985 (Golden Bear award, 1985); (screenplay) Plenty, 1985. *Publications:* Slag, 1970; The Great Exhibition, 1972; Knuckle, 1974; Brassneck, 1974; Fanshen, 1976; Teeth 'n' Smiles, 1976; Plenty, 1978; Licking Hitler, 1978; Dreams of Leaving, 1980; A Map of the World, 1982; Saigon, 1983; The History Plays, 1984; Pravda, 1985; Wetherby, 1985; The Asian Plays, 1986; The Bay at Nice, 1986; Wrecked Eggs, 1986. *Address:* 33 Ladbroke Road, W11.

HARE, Prof. Frederick Kenneth, OC 1978; PhD; FRSC 1968; Professor of Geography and Physics, 1969–84, and Director, Institute for Environmental Studies, 1974–79, now University Professor Emeritus in Geography, University of Toronto; Provost, University of Trinity College, Toronto, 1979–86; *b* Wylye, Wilts, 5 Feb. 1919; *s* of Frederick Eli Hare and Irene Smith; *m* 1st, 1941, Suzanne Alice Bates (marr. diss. 1952); one *s*; 2nd, 1953, Helen Neilson Morrill; one *s* one *d*. *Educ:* Windsor Grammar Sch.; King's Coll., University of London (BSc); Univ. of Montreal (PhD). Lectr in Geography, Univ. of Manchester, 1940–41; War service in Air Min., Meteorological Office, 1941–45; McGill University: Asst and Assoc. Prof. of Geography, 1945–52; Prof. of Geography and Meteorology, 1952–64; Chm. of Dept, 1950–62; Dean of Faculty of Arts and Science, 1962–64; Prof. of Geography, Univ. of London (King's Coll.), 1964–66; Master of Birkbeck Coll., Univ. of London, 1966–68; Pres., Univ. of British Columbia, 1968–69. Vis. Centenary Prof., Univ. of Adelaide, 1974. FKC 1967. Sci. Advr, Dept of the Environment, Canada, 1972–74. Mem. Nat. Research Council of Canada, 1962–64; Chm. of Bd, Arctic Inst. of N America, 1963; Mem., NERC, 1965–68; Dir, Resources for the Future, 1968–80; Member: SSRC, Canada, 1974–76; Adv. Council, Electric Power Res. Inst., 1978–80; Bd of Dirs, CIMMYT. Chairman: Adv. Cttee on Canadian Demonstration Projects, 1974–75, for 1976 UN Conf. on Human Settlements; Special Prog. Panel on Ecoscis, NATO, 1975; Federal Study Gp on Nuclear Waste Disposal, 1977; Climate Programme Planning Bd, Govt of Canada, 1979–; Commn on Lead in the Environment, RSC, 1984–; Section W, AAAS, 1985–86. President: Canadian Assoc. of Geographers, 1963–64; RMetS, 1967–68 (Vice-Pres., 1968–70); Sigma Xi, 1986–87; Fellow, Amer. Meteorological Soc., 1969; Hon. Fellow, Amer. Geographical Soc., 1963; Hon. Pres., Assoc. of Amer. Geographers, 1964. Hon. Life Mem., Birkbeck Coll., 1969. Hon. LLD: Queen's (Canada) Univ., 1964; Univ. of W Ontario, 1968; Trent Univ., 1979; Memorial Univ., 1985; Hon. DSc: McGill, 1969; York (Canada), 1978; DSc *ad eund.* Adelaide, 1974; Hon. DSLitt Thorneloe Coll., Sudbury (Canada), 1984. Hon. Cert. Graduation, Nat. Defence Coll., Kingston, Canada, 1986. Meritorious Achievement Citation, Assoc. Amer. Geographers, 1961; President's Prize, RMetS (Can.), 1961, 1962; Patterson Medal, Can. Met. Service, 1973; Massey Medal, Royal Can. Geographical Soc., 1974; Patron's Medal, RGS, 1977; Award for Scholarly Distinction, Canadian Assoc. of Geographers, 1979; Univ. of Toronto Alumni Assoc. Faculty Award, 1982. *Publications:* The Restless Atmosphere, 1953; On University Freedom, 1968; (with M. K. Thomas) Climate Canada, 1974, 2nd edn 1979; numerous articles in Quarterly Jl Royal Meteorological Soc., Geography, and other learned jls. *Recreation:* music. *Address:* 301 Lakeshore Road West, Oakville, Ont L6K 1G2, Canada. *Clubs:* McGill Faculty (Montreal) (Hon. Life Mem.); Toronto Faculty, York (Toronto).

HARE, Geoffrey; Chief Executive, Scottish Tourist Board, since 1986; *b* 28 Dec. 1940; *s* of Leslie and Greta Hare; *m* 1971, Joy Margaret Beckley; one *d*. *Educ:* José Pedro Varela School, Montevideo, Uruguay; Lawrence Sheriff Grammar School, Rugby. Management Trainee, Savoy Hotel, London, Spain, Canary Isles, 1957–59; Hotel Management Trainee, Paris, Jersey, UK, 1960–63; Agricultural/Hotel studies, Israel, 1964–65; Universal Sky Tours, Majorca, 1965–66; Area Manager, Wallace Arnold Tours, Portugal, 1966–67; Trust House Forte Hotels, 1967–77; Dir of Tourism, NW Tourist Bd, 1977–86. *Recreations:* philately, driving, walking, sketching. *Address:* 10/4 Damside, Dean Village, Edinburgh EH4 3BB.

HARE, Kenneth; *see* Hare, F. K.

HARE, Hon. Mrs Richard; *see* Gordine, Dora.

HARE, Rt. Rev. Richard; *see* Hare, Rt Rev. Thomas Richard.

HARE, Prof. Richard Mervyn, FBA 1964; Graduate Research Professor of Philosophy, University of Florida at Gainesville, since 1983; *b* 21 March 1919; *s* of late Charles Francis Aubone Hare and late Louise Kathleen (*née* Simonds); *m* 1947, Catherine, *d* of Sir Harry

Verney, 4th Bt, DSO; one *s* three *d*. *Educ:* Rugby (Schol.); Balliol Coll., Oxford (Schol.). Commissioned Royal Artillery, 1940; Lieut, Indian Mountain Artillery, 1941; Prisoner of War, Singapore and Siam, 1942–45. 1st Lit. Hum. 1947. Fellow and Tutor in Philosophy, Balliol Coll., Oxford, 1947–66, Hon. Fellow, 1974; White's Prof. of Moral Philosophy and Fellow of Corpus Christi Coll., Oxford, 1966–83, Hon. Fellow, 1983. Visiting Fellow: Princeton, 1957; ANU, 1966; Center for Advanced Study in Behavioral Sciences, Stanford, 1980; Wilde Lectr in Natural Religion, Oxford, 1963–66; Visiting Professor: Univ. of Michigan, 1968; Univ. of Delaware, 1974. Pres., Aristotelian Soc., 1972–73. Member: Nat. Road Safety Advisory Council, 1966–68; C of E Working Parties on Medical Questions, 1964–75. Hon. Fellow, Inst. of Life Scis, Hastings Center, 1974; For. Hon. Mem., American Acad. of Arts and Sciences, 1975. Tanner Award, 1979. *Publications:* The Language of Morals, 1952; Freedom and Reason, 1963; Essays on Philosophical Method, 1971; Practical Inferences, 1971; Essays on the Moral Concepts, 1972; Applications of Moral Philosophy, 1972; Moral Thinking, 1981; Plato, 1982. *Recreations:* music, gardening. *Address:* Saffron House, Ewelme, Oxford.

HARE, Sir Thomas, 5th Bt *cr* 1818; *b* 27 July 1930; *s* of Sir Ralph Leigh Hare, 4th Bt, and Doreen Pleasance Anna (*d* 1985), *d* of late Sir Richard Bagge, DSO; *S* father, 1976; *m* 1961, Lady Rose Amanda Bligh, *d* of 9th Earl of Darnley; two *d*. *Educ:* Eton; Magdalene College, Cambridge (MA). ARICS. *Heir: cousin* Philip Leigh Hare [*b* 13 Oct. 1922; *m* 1950, Anne Lisle, *d* of Major Geoffrey Nicholson, CBE, MC; one *s* one *d*]. *Address:* Stow Bardolph, King's Lynn, Norfolk PE34 3HU.

HARE, Rt. Rev. Thomas Richard; *see* Pontefract, Bishop Suffragan of.

HARE DUKE, Rt. Rev. Michael Geoffrey; *see* St Andrews, Dunkeld and Dunblane, Bishop of.

HARES, Phillip Douglas George, CBE 1985; Chairman and Chief Executive since 1986, and Board Member for Finance, since 1981, British Shipbuilders (Deputy Chief Executive, 1983–86); *b* 31 Dec. 1926; *s* of Edgar Sidney George and Edith Winifred Frances Hares; *m* 1955, Violet May Myers; one *s* one *d*. *Educ:* Richmond and East Sheen Grammar Sch. FIAM; FBCS; FBIM. Involved with management sciences and computing in various commercial, industrial, and consulting organisations, 1952–69, dating from early application of computers in 1952 with J. Lyons & Co. Ltd; Asst Man. Dir (Ops), British Mail Order Corp. Ltd (Great Universal Stores), 1969–77; Man. Dir (Finance), British Shipbuilders, 1978–81, Corporate Man. Dir, 1982–83; Chairman: Falmouth Shiprepair Ltd, 1983–85; Vosper Shiprepairers Ltd, 1983–85; Dir, Iron Trades Insce Gp, 1985–. Mem. Council, CBI, 1983– (Mem., Economic Situation Cttee, 1983–). Freeman, City of London, 1983; Liveryman, Worshipful Co. of Shipwrights, 1984–. *Address:* Garden Court, Ince Road, Burwood Park, Walton-on-Thames, Surrey KT12 5BJ. *Recreations:* reading, genealogy. *Club:* City Livery.

HAREWOOD, 7th Earl of, *cr* 1812; **George Henry Hubert Lascelles,** KBE 1986; Baron Harewood, 1796; Viscount Lascelles, 1812; a Governor of BBC, since 1985; President, British Board of Film Classification, since 1985; Artistic Director, 1988 Adelaide Festival, since 1986; *b* 7 Feb. 1923; *er s* of 6th Earl of Harewood, KG, GCVO, DSO, and HRH Princess Mary (Princess Royal; who *d* 28 March 1965); *S* father, 1947; *m* 1st, 1949, Maria Donata (marr. diss. 1967; she *m* 1973, Rt Hon. (John) Jeremy Thorpe), *d* of late Erwin Stein; three *s*; 2nd, 1967, Patricia Elizabeth, *d* of Charles Tuckwell, Australia; one *s* and one step *s*. *Educ:* Eton; King's Coll., Cambridge (MA; Hon. Fellow, 1984). Served War of 1939–45, Capt. Grenadier Guards (wounded and prisoner, 1944, released May 1945); ADC to Earl of Athlone, 1945–46, Canada. Editor of magazine "Opera" 1950–53; Royal Opera House, Covent Garden: a Dir, 1951–53; on staff, 1953–60; a Dir, 1969–72; Chm. Bd, ENO (formerly Sadler's Wells Opera), 1986– (Man. Dir, 1972–85); Artistic Director: Edinburgh Internat. Festival, 1961–65; Leeds Festival, 1958–74; Artistic Advr, New Philharmonia Orch., London, 1966–76; Man. Dir, English Nat. Opera North, 1978–81. Chm., Music Advisory Cttee of British Council, 1956–66; Chancellor of the Univ. of York, 1963–67; Member: Arts Council, 1966–72; Gen. Adv. Council of BBC, 1969–77. President: English Football Assoc., 1963–72; Leeds United Football Club. Hon. RAM, 1983; Hon. LLD: Leeds, 1959; Aberdeen, 1966; Hon. DMus Hull, 1962; DUniv York, 1982. Janáček Medal, 1978. *Publications:* (ed) Kobbé's Complete Opera Book, 1953, 3rd edn 1987; The Tongs and the Bones (autobiog.), 1981. *Heir: s* Viscount Lascelles, *qv*. *Address:* Harewood House, Leeds LS17 9LG.

HARFORD, Sir James (Dundas), KBE 1956; CMG 1943; *b* Great Yarmouth, 7 Jan. 1899; *s* of late Rev. Dundas Harford, MA; *m* 1st, 1932, Countess Thelma, *d* of Count Albert Metaxa; one *s*; 2nd, 1937, Lilias Madeline, *d* of Major Archibald Campbell; two *d*. *Educ:* Repton; Balliol Coll., Oxford (Hon. Scholar, MA). Served European War, France and Belgium, 1917–19; Asst Master, Eton Coll., 1922–25; Administrative Service, Nigeria, 1926; District administration, Bornu Province, 1926–29; Asst Sec., Nigerian Secretariat, 1930–34 and Clerk to Exec. and Legislative Councils; seconded to Colonial Office, 1934–36; Administrator of Antigua and Federal Sec. of the Leeward Islands, 1936–40; Administrator, St Kitts-Nevis, 1940–47; administered Government of Leeward Islands, on various occasions; seconded to Colonial Office, 1947–48; administered Government of Mauritius, on various occasions; Colonial Sec., Mauritius, 1948–53; Governor and Commander-in-Chief of St Helena, 1954–58. Conference Organiser, Commonwealth Institute, 1959–64. *Address:* Links Cottage, Rother Road, Seaford, East Sussex.

HARFORD, Sir (John) Timothy, 3rd Bt *cr* 1934; Director, Singer & Friedlander Ltd, since 1970 (Local Director, 1967–69); Deputy Chairman, Wolseley-Hughes Group plc, since 1983; Vice-Chairman, Wesleyan & General Assurance Society, since 1985; *b* 6 July 1932; *s* of Sir George Arthur Harford, 2nd Bt and Anstice Marion, *d* of Sir Alfred Tritton, 2nd Bt; *S* father, 1967; *m* 1962, Carolyn Jane Mullens; two *s* one *d*. *Educ:* Harrow Sch.; Oxford Univ.; Harvard Business Sch. Philip Hill Higginson Erlangers Ltd, 1960–63; Dir, Birmingham Industrial Trust Ltd, 1963–67. *Recreations:* wine and food, travel. *Heir: s* Mark John Harford, *b* 6 Aug. 1964. *Address:* South House, South Littleton, Evesham, Worcs. *T:* Evesham 830478. *Club:* Boodle's.

HARGREAVES, David Harold, PhD; Chief Inspector, Inner London Education Authority, since 1984; *b* 31 Aug. 1939; *s* of Clifford and Marion Hargreaves. *Educ:* Bolton School; Christ's College, Cambridge. MA, PhD. Asst Master, Hull Grammar Sch., 1961–64; Research Associate, Dept. of Sociology and Social Anthropology, Univ. of Manchester, 1964–65; Lectr, Senior Lectr then Reader, Dept. of Education, Univ. of Manchester, 1965–79; Reader in Education and Fellow of Jesus College, Oxford, 1979–84. FRSA 1984. *Publications:* Social Relations in a Secondary School, 1967; Interpersonal Relations and Education, 1972; (jtly) Deviance in Classrooms, 1975; The Challenge for the Comprehensive School, 1982. *Recreations:* opera, British watercolours, parks. *Address:* Room 273, ILEA, County Hall, SE1. *T:* 01–633 3317. *Club:* Athenæum.

HARGREAVES, Prof. John Desmond; Professor of History, University of Aberdeen, 1962–85; *b* 25 Jan. 1924; *s* of Arthur Swire Hargreaves and Margaret Hilda (*née* Duckworth); *m* 1950, Sheila Elizabeth (*née* Wilks); one *s* two *d*. *Educ:* Skipton Grammar Sch.; Bootham; Manchester Univ. War service, 1943–46. Asst Princ., War Office, 1948; Lectr in History: Manchester Univ., 1948–52; Fourah Bay Coll., Sierra Leone, 1952–54; Aberdeen Univ., 1954–62. Vis. Prof., Union Coll. Schenectady, New York, 1960–61; Univ. of Ibadan, 1970–71. Mem., Kidd Cttee on Sheriff Court Records, 1966. Pres., African Studies Assoc. (UK), 1972–73. Hon. DLitt Sierra Leone, 1984. *Publications:* Life of Sir Samuel Lewis, 1958; Prelude to the Partition of West Africa, 1963; West Africa: the Former French States, 1967; France and West Africa, 1969; West Africa Partitioned: Vol. I, The Loaded Pause, 1974, Vol. II, The Elephants and the Grass, 1985; The End of Colonial Rule in West Africa, 1979; Aberdeenshire to Africa, 1981; many articles and chapters in jls and collaborative volumes. *Recreations:* hill-walking, theatre, lawn tennis. *Address:* Balcluain, Raemoir Road, Banchory, Kincardine AB3 3UJ. *T:* Banchory 2655. *Club:* Royal Commonwealth Society.

HARGREAVES, (Joseph) Kenneth; MP (C) Hyndburn, since 1983; *b* 1 March 1939; *s* of James and Mary Hargreaves. *Educ:* St Mary's Coll., Blackburn; Manchester Coll. of Commerce. ACIS. Standard Cost/Wages Clerk, NCB, 1957–61; Audit Asst, Treasurer's Dept, Lancs CC, 1961–63; Office Manager, Shopfitters (Lancashire) Ltd, Oswaldtwistle, 1963–83. *Recreations:* Gilbert and Sullivan, classical music, travel. *Address:* 31 Park Lane, Oswaldtwistle, Accrington, Lancs. *T:* Accrington 396184; (office) 01–219 5138.

HARGREAVES, Brig. Kenneth, CBE 1956 (MBE (mil.) 1939); TD 1942; DL; Lord-Lieutenant, West Yorkshire, 1974–78 (West Riding of Yorkshire and City of York, 1970–74); Hon. President, Hargreaves Group Ltd, since 1974 (Managing Director, 1938–64, Chairman, 1964–74); *b* 23 Feb. 1903; *s* of late Henry Hargreaves, Leeds, and late Hope Hargreaves; *m* 1st, 1958, Else Margareta Allen (*d* 1968); one step *s* one step *d* (both adopted); 2nd, 1969, Hon. Mrs Margaret Packe; two step *d*. *Educ:* Haileybury Coll. Lieut-Col comdg 96th HAA Regt RA, 1939–41; Brig. comdg 3rd Ind. AA Bde, 1942–45; Hon. Col, several TA regiments, 1947–66; Vice-Pres., Yorks TAVR, 1970–78. Director: Lloyds Bank Ltd, 1965–73 (Chm., Yorkshire Regional Bd, 1967–73); Yorkshire Bank, 1969–79; Sadler's Wells Trust Ltd, 1969–75; ENO, 1975–80; Opera North, 1981–84; Pres., Friends of Opera North, 1978–. Mem., Royal Commn on Historical Monuments, 1971–74. Pres., Queen's Silver Jubilee Appeal, W Yorks, 1977–78. Chairman: Coal Industry Soc., 1933–34, Pres. 1973–75; Coal Trade Benevolent Assoc., 1958; British Railways (Eastern) Bd, 1970–73 (Dir, 1964–73). President: Chartered Inst. of Secretaries, 1956 (FCIS 1930); W Yorks Branch, BRCS, 1965–74, now Patron; St John Council (W Yorks), 1970–74, W and S Yorks, 1974–78; Yorks Agricultural Soc., 1972–73; Haileybury Soc., 1974–75; Vice-Pres., Leeds Chamber of Commerce, 1946–47; Dep. Chm., Leeds Musical Festival, 1961–70; Mem. Court, University of Leeds, 1950– (Hon. LLD 1970); Trustee, York Minster, 1970–; High Steward, Selby Abbey, 1974–; Patron, Central Yorkshire Scouts, 1978 (former Chm. and Pres.). Contested: Pontefract, 1945; Keighley, 1950 and 1951; Hon. Treasurer, Yorks Provincial Area Conservative and Unionist Assoc., 1946–54; Governor, Swinton Conservative Coll., 1952–70; Lay Reader, Ripon Diocese, 1954–. Liveryman, Clothworkers' Co., 1938, Master, 1969–70. High Sheriff of Yorks, 1962–63; DL WR Yorks 1956–70, West Yorks, 1978–. KStJ 1970. *Recreations:* gardening, music. *Address:* Easby House, Great Ouseburn, York YO5 9RQ. *T:* Green Hammerton 30548. *Clubs:* Army and Navy, Carlton.

HARGREAVES, Maj.-Gen. William Herbert, CB 1965; OBE 1945; FRCP; *b* 5 Aug. 1908; *s* of Arthur William Hargreaves; *m* 1946, Pamela Mary Westray; one *s* one *d*. *Educ:* Merchant Taylors' Sch.; St Bartholomew's Hospital. FRCP 1950; FRCPE 1965. Served War of 1939–45. Medical Liaison Officer to Surgeon-Gen., US Army, Washington, DC, 1946–48; Prof. of Medicine, Univ. of Baghdad, 1951–59; Physician to late King Faisal II of Iraq, 1951–58; Hon. Consulting Physician, Iraqi Army, 1953–59; Consulting Physician to the Army, 1960–65; retd 1965. Lectr in Tropical Medicine, Middlesex Hosp. Med. Sch., 1960–65, and London Hosp. Med. Sch., 1963–65; Hon. Consulting Physician, Royal Hosp., Chelsea, 1961–65; Chief Med. Advr, Shell Internat. Petroleum Co. Ltd, 1965–72. Examiner: RCP, 1964–66; Soc. Apothecaries, 1966–73. Mem. of Council, Royal Society of Medicine, 1966–69, Vice-Pres., Library (Scientific Research) Section, 1967–69. Counsellor, Royal Soc. of Tropical Med. and Hygiene, 1961–65; Member: Hosp. Cttee, St John's Ophthalmic Hosp., Jerusalem, 1968–71; Finance Cttee, RCP. OStJ 1965. Iraq Coronation Medal, 1953. *Publications:* The Practice of Tropical Medicine (with R. J. G. Morrison), 1965; chapters in: Textbook of Medicine (Conybeare), 16th edn 1975; Modern Trends in Gastro-Enterology (Avery Jones), 1951; Medicine in the Tropics (Woodruff), 1974; numerous articles in med. jls. *Recreations:* art and music. *Address:* 6/3 Gladswood Gardens, Double Bay, NSW 2028, Australia.

HARINGTON, Gen. Sir Charles (Henry Pepys), GCB 1969 (KCB 1964; CB 1961); CBE 1957 (OBE 1953); DSO 1944; MC 1940; ADC (General) to the Queen, 1969–71; *b* 5 May 1910; *s* of Lt-Col H. H. Harington and Dorothy Pepys; *m* 1942, Victoire Marion Williams-Freeman; one *s* two *d*. *Educ:* Malvern; Sandhurst. Commissioned into 22nd (Cheshire) Regt, 1930. Served War of 1939–45: France and Belgium, 2nd Bn Cheshire Regt, 1939–40; CO, 1st Bn Manchester Regt and GSO1, 53 (Welch) Div., NW Europe, 1944–45. DS Staff Coll., 1946; GSO1 Mil. Mission Greece, 1948; CO 1st Bn The Parachute Regt, 1949; Mil. Asst to CIGS, 1951; SHAPE, 1953; Comdr 49 Inf. Bde in Kenya, 1955; idc 1957; Comdt Sch. of Infantry, 1958; GOC 3rd Div., 1959; Comdt, Staff Coll., Camberley, 1961; C-in-C Middle East, 1963; DCGS, 1966; Chief of Personnel and Logistics, to the three Services, 1968–71, retired; Col The Cheshire Regt, 1962–68. Col Comdt, Small Arms Sch. Corps, 1964–70; Col Comdt, The Prince of Wales Div., 1968–71. President: Combined Cadet Force Assoc., 1971–80; Milocarian (Tri-Service) Athletic Club. Chm. Governors, Royal Star and Garter Home, 1972–80. Comr, Duke of York's Royal Military Sch. Knight Officer with swords, Order of Orange Nassau (Netherlands), 1945. *Recreations:* sailing, English watercolours. *Address:* 19 Rivermead Court, SW6 3RT. *Clubs:* Army and Navy, Hurlingham (Pres.).

HARINGTON, (Edward Henry) Vernon; *b* 13 Sept. 1907; *er s* of late His Honour Edward Harington; *m* 1st, 1937, Mary Elizabeth (marr. diss. 1949), *d* of late Louis Egerton; one *d* (and one *d* decd); 2nd, 1950, Mary Johanna Jean, JP, *d* of late Lt-Col R. G. S. Cox, MC; two *d*. *Educ:* Eton. Called to Bar, Inner Temple, 1930. Private Sec. to Lord Chancellor and Dep. Serjeant-at-Arms, House of Lords, 1934–40; served with HM Forces, 1940–45 (Major, Coldstream Guards); WO, 1944–45; Austrian Control Commn, Legal Div., 1945; Asst Sec. to Lord Chancellor for Commns of the Peace, 1945; Dep. Judge Advocate, 1946; Asst Judge Advocate Gen., 1954–73. Dep. Chm., Herefordshire QS, 1969–71; a Recorder of the Crown Court, 1972–75. Chm., Hereford, Worcester, Warwicks and W Midlands Regional Agricl Wages Cttee, 1976–82. Councillor, Malvern Hill DC, 1979–. JP Herefordshire, 1969–71. *Recreations:* shooting, fishing. *Address:* Woodlands House, Whitbourne, Worcester. *T:* Knightwick 21437.

HARINGTON, Maj.-Gen. John, CB 1967; OBE 1958; *b* 7 Nov. 1912; *s* of late Col Henry Harington, Kelston, Folkestone, Kent; *m* 1943, Nancy, *d* of late Stanley Allen, Denne Hill, Canterbury; one *s*. *Educ:* Lambrook, Bracknell; Aldenham Sch.; RMA Woolwich. Commnd RA, 1933. Served War of 1939–45: BEF, 1939–40; Capt., RHA, France and Germany; Major 1943; 1st Airborne Corps; Lt-Col 1945. GSO1, British and Indian Div., Japan, 1946–47; CO 18th Regt RA, 1954–55; College Comdr, RMA,

Sandhurst, 1956–57; Head of Defence Secretariat, Middle East, 1958–59; commanded 1st Artillery Brigade, 1960–61; BRA, Far East Land Forces, 1962; DMS (2), War Office, 1962–64 (Min. of Defence, 1964); Chief of Staff to C-in-C, Far East Comd, 1964–67, retired. *Recreations:* ski-ing, shooting, golf, tennis. *Address:* Harkaway, Goodworth Clatford, Andover, Hants. *Clubs:* Army and Navy, Ski Club of Great Britain.

HARINGTON, Kenneth Douglas Evelyn Herbert; Metropolitan Magistrate, 1967–84; *b* 30 Sept. 1911; *yr s* of late His Honour Edward Harington; *m* 1st, 1939, Lady Cecilia Bowes-Lyon (*d* 1947), *er d* of 15th Earl of Strathmore; 2nd, 1950, Maureen Helen McCalmont, *d* of Brig.-Gen. Sir Robert McCalmont, KCVO, CBE, DSO; two *s. Educ:* Stowe. War of 1939–45: Served NW Europe (Major, Coldstream Guards). Hon. Attaché, British Legation, Stockholm, 1930–32; Barrister, Inner Temple, 1952; Acting Deputy Chm., Inner London and NE London Quarter Sessions, 1966–67. *Recreations:* shooting, fishing. *Address:* Orchard End, Upper Oddington, Moreton-in-Marsh, Glos. *T:* Stow on the Wold 30989. *Club:* Cavalry and Guards.

HARINGTON, Sir Nicholas (John), 14th Bt *cr* 1611; Senior Legal Assistant, Treasury Solicitor's Department, since 1977; *b* 14 May 1942; *s* of His Honour John Charles Dundas Harington, QC (*d* 1980) (*yr s* of 12th Bt) and Lavender Cecilia Harington (*d* 1982), *d* of late Major E. W. Denny, Garboldisham Manor, Diss; *S* uncle, 1981. *Educ:* Eton; Christ Church, Oxford (MA Jurisprudence). Called to the Bar, 1969. Employed in Persian Gulf, 1971–72. Joined Civil Service, 1972. *Recreations:* numerous. *Heir: b* David Richard Harington [*b* 27 June 1944; *m* 1983, Deborah (*née* Catesby); one *s*]. *Address:* The Ring o'Bells, Whitbourne, Worcester WR6 5RT. *T:* Knightwick 21819.

HARINGTON, Vernon; *see* Harington, E. H. V.

HARINGTON HAWES, Derrick Gordon; *b* 22 May 1907; *s* of late Col Charles Howard Hawes, DSO, MVO, Indian Army; *m* 1932, Drusilla Way; one *s* two *d. Educ:* Wellington Coll.; RMC Sandhurst. 14th Punjab Regt, IA, 1927–34; Indian Political Service, 1934–47; King Edward's Hospital Fund for London, 1949–62; Dir Gen., Internat. Hospital Fedn, 1962–75. *Address:* 8 Northbrook Road, Aldershot, Hants GU11 3HE. *Club:* Oriental.

HARKIN, Brendan; Chairman and Chief Executive, Labour Relations Agency, since 1976; *b* 21 April 1920; *s* of Francis and Catherine Harkin; *m* 1949, Maureen Gee; one *s* two *d. Educ:* St Mary's Christian Brothers' Primary and Grammar Schs, Belfast. Apprentice Electrician, 1936. Asst Sec. 1953, Gen. Sec. 1955–76, NI Civil Service Assoc. (which after amalgamations became Public Service Alliance, 1971). Chm., Strathearn Audio Ltd, 1974–76; Deputy Chairman: NI Finance Corp., 1972–76; NI Development Agency, 1976. Mem., EEC Economic and Social Cttee, 1973–76. Chm., Industry Year. Pres., Irish Congress of Trade Unions, 1976. Member: Council, NUU, now Univ. of Ulster, 1982–; Co-operation North. Pres., NI Hospice; Dep. Chm., Bd of Govs, St Louise's Comprehensive Coll. MUniv Open. Regular television and radio broadcaster, and contributor to several publications, particularly on industrial relations. *Recreations:* theatre, music, reading. *Address:* 113 Somerton Road, Belfast 15, Northern Ireland. *T:* 771154.

HARKNESS, Lt-Col Hon. Douglas Scott, OC 1978; GM 1943; ED 1944; PC (Canada) 1957; Minister of National Defence, Canada, 1960–63; *b* 29 March 1903; *s* of William Keefer and Janet Douglas Harkness (*née* Scott); *m* 1932, Frances Elisabeth, *d* of James Blair McMillan, Charlottetown and Calgary; one *s. Educ:* Central Collegiate, Calgary; University of Alberta (BA). Served overseas in War (Italy and NW Europe), 1940–45; Major and Lt-Col, Royal Canadian Artillery; with Reserve Army, CO 41st Anti-Tank Regt (SP), Royal Canadian Artillery. MP (Calgary E) gen. elecs, 1945, 1949; Re-elected: (Calgary N) gen. elecs, 1953, 1957, 1958, 1962, 1963, 1965, (Calgary Centre) 1968, retired 1972; Min. for Northern Affairs and Nat. Resources and Actg Minister of Agric., June 1957; Minister of Agric., Aug. 1957; relinquished portfolios of Northern Affairs and Nat. Resources, Aug. 1957, of Agriculture, Oct. 1960. Mem. Alta Military Institute. Hon. LLD Calgary, 1975. *Address:* 716 Imperial Way SW, Calgary, Alta T2S 1N7, Canada. *T:* Calgary (403) 243–0825. *Clubs:* Ranchmen's, Calgary Petroleum (Calgary).

HARKNESS, Ven. James, OBE 1978; QHC 1982; Chaplain General to the Forces, since 1987; *b* 20 Oct. 1935; *s* of James and Jane Harkness; *m* 1960, Elizabeth Anne Tolmie; one *s* one *d. Educ:* Univ. of Edinburgh (MA). Asst Minister, North Morningside Parish Church, Edinburgh, 1959–61; joined RAChD, 1961: Chaplain: 1 KOSB, 1961–65; 1 Queen's Own Highlanders, 1965–69; Singapore, 1969–70; Dep. Warden, RAChD Centre, 1970–74; Senior Chaplain: N Ireland, 1974–75; 4th Div., 1975–78; Asst Chaplain Gen., Scotland, 1980–81; Senior Chaplain: 1st British Corps, 1981–82; BAOR, 1982–84; Dep. Chaplain Gen. to the Forces, 1985–86. *Recreations:* general pursuits. *Address:* MoD Chaplains (Army), Bagshot Park, Bagshot, Surrey GU19 5PL. *T:* Bagshot 71717.

HARKNESS, Rear-Adm. James Percy Knowles, CB 1971; *b* 28 Nov. 1916; *s* of Captain P. Y. Harkness, West Yorkshire Regt, and Gladys Dundas Harkness (*née* Knowles); *m* 1949, Joan, *d* of late Vice-Adm. N. A. Sulivan, CVO; two *d.* Dir-Gen., Naval Manpower, 1970; retired 1972. *Recreation:* sailing.

HARKNESS, Captain Kenneth Lanyon, CBE 1963; DSC 1940; Royal Navy; *b* 24 Aug. 1900; *s* of late Major T. R. Harkness, RA, and late Mrs G. A. de Burgh; *m* 1st, 1932, Joan Phyllis Lovell (*d* 1979); one *d*; 2nd, 1979, Mary Isabel Powell (*née* Stroud), Brettenham, Suffolk. *Educ:* RN Colls, Osborne and Dartmouth; Cambridge Univ. Midshipman, HMS Bellerophon, 1917; Cambridge Univ., 1922; Qual. Gunnery, 1926; Comdr Admty, 1935; Sqdn Gunnery Off., 2nd Battle Sqdn, 1937; Comd HMS Winchelsea, 1938; Comd HMS Fearless, 1939–40; Capt. 1940; Chief of Intell. Service, Far East, 1940–42; Dep. Dir of Naval Ordnance, Admty, 1943–44; Comd HMS Ceylon, 1945; Comd HMS Sheffield, 1946; Chief of Staff to C-in-C Portsmouth, 1947; retired from RN, 1949. Civil Defence Officer, Portsmouth, 1949; Home Office, Asst Chief Trg Off. (CD), 1952; Prin. Off., later Reg. Dir of CD, London Reg., 1954; Temp. seconded as CD Adviser, Cyprus, 1956; later Regional Dir of Civil Defence, London Region, 1954–65. *Recreation:* gardening. *Address:* Far Rockaway, Durford Wood, Petersfield, Hants GU31 5AW. *T:* Liss 893173.

HARLAND, Bryce; *see* Harland, W. B.

HARLAND, Rt. Rev. Ian; *see* Lancaster, Bishop Suffragan of.

HARLAND, Air Marshal Sir Reginald (Edward Wynyard), KBE 1974; CB 1972; engineering and management consultant; *b* 30 May 1920; *s* of Charles Cecil Harland and Ida Maud (*née* Bellhouse); *m* 1942, Doreen Rosalind, *d* of late W. H. C. Romanis; two *s* two *d* (and one *s* decd). *Educ:* Summer Fields, Oxford; Stowe; Trinity Coll., Cambridge (MA). Served War of 1939–45: RAE Farnborough, 1941–42; N Africa, Italy and S France, 1942–45. Techn. trng, techn. plans and manning depts, Air Min., 1946–49; pilot trng, 1949–50; Chief Engrg Instructor, RAF Coll., Cranwell, 1950–52; Guided Weapon trng, RMCS Shrivenham, 1952–53; Thunderbird Project Officer: RAE Farnborough, 1953–55; Min. of Supply, 1955–56; psa 1957; Ballistic Missile Liaison Officer, (BJSM) Los Angeles, 1958–60; CO, Central Servicing Develt Estab., Swanton Morley, 1960–62; STSO, HQ No 3 (Bomber) Gp, Mildenhall, 1962–64; AO i/c Engrg, HQ Far East Air Force, Singapore, 1964–66; Harrier Project Dir, HQ Min. of Technology, 1967–68; idc 1969; AOC No 24 Group, RAF, 1970–72; AO Engineering, Air Support Command, 1972; AOC-in-C, RAF Support Command, 1973–77. Technical Dir, W. S. Atkins & Partners, 1977–82; Consultant to Short Brothers Ltd, 1983–. Member Council: BIM, 1973–78, 1980–; Assoc. of Project Managers, 1982–; Pres., Soc. Environmental Engrs, 1974–78; Vice-Chm., CEI, 1983–84. Contested (SDP) Bury St Edmunds, 1983. CEng 1966; FIMechE 1967; FIEE 1964; FRAeS 1967; CBIM (FBIM 1974); FIE (Singapore) 1967; MIE (Malaysia) 1966. *Publications:* occasional articles in engrg jls. *Recreations:* better management, better government. *Address:* 49 Crown Street, Bury St Edmunds, Suffolk IP33 1QX. *T:* Bury St Edmunds 63078. *Club:* Royal Air Force.

HARLAND, (William) Bryce; High Commissioner for New Zealand in the United Kingdom, since 1985; *b* 11 Dec. 1931; *s* of Edward Dugard Harland and Annie McDonald Harland (*née* Gordon); *m* 1st, 1957, Rosemary Anne Gordon (marr. diss. 1977); two *s* (and one *s* decd); 2nd, 1979, Margaret Anne Blackburn; one *s. Educ:* Victoria Univ., Wellington, NZ (MA Hons); Fletcher School of Law and Diplomacy, Boston, Mass, USA (AM). Joined NZ Dept of External Affairs, 1953; diplomatic postings: Singapore, 1956; Bangkok, 1957; NY, 1959; Wellington, 1962; Washington, 1965; Wellington, 1969; First NZ Ambassador to China, 1973–75; Ministry of Foreign Affairs, Wellington: Asst Sec., 1977–82; Head of African and European Divs, 1976–77; Perm. Rep. of NZ to the UN, NY, 1982–85 (Chm., Economic and Financial Cttee, Gen. Assembly, 1983). KStJ 1985. *Recreations:* reading history, walking. *Address:* 43 Chelsea Square, SW3 6LH. *T:* 01–930 8422. *Clubs:* Brooks's, East India, Royal Automobile.

HARLE, James Coffin, DPhil; Keeper, Department of Eastern Art, Ashmolean Museum, Oxford, since 1967; Student of Christ Church, Oxford, since 1970; *b* 5 April 1920; *s* of James Wyly Harle and Elfrieda Frances (*née* Baumann); *m* 1st, 1949, Jacqueline Thérèse Ruch (marr. diss. 1966, she *d* 1968); 2nd, 1967, Mrs Carola Sybil Mary Fleming (*d* 1971); 3rd, 1973, Lady (Betty) Hulbert. *Educ:* St George's Sch., Newport, RI; Princeton Univ. (BA 1942, Phi Beta Kappa); Oxford Univ. (BA 1st cl. Sanskrit and Pali, 1956, DPhil 1959). Served War, 1942–46, USNR (Aviation Br.), retd as Lieut; DFC (US). Asst to Dean of the College, Princeton, 1947; Part-time instructor in English, Princeton, 1948–49; Fulbright Lectr, Philippines, 1953–54; Ashmolean Museum: Asst Keeper, 1960; Sen. Asst Keeper, 1962. *Publications:* Tower Gateways in South India, 1963; Gupta Sculpture, 1974; articles in periodicals on Indian Art. *Address:* Hawkswell, Portland Road, Oxford. *T:* Oxford 55236. *Club:* Princeton (New York).

HARLECH, 6th Baron *cr* 1876; **Francis David Ormsby-Gore;** *b* 13 March 1954; *s* of 5th Baron Harlech, KCMG, PC, and Sylvia (*d* 1967), *d* of Hugh Lloyd Thomas, CMG, CVO; *S* father, 1985; *m* 1986, Amanda Jane Grieve. *Educ:* Worth. *Heir: uncle* Hon. John Julian Stafford Ormsby-Gore, *b* 12 April 1925. *Address:* The Mount, Racecourse Road, Oswestry, Shropshire SY10 7PH.

HARLEY, Prof. John Laker, CBE 1979; FRS 1964; FLS; FIBiol; MA, DPhil Oxon; Professor of Forest Science, Oxford University, 1969–79, now Emeritus Professor; Fellow of St John's College, Oxford, 1969–79, now Emeritus Fellow; *b* 17 Nov. 1911; *s* of late Charles Laker Harley and Edith Sarah (*née* Smith); *m* 1938, Elizabeth Lindsay Fitt; one *s* one *d. Educ:* Leeds Grammar Sch.; Wadham Coll., Oxford. Open Exhibition, Wadham Coll., 1930, Hon. Scholar 1933, Hon. Fellow, 1972; Christopher Welch Scholar, Oxford, 1933–37; Senior Student 1851 Exhibition, 1937–38. Departmental Demonstrator, Oxford, 1938–44. Served in Royal Signals, 1940–45: attached Operation Research Group No. 1, India, Lieut-Col GSO1. University Demonstrator, Oxford, 1945–62; Browne Research Fellow, Queen's Coll., Oxford, 1946–52; Official Fellow, Queen's Coll., Oxford, 1952–65; Reader in Plant Nutrition, Oxford Univ., 1962–65; Prof. of Botany, Sheffield Univ., 1965–69. Mem., ARC, 1970–80. President: British Mycological Soc., 1967 (Hon. Mem. 1980); British Ecological Soc., 1970–72 (Hon. Mem. 1983); Inst. of Biology, 1984–86. Hon. Fellow: Nat. Acad. of Scis, India, 1981; Wye Coll., 1983. Hon. FilDr Uppsala, 1981. Editor, New Phytologist, 1961–83. *Publications:* Biology of Mycorrhiza, 1969; (with S. E. Smith) Mycorrhizal Symbiosis, 1983; scientific papers in New Phytologist, Annals of Applied Mycology, Annals of Botany, Biochemical Jl, Plant Physiology, Proc. Royal Soc., Jl of Ecology. *Recreation:* gardening. *Address:* The Orchard, Old Marston, Oxford OX3 0PQ.

HARLEY, Sir Thomas (Winlack), Kt 1960; MBE 1944; MC 1918; DL; Consultant with Simpson North Harley & Co., solicitors, Liverpool and with Stanleys & Simpson North, London, admitted 1922; *b* 27 June 1895; *o s* of George Harley and Annie Thomson (*née* Macwatty); *m* 1924, Margaret Hilda (*d* 1981), 2nd *d* of late Canon J. U. N. Bardsley; three *s. Educ:* Birkenhead Sch.; Eton. Served European War, 1914–19, France and Balkans, Major The King's Own Regt (despatches, MC); War of 1939–45, Major RA (TA); comd (HG) AA Battery (MBE). Mem., Liverpool Regional Hosp. Bd, 1947– (Chm., 1959–68). Mem. Board of Governors, United Liverpool Hosps, 1955–69; Pres., Bebington and Ellesmere Port Conservative Assoc., etc. DL Cheshire (formerly County of Chester), 1962. *Recreation:* gardening. *Address:* Hesketh Hey, Thornton Hough, Wirral, Merseyside L63 1JA. *T:* 051–336 3439. *Clubs:* Royal Over-Seas League; Royal Liverpool Golf.

HARMAN, Sir Cecil W. F. S. K.; *see* Stafford-King-Harman.

HARMAN, Ernest Henry, CBE 1973 (OBE 1961); Chairman, South Western Gas Region (formerly South Western Gas Board), 1964–73; *b* 1908; *m* 2nd, 1958, Dorothy Anne Parsons; (two *d* by 1st *m*). *Educ:* London Univ. BSc (Hons). Sec., 1936, Gen. Manager, 1944, Commercial Gas Co.; Gen. Manager, Sheffield and Rotherham Div., East Midlands Gas Board, 1949; Dep. Chm., East Midlands Gas Board, 1952. *Recreations:* tennis, motoring, music. *Address:* Tall Trees, Court Hill, Church Lench, Evesham, Worcs WR11 4UH.

HARMAN, Harriet; MP (Lab) Peckham, since Oct. 1982; *b* 30 July 1950; *d* of John Bishop Harman, *qv* and Anna Charlotte Harman; *m* 1982, Jack Dromey; two *s. Educ:* St Paul's Girls' Sch.; York Univ. Brent Community Law Centre, 1975–78; Legal Officer, NCCL, 1978–82. *Publications:* Sex Discrimination in Schools, 1977; Justice Deserted: the subversion of the jury, 1979. *Address:* House of Commons, SW1A 0AA.

HARMAN, Gen. Sir Jack (Wentworth), GCB 1978 (KCB 1974); OBE 1962; MC 1943; Deputy Supreme Allied Commander, Europe, 1978–81, retired; *b* 20 July 1920; *s* of late Lt-Gen. Sir Wentworth Harman, KCB, DSO, and late Dorothy Harman; *m* 1947, Gwladys May Murphy (*widow* of Lt-Col R. J. Murphy), *d* of Sir Idwal Lloyd; one *d* and two step *d. Educ:* Wellington Coll.; RMC Sandhurst. Commissioned into The Queen's Bays, 1940, Bt Lt-Col, 1958; Commanding Officer, 1st The Queen's Dragoon Guards, 1960–62; commanded 11 Infantry Bde, 1965–66; attended IDC, 1967; BGS, HQ Army Strategic Command, 1968–69; GOC, 1st Div., 1970–72; Commandant, RMA, Sandhurst, 1972–73; GOC 1 (British) Corps, 1974–76; Adjutant-General, 1976–78. ADC Gen. to the Queen, 1977–80. Col, 1st The Queen's Dragoon Guards, 1975–80; Col Comdt, RAC, 1977–80. Dir, Wilsons (Insurance Brokers), 1982–. Vice-Chm., Nat. Army Museum,

1980–; Mem. Cttee, AA, 1981–. *Address:* Sandhills House, Dinton, near Salisbury, Wilts. *T:* Teffont 288. *Club:* Cavalry and Guards.

HARMAN, Hon. Sir Jeremiah (LeRoy), Kt 1982; **Hon. Mr Justice Harman;** a Judge of the High Court of Justice, Chancery Division, since 1982; *b* 13 April 1930; *er s* of late Rt Hon. Sir Charles Eustace Harman; *m* 1960, Erica Jane, *e d* of late Hon. Sir Maurice Richard Bridgeman, KBE; two *s* one *d. Educ:* Horris Hill Sch.; Eton Coll. Served Coldstream Guards and Parachute Regt, 1948–51; Parachute Regt (TA), 1951–55. Called to the Bar, Lincoln's Inn, 1954, Bencher, 1977; QC 1968; called to Hong Kong Bar, 1978, Singapore Bar, 1980; Mem., Bar Council, 1963–67. Dir, Dunford & Elliott Ltd, 1972–79. *Recreations:* fishing, shooting, stalking, watching birds. *Address:* Royal Courts of Justice, The Strand, WC2A 2LL.

HARMAN, John Bishop, FRCS, FRCP; Honorary Consulting Physician, since 1972; *b* 10 Aug. 1907; *s* of late Nathaniel Bishop Harman and of Katharine (*née* Chamberlain); *m* 1946, Anna Charlotte Malcolm Spicer; four *d. Educ:* Oundle; St John's Coll., Cambridge (Scholar); St Thomas's Hospital (Scholar). Fearnsides Scholar, Cantab, 1932; 1st Cl. Nat. Sci. Tripos Pt I, 2nd Cl. Pt II, Cantab; MA 1933; MD 1937; FRCS 1932; FRCP 1942. Physician: St Thomas' Hospital, 1938–72; Royal Marsden Hospital, 1947–72. Pres., Medical Defence Union, 1976–; 2nd Vice Pres., RCP, 1981–82. Late Lt-Col RAMC (despatches). *Publications:* contribs to medical literature. *Recreation:* horticulture. *Address:* 108 Harley Street, W1. *T:* 01–935 7822.
See also H. Harman.

HARMAN, Robert Donald, QC 1974; a Recorder of the Crown Court, since 1972; *b* 26 Sept. 1928; *o s* of late Herbert Donald Harman, MC; *m* 1st, 1960, Sarah Elizabeth (*d* 1965), *o d* of late G. C. Cleverly; two *s*; 2nd, 1968, Rosamond Geraldine, JP, 2nd *d* of late Cmdr G. T. A. Scott, RN; two *d. Educ:* privately; St Paul's Sch.; Magdalen Coll., Oxford. Called to Bar, Gray's Inn, 1954, Bencher, 1984; South-Eastern Circuit; a Junior Prosecuting Counsel to the Crown at Central Criminal Court, 1967–72; a Senior Treasury Counsel, 1972–74. Mem., Senate of the Inns of Court and the Bar, 1985–. Jt Hon. Sec., Barristers' Benevolent Assoc. Appeal Steward, BBB of C. Liveryman, Goldsmiths' Co. *Address:* 2 Harcourt Buildings, Temple, EC4. *T:* 01–353 2112; 17 Pelham Crescent, SW7 2NR. *T:* 01–584 4304. *Clubs:* Garrick, Beefsteak, Pratt's; Swinley Forest Golf.

HARMAR-NICHOLLS, family name of **Baron Harmar-Nicholls.**

HARMAR-NICHOLLS, Baron *cr* 1974 (Life Peer), of Peterborough, Cambs; **Harmar Harmar-Nicholls,** JP; Bt 1960; Member (C) Greater Manchester South, European Parliament, 1979–84; *b* 1 Nov. 1912; 3rd *s* of Charles E. C. Nicholls and Sarah Anne Nicholls, Walsall; *m* 1940, Dorothy Elsie, *e d* of James Edwards, Tipton; two *d. Educ:* Dorsett Road Sch., Darlaston; Queen Mary's Gram. Sch., Walsall. Mem. Middle Temple Inn of Court. Chairman: Nicholls and Hennessy (Hotels) Ltd; Malvern Festival Theatre Trust Ltd; Radio Luxembourg (London) Ltd, 1983– (Dir, 1963–); Dir, J. & H. Nicholls & Co., Paints, etc, 1945–. Mem. of Syndicate at Lloyd's. Mem. Darlaston UDC at age of 26 (Chm., 1949–50); County Magistrate, 1946. Vice-Chm. W Midland Fedn, Junior Imperial League, 1937; contested (C): Nelson and Colne, 1945; Preston by-election, 1946; MP (C) Peterborough Div. of Northants, 1950–Sept. 1974; PPS to Asst Postmaster-Gen., 1951–April 1955; Parly Sec., Min. of Agriculture, Fisheries and Food, April 1955–Jan. 1957; Parliamentary Sec., Min. of Works, 1957–60; Mem. Conservative Housing Cttee; Sec. of Parly Road Safety Cttee (Conservative); Jt Sec. All party Parly Group Empire Migration; Mem. Govt Overseas Settlement Board on migration to Commonwealth. War of 1939–45: volunteered as sapper, commnd Royal Engineers; served India and Burma. *Recreations:* gardening, reading, walking, theatre. *Address:* Abbeylands, Weston, Stafford. *T:* Weston 252. *Clubs:* St Stephen's Constitutional; (Pres.) Unionist, City and Counties (Peterborough); Conservative (Darlaston); Unionist (Walsall).

HARMER, Sir Dudley; *see* Harmer, Sir J. D.

HARMER, Sir Frederic (Evelyn), Kt 1968; CMG 1945; *b* 3 Nov. 1905; *yr s* of late Sir Sidney Frederic Harmer, KBE, FRS; *m* 1st, 1931, Barbara Susan (*d* 1972), *er d* of late Major J. A. C. Hamilton, JP, Fyne Court, Bridgwater, Som.; one *s* two *d* (and one *d* decd); 2nd, 1973, Daphne Shelton Agar. *Educ:* Eton (KS); King's Coll., Cambridge (Scholar). Wrangler, Maths Tripos Part II, 1926; Class 1, Div. 1, Econs Tripos Part II 1927; BA 1927; MA 1934. Entered Treasury, Sept. 1939; Temp. Asst Sec., 1943–45; served in Washington, March-June 1944 and again in Sept.-Dec. 1945 for Anglo-American economic and financial negotiations; resigned Dec. 1945 and joined New Zealand Shipping Co. (Chm., 1953–65). Dep. Chm., P&OSN Co., 1957–70. Chairman: Cttee of European Shipowners, 1965–68; Internat. Chamber of Shipping, 1968–71; HM Govt Dir, British Petroleum Co. Ltd, 1953–70. Hon. Fellow, LSE, 1970. *Recreations:* sailing, golf. *Address:* Tiggins Field, Kelsale, Saxmundham, Suffolk. *T:* Saxmundham 3156.

HARMER, Sir (John) Dudley, Kt 1972; OBE 1963; JP; company director; *b* 27 July 1913; *s* of Ernest George William Harmer and Germaine Stuart Harmer (*née* Wells); *m* 1947, Erika Minder-Lanz, Switzerland; two *s. Educ:* Merchant Taylors' Sch.; Wye College. Certif. Agriculture. Mem. 1956, Dep. Chm. 1964–72, Kent Agric. Exec. Cttee; Mem., Kent CC Agric. and Smallholdings Cttee, 1958 (Chm. of Selection of Tenants and Loans Sub-Cttee); Vice-Chm. 1964–66, Chm. 1966–71, SE Area Conservative Provincial Council; Pres., Kent East Euro Cons. Council, 1983–. Service connected with Home Guard, 1952–56: Hon. Major 1956. Trustee, Develt and Endowment Fund of Kent Inc. Soc. for Promoting Experiments in Horticulture, 1979–. JP Kent, 1962. *Recreations:* gardening, travel. *Address:* Stone Hill, Egerton, Ashford, Kent. *T:* Egerton 241. *Club:* Royal Commonwealth Society.

HARMER, Michael Hedley, MA, MB Cantab, FRCS; Consulting Surgeon, Royal Marsden Hospital and Paddington Green Children's Hospital (St Mary's Hospital); *b* 6 July 1912; *y s* of late Douglas Harmer, MC, FRCS, and May (*née* Hedley); *m* 1939, Bridget Jean, *d* of late James Higgs-Walker, MA, and of Muriel Jessie, *e d* of Rev. Harold Smith; one *s* one *d. Educ:* Marlborough; King's Coll., Cambridge; St Bartholomew's Hosp., London. Surgical Specialist, RAFVR, 1943–46. Bellman Snark Club, Cambridge, 1934–. Freeman of Norwich by Patrimony, 1935. *Publications:* A Handbook of Surgery, 1951; Aids to Surgery, 1962; (Jt Editor) Rose and Carless's Manual of Surgery, 19th edn, 1959; The Forgotten Hospital, 1982; papers on the surgery and classification of malignant disease. *Recreations:* music, the country. *Address:* Perrot Wood, Graffham, Petworth, Sussex GU28 0NZ. *T:* Graffham 307.

HARMOOD-BANNER, Sir George Knowles, 3rd Bt, *cr* 1924; *b* 9 Nov. 1918; *s* of Sir Harmood Harmood-Banner, 2nd Bt, and Frances Cordelia (*d* 1975), *d* of late George Duberly, JP, Plansworth, Co. Durham; *S* father 1950; *m* 1947, Rosemary Jane, *d* of Col M. L. Treston, CBE, FRCS, FRCOG, late IMS, and late Mrs Sheila Treston; two *d. Educ:* Eton; University of Cambridge. Served War of 1939–45; 2nd Lieut Royal Welch Fusiliers, 1942, attached to East African Engineers (SEAC); transferred RASC, 1945. *Recreations:* tennis, ski-ing and swimming. *Heir:* none. *Address:* c/o The Bank of Nova Scotia, 62–63 Threadneedle Street, EC2P 2LS.

HARMSWORTH, family name of **Viscount Rothermere** and **Baron Harmsworth.**

HARMSWORTH, 2nd Baron, *cr* 1939, of Egham; **Cecil Desmond Bernard Harmsworth;** painter; *b* 1903; *e s* of 1st Baron Harmsworth and Emilie Alberta (*d* 1942), *d* of William Hamilton Maffett, Finglas, Co. Dublin; *S* father, 1948; *m* 1926, Dorothy Alexander, *d* of late Hon. J. C. Heinlein, Bridgeport, Ohio, USA; one *d. Educ:* Eton Coll.; Christ Church, Oxford (MA); (in drawing) Académie Julian, Paris; (in painting) public galleries. Was successively newspaperman and book publisher before becoming a painter. Exhibitions: Galerie des Quatre-Chemins, Paris, 1933; Wildenstein Gall., London, 1938; Bonestell Gall., New York, 1944; Swedish Modern, Dallas, Texas, 1950; Messrs Roland, Browse & Delbanco, London, 1954. Has been regular contributor to Salon d'Automne and group exhibitions in Paris; has exhibited in many London and New York galleries, and at the Phillips Memorial Gallery, Washington, DC. Portraits of Norman Douglas, Havelock Ellis, Lord Inverchapel, James Joyce, Consuelo de Saint-Exupéry, Sir Osbert Sitwell, Swami Nikhilananda, etc. Chairman, Dr Johnson's House Trust. Served in British Information Services, New York, 1940–46. *Publications:* occasional prose and verse contributions to English, Irish, and US periodicals, inc. verse translation of Paul Valéry, Le Cimetière Marin (Adam Internat. Review nos 334–336, 1969); drawings and paintings reproduced in US magazines. *Heir:* *b* Hon. Eric Beauchamp Northcliffe Harmsworth [*b* 28 Aug. 1905; *m* 1935, Hélène (*d* 1962), *d* of Col Jules-Raymond Dehove, Paris; one *s* one *d*; *m* 1964, Mrs Helen Hudson, London. *Educ:* Eton Coll.; Christ Church, Oxford (MA)]. *Address:* Lime Lodge, Egham, Surrey. *T:* Egham 2379.

HARMSWORTH, Sir Hildebrand Harold, 3rd Bt *cr* 1922; *b* 5 June 1931; *s* of Sir Hildebrand Alfred Beresford Harmsworth, 2nd Bt, and Elen, *d* of Nicolaj Billenstein, Randers, Denmark; *S* father, 1977; *m* 1960, Gillian Andrea, *o d* of William John Lewis; one *s* two *d. Educ:* Harrow; Trinity College, Dublin. *Heir:* *s* Hildebrand Esmond Miles Harmsworth, *b* 1 Sept. 1964. *Address:* Ewlyn Villa, 42 Leckhampton Road, Cheltenham.

HARMSWORTH, St John Bernard Vyvyan; a Metropolitan Magistrate, 1961–85; *b* 28 Nov. 1912; *e s* of Vyvyan George Harmsworth and Constance Gwendolen Mary Catt; *m* 1937, Jane Penelope (*d* 1984), *er d* of Basil Tanfield Berridge Boothby; three *d. Educ:* Harrow; New Coll., Oxford. Called to the Bar, Middle Temple, 1937. Served in RNVR, Lieut-Comdr, Oct. 1939–Feb. 1946. *Recreations:* fly fishing, tennis. *Address:* 25 Whitelands House, SW3. *Clubs:* Boodle's, Pratt's, Beefsteak.

HARNDEN, Lt-Col Arthur Baker, CB 1969; BSc, CEng, FIEE, FBIM; Chairman, Appeals Tribunals, Supplementary Benefits Commission, 1970–82; *b* 6 Jan. 1909; *s* of Cecil Henry Harnden and Susan (*née* Baker); *m* 1st, 1935, Maisie Elizabeth Annie (*d* 1970), *d* of A. H. Winterburn, LRIBA; one *s*; 2nd, 1971, Jean Kathleen, *d* of H. F. Wheeler and *widow* of Eric J. Dedman; one step *s. Educ:* various state schools. Exec. Engr, GPO, 1933; Royal Corps of Signals, 1939–45; GSO1, WO, 1942; DCSO Antwerp, 1944, Hamburg 1945. Dir, London Telecommunications Region, GPO, 1962; Senior Dir, Operations, PO (Telecommunications), 1967–69. Principal, Comrie House Sch., Finchley, 1971–72. *Recreations:* painting and potting. *Address:* Comrie, Park Street, Fairford, Glos GL7 4JL. *T:* Cirencester 712805.

HARNDEN, Prof. David Gilbert, PhD, FRSE 1982, FIBiol, FRCPath; Director, Paterson Laboratories, Christie Hospital and Holt Radium Institute, since 1983; *b* 22 June 1932; *s* of William Alfred Harnden and Anne McKenzie Wilson; *m* 1955, Thora Margaret Seatter; three *s. Educ:* George Heriot's School, Edinburgh; University of Edinburgh. BSc. Lectr, Univ. of Edinburgh, 1956–57; Sci. Mem., Radiobiology Unit, MRC, Harwell, 1957–59; Sci. Mem., Clinical and Population Cytogenetics Unit, MRC, Edinburgh, 1959–69; Prof. of Cancer Studies, Univ. of Birmingham, 1969–83; Hon. Prof. of Experimental Oncology, Univ. of Manchester, 1983–. *Publications:* papers on cancer research and human genetics in learned jls. *Recreation:* sketching people and places. *Address:* Tanglewood, Ladybrook Road, Bramhall, Stockport, Cheshire SK7 3NE. *T:* 061–485 3214.

HARNIMAN, John Phillip, OBE 1984; British Council Representative in Belgium, since 1984; *b* 7 May 1939; *s* of William Thomas Harniman and Maud Kate Florence (*née* Dyrenfurth); *m* 1961, Avryl (*née* Hartley); one *s* one *d. Educ:* Leyton County High School; Culham College, Oxon (DipEd); London University (BA Hons); Université de la Sorbonne. William Morris School, Walthamstow, 1960–62; Ecole Normale Supérieure de Saint-Cloud, 1962–67; British Council: Algeria, 1967–70; Specialist Careers Officer, Personnel, 1970–73; Head, Overseas Careers, Personnel, 1973–76; Representative, Singapore, 1976–81; Cultural Attaché, Romania, 1981–84. *Recreations:* reading, listening to English classical and church music, letter-writing, cats. *Address:* Riverway, Mill Lane, Cookham-on-Thames, Berks; 76/77 High Street, Lavenham, Suffolk. *Clubs:* Anglo-Belgian; Cricket (Singapore).

HARPER, Alfred Alexander, MA, MD; Professor of Physiology, University of Newcastle upon Tyne, 1963–72; *b* 19 June 1907; *er s* of James and Elizabeth Harper. *Educ:* Aberdeen Grammar Sch.; Aberdeen Univ. Lecturer in Physiology, University of Leeds, 1935–36; Demonstrator in Physiology, St Thomas's Hosp., London, 1936–39; Lectr, later Reader, in Human Physiology, Univ. of Manchester, 1939–49; Prof. of Physiology, Univ. of Durham, 1949–63. *Publications:* papers in Jl of Physiology mostly on physiology of digestion. *Address:* Wellburn House, Benwell Lane, Newcastle upon Tyne NE15 6LX. *T:* Tyneside 2748178.

HARPER, Prof. Denis Rawnsley, CBE 1975; BArch, PhD, MSc Tech, FRIBA, MRTPI, PPIOB; building consultant; Professor of Building at the University of Manchester Institute of Science and Technology, 1957–74, now Emeritus; *b* 27 May 1907; *s* of James William Harper, Harrogate; *m* 1st, 1934, Joan Mary Coggin (*d* 1968); one *s* one *d*; 2nd, 1971, Dora Phylis Oxenham (widow). *Educ:* Harrogate Grammar Sch.; Univ. of Liverpool Sch. of Architecture. Asst Architect in Hosp. practice in London, 1930–38; RIBA Saxon Snell Prizeman, 1939; Lectr in Sch. of Architecture, University of Cape Town, 1939–49. In private practice (with Prof. Thornton White), in Cape Town, as architect and town planner, 1940–50; Associate Architect in BBC TV Centre, 1950–52; Chief Architect to Corby New Town, Northants, 1952–57. Hanson Fellow, The Master Builder Fedn of South Africa, 1972. Cttee Mem., CNAA. Mem., Summerland Fire Commn, 1973–74. *Publications:* Building: process and product, 1978; various contribs to technical jls. *Recreations:* gardening, boating. *Address:* 2 Glenfield Drive, Great Doddington, Wellingborough, Northants NN9 7TE. *T:* Wellingborough 223841.

HARPER, Donald John; Aerospace Systems and Defence Procurement consultant; *b* 6 Aug. 1923; *s* of Harry Tonkin and Caroline Irene Harper; *m* 1947, Joyce Beryl Kite-Powell; two *d. Educ:* Purley County Grammar Sch. for Boys; Queen Mary Coll., London. 1st cl. BSc (Eng) 1943; CEng, FRAeS. Joined Aero Dept, RAE Farnborough, 1943; Scientific Officer, Spinning Tunnel, 1947–49; High Speed and Transonic Tunnel, 1950–59; Sen. Scientific Officer; Principal Scientific Officer, 1955; Dep. Head of Tunnel, 1958–59; Space Dept RAE, Satellite Launching Vehicles, 1960–62; Senior Principal Scientific Officer, MoD, Central Staff, 1963–65; Head of Assessment Div., Weapons Dept RAE, 1966–68; Dir of Project Time and Cost Analysis, MoD (PE), 1968–71; Dir-Gen.,

Performance and Cost Analysis, MoD (PE), 1972–77; Dir-Gen. Research C, MoD (PE), 1978–83, and Chief Scientist, RAF, 1980–83. *Publications:* contrib. Aeronautical Res. Council reports and memoranda and techn. press. *Recreations:* music, especially choral singing; gardening; home improvement. *Address:* Beech Cottage, Beech Gardens, Woking, Surrey. *T:* Woking 60541.

HARPER, Heather (Mary), (Mrs E. J. Benarroch), CBE 1965; soprano; Director of Singing Studies, Britten-Pears School, Aldeburgh, since 1986; *b* 8 May 1930; *d* of late Hugh Harper, Belfast; *m* 1973, Eduardo J. Benarroch. *Educ:* Trinity Coll. of Music, London. Has sung many principal roles incl. Arabella, Ariadne, Marschallin, Chrysothemis, Elsa and Kaiserin, at Covent Garden, Glyndebourne, Sadler's Wells, Bayreuth, Teatro Colon (Buenos Aires), Edinburgh Fest., La Scala, NY Met, San Francisco, Deutsche Oper (Berlin), Frankfurt, Netherlands Opera, Canadian Opera Co., Toronto, and has sung at every Promenade Concert season since 1957; created the soprano role in Benjamin Britten's War Requiem in Coventry Cathedral in 1962; soloist at opening concerts: Maltings, Snape, 1967; Queen Elizabeth Hall, 1967. Toured USA, 1965, and USSR, 1967, with BBC SO; has toured USA annually, 1967–, and appears regularly at European music fests; toured: Japan and S Korea as Principal Soloist Soprano with Royal Opera Co., 1979; Australia and Hong Kong with BBC Symph. Orch., 1982; has also sung in Asia, Middle East, Australia and S America; Principal Soloist Soprano with Royal Opera House Co., visit to Los Angeles Olympic Games, 1984. Has made many recordings, incl. works of Britten, Beethoven, Berg, Mahler, Mozart and Verdi; broadcasts frequently throughout the world, and appears frequently on TV; Masterclasses for advanced students and young professionals, Britten-Pears Sch.; retired from operatic stage, 1984. FTCL; Hon. RAM, 1972. Hon. DMus, Queen's Univ., Belfast, 1966. Edison Award, 1971; Grammy Nomination, 1973; Grammy Award, 1979, 1984, Best vocal performance for Ravel's Scheherezade. *Recreations:* gardening, painting, cooking. *Address:* c/o 20 Milverton Road, NW6 7AS.

HARPER, James Norman; barrister; a Recorder of the Crown Court, 1980–84; *b* 30 Dec. 1932; *s* of late His Honour Judge Norman Harper and of Iris Irene Harper; *m* 1956, Blanka Miroslava Eva Sigmund; one *s* one *d. Educ:* Marlborough Coll.; Magdalen Coll., Oxford (BA Hons). Called to the Bar, Gray's Inn, 1957. Pres., Northumberland County Hockey Assoc., 1982–. *Recreations:* cricket, hockey, painting. *Address:* 51 Westgate Road, Newcastle upon Tyne NE1 1SS. *T:* Tyneside 2320541. *Club:* MCC.

HARPER, Prof. John Lander, DPhil; FRS 1978; Head, Unit of Plant Population Biology, School of Plant Biology, Bangor, since 1982; *b* 27 May 1925; *s* of John Hindley Harper and Harriett Mary (*née* Archer); *m* 1954, Borgny Lerø; one *s* two *d. Educ:* Lawrence Sheriff Sch., Rugby; Magdalen Coll., Oxford (BA, MA, DPhil). Demonstr, Dept of Agriculture, Univ. of Oxford, 1951, Lectr 1953; Rockefeller Foundn Fellow, Univ. of Calif, 1960–61; Prof. of Agricultural Botany, 1960, Prof. of Botany, 1977–82 and Head of Sch. of Plant Biology, 1967–82, University Coll. of North Wales, Bangor; now Emeritus Professor. For. Assoc., US Nat. Acad. of Sciences, 1984. Hon. DSc Sussex, 1984. *Publications:* Biology of Weeds, 1960; Population Biology of Plants, 1977; (with M. Begon and C. Townsend) Ecology: organism, population and communities, 1985; papers in Jl of Ecol., New Phytologist, Annals of Applied Biol., and Evolution. *Recreation:* gardening. *Address:* Cae Groes, Glan y Coed Park, Dwygyfylchi, near Penmaenmawr, N Wales. *T:* Penmaenmawr 622362. *Club:* Farmers'.

HARPER, John Mansfield; Special Advisor to the Board, NEC Business Systems (Europe) Ltd, since 1985; *b* 17 July 1930; *s* of late T. J. Harper and May (*née* Charlton); *m* 1956, Berenice Honorine, *d* of Harold Haydon; one *s* one *d. Educ:* Merchant Taylors' Sch.; St John's Coll., Oxford. 2nd Lieut Royal Corps of Signals, 1948–49. Asst Principal, Post Office, 1953; Private Sec. to Dir-Gen., 1956–58; Principal, 1958–66; Asst Sec., Reorganization Dept, 1966–69; Dir, North-Eastern Telecommunications Region, 1969–71; Dir, Purchasing and Supply, 1972–75; Sen. Dir, Planning and Provisioning, 1975–77; Asst Man. Dir, Telecommunications, 1978–79; Dep. Man. Dir, British Telecommunications (Post Office), 1979–81; Man. Dir, Inland Division, BT, 1981–83, retired. Comp IEE; CBIM; FRSA. *Publication:* Telecommunications and Computing: the uncompleted revolution, 1986. *Recreations:* music, gardening, electronics. *Address:* 34 Longfield Drive, Amersham, Bucks. *T:* Amersham 5443.

HARPER, William Ronald; Managing Director, Thames Water Authority, since 1986; *b* 5 June 1944; *s* of William and Dorothy Harper; *m* 1969, Susan Penelope (*née* Rider); two *d. Educ:* Barton Peveril Grammar Sch., Eastleigh, Hants. IPFA 1965. Hampshire CC, 1960–64; Eastbourne CBC, 1964–68; Chartered Inst. of Public Finance and Accountancy, 1968–70; Greenwich London BC, 1970–74; Thames Water Authority: joined 1974; Dir of Finance, 1982; Dir of Corporate Strategy, 1984. *Address:* Nugent House, Vastern Road, Reading, Berks RG1 8DB. *T:* Reading 593536.

HARPER GOW, Sir (Leonard) Maxwell, Kt 1985; MBE 1944; CBIM; Vice-Chairman, since 1981, and Director, since 1952, Christian Salvesen PLC (Chairman, 1964–81); *b* 13 June 1918; *s* of late Leonard Harper Gow and Eleanor Amalie (*née* Salvesen); *m* 1944, Lillan Margaret Kiaer; two *s* one *d. Educ:* Cargilfield; Rugby; Corpus Christi Coll., Cambridge Univ. (BA). CBIM (FBIM 1976). Served War, 1939–46: Major RA 1st Commando Bde. 3 seasons with Antarctic Whaling Fleet, 1946–47, 1948–49 and 1952–53. Director: Royal Bank of Scotland plc, 1965–87; Royal Bank of Scotland Group plc, 1978–87; DFM Holdings Ltd, 1985– (Chm.); Radio Forth Ltd, 1973– (Chm.). Mem. Council, Inst. of Directors, 1983–; Vice-Pres., Scottish Council of Develt and Industry, 1985–; Pres., Economic League (Scotland area), 1985–; Lloyd's Underwriter. Member, Queen's Body Guard for Scotland, the Royal Co. of Archers. Liveryman, Royal Co. of Shipwrights. Pres., Norwegian-Scottish Assoc., Edinburgh; Hon. Consul for Norway in Edinburgh/Leith. Comdr, Order of St Olav, Norway. *Recreations:* hill farming, shooting, fishing. *Address:* Eventyr, Lyars Road, Longniddry, East Lothian. *T:* Longniddry 52142. *Clubs:* Caledonian; New (Edinburgh).

HARPHAM, Sir William, KBE 1966 (OBE 1948); CMG 1953; HM Diplomatic Service, retired; Director, Great Britain-East Europe Centre, 1967–80; *b* 3 Dec. 1906; *o s* of W. Harpham and N. Harpham (*née* Stout); *m* 1943, Isabelle Marie Sophie Droz; one *s* one *d. Educ:* Wintringham Secondary Sch., Grimsby; Christ's Coll., Cambridge. Entered Dept of Overseas Trade, 1929; transferred to Embassy, Brussels, 1931, Rome, 1934; Private Sec. to Parliamentary Sec. for Overseas Trade, 1936; seconded to League of Nations, 1937; reverted to Dept of Overseas Trade, 1939; served: Cairo, 1940–44; Beirut, 1944–47; appointed Counsellor (Commercial) at Berne, 1947; Head of Gen. Dept, Foreign Office, 1950–53; Dep. to UK Delegate to OEEC, 1953–56; Minister, British Embassy, Tokyo, 1956–59; Minister (Economic), Paris, 1959–63; Ambassador to Bulgaria, 1964–66; retd 1967. Order of Madara Horseman, Bulgaria, 1969; Order of Stara Planina, Bulgaria, 1976. *Address:* 9 Kings Keep, Putney Hill, SW15 6RA. *T:* 01–788 1383. *Club:* Royal Automobile.

HARPLEY, Sydney Charles, RA 1981 (ARA 1974); sculptor since 1956; *b* 19 April 1927; *s* of Sydney Frederick Harpley, electrical engr and cabinet maker, and Rose Isabel Harpley, milliner; *m* 1956, Sally Holliday (marr. diss. 1968), illustrator; two *s* one *d. Educ:* Royal Coll. of Art. ARCA 1956. Realist sculptor, portraits and figure; commnd Smuts Memorial, Cape Town, 1963; sculpture in collections of Nat. Gallery, NZ; Nat. Gallery, Cape Town; Paul Mellon, USA; Anton Rupert, SA; Princess Grace of Monaco; Fleur Cowles Meyer, London; S. & D. Josefowitz, Geneva; Lady Verulam; Lord Jersey; Portraits: Edward Heath for Constitutional Club, 1973; Lee Kwan Yew, Singapore, 1983. Visitors' Choice Prize, RA Summer Exhibition, 1978, 1979. *Recreations:* chess, music. *Address:* Mill House, Chapel Lane, Clipston, Market Harborough, Leics. *T:* Market Harborough 86402.

HARRER, Prof. Heinrich; author and explorer; (awarded title of Professor by President of Austrian Republic, 1964); *b* Hüttenberg, 6 July 1912; *m*; one *s*; *m* 1953, Margaretha Truxa (marr. diss. 1958); *m* 1962, Katharina Haarhaus. *Educ:* University of Graz, Austria (graduated in Geography, 1938). First ascent, Eiger North Wall, 1938; Himalayan Expedition, 1939; interned in India, 1939–44; Tibet, 1944–51; Himalayan Expedition, 1951; expeditions: to the Andes, 1953; to Alaska, 1954; to Ruwenzori (Mountains of the Moon), Africa, 1957; to West New Guinea, 1961–62; to Nepal, 1965; to Xingu Red Indians in Mato Grosso, Brazil; to Bush Negroes of Surinam (Surinam Expedn with King Leopold of Belgium), 1966; to the Sudan, 1970; to North Borneo (Sabah) (with King Leopold of Belgium), 1971; N-S crossing of Borneo, 1972; Valley of Flowers (Alaknanda), 1974; Andaman Islands, 1975; Zangkar-Ladakh, 1976. 35 short films on expeditions; Prize for best documentary book, Donanland, 1982; 70th birthday Orders from Germany, Austria, Carinthia, Styria, 1982; Golden medal, Humboldt Soc., 1985. Hon. Citizen, Hüttenberg, 1983. Austrian National Amateur Golf Champion, 1958; Austrian National Seniors Golf Champion, 1970. Pres., Austrian Golf Association, 1964. *Publications:* Seven Years in Tibet, 1953 (Great Britain, and numerous other countries); Meine Tibet-Bilder, 1953 (Germany); The White Spider, History of the North Face of the Eiger, 1958; Tibet is My Country: Biography of Thubten Jigme Norbu, *e b* of Dalai Lama, 1960 (Eng.); I Come from the Stone Age, 1964 (London); The Last 500, 1975; The Last Caravan, 1976; Return to Tibet, 1984. *Address:* Neudorf 577, 9493–Mauren, Liechtenstein.

HARRIES, Rev. Richard Douglas; Dean, King's College, London, since 1981; *b* 2 June 1936; *s* of Brig. W. D. J. Harries, CBE and Mrs G. M. B. Harries; *m* 1963, Josephine Bottomley, MA, MB, BChir, DCH; one *s* one *d. Educ:* Wellington Coll.; RMA, Sandhurst; Selwyn Coll., Cambridge (MA 1965); Cuddesdon Coll., Oxford. Lieut, Royal Corps of Signals, 1955–58. Curate, Hampstead Parish Church, 1963–69; Chaplain, Westfield Coll., 1966–69; Lectr, Wells Theol Coll., 1969–72; Warden of Wells, Salisbury and Wells Theol Coll., 1971–72; Vicar, All Saints, Fulham, 1972–81. GOE examnr in Christian Ethics, 1972–76; Dir, Post Ordination Trng for Kensington Jurisdiction, 1973–79. Vice-Chairman: Council of Christian Action, 1979–; Council for Arms Control, 1982–; Mem., Home Office Adv. Cttee for reform of law on sexual offences, 1981–85; Chairman: Southwark Ordination Course; Shalom; ELSTA (End Loans to Southern Africa). Radio and TV work. Lectures: Hockerill, 1982; Drawbridge, 1982. FKC 1983. *Publications:* Prayers of Hope, 1975; Turning to Prayer, 1978; Prayers of Grief and Glory, 1979; Being a Christian, 1981; Should Christians Support Guerrillas?, 1982; The Authority of Divine Love, 1983; Praying Round the Clock, 1983; (ed with K. Ware and G. Every) Seasons of the Spirit, 1984; Prayer and the Pursuit of Happiness, 1985; (ed) Reinhold Niebuhr and the Issues of Our Time, 1986; contributed to: Teaching Christian Ethics, 1974; Stewards of the Mysteries of God, 1979; What Hope in an Armed World?, 1982; Unholy Warfare, 1983; The Cross and the Bomb, 1983; Dropping the Bomb, 1985; Julian Woman of our Day, 1985; If Christ be not Risen, 1986; articles in Theology, The Times, The Observer and various other periodicals. *Recreations:* theatre, literature, sport. *Address:* King's College, The Strand, WC2 2LS. *T:* 01–836 5454.

HARRINGTON, 11th Earl of, *cr* 1742; **William Henry Leicester Stanhope;** Viscount Stanhope of Mahon and Baron Stanhope of Elvaston, Co. Derby, 1717; Baron Harrington, 1729; Viscount Petersham, 1742; late Captain 15th/19th Hussars; *b* 24 Aug. 1922; *o s* of 10th Earl and Margaret Trelawney (Susan) (*d* 1952), *d* of Major H. H. D. Seaton; *S* father, 1929; *m* 1st, 1942, Eileen (from whom he obtained a divorce, 1946), *o d* of late Sir John Grey, Enville Hall, Stourbridge; one *s* one *d* (and one *d* decd); 2nd, 1947, Anne Theodora (from whom he obtained a divorce, 1962), *o d* of late Major Richard Arenbourg Blennerhassett Chute; one *s* two *d*; 3rd, 1964, Priscilla Margaret, *d* of Hon. A. E. Cubitt and Mrs Ronald Dawnay; one *s* one *d. Educ:* Eton; RMC, Sandhurst. Served War of 1939–45, demobilised 1946. Owns about 700 acres. Became Irish Citizen, 1965. *Heir: s* Viscount Petersham, *qv. Address:* Greenmount Stud, Patrickswell, Co. Limerick, Eire.

See also Baron Ashcombe.

HARRINGTON, Dr Albert Blair, CB 1979; Head of Civil Service Department Medical Advisory Service, 1976–79; *b* 26 April 1914; *s* of late Albert Timothy Harrington and Lily Harrington; *m* 1939, Valerie White; one *d. Educ:* Brisbane Grammar Sch., Qld; Aberdeen Univ. MB, ChB 1938, MD 1944. House Phys., Woodend Hosp., Aberdeen, 1938–39; service in RAMC (Field Amb., Blood Transfusion Phys., Neurologist), 1940–45; MO (Head Injuries) and Dep. Supt, Stoke Mandeville Hosp., 1946–48; Med. Supt, Dunston Hill Hosp., Gateshead, 1948–50; SMO (Pensions), Cleveleys, 1950–53; Med. Supt, Queen Mary's Hosp., Roehampton, 1954–56; SMO, Dept of Health (Hosp. Bldg and later Regional Liaison Duties), 1956–68; PMO (Hosp. Bldg), 1968–73; SPMO (Under-Sec.), DHSS, 1973–76. FFCM (Foundn Fellow) 1972. *Publications:* articles on Sjögren's Disease, paralytic poliomyelitis, and hospital planning, medical care and the work of the Medical Advisory Service. *Recreations:* gardening, country life; formerly tennis. *Address:* 59 Lauderdale Drive, Petersham, Richmond, Surrey TW10 7BS. *T:* 01–940 1345. *Club:* Athenæum.

HARRINGTON, Illtyd, JP; DL; Co-ordinator of The Big Strawberry (London) Company; *b* 14 July 1931; *s* of Timothy Harrington and Sarah (*née* Burchell); unmarried. *Educ:* St Illtyd's RC Sch., Dowlais; Merthyr County Sch.; Trinity Coll., Caermarthen. Member: Paddington Borough Council, 1959–64; Westminster City Council, 1964–68 and 1971–78, Leader, Lab. Gp, 1972–74; GLC, 1964–67 and for Brent S, 1973–86: Alderman, 1970–73; Chairman, Policy and Resources Cttee, 1973–77, Special Cttee, 1985–86; Dep. Leader, 1973–77, 1981–84; Dep. Leader of the Opposition, 1977–81; Chm. of the Council, 1984–85. JP Willesden 1968. First Chairman, Inland Waterways Amenity Adv. Council, 1968–71; Chm., London Canals Consultative Cttee, 1965–67, 1981–; Member: British Waterways Bd, 1974–82; BTA, 1976–80. Chm., Kilburn Skills, 1977–. Member: Bd, Theatre Royal, Stratford E, 1978–; Bd, Wiltons Music Hall, 1979–; Nat. Theatre Bd, 1975–77; Bd, National Youth Theatre, 1982–; Chm., Half Moon Theatre, 1978–; Director: Soho Poly Theatre, 1981–; The Young Vic, 1981–. Pres., Grand Union Canal Soc., 1974–; Vice Pres., Coventry Canal Soc., 1970–. Patron, Westminster Cathedral Appeal, 1977–. Trustee: Kew Bridge Pumping Mus., 1976–; Chiswick Family Rescue, 1978–; Managing Trustee, Mutual Municipal Insurance Co., 1985–. Governor, Brunel Univ., 1981–. DL Greater London, 1986. *Recreations:* a slave to local government; laughing, singing and incredulity. *Address:* 16 Lea House, Salisbury Street, NW8 8BJ. *T:* 01–402 6356. *Club:* Paddington Labour.

HARRIS, family name of **Barons Harris, Harris of Greenwich, Harris of High Cross** and of **Earl of Malmesbury.**

HARRIS, 6th Baron *cr* 1815, of Seringapatam and Mysore, and of Belmont, Kent; **George Robert John Harris;** Captain RA, retired; *b* 17 April 1920; *s* of 5th Baron Harris, CBE, MC, and Dorothy Mary (*d* 1981), *d* of Rev. W. J. Crookes; *S* father, 1984. *Educ:* Eton; Christ Church, Oxford. *Heir: cousin* Derek Marshall Harris [*b* 23 July 1916; *m* 1938, Laura Cecilia, *e d* of late Major Edmund Thomas William McCausland, Gurkha Rifles; one *s* one *d*]. *Address:* Huntingfield, Eastling, near Faversham, Kent.

HARRIS OF GREENWICH, Baron *cr* 1974 (Life Peer), of Greenwich; **John Henry Harris;** director of companies; *b* Harrow, Middlesex, 5 April 1930; *s* of late Alfred George and May Harris; *m* 1st, 1952, Patricia Margaret Alstrom (marr. diss. 1982); one *s* one *d*; 2nd, 1983, Angela Smith. *Educ:* Pinner County Grammar Sch., Middlesex. Journalist on newspapers in Bournemouth, Leicester, Glasgow and London. National Service with Directorate of Army Legal Services, WO. Personal assistant to Rt Hon. Hugh Gaitskell when Leader of the Opposition, 1959–62; Director of Publicity, Labour Party, 1962–64; Special Assistant: to Foreign Secretary, 1964–65; to Rt Hon. Roy Jenkins as Home Secretary, 1965–Nov. 1967, and as Chancellor, Nov. 1967–1970. Staff of Economist newspaper, 1970–74. Minister of State, Home Office, 1974–79. Chm., Parole Bd for England and Wales, 1979–82; Pres., Nat. Assoc. of Senior Probation Officers, 1983–; Trustee, Police Foundn (Chm., Exec. Cttee), 1980–. Eisenhower Exchange Fellow from UK, 1972. Mem. Council, Harlow, Essex, 1957–63, Chm. Council 1960–61, Leader of Labour Gp, 1961–63. Mem. Exec. Cttee, Britain in Europe, referendum campaign, 1975 (Jt Chm., Publicity Cttee). Joined Social Democratic Party, 1981. *Address:* House of Lords, SW1. *Clubs:* Reform, MCC.

HARRIS OF HIGH CROSS, Baron *cr* 1979 (Life Peer), of Tottenham in Greater London; **Ralph Harris;** Chairman, Institute of Economic Affairs, since 1986 (General Director, 1957–86); *b* 10 Dec. 1924; *m* 1949, Jose Pauline Jeffery; one *s* one *d* (and one *s* decd). *Educ:* Tottenham Grammar Sch.; Queens' Coll., Cambridge (Exhibr, Foundn Schol.). 1st Cl. Hons Econs, MA Cantab. Lectr in Polit. Economy, St Andrews Univ., 1949–56. Contested (C): Kirkcaldy, 1951; Edinburgh Central, 1955. Leader-writer, Glasgow Herald, 1956. Trustee, Wincott Foundn; Trustee and Hon. Treasurer, Ross McWhirter Foundn. Mem. Council, Univ. of Buckingham; Dir, Churchill Press. Free Enterprise Award, 1976. Hon. DSc Buckingham, 1984. *Publications:* Politics without Prejudice, a biography of R. A. Butler, 1956; Hire Purchase in a Free Society, 1958, 3rd edn 1961; (with Arthur Seldon) Advertising in a Free Society, 1959; Advertising in Action, 1962; Advertising and the Public, 1962; (with A. P. Herbert) Libraries: Free for All?, 1962; Choice in Welfare, 1963; Essays in Rebirth of Britain, 1964; Choice in Welfare, 1965; Right Turn, 1970; Choice in Welfare, 1970; Down with the Poor, 1971; (with Brendan Sewill) British Economic Policy 1970–74, 1975; Crisis '75, 1975; Catch '76, 1976; Freedom of Choice: consumers or conscripts, 1976; (with Arthur Seldon) Pricing or Taxing, 1976; Not from Benevolence, 1977; (ed, with Arthur Seldon) The Coming Confrontation, 1978; (with Arthur Seldon) Over-ruled on Welfare, 1979; End of Government, 1980; Challenge of a Radical Reactionary, 1981; No, Minister!, 1985; columnist in Truth, Statist, etc. *Recreations:* conjuring and devising spells against over-government. *Address:* 4 Walmar Close, Beech Hill, Hadley Wood, Barnet, Herts. *Clubs:* Political Economy, Mont Pelerin Society.

HARRIS, Prof. Sir Alan (James), Kt 1980; CBE 1968; BScEng, FEng, FICE, FIStructE, MConsE; Senior Partner, Harris & Sutherland, Consulting Engineers, 1955–81, consultant since 1981; Professor of Concrete Structures, Imperial College, London, 1973–81, now Emeritus; *b* 8 July 1916; *s* of Walter Herbert Harris and Ethel Roach, Plymouth; *m* 1948, Marie Thérèse, *d* of Prof. Paul Delcourt, Paris; two *s. Educ:* Owen's Sch., Islington; Northampton Polytechnic (London Univ.). Local Government engineer, 1933–40; served Royal Engineers (Mulberry, Rhine Bridges) (despatches), 1940–46; with Eugène Freyssinet in Paris studying prestressing, 1946–49; Director, Prestressed Concrete Co. Ltd, 1949–55; in private practice, 1955–81. Member: Council, Agrément Board, 1968–81; Engrg Council, 1981–84; part-time Board Mem., Property Services Agency, 1974–78; Chm., Hydraulics Research Station, 1982–. President, Instn of Structural Engineers, 1978–79. Trustee, Imperial War Museum, 1983–. Hon. DSc: City; Aston; Exeter. Croix de Guerre (France) 1945; Ordre de Mérite (France) 1975. *Publications:* numerous papers in learned jls. *Recreation:* sailing. *Address:* 128 Ashley Gardens, Thirleby Road, SW1P 1HL. *T:* 01–834 6924.

HARRIS, Anne Macintosh, (Mrs H. J. L. Harris), CBE 1985; National Chairman, National Federation of Women's Institutes, 1981–85; *b* 17 April 1925; *d* of Montague Macintosh Williams and Marguerite Anne Williams (*née* Barrington); *m* 1950, Henry John Leshley Harris; one *s* three *d. Educ:* Battle Abbey Sch.; Swanley Horticultural Coll. and Wye Coll. (Swanley Dip. in Horticulture, 1946). Owned and ran nursery/market garden and shop, 1946–53. Mem., WI, 1947–; Mem., NFWI Exec. Cttee, 1973–85 (Vice-Chm., 1979–81); Chm., NFWI Markets Sub-Cttee, 1972–79; WI representative: on Women's National Commn, 1982–85; on Advertising Adv. Cttee, IBA, 1984–. Mem. Council Nat. Trust, 1981–85. Trustee, Help the Aged, 1985–. Chm., Tunbridge Wells East District Local Assoc. Girl Guides, 1963–79; Vice-Chm., Brenchley PCC, 1978–82. *Recreations:* gardening, walking, reading, music. *Address:* The Old Vicarage, Brenchley, Tonbridge, Kent TN12 7NQ. *T:* Brenchley 2040. *Club:* Agricola Club and Swanley Guild (Wye).

HARRIS, Anthony David, LVO 1979; HM Diplomatic Service; Counsellor, Cairo, since 1987; *b* 13 Oct. 1941; *s* of Reginald William Harris and Kathleen Mary Harris (*née* Daw); *m* 1970, Patricia Ann Over; one *s. Educ:* Plymouth College; Exeter College, Oxford (BA, 2nd cl. Hons Lit. Hum.). Third Sec., Commonwealth Relations Office, 1964; Middle East Centre for Arab Studies, Lebanon, 1965; Third, later Second Sec., and Vice-Consul, Jedda, 1967; Second Sec. (Inf.), Khartoum, 1969; First Sec., FCO, 1972; First Sec., Head of Chancery and Consul, Abu Dhabi, 1975; First Sec., UK Mission to UN, Geneva, 1979; Counsellor, FCO, 1982; seconded to MoD as Regl Marketing Dir 1 (Arabian Peninsula and Pakistan), 1983. *Recreations:* shooting (HM the Queen's Prize, Bisley, 1964; British team to Canada, 1974), skiing, climbing. *Address:* 13A Elm Bank Mansions, The Terrace, Barnes, SW13 0NS. *T:* 01–876 0081. *Clubs:* North London Rifle; Commonwealth Rifle (Bisley).

HARRIS, Anthony Geoffrey S.; *see* Stoughton-Harris.

HARRIS, Sir Anthony (Travers Kyrle), 2nd Bt *cr* 1953; retired; *b* 18 March 1918; *s* of Marshal of the RAF Sir Arthur Travers Harris, 1st Bt, GCB, OBE, AFC, and Barbara Kyrle, *d* of Lt-Col E. W. K. Money, 85th KSLI; *S* father, 1984. *Educ:* Oundle. Served European War, 1939–45 with Queen Victoria's Rifles and Wiltshire Regt; Auxiliary Units, 1941; ADC to GOC-in-C Eastern Command, 1944. Reader for MGM, 1951–52; subsequently work with antiques and objets d'art. *Recreations:* music, horology. *Heir:* none. *Address:* 33 Cheyne Court, Flood Street, SW3.
See also R.J. Harris.

HARRIS, Rt. Rev. Augustine; *see* Middlesbrough, Bishop of, (RC).

HARRIS, Basil Vivian, CEng, MIEE; Chief Engineer, Communications Division, Foreign and Commonwealth Office, 1979–81, retired; *b* 11 July 1921; *s* of late Henry William and Sarah May Harris; *m* 1943, Myra Winifred Mildred Newport. *Educ:* Watford Grammar School. GPO Engineering Dept (Research), 1939; served RAF, 1943–46; GPO Engineering Dept (Radio Branch), 1946; Diplomatic Wireless Service, FCO, 1963; Dep. Chief Engineer, Communications Division, FCO, 1971. *Publications:* contribs to technical jls on communications. *Recreations:* golf, photography, travel. *Address:* 13 Decoy Drive, Eastbourne, Sussex BN22 0AB. *T:* Eastbourne 505819. *Club:* Royal Eastbourne Golf.

HARRIS, Ven. Brian; *see* Harris, Ven. R. B.

HARRIS, Brian Thomas, OBE 1983; QC 1982; Director, Professional Conduct Department, Institute of Chartered Accountants in England and Wales; *b* 14 Aug. 1932; *s* of Thomas and Eleanor Harris; *m* 1957, Janet Rosina Harris (*née* Hodgson); one *s* one *d. Educ:* Henry Thornton Grammar Sch.; King's Coll., Univ. of London. LLB (Hons). Called to the Bar, Gray's Inn, 1960; joined London Magistrates' Courts, 1963; Clerk to the Justices, Poole, 1967–85. Member: Juvenile Courts Committee, Magistrates' Assoc., 1973–; NACRO Juvenile Crime Adv. Cttee, 1982–; former member: CCETSW working party on legal trng of social workers (report, 1974); NACRO cttee on diversion (Zander report, 1975); HO/DHSS working party on operation of Children and Young Persons' Act 1969 (report, 1978); ABAFA working party on care proceedings (report, 1979). Pres., Justices' Clerks Soc., 1981–82. Editor, Justice of the Peace Review, 1982–85 (Legal Editor, 1973; Jt Editor, 1978). *Publications:* Criminal Jurisdiction of Magistrates, 1969, 9th edn 1984; Warrants of Search and Entry, 1973; The Courts, the Press and the Public, 1976; The Rehabilitation of Offenders Act 1974, 1976; New Law of Family Proceedings in Magistrates' Courts, 1979; (ed jtly) Clarke Hall and Morrison on Children; (ed) entry on Magistrates in Halsbury's Laws of England, 4th edn 1979; contribs to legal jls. *Recreation:* the contemplation of verse. *Address:* Church Barn, High Street, Yardley Hastings, Northants NN7 1ER. *T:* Yardley Hastings 387.

HARRIS, Cecil Rhodes, FCIS, FSCA; Chief Executive, Commercial Union Assurance Company Ltd, 1982–85; *b* 4 May 1923; *s* of Frederick William Harris and Dorothy Violet Plum; *m* 1946, Gwenyth Evans; one *s* two *d. Educ:* private schools. FCIS 1950; FSCA 1951. Joined Employers Liability Assurance, 1949, Asst Sec., 1961–64, Overseas Manager, Northern & Employers, 1965–68; Commercial Union Assurance Co. Ltd: Asst Gen. Man., 1969–73; Dep. Gen. Man., 1974; Dir and Sec., 1975–78; Exec. Dir, 1979; Dep. Chief Gen. Man., 1980–82. *Recreations:* tennis, study of the Scriptures. *Address:* Ashley, 35a Plough Lane, Purley, Surrey CR2 3QJ. *T:* 01–668 2820.

HARRIS, Sir Charles Herbert S.; *see* Stuart-Harris.

HARRIS, Colin Grendon, CMG 1964; HM Diplomatic Service, retired; *b* 25 Oct. 1912; *m* 1941, Adelaide Zamoiska (decd); *m* 1947, Monique Jacqueline Marcuse-Baudoux; four *s* two *d. Educ:* Rossall Sch.; Pembroke Coll., Cambridge. Entered Foreign (subseq. Diplomatic) Service, 1935; served San Francisco, Antwerp, Elisabethville, Leopoldville, Lisbon, Montevideo, Rio de Janeiro, Vienna, Tokyo, Oslo, retired 1969. *Address:* 263 Avenue Defré, Brussels, Belgium.

HARRIS, David; Director, Commission of the European Communities, Directorate for Social and Demographic Statistics, since 1973; *b* 28 Dec. 1922; *s* of David and Margaret Jane Harris; *m* 1946, Mildred Alice Watson; two *d. Educ:* Bootle Grammar Sch.; LSE (BScEcon). FSS. Statistician, BoT, 1960; Statistician 1966 and Chief Statistician 1968, HM Treasury; Chief Statistician, Central Statistical Office, Cabinet Office, 1969. *Recreations:* tennis, swimming, economics. *Address:* 41 Boulevard Napoleon Ier, Luxembourg. *T:* Luxembourg 445223; 3 Amberwood Drive, Camberley, Surrey. *T:* Camberley 20213.

HARRIS, David Anthony; MP (C) St Ives, since 1983; *b* 1 Nov. 1937; *s* of late E. C. Harris and Betty Harris; *m* 1962, Diana Joan Hansford; one *s* one *d. Educ:* Mount Radford Sch., Exeter. Jun. Reporter, Express and Echo, Exeter, 1954–58. Nat. Service, commnd Devonshire and Dorset Regt, 1958; Staff Captain (Public Relns) GHQ, MELF, 1959. Reporter, Western Morning News, 1960–61; joined Daily Telegraph, Westminster Staff, 1961; Political Correspondent, Daily Telegraph, 1976–79; MEP (C) Cornwall and Plymouth, 1979–84. Chm., Parly Lobby Journalists, 1977–78. Mem. (C) Bromley, and Bromley, Ravensbourne, GLC, 1968–77; Chm. Thamesmead Cttee, 1971–73. Contested (C), Mitcham and Morden, Feb. 1974. Mem., Commons Select Cttee on Agriculture, 1983–. *Recreations:* gardening, walking the dog. *Address:* Trewedna Farm, Perranwell, near Truro, Cornwall. *T:* Truro 86300. *Club:* Farmers'.

HARRIS, Dame Diana R.; *see* Reader Harris.

HARRIS, Rev. Donald Bertram; Vicar of St Paul's, Knightsbridge, 1955–78; *b* 4 Aug. 1904; unmarried. *Educ:* King's Coll. Choir Sch., Cambridge; Haileybury Coll.; King's Coll., Cambridge; Cuddesdon Coll., Oxford. Chorister, King's Coll. Choir, 1915–19; Choral Scholar, King's Coll., Cambridge, 1923–26; BA 1925; MA 1929; Ordained Deacon, 1927; Priest, 1928; Curate of Chesterfield Parish Church, 1927–31; St Mary the Less, Cambridge, 1931–36. Chaplain of King's Coll., Cambridge, 1932–33; Examg Chaplain to Bishop of Wakefield, 1932–36; Rector of Great Greenford, Middx, 1936–45; Archdeacon of Bedford 1946–55, and Rector of St Mary's Bedford, 1945–55, Life Governor, Haileybury and Imperial Service Coll., 1946–. Pres., Assoc. for Promoting Retreats, 1968–71. *Address:* 105 Marsham Court, Marsham Street, SW1. *T:* 01–828 1132. *Club:* Royal Thames Yacht.

HARRIS, Dr Edmund Leslie, CB 1981; FRCP, FRCPE, FFCM; Deputy Chief Medical Officer (Deputy Secretary), Department of Health and Social Security, since 1977; *b* 11 April 1928; *s* of late M. H. and S. Harris; *m* 1959, Robina Semple (*née* Potter). *Educ:* Univ. of Witwatersrand. MB, BCh 1952; MRCPE 1959, FRCPE 1971, MRCP 1959, FRCP 1975; MFCM 1978, FFCM 1980. Gen. practice, Benoni, S Africa, 1954; various NHS posts, 1955–61; Medical Dir, pharmaceutical industry, 1962–68; SMO, DHSS, 1969–72; PMO, Cttee on Safety of Medicines and Medicines Commn, 1973; SPMO, Under-Sec., and Head of Medicines Div., DHSS, 1974–77. Examiner for Dip. Pharm. Med., Royal Colls of Physicians, 1976–84. Chairman: Assoc. of Med. Advisers in Pharmaceutical Industry, 1966; Adv. Cttee on Nat. Blood Transfusion Service, 1980–; Expert Gp on Viral Haemorrhagic Fevers, 1984–; Adv. Cttee, NHS Drugs, 1985–. Member: Nat. Biol. Bd, 1975–77; Bd, Public Health Lab. Service, 1977–; Central Blood Products Authority, 1982–85; Adviser to WHO, 1970–. Rep. Governor, Imperial Cancer Res. Fund, 1977–. *Publications:* various, mainly on aspects of clinical pharmacology and control of medicines. *Recreations:* walking, photography. *Address:* Department of Health and Social Security, Alexander Fleming House, Elephant and Castle, SE1. *T:* 01–407 5522.

HARRIS, Euan Cadogan; Deputy Legal Adviser, Ministry of Agriculture, Fisheries and Food, 1964–71; *b* 6 June 1906; *s* of late Charles Poulett Harris, MD and Violet Harris; *m* 1931, Brenda (*d* 1986), *er d* of late William Turnbull Bowman, OBE and Jessie Bowman; two *d. Educ:* Epsom Coll.; Clare Coll., Cambridge. BA 1927; LLM 1928. Admitted Solicitor (Edmund Thomas Child Prize), 1930. Entered Legal Dept of Min. of Agric. and

Fisheries, 1935; Asst Solicitor, 1949–64. *Recreations:* walking, swimming, gardening; reading, especially history and literature of psychical research. *Address:* 6 Newlands Road, Rottingdean, East Sussex BN2 7GD. *T:* Brighton 32019.

See also Sir A. K. Rothnie.

HARRIS, Frank; *see* Harris, W. F.

HARRIS, Geoffrey (Herbert); Member, Transport Users' Consultative Committee for London, 1961–77 (Chairman, 1972–77, Deputy Chairman, 1971–72); Chairman, London Transport Passengers' Committee, 1972–74; *b* 31 Jan. 1914.; *s* of late W. Leonard Harris and late Sybil M. Harris; *m* 1945, Eve J. Orton; two *d. Educ:* Colchester Royal Grammar School. FCIS. Commercial Union Gp of Cos, 1932–37; Shell Gp of Cos, 1937–73; Manager Office Administration, London, 1963–73. Royal Artillery, 1937–45. *Recreations:* music, architecture, travel. *Address:* Garden End, Spinfield Lane, Marlow, Bucks. *T:* Marlow 72550. *Club:* Phyllis Court (Henley-on-Thames).

HARRIS, Prof. Harry, FRCP; FRS 1966; Harnwell Professor of Human Genetics, University of Pennsylvania, since 1976; *b* 30 Sept. 1919; *m* 1948, Muriel Hargest; one *s. Educ:* Manchester Gram. Sch.; Trinity Coll., Cambridge. (MA, MD); FRCP 1973. Research Asst, Galton Laboratory, Dept of Eugenics, Biometry, and Genetics UC, London, 1947–50; Leverhulme Scholar, RCP, 1947–48; Lund Research Fellow, Diabetic Assoc., 1949; Lectr, Dept of Biochem., UC, London, 1950–53; Sen. Lectr, 1953–58, Reader in Biochem. Genetics, 1958–60, Dept of Biochem., The London Hosp. Med. Coll.; Prof. of Biochem., University of London, at King's Coll., 1960–65; Galton Prof. of Human Genetics, London Univ. at UCL, 1965–76. Hon. Lectr, 1950–55, Hon. Research Associate, 1955–60, Dept of Eugenics, Biometry, and Genetics, UCL; Hon. Dir, MRC Human Biochem. Genetics Res. Unit, 1962–76; Hon. Consulting Geneticist, UCH, 1966–76. Joint Editor: Annals of Human Genetics, 1965–79; Advances in Human Genetics, 1970–. Nat. Research Coun. of Canada and Nuffield Foundation Vis. Lectr, British Columbia and McGill, 1967; Fogarty Scholar, Nat. Insts of Health, USA, 1972; Rock Carling Fellowship, Nuffield Provincial Hosps Trust, 1974. Lectures: Thomas Young, St George's Hosp. Med. Sch., 1966; De Frees, University Penna, 1966; Walter R. Bloor, Univ. Rochester, 1967; Langdon Brown, RCP, 1968; Sir William Jackson Pope, RSA, 1968; Darwin, Inst. Biol., 1969; Leonard Parsons, Birmingham Univ., 1969; Sidney Ringer, UCH Med. Sch., 1970; T. H. Huxley, Birmingham Univ., 1971; George Frederic Still, British Paediatric Assoc., 1971; L. S. Penrose Meml, Genetical Soc., 1973; Bicentennial, Coll. of Physicians of Pa, 1976; Noble Wiley Jones, Univ. of Oregon, 1978; Rhodes, Emory Univ., 1978; Thomas S. Hall, Washington Univ., St Louis, 1979; Harvey, Harvey Soc., NY, 1981; Karl Beyer, Wisconsin, 1983. For. Associate, Nat. Acad. of Scis, USA, 1976. Hon. Dr Univ. René Descartes, Paris, 1976. William Allan Meml Award, Amer. Soc. of Human Genetics, 1968. *Publications:* An Introduction to Human Biochemical Genetics (Eugenics Laboratory Memoir Series), 1953; Human Biochemical Genetics, 1959; The Principles of Human Biochemical Genetics, 1970, 3rd edn 1980; Prenatal Diagnosis and Selective Abortion, 1975; (with D. A. Hopkinson) Handbook of Enzyme Electrophoresis in Human Genetics, 1976. *Address:* 4050 Irving Street, Philadelphia, Pa 19104, USA. *T:* (215) 387–0245.

HARRIS, Prof. Henry, FRCP; FRCPath; FRS 1968; Regius Professor of Medicine, University of Oxford, since 1979; Head of the Sir William Dunn School of Pathology, since 1963; Hon. Director, Cancer Research Campaign, Cell Biology Unit, since 1963; Fellow of Lincoln College, 1963–79, Hon. Fellow 1980; Student of Christ Church; *b* 28 Jan. 1925; *s* of late Sam and late Ann Harris; *m* 1950, Alexandra Fanny Brodsky; one *s* two *d. Educ:* Sydney Boys' High Sch. and University of Sydney, Australia; Lincoln Coll., Oxford. Public Exhibnr, University of Sydney, 1942; BA Mod. Langs, 1944; MB BS 1950; Travelling Schol. of Austr. Nat. Univ. at Univ. of Oxford, 1952; MA; DPhil (Oxon.), 1954, DM 1979. Dir of Research, Brit. Empire Cancer Campaign, at Sir William Dunn Sch. of Pathology, Oxford, 1954–59; Visiting Scientist, Nat. Institutes of Health, USA, 1959–60; Head of Dept of Cell Biology, John Innes Inst., 1960–63; Prof. of Pathology, Univ. of Oxford, 1963–79. Vis. Prof., Vanderbilt Univ., 1968; Walker-Ames Prof., University of Washington, 1968; Foreign Prof., Collège de France, 1974. Member: ARC, 1968–78 (Chm., Animals Res. Bd, 1976–78); Council, European Molecular Biology Organization, 1974–76; Council, Royal Society, 1971–72; Scientific Adv. Cttee, CRC, 1961–; Governor, European Cell Biology Organization, 1973–75. Lectures: Almroth Wright, 1968; Harvey, Harvey Soc. NY, 1969; Dunham, Harvard, 1969; Jenner Meml, 1970; Croonian, Royal Soc., 1971; Nat. Insts of Health, USA, 1971; Foundation, RCPath, 1973; Woodhull, Royal Instn, 1975; Rotherham, Lincoln Coll., Oxford, 1979; Herbert Spencer, Oxford Univ., 1979; Opening Plenary, Internat. Congress of Cell Biology, 1980; First Distinguished, in Experimental Pathology, Pittsburgh Univ., 1982; Louis Gross Meml, NY, 1983; Claude Bernard, Acad. des Sciences, Paris, 1984. Foreign Hon. Mem., Amer. Acad. Arts and Sciences; Foreign Mem., Max-Planck Soc.; Hon. Member: Amer. Assoc. of Pathologists; German Soc. of Cell Biology; Corresp. Member: Amer. Assoc. for Cancer Res.; Aust. Acad. of Science. Hon. Fellow, Cambridge Philosophical Soc. Hon. FRCPath Aust. Hon. DSc Edinburgh, 1976; Hon. MD: Geneva, 1982; Sydney, 1983. Feldberg Foundn Award, Ivison Macadam Meml Prize, RCSE; Prix de la Fondation Isabelle Decazes de Noüe for cancer research; Madonnina Prize for medical scis (City of Milan), 1979; Royal Medal, Royal Soc., 1980; Osler Medal, RCP, 1984. *Publications:* Nucleus and Cytoplasm, 1968, 3rd edn, 1974; Cell Fusion, 1970; La Fusion cellulaire, 1974; The Balance of Improbabilities, 1986; papers on cellular physiology and biochemistry, in scientific books and jls. *Recreation:* history. *Address:* Sir William Dunn School of Pathology, South Parks Road, Oxford OX1 3RE. *T:* Oxford 57321.

HARRIS, Lt-Gen. Sir Ian (Cecil), KBE 1967 (CBE 1958); CB 1962; DSO 1945; Member of Family Partnership and Manager, Ballykisteen Stud, Tipperary, and Owner, Victor Stud, Golden, Cashel, Tipperary; Chairman: Irish Bloodstock Breeders Association, since 1977; Irish Bloodstock Breeders Federation, since 1978; *b* 7 July 1910; *y s* of late J. W. A. Harris, Victor Stud, Golden, Tipperary; *m* 1945, Anne-Marie Desmotreux; two *s. Educ:* Portora Royal Sch., Enniskillen, Northern Ireland; RMC, Sandhurst. 2nd Lt Royal Ulster Rifles, 1930; served War of 1939–45, NW Frontier of India, 1939 (despatches); comd 2nd Bn Royal Ulster Rifles, 1943–45; GSO1, 25 Ind. Div. and 7 Div. in Burma and Malaya, 1945–46 (despatches), India and Pakistan, 1946–47; AQMG Scottish Comd, 1949–51, comd 6th Bn Royal Ulster Rifles (TA), 1951–52; Chief of Staff, Northern Ireland, 1952–54; Comdr 1 Federal Infantry Bde, Malaya, 1954–57 (despatches); Dep. Dir of Staff Duties (A), WO, 1957–60; GOC Singapore Base District, 1960–62; Chief of Staff, Contingencies Planning, Supreme HQ, Allied Powers, Europe, 1963–66; GOC-in-C, then GOC, N Ireland, 1966–69. Colonel: Royal Ulster Rifles, 1962–68; Royal Irish Rangers, 1968–72. *Recreations:* riding and tennis. *Address:* Acraboy House, Monard, Co. Tipperary. *T:* Tipperary 51564. *Club:* Army and Navy.

HARRIS, Air Cdre Irene Joyce, CB 1984; RRC 1976; SRN, SCM; Director, Nursing Services (RAF), and Matron-in-Chief, Princess Mary's Royal Air Force Nursing Service, 1981–84; *b* 26 Sept. 1926; *d* of late Robert John Harris and Annie Martha Harris (*née* Breed). *Educ:* Southgate County Sch.; Charing Cross Hosp.; The London Hosp.; Queen Mary's Maternity Home, Hampstead. SRN 1947, SCM 1950. Joined Princess Mary's RAF Nursing Service, 1950; gen. nursing and midwifery duties in UK, Singapore, Germany and Cyprus; Dep. Matron, 1970; Sen. Matron, 1975; Principal Matron, 1978; Dep. Dir, Nursing Services (RAF), 1981. QHNS 1981–84. *Recreations:* travel, cine-photography, ornithology, Thames sailing barges, music. *Address:* 51 Station Road, Haddenham, Ely, Cambs CB6 3XD. *Club:* Royal Air Force.

HARRIS, Sir Jack A. S.; *see* Sutherland-Harris.

HARRIS, Sir Jack Wolfred Ashford, 2nd Bt, *cr* 1932; Chairman, Bing Harris & Co. Ltd, Wellington, NZ, 1935–78 (Director until 1982), retired; *b* 23 July 1906; *er s* of Rt Hon. Sir Percy Harris, 1st Bt, PC, and Frieda Bloxam (*d* 1962); *S* father 1952; *m* 1933, Patricia, *o d* of A. P. Penman, Wahroonga, Sydney, NSW; two *s* one *d. Educ:* Shrewsbury Sch.; Trinity Hall, Cambridge. BA (Cantab) History; then one year's study in Europe. Joined family business in New Zealand, 1929, and became director shortly afterwards. Past Pres. Wellington Chamber of Commerce. Served during War of 1939–45, for three years in NZ Home Forces. *Recreations:* gardening, fishing, swimming. *Heir: s* Christopher John Ashford Harris [*b* 26 Aug. 1934; *m* 1957, Anna, *d* of F. de Malmanche, Auckland, NZ; one *s* two *d*]. *Address:* Te Rama, Waikanae, near Wellington, NZ. *Clubs:* Royal Automobile; Wellington (Wellington); Northern (Auckland).

HARRIS, John Charles; solicitor; Adviser and Director, South Yorkshire Residuary Body, since 1985; *b* 25 April 1936; *s* of Sir Charles Joseph William Harris, KBE; *m* 1961, Alison Beryl Sturley; one *s* one *d. Educ:* Dulwich College; Clare College, Cambridge. MA, LLM. 2nd Lieut, Intelligence Corps, 1954–56. UKAEA (seconded to OECD), 1959–63; articled to Town Clerk, Poole, 1963–66; Asst Sol., then Senior Asst Sol., Poole BC, 1966–67; Asst Sol., then Principal Asst to Chief Exec. and Town Clerk, 1967–71, Dep. Town Clerk, 1972–73, County Borough of Bournemouth; County Sec., 1973–83, Chief Exec. and County Clerk, 1983–86, S Yorks CC; Dir, S Yorks Passenger Transport Exec., 1984–86; Clerk to Lord Lieutenant of S Yorks, 1984–86. Adviser to AMA Police and Fire Cttee, 1976–86; Mem., Home Office Tripartite Working Party on Police Act 1964, 1983–86; Chm., Soc. of County Secretaries, 1983–84; Mem. Exec. Council, Soc. of Local Authority Ch. Executives (Solace), 1984–86; Mem., Law Society. Hon. PR Officer, S Yorks and Humberside Region, Riding for Disabled Assoc.; Trustee, S Yorks Charity Inf. Service; Founder Mem./Sec., Barnsley Rockley Rotary Club, 1976–79; Vice-Chm. and Sec., Friends of Opera North; Member: Council, Opera North; Guild of Freemen, City of London; Justice; European Movement. DL S Yorks, 1986. FRSA 1984. *Recreations:* being with family and friends; competitive trail riding; riding Welsh cobs; opera, foreign travel. *Address:* Long Lane Close, High Ackworth, Pontefract, Yorks WF7 7EY.

HARRIS, John Frederick, OBE 1986; FSA; Curator, British Architectural Library's Drawing Collection and Heinz Gallery, 1960–86; *b* 13 Aug. 1931; *s* of Frederick Harris and Maud (*née* Sellwood); *m* 1960, Eileen Spiegel, New York; one *s* one *d. Educ:* Cowley C of E School. Itinerant before 1956; Library of Royal Inst. of Architects, 1956. Mem., Mr Paul Mellon's Adv. Bd, 1966–78; Trustee, Amer. Mus. in Britain, 1974–; Chm., Colnaghi & Co., 1982–. President: Internat. Confedn on Architectural Museums, 1981–84 (Chm., 1979–81; Hon. Pres., 1984–); Marylebone Soc., 1978–80; Member: Council, Drawing Soc. of America, 1962–68; Council, Victorian Soc., 1974–; Nat. Council, Internat. Council of Monuments and Sites, 1976–83; Soc. of Dilettanti, 1977–; Mem. Committee: Soc. of Architectural Historians of GB, 1958–66; Georgian Gp, 1970–74; Save Britain's Heritage, 1970–; Thirties Soc., 1979–; Stowe Landscape, 1980– (Patron, Stowe Gardens Buildings Trust, 1986–); Bldg Museum Proj., 1980–; Garden History, 1980–; Jl of Garden History, 1980–. Member: Adv. Council, Drawings Center, NY, 1983–; Adv. Bd, Centre Canadienne d'Architecture, Montreal, 1983–; Management Cttee, Courtauld Inst. of Art, 1983–; Somerset House Building Cttee, 1986–; Council, Royal Archaeol. Inst., 1984–; Adv. Cttees, Historic Bldgs and Monuments Commn, 1984–; Ashton Meml Steering Gp, 1984–; GLC Historic Buildings Panel, 1984–86; Architecture Club. Mem., Ambrose Congreve Award, 1980–82; Ashmole Archive Comm., 1985–. Andrew W. Mellon Lectr in Fine Arts, Nat. Gall., Washington, 1981; Slade Prof. of Fine Art, Univ. of Oxford, 1982–83. Exhibitions Organizer: The King's Arcadia, 1973; The Destruction of the Country House (with Marcus Binney), 1974; The Garden, 1979; Dir, British Country House Exhibn, Nat. Gall., Washington, 1982–83; many exhibns in Heinz Gall.; travelling exhibns and catalogues: Italian Architectural Drawings, 1966; Sir Christopher Wren, 1970. FSA 1968; FRSA 1975; Hon. FRIBA 1972; Hon. MA Oxon. 1982; Hon. Brother Art Workers' Guild, 1972. Editor, Studies in Architecture, 1976–. *Publications:* English Decorative Ironwork, 1960; Regency Furniture Designs, 1961; ed, The Prideaux Collection of Topographical Drawings, 1963; (jtly) Lincolnshire, 1964; contrib. The Making of Stamford, 1965; (jtly) Illustrated Glossary of Architecture, 1966, 2nd edn 1969; (jtly) Buckingham Palace, 1968; Georgian Country Houses, 1968; contrib., Concerning Architecture, 1968; Sir William Chambers, Knight of the Polar Star, 1970 (Hitchcock Medallion 1971); ed, The Rise and Progress of the Present State of Planting, 1970; ed (jtly) The Country Seat, 1970; Catalogue of British Drawings for Architecture, Decoration, Sculpture and Landscape Gardening in American Collections, 1971; A Country House Index, 1971, 2nd edn 1979; Catalogue of the Drawings Collection RIBA: Inigo Jones and John Webb, 1972; contrib., Guide to Vitruvius Britannicus, 1972; (jtly) The King's Arcadia: Inigo Jones and The Stuart Court, 1973; Catalogue of the Drawings Collection RIBA: Colin Campbell, 1973; Headfort House and Robert Adam, 1973; (jtly) The Destruction of the Country House, 1974; Gardens of Delight, The Art of Thomas Robins, 1976; Gardens of Delight, The Rococo English Landscape of Thomas Robins, 1978; (jtly) Catalogue of Drawings by Inigo Jones, John Webb and Isaac de Caus in Worcester College, Oxford, 1979; A Garden Alphabet, 1979; ed, The Garden Show, 1979; The Artist and the Country House, 1979 (Sir Banister Fletcher prize, 1979); contrib., Village England, 1980; (contrib.) Lost Houses of Scotland, 1980; The English Garden 1530–1840: a contemporary view, 1981; contrib., John Claudius Loudon and the Early Nineteenth Century in Great Britain, Washington, 1980; (jtly) Interiors, 1981; The Palladians, 1981; Die Hauser der Lords und Gentlemen, 1982; William Talman, Maverick Architect, 1982; contrib., Gibraltar: an architectural appreciation, 1982; Architectural Drawings in the Cooper Hewitt Museum, New York, 1982; (contrib.) Vanishing Houses of England, 1982; (contrib.) Macmillan Encyclopedia of Architecture, 1982; (contrib.) Great Drawings from the Collection of Royal Institute of British Architects, 1983; (jtly) Britannia Illustrata Knyff & Kip, 1984; The Design of the British Country House, 1985; (contrib.) In Honor of Paul Mellon, Collector and Benefactor, 1986; articles in Country Life, Arch. Rev., Arch. Hist., and other jls. *Recreations:* grand hotels, history of World War I and flinting. *Address:* 16 Limerston Street, SW10 0HH.

HARRIS, John Frederick, CEng, FIEE; Chairman, East Midlands Electricity Board, since 1982; *b* 9 Dec. 1938; *s* of Jack Harris and Lily Harris; *m* 1960, Diana Joyce Brown; one *s* two *d. Educ:* Central Grammar School, Birmingham. Technical posts, Midlands Electricity, 1955–70; managerial posts, Southern Electricity, 1970–78; Chief Engineer, NW Electricity Board, 1978–79, Dep. Chm., 1979–82; Dir, BEI Ltd, 1982–. Pres., Nottingham VSO, 1984–. CBIM. *Recreation:* golf. *Address:* 57 Sheepwalk Lane, Ravenshead, Nottingham. *Club:* Royal Commonwealth Society.

HARRIS, John Percival, DSC 1945; QC 1974; **His Honour Judge Harris;** a Circuit Judge, since 1980; *b* 16 Feb. 1925; *o s* of late Thomas Percival Harris and Nora May

Harris; *m* 1959, Janet Valerie Douglas; one *s* two *d*. *Educ*: Wells Cathedral Sch.; Pembroke Coll., Cambridge. BA 1947. Served in RN, 1943–46: Midshipman, RNVR, 1944, Sub-Lt 1945. Called to Bar, Middle Temple, 1949, Bencher 1970. A Recorder of the Crown Court, 1972–80; Dep. Sen. Judge, Sovereign Base Areas, Cyprus, 1983–. *Recreations*: golf, reading, Victorian pictures. *Address*: Tudor Court, Fairmile Park Road, Cobham, Surrey. *T*: Cobham 4756; 12 King's Bench Walk, Temple, EC4Y 7EL. *T*: 01–353 5892. *Clubs*: United Oxford & Cambridge University; Woking Golf, Rye Golf.

HARRIS, John Robert, FRIBA; architect; Founder and Senior Partner, John R. Harris Architects, London, since 1949 (also Founder and Senior Partner of associated firms in Brunei, Oman, Qatar, Dubai and Hong Kong); Partner, Courbe Duboz et Harris, Paris, since 1978; *b* 5 June 1919; *s* of Major Alfred Harris, CBE, DSO and Rosa Alfreda Alderson; *m* 1950, Gillian, *d* of Col C. W. D. Rowe, CB, MBE, TD, DL, JP; one *s* one *d*. *Educ*: Harrow Sch.; Architectural Assoc. Sch. of Architecture (AA Dipl. Hons). FRIBA 1949; HKIA 1982; Membre de l'Ordre des Architectes Français, 1978. Served War, TA and Active Service, 1939–45 (TEM 1945); Lieut RE, Hong Kong, 1940–41; POW of Japanese, 1941–45; Mem., British Army Aid Gp, China, 1943–45; Hong Kong Resistance, 1942–45. Projects won in internat. competition: State Hosp., Qatar, 1953; New Dubai Hosp., 1976; Corniche Develt and Traffic Intersection, Dubai, 1978; HQ for Min. of Social Affairs and Labour, Oman, 1979; Tuen Mun Hosp., Hong Kong, 1981 (internat. assessment); Ruler's Office develt, Dubai, 1985. Architects and planners for Zhuhai New Town, Economic Zone, People's Republic of China, 1984. Major works in UK include: hospitals: Royal Northern, London, 1973; Ealing, 1976; RAF Upper Heyford, 1982; RAF Bentwaters, 1982; Park Hosp., Nottingham, 1983; Stoke Mandeville, 1983; Wellesley House and St Peter's Court school re-develt, 1975; apartments, Hyde Park, 1983; dept stores in Barnstaple, Basildon, Cwmbran, Eltham, Harlow, Hammersmith, Sutton Coldfield and Worthing. Major works overseas include: Internat. Trade Centre, Dubai, 1982; British Embassy, Chancery Offices and Ambassador's Residence, Abu Dhabi, 1982; shopping centres, Oman, 1978 and 1984; National Bank of Dubai HQ Bldg, 1968; Grindlay's Bank, Muscat, 1969; British Bank of the ME, Salalah, Oman, 1983; Sulaibikhat Hosp., Kuwait, 1968; University Teaching Hosp., Maiduguri, Nigeria, 1982; Caritas Hosp., Hong Kong, 1983; Rashid Hosp., Dubai, 1983; Women's Hosp., Doha, 1984; Shell Recreation Centre, Brunei, 1984; dept stores in Antwerp, Brussels, Lille, Paris and Strasbourg, 1973–83. FRSA 1982. Silver Jubilee Medal, 1977. *Publications*: (jtly) John R. Harris Architects, 1984; contrib. to books and architectural and technical jls. *Recreations*: architecture, sailing, travel. *Address*: 24 Devonshire Place, W1N 2BX. *T*: 01–935 9353. *Clubs*: Athenæum, Royal Thames Yacht.

HARRIS, Leonard John; Commissioner of Customs and Excise, since 1983; *b* 4 July 1941; *s* of Leonard and May Harris; *m* 1965, Jill Christine Tompkins (marr. diss.); one *s* two *d*. *Educ*: Westminster City Sch.; St John's Coll., Cambridge. BA 1964 (Eng. Lit.), MA 1967. HM Customs and Excise: Asst Principal, 1964; Private Sec. to Chairman, 1966–68; Principal, 1968; CS Selection Bd, 1970; HM Customs and Excise, 1971; Cabinet Office, 1971–74; First Sec., UK Rep. to EEC, 1974–76, Counsellor, 1976–77; Asst Sec., HM Customs and Excise, 1977–80, Cabinet Office, 1980–83; Under Sec., 1983. *Address*: Elm Cottage, Reading Road, Harwell, Oxon. *T*: Harwell 615.

HARRIS, Brigadier Lewis John, CBE 1961 (OBE 1949; MBE 1943); consultant, surveys and mapping; *b* 19 Dec. 1910; *e s* of late David Rees and of Cecilia Harris; *m* 1975, Thelma Opal, *d* of James Marshall Carr and Zettie Lou Witt, and *widow* of Lt-Col A. L. Nowicki, US Corps of Engineers. *Educ*: Christ Coll., Brecon; RMA, Woolwich; Pembroke Coll., Cambridge (Exhibitioner), Mech. Sci. Tripos, MA. Commissioned RE 1930; Triangulation of Jamaica, 1937–39; served War of 1939–45: British Expeditionary Force, 1939–40 (despatches); First Army in North Africa, 1942–43, AFHQ and American Seventh Army, Italy, 1944; Land Forces SE Asia, India, Burma and Malaya, 1944–46; Chief Instructor, Sch. of Mil. Survey, 1946–49; War Office, Geog. Section GS, 1949–52; Ordnance Survey, 1952–53; Dir, Survey GHQ, Middle East, and GHQ, E Africa, 1953–55; Land Survey Adviser, Allied Forces, Mediterranean, 1954–55; Ordnance Survey of Great Britain, 1955–61; Brig. 1956; Dir, Map Production and Publication, 1956–59; Dir, Field Surveys, 1959–61; Dir of Mil. Survey, MoD and Chief of Geographical Section Gen. Staff, 1961–65. Consultant, Federal Surveys and Mapping, Canada, 1967–85. Hon. Col 135 Survey Engineer Regt, TA, 1965–67. Chm., Nat. Cttee for Cartography, Royal Society, 1961–67. Hon. Foreign Sec., Royal Geographical Soc., 1964–67; Vice-Pres., Internat. Cartographic Assoc., 1958–61. Hon. Vice-Pres., Army Rugby Union. FRAS, FRGS, FRICS. *Publications*: various papers on cartography in learned jls. *Recreations*: outdoor sports, travelling. *Address*: 12410 Hound Ears Point, Fox Den, PO Box 22129, Knoxville, Tenn 37933, USA. *Clubs*: Naval and Military, MCC; Hawks (Cambridge); Royal Ottawa Golf; IZ, FF, BB.

HARRIS, Lyndon Goodwin, RI 1958; RSW 1952; RWA 1947; artist in oil, water-colour, stained glass, and etching; *b* 25 July 1928; *s* of late S. E. Harris, ACIS and late Mary Elsie Harris. *Educ*: Halesowen Grammar Sch. Studied Art at: Birmingham Coll. of Art; Slade Sch. of Fine Art, 1946–50; University of London Inst. of Education, 1950–51; Courtauld Inst.; Central Sch. of Art and Crafts, London. Leverhulme Schol., Pilkington Schol., Slade Schol., and Slade Anatomy Prizeman; Dip. Fine Art (London) 1949; Courtauld Certificate, 1950; ATD 1951. *Works exhibited*: Paris Salon (Gold Medal, Oil Painting; Honourable Mention, Etching); RA (first exhibited at age of 13), RSA, RI, RSW, NEAC, RBA, RGI, RWA, and principal provincial galleries. *Works in permanent collections*: Ministry of Works; University Coll., London; Birmingham and Midland Inst.; City of Worcester; (stained glass) Gorsty Hill Methodist Church, Halesowen. *Recreation*: music (organ and pianoforte). *Address*: The Uplands, Waxland Road, Halesowen, West Midlands.

HARRIS, Margaret Frances, OBE 1975; Director of Theatre Design Course at Riverside (formerly, the English National Opera and Sadler's Wells Design Course); *b* 28 May 1904; *d* of William Birkbeck Harris and Kathleen Marion Carey. *Educ*: Downe House. In partnership with Elizabeth Montgomery and late Sophie Devine as firm of Motley, 1931–. Has designed many productions in London and New York of drama, opera and ballet: first notable production, Richard of Bordeaux, for John Gielgud, 1932; recently, sets and costumes for: Prokofiev's War and Peace, Coliseum, 1972; (with Elizabeth Montgomery) Unknown Soldier and His Wife, New London, 1973; A Family and a Fortune, 1975; Tosca, English Nat. Opera, 1976; Paul Bunyan, English Music Theatre, 1976; The Consul, Coliseum, 1978. *Publications*: Designing and Making Costume, by Motley, 1965; Theatre Props, by Motley, 1976. *Address*: 40 Smith Square, SW1. *T*: 01–222 5431.

HARRIS, Prof. Martin Best; Professor of Romance Linguistics since 1976, Pro-Vice-Chancellor since 1981, University of Salford; *b* 28 June 1944; *s* of William Best Harris and Betty Evelyn (*née* Martin); *m* 1966, Barbara Mary (*née* Daniels); two *s*. *Educ*: Devonport High Sch. for Boys, Plymouth; Queens' Coll., Cambridge (BA, MA); Sch. of Oriental and African Studies, London (PhD). Lecturer in French Linguistics, Univ. of Leicester, 1967; University of Salford: Sen. Lectr in Fr. Ling., 1974; Dean of Social Sciences and Arts, 1978–81. Member: Internat. Cttee for Historical Linguistics, 1979–; UGC, 1984–; Chm., UGC NI Working Party, 1985–. Mem. Council, Philological Soc., 1979–. Vice Chm. of Governors, Parrs Wood High Sch., 1982–86. Mem. Editorial Board: Journal Linguistics, 1982–; Diachronica, 1983–; Jt Gen. Editor, Longman Linguistics Library, 1982–. *Publications*: (ed) Romance Syntax: synchronic and diachronic perspectives, 1976; The Evolution of French Syntax: a comparative approach, 1978; (ed with N. Vincent) Studies in the Romance Verb, 1982; about 30 articles in appropriate jls and collections. *Recreations*: gardening, travel, wine. *Address*: 25 Parkfield Road South, Didsbury, Manchester M20 0DB. *T*: 061–445 7617; Department of Modern Languages, University of Salford, Salford M5 4WT. *T*: 061–736 5836 5843, ext. 7016.

HARRIS, Martin Richard; Director: National Westminster Bank PLC, since 1977; County Bank Ltd, since 1977; De La Rue Co. plc, since 1981; Equity & Law Life Assurance Soc. Plc, since 1981 (Deputy Chairman, since 1983); TR Industrial & General Trust plc, since 1983; Chairman, Nineteen Twenty-Eight Investment Trust plc, since 1984; *b* 30 Aug. 1922; *m* 1952, Diana Moira (*née* Gandar Dower) JP, Mayor of Merton, 1985–86; four *s*. *Educ*: Wellington Coll. FCA. Captain, RE, ME and Italy, 1941–46. Joined Price Waterhouse & Co., 1946, Partner, 1956–74; Dir Gen., Panel on Take-Overs and Mergers, 1974–77; Director: Reckitt and Colman, 1977–82 (Dep. Chm., 1979–82); Inmos International, 1980–84; Westland plc, 1981–85. Inst. of Chartered Accountants in England and Wales: Mem. Council, 1971–79; Chm., Parly and Law Cttee, 1973–74; Chm., Prof. Standards Cttee, 1977–79; Mem., Accountants Internat. Study Gp, 1972–74. Mem., DTI's Company Law Consultative Gp, 1972–74. Member: Court, Drapers' Co., 1978–; Court, Co. of Chartered Accountants, 1977– (Master, 1983). Mem. Council, RCM, 1985– (Chm. Development Fund, 1984–); Governor, QMC, London Univ., 1979–. US Silver Star 1945. *Recreations*: music and opera, philately, antique furniture and china, keeping busy. *Address*: 29 Belvedere Grove, Wimbledon, SW19 7RQ. *T*: 01–946 0951. *Clubs*: Carlton, MCC.

HARRIS, Maurice Kingston, CB 1976; formerly Secretary, Northern Ireland Ministry of Home Affairs, Jan. 1973, seconded to Northern Ireland Office, 1974–76; *b* 5 Oct. 1916; *s* of late Albert Kingston Harris and late Annie Rebecca Harris; *m* 1948, Margaret McGregor, *d* of Roderick Fraser McGregor; one *s* three *d*. *Educ*: The Perse Sch.; London Univ. 1st cl. Hons Mod. Langs, 1939. Served in Indian Army, 8th Punjab Regt, 1942–46. Colonial Office, 1946–47. Entered Northern Ireland Civil Service, 1947, and served in various Ministries; retired 1976. *Recreations*: music, walking. *Address*: 27 Strangford Avenue, Belfast BT9 6PG. *T*: Belfast 681409.

HARRIS, Noël H. V.; *see* Vicars-Harris.

HARRIS, Rt. Rev. Patrick Burnet; Secretary, Partnership for World Mission, since 1986; *b* 30 Sept. 1934; *s* of Edward James Burnet Harris and Astrid Kendall; *m* 1968, Valerie Margaret Pilbrow; two *s* one *d*. *Educ*: St Albans School; Keble Coll., Oxford (MA). Asst Curate, St Ebbe's, Oxford, 1960–63; Missionary with S American Missionary Soc., 1963–73; Archdeacon of Salta, Argentina, 1969–73; Diocesan Bishop of Northern Argentina, 1973–80; Rector of Kirkheaton and Asst Bishop, Dio. Wakefield, 1981–85. *Recreations*: ornithology, S American Indian culture, music. *Address*: Victoria Lodge, 91 Waverley Road, Reading, Berks RG3 2QB; (office) Partnership for World Mission, 157 Waterloo Road, SE1 8UU.

HARRIS, Prof. Peter Charles, MD, PhD, FRCP; Simon Marks Professor of Cardiology, University of London, since 1966; Physician, National Heart Hospital; *b* 26 May 1923; *s* of late David Jonathan Valentine and Nellie Dean Harris; *m* 1952, Felicity Margaret Hartridge (marr. diss. 1982); two *d*. *Educ*: St Olave's Grammar Sch.; Univ. of London. MB, BS (London) 1946; MRCP 1950; MD (Univ. medal) 1951; PhD 1955; FRCP 1965. House appts at King's Coll. Hospital, and elsewhere, 1946–55. Nuffield Fellow, Columbia Univ., New York, 1955–57; Lectr, Sen. Lectr and Reader in Medicine, Univ. of Birmingham, 1957–66; Dir, Inst. of Cardiology, Univ. of London, 1966–73. Pres., Internat. Soc. for Heart Research, 1981–83. Hon. FACC, 1976. *Publications*: The Human Pulmonary Circulation (with D. Heath), 1962, 3rd edn 1986; articles to jls, etc, on cardio-pulmonary physiology and biochemistry. *Recreation*: chamber music. *Address*: 2 Beaumont Street, W1. *T*: 01–486 3043.

HARRIS, Group Captain Peter Langridge, AE 1961, Clasp 1971; CEng, FIEE; DL; ADC to the Queen, since 1984; Assistant General Manager, GEC (formerly Marconi) Avionics Ltd, since 1969; Inspector, Royal Auxiliary Air Force, since 1983; *b* 6 Sept. 1929; *s* of Arthur Langridge Harris and Doris Mabel (*née* Offen); *m* 1955, (Yvonne) Patricia Stone; two *d*. *Educ*: St Edward's Sch., Oxford; Univ. of Birmingham (BSc). CEng, FIEE 1976; MBIM 1969. Served: RAF, 1947–49; RAFVR, 1949–60; RAuxAF, 1960–78 and 1982–; commanded 1 (Co. Hertford) Maritime HQ Unit, 1973–77; Air Force Mem., TA&VRA for Greater London, 1978–; Gp Captain 1983. Elliott Bros (London) Ltd, 1952–55; Decca Navigator Co. Ltd, 1955–59; GEC (formerly Marconi) Avionics Ltd, 1959–. Chm., Hatfield Dist IEE, 1979–80. DL Greater London, 1986. *Recreations*: skiing, travel, gardening. *Address*: 29 Davenham Avenue, Northwood, Mddx HA6 3HW. *T*: Northwood 24291. *Club*: Royal Air Force.

HARRIS, Peter Michael; Circuit Administrator, Northern Circuit, Lord Chancellor's Department, since 1986; *b* 13 April 1937; *s* of Benjamin Warren Harris and Ethel Evelyn Harris (*née* Mabbutt); *m* 1963, Bridget Burke; one *s* two *d*. *Educ*: Cirencester Grammar School; Britannia Royal Naval College, Dartmouth. Cadet, RN, 1953; Lieut Comdr 1967; retired from RN 1972. Called to the Bar, Gray's Inn, 1970; Lord Chancellor's Department: Legal Asst, 1974; Sen. Legal Asst, 1977; Asst Sol., 1980; Dep. Circuit Administrator, Midland and Oxford Circuit, 1980; Head of Property and Family Law Div., 1982; Head of Civil Courts Div., 1985. Asst Editor, County Court Practice. *Recreations*: reading, walking, swimming, gardening. *Address*: 5 Myton Gardens, Warwick CV34 6BH. *T*: Warwick 498787.

HARRIS, Philip; Principal, Monopolies and Mergers Commission, 1977–85; *b* Manchester, 15 Dec. 1915; *er s* of S. D. Harris and Sarah Chazan; *m* 1939, Sarah Henriques Valentine; three *d*. *Educ*: Manchester Grammar Sch.; Trinity Hall, Cambridge (Open Scholarship, BA 1st Cl (with dist.), Historical Tripos, MA 1970). Asst Principal, Board of Trade, 1938–40. Served War, 1940–45; Anti-Aircraft Command and Western Europe; 2nd Lieut RA, 1941; Lieut, 2/8th Lancs Fusiliers, 1944; Capt., 6th Royal Welch Fusiliers, 1945. Principal, Board of Trade, 1946; Asst Sec., Board of Trade, 1948–64; Asst Registrar, Office of the Registrar of Restrictive Trading Agreements, 1964–66, Principal Asst Registrar, 1966–73; Principal Asst Registrar, Fair Trading Div. I, DTI, 1973; Dir, Restrictive Trade Practices Div., Office of Fair Trading, 1973–76. Nuffield Travelling Fellowship, 1956–57 (study of Indian Industrial Development). UK Mem., EEC Adv. Cttee on Cartels and Monopolies, 1973–76. Leader, UK Delgn to Internat. Cotton Advisory Cttee, 1960, 1963. *Recreation*: history. *Address*: 23 Court House Gardens, Finchley, N3 1PU. *T*: 01–346 3138.

HARRIS, Sir Philip (Charles), Kt 1985; Chairman, Harris Queensway PLC, since 1964; *b* 15 Sept. 1942; *s* of Charles William Harris and Ruth Ellen (*née* Ward); *m* 1960, Pauline Norma (*née* Chumley); three *s* one *d*. *Educ*: Streatham Grammar School. Non-exec. Dir, Fisons Plc, 1986–. Mem., British Show Jumping Assoc., 1974. Member: Council of

Governors, Utd Med. and Dental Schs of Guy's and St Thomas's Hosps, 1984–; Court of Patrons, RCOG, 1984–; Chm., Generation Trust, 1984–; Governor, Nat. Hosp. for Nervous Diseases, 1985–. Hambro Business Man of the Year, 1983. *Recreations:* football, cricket, show jumping, tennis. *Address:* Harris House, 76 High Street, Orpington, Kent BR6 0LX.

HARRIS, Phillip, FRCSE, FRCPE, FRCS(Glas); FRS(Ed); Consultant Neurosurgeon, Department of Surgical Neurology, Royal Infirmary and Western General Hospital, Edinburgh, and Spinal Unit, Edenhall Hospital, Musselburgh, since 1955; Senior Lecturer, Department of Neurological Surgery, Edinburgh University, since 1975; Member, MRC Brain Metabolism Unit, University of Edinburgh, since 1952; Chairman: Professional and Linguistic Assessments Board, General Medical Council; Committee of Management, School of Occupational Therapy, Edinburgh; Member, Advisory Council, Society of British Neurological Surgeons; *b* Edinburgh, 28 March 1922; *s* of late Simon Harris, Edinburgh; *m* 1949, Sheelagh Shèna (*née* Coutts); one *s* one *d*. *Educ:* Royal High Sch., Edinburgh; Edinburgh Univ.; Sch. of Med. of Royal Colls, Edinburgh. Medallist in Anatomy, Physiol., Physics, Materia Medica and Therapeutics, Med., Midwifery and Gynaec., and Surgery. LRCP and LRCSEd, LRFP and SG 1944; FRCSE 1948; MRCPE 1954; FRCPE 1959; FRCS(Glas) 1964 (*ad eundem*). Sydney Watson-Smith Lectr, RCPE, 1967; Honeyman-Gillespie Lectr, Edinburgh Univ., 1968; Visiting Prof.: Columbus, Ohio; Cincinnati, Ohio; Phoenix, Arizona; UCLA; Montreal Neurological Inst., Montreal; Chicago; Rangoon; Bangkok; Buenos Aires; La Paz. Guest Chief and Vis. Lectr in Univs in Canada, USA, Japan, Israel, Denmark, Peru, Hong Kong, Uruguay. Member: Amer. Assoc. of Neurolog. Surgeons; Burmese Med. Assoc.; Hong Kong Surg. Soc.; Middle East Neurosurg. Soc.; Brazilian Coll. Surgeons. Chm., Epilepsy Soc. of Edinburgh and SE Reg.; Trustee and Mem. Exec., Scottish Trust for the Physically Disabled Ltd. Pres., Royal High Sch. FP Club, Edinburgh. Captain RAMC, 1945–48. *Publications:* Spinal Injuries, RCSE, 1965; (ed jtly) Epilepsy, 1971; (ed jtly) Head Injuries, 1971; chapters in books on neurological surgery; over 60 papers in scientific jls on various neurosurgical topics. *Recreations:* sport, music, travel. *Address:* 4/5 Fettes Rise, Edinburgh EH4 1QH. *T:* 031–552 8900. *Clubs:* New (Edinburgh); Royal Scottish Automobile (Glasgow); University Staff (Edinburgh).

HARRIS, Ven. (Reginald) Brian; Archdeacon of Manchester, since 1980; a Residentiary Canon of Manchester Cathedral, since 1980, Sub-Dean since 1986; *b* 14 Aug. 1934; *s* of Reginald and Ruby Harris; *m* 1959, Anne Patricia Hughes; one *s* one *d*. *Educ:* Eltham College; Christ's College Cambridge (MA); Ridley Hall, Cambridge. Curate of Wednesbury, 1959–61; Curate of Uttoxeter, 1961–64; Vicar of St Peter, Bury, 1964–70; Vicar of Walmsley, Bolton, 1970–80; RD of Walmsley, 1970–80. *Recreations:* walking, painting, music. *Address:* 4 Victoria Avenue, Eccles, Manchester M30 9HA. *T:* 061–707 6444.

HARRIS, Richard Reader; *b* 4 June 1913; *s* of Richard Reader Harris; *m* 1940, Pamela Rosemary Merrick Stephens; three *d*. *Educ:* St Lawrence Coll., Ramsgate. Called to the Bar, 1941. Fire Service, 1939–45. MP (C) Heston and Isleworth, 1950–70. *Recreations:* squash, tennis.

HARRIS, Richard Travis; Director: Gallaher Ltd, since 1970; Burton Group plc, since 1984; *b* 15 April 1919; 2nd *s* of Douglas Harris and Emmeline Harris (*née* Travis); *m* 1st, 1941, June Constance Rundle (marr. diss. 1953); two *d*; 2nd, 1953, Margaret Sophia Nye (*née* Aron); one *s* one *d*. *Educ:* Charterhouse; RMA Woolwich. Served War of 1939–45, France, Western Desert, Tunisia, Italy (despatches twice); BAOR, 1945–46; Sudan Defence Force Signal Regt, 1947–50 (CO, 1948–50); retired from Royal Signals, 1950, Lt-Col. Man. Dir, Rediffusion (Nigeria) Ltd and Gen. Manager, Rediffusion in Africa, 1951–54; Dep. Gen. Manager, Associated-Rediffusion Ltd, 1954–57; Man. Dir, Coates & Co. (Plymouth) Ltd, 1957–64 (Dir, 1957–68); Man. Dir, 1964–78, Chm., 1970–78, Dollond & Aitchison Ltd; Chm., Dollond & Aitchison Group Ltd (formerly TWW Enterprises Ltd), 1970–78 (Dir, 1968–85); Director: Dollond International Ltd, 1973–83; Filotechnica Salmoiraghi SpA, 1974–83; Istituto Ottico Vigano SpA, 1974–83; Saunders Valve Co. Ltd, 1978–84; Mono Pumps Ltd, 1978–84; Formatura Iniezione Polimeri SpA, 1978–84; Tobacco Kiosks Ltd, 1978–84; Gallaher Pensions Ltd, 1975–84. Chairman: Fedn of Optical Corporate Bodies, 1970–82; Fedn of Opthalmic & Dispensing Opticians, 1985–; Chm. Council, Inst. of Dirs, 1982–85 (Vice-Pres., 1985–); Mem. Council, Univ. of Birmingham, 1978–, Life Mem., Court, 1981. Governor, Royal Shakespeare Theatre, 1980–; Master, Coachmakers and Coach Harness Makers, 1963–64. *Recreations:* fishing, theatre. *Address:* 21 Lucy's Mill, Stratford-upon-Avon, Warwickshire CV37 6DE. *T:* Stratford-upon-Avon 66016. *Clubs:* Athenæum; Royal Western Yacht (Plymouth).

HARRIS, Robert; actor since 1922; *b* 28 March 1900; *s* of Alfred H. Harris and Suzanne Amelie (*née* Anstie). *Educ:* Sherborne; New Coll., Oxford. Has appeared in Shakespearean rôles with the Old Vic-Sadler's Wells Company and at Stratford-on-Avon, and in the West End (Hamlet, Oberon, Prospero, Angelo, Henry IV, King John, Shylock and Dr Faustus. Other parts include: St Bernard, in The Marvellous History of St Bernard; Charles Tritton, in The Wind and The Rain; Eugene Marchbanks, in Candida (NY); Orin Mannon, in Mourning Becomes Electra; Thomas More, in A Man for all Seasons (USA); Pope Pius XII in The Deputy (NY); 40 Years On (Canada); J. Robert Oppenheimer, Fortune Theatre; films include: How he lied to her Husband; Decline and Fall; Morta in Roma; Ransom; Love Among the Ruins. Television and radio plays incl.: Old Jolyon in The Forsyte Saga; Prof. Gay in C. P. Snow's Strangers and Brothers (serials); Archdeacon Grantly in The Barchester Chronicles; The Mysterious Death of Charles Bravo; Edward and Mrs Simpson (TV serial). *Recreation:* travel. *Clubs:* Garrick, Chelsea Arts.

HARRIS, Sir Ronald (Montague Joseph), KCVO 1960 (MVO 1943); CB 1956; First Church Estates Commissioner, 1969–82; Chairman, Central Board of Finance of Church of England, 1978–82; *b* 6 May 1913; *o s* of late Rev. J. Montague Harris and Edith Annesley Harris (*née* Malcolmson); *m* 1st, 1939, Margaret Julia Wharton (*d* 1955); one *s* three *d*; 2nd, 1957, Marjorie, *widow* of Julian Tryon, and *e d* of late Sir Harry Verney, 4th Bt, DSO, and late Lady Rachel Verney; one step *d* (one step *s* decd). *Educ:* Harrow; Trinity Coll., Oxford. India Office and Burma Office, 1936–38, Private Sec. to Sec. of Cabinet, 1939–43; India Office and Burma Office, 1944–47; Imperial Defence Coll., 1948; HM Treasury, 1949–52; Cabinet Office, 1952–55; Second Crown Estate Commissioner, 1955–60; Third Sec., HM Treasury, 1960–64; Sec. to Church Commissioners, 1964–68. Director: Yorks Insurance Co., 1966–69; Yorkshire General Life Assurance Co., 1969–84; General Accident Fire and Life Assurance Corp. Ltd, 1970–84. Chairman: Benenden Sch. Council, 1971–77; Friends of Yehudi Menuhin Sch., 1972–, Governor, 1976–, Vice-Chm. of Governors, 1984–. *Address:* Slyfield Farm House, Stoke D'Abernon, Cobham, Surrey KT11 3QE. *Club:* Boodle's.

HARRIS, Rosemary Jeanne; author; *b* 1923; *yr d* of Marshal of the RAF Sir Arthur Harris, 1st Bt, GCB, OBE, AFC, LLD, and of Barbara Kyrle Money. *Educ:* privately; Thorneloe Sch., Weymouth; St Martin's, Central and Chelsea Schs of Art. Red Cross Nursing Auxiliary, London, Westminster Div., from 1941. Student, 1945–48; picture restorer, 1949; student at Courtauld Inst. (Dept of Technology), 1950; Reader, MGM, 1951–52; subseq. full-time writer. Reviewer of children's books for The Times, 1970–73. Television plays: Peronik, 1976; The Unknown Enchantment, 1981. *Publications:* The Summer-House, 1956; Voyage to Cythera, 1958; Venus with Sparrows, 1961; All My Enemies, 1967; The Nice Girl's Story, 1968; A Wicked Pack of Cards, 1969; The Double Snare, 1975; Three Candles for the Dark, 1976; *for children:* The Moon in the Cloud, 1968 (Carnegie Medal); The Shadow on the Sun, 1970; The Seal-Singing, 1971; The Child in the Bamboo Grove, 1971; The Bright and Morning Star, 1972; The King's White Elephant, 1973; The Lotus and the Grail, 1974; The Flying Ship, 1974; The Little Dog of Fo, 1976; I Want to be a Fish, 1977; A Quest for Orion, 1978; Beauty and the Beast, 1979; Greenfinger House, 1979; Tower of the Stars, 1980; The Enchanted Horse, 1981; Janni's Stork, 1982; Zed, 1982; (adapted) Heidi, by Johanna Spyri, 1983. *Recreations:* music, theatre, photography, gardening. *Address:* c/o A. P. Watt Ltd (Literary Agents), 26/28 Bedford Row, WC1R 4HE.

See also Sir A. T. K. Harris, Bt.

HARRIS, Rosina Mary; Partner, Joynson-Hicks, Solicitors, since 1954 (Senior Partner, 1977–86); Deputy Chairman, Blundell-Permoglaze Holdings plc, 1981–86 (non-executive Director, 1979–86); *b* 30 May 1921; *d* of Alfred Harris, CBE, DSO, and Rosa Alfreda Harris. *Educ:* St Swithun's Sch., Winchester; Oxford Univ. (BA 1946, MA; BCL). Joined American Ambulance of Gt Britain, 1940. Member, Whitford Committee (a Cttee set up under the Chairmanship of Hon. Mr Justice Whitford to enquire into and report as to copyright law), 1973. The Queen's Silver Jubilee Medal, 1977. *Recreations:* theatre, riding. *Address:* 23 Devonshire Place, W1N 1PD. *T:* (office) 01–836 8456.

HARRIS, Prof. Roy, MA, DPhil, PhD; FRSA; Professor of General Linguistics, University of Oxford, since Jan. 1978; Fellow of Worcester College, Oxford; *b* 24 Feb. 1931; *s* of Harry and Emmie J. Harris; *m* 1955, Rita Doreen Shulman; one *d*. *Educ:* Queen Elizabeth's Hospital, Bristol; St Edmund Hall, Oxford (MA, DPhil); SOAS, London (PhD). Lecteur, Ecole Normale Supérieure, Paris, 1956–57; Asst Lectr, 1957–58, Lectr, 1958–60, Univ. of Leicester; Exeter Coll., Oxford, 1960–76; Keble Coll., Oxford, 1960–67; Magdalen Coll., Oxford, 1960–76; New Coll., Oxford, 1960–67; Faculty of Medieval and Modern Languages, Oxford, 1961–76; Fellow and Tutor in Romance Philology, Keble Coll., Oxford, 1967–76; Prof. of the Romance Langs, Oxford Univ., 1976–77. Council Member, Philological Soc., 1978–82. Editor, Language & Communication, 1980–. Scott Moncrieff prize, Translators' Assoc. (Soc. of Authors), 1984. *Publications:* Synonymy and Linguistic Analysis, 1973; Communication and Language, 1978; The Language-Makers, 1980; The Language Myth, 1981; (trans.) F. de Saussure: Course in General Linguistics, 1983; (ed) Approaches to Language, 1983; (ed) Developmental Mechanisms of Language, 1985; The Origin of Writing, 1986; contribs to Analysis, French Studies, Jl of Linguistics, Language Sciences, Linguistics, Medium Ævum, Revue de linguistique romane, Semiotica, Theoria, TLS, Zeitschrift für romanische Philologie. *Recreations:* cricket, modern art and design. *Address:* Worcester College, Oxford OX1 2HB. *T:* Oxford 247251.

HARRIS, (Theodore) Wilson; *b* 24 March 1921; *m* 1st, 1945, Cecily Carew; 2nd, 1959, Margaret Whitaker (*née* Burns). *Educ:* Queen's Coll., Georgetown, British Guiana. Studied land surveying, British Guiana, 1939, and subseq. qualified to practise; led many survey parties (mapping and geomorphological research) in the interior; Senior Surveyor, Projects, for Govt of British Guiana, 1955–58. Came to live in London, 1959. Writer in Residence, Univ. of West Indies and Univ. of Toronto, 1970; Commonwealth Fellow, Leeds Univ., 1971; Vis. Prof., Univ. of Texas at Austin, 1972; Guggenheim Fellow, 1973; Henfield Fellow, UEA, 1974; Southern Arts Writer's Fellowship, 1976; Guest Lectr, Univ. of Mysore, 1978; Vis. Lectr, Yale Univ., 1979; Writer in Residence: Univ. of Newcastle, Australia, 1979; Univ. of Qld, Australia, 1986; Vis. Prof., Univ. of Texas at Austin, 1981–82; Regents' Lectr, Univ. of California, 1983. Hon. DLit Univ. of West Indies, 1984. *Publications:* Eternity to Season (poems, privately printed), 1954; Palace of the Peacock, 1960; The Far Journey of Oudin, 1961; The Whole Armour, 1962; The Secret Ladder, 1963; Heartland, 1964; The Eye of the Scarecrow, 1965; The Waiting Room, 1967; Tradition, the Writer and Society: Critical Essays, 1967; Tumatumari, 1968; Ascent to Omai, 1970; The Sleepers of Roraima (a Carib Trilogy), 1970; The Age of the Rainmakers, 1971; Black Marsden, 1972; Companions of the Day and Night, 1975; Da Silva da Silva's Cultivated Wilderness, and Genesis of the Clowns, 1977; The Tree of the Sun, 1978; Explorations (essays), 1981; The Angel at the Gate, 1982; The Womb of Space: the cross-cultural imagination, 1983; Carnival, 1985. *Address:* c/o Faber and Faber, 3 Queen Square, WC1N 3AU.

HARRIS, Thomas George; Counsellor (Commercial), British Embassy, Washington, since 1983; *b* 6 Feb. 1945; *s* of Kenneth James Harris and Dorothy Harris; *m* 1967, Mei-Ling Hwang; three *s*. *Educ:* Haberdashers' Aske's School; Gonville and Caius College, Cambridge. MA. Board of Trade, 1966–69; British Embassy, Tokyo, 1969–71; Asst Private Sec. to Minister for Aerospace, 1971–72; Dept. of Trade, 1972–76; Cabinet Office, 1976–78; Principal Private Sec. to Sec. of State for Trade and Industry, 1978–79; Asst Sec., Dept of Trade, 1979–83. *Address:* 8 Oakeshott Avenue, Highgate, N6 6NS. *T:* 01–340 2495.

HARRIS, Hon. Walter Edward, PC (Canada), QC (Canada); DCL; Director, Homewood Sanitarium Ltd; *b* 14 Jan. 1904; *s* of Melvin Harris and Helen (*née* Carruthers); *m* 1933, Grace Elma Morrison; one *s* two *d*. *Educ:* Osgoode Hall, Toronto. Served War of 1939–45. First elected to House of Commons, Canada, 1940 (re-elected 1945, 1949, 1953), MP (Canada) until 1957. Parliamentary Asst to Sec of State for External Affairs, 1947; Parly Asst to Prime Minister, 1948; Minister of Citizenship and Immigration, 1950; of Finance, 1954–57. Mem. of the firm of Harris & Dunlop, Barristers, Markdale. *Address:* Markdale, Ontario, Canada.

HARRIS, (Walter) Frank; retired 1982; *b* 19 May 1920; *m* Esther Blanche Hill; two *s* two *d*. *Educ:* King Edward's Sch., Birmingham; University of Nottingham. Served Royal Air Force, 1939–46. University, 1946–49. Ford Motor Company, 1950–65; Principal City Officer and Town Clerk, Newcastle upon Tyne, 1965–69. Comptroller and Dir, Admin, Massey-Ferguson (UK), 1969–71; Financial Dir, Dunlop SA Ltd, 1972–79; Business Planning Exec., Dunlop Ltd (UK Tyre Gp), 1979–81. *Recreations:* astrophysics (undergraduate at Univ. of S Africa and at Open Univ.), fell walking, gardening. *Address:* Acomb High House, Northumberland NE46 4PH. *T:* Hexham 602844.

HARRIS, William Barclay, QC 1961; *b* 25 Nov. 1911; *s* of W. Cecil Harris, Moatlands, E Grinstead, Sussex; *m* 1937, Elizabeth, 2nd *d* of Capt. Sir Clive Milnes-Coates, 2nd Bt, and of Lady Celia Milnes-Coates; one *s* two *d*. *Educ:* Harrow; Trinity Coll., Cambridge (MA). Served 1940–45: with Coldstream Guards, N Africa, Italy, Germany (despatches), Major. Barrister, Inner Temple, 1937. Chm., Rowton Hotels, 1965–83. A Church Commissioner, 1966–82 (Chm., Redundant Churches Cttee, 1972–82); Mem., Bd of Governors, 1972–82). Chm., Georgian Group, 1985–. Liveryman, Worshipful Co. of Merchant Taylors. *Address:* Moatlands, East Grinstead, West Sussex. *T:* Sharpthorne 810228; 29 Barkston Gardens, SW5. *T:* 01–373 8793. *Clubs:* Athenæum, MCC, Brooks's.

HARRIS, Sir William (Gordon), KBE 1969; CB 1963; MA (Cantab); FEng; FICE; Chairman, B & CE Holiday Management Co., since 1978; *b* 10 June 1912; *s* of late Capt. James Whyte Harris, Royal Naval Reserve, and Margaret Roberta Buchanan Forsyth; *m* 1938, Margaret Emily Harvie; three *s* one *d*. *Educ:* Liverpool Coll.; Sidney Sussex Coll., Cambridge. Mechanical Sciences Tripos and BA 1932, MA 1937. London Midland & Scottish Railway, 1932–35; Sudan Irrigation Dept, 1935–37; Joined Civil Engineer in Chief's Dept, Admiralty, 1937; Asst Civil Engineer in Chief, 1950; Deputy Civil Engineer in Chief, 1955; Civil Engineer in Chief, 1959; Dir-Gen., Navy Works, 1960–63; Dir-Gen. of Works, MPBW, 1963–65; Dir-Gen., Highways, MoT, later DoE, 1965–73. Partner, Peter Fraenkel & Partners, 1973–78. Dir, British Sch. of Osteopathy, 1982–. Chief British Delegate to: Perm. Internat. Assoc. of Navigation Congresses, 1969–June 1985 (Vice-Pres., 1976–79); Perm. Internat. Assoc. of Road Congresses, 1970–73; Mem., Dover Harbour Bd, 1959–82 (Dep. Chm., 1975–79; Chm., 1980–82); Chm., Construction Industry Manpower Bd, 1976–79. Commonwealth Fund (of New York) Fellowship, 1950–51. A Vice-Pres., Instn Civil Engineers, 1971–74, Pres. 1974–75. FEng, 1977. Mem., Smeatonian Soc. of Civil Engineers, 1966– (Pres., 1984). Hon. DSc City, 1977. *Recreations:* gardening, ten grand-children, walking dog. *Address:* 3 Rofant Road, Northwood, Mddx. *T:* Northwood 25899.

HARRIS, Sir William (Woolf), Kt 1974; OBE 1961; JP; surveyor and public company director; *b* London, 19 Aug. 1910; *e s* of Simon Harris and Fanny Harris, London; *m* 1952, Beverly Joyce, *y d* of Howard Bowden, Minneapolis, USA; one *s* two *d*. *Educ:* King's Coll.; Princeton Univ. Chm. of number of companies concerned with residential and industrial building construction. Chm., Bow Street Magistrates Court, 1955–80; Chm., Inner London Juvenile Courts, 1955–75; Member: Inner London Sessions Appeals Court; London Probation Cttee and Home Office Juvenile Courts Consultative Cttee, 1955–72; a General Commissioner of Taxes; Vice-Pres. (former Chm.), Royal Soc. of St George (City of London); former jt Nat. Treas., Trades Adv. Council; Founder 1951, and Chm. until 1963, Addison Boys Club, Hammersmith; Conservative Party: Chairman: Nat. Union of Conservative Assocs, 1971–73; Party Conf., 1972; Standing Adv. Cttee on Candidates, 1971–73; Greater London Area, 1966–69; former London Area, 1963; Mem., Adv. Cttee on Policy, 1965–75 and of other nat. adv. cttees; Mem., Nat. Exec. Cttee and Gen. Purpose Cttee, 1963–75; Chm., S Battersea Conservative Assoc., 1956–63; former Pres. and Chm., Battersea Chamber of Commerce; Branch Chm., NSPCC, 1956–65; Founder and Nat. Chm., Leasehold Reform Assoc., 1956–67. Mem. Council and Ct, City Univ., 1979–. Mem. Council, Imperial Soc. of Knights Bachelor, 1978–. Prime Warden, Worshipful Co. of Basketmakers, 1984–85. Freeman, City of London; High Sheriff of Greater London, 1971–72; JP Bow Street, 1952. *Publications:* papers on problems of juvenile delinquency, child welfare, mental health and penal reform in various jls. *Recreations:* reading history, theatre, travel. *Address:* 6 London House, Avenue Road, NW8 7PX. *T:* 01–586 0707. *Clubs:* Carlton, St Stephen's Constitutional, City Livery.

HARRIS, Wilson; *see* Harris, T. W.

HARRISON; *see* Graham-Harrison.

HARRISON, (Alastair) Brian (Clarke); DL; farmer; *b* 3 Oct. 1921; *s* of late Brig. E. F. Harrison, Melbourne; *m* 1952, Elizabeth Hood Hardie, Oaklands, NSW, Aust.; one *s* one *d*. *Educ:* Geelong Grammar Sch.; Trinity Coll., Cambridge. Capt. AIF. MP (C) Maldon, Essex, 1955–Feb. 1974; Parliamentary Private Secretary to: Min. of State, Colonial Office, 1955–56; Sec. of State for War, 1956–58; Min. of Agriculture, Fisheries and Food, 1958–60. Mem. Victoria Promotion Cttee (London); Mem. One Nation Gp which published The Responsible Society, and One Europe; toured USA on E-SU Ford Foundation Fellowship, 1959; Commonwealth Parliamentary Assoc. Delegations: Kenya and Horn of Africa, 1960; Gilbert and Ellice Islands, New Hebrides and British Solomon Islands Protectorate. Chm., Standing Conf. of Eastern Sport and Physical Recreation, 1974–80. Organizer (with Univ. of WA), expedns to Nepal studying human physiol., 1979–84. High Sheriff, 1979, DL 1980, Essex. *Recreations:* photography, gardening. *Address:* Green Farm House, Copford, Colchester, Essex; Mundethana, Kojonup, WA 6395, Australia. *Clubs:* Pratt's; Melbourne (Melbourne); Weld (Perth).

HARRISON, Albert Norman, CB 1966; CVO 1955; OBE 1946; RCNC; Hon. Vice-President RINA; *b* 12 July 1901; *s* of William Arthur and Sarah Jane Harrison, Portsmouth, Hants; *m* 1941, Queenie Perpetua Parker, Luton, Beds; one *d*. *Educ:* Portsmouth; Royal Naval Coll., Greenwich. Asst Constructor, Royal Corps of Naval Constructors, 1926; Constructor, 1937; Principal Ship Overseer. Vickers-Armstrong, Barrow-in-Furness, 1936–39; Staff of RA (D), Home Fleet, 1940–41; Naval Constructor-in-Chief, Royal Canadian Navy, 1942–48; Chief Constructor, Admiralty, 1948–51; Asst Dir of Naval Construction, Admiralty, 1951–61; Dir of Naval Construction, Min. of Defence (N) (formerly Admiralty), 1961–66. *Address:* Whiteoaks, 126 Bloomfield Road, Bath, Avon BA2 2AS. *T:* Bath 29145. *Club:* Bath and County (Bath).

HARRISON, Alexander, CBE 1955; CA; Vice-President, Trustee Savings Bank Association (Deputy-Chairman, 1947–59); *b* 26 Feb. 1890; *s* of John Harrison, CBE, LLD, FRSE, DL, and Helen Georgina Roberts; *m* 1931, Jean Muriel Small; one *s* three *d*. *Educ:* Merchiston Castle Sch. Chartered Accountant, 1914 (Distinction). Chairman: Edinburgh Savings Bank, 1945–54; Edinburgh Investment Trust, 1945–60; Standard Life Assurance Co., 1955–57; Dir, British Linen Bank, 1945–68; Alex Cowan & Sons. Mem. Edinburgh Town Council, 1946–48. Served European War, 1914–18; temp. Major, Royal Scots, attached Machine Gun Corps in France and Italy, FRSGS. Hon. Pres., Scottish Mountaineering Club. *Address:* 3a Tipperlinn Road, Edinburgh EH10 5ET. *T:* 031–447 7434. *Clubs:* Alpine; New (Edinburgh).

HARRISON, Brian; *see* Harrison, A. B. C.

HARRISON, Prof. Charles Victor; retired; Professor of Pathology, University of Ife, Nigeria, 1972–75; *b* Newport, Mon, 1907; *s* of Charles Henry Harrison, LDS, and Violet Harrison (*née* Witchell); *m* 1937, Olga Beatrice Cochrane; one *s* one *d*. *Educ:* Dean Close Sch., Cheltenham; University Coll., Cardiff; University Coll. Hosp., London. MB, BCh, BSc (Wales), 1929; MB, BS (London), 1929; MD (London), 1937; FRCPath 1965; FRCP 1967. Demonstrator in Pathology, Welsh National School of Medicine, 1930; Asst Morbid Anatomist, British Postgraduate Medical Sch., 1935; Senior Lecturer, Liverpool Univ., 1939; Reader in Morbid Anatomy, Postgraduate Medical Sch. of London, 1946; Prof., Royal Postgrad. Med. Sch., Univ. of London, 1955–72. Hon. DSc Wales, 1972. Willie Seager Gold Medal in Pathology, 1927. *Publications:* (ed) Recent Advances in Pathology, 1973; various scientific papers in Jl of Pathology and Bacteriology, British Heart Journal, Jl Clin. Pathology, etc. *Recreations:* carpentry and gardening. *Address:* 8 Wattleton Road, Beaconsfield, Bucks HP9 1TS. *T:* Beaconsfield 2046.

HARRISON, Claude William, RP 1961; Artist; portrait painter and painter of conversation pieces, imaginative landscapes and murals, etc; *b* Leyland, Lancs, 31 March 1922; *s* of Harold Harrison and Florence Mildred Ireton; *m* 1947, Audrey Johnson; one *s*. *Educ:* Hutton Grammar Sch., Lancs. Served in RAF, 1942–46. Royal Coll. of Art, 1947–49; Studio in Ambleside, 1949–52. Exhibited since 1950 at: RA; RSA; Royal Society Portrait Painters; New English Art Club, etc. *Publication:* The Portrait Painter's handbook, 1968. *Recreation:* painting. *Address:* Barrow Wife, Cartmel Fell, near Grange over Sands, Cumbria. *T:* Newby Bridge 31323.

HARRISON, Sir Colin; *see* Harrison, Sir R. C.

HARRISON, David, ScD; Vice-Chancellor, University of Exeter, since 1984; Fellow of Selwyn College, Cambridge, since 1957; *b* 3 May 1930; *s* of Harold David Harrison and Lavinia Wilson; *m* 1962, Sheila Rachel Debes; one *s* one *d* (and one *s* decd). *Educ:* Bede Sch., Sunderland; Clacton County High Sch.; Selwyn Coll., Cambridge (1st Cl. Pts I and II Natural Sciences Tripos, BA 1953, PhD 1956, MA 1957, ScD 1979). CEng; FRSC (FRIC 1961), FIChemE 1968. 2nd Lieut, REME, 1949. Research student, Dept of Physical Chemistry, Cambridge, 1953–56; Univ. Asst Lectr in Chem. Engrg, 1956–61; Univ. Lectr, 1961–79; Sen. Tutor, Selwyn Coll., Cambridge, 1967–79; Vice-Chancellor, Univ. of Keele, 1979–84. Visiting Professor of Chemical Engineering: Univ. of Delaware, USA, 1967; Univ. of Sydney, 1976. Member, Council of the Senate, Univ. of Cambridge, 1967–75; Chm. of Faculty Bd of Educn, 1976–78; Member Council: Lancing Coll., 1970–82; Haileybury, 1974–84; St Edward's, Oxford, 1977–; Bolton Girls' Sch., 1981–84; Shrewsbury Sch., 1983–; Taunton Sch., 1986–; Fellow, Woodard Corporation of Schools, 1972–; Chairman: Bd of Trustees, Homerton Coll., Cambridge, 1979–; UCCA, 1984–; Voluntary Sector Consultative Council, 1984–; Mem., Marshall Aid Commemoration Commn, 1982–. FRSA 1985. Hon. Editor, Trans Instn of Chemical Engrs, 1972–78. *Publications:* (with J. F. Davidson) Fluidised Particles, 1963; (also with J. F. Davidson) Fluidization, 1971, rev. edn (with J. F. Davidson and R. Clift) 1985; numerous articles in scientific and technological jls. *Recreations:* music, tennis, hill walking, good food. *Address:* Northcote House, The Queen's Drive, Exeter EX4 4QJ. *T:* Exeter 263263. *Clubs:* Athenæum; Federation House (Stoke-on-Trent).

HARRISON, Denis Byrne; JP; a Local Commissioner for Administration in England, 1974–81, and Vice-Chairman of the Commission for Local Administration, 1975–81; *b* 11 July 1917; *y s* of late Arthur and Priscilla Harrison; *m* 1956, Alice Marion Vickers, *e d* of late Hedley Vickers. *Educ:* Birkenhead Sch.; Liverpool Univ. (LLM). Articled to late E. W. Tame, OBE (Town Clerk of Birkenhead). Admitted Solicitor, 1939; Asst Solicitor to Birkenhead Corp., 1939. Served War, 1939–46: 75th Shropshire Yeo. (Medium Regt) RA, Combined Ops Bombardment Unit; Staff Captain at HQ of OC, Cyprus. First Asst Solicitor, Wolverhampton Co. Borough, 1946–49; Dep. Town Clerk of Co. Boroughs: Warrington, 1949–57; Bolton, 1957–63; Sheffield, 1963–66; Town Clerk and Chief Exec. Officer, Sheffield, 1966–74. Mem., Advisory Council on Noise, 1970–79. Mem. Council, 1975–82, Pro-Chancellor, 1980–82, Univ. of Sheffield. JP City of London, 1976. *Recreations:* reading, music, golf. *Address:* 108A Whitehall Court, SW1. *T:* 01–930 6394; 2 Leicester Close, Henley-on-Thames, Oxon RG9 2LD. *T:* Henley-on-Thames 572782.

HARRISON, Prof. Donald Frederick Norris, MD, PhD, FRCS; Professor of Laryngology and Otology (University of London), at the Institute of Laryngology, Gray's Inn Road, WC1, since 1963; Surgeon, Royal National Throat, Nose and Ear Hospital; Civilian Consultant on ENT to RN; *b* 9 March 1925; *s* of Frederick William Rees Harrison, OBE, JP, and Florence, *d* of Robert Norris, Portsmouth, Hants; *m* 1949, Audrey, *o d* of Percival Clubb, Penarth, Glam.; two *d*. *Educ:* Newport High Sch., Mon.; Guy's Hosp. MD (London) 1960; MS (London) 1959; PhD (London) 1983; FRCS 1955. Ho. Surg., Guy's Hosp. and Royal Gwent Hospital, Newport; Surg. Registrar, Shrewsbury Eye and Ear Hosp.; Senior Registrar, Throat and Ear Dept, Guy's Hosp.; University Reader in Laryngology, Inst. of Laryngol. and Otol. Hunterian Prof., RCS, 1962; Eramus Wilson Demonstrator, RCS, 1971; Lectures: Chevalier Jackson, 1964; Yearsley, 1972; Wilde, 1972; Litchfield, 1973; Semon, 1974; Colles, RCSI, 1977; Jobson Horne, BMA, 1979; Conacher, Toronto, 1978; Harris, USA, 1984; Putney, USA, 1985; Baker, 1986. W. J. Harrison Prize, RSM, 1978; Gold medal, Internat. Fedn of Oto Rhino Laryngological Socs, 1985. Mem. of Court of Examiners, RCS; Examr, NUI; External Examr, Univs of Melbourne, Sydney, Manchester, Liverpool, Glasgow, Hong Kong and Cambridge; Fellow Medical Soc. London; Scientific Fellow, Royal Zoological Soc. of London; FRSM (Pres., Sect. of Laryngology, 1984, former Vice-Pres.); Mem. Council, Sect. of Oncology); Mem. BMA; Mem. Council: Brit. Assoc. of Otolaryngologists; Brit. Assoc. of Head and Neck Oncologists (Pres.); Former Chairman: Special Adv. Cttee on Human Communication; Bd Postgrad. Med. Studies, London Univ.; Chm., Centennial Conf., Laryngeal Cancer, 1974; Asst Sec., Collegium Oto-Rhino-Laryngologium; Member: Anatomical Soc. of Great Britain; Cttee of Management, Institute of Cancer Research; Internat. Cttee for Cancer of Larynx; Chm., NE Thames Region Postgrad. Cttee. Editorial Board: Acta Otolaryngologica; Practica Oto-Rhino-Laryngologica; Annals of Oto-Rhino-Laryngology; Excerpta Medica (Sect. II); Otolaryngological Digest. Hon. FRCSE 1981; Hon. Fellow: Acad. ENT, America, 1976; Triol. Soc., USA, 1977; Amer. Laryngol Assoc., 1979; Hon. FRACS, 1977. Hon. Member: NZ ENT Soc.; Jamaican ENT Soc.; Polish ENT Soc.; Egyptian ENT Soc.; Otolaryngological Soc., Australia; Spanish ENT Soc., For. Mem., Internat. Broncho-œsophagological Soc.; Corresp. Member: Amer. Head and Neck Soc.; Soc. Française d'Otorhinolaryngologie; Otolaryngological Soc., Denmark; Amer. Acad. of Facial Plastic Reconstr. Surgery; Pacific Coast Oto-Ophthalmological Soc.; Amer. Laryngological Soc.; Yeoman, Soc. of Apothecaries. *Publications:* (ed jtly) Scientific Basis of Otolaryngology, 1976; articles on familial hæmorrhagic telangiectases, meatal oseomata, cancer chemotherapy, head and neck surgery in learned jls; chapters in Text Books on Ent. and Gen. Surgery. *Recreation:* heraldry. *Address:* Institute of Laryngology and Otology, Gray's Inn Road, WC1. *T:* 01–837 8855; Springfield, Fisher's Farm, Horley, Surrey. *T:* Horley 4307.

HARRISON, Douglas Creese, DSc London, PhD Cantab, ARIC; Professor of Biochemistry, Queen's University, Belfast, 1935–67, now Professor Emeritus; *b* 29 April, 1901; *s* of Lovell and Lillian E. Harrison, MBE, JP; *m* 1926, Sylva Thurlow, MA, PhD, Philadelphia, USA; one *s*. *Educ:* Highgate Sch.; King's Coll., London; Emmanuel Coll., Cambridge. Keddey Fletcher-Warr Research Studentship, 1925–28; Lecturer at Sheffield Univ., 1926–35. *Publications:* various papers in the Biochemical Journal, Proc. Royal Society, Lancet, etc. *Address:* 4 Broomhill Park Central, Belfast. *T:* Belfast 665685.

HARRISON, Maj.-Gen. Eric George William Warde, CB 1945; CBE 1943; MC 1915; MA (hon.) Oxford; *b* 23 March 1893; *s* of Major W. C. Warde Harrison, Indian Army; *m* 1961, Mrs Roza M. Stevenson, *widow* of J. B. Stevenson (she *d* 1967). *Educ:* Royal Military Academy, Woolwich. Commissioned Royal Artillery, 1913; European War, France and Belgium, 1914–19, GSOII 58 Div. and III Corps (despatches four times, MC, Crown of Italy, Bt Major); Staff Coll. Camberley, 1925–26; GSOII Lahore District, India, 1928–32; shot in Tanganika, 1930; in Baltistan, British Lahaul, Chamba in Himalayas, and in forests of United and Central Provinces in India; Major, 1932; Bt Lieut-Col 1931; Commanding Oxford Univ. OTC 1934–38; Lieut-Col 1939; Col 1939. War of 1939–45, CRA 12 Div., BRA Northern Ireland, CCRA 9 Corps, MGRA AFHQ, Comdr Surrey and Sussex District. War Service North Africa and Italy, 1943–45 (despatches, CBE, CB); Temp. Maj.-Gen. 1944; ADC to the King, 1945–46; retired pay, 1946. JP 1951, DL 1955, High Sheriff 1958, Cornwall. Chm. St Lawrence's Hospital Management Cttee, 1952–66. *Publications:* Riding, 1949; To Own a Dog, 1951; Gunners,

Game and Gardens, 1979. *Recreations:* gardening, painting; Rugby football Mother Country XV 1919, Army 1920; Athletics, represented England in 120 yds Hurdles, 1914 and 1920, Olympic Games, 1924; Master RA Harriers, 1920–24, Staff Coll. Drag 1925–26, Lahore Hounds 1928–31, South Oxon Foxhounds, 1935–38, North Cornwall Foxhounds, 1940–48. *Address:* Swallowfield Park, near Reading, Berks. *Club:* Army and Navy.

HARRISON, Sir Ernest (Thomas), Kt 1981; OBE 1972; FCA; Chairman and Chief Executive, Racal Electronics Plc, since 1966; Chairman and Chief Executive, Decca Ltd, since 1980; Chairman, Racal-Chubb Ltd, since 1984; *b* 11 May 1926; *s* of Ernest Horace Harrison and Gertrude Rebecca Gibbons Harrison; *m* 1960, Phyllis Brenda Knight (Janie); three *s* two *d. Educ:* Trinity Grammar Sch., Wood Green, London. Qualified as Chartered Accountant, 1950; served Articles with Harker Holloway & Co.; joined Racal Electronics as Secretary and Chief Accountant, when company commenced manufacturing, 1951; Director, 1958, Dep. Man. Dir, 1961. Active in National Savings movement, 1964–76, for which services awarded OBE. Mem., RSA; Liveryman, Scriveners' Co. CompIERE 1975; CBIM; CompIEE 1978. Hon. DSc: Cranfield, 1981; City, 1982; DUniv: Surrey, 1981; Edinburgh, 1983. Businessman of the Year, 1981. *Recreations:* horse racing (owner), gardening, sport, espec. soccer. *Address:* Racal Electronics Plc, Western Road, Bracknell, Berkshire RG12 1RG.

HARRISON, Sir Francis Alexander Lyle, (Sir Frank Harrison), Kt 1974; MBE 1943; QC (NI); DL; President, Lands Tribunal for Northern Ireland, 1964–83; District Electoral Areas Commissioner, 1984; *b* 19 March 1910; *s* of Rev. Alexander Lyle Harrison and Mary Luise (*née* Henderson), Rostrevor, Co. Down; *m* 1940, Norah Patricia (*née* Rea); two *d. Educ:* Campbell Coll., Belfast; Trinity Coll., Dublin. BA (Moderator in Legal Sci.), LLB (Hons). Called to Bar of NI, 1937. Served War: commissioned Gen. List, Oct. 1939; ADC to GOC, NI, 1939–40; Major, Dep. Asst Adjt-Gen., HQ, NI, 1941–45 (MBE). Apptd to determine Industrial Assurance disputes in NI, 1946–62; Counsel to Attorney-Gen., NI, 1946–48; KC 1948. Legal Adviser to Min. of Home Affairs, 1949–64; Sen. Crown Prosecutor, Co. Fermanagh, 1948–54; subseq. for Counties Tyrone, Londonderry and Antrim, 1954–64; Chm., Mental Health Review Tribunal, 1948–64; Counsel to the Speakers of House of Commons and Senate of NI, 1953–64; Mem. Statute Law Cttee, NI, 1953–64; Chm., Advisory Cttee under Civil Authorities Special Powers Acts (NI), 1957–62; Bencher, Inn of Court of NI, 1961; Chm., Shaftesbury Sq. Hosp. Management Cttee, 1964–73; Chm., Glendhu Children's Hostel, 1968–81; Founder Mem., NI Assoc. of Mental Health, 1959. Boundary Comr under Local Govt (Boundaries) Act (NI), 1971 and 1982–84. DL Co. Down, 1973. *Publications:* Report of Working Party on Drug Dependence, 1968; Recommendations as to Local Government Boundaries and Wards in Northern Ireland, 1972, 1984; Recommendations as to District Electoral Areas in Northern Ireland, 1985. *Recreations:* hybridisation of narcissi, country pursuits, social service. *Address:* Ballydorn Hill, Killinchy, Newtownards, Co. Down, Northern Ireland. *T:* Killinchy 541 250.

HARRISON, Francis Anthony Kitchener; *b* 28 Aug. 1914; *s* of late Fred Harrison, JP, and Mrs M. M. Harrison (*née* Mitchell); *m* 1955, Sheila Noëlle, *d* of late Lt-Col N. D. Stevenson and of Lady Nye; three *s* one *d. Educ:* Winchester; New Coll., Oxford. Asst Principal, India Office, Nov. 1937; 1st Sec., UK High Commn, New Delhi, 1949–51; Commonwealth Relations Office, 1951–56; Asst Sec., 1954; Dep. High Comr for the UK at Peshawar, 1956–59; Asst Sec., CRO, 1959–61; British Dep. High Comr, New Zealand, 1961–64; Asst Sec., Cabinet Office, 1965–67; Asst Dir, Civil Service Selection Bd, 1967–79. *Recreations:* golf, gardening. *Address:* Lea Farm, Bramley, near Guildford, Surrey. *T:* Guildford 893138.

HARRISON, Prof. Francis Llewelyn, FBA 1965; Professor of Ethnomusicology, University of Amsterdam, 1970–76, now Emeritus; *b* Dublin, 29 Sept. 1905; *s* of Alfred Francis and Florence May Harrison; *m* 1966, Joan Rimmer; (two *d* of a former marriage). *Educ:* St Patrick's Cathedral Gram. Sch., Dublin; Mountjoy Sch., Dublin; Trinity Coll., Dublin; Oxford Univ. MusB Dublin, 1926; MusD Dublin, 1929; MA, DMus Oxon, 1952; Hon. LLD Queen's (Canada), 1974. Organist, St Canice's Cath., Kilkenny, 1927; Prof. of Music: Queen's Univ., Kingston, Ontario, 1935; Colgate Univ., 1946; Washington Univ., St Louis, 1947; Lectr in Music, 1952, Sen. Lectr, 1956, Reader in History of Music, 1962–70, University of Oxford; Senior Research Fellow, Jesus Coll., 1965–70. Visiting Professor of Musicology: Yale Univ., 1958–59; Utrecht Univ., 1976–79; Mellon, Univ. of Pittsburg, 1981; Vis. Prof. of Music, Princeton Univ., 1961, 1968–69; Vis. Mem., Inst. for Advanced Study, Princeton, 1957; Vis. Scholar, Queen's Univ, Kingston, 1980; Fellow of Center for Advanced Study in the Behavioral Sciences, Stanford, Calif, 1965–66. General Editor: Early English Church Music, 1961–73; Polyphonic Music of the Fourteenth Century, 1963–73. *Publications:* The Eton Choirbook (3 vols), 1956–61; Music in Medieval Britain, 1958; Collins Music Encyclopaedia (with J. A. Westrup), 1956; Musicology (with M. Hood and C. V. Palisca), 1963; European Musical Instruments (with J. Rimmer), 1964; Polyphonic Music of the Fourteenth Century, vol. V (Motets of French Provenance), 1969, vol. XV (Motets of English Provenance), 1980, (with E. Sanders and P. J. Lefferts) vol. XVI (English Music for Mass and Office), 1983, vol. XVII (Votive Sequences etc.), 1986; Time, Place and Music, 1974; (with E. J. Dobson) Medieval English Songs, 1979; edns of music by William Mundy, John Sheppard and others; contribs to New Oxford History of Music, and to musical jls, etc. *Recreation:* travel. *Address:* 3 Gore Mews, Canterbury, Kent CT1 1JB. *T:* Canterbury 59752.

HARRISON, Sir Frank; *see* Harrison, Sir Francis A. L.

HARRISON, Fred Brian, CBE 1982; FCA; Member, British Coal (formerly National Coal Board), since 1976; *b* 6 March 1927; *s* of Fred Harrison and Annie Harrison; *m* 1950, Margaret Owen; two *s. Educ:* Burnley Grammar Sch. FCA 1960. East Midlands Div., National Coal Board: Divnl Internal Auditor, 1953–55; Financial Accountant, No 3 Area, 1955–57, Cost Accountant, 1957–62; Chief Accountant, No 1 Area, 1962–67; Chief Accountant, N Derbyshire Area, NCB, 1967–68; Finance Dir, Coal Products Div., NCB, 1968–71, Dep. Man. Dir, 1971–73; Dep. Chief Exec., NCB (Coal Products) Ltd, 1973–76, Chm., 1978–83. Chm., British Investment Trust, 1978–85. *Recreations:* music, theatre. *Address:* 11 Birch Tree Walk, Watford, Herts. *T:* Watford 31967.

HARRISON, Sir Geoffrey (Wedgwood), GCMG 1968 (KCMG 1955; CMG 1949); KCVO 1961; HM Diplomatic Service, retired; *b* Southsea, 18 July 1908; *s* of late Lieut-Comdr Thomas Edmund Harrison, Royal Navy, and Maud, *d* of Percy Godman; *m* 1936, Amy Katharine, *d* of late Rt Hon. Sir R. H. Clive, PC, GCMG; three *s* one *d. Educ:* Winchester; King's Coll., Cambridge. Entered FO, 1932; served HM Embassy, Tokyo, 1935–37; HM Embassy, Berlin, 1937–39; Private Sec. to Parly Under-Sec., FO, 1939–41; First Sec., FO, 1941–45; Counsellor, HM Embassy, Brussels, 1945–47; Brit. Minister in Moscow, 1947–49; Head of Northern Dept, FO, 1949–51; Asst Under-Sec., FO, 1951–56; Ambassador: to Brazil, 1956–58; to Persia, 1958–63; Dep. Under-Sec. of State, FO, 1963–65; Ambassador to the USSR, 1965–68. Mem., West Sussex CC, 1970–77. Order of Homayoun (1st Class), 1959. *Recreations:* music, gardening. *Address:* West Wood, Mannings Heath, near Horsham, Sussex. *T:* Horsham 40409; 6 Ormonde Gate, SW3. *T:* 01-352 9488.

See also J. C. Harrison.

HARRISON, George Anthony; DL; solicitor; Clerk to the Lieutenancy of Greater Manchester; Chairman and Director, Central Station Properties Ltd; Director of various companies; *b* 20 Aug. 1930; *s* of John and Agnes Catherine Harrison; *m* 1957, Jane Parry; two *s* one *d. Educ:* Roundhay Sch., Leeds; Trinity Coll., Cambridge (MA, LLB). Asst Solicitor, Wolverhampton, 1955–58; ICI, 1958–59; Dep. Town Clerk, Wallasey and Bolton, 1962–65; Town Clerk and Clerk of the Peace, Bolton, 1965–69; Dir-Gen., Greater Manchester Transport Exec., 1969–76; Chief Exec., Greater Manchester Council, 1976–86. DL Manchester, 1978. *Recreations:* music, squash, sailing. *Address:* 2 Clarebank, Chorley New Road, Bolton. *T:* Bolton 43545.

HARRISON, George Bagshawe, MA Cantab; PhD London; Emeritus Professor of English, University of Michigan, 1964 (Professor, 1949–64); *b* 14 July 1894; *s* of late Walter Harrison, Brighton; *m* 1919, Dorothy Agnes, *o d* of late Rev. Thomas Barker; one *d* (three *s* decd). *Educ:* Brighton Coll.; Queens' Coll., Cambridge (Classical Exhibitioner); 1st Class English Tripos, 1920. Commnd to 5th Bn The Queen's Royal Regt, and served in India and Mesopotamia, 1914–19; Staff Capt. 42nd Indian Infantry Brigade (despatches); War of 1939–45, RASC and Intelligence Corps, 1940–43. Asst Master, Felsted Sch., 1920–22; Senior Lecturer in English, St Paul's Training Coll., Cheltenham, 1922–24; Asst Lecturer in English Literature, King's Coll., University of London, 1924–27; Lecturer, 1927–29; Frederic Ives Carpenter Visiting Prof. of English, University of Chicago, 1929; Reader in English Literature, University of London, 1929–43; Head of English Dept and Prof. of English, Queen's Univ., Kingston, Ont., Canada, 1943–49; lectured at Sorbonne, 1933, in Holland, 1940; Alexander Lecturer, University of Toronto, Canada, 1947. Mem., Internat. Commn on English in the Liturgy. Hon. LittD Villanova, 1960, Holy Cross, 1961; Marquette, 1963; Hon. LLD Assumption, 1962. KSG 1981. Campion Award for long and eminent service in cause of Christian literature, 1970. *Publications:* Shakespeare: the Man and his Stage (with E. A. G. Lamborn), 1923; Shakespeare's Fellows, 1923; John Bunyan: a Study in Personality, 1928; England in Shakespeare's Day; An Elizabethan Journal, 1591–94, 1928; A Second Elizabethan Journal 1595–98, 1931; A Last Elizabethan Journal, 1599–1603, 1933; Shakespeare at Work, 1933; The Life and Death of Robert Devereux, Earl of Essex, 1937; The Day before Yesterday (a Journal of 1936), 1938; Elizabethan Plays and Players, 1940; A Jacobean Journal, 1603–1606, 1941; A Second Jacobean Journal, 1607–1610, 1950; Shakespeare's Tragedies, 1951; Profession of English, 1962; The Fires of Arcadia, 1965; (with John McCabe) Proclaiming the Word: a handbook for church speaking, 1976; One Man in His Time 1894–1984, 1985, etc.; Editor: The Bodley Head Quartos, 1922–26; The New Readers' Shakespeare (with F. H. Pritchard); The Pilgrim's Progress and Mr Badman; The Church Book of Bunyan Meeting, 1928; Breton's Melancholike Humours, 1929; The Trial of the Lancaster Witches, 1612, 1929; The Earl of Northumberland's Advice to his son; translated and edited The Journal of De Maisse (with R. A. Jones), 1931; A Companion to Shakespeare Studies (with Harley Granville-Barker), 1934; The Letters of Queen Elizabeth, 1935; The Penguin Shakespeares, 1937–59; Contributor to The Road to Damascus, 1949; etc. *Address:* 36A Manson Street, Palmerston North, New Zealand. *T:* 75–895.

HARRISON, (George) Michael (Antony), CBE 1980; Chief Education Officer, City of Sheffield, 1967–85; Special Adviser, TVEI Programme, Manpower Services Commission, since 1985; Chairman, British Thornton Harrison Ltd, since 1985; *b* 7 April 1925; *s* of George and Kathleen Harrison; *m* 1951, Pauline (*née* Roberts); two *s* one *d. Educ:* Manchester Grammar Sch.; Brasenose Coll., Oxford. MA (LitHum); DipEd. Military service, Lieut, Parachute Regt, 1947. Asst Master, Bedford Modern Sch., 1951–53; Admin. Asst, W Riding CC, Education Dept, 1953–55; Asst Educn Officer, Cumberland CC Educn Dept, 1955–64; Dep. Educn Officer, Sheffield, 1965–67. Hon. Research Fellow, Leeds Univ., 1985–. Member various cttees, incl.: Taylor Cttee of Enquiry on Govt in Schools, 1975–77; UK Nat. Commn for Unesco Educn Adv. Cttee, 1977–83; Yorkshire and Humberside Econ. Planning Council, 1978–79; Technician Educn Council, 1979–83; Engineering Council, 1982–; Board, Nat. Adv. Body on Local Authority Higher Educn, 1981–83. Pres., Soc. of Educn Officers, 1976; Vice-Pres., Standing Conf. on Schools' Science and Technology, 1980– (Chm. 1975–79). *Recreations:* sailing, gardening, music. *Address:* Audrey Cottage, 83 Union Road, Sheffield S11 9EH. *T:* Sheffield 53783. *Club:* Royal Over-Seas League.

HARRISON, Maj.-Gen. Ian Stewart, CB 1970; Captain of Deal Castle, since 1980; Director, British Consultants Bureau, since 1977; *b* 25 May 1919; *s* of Leslie George Harrison and Evelyn Simpson Christie; *m* 1942, Winifred Raikes Stavert; one *s* one *d. Educ:* St Albans Sch. Commissioned, Royal Marines, 1937; service at sea, in Norway, Middle East, Sicily, BAOR, 1939–45; Staff Coll., Camberley (student), 1948; HQ 3rd Commando Bde, 1949–51 (despatches); Staff of Comdt-Gen., RM, 1951–52; Staff Coll., Camberley (Directing Staff), 1953–55; Commandant, RM Signal Sch., 1956–58; Joint Services Staff Coll. (Student), 1958; CO 40 Commando, RM, 1959–61; Dir, Royal Marines Reserves, 1962; Staff of Comdt-Gen., RM, 1963–64; Joint Warfare Estabt, 1965–67; British Defence Staff, Washington, DC, 1967–68; Chief of Staff to Comdt-Gen., RM, 1968–70, retired. ADC to HM the Queen, 1967–68. Representative Col Comdt, Royal Marines, 1981–82. Dir-Gen. British Food Export Council, 1970–77. *Recreations:* sailing, real tennis, lawn tennis, golf. *Address:* Manor Cottage, Runcton, Chichester, W Sussex PO20 6PU. *T:* Chichester 785480. *Clubs:* Army and Navy, St Stephen's Constitutional; Royal Yacht Squadron, Royal Naval Sailing Association, Royal Marines Sailing (Commodore, 1968–70), Itchenor Sailing; Royal St George's Golf.

HARRISON, Jessel Anidjah; Chairman, Slimma Group Holdings Ltd (formerly Emu Wool Industries Ltd), since 1973; *b* 28 May 1923; *s* of Samuel Harrison and Esta (*née* Romain); *m* 1st, 1943, Irene (*née* Olsberg) (marr. diss. 1956); one *s* one *d*; 2nd, 1961, Doreen Leigh. *Educ:* Vernon House Preparatory Sch.; Brondesbury Coll.; Macauley Coll., Cuckfield, Sussex. Chairman: Slimma Ltd, 1964; Slimma (Wales) Ltd, 1971; Dir, Tootals Clothing Div., 1977–. Member: European Trade Cttee, 1975–; Clothing Industry Productivity Resources Agency, 1978–; British Overseas Trade Adv. Council, 1978–. Vice Pres., Clothing Export Council of Great Britain, 1977 (Chm., 1973); Chm., British Overseas Trade Group for Israel, 1978–83. Pres., Clothing Institute, 1978. *Recreations:* golf, walking. *Address:* 113 Abbotsbury Road, W14 8EP. *T:* 01–603 7468. *Club:* Royal Automobile.

HARRISON, Surgeon Vice-Adm. Sir John (Albert Bews), KBE 1982; FRCP, FRCR; Medical Director General (Naval), 1980–83; *b* 20 May 1921; *s* of late Albert William Harrison and Lilian Eda Bews, Dover, Kent; *m* 1943, Jane (*née* Harris); two *s. Educ:* Queens' Coll., Cambridge; St Bartholomew's Hosp. Joined RNVR, 1947 and RN 1953; served: RM Infirmary, Deal, 1948; HMS Sparrow, Amer. WI stn, 1949; RN Hosp., Plymouth, 1951; HMS Ganges, 1952; Admiralty Med. Bd and St Bartholomew's Hosp., 1953; RN Hosps, Hong Kong, 1955, Chatham, 1958, Haslar, 1959; St Bart's and Middlesex Hosps, 1961; RN Hosps Malta, 1962, Haslar, 1964–75; Adviser in Radiol., 1967–79; Dep. Med. Dir Gen. and Dir Med. Personnel and Logistics, 1975–77; Dean of

Naval Medicine and Surgeon Rear-Adm., Inst. of Naval Medicine, 1977–80. Mem., Council for Med. Postgrad. Educn of Eng. and Wales, 1977–79. Pres., Section of Radiology, RSM, 1984–85. Fellow: RSM; MedSocLond (Pres. 1985–86). CStJ 1983. QHP 1976–83. *Publications:* Hyperbaric Osteonecrosis et al, 1975; articles in med. press on sarcoidosis, tomography, middle ear disease, and dysbaric osteonecrosis. *Recreations:* fishing, cricket, countryman. *Address:* Alexandra Cottage, Swanmore, Hampshire SO3 2PB. *Clubs:* Naval and Military, MCC.

HARRISON, John Audley, CB 1976; a Director, Ministry of Defence, 1969–76; *b* 13 May 1917; *s* of John Samuel Harrison and Florence Rose (*née* Samways); *m* 1940, Dorothea Pearl (*née* West); two *s* one *d. Educ:* Caterham Sch., Surrey. Prudential Assce Co. Ltd, 1935–39. London Rifle Bde (TA), 1939–40; York and Lancaster Regt (emergency commn), 1940–46. Attached War Office (later MoD), 1946–76, retd, May 1976. *Recreations:* golf, bridge. *Address:* 23 Benfield Way, Portslade, Sussex. *T:* Brighton 418302. *Club:* Dyke Golf (Brighton).

HARRISON, John Clive, LVO 1971; HM Diplomatic Service; Head of Consular Department, Foreign and Commonwealth Office, since 1985; *b* 12 July 1937; *s* of Sir Geoffrey Harrison, *qv*; *m* 1967, Jennifer Heather Burston; one *s* two *d. Educ:* Winchester Coll.; Jesus Coll., Oxford. BA. Entered Foreign Office, 1960; Rangoon, 1961; Vientiane, 1964; FO, 1964; Second, later First, Sec. (Information), Addis Ababa, 1967; Ankara, 1971; seconded to Cabinet Office, 1973; First Sec., FCO, 1976; First Sec., Head of Chancery and Consul, Luxembourg, 1978; Counsellor and Head of Chancery, Lagos, 1981–84; Counsellor, attached to Protocol Dept, FCO, 1984. *Recreations:* gardening, tennis, golf, family holidays. *Address:* c/o Foreign and Commonwealth Office, King Charles Street, SW1A 2AH; 4 Woodend Park, Cobham, Surrey KT11 3BX. *T:* Cobham 64637. *Club:* Mannings Heath Golf (Sussex).

HARRISON, Prof. John Fletcher Clews, PhD; Emeritus Professor of History, University of Sussex, since 1985 (Professor of History, 1970–82; Hon. Professor of History, 1982–85); *b* 28 Feb. 1921; *s* of William Harrison and Mary (*née* Fletcher); *m* 1945, Margaret Ruth Marsh; one *s* one *d. Educ:* City Boys' Sch., Leicester; Selwyn Coll., Cambridge (Schol. and Prizeman; Goldsmiths' Open Exhibnr in History, BA 1st Cl. Hons 1942, MA 1946); PhD Leeds. Served Army, 1941–45 (overseas 1942–45): commnd, Royal Leics Regt and seconded to KAR, 1942; Captain and Adjt, 17th Bn, KAR, 1943–44; Staff Captain, GSOIII, E Africa Comd, 1944–45. Lectr, Dept of Adult Educn and Extra-Mural Studies, Univ. of Leeds, 1947–58; Dep. Dir, Extra-Mural Studies and Dep. Head of Dept, Univ. of Leeds, 1958–61; Prof. of History, Univ. of Wisconsin, USA, 1961–70. Research and teaching (Fulbright Award), Univ. of Wisconsin, 1957–58; Faculty Res. Fellow, SSRC, USA, 1963–64; Vis. Professorial Res. Fellow, ANU, 1968–69 and 1977; Res. Fellow, Harvard Univ., 1972–73; Social Sci. Res. Fellow, Nuffield Foundn, 1975; Vice-Chancellor's Cttee Visitor, NZ, 1977; Herbert F. Johnson Res. Prof., Univ. of Wisconsin, 1977–78. Vice-Pres., Soc. for Study of Labour History, 1984– (Sec., 1960–61; Chm., 1974–81); Mem., Adv. and Editorial Bds, Victorian Studies, 1963–. Hon. Mem., Phi Beta Kappa, Wisconsin, 1978. *Publications:* A History of the Working Men's College 1854–1954, 1954; Social Reform in Victorian Leeds: The Work of James Hole 1820–1895, 1954; Learning and Living 1790–1960: A Study in the History of the English Adult Education Movement, 1961, Toronto 1961; ed, Society and Politics in England 1780–1960, NY 1965; ed, Utopianism and Education: Robert Owen and the Owenites, NY 1968; Quest for the New Moral World: Robert Owen and the Owenites in Britain and America, 1969, NY 1969 (Walter D. Love Meml Prize, USA, 1969); The Early Victorians 1832–1851, 1971, NY 1971; The Birth and Growth of Industrial England 1714–1867, 1973; ed, Eminently Victorian, BBC 1974; (with Dorothy Thompson) Bibliography of the Chartist Movement 1837–1976, 1978; The Second Coming: Popular Millenarianism 1780–1850, 1979, NJ 1979; The Common People, 1984; articles and reviews in Victorian Studies, TLS and usual academic history jls. *Recreations:* walking, gardening, book collecting. *Address:* 13 Woodlands, Barrowfield Drive, Hove, Sussex BN3 6TJ. *T:* Brighton 554145.

HARRISON, John H.; *see* Heslop-Harrison.

HARRISON, Hon. Sir (John) Richard, Kt 1980; ED; farmer and company director; *b* 23 May 1921; *s* of William Harrison and Jean (*née* Bell); *m* 1948, Margaret Kelly; three *s* one *d. Educ:* Wanganui Collegiate Sch.; Canterbury University Coll. (BA). CO, Hawke's Bay Regt, 1956–59. MP (Nat) for Hawke's Bay, 1963–84; Govt Whip, 1970–71; Opposition Whip, 1974–75; Chm. of Cttees, 1972, 1976–77; Speaker, House of Representatives, 1978–84. Pres., Commonwealth Parly Assoc., 1978–79. Pres., Nat. Soc. on Alcoholism and Drug Dependence, 1986–. *Recreations:* gardening, Rotary. *Address:* Springfield, Takapau, New Zealand. *Club:* Hastings.

HARRISON, Kathleen, (Mrs J. H. Back); leading character actress, stage and films; *d* of Arthur Harrison, MICE, Civil Engineer, and Alice Harrison; *m* 1916, John Henry Back; two *s* one *d. Educ:* Clapham High Sch. Trained at RADA. *Notable plays include:* Badger's Green, Prince of Wales Theatre, 1930; Night Must Fall, Duchess, 1935; The Corn is Green, Duchess, 1938; Flare Path, Apollo, 1942; The Winslow Boy, Lyric, 1946; All for Mary, Duke of York's, 1955; Nude with Violin, Globe, 1956; How Say You?, Aldwych, 1959; Watch it, Sailor!, Aldwych, 1960; The Chances, Chichester Festival, 1962; Norman, Duchess, 1963; title role in Goodnight Mrs Puffin, New Theatre, Bromley; Harvey, Richmond Theatre, 1971; She Stoops to Conquer, Young Vic, 1972; toured in All for Mary and Goodnight Mrs Puffin, 1970. *Films include:* In Which We Serve; The Huggett films; Alive and Kicking; The Winslow Boy; Bank Holiday; Holiday Camp; Barabbas; West 11; Scrooge; The London Affair. *TV includes:* Martin Chuzzlewit serial (Betsy Prig); title role in Mrs Thursday series; Waters of the Moon; The Coffee Lace; Spring and Autumn, 1973; The Defence, in Shades of Greene, 1975; Mrs Boffin, in Our Mutual Friend, 1976; Danger UXB. *Address:* c/o T. Plunket Greene, 91 Regent Street, W1. *T:* 01–734 7311.

HARRISON, Kenneth Cecil, OBE 1980 (MBE mil. 1946); FLA; City Librarian, Westminster, 1961–80, retired; Consultant Librarian, Ranfurly Library Service, since 1983; *b* 29 April 1915; *s* of Thomas and Annie Harrison; *m* 1941, Doris Taylor; two *s. Educ:* Grammar Sch., Hyde. Asst, Hyde Public Library, 1931–37; Branch Librarian, Coulsdon and Purley Public Libraries, 1937–39; Borough Librarian: Hyde, 1939–47; Hove (also Curator), 1947–50; Eastbourne, 1950–58; Hendon, 1958–61. HM Forces, 1940–46; Commnd RMC Sandhurst, 1942; served with E Yorks Regt in Middle East, Sicily and NW Europe (wounded, 1944; Major 1944–46). President: Library Assoc., 1973; Commonwealth Library Assoc., 1972–75, Exec. Sec., 1980–83; Vice-President: Internat. Assoc. Metropolitan Libraries; Westminster Arts Council (Hon. Sec. 1965–80). Member: IFLA Public Libraries Cttee, 1969–81; Central Music Library Council, 1961–80; Library Assoc. Council, 1953–79; MCC Arts and Library Cttee, 1973–; Chm. Jt Organising Cttee for Nat. Library Week, 1964–69. British Council: Cultural Exchange Scholar to Romania, 1971; Mem., Library Adv. Panel, 1974–80; Consultant to Sri Lanka, 1974, to India, 1981. UNESCO Consultant to the Seychelles and Mauritius, 1977–78; Commonwealth Relations Trust Consultant to Ghana, Sierra Leone and The Gambia, 1979; Library Consultant, Bermuda, 1983. Commonwealth Foundn Scholar, E and Central Africa, 1975. C. C. Williamson Meml Lectr, Nashville, Tenn, 1969. Governor, Westminster College, 1962–80. Editor, The Library World, 1961–71. Knight, First Class, Order of the Lion (Finland), 1976. *Publications:* First Steps in Librarianship, 1950, 5th edn 1980; Libraries in Scandinavia, 1961, 2nd edn 1969; The Library and the Community, 1963, 3rd edn 1977; Public Libraries Today, 1963; Facts at your Fingertips, 1964, 2nd edn 1966; British Public Library Buildings (with S. G. Berriman), 1966; Libraries in Britain, 1968; Public Relations for Librarians, 1973, 2nd edn 1982; (ed) Prospects for British Librarianship, 1976; Public Library Policy, 1981; Public Library Buildings 1975–83, 1986; contribs to many British and foreign jls and encyclopædias. *Recreations:* reading, writing, travel, wine, cricket, crosswords, zoo visiting. *Address:* 5 Tavistock, Devonshire Place, Eastbourne, E Sussex BN21 4AG. *T:* Eastbourne 26747. *Clubs:* Royal Commonwealth Society, MCC.

HARRISON, Michael; *see* Harrison, G. M. A.

HARRISON, Michael Guy Vicat, QC 1983; *b* 28 Sept. 1939; *s* of Hugh Francis Guy Harrison and Elizabeth Alban Harrison (*née* Jones); *m* 1966, Judith (*née* Gist); one *s* one *d. Educ:* Charterhouse; Trinity Hall, Cambridge (MA). Called to the Bar, Gray's Inn, 1965. *Recreations:* tennis, squash, sailing. *Address:* 2 Harcourt Buildings, Temple, EC4. *T:* 01–353 8415.

HARRISON, Michael Jackson; Director, The Polytechnic, Wolverhampton, since 1985; *b* 18 Dec. 1941; *s* of Jackson Harrison and Norah (*née* Lees); *m* 1974, Marie Ghislaine Félix. *Educ:* Guildford Tech. Coll.; Univ. of Leicester (BA, MA). Lecturer in Sociology: Enfield Coll. of Technol., 1966–67; Univ. of Leeds, 1967–68; Sen. Lectr, Enfield Coll. of Technol., 1968–72; Principal Lectr, Sheffield City Polytechnic, 1972–76; Head of Dept, Hull Coll. of Higher Educn, 1976–81; Asst Dir, 1982–84, Dep. Dir, 1985, The Polytechnic, Wolverhampton. Vis. Lectr, Univ. of Oregon, 1971. FBIM 1983. *Publications:* (jtly) A Sociology of Industrialisation, 1978; contribs to learned jls. *Recreations:* weight training, cinema, travelling, music. *Address:* 33 Alexandra Road, Penn, Wolverhampton WV4 5UA. *T:* Wolverhampton 339815.

HARRISON, Sir Michael James Harwood, 2nd Bt *cr* 1961, of Bugbrooke; Director of private companies; *b* 28 March 1936; *s* of Sir (James) Harwood Harrison, 1st Bt, TD, MP (C) Eye, Suffolk 1951–79, and of Peggy Alberta Mary, *d* of late Lt-Col V. D. Stenhouse, TD; *S* father, 1980; *m* 1967, Rosamund Louise, *d* of Edward Clive; two *s* two *d. Educ:* Rugby. Served with 17th/21st Lancers, 1955–56. Member of Lloyds. Mem. Council, Sail Training Assoc.; Vice-Pres., Assoc. of Combined Youth Clubs. Master, Mercers' Co., 1986–87; Freeman of the City of London. *Recreations:* sailing, ski-ing, riding (horse and bicycle), Daily Telegraph crossword. *Heir:* *s* Edwin Michael Harwood Harrison, *b* 29 May 1981. *Address:* 35 Paulton's Square, SW3. *T:* 01–352 1760. *Clubs:* Boodle's, MCC, Ski Club of GB; Royal Harwich Yacht.

HARRISON, Mrs Molly, MBE 1967; Curator, Geffrye Museum, 1941–69; *b* Stevenage, 1909; *d* of late Ethel and late Ernest Charles Hodgett; *m* 1940, Gordon Frederick Harrison; three *d. Educ:* Friends Sch., Saffron Walden; Convent in Belgium; Sorbonne. Teaching in various Schs, 1934–39; Asst to Curator, Geffrye Museum, 1939–41. FMA 1952; Member: Council Museums Assoc., 1953–56; Council of Industrial Design, 1958–61; Cttee of Management, Society of Authors, 1967. Lectr on varied educational topics. FRSA 1968. Editor, Local Search Series, 1969–77. *Publications:* Museum Adventure, 1950; Picture Source Books for Social History, 1951, 1953, 1955, 1957, 1958, 1960 and 1966; Furniture 1953; Learning out of School, 1954; Food, 1954; Homes, 1960; Children in History, 1958, 1959, 1960, 1961; Your Book of Furniture, 1960; Shops and Shopping, 1963; How They Lived, 1963; Changing Museums, 1967; Hairstyles and Hairdressing, 1968; The English Home, 1969; People and Furniture, 1971; The Kitchen in History, 1972; Homes, 1973; Museums and Galleries, 1973; On Location: Museums, 1974; People and Shopping, 1975; Home Inventions, 1975; Homes in Britain, 1975; Markets and Shops, 1979; Growing Up in Victorian Times, 1980; Homes in History, 1983; The Story of Travelling (4 vols), 1983, 1984; numerous articles and reviews. *Recreations:* writing, gardening. *Address:* The Coach House, Horse Leas, Bradfield, Berks. *T:* Reading 744437.

HARRISON, Patrick Kennard, CBE 1982; Secretary, Royal Institute of British Architects, since 1968; *b* 8 July 1928; *e s* of late Richard Harrison and Sheila Griffin; *m* 1955, Mary Wilson, *y d* of late Captain G. C. C. Damant, CBE, RN; one *d. Educ:* Lord Williams's Sch., Thame; Downing Coll., Cambridge (Exhbnr). Asst Principal, Dept of Health for Scotland, 1953; Private Sec. to Deptl Sec. and to Parly Secs, Scottish Office, 1958–60; Principal, Scottish Develt Dept and Regional Develt Div., Scottish Office, 1960–68. Hon. Mem., Amer. Inst. of Architects, 1978. *Address:* 63 Princess Road, NW1. *T:* 01–722 8508. *Clubs:* Reform; New (Edinburgh).

HARRISON, Rex Carey; Commendatore, Order of Merit of the Republic of Italy, 1967; actor; *b* 5 March 1908; *s* of William Reginald and Edith Carey Harrison; *m* 1st, 1934, Marjorie Noel Collette Thomas; one *s*; 2nd, 1943, Lilli Palmer (marr. diss. 1957); one *s*; 3rd, 1957, Kay Kendall (*d* 1959); 4th, 1962, Rachel Roberts (marr. diss. 1971); 5th, Hon. Elizabeth Rees Harris (marr. diss. 1976), *d* of 1st Baron Ogmore, PC, TD; 6th, 1978, Mercia Tinker. *Educ:* Birkdale Preparatory Sch.; Liverpool Coll. Made first appearance on the stage at Liverpool Repertory Theatre, 1924; remained until 1927. Toured with Charley's Aunt playing Jack, 1927; also toured at intervals during subsequent years until 1935, and appeared with Cardiff Repertory, and in the West End. First appearance on London stage as Rankin in The Ninth Man, Prince of Wales Theatre, 1931; First appearance on New York stage at Booth Theatre, 1936, as Tubbs Barrow in Sweet Aloes. Played in French Without Tears at Criterion, 1936–37–38, and at Haymarket Theatre, 1939–41, in Design for Living (Leo) and No Time for Comedy (Gaylord Esterbrook). Volunteered RAFVR, 1941, and served till 1944. Released from Forces to make Blithe Spirit (film), and, 1945, Rake's Progress (film). Filmed in Hollywood, 1945–46–47. (Maxwell Anderson's) Anne of the Thousand Days, Schubert Theatre, NY, 1948–49 (Antoinette Perry Award, best actor); in The Cocktail Party, New Theatre, London, 1950; acted in and produced Bell, Book and Candle, Ethel Barrymore Theatre, NY, 1951, and Phœnix Theatre, London, 1954; in Venus Observed, Century Theatre, NY, 1952; directed and played in Love of Four Colonels, Schubert Theatre, NY, 1953; produced Nina, Haymarket Theatre, London, 1955; acted in: My Fair Lady (Henry Higgins), Mark Hellinger Theatre, NY, 1956–57 (Antoinette Perry Award, best actor), and Drury Lane, London, 1958–59; The Fighting Cock, Anta Theatre, NY, 1959; Platonov, Royal Court, 1960 (Evening Standard Award, best actor); August for the People, Edinburgh Festival, 1961, and Royal Court Theatre; The Lionel Touch, Lyric, 1969; Henry IV, Her Majesty's, 1974; Perrichon's Travels, Chichester, 1976; Caesar and Cleopatra, NY, 1977; The Kingfisher, NY, 1978–79; Heartbreak House, Haymarket, 1983, NY, 1983; Aren't We All?, Haymarket, 1984–85, NY and US tour, 1986. Began acting in films in 1929. Best known films: Storm in a Teacup, 1936; St Martin's Lane, 1937; Over the Moon, 1938; Night Train to Munich, Major Barbara, 1940–41; Blithe Spirit, 1944; I Live in Grosvenor Square, 1944; The Rake's Progress, 1945; (Hollywood, 1945) Anna and the King of Siam, 1946; The Ghost and Mrs Muir, 1947; The Foxes of Harrow, 1947; (Galsworthy's)

Escape (in England), 1948; Unfaithfully Yours (in America), 1948; The Long Dark Hall, 1951; King Richard and the Crusaders, 1954; The Constant Husband, 1955; The Reluctant Debutante, 1958; Midnight Lace, 1960; The Happy Thieves, 1961; Cleopatra (Julius Caesar), 1962; My Fair Lady, 1964 (Academy Award, best actor); The Yellow Rolls Royce, 1965; The Agony and the Ecstacy, 1965; The Honey Pot, 1967; Doctor Dolittle, 1967; A Flea in her Ear, 1967; Staircase, 1968; The Prince and the Pauper, 1976; Man in the Iron Mask, 1977; Ashanti, 1979. *Publication:* Rex (autobiog.), 1974. *Recreations:* golf, yachting, fishing. *Address:* 5 Impasse de la Fontaine, Monte Carlo, Monaco 98000. *Clubs:* Beefsteak, Green Room, Garrick; Players' (New York); Travellers' (Paris).

HARRISON, Hon. Sir Richard; *see* Harrison, Hon. Sir J. R.

HARRISON, Prof. Sir Richard (John), Kt 1984; MD, DSc; FRS 1973; Professor of Anatomy, Cambridge University, 1968–82, now Emeritus; Fellow of Downing College, Cambridge, 1968–82, Hon. Fellow, 1982; *b* 8 Oct. 1920; *er s* of late Geoffrey Arthur Harrison, MD, and Theodora Beatrice Mary West; *m* Barbara, *o d* of late James and Florence Fuller, Neston, Cheshire. *Educ:* Oundle; Gonville and Caius Coll., Cambridge (Scholar); St Bartholomew's Hosp. Medical Coll. LRCP, MRCS, 1944. House Surgeon, St Bartholomew's Hosp., 1944. MB, BChir, 1944; MA 1946; MD Cantab 1954. Demonstrator in Anatomy, St Bartholomew's Hosp. Medical Coll., 1944; Lectr in Anatomy, Glasgow Univ., 1946, DSc Glasgow 1948; Sen. Lectr, 1947, and Reader in Anatomy, 1950, Charing Cross Hosp. Medical Sch. (Symington Prize for research in Anatomy); Reader in charge of Anatomy Dept, London Hosp. Medical Coll., 1951–54; Prof. of Anatomy, University of London, at London Hosp. Medical Coll., 1954–68; Fullerian Prof. of Physiology, Royal Institution, 1961–67. Wooldridge Lectr, BVA, 1983. Chairman: Farm Animal Welfare Adv. Cttee, MAFF, 1974–79; Farm Animal Welfare Council, 1979–. President: European Assoc. for Aquatic Mammals, 1974–76; Anat. Soc. of GB and Ireland, 1978–79. XIIth Internat. Congress of Anatomists, London, 1985; Internat. Fedn of Assocs of Anatomists, 1985–. A Trustee, British Museum (Natural History), 1978– (Chm. Trustees, 1984–); Member Council: Royal Soc., 1981–82; Zool. Soc., 1974–78, 1980–83; Nat. Trust, 1984–85. Hon. Member: American Assoc. of Anatomists; Societa Italiana Anatomia. *Publications:* Man the Peculiar Animal, 1958; (with J. E. King) Marine Mammals, 1965, 2nd edn 1979; Reproduction and Man, 1967; (with W. Montagna) Man, 2nd edn 1972; Functional Anatomy of Marine Mammals, vol. I, 1972, vol. II, 1974, vol. III, 1977; (with S. H. Ridgway) Handbook of Marine Mammals, vols I and II, 1981, vol. III, 1985; (with M. M. Bryden) Research on Dolphins, 1986; numerous papers on embryology, comparative and human anatomy. *Recreations:* marine biology, painting, golf. *Address:* The Beeches, 8 Woodlands Road, Great Shelford, Cambs. *T:* Cambridge 843287. *Clubs:* Garrick; Sheringham Golf.

HARRISON, Prof. Richard Martin; Professor of Archaeology of the Roman Empire and Fellow, All Souls College, University of Oxford, since 1985; Vice-President, Society of Antiquaries, since 1984; *b* 16 May 1935; *s* of George Lawrance Harrison and Doris Waring (*née* Ward); *m* 1959, Elizabeth Anne Harkness Browne; one *s* three *d*. *Educ:* Sherborne Sch.; Lincoln Coll., Oxford (BA Greats 1958, MA 1961). FSA 1965. Scholar 1959, and Fellow 1960, Brit. Inst. of Archaeol., Ankara; Rivoira Scholar, Brit. Sch. at Rome, 1960; Controller of Antiquities, Provincial Govt of Cyrenaica, 1960–61; Lectr in Class. Archaeol., Bryn Mawr Coll., 1961–62; Glanville Res. Student, Lincoln Coll., Oxford, 1962–64; Newcastle upon Tyne University: Lectr in Roman and Romano-British History and Archaeol., 1964–68; Prof. of Roman Hist. and Archaeol., 1968–72; Prof. of Archaeology, 1972–85. Vis. Fellow, Dumbarton Oaks, 1969. Dir, Excavations at Saraçhane (Istanbul), 1964–69. Corresp. Mem., German Archaeol. Inst., 1973. *Publications:* Excavations at Saraçhane in Istanbul, 1986; articles on Roman and Byzantine archaeol. in Anatolian Studies, Dumbarton Oaks Papers, Jl of Roman Studies. *Recreation:* hill-walking in Northumberland and Turkey. *Address:* 10 Norham Gardens, Oxford OX2 6QB; Institute of Archaeology, 36 Beaumont Street, Oxford; All Souls College, Oxford.

HARRISON, Sir (Robert) Colin, 4th Bt, *cr* 1922; *b* 25 May 1938; *s* of Sir John Fowler Harrison, 2nd Bt, and Kathleen, *yr d* of late Robert Livingston, The Gables, Eaglescliffe, Co. Durham; *S* brother, 1955; *m* 1963, Maureen, *er d* of E. Leonard Chiverton, Garth Corner, Kirkbymoorside, York; one *s* two *d*. *Educ:* St Peter's Coll., Radley; St John's Coll., Cambridge. Commissioned with Fifth Royal Northumberland Fusiliers (National Service), 1957–59. Chm., Young Master Printers Nat. Cttee, 1972–73. *Heir: s* John Wyndham Fowler Harrison, *b* 14 Dec. 1972. *Address:* The Grange, Rosedale Abbey, Pickering, N Yorks YO18 8RD. *T:* Lastingham 329.

HARRISON, Terence, CEng; FIMechE; FIMarE; Executive Chairman, Northern Engineering Industries plc, since 1986; *b* 7 April 1933; *s* of late Roland Harrison and of Doris (*née* Wardle); *m* 1956, June (*née* Forster); two *s*. *Educ:* A. J. Dawson Grammar Sch., Co. Durham; West Hartlepool and Sunderland Tech. Colls. BSc(Eng) Durham. CEng 1964; FIMechE 1984; FIMarE 1973. Marine engrg apprenticeship, Richardson's Westgarth, Hartlepool, 1949–53; commnd REME, service in Nigeria, 1955–57; Clarke Chapman, Gateshead (Marine Division): Res. Engr, 1957; Chief Mechanical Engr, 1967; Man. Dir, 1969; Man. Dir, Clarke Chapman Ltd, Gateshead, 1976; Northern Engineering Industries plc: Dir, 1977; Man. Dir, UK Ops, 1980–83; Chief Exec., 1983–86. Director: NEB (Northern Region), 1980–84; British Nuclear Associates, 1984–; National Nuclear Corporation, 1986. *Publications:* technical papers to mechanical, marine and mining societies. *Recreations:* golf, music. *Address:* South Lodge, Hepscott, Morpeth, Northumberland NE3 3SB. *T:* Morpeth 519228; (office) Northern Engineering Industries plc, NEI House, Regent Centre, Newcastle upon Tyne NE3 3SB. *T:* Tyneside 2843191.

HARRISON, Theophilus George, OBE 1971; JP; Member, Greater Manchester Council, 1973–77 (Chairman, 1973–1974 and 1974–1975, Deputy Chairman, 1975–76); General Secretary, National Association of Powerloom Overlookers, 1947–76, now Life Member; Member Executive, General Union of Associations of Loom Overlookers, 1947–76, now Life Member (President, 1964–66); *b* 30 Jan. 1907; *s* of Alfred and Emma Harrison; *m* 1935, Clarissa Plevin; one *s* one *d*. Swinton and Pendlebury Borough Council: Mem., 1941–56; Alderman, 1956–74; Mayor, 1954–55; Chairman: Housing Cttee; Highways and Lighting Cttee; Mem., Div. Planning Cttee; Lancs CC: Mem. Educn Cttee, 1946–74 (Vice-Chm. 1951–53, Chm. 1953–74); Chm., Road Safety Cttee, Vice-Chairman: Public Health and Housing Cttee; Greater Manchester Transport Cons. Cttee; Pres., Lancs Non-County Boroughs Assoc., 1960–62; Chairman: Swinton and Pendlebury Youth Employment Cttee; Youth Adv. Cttee and Youth Centres; Mem., Div. Exec., Educn Cttee; Member: Gen. Council, Lancs and Merseyside Ind. Develt Corp.; N Counties Textile Trades Fedn Central Board; Life Member: Salford Trades Council (formerly Mem., Swinton and Pendlebury Trades Council); Swinton Labour Club. Member: Manchester Reg. Hosp. Bd, 1961–74; Mental Health Review Tribunals, 1961–70; W Manchester HMC, 1957–74 (Chm. 1963–74); Wrightington HMC, 1957–74; Salford Community Health Council, 1973–83 (former Vice-Chm. and Chm., Develt Cttee); Assoc. of Community Health Councils, 1973–83 (former Vice-Chm., NW Region). Hon. Vice-Pres., Greater Manchester Council for Voluntary Service. Past Chm. or Mem. many other Co. or local organizations and cttees. Former Pres., SE Lancs and Cheshire Accident Prevention Fedn; Dir, RoSPA; Freeman of Swinton and Pendlebury, 1973 (now Salford DC). JP 1949. *Recreations:* reading, Rugby League football (spectator); much of his political and public activities. *Address:* 271 Rivington Crescent, Bolton Road, Pendlebury, Swinton, Manchester M27 2TQ. *T:* 061–794 1112.

HARRISON, Tony; poet; *b* 30 April 1937; *s* of Harry Ashton Harrison and Florrie (*née* Wilkinson-Horner); *m* 1st, 1960, Rosemarie Crossfield (*née* Dietzsch); one *s* one *d*; 2nd, 1984, Teresa Stratas. *Educ:* Cross Flatts County Primary Sch.; Leeds Grammar Sch.; Univ. of Leeds (BA, Dip.Linguistics). Lecturer in English: Ahmadu Bello Univ., Zaria, N Nigeria, 1962–66; Charles Univ., Prague, 1966–67; Northern Arts Fellow in Poetry, Univs of Newcastle and Durham, 1967–68 and 1976–77; UNESCO Fellow in Poetry, Cuba, Brazil, Senegal, Gambia, 1969; Gregynog Arts Fellow, Univ. of Wales, 1973–74; Resident Dramatist, National Th., 1977–79; UK/US Bi-Centennial Fellow, New York, 1979–80. *Publications:* Earthworks, 1964; Aikin Mata, 1966; Newcastle is Peru, 1969; The Loiners, 1970; The Misanthrope, 1973; Phaedra Britannica, 1975; Palladas: poems, 1975; The Passion, 1977; Bow Down, 1977; From The School of Eloquence and other poems, 1978; The Bartered Bride, 1978; Continuous, 1981; A Kumquat for John Keats, 1981; US Martial, 1981; The Oresteia, 1981; Selected Poems, 1984; The Mysteries, 1985; Dramatic Verse 1973–85, 1985; v., 1985; The Fire-Gap, 1985. *Address:* c/o Fraser & Dunlop (Scripts) Ltd, 91 Regent Street, W1R 8RU. *T:* 01–734 7311.

HARRISON, Rt. Hon. Walter, PC 1977; JP; MP (Lab) Wakefield, since 1964; *b* 2 Jan. 1921; *s* of Henry and Ada Harrison; *m* 1948, Enid Mary (*née* Coleman); one *s* one *d*. *Educ:* Dewsbury Technical and Art Coll. Electrical Inspector and Electrical Foreman, Electricity Supply Industry, 1937–64. Asst Govt Whip, 1966–68; a Lord Comr of the Treasury, 1968–70; Dep. Chief Opposition Whip, 1970–74 and 1979–83; Treasurer of HM Household and Dep. Chief Govt Whip, 1974–79. West Riding CC, 1958–64; Alderman, Castleford Borough Council, 1959–66 (Councillor, 1952–59); JP West Riding Yorks, 1962. *Address:* House of Commons, SW1. *T:* 01–219 3000.

HARRISON-CHURCH, Prof. Ronald James; Professor of Geography, University of London, at London School of Economics, 1964–77; *b* 26 July 1915; *s* of late James Walter Church and late Jessie May Church; *m* 1944, Dorothy Violet, *d* of late Robert Colchester Harrison and late Rose Harrison; one *s* one *d*. *Educ:* Westminster City Sch.; Universities of London and Paris. BSc (Econ) 1936, PhD 1943, London. LSE: Asst Lectr, 1944–47; Lectr, 1947–58; Reader, 1958–64. Consultant to UN Economic Commn for Africa on large scale irrigation schemes, 1962. Visiting Professor: University of Wisconsin, 1956; Indiana Univ., 1965; Tel Aviv and Haifa Univs, 1972–73. Has lectured in many other univs in Brazil, US, Canada, West Africa, Belgium, France, Germany, Poland and Sweden. Member: Cttee for Staff Fulbright Awards, US-UK Educnl Commn, 1958–61 and 1972–75; Cttee, British Fulbright Schols Assoc., 1981–83; Africa Field Cttee, Oxfam, 1974–80. Chm., Firbank Housing Soc., 1977–83. Vice-Pres., Royal Afr. Soc. (Speakers and Publics Cttee, 1972–85); Back Award, RGS, 1957; Reg. Conf. IGU Award, 1978. *Publications:* Modern Colonization, 1951; West Africa, 1957, 8th edn, 1980; Environment and Policies in West Africa, 1963, 2nd edn 1976; Looking at France, 1970, rev. repr. 1976, French edn 1969, Spanish edn 1973; (jtly) Africa and the Islands, 1964, 4th edn, 1979; (jtly) An Advanced Geography of Northern and Western Europe, 1967, 3rd edn 1980; contribs to Geograph. Jl, W Africa, etc. *Recreations:* reading, travel, television documentaries. *Address:* 40 Handside Lane, Welwyn Garden City, Herts. *T:* Welwyn Garden 323293.

HARRISON-HALL, Michael Kilgour; DL; **His Honour Judge Harrison-Hall;** a Circuit Judge, since 1972; *b* 20 Dec. 1925; *s* of late Arthur Harrison-Hall, Oxford; *m* 1951, Jessie Margaret, *d* of late Rev. Arthur William Brown, Collingbourne Ducis, Wilts; two *s* two *d*. *Educ:* Rugby; Trinity College, Oxford. Called to Bar, Inner Temple, 1949. Dep. Chm., Warwickshire QS, 1968–71; a Recorder of the Crown Court, 1972. DL Warwicks, 1985. *Address:* Ivy House, Church Street, Barford, Warwick. *T:* Barford 624272. *Clubs:* United Oxford & Cambridge University; Leander.

HARROD, Maj.-Gen. Lionel Alexander Digby, OBE 1969; Inspector of Recruiting (Army), since 1979; *b* 7 Sept. 1924; *s* of Frank Henry Harrod, CBE, and Charlotte Beatrice Emmeline (*née* David); *m* 1952, Anne Priscilla Stormont Gibbs; one *s* two *d*. *Educ:* Bromsgrove Sch. Grenadier Guards, 1944–63; Bde Major, 19 Bde, 1956–58; WO staff, 1959–60; CO 1 Welch, 1966–69; Brit. Def. Staff, Washington, 1969–70; Military Attaché, Baghdad, 1971; Staff HQ UKLF, 1972–73; Chief, Brit. Mission to Gp of Soviet Forces, Germany, 1974–76; ACOS (Intelligence), SHAPE, 1976–79, retired. Col, Royal Regt of Wales, 1977–82. Vice Chm., N Dorset Conservative Assoc.; Cttee, Military Commentators Circle; Member: British Atlantic Cttee; Peace Through NATO; European Atlantic Gp; Pilgrims. *Recreations:* sport, country life. *Address:* The Grange, Marnhull, Dorset. *T:* Marnhull 820256. *Clubs:* Army and Navy, MCC, Pratt's.

HARROLD, Roy Mealham; farmer, since 1947; *b* 13 Aug. 1928; *s* of John Frederick Harrold and Ellen Selena Harrold (*née* Mealham); *m* 1968, Barbara Mary, *yr d* of William and Florence Andrews; one *s* one *d*. *Educ:* Stoke Holy Cross Primary Sch.; Bracondale Sch., Norwich. County Chm., Norfolk Fedn of Young Farmers' Clubs, 1956–57; Mem., Nat. Council of Young Farmers, 1957–60; Mem. Council, Royal Norfolk Agric. Assoc., 1972–75, 1980–83; Mem., Press Council, 1976–83. Lay Chm., Norwich East Deanery Synod, 1970–79; Mem., Norwich Dio. Synod, 1970–; Mem., Norwich Dio. Bd of Patronage, 1970–82; Norwich Dio. Bd of Finance, 1983–; Church Warden, St Peter Mancroft, Norwich, 1978–82. *Recreations:* music, opera, ballet. *Address:* Salamanca Farm, Stoke Holy Cross, Norwich NR15 8QJ. *T:* Framingham Earl 2322.

HARROP, Sir Peter (John), KCB 1984 (CB 1980); Second Permanent Secretary, Department of the Environment, 1981–86; *b* 18 March 1926; *s* of late Gilbert Harrop; *m* 1975, Margaret Joan, *d* of E. U. E. Elliott-Binns, *qv*; two *s*. *Educ:* King Edward VII Sch., Lytham, Lancs; Peterhouse, Cambridge. MA (Hist. Tripos). Served RNVR, 1945–47 (Sub-Lt). Min. of Town and Country Planning, 1949; Min. of Housing and Local Govt, 1951; Dept of the Environment, 1970 (Chm., Yorks and Humberside Economic Planning Bd, and Regional Dir, 1971–73); Under Sec., HM Treasury, 1973–76; Deputy Secretary: DoE, 1977–79, 1980–81; Cabinet Office, 1979–80. *Recreations:* sailing, skiing, travelling by train. *Address:* 19 Berwyn Road, Richmond, Surrey. *Clubs:* United Oxford & Cambridge University, Roehampton; Ski Club of Great Britain; Island Cruising (Salcombe).

HARROWBY, 6th Earl of, *cr* 1809; **Dudley Ryder;** Baron Harrowby, 1776; Viscount Sandon, 1809; Major, late RFA (TAR); *b* 11 Oct. 1892; *e s* of 5th Earl of Harrowby and Hon. Mabel Danvers Smith, DBE (*d* 1956), *y d* of late Rt Hon. W. H. Smith, MP, and 1st Viscountess Hambleden; *S* father 1956; *m* 1922, Lady Helena Blanche Coventry (*d* 1974), *e d* of late Viscount Deerhurst; two *s* one *d*. *Educ:* Eton; Christ Church, Oxford (BA). Asst Private Sec. to Viscount Milner, Sec. of State for the Colonies, Jan. 1919–Aug. 1920; MP (U) Shrewsbury Division of Salop, Nov. 1922–Nov. 1923, and Oct. 1924–May 1929; Parliamentary Private Sec. to Sir S. Hoare, Sec. of State for Air, Dec. 1922–Nov. 1923; Alderman LCC, 1932–37, Mem. for Dulwich, 1937–40; served European War, Major RA, 1914–19 (wounded); served War of 1939–45. Col Commandant Staffs Army Cadet Force, 1946–50. DL Staffs, 1925; JP Staffs, 1929; Mem. of Royal Commission on

Historical Manuscripts, 1935–66. Hon. DLitt Oxon, 1964. *Publications:* England at Worship; (joint) Geography of Everyday Things. *Heir: s* Viscount Sandon, *qv. Address:* Sandon Hall, Stafford; Burnt Norton, Chipping Campden, Gloucestershire. *Club:* Travellers'.

HARSCH, Joseph Close, CBE (Hon.) 1965; writer and broadcaster; columnist, Christian Science Monitor, Boston; *b* Toledo, Ohio, 25 May 1905; *s* of Paul Arthur Harsch and Leila Katherine Close; *m* 1932, Anne Elizabeth Wood; three *s. Educ:* Williams Coll., Williamstown, Mass (MA); Corpus Christi Coll., Cambridge (MA). Joined staff Christian Science Monitor, 1929; Washington corresp., then foreign corresp.; Asst Dir, Intergovt Cttee, London, 1939; Monitor Corresp. in Berlin, 1940, SW Pacific area, 1941 and 1942. Began radio broadcasting, 1943; Senior European Correspondent, NBC, 1957–65; Diplomatic Correspondent, NBC, 1965–67; Commentator, American Broadcasting Co., 1967–71; Chief Editorial Writer, Christian Science Monitor, 1971–74. Edward Weintal award for writing on foreign affairs, 1979. *Publications:* Pattern of Conquest, 1941; The Curtain Isn't Iron, 1950. *Address:* 275 Highland Drive, Jamestown, RI 02835, USA; c/o Christian Science Monitor, 1 Norway Street, Boston, Mass 02115, USA. *Clubs:* Garrick; Metropolitan, Cosmos (Washington, DC); Century (New York); St Botolph (Boston).

HARSTON, Julian John Robert Clive; HM Diplomatic Service; Counsellor, Harare, since 1984; *b* 20 Oct. 1942; *s* of Col Clive Harston and Kathleen Harston; *m* 1966, Karen Howard Oake Harston (*née* Longfield); one *s. Educ:* King's Sch., Canterbury; Univ. of London (BSc). British Tourist Authority, 1965–70; FCO, 1970; Consul, Hanoi, 1973; 1st Secretary: Blantyre, 1975; Lisbon, 1982. *Recreations:* photography, travel. *Address:* c/o Foreign and Commonwealth Office, SW1; 33 Rosemont, Richmond, Surrey. *T:* 01–940 6997. *Clubs:* East India, Devonshire, Sports and Public Schools; Gremio Literario (Lisbon); Harare (Zimbabwe).

HART, Alan; Controller, International Relations, BBC Television, since 1986; *b* 17 April 1935; *s* of Reginald Thomas Hart and Lillian Hart; *m* 1961, Celia Mary Vine; two *s* one *d. Educ:* Pinnerwood Primary Sch.; University College Sch., Hampstead. Reporter: Willesden Chronicle and Kilburn Times, 1952–58; Newcastle Evening Chronicle, 1958; London Evening News, 1958–59; Editorial Asst, BBC Sportsview, 1959–61; Television Sports Producer, BBC Manchester, 1962–64; Asst Editor, Sportsview, 1964–65; Editor, Sportsview, 1965–68; Editor, Grandstand, 1968–77; Head of Sport, BBC Television, 1977–81; Controller, BBC1 Television, 1981–84. FRTS 1983. *Recreations:* sport, music, walking. *Address:* Old Stocks, Halfacre Hill, Chalfont St Peter, Bucks SL9 7PB. *T:* 01–580 4468.

HART, Alan Edward; Chief Executive, Equal Opportunities Commission, since 1985; *b* 28 July 1935; *m* 1961, Ann Derbyshire; one *s* one *d. Educ:* Varndean County Grammar Sch., Brighton; Lincoln Coll., Univ. of Oxford (MA). Solicitor. Dep. Town Clerk, City of Salford, 1970–73; Dir of Admin, 1973–75, Chief Exec., 1975–85, Wigan MBC. *Address:* c/o Equal Opportunities Commission, Overseas House, Quay Street, Manchester M3 3HN.

HART, Alexander Hendry, QC (Canada) 1969; Agent General for British Columbia in the United Kingdom and Europe, since 1981; *b* Regina, Sask., 17 July 1918; *s* of Alexander Hart and Mary (*née* Davidson); *m* 1948, Janet MacMillan Mackay; three *s* one *d. Educ:* Dalhousie Law School (LLB). Served War, Royal Canadian Artillery, 1939–45; retired with rank of Major. Read law with McInnis, Mcquarrie and Cooper; called to Bar of Nova Scotia, 1947. Vice-Pres., Marketing, 1967–71; Sen. Vice-Pres., Canadian Nat. Rlwys, 1971–81. Dep. Internat. Pres., Pacific Basin Economic Council, 1980–81; Pres., Canada-UK Chamber of Commerce, 1983; Past Pres., Vancouver Board of Trade; Past Chm., Western Transportation Adv. Council; Past Mem., University Council of British Columbia; Past Pres., Canada Japan Soc. of Vancouver. *Recreation:* golf. *Address:* British Columbia House, 1 Regent Street, SW1Y 4NS. *T:* 01–930 6857. *Clubs:* East India, Devonshire, Sports and Public Schools, Royal Automobile; Royal & Ancient Golf (St Andrews); Vancouver, Men's Canadian, Shaughnessy Golf and Country (Vancouver); Pine Valley (Clementon, NJ).

HART, Anelay Colton Wright; Partner in Appleby, Hope & Matthews, since 1963; *b* 6 March 1934; *s* of Anelay Thomas Bayston Hart and Phyllis Marian Hart; *m* 1979, Margaret Gardner (*née* Dewing). *Educ:* Stamford Sch.; King's Coll., London (LLB). Solicitor. Advisory Director, World Society for the Protection of Animals, 1982–; RSPCA: Mem. Council, 1969–; Hon. Treasurer, 1974–81; Chm. of Council, 1981–83, 1985–86; Vice-Chm. Council, 1983–84, 1986–87; Queen Victoria Silver Medal, 1984. President, Rotary Club of South Bank and Eston, 1972–73. *Recreations:* walking, gardening. *Address:* Chequers, High Street, Normanby, Middlesbrough, Cleveland TS6 0LD. *T:* Eston Grange 465444. *Club:* Royal Over-Seas League.

HART, Anthony; *see* Hart, T. A. A.

HART, Anthony Bernard, PhD; Head of Chemistry Division, Research Division of Central Electricity Generating Board, 1976–82; *b* 7 July 1917; *s* of late Oliver and Jessie Hart; *m* 1946, Judith Ridehalgh (*see* Rt Hon. Dame Judith Hart); two *s. Educ:* Enfield Grammar Sch.; Queen Mary Coll., London. BSc, PhD; CEng, CChem, FRSC, MInstE. RN Cordite Factories, 1940–46; RN Scientific Service, 1946–50; Lectr in Physical Chem., Royal Coll. of Sci. and Technol., Glasgow (now Strathclyde Univ.), 1950–60; Res. Div., CEGB, 1960–82. Exec. Mem., later Chm., Glasgow Trades Council, 1952–60; Nat. Exec. Mem., AUT, 1954–59. Co-Chm. Steering Cttee, World Disarmament Campaign, 1986– (Mem., 1980–81); Exec. Mem. and Co-Founder, Scientists Against Nuclear Arms, 1981–. Mem., Barnes BC, 1962–64; Mem. and Leader of Opposition, Richmond upon Thames Council, 1964–68 and 1971–74; Chm., Richmond upon Thames Local Govt Cttee, 1968–77; Mem. for Hornsey, GLC, 1981–86 (Chm., F & GP Cttee, 1981–82, Dep. Chief Whip, 1983–86). *Publications:* (with G. J. Womack) Fuel Cells, 1967; (with A. J. B. Cutler) Deposition and Corrosion in Gas Turbines, 1973; contribs to scientific jls. *Recreation:* campaigning for peace and socialism. *Address:* 3 Ennerdale Road, Kew, Richmond, Surrey TW9 3PG. *T:* 01–948 1989.

HART, Anthony John, DSC 1945; JP; Chairman, Cunningham Hart & Co. Ltd, since 1985 (Senior Partner, 1972–85); *b* 27 Dec. 1923; *s* of Cecil Victor Hart and Kate Winifred Hart (*née* Boncey); *m* 1947, E. Penelope Morris; one *s* one *d. Educ:* King's College Sch., Wimbledon; Dauntsey's Sch. ACII, FCILA. RN 1942–46 (Ordinary Seaman to Lieut). Joined Hart & Co., 1946, Partner 1952, Senior Partner 1969; on merger name changed to Cunningham Hart & Co. Mem. Council, CILA, 1964, Pres., 1970–71. Chm., Medic Alert Foundn in UK, 1971–83; Governor, Dauntsey's Sch.; Mem. Council, Mansfield House University Settlement. Liveryman, 1960, Master, 1976–77, Broderers' Co.; Liveryman, 1979, Mem. Court, 1986, Insurers' Co. Alderman, Ward of Cheap, City of London, 1977–84. FRSA. JP City of London, 1977. *Recreation:* golf. *Address:* 7 Dickens Close, Petersham, Surrey. *T:* 01–948 0587. *Clubs:* City Livery, Richmond Golf.

HART, Sir Byrne, Kt 1974; CBE 1968; MC; chartered accountant; *b* Brisbane, 6 Oct. 1895; *s* of F. McD. Hart; *m* 1922, Margaret H., *d* of D. Cramond; two *s. Educ:* Southport Sch.; Brisbane Grammar Sch. FCA. Served Wars of 1914–18 and 1939–45. *Address:* 14

Gerald Street, Ascot, Brisbane, Queensland 4007. *Clubs:* Queensland, Queensland Turf (Brisbane); Union (Sydney).

HART, David Michael; General Secretary, National Association of Head Teachers, since 1978; *b* 27 Aug. 1940; *s* of Edwin Henry Hart and Freda Muriel Hart; *m* 1963, Mary Chalmers; two *s. Educ:* Hurstpierpoint Coll., Sussex. Solicitor 1963, Herbert Ruse Prizeman. *Recreations:* tennis, bridge. *Address:* Barn Cottage, Fairmile Lane, Cobham, Surrey. *T:* Cobham 62884. *Clubs:* MCC, Wig and Pen.

HART, Donald; QC 1978; a Recorder of the Crown Court, since 1978; *b* 6 Jan. 1933; *s* of Frank and Frances Hart; *m* 1958, Glenys Thomas; two *s* two *d. Educ:* Altrincham Grammar Sch.; Magdalen Coll., Oxford. MA. Macaskie Scholar, Arden and Atkin Prize, Lee Essay Prize (Gray's Inn), 1956. Called to the Bar, Gray's Inn, 1956; Northern Circuit, 1956–. *Recreations:* opera, Manchester City FC. *Address:* 7 Bunkers Hill, Romiley, Cheshire. *T:* 061–430 3998; (chambers) 18 St John Street, Manchester. *T:* 061–834 9843.

HART, Dr Everard Peter, CChem, FRSC; Rector, Sunderland Polytechnic, since 1981; *b* 16 Sept. 1925; *s* of Robert Daniel Hart and Margaret Stokes; *m* Enid Mary Scott; three *s* one *d. Educ:* Wyggeston Grammar Sch., Leicester; Loughborough Coll.; London Univ. (BSc, PhD). Asst Lectr, Lectr and Sen. Lectr, Nottingham and Dist Technical Coll., 1951–57; Sunderland Technical College, later Sunderland Polytechnic: Head of Dept of Chemistry and Biology, 1958–69; Vice-Principal, 1963–69; Dep. Rector, 1969–80. Member: Cttee for Sci. and Technol., CNAA, 1974–77; Gen. Council, Northern Arts, 1982–. Royal Institute of Chemistry: Mem. Council, 1963–65, 1970–73; Vice-Pres., 1973–75. FRSA 1985. *Recreations:* music, opera, theatre, travel. *Address:* Redesdale, The Oval, North End, Durham City. *T:* Durham 48305; (office) Langham Tower, Ryhope Road, Sunderland. *T:* Sunderland 76233.

HART, F(rancis) Dudley, FRCP; Physician, and Physician-in-charge Rheumatism Unit, Westminster Hospital, SW1, 1946–74; Consulting Physician: Hospital of St John and St Elizabeth, London; Westminster Hospital; Chelsea Hospital for Women; lately Consulting Rheumatologist, The Star and Garter Home for Disabled Sailors, Soldiers and Airmen, Richmond; lately Hon. Consulting Physician (Civilian) to the Army; *b* 4 Oct. 1909; *s* of Canon C. Dudley Hart and Kate Evelyn Bowden; *m* 1944, Mary Josephine, *d* of late Luke Tully, Carrigaline, Co. Cork; one *s* two *d. Educ:* Grosvenor Sch., Nottingham; Edinburgh Univ. MB, ChB Edinburgh 1933, MD 1939; MRCP 1937, FRCP 1949. House physician and clinical asst, Brompton Hosp., 1937; Med. Registrar, Royal Northern Hosp., 1935–37; Med. Registrar, Westminster Hosp., 1939–42; Med. Specialist and Officer i/c Med. Div., RAMC, 1942–46. Mem., Cttee on Review of Medicines, 1975–82. Ex-Pres. Heberden Soc.; Member: BMA; RSM; Med. Soc. of London. Arris and Gale Lectr, RCS, 1955; Ellman Lectr, RCP, 1969; Stanley Davidson Lectr, Univ. of Aberdeen, 1970; Bradshaw Lectr, RCP, 1975; Alexander Brown Meml Lectr, Univ. of Ibadan, Nigeria, 1979; Bernadine Becker Lectr, NY, 1984. Exec. Mem., Arthritis and Rheumatism Council; Hon. Member: Ligue Française contre le Rheumatisme; La Societa di Rheumatologia Italia; American Rheumatism Association; Australian Rheumatism Association. *Publications:* (co-author) Drugs: actions, uses and dosage, 1963; (ed) French's Differential Diagnosis, 10th edn, 1973, 12th edn, 1985; (ed) The Treatment of Chronic Pain, 1974; Joint Disease: all the arthropathies, 1975, 3rd edn 1978; (ed) Drug Treatment of the Rheumatic Diseases, 1978, 2nd edn 1982; contributions to: Pye's Surgical Handicraft, 1939–72; Cortisone and ACTH, 1953; Miller's Modern Medical Treatment, 1962; Copeman's Textbook of the Rheumatic Diseases (ed J. T. Scott), 3rd edn 1964, 5th edn 1978; Encyclopedia of General Practice, 1964; Chambers's Encyclopædia, 1964; Drug Treatment, 1976; Butterworth's Medical Dictionary (all rheumatological sections), 1978; Overcoming Arthritis, 1981; Practical Problems in Rheumatology, 1983; articles and broadcasts on general medicine and rheumatism. *Recreations:* multi-track recording, travelling. *Address:* 24 Harmont House, 20 Harley Street, W1N 1AN. *T:* 01–935 4252; (private) 19 Ranulf Road, Hampstead, NW2. *T:* 01–794 2525.

HART, Sir Francis Edmund T.; *see* Turton-Hart.

HART, (Frank) Donald; *see* Hart, Donald.

HART, Frank Thomas, BA; JP; *b* London, 9 Nov. 1911; *s* of late Samuel Black and Ada Frances Laura Hart; *m* 1938, Eveline Brenda Deakin, Leek, Staffs; three *s. Educ:* Gravesend and Sheerness Junior Technical Schs. DPA (London); Diploma of Economics (London); BA Open, 1982. Asst Sec., Buchanan Hospital, St Leonards-on-Sea, 1931–34; Sec., 1934–42; Sec., Central London Eye Hospital, 1942–44; Sec.-Superintendent, Princess Louise Hospital, 1944–48; Superintendent, Royal Infirmary, Sheffield, 1948–52; House Governor and Sec. to the Bd, Charing Cross Hospital, 1952–73; Hospital Manager, Zambia Medical Aid Soc., 1973–75. Mem. Tribunal set up by President of Zambia to hear applications for release from political detainees. Pres., League of Friends, Charing Cross Hosp., 1985–; Past Pres., Assoc. of Hosp. Secretaries; Past Pres. of the Hospital Officers' Club. Chm., Hastings Bowls Assoc. JP: Co. Mddx, 1955–65; Co. Surrey, 1965–77, East Sussex, 1978–81. Freeman, City of London, 1959; Mem., Worshipful Soc. of Apothecaries. *Publications:* (jointly) A Study of Hospital Administration, 1948; Roots of Service (A History of Charing Cross Hospital), 1985. *Recreations:* all games, walking, reading. *Address:* St Alban, 4/11 The Mount, St Leonards on Sea, East Sussex TN38 0HR.

HART, George Vaughan; Consultant, Law Reform Division, Department of Justice, Dublin, since 1972; *b* 9 Sept. 1911; *e s* of George Vaughan Hart and Maude (*née* Curran); *m* 1949, Norah Marie, *d* of Major D. L. J. Babington; one *s* one *d. Educ:* Rossall; Corpus Christi Coll., Oxford. Called to Bar, Middle Temple, 1937. Served Royal Irish Fusiliers, 1940–45. Entered Home Office as Legal Asst, 1946; Principal Asst Legal Advr, 1967–72. Sec., Criminal Law Revision Cttee, 1959–72. *Recreations:* walking, bird-watching. *Address:* 1 Mount Salus, Knocknacree Road, Dalkey, Co. Dublin. *T:* Dublin 850420. *Clubs:* Athenæum; Kildare Street and University (Dublin).

HART, Graham Allan; Deputy Secretary, Department of Health and Social Security, since 1984; *b* 13 March 1940; *s* of Frederick and Winifred Hart; *m* 1964, Margaret Aline Powell; two *s. Educ:* Brentwood Sch.; Pembroke Coll., Oxford. Assistant Principal, 1962, Principal, 1967, Ministry of Health; Asst Registrar, General Medical Council, 1969–71; Principal Private Sec. to Secretary of State for Social Services, 1972–74; Asst Sec., 1974, Under Sec., 1979, DHSS; Under Sec., Central Policy Review Staff, 1982–83. *Address:* 68 Kings Avenue, Bromley, Kent BR1 4HL. *T:* 01–464 9456.

HART, Prof. Herbert Lionel Adolphus; QC 1984; FBA 1962; Principal, Brasenose College, Oxford, 1973–78. Hon. Fellow 1978; Delegate of the Oxford University Press, 1960–74; *b* 18 July 1907; 3rd *s* of Simeon Hart and Rose (*née* Samson); *m* 1941, Jenifer, 3rd *d* of Sir John Fischer Williams, CBE, KC; three *s* one *d. Educ:* Cheltenham Coll.; Bradford Grammar Sch.; New Coll., Oxford (Hon. Fellow 1968). Open Classical Scholar, New Coll., Oxford, 1926; First Class Lit. Hum., 1929. Practised at the Chancery Bar, 1932–40. Served War of 1939–45, in War Office, 1940–45. Fellow and Tutor in Philosophy, New Coll., Oxford, 1945; University Lecturer in Philosophy, Oxford, 1948; Prof. of Jurisprudence, Oxford, 1952–68; Fellow, University Coll., Oxford, 1952–68; Res. Fellow 1969–73, Hon. Fellow, 1973; Sen. Res. Fellow, Nuffield Foundn, 1969–73.

Visiting Professor: Harvard Univ., 1956–57; Univ. of California, LA, 1961–62. Mem., Monopolies Commn, 1967–73. Pres., Aristotelian Soc., 1959–60; Vice-Pres., British Acad., 1976–77. Hon. Master of the Bench, Middle Temple, 1963. For. Mem., Amer. Acad. of Arts and Sciences, 1966. Hon. Dr of Law: Stockholm, 1960; Hebrew Univ. of Jerusalem, 1985; Hon. LLD: Glasgow, 1966; Chicago, 1966; Cambridge, 1978; Harvard, 1980; Edinburgh, 1980; Georgetown, 1982; Hon. DLitt: Kent, 1969; Hull, 1979; Bradford, 1980; Hon. Dr, Nat. Autonomous Univ. of Mexico, 1979; Hon. PhD Tel Aviv, 1983. Fellow, Accademia delle Scienze, Turin, 1964; Commonwealth Prestige Fellow (Govt of NZ), 1971. *Publications:* (with A. M. Honoré) Causation in the Law, 1959, 2nd edn 1984; The Concept of Law, 1961; Law Liberty and Morality, 1963; The Morality of the Criminal Law, 1965; Punishment and Responsibility, 1968; (ed, with J. H. Burns) Jeremy Bentham: An Introduction to the Principles of Morals and Legislation, 1970; (ed) Jeremy Bentham: Of Laws in General, 1970; (ed jtly) Jeremy Bentham: A Comment on the Commentaries and A Fragment on Government, 1977; Essays on Bentham: jurisprudence and political theory, 1982; Essays in Jurisprudence and Philosophy, 1983; articles in philosophical and legal journals. *Address:* University College, Oxford; 11 Manor Place, Oxford. *T:* 242402.

HART, Rt. Hon. Dame Judith (Constance Mary), DBE 1979; PC 1967; MP (Lab) Clydesdale, since 1983 (Lanark Division of Lanarkshire, 1959–83); *d* of late Harry Ridehalgh and Lily Ridehalgh; *m* 1946, Anthony Bernard Hart, *qv*; two *s*. *Educ:* Clitheroe Royal Grammar Sch.; London School of Economics, London University (BA Hons 1945). Contested (Lab) Bournemouth West, 1951, and South Aberdeen, 1955. Jt Parly Under-Sec. of State for Scotland, 1964–66; Minister of State, Commonwealth Office, 1966–67; Minister of Social Security, 1967–68; Paymaster-General (in the Cabinet), 1968–69; Minister of Overseas Develt, 1969–70, 1974–75; Minister for Overseas Develt, 1977–79; front bench opposition spokesman on overseas aid, 1979–80. Govt Co-Chm., Women's Nat. Commn, 1969–70. Labour Party: Mem., Nat. Executive, 1969–83; Vice-Chm., 1980–81, Chm., 1981–82. Hon. Fellow, Inst. of Development Studies, Sussex Univ., 1985. *Publication:* Aid and Liberation, 1973. *Recreations:* theatre, gardening, spending time with her family. *Address:* 3 Ennerdale Road, Kew Gardens, Richmond-upon-Thames.

HART, Michael, MA; FRSA; Headmaster of European School, Luxembourg, since 1980; *b* 1 May 1928; *yr s* of late Dr F. C. Hardt; *m* 1956, Lida Dabney Adams, PhD (Wisconsin Univ.). *Educ:* Collège Français, Berlin; Landerziehungsheim Schondorf; Keble Coll., Oxford (Exhib.). 1st Cl. Hons History, 1951. Administrative Asst, UNRRA, 1945–47; Asst Master and Head of History, Sherborne Sch., 1951–56; Head of History, 1956–61, and Housemaster of School House, 1961–67, Shrewsbury Sch.; Headmaster of Mill Hill Sch., 1967–74; HM Inspector of Schs, DES, 1974–76; Headmaster, European Sch., Mol, Belgium, 1976–80. *Publications:* The EEC and Secondary Education in the UK, 1974; contrib. to Reader's Digest World Atlas and Atlas of British Isles. *Recreations:* travel, climbing. *Address:* 10 rue Jean Engling, Dommeldange, Luxembourg.

HART, Prof. Michael, FRS 1982; CPhys, FInstP; Professor of Physics, University of Manchester, since 1984; Science Programme Co-ordinator (part-time, on secondment), Daresbury Laboratory, Science and Engineering Research Council, since 1985; *b* 4 Nov. 1938; *s* of Reuben Harold Victor Hart and Phyllis Mary (*née* White); *m* 1963, Susan Margaret (*née* Powell); three *d*. *Educ:* Cotham Grammar Sch., Bristol; Bristol Univ. (BSc, PhD, DSc). FInstP 1971. Research Associate: Dept of Materials Science and Engrg, Cornell Univ., 1963–65; Dept of Physics, Bristol Univ., 1965–67; Lectr in Physics, 1967–72, Reader in Physics, 1972–76, Bristol Univ.; Sen. Resident Res. Associate of Nat. Research Council, Nat. Aeronautics and Space Admin Electronics Research Center, Boston, Mass, 1969–70; Special Advisor, Central Policy Review Staff, Cabinet Office, 1975–77; Wheatstone Prof. of Physics and Head of Physics Dept, KCL, 1976–84. Amer. Crystallographic Assoc.'s Bertram Eugene Warren Award for Diffraction Physics (jtly with Dr U. Bonse), 1970; Charles Vernon Boys Prize of Inst. of Physics, 1971. *Publications:* numerous contribs to learned jls on x-ray optics, defects in crystals and synchrotron radiation. *Recreations:* weaving, flying kites. *Address:* 54 Manor Park South, Knutsford, Cheshire WA16 8AN. *T:* Knutsford 2893. *Club:* Athenæum.

HART, Prof. Oliver Simon D'Arcy, PhD; Professor of Economics, Massachusetts Institute of Technology, since 1985; *b* 9 Oct. 1948; *s* of Philip Montagu D'Arcy Hart, *qv* and Ruth Hart; *m* 1974, Rita Goldberg (who retains maiden name); two *s*. *Educ:* University Coll. Sch.; Univ. of Cambridge (BA 1969); Univ. of Warwick (MA 1972); Princeton Univ. (PhD 1974). Lectr in Econs, Univ. of Essex, 1974–75; Asst Lectr in Econs, subseq. Lectr, Univ. of Cambridge, 1975–81; Fellow of Churchill Coll., Cambridge, 1975–81; Prof. of Economics, LSE, 1982–85; Prog. Dir, Centre for Economic Policy Res., 1983–84. Fellow, Econometric Soc., 1979 (Mem. Council, 1982–). Editor, Review of Economic Studies, 1979–83. *Publications:* articles on economic theory in Econometrica, Rev. of Econ. Studies, Jl of Pol Economy. *Recreations:* playing and watching tennis. *Address:* Department of Economics, Massachusetts Institute of Technology, Cambridge, Mass 02139, USA.

HART, P(hilip) M(ontagu) D'Arcy, CBE 1956; MA, MD (Cambridge), FRCP; Medical Research Council grant holder, National Institute for Medical Research, since 1965 (Director, Tuberculosis Research Unit, Medical Research Council, 1948–65); *b* 25 June 1900; *s* of late Henry D'Arcy Hart and late Hon. Ethel Montagu; *m* 1941, Ruth, *d* of late Herbert Meyer and late Grete Meyer-Larsen; one *s*. *Educ:* Clifton Coll.; Gonville and Caius Coll., Cambridge; University Coll. Hospital. Dorothy Temple Cross Fellowship to USA, 1934–35; Consultant Physician, UCH, 1934–37; Mem. Scientific Staff, MRC, 1937–48; Mem. Expert Cttee on Tuberculosis, WHO, 1947–64. Goldsmith Entrance Exhibnr, Filliter Exhibnr, Magrath Scholarship, Tuke Medals, UCH Medical Sch., 1922–25; Horton Smith MD Prize, Cambridge, 1930; Royal College of Physicians: Milroy Lecture, 1937; Mitchell Lecture, 1946; Weber-Parkes Prize, 1951; Marc Daniels Lecture, 1967; Stewart Prize, BMA, 1964. *Publications:* scientific papers on respiratory disease, epidemiology and cell biology. *Address:* National Institute for Medical Research, Mill Hill, NW7. *T:* 01–959 3666; 37 Belsize Court, NW3 5QN. *Club:* Athenæum.
See also O. S. D'A. Hart.

HART, Captain Raymond, CBE 1963; DSO 1945; DSC 1941, Bar 1943; Royal Navy; *b* 24 June 1913; *o s* of late H. H. Hart, Bassett, Southampton; *m* 1945, Margaret Evanson, *o d* of Capt. S. B. Duffin, Danesfort, Belfast; two *s* one *d*. *Educ:* Oakmount Preparatory Sch.; King Edward VI Sch. Joined Merchant Navy, 1929; Joined Royal Navy, 1937; HMS Hasty, 2nd Destroyer Flotilla, 1939–42; in command: HMS Vidette, 1942–44 (despatches); HMS Havelock, 1944; Sen. Officer, 21st Escort Gp, 1944–45; served in HMS Vanguard during Royal Tour of S Africa, 1947. RN Staff Course, 1949–52; in command, HMS Relentless, 1952–53; Joint Services Staff Course, 1953–54; Staff C-in-C Allied Forces Mediterranean, as Liaison Officer to C-in-C Allied Forces Southern Europe, HQ Naples, Italy, 1954–56; in command, HMS Undine, and Capt. 6th Frigate Sqdn, 1957–58; Cdre Naval Drafting, 1960–62; retd from RN, 1963. Nautical Advr, British & Commonwealth Shipping Co., 1963–72; Fleet Manager, Cayzer, Irvine & Co. Ltd, 1972–76; Director: Union-Castle Mail Steamship Co. Ltd; Clan Line Steamers Ltd, 1964–76; Cayzer, Irvine & Co. Ltd, 1966–76; British & Commonwealth Shipping Co. Ltd, 1966–76. Council, Missions to Seamen; Mem., Cttee of Management, Marine Soc. FRIN; FNI. Officer Order of Merit of Republic of Italy, 1958. *Recreations:* swimming, golf, gardening. *Address:* Three Firs Cottage, Bramshott Chase, Hindhead, Surrey. *T:* Hindhead 4890.

HART, (Thomas) Anthony (Alfred), MA; Headmaster, Cranleigh School, since 1984; *b* 4 March 1940; *er s* of Rev. Arthur Reginald Hart and Florence Ivy Hart; *m* 1971, Daintre Margaret Withiel (*née* Thomas); one *s* one *d*. *Educ:* City of Bath Sch.; New Coll., Oxford (2nd Cl. Hons PPE; MA); Pres., Oxford Union, 1963. Served with VSO, Mzuzu Secondary Sch., Nyasaland, 1959–60. Asst Principal and Principal, Min. of Transport, 1964–69; seconded to Govt of Malaŵi as Transport Adviser, 1969–70; Principal, DoE and CSD, 1970–73; Head, Voluntary Services Unit, Home Office, 1973–75; Asst Sec., CSD and HM Treasury, 1975–84. *Recreations:* reading, travel, listening to music, dining out. *Address:* The Headmaster's House, Cranleigh School, Cranleigh, Surrey GU6 8QQ. *T:* Cranleigh 276377. *Club:* Travellers'.

HART, Thomas Mure, CMG 1957; *b* 1 March 1909; *s* of late Maxwell M. Hart and of Elizabeth Watson, Aiknut, West Kilbride; *m* 1936, Eileen Stewart Lawson; one *s* one *d*. *Educ:* Strathallan; Glasgow Univ.; Brasenose Coll., Oxford. Colonial Administrative Service, 1933; seconded Colonial Office, 1933–36; Malayan Civil Service, 1936; Dir of Commerce and Industry, Singapore, 1953; Financial Sec., Singapore, 1954; retired, 1959. Bursar, Loretto Sch., Musselburgh, 1959–69. *Recreation:* golf. *Address:* 44 Frogston Road West, Edinburgh EH10 7AJ. *T:* 031–445 2152. *Clubs:* Royal and Ancient (St Andrews); Honourable Company of Edinburgh Golfers.

HART, Maj.-Gen. Trevor Stuart, CB 1982; MRCS, LRCP; FFCM; Hospital and Medical Director, National Guard King Khalid Hospital, Jeddah, 1983–84; *b* 19 Feb. 1926; *s* of R. J. Hart and C. G. Hart (*née* Blyfield); *m* 1954, P. G. Lloyd; two *s* one *d*. *Educ:* Dulwich Coll.; Guy's Hosp. MB, BS; FFCM; DPH, DTM&H. DDMS HQ 1 (BR) Corps, 1975–78; DMS: UKLF, 1978–81; BAOR, 1981–83. Mem., Wessex RHA, 1984–. Col Comdt, RAMC, 1984–. OStJ 1973. *Recreations:* gardening, growing orchids (more leaves than blooms). *Address:* c/o Barclays Bank, 72 Cheapside, EC2.

HART, Rt. Rev. Mgr William Andrew; *b* Dumbarton, 9 Sept. 1904; *s* of Daniel Hart and Margaret Gallagher. *Educ:* St Mungo's Academy, Glasgow; St Mary's Coll., Blairs, Aberdeen; Royal Scots Coll. and Pontifical Univ., Valladolid, Spain. Asst Priest, St Mary's, Hamilton, 1929–33; St John's, Glasgow, 1933–39; Army Chaplain, 1939–45; Asst Priest, St Michael's, Glasgow, 1945–48; Vice-Rector, Royal Scots Coll., Valladolid, 1948–49; Parish Priest, St Nicholas', Glasgow, 1949–51, St Saviour's, Glasgow, 1951–55; Bishop of Dunkeld, 1955–81. *Address:* Birchwood House, Birnam, Dunkeld, Perthshire. *T:* Dunkeld 267.

HART-DAVIS, Sir Rupert (Charles), Kt 1967; author, editor and former publisher; Director of Rupert Hart-Davis, Ltd, Publishers, 1946–68; Vice-President, Committee of the London Library, since 1971 (Chairman 1957–69); *b* 28 Aug. 1907; *o s* of Richard Vaughan Hart-Davis and Sybil Mary Cooper, *er sister* of 1st Viscount Norwich; *m* 1st, 1929, Peggy Ashcroft (now Dame Peggy Ashcroft) (marr. diss.); 2nd, 1933, Catherine Comfort Borden-Turner (marr. diss.), *d* of Mary Borden and George Douglas Turner; two *s* one *d*; 3rd, 1964, Winifred Ruth (*d* 1967), *d* of C. H. Ware, Bromyard, and *widow* of Oliver Simon; 4th, 1968, June (*née* Clifford), *widow* of David Williams. *Educ:* Eton; Balliol Coll., Oxford. Student at Old Vic, 1927–28; Actor at Lyric Theatre, Hammersmith, 1928–29; office boy at William Heinemann Ltd, 1929–31; Manager of Book Soc., 1932; Dir of Jonathan Cape Ltd, 1933–40. Served in Coldstream Guards, 1940–45. Founded Rupert Hart-Davis Ltd, 1946. Hon. DLitt: Reading, 1964; Durham, 1981. *Publications:* Hugh Walpole: a biography, 1952; The Arms of Time: a memoir, 1979; *edited:* The Essential Neville Cardus, 1949; E. V. Lucas: Cricket all his Life, 1950; George Moore: Letters to Lady Cunard, 1957; The Letters of Oscar Wilde, 1962; Max Beerbohm: Letters to Reggie Turner, 1964; Max Beerbohm: More Theatres, 1969; Max Beerbohm: Last Theatres, 1970; Max Beerbohm: A Peep into the Past, 1972; A Catalogue of the Caricatures of Max Beerbohm, 1972; The Autobiography of Arthur Ransome, 1976; William Plomer: Electric Delights, 1978; The Lyttelton Hart-Davis Letters, vol. I, 1978, vol. II, 1979, vol. III, 1981, vol. IV, 1982, vol. V, 1983, vol. VI, 1984; Selected Letters of Oscar Wilde, 1979; Two Men of Letters, 1979; Siegfried Sassoon Diaries: 1920–1922, 1981, 1915–1918, 1983, 1923–25, 1985; The War Poems of Siegfried Sassoon, 1983; A Beggar in Purple: commonplace book, 1983; More Letters of Oscar Wilde, 1985; Siegfried Sassoon: Letters to Max Beerbohm, 1986. *Recreations:* reading, book-collecting, watching cricket. *Address:* The Old Rectory, Marske-in-Swaledale, Richmond, N Yorks.
See also Baron Silsoe.

HART DYKE, Sir Derek William, 9th Bt *cr* 1677; *b* 4 Dec. 1924; *s* of Sir Oliver Hamilton Augustus Hart Dyke, 8th Bt, and Millicent Zoë (*d* 1975), *d* of Dr Mayston Bond; *S* father, 1969; *m* 1st, 1953, Dorothy Moses, Hamilton, Ont (marr. diss. 1963); one *s* one *d*; 2nd, 1964, Margaret Dickson Elder, Ottawa (marr. diss. 1972). Mem., Royal Canadian Military Inst. *Educ:* Harrow; Millfield. *Heir:* *s* David William Hart Dyke, *b* 5 Jan. 1955. *Address:* 30 West Avenue North, Apt 611, Hamilton, Ontario L8L 5B8, Canada. *Club:* Hamilton Press.

HART-LEVERTON, Colin Allen; QC 1979; a Recorder of the Crown Court, since 1979; *b* 10 May 1936; *s* of Monty Hart-Leverton and Betty (*née* Simmonds). *Educ:* Stowe; self-taught thereafter. Mem., Inst. of Taxation, 1957 (youngest to have ever qualified); called to the Bar, Middle Temple, 1957 (youngest to have ever qual.). Contested (L): Bristol West, 1959 (youngest cand.); Walthamstow West, 1964. Prosecuting Counsel, Central Criminal Court, 1974–79; Dep. Circuit Judge, 1975; Attorney-at-Law, Turks and Caicos Islands, Caribbean, 1976. Occasional television and radio broadcasts. *Recreations:* table-tennis, jazz. *Address:* 10 King's Bench Walk, EC4Y 7EB. *T:* 01–353 2501; 9533 Brighton Way, Beverly Hills, Calif, USA.

HARTE, Julia Kathleen; *see* McKenzie, J. K.

HARTE, Dr Michael John; Assistant Under Secretary of State (Dockyard Planning Team), Ministry of Defence, since 1985; *b* 15 Aug. 1936; *s* of Harold Edward Harte and Marjorie Irene Harte; *m* 1st, 1962, Diana Hayes (marr. diss. 1971); 2nd, 1975, Mary Claire Preston; four step *d*. *Educ:* Charterhouse; Trinity Coll., Cambridge (BA); University Coll., London (PhD; Dip. in Biochem. Engrg). Sen. Scientific Officer, Microbiol Res. Estab., MoD, 1963; Principal, MoD, 1967; Private Sec. to Minister of State for Def., 1972; Asst Sec., Central Policy Rev. Staff, 1973; Asst Sec., MoD, 1975–77; Counsellor, Budget and Infrastructure, UK Delegn to NATO, 1977–81; Chm., NATO Civil and Mil. Budget Cttees, 1981–83; Asst Sec., MoD, 1983–85. *Recreation:* wine: tasting, buying, drinking, keeping. *Address:* Greenman Farm, Wadhurst, E Sussex TN5 6LE. *T:* Wadhurst 3292.

HARTHAN, John Plant, MA, FLA; Keeper of the Library, Victoria and Albert Museum, 1962–76; *b* 15 April 1916; *y s* of late Dr George Ezra Harthan, Evesham, Worcs, and Winifred May Slater. *Educ:* Bryanston; Jesus Coll., Cambridge; University Coll., London. Asst-Librarian, Southampton Univ., 1940–43; Royal Society of Medicine Library,

1943–44; Asst Under-Librarian, Cambridge Univ. Library, 1944–48; Asst-Keeper of the Library, Victoria and Albert Museum, 1948. FLA 1939. *Publications*: Bookbindings in the Victoria and Albert Museum, 1950, 3rd edn 1985; co-editor, F.D. Klingender, Animals in Art and Thought, 1971; Books of Hours, 1977; The History of the Illustrated Book, 1981; Introduction to Illuminated Manuscripts, 1983. *Recreations*: history of religion, royalty, music, botany, writing. *Address*: 15 Palliser Court, Palliser Road, W14 9ED.

HARTILL, Edward Theodore, FRICS; City Surveyor, Corporation of London, since 1985; *b* 23 Jan. 1943; *s* of Clement Augustus Hartill and Florence Margarita Hartill; *m* 1975, Gillian Ruth (*née* Todd); two *s*, and two *s* from previous marr. *Educ*: Priory Sch. for Boys, Shrewsbury; Coll. of Estate Management, London Univ. BSc (Estate Management); FRICS 1978. Joined Messrs Burd and Evans, Land Agents, Shrewsbury, 1963; Estates Dept, Legal and Gen. Assce Soc., 1964–73; Property Investment Dept, Guardian Royal Exchange Assce Gp, 1973–85. Vis. Lectr in Law of Town Planning and Compulsory Purchase, Hammersmith and W London Coll. of Advanced Business Studies, 1968–78. Mem., British Schs Exploring Soc. Liveryman, Chartered Surveyors' Co., 1985–. *Publications*: occasional lectures and articles on professional topics. *Recreations*: travel, hill walking, cinema, family. *Address*: 215 Sheen Lane, East Sheen, SW14 8LE. *T*: 01–878 4494.

HARTINGTON, Marquess of; Peregrine Andrew Morny Cavendish; *b* 27 April 1944; *s* of 11th Duke of Devonshire, *qv*; *m* 1967, Amanda Carmen, *d* of late Comdr E. G. Heywood-Lonsdale, RN, and of Mrs Heywood-Lonsdale; one *s* two *d. Educ*: Eton; Exeter Coll., Oxford. *Heir*: *s* Earl of Burlington, *qv. Address*: Beamsley Hall, Skipton, N Yorks.

HARTLAND-SWANN, Julian Dana Nimmo; HM Diplomatic Service; Consul General, Frankfurt, since 1986; *b* 18 Feb. 1936; *s* of late Prof. J. J. Hartland-Swann and of Mrs Kenlis Hartland-Swann (*née* Taylour); *m* 1960, Ann Deirdre Green; one *s* one *d. Educ*: Stowe; Lincoln Coll., Oxford (History). HM Forces, 1955–57. Entered HM Diplomatic Service, 1960; 3rd Sec., Brit. Embassy, Bangkok, 1961–65; 2nd, later 1st Sec., FO, 1965–68; 1st Sec., Berlin, 1968–71; 1st Sec. and Head of Chancery, Vienna, 1971–74; FCO, 1975–77; Counsellor, 1977; Ambassador to Mongolian People's Republic, 1977–79; Counsellor and Head of Chancery, Brussels, 1979–83; Head of SE Asian Dept, FCO, 1983–85. *Recreations*: French food, sailing, restoring ruins. *Address*: c/o Foreign and Commonwealth Office, SW1A 2AH.

HARTLEY, Arthur Coulton, CIE 1946; OBE 1943; ICS (retired); *b* 24 March 1906; *s* of late John Aspinall Hartley and Jennie Hartley; *m* 1943, Mrs Cecilie Leslie; one *s. Educ*: Cowley Grammar Sch.; Manchester Univ.; Balliol Coll., Oxford. Entered Indian Civil Service, 1929; Asst Magistrate, Comilla, Bengal, 1929–30; Subdivisional Magistrate, Sirajganj, Bengal, 1930–32; Asst Settlement Officer, Rangpur, Bengal, 1932–34; Settlement Officer, Rangpur, Bengal, 1934–37; Asst Sec. to Governor of Bengal, 1938–40; District Magistrate, Howrah, Bengal, 1940–43; Controller of Rationing, Calcutta, Bengal, 1943–45; Dir-Gen. of Food, Bengal, India, 1945–47. *Publication*: Report on Survey and Settlement Operations of Rangpur, 1938. *Recreations*: hill walking, painting. *Address*: 12 Grange Road, Lewes, E Sussex BN7 1TR.

HARTLEY, Brian Joseph, CMG 1950; OBE 1945 (MBE 1934); Consultant, Oxfam East Africa, 1981–85; *b* 1907; *s* of late John Joseph Hartley, Tring, Herts; *m* 1951, Doreen Mary, *d* of Col R. G. Sanders; three *s* one *d. Educ*: Loughborough; Midland Agricultural Coll.; Wadham Coll., Oxford; Imperial Coll. of Tropical Agriculture, Trinidad. Entered Colonial Service; Agricultural Officer, Tanganyika, 1929; Aden Protectorate: Agricultural Officer, 1938; Agricultural Adviser, 1944; Dir of Agriculture, 1946–54; retd 1954; Chief, FAO(UN), mission in Iraq, 1955; Mem., Tanganyika Agricultural Corporation, 1956–62; Trustee, Tanganyika Nat. Parks, 1957–64; Mem., Ngorongoro Conservation Authority Advisory Board, 1963–64. UN (Special Fund) Consultant Team Leader: Kafue Basin Survey, N Rhodesia, 1960; Livestock Develt Survey, Somalia, 1966; Chief Livestock Adviser, FAO, Somalia, 1967–70; Project Manager, UNSF Survey of Northern Rangelands Project, Somalia, 1970–72; Consultant, FAO-IBRD Project, Anatolia, Turkey, 1972–73; Consultant, ODA, Wadi Rima and Montane Plains, Yemen Arab Republic, 1975; Consultant, 1973–76, Technical Manager, 1976–79, World Bank Nomadic Rangelands Project, Ethiopia; Consultant, Oxfam Karamoja Relief Prog. in Uganda, 1980. *Publication*: Camels in the Horn of Africa. *Address*: Box 337, Malindi, Kenya.

HARTLEY, Prof. Brian Selby, PhD; FRS 1971; Professor of Biochemistry, Imperial College, University of London, since 1974 and Director, Centre for Biotechnology, since 1982; *b* 16 April 1926; *s* of Norman and Hilda Hartley; *m* 1949, Kathleen Maude Vaughan; three *s* one *d. Educ*: Queens' Coll., Cambridge; Univ. of Leeds. BA 1947, MA 1952, Cantab; PhD 1952, Leeds. ICI Fellow, Univ. of Cambridge, 1952; Helen Hay Whitney Fellow, Univ. of Washington, Seattle, USA, 1958; Fellow and Lectr in Biochemistry, Trinity Coll., Cambridge, 1964; Scientific Staff, MRC Laboratory of Molecular Biology, 1961–74. Mem. Council: EMBO (European Centre for Molecular Biology), 1978–84; Royal Soc., 1982–84. Hon. Mem., Amer. Soc. of Biological Chemists, 1977. British Drug Houses Medal for Analytical Biochemistry, 1969. *Publications*: papers and articles in scientific jls and books. *Recreations*: fishing, gardening. *Address*: Imperial College of Science and Technology, SW7 2AZ.

HARTLEY, Air Marshal Sir Christopher (Harold), KCB 1963 (CB 1961); CBE 1957 (OBE 1949); DFC 1945; AFC 1944; BA Oxon; *b* 31 Jan. 1913; *s* of late Brig.-Gen. Sir Harold Hartley, GCVO, CH, CBE, MC, FRS; *m* 1st, 1937, Anne Sitwell (marr. diss., 1943); 2nd, 1944, Margaret Watson; two *s. Educ*: Eton; Balliol Coll., Oxford (Williams Exhibnr); King's Coll., Cambridge. Zoologist on Oxford Univ. expeditions: to Sarawak, 1932; Spitsbergen, 1933; Greenland, 1937. Asst Master at Eton Coll., 1937–39. Joined RAFVR, 1938. Served War of 1939–45: 604 Sqdn, 256 Sqdn, Fighter Interception Unit, Central Fighter Establishment. Permanent Commission, 1945; AOC 12 Group, Fighter Command, 1959; ACAS (Operational Requirements), Air Min., 1961; DCAS, 1963–66; Controller of Aircraft, Min. of Aviation and Min. of Technology, 1966–70, retired. Dep. Chm., British Hovercraft Corporation, 1979– (Chm., 1974–78); Dir, Westland Aircraft Ltd, 1971–83. *Recreation*: fishing. *Address*: c/o Marex (Whitehall) Associates, Whitehall House, 41 Whitehall, SW1. *Club*: Travellers'.

HARTLEY, David Fielding, PhD; FBCS; Director, University Computing Service, University of Cambridge, since 1970; Fellow of Darwin College, Cambridge, since 1969; *b* 14 Sept. 1937; *s* of late Robert M. Hartley and late Sheila E. Hartley, LRAM; *m* 1960, Joanna Mary, *d* of Stanley and Constance Bolton; one *s* two *d. Educ*: Rydal Sch.; Clare Coll., Cambridge (MA, PhD). Mathematical Laboratory, Univ. of Cambridge: Sen. Asst in Research, 1964–65; Asst Dir of Research, 1966–67; Univ. Lectr, 1967–70; Jun. Research Fellow, Churchill Coll., Cambridge, 1964–67. British Computer Society: Mem. Council, 1970–73, 1977–80, 1985–; Vice Pres. (Technical), 1985–. Chm., Inter-University Cttee on Computing, 1972–74; Mem., Computer Board for Univs and Research Councils, 1979–83; Mem. Council of Management, Numerical Algorithms Gp Ltd, 1979– (Chm., 1986–); adviser to Prime Minister, Information Technology Adv. Panel, 1981–86; DTI Hon. Adviser in Information Technology (on sabbatical leave), 1983; Mem. various

Govt, Res. Council and Industry cttees and consultancies. Mem., BBC Science Consultative Gp, 1984–. Director: CADCentre Ltd, 1983–; Cambridge Control Ltd. Governor, Rydal Sch., 1982–. Medal of Merits, Nicholas Copernicus Univ., Poland, 1984. *Publications*: papers in scientific jls on operating systems, programming languages, computing service management. *Address*: 26 Girton Road, Cambridge CB3 0LL. *T*: Cambridge 276975.

HARTLEY, Sir Frank, Kt 1977; CBE 1970; PhD London, CChem, FPS, FRSC; Vice-Chancellor, University of London, 1976–78; Dean of the School of Pharmacy, University of London, 1962–76; *b* 5 Jan. 1911; *s* of late Robinson King Hartley and Mary Hartley (*née* Holt); *m* 1937, Lydia May England; two *s. Educ*: Municipal Secondary (later Grammar) Sch., Nelson, Lancs; Sch. of Pharmacy (Fellow, 1977), University Coll. (Fellow, 1972), and Birkbeck Coll. (Fellow, 1970), University of London. Jacob Bell Schol., 1930, Silver Medallist in Pharmaceutics, Pharmaceut. Chem. and Pharmacognosy, 1932. Pharmaceutical Chemist, 1932, Demonstrator and Lectr, 1932–40, at Sch. of Pharmacy; 1st cl. hons BSc (Chem.), University of London, 1936, and PhD, 1941; Chief Chemist, Organon Laboratories Ltd, 1940–43; Sec., Therapeutic Research Corp., 1943–46; Sec., Gen. Penicillin Cttee (Min. of Supply), 1943–46; Dir of Research and Sci. Services, The British Drug Houses, Ltd, 1946–62; Chm. Brit. Pharmaceut. Conf., 1957, and of Sci. Adv. Cttee of Pharmaceut. Soc. of Great Britain, 1964–66; Mem. Council, 1955–58, 1961–64, Vice-Pres., 1958–60, 1964–65, 1967–69, Pres., 1965–67, of Royal Institute of Chemistry; Hon. Treasurer, 1956–61, Chm. 1964–68 of Chem. Council; Mem. 1953–80, Vice-Chm. 1963–68, Chm. 1970–80, of British Pharmacopoeia Commn, and a UK Deleg., 1964–80, to European Pharmacopoeia Commn; Mem., 1970–84, Vice-Chm., 1977–84, Medicines Commn; Member: Poisons Bd (Home Office), 1958–66; Cttee on Safety of Drugs (Min. of Health), 1963–70; Cttee on Prevention of Microbiol Contamination of Medicinal Products, 1972–73; Nat. Biological Standards Bd, 1975–83; Cttee of Enquiry on Contaminated Infusion Fluids, 1972; Chairman: Bd of Studies in Pharmacy, Univ. of London, 1964–68; Pharmacy Bd, CNAA, 1965–77; Collegiate Council, 1969–73; Panel on Grading of Chief Pharmacists in Teaching Hosps, 1972–74, Qualified Person Adv. Cttee, DHSS, 1979; Comrs for Lambeth, Southwark and Lewisham Health Area, 1979–80; Pharmacy Working Gp, Nat. Adv. Bd for Higher Educn, Local Authorities, 1982–84; Health Care Sci. Adv. Cttee, Council of Science and Technol. Insts, 1982–; Mem., Academic Council, 1969–73. Co-opted Mem. Senate, 1968–76, 1978–, ex officio Mem., 1976–78, Senate Mem. of Court, 1970–76, 1978–, ex officio Mem., 1976–78, Dep. Vice-Chancellor, 1973–76, University of London; Member Council: St Thomas's Hosp. Medical Sch., University of London, 1968–80; Royal Free Hosp. Med. Sch., 1970–; Member Bd of Governors: Royal Free Hosp. Gp, 1970–74; Kingston Polytechnic, 1970–75; British Postgrad. Med. Fedn, London Univ., 1972–; Royal Postgrad. Med. Sch., 1972–; Inst. of Basic Med. Sci, 1973–. Chm., Consortium of Charing Cross and Westminster Med. Schs London Univ., 1981–84. Lectures: Sir William Pope Meml, RSA, 1962; Wilkinson, Inst. of Dental Surg., 1978; Astor, Middlesex Hosp. Med. Sch., 1980; Bernal, Birkbeck Coll., 1982. Hon. FRCP 1979, Hon. FRCS 1980, Hon. FRSC 1981. Liveryman, Worshipful Soc. of Apothecaries of London. Hon. DSc Warwick, 1978; Hon. LLD Strathclyde, 1980. Charter Gold Medal, Pharm. Soc. of GB, 1974. *Publications*: papers on chem. and pharmaceut. research in Quarterly Jl of Pharmacy, Jl of Pharmacy and Pharmacology and Jl of Chem. Soc. Reviews and articles in sci. and tech. jls. *Recreations*: reading, gardening. *Address*: 24 Old School Close, St Mary's Mead, Merton Park, SW19 3HY. *T*: 01–542 7198. *Clubs*: Athenæum, Savage.

See also F. R. Hartley.

HARTLEY, Prof. Frank Robinson, CChem, FRSC; Principal and Dean, Royal Military College of Science, Shrivenham, since 1984 (Acting Dean, 1982–84); *b* 29 Jan. 1942; *s* of Sir Frank Hartley, *qv*; *m* 1964, Valerie Peel; three *d. Educ*: King's College, Sch., Wimbledon (Sambrooke Schol.); Magdalen Coll., Oxford (Demy; BA, MA, DPhil). Post-doctoral Fellow, Commonwealth Scientific and Industrial Research Organisation, Div. of Protein Chemistry, Melbourne, Aust., 1966–69; Imperial Chemical Industries Research Fellow and Tutor in Physical Chemistry, University Coll. London, 1969–70; Lectr in Inorganic Chemistry, Univ. of Southampton, 1970–75; Professor of Chemistry and Head of Dept of Chemistry and Metallurgy, Royal Military Coll. of Science, Shrivenham, 1975–82. Sen. Travelling Fellow, ACU, 1986. Gov.; Welbeck Coll. Mem., Oxford Union. *Publications*: The Chemistry of Platinum and Palladium (Applied Science), 1973; Elements of Organometallic Chemistry (Chemical Soc.), 1974, Japanese edn 1981; (with C. Burgess and R. M. Alcock) Solution Equilibria, 1980, Russian edn 1983; (with S. Patai) The Chemistry of the Metal—Carbon Bond, vol. 1 1983, vol. 2 1984, vol. 3 1985; Supported Metal Complexes, 1985; papers in inorganic, coordination and organometallic chemistry in major English, Amer. and Aust. chemical jls. *Recreations*: Rugby refereeing, golf, swimming, squash, gardening, cliff walking, reading. *Address*: 9 Curtis Road, Shrivenham, Wiltshire SN6 8AY. *Club*: Shrivenham.

HARTLEY, His Honour Gilbert Hillard; a Circuit Judge (formerly Judge of County Courts), 1967–82; *b* 11 Aug. 1917; *s* of late Percy Neave Hartley and late Nellie Bond (*née* Hillard); *m* 1948, Jeanne, *d* of late C. W. Gall, Leeds; one *s* two *d. Educ*: Ashville, Harrogate; Exeter Coll. Oxford. Called to Bar, Middle Temple, 1939. Served with Army, 1940–46. Recorder of Rotherham, 1965–67; Dep. Chm., WR of Yorkshire QS, 1965–71. *Address*: South Lawn, East Keswick, Leeds LS17 9DB.

HARTLEY, Ven. Peter Harold Trahair; Archdeacon of Suffolk, 1970–75, now Archdeacon Emeritus; *b* 11 July 1909; *m* 1938, Ursula Mary Trahair; two *d. Educ*: Leys School; University of London (BSc 1935); Queen's College, Oxford (MA 1948); Cuddesdon Theological College. Deacon 1953, Priest 1954, Diocese of St Edmundsbury; Curate of Dennington and Badingham, 1953–55; Rector of Badingham, 1955, with Bruisyard, 1960, and Cransford, 1974; Priest-in-Charge, Badingham with Bruisyard and Dennington, 1976–85. Rural Dean of Loes, 1967–70. *Publications*: papers in zoological journals. *Recreations*: natural history, naval and military history. *Address*: 26 Double Street, Framlingham, Woodbridge, Suffolk. *T*: Framlingham 723604.

HARTLEY, Richard Leslie Clifford, QC 1976; *b* 31 May 1932; *s* of late Arthur Clifford Hartley, CBE and late Nina Hartley. *Educ*: Marlborough Coll.; Sidney Sussex Coll., Cambridge (MA). Called to the Bar, Gray's Inn, 1956. *Recreations*: golf, tennis. *Address*: 15 Chesham Street, SW1. *T*: 01–235 2420. *Clubs*: Garrick, MCC; Woking Golf, Rye Golf, St Enodoc Golf.

HARTLING, Poul; Grand Cross of Dannebrog; United Nations High Commissioner for Refugees, 1978–85; Member of Folketing, Denmark, 1957–60 and 1964–78; *b* 14 Aug. 1914; *s* of Mads Hartling and Mathilde (*née* Nielsen); *m* 1940, Elsebeth Kirkemann; three *s* one *d. Educ*: Univ. of Copenhagen (Master of Divinity 1939). Curate, Frederiksberg Church, 1941–45; Chaplain, St Luke Foundn, 1945–50; Principal, Zahle's Teachers' Trng Coll., 1950–68. Chm., Liberal Party Parly Group, 1965–68; Mem., Nordic Council, 1964–68 (Pres., 1966–68); Minister of Foreign Affairs, 1968–71; Prime Minister, 1973–75; Chm., Liberal Party, 1964–78. Secretary: Christian Academic Soc., 1934–35; Christian Movement of Sen. Secondary Students, 1939–43. Dr *hc* Valparaiso Univ., Indiana, 1981. Grand-Croix: l'Ordre de la Couronne, Belgique; l'Ordre de Mennlik II, Ethiopie; Grosskreuz des Verdienstordens der Bundesrep. Deutschland; Royal Order of St

Olav, Norway; Falcon of Iceland; Merit of Luxembourg; Yugoslovenske Zvezde. *Publications:* Sursum Corda, 1942; Growth of church idea in the missionary field, 1945; (ed) Church, School, Culture, 1963; The Danish Church, 1964 (2nd edn 1967); From 17 Years in Danish Politics, 1974; Autobiography vol. I, 1980, vol. II, 1981, vol. III, 1983, vol. IV, 1985. *Recreation:* music. *Address:* Emilievej 6 E, DK 2920 Charlottenlund, Denmark.

HARTMAN, (Gladys) Marea, CBE 1978 (MBE 1967); Head of Delegation, English International Athletics Teams and Commonwealth Games Athletics Teams, since 1978; *b* 1920. Competed as a runner for Spartan Athletic Club and Surrey County; team manager, British athletics team at Olympic and European Games and English athletics team at Commonwealth Games, 1956–78. Mem., Women's Commn of Internat. Amateur Athletic Fedn, 1958– (Chm., 1968–81); Hon. Treasurer, British Amateur Athletic Bd, 1972–84; Hon. Sec., Women's AAA, 1960– (Hon. Treasurer, 1950–60; Life Vice-Pres., 1980; Vice-Chm., 1981–); Hon. Treasurer, CCPR, 1984– (Dep. Chm., 1981–83). *Recreations:* music, reading, theatre. *Address:* c/o Women's Amateur Athletic Association, Francis House, Francis Street, SW1P 1DE. *T:* 01–828 4731.

HARTOG, Harold Samuel Arnold; Knight, Order of the Netherlands Lion; KBE (Hon.) 1970; Advisory Director, Unilever NV, 1971–75; *b* Nijmegen, Holland, 21 Dec. 1910; *m* 1963, Ingeborg Luise Krahn. *Educ:* Wiedemann Coll., Geneva. Joined Unilever, 1931. After service with Dutch forces during War of 1939–45 he joined management of Unilever interests in France, and subseq. took charge of Unilever cos in the Netherlands; elected to Bds of Unilever, 1948; Mem. Rotterdam Group Management and responsible for Unilever activities in Germany, Austria and Belgium, 1952–60; subseq. Mem. Cttee for Unilever's overseas interests, in London; became, there, one of the two world co-ordinators of Unilever's foods interests, 1962; Chm., Unilever NV, 1966–71. *Recreations:* history of art; collecting Chinese pottery and porcelain. *Address:* Kösterbergstrasse 40B, 2000 Hamburg (Blankensee), Germany. *Clubs:* Dutch; Ubersee (Hamburg); Golf (Falkenstein).

HARTOPP, Sir John Edmund Cradock-, 9th Bt, *cr* 1796; TD; *b* 8 April 1912; *s* of late Francis Gerald Cradock-Hartopp, Barbrook, Chatsworth, Bakewell, Derbyshire (kinsman of 8th Bt) and Elizabeth Ada Mary (*née* Stuart); *S* kinsman, Sir George Francis Fleetwood Cradock-Hartopp, 1949; *m* 1953, Prudence, 2nd *d* of Sir Frederick Leith-Ross, GCMG, KCB; three *d*. *Educ:* Summer Fields, Oxford; Uppingham Sch. Travelled in United States of America before joining at age of 18, Staff of Research Laboratories, Messrs Thos Firth & John Brown Ltd, Steel Makers, Sheffield, 1930; travelled in India and the Far East, 1948–49; Dir, Firth Brown Tools Ltd, 1961–76. War of 1939–45 (despatches twice); joined TA and served with Royal Engineers in UK; Norway, 1940; North Africa (1st Army), 1943; Italy, 1943–45; released, 1945, with rank of Major. Mem. Council: Machine Tool Research Assoc., 1965–70; Machine Tool Trades Assoc., 1970–73. *Recreations:* golf (semi-finalist English Golf Champ., 1935; first reserve, Eng. *v* France, 1935); cricket, tennis, motoring. *Heir: cousin* Lt-Comdr Kenneth Alston Cradock-Hartopp, MBE, DSC, RN [*b* 26 Feb. 1918; *m* 1942, Gwendolyn Amy Lilian Upton; one *d*]. *Address:* The Cottage, 27 Wool Road, Wimbledon Common, SW20. *Clubs:* East India, MCC; Royal and Ancient (St Andrews).

HARTWELL, Baron, *cr* 1968 (Life Peer), of Peterborough Court in the City of London; **(William) Michael Berry,** MBE 1944; TD; Chairman and Editor-in-Chief of The Daily Telegraph and Sunday Telegraph; *b* 18 May 1911; 2nd *s* of 1st Viscount Camrose and Mary Agnes, *e d* of late Thomas Corns, London; *m* 1936, Lady Pamela Margaret Elizabeth Smith (*d* 1982), *yr d* of 1st Earl of Birkenhead, PC, GCSI, KC; two *s* two *d*. *Educ:* Eton; Christ Church, Oxford (MA). 2nd Lieut 11th (City of London Yeo.) Light AA Bde, RA (TA), 1938; served War of 1939–45; Capt. and Major, 1940; Lieut-Col 1944 (despatches twice, MBE). Editor, Sunday Mail, Glasgow, 1934–35; Managing Editor, Financial Times, 1937–39; Chm. Amalgamated Press Ltd, 1954–59. *Publication:* Party Choice, 1948. *Address:* 18 Cowley Street, Westminster, SW1. *T:* 01–222 4673; Oving House, Whitchurch, near Aylesbury, Bucks. *T:* Aylesbury 641307. *Clubs:* White's, Beefsteak; Royal Yacht Squadron.

See also Col Hon. J. Berry, Viscount Camrose.

HARTWELL, Benjamin James, OBE 1959; Clerk to Southport Borough Justices, 1943–73; *b* Southport, 24 June 1908; *s* of late Joseph Hartwell, Bucks, and late Margaret Ann Hartwell; *m* 1937, Mary (*née* Binns) (*d* 1986), Southport; one *s* one *d*. *Educ:* Kirkcudbright Acad.; King George V Sch., Southport; London Univ. (LLM). Admitted a Solicitor of the Supreme Court, 1936; Hon. Sec. Justices' Clerks' Soc., 1947–59; Pres. Lancs and Cheshire Dist of Boys' Brigade, 1950–63; Chm. Council, Congregational Union of England and Wales, 1952–58; Chm. Congregational Union of England and Wales 1959–60. Member: Central Cttee, World Council of Churches, 1954–61; Home Secretary's Advisory Council on the Treatment of Offenders, 1955–63. *Address:* 101 Ewell Way, Totton, Southampton SO4 3PQ.

HARTWELL, Sir Brodrick William Charles Elwin, 5th Bt, *cr* 1805; *b* 7 Aug. 1909; *s* of Sir Brodrick Cecil Denham Arkwright Hartwell, 4th Bt, and Joan Amy (*d* 1962), *o d* of Robert Milne Jeffrey, Esquimault, Vancouver; *S* father, 1948; *m* 1st, 1937, Marie Josephine, *d* of late S. P. Mullins (marriage dissolved 1950); one *s*; 2nd, 1951, Mary Maude, MBE, *d* of J. W. Church, Bedford; one *d* decd. *Educ:* Bedford Sch. Sometime Pilot Officer RAF. Served War of 1939–45; Capt. Leics Regt, 1943. *Heir: s* Francis Antony Charles Peter Hartwell [*b* 1 June 1940; *m* 1968, Barbara Phyllis Rae, *d* of H. Rae Green; one *s*]. *Address:* Little Dale, 50 High Street, Lavendon, Olney, Bucks.

HARTWELL, Eric, CBE 1983; Vice-Chairman, Trusthouse Forte plc, since 1972 (Chief Executive, 1979–82, Joint Chief Executive, 1982–83); *b* 10 Aug. 1915; *m* 1st, 1937, Gladys Rose Bennett (marr. diss.); one *s* one *d*; 2nd, 1952, Dorothy Maud Mowbray; one *s* one *d*. *Educ:* Mall Sch., Twickenham; Worthing High School. FHCIMA; CBIM. Electrical industry, 1932–37; Dir, Fortes & Co. Ltd, 1938; HM Forces, 1940–45; Jt Man. Dir, Forte Holdings Ltd, 1962; Dep. Man. Dir, Trust Houses Forte Ltd, 1970; Dep. Chief Exec., Trust Houses Forte Ltd, 1972–75, Jt Chief Exec., 1975–78. Chm., BHRCA, 1981–85. Vice-Chm., Thames Heritage Trust Ltd, 1983–; Mem. Cttee, Nuffield Hosp., Enfield; Dir, LV Catering Educn Trust Ltd. Liveryman, Upholders' Co., 1952–. FRSA 1984. *Recreations:* yachting, painting, photography. *Address:* Tall Trees, 129 Totteridge Lane, N20 8NS. *T:* 01–445 2321. *Clubs:* National Sporting, River Emergency Service Association, Inner Magic Circle; Thames Motor Yacht; South Herts Golf.

HARTY, Bernard Peter; Chamberlain, City of London Corporation, since 1983; *b* 1 May 1943; *s* of William Harty and Eileen Nora (*née* Canavan); *m* 1965, Glenys Elaine Simpson; one *d*. *Educ:* Ullathorne Grammar Sch., Coventry. CIPFA 1966; MBCS 1983. Accountant, Coventry CBC, 1961–69; Forward Budget Planning Officer, Derbyshire CC, 1969–72; Chief Accountant, Bradford CBC, 1972–74; Chief Finance Officer, Bradford MDC, 1973–76; County Treasurer, Oxfordshire CC, 1976–83. Mem. Nat. Cttee, Information Technol. Year 1982 (IT82); Chm., IT82 Local Govt Cttee, 1982. Freeman, City of London, 1983; Liveryman, Worshipful Co. of Tallow Chandlers, 1984. *Publications:* papers in professional jls. *Recreations:* theatre, music, National Trust, cricket. *Address:* Chamber of London, PO Box 270, Guildhall, EC2P 2EJ. *T:* 01–606 3030.

HARTY, Most Rev. Michael; *see* Killaloe, Bishop of, (RC).

HARUNA, Alhaji; *see* Gwandu, Emir of.

HARVEY, family name of **Barons Harvey of Prestbury** and **Harvey of Tasburgh.**

HARVEY OF PRESTBURY, Baron *cr* 1971 (Life Peer), of Prestbury in the County Palatine of Chester; **Arthur Vere Harvey,** Kt 1957; CBE 1942; FRAeS; *b* 31 Jan. 1906; *e s* of A. W. Harvey, Kessingland, Suffolk; *m* 1st, 1940, Jacqueline Anne (marr. diss., 1954), *o d* of W. H. Dunnett; two *s*; 2nd, 1955, Mrs Hilary Charmian Williams (marr. diss. 1977); 3rd, 1978, Mrs Carol Cassar Torreggiani. *Educ:* Framlingham Coll. Royal Air Force 1925–30, qualified as flying instructor; Dir of Far East Aviation Co. Ltd and Far East Flying Training Sch. Ltd, Hong-Kong, 1930–35; Adviser to Southern Chinese Air Forces with hon. rank of Maj.-Gen., 1932–35; Sqdn Leader AAF, 1937, and founded 615 County of Surrey Squadron and commanded the Squadron in France, 1939–40 (despatches twice); Group Captain 1942; Air Commodore 1944. MP (C) Macclesfield Div. of Cheshire, 1945–71; Chairman Cons. Members' 1922 Cttee, 1966–70. Dir, Tradewinds Airways Ltd. Vice-Pres. British Air Line Pilots' Assoc., 1965. FRAeS. Hon. Freeman: Macclesfield, 1969; Congleton, 1970. Hon. DSc Salford, 1972. Comdr, Order of Oranje Nassau, 1969. *Recreations:* private flying (4th King's Cup Race, 1937), sailing. *Address:* Rocklands, Les Vardes, St Peter Port, Guernsey, CI. *Clubs:* Buck's, Royal Air Force; Royal Yacht Squadron (Cowes).

HARVEY OF TASBURGH, 2nd Baron, *cr* 1954, of Tasburgh, Norfolk; **Peter Charles Oliver Harvey;** Bt 1868; Chartered Accountant; *b* 28 Jan. 1921; *er s* of 1st Baron Harvey of Tasburgh, GCMG, GCVO, CB, and Maud Annora (*d* 1970), *d* of late Arthur Watkin Williams-Wynn; *S* father, 1968; *m* 1957, Penelope Anne, *d* of Lt-Col Sir William Makins, 3rd Bt; two *d*. *Educ:* Eton; Trinity College, Cambridge. Served 1941–46 with Royal Artillery, Tunisia, Italy. Bank of England, 1948–56; Binder Hamlyn & Co., 1956–61; Lloyds Bank International Ltd (formerly Bank of London and South America), 1961–75; English Transcontinental Ltd, 1975–78; Brown, Shipley & Co., 1978–81. *Recreations:* sailing, music. *Heir: b* Hon. John Wynn Harvey [*b* 4 Nov. 1923; *m* 1950, Elena Maria-Teresa, *d* of late Marchese Giambattista Curtopassi, Rome; two *s* one *d*]. *Address:* Crownick Woods, Restronguet, Mylor, Falmouth, Cornwall. *Clubs:* Brooks's; Royal Cornwall Yacht, Royal Fowey Yacht.

HARVEY, Alan Frederick Ronald, OBE 1970; HM Diplomatic Service, retired; *b* 15 Dec. 1919; *s* of Edward Frederick and Alice Sophia Harvey; *m* 1946, Joan Barbara (*née* Tuckey); one *s*. *Educ:* Tottenham Grammar Sch. Air Ministry, 1936–40 (Civil Service appt). Served War, RAF, 1940–46. Air Min., 1946–49; Foreign Office, 1949–52 (on transfer to Diplomatic Service); HM Vice-Consul, Turin, 1953–55; Second Sec.: Rome, 1956; Tokyo, 1957–59; HM Consul (Information): Chicago, 1959–62; FO, 1963–65; First Sec. (Commercial): Belgrade, 1965–67; Tokyo, 1967–72; Commercial Counsellor: Milan, 1973–74; Rome, 1975–76; Consul-General in Perth, 1976–78. *Recreations:* tennis, golf. *Address:* Ken Hill House, Cricket St Thomas, Chard, Somerset TA20 4DE. *Club:* Royal Commonwealth Society, Civil Service; Windwhistle Gold, Squash and Country.

HARVEY, Alexander, PhD, BSc, FInstP; Principal, University of Wales Institute of Science and Technology, 1946–68 (formerly Cardiff Technical College, later Welsh College of Advanced Technology); Pro-Vice-Chancellor, University of Wales, 1967–68; *b* 21 Sept. 1904; *s* of Andrew Harvey, Bangor, Co. Down; *m* 1933, Mona Anderson, Newcastle upon Tyne; one *s* two *d*. *Educ:* Gateshead Grammar Sch.; Armstrong (King's) Coll., Univ. of Durham. Commonwealth Fund Fellowship, Univ. of California, 1929–31; Scientific Asst, Adam Hilger Ltd, London, 1931–33; Asst Lecturer, Physics Dept, University of Manchester, 1933–34; Head of Physics Dept, Wigan and District Mining and Tech. Coll., 1934–42; Principal, Scunthorpe Tech. Sch., 1942–46. President: Assoc. of Principals of Technical Instns, 1957–58; South Wales Instn of Engineers, 1970–71; Chm. Council of Assoc. of Technical Instns, 1961–62. Hon. LLD Wales, 1970. *Publications:* Science for Miners, 1938; One Hundred Years of Technical Education, 1966; various papers on optical, spectroscopic and educational subjects. *Address:* 110 Pencisely Road, Llandaff, Cardiff. *T:* Cardiff 563795.

HARVEY, Rev. Canon Anthony Ernest, DD; Canon of Westminster since 1982; *b* 1 May 1930; *s* of Cyril Harvey, QC, and Nina (*née* Darley); *m* 1957, Julian Elizabeth McMaster; four *d*. *Educ:* Dragon Sch., Oxford; Eton Coll.; Worcester Coll., Oxford (BA, MA, DD 1983); Westcott House, Cambridge. Curate, Christ Church, Chelsea, 1958; Research Student, Christ Church, Oxford, 1962; Warden, St Augustine's Coll., Canterbury, 1969; Univ. Lectr in Theology and Fellow of Wolfson Coll., Oxford, 1976; Chaplain, The Queen's Coll., 1977. Examining Chaplain to Archbishop of Canterbury, 1975; Six Preacher, Canterbury Cathedral, 1977; Bampton Lectr, 1980. Mem., Archbishops' Commn on Urban Priority Areas, 1984. *Publications:* Companion to the New Testament (New English Bible), 1970, 2nd edn 1980; Priest or President?, 1975; Jesus on Trial, 1976; Something Overheard, 1977; (ed) God Incarnate: story and belief, 1981; Jesus and the Constraints of History, 1982; Believing and Belonging, 1984; (ed) Alternative Approaches to New Testament Study, 1985; articles in classical and theological jls. *Recreations:* music, walking. *Address:* 3 Little Cloister, Westminster Abbey, SW1. *T:* 01–222 4174.

HARVEY, Anthony Peter; Head, Department of Library Services, since 1981, and Co-ordinator of Planning and Development, since 1985, British Museum (Natural History); *b* 21 May 1940; *s* of Frederick William Henry Harvey and late Fanny Evelyn Harvey (*née* Dixon); *m* 1963, Margaret Hayward; three *s* one *d*. *Educ:* Hertford Grammar Sch. MIInfS. Dept of Oriental Printed Books, British Museum, 1958–60; Dept of Palaeontology, BM (Nat. Hist.), 1960–75, Librarian, 1963–75. Member: Geolog. Soc., 1973 (Chm., Geolog. Inf. Gp, 1975–78; Chm., Liby Cttee, 1981–84); Bibliog. Soc., 1962; Printing Hist. Soc., 1965; RGS (Mem. Liby Cttee, 1985–). Mem., Guild of Freemen, City of London, 1986. *Publications:* (ed) Secrets of the Earth, 1967; (ed) Directory of Scientific Directories, 1969, 4th edn 1986; Prehistoric Man, 1972; Guide to World Science, vol. 1, 1974; (ed) Encyclopedia of Prehistoric Life, 1979; European sources of scientific and technical information, 6th edn 1984; numerous contribs to learned jls, ref. works and periodicals. *Recreations:* music, books, the countryside. *Address:* Ragstones, Broad Oak, Heathfield, East Sussex TN21 8UD. *T:* Heathfield 2012.

HARVEY, Arthur Douglas; Assistant Under-Secretary of State, Ministry of Defence, 1969–76; *b* 16 July 1916; *o s* of late William Arthur Harvey and Edith Alice; *m* 1940, Doris Irene Lodge; one *s* (and one *s* decd). *Educ:* Westcliff High Sch.; St Catharine's Coll., Cambridge. Wrangler, Maths Tripos, 1938. Entered War Office, 1938; served in Army, 1940–45; Princ. 1945; Registrar, Royal Military College of Science, 1951–54; Asst Sec. 1954; Under-Sec. 1969. *Address:* 36b Lovelace Road, Long Ditton, Surrey. *T:* 01–399 0587.

HARVEY, Barbara Fitzgerald, FSA 1964; FBA 1982; Fellow of Somerville College, Oxford, since 1956; *b* 21 Jan. 1928; *d* of Richard Henry Harvey and Anne Fitzgerald (*née* Julian). *Educ:* Teignmouth Grammar Sch.; Bishop Blackall Sch., Exeter; Somerville Coll., Oxford (Schol.). First Cl. Final Honour Sch. of Modern History, Oxford, 1949; Bryce Student, Oxford Univ., 1950–51; BLitt Oxon 1953. Assistant, Dept of Scottish History, Edinburgh Univ., 1951–52; Asst Lectr, subseq. Lectr, Queen Mary Coll., London Univ., 1952–55; Tutor, Somerville Coll., Oxford, 1955–; Vice-Principal, 1976–79, 1981–83. Assessor, Oxford Univ., 1968–69. *Publications:* Documents Illustrating the Rule of Walter de Wenlok, Abbot of Westminster 1283–1307, 1965; Westminster Abbey and its Estates in the Middle Ages, 1977; (ed, with L. C. Hector) The Westminster Chronicle 1381–94, 1982; contribs to Economic History Rev., Trans Royal Historical Soc., Bulletin of Inst. of Historical Research, etc. *Address:* Somerville College, Oxford OX2 6HD. *T:* Oxford 57595.

HARVEY, Benjamin Hyde, OBE 1968; FCA; IPFA; DPA; General Manager, Harlow Development Corporation, 1955–73; *b* 29 Sept. 1908; *s* of Benjamin Harvey and Elizabeth (*née* Hyde); *m* 1938, Heather Frances Broome; one *d. Educ:* Stationers' Company's Sch. Local Govt, 1924–40; Treas., Borough of Leyton, 1940–47; Comptroller, Harlow Develt Corp., 1947–55. Hon. LLD Newfoundland, 1985. *Publication:* (jtly) Harlow: the story of a new town, 1980. *Recreations:* books, sport. *Address:* Brick House, Broxted, Essex. *T:* Harlow 850233.

HARVEY, Prof. Brian Wilberforce; Professor of Property Law, since 1973, and Pro-Vice-Chancellor, since 1986, University of Birmingham; *b* 17 March 1936; *s* of Gerald and Noelle Harvey; *m* 1962, Rosemary Jane Brown; two *s* two *d. Educ:* Clifton Coll., Bristol; St John's Coll., Cambridge (Choral Schol., MA, LLM). Solicitor, 1961. Lectr, Birmingham Univ., 1962–63; Sen. Lectr, Nigerian Law Sch., 1965–67; Lectr, Sen. Lectr and Prof. of Law, QUB, 1967–73; Univ. of Birmingham: Dir, Legal Studies, 1973–76; Dean, Faculty of Law, 1982–85. Vis. Prof., Univ. of Singapore, 1985–86. Chairman: Gtr Birmingham Social Security Appeal Tribunals, 1982–; Medical Appeals Tribunals, 1985–. Member: Statute Law Cttee (NI), 1972–73; Cttee on Legal Educn (NI), 1972–73; Adviser, Council of Legal Educn, NI, 1976–79. *Publications:* Law of Probate Wills and Succession in Nigeria, 1968; (jtly) Survey of Northern Ireland Land Law, 1970; Settlements of Land, 1973; (ed) Vocational Legal Training in UK and Commonwealth, 1975; (ed) The Lawyer and Justice, 1978; The Law of Consumer Protection and Fair Trading, 1978, 2nd edn 1982; (jtly) Consumer and Trading Law Cases and Materials, 1985; (jtly) Law and Practice of Auctions, 1985. *Recreations:* performing and listening to music. *Address:* c/o Faculty of Law, The University, Birmingham B15 2TT.

See also J. D. Harvey.

HARVEY, Bryan Hugh, CBE 1978; Adviser, Ministry of Defence, since 1985; Chairman, Advisory Committee on Major Hazards, 1975–83; *b* 17 Oct. 1914; *y s* of late Oliver Harvey and Ellen Harvey (*née* Munn); *m* 1941, Margaret (*d* 1986), 2nd *d* of late E. G. Palmer; one *d. Educ:* KES Birmingham; Bristol Grammar Sch.; Corpus Christi Coll., Oxford; Harvard Univ. BA 1936; MA 1945; MSc 1953 (Industrial Hygiene). RAF, 1943–45. Printing industry until 1938, when joined Inspectorate of Factories; Dep. Chief Inspector, 1965; Chief Inspector, 1971–74; Dep. Dir Gen. (Dep. Sec.), Health and Safety Exec., 1975–76. Advr to Employment Cttee, H of C, 1980–83. Rockefeller Foundn Fellow, 1952–53; Hon. Lectr, Dept of Occupational Health, Univ. of Manchester, 1954–59; Vis. Prof., Univ. of Aston in Birmingham, 1972–79; External Examiner, Loughborough Univ. of Technology, 1984–. Hon. Mem., British Occupational Hygiene Soc. (Pres. 1976–77). FSA 1964; Hon. Fellow, Instn of Occupational Safety and Health. *Publications:* (with R. Murray) Industrial Health Technology, 1958; (ed) Handbook of Occupational Hygiene, 1980; many articles in jls on industrial safety and hygiene, and industrial archaeology. *Recreations:* industrial archaeology, Georgian architecture, steam engines. *Address:* 2 Surley Row, Caversham, Reading, Berks RG4 8LY. *T:* Reading 479453. *Clubs:* Army and Navy; Leander.

HARVEY, Charles Richard Musgrave; (3rd Bt *cr* 1933, but does not use the title); *b* 7 April 1937; *s* of Sir Richard Musgrave Harvey, 2nd Bt, and Frances Estelle (*d* 1986), *er d* of late Lindsay Crompton Lawford, Montreal; *S* father, 1978; *m* 1967, Celia Vivien, *d* of George Henry Hodson; one *s* one *d. Educ:* Marlborough; Pembroke Coll., Cambridge (BA 1960, MA 1964). Fellow, Institute of Development Studies, Sussex. *Heir: s* Paul Richard Harvey, *b* 1971.

HARVEY, Colin Stanley, MBE 1964; TD 1962; DL; a Recorder of the Crown Court, Western Circuit, since 1975; a Solicitor of the Supreme Court; *b* 22 Oct 1924; *s* of Harold Stanley and Lilian May Harvey; *m* 1949, Marion Elizabeth (*née* Walker); one *s* one *d. Educ:* Bristol Grammar Sch.; University Coll., Oxford (BA). Served 1939–45 war in Queen's Regt and RA, India, Burma, Malaya, Java. In private practice as a solicitor. Bt Lt-Col TAVR, 1973. DL Avon, 1977. *Recreations:* TAVR, riding, beagling. *Address:* 12 Southfield Road, Westbury-on-Trym, Bristol BS9 3BH. *T:* Bristol 620404. *Clubs:* Royal Commonwealth Society; Clifton (Bristol); Royal Western Yacht (Plymouth).

HARVEY, Ven. Francis William; Archdeacon of London and Canon Residentiary of St Paul's Cathedral, since 1978; *b* 28 Sept. 1930; *s* of Frank and Clara Harvey; *m* 1955, Mavis Wheeler; one *s* three *d. Educ:* Chester College; Lichfield Theological Coll. Mil. service, RAOC, 1948–50. Teaching service, 1952–60; Curate, St Ann, Rainhill, Liverpool, 1962–65; Vicar, St Mark, Edge Lane, Liverpool, 1965–68; Liverpool Diocesan Planning Adviser, 1967–71; Area Sec., London Diocesan Fund, 1971–75; Pastoral Sec., Diocese of London, 1975–78; Prebendary of St Paul's Cathedral, 1975–78. Examining Chaplain to Bishop of London, 1981–. Member: Gen. Synod Commn on Faculty Jurisdiction, 1980; Gen. Synod, 1984–. Trustee, City Parochial Foundn, 1979–. Freeman, City of London, 1979; Hon. Liveryman, Masons' Co., 1984. MA Lambeth, 1982. *Recreations:* music, reading, photography. *Address:* 2 Amen Court, EC4M 7BU. *T:* 01–248 3312.

HARVEY, Ian Douglas, TD 1950; psc 1944; author; public relations consultant; free-lance journalist; Associate, Douglas Stephens Associates Ltd, Management Consultants, 1970–80; *b* 25 Jan. 1914; *s* of late Major Douglas Harvey, DSO, and of late Mrs Bertram Bisgood (*née* Dorothy Cundall); *m* 1949, Clare (legally separated), *y d* of late Sir Basil E. Mayhew, KBE; two *d. Educ:* Fettes Coll.; Christ Church, Oxford. BA, 1937; MA, 1941. President: Oxford Univ. Cons. Assoc., 1935; Oxford Carlton Club, 1936; Oxford Union Soc., 1936. Served War of 1939–45, Adjutant, 123 LAA Regt, RA, 1940; Bde Major, 38 AA Bde, RA, 1943; GSO2 (ops), HQ AA command, 1944; Staff Coll. Camberley, 1944; Bde Major 100 AA Bde, NW Europe, 1945; Lieut-Col Comdg 566 LAA Regt, RA (City of London Rifles) TA, 1947–50. Contested Spelthorne Div. of Mddx, 1945; MP (C) Harrow East, 1950–58; Mem., Parly Select Cttee for reform of Army and Air Force Acts, 1952–54; Sec., 1922 Cttee, 1955–57; Parly Sec., Min. of Supply, 1956–57; Jt Parly Under-Sec. of State, FO, 1957–58. Mem. of Council, Royal Borough of Kensington, 1947–52; Mem. of LCC for S Kensington, 1949–52; Rep. of LCC on County of London TA Assoc. 1949–52; Chairman: Paddington Cons. Assoc., 1980–83; Westminster N Cons. Assoc., 1983; ILEA Tertiary Educn Bd, Div. 1, 1985–; contested (C) Westminster N, ILEA, 1986. Deleg. Advertising Assoc. to Advertising Fedn of America Convention (Detroit), 1950; Chm. Press Relations Cttee of Internat. Advertising Conference (Great Britain), 1951; Member: Advertising Assoc.; Inst. of Public Relations; Adv. Cttee on Publicity and Recruitment for Civil Defence, 1952–56; London Soc. of Rugby Union Football Referees; Rep. of Church Assembly on Standing Cttee of Nat. Soc., 1951–55; Vice-Pres., Campaign for Homosexual Equality, 1972–; Pres., Cons. Gp for Homosexual Equality, 1980–. Director: W. S. Crawford Ltd, 1949–56; Colman, Prentis and Varley Ltd, 1962–63; Advertising Controller, Yardley of London Ltd, 1963–64 (Advertising Dir, 1964–66). Chairman: Coningsby Club, 1946–47; London Old Fettesian Assoc., 1953–54 (Vice-Pres., 1981–); Dep. Chm., Westminster Play Assoc., 1980–; Secretary: Iain Macleod Meml Trust, 1974–; Selwyn-Lloyd Meml Library Appeal, 1980–81; Subscriptions Manager, Middle East International, 1978–80. Governor: Birkbeck Coll., 1949–52; St George's Sch. (RC), Maida Vale, 1977– (Chm., 1983); Paddington Coll., 1979–; St Mary of the Angels (RC) Sch., 1983–; St Augustine's Sch., Kilburn, 1984–; Quintin Kynaston Sch., St John's Wood, 1985–. Editor, Westminster North Gazette, 1984–. *Publications:* Talk of Propaganda, 1947; The Technique of Persuasion, 1951; Arms and To-morrow, 1954; To Fall Like Lucifer, 1971. *Recreations:* squash, cycling, swimming, tennis. *Address:* 62D St Michael's Street, W2 1QR.

HARVEY, John Edgar; consultant in energy policy and public affairs; Director, Burmah Oil Trading Ltd and subsidiary companies in Burmah Oil Group, 1974–80; *b* 24 April 1920; *s* of John Watt Harvey and Charlotte Elizabeth Harvey; *m* 1945, Mary Joyce Lane, BA, JP; one *s. Educ:* Xaverian Coll., Bruges, Belgium; Lyme Regis Grammar Sch. Radio Officer, in the Merchant Navy, 1939–45. Contested (C): St Pancras North, 1950; Walthamstow East, 1951; Mem. Nat. Exec. Cttee., Conservative Party, 1950–55; Chm., Woodford Conservative Assoc., 1954–56. MP (C) Walthamstow East, 1955–66. Mem., NSPCC Central Executive Cttee, 1963–68. Governor, Forest Sch., 1966–78. Verderer of Epping Forest, 1970–. Past Master, Guild of Freemen of City of London. *Recreations:* various in moderation. *Address:* 43 Traps Hill, Loughton, Essex. *T:* 01–508 8753. *Clubs:* Carlton, City of London, City Livery.

HARVEY, Prof. Jonathan Dean; composer; Professor of Music, University of Sussex, since 1980; *b* 3 May 1939; *s* of Gerald and Noelle Harvey; *m* 1960, Rosaleen Marie Barry; one *s* one *d. Educ:* St Michael's Coll., Tenbury; Repton; St John's Coll., Cambridge (MA, DMus); Glasgow Univ. (PhD). Lectr, Southampton Univ., 1964–77; Reader, Sussex Univ., 1977–80. Harkness Fellow, Princeton Univ., 1969–70. Works performed at many festivals and international centres. *Publications:* The Music of Stockhausen, 1975; compositions: Persephone Dream, for orch., 1972; Inner Light (trilogy), for performers and tape, 1973–77; Smiling Immortal, for chamber orch., 1977; String Quartet, 1977; Veils and Melodies, for tapes, 1978; Magnificat and Nunc Dimittis, for choir and organ, 1978; Album, for wind quintet, 1978; Hymn, for choir and orch., 1979; Be(com)ing, for clarinet and piano, 1979; Concelebration, instrumental, 1979, rev. 1981; Mortuos Plango, Vivos Voco, for tape, 1980; Passion and Resurrection, church opera, 1981; Resurrection, for double chorus and organ, 1981; Whom Ye Adore, for orch., 1981; Bhakti, for 15 insts and tape, 1982; Easter Orisons, for chamber orch., 1983; The Path of Devotion, for choir and orch., 1983; Nachtlied, for soprano, piano and tape, 1984; Gong-Ring, for ensemble with electronics, 1984; Song Offerings, for soprano and players, 1985; Madonna of Winter and Spring, for orch., synthesizers and electronics, 1986. *Recreations:* tennis, walking, meditation. *Address:* 35 Houndean Rise, Lewes, Sussex BN7 1EQ. *T:* Brighton 471241.

See also B. W. Harvey.

HARVEY, Prof. Leonard Patrick; Cervantes Professor of Spanish, King's College, University of London, 1973–84, now Professor Emeritus; *b* 25 Feb. 1929; *s* of Francis Thomas Harvey and Eva Harvey; *m* 1954, June Rawcliffe; two *s. Educ:* Alleyn's Sch., Dulwich; Magdalen Coll., Oxford. 1st cl. hons BA Mod. Langs 1952; 2nd cl. Oriental Studies 1954; MA 1956; DPhil 1958. Lectr in Spanish, Univ. of Oxford, 1957–58; Univ. of Southampton, 1958–60; Queen Mary Coll., Univ. of London: Lectr, 1960–63; Reader and Head of Dept, 1963; Prof. of Spanish, 1967–73; Dean of Faculty of Arts, 1970–73; Dean of Faculty of Arts, KCL, 1979–81. Vis. Prof., Univ. of Victoria, BC, 1966. Mem. UGC, 1979–83. Chm., Educn Cttee, Hispanic and Luso-Brazilian Council, 1984–. *Publications:* articles in Al-Andalus, Bulletin of Hispanic Studies, Jl of Semitic Studies, Modern Philology, Revista de Filología Española, etc. *Address:* Tree Tops, Yester Park, Chislehurst BR7 5DQ. *T:* 01–467 3565.

HARVEY, Mary Frances Clare, MA; Headmistress, St Mary's Hall, Brighton, since 1981; *b* 24 Aug. 1927; *d* of Rev. Oliver Douglas Harvey, West Malling, Kent. *Educ:* St Mary's Sch., Colchester; St Hugh's Coll., Oxford. BA Oxon, Final Honour Sch. of Mod. Hist., 1950; Diploma in Educn, 1951; MA 1954. History Mistress, St Albans High Sch., 1951; Head of History Dept, Portsmouth High Sch., GPDST, 1956; Headmistress: Sch. of St Clare, Penzance, 1962–69; Badminton Sch., Westbury on Trym, Bristol, 1969–81. Governor, Bristol Cathedral Sch., 1978–81. *Recreations:* music, travel, reading, needlework. *Address:* 233 Eastern Road, Brighton BN2 5JF. *T:* Brighton 683028.

HARVEY, Michael Llewellyn Tucker, QC 1982; a Recorder, since 1986; *b* 22 May 1943; *s* of Rev. Victor Llewellyn Tucker Harvey and Pauline Harvey (*née* Wybrow); *m* 1972, Denise Madeleine Neary; one *s* one *d. Educ:* St John's Sch., Leatherhead; Christ's Coll., Cambridge (BA Hons Law, LLB, MA). Called to the Bar, Gray's Inn, 1966 (Uthwatt Schol. 1965, James Mould Schol. 1966). *Publication:* joint contributor of title 'Damages' in Halsbury's Laws of England, 4th edn 1975. *Recreations:* shooting, golf. *Address:* 2 Crown Office Row, Temple, EC4Y 7HJ. *T:* 01–353 9337. *Clubs:* Athenæum, United Oxford & Cambridge University; Hawks (Cambridge).

HARVEY, Neil; Under Secretary, Statistics Division 1, Department of Trade and Industry, since 1984; *b* 10 Feb. 1938; *s* of Edward Felters and Lucy Felters (*née* Graves; she *m* 2nd, Frederick Harvey); *m* 1963, Clare Elizabeth Joscelyne; two *s. Educ:* Eton House Sch., Essex; LSE. BSc(Econ). Economist/Statistician, Kuwait Oil Co., 1959–62; Statistician, Midland Bank Economics Dept, 1962–65; Asst Statistician/Statistician, DEA, 1965–69; Statistician, HM Treasury, 1969–73; Chief Statistician, Inland Revenue, 1973–77; Controller, Statistical Office, HM Customs and Excise, 1977–84. *Recreations:* reading, gardening. *Address:* Department of Trade and Industry, Millbank Tower, Millbank, SW1P 4QU.

HARVEY, Prof. Paul Dean Adshead, FSA, FRHistS; Emeritus Professor, University of Durham, since 1985; Member, Advisory Council on Public Records, since 1984; *b* 7 May 1930; *s* of John Dean Monroe Harvey and Gwendolen Mabel Darlington (*née* Adshead); *m* 1968, Yvonne Crossman. *Educ:* Bishop Feild Coll., St John's, Newfoundland; Warwick Sch.; St John's Coll., Oxford (BA 1953; MA; DPhil 1960); FRHistS 1961, FSA 1963. Asst Archivist, Warwick County Record Office, 1954–56; Asst Keeper, Dept of Manuscripts, British Museum, 1957–66; Lectr, 1966–70, Sen. Lectr, 1970–78, Dept of History, Univ. of Southampton; Prof. of Mediaeval Hist., Univ. of Durham, 1978–85. Vice-Pres., Surtees Soc., 1978–. Jt Gen. Editor, Southampton Records Series, 1966–78; Gen. Editor, Portsmouth Record Series, 1969–. *Publications:* The printed maps of Warwickshire 1576–1900 (with H. Thorpe), 1959; A Medieval Oxfordshire Village:

Cuxham 1240–1400, 1965; (with W. Albert) Portsmouth and Sheet Turnpike Commissioners' minute book 1711–1754, 1973; Manorial records of Cuxham, Oxfordshire, circa 1200–1359, 1976; The history of topographical maps: symbols, pictures and surveys, 1980; (ed) The peasant land market in medieval England, 1984; Manorial records, 1984; (ed with R. A. Skelton) Local maps and plans from medieval England, 1986; (contrib) The Victoria History of the County of Oxford, vol. 10, 1972; articles in learned jls and periodicals. *Recreations:* British topography and topographical writings. *Address:* Lyndhurst, Farnley Hey Road, Durham DH1 4EA. *T:* Durham 3869396.

HARVEY, Peter, CB 1980; Assistant to Speaker's Counsel, House of Commons, since 1986; *b* 23 April 1922; *o s* of Rev. George Leonard Hunton Harvey and Helen Mary (*née* Williams); *m* 1950, Mary Vivienne, *d* of John Osborne Goss and Elsie Lilian (*née* Bishop); one *s* one *d*. *Educ:* King Edward VI High Sch., Birmingham; St John's Coll., Oxford (MA, BCL). RAF, 1942–45. Called to the Bar, Lincoln's Inn, 1948. Entered the Home Office as a Legal Assistant, 1948; Principal Asst Legal Advr, 1971–77; Legal Advr, DES, 1977–83; Consultant, Legal Advr's Br., Home Office, 1983–86. *Publications:* contributor to Halsbury's Laws of England (3rd and 4th edns). *Recreations:* history, and walking. *Address:* Mannamead, Old Avenue, Weybridge, Surrey KT13 0PS. *T:* Weybridge 45133.

HARVEY, Rt. Rev. Philip James Benedict, OBE 1973; Auxiliary Bishop of Westminster (Bishop in North London) (RC), since 1977; Titular Bishop of Bahanna; *b* 6 March 1915; *s* of William Nathaniel and Elizabeth Harvey. *Educ:* Cardinal Vaughan Sch., Kensington; St Edmund's Coll., Ware, Herts. Ordained Priest, Westminster, 1939; Assistant Priest: Cricklewood, 1929–45; Kentish Town, 1945–46; Fulham, 1946–53; Asst Administrator, Crusade of Rescue, 1953–63, Administrator 1963–77. *Address:* 4 Egerton Gardens, NW4 4BA. *T:* 01-202 9012.

HARVEY, Robert Lambart; MP (C) South West Clwyd, since 1983; *b* 21 Aug. 1953; *s* of Hon. John and Elena Harvey; *m* 1981, Jane Roper. *Educ:* Eton; Christ Church, Oxford (BA 1974, MA 1978). Staff Correspondent, The Economist, 1974–81, Asst Editor, 1981–83. *Publication:* Portugal: birth of a democracy, 1978. *Recreations:* the arts, films, music, swimming, walking. *Address:* House of Commons, SW1A 0AA. *Clubs:* Brooks's, Travellers', Lansdowne.

HARVEY, Major Thomas Cockayne, CVO 1951; DSO 1945; Extra Gentleman Usher to the Queen, since 1952 (to King George VI, 1951–52); *b* 22 Aug. 1918; *s* of late Col John Harvey, DSO; *m* 1940, Lady Katharine Mary Coke (Woman of the Bedchamber to Queen Elizabeth the Queen Mother, 1961–63), *yr d* of 3rd Earl of Leicester; one *s* two *d*. *Educ:* Radley; Balliol Coll., Oxford. Joined Scots Guards SRO, 1938. Served Norway, 1940, Italy, 1944; Private Sec. to the Queen, 1946–51. *Recreations:* golf, shooting. *Address:* Warham House, Warham, Wells, Norfolk NR23 1NG. *T:* Fakenham 710457. *Clubs:* White's, Beefsteak.

HARVEY-JAMIESON, Lt-Col Harvey Morro, OBE 1969; TD; DL; WS; Member, Queen's Body Guard for Scotland (Royal Company of Archers), since 1934; *b* 9 Dec. 1908; *s* of late Major A. H. Morro Jamieson, OBE, RGA, Advocate, Edinburgh, and Isobel, *d* of late Maj.-Gen. Sir Robert Murdoch Smith, KCMG; *m* 1936, Frances, *o c* of late Col. J. Y. H. Ridout, DSO; three *s*; assumed additional surname of Harvey, with authority of Lord Lyon King of Arms, 1958. *Educ:* Edinburgh Acad.; RMC Sandhurst (Prize Cadetship); Edinburgh Univ. (BL). Commissioned 1st Bn KOSB, 1928; Capt. RARO 1938; Major, 1939, to raise 291 HAA Battery RA (TA). Served War of 1939–45, Belgium, Holland and Germany, RA and Staff, Lieut-Col, 1942; Comd 3rd Edinburgh HG Bn, 1954–57. France and Germany Star, General Service and Home Defence Medals; Jubilee Medals 1935 and 1977; Coronation Medals, 1937 and 1953. Secretary and Legal Adviser, Co. of Merchants of City of Edinburgh, 1946–71; former Mem., Cttee on Conveyancing Legislation and Practice (apptd by Sec. of State for Scotland, 1964). Mem. Council, Cockburn Assoc. (Edinburgh Civic Trust), 1958–78; Hon. Manager, Edinburgh and Borders Trustee Savings Bank, 1957–78. Chairman, Scottish Committee: HMC; Assocs of Governing Bodies of Boys' and Girls' Public Schs, 1966–71. DL, County of the City of Edinburgh, 1968–84. *Publications:* The Historic Month of June, 1953; contrib. to Juridical Review, Scots Law Times and Yachting Monthly. *Address:* Walhampton Cottage, Walhampton, Lymington, Hants SO41 5SB. *T:* Lymington 74589. *Clubs:* Royal Forth Yacht (Granton); Royal Lymington Yacht; Army Sailing Association.

HARVEY-JONES, Sir John (Henry), Kt 1985; MBE 1952; Chairman, Imperial Chemical Industries PLC, 1982–March 1987; *b* 16 April 1924; *s* of Mervyn Harvey-Jones, OBE, and Eileen Harvey-Jones; *m* 1947, Mary Evelyn Atcheson, *er d* of F. F. Bignell and Mrs E. Atcheson; one *d*. *Educ:* Tormore Sch., Deal, Kent; RNC, Dartmouth, Devon. RN, 1937–56: specialised in submarines; qual. as Russian interpreter, 1946, and subseq. as German interpreter; appts in Naval Intell. (MBE); resigned, 1956, Lt-Comdr. Joined ICI as Work Study Officer, Wilton, 1956; commercial appts at Wilton and Heavy Organic Chemicals Div. until apptd Techno-Commercial Dir, 1967; Dep. Chm., HOC Div., 1968; Chm., ICI Petrochemicals Div., 1970–73; Main Bd, ICI, 1973, Dep. Chm., 1978–82. Chm., Phillips-Imperial Petroleum, 1973–75; Non-Exec. Director: Carrington Viyella Ltd, 1974–79 and 1981–82; Reed International PLC, 1975–84; Grand Metropolitan plc, 1983–; Mem. Bd, Fiber Industries Inc., 1975–78. Member: Tees & Hartlepool Port Authority, 1968–73; NE Develt Bd, 1971–73; Soc. Chemical Industry, 1978–; RSA, 1979–; Court, British Shippers' Council, 1982–; Council, British-Malaysian Soc., 1983–. Vice-Chairman: PSI, 1980–85; BIM, 1980–85; Vice-Pres., Industrial Participation Assoc., 1983. Hon. Vice-Pres., Inst. of Marketing, 1982–; Pres., Conseil Européen des Fédérations de l'Industrie Chimique (CEFIC), 1984–86 (Vice-Pres., 1982–84). Vice-Pres., Hearing & Speech Trust, 1985–; Vice-Chm., Gt Ormond St Redevelt Appeal, 1986–. Trustee: Police Foundn, 1983– (Chm., 1984–); Science Museum, 1984–. Chancellor, University of Bradford, 1986–. Dimbleby Lectr, BBC TV, 1986. Hon. FRSC 1985; Hon. FIChemE 1985. Hon. LLD Manchester, 1985; DUniv Surrey, 1985; Hon. DSc: Bradford, 1986; Leicester, 1986. BIM Gold Medal, 1986. Comdr's Cross, Order of Merit (FRG), 1985. *Recreations:* ocean sailing, swimming, countryside, cooking, contemporary literature, pony driving. *Address:* c/o Imperial Chemical House, Millbank, SW1P 3JF. *T:* 01–834 4444. *Club:* Athenæum.

HARVIE-CLARK, Ven. Sidney, MA; Archdeacon of Stow, 1967–75 and Vicar of Hackthorn and Rector of Cold Hanworth, 1967–75; now Archdeacon Emeritus; *b* 26 July 1905; *s* of John Harvie Clark and Minnie Young Hunter, Glasgow and Chiswick, London; *m* 1936, Sheilah Marjorie, *d* of late Dr G. C. L. Lunt, Bishop of Salisbury; one *s* one *d* (one *d* decd). *Educ:* St Paul's Sch., London; Jesus Coll. and Westcott House, Cambridge. Deacon, 1930; Priest, 1931; Curate, St Mary's, Gateshead, Co. Durham, 1930–34; St Mary's, Portsea, 1934–36; Rector, Jarrow-on-Tyne, 1936–40; St John's, Edinburgh, 1940–47; Rector of Wishaw, 1947–48; Archdeacon of Birmingham, 1947–67; Vicar of Harborne, 1948–67. *Recreations:* walking, camping. *Address:* Stow House, Skillington, Grantham, Lincs NG33 5HQ. *T:* Grantham 860447.

HARVIE-WATT, Sir George Steven, 1st Bt, *cr* 1945, of Bathgate; QC 1945; TD 1942 (with three Bars); *b* 23 Aug. 1903; *s* of late James McDougal Watt of Armadale; *m* 1932, Bettie, *o d* of late Paymaster-Capt. Archibald Taylor, OBE, RN; two *s* one *d*. *Educ:* George Watson's Coll., Edinburgh; Glasgow Univ.; Edinburgh Univ. Called to Bar, Inner Temple, 1930; practised in London and on North Eastern Circuit. Commissioned RE TA 1924, 52nd (Lowland) Scottish Div., 1924–29; 56th (1st London) Div., 1929–38; Bt Major, 1935; Lt-Col Commanding 31st Bn RE TA, 1938–41; promoted Brig. to command 6th AA Bde, 1941; Brig. Commanding 63rd AA Bde TA, 1948–50; Hon. Col 566 LAA Regt, 1949–62. ADC to King George VI, 1948–52; ADC to the Queen, 1952–58; MP (U) Keighley Div. of Yorks, 1931–35; (U) Richmond, Surrey, Feb. 1937–Sept. 1959; PPS to late Rt Hon. Euan Wallace when Parly Sec. to Board of Trade, 1937–38; Asst Government Whip, 1938–40; PPS to Rt Hon. Winston S. Churchill when Prime Minister, July 1941–July 1945; Hon. Treas. UK Branch of Commonwealth Parly Assoc., 1945–51; Mem. UK Deleg. to CPA Confs, Ottawa and Washington, 1949, Australia and New Zealand, 1950; Mem. of Borough Council, Royal Borough of Kensington, 1934–45. Formerly Mem. of City of London TA Association; TA Rep. Council of RUSI, 1948–57; DL: Surrey, 1942; Greater London, 1966–78; JP County of London, 1944–56. President: Consolidated Gold Fields Ltd, 1973–81 (Chief Executive, 1954–69, Dep. Chm., 1954–60, Chm., 1960–69); Printers' Pension Corp., 1956–57; formerly: Chm., Monotype Corp. Ltd; Director: Eagle Star Insce Co.; Standard Bank Ltd; Midland Bank Ltd; Clydesdale Bank Ltd; Great Western Rly Co.; North British Steel Gp. Member of Queen's Body Guard for Scotland, Royal Company of Archers; Hon. Freeman, City of London, 1976. FRSA 1973. Gold Medal, Inst. Mining and Metallurgy (for distinguished service to world-wide mining), 1969. *Publication:* Most of My Life, 1980. *Heir: s* James Harvie-Watt, *qv*. *Recreation:* Territorial Army. *Address:* Sea Tangle, Earlsferry, Leven, Fife KY9 1AD. *T:* Elie 330506. *Club:* Caledonian (Chm. 1953–61, Vice-Pres. 1961–85).

HARVIE-WATT, James, FCA; company director; *b* 25 Aug. 1940; *s* and *heir* of Sir George Harvie-Watt, *qv*; *m* 1966, Roseline, *d* of late Baron Louis de Chollet, Fribourg, Switzerland, and Frances Tate, Royal Oak, Maryland, USA; one *s* one *d*. *Educ:* Eton; Christ Church, Oxford (MA). FCA 1975 (ACA 1965). Lieut London Scottish (TA), 1959–67. With Coopers & Lybrand, 1962–70; Executive, British Electric Traction Co. Ltd, and Director of subsid. companies, 1970–78; Man. Dir, Wembley Stadium Ltd, 1973–78; director of private companies. Mem. Executive Cttee, London Tourist Board, 1977–80; Member: Sports Council, 1980– (Vice-Chm., 1985–; Mem. Sports Council enquiries into: Financing of Athletics in UK, 1983; Karate, 1986); Chm., Crystal Palace Nat. Sports Centre, 1984–; Member Managment Cttee: Nat. Coaching Foundn, 1984–; Holme Pierrepont Nat. Water Sports Centre, 1985–; Mem. Council, NPFA, 1985–. OStJ 1964, and Mem. London Council of the Order, 1975–84. *Recreations:* shooting, tennis, reading, philately. *Address:* 15 Somerset Square, W14 8EE. *T:* 01–602 6944. *Clubs:* White's, Pratt's, Queen's Tennis; Sunningdale Golf.

HARVINGTON, Baron *cr* 1974 (Life Peer), of Nantwich; **Robert Grant Grant-Ferris,** PC 1971; Kt 1969; AE; *b* 30 Dec. 1907; *s* of late Robert Francis Ferris, MB, ChB; *m* 1930, Florence, *d* of Major W. Brennan De Vine, MC; one *s* one *d*. *Educ:* Douai Sch. Called to Bar, Inner Temple, 1937; joined RAuxAF, 1933, 605 (County of Warwick) Fighter Sqdn; Flight Comdr 1939–40; Wing Comdr, 1941; Air Efficiency Award, 1942. MP (C) North St Pancras, 1937–45; MP (C) Nantwich, Cheshire, 1955–Feb. 1974; PPS to Minister of Town and Country Planning (Rt Hon. W. S. Morrison, KC, MP), 1944–45; Temp. Chm. House of Commons and Chairman of Cttees, 1962–70; Chm. of Ways and Means and the Dep. Speaker, House of Commons, 1970–74. Contested Wigan, 1935, North St Pancras, 1945, Central Wandsworth, 1950, 1951. Chm., Bd of Management, Hosp. of St John and St Elizabeth, 1963–70. Pres. Southdown Sheep Soc. of England, 1950–52, 1959–60, 1973; Pres. Nat. Sheep Breeders' Assoc., 1956–58; a Vice-Pres. Smithfield Club, 1964, Pres. 1970. Mem. Council, Imperial Soc. of Knights Bachelor, 1973–. Knight Grand Cross of Magistral Grace, with Riband, 1985, the Sovereign and Military Order of Malta; holds Grand Cross of Merit with Star of same Order, 1953; Comdr, Order of Leopold II (Belgium), 1964. *Recreations:* formerly hunting, golf, yachting (sometime Hon. Admiral, House of Commons Yacht Club). *Address:* La Vielle Maison, The Bulwarks, St Aubin, Jersey, Channel Islands. *T:* Jersey 45418. *Clubs:* Carlton, MCC, Royal Thames Yacht; Royal Yacht Squadron (Cowes); Royal and Ancient Golf.
See also Sir T. G. R. Brinckman, Bt.

HARWOOD, Basil Antony, MA; QC 1971; Barrister; a Master of the Supreme Court (Queen's Bench Division), 1950–70; Senior Master and Queen's Remembrancer, 1966–70; 2nd *s* of late Basil Harwood, DMus, Woodhouse, Olveston, Glos; *m* 1929, Enid Arundel, *d* of late Philip Grove, Quorn House, Leamington; two *s*. *Educ:* Charterhouse; Christ Church, Oxford (MA). Called to the Bar, Inner Temple, 1927. Served War of 1939–45 in Italy. Prosecuting Counsel to Post Office, Western Circuit, 1948–50. Pres. Medico-Legal Soc., 1967–69; Hon. Mem., Epée Club, 1970 (Mem., 1928–70). *Publication:* Circuit Ghosts, 1980. *Address:* 1 The Mount, Whitchurch, Hants RG28 7AT.

HARWOOD, Elizabeth Jean, (Mrs J. A. C. Royle); international opera singer; *b* 27 May 1938; *d* of Sydney and Constance Harwood; *m* 1966, Julian Adam Christopher Royle; one *s*. *Educ:* Skipton Girls' High Sch.; Royal Manchester Coll. of Music. FRMCM, GRSM, LRAM. Kathleen Ferrier Memorial Schol., 1960; jt winner, Verdi Competition (Busetto), 1965. Principal operatic roles at Glyndebourne, Sadler's Wells, Covent Garden, Scottish Opera, principal opera houses in Europe incl. Salzburg, Paris and La Scala; toured Australia, 1965, with Sutherland-Williamson Internat. Opera Co. singing principal roles in Lucia de Lammermoor, La Sonnambula and L'Elisir d'Amore; Così Fan Tutte, NY Met. Opera, 1975 (début), 1982; Don Giovanni, 1978; Rosenkavalier, Glyndebourne, 1980; took part in exchange visit to La Scala with Covent Garden Opera, 1976; ABC recital and concert tour, 1986. Has made numerous recordings of oratorio, opera and English songs. *Recreations:* swimming, horse riding. *Address:* Masonetts, Fryerning, Ingatestone, Essex. *T:* Ingatestone 353024. *Club:* Oriental.

HARWOOD, Ronald, FRSL; writer since 1960; *b* 9 Nov. 1934; *s* of late Isaac Horwitz and Isobel Pepper; *m* 1959, Natasha Riehle; one *s* two *d*. *Educ:* Sea Point Boys' High Sch., Cape Town; RADA. FRSL 1974. Actor, 1953–60. Artistic Dir, Cheltenham Festival of Literature, 1975; Presenter: Kaleidoscope, BBC, 1973; Read All About It, BBC TV, 1978–79. Chm., Writers Guild of GB, 1969; Mem., Lit. Panel, Arts Council of GB, 1973–78. Visitor in Theatre, Balliol Coll., Oxford, 1986. TV plays incl.: The Barber of Stamford Hill, 1960; (with Casper Wrede) Private Potter, 1961; The Guests, 1972; adapted several of Roald Dahl's Tales of the Unexpected for TV, 1979–80; TV series, All the World's a Stage, 1984; screenplays incl.: A High Wind in Jamaica, 1965; One Day in the Life of Ivan Denisovich, 1971; Evita Perón, 1981; The Dresser, 1983. *Publications: novels:* All the Same Shadows, 1961; The Guilt Merchants, 1963; The Girl in Melanie Klein, 1969; Articles of Faith, 1973; The Genoa Ferry, 1976; Cesar and Augusta, 1978; *short stories:* One. Interior. Day.—adventures in the film trade, 1978; (co-ed) New Stories 3, 1978; *biography:* Sir Donald Wolfit, CBE—his life and work in the unfashionable theatre, 1971; (ed) The Ages of Gielgud, 1984; *essays:* (ed) A Night at the Theatre, 1983; *plays:* Country Matters, 1969; The Ordeal of Gilbert Pinfold (from Evelyn Waugh), 1977; A Family, 1978; The Dresser, 1980 (New Standard Drama Award; Drama Critics

Award); After the Lions, 1982; Tramway Road, 1984; The Deliberate Death of a Polish Priest, 1985; Interpreters, 1986; *musical libretto:* The Good Companions, 1974; *historical:* All the World's a Stage, 1983. *Recreations:* tennis, cricket. *Address:* c/o Judy Daish Associates, 83 Eastbourne Mews, W2 6LQ. *T:* 01–262 1101. *Clubs:* Garrick, MCC.

HASELDEN, Edward Christopher, CMG 1952; *b* 14 Aug. 1903; *s* of E. N. Haselden, Minieh, Upper Egypt; *m* 1929, Lily Jewett Foote; two *d.* *Educ:* Cheltenham Coll.; Pembroke Coll., Cambridge. Joined Sudan Political Service, 1925; Sudan Agent in Cairo, 1945–53; retired, 1953. Chm. of Anglo-Egyptian Aid Soc. Cttee, 1960. Order of the Nile (4th Class), 1936. *Address:* 14 Gilston Road, SW10. *Club:* Athenæum.

HASELDEN, Prof. Geoffrey Gordon; Brotherton Professor of Chemical Engineering, University of Leeds, since 1960; *b* 4 Aug. 1924; *s* of George A. Haselden and Rose E. (*née* Pleasants); *m* 1945, Eileen Doris Francis; three *d.* *Educ:* Sir Walter St John's Sch.; Imperial Coll. of Science and Technology. BScChemEng London 1944; FCGI; PhD (Eng) Chem Eng London, 1947; DScEng London, 1962; DIC; CEng; FIMechE; FIChemE; MInstR. Mem. Gas Research Bd, 1946–48; Lectr in Low Temperature Technology, Chemical Engrg Dept, 1948–57, Senior Lectr in Chemical Engrg, 1957–60, Imperial Coll. Chm., British Cryogenics Council, 1967–71. President: Commn A3, Internat. Inst. of Refrigeration, 1971–79; Inst. of Refrigeration, 1981–84; Vice-Pres., IChemE, 1984–85. Gen. Editor, Internat. Jl of Refrigeration, 1978–. *Publications:* Cyrogenic Fundamentals, 1971; research papers in Trans Inst. Chem. Eng., etc. *Recreation:* Methodist lay preacher. *Address:* 12 High Ash Drive, Wigton Lane, Leeds LS17 8RA. *T:* Leeds 687047; The University, Leeds. *T:* Leeds 431751.

HASELDINE, (Charles) Norman; public relations consultant; *b* 25 March 1922; *s* of Charles Edward Haseldine and Lily White; *m* 1946, Georgette Elise Michelle Bernard; four *s.* *Educ:* Nether Edge Grammar Sch., Sheffield. Education Officer, Doncaster Co-operative Soc., 1947–57; PRO, Sheffield & Ecclesall Co-op. Soc., 1957–70. MP (Lab and Co-op) Bradford West, 1966–70; PPS to Minister of Power, 1968–69; PPS to Pres. Bd of Trade, 1969–70; Mem. Select Cttee on Nationalised Inds. *Recreation:* classical music. *Address:* 115 Psalter Lane, Sheffield S11 8YR. *T:* Sheffield 585974.

HASELER, Dr Stephen Michael Alan; author and Professor of Government; *b* 9 Jan. 1942; *m* 1967, Roberta Alexander. *Educ:* London School of Economics. BSc(Econ), PhD. Contested (Lab): Saffron Walden, 1966; Maldon, 1970. Chm., Labour Political Studies Centre, 1973–78. Mem. GLC, 1973–77, Chm. General Purposes Cttee, 1973–75. Founder Mem., SDP, 1981. Visiting Professor: Georgetown Univ., Washington DC, 1978; Johns Hopkins Univ., 1984. *Publications:* The Gaitskellites, 1969; Social-Democracy—Beyond Revisionism, 1971; The Death of British Democracy, 1976; Eurocommunism: implications for East and West, 1978; The Tragedy of Labour, 1980; Anti-Americanism, 1985. *Address:* 2 Thackeray House, Ansdell Street, W8. *T:* 01–937 3976.

HASELGROVE, Dennis Cliff, CB 1963; MA; FSA; Under Secretary, Department of the Environment, 1970–75; *b* 18 Aug. 1914; *s* of late H. Cliff Haselgrove, LLB, Chingford; *m* 1941, Evelyn Hope Johnston, MA, *d* of late R. Johnston, Edinburgh; one *s.* *Educ:* Uppingham Sch.; King's Coll., Cambridge. 1st Class, Classical Tripos, Parts I and II. Entered Ministry of Transport, Oct. 1937; Private Sec. to Permanent Sec., and Asst Priv. Sec. to Minister, 1941. Served in Intelligence Corps and 10th Baluch Regt, IA, 1941–45. Min. of Transport: Asst Sec., 1948; Under-Sec., 1957–70. Govt Delegate to: ILO Asian Maritime Conf., 1953; Internat. Conf. on Oil Pollution of the Sea, 1954, 1962; Internat. Lab. Conf. (Maritime Session), 1958; Internat. Conf. on Safety of Life at Sea, 1960. Imperial Defence Coll., 1955. *Recreations:* archæology, travel, philately. *Address:* 10 Church Gate, SW6 3LD. *T:* 01–736 5213.

HASELHURST, Alan Gordon Barraclough; MP (C) Saffron Walden, since July 1977; *b* 23 June 1937; *s* of John Haselhurst and Alyse (*née* Barraclough); *m* 1977, Angela (*née* Bailey); two *s* one *d.* *Educ:* King Edward VI Sch., Birmingham; Cheltenham Coll.; Oriel Coll., Oxford. Pres., Oxford Univ. Conservative Assoc., 1958; Sec., Treas. and Librarian, Oxford Union Soc., 1959–60; Nat. Chm., Young Conservatives, 1966–68. MP (C) Middleton and Prestwich, 1970–Feb. 1974. PPS to Sec. of State for Educn, 1979–82. Chm., Rights of Way Review Cttee, 1983–. Chairman: Manchester Youth and Community Service, 1974–77; Commonwealth Youth Exchange Council, 1978–81; Chm. Trustees, Community Projects Foundn, 1986–. *Recreations:* gardening, theatre, music. *Address:* House of Commons, SW1A 0AA. *Club:* MCC.

HASHMI, Dr Farrukh Siyar, OBE 1974; FRCPsych; Consultant Psychiatrist, All Saints' Hospital, Birmingham, since 1969; Psychotherapist, HM Prison, Stafford, since 1973; *b* Gujrat, Pakistan, 12 Sept. 1927; *s* of Dr Ziaullah Qureshi and Majida Qureshi; *m* 1972, Shahnaz; one *s* two *d.* *Educ:* King Edward Med. Coll., Lahore (Punjab Univ.). MB, BS; MRCPsych; DPM; FRCPsych 1979. Mayo Hosp. and King Edward Med. Coll., Lahore, March-Sept. 1953; New End Hosp., Hampstead, 1954; Children's Hosp., Birkenhead, 1954–55; Sen. House Officer, Brook Gen. Hosp., Woolwich, 1955–56; Snowdon Road Hosp., Bristol, 1956; Asst MOH, Co. Berwicks, 1957; Scholar, Volkart Foundn, Switzerland, 1958–60; psychiatric medicine: Registrar, Uffculme Clinic and All Saints Hosp., Birmingham, 1960–63, Sen. Registrar, 1966–69; Research Fellow, Dept of Psychiatry, Birmingham Univ., 1963–66. Chm., Psychiatric Div., West Birmingham Health Dist., 1977–83; Member: Race Relations Bd, W Midlands Conciliation Cttee, 1968–81; Community Relations Working Party, NAYC, 1968–81; Home Secretary's Adv. Cttee on Race, 1976–81 (formerly Mem., HO Adv. Cttee on Race Relations Research); CRE, 1980–86; Working Party on Community and Race Relations Trng, HO Police Trng Council, 1982–; Wkg Gp on Ethnic Minorities, W Midlands RHA, 1982–; Mental Health Services Cttee, RHA, 1976–; SSRC Project, Univ. of East Anglia, 1974–81; Council, Mind (NAMH), 1976–81; UK Cttee, World Fedn for Mental Health, 1978–; Health and Welfare Adv. Panel, NCCI, 1966–81; Cttee of Inquiry into Educn of Children from Ethnic Minority Gps (Swann Cttee), 1982–85; Warley Area Social Services Sub-Cttee, 1973–81; Central DHA, Birmingham, 1982–; BBC Regl Adv. Council, 1970–77; GMC, 1979–84 (GMC Mem., Tribunal on Misuse of Drugs, 1983–84); Parole Board, 1981–85; Advisory Consultant, C of E Bd for Social Responsibility, 1984–. President: Pakistan Med. Soc., UK, 1974–76; Overseas Doctors Assoc., UK, 1975–79; Founder and Chm., Iqbal Acad., Coventry Cathedral, 1972–. Mem. Editl Bd, Medicos, 1977–81. *Publications:* Pakistan Family in Britain, 1965; Mores, Migration and Mental Illness, 1966; Psychology of Racial Prejudice, 1966; Community Psychiatric Problems among Birmingham Immigrants, 1968; In a Strange Land, 1970; Measuring Psychological Disturbance in Asian Immigrants to Britain, 1977. *Recreations:* writing, reading, music. *Address:* 5 Woodbourne Road, Edgbaston, Birmingham B15 3QJ. *T:* 021–455 0011. *Clubs:* Oriental; Rotary, Edgbaston Priory (Birmingham).

HASKARD, Sir Cosmo (Dugal Patrick Thomas), KCMG 1965 (CMG 1960); MBE 1945; *b* 25 Nov. 1916; *o c* of late Brig.-Gen. J. McD. Haskard, CMG, DSO; *m* 1957, Phillada, *o c* of Sir Robert Stanley, KBE, CMG; one *s.* *Educ:* Cheltenham; RMC Sandhurst; Pembroke Coll., Cambridge (MA). Served War of 1939–45 (MBE); 2nd Lieut, TA (Gen. List), 1938; emergency Commn, Royal Irish Fusiliers, 1939; seconded KAR, 1941; served 2nd Bn, E Africa, Ceylon, Burma; Major 1944. Cadet, Tanganyika, 1940; transf. Nyasaland, 1946; Dist Comr, 1948; Provincial Commissioner, 1955; acting Secretary for African Affairs, 1957–58; Sec. for Labour and Social Development, 1961; Sec. for Local Government, 1962; Sec. for Natural Resources, 1963; Governor and C-in-C, Falkland Islands, and High Comr for the British Antarctic Territory, 1964–70. Served on Nyasaland-Mozambique Boundary Commission, 1951–52. Trustee, Beit Trust, 1976–. *Address:* Tragariff, Bantry, Co. Cork, Ireland.

HASKELL, Donald Keith, CVO 1979; HM Diplomatic Service; Head of Chancery, Bonn, since 1985; *b* 9 May 1939; *s* of Donald Eric Haskell and Beatrice Mary Haskell (*née* Blair); *m* 1966, Maria Luisa Soeiro Tito de Morais; two *s* two *d* (and one *s* one *d* decd). *Educ:* Portsmouth Grammar Sch.; St Catharine's Coll., Cambridge (BA 1961, MA 1964). Joined HM Foreign Service, 1961; served in: London, Lebanon, Iraq, Libya; HM Consul, Benghazi, 1969–70; First Sec., Tripoli, 1970–72; Foreign and Commonwealth Office, 1972–75; Chargé d'Affaires and Consul-Gen., Santiago, 1975–78; Counsellor and Consul-Gen., Dubai, 1978–81; Hd, Nuclear Energy Dept, FCO, 1981–83; Hd, Middle East Dept, FCO, 1983–84. Foundation Medal, Soka Univ. of Japan, 1975. *Recreations:* rifle shooting (captained Cambridge Univ. Rifle Assoc., 1960–61; represented England and GB in shooting competitions on various occasions), squash, tennis, wine and food. *Address:* c/o Foreign and Commonwealth Office, SW1A 2AL. *Club:* Hawks (Cambridge).

HASKELL, Francis James Herbert, FBA 1971; Professor of Art History, Oxford University and Fellow of Trinity College, Oxford, since October 1967; *b* 7 April 1928; *s* of late Arnold Haskell, CBE, and Vera Saitzoff; *m* 1965, Larissa Salmina. *Educ:* Eton Coll.; King's Coll., Cambridge. Junior Library Clerk, House of Commons, 1953–54; Fellow of King's Coll., Cambridge, 1954–67; Librarian of Fine Arts Faculty, Cambridge Univ., 1962–67. Mem., British Sch. at Rome, 1971–74. A Trustee, Wallace Collection, 1976–. Mem. Exec. Cttee, Nat. Art Collections Fund, 1976–. Foreign Hon. Mem., Amer. Acad. of Arts and Scis, 1979; Corresp. Mem., Accad. Pontaniana, Naples, 1982; Foreign Mem., Ateneo Veneto, 1986. Serena medal for Italian studies, British Acad., 1985. *Publications:* trans., Venturi, Roots of Revolution, 1960; Patrons and Painters: a study of the relations between Art and Society in the Age of the Baroque, 1963, 2nd edn 1980 (trans. Italian and Spanish); Géricault (The Masters), 1966; An Italian Patron of French Neo-Classic Art, 1972; (ed jtly) The Artist and Writer in France, 1975; Rediscoveries in Art, 1976, 2nd edn 1980 (trans. Italian and French) (Mitchell Prize for Art History, 1977); L'arte e il linguaggio delta politica (Florence), 1977; (with Nicholas Penny) Taste and the Antique, 1981, 2nd edn 1982; articles in Burlington Mag., Jl Warburg Inst., etc; reviews in New Statesman, NY Review of Books, etc. *Recreation:* foreign travel. *Address:* 7 Walton Street, Oxford; Trinity College, Oxford OX1 2HG; 35 Beaumont Street, Oxford.

HASKELL, Peter Thomas, CMG 1975; PhD, FRES, FIBiol; Director, Cleppa Park Field Research Station, University College, Cardiff, since 1984; *b* 21 Feb. 1923; *s* of late Herbert James and Mary Anne Haskell; *m*; one *s.* *Educ:* Portsmouth Grammar Sch.; Imperial Coll., London. BSc, ARCS, PhD. Asst Lectr, Zoology Dept, Imperial Coll., London, 1951–53; Lectr, 1953–55; Sen. Sci. Officer, Anti-Locust Research Centre, Colonial Office, 1955–57; Principal Sci. Officer, 1957–59; Dep. Dir, 1959–62; Dir, Anti-Locust Research Centre, ODM, 1962–71; Dir, Centre for Overseas Pest Res. and Chief Advr on Pest Control, ODA, 1971–83. Consultant: FAO, UN, 1962–; UNDP, 1970–; WHO, 1973–; OECD, 1975–; UNEP, 1976–; Agricl and Vet. Adv. Cttee, British Council, 1976–. Vice-Pres., Inst. of Biology, 1982. Professorial Res. Fellow, University Coll., Cardiff, 1971–83. Mem., Bd of Governors, Internat. Centre for Insect Physiology and Ecology, Kenya, 1972– (Vice-Chm., 1978; Chm., 1979–). Vis. Prof., Univ. of Newcastle, 1977. Thamisk Lectr, Royal Swedish Acad. of Scis, 1979. Van Den Brande Internat. Prize, 1982. Chief Editor, Tropical Pest Management, 1985–. *Publications:* Insect Sounds, 1962; The Language of Insects, 1962; Pesticide Application: principles and practice, 1985; many papers and articles in scientific and literary jls. *Recreations:* gardening, reading. *Address:* Nyali, Castle Precinct, Llandough, Cowbridge, Glam. *T:* Cowbridge 3564.

HASKINS, Sam, (Samuel Joseph), FRPS, FSIAD; photographer; *b* 11 Nov. 1926; *s* of Benjamin G. Haskins and Anna E. Oelofse; *m* 1952, Alida Elzabé van Heerden; two *s.* *Educ:* Helpmekaar Sch.; Witwatersrand Technical Coll.; Bolt Court Sch. of Photography. Freelance work: Johannesburg, 1953–68; London, 1968–. One-man Exhibitions: Johannesburg, 1953, 1960; Tokyo, 1970, 1973, 1976, 1981, 1985; London, 1972, 1976, 1978, 1980; Paris, 1973; Amsterdam, 1974; NY, 1981; San Francisco, 1982; Toronto, 1982; Bologna, 1982. *Publications:* Five Girls, 1962; Cowboy Kate and other stories, 1964 (Prix Nadar, France, 1964); November Girl, 1966; African Image, 1967 (Silver Award, Internat. Art Book Contest, 1969); Haskins Posters, 1972 (Gold Medal, New York Art Directors Club, 1974); Photo-Graphics, 1980 (Kodak Book Award); portfolios in most major internat. photographic magazines. *Recreations:* sculpting, books, music. *Address:* 9A Calonne Road, SW19 5HH. *T:* 01–946 9660.

HASLAM, Hon. Sir Alec (Leslie), Kt 1974; Judge of the Supreme Court of New Zealand, 1957–76, Senior Puisne Judge, 1973–76; *b* 10 Feb. 1904; *s* of Charles Nelson Haslam and Adeline Elsie Haslam; *m* 1933, Kathleen Valerie Tennent (*d* 1985); two *s* two *d.* *Educ:* Waitaki Boys' High Sch.; Canterbury UC; Oriel Coll., Oxford. Rhodes Scholar 1927; 1st cl. hons LLM NZ; DPhil, BCL Oxon. Served with 10th Reinf. 2 NZEF, ME and Italy, 1943–46. Barrister and Solicitor, 1925; in private practice, 1936–57. Lectr in Law, Canterbury Univ., 1936–50 (except while overseas). Chm. Council of Legal Educn, 1962–75 (Mem. 1952); Mem., Rhodes Scholarship Selection Cttee, 1936–74; NZ Sec. to Rhodes Scholarships, 1961–74; Mem., Scholarships (Univ. Grants) Cttee, 1962–80; Pres., Canterbury District Law Soc., 1952–53; Vice-Pres., NZ Law Soc., 1954–57; Mem., Waimairi County Council, 1950–56; Mem., NZ Univ. Senate, 1956–61. Sen. Teaching Fellow, Univ. of Canterbury, 1977–81. Hon. LLD Canterbury, 1973. *Publication:* Law Relating to Trade Combinations, 1931. *Recreations:* reading, walking, bowls; formerly athletics (rep. Canterbury Univ. and Oriel Coll.) and rowing (rep. Oriel Coll.). *Address:* 22 Brackendale Place, Burnside, Christchurch 4, NZ. *T:* 588–589.

HASLAM, Rear Adm. Sir David William, KBE 1984 (OBE 1964); CB 1979; Hydrographer of the Navy, 1975–85; Acting Conservator of the River Mersey, since 1985; *b* 26 June 1923; *s* of Gerald Haigh Haslam and Gladys Haslam (*née* Finley). *Educ:* Ashe Prep. Sch., Etwall; Bromsgrove Sch., Worcs. FRGS, FRIN, FRICS, FNI. Special Entry Cadet, RN, 1941; HMS Birmingham, HMAS Quickmatch, HMS Resolution (in Indian Ocean), 1942–43; specialised in hydrographic surveying, 1944; HMS White Bear (surveying in Burma and Malaya), 1944–46; comd Survey Motor Launch 325, 1947; RAN, 1947–49; HMS Scott, 1949–51; HMS Dalrymple, 1951–53; i/c RN Survey Trng Unit, Chatham, 1953–56; HMS Vidal, 1956–57; comd, HMS Dalrymple, 1958; comd, HMS Dampier, 1958–60; Admty, 1960–62; comd, HMS Owen, 1962–64; Exec. Officer, RN Barracks, Chatham, 1964–65; Hydrographer, RAN, 1965–67; comd, HMS Hecla, 1968–70; Asst Hydrographer, MoD, 1970–72; comd, HMS Hydra, 1972–73; Asst Dir (Naval) to Hydrographer, 1974–75; sowc 1975. Lt-Comdr 1952; Comdr 1957; Captain 1965; Rear Adm. 1975. Pres., Hydrographic Soc., 1977–79. Underwriting Mem., Lloyd's. Governor, Bromsgrove Sch., 1977–. Liveryman, Chartered Surveyors' Co. FRSA. *Recreations:* most team games (Pres., English Schs Basketball Assoc.), supporting youth organisations. *Address:* c/o National Westminster Bank, 28 Iron Gate, Derby DE1 3HP.

HASLAM, Geoffrey; *see* Haslam, W. G.

HASLAM, Sir Robert, Kt 1985; CEng, MInstME; Chairman, British Coal, since 1986 (Non-executive Deputy Chairman, 1985–86; Deputy Chairman, 1986); a Director, Bank of England, since 1985; *b* 4 Feb. 1923; *s* of Percy and Mary Haslam; *m* 1947, Joyce Quin; two *s*. *Educ:* Bolton Sch.; Birmingham Univ. (BSc Coal Mining, 1st Cl.). Joined Manchester Collieries Ltd, 1944; National Coal Board, Jan. 1947; Mining Engr, Oct. 1947, Personnel Director, 1960, ICI Nobel Division; Director, 1963, Dep. Chm., 1966, ICI Plastics Div.; Dep. Chm., 1969, Chm., 1971, ICI Fibres Div.; Director, ICI Ltd, 1974; Chairman: ICI Americas Inc., 1978–81; ICI Canada Ltd, 1979–80; Dep. Chm., ICI plc, 1980–83; Chairman: British Steel Corporation, 1983–86; Tate & Lyle plc, 1983–86 (non-exec. Dep. Chm., 1982; Dir, 1978–86); Director: Fibre Industries, Inc., 1971–75; Imperial Metal Industries, 1975–77; AECI Ltd, 1978–79; Carrington Viyella, 1982–83; Cable and Wireless, 1982–83. Chairman: Man-Made Fibres Producers Cttee, 1972–74; Common Market Group of CIRFS, 1973–75; Nationalized Industries Chairmen's Group, 1985–86 (Mem., 1983–); Member: BOTB, 1981–85 (Chm., N America Adv. Gp, 1982–85); NEDC, 1985–; Vice-Pres., British Textile Confedn, 1972–74. Chm. Council, Manchester Business Sch., 1985–. Freeman, City of London, 1985. *Recreations:* golf, travel. *Address:* c/o British Coal, Hobart House, Grosvenor Place, SW1X 7AE. *T:* 01–235 2020. *Clubs:* Brooks's; Wentworth.

HASLAM, (William) Geoffrey, OBE 1985; DFC 1944; Director, Prudential Corporation PLC, since 1980 (Deputy Chairman, 1980–84); *b* 11 Oct. 1914; *yr s* of late William John Haslam and late Hilda Irene Haslam; *m* 1941, Valda Patricia Adamson; two *s* one *d*. *Educ:* New Coll. and Ashville Coll., Harrogate. War Service with RAF, No 25 Sqdn (night fighters), 1940–46. Joined Prudential Assurance Co. Ltd, 1933: Dep. Gen. Manager, 1963; Gen. Manager, 1969; Chief Gen. Manager, 1974–78; Chief Exec., 1979; Dep. Chm., 1980–84. Chairman: Industrial Life Offices Assoc., 1972–74; British Insurance Assoc., 1977–78. Chm., St Teresa's Hospital, Wimbledon, 1983–; Vice Pres., NABC, 1983–. *Recreation:* golf. *Address:* 6 Ashbourne Road, W5 3ED. *T:* 01–997 8164. *Clubs:* City of London, MCC.

HASLEGRAVE, Herbert Leslie, WhSch (Sen.), MA Cantab, PhD London, MSc (Eng), CEng, FIMechE, FIEE, FIProdE; formerly Vice-Chancellor, Loughborough University of Technology; *b* 16 May 1902; *s* of late George Herbert Haslegrave and Annie (*née* Totty), Wakefield; *m* 1938, Agnes Mary, *er d* of Leo Sweeney, Bradford; one *d*. *Educ:* Wakefield Gram. Sch.; Bradford Technical Coll.; Trinity Hall Cambridge (Scholar). Rex Moir Prizeman, John Bernard Seeley Prizeman, Ricardo Prizeman, 1928; 1st Cl. Mechanical Sciences Tripos, 1928. English Electric Co. Ltd: Engineering Apprentice, 1918–23; Asst Designer, Stafford, 1928–30; Lecturer: Wolverhampton and Staffs Technical Coll., 1931; Bradford Technical Coll., 1931–35; Head of Continuative Education Dept, Loughborough Coll., 1935–38; Principal: St Helens Municipal Technical Coll., 1938–43; Barnsley Mining and Technical Coll., 1943–46; Leicester Coll. of Technology, 1947–53; Loughborough Coll. of Technology, 1953–66. Bernard Price Lectr, SA Inst. of Electrical Engrs, 1971. Member of: Productivity Team on Training of Supervisors, visiting USA, 1951; Delegation on Education and Training of Engineers visiting USSR, 1956; Council, IMechE, 1965–66; Council, IEE, 1956–58. Chairman: Council, Assoc. of Technical Institutions, 1963–64; Cttee on Technician Courses and Examinations, 1967–69; Pres., Whitworth Soc., 1972–73. Hon. DTech Loughborough Univ. of Technology. *Publications:* various on engineering, education and management in proceedings of professional engineering bodies and educational press; chapter in Management, Labour and Community. *Recreations:* motoring, swimming, music. *Address:* 19 Lands Road, Brixham, Devon.

HASLEGRAVE, Neville Crompton; Town Clerk, 1965–74, and Chief Executive Officer, 1969–74, Leeds; Solicitor; *b* 2 Aug. 1914; *o s* of late Joe Haslegrave, Clerk of Council, and late Olive May Haslegrave; *m* 1943, Vera May, *o d* of late Waldemar Julius Pedersen, MBE, and Eva Pedersen; two *d*. *Educ:* Exeter Cathedral Choristers School; Leeds Univ. Asst Examr, Estate Duty Office, Bd of Inland Revenue, 1940–44; Asst Solicitor, Co. Borough of Leeds, 1944–46. Chief Prosecuting Solicitor, Leeds, 1946–51; Principal Asst Solicitor, Leeds, 1951–60; Dep. Town Clerk, Leeds, 1960–65. Pres., Leeds Law Soc., 1972–73. Mem., IBA Adv. Council, 1969–73. *Recreations:* cricket, music, walking. *Address:* 37 West Court, West Avenue, Roundhay, Leeds LS8 2SP. *Club:* Headingley Taverners'.

HASLEWOOD, Prof. Geoffrey Arthur Dering; Professor of Biochemistry at Guy's Hospital Medical School, University of London, 1949–77, now Emeritus; *b* 9 July 1910; *s* of N. A. F. Haslewood, Architect, and Florence (*née* Hughes); *m* 1943, B. W. Leeburn (*d* 1949); two *d*; *m* 1953, E. S. Blakiston, Geelong, Vic, Australia. *Educ:* St Marylebone Grammar Sch.; University Coll., London. Research on polycyclic aromatic hydrocarbons, etc, at Royal Cancer Hosp. (Free), 1933–35; Asst in Pathological Chemistry at British Postgraduate Med. Sch., 1935–39; Reader in Biochemistry at Guy's Hosp. Med. Sch., 1939–49. Mem., Zaire River Expedition, 1974–75. MSc 1932, PhD 1935, DSc 1946, London. FRSC (FRIC 1946). *Publications:* Bile Salts, 1967; The Biological Importance of Bile Salts, 1978; various articles and original memoirs in scientific literature, mainly on steroids in relation to evolution. *Recreation:* conservation, especially of amphibians and reptiles. *Address:* 28 Old Fort Road, Shoreham-by-Sea, Sussex BN4 5RJ. *T:* Brighton 453622.

HASLIP, Joan; author; *b* 27 Feb. 1912; *yr d* of late George Ernest Haslip, MD, original planner of the Health Service. *Educ:* privately in London and on the continent. Grew up in Florence. Sub-editor, London Mercury, 1929–39, contributed verse, reviews, etc; travelled extensively Europe, USA, Middle East; Editor, European Service, BBC, 1941–45 (Italian Section); lectured for British Council, Italy and Middle East; broadcast and contributed articles to BBC and various publications and newspapers. FRSL 1958. *Publications:* (several translated); Out of Focus (novel), 1931; Grandfather Steps (novel), 1932 (USA 1933); Lady Hester Stanhope, 1934; Parnell, 1936 (USA 1937); Portrait of Pamela, 1940; Lucrezia Borgia, 1953 (USA 1954); The Sultan, Life of Abdul Hamid, 1958, repr. 1973; The Lonely Empress, a life of Elizabeth of Austria, 1965 (trans. into ten languages); Imperial Adventurer, 1971 (Book of Month choice, USA, 1972); Catherine the Great, 1976; The Emperor and the Actress, 1982. *Recreations:* travelling and conversation. *Address:* 8 Via Piana, Bellosguardo, Florence, Italy.

HASLUCK, Rt. Hon. Sir Paul (Meernaa Caedwalla), KG 1979; GCMG 1969; GCVO 1970; PC 1966; Governor-General of Australia, 1969–74; *b* 1 April 1905; *s* of E. M. C. Hasluck and Patience (*née* Wooler); *m* 1932, Alexandra Margaret Martin Darker, AD 1978, DStJ 1971; one *s* (and one *s* decd). *Educ:* University of Western Australia (MA). Journalist until 1938. Lectr in History, University of Western Australia, 1939–40; Australian Diplomatic Service, 1941–47; Head of Australian Mission to United Nations, 1946–47; Representative on Security Council, Atomic Energy Commn, General Assembly, etc. Research Reader in History, University of Western Australia, 1948. Official War Historian. Mem. (L) House of Representatives, 1949–69; Minister for Territories in successive Menzies Governments, 1951–63; Minister for Defence, 1963–64; Minister for External Affairs, 1964–69. Fellow, Aust. Acad. of Social Scis. Hon. Fellow, Aust. Acad. of Humanities; Hon. FRAIA; Hon. FRAHS. KStJ 1969. *Publications:* Black Australians, 1942; Workshop of Security, 1946; The Government and the People (Australian Official War History), vol. 1, 1951, vol. 2, 1970; Collected Verse, 1970; An Open Go, 1971; The Office of the Governor-General (Queale Meml Lecture), 1973, rev. edn, 1979; The Poet in Australia, 1975; A Time for Building: Australian administration in Papua New Guinea, 1976; Mucking About (autobiog.), 1977; Sir Robert Menzies (Mannix Lecture), 1980; Diplomatic Witness, 1980; Dark Cottage (verse), 1984. *Recreation:* book collecting (Australiana). *Address:* 2 Adams Road, Dalkeith, WA 6009, Australia. *Clubs:* Weld (Perth); Claremont Football.

HASSALL, Anthony Frank Albert; Group Managing Director and Chief Executive, Torvale Group, since 1979; *b* 6 Aug. 1930; *s* of late Frank Armitage Hassall and Ena Dorothy (*née* Andrews); *m* 1954, Brenda, *d* of late Thomas Harry Freeman; two *s* one *d*. *Educ:* Derby Grammar Sch.; Loughborough Coll. (BSc MechEng, DLC). CEng. Instr Lieut RN, 1954. British Celanese Ltd, 1952; H. C. Slingsby Ltd, 1957; NRDC, 1960; British Technical Service Corp., Washington, DC, 1963; Marketing Dir, Bridon Fibres & Plastics Ltd, 1966–77; Regional Industrial Dir (Under Sec.), Yorks and Humberside, DoI, 1977–78. *Recreations:* squash, golf. *Address:* c/o Torvale Group, Pembridge, Herefordshire. *T:* Pembridge 383. *Club:* Farmers'.

HASSALL, Prof. Cedric Herbert, FRS 1985; CChem; Hon. Visiting Professor: University of Warwick, since 1985; University College, Cardiff, since 1985; *b* 6 Dec. 1919; *s* of late H. Hassall, Auckland, NZ; *m* 1st, 1946, H. E. Cotti (marr. diss. 1982); one *d* (and one *s* decd); 2nd, 1984, J. A. Mitchelmore. *Educ:* Auckland Grammar Sch., NZ; Auckland Univ. (MSc); Univ. of Cambridge (PhD, ScD). Lectr, Univ. of Otago, NZ, 1943–45; Sen. studentship, Royal Commn for 1851, Cambridge, 1946–48; Foundn Prof. of Chem., Univ. of WI, 1948–56; Carnegie and Rockefeller Fellowships in USA, 1950, 1956; Head, Dept of Chemistry, Univ. Coll., of Swansea, UCW, 1957–71; Dir of Research, Roche Products Ltd, 1971–84. Comr, Royal Univ. of Malta, 1964–71; Planning Adviser: Univ. of Jordan, 1965–71; Univ. of Aleppo, 1965; Abdul Aziz Univ., Jedda, 1966, 1968. Vis. Professor: Univ. of Kuwait, 1969, 1979; Aligarh Univ., India (Royal Soc.), 1969–70; Univ. of Liverpool, 1971–79. Pres., Chem. Section of British Assoc., 1987; Member: various cttees of Royal Soc. Chem., 1959–; Pres., Perkin Div. of RSC, 1985–; various Govt cttees relating to sci. affairs. Hon. Fellow, UC of Swansea, 1986; Hon. DSc West Indies, 1975. *Publications:* papers on aspects of organic chemistry, largely in Jl of Chemical Soc. *Recreations:* tennis, watching Rugby football, exploring countryside. *Address:* 6 Ashcroft Close, Harpenden, Herts AL5 1JJ. *T:* Harpenden 3377.

HASSALL, Joan, RE 1948; FSIAD 1958; painter and wood engraver; *b* 3 March 1906; *d* of late John Hassall, RI, RWA, and late Constance Brooke-Webb. *Educ:* Parsons Mead, Ashtead; Froebel Educational Institute, Roehampton. Sec. to London Sch. of Art, 1925–27; studied Royal Academy Schs, 1928–33; studied Wood Engraving, LCC Sch. of Photo-engraving and Lithography. Teacher of Book Production (deputy), Edinburgh Coll. of Art, 1940; resumed her own work in London, chiefly wood engraving, 1945. Work represented in: British Museum, Victoria and Albert Museum and collections abroad. Designed the Queen's Invitation Card to her guests for Coronation, 1953. Master, Art Workers Guild, 1972 (Mem., 1964–); Bronze Medal, Paris Salon, 1973. *Publications:* first published engraving in Devil's Dyke, by Christopher Hassall, 1935; The Wood Engravings of Joan Hassall, 1960; Joan Hassall: Engravings and Drawings, 1985. Her engraved and drawn work appears in many classic and contemporary books of prose and poetry, and in advertising. *Recreations:* music, literature and printing. *Address:* Priory Cottage, Malham, Skipton, N Yorks BD23 4DD. *T:* Airton 356.

HASSALL, Tom Grafton, FSA 1971; MIFA; Secretary, Royal Commission on Historical Monuments of England, since 1986; Fellow, St Cross College, Oxford, since 1974; *b* 3 Dec. 1943; *s* of William Owen Hassall, *qv*; *m* 1967, Angela Rosaleen Goldsmith; three *s*. *Educ:* Dragon Sch., Oxford; Lord Williams's Grammar Sch., Thame; Corpus Christi Coll., Oxford (BA History). Assistant local editor, Victoria County History of Oxford, 1966–67; Director, Oxford Archaeological Excavation Cttee, 1967–73; Dir, Oxfordshire (now Oxford) Archaeological Unit, 1973–85; Associate Staff Tutor, Oxford Univ. Dept for External Studies, 1978–85. Trustee, Oxford Preservation Trust, 1973–; Chairman: Standing Conf. of Unit Managers, 1980–83; British Archaeological Awards, 1983–; President: Council for British Archaeology, 1983–86; Oxfordshire Architectural and Historical Soc., 1984–; Mem., Ancient Monuments Adv. Cttee, Historic Buildings and Monuments Commn, 1984–. *Publications:* Oxford: the city beneath your feet, 1972; specialist articles on archaeology. *Recreations:* gardening, Norfolk Cottage. *Address:* The Manor House, Wheatley, Oxford OX9 1XX. *T:* Wheatley 4428.

HASSALL, William Owen; Librarian to Earl of Leicester, Holkham, 1937–83; Bodleian Library, Oxford, 1938–80 (Senior Assistant Librarian); *b* 4 Aug. 1912; *s* of Lt-Col Owen Hassall and Bessie Florence Hassall (*née* Cory); *m* 1936, Averil Grafton Beaves; three *s* one *d*. *Educ:* Twyford Sch., Hants; Wellington Coll., Berks; (Classical scholar) Corpus Christi Coll., Oxford. Hon. Mods, 1st cl. Modern History, 1936, DPhil 1941. Lent by RA to Min. Economic Warfare, 1942–46. Formerly: External Examnr in History, Univs of Bristol, Durham, Leicester and Oxford Insts of Educn (Trng Colls); Hon. Editorial Sec., British Records Assoc.; Mem. Council, Special Libraries and Information Bureaux. Hon. Sec., Oxfordshire Record Soc., 1947–76. FSA 1942; FRHistS. *Publications:* A Cartulary of St Mary Clerkenwell, 1949; A Catalogue of the Library of Sir Edward Coke, 1950; The Holkham Bible Picture Book, 1954; Wheatley Records, 956–1956, 1956; They saw it happen: an anthology of eye-witnesses' accounts for events in British history, 55BC-AD1485, 1957; Who's Who in History, vol. I, British Isles, 55BC-1485, 1960; (with A. G. Hassall) The Douce Apocalypse, 1961; How they Lived: an anthology of original accounts written before 1485, 1962; Index of Names in Oxfordshire Charters, 1966; History Through Surnames, 1967; The Holkham Library Illuminations and Illustrations in the Manuscript Library of the Earl of Leicester (printed for presentation to the Members of the Roxburghe Club), 1970; (with A. G. Hassall) Treasures from the Bodleian, 1975; contrib. to various learned publications; work on Holkham records, 1250–1350. *Recreation:* grandchildren. *Address:* Manor House, Wheatley, Oxford. *T:* Wheatley 2333.
See also T. G. Hassall.

HASSAN, Sayed Abdullah El; Order of Sudanese Republic; Golden Order of Regional Government; Ambassador of Democratic Republic of the Sudan to the Court of St James's, 1971–72 and 1983–85; *b* 1925; *m* Madame Khadiga Diglal; four *s* one *d*. Diploma in Arts and Public Administration. District Officer, Min. of Interior and Min. of Local Govt, 1949–56; Consul Gen., Uganda and Kenya, 1956–58; Head of Political Section, Min. of Foreign Affairs, 1958–60; Ambassador to Ghana, 1960–64; Dir Gen., Min. of Information, 1964–65; Ambassador to France, 1965–67, to Ethiopia, 1967–69; Under Sec., Ministry of Foreign Affairs, 1969–70; Ambassador to Soviet Union, 1970–71; Mem., Political Bureau, Sudanese Socialist Union, 1972–77; Minister of Rural Develt, 1972–73; Minister of Interior, 1973–75; Sec. Gen. to the Presidency, 1975–76; Minister for Cabinet Affairs, 1976–77; Mem., Nat. Assembly (3rd) and Chm., Foreign Relations Cttee, 1979–80; Governor designate, Eastern Region, March-Nov. 1980; Ambassador to Tunisia and

Perm. Rep. to Arab League, 1982–83. Sec. Gen., Nat. Council for Friendship, Solidarity and Peace, 1973–; Mem., Sudan delegations to UN, OAU, UNHCR and numerous assemblies, conferences and visits. Holds numerous foreign decorations. *Address:* c/o Foreign Office, Khartoum, Sudan.

HASSAN, Sir Joshua (Abraham), KCMG 1986; Kt 1963; CBE 1957; LVO 1954; QC (Gibraltar) 1961; JP; Chief Minister of Gibraltar, 1964–69, and since 1972; *b* 1915; *s* of late Abraham M. Hassan, Gibraltar; *m* 1945, Daniela (marr. diss. 1969), *d* of late José Salazar; two *d*; *m* 1969, Marcelle, *d* of late Joseph Bensimon; two *d*. *Educ:* Line Wall Coll., Gibraltar. Called to Bar, Middle Temple, 1939; Hon. Bencher, 1983. HM Deputy Coroner, Gibraltar, 1941–64; Mayor of Gibraltar, 1945–50 and 1953–69; Mem. Executive Council, Chief Mem. Legislative Council, Gibraltar, 1950–64; Leader of the Opposition, Gibraltar House of Assembly, 1969–72. Chairman: Cttee of Management, Gibraltar Museum, 1952–65; Gibraltar Govt Lottery Cttee, 1955–70; Central Planning Commn, 1947–70. Hon. LLD Hull Univ., 1985. *Address:* 11/18 Europa Road, Gibraltar. *T:* 77295. *Clubs:* United Oxford & Cambridge University; Royal Gibraltar Yacht.

HASSAN, Mamoun Hamid; independent producer/director; *b* Jedda, 12 Dec. 1937; *s* of late Dr Hamid Hassan and of Fatma Hassan (*née* Sadat); *m* 1966, Moya Jacqueline Gillespie, MA Oxon; two *s*. Formerly script writer, editor and director; Head of Production Board, British Film Inst., 1971–74; Head of Films Branch, UNRWA, Lebanon, 1974–76; Bd Mem., 1978–84, Man. Dir, 1979–84, Nat. Film Finance Corp. Member: Cinematograph Films Council, 1977–78; Scottish Film Production Fund, 1983–; Governor, Nat. Film and Television Sch., 1983–. Films produced include: No Surrender, 1985. *Address:* High Ridge, 9 High Street, Deddington, Oxford OX5 4SJ.

HASSETT, Gen. Sir Francis (George), AC 1975; KBE 1976 (CBE 1966; OBE 1945); CB 1970; DSO 1951; LVO 1954; Chief of the Defence Force Staff, 1975–77, retired; *b* 11 April 1918; *s* of John Francis Hassett, Sydney, Australia; *m* 1946, Margaret Hallie Roberts, *d* of Dr Edwin Spencer Roberts, Toowoomba, Qld; one *s* two *d* (and one *s* decd). *Educ:* RMC, Duntroon, Australia. Graduated RMC, 1938. Served War of 1939–45, Middle East and South West Pacific Area (Lt-Col; despatches twice); CO 3 Bn Royal Australian Regt, Korea, 1951–52; Marshal for ACT Royal Tour, 1954; Comd 28 Commonwealth Bde, 1961–62; idc, 1963; DCGS, 1964–65; Head of Aust. Jt Services Staff, Australia House, 1966–67; GOC Northern Comd, Australia, 1968–70; Chm., Army Rev. Cttee, 1969–70; Vice Chief of Gen. Staff, Australia, 1971–73; CGS, Australia, 1973–75. Extra Gentleman Usher to the Queen, 1966–68. *Recreations:* fishing, boating. *Address:* 42 Mugga Way, Red Hill, Canberra, ACT 2603, Australia. *Clubs:* Commonwealth, Queensland.

HASSETT, Maj.-Gen. Ronald Douglas Patrick, CB 1978; CBE 1975; Director, Orient: New Zealand Trading Co. Ltd, since 1979; *b* 27 May 1923; *s* of Edmond Hassett and Elinor Douglas; *m* 1953, Lilian Ivy Gilmore; two *s* one *d*. *Educ:* St Patrick's Coll., Wellington; RMC Duntroon. psc, G, rcds. 2nd NZ Expeditionary Force, Italy, 1944–46; NZ Army Liaison Staff, London, 1948–50; served Korea, NZ and Malaya, 1952–62; NZ Instructor, Australian Staff Coll., 1963–65; Dir of Equipment, NZ Army, 1966–67; DQMG, 1967–69; Comdr NZ Inf. Brigade Group, 1969; DCGS, 1970; RCDS, 1971; ACDS (Policy), 1972–74; Dep. Chief of Defence Staff, 1974–76; Chief of General Staff, NZ Army, 1976–78. *Recreations:* gardening, golf. *Address:* (office) Suite 5.98 5th Floor, Wisma Central, Jalan Ampang, PO Box 2197, Kuala Lumpur, Malaysia; (home) 70 Lorong Chong Khoon Lin 3, Ukay Heights, Kuala Lumpur, Malaysia.

HASTERT, Roger Joseph Leon; Commandeur, Order of Adolphe de Nassau, Luxembourg; Hon. CMG 1972; Dr-en-Droit; Maréchal de la Cour, Luxembourg, since 1985; *b* Luxembourg City, 10 July 1929; *m* Eléonore Heijmerink; one *s* one *d*. Barrister-at-law, Luxembourg, 1956–59; joined Diplomatic Service, 1959 (Political Affairs); First Sec. and Consul Gen., Brussels, 1963–69; Dir of Protocol and Juridical Affairs, Min. of Foreign Affairs; Pres., Commn Internationale de la Moselle; and Mem., Commn de Contrôle des Comptes des Communautés Européennes, 1969–73; Ambassador to The Netherlands, 1973–1978; Ambassador to UK and Perm. Rep. to Council of WEU, 1978–85, concurrently Ambassador to Ireland and Iceland. *Address:* Palais Grand Ducal, 2 rue du Rost, Luxembourg.

HASTIE, Robert Cameron, CBE 1983; RD 1968 (Bar 1978); DL; Chairman: Bernard Hastie & Co. Ltd, UK and Australia, since 1973; *b* Swansea, 24 May 1933; *s* of B. H. C. Hastie and M. H. Hastie; *m* 1961, Mary Griffiths; two *s* one *d*. *Educ:* Bromsgrove School. Joined RN, National Service, 1951; Midshipman 1953, Lieut 1957, RNVR; qual. RNR Ocean comd, 1963; progressive ranks to Captain RNR, 1974, in comd HMS Cambria, 1974–77; Captain Sea Trng RNR, 1977–79; Aide-de-Camp to the Queen, 1977; Commodore RNR 1979. Pres., Swansea Unit Sea Cadet Corps, 1982–. Member: Inst. of Directors, 1960–; W Wales Cttee, CBI, 1982–. Vice-Chairman: (Navy), Council of TA & VRA, 1983–; TA & VRA, Wales, 1984–. DL West Glamorgan, 1974; High Sheriff of W Glamorgan County, 1977–78. *Recreations:* sailing, shooting, skiing, tennis. *Address:* Upper Hareslade Farm, Bishopston, Swansea SA3 3BU. *T:* Bishopston 2957; (day) Swansea 51541. *Clubs:* Naval; Cardiff and County (Cardiff); Royal Naval Sailing Association (Portsmouth); Bristol Channel Yacht (Swansea); Royal Sydney Yacht Squadron (Sydney, Aust.).

HASTIE-SMITH, Richard Maybury, CB 1984; FIPM 1986; Deputy Under-Secretary of State, Ministry of Defence, since 1981; *b* 13 Oct. 1931; *s* of Engr-Comdr D. Hastie-Smith and H. I. Hastie-Smith; *m* 1956, Bridget Noel Cox; one *s* two *d*. *Educ:* Cranleigh Sch. (Schol.); Magdalene Coll., Cambridge (Schol.; MA). HM Forces, commnd Queen's Royal Regt, 1950–51. Entered Administrative Class, Home CS, War Office, 1955; Private Sec. to Permanent Under-Sec., 1957; Asst Private Sec. to Sec. of State, 1958; Principal, 1960; Asst Private Sec. to Sec. of State for Defence, 1965; Private Sec. to Minister of Defence (Equipment), 1968; Asst Sec., 1969; RCDS, 1974; Under-Sec., MoD, 1975, Cabinet Office, 1979–81. Chm., Magdalene Coll. Assoc., 1983–. Governor: Cranleigh Sch., 1963–; St Catherine's Sch., Bramley, 1972–. *Address:* 18 York Avenue, East Sheen, SW14. *T:* 01–876 4597. *Club:* Army and Navy.

HASTILOW, Michael Alexander; Director, Glynwed Ltd, 1969–81; *b* 21 Sept. 1923; *s* of late Cyril Alexander Frederick Hastilow, CBE, MSc, BCom, FRIC, and Doreen Madge, MA; *m* 1953, Sheila Mary Tipper (*née* Barker); one *s* two *d*. *Educ:* Mill Hill Sch.; Birmingham Univ. (Pres., Guild of Undergrads; BSc Civil Engrg, BCom). Served in Fleet Air Arm, RNVR, 1944–46. Commercial Manager, J. H. Lavender & Co. Ltd, 1948–54; Birmid Industries Ltd, 1954–57: Asst Gen. Man., Birmidal Developments Ltd, 1956–57; Commercial Man., Birmetals Ltd, 1957; Commercial and Gen. Sales Man., Bilston Foundries Ltd, 1957–63; Dir, Cotswold Buildings Ltd, 1963–64; Glynwed Ltd, 1964–81: Dir, The Wednesbury Tube Co. Ltd, 1966–81 (Man. Dir, 1968–74; Chm., 1973–76); dir or chm. of various Glynwed divs and subsids. British Non-Ferrous Metals Federation: Mem. Council, 1973–81; Vice Pres., 1975–79; Pres., 1979–80; Chm., Tube Gp, 1975–77. National Home Improvement Council: Mem. Council, 1975–84; Mem. Bd, 1975–84; Vice Chm., 1979–80; Chm., 1980–81. Member: Commn for New Towns, 1978–; Construction Exports Adv. Bd, 1975–78; Exec. Cttee, 1973–84, and Council,

1974–84, Nat. Council for Bldg Material Producers; EDC for Building, 1980–82. Hon. Treasurer, Midlands Club Cricket Conf., 1969–81, Pres., 1981–82. *Recreations:* cricket, railways. *Address:* The Mount, 3 Kendal End Road, Rednal, Birmingham B45 8PX. *T:* 021–445 2007. *Clubs:* Royal Automobile, Old Millhillians.

HASTINGS, family name of **Earl of Huntingdon.**

HASTINGS; *see* Abney-Hastings, family name of Countess of Loudoun.

HASTINGS, 22nd Baron, *cr* 1290; **Edward Delaval Henry Astley,** Bt 1660; *b* 14 April 1912; *s* of 21st Baron and Lady Marguerite Nevill (*d* 1975), *d* of 3rd Marquess of Abergavenny; *S* father 1956; *m* 1954, Catherine Rosaline Ratcliffe Coats, 2nd *d* of late Capt. H. V. Hinton; two *s* one *d*. *Educ:* Eton and abroad. Supplementary Reserve, Coldstream Guards, 1934; served War of 1939–45, Major 1945; farming in Southern Rhodesia, 1951–57. Mem. of Parliamentary delegation to the West Indies, 1958; a Lord in Waiting, 1961–62; Jt Parly Sec., Min. of Housing and Local Govt, 1962–64. Chairman: British-Italian Soc., 1957–62 (Pres., 1972–); Italian People's Flood Appeal, 1966–67; Governor: Brit. Inst. of Florence, 1959–; Royal Ballet, 1971–; Chm., Royal Ballet Benevolent Fund, 1966–84; Pres., British Epilepsy Assoc., 1965–. Grand Officer, Order of Merit (Italy), 1968. *Recreations:* riding, ballet, foreign travel. *Heir: s* Hon. Delaval Thomas Harold Astley, *b* 25 April 1960. *Address:* Fulmodeston Hall, Fakenham, Norfolk. *T:* Thursford 231; Seaton Delaval Hall, Northumberland. *Clubs:* Brooks's, Army and Navy; Northern Counties (Newcastle); Norfolk (Norwich).

HASTINGS, Bernard Ratcliffe; Chairman, North Western Electricity Board, since 1985; *b* 16 March 1930; *s* of Robert Patrick and Mary Frances Hastings; *m* 1956, Mary Roddick Murdoch, BA; one *s* one *d*. *Educ:* Glasgow Univ. BSc Hons. Various posts, latterly Head of Industrial Engrg Dept, Mullard Radio Valve Co., 1955–67; Management Services Controller, South of Scotland Electricity Bd, 1967–74; Dep. Chm., 1974–77, Chm., 1978–85, Merseyside and N Wales Electricity Bd. *Recreations:* golf, piano, gardening. *Address:* Ranfurly, 2 Walnut Croft, Churton, Chester CH3 6NB. *T:* Farndon 270788.

HASTINGS, Hubert De Cronin; Chairman, Architectural Press, 1927–74; Editor, Architectural Review, 1927–73; Editor, Architects' Journal, 1932–73; *b* 18 July 1902; *s* of Percy Hastings and Lilian Bass; *m* 1927, Hazel Rickman Garrard; one *s* one *d*. Royal Gold Medal for Architecture, 1971. *Publications:* The Italian Townscape, 1963; Civilia—The End of Sub-Urban Man, 1971; The Alternative Society, 1980. *Address:* 9/13 Queen Anne's Gate, Westminster, SW1. *Clubs:* Arts, National, ICA.

HASTINGS, Max Macdonald; author, journalist and broadcaster; Editor, The Daily Telegraph, since 1986; *b* 28 Dec. 1945; *s* of Macdonald Hastings and Anne Scott-James, *qv; m* 1972, Patricia Mary Edmondson; two *s* one *d*. *Educ:* Charterhouse (Scholar); University Coll., Oxford (Exhibnr). Served TA Parachute Regt, 1963. Researcher, BBC TV Great War series, 1963–64; Reporter, Evening Standard, 1965–67; Fellow, US World Press Inst., 1967–68; Roving Correspondent, Evening Standard, 1968–70; Reporter, BBC TV Current Affairs, 1970–73; freelance journalist and broadcaster, 1973–; Editor, Evening Standard Londoner's Diary, 1976–77; Columnist, Daily Express, 1981–83; contributor, Sunday Times, 1985–86. As War Correspondent, covered Middle East, Indochina, Angola, India-Pakistan, Cyprus, N Ireland and S Atlantic. TV documentaries for BBC and Central TV, 1970–. Dir, Hereward Radio plc, 1984–86. Journalist of the Year, British Press Awards, 1982 (cited 1973 and 1980); What The Papers Say Reporter of the Year, Granada TV, 1982. *Publications:* America 1968: the fire this time, 1968; Ulster 1969: the struggle for civil rights in Northern Ireland, 1970; Montrose: the King's champion, 1977; Yoni: the hero of Entebbe, 1979; Bomber Command, 1979 (Somerset Maugham Prize for Non-Fiction, 1980); (contrib.) The Battle of Britain, 1980; Das Reich, 1981; (with Simon Jenkins) The Battle for The Falklands, 1983 (Yorkshire Post Book of the Year Award); Overlord: D-Day and the battle for Normandy, 1984 (Yorkshire Post Book of the Year Award); Victory in Europe, 1985; (ed) Oxford Book of Military Anecdotes, 1985; contrib. The Standard, The Spectator, The Field. *Recreations:* shooting, fishing. *Address:* Guilsborough Lodge, Guilsborough, Northants; (office) The Daily Telegraph, 135 Fleet Street, EC4. *T:* 01–353 4242. *Clubs:* Brooks's, Beefsteak, Saintsbury.

HASTINGS, Michael; playwright; *b* 2 Sept. 1938; *s* of Max Emmanuel Gerald and Marie Katherine Hastings; *m* 1975, Victoria Hardie; two *s* and one *d* by previous *m*. *Educ:* various South London schools. Bespoke tailoring apprenticeship, London, 1953–56. FRGS. *Publications:* plays: Don't Destroy Me, 1956; Yes and After, 1957; The World's Baby, 1962; Lee Harvey Oswald: 'a far mean streak of indepence brought on by negleck', 1966; The Cutting of the Cloth (unperformed autobiographical play), 1969; The Silence of Saint-Just, 1971; For the West (Uganda), 1977; Gloo Joo, 1978; Full Frontal, 1979; Carnival War a Go Hot, 1980; Midnite at the Starlite, 1980; Molière's The Miser (adaptation), 1982; Tom and Viv, 1984, rev. edn 1985 (incl. introductory critical essay); novels: The Game, 1957; The Frauds, 1960; Tussy is Me, 1968; The Nightcomers, 1971; And in the Forest the Indians, 1975; poems: Love me Lambeth, 1959; stories: Bart's Mornings and other Tales of Modern Brazil, 1975; criticism: Rupert Brooke, The Handsomest Young Man in England, 1967; Sir Richard Burton: a biography, 1978; for film and television: For the West (Congo), 1963; Blue as his Eyes the Tin Helmet He Wore, 1966; The Search for the Nile, 1972; The Nightcomers, 1972; Auntie Kathleen's Old Clothes, 1977; Murder Rap, 1980; Midnight at the Starlight, 1980; Michael Hastings in Brixton, 1980; Stars of the Roller State Disco, 1984. *Address:* 2 Helix Gardens, Brixton Hill, SW2.

HASTINGS, Lt-Col Robin Hood William Stewart, DSO 1944 (and Bar 1945); OBE (mil.) 1946; MC 1943; despatches twice; Chairman, British Bloodstock Agency Ltd, 1968–86, President, since 1986; *b* 16 Jan. 1917; *s* of Hon. Osmond Hastings and Mary Caroline Campbell Hastings; *c* and *heir-pres.* to 15th Earl of Huntingdon, *qv; m* 1950, Jean Suzanne Palethorpe; one *d*. *Educ:* Stowe Sch.; Christ Church Oxford (Hons History, MA). Commissioned Rifle Brigade, 1939; Commanded: 6th Bn The Green Howards, 1943–44; 2nd Bn KRRC, 1944; GSOI 11th Armoured Div., 1945; commanded 1 Rifle Bde, 1945–46. Employed by BBA Ltd, 1952–; Director, 1954. Rode steeplechasing, 1945–52. *Publications:* The Rifle Brigade 1939–45, 1950; (jtly) The London Rifle Brigade 1919–50, 1952. *Recreations:* hunting, shooting. *Address:* The Malt House, Bramdean, Alresford, Hampshire SO24 0LN. *T:* Bramdean 243. *Club:* White's.

HASTINGS, Sir Stephen (Lewis Edmonstone), Kt 1983; MC 1944; *b* 4 May 1921; *s* of late Lewis Aloysius MacDonald Hastings, MC, and of Edith Meriel Edmonstone; *m* 1st, 1948, Harriet Mary Elisabeth (marr. diss. 1971), *d* of Col Julian Latham Tomlin, CBE, DSO; one *s* one *d*; 2nd, 1975, Hon. Elisabeth Anne Lady Naylor-Leyland, *yr d* of late Viscount FitzAlan of Derwent and of Countess Fitzwilliam. *Educ:* Eton; RMC, Sandhurst. Gazetted Ensign, Scots Guards, 1939; served 2nd Bn, Western Desert, 1941–43 (despatches); SAS Regt, 1943. Joined Foreign Office, 1948. British Legation, Helsinki, 1950–52; British Embassy, Paris, 1953–58; First Sec., Political Office, Middle East Forces, 1959–60. MP (C) Mid-Bedfordshire, Nov. 1960–1983. Chm., BMSS (Shrewsbury) Ltd, 1978–; Dir, Fitzwilliam Estates Co., 1980–. Chm., British Field Sports Soc., 1982–. Jt

Master, Fitzwilliam Hounds. *Publication:* The Murder of TSR2, 1966. *Recreations:* fieldsports, skiing. *Address:* Milton, Peterborough PE6 7AF; 12A Ennismore Gardens, SW7. *Clubs:* White's, Pratt's, Buck's.

HASWELL, (Anthony) James (Darley), OBE 1985; Insurance Ombudsman, since 1981; *b* 4 Aug. 1922; *s* of Brig. Chetwynd Henry Haswell, CIE, and Dorothy Edith (*née* Berry); *m* 1957, Angela Mary (*née* Murphy); three *s* one *d. Educ:* Winchester Coll.; St John's Coll., Cambridge (MA). Solicitor of the Supreme Court. Admitted Solicitor, 1949; RAC Legal Dept, 1949; private practice, London and Cornwall, 1950–51; commnd, Army Legal Services Staff List (Captain), 1952; Temp. Major 1956; Lt-Col 1967; retired from Army Legal Corps, 1981. *Publications:* Insurance Ombudsman Bureau annual reports for years 1981–; miscellaneous articles in industry jls. *Recreations:* chamber music, theatre, painting, woodwork, Insurance Orchestra (Chm. and playing member). *Address:* 31 Chipstead Street, SW6 3SR. *T:* 01–736 1163.

HASZELDINE, Dr Robert Neville, ScD; FRS 1968; CChem, FRSC; Professor of Chemistry, 1957–82, Head of Department of Chemistry, 1957–76, and Principal, 1976–82, University of Manchester Institute of Science and Technology (Faculty of Technology, The University of Manchester); *b* Manchester, 3 May 1925; *s* of late Walter Haszeldine and late Hilda Haszeldine (*née* Webster); *m* 1954, Pauline Elvina Goodwin; two *s* two *d. Educ:* Stockport Grammar Sch.; University of Birmingham (John Watt Meml Schol., 1942; PhD 1947; DSc 1955); Sidney Sussex Coll., Cambridge (MA, PhD 1949); Queens' Coll., Cambridge (ScD 1957). University of Cambridge: Asst in Research in Organic Chemistry, 1949; University Demonstrator in Organic and Inorganic Chemistry, 1951; Asst Dir of Research, 1956; Fellow and Dir of Studies, Queens' Coll., 1954–57, Hon. Fellow, 1976. Mem. various Govt Cttees, 1957–. Former Vice-Pres., Perkin Div., Chemical Soc. Tilden Lectr, 1968; Vis. Lectr at universities and laboratories in the USA, Russia, Switzerland, Austria, Germany, Japan, China, Israel, S America and France. Meldola Medal, 1953; Corday-Morgan Medal and Prize, 1960. *Publications:* numerous scientific publications in chemical jls. *Recreations:* mountaineering, gardening, natural history, good food, wine. *Address:* Copt Howe, Chapel Stile, Great Langdale, Cumbria LA22 9JR. *T:* Langdale 685.

HATCH, family name of **Baron Hatch of Lusby.**

HATCH OF LUSBY, Baron *cr* 1978 (Life Peer), of Oldfield in the County of W Yorks; **John Charles Hatch;** author, lecturer, broadcaster; *b* 1 Nov. 1917; *s* of John James Hatch and Mary White. *Educ:* Keighley Boys' Grammar School; Sidney Sussex Coll., Cambridge (BA). Tutor, Nat. Council of Labour Colls, 1942–44; Nat. Organiser, Independent Labour Party, 1944–48, Lectr, Glasgow Univ., 1948–53; Sec., Commonwealth Dept, Labour Party, 1954–61; Dir, Extra-Mural Dept, Univ. of Sierra Leone, 1961–62; Director: African Studies Programme, Houston, Texas, 1964–70; Inst. of Human Relations, Zambia Univ., 1980–82. Commonwealth Correspondent, New Statesman, 1950–70. Hon. Fellow, School of Peace Studies, Univ. of Bradford, 1976. Hon. DLitt, Univ. of St Thomas, Houston, 1981. *Publications:* The Dilemma of South Africa, 1953; New from Africa, 1956; Everyman's Africa, 1959; Africa Today and Tomorrow, 1960; A History of Post-War Africa, 1964; The History of Britain in Africa, 1966; Africa: The Re-Birth of Self-Rule, 1968; Tanzania, 1969; Nigeria, 1971; Africa Emergent, 1974; Two African Statesmen, 1976. *Recreations:* cricket, music. *Address:* Jasmine Cottage, East Bank, Winster, near Matlock, South Derbyshire DE4 2DT. *T:* Winster 705. *Clubs:* Royal Commonwealth Society, MCC.

HATCH, David Edwin; Director of Programmes, BBC Radio, since 1986; *b* 7 May 1939; *s* of Rev. Raymond Harold Hatch and Winifred Edith May (*née* Brookes); *m* 1964, Ann Elizabeth Martin; two *s* one *d. Educ:* St John's Sch., Leatherhead; Queens' Coll., Cambridge (MA, DipEd). Actor, Cambridge Circus, 1963; BBC: I'm Sorry I'll Read That Again, 1964; Producer, Light Entertainment Radio, 1964, Executive Producer, 1972; Network Editor Radio, Manchester, 1974; Head of Light Entertainment Radio, 1978; Controller: Radio Two, 1980–83; Radio 4, 1983–86. Mem. Bd of Management, Services Sound and Vision Corp., 1981–. *Recreations:* winemaking, laughing, family. *Address:* The Windmill, Ray's Hill, Cholesbury, near Chesham, Bucks HP5 2UJ. *T:* Cholesbury 542. *Clubs:* Rugby, Lords' Taverners'.

HATCH, Dr Marshall Davidson, AM 1981; FRS 1980; FAA; Chief Research Scientist, Division of Plant Industry, CSIRO, Canberra, since 1970; *b* 24 Dec. 1932; *s* of Lloyd Davidson Hatch and Alice Endesby Hatch (*née* Dalziel); divorced; two *s. Educ:* Newington Coll., Sydney; Univ. of Sydney (BSc, PhD). FAA. Res. Scientist, Div. of Food Res., CSIRO, 1955–59; Post Doctoral Res. Fellow, Univ. of Calif., Davis, 1959–61; Res. Scientist, Colonial Sugar Refining Co. Ltd, Brisbane, 1961–66 and 1968–69 (Reader in Plant Biochemistry, Univ. of Queensland, Brisbane, 1967). Rank Prize, 1981. *Publications:* 121 papers, reviews and chaps in scientific jls and text books in field of photosynthesis and other areas of plant biochemistry. *Recreations:* skiing, squash, running. *Address:* (office) Division of Plant Industry, CSIRO, PO Box 1600, Canberra City, ACT 2601, Australia.

HATCHARD, Frederick Henry; Stipendiary Magistrate for Metropolitan County of West Midlands (Birmingham), since 1981; *b* 22 April 1923; *s* of Francis and May Hatchard; *m* 1955, Patricia Egerton; two *s. Educ:* Yardley Grammar Sch., Birmingham. Justices Clerk: Sutton Coldfield and Coleshill, 1963–67; Walsall, 1967–81. *Recreations:* walking, gardening. *Address:* 3(B) Manor Road, Streetly, Sutton Coldfield B74 3NQ.

HATENDI, Rt. Rev. Ralph Peter; *see* Harare, Bishop of.

HATFIELD, Rt. Rev. Leonard Fraser; Bishop of Nova Scotia, 1980–84, retired; *b* 1 Oct. 1919; *s* of Otto Albert Hatfield and Ada Hatfield (*née* Tower). *Educ:* Port Greville and Amherst High School; King's and Dalhousie Univ., Halifax (BA 1940, MA 1943, Sociology). Deacon 1942, priest 1943; Priest Assistant, All Saints Cathedral, Halifax, NS, 1942–46; Rector of Antigonish, NS, 1946–51; Asst. Sec., Council for Social Service of Anglican Church of Canada, 1951–54; Gen. Sec., 1955–61; Rector: Christ Church, Dartmouth, NS, 1961–71; St John's, Truro, NS, 1971–76. Canon of All Saints Cathedral, Halifax, 1969; Bishop Suffragan, Dio. NS, 1976. Has served: Dio. Council, NS Synod; Corpn of Anglican Dio. Centre; Dean and Chapter, All Saints Cathedral; Bd of Governors, King's Coll.; Program Cttee and Unit of Public Social Responsibility, Gen. Synod; Council of Churches on Justice and Corrections; Anglican Cons. Council, and various cttees of WCC; Organizing Sec., Primate's World Relief and Develt Fund; founding mem., Vanier Inst. of the Family, Ottawa; convened Primate's Task Force on Ordination of Women to the Priesthood; rep. Anglican Church of Canada at Internat. Bishops' Seminar, Anglican Centre in Rome, 1980. Hon. DD: Univ. of King's Coll., Halifax, NS, 1956; Atlantic Sch. of Theology, 1985. *Publication:* He Cares, 1958. *Recreations:* fishing, gardening, travelling, and playing bridge. *Address:* Port Greville, Site 31, Box 1, RR#3, Parrsboro, Nova Scotia B0M 1S0, Canada.

HATFIELD, Hon. Richard Bennett; PC (Can.) 1982; Premier of New Brunswick since 1970; MLA (Progressive C) Carleton County since 1961, New Brunswick; *b* 9 April 1931; single. *Educ:* Rothesay Collegiate Sch.; Hartland High Sch.; Acadia Univ.; Dalhousie Univ. BA Acadia 1952; LLB Dalhousie 1956. Admitted to Bar of NS, 1956. Joined law firm of Patterson, Smith, Matthews & Grant in Truro, NS, 1956; Exec. Asst to Minister of Trade and Commerce, Ottawa, 1957–58; Sales Man., Hatfield Industries Ltd, 1958–65. Leader, PC Party of New Brunswick, 1969. Mem. Bd Dirs, Canadian Council of Christians and Jews. Hon. LLD: Moncton, 1971; New Brunswick, 1972; St Thomas, 1973; Mount Allison, 1975; Hon. Dr Pol. Sci. Université Sainte-Anne, NS, 1983. Hon. Chief, Micmac and Maliseet Tribes, 1970. Canada-Israel Friendship Award, 1973; Aboriginal Order of Canada, 1985. *Address:* Office of the Premier, PO Box 6000, Fredericton, New Brunswick E3B 5H1, Canada. *T:* (506) 453–2144.

HATFULL, Alan Frederick; Counsellor (Labour), Bonn, since 1981; *b* 12 June 1927; *s* of Frederick George Hatfull and Florence May Hatfull (*née* Dickinson); *m* 1951, Terttu Kaarina Wahlroos; one *s* one *d. Educ:* St Olave's and St Saviour's Grammar School; London School of Economics. BSc (Econ) 1951. Assistant Principal, Min. of Labour, 1951, Principal 1957, Assistant Sec., 1965; Director, Commn on Industrial Relations, 1970–73; Counsellor (Labour), Paris, 1977–81. *Address:* c/o British Embassy, Bonn, BFPO 19.

HATHERTON, 8th Baron *cr* 1835; **Edward Charles Littleton;** *b* 24 May 1950; *s* of Mervyn Cecil Littleton (*d* 1970) (*g s* of 3rd Baron) and of Margaret Ann, *d* of Frank Sheehy; *S* cousin, 1985; *m* 1974, Hilda Maria, *d* of Rodolfo Robert; one *s* two *d. Heir: s* Hon. Thomas Edward Littleton, *b* 1977. *Address:* PO Box 3358, San José, Costa Rica.

HATTERSLEY, Edith Mary, (Molly Hattersley); Assistant Education Officer, Inner London Education Authority, since 1983; *b* 5 Feb. 1931; *d* of Michael and Sally Loughran; *m* 1956, Rt Hon. Roy Sydney George Hattersley, *qv. Educ:* Consett Grammar Sch.; University College of Hull. BA Hons English (London), CertEd (Hull). Assistant Mistress at schools in Surrey and Yorkshire, 1953–61; Sen. Mistress, Myers Grove Sch., Sheffield, 1961–64; Dep. Headmistress, Kidbrooke Sch., SE3, 1965–69; Headmistress, Hurlingham Sch., SW6, 1969–74; Headmistress, Creighton Sch., N10, 1974–82. Advr on educnl matters to Trustees of BM, 1978–. Chairman of Cttee, Assoc. of Head Mistresses, 1975–77; Pres., Secondary Heads Assoc., 1980–81. Mem. Ct of Governors, LSE, 1970–. FRSA 1982. *Recreation:* reading. *Address:* 14 Gayfere Street, SW1P 3HP.

HATTERSLEY, Rt. Hon. Roy Sydney George, PC 1975; BSc (Econ.); MP (Lab) Sparkbrook Division of Birmingham since 1964; Deputy Leader of the Labour Party, since 1983; *b* 28 Dec. 1932; *s* of Frederick Roy Hattersley, Sheffield; *m* 1956, Molly Hattersley, *qv. Educ:* Sheffield City Grammar Sch.; Univ. of Hull. Journalist and Health Service Executive, 1956–64; Mem. Sheffield City Council, 1957–65 (Chm. Housing Cttee and Public Works Cttee). PPS to Minister of Pensions and National Insurance, 1964–67; Jt Parly Sec., DEP (formerly Min. of Labour), 1967–69; Minister of Defence for Administration, 1969–70; Labour Party spokesman: on Defence, 1972; on Educn and Sci., 1972–74; Minister of State, FCO, 1974–76; Sec. of State for Prices and Consumer Protection, 1976–79; principal opposition spokesman on environment, 1979–80, on home affairs, 1980–83, on Treasury and economic affairs, 1983–. Visiting Fellow: Inst. of Politics, Univ. of Harvard, 1971, 1972; Nuffield Coll., Oxford, 1984–. Dir, Campaign for a European Political Community 1966–67. Columnist: Punch; The Guardian; The Listener, 1979–82; Columnist of the Year, Granada, 1982. *Publications:* Nelson, 1974; Goodbye to Yorkshire (essays), 1976; Politics Apart, 1982; Press Gang, 1983; A Yorkshire Boyhood, 1983. *Address:* House of Commons, SW1. *Club:* Reform.

HATTO, Prof. Arthur Thomas, MA; Head of the Department of German, Queen Mary College, University of London, 1938–77; *b* 11 Feb. 1910; *s* of Thomas Hatto, LLB and Alice Walters; *m* 1935, Margot Feibelmann; one *d. Educ:* Dulwich Coll.; King's Coll., London (Fellow, 1971); University Coll., London. BA (London) 1931; MA (with Distinction), 1934. Lektor für Englisch, University of Berne, 1932–34; Asst Lectr in German, KCL, 1934–38; Queen Mary Coll., University of London, 1938 (Head of Dept of German). Temp. Sen. Asst, Foreign Office, 1939–45; Part-time Lectr in German, University Coll., London, 1944–45; returned to Queen Mary Coll., 1945; Reader in German Language and Literature, 1946, Prof. of German Language and Literature, 1953, University of London. Governor: SOAS, Univ. of London, 1960 (Foundn Day Lecture, 1970; Hon. Fellow, 1981); QMC, Univ. of London, 1968–70. Chairman: London Seminar on Epic; Cttee 'A' (Theol. and Arts), Central Research Fund, Univ. of London, 1969. Fellow: Royal Anthropological Institute; Royal Asiatic Society (lecture: Plot and character in Kirghiz epic poetry of the mid 19th cent., 1976); Leverhulme Emeritus Fellow (heroic poetry in Central Asia and Siberia), 1977–. Corresp. Mem., Finno-Ugrian Soc., 1978; Invited Mem., Rundgespräch, Seminar für Sprach-und Kulturwissenschaft Zentralasiens, Univ. of Bonn, 1978, 1979, 1980, 1983, 1985, Associate Mem., 1984. *Publications:* (with R. J. Taylor) The Songs of Neidhart von Reuental, 1958; Gottfried von Strassburg, Tristan (trans. entire for first time) with Tristran of Thomas (newly trans.) with an Introduction, 1960; The Niblungenlied: a new translation, with Introduction and Notes, 1964; editor of Eos, an enquiry by fifty scholars into the theme of the alba in world literature, 1965; (ed for first time with translation and commentary) The Memorial Feast for Kökötöy-khan: a Kirghiz epic poem, 1977; Essays on Medieval German and Other Poetry, 1980; Parzival, Wolfram von Eschenbach, a new translation, 1980; gen. editor, Traditions of Heroic and Epic Poetry, vol. I, 1980; articles in learned periodicals. *Recreations:* reading, gardening, walking.

HATTON; *see* Finch Hatton, family name of Earl of Winchilsea.

HATTON, Thomas Fielding; His Honour Judge Hatton; a Circuit Judge, since 1984; *b* 13 Jan. 1931; *s* of late Dr John Hatton, MD, DPH, and Margaret Louise Hatton, RRC (*née* Dixon); *m* 1959, Elizabeth Mary, *d* of late William Edwin Metcalfe and Kathleen Elizabeth Mary Metcalfe, Clifton, York; one *s* three *d. Educ:* Epsom College; Worcester College, Oxford (MA). Nat. Service, RA; commissioned 1950, served RA TA (Captain). Called to the Bar, Middle Temple, 1956 (Garraway Rice Prize; Harmsworth Scholar); in practice, Northern Circuit, 1956–84. Mem., County Court Rules Cttee, 1978–82. *Recreations:* reading, walking. *Address:* Warren Cottage, Stanley Road, Hoylake, Wirral. *T:* 051–632 4048; Hilltop, High Road, Chigwell, Essex. *Club:* Royal Liverpool Golf.

HATTY, Hon. Sir Cyril (James), Kt 1963; Minister of Finance, Bophuthatswana, 1979–82; *b* 22 Dec. 1908; *o s* of James Hatty and Edith (*née* Russen); *m* 1937, Doris Evelyn, *o d* of James Lane Stewart and Mable Grace Stewart; two *s. Educ:* Westminster City Sch. Deputy Dir, O and M Division, UK Treasury, until Jan. 1947; emigrated to S Africa, in industry, Feb. 1947; moved to Bulawayo, in industry, Jan. 1948. MP for Bulawayo North, Sept. 1950–Dec. 1962; Minister of Treasury, Jan. 1954–Sept. 1962, also Minister of Mines, Feb. 1956–Dec. 1962. FCIS; Fellow, Inst. of Cost and Management Accountants; FBIM. *Publication:* Digest of SR Company Law, 1952. *Recreations:* painting, music. *Address:* Merton Park, Norton, Zimbabwe. *Clubs:* Harare, New (Harare, Zimbabwe).

HAUGHEY, Charles James, Teachta Dala (TD) (FF) for Dublin North Central; Leader of the Opposition, Ireland, since 1982; *b* 16 Sept. 1925; *s* of John Haughey and Sarah Ann (*née* McWilliams); *m* 1951, Maureen Lemass; three *s* one *d. Educ:* Scoil Mhuire, Marino, Dublin; St Joseph's Christian Brothers' Sch., Fairview, Dublin; University College Dublin (BCom); King's Inns, Dublin. Called to Irish Bar, 1949. Member, Dublin Corporation,

1953–55; Member (FF) Dail Eireann for a Dublin constituency, 1957–, now representing Dublin North Central; Parliamentary Secretary to Minister for Justice, 1960–61; Minister: for Justice, 1961–64; for Agriculture, 1964–66; for Finance, 1966–70; Chairman, Jt Cttee on the Secondary Legislation of the European Communities, 1973–77; Minister for Health and Social Welfare, 1977–79; Taoiseach (Prime Minister of Ireland), 1979–81 and Feb.-Dec. 1982. President, Fianna Fail Party, 1979–. Hon. Fellow, RHA. *Recreations:* music, sailing, riding, swimming. *Address:* Abbeville, Kinsaley, Co. Dublin, Ireland. *T:* (01) 450111. *Clubs:* St Stephen's Green, Ward Union Hunt (Dublin).

HAUGHTON, Daniel Jeremiah; *b* Dora, Walker County, Ala, 7 Sept. 1911; *s* of Gayle Haughton and Mattie Haughton (*née* Davis); *m* 1935, Martha Jean, *d* of Henry Oliver, Kewanee, Ill, a farmer; no *c. Educ:* Univ. of Alabama. BS degree in commerce and business administration, 1933. Lockheed Aircraft Corp., 1939–76: first as systems analyst; Works Manager, Vega Aircraft Corp. (a subsidiary), 1943; General Manager, Lockheed-Georgia Co. (a div.), 1952–56; elected: a Lockheed Vice-Pres., 1952, Exec. Vice-Pres., 1956; a Dir, 1958; Pres. of Corp., 1961; Chm. of Bd, 1967–76. Member of many professional societies; active in community and national affairs, including, 1967, Chm. of US Treasury Dept's industrial payroll savings bonds campaign. Chm., Nat. Multiple Sclerosis Soc.; Bd of Trustees, Nat. Security Industrial Assoc. Employer of the Year, Nat. Ind. Recreation Assoc., 1973; Management Man of the Year, Nat. Managing Assoc., 1966; Award of Achievement, Nat. Aviation Club, 1969; 16th Annual Nat. Transportation Award, Nat. Defense Transportation Assoc.; Tony Jannus Award, 1970; Salesman of the Year, Sales and Marketing Assoc., Los Angeles, 1970. Hon. LLD: Univ. of Alabama, 1962; George Washington Univ., 1965; Hon. DSc (Business Admin) Clarkson Coll. of Tech., 1973; Hon. LLD Pepperdine Univ., 1975. *Recreation:* fishing. *Address:* 1890 Battlefield Road SW, Marietta, Ga 30064, USA. *T:* (404) 422 9957. *Club:* Capital City (Atlanta).

HAUGHTON, Surgeon Rear-Adm. John Marsden, LVO 1964; FFARCS; retired, 1982; *b* 27 Oct. 1924; *s* of Col Samuel George Steele Haughton, CIE, OBE, IMS, and Marjory Winifred Haughton (*née* Porter); *m* 1956, Lucy Elizabeth Lee, Tackley, Oxon; three *s* one *d. Educ:* Winchester Coll.; St Thomas' Hosp., 1942–48 (MRCS, LRCP, DA). Joined Royal Navy, 1949; 45 Commando RM, Malaya, 1950; Anaesthetic Specialist, RN Hosp., Plymouth, 1952; HMS Superb, 1954; RN Hosps, Haslar, 1956, Chatham, 1958; Sen. Anaesthetist, RN Hosp., Malta, 1959; PMO, Royal Yacht Britannia, 1962; Consultant Anaesthetist, RN Hospital: Haslar, 1964; Malta, 1968; Haslar, 1970; Comd MO and MO in charge RN Hosp., Malta, 1975; MO in charge RN Hosp., Plymouth, 1978; Surg. Rear-Adm. (Naval Hosps), Haslar, 1980–82. QHP 1978–82. *Recreations:* fishing, gardening, walking. *Address:* Footaway, Chagford, Devon TQ13 8JF.

HAUSER, Frank Ivor, CBE 1968; free-lance director; *b* 1 Aug. 1922; *s* of late Abraham and of Sarah Hauser; unmarried. *Educ:* Cardiff High Sch.; Christ Church, Oxford. Oxford, 1941–42; RA, 1942–45; Oxford, 1946–48. BBC Drama Producer, 1948–51; Director: Salisbury Arts Theatre, 1952–53; Midland Theatre Co., 1945–55. Formed Meadow Players Ltd, which re-opened the Oxford Playhouse, 1956, Dir of Productions, 1956–73; took Oxford Playhouse Co. on tour of India, Pakistan and Ceylon, 1959–60. Produced at Sadler's Wells Opera: La Traviata, 1961; Iolanthe, 1962; Orfeo, 1965; produced: at Oxford Playhouse: Antony and Cleopatra, 1965; Phèdre, 1966; The Promise, 1966; The Silent Woman, 1968; Pippa Passes, 1968; Uncle Vanya, 1969; Curtain Up, 1969; The Merchant of Venice, 1973; also: Il Matrimonio Segreto, Glyndebourne, 1965; A Heritage and its History, Phoenix, 1965; The Promise, Fortune, 1967; Volpone, Garrick, 1967; The Magic Flute, Sadler's Wells, 1967; Kean, Globe, 1971; The Wolf, Apollo, 1973; Cinderella, Casino, 1974; On Approval, Haymarket, 1975; All for Love, Old Vic, 1977; The Importance of Being Earnest, Old Vic, 1980; Captain Brassbound's Conversion, Haymarket, 1982; An Enemy of the People, NY, 1985. *Recreation:* piano. *Address:* 5 Stirling Mansions, Canfield Gardens, NW6. *T:* 01–624 4690.

HAVARD, John David Jayne, MD; Secretary, British Medical Association, since 1980; *b* 5 May 1924; *s* of Dr Arthur William Havard and Ursula Jayne Vernon Humphrey; *m* 1st, 1950, Margaret Lucy Lumsden Collis (marr. diss. 1982); two *s* one *d*; 2nd, 1982, Audrey Anne Boutwood, FRCOG, *d* of Rear Adm. L. A. Boutwood, CB, OBE. *Educ:* Malvern Coll.; Jesus Coll., Cambridge (MA, MD, LLM); Middlesex Hosp. Med. Sch. Called to the Bar, Middle Temple, 1953. Professorial Med. Unit, Middlesex Hosp., 1950; National Service, RAF, 1950–52; general practice, Lowestoft, 1952–58 (Sec., E Suffolk LMC, 1956–58). British Medical Assoc.: Asst Sec., 1958–64; Under-Sec., 1964–76; Dep. Sec., 1976–79. Short-term Cons., Council of Europe, 1964–67, OECD 1964–69, WHO 1967–, on Road Accident Prevention. Dep. Chm., Staff Side, Gen. Whitley Council for the Health Services, 1975–; Sec., Managerial, Professional and Staffs Liaison Gp, 1978–; Member: various Govt Working Parties on Coroners' Rules, Visual Standards for Driving, Licensing of Professional Drivers, etc. Pres., British Acad. of Forensic Scis, 1984–85. Governor, Malvern Coll., 1984. Gold Medal, Inter-Scandinavian Union for Non-Alcoholic Traffic, 1962. Pres., CUAC, 1945–46; Captain United Hosps AC, 1946–47; London Univ. Record for 100 yards, 1947. *Publications:* Detection of Secret Homicide (Cambridge Studies in Criminology), 1960; Research on Effects of Alcohol and Drugs on Driving Behaviour (OECD), 1968; chapters in textbooks on legal medicine, research advances on alcohol and drugs, etc; many articles in med., legal and sci. periodical lit.; several WHO reports. *Recreations:* Bach Choir, history, English countryside. *Address:* 1 Wilton Square, N1. *T:* 01–359 2802. *Clubs:* United Oxford & Cambridge University; Achilles.

HAVARD-WILLIAMS, Peter; (foundation) Professor and Head of the Department of Library and Information Studies since 1972, and Warden of Royce Hall since 1978, Loughborough University; *b* 1922; *s* of Graham Havard-Williams and Elizabeth (*née* James); *m* 1st, 1964, Rosine (*d* 1973), *d* of late Paul Cousin, Croix de Guerre; two *d*; 2nd, 1976, Eileen Elizabeth, *d* of Oliver Cumming; one *d. Educ:* Bishop Gore Grammar Sch., Swansea; University Coll. of Swansea (Smith's Charity Scholar; MA Wales); Oxford Univ.; PhD Loughborough Univ. FBIM, FRSA, FLAI, FIInfSc, FLA, ANZLA. Sub-Librarian, Univ. of Liverpool, 1951–56; Libr. and Keeper of Hocken Collection, Univ. of Otago, 1956–60; Fellow, Knox Coll., Dunedin, 1958–60; Dep. Libr., Univ. of Leeds, 1960–61; Libr., QUB, 1961–71 (Dir, Sch. of Lib. and Inf. Studies, 1964–70); Dean and Prof., Lib. Sch., Ottawa Univ., 1971–72; Loughborough University: Dean of Educn and Humanities, 1976–79; Project Head, Centre for Library and Information Management, 1979–; Public Orator, 1980–. Library Association: Vice-Pres., 1970–82; Chm. Council, 1970–71 and 1974–75; Chm. Exec. Cttee, 1976–78; Chm., Cons. Cttee on Nat. Library Co-ordination 1978–80; Chm., Bd of Assessors, 1981; Chm., NI Br., 1963 (when first all-Ireland lib. conf. held at Portrush). President: Internat. Colloquium on Univ. Lib. Bldgs, Lausanne, 1971; Internat. Seminar on Children's Lit., Loughborough, 1976; Vice-Pres., Internat. Fedn of Lib. Assocs, 1970–77. Member: Adv. Cttee on Public Lib. Service, NI, 1965; Lib. Adv. Council, 1976–78; Hon. Soc. of Cymmrodorion, 1970–; Ct of Governors, UWIST, 1979–. Lib. bldg consultant, UK and abroad, 1961–; Cons. and Mem. Brit. Delegn, Unesco Inter-govtl Conf. on Nat. Inf. Systems, Paris, 1974; Consultant to Unesco, EEC, Council of Europe, British Council and foreign govts and instns, 1974–. Ext. Examr, London, Sheffield, Strathclyde, NUI, CNAA, Kenyatta Univ. Coll. and Univs of Ibadan, WI, Zambia; Lectr, European Inst. of Inf. Management, 1983–; has lectured in Brazil, China, Finland, France, India, Kenya, Mexico, Poland, Sweden, Morocco, Algiers, Tunisia. Editor, IFLA Communications and Publications, 1971–78; Editorial Consultant, Internat. Library Review, 1969–; Consultant Editor: Library Progress Internat., 1981–; Library Waves, 1986–. Hon. FLA 1986. Hon. Dr Confucian Univ., Seoul, 1982. *Publications:* (ed) Marsden and the New Zealand Mission, 1961; Planning Information Manpower, 1974; Departmental Profile, 1981; Development of Public Services in Sierra Leone, 1984; articles in Jl of Documentation, Libri, Internat. Lib. Rev., Unesco Bull. for Libs, Eng. Studies, Essays in Crit., and Monthly Mus. Record, etc. *Recreations:* collecting Bloomsbury first editions, bears (esp. Winnie the Pooh), music, idling. *Address:* Department of Library and Information Studies, Loughborough University, Loughborough, Leics LE11 3TU. *T:* Loughborough 263171. *Clubs:* Athenæum, Royal Commonwealth Society.

HAVELOCK, Sir Wilfrid (Bowen), Kt 1963; *b* 14 April 1912; *s* of late Rev. E. W. Havelock and Helen (*née* Bowen); *m* 1st, 1938, Mrs M. E. Pershouse (*née* Vincent) (marr. diss. 1967); one *s*; 2nd, 1972, Mrs Patricia Mumford, *widow* of Major Philip S. Mumford. *Educ:* Imperial Service Coll., Windsor, Berks. Elected to Kenya Legislative Council, 1948; Chairman, European Elected Members, 1952; Mem., Kenya Executive Council, 1952; Minister for Local Government, Kenya, 1954; Minister for Agriculture, Kenya, 1962–63. Dep. Chm., Agricl Finance Corp., Kenya, 1964–84; Member: Nat. Irrigation Bd, 1974–79; Hotels and Restaurant Authority, 1975–81. Dir, Bamburi Portland Cement Co., 1974–. Chm., Kenya Assoc. of Hotelkeepers and Caterers, 1974, 1975, 1976. *Address:* PO Box 30181, Nairobi, Kenya. *T:* Nairobi 749806. *Clubs:* Royal Commonwealth Society; Mombasa, Muthaiga Country, Nairobi (Kenya).

HAVELOCK-ALLAN, Sir Anthony James Allan, 4th Bt *cr* 1858; film producer; *b* 28 Feb. 1905; *s* of Allan (2nd *s* of Sir Henry Havelock-Allan, 1st Bt, VC, GCB, MP), and Annie Julia, *d* of Sir William Chaytor, 3rd Bt; *S* brother, 1975; *m* 1st, 1939, Valerie Louise Hobson, *qv* (marr. diss. 1952), *d* of late Comdr Robert Gordon Hobson, RN; two *s*; 2nd, 1979, Maria Theresa Consuela (Sara) Ruiz de Villafranca, *d* of late Don Carlos Ruiz de Villafranca (formerly Ambassador to Chile and to Brazil), and Doña Julia Ruiz de Villafranca y Osuño, Villafranca, prov. Madrid. *Educ:* Charterhouse; Switzerland. Artists and Recording Manager, Brunswick Gramophone Co., London and Vox AG, Berlin, 1924–29; entered films as Casting Dir and Producer's Asst, 1933; produced quota films for Paramount; produced for Pinebrook Ltd and Two Cities Films, 1938–40; Assoc. Producer to Noel Coward, 1941; with David Lean and Ronald Neame, formed Cineguild, 1942; Producer, Assoc. Producer or in charge of production for Cineguild, 1942–47; formed Constellation Films, independent co. producing for Rank Org. and British Lion, 1949; Mem. Cinematographic Films Council and Nat. Film Production Council, 1948–51; Mem. Home Office Cttee on Employment of Children in Entertainment; Chm. British Film Academy, 1952; formed with Lord Brabourne and Major Daniel Angel British Home Entertainment to introduce Pay TV, 1958; Chm. Council of Soc. of Film and Television Arts (now BAFTA), 1962, 1963; Mem. Nat. Film Archive Cttee; a Gov. British Film Inst. and Mem. Institute's Production Cttee, 1958–65; Mem. US Academy of Motion Pictures Arts and Sciences, 1970. Films include: This Man is News, This Man in Paris, Lambeth Walk, Unpublished Story, From the Four Corners (documentary prod and dir), Brief Encounter (shared Academy script nomination), Great Expectations (shared Academy script nomination), Take my Life, Blanche Fury, Shadow of the Eagle, Never Take No for an Answer, Interrupted Journey, Young Lovers (dir Anthony Asquith), Orders to Kill (dir Anthony Asquith), Meet Me Tonight, The Quare Fellow, An Evening with the Royal Ballet (directed two ballets); (for television): National Theatre's Uncle Vanya, Olivier's Othello, Zeffirelli's Romeo and Juliet, David Lean's Ryan's Daughter. *Heir: s* Simon Anthony Henry Havelock-Allan, *b* 6 May 1944. *Address:* c/o Lloyds Bank, Berkeley Square, W1.

HAVERGAL, Henry MacLeod, OBE 1965; MA Oxon, BMus Edinburgh; FRCM; FRSAMD; Hon. RAM; *b* 21 Feb. 1902; *er s* of Rev. Ernest Havergal; *m* 1st, 1926, Hyacinth (*d* 1962), *er d* of Arthur Chitty; two *s*; 2nd, 1964, Nina Davidson, Aberdeen. *Educ:* Choristers Sch., Salisbury; St Edward's Sch. and St John's Coll., Oxford. Dir of Music, Fettes Coll., Edinburgh, 1924–33; Haileybury Coll., 1934–36; Harrow Sch., 1937–45; Master of Music, Winchester Coll., 1946–53; Principal, Royal Scottish Academy of Music (later Royal Scottish Academy of Music and Drama), 1953–69; Dir, Jamaica Sch. of Music, 1973–75. Hon. DMus Edinburgh, 1958; Hon. LLD Glasgow, 1969. *Recreation:* fishing. *Address:* 3 East Claremont Street, Edinburgh EH7 4HT. *T:* 031–556 6525. *Club:* New (Edinburgh).

HAVERS, Rt. Hon. Sir (Robert) Michael (Oldfield), PC 1977; Kt 1972; QC 1964; QC (NI) 1973; MP (C) Wimbledon, since 1970; Attorney General, since 1979; *b* 10 March 1923; 2nd *s* of Sir Cecil Havers, QC, and late Enid Snelling; *m* 1949, Carol Elizabeth, *d* of Stuart Lay, London; two *s. Educ:* Westminster Sch.; Corpus Christi Coll., Cambridge. Lieut RNVR, 1941–46. Called to Bar, Inner Temple, 1948; Master of the Bench, 1971. Recorder: of Dover, 1962–68; of Norwich, 1968–71; a Recorder, 1972; Chm., West Suffolk QS, 1965–71 (Dep. Chairman 1961–65). Chancellor of Dioceses of St Edmundsbury and Ipswich, 1965–73, of Ely, 1969–73. Solicitor-General, 1972–74; Shadow Attorney-General and Legal Adviser to Shadow Cabinet, 1974–79. Chm., Lakenheath Anglo-American Community Relations Cttee, 1966–71; Mem., Privileges Cttee, 1978–. *Publications:* (jtly) The Poisoned Life of Mrs Maybrick, 1977; The Royal Baccarat Scandal, 1977; (jtly) Tragedy in Three Voices: the Rattenbury murder, 1980. *Recreations:* writing, photography, reading. *Address:* 5 King's Bench Walk, Temple, EC4. *T:* 01–353 4713. *Clubs:* Garrick, Pratt's, Beefsteak.

See also Hon. Dame A. E. O. Butler-Sloss.

HAVERY, Richard Orbell, QC 1980; a Recorder of the Crown Court, since 1986 (an Assistant Recorder, 1982–86); *b* 7 Feb. 1934; *s* of Joseph Horton Havery and Constance Eleanor (*née* Orbell). *Educ:* St Paul's; Magdalen Coll., Oxford (MA 1961). Called to the Bar, Middle Temple, 1962. *Publication:* (with D. A. McI. Kemp and M. S. Kemp) The Quantum of Damages: personal injury claims, 3rd edn, 1967. *Recreations:* music, croquet, steam locomotives. *Address:* Gray's Inn Chambers, Gray's Inn, WC1R 5JA. *T:* 01–405 7211. *Clubs:* Garrick, Hurlingham.

HAVILAND, Denis William Garstin Latimer, CB 1957; MA; CBIM; FIIM; FRSA; idc; Director, Organised Office Designs Ltd, since 1972; *b* 15 Aug. 1910; *s* of late William Alexander Haviland and of Edyth Louise Latimer. *Educ:* Rugby Sch., St John's Coll., Cambridge (MA, exam. of AMInstT). LMS Rly, 1934–39. Army, RE (Col), 1940–46. Prin., Control Office for Germany and Austria, 1946; Asst Sec., 1947; transf. FO (GS), 1947; seconded to IDC, 1950; transf. Min. of Supply, 1951; Under Sec., 1953; Dep. Sec., 1959; trans. Min. of Aviation, 1959, Deputy Sec., 1959–64. Chm., Preparatory Commn European Launcher Develt Organisation, 1962–64. Jt Man. Dir and Dep. Chm., 1964, Chm. and Man. Dir, 1965–69, Staveley Industries Ltd; Dir, Short Bros Ltd, 1964–81; Chm., Technology and Innovation Exchange, 1981–82; consultant. Member, Council, BIM, 1967–83 (Vice-Chm., 1973–74; Chm., Professional Standards Cttee, 1975–82). Member: Management Studies Bd, CNAA, 1974–79; Business and Management Cttee and

Academic Cttee, CNAA, 1979–83; Ct, Cranfield Inst. of Technology, 1970–83. Chairman: Confedn of Healing Organisations, 1981–; Holistic Cancer Council, 1984–86. Liveryman, Coachmakers' Co. Verulam Gold Medal, BIM, 1984. *Address:* 113 Hampstead Way, NW11. *T:* 01–455 2638. *Club:* Naval and Military.

HAVILLAND; *see* de Havilland.

HAWAII, Bishop of, (Episcopal Church in the USA); *see* Browning, Rt Rev. E. L.

HAWARDEN, 8th Viscount, *cr* 1791; **Robert Leslie Eustace Maude;** farming his own estate since 1952; *b* 26 March 1926; *s* of 7th Viscount Hawarden and Viscountess Hawarden (*née* Marion Wright) (*d* 1974); *S* father 1958; *m* 1957, Susannah Caroline Hyde Gardner; two *s* one *d*. *Educ:* Winchester; Christ Church, Oxford. Cirencester Agricultural Coll., 1948–50. Served for a short time in the Coldstream Guards and was invalided out, 1945–46. *Recreation:* shooting. *Heir: s* Hon. Robert Connan Wyndham Leslie Maude, *b* 23 May 1961. *Address:* Wingham Court, near Canterbury, Kent. *T:* Canterbury 720222. *Club:* Farmers'.

HAWES, Derrick Gordon H.; *see* Harington Hawes.

HAWKE, family name of **Baron Hawke.**

HAWKE, 10th Baron, *cr* 1776, of Towton; **Julian Stanhope Theodore Hawke;** *b* 19 Oct. 1904; *s* of 8th Baron Hawke and Frances Alice (*d* 1959), *d* of Col J. R. Wilmer, Survey of India; *S* brother, 1985; *m* 1st, 1933, Griselda (marr. diss. 1946; she *d* 1984), *d* of late Capt. Edmund W. Bury; two *d*; 2nd, 1947, Georgette Margaret, *d* of George S. Davidson; one *s* three *d*. *Educ:* Eton; King's College, Cambridge (BA). With Glazebrook Steel & Co. Ltd, 1926–69, Director 1933–69. Served War of 1939–45 with AAF; Wing Comdr, W Africa. A Commissioner of Taxes, Manchester, for about 25 years until 1974 (for some years Head of Manchester Central Section). *Recreations:* golf (½ Blue Cambridge), shooting. *Heir: s* Hon. Edward George Hawke, ARICS, *b* 25 Jan. 1950. *Address:* The Old Mill House, Cuddington, Northwich, Cheshire. *T:* Northwich 882248. *Club:* Royal Liverpool Golf.

HAWKE, Hon. Robert James Lee, AC 1979; MP (Lab) Wills, Melbourne, since 1980; Prime Minister of Australia, since 1983; *b* 9 Dec. 1929; *m* 1956, Hazel Masterson; one *s* two *d*. *Educ:* Univ. of Western Australia (LLB, BA(Econ)); Oxford Univ. (BLitt; Hon. Fellow, University Coll., 1984). Research Officer and Advocate for Aust. Council of Trade Unions, 1958–69. Pres., ACTU, 1970–80. Australian Labor Party: Mem., Nat. Exec., 1971–; Pres., 1973–78; Leader, 1983–. Leader of the Opposition, Feb.-March 1983. Member: Governing Body of Internat. Labour Office, 1972–80; Board, Reserve Bank of Australia, 1973–80; Aust. Population and Immigration Council, 1976–80; Aust. Manufacturing Council, 1977–80. *Recreations:* tennis, cricket, reading. *Address:* Parliament House, Canberra, ACT 2600, Australia.

HAWKEN, Lewis Dudley, CB 1983; a Deputy Chairman of the Board of Customs and Excise, since 1980; *b* 23 Aug. 1931; *s* of Richard and Doris May Evelyn Hawken; *m* 1954, Bridget Mary Gamble; two *s* one *d*. *Educ:* Harrow County Sch. for Boys; Lincoln Coll., Oxford (MA). Comr of Customs and Excise, 1975. *Recreations:* collecting Victorian books, tennis. *Address:* 19 Eastcote Road, Ruislip, Mddx. *T:* Ruislip 32405. *Clubs:* United Oxford & Cambridge University, MCC.

HAWKER, Albert Henry, CMG 1964; OBE 1960; *b* 31 Oct. 1911; *s* of late H. J. Hawker, Cheltenham and late Mrs G. A. Hawker, Exeter; *m* 1944, Margaret Janet Olivia (*d* 1980), *d* of late T. J. C. Acton (ICS) and Mrs M de C. Acton, BEM, Golden Furlong, Brackley, Northants; two *s*. *Educ:* Pate's Sch., Cheltenham. Served War of 1939–45: Bde Major 12th Bde, 1941–43; Staff Coll., Camberley, 1943–44; Lieut-Col Mil. Asst to CGS in India, 1944–46. RARO; Lieut-Col The Gordon Highlanders, 1946–61. Barclays Bank Ltd, Birmingham and Oxford Local Districts, 1929–39. Joined HM Overseas Civil Service, 1946; served in: Palestine, 1946–48; N Rhodesia, 1948–52; Zanzibar, 1952–64 (Development Sec., Admin. Sec., Perm. Sec. in Min. of Finance, Prime Minister's Office, Vice-President's Office and President's Office); retd, 1964. Director: Thomson Regional Newspapers Ltd, 1965–69; The Times Ltd and The Sunday Times Ltd, 1968–69; The Thomson Organization, 1969–76. Gold Cross, Royal Order of George I of Greece, 1948; Brilliant Star of Zanzibar, 1957. *Recreations:* sailing (Cdre, Zanzibar Sailing Club, 1955 and 1961), gardening, photography. *Address:* Bowling Green Farm, Cottered, near Buntingford, Herts. *T:* Cottered 234. *Clubs:* Royal Commonwealth Society, Royal Yachting Association.

HAWKER, Rt. Rev. Dennis Gascoyne; *see* Grantham, Bishop Suffragan of.

HAWKER, Sir (Frank) Cyril, Kt 1958; Chairman: The Chartered Bank, 1973–74; The Standard Bank Ltd, 1962–74; Standard and Chartered Banking Group, 1969–74; The Bank of West Africa, 1965–73; Union Zairoise de Banques, 1969–74; Director: Head Wrightson & Co. Ltd, 1962–79; Davy Corporation Ltd, 1977–79; Deputy-Chairman, Midland and International Banks, 1964–72; Vice President, National Playing Fields Association, since 1976 (Hon. Treasurer and Chairman, Finance Committee, 1958–76); *b* 21 July 1900; *s* of late Frank Charley and Bertha Mary Hawker; *m* 1931, Marjorie Ann, *d* of late Thomas Henry and Amelia Harriett Pearce; three *d*. *Educ:* City of London Sch. Entered service Bank of England, 1920; Dep. Chief Cashier, 1944–48; Chief Accountant, 1948–53; Adviser to Governors, 1953–54; Executive Director, Bank of England, 1954–62. Dep. Chm., Agricultural Mortgage Corporation, 1962–73. High Sheriff of County of London, 1963. President: MCC, 1970–71; Minor Counties Cricket Assoc., 1968–; Amateur Football Alliance; Hon. Vice-Pres., Football Assoc. *Recreation:* cricket. *Address:* Hadlow Lodge, Burgh Hill, Etchingham, E Sussex TN19 7PE. *T:* Hurst Green 341. *Clubs:* Athenæum, MCC (Hon. Life Mem.).

HAWKES, (Charles Francis) Christopher, FBA, FSA; Professor of European Archaeology in the University of Oxford, and Fellow of Keble College, 1946–72, Professor Emeritus, since 1972; Hon. Fellow of Keble College, since 1972; Secretary, Committee of Research Laboratory for Archæology and History of Art, 1955–72; *b* 5 June 1905; *o s* of late Charles Pascoe Hawkes; *m* 1st, 1933, Jacquetta (from whom he obtained a divorce 1953) (*see* Jacquetta Hawkes), *yr d* of late Sir Frederick Gowland Hopkins, OM; one *s*; 2nd, 1959, Sonia Elizabeth, *o d* of late Albert Andrew Chadwick. *Educ:* Winchester Coll. (Scholar); New Coll. Oxford (Scholar). 1st in Classical Hon. Mods 1926, in Final Lit. Hum. 1928; BA 1928; MA 1931; entered British Museum, Dept. of British and Medieval Antiquities, 1928; Asst Keeper 1st Class, 1938; in charge of Prehistoric and Romano-British Antiquities, 1946. Principal in Ministry of Aircraft Production, 1940–45. Retired from British Museum, 1946. I/c Inst. of Archæology, Oxford, 1961–67, 1968–72. FBA, 1948; FSA 1932; Fellow of Royal Archæological Institute, Hon. Sec. 1930–35, and Hon. Editor of Archæological Journal, 1944–50; Pres., Prehistoric Soc., 1950–54; a National Sec. for Great Britain, 1931–48, Mem. of Permanent Council, 1948–71, and Mem. Cttee of Honour, 1971–, International Union of Prehistoric and Protohistoric Sciences; Hon. Sec. of Colchester Excavation Cttee and in joint charge of its excavations, 1930–62; in charge of, or associated with various excavations, 1925–64, on Roman and prehistoric sites, especially for the Hants Field Club, and near Oxford; conducted archæological expedns in N Portugal, 1958–59. Vis. Lectr, Univ. of Manchester, 1947–49; Lectures: Dalrymple, Univ. of Glasgow, 1948; George Grant McCurdy, Harvard Univ., 1953; Davies, Belfast, 1974; Myres Meml, Oxford, 1975; British Acad., and Accad. Naz. Lincei, Rome, 1975; Mortimer Wheeler, 1975; travelled in Europe as Leverhulme Research Fellow, 1955–58, and as Leverhulme Emeritus Fellow, 1972–73; Guest Academician, Budapest, 1971; Guest Prof., Univ. of Munich, 1974; a Visitor, Ashmolean Museum, 1961–67. President: Section H., Brit. Assoc., 1957; Hants Field Club, 1960–63; Member: Council for British Archæology 1944–72 (Pres., 1961–64; Group 9 Convener, 1964–67); Ancient Monuments Board for England, 1954–69. Mem., German Archaeological Inst.; Corresp. Mem., RIA; Swiss Soc. for Prehistory; Patronal Mem., Univ. of Barcelona Inst. of Archaeology and Prehistory. Editor of Inventaria Archæologica for Great Britain, 1954–76. Hon. Dr Rennes, 1971; Hon. DLitt NUI, 1972. Various British Acad. awards, 1963–; Gold Medal, Soc. of Antiquaries, 1981. *Publications:* St Catharine's Hill, Winchester (with J. N. L. Myres and C. G. Stevens), 1931; Archæology in England and Wales, 1914–31 (with T. D. Kendrick), 1932; Winchester College: An Essay in Description and Appreciation, 1933; The Prehistoric Foundations of Europe, 1940, 1974; Prehistoric Britain (with Jacquetta Hawkes), 1943, 1947, 1957; Camulodunum: The Excavations at Colchester, 1930–39 (with M. R. Hull), 1947; (contrib. and ed with Sonia Hawkes) Archaeology into History, vol I, 1973; (contrib. and ed with P. M. Duval) Celtic Art in Ancient Europe, 1976; (ed. and co-author with late M. R. Hull) Corpus of Ancient Brooches in Britain, vol. I, 1986; articles in encyclopædias, collaborative books, congress proceedings, and many archæological journals; received complimentary vol. by British and foreign colleagues, 1971. *Recreations:* archæology, travelling, music. *Address:* Keble College, Oxford; 19 Walton Street, Oxford.

HAWKES, David, MA, DPhil; Research Fellow, All Souls College, Oxford, 1973–83, now Emeritus; *b* 6 July 1923; *s* of Ewart Hawkes and Dorothy May Hawkes (*née* Davis); *m* 1950, Sylvia Jean Perkins; one *s* three *d*. *Educ:* Bancroft's Sch. Open Scholarship in Classics, Christ Church, Oxford, 1941; Chinese Hons Sch., Oxford, 1945–47; Research Student, National Peking Univ., 1948–51. Formerly University Lecturer in Chinese, Oxford; Prof. of Chinese, Oxford Univ., 1959–71. *Publications:* Ch'u Tz'ŭ, Songs of the South, 1959, rev. edn as The Songs of the South: an Ancient Chinese Anthology of Poems by Qu Yuan and Other Poets, 1985; A Little Primer of Tu Fu, 1967; The Story of the Stone, vol. 1, 1973, vol. 2, 1977, vol. 3, 1980.

HAWKES, Jacquetta, OBE 1952; author and archaeologist; *b* 1910; *yr d* of Sir Frederick Gowland Hopkins, OM and Jessie Anne Stephens; *m* 1st, 1933, Christopher Hawkes (*see* Prof. C. F. C. Hawkes) (marr. diss. 1953); one *s*; 2nd, 1953, J. B. Priestley, OM (*d* 1984). *Educ:* Perse Sch.; Newnham Coll., Cambridge. MA. Associate, Newnham Coll., 1951. Research and excavation in Great Britain, Eire, France and Palestine, 1931–40; FSA, 1940. Asst Principal, Post-War Reconstruction Secretariat, 1941–43; Ministry of Education, becoming established Principal and Sec. of UK National Commn for UNESCO, 1943–49; retired from Civil Service to write, 1949. John Danz Vis. Prof., Univ. of Washington, 1971. Vice-Pres. Council for Brit. Archæology, 1949–52; Governor, Brit. Film Inst., 1950–55. Archæological adviser, Festival of Britain, 1949–51. Mem., UNESCO Culture Advisory Cttee, 1966–79. Life Trustee, Shakespeare Birthplace Trust, 1985. Hon. DLitt Warwick, 1986. *Publications:* Archæology of Jersey, 1939; Prehistoric Britain (with Christopher Hawkes), 1944; Early Britain, 1945; Symbols and Speculations (poems), 1948; A Land, 1951 (£100 Kemsley Award); Guide to Prehistoric and Roman Monuments in England and Wales, 1951; Dragon's Mouth, (play) (with J. B. Priestley); Fables, 1953; Man on Earth, 1954; Journey Down a Rainbow (with J. B. Priestley), 1955; Providence Island, 1959; Man and the Sun, 1962; Unesco History of Mankind, Vol. I, Part 1, 1963; The World of the Past, 1963; King of the Two Lands, 1966; The Dawn of the Gods, 1968; The First Great Civilizations, 1973; (ed) Atlas of Ancient Archaeology, 1975; The Atlas of Early Man, 1976; A Quest of Love, 1980; Mortimer Wheeler: Adventurer in Archaeology, 1982; Shell Guide to British Archaeology, 1986; contrib. learned jls and national periodicals. *Recreation:* natural history. *Address:* Kissing Tree House, Alveston, Stratford-on-Avon, Warwicks.

HAWKES, Prof. John Gregory; Mason Professor of Botany, University of Birmingham, 1967–82, now Emeritus; *b* 27 June 1915; *s* of C. W. and G. M. Hawkes; *m* 1941, Ellen Barbara Leather; two *s* two *d*. *Educ:* Univ. of Cambridge. BA, MA, PhD, ScD. Botanist, Potato Res. Station of Commonwealth Agricultural Bureaux, 1939–48, 1951–52; Dir of Potato Research Project, Min. of Ag., Colombia, S America, 1948–51; Lectr and Sen. Lectr in Taxonomic Botany, 1952–61; Prof. of Taxonomic Botany (Personal Chair), 1961–67. *Publications:* The Potatoes of Argentina, Brazil, Paraguay, and Uruguay (with J. P. Hjerting), 1969; A Computer-Mapped Flora (with D. A. Cadbury and R. C. Readett), 1971; (with O. H. Frankel) Crop Genetic Resources for Today and Tomorrow, 1975; Conservation and Agriculture, 1978; (with R. N. Lester and A. D. Skelding) The Biology and Taxonomy of the Solanaceae, 1979; The Diversity of Crop Plants, 1983; contribs to various botanical and plant breeding jls. *Recreations:* walking, gardening, travel, art, archaeology. *Address:* 66 Lordswood Road, Birmingham B17 9BY. *T:* 021–427 2944.

HAWKES, Michael John; Chairman, Kleinwort, Benson Ltd, since 1983; *b* 7 May 1929; *s* of Wilfred Arthur Hawkes and Anne Maria Hawkes; *m* 1st, 1957, Gillian Mary Watts; two *s* two *d*; 2nd, 1973, Elizabeth Anne Gurton. *Educ:* Bedford School; New College, Oxford (Exhibnr; MA); Gray's Inn. Kleinwort Sons & Co. Ltd, 1954; Kleinwort, Benson Ltd: Director, 1967; Vice Chm., 1974; Dep. Chm., 1982; Director, Kleinwort, Benson, Lonsdale Ltd, 1974–; Chairman, Sharps Pixley Ltd, 1971–. *Address:* Brookfield House, Burghfield Common, Berks. *T:* Burghfield Common 2912; 78 Denbigh Street, SW1. *T:* 01–834 5478. *Club:* Leander (Henley on Thames).

HAWKES, Raymond; Deputy Director, Naval Ship Production, 1977–78, retired; *b* 28 April 1920; *s* of Ernest Hawkes; *m* 1951, Joyce Barbara King; one *s* one *d*. *Educ:* RNC Greenwich. 1st cl. Naval Architecture, RCNC; CEng; FRINA. Ship design, Bath, 1942–45 and 1954–56; aircraft carrier research at RAE Farnborough, 1945–49; hydrodynamic research at A.E.W. (Admiralty Experiment Works) Haslar, 1949–54; Principal Admty Overseer, Birkenhead, 1956–58; ship prodn, Bath, 1958–62; Chief Cons. Design, assault ships, survey fleet, small ships and auxiliaries, 1962–69; Senior Officers War Course 1966; Asst Dir Warship Design and Project Man. for Through Deck Cruiser, 1969–72; Dep. Dir, Warship Design, 1972–77. *Recreation:* golf. *Address:* Wood Meadow, Beechwood Road, Combe Down, Bath. *T:* Combe Down 832885.

HAWKESBURY, Viscount; Luke Marmaduke Peter Savile Foljambe; *b* 25 March 1972; *s* and *heir* of 5th Earl of Liverpool, *qv*.

HAWKESWORTH, John Stanley; film and television producer and dramatist; *b* 7 Dec. 1920; *s* of Lt-Gen. Sir John Hawkesworth, KBE, CB, CBE, DSO, and Lady (Helen Jane) Hawkesworth; *m* 1943, Hyacinthe Gregson-Ellis; one *s*. *Educ:* Rugby Sch.; Oxford Univ. (BA war degree). Joined Grenadier Guards, 1940; commnd 1941; demobilised 1946 (Captain). Entered film industry as Designer: The Third Man, The Man Who Never Was, The Prisoner, Father Brown; became Producer/Dramatist, Tiger Bay; TV creations include: Upstairs, Downstairs; The Duchess of Duke Street; Danger UXB; The Flame Trees of Thika; The Tale of Beatrix Potter; By the Sword Divided; Oscar. Many television awards, incl. Peabody Award, Univ. of Georgia, 1977. *Publications:* Upstairs, Downstairs, 1972; In My Lady's Chamber, 1973. *Recreations:* tennis, hunting, gardening. *Address:* Fishponds House, Knossington, Oakham, Rutland LE15 8LX. *T:* Somerby 339; Flat 2, 24 Cottesmore Gardens, W8. *T:* 01–937 4869.

HAWKESWORTH, Thomas Simon Ashwell; QC 1982; a Recorder of the Crown Court, since 1982; *b* 15 Nov. 1943; *s* of Charles Peter Elmhirst Hawkesworth and Felicity Hawkesworth; *m* 1970, Jennifer Lewis; two *s. Educ:* Rugby Sch.; The Queen's Coll., Oxford. MA. Called to the Bar, Gray's Inn, 1967. Asst Recorder, 1980–82. *Recreations:* gardening, amateur dramatics. *Address:* The Lodge, Kirkby Overblow, Harrogate, N Yorks HG3 1HH. *T:* Harrogate 879355.

HAWKEY, Rt. Rev. Ernest Eric; *b* 1 June 1909; *s* of Richard and Beatrice Hawkey; *m* 1943, Patricia Spark. *Educ:* Trinity Grammar Sch., Sydney, NSW. Deacon, 1933; Priest, 1936. Curate: St Alban's, Ultimo, 1933–34; St Paul, Burwood, 1934–40; Priest-in-charge, Kandos, 1940–46, Rector, 1946–47; Aust. Bd of Missions: Actg Organising Sec., 1947–50; Organising Sec., 1950–68; Canon Residentiary, Brisbane, 1962–68; Bishop of Carpentaria, 1968–74. *Recreations:* music, gardening. *Address:* 2/12 Wellington Street, Clayfield, Queensland 4011, Australia. *T:* 262–2108.

HAWKING, Prof. Stephen William, CBE 1982; FRS 1974; Fellow of Gonville and Caius College, Cambridge; Lucasian Professor of Mathematics, Cambridge University, since 1979; *b* 8 Jan. 1942; *s* of Dr F. and Mrs E. I. Hawking; *m* 1965, Jane Wilde; two *s* one *d. Educ:* St Albans Sch.; University Coll., Oxford (BA), Hon. Fellow 1977; Trinity Hall, Cambridge (PhD), Hon. Fellow 1984. Research Fellow, Gonville and Caius Coll., 1965–69; Fellow for distinction in science, 1969–; Mem. Inst. of Theoretical Astronomy, Cambridge, 1968–72; Research Asst, Inst. of Astronomy, Cambridge, 1972–73; Cambridge University: Research Asst, Dept of Applied Maths and Theoretical Physics, 1973–75; Reader in Gravitational Physics, 1975–77, Professor, 1977–79. Fairchild Distinguished Schol., Calif Inst. of Technol., 1974–75. Mem., Pontifical Acad. of Scis, 1986–; Foreign Member: Amer. Acad. of Arts and Scis, 1984; Amer. Philosophical Soc., 1985. Hon. Mem., RAS (Can), 1985. Hon. DSc Oxon, 1978. (Jtly) Eddington Medal, RAS, 1975; Pius XI Gold Medal, Pontifical Acad. of Scis, 1975; Dannie Heinemann Prize for Math. Phys., Amer. Phys. Soc. and Amer. Inst. of Physics, 1976; William Hopkins Prize, Cambridge Philosoph. Soc., 1976; Maxwell Medal, Inst. of Physics, 1976; Hughes Medal, Royal Soc., 1976; Albert Einstein Award, 1978; Albert Einstein Medal, Albert Einstein Soc., Berne, 1979; Franklin Medal, Franklin Inst., USA, 1981; Gold Medal, RAS, 1985. Hon. Degrees: Chicago, 1981; Leicester, New York, Notre Dame, Princeton, 1982. *Publications:* (with G. F. R. Ellis) The Large Scale Structure of Space-Time, 1973; (ed W. W. Israel) General Relativity: an Einstein centenary survey, 1979; (ed with M. Roček) Superspace and Supergravity, 1981; (ed jtly) The Very Early Universe, 1983. *Address:* 5 West Road, Cambridge. *T:* Cambridge 351905.

HAWKINGS, Sir (Francis) Geoffrey, Kt 1978; Chairman: Stone-Platt Industries Ltd, 1974–80 (Director, 1962; Managing Director, 1967); Chloride Group Ltd, 1977–79 (Director, 1975; Deputy Chairman, 1976); Director, Alliance Investment Co., 1976–81; *b* 13 Aug. 1913; *s* of Harry Wilfred Hawkings and Louise Hawkings, Lymington, Hants; *m* 1940, Margaret Mary, *d* of Alexander Wilson, OBE, MD, DL; one *s* one *d. Educ:* Wellington; New Coll., Oxford (MA). Commissioned into Lancashire Fusiliers (TA), 1939; Camberley sc, 1943; Bde Major, Inf. and Air-borne Bdes. Administrative appt, Stewarts & Lloyds Ltd, 1946–49; joined Textile Machinery Makers Ltd, 1950, Dir, 1959, Man. Dir, 1961. Mem., Court of Governors, Manchester Univ., 1964–79; Pres., Engrg Employers' Fedn, 1978–80. *Recreations:* fishing, racing.

HAWKINS, Sir Arthur (Ernest), Kt 1976; BSc (Eng); CEng, FIMechE, FIEE, FInstE; Chairman 1972–77, Member, 1970–77, Central Electricity Generating Board; *b* 10 June 1913; *s* of Rev. H. R. and Louisa Hawkins; *m* 1939, Laura Judith Tallent Draper; one *s* two *d. Educ:* The Grammar Sch., Gt Yarmouth; City of Norwich Technical Coll. Served (prior to nationalisation) with Gt Yarmouth Electricity Dept, Central Electricity Bd and Islington Electricity Dept (Dep. Engr and Gen. Manager); Croydon Dist Manager of SE Elec. Bd, 1948; joined Brit. Electricity Authority as Chief Asst Engr in System Operation Br., 1951; Personal Engrg Asst to Chief Engr, 1954. With the CEGB since its formation in 1957, at first as System Planning Engr and then as Chief Ops Engr, 1959–64; Midlands Regional Dir, 1964–70. Mem., Nuclear Power Adv. Bd, 1973–. Chm., F International Ltd, 1978–79. CBIM. *Publications:* contrib. Jl of Management Studies; various papers to technical instns. *Recreations:* fell walking, swimming, motoring. *Address:* 61 Rowan Road, W6. *Club:* Royal Automobile.

HAWKINS, Catherine Eileen; Regional General Manager, South Western Regional Health Authority, since 1984; *b* 16 Jan. 1939; *d* of Stanley Richard Hawkins and Mary-Kate Hawkins. *Educ:* La Retraite High Sch., Clifton. SRN, CMB (Pt 1), HVCert, DN London, Queen's Inst. of Nursing Cert, IRCert. General nursing, student, 1956–60; Staff Nursing, Charing Cross Hosp., SRN, 1960–61; Pt 1 midwifery, St Thomas' Hosp., 1961; Health Visitor Student, LCC, RCN, 1961–62; LCC Health Visitor, 1962–63; Bristol CC HV, 1963–64; Project Leader, Bahrain Public Health Service, 1964–66; Field Work Teacher, HV, 1966–68; Health Centre Administrator, 1968–71; Administrator, Res. Div., Health Educn Council, 1971–72; Sen. Nursing Officer, Community Services, 1972–74; Area Nurse Service Capital Planning, Avon AHA, 1974–79; Dist Nursing Officer, Bristol and Weston DHA, 1979–82; Chief Nursing Officer, Southmead DHA, 1982–84; Regional Nursing Officer, SW RHA, 1984. *Recreations:* travel, badminton, 2½ acre smallholding: ducks, chickens, geese, goats, horses, orchard, vegetables. *Address:* Greenfield Farm, Severn Road, Northwick, Pilning, Avon BS12 3HW.

HAWKINS, Christopher James; MP (C) High Peak, since 1983; *b* 26 Nov. 1937; *s* of Alec Desmond Hawkins and Christina Barbara; *m* Susan Ann Hawkins; two *d. Educ:* Bristol Grammar Sch.; Bristol Univ. BA (Hons) Economics. Joined Courtaulds Ltd, Head Office Economics Dept, 1959; seconded to UK aid financed industrial and economic survey of Northern Nigeria, 1960; similar mission to Tunisia to work on 5 year plan, 1961; Research Div. Economist, Courtaulds Ltd, 1961–66, Building Develt Manager, 1965–66; Lectr in Economics, 1966, Sen. Lectr, 1973–83, Univ. of Southampton. *Publications:* Capital Investment Appraisal, 1971; Theory of the Firm, 1973; The British Economy: what will our children think?, 1982; Britain's Economic Future: an immediate programme for revival, 1983; articles in Jl of Industrial Economics, Amer. Economic Review. *Recreations:* reading, music, sailing. *Address:* House of Commons, SW1A 0AA.

HAWKINS, Desmond, OBE 1963; BBC Controller, South and West, 1967–69; *b* 1908; *m* Barbara Hawkins (*née* Skidmore); two *s* two *d.* Novelist, critic and broadcaster, 1935–45; Literary Editor of New English Weekly and Purpose Quarterly; Fiction Chronicler of The Criterion; Features Producer, BBC West Region, 1946; Head of Programmes, 1955; founded BBC Natural History Unit, 1957. FRSL 1977. Hon. LLD Bristol, 1974. Silver Medal, RSPB, 1959; Imperial Tobacco Radio Award for best dramatisation, 1976 and 1978. *Publications:* Poetry and Prose of John Donne, 1938; Hawk among the Sparrows, 1939; Stories, Essays and Poems of D. H. Lawrence, 1939; Lighter than Day, 1940; War Report, 1946 rev. edn (as BBC War Report), 1985; Sedgemoor and Avalon, 1954; The BBC Naturalist, 1957; Hardy the Novelist, 1965; Wild Life in the New Forest, 1972; Avalon and Sedgemoor, 1973; Hardy, Novelist and Poet, 1976; preface to Richard Jefferies' Wild Life in a Southern County, 1978; Cranborne Chase, 1980; Concerning Agnes, 1982; Hardy's Wessex, 1983; (ed and introd) Wake Smart's Chronicle of Cranborne, 1983; The Tess Opera, 1984. *Address:* 2 Stanton Close, Blandford Forum, Dorset DT11 7RT. *T:* Blandford 54954. *Club:* BBC.

HAWKINS, Air Vice-Marshal Desmond Ernest, CB 1971; CBE 1967; DFC and Bar, 1942; *b* 27 Dec. 1919; *s* of Ernest and Lilian Hawkins; *m* 1947, Joan Audrey (*née* Munro); one *s,* and one step *s. Educ:* Bancroft Sch. Commissioned in RAF, 1938. Served War of 1939–45: Coastal Command and Far East, commanding 36, 230 and 240 Sqdns, 1940–46 (despatches). Commanded RAF Pembroke Dock, 1946–47 (despatches). Staff appts, 1947–50; RAF Staff Coll., 1950; Staff appts, 1951–55; commanded 38 Sqdn, OC Flg, RAF Luqa, 1955–57; jssc, 1957; Staff appts, 1958–61; SASO 19 Gp, 1961–63; commanded RAF Tengah, 1963–66; idc 1967; commanded RAF Lyneham, 1968; SASO, HQ, RAF Strike Command, 1969–71; Dir-Gen., Personal Services (RAF), MoD, 1971–74; Dep. Man. Dir, Services Kinema Corp., 1974–80. *Recreations:* sailing, fishing. *Address:* c/o Barclays Bank, Lymington, Hants. *Clubs:* Royal Air Force; Cruising Association; Royal Lymington Yacht.

HAWKINS, Prof. Eric William, CBE 1973; Director, Language Teaching Centre, University of York, 1965–79, now Professor Emeritus; *b* 8 Jan. 1915; *s* of James Edward Hawkins and Agnes Thompson (*née* Clarie); *m* 1938, Ellen Marie Thygesen, Copenhagen; one *s* one *d. Educ:* Liverpool Inst. High Sch.; Trinity Hall, Cambridge (Open Exhibn). MA, CertEd, (Hon.) FIL. War Service, 1st Bn The Loyal Regt, 1940–46 (despatches 1945); wounded N Africa, 1943; Major 1945. Asst Master, Liverpool Coll., 1946–49; Headmaster: Oldershaw Grammar Sch., Wallasey, 1949–53; Calday Grange Grammar Sch., Ches, 1953–65. Member: Central Adv. Council for Educn (England) (Plowden Cttee), 1963–66; Rampton Cttee (educn of ethnic minorities), 1979–81. Hon. Professorial Fellow, University Coll. of Wales, Aberystwyth, 1979–. Gold Medal, Inst. Linguists, 1971. Comdr, Ordre des Palmes Académiques (France), 1986. *Publications:* (ed) Modern Languages in the Grammar School, 1961; (ed) New Patterns in Sixth Form Modern Language Studies, 1970; A Time for Growing, 1971; Le français pour tout le monde, vols 1–5, 1974–79; Modern Languages in the Curriculum, 1981; Awareness of Language: an Introduction, 1984. *Recreations:* walking, cello. *Address:* 9 Tower View, Tranby Lane, Anlaby, Hull HU10 7EG. *Club:* Royal Commonwealth Society.

See also M. R. Jackson.

HAWKINS, Frank Ernest; Chairman, 1959–73, and Managing Director, 1956–73, International Stores Ltd, Mitre Square, EC3; *b* 12 Aug. 1904; 2nd *s* of late George William and Sophie Hawkins; *m* 1933, Muriel, *d* of late Joseph and Isabella Sinclair; two *s* one *d. Educ:* Leyton County High Sch. Joined staff of International Stores Ltd as boy clerk, 1919; apptd: Asst Sec., 1934; Sec., 1935; Director, 1949; Managing Dir, 1956; Vice-Chm., 1958; Chairman, 1959. *Recreation:* golf. *Address:* Flat 7, The Croft, Page's Croft, Wokingham, Berks RG11 2HN. *Club:* East Berkshire Golf.

HAWKINS, Sir Humphry (Villiers) Cæsar, 7th Bt, *cr* 1778; MB, ChB; Medical Practitioner; *b* 10 Aug. 1923; *s* of Sir Villiers Geoffry Caesar Hawkins, 6th Bt and Blanche Hawkins, *d* of A. E. Hampden-Smithers; *S* father 1955; *m* 1952, Anita, *d* of C. H. Funkey, Johannesburg; two *s* three *d. Educ:* Hilton Coll.; University of Witwatersrand. Served War of 1939–45 with 6th SA Armoured Div. *Heir: s* Howard Cæsar Hawkins, *b* 17 Nov. 1956. *Address:* 41 Hume Road, Dunkeld, Johannesburg, S Africa. *Club:* Johannesburg Country.

HAWKINS, Sir Paul (Lancelot), Kt 1982; TD 1945; MP (C) South West Norfolk since 1964; *b* 7 Aug. 1912; *s* of L. G. Hawkins and of Mrs Hawkins (*née* Peile); *m* 1st, 1937, E. Joan Snow (*d* 1984); two *s* one *d*; 2nd, 1985, Tina Daniels. *Educ:* Cheltenham Coll. Joined Family Firm, 1930; Chartered Surveyor, 1933. Served in TA, Royal Norfolk Regt, 1933–45; POW Germany, 1940–45. An Asst Govt Whip, 1970–71; a Lord Comr of the Treasury, 1971–73; Vice-Chamberlain of HM Household, 1973–74. Mem., H of C (Services) Select Cttee, 1976–. Mem., Delegn to Council of Europe and WEU, 1976–. CC Norfolk, 1949–70, Alderman, 1968–70. *Recreations:* walking, gardening, travel. *Address:* Stables, Downham Market, Norfolk. *Club:* Carlton.

HAWKINS, Rt. Rev. Ralph Gordon, CMG 1977; ThD; *b* St John's, Newfoundland, 1911; *s* of late Samuel J. and Alfreda Hawkins; *m* 1938, Mary Edna, *d* of late William James and Grace Leslie, Newport, Mon.; one *s* one *d. Educ:* Univ. Memorial Coll., St John's; St Boniface Coll., Warminster; Durham Univ. (Hatfield Coll.). BA, LTh 1934; deacon, 1935, priest, 1936, Bristol. Curate of St Anne's, Brislington, 1935–38; Rector of Morawa, 1938–43; Rector of Wembley-Floreat Park, 1943–49; Chaplain, RAAF, 1943–45; Rector of St Hilda's, N Perth, 1949–56; Canon of Perth, 1954; Archdeacon of Perth, 1957; Bishop of Bunbury, 1957–77. *Address:* 9 Cross Street, Bunbury, WA 6230, Australia.

HAWKINS, Vice-Adm. Sir Raymond (Shayle), KCB 1965 (CB 1963); *b* 21 Dec. 1909; *s* of late Thomas Hawkins and Dorothy Hawkins, Bedford; *m* 1936, Rosalind (marr. diss. 1980), *d* of late Roger and Ada Ingpen; three *s* one *d. Educ:* Bedford Sch. Entered Royal Navy, 1927; HMS Iron Duke 1932; HMS Resolution, 1933; served with Submarines, 1935–43; HMS Orion, 1943. Asst Naval Attaché, Paris, 1954; Commanding Officer, HMS St Vincent, 1957; Rear-Adm., Nuclear Propulsion, 1959; Dir of Marine Engineering, 1961–63; Chief Naval Engineering Officer, 1962–63; Vice-Adm., 1964; a Lord Comr of the Admiralty, Fourth Sea Lord and Vice-Controller, 1963–64; Chief of Naval Supplies and Transport and Vice-Controller of the Navy, MoD, 1964–67; retd, 1967. *Address:* The Old Garden, All Saints Road, Lansdown, Bath, Avon.

HAWKINS, Richard Graeme; QC 1984; a Recorder, since 1985; *b* 23 Feb 1941; *s* of Denis William Hawkins and of late Norah Mary (*née* Beckingsale); *m* 1969, Anne Elizabeth, *d* of Dr and Mrs Glyn Edwards, The Boltons, Bournemouth; one *s* one *d. Educ:* Hendon County Sch.; University College London (LLB Hons 1962). Called to the Bar, Gray's Inn, 1963. Mem., Hon. Soc. of Gray's Inn, 1959–. *Recreation:* sailing. *Address:* 3 Temple Gardens, EC4Y 9AU. *T:* 01–353 3533.

HAWKINS, Ven. Richard Stephen; Archdeacon of Totnes, since 1981; Priest-in-charge of Whitestone with Oldridge, since 1981; *b* 2 April 1939; *s* of late Ven. Canon John Stanley Hawkins and of Elsie Hawkins (*née* Briggs); *m* 1966, Valerie Ann Herneman; one *s* one *d* (and one *s* one *d* decd). *Educ:* Exeter School; Exeter Coll., Oxford; St Stephen's House, Oxford. MA (Oxon); BPhil (Exeter Univ.); CQSW. Asst Curate, St Thomas, Exeter, 1963–66; Team Vicar of Clyst St Mary, Clyst Valley Team Ministry, 1966–78; Bishop's Officer for Ministry and Joint Director, Exeter-Truro Ministry Training Scheme, 1978–81; Team Vicar, Central Exeter Team Ministry, 1978–81; Diocesan Director of Ordinands, 1979–81. *Address:* The Rectory, Whitestone, Exeter EX4 2JT. *T:* Longdown 406.

HAWKINS, Rev. Robert Henry; *b* 3 March 1892; *s* of Rev. Francis Henry Albert Hawkins and Mary Anna Ridley Hawkins (*née* Morris); *m* 1917, Margaret (*d* 1977), *e d* of Rev. T. A. Lacey, DD, Canon of Worcester; two *s* three *d*. *Educ:* Forest Sch., Essex; St Edmund Hall, Oxford. BA 1913, MA 1919. Served European War: commissioned 3rd S Staffs Regt, 1914; France and Salonika, 1915–17; RFC (Flight Comdr), 1917–19. Ordained Deacon, 1919, Priest, 1920; Vicar of: Maryport, Dio. Carlisle, 1923–27; St George, Barrow in Furness, 1927–34; Dalston, 1934–43; Vicar of St Mary, Nottingham, Rural Dean of Nottingham and Hon. Canon of Southwell, 1943 58; Canon of St George's, Windsor, 1958–70. *Address:* Manormead, Tilford Road, Hindhead, Surrey. *T:* Hindhead 6493.

HAWKSLEY, John Callis, CBE 1946; PhD, MD, FRCP; formerly Physician, University College Hospital and St Peter's, St Paul's and St Philip's Hospitals, London; *b* 30 Nov. 1903; *s* of late Joseph Hawksley, Great Yarmouth; *m* 1933, Margaret (*d* 1985), *er d* of late Engineer Vice-Adm. Sir Reginald Skelton, KCB, CBE, DSO; two *s* two *d*. *Educ:* Dulwich Coll.; University Coll., London; University Coll. Hospital. Appts on resident staff, University Coll. Hosp., 1926–28; ship's surg., BISN Co., 1929; research appts, Birmingham Children's Hosp., 1930–32; Sebag-Montefiore Research Fellow, Hospital for Sick Children, Gt Ormond Street, 1933–34; Bilton Pollard Travelling Fellowship, University Coll. Hosp., 1935, devoted to work at Bispebjerg Hosp., Copenhagen; Asst Physician, University Coll. Hosp., 1936–39; Physician to University Coll. Hosp., 1940; retd, 1969. Temp. commission RAMC 1939; served with rank of Lieut-Col in MEF, 1941–44 (despatches); Consulting Physician, local Brig., with South East Asia Command, 1945. Fellow of University Coll., London, 1946; Dean of University Coll. Hosp. Med. Sch., 1949–54; Senior Vice-Pres., RCP, 1966. *Publications:* contributions to various medical journals. *Recreations:* mountaineering, music. *Address:* The Old Vicarage, East Kennett, Wilts. *T:* Lockeridge 237. *Club:* Alpine.

HAWKSLEY, (Philip) Warren; MP (C) The Wrekin, since 1979; *b* 10 March 1943; *s* of late Bradshaw Warren Hawksley and Monica Augusta Hawksley. *Educ:* Denstone Coll., Uttoxeter. Employed by Lloyd's Bank since leaving school. Member: Salop County Council, 1970–81; West Mercia Police Authority, 1977–81. *Recreations:* badminton, reading, travel, beagling. *Address:* House of Commons, SW1A 0AA.

HAWLEY, Major Sir David Henry, 7th Bt, *cr* 1795; MA; FRICS; DL; late KRRC; formerly with firm of Jas Martin & Co., Chartered Surveyors, Land Agents and Valuers, 8 Bank Street, Lincoln; *b* 13 May 1913; *e s* of Capt. Cyril Francis Hawley and Ursula Mary, *d* of Henry Percy St John; *S* uncle, 1923; *m* 1938, Hermione, 2nd *d* of late Col L. Gregson; one *s* two *d*. *Educ:* Eton; Magdalene Coll., Cambridge. Served Palestine, 1936–39 (medal and clasp), War of 1939–45 (prisoner, 1939–45 Star, despatches). Hon. Life Mem., Nat. Trust. Chm., Lincoln Dio. Adv. Cttee, 1978–81. Vice-Pres., Lincs Branch, CLA. DL 1952, High Sheriff, 1962–63, Lincs. *Recreations:* shooting, letter writing. *Heir:* *s* Henry Nicholas Hawley, *b* 26 Nov. 1939. *Address:* Tumby Lawn, Boston, Lincs PE22 7TA. *T:* Coningsby 42337.

HAWLEY, Sir Donald (Frederick), KCMG 1978 (CMG 1970); MBE 1955; HM Diplomatic Service, retired; British High Commissioner in Malaysia, 1977–81; Barrister-at-law; *b* 22 May 1921; *s* of late Mr and Mrs F. G. Hawley, Little Gaddesden, Herts; *m* 1964, Ruth Morwenna Graham Howes, *d* of late Rev. P. G. Howes and of Mrs Howes, Charmouth, Dorset; one *s* three *d*. *Educ:* Radley; New Coll., Oxford (MA). Served in HM Forces, 1941. Sudan Political Service, 1944; joined Sudan Judiciary, 1947. Called to Bar, Inner Temple, 1951. Chief Registrar, Sudan Judiciary, and Registrar-Gen. of Marriages, 1951; resigned from Sudan Service, 1955; joined HM Foreign Service, 1955; FO, 1956: Political Agent, Trucial States, in Dubai, 1958; Head of Chancery, British Embassy, Cairo, 1962; Counsellor and Head of Chancery, British High Commission, Lagos, 1965; Vis. Fellow, Dept of Geography, Durham Univ., 1967; Counsellor (Commercial), Baghdad, 1968; HM Consul-General, Muscat, 1971; HM Ambassador to Oman, 1971–75; Asst Under Sec. of State, FCO, 1975–77. Special Adviser to Hongkong and Shanghai Banking Corp.; Chm., Ewbank Preece Ltd; consultant. Vice-Pres., Anglo-Omani Soc.; Chm., British Malaysian Soc. Mem. Council, Reading Univ. *Publications:* Handbook for Registrars of Marriage and Ministers of Religion, 1963 (Sudan Govt pubn); Courtesies in the Trucial States, 1965; The Trucial States, 1971; Oman and its Renaissance, 1977; Courtesies in the Gulf Area, 1978; Manners and Correct Form in the Middle East, 1984. *Recreations:* tennis, squash, sailing, book collecting; Hon. Sec., Sudan Football Assoc., 1952–55. *Address:* Little Cheverell House, near Devizes, Wilts. *T:* Lavington 3322. *Clubs:* Athenæum, Travellers', Beefsteak.

HAWORTH, Sir (Arthur) Geoffrey, 2nd Bt, *cr* 1911; MA; farmer; *b* 5 April 1896; *s* of Sir Arthur Haworth, 1st Bt, and Lily (*d* 1952), *y d* of late John Rigby, Altrincham; *S* father, 1944; *m* 1926, Emily Dorothea (*d* 1980), *er d* of H. E. Gaddum, The Priory, Bowdon; two *s* two *d*. *Educ:* Rugby Sch.; New Coll., Oxford. Served European War, 1914–19, Lieut Queen's Own Royal West Kent Regiment and Machine Gun Corps (despatches). Chm., Hallé Concert Soc., 1965–77; Pres., Manchester Palace Theatre Trust Ltd, 1980– (Chm., 1978–80). FRSA 1969. JP Chester, 1937–70. Hon. MA Manchester, 1972. *Recreation:* music. *Heir:* *s* Philip Haworth [*b* 17 Jan. 1927; *m* 1951, Joan Helen, *d* of late S. P. Clark, Ipswich; four *s* one *d*]. *Address:* The Red Brook, Lower Peover, Cheshire. *Club:* Farmers'.

HAWORTH, Mrs Betsy Ellen; Deaconess; Third Church Estates Commissioner, since 1981; *b* 23 July 1924; *d* of Ambrose and Annie Kenyon; *m* 1953, Rev. Fred Haworth (*d* 1981); one *s* two *d*. *Educ:* William Temple Coll. IDC (C of E). Licensed as lay worker, dio. Manchester, 1952, dio. Blackburn, 1965; elected Mem., Church Assembly, 1965–70, Gen. Synod, 1970–75, 1975–80, 1980–85, Ex-officio Mem., 1985–. Advr for Women's Ministry, dio. Manchester, 1971–81. Deaconess 1980. Examining Chaplain to Bishop of Manchester, 1981–. *Address:* 5 The Cottages, Lambeth Palace, SE1 7JU. *T:* 01–928 5407.

HAWORTH, Sir Geoffrey; *see* Haworth, Sir A. G.

HAWORTH, John Liegh W.; *see* Walker-Haworth.

HAWORTH, Very Rev. Kenneth William; Dean of Salisbury, 1960–71, Dean Emeritus, since 1971; *b* 21 Jan. 1903; *s* of William Bell and Helen Haworth; *m* 1937, Sybil Mavrojani (*d* 1982); two *s* two *d*. *Educ:* Cheltenham Coll.; Clare Coll., Cambridge; Wells Theological Coll. Curate of St Giles, Willenhall, 1926; Domestic Chaplain 1931, Examining Chaplain, 1937, to Bp of Lichfield; Chaplain of Wells Theological Coll., 1938; CF (4th cl.), 1939; Rector of Stratton w. Baunton, Dio., Gloucester, 1943; Vice-Principal of Wells Theol. Coll., 1946, Principal, 1947–60; Prebendary of Combe II in Wells Cathedral, 1947–60; Exam. Chap. to Bishop of Bath and Wells, 1947; Proctor in Convocation, 1956–59; Exam. Chap. to Bishop of Salisbury, 1962. *Address:* The Common, Woodgreen, Fordingbridge, Hants. *T:* Downton 22239.

HAWORTH, Lionel, OBE 1958; FRS 1971; RDI; FEng; Senior Partner, Lionel Haworth and Associates; *b* 4 Aug. 1912; *s* of John Bertram Haworth and Anna Sophia Ackerman; *m* 1956, Joan Irene Bradbury; one *s* one *d*. *Educ:* Rondebosch Boys' High Sch.; Univ. of Cape Town. Cape Town Corp's Gold Medal and schol. tenable abroad. BSc (Eng); FIMechE; FRAeS. Graduate Apprentice, Associated Equipment Co., 1934; Rolls-Royce Ltd, Derby: Designer, 1936; Asst Chief Designer, 1944; Dep. Chief Designer, 1951; Chief Designer (Civil Engines), 1954; Chief Engr (Prop. Turbines), 1962; Bristol Siddeley Engines Ltd: Chief Design Consultant, 1963; Chief Designer, 1964; Dir of Design, Aero Div., 1965, Dir of Design, Aero Div., Rolls-Royce Ltd, 1968–77. Brit. Gold Medal for Aeronautics, 1971; RDI 1976; Founder Fellow, Fellowship of Engineering, 1976. *Recreation:* sailing. *Address:* 10 Hazelwood Road, Sneyd Park, Bristol BS9 1PX. *T:* Bristol 683032.

HAWORTH, Robert Downs, DSc, PhD Victoria, BSc Oxon; FRS 1944; FRSC; Firth Professor of Chemistry, University of Sheffield, 1939–63, now Emeritus; *b* 15 March 1898; *s* of J. T. and Emily Haworth, Cheadle, Cheshire; *m* 1930, Dorothy, *d* of A. L. Stocks, Manchester; one *d*. *Educ:* Secondary Sch., Stockport; University of Manchester, Mercer Scholar, 1919; Beyer Fellow, 1920; 1851 Exhibition Scholar, 1921–23; 1851 Exhibition Sen. Student, 1923–25; Demonstrator in Organic Chemistry, Oxford, 1925–26; Lecturer in Chemistry, King's Coll., Newcastle upon Tyne, 1927–39. Visiting Prof. of Organic Chemistry, University of Madras, 1963–64. Davy Medal, Royal Society, 1956. Hon. DSc Sheffield, 1974. *Publications:* papers on organic chemistry in Journal of Chemical Society. *Address:* 11 Cedar Grove, Bexley, Kent DA5 3DB. *T:* 01–303 9829.

HAWSER, Cyril Lewis, QC 1959; **His Honour Judge Hawser;** a Circuit Judge, since 1978; Senior Official Referee, since 1985; *b* 5 Oct. 1916; *s* of Abraham and Sarah Hawser; *m* 1940, Phyllis Greatrex; one *s* one *d*. *Educ:* Cardiff High Sch.; Balliol Coll., Oxford (Williams Law Scholar; MA). Called to the Bar, 1938, Bencher, 1966, Reader, 1985, Inner Temple. Recorder of Salisbury, 1967–69; Recorder of Portsmouth, 1969–71; a Recorder of the Crown Court, 1972–78; Official Referee, 1978. Mem. Council and Vice-Chm. of Exec. Cttee of Justice. *Publication:* (report) Case of James Hanratty, 1975. *Recreations:* tennis, chess, conversation. *Address:* 1 Harcourt Buildings, Middle Temple Lane, EC4. *T:* 01–353 8131.

HAWTHORNE, James Burns, CBE 1982; Controller, BBC Northern Ireland, since 1978; *b* 27 March 1930; *s* of Thomas Hawthorne and Florence Hawthorne (*née* Burns); *m* 1958, Patricia King; one *s* two *d*. *Educ:* Queen's Univ., Belfast (BA); Stranmillis Coll. of Educn. Master at Sullivan Upper Sch., Holywood, 1951–60; joined Educn Dept, BBC, 1960; Schools Producer in charge, N Ireland, 1967; Chief Asst, N Ireland, 1969–70; seconded to Hong Kong Govt, as Controller Television, 1970; Dir of Broadcasting, Hong Kong, 1972–77 (resigned from BBC staff, 1976, *ie* seconded status ended; rejoined BBC, Jan. 1978, on appt as Controller, NI). Mem., NI Council for Educn Develt, 1980–85. JP Hong Kong, 1972–77. Queen's Univ. New Ireland Soc. award for community relations work, 1967; Winston Churchill Fellowship, 1968; Cyril Bennett Award, RTS, 1986. *Publications:* (ed) Two Centuries of Irish History, 1966, repr. 1967, 1969, rev. edn 1974; Reporting Violence: lessons from Northern Ireland, 1981. *Recreations:* angling, music. *Address:* c/o BBC, Belfast, Northern Ireland BT2 8HQ.

HAWTHORNE, Nigel Barnard; self-employed actor and writer; *b* Coventry, 5 April 1929; *s* of Charles Barnard Hawthorne and Agnes Rosemary (*née* Rice). *Educ:* Christian Brothers' Coll., Cape Town, S Africa. Entered theatre professionally, 1950; returned to England, 1951, where he has worked ever since, with the exception of a small number of engagements abroad. *Stage:* Otherwise Engaged, 1976; Privates on Parade, 1978 (Best Supporting Actor, SWET and Clarence Derwent awards); Peer Gynt, and Tartuffe, with RSC, 1983–84 (Tartuffe televised 1985); Across from the Garden of Allah, 1986; Jacobowski and the Colonel, NT, 1986; The Magistrate, NT, 1986; *television:* Marie Curie, 1977; Destiny, 1978; Edward and Mrs Simpson, 1978; The Knowledge, 1979; Rod of Iron, 1980; Yes Minister (series), annually 1980–83, 1985–86 (Broadcasting Press Guild and BAFTA (Best Actor in Light Entertainment) awards, 1982; BAFTA Award, 1983); Yes, Prime Minister (series), 1986; The Critic, 1982; The Barchester Chronicles, 1982; Mapp and Lucia, 1984–86; Jenny's War, 1985; *films:* Firefox, 1981; Gandhi, 1981; Golda, 1981; John Paul II, 1983; The House, 1984; Turtle Diary, 1984; The Chain, 1985. *Recreations:* swimming, gardening, painting.

HAWTHORNE, Prof. Sir William (Rede), Kt 1970; CBE 1959; MA; ScD; FRS 1955; FEng; FIMechE; Master of Churchill College, Cambridge, 1968–83; Hopkinson and ICI Professor of Applied Thermodynamics, University of Cambridge, 1951–80; Head of Department of Engineering, 1968–73; *b* 22 May 1913; *s* of William Hawthorne, MInstCE, and Elizabeth C. Hawthorne; *m* 1939, Barbara Runkle, Cambridge, Massachusetts, USA; one *s* two *d*. *Educ:* Westminster Sch.; Trinity Coll., Cambridge; Massachusetts Institute of Technology, USA. Development Engineer, Babcock & Wilcox Ltd, 1937–39; Scientific Officer, Royal Aircraft Establishment, 1940–44; British Air Commission, Washington, 1944; Dep. Dir Engine Research, Min. of Supply, 1945; Massachusetts Institute of Technology: Associate Prof. of Mechanical Engineering, 1946; George Westinghouse Prof. of Mechanical Engineering, 1948–51; Jerome C. Hunsaker Prof. of Aeronautical Engineering, 1955–56; Vis. Inst. Prof., 1962–63; Mem. Corporation, 1969–74. Chairman: Home Office Scientific Adv. Council, 1967–76; Defence Scientific Adv. Council, 1969–71; Adv. Council for Energy Conservation, 1974–79; Member: Energy Commn, 1977–79; Standing Commn on Energy and the Environment, 1978–81. Director: Dracone Developments Ltd, 1958–; Cummins Engine Co. Inc., 1974–86. Governor, Westminster Sch., 1956–76. A Vice-Pres., Royal Soc., 1969–70 and 1979–81; Mem. Council, 1968–70, 1979–81 (Royal Medal, 1982). Foreign Associate: US Nat. Acad. of Sciences, 1965; US Nat. Acad. of Engrg, 1976. Fellow, Imperial Coll., London Univ., 1983. Hon. FAIAA; Hon. FRAeS; Hon. FRSE 1983. Hon. DEng: Sheffield, 1976; Liverpool 1982; Hon. DSc: Salford, 1980; Strathclyde, 1981; Bath, 1981; Oxon, 1982; Sussex, 1984. Medal of Freedom (US), 1947. *Publications:* papers in mechanical and aeronautical journals. *Address:* Churchill College, Cambridge. *Club:* Athenæum.

See also J. O'Beirne Ranelagh.

HAWTREY, John Havilland Procter, CBE 1958; FICE; *b* 16 Feb. 1905; *e s* of late Edmond Charles Hawtrey and late Helen Mary Hawtrey (*née* Durand); *m* 1947, Kathleen Mary, *d* of late Captain M. T. Daniel, RN, Henley-on-Thames; one *s* one *d*. *Educ:* Eton; City and Guilds Engineering Coll., London (BSc 1927). Asst Engineer, later Dist Engineer, Burma Railways, 1927–47. Served War of 1939–45: with RE, 1940–46; Major 1942, in India and Burma, 1942–46 (despatches). Entered office of Crown Agents for Oversea Govts and Administrations, 1948: Chief Civil Engineer, 1956; Crown Agent and Engineer-in-Chief, 1965; retired, 1969. *Address:* 76 Makins Road, Henley-on-Thames, Oxon RG9 1PR. *T:* Henley-on-Thames 574896.

See also S. C. Hawtrey.

HAWTREY, Stephen Charles, CB 1966; Clerk of the Journals, House of Commons, 1958–72; *b* 8 July 1907; *s* of Edmond C. Hawtrey; *m* 1934, Leila Winifred (*d* 1982), *e d* of late Lieut-Col Wilmot Blomefield, OBE; two *s* one *d*. *Educ:* Eton; Trinity Coll., Cambridge (MA). Asst Clerk, House of Commons, 1930; Senior Clerk, 1944. Temporarily attached: to Min. of Home Security, 1939; to Secretariat of Council of Europe, Strasbourg, France, at various sessions between 1950 and 1964. *Publication:* (With L. A. Abraham) A Parliamentary Dictionary, 1956 and 1964; 3rd edn (with H. M. Barclay), 1970. *Address:*

52 New Street, Henley-on-Thames, Oxon. *T:* Henley 574521. *Clubs:* United Oxford & Cambridge University; Railway.
See also J. H. P. Hawtrey.

HAY, family name of **Earls of Erroll** and **Kinnoull,** and of **Marquis of Tweeddale.**

HAY, Lord; Harry Thomas William Hay; *b* 8 Aug. 1984; *s* and *heir* of Earl of Erroll, *qv.*

HAY, Allan Stuart, PhD; FRS 1981; Research and Development Manager, Chemical Laboratories, General Electric Research & Development Center, Schenectady, New York, since 1980; *b* 23 July 1929; *s* of Stuart Lumsden and Verna Emila Hay; *m* 1956, Janet Mary Keck; two *s* two *d. Educ:* Univ. of Alberta (BSc Hon, MSc); Univ. of Illinois (PhD). Research Associate, General Electric Res. & Develt Center, 1955; Manager, Chemical Laboratory, General Electric, 1968. Adjunct Professor, Polymer Science and Engineering Dept, Univ. of Massachusetts, 1975. Soc. of Plastics Engrs Internat. award in Plastics Science and Engineering, 1975; Achievement award, Industrial Res. Inst., 1984. *Publications:* numerous papers and contribs to learned jls. *Recreations:* philately, reading, swimming. *Address:* 2306 Pine Ridge Road, Schenectady, New York 12309, USA. *T:* 518 393 4087.

HAY, Sir Arthur Thomas Erroll, 10th Bt of Park, *cr* 1663; ISO 1974; DiplArch; ARIBA 1935; retired Civil Servant; *b* 13 April 1909; *o s* of 9th Bt and Lizabel Annie (*d* 1957), *o d* of late Lachlan Mackinnon Macdonald, Skeabost, Isle of Skye; *S* father, 1923; *m* 1st, 1935, Hertha Louise (who was granted a divorce, 1942), *d* of late Herr Ludwig Stölzle, Nagelberg, Austria, and of H. E. Frau Vaugoin, Vienna; one *s*; 2nd, 1942, Rosemarie Evelyn Anne, *d* of late Vice-Adm. Aubrey Lambert and of Mrs Lambert. *Educ:* Fettes Coll., Edinburgh. Student of architecture, University of Liverpool, 1927–31; Diploma in Architecture, Architectural Assoc., July 1934. Served War of 1939–45; 2nd Lieut RE 1943; Lieut 1944; service in Normandy, Belgium, Holland and Germany in 21 Army Group. *Heir: s* John Erroll Audley Hay, *b* 3 Dec. 1935. *Address:* c/o Lloyds Bank, Castle Street, Farnham, Surrey.

HAY, Sir David (Osborne), Kt 1979; CBE 1962; DSO 1945; retired public servant; *b* 29 Nov. 1916; 2nd *s* of late H. A. Hay, Barwon Heads, Victoria; *m* 1944, Alison Marion Parker Adams; two *s. Educ:* Geelong Grammar Sch.; Brasenose Coll., Oxford; Melbourne Univ. Joined Commonwealth Public Service, 1939. Australian Imperial Force, 1940–46: Major, 2nd Sixth Infantry Bn; served in Western Desert, Greece, New Guinea. Rejoined External Affairs Dept, 1947; Imp. Def. Coll., 1954; Minister (later Ambassador) to Thailand, 1955–57; High Comr in Canada, 1961–64; Ambassador to UN, New York, 1964–65; First Asst Secretary, External Affairs, 1966; Administrator of Papua and New Guinea, 1967–70; Sec., Dept of External Territories, Canberra, 1970–73; Defence Force Ombudsman, 1974–76; Sec., Dept of Aboriginal Affairs, 1977–79. *Publications:* The Delivery of Services financed by the Department of Aboriginal Affairs, 1976; Nothing Over Us: the story of the 2nd Sixth Battalion, 1985. *Address:* 10 Hotham Crescent, Deakin, ACT 2600, Australia. *Clubs:* Australian, Melbourne (Melbourne); Commonwealth (Canberra).

HAY, Dr David Russell, CBE 1981; FRCP; FRACP; (first) Medical Director, National Heart Foundation of New Zealand, since 1977; Cardiologist, Canterbury Hospital (formerly North Canterbury Hospital) Board, since 1964; *b* 8 Dec. 1927; twin *s* of Sir James Lawrence Hay, OBE, and Lady (Davidina Mertel) Hay; *m* 1958, Dr Jocelyn Valerie Bell; two *d. Educ:* St Andrew's Coll., Christchurch; Otago Univ. (MB, ChB; MD). FRACP 1965; FRCP 1971. Resident appts, Christchurch, Royal South Hants, Hammersmith, Brompton and National Heart Hosps, 1951–55; Sen. Registrar, Dunedin and Christchurch Hosps, 1956–59; Physician, N Canterbury Hosp. Bd, 1959–64; Head of Dept of Cardiology, 1969–78; Chm. of Medical Services and Hd of Dept of Medicine, 1978–84. Chm., Christchurch Hosps Med. Staff Assoc., 1983–85 (Dep. Chm., 1982–83); Clin. Lectr, Christchurch Clinical Sch., Univ. of Otago, 1973–80; Clin. Reader, 1980–; Foundn Councillor, Nat. Heart Foundn of NZ, 1968–; Mem. Scientific Cttee, 1968–; Sec., 1974–77; Councillor, RACP, 1964–66; Examiner, 1974–75; Censor, 1975–79; Mem. Specialist Adv. Cttee on Cardiology, 1980–; Chm., Central Specialists Cttee of BMA, 1967–68; Pres., Canterbury Div. of BMA, 1972. Chm., NZ Region of Cardiac Soc. of Australia and NZ, and Councillor, 1977–81. Member: Resuscitation Cttee of Nat. Cttee on Emergency Care, 1979–; Nat. Forum on Health Educn and Health Promotion, 1984–; NZ Govt Adv. Cttee on Prevention of Cardiovascular Disease, 1985–; NZ Adv. Cttee on Smoking and Health, 1974–; WHO Expert Adv. Panel on Smoking and Health, 1977–. Speaker: World Conf. on Smoking and Health, Stockholm, 1979; Internat. Soc. and Fedn of Cardiology Workshop, Jakarta, 1982. Trustee: J. L. Hay Charitable Trust; W. H. Nicholls Charitable Trust; Edna and Winifred White-Parsons Charitable Trust. *Publications:* (ed) Coronary Heart Disease: prevention and control in 1983, 1983; editor of technical report series of National Heart Foundn and author of numerous NHF pubns; over seventy sci. papers in various med. jls, mostly on smoking and health and preventive cardiology. *Recreations:* golf, tennis. *Address:* 20 Greers Road, Christchurch 4, New Zealand. *T:* 585–482. *Club:* Christchurch Golf.
See also Sir Hamish Hay.

HAY, Prof. Denys, MA; FBA 1970; FRSE 1977; Emeritus Professor of Medieval History, University of Edinburgh; *b* 29 Aug. 1915; *s* of Rev. W. K. Hay and Janet Waugh; *m* 1937, Sarah Gwyneth, *d* of S. E. Morley; one *s* two *d. Educ:* Royal Grammar Sch., Newcastle upon Tyne; Balliol Coll., Oxford. 1st Cl. hons, Modern History, 1937; senior demy, Magdalen Coll., 1937. Temporary Lecturer, Glasgow Univ., 1938; Bryce Studentship, Oxford Univ., 1939; Asst Lecturer, University Coll., Southampton, 1939; RASC 1940–42; War Historian (Civil Depts), 1942–45; Lecturer, 1945, Professor of Medieval History, 1954–80, Emeritus Professor 1980, Edinburgh Univ., Vice-Principal, 1971–75. Literary Dir, RHistS, 1955–58 (Hon. Life Vice-Pres., 1981–); Lectures: Italian, British Acad., 1959; Wiles, QUB, 1960; Birkbeck, Trinity Coll., Cambridge, 1971–72; David Murray, Glasgow Univ., 1983; Visiting Professor: Cornell Univ., 1963; Univ. of Virginia, 1980; Prof. of History, European Univ. Inst., Badia Fiesolana, 1980–82; Senior Fellow, Newberry Library, Chicago, 1966; Trustee, Nat. Library of Scotland, 1966–; President: Historical Association, 1967–70; Ecclesiastical Hist. Soc., 1980–81; Mem., Reviewing Cttee on Export of Works of Art, 1976–80. Editor, English Historical Review, 1958–65. Hon. For. Mem., Amer. Acad. of Arts and Scis, 1974. Hon. DLitt Newcastle, 1970; Hon. Dr Tours Univ., 1982. Comdr, Order of Merit, Italy, 1980. *Publications:* Anglica Historia of P. Vergil, 1950; Polydore Vergil, 1952; From Roman Empire to Renaissance Europe, 1953 (The Medieval Centuries, 1964); ed. R. K. Hannay's Letters of James V, 1954; Europe: the emergence of an idea, 1957, new edn 1968; (ed) New Cambridge Modern History, Vol. I: The Renaissance, 1493–1520, 1957, new edn 1976; Italian Renaissance in its Historical Background, 1961, new edn 1976; Design and Development of Weapons (History of Second World War) (with M. M. Postan and J. D. Scott), 1964; Europe in the 14th and 15th Centuries, 1966; (ed with W. K. Smith) Aeneas Sylvius Piccolomini, *De Gestis Concilii Basiliensis,* 1967; (ed) The Age of the Renaissance, 1967; Annalists and Historians, 1977; Italian Church in the 15th Century, 1977; articles in historical journals. *Address:* 31 Fountainhall Road, Edinburgh EH9 2LN. *T:* 031–667 2886. *Club:* United Oxford & Cambridge University.
See also Richard Hay.

HAY, Frances Mary, (Mrs Roy Hay); *see* Perry, F. M.

HAY, Rt. Rev. Mgr George Adam; Parish Priest, Sacred Heart and St Teresa, Paignton, since 1984; *b* 14 Nov. 1930; *s* of late Sir William Rupert Hay, KCMG, KCIE, CSI, and late Sybil Ethel, *d* of Sir Stewart Abram. *Educ:* Ampleforth College, York; New Coll., Oxford (BA History, MA); Venerable English Coll., Rome (STL). National Service as Midshipman RNVR, 1949–50; student, Oxford, 1950–53; Venerable English Coll., Rome, 1953–60. Ordained priest at Rome, 1959; Curate, Sacred Heart Church, Exeter, and part-time RC Chaplain to students at Exeter Univ., 1960; Chaplain to students at Exeter Univ. and Priest-in-charge, Crediton, 1966–78; Rector, Venerable English Coll., Rome, 1978–84; Parish Priest, St John the Baptist, Dartmouth, 1984. *Recreations:* fly fishing, squash, mountain walking. *Address:* 24 Cecil Road, Paignton, Devon TQ3 2SH. *T:* Paignton 557518.

HAY, Sir Hamish (Grenfell), Kt 1982; Mayor of Christchurch, New Zealand, since 1974; Director: Canterbury Development Corporation, since 1983; Mutual Funds, since 1983; NZ Municipalities Co-op Insurance Co. Ltd, since 1982; *b* 8 Dec. 1927; twin *s* of Sir James Lawrence Hay, OBE, and Lady (Davidina) Hay; *m* 1955, Judith Leicester Gill; one *s* four *d. Educ:* St Andrew's Coll., Christchurch; Univ. of Canterbury, NZ (BCom). FCA(NZ). Councillor, Christchurch City Council, 1959–74. Member: Victory Park Bd, 1974–; Lyttelton Harbour Bd, 1983–. Chairman: Christchurch Town Hall Board of Management, 1968–; Canterbury Museum Trust Bd, 1981–84; Canterbury United Council, 1983–; President: Christchurch Aged People's Welfare Council, 1974–; Christchurch Civic Music Council, 1974–; Christchurch Symphony Orchestra, 1982–; Chm., Christchurch Arts Festival, 1965–74; past Mem., Queen Elizabeth II Arts Council. Chm., New Zealand Soc. of Accountants (Canterbury Br.), 1958; Dep. Man. Dir, Haywrights Ltd, 1962–74. Mem. Council, Univ. of Canterbury, 1974–; Chm. of Governors, McLean Inst., 1974–. Vice-Pres., Municipal Assoc. of NZ, 1974–; Trustee, Canterbury Savings Bank, 1962– (Pres., 1974–75). Hon. Rangitira, Ngai Tahu S Island Maori Tribe, 1980. *Recreations:* golf, gardening, listening to good music. *Address:* 70 Heaton Street, Merivale, Christchurch 5, New Zealand. *T:* 557–244. *Club:* Christchurch (New Zealand).
See also D. R. Hay.

HAY, Sir James B. D.; *see* Dalrymple-Hay.

HAY, John Albert; Managing Director, Walport Group, 1968–84; *b* 24 Nov. 1919; *er s* of Alderman J. E. Hay; *m* 1st, 1947, Beryl Joan (marr. diss. 1973), *o d* of Comdr H. C. Found, RN (retired); one *s* one *d*; 2nd, 1974, Janet May, *y d* of A. C. Spruce. *Educ:* Brighton, Hove and Sussex Grammar Sch. Solicitor admitted May 1945. Chairman: Brighton and Hove Young Conservatives, 1945–47; Sussex Federation of Young Conservatives, 1945–47; Young Conservative and Unionist Central Cttee, 1947–49; Conservative Party Housing and Local Govt Cttee, 1956–59; formerly Dir London Municipal Soc.; formerly Vice-Pres. Urban District Councils Assoc.; Hon. Sec. UK Council of the European Movement, 1965–66; Mem. of Exec. Cttee, Nat. Union of Conservative and Unionist Assoc., 1947–49 and 1950–51. Served War of 1939–45, in RNVR; temp. Sub-Lieut, RNVR, 1940–44; temp. Lieut, RNVR, 1944; invalided 1944. Member: British Delegn, Congress of Europe, 1948, and 1973; UK Delegns, Council of Europe and Western European Union, 1956–59. MP (C) Henley, Oxon, 1950–Feb. 1974; PPS to Pres. of BoT, 1951–56; Parly Sec., MoT, 1959–63; Civil Lord of the Admiralty, 1963–64; Parly Under-Sec. of State for Defence for the Royal Navy, April-Oct. 1964. Chm., British Section, Council of European Municipalities, 1971–76, Vice-Chm., 1976–77, Pres., 1977–81, Vice-Pres., 1981–. Mem. Court, Reading Univ., 1968–. Fellow, Royal Philharmonic Soc., 1976. *Recreations:* gardening, music, travel, historical study. *Address:* 6 Elmwood Road, W4. *T:* 01–994 3022.

HAY, Prof. John Duncan, MA, MD, FRCP; Professor of Child Health, University of Liverpool, 1957–74, now Professor Emeritus; *b* 6 Feb. 1909; *s* of late Prof. John Hay; *m* 1936, Jannett Ceridwen Evans; one *s* two *d. Educ:* Liverpool Coll.; Sidney Sussex Coll., Cambridge; Liverpool Univ. MB, ChB, 1st Cl. Hons, Liverpool, 1933; MA 1934, MB 1935, Cambridge; MD Liverpool, 1936; DCH London, MRCP 1939; FRCP 1951. Holt Fellowship in Pathology, Liverpool, 1935; Cons. Pædiatrician to: Royal Liverpool Children's Hospital, 1939–74; Royal Liverpool Babies' Hospital, 1939–61; Birkenhead Children's Hosp., 1937–54; Liverpool Maternity Hosp. 1946–74; Lancashire County Hosp., Whiston, 1942–51; Liverpool Open-Air Hospital, Leasowe, and Mill Road Maternity Hosp., 1947–74; Alder Hey Children's Hosp., 1957–74; Liverpool Education Cttee, 1951–72. Demonstrator in Pathology, University of Liverpool, 1935 and 1938; Asst Lectr in Clinical Pædiatrics, University of Liverpool, 1948–57. Brit. Paediatric Association: Treasurer, 1964–71; Pres., 1972–73; Hon. Mem., 1973–; President: Liverpool Med. Instn, 1972–73; Liverpool Paediatric Club, 1975–; Hon. Mem. Assoc. European Paediatric Cardiologists, 1975–. RAMC (Major and Lieut-Col), 1942–46. *Publications:* contribs to Archives of Disease in Childhood, British Heart Journal, BMJ, Lancet, Practitioner, Brit. Encyclopædia of Medical Practice, Medical Progress, 1957, Cardiovascular Diseases in Childhood. *Recreations:* music, fell walking. *Address:* Fairfield, Cedarway, Gayton, Merseyside L60 3RH. *T:* 051–342 2607.

HAY, Richard; Deputy Director-General, Directorate-General for Personnel and Administration, European Commission, since 1981; *b* 4 May 1942; *s* of Prof. Denys Hay, *qv; m* 1969, Miriam Marguerite Alvin England; two *s. Educ:* George Watson's Coll., Edinburgh; Edinburgh Univ.; Balliol Coll., Oxford (BA Hons, Mod. Hist.). Assistant Principal, HM Treasury, 1963–68; Secretary, West Midlands Economic Planning Council, 1966–67; Private Sec. to Financial Sec., Treasury, 1967–68; Principal, Treasury, 1968–73; Member, Cabinet of Sir Christopher (now Lord) Soames, Vice-Pres., European Commn, 1973–75; Dep. Chef de Cabinet, 1975–77; Chef de Cabinet to Mr Christopher Tugendhat, Member, European Commn, 1977–79; Dir, Economic Structures and Community Interventions, Directorate-Gen. for Economic and Financial Affairs, European Commn, 1979–81. *Address:* c/o European Commission, 200 rue de la Loi, 1049 Brussels, Belgium. *T:* (02) 235 4580. *Club:* United Oxford & Cambridge University.

HAY, Maj.-Gen. Robert Arthur, CB 1970; MBE 1946; Executive Officer, Australian Centre for Publications acquired for Development, since 1982; Australian Army Officer, retired 1977; *b* 9 April 1920; *s* of Eric Alexander Hay and Vera Eileen Hay (*née* Whitehead); *m* 1944, Endrée Patricia Hay (*née* McGovern); two *s* one *d. Educ:* Brighton Grammar Sch., Melbourne, Victoria; RMC Duntroon, ACT (graduated Dec. 1939); Australian Staff Coll., 1944; USA Staff Coll., Fort Leavenworth, 1944. Lt-Col, 1945; Col, 1955; Col GS HQ Eastern Comd; Military Attaché, Washington, DC, 1956; Dir Administrative Planning, AHQ, 1959; Defence Representative, Singapore and Malaya, 1962; Brig., 1964; IDC London, 1965; Dir Military Ops and Plans, AHQ, 1966; Maj.-Gen., 1967; Dep. Chief of the General Staff, AHQ; Comdr, Australian Forces, Vietnam, 1969; Comdr, First Australian Div., 1970; Chief, Mil. Planning Office, SEATO, 1971–73;

Comdt, Royal Military Coll., Duntroon, 1973–77. Sec., Australian Council of Professions, 1978–86. Pres., Veterans Tennis Assoc. of Australia, 1981–. *Recreations:* tennis, golf. *Address:* 5 Borrowdale Street, Red Hill, ACT 2603, Australia. *Clubs:* Melbourne Cricket; Commonwealth, Royal Canberra Golf (Canberra); Tanglin (Singapore).

HAY, Robert Colquhoun, WS; President, Industrial Tribunals for Scotland, since 1981 (Chairman, 1976–81); *b* 22 Sept. 1933; *s* of late Mr and Mrs J. B. Hay; *m* 1958, Olive Black; two *s* two *d. Educ:* Univ. of Edinburgh (MA, LLB). Depute Procurator Fiscal, Edinburgh, 1963–68; Partner, Bonar Mackenzie, WS, 1968–76; Temp. Sheriff, 1984–. *Address:* Central Office of Industrial Tribunals (Scotland), St Andrew House, 141 West Nile Street, Glasgow G1 2RU. *T:* 041–331 1601. *Club:* Caledonian.

HAY, Robert Edwin, (Roy Hay), MBE 1970; VMH 1971; formerly Editor, Gardeners' Chronicle (1954–64); *b* 20 Aug. 1910; *o s* of late Thomas Hay, CVO, sometime Superintendent Central Royal Parks; *m* 1st, 1946, Elizabeth Jessie (*d* 1976), *d* of late Rev. H. C. Charter; two *d*; 2nd, 1977, Mrs Frances Perry, *qv. Educ:* Marylebone Grammar Sch. Horticultural seed trade, 1928; Asst Editor, Gardeners' Chronicle, 1936; Editor, Royal Horticultural Soc.'s publications, 1939; Min. of Agriculture, 1940; Horticultural Officer, Malta, 1942; Controller of Horticulture and Seed Divs, British zone of Germany, 1945. Officier du Mérite Agricole: Belgium, 1956; France, 1959. *Publications:* Annuals, 1937; In My Garden, 1955; Gardening the Modern Way, 1962; (with P. M. Synge) The Dictionary of Garden Plants, 1969; (jtly) The Dictionary of Indoor Plants in Colour, 1975; (ed) The Complete Guide to Fruit and Vegetable Growing, 1978; (with Frances Perry) Tropical and Subtropical Plants, 1982; Gardener's Calendar, 1983. *Recreation:* foreign travel. *Club:* Farmers'.

HAY, Robin William Patrick Hamilton; Recorder, since 1985; barrister; *b* 1 Nov. 1939; *s* of William R. Hay and Dora Hay; *m* 1969, Lady Olga Maitland, *d* of Earl of Lauderdale, *qv*; two *s* one *d. Educ:* Eltham; Selwyn Coll., Univ. of Cambridge (MA, LLM). Called to the Bar, Inner Temple, 1964. *Recreations:* church tasting, gastronomy, choral singing. *Address:* 21 Cloudesley Street, N1.

HAY, Sir Ronald Nelson, 11th Bt *cr* 1703, of Alderston; *b* 9 July 1910; *s* of Frederick Howard Hay (*d* 1934) (*g s* of 6th Bt); *S* brother, 1985; *m* 1940, Rita, *d* of John Munyard; one *s* one *d. Heir: s* Ronald Frederick Hamilton Hay, *b* 1941.

HAY DAVISON, Ian Frederic; *see* Davison, I. F. H.

HAYBALL, Frederick Ronald, CMG 1969; *b* 23 April 1914; *s* of late Frederick Reuben Hayball and late Rebecca Hayball; *m* 1938, Lavinia Violet Palmer; one *s* one *d. Educ:* Alleyn's Sch., Dulwich. Accountant, Myers, Gondouin & Co. Ltd, 1932–39. Flying Officer, RAF, 1939–45. Foreign and Commonwealth Office, 1945–69 (Counsellor, retired); Asst Sec., Longman Gp Ltd, 1969–81. *Recreations:* cricket, angling, motoring. *Address:* 50 Theydon Park Road, Theydon Bois, Essex. *T:* Theydon Bois 2195.

HAYCRAFT, Colin Berry; Chairman, Managing Director and controlling shareholder, Gerald Duckworth & Co. Ltd, publishers, since 1971; *b* 12 Jan. 1929; *yr s* of Major W. C. S. Haycraft, MC and Bar, 5/8 Punjab Regt (killed 1929), and late Olive Lillian Esmée (*née* King); *m* 1957, Anna Margaret Lindholm (novelist, under the pseudonym Alice Thomas Ellis); four *s* one *d* (and one *s* one *d* decd). *Educ:* Wellington Coll. (schol.); The Queen's Coll., Oxford (Open Schol. in Classics; 1st Cl. Classical Mods, 1st Cl. Lit.Hum., MA). Nat. service (army), 1947–49. Personal Asst to Chm., Cecil H. King, Daily Mirror Newspapers Ltd; Dir, Weidenfeld & Nicolson Ltd and Weidenfeld (Publishers) Ltd (original editor and subseq. Man. Dir, World University Library Ltd); joined Duckworth, 1968. Public Schs Rackets Champion (singles and pairs), 1946; Oxford blue for Squash Rackets (4 years, Captain OUSRC, Eng. internat.), Lawn Tennis (Devon Co. player) and Rackets. *Address:* 22 Gloucester Crescent, NW1 7DY. *Clubs:* Beefsteak; Vincent's (Oxford); Jesters; Queen's.

See also J. S. Haycraft.

HAYCRAFT, John Stacpoole, CBE 1982; Director General, English International (International House), since 1975; *b* 11 Dec. 1926; *s* of late Major W. C. S. Haycraft and Olive Haycraft; *m* 1953, Brita Elisabeth Langenfelt; two *s* one *d. Educ:* Wellington Coll.; Jesus Coll., Oxford (Open Exhibnr; MA). E-SU Fellowship. Yale Univ., 1951–52. Founder and Dir, Academia Britanica, Córdoba, 1953; Founder and Principal: International Language Centre, London, 1960; International Teacher Trng Inst., 1963; Founder and Director: International House, London, 1964; International House, Rome, 1967–68; Dir, International House, Paris, 1971–72; Founder: English Teaching Theatre, 1970; English International (International House), 1975. *Publications:* Babel in Spain, 1958, 2nd edn 1958; Getting on in English, 1964, 7th edn 1982 (trans. 9 langs); Babel in London, 1965; George and Elvira, 1970; Choosing Your English, 1972, 8th edn 1982; Action, 1977; Introduction to English Language Teaching, 1978; Think, Then Speak, 1984; Italian Labyrinth, 1985; contrib. Modern English Teacher, etc. *Recreations:* squash, tennis, swimming, chess, cinema, theatre, history, travel. *Address:* 81 Lee Road, SE3. *T:* 01–852 5495. *Club:* Canning.

See also C. B. Haycraft.

HAYDAR, Dr Loutof Allah; Syrian Ambassador to the Court of St James's, since 1982; *b* 22 March 1940; *s* of Haydar and Mary; *m* 1968, Hayat Hassan; one *s* three *d. Educ:* Damascus Univ. (BA English Literature 1964); Moscow State Univ. (PhD 1976). Joined Foreign Office, 1965; served at Syrian Embassy: London, 1965–67; Bonn, 1967–68; Moscow, 1970–75; served with Syrian Delegation to UN, New York, 1978–82. *Publication:* The Ancient History of Palestine and the Middle East (PhD Thesis), 1976. *Address:* Embassy of the Syrian Arab Republic, 8 Belgrave Square, SW1X 8PH. *T:* 01–245 9012.

HAYDAY, Anthony Victor; HM Diplomatic Service; Consul General, Cleveland, since 1985; *b* 1 June 1930; *s* of Charles Leslie Victor Hayday and Catherine (*née* McCarthy); *m* 1966, Anne Heather Moffat; one *s* one *d. Educ:* Beckenham and Penge Grammar School. Royal Air Force, 1949–50; HM Foreign (later Diplomatic) Service, 1950; Brazzaville, 1953; British Information Services, New York, 1955; FO, 1958; Vice Consul, Houston, 1961; 2nd Secretary, Algiers, 1962; FO (later FCO), 1966; 1st Secretary, New Delhi, 1969; Head of Chancery, Freetown, 1973; on secondment to Commonwealth Secretariat, 1976–80. Dep. High Comr, Calcutta, 1981–85. *Recreations:* birdwatching, athletics. *Address:* c/o Foreign and Commonwealth Office, SW1. *Clubs:* Brooks's, Blackheath Harriers, Mensa; Bengal (Calcutta).

HAYDAY, Sir Frederick, Kt 1969; CBE 1963; National Industrial Officer, National Union of General and Municipal Workers, 1946–71; Chairman, International Committee, Trades Union Congress; *b* 26 June 1912; *s* of late Arthur Hayday, MP for W Notts; *m*. Member: General Council of the Trades Union Congress, 1950–72 (Chairman, 1962–63, Vice-Chairman, 1964–69); IBA (formerly ITA), 1969–73; British Railways Board, 1962–76. Mem., Police Complaints Bd, 1977–83. *Address:* 42 West Drive, Cheam, Surrey. *T:* 01–642 8928.

HAYDEN, Hon. William George; MHR (Lab) for Oxley, Qld, since 1961; Minister of Foreign Affairs, Australia, since 1983; *b* Brisbane, 23 Jan. 1933; *s* of G. Hayden, Oakland, Calif, USA; *m* 1960, Dallas, *d* of W. Broadfoot; one *s* two *d. Educ:* Brisbane State High Sch. BEcon (Q). Police Constable in Queensland, 1953–61. Parly Spokesman on Health and Welfare, 1969–72; Minister for Social Security, Australian Commonwealth Govt, 1972–75; Federal Treasurer, June-Nov. 1975; Leader of Australian Labor Party and the Opposition, 1977–83; spokesman on defence, 1976–83 and on economic management, 1977–83. *Address:* Parliament House, Canberra, ACT, Australia; (home) 16 East Street, Ipswich, Queensland 4305, Australia.

HAYDON, Prof. Denis Arthur, FRS 1975; Professor of Membrane Biophysics, University of Cambridge, since 1980; Fellow, since 1965, Vice-Master, 1978–82, Trinity Hall, Cambridge; *b* 21 Feb. 1930; *s* of late Ernest George Haydon and Grace Violet (*née* Wildman); *m* 1958, Ann Primrose Wayman (marr. diss. 1986); two *s* one *d. Educ:* Dartford Grammar Sch.; King's Coll., Univ. of London (BSc, PhD). MA Cantab. ICI Res. Fellow, Imperial Coll., London, 1956–58; Asst Dir of Res., Univ. of Cambridge, Dept of Colloid Science, 1959–70, and Dept of Physiology, 1970–74; Dir of Studies in Natural Scis, Trinity Hall, 1965–78; Asst Tutor, Trinity Hall, 1968–73; Tutor for Natural Scientists, Trinity Hall, 1973–74; Reader in Surface and Membrane Biophysics, Univ. of Cambridge, 1974–80. Chem. Soc. Medal for Surface and Colloid Chem., 1976. *Publications:* (with R. Aveyard) An Introduction to the Principles of Surface Chemistry, 1973; papers on surface chemistry and membrane biophysics in Proc. Royal Soc., Trans Faraday Soc., Jl Chem. Soc. and other sci. jls. *Recreations:* climbing, sailing, music. *Address:* Westgate Cottage, 7 Orwell Road, Barrington, Cambridge CB2 5SE. *T:* Cambridge 871305.

HAYDON, Francis Edmund Walter; HM Diplomatic Service; Counsellor, Foreign and Commonwealth Office, since 1981; *b* 23 Dec. 1928; *s* of late Surgeon Captain Walter T. Haydon, RN and Maria Christina Haydon (*née* Delahoyde); *m* 1959, Isabel Dorothy Kitchin; two *s* two *d. Educ:* Downside School; Magdalen College, Oxford. BA (1st cl. Modern History) 1949. Asst London correspondent, Agence France-Presse, 1951–52; Asst diplomatic correspondent, Reuters, 1952–55; joined Foreign Office, 1955; Second Sec., Benghazi, 1959, Beirut, 1962; First Sec., Blantyre, 1969, Ankara, 1978. *Recreations:* lawn tennis, cricket, enjoying the countryside. *Address:* Broadmeads, Coronation Road, Ascot, Berks. *T:* Ascot 21005.

HAYDON, Sir Walter Robert, (Sir Robin Haydon), KCMG 1980 (CMG 1970); HM Diplomatic Service, retired; Director, Imperial Tobacco Ltd, since 1984; *b* 29 May 1920; *s* of Walter Haydon and Evelyn Louise Thom; *m* 1943, Joan Elizabeth Tewson; one *d* (and one *s* one *d* decd). *Educ:* Dover Grammar Sch. Served in Army in France, India and Burma, 1939–46. Entered Foreign Service, 1946; served at London, Berne, Turin, Sofia, Bangkok, London, Khartoum, UK Mission to UN (New York), Washington; Head of News Dept, FCO, 1967–71; High Comr, Malaŵi, 1971–73; Chief Press Sec., 10 Downing Street, 1973–74; High Comr, Malta, 1974–76; Ambassador to Republic of Ireland, 1976–80. Dir of Gp Public Affairs, Imperial Gp, 1981–84. Member: Reviewing Cttee on Export of Works of Art, 1984–; Tobacco Adv. Council, 1984–. Governor: E-SU, 1980–; Dover Grammar Sch., 1982–. *Recreations:* walking, swimming, tennis. *Address:* c/o Lloyds Bank, Cox's & King's Branch, 6 Pall Mall, SW1Y 5NH. *Club:* Travellers'.

HAYE, Colvyn Hugh, CBE 1983; JP; Commissioner for Hong Kong, 1984–April 1987; *b* 7 Dec. 1925; 3rd *s* of Colvyn Hugh Haye and Avis Rose Kelly; *m* 1949, Gloria Mary Stansbury; two *d. Educ:* Sherwood Coll.; Univ. of Melbourne (BA, Teachers' Cert.); Christchurch Coll., Oxford (Overseas Service Trng Course). Served War, RNVR, Midshipman and Sub-Lt, 1944–46. Victorian State Educn Service, 1947–52; joined Colonial Service, now HMOCS, Hong Kong Government: Educn Officer, 1953; Sen. Educn Officer, 1962; Asst Dir and Head of Educnl Television Service, 1969; Dep. Dir, 1975; Dir of Educn and Official Mem., Legislative Council, 1980; Sec., Administrative Service and Comr, London Office, 1984. JP Hong Kong, 1971–87. *Recreations:* reading, writing, talking, walking. *Address:* (until April 1987) Hong Kong Government Office, 6 Grafton Street, W1X 3LB. *T:* 01–493 4760; Wymering, Sheet Common, near Petersfield, Hants GU32 5AT. *T:* Petersfield 68480. *Clubs:* Hong Kong, Tripehounds, Toastmasters (Hong Kong).

HAYEK, Friedrich August (von), CH 1984; FBA 1944; Dr Jur, DrScPol, Vienna; DSc (Econ.) London; *b* Vienna, 8 May 1899; *s* of late August von Hayek, Prof. of Botany at University of Vienna; certificate of naturalisation, 1938; *m* 1st, Hella von Fritsch (*d* 1960); one *s* one *d*; 2nd, Helene Bitterlich. *Educ:* University of Vienna. Austrian Civil Service, 1921–26; Dir, Austrian Institute for Economic Research, 1927–31; Lecturer in Economics, University of Vienna, 1929–31; Tooke Prof. of Economic Science and Statistics in University of London, 1931–50; Prof. of Social and Moral Science, University of Chicago, 1950–62; Prof. of Economics, Univ. of Freiburg i B, 1962–69. Chm., Adam Smith Inst. Hon. Fellow: LSE; Austrian Acad. of Scis; American Economic Assoc.; Hoover Inst. on War, Revolution and Peace; Argentine Acad. of Economic Sci.; Academia Sinica. Dr jur *hc* Rikkyo Univ., Tokyo, 1964; Dr jur *hc* Univ. of Salzburg, 1974; Dr Lit. Hum. *hc* Univ. of Dallas, 1975; Hon. Dr Soc. Sci., Marroquin Univ., Guatemala, 1977; Hon. Dr: Santa Maria Univ., Valparaiso, 1977; Univ. of Buenos Aires, 1977; Univ. of Giessen, 1982. Nobel Prize in Economic Science (jtly), 1974. Austrian Distinction for Science and Art, 1975; Mem., Orden pour le Mérite für Wissenschaften und Künste, Fed. Rep. of Germany, 1977; Medal of Merit, Baden-Württemberg, 1981; Ring of Honour, City of Vienna, 1983; Gold Medal, City of Paris, 1984. *Publications:* Prices and Production, 1931; Monetary Theory and the Trade Cycle, 1933 (German edition, 1929); Monetary Nationalism and International Stability, 1937; Profits, Interest, and Investment, 1939; The Pure Theory of Capital, 1941; The Road to Serfdom, 1944; Individualism and Economic Order, 1948; John Stuart Mill and Harriet Taylor, 1950; The Counter-revolution of Science, 1952; The Sensory Order, 1952; The Political Ideal of the Rule of Law, 1955; The Constitution of Liberty, 1960; Studies in Philosophy, Politics and Economics, 1967; Freiburger Studien, 1969; Law, Legislation & Liberty, vol. I: Rules and Order, 1973, Vol II: The Mirage of Social Justice, 1976, Vol. III: The Political Order of a Free People, 1979; De-Nationalisation of Money, 1976; New Studies in Philosophy, Politics, Economics and the History of Ideas, 1978; edited: Beiträge zur Geldtheorie, 1933; Collectivist Economic Planning, 1935; Capitalism and the Historians, 1954; and the works of H. H. Gossen, 1927; F. Wieser, 1929; C. Menger, 1933–36; and H. Thornton, 1939; articles in Economic Journal, Economica, and other English and foreign journals. *Address:* Urachstrasse 27, D-7800 Freiburg i. Brg, West Germany. *Club:* Reform (London).

HAYES, Brian, QPM 1985; Chief Constable, Surrey Constabulary, since 1982; *b* 25 Jan. 1940; 2nd *s* of James and Jessie Hayes; *m* 1960, Priscilla Rose Bishop; one *s* three *d. Educ:* Plaistow County Grammar Sch.; Sheffield Univ. (BA Hons 1st Cl. Mod. Langs); MIL 1972. FBIM. Metropolitan Police, 1959–77; seconded Northern Ireland, 1971–72; Police Adviser, Mexico, 1975 and 1976, Colombia, 1977; British Police representative, EEC, 1976–77; Asst Chief Constable, Surrey Constabulary, 1977–81; Dep. Chief Constable, Wiltshire Constabulary, 1981–82. Nat. Sec., Police Athletic Assoc., 1984–. Police Long

Service and Good Conduct Medal, 1981. *Recreations:* martial arts, running, sailing. *Address:* Mount Browne, Sandy Lane, Guildford, Surrey GU3 1HG. *T:* Guildford 571212.

HAYES, Sir Brian (David), KCB 1980 (CB 1976); Permanent Secretary, Department of Trade and Industry, since 1985 (Joint Permanent Secretary, 1983–85); *b* 5 May 1929; *s* of late Charles and Flora Hayes, Bramerton, Norfolk; *m* 1958, Audrey Jenkins; one *s* one *d*. *Educ:* Norwich Sch.; Corpus Christi Coll., Cambridge. BA (Hist.) 1952, PhD (Cambridge) 1956. RASC, 1947–49. Joined Min. of Agriculture, Fisheries and Food, 1956; Asst Private Sec. to the Minister, 1958; Asst Sec., 1967; Under-Sec., Milk and Poultry Gp, 1970–73; Dep. Sec., 1973–78; Permanent Sec., 1979–83. *Recreations:* reading, watching cricket. *Address:* c/o Department of Trade and Industry, 1 Victoria Street, SW1H 0ET.

HAYES, Sir Claude (James), KCMG 1974 (CMG 1969); MA, MLitt; Chairman, Crown Agents for Oversea Governments and Administrations, 1968–74; *b* 23 March 1912; *er s* of late J. B. F. Hayes, West Hoathly, Sussex; *m* 1940, Joan McCarthy (*d* 1984), *yr d* of Edward McCarthy Fitt, Civil Engineer; two *s* one *d*. *Educ:* Ardingly Coll.; St Edmund Hall, Oxford (Scholar); Sorbonne; New Coll., Oxford (Sen. Scholar). Heath Harrison Travelling Scholarship; Zaharoff Travelling Fellowship; Paget Toynbee Prize; MA, MLitt. Asst Dir of Examinations, Civil Service Commn, 1938. Captain RASC 1st Inf. Div. BEF, 1939; Major 1940, Combined Ops; Lieut-Col, 1942–45 (N Africa, Sicily, Italy, NW Europe). Dep. Dir of Examinations, Civil Service Commn, 1945; Dir and Comr, 1949, also Sec., 1955; Nuffield Foundn Fellowship, 1953–54, toured Commonwealth studying public service recruitment and management. Asst Sec., HM Treasury, 1957; British Govt Mem., Cttee on Dissolution of Central African Fedn, 1963; Under-Sec., HM Treasury, 1964–65; Prin. Finance Officer, Min. of Overseas Development, 1965–68. *Recreations:* music; unaided gardening; antique furniture; 18th century bourgeois chattels; getting value for money from shops. *Address:* Prinkham, Chiddingstone Hoath, Kent. *T:* Cowden 335.

HAYES, Colin Graham Frederick, MA; RA 1970 (ARA 1963); painter; *b* 17 Nov. 1919; *s* of Gerald Hayes and Winifred (*née* Yule); *m* 1949, Jean Westbrook Law; three *d*. *Educ:* Westminster Sch.; Christ Church, Oxford. Served Royal Engineers, 1940–45 (Middle East) (Capt.). Ruskin Sch. of Drawing, 1946–47. Tutor, Sen. Tutor and Reader, Royal College of Art, 1949–84; Hon. ARCA, 1960; Fellow, RCA, 1960–84 (Hon. Fellow, 1984). Work in Collections: Arts Council; British Council; Carlisle Museum, etc. *Publications include:* Renoir, 1961; Stanley Spencer, 1963; Rembrandt, 1969; many articles on painting in jls. *Address:* 26 Cleveland Avenue, W4. *T:* 01–994 8762.

HAYES, Helen, (Mrs Charles MacArthur); actress; *b* Washington, DC 10 Oct. 1900; *d* of Francis Van Arnum Brown and Catherine Estelle Hayes; *m* 1928, Charles MacArthur (*d* 1956); one *s* one *d*. *Educ:* Sacred Heart Academy, Washington, DC. As actress has appeared in USA in stage plays, among others: Pollyanna, Dear Brutus, Clarence, Bab, Coquette, The Good Fairy, To the Ladies, Young Blood, Mary of Scotland, Victoria Regina, Ladies and Gentlemen, Twelfth Night, Harriet, Happy Birthday; The Wisteria Trees, 1950; Mrs McThing, 1952. First appearance in England in The Glass Menagerie, 1948. Is also radio actress. Has appeared in films: Farewell to Arms, The Sin of Madelon Claudet, Arrowsmith, The Son-Daughter, My Son John, Anastasia, Airport (Best Supporting Actress Award, 1971), Candleshoe, etc. Awarded gold statuette by Motion Picture Academy of Arts and Sciences, 1932, as outstanding actress, based on performance in the Sin of Madelon Claudet; Hon. degrees: Smith Coll., Hamilton Coll., Columbia Univ., Princeton Univ., St Mary's Coll. Medal of Freedom, 1986. *Publications:* A Gift of Joy, 1965; On Reflection, 1968; (with Anita Loos) Twice Over Lightly, 1971; (with Marion Glasserow Gladney) Our Best Years, 1984; *relevant publication:* Front Page Marriage: Helen Hayes and Charles MacArthur, by Jhan Robbins, 1982. *Address:* Nyack, New York, NY 10960, USA. *Clubs:* Cosmopolitan, River, etc.

HAYES, Most Rev. James Martin; *see* Halifax (NS), Archbishop of, (RC).

HAYES, Jeremy Joseph James; MP (C) Harlow, since 1983; barrister; *b* 20 April 1953; *s* of Peter and Daye Hayes; *m* 1979, Alison Gail Mansfield; one *d*. *Educ:* Oratory Sch.; Chelmer Inst. LLB London. Called to the Bar, Middle Temple, 1977. Proposer, Parents Aid (No 2) Bill; Sponsor, Video Recordings Bill. Jt Sec., Cons. Cttee on Constitutional Affairs, 1983–; Member: All Party Parly Gp on Human Rights; All Party Parly Gp on Race Relations. Pres., Eastern Area YCs; Vice-Pres., Epping Forest YCs. Member: FRAME; Amnesty Internat. Freeman, City of London; Liveryman, Fletchers' Co.; Freeman, Co. of Watermen and Lightermen. *Recreations:* Sunday afternoons at the Bell, Wendens Ambo; changing nappies and slumping in front of the TV with my wife. *Address:* Chestnut Cottage, Royston Road, Wendens Ambo, Saffron Walden, Essex CB11 4JX. *T:* Saffron Walden 40457. *Clubs:* Carlton; Essex.

HAYES, Vice-Admiral Sir John (Osler Chattock), KCB 1967 (CB 1964); OBE 1945; Lord-Lieutenant of Ross and Cromarty, Skye and Lochalsh, since 1977; *b* 9 May 1913; *er s* of late Major L. C. Hayes, RAMC and Mrs Hayes; *m* 1939, Hon. Rosalind Mary Finlay, *o d* of 2nd and last Viscount Finlay of Nairn; two *s* one *d*. *Educ:* RN Coll., Dartmouth. Entered RN, 1927. Served War of 1939–45; Atlantic, HMS Repulse, Singapore, Russian Convoys, Malta. The Naval Sec., 1962–64; Flag Officer: Flotillas, Home Fleet, 1964–66; Scotland and NI, 1966–68; retd. Comdr 1948; Capt. 1953; Rear-Adm. 1962; Vice-Adm. 1965. Chm., Cromarty Firth Port Authority, 1974–77. Mem., Queen's Body Guard for Scotland (Royal Company of Archers), 1969. Pres., Scottish Council, King George's Fund for Sailors, 1968–78. Dep. Chm. Bd of Governors, Gordonstoun Sch. King Gustav V of Sweden Jubilee Medal, 1948. *Recreations:* walking, music, writing. *Address:* Arabella House, by Tain, Ross and Cromarty. *T:* Nigg Station 293.

HAYES, John Philip, CB 1984; Senior Fellow, Trade Policy Research Centre, since 1984; *b* 1924; *s* of late Harry Hayes and late Mrs G. E. Hayes (*née* Hallsworth); *m* 1956, Susan Elizabeth, *d* of Sir Percivale Liesching, GCMG, KCB, KCVO; one *s* one *d*. *Educ:* Cranleigh Sch.; Corpus Christi Coll., Oxford. RAFVR, 1943–46. Barnett Memorial Fellowship, 1948–49; Political and Economic Planning, 1950–53; OEEC, 1953–58; Internat. Bank for Reconstruction and Develt, 1958–64; Head, Economic Develt Div., OECD, 1964–67; Dir, World Economy Div., Economic Planning Staff, ODM, 1967–69; Dep. Dir Gen. of Economic Planning, ODM, later ODA, 1969–71; Dir, Econ. Program Dept, later Econ. Analysis and Projections Dept, IBRD, 1971–73; Dir, Trade and Finance Div., Commonwealth Secretariat, 1973–75; Asst Under-Sec. of State (Economics), FCO, 1975–84. *Recreations:* music, travel. *Address:* 51 Enfield Road, Brentford, Mddx TW8 9PA. *T:* 01–568 7590.

HAYES, John Trevor, CBE 1986; MA Oxon, PhD London; FSA; Director of the National Portrait Gallery, London, since 1974; *b* 21 Jan. 1929; *er s* of late Leslie Thomas Hayes and late Gwendoline (*née* Griffiths), London. *Educ:* Ardingly; Keble Coll. Oxford (Open Exhibr; Hon. Fellow, 1984); Courtauld Inst. of Art, London; Inst. of Fine Arts, New York. Asst Keeper, London Museum, 1954–70, Dir, 1970–74; Commonwealth Fund Fellow, 1958–59 (NY Univ.); Vis. Prof. in History of Art, Yale Univ., 1969. Chm., Walpole Soc., 1981–. *Publications:* London: a pictorial history, 1969; The Drawings of Thomas Gainsborough, 1970; Catalogue of Oil Paintings in the London Museum, 1970; Gainsborough as Printmaker, 1971; Rowlandson: Watercolours and Drawings, 1972; Gainsborough: Paintings and Drawings, 1975; The Art of Graham Sutherland, 1980; The Landscape Paintings of Thomas Gainsborough, 1982; various London Museum and Nat. Portrait Gall. pubns; numerous articles in The Burlington Magazine, Apollo and other jls. *Recreations:* music, walking, gardening, travel. *Address:* c/o The National Portrait Gallery, St Martin's Place, WC2H 0HE. *T:* 01–930 1552. *Clubs:* Beefsteak, Arts.

HAYES, John William; Secretary General, Law Society, since 1987; *b* 10 Feb. 1945; *s* of late Dick Hayes and of Bridget Isobel Hayes; *m* 1970, Jennifer Hayes (*née* Harvey); two *s* one *d*. *Educ:* Nottingham High Sch.; Morecambe Grammer Sch.; Victoria Univ. of Manchester (LLB). Solicitor. Articled Thomas Foord, 1966–69; Worthing Borough Council, 1966–69; Nottingham County Borough Council, 1969–71; Somerset CC, 1971–74; Asst, Dep. Clerk and Dep. Chief Exec., Notts CC, 1974–80; Clerk and Chief Exec., Warwicks CC, 1980–86. Chm., Local Govt Gp, Law Soc., 1981–82; Sec., Warwicks Probation Cttee, 1983–86; Clerk to Warwicks Magistrates' Courts' Cttee, 1983–86; Clerk to Lord Lieut of Warwicks, 1980–86. Member: Council, Warwick Univ., 1980–86; Bishop of Coventry's Board of Social Responsibility, 1981–86; Inner Cities' Task Force, 1985–86. *Recreations:* cooking, cricket, music, idleness. *Address:* Law Society, 113 Chancery Lane, WC2A 1LP. *T:* 01-242 1222.

HAYES, Thomas William Henry; *b* 1 Aug. 1912; *s* of Henry Daniel and Joanna Hayes; *m* 1933, Alice Frances; one *s*. *Educ:* Central Foundation Sch., London; London Univ. After 3 years in teaching and 2 in industry joined Prison Service, 1937, as Borstal Housemaster. Served in RA, 1940–45. Dep. Gov. Rochester Borstal, 1945–48; Staff Officer, with British Police and Prisons Mission to Greece, 1948–51; Governor, subseq. of Lewes Prison, Hatfield and Lowdham Grange Borstals, Ashford Remand Centre and Wormwood Scrubs Prison; Asst Dir of Borstals, Home Office, 1964–69; Regional Dir of Prisons, SW Region, 1969–72; Advr to Dir of Prisons, Botswana, 1975–77; Regional Prisons Adviser, British Develt Div., Caribbean, 1978–79, retired. *Recreations:* gardening, contract bridge. *Address:* 5 Squitchey Lane, North Oxford OX2 7LD.

HAYES, Walter, CBE 1980; Vice Chairman, Ford of Europe Inc., since 1984; Vice President, Ford Motor Company, since 1977; *b* 12 April 1924; *s* of Walter and Hilda Hayes; *m* 1949, Elizabeth (*née* Holland); two *s* one *d*. *Educ:* Hampton Grammar Sch.; Royal Air Force. Editor, Sunday Dispatch, 1956; Associate Editor, Daily Mail, 1959; Director, Ford of Britain, 1965; Vice-Pres., Ford of Europe Incorporated, 1968; Director: Ford Motor Co. Ltd; Ford Werke A.G.; Ford Advanced Vehicles Ltd, 1963–70. Vice-Pres., Public Affairs, Ford Motor Co. in the United States, 1980–84. *Publications:* Angelica: a story for children, 1968; The Afternoon Cat and Other Poems, 1976. *Recreations:* old books, cricket. *Address:* 4 Grafton Street, W1. *Clubs:* MCC, Royal Automobile.

HAYES, Prof. William, FRS 1964; FRSE 1968; FAA 1976; Professor and Head of the Department of Genetics, Research School of Biological Sciences, Australian National University, 1974–78, now Emeritus; *b* 18 Jan. 1913; *s* of William Hayes and Miriam (*née* Harris), Co. Dublin, Ireland; *m* 1941, Honora Lee; one *s*. *Educ:* College of St Columba, Rathfarnham, Co. Dublin; Dublin Univ. BA (1st Cl. Mods. Nat. Sci.) Dublin, 1936; MB, BCh, Dublin, 1937; FRCPI 1945; ScD, Dublin, 1949. Served in India as Major, RAMC, Specialist in Pathology, 1942–46. Lectr in Bacteriology, Trinity Coll., Dublin, 1947–50; Sen. Lectr in Bacteriology, Postgraduate Medical Sch. of London, 1950–57, later Hon. Senior Lectr; Dir, MRC Molecular Genetics Unit, 1957–68, Hon. Dir 1968–73; Prof. of Molecular Genetics, Univ. of Edinburgh, 1968–73; Sherman Fairchild Dist. Scholar, Div. of Biology, California Inst. of Technology, 1979–80; Vis. Fellow, Botany Dept, ANU, 1980–. Hon. Fellow, RPMS, 1985; Hon. DSc: Leicester, 1966; NUI, 1973; Kent, 1973; Hon. LLD Dublin, 1970. *Publication:* The Genetics of Bacteria and their Viruses, 1964. *Recreations:* painting, reading or doing nothing. *Address:* 17 MacPherson Street, O'Connor, ACT 2601, Australia.

HAYES, Prof. William; Official Fellow and Tutor, since 1960, Principal Bursar, 1977–Aug. 1987, President, from Aug. 1987, St John's College, University Lecturer, since 1962 and Director and Head of the Clarendon Laboratory, since 1985, Oxford University; *b* 12 Nov. 1930; *s* of Robert Hayes and Eileen Tobin; *m* 1962, Joan Ferriss; two *s* one *d*. *Educ:* University Coll., Dublin (MSc, PhD); Oxford Univ. (MA, DPhil). 1851 Overseas Schol., St John's Coll., Oxford, 1955–57; temporary research appointments at: Argonne Nat. Lab., 1957–58; Purdue Univ., 1963–64; RCA Labs, Princeton, 1968; Univ. of Illinois, 1971; Bell Labs, 1974. Mem., Physics Cttee, SERC, 1982–85. *Publications:* (ed) Crystals with the Fluorite Structure, 1974; (with R. Loudon) Scattering of Light by Crystals, 1978; (with A. M. Stoneham) Defects and Defect Processes in non-metallic Solids, 1985; contribs to Procs of Royal Soc., Jl of Physics, Physical Rev., etc. *Recreations:* walking, reading, listening to music. *Address:* 91 Woodstock Road, Oxford OX2 6HL. *T:* Oxford 59112.

HAYHOE, Rt. Hon. Bernard John, (Barney), PC 1985; CEng, FIMechE; MP (C) Brentford and Isleworth, since 1974 (Heston and Isleworth, 1970–74); *b* 8 Aug. 1925; *s* of Frank Stanley and Catherine Hayhoe; *m* 1962, Anne Gascoigne Thornton, *o d* of Bernard William and Hilda Thornton; two *s* one *d*. *Educ:* State schools; Borough Polytechnic. Tool Room Apprentice, 1941–44; Armaments Design Dept, Ministry of Supply, 1944–54; Inspectorate of Armaments, 1954–63; Conservative Research Dept, 1965–70. PPS to Lord President and Leader of House of Commons, 1972–74; an additional Opposition Spokesman on Employment, 1974–79; Parly Under Sec. of State for Defence for the Army, 1979–81; Minister of State: CSD, 1981; HM Treasury, 1981–85; (Minister for Health) DHSS, 1985–86. Hon. Sec., 1970–71, Vice-Chm., 1974, Cons. Parly Employment Cttee; Jt Hon. Sec., 1970–73, Vice-Chm., 1973–76, Cons. Gp for Europe; Vice-Chm., Cons. Party Internat. Office, 1973–79; Mem., Select Cttee on Race Relations and Immigration, 1971–73. Mem., Trilateral Commn, 1977–79. Governor, Birkbeck Coll., 1976–79. *Address:* 20 Wool Road, SW20 0HW. *T:* 01–947 0037.

HAYHOE, Prof. Frank George James, MD, FRCP, FRCPath; Leukaemia Research Fund Professor of Haematological Medicine, University of Cambridge, since 1968; Fellow, Darwin College, Cambridge, since 1964, Vice-Master, 1964–74; *b* 25 Oct. 1920; *s* of Frank Stanley and Catharine Hayhoe; *m* 1945, Jacqueline Marie Marguerite (*née* Dierkx); two *s*. *Educ:* Selhurst Grammar Sch.; Trinity Hall, Cambridge; St Thomas's Hospital Medical Sch. BA Cantab 1942; MRCS, LRCP 1944; MB, BChir Cantab 1945; MRCP 1949; MA Cantab 1949; MD Cantab 1951; FRCP 1965; FRCPath 1971. Captain RAMC, 1945–47. Registrar, St Thomas' Hosp., 1947–49. Elmore Research Student, Cambridge Univ., 1949–51; Royal Soc. Exchange Res. Schol., USSR, 1962–63; Lectr in Medicine, Cambridge Univ., 1951–68; Mem. Council of Senate, 1967–71. Member: Bd of Governors, United Cambridge Hospitals, 1971–74; Cambs AHA, 1974–75; GMC, 1982–. Lectures: Langdon Brown, RCP, 1971; Cudlip Meml, Ann Arbor, 1967; vis. lectr at med. schs in N and S America, Europe, Middle East, Africa, India. G. F. Götz Foundn Prize, Zürich Univ., 1974; Suniti Rana Panja Gold Medal, Calcutta Sch. of Trop. Med., 1979. *Publications:* (ed) Lectures in Haematology, 1960; Leukaemia: Research and Clinical Practice, 1960; (jtly) Cytology and Cytochemistry of Acute Leukaemia, 1964; (ed) Current Research in Leukaemia, 1965; (with R. J. Flemans) An Atlas of Haematological

Cytology, 1969, 2nd edn 1982; (with J. C. Cawley) Ultrastructure of Haemic Cells, 1973; (jtly) Leukaemia, Lymphomas and Allied Disorders, 1976; (jtly) Hairy Cell Leukaemia, 1980; (with D. Quaglino) Haematological Cytochemistry, 1980, 2nd edn 1987; (ed with D. Quaglino) The Cytobiology of Leukaemias and Lymphomas, 1985; contribs to med. and scientific jls, on haematological topics, especially leukaemia. *Address:* Department of Haematological Medicine, University of Cambridge, Cambridge. *T:* Cambridge 245171. *See also B. J. Hayhoe.*

HAYMAN, Mrs Helene (Valerie); broadcaster; *b* 26 March 1949; *d* of Maurice Middleweek and Maude Middleweek; *m* 1974, Martin Hayman; four *s. Educ:* Wolverhampton Girls' High Sch.; Newnham Coll., Cambridge (MA). Pres., Cambridge Union, 1969. Worked with Shelter, Nat. Campaign for the Homeless, 1969; Camden Council Social Services Dept, 1971; Dep. Dir, Nat. Council for One Parent Families, 1974. Contested (Lab) Wolverhampton SW, Feb. 1974; MP (Lab) Welwyn and Hatfield, Oct. 1974–1979. Chairperson, Maternity Alliance, 1984–; Member: RCOG Ethics Cttee, 1982–; Bloomsbury HA, 1985–.

HAYMAN, John David Woodburn; His Honour Judge Hayman; a Circuit Judge, since 1976; *b* 24 Aug. 1918; *m*; two *s* four *d. Educ:* King Edward VII Sch., Johannesburg; St John's Coll., Cambridge (MA, LLM). Served with S African Forces, 1940–42. Called to the Bar, Middle Temple, 1945. Sometime Lecturer in Law: University Coll. of Wales, Aberystwyth; Leeds Univ.; Cambridge Univ.

HAYMAN, Sir Peter (Telford), KCMG 1971 (CMG 1963); CVO 1965; MBE 1945; HM Diplomatic Service, retired; *b* 14 June 1914; *s* of C. H. T. Hayman, The Manor House, Brackley, Northants; *m* 1942, Rosemary Eardley Blomefield; one *s* one *d. Educ:* Stowe; Worcester Coll., Oxford. Asst Principal: Home Office, 1937–39; Min. of Home Security, 1939–41; Asst Priv. Sec. to Home Sec. (Rt Hon. Herbert Morrison, MP), 1941–42; Principal, Home Office, 1942. Served War, 1942–45, Rifle Bde, Major. Principal, Home Office, 1945–49; transf. to Min. of Defence as Personal Asst to Chief Staff Officer to the Minister, 1949–52; Asst Sec, Min. of Defence, 1950; UK Delegation to NATO, 1952–54; transf. to FO, 1954; Counsellor, Belgrade, 1955–58; seconded for temp. duty with Governor of Malta, 1958; Couns., Baghdad, 1959–61; Dir-Gen. of British Information Services, New York, 1961–64; Minister and Dep. Comdt, Brit. Milit. Govt in Berlin, 1964–66; Asst Under-Sec., FO, 1966–69; Dep. Under-Secretary of State, FCO, 1969–70; High Comr in Canada, 1970–74. *Recreations:* shooting, fishing, travel. *Address:* Uxmore House, Checkendon, Oxon. *T:* Checkendon 680 658. *Club:* MCC.

HAYMAN, Prof. Walter Kurt, FRS 1956; MA; ScD (Cambridge); Hon. ARCS (Imperial College); Professor of Pure Mathematics, University of York, since 1985; Professor of Pure Mathematics, 1956–85, and Dean of the Royal College of Science, 1978–81, at the Imperial College of Science and Technology, London; *b* 6 Jan. 1926; *s* of late Franz Samuel Haymann and Ruth Therese (*née* Hensel); *m* 1947, Margaret Riley Crann, MA Cantab, *d* of Thomas Crann, New Earswick, York; three *d. Educ:* Gordonstoun Sch.; St John's Coll., Cambridge. Lecturer at King's Coll., Newcastle upon Tyne, 1947, and Fellow of St John's Coll., Cambridge, 1947–50; Lecturer, 1947, and Reader, 1953–56, Exeter. 1st Smiths prize, 1948, shared Adams Prize, 1949, Junior Berwick Prize, 1955; Senior Berwick Prize, 1964. Visiting Lecturer at Brown Univ., USA, 1949–50, at Stanford Univ., USA (summer) 1950 and 1955, and to the American Mathematical Soc., 1961. Co-founder with Mrs Hayman of British Mathematical Olympiad; Vice-Pres., London Mathematical Soc., 1982–84. Foreign Member: Finnish Acad. of Science and Letters; Accademia Nazionale dei Lincei, Rome; Corresp. Mem., Bavarian Acad. of Science. Hon. DSc: Exeter, 1981; Birmingham, 1985. *Publications:* Multivalent Functions (Cambridge, 1958) Meromorphic Functions (Oxford, 1964); Research Problems in Function Theory (London, 1967); Subharmonic Functions, vol I, 1976; papers in various mathematical journals. *Recreations:* music, travel. *Address:* University of York, Heslington, York YO1 5DD. *T:* York 59861.

HAYMAN, Rev. Canon William Samuel; Chaplain to The Queen's Household, 1961–73; *b* 3 June 1903; *s* of late Rev. William Henry Hayman, Rector of Leckford, and late Louise Charlotte Hayman; *m* 1930, Rosemary Prideaux Metcalfe; one *s* one *d. Educ:* Merchant Taylors' Sch.; St John's Coll., Oxford (MA). Deacon, 1926; Priest, 1927; Curate: St Matthew, Brixton, 1926–32; Wimbledon (in charge of St Mark), 1932–34; Vicar of Finstall, Worcs, 1934–38; Rector of Cheam, 1938–72. Hon. Canon of Southwark, 1952–60, Canon Emeritus, 1972. Rural Dean of Beddington, 1955–60; Archdeacon of Lewisham, 1960–72. Scouts Silver Acorn, 1971. *Recreations:* fly-fishing, photography, music. *Address:* 8 Black Jack Mews, Cirencester, Glos GL7 2AA. *T:* Cirencester 5024.

HAYNES, David Francis, (Frank); JP; MP (Lab) Ashfield, since 1979; *b* London, March 1926; *m*; one *s* two *d. Educ:* secondary schs in London. Fireman, Southern Railway; then coalminer. Member: Notts CC, 1965–; Mansfield DC; Chm., Central Notts Community Health Council. Mem., NUM. *Address:* House of Commons, SW1; 27 Lawns Road, Annesley Woodhouse, Kirkby in Ashfield, Notts.

HAYNES, Denys Eyre Lankester; Keeper of Greek and Roman Antiquities, British Museum, 1956–76; *b* 15 Feb. 1913; 2nd *s* of late Rev. Hugh Lankester Haynes and late Emmeline Marianne Chaldecott; *m* 1951, Sybille Edith Overhoff. *Educ:* Marlborough; Trinity Coll., Cambridge. Scholar, British School at Rome, 1936; Asst Keeper: Victoria and Albert Museum, 1937; British Museum, 1939–54 (released for war service, 1939–45); Dep. Keeper, British Museum, 1954. Geddes-Harrower Prof. of Greek Art and Archaeology, Univ. of Aberdeen, 1972–73. Chm., Soc. for Libyan Studies, 1974. Corr. Mem., German Archæological Inst., 1953; Ordinary Mem., 1957. Visitor, Ashmolean Museum, 1979. Lectures: Burlington, 1976; Brown and Hayley, Univ. of Puget Sound, 1977. *Publications:* Porta Argentariorum, 1939; Ancient Tripolitania, 1946; Antiquities of Tripolitania, 1956; The Parthenon Frieze, 1958; The Portland Vase, 1964; Fifty Masterpieces of Classical Art, 1970; The Arundel Marbles, 1975; Greek Art and the Idea of Freedom, 1981. *Address:* Flat 17, Murray Court, 80 Banbury Road, Oxford OX2 6LQ.

HAYNES, Edwin William George, CB 1971; *b* 10 Dec. 1911; *s* of Frederick William George Haynes and Lilian May Haynes (*née* Armstrong); *m* 1942, Dorothy Kathleen Coombs; one *s* one *d. Educ:* Regent Street Polytechnic Secondary Sch.; University of London (BA, LLM). Barrister-at-law, Lincoln's Inn, 1946. Estate Duty Office, Inland Revenue, 1930–39; Air Min., 1939; Min. of Aircraft Production, 1940; Min. of Supply, 1946; Min. of Aviation, 1959; Under-Sec., 1964; Under-Sec., DTI (formerly Min. of Technology), 1968–71. Covent Garden Market Authority, 1971–81. *Address:* 92 Malmains Way, Beckenham, Kent. *T:* 01–650 0224.

HAYNES, Ernest Anthony, (Tony), CIGasE; Regional Chairman, East Midlands Region, British Gas Corporation, since 1983; *b* 8 May 1922; *s* of Joseph Ernest Haynes and Ethel Rose (*née* Toomer); *m* 1946, Sheila Theresa (*née* Blane); two *s* two *d. Educ:* King Edward Sixth Grammar Sch., Totnes, S Devon. Joined gas industry with Torquay and Paignton Gas Co., following demobilisation from Royal Hampshire Regt; with Northern Gas Board for eleven years; held number of appts, finally as Commercial Manager; Asst Dir of Marketing, Gas Council; Dir of Marketing, Eastern Gas, 1974; Deputy Chairman: North Eastern Gas, 1977; North Thames Gas, 1979. Vice-Pres., Internat. Colloquium about Gas Marketing, 1983–84. *Publications:* papers to Instn of Gas Engineers and Internat. Colloquium about Gas Marketing (Silver Medal, IGasE, for paper, Energy Conservation—a marketing opportunity). *Recreations:* golf, flyfishing. *Address:* 1 Aldworth Gardens, The Avenue, Crowthorne, Berkshire RG11 6PQ.

HAYNES, Frank; *see* Haynes, D. F.

HAYNES, Very Rev. Peter; Dean of Hereford since 1982; Vicar, St John Baptist, Hereford, since 1983; *b* 24 April 1925; *s* of Francis Harold Stanley Haynes and Winifred Annie Haynes; *m* 1952, Ruth, *d* of late Dr Charles Edward Stainthorpe, MRCS, LRCP, Brunton Park, Newcastle upon Tyne; two *s. Educ:* St Brendan's Coll., Clifton; Selwyn Coll., Cambridge (MA); Cuddesdon Theol Coll., Oxford. Staff of Barclays Bank, 1941–43; RAF, 1943–47. Deacon 1952, Priest 1953. Asst Curate, Stokesley, 1952–54; Hessle, 1954–58; Vicar, St John's Drypool, Hull, 1958–63; Bishop's Chaplain for Youth and Asst Dir of Religious Educn, Dio. Bath and Wells, 1963–70; Vicar of Glastonbury, 1970–74 (with Godney from 1972); Archdeacon of Wells, Canon Residentiary and Prebendary of Huish and Brent in Wells Cathedral, 1974–82. Proctor in Convocation, 1976–82. Mem., Dioceses Commn, 1978–86. *Recreations:* sailing, model engineering. *Address:* The Deanery, Hereford HR1 2NG. *T:* Hereford 272525.

HAYNES-DIXON, Margaret Rumer; *see* Godden, Rumer.

HAYR, Air Vice-Marshal Kenneth William, CB 1982; CBE 1976; AFC 1963 and Bar 1972; Commander British Forces Cyprus and Administrator Sovereign Base Areas, since 1985; *b* 13 April 1935; *s* of Kenneth James and Jean Templeton Hayr; *m* 1961, Joyce Gardner; three *s. Educ:* Auckland Grammar Sch.; RAF Coll. Cranwell. Served Hunter and Lightning Sqns, 1957–64; Central Fighter Estabt/Fighter Comd Trials Unit, 1964–67; Phantom OCU Sqn Comdr, 1968–69; OC 1 (F) Sqn (Harriers), 1970–71; RAF Staff Coll., 1972; OC RAF Binbrook (Lightnings), 1973–76; Inspector of Flight Safety (RAF), 1976–79; RCDS 1980; Asst Chief of Air Staff (Ops), 1980–82; AOC No 11 Group, RAF, 1982–85. Freeman, City of London, 1984. *Recreations:* flying, wind surfing, tennis, golf. *Address:* c/o Lloyds Bank, Cox's & King's Branch, 6 Pall Mall, SW1Y 5NH. *Club:* Royal Air Force.

HAYTER, 3rd Baron *cr* 1927 of Chislehurst, Kent; **George Charles Hayter Chubb,** KCVO 1977; CBE 1976; Bt 1900; a Deputy Chairman, House of Lords, since 1981; Managing Director, 1941–71, Chairman, 1957–81, Chubb & Son's Lock & Safe Co. Ltd; *b* 25 April 1911; *e s* of 2nd Baron Hayter and Mary (*d* 1948), *d* of J. F. Haworth; *S* father, 1967; *m* 1940, Elizabeth Anne Rumbold, MBE 1975, JP; three *s* one *d. Educ:* Leys Sch., Cambridge; Trinity Coll., Cambridge (MA). Chairman: Royal Society of Arts, 1965–66; Management Cttee, King Edward's Hospital Fund for London, 1965–82; Executives Assoc. of GB, 1960; Duke of Edinburgh's Countryside in 1970 Cttee. President: Canada-United Kingdom Chamber of Commerce, 1966–67; Royal Warrant Holders Association, 1967; Business Equipment Trades Association, 1954–55. Mem., CoID, 1964–71; Chairman: EDC International Freight Movement, 1972–79; British Security Industry Assoc., 1973–77. Worshipful Company of Weavers': Liveryman, 1934–; Upper Bailiff, 1961–62. *Publication:* Security offered by Locks and Safes (Lecture, RSA), 1962. *Heir: s* Hon. George William Michael Chubb [*b* 9 Oct. 1943; *m* 1983, Waltraud, *yr d* of J. Flackl, Sydney, Australia; one *s*]. *Address:* Ashtead House, Ashtead, Surrey. *T:* Ashtead 73476.

HAYTER, Dianne, JP; Director: Alcohol Concern, since 1984; Galleon World Travel, since 1982; *b* 7 Sept. 1949; *d* of late Alec Hayter and late Nancy Hayter. *Educ:* Trevelyan Coll., Durham Univ. (BA Hons Sociology and Social Admin). Research Assistant: General and Municipal Workers Union, 1970–72; European Trade Union Confedn (ETUC), Brussels, 1973; Research Officer, Trade Union Adv. Cttee to OECD (TUAC-OECD), Paris, 1973–74; Asst Gen. Sec., Fabian Soc., 1974–76, Gen. Sec., 1976–82; Journalist, A Week in Politics, Channel Four, 1982–84. Mem. Exec. Cttee, London Labour Party, 1977–83; Mem., Royal Commn on Criminal Procedure, 1978–80. Member: Labour Parliamentary Assoc.; Labour Party; Soc. of Labour Lawyers; Socialist Health Assoc.; NUJ; GMBTU; Justice. JP Inner London, 1976–. *Publications:* The Labour Party: crisis and prospects (Fabian Soc.), 1977; (contrib.) Labour in the Eighties, 1980. *Recreations:* reading, politics. *Address:* 305 Gray's Inn Road, WC1X 8QF. *T:* (office) 01–833 3471.

HAYTER, Paul David Grenville; Principal Clerk of Committees, House of Lords, since 1985; *b* 4 Nov. 1942; *s* of Rev. Canon Michael George Hayter and Katherine Patricia Hayter (*née* Schofield); *m* 1973, Hon. Deborah Gervaise, *d* of Baron Maude of Stratford-upon-Avon, *qv*; two *s* one *d. Educ:* Eton (King's Scholar); Christ Church, Oxford (MA). Clerk, Parlt Office, House of Lords, 1964; seconded as Private Sec. to Leader of House and Chief Whip, House of Lords, 1974–77; Clerk of Cttees, 1977. Sec., Assoc. of Lieutenants of Counties and Custodes Rotulorum, 1977–. *Recreations:* music, gardening, botanising, archery, painting. *Address:* Williamscot, Banbury, Oxon.

HAYTER, Stanley William, CBE 1967 (OBE 1959); Hon. RA 1982; artist; *b* 27 Dec. 1901; *s* of William Harry Hayter and Ellen Mercy Palmer; *m* 1st, 1926, Edith Fletcher (marriage dissolved at Reno, Nevada, 1929); one *s* decd; 2nd, 1940, Helen Phillips (marr. diss., Paris, 1971); two *s. Educ:* Whitgift Middle Sch.; King's Coll., London. Chemist, Anglo-Iranian Oil Co., Abadan, Iran, 1922–25. Founded Atelier 17, Paris, 1927. Has exhibited since 1927 in various cities of Europe, America and Japan (incl. London: 1928, 1938, 1957, 1962, 1967). Paintings and prints in principal museums in Gt Britain, France, Belgium, Switzerland, Sweden, Italy, Canada, USA, Japan. Foreign Mem., Amer. Acad. of Arts and Scis, 1978. Hon. Dr: Hamline Univ., Minn.; New Sch. for Social Research, NY, 1983. Legion of Honour, 1951; Commandeur des Arts et Lettres, 1986 (Chevalier, 1967). *Publications:* New Ways of Gravure, 1949 (New York also) (revised edn 1983); Nature and Art of Motion, New York, 1964; About Prints, 1962. *Address:* 12 rue Cassini, 75014 Paris, France. *T:* 43 26 26 60.

HAYTER, Sir William Goodenough, KCMG 1953 (CMG 1948); Warden of New College, Oxford, 1958–76, Hon. Fellow, 1976; *b* 1 Aug. 1906; *s* of late Sir William Goodenough Hayter, KBE; *m* 1938, Iris Marie, *d* of late Lieut-Col C. H. Grey (formerly Hoare), DSO; one *d. Educ:* Winchester; New Coll., Oxford. Entered HM Diplomatic Service, 1930; served Foreign Office, 1930; Vienna, 1931; Moscow, 1934; Foreign Office, 1937; China, 1938; Washington, 1941; Foreign Office, 1944 (Asst Under-Sec. of State, 1948); HM Minister, Paris, 1949; Ambassador to USSR, 1953–57; Deputy Under-Sec. of State, Foreign Office, 1957–58. Fellow of Winchester Coll., 1958–76. Trustee, British Museum, 1960–70. Hon. DL Bristol, 1976; Grosses Goldenes Ehrenzeichen mit dem Stern für Verdienste (Austria), 1967. *Publications:* The Diplomacy of the Great Powers, 1961; The Kremlin and the Embassy, 1966; Russia and the World, 1970; William of Wykeham, Patron of the Arts, 1970; A Double Life (autobiog.), 1974; Spooner, 1977. *Address:* Bassetts House, Stanton St John, Oxford. *T:* Stanton St John 598.

HAYWARD, Sir Alfred, KBE 1961 (CBE 1960); retired; *b* England, 14 Jan. 1896; *s* of Thomas and Minnie Hayward, Sudbourne, Suffolk; *m* 1923, Margaret Fromm; one *s* two *d.* Came to New Zealand, 1911. Served European War, 1914–18, in France, 1916–18. Took up farming in Waikato district. Dir, NZ Co-op. Dairy Co., 1933–61. Chm.,

1947–61; Deputy Chm., NZ Dairy Board, 1958. JP 1957. *Address:* 34 Melrose House, 159 Waiki Road, Tauranga, New Zealand.

HAYWARD, Sir Anthony (William Byrd), Kt 1978; Deputy Chairman and Acting Chairman, Elders Keep Holdings, since 1985; Director of various overseas companies; *b* 29 June 1927; *s* of Eric and Barbara Hayward; *m* 1955, Jenifer Susan McCay; two *s* two *d. Educ:* Stowe Sch., Buckingham; Christ Church, Oxford. Served RNVR, 1945–48. With family business in Calcutta, 1948–57; Shaw Wallace & Co. Ltd, India, 1957–78; Man. Dir, Guthrie Berhad, Singapore, 1978–81; Pres. and Chief Exec. Officer, Private Investment Co. for Asia (PICA) SA, 1982–84. Pres., Associated Chambers of Commerce and Industry of India, 1977–78. *Recreations:* shooting, fishing, golf, photography. *Address:* Dane Street House, Chilham, near Canterbury, Kent. *T:* Canterbury 730221. *Clubs:* Oriental; Rye Golf.
See also Ven. J. D. R. Hayward.

HAYWARD, Brian Robin, FCIT; Chairman, Mark IV Management Ltd; *b* 11 Jan. 1937; *s* of Henry Albert and Jesse Agness Hayward; *m* 1954, Kathleen Mary Scott; three *s. Educ:* Woodlands, Gillingham, Kent. CBIM; MInstM. Depot Manager, Pickfords, 1963–66; Transport Manager, Hotpoint, 1966–69; Director and General Manager, Carryfast Ltd, 1969–72; Supplies Director, British Domestic Appliances, 1972–75; Managing Director, Southern BRSL, 1975–76; Gp Man. Dir, National Carriers Ltd, 1976–83 (Founder mem., Nat. Freight Consortium Bd, 1982); Chm., Fashion Flow Ltd, 1976–83. *Recreation:* golf. *Address:* 34 Audley Gate, Peterborough. *T:* Peterborough 263711. *Club:* Royal Automobile.

HAYWARD, Maj.-Gen. George Victor, BSc; CEng, FICE, FIMechE; Senior Planning Inspector, Department of the Environment; *b* 21 June 1918; *e s* of late G. H. Hayward; *m* 1953, Gay Benson, *d* of late H. B. Goulding, MB, BCh, FRCSI; one *s* one *d. Educ:* Blundells; Birmingham Univ. (BSc). War of 1939–45: commissioned, 1940; transf. to REME, 1942; GSO1 REME Training Centre, 1958; Comdr, REME 2nd Div., 1960; Asst Mil. Sec., War Office, 1962; Col, RARDE, Fort Halstead, 1963; CO, 38 Central Workshop, 1965; Dep. Comdt, Technical Group, REME, 1966; Comdt, REME Training Centre, 1969; Comdt, Technical Gp, REME, 1971–73, retired. Col Comdt, REME, 1973–78. *Recreations:* sailing, ski-ing, shooting. *Address:* Chart Cottage, Chartwell, Westerham, Kent. *T:* Edenbridge 866253. *Club:* Army and Navy.

HAYWARD, Gerald William; HM Diplomatic Service, retired; *b* 18 Nov. 1927; *s* of late Frederick William Hayward and Annie Louise (*née* Glasscock); *m* 1956, Patricia Rhonwen (*née* Foster Hall); one *s* three *d. Educ:* Tottenham Grammar School; London and Hong Kong Univs. HM Forces, 1946–57. Joined HM Foreign (now HM Diplomatic) Service, 1957; British High Commn, Kuala Lumpur, 1958–60; HM Embassy, Bangkok, 1960–62; Hong Kong, 1962–64; FO, 1964–67; Copenhagen, 1967–71; FCO, 1971–76; Counsellor: Kuala Lumpur, 1976–79; FCO, 1980–82. *Recreations:* golf, ski-ing. *Address:* White Mill End, 5 Granville Road, Sevenoaks, Kent TN13 1ES. *T:* Sevenoaks 451227. *Club:* Naval and Military.

HAYWARD, Sir Jack (Arnold), Kt 1986; OBE 1968; Chairman, Grand Bahama Development Co. Ltd and Freeport Commercial and Industrial Ltd, since 1976; *b* 14 June 1923; *s* of late Sir Charles Hayward, CBE and Hilda, *d* of John and Alexandra Arnold; *m* 1948, Jean Mary Forder; two *s* one *d. Educ:* Northaw Prep Sch.; Stowe Sch., Buckingham. Joined RAF, 1941; flying training in Florida, USA; active service as officer pilot in SE Asia Comd, demobilised as Flt-Lt, 1946. Joined Rotary Hoes Ltd, 1947; served S Africa branch until 1950. Founded USA operations Firth Cleveland Gp of Companies, 1951; joined Grand Bahama Port Authority Ltd, Freeport, Grand Bahama Island, 1956. Hon. LLD Exeter, 1971. *Recreations:* promoting British endeavours, mainly in sport; watching cricket; amateur dramatics; preserving the British landscape, keeping all things bright, beautiful and British. *Address:* Seashell Lane (PO Box F-99), Freeport, Grand Bahama Island, Bahamas. *T:* Freeport 373–1528. *Clubs:* MCC, Pratt's, Royal Air Force, Durban Country (S Africa).

HAYWARD, Ven. John Derek Risdon; Vicar of Isleworth, since 1964; General Secretary, Diocese of London, since 1975; Archdeacon of Middlesex, 1974–75, now Archdeacon Emeritus; *b* 13 Dec. 1923; *s* of late Eric Hayward and of Barbara Olive Hayward; *m* 1965, Teresa Jane Kaye; one *s* one *d. Educ:* Stowe; Trinity Coll., Cambridge (BA 1956, MA 1964). Served War of 1939–45, Lieut 27th Lancers, Middle East and Italy, 1943–45 (twice wounded). Man. Dir, Hayward Waldie & Co., Calcutta (and associated cos), 1946–53. Trinity Coll., Cambridge, 1953–56, Westcott House, Cambridge, 1956–57. Asst Curate, St Mary's Bramall Lane, Sheffield, 1957–58; Vicar, St Silas, Sheffield, 1959–63. Mem., General Synod, 1975. Dir, SCM Press, 1985–. Bronze Star (US) 1945. *Recreations:* riding, skiing, sailing (when opportunity offers). *Address:* 61 Church Street, Isleworth, Mddx TW7 6BE. *T:* 01-560 6662.
See also Sir Anthony Hayward.

HAYWARD, Sir Richard (Arthur), Kt 1969; CBE 1966; *b* 14 March 1910; *m* 1936, Ethel Wheatcroft; one *s* one *d. Educ:* Catford Central Sch. Post Office: Boy Messenger; Counter Clerk; Union of Post Office Workers: Assistant Secretary, 1947; Deputy General Secretary, 1951. Secretary General, Civil Service National Whitley Council (Staff Side), 1955–66; Chm., Supplementary Benefits Commn, 1966–69; Member, Post Office Board, 1969–71; Chairman: NHS Staff Commn, 1972–75; New Towns Staff Commn, 1976–77; Member: Civil Service Security Appeals Panel, 1967–82; Home Office Adv. Panel on Security (Immigration Act 1972), 1972–81; Parole Board, England and Wales, 1975–79; Solicitors' Disciplinary Tribunal, 1975–82. UK Rep., Meeting of Experts on Conditions of Work and Service of Public Servants, ILO, 1963; overseas visits, inc. Israel, Mauritius, Canada, to advise on Trade Unionism in Public Services. Life Vice-President: Civil Service Sports Council, 1973 (Chm., 1968–73); Nat. Assoc. of Young Cricketers, 1975; Assoc. of Kent Cricket Clubs, 1984 (Pres., 1970–84); President: Civil Service Cricket Assoc., 1966–; Civil Service Assoc. Football, 1974–. Governor, Guy's Hosp., 1949–72. Freedom, City of London, 1980. *Recreations:* topography of Southwark, watching sport. *Address:* 10 Birchwood Avenue, Southborough, Tunbridge Wells, Kent TN4 0UD. *T:* Tunbridge Wells 29134. *Clubs:* MCC, Civil Service.

HAYWARD, Robert Antony; MP (C) Kingswood, since 1983; *b* 11 March 1949; *s* of Ralph and Mary Hayward; *m* 1981, Gillian Mary. *Educ:* Abingdon Sch.; Maidenhead Grammar Sch.; University Coll. of Rhodesia (BSc Econ Hons London). Personnel Officer, Esso Petroleum, 1971–75; Personnel Manager: Coca Cola Bottlers (S & W) Ltd, 1975–79; GEC Large Machines, 1979–82. PPS to Minister for Corporate and Consumer Affairs, 1985–. Mem., Commons Select Cttee on Energy, 1983–85. *Recreations:* Rugby referee; psephology. *Address:* Thistledown, Sunnyvale Drive, Longwell Green, Bristol BS15 6YH. *T:* Bristol 327005.

HAYWARD, Ronald George, CBE 1970; General Secretary of the Labour Party, 1972–82; *b* 27 June 1917; *s* of F. Hayward, small-holder, Oxon; *m* 1943, Phyllis Olive (*née* Allen); three *d. Educ:* Bloxham C of E Sch.; RAF Technical Schools, Halton, Cosford, Locking. Apprenticed Cabinet-maker, 1933–36. NCO, RAF: Technical Training Instructor, 1940–45. Labour Party: Secretary-Agent: Banbury Constituency, 1945–47; Rochester and Chatham Constituency, 1947–50; Asst Regional Organiser, 1950–59; Regional Organiser, 1959–69; National Agent, 1969–72. Vice-Pres., Nat. Union of Labour and Socialist Clubs. *Address:* Haylens, 1 Sea View Avenue, Birchington, Kent.

HAYWARD ELLEN, Patricia Mae; *see* Lavers, P. M.

HAYWOOD, Thomas Charles Stanley, OBE 1962; JP; Lieutenant of Leicestershire, 1974–84 (Lord Lieutenant of Rutland, 1963–74); *b* 10 March 1911; *s* of late Charles B. Haywood, Woodhatch, Reigate, Surrey; *m* 1937, Anne, *d* of J. B. A. Kessler, London; two *s* one *d. Educ:* Winchester; Magdalene Coll., Cambridge. Served 1939–42 with Leics Yeomanry, Capt. 1940, Hon. Col, 1970–77. Chm. Trustees, Oakham Sch., 1964–81. DL 1962, JP 1957, High Sheriff 1952, County of Rutland. *Address:* Gunthorpe, Oakham, Rutland. *T:* Manton 203.

HAZAN, John Boris Roderick, QC 1969; **His Honour Judge Hazan;** a Circuit Judge assigned to the Central Criminal Court, since 1982; *b* 3 Oct. 1926; *s* of Selik and Eugenie Hazan. *Educ:* King's Coll., Taunton; King's Coll., Univ. of London (LLB 1946). Called to Bar, Lincoln's Inn, 1948, Bencher 1977. Prosecuting Counsel to Inland Revenue, South Eastern Circuit, 1967–69. Dep. Chm., Surrey QS, 1969–71; a Recorder of the Crown Court, 1972–82. Member: Criminal Law Revision Cttee, 1971–; Home Secretary's Policy Adv. Cttee on Sexual Offences, 1976–84; Lord Chancellor's and Home Secretary's Cttee on Fraud Trials, 1984–86; Dept of Trade Inspector, Hartley Baird Ltd, 1973–76. JP Surrey, 1969. Freeman, City of London; Liveryman, Musicians' Co. *Recreations:* music, opera, walking. *Address:* 43 Marlborough Mansions, Cannon Hill, NW6 1JS. *Club:* Savile.

HAZELL, Bertie, CBE 1962 (MBE 1946); Chairman, Special Programme Board, North Yorkshire, Manpower Services Commission, 1978–83; *b* 18 April 1907; *s* of John and Elizabeth Hazell; *m* 1936, Dora A. Barham; one *d. Educ:* various elementary schs in Norfolk. Agricultural worker, 1921; apptd Sec. and Agent to E Norfolk Divisional Labour Party, Sept. 1933; District Organiser, Nat. Union of Agricl Workers, 1937–64, Pres., 1966–78; Mem. W Riding of Yorks, War Agricultural Executive Cttee, 1939 (Chm. several of its Cttees, throughout war period). Contested (Lab) Barkston Ash Parliamentary Division, 1945 and 1950 Gen. Elections; MP (Lab) North Norfolk, 1964–70. Chairman: E and W Ridings Regional Bd for Industry, 1954–64; N Yorks AHA, 1974–82; York DHA, 1981–84; Vice-Chm., Agricultural, Horticultural and Forestry Trng Bd, 1972–74; Member: E Riding Co. Agricultural Exec. Cttee, 1946–64; Agricultural Wages Board, 1946–78; Leeds Regional Hosp. Board, 1948–74 (Chm. Works and Buildings Cttee); Potato Marketing Bd, 1970–79. Magistrate, City of York, 1950–; Chairman: York and District Employment Cttee, 1963–74; N Yorks District Manpower Cttee, 1975–80; Vice-Chm., Leeds Regional Hosp. Bd, 1967–74. Mem. Council, Univ. of E Anglia. MUniv York, 1984. *Recreation:* gardening. *Address:* 42 Fellbrook Avenue, Beckfield Lane, Acomb, York. *T:* York 78443.

HAZELL, Ven. Frederick Roy; Archdeacon of Croydon, since 1978; *b* 12 Aug. 1930; *s* of John Murdoch and Ruth Hazell; *m* 1956, Gwendoline Edna Armstrong (*née* Vare), *widow* of Major J. W. D. Armstrong; one step-*s. Educ:* Hutton Grammar School, near Preston; Fitzwilliam Coll., Cambridge (MA); Cuddesdon Coll., Oxford. HM Forces, 1948–50. Asst Master, Kingham Hill School, 1953–54; Asst Curate, Ilkeston Parish Church, 1956–59; Priest-in-Charge, All Saints', Marlpool, 1959–62; First Vicar of Marlpool, 1962–63; Chaplain, Univ. of the West Indies, 1963–66; Asst Priest, St Martin-in-the-Fields, 1966–68; Vicar of Holy Saviour, Croydon, 1968–84; Rural Dean of Croydon, 1972–78. Hon. Canon of Canterbury, 1973–84. *Recreations:* music, numismatics. *Address:* St Matthew's House, 100 George Street, Croydon CR0 1PE.

HAZELL, Quinton, CBE 1978 (MBE 1961); DL; Director: Foreign and Colonial Investment Trust, since 1978; Hawker-Siddeley Group, since 1979; *b* 14 Dec. 1920; *s* of late Thomas Arthur Hazell and Ada Kathleen Hazell; *m* 1942, Morwenna Parry-Jones; one *s. Educ:* Manchester Grammar School. FIMI 1964. Management Trainee, Braid Bros Ltd, Colwyn Bay, 1936–39; Royal Artillery, 1939–46; formed Quinton Hazell Ltd, 1946; Chm., 1946–73; Chairman: Edward Jones (Contractors) Ltd, 1973–74; Supra Group plc, 1973–82 (Pres., 1983–). Chm., W Midlands Econ. Planning Council, 1971–77. Mem., Welsh Adv. Cttee for Civil Aviation, 1961–67; Director: Wales Gas Bd, 1961–65; Winterbottom Energy Trust, 1978–82; Phoenix Assurance Co. plc, 1968–85; Banro Industries plc, 1985–; British Law Executor & Trustee Co., 1986–; Non-Exec. Chm., F&C Enterprise Trust plc, 1981–86; Dep. Chm., Warwickshire Private Hosp., Leamington Spa, 1981–; Governor, Lord Leycester Hosp., Warwick, 1971–. Member Council: UC Bangor, 1966–68; Univ. of Birmingham. Freeman, City of London, 1960; Liveryman, Coachmakers' and Coach Harness Makers' Co., 1960. DL Warwicks, 1982. *Recreations:* antiques, horology, water ski-ing. *Address:* Watchbury Hill, Barford, Warwicks CV35 8DD. *T:* Leamington Spa 624341.

HÁZI, Dr Vencel; Hungarian Ambassador to United States of America, since 1983; *b* 3 Sept. 1925; *m* 1952, Judit Zell; one *d. Educ:* Technical Univ. and Univ. of Economics, Budapest. Entered Diplomatic Service, 1950; served in Min. of Foreign Affairs, Budapest, 1950; Press Attaché, Hungarian Legation, London, 1951–53; Counsellor, Legation, Stockholm, 1957–58; Ambassador: to Iraq, and to Afghanistan, 1958–61; to Greece, and to Cyprus, 1962–64; Head of Western Dept, Min. of For. Affairs, Budapest, 1964–68; Dep. For. Minister, Budapest, 1968–70, 1976–83; Ambassador to Court of St James's, 1970–76. Golden Grade of Order of Merit for Labour, 1962, and of Medal of Merit of Hungarian People's Republic, 1953; Grand Cordon of Order of Omayoum, 1st Class, Iran. *Recreations:* reading, music, swimming, chess. *Address:* Hungarian Embassy, 3910 Shoemaker Street NW, Washington, DC 20008, USA. *Club:* Opera Fans (Budapest).

HAZLERIGG, family name of **Baron Hazlerigg.**

HAZLERIGG, 2nd Baron, *cr* 1945, of Noseley; **Arthur Grey Hazlerigg,** Bt, *cr* 1622; MC 1945; TD 1948; DL, JP; *b* 24 Feb. 1910; *e s* of 1st Baron and Dorothy Rachel (*d* 1972), *e d* of John Henry Buxton, Easneye, Ware, Herts; *S* father 1949; *m* 1945, Patricia (*d* 1972), *e d* of late John Pullar, High Seat, Fields Hill, Kloof, Natal, SA; one *s* two *d. Educ:* Eton; Trinity Coll., Cambridge. BA 1932. FRICS 1946. Served War of 1939–45, Leics Yeomanry (MC); Major, 1941; served in Italy. DL Leics 1946; JP 1946. *Recreations:* golf, shooting. *Heir: s* Hon. Arthur Grey Hazlerigg [*b* 5 May 1951; *m* 1986, Laura, *e d* of Sir William Dugdale, Bt, *qv*]. *Address:* Noseley Hall, Leicester LE7 9EH. *Clubs:* Army and Navy, MCC.

HAZLEWOOD, Air Vice-Marshal Frederick Samuel, CB 1970; CBE 1967 (OBE 1960); AFC 1951 (Bar to AFC, 1954); retired; *b* 13 May 1921; *s* of Samuel Henry and Lilian Hazlewood; *m* 1943, Isabelle Mary (*née* Hunt); one *s. Educ:* Kimbolton Sch. Served War of 1939–45: joined RAF, 1939; ops with Bomber Command, 1941; MEAF and UK Coastal Command, 1940–45. Lancaster Units, 1948–53; Comdg Officer, No 90 Valiant Sqdn, 1958–61; HQ, Bomber Comd, 1961–63; HQ, RAF, Germany, 1963–64; OC RAF Lyneham, 1965–67; HQ, RAF, Germany, 1968–69; AOC and Commandant, Central Flying School, 1970–72; AOC 38 Gp, RAF, 1972–74; Comdt, Jt Warfare Estab., 1974–76.

Recreations: golf, tennis, rough shooting. *Address:* Holly Ditch Farm, Calne, Wilts. *Club:* Royal Air Force.

HAZLEWOOD, Rt. Rev. John; *see* Ballarat, Bishop of.

HEAD, family name of **Viscount Head.**

HEAD, 2nd Viscount *cr* 1960, of Throope; **Richard Antony Head;** *b* 27 Feb. 1937; *s* of 1st Viscount Head, GCMG, CBE, MC, PC, and of Dorothea, Viscountess Head, *d* of 9th Earl of Shaftesbury, KP, GCVO, CBE, PC; *S* father, 1983; *m* 1974, Alicia Brigid, *er d* of Julian Salmond; two *s* one *d.* *Educ:* Eton; RMA Sandhurst. The Life Guards, 1957–66 (Captain), retd. Trainer of racehorses, 1968–83. *Recreations:* hunting, sailing, golf. *Heir: s* Hon. Henry Julian Head, *b* 30 March 1980. *Address:* Throope Manor, Bishopstone, Salisbury, Wilts. *T:* Coombe Bissett 318. *Clubs:* White's, Cavalry and Guards.

HEAD, Adrian Herbert; His Honour Judge Head; a Circuit Judge since 1972; *b* 4 Dec. 1923; *s* of late Judge Head and late Mrs Geraldine Head (*née* Pipon); *m* 1947, Ann Pamela, *d* of late John Stanning and late Mrs A. C. Lewin, of Leyland and Njoro, Kenya; three *s.* *Educ:* RNC Dartmouth (invalided, polio); privately; Magdalen Coll., Oxford (MA). Arden Scholar, Gray's Inn, 1947. Called to Bar, Gray's Inn, 1947 (subseq. ad eundem Inner Temple). Chm., Agricultural Land Tribunals (SE Region), 1971; Dep. Chm., Middlesex QS, 1971. Dir, later Chm., Norfolk Lavender Ltd, 1953–71. Tredegar Memorial Lectr, RSL, 1948. *Publications:* (contrib.) Oxford Poetry 1942–1943, 1943; The Seven Words and The Civilian, 1946; contrib. Essays by Divers Hands, 1953; Safety Afloat (trans. from Dutch of W. Zantvoort), 1965; Consumer Credit Act Supplement to McCleary's County Court Precedents, 1979; Poems in Praise, 1982, 2nd edn 1987; (general ed. and contrib.) Butterworths County Court Precedents and Pleadings, 1985. *Recreations:* painting, sailing, writing, trees. *Address:* Overy Staithe, Kings Lynn, Norfolk PE31 8TG. *T:* Fakenham (0328) 738312; 5 Raymond Buildings, Gray's Inn, WC1R 5BP. *T:* 01–405 7146. *Clubs:* Norfolk (Norwich); Royal Naval Sailing Association, Cruising Association.

HEAD, Audrey May; Member, Monopolies and Mergers Commission, since 1986; Director, 1973–85, Managing Director, 1976–85, Hill Samuel Unit Trust Managers Ltd; *b* 21 Jan. 1924; *d* of Eric Burton Head and Kathleen Irene Head. *Educ:* St Catherine's Sch., Bramley, Surrey. Chartered Auctioneers' and Estate Agents' Institute, 1949–58; Hill Samuel Group, 1958–86, a Manager, 1968; Director: Hill Samuel Investment Management, 1974–86; Hill Samuel Life Assurance, 1983–86; Trade Unions Unit Trust Managers Ltd, 1986–. Chm., Unit Trust Assoc., 1983–85. Governor, St Catherine's Sch., Bramley, Surrey, 1979–. Nominated as Business Woman of the Year, 1976. Silver Jubilee Medal, 1977. *Recreations:* golf, gardening. *Address:* West Chantry, 4 Clifford Manor Road, Guildford, Surrey GU4 8AG. *T:* Guildford 61047. *Club:* Sloane.

HEAD, Dennis Alec, CBE 1979; CEng, FRAeS, CBIM; Divisional Director (Northern Ireland), STC Defence Systems, since 1986; *b* 8 Nov. 1925; *s* of late Alec Head and Florence Head; *m* 1966, Julia Rosser-Owen, BA; one *s.* *Educ:* Whitgift Sch.; Peterhouse, Cambridge (Mech. Sciences Tripos, MA); Royal Naval Engrg Coll., Manadon. Served FAA, RN, 1943–47: Sub-Lt (A) RNVR, 1945; Air Engr Officer. Rolls-Royce Ltd: grad. apprentice, 1949; Manager, Design Services, Aero Engine Div., 1962, Dir of Personnel and Admin, 1967; Dir and Gen. Man., subseq. Man. Dir, Derby Engine Div., 1973; Man. Dir Aero Div., 1976; Man. Dir Operations, 1980–82; Member Board: Rolls-Royce Ltd, 1973–82; Rolls-Royce Turbomeca, 1973–82 (Chm., 1981–82); Turbo-Union, 1979–82; Chm., Rolls-Royce & Associates, 1981–82; Mem. Bd and Dir Operations, Short Brothers, 1982–86. Member: Reg. Adv. Council for Further Educn, 1968–73; Engrg Employers' Fedn Policy Cttee, 1978–82. *Recreations:* photography, history, music.

HEAD, Major Sir Francis (David Somerville), 5th Bt, *cr* 1838; late Queen's Own Cameron Highlanders; *b* 17 Oct. 1916; *s* of 4th Bt and Grace Margaret (*d* 1967), *d* of late David Robertson; *S* father, 1924; *m* 1st, 1950, Susan Patricia (marr. diss. 1965), *o d* of A. D. Ramsay, OBE; one *s* one *d;* 2nd, 1967, Penelope, *d* of late Wilfred Alexander. *Educ:* Eton; Peterhouse, Cambridge, BA 1937. Served War of 1939–45 (wounded and prisoner); retired 1951. *Heir: s* Richard Douglas Somerville Head [*b* 16 Jan. 1951. *Educ:* Eton; Magdalene Coll., Cambridge]. *Address:* 63 Chantry View Road, Guildford, Surrey GU1 3XU. *Club:* Naval and Military.

HEAD, Michael Edward; Assistant Under Secretary of State, Home Office, since 1984; Registrar of the Baronetage, since 1984; *b* 17 March 1936; *s* of Alexander Edward Head and Wilhelmina Head; *m* 1963, Wendy Elizabeth, *d* of R. J. Davies; two *s* two *d.* *Educ:* Leeds, Kingston, and Woking Grammar Schools; University College London (BA; Pollard Prize); Univ. of Michigan (MA). 2nd Lieut, Royal Artillery (Nat. Service), 1958–60. Home Office, 1960; Private Sec. to Parly Under Secs of State, 1964–66; Sec., Deptl Cttee on Liquor Licensing (Erroll), 1971–72; Asst Sec., 1974–84: Probation and After Care Dept; Community Programmes and Equal Opportunities Dept; Criminal Dept; Asst Under Sec. of State, General Dept, 1984, Criminal Justice and Constitutional Dept, 1986. *Recreations:* theatre, reading. *Address:* Byways, The Ridge, Woking, Surrey. *T:* Woking 72929. *Clubs:* Reform; Rotary (Woking).

HEAD, Mildred Eileen, OBE 1971; owner, director and partner in several furniture and drapery shops, 1950–83; *b* 13 June 1911; *d* of Philip Strudwick Head and Katie Head. *Educ:* Sudbury Girls' Secondary Sch.; Chelsea Coll. of Physical Educn (Dipl.). MCSP. Teacher, Lectr and Organiser of Physical Educn, 1933–50. Pres., Nat. Fedn of Business and Professional Women of Gt Britain and N Ireland, 1966–69; Pres., Nat. Chamber of Trade, 1977–79 (Chm. Bd of Management, 1971–77). Mayor of Borough of Sudbury, 1970–71; Member: Price Commn, 1973–77; Nat. Economic Cttee for Distributive Trades, 1974–84; Retail Consortium, 1971–83; Davignon/Narjes Cttee for Commerce and Distribution (EEC), 1979–86; Discip. Cttee of Assoc. of Certified Accountants, 1980–83; Assessor, Auld Cttee of Inquiry into Shops Hours, 1984–85. Comr of Inland Revenue, 1959–86. Pres., Internat. Fedn of Business and Professional Women, 1977–80 (First Vice-Pres., 1974–77). Chm., Management Cttee, Quay Theatre, Sudbury, 1982–. *Recreations:* theatre, gardening, bridge. *Address:* Rosebank, Ingrams Well Road, Sudbury, Suffolk CO10 6RT. *T:* Sudbury 72185.

HEADFORT, 6th Marquis of, *cr* 1800; **Thomas Geoffrey Charles Michael Taylour,** FRICS; Bt 1704; Baron Headfort, 1760; Viscount Headfort, 1762; Earl of Bective, 1766; Baron Kenlis (UK), 1831; *b* 20 Jan. 1932; *o s* of 5th Marquis and Elsie Florence (*d* 1972), *d* of J. Partridge Tucker, Sydney, NSW, and *widow* of Sir Rupert Clarke, 2nd Bt of Rupertswood; *S* father, 1960; *m* 1st, 1958, Hon. Elizabeth Nall-Cain (from whom he obtained a divorce, 1969), *d* of 2nd Baron Brocket; one *s* two *d;* 2nd, 1972, Virginia, *d* of late Mr Justice Nable, Manila. *Educ:* Stowe; Christ's Coll., Cambridge (MA; Cert. of Proficiency in Rural Estate Management). 2nd Lieut Life Guards, 1950; acting Pilot Officer, RAFVR, 1952. Dir, Bective Electrical Co. Ltd, 1953; Sales Manager and Chief Pilot, Lancashire Aircraft Co. Ltd, 1959. Freeman, Guild of Air Pilots and Air Navigators, 1958. Piloted Prospector aircraft around Africa, 1960, etc. FRICS; FCIArb; Mem., Irish Auctioneers and Valuers Inst. Council, Royal Agricultural Society of England, 1961. Inspector, Royal Hongkong Auxiliary Police. Holds commercial pilot's licence. Underwriting Mem. of Lloyds. *Heir: s* Earl of Bective, *qv.* *Address:* Ellerslie, Crosby, Isle of Man. *T:* Marown 851521; 1425 Figueroa Street, Paco, Manila, Philippines. *T:* Manila 59–38–29; telex 64792 HDFT PN; Affix Ltd, 603 Kam Chung Building, 54 Jaffe Road, Wanchai, Hong Kong. *T:* Hong Kong 5–286011; telex 75204 AFFIX HX. *Clubs:* Cavalry and Guards, Lansdowne, Little Ship, Lloyds Yacht, House of Lords Yacht, Kildare Street and University (Dublin); Ellan Vannin (Isle of Man); Manila, Manila Polo (Philippines); Hong Kong, Foreign Correspondents (Hong Kong).

HEADLEY, 7th Baron *cr* 1797; **Charles Rowland Allanson-Winn;** Bt 1660 and 1776; retired; *b* 19 May 1902; *s* of 5th Baron Headley and Teresa (*d* 1919), *y d* of late W. H. Johnson; *S* brother, 1969; *m* 1927, Hilda May Wells-Thorpe; one *s* three *d.* *Educ:* Bedford School. *Recreations:* golf, fishing. *Heir: s* Hon. John Rowland Allanson-Winn, *b* 14 Oct. 1934. *Address:* Dreys, 7 Silverwood, West Chiltington, Pulborough, W Sussex RH20 2NG. *T:* West Chiltington 3083.

HEADLY, Derek, CMG 1957; lately Malayan Civil Service; Midlands Secretary, Independent Schools Careers Organisation (formerly Public Schools Appointments Bureau), 1966–77; *b* 1908; *s* of L. C. Headly, The House-on-the-Hill, Woodhouse Eaves, Leics; *m* 1946, Joyce Catherine (marr. diss. 1975), *d* of C. F. Freeman; one *s* one *d.* *Educ:* Repton Sch.; Corpus Christi Coll., Cambridge (BA). Military Service, 1944–46, Lieut-Col, Special Ops Exec., Force 136 (despatches). Cadet, Malaya, 1931; served Muar, Trengganu, etc; Palestine, 1938–44; Resident N Borneo, 1949; ret. as Brit. Adv., Kelantan, 1957. Dir, Vipan & Headly Ltd, 1957–66. Mem. Melton and Belvoir RDC, 1958–67. Officer (Brother) Order of St John. *Publication:* From Learning to Earning (Independent Schools Careers Organisation Careers Guide), 1977. *Recreations:* hill walking, gardening. *Address:* Rooftree Cottage, Hoby, Melton Mowbray, Leics. *T:* Rotherby 214. *Club:* Special Forces.

HEAF, Peter Julius Denison, MD, FRCP; formerly Consultant Physician, University College Hospital, now retired; *b* 1922; *s* of late Prof. F. R. G. Heaf, CMG; *m* 1947, Rosemary Cartledge; two *s* two *d.* *Educ:* Stamford Sch., Lincs; University Coll., London, Fellow 1973. MB, BS 1946; MD London 1952; MRCP 1954; FRCP 1965. House Physician and Surg., also RMO, University Coll. Hosp., and Capt. RAMC, 1946–51; Research Asst, Brompton Hosp., 1953–54; Sen. Registrar, St Thomas' Hosp., 1955–58. *Publications:* papers on chest disease and pulmonary physiology, in Lancet, etc. *Recreations:* painting, sailing. *Address:* Ferrybrook House, Chalmore Gardens, Wallingford, Oxon OX10 9EP. *T:* Wallingford 39176.

HEAKES, Air Vice-Marshal Francis Vernon, CB 1944; Commander, Legion of Merit (US); RCAF retired; *b* 27 Jan. 1894; *s* of Frank R. Heakes, Architect, and Susie Pemberton Heakes; *m* 1920, Edna Eulalie Watson, BA; one *s* three *d.* *Educ:* University of Toronto. Canadian Expeditionary Force, Lieut 1916–17; RFC (seconded), 1917–18; RAF 1918–19; CAF 1919; CAF and RCAF since 1923; Air Mem. Permanent Joint Board, Canada and US; Dir Air Personnel, RCAF; Dir Plans & Operations; AOC, RCAF, Newfoundland; AOC Western Air Command, Canada. *Recreations:* sports, all kinds, writing prose and verse, oil painting, musical composition. *Address:* 1449 West 40 Avenue, Vancouver, BC V6M 1V5, Canada.

HEAL, Anthony Standerwick; Head of the Business, Heal & Son Holdings plc, 1981–84; *b* 23 Feb. 1907; *s* of Sir Ambrose Heal and Lady Edith Florence Digby Heal; *m* 1941, Theodora Caldwell (*née* Griffin); two *s.* *Educ:* Leighton Park Sch., Reading. Joined Heal & Son Ltd 1929; Dir 1936; Chm., Heal & Son, later Heal & Son Hldgs, Ltd, 1952–81. Chm. Council, London and S Eastern Furniture Manufrs Assoc., 1947–48; Master, Furniture Makers Guild (now Worshipful Co. of Furniture Makers), 1959–60; Mem. Council of Industrial Design, 1959–67; Mem. Council, City and Guilds of London Inst., 1969–81, Chm., Licentiateship Cttee, 1976–79; Pres., Design and Industries Assoc., 1965; Chm. Indep. Stores Assoc., 1970–72. Hon. FSIAD (Hon. FSIA 1974); Hon. FCGI 1981. RSA Bi-Centenary Medal, 1964. Order of White Rose of Finland, 1970; Chevalier (First Class) Order of Dannebrog, 1974. *Recreations:* vintage cars and steam engines. *Address:* Baylins Farm, Knotty Green, Beaconsfield, Bucks. *Clubs:* Vintage Sports Car, National Traction Engine.

See also O. S. Heal.

HEAL, Oliver Standerwick; Chairman, Heal Textil GmbH, since 1984; *b* 18 April 1949; *s* of Anthony Standerwick Heal, *qv.* *Educ:* Leighton Park Sch., Reading. Joined Heal's, 1970; Dir, Heal & Son Ltd, 1974–83, Chm., 1977–83; Chm., Heal & Son Holdings PLC, 1981–83 (Dir, 1975–83); Dir, Staples & Co. Ltd, 1981–84. *Recreation:* vintage cars. *Address:* Reinsburgstrasse 171, D7000 Stuttgart 1, West Germany. *Clubs:* Winnowing; Vintage Sports Car (Newbury).

HEALD, Mervyn; QC 1970; a Recorder, since 1985; *b* 12 April 1930; *s* of Rt Hon. Sir Lionel Heald, QC, and of Daphne Constance, CBE 1976, *d* of late Montague Price; *m* 1954, Clarissa Bowen; one *s* three *d.* *Educ:* Eton College; Magdalene College, Cambridge. Called to the Bar, Middle Temple, 1954; Bencher, 1978. *Recreations:* country pursuits. *Address:* Headfoldswood, Loxwood, Sussex. *T:* Loxwood 752 248.

HEALD, Thomas Routledge; His Honour Judge Heald; a Circuit Judge (formerly County Court Judge), since 1970; *b* 19 Aug. 1923; *s* of late John Arthur Heald and Nora Marion Heald; *m* 1950, Jean, *d* of James Campbell Henderson; two *s* two *d.* *Educ:* Merchant Taylors' Sch.; St John's Coll., Oxford. Fish Schol., St John's Coll., Oxford, 1941; Lieut, RAC, 1943–45; BA (Jurisprudence) 1947; MA 1949. Called to Bar, Middle Temple, 1948; Midland Circuit; Prosecuting Counsel to Inland Revenue (Midland Circuit), 1965–70; Deputy Chairman, QS: Lindsey, 1965–71; Notts, 1969–71. Council of HM Circuit Judges: Asst Sec., 1980–83; Sec., 1984–85; Vice-Pres., 1986–87; Member: Matrimonial Rules Cttee, 1980–83; President's Cttee on Adoption, 1983–; President's Family Cttee, 1984–. Mem., Senate of Inns of Court, 1984–. Mem. Council, Nottingham Univ., 1974– (Chm., Physical Recreation Adv. Cttee, 1979–85; Chm., Law Adv. Cttee, 1976–84; Chm., Estates and Buildings Cttee, 1985–); Chm., Law Adv. Cttee, Trent Polytechnic, 1979–84. *Recreations:* golf, local history, family history. *Address:* Rebbur House, Nicker Hill, Keyworth, Nottingham NG12 5ED. *T:* Plumtree 2676. *Clubs:* United Services (Nottingham); Notts Golf, Woking Golf.

HEALEY, Sir Charles Edward C.; *see* Chadwyck-Healey.

HEALEY, Rt. Hon. Denis Winston, CH 1979; MBE 1945; PC 1964; MP (Lab) South East Leeds, Feb. 1952–55, Leeds East since 1955; Deputy Leader of the Labour Party, 1980–83; *b* 30 Aug. 1917; *s* of late William Healey, Keighley, Yorks; *m* 1945, Edna May Edmunds (*see* E. M. Healey); one *s* two *d.* *Educ:* Bradford Grammar Sch.; Balliol Coll., Oxford (Hon. Fellow, 1979). First Cl. Hons Mods 1938; Jenkyns Exhib. 1939; Harmsworth Sen. Schol., First Cl. Lit. Hum., BA 1940; MA 1945. War of 1939–45; entered Army, 1940; served N Africa, Italy. Major RE 1944 (despatches). Contested (Lab) Pudsey and Otley Div., 1945; Sec., International Dept, Labour Party, 1945–52. Shadow Cabinet, 1959–64, 1970–74, 1979–; Secretary of State for Defence, 1964–70; Chancellor of the Exchequer, 1974–79; opposition spokesman on Foreign and Commonwealth Affairs, 1980–. Mem. Brit. Delegn to Commonwealth Relations Conf., Canada, 1949;

British Delegate to: Consultative Assembly, Council of Europe, 1952–54; Inter Parly Union Conf., Washington, 1953; Western European Union and Council of Europe, 1953–55. Chm., IMF Interim Cttee, 1977–79. Mem. Exec. Fabian Soc., 1954–61. Mem., Labour Party Nat. Exec. Cttee, 1970–75. Councillor: RIIA, 1948–60; Inst. of Strategic Studies, 1958–61. Grand Cross of Order of Merit, Germany, 1979. *Publications:* The Curtain Falls, 1951; New Fabian Essays, 1952; Neutralism, 1955; Fabian International Essays, 1956; A Neutral Belt in Europe, 1958; NATO and American Security, 1959; The Race Against the H Bomb, 1960; Labour Britain and the World, 1963; Healey's Eye, 1980; Labour and a World Society, 1985; Beyond Nuclear Deterrence, 1986. *Recreations:* travel, photography, music, painting. *Address:* House of Commons, SW1. *T:* 01–219 4060.

HEALEY, Deryck John; FRSA 1978, FSIAD; photographic designer and stylist, since 1985; Chairman, Dreamshire Ltd, since 1985; Chairman and Managing Director, Routes Group Ltd, since 1985; Managing Director: Routes Tours Ltd, since 1985; Routes Design and Education Ltd, since 1985; Design Consultant, Wedgwood PLC, since 1984; *b* 30 Jan. 1937; *s* of Leonard Melvon Healey and Irene Isabella Healey (*née* Ferguson); *m* 1962, Mary Elizabeth Pitt Booth (decd); two *s*. *Educ:* Northlands High Sch., Natal, SA (Victoria League Empire Scholar; DipAD, SA, 1955; Golden Jubilee Cert. of Merit, 1957); Manchester Polytechnic (DipAd 1958, Textile Design Prize, 1957, 1958; Design Travel Bursary, 1958; Royal Manch. Inst. Cert. of Merit, 1958; Calico Printers' Assoc. Fellow, 1961–62). Design Man., Good Hope Textiles, SA, 1959–66; Chairman: Deryck Healey Associates, London, 1966–85; Deryck Healey International, 1969–85; Design Man., WPM London (Wallpaper mfrs), 1966–68; ICI Design Studio Manager, Asst to Elsbeth Juda, 1968–80; Consultant, D. H. I. Interiors Ltd, 1983–85. Chm., CNAA Textile and Fashion Bd, 1971–81; Member: Design working party, Clothing and Allied Products Trng Bd, 1980; CNAA Art and Design Cttee, 1971–81; Design Council Textile Design Selection Ctte, 1978–85; Craft Council Bd, 1983–85 (Textile Panel, 1980; Finance and Gen. Purposes Cttee, 1983–85; Chairman: Textile Develt Group, 1982–84; Projects and Organisations Cttee, 1983–85). RSA: Annual Sponsor, D. Healey Fashion and Colour Bursaries, 1978–85; Mem. Bursary Bd, 1982–. Patron, New Art Tate Gall., 1983–. Dir, On the Wall Art Gall., 1985–. Member: Contemp. Art Soc., 1982–; ICA, 1970–; Chelsea Arts Club, 1982–; Friend of RA, 1980–. SIAD: Mem., British Design Export Gp, 1980; Chm., Textile and Fashion Gp, 1966–67. Governor, London Coll. of Fashion, 1978. External Examiner, Textile and Fashion courses: CNAA BA and MA; Liverpool, BA, 1978–80; Manchester, MA, 1976–79; Kingston, BA, 1978–80; St Martin's, BA, 1978–80; Glasgow, BA, 1979–82; RCA, Textiles, 1980; Adviser and External Examiner, Middx Polytechnic, BA, 1982–86; External Examnr, London Coll. of Furniture, BTEC, 1985. FSIAD 1964. CoID Design Award, 1964; Queen's Award to Industry for Export, 1974; RSA Bicentenary Medal, 1981; Textile Institute Design Medal, 1982. *Publications:* Colour, 1980 (Mem. Editorial Bd and contrib.); Living with Colour, 1982; The New Art of Flower Design, 1986. *Recreations:* drawing, painting, photography, sculpture, gardening, Deryck Healey Trust for the encouragement of Art, Design and Craft graduates. *Address:* 20 Tedworth Square, SW3 4DR. *Clubs:* various.

HEALEY, Donald Mitchell, CBE 1973; Director, Healey Automobile Consultants Ltd, since 1955; *b* 3 July 1898; *s* of John Frederick and Emmie Mitchell Healey; *m* 1921, Ivy Maud James; three *s*. *Educ:* Newquay Coll. Pupil, Sopwith Aviation Co., 1914; RFC and RAF, 1915–18; Aeronautical Inspection Dept, Air Ministry, 1918–20; self-employed automobile engr and competitions driver, 1920; Experimental Manager and Technical Dir, Triumph Motor Co. Ltd, 1933–39; Gen. Man., Air Min. Carburettor Co., Humber Co., and RAF, 1939–45; formed Donald Healey Motor Co. Ltd, Manufacturers, Healey, Nash Healey and Austin Healey cars, 1945–73; Chm., Jensen Motors Ltd, 1973. Médaille de l'Education Physique et Sports (ler Cl.), Monaco, 1962. *Recreations:* swimming, motor sport. *Address:* Bridge House, Perranporth, Cornwall TR6 0ES. *T:* Perranporth 3521. *Club:* Royal Air Force.

HEALEY, Edna May; writer; *b* 14 June 1918; *d* of Rose and Edward Edmunds; *m* 1945, Right Hon. Denis Healey, *qv*: one *s* two *d*. *Educ:* Bell's Grammar School, Coleford, Glos; St Hugh's College, Oxford (BA, Dip Ed). Taught English and History, Keighley Girls' Grammar School, 1940–44; freelance lecturer, England and America; television writer and presenter; radio writer and broadcaster. *Publications:* Lady Unknown: life of Angela Burdett-Coutts, 1978; Wives of Fame, 1986. *Recreations:* gardening, listening to music. *Address:* Pingles Place, Alfriston, East Sussex.

HEALY, Prof. John Francis, MA, PhD; Professor of Classics, London University, since 1966; Chairman of Department at Royal Holloway and Bedford New College, since 1985 (Head of Department, Royal Holloway College, 1966–85); *b* 27 Aug. 1926; *s* of late John Healy and Iris Maud (*née* Cutland); *m* 1st, 1957, Carol Ann McEvoy; one *s*; 2nd, 1985, Barbara Edith Henshall. *Educ:* Trinity Coll., Cambridge (Open Exhbn in Classics 1943; Classical Prelim. Cl. 1 1944; Classical Tripos: 1st Cl. Pt I 1949, 1st Cl. Pt II 1950 (dist. Cl. Archaeol.); Sen. Schol. 1950; BA 1950, MA 1952, PhD 1955). War service, 1944–48; Captain, Intelligence Corps, 1946–48. Walston student, Brit. Sch. of Archaeol., Athens, 1950; G. C. Winter Warr Schol., Cambridge, 1951; Manchester University: Asst Lectr in Classics, 1953–56; Lectr in Classics and Class. Archaeol., 1956–61; London University: Reader in Greek, Bedford Coll., 1961–66; Chm., Bd of Studies in Classics, 1979–81; Dean of Faculty of Arts, Royal Holloway Coll., 1978–81. Chm. Finance Cttee, Inst. of Classical Studies, London, 1967–. FRNS 1950; FRSA 1971; MRI 1979. *Publications:* contrib. (A. Rowe) Cyrenaican Expeditions of the University of Manchester, 1955–57; Mining and Metallurgy in the Greek and Roman World, 1978; Sylloge Nummorum Graecorum, vol. VII, The Raby and Güterbock collections in Manchester University Museum, 1986; articles and reviews in Jl of Hellenic St., Numismatic Chron., Nature, Amer. Num. Soc.'s Mus. Notes, Jl of Metals, Class. Rev., Gnomon. *Recreations:* travel, music, creative gardening. *Address:* Department of Classics, Royal Holloway and Bedford New College, Egham Hill, Egham, Surrey TW20 0EX. *T:* Egham 34455. *Club:* Cambridge Union Society.

HEALY, Tim T.; *see* Traverse-Healy.

HEANEY, Henry Joseph, MA, FLA; University Librarian and Keeper of the Hunterian Books and Manuscripts, Glasgow, since 1978; *b* 2 Jan. 1935; *s* of late Michael Heaney and Sarah (*née* Fox); *m* 1976, Mary Elizabeth Moloney. *Educ:* Abbey Grammar Sch., Newry; Queen's Univ. of Belfast (MA). FLA 1967. Asst Librarian, QUB, 1959–62; Libr., Magee University Coll., Londonderry, 1962–67; Dep. Libr., New Univ. of Ulster, 1967–69; Asst Sec., Standing Conf. of National and Univ. Libraries, 1969–72; Librarian: QUB, 1972–74; University Coll., Dublin, 1975–78. Member: Adv. Cttee on Public Lib. Service, NI, 1965; Standing Cttee, Univ. Libraries Sect. IFLA, 1985–; Chm., NI Branch, Lib. Assoc., 1966, 1973. Trustee, Nat. Lib. of Scotland, 1980–. *Publication:* (ed) IFLA Annual, 1971. *Address:* Glasgow University Library, Glasgow G12 8QE. *T:* 041–339 8855.

HEANEY, Leonard Martin, CMG 1959; Overseas Civil Service, retired; *b* 28 Nov. 1906; *s* of Alexander John and Lilian Heaney; *m* 1947, Kathleen Edith Mary Chapman; no *c*. *Educ:* Bristol Grammar Sch.; Oriel Coll., Oxford. Joined Colonial Service on leaving Oxford, 1929; served in Tanganyika, retiring as a Senior Provincial Commissioner, 1959. Military service with East African Forces in Abyssinia, Madagascar, Ceylon, Burma, 1940–45. *Recreations:* reading and golf. *Address:* Flat No 9, Salcombe Court, Salcombe Hill Road, Sidmouth, Devon.

HEANEY, Seamus Justin; Member of Irish Academy of Letters; Boylston Professor of Rhetoric and Oratory at Harvard University (formerly Visiting Professor), since 1985; *b* 13 April 1939; *s* of Patrick and Margaret Heaney; *m* 1965, Marie Devlin; two *s* one *d*. *Educ:* St Columb's College, Derry; Queen's University, Belfast. BA first cl. 1961. Teacher, St Thomas's Secondary Sch., Belfast, 1962–63; Lectr, St Joseph's Coll. of Educn, Belfast, 1963–66; Lectr, Queen's Univ., Belfast, 1966–72; free-lance writer, 1972–75; Lectr, Carysfort Coll., 1975–81. Bennett Award, 1982. *Publications:* Eleven Poems, 1965; Death of a Naturalist, 1966 (Somerset Maugham Award, 1967; Cholmondeley Award, 1968); Door into the Dark, 1969; Wintering Out, 1972; North, 1975 (W. H. Smith Award; Duff Cooper Prize); Field Work, 1979; Preoccupations: Selected Prose, 1968–1978, 1980; Selected Poems, 1965–1975, 1980; (ed with Ted Hughes) The Rattle Bag, 1982; Sweeney Astray, 1984; Station Island, 1984. *Address:* c/o Faber & Faber, 3 Queen Square, WC1N 3RU.

HEANEY, Brig. Sheila Anne Elizabeth, CB 1973; MBE 1955; TD; Chairman, Women's Royal Voluntary Service, Scotland, 1977–81; *b* 11 June 1917; 2nd *d* of late Francis James Strong Heaney, MA, MD, FRCSI, Liverpool and Anne Summers McBurney. *Educ:* Huyton Coll.; Liverpool University. BA 1938. Joined ATS, 1939, WRAC, 1949; Director, WRAC, and Hon. ADC to the Queen, 1970–73. *Address:* c/o Midland Bank, 32 Rodney Street, Liverpool L1 2TP.

HEANLEY, Charles Laurence, TD 1950; FRCS; Consulting Surgeon; Member of Lloyd's; *b* 28 Feb. 1907; *e s* of Dr C. M. Heanley; *m* 1935; three *s*. *Educ:* Epsom Coll.; Downing Coll., Cambridge (Exhib., Schol.); London Hosp. BA Cambridge (Nat. Sci. Tripos) 1929, MA 1934; MRCS, LRCP 1932; MB, BCh Cambridge 1934; FRCS 1933; MRCP 1935. London Hosp., 1929; Surg. First Asst, 1936. Served War of 1939–45; France, Surgical Specialist, 17th Gen. Hosp., 1939–40; Surgeon Specialist, RAMC Park Prewitt Plastic Unit, 1941–42; India, OC No 3 British Maxillo-Facial Surgical Unit and Lieut-Col OC Surgical Div., 1942–45; Surg. in charge of Dept of Plastic Surg., London Hosp., 1946–64. Cons. Surg. Worthing Hosp., Bethnal Green Hosp., and Plastic Unit Queen Victoria Hosp., East Grinstead, 1945; Plastic Surg. London Hosp.; Hon. Cons. Plastic Surg. Royal National and Golden Square Hosps, 1969. *Publications:* varied medical articles. *Recreations:* swimming, archæology. *Address:* Vainona, St George, Woodmancote, Henfield, West Sussex BN5 9ST. *T:* Brighton 492947.

HEAP, Sir Desmond, Kt 1970; LLM, Hon. LLD, PPRTPI; solicitor; *b* 17 Sept. 1907; *o s* of late William Heap, Architect, Burnley, Lancs, and of Minnie Heap; *m* 1945, Adelene Mai, *o d* of late Frederick Lacey, Harrogate, and of Mrs F. N. Hornby; one *s* two *d*. *Educ:* The Grammar Sch., Burnley; Victoria University of Manchester. LLB Hons 1929; LLM 1936; Hon. LLD 1973; admitted Solicitor, 1933; Hons Final Law Examination; Pres., Law Soc., 1972–73 (Mem. Council, 1954–78, Chm. Law Reform Cttee, 1955–60, and Chm., Town Planning Cttee, 1964–70). Senior Past Master, Worshipful Company of Solicitors; Liveryman of Worshipful Company of Carpenters. Hon. Mem., Court of Worshipful Co. of Chartered Surveyors; Legal Mem., RTPI (formerly TPI), 1935–, Mem. of Council, 1947–77, Pres., 1955–56; Assoc. Mem. Royal Institute of Chartered Surveyors, 1953–, Mem. of Council, 1957–84; Mem. of Colonial Office Housing and Town Planning Adv. Panel, 1953–65; Prosecuting Solicitor, 1935–38 and Chief Asst Solicitor for City of Leeds, 1938–40; Dep. Town Clerk of Leeds, 1940–47; Lecturer in the Law of Town and Country Planning and Housing, Leeds Sch. of Architecture, 1935–47; Comptroller and City Solicitor to the Corporation of London, 1947–73. Mem. of Editorial Board of Journal of Planning and Environment Law, 1948–; Mem., Council on Tribunals, 1971–77; Vice-Pres., Statute Law Soc., 1982–. Dep. Pres., City of London Branch, British Red Cross Soc., 1956–76. Chm. of Governors, Hurstpierpoint Coll., 1975–82. FRSA (Mem. Council, 1974–78). Hon. Member: Amer. Bar Foundn, 1971–; Hawaii Chapter, Phi Beta Kappa; Hon. Fellow, Inc. Soc. of Valuers and Auctioneers, 1979–. Gold Medal, RTPI, 1983; Gold Medal, Lincoln Inst. of Land Policy, Cambridge, Mass, 1983. *Publications:* Planning Law for Town and Country, 1938; Planning and the Law of Interim Development, 1944; The Town and Country Planning Act, 1944, 1945; An Outline of Planning Law, 1943 to 1945, 1945; The New Towns Act, 1946, 1947; Introducing the Town and Country Planning Act, 1947, 1947; Encyclopædia of Planning, Compulsory Purchase and Compensation, Vol. 1, 1949; An Outline of Planning Law, 1949, 9th edn 1986; Heap on the Town and Country Planning Act, 1954, 1955; Encyclopædia of Planning Law and Administration, 4 vols, 1960; Introducing the Land Commission Act 1967, 1967; Encyclopædia of Betterment Levy, 1967; The New Town Planning Procedures, 1969; How to Control Land Development, 1974, 2nd edn 1981; The Land and the Development; or, the Turmoil and the Torment (Hamlyn Lectures), 1975; Lectures on tape: The Community Land Act, 1975; articles in legal jls. *Recreations:* swimming, pedal biking, the amateur theatre. *Address:* 30 Andrewes House, Barbican, EC2Y 8AX. *T:* 01–588 2645; Last, Suddards & Co., 128 Sunbridge Road, Bradford. *T:* Bradford 33571. *Clubs:* Athenæum, City Livery, Guildhall.

HEAP, Peter William; HM Diplomatic Service; Deputy High Commissioner, Lagos, since 1986; *b* 13 April 1935; *s* of Roger and Dora Heap; *m* 1st, 1960, Helen Cutting Wilmerding (marr. diss.); two *s* two *d*; 2nd, 1977, Dorrit Breitenstein. *Educ:* Bristol Cathedral Sch.; Merton Coll., Oxford. 2nd Lt Glos Regt and RWAFF, 1954–56. CRO, 1959; Third Sec., Dublin, 1960; Third and Second Sec., Ottawa, 1960; First Sec., Colombo, 1963–66; seconded to MoD, 1966–68; FO, 1968–71; Dep. Dir-Gen., British Information Services, New York, 1971–76; Counsellor (Political and Economic), 1976–78, Counsellor (Commercial), 1978–80, Caracas; Head of Energy, Science and Space Dept, FCO, 1980–83; High Comr to the Bahamas, 1983–86. *Address:* c/o Foreign and Commonwealth Office, King Charles Street, SW1A 2AL.

HEARD, Peter Graham, FRICS; FRVA; Deputy Chief Valuer, Board of Inland Revenue, since 1983; *b* 22 Dec. 1929; *s* of late Sidney Horwood Heard and Doris Winifred Heard, MBE; *m* 1953, Ethne Jean Thomas; two *d*. *Educ:* Exmouth Grammar School. Articled to W. W. Needham, 1946; joined Valuation Office, 1950; served in Exeter, Kidderminster, Dudley, Leeds; District Valuer, Croydon, 1971; Superintending Valuer, Chief Valuer's Office, 1973; Asst Sec., Bd of Inland Revenue, 1975; Superintending Valuer, Midlands, 1977; Asst Chief Valuer, 1978. *Recreations:* cricket, golf, countryside, walking the dog, theatre. *Address:* Romany Cottage, High Street, Lindfield, Sussex. *T:* Lindfield 2095. *Clubs:* MCC, Civil Service.

HEARN, David Anthony; Joint General Secretary, Broadcasting and Entertainment Trades Alliance, since 1984; *b* 4 March 1929; *s* of James Wilfrid Laurier Hearn and Clara (*née* Barlow); *m* 1952, Anne Beveridge; two *s*. *Educ:* Trinity Coll., Oxford (MA). Asst to Gen. Sec., Assoc. of Broadcasting Staff, 1955; subseq. Asst Gen. Sec., then Dep. Gen. Sec.; Gen. Sec., Assoc. of Broadcasting and Allied Staffs, 1972–84. Sen. Res. Fellow, Nuffield

Coll., Oxford, 1970–71. *Address:* 4 Stocks Tree Close, Yarnton, Oxford OX5 1LU. *T:* Kidlington 4613.

HEARN, Rear-Adm. Frank Wright, CB 1977; Assistant Chief of Personnel and Logistics, Ministry of Defence, 1974–77; *b* 1 Oct. 1919; *s* of John Henry Hearn, Civil Servant, and Elsie Gertrude Hearn; *m* 1st, 1947, Ann Cynthia Keeble (*d* 1964); two *d*; 2nd, 1965, Ann Christina June St Clair Miller. *Educ:* Abbotsholme Sch., Derbyshire. Joined RN, 1937; HMS Hood, 1937–39. Served War of 1939–45 in various HM Ships in Atlantic, Mediterranean and East Indies. Staff of CinC, Home Fleet, 1951–53; Sec. to Flag Officer, Submarines, 1954–56; after service in USA became Sec. to Dir of Naval Intell., 1958–60, when joined HMS Tiger as Supply Officer; Fleet Supply Officer, Western Fleet, 1962–64; subseq. service in Plans Div, MoD (Navy) and CSO (Admin.) to Flag Officer, Submarines; IDC 1969; commanded HMS Centurion in rank of Cdre, 1970–73; Chm., Review of Officer Structure Cttee, 1973–74. *Recreations:* golf, tennis, gardening, wine-making. *Address:* Hurstbrook Cottage, Hollybank Lane, Emsworth, Hants PO10 7UE. *T:* Emsworth 372149.

HEARN, Rt. Rev. George Arthur; see Rockhampton, Bishop of.

HEARN, Prof. John Patrick; Director of Science and Director of Institute of Zoology, The Zoological Society of London, since 1980; Visiting Professor in Zoology, University College London, since 1979; Director, MRC/AFRC Comparative Physiology Research Group, since 1983; *b* Limbdi, India, 24 Feb. 1943; *s* of Lt-Col Hugh Patrick Hearn , Barrister, and Cynthia Ellen (*née* Nicholson); *m* 1967, Margaret Ruth Patricia McNair; four *s* one *d*. *Educ:* Crusaders' Sch., Headley, Hants; St Mary's Sch., Nairobi, Kenya; University Coll., Dublin (BSc, MSc); ANU, Canberra (PhD). Sen. Demonstrator in Zool., University Coll., Dublin, 1966–67; Lectr in Zool., 1967–69, and Dean of Science, 1968–69, Strathmore Coll., Nairobi; Res. Scholar, ANU, 1969–72; Staff Mem., MRC Reproductive Biology Unit, Edinburgh, 1972–79; Hon. Fellow, Univ. of Edinburgh, 1974–79. Consultant Scientist, WHO Special Prog. of Res. in Human Reproduction, Geneva, 1978–79; Dir, Wellcome Labs of Comparative Physiology, Zoological Soc. London, 1979–80. Pres., Internat. Primatological Soc., 1985–. Scientific Medal, Zool Soc. London, 1983; Osman Hill Medal, Primate Soc. of GB, 1986. *Publications:* (ed with H. Rothe and H. Wolters) The Biology and Behaviour of Marmosets, 1978; (ed) Immunological Aspects of Reproduction and Fertility Control, 1980; (ed) Reproduction in New World Primates, 1982; (ed) Advances in Animal Conservation, 1985; papers on develtl and reproductive physiol. in scientific jls. *Recreations:* music, travel, wildlife, squash, running, swimming. *Address:* The Institute of Zoology, The Zoological Society of London, Regent's Park, NW1 4RY. *T:* 01–722 3333.

HEARNE, Graham James; Chief Executive, Enterprise Oil plc, since 1984; *b* 23 Nov. 1937; *s* of Frank Hearne and Emily (*née* Shakespeare); *m* 1961, Carol Jean (*née* Brown); one *s* three *d*. *Educ:* George Dixon Grammar Sch., Birmingham. Admitted solicitor, 1959: Pinsent & Co., Solicitors, 1959–63; Fried, Frank, Harris, Shriver & Jacobson, Attorneys, NYC, 1963–66; Herbert Smith & Co., Solicitors, 1966–67; IRC, 1967–70; N. M. Rothschild & Sons Ltd, 1970–77; Finance Dir, Courtaulds Ltd, 1977–81; Chief Exec., Tricentrol, 1981–83; Gp Man. Dir, Carless, Capel and Leonard, 1983–84. Non-exec. Director: N. M. Rothschild & Sons Ltd, 1973–; Northern Foods, Ltd, 1976–82; BPB Industries, 1982–; part-time Member: British National Oil Corp., 1975–78; Dover Harbour Bd, 1976–78. *Address:* 1 East Heath Road, NW3 1BN. *T:* 01–794 4987. *Club:* Reform.

HEARNE, Peter Ambrose; FEng 1984; Director and General Manager, GEC (formerly Marconi) Avionics, since 1970; *b* 14 Nov. 1927; *e s* of late Arthur Ambrose Hearne, MD, and Helen Mackay Hearne; *m* 1952, Georgina Gordon Guthrie; three *s*. *Educ:* Sherborne Sch., Dorset; Loughborough Coll. of Technol. (DLC); Cranfield Inst. of Technol. (MSc); MIT. Design Engr, Saunders Roe, 1946–47; Ops Develt Engr, BOAC, 1949–54; Helicopter Proj. Engr, BEA, 1954–58; Marketing Manager, British Oxygen, 1958–59; Divl Man., Guided Weapons, Elliott Flt Automation, 1959; Asst Gen. Man., 1960; Dir and Gen. Man., 1965–70. Vis. Prof., Cranfield Inst. of Technol., 1981–82. Chm., Cranfield Soc., 1965–67, Pres., 1981; Pres., Royal Aeronautical Society, 1980–81 (Vice-Pres., 1976–79). John Curtis Sword, Aviation Week, 1982. *Publications:* papers in Jl of RAeS and NATO Agard series. *Recreations:* flying with and without engines, sailing, models. *Address:* The Limes, Wateringbury, Kent. *T:* Maidstone 812385. *Clubs:* Surrey and Hants Gliding, Tiger (Redhill); Whitstable Yacht, Southwold Sailing.

HEARNSHAW, Prof. Leslie Spencer; Professor of Psychology, University of Liverpool, 1947–75, now Emeritus; *b* Southampton, 9 Dec. 1907; *o s* of late Prof. F. J. C. Hearnshaw, Prof. of History, King's Coll., London; *m* 1937, Gwenneth R. Dickins, Perth, Western Australia; one *s* three *d*. *Educ:* King's Coll. Sch., Wimbledon; Christ Church, Oxford; King's Coll., London. 1st Class Lit Hum, 1930; 1st Class Psychology Hons (London), 1932. Investigator, Nat. Institute of Industrial Psychology, London, 1933–38; Lecturer in Psychology, Victoria Univ., Coll., Wellington, NZ, 1939–47; Dir, Industrial Psychology Div., DSIR, Wellington, NZ, 1942–47; Mem. of Council, British Psychological Soc., 1949–57; Chm., Industrial Section, 1953–54; Pres., British Psychological Soc., 1955–56. Pres. Section J (Psychology), Brit. Assoc., 1954; Hon. Dir, Medical Research Council, Research Group into occupational aspects of ageing, 1955–59, 1963–70. Hobhouse Memorial Lecturer, 1966. Vice-Pres., International Assoc. of Applied Psychology, and Editor of its Journal, 1964–74. *Publications:* (with R. Winterbourn) Human Welfare and Industrial Efficiency, 1945; A Short History of British Psychology, 1840–1940, 1964; Cyril Burt, psychologist, 1979; The Shaping of Modern Psychology, 1986; articles on industrial psychology and the psychology of thinking. *Address:* 1 Devonshire Road, West Kirby, Wirral L48 7HR. *T:* 051–625 5823.
See also C. T. C. Wall.

HEARST, Stephen, CBE 1980; FRSA; Special Adviser to the Director-General, BBC, since 1982; *b* Vienna, Austria, 6 Oct. 1919; *m* 1948, Lisbeth Edith Neumann; one *s* one *d*. *Educ:* Vienna Univ.; Reading Univ. (Dip. Hort.); Brasenose Coll., Oxford (MA). Free lance writer, 1949–52; joined BBC as producer trainee, 1952; Documentary television: script writer, 1953–55; writer producer, 1955–65; Exec. Producer, Arts Programmes Television, 1965–67; Head of Arts Features, Television, 1967–71; Controller, Radio 3, 1972–78; Controller, Future Policy Gp, 1978–82. FRSA 1980. *Publications:* Two Thousand Million Poor, 1965; Artistic Heritage and its Treatment by Television, 1982; contrib. to The Third Age of Broadcasting (ed Wenham), 1982. *Recreations:* gardening, swimming, reading, listening to music. *Address:* c/o British Broadcasting Corporation, Broadcasting House, W1A 1AA.

HEARST, William Randolph, Jun.; journalist; Editor-in-Chief, The Hearst Newspapers, and Chairman of the Executive Committee, The Hearst Corporation; *b* NYC, 27 Jan. 1908; *s* of William Randolph Hearst and Millicent Veronica (*née* Willson); *m* 1st, 1928, Alma Walker (marr. diss., 1932); 2nd, 1933, Lorelle McCarver (marr. diss., 1948); 3rd, 1948, Austine McDonnell; two *s*. *Educ:* Collegiate Sch.; St John's Manlius Mil. Acad., Syracuse; Berkeley High Sch., Berkeley, Calif.; Hitchcock Mil. Acad., San Rafael, Calif; University of Calif. Began career with New York American, NYC, as a reporter, 1928;

publisher, 1936–37; publisher, NY Journal-American, 1937–56; The American Weekly, 1945–56; War Correspondent, 1943–45. Mem. Bd, USO, NY; Permanent Charter Mem., For. Correspondents Club of Japan, 1945–; Hon. Co-Chm., Damon Runyon-Walter Winchell Cancer Fund Bd of Dirs. *Address:* (home) 810 Fifth Avenue, New York, NY 10021, USA; (office) 959 Eighth Avenue, New York, NY 10019, USA. *Clubs:* Overseas Press, Marco Polo, Brook, Madison Square Garden (New York City); F Street, Sulgrave, National Press, Metropolitan, Burning Tree, International (Washington), Bohemian, Pacific Union (San Francisco); London Press; Alaska Press; Tokyo Press.

HEARTH, John Dennis Miles, CBE 1983; Chief Executive, Royal Agricultural Society of England, since 1972; *b* 8 April 1929; *s* of late Cyril Howard Hearth, MC, and of Dr Pauline Kathleen Hearth, MB, BSc; *m* 1959, Pamela Anne (*née* Bryant); two *s*. *Educ:* The King's Sch., Canterbury; Brasenose Coll., Oxford (MA). Called to the Bar, Gray's Inn, 1962. Administrative Officer, HM Overseas Civil Service, 1953–61; Editor, Fairplay Shipping Journal, Fairplay Publications Ltd, 1961–66; Cunard Steam-Ship Co. Ltd, 1966–71 (various appts and Main Board Joint Ventures Director, 1969–71). Mem. Council, Warwick Univ., 1985. CBIM 1980. *Recreations:* travel, history, theatre, golf. *Address:* Bayard's, Fenny Compton, near Leamington Spa, Warwicks CV33 0XY. *T:* Fenny Compton 370. *Clubs:* Farmers', Anglo-Belgian.

HEASLIP, Rear-Adm. Richard George, ADC 1984; Flag Officer Submarines, and Commander Submarine Forces Eastern Atlantic, since 1984; *b* 30 April 1932; *s* of Eric Arthur Heaslip and Vera Margaret (*née* Bailey); *m* 1959, Lorna Jean Grayston, Halifax, NS, Canada; three *s* one *d* (incl. twin *s* and *d*). *Educ:* Royal Naval Coll., Dartmouth. CO HMS Sea Devil, 1961–62; Exec. Officer, HMS Dreadnought (1st British nuclear submarine), 1965–66; CO HMS Conqueror (nuclear submarine), 1971–72; CO Second Submarine Sqdn, 1975–77; Staff, SACLANT, 1980–82; Staff, CDS, 1982–84; Dep. Asst COS (Ops), Staff of SACEUR, 1984. Chm., RN Football Assoc., 1976–. *Recreations:* walking, music, gardening. *Address:* Wade Cottage, Wade Court, Havant, Hants PO9 2SU. *T:* Havant 484596.

HEATH, Sir Barrie, Kt 1978; DFC 1941; Director: Smiths Industries Ltd, since 1970; RTZ Cement Ltd, since 1980; *b* 11 Sept. 1916; *s* of George Heath and Florence Amina Heath (*née* Jones); *m* 1st, 1939, Joy Anderson (*d* 1980); two *s*; 2nd, 1981, Joan Elizabeth McKee. *Educ:* Wrekin; Pembroke Coll., Cambridge. Trained with Rootes Securities Ltd, 1938–39; fighter pilot, RAF, 1939–45 (Wing Comdr, despatches); Dir, Hobourn Aero Components, Rochester, 1946–50; Man. Dir, Powell Duffryn Carbon Products Ltd, 1950–60; Man. Dir, Triplex Safety Glass Co. Ltd, 1960–68, Chm., 1965–74; non-exec. Dir, GKN Ltd, 1972–74; Group Chm., GKN Ltd, 1975–79; Chm., Hesketh Motorcycles, 1980–82; Director: Pilkington Brothers Ltd, 1967–84; Barclays Bank UK Ltd, 1975–84; Barclays Bank Ltd, 1976–84. Dep. Pres., Soc. of Motor Manufacturers and Traders, 1980–81 (Vice-Pres., 1973–78, Pres., 1978–80); Vice-President: Engineering Employers' Fedn, 1975–80; Inst. of Motor Industry, 1975–; Pres., German Chamber of Industry and Commerce in UK, 1977–80; Founder Mem., Engineering Industries Council, 1975–80; Chm., Commonwealth Games UK Jt Appeal Cttee, 1977–78; Member: Industrial Democracy Cttee, 1975–77; British Overseas Trade Adv. Council, 1977–80; BOTB, 1977–80; Tenneco European Adv. Council, 1980–84. Governor, and Chm. Vehicle Cttee, Motability, 1977–85. Trustee: Nat. Motor Mus., 1975–; RAF Mus., 1976–; Beaverbrook Foundn, 1984–. Freeman of City of London; Liveryman, Coachmaker and Coach Harness Makers' Co. *Recreations:* yachting, shooting. *Address:* Watercroft, Penn, Bucks HP10 8NX. *Clubs:* Royal Air Force, Royal Ocean Racing, Royal Thames Yacht; Royal Yacht Squadron, Royal London Yacht.

HEATH, Prof. Bernard Oliver, OBE 1980; CEng, FRAeS; Professor of Aeronautical Engineering (British Aerospace Integrated Chair), Salford University, since 1983; *b* 8 March 1925; *s* of Bernard Ernest Heath and Ethel May Heath; *m* 1948, Ethel Riley; one *s*. *Educ:* Derby Sch.; Bemrose Sch., Derby; University Coll. of Nottingham (BSc Univ. of London 1944); Imperial Coll. of Science and Technology (DIC 1945). CEng 1966; FRAeS 1978; HMIED 1975. English Electric Co.: Stressman (loading and stressing of Canberra), 1945; Aerodynamicist, Lightning, 1948; Aerostructures Gp Leader, 1951; Chief Proj. Engr, 1957; Asst Chief Engr, Canberra and TSR2, 1959; British Aircraft Corporation: TSR2 Proj. Manager (Develt), 1963; Special Dir, 1965; Leader, Jaguar Technical Team, 1965; Proj. Manager, AFVG, 1966; Panavia: Dir, Systems Engrg (Warton), 1969–81; Dir, MRCA, 1970; Dir of Engrg, 1974; British Aerospace: Technical Dir, Warton Div., 1978–81; Divisional Dir of Advanced Engrg, 1981–84. Chm., SBAC Technical Bd, 1980–82. RAeS Silver Medal (for outstanding work over many yrs on design and develt of mil. aircraft), 1977; (jtly) Internat. Council of Aeronautical Sciences Von Karman Award (for successful internat. co-operation on Tornado), 1982. *Publications:* papers to Internat. Council of Aeronautical Sciences Congresses; contrib. RAeS Jl, Flight, The Times, R & D Mgt and Aircraft Engrg. *Recreation:* history of transport. *Address:* Department of Aeronautical and Mechanical Engineering, University of Salford, Salford M5 4WT. *T:* 061–736 5843.

HEATH, Edward Peter, OBE 1946; *b* 6 June 1914; a Deputy Chairman, Inchcape & Co. Ltd, 1976–79; *m* 1953, Eleanor Christian Peck; one *s* three *d*. *Educ:* St Lawrence Coll., Ramsgate. Joined Borneo Co. Ltd, 1934; interned in Thailand, 1941–45. Gen. Manager, Borneo Co. Ltd, 1953–63; a Man. Dir, 1963–67; a Man. Dir, Inchcape & Co. Ltd, 1967–75. Director: Mann Egerton & Co. Ltd, 1973–79; Dodwell & Co. Ltd, 1974–79; Inchcape Far East Ltd, 1972–79; Chairman: Toyota GB and Pride & Clark, 1978–79; Anglo-Thai Corp. Ltd, 1978–79; Dep. Chm., Bewac Motor Corp., 1970–79. Consultant, Matheson & Co. Ltd, 1980–83; Director: Matheson Motor Hldgs, 1981–83; Lancaster Gp Hldgs, 1981–83. Dep. Chairman: Hong Kong Assoc., 1975–79; Anglo Thai Soc., 1975–85. Order of White Elephant (5th Cl.) (Thailand); Officer, Order of Orange Nassau (Netherlands). *Recreations:* hunting, gardening, motoring. *Address:* Cooks Place, Albury, Guildford, Surrey GU5 9BJ. *T:* Shere 2698. *Clubs:* Boodle's, City of London.

HEATH, Rt. Hon. Edward Richard George, PC 1955; MBE 1946; MP (C) Old Bexley and Sidcup, since 1983 (Bexley, 1950–74; Bexley, Sidcup, 1974–83); Member, Public Review Board, Arthur Andersen & Co., since 1978; *b* Broadstairs, Kent, 9 July 1916; *s* of late William George and Edith Anne Heath. *Educ:* Chatham House Sch., Ramsgate; Balliol Coll., Oxford (Scholar; Hon. Fellow, 1969). Scholar, Gray's Inn, 1938 (Hon. Bencher, 1972). Pres. Oxford Univ. Conservative Assoc., 1937; Chm. Federation of Univ. Conservative Assocs, 1938; Pres. Oxford Union, 1939; Oxford Union debating tour of American Univs, 1939–40; Pres. Federation of University Conservative and Unionist Associations, 1959–77, Hon. Life Patron, 1977. Served War of 1939–45 (despatches, MBE); in Army, 1940–46, in France, Belgium, Holland and Germany; gunner in RA, 1940; Major 1945. Lieut-Col comdg 2nd Regt HAC, TA, April 1947–Aug. 1951; Master Gunner within the Tower of London, 1951–54. Administrative Civil Service, 1946–47 resigning to become prospective candidate for Bexley. Asst Conservative Whip, Feb. 1951; Lord Commissioner of the Treasury, Nov. 1951, and Joint Deputy Govt Chief Whip, 1952, and Dep. Govt Chief Whip, 1953–55; Parliamentary Sec. to the Treasury, and Government Chief Whip, Dec. 1955–Oct. 1959; Minister of Labour, Oct. 1959–July 1960; Lord Privy Seal, with Foreign Office responsibilities, 1960–63; Sec. of

State for Industry, Trade, Regional Development and Pres. of the Board of Trade, Oct. 1963–Oct. 1964; Leader of the Opposition, 1965–70; Prime Minister and First Lord of the Treasury, 1970–74; Leader of the Opposition, 1974–75. Chm., Commonwealth Parly Assoc., 1970–74. Mem., Indep. Commn on Internat. Development Issues, 1977–79. Mem. Council, Royal College of Music, 1961–70; Chm., London Symphony Orchestra Trust, 1963–70; Vice-Pres., Bach Choir, 1970–; Pres., European Community Youth Orchestra, 1977–80; Hon. Mem., LSO, 1974–. Smith-Mundt Fellowship, USA, 1953; Vis. Fellow, Nuffield Coll., Oxford, 1962–70, Hon. Fellow, 1970; Chubb Fellow, Yale, 1975; Montgomery Fellow, Dartmouth Coll., 1980. Lectures: Cyril Foster Meml, Oxford, 1965; Godkin, Harvard, 1966; Montagu Burton, Leeds, 1976; Edge, Princeton, 1976; Romanes, Oxford, 1976; Ishizaka, Japan, 1979; Felix Neubergh, Gothenburg, 1979, 10th STC Communication, London, 1980, Noel Buxton, Univ. of Essex, 1980; Alastair Buchan Meml, London, 1980; Hoover, Univ. of Strathclyde, 1980; Stanton Griffis Disting., Cornell Univ., 1981; Edwin Stevens, RSM, 1981; William Temple, York, 1981; City of London, Chartered Insce Inst., 1982; John Findley Green, Westminster Coll., Missouri, 1982; Mizuno, Tokyo, 1982; ITT European, Brussels, 1982; Bruce Meml, Keele Univ., 1982; Gaitskell, Univ. of Nottingham, 1983; Trinity Univ., San Antonio, 1983; lect. to mark opening Michael Fowler Centre, Wellington, NZ, 1983; Bridge Meml, Guildhall, 1984; David R. Calhoun Jr Meml, Washington Univ., St Louis, 1984; Corbishley Meml, RSA, 1984; John Rogers Meml, Llandudno, 1985; George Woodcock, Univ. of Leicester, 1985. Liveryman, Goldsmiths' Co., 1966; Hon. Freeman, Musicians' Co., 1973. Hon. FRCM; Hon. FRCO; Hon. Fellow, Royal Canadian Coll. of Organists. Hon. DCL Oxon, 1971; Hon. DTech Bradford, 1971; Hon. LLD Westminster Coll., Salt Lake City, 1975; Dr *hc* Univ. of Paris, Sorbonne, 1976; Hon. Dr of Public Admin, Wesleyan Coll., Macon, Ga, 1981; Hon. DL, Westminster Coll., Fulton, Missouri, 1982. Freiherr Von Stein Foundn Prize; Charlemagne Prize, 1963; Estes J. Kefauver Prize 1971; Stresseman Gold Medal, 1971; Gold Medal of City of Paris, 1978; World Humanity Award, 1980; Gold Medal, European Parlt, 1981. Winner, Sydney to Hobart Ocean Race, 1969; Captain: Britain's Admiral's Cup Team, 1971, 1979; Britain's Sardinia Cup Team, 1980. *Publications:* (joint) One Nation—a Tory approach to social problems, 1950; Old World, New Horizons (Godkin Lectures), 1970; Sailing: a course of my life, 1975; Music: a joy for life, 1976; Travels: people and places in my life, 1977; Carols: the joy of Christmas, 1977. *Recreations:* sailing, music. *Address:* House of Commons, SW1. *Clubs:* Buck's, Carlton, St Stephen's Constitutional (Jt Pres., 1979); Royal Yacht Squadron.

HEATH, Henry Wylde Edwards, CMG 1963; QPM; Commissioner of Police, Hong Kong, 1959–67, retired; *b* 18 March 1912; *s* of late Dr W. G. Heath and late Mrs L. B. Heath; *m* Joan Mildred Crichett; two *s* one *d. Educ:* Dean Close Sch.; HMS Conway. Probationer Sub-Inspector of Police, Leeward Islands, 1931; Asst Supt, Hong Kong, 1934; Superintendent, 1944; Asst Commissioner, 1950. Colonial Police Medal, 1953; QPM, 1957. *Recreations:* golf, ski-ing. *Address:* Quintynes Cottage, 4 Firle Drive, Seaford, Sussex. *Clubs:* Seaford Golf; Kandahar Ski.

HEATH, Prof. John Baldwin; Professor of Economics, London Graduate School of Business Studies, since 1970; Director of the London Sloan Fellowship Programme (formerly of the Master's Programme), since 1983; *b* 25 Sept. 1924; *s* of late Thomas Arthur Heath and late Dorothy Meallin; *m* 1953, Wendy Julia Betts; two *s* one *d. Educ:* Merchant Taylors' Sch.; St Andrews Univ.; Cambridge Univ. RNVR, 1942–46. Spicers Ltd, 1946–50; Lecturer in Economics, Univ. of Manchester, 1956–64; Rockefeller Foundation Fellowship, 1961–62; Dir, Economic Research Unit, Bd of Trade, 1964–67; Dir, Economic Services Div., BoT, 1967–70. Member: Mechanical Engrg EDC, 1971–76; British Airports Auth., 1980–; Economic Adviser, CAA, 1972–78. *Publications:* articles in many learned jls on competition and monopoly, productivity, cost-benefit analysis. *Recreations:* music, walking. *Address:* 25 Chalcot Square, NW1. *T:* 01–722 4301.

HEATH, John Moore, CMG 1976; HM Diplomatic Service, retired; Director General, Canning House, since 1982; *b* 9 May 1922; *s* of late Philip George and Olga Heath; *m* 1952, Patricia Mary Bibby; one *s* one *d. Educ:* Shrewsbury Sch.; Merton Coll., Oxford (MA). Served War of 1939–45, France, Belgium and Germany: commnd Inns of Court Regt, 1942; Capt. GSO3 11th Armoured Div., 1944–45 (despatches). Merton Coll., 1940–42, 1946–47. Entered Foreign Service, 1950; 2nd Sec., Comr-Gen.'s Office, Singapore, 1950–52; 1st Sec. (Commercial), Jedda, 1952–56; 1st Sec., FO, 1956–58; Nat. Def. Coll., Kingston, Ont., 1958–59; Head of Chancery and HM Consul, Brit. Embassy, Mexico City, 1959–62; Head of Chancery, Brit. Embassy, Kabul, Afghanistan, 1963–65; Counsellor and Head of Establishment and Organisation Dept, FCO (formerly DSAO), 1966–69; Counsellor (Commercial), Brit. Embassy, Bonn, 1969–74; Overseas Trade Advr, Assoc. of British Chambers of Commerce, on secondment, 1974; Consul-Gen., Chicago, 1975–79; Ambassador to Chile, 1980–82. Orden al Merito por Servicios Distinguidos, Peru, 1984. *Recreations:* walking, travel. *Address:* 6 Cavendish Crescent, Bath, Avon. *Club:* Naval and Military.

HEATH, Sir Mark (Evelyn), KCVO 1980; CMG 1980; Director of Protocol, Government of Hong Kong, since 1985; *b* 22 May 1927; *m* 1954, Margaret Alice Bragg; two *s* one *d. Educ:* Marlborough; Queens' Coll., Cambridge. RNVR, 1945–48. HM Foreign (subseq. Diplomatic) Service, 1950–85; served in Indonesia, Denmark, Bulgaria, Canada, France; Ambassador to the Holy See, 1982–85. *Address:* A101 Tregunter Path 14, Hong Kong. *Clubs:* Athenæum, Nikaean; Foreign Correspondents (Hong Kong).

HEATH, Air Marshal Sir Maurice (Lionel), KBE 1962 (OBE 1946); CB 1957; CVO 1978; DL; Gentleman Usher to the Queen, 1966–79, Extra Gentleman Usher to the Queen since 1979; *b* 12 Aug. 1909; *s* of Lionel Heath, Artist and Principal of the Mayo Sch. of Arts, Lahore, India; *m* 1938, Kathleen Mary *d* of Boaler Gibson, Bourne, Lincs; one *s* one *d. Educ:* Sutton Valence Sch.; Cranwell. Commissioned RAF, 1929; service with Nos 16 and 28 Squadrons; Specialist Armament duties, 1933–42; Chief Instructor, No 1 Air Armament Sch., 1942; Station Commander, Metheringham, No 5 Group, Bomber Comd, 1944 (despatches). Dep. to Dir-Gen. of Armament, Air Min., 1946–48; CO Central Gunnery Sch., 1948–49; Sen. Air Liaison Officer, Wellington, NZ, 1950–52; CO Bomber Comd Bombing Sch., 1952–53; idc, 1954; Dir of Plans, Air Min., 1955; Deputy Air Secretary, Air Ministry, 1955–57; Commander, British Forces, Arabian Peninsula, 1957–59; Commandant, RAF Staff Coll., 1959–61; Chief of Staff, HQ Allied Air Forces Central Europe, 1962–65, retd. Dir, Boyd and Boyd, Estate Agents, 1971–76; Private Agent, Henderson Financial Management, 1980–. Chief Hon. Steward, Westminster Abbey, 1965–74. Appeal Dir, 1977–79, Appeal Consultant, 1979–84, Voluntary Research Trust Nat. Appeal, King's Coll. Hosp. and Med. Sch. Pres., Storrington Br., RAFA, 1966–84, Life Vice Pres., 1984–. DL West Sussex, 1977. *Recreations:* sailing, golf and travel. *Address:* Heronscroft, Rambledown Lane, West Chiltington, Pulborough, Sussex RH20 2NW. *Clubs:* Royal Air Force; West Sussex Golf (Pulborough).

HEATH, Oscar Victor Sayer, FRS 1960; DSc (London); Professor of Horticulture, University of Reading, 1958–69, now Emeritus; *b* 26 July 1903; *s* of late Sir (Henry) Frank Heath, GBE, KCB, and Frances Elaine (*née* Sayer); *m* 1930, Sarah Margery, (*d* 1984), *d* of Stephen Bumstead, Guestling, Hastings; two *s* one *d. Educ:* Imperial Coll., London (Forbes Medallist), Fellow, 1973. Asst Demonstrator in Botany, Imperial Coll., 1925–26; Empire Cotton Growing Corp. Sen. Studentship, Imperial Coll. of Tropical Agriculture, Trinidad, 1926–27; Plant Physiologist, Empire Cotton Growing Corp., Cotton Experiment Station, Barberton, S Africa, 1927–36; Research Student, Imperial Coll., London, 1936–39; Leverhulme Research Fellow, 1937–39; Research Asst, 1939–40, and Mem. of Staff, Research Inst. of Plant Physiology of Imperial Coll., Rothamsted, 1940–46, London, 1946–58; Sen. Principal Scientific Officer, 1948–58; Special Lectr in Plant Physiology, Imperial Coll., 1945–58; Dir, ARC Unit of Flower Crop Physiology, 1962–70; Mem. ARC, 1965–70; Leverhulme Emeritus Res. Fellow, 1970–72. *Publications:* chapters on physiology of leaf stomata in Encyclopædia of Plant Physiology (ed Ruhland) 1959, in Plant Physiology: a Treatise (ed Steward), 1959, and (with T. A. Mansfield) in Physiology of Plant Growth (ed Wilkins), 1969; The Physiological Aspects of Photosynthesis, 1969 (trans. German, 1972, Russian, 1972); Investigation by Experiment, 1970 (trans. Spanish, 1977, Portuguese, 1981); Stomata, 1975, 2nd edn 1981; papers in scientific jls. *Address:* 10 St Peter's Grove, W6 9AZ. *T:* 01–748 0471.

HEATH-GRACIE, George Handel, BMus (Dunelm), 1932; FRCO 1915; Organist and Master of the Choristers, Derby Cathedral, 1933–57; Diocesan Choirmaster, 1936–57; Founder and Conductor, Derby Bach Choir, 1935; Special Commissioner, Royal School of Church Music, 1951–66; *m* 1922, Marjory Josephine Knight (*d* 1986). *Educ:* Bristol Grammar Sch.; Bristol Cathedral. Organist of various Bristol Churches, 1909–14; of St John's, Frome, 1914–15; Service with HM forces, 1915–19; Organist of St Peter, Brockley, SE, 1918–33; Conductor South London Philharmonic Soc., 1919–21; Broadcast Church Music Series, 1936–38; Music Dir, Derby Sch., 1938–44; Mem. panel of examnrs, Associated Bd of Royal Schs of Music, 1946–82; Sch. Music Adviser, Derbyshire Educn Cttee, 1944–57; Mem. Council, Incorporated Soc. of Musicians for SW England, 1964–67; Mem. Diocesan Adv. Cttee, to 1957; Mem., Artist selection panel, BBC, 1946–74. Extra-mural Lectr, University Coll., Nottingham; Festival Adjudicator and Lectr. Toured Canada and USA as adjudicator, lecturer and performer, 1949, return visit, 1953; travelled in Asia, and African Tour, 1959; Eastern Tour, Ceylon, Singapore, Malaya, 1960; Tour of W Indies, N and S America and New Zealand, 1966, and New Zealand, 1968. *Publications:* various Church Music and press articles. *Recreations:* gossip, brewing. *Address:* Woodhouse, Uplyme, Lyme Regis, Dorset. *Clubs:* Savage; Exeter and County; (Hon.) Kiwanis (Peterborough, Ont).

HEATH-STUBBS, John (Francis Alexander); poet; Lecturer in English Literature, College of St Mark and St John, Chelsea, 1963–73; *b* 1918; *s* of Francis Heath Stubbs and Edith Louise Sara (*née* Marr). *Educ:* Bembridge School; Worcester Coll. for the Blind, and privately; Queen's Coll., Oxford. English Master, Hall Sch., Hampstead, 1944–45; Editorial Asst, Hutchinson's, 1945–46; Gregory Fellow in Poetry, Leeds Univ., 1952–55; Vis. Prof. of English: University of Alexandria, 1955–58; University of Michigan, 1960–61. FRSL 1953. Queen's Gold Medal for Poetry, 1973; Oscar Williams/Jean Durwood Award, 1977. *Publications: verse:* Wounded Thammuz; Beauty and the Beast; The Divided Ways; The Swarming of the Bees; A Charm against the Toothache; The Triumph of the Muse; The Blue Fly in his Head; Selected Poems; Satires and Epigrams; Artorius; A Parliament of Birds; The Watchman's Flute; Birds Reconvened; Buzz Buzz; Naming the Beasts; The Immolation of Aleph; *drama:* Helen in Egypt; *criticism:* The Darkling Plain; Charles Williams; The Pastoral; The Ode; The Verse Satire; *translations:* (with Peter Avery) Hafiz of Shiraz; (with Iris Origo) Leopardi, Selected Prose and Poetry; (with Carol A. Whiteside) The Poems of Anyte; (with Peter Avery) The Rubaiyat of Omar Khayyam; *edited:* Selected Poems of Jonathan Swift; Selected Poems of P. B. Shelley; Selected Poems of Tennyson; Selected Poems of Alexander Pope; (with David Wright) The Forsaken Garden; Images of Tomorrow; (with David Wright) Faber Book of Twentieth Century Verse; (with Martin Green) Homage to George Barker on his Sixtieth Birthday; Selected Poems of Thomas Gray; (with Phillips Salman) Poems of Science. *Recreation:* taxonomy. *Address:* 35 Sutherland Place, W2. *T:* 01–229 6367.

HEATHCOAT-AMORY, David Philip, FCA; MP (C) Wells, since 1983; *b* 21 March 1949; *s* of Roderick and Sonia Heathcoat-Amory; *m* 1978, Linda Adams; two *s. Educ:* Eton Coll.; Oxford Univ. (MA PPE). Qual. as Chartered Accountant with Price Waterhouse & Co., 1974; FCA 1980. Worked in industry, becoming Asst Finance Dir of British Technology Gp, until 1983 when resigned to fight Gen. Election. PPS to the Minister of State for Defence Procurement, 1985–. *Recreations:* fishing, shooting, music, growing trees. *Address:* 12 Lower Addison Gardens, W14 8BQ. *T:* 01–603 3083. *Clubs:* Avalon (Glastonbury); Shepton Mallet Conservative; Wells Conservative.

HEATHCOAT AMORY, Sir Ian, 6th Bt *cr* 1874; JP; DL; *b* 3 Feb. 1942; *s* of Sir William Heathcoat Amory, 5th Bt, DSO, and of Margaret Isabel Dorothy Evelyn, *yr d* of Sir Arthur Havelock James Doyle, 4th Bt; *S* father, 1982; *m* 1972, Frances Louise, *d* of J. F. B. Pomeroy; four *s. Educ:* Eton. Chairman: Lowman Manufacturing Co. Ltd, 1976–; DevonAir Radio Ltd, 1983–; Dir, Watts Blake Bearne & Co. PLC, 1984–. Mem., Devon CC, 1973–85. JP, DL Devon. *Heir: s* William Francis Heathcoat Amory, *b* 19 July 1975. *Address:* Calverleigh Court, Tiverton, Devon.

HEATHCOTE, Brig. Sir Gilbert (Simon), 9th Bt *cr* 1733; CBE 1964 (MBE 1941); *b* 21 Sept. 1913; *s* of Col R. E. M. Heathcote, DSO (*d* 1970), Manton Hall, Rutland and Millicent Heathcote (*d* 1977), *d* of William Walton, Horsley Priory, Nailsworth, Glos; *S* to baronetcy of 3rd Earl of Ancaster, KCVO, 1983; *m* 1st, 1939, Patricia Margaret (*née* Leslie) (marr. diss. 1984); one *s* one *d*; 2nd, 1984, Ann, *widow* of Brig. J. F. C. Mellor. *Educ:* Eton; RMA Woolwich. Commnd RA, 1933, War Service in Europe, 1939–44; Comdr RA, 1960–62; Chief of Staff, Middle East Comd, 1962–64; retd. *Recreations:* sailing, ski-ing, equitation. *Heir: s* Mark Simon Robert Heathcote, *b* 1 March 1941. *Address:* The Coach House, Tillington, near Petworth, Sussex. *Clubs:* Army and Navy, Royal Cruising; Royal Yacht Squadron.

HEATHCOTE, Sir Michael Perryman, 11th Bt, *cr* 1733; *b* 7 Aug. 1927; *s* of Leonard Vyvyan Heathcote, 10th Bt, and Joyce Kathleen Heathcote (*d* 1967); *S* father, 1963; *m* 1956, Victoria Wilford, *e d* of Comdr J. E. R. Wilford, RN, Retd; two *s* one *d. Educ:* Winchester Coll.; Clare Coll., Cambridge. Started farming in England, 1951, in Scotland, 1961. Is in remainder to Earldom of Macclesfield. *Recreations:* fishing, shooting and farming. *Heir: s* Timothy Gilbert Heathcote, *b* 25 May 1957. *Address:* Warborne Farm, Boldre, Lymington, Hants. *T:* Lymington 73478; Carie and Carwhin, Lawers, by Aberfeldy, Perthshire.

HEATHCOTE-DRUMMOND-WILLOUGHBY, family name of **Baroness Willoughby de Eresby.**

HEATHCOTE-SMITH, Clifford Bertram Bruce, CBE 1963; HM Diplomatic Service, 1936–72; acting Senior Clerk, Department of Clerk of House of Commons, 1973–77; *b* 2 Sept. 1912; *s* of late Sir Clifford E. Heathcote-Smith, KBE, CMG; *m* 1940, Thelma Joyce Engström; two *s. Educ:* Malvern; Pembroke Coll., Cambridge. Entered Consular Service, 1936; served in China, 1937–44; Foreign Office, 1944–47; Political Adviser, Hong-Kong, 1947–50, Montevideo, 1951–56; Commercial Counsellor: Ankara, 1956–60; Copenhagen, 1960–64; Washington, 1964–65; Dep. High Comr, Madras,

1965–68; a Diplomatic Service Inspector, 1969–72. *Address:* Lampool Lodge, Maresfield, East Sussex. *T:* Nutley 2849.

HEATHER, Stanley Frank, CBE 1980; Comptroller and City Solicitor, City of London Corporation, 1974–80; Attorney and General Counsel, City of London (Arizona) Corporation, 1974–81; *b* 8 Jan. 1917; *s* of Charles and Jessie Heather; *m* 1946, Janet Roxburgh Adams, Perth; one *s* one *d.* *Educ:* Downhills Sch.; London Univ. Commnd Reconnaissance Corps, RAC, 1941; India/Burma Campaign, 1942–45. Admitted Solicitor, 1959. Asst Solicitor, City of London, 1963; Dep. Comptroller and City Solicitor, 1968. FRSA 1981. *Recreations:* golf, fishing. *Address:* Kinnoull, 14 Morrell Avenue, Horsham, West Sussex. *T:* Horsham 60109. *Clubs:* City Livery, Guildhall; Ifield Golf and Country (W Sussex).

HEATLY, Peter, CBE 1971; DL; Director, Peter Heatly & Co. Ltd, since 1958; Chairman: Scottish Sports Council, since 1975; Commonwealth Games Federation, since 1982; *b* 9 June 1924; *s* of Robert Heatly and Margaret Ann Heatly; *m* 1st, 1948, Jean Robertha Hermiston (*d* 1979); two *s* two *d*; 2nd, 1984, Mae Calder Cochrane. *Educ:* Leith Academy; Edinburgh Univ. (BSc). CEng, FICE. DL City of Edinburgh, 1984–. *Recreations:* swimming, golf, gardening. *Address:* Lanrig, Balerno, Edinburgh EH14 7AJ. *T:* 031–449 3998.

HEATON, David; Assistant Under Secretary of State, Home Office, 1976–83; *b* 22 Sept. 1923; *s* of late Dr T. B. Heaton, OBE, MD; *m* 1961, Joan, *d* of Group Captain E. J. Lainé, CBE, DFC; two *s* one *d.* *Educ:* Rugby Sch. Served RNVR, 1942–46. Ghana, 1948–58; Cabinet Office, 1961–69; Home Office, 1969–83. *Address:* 53 Murray Road, SW19 4PF. *T:* 01–947 0375.

HEATON, Very Rev. Eric William; Dean of Christ Church, Oxford, since 1979; Pro-Vice-Chancellor, Oxford University, since 1984; *b* 15 Oct. 1920; *s* of late Robert William Heaton and late Ella Mabel Heaton (*née* Brear); *m* 1951, Rachel Mary, *d* of late Rev. Charles Harold Dodd, CH, FBA; two *s* two *d.* *Educ:* Ermysted's, Skipton; (Exhibnr) Christ's Coll., Cambridge (MA). English Tripos, Part I; Theological Tripos, Part I (First Class). Deacon, 1944; Priest, 1945; Curate of St Oswald's, Durham, 1944–45; Staff Sec., Student Christian Movement in University of Durham, 1944–45; Chaplain, Gonville and Caius Coll., Cambridge, 1945–46; Dean and Fellow, 1946–53; Tutor, 1951–53; Bishop of Derby's Chaplain in University of Cambridge, 1946–53; Canon Residentiary, 1953–60, and Chancellor, 1956–60, Salisbury Cathedral; Tutor in Theology, Official Fellow and Chaplain, 1960–74, Senior Tutor, 1967–73, St John's College, Oxford; Dean of Durham, 1974–79. Chm. Council, Headington Sch., Oxford, 1968–74; Chm. Governors, High Sch., Durham, 1975–79. Moderator, Gen. Ordination Exam., 1971–81. Examining Chaplain to: Archbishop of York, 1951–56; Bishop of Portsmouth, 1947–74; Bishop of Salisbury, 1949–64; Bishop of Norwich, 1960–71; Bishop of Wakefield, 1961–74; Bishop of Rochester, 1962–74. Select Preacher: Cambridge University, 1948, 1958; Oxford Univ., 1958–59, 1967, 1971. Hon. Lectr, Univ. of Durham, 1975–79. Hon. Fellow, Champlain Coll., Univ. of Trent, Ont, Canada, 1973–; Hon. Fellow: St John's Coll., Oxford, 1979; Christ's Coll., Cambridge, 1983. *Publications:* His Servants the Prophets, 1949 (revised and enlarged Pelican edn, The Old Testament Prophets, 1958, 2nd rev. edn, 1977); The Book of Daniel, 1956; Everyday Life in Old Testament Times, 1956; Commentary on the Sunday Lessons, 1959; The Hebrew Kingdoms, 1968; Solomon's New Men, 1974; articles in Jl of Theological Studies, Expository Times, etc. *Address:* Christ Church, Oxford. *T:* (office) Oxford 247122, (private) Oxford 243815.

HEATON, Ralph Neville, CB 1951; *b* 4 June 1912; *s* of late Ernest Heaton; *m* 1939, Cecily Margaret Alabaster; three *s* one *d.* *Educ:* Westminster; Christ Church, Oxford. Formerly Deputy Secretary various Govt Depts, including Education, Transport, and Economic Affairs. Commonwealth Fund Fellow, 1951–52. *Address:* 38 Manor Park Avenue, Princes Risborough, Bucks.

HEATON, Sir Yvo (Robert) Henniker-, 4th Bt *cr* 1912; *b* 24 April 1954; *s* of Sir (John Victor) Peregrine Henniker-Heaton, 3rd Bt, and of Margaret Patricia, *d* of late Lieut Percy Wright, Canadian Mounted Rifles; *S* father, 1971; *m* 1978, Freda, *d* of B. Jones. *Heir:* *cousin* John Lindsey Henniker-Heaton [*b* 19 June 1946; *m* 1970, Elisabeth Gladswell; two *s*]. *Address:* 34 High Street, Kegworth, Derby DE7 2DA.

HEATON-WARD, Dr William Alan, FRCPsych; Lord Chancellor's Medical Visitor, since 1978; *b* 19 Dec. 1919; *s* of Ralph Heaton-Ward, MA, and Mabel Orton; *m* 1945, Christine Edith Fraser; two *d.* *Educ:* Queen Elizabeth's Hosp., Bristol; Univ. of Bristol Med. Sch. MB, ChB, 1944; DPM 1948; FRCPsych 1971. Jun. Clerk, Messrs W. D. & H. O. Wills, 1936–38; House Phys., Bristol Royal Inf., 1944–45; MO, Littlemore Mental Hosp., 1945–46; served RNVR, 1946–48: Surg. Lt-Comdr; Neuropsychiatrist, Nore Comd; Sen. Registrar, St James Hosp., Portsmouth, 1948–50; Dep. Med. Supt, Hortham Brentry Gp, 1950–54; Stoke Park Hosp. Group: Consultant Psych., 1954–78, Hon. Consultant, 1978–; Med. Supt, 1954–61; Cons. Psych. i/c, 1963–74; Clinical Teacher in Mental Health, Univ. of Bristol, 1954–78; Cons. Psych., Glos Royal Hosp., 1962–67. Hon. Cons. Adviser: NAMH, 1966–73; CARE, 1970–78; British Council Vis. Lectr, Portugal, 1971. Royal Coll. of Psychiatrists: Vice Pres., 1976–78; Blake Marsh Lectr, 1976; Burden Res. Gold Medal and Prize Winner, 1978. Pres., Brit. Soc. for Study of Mental Subnormality, 1978–79; Vice-Pres., Fortune Centre, Riding for the Disabled, 1980–; Mem. Council, Inst. of Mental Subnormality, 1972–76; Hon. Mem., Amer. Assoc. of Physician Analysts, 1976–. *Publications:* Notes on Mental Deficiency (jtly), 1952, 3rd edn 1955; Mental Subnormality, 1960, 5th edn, (jtly) as Mental Handicap, 1984; Left Behind, 1977; papers on all aspects of care and treatment of mentally handicapped and on gen. psychiatric topics; book revs. *Recreations:* following all forms of outdoor sport, gardening, seeking the sun, philately. *Address:* Flat 2, 38 Apsley Road, Clifton, Bristol BS8 2SS. *T:* Bristol 738971. *Club:* Savages (Bristol).

HEAUME, Sir Francis H. du; *see* du Heaume.

HEAVENER, Rt. Rev. Robert William; Bishop of Clogher, 1973–80. *b* 28 Feb. 1906; *s* of Joseph and Maria Heavener; *m* 1936, Ada Marjorie, *d* of Rev. Chancellor Thomas Dagg; one *s* one *d.* *Educ:* Trinity Coll., Dublin (MA). Ordained, 1929; Curate, Clones; Diocesan Curate, 1930; Curate-in-charge, Lack, 1933–38; Rector, Derryvullen N. 1938–46; Rector, Monaghan, 1946–73; Rural Dean, 1946. Examining Chaplain and Canon of Clogher, 1951–62; Canon of St Patrick's Cathedral, Dublin, 1962–68; Archdeacon of Clogher, 1968–73. OCF, 1938–43; Member of Staff of Command Welfare Officer, NI District, 1938–43. *Publications:* Co. Fermanagh, 1940 (a short topographical and historical account of NI); Diskos, 1970 (a collection of material for Adult Education); (as Robert Cielou) Spare My Tortured People, 1983 (an attempt to understand the Ulster situation today). *Recreations:* tennis, rare book collecting. *Address:* Fardross, Clogher, Co. Tyrone BT76 0HG. *T:* Clogher 48228. *Club:* Friendly Brother House (Dublin).

HEBBLETHWAITE, Peter; Vatican Affairs Writer for The National Catholic Reporter (USA), since 1979; *b* 30 Sept. 1930; *s* of Charles and Elsie Ann Hebblethwaite; *m* 1974, Margaret I. M. Speaight; two *s* one *d.* *Educ:* Xaverian Coll., Manchester; Campion Hall, Oxford; Heythrop Coll., Oxon. MA (1st Cl.) Oxford; LTh. Editor, The Month, a Jesuit review of Church and world affairs, 1965–73; Asst Editor, Frontier, 1974–76; Lectr in French, Wadham Coll., Oxford, 1976–79; thence to Rome as free-lance and Vatican Affairs Writer, for National Catholic Reporter, 1979–. *Publications:* Georges Bernanos, 1965; The Council Fathers and Atheism, 1966; Theology of the Church, 1968; The Runaway Church, 1975; Christian-Marxist Dialogue and Beyond, 1977; The Year of Three Popes, 1978; The New Inquisition?, 1981; The Papal Year, 1981; Introducing John Paul II, the Populist Pope, 1982; John XXIII, Pope of the Council, 1984; Synod Extraordinary, 1986; In the Vatican, 1986; contribs to TLS. *Recreations:* singing songs, Lieder and chansons. *Address:* 45 Marston Street, Oxford OX4 1JU. *T:* Oxford 723771.

HEBBLETHWAITE, Sidney Horace, CMG 1964; HM Diplomatic Service, retired; Hon. Vice-Consul at Florence, since 1978; *b* 15 Nov. 1914; *s* of Sidney Horace Hebblethwaite and Margaret Bowler Cooke; *m* 1942, May Gladys Cook; two *d.* *Educ:* Reale Ginnasio-Liceo, Francesco Petrarca, Trieste, Italy; Pembroke Coll., Cambridge. Third Sec., FO, 1939; transferred to: Rome, 1939; FO, 1940; Lisbon, 1942; Second Sec. 1944; transferred to FO, 1945; Foreign Service Officer, 1948; 1st Sec. (Information), Athens, 1949; transferred to: Rome, 1951; FO, 1955; seconded to Treasury, 1957; transferred to Brussels, 1958; Counsellor: HM Embassy, Stockholm, 1958–62, Rangoon, 1962–65; Counsellor (Information), Washington, 1965–68; retired, in order to take up appt as HM Consul, Florence, 1970–74. *Recreations:* music, reading. *Address:* 10 Via San Egidio, Florence, Italy.

HEBDITCH, Maxwell Graham; Director, Museum of London, since 1977 (Deputy Director, 1974–77); *b* 22 Aug. 1937; *s* of late Harold Hebditch, motor engr, Yeovil, and Lily (*née* Bartle); *m* 1963, Felicity Davies; two *s* one *d.* *Educ:* Yeovil Sch.; Magdalene Coll., Cambridge. MA, FSA, FMA. Field Archaeologist, Leicester Museums, 1961–64; Asst Curator in Archaeology, later Curator in Agricultural and Social History, City Museum, Bristol, 1965–71; Dir, Guildhall Mus., London, 1971–74. Chm., UK Nat. Cttee, ICOM, 1981–87. *Publications:* contribs to Britannia, Museums Jl, County Archaeological Jls. *Recreation:* archaeology. *Address:* Museum of London, London Wall, EC2Y 5HN. *T:* 01–600 3699.

HECTOR, Gordon Matthews, CMG 1966; CBE 1961 (OBE 1955); Secretary to the Assembly Council, General Assembly of the Church of Scotland, 1980–85; *b* 9 June 1918; *m* 1954, Mary Forrest, MB, ChB, *o d* of late Robert Gray, Fraserburgh, Aberdeenshire; one *s* two *d.* *Educ:* Edinburgh Academy; Lincoln Coll., Oxford. Military Service with East Africa Forces, 1940–45. Apptd Dist Officer, Kenya, 1946; Asst Sec., 1950; Sec. to Road Authority, 1951; Sec. to Govt of Seychelles, 1952; Acting Governor, 1953; Dep. Resident Comr and Govt Sec., Basutoland, 1956; Chief Sec., Basutoland, 1964; Deputy British Government Representative, Lesotho (lately Basutoland), 1965. Sec., Basutoland Constitutional Commn, 1957–58. Clerk to the Univ. Court, Aberdeen, 1967–76; Dep. Sec. and Establishment Officer, Aberdeen Univ., 1976–80. Fellow of the Commonwealth Fund, 1939. Chm., Council of Victoria League in Scotland, 1983–; Vice-Pres., St Andrew Soc., 1983–. Mem., West End Community Council, 1983–. Mem. Bd of Governors, Oakbank D List Sch. Burgess of Guild, Aberdeen City. *Recreation:* railways ancient and modern. *Address:* 18 Magdala Crescent, Edinburgh EH12 5BD. *T:* 031–346 2317. *Clubs:* Royal Over-Seas League; New (Edinburgh); Vincent's (Oxford).

HEDDLE, (Bentley) John; MP (C) Mid Staffordshire, since 1983 (Lichfield and Tamworth, 1979–83); Consultant Surveyor (partner Elliott Son and Boyton, Chartered Surveyors, since 1980); Underwriting Member of Lloyd's, and director of public and private companies; *b* 15 Sept. 1941; *s* of Oliver Heddle and late Lilian Heddle; *m* 1964, Judith (marr. diss. 1985), *d* of Dr R. H. M. Robinson, Hyde Hall, Rettendon, Essex, and Joy Robinson, Hothfield, Kent; two *s* two *d*; *m* 1986, Janet (*née* Stokes), of Hythe, Kent, and Chalvington, Sussex. *Educ:* Bishop's Stortford Coll.; College of Estate Management, London Univ., 1962–64. FCIArb; FInstD, FRSA, and other professional instns. Partner, Heddle Butler & Co., Cons. Surveyors, 1966–70; John Heddle & Co., 1970–80. Member: Internat. Real Estate Fedn, 1972–; Bd of Management, UK Housing Assoc., 1980–. Vice-Pres., Building Socs Assoc. Councillor, Kent CC, 1973–80. Contested (C): Gateshead West, Feb. 1974; Bolton East, Oct. 1974; adopted as parly cand., Lichfield and Tamworth, Nov. 1975. Mem., H of C Select Cttee on the Environment, 1982; Chm., Cons. Parly Environment Cttee, 1983– (Jt Sec., 1979–83). Chairman: Bow Gp Environment Cttee, 1980; Cons. Nat. Local Govt Adv. Cttee, 1984–; Mem., Cons. Party Nat. Union Exec, 1984–. Industry and Parlt Trust Fellowship, 1979. Deleg. to CPA Conf., Gibraltar, 1981. Freeman, City of London, 1979. *Publications:* The Way Through the Woods, 1973; St Cuthbert's Village—an urban disaster, 1976; A New Lease of Life—a solution to Rent Control (CPC), 1975; The Great Rate Debate (CPC), 1980; No Waiting?—a solution to the hospital waiting list problem (CPC), 1982; various contribs on housing, rating, planning and environmental subjects to nat. and profess. press and political jls. *Recreation:* relaxing with family. *Address:* House of Commons, SW1A 0AA. *T:* 01–219 5074; The Old College House, Lichfield, Staffs. *Club:* Carlton.

HEDDY, Brian Huleatt; HM Diplomatic Service, retired; Regional Co-ordinator and Resettlement Officer, British Refugee Council, 1979–82; *b* 8 June 1916; *o s* of late Dr William Reginald Huleatt Heddy, Barrister-at-Law, and Ruby Norton-Taylor; *m* 1st, 1940, Barbara Ellen Williams (*d* 1965); two *s* one *d*; 2nd, 1966, Ruth Mackarness (*née* Hogan) (*d* 1967); (one step *s* two step *d*); 3rd, 1969, Horatia Clare Kennedy. *Educ:* St Paul's Sch.; Pembroke Coll., Oxford. Commissioned in 75th (Highland) Field Regt, Royal Artillery, Nov. 1939; served in France 1940; WA, 1943; War Office and France, 1944–45; Mem. of Gray's Inn. Entered Foreign Service, 1945. Appointed to Brussels, 1946; Denver, 1948; Foreign Office, 1952; Tel Aviv, 1953; UK Delegation to ECSC, Luxembourg, 1955; Foreign Office, 1959; promoted Counsellor, 1963; Consul-Gen. at Lourenço Marques, 1963–65; Head of Nationality and Consular Dept, Commonwealth Office, 1966–67; Head of Migration and Visa Dept, FCO, 1968–71; Consul-Gen. in Durban, 1971–76. *Recreations:* tennis, golf. *Address:* Wynyards, Winsham, near Chard, Somerset. *T:* Winsham 260. *Clubs:* East India, Devonshire, Sports and Public Schools, MCC.

HEDGECOE, Prof. John, Dr RCA; FSIAD; Professor of Photography, Royal College of Art, London; Pro Rector, since 1981, Acting Rector, 1983–84; *b* 24 March 1937; *s* of William Hedgecoe and Kathleen Don; *m* 1960, Julia Mardon; two *s* one *d.* *Educ:* Gulval Village Sch., Cornwall; Guildford Sch. of Art. Staff Photographer, Queen Magazine, 1957–72; Freelance: Sunday Times and Observer, 1960–70; most internat. magazines, 1958–; Portrait, HM the Queen, for British and Australian postage stamps, 1966; photographed The Arts Multi-Projection, British Exhibn, Expo Japan Show, 1970. Started Photography Sch. at RCA, 1965: Head of Dept and Reader in Photography, 1965–74; Fellow, 1973; awarded Chair of Photography, 1975; started Audio/Visual Dept, 1980; started Holography Unit, 1982; Managing Trustee, RCA, 1983. Vis. Prof., Norwegian Nat. Television Sch., Oslo, 1985. Chm., Mobius International Ltd, 1985; Man. Dir, Lion & Unicorn Press Ltd, 1986; Director: John Hedgecoe Ltd, 1965–; Perennial Pictures Ltd, 1980. Mem. Photographic Bd, CNAA, 1976–78; Gov., W Surrey Coll. of Art (and Mem. Acad. Adv. Bd), 1975–; Acad. Gov., Richmond Coll., London; Trustee, The Minories Victor Batte-Lay Trust, 1985–. Has illustrated numerous books, 1958–; has contributed to several radio broadcasts. Television: Tonight, Aust. TV, 1967; Folio, Anglia, 1980; 8 progs on Photography, Channel Four, 1983, repeated 1984; Winners, Channel Four, 1984; Light and Form, US Cable TV, 1985. Exhibitions: London, Sydney, Toronto, Edinburgh, Venice, Prague; Collections: V&A Museum; Art Gall. of Ontario; Nat. Portrait Gall., London; Citibank, London; Henry Moore Foundn; Museum of Modern Art, NY; Leeds City Art Gall. Publications: Henry Moore, 1968 (prize best art book, world-wide, 1969); (jtly) Kevin Crossley-Holland book of Norfolk Poems, 1970; (jtly) Photography, Material and Methods, 1971–74 edns; Henry Moore, Energy in Space, 1973; The Book of Photography, 1976; Handbook of Photographic Techniques, 1977, 2nd edn 1982; The Art of Colour Photography, 1978 (Kodak Photobuchpreis Stuttgart 1979; Grand Prix Technique de la Photographie, Musée Français de la Photographie, Paris 1980); Possessions, 1978; The Pocket Book of Photography, 1979; Introductory Photography Course, 1979; Master Classes in Photography: Children and Child Portraiture, 1980; (illus.) Poems of Thomas Hardy, 1981; (illus.) Poems of Robert Burns, 1981; The Book of Advanced Photography, 1982; What a Picture!, 1983; The Photographer's Work Book, 1983; Aesthetics of Nude Photography, 1984; The Workbook of Photo Techniques, 1984; The Workbook of Darkroom Techniques, 1984; Pocket Book of Travel and Holiday Photography, 1986; Henry Moore: his ideas, inspirations and life as an artist, 1986; The Three Dimensional Pop-up Photography Book, 1986; (with A. L. Rowse) Shakespeare's Land, 1986; Photographer's Manual of Creative Ideas, 1986. Recreations: sculpture, building, gardening. Address: Burgates, Little Dunmow, Essex CM6 3HT. T: Great Dunmow 820328.

HEDGELAND, Air Vice-Marshal Philip Michael Sweatman, CB 1978; OBE 1957 (MBE 1948); CEng, FIEE; Consultant in Communications and Electronics; b 24 Nov. 1922; s of Philip and Margaret Hedgeland, Maidstone, Kent; m 1946, Jean Riddle Brinkworth, d of Leonard and Anne Brinkworth, Darlington, Co. Durham; two s. Educ: Maidstone Grammar Sch.; City and Guilds Coll., Imperial Coll. of Science and Technology, London. BSc(Eng), ACGI (Siemens Medallist). Served War: commnd into Technical Br., RAF, 1942; Radar Officer, Pathfinder Force and at TRE, Malvern. Radar Develt Officer, Central Bomber Estabt, 1945–48; Radio Introd. Unit Project Officer for V-Bomber Navigation and Bombing System, 1952–57; Wing Comdr Radio (Air) at HQ Bomber Comd, 1957–60; jssc 1960; Air Ministry Technical Planning, 1961–62; aws 1963; Dir of Signals (Far East), Singapore, 1963–65; commanded RAF Stanbridge (Central Communications Centre), 1966–67; SASO, HQ Signals Comd/90 Gp, 1968–69; IDC, 1970; MoD Procurement Exec., Project Dir for Airborne Radar, 1971–74; Vice-Pres., Ordnance Bd, 1975–77, Pres., 1977–78. FCGI 1977. Pres., Pathfinder Assoc. 1985–87. Recreations: audio engineering, horticulture, amateur radio. Address: 16 Amersham Hill Gardens, High Wycombe, Bucks HP13 6QP. T: High Wycombe 25266. Club: Royal Air Force.

HEDGER, Eric Frank, CB 1979; OBE 1960; Director General of Defence Contracts, Under Secretary, Ministry of Defence, 1969–80; b 15 Sept. 1919; s of Albert Frank Hedger and late Ellen Agnes Hedger (née Laffey); m 1945, Joan Kathleen Bernas; two s one d. Educ: St Luke's, Southsea. War Service, 1939–46 (despatches 1945): Adjutant, 10 Air Formation Signals; Adjutant, then 2nd i/c, 7 Indian Air Formation Signals. Secretary, Admiralty Awards Council, 1946–49; Admin. Staff Coll., 1958; Dir of Navy Contracts, 1968. Mem. of Council and Bd of Management, Inst. of Purchasing and Supply, 1974–75. FInstPS. Recreations: music, reading, doing something. Address: 5 Maywood Close, Beckenham Place Park, Beckenham, Kent. T: 01–650 3250.

HEDGES, Anthony (John); Reader in Composition, University of Hull, since 1978; b 5 March 1931; s of late S. G. Hedges; m 1957, Delia Joy Marsden; two s two d. Educ: Bicester Grammar Sch.; Keble Coll., Oxford. MA, BMus, LRAM. National Service as solo pianist and arranger Royal Signals Band, 1955–57. Teacher and Lecturer, Royal Scottish Academy of Music, 1957–63. During this period became a regular contributor to Scotsman, Glasgow Herald, Guardian, Musical Times, etc. Lecturer in Music, Univ. of Hull, 1963, Sen. Lectr, 1968. The Composers' Guild of Great Britain: Chm., Northern Br., 1966–67; Mem. Exec. Cttee of Guild, 1969–73, 1977–81, 1982–; Chm. of Guild, 1972, Jt Chm., 1973. Member: Council, Central Music Library, Westminster, 1970; Council, Soc. for Promotion of New Music, 1974–81; Music Bd, CNAA, 1974–77; Music Panel, Yorks Arts Assoc., 1974–75, Lincs and Humberside Arts Assoc., 1975–78; Founder-conductor, The Humberside Sinfonia, 1978–81. Wrote regularly for Yorkshire Post, 1963–78, and contributed to many jls, incl. Composer, Current Musicology, etc, and also broadcast on musical subjects. Publications include: (works): orchestral: Comedy Overture, 1962 (rev. 1967); Overture, October '62, 1962 (rev. 1968); Sinfonia Semplice, 1963; Expressions for Orchestra, 1964; Prelude, Romance and Rondo, strings, 1965; Concertante Music, 1965; Four Miniature Dances, 1967; A Holiday Overture, 1968; Variations on a theme of Rameau, 1969; Kingston Sketches, 1969; An Ayrshire Serenade, 1969; Four Diversions, strings, 1971; Celebrations, 1973; Symphony, 1972–73; Festival Dances, 1976; Overture, Heigham Sound, 1978; Four Breton Sketches, 1980; Sinfonia Concertante, 1980; Scenes from the Humber, 1981; A Cleveland Overture, 1984; choral: Gloria, unaccompanied, 1965; Epithalamium, chorus and orch. (Spencer), 1969; To Music, chorus and orch. (various texts), 1972; Psalm 104, 1973; A Manchester Mass, chorus, orch. and brass band, 1974; A Humberside Cantata, 1976; Songs of David, 1978; The Temple of Solomon, 1979; I Sing the Birth: canticles for Christmas, 1985; chamber music: Five Preludes, piano, 1959; Four Pieces, piano, 1966; Rondo Concertante, v, cl. hn, vc, 1967; Sonata for violin and harpsichord, 1967; Three Songs of Love, s, pf (from Song of Songs), 1968; String Quartet, 1970; Rhapsody, v, pf, 1971; piano sonata, 1974; Song Cycle, 1977; Fantasy for Violin and Piano, 1981; Sonatinas for Flute, Viola, Cello, 1982; Wind Quintet, 1984; opera: Shadows in the Sun (lib. Jim Hawkins), 1976; musical: Minotaur (lib. Jim Hawkins), 1978; miscellaneous: many anthems, partsongs, albums of music for children; music for television, film and stage. Recreations: family life, reading, walking. Address: Malt Shovel Cottage, 76 Walkergate, Beverley, HU17 9ER. T: Beverley 860580.

HEDLEY, Prof. Anthony Johnson, MD; FRCPE, FRCPGlas, FFCM; Henry Mechan Professor of Public Health, University of Glasgow, since 1984; b 8 April 1941; s of Thomas Johnson Hedley and Winifred Duncan; m 1967, Elizabeth-Anne Walsh. Educ: Rydal Sch.; Aberdeen Univ. (MB, ChB 1965; MD 1972); Edinburgh Univ. (Dip. Soc. Med. 1973). MRCP 1973; FRCPE 1981; FRCPGlas, 1985; FFCM 1981 (MFCM 1975). Lectr in Community Medicine, Univ. of Aberdeen, 1974–76; Sen. Lectr in Community Health, Univ. of Nottingham, 1976–83; Prof.-Designate in Community Medicine, Univ. of Glasgow, 1983–84. Med. Adviser (Thailand), ODA, 1977–. Hon. MD Khon Kaen Univ., 1983. Publications: papers and chapters on endocrine disease, surveillance of chronic disease and on med. educn. Recreations: long-distance running, photography, rifle shooting. Address: 23 Ninian Avenue, Houston, Renfrewshire. T: Bridge of Weir 613038. Clubs: Rydal Veterans (Colwyn Bay); Freelancers (Nottingham).

HEDLEY, Hilda Mabel, CB 1975; Under-Secretary, Department of Health and Social Security (formerly Ministry of Health), 1967–75; b 4 May 1918; d of late George Ward Hedley, Cheltenham, and late Winifred Mary Hedley (née Cockshott). Educ: Cheltenham Ladies' Coll.; Newnham Coll., Cambridge. Uncommon Languages Dept., Postal Censorship, 1940–42; Foreign Office, 1942–46; Min. of Health, later DHSS, 1946–75. Sec. to Royal Commn on Mental Health, 1954–57. Nuffield Foundation Travelling Fellowship, 1960–61. Gen. Sec., Cheltenham Ladies' Coll. Guild, 1976–82. Recreations: gardening, bird-watching, cooking. Address: The Anchorage, Castle Street, Winchcombe, Cheltenham GL54 5JA. T: Winchcombe 602314.

HEDLEY, Prof. Ronald; Director, Trent Polytechnic, Nottingham, 1970–80, Emeritus Professor, 1980; b 12 Sept. 1917; s of Francis Hedley, Hebburn, Co. Durham; m 1942; one s one d. Educ: Jarrow Grammar Sch.; Durham Univ. (MA, DipEd); Ecole Normale d'Instituteurs, Evreux. Various appts in teaching and educational administration, 1947–64; Dep. Dir of Education, Nottingham, 1964–70. Chm., Regional Acad. Bd, Regional Adv. Council for Further Educn in E Midlands, 1972–76; Member: Central Council for Educn and Trng in Social Work, 1971–77; Nat. Adv. Council for Educn for Ind. and Commerce, 1973–77; Central Council for Educn and Trng of Health Visitors, 1972–77; Cttee for Arts and Social Studies, CNAA, 1974–76; Personal Social Services Council, 1974–78; Cttee on Recreation Management Training, 1977–80; Local Govt Trng Bd, 1978–81; Adv. Cttee for Supply and Educn of Teachers, 1980–81, Chm., Local Cttee for Teacher Educn, King Alfred's Coll., Winchester, 1986–. FRSA 1970. Hon. Fellow, Trent Polytechnic, 1980. Hon. Senator, Fachhochschule, Karlsruhe, Germany, 1980. Hon. LlD Nottingham, 1981. Address: 5 Branksome Close, Pitt Manor, Winchester, Hants. T: Winchester 65546.

HEDLEY, Ronald Henderson, CB 1986; DSc, PhD; FIBiol; Director, British Museum (Natural History), since 1976; b 2 Nov. 1928; s of Henry Armstrong Hedley and Margaret Hopper; m 1957, Valmai Mary Griffith, New Zealand; one s. Educ: Durham Johnston Sch.; King's Coll., Univ. of Durham. Commissioned in Royal Regt of Artillery, 1953–55. Sen. Scientific Officer, British Museum (Natural History), 1955–61; New Zealand Nat. Research Fellow, 1960–61; Principal Scientific Officer, 1961–64; Dep. Keeper of Zoology, 1964–71; Dep. Dir, 1971–76. Vis. Lectr in Microbiology, Univ. of Surrey, 1968–75. Mem. Council, Fresh Water Biological Assoc., 1972–76; Trustee, Percy Sladen Meml Fund, 1972–77; Pres., British Section, Soc. of Protozoology, 1975–78; Member Council: Marine Biolog. Assoc., 1976–79, 1981–; Zoological Soc., London, 1981–85 (Hon. Sec., 1977–80; Vice-Pres., 1980–85); Mem., Internat. Trust for Zoological Nomenclature, 1977–. Member: Council, Royal Albert Hall, 1982–; National Trust, 1985–. Publications: (ed with C. G. Adams) Foraminifera, vols 1–3, 1974, 1976, 1978; (with C. G. Ogden) Atlas of Testate Amoebae, 1980; technical papers, mainly on biology, cytology and systematics of protozoa, 1956–. Address: British Museum (Natural History), Cromwell Road, SW7 5BD. T: 01–589 6323. Club: Athenæum.

HEDLEY-MILLER, Mrs Mary Elizabeth, CB 1983; Ceremonial Officer, Cabinet Office, since 1983; b 5 Sept. 1923; d of late J. W. Ashe; m 1950, Roger Latham Hedley-Miller; one s two d. Educ: Queen's Sch., Chester; St Hugh's Coll., Oxford (MA). Joined HM Treasury, 1945; served in UK Treasury Delegn, Washington DC, 1947–49; Under-Sec., HM Treasury, 1973–83. Alternate Dir, Monetary Cttee, EEC, and Alternate Exec. Dir, European Investment Bank, 1977–83. Recreations: family, including family music; reading. Address: 108 Higher Drive, Purley, Surrey. T: 01–660 1837. Club: United Oxford & Cambridge University.

HEENAN, Maurice, CMG 1966; QC (Hong Kong) 1962; The General Counsel, United Nations Relief and Works Agency for Palestine Refugees in the Near East, 1973–77; b NZ, 8 Oct. 1912; 2nd s of late David Heenan and of Anne Frame; m 1951, Claire, 2nd d of late Emil Ciho and Iren Rotbauer, Trenčín, Bratislava, Czechoslovakia; two d. Educ: Canterbury Coll., University of New Zealand. Law Professional, LLB, Barrister and Solicitor of Supreme Court of New Zealand, Practised law in NZ, 1937–40. War of 1939–45; Major, 2nd NZEF; active service Western Desert, Libya, Cyrenaica and Italy, 1940–45 (despatches). Crown Counsel, Palestine, 1946–48. Solicitor-Gen., Hong Kong, 1961; HM's Attorney-Gen., Hong Kong, and ex officio MEC and MLC, Hong Kong, 1961–66; Dep.-Dir, Gen. Legal Div., Office of Legal Affairs, Offices of the Sec.-Gen., UN, NY, 1966–73. Recreations: Rugby football, tennis, squash, ski-ing, golf. Address: Plane Trees, West Road, New Canaan, Conn 06840, USA. Clubs: Hong Kong; Country (New Canaan).

HEEPS, William; Chairman and Chief Executive, Thomson Regional Newspapers Ltd, since 1984; Director, International Thomson Organisation plc, Thomson Television, and The Thomson Organisation Ltd, since 1984; b 4 Dec. 1929; er s of late William Headrick Heeps and Margaret Munro Heeps; m 1st, 1956, Anne Robertson Paton (d 1974); two d; 2nd, 1983, Jennifer Rosemary Bartlett; one step d. Educ: Graeme High School, Falkirk. Journalist, Falkirk Mail, Linlithgowshire Jl and Gazette, Daily Record, Evening News and Dispatch, Edinburgh; Editor, Evening Gazette, Middlesbrough, 1966–68; Managing Director: Celtic Newspapers, 1968–71; North Eastern Evening Gazette, Middlesbrough, 1972–75; Evening Post-Echo, Hemel Hempstead, 1976–78; Thomson Magazines, 1978–80; Thomson Data, 1980–82; Editorial Dir, Thomson Regional Newspapers, 1982, Man. Dir and Editor-in-Chief, 1983. Director: Chester Chronicle; Teesside Communications; Celtic Newspapers; Glamorgan Gazette; Reading Standard; Belfast Telegraph Newspapers Ltd; Cheshire and North Wales Newspaper Co. Ltd; Thomson International Press Consultancy Ltd. Vice Pres., Newspaper Soc., 1986 (Mem. Council, 1984–). Trustee, Thomson Foundn. Dep. Chm., Royal Caledonian Schools, 1985. Elder, Church of Scotland. FBIM 1984. Recreations: golf, badminton. Address: Jollivers, Longcroft Lane, Felden, Hemel Hempstead, Herts. T: Hemel Hempstead 53524. Club: Caledonian.

HEES, Hon. George H., PC (Canada) 1957; MP (Canada) (Progressive C) Northumberland, Ontario, since Nov. 1965 (formerly Prince Edward-Hastings Riding); Minister of Veterans Affairs, since 1984; b Toronto, 17 June 1910; s of Harris Lincoln Hees, Toronto, and Mabel Good, New York; m 1934, Mabel, d of late Hon. E. A. Dunlop; three d. Educ: Trinity Coll. Sch., Port Hope, Ont; RMC, Kingston, Ont; University of Toronto; Cambridge Univ. Formerly Dir, George H. Hees & Son & Co. Served War of 1939–45: Royal Canadian Artillery, 1941–44; 3rd Anti-Tank Regt, Royal Canadian Artillery; Bde Major, 5th Infantry Bde, Holland (wounded); retd as Major. Contested (Prog. C) Spadina Riding, 1945; MP (Prog. C) Toronto–Broadview, May 1950–1963; Minister of Transport, Canada, 1957–60; Minister of Trade and Commerce, 1960–63. Pres., Montreal and Canadian Stock Exchanges, 1964–65. Executive with George H. Hees Son & Co., Toronto; Dir, Expo 67. Hon. Dr of Laws, 1961. Recreations: reading, ski-ing, swimming, golf, tennis, riding, bridge; formerly boxing. Address: 7 Coltrin Place, Ottawa, Ontario K1M 0A5, Canada; Rathbunwood, Cobourg, Canada. Clubs: Toronto Golf, Toronto Badminton and Racquet, Osler Bluff Ski (Toronto); Royal Ottawa Golf.

HEFFER, Eric Samuel; MP (Lab) Walton Division of Liverpool since 1964; b 12 Jan. 1922; s of William George Heffer and Annie Heffer (née Nicholls); m 1945, Doris Murray. Educ: Bengeo Junior Sch. and Longmore Senior Sch., Hertford. Apprenticed carpenter/joiner, 1936, and worked at the trade until 1964. Served RAF, 1942–45. Pres. Liverpool Trades Council and Labour Party, 1959–60, 1964–65, and Vice-Pres., 1960 and 1964. Liverpool City Councillor, 1960–66. Member: Council of Europe, 1965–68;

WEU, 1965–68 (served on political, social and financial cttees). Labour front bench spokesman on Industrial Relations, 1970–72; Minister of State, Dept of Industry, 1974–75; Mem., Shadow Cabinet, 1981–; Labour spokesman on European affairs, 1981–83, on housing and construction, 1983–. Mem., Lab. Party Nat. Exec. Cttee, 1975–86; Vice-Chm., Labour Party, 1982–83, Chm., 1983–84. *Publications:* (part author) The Agreeable Autocracies, 1961, (USA); (part author) Election 70, 1970; The Class Struggle in Parliament, 1973; articles in Tribune, Liverpool Daily Post, The Times, Guardian, Daily Telegraph, New Statesmen, Spectator, New Outlook, Labour Voice, New Left Review, and in foreign jls. *Recreations:* hill-walking, mountaineering. *Address:* House of Commons, SW1.

HEGARTY, Most Rev. Séamus; *see* Raphoe, Bishop of, (RC).

HEGGS, Geoffrey Ellis; Chairman of Industrial Tribunals, London Central Region, since 1977; a Recorder of the Crown Court, since 1983; *b* 23 Oct. 1928; *s* of George Heggs, MBE and Winifred Grace Heggs; *m* 1953, Renata Fanny Madeleine Calderan (*see* R. F. M. Heggs); two *s* one *d*. *Educ:* Elizabeth Coll., Guernsey; LLB London. Admitted Solicitor, 1952. Rotary Foundn Fellow, Yale Univ., 1953–54; LLM Yale; Asst Sec., Law Soc., 1956–58; practised as solicitor in London, 1958–77. Member: Law Society; City of London Solicitors' Company. *Recreations:* military history, music, painting. *Address:* 93 Ebury Bridge Road, SW1W 8RE. *T:* 01–730 9161.

HEGGS, Renata Fanny Madeleine; a Social Security Commissioner, since 1981; *b* 29 Nov. 1929; *d* of E. and G. Calderan; *m* 1953, Geoffrey Ellis Heggs, *qv*; two *s* one *d*. *Educ:* Notting Hill and Ealing High Sch., GPDST; London Univ. (LLB 1952). Admitted Solicitor, 1955; practising Solicitor, 1955–81. Chm., Nat. Insce Local Tribunal, 1976–81; pt-time Chm. of Industrial Tribunals, 1978–81; Pres., Appeal Tribunal under London Building Acts, 1979–81. *Recreations:* music, travelling. *Address:* (office) 6 Grosvenor Gardens, SW1W 0DH. *T:* 01–730 9236.

HEGINBOTHAM, Christopher John; National Director, MIND (National Association for Mental Health), since 1982; *b* 25 March 1948; *s* of Joseph William and Marjorie Heginbotham. *Educ:* Univ. of Birmingham (BSc Hons); Univ. of Essex (MSc). Area Manager, Circle Thirty Three Housing Trust, 1977–80; Assistant Borough Housing Officer, London Borough of Haringey, 1980–82. Member: Hampstead DHA, 1981–; Nat. Adv. Council on Employment of Disabled People, 1983–. *Publications:* Housing Projects for Mentally Handicapped People, 1981; Promoting Residential Services for Mentally Handicapped People, 1982; Webs and Mazes: approaches to community care, 1984. *Recreations:* writing, painting, sailing. *Address:* 22 Harley Street, W1. *T:* 01–637 0741.

HEGINBOTHAM, Prof. Wilfred Brooks, OBE 1978; FEng 1985; Director General, Production Engineering Research Association of Great Britain (PERA), Melton Mowbray, 1979–84; *b* 9 April 1924; *s* of Fred and Alice Heginbotham; *m* 1957, Marjorie Pixton; three *d*. *Educ:* Manchester Univ. (UMIST). BScTech 1949; MScTech 1950; PhD (Manchester) 1956; DSc (Manchester) 1979. FIProdE; MIMechE; FRSA. Started in industry as wood pattern maker; part-time courses to HNC, 1938–46; Walter Preston Schol., Manchester Coll. of Tech., 1946; joined staff, 1951; Lectr in Production Engineering subjects, UMIST, 1951–58; industrial experience for 10 years; Nottingham University: Sen. Lectr, 1958; started first BSc course in Prod. Engrg in UK, 1961; Head of Dept of Prod. Engrg and Prod. Management, 1961–63; Cripps Prof., 1963–79; Dean, Faculty of Applied Science, 1967–71; Special Prof. of Prodn Engrg, 1983–86; Hon. Prof., Dept of Engrg, Univ. of Warwick, 1984–. Developed group to study Automatic Assembly Systems and Industrial Robot devices, including computer vision and tactile sense, and co-operated with industry in development of advanced automation equipment. Chm. Org. Cttee for establishment of Brit. Robot Assoc., 1977, Chm. of Council, 1977–80, Pres., 1980–84. Editor-in-Chief: The Industrial Robot; Assembly Automation; Advanced Manufacturing Technology Journal. Hon. DTech Scis Eindhoven, 1981; Hon. DSc Aston, 1983. Engelberger Award, Robot Inst. of America, 1983. *Publications:* Programmable Assembly, 1984; (ed with D. T. Pham) Robot Grippers, 1986; contribs to Encyc. Brit. on Robot Devices and to prof. pubns on metal cutting, automated assembly, industrial robots, artificial intelligence and production processes. *Recreations:* gliding, model aircraft construction and operation (radio controlled). *Address:* Bardsley Brow, 14 Middleton Crescent, Beeston, Notts NG9 2TH. *T:* Nottingham 257796.

HEGLAND, David Leroy, DFC 1944; Director: Kemtron Ltd; Galena; Massey-Ferguson Holdings (Australia) Ltd; Carlton and United Breweries Holdings Ltd; Plessey Pacific Pty Ltd; cattle grazier; *b* 12 June 1919; *s* of Lee and Jennie Hegland; *m* 1944, Dagmar Cooke; two *s* one *d*. *Educ:* Whitman Coll., Washington, USA (BA). Served War, 1942–45; USN aircraft pilot in Pacific Ocean areas; Lt Comdr USNR, 1945. Managing Director: GM International, Copenhagen, 1956–58; GM South African, Port Elizabeth, 1958–61; GM Holden's Pty Ltd, Melbourne, 1962–65; Chm. and Man. Dir, Vauxhall Motors Ltd, Luton, 1966–70; Dir, General Motors Ltd, London, 1966–70; Chm., GKN Australia Ltd, and Dir, Ajax GKN Holdings Pty Ltd, and Guest, Keen & Nettlefolds (Overseas) Ltd, 1972–80. Member: Albury-Wodonga Develt Corp., 1980–81; Industry Forum, Aust. Acad. of Science, 1972–; Aust. Inst. of Dirs; Delta Sigma Rho. FIMI. Richard Kirby medal for production engrg, 1964. *Recreations:* flying, tennis, riding. *Address:* c/o Galena Hills, Holbrook, NSW 2644, Australia. *Clubs:* Royal & Ancient Golf (St Andrews); Melbourne, Victoria Racing (Melbourne); Albury (Albury, NSW).

HEIFETZ, Jascha; Commander, Legion of Honour, 1957; violinist, soloist; 1st Vice-President of American Guild of Musical Artists, Inc., New York City; Hon. Member: Society of Concerts of Paris Conservatoire; Association des Anciens Elèves du Conservatoire; Cercle International de la Jeunesse Artistique; Hon. Vice-President of Mark Twain Society, USA; Hon. President, Musicians' Fund of America; on music department staff, University of Southern California, Los Angeles; *b* Vilna, Russia, 2 Feb. 1901; father professional violinist and music teacher. *Recreations:* sailing, ping-pong (table tennis), motoring, reading and dancing. *Address:* Beverly Hills, Calif, USA. *Clubs:* Royal Automobile, Savage; Bohemian (New York); Beaux Arts, Inter-Allied (Paris).

HEILBRON, Hon. Dame Rose, DBE 1974; **Hon. Mrs Justice Heilbron;** a Judge of the High Court of Justice, Family Division, since 1974; *b* 19 Aug. 1914; *d* of late Max and Nellie Heilbron; *m* 1945, Dr Nathaniel Burstein; one *d*. *Educ:* Belvedere Sch., GPDST; Liverpool University, LLB 1st Class Hons, 1935; Lord Justice Holker Scholar, Gray's Inn, 1936; LLM 1937. Called to Bar, Gray's Inn, 1939, Bencher, 1968, Treasurer, 1985; joined Northern Circuit, Leader, 1973–74, Presiding Judge, 1979–82; QC 1949; Recorder of Burnley, 1956–71, a Recorder, and Hon. Recorder of Burnley, 1972–74. Mem., Bar Council, 1973–74. Chm., Home Sec's Adv. Gp on Law of Rape, 1975–. Hon. Fellow: Lady Margaret Hall, Oxford, 1976; UMIST, 1986; Hon. LLD: Liverpool, 1975; Warwick, 1978; Manchester, 1980. Hon. Col, WRAC(TA). *Address:* Royal Courts of Justice, Strand, WC2.

HEIM, Most Rev. Bruno Bernard, PhD, JCD; Apostolic Pro-Nuncio to the Court of St James's, 1982–85 (Apostolic Delegate, 1973–82); *b* Olten, Switzerland, 5 March 1911; *s* of Bernard and Elisabeth Heim-Studer. *Educ:* Olten, Engelberg and Schwyz; St Thomas of Aquino Univ.; Gregorian Univ.; Univ. of Fribourg; Papal Acad. of Diplomacy. Priest 1938; Vicar in Basle and Arbon, 1938–42; Chief Chaplain for Italian and Polish Internees in Switzerland, 1943–45; Sec., Papal Nunciature in Paris; Auditor at Nunciature in Vienna; Counsellor and Chargé d'affaires at Nunciature in Germany; titular Archbp of Xanthos, 1961; Apostolic Delegate to Scandinavia, 1961–69; Apost. Pro-Nuncio (Ambassador): to Finland, 1966–69; to Egypt, 1969–73; President of Caritas Egypt, 1969–73. Lauréat, French Acad.; Corresp. Mem., Real Academia de la Historia, Madrid, 1950; Mem. Council, Internat. Heraldic Acad.; Grand Cross: Order of Malta, 1950; Teutonic Order, 1961; Order of Finnish Lion, 1969; Order of St Maurice and Lazarus, 1973; (1st Class) Order of the Republic, Egypt, 1975; Constantinian Order of St George; Sub-Prelate, Order of St John; Comdr, Order of Isabel la Catolica; Gr. Officer Order of Holy Sepulchre; Orders of Merit: Germany, Italy, Austria; Officier Légion d'honneur, etc. *Publications:* Die Freundschaft nach Thomas von Aquin, 1934; Wappenbrauch und Wappenrecht in der Kirche, 1947; Coutumes et droit heraldiques de l'Eglise, 1949; L'oeuvre héraldique de Paul Boesch, 1973; Heraldry in the Catholic Church, 1978; Armorial Liber Amicorum, 1981; contrib. Adler, Zeitschrift f. Heraldik und Genealogie, Heraldisk Tidskrift. *Recreations:* heraldry, heraldic painting, cooking, gardening. *Address:* Zehnderweg 31, CH–4600 Olten, Switzerland.

HEIM, Paul Emil; Registrar, Court of Justice of the European Communities, since 1982; *b* 23 May 1932; *s* of George Heim and Hedy Heim (*née* Herz); *m* 1962, Elizabeth, *er d* of late Lt-Col G. M. Allen, MBE; one *s* two *d*. *Educ:* Prince of Wales School, Nairobi; King's Coll., Univ. of Durham (LLB). Called to the Bar, Lincoln's Inn, 1955; Dep. Registrar, Supreme Court of Kenya, then Sen. Dep. Registrar, Magistrate and Acting Registrar (HMOCS), 1954–65; Administrator, European Court of Human Rights, Strasbourg, 1965, European Commn of Human Rights, Strasbourg, 1966; Principal Administrator, Political Directorate, Council of Europe, 1967, Dep. Head, Private Office, 1969; Head of Div., then Dir, European Parlt, 1973–81. *Recreations:* tennis, poetry. *Address:* 11 rue du Village, Schuttrange, Luxembourg; Wearne Wych, Langport, Somerset.

HEINE, Prof. Volker, FRS 1974; Professor of Theoretical Physics, University of Cambridge, since 1976; Fellow of Clare College, Cambridge, since 1960; *b* 19 Sept. 1930; *m* 1955, M. Daphne Hines; one *s* two *d*. *Educ:* Otago Univ. (MSc, DipHons); Cambridge Univ. (PhD). FInstP. Demonstrator, Cambridge Univ., 1958–63, Lectr 1963–70; Reader in Theoretical Physics, 1970–76. Vis. Prof., Univ. of Chicago, 1965–66; Vis. Scientist, Bell Labs, USA, 1970–71. *Publications:* Group Theory in Quantum Mechanics, 1960; (jtly) Solid State Physics Vol. 24, 1970, Vol. 35, 1980; articles in Proc. Royal Soc., Jl Physics, Physical Review, etc. *Address:* Cavendish Laboratory, Madingley Road, Cambridge CB3 0HE.

HEINZ, Henry John, II, Hon. KBE 1977; Chairman, H. J. Heinz Company, since 1959 (President, 1941–59); *b* Sewickley, Pa, USA, 10 July 1908; *s* of Howard and Elizabeth Rust Heinz; *m* 1st, 1935, Joan Diehl (marr. diss. 1942); one *s*; *m* 1953, Drue English Maher. *Educ:* Yale (BA 1931); Trinity Coll., Cambridge. Salesman, H. J. Heinz Co., Ltd, London, 1932; with H. J. Heinz Co., Pittsburgh, Pa, Pres., 1941–59; Chm., 1959–. Chm., Governing Bd, Yale Univ. Art Gallery; Member: Adv. Cttee, Yale Univ. Economic Growth Centre; Council of Management, British-Ditchley Foundn; Business Cttee for the Arts; Nat. Council (US), WWF; Director: Pittsburgh Symphony Soc.; World Affairs Council, Pittsburgh; Trustee: Carnegie Inst.; Carnegie-Mellon Univ.; Internat. Life Science Inst.; Nutrition Foundn; Cttee for Econ. Develt; US Council, ICC. Commander, Royal Order of the Phœnix, Greece, 1950; Chevalier de la Légion d'Honneur, France, 1950; Comdr of Order of Merit, Italian Republic. OStJ. *Recreation:* ski-ing. *Address:* (residence) Goodwood, Sewickley, Pa 15143, USA. *Clubs:* Buck's, White's; The Brook, River (New York); Duquesne, Rolling Rock, Allegheny Country (Pittsburgh).

HEISBOURG, Georges; Ambassador of Luxembourg, retired; *b* 19 April 1918; *s* of Nicolas Heisbourg and Berthe (*née* Ernsterhoff); *m* 1945, Hélène Pinet; two *s* one *d*. *Educ:* Athénée, Luxembourg; Univs of Grenoble, Innsbruck and Paris. Head of Govt Press and Information Office, Luxembourg, 1944–45; Attaché 1945–48, Sec. 1948–51, of Legation, London; Head of Internat. Organisations Section, Dir of Political Affairs, Min. of For. Affairs, Luxembourg, 1951–58; Luxembourg Ambassador to USA, Canada and Mexico, 1958–64; Perm. Rep. to UN, 1958–61; Luxembourg Ambassador: to Netherlands, 1964–67; to France, 1967–70; Perm. Rep. to OECD, 1967–70; Sec. Gen., WEU, 1971–74; Ambassador to USSR, Finland, Poland and Outer Mongolia, 1974–77; Perm. Rep. to Council of Europe, 1978–79; Ambassador to Fed. Rep. of Germany and to Denmark, 1979–83. Grand Officer, Nat. Order of Crown of Oak, 1980 (Chevalier, 1958), Comdr, Order of Adolphe de Nassau, 1963, and Grand Officer, Order of Merit, 1976, Luxembourg; also holds decorations from Austria, Belgium, France, Germany, Italy, Mexico, and the Netherlands. *Publication:* Le gouvernement Luxembourgeois en exil 1940, 1986. *Recreations:* tennis, swimming. *Address:* J.-P. Brasseur 32, 1258–Luxembourg.

HEISER, Terence Michael, CB 1984; Permanent Secretary, Department of the Environment, since 1985; *b* 24 May 1932; *s* of David and Daisy Heiser; *m* 1957, Kathleen Mary Waddle; one *s* two *d*. *Educ:* Grafton Road Primary Sch., Dagenham; London Evacuee Sch., Sunninghill, Berks; Windsor County Boy's Sch., Berks; Birkbeck Coll., Univ. of London; BA (Hons English). Served in RAF, 1950–52; joined Civil Service 1949, served with Colonial Office, Min. of Works, Min. of Housing and Local Govt; Principal Private Sec. to Sec. of State for the Environment, 1975–76; Under Secretary: Housing Directorate, 1976–79; Local Govt Finance Directorate, 1979–81; Dep. Sec., DoE, 1981–85. *Recreations:* reading, walking, talking.

HEISKELL, Andrew; Chairman, President's Committee on the Arts and the Humanities, since 1982; Chairman of the Board, Time Inc., 1960–80; *b* Naples, 13 Sept. 1915; *s* of Morgan Heiskell and Ann Heiskell (*née* Hubbard); *m* 1937, Cornelia Scott (marr. diss.); one *s* one *d*; *m* 1950, Madeleine Carroll (marr. diss.); one *d*; *m* 1965, Marian, *d* of Arthur Hays Sulzberger, and *widow* of Orvil E. Dryfoos. *Educ:* Switzerland; France; University of Paris. Science teacher, Ecole du Montcel, Paris, 1935. Life Magazine: Science and Medicine Editor, 1937–39; Asst Gen. Manager, 1939–42; Gen. Manager, 1942–46; Publisher, 1946–60; Vice-Pres., Time, Inc., 1949–60. Director: Amer. TV & Communications Corp.; Book-of-the-Month Club Inc.; Vivian Beaumont Theater Inc. Director: Internat. Executive Service Corps; Enterprise Foundn, Independent Sector, People for the American Way. Mem. Bd of Advisors, Dumbarton Oaks Research Library and Collection. Trustee: New York Public Library (Chm.); Trust for Cultural Resources of the City of New York; Chm., Bryant Park Restoration Corp. Vice Chm., and Chm. Exec. Cttee, The Brookings Instn. Fellow, Harvard Coll. Wharton Sch. Alumni Soc., Univ. of Pennsylvania, Gold Medal Award of Merit, 1968. Hon. LLD: Shaw Univ., 1968; Lake Erie Coll., 1969; Hofstra Univ., 1972; Hobart and William Smith Colls, 1973; Hon. DLitt Lafayette Coll., 1969. *Address:* Time and Life Building, Rockefeller Center, New York, NY 10020; 870 United Nations Plaza, New York, NY 10017; Darien, Conn, USA.

HELAISSI, Sheikh Abdulrahman Al-; Hon. GCVO; Saudi Arabian Ambassador to the Court of St James's, 1966–76; *b* 24 July 1922. *Educ:* Universities of Cairo and London.

Secretary to Embassy, London, 1947–54; Under-Sec., Min. of Agriculture, 1954–57; Head of Delegn to FAO, 1955–61; Ambassador to Sudan, 1957–60; Representative to UN, and to various confs concerned with health and agriculture; Delegate to Conf. of Non-aligned Nations, Belgrade, 1961; Ambassador: Italy and Austria, 1961–66; UK and Denmark (concurrently), 1966–70. Versed in Islamic Religious Law. *Publication*: The Rehabilitation of the Bedouins, 1959. *Address*: c/o Olaya, Division 3, Riyadh, POB 8062, Saudi Arabia.

HELE, Desmond George K.; *see* King-Hele.

HELE, Sir Ivor (Henry Thomas), Kt 1983; CBE 1969 (OBE 1954); artist; *b* 13 June 1912; *s* of Arthur Hele and Ethel May Hele; *m* 1957, May E. Weatherly. *Educ*: Prince Alfred Coll., Adelaide. Studied art in Paris, Munich and Italy, 1929–32. Enlisted AIF, 1940; War Artist: ME and New Guinea, 1941–46; Korea, 1952. Work represented in: National War Meml, Canberra; King's Hall, Parlt House, Canberra; various national galls. Archibald Prize, 1951, 1953, 1954, 1955 and 1957. *Publication*: The Art of Ivor Hele, 1966. *Recreations*: swimming, gardening. *Address*: Box 35, Aldinga, SA 5173, Australia.

HELE, James Warwick, CBE 1986; High Master of St Paul's School 1973–86; *b* 24 July 1926; *s* of John Warwick Hele, Carlisle; *m* 1948, Audrey Whalley; four *d*. *Educ*: Sedbergh Sch.; Hertford Coll., Oxford; Trinity Hall, Cambridge (Schol., MA). 1st cl. hons History Tripos 1951. 5th Royal Inniskilling Dragoon Guards, 1946–48. Asst Master, Kings College Sch., Wimbledon, 1951–55; Rugby School: Asst Master, 1955–73; Housemaster, Kilbracken, 1965–73; 2nd Master, 1970–73. Chairman: Headmasters' Conference, 1982 (Chm., Acad. Cttee, 1979–81); Indep. Schs Jt Adv. Cttee, 1983–; Mem., Secondary Exams Council, 1986–. *Recreations*: Rugby football (Oxford Univ. XV 1944), hill walking, Brathay Exploration Group. *Address*: Hillside, Hawkesdene Lane, Shaftesbury, Dorset. *T*: Shaftesbury 4205. *Club*: East India, Devonshire, Sports and Public Schools.

HELLABY, Sir (Frederick Reed) Alan, Kt 1981; Chairman, P & O New Zealand, since 1986; Managing Director, 1963–83, and Chairman, 1983–85, R. & W. Hellaby Ltd.; *b* 21 Dec. 1926; *s* of Frederick Allan Hellaby and Mavis Reed; *m* 1954, Mary Dawn Trotter; three *s* one *d*. *Educ*: King's Coll., Auckland; Auckland Univ. Joined R. & W. Hellaby Ltd, 1948, Dir, 1960–, Dep. Chm., 1969–. Chairman: NZ Steel Ltd, 1974–86 (Dir, 1964–); NZ Insurance Co., 1979– (Dir, 1966–); NZI Corp. (formerly NZ S British Insurance Gp), 1981–; NZ Steel Develt Co. Ltd, 1981–86; Director: Rheem NZ Ltd; IBM (NZ) Ltd; Alcan NZ Ltd, 1985–; former Director: NZ Steel Mining; Pacific Steel Ltd. Mem., Commn of Inquiry into Meat Industry, 1973. Chm., NZ Export Year Cttee, 1978–79. Pres., Auckland Chamber of Commerce, 1985–. Chm. Bd of Governors, King's Coll.; Chm. and Trustee, NZ Police Centennial Trust, 1986; Trustee: Massey Univ. Agricl Res. Foundn; NZ Red Cross Foundn. Hon. DSc Massey, 1982. *Recreation*: weekend farming. *Address*: 519 Remuera Road, Auckland, New Zealand. *T*: 547423. *Clubs*: Northern, Royal NZ Yacht Squadron, Auckland Golf (all Auckland).

HELLIER, Maj. Gen. Eric Jim, CBE 1977 (OBE 1970, MBE 1967); General Manager, International Military Services, since 1982; *b* 23 July 1927; *s* of Harry and Elizabeth Hellier; *m* 1952, Margaret Elizabeth Leadeham; one *s* one *d* (and one *s* decd). *Educ*: Hugh Saxons Sch.; Cardiff Univ. Served, 1945–66: Navigating Officer, RNVR; regtl duty, Royal Signals; Staff Coll. and Jt Services Staff Coll; GSO2 WO; DAA&QMG 39 Inf. Bde; CO, 24 Signals Regt, 1967–69; GSO1 Plans (Operational Requirements) MoD, 1970; Col A/Q HQ 4 Div, 1971–72; Comd Bde Royal Signals and Catterick Garrison, 1973–74; RCDS, 1975; Brig A/Q HQ 1(BR), Corps, 1976–79; Maj. Gen. Admin, UKLF, 1979–81. Col Comdt, 1981–, Rep. Col Comdt, 1983, Royal Corps of Signals. Chairman: Gen. Purposes Cttee, Regular Forces Employment Assoc., 1983–; Royal Signals Instn, 1984–. *Recreations*: squash, tennis, sailing. *Address*: Wayside, West Hatch, Taunton TA3 5RJ. *T*: Taunton 480099. *Club*: Army and Navy.

HELLINGS, Gen. Sir Peter (William Cradock), KCB 1970 (CB 1966); DSC 1940; MC 1943; DL; *b* 6 Sept. 1916; *s* of Stanley and Norah Hellings; *m* 1941, Zoya, *d* of Col Bassett; one *d* (one *s* decd). *Educ*: Naut. Coll., Pangbourne. Joined Royal Marines, 1935; Company Cmdr, 40 Commando, 1942; GSO 2, Commando Group, 1944; Comdr 41 and 42 Commandos, 1945–46; Brigade Major, 3 Commando Bde in Malaya, 1949–51; joined Directing Staff of Marine Corps Schs, Quantico, USA, 1954; Comdr 40 Commando, 1958; Brigade Comdr, 3 Commando Bde, 1959; Comdr Infantry Training Centre, Royal Marines, 1960; idc 1962; Dep. Dir, Joint Warfare Staff, 1963; Maj.-Gen., 1964; Chief of Staff to Commandant-Gen., RM, 1964; Group Comdr, HQ Portsmouth Group RM, 1967–68; Lt-Gen., 1968; Comdt-Gen., RM, 1968–71; General, 1970. Col Comdt, Royal Marines, 1977–79, Representative Col Comdt, 1979–80. DL Devon 1973. *Recreations*: shooting, fishing. *Address*: The Leys, Milton Combe, Devon. *T*: Yelverton 3355.

HELLYER, Arthur George Lee, MBE 1967; FLS; Gardening Correspondent to the Financial Times; Editor of Amateur Gardening, 1946–67; Editor of Gardening Illustrated, 1947–56; *b* 16 Dec. 1902; *s* of Arthur Lee Hellyer and Maggie Parlett; *m* 1933, Grace Charlotte Bolt (*d* 1977); two *s* one *d*. *Educ*: Dulwich Coll. Farming in Jersey, 1918–21; Nursery work in England, 1921–29; Asst Editor of Commercial Horticulture, 1929; Asst Editor of Amateur Gardening, 1929–46. Associate of Hon. of Royal Horticultural Society; Victoria Medal of Honour in Horticulture. *Publications*: Your New Garden, 1937; Your Garden Week by Week, 1938; Amateur Gardening Pocket Guide, 1941, 4th rev. edn 1971; The Amateur Gardener, 1948, 4th rev. edn 1972; Encyclopaedia of Plant Portraits, 1953; Encyclopaedia of Garden Work and Terms, 1954; Flowers in Colour, 1955; English Gardens Open to the Public, 1956; Amateur Gardening Popular Encyclopaedia of Flowering Plants, 1957; Garden Plants in Colour, 1958; Garden Pests and Diseases, 1966; Starting with Roses, 1966; Shrubs in Colour, 1966, rev. edn as The Collingridge Book of Ornamental Garden Shrubs, 1981; Find Out About Gardening, 1967; Gardens to Visit in Britain, 1970; Your Lawn, 1970; Carter's Book for Gardeners, 1970; All Colour Gardening Book, 1972; All Colour Book of Indoor and Greenhouse Plants, 1973; Picture Dictionary of Popular Flowering Plants, 1973; Bulbs Indoors, 1976; The Collingridge Encyclopaedia of Gardening, 1976; Shell Guide to Gardens, 1977; Gardens of Genius, 1980; The Dobies Book of Greenhouses, 1981; Gardening Through the Year, 1981; Garden Shrubs, 1982. *Recreations*: gardening, photography, travelling. *Address*: Orchard Cottage, Rowfant, near Crawley, West Sussex. *T*: Copthorne 714838.

HELLYER, Hon. Paul Theodore, PC (Canada) 1957; FRSA 1973; Syndicated Columnist, Toronto Sun, 1974–84; *b* Waterford, Ont, Canada, 6 Aug. 1923; *s* of A. S. Hellyer and Lulla M. Anderson; *m* 1945, Ellen Jean, *d* of Henry Ralph, Toronto, Ont; two *s* one *d*. *Educ*: Waterford High Sch., Ont; Curtiss-Wright Techn. Inst. of Aeronautics, Glendale, Calif; University of Toronto (BA). Fleet Aircraft Mfg Co., Fort Erie, Ont. Wartime service, RCAF and Cdn Army. Propr Mari-Jane Fashions, Toronto, 1945–56; Treas., Curran Hall Ltd, Toronto, 1950 (Pres., 1951–62). Elected to House of Commons, 1949; re-elected, 1953; Parly Asst to Hon. Ralph Campney, Minister of Nat. Defence, 1956; Associate Minister of Nat. Defence, 1957; defeated in gen. elections of June 1957 and March 1958; re-elected to House of Commons in by-election Dec. 1958 and again re-elected June 1962, April 1963, Nov. 1965, June 1968, and Oct. 1972; defeated gen. election July 1974; Minister of National Defence, 1963–67; Minister of Transport, 1967–69, and Minister i/c Housing, 1968–69; resigned 1969 on question of principle relating to housing. Chm., Federal Task Force on Housing and Urban Develt, 1968. Served as a Parly Rep. to NATO under both L and C administrations. Joined Parly Press Gallery, Oct. 1974. Distinguished visitor, York Univ., 1969–70. Founder and Leader, Action Canada, 1971; joined Progressive Cons. Party, 1972; Candidate for leadership of Progressive Cons. Party, Feb. 1976; re-joined Liberal Party, Nov. 1982. *Publications*: Agenda: a Plan for Action, 1971; Exit Inflation, 1981; Jobs for All—Capitalism on Trial, 1984. *Recreations*: philately, music. *Address*: Suite 506, 65 Harbour Square, Toronto, Ont M5J 2L4, Canada. *Club*: Ontario.

HELMORE, Roy Lionel, CBE 1980; Principal, Cambridgeshire College of Arts and Technology, 1977–86; Fellow of Hughes Hall, Cambridge, since 1982; *b* 8 June 1926; *s* of Lionel Helmore and Ellen Helmore (*née* Gibbins); *m* 1969, Margaret Lilian Martin. *Educ*: Montrose Academy; Edinburgh Univ. (BScEng); MA (Cantab). FIEE, FBIM. Crompton Parkinson Ltd, 1947–49; Asst Lectr, Peterborough Techn. Coll., 1949–53; Lectr, subseq. Sen. Lectr, Shrewsbury Techn. Coll., 1953–57; Head of Electrical Engrg and Science, Exeter Techn. Coll., 1957–61; Principal, St Albans Coll. of Further Education, 1961–77. Association of Principals of Colleges: Hon. Sec., 1968–71; Pres., 1972–73; Hon. Treasurer, 1983–86. Member: BBC Further Educn Adv. Council, 1967–73; Air Transport and Travel ITB, 1967–73; Technician Educn Council, 1973–79 (Vice-Chm.); Manpower Services Commn, 1974–82; RAF Trng and Educn Adv. Cttee, 1976–79; Chm., Trng and Further Educn Cons. Gp, 1977–82. JP St Albans, 1964–78. *Recreations*: gardening, travel, opera. *Address*: 83 Chishill Road, Heydon, Royston, Herts SG8 8PN. *T*: Royston 838570. *Club*: Royal Commonwealth Society.

HELMSING, Most Rev. Charles H.; Former Bishop (RC) of Kansas City-St Joseph (Bishop, 1962–77, retired); *b* 23 March 1908; *s* of George Helmsing and Louise Helmsing (*née* Boschert). *Educ*: St Michael's Parochial Sch.; St Louis Preparatory Seminary; Kenrick Seminary. Sec. to Archbishop of St Louis, 1946–49; Auxiliary Bishop to Archbishop of St Louis, and Titular Bishop of Axum, 1949; first Bishop, Diocese of Springfield-Cape Girardeau, Mo, 1956–62. Member: Secretariat of Christian Unity, 1963–76; US Bishops Cttee for Ecumenical Affairs, 1964–76; Preparatory Cttee for Dialogue between Anglican Communion and Roman Catholic Church, 1966–67 (Chm., Roman Catholic Members); Chm., Special Cttee for Dialogue with Episcopal Church, US, 1964–76. Hon. Doctorates: Letters: Avila Coll. 1962; Humanities, Rockhurst Coll., 1963. Law: St Benedict's Coll. 1966. Order of Condor, Bolivia, 1966. *Address*: Cathedral House, 416 West 12th, Kansas City, Missouri 64105, USA.

HELY, Brig. Alfred Francis, CB 1951; CBE 1945; DSO 1943; TD 1944; DL; Chief Dental Officer, Cheshire County Council, 1957–68; *b* 3 Aug. 1902; *s* of Alfred Francis Hely; unmarried. *Educ*: St Edward's Coll., Liverpool; Liverpool Univ. Qualified as a Dental Surg., 1923; in private practice, 1923–26. Liverpool Univ. OTC, 1921–25; Cadet Corporal, Duke of Lancaster's Own Imperial Yeomanry, 1925–26; 106 (Lancs Hussars), RHA, 1926–41 (comd, 1937–41); served War of 1939–45 (despatches twice); 60th Field Regt, RA, 1941–42; CRA 7 Ind. Div., 1942–45; Comd 7 Ind. Div. 1945 until end of hostilities in Burma (3 months); war service in Palestine, Western Desert, Greece, Crete, Syria, 1940–42, North-West Frontier, India, 1942, Burma, 1943–45. CRA 42 (Lancs) Inf. Div. (TA), 1947–50. DL Merseyside (formerly County Palatine of Lancaster), 1951. *Recreations*: outdoor country pursuits. *Address*: 27 Bidston Court, Upton Road, Oxton, Birkenhead, Merseyside L43 7PA.

HELY, Air Commodore Arthur Hubert McMath, CB 1962; OBE 1945; Air Commodore Operations, HQ Maintenance Command, 1961–64, retired; *b* 16 Feb. 1909; *s* of Hamilton McMath Hely, OBE, RD and Lubie Thrine Hely (*née* Jörgensen); *m* 1935, Laura Mary Sullivan, 6th *d* of Serjeant A. M. Sullivan, QC; two *s* two *d*. *Educ*: Truro Sch.; Mt Albert GS, Auckland, NZ; Auckland University. Joined Royal Air Force, 1934; Staff Coll., 1942; HQ SACSEA, 1944, 1945; Joint Chiefs of Staff, Australia, 1946–48; Joint Services Staff Coll., 1948; Group Capt. 1950; HQ Fighter Command, 1953–56; HQ Far East Air Force, 1956, 1958; Air Ministry (acting Air Commodore), 1958; Air Commodore, 1959. *Recreations*: golf, painting. *Address*: Windrush, Harborough Hill, West Chiltington, West Sussex. *Club*: West Sussex Golf.

HELY-HUTCHINSON, family name of **Earl of Donoughmore.**

HEMANS, Simon Nicholas Peter, CVO 1983; HM Diplomatic Service; Head of Chancery, Moscow, since 1985; *b* 19 Sept. 1940; *s* of Brig. P. R. Hemans, CBE, and Mrs M. E. Hemans (*née* Melsome); *m* 1970, Ursula Martha Naef; three *s* one *d*. *Educ*: Sherborne; London School of Economics (BScEcon). Joined Foreign Office, 1964; British Embassy, Moscow, 1966–68; FO, 1968–69; Dep. Commissioner, Anguilla, March-Oct. 1969; FO, 1969–71; UK Mission to UN, New York, 1971–75; British Embassy, Budapest, 1975–79; FO, 1979–81; Dep. High Comr, Nairobi, 1981–84. *Recreation*: travel. *Address*: c/o Foreign and Commonwealth Office, SW1.

HEMINGFORD, 3rd Baron; *see* Herbert, D. N.

HEMINGWAY, Albert, MSc, MB, ChB; Emeritus Professor, University of Leeds (Professor of Physiology, 1936–67); *b* 27 July 1902; *s* of Herbert Hemingway, Leeds; *m* 1930, Margaret Alice Cooper; one *d*. *Educ*: University of Leeds. Demonstrator in Physiology, King's Coll., London, 1925; Senior Asst in Physiology, University Coll., London, 1926; Lecturer in Experimental Physiology, Welsh National Sch. of Medicine, 1927. Vis. Prof., Makerere University Coll., Uganda, 1968. Examiner in Physiology, Universities of St Andrews, Birmingham, Bristol, Cambridge, Durham, Glasgow, Liverpool, London, Manchester, Wales and RCS. Mem. various cttees of MRC on work and exercise physiology; Mem. Cttee, Physiological Soc. (Editor, Jl Physiology); Pres., Section I, British Assoc., 1959. *Publications*: original papers on the physiology of the circulation, exercise and the kidney in scientific and medical journals. *Recreation*: travel. *Address*: 4 Helmsley Drive, Leeds LS16 5HY. *T*: Leeds 785720.

HEMINGWAY, Peter, FCA; Director and Chief General Manager, Leeds Permanent Building Society, since 1982; *b* 19 Jan. 1926; *s* of William Edward and Florence Hemingway; *m* 1952, June Maureen, *d* of Maurice and Lilian A. Senior. *Educ*: Leeds College of Commerce. With John Gordon, Walton & Co., Chartered Accountants, Leeds, 1941–62, Partner 1959–62; Director, Provincial Registrars Ltd, 1955–62; joined Leeds Permanent Bldg Soc. as Secretary, 1962. Local Dir (Leeds), Royal Insurance (UK) Ltd, 1983–; Dir, Homeowners Friendly Soc., 1983–. Hon. Sec. 1970–82, Vice-Chm. 1982–84, Chm. 1984–86, Yorkshire and North Western Assoc. of Building Societies; Mem. Council: Building Societies Assoc., 1981–; Chartered Building Societies Inst., 1982–. *Recreations*: travel, motor racing, music, gardening. *Address*: Old Barn Cottage, Kearby, near Wetherby, Yorks LS22 4BU. *T*: Harewood 886380.

HEMLOW, Prof. Joyce; Professor Emerita, McGill University, Montreal, Canada; author; *b* 30 July 1906; *d* of William Hemlow and Rosalinda (*née* Redmond), Liscomb, NS. *Educ*: Queen's Univ., Kingston, Ont (MA; Hon. LLD 1967); Harvard Univ.,

Cambridge, Mass (AM, PhD). Preceding a univ. career, period of teaching in Nova Scotia, Canada; lecturer in English Language and Literature at McGill Univ.; Prof. of English Language and Literature, McGill Univ., 1955, Greenshields Professor 1965. FRSC 1960. Guggenheim Fellow, 1951–52, 1960–62 and 1966. Member, Phi Beta Kappa, The Johnsonians, and of other literary and professional organizations. Hon. LLD Dalhousie, 1972. James Tait Black Memorial Book Prize, 1958; Brit. Academy Award (Crawshay Prize), 1960. *Publications:* The History of Fanny Burney, 1958 (GB); (ed with others) The Journals and Letters of Fanny Burney (Madame d'Arblay), vols i-xii, 1972–84; (ed) Fanny Burney: selected letters and journals, 1986; articles in learned jls on Fanny Burney's novels and unpublished plays. *Address:* (home) Liscomb, Nova Scotia, Canada; 1521 Le Marchant Street, Halifax, NS B3H 3R2, Canada. *Club:* English-Speaking Union (Canadian Branch).

HEMMING, Air Commodore Idris George Selvin, CB 1968; CBE 1959 (OBE 1954); retired; *b* 11 Dec. 1911; *s* of late George Hemming, Liverpool; *m* 1939, Phyllis, *d* of Francis Payne, Drogheda, Eire; two *s*. *Educ:* Chalford, Glos.; Wallasey, Cheshire. Joined RAF, 1928; served War of 1939–45, UK, India and Burma; Gp Capt. 1957; Air Cdre 1962; Dir of Equipment (Pol.) (RAF), MoD, 1962–66; Dir of Equipment (1) (RAF), MoD, Harrogate, 1966–68. *Recreations:* cricket, golf. *Address:* Ash House, St Chloe Green, Amberley, near Stroud, Glos GL5 5AP. *T:* Amberley 3581. *Club:* Royal Air Force.

HEMMING, John Henry, DLitt; Joint Chairman, Municipal Journal Ltd, since 1976 (Director, since 1962; Deputy Chairman, 1967–76); Director and Secretary, Royal Geographical Society, since 1975; *b* 5 Jan. 1935; *s* of late Henry Harold Hemming, OBE, MC, and of Alice Louisa Weaver, OBE; *m* 1979, Sukie, *d* of late M. J. Babington Smith, CBE; one *s* one *d*. *Educ:* Eton College; McGill University; Oxford University (DLitt 1981). Chairman: Brintex Ltd, 1979– (Man. Dir, 1963–70, Dep. Chm. 1976–78); Newman Books, 1979–. Member, Iriri River Expedition, Brazil, 1961. Member Council: Lepra; Anglo-Brazilian Soc.; Mem., CNAA (Geography). Corres. Mem., Academia Nacional de la Historia, Venezuela. Sponsor, Survival International; Trustee: L. S. B. Leakey Trust; Gilchrist Educnl Trust. *Publications:* The Conquest of the Incas, 1970 (Robert Pitman Literary Prize, 1970, Christopher Award, NY, 1971); (jt) Tribes of the Amazon Basin in Brazil, 1972; Red Gold: The Conquest of the Brazilian Indians, 1978; The Search for El Dorado, 1978; Machu Picchu, 1981; Monuments of the Incas, 1982; The New Incas, 1983; (ed) Change in the Amazon Basin (2 vols), 1985. *Recreations:* writing, travel. *Address:* 10 Edwardes Square, W8 6HE. *Clubs:* Travellers', Beefsteak, Geographical (Mem. Council).
See also L. A. Service.

HEMMINGS, David Leslie Edward; actor, director and producer; engaged in entertainment industry since 1949; *b* 18 Nov. 1941; *m* 1st, 1960, Genista Ouvry; one *d*; 2nd, 1969, Gayle Hunnicutt (marr. diss. 1975); one *s*; 3rd, 1976, Prudence J. de Casembroot; two *s*. *Educ:* Glyn Coll., Epsom, Surrey. The Turn of the Screw, English Opera Group, 1954; Five Clues to Fortune, 1957; Saint Joan, 1957; The Heart Within, 1957; Men of Tomorrow, 1958; In the Wake of a Stranger, 1958; No Trees in the Street, 1959; Some People, 1962; Play it Cool, 1962; Live it Up, 1963; Two Left Feet, 1963; The System, 1964; Be my Guest, 1965; Eye of the Devil, 1966; Blow Up, 1966; Camelot, 1967; Barbarella, 1967; Only When I Larf, 1968; The Charge of the Light Brigade, 1968; The Long Day's Dying, 1968; The Best House in London, 1968; Alfred the Great, 1969; Fragment of Fear, 1970; The Walking Stick, 1970; Unman, Wittering & Zigo, 1971; The Love Machine, 1971; Voices, 1973; Don't Worry Momma, 1973; Juggernaut, 1974; Quilp, 1974; Profundo Rosso, 1975; Islands in the Stream, 1975; The Squeeze, 1976; Jeeves (musical), Her Majesty's, 1975; Power Play, 1978; Thirst, 1979; Beyond Reasonable Doubt, 1980; Jekyll and Hyde, 1980; Harlequin, 1980. BBC TV, Scott Fitzgerald, 1975; ITV, The Rime of the Ancient Mariner, 1978; ITV, Charlie Muffin, 1979. Directed: Running Scared, 1972; The 14, 1973 (Silver Bear Award, Berlin Film Festival, 1973); Disappearance, 1977; Power Play, 1977; Just a Gigolo, 1978; David Bowie Stage, 1979; Murder By Decree, 1979; Survivor, 1979; Race to the Yankee Zephyr, 1980; also in Australia, NZ etc. Produced: Strange Behaviour, 1981; Turkey Shoot, 1981. Director: International Home Video FGH Pty Ltd (Melbourne); Film and General Holdings Inc. (California). *Recreation:* painting. *Address:* c/o Michael Whitehall Ltd, 125 Gloucester Road, SW7. *Clubs:* Turf, Chelsea Arts, Magic Circle.

HEMP, Prof. William Spooner, MA, FRAeS; Stewarts and Lloyds Professor of Structural Engineering, Oxford University, 1965–83; Emeritus Fellow of Keble College, Oxford, since 1984 (Professorial Fellow, 1965–83); *b* 21 March 1916; *s* of late Rev. William James Hemp and Daisy Lilian Hemp; *m* 1938, Dilys Ruth Davies; one *s*. *Educ:* Paston Grammar Sch., North Walsham; Jesus Coll., Cambridge (Scholar, MA). Aeronautical Engineer, Bristol Aeroplane Co., 1938–46. Coll. of Aeronautics: Senior Lecturer, 1946–50; Prof. of Aircraft Structures and Aeroelasticity, 1950–65; Head of Dept of Aircraft Design, 1951–65; Dep. Principal, 1957–65. Mem. of various cttees of Aeronautical Research Council since 1948. Visiting Prof., Stanford Univ., Calif, 1960–61. *Publications:* Optimum Structures, 1973; research papers in the Theory of Structures, Solid Mechanics and Applied Mathematics. *Recreations:* mountain walking, music. *Address:* Duffryn House, Church Lane, Horton-cum-Studley, Oxford.

HEMPHILL, 5th Baron *cr* 1906, of Rathkenny and Cashel; **Peter Patrick Fitzroy Martyn Martyn-Hemphill;** *b* 5 Sept. 1928; *o s* of 4th Baron Hemphill and Emily, *d* of F. Irving Sears, Webster, Mass; *S* father 1957; *m* 1952, Olivia Anne, *er d* of Major Robert Francis Ruttledge, MC, Cloonee, Ballinrobe, County Mayo; one *s* two *d*; assumed surname of Martyn in addition to Hemphill, 1959. *Educ:* Downside; Brasenose Coll., Oxford (MA). *Heir:* *s* Hon. Charles Andrew Martyn Martyn-Hemphill [*b* 8 Oct. 1954; *m* 1985, Sarah J. F., *e d* of Richard Lumley; one *d*]. *Address:* Raford, Kiltulla, Co. Galway, Eire. *Clubs:* Royal Automobile, White's; Kildare Street and University (Dublin); County (Galway).

HEMSLEY, Thomas Jeffrey; free-lance opera and concert singer; *b* 12 April 1927; *s* of Sydney William Hemsley and Kathleen Annie Hemsley (*née* Deacon); *m* 1960, Hon. Gwenllian Ellen James, *d* of 4th Baron Northbourne; three *s*. *Educ:* Ashby de la Zouch Grammar Sch.; Brasenose Coll., Oxford (MA). Vicar Choral, St Paul's Cathedral, 1950–51; Prin. Baritone, Stadttheater, Aachen, 1953–56; Deutsche Oper am Rhein, 1957–63; Opernhaus, Zurich, 1963–67; Glyndebourne, Bayreuth, Edinburgh Festivals, etc. Hon. RAM 1974. *Address:* 10 Denewood Road, N6. *T:* 01–348 3397.

HENAO, Rev. Sir Ravu, Kt 1982; OBE 1975; Executive Secretary, Bible Society of Papua New Guinea, since 1980; *b* 27 March 1927; *s* of Boga Henao and Gaba Asi; *m* 1944, Lahui Peri; four *s* five *d*. *Educ:* Port Moresby (completed standard 5); Lawes Theol Coll., Fife Bay, Milne Bay Province. Primary sch. teacher, various schs in Central Dist, 1944–66 (pastor as well as teacher, 1946); Chm. (full-time), Papua Ekalesia (national church related to London Missionary Soc.), 1967; Bishop of United Church for Papua Mainland Region, 1968–80. *Publications:* (with Raymond Perry) Let's Discuss These Things, 1966; (with Alan Dunstan) Paul's Letter to the Galatians, 1974. *Recreations:* fishing, hunting, gardening. *Address:* PO Box 18, Port Moresby, Papua New Guinea. *T:* (office) 21–7893, (home) 21–4367.

HENARE, Sir James Clendon Tau, KBE 1978 (CBE 1966); DSO 1945; retired farmer, New Zealand; *b* Motatau, NZ, 18 Nov. 1911; *s* of Tau Henare, MP; *m* 1933, Rosie, *d* of Johnson Cherrington; three *s* three *d*. *Educ:* Motatau Sch., Awanui, Takapuna; Thorndon Normal Sch.; Sacred Heart Coll., Auckland; Massey Coll. (later Univ.). Served War, 2nd NZEF; Private, 1939; commissioned, 1940; finally CO (Lt-Col) Maori Bn (despatches). Member: Waitangi Nat. Trust Bd; Bay of Islands CC; Bay of Islands Maritime and Historic Park Bd; Chm., Taitokerau Trust Bd. Former Member: Rehabilitation Bd; Geographic Bd; Bd of Maori Affairs; Auckland Diocese Synod; Maori Language Runanga, and many other organisations. Awarded KBE for service to the community, especially Maori affairs, New Zealand. *Address:* Moerewa Road 3, Bay of Islands, New Zealand.

HENBEST, Harold Bernard; *see* Herbert, H. B.

HENDER, John Derrik, CBE 1986; DL; public sector consultant; Chief Executive, West Midlands Metropolitan County Council, 1973–86; *b* 15 Nov. 1926; *s* of late Jessie Peter and late Jennie Hender; *m* 1949, Kathleen Nora Brown; one *d*. *Educ:* Great Yarmouth Grammar School. IPFA, FCA, FBIM. Deputy Borough Treasurer: Newcastle-under-Lyme, 1957–61; Wolverhampton County Borough, 1961–64; City Treas. 1965–69, Chief Exec. and Town Clerk 1969–73, Coventry County Borough. DL West Midlands, 1975. *Publications:* numerous articles relating to various aspects of local govt and related matters. *Recreation:* gardening. *Address:* 10 Barns Croft, Little Aston, Sutton Coldfield, West Midlands B74 3BW.

HENDERSON, family name of **Barons Faringdon** and **Henderson of Brompton.**

HENDERSON OF BROMPTON, Baron *cr* 1984 (Life Peer), of Brompton in the Royal Borough of Kensington and Chelsea and of Brough in the County of Cumbria; **Peter Gordon Henderson,** KCB 1975; Clerk of the Parliaments, 1974–83; *b* 16 Sept. 1922; *m* 1950, Susan Mary Dartford; two *s* two *d*. *Educ:* Stowe Sch.; Magdalen Coll., Oxford (Demy). Served War, Scots Guards, 1942–44. Clerk, House of Lords, 1954–60; seconded to HM Treasury as Sec. to Leader and Chief Whip, House of Lords, 1960–63; Reading Clerk and Clerk of Public Bills, 1964–74; Clerk Asst, 1974. Mem., Cttee on Preparation of Legislation, 1973–74. Governor, Godolphin and Latymer Sch. *Address:* 16 Pelham Street, SW7 2NG; Helbeck Cottage, Brough, Kirkby Stephen, Cumbria CA17 4DD. *Club:* Pratt's.

HENDERSON, Barry; *see* Henderson, J. S. B.

HENDERSON, Charles Edward, FIA; Principal Establishment and Finance Officer, Department of Energy, since 1986; *b* 19 Sept. 1939; *s* of late David Henderson and of Giorgiana Leggatt Henderson; *m* 1966, Rachel Hilary Hall; one *s* one *d*. *Educ:* Charterhouse; Pembroke Coll., Cambridge (MA). FIA 1965. Actuarial Trainee, subseq. Asst Investment Sec., Equity & Law Life Assurance Soc., 1960–70; ECGD, 1971–73; DTI, 1973–74; Dept of Energy, 1974–: Asst Sec., 1975; Under Sec., 1982; Atomic Energy Div., 1982; Oil Div., 1985. Dir, Aluminium Corp. Ltd, 1981–84. *Recreations:* making and listening to music, mountaineering, golf. *Address:* 33 Fairfax Road, Bedford Park, W4 1EN. *T:* 01–994 1345.

HENDERSON, Rt. Rev. Charles Joseph; Auxiliary Bishop in Southwark, (RC), since 1972; Titular Bishop of Tricala, since 1972; Area Bishop with responsibility for South East Metropolitan London, since 1980; *b* 14 April 1924; *s* of Charles Stuart Henderson and Hanora Henderson (*née* Walsh). *Educ:* Mount Sion Sch., Waterford; St John's Seminary, Waterford. Priest, 1948; Curate, St Stephen's, Welling, Kent, 1948–55; English Martyrs, Streatham, SW16, 1955–58; Chancellor, RC Diocese of Southwark, 1958–70; Vicar General, RC Diocese of Arundel and Brighton, 1965–66; Episcopal Vicar for Religious, Southwark, 1968–73; Vicar General, RC Archdiocese of Southwark, 1969; Parish Priest, St Mary's, Blackheath, 1969–82; Canon of Cathedral Chapter, 1972; Provost of Cathedral Chapter, 1973. Member: Ecumenical Commn for England and Wales, 1976–; Nat. Catholic Commn for Racial Justice, 1978–81; English Anglican/RC Cttee, 1982–, Co. Chm. 1983–; Methodist/RC Nat. Ecumenical Cttee, 1983 and Co. Chm. 1984–; Chm., RC Cttee for Dialogue with Other Faiths, 1984–; RC Consultant-Observer, BCC, 1982–86. Papal Chamberlain, 1960; Prelate of Papal Household, 1965. Freeman, City of Waterford, 1973. Kt Comdr with Star of Equestrian Order of Holy Sepulchre, Jerusalem, 1973. *Recreation:* special interest in sport. *Address:* Park House, 6A Cresswell Park, Blackheath, SE3 9RD. *T:* 01–318 1094.

HENDERSON, David; *see* Henderson, P. D.

HENDERSON, Denys Hartley; Deputy Chairman, Imperial Chemical Industries, since 1986, Chairman, from April 1987; *b* 11 Oct. 1932; *s* of John Hartley Henderson and Nellie Henderson (*née* Gordon); *m* 1957, Doreen Mathewson Glashan, *o d* of Robert and Mary Glashan; two *d*. *Educ:* Aberdeen Grammar School; Univ. of Aberdeen (MA, LLB). Solicitor; Mem., Law Soc. of Scotland. Joined ICI as lawyer in Secretary's Dept, London, 1957; commercial appts at Agricl Div. and Nobel Div.; Dir, Fertiliser Sales and Marketing, Agricl Div., 1972; Corporate Gen. Manager, Commercial, 1974; Chm., ICI Paints Div., 1977; ICI Main Bd Dir, 1980. Non-Exec. Director: Dalgety plc, 1981–; Barclays Bank, 1983–; Barclays, 1983–; Barclays International, 1981–. Mem., BBC's Consultative Group on Industrial and Business Affairs, 1985–. *Recreations:* family life, swimming, reading, travel, minimal gardening, unskilled but enjoyable golf. *Address:* ICI, Imperial Chemical House, Millbank, SW1P 3JF. *T:* 01-834 4444. *Club:* Royal Automobile.

HENDERSON, Derek, FDSRCS; Senior Consultant Oral and Maxillo-facial Surgeon, St Thomas' Hospital, since 1975; Consultant, St George's Hospital, since 1975; Hon. Consultant, Charing Cross Hospital, since 1977; Recognised Teacher, University of London, since 1977; Hon. Civilian Consultant in Dental Surgery: Royal Navy, since 1971; Army, since 1981; *b* 9 April 1935; *s* of Robert Henderson and Dorothy Edith Henderson; *m* 1961, Jennifer Jill Anderson; one *s* one *d*. *Educ:* Dulwich Coll.; London Univ. (BDS Hons 1956, MB, BS Hons 1963). FDSRCS (Eng) 1960 (LDS 1956); MRCS, LRCP 1963. Dental and med. trng, KCH, London, 1952–56 and 1959–63 (Prizeman); house surg. appts, KCH and Royal Dental Hosp., 1956–59; King's Coll. Hospital: Lectr in Dental Materials, 1958–65; ENT House Officer, and Casualty Off., 1964; Registrar in Oral Surg., Queen Mary's Hosp., Roehampton, and Westminster Hosp., 1965; Sen. Registrar in Oral Surg., United Cardiff Hosps, 1965–67; Consultant Oral Surgeon to Eastern Reg. Hosp. Bd, Scotland, and Dundee Dental Hosp., 1967–69 (Hon. Sen. Lectr, Univ. of Dundee); Consultant i/c Reg. Maxillo-facial Service to Glasgow and West of Scotland, based on Canniesburn Plastic and Oral Surg. Unit, Glasgow, 1969–75 (Hon. Clinical Teacher, Glasgow Univ.); Consultant, Royal Dental Hosp., 1975–85. Hon. Civilian Consultant, Queen Elizabeth Mil. Hosp., Woolwich (formerly Queen Alexandra Mil. Hosp., Millbank), 1976–81; Hon. Sen. Lectr in Oral Surg., Royal Dental Sch., London, 1977–85. Vis. Prof. and Lectr, Brazil, Argentina, Chile, USA, Spain, Venezuela, Australia, Holland, Saudi Arabia, Uruguay, SA. Royal College of Surgeons: Hunterian Prof., 1975–76; Mem. Council, 1984–; Kelsey Fry Adviser in Postgraduate Educnl Trng, 1975–80, Mem. Bd, 1978–, Mem. Exec. Cttee, 1983–, and Vice-Dean, 1984–85, Faculty of Dental Surgery (also Examr, FDSRCS). Member: Central Cttee for Hospital Dental Services, 1978–85 (Mem. Exec. Cttee, 1980–85); Central Cttee for Univ. Dental Teachers and Research Workers, 1978–81; Negotiating Subcttee, CCHMS, 1980–85; European Assoc. for Maxillo-Facial Surg.; BMA; BDA; Craniofacial Soc. (Mem. Council, 1973–77); Oral Surgery Club GB. Fellow: BAOMS (Mem. Council, 1974–76, 1977–80, 1984–); Internat. Assoc. of Oral Surgeons. Hon. Mem., Amer. Assoc. of Oral Surgeons in Europe; Hon. Associate Life Mem., Soc. of Maxillo-facial and Oral Surgeons of SA; Hon. Pres., Inst. of Maxillo-Facial Technol., 1977–78. *Publications:* An Atlas and Textbook of Orthognathic Surgery, 1985; contribs on general oral surgery to British Jl of Oral Surgery and British Dental Jl, and especially on surgery of facial and jaw deformity to Brit. Jl of Oral Surg. and Brit. Jl of Plastic Surg. *Recreation:* fly fishing. *Address:* Mallington, Headley Road, Leatherhead, Surrey KT22 8PU. *T:* Leatherhead 378513; 107 Harley Street, W1N 1DG. *T:* 01–935 6906. *Clubs:* Savage, Flyfishers'; Royal Navy Medical; Piscatorial Soc.

HENDERSON, Dr Derek Scott; Principal and Vice-Chancellor, Rhodes University, Grahamstown, South Africa, since 1975; *b* 28 Oct. 1929; *s* of Ian Scott and Kathleen Elizabeth Henderson; *m* 1958, Thelma Muriel Mullins; two *d. Educ:* Rhodes University Coll. (BSc); Oxford Univ. (MA); Cambridge Univ. (MA); Harvard Univ. (PhD). Exec. Trainee, Anglo American Corp. of S Africa, 1953–56; Lectr in Maths, Univ. of the Witwatersrand, Johannesburg, 1957; Associate Engr, IBM Corp., Poughkeepsie, NY, 1960–62; Univ. of the Witwatersrand, 1962–75: Sen. Lectr, then Dir of Computer Centre; Prof. of Computer Science; Head of Dept of Applied Maths; Dean of Science Faculty. *Publications:* seventeen articles in learned jls. *Recreation:* golf. *Address:* Rhodes University, PO Box 94, Grahamstown, 6140, S Africa. *T:* 0461–3639. *Club:* Port Elizabeth (Port Elizabeth, S Africa).

HENDERSON, Douglas Mackay, CBE 1985; FRSE 1966; FLS; Regius Keeper, Royal Botanic Garden, Edinburgh, since 1970; *b* 30 Aug. 1927; *s* of Captain Frank Henderson and Adine C. Mackay; *m* 1952, Julia Margaret Brown; one *s* two *d. Educ:* Blairgowrie High Sch.; Edinburgh Univ. (BSc). Scientific Officer, Dept of Agriculture and Fisheries for Scotland, 1948–51. Royal Botanic Garden, Edinburgh, 1951–. Hon. Prof., Edinburgh Univ., 1983–. Sec., Internat. Assoc. of Botanical Gardens, 1969–81. Curator of Library and Museum, Royal Soc. of Edinburgh, 1978–. VMH, 1985. *Publications:* British Rust Fungi (with M. Wilson), 1966; many papers on taxonomy of cryptogams. *Recreations:* music, art, hill walking, field natural history, sailing. *Address:* 12 Afton Terrace, Edinburgh EH5 3NG. *T:* 031–552 3457.

HENDERSON, Ven. Edward Chance, BD, ALCD; Archdeacon of Pontefract, 1968–81, now Archdeacon Emeritus; *b* 15 Oct. 1916; *s* of William Edward and Mary Anne Henderson; *m* 1942, Vera Massie Pattison; two *s* three *d. Educ:* Heaton Grammar Sch.; London University. Asst Curate, St Stephen, Newcastle upon Tyne, 1939–42; Organising Sec., CPAS, 1942–45; Vicar of St Mary of Bethany, Leeds, 1945–51; Priest i/c: Armley Hall, Leeds, 1948–51; St John, New Wortley, Leeds, 1949–51; Vicar of: All Souls, Halifax, 1951–59; Dewsbury, 1959–68; Darrington with Wentbridge, 1968–75. Examining Chaplain to Bishop of Wakefield, 1972–81. *Address:* 12 Park Lane, Balne, Goole, North Humberside DN14 0EP. *T:* Goole 85284.

HENDERSON, Edward Firth, CMG 1972; HM Diplomatic Service, retired; *b* 12 Dec. 1917; *m* 1960, Jocelyn (*née* Nenk), MBE; two *d. Educ:* Clifton Coll.; BNC, Oxford. Served War of 1939–45 in Army (despatches); served in Arab Legion, 1945–47. With Petroleum Concessions Ltd, in Arabian Gulf, 1948–56; Foreign Service, 1956; served in Middle East posts and in Foreign Office; Political Agent, Qatar, 1969–71, and Ambassador there 1971–74. Lectr and Res. Schol., Sch. of Advanced Internat. Studies, Johns Hopkins Univ., 1976, 1977 and 1979; Lectr, Univs of Texas, NY and Princeton, 1979; Hon. Fellow, LSE, 1980–81. Research specialist, Centre for Documentation and Res., Presidential Court, Abu Dhabi, 1976–81; Dir, Council for the Advancement of Arab-British Understanding, 1981–82; Chm., Amer. Educal Trust, Washington, DC, 1982–83. Returned to Abu Dhabi, 1984. *Address:* 4 Purcell Close, Tewin Wood, near Welwyn, Herts AL6 0NN. *Club:* Travellers'.

HENDERSON, Prof. George David Smith, FSA; Professor of Medieval Art, Cambridge, since 1986; Fellow of Downing College, Cambridge, since 1974; *b* 7 May 1931; *yr s* of late Very Rev. Prof. George David Henderson, DLitt, DTh, DD and Jenny Holmes McCulloch Henderson (*née* Smith); *m* 1957, Isabel Bisset Murray; one *s* one *d. Educ:* Aberdeen Grammar Sch.; Univ. of Aberdeen (MA 1953); Courtauld Inst., Univ. of London (BA 1956); Trinity Coll., Cambridge (MA, PhD 1961). Research Fellow, Barber Inst. of Art, Univ. of Birmingham, 1959–60; Graham Robertson Research Fellow, Downing Coll., Cambridge, 1960–63; Univ. of Manchester: Asst Lectr in History of Art, 1962–64; Lectr, 1964–66; Univ. of Edinburgh: Lectr in Fine Arts, 1966–71; Reader in Fine Arts, 1971–73; Univ. of Cambridge: Lectr in History of Art, 1974–79; Head of Dept, 1974–; Reader in Medieval Art, 1979–86; a Syndic, Fitzwilliam Museum, 1974–. *Publications:* Gothic, 1967; Chartres, 1968; Early Medieval, 1972; (ed with Giles Robertson) Studies in Memory of David Talbot Rice, 1975; Bede and the Visual Arts (Jarrow Lect.), 1980; Losses and Lacunae in Early Insular Art (Garmonsway Lect.), 1982; Studies in English Bible Illustration, 1985; From Durrow to Kells, 1987; articles in UK and Amer. jls. *Recreations:* listening to Wagner, looking for agates. *Address:* Downing College, Cambridge. *T:* Cambridge 334800. *Club:* United Oxford & Cambridge University.

HENDERSON, Rt. Rev. George Kennedy Buchanan; *see* Argyll and the Isles, Bishop of.

HENDERSON, Prof. George Patrick, FRSE 1980; Professor of Philosophy in the University of Dundee (formerly Queen's College, Dundee), 1959–80, Dean, Faculty of Arts and Social Sciences, 1973–76; *b* 22 April 1915; *e s* of Rev. George Aitchison Henderson, MA, and Violet Margaret Mackenzie; *m* 1939, Hester Lowry Douglas McWilliam, BSc (*d* 1978), *d* of Rev. John Morell McWilliam, BA. *Educ:* Elgin Academy; St Andrews Univ. (Harkness Scholar); Balliol Coll., Oxford. 1st Class Hons in Philosophy, University of St Andrews, 1936; Miller Prize and Ramsay Scholarship; MA 1936; Ferguson Scholarship in Philosophy, 1936; 2nd Class Lit Hum, University of Oxford, 1938; BA 1938. Asst in Logic and Metaphysics, University of St Andrews, 1938; Shaw Fellow in Mental Philosophy, University of Edinburgh, 1938. MA Oxon, 1943. Army Service, 1940–46; Royal Artillery (commissioned 1940, Adjutant 1942–43) and Gen. Staff (GSO 3 1945); served in UK, Italy and Greece. Lecturer in Logic and Metaphysics, University of St Andrews, 1945; Senior Lecturer, 1953. Corresp. Member: Acad. of Athens, 1973; Ionian Acad., 1975. Editor of the Philosophical Quarterly, 1962–72. *Publications:* The Revival of Greek Thought, 1620–1830, 1970; The Ionian Academy (in Greek trans.), 1980; E. P. Papanoutsos, 1983; numerous articles and reviews in principal philosophical periodicals. *Recreations:* modern Greek studies, gardening. *Address:* The Pendicle, Invergowrie, Dundee DD2 5DQ.

HENDERSON, Sir Guy (Wilmot McLintock), Kt 1956; BA, LLM Cantab; QC (Uganda) 1949; Chief Justice of the Bahamas, 1951–60, retired; *b* 13 July 1897; *e s* of late Arthur James and Charlotte West Henderson; *m* 1930, Ann (*d* 1980), *d* of late George and Elizabeth Dring-Campion; two *s* one *d. Educ:* Blundell's, Tiverton; Collegiate Sch., Wanganui, NZ; Trinity Coll., Cambridge. Served European War, 1914–18, Lieut RFA

(SR). Barrister-at-Law, Inner Temple, 1923; private practice, Rangoon, Burma, 1924–29; professional clerk, prosecuting staff GPO, London, 1930–32; stipendiary and circuit magistrate, Bahamas, 1932–37; Crown Counsel, Tanganyika Territory, 1937–40; legal draftsman, Nigeria, 1940–45; dep. Chief Legal Adviser, British Military Administration, Malaya, 1945–46; Solicitor-Gen., Colony of Singapore, 1946–48; Attorney-Gen., Uganda Protectorate, 1948–51. *Address:* PO Box N 7776, Nassau, Bahamas.

HENDERSON, Ian Dalton, ERD 1960 (1st clasp 1966, 2nd clasp 1972); FRCS; Consultant Surgeon, Tunbridge Wells District, 1956–82, now Honorary Consultant Surgeon; *b* 4 Nov. 1918; *s* of Stewart Dalton Henderson and Grace Aird (*née* Masterson); *m* 1951, Rosa Hertz, MB, BS, MRCOG; two *d. Educ:* Fettes Coll., Edinburgh; Guy's Hosp., Univ. of London (MB, BS 1943). LMSSA 1943; FRCS 1949. Served War, RAMC, 1943–46: served India; Major, 1945–46. Lectr in Anatomy and Surg. Registrar, Guy's Hosp., 1947–50; Sen. Surg. Registrar, Royal Postgrad. Med. Sch. of London, 1952–56. Hon. Surgeon to the Queen, 1971–73. Member: Kent AHA, 1973–82; Société Internat. de Chirurgie, 1972–. FRSM 1947–. Served TA and AER, subseq. T&AVR, 1948–79; former Hon. Col and OC 308 Gen. Hosp., T&AVR. Silver Jubilee Medal, 1978. *Recreations:* archaeology, skiing, golf, photography. *Address:* 5 Thornbury Court, Chepstow Villas, W11 2QZ. *T:* 01–221 3822.

HENDERSON, James Ewart, MA, DSc; Managing Director since 1982 and Chairman since 1985, Mastiff Electronic Systems Ltd; President and Chief Executive, Mastiff Systems US Inc., since 1982; *b* 29 May 1923; *s* of late Rev. James Ewart Henderson, MA, BD and Agnes Mary (*née* Crawford); *m* 1st, 1949, Alice Joan Hewlitt; one *d*; 2nd, 1966, Nancy Maude Dominy; two *s. Educ:* private sch.; Glasgow Univ.; Edinburgh Univ. Research on air rockets and guns, MAP, 1943–44; hon. commn in RAFVR, 1944–46; operational assessment of air attacks in Belgium, Holland and Germany, 2TAF, 1944–45; exper. research on fighter and bomber capability, and on the use of radar and radio aids: RAF APC Germany, 1945–46, Fighter Comd, 1946–49 and CFE, 1949–52; research on weapons effects and capability: Air Min., 1952–54, AWRE 1955, Air Min., 1955–58; Asst Scientific Adviser (Ops), Air Min., 1958–63; Dep. Chief Scientist (RAF), MoD, 1963–69; Chief Scientist (RAF) and Mem., Air Force Bd, 1969–73. Aviation Consultant, Hawker Siddeley Aviation Ltd, 1973–77; Financial Consultant, Charles Stapleton & Co. Ltd, 1973–78; freelance Operational Res. and Management Consultant, 1975–78; Director: Lewis Security Systems Ltd, 1976–77; Mastiff Security Systems Ltd, 1977–82; Chm., TIB Netherlands, 1982–86. Scientific Advr, BAe, 1978–82. Chairman: Air League, 1981– (Mem. Council, 1979–80); Air League Educational Trust, 1983–. FInstD 1978. *Publications:* technical papers on operational capability of aircraft and weapons; UK manual on Blast Effects of Nuclear Weapons. *Recreations:* flying (private pilot's licence), sailing, golf, opera, photography. *Address:* Mastiff Electronic Systems Ltd, Little Mead, Cranleigh, Surrey GU6 8ND. *Clubs:* Naval and Military; Royal Scottish Automobile (Glasgow); Moor Park Golf; New Zealand Golf.

HENDERSON, (James Stewart) Barry; MP (C) North East Fife, since 1983 (East Fife, 1979–83); management consultant, since 1975; *b* 29 April 1936; *s* of James Henderson, CBE and Jane Stewart McLaren; *m* 1961, Janet Helen Sprot Todd; two *s. Educ:* Lathallan Sch.; Stowe Sch. Mem. British Computer Soc. Nat. Service, 1954–56; electronics and computer industries, 1957–65; Scottish Conservative Central Office, 1966–70; computer industry, 1971–74; MP (C) East Dunbartonshire, Feb.-Sept. 1974. Member: Select Cttee on Scottish Affairs, 1979–; H of C Chairmen's Panel, 1981–83; Chm., Scottish Cons. Back Bench Cttee, 1983–84; PPS to Economic Sec. to the Treasury, 1984–. Trustee, St Andrews Links Trust, 1979–. *Address:* Old Gillingshill, by Anstruther, Fife.

HENDERSON, Sir James Thyne, KBE 1959; CMG 1952; *b* 18 Jan. 1901; *s* of late Sir Thomas Henderson; *m* 1930, Karen Margrethe Hansen; one *s* four *d. Educ:* Warriston, Moffat; Sedbergh Sch.; Queen's Coll., Oxford. Entered Diplomatic Service, 1925, apptd to FO; transf. to Tehran, 1927; Athens, 1929; Helsinki, 1932, where acted as Chargé d'Affaires in 1932, 1933, 1934 and 1935; Foreign Office, 1935. First Sec., 1936; attached to Representative of Finland at the Coronation of King George VI, 1937; Tokyo, 1938; Santiago, 1941; Foreign Office, 1944; Stockholm, 1946, Chargé d'Affaires there in 1946 and 1947; Counsellor, 1947; Consul-Gen., Houston, 1949; HM Minister to Iceland, 1953–56; HM Ambassador to Bolivia, 1956–60, retired. *Recreation:* gardening. *Address:* 43/14 Gillespie Crescent, Edinburgh EH10 4HY. *T:* 031–229 8191.

HENDERSON, Dame Joan; *see* Kelleher, Dame Joan.

HENDERSON, Sir (John) Nicholas, GCMG 1977 (KCMG 1972; CMG 1965); HM Diplomatic Service, retired; re-appointed, Ambassador to Washington, 1979–82; Lord Warden of the Stannaries and Keeper of the Privy Seal of the Duke of Cornwall, since 1985; Director: Foreign & Colonial Investment Trust, since 1982; M&G Reinsurance, since 1982; Hambros, since 1983; Tarmac, since 1983; F & C Eurotrust, since 1984; *b* 1 April 1919; *s* of Prof. Sir Hubert Henderson; *m* 1951, Mary Barber (*née* Cawadias); one *d. Educ:* Stowe Sch.; Hertford Coll., Oxford (Hon. Fellow 1975). Mem. HM Diplomatic Service. Served Minister of State's Office, Cairo, 1942–43; Asst Private Sec. to the Foreign Sec., 1944–47; HM Embassy, Washington, 1947–49; Athens, 1949–50; Permanent Under Secretary's Dept, FO, 1950–53; HM Embassy, Vienna, 1953–56; Santiago, 1956–59; Northern Dept, FO, 1959–62; Permanent Under Secretary's Dept, 1962–63; Head of Northern Dept, Foreign Office, 1963; Private Sec. to the Sec. of State for Foreign Affairs, 1963–65; Minister in Madrid, 1965–69; Ambassador to Poland, 1969–72, to Federal Republic of Germany, 1972–75, to France, 1975–79. Mem., BBC General Adv. Council, 1983–; Chm., Channel Tunnel Gp, 1985–86. Mem. Council, Duchy of Cornwall, 1985–. Trustee, Nat. Gallery, 1985–. Pres., Hertford Soc., 1984–. Romanes Lectr, 1986. *Publications:* Prince Eugen of Savoy (biography), 1964; The Birth of Nato, 1982; The Private Office, 1984; various stories and articles in Penguin New Writing, Horizon, Apollo, Country Life, The Economist and History Today. *Recreations:* tennis, gardening. *Address:* 6 Fairholt Street, SW7 1EG. *T:* 01–589 4291; School House, Combe, near Newbury, Berks. *T:* Inkpen 330. *Clubs:* Brooks's, Garrick, Beefsteak.
See also Viscount Moore.

HENDERSON, John Ronald, CVO 1985; OBE 1985 (MBE 1945); Vice-Lord-Lieutenant of Berkshire, since 1979; Chairman, Henderson Administration (Group), since 1983; *b* 6 May 1920; *s* of Major R. H. W. Henderson and Mrs Marjorie Henderson (*née* Garrard); *m* 1st, 1949, Sarah Katherine Beckwith-Smith (*d* 1972); two *s* one *d*; 2nd, 1976, Catherine Christian; one step *s* two step *d. Educ:* Eton; Cambridge Univ. Served War: ADC to Field Marshal Montgomery, 1942–46; retd Major, 12th Royal Lancers, 1946. Director: Barclays Bank, 1978–; Barclays International, 1972–. *Recreations:* racing, shooting, golf, tennis. *Address:* West Woodhay House, Newbury, Berks. *T:* Inkpen 271. *Club:* White's.

HENDERSON, John Stuart Wilmot; Under Secretary, Minister of Defence, and Director General of Ordnance Factories, Finance, Procurement and Administration, retired 1976; *b* 31 March 1919; *s* of Bruce Wilmot Henderson and Sarah (*née* Marchant); *m* 1st, 1941, Elsie Kathleen (*née* Rose) (*d* 1981); one *s* three *d*; 2nd, 1984, Yvonne Crawley (*née* Smith), *widow* of Victor James Crawley. *Educ:* Wade Deacon Grammar Sch., Widnes.

Exec. Officer, Royal Ordnance Factories, 1938–39; served War of 1939–45: Royal Fusiliers, 1939–43; Intell. Corps, 1944–47; various appts in Ministries of Supply, Aviation, Technology and Defence, 1947–76. *Recreations:* gardening, enjoying music. *Address:* Broadlands, 125 Aylestone Hill, Hereford HR1 1JJ. *T:* Hereford 53976.

HENDERSON, Kenneth David Druitt, CMG 1951; Vice-President, World Congress of Faiths, since 1966; *b* 4 Sept. 1903; *s* of late George Gilfillan Henderson, MA, MB, CM (Edinburgh); *m* 1935, Margery Grant, *d* of John Atkinson, Sydney, NSW; one *s* two *d*. *Educ:* Glenalmond; University Coll., Oxford. Entered Sudan Political Service, 1926; Dept Asst Civil Sec., 1938–44; Sec. to Governor-General's Council, 1939–44, to N Sudan Advisory Council, 1944; Principal Sch. of Administration and Police, Omdurman, 1944; Deputy-Governor, Kassala Province, Sudan, 1945; Asst Civil Sec., 1946–49; Governor, Darfur Province, Sudan, 1949–53. Sec., Spalding Educnl Trust, 1953–86. Officer, Order of the Nile, 1937. *Publications:* History of the Hamar Tribe, 1935; Survey of the Anglo-Egyptian Sudan, 1898–1944, 1945; The Making of The Modern Sudan, 1952; Sudan Republic, 1965; Account of the Parish of Langford, 1973; Younghusband Memorial Lecture (inaugural), 1976; Is Religion Necessary? (Farmington Paper), 1977; contribs to Chambers's Encyclopædia, Encyclopædia Britannica, and Encyclopædia Americana. *Address:* Orchard House, Steeple Langford, Salisbury, Wilts SP3 4NQ. *T:* Salisbury 790388. *Club:* Caledonian.

HENDERSON, Leslie Edwin, CBE 1982; Director of Contracts, Property Services Agency, 1978–82, retired; *b* 16 Dec. 1922; *s* of Thomas Edwin and Mabel Mary Henderson; *m* 1946, Marjorie (*née* Austin); two *s*. *Educ:* Ealing County Sch., London. Entered Civil Service (BoT) as Clerical Officer, 1939; Min. of Shipping, 1939; served in RAF, 1941–46; Min. of War Transport, 1946; subsequently in: Min. of Transport and Civil Aviation, MoT, DoE; Head of Contracts, Highways, Dept of Transport, 1968–78. *Recreations:* gardening, do-it-yourself. *Address:* 61 Greenacres Avenue, Ickenham, Mddx UB10 8HH. *T:* Ruislip 72536.

HENDERSON, Sir Nicholas; *see* Henderson, Sir J. N.

HENDERSON, Admiral Sir Nigel Stuart, GBE 1968 (OBE 1944); KCB 1962 (CB 1959); DL; *b* 1 Aug. 1909; *s* of late Lt-Col Selby Herriott Henderson, IMS; *m* 1939, Catherine Mary Maitland; one *s* two *d*. *Educ:* Cheltenham Coll. Entered RN, 1927; served War of 1939–45 in HM Ships and as Fleet Gunnery Officer, Mediterranean; Comdr 1942; Capt. 1948; Naval Attaché, Rome, 1949–51; in comd HMS Protector, 1951; in comd RN Air Station, Bramcote, 1952; Imperial Defence Coll., 1954; in command HMS Kenya, 1955; Rear-Admiral, 1957; Vice-Naval Dep. to Supreme Allied Comdr, Europe, 1957–Dec. 1959; Vice-Adm. 1960; Dir-Gen. of Training, Admiralty, 1960–62; C-in-C Plymouth, 1962–65; Adm. 1963; Head of British Defence Staffs, Washington, and UK Rep., Mil. Cttee, NATO, 1965–68; Chm., Mil. Cttee, NATO, 1968–71; retired 1971. Rear-Admiral of the United Kingdom, 1973–76; Vice-Admiral of the United Kingdom, and Lieutenant of the Admiralty, 1976–79. Pres., Royal British Legion, Scotland, 1974–80. DL Stewartry of Kirkcudbright, 1973. *Address:* Hensol, Mossdale, Castle Douglas, Kirkcudbrightshire. *T:* Laurieston 207.

HENDERSON, (Patrick) David; Head of Economics and Statistics Department, Organization for Economic Co-operation and Development, since 1984; *b* 10 April 1927; *s* of late David Thomson Henderson and late Eleanor Henderson; *m* 1960, Marcella Kodicek; one *s* one *d*. *Educ.* Ellesmere Coll., Shropshire; Corpus Christi Coll., Oxford. Fellow and Tutor in Economics, Lincoln Coll., Oxford, 1948–65; Univ. Lectr in Economics, Oxford, 1950–65; Commonwealth Fund Fellow (Harvard), 1952–53; Junior Proctor, Oxford Univ., 1955–56; Economic Adviser, HM Treasury, 1957–58; Chief Economist, Min. of Aviation, 1965–67; Adviser Harvard Development Advisory Service (Athens and Kuala Lumpur), 1967–68; Vis. Lectr, World Bank, 1968–69; Economist, World Bank, 1969–75, Dir of Economics Dept 1971–72; Prof. of Political Economy, UCL, 1975–83. Mem., Commn on Environmental Pollution, 1977–80; Special Adviser, Sec. of State for Wales, 1978–79; Member: Nat. Ports Council, 1979–81; Bd, Commonwealth Develt Corp., 1980–83. Reith Lectr, BBC, 1985. *Publications:* India: the energy sector, 1975; Innocence and Design: the influence of economic ideas on policy, 1986; (jointly) Nyasaland: The Economics of Federation, 1960; ed and contrib.: Economic Growth in Britain, 1965; contrib: The British Economy in the 1950's, 1962; Public Enterprise, 1968; Public Economics, 1969; Unfashionable Economics, 1970; The World Bank, Multilateral Aid and the 1970's, 1973; The Economic Development of Yugoslavia, 1975; Protectionism and Growth, 1985; articles in economic and other jls. *Address:* OECD, 2 rue André-Pascal, 75775 Paris, Cedex 16, France.

HENDERSON, Dr Richard, FRS 1983; Member of Scientific Staff, Medical Research Council Laboratory of Molecular Biology, Cambridge, since 1973; Fellow of Darwin College, Cambridge, since 1981; *b* 19 July 1945; *s* of John and Grace Henderson; *m* 1969, Penelope FitzGerald; one *s* one *d* (and one *d* decd). *Educ:* Hawick High Sch.; Boroughmuir Secondary Sch.; Edinburgh Univ. (BSc); Cambridge Univ. (PhD). Helen Hay Whitney Fellow, Yale, 1970–73. William Bate Hardy Prize, Cambridge Phil Soc., 1978; Ernst Ruska Prize for Electron Microscopy, Ernst Ruska Foundn, 1981. *Publications:* research pubns and reviews in scientific jls. *Recreations:* canoeing, wine-tasting. *Address:* MRC Laboratory of Molecular Biology, Hills Road, Cambridge CB2 2QH. *T:* Cambridge 248011.

HENDERSON, Robert Alistair; Chairman: Kleinwort, Benson, Lonsdale plc, since 1978; Cross Investment Trust Ltd, since 1969; Merchants Trust PLC, since 1985; MT Oil & Gas Ltd, since 1985; Deputy Chairman: Cadbury Schweppes plc, since 1983 (Director, since 1977); British Airways, since 1985 (Director, since 1981); Director: Hamilton Brothers Oil and Gas Ltd; Hamilton Oil (Great Britain) PLC (formerly Hamilton Brothers Oil Co. (Great Britain) Ltd); Hamilton Oil Corporation, since 1984; Inchcape PLC; *b* 4 Nov. 1917; *s* of Robert Evelyn Henderson and Beatrice Janet Elsie Henderson; *m* 1947, Bridget Elizabeth, *d* of late Col J. G. Lowther, CBE, DSO, MC, TD, and Hon. Lilah White, *er d* of 3rd Baron Annaly; two *s* one *d*. *Educ:* Eton; Magdalene Coll., Cambridge. Hons degree in History. Served War: 60th Rifles, 1940–45, Captain. Jessel Toynbee & Co. Ltd, 1945–48; Borneo Co. Ltd, 1948–51; Robert Benson, Lonsdale & Co. Ltd, 1951 (Dir, 1957); Dir, Kleinwort, Benson Ltd, 1961 (on merger of Robert Benson, Lonsdale & Co. Ltd with Kleinwort Sons & Co.; Vice-Chm., 1970–71, Dep. Chm., 1971–75, Chm., 1975–83). Dir, Equitable Life Assurance Soc., 1958–81. *Recreations:* gardening, shooting, fishing. *Address:* 7 Royal Avenue, Chelsea, SW3 4QE; North Ecchinswell Farm, Ecchinswell, near Newbury, Berks RG15 8UJ. *T:* Headley 244. *Clubs:* White's, Brooks's.

HENDERSON, Robert Brumwell, CBE 1979; Chairman, Ulster Television, since 1983 (Managing Director, 1959–83, Deputy Chairman, 1977–83); *b* 28 July 1929; *s* of late Comdr Oscar Henderson, CVO, CBE, DSO, RN, and of Mrs Henderson; *m*; two *d*; *m* 1970, Patricia Ann Davison. *Educ:* Brackenber House Sch., Belfast; Bradfield Coll., Berks; Trinity Coll., Dublin. BA (Hons) 1951, MA 1959. Journalism: London, Liverpool, Glasgow and Belfast, 1951–59. Director: ITN, 1964–68; Independent Television Publications, 1969–; Chm., Publicity Assoc. of NI, 1959–60; Vice-Chm., Co-operation North, 1984–; President: Radio Industries Club of NI, 1963–70, 1972–; NI Chamber of Commerce and Industry, 1980–81; NI Br., Inst. of Marketing 1984–; Member: Exec. Council, Cinema and Television Benevolent Fund, 1980–84; Council for Continuing Educn, 1975–85; NI Council for Educnl Develt, 1980–; Cttee to Review Higher Educn in NI, 1964; various cttees of Trinity Coll. Dublin, Univ. of Ulster; Senate, Queen's Univ. of Belfast, 1980–; Council, Inst. of Dirs, 1981– (Chm., NI Br., 1973–79); Governor, Ulster Polytechnic, 1979–84. FRTS 1977 (Mem. Council, 1981–84, Chm., 1982–84, Vice Pres., 1986–). Hon. DLitt Ulster, 1982. *Publications:* Midnight Oil, 1961; A Television First, 1977; Amusing, 1984. *Recreations:* reading, theatre and cinema, golf. *Address:* Ulster Television, Havelock House, Ormeau Road, Belfast BT7 1EB. *Clubs:* Naval and Military; Royal County Down Golf; Malone Golf.

HENDERSON, Robert Ewart, QC (Scot.) 1982; *b* 29 March 1937; *s* of William Ewart Henderson and Agnes Ker Henderson; *m* 1st, 1958, Olga Sunter; two *s* two *d*; 2nd, 1982, Carol Black. *Educ:* Larchfield Sch., Helensburgh; Morrison's Acad., Crieff; Glasgow Univ. (BL 1962). Admitted to Faculty of Advocates, 1963. National Service, 2nd Lieut RA, 1956–58. Hon. Sheriff-Substitute, Stirling, Dunbarton and Clackmannan, 1968; Standing Jun. Counsel in Scotland, DTI, 1970–74, Dept of Trade, 1974–77; Temp. Sheriff, 1978. Pres., Glasgow Univ. Law Soc., 1961–62; Chairman: NHS Appeal Tribunal, 1972; Medical Appeal Tribunal (Scotland), 1985–. Contested (C) Inverness-shire, Feb. and Oct. 1974. *Recreations:* golf, sailing. *Address:* The Old Schoolhouse, Gullane, East Lothian EH31 2AF. *T:* Gullane 842012. *Clubs:* New (Edinburgh); Hon. Company of Edinburgh Golfers (Muirfield); Royal St George's Golf (Sandwich).

HENDERSON, Roger Anthony, QC 1980; a Recorder of the Crown Court, since 1983; *b* 21 April 1943; *s* of late Dr Peter Wallace Henderson and of Dr Stella Dolores Henderson; *m* 1968, Catherine Margaret Williams; three *d* (and one *d* decd). *Educ:* Radley Coll.; St Catharine's Coll., Cambridge (Scholar; 1st Cl. Hons degree in Law, MA; Adderley Prize for Law, 1964). Inner Temple: Duke of Edinburgh Award, 1962; Major Scholarship, 1964; called to the Bar, 1964; Pupil Studentship, 1965; Bencher, 1985; Mem., Senate of Inns of Court and the Bar, 1983–86. Member: Exec. Council, British Acad. of Forensic Sciences, 1977– (Pres., 1986–87); Council of Legal Educn, 1983–86. *Recreations:* fly-fishing, shooting. *Address:* 2 Harcourt Buildings, Temple, EC4Y 9DB. *T:* 01–583 9020; 9 Brunswick Gardens, W8.

HENDERSON, Roy (Galbraith), CBE 1970; FRAM; retired baritone and Teacher of Singing (private); Professor of Singing, RAM, London, 1940–74; *b* Edinburgh, 4 July 1899; *er s* of late Rev. Dr Alex. Roy Henderson, formerly Principal of Paton Coll., Nottingham; *m* 1926, Bertha Collin Smyth (*d* 1985); one *s* two *d*. *Educ:* Nottingham High Sch.; Royal Academy of Music, London (Worshipful Company of Musicians Medal). Debut as baritone singer, Queen's Hall, London, 1925; has sung at all leading Festivals in England, Internat. Festival for contemporary music, Amsterdam, 1933; recitals at first two Edinburgh Festivals, 1947 and 1948; principal parts in all Glyndebourne Opera festivals, 1934–40, associated chiefly with works of Delius, Elgar and Vaughan Williams, and sang many first performances of contemp. music. Retired from concert platform, 1951, to devote his whole time to teaching (among his pupils was late Kathleen Ferrier). Conductor, Huddersfield Glee and Madrigal Soc., 1932–39; Founder and Conductor, Nottingham Oriana Choir, 1937–52. Conductor of Bournemouth Municipal Choir, 1942–53. Adjudicator at International Concours, Geneva, 1952, and Triennially, 1956–65. Mem. of the Jury of the International Muziekstad s'Hertogenbosch, Holland, 1955–62, 1965, and Barcelona, 1965. Master classes in singing: Royal Conservatory of Music, Toronto, 1956; Toonkunst Conservatorium, Rotterdam, 1957, 1958; s'Hertogenbosch, 1967. Awarded the Sir Charles Santley memorial by Worshipful Company of Musicians for distinguished services to the art of singing, 1958. *Publications:* contributed to: Kathleen Ferrier, ed Neville Cardus, 1954; Opera Annual, 1958; The Voice, ed Sir Keith Falkner, 1983. *Recreations:* fishing, gardening and cricket. *Address:* 90 Burbage Road, SE24 9HE. *T:* 01–274 9004.

HENDERSON, William Crichton; Advocate; Sheriff of Tayside, Central and Fife (formerly Stirling, Dunbarton and Clackmannan) at Stirling, since 1972 (also at Alloa, 1972–81); *b* 10 June 1931; *s* of late William Henderson, headmaster, and late Helen Philp Henderson (*née* Crichton); *m* 1962, Norma Sheila Hope Henderson (*née* Grant) (marr. diss. 1985); two *d*. *Educ:* George Watson's Boys' Coll., Edinburgh; Edinburgh Univ. MA Edinburgh 1952, LLB Edinburgh 1954. Admitted Solicitor, 1954; Diploma in Administrative Law and Practice, Edinburgh, 1955; called to Scottish Bar, 1957; practised as Advocate, 1957–68; Sheriff of Renfrew and Argyll at Paisley, 1968–72. Chm., Supreme Court Legal Aid Cttee, 1967–68. *Recreations:* gardening, travel. *Club:* New (Edinburgh).

HENDERSON, Sir William (MacGregor), Kt 1976; FRS 1976; FRSE 1977; President, Zoological Society of London, since 1984; *b* 17 July 1913; *s* of late William Simpson Henderson and late Catherine Alice Marcus Berry; *m* 1941, Alys Beryl Goodridge; four *s*. *Educ:* George Watson's Coll., Edinburgh; Royal (Dick) Veterinary Coll., Edinburgh (MRCVS); Univ. of Edinburgh (BSc, DSc). Assistant, Dept of Medicine, Royal (Dick) Veterinary Coll., Edinburgh, 1936–38; Member Scientific Staff, Animal Virus Research Inst., Pirbright, 1939–56, Dep. Dir, 1955–56; Director, Pan American Foot-and-Mouth Disease Center, Rio de Janeiro, 1957–65; Head, Dept of Microbiology, ARC Inst. for Research on Animal Diseases, Compton, 1966–67, Director, 1967–72; Sec., ARC, 1972–78. Visiting Prof., Univ. of Reading, 1970–72. Chm., Genetic Manipulation Adv. Gp, 1979–81. Mem., Science Council, 1980–82, Bd Mem., 1982–84, Celltech Ltd; Bd Mem., Wellcome Biotechnology Ltd, 1983–. Pres., Royal Assoc. of British Dairy Farmers, 1985–87. Corresp. Member: Argentine Assoc. of Microbiology, 1959; Argentine Soc. of Veterinary Medicine, 1965; Foreign Mem., Argentine National Acad. of Agronomy and Veterinary Science, 1980; Hon. Mem. Brasilian Soc. of Veterinary Medicine, 1965; FRCVS, by election, 1973; FIBiol; Hon. Fellow, RASE, 1979. Hon. DVMS Edinburgh, 1974; Hon. DVSc Liverpool, 1977; Hon. DSc Bristol,. 1985. Orden de Mayo, Argentina, 1962. Dalrymple-Champneys Award, 1974; Massey-Ferguson National Award, 1980; Underwood-Prescott Award, 1981. *Publications:* Quantitative Study of Foot-and-Mouth Disease Virus, 1949; Man's Use of Animals, 1981; British Agricultural Research and the Agricultural Research Council, 1981; contribs to scientific jls principally on foot-and-mouth disease. *Recreation:* gardening. *Address:* Yarnton Cottage, Streatley, Berks. *Clubs:* Athenæum; New (Edinburgh).

HENDERSON, William Ross, TD 1972, clasps 1978, 1984; Director, Scottish Conservative and Unionist Central Office, since 1984; *b* 15 Sept. 1936; *s* of Major William Ross Henderson and Jean Elizabeth Doxford Henderson; *m* 1969, Valerie Helen Thomas; one *s* one *d*. *Educ:* Argyle House School, Sunderland. Agent and Secretary, Newcastle upon Tyne West Cons. Assoc., 1961–68; Dep. Central Office Agent, Greater London Area, 1968–76; Cons. Party Training Officer, 1976–80; Central Office Agent, East of England Area, 1980–84. Cross of Merit, Gold Class, Poland, 1972. *Recreations:* gardening, reading. *Address:* Scottish Conservative and Unionist Central Office, 3 Chester Street, Edinburgh EH3 7RF. *T:* 031–226 4426. *Clubs:* St Stephen's Constitutional; Caledonian (Edinburgh).

HENDERSON-STEWART, Sir David (James), 2nd Bt *cr* 1957; *b* 3 July 1941; *s* of Sir James Henderson-Stewart, 1st Bt, MP, and of Anna Margaret (*née* Greenwell); *S* father, 1961; *m* 1972, Anne, *d* of Count Serge de Pahlen; three *s* one *d*. *Educ:* Eton Coll.; Trinity Coll., Oxford. *Heir: s* David Henderson-Stewart, *b* 2 Feb. 1973. *Address:* 3 Chepstow Crescent, W11 3EA. *T:* 01–221 6255.

HENDRIE, Prof. Gerald Mills; Professor of Music, The Open University, since 1969; *b* 28 Oct. 1935; *s* of James Harold Hendrie and Florence Mary MacPherson; *m* 1962, Dinah Florence Barsham (*d* 1985); two *s*. *Educ:* Framlingham Coll., Suffolk; Royal Coll. of Music; Selwyn Coll., Cambridge (MA, MusB, PhD). FRCO, ARCM. Director of Music, Homerton Coll., Cambridge, 1962–63; Lectr in the History of Music, Univ. of Manchester, 1963–67; Prof. and Chm., Dept of Music, Univ. of Victoria, BC, Canada, 1967–69; Reader in Music, subseq. Prof., The Open Univ., 1969–; Dir of Studies in Music, St John's Coll., Cambridge, 1981–84, Supervisor, 1977–84. Secretary, Spalding Educational Trust, since 1953; Vis. Fellow in Music, Univ. of WA, 1985. FRSA. *Publications:* Musica Britannica XX, Orlando Gibbons: Keyboard Music, 1962 (2nd rev. edn, 1967); The Chandos and Related Anthems of George Frideric Handel (4 vols and critical commentary for the Halle Handel Society's complete edn of Handel's works, in progress), vol. 1 1985; vol. 2 1986; articles for Die Musik in Geschichte und Gegenwart; various others including musical compositions, recordings for TV, radio and disc. *Address:* The Open University, Walton Hall, Milton Keynes, Bucks MK7 6AA. *T:* Milton Keynes 653280.

HENDRY, Prof. Arnold William; Professor of Civil Engineering, University of Edinburgh, since 1964; *b* 10 Sept. 1921; *s* of late Dr George Hendry, MB, ChB, Buckie, Scotland; *m* 1st, 1946, Sheila Mary Cameron Roberts (*d* 1966), Glasgow; one *s* one *d* (and one *s* decd); 2nd, 1968, Elizabeth Lois Alice Inglis, Edinburgh. *Educ:* Buckie High Sch.; Aberdeen Univ. Civil engineer with Sir William Arrol & Co. Ltd, Bridge builders and Engineers, Glasgow, 1941–43; Asst in Engineering, University of Aberdeen, 1943–46; Lecturer in Civil Engineering, 1946–49; Reader in Civil Engineering, Univ. of London, King's Coll., 1949–51; Prof. of Civil Engrg and Dean of Fac. of Engrg, Univ. of Khartoum, 1951–57; Prof. of Building Science, University of Liverpool, 1957–63. *Publications:* An Introduction to Photo-Elastic Analysis, 1948; (with L. G. Jaeger) The Analysis of Grid Frameworks, 1958; The Elements of Experimental Stress Analysis, 1964, 2nd edn 1977; Structural Brickwork, 1981; An Introduction to the Design of Load Bearing Brickwork, 1981; about 100 papers and articles in professional and technical jls. *Address:* Department of Civil Engineering, University of Edinburgh, Edinburgh EH9 3JL.

HENDRY, Prof. David Forbes, PhD; Professor of Economics, University of Oxford, since 1982; Fellow, Nuffield College, Oxford, since 1982; *b* 6 March 1944; *s* of Robert Ernest Hendry and Catherine Helen (*née* Mackenzie); *m* 1966, Evelyn Rosemary (*née* Vass); one *d*. *Educ:* Aberdeen Univ. (MA 1st Cl. Hons); LSE (MSc Distinction, PhD). Fellow, Econometric Soc., 1975. Lectr, LSE, 1969, Reader, 1973, Prof. of Econometrics, 1977. Vis. Professor: Yale Univ., 1975; Univ. of Calif, Berkeley, 1976; Catholic Univ. of Louvain, 1980; Univ. of Calif, San Diego, 1981. Editor: Rev. of Econ. Studies, 1971–75; Econ. Jl, 1976–80. *Publications:* (ed with K. F. Wallis) Econometrics and Quantitative Economics, 1984; papers in econometrics, statistics and economics jls. *Recreations:* squash, cricket. *Address:* Nuffield College, Oxford OX1 1NF; 26 Northmoor Road, Oxford. *T:* Oxford 55588.

HENHAM, John Alfred; His Honour Judge Henham; a Circuit Judge, since 1983; *b* 8 Sept. 1924; *s* of Alfred and Daisy Henham; *m* 1946, Suzanne Jeanne Octavie Ghislaine Pinchart (*d* 1972); two *s*. Stipendiary Magistrate for S Yorks, 1975–82; a Recorder of the Crown Court, 1979–82. *Address:* Crown Court, Castle Street, Sheffield S3 8LW.

HENIG, Prof. Stanley; Professor of European Politics, since 1982 and Dean of Faculty of Social Studies, since 1985, Preston Polytechnic; *b* 7 July 1939; *s* of Sir Mark Henig and Grace (*née* Cohen); *m* 1966, Ruth Beatrice Munzer; two *s*. *Educ:* Wyggeston Grammar Sch.; Corpus Christi Coll., Oxford. BA 1st Cl. Hons, 1961; MA 1965 Oxon. Teaching Asst, Dept of Politics, Univ. of Minnesota, 1961; Research Student, Nuffield Coll., 1962; Lecturer in Politics, Lancaster Univ., 1964–66. MP (Lab) Lancaster, 1966–70; Lectr in Politics, Warwick Univ., 1970–71; Lectr, Civil Service Coll., 1972–75. Governor, British Inst. of Recorded Sound, 1975–80. Secretary: Historic Masters Ltd, 1983–; Historic Singers Trust, 1985–. Asst Editor, Jl of Common Market Studies, 1964–72, Editor, 1973–76. *Publications:* (ed) European Political Parties, 1969; External Relations of the European Community, 1971; (ed) Political Parties in the European Community, 1979; Power and Decision in Europe, 1980. *Recreation:* collector of old gramophone records. *Address:* 10 Yealand Drive, Lancaster LA1 4EW. *T:* 69624.

HENLEY, 8th Baron (Ire.), *cr* 1799; **Oliver Michael Robert Eden;** Baron Northington (UK) 1885; *b* 22 Nov. 1953; *er s* of 7th Baron Henley and of Nancy Mary, *d* of Stanley Walton, Gilsland, Cumbria; *S* father, 1977; *m* 1984, Caroline Patricia, *d* of A. G. Sharp, Mackney, Oxon. *Educ:* Clifton; Durham Univ. (BA 1975). Called to the Bar, Middle Temple, 1977. Mem., Cumbria CC, 1986–. Pres., Cumbria Assoc. of Local Councils, 1981–. *Heir: b* Hon. Andrew Francis Eden, *b* 4 Sept. 1955. *Address:* Scaleby Castle, Carlisle, Cumbria CA6 4LN. *Clubs:* Brooks's, Pratt's.

HENLEY, Sir Douglas (Owen), KCB 1973 (CB 1970); Comptroller and Auditor General, 1976–81; Advisor to Deloitte, Haskins and Sells, since 1981; *b* 5 April 1919; *m* 1942, June Muriel Ibbetson; four *d*. *Educ:* Beckenham County Sch.; London Sch. of Economics (Hon. Fellow, 1974). BSc (Econ.), 1939; Gerstenberg Studentship and Leverhulme Res. Studentship (not taken up). Served Army, 1939–46; Queen's Own Royal West Kent Regt and HQ 12th Inf. Bde (despatches twice, 1945). Treasury, 1946; Treas. rep. (Financial Counsellor) in Tokyo and Singapore, 1956–59; Asst Under-Sec. of State, DEA, 1964–69, Dep. Under-Sec. of State, 1969; Second Permanent Sec., HM Treasury, 1972–76. Mem. Council, GPDST, 1982–; Chm., London Small Business Property Trust; Gov., Alleyn's Coll. of God's Gift, Dulwich, 1983–. Hon. LLD Bath, 1981. *Address:* Walwood House, Park Road, Banstead, Surrey SM7 3ER. *T:* Burgh Heath 52626.

HENLEY, Rear-Adm. Sir Joseph (Charles Cameron), KCVO 1963; CB 1962; *b* 24 April 1909; *e s* of Vice-Adm. J. C. W. Henley, CB; *m* 1934, Daphne Ruth (marr. diss. 1965), *d* of late A. A. H. Wykeham, of Pitt Place, Brighstone, IW; one *s* three *d*; *m* 1966, Patricia Sharp, MBE 1952, *d* of late Roy Eastman, Alberta, Canada. *Educ:* Sherborne. Joined Royal Navy, 1927. Served War of 1939–45, in HMS Birmingham and King George V. Capt., 1951, in command HMS Defender, 1954–55; Naval Attaché, Washington (as Commodore), 1956–57; Dir, Royal Naval Staff Coll., 1958; Chief of Staff, Mediterranean Station, 1959–61, as Commodore; Rear-Adm. 1960; Flag Officer, Royal Yachts and Extra Naval Equerry to the Queen, 1962–65; retd 1965. *Address:* 11a Hopewood Gardens, Darling Point, Sydney, NSW 2027, Australia. *T:* 321068. *Clubs:* Royal Yacht Squadron; Royal Sydney Golf.

HENMAN, Philip Sydney, DL; Founder of Transport Development Group Ltd; FCIT. DUniv Surrey, 1974. Farmer. High Sheriff, Surrey, 1971–72; DL Surrey, 1979. *Address:* 25 Elm Place, Rustington, W Sussex.

HENN, Charles Herbert; Assistant Under Secretary of State, Ministry of Defence, since 1979; *b* 11 July 1931; *s* of Herbert George Henn and Ellen Anne Henn; *m* 1955, Ann Turner; one *s* one *d*. *Educ:* King's Coll. Sch., Wimbledon; Queen's Coll., Oxford (BA). National Service, REME, 1952–54 (2/Lieut). Scientific Officer, WO, 1954; Sen. Scientific Officer, 1957; Principal, 1964; Private Sec. to Minister of State for Defence, 1969; Asst Sec., 1972. *Recreations:* walking, running, listening to music.

HENNELL, Rev. Canon Michael Murray; Residentiary Canon, Manchester Cathedral, 1970–84, Canon Emeritus, since 1984; *b* 11 Sept. 1918; *s* of Charles Murray and Jessie Hennell; *m* 1950, Peggy Glendinning; four *s*. *Educ:* Bishops Stortford Coll. (Prep.); Royal Masonic Sch.; St Edmund Hall and Wycliffe Hall, Oxford. MA Oxon and, by incorporation, MA Cantab. Asst Curate: St Stephen's With St Bartholomew's, Islington, N1, 1942–44; All Saints, Queensbury, Middx, 1944–48; Tutor, Ridley Hall, Cambridge, 1948–51. St Aidan's Coll., Birkenhead: Sen. Tutor, 1951; Vice-Principal, 1952–59; Principal, 1959–63; Principal, Ridley Hall, Cambridge, 1964–70. Examining Chaplain to the Bishops of Derby and Manchester (Chelmsford, 1964–70; Liverpool, 1964–75). Commissary to the Bishop on the Niger, 1975–84. *Publications:* John Venn and the Clapham Sect, 1958; Popular Belief and Practice, 1972; Sons of the Prophets, 1979; ed and contrib., Charles Simeon, 1759–1836, 1959; contribs to: The Anglican Synthesis, 1964; A Dictionary of Christian Spirituality, 1983. *Address:* 53 Cleveley Road, Meols, Wirral, Merseyside L47 8XN.

HENNESSEY, Robert Samuel Fleming, CMG 1954; Assistant Research Director, Wellcome Foundation, 1967–70, retired; *b* 8 May 1905; *s* of late W. R. H. Hennessey and late Elizabeth Fleming; *m* 1930, Grace Alberta Coote (*d* 1980); one *s* one *d*. *Educ:* St Andrew's Coll., Dublin; Dublin and London Universities. MD, FRCPI, DipBact, DTM&H. Pathologist, Uganda, 1929; Dep. Director (Laboratories), Palestine, 1944; Dep. Director, Medical Services, Palestine, 1946; Asst Medical Adviser, Colonial Office, 1947; Director of Medical Services, Uganda, 1949–55; Head of the Wellcome Laboratories of Tropical Medicine, London, 1956–58; Head of Therapeutic Research Division, Wellcome Foundation, 1958–66. *Publications:* papers on pathology in scientific jls. *Recreations:* music, literature. *Address:* 51 Stone Park Avenue, Beckenham, Kent. *T:* 01–650 5336.

HENNESSY, family name of **Baron Windlesham.**

HENNESSY, Christopher; journalist; Chairman, Associated Catholic Newspapers (1912) Ltd, 1970–79; Trustee, The Universe, since 1979 (Editor, 1954–72); *b* 29 Dec. 1909; *e s* of Daniel and Anne Hennessy; *m* 1942, Kathleen Margaret Cadley, Liverpool. *Educ:* St Edward's Coll., Liverpool. Served War of 1939–45 as Commissioned Officer in British and Indian Armies; commanded a Territorial Army Unit in the North-West, 1950–55. KCSG 1975. *Recreation:* travel. *Address:* Beech House, Montreal Road, Riverhead, Sevenoaks, Kent TN13 2EP. *T:* Sevenoaks 454117.

HENNESSY, Denis William, OBE 1967; HM Diplomatic Service, retired; *b* 5 Dec. 1912; *s* of Daniel Hennessy and Rosina Gertrude Hennessy (*née* Griffiths); *m* 1937, Lorna McDonald Lappin; three *s* one *d*. *Educ:* private sch. Joined Foreign Office, 1930; served in the Foreign Office and in Prague, Washington, New York, Zürich, Bremen, Miami, Düsseldorf, Accra, and as Consul-Gen., Hanover; Counsellor, Bonn, 1969–72. *Address:* 37 Dean Road, Bateman, WA 6153, Australia. *Club:* Travellers'.

HENNESSY, Sir James (Patrick Ivan), KBE 1982 (OBE 1968; MBE 1959); CMG 1975; HM Diplomatic Service, retired; HM Chief Inspector of Prisons for England and Wales, since 1982; *b* 26 Sept. 1923; *s* of late Richard George Hennessy, DSO, MC; *m* 1947, Patricia, *o d* of late Wing Comdr F. H. Unwin, OBE; five *d* (one *s* decd). *Educ:* Bedford Sch.; Sidney Sussex Coll., Cambridge. Served RA, 1942–44; seconded IA, 1944–46, Adjt and Battery Comdr, 6th Indian Field Regt. Apptd to HM Overseas Service, Basutoland, District Officer, 1948; Judicial Comr, 1953; Dist Comr, 1954–56; Jt Sec., Constitutional Commn, 1957–59; Supervisor of Elections, 1959; Sec. to Exec. Council, 1960; seconded to Office of High Comr, Cape Town/Pretoria, 1961–63; Perm. Sec. for local govt, 1964; MLC, 1965; Sec. for External Affairs, Defence and Internal Security, 1967; Prime Minister's Office, and Head of Civil Service, 1968. Retired, later apptd to HM Diplomatic Service; FO, 1968–70; Montevideo, 1970; (Chargé d'Affaires 1971–72); Acting, later High Comr to Uganda and Ambassador (non-resident), Rwanda, 1973–76; Consul-Gen., Cape Town, 1977–80; Governor and C-in-C, Belize, 1980–81. *Address:* Home Office, 50 Queen Anne's Gate, SW1H 9AT. *Clubs:* Naval and Military, Royal Commonwealth Society.

HENNESSY, Sir John Wyndham P.; *see* Pope-Hennessy.

HENNESSY, Brig. Mary Brigid Teresa, (Rita), MBE 1967; RRC 1982; QHNS 1985; Matron-in-Chief, Queen Alexandra's Royal Army Nursing Corps, since 1985 and Director of Defence Nursing Service, since 1986; *b* 27 Jan. 1933; *d* of late Bartholomew and Nora Agnes Hennessy. *Educ:* Convent of Mercy, Ennis, Co. Clare; Whittington Hosp., Highgate, London; Victoria Maternity Hosp., Barnet. SRN; SCM. Joined QARANC, 1959; service in Britain, Singapore, Malaya, Germany; various hosp. appts, 1959–74; seconded to office of Chargé d'affaires, Peking, 1965–67; Dep. Matron, Hongkong, 1976; Lt-Col 1979; Col 1982; Brig., Matron-in-Chief and Dir of Army Nursing Services, 1985. *Recreations:* music, theatre, gardening. *Address:* 28 Wulwyn Court, Edgcumbe Park, Crowthorne, Berks. *T:* Crowthorne 771030.

HENNIKER, 8th Baron *cr* 1800; **John Patrick Edward Chandos Henniker-Major,** KCMG 1965 (CMG 1956); CVO 1960; MC 1945; Bt 1765; Baron Hartismere (UK) 1866; Director, Wates Foundation, 1972–78; *b* 19 Feb. 1916; *s* of 7th Baron Henniker, and Molly (*d* 1953), *d* of Sir Robert Burnet, KCVO; *S* father, 1980; *m* 1946, Margaret Osla Benning (*d* 1974); two *s* one *d*; *m* 1976, Julia Marshall Poland (*née* Mason). *Educ:* Stowe; Trinity Coll., Cambridge. HM Foreign Service, 1938; served 1940–45, Army (Major, The Rifle Brigade). HM Embassy Belgrade, 1945–46; Asst Private Secretary to Secretary of State for Foreign Affairs, 1946–48; Foreign Office, 1948–50; HM Embassy, Buenos Aires, 1950–52; Foreign Office, 1952–60 (Counsellor and Head of Personnel Dept, 1953); HM Ambassador to Jordan, 1960–62; to Denmark, 1962–66; Civil Service Commission, 1966–67; Asst Under-Secretary of State, FO, 1967–68. Dir-Gen., British Council, 1968–72. Lay Mem., Mental Health Review Tribunal (Broadmoor), 1975–81; Member: Parole Bd, 1979–83; Council and Finance Bd, Univ. of E Anglia, Norwich, 1979–; Council, Toynbee Hall, 1978–, Dep. Chm., 1982–86. Trustee: City Parochial Foundn, 1973; London Festival Ballet, 1975–85. Governor: Cripplegate Foundn, 1979–; Stowe Sch., 1982–. Hon. (Lay) Canon of St Edmundsbury Cathedral, 1986. *Recreations:* gardening, bridge, ornithology. *Heir: s* Hon. Mark Ian Philip Chandos Henniker-Major [*b* 29 Sept. 1947; *m* 1973, Mrs Lesley Antoinette Masterton-Smith, *d* of Wing Comdr G. W. Foskett; two *s* three *d*]. *Address:* Red House, Thornham Magna, Eye, Suffolk. *Club:* Special Forces.

HENNIKER, Brig. Sir Mark Chandos Auberon, 8th Bt, *cr* 1813; CBE 1953 (OBE 1944); DSO 1944; MC 1933; DL; retired, 1958; *b* 23 Jan. 1906; *s* of late F. C. Henniker, ICS, and of Ada Russell (*née* Howell); *S* cousin (Lieut-Col Sir Robert Henniker, 7th Bt, MC) 1958; *m* 1945, Kathleen Denys (*née* Anderson); one *s* one *d*. *Educ:* Marlborough

Coll.; Royal Military Academy, Woolwich; King's Coll., Cambridge. Royal Engineers, 1926; served India, 1928–34 (MC); Aldershot, 1937–39; BEF, 1939–40; North Africa, 1943; Sicily, 1943 (wounded); Italy, 1943 (OBE); NW Europe, 1944–45 (immediate award of DSO, Oct. 1944); India, 1946–47; Malaya, 1952–55 (CBE); Port Said, 1956 (despatches). Hon. Col, Parachute Engineer Regt (TA), 1959–68; Hon. Col, REME (TA), 1964–68. DL Gwent (formerly County of Mon), 1963. *Publications:* Memoirs of a Junior Officer, 1951; Red Shadow over Malaya, 1955; Life in the Army Today, 1957. *Recreations:* appropriate to age and rank. *Heir: s* Adrian Chandos Henniker [*b* 18 Oct. 1946; *m* 1971, Ann, *d* of Stuart Britton; twin *d*]. *Address:* c/o Lloyds Bank, Cox's & King's Branch, 6 Pall Mall, SW1. *Club:* Athenæum.

HENNIKER HEATON, Sir Yvo Robert; *see* Heaton.

HENNIKER-MAJOR, family name of **Baron Henniker.**

HENNING, Prof. Basil Duke, PhD; *b* 16 April 1910; *s* of late Samuel C. Henning and Julia, *d* of Gen. Basil Duke, CSA; *m* 1939, Alison Peake; two *s* one *d*. *Educ:* Yale Univ. (BA 1932, PhD 1937). Served War: Pacific War, 1943–45; Lieut (JG) USNR, 1942–44; Lieut, 1944–47; Lt-Comdr, 1947–55. Commendation Medal, USA, 1944 and 1945. Yale University: Instr, 1935–39; Sterling Fellow, 1939–40; Instr, 1940–42; Asst Prof., 1945–46; Associate Prof., 1946–70; Master, Saybrook Coll., 1946–75; Colgate Prof. of History, 1970–78. FRHistS 1963. Yale Medal, 1979; William C. de Vane Medal, Phi Beta Psi Soc. (Yale chapter), 1981. *Publications:* (ed) The Parliamentary Diary of Sir Edward Dering, 1670–1673, 1940; (jtly) Ideas and Institutions in European History, 800–1715, 1948; The Quest for a Principle of Authority, 1715 to Present, 1948; Crises in English History, 1066–1945: select problems in historical interpretation, 1952; The Dynamic Force of Liberty in Modern Europe, 1952; Foundations of the Modern State, 1952; Select Problems in Western Civilization, 1956; (ed) Conflict in Stuart England: essays in honour of Wallace Notestein, 1960; (ed) History of Parliament 1660–1690, 1983. *Recreations:* reading, music. *Address:* 34 Tavistock Square, WC1H 9EZ. *T:* 01–636 0272; 223 Bradley Street, New Haven, Conn 06511, USA. *T:* 203–777–0123. *Clubs:* Garrick; Yale (NY); Lawn (New Haven, Conn).

HENNINGS, Richard Owen, CMG 1957; retired as Deputy Chief Secretary, Kenya (1960–63); *b* 8 Sept. 1911; *s* of W. G. Hennings; *m* 1939, Constance Patricia Milton Sexton; one *d*. *Educ:* Cheltenham; New Coll., Oxford. Newdigate Prize Poem, 1932. District Officer, Kenya, 1935; Political Officer, Ethiopia, 1941; Secretary for Agriculture, Kenya, 1953; Permanent Secretary, Ministry of Agriculture, Animal Husbandry and Water Resources, Kenya, 1956. Nominated Member of Kenya Legislative Council, 1960, and of East African Central Legislative Assembly, 1960. Hon. Editor, Ski Notes and Queries, 1964–71; Editor, Ski Survey, 1972–73. *Publications:* Arnold in Africa, 1941; African Morning, 1951; articles in The Geographical Magazine, Journal of African Administration, Corona, British Ski Year Book, Ski Notes and Queries. *Recreations:* ski-ing, tennis, gardening, reefing. *Address:* July Farm House, Great Chesterford, Saffron Walden, Essex. *Clubs:* Ski Club of Great Britain; Nairobi (Nairobi).

HENREY, Mrs Robert; authoress; *b* Paris, 13 Aug. 1906; maiden name Madeleine Gal; *m* 1928, Robert Selby Henrey (*d* 1982), *o s* of Rev. Thomas Selby Henrey, Vicar of Old Brentford, Mddx, and Euphemia, *d* of Sir Coutts and Lady Lindsay of Balcarres; one *s*. *Educ:* Protestant Girls' Sch., Clichy; Convent of The Holy Family, Tooting, SW. *Publications:* autobiographical sequence in the following chronological order: The Little Madeleine, 1951, New York, 1953; An Exile in Soho, 1952; Julia, 1971; A Girl at Twenty, 1974; Madeleine Grown Up, 1952, New York 1953; Green Leaves, 1976; Madeleine Young Wife, New York 1954, London 1960; London under Fire 1940–45, 1969; A Month in Paris, 1954; Milou's Daughter, 1955, New York 1956; Her April Days, 1963; Wednesday at Four, 1964; Winter Wild, 1966; She Who Pays, 1969; The Golden Visit, 1979 (read in the above order these volumes make one consecutive narrative); *other books:* A Farm in Normandy, 1941; A Village in Piccadilly, 1943; The Incredible City, 1944; The Foolish Decade, 1945; The King of Brentford, 1946; The Siege of London, 1946; The Return to the Farm, 1947; London (with illustrations by Phyllis Ginger RWS) 1948, New York, 1949; A Film Star in Belgrave Square, 1948; A Journey to Vienna, 1950; Matilda and the Chickens, 1950; Paloma, 1951, New York, 1955; A Farm in Normandy and the Return, 1952; Madeleine's Journal, 1953; This Feminine World, 1956; A Daughter for a Fortnight, 1957; The Virgin of Aldermanbury (illustrations by Phyllis Ginger), 1958; Mistress of Myself, 1959; The Dream Makers, 1961; Spring in a Soho Street, 1962. *Recreations:* most feminine occupations: sewing, knitting, ironing, gardening. *Address:* c/o J. M. Dent & Sons, Aldine House, 33 Welbeck Street, W1M 8LX; Ferme Robert Henrey, 14640 Villers-sur-Mer, Calvados, France. *T:* Calvados (31) 87 03 88.

HENRI, Adrian Maurice; President, Liverpool Academy of Arts, 1972–81; *b* Birkenhead, 10 April 1932; *s* of Arthur Maurice Henri and Emma Johnson; *m* 1957, Joyce Wilson. *Educ:* St Asaph Grammar Sch., N Wales; Dept of Fine Art, King's Coll., Newcastle upon Tyne, 1951–55. Hons BA Fine Art (Dunelm) 1955. Worked for ten seasons in Rhyl fairground, later as a scenic-artist and secondary school teacher; taught at Manchester then Liverpool Colls of Art, 1961–67. Led the poetry/rock group, Liverpool Scene, 1967–70; since then, freelance poet/painter/singer/songwriter/lecturer. Tour of USA, 1973; Bicentennial Poetry Tour of USA, 1976; exchange tour of Canada, 1980. Pres., Merseyside Arts Assoc., 1978–80; Writer-in-Residence, Tattenhall Centre, Cheshire, 1980–82. *Exhibitions:* include: Biennale della Giovane Pintura, Milan, 1968; Pen as Pencil, Brussels, 1973; John Moores Liverpool Exhibns, 1962, 1965, 1974, 1978, 1980; Peter Moores Project, Real Life, Liverpool, 1977; Art and the Sea, 1980–81; Hedgerow mural, 1980, Summer Terrace mural, 1983. Royal Liverpool Hosp. John Moores Liverpool £2000 prize, 1972. *Major One-Man Shows:* ICA, London, 1968; ArtNet, London, 1975; Williamson Art Gall., Birkenhead, 1975; Retrospective 1960–76, Wolverhampton City Art Gall., 1976; Demarco Gall., Edinburgh, 1978; Touring Retrospective, The Art of Adrian Henri, South Hill Park and elsewhere, 1986. Various recordings. *Publications:* Tonight at Noon, 1968; City, 1969 (out of print); Autobiography, 1971; (with Nell Dunn) I Want (novel), 1972; World of Art Series. Environments and Happenings, 1974; The Best of Henri, 1975; City Hedges 1970–76, 1977; From The Loveless Motel, poems 1976–79, 1980; (for children) Eric, the Punk Cat, 1982; Penny Arcade, poems 1978–82, 1983; Collected Poems, 1986; (for children) Eric and Frankie in Las Vegas, 1986; (for children) The Phantom Lollipop-Lady, 1986; *anthologies:* The Oxford Book of Twentieth Century Verse, 1973; The Liverpool Scene (ed Edward Lucie-Smith), 1967; Penguin Modern Poets No 10: The Mersey Sound, 1967, rev. and enlarged edn, 1974, rev. edn, 1983; British Poetry since 1945 (ed Edward Lucie-Smith: Penguin), 1970; New Volume, 1983; *plays:* I Wonder, a Guillaume Apollinaire Show (with Mike Kustow), 1968; Yesterday's Girl (a play with music for Granada TV), 1973; (with Nell Dunn) I Want, 1983; The Husband, the Wife and the Stranger (for BBC TV), 1986. *Recreations:* watching Liverpool FC; visiting Shropshire and Normandy; old movies; SF, Gothic and crime novels. *Address:* 21 Mount Street, Liverpool L1 9HD. *T:* 051–709 6682; (literary agent) Deborah Rogers Ltd, 49 Blenheim Crescent, W11. *Clubs:* Chelsea Arts; Private Chauffeurs' (Liverpool).

HENRION, Frederic Henri Kay, OBE 1985 (MBE 1951); RDI; PPSIAD; general consulting designer and lecturer; Consultant to Henrion, Ludlow and Schmidt, since 1982; *b* 18 April 1914; *m*; two *s* one *d*. Textile design in Paris, 1932–33; worked in Paris and London, 1936–39; designed Smoke Abatement Exhibition, Charing Cross Station, and worked on Glasgow Empire Exhibition, 1939, and New York World Fair, 1940–45. Design of all exhibitions for Ministry of Agriculture through Ministry of Information and exhibitions for Army Bureau of Current Affairs (WO), etc., 1943–45. Consultant Designer to US Embassy and US Office of War Information, 1945; Chief Cons. Designer to Sir William Crawford and Partners, 1946–47; Art Editor of Contact Publication, 1947–48; Art Director BOAC Publications, 1949–51, and of Future Magazine, 1951; Designer, Festival of Britain pavilions (Agriculture and Natural History), 1950–51–54; Art Editor and Designer of the Bowater Papers, 1951–53; subseq. Cons. Designer for many firms. Posters for: GPO; BOAC; LPTB; Council of Industrial Design; exhibitions and permanent collections in Europe, USA and S America. One-man show, Designing Things and Symbols, at Institute of Contemporary Arts, 1960. Vis. Lectr, RCA, 1950–60; Member Council and Vice-President, SIAD (President, 1961–63); Member: Council of Industrial Design, 1963–66; Advisory Council to Governors of London School of Printing; Council, CNAA (Chm. Bd of Graphic Design; Mem. Cttee of Art and Design, 1973–78); Court, RCA, 1975; President: Alliance Graphique Internationale, 1962–67; ICOGRADA, 1968–70; Past Governor, Central School of Art; Outside Assessor, Scottish Schools of Art; Consultant Designer to: BTC; KLM Royal Dutch Airlines; British Olivetti Ltd; Tate & Lyle Ltd; The Postmaster General; BEA; Blue Circle Group; Courage, Barclay & Simonds Ltd; Financial Times; Volkswagen, Audi, NSU, Porsche, LEB, Penta Hotels, Braun AG. Co-ordinating graphics designer for British Pavilion, Expo 67. Master of Faculty, RDI, 1971–73; Head of Faculty of Visual Communication, London Coll. of Printing, 1976–79. Visiting Professor: Cooper Union, NY, 1984–86; Univ. of Essen, 1984–85; lectured in the UK, USA, Canada, Mexico, Israel, Germany, and Italy, 1982–85. Hon. Dip. Manchester, 1962. SIAD Design Medal, 1976. *Publications:* Design Co-ordination and Corporate Image, 1967 (also USA); Top Graphic Designers, 1983; contributor to: Graphis, Gebrauchgraphik, Design Magazine, Architectural Review, Art and Industry, Penrose Annual, Format, Novum Gebrauchsgraphik, The Designer, Print Magazine (USA), Graphic Design, Idea (Tokyo). *Address:* 35 Pond Street, NW3 2PN. *T:* 01–435 7402.

HENRIQUES, Richard Henry Quixano; QC 1986; barrister; a Recorder of the Crown Court, since 1983; *b* 27 Oct. 1943; *s* of Cecil Quixano Henriques and late Doreen Mary Henriques; *m* Joan Hilary (*née* Senior); one *s*. *Educ:* Bradfield Coll., Berks; Worcester Coll., Oxford (BA). Called to the Bar, Inner Temple, 1967. *Recreations:* bridge, golf. *Address:* Ilex House, Woodhouse Road, Thornton-Cleveleys, Lancs FY5 5LQ. *T:* Cleveleys 826199. *Clubs:* The Manchester (Manchester); North Shore Golf (Blackpool).

HENRISON, Dame (Anne) Rosina (Elizabeth), DBE 1984; *b* 7 Dec. 1902; *d* of Amelina Marie (*née* Malepa) and Julius Marie; *m* 1st, 1931, Charles Duval; three *s* one *d*; 2nd, 1943, Edward Henrison. *Educ:* Loreto Convent, Port Louis. Hon. Citizen, Town of Bangui, Central Africa, 1975; Ordre de Mérite, Centre Africaine; Mother Gold Medal. *Recreations:* reading, travelling. *Address:* Melville, Grandgaube, Mauritius. *T:* 039–518. *Club:* Port Louis Tennis (Mauritius).

HENRY, David; Senior Director, Postal Services, 1978–82, retired; *b* 19 April 1925; *s* of Thomas Glanffrwd Henry and Hylda Frances Henry. *Educ:* Midhurst Grammar Sch.; St John's Coll., Cambridge (MA Hons). Assistant Postal Controller, 1950; Head Postmaster, Norwich, 1961; Postal Controller, 1966; Controller Operations, 1968; Director, Midlands Postal Region, 1969; Chairman, Midlands Postal Board, 1974; Dir, London Postal Region, 1977. *Recreations:* Rugby football, cricket. *Clubs:* City Livery, Civil Service.

HENRY, Sir Denis (Aynsley), Kt 1975; OBE 1962; QC Grenada 1968; barrister-at-law; Senior Partner, Henry, Henry & Bristol, St George's, Grenada, WI; *b* 3 Feb. 1917; *s* of Ferdinand H. Henry and Agatha May Henry; *m* 1966, Kathleen Carol (*née* Sheppard); two *s* three *d*. *Educ:* Grenada Boys' Secondary Sch.; King's Coll., London (LLB Hons). Called to Bar, Inner Temple (Certif. of Honour), 1939. In practice at Bar, Grenada, 1939–. Served three terms as nominated MLC, Grenada, 1952–65; Sen. nominated Mem. Exec. Council, 1956–65; Senator in First Parlt of Associated State of Grenada, 1966–67. Mem. Council, Univ. of West Indies, 1956–68. Pres. and Dir, Windward Islands Banana Growers Assoc., 1957–75; Pres., Commonwealth Banana Exporters Assoc., 1973–75; Chairman: Grenada Banana Co-operative Soc., 1953–75; Grenada Cocoa Assoc., 1973–75. Vice-Pres., Commonwealth Caribbean Society for the Blind, 1972–75; Mem. Exec., West India Cttee, London, 1972–75. *Recreations:* golf, swimming, tennis. *Address:* Mount Parnassus, St George's, Grenada, WI. *T:* 2370. *Clubs:* Royal Commonwealth Society; Grenada Golf, Richmond Hill Tennis (Grenada).

HENRY, Hon. Sir Denis Robert Maurice; Kt 1986; **Hon. Mr Justice Henry;** a Judge of the High Court of Justice, Queen's Bench Division, since 1986; *b* 19 April 1931; *o s* of late Brig. Maurice Henry and of Mary Catherine (*née* Irving); *m* 1963, Linda Gabriel Arthur; one *s* one *d* (and one *d* decd). *Educ:* Shrewsbury; Balliol Coll., Oxford (MA). 2nd Lieut, KORR, 1950–51. Called to the Bar, Inner Temple, 1955, Bencher, 1985; QC 1977; a Recorder, 1979–86. *Recreations:* history, golf. *Address:* Royal Courts of Justice, Strand, WC2.

HENRY, (Ernest James) Gordon, FCIB; Chairman: Adam & Company PLC, Edinburgh, since 1983; New Scotland Insurance Group, since 1986; *b* 16 June 1919; *s* of Ernest Elston Henry and Dolina Campbell (*née* Smith); *m* 1950, Marion Frew Allan; three *d*. *Educ:* Bellahouston Acad., Glasgow. FCIB 1957. Served War, Army (No 5 Commando), 1939–46. Began career in insurance broking, Glasgow, 1937; founded Gordon Henry & Co., Insurance Brokers, 1952; merged with Matthews Wrightson, 1957; Dep. Chm., Matthews Wrightson Hldgs, 1974; Chm., Stewart Wrightson Holdings Ltd (formerly Matthews Wrightson Holdings Ltd), 1978–81, retd. Dir, Norscot Hotels PLC, 1985–. Dir, Royal Caledonian Schs, Herts. Member: Worshipful Co. of Insurers; Incorporation of Bakers, Glasgow; Merchants House, Glasgow. *Recreations:* golf, fishing, writing. *Address:* Rannoch, Gryffe Road, Kilmacolm, Renfrewshire. *T:* Kilmacolm 3382; 4 Johnstone Court, North Street, St Andrews. *T:* St Andrews 77164. *Clubs:* The Western (Glasgow); Royal & Ancient Golf (St Andrews, Fife); Western Gailes Golf (Ayrshire); Kilmacolm Golf (Renfrewshire).

HENRY, Sir James Holmes, 2nd Bt, *cr* 1922; CMG 1960; MC 1944; TD 1950; QC (Tanganyika) 1953, (Cyprus) 1957; Chairman, Foreign Compensation Commission, 1977–83 (Commissioner, 1960–77); *b* 22 Sept. 1911; *er s* of Rt Hon. Sir Denis Stanislaus Henry, 1st Baronet, Cahore, Draperstown, Co. Londonderry, 1st Lord Chief Justice of Northern Ireland, and Violet (*d* 1966), 3rd *d* of late Rt Hon. Hugh Holmes, Court of Appeal, Ireland; *S* father, 1925; *m* 1st, 1941 (marriage terminated by divorce and rescript of Holy Office in Rome); 2nd, 1949, Christina Hilary, *widow* of Lieut-Commander Christopher H. Wells, RN, and *e d* of late Sir Hugh Holmes, KBE, CMG, MC, QC (formerly Mixed Courts, Egypt); three *d*. *Educ:* Mount St Mary's Coll., Chesterfield;

Downside Sch.; University College, London. BA (Hons) Classics (1st Class), University Scholarships. Called to Bar, Inner Temple, 1934; practised, London, 1934–39. Served War of 1939–45, London Irish Rifles (wounded). Crown Counsel, Tanganyika, 1946; Legal Draftsman, 1949; jt comr, Revised Edn of Laws of Tanganyika (1947–49), 1950; Solicitor-General, 1952; Attorney-General, Cyprus, 1956–60. *Heir: nephew* Patrick Denis Henry, *b* 20 Dec. 1957. *Address:* Kandy Lodge, 18 Ormond Avenue, Hampton on Thames, Mddx. *Clubs:* Travellers', Royal Commonwealth Society.

HENRY, Thomas Cradock, FDS, RCS; MRCS; LRCP; retired; Hon. Consultant Oral Surgeon, Hospital for Sick Children, Great Ormond Street; Consultant Maxillo-Facial Surgeon, Royal Surrey County Hospital; Consultant Oral Surgeon, Italian Hospital, London; *b* 30 Dec. 1910; *s* of late Thomas Henry and Rose Emily Bowdler, Moorgate, Park Retford; *m* 1939, Claire Mary, 7th *c* of late R. A. Caraman, The Grange, Elstree; two *s*. *Educ:* King Edward VI Grammar Sch., Retford; King's Coll., University of London; Middlesex and Royal Dental Hospital; Saunders Scholar; qualified as Doctor, 1935. Formerly: House Physician, House Surgeon and Resident Anæsthetist St James's Hosp., London; Dental House Surgeon, St Bartholomew's Hosp.; Squadron Leader and Surgical Specialist, RAFVR, 1939–46; Surgical Registrar, Plastic and Jaw Injuries Centre, East Grinstead, 1941–42; Surgeon in charge of Maxillo-Facial and Burns Unit, RAF Hosp., Cosford, 1942–46; Hunterian Prof., RCS, 1944–45. FRSocMed; Founder Fellow and Pres., British Assoc. of Oral Surgeons; Member: British Assoc. of Plastic Surgeons (Mem. Council); BMA. *Publications:* Fracture of the Facial Bones (chapter in Fractures and Dislocations in General Practice, 1949); Labial Segment Surgery (chapter in Archer's Oral Surgery, 1971); Melanotic Ameloblastoma (in Trans 3rd ICOS); numerous contrib. to leading medical and dental journals, including BMJ and Jl of Bone and Joint Surgery. *Recreations:* shooting and fishing. *Address:* Redwing Cottage, Bridge Road, Cranleigh, Surrey GU6 7HH. *T:* Cranleigh 277730.

HENRY, Hon. Sir Trevor (Ernest), Kt 1970; Judge, Fiji Court of Appeal, since 1974; *b* 9 May 1902; *s* of John Henry and Edith Anna (*née* Eaton); *m* 1930, Audrey Kate Sheriff; one *s* one *d*. *Educ:* Rotorua District High Sch.; Univ. of New Zealand (Auckland). LLB 1925, LLM Hons 1926, NZ. Solicitor of Supreme Court of NZ, 1923, Barrister, 1925. Judge of the Supreme Court of NZ, 1955–77. *Recreation:* fishing. *Address:* 16 Birdwood Crescent, Parnell, Auckland 1, New Zealand. *Club:* Northern (Auckland).

HENRY, William Robert, CBE 1979; Chairman: Coats Patons Ltd, 1975–81; Scottish Amicable Life Assurance Society, 1981–84; *b* 30 April 1915; *s* of William Henry and Sarah (*née* Lindsay); *m* 1947, Esther Macfayden; two *s* one *d*. *Educ:* Govan High Sch.; London Univ. Entered Company's service, 1934; Head of Financial Dept, 1953; Asst Accountant, 1957; Dir, J. & P. Coats Ltd (Parent Co.), 1966; Dep. Chm., Coats Patons Ltd, 1970. FBIM 1976. *Recreations:* golf, gardening. *Address:* Hawkstone Lodge, Ascog, Isle of Bute, Scotland.

HENSHALL, Rt. Rev. Michael; *see* Warrington, Bishop Suffragan of.

HENSLEY, John; *b* 28 Feb. 1910; *s* of late Edward Hutton and Marion Hensley; *m* 1st, 1940, Dorothy Betty (*d* 1969), *d* of Percy George and Dorothy Coppard; one *s*; 2nd, 1971, Elizabeth, *widow* of Charles Cross and *d* of Harold and Jessie Coppard. *Educ:* Malvern; Trinity Coll., Cambridge (Chancellor's Classical Medal, MA). Entered Min. of Agriculture and Fisheries, 1933; Priv. Sec. to Chancellor of Duchy of Lancaster and Minister of Food, 1939; Priv. Sec. to Minister of Agriculture and Fisheries, 1945; Asst Sec., 1946; Under Sec., 1957. Member: Agricultural Research Council, 1957–59; Council, Nat. Inst. of Agricultural Botany, 1970–73; Sec., Cttee of Inquiry into Veterinary Profession, 1971–75; retired 1975. *Recreations:* theatre, opera, genealogy, gardening. *Address:* 109 Markfield, Courtwood Lane, Croydon CR0 9HP. *T:* 01-657 6319.

HENSON, Marguerite Ann, (Mrs Nicky Henson); *see* Porter, M. A.

HENSON, Ronald Alfred, MD, FRCP; Physician and Neurologist, The London Hospital, 1949–81, Chairman, Section of Neurological Sciences, 1968–81; Physician, National Hospitals for Nervous Diseases, Maida Vale Hospital, 1952–81; Member: Medical Appeals Tribunal, since 1980; Attendance Allowance Board, since 1981; *b* 4 Oct. 1915; *s* of Alfred and Nellie Henson, Chippenham, Wilts; *m* 1941, Frances, *d* of A. Francis and Jessie Sims, Bath; three *d*. *Educ:*King Edward VI Sch., Bath; London Hospital Medical Coll.; Univ. of London (Dip. Hist. Music). Major, RAMC, 1940–46. Mem., Archbishops' Commission on Divine Healing, 1953–57. Dir of Studies, Institute of Neurology, University of London, 1955–64, Chm. Academic Bd, 1974–77; Dir, Cancer Res. Campaign Neuropathological Res. Unit, London Hosp. Med. Coll., 1967–71, Chm. Council, 1974–77. Examiner: RCP, 1965–68, 1969–75; Univ. of London, 1971–74; Langdon-Brown Lectr, RCP, 1977; Fest. lectr, Univ. of Bergen, 1981; Vis. lectr at med. schs and neurological socs in N America, Europe, India, Thailand, Australia, NZ, 1959–86. Hon. Consulting Neurologist, Royal Soc. Musicians, GB, 1966–81; formerly Mem. Board of Governors: The London Hosp.; Nat. Hosps for Nervous Diseases. Chairman: Advance in Medicine, 1976–83; Scientific Adv. Panel, Action Research, 1983 (Mem., 1977; Vice-Chm., 1981); President: Neurological Section, RSM, 1976–77 (Sec., 1956–58; Vice-Pres. 1974); Assoc. of British Neurologists, 1976–77 (Sec., 1964–68). Commonwealth Fellow 1964. Special Trustee, The London Hosp., 1974–82. Member: Assoc. of Physicians of Great Britain and Ireland; British Neuropathological Soc.; Hon. Corresponding Mem. Amer. Neurological Assoc., 1966; Hon. Member: Canadian Neurological Soc., 1971; Belgian Neurological Soc., 1976; Assoc. of British Neurologists, 1983. Chm., London Bach Soc., 1977–85; Arts Council of GB: Mem., 1981–85; Vice-Chm., Regional Adv. Cttee, 1982–86; Chm., Study Gp on Opera Provision Outside London, 1985. Vice-Chm., Cheltenham Internat. Music Fest., 1983–; Chm., Glos Arts Cttee, 1984–; Member: Exec. Cttee, Southern Arts, 1982–; Management Cttee, SW Arts, 1983–. Mem. Bd of Governors, King Edward's Sch., Bath, 1983–. Dep. Editor, Brain, 1974–81. *Publications:* Music and the Brain (ed jtly), 1977; Cancer and the Nervous System (jtly), 1982; various contributions to the neurological literature. *Address:* The Nab, Church Road, Newnham-on-Severn, Glos GL14 1AY. *Clubs:* Athenæum, MCC.

HENZE, Hans Werner; composer; *b* 1 July 1926; *s* of Franz Gebhard Henze and Margarete Geldmacher. *Educ:* Bünde i/W; Bielefeld i/W; Braunschweig. Studying music in Heidelberg, 1945; First Work performed (Chamber Concerto), at Darmstadt-Kranichstein, 1946; Musical Dir, Municipal Theatre, Constance, 1948; Artistic Dir of Ballet, Hessian States Theatre, Wiesbaden, 1950; Prof. of Composition, Acad. Mozarteum, Salzburg, 1961. Definite departure for Italy, living first in Forio d'Ischia, then Naples, then Castelgandolfo as a composer; Artistic Director: Internat. Art Workshop, Montepulciano, Tuscany, 1976–80; Philharmonic Acad., Rome, 1981–; Prof. of Composition, Hochschule für Musik, Cologne, 1980–. Frequent international conducting tours. Member: German Acad. of Arts, E Berlin; Philharmonic Acad., Rome. Hon. DMus Edinburgh, 1970. Robert Schumann Prize, 1952; Prix d'Italia, 1953; Nordrhein-Westphalien Award, 1955; Berlin Prize of Artists, 1958; Great Prize for Artists, Hanover, 1962; Louis Spohr Prize, Brunswick, 1977. *Publications:* a book of Essays; 6 symphonies; 9 full length operas, 3 one-act operas, 1 children's opera; 6 normal ballets and 5 chamber ballets; chamber music; choral works; concerti for violin, viola, violoncello, double bass, oboe, clarinet and harp; various symphonic works; song cycle; music theatre works incl. El Cimarrón, La Cubana, Natascha Ungeheuer, and El Rey de Harlem. *Address:* B. Schott's Soehne, 6500 Mainz, Weihergarten 1–5, West Germany.

HEPBURN, Audrey; actress; *b* Brussels, 4 May 1929; *d* of J. A. Hepburn; *m* 1st, 1954, Mel Ferrer (marr. diss. 1968); one *s*; 2nd, 1969, Dr Andrea Dotti; one *s*. Studied ballet in Amsterdam and in Marie Rambert's ballet sch. First stage part in musical production, High Button Shoes; first film appearance in Laughter in Paradise. Played leading rôles in Gigi (play), New York, 1951 (tour of America, Oct. 1952–May 1953); Ondine (play by Jean Giraudoux), 1954. *Films:* One Wild Oat; The Lavender Hill Mob; The Young Wives' Tale; The Secret People; Nous Irons à Monte Carlo; Roman Holiday, 1952; Sabrina Fair, 1954; War and Peace, 1956; Funny Face, 1957; Love in the Afternoon, 1957; The Nun's Story, 1958, also Green Mansions; The Unforgiven, 1960; Breakfast at Tiffany's, 1961; Paris When it Sizzles, 1962; Charade, 1962; My Fair Lady, 1964; How to Make a Million, 1966; Two for the Road, 1967; Wait Until Dark, 1968; Robin Hood and Maid Marion, 1975; Bloodline, 1979; They All Laughed, 1980. *Address:* c/o Kurt Frings, 415 North Crescent Drive, Beverly Hills, Calif 90210, USA.

HEPBURN, Bryan Audley St John, CMG 1962; Financial Secretary, Sarawak, 1958–63; Member, Sarawak Legislative and Executive Councils, 1955–63; Member, Inter-Governmental Committee which led to establishment of Federation of Malaysia; *b* 24 Feb. 1911; *m* 1940, Sybil Isabel Myers; two *d*. *Educ:* Cornwall Coll., Jamaica. Jamaica Civil Service, 1930; Asst Sec., Colonial Service, 1944; Principal Asst Sec., Sarawak, 1947; Development Sec., 1951. Chm., Sarawak Develt Finance Corp., 1958–63; Chm., Sarawak Electricity Supply Co. Ltd, 1955–63; Dir, Malayan Airways Ltd, 1959–63; Dir, Borneo Airways Ltd, 1958–63; Dep. Chm., Malaysian Tariff Adv. Bd, 1963–65. Ministry of Overseas Development, 1966–73. *Recreations:* golf, fishing. *Address:* 7 Weald Rise, Haywards Heath, West Sussex. *Clubs:* Royal Over-Seas League; Haywards Heath Golf; Sarawak (Sarawak).

HEPBURN, John William; Under Secretary, Ministry of Agriculture, Fisheries and Food, since 1982; *b* 8 Sept. 1938; *s* of late Dugald S. Hepburn and of Margarita R. Hepburn; *m* 1972, Isla Marchbank; one *s*. *Educ:* Hutchesons' Grammar Sch., Glasgow Univ. (MA); Brasenose Coll., Oxford. Assistant Principal, 1961, Principal, 1966, MAFF; First Secretary, UK Delegn to European Communities, Brussels, 1969–71; Private Sec. to Minister of Agriculture, Fisheries and Food, 1971–73; Asst Sec., MAFF, 1973–81. *Recreation:* golf. *Address:* c/o Ministry of Agriculture, Fisheries and Food, SW1.

HEPBURN, Katharine; actress; *b* 9 Nov. 1909; *d* of late Dr Thomas N. Hepburn and Katharine Houghton; *m* Ludlow Ogden Smith (marr. diss.). *Educ:* Hartford; Bryn Mawr College. First professional appearance on stage, Baltimore, 1928, in Czarina; first New York appearance, 1928, in Night Hostess (under name Katherine Burns), The Millionairess, New Theatre, London, 1952. Entered films, 1932; notable films: A Bill of Divorcement; Morning Glory; Little Women; The Little Minister; Mary of Scotland; Quality Street; Stage Door; The Philadelphia Story; Keeper of the Flame; Dragon Seed; Woman of the Year; Under-current; Without Love; Sea of Grass; Song of Love; State of the Union; Adam's Rib; The African Queen; Pat and Mike; Summer Madness; The Iron Petticoat; The Rainmaker; His Other Woman; Suddenly, Last Summer; Long Day's Journey into Night; Guess Who's Coming to Dinner; The Madwoman of Chaillot; The Lion in Winter; The Trojan Women; A Delicate Balance; Rooster Cogburn; On Golden Pond. *Stage:* Warrior's Husband; The Philadelphia Story; Without Love; As You Like It; Taming of the Shrew; Merchant of Venice; Measure for Measure, Australia, 1955; Coco, 1970; A Matter of Gravity, NY, 1976, tour, 1977; The West Side Waltz, NY, 1981. Academy Awards for performances in Morning Glory, Guess Who's Coming to Dinner, The Lion in Winter, On Golden Pond.

HEPBURN, Surg. Rear-Adm. Nicol Sinclair, CB 1971; CBE 1968; *b* 2 Feb. 1913; *s* of late John Primrose and Susan Hepburn, Edinburgh; *m* 1939, Dorothy Blackwood; two *s*. *Educ:* Broughton; Edinburgh Univ. MB, ChB 1935; DPH London, 1948; DIH London, 1952. Barrister-at-law, Gray's Inn, 1956. Joined RN, 1935; served during war in Atlantic and Pacific Stations; SMO, HM Dockyard: Plymouth, 1952; Portsmouth, 1955; Naval Medical Officer of Health: Portsmouth, 1959; Malta, 1962; Surg. Cdre and Dep. Med. Dir-Gen., 1966; Surg. Rear-Adm. 1969; MO i/c, RN Hosp., Haslar, 1969–72; retd. MO, DHSS, 1972–80. FRSM; FFCM 1973. *Address:* Mallows, 10 Chilbolton Avenue, Winchester, Hants SO22 5HD.

HEPBURN, Sir Ninian B. A. J. B.; *see* Buchan-Hepburn.

HEPBURN, Prof. Ronald William; Professor of Moral Philosophy, University of Edinburgh, since 1975 (Professor of Philosophy, 1964–75); *b* 16 March 1927; *s* of late W. G. Hepburn, Aberdeen; *m* 1953, Agnes Forbes Anderson; two *s* one *d*. *Educ:* Aberdeen Grammar Sch.; University of Aberdeen. MA 1951, PhD 1955 (Aberdeen). National service in Army, 1944–48. Asst, 1952–55, Lecturer, 1955–60, Dept of Moral Philosophy, University of Aberdeen; Visiting Associate Prof., New York University, 1959–60; Prof. of Philosophy, University of Nottingham, 1960–64. Stanton Lecturer in the Philosophy of Religion, Cambridge, 1965–68. *Publications:* (jointly) Metaphysical beliefs, 1957; Christianity and Paradox, 1958; Wonder and Other Essays: eight studies in aesthetics and neighbouring fields, 1984; contrib. to learned journals; broadcasts. *Recreations:* music, hill-walking. *Address:* Department of Philosophy, University of Edinburgh, David Hume Tower, George Square, Edinburgh EH8 9JX.

HEPBURNE-SCOTT, family name of **Lord Polwarth.**

HEPHER, Michael Leslie; Chairman and Managing Director, Abbey Life Group, since 1980; *b* 17 Jan. 1944; *s* of Leslie and Edna Hepher; *m* 1971, Janice Morton; one *s* two *d*. *Educ:* Kingston Grammar School. FIA; Associate, Soc. of Actuaries; FLIA. Provident Life Assoc., UK, 1961–67; Commercial Life Assurance, Canada, 1967–70; Maritime Life Assurance Co., Canada, 1970–79; Abbey Life Group, UK, 1979–. *Recreations:* tennis, reading. *Address:* Little Maples, St Aldhems Road, Branksome Park, Poole, Dorset. *T:* Poole 764680.

HEPPEL, Richard Purdon, CMG 1959; HM Diplomatic Service, retired; *b* 27 Oct. 1913; 2nd *s* of late Engineer Rear-Admiral Walter George Heppel and Margaret, *d* of late Robert Stevens Fraser; *m* 1949, Ruth Theodora, *d* of late Horatio Matthews, MD; two *s* one *d*. *Educ:* Rugby Sch.; Balliol Coll., Oxford. Laming Travelling Fellow, Queen's Coll., 1935. Entered Diplomatic Service, 1936; Third Sec., Rome, 1939; Second Sec., Tehran, 1942; First Sec., Athens, 1944; Private Sec. to Min. of State, 1946; First Sec., Karachi, 1948, Madrid, 1951; Counsellor, HM Legation, Saigon, 1953–54; Ambassador to Cambodia, 1954–56; Minister at Vienna, 1956–59; Head of South East Asia Dept, Foreign Office, 1959; Head of Consular Dept, Foreign Office, 1961–63; Imperial Defence Coll., 1960; Consul-Gen. at Stuttgart, 1963–69. Administrative Officer, The City Univ. Grad. Business Centre, 1969–70; Appeals Sec. for Beds, Bucks and Herts, Cancer Res. Campaign, 1970–79. MIL 1985. Freeman, Skinners' Company, 1961, Liveryman 1969. *Address:* Barns Piece, Nether Winchendon, Aylesbury, Bucks. *Club:* Travellers'.

HEPPELL, (Thomas) Strachan, CB 1986; Deputy Secretary, Department of Health and Social Security, since 1983; *b* 15 Aug. 1935; *s* of Leslie Thomas Davidson Heppell and Doris Abbey Heppell (*née* Potts); *m* 1963, Felicity Ann Rice; two *s*. *Educ:* Acklam Hall Grammar Sch., Middlesbrough; The Queen's Coll., Oxford. National Assistance Board, Ministry of Social Security/DHSS: Asst Principal, 1958; Principal, 1963–73 (seconded to Cabinet Office, 1967–69); Asst Director of Social Welfare, Hong Kong, 1971–73; Asst Sec., DHSS, 1973–78 (Social Security Adviser, Hong Kong Govt, 1977); Under Sec., DHSS, 1979–83. *Publications:* contribs to social administration jls. *Recreations:* gardening, travelling. *Address:* 61 Tor Bryan, Ingatestone, Essex CM4 9HN. *T:* Ingatestone 353418.

HEPPER, Anthony Evelyn, CEng, FIMechE; CBIM; Chairman: Hyde Sails Ltd, since 1984; Lamont and Partners, since 1986; *b* 16 Jan. 1923; *s* of Lieut-Col J. E. Hepper; *m* 1970, Jonquil Francisca Kinloch-Jones. *Educ:* Wellington Coll., Berks. Royal Engrs, 1942–47 (retd as Hon. Major); Courtaulds Ltd, 1947–53; Cape Asbestos Co. Ltd 1953–57; Thomas Tilling Ltd, 1957–68 (Dir from 1963 until secondment), seconded as Industrial Adviser, DEA, 1966–67, and Mem., SIB, 1967; Chairman: Upper Clyde Shipbuilders Ltd, 1968–71; Henry Sykes Ltd, 1972–81; Richardsons Westgarth plc, 1982–85; Director: Cape Industries plc, 1968–; Cardinal Investment Trust plc, 1982–84; General Investors Trustees plc, 1982–84; F. & Pacific Investment Trust PLC, 1984–. *Recreation:* golf. *Address:* 70 Eaton Place, SW1X 8AT. *T:* 01–235 7518. *Club:* Boodle's.

HEPPLE, Prof. Bob Alexander; Professor of English Law, University College, London, since 1982; a part-time Chairman of Industrial Tribunals (England and Wales), 1975–77 and since 1982 (full-time, 1977–82); *b* 11 Aug. 1934; *s* of late Alexander Hepple and of Josephine Zwarenstein; *m* 1960, Shirley Goldsmith; one *s* one *d*. *Educ:* Univ. of Witwatersrand (BA 1954, LLB *cum laude* 1957); Univ. of Cambridge (LLB 1966, MA 1968). Attorney, S Africa, 1958; Lectr in Law, Univ. of Witwatersrand, 1959–62; Advocate, S Africa, 1962–63. Left S Africa after detention without trial for anti-apartheid activities, 1963. Called to Bar, Gray's Inn, 1966; Lectr in Law, Nottingham Univ., 1966–68; Fellow of Clare Coll., Cambridge and Univ. Lectr in Law, 1968–76; Prof. of Comparative Social and Labour Law, Univ. of Kent, 1976–77 (Hon. Prof., 1978–83). Mem., CRE, 1986–. *Publications:* various books and articles on labour law, race relations, law of tort, etc; Founding Editor, Industrial Law Jl, 1972–77; Gen. Ed (jtly) Encyclopedia of Labour Relations Law, 1972–; Chief Editor, International Encyclopedia of Comparative Law, Vol. XV, Labour Law, 1979–. *Address:* Faculty of Laws, University College, 4–8 Endsleigh Gardens, WC1H 0EG.

HEPPLE, (Robert) Norman, RA 1961 (ARA 1954); RP 1948; NEAC 1950; *b* 18 May 1908; *s* of Robert Watkin Hepple and Ethel Louise Wardale; *m* 1948, Jillian Constance Marigold Pratt; one *s* one *d*. *Educ:* Goldsmiths' Coll.; Royal Acad. Schools. Figure subject and portrait painter. Pres., Royal Soc. of Portrait Painters, 1979–83. *Address:* (studio) 16 Cresswell Place, South Kensington, SW10; (home) 10 Sheen Common Drive, Richmond, Surrey. *T:* 01–878 4452.

HEPPLESTON, Prof. Alfred Gordon; Professor of Pathology, University of Newcastle upon Tyne (formerly Durham), 1960–77, now Emeritus Professor; *b* 29 Aug. 1915; *s* of Alfred Heppleston, Headmaster, and Edith (*née* Clough); *m* 1942, Eleanor Rix Tebbutt; two *s*. *Educ:* Manchester Grammar Sch. Chief Asst, Professorial Medical Unit, University of Manchester; Asst Lecturer in Pathology, Welsh Nat. Sch. of Medicine, Univ. of Wales, 1944–47; Dorothy Temple Cross Research Fellow, Univ. of Pennsylvania, 1947–48; Sen. Lectr in Pathology, Univ. of Wales, 1948–60. *Publications:* on pathological topics, largely in reference to pulmonary disorders. *Recreations:* ornithology, cricket and music. *Address:* Bridgeford Gate, Bellingham, Hexham, Northumberland NE48 2HU.

HEPTINSTALL, Leslie George; HM Diplomatic Service, retired; *b* 20 Aug. 1919; *s* of late Victor George Heptinstall and of Maud Maunder; *m* 1949, Marion Nicholls; one *d*. *Educ:* Thames Valley County Sch.; London Univ. (BSc Econ.). Served War of 1939–45: Capt., Royal Artillery; Middle East, Mediterranean, North-West Europe. Asst Principal, Colonial Office, 1948; Principal, 1951; seconded to West African Inter-Territorial Secretariat, Accra, 1955; Acting Chief Sec., 1958; Acting Administrator, W African Research Office, 1959; Principal, CRO, 1961; First Sec. on Staff of Brit. High Comr, Wellington, NZ, 1962–64; Brit. Dep. High Comr, Lahore, 1964–65; Head of South Asia Dept, ODM, 1966–68; Dep. Senior Trade Comr, Montreal, 1968–70; Internat. Coffee Orgn, 1971–73. *Recreations:* sailing, golf and tennis. *Address:* 63 Richmond Way, Great Bookham, Surrey.

HEPWORTH, Rear-Adm. David, CB 1976; retired from RN, 1976; naval consultant; *b* 6 June 1923; *s* of Alfred Ernest Hepworth and Minnie Louisa Catherine Bennet Tanner (*née* Bowden); *m* 1st, 1946, Brenda June Case (marr. diss. 1974); one *s* one *d*; 2nd, 1975, Eileen Mary Macgillivray (*née* Robson). *Educ:* Banbury Grammar School. Boy Telegraphist, RN, 1939; HMS Ganges, 1939–40; served in Atlantic, Mediterranean and E Indies Fleets; commnd 1944; submarines and midget submarines, 1945–50; Home, Australian and Far East Stns, 1951–58; Sen. Officer Submarines Londonderry, 1959–61; CO HMS Ashanti, 1961–64; jssc 1964; Dep. Dir Undersea Warfare, MoD, 1964–66; idc 1967; CO HMS Ajax and Captain (D) 2nd Far East Destroyer Sqdn, 1968–69; Dir RN Tactical Sch. and Maritime Tactical Sch., 1969–71; Dir Naval Warfare, MoD, 1971–73; Staff of Vice-Chief of Naval Stuff, 1973–76. Lt-Comdr 1952; Comdr 1958; Captain 1964; Rear-Adm. 1974. Naval Advr to Internat. Military Services Ltd, 1977–83. *Recreations:* home and garden. *Address:* Darville House, Lower Heyford, Oxon. *T:* Steeple Aston 47460.

HEPWORTH, Noel Peers, OBE 1980; Director, Chartered Institute of Public Finance and Accountancy, since 1980; *b* 22 Dec. 1934; *m* 1963, Jean Margaret Aldcroft; one *s* three *d*. *Educ:* Crewe County Grammar Sch.; London Univ. IPFA 1958; DPA 1963. Nat. Service, RAF, 1953–55. NW Gas Bd, 1951–58; Asst City Treasurer, Manchester, 1965–72; Dir of Finance, Croydon, 1972–80. Financial Advr to London Boroughs Assoc. and AMA, 1972–80; Mem., London Treasurers' Adv. Body, 1972–80; Member: Dept of Envt Property Adv. Group, 1980–; Audit Commn, 1983–. FRSA 1985. *Publications:* Finance of Local Government, 1970, 7th edn 1983, Japanese edn 1983; Housing Rents, Costs and Subsidies, 1978, 2nd edn 1981; contribs to technical and financial jls, local govt press and nat. press. *Recreations:* gardening, walking. *Address:* Chartered Institute of Public Finance and Accountancy, 2–3 Robert Street, WC2N 6BH. *T:* 01–930 3456.

HERBECQ, Sir John (Edward), KCB 1977; a Church Commissioner, since 1982; *b* 29 May 1922; *s* of late Joseph Edward and Rosina Elizabeth Herbecq; *m* 1947, Pamela Filby; one *d*. *Educ:* High Sch. for Boys, Chichester. Clerical Officer, Colonial Office, 1939; Asst Principal, Treasury, 1950; Private Sec. to Chm., UK Atomic Energy Authority, 1960–62; Asst Sec., Treasury, 1964; Asst Sec., 1968, Under Sec., 1970, Dep. Sec., 1973, Second Permanent Sec., 1975–81, CSD. Mem., Review Body for Nursing Staff, Midwives, Health Visitors and Professions Allied to Medicine, 1983–; Chm., Malawi Civil Service Review Commn, 1984–85. Member: C of E Pensions Bd, 1985–; Chichester Diocesan Bd of Finance, 1983–. *Recreations:* Scottish country dancing (ISTD Supreme Award with Hons), walking, watching cricket. *Address:* Maryland, Ledgers Meadow, Cuckfield, Haywards Heath, West Sussex RH17 5EW. *T:* Haywards Heath 413387.

HERBERT, family name of **Earls of Carnarvon, Pembroke,** and **Powis,** and **Baron Hemingford.**

HERBERT, Lord; William Alexander Sidney Herbert; *b* 18 May 1978; *s* and *heir* of Earl of Pembroke and Montgomery, *qv*.

HERBERT, Alfred James; British Council Representative, Portugal, 1980–84, retired; *b* 16 Oct. 1924; *s* of Allen Corbyn Herbert and Betty Herbert; *m* 1st, 1958, Helga Elberling (*d* 1981); two *s*; 2nd, 1982, Dr Wanda Wolska. *Educ:* Royal Masonic Schs; University Coll. London (BA 1950, MA 1952). Guest Prof. of English Lit., Univs of Yokohama and Tokyo, 1958–60; Lectr, English Dept, Birmingham Univ., 1960–62; joined British Council, 1962: Sierra Leone, 1962–65; Brazil, 1965–68; Representative: Somalia, 1968–70; Pakistan, 1974–77; Poland, 1977–80. *Publications:* Modern English Novelists, (Japan), 1960; Structure of Technical English, 1965. *Recreations:* travelling, reading. *Address:* Quinta do Val do Riso, São Simão, Azeitão, 2900 Setubal, Portugal.

HERBERT, Christopher Alfred, CB 1973; retired; *b* 15 June 1913; *s* of Alfred Abbot Herbert and Maria Hamilton (*née* Fetherston); *m* 1941, Evelyn Benson Scott (*née* Ross) (*d* 1972); one *s* one *d*. *Educ:* Mountjoy Sch., Dublin; Trinity Coll., Dublin (BA (Hons)). Indian Civil Service, 1937–47; Eastern Manager, May & Baker (India) Ltd, 1947–50. MoD, 1950–77, Under Sec., 1971–77. *Recreations:* walking, gardening, reading. *Address:* 41 Woodcote Avenue, Wallington, Surrey. *T:* 01–647 5223. *Club:* East India, Devonshire, Sports and Public Schools.

HERBERT, (Dennis) Nicholas; (3rd Baron Hemingford, *cr* 1943, of Watford); Editorial Director, Westminster Press, since 1974; *b* 25 July 1934; *s* of 2nd Baron Hemingford and Elizabeth McClare (*d* 1979), *d* of Col J. M. Clark, Haltwhistle, Northumberland; *S* father, 1982; remains known professionally as Nicholas Herbert; *m* 1958, Jennifer Mary Toresen Bailey, *d* of F. W. Bailey, Harrogate; one *s* three *d*. *Educ:* Oundle Sch.; Clare Coll., Cambridge (MA). Reuters Ltd, 1956–61; The Times: Asst Washington Corresp., 1961–65; Middle East Corresp., 1965–68; Dep. Features Editor, 1968–70; Editor, Cambridge Evening News, 1970–74. Vice-Pres., Guild of British Newspaper Editors, 1979, Pres., 1980–81. Sec., Assoc. of British Editors, 1985–. *Heir: s* Hon. Christopher Dennis Charles Herbert, *b* 4 July 1973. *Address:* Old Rectory, Hemingford Abbots, Huntingdon PE18 9AH. *T:* St Ives (Hunts) 66234. *Clubs:* Royal Commonwealth Society, City Livery.

HERBERT, Frederick William; Parliamentary Correspondent, Eurotunnel (UK), since 1986; Emeritus Fellow in Industrial Relations, International Management Centre, Buckingham, since 1985; Chairman, NALGO Insurance Association Ltd, since 1981; *b* London, 18 Dec. 1922; *s* of late William Herbert and Alice Herbert; *m* 1948, Nina Oesterman; two *d*. *Educ:* Ealing Boys' Grammar Sch. Served RAFVR, 1942–46. Local Govt Finance, Mddx CC, 1939–65; Greater London Council: Local Govt Finance, 1965–72; Personnel Management, Estabt Officer, 1972–77; Asst Dir of Personnel, 1977–80; Head of Industrial Relations, 1980–82; Controller of Personnel, 1982–84. *Recreations:* cricket, music (classical and jazz), theatre, Antient Society of Cogers (debating). *Address:* 20 Priory Hill, Wembley, Mddx HA0 2QF. *T:* 01–904 8634. *Clubs:* Royal Over-Seas League, MCC.

HERBERT, Prof. Harold Bernard; engaged in educational research; *b* 10 March 1924; *s* of late A. Bernard Henbest and Edith Winifred Henbest (*née* Herbert); *m* 1948, Rosalind Eve Skone James; two *s* one *d*. *Educ:* Barking Abbey Sch.; Imperial Coll. of Science, London. Beit Research Fellow, 1947–48; Lectr, University of Manchester, 1948–56; Research Fellow, Harvard Univ., 1953–54; Vis. Prof., UCLA, 1954; Reader, KCL, 1956–57; Prof of Organic Chemistry, QUB, 1958–73. *Publications:* Organic Chemistry (with M. F. Grundon), 1968; contribs to Jl of Chemical Soc. *Address:* 5 Witley Court, Coram Street, WC1N 1HD. *T:* 01–278 0888.

HERBERT, Jocelyn, Hon. ARCA 1964; RDI 1971; *b* 22 Feb. 1917; *d* of Sir Alan Patrick Herbert, CH, and Gwendolen (*née* Quilter); *m* 1937, Anthony Lousada (marr. diss. 1960); one *s* three *d*. *Educ:* St Paul's Girls' Sch.; Paris and Vienna; London Theatre Studio; Slade School of Art. Started painting at André L'Hote's Sch., Paris, 1932–33; studied drawing and painting with Leon Underwood, 1934; trained as theatre designer with Michel St Denis and George Devine, London Th. Studio, 1936–37; joined staff of English Stage Co., Royal Court Th., 1956; became freelance designer, 1958, centred largely on Royal Court. *Plays designed*, 1957–: Royal Court Theatre: Ionesco: The Chairs, The Lesson, Exit the King; W. B. Yeats: Purgatory; Ann Jellico: Sport of My Mad Mother; Samuel Beckett: Krapp's Last Tape, Happy Days, Not I, Footfalls, That Time; Arnold Wesker: Roots, The Kitchen, I'm Talking about Jerusalem, Chips with Everything, The Merchant; Arden: Serjeant Musgrave's Dance; Christopher Logue: Trials by Logue, Antigone, The Trial of Cob and Leach; Middleton: The Changeling; Shakespeare: Richard III, Midsummer Night's Dream, Julius Caesar; John Osborne: Luther, A Patriot for Me, Inadmissible Evidence; Barry Reckford: Skyvers; W. Solvonka: The Lion and the Jewel; O'Neil and Seabrook: Life Price; Donald Howarth: Three Months Gone; David Storey: Home, The Changing Room, Cromwell, Life Class, Early Days; Christopher Hampton: Savages, The Portage to San Cristobal of A. H.; Joe Orton: What the Butler Saw; David Hare: Teeth 'n' Smiles; Mustapha Matura: Rum and Coca Cola; RSC: Richard III; Ibsen's Ghosts; Phoenix: Brecht's Baal; National Theatre: Othello; Brecht's Mother Courage and Life of Galileo; A Woman Killed with Kindness; Adrian Mitchell's Tyger; David Storey's Early Days; Aeschylus' The Oresteia; Queen's Theatre: The Seagull; Brecht's Joan of the Stockyard; Round House: Hamlet; Albery Theatre: Pygmalion; Aldwych: Saratoga; (New York) Wesker's The Merchant; Haymarket: Heartbreak House; Lyric, Hammersmith: The Devil and the Good Lord; Lyric, Shaftesbury Ave: Gigi. *Opera*, 1967, and 1975–: Sadler's Wells: Gluck's Orpheus and Euridice; Paris Opera: Verdi's The Force of Destiny, 1975; Metropolitan, NY: Alban Berg's Lulu, 1977; Mozart's The Abduction, 1979; Brecht and Weil's Rise and Fall of the City of Mahagonny, 1979; Coliseum: The Mask of Orpheus, 1986. *Films:* Tony Richardson: (colour cons. and costumes) Tom Jones, (prodn designer) Hamlet, Ned Kelly, Hotel New Hampshire; Karel Reisz: (prodn designer) Isadora; Lindsay Anderson: (prodn designer) If . . ., O Lucky Man!. *Recreations:* the country, painting. *Address:* 45 Pottery Lane, W11. *T:* 01–727 1104.

HERBERT, Nicholas; *see* Herbert, D. N.

HERBERT, Adm. Sir Peter (Geoffrey Marshall), KCB 1983; OBE 1969; Consultant; Chairman of Council, Soldiers', Sailors', and Airmen's Families Association, since 1985; *b* 28 Feb. 1929; *s* of A. G. S. Herbert and P. K. M. Herbert; *m* 1953, Ann Maureen (*née* McKeown); one *s* one *d*. *Educ:* Dunchurch Hall; RN Coll., Dartmouth. Specialised in submarines, 1949; Comd HM Submarine Scythian, 1957–58; nuclear course, RN Coll., Greenwich, 1959; Comd HM Submarine Porpoise, 1960–62; Comd nuclear submarine, HMS Valiant, 1963–68; Comd HMS Venus, 1964; Dep. Dir, Naval Equipment, 1969; Comd 10th (Polaris) Submarine Squadron, 1970–72; COS to Flag Officer Submarines, 1972–74; Comd HMS Blake, 1974–75; Dep. Chief, Polaris Exec., 1976–78; Flag Officer Carriers and Amphibious Ships, 1978–79; Dir Gen., Naval Manpower and Training, 1980–81; Flag Officer Submarines and Comdr Submarines Eastern Atlantic, 1981–83;

VCDS (Personnel and Logistics), 1983–84. Chm. Trustees, RN Submarine Museum. FBIM, MINucE. *Recreations:* woodwork, gardening, golf, swimming. *Address:* Dolphin Square, SW1. *T:* 01–798 8330. *Club:* Army and Navy.

HERBERT, Prof. Robert Louis, PhD; Robert Lehman Professor of the History of Art, Yale University, since 1974; *b* 21 April 1929; *s* of John Newman Herbert and Rosalia Harr Herbert; *m* 1953, Eugenia Randall Warren; one *s* two *d. Educ:* Wesleyan Univ., Middletown, Conn (BA 1951); Yale Univ. (MA 1954, PhD 1957). Fulbright Scholar, Paris, 1951–52; Faculty, Yale Univ., 1956–: Associate Prof., 1963; Prof., 1966; Departmental Chm., 1965–68. Guggenheim Fellow, 1971–72; Slade Prof. of Fine Art, Oxford, 1978. Organizer of exhibitions: Barbizon Revisited, Boston Museum of Fine Arts and others, 1962–63; Neo-Impressionism, Solomon R. Guggenheim Mus., 1968; J. F. Millet, Musées Nationaux, Paris, and Arts Council, London, 1975–76; Léger's Le Grand Déjeuner, Minneapolis Inst. of Arts and Detroit Inst. of Arts, 1980. Fellow, Amer. Acad. of Arts and Sciences, 1978. Chevalier, Ordre des Arts et des Lettres, 1976. *Publications:* Barbizon Revisited, 1962–63; Seurat's Drawings, 1963; The Art Criticism of John Ruskin, 1964; Modern Artists on Art, 1964; Neo-Impressionism, 1968; David, Voltaire, 'Brutus' and the French Revolution, 1972; J. F. Millet, 1975; (ed jtly) Société Anonyme and Dreier Bequest at Yale University: a catalogue raisonné, 1984; articles in learned jls. *Address:* Department of the History of Art, Yale University, Box 2009, 56 High Street, New Haven, Conn 06520, USA. *T:* 436–8347.

HERBERT, Robin Arthur Elidyr, DL; JP; Chairman, Leopold Joseph Holdings PLC, since 1978; a Director: National Westminster Bank PLC (Chairman, SW Regional Board); Equity and Law Life Assurance; Agricultural Mortgage Corporation, since 1985; Marks & Spencer plc, since 1986; President and Chairman of Council, Royal Horticultural Society, since 1984 (Member Council, 1971–74 and since 1979); *b* 5 March 1934; *s* of late Sir John Arthur Herbert, GCIE and Lady Mary Herbert; *m* 1960, Margaret Griswold Lewis; two *s* two *d. Educ:* Eton; Christ Church, Oxford (MA); Harvard Business School (MBA). ARICS. 2nd Lieut Royal Horse Guards, 1953–54; Captain Royal Monmouthshire RE, 1962–68. Dep. Chm., Countryside Commn, 1971–80; Member: Council, National Trust, 1969– (Mem., Exec. Cttee, 1969–84; Chm. Cttee for Wales, 1969–84); Nat. Water Council, 1980–83; Welsh Develt Agency, 1980–86. Financial Advr, Water Superanuation Fund, 1986–. DL 1968, JP 1964, High Sheriff 1972, Monmouthshire. *Recreations:* dendrology, walking. *Address:* Llanover, Abergavenny, Gwent. *T:* Nantyderry 880232. *Clubs:* Brooks's, Pratt's.

HERBERT, Walter William, (Wally Herbert); *b* 24 Oct. 1934; *s* of Captain W. W. J. Herbert and Helen (*née* Manton); *m* 1969, Marie, *d* of Prof. C. A. McGaughey; two *d*. Trained as surveyor in RE; Egypt, 1953–54, demob. 1955; travelled in Middle East, 1955; Surveyor with Falkland Is Dependencies Survey; Hope Bay, Antarctica, 1955–58; travelled in S America, 1958–59; Mem. expedn to Lapland and Spitzbergen, 1960; travelled in Greenland, 1960; Surveyor, NZ Antarctic Expedn, 1960–62; leader Southern Party; mapped 26,000 sq. miles of Queen Maud Range and descended Amundsen's route to Pole on 50th anniv.; led expedn to NW Greenland, 1966–67; dog-sledged 1,400 miles Greenland to Canada in trng for trans-Arctic crossing; led British Trans-Arctic Expedn, 1968–69, which made 3,800–mile first surface crossing of Arctic Ocean from Alaska via North Pole to Spitzbergen (longest sustained sledging journey in history of Polar exploration); led Ultima Thule expedn (filming Eskimos, Thule District), 1971–73; led expedn to Lapland, 1975; led expedn to Greenland, 1978–82 (attempting first circumnavigation by dog sledge and skin boat). Hon. Mem., British Schools Exploring Soc.; Jt Hon. Pres., World Expeditionary Assoc. FRGS. Polar Medal 1962, and clasp 1969; Livingstone Gold Medal, RSGS, 1969; Founder's Gold Medal, RGS, 1970; City of Paris Medal, 1983; French Geog. Soc. Medal, 1983; Explorers' Medal, Explorers' Club, 1985; Finn Ronne Award, 1985. *Publications:* A World of Men, 1968; Across the Top of the World, 1969; (contrib.) World Atlas of Mountaineering, 1969; The Last Great Journey on Earth, 1971; Polar Deserts, 1971; Eskimos, 1976 (Jugendbuchpreis, 1977); North Pole, 1978; (contrib.) Expeditions the Expert's Way, 1977; (contrib.) Bell House Book, 1978; Hunters of the Polar North, 1982; The Noose of Laurels. *Recreation:* painting. *Address:* c/o Royal Geographical Society, SW7. *Clubs:* Lansdowne; Explorers (NY).

HERBERT-JONES, Hugh (Hugo) Jarrett, CMG 1973; OBE 1963; HM Diplomatic Service, retired; International Affairs Director, Confederation of British Industry, since 1979; *b* 11 March 1922; *s* of late Dora Herbert-Jones (*née* Rowlands), and Captain Herbert-Jones; *m* 1954, Margaret, *d* of Rev. J. P. Veall; one *s* two *d. Educ:* Bryanston; Worcester Coll., Oxford. History Scholar. Commnd Welsh Guards, 1941; served NW Europe and Middle East; wounded 1944; demobilised 1946 (Major). Entered Foreign (later Diplomatic) Service, 1947; served: Hamburg, 1947; Berlin, 1949; Hong Kong, 1951; Phnom Penh, 1955; Saigon, 1956; Nairobi, 1959; Pretoria/Cape Town, 1963; FCO, 1966; Paris, 1973; FCO, 1975–79. *Recreations:* sailing, golf, music, spectator sports. *Address:* Prior's Hill, Park Road, Aldeburgh, Suffolk IP15 5ET. *T:* Aldeburgh 3335; 401 Hawkins House, Dolphin Square, SW1. *T:* 01–821 1183. *Clubs:* Garrick, MCC; London Welsh Rugby Football; Aldeburgh Golf; Aldeburgh Yacht.

HERBISON, Dame Jean (Marjory), DBE 1985; CMG 1976; Associate Director, Christchurch Polytechnic, New Zealand, 1975–84; *b* 29 April 1923; *d* of William Herbison and Sarah Jane Herbison (*née* McKendry). *Educ:* Univ. of Canterbury (BA); Auckland Teachers' Coll. (Dip Teaching); Univ. of Northern Iowa (MA); Inst. of Education, Univ. of London. AIE 1984. Teaching, Avonside Girls' High School, Christchurch, 1952–59; Dean, 1960–68, Vice-Principal, 1968–74, Christchurch Teachers' Coll.; Assoc. Dir, Christchurch Polytechnic, 1975–84; Mem. Council, 1970–84, Chancellor, 1979–84, Univ. of Canterbury. Member: NZ Council for Educnl Research, 1977–; UGC, 1985–; Ministerial Cttee of Inquiry into Curriculum, Assessment and Qualifications in the Senior Secondary Sch., 1985–; Vice-Pres., Commonwealth Council for Educnl Admin, 1982–. Hon. Fellow: NZ Educnl Inst.; NZ Inst. of Management. Queen's Silver Jubilee Medal, 1977. *Recreations:* gardening, walking, reading. *Address:* 2/172 Soleares Avenue, Christchurch 8, New Zealand. *T:* Christchurch 849–086.

HERBISON, Rt. Hon. Margaret McCrorie, PC 1964; Lord High Commissioner to the General Assembly of the Church of Scotland, 1970–71; *b* 11 March 1907. *Educ:* Dykehead Public Sch., Shotts; Bellshill Acad.; Glasgow Univ. Teacher of English and History in Glasgow Schs; MP (Lab) North Lanark, 1945–70; Jt Parly Under-Sec. of State, Scottish Office, 1950–51; Minister of Pensions and National Insurance, Oct. 1964–Aug. 1966, of Social Security, 1966–67. Chm., Select Cttee on Overseas Aid, 1969–. Member National Executive Cttee, Labour Party; Chm. Labour Party, 1957. Mem., Royal Commn on Standards of Conduct in Public Life, 1974–. Scotswoman of the Year, 1970. Hon. LLD Glasgow, 1970. *Recreations:* reading, gardening. *Address:* 8 Mornay Way, Shotts, Lanarkshire ML7 4EG. *T:* Shotts 21944.

HERD, Frederick Charles; Assistant Under-Secretary of State (Civilian Management, General), Ministry of Defence, 1970–75; *b* 27 April 1915. *Educ:* Strode's Sch., Egham; Sidney Sussex Coll., Cambridge. Asst Principal, Admiralty, 1937; Principal, 1941; Asst. Sec., 1950; Asst Under-Sec. of State, 1964. *Recreations:* music, lawn tennis, bridge. *Address:* 11 Bloemfontein Avenue, W12.

HERDON, Christopher de Lancy, OBE 1971; HM Diplomatic Service, retired; Leader-writer, The Tablet, since 1983; Roman Catholic Observer to the British Council of Churches, since 1984; *b* 24 May 1928; *s* of Wilfrid Herdon and Clotilde (*née* Parsons); *m* 1953, Virginia Grace; two *s* two *d* (and one *s* decd). *Educ:* Ampleforth; Magdalen Coll., Oxford. Foreign Office, 1951; Vienna, 1953; 2nd Sec., Baghdad, 1957; Beirut, 1961; 1st Sec., Amman, 1962; FO, 1965; Aden, 1967; FCO, 1970; Counsellor: Rome, 1973; FCO, 1977; retired 1983. *Recreations:* painting, music, sailing, long-distance walking. *Address:* Moses Farm, Lurgashall, Petworth, W Sussex GU28 9EP. *T:* North Chapel 323. *Clubs:* Reform, Special Forces; Thorney Island Sailing.

HEREFORD, 18th Viscount *cr* 1550; **Robert Milo Leicester Devereux;** Bt 1611; Premier Viscount of England; *b* 4 Nov. 1932; *o s* of Hon. Robert Godfrey de Bohun Devereux (*d* 1934) and Audrey Maureen Leslie, DStJ 1963 (*d* 1978) (she *m* 2nd 1961, 7th Earl of Lisburne, who *d* 1965), *y d* of late James Meakin, Westwood Manor, Staffs and of late Countess Sondes; *S* grandfather, 1952; *m* 1969, Susan Mary (marr. diss. 1982), *o c* of Major Maurice Godley, Ide Hill, Sevenoaks, Kent, and of Mrs Glen Godley, Ascott, Shipston-on-Stour, Warwicks; two *s*. *Educ:* Eton. Served Royal Horse Guards (The Blues), 1960–63. Member: Royal Philharmonic Soc.; Royal Philharmonic Orchestra Assoc. OStJ. *Heir:* *s* Hon. Charles Robin de Bohun Devereux, *b* 11 Aug. 1975. *Address:* The Lyford Cay Club, PO Box N7776, Nassau, Bahamas. *Clubs:* House of Lords Yacht, Lloyd's Yacht.

HEREFORD, Bishop of, since 1973; **Rt. Rev. John (Richard Gordon) Eastaugh;** *b* 11 March 1920; *s* of Gordon and Jessie Eastaugh; *m* 1963, Bridget Nicola, *y d* of Sir Hugh Chance, CBE; two *s* one *d. Educ:* Leeds Univ.; Mirfield. Curate of All Saints, Poplar, 1944; Rector: of W. Hackney, 1951; of Poplar, 1956; Commissary of Bp of Polynesia, 1962; Vicar of Heston, 1963; Archdeacon of Middlesex, 1966–73; Vicar of St Peter, Eaton Square, 1967–74. Sub Prelate, Order of St John, 1978–. *Recreations:* theatre, music. *Address:* Bishop's House, The Palace, Hereford HR4 9BN.

HEREFORD, Dean of; *see* Haynes, Very Rev. Peter.

HEREFORD, Archdeacon of; *see* Woodhouse, Ven. A. H.

HEREN, Louis Philip, FRSL; journalist and author; *b* 6 Feb. 1919; *s* of William Heren and Beatrice (*née* Keller); *m* 1948, Patricia Cecilia O'Regan (*d* 1975); one *s* three *d. Educ:* St George's Sch., London. FRSL 1974. Army, 1939–46. Foreign Corresp. of The Times, 1947–70; India, 1947–48; Israel and Middle East, 1948–50; Southeast Asian Corresp., 1951–53; Germany, 1955–60; Chief Washington Corresp. and American Editor, 1960–70; Co-Dep. Editor (Foreign), 1970–73; Dep. Editor and Foreign Editor, 1973–78; Dep. Editor, 1978–81; Associate Editor, and Dir, Times Newspapers Hldgs Ltd, 1981. War Correspondent: Kashmir, 1947; Israel-Arab war, 1948; Korean war, 1950. Hannan Swaffer Award for Internat. Reporting, 1967; John F. Kennedy Memorial Award, 1968. *Publications:* New American Commonwealth, 1968; No Hail, No Farewell, 1970; Growing Up Poor in London, 1973; The Story of America, 1976; Growing Up on The Times, 1978; Alas, Alas for England, 1981; The Power of the Press?, 1985. *Address:* Fleet House, Vale of Health, NW3. *T:* 01–435 0902. *Club:* Garrick.

HERFORD, Geoffrey Vernon Brooke, CBE 1956 (OBE 1946); MSc; FIBiol; Director of Pest Infestation Research, Agricultural Research Council, 1940–68, retired; *b* 1905; *s* of late Henry J. R. Herford, Hampstead; *m* 1933, Evelyn Cicely (*d* 1969), *d* of W. G. Lambert. *Educ:* Gresham's School, Holt; Magdalen College, Oxford (BA); Minnesota University (MSc). *Address:* Rose Cottage, Wells Road, Eastcombe, Stroud, Glos.

HERIOT, Alexander John, MS, FRCS, FDS; Senior Surgeon, King's College Hospital, 1969–79; Postgraduate Regional Dean, South East Thames Regional Health Authority, 1973–79; *b* 28 May 1914; *s* of Robert Heriot; *m* 1940, Dr Christine Stacey (*d* 1958); two *s*; *m* 1959, Dr Cynthia Heymeson; one *s* one *d*. Major RAMC. *Address:* 261 Trinity Road, SW18.

HERITAGE, John Langdon; Circuit Administrator, South Eastern Circuit, since 1983; *b* 31 Dec. 1931; *s* of Frank and Elizabeth Heritage; *m* 1956, Elizabeth Faulkner, *d* of Charles and Ethel Robertson; two *s* one *d. Educ:* Berkhamsted Sch., Exeter Coll., Oxford (MA). Called to the Bar, Middle Temple, 1956. National Service, Royal Hampshire Regt and Royal W African Frontier Force. Legal Asst, Treasury Solicitor's Office, 1957, Sen. Legal Asst 1964; Asst Solicitor, Lord Chancellor's Dept, 1973; Sec., Royal Commn on Legal Services, 1976–79; Under Sec., 1983. *Publications:* articles in legal jls. *Recreation:* making things. *Address:* Hurdle House, 1 Chestnut Lane, Amersham, Bucks HP6 6EN. *T:* Amersham 5165. *Club:* United Oxford & Cambridge University.

HERITAGE, Robert, CBE 1980; RDI, DesRCA, FSIA; Professor, School of Furniture Design, Royal College of Art, 1974–85; *b* 2 Nov. 1927; *m* Dorothy; two *s* one *d. Educ:* Royal College of Art, RCA, 1950; freelance designer, 1961. RDI 1963. *Recreations:* tennis, fishing. *Address:* 12 Jay Mews, Kensington Gore, SW7 2EP. *Club:* Chelsea Arts.

HERITAGE, Rev. Canon Thomas Charles; Canon Residentiary of Portsmouth Cathedral, 1964–76, now Canon Emeritus; *b* 3 March 1908; *s* of Thomas and Sarah Ellen Heritage; *m* 1934, Frances Warrington (*d* 1979); twin *d. Educ:* The King's Sch., Chester; St Edmund Hall, Oxford. BA 1929; MA 1944; Diploma in Education (Oxford), 1930; ATCL 1931. Deacon, 1934; Priest, 1938. Curate of Christ Church, Chesterfield and Asst Master, Chesterfield Grammar Sch., 1934–38; Asst Master, Portsmouth Grammar Sch., 1938–64; Curate of St Mark, Portsmouth, 1938–40, St Christopher, Bournemouth, 1940–44; Chaplain of Portsmouth Cathedral, 1945–64. Hon. Canon, 1958–64. Examining Chaplain to the Bishop of Portsmouth, 1965–74. Warden, Portsmouth Diocesan Readers' Assoc., 1966–76. *Publications:* A New Testament Lectionary for Schools, 1943; The Early Christians in Britain (with B. E. Dodd), 1966. *Recreations:* music, the theatre, reading, travel. *Address:* 117 The Close, Salisbury, Wilts SP1 2EY. *T:* Salisbury 29104.

HERLIE, Eileen; actress; *b* 8 March 1920; *d* of Patrick Herlihy (Irish) and Isobel Cowden (Scottish); *m* 1st, 1942, Philip Barrett; 2nd, 1951, Witold Kuncewicz. *Educ:* Shawlands Academy, Glasgow. Varied repertoire with own company, 1942–44; Old Vic, Liverpool, 1944–45; Lyric Theatre, Hammersmith, 1945–46; Andromache in Trojan Women, Alcestis in Thracian Horses, Queen in Eagle has Two Heads, 1946–47; Gertrude in Hamlet (film), 1948; Medea, 1949; Angel with the Trumpet (film), 1949; Paula in The Second Mrs Tanqueray, Haymarket, 1950–51; Helen D'Oyly Carte in Gilbert and Sullivan (film), 1952; Mother in Isn't Life Wonderful? (film), 1952; John Gielgud Season, 1953: Mrs Marwood in The Way of the World; Belvidera in Venice Preserv'd; Irene in Sense of Guilt, 1953; Mrs Molloy in The Matchmaker, 1954; She Didn't Say No! (film), 1958; acted in George Dillon (New York), 1958; Take Me Along (New York), 1959; All America (New York), 1963; The Queen in Hamlet (New York), 1964; Halfway up the Tree, 1967; Emperor Henry IV, NY, 1973; Crown Matrimonial, 1973; The Seagull (film). *Recreations:* riding, reading, music.

HERMAN, Josef, OBE 1980; painter; *b* 3 Jan. 1911; *m* 1955, Eleanor Ettlinger; one *s* (one *d* decd). *Educ:* Warsaw. First exhibition, Warsaw, 1932; left for Belgium, 1938; arrived in Britain, June 1940; lived in: Glasgow, 1940–43; Ystradgynlais (mining village, Wales), 1944–53. Exhibitions include: Glasgow, 1942; Edinburgh, 1942; London, 1943; Roland, Browse and Delbanco Gallery, 1946–; British Council; Arts Council; (retrospective) Whitechapel Art Gallery, 1956; (retrospective) Camden Arts Centre, 1980; contrib. to British Mining exhbn, Science Museum, 1983. Work in permanent collections: Arts Council; British Council; British Museum; National Museum, Cardiff; Contemporary Art Society; National Museum Bezalel, Jerusalem; National Gallery, Johannesburg; Tate Gallery, London; Victoria and Albert Museum, London; National Gallery, Melbourne; National Gallery, Ottawa; National Gallery, Wellington, etc. Gold Medal, Royal National Eisteddfod, Llanelly, 1962; Contemporary Art Society prize, 1952 and 1953; prize, John Moore Exhibition, 1956; Trust House Award, 1962. *Publication:* Related Twilights (autobiog.), 1975. *Address:* 120 Edith Road, W14.

HERMANN, Alexander Henry Baxter; HM Diplomatic Service, retired; *b* 28 Dec. 1917; *m* 1944, Eudoksia Eugenia Domnina; one *d.* Joined Foreign Service, 1939; served 1942–55; Peking, Ahwaz, Chengtu, Chungking, Shanghai, Quito, Panama, Tamsui; Foreign Office, 1956; Commercial Counsellor and Consul-General, Rangoon, 1957–61; HM Consul-General at Marseilles, also to Monaco, 1961–65; Diplomatic Service Inspector, 1965–66; Counsellor, Hong Kong Affairs, Washington, 1967–70, 1974–77; Consul-General, Osaka, 1971–73. *Address:* 6 Church Farm Lane, Sidlesham, Sussex.

HERMON, Sir John (Charles), Kt 1982; OBE 1975; Chief Constable, Royal Ulster Constabulary, since 1980; *b* 23 Nov. 1928; *s* of late William Rowan Hermon and Agnes Hermon; *m* 1954, Jean Webb; one *s* one *d. Educ:* Larne Grammar Sch. Accountancy training and business, 1946–50; joined RUC, 1950. CStJ 1984. *Recreations:* boating, reading, walking. *Address:* Brooklyn, Knock Road, Belfast, N Ireland BT5 6LE. *T:* Belfast 652062. *Clubs:* Garrick, Royal Commonwealth Society; Royal Ulster Yacht (Bangor, Co. Down).

HERMON, Peter Michael Robert; Informations Systems Director, Harris Queensway PLC, since 1986; *b* 13 Nov. 1928; British; *m* 1954, Norma Stuart Brealey; two *s* two *d. Educ:* Nottingham High Sch.; St John's and Merton Colls, Oxford. 1st cl. hons Maths Oxon. Leo Computers Ltd, 1955–59; Manager, Management and Computer Divs, Dunlop Co., 1959–65; Information Handling Dir, BOAC, 1965–68; Management Services Dir, BOAC, and Mem. Bd of Management, 1968–72; Mem. of Board, BOAC, 1972; British Airways: Gp Management Services Dir, 1972–78; Board Mem., 1978–83; Management Services Dir, 1978–82; Man. Dir, European Services Div., 1982–83. Man. Dir, Tandem Computers Ltd, 1983–84; Dir, Tandem UK, 1983–85; Head of Systems and Communications, Lloyd's of London, 1984–86. Mem. Bd of Dirs, Internat. Aeradio Ltd, 1966–83, Chm., 1982–83; Chm., Internat. Aeradio (Caribbean) Ltd, 1967–83; Mem. Bd, SITA, 1972–83, Chm., 1981–83. *Recreations:* hill walking, music, cats. *Address:* White Flints, Quentin Way, Wentworth, Virginia Water, Surrey.

HERMON-HODGE, family name of **Baron Wyfold.**

HERN, Major William Richard, (Dick), CVO 1980; racehorse trainer; *b* Holford, Somerset, 20 Jan. 1921. Served War of 1939–45, North Irish Horse. Asst Trainer to Major M. B. Pope, MC, 1952–57; licence to train under Jockey Club rules, 1957–; leading trainer, 1962, 1972, 1980, 1983. Races won include: Derby, 1979, 1980 (Troy, Henbit); 2,000 Guineas, 1971 (Brigadier Gerard); 1,000 Guineas, 1974 (Highclere); St Leger, 1962, 1965, 1974, 1977, 1981, 1983 (Hethersett, Provoke, Bustino, Dunfermline, Cut Above, Sun Princess); Epsom Oaks, 1977, 1980, 1983 (Dunfermline, Bireme, Sun Princess); King George VI and Queen Elizabeth Diamond Stakes, 1972, 1979, 1980, 1985 (Brigadier Gerard, Troy, Ela-Mana-Mou, Petoski); Champion Stakes, 1971, 1972 (Brigadier Gerard); Eclipse Stakes, 1972, 1980 (Brigadier Gerard, Ela-Mana-Mou); Coronation Cup, 1974, 1975 (Buoy, Bustino). Leading Trainer, Flat Seasons, 1962, 1972, 1980, 1983. *Address:* West Ilsley Stables, West Ilsley, Newbury, Berks RG16 0AE. *T:* (office) East Ilsley 219; (home) East Ilsley 251.

HERNIMAN, Ven. Ronald George; Archdeacon of Barnstaple since 1970; *b* 18 April 1923; *s* of George Egerton and Rose Herniman; *m* 1949, Grace Jordan-Jones; one *s* two *d. Educ:* Geneva; Bideford, Devon. Served RAF, 1941–46. Birkbeck Coll., London Univ., 1948–51 (BA); Oak Hill Theological Coll., 1951–53; Tutor, Oak Hill Coll., 1953–54; Asst Curate, Christ Church, Cockfosters, 1954–56; Dir of Philosophical Studies, Oak Hill, 1956–61; Rector of Exe Valley Group of Churches (Washfield, Stoodleigh, Withleigh, Calverleigh Oakford, Morebath, Rackenford, Loxbeare and Templeton), 1961–72; Rector of Shirwell with Loxhore, 1972–82. *Recreations:* sailing; making and mending things. *Address:* Stage Cross, Whitemoor Hill, Bishop's Tawton, Barnstaple, N Devon EX32 0BE. *T:* Barnstaple 75475.

HERON, Sir Conrad (Frederick), KCB 1974 (CB 1969); OBE 1953; Permanent Secretary, Department of Employment, 1973–76; *b* 21 Feb. 1916; *s* of Richard Foster Heron and Ida Fredrika Heron; *m* 1948, Envye Linnéa Gustafsson; two *d. Educ:* South Shields High Sch.; Trinity Hall, Cambridge. Entered Ministry of Labour, 1938; Principal Private Secretary to Minister of Labour, 1953–56; Under-Secretary, Industrial Relations Dept, 1963–64 and 1965–68, Overseas Dept, 1964–65; Dep. Under-Sec. of State, Dept of Employment, 1968–71; Dep. Chm., Commn on Industrial Relations, 1971–72; Second Permanent Sec., Dept of Employment, 1973. *Address:* Old Orchards, West Lydford, Somerton, Somerset. *T:* Wheathill 387.

HERON, Patrick, CBE 1977; painter; *b* 30 Jan. 1920; *e s* of late T. M. and Eulalie Heron; *m* 1945, Delia Reiss (*d* 1979); two *d. Educ:* St Ives, Cornwall; Welwyn Garden City; St Georges, Harpenden; Slade School. Art criticism in: New English Weekly, 1945–47; New Statesman and Nation, 1947–50 (Art Critic); London correspondent, Arts (NY), 1955–58. John Power Lectr, Sydney Univ., 1973; Doty Prof., Univ. of Texas at Austin, 1978. Trustee, Tate Gall., 1980–. One-man exhibitions: Redfern Gallery, London, 1947, 1948, 1950, 1951, 1954, 1956 and 1958; Waddington Galleries, London, 1959, 1960, 1963, 1964, 1965, 1967, 1968, 1970 (canvases), 1970 (prints), 1973, 1975, 1977, 1979; Rutland Gallery, London, 1975; Waddington Fine Arts, Montreal, 1970; Bertha Schaefer Gallery, NY, 1960, 1962 and 1965; Galerie Charles Lienhard, Zurich, 1963; Traverse Theatre Gallery, Edinburgh, 1965; São Paulo Bienal VIII, 1965 (Silver Medal) (exhibn toured S Amer., 1966); Harrogate Festival, 1970; Rudy Komon Gall., Sydney, 1970; Whitechapel Gallery, 1972; Bonython Art Gall., Sydney, 1973; Galerie le Balcon des Arts, Paris, 1977; Retrospective exhibitions: Wakefield City Art Gallery, Leeds, Hull, Nottingham, 1952; Richard Demarco Gallery, Edinburgh, 1967; Museum of Modern Art, Oxford, 1968; Kunstnernes Hus, Oslo, 1967; Univ. of Texas at Austin Art Mus., 1978 (69 works); Oriel Gallery, Cardiff, 1979; Barbican, 1985. Twelve paintings shown at São Paulo Bienal II, Brazil, 1953–54. Carnegie International, Pittsburgh, 1961; British Art Today, San Francisco, Dallas, Santa Barbara, 1962–63; Painting and Sculpture of a Decade, 1954–64, Tate Gallery, 1964; British Painting and Sculpture, 1960–70, National Gallery of Art, Washington DC; British Painting 1952–1977, RA, 1977; Color en la Pintura Británica (tour of S Amer.), 1977–78. Exhibited in group and British Council exhibitions in many countries; works owned by: Tate Gallery; Arts Council; British Council; V&A Museum; British Museum; Gulbenkian Foundation; Leeds City Art Gallery; Stuyvesant Foundation; National Portrait Gallery; Broadcasting House; Warwick Univ.; Wakefield City Art Gallery; Manchester City Art Gallery; Contemporary Art Society; Oldham Art Gallery; CEMA, N Ireland; Abbot Hall Art Gallery, Kendal; The Art Gallery, Aberdeen; National Gallery of Wales, Cardiff; Toronto Art Gallery; Montreal Museum of Fine Art; Vancouver Art Gallery; Toledo Museum of Art, Ohio; Smith College Museum of Art, Mass; Brooklyn Museum, NY; Albright-Knox Art Gallery, Buffalo, NY; Univ. of Michigan Museum of Art; Univ. of Texas at Austin Art Museum; Museum of Art, Carnegie Inst., Pittsburgh; Stuyvesant Foundn, Holland; Boymans Museum, Rotterdam; Musée d'Art Contemporain, Montreal; Western Australian Art Gallery, Perth; Pembroke and Nuffield Colleges, Oxford; Stirling Univ.; Bristol City Art Gall.; Exeter Art Gallery; Exeter Univ. (Cornwall House); Plymouth City Art Gallery; Power Collection, Sydney; London Art Gall., London, Ont.; Hatton Art Gall., Newcastle Univ.; Southampton Art Gall.; Norwich Art Gall; also represented in Fitzwilliam Museum, Cambridge, and in municipal collections at Glasgow, Reading and Sheffield. Hon. DLitt Exeter, 1982. Awarded Grand Prize by international jury, John Moores' 2nd Liverpool Exhibition, 1959. *Publications:* Vlaminck: Paintings, 1900–1945, 1947; The Changing Forms of Art, 1955; Ivon Hitchens, 1955; Braque, 1958; The Shape of Colour, 1973; Paintings by Patrick Heron 1965–1977, 1978; The Colour of Colour, 1978; contrib. The Guardian, Studio International, etc. *Address:* Eagles Nest, Zennor, near St Ives, Cornwall. *T:* Penzance 796921; 12 Editha Mansions, Edith Grove, SW10. *T:* 01–352 1787.

HERON, Raymond, CBE 1984; retired; Deputy Director, Propellants, Explosives and Rocket Motor Establishment, Ministry of Defence (Procurement Executive), 1977–84; *b* 10 April 1924; *s* of Lewis and Doris Heron; *m* 1948, Elizabeth MacGathan; one *s* one *d. Educ:* Heath Grammar Sch., Halifax; Queen's Coll., Oxford (BA Physics). Shell Refining and Marketing Co., 1944–47; RN, Instructor Branch, 1947–52; Rocket Propulsion Estabt, Min. of Supply (later Min. of Technology), 1952–67; Cabinet Office, 1967; Asst Dir, Min. of Technology, 1967–73; Dep. Dir, Explosives Research and Development Estabt, MoD, 1973; Special Asst to Sec. (Procurement Exec.), MoD, 1973–74; Head of Rocket Motor Exec. and Dep. Dir/2, Rocket Propulsion Estabt, MoD (PE), 1974–76. *Publications:* articles in scientific and technical jls. *Recreations:* music, hill walking, golf. *Address:* 9 Grange Gardens, Wendover, Aylesbury, Bucks HP22 6HB. *T:* Wendover 622921. *Club:* Ashridge Golf.

HERON, Robert, MA; Director, Duke of Edinburgh's Award Scheme, since 1978; *b* 12 Oct. 1927; *s* of James Riddick Heron and Sophie Leathem; *m* 1953, Patricia Mary Pennell; two *s* one *d. Educ:* King Edward's Sch., Birmingham; St Catharine's Coll., Cambridge. Housemaster: Strathallan, Perthshire, 1952–59; Christ Coll., Brecon, 1959–62; Headmaster, King James I Sch., IOW, 1962–66. Head of Educational Broadcasting, ATV Network Ltd, 1966–69, responsible for production of TV programme series in the scis, langs, soc. documentary, leisure interests, music, drama; Deleg., EBU study gps on educnl broadcasting, 1967–69; Programme Dir, The Electronic Video Recording Partnership (CBS Inc. USA/ICI/Ciba-Geigy UK), 1970–77; Managing Dir, EVR Ltd, 1974–77, and of EVR Enterprises Ltd, 1975–77. Freeman, City of London, 1981. Formerly 6/7th Bn, The Black Watch (RHR) TA. *Recreations:* shooting, hill walking, sport. *Address:* The Oast, Ingledon Park, Tenderden, Kent. *Clubs:* Rugby; ISC (Cowes); Achilles; Hawks (Cambridge).

HERON-MAXWELL, Sir Nigel (Mellor), 10th Bt *cr* 1683; *b* 30 Jan. 1944; *s* of Sir Patrick Ivor Heron-Maxwell, 9th Bt and of D. Geraldine E., *yr d* of late Claud Paget Mellor; *S* father, 1982; *m* 1972, Mary Elizabeth Angela, *o d* of W. Ewing, Co. Donegal; one *s* one *d. Educ:* Milton Abbey. *Heir: s* David Mellor Heron-Maxwell, *b* 22 May 1975. *Address:* 105 Codicote Road, Welwyn, Herts.

HERRIDGE, Geoffrey Howard, CMG 1962; Chairman, Iraq Petroleum Co. Ltd and Associated Companies, 1965–70, retired (Managing Director, 1957–63; Deputy Chairman, 1963–65); *b* 22 Feb. 1904; 3rd *s* of late Edward Herridge, Eckington, Worcestershire; *m* 1935, Dorothy Elvira Tod; two *s* two *d. Educ:* Crypt Sch., Gloucester; St John's Coll., Cambridge. Joined Turkish Petroleum Co. Ltd (later Iraq Petroleum Co. Ltd), Iraq, 1926; served in Iraq, Jordan, Palestine, 1926–47; General Manager in the Middle East, Iraq Petroleum Co. and Associated Companies, 1947–51; Executive Director, 1953–57; Member of London Cttee, Ottoman Bank, 1964–79. Chairman, Petroleum Industry Training Board, 1967–70. *Recreation:* sailing. *Address:* Flint, Sidlesham Common, Chichester, West Sussex. *T:* Sidlesham 357. *Club:* Oriental.

HERRIES OF TERREGLES, Lady (14th in line, of the Lordship *cr* 1490); **Anne Elizabeth Fitzalan-Howard;** *b* 12 June 1938; *e d* of 16th Duke of Norfolk, EM, KG, PC, GCVO, GBE, TD, and of Lavinia Duchess of Norfolk, *qv*; *S* to lordship upon death of father, 1975; *m* 1985, Colin Cowdrey, *qv.* Racehorse trainer. *Recreations:* riding, golf, breeding spaniels. *Heir: sister* Lady Mary Katharine Fitzalan-Howard, CVO 1982, *b* 14 Aug. 1940. *Address:* Angmering Park, Littlehampton, West Sussex.

HERRIES, Sir Michael Alexander Robert Young-, Kt 1975; OBE 1968; MC 1945; DL; Chairman: The Royal Bank of Scotland plc, since 1976 (Director since 1972; Vice-Chairman, 1974–75; Deputy Chairman, 1975–76); The Royal Bank of Scotland Group plc (formerly National and Commercial Banking Group Ltd), since 1978 (Director since 1976); Scottish Mortgage and Trust PLC, since 1984 (Director, since 1975); Director: Matheson & Co. Ltd (Chairman, 1971–75); Jardine Matheson (Holdings) Ltd; Scottish Widows' Fund and Life Assurance Society, since 1974 (Chairman, 1981–84, Deputy Chairman, 1979–81 and 1984–85); *b* 28 Feb. 1923; *s* of Lt-Col William Dobree Young-Herries and Ruth Mary (*née* Thrupp); *m* 1949, Elizabeth Hilary Russell (*née* Smith); two *s* one *d. Educ:* Eton; Trinity Coll., Cambridge (MA). Served KOSB, 1942–47; Temp. Captain, Actg Maj., Europe and ME; Adjt 5th (Dumfries and Galloway) Battalion and 1st Battalion TARO, 1949. Joined Jardine Matheson & Co. Ltd, 1948; served in Hong Kong, Japan and Singapore; Director, 1959; Managing Director, 1962; Chm. and Man. Dir, 1963–70; Chairman: Jardine Japan Investment Trust Ltd, 1972–76; Crossfriars Trust Ltd, 1972–76; Dep. Chm., Williams & Glyn's Bank, 1978–85. Formerly Mem., Exec. Legislative Council, Hong Kong; Chm., Hong Kong Univ. and Polytechnics Grant Cttee, 1965–73. Former Mem. Council, London Chamber of Commerce and Industry, Hon. Mem., 1980–; Chairman: Scottish Trust for the Physically Disabled, 1981–83; Scottish Disability Foundn, 1982–; Mem. Council, Missions to Seamen. Mem., Royal Company of Archers (Queen's Body Guard for Scotland), 1973–. DL Dumfries and Galloway, 1983. Hon. LLD: Chinese Univ. of Hong Kong, 1973; Univ. of Hong Kong, 1974. Hon. DLitt Heriot-Watt, 1984. *Recreations:* shooting, walking, swimming, tennis. *Address:* (office) The Royal Bank of Scotland plc, 42 St Andrew Square, Edinburgh EH2 2YE. *T:* 031–556 8555; Spottes, Castle Douglas, Stewartry of Kirkcudbright. *T:* Haugh of Urr 202; 30 Heriot Row, Edinburgh. *T:* 031–226 2711; Flat 14, Lochmore House, Cundy Street, SW1W 9JX. *T:* 01–730 1119. *Clubs:* Caledonian, Farmers', City of London; New (Edinburgh).

HERRING, Cyril Alfred; Chairman and Managing Director, Southern Airways Group, since 1978; *b* Dulwich, 17 Jan. 1915; *s* of Alfred James Herring and Minnie Herring (*née* Padfield); *m* 1939, Helen (*née* Warnes); three *s. Educ:* Alleyn's Sch.; London School of Economics. BSc(Econ); FCMA; JDipMA; IPFA; FCIT. Chief Accountant, Straight Corporation Ltd, 1936–46; joined BEA, 1946; Chief Accountant, 1951–57; Personnel Director, 1957–65; Financial Director, 1965–71; Executive Board Member, 1971–74; Mem., BAB, 1972–78; Chief Executive, British Airways Regional Div., 1972–74; Finance Dir, 1975–78; Chm. and Man. Dir, British Air Services Ltd, 1969–76; Chairman: Northeast Airlines Ltd, 1969–76; Cambrian Airways Ltd, 1973–76; London Rail Adv. Cttee, 1976–80; CIPFA Public Corporations Finance Group, 1976–78. Member Council: Chartered Inst. of Transport, 1971–74; Inst. of Cost and Management Accountants, 1967–77 (Vice-Pres., 1971–73, Pres., 1973–74); CBI, 1975–78 (Mem. Financial Policy Cttee, 1975–78, Finance and General Purposes Cttee, 1977–78). Freeman, City of London; Liveryman, Guild of Air Pilots and Air Navigators. *Recreations:* flying, motoring, boating. *Address:* Cuddenbeake, St Germans, Cornwall. *Clubs:* Reform, Royal Aero.

HERRINGTON, Air Vice-Marshal Walter John, CB 1982; RAF retd; Aviation Adviser, International Military Services, since 1982; *b* 18 May 1928; *s* of Major H. Herrington, MBE, MM and Daisy Restal Gardiner; *m* 1958, Joyce Maureen Cherryman; two *s. Educ:* Peter Symonds, Winchester; Woking Grammar Sch.; RAF Coll., Cranwell. FBIM. Commnd RAF, 1949, Pilot; 1950–69: Long Range Transp. Sqdns; ADC to C-in-C Bomber Comd; Reconnaissance Sqdns; RAF Staff Coll.; Exchange Officer, USAF Acad., Colo; Comd 100 Sqdn; Jt Services Staff Coll.; Air Sec.'s Dept; Stn Comdr RAF Honnington, 1969–71; Ops Dept, MoD, 1971–73; RCDS (student) 1974; Defence Attaché, Paris, 1975–77. Hon. ADC to the Queen, 1971–74; Senior RAF Mem., Directing Staff, RCDS, 1978–80; Dir of Service Intelligence, 1980–82. Mem. Council, TA&VRA, 1984–. Mem., European Security Study, 1982–83. *Publications:* text books for courses on air power for USAF Academy. *Recreations:* reading, international affairs, sport. *Address:* c/o Lloyds Bank, Obelisk Way, Camberley, Surrey. *Club:* Royal Air Force.

HERRIOT, James; *see* Wight, J. A.

HERROD, Donald, QC 1972; **His Honour Judge Herrod;** a Circuit Judge, since 1978; *b* 7 Aug. 1930; *o s* of Wilfred and Phyllis Herrod, Doncaster; *m* 1959, Kathleen Elaine Merrington, MB, ChB; two *d. Educ:* grammar schs, Doncaster and Leeds. Called to Bar, 1956. A Recorder of the Crown Court, 1972–78. Member: Parole Bd, 1978–81; Judicial Studies Bd, 1982–86. *Recreations:* lawn tennis, golf. *Address:* The Crown Court, 1 Oxford Row, Leeds LS1 3BE.

HERRON, Very Rev. Andrew; Clerk to the Presbytery of Glasgow, 1959–81; *b* 29 Sept. 1909; *s* of John Todd Herron and Mary Skinner Hunter; *m* 1935, Joanna Fraser Neill; four *d. Educ:* Glasgow Univ. (MA, BD, LLB). ATCL 1930. Minister: at Linwood, 1936–40, at Houston and Killellan, 1940–59; Clerk to the Presbytery of Paisley, 1953–59; Moderator of General Assembly of Church of Scotland, 1971–72. Convener: Dept of Publicity and Publications, 1959–68; Gen. Admin Cttee; Business Cttee, Gen. Assembly, 1972–76, 1978; Gen. Trustee, Church of Scotland. Hon. DD St Andrews, 1975; Hon. LLD Strathclyde, 1983. Editor, Church of Scotland Year-Book, 1961–. *Publications:* Record Apart, 1974; Guide to the General Assembly of the Church of Scotland, 1976; Guide to Congregational Affairs, 1978; Guide to Presbytery, 1983; Kirk by Divine Right (Baird lectures), 1985. *Address:* 36 Darnley Road, Glasgow G41 4NE. *T:* 041–423 6422. *Club:* Caledonian (Edinburgh).

HERRON, Henry, CBE 1975; Procurator-Fiscal, Glasgow, 1965–76, retired; Deputy Chairman of Traffic Commissioners and Licensing Authority for Scottish Traffic Area, 1978–81; *b* 6 May 1911; *s* of William and Jessie Herron; *m* 1942, Dr Christina Aitkenhead Crawford; one *s* two *d. Educ:* Hamilton Academy; Glasgow Univ. (MA, LLB). Solicitor. Depute Procurator-Fiscal, Glasgow, 1946; Procurator-Fiscal, Banff, 1946–51; Asst Procurator-Fiscal, Glasgow, 1951–55; Procurator-Fiscal, Paisley, 1955–65. *Recreations:* gardening, jurisprudence, criminology. *Address:* 51 Craw Road, Paisley. *T:* 041–889 3091.

HERRON, Shaun; novelist; *m*; two *s* two *d*. Northern Irish. Ordained to Ministry of Scottish Congregational Churches, 1940; Minister, United Church of Canada, 1958. Editor, British Weekly, 1950–58; Correspondent in USA, 1960–64, Sen. Leader Writer, 1964–76, Winnipeg Free Press. Has held various lectureships in US and Canada. Finds entries in reference books too dreary to read. *Publications: novels:* Miro, 1968; The Hound and The Fox and The Harper, 1970; Through the Dark and Hairy Wood, 1972; The Whore-Mother, 1973; The Bird in Last Year's Nest, 1974; The Mac Donnell, 1976; Aladale, 1978; The Blacksmith's Daughter, 1987. *Recreations:* travelling, writing. *Address:* c/o A. P. Watt Ltd, 26/28 Bedford Row, WC1R 4HL.

HERSCHELL, family name of **Baron Herschell.**

HERSCHELL, 3rd Baron, *cr* 1886; **Rognvald Richard Farrer Herschell;** late Captain Coldstream Guards; *b* 13 Sept. 1923; *o s* of 2nd Baron and Vera (*d* 1961), *d* of Sir Arthur Nicolson, 10th Bt, of that Ilk and Lasswade; *S* father, 1929; *m* 1948, Heather, *d* of 8th Earl of Dartmouth, CVO, DSO; one *d. Educ:* Eton. Page of Honour to the King, 1935–40. *Heir:* none. *Address:* Westfield House, Ardington, Wantage, Oxon. *T:* Abingdon 833224.

HERSEY, David Kenneth; lighting designer; founder Chairman, DHA Lighting, since 1972; *b* 30 Nov. 1939; *s* of Ella Morgan Decker and C. Kenneth Hersey; *m* Demetra Maraslis; one *s* two *d. Educ:* Oberlin Coll., Ohio. Left NY for London, 1968; lighting designer for theatre, opera and ballet cos, incl. Royal Opera House, ENO, Glyndebourne, Ballet Rambert, London Contemporary Dance, Scottish Ballet; lighting consultant to Nat. Theatre, 1974–84; many productions for RSC. Chm., Assoc. of Lighting Designers, 1984–. *Designs include:* Evita, 1978 (Tony award, 1980); Nicholas Nickleby, 1980; Cats, 1981 (Tony and Drama Desk awards, 1983); Song and Dance, 1982; Guys and Dolls, 1982; Starlight Express, 1984; Albert Herring, 1985; Les Misérables, 1985. *Recreation:* sailing. *Address:* 29 Rotherwick Road, Hampstead Garden Suburb, NW11 7DG. *T:* 01–458 9022.

HERSEY, John; writer; *b* 17 June 1914; *s* of Roscoe M. and Grace B. Hersey; *m* 1st, 1940, Frances Ann Cannon (marr. diss. 1958); three *s* one *d*; 2nd, 1958, Barbara Day Kaufman; one *d. Educ:* Yale Univ.; Clare Coll., Cambridge. Secretary to Sinclair Lewis, 1937; Editor Time, 1937–42; War and Foreign Correspondent, Time, Life, New Yorker, 1942–46. Mem. Council, Authors' League of America, 1946–70 (Vice-Pres., 1948–55, Pres., 1975–80). Fellow, Berkeley Coll., Yale Univ., 1950–65; Master, Pierson Coll., Yale Univ., 1965–70, Fellow, 1965–. Writer in Residence, Amer. Acad. in Rome, 1970–71. Lectr, Yale Univ., 1971–75, Vis. Prof., 1975–76, Adjunct Prof., 1976–84, now Emeritus; Lectr, Salzburg Seminars in Amer. Studies, 1975; Vis. Prof., MIT, 1975. Chm., Connecticut Cttee for the Gifted, 1954–57; Member: Amer. Acad. Arts and Letters, 1953 (Sec., 1962–76; Chancellor, 1981–84); Nat. Inst. Arts and Letters, 1950; Amer. Acad. of Arts and Scis, 1978; Council, Authors' Guild, 1946– (Chm., Contract Cttee, 1963–); Yale Univ. Council cttees on the Humanities, 1951–56, and on Yale Coll., 1959–69 (Chm., 1964–69) and 1981–; Vis. Cttee, Harvard Grad. Sch. of Educn, 1960–65; Vis. Cttee, Loeb Drama Center, 1980–; Nat. Citizens' Commn for the Public Schs, 1954–56; Bd of Trustees, Putney Sch., 1953–56; Trustee: Nat. Citizens' Council for the Public Schs, 1956–58; Nat. Cttee for the Support of the Public Schs, 1962–68. Delegate: to White House Conf. on Educn, 1955; to PEN Congress, Tokyo, 1958. Comr, Nat. Commn on New Technological Uses of Copyrighted Works, 1975–78. Hon. Fellow, Clare Coll., Cambridge, 1967. Hon. MA Yale Univ., 1947; Hon. LLD: Washington and Jefferson Coll., 1946; Univ. of New Haven, 1975; Hon. LHD: New Sch. for Social Research, 1950; Syracuse Univ., 1983; Hon. DHL Dropsie Coll., 1950; Hon. LittD: Wesleyan Univ., 1957; Bridgeport Univ., 1959; Clarkson Coll. of Technology, 1972; Yale Univ., 1984; Monmouth Coll., 1985. Pulitzer Prize for Fiction, 1945; Sidney Hillman Foundn Award, 1951; Howland Medal, Yale Univ., 1952. *Publications:* Men on Bataan, 1942; Into the Valley, 1943; A Bell for Adano, 1944; Hiroshima, 1946; The Wall, 1950; The Marmot Drive, 1953; A Single Pebble, 1956; The War Lover, 1959; The Child Buyer, 1960; Here to Stay, 1962; White Lotus, 1965; Too Far to Walk, 1966; Under the Eye of the Storm, 1967; The Algiers Motel Incident, 1968; The Conspiracy, 1972; The Writer's Craft, 1974; My Petition for More Space, 1974; The President, 1975; The Walnut Door, 1977; Aspects of the Presidency, 1980; The Call, 1985.

HERSHEY, Dr Alfred Day; Director, Genetics Research Unit, Carnegie Institution of Washington, 1962–74, retired; *b* 4 Dec. 1908; *s* of Robert D. Hershey and Alma (*née* Wilbur); *m* 1945, Harriet Davidson; one *s. Educ:* Michigan State Coll. (now Univ.). BS 1930; PhD 1934. Asst Bacteriologist, Washington Univ. Sch. of Medicine, St Louis Missouri, 1934–36; Instructor, 1936–38; Asst Prof., 1938–42; Assoc. Prof., 1942–50; Staff Mem., Dept of Genetics (now Genetics Research Unit), Carnegie Instn of Washington, 1950–. Albert Lasker Award, Amer. Public Health Assoc., 1958; Kimber Genetics Award, Nat. Acad. Sci., US, 1965. Hon. DSc, Chicago, 1967; Hon. Dr Med. Science, Michigan State, 1970. Nobel Prize for Physiology or Medicine (jtly), 1969. *Publications:* numerous articles in scientific jls or books. *Address:* RD Box 1640, Moores Hill Road, Syosset, NY 11791, USA. *T:* 516 692 6855.

HERTFORD, 8th Marquess of, *cr* 1793; **Hugh Edward Conway Seymour;** Baron Conway of Ragley, 1703; Baron Conway of Killultagh, 1712; Earl of Hertford, Viscount Beauchamp, 1750; Earl of Yarmouth, 1793; DL Warwick, 1959; formerly Lieutenant Grenadier Guards; *b* 29 March 1930; *s* of late Brig.-General Lord Henry Charles Seymour, DSO (2nd *s* of 6th Marquess) and Lady Helen Frances Grosvenor (*d* 1970), *d* of 1st Duke of Westminster; *S* uncle, 1940; *m* 1956, Comtesse Louise de Caraman Chimay, *o d* of late Lt-Col Prince Alphonse de Chimay, TD; one *s* three *d. Educ:* Eton. Chm., Hertford Public Relations Ltd, 1962–73. Chief interests are estate management (Diploma, Royal Agricultural Coll., Cirencester, 1956) and opening Ragley to the public. *Heir: s* Earl of Yarmouth, *qv. Address:* Ragley Hall, Alcester, Warwickshire. *T:* Alcester 762455/762090/762845. *Clubs:* White's, Pratt's, Turf.

HERTFORD, Bishop Suffragan of, since 1982; **Rt. Rev. Kenneth Harold Pillar;** *b* 10 Oct. 1924; *s* of Harold and Mary Pillar; *m* 1955, Margaret Elizabeth Davies; one *s* three *d. Educ:* Devonport High School; Queens' Coll., Cambridge (MA); Ridley Hall, Cambridge. Asst Curate, Childwall, Liverpool, 1950–53; Chaplain, Lee Abbey, Lynton, N Devon, 1953–57; Vicar: St Paul's, Beckenham, 1957–62; St Mary Bredin, Canterbury, 1962–65; Warden of Lee Abbey, Lynton, N Devon, 1965–70; Vicar of Waltham Abbey, Essex, 1970–82; RD of Epping Forest, 1976–82. *Recreation:* walking. *Address:* Hertford House, Abbey Mill Lane, St Albans, Herts AL3 4HE. *T:* St Albans 66420.

HERTFORDSHIRE, Bishop in, (RC); *see* O'Brien, Rt Rev. J. J.

HERVEY, family name of **Marquess of Bristol.**

HERVEY, Rear Adm. John Bethell, CB 1982; OBE 1970; independent naval consultant; *b* 14 May 1928; *s* of late Captain Maurice William Bethell Hervey, RN, and Mrs Joan Hervey (*née* Hanbury); *m* 1950, (Audrey) Elizabeth Mote; two *s* one *d. Educ:* Marlborough Coll., Wilts. Joined RN, 1946; specialised in submarines, 1950, nuclear submarines, 1968; command appointments: HMS Miner VI, 1956; HMS Aeneas, 1956–57; HMS Ambush, 1959–62; HMS Oracle, 1962–64; Sixth Submarine Div., 1964–66; HMS Cavalier, 1966–67; HMS Warspite, 1968–69; Second Submarine Sqdn, 1973–75; HMS Kent, 1975–76; staff appointments: Course Officer, Royal Naval Petty Officers Leadership Sch., 1957–59; Submarine Staff Officer to Canadian Maritime Comdr, Halifax, NS, 1964–66; Ops Officer to Flag Officer Submarines, 1970–71; Def. Op. Requirements Staff, 1971–73; Dep. Chief of Allied Staff to C-in-C Channel and C-in-C Eastern Atlantic (as Cdre), 1976–80; Comdr British Navy Staff, and British Naval Attaché, Washington, and UK Nat. Liaison Rep. to SACLANT, 1980–82, retired. Comdr 1964, Captain 1970, Rear Adm. 1980. Marketing Vice-Pres., Western Hemisphere, MEL, 1982–86. FBIM 1983. *Recreations:* walking, talking, reading. *Address:* c/o National Westminster Bank, 26 Haymarket, SW1Y 4ER. *Clubs:* Army and Navy, Royal Navy of 1765 and 1785.

HERVEY-BATHURST, Sir F.; *see* Bathurst.

HERWARTH von BITTENFELD, Hans Heinrich; Grand Cross (2nd Class), Order of Merit, Federal Republic of Germany, 1963; Hon. GCVO 1958; State Secretary, retired; *b* Berlin, 14 July 1904; *s* of Hans Richard Herwarth von Bittenfeld and Ilse Herwarth von Bittenfeld (*née* von Tiedemann); *m* 1935, Elisabeth Freiin von Redwitz; one *d. Educ:* Universities of Berlin, Breslau and Munich (Law and Nat. Econ.). Entered Auswärtiges Amt, Berlin, 1927; Attaché, Paris, 1930; Second Secretary and Personal Secretary to Ambassador, Moscow, 1931–39. Military Service, 1939–45. Oberregierungsrat, Regierungsdirektor, Bavarian State Chancellery, 1945–49; Ministerialdirigent and Chief of Protocol, Federal Government, 1950, Minister Plenipotentiary, 1952; German Ambassador to Court of St James's, 1955–61; State Secretary and Chief of German Federal Presidential Office, 1961–65; German Ambassador to Republic of Italy, 1965–69; Pres., Commn for Reform of German Diplomatic Service, 1969–71. Chm., Supervisory Council, Unilever, Germany, 1969–77. Chm., Venice Cttee, German Unesco Commn; Pres., Internat. Adv. Cttee for Venice. Pres., Goethe Institut, Munich, 1971–77. *Publication:* Against Two Evils: memoirs of a diplomat-soldier during the Third Reich, 1981. *Recreations:* ski-ing, antiques. *Address:* Schloss, 8643 Küps, Germany. *T:* 09264 7174.

HERZBERG, Charles Francis; Director: Industrial Planning, NEI International Ltd, since 1984; Northern Investors Co. Ltd, since 1984; *b* 26 Jan. 1924; *s* of Dr Franz Moritz Herzberg and Mrs Marie Louise Palache; *m* 1956, Ann Linette Hoare; one *s* two *d. Educ:* Fettes Coll., Edinburgh; Sidney Sussex Coll., Cambridge (MA). CEng, FIMechE, MIGasE. Alfred Herbert Ltd, 1947–51; Chief Engr and Dir, Hornflowa Ltd, Maryport, 1951–55; Chief Engr, Commercial Plastics Gp of Cos, and Dir, Commercial Plastics Engrg Co. at Wallsend on Tyne, North Shields, and Cramlington, Northumberland, 1955–66; Corporate Planning Dir, Appliance Div., United Gas Industries, and Works Dir, Robinson Willey Ltd, Liverpool, 1966–70; Man. Dir and Chief Exec., Churchill Gear Machines Ltd, Blaydon on Tyne, 1970–72; Regional Industrial Director, Dept of Industry, N Region, 1972–75; Dir of Corporate Devel, Clarke Chapman Ltd, 1975–77; Gp Industrial Planning Adviser, Northern Engineering Industries plc, 1977–84. *Recreation:* shooting.

Address: 3 Furzefield Road, Gosforth, Newcastle upon Tyne NE3 4EA. *T:* Tyneside 285 5202. *Club:* East India, Devonshire, Sports and Public Schools.

HERZBERG, Gerhard, CC (Canada), 1968; FRS 1951; FRSC 1939; Director, Division of Pure Physics, National Research Council of Canada, 1949–69, now Distinguished Research Scientist, National Research Council of Canada; *b* Hamburg, Germany, 25 Dec. 1904; *s* of late Albin Herzberg and Ella Herzberg; *m* 1929, Luise Herzberg, *née* Oettinger (*d* 1971); one *s* one *d*; *m* 1972, Monika Herzberg, *née* Tenthoff. *Educ:* Inst. of Technology, Darmstadt, Germany; Univ. of Göttingen, Germany; Univ. of Bristol, England. Lecturer, Darmstadt Inst. of Technology, 1930; Research Professor, Univ. of Saskatchewan, 1935; Prof. of Spectroscopy, Yerkes Observatory, Univ. of Chicago, 1945; Principal Research Officer, National Research Council of Canada, 1948. University Medal, Univ. of Liège, Belgium, 1950; President, RSC, 1966 (Henry Marshall Tory Medal, 1953). Joy Kissen Mookerjee Gold Medal of Indian Association for Cultivation of Science, 1954 (awarded 1957). Gold Medal of Canadian Association Phys., 1957; Bakerian Lecture, Royal Society, 1960; Faraday Lecture and Medal, Chem. Soc., 1970; Nobel Prize for Chemistry, 1971; Royal Medal, Royal Soc., 1971. Hon. Fellow: Indian Academy of Science, 1954; Indian Physical Society, 1957; Chemical Society of London, 1968. Hon. Member: Hungarian Academy of Sciences, 1964; Optical Society of America, 1968; Royal Irish Acad., 1970; Japan Acad., 1976; Chem. Soc. of Japan, 1978; Hon. Foreign Member American Academy Arts and Sciences, 1965; Foreign Associate, National Academy of Sciences, US, 1968; Foreign Mem. (Physics), Royal Swedish Acad. of Sciences, 1981. President, Canadian Association of Physicists, 1956; Vice-Pres., International Union of Pure and Applied Physics, 1957–63. Holds numerous hon. degrees, including Hon. ScD Cantab, 1972. *Publications:* Atomic Spectra and Atomic Structure, 1st edition (USA) 1937, 2nd edition (USA) 1944; Molecular Spectra and Molecular Structure: I, Spectra of Diatomic Molecules, 1st edition (USA), 1939, 2nd edition (USA), 1950; II, Infra-red and Raman Spectra of Polyatomic Molecules (USA), 1945; III, Electronic Spectra and Electronic Structure of Polyatomic Molecules (USA), 1966; IV, (with K. P. Huber) Constants of Diatomic Molecules (USA), 1979; The Spectra and Structures of Simple Free Radicals: an introduction to Molecular Spectroscopy (USA), 1971; original research on atomic and molecular spectra published in various scientific journals. *Address:* National Research Council, Ottawa, Ontario K1A 0R6, Canada. *T:* 99–00917; 190 Lakeway Drive, Rockcliffe Park, Ottawa, Ontario K1L 5B3, Canada. *T:* 746–4126.

HERZIG, Christopher; Director, External Relations, International Atomic Energy Agency, Vienna, since 1981; *b* 24 Oct. 1926; *s* of late L. A. Herzig and late Mrs Elizabeth Herzig (*née* Hallas); *m* 1952, Rachel Katharine Buxton; four *s* one *d*. *Educ:* Christ's Hosp.; Selwyn Coll., Cambridge (MA). Asst Principal, Min. of Fuel and Power, 1951–56; Principal, Min. of Supply, 1956–58; Min. of Aviation, 1959–61; Private Sec. to Lord President of the Council, 1961–64; Private Sec. to Minister of Technology, 1964–66; Asst Sec., Min. of Technology, 1966–70; Dept of Trade and Industry, 1970–71, Under-Sec., DTI, 1972–73; Under Sec., Dept of Energy, 1974–81. UK Governor, IAEA, 1972–78. *Address:* 13a The Causeway, Horsham, West Sussex RH12 1HE. *T:* Horsham 65239; Wasagasse 4/8, 1090 Vienna.

HERZOG, Chaim, Hon. KBE 1970; President of Israel, since 1983; *b* Ireland, 17 Sept. 1918; *s* of Rabbi Isaac Halevy Herzog, first Chief Rabbi of Israel and formerly of Ireland, and Sarah Herzog (*née* Hillman); *m* 1947, Aura (*née* Ambache); three *s* one *d*. *Educ:* Univ. of London (LLB). Called to the Bar, Lincoln's Inn, 1942; Advocate, Israel Bar. Immigrated to Palestine, 1935; Army service: Jerusalem, 1936–38; British Army, war of 1939–45; RMC; served 2nd Army, NW Europe; Israel Defence Forces: Defence Attaché, USA, 1950–54; Dir of Mil. Intell., 1948–50 and 1959–62; Comdr, Jerusalem Brigade, 1954–57; Chief of Staff, Southern Comd, 1957–59; retired 1962 (Maj.-Gen.); 1st Mil. Governor, W Bank and Jerusalem, 1967. Ambassador and Perm. Rep. to UN, 1975–78; Mem. Tenth Knesset, 1981–83. Director, 1962–83: Israel Aircraft Industries; Industrial Development Bank of Israel; Israel Discount Bank; Man. Dir, G. U. S. Industries, 1962–72; Senior Partner, Herzog, Fox and Neeman, 1972–83. President: Variety Club of Israel, 1967–72; ORT Israel, 1968–83; World ORT Union, 1980–83. Hon. degrees from home and overseas univs. *Publications:* Israel's Finest Hour, 1967; Days of Awe, 1973; (ed) Judaism, Law and Ethics, 1974; The War of Atonement, 1975; Who Stands Accused?, 1978; (with Mordechai Gichon) Battles of the Bible, 1978; The Arab–Israeli Wars, 1982. *Recreations:* sailing, flying light aircraft, golf. *Address:* Office of the President, Jerusalem, Israel.

HERZOG, Frederick Joseph, MC; farmer, retired; *b* 8 Dec. 1890; *s* of late F. C. Herzog, formerly of Mossley Hill, Liverpool; *m* 1918, Constance Cicely Broad (*d* 1983); two *s* one *d*. *Educ:* Charterhouse; Trinity Coll., Cambridge. BA, Economics tripos, 1911. Served European War in Royal Artillery, 1914–19 (MC); retired with rank of Major. High Sheriff of Denbighshire, 1942; JP Denbighshire since 1946. *Recreations:* sketching, gardening. *Address:* The Grange, Ruthin, North Wales. *T:* Ruthin 2124.

HESELTINE, Rt. Hon. Michael (Ray Dibdin); PC 1979; MP (C) Henley, since 1974 (Tavistock, 1966–74); *b* 21 March 1933; *s* of late Col R. D. Heseltine, Swansea, Glamorgan; *m* 1962, Anne Harding Williams; one *s* two *d*. *Educ:* Shrewsbury Sch.; Pembroke Coll., Oxford. BA PPE; Pres. Oxford Union, 1954. National Service (commissioned), Welsh Guards, 1959. Contested (C): Gower, 1959; Coventry. North, 1964. Director of Bow Publications, 1961–65; Chm., Haymarket Press, 1966–70. Vice-Chm., Cons. Parly Transport Cttee, 1968; Opposition Spokesman on Transport, 1969; Parly Sec., Min. of Transport, June-Oct. 1970; Parly Under-Sec. of State, DoE, 1970–72; Minister for Aerospace and Shipping, DTI, 1972–74; Opposition Spokesman on: Industry, 1974–76; Environment, 1976–79; Sec. of State for the Environment, 1979–83, for Defence, 1983–86. Pres., Assoc. of Conservative Clubs, 1978; Vice-Pres., 1978, Pres., 1982–, Nat. Young Conservatives. *Publication:* Reviving the Inner Cities, 1983. *Address:* c/o House of Commons, SW1A 0AA. *Club:* Carlton.

HESELTINE, Rt. Hon. Sir William (Frederick Payne), KCB 1986 (CB 1978); KCVO 1982 (CVO 1969; MVO 1961); PC 1986; Private Secretary to the Queen and Keeper of the Queen's Archives, since 1986; *b* E Fremantle, W Australia, 17 July 1930; *s* of late H. W. Heseltine; *m* 1st, Ann Elizabeth (*d* 1957), *d* of late L. F. Turner, Melbourne; 2nd, Audrey Margaret, *d* of late S. Nolan, Sydney; one *s* one *d*. *Educ:* Christ Church Grammar Sch., Claremont, WA; University of Western Australia (1st class hons, History). Prime Minister's dept, Canberra, 1951–62; Private Secretary to Prime Minister, 1955–59; Asst Information Officer to The Queen, 1960–61; Acting Official Secretary to Governor-General of Australia, 1962; Asst Federal Director of Liberal Party of Australia, 1962–64; attached to Household of Princess Marina for visit to Australia, 1964; attached to Melbourne Age, 1964; Asst Press Secretary to the Queen, 1965–67, Press Secretary, 1968–72; Assistant Private Secretary to the Queen, 1972–77, Dep. Private Secretary, 1977–86. *Address:* The Old Stables, Kensington Palace, W8 4PU. *Club:* Boodle's.

HESKETH, 3rd Baron, *cr* 1935, of Hesketh; **Thomas Alexander Fermor-Hesketh,** Bt 1761; a Lord in Waiting (Government Whip), since 1986; *b* 28 Oct. 1950; *s* of 2nd Baron and Christian Mary, OBE 1984, *o d* of Sir John McEwen, 1st Bt of Marchmont, DL, JP; *S* father 1955; *m* 1977, Hon. Claire, *e d* of 3rd Baron Manton, *qv*; two *d*. *Educ:* Ampleforth.

Heir: b Hon. Robert Fermor-Hesketh [*b* 1 Nov. 1951; *m* 1979, Jeanne, *d* of Patrick McDowell]. *Address:* Easton Neston, Towcester, Northamptonshire. *T:* Towcester 50445. *Clubs:* White's, Turf.

HESKETH, Roger Fleetwood, OBE 1970; TD 1942; *b* 28 July 1902; *e s* of Charles Hesketh Fleetwood-Hesketh, DL; *m* 1952, Lady Mary Lumley, OBE, DStJ, *e d* of 11th Earl of Scarbrough, KG, PC, GCSI, GCIE, GCVO; one *s* two *d*. *Educ:* Eton; Christ Church, Oxford (MA) Joined Duke of Lancaster's Own Yeomanry, 1922. Called to the Bar, Inner Temple, 1928. MP (C) for Southport, 1952–59. High Sheriff, Lancs, 1947; DL 1950, Vice-Lieutenant, 1972–77; JP 1950, Lancs; Mayor of Southport, 1950; Freeman of the Borough, 1966. Chairman, Lancashire Agricultural Executive Cttee, 1965–72. Trustee, Historic Churches Preservation Trust. Served War of 1939–45 (despatches, Bronze Star Medal, USA). Hon. Colonel, Duke of Lancaster's Own Yeomanry, 1956–67. *Address:* Meols Hall, Southport, Merseyside. *T:* Southport 28171; H4 Albany, Piccadilly, W1. *T:* 01–734 5320. *Club:* Travellers'.

HESLOP-HARRISON, Prof. John, MSc, PhD, DSc; FRS 1970; FRSE, MRIA, FRSA, FLS; Royal Society Research Professor, University College of Wales, Aberystwyth, 1977–85; *b* 10 Feb. 1920; *s* of late Prof. J. W. Heslop-Harrison, FRS; *m* 1950, Yolande Massey; one *s*. *Educ:* Grammar School, Chester-le-Street, King's Coll. (University of Durham), Newcastle upon Tyne. MSc (Dunelm), PhD (Belfast), DSc (Dunelm). Army service, 1941–45. Lecturer in Agricultural Botany, King's Coll., Univ. of Durham, 1945–46; Lecturer in Botany: Queen's Univ., Belfast, 1946–50; UCL, 1950–53; Reader in Taxonomy, UCL, 1953–54; Prof. of Botany, Queen's Univ., Belfast, 1954–60; Mason Prof. of Botany, Univ. of Birmingham, 1960–67; Prof. of Botany, Inst. of Plant Develt, Univ. of Wisconsin, 1967–71; Dir, Royal Botanic Gardens, Kew, 1971–76. Visiting Professor: (Brittingham) Univ. of Wisconsin, 1965; US Dept of Agriculture Institute of Forest Genetics, Rhinelander, Wis, 1968; Univ. of Massachusetts, Amherst, Mass, 1976–77, 1978–79; Lectures: Sigma Xi, Geneva, NY, 1969; William Wright Smith, Edinburgh, 1972; George Bidder, Soc. Exptl Biol., Leeds, 1973; Ghosh, Univ. of Calcutta, 1973; Kennedy Orton Meml, UCW, Bangor, 1974; Croonian, Royal Society, 1974; Amos Meml, E Malling, 1975; Holden, Univ. of Nottingham, 1976; Bewley, Glasshouse Crops Res. Inst., 1978; Hooker, Linnean Soc., 1979; Bateson, John Innes Inst., 1979; Waller Meml, Univ. of Ohio, 1980; Blackman, Univ. of Oxford, 1980. Mem., ARC, 1977–82; Vice-President: Botanical Soc. of British Isles, 1972; Linnean Soc., 1973; President: Inst. of Biology, 1974–75; Sect. K, British Assoc. for Advancement of Science, 1974. Editor, Annals of Botany, 1961–67. Corresp. Mem., Royal Netherlands Botanical Soc., 1968; For. Fellow, Indian Nat. Sci. Acad., 1974; For. Associate, National Acad. of Sciences, USA, 1983; Mem., German Acad. of Science, 1975; For. Mem., American Botanical Soc., 1976; For. Hon. Mem., Amer. Acad. Arts and Scis., 1982; For. Mem., Acad. Royale de Belgique (Sci. Div.), 1985. Hon. DSc: Belfast, 1971; Bath, 1982; Edinburgh, 1984; Hull, 1986. Trail-Crisp Award, Linnean Soc., 1967; Univ. of Liège Medal, 1967; Erdtman Internat. Medal for Palynology, 1971; Cooke Award, Amer. Acad. of Allergy, 1974; Darwin Medal, Royal Soc., 1983; Keith Medal, RSE, 1984. *Publications:* papers and monographs on botanical subjects in various British and foreign journals. *Recreations:* hill walking, photography and painting. *Address:* The Pleasaunce, 137 Bargates, Leominster, Herefordshire HR6 8QS; Welsh Plant Breeding Station, Plas Gogerddan, near Aberystwyth SY23 3EB.

HESS, Ellen Elizabeth, NDH; Administrator, Studley College Trust, 1970–80; Principal, Studley College, Warwickshire, 1956–69; *b* 28 Dec. 1908; *d* of Charles Michael Joseph Hess and Fanny Thompson Hess (*née* Alder). *Educ:* Grammar School for Girls, Dalston; Royal Botanic Society, Regents Park. Lecturer in Horticulture, Swanley Horticultural College for Women, 1934–39; Agricultural Secretary, National Federation of Women's Institutes, 1939–46; Ellen Eddy Shaw Fellowship, Brooklyn Botanic Gardens, New York, USA, 1946–47; School of Horticulture, Ambler, Pa., USA, 1947–48; HM Inspector of Schools (Agriculture and Further Education), 1948–56. Veitch Meml Medal, RHS, 1967. *Recreations:* travel, photography, walking. *Address:* The Croft, 54 Torton Hill Road, Arundel, West Sussex BN18 9HH.

HESSAYON, Dr David Gerald; horticultural and agricultural author; Chairman: Pan Britannica Industries Ltd, since 1972; Turbair Ltd, since 1972; Director, Tennants Consolidated Ltd, since 1982; *b* 13 Feb. 1928; *s* of Jack and Lena Hessayon; *m* 1951, Joan Parker Gray; two *d*. *Educ:* Salford Grammar Sch.; Leeds Univ. (BSc 1950); Manchester Univ. (PhD 1954). FRMS 1960; FRES 1960; FRSA 1970; FIBiol 1971; FBIM 1972; FIHort 1986. Res. Fellow, UC of Gold Coast, 1953; entered Pan Britannica Industries Ltd, 1955; Technical Manager, 1955; Technical Dir, 1960; Man. Dir, 1964. Chm., British Agrochemicals Assoc., 1980–81. Mem., Guild of Freemen, City of London, 1977–; Liveryman, Gardeners' Co., 1985. *Publications:* Be Your Own Gardening Expert, 1959, revd edn 1977; Be Your Own House Plant Expert, 1960, revd edn 1980; Potato Growers Handbook, 1961; Silage Makers Handbook, 1961; Be Your Own Lawn Expert, 1962, revd edn 1979; Be Your Own Rose Expert, 1964, revd edn 1977; (with J. P. Hessayon) The Garden Book of Europe, 1973; Vegetable Plotter, 1976; Be Your Own House Plant Spotter, 1977; Be Your Own Vegetable Doctor, 1978; Be Your Own Garden Doctor, 1978; The House Plant Expert, 1980; The Rose Expert, 1981; The Lawn Expert, 1982; The Cereal Disease Expert, 1982; The Tree and Shrub Expert, 1983; The Armchair Book of the Garden, 1983; The Flower Expert, 1984; The Vegetable Expert, 1985; The Indoor Plant Spotter, 1985; The Garden Expert, 1986. *Recreations:* American folk music, thinking about the book I should be writing. *Address:* Hilgay, Mill Lane, Broxbourne, Herts. *Club:* Press.

HESSE, Mary Brenda, MA, MSc, PhD; FBA 1971; Professor of Philosophy of Science, University of Cambridge, 1975–85; Fellow of Wolfson College (formerly University College), Cambridge, since 1965; *b* 15 Oct. 1924; *d* of Ethelbert Thomas Hesse and Brenda Nellie Hesse (*née* Pelling). *Educ:* Imperial Coll., London; University Coll., London. MSc, PhD (London); DIC; MA (Cantab). Lecturer: in Mathematics, Univ. of Leeds, 1951–55; in Hist. and Philosophy of Science, UCL, 1955–59; in Philosophy of Science, Univ. of Cambridge, 1960–68; Reader in Philosophy of Sci., Cambridge Univ., 1968–75; Vice-Pres., Wolfson Coll., 1976–80. Member: Council, British Acad., 1979–82; UGC, 1980–85. Visiting Prof.: Yale Univ., 1961; Univ. of Minnesota, 1966; Univ. of Chicago, 1968. Stanton Lectr, Cambridge, 1977–80; Joint Gifford Lectr, Edinburgh, 1983. Hon. DSc Hull, 1984. Editor, Brit. Jl for the Philosophy of Science, 1965–69. *Publications:* Science and the Human Imagination, 1954; Forces and Fields, 1961; Models and Analogies in Science, 1963; The Structure of Scientific Inference, 1974; Revolutions and Reconstructions in the Philosophy of Science, 1980; articles in jls of philosophy and of the history and the philosophy of science. *Recreations:* walking, Roman roads. *Address:* Department of History and Philosophy of Science, Free School Lane, Cambridge CB2 3RH.

HESTER, Rev. Canon John Frear; Canon Residentiary and Precentor of Chichester Cathedral, since 1985; Chaplain to HM the Queen, since 1984; *b* 21 Jan. 1927; *s* of William and Frances Mary Hester; *m* 1959, Elizabeth Margaret, *d* of Sir Eric Riches, *qv*; three *s*. *Educ:* West Hartlepool Grammar School; St Edmund Hall, Oxford (MA);

Cuddesdon Coll., Oxford. Captain RAEC, 1949–50. Personal Asst to Bishop of Gibraltar, 1950; Deacon, 1952; Priest, 1953; Assistant Curate: St George's, Southall, 1952–55; Holy Redeemer, Clerkenwell, 1955–58; Sec., Actors' Church Union, 1958–63; Chaplain, Soc. of the Sisters of Bethany, Lloyd Sq., 1959–62; Dep. Minor Canon of St Paul's Cathedral, 1962–75; Rector of Soho, 1963–75; Priest-in-charge of St Paul's, Covent Garden, 1969–75; Vicar of Brighton, 1975–85; Senior Chaplain, Actors' Church Union, 1970–75; Chaplain to Lord Mayor of Westminster, 1970–71; in residence at St George's Coll. and the Ecumenical Inst., Tantur, Jerusalem, 1973; Chm., Covent Garden Conservation Area Adv. Ctee, 1971–75; Canon and Prebendary of Chichester Cathedral, 1976–85; RD of Brighton, 1976–85. Editor, Christian Drama, 1957–59. Lectr and preacher, US, 1961–; Leader of Pilgrimages to the Holy Land, 1962–. Mem., Worshipful Co. of Parish Clerks, 1970–86; Chaplain, Brighton and Hove Albion FC, 1979–; Hon. Mem., British Actors' Equity Assoc. *Publication:* Soho Is My Parish, 1970. *Recreations:* sitting down; pulling legs; watching soccer and other drama; Middle Eastern studies. *Address:* The Residentiary, Canon Lane, Chichester PO19 1PX. *T:* Chichester 782961.

HESTON, Charlton; actor (films, stage and television), USA; *b* Evanston, Ill, 4 Oct. 1924; *s* of Russell Whitford Carter and Lilla Carter (*née* Charlton); *m* 1944, Lydia Marie Clarke (actress), Two Rivers, Wisconsin; one *s* one *d*. *Educ:* New Trier High Sch., Ill; Sch. of Speech, Northwestern Univ., 1941–43. Served War of 1939–45, with 11th Army Air Forces in the Aleutians. Co-Dir (with wife), also both acting, Thomas Wolfe Memorial Theatre, Asheville, NC (plays: the State of the Union, The Glass Menagerie, etc.). In Antony and Cleopatra, Martin Beck Theatre, New York, 1947; also acting on Broadway, 1949 and 1950, etc.; London stage début (also dir.), The Caine Mutiny Court Martial, Queen's, 1985. *Films:* (1950–) include: Dark City, Ruby Gentry, The Greatest Show on Earth, Arrowhead, Bad For Each Other, The Savage, Pony Express, The President's Lady, Secret of the Incas, The Naked Jungle, The Far Horizons, The Private War of Major Benson, The Ten Commandments (Moses), The Big Country, Ben Hur (Acad. Award for best actor, 1959), The Wreck of the Mary Deare, El Cid, 55 Days at Peking, The Greatest Story Ever Told, Major Dundee, The Agony and the Ecstacy, Khartoum, Will Penny, Planet of the Apes, Soylent Green, The Three Musketeers, Earthquake, Airport 1975, The Four Musketeers, The Last Hard Men, Battle of Midway, Two-Minute Warning, Gray Lady Down, Crossed Swords, The Mountain Men, The Awakening, Mother Lode. TV appearances, esp. in Shakespeare. Mem., Screen Actors' Guild (Pres., 1966–69); Mem., Nat. Council on the Arts, 1967–; Chm., Amer. Film Inst., 1961–; Chm., Center Theatre Group, LA, 1963; Chm. on the Arts for Presidential Task Force on the Arts and Humanities, 1981–. Is interested in Shakespearian roles. Academy Award, 1978; Jean Hersholt Humanitarian Award, 1978. *Publication:* (ed Hollis Alpert) The Actor's Life: Journals 1956–1976, 1979. *Address:* c/o Mrs Carol M. Lanning, 1369 Avenida de Cortez, Pacific Palisades, Calif 90272, USA. *Club:* All England Lawn Tennis.

HETHERINGTON, Alastair; *see* Hetherington, H. A.

HETHERINGTON, (Arthur) Carleton, CBE 1971 (MBE 1945); Secretary of Association of County Councils, 1974–80; *b* 13 Feb. 1916; *s* of late Arthur Stanley and Mary Venters Hetherington, Silloth, Cumberland; *m* 1941, Xenia, *d* of late Nicholas Gubsky, Barnes; three *s*. *Educ:* St Bees Sch. Admitted Solicitor 1938. Asst Solicitor: Peterborough, 1938–39; Stafford, 1939. Served Royal Artillery, 1939–46 (Hon. Lt-Col); Temp. Lt-Col 1944–46. Dep. Clerk of the Peace and Dep. Clerk of County Council: of Cumberland, 1946–52; of Cheshire, 1952–59; Clerk of the Peace and Clerk of County Council of Cheshire, 1959–64. Sec., County Councils Assoc., 1964–74. Mem., Departmental Cttee on Jury Service, 1963–64; Sec., Local Authorities Management Services and Computer Cttee, 1965–80. *Recreations:* music, golf, family. *Address:* 33 Campden Hill Court, W8 7HS. *Club:* Royal Automobile.

HETHERINGTON, Sir Arthur (Ford), Kt 1974; DSC 1944; FEng 1976; Chairman, British Gas Corporation, 1973–76 (Member 1967, Deputy Chairman 1967–72, Chairman 1972, Gas Council); *b* 12 July 1911; *s* of late Sir Roger Hetherington and Lady Hetherington; *m* 1937, Margaret Lacey; one *s* one *d*. *Educ:* Highgate Sch.; Trinity Coll., Cambridge (BA). Joined staff of Gas Light & Coke Company, 1935. Served War, RNVR, 1941–45. North Thames Gas Board, 1949–55; joined staff of Southern Gas Board, 1955; Deputy Chairman, 1956; Chairman 1961–64; Chairman, E Midlands Gas Board, 1964–66. Hon. FIGasE. Hon. DSc London, 1974. *Address:* 32 Connaught Square, W2. *T:* 01–723 3128. *Clubs:* Athenæum; Royal Southampton Yacht.

See also R. le G. Hetherington.

HETHERINGTON, Carleton; *see* Hetherington, A. C.

HETHERINGTON, Rear-Adm. Derick Henry Fellowes, CB 1961; DSC 1941 (2 Bars 1944, 1945); MA (Oxon), 1963; Domestic Bursar and Fellow of Merton College, Oxford, 1963–76; Emeritus Fellow, 1976; *b* 27 June 1911; *s* of Commander H. R. Hetherington, RD, Royal Naval Reserve, and Hilda Fellowes; *m* 1942, Josephine Mary, *d* of Captain Sir Leonard Vavasour, 4th Bt, RN; one *s* three *d* (and one *s* decd). *Educ:* St Neot's, Eversley, Hants; RNC Dartmouth. Cadet, HMS Barham, 1928–29; Midshipman-Comdr (HMS Effingham, Leander, Anthony, Wildfire, Kimberley, Windsor, Lookout, Royal Arthur, Cheviot), 1929–50; Captain 1950; Chief of Staff, Canal Zone, Egypt, 1950–52; Senior British Naval Officer, Ceylon, 1953–55; Captain (D) 4th Destroyer Squadron, 1956–57; Director of Naval Training, Admiralty, 1958–59; Flag Officer, Malta, 1959–61; retired 1961. Croix de Guerre (France) 1945. *Address:* Magpie Cottage, Christmas Common, Oxford OX9 5HR.

HETHERINGTON, (Hector) Alastair; journalist; Research Professor, Stirling University, since 1982; former Editor of The Guardian; *b* Llanishen, Glamorganshire, 31 Oct. 1919; *yr s* of late Sir Hector Hetherington and Lady Hetherington; *m* 1st, 1957, Miranda (marr. diss. 1978), *d* of Professor R. A. C. Oliver, *qv*; two *s* two *d*; 2nd, 1979, Sheila Janet Cameron, *widow* of Hamish Cameron; one step *s* two step *d*. *Educ:* Gresham's Sch., Holt; Corpus Christi Coll., Oxford (Hon. Fellow, 1971). Royal Armoured Corps, 1940–46. Editorial staff, The Glasgow Herald, 1946–50; joined Manchester Guardian, 1950, Asst Editor and Foreign Editor, 1953–56, Editor, 1956–75; Director: Guardian and Manchester Evening News Ltd, 1956–75; Guardian Newspapers Ltd, 1967–75; Controller, BBC Scotland, 1975–78; Manager, BBC Highland, 1979–80. Member, Royal Commission on the Police, 1960–62. Vis. Fellow, Nuffield Coll., Oxford, 1973–79. Trustee, Scott Trust, 1970– (Chm., 1984–). Journalist of the Year, Nat. Press awards, 1970. *Publications:* Guardian Years, 1981; News, Newspapers and Television, 1985. *Recreations:* hill walking, golf. *Address:* 38 Chalton Road, Bridge of Allan, Stirling FK9 4EF. *T:* Stirling 832168; Tigh na-Fraoich, High Corrie, Isle of Arran KA27 8JB. *T:* Brodick 81652. *Clubs:* Athenæum, Caledonian.

HETHERINGTON, Roger le Geyt, CBE 1974 (OBE 1945); retired; *b* 20 Dec. 1908; *s* of late Sir Roger and Lady Hetherington; *m* 1945, Katharine Elise Dawson; one *d*. *Educ:* Highgate Sch.; Trinity Coll., Cambridge (MA). FEng, FICE, FIWES. Joined Binnie Deacon & Gourley (now Binnie & Partners), as pupil, 1930. Served War, RE, 1940–45. Taken into partnership, Binnie & Partners, 1947, Sen. Partner, 1973. President: Institution of Civil Engineers, 1972–73; Pipeline Industries Guild, 1975–77; Mem., Smeatonian Soc. of Civil Engineers. *Address:* 38 North Road, Highgate N6 4AX. *T:* 01–340 4203. *Club:* United Oxford & Cambridge University.

See also Sir A. F. Hetherington.

HETHERINGTON, Sir Thomas Chalmers, (Tony), KCB 1979; CBE 1970; TD; QC 1978; Director of Public Prosecutions, since 1977; Head of the Crown Prosecution Service, since 1986; *b* 18 Sept. 1926; *er s* of William and Alice Hetherington; *m* 1953, June Margaret Ann Catliff; four *d*. *Educ:* Rugby Sch.; Christ Church, Oxford. Served in Royal Artillery, Middle East, 1945–48; Territorial Army, 1948–67. Called to Bar, Inner Temple, 1952; Bencher, 1978. Legal Dept, Min. of Pensions and Nat. Insce, 1953; Law Officers' Dept, 1962, Legal Sec., 1966–75; Dep. Treasury Solicitor, 1975–77. *Address:* 4/12 Queen Anne's Gate, SW1.

HETZEL, Phyllis Bertha Mabel, (Mrs R. D. Hetzel, jr); President, Lucy Cavendish College, Cambridge, 1979–84; *b* 10 June 1918; *d* of Stanley Ernest and Bertha Myson; *m* 1st, 1941, John Henry Lewis James (*d* 1962); one *d*; 2nd, 1974, Baron Bowden, *qv* (marr. diss. 1983); 3rd, 1985, Ralph Dorn Hetzel. *Educ:* Wimbledon High Sch.; Newnham Coll., Cambridge (MA). Commonwealth (now Harkness) Fellow, 1957–58. BoT, 1941; Principal 1947; Asst Sec., 1960; DEA, 1964–69; Min. of Technology, 1969–70; Dept of Trade and Industry, 1970–75; Asst Under-Sec. of State 1972; Regional Dir, NW Region, DTI, subseq. DoI, 1972–75. Member: Monopolies and Mergers Commn, 1975–78; Local Govt Boundary Commn for England, 1977–81; W Midlands Cttee, National Trust, 1976–81. Chm., Manchester, Marriage Guidance Council, 1976–79. Member: Court, Manchester Univ., 1976–83; Court and Council, UMIST, 1978–80; Council of Senate, Cambridge Univ., 1983–84; Bd, American Friends of Cambridge University Inc., 1985–. *Publications:* The Concept of Growth Centres, 1968; Gardens through the Ages, 1971; Regional Policy in Action, 1980; contrib. Public Administration, Encycl. Britannica. *Recreations:* landscape architecture, collecting art nouveau. *Address:* 4411 Gloria Avenue, Encino, Calif 91436, USA. *T:* 818 990 5224; Lucy Cavendish College, Cambridge CB3 0BU; 18 Trafalgar Road, Cambridge.

HEUSTON, Prof. Robert Francis Vere, DCL Oxon 1970; MRIA 1978; Regius Professor of Laws, Trinity College, Dublin, 1970–83; Arthur Goodhart Professor of Legal Science and Fellow, Jesus College, Cambridge, Oct. 1986–87; *b* Dublin, 17 Nov. 1923; *e s* of late Vere Douglas Heuston and late Dorothy Helen Coulter; *m* 1962, Bridget Nancy (*née* Bolland), *widow* of Neville Ward-Perkins; four step *c*. *Educ:* St Columba's Coll.; Trinity Coll., Dublin; St John's Coll., Cambridge. Barrister, King's Inns, 1947 (Hon. Bencher, 1983), Gray's Inn, 1951; Hon. Member, Western Circuit, 1966. Fellow, Pembroke Coll., Oxford, 1947–65 (Hon. Fellow, 1982), Dean, 1951–57, Pro-Proctor, 1953; Professor of Law, Univ. of Southampton, 1965–70. Member, Law Reform Cttee (England), 1968–70, (Ireland), 1975–81. Visiting Professor: Univ. of Melbourne, 1956; Univ. of British Columbia, 1960, 1985; ANU, 1977; Gresham Professor in Law, 1964–70. *Publications:* (ed) Salmond and Heuston on Torts, 18th edn 1981; Essays in Constitutional Law, 2nd edn 1964; Lives of the Lord Chancellors, vol. I, 1885–1940, 1964, vol. II, 1940–70, 1987; various in learned periodicals. *Address:* Kentstown House, Brownstown, Navan, Co. Meath, Ireland. *T:* Drogheda 25195. *Clubs:* United Oxford & Cambridge University; Royal Irish Yacht.

HEWAN, Gethyn Elliot; Hon. Secretary, Surrey Golf Union, since 1977; *b* 23 Dec. 1916; *s* of late E. D. Hewan and Mrs L. Hewan; *m* 1943, Peggy (*née* Allen); one *s* two *d*. *Educ:* Marlborough Coll., Wilts; Clare Coll., Cambridge (Exhibitioner); Yale Univ., USA (Mellon Schol). BA Hons 1938; MA 1943, Cambridge. Served War of 1939–45 (despatches): Middle East; Capt. 3rd Regt RHA 1943; Staff Coll., Camberley, psc 1944; BMRA 51st Highland Div., 1944–45. Asst Master, Wellington Coll., 1946–50; Headmaster, Cranbrook Sch., Bellevue Hill, NSW, 1951–63; Acting Bursar, Marlborough Coll., Wilts, 1963; Asst Master, Winchester Coll., 1963–64, Charterhouse Sch., 1964–65; Headmaster, Allhallows Sch., Rousdon, 1965–74. Sec., NSW branch of HMC of Aust., 1956–63; Standing Cttee of HMC of Aust., 1958–63; Foundation Member, Aust. Coll. of Education, 1958; Exec. Cttee, Australian Outward Bound Foundation, 1958–63. *Recreations:* cricket (Cambridge blue, 1938), golf, fishing; formerly hockey (blue, 1936–37–38, Captain) and billiards (½-blue, 1938). *Address:* Newquay, Nursery Close, Horsell, Woking, Surrey. *T:* Woking 62597. *Clubs:* I Zingari; Free Foresters; Oxford and Cambridge Golfing Society; Worplesdon Golf; Senior Golfers'.

HEWARD, Air Chief Marshal Sir Anthony Wilkinson, KCB 1972 (CB 1968); OBE 1952; DFC and bar; AFC; Air Member for Supply and Organisation, Ministry of Defence, 1973–76; *b* 1 July 1918; *s* of late Col E. J. Heward; *m* 1944, Clare Myfanwy Wainwright, *d* of late Maj.-Gen. C. B. Wainwright, CB; one *s* one *d*. Gp Captain RAF, 1957; IDC 1962; Air Cdre 1963; Dir of Operations (Bomber and Reconnaissance) MoD (RAF), 1963; Air Vice-Marshal 1966; Dep. Comdr, RAF Germany, 1966–69; AOA, HQ RAF Air Support Command, 1969–70; Air Marshal 1970; Chief of Staff, RAF Strike Command, 1970–72; AOC, No 18 (Maritime) Group, 1972–73; Air Chief Marshal, 1974. County Councillor, Wilts, 1981–. *Address:* Home Close, Donhead St Mary, near Shaftesbury, Dorset. *Clubs:* Royal Air Force, Flyfishers'.

HEWARD, Edmund Rawlings, CB 1984; Chief Master of the Supreme Court (Chancery Division), 1980–85 (Master, 1959–79); *b* 19 Aug. 1912; *s* of late Rev. Thomas Brown Heward and Kathleen Amy Rachel Rawlings; *m* 1945, Constance Mary Sandiford, *d* of late George Bertram Crossley, OBE. *Educ:* Repton; Trinity Coll., Cambridge. Admitted a solicitor, 1937. Enlisted Royal Artillery as a Gunner, 1940; released as Major, DAAG, 1946. Partner in Rose, Johnson and Hicks, 9 Suffolk St, SW1, 1946. LLM 1960. *Publications:* Guide to Chancery Practice, 1962 (5th edn 1979); Matthew Hale, 1972; (ed) Part 2, Tristram and Coote's Probate Practice, 24th edn, 1973, 26th edn, 1983; (ed) Judgments and Orders in Halsbury's Laws of England, 4th edn; Lord Mansfield, 1979, paperback 1985; Chancery Practice, 1983; (ed) Chancery Orders, 1986. *Address:* 36a Dartmouth Row, Greenwich, SE10 8AW. *T:* 01–692 3525. *Clubs:* United Oxford & Cambridge University, Travellers'.

HEWER, Thomas Frederick, MD (Bristol); FRCP, FLS; Professor of Pathology, 1938–68, and Pro-Vice-Chancellor, 1966–68, University of Bristol; Professor Emeritus, 1968; *b* 12 April 1903; *s* of William Frederick Hewer and Kathleen Braddon Standerwick; *m* 1941, Anne Hiatt Baker, OBE 1977; two *s* two *d*. *Educ:* Bristol Gram. Sch.; University of Bristol. Commonwealth Fund Fellow and Asst Pathologist, Johns Hopkins Univ., USA, 1927–29; Bacteriologist Sudan Government, 1930–35; Sen. Lectr in Pathology, University of Liverpool, 1935–38. Botanical explorer, FAO/UN, 1975–80; consultant, WHO, investigating causation of cancer among Turkoman, NE Iran, making botanical exploration of desert E of Caspian Sea, 1976–77. Mem. Council and Chm. Animal Cttee, Bristol Zoo, 1953–83. Vice-Pres., Bristol Br., E-SU, 1967– (Chm., 1942–67). *Publications:* articles in medical and horticultural journals. *Recreations:* gardening and travel. *Address:* Vine House, Henbury, Bristol BS10 7AD. *T:* Bristol 503573. *Club:* English-Speaking Union.

HEWETSON, Sir Christopher (Raynor), Kt 1984; TD 1967; DL; Partner, Laces & Co., Solicitors, Liverpool, since 1961; President, Law Society, 1983–84; *b* 26 Dec. 1929; *s* of Harry Raynor Hewetson and Emma Hewetson; *m* 1962, Alison May Downie, *d* of Prof. A. W. Downie, *qv*; two *s* one *d. Educ:* Sedbergh Sch.; Peterhouse, Cambridge (MA). National Service, 2nd Lieut 4th RHA, 1951–53; Territorial Service, 1953–68: Lt-Col commanding 359 Medium Regt, RA, TA, 1965–68. Qualified as solicitor, 1956. Mem. Council, Law Society, 1966–; Vice-Pres., 1982–83; President, Liverpool Law Society, 1976. DL Merseyside, 1986. *Recreations:* golf, walking. *Address:* 24c Westcliffe Road, Birkdale, Southport, Merseyside PR8 2BU, *T:* Southport 67179. *Clubs:* Army and Navy; Athenæum (Liverpool); Royal Birkdale Golf (Southport).

HEWETSON, Gen. Sir Reginald (Hackett), GCB 1966 (KCB 1962; CB 1958); CBE 1945 (OBE 1943); DSO 1944; Adjutant-General, Ministry of Defence (Army), 1964–67; retired; *b* Shortlands, Kent, 4 Aug. 1908; *s* of late J. Hewetson, ICS, and E. M. M. Hackett-Wilkins; *m* 1935, Patricia Mable, *y d* of late F. H. Burkitt, CIE; one *s* one *d. Educ:* Repton; RMA, Woolwich. Regular Commission in RA, 1928; Service in India (including Active Service, 1930–32), 1929–35; RA depot and home stations, 1935–39; psc 1939; Staff Capt. RA 4 Div., 1938; Adjt 30 Fd Regt and Capt. 1939; France, Oct. 1939–Jan. 1940; 2nd war course at Staff Coll., Camberley, Jan.-April 1940; Brigade Major RA 43 (Wessex) Div. May-Sept. 1940. Temp. Major; various GSO2 jobs incl. instructor Senior Officers Sch., 1940–42; GSO1 (Lieut-Col) HQ L of C North Africa, Sept.-Nov. 1942; 78 Div. (in North Africa), 1942–43 (OBE); Lieut-Col Comdg Fd Regt in 56 (London) Div. in Italy, 1943–44 (DSO); BGS HQ 10 Corps, 1944–45; BGS, British Troops, Austria, 1945–47; Student, IDC, 1949; Dep. Dir Staff Duties, WO, 1950–52; CRA 2nd Infantry Div., BAOR, 1953–55; GOC 11th Armoured Div., March 1956; GOC, 4th Infantry Div. 1956–58; Commandant, Staff Coll., Camberley, 1958–61; Commander, British Forces, Hong Kong, Dec. 1961–March 1963; GOC-in-C, Far East Land Forces, 1963–64. Col Comdt, RA, 1962–73; Col Comdt, APTC, 1966–70; ADC (Gen.), 1966–67. Chm., Exec. Cttee, Army Benevolent Fund, 1968–76. Governor and Mem. Administrative Bd, Corps of Commissionaires, 1964–84 (Pres., 1980–84); retd. *Recreations:* cricket (Army and Kent 2nd XI MCC, IZ), hockey (Norfolk and RA), golf. *Address:* Cherry Orchard, Fairwarp, near Uckfield, East Sussex. *Club:* MCC.

HEWETT, Sir John George, 5th Bt, *cr* 1813; MC 1919; Captain KAR; *b* 23 Oct. 1895; *e surv. s* of Sir Harold George Hewett, 4th Bt, and Eleanor (*d* 1946), *d* of Capt. Studdy, RN, and Mrs W. T. Summers; *S* father, 1949; *m* 1926, Yuilleen Maude (*d* 1980), *o c* of Samuel F. Smithson, Lauriston, Camberley; two *s. Educ:* Cheltenham. Served European War, 1914–18, British East Africa, 1914–19. *Heir: er s* Peter John Smithson Hewett, MM [*b* 27 June 1931; *m* 1958, Jennifer Ann Cooper, *o c* of Emrys Thomas Jones, Bexhill-on-Sea; two *s* one *d. Educ:* Bradfield Coll.; Jesus Coll., Cambridge. Called to the Bar, Gray's Inn, 1954; now a practising Advocate in Kenya. Kenya Regt attached Special Branch, Kenya Police, 1957]. *Address:* Lamwia Road, Langata, PO Box 40763, Nairobi, Kenya.

HEWETT, Major Richard William; Vice President and Director, International Operations, Reader's Digest Association Inc., since 1986; *b* 22 Oct. 1923; *s* of late Brig. W. G. Hewett, OBE, MC, and Louise S. Hewett (*née* Wolfe); *m* 1954, Rosemary Cridland; two *d. Educ:* Wellington Coll., Berks. Enlisted RA, 1941; commnd RA, 1943; regular commn 1944: served Normandy, India, UK, Malaya; regtl duty, flying duties Air OP, Instr, OCTU, Mons, 1954; sc 1955; Staff and regtl duties, Germany, 1956–59; Mil. Mission, USA, 1959–61. Joined Reader's Digest Assoc. Ltd, 1962; Dir 1976; Man. Dir, 1981–84; Chm. and Man. Dir, 1984–86. *Recreations:* tennis, fishing, travelling. *Address:* c/o 25 Berkeley Square, W1X 6AB. *Club:* Annabel's.

HEWISH, Prof. Antony, MA, PhD; FRS 1968; Professor of Radioastronomy, University of Cambridge, since 1971 (Reader, 1969–71); Fellow of Churchill College since 1962; Director, Mullard Radio Astronomy Observatory, Cambridge, since 1982; *b* 11 May 1924; *s* of Ernest William Hewish and late Frances Grace Lanyon Pinch; *m* 1950, Marjorie Elizabeth Catherine Richards; one *s* one *d. Educ:* King's Coll., Taunton; Gonville and Caius Coll., Cambridge (Hon. Fellow, 1976). BA (Cantab.) 1948, MA 1950, PhD 1952; Hamilton Prize, Isaac Newton Student, 1952. RAE Farnborough, 1943–46; Research Fellow, Gonville and Caius Coll., 1952–54; Asst Dir of Research, 1954–62; Fellow, Gonville and Caius Coll., 1955–62; Lectr in Physics, Univ. of Cambridge, 1962–69. Visiting Prof. in Astronomy, Yale, 1963; Prof. of the Royal Instn, 1977; Halley Lectr, Oxford, 1979; Karl Schwarzschild Lectr, Bonn, 1971. Hon. DSc: Leicester, 1976; Exeter, 1977. Foreign Hon. Mem., Amer. Acad. of Arts and Sciences; Foreign Fellow, Indian Nat. Sci. Acad., 1982; Hon. Fellow, Instn of Electronics and Telecommunication Engrs, India, 1985. Eddington Medal, Royal Astronomical Soc., 1969; Charles Vernon Boys Prize, Inst. of Physics and Physical Soc., 1970; Dellinger Gold Medal, Internat. Union of Radio Science, 1972; Michelson Medal, Franklin Inst., 1973; Hopkins Prize, Cambridge Phil Soc., 1973; Holweck Medal and Prize, Soc. Française de Physique, 1974; Nobel Prize for Physics (jtly), 1974; Hughes Medal, Royal Soc., 1977. *Publications:* Papers in Proc. Royal Society, Phys. Soc., Mon. Not. Royal Astr. Soc., etc. *Recreations:* music, gardening, sailing. *Address:* Pryor's Cottage, Kingston, Cambridge. *T:* Comberton 2657.

HEWITT, family name of **Viscount Lifford.**

HEWITT, Cecil Rolph; *see* Rolph, C. H.

HEWITT, Sir (Cyrus) Lenox (Simson), Kt 1971; OBE 1963; company chairman and director; Director, Ansett Transport Industries Ltd, since 1982; *b* 7 May 1917; *s* of Cyrus Lenox Hewitt and Ella Louise Hewitt; *m* 1943, Alison Hope (*née* Tillyard); one *s* three *d. Educ:* Scotch Coll., Melbourne; Melbourne Univ. (BCom). FASA, FCIS, LCA. Broken Hill Proprietary Co. Ltd, 1933–39; Asst Sec., Commonwealth Prices Br., Canberra, 1939–46; Economist, Dept of Post War Reconstruction, 1946–49; Official Sec. and Actg Dep. High Comr, London, 1950–53; Commonwealth Treasury: Asst Sec., 1953–55; 1st Asst Sec., 1955–62; Dep. Sec., 1962–66; Chm., Australian Univs Commn, 1967; Secretary to: Prime Minister's Dept, 1968–71; Dept of the Environment, Aborigines and the Arts, 1971–72; Dept of Minerals and Energy, 1972–75. Lectr, Econs and Cost Accountancy, Canberra UC, 1940–49, 1954. Acting Chairman: Pipeline Authority, 1973–75; Petroleum and Minerals Authority, 1974–75; Chairman: Qantas Airways Ltd, 1975–80 (Dir, 1973–80); Qantas Wentworth Hldgs Ltd, 1975–80; QH Tours Ltd, 1975–80 (Dir, 1974–80); Petroleum and Minerals Co. of Aust. Pty Ltd, 1975–; Austmark Internat. Ltd, 1983–; Northern Mining Corp. NL, 1984–85; State Rail Authority of NSW, 1985–; Director: East/Aust. Pipeline Corp. Ltd, 1974–75; Mary Kathleen Uranium Ltd, 1975–80; Aust. Industry Develt Corp., 1975; Santos Ltd, 1981–82; Pontello Constructions Ltd, 1980–82; Aberfoyle Ltd, 1981–; Endeavour Resources Ltd, 1982–; Short Brothers (Australia) Ltd, 1981–; Airship Industries PLC, 1984–; Industrial & Pastoral Holdings Ltd, 1984–; British Midland Airways (Australia) Pty Ltd, 1985–; Universal Telecasters Securities Ltd, 1986–. Dep. Chm., Aust. Atomic Energy Commn, 1972–77; Chairman: Exec. Cttee, IATA, 1976–77 (Mem , 1975–); Orient Airlines Assoc., 1977. *Recreations:* tennis, farming. *Address:* 9 Torres Street, Red Hill, Canberra, ACT 2603, Australia. *T:* 952446; (office) PO Box 33, Redfern, NSW 2016, Australia. *T:* 699 2222. *Clubs:* Brooks's; Melbourne (Melbourne); Union (Sydney).

See also P. H. Hewitt.

HEWITT, Eric John, PhD, DSc; FRS 1982; Head of Biochemistry Group in Plant Sciences Division, Long Ashton Research Station, and Reader in Plant Physiology, University of Bristol, 1967–84, retired; *b* London, 27 Feb. 1919; *s* of Harry Edward Hewitt, OBE, MD, DPH, and Blanche (*née* Du Roveray); *m* 1943, Hannah Eluned (*née* Williams); one *s. Educ:* Whitgift Sch., S Croydon; King's Coll., Univ. of London, 1936–40 (BSc 1st Cl., AKC; DipEd); PhD, DSc Bristol; FIBiol. Asst Chemist/Chemist, MoS, 1940–42; Long Ashton Research Station: ARC Res. Grant Research Asst, 1942–45, Sen. Plant Physiologist, 1945–84; seconded to ARC Unit of Plant Nutrition (Micronutrients), 1952–59; SPSO (merit promotion), 1967. *Publications:* Sand and Water Culture Methods Used in the Study of Plant Nutrition, 1952, 2nd edn 1966; (with T. A. Smith) Plant Mineral Nutrition, 1975; (ed, with C. V. Cutting): (sympos.) Nitrogen Metabolism in Plants, 1968; (sympos.) Nitrogen Assimilation of Plants, 1979; approx. 150 research contribs to jls. *Recreations:* squash, gardening, fell walking, TV and records. *Address:* Langdales, 63 Ridgeway Road, Long Ashton, Bristol BS18 9EZ. *T:* Long Ashton 392274. *Club:* Chesham (King's College Assoc.).

HEWITT, Gavin Wallace; HM Diplomatic Service; Counsellor, on loan to the Home Civil Service, since 1984; *b* 19 Oct. 1944; *s* of George Burrill and Elisabeth Murray Hewitt; *m* 1973, Heather Mary Clayton; two *s* two *d. Educ:* George Watson's Boys' Coll., Edinburgh; Edinburgh Univ. (MA). Min. of Transport, 1967–70; on secondment from MoT as Third, later Second, Sec. to UK Delegn, EEC, Brussels, 1970–72; FCO, 1972–73; First Sec., British High Commn, Canberra, 1973–78; FCO, 1978–81; First Sec. and Head of Chancery, HM Embassy, Belgrade, 1981–84; Mem., Jt FCO/BBC Review Gp, BBC External Services, 1984. *Recreations:* music, squash, tinkering. *Address:* c/o Foreign and Commonwealth Office, SW1.

HEWITT, Rev. Canon George Henry Gordon; Residentiary Canon, Chelmsford Cathedral, 1964–78, Canon Emeritus since 1978; *b* 30 May 1912; *s* of Rev. G. H. Hewitt; *m* 1942, Joan Ellen Howden; two *s* one *d. Educ:* Trent Coll.; Brasenose, Oxford; Wycliffe Hall, Oxford. Asst Curate, St Clement, Leeds, 1936–39; Chaplain, Ridley Hall, Cambridge, 1939–41; Asst Curate, Leeds Parish Church, 1941–43; Religious Book Editor, Lutterworth Press, 1943–52; Diocesan Education Sec., Sheffield, 1952–58; Residentiary Canon, Sheffield Cathedral, 1953–58; Vicar of St Andrew, Oxford, 1958–64. Chaplain to the Queen, 1969–82. *Publications:* Let the People Read, 1949; The Problems of Success: a history of the Church Missionary Society, 1910–1942, vol. I, 1971, vol. II, 1977. *Address:* 8 Rainsford Avenue, Chelmsford, Essex.

HEWITT, Harold; His Honour Judge Hewitt; a Circuit Judge, since 1980; *b* 14 March 1917; *s* of George Trueman Hewitt and Bertha Lilian Hewitt; *m* 1946, Doris Mary Smith; two *s. Educ:* King James I Grammar Sch., Bishop Auckland. Admitted solicitor (Hons), 1938; HM Coroner, S Durham, 1948–80; a Recorder of the Crown Court, 1974–80. Chm. (part-time), Industrial Tribunal, 1975–80. Member Council, Law Society, 1976–80. *Recreations:* gardening, French literature, bird-watching. *Address:* Longmeadows, Etherley, Bishop Auckland, Co. Durham. *T:* Bishop Auckland 832386; Saltings Cottage, Bowness-on-Solway, Cumbria. *Clubs:* Carlton, Lansdowne.

HEWITT, Harold; solicitor; consultant since 1973; *b* 1 Jan. 1908; *m* 1949, Jeannette Myers; one *d. Educ:* Bede Collegiate Sch., Sunderland; Armstrong Coll., Univ. of Durham. Solicitor, admitted 1930. Legal Adviser, High Commissioner for Austria, Allied Commission, 1946–49. Member, Law Society; Past Pres., Bexley and Dartford Law Soc. *Recreation:* social welfare work. *Address:* 121 Dorset House, Gloucester Place, NW1 5AQ.

HEWITT, Harry Ronald, FEng; Chairman, Johnson Matthey PLC, 1983–84; retired; *b* 12 April 1920; *s* of Charles William Hewitt and Florence Hewitt; *m* 1954, Rosemary Olive, *d* of Walter George Hiscock and Olive Mary Hiscock; two *s* one *d. Educ:* City of Leeds High Sch.; Leeds Coll. of Technol. (BSc London 1941). FEng 1982; MIChemE 1949; MRSC 1944; CBIM 1983 (MBIM 1947). Jun. Chemist, Joseph Watson & Sons, soap manufrs, Leeds, 1936–41; Chemist, Royal Ordnance Factories (explosive manuf.), 1941–45; Control Officer, Chemical Br., Control Commn, Germany, 1945–47; Works Manager, Consolidated Zinc Corp., Avonmouth and Widnes, 1947–58; Johnson Matthey: Gen. Man., 1958–62; Exec. Dir, 1962–76; Gp Man. Dir, 1976–83. Freeman, City of London, 1979; Liveryman, Worshipful Co. of Clockmakers, 1979. FRSA. *Recreations:* golf, tennis, skiing, music. *Address:* 6 Loom Lane, Radlett, Herts WD7 8AD. *T:* Radlett 5243.

HEWITT, Capt. John Graham, DSO 1940; RN (retired); *b* 15 Oct. 1902; *s* of J. G. L. Hewitt, SM, Marton, NZ; two *s; m* 1947, Mrs Rooney, *widow* of Col J. J. Rooney, IMS. *Educ:* RN Colls, Osborne and Dartmouth. Midshipman, 1919; Comdr, 1936; commanded HMS Winchelsea, 1937, HMS Auckland, 1940–41; HMS Dauntless, 1941–42; Capt. 1942; HMS Royalist, 1944; HMS Frobisher, 1945–46; Second Naval Member of NZ Navy Board, 1947; Director Tactical Sch., Woolwich, 1949–52; retired list, 1952. Norwegian War Cross, 1942. *Recreation:* fishing. *Address:* 16 Royston Court, Kew Gardens, Richmond, Surrey.

HEWITT, Sir Lenox; *see* Hewitt, Sir C. L. S.

HEWITT, Margaret, PhD; Reader in Social Institutions, University of Exeter, since 1970; *b* 25 Oct. 1928; *d* of Robert Henry Hewitt and Jessie Hewitt. *Educ:* Bedford Coll., London; London Sch. of Economics. BA Hons Sociology (1st Cl.) 1950, PhD Sociology 1953. Univ. of London Postgrad. Studentship in Sociology, 1950–52; Asst Lectr in Sociology, University Coll. of the South West, 1952–54; Lectr in Sociology, Univ. of Exeter, 1954–65, Sen. Lectr, 1965–70. Mem. Council, Univ. of Exeter, 1964–70; Governor: Bedford Coll., 1968–; St Luke's Coll., Exeter, 1969–78. Member: Church Assembly, 1961–70; Gen. Synod of Church of England, 1970–; Standing Cttee of Gen. Synod, 1976–; Church Commn on Crown Appts, 1977–. Pres., William Temple Assoc., 1983–. Rep. of Univ. of London on Council of Roedean Sch., 1974–84. *Publications:* Wives and Mothers in Victorian Industry, 1958; (with Ivy Pinchbeck) Children in English Society, Vol. I 1969, Vol. II 1973. *Recreation:* doing nothing. *Address:* 14 Velwell Road, Exeter, Devon EX4 4LE. *T:* Exeter 54150. *Club:* Royal Over Seas League.

HEWITT, Sir Nicholas Charles Joseph, 3rd Bt *cr* 1921; *b* 12 Nov. 1947; *s* of Sir Joseph Hewitt, 2nd Bt and of Marguerite, *yr d* of Charles Burgess; *S* father, 1973; *m* 1969, Pamela Margaret, *o d* of Geoffrey J. M. Hunt, TD; two *s* one *d. Heir: s* Charles Edward James Hewitt, *b* 15 Nov. 1970. *Address:* The Forge, Hutton Buscel, Scarborough, North Yorks. *T:* Scarborough 862307.

HEWITT, Patricia Hope; Press and Broadcasting Secretary to the Leader of the Opposition, since 1983; *b* 2 Dec. 1948; *d* of Sir (Cyrus) Lenox (Simson) Hewitt, *qv*, and Alison Hope Hewitt; *m* 1981, William Birtles; one *d. Educ:* C of E Girls' Grammar Sch., Canberra; Australian Nat. Univ.; Newnham Coll., Cambridge. BA, AMusA (piano). Public Relations Officer, Age Concern (Nat. Old People's Welfare Council), 1971–73; Women's Rights Officer, Nat. Council for Civil Liberties, 1973–74, Gen. Secretary 1974–83. Trustee: Cobden Trust, 1974–83; Areopagitica Trust, 1981–84; Member: Sec. of State's Adv. Cttee on Employment of Women, 1977–84; Unofficial Cttee of Enquiry into Southall, 23 April 1979; National Labour Women's Cttee, 1979–83; Labour Party

Enquiry into Security Services, 1980–81; Council, Campaign for Freedom of Information, 1983–; Bd, Internat. League for Human Rights, 1984–; Co-Chm., Human Rights Network, 1979–81. Contested (Lab) Leicester East, 1983. Mem., Editorial Adv. Panel, New Socialist, 1980–. *Publications:* Your Rights (Age Concern), 1973, 14th edn 1986; Rights for Women (NCCL), 1975; Civil Liberties, the NCCL Guide (co-ed 3rd edn), 1977; The Privacy Report (NCCL), 1977; Your Rights at Work (NCCL), 1978, 2nd edn 1981; The Abuse of Power, 1981; A Fair Cop (NCCL), 1982. *Recreations:* reading, theatre, music, politics, gardening. *Address:* 21 Rochester Square, NW1 9SA. *T:* 01–267 2567.

HEWITT, Peter McGregor, OBE 1967; Regional Director, East Midlands, Departments of the Environment and Transport, since 1984; *b* 6 Oct. 1929; *e s* of late Douglas McGregor Hewitt and of Audrey Vera Hewitt; *m* 1962, Joyce Marie Gavin; three *d*. *Educ:* De Aston Sch., Market Rasen, Lincs; Keble Coll., Oxford (MA). National Service (Army), 1947–49. HM Overseas Civil Service, 1952–64: served in Malaya and N Borneo; HM Diplomatic Service, 1964–71: served in FO, Shanghai and Canberra; Home Civil Service: Principal, 1971–77; Asst Sec., 1977–83; Grade 4, 1984. *Recreations:* cricket, music, gardening. *Address:* c/o Departments of the Environment and Transport, Cranbrook House, Cranbrook Street, Nottingham NG1 1FB.

HEWITT, Richard Thornton, OBE 1945; retired; Executive Director, Royal Society of Medicine, 1952–82; Vice-President, The Royal Society of Medicine Foundation, Inc., New York, since 1969; *b* 1917; *yr s* of late Harold and Elsie Muriel Hewitt, Bramhall, Cheshire. *Educ:* King's Sch., Macclesfield; Magdalen Coll., Oxford (Exhibitioner). Served War, Lt-Col, infantry and special forces, 1939–46. Asst Registrary, Cambridge Univ., 1946. Incorporated MA, Magdalene Coll., Cambridge, 1946. Sec., Oxford Univ. Medical Sch., 1947–52. FKC 1985. Hon. Fellow: Swedish Med. Soc., 1968; RSocMed, 1985; Chelsea Coll., 1985. Liveryman, Worshipful Society of Apothecaries of London, 1954. Freeman of the City of London, 1954. *Recreations:* gentle golf and gardening, music. *Address:* 84 Dorset House, NW1. *T:* 01–935 4014; The White House, Iffley, Oxford. *T:* Oxford 779263. *Clubs:* MCC, Royal Automobile; Frewen (Oxford); Royal and Ancient (St Andrews).

HEWLETT-DAVIES, Mrs Janet Mary; Director of Public Affairs, Pergamon, BPCC and Mirror Group of Companies, since 1986; *b* 13 May 1938; *d* of Frederick Charles and Margaret Ellen Hewlett; *m* 1964, Barry Davies. *Educ:* King Edward VI High School for Girls, Birmingham. Journalist, West Midlands 1956–59; BBC, 1959–65; Films Division, Central Office of Information, 1966–67; Press Officer: Prime Minister's Office, 1967–72; HM Customs and Excise, 1972–73; Principal Information Officer, Dept of Trade and Industry, 1973–74; Dep. Press Secretary to Prime Minister, 1974–76; Head of Information, Dept of Transport, 1976–79; Director of Information: DoE, 1979–82; DHSS, 1982–86. Vice-Chm., WHO Working Gp on Information and Health, 1983. FRSA 1985. *Recreations:* cooking, theatre, needlework, Radio 4. *Address:* 131a Ashley Gardens, SW1P 1HL. *T:* 01–834 3738. *Club:* Reform.

HEWS, (Gordon) Rodney (Donald), MC 1945; TD 1950; DL; Chairman, Kent Messenger Ltd, 1982–86 (Deputy Chairman, 1980–82); *b* 10 May 1917; *yr s* of late G. R. Hews and Alderman Mrs Evelyn Hews, CBE; *m* 1944, Maureen Sydney Smith, *d* of late Air Cdre Sydney Smith, OBE, DL; two *s* one *d*. *Educ:* Kent Coll., Canterbury. Joined family newspaper, Kentish Gazette, 1935; Editor, 1950–63; Man. Dir, T. F. Pain & Sons Ltd (publishers of East Kent Mercury, Deal), 1953–80; Chm. and Man. Dir, Kent County Newspapers Ltd, 1963–80. Gazetted 2nd Lieut 4th Bn The Buffs, TA, 1936; served War, 1939–45, on Staff and with 2nd Bn The Buffs: France, 1940; ME, Persia/Iraq, 1941–43 (ME Staff Coll., 1942); Burma, 1944–45 (MC); commanded 4th Bn The Buffs, 1953–55, 5th Bn The Buffs, 1955–57; Col 133 Infantry Bde, 1957–66. Gen. Comr of Income Tax, Canterbury Div., 1961– (Chm., 1967–). Mem., Immigration Appeals Tribunal, 1963–65. JP Canterbury, 1955–85 (Chm., 1972–81); Vice Chm., Kent Magistrates' Courts Cttee, 1980–83; DL Kent, 1980. Comdr, Order of the Dannebrog, Denmark, 1955. *Address:* 4 Derringstone Street, Barham, near Canterbury, Kent CT4 6QB. *T:* Canterbury 831238.

HEXHAM AND NEWCASTLE, Bishop of, (RC), since 1974; **Rt. Rev. Hugh Lindsay;** *b* 20 June 1927; *s* of William Stanley Lindsay and Mary Ann Lindsay (*née* Warren). *Educ:* St Cuthbert's Grammar Sch., Newcastle upon Tyne; Ushaw Coll., Durham. Priest 1953. Asst Priest; St Lawrence's, Newcastle upon Tyne, 1953; St Matthew's, Ponteland, 1954; Asst Diocesan Sec., 1953–59; Diocesan Sec., 1959–69; Chaplain, St Vincent's Home, West Denton, 1959–69; Auxiliary Bishop of Hexham and Newcastle and Titular Bishop of Chester-le-Street, 1969–74. *Recreation:* walking. *Address:* Bishop's House, East Denton Hall, 800 West Road, Newcastle upon Tyne NE5 2BJ.

HEXHAM AND NEWCASTLE, Auxiliary Bishop of, (RC); *see* Swindlehurst, Rt Rev. O. F.

HEXT, Maj.-Gen. Frederick Maurice, CB 1954; OBE 1945; CEng; FIMechE; FIEE; *b* 5 May 1901; *s* of Frederick Robert Hext; *m* 1924, Kathleen Goulden; one *s*. *Educ:* Portsmouth Gram. Sch.; RMA, Woolwich. Commissioned RE 1921; served in India, 1925–28, and 1931–34; Instructor, Sch. of Military Engineering, 1939–42; served NW Europe Campaign (despatches) Comdr, REME, 53rd (Welsh) Div., and Dep. Dir of Mechanical Engineering, 12 Corps; DDME, 1 Corps, 1945–46; DDME, Burma Command, 1946–48; AAG, AG 21, War Office, 1949–51; DME, BAOR, 1951–53; Inspector of REME, 1953–56, retired 1956. Hon. Col 53 (Welsh) Inf. Div. REME, 1956–61. Maj.-Gen., 1953. Formerly Member Wessex RHB; Chm. Isle of Wight Group Hospital Management Cttee, 1961–72. FRSA. *Address:* 17 Brettingham Court, Hinton St George, Crewkerne, Somerset. *T:* Crewkerne 73059.

HEY, Donald Holroyde, DSc, PhD; FRS 1955; FRSC; Daniell Professor of Chemistry, University of London, 1950–71, now Emeritus Professor; President, Section B, British Association for the Advancement of Science, 1965; *b* Swansea, 1904; 2nd *s* of Arthur Hey, MusB, FRCO, LRAM, and Frances Jane Hey; *m* 1931, Jessie (*d* 1982), MSc (Wales), *d* of Thomas and Katharine Jones; one *s* one *d*. *Educ:* Magdalen Coll. Sch., Oxford; University Coll., Swansea, BSc, MSc Wales; PhD London; DSc Manchester. Asst Lecturer in Chemistry, University of Manchester, 1928–30; Lecturer in Chemistry, University of Manchester, 1930–38; Lecturer in Chemistry, Imperial Coll. of Science and Technology, London, 1939–41; Dir of British Schering Research Institute, 1941–45; University Prof. of Chemistry at King's Coll., London, 1945–50; Asst Principal, King's Coll., 1962–68. Scientific Advr for Civil Defence, SE Region, 1952–58. Vice-Pres. of Chemical Soc. 1951–54 (Tilden Lectr, 1951, Pedler Lectr, 1970, Hon. Secretary, 1946–51, Vice-Pres., Perkin Div., 1971). Reilly Lectr, University of Notre Dame, Indiana, 1952; Visiting Prof. University of Florida, 1967. FKC; Fellow Imp. Coll. of Science and Technology, 1968; Hon. Fellow: Chelsea Coll., 1973; Univ. Coll. Swansea, 1986. Member: Council, KCL, 1955–78; Adv. Council RMCS, 1961–73. Hon. DSc Wales, 1970. Defence Medal 1945. Intra-Science Res. Conf. Award and Medal, Santa Monica, Calif., 1968; Hon. Fellow, Intra-Science Res. Foundn, 1971. *Publications:* articles in scientific journals, mainly in Jl of Chem. Soc. *Recreations:* music, gardening. *Address:* 78 Doods Road, Reigate, Surrey.

HEY, Air Vice-Marshal Ernest, CB 1967; CBE 1963 (OBE 1954); CEng; Air Member for Technical Services, Department of Air, Canberra, 1960–72, retired; *b* Plymouth, Devon, 29 Nov. 1912; *s* of Ernest Hey, Terrigal, NSW; *m* 1936, Lorna, *d* of Sqdn Ldr A. Bennett, Melbourne; one *s* one *d*. *Educ:* Sydney Technical High Sch.; Sydney University. RAAF cadet, 1934; served War of 1939–45; Dir Technical Services, 1947–54; AOC Maintenance Comd, 1956–57; Imp. Defence Coll., 1957; Liaison Air Materiel Comd, USAF, 1958–59. *Recreations:* painting, lawn bowls.

HEY, James Stanley, MBE 1945; DSc; FRS 1978; retired; Research Scientist at Royal Radar Establishment, 1952–69; Chief Scientific Officer, 1966–69; *b* 3 May 1909; *s* of William Rennie Hey and Barbara Elizabeth Hey (*née* Matthews); *m* 1934, Edna Heywood. *Educ:* Rydal Sch.; Manchester Univ. BSc (Physics), 1930; MSc (X-ray Crystallography), 1931; DSc (Radio Astronomy and Radar Research), 1950. Army Operational Research Group, 1940–52 (Head of Estab., 1949–52). Hon. DSc: Birmingham, 1975; Kent, 1977. Eddington Medal, RAS, 1959. *Publications:* The Radio Universe, 1971, rev. 3rd edn 1983; The Evolution of Radio Astronomy, 1973; research papers in scientific jls (RAS, Royal Society, Phys Soc., Philosophical Magazine, Nature, etc) including pioneering papers in radio astronomy. *Address:* 4 Shortlands Close, Willingdon, Eastbourne, East Sussex BN22 0JE.

HEYCOCK, Baron *cr* 1967 (Life Peer), of Taibach; **Llewellyn Heycock,** CBE 1959; DL, JP; *b* 12 Aug. 1905; *s* of William Heycock and late Mary Heycock; *m* 1930, Olive Elizabeth (*née* Rees); one *s* (and one *s* decd). *Educ:* Eastern Sch., Port Talbot. Engine Driver, Dyffryn Yard Loco Sheds, Port Talbot. Glam County Council: Mem., 1937–74; Chm. 1962–63; Chm., Educn Cttee, 1944–74; Chm., West Glamorgan CC, 1973–75. Pres., UWIST, 1968–75; Mem., Council and Court, University of Wales. Formerly: Mem., Council and Court, University Coll. of S Wales and Mon.; Chairman: Schools Museum Service for Wales; Celtic Sea Adv. Cttee; Exec. Cttee, Royal National Eisteddfod of Wales, Port Talbot (1966); Welsh Jt Educn Cttee; President: Coleg Harlech; Assoc. of Educn Cttees (1964–65); Nat. Assoc. of Div. Execs for England and Wales (1954–55, 1965–66); Exec. Mem., County Councils Assoc.; Mem., Adv. Cttee for Educn in Wales under 1944 Butler Act. Hon. Druid, Nat. Eisteddfod of Wales, 1963; Vice-Pres., Nat. Theatre Co. for Wales. Hon. LLD, University of Wales, 1963. Hon. Freedom of Port Talbot, 1961. CStJ. JP Glam; JP Port Talbot; DL Glam 1963. *Recreation:* Rugby football. *Address:* 1 Llewellyn Close, Taibach, Port Talbot, West Glam. *T:* Port Talbot 2565.

HEYERDAHL, Thor; author and anthropologist, since 1938; *b* 6 Oct. 1914; *s* of Thor Heyerdahl and Alison Heyerdahl (*née* Lyng); *m* 1st, 1936, Liv Coucheron Torp (*d* 1969); two *s*; 2nd, 1949, Yvonne Dedekam-Simonsen; three *d*. *Educ:* University of Oslo, 1933–36. Researches in the Marquesas Islands (Pacific), 1937–38; Researches among Coast Indians of Brit. Columbia, 1939–40. Active service Free Norwegian Army-Air Force parachute unit, 1942–45. Organised and led Kon-Tiki expedition, 1947. Continued research in USA and Europe, with authorship, 1948–. Organised and led Norwegian Archæological Expedition to the Galapagos Islands, 1952; experiments revealing tacking principles of balsa raft in Ecuador, 1953; field research, Bolivia, Peru, Colombia, 1954. Organised and led Norwegian Archæological Expedition to Easter Island and the East Pacific, 1955–56. Continued research, 1957–59. Made crossing from Safi, Morocco, to W Indies in papyrus boat, Ra II, 1970; sailed from Qurna, Iraq, to Djibouti in reed boat, Tigris, 1977–78; organised and led two archaeol expedns to Maldive Islands, 1982–84; leader, organiser jt Norwegian/Chilean archaeol expedn, Easter Island, 1986. Participation in: Internat. Congress of Americanists, 1952–; Pacific Science Congresses, 1961–, all with lectures subseq. publ. in Proc. Congress. Chm. Bd, Kon-Tiki Museum, Oslo; Vice-Pres., World Assoc. of World Federalists, 1966–; Trustee, Internat. Bd, World Wildlife Fund, 1977–; Internat. Patron, United World Colls, 1980. Mem., Royal Norwegian Acad. of Science, 1958; Fellow: New York Acad. of Sciences, 1960; Amer. Anthropological Assoc., 1966. Hon. Prof., Inst. Politecnico Nacional, Mexico, 1972. Hon. Dir, Explorers' Club, NY, 1982. Hon. Mem. Geog. Soc.: Peru, 1953; Norway, 1953; Brazil, 1954; USSR, 1964. Hon. Doctor: Oslo, 1961; USSR Acad. of Scis, 1980. Retzius Medal, Swedish Soc. for Anthropology and Geography, 1950; Mungo Park Medal, Royal Scottish Geographical Society, 1951; Prix Bonaparte-Wyse from Société de Géographie, Paris, 1951; Elish Kent Kane Gold Medal, Geog. Soc. of Philadelphia, 1952; Vega Medal, Swedish Soc. of Anthropology and Geography, 1962; Lomonosov Medal, Moscow Univ., 1962; Royal Gold Medal, Royal Geog. Society, London, 1964; Officer of El Order por Meritos Distinguidos, Peru, 1953; Gold Medal City of Lima; Gr.-Officer, Order Al Merito della Repubblica Italiana, Italy, 1965; Comdr, Knights of Malta, 1970; Comdr with Star, Order of St Olav, Norway, 1970; Order of Merit, Egypt, 1971; Grand Officer, Royal Alaouites Order, Morocco, 1971; Hon. Citizen, Larvik, Norway, 1971; Kiril i Metodi Order, Bulgaria, 1972; Internat. Pahlavi Environment Prize, UN, 1978; Order of Golden Ark, Netherlands, 1980; Bradford Washburn Award, Boston Mus. of Science, USA, 1982. *Films:* The Kon-Tiki Expedition (Oscar award for camera achievement, Nat. Acad. Motion Picture Arts and Scis, 1951); Galapagos Expedition; Aku-Aku, The Secret of Easter Island; The Ra Expeditions; The Tigris Expedition; The Maldive Mystery. *Publications:* Paa Jakt efter Paradiset, 1938; The Kon-Tiki Expedition, 1948; American Indians in the Pacific: the theory behind the Kon-Tiki expedition, 1952; (with A. Skjolsvold) Archæological Evidence of Pre-Spanish Visits to the Galapagos Islands, 1956; Aku-Aku: The Secrets of Easter Island, 1957; Co-editor (with E. N. Ferdon, Jr) Reports of the Norwegian Achæological Expedition to Easter Island and the East Pacific, Vol. I: The Archæology of Easter Island, 1961, vol. II: Miscellaneous Papers, 1965; Navel of the World (Chapter XIV) in Vanished Civilizations, 1963; Indianer und Alt-Asiaten im Pazifik: Das Abenteuer einer Theorie, 1965 (Vienna); Sea Routes to Polynesia, 1968; The Ra Expeditions, 1970; Chapters in Quest for America, 1971; Fatu-Hiva Back to Nature, 1974; Art of Easter Island, 1975; Zwischen den Kontinenten, 1975; Early Man and the Ocean, 1978; The Tigris Expedition, 1980; The Mystery of the Maldives, 1986; contrib. National Geographical Magazine, Royal Geographical Journal, The Geographical Magazine, Archiv für Völkerkunde, Ymer, Swedish Geogr. Year-book, South-western Journal of Anthropology, Russian Academy of Sciences Yearbook, American Antiquity, Antiquity (Cambridge); works trans. into numerous languages; *relevant publication:* Senor Kon-Tiki, by Arnold Jacoby, 1965. *Recreations:* outdoor life, travelling. *Address:* Colla Micheri, 17020 Laigueglia, Italy.

HEYGATE, Sir George Lloyd, 5th Bt *cr* 1831; *S* father, 1976. *Heir:* *b* Richard John Gage Heygate.

HEYHOE FLINT, Rachael, MBE 1972; public relations consultant; journalist, broadcaster, public speaker, sportswoman; *b* 11 June 1939; *d* of Geoffrey Heyhoe and Roma (*née* Crocker); *m* 1971, Derrick Flint, BSc; one *s* and one step *s* two step *d*. *Educ:* Wolverhampton High Sch. for Girls; Dartford Coll. of Physical Educn (Dip. in Phys. Educn). Head of Phys. Education: Wolverhampton Municipal Grammar Sch., 1960–62; Northicote Sch., 1962–64; US Field Hockey Assoc. Coach, 1964 and 1965; Journalist, Wolverhampton Express & Star, 1965–72; Sports Editor, Wolverhampton Chronicle, 1969–71; first woman Sports Reporter, ITV, 1972; Daily Telegraph Sports Writer, 1967–; Vice-Chm., 1981–86, and Public Relations Officer, 1982–86, Women's Cricket

Assoc.; Marketing and Promotions Consultant: Godfrey Davis (Holdings) Ltd, Bushey, Herts, 1982–; National Mutual Life Assurance Soc., Hitchin, Herts, 1983–; European Ferries, 1983; La Manga Country Club, Southern Spain, 1983–; Promotions consultant, Wolves FC, 1985. Mem., Sportswriters Assoc., 1967. England Hockey rep., 1964 (goalkeeper); Mem., England Women's Cricket team, 1960–83, Captain, 1966–77. Hit first 6 in Women's Test Cricket 1963 (England *v* Australia, Oval); scored highest test score in England and 2nd highest in world, 1976 (179 runs for England *v* Australia, Oval). Best After Dinner Speakers Award, Guild of Professional Toastmasters, 1972. *Publications:* Just for Kicks, (Guide to hockey goalkeeping), 1966; Women's Hockey, 1975; (with Netta Rheinberg) Fair Play, The Story of Women's Cricket, 1976; (autobiog.) "Heyhoe!", 1978. *Recreations:* golf, hockey, cricket; former county squash player (Staffs). *Address:* Danescroft, Wergs Road, Tettenhall, Wolverhampton, West Midlands. *T:* Wolverhampton 752103. *Clubs:* Lord's Taverners; Wolverhampton Lawn Tennis & Squash; South Staffs Golf.

HEYMAN, Allan, QC 1969; *b* 27 Feb. 1921; *e s* of late Erik Heyman and Rita Heyman (*née* Meyer); *m* 1958, Anne Marie (*née* Castenschiold); one *d*. *Educ:* Stenhus Kostskole, Denmark; Univ. of Copenhagen. Master of Law (Univ. of Copenhagen), 1947. Called to Bar, Middle Temple, 1951, Bencher 1975. Pres., Internat. Lawn Tennis Fedn, 1971–74, Hon. Life Vice-Pres., 1979. Kt of Dannebrog (Denmark). *Recreations:* shooting, stalking, reading, music. *Address:* 1 New Square, Lincoln's Inn, WC2; Marshland House, Iken, Woodbridge, Suffolk. *Clubs:* Naval and Military, Shikar; All England Lawn Tennis and Croquet.

HEYMAN, Sir Horace (William), Kt 1976; BSc; CEng, FIEE; Chartered Engineer and business consultant; Chairman, English Industrial Estates Corporation, 1970–77; Director, Supervisory Board, Zurich, 1955–84, UK Group, 1965–86, Hotelplan International; *b* 13 March 1912; *m* 1st, 1939; one *s* one *d*; 2nd, 1966, Dorothy Forster Atkinson. *Educ:* Ackworth Sch.; Technische Hochschule, Darmstadt; Birmingham Univ. BSc hons, electrical engrg, 1936. Electricars Ltd, 1936–40; Metropolitan Vickers Ltd, Sheffield, 1940–45; Smith's Electric Vehicles Ltd and Subsids, 1945–64 (Man. Dir, 1949–64); Co-Founder, Sevcon Engineering Ltd, 1960; Vice-Pres., Battronic Corp., Philadelphia, 1960–64. Export Marketing Adviser for Northern Region, BoT, 1969–70; Consultant: DoI Invest in Britain Bureau, 1977–79; Elmwood Sensors Ltd, 1977–; Thermal Quarz Schmelz GmbH, 1983–; Chm., Newcastle Polytechnic Products Ltd, 1983–86. Newcastle Polytechnic: Governor, 1974–86; Vice-Chm., 1983–86; Hon. Fellow, 1985. Mem. Council, Soc. of Motor Manufrs and Traders, 1949–64 (Man. Cttee, 1952–64); Chm., Electric Vehicle Assoc. of Gt Britain, 1953–55. Witness at US Senate hearings on air and water pollution, 1967. Chairman: N Region Energy Conservation Group, 1973–77; NEDO Working Party on House Bldg Performance, 1976–79. Pres., Northumbria Tourist Bd, 1983–86. FIEE 1952; FRSA 1969. *Address:* 20 Whitburn Hall, Whitburn, Sunderland SR6 7JQ. *T:* Whitburn 294957.

HEYMAN, Prof. Jacques, MA, PhD; FICE; FSA; FEng; Professor of Engineering, since 1971, and Head of Department of Engineering, since 1983, University of Cambridge; Fellow of Peterhouse, 1949–51, and since 1955; Consultant Engineer: Ely Cathedral, since 1972; St Albans Cathedral, since 1978; *b* 8 March 1925; *m* 1958, Eva Orlans (*d* 1982); three *d*. *Educ:* Whitgift Sch.; Peterhouse, Cambridge. Senior Bursar, Peterhouse, 1962–64; University Demonstrator, Engineering Dept, Cambridge Univ., 1951, University Lectr, 1954, Reader, 1968. Vis. Professor: Brown Univ., USA, 1957–58; Harvard Univ., 1966. Member: Architectural Adv. Panel, Westminster Abbey, 1973–; Cathedrals Advisory Commn for England, 1981–; Council, ICE, 1960–63 and 1975–78; Smeatonian Soc. of Civil Engrs, 1982–. Hon. DSc Sussex, 1975. James Watt Medal, 1973. *Publications:* The Steel Skeleton, vol. 2 (with Lord Baker, M. R. Horne), 1956; Plastic Design of Portal Frames, 1957; Beams and Framed Structures, 1964, 2nd edn 1974; Plastic Design of Frames, vol. 1, 1969 (paperback 1980), vol. 2, 1971; Coulomb's Memoir on Statics, 1972; Equilibrium of Shell Structures, 1977; Elements of Stress Analysis, 1982; The Masonry Arch, 1982; articles on plastic design, masonry construction and general structural theory. *Address:* Engineering Laboratory, Trumpington Street, Cambridge. *T:* Cambridge 332617.

HEYMANN, Prof. Franz Ferdinand, PhD; CPhys, FInstP; Quain Professor of Physics, and Head of Department of Physics and Astronomy, University College, University of London, since 1975; *b* 17 Aug. 1924; *s* of Paul Gerhard Heymann and Magdalena Petronella Heymann; *m* 1950, Marie Powell. *Educ:* Univ. of Cape Town (BScEng with Distinction, 1944); Univ. of London (PhD 1953). FInstP 1966. Engr, Cape Town, 1944–45; Jun. Lectr in Engrg, Univ. of Cape Town, 1945–47; Special Trainee, Metropolitan Vickers, Manchester, 1947–50; University Coll. London: Asst Lectr in Physics, 1950–52; Lectr, 1952–60; Reader, 1960–66; Prof. of Physics, 1966–75. *Publications:* scientific papers on res. done mainly in fields of particle accelerators and elementary particle physics. *Recreations:* music, gemmology, gardening. *Address:* Department of Physics and Astronomy, University College, Gower Street, WC1E 6BT; 59 The Gateway, Woking, Surrey. *T:* Woking 72304.

HEYTESBURY, 6th Baron *cr* 1828; **Francis William Holmes à Court;** Bt 1795; *b* 8 Nov. 1931; *s* of 5th Baron Heytesbury and Beryl (*d* 1968), *y d* of late A. E. B. Crawford, LLD, DCL, Aston Clinton House, Bucks; *S* father, 1971; *m* 1962, Alison, *e d* of Michael Graham Balfour, CBE; one *s* one *d*. *Educ:* Bryanston; Pembroke College, Cambridge (BA 1954). *Heir: s* Hon. James William Holmes à Court, *b* 30 July 1967.

HEYWARD, Rt. Rev. Oliver Spencer; *see* Bendigo, Bishop of.

HEYWOOD, Francis Melville, MA; Warden of Lord Mayor Treloar College, 1952–69, retired 1969; *b* 1 Oct. 1908; 4th *s* of late Rt Rev. B. O. F. Heywood, DD; *m* 1937, Dorothea Kathleen (*d* 1983), *e d* of late Sir Basil Mayhew, KBE; one *s* two *d* (and one *s* decd). *Educ:* Haileybury Coll. (Scholar); Gonville and Caius Coll. Cambridge (Scholar), 1st Class Hons, Classical Tripos, Part I, 1929; Part II, 1931; Rugby Football blue, 1928. Asst Master, Haileybury Coll., 1931–35; Fellow, Asst Tutor and Praelector, Trinity Hall, Cambridge, 1935–39; Master of Marlborough Coll., 1939–52. *Publication:* A Load of New Rubbish, 1985. *Recreations:* walking, writing. *Address:* 30 The Bayle, Folkestone, Kent.

HEYWOOD, Geoffrey, MBE (mil.) 1945; JP; Consulting Actuary; *b* 7 April 1916; *s* of Edgar Heywood and Annie (*née* Dawson), Blackpool; *m* 1941, Joan Corinna Lumley; one *s* one *d*. *Educ:* Arnold Sch., Blackpool. Served War, 1940–46: Royal Artillery, N Africa, Italy, Greece; commissioned, 1941, Major, 1944; despatches, 1945. Refuge Assce Co. Ltd, 1933–40; Duncan C. Fraser & Co. (Consulting Actuaries), 1946–86 (Sen. Partner, 1952–86). Pres., Manchester Actuarial Soc., 1951–53; Chm., Assoc. of Consulting Actuaries, 1959–62; Chm., Internat. Assoc. of Consulting Actuaries, 1968–72; Pres., Inst. of Actuaries, 1972–74 (Vice-Pres., 1964–67). Mem. Page Cttee to Review National Savings. Dep. Chm., Mersey Docks & Harbour Co., 1975–85; Mem., Nat. Bus Co., 1978–85. Chm., Merseyside CableVision, 1982–; Director: Barclays Bank Trust Co., 1967–86; Liverpool Bd Barclays Bank, 1972–86; Barclays Unicorn Gp, 1977–85; Universities Superannuation Scheme, 1974–86. FFA 1939; FIA 1946; FRAS 1982. Founder Master, Actuaries Co., 1979; Liveryman, Clockmakers' Co. JP Liverpool 1962. *Publications:* contribs to Jl Inst. Actuaries. *Recreations:* golf, tennis, antiquarian horology. *Address:* Drayton, Croft Drive East, Caldy, Wirral, Merseyside L48 1LS. *T:* 051–625 6707. *Clubs:* Army and Navy, Royal Automobile.

HEYWOOD, Very Rev. Hugh Christopher Lempriere, MA; Provost Emeritus of Southwell; *b* 5 Nov. 1896; *s* of late Charles Christopher Heywood; *m* 1920, Margaret Marion (*d* 1982), *d* of Herbert Vizard; one *s* one *d*. *Educ:* Haileybury; Trinity Coll., Cambridge (Scholar and Stanton Student). Manchester Regt 1914–17 (wounded, despatches); 74th Punjabis IA 1917–23 (Staff Capt., 1919–22); Ordained, 1926; Curate of St Andrew's the Great, Cambridge, 1926–27; of Holy Cross, Greenford, 1927–28; Fellow and Dean, Gonville and Caius Coll., Cambridge, 1928–45; University Lecturer in Divinity, Cambridge, 1937–45; Provost of Southwell and Rector of S Mary, Southwell, 1945–69; Priest-in-charge of Upton, Diocese of Southwell, 1969–76. Examining Chaplain to Bishop of Southwark, 1932–41, and to Bishop of Southwell, 1941–69. Junior Proctor, Cambridge, 1934–35 and 1942–43. *Publications:* The Worshipping Community, 1938; On a Golden Thread, 1960; Finding Happiness in Remembering, 1978; Still on a Golden Thread, 1980; And Still on that Thread, 1982. *Address:* 26 Lyndewode Road, Cambridge.

HEYWOOD, Sir Oliver Kerr, 5th Bt, *cr* 1838; *b* 30 June 1920; *s* of late Maj.-Gen. C. P. Heywood, CB, CMG, DSO (2nd *s* of 3rd Bt) and late Margaret Vere, *d* of late Arthur Herbert Kerr; *S* uncle 1946; *m* 1947, Denise Wymondham, 2nd *d* of late Jocelyn William Godefroi, MVO; three *s*. *Educ:* Eton; Trinity Coll. Cambridge (BA). Served in Coldstream Guards, 1940–46 (despatches). Profession: artist. *Heir: s* Peter Heywood [*b* 10 Dec. 1947; *m* 1970, Jacqueline Anne, *d* of Sir Robert Hunt, *qv*; two *d*]. *Address:* Rose Cottage, Elcombe, Stroud, Glos.

HEYWOOD, Prof. Vernon Hilton; Professor and Head of Department of Botany, University of Reading, since 1968; *b* 24 Dec. 1927; *s* of Vernon William and Marjorie Elizabeth Heywood; *m* 1st, 1952, María de la Concepción Salcedo Manrique; four *s*; 2nd, 1980, Christine Anne Brighton. *Educ:* George Heriot's Sch., Edinburgh; Edinburgh Univ. (BSc, DSc); Pembroke Coll., Cambridge (PhD). Lecturer 1955–60, Sen. Lectr 1960–63, Reader 1963–64, Professor 1964–68, Dept of Botany, Univ. of Liverpool; Dean, Faculty of Science, Univ. of Reading, 1978–81. Chm., European Plants Specialist Gp, Species Survival Commn of IUCN, 1984–. Trustee, Royal Botanic Gardens, Kew, 1983–. Councillor of Honour, Consejo Superior de Investigaciones Científicas, Spain, 1970. *Publications:* Principles of Angiosperm Taxonomy (with P. H. Davis), 1963, 2nd edn 1965; Plant Taxonomy, 1967, 2nd edn 1976; Flowering Plants of the World, 1978, 2nd edn 1985; (jtly) Our Green and Living World, 1984; Las Plantas con Flores, 1985; nearly 200 papers in sci. jls. *Recreations:* cooking, travel, music, writing. *Address:* White Mead, 22 Wiltshire Road, Wokingham RG11 1TP. *T:* Wokingham 780185.

HEYWORTH, Peter Lawrence Frederick; Music Critic of The Observer since 1955; *b* 3 June 1921; *er s* of Lawrence Ormerod Heyworth and Ellie Stern. *Educ:* Charterhouse; Balliol Coll., Oxford. HM Forces, 1940–46; Balliol, 1947–50; University of Göttingen, 1950. Music critic of Times Educational Supplement, 1952–56; Record reviewer for New Statesman, 1956–58; Guest of the Ford Foundation in Berlin, 1964–65. Critic of the Year, British Press Awards, 1980, commendation 1979. *Publications:* (ed) Berlioz, Romantic and Classic: selected writings by Ernest Newman, 1972; (ed) Conversations with Klemperer, 1973; Otto Klemperer: his life and times, Vol. 1 1885–1933, 1983. *Address:* 32 Bryanston Square, W1H 7LS. *T:* 01–262 8906; Yew Tree Cottage, Hinton St Mary, Sturminster Newton, Dorset. *T:* Sturminster Newton 72203.

HEZLET, Vice-Admiral Sir Arthur Richard, KBE 1964; CB 1961; DSO 1944 (Bar 1945); DSC 1941; *b* 7 April 1914; *s* of late Maj.-Gen. R. K. Hezlet, CB, CBE, DSO; *m* 1948, Anne Joan Patricia, *e d* of late G. W. N. Clark, Carnabane, Upperlands, Co. Derry; two adopted *d*. *Educ:* RN College, Dartmouth. Comd HM Submarines: H44, Ursula, Trident, Thrasher and Trenchant, 1941–45; comd HMS Scorpion, 1949–50; Chief Staff Officer to Flag Officer (Submarines), 1953–54; Capt. (D), 6th Destroyer Squadron 1955–56; Dir, RN Staff Coll., Greenwich, 1956–57; comd HMS Newfoundland, 1958–59; Rear-Adm. 1959; Flag Officer (Submarines), 1959–61; Flag Officer, Scotland, 1961–62; Vice-Adm. 1962; Flag Officer, Scotland and Northern Ireland, 1963–64; retired 1964. Legion of Merit (Degree of Commander) (US), 1945. *Publications:* The Submarine and Sea Power, 1967; Aircraft and Sea Power, 1970; The 'B' Specials, 1972; Electron and Sea Power, 1975. *Address:* Bovagh House, Aghadowey, Co. Derry, N Ireland. *Clubs:* Army and Navy, Royal Ocean Racing.

HIBBARD, Prof. Bryan Montague, MD, PhD; FRCOG; Professor of Obstetrics and Gynaecology, University of Wales College of Medicine (formerly Welsh National School of Medicine), since 1973; Consultant Obstetrician and Gynaecologist, University Hospital of Wales; *b* 24 April 1926; *s* of Montague Reginald and Muriel Irene Hibbard; *m* 1955, Elizabeth Donald Grassie. *Educ:* Queen Elizabeth's Sch., Barnet; St Bartholomew's Hosp. Med. Coll., London (MD); PhD (Liverpool). MRCS. Formerly: Sen. Lectr, Liverpool Univ.; Consultant Obstetrician and Gynaecologist, Liverpool RHB. Member: Cttee on Safety of Medicines, 1979–83; Maternity Services Adv. Cttee, 1981–85; Medicines Commn, 1986–. *Publications:* numerous contribs to world medical literature. *Recreations:* collecting 18th century drinking glasses, fell walking, coarse gardening. *Address:* The Clock House, Cathedral Close, Llandaff, Cardiff CF5 2ED. *T:* Cardiff 564565.

HIBBERD, Prof. George, PhD; ARTC, CEng, Hon. FIMinE; FRSE; Dixon Professor of Mining, University of Glasgow, and Professor of Mining, University of Strathclyde, Glasgow, 1947–67, now Emeritus; *b* Muirkirk, NB, 17 May 1901; *e s* of Charles Hibberd and Helen Brown; *m* 1931, Marion Dalziel Robb Adamson; two *s* two *d*. *Educ:* Muirkirk Public Sch.; Royal Tech. Coll., Glasgow. Walter Duncan Res. Scholar. Mining official, 1926–28; Coll. Lectr, 1928–46. Past Pres. Mining Inst. of Scotland. Mem. Council, Inst. Mining Engineers. *Publications:* A Survey of the Welsh Slate Industry; A Survey of The Caithness Flagstone Industry; numerous papers on mining and scientific subjects in technical press. (Jointly) A Survey of the Scottish Slate Industry and A Survey of the Scottish Free-Stone Quarrying Industry. *Recreations:* golf, gardening. *Address:* 120 Kings Park Avenue, Glasgow G44 4HS. *T:* 041–632 4608.

HIBBERT; *see* Holland-Hibbert, family name of Viscount Knutsford.

HIBBERT, Christopher, MC 1945; author; *b* 5 March 1924; *s* of late Canon H. V. Hibbert; *m* 1948, Susan Piggford; two *s* one *d*. *Educ:* Radley; Oriel Coll., Oxford (MA). Served in Italy, 1944–45; Capt., London Irish Rifles. Partner in firm of land agents, auctioneers and surveyors, 1948–59. Fellow, Chartered Auctioneers' and Estate Agents' Inst., 1948–59. Pres., Johnson Soc., 1980. Won Heinemann Award for Literature, 1962. FRSL, FRGS. *Publications:* The Road to Tyburn, 1957; King Mob, 1958; Wolfe at Quebec, 1959; The Destruction of Lord Raglan, 1961; Corunna, 1961; Benito Mussolini, 1962; The Battle of Arnhem, 1962; The Roots of Evil, 1963; The Court at Windsor, 1964; Agincourt, 1964; (ed) The Wheatley Diary, 1964; Garibaldi and His Enemies, 1965; The Making of Charles Dickens, 1967; (ed) Waterloo: Napoleon's Last Campaign, 1967; (ed) An American in Regency England: The Journal of Louis Simond, 1968;

Charles I, 1968; The Grand Tour, 1969; London: Biography of a City, 1969; The Search for King Arthur, 1970; (ed) The Recollections of Rifleman Harris, 1970; Anzio: the bid for Rome, 1970; The Dragon Wakes: China and the West, 1793–1911, 1970; The Personal History of Samuel Johnson, 1971; (ed) Twilight of Princes, 1971; George IV, Prince of Wales, 1762–1811, 1972; George IV, Regent and King, 1812–1830, 1973; The Rise and Fall of the House of Medici, 1974; (ed) A Soldier of the Seventy-First, 1975; Edward VII: a portrait, 1976; The Great Mutiny: India 1857, 1978; Disraeli and His World, 1978; The Court of St James's, 1979; (ed) Boswell's Life of Johnson, 1979; The French Revolution, 1981; (ed) Greville's England, 1981; Africa Explored: Europeans in the Dark Continent, 1769–1889, 1982; (ed with Ben Weinreb) The London Encyclopaedia, 1983; Queen Victoria in Her Letters and Journals, 1984; Rome, Biography of a City, 1985; Cities and Civilizations, 1986. *Recreations:* gardening, travel, cooking. *Address:* The Old Post Office, Stonor, near Henley-on-Thames, Oxon RG9 6HE. *Club:* Army and Navy.

HIBBERT, Eleanor; author; *b* London. *Educ:* privately. *Publications: as Jean Plaidy:* Together They Ride, 1945; Beyond The Blue Mountains, 1947; Murder Most Royal (and as The King's Pleasure, USA), 1949; The Goldsmith's Wife, 1950; Madame Serpent, 1951; Daughter of Satan, 1952; The Italian Woman, 1952; Sixth Wife, 1953, new edn 1969; Queen Jezebel, 1953; St Thomas's Eve, 1954; The Spanish Bridegroom, 1954; Gay Lord Robert, 1955; The Royal Road to Fotheringay, 1955, new edn 1968; The Wandering Prince, 1956; A Health Unto His Majesty, 1956; Here Lies Our Sovereign Lord, 1956; Flaunting Extravagant Queen, 1956, new edn 1960; Triptych of Poisoners, 1958, new edn 1970; Madonna of the Seven Hills, 1958; Light on Lucrezia, 1958; Louis the Wellbeloved, 1959; The Road to Compiegne, 1959; The Rise of the Spanish Inquisition, 1959; The Growth of the Spanish Inquisition, 1960; Castile For Isabella, 1960; Spain for the Sovereigns, 1960; The End of the Spanish Inquisition, 1961; Daughters of Spain, 1961; Katherine, The Virgin Widow, 1961; Meg Roper, Daughter of Sir Thomas More (for children), 1961; The Young Elizabeth (for children), 1961; The Shadow of the Pomegranate, 1962; The King's Secret Matter, 1962; The Young Mary, Queen of Scots, 1962; The Captive Queen of Scots, 1963; Mary, Queen of France, 1964; The Murder in the Tower, 1964; The Thistle and the Rose, 1965; The Three Crowns, 1965; Evergreen Gallant, 1965; The Haunted Sisters, 1966; The Queen's Favourites, 1966; The Princess of Celle, 1967; Queen in Waiting, 1967; The Spanish Inquisition, its Rise, Growth and End (3 vols in one), 1967; Caroline The Queen, 1968; Katharine of Aragon (3 vols in one), 1968; The Prince and the Quakeress, 1968; The Third George, 1969; Catherine de Medici (3 vols in one), 1969; Perdita's Prince, 1969; Sweet Lass of Richmond Hill, 1970; The Regent's Daughter, 1971; Goddess of the Green Room, 1971; Victoria in the Wings, 1972; Charles II (3 vols in one), 1972; The Captive of Kensington Palace, 1972; The Queen and Lord M, 1973; The Queen's Husband, 1973; The Widow of Windsor, 1974; The Bastard King, 1974; The Lion of Justice, 1975; The Passionate Enemies, 1976; The Plantagenet Prelude, 1976; The Revolt of the Eaglets, 1977; The Heart of the Lion, 1977; The Prince of Darkness, 1978; The Battle of the Queens, 1978; The Queen from Provence, 1979; Edward Longshanks, 1979; The Follies of the King, 1980; The Vow on the Heron, 1980; Passage to Pontefract, 1981; Star of Lancaster, 1981; Epitaph for Three Women, 1981; Red Rose of Anjou, 1982; The Sun in Splendour, 1982; Uneasy Lies the Head, 1982; Myself My Enemy, 1983; Queen of this Realm, 1984; Victoria Victorious, 1986; *as Eleanor Burford:* Daughter of Anna, 1941; Passionate Witness, 1941; Married Love, 1942; When All The World Was Young, 1943; So The Dreams Depart, 1944; Not In Our Stars, 1945; Dear Chance, 1947; Alexa, 1948; The House At Cupid's Cross, 1949; Believe The Heart, 1950; Love Child, 1950; Saint Or Sinner?, 1951; Dear Delusion, 1952; Bright Tomorrow, 1952; When We Are Married, 1953; Leave Me My Love, 1953; Castles in Spain, 1954; Hearts Afire, 1954; When Other Hearts, 1955; Two Loves In Her Life, 1955; Married in Haste, 1956; Begin To Live, 1956; To Meet A Stranger, 1957; Pride of the Morning, 1958; Blaze of Noon, 1958; Dawn Chorus, 1959; Red Sky At Night, 1959; Night of Stars, 1960; Now That April's Gone, 1961; Who's Calling?, 1962; *as Ellalice Tate:* Defenders of The Faith, 1956 (under name of Jean Plaidy, 1970); Scarlet Cloak, 1957 (2nd edn, under name of Jean Plaidy, 1969); Queen of Diamonds, 1958; Madame Du Barry, 1959; This Was A Man, 1961; *as Elbur Ford:* The Flesh and The Devil, 1950; Poison in Pimlico, 1950; Bed Disturbed, 1952; Such Bitter Business, 1953 (as Evil in the House, USA 1954); *as Kathleen Kellow:* Danse Macabre, 1952; Rooms At Mrs Oliver's, 1953; Lilith, 1954 (2nd edn, under name of Jean Plaidy, 1967); It Began in Vauxhall Gardens, 1955 (2nd edn under name of Jean Plaidy, 1968); Call of the Blood, 1956; Rochester-The Mad Earl, 1957; Milady Charlotte, 1959; The World's A Stage, 1960; *as Victoria Holt:* Mistress of Mellyn, 1961; Kirkland Revels, 1962; The Bride of Pendorric, 1963; The Legend of the Seventh Virgin, 1965; Menfreya, 1966; The King of the Castle, 1967; The Queen's Confession, 1968; The Shivering Sands, 1969; The Secret Woman, 1971; The Shadow of the Lynx, 1972; On the Night of the Seventh Moon, 1973; The Curse of the Kings, 1973; The House of a Thousand Lanterns, 1974; Lord of the Far Island, 1975; The Pride of the Peacock, 1976; My Enemy the Queen, 1978; The Spring of the Tiger, 1979; The Mask of the Enchantress, 1980; The Judas Kiss, 1981; The Demon Lover, 1982; The Time of the Hunter's Moon, 1983; The Landower Legacy, 1984; The Road to Paradise Island, 1985; *as Philippa Carr:* The Miracle at St Bruno's, 1972; Lion Triumphant, 1974; The Witch from the Sea, 1975; Saraband for Two Sisters, 1976; Lament for a Lost Lover, 1977; The Love Child, 1978; The Song of the Siren, 1979; The Drop of the Dice, 1980; The Adulteress, 1981; Zipporah's Daughter, 1983; Voices in a Haunted Room, 1984; Midsummer's Eve, 1986. *Address:* c/o Robert Hale Ltd, 45/47 Clerkenwell Green, EC1.

HIBBERT, Maj.-Gen. Hugh Brownlow, DSO 1940; *b* 10 Dec. 1893; *s* of late Adm. H. T. Hibbert, CBE, DSO; *m* 1926, Susan Louisa Mary Feilding (*d* 1975); one *s* one *d*. *Educ:* Uppingham; RMC, Sandhurst. Retired pay, 1946. *Address:* Kilsall Hall, Shifnal, Salop.

HIBBERT, Jack; Director, Central Statistical Office, and Head of Government Statistical Service, since 1985; *b* 14 Feb. 1932; *s* of late William Collier Hibbert and Ivy Annie (*née* Wigglesworth); *m* 1957, Joan Clarkson; two *s* one *d*. *Educ:* Leeds Grammar Sch.; London Sch. of Economics (BScEcon). Served Royal Air Force, 1950–52. Exchequer and Audit Dept, 1952–60; Central Statistical Office, 1960–65; LSE, 1965–66; CSO, 1966; Chief Statistician, 1970; Asst Dir, 1977; OECD and EUROSTAT Consultant 1981; Under Sec., DTI, 1982–85. *Publications:* Measuring the Effects of Inflation on Income, Saving and Wealth (OECD), 1983; articles in Economic Trends, Rev. of Income and Wealth. *Recreations:* bridge, walking. *Address:* Central Statistical Office, Great George Street, SW1P 3AQ. *Club:* Reform.

HIBBERT, Sir Reginald (Alfred), GCMG 1982 (KCMG 1979; CMG 1966); HM Diplomatic Service, retired; Director, Ditchley Foundation, since 1982; *b* 21 Feb. 1922; *s* of Alfred Hibbert, Sawbridgeworth, Herts; *m* 1949, Ann Alun Pugh, *d* of late Sir Alun Pugh; two *s* one *d*. *Educ:* Queen Elizabeth's Sch., Barnet; Worcester Coll., Oxford. Served with SOE and 4th Hussars in Albania and Italy, 1943–45. Entered Foreign Service, 1946; served in Bucharest, Vienna, Guatemala, Ankara, Brussels; Chargé d'Affaires, Ulan Bator, 1964–66; Research Fellow, Leeds Univ., 1966–67; Political Adviser's Office, Singapore, 1967–69; Political Adviser to C-in-C Far East, 1970–71; Minister, Bonn, 1972–75; Asst Under-Sec. of State, FCO, 1975–76; Dep. Under-Sec. of State, FCO, 1976–79; Ambassador to France, 1979–82. Vis. Fellow, Nuffield Coll., Oxford, 1984–. *Address:* Ditchley Park, Enstone, Oxon OX7 4ER. *T:* Enstone 346; Frondeg, Pennal, Machynlleth, Powys SY20 9JX. *T:* Pennal 220. *Club:* Reform.

HICK, Prof. John Harwood; Danforth Professor since 1979, and Director of Blaisdell Programs in World Religions and Cultures since 1983, Claremont Graduate School, California; *b* 20 Jan. 1922; *s* of Mark Day Hick and Mary Aileen (Hirst); *m* 1953, (Joan) Hazel, *d* of F. G. Bowers, CB, CBE, and Frances Bowers; three *s* one *d*. *Educ:* Bootham Sch., York; Edinburgh Univ. (MA 1948 (1st cl. hons Philos); DLitt 1974); Oriel Coll., Oxford (Campbell-Fraser schol.; DPhil 1950); Westminster Coll., Cambridge. Friends' Ambulance Unit, 1942–45. Ordained, Presb. C of E, 1953; Minister, Belford Presb. Church, Northumberland, 1953–56; Asst Prof. of Philosophy, Cornell Univ., 1956–59; Stuart Prof. of Christian Philosophy, Princeton Theolog. Seminary, 1959–64; S. A. Cook Bye-Fellow, Gonville and Caius Coll., Cambridge, 1963–64; PhD by incorporation; Lectr in Divinity, Cambridge Univ., 1964–67; H. G. Wood Prof. of Theology, Univ. of Birmingham, 1967–82. Guggenheim Fellow, 1963–64, and 1985–86; Leverhulme Res. Fellow, 1976; Scholar-in-residence, Rockefeller Foundn Research Center, Bellagio, Italy, 1986. Lectures: Mead-Swing, Oberlin Coll., USA, 1962–63; Mary Farnum Brown, Haverford Coll., USA 1964–65; James W. Richard, Univ. of Virginia, 1969; Distinguished Vis., Univ. of Oregon, 1969; Arthur Stanley Eddington Meml, 1972; Stanton, Cambridge Univ., 1974–77; Teape, Delhi and Madras, 1975; Ingersoll, Harvard, 1977; Hope, Stirling, 1977; Younghusband, London, 1977; Mackintosh, East Anglia, 1978; Riddell, Newcastle, 1978–79; Berkeley, TCD, 1979; Greenhoe, Louisville Pres. Sem., 1979; Potter, Washington State Univ., 1980; Montefiore, London, 1980; Brooks, Univ. of S California, 1982; Mars and Shaffer, Northwestern Univ., 1983; Niebuhr, Elmhurst Coll., 1986; Gifford, Edinburgh, 1986–87. Visiting Professor: Banares Hindu Univ., 1971; Visva Bharati Univ., 1971; Punjabi Univ., Patiala, 1971; Visiting Fellow: British Acad. Overseas, 1974; Univ. of Ceylon, 1974. Hulsean Preacher, Cambridge Univ., 1969; Select Preacher, Oxford Univ., 1970. Chairman: Religious and Cultural Panel, Birmingham Community Relations Cttee, 1969–74; Coordinating Working Party, Statutory Conf. for Revision of Agreed Syllabus of Religious Educn, Birmingham, 1971–74; Birmingham Inter-Faiths Council, 1975; President: Soc. for the Study of Theology, 1975–76; All Faiths for One Race, 1980–85 (Chm., 1972–73, 1978–80); Member: Amer. Soc. for the Study of Religion, 1983–; Amer. Philosophical Assoc., 1980–; Amer. Acad. of Religion, 1980–. Mem. Council, Selly Oak Colls, 1967–80; Governor, Queen's Coll., Birmingham, 1972–80. Member Editorial Board: The Encyclopedia of Philosophy; Religious Studies; Jl of Religion; Studies in Religion; Modern Theology. Hon. Teol. Dr Uppsala, 1977. *Publications:* Faith and Knowledge, 1957, 2nd edn 1966; Philosophy of Religion, 1963, 3rd edn 1983 (Spanish, Portuguese, Chinese, Japanese, Korean, Finnish and Swedish edns); (ed) Faith and the Philosophers, 1963; (ed) The Existence of God, 1963; (ed) Classical and Contemporary Readings in the Philosophy of Religion, 1963, 2nd edn 1970; Evil and the God of Love, 1966, 2nd edn 1977; (ed) The Many-Faced Argument, 1967; Christianity at the Centre, 1968, 2nd edn as The Centre of Christianity, 1977 (trans. Dutch and Chinese); Arguments for the Existence of God, 1971; Biology and the Soul, 1972; God and the Universe of Faiths, 1973; (ed) Truth and Dialogue, 1974; Death and Eternal Life, 1976 (trans. Dutch); (ed) The Myth of God Incarnate, 1977 (trans. German and Arabic); God has Many Names, 1980; (ed with Brian Hebblethwaite) Christianity and Other Religions, 1980; The Second Christianity, 1983; (with Michael Goulder) Why Believe in God?, 1983; Problems of Religious Pluralism, 1985; (ed with Hasan Askari) The Experience of Religious Diversity, 1985. *Address:* Department of Religion, Claremont Graduate School, Claremont, Calif 91711, USA; 21 Greening Drive, Edgbaston, Birmingham B15 2XA.

HICKEY, Sir Justin, Kt 1979; Chairman and Managing Director, Bartinon Securities Ltd (formerly Accident Insurance Mutual Ltd), since 1968; *b* 5 April 1925; *s* of Hon. Simon Hickey, Speaker, New South Wales Parliament, and Hilda Ellen Hickey (*née* Dacey); *m* 1964, Barbara Standish Thayer; one *s* four *d*. *Educ:* De La Salle College, Sydney. Chairman: Australian Family Trust, 1965; Thayer Foundation (US), 1972; Queensland Science & Technology Ltd, 1984–; Mem., Lloyd's of London, 1979. FRSA 1978. JP 1950. *Recreations:* yachting, art collection. *Address:* Bartinon, 20 Marseille Court, Sorrento, Qld 4217, Australia. *Club:* Royal Motor Yacht (Sydney).

HICKINBOTHAM, Rev. James Peter, DD Lambeth, 1979; *b* 16 May 1914; *s* of late F. J. L. Hickinbotham, JP and late Mrs Hickinbotham; *m* 1948, Ingeborg Alice Lydia Manger; two *s* one *d*. *Educ:* Rugby Sch.; Magdalen Coll., Oxford; Wycliffe Hall, Oxford. Deacon, 1937; priest, 1938; curate: St John, Knighton, Leicester, 1937–39; St Paul, S Harrow, 1940–42; Chaplain, Wycliffe Hall, Oxford, 1942–45; Vice-Principal, 1945–50. Prof. of Theology, University Coll. of the Gold Coast, 1950–54. Principal, St John's Coll. and Cranmer Hall, Durham, 1954–70; Principal of Wycliffe Hall, Oxford, 1970–79. Examining Chaplain: to Bishop of Manchester, 1947–50; to Bishop of Leicester, 1948–53; to Bishop of Durham, 1955–70. Proctor in Convocation, 1957–70. Hon. Canon, Durham Cathedral, 1959–70. Hon. Curate, Christ Church, Dowend, 1979–84. *Address:* 23 St George's View, Cullompton, Devon EX15 1BA. *T:* Cullompton 33326.

HICKLIN, Denis Raymond, OBE 1969; Member (part-time), Forestry Commission, 1978–81; *b* 15 April 1918; *s* of Joseph Herbert and Florence May Hicklin; *m* 1949, Joyce Grisdale Smith; two *s*. *Educ:* Merchant Taylors' Sch. Served War, 1939–46, RA (Major). John Dickinson, 1936–48; St Anne's Board Mill Co. Ltd, 1948–78 (Chm. and Man. Dir, 1966–78). *Recreations:* tennis, golf. *Address:* 1 Bumpers Batch, Midford Road, Bath BA2 5SQ. *T:* Bath 833123.

HICKLING, Rev. Canon Colin John Anderson; Canon Theologian, Leicester Cathedral, since 1983; *b* 10 July 1931; *s* of late Charles Frederick Hickling, CMG, ScD, and late Marjorie Ellerington, *d* of late Henry Blamey. *Educ:* Taunton Sch.; Epsom Coll.; King's Coll., Cambridge; Chichester Theol Coll. BA 1953, MA 1957. Deacon 1957, Priest 1958. Asst Curate, St Luke's, Pallion, Sunderland, 1957–61; Asst Tutor, Chichester Theol Coll., 1961–65; Asst Priest Vicar, Chichester Cath., 1964–65; Asst Lectr in New Testament Studies, King's Coll., Univ. of London, 1965–68, Lectr, 1968–84; Dep. Minor Canon, St Paul's Cath., 1969–78; Dep. Priest in Ordinary to the Queen, 1971–74; Priest in Ordinary to the Queen, 1974–84; Subwarden of King's Coll. Hall, 1969–78; Warden of King's Coll. Hostel, 1978–81; Tutor in Biblical Studies, Queen's Coll., Birmingham, 1984–85; E. W. Benson Fellow, Lincoln Theol Coll., 1985–86. Mem., Liturgical Commn, 1981–86. Boyle Lectr, 1973–76; Select Preacher: Univ. of Cambridge, 1979; Univ. of Oxford, 1983. *Publications:* contributed to: Church without Walls, 1968; Catholic Anglicans Today, 1968; Bible Bibliography 1967–73, 1974; (also ed jtly) What About the New Testament?, 1975; St Paul: Teacher and Traveller, 1975; L'Evangile de Jean, 1977; Les Actes des Apôtres, 1979; The Ministry of the Word, 1979; This is the Word of the Lord, 1980; Studia Biblica 1978, Vol. III, 1980; Logia: the sayings of Jesus, 1982; Studia Evangelica, Vol. VII, 1982; reviews and articles. *Recreation:* music. *Address:* c/o Lincoln Theological College, Drury Lane, Lincoln LN1 3BP.

HICKLING, Reginald Hugh, CMG 1968; PhD (London); QC (Gibraltar) 1970; *b* 2 Aug. 1920; *er s* of late Frederick Hugh Hickling and Elsie May Hickling, Malvern,

Worcs; *m* 1945, Beryl Iris (*née* Dennett); two *s* one *d* (and one *s* decd). *Educ:* Buxton Coll.; Nottingham Univ. RNVR, 1941–46. Dep. Solicitor, Evening Standard, London, 1946–50; Asst Attorney-Gen., Sarawak, 1950–55; Legal Adviser, Johore, 1956; Legal Draftsman, Malaya, 1957; Parly Draftsman, Malaya, 1959; Comr of Law Revision, Malaya, 1961; Commonwealth Office, 1964; Legal Adviser to High Comr, Aden and Protectorate of S Arabia, 1964–67; Maritime Law Adviser: Thailand, 1968–69; Malaysia, 1969; Ceylon, 1970; Yemen Arab Republic, 1984, 1986; Attorney-General, Gibraltar, 1970–72. Lectr in SE Asian Law, SOAS, 1976–78, 1981–, Vis. Professor, Faculty of Law: Univ. of Singapore, 1974–76 and 1978–80; Univ. of Malaya, 1983–84, 1986–. Hon. JMN (Malaya), 1960. *Publications:* The Furious Evangelist, 1950; The English Flotilla, 1954 (US as Falconer's Voyage, 1956); Sarawak and Its Government, 1955; Festival of Hungry Ghosts, 1957; An Introduction to the Federal Constitution, 1960; Lieutenant Okino, 1968; A Prince of Borneo, 1985; The Ghost of Orchard Road, 1985. *Recreation:* not watching TV. *Address:* 1 Highfield Road, Malvern, Worcs. *T:* Malvern 68197.

HICKMAN, Sir Glenn; *see* Hickman, Sir R. G.

HICKMAN, John Kyrle, CMG 1977; HM Diplomatic Service; Ambassador to Chile, since 1982; *b* 3 July 1927; *s* of late J. B. Hickman and Joan Hickman; *m* 1956, Jennifer Love; two *s* one *d*. *Educ:* Tonbridge; Trinity Hall, Cambridge. Served in RA, 1948–50. Asst Principal, WO, 1950; Principal, 1955; transf. to CRO, 1958; UK High Commn, Wellington, 1959–62; HM Diplomatic Service, 1965; British Embassy, Madrid, 1966; Counsellor and HM Consul-General, Bilbao, 1967; Dep. High Comr, Singapore, 1969–71; Head of SW Pacific Dept, FCO, 1971–74; Counsellor, Dublin, 1974–77; Ambassador to Ecuador, 1977–81. *Publications:* The Enchanted Islands: the Galápagos Discovered, 1985; occasional historical articles. *Recreations:* history, golf. *Address:* c/o Foreign and Commonwealth Office, SW1; 3 Weltje Road, W6. *Club:* Garrick.

HICKMAN, Michael Ranulf; His Honour Judge Hickman; a Circuit Judge, since 1974; *b* 2 Oct. 1922; *s* of John Owen Hickman and Nancy Viola Hickman (*née* Barlow); *m* 1943, Diana Richardson; one *s* one *d*. *Educ:* Wellington; Trinity Hall, Cambridge. 2nd cl. Hons in Law. Served War, RAFVR, 1940–46. Cambridge Univ., 1946–48; called to Bar, Middle Temple, 1949. Actg Dep. Chm., Hertfordshire QS, 1965–72; a Recorder of Crown Court, 1972–74. *Recreations:* shooting, fishing, gun dog training. *Address:* The Acorn, Bovingdon, Herts. *T:* Hemel Hempstead 832226.

HICKMAN, Sir (Richard) Glenn, 4th Bt *cr* 1903; *b* 12 April 1949; *s* of Sir Alfred Howard Whitby Hickman, 3rd Bt, and of Margaret D., *o d* of Leonard Kempson; *S* father, 1979; *m* 1981, Heather Mary Elizabeth, *er d* of late Dr James Moffett, Swindon, and late Dr Gwendoline Moffett; one *s* one *d*. *Educ:* Eton. *Heir:* *s* Charles Patrick Alfred Hickman, *b* 5 May 1983. *Address:* Twin Cottage, Batlers Green, Radlett, Herts. *Club:* Turf.

HICKMET, Richard Saladin; MP (C) Glanford and Scunthorpe, since 1983; barrister-at-law; *b* 1 Dec. 1947; *s* of Ferid and Elizabeth Hickmet; *m* 1973, Susan (*née* Ludwig); three *d*. *Educ:* Millfield Sch.; Sorbonne; Hull Univ. (BA). Dir, private hotel group, 1972–74. Called to the Bar, Inner Temple, 1974. Mem., Wandsworth Borough Council, 1978–83 (Chm., Leisure and Amenities Cttee, 1980–83; privatised street cleansing, refuse collection, parks maintenance). Mem. Management Cttee, and Trustee, Battersea Arts Centre. *Recreations:* squash, hunting. *Address:* House of Commons, SW1A 0AA. *T:* 01–219 3000; 3 Dr Johnson's Buildings, Temple, EC4. *T:* 01–353 8778.

HICKOX, Richard Sidney, FRCO(CHM); conductor; Music Director: City of London Sinfonia, since 1971; Richard Hickox Singers, since 1971; London Symphony Chorus, since 1976; Bradford Festival Choral Society, since 1978; Artistic Director, Northern Sinfonia, since 1982; Associate Conductor, London Symphony Orchestra, since 1985; *b* Stokenchurch, Bucks, 5 March 1948; *m* 1976, Frances Ina Sheldon-Williams; one *s*. *Educ:* in organ, piano and composition, Royal Acad. of Music (LRAM); Organ Scholar, Queens' Coll., Cambridge (MA). Début as professional conductor, St John's Smith Square, 1971; Organist and Master of the Music, St Margaret's, Westminster, 1972–82; Prom début, 1973. Artistic Director: Wooburn Fest., 1967–; St Endellion Fest., 1974–; Christ Church Spitalfields Fest., 1978–; Truro Fest., 1981–; Principal Guest Conductor, Dutch Radio Orch., 1980–; Assoc. Conductor, San Diego Symphony Orch., 1983–84; also regularly conducts LSO, RPO, Bournemouth Symphony Orch. and Sinfonietta, Royal Liverpool Phil. Orch., BBC Symphony, Concert, Scottish and Welsh Orchs, BBC Singers, Aarhus and Odens Orchs, Hallé Orch.; San Francisco Symphony Orch.; Detroit Symphony Orch.; Houston Symphony Orch.; Suisse Romande; Stockholm Philharmonic. Conducted: ENO, 1979; Opera North, 1982, 1986; Scottish Opera, 1985, 1987; Royal Opera, 1985; has appeared at many music festivals incl. Proms, Flanders, Bath and Cheltenham. Co-founder, Opera Stage, 1985. Many recordings of choral and orchestral music. *Address:* 35 Ellington Street, N7. *T:* 01–607 8984.

HICKS; *see* Joynson-Hicks.

HICKS, David (Nightingale); interior decorator, designer and author; Director: David Hicks International, since 1976; David Hicks Ltd, since 1960; *b* 25 March 1929; 3rd surv. *s* of late Herbert Hicks (stockbroker and twice past Master Salter's Company) and late Mrs Hicks; *m* 1960, Lady Pamela Carmen Louise Mountbatten, *yr d* of Admiral of the Fleet Earl Mountbatten of Burma, KG, GCB, OM, GCSI, GCIE, GCVO, DSO, PC, FRS; one *s* two *d*. *Educ:* Charterhouse; Central School of Arts and Crafts, London. Interiors for: Helena Rubinstein; QE2; HRH the Prince of Wales; Govt of NSW; British Steel Corp.; Aeroflot Offices; Marquess of Londonderry; Library in British Embassy, Washington, and Royal Yacht for HM King Fahd. Associate offices in: Brussels, Geneva, Karachi, Paris, Tokyo, Sydney. Designer of fabrics, carpets, furniture, women's wear, etc. Master, Salters' Co., 1977–78. FRSA. CoID (now Design Council) design award, 1970. *Publications:* David Hicks on Decoration, 1966; David Hicks on Living—with taste, 1968; David Hicks on Bathrooms, 1970; David Hicks on Decoration—with fabrics, 1971; David Hicks on Decoration—5, 1972; David Hicks Book of Flower Arranging, 1976; David Hicks Living with Design, 1979; David Hicks Garden Design, 1982. *Recreations:* shooting, riding, gardening, preservation. *Address:* Albany, Piccadilly, W1. *T:* (office) 01–627 4400.

HICKS, Col Sir Denys (Theodore), Kt 1961; OBE 1950; TD 1943; DL; Member Council of The Law Society, 1948–69; *b* 2 May 1908; *s* of late Cuthbert Hicks, Bristol; *m* 1941, Irene Elizabeth Mansell Leach; four *d*. *Educ:* Clifton. Admitted a Solicitor of Supreme Court of Judicature, 1931. Served War of 1939–45; with RA in UK and on staff; Col 1953; Hon. Col, 266 (Gloucester Vol. Artillery) Bty RA (Vols), 1972–75. Vice-President of The Law Society, 1959, Pres., 1960; Chm., Internat. Bar Assoc., 1966–70, Pres., 1970–74, Hon. Life Pres., 1974. Dep. Chm., Horserace Betting Levy Board, 1961–76; Mem., Royal Commission on Assizes and QS, 1967. Hon. Member: Amer. Bar Assoc., 1960; Il Ilustre y Nacional Collegio de Abagados de Mexico, 1964; Virginia State Bar Assoc., 1966. DL Avon (formerly Glos), 1957. *Address:* Damson Cottage, Hunstrete, Pensford, Bristol BS18 4NY. *T:* Compton Dando 464.

HICKS, Howard Arthur, CBE 1981; Founder and Chairman, IDC Group plc, since 1957; *b* 3 May 1914; *s* of Ivor Lewis Hicks and Gertrude Freda (*née* Shaw); *m* 1940, Anne Maureen (*née* Lang); one *s* one *d*. *Educ:* Pontypridd; Polytechnic of Wales (Fellow 1984). DSc Aston in Birmingham, 1976. CEng, FICE, FIProdE, FCIOB, FAmSCE, MSocIS, FIMH, FRSA, CBIM. Civil Engineer, Bridge Dept, Glamorgan CC, 1934–39; served War, Royal Engineers, 1939–46 (Major); Man. Dir, Beecham Reinforced Concrete Engineers, 1947–56; Director: Candover Investments plc, 1980–; Matthew Hall plc, 1984–. Chm., Aston Technical Management & Planning Services (Aston Univ.) Ltd, 1970–82; President: Inst. of Materials Handling, 1977–80; Instn of Production Engrs, 1980–81. Internat. Engrg Achievements Award, Inst. for the Advancement of Engrg, 1981; Distinguished Internat. Archimedes Engrg Achievements Award, Nat. Soc. of Professional Engrs of America, 1980; SME Engrg Citation, Soc. of Manufacturing Engrs of United States, 1982; Internat. Engr of the Year, Inst. for the Advancement of Engrg, LA, Calif, 1983; Space Shuttle Technol. Award, NASA, 1984. *Recreations:* (patron) Pontypridd Rugby Football Club; theatre. *Address:* Avonfield, Stratford upon Avon, Warwickshire CV37 6BJ. *T:* Stratford upon Avon 293594. *Clubs:* Athenæum; Cardiff and County; Phoenix (Lima, Peru).

HICKS, John Charles; QC 1980; a Recorder of the Crown Court, Western Circuit, since 1978; *b* 4 March 1928; *s* of late Charles Hicks and late Marjorie Jane Hicks; *m* 1957, Elizabeth Mary, *o d* of late Rev. J. B. Jennings; one *d* (one *s* decd). *Educ:* King Edward VI Grammar Schs, Chelmsford and Totnes; London Univ. LLM 1954. Served RA (National Service), 1946–48. Admitted solicitor, 1952; called to the Bar, Middle Temple, 1966. Legal Dept, Thomas Tilling Ltd, 1953–54; Partner in Messrs Burchells, solicitors, 1955–65; Methodist Missionary Soc., Caribbean, 1965–66. *Publications:* (ed jtly) The Constitution and Discipline of the Methodist Church in the Caribbean and the Americas, 1967, with annual supplements to date; articles in Mod. Law Rev., Cambridge Law Jl, and Epworth Rev. *Recreations:* squash rackets, music, theatre, opera, the Methodist Constitution. *Address:* 14 St Alban's Avenue, W4 5JP. *T:* 01–994 0315.

HICKS, Sir John (Richard), Kt 1964; FBA 1942; Fellow of All Souls College, since 1952; *b* 1904; *s* of late Edward Hicks, Leamington Spa; *m* 1935, Ursula K. Webb (*d* 1985). *Educ:* Clifton Coll.; Balliol Coll., Oxford. Lectr, London Sch. of Economics, 1926–35; Fellow of Gonville and Caius Coll., Cambridge, 1935–38, Hon. Fellow, 1971; Prof. of Political Economy, University of Manchester, 1938–46; Official Fellow of Nuffield Coll., Oxford, 1946–52; Drummond Prof. of Political Economy, University of Oxford, 1952–65; Member: Revenue Allocation Commn, Nigeria, 1950; Royal Commn on the Taxation of Profits and Income, 1951. Hon. Fellow, LSE, 1969. (Jtly) Nobel Memorial Prize for Economics, 1972. *Publications:* The Theory of Wages, 1932 (revised edn, 1963); Value and Capital, 1939; The Taxation of War Wealth (with U. K. Hicks and L. Rostas), 1941; The Social Framework, 1942 (4th edn, 1971); Standards of Local Expenditure (with U. K. Hicks), 1943; The Problem of Valuation for Rating (with U. K. Hicks and C. E. V. Leser), 1944; The Incidence of Local Rates in Great Britain (with U. K. Hicks), 1945; The Problem of Budgeting Reform, 1948; A Contribution to the Theory of the Trade Cycle, 1950; (with U. K. Hicks) Report on Finance and Taxation in Jamaica, 1955; A Revision of Demand Theory, 1956; Essays in World Economics, 1960; Capital and Growth, 1965; Critical Essays in Monetary Theory, 1967; A Theory of Economic History, 1969; Capital and Time, 1973; The Crisis in Keynesian Economics, 1974; Economic Perspectives, 1977; Causality in Economics, 1979; Collected Papers, 3 vols, 1981–83. *Address:* All Souls College, Oxford.

HICKS, Maj.-Gen. Michael; *see* Hicks, Maj.-Gen. W. M. E.

HICKS, Robert; MP (C) Cornwall South-East, since 1983 (Bodmin, 1970–Feb. 1974 and Oct. 1974–1983); *b* 18 Jan. 1938; *s* of W. H. Hicks; *m* 1962, Maria Elizabeth Ann Gwyther; two *d*. *Educ:* Queen Elizabeth Grammar Sch., Crediton; University Coll., London; Univ. of Exeter. Taught at St Austell Grammar Sch., 1961–64; Lecturer in Regional Geography, Weston-super-Mare Technical Coll., 1964–70. An Asst Govt Whip, 1973–74; Mem., Select Cttee of House of Commons, European Legislation, 1973, 1976–; Vice-Chairman, Cons. Parly Cttees for: Agriculture, 1972–73 (Chm., Horticultural Sub-Cttee), and 1974–82; European Affairs, 1979–80; Chairman: Westcountry Gp of Cons. MPs, 1976–77; UK Gp, Parly Assoc. for Euro-Arab Co-operation, 1982–; Treasurer, Cons. Party ME Council, 1980–; Parly Adviser to British Hotels, Restaurants and Caterers Assoc., 1974–, to Milk Marketing Bd, 1985–. *Recreations:* cricket, gardening. *Address:* Little Court, St Ive, Liskeard, Cornwall. *Club:* MCC.

HICKS, Thomas; *see* Steele, Tommy.

HICKS, Maj.-Gen. (William) Michael (Ellis), CB 1982; OBE 1967; Secretary, Royal College of Defence Studies, since 1983; *b* 2 June 1928; *s* of late Group Captain William Charles Hicks, AFC, and Nellie Kilbourne (*née* Kay); *m* 1950, Jean Hilary Duncan; three *s*. *Educ:* Eton Coll.; RMA Sandhurst. Commnd 2 Lieut Coldstream Guards, 1948; served, 1948–67: regtl service, UK, Tripoli and Canal Zone; Instr, Sch. of Inf. (Captain); Staff Coll. (Major); GSO2 (Ops) HQ 4 Div.; regtl service, BAOR, UK and Kenya; JSSC; GSO (DS) Staff Coll.; GSO1 MO1, MoD, 1967–70 (Lt-Col); CO 1st Bn Coldstream Guards, 1970–72; RCDS, 1973 (Col); comd 4th Guards Armoured Bde, 1974–76 (Brig.); BGS Trng HQ UKLF, 1977–79; BGS (Author) attached to DMO, MoD, 1979; GOC NW Dist, 1980–83, retd. *Recreations:* golf, gardening. *Address:* c/o Lloyds Bank, Cox's & King's Branch, 6 Pall Mall, SW1Y 5NH.

HICKS BEACH, family name of **Earl St Aldwyn.**

HIDAYATULLAH, Mohammed, OBE 1946; Vice-President of India, 1979–84 (Acting President, 1969 and 1982); *b* 17 Dec. 1905; *y s* of Khan Bahadur Hafiz M. Wilayatullah, ISO; *m* 1948, Pushpa Shah, *d* of A. N. Shah, ICS; one *s* (one *d* decd). *Educ:* Govt High Sch., Raipur; Morris Coll., Nagpur (Phillips Schol.; BA; Malak Gold Medal); Trinity Coll., Cambridge (MA); Lincoln's Inn; Bencher 1968. Nagpur High Court: Advocate, 1930–46; Govt Pleader, 1942–43; Advocate General, CP & Berar, 1943–46; Puisne Judge, 1946–54; Chief Justice, 1954–56; Chief Justice, Madhya Pradesh High Court, 1956–58; Puisne Judge, Supreme Court of India, 1958–68, Chief Justice, 1968–70. Dean, Faculty of Law, Nagpur Univ., 1950–54; Mem., Faculty of Law, Sagar, Vikram and Aligarh Univs; President: Indian Law Inst., 1968–70; Internat. Law Assoc. (Indian Br.), 1968–70; Indian Soc. of Internat. Law, 1968–70; Member: Internat. Inst. of Space Law, Paris; British Inst. of Internat. and Comparative Law, 1982–; Exec. Coun., World Assembly of Judges; Advr, Council for World Peace through Law; rep. India at Internat. Confs at Bangkok, Helsinki, Durham, Geneva, Port of Spain, Belgrade, Venice, Canberra, Melbourne, Washington, New York, Tunis, Tokyo and Stockholm. Chancellor: Muslim Nat. Univ., New Delhi; Delhi Univ.; Punjab Univ., until 1985; Hyderabad Central Univ., 1986. Assoc. Mem., Royal Acad. of Morocco. Pres., Indian Red Cross Soc., 1982–; Mem., Internat. Council of Former Scouts and Guides (awarded Silver Elephant, 1948); Chief Scout, All India Boy Scouts Assoc. (awarded Bronze Medal for Gallantry, 1969). Kt of Mark Twain, 1985. Fellow, Indian Law Inst., 1986. Hon. LLD: Univ. of Philippines, 1970; Ravishankar Univ., 1970; Rajasthan Univ., 1976; Benares Hindu Univ.; Berhampore Univ.; Punjab Univ.; Nagpur Univ., 1985; Hon. DLitt: Bhopal Univ.; Kakatiya Univ.; Hon. DCL Delhi Univ. Medallion and plaque of Merit, Philconsa, Manila; Order of Jugoslav Flag with Sash, 1972. *Publications:* Democracy in India and the

Judicial Process, 1966; The South-West Africa Case, 1967; Judicial Methods, 1969; A Judge's Miscellany, vol. 1 1972, second series 1979, third series 1983, fourth series, 1985; USA and India, 1977; 5th and 6th Schedules to Constitution of India 1979; My Own Boswell (memoirs), 1980; (ed) Mulla's Mohamedan Law, 16th, 17th and 18th edns; Taqrir-o Tabir (Urdu), Right to Property and the Indian Constitution, The Indian Constitution (ed, 3 vols); numerous monographs and articles. *Recreations:* golf, bridge. *Address:* A-10 Rockside, 112 Walkeshwar Road, Bombay 6, India. *T:* 8129798. *Clubs:* Delhi Gymkhana (New Delhi); Willingdon (Bombay).

HIDDEN, Anthony Brian, QC 1976; a Recorder of the Crown Court, since 1977; *b* 7 March 1936; *s* of late James Evelyn Harold Hidden, GM and of Gladys Bessie (*née* Brooks); *m* 1982, Mary Elise Torriano Pritchard, *d* of R. C. Pritchard of Barton Abbotts, Tetbury, Glos; one *s* one *d*. *Educ:* Reigate Grammar Sch.; Emmanuel Coll., Cambridge (BA Hons 1957, MA 1960). 2nd Lieut, 1st Royal Tank Regt, Far East Land Forces, Hong Kong, 1958–59. Called to the Bar, Inner Temple, 1961, Bencher, 1985; Mem., Hon. Soc. of Inner Temple, 1956–, and of Lincoln's Inn (*ad eundem*), 1973–. Leader, SE Circuit, 1986–. *Recreations:* reading, playing bad golf, watching football. *Address:* 8 New Square, Lincoln's Inn, WC2A 3QP. *T:* 01–242 4986.

HIDE, Dr Raymond, FRS 1971; Head of Geophysical Fluid Dynamics Laboratory (Chief Scientific Officer), Meteorological Office, Bracknell, since 1967; Senior Research Fellow, Jesus College, Oxford, since 1983; *b* 17 May 1929; *s* of late Stephen Hide and Rose Edna Hide (*née* Cartlidge); *m* 1958, (Phyllis) Ann Licence; one *s* two *d*. *Educ:* Percy Jackson Grammar Sch., near Doncaster; Manchester Univ.; Caius Coll., Cambridge. BSc 1st cl. hons Physics Manchester, 1950; PhD 1953, ScD 1969, Cantab. Res. Assoc. in Astrophysics, Univ. of Chicago, 1953–54; Sen. Res. Fellow, AERE Harwell, 1954–57; Lectr in Physics, Univ. of Durham (King's Coll., Newcastle), 1957–61; Prof. of Geophysics and Physics, MIT, 1961–67. Short-term vis. appts at Princeton Inst. for Advanced Study, 1954 and at MIT and UCLA, 1960; Visiting Professor: Dept of Maths, UCL, 1967–84; Dept of Meteorol., Reading Univ., 1976–; Gresham Prof. of Astronomy, 1985–; Adrian Fellow, Univ. of Leicester, 1980–83. Mem. NERC, 1972–75. Mem. Council: RAS, 1969–72 and 1983–86 (Vice-Pres., 1970–72; Pres., 1983–85); Royal Meteorological Soc., 1969–72 and 1974–77 (Pres., 1974–76); Eur. Geophysical Soc., 1981–85 (Pres., 1982–84). Lectures: Symons Meml, RMetS, 1970; R. A. Fisher Meml, 1977; Halley, Oxford, 1980; Jeffreys, RAS, 1981; Union, Internat. Union of Geodesy and Geophysics Gen. Assembly, Hamburg, 1983; Scott, Cambridge, 1984; Thompson, Toronto, 1984. Fellow, Amer. Acad. of Arts and Sciences, 1964. Hon. DSc Leicester, 1985. Charles Chree Medal, Inst. Physics, 1975; Holweck Medal, Soc. Franç. de Physique, 1982. *Publications:* papers in scientific jls. *Address:* Geophysical Fluid Dynamics Laboratory, Meteorological Office (21), Bracknell, Berks RG12 2SZ. *T:* Bracknell 420242, ext. 2592.

HIEGER, Izrael, DSc (London); Biochemist, Royal Marsden Hospital, 1924–66; *b* Siedletz, Russian-Poland, June 1901; *s* of F. E. Hieger. *Educ:* Birkbeck Coll. and University Coll., London. With colleagues, Anna Fuller Memorial Prize for Cancer Research, 1939. *Publications:* One in Six: An Outline of the Cancer Problem, 1955; Carcinogenesis, 1961; papers on the discovery of cancer producing chemical compounds. *Address:* Chester Beatty Research Institute, Royal Marsden Hospital, Fulham Road, SW3.

HIGGINBOTTOM, Donald Noble; HM Diplomatic Service, retired; Counsellor, Foreign and Commonwealth Office, 1976–79; *b* 19 Dec. 1925; *s* of late Harold Higginbottom and Dorothy (*née* Needham); *m* 1950, Sarah Godwin. *Educ:* Calday Grange Grammar Sch., Cheshire; King's Coll., Cambridge (1st Cl. Hons Hist.); Yale Univ., USA (MA Hist.). Lectr in Humanities, Univ. of Chicago, 1951. Entered Foreign Office, 1953; Buenos Aires, 1955; Peking, 1958; Saigon, 1960; Phnom Penh, 1962; Singapore, 1964; Bangkok, 1971; Buenos Aires, 1974. *Recreations:* electronic clocks, power boating. *Address:* 91 Dora Road, Wimbledon, SW19 7JT. *T:* 01–946 8890. *Clubs:* Athenæum; Yacht Club Olivos (Buenos Aires).

HIGGINS; *see* Longuet-Higgins.

HIGGINS, Alec Wilfred, MBE 1944; MC 1940; TD 1945; JP, DL; Deputy Chairman of Lloyd's, 1975, 1976, 1980 and 1981; Chairman: Higgins & Doble Ltd, since 1962; Crowe Underwriting Agency Ltd, since 1978; M. J. Marchant Underwriting Agency Ltd, since 1982; *b* 1 Nov. 1914; *s* of late Frederick Gladstone Higgins and Beatrice Louisa Scriven; *m* 1939, Denise May Philcox; two *s* one *d*. *Educ:* Merton Court Sch., Sidcup; Sutton Valence Sch. Joined Woods & Maslen Ltd, 1937, Chm., 1963–80. Underwriting Mem. of Lloyd's, 1948 (Mem. Cttee, 1967–73, 1975–77, 1980–83); Mem. Cttee, Lloyd's Insce Brokers Assoc., 1960–63 and 1965–68 (Dep. Chm. 1965, Chm. 1966); Mem., Gen. Cttee, Lloyd's Register of Shipping, 1978–81; Chm., Insce Section, London Chamber of Commerce, 1963–64; Vice-Pres., Insce Inst. of London, 1967; Member: Council, Chartered Insce Inst., 1972–80; Insce Industry Trng Council, 1969; Export Guarantee Adv. Council, 1977–83 (Dep. Chm., 1982–83). Mem., Court of Assistants, Insurers' Co., 1980, Master 1984. Councillor, Chislehurst and Sidcup UDC, 1962–65 (Vice-Chm. of Council, 1964); Alderman, London Borough of Bexley, 1968–78; JP Bexley, 1967–84; DL Greater London, 1973, Representative DL, Havering, 1978. *Recreation:* swimming. *Address:* Somersby, 12 Priestlands Park Road, Sidcup, Kent DA15 7HR. *T:* 01–300 3792. *Clubs:* City of London, Royal Automobile.

HIGGINS, Sir Christopher (Thomas), Kt 1977; Chairman, Peterborough Development Corporation, 1968–81; *b* 14 Jan. 1914; *s* of late Thomas Higgins and Florence Maud Higgins; *m* 1936, Constance Joan Beck; one *s* one *d*. *Educ:* West Kensington Central Sch.; London Univ. Executive with Granada Group Ltd, 1939–68. Served War of 1939–45: with RA, 1940–46. Member: Acton Borough Council, 1945–65; GLC, 1964–67; Hemel Hempstead Develt Corp., 1947–52; Bracknell Develt Corp., 1965–68. Chm., North Thames Gas Consumers' Council, 1969–79. *Recreations:* reading, gardening, walking; watching most sports. *Address:* Coronation Cottage, Wood End, Little Horwood, Milton Keynes, Bucks MK17 0PE. *T:* Winslow 2636.

HIGGINS, Frank, FCIT 1979; *b* 30 Aug. 1927; *s* of Wilfred and Hilda Higgins; *m* 1948, Betty Pulford; one *s* one *d*. *Educ:* Hanley High Sch., Stoke-on-Trent; St Paul's Coll., Cheltenham. Teacher: Stoke-on-Trent, 1946; Notts, 1948–58; Organising Sec., Youth Gp, 1958–60; Teacher, Nottingham, Derby, 1960–73; Mem. Nat. Bus Co., 1974–79. Contested (Lab) Harborough 1966, Grantham 1970. Mem., Nottingham City Council, 1971–74, 1979– (Chm. Transportation Cttee, 1972–74, 1979–81); Lord Mayor of Nottingham, 1986–87; Mem., Notts CC, 1973–77 and 1981– (Chm. Environment Cttee, 1973–77; Chm. Resources Cttee, 1981–86); Chm., E Midlands Airport Jt Cttee, 1986–. Chm., Central Transport Consultative Cttee, 1977–80. *Recreations:* travelling, talking. *Address:* 23 Glendale Close, Carlton, Nottingham. *T:* Nottingham 616802.

HIGGINS, Jack; *see* Patterson, Harry.

HIGGINS, Prof. John Christopher, CEng, FIEE; CBIM; Director of Management Centre, University of Bradford, and Professor of Management Sciences, since 1972; *b* 9 July 1932; *s* of Sidney James Higgins and Margaret Eileen Higgins (*née* Dealtrey); *m* 1960, Margaret Edna Howells; three *s*. *Educ:* Gonville and Caius Coll., Cambridge (MA); Univ. of London (BSc, MSc); PhD Bradford. Short service commission, RAF, 1953–56; 1956–70: Electronics Industry; Dept of Chief Scientist (RAF) in MoD; management consultancy; Director of Economic Planning and Research for IPC Newspapers Ltd. Member: Final Selection Bd for Civil Service Commn, 1976–; Defence Scientific Adv. Council's Assessments Bd, 1976–83 (Chm. of its Cttee on Operational Analysis, 1980–83); UGC Sub-Cttee on Management and Business Studies, 1979–85; Chm., Social Sciences Res. Council's Accountancy Steering Cttee and Member of its Management and Industrial Relns Cttee, 1976–80. Vis. Fellow, Wolfson Coll., Cambridge, 1985. *Publications:* Information Systems for Planning and Control: concepts and cases, 1976; Strategic and Operational Planning Systems: Principles and Practice, 1980; Computer-Based Planning Systems, 1985; numerous papers and articles on corporate planning, information systems and management educn. *Recreations:* violin/viola (ex National Youth Orchestra of Great Britain), cricket, fell-walking. *Address:* Woodfield, 36 Station Road, Baildon, West Yorkshire BD17 5NW. *T:* Bradford 592836.

HIGGINS, Hon. John Patrick Basil; Hon. Mr Justice Higgins; a Judge of the High Court of Northern Ireland, since 1984; *b* 14 June 1927; *e s* of late John A. and Mary Philomena Higgins, Magherafelt; *m* 1960, Bridget, *e d* of late Dr Matthew F. O'Neill, Hollingwood, Chesterfield; two *s* three *d*. *Educ:* St. Columb's Coll., Derry; Queen's Univ., Belfast (LLB). Called to Bar of N Ireland, 1948, Bencher, 1969–71 and 1983–; QC (N Ire.) 1967; County Court Judge, 1971–84: Armagh and Fermanagh, 1976–79; S Antrim, 1979–82; Recorder of Belfast, 1982–84. Chairman: Mental Health Review Tribunal for NI, 1963–71; Legal Aid Adv. Cttee (NI), 1975–82; Council of HM County Court Judges, 1978–84; Member: County Court Rules Cttee (NI), 1973–82 (Chm., 1982–84); Statute Law Cttee of NI, 1975–; Lowry Cttee on Registration of Title in NI, 1958–67; Jones Cttee on County Courts and Magistrates' Courts in NI, 1972–73; Gardiner Cttee on measures to deal with terrorism in NI, 1974. Chm., Voluntary Service, Belfast, 1975–85. Member: Community Peace Conf., 1969; Bd of Management, St Joseph's Coll. of Educn, Belfast, 1969–85; Bd of Governors, Dominican Coll., Portstewart, 1974–84. *Address:* The Royal Courts of Justice (Ulster), Belfast, Northern Ireland.

HIGGINS, Prof. Peter Matthew; Bernard Sunley Professor and Chairman of Department of General Practice, United Medical Schools of Guy's and St Thomas' Hospitals (formerly Guy's Hospital Medical School), University of London, since 1974; *b* 18 June 1923; *s* of Peter Joseph Higgins and Margaret Higgins; *m* 1952, Jean Margaret Lindsay Currie; three *s* one *d*. *Educ:* St Ignatius' Coll., London; UCH, London. MB, BS; FRCP, FRCGP. House Phys., Medical Unit, UCH, 1947; RAMC, 1948–49; House Phys., UCH, St Pancras, 1950; Resident MO, UCH, 1951–52; Asst Med. Registrar, UCH, 1953; Gen. Practice, Rugeley, Staffs, 1954–66, and Castle Vale, Birmingham, 1966–68; Sen. Lectr, Guy's Hosp. Med. Sch., 1968–74. Vice-Chm., SE Thames RHA, 1976–. Vice-Chm., Governors, Linacre Centre. *Publications:* articles in Lancet, BMJ, Jl RCGP. *Recreations:* squash, swimming, sailing. *Address:* Wallings, Heathfield Lane, Chislehurst, Kent. *T:* 01–467 2756.

HIGGINS, Reynold Alleyne, LittD; FBA 1972; FSA; *b* Weybridge, 26 Nov. 1916; *er s* of late Charles Alleyne Higgins and late Marjorie Edith (*née* Taylor); *m* 1947, Patricia Mary, *d* of J. C. Williams; three *s* two *d*. *Educ:* Sherborne Sch.; Pembroke Coll., Cambridge (Scholar). First Cl., Classical Tripos pts I and II, 1937, 1938; MA, 1960; LittD, 1963. Served War: Queen Victoria's Rifles, KRRC, 1939–46 (Captain, PoW). Asst Keeper, Dept of Greek and Roman Antiquities, British Museum, 1947, Dep. Keeper, 1965–77, Acting Keeper, 1976. Visiting Fellow, British School of Archaeology at Athens, 1969, Chm., Managing Cttee, 1975–79; Norton Lectr, Archaeol Inst. of America, 1982–83. Corr. Mem., German Archaeological Inst. *Publications:* Catalogue of Terracottas in British Museum, vols I and II, 1954, 1959; Greek and Roman Jewellery, 1961, 2nd edn 1980; Greek Terracotta Figures, 1963; Jewellery from Classical Lands, 1965; Greek Terracottas, 1967; Minoan and Mycenaean Art, 1967, 2nd edn 1981; The Greek Bronze Age, 1970; The Archaeology of Minoan Crete, 1973; The Aegina Treasure, 1979; also articles and reviews in British and foreign periodicals. *Recreation:* travel. *Address:* Hillside Cottage, Chiddingfold Road, Dunsfold, near Godalming, Surrey GU8 4PB. *T:* Dunsfold 400.

HIGGINS, Prof. Rosalyn, JSD; QC 1986; Professor of International Law at the London School of Economics, University of London, since 1981; *b* 2 June 1937; *d* of Lewis Cohen and Fay Inberg; *m* 1961, Rt Hon. Terence Langley Higgins, *qv*; one *s* one *d*. *Educ:* Burlington Grammar Sch., London; Girton Coll., Cambridge (Scholar; BA 1958, 1st Cl. Law Qualifying 1, 1st Cl. Tripos Pt II; 1st Cl. LLB 1959); Yale Law Sch., (JSD 1962). UK Intern, Office of Legal Affairs, UN, 1958; Commonwealth Fund Fellow, 1959; Vis. Fellow, Brookings Instn, Washington, DC, 1960; Jun. Fellow in Internat. Studies, LSE, 1961–63; Staff Specialist in Internat. Law, RIIA, 1963–74; Vis. Fellow, LSE, 1974–78; Prof. of Internat. Law, Univ. of Kent at Canterbury, 1978–81. Vis. Prof. of Internat. Law: Stanford Univ., 1975; Yale Univ., 1977. Mem., UN Cttee on Human Rights, 1985–. Sidgwick Meml Lecture, Cambridge, 1977; Montague Burton Lecture, Leeds Univ., 1979; Hague Lectures on Internat. Law, 1982. Vice Pres., Amer. Soc. of Internat. Law, 1972–74 (Certif. of Merit, 1971). Dr *hc* Univ. of Paris XI, 1980. Mem. Board of Editors: International Organization, 1972–78; American Journal of International Law; British Yearbook of International Law. *Publications:* The Development of International Law through the Political Organs of the United Nations, 1963; Conflict of Interests: international law in a divided world, 1965; The Administration of the United Kingdom Foreign Policy through the United Nations, 1966; (ed with James Fawcett) Law in Movement—essays in memory of John McMahon, 1974; UN Peacekeeping: documents and commentary: Vol. I, Middle East, 1969; Vol. II, Asia, 1971; Vol. III, Africa, 1980; Vol. IV, Europe, 1981; articles for law jls and jls of internat. relations. *Recreations:* sport, cooking, eating. *Address:* London School of Economics, Houghton Street, WC2A 2AE; 4 Essex Court, Temple, EC4Y 9AJ. *T:* 01–583 9191.

HIGGINS, Rt. Hon. Terence (Langley); PC 1979; MP (C) Worthing since 1964; *b* 18 Jan. 1928; *s* of Reginald Higgins, Dulwich; *m* 1961, Prof. Rosalyn Higgins, *qv*; one *s* one *d*. *Educ:* Alleyn's Sch., Dulwich; Gonville and Caius Coll., Cambridge. Brit. Olympic Team (athletics) 1948, 1952; BA (Hons) 1958. MA 1963; Pres. Cambridge Union Soc., 1958. NZ Shipping Co., 1948–55; Lectr in Economic Principles, Dept of Economics, Yale Univ., 1958–59; Economist with Unilever, 1959–64. Dir, Lex Service Group, 1980–. Sec., Cons. Parly Finance Cttee, 1965–66; Opposition Spokesman on Treasury and Economic Affairs, 1966–70; Minister of State, Treasury, 1970–72; Financial Sec. to Treasury, 1972–74; Opposition Spokesman: on Treasury and Econ. Affairs, 1974; for Trade, 1974–76; Chairman: Cons. Parly Cttees, on Sport, 1979–81, Transport, 1979–; Select Cttee on Procedure, 1980–83; House of Commons Liaison Cttee, 1984–; Member: Select Cttee on Treasury and Civil Service, 1980–86 (Chm., 1983–86); Public Accounts Commn, 1984–; Exec. Cttee, 1922 Cttee, 1980–. Member: Council, RIIA, 1979–; Council, IAM, 1979. Governor, Dulwich Coll., 1980–. *Address:* c/o House of Commons, SW1A 0AA. *Clubs:* Yale; Hawks (Cambridge).

HIGGINS, Wilfred Frank; *see* Higgins, Frank.

HIGGINS, Rear-Adm. William Alleyne, CB 1985; CBE 1980; Secretary, Defence, Press and Broadcasting Committee, since 1986; *b* 18 May 1928; *s* of Comdr H. G.

Higgins, DSO, RN, and Mrs L. A. Higgins; *m* 1963, Wiltraud Hiebaum; two *s* one *d*. *Educ:* Wellington College. Joined Royal Navy, 1945; Commander 1965; Captain 1973; Commodore, HMS Drake, 1980–82; Flag Officer Medway and Port Adm. Chatham, 1982–83; Dir. Gen. Naval Personal Services, 1983–86; Chief Naval Supply and Secretariat Officer, 1983–86. *Recreations:* skiing, rock climbing and mountaineering. *Address:* c/o National Westminster Bank, 48 Blue Boar Row, Salisbury, Wilts. *Club:* Royal Naval and Royal Marines Mountaineering.

HIGGINSON, Dr Gordon Robert; Vice-Chancellor, University of Southampton, since 1985; *b* 8 Nov. 1929; *s* of Frederick John and Letitia Higginson; *m* 1954, Marjorie Forbes Rannie; three *s* two *d*. *Educ:* Leeds Univ. BSc, PhD. FICE; FIMechE. Scientific Officer, then Sen. Scientific Officer, Min. of Supply, 1953–56; Lectr, Leeds Univ., 1956–62; Associate Prof., RMCS, Shrivenham, 1962–65; Durham University: Prof. of Engrg, 1965–85; Dean of Faculty of Science, 1972–75. Mem., Engineering Council, 1986–. IMechE James Clayton Fund Prize, 1963 and 1979. Gold Medal, Brit. Soc. of Rheology, 1969. *Publications:* Elastohydrodynamic Lubrication (with D. Dowson), 1966, 2nd edn 1977; Foundations of Engineering Mechanics, 1974; papers on mechanics in various jls. *Address:* The University, Southampton SO9 5NH. *T:* Southampton 559122.

HIGGON, Col Laurence Hugh, CBE 1958; MC 1916 and Bar 1917; *b* 3 Sept. 1884; 4th (and *o* surv.) *s* of late Capt. J. D. G. Higgon, RA, DL, JP, Scolton, Pembrokeshire; *m* 1922, Neda Kathleen C., *er d* of Lieut-Col F. Rennick (killed 1915); two *d*. *Educ:* Cheltenham; RMA, Woolwich. Entered RA 1903; retired, 1927; comd 102nd (Pembroke Yeo.) Bde RA, 1930–35 (Bt Col); Hon. Col 1948; Hon. Comr Toc H in Wales, 1931. Rejoined RA (Lieut-Col), 1939. Home Guard, Pembs (Lieut-Col), 1942–45. DL, JP, Pembrokeshire; JP Haverfordwest. Served European War, 1914–19, France and Flanders (despatches twice, MC and Bar). Chm. Pembroke County War Memorial Hospital 1934–53; Mem. West Wales Hosps Management Cttee, 1948–53; Chm. Standing Joint Cttee, 1949–54; Chm., Pembroke TA Assoc., 1944–47; Lord Lieutenant, Pembrokeshire, 1944–54. OStJ. *Address:* c/o Brig. D. W. H. Birch, CBE, Five Elms Cottage, Woodcutts, Salisbury, Wilts. *Club:* Army and Navy.

HIGGS, Air Vice-Marshal Barry, CBE 1981; Assistant Chief of Defence Staff (Overseas), since 1985; *b* 22 Aug. 1934; *s* of late Percy Harold Higgs and of Ethel Eliza Higgs; *m* 1957, Sylvia May Wilks; two *s*. *Educ:* Finchley County Secondary Grammar Sch. Served with Nos 207, 115, 138, 49 and 51 Sqdns, 1955–70; sc 1968; Forward Policy (RAF), 1971–73; ndc 1974; Comd No 39 (PR) Sqdn, 1975–77; Asst Dir Defence Policy, 1978–79; Comd RAF Finningley, 1979–81; RCDS 1982; Dep. Dir of Intelligence, 1983–85. *Recreations:* bridge, gardening, the outdoors, theatre. *Address:* 33 Parsonage Street, Cambridge CB5 8DN. *T:* Cambridge 69062. *Club:* Royal Air Force.

HIGGS, Brian James, QC 1974; a Recorder of the Crown Court, since 1974; Barrister-at-Law; *b* 24 Feb. 1930; *s* of James Percival Higgs and Kathleen Anne Higgs; *m* 1st, 1953, Jean Cameron DuMerton; two *s* three *d*; 2nd, 1980, Vivienne Mary Johnson; one *s*. *Educ:* Wrekin Coll.; London Univ. Served RA, 1948–50. Called to Bar, Gray's Inn, 1955. Contested (C) Romford, 1966. *Recreations:* gardening, golf, wine, chess, bridge. *Address:* Navestock Woodhouse, Navestock Side, Brentwood, Essex. *T:* Coxtie Green 72032; 9 King's Bench Walk, Temple, EC4Y 7DX. *T:* 01–353 5638. *Club:* Thorndon Park Golf.

HIGGS, Rt. Rev. Hubert Laurence, MA Cantab; *b* 23 Nov. 1911; *s* of Frank William and Mary Ann Higgs; *m* 1936, Elizabeth Clare (*née* Rogers); one *s* one *d*. *Educ:* University Coll. Sch.; Christ's Coll., Cambridge; Ridley Hall, Cambridge. Curate: Holy Trinity, Richmond, 1935; St Luke's, Redcliffe Square, London, 1936–38; St John's, Boscombe (and Jt Sec. Winchester Youth Council), 1938–39. Vicar, Holy Trinity, Aldershot, 1939–45; Editorial Sec., Church Missionary Soc., 1945–52; Vicar, St John's, Woking, 1952–57 (Rural Dean, 1957); Archdeacon of Bradford and Canon Residentiary of Bradford Cathedral, 1957–65; Bishop Suffragan of Hull, 1965–76; RD of Hull, 1972–76. *Recreations:* history, music-listening, gardening. *Address:* The Farmstead, Chediston, Halesworth, Suffolk IP19 0AS. *T:* Halesworth 2621.

HIGGS, Sir (John) Michael (Clifford), Kt 1969; DL; solicitor, retired; *b* 30 May 1912; *s* of late Alderman A. W. Higgs, Cranford House, Stourton, Staffs; *m* 1st, 1936, Diana Louise Jerrams (*d* 1950); two *d*; 2nd, 1952, Rachel Mary Jones, OBE; one *s* one *d*. *Educ:* St Cuthberts, Malvern; Shrewsbury. LLB (Birmingham), 1932. Admitted solicitor, 1934. Served War of 1939–45 with 73 HAA Regt RA (TA), 1939–42; JAG Staff, 1942–46; demobilised, 1946, with rank of Lieut-Col. Mem. of Staffs County Council, 1946–49; MP (C) Bromsgrove Div. of Worcs, 1950–55; Member: Worcs CC, 1953–73 (Chm. 1959–73; Alderman, 1963); Hereford and Worcester CC, 1973–85 (Chm., 1973–77); West Midlands Economic Planning Council, 1965–79; Chm., W Midlands Planning Authorities' Conf., 1969–73. DL Worcs 1968, Hereford and Worcester, 1974. *Address:* Pixham Cottage, Callow End, Worcester WR2 4TH. *T:* Worcester 830645.

HIGGS, Sir Michael; *see* Higgs, Sir J. M. C.

HIGGS, Prof. Peter Ware, PhD; FRS 1983; FRSE; Professor of Theoretical Physics, University of Edinburgh, since 1980; *b* 29 May 1929; *s* of Thomas Ware Higgs and Gertrude Maud (*née* Coghill); *m* 1963, Jo Ann, *d* of Jo C. and Meryl Williamson, Urbana, Ill; two *s*. *Educ:* Cotham Grammar Sch., Bristol; King's Coll., Univ. of London (BSc, MSc; PhD 1954). FRSE 1974. Royal Commn for Exhibn of 1851 Sen. Student, KCL, 1953–54 and Univ. of Edinburgh, 1954–55; Sen. Res. Fellow, Univ. of Edinburgh, 1955–56; ICI Res. Fellow, UCL, 1956–57 and Imperial Coll., 1957–58; Lectr in Maths, UCL, 1958–60; Lectr in Mathematical Physics, 1960–70, and Reader in Math. Physics, 1970–80, Univ. of Edinburgh. Hughes Medal, Royal Soc., 1981; Rutherford Medal, Inst. of Physics, 1984. *Publications:* papers on molecular vibrations and spectra, classical and quantum field theories, and on spontaneous breaking of gauge symmetries in theories of elementary particles. *Recreations:* walking, swimming, listening to music. *Address:* 2 Darnaway Street, Edinburgh EH3 6BG. *T:* 031–225 7060.

HIGHAM, John Drew, CMG 1956; *b* 28 Nov. 1914; *s* of Richard and Margaret Higham, Pendleton, Lancs; *m* 1st, 1936, Mary Constance Bromage (*d* 1974); three *d*; 2nd, 1976, Katharine Byard Pailing. *Educ:* Manchester Grammar Sch.; Gonville and Caius Coll., Cambridge (Scholar). Asst Principal, Admiralty, 1936; Asst Private Sec. to First Lord, 1939; Private Sec. to Parliamentary Sec. and Parliamentary Clerk, 1940; Principal, Admiralty, 1941; transferred to Colonial Office, 1946; Asst Sec. Colonial Office, 1948; seconded to Singapore as Under Sec., 1953, and as Dir of Personnel, 1955–57 (acted on various occasions as Chief Sec.); Asst Sec., Min. of Housing and Local Govt, 1965; Head of Development Control Div., DoE, 1970–74. Vice-Chm., Bredon Parish Council, 1985–. Chevalier 1st Cl. Order of St Olaf (Norway), 1948. *Recreations:* history of art, gardening. *Address:* Avonside, Bredon, Tewkesbury, Glos. *T:* Bredon 72468.

HIGHAM, Rear-Adm. Philip Roger Canning, CB 1972; *b* 9 June 1920; *s* of Edward Higham, Stoke Bishop, Bristol; *m* 1942, Pamela Bracton Edwards, *er d* of Gerald Edwards, Southport, Lancs; two *s*. *Educ:* RNC Dartmouth. Cadet, 1937; Midshipman, 1938; Sub-Lt 1940; Lieut 1942; qual. Gunnery Officer, 1944; Second Gunnery Off., HMS Vanguard, Royal Tour of S Africa, 1947; psc 1948; Exper. Dept, HMS Excellent, 1951–52; Comdr, Devonport Gunnery Sch., 1953; Trials Comdr, RAE Aberporth, 1954–55; jssc 1956; Exper. Comdr, HMS Excellent, 1957–59; Admty (DTWP), 1960–61; Naval Attaché, Middle East, 1962–64; idc 1965; Dep. Chief Polaris Exec., 1966–68; Cdre i/c Hong Kong, 1968–70; Asst Chief of Naval Staff (Op. Requirements), 1970–72; retired list 1973; Dir, HMS Belfast Trust, 1973–78; Keeper, HMS Belfast, Imperial War Mus., 1978–83. Trustee, Portsmouth Naval Base Property Co., 1985–. *Recreations:* gardening, fishing. *Address:* Apple Tree Farm, Prinsted, Emsworth, Hants. *T:* Emsworth 372195. *Club:* Naval and Military.

HIGHET, Helen Clark; *see* MacInnes, H. C.

HIGHSMITH, Patricia; writer since 1942; *b* 19 Jan. 1921; *o c* of Jay Bernard Plangman and Mary Coates (of German and English-Scots descent respectively); name changed to Highsmith on mother's 2nd marriage; unmarried. *Educ:* Barnard Coll., Columbia Univ., New York. For a year after univ. had a mediocre writing job; after that free-lance until publication of first novel. Lived in Europe and America alternately from 1951, and now has been some years in France. *Publications: novels:* Strangers on a Train, 1950; The Blunderer, 1955; The Talented Mr Ripley, 1956; Deep Water, 1957; A Game for the Living, 1958; This Sweet Sickness, 1960 (filmed 1979); The Cry of the Owl, 1962; The Two Faces of January, 1964; The Glass Cell, 1965; A Suspension of Mercy, 1965; Those Who Walk Away, 1967; The Tremor of Forgery, 1969; Ripley Under Ground, 1971; A Dog's Ransom, 1972; Ripley's Game, 1974 (filmed as The American Friend, 1978); Edith's Diary, 1977; The Boy Who Followed Ripley, 1980; People Who Knock on the Door, 1983; Found in the Street, 1986; *short stories:* The Animal-Lover's Book of Beastly Murder, 1975; Little Tales of Misogyny, 1977; Slowly, Slowly in the Wind, 1979; The Black House, 1981; Mermaids on the Golf Course, 1985; Plotting and Writing Suspense Fiction, 1966, 2nd edn, 1983. *Recreations:* drawing, some painting, carpentering, snail-watching, travelling by train. *Club:* Detection.

HIGHTON, Rear-Adm. Jack Kenneth, CB 1959; CBE 1952; *b* 2 Sept. 1904; *s* of John Henry Highton and Kate (*née* Powers); *m* 1933, Eileen Metcalfe Flack; one *s* two *d*. *Educ:* Bedford Modern Sch. Joined Royal Navy, 1922; Captain 1951; Dir of Welfare and Service Conditions, 1955–57; Rear-Adm. 1957; Chief Staff Officer (Administration) to Commander-in-Chief, Plymouth, 1957–60; retired, 1960. *Recreations:* walking, sailing, gardening. *Address:* c/o National Westminster Bank, Woodbridge, Suffolk.

HIGMAN, Prof. Graham, MA, DPhil; FRS 1958; Waynflete Professor of Pure Mathematics, Oxford University, and Fellow of Magdalen College, Oxford, 1960–84; *b* 1917; 2nd *s* of Rev. Joseph Higman; *m* 1941, Ivah May Treleaven (*d* 1981); five *s* one *d*. *Educ:* Sutton Secondary Sch., Plymouth; Balliol Coll., Oxford (Hon. Fellow 1984). Meteorological Office, 1940–46; Lecturer, University of Manchester, 1946–55; Reader in Mathematics at Oxford Univ., 1955–60; Senior Research Fellow, Balliol Coll., Oxford, 1958–60. George A. Miller Vis. Prof., Univ. of Illinois, 1984–86. Hon. DSc Exeter, 1979. De Morgan Medal, London Mathematical Soc., 1974; Sylvester Medal, Royal Soc., 1979. *Publications:* papers in Proc. London Math. Soc., and other technical jls.

HIGNETT, John Mulock, FCA; a Managing Director, Lazard Brothers since 1984; *b* 9 March 1934; *s* of Reginald and Marjorie Hignett; *m* 1961, Marijke Inge de Boer; one *s* one *d*. *Educ:* Harrow Sch.; Magdalene Coll., Cambridge (MA). Kemp Chatteris & Co., 1958–61; Deloitte & Co., 1961–63; joined Lazard Brothers & Co. Ltd, 1963; Manager, Issues Dept, 1971; Dir, 1972; Head of Corporate Finance Div., 1980. Director-General: Panel on Take-Overs and Mergers, 1981–83; Council for the Securities Industry, 1983. *Address:* 61 Roehampton Lane, SW15 5NE. *T:* 01–876 2902. *Clubs:* MCC; Hawks (Cambridge).

HIGNETT, Peter George; Regional Veterinary Officer, People's Dispensary for Sick Animals, since 1982; *b* 3 June 1925; *s* of Harry Sutton Hignett and Annie Hignett; *m* 1948, Patricia Bishop; two *s* one *d*. *Educ:* Pontesbury C of E Sch.; King Edward VI Sch., Birmingham; Univ. of Liverpool (MRCVS). General practice, 1947–49; Wellcome Veterinary Res. Station, 1949–54; Reader in Veterinary Reproduction, Univ. of Glasgow, 1954–76; Gen. Man., Hampshire Cattle Breeders' Soc., 1976–82. Mem. Council, RCVS, 1972–, Pres., 1981–82; President: Soc. for Study of Animal Breeding, 1966–68; Southern Counties Veterinary Soc., 1983–84; Secretary: Associated AI Centres, 1977–82; Edgar Meml Trust, 1977–82; Member: Trehane Cttee, 1979–82; Scientific Adv. Cttee, Animal Health Trust, 1983–85. *Publications:* scientific papers on fertility in domestic animals. *Recreations:* gardening, sailing, music. *Address:* Qaisik, Sway Road, Brockenhurst, Hants SO4 7SG. *T:* Lymington 22066. *Club:* Farmers'.

HIGTON, Dennis John, CEng, FIMechE, FRAeS; company director and consultant; Chairman, Technology Division, Civil Service Commission, since 1984; *b* 15 July 1921; *s* of John William and Lillian Harriett Higton; *m* 1945, Joy Merrifield Pickett; one *s* one *d*. *Educ:* Guildford Technical Sch.; RAE Farnborough Technical Sch. Mid-Wessex Water Co., 1937. RAE Engineering Apprentice, 1938–42; RAE Aerodynamics Dept (Aero Flight), 1942–52; learned to fly at No 1 EFTS RAF Panshangar, 1946; A&AEE Boscombe Down, Head of Naval Test and Supt of Performance, 1953–66; British Defence Staff, Washington DC, USA, 1966–70; MoD(PE) Anglo-French Helicopter Production, 1970–72; Director Aircraft Production, 1972–75; Under-Sec. and Dir-Gen. of Mil. Aircraft Projects, MoD, 1976–79, of Aircraft 4, 1979–80, of Aircraft 3, 1980–81. Mem., Fleet Air Arm Officers Assoc., 1960–. Chm., S Wilts and Salisbury Br., NSPCC, 1982–. *Publications:* research and memoranda papers mainly on aerodynamic flight testing. *Recreations:* beekeeping, skiing, sailing, gardening, walking on Salisbury Plain, shooting, water-colour painting. *Address:* Jasmine Cottage, Rollestone Road, Shrewton, Salisbury, Wiltshire SP3 4HG. *T:* Shrewton 620276.

HILALY, Agha, HQA, SPk; Chairman, Board of Governors, Pakistan Institute of Strategic Studies, since 1973; *b* 20 May 1911; *s* of late Agha Abdulla; *m* 1938, Malek Taj Begum, *d* of Mirza Kazim, Bangalore; three *s*. *Educ:* Presidency Coll., Madras (MA); King's Coll., Cambridge (MA). Entered former ICS (Bengal cadre), 1936; Under-Sec., Govt of Bengal, 1939–41; Govt of India, 1941–47; entered Pakistan Foreign Service at time of Partition; Jt Sec., Min. of Foreign Affairs, 1951; Imp. Def. Coll., 1955; Ambassador to Sweden, Norway, Denmark and Finland, 1956; Delegate to UN Gen. Assembly, 1958; Ambassador to USSR and Czechoslovakia, 1959; High Commissioner in India and Ambassador to Nepal, 1961; High Commissioner for Pakistan in the UK and Ambassador to Ireland, 1963–66; Ambassador for Pakistan to the United States, 1966–71, also accredited to Mexico, Venezuela and Jamaica. Dir, State Bank of Pakistan, 1972–. Hilal-i-Quaid-i-Azam, Pakistan; Star of Pakistan; Grand Cross, Order of the North Star, Sweden; Grand Cross, Prabol Gurkha Dakshana Bahu (Nepal). *Recreations:* colour photography, shooting. *Address:* No 48 Fifteenth Street, Phase 5, Defence Housing Society, Karachi 6, Pakistan. *Clubs:* Travellers'; International (Washington); Sind (Karachi).

HILARY, David Henry Jephson; Assistant Under Secretary of State, Home Office, since 1975; *b* 3 May 1932; *s* of late Robert and Nita Hilary; *m* 1957, Phœbe Leonora, *d* of John J. Buchanan; two *s* two *d*. *Educ:* Tonbridge Sch.; King's Coll., Cambridge (Sandys Student

1954, Craven Student 1955; MA). Royal Artillery, 1953–54. Entered Home Office, 1956. *Recreations:* cricket, squash, bridge. *Address:* 17 Victoria Square, SW1. *Clubs:* RAC, MCC.

HILD, Maj.-Gen. John Henry, MBE 1969; CEng, FIEE; FBIM; Director, Siemens (UK) Ltd, since 1984; consultant, since 1984; *b* 28 March 1931; *m* 1954, Janet Macdonald Brown; one *s* one *d*. *Educ:* Blackfriars; Laxton; Sandhurst. Joined Army, 1949; commissioned, 1952; Korea, 1952–53; sc 1961; MoD, DAQMG, 1962–64; Borneo, 1965; Hong Kong, 1966–67; 1 (BR) Corps, DAQMG, 1968–69; CO 18 Sig. Regt, 1969–71; DS, Staff Coll., 1972–73; Comd 1 Sig. Gp, 1974–76; Comdt, Sch. of Sigs, 1976–78; RCDS 1979; HQ BAOR, DQMG and CSO, 1980–84. Col Comdt, RCS, 1986–. Caravan Club Council, 1985–. *Recreations:* entertaining friends, travel, sport. *Address:* c/o Lloyds Bank, Cox's and King's Branch, 6 Pall Mall, SW1. *Club:* Army and Navy.

HILDER, Rev. Geoffrey Frank; Archdeacon of Taunton, 1951–71; Prebendary of Wells Cathedral, 1951–73; Provost of Western Division of Woodard Corporation, 1960–70; *b* 17 July 1906; *s* of Albert Thomas and Lilian Ethel Hilder; *m* 1939, Enid (*d* 1985), *d* of Rev. F. E. Coggin. *Educ:* Uppingham Sch.; Lincoln Coll., Oxford; Inner Temple; Ely Theological Coll. Called to the Bar, 1930. Deacon, 1931; Priest, 1932; Rector of Ruardean, Glos., 1937–41; Vicar of St Stephen's, Cheltenham, 1941–48; Vicar of Hambridge, 1948–59. Prolocutor of Lower House of Convocation of Canterbury, 1955–70; Dir of Ecclesiastical Insurance Office Ltd, 1957–61. *Recreations:* music, gardening. *Address:* 4 Falcon Terrace, Bude, Cornwall EX23 8LJ. *T:* Bude 4532.

HILDER, Rowland, OBE 1986; RI 1938; painter; *b* Greatneck, Long Island, USA, 28 June 1905, British parents; *m* 1929, Edith Blenkiron; one *s* one *d*. *Educ:* Goldsmiths' Coll. Sch. of Art, London. Exhibited, Hayward Gall., 1983. PRI 1964–74. *Publications:* Illustrated editions of: Moby Dick, 1926; Treasure Island, 1929; Precious Bane, 1930; The Bible for To-day, 1940; The Shell Guide to Flowers of the Countryside (with Edith Hilder), 1955; (jointly) Sketching and Painting Indoors, 1957; Starting with Watercolour, 1966; Painting Landscapes in Watercolour, 1983 (USA, as Expressing Land, Sea and Sky in Watercolour, 1982); *relevant publications:* Rowland Hilder: painter and illustrator, by John Lewis, 1978; Rowland Hilder's England, by Denis Thomas, 1986. *Address:* 5 Kidbrooke Grove, Blackheath, SE3 0PG. *T:* 01–858 3072.

HILDITCH, Clifford Arthur; Director of Social Services, Manchester City Council, 1970–74, Manchester District Council, 1974–83, retired; *b* 3 Feb. 1927; *s* of late Arthur Clifford Hilditch and of Lilian Maud Hilditch (*née* Brockman); *m* 1953, Joyce Hilditch (*née* Burgess); one *s*. *Educ:* Huntingdon Grammar Sch.; London Univ. Dip. in Applied Social Studies. Army Service, 1944–48 (commissioned into Indian Army, 1945). Service as an Administrative Officer, LCC (Welfare Services) until 1961; Manchester City Council: Dep. Chief Welfare Officer, 1962–64; Chief Welfare Officer, 1965–70. Chm., E Cheshire Hospice Council, 1984–; Mem., Industrial Tribunals, 1983–. Hon. Fellow, Manchester Polytechnic, 1976. *Publications:* contributor to various hosp. and social services jls. *Recreations:* various. *Address:* 14 Priory Road, Wilmslow, Cheshire. *T:* Wilmslow 522109.

HILDRED, Sir William (Percival), Kt 1945; CB 1942; OBE 1936; Grand Officer, Order of Orange-Nassau, 1946; Commander Order of Crown of Belgium; MA; Director-General Emeritus International Air Transport Association (Director-General, 1946–66); *b* 13 July 1893; *s* of late William Kirk Hildred; *m* 1920, Constance Mary Chappell, MB, ChB (*d* 1985); two *s* one *d*. *Educ:* Boulevard Sch., Hull; University of Sheffield. Served European War, 1st York and Lancaster Regt, 1914–17; entered Treasury, 1919; Finance Officer, Empire Marketing Board, 1926–34; Head of Special Measures Branch, Ministry of Agriculture and Fisheries, 1934–35; Deputy General Manager, Export Credits Guarantee Dept, 1935–38; Deputy Dir-Gen. of Civil Aviation, Air Ministry, 1938; Principal Asst Sec., Ministry of Aircraft Production, 1940; assisted in formation of RAF Ferry Command, Montreal, 1941; Director-Gen. of Civil Aviation, Ministry of Civil Aviation, 1941–46. Edward Warner Award of ICAO, 1965. Hon. LLD: Sheffield; McGill Univ.; FRSA. Hon. FRAeS. *Recreations:* cycling, music, carpentry. *Address:* Spreakley House, Frensham, Surrey.

HILDRETH, Maj.-Gen. Sir (Harold) John (Crossley), KBE 1964 (CBE 1952; OBE 1945); *b* 12 June 1908; *s* of late Lt-Col H. C. Hildreth, DSO, OBE, FRCS, and late Mrs Hildreth; *m* 1950, Mary, *d* of late G. Wroe; two *s* three *d*. *Educ:* Wellington Coll., Berks; RMA, Woolwich. 2nd Lieut, RA, 1928; transferred to RAOC, 1935, as Captain; Major 1944; Lieut-Col 1948; Col 1952; Brig. 1958; Maj.-Gen. 1961. War Office: Col 1942–44; Brig. 1944–47; Inspector of Establishments, 1947–50; Controller of Army Statistics, 1950–51; Comdr RAOC, Ammunition Org., 1951–53; Comdr, Bicester, 1953–57; DOS, BAOR, 1957–60; Inspector, RAOC, War Office, 1960–61; Dir of Ordnance Service, War Office, 1961–64; retired, Dec. 1964. Man. Dir, Army Kinema Corp., 1965–70, Services Kinema Corp., 1970–75. Chm. Greater London Br., SS&AFA, 1977–81. Col Commandant, RAOC, 1963–70. Legion of Merit (degree of Officer), USA. *Recreations:* shooting, sailing. *Address:* 56 The Cottages, North Street, Emsworth, Hants PO10 7PJ. *T:* Emsworth 373466. *Club:* Emsworth Sailing.

HILDRETH, (Henry) Jan (Hamilton Crossley); independent consultant; Executive Director, Minster Trust Ltd; non-executive Director, Monument Oil PLC, and other companies; *b* 1 Dec. 1932; *s* of Maj.-Gen. Sir (Harold) John (Crossley) Hildreth, KBE, and late Mrs Joan Elise Hallett (*née* Hamilton); *m* 1958, Wendy Moira Marjorie, *d* of late Arthur Harold Clough, CMG; two *s* one *d*. *Educ:* Wellington Coll.; The Queen's Coll., Oxford. National Service in RA, BAOR, 1952–53; 44 Parachute Bde (TA), 1953–58. Oxford, Hon. Mods (Nat. Sci.), BA (PPE) 1956, MA. Baltic Exchange, 1956; Royal Dutch Shell Group, 1957: served Philippines (marketing) and London (finance); Kleinwort, Benson Ltd, 1963; NEDO, 1965; Member of Economic Development Cttees for the Clothing, the Hosiery and Knitwear, and the Wool Textile industries; Mem., London Transport Bd, subseq. LTE, 1968–72: main responsibilities Finance, Marketing, Corp. Plan, Data Processing, and Estates; Asst Chief Exec., John Laing & Son Ltd, 1972–74; Dir-Gen., Inst. of Directors, 1975–78. Member: Cttee, GBA, 1978–86; Council, ISIS, 1979–; Exec. Cttee, Industrial Soc., 1973–84; Council, British Exec. Service Overseas; Council, 1980–83, 1985–, and Finance Cttee, 1980–, Spastic Soc.; Hon. Treasurer, Contact A Family. Constituency Chm., Wimbledon Cons. Assoc. Governor: Wellington Coll.; Eagle House Sch. FCIT. FRSA. *Recreations:* cross-country running, photography, water mills, and others. *Address:* 50 Ridgway Place, Wimbledon, SW19. *Clubs:* Athenæum; Vincent's (Oxford); Thames Hare and Hounds.

HILDREW, Bryan, CBE 1977; FEng 1976; Managing Director, Lloyds Register of Shipping, 1977–85; *b* 19 March 1920; *s* of Alexander William Hildrew and Sarah Jane (*née* Clark); *m* 1950, Megan Kathleen Lewis; two *s* one *d*. *Educ:* Bede Collegiate Sch., Sunderland; Technical Coll., Sunderland; City and Guilds, Imperial Coll., London (MSc, DIC). FIMechE, FIMarE. Engineer Officer, RN, 1941–46. Lloyds Register of Shipping: Research Surveyor, 1948–67 (Admiralty Nuclear Submarine Project, 1956–61); Chief Engineer Surveyor, 1967–70; Technical Dir, 1970–77. Chm., Abbeyfield, Orpington, 1985–. President: IMechE, 1980–81; IMarE, 1983–85; Chm., CEI, 1981–82. *Recreations:* orienteering, walking. *Address:* 8 Westholme, Orpington, Kent. *T:* Orpington 25451.

HILDYARD, Rev. Christopher, LVO 1966; MA; *b* 28 April 1901; *s* of Lyonel D'Arcy and Dora Hildyard. *Educ:* St George's, Windsor Castle; Repton; Magdalene Coll., Cambridge; Cuddesdon Theological Coll. Curate at Glass Houghton, West Yorks, 1925–27; Curate at Gisborough, North Yorks, 1927–28; Asst Minor Canon, Westminster Abbey, 1928–32; Minor Canon, Westminster Abbey, 1932–73; Chaplain of Westminster Hospital, 1937–58; Custodian, Westminster Abbey, 1945–55; Sacrist, Westminster Abbey, 1958–73, Sacrist Emeritus, 1977. Chairman, Royal Asylum of St Ann's Soc., 1952–76. Patron of the Living of Rowley, E Yorks. *Recreation:* painting. *Address:* 2 The Cloisters, Westminster, SW1P 3PA. *T:* 01–222 4982.

HILDYARD, Sir David (Henry Thoroton), KCMG 1975 (CMG 1966); DFC 1943; HM Diplomatic Service, retired; *b* 4 May 1916; *s* of late His Honour G. M. T. Hildyard, QC, and Sybil, *d* of H. W. Hamilton Hoare; *m* 1947, Millicent (*née* Baron), *widow* of Wing Commander R. M. Longmore, OBE; one *s* one *d*. *Educ:* Eton; Christ Church, Oxford. Served with RAF, 1940–46. Entered HM Foreign (subseq. Diplomatic) Service, 1948; Montevideo, 1950; Madrid, 1953; FO, 1957; Counsellor, Mexico City, 1960–65; Head of Economic Relations Dept, FO, 1965–68; Minister and Alternate UK Rep. to UN, 1968–70; Ambassador to Chile, 1970–73; Ambassador and Permanent UK Rep. to UN and other International Organisations, Geneva, 1973–76. *Recreations:* tennis, golf. *Address:* 97 Onslow Square, SW7. *Clubs:* Reform, Hurlingham.

HILEY, Joseph; DL; *b* 18 Aug. 1902; *s* of Frank Hiley of Leeds; *m* 1932, Mary Morrison, *d* of Dr William Boyd; three *d*. *Educ:* West Leeds High Sch.; Leeds Univ., 1920–23. Formerly family business, Hiley Brothers, took over firm of J. B. Battye & Co. Ltd, 1924, Managing Dir 1927–59; Dir, Irish Spinners Ltd, 1952–74. Mem. of Lloyd's, 1966–. MP (C) Pudsey, Oct. 1959–Feb. 1974. Leeds City Councillor, 1930, Alderman, 1949, resigned, 1960; Lord Mayor of Leeds, 1957–58; President: West Leeds Conservative Assoc.; Leeds & District Spastics Soc.; Leeds YMCA; Central Yorks Scout Council; Past President: Hand-Knitting Assoc.; Leeds Chamber of Commerce; Chm., Northorpe Hall Trust. DL West Yorks, 1971. *Recreations:* cricket, theatre. *Address:* Elmaran, Layton Road, Horsforth, Leeds. *T:* Horsforth 4787. *Clubs:* Leeds (Leeds); Pudsey Conservative (Pudsey).

HILEY, Sir Thomas (Alfred), KBE 1966; Chartered Accountant, Australia, since 1932; *b* 25 Nov. 1905; *s* of William Hiley and Maria (*née* Savage); *m* 1929, Marjory Joyce (*née* Jarrott) (*d* 1972); two *s*. *Educ:* Brisbane Grammar Sch.; University of Qld. State Public Service, 1921; Public Accountancy, 1923; in practice (Public Accountant), 1925. Qld Parliament, 1944; Dep. Leader of Opposition, 1950; Treasurer of Qld and Minister for Housing, 1957; Treasurer, 1963; Deputy Premier, 1965; retired from Parliament, 1966. Pres., Inst. of Chartered Accts in Aust., 1946–47. Hon. MCom, University of Qld, 1960. *Recreations:* shooting, fishing, cricket. *Address:* Illawong, 39 The Esplanade, Tewantin, Qld 4565, Australia. *T:* 471–175. *Club:* Queensland (Brisbane).

HILGENDORF, Sir Charles, Kt 1981; CMG 1971; JP; farmer; *b* 1908; *s* of Prof. Frederick William Hilgendorf and Frances Elizabeth (*née* Murray); *m* 1936, Rosemary Helen Mackenzie; one *s* one *d*. *Educ:* Christ's College, Christchurch; Univ. of Canterbury, NZ (MA; Hon. LLD 1978). Held various positions in Federated Farmers of NZ, 1946–61. Member: NZ Meat Producers Board, 1961–80 (Chm., 1972–80); University Grants Cttee (of NZ), 1961–74. *Address:* Sherwood, Ashburton, NZ. *T:* Winchmore 643. *Clubs:* Farmers'; Christchurch, Wellington (both in New Zealand).

HILL, family name of **Marquess of Downshire, Baron Hill of Luton** and **Baron Sandys.**

HILL; *see* Clegg-Hill, family name of Viscount Hill.

HILL, 8th Viscount *cr* 1842; **Antony Rowland Clegg-Hill;** Bt 1726–27; Baron Hill 1814; *b* 19 March 1931; *s* of 7th Viscount Hill and Elisabeth Flora (*d* 1967), *d* of Brig.-Gen. George Nowell Thomas Smyth-Osbourne, CB, CMG, DSO; *S* father, 1974; *m* 1963, Juanita Phyllis (marr. diss. 1976), *d* of John W. Pertwee, Salfords, Surrey. *Educ:* Kelly Coll.; RMA, Sandhurst. Formerly Captain, RA. Freeman of Shrewsbury, 1957. *Heir: cousin* Peter David Raymond Charles Clegg-Hill [*b* 17 Oct. 1945; *m* 1973, Sharon Ruth Deane, Kaikohe, NZ; one *s* three *d*]. *Address:* House of Lords, SW1A OPW.

HILL OF LUTON, Baron, *cr* 1963 (Life Peer); **Charles Hill,** PC 1955; MA, MD, DPH, LLD; *b* 15 Jan. 1904; *s* of late Charles Hill and Florence M. Cook; *m* 1931, Marion Spencer Wallace; two *s* three *d*. *Educ:* St Olave's Sch.; Trinity Coll., Cambridge; London Hosp. Formerly: House Physician and Receiving Room Officer, London Hospital; London University Extension Lecturer in Biology; Deputy Medical Supt, Coppice Mental Hospital, Nottingham; Deputy MOH, City of Oxford; Sec., BMA, 1944–50: Pres., World Medical Assoc.; Chm., Central Council for Health Educn; Hon. Sec., Commonwealth Medical Conf. Chm., Chest, Heart and Stroke Assoc., 1974–83 (Vice-Pres., 1983–). MP (L and C) Luton, 1950–63; Parly Sec., Min. of Food, 1951–April 1955; Postmaster-Gen., April 1955–Jan. 1957; Chancellor of the Duchy of Lancaster Jan. 1957–Oct. 1961; Minister of Housing and Local Government and Minister for Welsh Affairs, Oct. 1961–July 1962. Chm., Nat. Jt Council for Local Authorities' Administrative, Professional, Technical and Clerical Services, 1963–78. Chm., Independent Television Authority, 1963–67; Chm. of Governors of the BBC, 1967–72. Chairman: Laporte Industries Ltd, 1965–70; Abbey National Building Soc., 1976–78 (Dir, 1964–78). Hon. Fellow Amer. Medical Assoc. *Publications:* What is Osteopathy? (jointly), 1937; Reprinted Broadcasts, 1941–50; Both Sides of the Hill, 1964; Behind the Screen, 1974. *Recreations:* fishing, walking. *Address:* 9 Borodale, Kirkwick Avenue, Harpenden, Herts AL5 2QW. *T:* Harpenden 64288. *Club:* Reform.

See also D. R. Fairbairn.

HILL, Prof. Alan Geoffrey, MA; Professor of English Language and Literature in the University of London at Royal Holloway and Bedford New College (formerly Royal Holloway College), since 1981; *b* 12 Dec. 1931; *yr s* of Thomas Murton Hill and Alice Marion Hill (*née* Nunn); *m* 1960, Margaret Vincent Rutherford, MA; three *d*. *Educ:* Dulwich Coll.; St Andrews Univ. (MA 1st Cl. Hons English Lang. and Lit.); Merton Coll., Oxford (BLitt). Asst Lectr/Lectr in English, Exeter Univ., 1958–62; Lectr in English, St Andrews Univ., 1962–68; Sen. Lectr in English, Dundee Univ., 1968–80. Vis. Professor of English, Univ. of Saskatchewan, 1973–74; Ext. Examr in English, Univ. of Buckingham, 1986–. Crowsley Lectr, Charles Lamb Soc., 1981; Warton Lectr, British Acad., 1986. Trustee, Dove Cottage Trust, 1969–; General Editor, The Letters of William and Dorothy Wordsworth, 1979–. *Publications:* The Letters of William and Dorothy Wordsworth, vol. III, The Middle Years, Part 2, 1812–1820, 2nd edn (rev. and ed with Mary Moorman), 1970; vol. IV, The Later Years, Part 1, 1821–1828, 2nd edn (rev. and ed), 1978; vol. V, The Later Years, Part 2, 1829–1834, 2nd edn (rev. and ed), 1979; vol. VI, The Later Years, Part 3, 1835–1839, 2nd edn (rev. and ed), 1982; (ed) Selected Letters of Dorothy Wordsworth, 1981; (ed) Selected Letters of William Wordsworth, 1984; (ed) John Henry Newman, Loss and Gain, 1986; articles and reviews in lit. and theological jls.

Recreations: music, fine arts, ecclesiology. *Address:* 1a Northcroft Road, Englefield Green, Surrey TW20 0DP. *T:* Egham 31659. *Club:* Savile.

HILL, Alan John Wills, CBE 1972; publishing consultant; Consultant to the Heinemann Group of Publishers, 1979–84 and since 1986; *b* 12 Aug. 1912; *s* of William Wills Hill and May Frances Hill; *m* 1939, Enid Adela Malin; two *s* one *d*. *Educ:* Wyggeston Sch., Leicester; Jesus Coll., Cambridge (Schol., MA). RAF, 1940–45: Specialist Armament Officer (Sqdn Ldr). Publishing Asst, Wm Heinemann Ltd, 1936–40; Dir, 1955; jt Man. Dir, 1959–61; Chm. and Man. Dir, Heinemann Educational Books Ltd, 1961–79; Man. Dir, Heinemann Group of Publishers Ltd, 1973–79; Chairman: Heinemann Educnl Books (Nigeria), 1969–83; World's Work Ltd, 1973–79; Hill MacGibbon Ltd, 1984; Pres., Heinemann Educational Books Inc. (USA), 1977–79; Man. Dir, Heinemann Computers in Education Ltd, 1981–84; Consultant to William Collins, 1985. Chm., Soc. of Bookmen, 1965–68; Chm., Educational Publishers' Council, 1969–71; Vice-Chm., Educn Technol. Project, 1985–; Member: Council, Publishers' Assoc., 1972–79; Exec. Cttee, National Book League, 1973–79; British Council Books Adv. Panel, 1973–83; CNAA (Business Studies Panel), 1975–82; UNESCO Cttee on Copyright in third world countries; Cttee, Friends of the Lake District. Governor, Nuffield-Chelsea Curriculum Trust, 1979–; Mem. Council, Chelsea Coll., London Univ., 1978–85 (Vice-Chm., 1981–85); Mem. Council and Hon. Fellow, KCL, 1985–. Pres., Keswick Amateur Athletic Club, 1977–. Closely involved with Commonwealth literature and educn. *Publications:* (with R. W. Finn) And So Was England Born, 1939; History in Action, 1962; articles in jls. *Recreations:* swimming, mountain-walking, gardening. *Address:* 56 Northway, NW11 6PA. *T:* 01–455 8388; New House, Rosthwaite, Borrowdale, Cumbria. *Clubs:* Athenæum, Garrick, Royal Air Force, PEN.

HILL, Alastair Malcolm; QC 1982; a Recorder of the Crown Court, since 1982; *b* 12 May 1936; *s* of Prof. Sir Ian George Wilson Hill, CBE, LLD, FRCP, FRSE and Lady (Audrey) Hill; *m* 1969, Elizabeth Maria Innes; one *s* one *d*. *Educ:* Trinity Coll., Glenalmond; Keble Coll., Oxford (Stevenson-Chatterton Schol.; BA Hons Jurisp. 1959). Nat. Service, RHA, 1954–56. Called to the Bar, Gray's Inn, 1961; South Eastern Circuit. *Recreations:* collecting prints and watercolours, opera, fly-fishing. *Address:* New Court, Temple, EC4Y 9BE. *T:* 01–583 6166.

HILL, (Arthur) Derek; artist, writer, and organiser of exhibitions; *b* Bassett, Hampshire, 6 Dec. 1916; *s* of A. J. L. Hill and Grace Lilian Mercer. *Educ:* Marlborough Coll. Has designed sets and dresses for Covent Garden and Sadler's Wells. *One-man exhibitions:* Nicholson Gall., London, 1943; Leicester Galls, London, 1947, 1950, 1953 and 1956. *Organised exhibitions:* 1934 onwards: Dégas Exhibn for Edinburgh Fest. and Tate Gall., London, 1952; Landseer exhibn (with John Woodward) at Royal Academy, 1961, etc. Represented in exhibns, Europe and USA, 1957–; exhibns in New York, 1966 and 1969; retrospective exhibitions: Whitechapel Gall., London, 1961; Arts Council of NI, Belfast, 1970; Municipal Gall., Dublin, 1971; portraits, Marlborough Fine Arts, London, 1978; King's Lynn Fest., 1986. *Pictures owned by:* Tate Gall.; Nat. Gall. of Canada; Arts Council; Fogg Museum, Harvard; Nat. Portrait Gall. of Denmark; Liechtenstein Gall., Vaduz; National Gall. of Ireland and Municipal Gall. of Dublin; Ulster Mus., Belfast; Walker Gall., Liverpool; City Art Galleries of: Southampton, Birmingham, Bradford, Coventry, Carlisle, Sheffield, etc. FRGS. *Publications:* Islamic Architecture and Its Decoration (with Prof. Oleg Grabar), 1965; Islamic Architecture in North Africa (with L. Golvin), 1976; articles in Illustrated London News, Apollo, Burlington Magazine, etc. *Recreations:* gardening, travelling.

HILL, Sir Austin Bradford, Kt 1961; CBE 1951; FRS 1954; PhD (Econ.), 1926, DSc, 1929 (London); Emeritus Professor of Medical Statistics, London School of Hygiene and Tropical Medicine, University of London, and Hon. Director, Statistical Research Unit of Medical Research Council, 1945–61; Dean of the London School of Hygiene and Tropical Medicine, 1955–57, Honorary Fellow, 1976; *b* 8 July 1897; 3rd *s* of late Sir Leonard Erskine Hill, FRS; *m* 1923, Florence Maud (*d* 1980), *d* of late Edward Salmon, OBE; two *s* one *d*. *Educ:* Chigwell Sch.; privately; University Coll., London. Flight Sub-Lieut in Royal Naval Air Service, 1916–18; on staff of Medical Research Council and its Industrial Health Research Board, 1923–33; Reader in Epidemiology and Vital Statistics, London Sch. of Hygiene and Tropical Medicine, 1933–45; seconded during the war to Research and Experiments Dept, Ministry of Home Security, 1940–42, and to Medical Directorate, RAF, 1943–45. Hon. Civil Consultant in Medical Statistics to RAF and mem. of Flying Personnel Research Cttee, 1943–78; Civil Consultant in Medical Statistics to RN, 1958–77; Mem., Cttee on Safety of Medicines, 1964–75; Pres. Royal Statistical Soc., 1950–52 (Hon. Sec. 1940–50); Gold Medallist, 1953; Pres. Section of Epidemiology, RSM, 1953–55, Section of Occupational Medicine, 1964–65; Member: Council, MRC, 1954–58; Cttee on Review of Medicines, 1975–78; Fellow of University Coll., London; Hon. FRCP; Hon. FFCM; Hon. FFOM; Hon. FIA; Hon FRSM; Hon. FAPHA; Hon. Fellow: Soc. of Community Medicine; Soc. of Occupational Medicine; Faculty of Medicine, University of Chile; Society for Social Medicine; Internat. Epidemiological Assoc.; Med. Research Club. Cutter Lecturer, Harvard, 1953; Harben Lecturer RIPH&H, 1957; Alfred Watson Memorial Lectr Inst. of Actuaries, 1962; Marc Daniels Lectr RCP, 1963. Hon. DSc Oxford, 1963; Hon. MD Edinburgh, 1968. Galen Medallist, Soc. of Apothecaries, 1959; Harben Gold Medallist, 1961; Jenner Medallist, RSM, 1965; Heberden Medallist, Heberden Soc., 1965. *Publications:* Internal Migration and its Effects upon the Death Rates, 1925; The Inheritance of Resistance to Bacterial Infection in Animal Species, 1934; Principles of Medical Statistics, 1937, 11th edn, as A Short Textbook of Medical Statistics, 1985; Statistical Methods in Clinical and Preventive Medicine, 1962; reports to Industrial Health Research Board on industrial sickness and numerous papers in scientific journals, especially studies of cigarette smoking and cancer of the lung and of the clinical trial of new drugs. *Recreations:* walking in the countryside, gardening. *Address:* April Cottage, Lower Hopton, Nesscliffe, Shropshire SY4 1DL. *T:* Nesscliffe 231.

HILL, Brian, DL; Chief Executive and Clerk, Lancashire County Council, since 1977; *b* 16 Oct. 1930; *m* 1954, Barbara (*née* Hickson); one *d*. *Educ:* Wigan Grammar Sch.; Univ. of Manchester (LLB). Solicitor. Asst Solicitor, Manchester Corp., 1953–56; Lancashire County Council: Sen. Solicitor appts, finally Second Dep. Clerk of CC, 1956–74; Dep. Clerk, 1974–76. Clerk of Lancs Lieutenancy, 1977–; County Electoral Returning Officer, 1977–. Secretary: Lancs Adv. Cttee, 1977–; Lord Chancellor's Adv. Cttee on Gen. Comrs of Income Tax, 1977–; Lancs Probation and After Care Cttee, 1977–; Adviser to Police Cttee, ACC, 1984–; Co. Sec., Lancashire Enterprises Ltd, 1982–; Mem., MSC Area Manpower Bd, 1983–86. Chairman: Local Govt Legal Soc., 1970–71; Soc. of County Secs, 1976–77; NW Br., SOLACE, 1985; Vice-Pres., Lancs Youth Clubs Assoc., 1977–; Clerk to Court, RNCM, Manchester, 1977– (Hon. RNCM 1979); Mem. Court, Univ. of Lancaster, 1977–. Sec., Lancs Cttee, Royal Jubilee and Prince's Trusts, 1985–. DL Lancs, 1977. FRSA 1983. *Recreation:* music. *Address:* The Cottage, Bruna Hill, Garstang, near Preston, Lancs. *Club:* Royal Over-Seas League.

HILL, Brian John, FRICS; FCIOB; Chairman and Chief Executive, Higgs and Hill plc, since 1983; *b* 19 Dec. 1932; *s* of Doris Winifred Hill and Gerald Aubrey Hill, OBE; *m* 1959, Janet J. Newman; two *s* one *d*. *Educ:* Stowe School; Emmanuel College, Cambridge. BA (Land Economy); MA. Managing Director, Higgs and Hill Building Ltd, 1966, Group Managing Dir, 1972. Pres., London Region, Nat. Fedn of Building Trades Employers, 1981–82; Chairman: Vauxhall Coll. of Building and Further Educn, 1979–86; Nat. Contractors Group, 1983–84; Dir, Building Centre; Senior Vice-Pres., Chartered Inst. of Building, 1986. Property Services Agency: Mem. Adv. Bd, 1981–86; Mem. Bd, 1986–. Mem. Cttee, Lazard Property Unit Trust, 1982–. Governor, Great Ormond Street Hosp. for Sick Children, 1985–. *Recreations:* travelling, tennis, gardening. *Address:* Barrow House, The Warren, Kingswood, Surrey. *T:* Mogador 832424. *Club:* Royal Automobile.

HILL, Christopher; *see* Hill, J. E. C.

HILL, Rev. Canon Christopher John; The Archbishop of Canterbury's Assistant for Ecumenical Affairs, since 1982, Hon. Canon of Canterbury Cathedral, since 1982; *b* 10 Oct. 1945; *s* of Leonard and Frances V. Hill; *m* 1976, Hilary Ann Whitehouse; three *s* one *d*. *Educ:* Sebright Sch., Worcs; King's Coll., London (BD Hons; Relton Prize for Theology, 1967; MTh 1968; AKC 1967). Deacon 1969, priest 1970. Asst Curate, Dio. of Lichfield: St Michael's, Tividale, 1969–73; St Nicholas, Codsall, 1973–74; Asst Chaplain to Archbp of Canterbury for Foreign Relations, 1974–81. Anglican Secretary: Anglican-RC Internat. Commn (I), 1974–81, Internat. Commn (II), 1983–; Anglican-Lutheran Eur. Commn, 1981–82. Guestmaster, Nikaean Club, 1982. *Publications:* miscellaneous ecumenical articles. *Recreations:* Radio 3, mountain walking, detective stories, Italian food, unaffordable wine. *Address:* Lambeth Palace, SE1 7LB. *T:* 01–928 4880. *Club:* Athenæum.

HILL, Colin de Neufville, CMG 1961; OBE 1959; Business Manager, University of Sussex, 1964–82; *b* 12 Jan. 1917; *s* of Philip Rowland and Alice May Hill; *m* 1950, Mary Patricia Carson Wilson; two *s*. *Educ:* Cheltenham Coll.; St Edmund Hall, Oxford. BA. hons in Mod. Langs, Oxford, 1938. Selected for appt to Colonial Service, 1938; Administrative Officer, Colonial Admin. Service, Eastern Nigeria, 1939; served with Provincial and Regional Administration, Eastern Nigeria, 1939–53; transferred to Tanganyika and apptd Sec. for Finance, 1954; Permanent Sec. to the Treasury, Tanganyika Government, 1959–64. *Recreations:* photography, gardening, music. *Address:* Mount Pleasant Farm, Barcombe, near Lewes, East Sussex.

HILL, Prof. David Keynes, ScD; FRS 1972; Professor of Biophysics, Royal Postgraduate Medical School, University of London, 1975–82; *b* 23 July 1915; *s* of late Prof. Archibald Vivian Hill, CH, OBE, ScD, FRS, and Margaret Neville, *d* of late Dr J. N. Keynes; *m* 1949, Stella Mary Humphrey; four *d*. *Educ:* Highgate Sch.; Trinity Coll., Cambridge. ScD Cantab 1965. Fellow, Trinity Coll., Cambridge, 1940–48; Physiologist on staff of Marine Biological Assoc., Plymouth, 1948–49; Sen. Lectr, 1949–62, Reader in Biophysics, 1962–75, Vice-Dean, 1969–74, Royal Postgrad. Med. Sch., London Univ. Physiological Society: Editor of Journal, 1969–76; Chm., Bd of Monographs, 1979–81. *Publications:* Scientific papers in Jl Physiology. *Recreations:* gardening, photography. *Address:* Ivy Cottage, Winksley, Ripon, N Yorks HG4 3NR. *T:* Kirkby Malzeard 562.

See also Polly Hill.

HILL, David Neil, MA, FRCO; Organist and Master of Music, Westminster Cathedral, since 1982; *b* 13 May 1957; *s* of James Brian Greatrex Hill and Jean Hill; *m* 1979, Hilary Llystyn Jones; one *s* one *d*. *Educ:* Chetham's School of Music, Manchester; St John's College, Cambridge (organ student; toured Aust. 1977, USA and Canada, 1978, Japan, 1979; MA). Conductor, Alexandra Choir, 1979–; Sub-Organist, Durham Cathedral, 1980–82. Recordings with Westminster Cathedral Choir (Gramophone award, 1985); concerts abroad; toured Aust. as organist, 1984; USA tour with Cathedral Choir, 1985. *Recreations:* wine, beer, cricket, reading, snooker. *Address:* 42 Francis Street, SW1P 1QW. *T:* 01–834 4008.

HILL, Derek; *see* Hill, A. D.

HILL, Prof. Dorothy, CBE 1971; FRS 1965; FAA 1956; Research Professor of Geology, University of Queensland, 1959–72, now Emeritus Professor; President, Professorial Board, 1971–72, Member of Senate, 1976–77; *b* 10 Sept. 1907; *d* of R. S. Hill, Brisbane; unmarried. *Educ:* Brisbane Girls' Grammar Sch.; Univs of Queensland and Cambridge. BSc (Qld) 1928, 1st Cl. Hons in Geol. and Univ. Gold Medal. Foundn Trav. Fellowship of Univ. of Queensland held at Newnham Coll., Cambridge, 1930–32; PhD Cantab 1932; Old Students' Res. Fellowship, Newnham Coll., Cambridge, 1932–35; Sen. Studentship (Exhibn of 1851) held at Cambridge, 1935–37; Coun. for Sci. and Indust. Res. Fellowship, held at Univ. of Queensland, 1937–42; DSc (Qld) 1942. WRANS, Second Off., 1942–45 (RAN Ops Staff). Univ. of Queensland: Lectr in Geol., 1946–56, Reader, 1956–59. Hon. Editor, Geol. Soc. of Aust., 1958–64; Mem. Council, Australian Acad. of Science, 1968–70, Pres. 1970; Pres., Geol Soc. of Aust., 1973–75. Lyell Medal, Geol. Soc. of London, 1964; Clarke Medal, Royal Society of NSW, 1966; Mueller Medal, ANZAAS, 1967; Foreign and Commonwealth Mem. Geol. Soc. London, 1967; Hon. Fellow, Geol Soc. of America, 1971. Hon. LLD Queensland, 1974. W. R. Browne Medal, Geol. Soc. of Australia, 1980; ANZAAS Medal, 1983. *Publications:* numerous, in geology and palæontology jls on fossil corals, archæocyatha, brachiopods, reef sediments and Australian geology and stratigraphy. *Recreations:* travel, reading. *Address:* University of Queensland, St Lucia, Brisbane, Qld 4067, Australia.

HILL, Col (Edward) Roderick, DSO 1944; JP; Lord-Lieutenant of Gwent, 1974–79 (HM Lieutenant for Monmouthshire, 1965–74); Patron, Chepstow Race Course Co. Ltd (Director, 1958–83; Chairman, 1964–81); *b* 1904; *s* of late Capt. Roderick Tickell Hill; *m* 1934, Rachel (*d* 1983), *e d* of Ellis Hicks Beach, Witcombe Park, Glos; one *s* one *d*. *Educ:* Winchester; Magdalen Coll., Oxford. Gazetted to Coldstream Guards, 1926; served War of 1939–45, with regt (despatches, DSO); commanded 5th Bn and 1st Bn Coldstream Guards and Guards Training Bn; comd Regt, 1949–52. JP Co. Monmouth; High Sheriff of Monmouthshire, 1956; DL Monmouthshire, 1957; Vice-Lieut, 1963–65. Chm. of the Curre Hunt, 1959–65. Chm. of Governors, Monmouth Sch. and Monmouth Sch. for Girls, 1961–66; Chm. Chepstow RDC, 1962–63. Hon. Col, 104 Light AD Regt RA(V), 1967–69. Freeman and Liveryman, Haberdashers Co., 1969. Pres., Royal Welsh Agric. Soc., 1970–71. Pres., TA&VRA for Wales and Monmouthshire, 1971–74. Officer, Order of Orange-Nassau (with swords), 1946. KStJ 1972. *Publication:* (with the Earl of Rosse) The Story of the Guards Armoured Division, 1941–1945, 1956. *Address:* Manor Farm Cottage, Stanford in the Vale, Faringdon, Oxfordshire SN7 8NN. *Club:* Cavalry and Guards.

See also Baron Raglan.

HILL, (Eliot) Michael, QC 1979; a Recorder of the Crown Court, since 1977; *b* 22 May 1935; *s* of Cecil Charles Hill and Rebecca Betty Hill; *m* 1965, Kathleen Irene (*née* Hordern); one *s* two *d*. *Educ:* Bancroft's Sch., Essex; Brasenose Coll., Oxford. Called to the Bar, Gray's Inn, 1958; Mem., Senate of the Inns of Court and the Bar, 1976–79 and 1982–. South-Eastern Circuit. Prosecuting Counsel to Crown, Inner London Sessions, 1969–74; Jun. Pros. Counsel to Crown, Central Criminal Court, 1974–77; a Sen. Pros. Counsel to Crown, 1977–79. Chm., Criminal Bar Assoc., 1982–86 (Sec., 1973–75; Vice-Chm., 1979–82); Member: Criminal Law Revision Cttee, 1983–; Council of Legal Educn,

1983–. *Recreations:* family, friends, riding, fishing and just living. *Address:* (chambers) 3 Temple Gardens, Temple, EC4Y 9AU. *T:* 01–353 1662.

HILL, Dame Elizabeth (Mary), DBE 1976; Emeritus Professor of Slavonic Studies, Cambridge; *b* 24 Oct. 1900; *m* 1984, Stojan J. Veljković. *Educ:* University and King's Colls, London Univ. BA London 1924, PhD London 1928; MA Cantab 1937. War of 1939–45: Slavonic specialist, Min. of Information. University Lecturer in Slavonic, 1936–48; Prof. of Slavonic Studies, Univ. of Cambridge, 1948–68; Andrew Mellon Prof. of Slavic Languages and Literatures, Pittsburgh Univ., 1968–70. Fellow of University Coll., London; Fellow, Girton Coll., Cambridge. Hon. LittD East Anglia, 1978. *Address:* 10 Croft Gardens, Cambridge.

HILL, Air Cdre Dame Felicity (Barbara), DBE 1966 (OBE 1954); Director of the Women's Royal Air Force, 1966–69; *b* 12 Dec. 1915; *d* of late Edwin Frederick Hill and late Mrs Frances Ada Barbara Hill (*née* Cocke). *Educ:* St Margaret's Sch., Folkestone. Joined WAAF, 1939; commnd, 1940; served in: UK, 1939–46; Germany, 1946–47; Far East Air Force, 1949–51; other appts included Inspector of WRAF, 1956–59; OC, RAF Hawkinge, 1959–60; OC, RAF Spitalgate, 1960–62; Dep. Dir, 1962–65. Hon. ADC to the Queen, 1966–69. *Address:* Worcester Cottage, Mews Lane, Winchester, Hants. *Club:* Royal Air Force.

HILL, Geoffrey (William), FRSL; University Lecturer in English and Fellow of Emmanuel College, University of Cambridge, since 1981; *b* 18 June 1932; *s* of late William George Hill and late Hilda Beatrice Hill (*née* Hands); *m* 1956, Nancy Whittaker (marr. diss.); three *s* one *d*. *Educ:* County High Sch., Bromsgrove; Keble Coll., Oxford (BA 1953, MA 1959; Hon. Fellow, 1981). Mem., academic staff, Univ. of Leeds, 1954–80 (Prof. of Eng. Lit., 1976–80). Churchill Fellow, Dept of English, Univ. of Bristol, 1980. Clark Lectr, Trinity Coll., Cambridge, 1986. FRSL 1972. English version of Ibsen's Brand produced at National Theatre, London, 1978. Whitbread Award, 1971; RSL Award (W. H. Heinemann Bequest), 1971; Loines Award, Amer. Acad. and Inst. of Arts and Letters, 1983; Ingram Merrill Foundn Award in Literature, 1985. *Publications: poetry:* For the Unfallen, 1959 (Gregory Award, 1961); King Log, 1968 (Hawthornden Prize, 1969; Geoffrey Faber Meml Prize, 1970); Mercian Hymns, 1971 (Alice Hunt Bartlett Award, 1971); Somewhere is Such a Kingdom: Poems 1952–1971, 1975; Tenebrae, 1978 (Duff Cooper Meml Prize, 1979); The Mystery of the Charity of Charles Péguy, 1983; Collected Poems, 1985; *poetic drama:* Henrik Ibsen, Brand: a version for the English Stage, 1978; *criticism:* The Lords of Limit: essays on literature and ideas, 1984. *Address:* Emmanuel College, Cambridge CB2 3AP.

HILL, George Geoffrey David, CMG 1971; late Assistant Secretary, Department of the Environment (Head of International Transport Division, Ministry of Transport, 1964); *b* 15 Aug. 1911; *o s* of late William George Hill, JP; *m* 1935, Elisabeth Wilhelmina (*née* Leuwer); one *d*. *Educ:* Manchester Grammar Sch.; Gonville and Caius Coll., Cambridge (BA (Hons)). Entered Ministry of Transport as Asst Principal, 1934; Principal, 1941; Asst Sec., 1954; retired 1972. *Recreations:* bridge, languages. *Address:* 125 Ember Lane, Esher, Surrey. *T:* 01–398 1851.

HILL, George Raymond, FCA, FCIT; FHCIMA; Director: Prince of Wales Hotels PLC, since 1985; Crest Hotels Investments Ltd (Vice-Chairman, since 1982); Sims Catering Butchers plc, since 1985 (Chairman); *b* 25 Sept. 1925; *s* of George Mark and Jill Hill; *m* 1948, Sophie (*née* Gilbert); two *d*. *Educ:* St Dunstan's Coll., London. Royal Marines, 1943–46 (Lieut). Distillers Co. Ltd (Industrial Group), 1952–66; BP Chemicals Ltd, 1967–69; British Transport Hotels Ltd: Chief Exec., 1970–76; Chm., 1974–76; Dir, Bass PLC, 1976–84 (Mem. Exec. Cttee); Chm., Bass UK Ltd, 1978–80; Chm., Howard Machinery PLC (later H. M. Holdings PLC), 1984–85; Associate, Korn-Ferry International Ltd, 1984–. Member Boards: British Railways (Scottish), and British Rail Hovercraft Ltd, 1972–76; British Tourist Auth., 1981–. Member: Hotel and Catering Industry Trng Bd, 1973–80; Civil Service Final Selection Bd, 1973–80; Cttee of Inquiry on Motorway Service Areas, 1978; BHRCA (Bd Chm., 1979–80; Nat. Council Chm., 1985–); Pres., Licensed Victuallers Schs, 1982–83. FRSA 1980. *Recreations:* music, theatre, works of art, country life. *Address:* 23 Sheffield Terrace, W8; The Paddocks, Chedworth, Glos. *Club:* Royal Automobile.

HILL, Gladys, MA, MD; FRCS, FRCOG; retired as Obstetrician and Gynæcologist, Royal Free Hospital (1940–59); *b* 28 Sept. 1894; *d* of late Arthur Griffiths Hill and Caroline Sutton Hill. *Educ:* Cheltenham Ladies' Coll.; Somerville Coll., Oxford; Royal Free Hosp. Med. Sch. MA Oxon, MD, BS London, FRCS 1936; FRCOG 1943. *Publications:* contribs to medical journals. *Recreations:* architecture, amateur dramatics, reading. *Address:* The Captain's Cottage, Bishops Lydeard, near Taunton, Som. *T:* Bishops Lydeard 432533.

HILL, Graham Starforth; Consultant: to Monaco office, Frere, Cholmeley, solicitors, since 1984; to Rodyk and Davidson, solicitors, Singapore, since 1985; *b* 22 June 1927; *s* of late Harold Victor John Hill and Helen Dora (*née* Starforth); *m* 1952, Margaret Elise Ambler (marr. diss.); one *s* one *d*. *Educ:* Dragon Sch., Oxford; Winchester Coll.; St John's Coll., Oxford (MA Hons). Called to the Bar, Grays Inn, 1951; admitted solicitor, 1961; also admitted solicitor Malaysia, Singapore and Hong Kong; Notary Public and Comr for Oaths, Singapore. Flying Officer, RAF, 1948–50. Crown Counsel, Colonial Legal Service, Singapore, 1953–56; Partner, subseq. Sen. Partner, Rodyk and Davidson, Advocates and Solicitors, Singapore, 1957–76. Chm., Guinness Mahon & Co. Ltd, 1979–83 (Dir, 1977–79); non-exec. Chm., Federal Finance and Credit Corp. Ltd, 1984–; non-exec. Dir, Phelan, Lewis and Peat Ltd, 1984–86. Mem., Malayan Bd of Income Tax, 1957–60. Formerly (all Singapore): Hon. Legal Adviser to High Commn; Law Reform Comr; dir of numerous cos; Member: Univ. Faculty of Law; Constitutional Commn; Council, Law Soc. (Pres., 1970–74, Hon. Mem. 1978); Courts Martial Mil. Ct of Appeal; Council, Internat. Bar Assoc.; Discip. Cttee and Appeal Cttee, ICA, 1980–86. Trustee: Southwark Cathedral Develt Trust Fund, 1980–85; Royal Opera House Trust, 1982–85. FRSA. Cavaliere dell'Ordine della Stella della Solidarieta, and Commendatore dell'Ordine al Merito, Italy. *Publications:* co-editor, The Laws of Singapore, revised edition 1970; report of Constitutional Commission of Singapore. *Recreations:* music, Italy. *Address:* Casa Claudia, Piccolo Pevero, 07020 Porto Cervo, Sardegna, Italy. *T:* Porto Cervo 92317; 28 St Petersburgh Place, W2 4LA. *T:* 01–221 6585. *Clubs:* Athenæum, Garrick; Singapore Turf (Singapore); Costa Smeralda Yacht (Italy).

See also I. S. Hill.

HILL, Harry, OBE 1986; FCCA, FCIS, FTII, CBIM; Director, Beecham Group, since 1979; Vice-Chairman, Beecham Products, since 1984; *b* 22 May 1924; *s* of James and Charlotte Hill; *m* 1944, Vera Brydon; two *d*. War service, 1942–45: flying duties, Fleet Air Arm; Lieut RNVR. John Marshall & Co., Newcastle upon Tyne, 1945–50: Professional accounting and auditing; articled clerk, subseq. managing clerk and partner; General Motors Ltd, London, 1950–69: sen. financial appts; Group Gen. Comptroller, 1966–69; Parkinson-Cowan Ltd, London, 1969–71; Dir of Finance and Admin; Beecham Products, Brentford, Mddx: Financial Dir, 1972–76; Admin Dir, 1976–77; Vice-Chm., Food and Drink Div., 1977–80; Chm., Internat. Div., 1977–84; Chm., Proprietaries Div., 1981–86. FCCA 1964 (ACCA 1949); FCIS 1970; FTII 1976; CBIM 1983. Pres., Assoc. of Certified Accountants, 1975–76; Mem., Price Commn, 1977–79; Chm., Apple and Pear Develt Council, 1983–86. *Recreations:* gardening, reading, motoring. *Address:* 77 Howards Thicket, Gerrards Cross, Bucks SL9 7NU. *T:* Gerrards Cross 883550.

HILL, Rt. Rev. Henry Gordon; on staff of Primate of Canada, episcopal liaison with non-Chalcedonian orthodox church; Co-Chairman, Anglican-Orthodox Joint Doctrinal Commission, since 1980; *b* 14 Dec. 1921; *s* of Henry Knox Hill and Kathleen Elizabeth (*née* Cunningham); unmarried. *Educ:* Queen's Univ., Kingston, Ont. (BA 1945); Trinity Coll., Toronto (LTh 1948); St John's Coll., Cambridge (MA 1952). Deacon, Dio. Ont., 1948; Priest (Bp of Ely for Ontario), 1949; Curate, Belleville, Ont., 1950; Rector of Adolphustown, Ont., 1951; Chaplain, St John's Coll., Cambridge, Eng., 1952; Curate, Wisbech, Cambs, 1955; Rector, St Thomas, Reddendale, Ont., 1957; Asst Prof., Canterbury Coll., Assumption Univ., Windsor, 1962–68; (Vice-Principal, 1965–68); Associate Prof. of History, Univ. of Windsor, Ont., 1968–74; Bishop of Ontario, 1975–81; Asst Bishop of Montreal, 1981–83. Warden, Sisters of St John the Divine, 1976; Vice-Pres., Fellowship of St Alban and St Sergius, 1980. Hon. DD: Trinity Coll., Toronto, 1976; Montreal Dio. Theol Coll., 1976; Hon. LLD Univ. of Windsor, 1976; Hon. Dr, Theological Inst., Bucharest, 1977. KLJ 1980. Patriarchal Cross of Romanian Orthodox Church, 1969. *Publications:* Contemplation and Ecumenism (Monastic Studies No 15), 1984; Light Out of the East: chapters on the life and worship of the ancient orthodox churches, 1986; articles in Cdn Jl of Theology, Sobornost, Jl Fellowship of St Alban and St Sergius. *Recreations:* walking, reading. *Address:* St John's Convent, 1 Botham Road, Willowdale, Ontario M2N 2JS, Canada.

HILL, Henry Howard E.; *see* Erskine-Hill.

HILL, Ian Macdonald, MS, FRCS; Consulting Cardiothoracic Surgeon, St Bartholomew's Hospital, since 1984 (Consultant Cardio-thoracic Surgeon, 1950–84); Hon. Consultant Thoracic Surgeon, SE Thames Regional Health Authority, since 1984 (Consultant Thoracic Surgeon, 1950–84); *b* 8 June 1919; British; *m* 1944, Agnes Mary Paice; three *s* one *d*. *Educ:* Stationers' Company Sch.; St Bartholomew's Hosp. Medical Coll. Undergrad. schols and medals, 1937–41; MB, BS (Hons) London, 1942; MRCS, LRCP 1942; FRCS 1944; MS London 1945. Demonstrator of Anatomy, St Bartholomew's, 1943; Surgical Chief Asst, St Bart's Hosp., 1944; RAF Medical Branch, 1946; Wing Comdr i/c Surg. Div. No 1 RAF Gen. Hosp., 1947; Senior Registrar, Thoracic Surg. Unit, Guy's Hosp., 1948; Surgical Chief Asst, Brompton Hosp. and Inst. of Diseases of the Chest, 1950. Sub-Dean, St Bart's Hosp. Med. Coll., 1964–73. FRSocMed. Member: Soc. of Apothecaries; Soc. of Thoracic Surgeons; Thoracic and Cardiac Socs. Governor, St Bartholomew's Hosp. Med. Coll., 1985–. Freeman of City of London. *Publications:* articles in professional jls, mainly relating to lung and cardiac surgery, 1942–61. *Recreations:* old cars, furniture, keyboard instruments; gardening and house care. *Address:* Bracken Wood, Church Lane, Fernham, Faringdon, Oxon SN7 7PB. *T:* Uffington 475.

HILL, (Ian) Starforth, QC 1969; **His Honour Judge Starforth Hill;** a Circuit Judge, since 1974; *b* 30 Sept. 1921; *s* of late Harold Victor John Hill; *m* 1st, 1950, Bridget Mary Footner; one *s* two *d*; 2nd, 1982, Greta Grimshaw; 3rd, 1986, Wendy Elizabeth Stavert. *Educ:* Shrewsbury Sch.; Brasenose Coll., Oxford (MA). 11th Sikh Regt, Indian Army, 1940–45, India, Africa, Italy (despatches). Called to Bar, Gray's Inn, 1949; Dep. Chm., Isle of Wight QS, 1968–71; Western Circuit; a Recorder of the Crown Court, 1972–74. Mem., Parole Bd, 1983–84. *Address:* 1 Crown Office Row, Temple, EC4. *T:* 01–353 9272; Tulls Hill, Preston Candover, Hants RG25 2EW. *T:* Preston Candover 309. *Club:* Hampshire (Winchester).

See also G. S. Hill.

HILL, Ivan Conrad, CBE 1960; Chairman, Industrial Coal Consumers Council, since 1965; *b* 22 Jan. 1906; *s* of Wilfred Lawson Hill and Annie Jane (*née* England); *m* 1st, 1931, Alexandrina Ewart (marr. diss. 1962); four *d*; 2nd, 1963, Sheila Houghton. *Educ:* Oakham Sch.; St John's Coll., Cambridge. Exhibitioner and Open Scholar of St John's Coll. 1st cl. Hons Law Tripos Cantab 1928. Apptd Jt Man. Dir, Kelsall & Kemp Ltd, 1933. Chm. Wool Industries Research Assoc., 1950–53; Mem. Monopolies and Restrictive Practices Commn, and Monopolies Commn, 1951–63; Chairman: British Rayon Research Assoc., 1956–61; Samuel Courtauld & Co. Ltd, 1962–66; Illingworth Morris & Co. Ltd, 1976–80; Convoy Woollen Co. Ltd, 1984–. Liveryman, Weavers' Company, 1938–. *Recreations:* travel, architecture, sport. *Address:* Crystal Spring, Duchy Road, Harrogate, N Yorks.

HILL, Brig. James; *see* Hill, Brig. S. J. L.

HILL, James; *see* Hill, S. J. A.

HILL, Sir James Frederick, 4th Bt *cr* 1917; Chairman, Sir James Hill & Sons Ltd; Director: Yorkshire Building Society; British Rail (Eastern Region); The Yorkshire General Unit Trust Ltd; *b* 5 Dec. 1943; *s* of Sir James Hill, 3rd Bt and of Marjory, *d* of late Frank Croft; *S* father, 1976; *m* 1966, Sandra Elizabeth, *o d* of J. C. Ingram; one *s* three *d*. *Heir:* *s* James Laurence Ingram Hill, *b* 22 Sept. 1973. *Address:* Roseville, Moor Lane, Menston, Ilkley, West Yorks LS29 6AP. *T:* Menston 74624. *Clubs:* Royal Automobile; Bradford (Yorks); Ilkley Golf.

HILL, James William Thomas, (Jimmy); Chairman, Jimmy Hill Ltd, since 1972; Soccer analyst to the BBC, since 1973; *m* 1st, 1950, Gloria Mary (marr. diss. 1961); two *s* one *d*; 2nd, 1962, Heather Christine (marr. diss. 1982); one *s* one *d*. *Educ:* Henry Thornton School, Clapham. Player, Brentford FC, 1949–52, Fulham FC, 1952–61; Gen. Manager, Coventry City FC, 1961–67, Managing Director, 1975–83, Chm., 1980–83. London Weekend Television: Head of Sport, 1967–72; Controller of Press, Promotion and Publicity, 1971–72; Deputy Controller, Programmes, 1972–73. Mem., Sports Council, 1971–76. Hon. Chm., The Professional Footballers Assoc., 1957–61. *Publications:* Striking for Soccer, 1961; Improve your Soccer, 1964; Football Crazy, 1985. *Recreations:* golf, riding, tennis, soccer, bridge. *Address:* c/o BBC Television, Kensington House, Richmond Way, W14 0AX. *Clubs:* The Sportsman, Queen's, All England Lawn Tennis and Croquet; The Berkshire.

HILL, Jimmy; *see* Hill, James William Thomas.

HILL, John; *see* Hill, F. J.

HILL, John; Hon. Lecturer, Institute of Local Government Studies, Birmingham University, since 1984; *b* 28 April 1922; *s* of William Hallett Hill and Emily Hill (*née* Massey); *m* 1952, Hilda Mary Barratt; one *s*. *Educ:* Merchant Taylors' Sch., Crosby; Liverpool Univ. (BCom); Inst. of Public Finance and Accountancy, 1954. City Treasurer of Liverpool, 1974–82. Mem., Merseyside Residuary Body, 1985–. *Recreation:* music. *Address:* 325 Northway, Lydiate, Merseyside L31 0BW. *T:* 051–526 3699.

HILL, John Edward Bernard; farming in Suffolk since 1946; *b* 13 Nov. 1912; *o s* of late Capt. Robert William Hill, Cambs Regt, and Marjorie Jane Lloyd-Jones, *d* of Edward Scott Miller; *m* 1944, Edith Luard, *widow* of Comdr R. A. E. Luard, RNVR, and 5th *d* of late John Maxwell, Cove, Dunbartonshire; one adopted *d*. *Educ:* Charterhouse; Merton

Coll., Oxford (MA). Various journeys; Middle East, Far East, India, USA, 1935–37; Far East, 1956–57; USA, 1958. Called to Bar, Inner Temple (Certificate of Honour), 1938. RA (TA), 1939; Air Observation Post Pilot, 1942; War Office, 1942; 651 (Air OP) RAF, Tunisia, 1942; wounded, 1943; invalided out, 1945. MP (C) South Norfolk, Jan. 1955–Feb. 1974; Mem. Parliamentary delegns: W Germany and Berlin, 1959; Ghana, 1965; IPU Conf., Teheran, 1966; CPA Conf., Uganda, 1967; Bulgaria, 1970; Council of Europe and WEU, 1970–72; Mem., European Parlt, 1973–74; Chm., Cons. Educn Cttee, 1971–73; Member: Select Cttee on Agriculture, 1967–69; Select Cttee on Procedure, 1970–71; Asst Govt Whip, 1959–60; a Lord Comr of the Treasury, 1960–64. Mem. East Suffolk and Norfolk River Board, 1952–62. Mem. Exec. Cttee, CLA, 1957–59, 1977–82. Member: Governing Body, Charterhouse Sch., 1958; Langley Sch., Norfolk, 1962–77; GBA Cttee, 1966–79, 1980–83; Council, Univ. of East Anglia, 1975–82. *Recreations:* association football (Blue; Sec., OUAFC 1934); shooting, concerts, picture galleries. *Address:* Watermill Farm, Wenhaston, Halesworth, Suffolk. *T:* Blythburgh 207. *Club:* Garrick.

HILL, Prof. (John Edward) Christopher, FBA 1966; DLitt; Master of Balliol College, Oxford, 1965–78; *b* 6 Feb. 1912; *m* 1st, 1944, Inez Waugh; one *d*; 2nd, 1956, Bridget Irene Sutton; one *s* one *d* (and one *d* decd). *Educ:* St Peter's Sch., York; Balliol Coll., Oxford. BA 1931, DLitt 1965. Fellow of All Souls Coll., Oxford, 1934; Asst Lectr, University Coll., Cardiff, 1936; Fellow and Tutor in Modern History, Balliol Coll., Oxford, 1938. Private in Field Security Police, commissioned Oxford and Bucks Light Inf., 1940, Major; seconded to Foreign Office, 1943. Returned to Balliol, 1945; University Lectr in 16th- and 17th-century history, 1959; Ford's Lectr, 1962. Vis. Prof., Open Univ., 1978–80. Hon. DLitt: Hull, 1966; E Anglia, 1968; Glasgow, 1976; Exeter, 1979; Wales, 1979; Hon. LittD Sheffield, 1967; Hon. LLD Bristol, 1976; DUniv York, 1978; Hon. Dr Sorbonne Nouvelle, 1979; DUniv Open, 1982. Foreign Hon. Member: Amer. Acad. of Sciences, 1973; Hungarian Acad. of Sciences, 1982. *Publications:* The English Revolution 1640, 1940; (under name K. E. Holme) Two Commonwealths, 1945; Lenin and the Russian Revolution, 1947; The Good Old Cause (ed jointly with E. Dell), 1949; Economic Problems of the Church, 1956; Puritanism and Revolution, 1958; Oliver Cromwell, 1958; The Century of Revolution, 1961; Society and Puritanism in Pre-Revolutionary England, 1964; Intellectual Origins of the English Revolution, 1965; Reformation to Industrial Revolution, 1967; God's Englishman, 1970; Antichrist in 17th Century England, 1971; The World Turned Upside Down, 1972; ed, G. Winstanley, The Law of Freedom and other writings, 1973; Change and Continuity in Seventeenth Century England, 1975; Milton and the English Revolution, 1978 (Heinemann award; Milton Soc. of America award); Some Intellectual Consequences of the English Revolution, 1980; (with B. Reay and W. M. Lamont) The World of the Muggletonians, 1983; The Experience of Defeat: Milton and some contemporaries, 1984; Collected Essays Vol. I: Writing and Revolution in 17th Century England, 1985, Vol. II: Religion and Politics in 17th Century England, 1986; articles in learned journals, etc. *Address:* Woodway House, Sibford Ferris, Banbury, Oxon OX15 5RA.

HILL, John Frederick Rowland, CMG 1955; *b* 20 April 1905; *s* of Judge William Henry Hill; *m* 1930, Phyllys Esmé (*née* Fryer); one *s* two *d. Educ:* Pinewood Sch., Farnborough; Marlborough Coll.; Lincoln Coll., Oxford. BA Oxon, Hon. Sch. Jurisprudence, 1927; Cadet Colonial Civil Service, Tanganyika, 1928; Asst District Officer, 1930; District Officer, 1940; Dep. Provincial Comr, 1947; Provincial Comr, 1948; Sen. Provincial Comr, 1950; Mem. for Communications, Works and Development Planning, Tanganyika Govt, 1951–56; Chm., Tanganyika Broadcasting Corp. and Dir of Broadcasting, 1956–57; Govt Liaison Officer, Freeport, Bahamas, 1957–58; Supervisor of Elections, Zanzibar, 1959–60. *Address:* 3 Melville Beach Road, Applecross, Perth, WA 6153, Australia. *T:* 3649897.

HILL, Sir John McGregor, Kt 1969; BSc, PhD; FRS 1981; FEng 1982; FInstP; FInstE; Chairman: Amersham International PLC, since 1975; Aurora Holdings PLC, since 1984; British Nuclear Fuels PLC, 1971–83; *b* 21 Feb. 1921; *s* of late John Campbell Hill and Margaret Elizabeth Park; *m* 1947, Nora Eileen Hellett; two *s* one *d. Educ:* King's Coll., London; St John's Coll., Cambridge. Flt Lieut, RAF, 1941. Cavendish Laboratory, Cambridge, 1946; Lecturer, London Univ., 1948. Joined UKAEA, 1950, Mem. for Production, 1964–67, Chm., 1967–81. Member: Advisory Council on Technology, 1968–70; Nuclear Power Adv. Bd, 1973–; Energy Commn, 1977–79. Pres., British Nuclear Forum, 1984–. Hon. FIChemE 1977; Hon. FIEE 1981; Foreign Associate, US Nat. Acad. of Engineering, 1976. Hon. DSc Bradford, 1981. Melchett Medal, Inst. of Energy, 1974; Sylvanus Thompson Medal, Inst. of Radiology, 1978. *Recreation:* golf. *Address:* Dominic House, Sudbrook Lane, Richmond, Surrey. *T:* 01–940 7221. *Club:* East India, Devonshire, Sports and Public Schools.

HILL, Sir John (Maxwell), Kt 1974; CBE 1969; DFC 1945; QPM; Chief Inspector of Constabulary, Home Office, 1972–75; *b* 25 March 1914; *s* of late L. S. M. Hill, Civil Servant, Plymouth; *m* 1939, Marjorie Louisa, *d* of late John Oliver Reynolds, Aylesbury, Bucks; one *s* one *d. Educ:* Plymouth Coll. Metropolitan Police Coll., Hendon, 1938–39; joined Metropolitan Police, 1933. Served with RAF, 1942–45. Dep. Comdr, New Scotland Yard, 1959; Metropolitan Police: Comdr, No 3 District, 1963, Comdr, No 1 District, 1964; HM Inspector of Constabulary, 1965; Asst Comr (Administration and Operations), 1966–68; Asst Comr (Personnel and Training), 1968–71; Dep. Comr, 1971–72. *Recreations:* walking, golf. *Address:* 23 Beacon Way, Banstead, Surrey. *T:* Burgh Heath 52771. *Clubs:* Royal Automobile, Royal Air Force.

HILL, Rear-Adm. John Richard; Under-Treasurer, Middle Temple, since 1984; *b* 25 March 1929; *s* of Stanley Hill and May Hill (*née* Henshaw); *m* 1956, Patricia Anne Sales; one *s* two *d. Educ:* Royal Naval College, Dartmouth. China Station as midshipman, 1946–47; Sub-Lieut's Courses, 1948–49; Lieut, HM Ships: Gambia, 1950; Chevron, 1950–52; Tintagel Castle, 1952–54; Dryad (Navigation Specialist), 1954; Cardigan Bay, 1954–56; Albion, 1956–58; Roebuck, 1958–59; Lt-Comdr, Pembroke Dock, 1959–60; HMS Duchess, 1960–62; Comdr, MoD, 1963–65 and 1967–69; IDC 1965–67; HMS Dryad, 1969–71; Captain, MoD, 1973–75; Defence and Naval Attaché, The Hague, 1975–77; Cdre, MoD, 1977–80; Rear-Adm. 1981; Flag Officer, Admiralty Interview Bd, 1981–83. Defence Fellow, University of London King's College, 1972. Editor, The Naval Review, 1983–. *Publications:* The Royal Navy Today and Tomorrow, 1981; Anti-Submarine Warfare, 1984; British Sea Power in the 1980s, 1985; Maritime Strategy for Medium Powers, 1986; articles in Survival, Navy International, Brassey's Annual, NATO's 15 Nations, Naval Review. *Recreation:* amateur theatre. *Address:* Cornhill House, The Hangers, Bishop's Waltham, Southampton SO3 1EF. *Club:* Royal Commonwealth Society.

HILL, Len; *see* Hill, R. K. L.

HILL, Martyn Geoffrey; tenor singer; *b* 14 Sept. 1944; *s* of Norman S. L. Hill and Gwendoline A. M. Hill (*née* Andrews); *m* 1974, Marleen M. J. B. (*née* De Maesschalck); three *s* one *d. Educ:* Sir Joseph Williamson's Mathematical School, Rochester, Kent; King's College, Cambridge; Royal College of Music (ARCM); vocal studies with Audrey

Langford. Concert, oratorio, recital and operatic appearances throughout the world with major orchestras, conductors and choirs; numerous radio, TV and gramophone recordings.

HILL, Michael; *see* Hill, E. M.

HILL, Michael William, CChem; Director, The British Library, Science Reference Library, since 1973; *b* 1928; *o s* of late Geoffrey William Hill, Ross on Wye and Torquay; *m* 1st, 1957, Elma Jack Forrest (*d* 1967); one *s* one *d*; 2nd, 1969, Barbara Joy Youngman. *Educ:* Nottingham High Sch.; Lincoln Coll., Oxford (BSc, MA). MRIC 1953; CChem; FIInfSc 1982. Research Chemist, Laporte Chemicals Ltd, 1953–56; Morgan Crucible Group: Laboratory Head, 1956; Asst Process Control Manager, 1958; Group Technical Editor, 1963. Asst Keeper, British Museum, 1964. Dep. Librarian, Patent Office Library, 1965; Keeper, Nat. Ref. Library of Science and Invention, 1968–73. Member: Exec. Cttee, Nat. Central Library, 1971–74; EEC/CIDST Working Parties on Patent documentation, 1973–, and on Information for Industry, 1976–; Board, UK Chemical Inf. Service, 1974–77; Adv. Cttee for Scottish Science Reference Library, 1983–; Chairman: Circle of State Librarians, 1977–79; Council, Aslib, 1979–81; Vice Pres., IATUL, 1976–81; Pres., Fédn Internat. de Documentation, 1985–. *Publications:* Patent Documentation (with Wittmann and Schiffels), 1979; papers on librarianship, documentation and information science in jls and conf. proceedings. *Address:* 137 Burdon Lane, Cheam, Surrey SM2 7DB. *T:* 01–642 2418. *Club:* United Oxford & Cambridge University.

HILL, Norman A.; *see* Ashton Hill.

HILL, Dr Polly; Fellow, Clare Hall, Cambridge, since 1965; Associate, Newnham College, Cambridge; *b* 10 June 1914; *d* of Prof. A. V. Hill, CH, OBE, FRS, and Margaret, *d* of Dr J. N. Keynes and F. A. Keynes; *m* 1953, Kenneth Humphreys (marr. diss. 1961; he *d* 1985); one *d. Educ:* Newnham Coll., Cambridge. PhD Cantab 1967. Editorial Asst, REconS, 1936–38; research, Fabian Soc., 1938–39; temp. civil servant, 1940–51; editorial staff, West Africa (weekly), 1951–53; Res. Fellow, then Sen. Res. Fellow, Econs Dept, followed by Inst. of African Studies, Univ. of Ghana, 1954–65; financed by Center for Research on Econ. Develt, Univ. of Mich, Ann Arbor, mainly working in Cambridge and northern Nigeria, 1965–70, and by SSRC, mainly working in northern Nigeria, 1970–72; Smuts Reader in Commonwealth Studies, Cambridge Univ., 1973–79; fieldwork in villages in Karnataka, S India, 1977–78, and (as Leverhulme Emeritus Fellow) in Kerala, S India, 1981–82. *Publications:* The Unemployment Services, 1940; The Gold Coast Cocoa Farmer, 1956; The Migrant Cocoa-Farmers of Southern Ghana, 1963, 3rd edn 1977; Rural Capitalism in West Africa, 1970, 2nd edn 1976; Rural Hausa, 1972; Population, Prosperity and Poverty: rural Kano, 1900 and 1970, 1977 (Amaury Talbot prize for African anthropology, 1977); Dry Grain Farming Families, 1982; Development Economics on Trial, 1986; articles on rural W Africa and India in learned jls; chapters in books. *Address:* The Stilts, Hemingford Abbots, Huntingdon, Cambs PE18 9AR. *T:* St Ives (Huntingdon) 63296.
See also D. K. Hill, J. H. Humphrey.

HILL, Sir Richard (George Rowley), 10th Bt *cr* 1779, of Brook Hall, Londonderry; MBE (mil.) 1974; retired; *b* 18 Dec. 1925; *s* of Sir George Alfred Rowley Hill, 9th Bt, and of Rose Ethel Kathleen, MBE, *d* of late William Richard Spratt; *S* father, 1985; *m* 1st, 1954, Angela Mary (*d* 1974), *d* of late Lt-Col Stanley Herbert Gallon, TD, Berwick-upon-Tweed; 2nd, 1975, Zoreen Joy MacPherson (marr. diss. 1986), *d* of late Norman Warburton Tippett, Kirkland, Berwick-upon-Tweed, and *widow* of Lieut Andrew David Wilson Marshall, KOSB; two *d*; 3rd, 1986, Elizabeth Margaret (*née* Tarbitt), *widow* of Laurence Sage, RNVR/FAA. *Recreations:* swimming, riding, reading. *Heir:* half-*b* John Rowley Hill, *b* 1940. *Address:* 5 Elmtree Court, Great Missenden, Bucks HP16 9AD. *T:* Great Missenden 3156.

HILL, Robert, ScD Cantab 1942; FRS 1946; biochemist; Member of Scientific Staff of Agricultural Research Council, 1943–66; *b* 2 April 1899; *s* of Joseph Alfred Hill and Clara Maud Jackson; *m* 1935, Amy Priscilla, *d* of Edgar Worthington; two *s* two *d. Educ:* Bedales Sch.; Emmanuel Coll., Cambridge (Scholar). Served European War, 1914–18: RE pioneer Anti-gas Dept, 1917–18. Emmanuel Coll., Cambridge, 1919–22; Senior Studentship (Exhibn of 1851), 1927; Beit Memorial Research Fellow, 1929; Senior Beit Memorial Research Fellow, 1935; Hon. Fellow of Emmanuel Coll., 1963. Royal Medal, Royal Society, 1963; 1st Award for photosynthesis, Soc. of American Plant Physiologists, 1963; Charles E. Kettering Research Award, 1963; Hon. Member: Amer. Soc. of Biological Chemists, 1964; Comité Internat. de Photobiologie, 1968; American Acad. Arts and Sciences, 1971; For. Associate, Nat. Acad. of Sciences, 1975; For. Mem., Accad. Nazionale dei Lincei, 1975. *Publication:* (with C. P. Whittingham) Photosynthesis, 1955. *Recreations:* growing plants and dyeing with traditional plant dyes, water-colour painting. *Address:* 1 Comberton Road, Barton, Cambridge CB3 7BA.

HILL, Sir Robert E.; *see* Erskine-Hill.

HILL, Robert Williamson, (Robin), CEng, FIGasE; Chairman, Scottish Region, British Gas Corporation, since 1982; *b* 8 Dec. 1936; *s* of William Hill and Mary Duncanson (*née* Williamson); *m* 1961, Janette Margaret (*née* Bald); one *s* two *d. Educ:* Dumbarton Acad.; Strathclyde Univ. (BSc 1st Cl. Hons). CEng, FIGasE 1958. Scottish Gas Board: various appts, 1958–70; Area Service Manager, subseq. Regional Service Manager, 1970–73; British Gas Corporation: Service Ops Manager, 1973–75; Asst Service Dir, 1975–76; Service Dir, 1977–82. Pres., Assoc. for Sci. Educn, Scotland, 1985–86. Hon. Mem., CGLI, 1981. Liveryman, Engineers' Co., 1984–. *Recreation:* golf. *Address:* 4 Hillpark Way, Edinburgh EH4 7SS. *T:* 031–336 4657.

HILL, Roderick; *see* Hill, Colonel E. R.

HILL, Rodney, FRS 1961; PhD; ScD; Professor of Mechanics of Solids, University of Cambridge, 1972–79 (Reader, 1969–72); Fellow, Gonville and Caius College, since 1972; *b* 11 June 1921; *o s* of Harold Harrison Hill, Leeds; *m* 1946, Jeanne Kathlyn, *yr d* of C. P. Wickens, Gidea Park; one *d. Educ:* Leeds Grammar Sch.; Pembroke Coll., Cambridge. MA, PhD, ScD Cambridge. Armament Research Dept, 1943–46; Cavendish Laboratory, Cambridge, 1946–48; British Iron and Steel Research Assoc., 1948–50; University of Bristol: Research Fellow, 1950–53, Reader, 1953; Univ. of Nottingham: Prof. of Applied Mathematics, 1953–62; Professorial Research Fellow, 1962–63; Berkeley Bye-Fellow, Gonville and Caius Coll., Cambridge, 1963–69. Hon. DSc: Manchester, 1976; Bath, 1978. Von Karman Medal, ASCE, 1978. Editor, Jl of Mechanics and Physics of Solids, 1952–68. *Publications:* Mathematical Theory of Plasticity, 1950; Principles of Dynamics, 1964. *Address:* Department of Applied Mathematics and Theoretical Physics, Silver Street, Cambridge.

HILL, Roy Kenneth Leonard, (Len), CBE 1983; JP; Chairman, South West Water Authority, since 1977; Chairman, Water Authorities Association, since 1983; *b* 28 May 1924; *m* 1944, Barbara May Kendall. Mem., ASLEF; Plymouth City Councillor, 1961–68, 1970–74 (formerly Dep. Lord Mayor); County Councillor, Devon, 1974 (formerly Leader of Labour Gp). Mem., SW Econ. Planning Council. Chm. Council, Coll. of St

Mark and St John, Plymouth; Governor, Plymouth Polytechnic; Mem. Bd of Visitors, Dartmoor Prison. JP Plymouth, 1968. *Address:* 5 Revell Park Road, Plympton, Plymouth PL7 4EH. *T:* Plymouth 339125.

HILL, (Stanley) James (Allen); MP (C) Southampton Test, 1970–Oct. 1974, and since 1979; company director; *b* 21 Dec. 1926; *s* of James and Florence Cynthia Hill; *m* 1958, Ruby Susan Evelyn Ralph; two *s* three *d. Educ:* Regents Park Sch., Southampton; Southampton Univ.; North Wales Naval Training Coll. Former Pilot. Mem., Southampton City Council, 1966–70, 1976–79, Chm. of Housing, 1967–70, 1976–79; Mem. Cttee, Southampton Conservative and Ratepayers Fedn. Secretary: Cons. Parly Cttee on Housing and Construction, 1971–73; Cons. Industry Cttee, 1979–81; Mem., Select Cttee on European Legislation, 1979–84. Mem., British Delegn to European Parlt, Strasbourg, and Chm., Regional Policy and Transport Cttee, 1973–75; Member: Hon. Cttee for Europe Day, Council of Europe, 1973–75; Scientific, Technol and Aerospace Cttee, Western European Defence, 1979–85; Political and Legal Affairs Cttee, Council of Europe, 1984–85; Govt Whip to Council of Europe and WEU, 1980–85. Pres., Motor Schools Assoc., 1980–85; Mem. Council, IAM, 1982–85. *Recreations:* private aviation, farming. *Address:* 51 Oakley Street, SW3; Gunsfield Lodge, Melchet Park, Plaitford, near Romsey, Hants. *Clubs:* Carlton, St Stephen's Constitutional.

HILL, Brig. (Stanley) James (Ledger), DSO 1942, and Bars, 1944, 1945; MC 1940; Vice-Chairman, Powell Duffryn Ltd, 1970–76 (Director, 1961–76); Chairman, Pauls & Whites Ltd, 1973–76 (Director, since 1970); Director: Lloyds Bank, 1972–79; Lloyds Bank UK Management Committee Ltd, 1979–81; *b* 14 March 1911; *s* of late Maj.-Gen. Walter Pitts Hendy Hill, CB, CMG, DSO, West Amesbury House, Wilts; *m* 1937, Denys, *d* of late E. Hubert Gunter-Jones, MC, JP, Gloucester House, Ledbury; one *d. Educ:* Marlborough; RMC Sandhurst. 2nd Bn, Royal Fusiliers, 1931–35; 2nd Bn, RF, BEF, 1939; DAAG, GHQ, BEF, 1940; comd 1st Bn, Parachute Regt, N Africa landing, 1942; comd 3rd Parachute Bde, 1943–45; took part in Normandy and Rhine crossing (wounded thrice); comdr 4th Parachute Bde (TA), 1947–48. Apptd to Bd of Associated Coal & Wharf Cos Ltd, 1948; Pres., Powell Duffryn Group of Cos in Canada, 1952–58. Legion of Honour (France), 1942; Silver Star (USA), 1945; King Haakon VII Liberty Cross (Norway), 1945. *Recreation:* birdwatching. *Address:* Hidden House, Guilden Road, Chichester PO19 4LA. *T:* Chichester 789083. *Clubs:* Army and Navy; Island Sailing (IoW).

HILL, Starforth; *see* Hill, Ian S.

HILL, Susan Elizabeth, (Mrs Stanley Wells); novelist and playwright; *b* 5 Feb. 1942; *d* of late R. H. and Doris Hill; *m* 1975, Dr Stanley W. Wells, *qv*; two *d* (and one *d* decd). *Educ:* grammar schs in Scarborough and Coventry; King's Coll., Univ. of London. BA Hons English 1963; Fellow, 1978. FRSL 1972. Literary critic, various jls, 1963–; numerous plays for BBC, 1970–. *Publications:* The Enclosure, 1961; Do me a Favour, 1963; Gentleman and Ladies, 1969; A Change for the Better, 1969; I'm the King of the Castle, 1970; The Albatross, 1971; Strange Meeting, 1971; The Bird of Night, 1972; A Bit of Singing and Dancing, 1973; In the Springtime of the Year, 1974; The Cold Country and Other Plays for Radio, 1975; (ed) The Distracted Preacher and other stories by Thomas Hardy, 1979; The Magic Apple Tree, 1982; The Woman in Black: a ghost story, 1983; (ed) Ghost Stories, 1983; (ed) People, an anthology, 1983; One Night at a Time (for children), 1984; Through the Kitchen Window, 1984; Through the Garden Gate, 1986; Mother's Magic (for children), 1986; *play:* The Ramshackle Company, 1981. *Recreations:* music, walking in the English countryside, friends, reading, broadcasting. *Address:* Midsummer Cottage, Church Lane, Beckley, Oxon.

HILL, Victor Archibald Lord, MA; *b* 3 July 1905; *o s* of W. E. Hill; *m* 1938, Jean Melicent, *e d* of Dr D. N. Seth-Smith, Bournemouth; two *s. Educ:* Chigwell Sch.; Queen Mary Coll., London (Open Exhibr; University Schol. in Classics; 1st cl. Hons BA); Hertford Coll., Oxford (Open Schol., 1st Cl. Hon. Mods, 3rd Cl. Lit. Hum.). MA (Oxon) 1934. Asst Master, Shrewsbury Sch., 1930–40, 1946–48; Headmaster, Allhallows Sch., 1948–65; Asst Master: Blundell's, 1965–66; Uppingham, 1966–67, 1968–69; Chigwell, 1969–70; Lectr in Classics, Exeter Univ., 1967–68. Served 1940–45, with KSLI and RA (Major). *Recreation:* music. *Address:* Beggars' Roost, Morchard Bishop, near Crediton, Devon. *T:* Morchard Bishop 315.

HILL, Prof. William George, FRS 1985; FRSE 1979; Professor of Animal Genetics, University of Edinburgh, since 1983; *b* 7 Aug. 1940; *s* of late William Hill and of Margaret Paterson Hill (*née* Hamilton); *m* 1971, Christine Rosemary Austin; one *s* two *d. Educ:* St Albans School; Wye Coll., Univ. of London (BSc 1961); Univ. of California, Davis (MS 1963); Iowa State Univ.; Univ. of Edinburgh (PhD 1965; DSc 1976). Asst Lectr, 1965–67, Lectr, 1967–74, Reader, 1974–83, in Genetics, Univ. of Edinburgh. Visiting Professor/Research Associate: Univ. of Minnesota, 1966; Iowa State Univ., 1967–78; N Carolina State Univ., 1979, 1985. Consultant Geneticist: Cotswold Pig Develt Co., 1965–85; British Friesian Cattle Soc., 1978–. Member: Scientific Study Group, Meat and Livestock Commn, 1969–72; Cattle Res. Consultative Cttee, 1985–86; AFRC Animals Res. Grant Bd, 1986–. *Publications:* Benchmark Papers in Quantitative Genetics (ed), 1984; numerous papers on quantitative and population genetics, biometrics and animal breeding, in sci. jls. *Recreations:* farming, bridge. *Address:* 4 Gordon Terrace, Edinburgh EH16 5QH. *T:* 031-667 3680.

HILL, William Sephton; European Affairs Adviser, British American Tobacco Co. Ltd, since 1985; *b* 24 July 1926; *s* of late William Thomas and Annie May Hill; *m* 1954, Jean, *d* of Philip Wedgwood; one *d. Educ:* Cowley Sch., St. Helens, Merseyside. BA, LLB Cantab. Served RAF, 1944–48, Japanese interpreter. Called to the Bar, Gray's Inn, 1951; practised Northern Circuit, 1951–54. Joined Solicitor's Office, HM Customs and Excise, 1954; Principal Asst Solicitor, 1980–85. *Recreations:* golf (ex-captain and ex-champion, Civil Service Golfing Society), bridge, listening to and playing piano. *Address:* 31 Hill Rise, Rickmansworth, Herts WD3 2NY. *T:* Rickmansworth 774756. *Club:* Moor Park Golf (Herts).

HILL-NORTON, family name of **Baron Hill-Norton.**

HILL-NORTON, Baron *cr* 1979 (Life Peer), of South Nutfield, Surrey; **Admiral of the Fleet Peter John Hill-Norton,** GCB 1970 (KCB 1967; CB 1964); Chairman, Military Committee of NATO, 1974–77; *b* 8 Feb. 1915; *s* of Capt. M. J. Norton and Mrs M. B. Norton; *m* 1936, Margaret Eileen Linstow; one *s* one *d. Educ:* RNC Dartmouth. Went to sea, 1932; commnd, 1936; specialised in Gunnery, 1939; War of 1939–45: Arctic Convoys; NW Approaches; Admiralty Naval Staff. Comdr 1948; Capt. 1952; Naval Attaché, Argentine, Uruguay, Paraguay, 1953–55; comd HMS Decoy, 1956–57; comd HMS Ark Royal, 1959–61; Asst Chief of Naval Staff, 1962–64; Flag Officer, Second-in-Command, Far East Fleet, 1964–66; Dep. Chief of the Defence Staff (Personnel and Logistics), 1966; Second Sea Lord and Chief of Naval Personnel, Jan.-Aug. 1967; Vice-Chief of Naval Staff, 1967–68; C-in-C Far East, 1969–70; Chief of the Naval Staff and First Sea Lord, 1970–71; Chief of the Defence Staff, 1971–73. President: Sea Cadets Assoc., 1977–84; Defence Manufacturers' Assoc., 1980–84; British Maritime League, 1982–85; Vice-Pres., RUSI, 1977. Liveryman, Shipwrights' Co., 1973, Mem. Court, 1979; Freeman, City of London, 1973. *Publications:* No Soft Options, 1978; Sea Power, 1982. *Recreations:* gardening, shooting. *Address:* Cass Cottage, Hyde, Fordingbridge, Hants. *Clubs:* Army and Navy; Royal Thames Yacht, Royal Navy of 1765.

HILL-SMITH, Derek Edward, VRD 1958; **His Honour Judge Hill-Smith;** a Circuit Judge, since 1972; *b* 21 Oct. 1922; *s* of Charles Hill-Smith and Ivy (*née* Downs); *m* 1950, Marjorie Joanna, *d* of His Honour Montague Berryman, QC; one *s* one *d. Educ:* Sherborne; Trinity Coll., Oxford (MA). RNVR, 1942–46; Lt-Comdr RNR. Trinity Coll., Oxford, 1941–42 and 1946–47 (MA, Classics and Modern Greats); BEA, 1947–48; business, 1948–50; teaching, 1950–54; called to Bar, Inner Temple, 1954; Dep. Chm., Kent QS, 1970; Recorder, 1972. *Publications:* contrib. Law Guardian. *Recreations:* the theatre, food and wine, collecting and restoring Old Masters. *Address:* c/o National Westminster Bank, North Street, Bishop's Stortford, Herts. *Clubs:* Garrick; Bar Yacht.

HILL-TREVOR, family name of **Baron Trevor.**

HILL-WOOD, Sir David (Basil), 3rd Bt *cr* 1921; Director, Guinness Mahon & Co. Ltd (Bankers), since 1977; *b* 12 Nov. 1926; *s* of Sir Basil Samuel Hill Hill-Wood, 2nd Bt, and Hon. Joan Louisa Brand, *e d* of 3rd Viscount Hampden; *S* father, 1954; *m* 1970, Jennifer, 2nd *d* of late Peter McKenzie Strang, Adelaide; two *s* one *d. Educ:* Eton. Served in Army (Grenadier Guards), 1945–48. Morgan Grenfell & Co. Ltd, 1948–55; Myers & Co., Stockbrokers, 1955–71, Sen. Partner, 1971–74; Dir, Capel-Cure Myers Ltd, 1974–77. Aust. Rep., FA Council, 1978–. High Sheriff Berks, 1982. *Recreations:* soccer, farming, forestry. *Heir: s* Samuel Thomas Hill-Wood, *b* 24 Aug. 1971. *Address:* Dacre Farm, Farley Hill, Reading, Berks. *T:* Eversley 733185; 58 Cathcart Road, SW10. *T:* 01-352 0389. *Clubs:* White's; Melbourne (Australia).

HILLABY, John; writer, naturalist and traveller; *b* 24 July 1917; *er s* of late Albert Ewart Hillaby, Pontefract, and Mabel Colyer; *m* 1940, Eleanor Riley, Leeds (marr. diss.); two *d*; *m* 1966, Thelma Gordon (*d* 1972), child analyst, London and Montreal; *m* 1981, Kathleen Burton, Easingwold, Yorks. *Educ:* Leeds; Woodhouse Grove, Yorkshire. Served War, RA, 1939–44. Local journalism up to 1939; magazine contributor and broadcaster, 1944–; Zoological Corresp., Manchester Guardian, 1949; European science writer, New York Times, 1951–; biological consultant, New Scientist, 1953–. Formerly a dir, Universities Fedn for Animal Welfare; Founder Pres., Backpackers Club. Has travelled on foot through parts of boreal Canada, Appalachian Trail, USA, Congo, traversed Ituri Forest and Mountains of the Moon (Ruwenzori), Sudan, Tanzania; three months foot safari with camels to Lake Rudolf, Kenya, and walked from Lands End to John o'Groats, from The Hague to Nice via the Alps, from Provence to Tuscany, from Lake District to London, and from Athens to Mt Olympos via the Pindos mountains. Woodward Lectr, Yale, 1973. Radio and TV series include: Men of the North, Expedition South, Alpine Venture, Hillaby Walks, Globetrotter, etc. FZS (scientific). *Publications:* Within The Streams, 1949; Nature and Man, 1960; Journey to the Jade Sea, 1964; Journey through Britain, 1968; Journey through Europe, 1972; Journey through Love, 1976; Journey Home, 1983; John Hillaby's Yorkshire: the moors and dales, 1986. *Recreations:* talking, reading, music, walking alone; observing peculiarities of man, beast, fowl and flora. *Address:* 85 Cholmley Gardens, NW6. *T:* 01-435 4626; Rosedale-by-Pickering, North Yorkshire. *Club:* Savage.

HILLARD, His Honour Richard Arthur Loraine, MBE 1946; a Circuit Judge (formerly a County Court Judge), 1956–72; *b* 1906; *e s* of Frederick Arthur Hillard, Puriton Manor, Bridgwater, Som; *m* 1st, 1936, Nancy Alford (*d* 1964), *d* of Dr Alford Andrews, Cambridge; one *s* one *d*; 2nd, 1969, Monica Constance, *er d* of John Healey Carus, Darwen, and *widow* of Paul Hillard; one step *s* one step *d. Educ:* Worcester Royal Grammar Sch.; Christ Church, Oxford. Barrister, Gray's Inn, 1931; South-Eastern circuit. Served, 1940–45: Military Dept, Judge Advocate General's Office, 1941–45, Lt-Col 1945. Asst Reader and Lecturer, Council of Legal Education, 1945–55. Chm. Agricultural Land Tribunal, South Eastern Province, 1955. *Recreation:* gardening. *Address:* Oakchurch House, Staunton-on-Wye, Hereford. *T:* Moccas 345. *Club:* United Oxford & Cambridge University.

HILLARY, Sir Edmund, KBE 1953; New Zealand High Commissioner to India, since 1984; author; lecturer; mountaineer; *b* 20 July 1919; *s* of Percival Augustus Hillary and Gertrude Hillary (*née* Clark); *m* 1953, Louise Rose (*d* 1975); one *s* one *d* (and one *d* decd). *Educ:* Auckland Grammar Sch., Auckland, New Zealand. Apiarist, 1936–43. RNZAF, navigator on Catalina flying boats in Pacific Area, 1944–45. Apiarist (in partnership with brother W. F. Hillary), 1951–70. Himalayan Expeditions: NZ Gawhal Expedition, 1951; British Everest Reconnaissance, 1951; British Cho Oyu Expedition, 1952; Everest Expedition, 1953; with Sherpa Tenzing reached summit of Mount Everest, May 1953 (KBE). Leader of NZ Alpine Club Expedition to Barun Valley, East of Everest, 1954. Appointed, 1955, leader of New Zealand Transantarctic Expedition; completed overland journey to South Pole, Jan. 1958. Expeditions in Everest region, 1960–61, 1963, 1964, 1965; built first hosp. for Sherpas in Everest Area, with public subscription and NZ doctor, 1966; led expedition to Antarctic for geological and mountaineering purposes incl. first ascent of Mt Herschel, 1967; expedition to E Nepal (explored Himalayan rivers with two jet boats; first ascent of 180 miles of Sun Kosi river from Indian border to Katmandu), 1968; jet boat expedition up the Ganges, 1977. Consultant to Sears Roebuck & Co., Chicago, on camping and outdoor equipment. Hon. LLD: Univ. of Victoria, BC, Canada, 1969; Victoria Univ., Wellington, NZ, 1970. Hubbard Medal (US), 1954; Star of Nepal 1st Class; US Gold Cullum Geographical Medal, 1954; Founder's Gold Medal, Royal Geographical Society, 1958; Polar Medal, 1958. *Publications:* High Adventure; East of Everest, 1956 (with George Lowe); The Crossing of Antarctica, 1958 (with Sir Vivian Fuchs); No Latitude for Error, 1961; High in the Thin Cold Air, 1963 (with Desmond Doig); School House in the Clouds, 1965; Nothing Venture, Nothing Win (autobiog.), 1975; From the Ocean to the Sky: jet boating up the Ganges, 1979; (with Peter Hillary) Two Generations, 1983. *Recreations:* mountaineering, ski-ing, camping. *Address:* New Zealand High Commission, 25 Golf Links, New Delhi 110003, India; 278a Remuera Road, Auckland, SE2, New Zealand. *Clubs:* New Zealand Alpine (Hon. Mem.; Pres. 1965–67); Explorers (New York) (Hon. Pres); Hon. Mem. of many other NZ and US clubs.

HILLER, Dame Wendy, DBE 1975 (OBE 1971); actress; *b* 1912; *d* of Frank Watkin and Marie Hiller, Bramhall, Cheshire; *m* 1937, Ronald Gow; one *s* one *d. Educ:* Winceby House, Bexhill. Manchester Repertory Theatre; Sir Barry Jackson's tour of Evensong; Sally Hardcastle in Love on the Dole, London and New York; leading parts in Saint Joan and Pygmalion at Malvern Festival, 1936. *Plays include:* Twelfth Night (war factory tour); Cradle Song (Apollo); The First Gentleman (Savoy); Tess of the d'Urbervilles (Piccadilly); The Heiress (Biltmore, NY, and Haymarket, London); Ann Veronica (Piccadilly); Waters of the Moon (Haymarket), 1951–53; The Night of the Ball (New), 1955; Old Vic Season, 1955–56; Moon for the Misbegotten (NY), 1957; Flowering Cherry (Haymarket), 1958; Toys in the Attic (Piccadilly), 1960; Aspern Papers (NY), 1962; The Wings of the Dove (Lyric), 1963; The Sacred Flame (Duke of York's), 1967; When We Dead Awaken (Edinburgh Festival), 1968; The Battle of Shrivings (Lyric),

1970; Crown Matrimonial (Haymarket), 1972; John Gabriel Borkman (National), 1975; Lies! (Albery), 1975; Waters of the Moon (Chichester), 1977, (Haymarket) 1978; The Old Jest, 1980; The Aspern Papers (Haymarket), 1984. *Films:* Pygmalion; Major Barbara; I Know Where I'm Going; Outcast of the Islands; Separate Tables (Academy Award); Sons and Lovers; Toys in the Attic; A Man for All Seasons; David Copperfield; Murder on the Orient Express; The Elephant Man, etc. *TV:* When We Dead Awaken, 1968; Peer Gynt, 1972; Clochemerle, 1973; Last Wishes, 1978; Richard II, 1979; Miss Morison's Ghosts, 1981; The Kingfisher, Witness for the Prosecution, Attracta, 1982; The Comedy of Errors, 1983; Death of the Heart, 1985; Darley's Folly, 1986. Hon. LLD Manchester, 1984. *Address:* c/o ICM, 388/396 Oxford Street, W1N 9HE.

HILLERY, Dr Patrick John; Uachtarán na hÉireann (President of Ireland), since Dec. 1976, re-elected for second term, Dec. 1983; *b* Miltown Malbay, Co. Clare, 2 May 1923; *s* of Dr Michael Joseph Hillery and Ellen (*née* McMahon); *m* 1955, Dr Mary Beatrice Finnegan; one *s* one *d*. *Educ:* Miltown Malbay National Sch.; Rockwell Coll.; University Coll., Dublin. BSc; MB BCh, BAO, DPH. Mem. Health Council, 1955–57; MO, Miltown Malbay, 1957–59; Coroner for West Clare, 1958–59; TD (Mem. Dáil Eireann), Clare, 1951–73; Minister: for Educn, 1959–65; for Industry and Commerce, 1965–66; for Labour, 1966–69; of Foreign Affairs, 1969–72 (negotiated Ireland's accession to European Communities); Comr for Social Affairs and a Vice-Pres., Commn of the European Communities, 1973–76. MRIA 1963. Hon. FRCSI 1977; Hon. FFDRCSI 1977; Hon. FRCPI 1978; Hon. FRCGP 1982; Hon. Fellow: Pharmaceutical Soc. of Ireland, 1984; All-India Inst. of Medical Sciences, 1978. Hon. LLD: NUI, 1962; Univ. of Dublin, 1977; Univ. of Melbourne, 1985. *Address:* Áras an Uachtaráin, Phoenix Park, Dublin 8, Ireland; Spanish Point, Co. Clare, Ireland.

HILLHOUSE, Robert Russell; Under Secretary, Scottish Education Department, since 1985; *b* 23 April 1938; *s* of Robert Hillhouse and Jean Russell; *m* 1966, Alison Janet Fraser; two *d*. *Educ:* Hutchesons' Grammar Sch., Glasgow; Glasgow Univ. (MA). Scottish Education Dept, 1962; HM Treasury, 1971; Asst Secretary, Scottish Office, 1974; Scottish Home and Health Dept, 1977; Under Sec. (Principal Finance Officer), Scottish Office, 1980. *Recreation:* making music. *Address:* 48 Dreghorn Loan, Colinton, Edinburgh. *T:* 031–441 1587.

HILLIER, Bevis; Associate Editor, Los Angeles Times, since 1984; *b* 28 March 1940; *s* of J. R. Hillier, *qv*. *Educ:* Reigate Grammar Sch.; Magdalen Coll., Oxford (demy). Gladstone Memorial Prize, 1961. Editorial staff, The Times, 1963–68 (trainee, Home News Reporter, Sale Room Correspondent); Editor, British Museum Society Bulletin, 1968–70; Antiques Correspondent, 1970–84, Dep. Literary Editor, 1981–84, The Times; Guest Curator, Minneapolis Inst. of Arts, USA, 1971; Editor, The Connoisseur, 1973–76. FRSA 1967. *Publications:* Master Potters of the Industrial Revolution: The Turners of Lane End, 1965; Pottery and Porcelain 1700–1914, 1968; Art Deco of the 1920s and 1930s, 1968; Posters, 1969; Cartoons and Caricatures, 1970; The World of Art Deco, 1971; 100 Years of Posters, 1972; introduction to A Boy at the Hogarth Press by Richard Kennedy, 1972; Austerity/Binge, 1975; (ed with Mary Banham) A Tonic to the Nation: The Festival of Britain 1951, 1976; The New Antiques, 1977; Greetings from Christmas Past, 1982; The Style of the Century 1900–1980, 1983; John Betjeman: a life in pictures, 1984; contributor to The Connoisseur, Apollo, Trans English Ceramic Circle, Proc. Wedgwood Soc., etc. *Recreations:* piano; collecting; awarding marks out of ten for suburban front gardens. *Address:* 527 South Fuller Avenue, Los Angeles, CA 90036, USA; Los Angeles Times, Times Mirror Square, Los Angeles, California 90053, USA. *Clubs:* Beefsteak, Garrick.

HILLIER, Jack Ronald; freelance writer and expert on Japanese art, since 1950; *b* 29 Aug. 1912; *s* of Charles Hillier and Minnie Hillier (*née* Davies); *m* 1938, Mary Louise Palmer; one *s* one *d*. *Educ:* Fulham Central School. Sotheby Consultant on oriental pictorial art, 1953–67. Uchiyama Susumu Award, Tokyo, 1982. *Publications:* Old Surrey Water Mills, 1951; Japanese Masters of the Colour Print, 1953; Hokusai Paintings, Drawings and Woodcuts, 1955; The Japanese Print: a new approach, 1957, 4th edn 1975; Utamaro: colour prints and paintings, 1961, 2nd edn 1979; Japanese Drawings: from the 17th to the end of the 19th century, 1965, 3rd edn 1975; Hokusai Drawings, 1966; Catalogue of Japanese Paintings and Prints in Collection of Richard P. Gale, 1970; The Harari Collection of Japanese Paintings and Drawings, 1970–73; Suzuki Harunobu, 1970; The Uninhibited Brush: Japanese art in the Shijō style, 1974; Japanese Prints and Drawings from the Vever Collection, 1976; The Art of Hokusai in Book Illustration, 1980; The Art of the Japanese Book. *Recreations:* wood engraving, water colour painting, classical music (esp. lieder), the English countryside. *Address:* 27 Whitepost Hill, Redhill, Surrey RH1 6DA. *T:* Redhill 61369.

See also Bevis Hillier.

HILLIER-FRY, (William) Norman, CMG 1982; HM Diplomatic Service, retired; High Commissioner in Uganda, 1980–83; *b* 12 Aug. 1923; *o s* of William Henry and Emily Hillier Fry; *m* 1948, Elizabeth Adèle Misbah; two *s* two *d*. *Educ:* Colfe's Grammar School, Lewisham; St Edmund Hall, Oxford (BA 1946). Served Army, 1942–45; commissioned, Loyal Regt, 1942. HM Foreign Service, 1946; served: Iran, 1947–52; Strasbourg (Delegation to Council of Europe), 1955–56; Turkey, 1956–59; Czechoslovakia, 1961–63; Counsellor, UK Disarmament Delegn, Geneva, 1968–71; Hd of ME Dept, ODA, 1971–74; Consul-Gen., Hamburg, 1974–79; Ambassador to Afghanistan, 1979–80. *Recreations:* music, theatre. *Address:* 127 Coombe Lane West, Kingston-upon-Thames, Surrey KT2 7HF.

HILLIS, Arthur Henry Macnamara, CMG 1961; Comptroller General, National Debt Office, 1961–68; *b* 29 Dec. 1905; *s* of late John David Hillis, FRCS, Dublin; *m* 1936, Mary Francis; no *c*. *Educ:* Trinity Coll., Dublin. Called to Bar, Inner Temple, 1931. HM Treasury, 1941; Harkness Fund Fellow, USA, 1950–51; Minister (Treasury Adviser), UK Permanent Mission to United Nations, 1958–61; Under-Sec., Treasury, 1961. Mem., Internat. CS Commn (UN), 1974–81. *Address:* 2 Hare Court, Temple, EC4. *T:* 01–353 3443. *Club:* Athenæum.

HILLMAN, Ellis Simon; Principal Lecturer in Environmental Studies, North East London Polytechnic, since 1972, and Head of International Office, since 1981; *b* 17 Nov. 1928; *s* of David and Annie Hillman; *m* 1967, Louise; one *s*. *Educ:* University Coll. Sch.; Chelsea Coll. of Science and Technol. (BSc). Scientific Technical Officer: Soil Mechanics Ltd; NCB Field Investigation Group; Architectural Assoc.; Organiser of Conference NELP/British Telecom on Rewiring Britain—Technical Challenge of Cable TV; Chm., London Subterranean Survey Assoc., 1968–. Elected to LCC, 1958; GLC Cllr, 1964–81; Councillor (Lab), Colindale, 1986–. Chairman: GLC Arts and Recreation Cttee, 1973–77; AMA Arts and Recreation Cttee, 1974–78; Further and Higher Educn Sub-Cttee, ILEA, 1977–81 (Bldgs Section, 1970–73); Vice-Chm., ILEA, 1980–81. Member: Lee Valley Reg. Park Authority, 1973–81; Sports Council, 1975–81; Water Space Amenity Commn, 1977–80; Inland Waterways Amenity Adv. Council, 1977–80; ARCUK Bd of Educn, 1973–82, 1986–. Member: Exec. Cttee, Greater London Arts Assoc., 1982–; Council, Science Fiction Foundn, 1986–; Vice-Pres., Hackney Soc., 1984–. Invited Mem., Green Alliance, 1984–. Founder and Hon. Pres., Lewis Carroll Soc., 1969–. Governor: Imperial Coll. of Science and Technol., 1971–, and Queen Mary Coll., 1973–82, Univ. of London; Museum of London; formerly Gov., Coombe Lodge Staff Further Educn Coll.; Chm. Governors, Hackney Coll., 1974–82, 1985–. Chm., Colson Trust and Mem. Editl Bd, Colson News: Two Way Numbers, 1984–. Guest Editor, The Built Environment (one edn), 1984. FRSA 1979. *Publications:* Essays in Local Government Enterprise, 1964–67; (ed) Towards a Wider Use, 1976; Novellae on the Scroll of Esther, 1982; (ed) Space for the Living or Space for the Dead, 1977; (jtly) London Under London, 1985; contrib. Underground Services; Architects Jl, Arch. Design, Municipal Rev., Municipal Jl and Structural Survey and the Environmentalist. *Recreations:* walking, gardening, allotment holding, classical music, reading, writing poetry. *Address:* 29 Haslemere Avenue, NW4 2PU. *T:* 01–202 7792.

HILLS, Air Vice-Marshal David Graeme Muspratt, CB 1985; OBE 1965; Director, Medical Policy and Plans, Ministry of Defence, 1983–85; *b* 28 Feb. 1925; *s* of late Arthur Ernest Hills and Muriel Steinman Hills (*née* Fisher); *m* 1960, Hilary Enid Mary, *d* of Rev. Raymond Morgan Jones and Mary Jones (*née* Ritson); two *s* one *d*. *Educ:* Salisbury Cathedral School; Epsom College; Middlesex Hosp. Medical School. MB BS 1949; MFCM, DPH, AFOM. Commissioned RAF Med. Branch, 1950; served UK, Korea (Casualty Evacuation and MO to 77 Sqn, RAAF), A&AEE, RAF Stanmore Park, RAF Tengah and MoD, 1951–68; OC RAF Hosp., Muharraq Bahrain, 1968–70; SMO RAF Cranwell, 1970–72; Dep. Dir Medical Personnel, RAF, 1972–75; PMO RAF Germany, 1975–78; Dep. Dir Gen., RAF Medical Services, 1979–83. QHS, 1980–85. CStJ. *Recreations:* music, painting, gardening, golf. *Address:* The Fourth Green, Sandwich Bay, Sandwich, Kent CT13 9PG. *T:* Sandwich 613064. *Club:* Royal Air Force.

HILLS, David Henry; Director of Economic and Logistic Intelligence, Ministry of Defence, since 1982; *b* 9 July 1933; *s* of Henry Stanford Hills and Marjorie Vera Lily Hills; *m* 1957, Jean Helen Nichols; one *s* two *d*. *Educ:* Varndean Sch., Brighton; Univ. of Nottingham (BA Econs). Served Army Intell. Corps, 1954–56. Entered MoD, 1956; other appointments include: NBPI, 1967–70; National Indust. Relations Court, 1971–73; Dir of Marketing, Defence Sales Orgn, MoD, 1979–82. *Recreation:* gardening. *Address:* Ministry of Defence, Metropole Building, Northumberland Avenue, WC2N 5BL. *T:* 01–218 5531. *Club:* Royal Commonwealth Society.

HILLS, Air Vice-Marshal Eric Donald, CB 1973; CBE 1968 (MBE 1941); SASO Maintenance Command, 1971–73, retired; *b* 26 Jan. 1917; *s* of late Henry James Hills; *m* 1945, Pamela Mary, *d* of late Col A. P. Sandeman, Cape Town; one *s* one *d*. *Educ:* Maidstone Grammar Sch. Joined RAF 1939; Group Captain 1962; Dir of Equipment 3 (RAF), 1968–69; Air Cdre 1969; Dir of Equipment (Policy) (RAF), MoD, 1969–71; Air Vice-Marshal 1971. *Recreations:* gardening, sport as spectator. *Address:* c/o National Westminster Bank, Stone, Staffs. *Club:* Royal Air Force.

HILLS, Graham John, PhD, DSc; FRSE, CChem, FRSC; Principal and Vice-Chancellor of the University of Strathclyde, since 1980; *b* 9 April 1926; *s* of Albert Victor Hills and Marjorie Hills (*née* Harper); *m* 1st, 1950, Brenda Stubbington (*d* 1974); one *s* three *d*; 2nd, 1980, Mary Jane McNaughton. *Educ:* Birkbeck Coll., London Univ. (BSc 1946, PhD 1950, DSc 1962; Hon. Fellow 1984). Lecturer in Physical Chemistry, Imperial College, 1949–62; Professor of Physical Chemistry, Univ. of Southampton, 1962–80; Visiting Professor: Univ. of Western Ontario, 1968; Case Western Reserve Univ., 1969; Univ. of Buenos Aires, 1977. Pres., Internat. Soc. of Electrochemistry, 1983–85. Member: Pay Rev. Bd for Nurses, Midwives and Professions Allied to Medicine, 1983–; Council, RSC, 1983–86. Hon. ScD Technical Univ. of Łodz, Poland, 1984; Hon. DSc Southampton, 1984; Hon. LLD Glasgow, 1985. Commander: Polish Order of Merit, 1984; Royal Norwegian Order of Merit, 1986. *Publications:* Reference Electrodes, 1961; Polarography, 1964; contrib. Faraday Transactions, on physical chemistry, espec. electrochemistry. *Recreations:* mountain walking, European political history, rocking the boat. *Address:* University of Strathclyde, McCance Building, 16 Richmond Street, Glasgow G1 1XQ. *T:* 041–552 4400. *Clubs:* Athenæum, Caledonian.

HILLS, Lawrence Donegan; President, Henry Doubleday Research Association, since 1986; *b* 2 July 1911; *s* of William Donegan and Mabel Annie Hills; *m* 1964, Mrs Hilda Cherry Brooke (*née* Fea). *Educ:* at home, owing to ill health. Took up horticulture on medical advice in 1927 and worked for many leading nurseries until 1940. Served War of 1939–45, RAF. Wrote first book, Miniature Alpine Gardening, in hospitals before invalided out on D-Day. Founded Henry Doubleday Research Assoc., 1954, and Director of this leading internat. body of gardeners and farmers without chemicals, 1954–86. Gardening Correspondent: Observer, 1958–66; Punch, 1966–70; Countryman, 1970; Garden News, 1981; Associate Editor, Ecologist, 1973. *Publications:* Miniature Alpine Gardening, 1944; Rapid Tomato Ripening, 1946; Propagation of Alpines, 1950; Alpines Without A Garden, 1953; Russian Comfrey, 1953; Alpine Gardening, 1955; Down To Earth Fruit and Vegetable Growing, 1960; Down to Earth Gardening, 1967; Lands of the Morning (Archaeology), 1970; Grow Your Own Fruit and Vegetables, 1971; Comfrey—Its Past, Present and Future, 1976; Organic Gardening, 1977; Fertility Gardening, 1981; Month by Month Organic Gardening, 1983. *Recreations:* reading, thinking, non-gardening writing, classical music. *Address:* Henry Doubleday Research Association, Ryton-on-Dunsmore, Coventry, Warwicks.

HILLYARD, Patrick Cyril Henry, OBE 1956; Head of Sound Light Entertainment BBC, 1952–64, retd Nov. 1964; *s* of Rev. Dr H. J. Hillyard and Louie Charlotte Robinson; *m* 1932, Ena Violet, *d* of late Rev. C. Porter-Brickwell; one *s*. *Educ:* The High Sch., Dublin. Studied stage production under Donald Calthrop. Stage directed and produced plays and musical comedies in England and America, including: A Midsummer Night's Dream, Twelfth Night, The Fake, Jolly Roger, No More Ladies, The Desert Song, Gay Divorce, On Your Toes, Lilac Time. Joined BBC Television Service as Dep. Productions Manager, 1937; Asst Dir of Variety, BBC, 1941; Actg Dir of Variety, BBC, 1946; Dir of Television Presentation, BBC, 1947; Head of Television Light Entertainment, BBC, 1948. Kt of Mark Twain, 1980. *Recreations:* going to the theatre, golf, tennis and swimming. *Address:* c/o Barclays Bank, 15 Langham Place, W1. *Club:* Malta Union.

HILSUM, Prof. Cyril, PhD; FRS 1979; FEng 1978; FInstP, FIEE; Director of Research, GEC plc, since 1985 (Chief Scientist, General Electric Co. Research Laboratories, 1983–85); Visiting Professor in Applied Physics and Electronics, University of Durham, since 1978; *b* 17 May 1925; *s* of Benjamin and Ada Hilsum; *m* 1947, Betty Cooper; two *d*. *Educ:* Raines Sch., London; University Coll., London (BSc, PhD). FIEE 1967; FIEEE 1984; FInstP 1960. Joined Royal Naval Scientific Service, 1945; Admiralty Res. Lab., 1947–50, and Services Electronics Res. Lab., 1950–64, working first on infra-red res., then on semiconductors; Royal Signals and Radar Estab., 1964–83, working first on compound semiconductors, later on flat panel electronic displays; CSO, 1974–83. Mem., SERC, 1984–. Foreign Associate, US National Acad. of Engrg, 1983. *Publications:* Semiconducting III-V Compounds, 1961; over 100 scientific and technical papers. *Recreations:* ballroom dancing, tennis. *Address:* GEC Research Laboratories, East Lane, Wembley, Mddx HA9 7PP.

HILTON, Brian James George; Head of Financial Services Division (Under Secretary), Department of Trade and Industry, since 1984; *b* 21 April 1940; *s* of Percival William Hilton and Gladys Hilton (*née* Haylett); *m* 1965, Mary Margaret Kirkpatrick; one *s* two *d*. *Educ:* St Marylebone Grammar Sch., London. Export Credits Guarantee Dept, 1958–68; Board of Trade, 1968–71; Foreign and Commonwealth Office, 1971–74: First Secretary to UK Delegn to OECD, Paris; Asst Sec., Dept of Industry, 1976–84; rcds 1981. Foundation Governor, Hampden Gurney Primary Sch., London W1, 1976–. *Recreations:* cricket, rugby, music, gardening. *Address:* Liongate, 8 Chilston Road, Tunbridge Wells, Kent TN4 9LT. *T:* Tunbridge Wells 24082.

HILTON, John Robert, CMG 1965; HM Diplomatic Service (appointed to Foreign Service, 1943), retired 1969; *b* 5 Jan. 1908; *s* of Oscar Hilton, MD, and Louisa Holdsworth Hilton; *m* 1933, Margaret Frances Stephens; one *s* three *d*. *Educ:* Marlborough Coll.; Corpus Christi Coll., Oxford (MA); Bartlett Sch. of Architecture; University Coll., London (Diploma). ARIBA. Dir of Antiquities, Cyprus, 1934–36; Architect to E. S. & A. Robinson Ltd and private practice, 1936–41. Capt. RE, 1941–43. Foreign Service, 1943; transferred to Istanbul, 1944; 2nd Sec., Athens, 1945; Foreign Office, 1947; 1st Sec., Istanbul, 1956; Foreign Office, 1960. Mem. Council, National Schizophrenia Fellowship, 1977–81, 1983– (Pres., 1985–). FRSA. *Publications:* articles in Architectural Review and other jls, Mind and Analysis; Memoir on Louis MacNeice (as appendix to his autobiography, The Strings are False), 1965. *Recreations:* philosophy, walking. *Address:* Hope Cottage, Nash Hill, Lacock, Wilts. *T:* Lacock 369.

HILTON, Col Peter, MC 1942 and Bars 1943 and 1944; JP; Managing Director, James Smith (Scotland Nurseries) Ltd; Lord-Lieutenant and Custos Rotulorum of Derbyshire, since 1978; *b* 30 June 1919; *er s* of late Maj.-Gen. R. Hilton, DSO, MC, DFC, and Phyllis Martha (*née* Woodin); *m* 1942, Winifred, *d* of late Ernest Smith, Man. Dir Scotland Nurseries, Tansley; one *s* (and one *s* decd). *Educ:* Malvern Coll.; RMA Woolwich; psc. Commnd RA, 1939; BEF, 1939–40, 1st Div. Dunkirk; Western Desert, 1942–43, 7th Armd Div. Alamein (RHA Jacket 1942); Italy, 1943–44, 5th American Army, Adjt 3rd Regt RHA; Normandy, 1944, OC J Bty RHA (wounded Falaise Gap); Greece, 1946–49 (despatches 1948); Instructor Royal Hellenic Staff Coll.; Col RA 1949, retd; RARO; recalled Korean Emergency, 1950; TA Commn, 1951; CO 528 W Notts Regt, RA (TA), 1951–54; ACF Commn, 1962; Comdt Derbyshire ACF, 1962–66, Hon. Col 1972–77. Vice-Pres., TA & VRA, E Midlands, 1978; Chm., Derbys War Pensions Cttee; Comdr, Derbys SJAB; Vice-Pres., Derbys Rural Community Council. Trustee: Derby New Theatre; Sherwood Foresters Museum; Crich Meml Trust; Vice-Pres., British Heart Foundn, Derbs; Chm. of Governors, Anthony Gell Sch., Wirksworth. JP 1967, High Sheriff 1970–71, DL 1972, Derbs; Mem. Wirksworth Div. Derbs CC, 1967–77. FRHS. KStJ 1979. Greek Order of Minerva, 1949. *Recreations:* ex-Service interests, local activities. *Address:* Alton Manor, Idridgehay, Derbs. *T:* Wirksworth 2435; James Smith (Scotland Nurseries) Ltd, Tansley, Matlock, Derbs DE4 5GF. *T:* Matlock 3036.

HILTON, Prof. Peter John, MA, DPhil Oxon, PhD Cantab; Distinguished Professor of Mathematics, State University of New York at Binghamton, since 1982; *b* 7 April 1923; *s* of late Dr Mortimer Hilton and Mrs Elizabeth Hilton; *m* 1949, Margaret (*née* Mostyn); two *s*. *Educ:* St Paul's Sch.; Queen's Coll., Oxford. Asst Lectr, Manchester Univ., 1948–51, Lectr, 1951–52; Lectr, Cambridge Univ., 1952–55; Senior Lecturer, Manchester Univ., 1956–58; Mason Prof. of Pure Mathematics, University of Birmingham, 1958–62; Prof. of Mathematics, Cornell Univ., 1962–71, Washington Univ., 1971–73; Beaumont Univ. Prof., Case Western Reserve Univ., 1972–82. Visiting Professor: Cornell Univ., USA, 1958–59; Eidgenössische Techn. Hochschule, Zürich, 1966–67, 1981–82; Courant Inst., NY Univ., 1967–68. Mathematician-in-residence, Battelle Research Center, Seattle, 1970–. Chairman: US Commn on Mathematical Instruction, 1971–74; NRC Cttee on Applied Maths Trng, 1977–; First Vice-Pres., Math. Assoc. of Amer., 1978–80. Corresp. Mem., Brazilian Acad. of Scis, 1979; Hon. Mem. Belgian Mathematical Soc., 1955. Hon. DHum N Michigan, 1977; Hon. DSc Meml Univ. of Newfoundland, 1983. Silver Medal, Univ. of Helsinki, 1975; Centenary Medal, John Carroll Univ., 1985. *Publications:* Introduction to Homotopy Theory, 1953; Differential Calculus, 1958; Homology Theory (with S. Wylie), 1960; Partial Derivatives, 1960; Homotopy Theory and Duality, 1965; (with H. B. Griffiths) Classical Mathematics, 1970; General Cohomology Theory and K-Theory, 1971; (with U. Stammbach) Course in Homological Algebra, 1971; (with Y.-C. Wu) Course in Modern Algebra, 1974; (with G. Mislin and J. Roitberg) Localization of Nilpotent Groups and Spaces, 1975; (with J. Pedersen) Fear No More, 1983; Nilpotente Gruppen und Nilpotente Räume, 1984; numerous research articles on algebraic topology, homological algebra and category theory in British and foreign mathematical journals. *Recreations:* travel, sport, reading, theatre, chess, bridge, broadcasting. *Address:* Department of Mathematics, State University of New York, Binghamton, NY 13901, USA.

HILTON, Prof. Rodney Howard, FBA 1977; Director, Institute for Advanced Research in the Humanities, University of Birmingham, since 1984; Professor of Medieval Social History, University of Birmingham, 1963–82, now Emeritus; *b* 1916; *s* of John James Hilton and Anne Hilton. *Educ:* Manchester Grammar Sch.; Balliol Coll. and Merton Coll., Oxford (BA, DPhil). Army, 1940–46; Lectr and Reader in Medieval History, Univ. of Birmingham, 1946–63. *Publications:* The Economic Development of Some Leicestershire Estates in the 14th and 15th Centuries, 1947; (with H. Fagan) The English Rising of 1381, 1950; (ed) Ministers' Accounts of the Warwickshire Estates of the Duke of Clarence, 1952; (ed) The Stoneleigh Leger Book, 1960; A Medieval Society, 1966, rev. edn 1983; The Decline of Serfdom in Medieval England, 1969, rev. edn 1983; Bondmen Made Free, 1973; The English Peasantry in the Later Middle Ages, 1975; (ed) Peasants, Knights and Heretics, 1976; (ed) The Transition from Feudalism to Capitalism, 1976; (ed with T. H. Aston) The English Rising of 1381, 1984; Class Conflict and the Crisis of Feudalism, 1985; articles and reviews in Past and Present, English Historical Review, Economic History Review, etc. *Address:* School of History, University of Birmingham, Birmingham B15 2TT. *T:* 021–472 1301.

HILTON, William (Samuel); Director, Master Builders' Federation, since 1969; National Director, Federation of Master Builders, since 1970; Managing Director: Trade Press (FMB) Ltd, since 1972; National Register of Warranted Builders Ltd, since 1980; *b* 21 March 1926; *m* 1948, Agnes Aitken Orr; three *s*. *Educ:* Kyleshill, Saltcoats; Ardrossan Academy. Railway Fireman until 1949; Labour Party Agent to late Lord Kirkwood, 1949–52; Research and Education Officer for Building Trade Operatives, 1952–66. MP (Lab and Co-op) Bethnal Green, 1966–Feb. 1974. Mem. Agrément Bd for Building Industry, 1965–66; Mem. Economic Development Council for Building Industry, 1964–66; Employers' Sec., Building and Allied Trades Jt Industrial Council, 1979–. Editor, Builders Standard, 1954–66. *Publications:* Building by Direct Labour, 1954; Foes to Tyranny, 1964; Industrial Relations in Construction, 1968. *Address:* The Roost, 1 Mavelstone Close, Bromley, Kent.

HIME, Martin; HM Diplomatic Service; Consul General, Houston, Texas, since 1985; *b* 18 Feb. 1928; *s* of Percy Joseph Hime and Esther Greta (*née* Howe); *m* 1st, 1960, Henrietta Fehling (marr. diss.); one *s* three *d*; 2nd, 1971, Janina Christine Majcher; one *d*. *Educ:* King's Coll. Sch., Wimbledon; Trinity Hall, Cambridge (MA). Served RA, 1946–48. Called to the Bar, Inner Temple, 1951; Marks and Spencer Ltd, 1952–58; joined HM Diplomatic Service, 1960; served in Tokyo, Kobe, Frankfurt and Buenos Aires, 1960–69; 2nd Sec., FCO, 1970–72; Consul, Johannesburg, 1972–74; 1st Sec. (Econ.), Pretoria, 1974–76; Asst Head, S Pacific Dept, FCO, 1976–79; Dep. High Comr in Bangladesh, 1979–82; Consul-Gen., Cleveland, Ohio, 1982–85. *Recreations:* golf, lawn tennis, books, table games. *Address:* c/o Foreign and Commonwealth Office, SW1; Field House, Dover House Road, Roehampton, SW15. *T:* 01–788 5070. *Clubs:* All England Lawn Tennis; Hawks (Cambridge).

HIMMELWEIT, Prof. Hilde T.; Professor of Social Psychology, London School of Economics, University of London, 1964–83, Emeritus Professor 1983; *b* Berlin; *d* of S. Litthauer and Feodore Litthauer (*née* Remak); *m* 1940, Prof. F. Himmelweit (*d* 1977), MD, FRCPEd; one *d*. *Educ:* Berlin; Hayes Court, Kent; Newnham Coll., Cambridge. Degrees in Mod. Langs and Psych.; qual. Educational and Clinical Psychologist, 1943; PhD London 1945; Clin. Psychologist, Maudsley Hosp., 1945–48; joined LSE, 1949; Reader in Social Psychology, 1954. Dir Nuffield Television Enquiry, 1954–58; Visiting Professor: Univ. of Calif, Berkeley, 1959; Hebrew Univ., Jerusalem, 1974; Stanford Univ., Calif, 1975; Fellowship to Centre for Advanced Study of Behavioral Sciences, Stanford, Calif, 1967 and 1983; Fellow, Van Leer Foundn, Jerusalem, 1978–79; Chm., Academic Adv. Cttee of Open Univ., 1969–74; FBPsS 1952; Member: Council, Brit. Psycholog. Soc., 1961–64; Editorial Bds, Brit. Jl of Soc. and Clin. Psychology, 1962–, Jl Communications Research, 1972–, Interdisciplinary Science Reviews, 1976; Research Bd, Inst. of Jewish Affairs, 1970–; US SSRC Cttee on TV and Social Behaviour, 1973–79; Annan Cttee on Future of Broadcasting, 1974–77; Adviser, House of Commons Select Cttee on ITA, 1972; Trustee: Internat. Broadcasting Inst., 1974–79; Centre for Contemporary Studies, 1980–; Vice-Pres., Internat. Soc. of Political Psychology (Nevitt Sanford Award, 1981). Hon. Dr Open Univ., 1976. *Publications:* Television and the Child, 1958; How Voters Decide, 1981, rev. edn 1985; articles and chapters on: rôle, structure and effects of broadcasting; attitude development and change; socialization, rôle of school and other instns; societal influences on outlook and behaviour; political attitudes and their change; voting behaviour. *Address:* London School of Economics, Houghton Street, WC2. *T:* 01–405 7686.

HIMSWORTH, Eric, CMG 1951; *b* 23 Nov. 1905; *s* of H. Himsworth and M. J. Macdonald; *m* 1941, Ethel Emily, *d* of Major Brook Pratt, DSO, Coldstream Guards; two *s*. *Educ:* Silcoates Sch., near Wakefield; Merton Coll., Oxford. MA, BCL Oxon; LLB, BSc (Econ.), DPA London. Colonial Administrative Service, 1928–55; Financial Sec., Malaya, 1952–55; UN Technical Assistance Administration, Nepal, 1956–64; IMF Financial Consultant, 1965–71; Consultant, Ta Hing Co., Hong Kong, 1972–84. *Recreation:* travelling. *Address:* 33 Ballachurry Avenue, Onchan, Isle of Man. *Club:* Royal Commonwealth Society.

HIMSWORTH, Sir Harold (Percival), KCB 1952; MD; FRS 1955; FRCP; Secretary, Medical Research Council, 1949–68, retired (Member and Deputy Chairman, 1967–68); *b* 19 May 1905; *s* of late Arnold Himsworth, Huddersfield, Yorks; *m* 1932, Charlotte, *yr d* of William Gray, Walmer, Kent; two *s*. *Educ:* King James' Grammar Sch., Almondbury, Yorks; University Coll. and University Coll. Hosp., London. Asst, Medical Unit, University Coll. Hosp., 1930; Beit Memorial Research Fellow, 1932–35; William Julius Mickle Fellow, University of London, 1935; Fellow of University Coll., London, 1936; Deputy Dir, Medical Unit, University Coll. Hospital, 1936; Goulstonian Lecturer, 1939; Oliver-Sharpey Lectr, 1949, RCP; Prof. of Medicine, Univ. of London and Dir of the Medical Unit, University Coll. Hospital, London, 1939–49; Mem. of Medical Research Council, 1948–49; Sydney Ringer Lecturer, 1949; Lowell Lecturer, Boston, Mass, 1947; Harveian Orator, Royal College of Physicians, 1962. Pres., Sect. of Experimental Medicine, Royal Society of Medicine, 1946–47. Chm., Bd of Management, London Sch. of Hygiene and Tropical Med., 1969–76. Prime Warden, Goldsmiths Co., 1975. Docteur *hc* Toulouse, 1950; Hon. LLD: Glasgow, 1953; London, 1956; Wales, 1959; Hon. DSc: Manchester, 1956; Leeds, 1968; Univ. of WI, 1968; Hon. ScD, Cambridge, 1964. New York Univ. Medallist, 1958; Conway Evans Prize, RCP, 1968. Member: Norwegian Med. Soc., 1954; Royal Soc. of Arts and Sciences, Göteborg, Sweden, 1957; Hon. Member: Med. Soc. of Sweden, 1949; Amer. Assoc. of Physicians, 1950; For. Mem., Amer. Philosoph. Soc., 1972; For. Hon. Member: Amer. Acad. of Arts and Sciences, 1957; Belgian Royal Acad. of Medicine, 1958. Hon. FRCR 1958; Hon. FRCPE 1960; Hon. FRSM 1961; Hon. FRCS 1965; Hon. FRCPath 1969; Hon. Fellow LSHTM, 1979; Hon. FRSTM, 1981. *Publications:* The Development and Organisation of Scientific Knowledge, 1970; Scientific Knowledge and Philosophic Thought, 1986; medical and scientific papers. *Recreation:* fishing. *Address:* 13 Hamilton Terrace, NW8. *T:* 01–286 6996. *Club:* Athenæum.
See also R. L. Himsworth.

HIMSWORTH, Prof. Richard Lawrence, MD; FRCP; Regius Professor of Medicine, University of Aberdeen, since 1985; *b* 14 June 1937; *s* of Sir Harold Himsworth, *qv*; *m* 1966, Sara Margaret Tattersall; two *s* one *d*. *Educ:* Westminster Sch.; Trinity Coll., Cambridge (MD 1971); University Coll. Hosp. Med. Sch. FRCP 1977. Lectr in Medicine, UCH Med. Sch., 1967–71; MRC Travelling Fellow, New York, 1969–70; MRC Scientific Staff, Clinical Res. Centre, 1971–85: Asst Dir, 1978–82; Head, Endocrinology Res. Gp, 1979–85; Consultant Physician, Northwick Park Hosp., 1972–85. Mem., NW Thames RHA, 1982–85. *Publications:* scientific and medical papers. *Recreation:* painting. *Address:* Mains of Kebbaty, Midmar, Inverurie AB3 7QL. *T:* Sauchen 430.

HINCHCLIFFE, Peter Robert Mossom, CVO 1979; HM Diplomatic Service; Head of Information Department, Foreign and Commonwealth Office, since 1985; *b* 9 April 1937; *s* of Herbert Peter and Jeannie Hinchcliffe; *m* 1965, Archbold Harriet Siddall; three *d*. *Educ:* Elm Park, Killylea, Co. Armagh, Prep. Sch.; Radley Coll.; Trinity Coll., Dublin (BA (Hons), MA). Military service, short service commission, W Yorks Regt, 1955–57; TCD, Dublin Univ., 1957–61; HMOCS: West Aden Protectorate, South Arabian Fedn, 1961–67; Admin. Asst, Birmingham Univ., 1968–69; FCO: 1st Sec., Near Eastern Dept, 1969–70; 1st Sec., UK Mission to UN, 1971–74; 1st Sec. and Head of Chancery, Kuwait, 1974–76; Asst Head of Science and Technology and Central and Southern African Depts, FCO, 1976–78; Dep. High Comr, Dar es Salaam, 1978–81; Consul-Gen., Dubai, 1981–85. *Recreations:* golf, tennis, philately. *Address:* c/o Foreign and Commonwealth Office, SW1A 2AH. *Clubs:* East India, Devonshire, Sports and Public Schools; North Middlesex Golf; Royal Co. Down Golf (Newcastle, Co. Down).

HINCHEY, Herbert John, CMG 1966; CBE 1955; Financial Adviser to Prime Minister of Mauritius, 1967–72; *b* 13 Feb. 1908; *s* of late Edward and late Mary A. Hinchey, Sydney, NSW; *m* 1944, Amy E., *d* of late William and late Caroline Beddows, Vuni Vasa Estate, Taveuni, Fiji; no *c*. *Educ:* Sydney Grammar Sch.; University of Sydney; London Sch. of Economics. Bank of New South Wales, Sydney and Brisbane, 1932–40; Colonial Administrative Service, later HMOCS, 1940–65; Financial Secretary: Western Pacific High Commn, 1948–52; Govt of Mauritius, 1952–57; E Africa High Commn/Common Services Organization, 1957–65. Sometime Member: Mauritius Legislative Coun.; E African Central Legislative Assembly; Chairman: E African Industrial Coun.; E African Industrial Research Bd; E African Currency Bd, E African Airways Bd, etc. *Recreations:*

reading, writing, walking. *Address:* 1/7 Sydney Street, Takapuna, Auckland 9, New Zealand. *Clubs:* East India, Devonshire, Sports and Public Schools; Corona; Nairobi (Nairobi).

HINCHINGBROOKE, Viscount; *see* Montagu, J. E. H.

HINCHLIFF, Rev. Canon Peter Bingham, MA, DD Oxon, PhD Rhodes; Chaplain and Fellow, Balliol College, Oxford, since 1972; *b* 25 Feb. 1929; *e s* of Rev. Canon Samuel Bingham Hinchliff and Brenda Hinchliff; *m* 1955, Constance, *d* of E. L. Whitehead, Uitenhage, S Africa; three *s* one *d*. *Educ:* St Andrew's Coll., Grahamstown, S Africa; Rhodes Univ., Grahamstown; Trinity Coll., Oxford. Deacon, 1952; Priest, 1953, in Anglican Church in S Africa; Asst in Parish of Uitenhage, 1952–55. Subwarden, St Paul's Theological Coll., Grahamstown, 1955–59; Lectr in Comparative Religion, Rhodes Univ., 1957–59; Prof. of Ecclesiastical History, Rhodes Univ., 1960–69; Canon and Chancellor, Grahamstown Cathedral, 1964–69; Sec., Missionary and Ecumenical Council of the General Synod (formerly the Church Assembly), 1969–72; Examng Chaplain to Bishop of Newcastle, 1973, to Bishop of Oxford, 1974–. Public Orator, Rhodes Univ., 1965; Hulsean Lectr, Cambridge Univ., 1975–76; Bampton Lectr, Oxford Univ., 1982. Provincial Hon. Canon, Cape Town Cathedral, 1959–; Hon. Canon, Grahamstown Cathedral, 1969–; Canon Theologian, Coventry Cathedral, 1972–. Pres., Oxford Soc. of Historical Theol., 1978–79. *Publications:* The South African Liturgy, 1959; The Anglican Church in South Africa, 1963; John William Colenso, 1964; The One-Sided Reciprocity, 1966; A Calendar of Cape Missionary Correspondence, 1967; The Church in South Africa, 1968; The Journal of John Ayliff, 1970; Cyprian of Carthage, 1974; (with D. Young) The Human Potential, 1981; Holiness and Politics, 1982; contributor to: Jl of Ecclesiastical History; Studia Liturgica, etc. *Recreations:* crossword puzzles, odd jobbery. *Address:* Balliol College, Oxford.

HINCHLIFF, Stephen, CBE 1976; Chairman, Dexion Group of Companies, since 1976; *b* 11 July 1926; *s* of Gordon Henry and Winifred Hinchliff; *m* 1951, Margaret Arrundale Crossland; one *s* one *d*. *Educ:* Almondbury Grammar Sch., Huddersfield; Boulevard Nautical Coll., Hull; Huddersfield Coll. of Technology; Cranfield Inst. of Technology (MSc). FIMechE, FIProdE. Production Engr, Dowty Auto Units Ltd, 1953–54; Dowty Seals Ltd: Chief Prodn Engr, 1953–54; Works Manager, 1954–56; Dir, 1956–76; Dep. Man. Dir, 1966–67; Man. Dir, 1967–76; Dep. Chm., Dowty Gp Ltd, 1973–76; Man. Dir, Dowty Gp Industrial Div., 1973–76; Man. Dir, Dexion-Comino Internat. Ltd, 1976–. CBIM; FRSA. *Recreations:* squash, badminton, tennis. *Address:* Bowmore Farm, Hawridge Common, near Chesham, Bucks HP5 2UH. *T:* Cholesbury 237.

HIND, Rev. Canon John William; Principal, Chichester Theological College, since 1982; Residentiary Canon and Bursalis Prebendary, Chichester Cathedral, since 1982; *b* 19 June 1945; *s* of Harold Hind and Joan Mary Hind; *m* 1966, Janet Helen McLintock; three *s*. *Educ:* Watford Grammar Sch.; Leeds Univ. (BA 1966). Asst Master, Leeds Modern Sch., 1966–69; Asst Lectr, King Alfred's Coll., Winchester, 1969–70; Cuddesdon Theol Coll.; Deacon 1972, Priest 1973; Asst Curate, St John's, Catford, 1972–76; Vicar, Christ Church, Forest Hill, 1976–82 and Priest-in-Charge, St Paul's, Forest Hill, 1981–82. *Recreations:* judo, languages. *Address:* The Theological College, Chichester, West Sussex PO19 3ES. *T:* Chichester 783367/783344.

HIND, Kenneth, ERD 1955; Senior Director, Employment and Industrial Relations, Post Office, 1973–80; *b* 14 March 1920; *er s* of late Harry and Edith Hind; *m* 1942, Dorothy Walton; one *s*. *Educ:* Central Sec. Sch., Sheffield; Queens' Coll., Cambridge (Munro Schol.). Army, 1940–48: Major, REME. General Post Office: Asst Principal, 1948; Principal, 1950; Asst Sec., 1960; Dir, Radio and Broadcasting, 1967; Central Services, 1969; Senior Dir, 1971. *Recreations:* cricket, gardening. *Address:* Flat 1, Florence Court, 22 Florence Road, Brighton BN1 6DJ. *T:* Brighton 507710.

HIND, Kenneth Harvard; MP (C) West Lancashire, since 1983; barrister; *b* 15 Sept. 1949; *s* of George Edward and Brenda Hind; *m* 1977, Patricia Anne (*née* Millar); one *d*. *Educ:* Woodhouse Grove Sch., Bradford; Leeds Univ. (LLB 1971); Inns of Court Sch. of Law. Pres., Leeds Univ. Union, 1971–72. Called to the Bar, Gray's Inn, 1973; practised North Eastern circuit, 1973–83. Member: Liverpool Univ. Senate; Soc. of Conservative Lawyers; Justice, Internat. Commn of Jurists; Hon. Mem., Anglo Hellenic Assoc. Hon. Vice-President: Merseyside Chamber of Commerce; Central and West Lancs Chamber of Industry and Commerce. *Recreations:* music, sailing Enterprise, collecting antiques, cricket; Hon. Vice-Pres. Headingley RUFC. *Address:* 8 Chestnut Close, Summerwood Lane, Halsall, Ormskirk, Lancs L39 8SY; 54 Red Post Hill, Dulwich, SE24 9JQ. *Clubs:* Farmers (Ormskirk); Ormskirk Conservative; Southport Sailing.

HINDE, Prof. Robert Aubrey, FRS 1974; Royal Society Research Professor, University of Cambridge, since 1963; Fellow of St John's College, Cambridge, since 1958; *b* 26 Oct. 1923; *s* of late Dr and Mrs E. B. Hinde, Norwich; *m* 1st, 1948, Hester Cecily (marr. diss. 1971), *d* of late C. R. V. Coutts; two *s* two *d*; 2nd, 1971, Joan Gladys, *d* of F. J. Stevenson; two *d*. *Educ:* Oundle Sch.; St John's Coll., Cambridge; Balliol Coll., Oxford (Hon. Fellow, 1986). Served Coastal Comd, RAF, Flt-Lt, 1941–45. Research Asst, Edward Grey Inst., Univ. of Oxford, 1948–50; Curator, Ornithological Field Station (now sub-Dept of Animal Behaviour), Madingley, Cambridge, 1950–65; St John's Coll., Cambridge: Research Fellow, 1951–54; Steward, 1956–58; Tutor, 1958–63. Hon. Dir, MRC Unit on Develt and Integration of Behaviour, 1970–. Hitchcock Prof., Univ. of California, 1979; Green Vis. Scholar, Univ. of Texas, 1983. Mem. Council, Royal Soc., 1985–86. For. Hon. Mem., Amer. Acad. of Arts and Sciences, 1974; For. Associate, Nat. Acad. of Scis, USA, 1978; Hon. Fellow, Amer. Ornithologists' Union, 1977; Hon FBPsS 1981. Hon. ScD: Univ. Libre, Brussels, 1974; Univ. of Paris (Nanterre), 1979. Scientific Medal, Zoological Soc., 1961; Leonard Cammer Medal in Psychiatry, Columbia Coll., NY, 1980. *Publications:* Animal Behaviour: a synthesis of Ethology and Comparative Psychology, 1966; (ed) Bird Vocalizations: their relations to current problems in biology and psychology, 1969; (ed jtly) Short Term Changes in Neural Activity and Behaviour, 1970; (ed) Non-Verbal Communication, 1972; (ed jtly) Constraints on Learning, 1973; Biological Bases of Human Social Behaviour, 1974; (ed jtly) Growing Points in Ethology, 1976; Towards Understanding Relationships, 1979; Ethology: its nature and relations with other sciences, 1982; (jtly) Defended to Death, 1982; (ed and contrib.) Primate Social Relationships: an integrated approach, 1983; (ed jtly) Social Relationships and Cognitive Development, 1985; sundry papers in biological and psychological journals. *Address:* Park Lane, Madingley, Cambridge. *T:* Madingley 210430.

HINDE, Thomas; *see* Chitty, Sir Thomas Willes.

HINDERKS, Prof. Hermann Ernst, MA, DrPhil; Professor of German in the Queen's University, Belfast, 1954–70; *b* 19 Dec. 1907; *s* of Elrikus Hinderks and Alma Charlotte Jane (*née* Hildebrand); *m* 1935, Ingeborg (*née* Victor); three *d*. *Educ:* Lichtwark Schule, Hamburg; Univs of Hamburg, Freiburg i.Br and Basle (MA, DrPhil 1938). Teacher St George's Cathedral Grammar Sch., Capetown, 1935–37; Head of German Dept, Rhodes University Coll., Grahamstown, S Africa, 1938–39; Lecturer in German, University of Cape Town, 1939–53. *Publications:* Friedrich Nietzsche, ein Menschenleben und seine Philosophie (with H. A. Reyburn and J. G. Taylor), 1st edn 1946, 2nd edn 1947 (Eng. version, Nietzsche, The Story of a Human Philosopher, 1948); Uber die Gegenstandsbegriffe in der Kritik der reinen Vernunft, 1948. *Recreations:* music and walking. *Address:* 8821 Gnotzheim, Spielberg 28, Mittelfranken, W Germany.

HINDLEY, Prof. Colin Boothman; Professor of Child Development since 1972, and Director of Centre for Study of Human Development since 1967, Institute of Education, London; *b* Bolton, 1923; *m* 1945; two *s*. *Educ:* Bolton Sch.; Manchester Univ.; University Coll., London. MB, ChB Manchester 1946; BSc London 1949 (1st cl. Psychol.). Asst Med. Officer, Hope Hosp., Salford; Res. Psychologist and subseq. Sen. Lectr, London Univ. Inst. of Educn, 1949–72; Head of Adolescent Development Dip. Course, 1968–72. Psychol. Adviser, Internat. Children's Centre Growth Studies, Paris, 1954–; Editor, Jl of Child Psychol. and Psychiat., 1959–69; Mem. Council, Brit. Psychol. Soc., 1970–73; Mem. Cttee, Internat. Soc. for Study Behavioural Develt, 1969–75; Mem. Assoc. Child Psychol. and Psychiat. (Chm. 1967–68). FBPsS. *Publications:* Conceptual and Methodological Issues in the Study of Child Development, 1980; chapters in Child Development: International Method of Study, ed Falkner, 1960; Learning Theory and Personality Development, in Psychosomatic Aspects of Paediatrics, ed Mackeith and Sandler, 1961; The Place of Longitudinal Methods in the Study of Development, in Determinants of Behavioural Development, ed Mönks, Hartup and de Wit, 1972; (jt ed. and contrib.) Development in Adolescence, 1983; contribs to jls. *Address:* Department of Child Development and Educational Psychology, Institute of Education, Bedford Way, WC1H 0AL.

HINDLEY, Henry Oliver Rait; *b* 19 June 1906; 3rd *s* of late Sir Clement Hindley; unmarried. *Educ:* Oundle; Trinity Coll., Cambridge; Dundee School of Economics. Industrial Consultant, 1936–40; Treasury, 1940; Air Min., 1940–45; Dir-Gen., Brit. Air Commission, later British Supply Office, USA, 1945–46; Chairman: Northern Divisional Board of National Coal Board, Sept. 1946–47; Raw Cotton Commission, 1947–51. Canadian Civil Servant, 1961; Sec., Adv. Cttee on Broadcasting, 1965; Asst Under-Sec. of State, 1965–69; Dept of Communications, 1969–75. Sec., Cttee on Telecommunications and Canadian Sovereignty, 1979. *Address:* 200 Rideau Terrace 1114, Ottawa, Ontario, K1M 0Z3, Canada.

HINDLEY, Michael John; Member (Lab) Lancashire East, European Parliament, since 1984; *b* 11 April 1947; *s* of John and Edna Hindley; *m* 1980, Ewa Agnieszka (*née* Leszczyc-Grabianka); one *d*. *Educ:* Clitheroe Royal Grammar School; London University (BA Hons); Lancaster University (MA); Free University of West Berlin. Labour Councillor, Hyndburn District Council, 1979–84 (Leader, 1981–84); contested (Lab) Blackpool North, 1983. Vice-Chm., External Economic Relations Cttee, European Parlt, 1984–. *Recreations:* swimming, walking, reading, music, travel. *Address:* 27 Commercial Road, Great Harwood, Lancs BB6 7HX. *T:* Great Harwood 887017.

HINDLEY-SMITH, David Dury, CBE 1972; Registrar, General Dental Council (formerly Dental Board of the UK), 1947–81; Chairman, Council of Royal Dental Hospital, London School of Dental Surgery, 1981–84 (Member, since 1976); Member, West Suffolk Health Authority, since 1982; (Chairman, Mental Health Committee, since 1982); *b* 20 Feb. 1916; *e s* of late James Dury Hindley-Smith; *m* 1947, Dorothy Westwood Legge, *e d* of Arthur Collins and Mary Fielding; two *d*. *Educ:* Uppingham; King's Coll., Cambridge (MA); Paris and Vienna. Passed examination for Diplomatic Service, 1939. War Service: Artists' Rifles, 1939; commissioned Royal Fus., 1940; liaison officer to Gén. Leclerc, 1942, to Gén. de Gaulle's first administration, 1944; Acting Col. Vice-Chm., Surrey Assoc. of Youth Clubs, 1950–70 (Vice-Pres., 1970–); Executive Chm., Nat. Assoc. of Youth Clubs, 1970–74 (Vice-Pres., 1974–); Chm., Sembal Trust, 1972–81; Vice-Pres., Suffolk Assoc. of Youth, 1984– (Chm., 1982–84). Hon. Mem., BDA, 1975; Hon. FDSRCSE 1977; Hon. FDSRCS, 1980. Cecil Peace Prize, 1938. *Recreations:* gardening, cooking. *Address:* The Ark House, Whepstead, Bury St Edmunds, Suffolk. *T:* Horringer 351.

HINDLIP, 5th Baron *cr* 1886; **Henry Richard Allsopp;** Bt 1880; *b* 1 July 1912; 2nd *s* of 3rd Baron Hindlip and Agatha (*d* 1962), 2nd *d* of late John C. Thynne; *S* brother, 4th Baron, 1966; *m* 1939, Cecily Valentine Jane, *o d* of late Lt-Col Malcolm Borwick, DSO, Hazelbech Hill, Northampton; two *s* one *d*. *Educ:* Eton; RMC Sandhurst. 2nd Lieut, Coldstream Guards, 1932; Major, 1941; retired, 1948. Served War of 1939–45; NW Europe, 1944. JP 1957, DL 1956, Wilts. Bronze Star Medal, USA, 1945. *Recreations:* travel, shooting. *Heir:* *s* Hon. Charles Henry Allsopp [*b* 5 Aug. 1940; *m* 1968, Fiona Victoria, *d* of Hon. William McGowan; one *s* three *d*]. *Address:* Tytherton House, East Tytherton, Chippenham, Wilts. *T:* Kelloways 207. *Club:* Turf.

See also Sir R. J. Hardy, Bt.

HINDMARSH, Frederick Bell; Under-Secretary, Department of Health and Social Security, 1973–79, retired; *b* 31 Jan. 1919; *yr s* of Frederick Hindmarsh and Margaret May Hindmarsh; *m* 1947, Mary Torrance Coubrough; one *d*. *Educ:* County Grammar Sch., Acton. Clerical Officer, Min. of Health, 1936; Exec. Officer, 1937. Served war, Army, 1939–46. Min. of Pensions and Nat. Insurance and Min. of Social Security: Higher Exec. Officer, 1946; Sen. Exec. Officer, 1947; Chief Exec. Officer, 1951; Sen. Chief Exec. Officer, 1959; Prin. Exec. Officer, 1964; Asst Sec., DHSS, 1969. *Recreation:* music. *Address:* 3 Hawthorn Close, Nascot Wood Road, Watford, Herts WD1 3SB. *T:* Watford 36769.

HINDMARSH, Irene, JP, MA; Principal, St Aidan's College, University of Durham, since 1970; Second Pro-Vice-Chancellor, University of Durham, 1982–85; *b* 22 Oct. 1923; *d* of Albert Hindmarsh and Elizabeth (*née* White). *Educ:* Heaton High Sch.; Lady Margaret Hall, Oxford (MA Hons French); King's Coll., Univ. of Durham (PGCE). Taught at St Paul's Girls' Sch., London, 1947–49, Rutherford High Sch., Newcastle upon Tyne, 1949–59; Interchange Teacher, Lycée de Jeunes Filles, Dax, Landes, France, 1954–55; Lectr in Educn and French, King's Coll., Durham, 1959–64; Headmistress, Birkenhead High Sch., GPDST, 1964–70. Vis. Prof., New York State Univ., Syracuse, Cornell, Harvard, 1962; Delegate of Internat. Fedn of Univ. Women to UNO, NY, to Commns on Human Rights and Status of Women, 1962, Vis. Professor, Fu-Dan Univ., Shanghai, 1979, and again, 1980; SW China Teachers' Univ., Beibei, Sichuan, and Fu-Dan Univ., Shanghai, 1986. Delegate/Translator to internat. confs of FIPESO, 1963–70; Chairman: Internat. Cttee of Headmistresses' Assoc., 1966–70; Internat. Panel of Joint Four, 1967–70. Editor, Internat. Bull. of AHM, 1966–70. JP Birkenhead 1966, Durham 1974. *Publications:* various articles on educnl topics in AGM papers of Assoc. of Head Mistresses; contribs to prelim. papers of FIPESO meetings; seminar papers to symposia on lit. topics, Sèvres, under auspices of Council of Europe; contrib. re St Aidan's to Durham History from the Air. *Recreations:* travel, music, theatre, films. *Address:* St Aidan's College, Durham DH1 3LJ. *T:* Durham 65011.

HINDSON, William Stanley, CMG 1962; BScEng, MIM, FIMechE; engineering and metallurgical consultant since 1974; *b* 11 Jan. 1920; *s* of late W. A. L. Hindson, Darlington; *m* 1944, Mary Sturdy (*d* 1961); one *s* one *d*; *m* 1965, Catherine Leikine, Paris, France; one *s*. *Educ:* Darlington Grammar Sch.; Coatham Sch., Redcar. With Dorman Long (Steel) Ltd, Middlesbrough, 1937–55; Metallurgical Equipment Export Co. Ltd and Indian

Steelworks Construction Co. Ltd, 1956–62; Wellman Engineering Corp. Ltd, 1963–69; Cementation Co. Ltd, 1970–71; Humphreys & Glasgow, 1971–74. Mem., Inst. of Directors. *Recreations:* chess, philately. *Address:* 36 Eresby House, Rutland Gate, SW7. *T:* 01–589 3194.

HINE, Air Chief Marshal Sir Patrick (Bardon), KCB 1983; Vice-Chief of the Defence Staff, since 1985; *b* 14 July 1932; *parents decd; m* 1956, Jill Adèle (*née* Gardner); three *s. Educ:* Peter Symonds Sch., Winchester. Served with Nos 1, 93 and 111 Sqdns, 1952–60; Mem., Black Arrows aerobatic team, 1957–59; commanded: No 92 Sqdn, 1962–64; No 17 Sqdn, 1970–71; RAF Wildenrath, 1974–75; Dir, Public Relations (RAF), 1975–77; RCDS 1978; SASO, HQ RAF, Germany, 1979; ACAS (Policy), 1979–83; C-in-C RAF Germany and Comdr, Second Allied Tactical Air Force, 1983–85. Queen's Commendation for Valuable Service in the Air, 1960. CBIM; FRAeS. Winner, Carris Trophy, Hants, IoW and Channel Islands Golf Championship, and Brabazon Trophy, 1949; English Schoolboy Golf Internat., 1948–49; Inter-Services Golf, 1952–57. *Recreations:* golf, squash, caravanning, photography. *Clubs:* Royal Air Force; Ashridge Golf.

HINES, Prof. Albert Gregorio; Professor of Economics, University of London, and Head of Department of Economics, Birkbeck College, 1972–83; *b* 8 Oct. 1935; Jamaican; *m* 1962, June Rosemary Chesney Carcas (marr. diss. 1976); two *s* one *d. Educ:* Victoria Town Sch., Manchester; London Sch. of Economics, Univ. of London (BSc Econ). Asst Lectr, Univ. of Bristol, 1962–64; Lectr, University Coll. London, 1964–68; Prof. of Economics, Univ. of Durham, 1968–72. Vis. Prof., Massachusetts Inst. of Technology, 1971–72. Vice-Pres., Section F, British Assoc. for the Advancement of Science, 1970–71. Economist, Overseas Development Ministry, 1965–66. Mem., Gen. Adv. Council, BBC, 1974–79; Chairman: Enquiry into Minority Arts in UK, 1975; Commn for Economic Stabilisation, Jamaica, 1975–. *Publications:* On the Reappraisal of Keynesian Economics, 1971; articles in: Economic Jl, Review of Economic Studies, Review of Economics and Statistics, Amer. Economic Review, The Times. *Recreations:* theatre, cinema, music, novels, cricket, walking.

HINES, Barry Melvin, FRSL; writer; *b* 30 June 1939; *s* of Richard and Annie Hines; *m* (marr. diss.); one *s* one *d. Educ:* Ecclesfield Grammar Sch.; Loughborough Coll. of Educn (Teaching Cert.). FRSL 1977. Teacher of Physical Educn, London, 1960–62 and S Yorks, 1962–72; Yorkshire Arts Fellow in Creative Writing, Sheffield Univ., 1972–74; E Midlands Arts Fellow in Creative Writing, Matlock Coll. of Higher Educn, 1975–77; Sheffield City Polytechnic: Arts Council Fellow in Creative Writing, 1982–84; Hon. Fellow in Creative Writing, 1984; Hon. Fellow, 1985. *Television scripts:* Billy's Last Stand, 1971; Speech Day, 1973; Two Men from Derby, 1976; The Price of Coal (2 films), 1977; The Gamekeeper, 1979; A Question of Leadership, 1981; Threads, 1984; *screenplays:* Kes, 1970; Looks and Smiles, 1981. *Publications:* (fiction): The Blinder, 1966; A Kestrel for a Knave, 1968; First Signs, 1972; The Gamekeeper, 1975; The Price of Coal, 1979; Looks and Smiles, 1981; Unfinished Business, 1983. *Recreations:* walking, supporting Sheffield United Football Club. *Address:* c/o Lemon and Durbridge Ltd, 24 Pottery Lane, Holland Park, W11 4LZ. *T:* 01–229 9216. *Club:* Hoyland Common Workingmen's (near Barnsley).

HINES, Sir Colin (Joseph), Kt 1976; OBE 1973; President: NSW Returned Services League Clubs Association, since 1971; NSW Branch, Returned Services League of Australia, since 1971; Deputy National President, Returned Services League of Australia, since 1974; *b* 16 Feb. 1919; *s* of J. Hines and Mrs Hines, Lyndhurst, NSW; *m* 1942, Jean Elsie, *d* of A. Wilson, Mandurama, NSW; two *s. Educ:* All Saints' Coll., Bathurst, NSW. Army, 1937–45. Farmer and grazier, 1946–71. Hon. Officer, Returned Services League of Aust., 1971–76. State Comr, Aust. Forces Overseas Fund, 1971–; Trustee, Anzac Meml Trust, 1971–. Chairman: War Veterans Homes, Narrabeen, 1971–; Clubs Mutual Services Ltd, 1972–. *Recreations:* rifle shooting, golf. *Address:* The Meadows, Lyndhurst, NSW 2741, Australia. *T:* Lyndhurst 17. *Club:* Imperial Services (Sydney, NSW).

HINES, Gerald; *see* Hines, V. G.

HINES, His Honour (Vivian) Gerald, QC 1964; a Circuit Judge, 1972–79, retired (Chairman, North East London Quarter Sessions, 1965–68, Greater London Quarter Sessions (Middlesex Area), 1969, Greater London Quarter Sessions (Inner London), 1969–71); *b* 24 Dec. 1912; 2nd *s* of late John Hines and Lizzie Emily (*née* Daniells), Essex; *m* 1st, 1950, Janet Graham, MA (*d* 1957), *e d* of late John Graham, Wigtownshire; 2nd, 1960, Barbara, *y d* of late Herbert Gunton, Colchester. *Educ:* Earls Colne Grammar Sch. Admitted Solicitor, 1935; private practice, 1935–42; Clerk to Colchester Borough Justices, 1942; called to Bar, Inner Temple, 1943; South-Eastern Circuit. Dep. Chairman: Essex QS, 1955–67; County of London QS, 1965; Judge of the Central Criminal Court, 1968–69. Mem., Home Office Adv. Council on the Penal System, 1970–. Member: Council, Magistrates' Assoc., 1967–70; Standing Joint Cttee, Essex, 1962–65. Governor, New Coll., London, 1963–65; Member: Court of Essex Univ., 1966–; Council of Boy Scouts' Assoc., 1961–66; Essex CC, 1946–49. JP Essex, 1955, Greater London, 1965–79. Freeman, City of London, 1975. Liveryman, Fan Makers' Co., 1976. *Publications:* Judicial Discretion in Sentencing, 1982; contrib. to Halsbury's Laws of England, 4th edn (Criminal Law Vol.); articles in British Jl of Criminology, The Magistrate, Reform and other jls. *Address:* 19 Cambridge Road, Colchester, Essex CO3 3NS. *T:* Colchester 576773.

HINGSTON, Lt-Col Walter George, OBE 1964; psc; FRGS; *b* Radcliffe on Trent, Notts, 15 Feb. 1905; *s* of late Charles Hingston, DL and late Mildred (*née* Pleydell Bouverie), Cotgrave, Nottingham; *m* 1939, Elizabeth Margaret, *d* of late Brig. Sir Clinton Lewis, OBE, and late Lilian Eyre (*née* Wace); two *d. Educ:* Harrow; RMC Sandhurst; and Staff Coll. 2nd Lieut, KOYLI, 1925; Nigeria Regt, RWAFF, 1931–36; 1st Punjab Regt, Indian Army, 1936. Served War of 1939–45: 4th Indian Div., North Africa, Eritrea (despatches); Dep. Dir Public Relations, GHQ India, 1942; Chief Information Officer to C-in-C, Ceylon, 1943; retired (invalided), 1945. Chief Information Officer, Dept of Scientific and Industrial Research, 1945–63; Editor, the Geographical Magazine, 1963–68. Mem., Marlborough and Ramsbury RDC, 1970–74. *Publications:* The Tiger Strikes, 1942; The Tiger Kills (with G. R. Stevens), 1944; Never Give Up, 1948. *Recreation:* fishing. *Address:* The Old Vicarage, Ramsbury, Marlborough, Wilts. *Club:* Army and Navy.

HINSLEY, Prof. Sir (Francis) Harry, Kt 1985; OBE 1946; FBA 1981; Master of St John's College, Cambridge since 1979 (Fellow, 1944–79; President, 1975–79); *b* 26 Nov. 1918; *s* of Thomas Henry and Emma Hinsley; *m* 1946, Hilary Brett, *d* of H. F. B. and Helena Brett-Smith, Oxford; two *s* one *d. Educ:* Queen Mary's Grammar Sch., Walsall; St John's Coll., Cambridge. HM Foreign Office, war service, 1939–46. University of Cambridge: Research Fellow, St John's Coll., 1944–50, Tutor, 1956–63; University Lectr in History, 1949–65; Reader in the History of International Relations, 1965–69; Prof., History of Internat. Relations, 1969–83; Vice-Chancellor, 1981–83; Chm., Faculty Bd of History, 1970–72; Lees-Knowles Lectr on Military Science, Trinity Coll., 1970–71. Lectures: Cecil Green, Univ. of BC, 1976; Sir Douglas Robb, Univ. of Auckland, and Yencken Meml, ANU, 1980; Martin Wight Meml, Univ. of Sussex, 1981; Lindsay Meml, Univ. of Keele, 1985; Chancellor's, Univ. of Witwatersrand, 1985; Earl Grey

Meml, Univ. of Newcastle-upon-Tyne, 1985. UK Rep., Provisional Academic Cttee for European Univ. Inst., 1973–75. Trustee, BM, 1984–. Hon. Fellow, TCD, 1981. Hon. DLitt Witwatersrand, 1985. Editor, The Historical Jl, 1960–71. *Publications:* Command of the Sea, 1950; Hitler's Strategy, 1951; (ed) New Cambridge Modern History, Vol. XI, 1962; Power and the Pursuit of Peace, 1963; Sovereignty, 1966, 2nd edn 1986; Nationalism and the International System, 1973; (ed) British Foreign Policy under Sir Edward Grey, 1977; (jtly) British Intelligence in the Second World War, vol. 1, 1979, vol. 2, 1981, vol. 3 (Pt 1), 1984, (Pt 2), 1986. *Address:* The Master's Lodge, St John's College, Cambridge. *T:* Cambridge 338635.

HINSLEY, Prof. Frederick Baden, DSc; FEng; Professor of Mining and Head of Department of Mining Engineering, University of Nottingham, 1947–67, now Emeritus; *b* 20 May 1900; *m* 1932, Doris Lucy Spencer; three *s* two *d. Educ:* Coalville Technical Coll.; University of Birmingham. Lecturer and Vice-Principal, County Technical Coll., Worksop, 1932–39; Lecturer in Dept of Mining, University Coll., Cardiff, 1939–47. Pres. IMinE, 1968. Silver medal, Warwicks and S Staffs Inst. of Mining Engineers, 1940; Gold medal, South Wales Inst. of Engineers, 1946; Silver medal, Midland Counties Instn of Engineers, 1951; Douglas Hay medal, 1955, Institution Medal, 1971, Instn of Mining Engineers; Van Waterschoot Van der Gracht medal, Royal Geol. and Mining Soc. of the Netherlands, 1962. *Publications:* contribs to: Proc. S Wales Inst. of Engineers; Proc. Nat. Assoc. of Colliery Managers; Trans Instn of Mining Engineers. *Recreations:* writing history of mining, gardening, reading. *Address:* 7 Puller Road, Boxmoor, Hemel Hempstead, Herts HP1 1QL. *T:* Hemel Hempstead 62011.

HINTON, Prof. Denys James, FRIBA; Chairman, Redditch New Town Development Corporation, 1978–85; *b* 12 April 1921; *s* of James and Nell Hinton; *m* 1971, Lynette Payne (*née* Pattinson); one *d. Educ:* Reading Sch.; Architectural Assoc. (MSc; AADip.). FRIBA. Asst, Wells Coates, 1950–52; Birmingham Sch. of Architecture: Lectr, 1952–57; Sen. Lectr, 1957–64; Dir, 1964–72; Prof. of Architecture, Univ. of Aston, 1966–81, now Emeritus. Sen. Partner, Hinton Brown Langstone, Architects, Warwick. Chm., Architects Registration Council of UK, 1983–86; Vice-Pres. (formerly Vice-Chm.), Exec. Cttee, Internat. New Towns Assoc., 1980–85. *Publications:* Performance Characteristics of the Athenian Bouleterion, RIBA Athens Bursary, 1962; Great Interiors: High Victorian Period, 1967; contrib. RIBA and Architects Jl, papers on architectural education, Inst. Bulletin (worship and religious architecture), Univ. of Birmingham. *Recreations:* travel, moving house, water colours. *Address:* 45 Park Hill, Moseley, Birmingham B13 8DR. *T:* 021–449 9909.

HINTON, Michael Herbert, JP; FCA; FICM; FRSA; FAAI; ACIArb; *b* 10 Nov. 1934; *s* of late Walter Leonard Hinton and of Freda Millicent Lillian Hinton; *m* 1st, 1955, Sarah Sunderland (marr. diss. 1982); one *s* two *d;* 2nd, 1984, Jane Margaret Manley, *d* of Arthur Crichton Howell. *Educ:* Ardingly Coll. Liveryman: Farmers' Co., 1964 (Master, 1981–82); Wheelwrights' Co. (Mem. Ct, 1971); Mem. Court of Common Council, 1970–71, Alderman, 1971–79, Ward of Billingsgate; Clerk to Wheelwrights' Co., 1965–71; Sheriff, City of London, 1977–78. JP City of London, 1971. *Recreations:* cricket, Association football, theatre, travel. *Address:* 9E Brechin Place, SW7 4QB. *T:* 01–373 7486. *Clubs:* Farmers, MCC, City Livery (Pres., 1976–77).

HINTON, Nicholas John, CBE 1985; Director-General, Save the Children Fund, since 1985; *b* 15 March 1942; *s* of Rev. Canon Hinton and late Mrs J. P. Hinton; *m* 1971, Deborah Mary Vivian; one *d. Educ:* Marlborough Coll., Wiltshire; Selwyn Coll., Cambridge (MA). Asst Dir, Northorpe Hall Trust, 1965–68; Nat. Assoc. for Care and Resettlement of Offenders, 1968–77, Dir, 1973–77; Dir, NCVO (formerly Nat. Council of Social Service), 1977–84. Member: Central Council for Educn and Trng in Social Work, 1974–79; Stonham Housing Assoc., 1976–79; Cttee of Inquiry into UK Prison Services, 1978–79; Exec Cttees, Councils of Social Service, NI, Scotland and Wales, 1977–84; Council, VSO, 1981–; Exec. Cttee, Business in the Community, 1982–; Trustee: Charities Aid Foundn, 1977–84. Dir, Edington Music Festival, 1965–70. Contested (SDP-Liberal Alliance) Somerton and Frome, 1983. FRSA 1981. *Recreation:* music. *Address:* Mary Datchelor House, 17 Grove Lane, SE5 8RD. *T:* 01–703 5400.

HIPKIN, John; Head of English, Meridian School, Royston, Herts, since 1977; *b* 9 April 1935; *s* of Jack Hipkin and Elsie Hipkin; *m* 1963, Bronwyn Vaughan Dewey; four *s* one *d. Educ:* Surbiton Grammar Sch. for Boys; LSE (BScEcon). Asst Teacher, 1957–65; Research Officer: King's Coll., Cambridge, 1965–68; Univ. of East Anglia, 1968–71; Sec., Schools Council Working Party on Whole Curriculum, 1973–74; Dir, Adv. Centre for Educn, 1974–77. *Publications:* (jtly) New Wine in Old Bottles, 1967; (ed jtly) Education for the Seventies, 1970; The Massacre of Peterloo (a play), 1968, 2nd edn 1974. *Recreations:* theatre, photography, history, modern music. *Address:* 82 Chesterton Road, Cambridge CB4 1ER. *T:* Cambridge 67038.

HIPPISLEY-COX, Peter Denzil John; solicitor and parliamentary agent; Senior Partner, Dyson, Bell & Co., London, since 1976; *b* 22 May 1921; *s* of late Col Sir Geoffrey Hippisley Cox, CBE, and Lady Hippisley Cox; *m* 1st, 1948, Olga Kay (marr. diss. 1956); one *d;* 2nd, 1956, Frieda Marion Wood; two *d. Educ:* Stowe; Trinity Coll., Cambridge (MA). Served War, RAF (Signals), 1941–46 (Flt Lieut). Admitted a solicitor, 1949. Dir, Equity & Law Life Assurance Soc., 1965– (Dep. Chm. 1973; Chm., 1977–85). Member: Council, Law Soc., 1956–81; Court, Drapers' Co., 1972– (Master, 1983–84). Governor, Bancroft's Sch., 1975–. *Recreation:* music. *Address:* 48D Whistlers Avenue, SW11 3TS. *T:* 01–585 2142. *Club:* Carlton.

HIPWELL, Hermine H.; *see* Vivenot, Baroness R. de.

HIRAHARA, Tsuyoshi; Ambassador of Japan to the Court of St James's, 1982–85; *b* 25 Oct. 1920; *m* Kiyo Nishi; two *d. Educ:* Faculty of Law, Tokyo Univ. Dep. Dir-Gen. for Gen. Affairs, Economic Affairs Bureau, Min. of For. Affairs, 1962; Consul-Gen., Milan, 1964; Minister, Brussels, 1966; Dep. Dir-Gen., 1969, Dir-Gen., 1970, Economic Affairs Bureau, Min. of For. Affairs; Ambassador to: Morocco, 1972; OECD, Paris, 1975–80. Commander: Legion of Honour (France); Ordre de la Couronne (Belgium); Grand Officer: Ordre de Leopold II (Belgium); Order of Ouissam Alaouit Cherifiam (Morocco). *Recreation:* golf. *Address:* c/o Ministry of Foreign Affairs, Kasumigaseki, Chiyoda-ku, Tokyo, Japan.

HIRSCH, Prof. Kurt August; Emeritus Professor of Pure Mathematics, University of London, Queen Mary College; *b* Berlin, 12 Jan. 1906; *s* of Dr Robert Hirsch and Anna (*née* Lehmann); *m* 1928, Elsa Brühl; one *s* two *d. Educ:* University of Berlin; University of Cambridge. Dr phil (Berlin), 1930; PhD (Cambridge), 1937. Asst Lecturer, later Lecturer, University Coll., Leicester, 1938–47; Lecturer, later Sen. Lecturer, King's Coll., Newcastle upon Tyne, 1948–51; Reader, University of London, Queen Mary Coll., 1951–57, Prof., 1957–73. Editor, Russian Mathematical Surveys. *Publications:* (with A. G. Kurosh) Theory of Groups, 2 vols, 2nd English edn 1954; (with F. R. Gantmacher) Theory of Matrices, 2 vols, English edn 1960; (with A. G. Kurosh) Lectures on General Algebra, English edn 1964; (with I. R. Shafarevich) Basic Algebraic Geometry, 1974;

contribs to learned jls. *Recreations:* chess, gardening. *Address:* 101 Shirehall Park, NW4 2QU. *T:* 01-202 7902.

HIRSCH, Prof. Sir Peter (Bernhard), Kt 1975; MA, PhD; FRS 1963; Isaac Wolfson Professor of Metallurgy in the University of Oxford since 1966; Fellow, St Edmund Hall, Oxford, since 1966; *b* 16 Jan. 1925; *s* of Ismar Hirsch and Regina Meyerson; *m* 1959, Mabel Anne Kellar (*née* Stephens), *widow* of James Noel Kellar; one step *s* one step *d*. *Educ:* Sloane Sch., Chelsea; St Catharine's Coll., Cambridge (Hon. Fellow, 1982). BA 1946; MA 1950; PhD 1951. Reader in Physics in Univ. of Cambridge, 1964–66; Fellow, Christ's Coll., Cambridge, 1960–66, Hon. Fellow, 1978. Has been engaged on researches with electron microscope on imperfections in crystalline structure of metals and on relation between structural defects and mechanical properties. Chairman: Metallurgy and Materials Cttee (and Mem., Eng. Bd), SRC, 1970–73; UKAEA, 1982–84 (pt-time Mem., 1982–86); Member: Elec. Supply Res. Council, 1969–82; Tech. Adv. Cttee, Advent, 1982–; Tech. Adv. Bd, Monsanto Electronic Mats, 1985–. Dir, Cogent Ltd, 1985–. Rosenhain Medal, Inst. of Metals, 1961; C. V. Boys Prize, Inst. of Physics and Physical Soc., 1962; Clamer Medal, Franklin Inst., 1970; Wihuri Internat. Prize, Helsinki, 1971; Royal Soc. Hughes Medal, 1973; Metals Soc. Platinum Medal, 1976; Royal Medal, Royal Soc., 1977; Arthur Von Hippel Award, Materials Res. Soc., 1983; (jtly) Wolf Prize in Physics, Wolf Foundn, 1983–84. Hon. Fellow: RMS, 1977; Japan Soc. of Electron Microscopy, 1979. Hon. DSc: Newcastle, 1979; City, 1979; Northwestern, 1982; Hon. ScD East Anglia, 1983. *Publications:* Electron Microscopy of Thin Crystals (with others), 1965; (ed) The Physics of Metals, vol. 2, Defects, 1975; numerous contribs to learned jls. *Recreation:* walking. *Address:* Department of Metallurgy and Science of Materials, Parks Road, Oxford OX1 3PH. *T:* Oxford 59981; 104A Lonsdale Road, Oxford OX2 7ET.

HIRSHFIELD, family name of **Baron Hirshfield.**

HIRSHFIELD, Baron *cr* 1967, of Holborn in Greater London (Life Peer); **Desmond Barel Hirshfield;** chartered accountant, as Lord Hirshfield, Chartered Accountants; Chairman, Horwath & Horwath (UK) Ltd, 1967–86; International President, Horwath & Horwath International, 1984–86 (President, 1977–84); Founder and Director, Foundation on Automation and Human Development, since 1962; *b* 17 May 1913; *s* of late Leopold Hirshfield and Lily Hirshfield (*née* Blackford); *m* 1951, Bronia Eisen. *Educ:* City of London Sch. Chartered Accountant, 1939; Founder and Chm., Trades Union Unit Trust Managers Ltd, 1961–83; Chm., MLH Consultants, 1981–83. Mem., Cttee on Consumer Credit, 1968–71; Dep. Chm., Northampton New Town Develt Corp., 1968–76; Member: Central Adv. Water Cttee, 1969–70; Top Salaries Review Body, 1975–84; Admin. Trustee, Chevening Estate, 1970–81; Pres., Brit. Assoc. of Hotel Accountants, 1969–83; Treasurer: UK Cttee of UNICEF, 1969–83; Nat. Council for the Unmarried Mother and her Child, 1970–71. President: Norwood Charitable Trust, 1960–83; Norwood Foundn, 1977–83. Capt., British Team, World Maccabi Games, Prague, 1934. *Publications:* pamphlets and reports on The Accounts of Charitable Institutions; Avoidance and Evasion of Income Tax; Scheme for Pay as You Earn; Investment of Trade Union Funds; Organisations and Methods Reviews; articles in periodicals and newspapers. *Recreations:* travel, painting, caricaturing. *Address:* 8 Baker Street, W1M 1DA. *T:* 01-486 5888.

HIRST, Hon. Sir David (Cozens-Hardy), Kt 1982; **Hon. Mr Justice Hirst;** a Judge of the High Court, Queen's Bench Division, since 1982; *b* 31 July 1925; *er s* of late Thomas William Hirst and Margaret Joy Hirst, Aylsham, Norfolk; *m* 1951, Pamela Elizabeth Molesworth Bevan, *d* of Col T. P. M. Bevan, MC; three *s* two *d*. *Educ:* Eton (Fellow, 1976); Trinity Coll., Cambridge. MA. Served 1943–47; RA and Intelligence Corps, Capt. 1946. Barrister, Inner Temple, 1951, Bencher, 1974; QC 1965; Vice-Chm. of the Bar, 1977–78, Chm., 1978–79. Member: Lord Chancellor's Law Reform Cttee; Council on Tribunals, 1966–80; Cttee to review Defamation Act, 1952, 1971–74; Hon. Life Mem., Amer. Bar Assoc. *Recreations:* shooting, lawn tennis, theatre and opera, growing vegetables. *Address:* Royal Courts of Justice, Strand, WC2A 2LL. *Clubs:* Boodle's, MCC.

HIRST, David Michael Geoffrey, FBA 1983; Reader in the History of Art, University of London at the Courtauld Institute, since 1980; *b* 5 Sept. 1933; *s* of Walter Hirst; *m* 1st, 1960, Sara Vitali (marr. diss. 1970); one *s*; 2nd, 1972, Jane Martineau. (marr. diss. 1984); 3rd, 1984, Diane Zervas. *Educ:* Stowe Sch.; New Coll., Oxford; Courtauld Inst. of Art. Lectr, Courtauld Inst., 1962–80. Fellow at Villa I Tatti, 1969–70; Mem., Inst. for Advanced Study, Princeton, 1975. *Publications:* Sebastiano del Piombo, 1981; many contribs to British and continental periodicals. *Address:* 3 Queensdale Place, W11.

HIRST, Prof. John Malcolm, DSC 1945; PhD; FRS 1970; FIBiol; Consultant on plant pathology and international agriculture; Director, Long Ashton Research Station, and Professor of Agricultural and Horticultural Science, Bristol University, 1975–84, now Professor Emeritus; *b* 20 April 1921; *s* of Maurice Herbert Hirst and Olive Mary (*née* Pank); *m* 1957, Barbara Mary Stokes; two *d*. *Educ:* Solihull Sch.; Reading University (BSc Hons Agric. Bot., 1950); PhD London 1955. Royal Navy (Coastal Forces), 1941–46. Rothamsted Exper. Stn, Harpenden, 1950–75, Hd of Plant Pathology Dept, 1967–75. Vice-Chm. Tech. Adv. Cttee, Consultative Gp, Internat. Agricl Research, 1981–82; Chm., Scientific Adv. Bd, Twyford Plant Labs. Jakob Eriksson Gold Medal (Internat. Botanical Congress), 1959; Research Medal, RASE, 1970. *Publications:* papers in scientific jls mainly in Trans British Mycological Soc., Annals of Applied Biology, Jl of General Microbiology. *Address:* The Cottage, Butcombe, Bristol BS18 6XQ. *T:* Lulsgate 2880. *Club:* Farmers'.

HIRST, Michael William, LLB, CA; MP (C) Strathkelvin and Bearsden, since 1983; *b* 2 Jan. 1946; *s* of late John Melville Hirst and of Christina Binning Torrance or Hirst; *m* 1972, Naomi Ferguson Wilson; one *s* two *d*. *Educ:* Glasgow Acad., Glasgow; Univ. of Glasgow (LLB). CA 1970. Exchange Student, Univ. of Iceland, 1967; Partner, Peat, Marwick Mitchell & Co., 1978–83; Consultant, Peat Marwick UK, 1983–. Pres., Glasgow Univ. Conservative Club, 1967; National Vice-Chm., Scottish Young Conservatives, 1971–73; Chm., Scottish Conservative Candidates Assoc., 1978–81; Vice-Chm., Pty Organisation Cttee, 1985–. Contested: Central Dunbartonshire, Feb. and Oct. 1974; E Dunbartonshire, 1979. PPS to Parly Under-Secs of State, DoE, 1985–. Mem., Select Cttee on Scottish Affairs, 1983–. *Recreations:* golf, walking, gardening. *Address:* Enderley, Baldernock Road, Milngavie, Glasgow G62 8DU. *T:* 041-956 1213. *Clubs:* Carlton; The Western (Glasgow).

HIRST, Prof. Paul Heywood; Professor of Education, University of Cambridge, and Fellow of Wolfson College (formerly University College), Cambridge, since 1971; *b* 10 Nov. 1927; *s* of late Herbert and Winifred Hirst, Birkby, Huddersfield. *Educ:* Huddersfield Coll.; Trinity Coll., Cambridge. BA 1948, MA 1952, Certif. Educn 1952, Cantab; DipEd 1955, London; MA Oxon (by incorporation), Christ Church, Oxford, 1955. Asst Master, William Hulme's Grammar Sch., Manchester, 1948–50; Maths Master, Eastbourne Coll., 1950–55; Lectr and Tutor, Univ. of Oxford Dept of Educn, 1955–59; Lectr in Philosophy of Educn, Univ. of London Inst. of Educn, 1959–65; Prof. of Educn, King's Coll., Univ. of London, 1965–71. Visiting Professor: Univ. of British Columbia, 1964, 1967; Univ. of Malawi, 1969; Univ. of Puerto Rico, 1984. De Carle Lectr, Univ. of Otago, 1976; Fink Lectr, Univ. of Melbourne, 1976. Vice-Pres., Philosophy of Educn Soc. of GB; Member: UGC Educn Sub-Cttee, 1971–80; Educn Cttee, 1972–82, and Academic Policy Cttee, 1981–, CNAA; Swann Cttee of Inquiry into Educn of Children from Ethnic Minorities, 1981–85. Chm., Univs Council for Educn of Teachers, 1985–. *Publications:* (with R. S. Peters) The Logic of Education, 1970; (ed with R. F. Dearden and R. S. Peters) Education and the Development of Reason, 1971; Knowledge and the Curriculum, 1974; Moral Education in a Secular Society, 1974; (ed) Educational Theory and its Foundation Disciplines, 1984; papers in: Philosophical Analysis and Education (ed R. D. Archambault), 1965, The Study of Education (ed J. W. Tibble), 1965; The Concept of Education (ed R. S. Peters), 1966; Let's Teach Them Right (ed C. Macy), 1969; also in Brit. Jl Educnl Studies, Jl Curriculum Studies, Jl of Philosophy of Educn. *Recreation:* music, especially opera. *Address:* Department of Education, 17 Trumpington Street, Cambridge CB2 1PT. *T:* Cambridge 332882. *Club:* Athenæum.

HIRST, Prof. Rodney Julian, MA; Professor of Logic and Rhetoric, University of Glasgow, 1961–81; *b* 28 July 1920; *s* of Rev. William Hirst and Elsie Hirst; *m* 1942, Jessica, *y d* of Charles Alfred Podmore; two *d*. *Educ:* Leeds Grammar Sch.; Magdalen Coll., Oxford. Demy, 1938–47; 1st Cl. Hons Classical Mods, 1940. War Service, 1940–45, mainly as REME Officer (Radar) at home and in Italy. First Class Hons Lit. Hum., Dec. 1947. Lectr in Logic and Metaphysics, St Andrews Univ., 1948; Glasgow University: Lectr, 1949, and Sen. Lectr, 1959, in Logic; Dean of Arts, 1971–73; Senate Assessor on Univ. Court, 1973–78; Vice-Principal, 1976–79. *Publications:* Problems of Perception, 1959; (co-author) Human Senses and Perception, 1964; Perception and the External World, 1965; Philosophy: an outline for the intending student, 1968; contribs to Encyclopedia of Philosophy and philosophical journals. *Address:* 55 Montgomerie Street, Eaglesham, Glasgow G76 0AU. *T:* Eaglesham 3386.

HISCOCKS, Prof. Charles Richard, MA, DPhil; Professor of International Relations, University of Sussex, 1964–72, now Emeritus; *b* 1 June 1907; *y s* of F. W. Hiscocks; unmarried. *Educ:* Highgate Sch.; St Edmund Hall, Oxford; Berlin University. Asst Master, Trinity Coll. Sch., Port Hope, Ont, 1929–32; Bradfield Coll., 1936–39; Marlborough Coll., 1939–40. Served with Royal Marines, 1940–45, Lieut-Col; seconded to army for mil. govt duties in Germany, 1945; Brit. Council Rep. in Austria, 1946–49, S India, 1949–50; Prof. of Polit. Sci. and Internat. Relations, Univ. of Manitoba, 1950–64. UK Mem., UN Sub-Commn for Prevention of Discrimination and Protection of Minorities, 1953–62. Pres., Winnipeg Art Gall., 1959–60. Vis. Fellow, Princeton Univ., 1970–71; Fellow, Adlai Stevenson Inst. of Internat. Affairs, Chicago, 1971–72. Vice-Pres., UNA 1977–. *Publications:* The Rebirth of Austria, 1953; Democracy in Western Germany, 1957; Poland: Bridge for the Abyss?, 1963; Germany Revived, 1966; The Security Council: a study in adolescence, 1973. *Recreations:* music, art, gardening. *Address:* Dickers, Hunworth, Melton Constable, Norfolk. *T:* Holt 2503. *Club:* Garrick.

HISLOP, George Steedman, CBE 1976; PhD; FEng, FIMechE; FRSE; Director: Caledonian Airmotive, since 1978; Inveresk Research Foundation, since 1980; *b* 11 Feb. 1914; *s* of George Alexander Hislop and Marthesa Maria Hay; *m* 1942, Joan Daphne, *d* of William Beer and Gwendoline Fincken; two *s* one *d*. *Educ:* Clydebank High Sch.; Royal Technical Coll., Glasgow (ARTC); Cambridge Univ. (PhD). BScEng London. CEng, FIMechE 1949; FRAeS 1955; Fellowship of Engrg, 1976; FRSE 1976; FRSA 1959. A&AEE, RAF Boscombe Down, 1939–45; RAE, Farnborough, 1945–46; BEA, 1947–53; Chief Engr/Dir, Fairey Aviation Ltd, 1953–60; Westland Aircraft Ltd, 1960–: Technical Dir (Develt), 1962–66; Dep. Man. Dir, 1966–68; Man. Dir, 1968–72; Vice-Chm., 1972–76. Chm., CEI, 1979–80 (Vice-Chm., 1978–79); Mem., Airworthiness Requirements Bd, CAA, 1976–83 (Chm., 1982–83). Mem. Council, RAeS, 1960–83 (Pres., 1973–74; Hon. FRAeS, 1983); Vis. Prof., Univ. of Strathclyde, 1978–84. Hon. DSc Strathclyde, 1976. *Publications:* contrib. R & M series and RAeS Jl. *Recreations:* hill walking, photography, bird watching. *Address:* Hadley, St John's Hill, Old Coulsdon, Surrey CR3 1HD. *T:* 01-660 1008. *Clubs:* Royal Air Force, MCC.

HISS, Alger; Commercial printing since 1959 (manufacturing, 1957–59); *b* 11 Nov. 1904; *s* of Charles Alger Hiss and Mary L. Hughes; *m* 1929, Priscilla Fansler Hobson; one *s*. *Educ:* Johns Hopkins Univ. (AB 1926, Hon. LLD 1947); Harvard Univ. (LLB 1929). Sec. and law clerk to Supreme Court Justice Holmes, 1929–30; law practice, 1930–33; asst to gen. counsel and asst gen. counsel, Agricultural Adjustment Admin., 1933–35; legal asst, special Senate cttee investigating munitions industry, 1934–35; special attorney, US Dept of Justice, 1935–36; asst to Asst Sec. of State, 1936; asst to Adviser on Political Relations, 1939; special asst to Dir, Office of Far Eastern Affairs, 1944; special asst to Dir, Office of Special Political Affairs, May 1944; Dep. Dir, Nov. 1944, Dir, 1945; accompanied Pres. Roosevelt and Sec. of State Stettinius to Malta and Yalta Conferences, Feb. 1945; exec. sec., Dumbarton Oaks Conversations, Aug.–Oct. 1944; sec.-gen., United Nations Conference on International Organization, San Francisco, 1945; Principal Adviser to US Delegation, Gen. Assembly of United Nations, London, 1946; elected Pres. and Trustee of Carnegie Endowment for Internat. Peace, Dec. 1946 (Pres. until 1949). Mem., Massachusetts Bar. Mem., Alpha Delta Phi, Phi Beta Kappa. *Publications:* The Myth of Yalta, 1955; In the Court of Public Opinion, 1957, new edn 1972; Holmes-Laski Letters (abridged edn), 1963. *Recreations:* tennis, swimming, ornithology.

HITCH, Brian, CMG 1985; CVO 1980; HM Diplomatic Service; Minister, Tokyo, since 1984; *b* 2 June 1932; *m* 1954, Margaret Kathleen Wooller; two *d*. *Educ:* Wisbech Grammar Sch. (FRCO, LRAM); Magdalene Coll., Cambridge. Joined FO, 1955; 3rd/2nd Sec., Tokyo, 1955–61; FO, 1961–62; 2nd/1st Sec., Havana, 1962–64; 1st Sec., Athens, 1965–68; 1st Sec. and Head of Chancery, Tokyo, 1968–72; Asst Head, Southern European Dept, FCO, 1972–73; Dep. Head, later Head, Marine and Transport Dept, FCO, 1973–75; Counsellor, Bonn, 1975–77 and Algiers, 1977–80; Consul-Gen., Munich, 1980–84. *Recreation:* music. *Address:* c/o Foreign and Commonwealth Office, SW1; (home) 1 Mount Ararat Road, Richmond, Surrey TW10 6PQ. *T:* 01-940 4737. *Club:* United Oxford & Cambridge University.

HITCHCOCK, Dr Anthony John Michael; Head of Safety and Transportation Department, Transport and Road Research Laboratory, Department of Transport, since 1978; *b* 26 June 1929; *s* of Dr Ronald W. Hitchcock and Hilda (*née* Gould); *m* 1953, Audrey Ellen (*née* Ashworth); one *s* two *d*. *Educ:* Bedales; Manchester Grammar Sch.; Trinity Coll., Cambridge; Univ. of Chicago. PhD, BA; MInstP; MCIT. Asst, Univ. of Chicago, 1951–52; AEA, 1953–67; Head of Traffic Dept, TRRL, 1967–71, 1971–75; Head, Res. Policy (Transport) Div., DoE/DoT, 1975–78. Vis. Prof., Transport Studies, Cranfield Inst. of Technology, 1978–81. *Publications:* Nuclear Reactor Control, 1960; articles in learned jls. *Recreation:* bridge. *Address:* Seal Point, Comeragh Close, Golf Club Road, Woking, Surrey GU22 0LZ. *T:* Woking 5219.

HITCHCOCK, Prof. Edward Robert, ChM, FRCS; FRCSE; Professor of Neurosurgery, University of Birmingham, since 1978; *b* 10 Feb. 1929; *s* of Edwin Robert and Martha Hitchcock; *m* 1953, Jillian Trenowath; three *s* one *d*. *Educ:* Lichfield Grammar Sch.; Univ. of Birmingham (MB ChB; ChM 1952). FRCS 1959; FRCSE, *ad eundem*, 1971. Leader, Univ. of Birmingham Spitzbergen Expedn, 1951. Lecturer in Anatomy, Univ. of Birmingham, 1953; Captain, RAMC, 1954–56; Registrar: Dept of Traumatic Surgery,

General Hosp., Birmingham, 1956; Professorial Surgical Unit, University College Hosp., London, 1957–59; Fellow in Clinical Research, MRC, 1960; 1961–65: Ho. Surg./Registrar/Sen. Registrar, Dept of Neurological Surgery, Radcliffe Inf., Oxford, and Dept of Neurosurgery, Manchester Royal Inf.; Research Fellow, Univ. of Oxford; Sen. Lectr and Reader, Dept of Surgical Neurology, Univ. of Edinburgh, 1966–78. Examiner, RCSE, Pt 1 1971–, Pt II 1975–, RCSE, Surgical Neurology, 1977. Member: Soc. of British Neurol Surgeons; Bd, World Soc. Stereo and Functional Neurosurgery, 1981–; Bd, Europ. Soc. of Functional and Stereotactic Surg., 1975–; Internat. Assoc. for Study of Pain. Hon. Specialist in Neurosurgery, Brazilian Neurosurg. Soc.; Corresp. Member: Amer. Assoc. of Neurol Surgeons; Scandinavian Neurosurg. Soc. *Publications:* (ed) Advances in Stereotactic and Functional Neurosurgery; Initial Management of Head Injuries (Folia Traumatologica), 1971; Management of the Unconscious Patient, 1971; papers on pain, neuroprosthetics, stereotactic surgery and tumours, in various jls. *Recreations:* history, capology, hedging, fishing. *Address:* Cubbold House, Ombersley, near Droitwich, Worcs WR9 0HJ. *T:* Worcester 620606.

HITCHCOCK, Geoffrey Lionel Henry, CBE 1975 (OBE 1957); External Relations Consultant, Bell Educational Trust, Cambridge, 1977–81; *b* 10 Sept. 1915; *s* of late Major Frank B. Hitchcock, MC, and Mrs Mildred Hitchcock (*née* Sloane Stanley), Danbury, Essex; *m* 1950, Rosemary, *d* of Albert de Las Casas, Tiverton; two *s* one *d*. *Educ:* Oratory Sch., Caversham; Hertford Coll., Oxford (Exhibr, MA). British Council, April-Sept. 1939. Commnd London Rifle Bde, 1939; served with KAR in E Africa and SE Asia; Major 1943. Returned to British Council, 1946; served in London; Germany, 1950–54; Representative in Austria, 1954–59; Representative in Yugoslavia, 1962–67; Controller Home Div., British Council, 1970–73; Rep. of British Council in France and Cultural Counsellor, British Embassy, Paris, 1973–76. *Recreations:* race-going, gardening. *Address:* The Old Post, Shipton-under-Wychwood, Oxfordshire OX7 6BP. *T:* Shipton-under-Wychwood 831474. *Club:* Travellers'.

HITCHCOCK, Prof. Henry-Russell; Adjunct Professor, Institute of Fine Arts, University of New York, since 1969; *b* 3 June 1903; *s* of Henry R. Hitchcock and Alice Whitworth Davis. *Educ:* Middlesex Sch., Concord, Mass, USA; Harvard Univ. MA 1927. Asst Prof. of Art, Vassar Coll., 1927–28; Asst, Assoc., Prof., Wesleyan Univ., 1929–48; Lectr in Architecture, Massachusetts Institute of Technology, 1946–48; Prof. of Art, Smith Coll., Mass, 1948–68; Prof. of Art, Univ. of Massachusetts, 1968. Dir, Smith Coll. Museum of Art, 1949–55; Lectr, Inst. of Fine Arts, New York Univ., 1951–57; Lectr in Architecture, Yale Univ., 1951–52, 1959–60, 1970, Cambridge Univ., 1962, 1964. Fellow Amer. Acad. of Arts and Sciences. Hon. Corr. Mem. RIBA; Franklin Fellow, RSA; Pres., Soc. of Architectural Historians, 1952–54; Fellow, Pilgrim Soc.; Founder-Mem., Victorian Soc.; Pres., Victorian Soc. in America, 1969–74. Hon. FRIBA 1986. Hon. DFA New York Univ., 1969; Hon. DLitt Glasgow, 1973; Hon. DHL: Pennsylvania, 1976; Wesleyan, 1979. Award of Merit, AIA, 1978; Benjamin Franklin Award, RSA, 1979. *Publications:* Modern Architecture, 1929, 2nd edn, 1970; J. J. P. Oud, 1931; The International Style (with Philip Johnson), 1932 (2nd edn 1966); The Architecture of H. H. Richardson, 1936 (3rd edn 1966); Modern Architecture in England (with others), 1937; Rhode Island Architecture, 1939 (2nd edn 1968); In the Nature of Materials, the Buildings of Frank Lloyd Wright, 1942 (2nd edn 1973); American Architectural Books, 1946; Painting towards Architecture, 1948; Early Victorian Architecture in Britain, 1954, 2nd edn 1972; Latin American Architecture since 1945, 1955; Architecture: Nineteenth and Twentieth Centuries, 1958 (4th edn 1977); German Rococo: The Brothers Zimmermann, 1968; Rococo Architecture in Southern Germany, 1968; (with William Seale) Temples of Democracy, 1977; Netherlandish Scrolled Gables of the 16th and early 17th Centuries, 1978; German Renaissance Architecture, 1981; *relevant publication:* In Search of Modern Architecture: a tribute to Henry-Russell Hitchcock (ed Helen Searing), 1982. *Address:* 152 E 62nd Street, New York, NY 10021, USA. *T:* 758–6554.

HITCHEN, Rt. Rev. Anthony; Titular Bishop of Othona and an Auxiliary Bishop of Liverpool, (RC), since 1979; *b* 23 May 1930. *Educ:* St Cuthbert's College, Ushaw. Priest, 1955; Administrator of St Mary's, Liverpool, 1969. *Address:* 55 Victoria Road, Freshfield, Liverpool L37 1LN.

HITCHEN, John David; a Recorder of the Crown Court, since 1978; *b* 18 July 1935; *s* of late Harold Samuel and Frances Mary Hitchen; *m* 1966, Pamela Ann Cellan-Jones. *Educ:* Woodhouse Grove Sch., nr Bradford; Pembroke Coll., Oxford (BA(Hons)). Called to Bar, Lincoln's Inn, 1961. *Recreations:* music, reading. *Address:* 39 Rutland Drive, Harrogate, Yorks. *T:* Harrogate 66236.

HITCHENS, Rear Adm. Gilbert Archibald Ford; Director General Ship Refitting, Ministry of Defence, since 1985; *b* 11 April 1932; *m* 1960, Patricia Hamilton; one *s* one *d*. BA (Open Univ.). Joined Royal Navy, 1950; Commander, 1968; Guided Weapons Staff Officer, Min. of Technology, 1968–70; Exec. Officer, RNEC, 1970–72; Senior Officer while building and Weapon Engineer Officer, HMS Sheffield, 1973–75; MoD (Navy), 1975–77; Naval Attaché, Tokyo and Seoul, 1977–79; Asst Dir, Manpower Requirements, MoD (Navy), 1979–80; Dir, Officers' Appts (Eng.), 1980–82; Captain, HMS Defiance, 1982–84; CSO Engrg to C-in-C Fleet, 1984–85. *Recreations:* any activity in the high hills (Pres., RN Ski Association).

HITCHIN, Prof. Aylwin Drakeford, CBE 1970; Boyd Professor of Dental Surgery, Director of Dental Studies, University of Dundee (formerly University of St Andrews), 1947–77 and Dean of Dundee Dental Hospital, 1947–73; Dental Consultant, Dundee Royal Infirmary, 1947–77; Civil Consultant Dental Surgeon to Royal Navy, 1957–77; *b* 31 Dec. 1907; *s* of Alfred Leonard Hitchin, FRPS, and Ruth Drakeford; *m* 1942, Alice Stella Michie; one *s* one *d*. *Educ:* Rutherford College, Newcastle upon Tyne; Durham University Coll. of Medicine. LDS (Dunelm) 1931, BDS 1932, MDS 1935; DDSc 1957; FDSRCS Edinburgh 1951; FFDRCS Ire 1964; FDSRCPS Glasgow 1967. Asst Hon. Dental Surgeon and Demonstrator of Dental Surgery, Newcastle upon Tyne Dental Hosp., 1932–36; Private Dental Practice, Newcastle upon Tyne, 1932–46 (except for 6 yrs with AD Corps during War of 1939–45); Dental Surgical Specialist, Scottish Command, 1943–45, with rank of Major. Chairman: Dental Educn Advisory Council, 1951–52; Dental Hosp. Assoc., 1959–60; Chm., Dental Cttee, Scot. Post-Grad. Med. Council, 1969–79; Member: Dental Cttee of MRC, 1966–72; Advisory Cttee on Medical Research (Scotland), 1967–71; Dental Adv. Cttee, Scottish Health Services Council, 1952–57, 1968–74; Convener, Dental Council, RCSE, 1971–74; Jt Cttee on Higher Training in Dentistry, 1969–74; East Scotland Regional Hosp. Bd, 1948–52; Dental Sub Cttee, UGC, 1969–73; Nominated Mem., Gen. Dent. Council, 1956–74; External Examiner Dental Subjects, Universities, Durham, Edinburgh, Queen's, Belfast, Dublin, Manchester, Liverpool, Birmingham, Leeds, Newcastle, Bristol, Wales, RCS in Ireland; Examiner, LDS, FDSRCS Edinburgh, FFDRCS Ire, and FDSRCPS Glasgow. William Guy Meml Lectr, RCSE, 1972; Founders and Benefactors Lectr, Univ. of Newcastle upon Tyne Dental Sch., 1973. President: Oral Surgery Club, 1956–57; Christian Dental Fellowship, 1966–69; Brit. Soc. Dental Radiology, 1961–63; Royal Odonto-Chir. Soc. of Scotland, 1969–70; Pres., Inter-Varsity Fellowship, 1966–67; Foundation Fellow of the British Assoc. of Oral Surgeons; Hon. Mem., Swedish Dental Soc. Dr Odont (*hc*) Lund, 1977; Hon. FDSRCPS Glasgow, 1979. *Publications:* contribs to dental periodical literature. *Address:* Coniston, Prieston Road, Bridge of Weir, Renfrewshire PA11 3AJ.

HITCHING, Alan Norman; barrister; a Recorder, since 1985; *b* 5 Jan. 1941; *s* of Norman Henry Samuel Hitching and Grace Ellen Hitching; *m* 1967, Hilda Muriel (*née* King); one *d* two *s*. *Educ:* Forest Sch., Snaresbrook; Christ Church, Oxford (BA 1962; Radcliffe Exhibnr and Dixon Scholar, 1962; BCL 1963; MA). Harmsworth Entrance Scholar, Middle Temple, 1960; Astbury Scholar and Safford Prize, Middle Temple, 1964; called to the Bar, Middle Temple, 1964. Second Prosecuting Counsel to Inland Revenue, SE Circuit, 1974, First Prosecuting Counsel, 1975. Chm., John Grooms Assoc. for the Disabled, 1981–. *Address:* 9 Monkhams Drive, Woodford Green, Essex IG8 0LG. *T:* 01–504 4260.

HIVES, family name of **Baron Hives.**

HIVES, 2nd Baron, *cr* 1950, of Duffield; **John Warwick Hives;** *b* 26 Nov. 1913; *s* of 1st Baron Hives and of Gertrude Ethel (*d* 1961), *d* of John Warwick; *S* father, 1965; *m* 1st, 1937, Olwen Protheroe Llewellin (*d* 1972); no *c*; 2nd, 1972, Gladys Mary Seals. *Educ:* Manor School, Mickleover, Derby. *Recreation:* shooting. *Heir: nephew* Matthew Peter Hives, *b* 25 May 1971. *Address:* Bendalls, Milton, Derby. *T:* Burton on Trent 703319. *Club:* Farmers'.

HO, Eric Peter, CBE 1981; Secretary for Trade and Industry, Hong Kong, since 1983; *b* 30 Dec. 1927; *s* of Sai-Ki Ho and Doris (*née* Lo); *m* 1956, Grace Irene, *d* of Mr and Mrs A. V. Young; two *s* one *d*. *Educ:* Univ. of Hong Kong (BA 1950). Inspector of Taxes (under training), London, 1950–53; Hong Kong Civil Service, 1954–: Inland Revenue, 1954–57; Admin. Service, 1957–; Sec. for Social Security, 1977–83. Overseas Service Course B, Cambridge Univ., 1961–62; RCDS, London, 1976. *Recreations:* swimming, lawn tennis. *Address:* 7 Wiltshire Road, Kowloon Tong, Hong Kong. *T:* 3–363567.

HOAD, Air Vice-Marshal Norman Edward, CVO 1972; CBE 1969; AFC 1951 and Bar, 1956; artist; *b* 28 July 1923; *s* of Hubert Ronald Hoad and Florence Marie (*née* Johnson); two *s*. *Educ:* Brighton. Joined RAF, 1941, pilot trng, S Rhodesia; Lancaster pilot until shot down and taken prisoner in Germany, 1944; various flying and instructional duties, 1945–51; Sqdn Ldr 1951; OC No 192 Sqdn, 1953–55; psc 1956; Wing Comdr, HQ 2 ATAF, 1957–59; pfc 1960; OC No 216 Sqdn, 1960–62; jssc 1963; Gp Capt., MoD, 1963–65; idc 1966; Stn Comdr: RAF Lyneham, 1967, RAF Abingdon, 1968; Defence and Air Attaché, British Embassy, Paris, 1969–72; Dir, Defence Policy (A), 1972–74; Chief of Staff, 46 Gp, RAF Strike Comd, April-Oct. 1974; AOC No 46 Group, and Comdr, UK Jt Airborne Task Force, 1974–75; Senior RAF Mem., RCDS, 1976–78. Director, Air League, 1978–82. Founder Mem., Guild of Aviation Artists; Chm., Soc. of Equestrian Artists. MBIM 1970. *Address:* Little Meadow, Stowupland, Stowmarket, Suffolk. *Club:* Royal Air Force.

HOARE, Prof. Charles Antony Richard, FRS 1982; Professor of Computation, Oxford University, since 1977; Fellow of Wolfson College, since 1977; Director, Oxford University Computing Laboratory, 1982–July 1987; *b* 11 Jan. 1934; *s* of Henry S. M. Hoare and Marjorie F. Hoare; *m* 1962, Jill Pym; one *s* one *d* (and one *s* decd). *Educ:* King's Sch., Canterbury; Merton Coll., Oxford (MA, Cert. Stats). Computer Div., Elliott Brothers, London, Ltd, 1959–68: successively Programmer, Chief Engr, Tech. Man., Chief Scientist; National Computer Centre, 1968; Prof. of Computer Science, QUB, 1968–77. Dist. FBCS 1978; Hon. DSc: Southern California, 1979; Warwick, 1985. A. M. Turing Award, Assoc. Comp. Mach., 1980; Harry Goode Meml Award, Amer. Fedn of Inf. Processing Socs, 1981; Faraday Medal, IEE, 1985. *Publications:* Structured Programming (with O.-J. Dahl and E. W. Dijkstra), 1972; Communicating Sequential Processes, 1985; articles in Computer Jl, Commun. ACM, and Acta Informatica. *Recreations:* walking, swimming, reading, listening to music. *Address:* 8–11 Keble Road, Oxford OX1 3QD. *T:* Oxford 54141 ext. 286.

HOARE, Rear-Adm. Desmond John, CB 1962; Vice President, United World Colleges, since 1969; *b* 25 June 1910; *s* of Capt. R. R. Hoare, OBE, Royal Navy; *m* 1941, Naomi Mary Gilbert Scott; one *s* two *d*. *Educ:* Wimbledon Coll.; King's Sch., Rochester. Joined RN, 1929; Engineering training, RNEC Keyham, 1930–33; Advanced engineering course, RNC Greenwich, 1934–36; HMS Exeter, 1936–39; Admiralty, 1939–41; HMS King George V, 1942–44; Admiralty, 1945–48; HMS Vanguard, 1949–51; HMS Condor (apprentice training), 1951–53; idc, 1955; Admiralty, 1956–59; Chief Staff Officer Technical to C-in-C Plymouth, 1960–62; retired, 1962. Headmaster, Atlantic Coll., 1962–69. *Recreations:* sailing, power boats. *Address:* Bally Island House, Skibbereen, Cork, Ireland.

HOARE, Sir Frederick (Alfred), 1st Bt, *cr* 1962; Kt 1958; Managing Partner of C. Hoare & Co., Bankers, of 37 Fleet Street, since 1947; Director: Messrs Hoare Trustees, since 1947; Mitre Court Securities Ltd, since 1963; Mitre Court Property Holding Co., since 1980; Grimersta Estate Ltd, since 1969; Tuscan Development Co., since 1972; Hoare's Bank Nominees Ltd, since 1936; *b* 11 Feb. 1913; *s* of late Frederick Henry Hoare, 37 Fleet Street, EC4; *m* 1st, 1939, Norah Mary, OBE (*d* 1973), *d* of A. J. Wheeler; two *d*; 2nd, 1974, Oonah Alice Dew (*d* 1980), *d* of late Brig.-Gen. David Ramsay Sladen, CMG, DSO, and Isabel Sladen (*née* Blakiston-Houston); 3rd, 1984, Sarah Lindsay Bamber (marr. diss. 1986), *widow* of James Henry Bamber and *d* of late Robert Irwin Herald, Glengyle, Belfast. *Educ:* Wellington Coll. Clerk to C. Hoare & Co., 1931; Bankers' Agent, 1936, Managing Partner 1947. Chm., General Practice Finance Corp., 1966–73; Deputy Chairman: Nat. Mutual Life Assurance Soc., 1969–72; St George Assurance Co. Ltd, 1969–73; Dir, TR Property Investment Trust plc, 1972–83. Common Councilman City of London, 1948; Alderman for Ward of Farringdon Without, 1950–71; Sheriff, City of London, 1956; Lord Mayor of London, 1961–62. Formerly one of HM Lieutenants for City of London; former Governor: Christ's Hosp.; Royal Bridewell Hosp.; Past Chm., St Bride's Institute; Mem., Court of Assistants and Prime Warden of Goldsmiths' Company, 1966–67; Liveryman, Spectacle Makers' Company, 1948–; Mem. Court, City Univ., 1974–. Pres., British Chess Federation, 1964–67; Past President: London Primary Schs Chess Assoc.; Cosmopolitan Banks Chess Assoc.; Upward Bound Young People's Gliding and Adventure Trust; Vice-Pres., Toc H. Trustee: Lady Hoare Thalidomide Appeal; Historic Churches Preservation Trust; Vice-Pres., Anglers' Co-operative Assoc. (Chm., 1977–82); Chm., John Eastwood Water Protection Trust Ltd, 1977–82; Member: Nat. Coun. for Voluntary Organisations; Nat. Council, Noise Abatement Soc.; Chm., Family Welfare Assoc., 1961–68; Vice-Pres., British Rheumatism and Arthritis Assoc., 1979–. Past Grand Deacon, United Grand Lodge of England. KStJ. Knight of Liberian Humane Order of African Redemption, 1962; Grand Officier de L'Ordre National de la République de Côte d'Ivoire, 1962. *Recreations:* chess, fishing, ornithology, photography, philately. *Heir:* none. *Address:* 34 Cadogan Square, SW1X 0JL. *Clubs:* Garrick, City Livery, Flyfishers', Pepys.

HOARE, John Michael; Regional General Manager, Wessex Regional Health Authority, since 1984 (Administrator, 1974–84); *b* 23 Oct. 1932; *s* of Leslie Frank Hoare and Gladys Hoare; *m* 1963, Brita Hjalte; one *s* one *d*. *Educ:* Raynes Park; Christ's Coll., Cambridge

(BA). Asst Sec., United Bristol Hosps, 1961; House Governor, St Stephen's Hosp., 1963; Asst Clerk, St Thomas' Hosp., 1965; Administrator, Northwick Park Hosp., 1967. Mem., Defence Medical Services Inquiry, 1971–73. *Recreations:* reading, walking, music, squash. *Address:* 24 Clausentum Road, Winchester, Hants SO23 9QE. *T:* Winchester 54192.

HOARE, Hon. Marcus Bertram, CMG 1965; Justice of Supreme Court of Queensland, 1966–80; *b* 3 March 1910; *s* of John George and Emma Hoare; *m* 1936, Eileen Parker; four *s*. *Educ:* Brisbane Grammar Sch. Solicitor, 1933; Barrister-at-Law, 1944; QC (Australia) 1960. *Address:* 97 Chelmer Street West, Chelmer, Brisbane, Qld 4068, Australia. *T:* 379–4181. *Club:* Johnsonian (Brisbane).

HOARE, Sir Peter Richard David, 8th Bt *cr* 1786; *b* 22 March 1932; *s* of Sir Peter William Hoare, 7th Bt, and of Laura Ray, *o d* of Sir John Esplen, 1st Bt, KBE; *S* father, 1973; *m* 1st, 1961, Jane (marr. diss. 1967), *o d* of Daniel Orme; 2nd, 1978, Katrin Alexa, Lady Hodson (marr. diss. 1982), *o d* of late Edwin Bernstiel; 3rd, 1983, Angela Francesca de la Sierra, *d* of Fidel Fernando Ayarza. *Educ:* Eton. *Recreations:* travelling, shooting, skiing. *Heir:* *b* David John Hoare [*b* 8 Oct. 1935; *m* 1st, 1965, Mary Vanessa (marr. diss. 1978), *y d* of Peter Gordon Cardew; one *s*; 2nd, 1984, Virginia Victoria Graham Labes, *d* of Michael Menzies]. *Address:* c/o Crèdit Andorrà, Andorra la Vella, Principality of Andorra. *Club:* Royal Automobile.

HOARE, Rev. Dr Rupert William Noel; Principal of Westcott House, Cambridge, since 1981; *b* 3 March 1940; *s* of Julian Hoare and Edith Hoare (*née* Temple); *m* 1965, Gesine (*née* Pflüger); three *s* one *d*. *Educ:* Rugby School; Trinity Coll., Oxford (BA 1961, MA 1967); Westcott House and Fitzwilliam House, Cambridge (BA 1964); Birmingham Univ. (PhD 1973). Deacon 1964, priest 1965, Dio. Manchester; Curate of St Mary, Oldham, 1964–67; Lecturer, Queen's Theological Coll., Birmingham, 1968–72; Rector, Parish of the Resurrection, Manchester, 1972–78; Residentiary Canon, Birmingham Cathedral, 1978–81. Canon Theologian of Coventry Cathedral, 1970–75. *Publications:* (trans. jtly) Bultmann's St John, 1971; (contrib.) Queen's Sermons, 1973, Queen's Essays, 1980; articles in Theology. *Recreations:* hill walking, sailing, gardening, listening to music. *Address:* Westcott House, Jesus Lane, Cambridge.

HOARE, Sir Timothy Edward Charles, 8th Bt *cr* 1784; Director: Career Plan Ltd; New Metals and Chemicals Ltd; *b* 11 Nov. 1934; *s* of Sir Edward O'Bryen Hoare, 7th Bt and of Nina Mary, *d* of late Charles Nugent Hope-Wallace, MBE; *S* father, 1969; *m* 1969, Felicity Anne, *o d* of Peter Boddington; one *s* twin *d*. *Educ:* Radley College; Worcester College, Oxford (BA Modern Hist.; MA); Birkbeck Coll., London (MA Manpower Studies). Mem., Gen. Synod of Church of England, 1970–. *Heir:* *s* Charles James Hoare, *b* 15 March 1971. *Address:* 10 Belitha Villas, N1.

HOBAN, Brian Michael Stanislaus; Head Master of Harrow, 1971–81; a part-time Chairman, Civil Service Executive Officer Selection Boards, since 1984; *b* 7 Oct. 1921; 2nd *s* of late Capt. R. A. Hoban; *m* 1947, Jasmine, 2nd *d* of J. C. Holmes, MC, Charterhouse, Godalming; one *s* one *d* (and one *d* decd). *Educ:* Charterhouse (Scholar); University Coll., Oxford (Sch.). 2nd Cl. Hon. Mods, 1947; 2nd Cl. Lit. Hum., 1949; BA 1949, MA 1957. Served War of 1939–45: Capt., Westminster Dragoons; NW Europe, 1944–45 (despatches); demobilised, Nov. 1945. Capt. Northants Yeomanry, TA, 1950–56. Asst Master: Uppingham Sch., 1949–52; Shrewsbury Sch., 1952–59; Headmaster, St Edmund's Sch., Canterbury, 1960–64; Head Master, Bradfield Coll., 1964–71. Hon. Associate Mem., HMC, 1981– (Hon. Treasurer, 1975–80). Governor, Wellington Coll., 1981–. JP Berks, 1967–71. *Publication:* (with Donald Swann) Jesu Parvule, 1965. *Recreations:* music, golf, walking, gardening. *Address:* Upcot, Wantage Road, Streatley, Berks RG8 9LD. *T:* Goring-on-Thames 873419. *Clubs:* East India, Devonshire, Sports and Public Schools; Vincent's (Oxford).

HOBAN, Russell Conwell; full-time writer, since 1967 (with some interruptions); *b* 4 Feb. 1925; *s* of Abram Hoban and Jenny Dimmerman; *m* 1st, 1944, Lillian Aberman (marr. diss. 1975); one *s* three *d*; 2nd, 1975, Gundula Ahl; three *s*. *Educ:* Lansdale High Sch.; Philadelphia Museum Sch. of Industrial Art. Served US Army, 1943–45: 339th Inf., 85th Div., Italy (Bronze Star Medal, 1945). Various jobs, 1945–56; free-lance illustration, 1956–65; copywriter with Doyle, Dane, Bernbach, New York, 1965–67; resident in London, 1969–. Drama: (television), Come and Find Me, 1980; The Carrier Frequency, 1984. *Publications: children's books:* What Does It Do and How Does It Work?, 1959; The Atomic Submarine, 1960; Bedtime for Frances, 1960; Herman the Loser, 1961; The Song in My Drum, 1962; London Men and English Men, 1963; Some Snow Said Hello, 1963; A Baby Sister for Frances, 1964; Nothing To Do, 1964; Bread and Jam for Frances, 1964; The Sorely Trying Day, 1964; Tom and the Two Handles, 1965; The Story of Hester Mouse, 1965; What Happened When Jack and Daisy Tried To Fool the Tooth Fairies, 1965; Goodnight, 1966; Henry and the Monstrous Din, 1966; Charlie the Tramp, 1966; The Little Brute Family, 1966; Save My Place, 1967; The Mouse and His Child, 1967; The Pedalling Man and Other Poems, 1968; The Stone Doll of Sister Brute, 1968; A Birthday for Frances, 1968; Ugly Bird, 1969; Best Friends for Frances, 1969; Harvey's Hideout, 1969; The Mole Family's Christmas, 1969; A Bargain for Frances, 1970; Emmet Otter's Jug-Band Christmas, 1971; Egg Thoughts and Other Frances Songs, 1972; The Sea-Thing Child, 1972; Letitia Rabbit's String Song, 1973; How Tom Beat Captain Najork and His Hired Sportsmen, 1974 (Whitbread Literary Award); Ten What?, 1974; Dinner at Alberta's, 1975; Crocodile and Pierrot, 1975; A Near Thing for Captain Najork, 1975; The Twenty-Elephant Restaurant, 1977; Arthur's New Power, 1978; The Dancing Tigers, 1979; La Corona and Other Tin Tales, 1979; Ace Dragon Ltd, 1980; Flat Cat, 1980; The Serpent Tower, 1981; The Great Fruit Gum Robbery, 1981; They Came from Aargh!, 1981; The Flight of Bembel Rudzuk, 1982; The Battle of Zormla, 1982; Jim Frog, 1983; Big John Turkle, 1983; Charlie Meadows, 1984; Lavinia Bat, 1984; The Rain Door, 1986; The Marzipan Pig, 1986; *novels:* The Lion of Boaz-Jachin and Jachin-Boaz, 1973; Kleinzeit, 1974; Turtle Diary, 1975 (filmed, 1985); Riddley Walker, 1980 (John W. Campbell Meml Award, 1981, Best Internat. Fiction, Aust. Sci. Fiction Achievement Award, 1983; adapted for stage, 1986); Pilgermann, 1983; articles and essays in books and magazines. *Recreations:* stones, short wave listening. *Address:* David Higham Associates Ltd, 5–8 Lower John Street, Golden Square, W1R 4HA. *T:* 01–437 7888.

HOBART, Archbishop of, (RC), since 1955; **Most Rev. Sir Guilford Young,** KBE 1978; DD (Rome); *b* Sandgate, Queensland, 10 Nov. 1916. Ordained, Rome, 1939; Auxiliary Bishop of Canberra and Goulburn, 1948; Co-Adjutor Archbishop of Hobart, 1954; succeeded to See of Hobart, Sept. 1955. *Address:* Archbishop's House, 31 Fisher Avenue, Sandy Bay, Hobart, Tasmania 7005, Australia; GPO Box 62a, Hobart, Tas 7001, Australia.

HOBART, Maj.-Gen. Patrick Robert Chamier, CB 1970; DSO 1945; OBE 1944; MC 1943; *b* 14 Nov. 1917; *s* of Robert Charles Arthur Stanley Hobart and Elsie Hinds. *Educ:* Charterhouse; Royal Military Academy Woolwich; 2nd Lieut, Royal Tank Corps, 1937; served in war of 1939–45 (despatches 4 times); France, Western Desert, Tunisia, Italy, with 2nd Royal Tank Regt, BM 9th Armd Bde, GSO2 30 Corps, GSO1 7th Armd Div; NW Europe, GSO1 Guards Armd Div. and CO 1st RTR; CO 2nd RTR, BAOR and N Africa, 1958–60; Comdr, 20th Armoured Brigade, BAOR, 1961–63; Chief of Staff, 1 (British) Corps, BAOR, 1964–66; Dir Military Operations, MoD, 1966–68; Chief of Staff Army Strategic Command, 1968–70; Dir, RAC, 1970–72; retired; Lieut-Governor, Royal Hosp., Chelsea, 1973–78. Col Comdt, Royal Tank Regt, 1968–78, Representative Col Comdt, 1971–74. ADC to the Queen, 1961–66. *Address:* c/o Royal Bank of Scotland, Kirkland House, Whitehall, SW1.

HOBART, Lt-Comdr Sir Robert (Hampden), 3rd Bt *cr* 1914; RN; *b* 7 May 1915; *o s* of Sir (Claud) Vere Cavendish Hobart, 2nd Bt, DSO, OBE and Violet Verve, MBE (*d* 1935), 2nd *d* of late John Wylie; *heir-pres.* to 10th Earl of Buckinghamshire; *S* father 1949; *m* 1st, 1942, Sylvia (*d* 1965), *d* of H. Argo, Durban, Natal; three *s* one *d*; 2nd, 1975, Caroline Fleur, *d* of Colonel H. M. Vatcher, MC, and *widow* of 11th Duke of Leeds. *Educ:* Wixenford; RN Coll., Dartmouth. Sub-Lieut, RN, 1935; Lieut-Comdr, 1945; served War of 1939–45 (wounded, two medals, four stars); retired, 1950. Contested (Nat Lib) Hillsborough Div. of Sheffield, 1945, (C and L) Itchen Div. of Southampton, 1950. *Heir:* *s* John Vere Hobart [*b* 9 April 1945; *m* 1982, Kate Iddles; one *s*]. *Address:* Gatcombe Park, Newport, Isle of Wight. *Clubs:* Travellers', Royal London Yacht; Royal Yacht Squadron; Royal Southern Yacht, Bembridge Sailing.

HOBART-HAMPDEN, family name of **Earl of Buckinghamshire.**

HOBBS, Herbert Harry, CB 1956; CVO 1972; Director, Ancient Monuments and Historic Buildings, 1970–72, retired; *b* 7 Nov. 1912; *s* of late Bertie Hobbs and Agnes Dora (*née* Clarke); *m* 1937, Joan Hazel Timmins (*d* 1979); two *s* one *d*. *Educ:* Bedford Sch.; Corpus Christi Coll., Oxford. Entered War Office, 1935; Comptroller of Lands and Claims, 1956–60; Asst Under-Sec. of State (Works), War Office, 1960–63; Under-Sec., MPBW, later DoE, 1963–72. Medal of Freedom with bronze palm (USA), 1946. *Recreations:* music, gardening. *Address:* 9 Hemp Garden, Minehead, Som.

HOBBS, John Charles; Chief Insurance Officer, Department of Health and Social Security, 1971–76; *b* 28 May 1917; British; *m* 1961, Doris Gronow. *Educ:* Portsmouth Southern Grammar Sch.; Portsmouth Coll. of Technology. 1st cl. hons BSc, 1936; 1st cl. hons BSc (Spec.) Maths, 1944. FIS 1950. Asst Principal, 1946; Principal, 1947; Asst Sec., 1957. *Recreations:* pianoforte, guitar, marquetry.

HOBBS, Ven. Keith; Archdeacon of Chichester, since 1981; *b* 3 March 1925; *s* of late Percival Frank and Gwennyth Mary Hobbs; *m* 1950, Mary, *d* of late Louis Lingg and Mary Elizabeth Ruderman; one *s* one *d*. *Educ:* St Olave's Grammar School; Exeter Coll., Oxford (MA); Wells Theological Coll. Instr Branch, RN, 1946; retired (Lt Comdr), 1956. Curate, Clewer St Stephen, 1958–60; Soho, 1960–62; St Stephen, S Kensington, 1962–78; Lectr and Co-ordinator of Counselling, Borough Road Coll., 1964–77; Actg Gen. Secretary, Church Union, 1977–78; Chaplain to Bishop of Chichester, 1978–81. *Address:* 4 Canon Lane, Chichester, W Sussex PO19 1PX. *T:* Chichester 784260.

HOBBS, Maj.-Gen. Michael Frederick, CBE 1982 (OBE 1979, MBE 1975); Commander, 4th Armoured Division, since 1985; *b* 28 Feb. 1937; *s* of late Brig. Godfrey Pennington Hobbs and Elizabeth Constance Mary Hobbs; *m* 1967, Tessa Mary Churchill; one *s* two *d*. *Educ:* Eton College. Served Grenadier Guards, 1956–80; Directing Staff, Staff Coll., 1974–77; MoD, 1980–82; Commander 39 Inf. Bde, 1982–84; Dir of PR (Army), 1984–85. *Recreations:* field sports, horticulture. *Clubs:* Army and Navy, MCC.

HOBDAY, Sir Gordon (Ivan), Kt 1979; Lord Lieutenant and Keeper of the Rolls for Nottinghamshire, since 1983; Chancellor, Nottingham University since 1979 (President of the Council, 1973–82); *b* 1 Feb. 1916; *s* of late Alexander Thomas Hobday and Frances Cassandra (*née* Meads); *m* 1940, Margaret Jean Joule; one *d*. *Educ:* Long Eaton Grammar Sch.; UC Nottingham. BSc, PhD London; FRSC. Joined Boots Co., 1939; Dir of Research, 1952–68; Man. Dir, 1970–72; Chm., 1973–81; Chm., Central Independent Television, 1981–85; Dir, Lloyds Bank, 1981–86. A Dep. Chm., Price Commn, 1977–78. DL Notts, 1981. KStJ 1983. Hon. LLD Nottingham, 1977. *Recreations:* handicrafts, gardening. *Address:* University of Nottingham, University Park, Nottingham NG7 2RD. *T:* Nottingham 56101. *Club:* Athenæum.

HOBDEN, Dennis Harry; *b* 21 Jan. 1920; *s* of Charles Hobden and Agnes Hobden (*née* Smith); *m* 1st, 1950, Kathleen Mary Hobden (*née* Holman) (marr. diss. 1970); two *s* two *d*; 2nd, 1977, Sheila Hobden, JP (*née* Tugwell). *Educ:* elementary sch. Entered GPO, 1934; retired 1982. Served as Air Crew, RAF, 1941–46 (Flt Lieut). MP (Lab) Kemptown Div. of Brighton, 1964–70. Member: Brighton Town Council, 1956–, Mayor of Brighton, 1979–80; E Sussex CC, 1973–85. *Recreations:* politics, gardening, music, reading, Spiritualism. *Address:* 3 Queens Park Terrace, Brighton, East Sussex BN2 2YA.

HOBDEN, Reginald Herbert, DFC 1944; HM Diplomatic Service, retired; *b* 9 Nov. 1919; *s* of William Richard and Ada Emily Hobden; *m* 1945, Gwendoline Ilma Vowles; two *s* one *d*. *Educ:* Sir William Borlase's Sch., Marlow. Apptd Colonial Office, Dec. 1936. Served War of 1939–45 (despatches, DFC): RAFVR, Sept. 1940–Jan. 1946 (Sqdn Ldr). Returned to Colonial Office, 1946; seconded to Dept of Technical Co-operation, 1961; First Sec., UK Commn, Malta, 1962–64; HM Diplomatic Service, Nov. 1964: CRO until April 1968; Head of British Interests Section, Canadian High Commn, Dar es Salaam, April 1968; British Acting High Comr, Dar es Salaam, July-Oct. 1968, and Counsellor, Dar es Salaam, Oct. 1968–69; Counsellor (Economic and Commercial), Islamabad, 1970–75; Inst. of Develt Studies, Sussex Univ., 1975; High Comr, Lesotho, 1976–78. Clerk in Clerk's Dept, House of Commons, 1978–84. *Recreations:* chess, bridge. *Address:* 14 Belmont Close, Uxbridge, Mddx. *T:* Uxbridge 34754.

HOBHOUSE, Sir Charles Chisholm, 6th Bt, *cr* 1812; TD; *b* 7 Dec. 1906; *s* of Sir Reginald A. Hobhouse, 5th Bt and Marjorie Chisholm Spencer (*d* 1967); *S* father, 1947; *m* 1st, 1946, Mary (*d* 1955), *widow* of Walter Horrocks, Salkeld Hall, Penrith; no *c*; 2nd, 1959, Elspeth Jean, *d* of T. G. Spinney, Mazagan, Morocco; one *s*. *Educ:* Eton. Commissioned North Somerset Yeomanry, 1926; Major 1940; Hon. Col 1966. *Recreations:* hunting, shooting. *Heir:* *s* Charles John Spinney Hobhouse, *b* 27 Oct. 1962. *Address:* The Manor, Monkton Farleigh, Bradford-on-Avon, Wilts. *T:* Bath 858558. *Clubs:* Brooks's, City of London.

HOBHOUSE, Hermione; *see* Hobhouse, M. H.

HOBHOUSE, (Mary) Hermione, MBE 1981; FSA; writer and conservationist; Editor, Survey of London, since 1983; *d* of late Sir Arthur Lawrence Hobhouse and Konradin Huth Hobhouse; *m* 1958, Henry Trevenen Davidson Graham; one *s* one *d*. *Educ:* Ladies' Coll., Cheltenham; Lady Margaret Hall, Oxford (Hons Mod. Hist.). Researcher/Writer, Associated-Rediffusion TV and Granada TV, 1957–65; Tutor in Architectural History, Architectural Assoc. Sch., London, 1973–; Sec., Victorian Soc., 1977–82. Member: Royal Commn for Exhibn of 1851, 1983–; Council, Nat. Trust, 1983–; Council, Soc. of Antiquaries, 1984–. *Publications:* Thomas Cubitt: Master Builder, 1971 (Hitchcock Medal, 1972); Lost London, 1971; History of Regent Street, 1975; Oxford and Cambridge, 1980; Prince Albert: his life and work, 1983; contrib. Architectural Design,

Architectural Review. *Recreations:* gardening, looking at buildings of all periods. *Address:* 61 St Dunstan's Road, W6. *T:* 01–741 2575. *Club:* Reform.

HOBKIRK, Col Elspeth Isabel Weatherley, CBE 1951; TD 1952; WRAC (retired); Governor of HM Prison and of HM Borstal for Girls, and of HM Young Offenders Institute, Greenock, 1955–69; also appointed Woman Adviser to Scottish Home and Health Department on conditions of detention of Women and Girls in Scotland, 1956, retired from Scottish Prison Service, Aug. 1969; *d* of late Brig.-Gen. C. J. Hobkirk, CMG, DSO, Cleddon Hall, Trellech, Mon., and Nora Louisa Hobkirk (*née* Bosanquet). *Educ:* Sandecotes, Dorset; London Sch. of Art. JP Monmouthshire, 1938–49. Joined FANY, 1938; enrolled ATS, 1939; served War of 1939–45, Sen. Comdr, 1942; Chief Comdr, 1945; Controller and Dep. Dir ATS, HQ London District, 1946; Dep. Dir ATS, War Office, 1947–49; commissioned into Women's Royal Army Corps, 1949; Dep. Dir WRAC, War Office, 1949; Dep. Dir WRAC, HQ Eastern Command, 1950–52; Vice-Pres. Regular Commissions Bd, 1950–52; retired, 1952. Head Warden, Bristol Royal Hospital, 1952–54; Governor, HM Prison, Duke Street, Glasgow, 1954–55 (prison moved to Greenock, 1955). Member: Govt Adv. Cttee on Drug Dependence, 1967–70; Parole Board for Scotland, 1970–73; (Chm.) Civil Service Commn Panel of Interviewers, 1969–73; Adv. Council on Social Work (Scotland), 1970–72; Emslie Cttee on Penalties for Homicide, 1970–72; Edinburgh Appeals Cttee, Campaign for Cancer Research, 1970–73; Bd of Governors and Exec. Cttee, St Columba's Hospice, 1976–80; an Hon. Sec., RUKBA, Edinburgh, 1974–75; Abbeyfield Edinburgh Exec. Cttee, 1975–76 (Chm. Extra Care House); Catholic Social Work Centre Exec. Cttee, 1974–77; Council, Scottish Soldiers', Sailors' and Airmen's Housing Assoc. and Mem., House Cttee, 1979–84. Hon. LLD Glasgow, 1976. *Recreations:* travel, painting, music, gardening; country pursuits generally. *Address:* 8 Moray Place, Edinburgh EH3 6DS.

HOBKIRK, Michael Dalgliesh; *b* 9 Dec. 1924; *s* of Roy and Phyllis Hobkirk; *m* 1952, Lucy Preble; two *d. Educ:* Marlborough Coll.; Wadham Coll., Oxford. BA (Social Studies), MA 1949. Served War of 1939–45: Army (RAC, RAEC, Captain), 1943–47. Civil Service: War Office, 1949–63; MoD, 1963–70; Directing Staff, Nat. Defence Coll., 1970–74; Brookings Instn, Washington, DC, USA, 1974–75; Lord Chancellor's Dept, 1975–80 (Principal Establishment and Finance Officer, 1977–80); Asst Under-Sec. of State, MoD, 1980–82. Sen. Fellow, Nat. Defense Univ., Washington, DC, USA, 1982–83. *Publication:* contrib. to The Management of Defence (ed L. Martin), 1976; The Politics of Defence Budgeting, 1984. *Address:* 48 Woodside Avenue, Beaconsfield, Bucks HP9 1JH. *Club:* United Oxford & Cambridge University.

HOBLER, Air Vice-Marshal John Forde, CB 1958; CBE 1943; *b* Rockhampton, Qld, Australia, 26 Sept. 1907; *s* of late L. E. Hobler, Rockhampton; *m* 1939, Dorothy Evelyn Diana Haines, Wilsford, Wilts; two *s* one *d. Educ:* Rockhampton, Qld. Served whole of War of 1939–45 in Bomber Command; commanded RAF Lossiemouth; Palestine, 1945; Staff Coll., 1946–48; Air Ministry, 1948–50; Comd Habbaniya, Iraq, 1950–52; HQ Flying Trg Comd, 1952–54; Air Ministry, 1954–56; AO i/c Administration, Middle East Air Force, 1956–58; Air Officer Commanding No 25 Gp, 1958–61; Air Officer i/c Administration, Far East Air Force, 1961–63, retd. Mem., RAF Escaping Soc. *Address:* Unit P8, The Domain Country Club, Ashmore, Qld 4214, Australia. *Club:* United Services (Brisbane).

HOBLEY, Brian; Chief Urban Archaeologist, City of London, since 1973; *b* 25 June 1930; *s* of William Hobley and Harriet (*née* Hobson); *m* 1953, Laurie Parkes; one *s* one *d. Educ:* Univ. of Leicester. BA Hons Leicester 1965; FSA 1969; AMA 1970. Field Officer, Coventry Corp., 1965; Keeper, Dept Field Archaeology, Coventry Museum, 1970. Lectr, Birmingham Univ. Extra-mural Dept, 1965–74. Chm. Standing Cttee, Arch. Unit Managers; Treasurer, Inst. of Field Archaeologists; Jt Sec., British Archaeologists and Developers Liaison Gp, 1986. MBIM 1978; MIFA 1982. *Publications:* (ed jtly) Waterfront Archaeology in Britain and Northern Europe, 1981; Roman Urban Defences in the West, 1983; Roman Urban Topography in Britain and the Western Empire, 1985; reports in learned jls incl. Proc. 7th, 8th, 9th and 12th Internat. Congresses of Roman Frontier Studies, Tel Aviv, Univ. Israel and Bucharest Univ., Rumania on excavations and reconstructions at The Lunt Roman fort, Baginton near Coventry and excavations in the City of London (report, Roman and Saxon London: a reappraisal, 1986). *Recreations:* classical music, chess. *Address:* Department of Urban Archaeology, Museum of London, London Wall, EC2Y 5HN. *T:* 01–600 3699.

HOBLEY, John William Dixon, CMG 1976; QC (Hong Kong); Senior Legal Adviser, Wigan Borough Council; *b* 11 June 1929; *s* of John Wilson Hobley and Ethel Anne Hobley; *m* 1953, Dorothy Cockhill; one *s* one *d. Educ:* University Sch., Southport, Lancs; Univ. of Liverpool (LLB). Called to the Bar, Gray's Inn, 1950; Northern Circuit, 1950–53; Hong Kong: Crown Counsel, 1953–62; Sen. Crown Counsel, 1962–65; Principal Crown Counsel, 1965–72; Attorney-Gen., Bermuda, 1972; Solicitor-Gen., 1973, Attorney-Gen., 1973–79, Hong Kong. *Recreations:* music, bridge. *Address:* 33 Sandringham Road, Ainsdale, Southport, Merseyside.

HOBMAN, David Burton, CBE 1983; Director, Age Concern England (National Old People's Welfare Council), since 1970; *b* 8 June 1927; *s* of J. B. and D. L. Hobman; *m* 1954, Erica Irwin; one *s* one *d. Educ:* University College Sch.; Blundell's. Community work, Forest of Dean, 1954–56; British Council for Aid to Refugees, 1957; Nat. Council of Social Service, 1958–67; Visiting Lectr in Social Admin, Nat. Inst. for Social Work, 1967; Dir, Social Work Adv. Service, 1968–70. Vis. Prof., Sch. of Social Work, McGill Univ., Montreal, 1977. Member: BBC/ITA Appeals Adv. Council, 1965–69; Steering Cttee, Enquiry into Homelessness, Nat. Asstce Bd, 1967–68; Adv. Council, Nat. Corp. for Care of Old People, 1970–74; Metrication Bd, 1974–80; Lord Goodman's Cttee Reviewing Law of Charity, 1975–76; Chairman: Social Welfare Commn Conf. of Bishops, 1968–71; Family Housing Assoc., 1969–70; Oftel Adv. Cttee for Disabled and Elderly Persons, 1984–; Home Concern Housing Assoc., 1985–; Consultant, UN Div. of Social Affairs, 1968–69; Observer, White House Congress on Ageing, 1971–; Pres., Internat. Fedn on Ageing, 1977–80, 1983– (Vice-Pres., 1974–77); Member: Personal Social Services Council, 1978–80; Exec. Cttee, Nat. Council of Voluntary Orgns, 1981–83; Anchor Housing, 1984–. Special Advr, British delegn to World Assembly on Ageing, 1982. Governor: Cardinal Newman Comp. Sch., Hove, 1971–76 (Chm); Volunteer Centre, 1975–79. KSG. *Publications:* A Guide to Voluntary Service, 1964, 2nd edn 1967; Who Cares, 1971; The Social Challenge of Ageing, 1978; The Impact of Ageing, 1981; numerous papers, broadcasts. *Recreations:* caravanning, travel, pebble polishing. *Address:* Robinswood, George's Lane, Storrington, Pulborough, W Sussex. *T:* Storrington 2987. *Club:* Reform.

HOBSBAWM, Prof. Eric John Ernest, FBA 1976; Emeritus Professor of Economic and Social History, University of London, since 1982; *b* 9 June 1917; *s* of Leopold Percy Hobsbawm and Nelly Grün; *m* 1962, Marlene Schwarz; one *s* one *d. Educ:* Vienna; Berlin; St Marylebone Grammar Sch.; Univ. of Cambridge (BA, PhD). Lectr, Birkbeck Coll., 1947; Fellow, King's Coll., Cambridge, 1949–55, Hon. Fellow, 1973; Reader, Birkbeck Coll., 1959, Prof., 1970–82. Hon. DPhil Univ. of Stockholm, 1970; Hon. Dr Hum. Let.: Univ. of Chicago, 1976; New Sch. of Social Res., 1982; Hon. LittD UEA, 1982. Foreign Hon. Mem., American Academy of Arts and Sciences, 1971; Hon. Mem., Hungarian Acad. of Sciences, 1979. *Publications:* Labour's Turning Point, 1948; Primitive Rebels, 1959; (*pseud.* F. Newton) The Jazz Scene, 1959; The Age of Revolution, 1962; Labouring Men, 1964; (ed) Karl Marx, Precapitalist Formations, 1964; Industry and Empire, 1968; (with G. Rudé) Captain Swing, 1969; Bandits, 1969; Revolutionaries, 1973; The Age of Capital, 1975; (with T. Ranger) The Invention of Tradition, 1983; Worlds of Labour, 1984; contribs to jls. *Recreation:* travel. *Address:* Birkbeck College, Malet Street, WC1. *T:* 01–580 6622.

HOBSLEY, Prof. Michael, TD 1969; PhD; FRCS; Director, Department of Surgical Studies, Middlesex Hospital Medical School, since 1983; David Patey Professor of Surgery, University of London, since 1986 (Professor of Surgery, since 1984); *b* 18 Jan. 1929; *s* of Henry Hobsley and Sarah Lily Blanchfield; *m* 1953, Jane Fairlie Cambell; one *s* three *d. Educ:* La Martinière Coll., Calcutta; Sidney Sussex Coll., Cambridge (MA, MB, MChir); Middlesex Hosp. Med. Sch. PhD London, 1961; FRCS 1958. Training posts in RAMC and at Middlesex, Whittington and Chace Farm Hosps, 1951–68; Comyns Berkeley Fellow, Gonville and Caius Coll., Cambridge and Mddx Hosp. Med. Sch., 1965–66; posts at Mddx Hosp. and Med. Sch., 1968–: Hon. Consultant Surgeon, 1969; Reader in Surgical Science, 1970–75; Prof. of Surg. Science, 1975–83. Howard C. Naffziger Surg. Res. Fellow, Univ. of Calif, 1966; Windermere Foundn Travelling Prof. of Surgery, 1984; Glaxo Visitor, Univ. of Witwatersrand, 1985; Vis. Professor: Univ. of Calif, 1980; Univ. of Khartoum, 1976; McMaster Univ., 1982; Monash Univ., 1984. Royal College of Surgeons: Hunterian Prof., 1962–63; Penrose May Tutor, 1973–78; Sir Gordon Taylor Lectr, 1980; Examr, 1968–. Examiner: Univ. of London, 1978–; Univ. of Nigeria, 1977–; Univ. of the WI, 1978–; Univ. of Bristol, 1986; Univ. of Cambridge, 1986. FRSM 1960. *Publications:* Pathways in Surgical Management, 1979, 2nd edn 1986; Disorders of the Digestive System, 1982; Colour Atlas of Parotidectomy, 1983; articles in BMJ, Lancet, British Jl of Surgery, Gut, Klinische Wochenschrift. *Recreation:* cricket. *Address:* Fieldside, Barnet Lane, Totteridge, N20 8AS. *T:* 01–445 6507. *Club:* MCC.

HOBSON, Anthony Robert Alwyn; bibliographical historian; *b* 5 Sept. 1921; *s* of Geoffrey Dudley Hobson, MVO and Gertrude Adelaide, *d* of Rev. Thomas Vaughan, Rector of Rhuddlan, Flintshire; *m* 1959, Elena Pauline Tanya, *d* of Igor Vinogradoff; one *s* two *d. Educ:* Eton Coll. (Oppidan Scholar); New Coll., Oxford (MA). Served Scots Guards, 1941–46, Captain; Italy, 1943–46 (mentioned in despatches). Joined Sotheby & Co., 1947: Dir, 1949–71, Associate, 1971–77. Sandars Reader in Bibliography, Univ. of Cambridge, 1974–75; Franklin Jasper Walls Lectr, Pierpont Morgan Library, NY, 1979; Vis. Fellow, All Souls Coll., Oxford, 1982–83. President: Bibliographical Soc., 1977–79; Association internationale de Bibliophilie, 1985–; Hon. Pres., Edinburgh Bibliographical Soc., 1971–; Trustee: Eton Coll. Collections Trust, 1977–; Lambeth Palace Library, 1984–. Hon. Fellow, Pierpont Morgan Library, 1983. Cavaliere Ufficiale, Al Merito della Repubblica Italiana, 1979. *Publications:* French and Italian Collectors and their Bindings, 1953; Great Libraries, 1970; Apollo and Pegasus, 1975; contrib. The Library, TLS, etc. *Recreations:* travel, opera, visiting libraries founded before 1800. *Address:* The Glebe House, Whitsbury, Fordingbridge, Hants. *T:* Rockbourne 221. *Clubs:* Brooks's, Roxburghe.

HOBSON, David Constable; Adviser to Prime Minister's Policy Unit, since 1983; Partner, Coopers & Lybrand, Chartered Accountants, 1953–84, Senior Partner, 1975–83; *b* 1 Nov. 1922; *s* of late Charles Kenneth and Eileen Isabel Hobson; *m* 1961, Elizabeth Anne Drury; one *s* one *d. Educ:* Marlborough Coll.; Christ's Coll., Cambridge (Scholar). MA. ACA 1950; FCA 1958. Served War, REME, 1942–47 (Captain). Joined Cooper Brothers & Co. (now Coopers & Lybrand), 1947; Mem., Exec. Cttee, Coopers & Lybrand (International), 1973–83 (Chm., 1975–76, 1978–79, 1981–82). Dir, The Laird Gp, 1985–. Inspector (for Dept of Trade), London & County Securities Group Ltd, 1974. Member: Accounting Standards Cttee, 1970–82; City Capital Markets Cttee, 1980–84; Nat. Biological Standards Bd, 1983–; Building Socs Commn, 1986–; Board Mem. (repr. UK and Ireland), Internat. Accounting Standards Cttee, 1980–85. Hon. Treasurer: Notting Hill Housing Trust, 1984–; Lister Inst., 1986–. Member of Council: Marlborough Coll., 1967–; Francis Holland Schools, 1975–. *Recreations:* travel, gardening, golf. *Address:* Magnolia, Chiswick Mall, W4 2PR. *T:* 01–994 7511. *Club:* Reform.

HOBSON, Sir Harold, Kt 1977; CBE 1971; Special Writer, The Sunday Times, since 1976 (Drama Critic, 1947–76); contributor to: Times Literary Supplement; Drama; *b* Thorpe Hesley, near Rotherham, 4 Aug. 1904; *o s* of late Jacob and Minnie Hobson; *m* 1st, 1935, Gladys Bessie (Elizabeth) (*d* 1979), *e d* of late James Johns; one *d*; 2nd, 1981, Nancy Penhale. *Educ:* privately; Oriel Coll., Oxford (Hon. Fellow, 1974). Asst Literary Editor, The Sunday Times, 1942–48; TV Critic, The Listener, 1947–51; for many years took part in BBC Radio programme The Critics. Mem., National Theatre Bd, 1976–79. Hon. DLitt Sheffield, 1977. Chevalier of the Legion of Honour, 1959. Knight of Mark Twain, 1976. *Publications:* The First Three Years of the War, 1942; The Devil in Woodford Wells (novel), 1946; Theatre, 1948; Theatre II, 1950; Verdict at Midnight, 1952; The Theatre Now, 1953; The French Theatre of Today, 1953; (ed) The International Theatre Annual, 1956, 1957, 1958, 1959, 1960; Ralph Richardson, 1958; (with P. Knightly and L. Russell) The Pearl of Days: an intimate memoir of The Sunday Times, 1972; The French Theatre since 1830, 1978; Indirect Journey (autobiog.), 1978; Theatre in Britain: a personal view, 1984. *Recreations:* reading the New Yorker, watching cricket. *Address:* 905 Nelson House, Dolphin Square, SW1. *Club:* La Casserole (Paris).

HOBSON, Lawrence John, CMG 1965; OBE 1960; with Arab-British Chamber of Commerce, since 1977; *b* 4 May 1921; *er s* of late John Sinton Hobson and Marion Adelaide Crawford; *m* 1946, Patricia Fiona Rosemary Beggs (*née* Green); one step *s* (one *s* decd). *Educ:* Taunton Sch.; St Catharine's Coll., Cambridge. BA 1946, MA 1950. Served War, 1941–42. ADC and Private Sec. to Gov., Aden, 1942; Political Officer, 1944; Asst Chief Sec., 1956; Aden govt Student Liaison Officer, UK, 1960–62; Political Adviser to High Comr, Aden, 1963–66; retired from HMOCS, 1966. With BP Ltd, 1966–77. Mem., Newbury DC, 1973–. *Address:* Saffron House, Stanford Dingley, near Reading, Berks. *T:* Bradfield 536.

HOBSON, Valerie Babette Louise, (Mrs Profumo); film and stage actress; *b* Larne, Ireland; *d* of Comdr R. G. Hobson, RN, and Violette Hamilton-Willoughby; *m* 1st, 1939, Sir Anthony James Allan Havelock-Allan, Bt (marr. diss. 1952), *qv*; two *s*; 2nd, 1954, John Dennis Profumo, *qv*; one *s. Educ:* St Augustine's Priory, London; Royal Academy of Dramatic Art. Was trained from early age to become ballet dancer; first stage appearance at Drury Lane in Ball at the Savoy, aged 15. The King and I, Drury Lane, 1953. First film, Badgers Green; went to Hollywood and appeared in Werewolf of London, Bride of Frankenstein, The Mystery of Edwin Drood, etc; at 18 returned to England. Films include: The Drum, This Man is News, This Man in Paris, The Spy in Black, Q Planes, Silent Battle, Contraband, Unpublished Story, Atlantic Ferry, The Adventures of Tartu, The Years Between, Great Expectations, Blanche Fury, The Small Voice, Kind Hearts and Coronets, Train of Events, Interrupted Journey, The Rocking Horse Winner, The Card,

Who Goes There?, Meet Me Tonight, The Voice of Merrill, Background, Knave of Hearts. *Recreations:* listening to music, writing, reading, painting.

HOCHHAUSER, Victor; impresario; *b* 27 March 1923; *m* 1949, Lilian Hochhauser (*née* Shields); three *s* one *d*. *Educ:* City of London Coll. Impresario for: David Oistrakh; Sviatoslav Richter; Mstislav Rostropovich; Gilels, Kogan; Margot Fonteyn; Natalia Makarova; Nureyev Festival; Bolshoi Ballet season at Covent Garden, 1963, 1969; Leningrad State Kirov Ballet, Covent Garden, 1961, 1966; Sunday Evening Concerts, Royal Albert Hall; Peking Opera and other Chinese companies, 1972–. *Recreations:* reading, swimming, sleeping. *Address:* 4 Oak Hill Way, NW3 7LR. *T:* 01–794 0987.

HOCKADAY, Sir Arthur (Patrick), KCB 1978 (CB 1975); CMG 1969; Secretary and Director-General, Commonwealth War Graves Commission, since 1982; *b* 17 March 1926; *s* of late William Ronald Hockaday and of Marian Camilla Hockaday, *d* of Rev. A. C. Evans; *m* 1955, Peggy, *d* of late H. W. Prince. *Educ:* Merchant Taylors' Sch.; St John's Coll., Oxford. BA (1st cl. Lit. Hum.) 1949, MA 1952. Apptd to Home Civil Service, 1949; Admty, 1949–62; Private Sec. to successive Ministers of Defence and Defence Secretaries, 1962–65; NATO Internat. Staff, 1965–69 (Asst Sec. Gen. for Defence Planning and Policy, 1967–69); Asst Under-Sec. of State, MoD, 1969–72; Under-Sec., Cabinet Office, 1972–73; Dep. Under-Sec. of State, MoD, 1973–76; 2nd Permanent Under-Sec. of State, MoD, 1976–82. *Publications:* (contrib.) Ethics and Nuclear Deterrence, 1982; The Strategic Defence Initiative, 1985; (contrib.) Ethics and European Security, 1986; occasional articles. *Recreation:* fell-walking. *Address:* 11 Hitherwood Court, Hitherwood Drive, SE19 1UX. *T:* 01–670 7940. *Clubs:* Naval and Military, Civil Service.

HOCKENHULL, Arthur James Weston, OBE 1966; HM Diplomatic Service, retired; *b* 8 Aug. 1915; *s* of late Frederick Weston Hockenhull and late Jessie Gibson Kaye Hockenhull (*née* Mitchell); *m* 1955, Rachel Ann Kimber; two *d*. *Educ:* Clifton Coll.; Exeter Coll., Oxford. HM Overseas Civil Service; various appts in Far East, Cyprus and British Guiana, 1936–57. Interned by Japanese, in Singapore, 1942–45; First Sec., UK Commn, Singapore, 1958–63; Counsellor, British High Commn, Malaysia, 1964–68; HM Consul-Gen., Houston, 1969–74. *Recreations:* golf, gardening, swimming. *Club:* United Oxford & Cambridge University.

HOCKER, Dr Alexander; Grosses Verdienstkreuz mit Stern des Verdienstordens der Bundesrepublik Deutschland, 1973; Director-General, European Space Research Organisation (ESRO), 1971–74; *m* 1940, Liselotte Schulze; five *s* one *d*. *Educ:* Univs of Innsbruck, Hamburg and Leipzig. Asst, Law Faculty, Leipzig Univ.; County Court Judge; Officer, Advanced Scientific Study Div., Min. of Educn, Hannover, 1947–49; Dep. of Sec.-Gen. of German Res. Assoc. (Deutsche Forschungsgemeinschaft), 1949–56; Ministerialrat and Ministerialdirigent (responsible for res., trng and sci. exchanges), Fed. Min. for Atomic Energy, 1956–61; Mem. Directorate, Nuclear Res. Centre (Kernforschungsanlage) Jülich, 1961–69; Sci. Adviser to Foundn Volkswagenwerk, 1969–71. German Deleg. to CERN, Geneva, 1952–61 (Chm. of Finance Cttee, 1960–61); Chm. of Legal, Admin. and Financial Working Gp of COPERS, 1961–63; Chm. of Council, ESRO, 1965–67 (Vice-Chm. 1964); Member: German Commn for Space Res., 1964–71; Kuratorium Max-Planck-Institut für Physik und Astrophysik, 1968–71; Max-Plank-Institut für Plasmaphysik, 1971–80, Hon. Member 1980–. *Publication:* (jtly) Taschenbuch für Atomfragen, 1968. *Address:* Bad Godesberg, Augustastrasse 63, 5300 Bonn 2, Germany. *T:* (0228) 363961.

HOCKING, Frederick Denison Maurice; formerly Cornwall County Pathologist; Consulting Biologist and Toxicologist, Devon River Board; late Consulting Pathologist, South-Western Regional Hospital Board; Acting Director Public Health Laboratory Service, Cornwall, and other hospitals in Cornwall; late Chemical Pathologist, Biochemist, and Assistant Pathologist, Westminster Hospital; Lecturer in General and Clinical Pathology, Westminster Hospital Medical School, University of London; *b* 28 Feb. 1899; *o s* of late Rev. Almund Trevosso Hocking and Gertrude Vernon Mary, *o d* of J. Parkinson; *m* 1st, 1927, Amy Gladys (*d* 1956), *y d* of A. T. Coucher; two *d*; 2nd, 1957, Kathleen, *e d* of Dr G. P. O'Donnell. *Educ:* High Sch., Leytonstone; City and Guilds of London Coll., Finsbury; Middlesex Hospital Medical Sch. RN Experimental and Anti-gas Station, 1917–18; Asst Laboratory Dir to the Clinical Research Assoc. MB, BS, BSc, MSc London, MRCS, LRCP, CChem, FRSC, FCS, FRMS; FRSA, MIBiol, FRSH. Associate of the City and Guilds of London Tech. Coll., Finsbury; Member: Pathological Soc. of Great Britain and Ireland; Association of Clinical Pathologists (Councillor, 1944–46); Society of Public Analysts; Medico-Legal Society; Brit. Assoc. in Forensic Medicine; former Mem. Court, Univ. of Exeter (representing Royal Institute of Chemistry); Pres. South-Western Branch, British Medical Association, 1946; Chm. South-Western Branch, RIC, 1955–57; Mem. Council, RIC, 1959–62, 1965–68. Mem. Brit. Acad. of Forensic Sciences; Mem. Soc. for Forensic Science. *Publications:* The Employment of Uranium in the Treatment of Malignant New Growths, British Empire Cancer Campaign International Conference, London, 1928; Disseminated Sclerosis (with Sir James Purves-Stewart), 1930; Seaside Accidents, 1958; Delayed Death due to Suicidal Hanging, 1961; Hanging and Manual Strangulation, 1966; Christmas Eve Crime in Falmouth (Murder in the West Country), 1975; The Porthole Murder: Gay Gibson (Facets of Crime), 1975; numerous scientific papers in medical journals, etc. *Recreations:* hotels, good food, wine, conversation. *Address:* Strathaven, Carlyon Bay, Cornwall. *Clubs:* National Liberal, English-Speaking Union.

HOCKING, Philip Norman; *b* 27 Oct. 1925; *s* of late Fred Hocking, FIOB; *m* 1950, Joan Mable, *d* of Horace Ernest Jackson, CBE, Birmingham; three *d*. *Educ:* King Henry VIII Sch., Coventry; Birmingham Sch. of Architecture. Dir, F. Hocking & Sons Ltd. Mem. Coventry City Council, 1955–60. Prominent Mem. Young Con. Movement. MP (C) Coventry South, 1959–64; PPS to Minister of State, FO, 1963–64. Contested Coventry S, 1964 and 1966. Chm., Conservative Back Benchers' Housing and Local Govt Cttee, 1962–64. *Recreations:* gardening and sailing.

HOCKLEY, Sir Anthony Heritage F.; *see* Farrar-Hockley.

HOCKLEY, Rev. Canon Raymond Alan; Canon Residentiary, Precentor, Succentor Canonicorum and Chamberlain of York Minster, since 1976; *b* 18 Sept. 1929; 2nd *s* of late Henry Hockley and Doris (*née* Stonehouse); unmarried. *Educ:* Firth Park School, Sheffield; Royal Academy of Music, London; Westcott House, Cambridge. MA, LRAM. Macfarren Schol., Royal Acad. of Music, 1951–54; Charles Lucas Medal, William Corder Prize, Cuthbert Nunn Prize, etc; Theodore Holland Award, 1955. Clements Memorial Prize for Chamber Music by a British subject, 1954. Curate of St Augustine's, Sheffield, 1958–61; Priest-in-charge of Holy Trinity, Wicker, with St Michael and All Angels, Neepsend, 1961–63; Chaplain of Westcott House, Cambridge, 1963–68; Fellow, Chaplain and Dir of Studies in Music, Emmanuel Coll., Cambridge, 1968–76. Works performed include: Songs for Tenor, Soprano; String Quartet; Divertimento for piano duet; Cantata for Easter and the Ascension; Symphony; My Enemies pictured within, a Bitter-Suite for Orchestra; various anthems and motets; incidental music for plays. Other works include: two more Symphonies, A Woman's Last Word for three sopranos; Oratorio on the Destruction and Salvation of the World. *Publications:* Six Songs of Faith; New Songs for the Church; Divertimento; Intercessions at Holy Communion; contribs to theological and musical jls. *Recreations:* cooking, talking, unfinished work. *Address:* 2 Minster Court, York. *T:* York 24965. *Club:* Yorkshire (York).

HOCKNEY, David, ARA 1985; artist; *b* Bradford, 9 July 1937; *s* of Kenneth and Laura Hockney. *Educ:* Bradford Grammar Sch.; Bradford Sch. of Art; Royal Coll. of Art. Lecturer: Maidstone Coll. of Art, 1962; Univ. of Iowa, 1964; Univ. of Colorado, 1965; Univ. of California, Los Angeles, 1966, Berkeley, 1967. One-man shows: Kasmin Ltd, London, 1963, 1965, 1966, 1968, 1969, 1970, 1972; Alan Gallery, New York, 1964–67, Museum of Modern Art, NY, 1964–68; Stedlijk Museum, Amsterdam, 1966; Whitworth Gallery, Manchester, 1969; Louvre, Paris, 1974; Galerie Claude Bernard, Paris, 1975 and 1985; Nicholas Wilder, LA, 1976; Galerie Neundorf, Hamburg, 1977; Warehouse Gall., 1979; Knoedler Gall., 1979, 1981, 1982, 1983, 1984 and 1986; André Emmerich Gall., 1979, 1980, 1982, 1983, 1984 and 1985; Tate, 1986; Hayward Gall., 1983 and 1985, etc; touring show of drawings and prints: Munich, Madrid, Lisbon, Teheran, 1977; USA and Canada, 1978; Tate, 1980. Retrospective Exhibn, Whitechapel Art Gall., 1970. Exhibn of photographs, Hayward Gall., 1983. 1st Prize, John Moores Exhibn, Liverpool, 1967. Designer: The Rake's Progress, Glyndebourne, 1975, La Scala, 1979; The Magic Flute, Glyndebourne, 1978; L'Enfant et les sortilèges and Nightingale, Double Bill, and Varii Capricci, Covent Garden, 1983; designing costumes and sets for the Metropolitan Opera House, NY, 1980. Film: A Bigger Splash, 1975. Shakespeare Prize, Hamburg Foundn, 1983. *Publications:* (ed and illustrated) 14 Poems of C. P. Cavafy, 1967; (illustrated) Six Fairy Tales of the Brothers Grimm, 1969; 72 Drawings by David Hockney, 1971; David Hockney by David Hockney, 1976; The Glue Guitar, 1977; David Hockney: Travels with Pen, Pencil and Ink: selected prints and drawings 1962–77, 1978; Paper Pools, 1980; (with Stephen Spender) China Diary, 1982; Hockney Paints the Stage, 1983; David Hockney: Cameraworks, 1984. *Address:* c/o Knoedler Kasmin Ltd, Knoedler Gallery, 22 Cork Street, W1.

HODDER, Prof. Bramwell William, PhD; Professor of Geography, School of Oriental and African Studies, University of London, 1970–83, now Emeritus; *b* 25 Nov. 1923; *s* of George Albert Hodder and Emily Griggs, Eastbourne; *m* 1971, Elizabeth (*née* Scruton); three *s* two *d* by previous marriages. *Educ:* Oldershaw, Wallasey; Oriel Coll., Oxford (MA, BLitt); PhD London. Served War, 1942–47, commissioned in Infantry (Cameronians), Lieut. Lecturer, Univ. of Malaya, Singapore, 1952–56; Lectr/Sen. Lectr, Univ. of Ibadan, Nigeria, 1956–63; Lectr, Univ of Glasgow, 1963–64; Lectr/Reader, Queen Mary Coll., Univ. of London, 1964–70. Chm., Commonwealth Geog. Bureau, 1968–72; Hon. Dir, 1981–82, Mem. Exec. Council, 1981–84, Internat. African Inst. Joint Hon. Pres., World Expeditionary Assoc., 1972–. *Publications:* Man in Malaya, 1959; Economic Development in the Tropics, 1968, 3rd edn 1980; (jtly) Markets in West Africa, 1969; (jtly) Africa in Transition, 1967; (jtly) Economic Geography, 1974; Africa Today, 1979; articles in various learned jls. *Recreations:* music, hill walking. *Address:* Maris House, Trumpington, Cambridge. *T:* Cambridge 841306.

HODDER-WILLIAMS, Paul, OBE 1945; TD; publisher; Consultant, Hodder & Stoughton Ltd, since 1975; *b* 29 Jan. 1910; *s* of late Frank Garfield Hodder Williams, sometime Dean of Manchester, and late Sarah Myfanwy (*née* Nicholson); *m* 1936, Felicity (*d* 1986), 2nd *d* of late C. M. Blagden, DD, sometime Bishop of Peterborough; two *s* two *d*. *Educ:* Rugby; Gonville and Caius Coll., Cambridge (MA). Joined Hodder & Stoughton Ltd, 1931; Dir, 1936, Chm., 1961–75. Served with HAC (Major, 1942), 99th (London Welsh) HAA Regt RA (Lt-Col Comdg, 1942–45). *Recreations:* gardening, walking. *Address:* Court House, Exford, Minehead, Somerset. *T:* Exford 268.

HODDINOTT, Prof. Alun, CBE 1983; DMus; Hon. RAM; FRNCM; Professor of Music, University College, Cardiff, since 1967 (Fellow, 1983); *b* 11 Aug. 1929; *s* of Thomas Ivor Hoddinott and Gertrude Jones; *m* 1953, Beti Rhiannon Huws; one *s*. *Educ:* University Coll. of S Wales and Mon. Lecturer: Cardiff Coll. of Music and Drama, 1951–59; University Coll. of S Wales and Mon, 1959–65; Reader, University of Wales, 1965–67. Member: BBC Music Central Adv. Cttee, 1971–78; Welsh Arts Council, 1968–74; Member Council: Welsh Nat. Opera, 1972–75; Composers' Guild of GB, 1972–; Nat. Youth Orchestra, 1972–. Chm., Welsh Music Archive, 1977–78, 1983–. Artistic Dir, Cardiff Music Festival. Governor, Welsh Nat. Theatre, 1968–74. Walford Davies Prize, 1954; Arnold Bax Medal, 1957; John Edwards Meml Award, 1967; Hopkins Medal, St David's Soc., NY, 1980. FRNCM 1981. *Publications: opera:* The Beach of Falesá, 1974; The Magician, 1975; What the Old Man does is always right, 1975; The Rajah's Diamond, 1979; The Trumpet Major, 1981; *choral:* Rebecca, 1961; oratorio, Job, 1962; Medieval Songs, 1962; Danegeld, 1964; Four Welsh Songs, 1964; Cantata: Dives and Lazarus, 1965; An Apple Tree and a Pig, 1968; Ballad, Black Bart, 1968; Out of the Deep, 1972; The Tree of Life, 1971; Four Welsh Songs, 1971; The Silver Swimmer, 1973; Sinfonia Fidei, 1977; Dulcia Iuventutis, 1978; Voyagers, 1978; Hymnus ante Somnum, 1979; Te Deum, 1982; Charge of the Light Brigade, 1983; In Parasceve Domini, 1983; King of Glory, 1984; Bells of Paradise, 1984; Jubilate, 1985; Lady and Unicorn, 1985; In Gravescentem Aetatem, 1985; Christ is Risen, 1986; Sing a New Song, 1986; Ballad of Green Broom; Flower Songs; In Praise of Music; *vocal:* Roman Dream, 1968; Ancestor Worship, 1972; Ynys Mon, 1975; A Contemplation upon Flowers, 1976; Six Welsh Songs, 1982; The Silver Hound, 1986; *orchestral:* Symphonies 1955, 1962, 1968, 1969, 1973, 1984; Nocturne, 1952; Welsh Dances I, 1958, II 1969; Folk Song Suite, 1962; Variations, 1963; Night Music, 1966; Sinfonietta I, 1968, II, 1969, III, 1970, IV, 1971; Fioriture, 1968; Investiture Dances, 1969; Divertimento, 1969; the sun, the great luminary of the universe, 1970; the hawk is set free, 1972; Welsh Airs and Dances for Symphonic Band, 1975; Landscapes, 1975; French Suite, 1977; Passaggio, 1977; Nightpiece, 1977; Lanterne des Morts, 1981; Five Studies, 1983; Four Scenes, 1983; Quodlibet, 1984; Hommage à Chopin, 1985; Welsh Dances–3rd Suite, 1985; Scena, 1986; Fanfare with Variants; Concerto for Orchestra; *concertos:* Clarinet, 1951; Oboe, 1954; Harp, 1958; Viola, 1958; Piano I, 1950, II, 1960, III, 1966; Violin, 1961; Organ, 1967; Horn, 1969; Nocturnes and Cadenzas (cello), 1969; Ritornelli (trombone), 1974; The Heaventree of Stars, for violin and orchestra, 1980; Doubles (oboe); Scenes and Interludes (trumpet), 1985; Violin, Cello, Piano (Triple Concerto); Divisions (horn); *chamber:* Septet, 1956; Sextet, 1960; Variations for Septet, 1962; Wind Quartet, 1963; String Quartet, 1965; Nocturnes and Cadenzas for Clarinet, Violin and Cello, 1968; Divertimento for 8 instruments, 1968; Piano Trio, 1970; Piano Quintet, 1972; Scena for String Quartet, 1979; Ritornelli for Brass Quintet, 1979; Ritornelli for four double basses, 1981; String Quartet no 2, 1984; Masks for oboe, bassoon, piano, 1985; Piano Trio no 2, 1985; Divertimenti for flute, bassoon, double-bass and percussion, 1985; Sonata for Four Clarinets; *instrumental:* sonatas for: piano, 1959, 1962, 1965, 1966, 1968, 1972, 1984, 1986; harp, 1964; clarinet and piano, 1967; violin and piano, 1969, 1970, 1971, 1976; cello and piano, 1970, 1977; horn and piano, 1971; organ, 1979; two pianos, 1986; sonatinas for: clavichord, 1963; 2 pianos, 1978; guitar, 1978; Suite for Harp, 1967; Fantasy for Harp, 1970; Italian Suite for Recorder and guitar, 1977; Nocturnes and Cadenzas for Solo Cello, 1983; Bagatelles for Oboe and Harp, 1983; Passacaglia and Fugue for Organ, 1986. *Address:* Maesawelon, Mill Road, Lisvane, Cardiff CF4 5UG.

HODGART, Prof. Matthew John Caldwell; Professor of English, Concordia University, Montreal, 1970–76; *b* 1 Sept. 1916; *s* of late Matthew Hodgart (Major RE), MC, and

Katherine Barbour Caldwell (née Gardner); m 1st, 1940, Betty Joyce Henstridge (d 1948); one s one d; 2nd, 1949, Margaret Patricia Elliott; one adopted d. Educ: Rugby Sch. (Scholar); Pembroke Coll., Cambridge (Scholar; BA 1938, MA 1945). Jebb Studentship, Cambridge, 1938–39. Served War, 1939–45: Argyll and Sutherland Highlanders and in Intelligence (mentioned in despatches). Cambridge University: Asst Lectr in English, 1945–49; Lectr in English, and Fellow of Pembroke Coll., 1949–64; Prof. of English, Sussex Univ., 1964–70. Vis. Professor: Cornell Univ., 1961–62 and 1969; Univ. of Calif, Los Angeles, 1977–78; Stanford Univ., 1979; La Trobe Univ., Australia, 1979–80; Hinckley Prof., Johns Hopkins Univ., 1982. Chevalier de la Légion d'honneur, and Croix de guerre, 1945. Publications: The Ballads, 1950; (with Prof. M. Worthington) Song in the Work of James Joyce, 1959; Samuel Johnson, 1962; (ed) Horace Walpole, Memoirs, 1963; (ed) Faber Book of Ballads, 1965; Satire, 1969 (trans. various languages); A New Voyage (fiction), 1969; James Joyce, Student Guide, 1978; contrib. Rev. of English Studies, and TLS. Recreations: travel, music, computers. Address: 13 Montpelier Villas, Brighton BN1 3DG. T: Brighton 26993.

HODGE, Alexander Mitchell, GC 1940; VRD; DL; Captain RNVR, retired; WS; Member of firm of Cowan & Stewart, WS, Edinburgh, 1946–84; Director, Standard Life Assurance Co. (Chairman, 1977–82); b 23 June 1916; y s of James Mackenzie Hodge, Blairgowrie, Perthshire; m 1944, Pauline Hester Winsome, o d of William John Hill, Bristol; one s two d. Educ: Fettes Coll.; Edinburgh Univ. (MA 1936, LLB 1938). Joined RNVR, 1938; served with Royal Navy, 1939–45 (despatches, GC). Comdr RNVR, 1949, Capt. RNVR, 1953; CO of the Forth Div. RNVR, 1953–57. Chm., Edinburgh Dist Sea Cadet Cttee, 1959–63; Chm., Lady Haig's Poppy Factory, 1961–67; Mem. Council, Earl Haig Fund (Scotland), 1963–67; Chm., Livingston New Town Licensing Planning Cttee, 1963–69; Dir, Edinburgh Western Gen. Hosp. Assoc. of Friends, 1962– (Chm., 1962–68); Trustee and Mem. Cttee of Management: Royal Victoria Hosp. Tuberculosis Trust, 1964– (Pres., 1970–); Royal Edinburgh Inst. for Sailors, Soldiers and Airmen, 1964–71; Chm. General Comrs of Income Tax, Edinburgh South Div., 1967–85; Pres., Edinburgh Chamber of Commerce, 1968–70; Chm., The Cruden Foundn, 1983– (Dir, 1969–72, 1973–). Governor, Fettes Coll., 1970–75; Mem. Court, Heriot-Watt Univ., 1982–. DL Edinburgh, 1972. Address: Springbank, Barnton, Edinburgh EH4 6DJ. T: 031–339 3054. Clubs: Royal Automobile; New (Edinburgh).

HODGE, David, CBE 1980; JP; DL; Lord Provost of Glasgow, and Lord Lieutenant of County of City of Glasgow, 1977–80; b 30 Sept. 1909; s of David Hodge and Sarah (née Crilly); m 1950, Mary Forbes Hodge (née Taylor); four d. Educ: St Mungo's Acad., Glasgow. Served War, RAF, 1940–46: air crew, Coastal Comd. On staff of Scottish Gas Bd, 1934–50; Prudential Assurance Co. Ltd, 1950–74, retd. Chm., Ruchill Ward and Maryhill Constituency for 20 yrs. Elected to Glasgow Corp., 1971; Magistrate, Corp. of Glasgow, 1972–74; Vice-Chm., Transport Cttee. Mem., City of Glasgow Dist Council, 1974: Chm., Licensing Court, Licensing Cttee, and Justices Cttee; Sec. of Admin; Council Rep., Convention of Scottish Local Authorities, 1974–77. JP, 1975, DL 1980, Glasgow. Hon. LLD Strathclyde, 1980. OStJ 1978. Recreations: interested in all sports (former professional footballer; winner of tennis championships; former swimming and badminton coach); theatre, ballet, music. Address: 59 Hillend Road, Glasgow G22 6NY. T: 041–336 8727. Clubs: Royal Automobile, Royal Air Forces Association; Art, Pres, Marist Centenary (Glasgow).

HODGE, James William; HM Diplomatic Service; Counsellor and Head of Chancery, Copenhagen, since 1986; b 24 Dec. 1943; s of William Hodge and late Catherine Hodge (née Carden); m 1970, Frances Margaret, d of Michael Coyne and Teresa Coyne (née Walsh); three d. Educ: Holy Cross Academy, Edinburgh; Univ. of Edinburgh (MA(Hons) English Lang. and Lit.). Commonwealth Office, 1966; Third Secretary, Tokyo, 1967; Second Secretary (Information), Tokyo, 1970; FCO, 1972; First Sec. (Development, later Chancery), Lagos, 1975; FCO, 1978; First Sec. (Economic), 1981, Counsellor (Commercial), 1982, Tokyo. Recreations: books, Scandinavian studies, tennis. Address: c/o Foreign and Commonwealth Office, SW1A 2AH. Clubs: MCC, Travellers'.

HODGE, John Dennis; Acting Associate Administrator for Space Station, NASA, Washington, since 1985; b 10 Feb. 1929; s of John Charles Henry Hodge and Emily M. Corbett Hodge; m 1952, Audrey Cox; two s two d. Educ: Northampton Engineering Coll., University of London (now The City Univ.). Vickers-Armstrong Ltd, Weybridge, England (Aerodynamics Dept), 1950–52; Head, Air Loads Section, Avro Aircraft Ltd, Toronto, Canada, 1952–59; Tech. Asst to Chief, Ops Div., Space Task Group, NASA, Langley Field, Va, USA, 1959; Chief, Flight Control Br., Space Task Group, NASA, 1961; Asst Chief of Flight Control, 1962, Chief, Flight Control Div., Flight Ops Directorate, NASA, MSC, 1963–68; Manager, Advanced Missions Program, NASA, Manned Spacecraft Centre, 1968–70; Dir, Transport Systems Concepts, Transport Systems Center, 1970; Vice-Pres., R&D, The Ontario Transportation Develt Corp., 1974–76; Department of Transportation, Washington, 1976–82; Chief, R&D Plans and Programs Analysis Div., 1976–77; Actg Dir, Office of Policy, Plans and Admin, 1977–79; Associate Administrator, for Policy, Plans and Program Management, Res. and Special programs Admin, 1979–82; Dir, Space Station Task Force, NASA, Washington, 1982–84; Dep. Associate Administrator for Space Station, NASA, Washington, 1984–85. Hon. ScD, The City Univ., London, Eng., 1966; NASA Medal for Exceptional Service, 1967 and 1969; Dept of Transportation Meritorious Achievement Award, 1974; Special Achievement Award, 1979; Presidential Rank Award of Meritorious Executive, NASA, 1985. Publications: contribs to NASA publications and various aerospace jls. Recreation: reading. Address: 1105 Challendon Road, Great Falls, Va 22066, USA.

HODGE, John Ernest, CMG 1962; CVO 1956; QPM 1955; Inspector-General of Police, Republic of Nigeria, 1962–64; b 3 Nov. 1911; s of late Rev. J. Z. Hodge, DD; m 1950, Margaret Henrietta, d of late Rev. Hugh Brady Brew, Wicklow; one s one d. Educ: Taunton Sch., Taunton, Som. Jamaica Constabulary, 1931–35; The Nigeria Police, 1935–64. Mem. East Lothian CC, 1972–75. OStJ 1961. CPM 1953. Recreation: golf. Address: Netherlea, Dirleton, East Lothian, Scotland. T: Dirleton 272. Club: North Berwick.

HODGE, Sir John Rowland, 2nd Bt cr 1921; MBE 1940; FRHS; company director; b 1 May 1913; s of Sir Rowland Hodge, 1st Bt, and Mabel (d 1923), d of William Edward Thorpe; S father, 1950; m 1936, Peggy Ann (marr. diss. 1939), o d of Sydney Raymond Kent; m 1939, Joan (marr. diss. 1961), o d of late Sydney Foster Wilson; three d; m 1967, Vivien Jill, d of A. S. Knightley; one s one d. Educ: Wrekin Coll.; Switzerland. Served War of 1939–45, RNVR; Lt-Comdr, RNVR, 1938; formerly Oxford and Bucks Light Infantry. Mem. Inst. of Directors. Dist Grand Master, Dist Grand Lodge of Freemasons, Malta. Freeman, City of Newcastle upon Tyne. Heir: s Andrew Rowland Hodge, b 3 Dec. 1968. Address: 16 Sutherland Drive, Gunton Park, Lowestoft NR32 4LP. T: Lowestoft 68943. Clubs: British Racing Drivers, Naval, Royal Malta Yacht, Royal Yachting Association, Cruising Association.

HODGE, Sir Julian Stephen Alfred, Kt 1970; Merchant banker; Chairman, Avana Group Ltd, 1973–81; Founder and Chairman, Commercial Bank of Wales, 1971–85;

Chairman, Commercial Bank of Wales (Jersey) Ltd; Director, Commercial Bank of Wales (IoM) Ltd; b 15 Oct. 1904; s of late Alfred and Jane Hodge; m 1951, Moira (née Thomas); two s one d. Educ: Cardiff Technical Coll. Certified Accountant, 1930. Fellow, Inst. of Taxation, 1941–. Founded Hodge & Co., Accountants and Auditors; Man. Dir, 1963–75, Exec. Chm., 1975–78, Hodge Group Ltd; former Chairman: Julian S. Hodge & Co. Ltd; Gwent Enterprises Ltd; Hodge Finance Ltd; Hodge Life Assurance Co. Ltd; Carlyle Trust Ltd, 1962–85; Dir, Standard Chartered Bank, 1973–75. Founder and Chairman: The Jane Hodge Foundation, 1962; Sir Julian Hodge Charitable Trust, 1964; Chairman: Aberfan Disaster Fund Industrial Project Sub-Cttee; Member: Welsh Economic Council, 1965–68; Welsh Council, 1968–79; Council, Univ. of Wales Inst. of Science and Technology (Treasurer, 1968–76; Pres., 1981–85); Foundation Fund Cttee, Univ. of Surrey; Pres., S Glamorgan Dist, St John Ambulance Bde; Trustee, Welsh Sports Trust. Former Governor, All Hallows (Cranmore Hall) Sch. Trust Ltd. FTII 1941. FRSA. Hon. LLD Univ. of Wales, 1971. KStJ 1977 (CStJ 1972); KSG 1978. Publication: Paradox of Financial Preservation, 1959. Recreations: golf, walking, reading, gardening. Address: Clos des Seux, Mont du Coin, St Aubin, St Brelade, Jersey, CI. Club: Victoria (St Helier, Jersey).

HODGES, C(yril) Walter; free-lance writer, book illustrator, theatrical historian and designer; b 18 March 1909; s of Cyril James and Margaret Mary Hodges; m 1936, Greta (née Becker); two s. Educ: Dulwich Coll.; Goldsmiths' Coll. Sch. of Art. Commenced as stage designer, 1929, then illustrator for advertising, magazines (esp. Radio Times) and children's books; began writing, 1937; served with Army, 1940–46 (despatches); has designed stage productions (Mermaid Theatre, 1951, 1964), permanent Elizabethan stage, St George's Theatre, 1976; exhibns (Lloyds, UK Provident Instn); mural decorations painted for Chartered Insce Inst., UK Provident Instn; Art Dir, Encyclopædia Britannica Films, 1959–61. Judith E. Wilson Lectr in Poetry and Drama, Cambridge, 1974; Co-ordinator, Symposium for the Reconstruction of Globe Playhouse, 1979, Adjunct Prof. of Theatre, 1980–83, Wayne State University, USA; Vis. Scholar, Univ. of Maryland, 1983. Hon. DLitt Sussex, 1979. Kate Greenaway Medal for illustration, 1965; Hons List, Hans Christian Andersen Internat. Award, 1966. Publications: Columbus Sails, 1939; The Flying House, 1947; Shakespeare and the Players, 1948; The Globe Restored, 1953 (rev. edn 1968); The Namesake, 1964; Shakespeare's Theatre, 1964; The Norman Conquest, 1966; Magna Carta, 1966; The Marsh King, 1967; The Spanish Armada, 1967; The Overland Launch, 1969; The English Civil War, 1972; Shakespeare's Second Globe, 1973; Playhouse Tales, 1974; The Emperor's Elephant, 1975; Plain Lane Christmas, 1978; The Battlement Garden, 1979; (ed) The Third Globe, 1981; contributor: Shakespeare Survey; Theatre Notebook; (illus.) The New Cambridge Shakespeare, 1984–. Recreations: music (listening), letters (writing), museums (visiting). Address: 36 Southover High Street, Lewes, East Sussex BN7 1HX. T: Lewes 6530.

HODGES, Elaine Mary, OBE 1975; HM Diplomatic Service; Counsellor, Foreign and Commonwealth Office, 1981–83; retired; b 12 Nov. 1928; d of late Lancelot James Hodges and of Edith Mary (née Crossland). Educ: Nottingham High School for Girls; St Anne's Coll., Oxford (BA Hons, MA). Joined Foreign Office, 1952; served in: Germany, 1952–53; Switzerland, 1955–56; Warsaw, 1959; New Delhi, 1963–64; Paris, 1967–69; Brussels, 1974–79. Recreations: gardening, antiques, travel. Address: 46 Westbridge Road, SW11 3PW. T: 01–228 3771.

HODGES, Gerald; Director of Finance, City of Bradford Metropolitan Council, 1974–85; b 14 June 1925; s of Alfred John Hodges and Gertrude Alice Hodges; m 1950, Betty Maire (née Brading); one s (and one s decd). Educ: King's Sch., Peterborough. IPFA. Accountancy Asst, Bexley Borough Council, 1941–48, and Eton RDC, 1948–49; Sen. Accountancy Asst, Newcastle upon Tyne, 1949–53; Chief Accountant, Hemel Hempstead, 1953–56; Dep. Treas., Crawley UDC, 1956–70; Treas., Ilkley UDC, 1970–74. Pres., Soc. of Metropolitan Treasurers, 1984–85. Hon. Treasurer: Yorkshire Arts, 1973–86; Univ. of Bradford, 1986–; Chm., Bradford Flower Fund Homes; Trustee, Bradford Disaster Appeal, 1985. Publications: occasional articles in professional jls. Recreations: travelling, ornithology, reading. Address: 23 Victoria Avenue, Ilkley, West Yorks. T: Ilkley 607346.

HODGES, Joseph Thomas Charles, FCA, FCIS; Director, Mark Loveday Underwriting Agencies Ltd, since 1984; b 25 July 1932; s of Joseph Henry Hodges and Hilda Ellen Susan (née Hermitage); m 1962, Joan Swan; two s one d. Educ: East Ham Grammar Sch. ACIS 1955, FCIS 1980; ACA 1960, FCA 1971. National Service, RAF, 1950–52. Accounts Dept, Corp. of Lloyd's, 1949–50 and 1953–55; articled to Gerard van de Linde & Son, Chartered Accountants, 1955–60; Corporation of Lloyd's: Audit Dept, 1960–66, Manager of Audit Dept, 1966–74; Head of Advisory and Legislation, 1974–80; Dep. Sec. Gen., 1980; Sec. Gen., 1980–84. Recreations: watching West Ham United, caravanning. Address: 246 Halfway Street, Sidcup, Kent DA15 8DW. T: 01–850 3927.

HODGES, Air Chief Marshal Sir Lewis (Macdonald), KCB 1968 (CB 1963); CBE 1958; DSO 1944 and Bar 1945; DFC 1942 and Bar 1943; b 1 March 1918; s of late Arthur Macdonald Hodges and Gladys Mildred Hodges; m 1950, Elizabeth Mary, e d of late G. H. Blackett, MC; two s. Educ: St Paul's Sch.; RAF Coll., Cranwell. Bomber Command, 1938–44; SE Asia (India, Burma, Ceylon), 1944–45; Palestine, 1945–47; Air Ministry and Min. of Defence, 1948–52; Bomber Command, 1952–59; Asst Comdt, RAF Coll., Cranwell, 1959–61; AO i/c Admin., Middle East Comd, Aden, 1961–63; Imperial Def. Coll., 1963; SHAPE, 1964–65; Ministry of Defence, Asst Chief of Air Staff (Ops), 1965–68; AOC-in-C, RAF Air Support Comd, 1968–70; Air Mem. for Personnel, MoD, 1970–73; Dep. C-in-C, Allied Forces Central Europe, 1973–76, retired. Air ADC to the Queen, 1973–76. Dir, Pilkington Bros Ltd (Optical Div.), 1979–83; Governor, BUPA, 1973–85; Chm. of Governors, Duke of Kent School, 1979–; Chm., RAF Benevolent Fund Educn Cttee, 1979–; Pres., RAF Escaping Soc., 1979–; Pres., Royal Air Forces Assoc., 1981–84. Légion d'Honneur (French) 1950; Croix de Guerre (French) 1944. Recreations: gardening, shooting, bee-keeping. Address: Allens House, Plaxtol, near Sevenoaks, Kent. Clubs: Royal Air Force, Special Forces.

HODGES, Mark Willie; Head of the Office of Arts and Libraries, 1982–84; b 23 Oct. 1923; s of William H. and Eva Hodges; m 1948, Glenna Marion (née Peacock); one s one d. Educ: Cowbridge Grammar Sch.; Jesus Coll., Oxford (MA 1948). Served War, RN, 1942–45. Lectr, Univ. of Sheffield, 1950–54; DSIR, 1954–56; Asst Scientific Attaché, Washington, 1956–61; Office of Minister for Science, 1961–64; Sec., Royal Commn on Med. Educn, 1965–68; Asst Sec., DES, 1968–79 (Arts and Libraries Br., 1977–79); Office of Arts and Libraries, 1979–84, Under Sec., 1982, Dep. Sec., 1983. Member: South Bank Theatre Bd, 1982– (Chm., 1984–); Council, Royal Albert Hall, 1983–; Council and Management Cttee, Eastern Arts Assoc., 1986–. Recreations: making and mending, listening to music. Address: The Corner Cottage, Church Way, Little Stukeley, Cambs PE17 5BQ. T: Huntingdon 59266. Clubs: Athenæum, United Oxford & Cambridge University.

HODGETTS, Robert Bartley; Clerk to Worshipful Company of Glaziers, 1978–85; b 10 Nov. 1918; s of late Captain Bartley Hodgetts, MN and Florence Hodgetts (née Stagg); m 1st, 1945, A. K. Jeffreys; one d; 2nd, 1949, Frances Grace, d of late A. J. Pepper,

Worcester; two *d*. *Educ:* Merchant Taylors' Sch., Crosby; St John's Coll., Cambridge (Scholar, MA). Served RNVR (A), 1940–45. Asst Principal, Min. of Nat. Insce, 1947; Principal 1951; Asst Sec. 1964; Under-Sec., DHSS, 1973–78. *Recreations:* watching cricket and Rugby football. *Address:* 9 Purley Bury Close, Purley, Surrey. *T:* 01–668 2827.

HODGINS, Ven. Michael Minden; Archdeacon of Hackney, 1951–71; Secretary of London Diocesan Fund, 1946–74; *b* 26 Aug. 1912; *yr s* of late Major R. Hodgins, Indian Army, and Margaret Hodgins (*née* Wilson); unmarried. *Educ:* Wellington; Cuddesdon Theological Coll. Deacon, 1939; Priest, 1940; Curate, S Barnabas, Northolt Park, 1939; Asst Secretary, London Diocesan Fund, 1943. MA Lambeth 1960. *Address:* 5 Up, The Quadrangle, Morden College, Blackheath, SE3 0PW. *T:* 01–858 4762.

HODGKIN, Sir Alan (Lloyd), OM 1973; KBE 1972; FRS 1948; MA, ScD Cantab; Master of Trinity College, Cambridge, 1978–84 (Fellow, 1936–78 and since 1984); Chancellor, University of Leicester, 1971–84; *b* 5 Feb. 1914; *s* of G. L. Hodgkin and M. F. Wilson; *m* 1944, Marion de Kay, *d* of late F. P. Rous; one *s* three *d*. *Educ:* Gresham's Sch., Holt; Trinity Coll., Cambridge. Scientific Officer working on Radar for Air Ministry and Min. of Aircraft Production, 1939–45. Lecturer and then Asst Dir of Research at Cambridge, 1945–52; Foulerton Research Prof., Royal Soc., 1952–69; John Humphrey Plummer Prof. of Biophysics, Univ. of Cambridge, 1970–81. Baly Medal, RCP, 1955; Royal Medal of Royal Society, 1958; Nobel Prize for Medicine (jointly), 1963; Copley Medal of Royal Society, 1965. Pres., Royal Society, 1970–75; Pres., Marine Biological Assoc., 1966–76. Foreign Member: Royal Danish Acad. of Sciences, 1964; Amer. Acad. of Arts and Sciences, 1962; Amer. Philosophical Soc.; Royal Swedish Acad. of Sciences; Member: Physiological Soc.; Leopoldina Acad., 1964; Pontifical Acad. of Sciences, 1968; Hon. Mem., Royal Irish Acad., 1974; Hon. For. Mem., USSR Acad. of Scis, 1976. Fellow, Imperial Coll. London, 1972; Hon. FRSE, 1974; Hon. Fellow: Indian National Science Acad., 1972; Girton Coll., Cambridge, 1979; Pharmaceutical Soc.; For. Assoc., Nat. Acad. of Scis, USA, 1974. Hon. MD: Berne 1956, Louvain 1958; Hon. DSc: Sheffield 1963, Newcastle upon Tyne 1965, E Anglia 1966, Manchester 1971, Leicester 1971, London 1971, Newfoundland 1973, Wales 1973, Rockefeller Univ., 1974, Bristol 1976; Oxford, 1977; Hon. LLD: Aberdeen 1973; Salamanca, 1984. Lord Crook Medal, 1983. *Publications:* scientific papers dealing with the nature of nervous conduction, muscle and vision, Jl Physiology, etc. *Recreations:* travel, ornithology and fishing. *Address:* Physiological Laboratory, Cambridge; 18 Panton Street, Cambridge. *T:* Cambridge 352707.

HODGKIN, Prof. Dorothy Mary Crowfoot, OM 1965; FRS 1947; Emeritus Professor, University of Oxford; Hon. Fellow: Somerville College, Oxford; Linacre College, Oxford; Girton College, Cambridge; Newnham College, Cambridge; Fellow, Wolfson College, Oxford, 1977–82; Chancellor, Bristol University, since 1970; *b* 1910; *d* of late J. W. Crowfoot, CBE; *m* 1937, Thomas Lionel Hodgkin (*d* 1982); two *s* one *d*. *Educ:* Sir John Leman Sch., Beccles; Somerville Coll., Oxford. Fellow, Somerville Coll., 1936–77, Royal Soc. Wolfson Research Prof., 1960–77, Oxford Univ. Pres., BAAS, 1977–78. Fellow: Australian Academy of Science, 1968; Akad. Leopoldina, 1968. Foreign Member: Royal Netherlands Academy of Science and Letters, 1956; Amer. Acad. of Arts and Sciences, Boston, 1958, and other learned bodies. Hon. Foreign Member: US Nat. Acad. of Scis, 1971; USSR Acad. of Scis, 1976; Bavarian Acad., 1980. Hon. DSc Leeds, Manchester and others; Hon. ScD Cambridge; LLD Bristol; DUniv Zagreb and York; Hon. Dr Medicine and Surgery Modena. First Freedom of Beccles, 1965. Royal Medallist of the Royal Society, 1956; Nobel Prize for Chemistry, 1964; Copley Medal, Royal Soc., 1976; Mikhail Lomonosov Gold Medal, Soviet Acad. of Science, 1982; Mem., Ehrenzeichens für Kunst and Wissenschaft, Austria, 1983. *Publications:* various, on the X-ray crystallographic analysis of structure of molecules, including penicillin, vitamin B_{12} and insulin. *Recreations:* archæology, walking, children. *Address:* Crab Mill, Ilmington, Shipston-on-Stour, Warwicks. *T:* Ilmington 233.

HODGKIN, Eliot; artist and writer; *b* 19 June 1905; *o s* of Charles Ernest Hodgkin and Alice Jane Brooke; *m* 1940, Maria Clara (Mimi) Henderson (*née* Franceschi); one *s*. *Educ:* Harrow; Royal Academy Schs. Exhibited at Royal Academy and bought under Chantrey Bequest, for Tate Gallery: October, 1936; Undergrowth, 1943; Pink and White Turnips, 1972; One Man Shows: London Leicester Galleries, 1956; New York, Durlacher, 1958; London, Arthur Jeffress Gallery, 1959; New York, Durlacher, 1962; London, Reid Gallery, 1963; Agnew's, 1966. *Publications:* She Closed the Door, 1931; Fashion Drawing, 1932; 55 London Views, 1948; A Pictorial Gospel, 1949. *Address:* 23 Hillcrest, 51–57 Ladbroke Grove, W11 3AX.

HODGKIN, Howard, CBE 1977; painter; *b* 6 Aug. 1932; *m* 1955, Julia Lane; two *s*. *Educ:* Camberwell Sch. of Art; Bath Academy of Art. Taught at Charterhouse Sch., 1954–56; taught at Bath Academy of Art, 1956–66; occasional tutor, Slade Sch. of Art and Chelsea Sch. of Art. Vis. Fellow in Creative Art, Brasenose Coll. Oxford, 1976–77. A Trustee: Tate Gall., 1970–76; National Gall., 1978–85. One-man exhibitions include: Arthur Tooth & Sons, London, 1961, 1962, 1964, 1967; Kasmin Gallery, 1969, 1971, 1976; Arnolfini Gall., Bristol, 1970, 1975; Dartington Hall, 1970; Galerie Müller, Cologne, 1971; Kornblee Gall., NY, 1973; Museum of Modern Art, Oxford, 1976, 1977; Serpentine Gall., London and provincial tour, Waddington Gall., 1976; André Emmerich Gall., Zürich and NY, 1977; Third Sydney Biennale, Art Gall. of NSW, 1979; Waddington Galls, 1972, 1980; Knoedler Gall. NY, 1981, 1982, 1984; Bernard Jacobson NY, 1980, 1981, LA, 1981, London, 1982; Tate Gall., 1982, 1985; Bath Fest., 1984; Phillips Collection, Washington DC, 1984; XLI Venice Biennale, 1984; Yale Centre for British Art, New Haven, 1985; Kestner-Gesellschaft, Hanover, 1985; Whitechapel Art Gall., 1985; Group Exhibitions include: The Human Clay, Hayward Gall., 1976; British Painting 1952–1977, RA, 1977; A New Spirit in Painting, RA, 1981; Hard Won Image, Tate Gall., 1984; An International Survey of Recent Paintings and Sculpture, Mus. of Mod. Art, 1984; NY, Carnegie International, Mus. of Art, Carnegie Inst., 1985–86; and in exhibns in: Australia, Austria, Belgium, Canada, Denmark, France, Germany, GB, Holland, India, Italy, Japan, Malta, Norway, Sweden, Switzerland, USA. Works in public collections: Arts Council of GB; British Council, London; Contemp. Arts Soc.; Kettering Art Gall.; Peter Stuyvesant Foundn; São Paulo Museum; Oldham Art Gall.; Tate; V&A Museum; Swindon Central Lib.; Bristol City Art Gall.; Walker Art Center, Minneapolis; Nat. Gall. of S Aust., Adelaide; Fogg Art Museum, Cambridge, Mass; BM; Louisiana Museum, Denmark; Museum of Modern Art, Edinburgh; Southampton Art Gall.; Museum of Modern Art, NY; Mus. of Art, Carnegie Inst.; Whitworth Art Gall., Manchester; City of Manchester Art Galls; Govt Picture Coll., London. 2nd Prize, John Moore's Exhibn, 1976 and 1980; Turner Prize, 1985. *Address:* 32 Coptic Street, WC1. *T:* 01–580 7970.

HODGKINS, David John; Director, Safety Policy and Information Service Division, Health and Safety Executive, since 1984; *b* 13 March 1934; *s* of Rev. Harold Hodgkins and Elsie Hodgkins; *m* 1963, Sheila Lacey; two *s*. *Educ:* Buxton Coll.; Peterhouse, Cambridge. BA 1956, MA 1960. Entered Min. of Labour as Asst Principal, 1956; Principal: Min. of Lab., 1961–65; Treasury, 1965–68; Manpower and Productivity Services, Dept of Employment, 1968–70; Assistant Secretary: Prices and Incomes Div., Dept of Employment, 1970–72; Industrial Relns Div., 1973–76; Under Secretary, Overseas and Manpower Divisions, Dept of Employment, 1977–84. *Address:* Four Winds, Batchelors Way, Amersham, Bucks HP7 9AJ. *T:* Amersham 5207. *Club:* Royal Commonwealth Society.

HODGKINSON, Rev. Canon Arthur Edward; Retired Priest-in-Charge of St Ebba's, Eyemouth, Diocese of Edinburgh, 1982–86; *b* 29 Oct. 1913; *s* of Arthur and Rose Hodgkinson. *Educ:* Glasgow High School, Edinburgh Theol College. LTh Durham 1942. Deacon 1939; Priest 1940. Curate, St George's, Maryhill, Glasgow, 1939–43; Choir Chaplain, 1943, and Precentor of St Ninian's Cath., Perth, 1944–47; Curate-in-Charge, St Finnian's, Lochgelly, 1947–52, and Rector, 1952–54; Rector, Holy Trinity, Motherwell, 1954–65; Provost of St Andrew's Cathedral, Aberdeen, 1965–78; Area Sec., Dioceses of Monmouth, Llandaff, Swansea and Brecon, and St Davids, USPG, 1978–82. Commissary to Bp of St John's, 1961–78; Mem., Anglican Consultative Council, 1971–77; Canon of St Mary's Cath., Glasgow, 1963–65. Hon. Canon of Christ Church Cathedral, Connecticut, 1965–78; Hon. Canon of Aberdeen, 1981. *Recreations:* motoring, travel. *Address:* The Vicarage, Penmark, near Barry, South Glam CF6 9BN.

HODGKINSON, Sir Derek; *see* Hodgkinson, Sir W. D.

HODGKINSON, Terence William Ivan, CBE 1958; Member, Editorial Board, The Burlington Magazine, since 1978 (Editor, 1978–81); *b* 7 Oct. 1913; *s* of late Ivan Tattersall Hodgkinson, Wells, Som, and of late Kathryn Van Vleck Townsend, New York (who *m* 2nd, 1929, Sir Gilbert Upcott, KCB; he *d* 1967); unmarried. *Educ:* Oundle Sch.; Magdalen Coll., Oxford. Served War of 1939–45 Major, Gen. Staff 1943. Joined staff of Victoria and Albert Museum (Dept of Architecture and Sculpture) 1946; Asst to the Dir, 1948–62; Secretary to the Advisory Council, 1951–67; Keeper, Dept of Architecture and Sculpture, 1967–74; Dir, Wallace Collection, 1974–78. Member: Exec. Cttee, Nat. Art Collections Fund, 1975–; Museums and Galleries Commn, 1981–. *Publications:* (part author) Catalogue of Sculpture in the Frick Collection, New York, 1970; Catalogue of Sculpture at Waddesdon Manor, 1970; articles in Burlington Magazine, Bulletin and Yearbook of the Victoria and Albert Museum and for Walpole Society. *Recreation:* music. *Address:* 9 The Grove, N6.

HODGKINSON, Air Chief Marshal Sir (William) Derek, KCB 1971 (CB 1969); CBE 1960; DFC; AFC; *b* 27 Dec. 1917; *s* of late E. N. Hodgkinson; *m* 1939, Heather Goodwin, *d* of late H. W. Goodwin, Southampton; one *s* one *d*. *Educ:* Repton. Commnd, 1937; Coastal Comd, 1938–42; POW Germany, 1942–45; Coastal Comd, 1946–61; Staff of Chief of Defence Staff, and ADC to the Queen, 1961–63; Comdt RAF Staff Coll., Andover, 1965; Asst Chief of the Air Staff, Operational Requirements, 1966–68; SASO, RAF Training Command, 1969–70; AOC-in-C, Near East Air Force, Commander British Forces Near East, and Administrator, Sovereign Base Areas, Cyprus, 1970–73; Air Secretary, 1973–76; retired 1976. *Recreations:* cricket, fishing. *Address:* Frenchmoor Lodge, West Tytherley, Salisbury, Wilts SP5 1NU. *Clubs:* Royal Air Force, MCC.

HODGSON, Adam Robin; Chief Executive, Hampshire County Council, since 1985; *b* 20 March 1937; *s* of Thomas Edward Highton Hodgson, CB; *m* 1962, Elizabeth Maureen Linda Bovenizer; one *s* two *d*. *Educ:* William Ellis Sch., London; Worcester Coll., Oxford (MA). Admitted Solicitor, 1964. Asst Solicitor, LCC and GLC, 1964–66; Sen. Asst Solicitor, Oxfordshire CC, 1966–71; Asst Clerk, Northamptonshire CC, 1972–74; Dep. County Sec., E Sussex CC, 1974–77; Dep. Chief Exec. and Clerk, Essex CC, 1977–85. *Recreations:* music, drama, geology. *Address:* The Castle, Winchester SO23 8UJ. *T:* Winchester 54411.

HODGSON, Alfreda Rose, (Mrs Paul Blissett); concert singer; *b* 7 June 1940; *d* of Alfred and Rose Hodgson; *m* 1963, Paul Blissett; two *d*. *Educ:* Northern School of Music (GNSM; Hon. Fellow 1972); LRAM. Won Kathleen Ferrier Memorial Scholarship, 1964; first professional concert with Royal Liverpool Philharmonic Orchestra, 1964; since then has sung with all major orchestras in Britain, also throughout Europe, USA, Canada, Mexico, and elsewhere; Covent Garden début, 1983–84 season (Le Rossignol, and L'Enfant et les Sortilèges). Sir Charles Santley Meml Gift, Worshipful Co. of Musicians, 1985. *Address:* 16 St Mary's Road, Prestwich, Manchester M25 5AP. *T:* 061–773 1541.

HODGSON, Arthur Brian, CMG 1962; Consultant, League of Red Cross Societies, since 1982; *b* 24 Aug. 1916; *s* of late Major Arthur H. F. Hodgson, Westfields, Iffley, Oxford; *m* 1945, Anne Patricia Halse, *d* of late Lt-Col E. M. Ley, DSO, KRRC; two *s* two *d*. *Educ:* Edinburgh Academy; Eton Coll.; Oriel Coll., Oxford; Trinity Coll., Cambridge. Colonial Civil Service, Tanganyika Administration, 1939–62, retiring as Principal Sec. and Dir of Establishments. British Red Cross Society: Sec., 1964; Dep. Dir-Gen., 1966–70; Dir-Gen., 1970–75; Counsellor, 1975–81. *Recreations:* rowing, rifle shooting, gardening, messing about in boats. *Address:* Chandlers, Furners Green, near Uckfield, Sussex TN22 3RH. *T:* Danehill 790310. *Clubs:* Naval; Leander.

HODGSON, Hon. Sir Derek; *see* Hodgson, Hon. Sir W. D. T.

HODGSON, George Charles Day, CMG 1961; MBE 1950; lately an Administrative Officer, Nyasaland; retired from HMOCS, Nov. 1964; Secretary, Old Diocesans' Union, Diocesan College, Rondebosch, Cape, South Africa, 1964–86; *b* 21 Sept. 1913; *s* of late P. J. Hodgson and of A. E. Joubert; *m* 1st, 1940, Edna Orde (*d* 1977), *d* of late G. H. Rushmere; one *s*; 2nd, 1978, Cecile Paston Dewar (*née* Foster). *Educ:* Diocesan Coll., Rondebosch, Capetown, S Africa; Rhodes Univ., Grahamstown, S Africa; Cambridge Univ. Joined Colonial Administrative Service as Cadet, 1939. Military Service, 1940–42; Lieut, 1st Bn King's African Rifles. Returned to duty as Distr. Officer, Nyasaland, 1943; seconded for special famine relief duties in Nyasaland, 1949–50; Provincial Commissioner, 1952; Adviser on Race Affairs to Govt of Federation of Rhodesia and Nyasaland, 1958–59; Nyasaland Govt Liaison Officer to Monckton Commn, 1960; Permanent Sec., Ministry of Natural Resources and Surveys, Nyasaland, 1961–62; Permanent Sec., Ministry of Transport and Communications, Nyasaland, 1963–64. *Recreations:* Rugby football, cricket, golf. *Address:* Little Barn, 86 Dean Street, Newlands, Cape, 7700, South Africa. *Clubs:* Royal Cape Golf, Western Province Cricket (Cape Town).

HODGSON, Gordon Hewett; Master of the Supreme Court, Queen's Bench Division, since 1983; *b* 21 Jan. 1929; *s* of late John Lawrence Hodgson and Alice Joan Hodgson (*née* Wickham); *m* 1958, Pauline Audrey Gray; two *s*. *Educ:* Oundle School; University College London. LLB (Hons). National Service, RAEC, 1947–49; called to the Bar, Middle Temple, 1953; private practice, South Eastern Circuit, 1954–83; Asst Boundary Commissioner, 1976; Asst Recorder, 1979. *Recreations:* sailing, enjoying Tuscany. *Address:* Journeys End, Shothanger Way, Bovingdon, Herts HP3 0DW. *T:* Hemel Hempstead 833200. *Clubs:* East India; Royal Corinthian Yacht.

HODGSON, James, CBE 1984; Vice-Chairman, British Telecom, 1983–85; Chairman, Printing Equipment Economic Development Committee, 1986; *b* 14 Oct. 1925; *s* of late Frederick and Lucy Hodgson; *m* Brenda Dawn (*née* Giles). *Educ:* Exeter Sch.; St John's Coll., Cambridge. Entered GPO, 1950; Private Sec. to Asst PMG, 1952–55 and to Dir

Gen. GPO, 1955–56; seconded to Cabinet Office, 1961–63; Head of Telephone Operating Div. of GPO Headquarters, 1965–67; Dir (later Sen. Dir Internat.), PO Telecommunications, 1969–81; Man. Dir, British Telecom Internat., 1981–83. Dir (non-exec.), Cable and Wireless Ltd, 1970–78. FRSA 1984. *Recreations:* travel, archaeology. *Address:* 48 Andrewes House, Barbican, EC2Y 8AX.

HODGSON, John Bury; Special Commissioner of Income Tax, 1970–78; *b* 17 March 1912; *s* of Charles Hodgson and Dorothy Hope Hodgson; *m* 1948, Helen Sibyl Uvedale Beaumont. *Educ:* Derbyshire Grammar Sch.; Manchester Univ. Solicitor, 1942; Asst Solicitor of Inland Revenue, 1956–70. *Publications:* (contrib.) Halsbury's Laws of England; (Consulting Editor) Sergeant on Stamp Duties. *Recreations:* sailing, beekeeping. *Address:* Five Thorns Cottage, Brockenhurst, Hants. *T:* Lymington 22653. *Clubs:* various yacht.

HODGSON, Ven. John Derek; Archdeacon of Auckland and Canon Residentiary of Durham Cathedral, since 1983; *b* 15 Nov. 1931; *s* of Frederick and Hilda Hodgson; *m* 1956, Greta Wilson; two *s* one *d. Educ:* King James School, Bishop Auckland; St John's Coll., Durham (BA Hons History); Cranmer Hall, Durham (Dip. Theology). Short service commission, DLI, 1954–57. Deacon 1959, priest 1960; Curate: Stranton, Hartlepool, 1959–62; St Andrew's, Roker, 1962–64; Vicar: Stillington, 1964–66; Consett, 1966–75; Rector of Gateshead, 1975–83; RD of Gateshead, 1976–83; Hon. Canon of Durham, 1978–83. *Recreations:* walking, music, theatre, country houses. *Address:* 15 The College, Durham DH1 3EQ. *T:* Durham 3847534.

HODGSON, Sir Maurice (Arthur Eric), Kt 1979; Chairman, British Home Stores plc, since 1982 (Chief Executive, 1982–85); Director, Storehouse PLC, since 1985; *b* 21 Oct. 1919; *s* of late Walter Hodgson and of Amy Hodgson (*née* Walker); *m* 1945, Norma Fawcett; one *s* one *d. Educ:* Bradford Grammar Sch.; Merton Coll., Oxford (Hon. Fellow, 1979). MA, BSc; FEng, FIChemE; CChem, FRSC. Joined ICI Ltd Fertilizer & Synthetic Products Gp, 1942; seconded to ICI (New York) Ltd, 1955–58; Head of ICI Ltd Technical Dept, 1958; Develt Dir, ICI Ltd Heavy Organic Chemicals Div., 1960, Dep. Chm., 1964; Gen. Man., Company Planning, ICI Ltd, 1966; Commercial Dir and Planning Dir, ICI Ltd, 1970; Dep. Chm., ICI Ltd, 1972–78, Chm., 1978–82; Director: Carrington Viyella Ltd, 1970–74; Imperial Chemicals Insce Ltd, 1970–78 (Chm. 1972); Dunlop Holdings plc, 1982–84 (Chm. 1984); Member: Internat. Adv. Bd, AMAX Inc., 1982–; European Adv. Council, Air Products and Chemicals Inc., 1982–84. Chm., Civil Justice Review Adv. Cttee, 1985–; Member: Court, British Shippers' Council, 1978–82; Council, CBI, 1978–82; Internat. Council, Salk Inst., 1978–; Court, Univ. of Bradford, 1979–. Vis. Fellow, Sch. of Business and Organizational Studies, Univ. of Lancaster, 1970–. CBIM 1980 (FBIM 1972). Governor, London Grad. Sch. of Business Studies, 1978–. Hon. DUniv Heriot-Watt, 1979; Hon. DTech Bradford, 1979; Hon. DSc Loughborough, 1981; Hon. FUMIST, 1979. Messel Medal, Soc. of Chemical Industry, 1980; George E. Davis Medal, IChemE, 1982. *Recreations:* horse-racing, swimming, fishing. *Address:* British Home Stores plc, Marylebone House, 129–137 Marylebone Road, NW1 5QD.

HODGSON, Patricia Anne, (Mrs George Donaldson); The Secretary of the BBC, since 1985; *b* 19 Jan. 1947; *d* of Harold Hodgson and Pat Smith; *m* 1979, George Donaldson; one *s. Educ:* Brentwood High Sch.; Newnham Coll., Cambridge (MA); LRAM (Drama) 1968. Conservative Res. Dept, briefing on public sector industries, 1968–70; freelance journalism and broadcasting in UK and USA during seventies; Chm., Bow Gp, 1975–76; Editor, Crossbow, 1976–80. Joined BBC as producer for Open Univ., specialising in history and philosophy, 1970; most of prodn career in educn, with spells in current affairs on Today and Tonight. BBC Secretariat, 1982–, Dep. Sec., 1983–85. *Television series* include: English Urban History, 1978; Conflict in Modern Europe, 1980; Rome in the Age of Augustus, 1981. *Recreation:* quietness. *Address:* Broadcasting House, Portland Place, W1A 0AA. *T:* 01–580 4468.

HODGSON, Prof. Phyllis; Professor of English Language and Mediæval Literature, Bedford College, University of London, 1955–72, retired; *b* 27 June 1909; *d* of late Herbert Henry Hodgson, MA, BSc, PhD, FRIC. *Educ:* Bolling Grammar Sch. for Girls, Bradford; Bedford Coll., University of London (BA); (Sen. Schol.) Lady Margaret Hall, Oxford (BLitt, DPhil). Tutor of St Mary's Coll., Durham Univ., 1936–38; Jex-Blake Fellow, Girton Coll., Cambridge (MA), 1938–40; Lecturer in English Language (Part-time), Queen Mary Coll., University of London, and Lecturer in English, Homerton Coll., Cambridge, 1940–42; Lecturer in English Language and Mediæval Literature, Bedford Coll., University of London, 1942–49; Reader in English Language in the University of London, 1949–55; External examiner for Reading Univ., 1955–57, 1961–63. Mem. Council of Early English Text Soc., 1959–79; Chm., Bd of Studies in English, 1964–66. Sir Israel Gollancz Prize, British Academy, 1971. *Publications:* The Cloud of Unknowing (EETS), 1944, 1958; Deonise Hid Divinite (EETS), 1955, 1958, 1973; The Franklin's Tale, 1960; The Orcherd of Syon and the English Mystical Tradition (Proc. Brit. Acad. 1964), 1965; The Orcherd of Syon (EETS), 1966; Three 14th Century English Mystics, 1967; The General Prologue to the Canterbury Tales, 1969; The Cloud of Unknowing and Related Treatises (Analecta Cartusiana), 1982; articles in Review of English Studies, Modern Language Review, Contemporary Review, etc. *Recreations:* music, walking, travel. *Address:* 25 Barton Croft, Barton-on-Sea, New Milton, Hants BH25 7BT. *T:* New Milton 612 349. *Club:* University Women's.

HODGSON, Robin Granville; Managing Director, Granville & Co. Ltd, since 1979 (Director, since 1972); Director, Johnson Bros & Co. Ltd, Walsall, since 1970; *b* 25 April 1942; *s* of Henry Edward and Natalie Beatrice Hodgson; *m* 1982, Fiona Ferelith, *o d* of K. S. Allom, Dorking, Surrey; one *s. Educ:* Shrewsbury Sch.; Oxford Univ. (BA Hons 1964); Wharton Sch. of Finance, Univ. of Pennsylvania (MBA 1969). Investment Banker, New York and Montreal, 1964–67; Industry in Birmingham, England, 1969–72; Dir, Community Hospitals plc, 1982–85. Contested (C) Walsall North, Feb. and Oct. 1974; MP (C) Walsall North, Nov. 1976–1979. Chm., Birmingham Bow Gp, 1972–73; Mem. Central Council, 1979–, Asst Treas., W Midlands Area, 1985–, Nat. Union of Cons. Assocs. Member: Council for the Securities Industry, 1980–; Securities and Investment Board, 1985–; Chm., Nat. Assoc. of Security Dealers and Investment Managers, 1979–85. Trustee, Friends of Shrewsbury Sch.; Associate, St. George's House, Windsor. Liveryman, Goldsmiths' Co., 1983. *Publication:* Britain's Home Defence Gamble, 1978. *Recreations:* squash, theatre. *Address:* 44 Charlwood Street, SW1. *T:* 01–834 7562; Astley Abbotts, Bridgnorth, Salop. *T:* Bridgnorth 3122.

HODGSON, Stanley Ernest, CBE 1974 (OBE 1966); retired; Education Adviser, British High Commission, New Delhi, 1971–77; *b* 11 July 1918; *s* of Harold Frederick Hodgson, MPS, and Winifred Caroline (*née* Gale); *m* 1945, Joan Beryl (*née* Ballard); two *d. Educ:* Brentwood Grammar Sch.; London Univ. Teacher's Certif., London, 1941; BA Hons Russian, London, 1949. RA, 1941–46. British Council: India, 1949–54; Uganda, 1956–60; Reg. Rep., South India, 1965–68; Controller Estabts, 1969–71. Dir, Fest. of India in Britain 1982. *Recreations:* reading, gardening, walking. *Address:* Clarendon, Netherfield Road, Battle, East Sussex TN33 OHJ. *T:* Battle 2631. *Club:* Royal Commonwealth Society.

HODGSON, Col Terence Harold Henry, DSO 1945; MC 1944; TD 1953; FSVA; FRSH; Vice Lord Lieutenant of Cumbria, since 1983; *b* 10 Dec. 1916; *s* of late Michael C. L. Hodgson, Grange-over-Sands; *m* 1st, 1942, Joan Winsome Servant (marr. diss. 1969; she *d* 1974); 2nd, 1972, Doreen Jacqueline Pollit Brünzel (*d* 1985); three *s* three *d*; 3rd, 1985, Elizabeth Robinson. *Educ:* Kendal Grammar Sch. FSVA 1953; FRSH 1954. Served War with Border Regt, Ceylon, India and Burma; Col TA, 1959; Hon. Colonel: King's Own Royal Border Regt, 1976–82; Cumbria Cadet Force, 1977–86. Chairman: Governors, Kirkbie Kendal Sch., 1970–86; Kendal Almshouse Charities, 1975–86. Past Pres., Cumberland and Westmorland Rugby Union. DL Westmorland, 1959. *Recreations:* shooting, Rugby football, horse racing. *Address:* School House, Winster, Windermere, Cumbria LA23 3PU. *T:* Windermere 5439. *Club:* Army and Navy.

HODGSON, Thomas Charles Birkett, CVO 1970; OBE 1966; QPM 1969; Chief Constable, Thames Valley Constabulary, 1968–70; *b* 8 Dec. 1907; *s* of late Thomas Edward Birkett Hodgson, Preston, Lancs; *m* 1936, Gwyneth Cosslett Bowles, *d* of Ivor Willans Bowles, Llandaff, Cardiff; one *s* one *d. Educ:* St Peter's, York. Served with Lancashire Constabulary, 1927–55; Asst Chief Constable, Birmingham, 1955–59; Chief Constable, Berkshire, 1959–68. *Address:* Little Newnham, Sutton Veny, near Warminster, Wilts. *T:* Sutton Veny 254.

HODGSON, Ven. Thomas Richard Burnham; Archdeacon of West Cumberland, since 1979; *b* 17 Aug. 1926; *s* of Richard Shillito Hodgson and Marion Thomasina Bertram Marshall; *m* 1952, Margaret Esther, *o d* of Evan and Caroline Margaret Makinson; one *s* one *d. Educ:* Harden House Prep. Sch.; Heversham Grammar School; London Coll. of Divinity, Univ. of London. BD, ALCD. Deacon 1952, priest 1953, dio. Carlisle; Curate of Crosthwaite, Keswick, 1952–55; Curate of Stanwix, Carlisle, 1955–59; Vicar of St Nicholas', Whitehaven, 1959–65; Rector of Aikton, 1965–67; Vicar of Raughtonhead with Gaitsgill, 1967–73; Hon. Canon of Carlisle, 1973–; Vicar of: Grange-over-Sands, 1973–79; Mosser, 1979–83. Mem., General Synod of C of E, 1983–. Domestic Chaplain to Bishop of Carlisle, 1967–73, Hon. Chaplain 1973–79; Director of Ordination Candidates, 1970–74; RD of Windermere, 1976–79; Surrogate, 1962–. *Recreations:* listening to music, watching drama, geology, meteorological observing. *Address:* Moorside, 50 Stainburn Road, Workington, Cumbria.

HODGSON, Hon. Sir (Walter) Derek (Thornley), Kt 1977; **Hon. Mr Justice Hodgson;** a Judge of the High Court of Justice, Queen's Bench Division, since 1977; *b* 24 May 1917; *s* of late Walter Hodgson, Whitefield, Manchester; *m* 1951, Raymonde Valda (*née* de Villiers) (*d* 1965); no *c. Educ:* Malvern Coll.; Trinity Hall, Cambridge. Scholar, Trinity Hall; Harmsworth Scholar, Middle Temple; 1st Cl. Law Tripos, Part II, 1938; 1st Cl. LLB, 1939. Served throughout War 1939–46, Royal Artillery; Burma 1942–45; released with rank of Captain, 1946. Called to Bar, Middle Temple, 1946 (Master of the Bench, 1967); QC 1961. Member: Senate of Inns of Court, 1966–69; Gen. Council of the Bar, 1965–69. Judge of the Salford Hundred Court of Record, 1965–71; a Law Comr, 1971–77; a Recorder of the Crown Court, 1972–77. Member: Lord Chancellor's Cttees on: Legal Educn, 1968–71; Contempt of Court, 1971–74; Butler Cttee on Mentally Abnormal Offenders, 1973–75; Parole Board, 1981–83 (Vice-Chm., 1982–83). Chm., Howard League Wkg Pty on Forfeiture (report published as The Profits of Crime and their Recovery, 1984). *Recreations:* fell walking, travel. *Address:* Royal Courts of Justice, Strand, WC2. *Clubs:* United Oxford & Cambridge University; Tennis and Racquets (Manchester); Hawks (Cambridge).

HODGSON, William Donald John; *b* 25 March 1923; *s* of James Samuel Hodgson and Caroline Maud Albrecht; *m* 1946, Betty Joyce Brown; two *s* six *d. Educ:* Beckenham Grammar School. Served Beds and Herts Regt, 1940–42; pilot, RAF and Fleet Air Arm, 1942–46. Documentary and feature film editor (with Jean Renoir on The River, Calcutta), 1946–50; Organiser, Festival of Britain Youth Programme, 1950–51; Asst Sec., Central Bureau for Educational Visits and Exchanges, 1951–54; Asst Gen. Man., Press Assoc., 1954–60; Gen. Man., ITN, 1960–82; Dir of Develt, ITN, 1982–86 (Dir, 1973–). Dir, UPITN Corp., 1967–73. Executive Producer: Battle for the Falklands, 1982; Theft of a Thoroughbred, 1983; Victory in Europe, 1985. *Recreations:* child and grandchildcare, private flying, cricket, swimming. *Address:* 38 Park Road, Beckenham, Kent. *T:* 01–650 8959.

HODIN, Prof. Josef Paul, LLD; author, art historian, art critic; *b* 17 Aug. 1905; *s* of Eduard D. Hodin and Rosa (*née* Klug); *m* 1945, Doris Pamela Simms; one *s* one *d. Educ:* Kleinseitner Realschule and Neustädter Realgymnasium, Prague; Charles Univ., Prague; London Univ.; Art Academies of Dresden and Berlin. Press Attaché to Norwegian Govt in London, 1944–45; Dir of Studies and Librarian, Inst. of Contemporary Arts, London, 1949–54; Hon. Mem. Editorial Council of The Journal of Aesthetics and Art Criticism, Cleveland, 1955–; Mem. Exec. Cttee British Soc. of Aesthetics; Pres., British Section, AICA; Editor: Prisme des Arts, Paris, 1956–59; Quadrum, Brussels, 1956–66. 1st internat. prize for art criticism, Biennale, Venice, 1954. Hon. PhD Uppsala, 1969; Hon. Prof. Vienna, 1975. DSM 1st cl. Czechoslovakia, 1947; St Olav Medal, Norway, 1958; Comdr, Order of Merit, Italy, 1966; Grand Cross, Order of Merit, Austria, 1968; Order of Merit, 1st cl., Germany, 1969; Silver Cross of Merit, Austria, 1972. *Publications:* Monographs on Sven Erixson (Stockholm), 1940; Ernst Josephson (Stockholm), 1942, Edvard Munch (Stockholm), 1948, (Frankfurt a/M), 1951; Isaac Grünewald (Stockholm), 1949; Art and Criticism (Stockholm), 1944; J. A. Comenius and Our Time (Stockholm), 1944; The Dilemma of Being Modern (London), 1956, (New York), 1959; Henry Moore (Amsterdam, Hamburg), 1956, (London, New York), 1958, (Buenos Aires), 1963; Ben Nicholson (London), 1957; Barbara Hepworth (Neuchatel, London, New York), 1961; Lynn Chadwick (Amsterdam, Hamburg, London, New York), 1961; Bekenntnis zu Kokoschka (Mainz), 1963; Edvard Munch (Mainz), 1963; Oskar Kokoschka: A Biography (London, New York), 1966; Walter Kern (Neuchatel, London), 1966; Ruszkowski (London), 1967; Bernard Leach (London), 1967; Oskar Kokoschka: Sein Leben Seine Zeit (Mainz), 1968; Kafka und Goethe (Hamburg), 1968; Die Brühlsche Terrasse, Ein Künstlerroman, 1970; Emilio Greco, Life and Work (London, New York), 1971; Edvard Munch (London, New York, Oslo), 1972; Modern Art and the Modern Mind (London, Cleveland), 1972; Alfred Manessier (London, NY, Paris), 1972; Bernard Stern (London), 1972; Ludwig Meidner (Darmstadt), 1973; Hilde Goldschmidt (Hamburg), 1974; Paul Berger-Bergner, Leben und Werk (Hamburg), 1974; Die Leute von Elverdingen (Hamburg), 1974; Kokoschka und Hellas (Vienna), 1977; John Milne (London), 1977; Else Meidner, 1979; Elisabeth Frink, 1984; Douglas Portway, 1983; Franz Luby (Vienna), 1983; Dieses Mütterchen hat Krallen, die Geschichte einer Prager Jugend (Hamburg), 1985; contribs on literary and art subjects to internat. periodicals. *Address:* 12 Eton Avenue, NW3 3EH. *T:* 01–794 3609. *Clubs:* Athenæum, Arts.

HODKIN, Rev. Canon Hedley; Residentiary Canon, Manchester Cathedral, 1957–70, Canon Emeritus, since 1970; Sub-Dean, 1966–70; *b* 3 Jan. 1902; *s* of Walter and Elizabeth Hodkin; *m* 1932, Mary M., *d* of Dr J. A. Findlay; one *s* one *d. Educ:* University of Sheffield; Christ's Coll. and Westcott House, Cambridge. Curate of: Morpeth, 1935–38; St George's, Newcastle, 1938–40; Vicar of: St Luke's, Newcastle, 1940–47; Holy Trinity, Millhouses, Sheffield, 1947–57. Examining Chaplain: to Bishop of Newcastle, 1939–47; to Bishop of Sheffield, 1951–57; to Bishop of Manchester, 1957. Hon. Canon of Sheffield,

1955–57. Select Preacher, Cambridge, 1968. *Recreation:* music. *Address:* 79 Folds Crescent, Sheffield S8 0EP. *T:* Sheffield 362155.

HODKINSON, Prof. Henry Malcolm, DM; FRCP; Barlow Professor of Geriatric Medicine, University College London, since 1985; *b* 28 April 1931; *s* of Charles and Olive Hodkinson; *m* (marr. diss.); four *d. Educ:* Brasenose Coll., Oxford (DM 1975); Middlesex Hospital. FRCP 1974. Consultant Physician in Geriatrics to: Enfield and Tottenham Gps of Hosps, 1962–70; Northwick Park Hosp., 1970–78 (also Mem., Scientific Staff of Clin. Res. Centre); Sen. Lectr in Geriatric Medicine, 1978–79, Prof. of Geriatric Medicine, 1979–84, RPMS. *Publications:* An Outline of Geriatrics, 1975, 2nd edn 1981 (trans. Spanish, Dutch, German, Italian and Japanese); Common Symptoms of Disease in the Elderly, 1976, 2nd edn 1980 (trans. Turkish), Biochemical Diagnosis of the Elderly, 1977; (ed) Clinical Biochemistry of the Elderly, 1984; approx. 100 papers in learned jls, 1961–. *Recreations:* English glass and ceramics. *Address:* 8 Chiswick Square, Burlington Lane, Chiswick, W4 2QG. *T:* 01–747 0239.

HODKINSON, William, CBE 1974 (OBE 1952); Part-time Member, British Gas Corporation, 1973–74; *b* 11 Aug. 1909; *s* of late William Hodkinson and late Ann Greenwood; *m* 1934, Ann, *d* of John Buxton; one *s. Educ:* St Anne's, Stretford; Salford Technical Coll. Stretford Gas Co.: Technical Asst, 1930–32; Asst Works Manager, 1932–35; UK Gas Corp. Ltd: Chief Technical Officer, 1935–39; Gen. Man., 1939–46; Tech. Dir and Gen. Man., 1946–49; North Western Gas Board (later North Western Gas Region): Chief Technical and Planning Officer, 1949–56; Dep. Chm., 1956–64; Chm., 1964–74. Pres., InstGasE, 1963–64. OStJ 1968. *Recreation:* golf. *Address:* 19 Harewood Avenue, Sale, Cheshire. *T:* 061–962 4653.

HODSON, Denys Fraser, CBE 1981; Director, Arts and Recreation, Thamesdown Borough Council, since 1974; *b* 23 May 1928; *s* of Rev. Harold Victor Hodson, MC and Marguerite Edmée Ritchie; *m* 1954, Julie Compton Goodwin; one *s* one *d. Educ:* Marlborough Coll.; Trinity Coll., Oxford (MA). After a career in commerce and industry, apptd first Controller of Arts and Recreation, Swindon Bor. Council, 1970. Chairman: Southern Arts Assoc., 1974–80 and 1985–; Council, Regional Arts Assocs, 1975–80; Chief Leisure Officers' Assoc., 1974 and 1982–84; a Dir, Oxford Playhouse Co., 1974–; a Governor: BFI, 1976–; Wyvern Arts Trust, 1984–. *Publications:* (contrib.) Arts Centres, 1981; conf. papers and articles. *Recreations:* bird-watching, fishing, the arts. *Address:* Manor Farm House, Fairford, Glos GL7 4AR. *T:* Cirencester 712462.

HODSON, Donald Manly; *b* 10 Sept. 1913; 2nd *s* of late Prof. T. C. Hodson; *m* 1940, Margaret Beatson Bell, *er d* of late Sir Nicholas Beatson Bell, KCSI, KCIE, three *s* one *d. Educ:* Gresham's Sch.; Balliol Coll., Oxford. Editorial staff, the Economist, 1935; Leader writer, Financial Times, 1936; Asst Leader Page Editor, News Chronicle, 1937–38; Leader Page Editor, News Chronicle, 1939. BBC European Services: Sub-Editor, 1940; Chief Sub-Editor, 1942; Duty Editor, 1943; European Talks Editor, 1945; Asst Head of European News Dept, 1946; Head of European Talks and English Dept, 1948–51; Asst Controller, European Services, 1951–58; Controller, Overseas Services, 1958–68; Controller of Programmes, External Broadcasting, 1968–70; Dir of Programmes, External Broadcasting, 1971–73, retired. *Address:* Scotland House, Scotland Street, Stoke by Nayland, Suffolk. *T:* Nayland 262102.

HODSON, Prof. Frank, BSc London 1949; PhD Reading 1951; Professor of Geology in the University of Southampton, 1958–81, now Emeritus; *b* 23 Nov. 1921; *s* of late Matthew and Gertrude Hodson; *m* 1945, Ada Heyworth; three *d. Educ:* Burnley Grammar Sch.; Reading Univ.; London Univ. (external student). Demonstrator, Reading Univ., 1947–49; Lecturer, Reading Univ., 1949–58. Dean, Faculty of Science, 1972–74, and 1976–77, Public Orator, 1970–73, Univ. of Southampton. Murchison Fund, Geol. Soc., 1962; Founder Mem. and first Hon. Sec., Palaeontol. Assoc., 1957. Pres. Sect. C (geology), British Assoc. for Adv. of Science, 1975; Mem., Mineralogical Soc. of GB. Hon. Mem. Geol. Soc. de Belg. *Publications:* geological papers in publications of learned societies. *Recreation:* book collecting. *Address:* Department of Geology, The University, Southampton SO9 5NH.

HODSON, Henry Vincent; Editor, The Annual Register (of world events), since 1973; *b* 12 May 1906; *er s* of late Prof. T. C. Hodson; *m* 1933, Margaret Elizabeth Honey, Sydney; four *s. Educ:* Gresham's Sch.; Balliol Coll., Oxford. Fellow of All Souls Coll., Oxford, 1928–35; Staff of Economic Advisory Council, 1930–31; Asst Editor of the Round Table, 1931, Editor, 1934–39; Director, Empire Div., Ministry of Information, 1939–41; Reforms Commissioner, Govt of India, 1941–42; Principal Asst Sec., and later head of Non-Munitions Div., Min. of Production, 1942–45; Asst Editor, Sunday Times, 1946–50, Editor, 1950–61; Provost of Ditchley, 1961–71. Sole Partner, Hodson Consultants, 1971–. Consultant Editor, The International Foundation Directory, 1974–. Past Master, Mercers' Co. *Publications:* Economics of a Changing World, 1933; (part) The Empire in the World, 1937; Slump and Recovery, 1929–37, 1938; The British Commonwealth and the Future, 1939; Twentieth Century Empire, 1948; Problems in Anglo-American Relations, 1963; The Great Divide: Britain-India-Pakistan, 1969 (reissued 1985); The Diseconomics of Growth, 1972; many articles in reviews, etc. *Address:* 23 Cadogan Lane, SW1X 9DP. *T:* 01–235 5509.

HODSON, Sir Michael (Robin Adderley), 6th Bt *cr* 1789; Captain, Scots Guards, retired; *b* 5 March 1932; *s* of Major Sir Edmond Adair Hodson, 5th Bt, DSO, and Anne Elizabeth Adderley (*d* 1984), *yr d* of Lt-Col Hartopp Francis Charles Adderley Cradock, Hill House, Sherborne St John; *S* father, 1972; *m* 1st, 1963, Katrin Alexa (marr. diss. 1978), *d* of late Erwin Bernstiel, Dinas Powis, Glamorgan; three *d*; 2nd, 1978, Catherine, *d* of John Henry Seymour, Wimpole St, W1. *Educ:* Eton. *Heir: b* Patrick Richard Hodson [*b* 27 Nov. 1934; *m* 1961, June, *o d* of H. M. Shepherd-Cross; three *s*]. *Address:* The White House, Awbridge, Romsey, Hants.

HODSON, Thomas David Tattersall; barrister; a Recorder of the Crown Court, since 1983; *b* 24 Sept. 1942; *s* of Thomas Norman Hodson and Elsie Nuttall Hodson; *m* 1969, Patricia Ann Vint; two *s* one *d. Educ:* Sedbergh Sch.; Manchester Univ. (LLB). Leader Writer, Yorkshire Post, 1964–65; called to the Bar, Inner Temple 1966; in practice on Northern Circuit, 1967–; Junior, 1969. *Recreations:* music, squash, fell-walking. *Address:* St James's Chambers, 68 Quay Street, Manchester M3 3EL. *T:* 061–834 7000.

HOFF, Harry Summerfield; see Cooper, William.

HOFFENBERG, Sir Raymond, (Bill), KBE 1984; PRCP; President, Wolfson College, Oxford, since 1985; *b* 6 March 1923; *er s* of Benjamin and Dora Hoffenberg; *m* 1949; two *s. Educ:* Grey High Sch., Port Elizabeth; Univ. of Cape Town. MB, ChB 1948, MD, PhD; MA Oxon. FRCPE, FRCPI; Hon. FRACP, Hon. FACP. Served with S African Armed Forces, N Africa and Italy, 1942–45. Sen. Lectr, Dept of Medicine, Univ. of Cape Town and Cons. Phys., Groote Schuur Hosp., 1955–67; Carnegie Corp. of NY Trav. Fellow, 1957–58; banned by S African Govt, 1967; emigrated to UK, 1968. Sen. Scientist, MRC (UK), attached Div. of Biophysics, Nat. Inst. of Med. Res., 1968–70 and Clinical Res. Centre, Harrow, 1970–72; Cons. Phys. (Endocrinology), New End Hosp. and Royal Free Hosp. Med. Sch., London, 1968–70; William Withering Prof. of Medicine, Univ. of

Birmingham, 1972–85. Member: West Midlands RHA, 1976–83; MRC, 1978–82. Member: Central and Exec. Cttee, Internat. Soc. for Endocrinology, 1976–; Royal Soc. Med., Endocr. Sect., 1970– (Pres., 1978–80); Med. Res. Soc. (Chm., 1978–83); Assoc. of Physicians (Pres., 1985–86); Amer. Assoc. of Physicians. Member Editorial Board: Clinical Science, 1968–72 (Chm. 1971–72), Clinical Endocrinology, 1971–77; Jl of Endocrinology, 1974–77; Qly Jl of Medicine, 1975–. Royal College of Physicians: Oliver-Sharpey Lectr, 1973; Procensor and Censor, 1977–79; Senior Censor and Vice Pres., 1981–82; Pres., 1983–. Freeman, City of London. Hon. DSc: Leicester; City. *Publications:* chapters and scientific papers on various aspects of endocrinology and metabolism in med. and biochem. jls. *Recreations:* (largely nostalgic) reading, walking, gardening, golf, tennis. *Address:* Wolfson College, Oxford OX2 6UD. *T:* Oxford 56711.

HOFFMAN, Dustin Lee; actor; *b* 8 Aug. 1937; *s* of Harry Hoffman and Lillian Hoffman; *m* 1st, 1969, Anne Byrne (marr. diss. 1980); two *d*; 2nd, 1980, Lisa Gottsegen; two *s* one *d. Educ:* Santa Monica City Coll.; Pasadena Playhouse. Stage debut in Sarah Lawrence Coll. prodn, Yes is For a Very Young Man; Broadway debut, A Cook for Mr General, 1961; appeared in: Harry, and Noon and Night, Amer. Place Theatre, NY, 1964–65; Journey of the Fifth Horse, and Star Wagon, 1965; Fragments, Berkshire Theatre Festival, Stockbridge, Mass, 1966; Eh?, 1966–67; Jimmy Shine, Broadway, 1968–69; Death of a Salesman, Broadway, 1984. Dir, All Over Town, Broadway, 1974. Films: The Graduate, 1967; Midnight Cowboy, 1969; John and Mary, 1969; Little Big Man, 1971; Who Is Harry Kellerman and Why Is He Saying Those Terrible Things About Me?, 1971; Straw Dogs, 1972; Alfredo, Alfredo, 1972; Papillon, 1973; Lenny, 1974; All The President's Men, 1975; Marathon Man, 1976; Straight Time, 1978; Agatha, 1979; Kramer vs Kramer, 1979 (Academy Award); Tootsie, 1983; Death of a Salesman, 1985. Record: Death of a Salesman. Obie Award as best off-Broadway actor, 1965–66, for Journey of the Fifth Horse; Drama Desk, Theatre World, and Vernon Rice Awards for Eh?, 1966; Oscar Award nominee for The Graduate, Midnight Cowboy, and Lenny. *Address:* Punch Productions, c/o Columbia Pictures, 711 Fifth Avenue, New York, NY 10022, USA.

HOFFMAN, Michael Richard, CEng; Chief Executive and Managing Director, Babcock International PLC, since 1983; *b* 31 Oct. 1939; *s* of Sydney William Hoffman and Ethel Margaret Hoffman (*née* Hill); *m* 1st, 1963, Margaret Edith Tregaskes (marr. diss. 1978); one *d*; 2nd, 1982, Helen Judith Peters. *Educ:* Hitchin Grammar Sch.; Univ. of Bristol (BScEng Hons). FIMechE, FIProdE. Rolls Royce, 1961; AE Ltd, 1973; Perkins Engines Group: Managing Director, 1976; Chairman, 1977; Massey Ferguson Ltd: Vice President, 1980; President, Farm Machinery Div., 1981. Vice Pres., IProdE, 1985–; Member: Technology Requirements Bd, 1985–; Council, Brunel Univ., 1984–. *Recreations:* squash, tennis, sailing. *Address:* 43 De Vere Gardens, W8 5AW. *T:* 01–580 4612. *Clubs:* Reform, Royal Automobile; Warwick Boat; Cambridge (Toronto).

HOFFMAN, Rev. Canon Stanley Harold, MA; Chaplain in Ordinary to the Queen, since 1976; Hon. Canon of Rochester Cathedral, 1965–80, now Emeritus; *b* 17 Aug. 1917; *s* of Charles and Ellen Hoffman, Denham, Bucks; *m* 1943, Mary Mifanwy Patricia, *d* of late Canon Creed Meredith, Chaplain to the Queen, and of Mrs R. Creed Meredith, Windsor; one *s* one *d. Educ:* The Royal Grammar Sch., High Wycombe, Bucks; St Edmund Hall, Oxford (BA 1939, MA 1943); Lincoln Theol. Coll., 1940–41. Deacon, 1941; Priest, 1942; Curate: Windsor Parish Ch., 1941–44; All Saints, Weston, Bath, 1944–47; Chertsey (in charge of All SS), 1947–50; Vicar of Shottermill, Haslemere, Sy, 1951–64; Diocesan Director of Education, Rochester, 1965–80; Warden of Readers, 1974–80. Proctor in Convocation, Church Assembly, 1969–70; Exam. Chaplain to Bp of Rochester, 1973–80. Member: Kent Educn Cttee, 1965–80; Bromley Educn Cttee, 1967–80; Kent Council of Religious Educn, 1965–80; Archbps' Commn on Christian Initiation, 1970. Vice-Chm., Christ Church Coll., Canterbury, 1973–80. Hon. MA Kent, 1982. *Publications:* (pt-author): A Handbook of Thematic Material, 1968; Christians in Kent, 1972; Teaching the Parables, 1974; contrib. various pubns on Preaching and Religious Educn; numerous Dio. study papers. *Recreations:* music, walking (in love with Cornwall). *Address:* Cedarwood, Holly Close, Grayshott Road, Headley Down, Bordon, Hants. *T:* Headley Down 713128.

HOFFMANN, Hon. Sir Leonard Hubert, Kt 1985; **Hon. Mr Justice Hoffmann;** a Judge of the High Court of Justice, Chancery Division, since 1985; *b* 8 May 1934; *s* of B. W. and G. Hoffmann; *m* 1957, Gillian Lorna Sterner; two *d. Educ:* South African College Sch., Cape Town; Univ. of Cape Town (BA); The Queen's Coll., Oxford (Rhodes Scholar; MA, BCL, Vinerian Law Scholar). Advocate of Supreme Court of S Africa, 1958–60. Called to the Bar, Gray's Inn, 1964, Bencher, 1984; QC 1977; a Judge, Courts of Appeal of Jersey and Guernsey, 1980–86. Stowell Civil Law Fellow, University Coll., Oxford, 1961–73. Member: Royal Commn on Gambling, 1976–78; Council of Legal Educn, 1983–. Dir, ENO, 1985–. *Publication:* The South African Law of Evidence, 1963. *Address:* Surrey Lodge, 23 Keats Grove, NW3 2RS.

HOFFMANN, Prof. Roald; John A. Newman Professor of Physical Science, Cornell University, since 1974; *b* 18 July 1937; *s* of Hillel Safran and Clara (*née* Rosen, who *m* 2nd, Paul Hoffmann); *m* 1960, Eva Börjesson; one *s* one *d. Educ:* Columbia Univ. (BA); Harvard Univ. (MA, PhD). Junior Fellow, Society of Fellows, Harvard Univ., 1962–65; Associate Professor, to Professor, Cornell Univ., 1965–74. Member: Nat. Acad. of Sciences; Amer. Acad. of Arts and Sciences. Foreign Member: Royal Soc., 1984; Indian Nat. Acad. of Sciences; Royal Swedish Acad. of Sciences. Hon. DTech Royal Inst. of Technology, Stockholm, 1977; Hon. DSc: Yale, 1980; Hartford, 1982; Columbia, 1982; City Univ. of NY, 1983; Puerto Rico, 1983; La Plata, 1984; Uruguay, 1984; State Univ. of NY at Binghamton, 1985; Colgate, 1985. Nobel Prize for Chemistry, 1981. *Publications:* many scientific articles. *Address:* Department of Chemistry, Cornell University, Ithaca, NY 14853, USA.

HOFFMEISTER, Maj.-Gen. Bertram Meryl, OC 1982; CB 1945; CBE 1944; DSO 1943; ED; *b* 15 May 1907; *s* of Flora Elizabeth Rodway and Louis George Hoffmeister; *m* 1935, Donalda Strauss; one *s* one *d. Educ:* Public Schs, Vancouver. Previous to war of 1939–45 employed by H. R. MacMillan Export Co. Ltd, Vancouver, BC. 1st Lieut Seaforth Highlanders of Canada, 1927; Capt. 1934; Major 1939 and given command of a rifle Co. Served with Seaforth Highlanders in England as Co. Comdr, 1939–40; returned to Canada, 1942, to attend Canadian Junior War Staff Course; given Command of Seaforth Highlanders of Canada and commanded this Bn in assault on Sicily in July 1943 (DSO); Brig. Oct. 1943 and assumed command 2 Canadian Infantry Brigade (Bar to DSO battle of Ortona); Maj.-Gen. and commanded 5 Cdn Armoured Div. March 1944; operations on Hitler Line, May-June 1944 (2nd Bar to DSO, CBE); in NW Europe until conclusion of hostilities (CB). GOC Canadian Army Pacific Force, 1945. Gen. Manager, Canadian White Pine Co. Ltd, and MacMillan Industries Ltd (Plywood Div.), 1945–47; H. R. MacMillan Export Co. Ltd; Gen. Mgr Prod., 1947–49 and Vice-Pres. Prod., 1949; Pres., 1949–51; MacMillan & Bloedel Ltd; Pres. 1951–56; Chm. Bd, 1956–57. Agent-Gen. for British Columbia, 1958–61. Pres., Council of the Forest Industries of BC, Vancouver, 1961–71. Chm., Nature Trust of BC (formerly Nat. Second Century Fund of BC, 1971–). *Recreations:* rugby, rowing, shooting, skiing. *Address:* 3040 Procter Avenue,

West Vancouver, BC V7V 1G1, Canada. *Clubs:* Vancouver, Capilano Golf and Country, Vancouver Rowing (Vancouver); Canadian.

HOFMEYR, Murray Bernard; Member, Executive Committee, Anglo American Corporation of South Africa Limited, since 1972; *b* 9 Dec. 1925; *s* of William and Margareta Hofmeyr; *m* 1953, Johanna Hendrika Hofmeyr (*née* Verdurmen); three *s* two *d. Educ:* BA (Rhodes), MA (Oxon). Joined Anglo American Corp., 1962; in Zambia, 1965–72; in England, 1972–80; Man. Dir, 1972–76, Chm. and Man. Dir, 1976–80, Charter Consolidated Ltd. *Recreations:* golf, tennis; Captain Oxford Univ. Cricket, 1951; played Rugby for England, 1950. *Address:* 54 Melville Road, Illovo, Johannesburg, South Africa.

HOFSTADTER, Prof. Robert; Max H. Stein Professor of Physics, Stanford University, 1971–85, now Emeritus; Director, High Energy Physics Laboratory, Stanford University, 1967–74; *b* Manhattan, New York, NY, 5 Feb. 1915; *s* of Louis and Henrietta Hofstadter; *m* 1942, Nancy Givan, Baltimore, Md; one *s* two *d. Educ:* City Coll. of New York (BS *magna cum laude*); Princeton Univ. (MA, PhD). Instructor in Physics: University of Pennsylvania, 1940–41; City Coll., New York, 1941–42; Associate Physicist and Physicist, Nat. Bureau of Standards, Washington DC, 1942–43; Asst Chief Physicist, Norden Laboratories Corp., New York, 1943–46; Asst Prof., physics, Princeton Univ., 1946–50; Associate Prof., physics, Stanford Univ., 1950–54; Prof., physics, 1954–. Member, Board of Governors: Weizmann Institute of Science, Rehovoth, Israel, 1967–; Technion, Haifa, Israel, 1977–85. Mem., Bd of Directors, John Fluke Manufacturing Co., Washington, 1979–. Associate Editor: Physical Review, 1951–53; Investigations in Physics, 1958–65; Review of Scientific Instruments, 1954–56; Reviews of Modern Physics, 1958–61. Has held various fellowships; Fellow American Physical Soc.; FPS (London); MNAS; Member: Amer. Acad. of Arts and Sciences; Inst. of Medicine; Amer. Phil Soc.; Amer. Acad. of Achievement. Sigma Xi; Phi Beta Kappa. Hon. LLD, City Univ. of NY, 1962; Hon. DSc: Gustavus Adolphus Coll., Minn, 1963; Carleton Univ., Ottawa, 1967; Seoul Nat. Univ., 1967; Technion, Haifa, Israel, 1985; *Laurea (hc)*, Padua, 1965; Dr Univ. (*hc*), Univ. of Clermont, 1967; Dr rer. nat. (*hc*) Julius-Maximilians Univ. of Würzburg, 1982; Dr rer. nat. (*hc*) Johannes Gutenberg Univ. of Mainz, 1982. (Jtly) Nobel Prize in Physics, 1961. *Publications:* (with Robert Herman) High Energy Electron Scattering Tables, 1960 (US); (ed) Nuclear and Nucleon Structure, 1963 (US); (co-ed with L. I. Schiff) Nucleon Structure (Proc. Internat. Conf. at Stanford Univ., 1963), 1964; numerous scientific papers on various aspects of molecular structure, solid state physics, nuclear physics, elementary particles, quantum electrodynamics, laser fusion and review articles on crystal counters, electron scattering, nuclear and nucleon structure and coronary angiography. *Recreations:* ranching, photography. *Address:* Department of Physics, Stanford University, Stanford, Calif 94305–2184, USA.

HOGAN, Air Vice-Marshal Henry Algernon Vickers, CB 1955; DFC 1940; retired; *b* 25 Oct. 1909; *s* of late Lt-Col Edward M. A. Hogan, IA; *m* 1939, Margaret Venetia, *d* of late Vice-Adm. W. Tomkinson, CB, MVO; one *s* one *d. Educ:* Malvern Coll.; RAF Coll., Cranwell. Commissioned 1930. Served in Fighter Sqdns and Fleet Air Arm; Instructor CFS, 1936–37; Mem. RAF Long Distance Flight (Vickers Wellesleys) to Australia, 1938; commanded No 501 Sqdn throughout Battle of Britain; USA, 1941–43 (Arnold Scheme and RAF Delegation Washington); Asst Comdt, Empire CFS, 1944; commanded No 19 Flying Training Sch., RAF Coll., Cranwell, 1945; Staff Coll., 1946; Air Ministry, 1947–48; SPSO, MEAF, 1949–50; commanded RAF, Wattisham 1951; Air Cdre 1953; Sector Comdr, Northern Sector, 1952–53; AOC No 81 Group, 1954; Air Vice-Marshal, 1956; AOC No 83 Group, 2nd ATAF, Germany, 1955–58; SASO, Flying Training Command, 1958–62. Led RAF Mission to Ghana, 1960, and Joint Services Mission to Ghana, 1961. Regional Dir, Civil Defence (Midland), 1964–68. USA Legion of Merit (Officer), 1945. *Recreation:* country pursuits. *Address:* Farlea, Stert, near Devizes, Wilts. *T:* Devizes 3113. *Club:* Royal Air Force.

HOGAN, Michael Henry; Secretary to the Gaming Board for Great Britain, 1980–86, retired; *b* 31 May 1927; *s* of James Joseph Hogan and Edith Mary Hogan; *m* 1st, 1953, Nina Spillane (*d* 1974); one *s* three *d*; 2nd, 1980, Mollie Burtwell. *Educ:* Ushaw Coll.; LSE. Certif. Social Sci., Certif. Mental Health. Asst Warden, St Vincent's Probation Hostel, 1949–50; London Probation Service, 1953–61; Home Office Inspectorate, 1961–80, Chief Probation Inspector, 1972–80. *Recreation:* golf. *Address:* Shrub Hill, Calvert Road, Dorking, Surrey. *T:* Dorking 885229.

HOGARTH, (Arthur) Paul, RA 1984 (ARA 1974); RDI 1979; FRSA 1984; painter, illustrator and draughtsman; *b* Kendal, Cumbria, 4 Oct. 1917; *s* of Arthur Hogarth and Janet Bownass; *m* 1963, one *s. Educ:* St Agnes Sch., Manchester; Coll. of Art, Manchester; St Martin's Sch. of Art, London. Travels in: Poland and Czechoslovakia, 1953; USSR and China, 1954; Rhodesia and S Africa, 1956; Ireland, with Brendan Behan, 1959; USA, 1961–79. Senior tutor of Drawing: Cambridge Sch. of Art, 1959–61; RCA, 1964–71; Associate Prof., Philadelphia Coll. of Art, 1968–69; Vis. Lectr, RCA, 1971–. Hon. Pres., Assoc. of Illustrators, 1982. Exhibitions: one-man, Leicester Gall., London, 1955; Agnews, London, 1957; Amer. Embassy, London, 1964; retrospectives, Time-Life Bldg, London, 1968; World of Paul Hogarth, Arts Council, RCA Gall., 1970; Travels through the Seventies, Kyle Gall., London; The Other Hogarth, Northern Arts Council, 1985–86. Dr RCA, 1971. *Publications:* Defiant People, 1953; Looking at China, 1956; People Like Us, 1958; (illus.) Brendan Behan's Island, 1962; Creative Pencil Drawing, 1964 (6th edn 1979); (illus.) Brendan Behan's New York, 1964; (with Robert Graves) Majorca Observed, 1965; (with M. Muggeridge) London à la Mode, 1966; Artist as Reporter, 1967, revised and enlarged edn, 1986; (with A. Jacob) Russian Journey, 1969; Drawing People, 1971; Artists on Horseback, 1972; Drawing Architecture, 1973; Paul Hogarth's American Album, 1974; Creative Ink Drawing, 1974 (5th edn 1979); Walking Tours of Old Philadelphia, 1976; Walking Tours of Old Boston, 1978; (with Stephen Spender) America Observed, 1979; Arthur Boyd Houghton, 1982; (with Graham Greene) Graham Greene Country, 1986; contrib. Graphis, Arts Rev., Design, Sports Illus., D. Tel. Mag., Illus. London News. *Recreation:* sailing. *Address:* c/o Tessa Sayle, 11 Jubilee Place, SW3 3TE. *T:* 01–352 4311. *Clubs:* Reform, Chelsea Arts.

HOGARTH, James, CB 1973; Under-Secretary, Scottish Home and Health Department, 1963–74, retired; *b* 14 Aug. 1914; *s* of George Hogarth; *m* 1940, Katherine Mary Cameron; two *s* one *d. Educ:* George Watson's, Edinburgh; Edinburgh Univ.; Sorbonne, Paris. Joined Dept of Health for Scotland as Asst Principal, 1938; Principal, 1944; Asst Sec., 1948; Under-Sec., 1963. *Publications:* Payment of the General Practitioner, 1963; translations from French, German, Russian, etc. *Recreation:* travel. *Address:* 6A Crawfurd Road, Edinburgh EH16 5PQ. *T:* 031–667 3878.

HOGARTH, Paul; *see* Hogarth, A. P.

HOGBEN, Ven. Peter Graham; Archdeacon of Dorking, since 1982; *b* 5 July 1925; *s* of Harold Henry and Winifred Minnie Hogben; *m* 1948, Audree Sayers; two *s. Educ:* Harvey Grammar School, Folkestone; Bishops' College, Cheshunt. Served Royal Engineers, 1943–47 (three years in Far East). Office Manager for two firms of Agricultural Auctioneers in Kent and Herts, 1948–59; theological college, 1960–61; ordained, 1961; Asst Curate of Hale, 1961–64; Vicar of Westborough, Guildford, 1964–71; Chaplain to WRAC, 1964–71; Vicar of Ewell, 1971–82; Editor, Guildford Diocesan Leaflet, 1978–82; Hon. Canon of Guildford, 1979–; RD of Epsom, 1980–82. *Recreations:* walking, gardening and photography. *Address:* Chesters, Reigate Road, Leatherhead KT22 8RB. *T:* Leatherhead 376266.

HOGG, family name of **Hailsham Viscountcy** and of **Baron Hailsham of Saint Marylebone.**

HOGG, Alexander Hubert Arthur, CBE 1973; Secretary, Royal Commission on Ancient Monuments in Wales and Monmouthshire, 1949–73; *b* 2 May 1908; *s* of A. F. Hogg; *m* 1943, Nellie, *d* of G. P. Henderson, MD; one *s* one *d. Educ:* Highgate Sch.; Sidney Sussex Coll., Cambridge (MA). Asst Engineer, Sir R. McAlpine & Sons, 1930–34; Junior Scientific Officer, Roads Research Laboratory, 1934–36; Lecturer, Engineering Dept, King's Coll., Newcastle upon Tyne, 1936–42; Temp. Experimental Officer, Admiralty Undex Works, Rosyth, 1942–45; ICI Fellowship, 1945–47; Lecturer Engineering Laboratory, University of Cambridge, 1947–49. FSA; FSAScot. Hon. DLitt Wales, 1974. *Publications:* Hill-Forts of Britain, 1975; British Hill-forts, an Index, 1979; Surveying for Field Archaeologists, 1980; papers in Philosophical Magazine and in Archæological periodicals. *Address:* Brynfield, Waun Fawr, Aberystwyth SY23 3PP. *T:* Aberystwyth 3479.

HOGG, Sir Arthur (Ramsay), 7th Bt *cr* 1846; MBE (mil.) 1945; retired; *b* 24 Oct. 1896; *s* of Ernest Charles Hogg (*d* 1907) (*g s* of 1st Bt) and Lucy (*d* 1924), *d* of late William Felton Peel; *S* cousin, Sir Kenneth Weir Hogg, 6th Bt, OBE, 1985; *m* 1924, Mary Aileen Hester Lee (*d* 1980), *d* of late P. H. Lee Evans; three *s* one *d. Educ:* Sherborne; Christ Church, Oxford (BA 1921; MA 1929). Served European War, 1914–18 (twice wounded), Captain Royal West Kent Regt; War of 1939–45 (MBE), Major, General List. *Heir: s* Michael David Hogg [*b* 19 Aug. 1925; *m* 1956, Elizabeth Anne Thérèse, *d* of Lt-Col Sir Terence Falkiner, Bt, *qv*; three *s*]. *Address:* 27 Elgin Road, Bournemouth BH3 7DH. *T:* Bournemouth 763287.

HOGG, Sir Christopher (Anthony), Kt 1985; Chairman: Courtaulds PLC, since 1980; Reuters Holdings PLC, since 1985 (Dir, since 1984); *b* 2 Aug. 1936; *s* of Anthony Wentworth Hogg and Monica Mary (*née* Gladwell); *m* 1961, Anne Patricia (*née* Cathie); two *d. Educ:* Marlborough Coll.; Trinity Coll., Oxford (MA; Hon. Fellow 1982); Harvard Univ. (MBA). National Service, Parachute Regt, 1955–57. Harkness Fellow, 1960–62; IMEDE, Lausanne, 1962–63; Hill, Samuel Ltd, 1963–66; IRC, 1966–68; Courtaulds PLC, 1968–. Member: Indust. Develt Adv. Bd, 1976–81; Cttee of Award for Harkness Fellowships, 1980–86. Hon. DSc Cranfield Inst. of Technol., 1986. *Publication:* Masers and Lasers, 1963. *Recreations:* theatre, reading, walking. *Address:* 18 Hanover Square, W1A 2BB. *T:* 01–629 9080.

HOGG, Douglas Martin; MP (C) Grantham, since 1979; barrister; Parliamentary Under-Secretary of State, Home Office, since 1986; *b* 5 Feb. 1945; *er s* of Baron Hailsham of Saint Marylebone, *qv*; *m* 1968, Sarah Boyd-Carpenter (*see* S. E. M. Hogg); one *s* one *d. Educ:* Eton (Oppidan Schol.); Christ Church, Oxford (Schol.; Pres., Oxford Union). Called to the Bar, Lincoln's Inn, 1968 (Kennedy Law Schol.). Mem., Agric. Select Cttees, 1979–82; PPS to Chief Sec., HM Treasury, 1982–83; an Asst Govt Whip, 1983–84. *Address:* House of Commons, SW1.

HOGG, Gilbert Charles; Secretary, British Gas Corporation, since 1984; *b* 11 Feb. 1933; *s* of Charles and Ivy Ellen Hogg; *m* 1st, Jeanne Whiteside; one *s* one *d*; 2nd, 1979, Angela Christina Wallace. *Educ:* Victoria University Coll., Wellington, NZ (LLB 1956). Called to the New Zealand Bar and admitted Solicitor, 1957; admitted Solicitor, GB, 1971. Served RNZAC (TF), 1955–62 (Lieut). Partner, Phillips, Shayle-George and Co., Solicitors, Wellington, 1960–66; Sen. Crown Counsel, Hong Kong, 1966–70; Editor, Business Law Summary, 1970–72; Divl Legal Adviser, BSC, 1974–79; Dir of Legal Services, British Gas, 1979–84. *Publication:* A Smell of Fraud (novel), 1974. *Address:* Rivermill House, 152 Grosvenor Road, SW1V 3JL. *T:* 01–821 1444. *Club:* Royal Automobile.

HOGG, Vice-Adm. Sir Ian (Leslie Trower), KCB 1968 (CB 1964); DSC 1941, Bar to DSC 1944; *b* 30 May 1911; 3rd *s* of Col John M. T. Hogg, IA, and Elma (*née* Brand); *m* 1945, Mary G. J., *e d* of Col and Mrs Marsden; two *s. Educ:* Cheltenham Coll. Entered Royal Navy, 1929; specialised in Navigation, 1937; HMS Cardiff, 1939; HMS Penelope, 1940; HMAS Napier, 1941–43; HMS Mauritius, 1944–45; Master of the Fleet, 1946–47; British Admiralty Delegation, Washington, DC, 1948–49; HMS Sluys, in comd, 1950–51; Staff of C-in-C Med., 1952–53; Captain RN, Dec. 1953; Brit. Joint Staff, Washington, DC, 1955–57; idc 1958; Staff of Chief of Defence Staff, 1959–60; Cdre, Cyprus, 1961–62; Dir, Chief of Defence Staff's Commonwealth Exercise, 1962–63; Rear-Adm. 1963; Flag Officer, Medway, and Admiral Superintendent, HM Dockyard, Chatham, 1963–66; Vice-Adm. 1966; Defence Services Sec., 1966–67; Vice-Chief of the Defence Staff, 1967–70, retired. FRSA 1971. *Address:* 32 Westbridge Road, SW11. *T:* 01–223 5770.

HOGG, Sir John (Nicholson), Kt 1963; TD 1946; Deputy Chairman: Williams & Glyn's Bank Ltd, 1970–83; Gallaher Ltd, 1964–78; Chairman, Banque Française de Crédit International Ltd, 1972–83; *b* 4 Oct. 1912; *o s* of late Sir Malcolm Hogg and of Lorna Beaman; *m* 1948, Barbara Mary Elisabeth, *yr d* of Capt. Arden Franklyn, Shedfield, Southampton and *widow* of Viscount Garmoyle (*d* of wounds, 1942); one *s* one *d. Educ:* Eton; Balliol Coll., Oxford. Joined Glyn, Mills and Co., 1934. Served War of 1939–45, with KRRC in Greece, Crete, Western Desert, Tunisia, NW Europe. Rejoined Glyn, Mills and Co. 1945, a Man. Dir., 1950–70, Dep. Chm. 1963–68, Chm. 1968–70; Director: Royal Bank of Scotland Gp Ltd, 1969–82; Prudential Corp. Ltd, 1964–85. Fellow of Eton Coll., 1951–70. Mem. of Commonwealth War Graves Commission, 1958–64; A Trustee Imperial War Graves Endowment Fund, 1965. Sheriff County of London, 1960; Chm., Export Credits Guarantee Department's Adv. Council, 1962–67. Chm., Abu Dhabi Investment Bd, 1967–75. Hon. Treasurer, Inst. of Child Health. *Recreations:* cricket, tennis, fishing. *Address:* The Red House, Shedfield, Southampton SO3 2HN. *T:* Wickham 832121. *Club:* Brooks's.

HOGG, Norman; MP (Lab) Cumbernauld and Kilsyth, since 1983 (Dunbartonshire East, 1979–83); Deputy Chief Opposition Whip, since 1983; *b* 12 March 1938; *s* of late Norman Hogg, CBE, LLD, DL, JP, and of Mary Wilson; *m* 1964, Elizabeth McCall Christie. *Educ:* Causewayend Sch., Aberdeen; Ruthrieston Secondary Sch., Aberdeen. Local Government Officer, Aberdeen Town Council, 1953–67; District Officer, National and Local Govt Officers Assoc., 1967–79. Secretary, Trade Unions' Cttee for the Electricity Supply Industry in Scotland, 1978–79; Member: Transport Users Consultative Cttee for Scotland, 1977–79; Select Cttee on Scottish Affairs, 1979–82; Scottish Labour Whip, 1982–83; Chm., Scottish Parly Lab Gp, 1981–82. *Recreation:* music. *Address:* House of Commons, SW1A 0AA. *T:* 01–219 5095.

HOGG, Rear-Adm. Peter Beauchamp, CB 1980; Head of British Defence Liaison Staff and Defence Adviser, Canberra, 1977–80, retired; Secretary, Winchester College Sixth Centenary Appeal, since 1980; *b* 9 Nov. 1924; *s* of Beauchamp and Sybil Hogg; *m* 1951,

Gabriel Argentine Alington; two *s* two *d. Educ:* Connaught House, Weymouth; Bradfield Coll., Berks; Royal Naval Engineering Coll., Keyham. Lieut, HMS Sirius, 1947–49; Advanced Engrg Course, RNC Greenwich, 1949–51; HMS Swiftsure and HMS Pincher, 1951–53; Lt Comdr, Loan Service with Royal Canadian Navy, 1953–56; Staff of RN Engrg Coll., Manadon, 1956–58; Comdr (Trng Comdr), HMS Sultan, 1959–62; Marine Engr Officer, HMS Hampshire, 1962–64; JSSC, Latimer, 1964; Ship Dept, Bath, 1965–67; Captain, Ship Dept, Bath, 1968–69; CO, HMS Tyne, 1970–71; RCDS, 1972; CO, HMS Caledonia, 1973–74; Dir of Naval Recruiting, 1974–76. *Address:* c/o National Westminster Bank, City Centre, Plymouth PL1 1DG.

HOGG, Rear-Adm. Robin Ivor Trower; Chief of Staff to Commander-in-Chief Fleet, since 1986; *b* 25 Sept. 1932; *s* of Dudley and Nancy Hogg; *m* 1st, 1958, Susan Bridget Beryl Grantham; two *s* two *d*; 2nd, 1970, Angela Sarah Patricia Kirwan. *Educ:* The New Beacon, Sevenoaks; Bedford School. Directorate of Naval Plans, 1974–76; RCDS 1977; Captain RN Presentation Team, 1978–79; Captain First Frigate Sqdn, 1980–82; Director Naval Operational Requirements, 1982–84; Flag Officer, First Flotilla, 1984–86. *Recreation:* private life. *Address:* c/o Coutts & Co., Chandos Branch, 440 Strand, WC2R 0QS. *T:* 01–379 6262.

HOGG, Sarah Elizabeth Mary; Assistant Editor, and Business and Finance Editor, The Independent, since 1986; *b* 14 May 1946; *d* of Baron Boyd-Carpenter, *qv*; *m* 1968, Douglas Martin Hogg, *qv*; one *s* one *d. Educ:* St Mary's Convent, Ascot; Lady Margaret Hall, Oxford University. 1st Cl. Hons PPE. Staff writer, Economist, 1967, Literary Editor, 1970, Economics Editor, 1977; Economics Editor, Sunday Times, 1981; Econs Editor and Dep. Exec. Editor, Finance and Industry, The Times, 1984–86. Presenter, Channel 4 News, 1982–83; Dir, London Broadcasting Co., 1982–. Govr, Centre for Economic Policy Research, 1985–. Wincott Foundation Financial Journalist of the Year, 1985. *Address:* The Independent, 40 City Road, EC1Y 2DB.

HOGG, Sir William Lindsay L.; *see* Lindsay-Hogg.

HOGGART, Richard, LittD; Warden, Goldsmiths' College, University of London, 1976–84; *b* 24 Sept. 1918; 2nd *s* of Tom Longfellow Hoggart and Adeline Emma Hoggart; *m* 1942, Mary Holt France; two *s* one *d. Educ:* elementary and secondary schs, Leeds; Leeds Univ. (MA, LittD 1978). Served 1940–46, RA; demobilised as Staff Capt. Staff Tutor and Sen. Staff Tutor, University Coll. of Hull and University of Hull, 1946–59; Sen. Lectr in English, University of Leicester, 1959–62; Prof. of English, Birmingham Univ., 1962–73, and Dir, Centre for Contemporary Cultural Studies, 1964–73; an Asst Dir-Gen., Unesco, 1970–75. Vis. Fellow, Inst. of Development Studies, Univ. of Sussex, 1975. Visiting Prof., University of Rochester (NY), USA, 1956–57; Reith Lectr, 1971. Member: Albemarle Cttee on Youth Services, 1958–60; (Pilkington) Cttee on Broadcasting, 1960–62; Arts Council, 1976–81 (Chm., Drama Panel, 1977–80; Vice-Chm., 1980–82); Statesman and Nation Publishing Co. Ltd, 1977–81 (Chm., 1978–81); Chairman: Adv. Council for Adult and Continuing Educn, 1977–83; European Museum of the Year Award, 1977–; Broadcasting Research Unit, 1981–. Governor, Royal Shakespeare Theatre. Pres., British Assoc. of Former UN Civil Servants, 1979–86. Hon. Professor: UEA, 1984; Univ. of Surrey, 1985; Hon. Fellow, Sheffield Polytechnic, 1983; DUniv: Open, 1973; Surrey, 1981; Hon D-ès-L Univ. of Bordeaux, 1975; Hon. LLD CNAA, 1982; Hon. LittD East Anglia, 1986. Mem. Editorial Board, New Universities Quarterly. *Publications:* Auden, 1951; The Uses of Literacy, 1957; W. H. Auden, 1957; W. H. Auden—A Selection, 1961; chap. in Conviction, 1958; chapter in Pelican Guide to English Literature, 1961; Teaching Literature, 1963; chapter in Of Books and Humankind, 1964; The Critical Moment, 1964; How and Why Do We Learn, 1965; The World in 1984, 1965; Essays by Divers Hands XXXIII; Guide to the Social Sciences, 1966; Technology and Society, 1966; Essays on Reform, 1967; Your Sunday Paper (ed), 1967; Speaking to Each Other: vol. I, About Society; vol. II, About Literature, 1970; Only Connect (Reith Lectures), 1972; An Idea and Its Servants, 1978; (ed with Janet Morgan) The Future of Broadcasting, 1982; An English Temper, 1982; Writers on Writing, 1986; numerous introductions, articles, pamphlets and reviews. *Recreation:* pottering about the house and garden. *Address:* Mortonsfield, Beavers Hill, Farnham, Surrey.

See also S. D. Hoggart.

HOGGART, Simon David; United States correspondent, The Observer, since 1985; *b* 26 May 1946; *s* of Richard Hoggart, *qv*; *m* 1983, Alyson Clare Corner; one *d. Educ:* Hymer's College, Hull; Wyggeston Grammar Sch., Leicester; King's College, Cambridge. MA. Reporter, The Guardian, 1968–71, N Ireland corresp., 1971–73, political corresp., 1973–81; feature writer, The Observer, 1981–85; political columnist, Punch, 1979–85. *Publications:* The Pact (with Alistair Michie), 1978; Michael Foot: a portrait (with David Leigh), 1981; On the House, 1981; Back on the House, 1982; House of Ill Fame, 1985; contribs to New Society. *Recreations:* reading, writing. *Address:* Suite 513, 2025 M Street NW, Washington, DC 20036, USA. *T:* 202 223 2910.

HOGGE, Maj.-Gen. (Arthur) Michael (Lancelot), CB 1979; General Manager, Regular Forces Employment Association, since 1981; *b* 4 Aug. 1925; *s* of late Lt-Col A. H. F. Hogge, Punjab Regt, Indian Army, and Mrs K. M. Hogge; *m* 1952, Gunilla Jeane Earley; two *s. Educ:* Wellington Coll.; Brasenose Coll., Oxford (war-time course). Commissioned, Oct. 1945; 6th Airborne Armoured Recce Regt and 3rd Hussars, Palestine, 1945–48; regimental appts, 3rd Hussars, BAOR, 1948–58; Queen's Own Hussars, BAOR, and Staff appts, 1958–65; comd Queen's Own Hussars, UK and Aden, 1965–67; Col GS, Staff Coll., 1969–71; Royal Coll. of Defence Studies, 1972; Dir of Operational Requirements, MoD, 1973–74, rank of Brig.; Dir Gen. Fighting Vehicles and Engineer Equipment, 1974–77; Dep. Master-General of the Ordnance, 1977–80. *Recreations:* sailing, horticulture. *Address:* c/o Lloyds Bank, Dorking, Surrey.

HOGGETT, Anthony John Christopher, PhD; QC 1986; *b* 20 Aug. 1940; *s* of Christopher Hoggett and Annie Marie Hoggett; *m* 1968, Brenda Marjorie Hale (*see* B. M. Hoggett); one *d. Educ:* Leeds Grammar Sch.; Hymers Coll., Hull; Clare Coll., Cambridge (MA, LLB); PhD Manchester. Asst Juridique, Inst. of Comparative Law, Paris, 1962–63; Lectr in Law, Univ. of Manchester, 1963–69; called to Bar, Gray's Inn, 1969, Head of Chambers, 1985; Asst Recorder, 1982. Res. Fellow, Univ. of Michigan, 1965–66. *Publications:* articles in Criminal Law Rev., Mod. Law Rev. and others. *Recreations:* swimming, music, walking. *Address:* Goyt Cliff, Strines Road, Marple, Cheshire SK6 7DT. *T:* 061–427 2945.

HOGGETT, Prof. Brenda Marjorie; Law Commissioner, since 1984; Professor of Law, University of Manchester, since 1986; *b* 31 Jan. 1945; *d* of Cecil Frederick Hale and Marjorie Hale (*née* Godfrey); *m* 1968, Anthony John Christopher Hoggett, *qv*; one *d. Educ:* Richmond High School for Girls, Yorks; Girton College, Cambridge. MA. Called to the Bar, Gray's Inn, 1969; Asst Lectr in Law, Univ. of Manchester, 1966, Lectr 1968, Senior Lectr 1976, Reader 1981–86. Barrister, Northern Circuit, 1969–; Legal Mem., Mental Health Review Tribunal for NW Region, 1979–80; Mem., Council on Tribunals, 1980–84; Editor, Jl of Social Welfare Law, 1978–84. *Publications:* Mental Health Law, 1976, 2nd edn 1984; Parents and Children, 1977, 2nd edn 1981; (with D. S. Pearl) The Family Law and Society: Cases and Materials, 1983; (with S. Atkins) Women and the Law, 1984; contribs to legal periodicals and other texts. *Recreations:* domesticity and drama. *Address:* Goyt Cliff, 63 Strines Road, Marple, Stockport, Cheshire SK6 7DT. *T:* 061–427 2945.

HOGUE, Oliver Alfred John, CVO 1954; literary staff, Mirror Newspapers, Sydney, 1962–75 and 1976; Associate News Editor, Daily Mirror, 1968–75; *b* 16 Sept. 1910; *s* of Frank Arthur Hogue and Vida C. Hogue (*née* Robinson), Sydney; *m* 1st, 1936, Mary Barbour May (marr. diss., 1966); four *s*; 2nd, 1966, Mary Elizabeth Mofflin (*d* 1976), *d* of Solomon Merkel, Lithuania. *Educ:* Newcastle (NSW) High Sch. Literary staff, Newcastle Herald, 1930; War Correspondent in Australia, 1940–43; Press Sec. to Hon. J. A. Beasley, Australian Minister for Supply, 1943–45; Political Corresp. for Sydney Sunday Sun, Canberra, 1945–53; literary staff, Sydney Sun, 1954–62. Pres., C'wealth Parly Press Gall., 1947–49. Aust. Govt PRO for Australian visit of the Queen and Prince Philip, 1954. *Address:* 7/34 Archer Street, Chatswood, NSW 2067, Australia. *T:* 4196614. *Club:* Journalists' (Sydney).

HOGWOOD, Christopher Jarvis Haley; harpsichordist, conductor, musicologist and broadcaster; Director, Academy of Ancient Music, since 1973; *b* 10 Sept. 1941; *s* of Haley Evelyn Hogwood and Marion Constance Higgott. *Educ:* Cambridge Univ. (MA); Charles Univ., Prague. Keyboard and orchestral recordings. Editor of books and music. Artistic Director: King's Lynn Festival, 1976–80; Handel and Haydn Soc., Boston, USA, 1986–. FRSA. *Publications:* Music at Court (Folio Society), 1977; The Trio Sonata, 1979; Haydn's Visits to England (Folio Society), 1980; (ed with R. Luckett) Music in Eighteenth-Century England, 1983; Handel, 1984. *Address:* 2 Claremont, Hills Road, Cambridge. *T:* Cambridge 63975.

HOHLER, Henry Arthur Frederick, CMG 1954; HM Diplomatic Service, retired; Ambassador to Switzerland 1967–70; *b* 4 Feb. 1911; *e s* of late Lt-Col Arthur Preston Hohler, DSO; *m* 1st, 1932, Mona Valentine (*d* 1944), *d* of late Lieut-Col Arthur Murray Pirie, DSO; two *s*; 2nd, 1945, Eveline Susan, *d* of late Lieut-Col Hon. Neville Albert Hood, CMG, DSO; two *d. Educ:* Eton; Sandhurst. 2nd Lieut Grenadier Guards, 1931. 3rd Sec. in Foreign Office, 1934; Budapest, 1936; 2nd Sec., 1939; Foreign Office, 1941; 1st Sec., 1945; Berne, 1945; Helsinki, 1948; Moscow, 1949; Counsellor, 1950; Head of Northern Dept, Foreign Office, 1951; Minister in Rome, 1956–60; Ambassador in Saigon, 1960–63; Minister in Paris, 1963–65; Asst Under-Sec., Foreign Office, 1966–67. Liveryman, Grocers' Company. *Address:* RR4, Box 216–A, Gloucester, Va 23061, USA. *Clubs:* Boodle's; Metropolitan (Washington).

See also T. S. Astell Hohler.

HOHLER, Thomas Sidney A.; *see* Astell Hohler.

HOLBOROW, Eric John, MD, FRCP, FRCPath; Emeritus Professor of Immunopathology and Honorary Consultant Immunologist, London Hospital Medical College, E1, retired 1983; *b* 30 March 1918; *s* of Albert Edward Ratcliffe Holborow and Marian Crutchley; *m* 1943, Cicely Mary Foister; two *s* one *d. Educ:* Epsom Coll.; Clare Coll., Cambridge; St Bart's Hosp. MA, MD (Cantab). Served War of 1939–45, Major, RAMC. Consultant Bacteriologist, Canadian Hosp., Taplow, 1953; Mem. Scientific Staff, MRC Rheumatism Unit, Taplow, 1957; Director, 1975; Head, MRC Group, Bone and Joint Res. Group, London Hosp. Med. Coll., 1976–83. Visiting Prof., Royal Free Hosp. Med. Sch., 1975. Bradshaw Lectr, RCP, 1982. Trustee, Smith Kline Foundn, 1977–. Editor, Jl Immunol. Methods, 1971–85. *Publications:* Autoimmunity and Disease (with L. E. Glynn), 1965; An ABC of Modern Immunology, 1968, 2nd edn 1973; (with W. G. Reeves) Immunology in Medicine, 1977, 2nd edn 1983; (with A. Maroudas) Studies in Joint Disease, vol. 1, 1981, vol. 2, 1983; books and papers on immunology. *Recreation:* glebe terriers.

HOLBROOK, David Kenneth, MA; author; Fellow and Director of English Studies, Downing College, Cambridge, since 1981; *b* 9 Jan. 1923; *o s* of late Kenneth Redvers and late Elsie Eleanor Holbrook; *m* 1949, Margot Davies-Jones; two *s* two *d. Educ:* City of Norwich Sch.; Downing Coll., Cambridge (Exhibr). Intell., mines and explosives officer, ER Yorks Yeo., Armd Corps, 1942–45. Asst Editor, Our Time, 1948; Asst Editor, Bureau of Current Affairs, 1949; Tutor organiser, WEA, 1952–53; Tutor, Bassingbourn Village Coll., Cambs, 1954–61; Fellow, King's Coll., Cambridge, 1961–65; Sen. Leverhulme Res. Fellow, 1965; College Lectr in English, Jesus Coll., Cambridge, 1968–70; Compton Poetry Lectr, Hull Univ., 1969 (resigned); Arts Council Writer's Grant, 1970; Writer in Residence, Dartington Hall, 1970–73 (grant from Elmgrant Trust); Asst Dir English Studies, Downing Coll., Cambridge, 1973–75; Hooker Distinguished Vis. Prof., McMaster Univ., Ontario, 1984; Arts Council Writers Grants, 1976, 1979. Mem. Editorial Bd, New Universities Qly, 1976–86. *Publications:* Children's Games, 1957; Imaginings, 1961; English for Maturity, 1961; Iron, Honey, Gold, 1961; Llareggub Revisited, 1962; People and Diamonds, 1962; Against the Cruel Frost, 1963; Lights in the Sky Country, 1963; Thieves and Angels, 1963; English for the Rejected, 1964; The Secret Places, 1964; Visions of Life, 1964; The Quest for Love, 1965; Flesh Wounds, 1966; Object Relations, 1967; The Exploring Word, 1967; Children's Writing, 1967; (with Elizabeth Poston) The Cambridge Hymnal, 1967; (with John Joubert) The Quarry (opera), 1967; Plucking the Rushes, 1968; Old World New World, 1969; Human Hope and the Death Instinct, 1971; The Masks of Hate, 1972; Sex and Dehumanization, 1972; Dylan Thomas, The Code of Night, 1972; ed, The Case Against Pornography, 1972; The Pseudo-revolution, 1973; English in Australia Now, 1973; Gustav Mahler and the Courage to Be, 1975; (with Christine Mackenzie) The Honey of Man, 1975; essay on Ted Hughes, in, The Black Rainbow, ed Peter Abbs, 1975; Sylvia Plath: poetry and existence, 1976; Lost Bearings in English Poetry, 1977; Education, Nihilism and Survival, 1977; essay on The Need for Meaning, in, Human Needs and Politics, ed Ross Fitzgerald, 1977; Chance of a Lifetime, 1978; A Play of Passion, 1978; Moments in Italy, 1978; essay on Magazines, in, Discrimination and Popular Culture, ed Denys Thompson; opera with Wilfred Mellers, The Borderline, perf. London 1958; operetta, The Wild Swans (with John Paynter), 1979; English for Meaning, 1980; Selected Poems, 1980; introduction to: Phantastes, 1983; The Old Wives' Tale, 1983; (contrib.) The Leavises, 1984; Evolution and the Humanities, 1986; The Novel and Authenticity, 1987; Education and Philosophical Anthropology, 1987; Nothing larger than life (novel), 1987. *Recreations:* painting in oils, cooking, gardening. *Address:* Denmore Lodge, Brunswick Gardens, Cambridge CB5 8DQ. *T:* Cambridge 315081.

HOLBURN, James; *b* 1 Dec. 1900; *s* of late Rev. James Holburn, Alyth, Perthshire; *m* 1931, Elizabeth Margaret (*d* 1972), *d* of late Rev. John McConnachie, DD, Dundee; three *s. Educ:* Harris Academy, Dundee; University of Glasgow (MA Hons). Editorial staff, the Glasgow Herald, 1921–34; joined The Times, 1934: asst correspondent and actg corresp. Berlin, 1935–39; correspondent Moscow, 1939–40; Ankara, 1940–41; War Correspondent, Middle East, 1941–42; Correspondent New Delhi, 1942–46; United Nations Headquarters, 1946–48; Diplomatic Corresp., 1948–51; Chief Corresp. Middle East, 1952–55; Editor, The Glasgow Herald, 1955–65. *Publications:* contributions to various periodicals. *Recreations:* golf, angling. *Address:* Pitnacree, Johnshill Road, Alyth, Perthshire PH11 8DX. *T:* Alyth 2476. *Club:* Western (Glasgow).

HOLCROFT, Sir Peter (George Culcheth), 3rd Bt *cr* 1921; JP; *b* 29 April 1931; *s* of Sir Reginald Culcheth Holcroft, 2nd Bt, TD, and Mary Frances (*d* 1963), *yr d* of late William Swire, CBE; *S* father, 1978; *m* 1956, Rosemary Rachel, *yr d* of late G. N. Deas; three *s* one *d*. *Educ:* Eton. High Sheriff of Shropshire, 1969; JP 1976. *Recreation:* the countryside. *Heir: s* Charles Antony Culcheth Holcroft [*b* 22 Oct. 1959; *m* 1986, Mrs Elizabeth Carter, *y d* of John Raper, Powys]. *Address:* Eaton Mascott Hall, Cross Houses, Shrewsbury.

HOLDEN, Basil Munroe; Rector, Glasgow Academy, 1959–75, retired; *b* 10 Nov. 1913; *m* 1951, Jean Watters; two *s* two *d*. *Educ:* Queen Elizabeth's Grammar Sch., Blackburn; King's Coll., Cambridge (Foundation Scholar). BA 1935, Maths Tripos (Wrangler), MA 1939. Mathematical Master, Highgate Sch., 1937. Instructor Lieut RN, 1940. Head of Mathematical Dept, Oundle Sch., 1947; Housemaster, Oundle Sch., 1956. *Address:* Brackenburn Lodge, Manesty, Keswick, Cumbria CA12 5UG. *T:* Borrowdale 637.

HOLDEN, Sir David (Charles Beresford), KBE 1972; CB 1963; ERD 1954; *b* 26 July 1915; *s* of Oswald Addenbrooke Holden and Ella Mary Beresford; *m* 1948, Elizabeth Jean Odling; one *s* one *d*. *Educ:* Rossall Sch.; King's Coll., Cambridge. Northern Ireland Civil Service, 1937–76; Permanent Sec., Dept of Finance, NI, and Head of NI Civil Service, 1970–76; Dir, Ulster Office, 1976–77. Royal Artillery, 1939–46. *Address:* Falcons, Wilsford Cum Lake, Amesbury, Salisbury SP4 7BL. *T:* Amesbury 22493.

HOLDEN, Derek; His Honour Judge Holden; a Circuit Judge, since 1984; *b* 7 July 1935; *s* of Frederic Holden and Audrey Holden (*née* Hayes); *m* 1961, Dorien Elizabeth Holden (*née* Bell); two *s*. *Educ:* Cromwell House, Staines Grammar Sch. Served Army; Lieut East Surrey Regt, 1953–56. Qualified as Solicitor, 1966; Derek Holden & Co., Staines, Egham, Camberley, Feltham and Ashford, 1966–84; Consultant, Batt Holden & Co., 1966–84. Partner: Dorien Property & Investment Co., 1970–84; Leisure Hire, 1974–79; Black Lake Securities, 1979–84; Dorien Leasing, 1979–84; a Recorder, 1980–84. Mem., Royal Yachting Assoc., 1975– (Dept of Trade Yachtmaster, Instr and Ocean certs). Principal, Chandor Sch. of Sailing, Lymington, 1978–85. President: Staines Amateur Regatta, 1980–; Staines Boat Club, 1984–. *Recreations:* sailing, ski-ing, photography. *Address:* Little Acorns, Queen Anne's Road, Windsor, Berks. *T:* Windsor 55164. *Clubs:* Law Society; Ski Club of Great Britain; Leander; Remenham (Henley); Burway Rowing (Laleham); Eton Excelsior Rowing (Windsor); Staines Boat; Royal Solent Yacht (Yarmouth, IoW); Queen Mary Sailing (Ashford); Westerly Association.

HOLDEN, Sir Edward, 6th Bt, *cr* 1893; Consultant Anæsthetist, Darlington & Northallerton Group Hospitals, 1957–74; *b* 8 Oct. 1916; *s* of Sir Isaac Holden Holden, 5th Bt, and Alice Edna Byrom (*d* 1971); *S* father, 1962; *m* 1942, Frances Joan, *e d* of John Spark, JP, Ludlow, Stockton-on-Tees; two adopted *s*. *Educ:* Leys Sch. and Christ's Coll., Cambridge (MA); St Thomas's Hosp. MRCS; LRCP 1942; DA Eng., 1946; FFA, RCS, 1958. Formerly Vis. Anæsth., Cumb. Infirm., Carlisle; Cons. Anæsth. W Cumb. Hospital Group. Mem. Council, Harlow Car Gardens. *Recreations:* fishing and gardening. *Heir: b* Paul Holden [*b* 3 March 1923; *m* 1950, Vivien Mary Oldham; one *s* two *d*]. *Address:* Moorstones, Osmotherley, Northallerton, N Yorks DL6 3BG. *Club:* Farmers'.

HOLDEN, Sir John David, 4th Bt *cr* 1919; *b* 16 Dec. 1967; *s* of David George Holden (*d* 1971) (*e s* of 3rd Bt), and of Nancy, *d* of H. W. D. Marwood, Foulrice, Whenby, Brandsby, Yorks; *S* grandfather, 1976. *Heir: uncle* Brian Peter John Holden [*b* 12 April 1944; *m* 1984, Bernadette Anne Lopez, *d* of George Gerard O'Malley].

HOLDEN, Maj.-Gen. John Reid, CB 1965; CBE 1960 (OBE 1953); DSO 1941; *b* 8 Jan. 1913; *s* of late John Holden, MA, Edinburgh; *m* 1939, Rosemarie Florence (*d* 1980), *d* of late William Henry de Vere Pennefather, Carlow; one *d*. *Educ:* Hamilton Academy; Glasgow Univ.; RMC, Sandhurst. 2nd Lieut Royal Tank Corps, 1937; Adjutant, 7th Royal Tank Regt, 1940–41 (despatches, DSO); Bde Major, 32nd Army Tank Bde, 1942; POW, 1942–45. GSO1, GHQ, Far ELF, Singapore, 1951–52 (OBE); CO 3rd Royal Tank Regt, BAOR, 1954–57; AAG, War Office, 1958. Comdr, 7th Armoured Bde Group, BAOR, 1958–61 (CBE). Royal Naval War Coll., 1961. Chief of Mission, British Comdrs-in-Chief Mission to the Soviet Forces in Germany, 1961–63; GOC 43 (Wessex) Div. Dist, 1963–65; Dir, RAC, 1965–68, retired 1968. Col Comdt, RTR, 1965–68. Hon. Col, The Queen's Own Lowland Yeomanry, RAC, T&AVR, 1972–75. *Recreations:* books, birds. *Address:* c/o Royal Bank of Scotland, Kirkland House, Whitehall, SW1.

HOLDEN, Kenneth Graham; retired; *b* 6 May 1910; *e s* of Norman Neill Holden; *m* 1937, Winifred Frances, *d* of Lt-Col T. F. S. Burridge; two *d*. *Educ:* Wellington Coll.; Pembroke Coll., Cambridge. Admitted Solicitor, 1935. Director: (and sometime Chm.) Hardman & Holden Ltd, Manchester, 1936–64; Williams & Glyn's Bank Ltd (formerly as Williams Deacon's Bank Ltd), 1949–78 (Chm., 1964–72); Royal Bank of Scotland Ltd, 1950–69; Geigy (Holdings) Ltd (later CIBA-Geigy (UK) Ltd), 1955–75; Borax Consolidated Ltd, 1961–64; Haden-Carrier Ltd, 1967–75; The Trustee's Corp. Ltd, 1967–80; Manchester Ship Canal Co., 1968–74; National Commercial Banking Group Ltd, 1969–76; Yorkshire Bank Ltd, 1970–78; The Industrial and General Trust Ltd, 1971–80. Part-time Mem., NW Gas Bd, 1965–72. Formerly Mem. Bd of Management (and sometime Jt Hon. Treasurer), Manchester Royal Infirmary. Governor, Manchester Grammar School. *Address:* 40 Lee Road, Aldeburgh, Suffolk. *T:* Aldeburgh 3159. *Club:* All England Lawn Tennis.

HOLDEN, Patrick Brian, MA, FCIS; Chairman, Steak Away Foods Ltd, since 1982; *b* 16 June 1937; *s* of Reginald John and Winifred Isabel Holden; *m* 1972, Jennifer Ruth (*née* Meddings), MB, BS. *Educ:* Allhallows Sch. (Major Schol.); St Catharine's Coll., Cambridge (BA Hons Law 1960, MA 1963). FCIS 1965. Served Royal Hampshire Regt, 1955–57 regular commn), seconded 1 Ghana Regt, RWAFF. Fine Fare Group: Sec., 1960–69; Legal and Property Dir, 1965–69; Pye of Cambridge Gp, 1969–74; Dir, Pye Telecom. Ltd, 1972–74; Dir and Sec., Oriel Foods Gp, 1975–81; Gp Sec., Fisons plc, 1981–83. Sec., New Town Assoc., 1974–75. FBIM. *Recreations:* bridge, sailing. *Address:* The Old School House, Lower Green, Tewin, Herts AL6 0LD. *T:* Tewin 7573. *Club:* Naval and Military.

HOLDEN, Philip Edward; an Underwriting Member of Lloyd's since 1954; *b* 20 June 1905. *Educ:* King Edward VI Schs, Birmingham. Qualified, CA, 1929; Managing Dir Amalgamated Anthracite Collieries, from 1940. Past Chm., Amalgamated Anthracite Holdings Group of Cos. Has served on Exec. of Monmouthshire and S Wales Coal Owners Assoc., and as Chm. of its Commercial Cttee; also served on Exec. Bd of S Wales Coal Mines Scheme. Pres. Swansea Chamber of Commerce, 1952–53; Vice-Chm. Chamber of Coal Traders, 1953–65; Vice-Chm. Nat. Council of Coal Traders (Chm. 1953–65); Pres. Brit. Coal Exporters' Assoc., 1958–63; Mem. Industrial Coal Consumers' Council, 1958. A Dir of public and private cos (coal, shipping, manufactures, electronics, electro-chemical and general engineering, etc). *Recreations:* Pres. Swansea City AFC Ltd; Vice-Pres. Clyne Golf Club, Ltd. *Address:* La Maison Blanche, Jerbourg Road, St Martin, Guernsey, CI. *T:* Guernsey 37985. *Club:* Royal Automobile.

HOLDEN-BROWN, Sir Derrick, Kt 1979; Chairman and Chief Executive, Allied-Lyons, PLC, since 1982; Director, Allied Breweries, since 1967 (Chairman, 1982–86); *b* 14 Feb. 1923; *s* of Harold Walter and Beatrice Florence (*née* Walker); *m* 1950, Patricia Mary Ross Mackenzie; one *s* one *d*. *Educ:* Westcliff. Mem., Inst of Chartered Accountants of Scotland. Served War, Royal Navy, 1941–46, Lt RNVR, Coastal Forces. Chartered Accountant, 1948; Hiram Walker & Sons, Distillers, 1949; Managing Director: Cairnes Ltd, Brewers, Eire, 1954; Grants of St James's Ltd, 1960; Dir, Ind Coope Ltd, 1962; Chm., Victoria Wine Co., 1964; Finance Dir, 1972, Vice-Chm., 1975–82, Allied Breweries; Director: Sun Alliance & London Insurance plc, 1977– (Vice Chm., 1983, Dep. Chm., 1985–); Midland Bank, 1984–. Chm., FDIC, 1984– (Dep. Chm. 1974–76). Chairman: Brewers' Soc., 1978–80; Water Decade Realisation Fund, 1985–; President: Food and Drink Fedn, 1985–; Food Manufacturers' Fedn Inc., 1985. *Recreations:* sailing, offshore cruising. *Address:* Copse House, Milford-on-Sea, Hants. *T:* Milford-on-Sea 2247. *Clubs:* Boodle's; Royal Yacht Squadron; Royal Lymington Yacht; Royal Naval Sailing Association.

HOLDER, Sir (John) Henry, 4th Bt *cr* 1898, of Pitsmaston, Moseley, Worcs; Production Director and Head Brewer, Elgood & Sons Ltd, North Brink Brewery, Wisbech, since 1975; *b* 12 March 1928; *s* of Sir John Eric Duncan Holder, 3rd Bt and of Evelyn Josephine, *er d* of late William Blain; *S* father, 1986; *m* 1960, Catharine Harrison, *yr d* of late Leonard Baker; twin *s* one *d*. *Educ:* Eton Coll.; Birmingham Univ. (Dip. Malting and Brewing); Dip. in Safety Management, British Safety Council. Diploma Mem., Inst. of Brewing. National Service, RAC; commnd 5th Royal Tank Regt, 1947. Shift Brewer, Mitchells & Butlers Ltd, 1951–53; Brewer, Reffels Bexley Brewery Ltd, 1953–56; Asst Manager, Unique Slide Rule Co., 1956–62; Brewer, Rhymney Brewery Co. Ltd, 1962–75. *Recreations:* dinghy sailing, computing. *Heir: er* twin *s* Nigel John Charles Holder, *b* 6 May 1962. *Address:* 47 St Paul's Road, Walton Highway, Wisbech, Cambs PE14 7DN. *T:* Wisbech 583493. *Clubs:* Ouse Amateur Sailing (King's Lynn); Snettisham Beach Sailing.

HOLDER, Air Marshal Sir Paul (Davie), KBE 1965; CB 1964; DSO 1942; DFC 1941; *b* 2 Sept. 1911; *s* of Hugh John and Frances Rhoda Holder; *m* 1940, Mary Elizabeth Kidd; two *s*. *Educ:* Bristol Univ.; University of Illinois, USA. MSc Bristol, 1933; Robert Blair Fellow, 1934; PhD Bristol, 1935. Commnd RAF, 1936; 84 Sqdn, Trng, 1938–39; RAF Staff Coll., 1946; Vice-Pres., RAF Selection Board, 1947–48; Student, Administrative Staff Coll., Henley on Thames, 1949; CO, RAF, Shallufa, Egypt, 1950–51; CO, RAF, Kabrit, Egypt, 1952; Dep. Dir, Air Staff Policy, Air Min., 1953–55; Student, Imperial Defence Coll., 1956; AOC, Singapore, 1957; AOC, Hong Kong, 1958–59; ACAS (Trng), Air Min., 1960–62; AOC No 25 Gp, RAF Flying Trng Comd, 1963–64; AOC-in-C, RAF Coastal Comd, NATO Comdr Maritime Air, Channel Comd, and Comdr Maritime Air, Eastern Atlantic Area, 1965–68, retired 1968. FRAeS 1966. *Recreations:* gardening, bridge. *Address:* Innisfree, Bramshott Chase, Hindhead, Surrey GU26 6DG. *T:* Hindhead 4579. *Club:* Royal Air Force.

HOLDERNESS, Baron *cr* 1979 (Life Peer), of Bishop Wilton in the County of Humberside; **Richard Frederick Wood;** PC 1959; DL; *b* 5 Oct. 1920; 3rd *s* of 1st Earl of Halifax, KG, PC, OM, GCSI, GCMG, GCIE, TD; *m* 1947, Diana, *d* of late Col E. O. Kellett, DSO, MP, and Hon. Mrs W. J. McGowan; one *s* one *d*. *Educ:* Eton; New College, Oxford. Hon. Attaché, British Embassy, Rome, 1940; served War of 1939–45 as Lieutenant, KRRC, 1941–43; retired, wounded, 1943; toured US Army hospitals, 1943–45; New College, Oxford, 1945–47. MP (C) Bridlington, Yorkshire, 1950–79; Parliamentary Private Secretary: to Minister of Pensions, 1951–53; to Minister of State, Board of Trade, 1953–54; to Minister of Agriculture and Fisheries, 1954–55; Joint Parliamentary Secretary: Ministry of Pensions and National Insurance, 1955–58; Ministry of Labour, 1958–59; Minister of Power, October 1959–63, of Pensions and National Insurance, Oct. 1963–64; Minister of Overseas Develt, ODM, June-Oct. 1970, FCO, 1970–74. Dir, Hargreaves Group Ltd, 1974–; Regional Dir, Yorkshire and Humberside regional board, Lloyds Bank, 1981–. Mem., Hansard Soc. Commn on Electoral Reform, 1975–76. Pres., Queen Elizabeth's Foundn for the Disabled, 1983–. DL E Riding Yorks, 1967. Hon. LLD: Sheffield Univ., 1962; Leeds, 1978; Hull, 1982. Hon. Colonel: Queen's Royal Rifles, 1962; 4th (Volunteer) Bn Royal Green Jackets, 1967–. *Address:* Flat Top House, Bishop Wilton, York YO4 1RY. *T:* Bishop Wilton 266; 49 Cadogan Place, SW1 9RT. *T:* 01–235 1597; 65 Les Collines de Guerrevieille, 83120 Ste Maxime, France.

See also Sir E. N. Brooksbank, Bt.

HOLDERNESS, Rt. Rev. George Edward, ERD (with 2 clasps) 1955; Dean Emeritus of Lichfield; an Assistant Bishop, Diocese of York, since 1980; *b* 5 March 1913; 2nd *s* of A. W. Holderness, Roundhay, Leeds; *m* 1940, Irene Mary, *er d* of H. G. Hird, Bedale, Yorkshire; one *s* two *d*. *Educ:* Leeds Grammar Sch.: Keble Coll., Oxford (MA); Westcott House, Cambridge. Assistant Curate of Bedale, 1936–39; Chaplain and Asst Master, Aysgarth School, Bedale, 1939–47. CF (RARO) 1940; SCF, 81st W African Div., 1943; DACG, India Command, 1945. Vicar of Darlington, 1947–55; Hon. Canon of Durham Cathedral, 1954; Suffragan Bishop of Burnley, 1955–70; Rector of Burnley, 1955–70; Canon of Blackburn Cathedral, 1955–70; Dean of Lichfield, 1970–79. DACG, TA, Northern Command, 1951–55. *Recreations:* shooting, fishing. *Address:* Riseborough Cottages, Marton, Sinnington, York YO6 6RD. *Clubs:* MCC, Forty, Lord's Taverners', I Zingari.

HOLDERNESS, Sir Richard William, 3rd Bt, *cr* 1920; Partner, Whiteheads, Estate Agents and Surveyors, since 1967; *b* 30 Nov. 1927; *s* of Sir Ernest William Elsmie Holderness, 2nd Bt, CBE, and Emily Carlton (*d* 1950), *y d* of late Frederick McQuade, Sydney, NSW; *S* father, 1968; *m* 1953, Pamela, *d* of Eric Chapman, CBE; two *s* one *d*. *Educ:* Dauntsey's Sch.; Corpus Christi Coll., Oxford. FRICS 1976. *Heir: s* Martin William Holderness, CA [*b* 24 May 1957; *m* 1984, Elizabeth, SRN, DipHV, *d* of Dr William and Dr Maureen Thornton, Belfast. *Educ:* Bradfield Coll., Berks]. *Address:* Rosetree House, Boxgrove, Chichester; (office) 12 Chapel Road, Worthing, West Sussex.

HOLDGATE, Martin Wyatt, CB 1979; PhD; FIBiol; Deputy Secretary, Environment Protection, and Chief Scientist, Department of the Environment, and Chief Scientific Adviser, Department of Transport, since 1985; *b* 14 Jan. 1931; *s* of late Francis Wyatt Holdgate, MA, JP, and of Lois Marjorie (*née* Bebbington); *m* 1963, Elizabeth Mary (*née* Dickason), widow of Dr H. H. Weil; two *s*. *Educ:* Arnold Sch., Blackpool; Queens' Coll., Cambridge. BA Cantab 1952; MA 1956; PhD 1955; FIBiol 1967. Senior Scientist, Gough Is Scientific Survey, 1955–56; Lecturer in Zoology, Manchester Univ., 1956–57; Lecturer in Zoology, Durham Colleges, 1957–60; Leader, Royal Society Expedition to Southern Chile, 1958–59; Asst Director of Research, Scott Polar Research Institute, Cambridge, 1960–63; Senior Biologist, British Antarctic Survey, 1963–66; Sec., Working Gp on Biology, Scientific Cttee on Antarctic Res., 1964–68; Dep. Dir (Research), The Nature Conservancy, 1966–70; Director: Central Unit on Environmental Pollution, DoE, 1970–74; Inst. of Terrestrial Ecology, NERC, 1974–76; Dir-Gen. of Res., Depts of the Environment and of Transport, 1976–79, Chief Scientist and Dep. Sec., 1979–85. Hon. Professorial Fellow, UC Cardiff, 1976–83. Member: NERC, 1976–; SERC (formerly SRC), 1976–86; ABRC, 1976–; Chm., Review of Scientific Civil Service, 1980. Chm.,

British Schools Exploring Society, 1967–78; Vice-Pres., Young Explorer's Trust, 1981– (Chm., 1972, 1979–81); Dir, World Resources Inst., Washington, DC, 1985–; Pres., Governing Council, UN Environment Prog., 1983–84. UNEP Silver Medal, 1983. *Publications:* A History of Appleby, 1956, 2nd edn 1970; Mountains in the Sea, The Story of the Gough Island Expedition, 1958; (ed jtly) Antarctic Biology, 1964; (ed) Antarctic Ecology, 1970; (with N. M. Wace) Man and Nature in the Tristan da Cunha Islands, 1976; A Perspective of Environmental Pollution, 1979; (ed jtly) The World Environment 1972–82, 1982; numerous papers in biological journals and works on Antarctic. *Address:* 35 Wingate Way, Trumpington, Cambridge CB2 2HD. *T:* Cambridge 840086. *Club:* Athenæum.

HOLDING, Malcolm Alexander; HM Diplomatic Service; Consul-General, Naples, since 1986; *b* 11 May 1932; *s* of Adam Anderson Holding and Mary Lillian (*née* Golding); *m* 1955, Pamela Eve Hampshire; two *d*. *Educ:* King Henry VIII Sch., Coventry. Foreign Office, 1949–51; HM Forces, 1951–53; FO, 1953–55; Middle East Centre for Arab Studies, 1956–57; Third Secretary (Commercial), Tunis, 1957–60; Second Sec. (Commercial), Khartoum, 1960–64; Second, later First Sec. (Commercial), Cairo, 1964–68; Consul, Bari, 1969; FCO, 1970–73; First Sec., British Dep. High Commission, Madras, 1973–75; FCO, 1976–78; Canadian National Defence Coll., Kingston, Ontario, 1978–79; Counsellor (Commercial), Rome, 1979–81; Consul-Gen., Edmonton, 1981–85. *Recreations:* sailing, skiing. *Address:* c/o Foreign and Commonwealth Office, SW1.

HOLDSWORTH, His Honour Albert Edward; QC 1969; a Circuit Judge, 1972–82; *b* 1909; *e s* of Albert Edward and Catherine Sarah Holdsworth; *m* 1st, 1941, Barbara Frances (*d* 1968), *e d* of Ernest Henry and Beatrice Maud Reeves; one *s*; 2nd, 1970, Brianne Evelyn Frances, *d* of Arthur James and Evelyn Lock; two *s*. *Educ:* Sir George Monoux Sch., Walthamstow; Gonville and Caius Coll., Cambridge (Exhibitioner). Pres., Cambridge Union, 1932; Economics and Politics tripos; MA. Formerly journalist: Financial News, 1932–33; Special Correspondent, World Economic Conf., 1933; Yorkshire Post, 1933–46, Polit. Correspondent, later London Editor. Broadcasts for BBC on current affairs topics, 1935–56. Called to Bar, Middle Temple, 1936. Conservative Candidate Ipswich, 1951; moved resolution in favour of UK entry into European Common Market, Conservative Conf., Llandudno, 1962. Dep.-Chm., SW Metropolitan Mental Health Tribunal, 1962–65. *Publication:* Forward Together, 1983. *Address:* 2 Middle Temple Lane, Temple, EC4Y 9AA. *T:* 01–353 7926; Sutton Gate, Sutton, Pulborough, West Sussex RH20 1PN. *T:* Sutton (West Sussex) 230. *Club:* Reform.

HOLDSWORTH, Lt-Comdr (Arthur) John (Arundell), CVO 1980; OBE 1962; Vice Lord Lieutenant for Devon, since 1982; an Extra Gentleman Usher to the Queen, since 1985 (Gentleman Usher, 1967–85); *b* 31 March 1915; *s* of Captain F. J. C. Holdsworth, JP, DL, Totnes, and M. W. Holdsworth (*née* Arundell); *m* 1940, Barbara Lucy Ussher, *d* of Col and Mrs W. M. Acton; one *s* one *d*. *Educ:* Stanmore Park Prep. Sch.; Royal Naval Coll., Dartmouth. Entered RN, 1928; served War at sea (despatches); Asst Naval Attaché Warsaw, 1947–49; BJSM Washington, 1950–51; Naval Staff, Germany, 1954–56; Flag Lieut to Bd of Admiralty, 1956–65; retired 1965. Steward, Newton Abbot Race Course, 1967–85; Dep. Pres., Devon Br., BRCS, 1971–85 (Patron, 1985–); Chm., Silver Jubilee Trust Council, Devon, 1978–85. DL 1973, High Sheriff, 1976–77, Devon. *Address:* Holbeam Mill, Ogwell, Newton Abbot, Devon TQ12 6LX. *T:* Newton Abbot 65547.

HOLDSWORTH, Sir (George) Trevor, Kt 1982; Chairman: GKN plc (formerly Guest, Keen & Nettlefolds plc), since 1980; Allied Colloids Group PLC, since 1983; Director: Midland Bank plc, since 1979; THORN EMI plc, since 1977; *b* 29 May 1927; *s* of late William Albert Holdsworth and Winifred Holdsworth (*née* Bottomley); *m* 1951, Patricia June Ridler; three *s*. *Educ:* Hanson Grammar Sch., Bradford; Keighley Grammar Sch. FCA 1950. Rawlinson, Greaves & Mitchell, Bradford, 1944–51; Bowater Paper Corp., 1952–63 (financial and admin. appts; Dir and Controller of UK paper-making subsids); joined Guest, Keen & Nettlefolds, 1963; Dep. Chief Accountant, 1963–64; Gp Chief Accountant, 1965–67; General Man. Dir, GKN Screws & Fasteners Ltd, 1968–70; Dir and Gp Controller, 1970–72; Gp Exec. Vice Chm., Corporate Controls and Services, 1973–74; Dep. Chm., 1974; Man. Dir and Dep. Chm., 1977. Dir, Equity Capital for Industry, 1976–84. Confederation of British Industry: Mem. Council, 1974–; Mem., Econ. and Financial Policy Cttee, 1978–80; Mem., Steering Gp on Unemployment, 1982; Mem., Special Programmes Unit, 1982; Chm., Tax Reform Working Party, 1984–. Mem., AMF Inc. Europ. Adv. Council, 1982–85; British Institute of Management: Mem. Council, 1974–; Vice-Chm., 1978; Mem., Bd of Fellows, 1979; Chm., 1980–82; a Vice-Pres., 1982–. Vice Pres., Engineering Employers' Fedn, 1980–; Dep. Chm., Adv. Bd, Inst. of Occupational Health, 1980; Member: Business and Commercial Enterprises Gp, and Overseas Panel, Duke of Edinburgh's Award, 1980–; Exec. Cttee, SMMT, 1980–83; Engineering Industries Council, 1980– (Chm., 1985); Court of British Shippers' Council, 1981–; British-North American Cttee, 1981–85; Council, RIIA, 1983–; Internat. Council of INSEAD, 1985; Eur. Adv. Cttee, New York Stock Exchange, 1985; Council, Royal Opera House Trust (Trustee, 1981–84); Council, Winston Churchill Meml Trust, 1985–. Trustee: Anglo-German Foundn for the Study of Industrial Society, 1980–; Brighton Fest. Trust, 1980– (Chm. 1982–); Philharmonia Trust, 1982–. Governor, Ashridge Management Coll., 1978. Vice-Pres., Ironbridge Gorge Museum Develt Trust, 1981–. Freeman, City of London, 1977; Liveryman, Worshipful Co. of Chartered Accountants in England and Wales, 1978. Hon. DTech Loughborough, 1981; Hon. DSc Aston, 1982; Hon. DEng Bradford, 1983. Chartered Accountants Founding Socs' Centenary Award, 1983. *Recreations:* music, theatre. *Address:* 7 Cleveland Row, St James's, SW1A 1DB. *T:* 01–930 2424. *Club:* Athenæum.

HOLDSWORTH, Lt-Comdr John; *see* Holdsworth, Lt-Comdr A. J. A.

HOLDSWORTH, Sir Trevor; *see* Holdsworth, Sir G. T.

HOLE, Rev. Canon Derek Norman; Vicar of St James the Greater, Leicester, since 1973; Chaplain to HM the Queen, since 1985; *b* 5 Dec. 1933; *s* of Frank Edwin Hole and Ella Evelyn Hole (*née* Thomas). *Educ:* Lincoln Theological College. Deacon, 1960; Priest, 1961; Asst Curate, St Mary Magdalen, Knighton, 1960–62; Domestic Chaplain to Archbishop of Cape Town, 1962–64; Asst Curate, St Nicholas, Kenilworth, 1964–67; Rector, St Mary the Virgin, Burton Latimer, 1967–73; Hon. Canon, Leicester Cathedral, 1983–. Rural Dean, Christianity South, Leicester, 1983–; Chaplain, Leicester High Sch., 1984–; Vice-Pres., Leicester Rotary Club, 1986–87. *Recreations:* music, walking. *Address:* St James the Greater Vicarage, 216 London Road, Leicester LE2 1NE. *T:* Leicester 542111. *Club:* Leicestershire (Leicester).

HOLE, George Vincer, CBE 1969; ICAO Consultant on Airport Affairs, since 1975; Chief Executive, British Airports Authority, 1965–72; *b* 26 Jan. 1910; *s* of George William Hole and Louisa Hole (*née* Vincer); *m* 1938, Gertraud Johanna Anna Koppe (Baroness von Broesigke); two *s*. *Educ:* Wilson's Grammar Sch., London; London Sch. of Economics. BSc (Econ.) 1933. Asst Auditor, Exchequer and Audit Dept, 1929; passed First Div. Exam., 1935; Under-Sec., 1958; Min. of Aviation, 1959–65; student Imperial Defence Coll., 1948; Chm. First Div. Assoc., 1949–50; Chm. OEEC Productivity Group, on Traffic Engineering and Control, in the United States, 1954; Chm. W European Airports Assoc., 1970; Member: Council, Internat. Bd of Airport Operators, 1970; Bd, Internat. Civil Airports Assoc. (Chm.); Bd, Airport Assocs Co-ordinating Council (first Chm.). FCIT. Hon. Treas., Caravan Club, 1960–66. Dir, J. E. Greiner Co. Ltd, Consulting Engineers, Edinburgh, 1972–75. ICAO Lectr on Airport Affairs, Beirut, 1972–75. Officer, Order of Orange Nassau, Netherlands, 1946; Officer, Order of the Crown, Belgium, 1946. *Recreation:* pottering. *Address:* 2 Macartney House, Chesterfield Walk, Greenwich, SE10 8HJ. *T:* 01–858 3917.

HOLFORD, Rear-Adm. Frank Douglas, CB 1969; DSC 1944; Director General of Naval Manpower, Ministry of Defence, 1967–69, retired 1970; *b* 28 June 1916; *y s* of late Capt. C. F. Holford, DSO, OBE, and Ursula Isobel Holford (*née* Corbett); *m* 1942, Sybil Priscilla, *d* of late Comdr Sir Robert and Lady Micklem; two *s*. *Educ:* RN Coll., Dartmouth. Cadet, 1929, Midshipman, HMS Hood, 1933; Sub-Lieut, HMS Wolverine, 1937; Lieutenant: HMS Kent, 1938; HMS Anson, 1941; HMS Sheffield, 1943; Lieut-Comdr: HMS Excellent, 1945; HMS Triumph, 1948; Commander: Admlty, Naval Ordnance Dept, 1951; British Joint Services Mission, USA, 1953; HMS Excellent, 1955; Captain: Admlty, Dir Guided Weapons, 1957; Naval and Mil. Attaché, Buenos Aires, 1960; Staff C-in-C Portsmouth, 1962; Cdre-i-C Hong Kong, 1965. Rear-Adm. 1967. jssc 1947. *Address:* Little Down Cottage, Shedfield, Hants. *T:* Wickham 832295.

HOLFORD, Surgeon Rear-Adm. John Morley, CB 1965; OBE 1954; Senior Principal Medical Officer, Department of Health and Social Security, 1973–74, retired; *b* 10 Jan. 1909; *o s* of late Rev. W. J. Holford and Amy Finnemore Lello; *m* 1935, Monica Peregrine, *d* of late Preb. P. S. G. Propert; two *s*. *Educ:* Kingswood, Bath; Trinity Hall, Cambridge. MA, MB, Cantab; FRCP; joined RN 1935. War service in HMS Nelson, 1940–42; RN Hosp. Plymouth, 1942–44; consultant in Medicine to RN, 1954–66; Surgeon Capt., 1957; Surgeon Rear-Adm. 1963; Medical Officer in Charge, RN Hosp. Haslar, 1963–66. Retired, 1966. MO, Min. of Health, 1966, SMO, 1967, SPMO, 1973. Gilbert Blanc Medal, 1956; F. E. Williams Prize in Geriatric Medicine, RCP, 1972. CStJ 1964. *Publications:* Articles in medical journals. *Recreations:* chess (jt champion of South Africa, 1946), bridge. *Address:* c/o Lloyds Bank, 84 Park Lane, W1. *Club:* Army and Navy.

HOLGATE, Hon. Harold Norman, MHA; Chairman, Parliamentary Labor Party, since 1986; *b* 5 Dec. 1933; *s* of late H. W. Holgate; *m* 1963, Rosalind, *d* of E. C. Wesley; two *s* two *d*. *Educ:* Maitland (NSW) High Sch.; Univ. of Tasmania (BA). Journalist: Sydney Morning Herald, 1952–55; Melbourne Herald, 1955–62; Political Journalist, Dep. Chief of Staff, Launceston Examiner, 1963–66; Public Relns Manager, Tasmanian Directorate of Industrial Development, 1966–70; Exec. Producer, ABC TV Public Affairs Programme, This Day Tonight, Hobart, 1970–73; Press Sec. to Dep. Prime Minister and Minister for Defence, Govt of Australia, Mr Lance Barnard, 1973–74; MHA (Lab) for Bass, Tasmania, 1974–; Speaker of House of Assembly, 1975–76; Minister (Govt of Tasmania): for Housing and Construction and Minister assisting the Dep. Premier, 1976–77; for Education, Recreation and the Arts and for Racing and Gaming, 1977–79; for Education, Recreation and the Arts, and for Police and Emergency Services, 1979–80; for Education, for Police and Emergency Services, for Racing and Gaming, 1980–81; for Police and Emergency Services, for Local Govt, for the Environment, for Water Resources, for Racing and Gaming, 1981; Premier of Tasmania, Treasurer and Minister for Racing and Gaming, 1981–82; Dep. Leader of the Opposition, Tasmanian House of Assembly, 1982–86. *Recreations:* horse racing, music, reading, swimming. *Address:* 145 Canning Street, Launceston, Tasmania 7250, Australia. *T:* 003. 317572.

HOLGATE, Dr Sidney, CBE 1981; Master of Grey College, University of Durham, 1959–80; Member, Academic Advisory Committee, Open University, 1969–81 (Vice-Chairman, 1972–75; Chairman, 1975–77); *b* Hucknall, Notts, 9 Sept. 1918; *e s* of late Henry and Annie Elizabeth Holgate; *m* 1942, Isabel Armorey; no *c*. *Educ:* Henry Mellish Sch., Nottingham; Durham Univ. Open Scholar, Hatfield Coll., Durham, 1937; Univ. Mathematical Scholarship, 1940; BA (1st Cl. Hons Mathematics) 1940; MA 1943; PhD 1945. Asst Master, Nottingham High Sch., 1941–42; Lecturer in Mathematics, University of Durham, 1942–46; Sec. of the Durham Colls, 1946–59; Pro-Vice-Chancellor, Univ. of Durham, 1964–69. Member: Schools Council Gen. Studies Cttee, 1967–70; Chm., BBC Radio Durham Council, 1968–72; Vice-Chm., BBC Radio Newcastle Council, 1972–74. Hon. DUniv. Open, 1980. *Publications:* mathematical papers in Proc. Camb. Phil. Soc. and Proc. Royal Soc. *Recreations:* cricket and other sports, railways, bridge. *Address:* 6 Howlcroft Villas, Neville's Cross, Durham DH1 4DU.

HOLGATE, Surgeon Rear-Adm. (D) William, CB 1962; OBE 1951; Chief Dental Officer, Ministry of Health, 1961–71, and Ministry of Education and Science, 1963–71; *b* 6 July 1906; *s* of Anthony and Jane Holgate; *m* 1933, Inga Ommanney Davis; one *s* one *d*. *Educ:* Scarborough Coll.; Guy's Hospital. LDS, RCS Eng., 1927; FDS, RCS Eng., 1963. Royal Navy, 1928–61; Director of Dental Services, 1960. *Address:* Upalong, The Highway, Luccombe, Shanklin, Isle of Wight. *Club:* Savage.

HOLLAMBY, Edward Ernest, OBE 1970; FRIBA, FRTPI, FSIAD; Chief Architect and Planner to London Docklands Development Corporation, 1981–85, retired; architectural consultant; *b* 8 Jan. 1921; *s* of Edward Thomas Hollamby and late Ethel May (*née* Kingdom); *m* 1941, Dori Isabel Parker; one *s* two *d*. *Educ:* School of Arts and Crafts, Hammersmith; University Coll. London. DipTP London. Served RM Engrs, 1941–46. Architect, Miners' Welfare Commn, 1947–49; Sen. Architect, LCC, 1949–62; Borough Architect, Lambeth, 1963–65, Bor. Architect and Town Planning Officer, 1965–69, Dir of Architecture, Planning and Develt, 1969–81. Works, 1957–, incl.: Christopher Wren and N Hammersmith Sec. Schs; Brandon Estate, Southwark; Housing at Elephant and Castle; study for Erith Township, Kent (prototype study for Thamesmead); pioneered rehabil. old houses, LCC Brixton Town Centre Develt Plan; housing schemes, Lambeth, 1965–, incl.: Lambeth Towers; Central Hill, Norwood; Stockwell; Brixton; flats, houses, old people's home, doctors' gp practice, Clapham. Area rehabil. and renewal schemes, Clapham Manor and Kennington; Norwood Libr. and Nettlefold Hall; schs for mentally retarded, Clapham and Kennington; rehabil. centre for disabled, Clapham; home for elderly, Kennington; offices for Tarmac; recreation centre, Brixton, study, Civic Centre, Brixton; holiday hotel for severely disabled, Netley, near Southampton; Girls' Secure Unit, Croydon, 1978; scheme for village development, Shirley Oaks, 1979; Isle of Dogs Urban Design Guide, 1982; framework for develt, Wapping, 1982; refurbishment of exterior and landscape, St George's in the East, 1983; Royal Docks Develt Strategy, 1984; overall layout, Western Dock, Wapping; Chm., Design Gp, Docklands Light Railway, 1982–84. External Examiner in Architecture, NE London Polytechnic, 1982–; assessor, numerous architectural competitions. Has lectured on architecture and environmental planning; numerous radio and TV appearances. RIBA: Mem. Council, 1961–70, Hon. Treas., 1967–70. Member: Historic Buildings Council, 1972–82; London Adv. Cttee, English Heritage; Founder Mem., William Morris Soc. Hon. ALI; FRSA. Numerous design and Civic Trust awards. *Publications:* contrib. architectural and town planning jls. *Recreations:* travel, classical music, opera, gardening. *Address:* Red House, Red House Lane, Upton, Bexleyheath, Kent DA6 8JF. *T:* 01–303 8808. *Club:* Arts.

HOLLAND, Rt. Rev. Alfred Charles; *see* Newcastle, NSW, Bishop of.

HOLLAND, Arthur David, CB 1973; TD 1947; Chief Highway Engineer, Department of the Environment, 1970–74; *b* 1 Nov. 1913; *o s* of Col. Arthur Leslie Holland, MC, TD, and Dora Helena Hassé; *m* 1938, Jean Moyra Spowart; two *s*. *Educ:* Malvern Coll.; University of Bristol (BSc(Eng)Hons). Asst Engineer, Great Western Railway Co, 1935–36; N Devon CC, 1936–37; Min. of Transport: Manchester, 1937–38; London, 1938–39. Served War: with RE, 1939–46; in Air Defence Gt Britain, 1939–42; with Middle East Forces, 1942–46, finally as Lt-Col RE (now Hon. Lt-Col), Sen. Staff Officer to Chief Engineer, Italy. Min. of Transport, Nottingham, 1946–47; Bridge Section, London, 1947–61; Divl Road Engr, E Midland Div., Nottingham, 1961–63; Asst Chief Engr (Bridges), 1963–65; Dep. Chief Engr, HQ London, 1965–70. FICE, FIStructE, FInstHE; Mem., Smeatonian Soc. of Civil Engrs. *Publications:* contribs to Proc. Instn of Civil Engineers and Instn of Highway Engineers. *Address:* Pine Tree Cottage, Pembroke Road, Woking, Surrey. *T:* Woking 62403.

HOLLAND, Brian Arthur; Solicitor to the Post Office, since 1981; *b* 14 June 1935; *s* of George Leigh Holland and Hilda Holland, MBE; *m* 1964, Sally Edwards; one *s* one *d*. *Educ:* Manchester Grammar Sch.; Manchester Univ. (LLB Hons). Admitted Solicitor, 1961. Joined Solicitor's Dept, GPO, 1961; Solicitor's Office, Post Office: Head of Civil Litigation Div., 1977–79; Dir, Litigation and Prosecution Dept, 1979–81. *Publication:* (contrib.) Halsbury's Laws of England, 4th edn, vol. 36. *Recreations:* scouting, photography, studying railways, sketching, gardening. *Address:* 23 Grasmere Road, Purley, Surrey CR2 1DY. *T:* 01-660 0479.

HOLLAND, Christopher John, QC 1978; barrister-at-law; *b* 1 June 1937; *er s* of late Frank and Winifred Mary Holland; *m* 1967, Jill Iona Holland; one *s* one *d*. *Educ:* Leeds Grammar Sch.; Emmanuel Coll., Cambridge (MA, LLB). National Service (acting L/Cpl), 3rd Royal Tank Regt, 1956–58. Called to the Bar, Inner Temple, 1963, Bencher, 1985; commenced practice on North Eastern Circuit. Vice Chm., Cttee of Inquiry into Outbreak of Legionnaires' Disease at Stafford, 1985. *Address:* Pearl Chambers, 22 East Parade, Leeds LS1 5BU. *T:* Leeds 452702; 2 Harcourt Buildings, Temple, EC4Y 9DB. *Clubs:* United Oxford & Cambridge University.

HOLLAND, Sir Clifton Vaughan, (Sir John), Kt 1973; BCE; FTS, FIE(Aust), FAIM, FAIB; Chairman, John Holland Holdings Limited, 1963–86; *b* Melbourne, 21 June 1914; *s* of Thomas and Mabel Ruth Elizabeth Holland; *m* 1942, Emily Joan Atkinson; three *s* one *d*. *Educ:* Flinders State Sch.; Frankston High Sch.; Queen's Coll., Univ. of Melbourne (BCE); Monash Univ. (Hon. DEng 1978). Junior Engineer, BP, 1936–39. Served War of 1939–45, RAE and 'Z' Special Force, Middle East, SW Pacific (Lt-Col). Construction Engr, BP Aust. 1946–49; Founder, John Holland (Constructions) Pty Ltd, 1949, Man. Dir 1949–73, Chm., 1949–81; Chm., Process Plant Constructions Pty Ltd, 1949–82; Director: T & G Life Soc., 1972–82; Aust. and NZ Banking Gp, 1976–81. Foundn Pres., Australian Fedn of Civil Contractors (Life Mem., 1971); Chm., Nat. Construction Industry Conf. Organising Cttee, 1982; Mem., Construction Industry Res. Bd, 1982. Chm., Econ. Consultative Adv. Gp to the Treasurer, 1975–81; Mem., Rhodes Scholar Selection Cttee, 1970–73; Mem. Bd, Royal Melbourne Hosp., 1963–79; Nat. Chm., Outward Bound, 1973–74, Chm. Victorian Div., 1964–77; Councillor, Inst. of Public Affairs, 1980; Mem., Churchill Fellowship Selection Cttee, 1968–82; Director: Winston Churchill Meml Trust, 1976–82 (Chm., Vic. Br., 1977–82); Child Accident Prevention Foundn of Australia, 1979–81; Chairman: La Trobe Centenary Commemoration Council, 1975–76; Matthew Flinders Bi-Centenary Council, 1973–75; History Adv. Council of Victoria, 1975–; Loch Ard Centenary Commemoration Cttee, 1976–78; Citizens' Council, 150th Anniversary Celebrations, Victoria, 1979–82; Victorian Cttee for Anzac Awards, 1982–; Nat. Chm., Queen's Silver Jubilee Trust for Young Australians, 1981– (Vic. Chm., 1977–80); Mem., Centenary Test Co-ordinating Cttee, 1976–77. Dep. Chm., Melbourne Univ. Engineering Sch. Centenary Foundn and Appeal Cttee, 1982–. Director: Corps of Commissionaires (Victoria) Ltd, 1978–; Australian Bicentenary Celebrations, 1980–82 (Vic. Chm., 1980–82). Pres., Stroke Res. Foundn, 1983–. Construction projects include: Jindabyne pumping station; Westgate Bridge; Tasman Bridge restoration. Foundation Fellow, Australian Acad. of Technological Scis. Peter Nicoll Russell Meml Medal, 1974; Kernot Meml Medal, Univ. of Melbourne, 1976. *Recreations:* golf, music, gardening, cricket. *Address:* 3/3 St Ninians Road, Brighton, Victoria 3186, Australia. *Clubs:* Australian, Naval and Military (Melbourne); Royal Melbourne Golf, Frankston Golf, Flinders Golf.

HOLLAND, David Cuthbert Lyall, CB 1975; Librarian of the House of Commons, 1967–76; *b* 23 March 1915; *yr s* of Michael Holland, MC, and Marion Holland (*née* Broadwood); *m* 1949, Rosemary Griffiths, *y d* of David Ll. Griffiths, OBE; two *s* one *d*. *Educ:* Eton; Trinity Coll., Cambridge (MA). War service, Army, 1939–46; PoW. Appointed House of Commons Library, 1946. Chm., Study of Parlt Gp, 1973–74. *Publications:* book reviews, etc. *Recreation:* book collecting. *Address:* The Barn, Milton Street, Polegate, East Sussex. *T:* Alfriston 870379. *Club:* Athenæum.

HOLLAND, David George, CMG 1975; Executive Director, The Group of Thirty, since 1986; *b* 31 May 1925; *s* of late Francis George Holland and Mabel Ellen Holland; *m* 1954, Marian Elizabeth Rowles; two *s* one *d*. *Educ:* Taunton Sch.; Wadham Coll., Oxford. Inst. of Economics and Statistics, Oxford, 1949–63; Internat. Bank for Reconstruction and Development, Washington, DC, 1963–65; Min. of Overseas Development, 1965–67; Chief Economic Adviser, FCO, 1967–75; Dep. Chief, Economic Intelligence and Overseas Depts, Bank of England, 1975–80; Chief Adviser, Bank of England, 1980–85. *Address:* 20 Woodside Avenue, N6.

HOLLAND, Rt. Rev. Edward; *see* Gibraltar in Europe, Bishop Suffragan of.

HOLLAND, Edward Richard Charles, OBE 1983 (MBE 1969); HM Diplomatic Service, retired; *b* 26 March 1925; *s* of Cecil Francis Richard Holland and Joyce Mary (*née* Pyne); *m* 1952, Dorothy Olive Branthwaite; two *s*. *Educ:* Launceston Coll. Served RAF, 1943–48. Joined FO, 1948; served in Batavia, Bangkok, Oslo, Prague and Helsinki, 1949–57; Consul, Saigon, 1957; FO, 1959; Cape Town, 1962; First Sec., Monrovia, 1964; Consul: Stuttgart, 1969; Düsseldorf, 1971; FCO, 1972; First Sec., Islamabad, 1977; Consul-Gen., Alexandria, 1981–82. *Recreations:* gardening, walking, reading, painting, listening to music. *Address:* 1 Prospect Cottages, Boughton Aluph, Ashford, Kent TN25 4JA. *T:* Ashford 28539. *Club:* Civil Service.

HOLLAND, Einion; *see* Holland, R. E.

HOLLAND, Frank Robert Dacre; Chairman: C. E. Heath & Co. PLC, 1973–84, Non-Executive Director, since 1984; C. E. Heath & Co. (Insurance Broking) Ltd, 1981–84; *b* 24 March 1924; *s* of Ernest Albert Holland and Kathleen Annie (*née* Page); *m* 1948, Margaret Lindsay Aird; one *d*. *Educ:* Whitgift Sch., Croydon. Joined C. E. Heath & Co. Ltd, 1941; entered Army, 1942; Sandhurst, 1943; commissioned 4th Queen's Own Hussars, 1944; served, Italy, 1944–45, Austria and Germany, 1945–47; returned to C. E. Heath & Co. Ltd, 1947; Joint Managing Director, North American Operation, 1965; Director, C. E. Heath & Co. Ltd, 1965, Dep. Chm., 1969. *Recreations:* travel, gardening. *Address:* Moatside, 68 Ashley Road, Walton-on-Thames, Surrey KT12 1HR. *T:* Walton-on-Thames 227591. *Club:* Oriental.

HOLLAND, Geoffrey; CB 1984; Second Permanent Secretary, since 1986, and Director, since 1981, Manpower Services Commission; *b* 9 May 1938; *s* of late Frank Holland, CBE and of Elsie Freda Holland; *m* 1964, Carol Ann Challen. *Educ:* Merchant Taylors' Sch., Northwood; St John's Coll., Oxford (BA 1st cl. Hons; MA). 2nd Lieut, RTR, 1956–58. Entered Min. of Labour, 1961, Asst Private Sec., 1964–65; Principal Private Sec. to Sec. of State for Employment, 1971–72; Manpower Services Commission: Asst Sec., Hd of Planning, 1973; Dir of Special Progs, 1977; Dep. Sec., 1981. Consultant, Industrial Cttee, C of E Bd of Social Responsibility. Hon. Fellow: Polytechnic of Wales, 1986; Inst. of Training Develt, 1986. Liveryman, Merchant Taylors' Co., 1967–. *Publications:* Young People and Work, 1977; many articles on manpower, educn, training, management etc in professional jls. *Recreations:* journeying, opera, exercising the dog. *Address:* c/o Manpower Services Commission, Moorfoot, Sheffield S1 4PQ. *Club:* East India, Devonshire, Sports and Public Schools.

HOLLAND, Sir Guy (Hope), 3rd Bt *cr* 1917; *b* 19 July 1918; *s* of Sir Reginald Sothern Holland, 1st Bt and Stretta Aimée Holland (*née* Price) (*d* 1949); *S* brother, 1981; *m* 1945, Joan Marianne Street, *d* of late Captain Herbert Edmund Street, XXth Hussars, and of Lady Tottenham; two *d*. *Educ:* privately and Christ Church, Oxford. Served War of 1939–45 (wounded); Captain, Royal Scots Greys; ADC to Gen. Sir Andrew Thorne, 1944. *Heir:* none. *Address:* Sheepbridge Barn, Eastleach, Cirencester, Gloucestershire GL7 3PS. *T:* Southrop 296. *Clubs:* Boodle's, Pratt's.

HOLLAND, Sir John; *see* Holland, Sir C. V.

HOLLAND, John Lewis; Director, The Birmingham Post and Evening Mail (formerly The Birmingham Post), since 1986 (Editor, 1982–86); *b* 23 May 1937; *s* of George James Holland and Esther Holland; *m* 1958, Maureen Ann Adams; one *s* one *d*. *Educ:* Nottingham Technical Grammar Sch. Trainee Reporter, Nottingham Evening News, subseq. Jun. Reporter, Mansfield Br. Office, 1953–55; Sports Reporter, Mansfield Reporter Co., 1955–56; Sports Reporter, subseq. Sports Editor, Aldershot News Group, 1956–59; News Editor, West Bridgford & Clifton Standard, Nottingham, 1959–61; Chief Sports Sub Editor, Bristol Evening Post, and Editor, Sports Green 'Un (sports edn), 1961–64; Editor, West Bridgford & Clifton Standard, Nottingham, and Partner, Botting & Turner Sports Agency, Nottingham, 1964–66; Birmingham Evening Mail: Dep. Sports Editor, 1966–71; Editor, Special Projects Unit (Colour Prodn Dept), 1971–75; Editor, 1975–79, and Gen. Man., 1979–81, Sandwell Evening Mail; Marketing/Promotions Gen. Man., Birmingham Post & Mail, 1981–82. *Recreations:* journalism, most sports (more recently watching soccer and playing squash), keeping horses, gardening, keep fit. *Address:* Windgarth, Lynn Lane, Shenstone, Lichfield, Staffs WS14 0EN. *Club:* Press (Birmingham).

HOLLAND, Rt. Rev. John Tristram, CBE 1975; *b* 31 Jan. 1912; *s* of Rt Rev. H. St B. Holland; *m* 1937, Joan Theodora Arundell, *d* of Dr R. Leslie Ridge, Carlton House, Enfield, Mddx; three *d*. *Educ:* Durham School; University College, Oxford; Westcott House, Cambridge. BA 1933, MA 1937, Oxford. Deacon, 1935; Priest, 1936; Curate of St Peter's, Huddersfield, 1935–37; Commissary to Bishop of Wellington, 1936–37; Vicar of Featherston, 1938–41; CF (2 NZEF), 1941–45; Vicar of: St Peter's, Upper Riccarton, 1945–49; St Mary's, New Plymouth, 1949–51; Bishop of Waikato, 1951–69; Bishop in Polynesia, 1969–75; Officiating Minister: Diocese of Canterbury, 1975–76; Diocese of Waiapu, 1976. *Address:* 8 Short Street, Tauranga, New Zealand.

HOLLAND, Sir Kenneth (Lawrence), Kt 1981; CBE 1971; QFSM 1974; Chairman, Loss Prevention Certification Board Ltd, since 1984; Consultant, Fire Safety Engineering, since 1981; Director, Gent Ltd, since 1981; *b* 20 Sept. 1918; *s* of Percy Lawrence and Edith Holland; *m* 1941, Pauline Keith (*née* Mansfield); two *s* one *d*. *Educ:* Whitcliffe Mount Grammar Sch., Cleckheaton, Yorks. Entered Fire Service, Lancashire, 1937; Divisional Officer: Suffolk and Ipswich, 1948; Worcestershire, 1952; Dep. Chief Fire Officer, Lancashire, 1955; Chief Fire Officer: Bristol, 1960; West Riding of Yorkshire, 1967; HM Chief Inspector of Fire Services, 1972–80. Fellow, Instn Fire Engineers. Hon. Treasurer, Poole Arts Fedn, 1985. OStJ 1964. Defence Medal; Fire Brigade Long Service and Good Conduct Medal. *Recreations:* motor sports, gardening, the Arts. *Address:* Melina, 1 Bessborough Road, Canford Cliffs, Poole, Dorset BH13 7JS. *Clubs:* Royal Over-Seas League, St John House.

HOLLAND, Norman James Abbott, TEng; FIElecIE; Standards Manager, Philips UK Group, since 1983; *b* 16 Dec. 1927; *s* of James George Holland and May Stuart Holland; *m* 1951, Barbara Florence Byatt; one *s* one *d*. *Educ:* Sir Walter St John's Grammar Sch.; Regent Street Polytechnic. TEng(CEI); MIEEE. Chairman: Internat. Electrotechnical Commn Adv. Cttee on Electronics and Telecommunications, 1984–; Electronic Engrg Assoc. Engrg Services Div., 1985–; Member: IEC Finance Cttee, 1985–; Engrg Council, 1985–. *Recreation:* golf. *Address:* 22 Mitchley Avenue, Riddlesdown, Purley, Surrey CR2 1DT.

HOLLAND, Sir Philip (Welsby), Kt 1983; MP (C) Gedling, since 1983 (Carlton, 1966–83); *b* 14 March 1917; *s* of late John Holland, Middlewich, Cheshire; *m* 1943, Josephine Alma Hudson; one *s*. *Educ:* Sir John Deane's Grammar Sch., Northwich. Enlisted RAF 1936; commissioned 1943. Factory Manager, Jantzen Knitting Mills, 1946–47; Management Research, 1948–49; Manufacturers' Agent in Engineering and Refractories Products, 1949–60. Contested (C) Yardley Div. of Birmingham, Gen. Election, 1955; MP (C) Acton, 1959–64; PPS: to Minister of Pensions and Nat. Insurance, 1961–62; to Chief Sec. to Treasury and Paymaster-Gen., 1962–64; to Minister of Aviation Supply, 1970; to Minister for Aerospace, 1971; to Minister for Trade, 1972. Pres., Cons. Trade Union Nat. Adv. Cttee, 1972–74. Personnel Manager, The Ultra Electronics Group of Companies, 1964–66; Personnel Consultant to Standard Telephones and Cables Ltd, 1969–81. Chm., Cttee of Selection, HofC, 1979–84; Standing Cttee Chm., 1983–. Councillor, Royal Borough of Kensington, 1955–59. *Publications:* The Quango Explosion (jtly), 1978; Quango, Quango, Quango, 1979; Costing the Quango, 1979; The Quango Death List, 1980; The Governance of Quangos, 1981; Quelling the Quango, 1982. *Recreations:* travel, hunting the quango. *Address:* House of Commons, SW1A 0AA.

HOLLAND, (Robert) Einion, FIA; Chairman, Pearl Assurance Co. Ltd, since 1983; *b* 23 April 1927; *s* of late Robert Ellis Holland and Bene Holland; *m* 1955, Eryl Haf Roberts; one *s* two *d*. *Educ:* University Coll. of N Wales, Bangor (BSc). FIA 1957. Joined Pearl Assurance Co. Ltd, 1953: Dir, 1973; Chief Gen. Manager, 1977–83. Chm., Industrial Life Offices Assoc., 1976–78; Director: Pearl American Corp., 1972–; Aviation & General Insurance Co. Ltd, 1972– (Chm. 1976–78, 1984–85); Community Reinsurance Corp. Ltd, 1973– (Chm., 1973–76); Monarch Insurance Co. of Ohio, 1977–85; First New York Syndicate Corp., 1979–; Property Holding & Investment Trust PLC, 1982–; Chm., London City Underwriters Ltd, 1978–85. Mem., Welsh Develt Agency, 1976–. Mem., CS Pay Research Unit Bd, 1980–81. *Recreations:* golf and Welsh literature. *Address:* 55 Corkscrew Hill, West Wickham, Kent BR4 9BA. *T:* 01-777 1861.

HOLLAND, Stuart (Kingsley); MP (Lab) Vauxhall, since 1979; *b* 25 March 1940; *y s* of Frederick Holland and May Holland, London; *m* 1976, Jenny Lennard; two *c*. *Educ:* state primary schs; Christ's Hosp.; Univ. of Missouri (Exchange Scholar); Balliol Coll., Oxford (Domus Scholar; 1st Cl. Hons Mod. History); St Antony's Coll., Oxford (Sen. Scholar; DPhil Econs). Econ. Asst, Cabinet Office, 1966–67; Personal Asst to Prime Minister, 1967–68; Res. Fellow, Centre for Contemp. European Studies, Univ. of Sussex, 1968–71, Assoc. Fellow and Lectr, 1971–79. Vis. Scholar, Brookings Instn, Washington, DC, 1970. Adviser to Commons Expenditure Cttee, 1971–72; Special Adviser to Minister of Overseas Develt, 1974–75. Opposition frontbench spokesman on overseas develt and co-operation, 1983–. Res. Specialist, RIIA, 1972–74; Associate, Inst. of Develt Studies, 1974–. Consultant: Econ. and Social Affairs Cttee, Council of Europe, 1973; Open Univ., 1973. Rapporteur, Trades Union Adv. Cttee, OECD, 1977. Chm., Public Enterprise Gp, 1973–75. Member: Council, Inst. for Workers' Control, 1974–; Expert Cttee on Inflation, EEC Commn, 1975–76; UN Univ. Working Party on Socio-Cultural Factors in Develt, Tokyo, 1977. Lubbock Lectr, Oxford Univ., 1975; Tom Mann Meml Lectr, Australia, 1977. Mem., Labour Party, 1962–; Mem. sub-cttees (inc. Finance and Econ. Policy, Indust. Policy, EEC, Economic Planning, Defence, Development Cooperation, Public Sector), Nat. Exec. Cttee, Labour Party, 1972–; Executive Member: Labour Coordinating Cttee, 1978–81; European Nuclear Disarmament Campaign, 1980–83; Mem., Economic Cttee, Socialist International, 1984–. Hon. MRTPI 1980. *Publications:* (jtly) Sovereignty and Multinational Corporations, 1971; (ed) The State as Entrepreneur, 1972; Strategy for Socialism, 1975; The Socialist Challenge, 1975; The Regional Problem, 1976; Capital versus the Regions, 1976; (ed) Beyond Capitalist Planning, 1978; Uncommon Market, 1980; (ed) Out of Crisis, 1983; (with Donald Anderson) Kissinger's Kingdom, 1984; (with James Firebrace) Never Kneel Down, 1984; contrib. symposia; articles in specialist jls and national and internat. press. *Recreation:* singing in the bath. *Address:* House of Commons, SW1. *T:* 01–219 4414.

HOLLAND, Rt. Rev. Thomas, DSC 1944; DD (Gregorian); retired Bishop of Salford; *b* 11 June 1908; *s* of John Holland and Mary (*née* Fletcher). *Educ:* Upholland; Valladolid; Rome. PhD Valladolid, 1929; DD Gregorian, Rome 1936. Taught theology: Spain, 1936–41; Lisbon, 1941–43. Chaplain, RN, 1943–46; Port Chaplain, Bombay, 1946–48; CMS, 1948–56; Secretary to Apostolic Delegate, 1956–60; Coadjutor Bp of Portsmouth, 1960–64; Bishop of Salford, 1964–83; Apostolic Administrator, 1983–84. Privy Chamberlain to the Pope, 1958. Member of Vatican Secretariat for Promoting Christian Unity, 1961–73, for Unbelievers, 1965–73; Mem., Vatican Synod, 1974. Hon. DLitt Salford, 1980. *Publications:* Great Cross, 1958. *Address:* Nazareth House, Scholes Lane, Prestwich, Manchester M25 8AP.

HOLLAND, Prof. Walter Werner, MD; FRCP, FRCGP, FFCM; Professor of Clinical Epidemiology, and Hon. Director, Social Medicine and Health Service Research Unit, United Medical and Dental Schools of Guy's and St Thomas's Hospitals (formerly St Thomas's Hospital Medical School), since 1968; *b* 5 March 1929; *s* of Henry Holland and Hertha Zentner; *m* 1964, Fiona Margaret Auchinleck Love; three *s*. *Educ:* St Thomas's Hosp. Med. Sch., London (BSc Hons 1951; MB, BS Hons 1954; MD 1964). FFCM 1972; FRCP 1973; FRCGP 1982. House Officer, St Thomas' Hosp., 1954–56; MRC Clin. Res. Fellow, London Sch. of Hygiene, 1959–61; Lectr, Johns Hopkins Univ., Md, USA, 1961–62; Sen. Lectr, Dept of Medicine, 1962–64, and Reader and Chm., Dept of Clin. Epidemiol. and Social Medicine, 1965–68, St Thomas's Hosp. Med. Sch. Fogarty Scholar-in-Residence, NIH, Bethesda, Md, 1984–85; Sawyer Scholar-in-Residence, Case Western Reserve Med. Sch., Cleveland, Ohio, 1985. Life Mem., Soc. of Scholars, Johns Hopkins Univ., 1970; Hon. Mem., Amer. Epidemiol Soc., 1985. Dr *hc* Univ. of Bordeaux, 1981. *Publications:* Data Handling in Epidemiology, 1970; Air Pollution and Respiratory Disease, 1972; Epidemiology and Health, 1977; Health Care and Epidemiology, 1978; Measurement of Levels of Health, 1979; Evaluation of Health Care, 1983; Chronic Obstructive Bronchopathies, 1983; Oxford Textbook of Public Health, 1984; pubns on health services res., epidemiol methods and on respiratory disease. *Recreations:* reading, swimming, walking. *Address:* Department of Community Medicine, St Thomas's Hospital UMDS, SE1 7EH. *T:* 01–928 9292, ext. 2010. *Club:* Athenæum.

HOLLAND-HIBBERT, family name of **Viscount Knutsford.**

HOLLAND-MARTIN, Robert George, (Robin); Consultant, Newmarket Company Ltd, since 1982; *b* 6 July 1939; *y s* of late Cyril Holland-Martin and of Rosa, *d* of Sir Gerald Chadwyck-Healey, 2nd Bt, CBE; *m* 1976, Dominique, 2nd *d* of Maurice Fromaget; two *d*. *Educ:* Eton. Cazenove & Co., 1960–74 (partner, 1968–74); Finance Director, Paterson Products Ltd, 1976–86. Hon. Dep. Treasurer, Cons. and Unionist Party, 1979–82. Member of Council: Metropolitan Hospital-Sunday Fund, 1963– (Chm. of Council, 1977–); Homoeopathic Trust, 1970– (Vice Chm. (formerly Dep. Chm.), 1975–). Victoria & Albert Museum: Mem. Adv. Council, 1972–83; Mem. Cttee, Associates of V&A, 1976–85 (Chm., 1981–85); Dep. Chm., Trustees, 1983–85. Mem., Visiting Cttee for Royal Coll. of Art, 1982– (Chm., 1984–). Trustee, Blackie Foundn Trust, 1971–. *Address:* 18 Tite Street, SW3 4HZ. *T:* 01–352 7871. *Clubs:* White's, Royal Automobile.

HOLLAND-MARTIN, Rosamund Mary, (Lady Holland-Martin), DBE 1983 (OBE 1947); DL; Chairman, National Society for the Prevention of Cruelty to Children, since 1969 (Member, Central Executive Committee, since 1947); *b* 26 June 1914; *d* of Charles Harry St John Hornby and Cicely Rachel Emily Barclay; *m* 1951, Adm. Sir Deric Holland-Martin, GCB, DSO, DSC (*d* 1977), Lord Lieutenant of Hereford and Worcester; one *s* one *d*. *Educ:* privately. WVS Administrator, South East, 1946–51; Vice-Chm., WRVS, 1978–81; Pres., Friends of Worcester Cathedral, 1978–; Pres., Worcester Sea Cadets, 1978–; Mem. Council, Malvern College, 1979–. DL Hereford and Worcester, 1983. *Recreations:* needlework, photography, gardening, collecting things. *Address:* Bells Castle, Kemerton, Tewkesbury, Glos GL20 7JW. *T:* Overbury 333.

See also M. C. St J. Hornby, Sir R. A. Hornby.

HOLLENDEN, 3rd Baron *cr* 1912; **Gordon Hope Hope-Morley;** I. & R. Morley Ltd, 1933–67, retired as Chairman; *b* 8 Jan. 1914; *s* of Hon. Claude Hope-Morley (*d* 1968) (*yr s* of 1st Baron) and Lady Dorothy Edith Isabel (*d* 1972), *d* of 7th Earl of Buckinghamshire; *S* uncle, 1977; *m* 1945, Sonja Sundt, Norway; three *s*. *Educ:* Eton. War medals of 1939–45; King Haakon of Norway Liberation medal. *Heir:* *s* Hon. Ian Hampden Hope-Morley [*b* 23 Oct. 1946; *m* 1972, Beatrice Saulnier, *d* of Baron Pierre d'Anchald, Paris; one *s* one *d*]. *Address:* Hall Place, Leigh, Tonbridge, Kent. *T:* Hildenborough 832255. *Clubs:* Brooks's, Beefsteak.

See also Sir Michael Hanley.

HOLLENWEGER, Prof. Walter Jacob; Professor of Mission, University of Birmingham, since 1971; *b* 1 June 1927; *s* of Walter Otto and Anna Hollenweger-Spörri; *m* 1951, Erica Busslinger. *Educ:* Univs. of Zürich and Basel. Dr theol Zürich 1966 (and degrees leading up to it). Stock Exchange, Zürich, and several banking appts, until 1948. Pastor, 1949–57; ordained, Swiss Reformed Church, 1961. Study Dir, Ev. Acad., Zürich, 1964–65; Research Asst, Univ. of Zürich, 1961–64; Exec. Sec., World Council of Churches, Geneva, 1965–71. *Publications:* Handbuch der Pfingstbewegung, 10 vols, 1965/66; (ed) The Church for Others, 1967 (also German, Spanish and Portuguese edns); (ed) Die Pfingstkirchen, 1971; Kirche, Benzin und Bohnensuppe, 1971; The Pentecostals, 1972 (also German and Spanish edns); Pentecost between Black and White, 1975 (also German and Dutch edns); Glaube, Geist und Geister, 1975; (ed) Studies in the Intercultural History of Christianity, 40 vols, 1975–; Evangelism Today, 1976 (also German edn); (with Th. Ahrens) Volkschristentum und Volksreligion in Pazifik, 1977; Interkulturelle Theologie, vol. I, 1979, vol. II, 1982; Erfahrungen in Ephesus, 1979; Wie Grenzen zu Brücken werden, 1980; Besuch bei Lukas, 1981; Conflict in Corinth—Memoirs of an Old Man, 1982 (also German, Italian, Indonesian and French edns); Jüngermesse/Gomer: Das Gesicht des Unsichtbaren, 1983; Zwingli zwischen Krieg und Frieden, 1983; Das Fest der Verlorenen, 1984; Der Handelsreisende Gottes, 1985; Das Wagnis des Glaubens, 1986; Weihnachtsoratorium, 1986. *Address:* Department of Theology, University of Birmingham, PO Box 363, Birmingham B15 2TT. *T:* 021–472 1301.

HOLLEY, Prof. Robert W., PhD; Resident Fellow, The Salk Institute, since 1968; *b* 28 Jan. 1922; *s* of Charles and Viola Holley, Urbana, Ill, USA; *m* 1945, Ann Dworkin; one *s*. *Educ:* Univ. of Illinois (AB); Cornell Univ. (PhD); Washington State Coll. Research Biochemist, Cornell Univ. Med. Coll., 1944–46; Instructor, State Coll. of Wash., 1947–48; Assistant Prof. and Associate Prof. of Organic Chemistry, NY State Agricultural Experimental Station, Cornell Univ., 1948–57; Research Chemist, US Plant, Soil and Nut. Lab., ARS, USDA, 1957–64; Prof. of Biochem. and Molecular Biol., Biol. Div., Cornell Univ., 1964–69. Various awards for research, 1965–. Hon. DSc Illinois, 1970. Nobel Prize in Physiology or Medicine, 1968. *Publications:* many contribs to: Jl Amer. Chem. Soc., Science, Jl Biol. Chem., Arch. Biochem., Nature, Proc. Nat. Acad. Sci., etc. *Recreations:* sculpture; family enjoys walks along ocean and trips to mountains. *Address:* The Salk Institute, PO Box 85800, San Diego, California 92138, USA. *T:* 453–4100 (ext. 341).

HOLLEY, Rear Adm. Ronald Victor, CEng; Director General Aircraft (Navy), since 1985; *b* 13 July 1931; *s* of late Mr and of Mrs V. E. Holley; *m* 1954, Sister Dorothy Brierley, QARNNS; two *s* twin *d*. *Educ:* Rondebosch, S Africa; RNEC Manadon; RAFC Henlow (post graduate). MIMechE, MIERE. Served HM Ships Implacable, Finisterre, Euryalus, Victorious, Eagle (899 Sqdn); NATO Defence Coll., Rome, 1968; Naval Plans, 1969–71; Aircraft Dept, 1971–73; Air Engr Officer, HMS Seahawk, 1973–75; Naval Asst to Controller of the Navy, 1975–77; RCDS, 1978; Seaman Officer Develt Study, 1979; Dir, Helicopter Projects, Procurement Exec., 1979–82; RNEC in command, 1982–84; Sen. Naval Mem., Directing Staff, RCDS, 1984–85. President: RN Volunteer Bands, 1983–; RN Amateur Fencing Assoc., 1986– (Chm., 1983–86). *Publications:* contribs to Naval Jls, and Seaford House Papers, 1978. *Recreations:* playing the bassoon; dinghy sailing, rowing, badminton.

HOLLEY, (William) Stephen, CBE 1979; General Manager, Washington Development Corporation, 1965–80; *b* 26 March 1920; *m* 1947, Dinah Mary Harper; three *s*. *Educ:* King William's Coll. Student Accountant, 1937–39. War service, RA (TA), 1939–45 (Major). Colonial Service, and Overseas Civil Service, 1945–64; Mem. Legislature and State Sec., Head of Civil Service, Sabah, Malaysia, 1964. Hon. ADK (Malaysia). DL Tyne and Wear, 1975–81. *Publications:* Washington—Quicker by Quango, 1983; contribs to Sarawak Museum Jl and press articles on New Town Development. *Recreations:* golf, writing, gardening, theatre. *Address:* Forge Cottage, The Green, Abthorpe, Northants. *Club:* Royal Commonwealth Society.

HOLLICK, Clive Richard; Chief Executive, MAI PLC (formerly Mills & Allen International PLC), since 1974; *b* 20 May 1945; *s* of Leslie George Hollick and Olive Mary (*née* Scruton); *m* 1977, Susan Mary (*née* Woodford); three *d*. *Educ:* Taunton's Sch., Southampton; Univ. of Nottingham (BA Hons). Joined Hambros Bank Ltd, 1968, Dir, 1973; Chairman: Shepperton Studios Ltd, 1976–84; Garban Ltd (USA), 1983–. Mem., Nat. Bus Co. Ltd, 1984–. *Recreations:* reading, theatre, cinema, tennis, countryside. *Address:* 14 Kensington Park Gardens, W11. *T:* 01–407 7624. *Club:* Royal Automobile.

HOLLIDAY, Prof. Frederick George Thomas, CBE 1975; DL; FRSE; Vice-Chancellor and Warden, University of Durham, since 1980; *b* 22 Sept. 1935; *s* of Alfred C. and Margaret Holliday; *m* 1957, Philippa Mary Davidson; one *s* one *d*. *Educ:* Bromsgrove County High Sch.; Sheffield Univ. BSc 1st cl. hons Zool. 1956; FIBiol 1970, FRSE 1971. Fisheries Research Trng Grant (Develt Commn) at Marine Lab., Aberdeen, 1956–58; Sci. Officer, Marine Lab., Aberdeen, 1958–61; Lectr in Zoology, Univ. of Aberdeen, 1961–66; Prof. of Biology, 1967–75, Dep. Principal, 1972, Acting Principal, 1973–75, Univ. of Stirling; Prof. of Zoology, Univ. of Aberdeen, 1975–79. Member: Scottish Cttee, Nature Conservancy, 1969; Council, Scottish Field Studies Assoc., 1970–78 (Pres., 1981–); Council, Scottish Marine Biol Assoc., 1967–85 (Pres., 1979–85); Scottish Wildlife Trust (Vice-Pres.); Council, Freshwater Biol Assoc., 1969–72; NERC Oceanography and Fisheries Research Grants Cttee, 1971; Council, NERC, 1973–79; Nature Conservancy Council, 1975–80 (Dep. Chm., 1976–77, Chm., 1977–80); Scottish Economic Council, 1975–80; Council, Marine Biol Assoc. UK, 1975–78; Oil Develt Council for Scotland, 1976–78; Standing Commn on Energy and the Environment, 1978–; Chm., Independent Review of Disposal of Radioactive Waste at Sea, 1984. Dir, Shell UK, 1980–; Chairman: British Rail (Eastern) Bd, 1986– (Mem., 1983–); Northern Regional Bd, Lloyd's Bank, 1986– (Mem., 1985–); Mem., Bd, Northern Investors Ltd, 1984–. Trustee, Nat. Heritage Meml Fund, 1980–; Vice-Pres., Civic Trust for NE. Member: Bd of Governors, Rowett Res. Inst., 1976–84; Scottish Civic Trust, 1984–. DUniv Stirling, 1984. DL Durham, 1985. *Publications:* (ed and contrib.) Wildlife of Scotland, 1979; numerous on fish biology and wildlife conservation in Adv. Mar. Biol., Fish Physiology, Oceanography and Marine Biology, etc. *Recreations:* walking, gardening. *Address:* Old Shire Hall, Durham. *T:* Durham 64466. *Club:* Royal Commonwealth Society.

HOLLIDAY, Leslie John, FCIOB, CBIM; Chairman and Chief Executive, John Laing plc, 1982–85 (Director, 1978); Chairman, John Laing Construction Ltd, since 1980 (Director, 1966); *b* 9 Jan. 1921; *s* of John and Elsie Holliday; *m* 1943, Kathleen Joan Marjorie Stacey; two *s*. *Educ:* St John's, Whitby. FCIOB 1969; CBIM 1982. Denaby & Cadby Colliery, 1937–40; served Merchant Navy, 1940–45; joined John Laing & Son Ltd, 1947, Dir 1977; Chairman: Laing Homes Ltd, 1978–81; Super Homes Ltd, 1979–81; Laing Management Contracting Ltd, 1980–81; John Laing Internat. Ltd, 1981–82; Director: Declan Kelly Holdings, 1985–; RM Douglas Holdings, 1986–. Mem., EDC for Bldg, 1979–82. *Recreations:* yachting, golf. *Address:* The White House, Frithsden Copse, Berkhamsted, Herts. *Clubs:* Royal Southern Yacht (Hamble); Porters Park Golf.

HOLLIDAY, Dr Robin, FRS 1976; Head, Division of Genetics, National Institute for Medical Research, since 1970; *b* 6 Nov. 1932; *s* of Clifford and Eunice Holliday; *m* 1957, Diana Collet (*née* Parsons); one *s* three *d*. *Educ:* Hitchin Grammar Sch.; Univ. of Cambridge (BA, PhD). Member, Scientific Staff: Dept of Genetics, John Innes Inst., Bayfordbury, Herts, 1958–65; Division of Microbiology, Nat. Inst. for Med. Research, 1965–70. *Publications:* The Science of Human Progress, 1981; Genes, Proteins and Cellular Aging, 1986; over 150 scientific papers on genetic recombination, repair, gene expression and cellular ageing. *Recreations:* travel, sculpture. *Address:* National Institute for Medical Research, Mill Hill, NW7 1AA. *T:* 01–959 3666.

HOLLIGER, Heinz; oboist and composer; *b* Langenthal, Switzerland, 1939; *m* Ursula Holliger, harpist. *Educ:* Berne Conservatoire; Paris; Basle; studied with Cassagnaud, Veress, Pierlot and Boulez. Played with Basle Orch., 1959–63; Prof. of oboe, Freiburg Music Acad., 1965–. Appeared at all major European music festivals. Has inspired compositions by Berio, Penderecki, Stockhausen, Henze, Martin and others. Compositions include: Der magische Tänzer, Trio, Dona nobis pacem, Pneuma, Psalm, Cardiophonie, Kreis, Siebengesang, H for wind quintet, string quartet Atembogen, Jahreszeiten, Come and Go. Has won many international prizes, incl. Geneva Competition first prize, 1959, and Munich Competition first prize, 1961. *Address:* c/o Ingpen & Williams Ltd, 14 Kensington Court, W8 5DN.

HOLLINGS, Hon. Sir (Alfred) Kenneth, Kt 1971; MC 1944; **Hon. Mr Justice Hollings;** Judge of the High Court of Justice, Family Division (formerly Probate, Divorce and Admiralty Division), since 1971; *b* 12 June 1918; *s* of Alfred Holdsworth Hollings and Rachel Elizabeth Hollings; *m* 1949, Harriet Evelyn Isabella, *d* of W. J. C. Fishbourne, OBE, Brussels; one *s* one *d*. *Educ:* Leys Sch., Cambridge; Clare Coll., Cambridge. Law Qualifying and Law Tripos, Cambridge, 1936–39; MA. Served RA (Shropshire Yeomanry), 1939–46. Called to Bar, Middle Temple, 1947 (Harmsworth Schol.); Master of the Bench, 1971. Practised Northern Circuit; QC 1966; Recorder of Bolton, 1968; Judge of County Courts, Circuit 5 (E Lancs), 1968–71; Presiding Judge, Northern Circuit, 1975–78. *Recreations:* walking, swimming, music. *Address:* Royal Courts of Justice, Strand, WC2. *Clubs:* Garrick, Hurlingham; Tennis and Racquets (Manchester).

HOLLINGS, Rev. Michael Richard, MC 1943; Parish Priest, St Mary of the Angels, Bayswater, since 1978; Dean of North Kensington, since 1980; *b* 30 Dec. 1921; *s* of Lieut-Commander Richard Eustace Hollings, RN, and Agnes Mary (*née* Hamilton-Dalrymple). *Educ:* Beaumont Coll.; St Catherine's Society, Oxford (MA). St Catherine's, 1939; Sandhurst, 1941. Served War of 1939–45 (despatches): commnd Coldstream Guards, 1941; served N Africa, Italy, Palestine, 1942–45; Major. Trained at Beda Coll., Rome, 1946–50. Ordained Rome, 1950; Asst Priest, St Patrick's, Soho Square, W1, 1950–54; Chaplain, Westminster Cathedral, 1954–58; Asst Chaplain, London Univ., 1958–59; Chaplain to Roman Catholics at Oxford Univ., 1959–70; Parish Priest, St Anselm's, Southall, Middx, 1970–78. Religious Adviser: ATV, 1958–59; Rediffusion, 1959–68; Thames Television, 1968; Advr, Prison Christian Fellowship, 1983–. Member: Nat. Catholic Radio and TV Commn, 1968; Westminster Diocesan Schools Commn, 1970–; Southall Chamber of Commerce, 1971–78; Oxford and Cambridge Catholic Educn Bd, 1971–78; Executive, Council of Christians and Jews, 1971–79, 1984–; Lay Mem., Press Council, 1969–75; Nat. Conf. of Priests Standing Cttee, 1974–76; Rampton Cttee, 1979–81; Swann Cttee, 1981–84; Exec., Ealing Community Relations Council, 1973–76; Exec., Notting Hill Social Council, 1980–; Chm., N Kensington Action Group, 1980–81. Mem. Bd, Christian Aid, 1984–. Chaplain: to Sovereign Military Order of Malta, 1957; to Nat. Council of Lay Apostolate, 1970–74; to Catholic Inst. of Internat. Relations, 1971–80. *Publications:* Hey, You!, 1955; Purple Times, 1957; Chaplaincraft, 1963; The One Who Listens, 1971; The Pastoral Care of Homosexuals, 1971; It's Me, O Lord, 1972; Day by Day, 1972; The Shade of His Hand, 1973; Restoring the Streets, 1974; I Will Be There, 1975; You Must Be Joking, Lord, 1975; The Catholic Prayer Book, 1976; Alive to Death, 1976; Living Priesthood, 1977; His People's Way of Talking, 1978; As Was His Custom, 1979; St Thérèse of Lisieux, 1981; Hearts not Garments, 1982; Chaplet of Mary, 1982; Path to Contemplation, 1983; Go In Peace, 1984; Christ Died at Notting Hill, 1985; Athirst for God, 1985; Prayers before and after Bereavement, 1986; By Love Alone, 1986; contrib. Tablet, Clergy Review, Life of the Spirit. *Recreations:* reading, walking, people. *Address:* St Mary of the Angels, Moorhouse Road, Bayswater, W2 5DJ. *T:* 01–229 0487.

HOLLINGSWORTH, Dorothy Frances, OBE 1958; *b* 10 May 1916; *d* of Arthur Hollingsworth and Dorothy Hollingsworth (*née* Coldwell). *Educ:* Newcastle upon Tyne Church High Sch.; Univ. of Durham (BSc 1937); Royal Infirmary, Edinburgh, Sch. of Dietetics (Dip. in Dietetics); FRIC 1956; State Registered Dietitian (SRD), 1963; FIBiol 1968. Hosp. Dietitian, Royal Northern Hosp., London, N7, 1939–41; Govt Service, 1941–70: mainly at Min. of Food until its merger with Min. of Agric. and Fisheries, 1955, to form present Min. of Agric., Fisheries and Food. Principal Scientific Officer and Head of a Scientific Br., 1949–70; Dir-Gen., British Nutrition Foundn, 1970–77. Chairman: British Dietetic Assoc., 1947–49; Internat. Cttee of Dietetic Assocs; 3rd Internat. Cong. Dietetics, 1961; Nutrition Panel, Food Gp, Soc. Chem. Ind., 1966–69 (Mem. Food Gp Cttee, 1969–72); Member: Nat. Food Survey Cttee, 1951–85; Dietetics Bd, Council for Professions Supp. to Med., 1962–74; Cttee on Med. Aspects of Food Policy, 1970–79; Physiological Systems and Disorders Bd, MRC, 1974–77; Environmental Medicine Res. Policy Cttee, MRC, 1975–76; Council, Inst. Food Sci. and Technol., 1970–; Council, Nutrition Soc., 1974–77; (Dep. Chm.) Adv. Cttee on Protein, ODA, FCO, 1970–73; Jt ARC/MRC Cttee on Food and Nutrition Res., 1970–74; Royal Soc. British Nat. Cttee for Nutritional Scis, 1970–; IBA Med. Adv. Panel, 1970–; Univ. of Reading Delegacy for Nat. Inst. for Res. in Dairying, 1973–85. Sec. Gen., Internat. Union of Nutritional Scis, 1978–85. Fellow, 1968, Vice-Pres., 1978–80, Inst. of Biology; Fellow, 1965, Vice-Pres., 1976–80, Hon. Fellow, 1985, Inst. of Food Science and Technology; Fellow, British Dietetic Assoc., 1979. *Publications:* The Englishman's Food, by J. C. Drummond and Anne Wilbraham (rev. and prod. 2nd edn), 1958; Hutchison's Food and the Principles of Nutrition (rev. and ed 12th edn with H. M. Sinclair), 1969; Nutritional Problems in a Changing World (ed, with Margaret Russell), 1973; (ed with E. Morse) People and Food Tomorrow, 1976; many papers in scientific jls. *Recreations:* talking with intelligent and humorous friends; appreciation of music, theatre and countryside; gardening. *Address:* 2 The Close, Petts Wood, Orpington, Kent BR5 1JA. *T:* Orpington 23168. *Clubs:* University Women's, Arts Theatre.

HOLLINGSWORTH, Michael Charles; Managing Director, Music Box Ltd, since 1986; Director: TV-am Ltd, since 1984; TV-am News Ltd, since 1984; Television Production and Management, since 1985; *b* 22 Feb. 1946; *s* of Albert George Hollingsworth and Gwendoline Marjorie Hollingsworth; *m* 1968, Patricia Margaret Jefferson Winn; one *d*. *Educ:* Carlisle Grammar Sch. Programme Editor, Anglia Television, 1964–67; Producer, BBC Local Radio, 1967–74; Northern Editor, Today, Radio Four, 1974–75; Editor, News and Current Affairs: Southern Television Ltd, 1975–79; ATV Network/Central, 1979–82; Sen. Producer, Current Affairs, BBC TV, 1982–84; Dir of Programmes, TV-am Ltd, 1984–85. Consultant on television matters to indep. television prodn cos. *Recreations:* DIY (house renovation), gardening, polo. *Address:* 21 Palmerston Road, SW14 7QA. *T:* 01–878 4299. *Clubs:* Royal Automobile; Guards' Polo (Windsor).

HOLLINGWORTH, John Harold; Director, Aba-Microfilm Ltd, since 1984; Governor, Cambridge Symphony Orchestra Trust, since 1982 (Director and General Manager, 1979–82); *b* 11 July 1930; *s* of Harold Hollingworth, Birmingham; *m* 1969, Susan Barbara (marr. diss. 1985), *d* of late J. H. Walters, Ramsey, IoM. *Educ:* Chigwell House Sch.; King Edward's Sch., Edgbaston. MP (C) All Saints Division of Birmingham, 1959–64. Chm., Edgbaston Div. Conservative Assoc., 1967–72; Vice-Chm., Birmingham Conservative Assoc., 1959–61, 1972–78 (Vice-Pres. 1960–66). Chm., Elmdon Trust Ltd, 1985–; dir of other cos. Mem., Cttee of ISSTIP. *Publications:* contributions to political journals. *Recreations:* cricket, tennis. *Address:* c/o Lloyds Bank, Sidney Street, Cambridge. *Club:* Lansdowne.

HOLLINS, Rear-Adm. Hubert Walter Elphinstone, CB 1974; marine consultant; General Manager, Middle East Navigation Aids Service, Bahrain, 1977–84; *b* 8 June 1923; *s* of Lt-Col W. T. Hollins; *m* 1963, Jillian Mary McAlpin; one *s* one *d*. *Educ:* Stubbington House; Britannia RNC Dartmouth. Cadet RN, 1937; Comdr 1957; Captain 1963; Rear-Adm. 1972; comd HM Ships Petard, Dundas, Caesar and Antrim; Flag Officer, Gibraltar, 1972–74; Admiral Commanding Reserves, 1974–77. Younger Brother of Trinity House; Mem., Trinity House Lighthouse Bd. Commodore, Bahrain Yacht Club, 1981–83. Master Mariner. Mem., RNVR Yacht Club. Trustee, Royal Merchant Navy Sch., Bearwood Coll.; Pres., Newbury Sea Cadet Corps. MNI, FBIM. *Recreations:* fishing, shooting. *Address:* Roselands, Bucklebury, Berks. *T:* Bradfield 744551.

HOLLIS, Hon. Sir Anthony Barnard, Kt 1982; **Hon. Mr Justice Hollis;** a Judge of the High Court of Justice, Family Division, since 1982; *b* 11 May 1927; *er s* of late Henry Lewis Hollis and of Gladys Florence Hollis (*née* Barnard); *m* 1956, Pauline Mary (*née* Skuce); one step *d*. *Educ:* Tonbridge Sch.; St Peter's Hall, Oxford. Called to Bar, Gray's Inn, 1951 (Bencher, 1979); QC 1969; a Recorder of the Crown Court, 1976–82. Chm., Family Law Bar Assoc., 1974–76. *Recreation:* golf. *Address:* Royal Courts of Justice, Strand, WC2. *Clubs:* Woking Golf; Royal St George's Golf (Sandwich).

HOLLIS, Daniel Ayrton, VRD; QC 1968; a Recorder of the Crown Court, since 1972; *b* 30 April 1925; *s* of Norman Hollis; *m* 1st, 1950, Gillian Mary Turner (marr. diss., 1961), *d* of J. W. Cecil Turner, Cambridge; one *s* one *d*; 2nd, 1963, Stella Hydleman, *d* of Mark M. Gergel; one *s*. *Educ:* Geelong Grammar Sch., Australia; Brasenose Coll., Oxford. Served N Atlantic and Mediterranean, 1943–46. Lieut-Commander, RNVR. Called to Bar, Middle Temple, 1949; Bencher, 1975. Standing Counsel to Inland Revenue at Central Criminal Court and London Sessions, 1965–68; Dep. Chm., Kent QS, 1970–71. *Recreation:* travel. *Address:* Queen Elizabeth Building, Temple, EC4.

HOLLIS, Ven. Gerald; Archdeacon of Birmingham, 1974–84; *b* 16 May 1919; *s* of Canon Walter Hollis and Enid (*née* Inchbold); *m* 1946, Doreen Emmet Stancliffe; one *s* three *d*. *Educ:* St Edward's Sch., Oxford; Christ Church, Oxford (MA); Wells Theological College. RNVR, 1940–45. Curate: All Saints, Stepney, E1, 1947–50; i/c St Luke's, Rossington, 1950–55; Rector, Armthorpe, 1955–60; Vicar of Rotherham and Rural Dean, 1960–74. Mem. Gen. Synod, C of E, 1975–84. *Publication:* Rugger: do it this way, 1946. *Recreation:* gardening. *Address:* 5 Bourchier Close, Sevenoaks, Kent TN13 1PD. *T:* Sevenoaks 457745. *Club:* Vincent's (Oxford).

HOLLIS, Posy; *see* Simmonds, P.

HOLLIS, Rt. Rev. Reginald; *see* Montreal, Bishop of.

HOLLMAN, Arthur, MD; FRCP; FLS; Consulting Cardiologist to: University College Hospital, London, since 1987 (Consultant Cardiologist, 1962–87); Hospital for Sick Children, London, since 1987 (Hon. Consultant Cardiologist, 1978–87); Fellow, University College London, since 1978; *b* 7 Dec. 1923; *s* of W. J. and I. R. Hollman; *m* 1949, Catharine Elizabeth Large; four *d*. *Educ:* Tiffin Boys' Sch., Kingston upon Thames; University Coll. London; UCH Med. Sch. (MD). FRCP 1967. FLS 1983. Jun. hosp. appts, London, Banbury and Taplow, 1946–57; Bilton Pollard Fellow of UCH Med. Sch. at Children's Meml Hosp., Montreal, 1951–52; Clinical Asst, National Heart Hosp., 1954–56; Sen. Registrar and Asst Lectr, Royal Postgraduate Med. Sch., 1957–62; Hon. Consultant Cardiologist, Kingston Hosp., 1964–87. Advisor in Cardiology: to Mauritius Govt, 1966–86; to Republic of Seychelles, 1974–. Councillor, RCP, 1976–79. Member: Cttee of Management, Chelsea Physic Garden, 1971–; Council, British Heart Foundn, 1975–80; British Cardiac Soc. (Mem. Council, Asst Sec., and Sec., 1971–76); Assoc. of Physicians of GB and Ireland. Pres., Osler Club, 1983–84. *Publications:* articles on cardiovascular subjects in British and Amer. jls. *Recreations:* gardening, especially medicinal plants; medical history. *Address:* Seabank, Chick Hill, Pett, Hastings, East Sussex TN35 4EQ. *T:* Hastings 813228; 208 Bryer Court, Barbican, EC2Y 8DE. *T:* 01–638 5062. *Club:* Athenæum.

HOLLOM, Sir Jasper (Quintus), KBE 1975; Chairman, Panel on Take-overs and Mergers, since 1980; President, Council of Foreign Bondholders, since 1983; Chairman: Eagle Star Holdings PLC, since 1985; Eagle Star Insurance Co. Ltd, since 1985; Director: BAT Industries plc, since 1980; Portals Holdings plc, since 1980; *b* 16 Dec. 1917; *s* of Arthur and Kate Louisa Hollom; *m* 1954, Patricia Elizabeth Mary Ellis. *Educ:* King's Sch., Bruton. Entered Bank of England, 1936; appointed Deputy Chief Cashier, 1956; Chief Cashier, 1962–66; Director, 1966–70, 1980–84; Deputy Governor, 1970–80. Chairman: Council for the Securities Industry, 1985–86; Commonwealth Develt Finance Co. Ltd, 1980–86. *Address:* High Wood, Selborne, Hants. *T:* Selborne 317.

HOLLOWAY, Hon. Sir Barry (Blyth), KBE 1984 (CBE 1974); MP (Pangu Pati) Eastern Highlands Provincial Electorate; Minister for Education, Papua New Guinea, since 1982; *b* 26 Sept. 1934; *s* of Archibald and Betty Holloway; *m* 1974, Ikini Aikel; three *s* four *d*. *Educ:* Launceston Church Grammar Sch., Tasmania; Sch. of Pacific Administration, Sydney, 1957; Univ. of Papua New Guinea. Dip., Pacific Admin. District Officer in Papua New Guinea, 1953–64. Elected to first PNG Parliament, 1964; Foundn Mem., Pangu Pati, 1966; Member of various parliamentary cttees, incl. Public Accounts; Speaker of Parliament, 1972–77; Finance Minister, 1977–80. Chairman of Constituent Assembly responsible for the formation of Constitution of the Independent State of Papua New Guinea, 1974–75. Director of various companies. *Recreations:* reading, agriculture. *Address:* PO Box 6361, Boroko, Papua New Guinea. *T:* Port Moresby 272338. *Club:* Papua (Port Moresby).

HOLLOWAY, David Richard; Literary Editor of The Daily Telegraph, since 1968 (Deputy Literary Editor, 1960–68); *b* 3 June 1924; *s* of W. E. Holloway and Margaret Boyd (*née* Schleselman); *m* 1952, Sylvia Eileen, (Sally), Gray; two *s* one *d*. *Educ:* Westminster; Birkbeck Coll., London; Magdalen Coll., Oxford. Served War, RAF, 1942–46 (navigator). Reporter: Middlesex County Times, 1940–41; Daily Sketch, 1941–42; Daily Mirror, 1949; News Chronicle: Reporter and Leader Writer, 1950–53; Asst Lit. Editor and novel reviewer, 1953–58; Book Page Editor, 1958–60. Chairman: Soc. of Bookmen, 1968–71; Booker Prize Judges, 1970. *Publications:* John Galsworthy, 1968; Lewis and Clark and the Crossing of America, 1971; Derby Day, 1975; Playing the Empire, 1979; (ed) Telegraph Year, 1–3, 1977–79; contrib. Folio Magazine and book trade jls. *Recreation:* listening. *Address:* 95 Lonsdale Road, SW13 9DA. *T:* 01–748 3711. *Clubs:* Reform, Groucho.

HOLLOWAY, Derrick Robert Le Blond; Registrar of the Family Division, Principal Registry, 1966–83; retired; *b* 29 May 1917; *s* of Robert Fabyan Le Blond and Mary

Beatrice Holloway; *m* 1942, Muriel Victoria Bower; one *s. Educ:* Brentwood; Univ. of London (LLB (Hons)). Principal Probate Registry, 1937. Served War of 1939–45: DCLI, RASC, Claims Commn. Sec., Cttee on Law of Intestate Succession, 1951; Sec., Cttee on Ancient Probate Records, 1953; Asst Sec., Royal Commn on Marriage and Divorce, 1952–56; Acting Registrar, Probate, Divorce and Admiralty Div., 1965. Gp Chm. (Amersham), Civil Service Retirement Fellowship. *Publications:* (ed jtly) Latey on Divorce (14th edn), 1952; Editor: Proving a Will (2nd edn), 1952; Obtaining Letters of Administration, 1954; Divorce Forms and Precedents, 1959; Probate Handbook (now Holloway's Probate Handbook), 1961, 7th edn 1984; Phillips' Probate Practice (6th edn), 1963; contrib. to Butterworths' Costs (4th edn), 1971; Acting in Person: how to obtain an undefended divorce, 1977. *Recreations:* marriage, gardening, foreign travel, music, photography. *Address:* 1 Chiltern Manor Park, Great Missenden, Bucks.

HOLLOWAY, Frank, FCA; CBIM; Managing Director, Supplies and Transport, 1980–83 and Board Member, 1978–83, British Steel Corporation; *b* 20 Oct. 1924; *s* of Frank and Elizabeth Holloway; *m* 1949, Elizabeth Beattie; three *d. Educ:* Burnage High Sch., Manchester. Served War, Royal Navy, 1943–46. Various senior finance appts in The United Steel Companies Ltd and later in British Steel Corp., 1949–72. Managing Director: Supplies and Production Control, 1973–76, Finance and Supplies, 1976–80, British Steel Corp. Director: Wogen Resources Ltd; Templeborough Rolling Mills Ltd. *Recreations:* cricket, collecting books.

HOLLOWAY, Prof. John, MA, DPhil, DLitt, LittD; Professor of Modern English, Cambridge, 1972–82 (Reader, 1966–72); Fellow of Queens' College, 1955–82, Life Fellow, 1982; *b* 1 Aug. 1920; *s* of George Holloway and Evelyn Astbury; *m* 1946, Audrey Gooding; one *s* one *d*; *m* 1978, Joan Black. *Educ:* County Sch., Beckenham, Kent; New Coll., Oxford (Open History Scholar). 1st class Modern Greats, 1941; DPhil Oxon 1947; DLitt Aberdeen 1954; LittD Cambridge, 1969. Served War of 1939–45, commnd RA, 1942; subsequently seconded to Intelligence. Temporary Lecturer in Philosophy, New Coll., 1945; Fellow of All Souls Coll., 1946–60; John Locke Scholar, 1947; University Lecturer in English: Aberdeen, 1949–54; Cambridge, 1954–66; Sec., 1954–56, Librarian, 1964–66, Chm., 1970, 1971, English Faculty. FRSL 1956. Lecture Tour: Ceylon, India, Pakistan, 1958; Middle East, 1965; Hong Kong, NZ, Fiji, 1984; Kyoto, 1986; Byron Professor, University of Athens, 1961–63; Alexander White Professor, Chicago, 1965; Hinkley Prof., Johns Hopkins Univ., 1972; Virginia Lectr, Charlottesville, 1979; Berg Prof., New York Univ., 1987. *Publications:* Language and Intelligence, 1951; The Victorian Sage, 1953; (ed) Poems of the Mid-Century, 1957; The Charted Mirror (Essays), 1960; (ed) Selections from Shelley, 1960; Shakespeare's Tragedies, 1961; The Colours of Clarity (essays), 1964; The Lion Hunt, 1964; Widening Horizons in English Verse, 1966; Blake, The Lyric Poetry, 1968; The Establishment of English, 1972; (ed with J. Black) Later English Broadside Ballads, vol. I, 1975, vol. II, 1979; The Proud Knowledge, 1977; Narrative and Structure, 1979; The Slumber of Apollo, 1983; contributions to journals; *verse:* The Minute, 1956; The Fugue, 1960; The Landfallers, 1962; Wood and Windfall, 1965; New Poems, 1970; Planet of Winds, 1977. *Recreation:* enjoyment. *Address:* Queens' College, Cambridge.

HOLLOWAY, Reginald Eric, CMG 1984; HM Diplomatic Service; Senior British Trade Commissioner, Hong Kong, since 1985, and Consul-General (non-resident), Macao, since 1986; *b* 22 June 1932; *s* of late Ernest and Beatrice Holloway; *m* 1958, Anne Penelope, *d* of late Walter Robert and Doris Lilian Pawley; one *d. Educ:* St Luke's, Brighton. Apprentice reporter, 1947–53; served RAF, 1953–55; journalist in Britain and E Africa, 1955–61; Press Officer, Tanganyika Govt, 1961–63; Dir, British Inf. Service, Guyana, 1964–67; Inf. Dept, FCO, 1967–69 (Anguilla, 1969); 2nd, later 1st Sec., Chancery in Malta, 1970–72; E African Dept, FCO, 1972–74; Consul and Head of Chancery, Kathmandu, 1974–77 (Chargé d'Affaires *ai*, 1975 and 1976); Asst Head, S Asian Dept, FCO, 1977–79; Counsellor, 1979; Inspector, 1979–81; Consul-Gen., Toronto, 1981–85. *Recreations:* woodworking, old wirelesses. *Address:* c/o Foreign and Commonwealth Office, SW1. *Club:* Royal Commonwealth Society.

HOLLOWAY, Rt. Rev. Richard Frederick; *see* Edinburgh, Bishop of.

HOLLOWAY, Dr Robin Greville; composer; Fellow of Gonville and Caius College, Cambridge, since 1969, and Lecturer in Music, University of Cambridge, since 1975; *b* 19 Oct. 1943; *s* of Robert Charles Holloway and Pamela Mary Jacob. *Educ:* St Paul's Cathedral Choir Sch.; King's Coll. Sch., Wimbledon; King's Coll., Cambridge (MA 1968; PhD 1972; MusD 1976); New Coll., Oxford. *Compositions* include: Garden Music, 1962; First Concerto for Orchestra, 1966–69; Scenes from Schumann, 1969–70; Evening with Angels, 1972; Domination of Black, 1973–74; Sea Surface full of Clouds, 1974–75; Clarissa, 1976; Romanza, 1976; The Rivers of Hell, 1977; Second Concerto for Orchestra, 1978–79; Serenade in C, 1979; Aria, 1980; Brand, 1981; Women in War, 1982; Second Idyll, 1983; Seascape and Harvest, 1984; Viola Concerto, 1984; Serenade in E flat, 1984; Ballad for harp and orch., 1985. *Publications:* Wagner and Debussy, 1978; numerous articles and reviews. *Recreation:* playing on two pianos. *Address:* Gonville and Caius College, Cambridge CB2 1TA. *T:* Cambridge 335424.

HOLLOWAY, Maj.-Gen. Robin Hugh Ferguson, CB 1976; CBE 1974; Referee, Small Claims Tribunal: Lower Hutt, since 1982; Wellington, since 1985; *b* Hawera, 22 May 1922; *s* of late Hugh Ferguson Holloway and Phyllis Myrtle Holloway; *m* 1947, Margaret Jewell, *d* of E. G. Monk, Temple Cloud, Somerset; one *s* two *d. Educ:* Hawera Technical High Sch.; RMC, Duntroon, Australia. Commnd NZ Staff Corps, 1942; served in 2nd NZEF, Solomon Is, Italy and Japan, 1943–47; qual. Air Observation Post Pilot, 1948–49; Staff Coll., Camberley, 1952; Jt Services Staff Coll., Latimer, 1958; Dir of Mil. Intelligence, 1959–61; Dep. Adjt Gen., 1962–63; Head, NZ Defence Liaison Staff, Singapore and Malaysia, 1964–65; ACDS, 1967–68; IDC, 1969; Comdr Northern Mil. Dist, and Comdr 1st Inf. Bde Gp, 1970; DCGS, 1971–73; CGS, 1973–76; R of O, March 1977. Dir of Civil Defence, NZ, 1977–83. Pres., Scout Assoc. of NZ, 1979–; Dep. Chief Scout, 1979–. *Recreations:* gardening, walking. *Address:* 435 Te Moana Road, Waikanae, New Zealand. *T:* Waikanae 34089. *Club:* Wellington (NZ).

HOLM, Ian; actor, since 1954; *b* 12 Sept. 1931; *s* of Dr James Harvey Cuthbert and Jean Wilson Cuthbert; *m* 1955, Lynn Mary Shaw (marr. diss. 1965); two *d*; and one *s* one *d*; *m* 1982, Sophie Baker; one *s. Educ:* Chigwell Grammar Sch., Essex. Trained RADA, 1950–53 (interrupted by Nat. Service); joined Shakespeare Memorial Theatre, 1954, left after 1955; Worthing Rep., 1956; tour, Olivier's Titus Andronicus, 1957; re-joined Stratford, 1958: roles include: Puck; Ariel; Gremio; Lorenzo; Prince Hal; Henry V; Duke of Gloucester; Richard III; The Fool in Lear; Lennie in The Homecoming (also on Broadway, 1966) (Evening Standard Actor of the Year, 1965); left RSC, 1967. Major film appearances include: Young Winston, The Fixer, Oh! What a Lovely War, The Bofors Gun, Alien, All Quiet on the Western Front, Chariots of Fire (Best Supporting Actor: Cannes, 1981; BAFTA, 1982); Return of the Soldier; Greystoke; Brazil; Laughterhouse; Dance With a Stranger; Wetherby; Dreamchild. TV series include: J. M. Barrie in BBC trilogy The Lost Boys (RTS Best Actor Award, 1979); We, the Accused, BBC 2, 1980; The Bell, BBC 2, 1981; other TV appearances include: Lech Walesa in

Strike, 1981; Goebbels in Inside the Third Reich, 1982; Mr and Mrs Edgehill, 1985; The Browning Version, 1986. *Recreations:* tennis, walking, general outdoor activities. *Address:* c/o Julian Belfrage Associates, 60 St James Street, SW1.

HOLMAN, Norman Frederick; *b* 22 Feb. 1914; *s* of late Walter John and Violet Holman, Taunton; *m* 1940, Louisa Young; one *s* two *d. Educ:* Huish's, Taunton. Entered Post Office as Exec. Officer, 1932; Higher Exec. Officer, 1942. Served in Royal Corps of Signals, 1942–46. Sen. Exec. Officer, 1950; Asst Accountant-Gen., 1953; Dep. Dir, 1956; Dir of Postal Finance, 1967; Dir of Central Finance and Accounts, PO, 1971–74. *Recreations:* bowls, bridge, The Observer crossword. *Address:* Crosswinds, 32 Richmond Road, Exmouth, Devon EX8 2NA. *T:* Exmouth 275298.

HOLMBERG, Eric Robert Reginald; Deputy Chief Scientist (Army), Ministry of Defence, 1972–77; *b* 24 Aug. 1917; *s* of Robert and May Holmberg; *m* 1940, Wanda Erna Reich; one *s* one *d. Educ:* Sandown (Isle of Wight) Grammar Sch.; St John's Coll., Cambridge (MA); Imperial Coll., London (PhD). Joined Mine Design Department, Admiralty, 1940; Admiralty Gunnery Establishment, 1945; Operational Research Department, Admiralty, 1950; appointed Chief Supt Army Operational Research Group, 1956; Dir, Army Operational Science and Res., subseq. Asst Chief Scientist (Army), MoD, 1961–72. *Publications:* The Trouble with Relativity, 1986; papers in Proc. Royal Astronomical Society. *Address:* 29 Westmoreland Road, Barnes, SW13 9RZ. *T:* 01–748 2568.

HOLME, Maj.-Gen. Michael Walter, CBE 1966; MC 1945; *b* 9 May 1918; *s* of Thomas Walter Holme and Ruth Sangster Holme (*née* Rivington); *m* 1948, Sarah Christian Van Der Gucht; one *s* two *d. Educ:* Winchester College. Directing Staff, Staff Coll., Camberley, 1952–55; Comdr 1st Bn 3rd East Anglian Regt, 1960–62; Comdr Land Forces Persian Gulf, 1963–66; Chief of Staff, Western Comd, 1966–67; Divisional Brig., The Queen's Div., 1968–69; GOC Near East Land Forces, 1969–72; retired; Dep. Col, The Royal Anglian Regiment, 1970–77. *Recreations:* various. *Address:* c/o C. Hoare & Co., 37 Fleet Street, EC4. *Club:* Army and Navy.

HOLME, Richard Gordon, CBE 1983; Chairman, Constitutional Reform Centre, since 1985; *b* 27 May 1936; *s* of J. R. Holme and E. M. Holme (*née* Eggleton); *m* 1958, Kathleen Mary Powell; two *s* two *d. Educ:* Royal Masonic Sch.; St John's Coll., Oxford; Harvard Business Sch. (PMD). Commnd 10th Gurkha Rifles, Malaya, 1954–56. Vice-Chm., Liberal Party Exec., 1966–67; Pres., Liberal Party, 1980–81; contested (L): East Grinstead, 1964 and by-election, 1965; Braintree, Oct. 1974; Cheltenham, 1983. Dir, Campaign for Electoral Reform, 1976–85; Sec., Parly Democracy Trust, 1977–; Hon. Treasurer, Green Alliance, 1978–. *Publications:* No Dole for the Young, 1975; A Democracy Which Works, 1978. *Address:* 89 St George's Road, Cheltenham, Glos. *Club:* Reform.

HOLMER, Paul Cecil Henry, CMG 1973; HM Diplomatic Service, retired; Ambassador to Romania, 1979–83; *b* 19 Oct. 1923; *s* of late Bernard Cecil and Mimi Claudine Holmer; *m* 1946, Irene Nora, *e d* of late Orlando Lenox Beater, DFC; two *s* two *d. Educ:* King's Sch., Canterbury; Balliol Coll., Oxford. Served in RA, 1942–46. Entered Civil Service, 1947; Colonial Office, 1947–49; transferred to HM Foreign Service, 1949; FO, 1949–51; Singapore, 1951–55; FO, 1955–56; served on Civil Service Selection Bd, 1956; FO, 1956–58; Moscow, 1958–59; Berlin, 1960–64; FO, 1964–66; Counsellor, 1966; Dep. High Comr, Singapore, 1966–69; Head of Security Dept, FCO, 1969–72; Ambassador, Ivory Coast, Upper Volta and Niger, 1972–75; Minister and UK Dep. Perm. Rep. to NATO, 1976–79. Dir, African Develt Fund, 1973–75. *Address:* Wincott House, Whichford, Shipston-on-Stour, Warwickshire CV36 5PG. *Club:* Royal Commonwealth Society.

HOLMES, Anthony, CBE 1982; Head of Passport Department, Home Office (formerly Chief Passport Officer, Foreign and Commonwealth Office), since 1980; *b* 4 Sept. 1931; *s* of Herbert and Jessie Holmes; *m* 1954, Sheila Frances Povall. *Educ:* Calday Grange Grammar School. Joined HM Customs and Excise, 1949; served HM Forces, 1950–52; Passport Office, 1955; Dep. Chief Passport Officer, 1977. *Recreations:* golf, sailing. *Address:* c/o Passport Department, Home Office, Clive House, 70 Petty France, SW1H 9HD. *Clubs:* Cowdray Park Golf (Midhurst); Royal Liverpool Golf.

HOLMES, Barry Trevor; HM Diplomatic Service; Consul-General, Atlanta, since 1985; *b* 23 Sept. 1933; *s* of Edwin Holmes and Marion (*née* Jones); *m* 1956, Dorothy Pitchforth; three *d. Educ:* Bishopshalt Grammar School. Entered HM Foreign Service, 1950; Wages Clerk, 1950–53; Foreign Office, 1955–58; Quito, 1958–62; FO, 1962–65; Vancouver, 1965–68; First Secretary, FCO, 1968–72; Nairobi, 1972–75; FCO, 1975–80; Commercial Counsellor, Helsinki, 1980–85. National Service: Captain, Royal Artillery, Egypt, 1953–55. *Recreations:* chess, lay-preaching when anyone will listen. *Address:* c/o Foreign and Commonwealth Office, SW1A 2AH.

HOLMES, Prof. Brian, PhD, FCP; Dean since 1980, Professor of Education since 1981, College of Preceptors; Editor, Education Today, since 1980; *b* 25 April 1920; *s* of Albert and Gertrude Maud Holmes; *m* 1st, 1945, Mary I. Refoy; two *s*; 2nd, 1971, Margaret Hon-Yin Wong; one *d. Educ:* Salt High School, Shipley; University College London (BSc Phys 1941); PhD Univ. of London Inst. of Educn 1962. RAFVR Radar Officer, 1941–45; schoolmaster, St Clement Dane's and King's College School, Wimbledon, 1946–51; Lectr in Educn, Univ. of Durham, 1951–53; Univ. of London Institute of Education: Asst Editor, 1953; Lectr, 1959; Senior Lectr, 1963; Reader, 1964; Professor of Comparative Educn, 1975–85, now Emeritus; Head of Dept of Comparative Educn, 1977–85; Pro-Director, 1983–85; Dean, Faculty of Educn, Univ. of London, 1982–85. Consultant: Unesco; Internat. Bureau of Educn; OECD; foreign govts. *Publications:* Problems in Education, 1965; (ed) Educational Policy and the Mission Schools, 1967; (ed) Diversity and Unity in Education, 1980; International Guide to Educational Systems, 1979; Comparative Education: some considerations of method, 1981; (ed) Equality and Freedom in Education, 1985; contribs to Internat. Review of Educn, Comparative Educn Review, Compare, Prospects, foreign periodicals. *Recreation:* antique British clocks. *Address:* 4 Sandwell Mansions, West End Lane, NW6 1XL. *T:* 01–794 3835. *Club:* Royal Commonwealth Society.

HOLMES, David, CB 1985; Deputy Secretary and Principal Finance Officer, Department of Transport, since 1982; *b* 6 March 1935; *s* of late George A. Holmes and Annie Holmes; *m* 1963, Ann Chillingworth; one *s* two *d. Educ:* Doncaster Grammar Sch.; Christ Church, Oxford (MA). Asst Principal, Min. of Transport and Civil Aviation, 1957; Private Sec. to Jt Parly Sec., 1961–63; HM Treasury, 1965–68; Principal Private Sec. to Minister of Transport, 1968–70; Asst Sec., 1970, Under Sec., 1976, Dept of Transport. *Recreation:* music. *Address:* 15 The Orchard, Winchmore Hill, N21 2DN. *T:* 01–360 7134.

HOLMES, David Vivian; garden designer; *b* 12 Oct. 1926; *s* of Vivian and Kathleen Holmes; *m* 1st, 1957, Rhoda Ann (marr. diss. 1978), *d* of late Col N. J. Gai; two *d*; 2nd, 1979, Linda Ruth Alexander, *d* of late G. L. Kirk and of Mrs M. M. Kirk. *Educ:* Ipswich Sch.; Allhallows Sch. Served KRRC, 1944–47. Entered journalism, 1948; Evening Standard, Londoner's Diary, 1951–56; Reporter, BBC News, 1956–61; various roles as BBC political reporter, 1961–72; Asst Head, BBC Radio Talks and Documentary

Programmes; launched Kaleidoscope arts programme, 1973; Presenter: News Extra, BBC2, 1973–75; Westminster, BBC2, intermittently, 1969–79; Political Editor, BBC, 1975–80; Chief Asst to Dir-Gen., BBC, 1980–83; Sec. of the BBC, 1983–85, retd. Chm., Parly Lobby Journalists, 1976–77. Member: Council, Hansard Soc., 1981–83; MoD Censorship Study Gp, 1983; Adv. Cttee, W Yorks Media in Politics Gp, Leeds Univ., 1985–. *Recreations:* conservation of the heritage, gardens and plants, music, the fine arts. *Address:* 21 Selwyn Road, Newnham, Cambridge CB3 9EA. *T:* Cambridge 329216.

HOLMES, Sir Frank (Wakefield), Kt 1975; JP; company director; consultant; Visiting Fellow, Institute of Policy Studies, Victoria University of Wellington; *b* 8 Sept. 1924; *s* of James Francis Wakefield and Marie Esme Babette Holmes; *m* 1947, Nola Ruth Ross; two *s*. *Educ:* Waitaki Boys' Jun. High Sch. (Dux 1936); King's High Sch. (Dux 1941); Otago Univ.; Auckland University Coll. (Sen. Schol. 1948); Victoria University Coll. MA (1st Cl. Hons) 1949. Flying Officer, Royal NZ Air Force, 1942–45 (despatches). Economic Div., Prime Minister's and External Affairs Depts 1949–52; Lectr to Prof., Victoria Univ. of Wellington, 1952–67; Macarthy Prof. of Economics, 1959–67; Dean, Faculty of Commerce, 1961–63; Economics Manager, Tasman Pulp & Paper Co Ltd, 1967–70; Victoria Univ. of Wellington: Prof. of Money and Finance, 1970–77; Vis. Prof. and Convener, Master of Public Policy Programme, 1982–85; Emeritus Prof., 1985. Adviser, Royal Commn on Monetary, Banking and Credit Systems, 1955; Consultant, Bank of New Zealand, 1956–58 and 1964–67; Chm., Monetary and Economic Council, 1961–64 and 1970–72; Jt Sec., Cttee on Universities, 1959; Mem., NZ Council Educnl Research, 1965–77 (Chm. 1970–74); Chairman: Adv. Council on Educnl Planning and Steering Cttee, Educnl Develt Conf., 1973–74; NZ Govt Task Force on Economic and Social Planning, 1976; NZ Planning Council, 1977–82; Dep. Chm., Inst. of Policy Studies, 1984–. President: NZ Assoc. of Economists, 1961–63; Economic Section, ANZAAS, 1967, Education Section, 1979; Central Council, Economic Soc. of Australia and NZ, 1967–68. Chairman: Equus Hldgs Ltd, 1983–; South Pacific Merchant Finance Ltd, 1985– (Dir, 1984–); Director: National Bank of NZ Ltd, 1982–; Norwich Union Life Insce Soc. 1983–. Mem., Internat. Organising Cttee, Pacific Trade and Develt Confs, 1982–. Life Mem., VUW Students' Assoc., 1967. JP 1960. FRSA. *Publications:* Money, Finance and the Economy, 1972; Government in the New Zealand Economy, 1977, 2nd edn 1980; pamphlets and articles on econs, finance, educn and internat. affairs. *Recreations:* touring, walking, swimming, music. *Address:* 61 Cheviot Road, Lowry Bay, Wellington, New Zealand. *T:* Wellington 684–719. *Club:* Wellington (Wellington).

HOLMES, Prof. Geoffrey Shorter, DLitt; FBA 1983; FRHistS; Professor of History, University of Lancaster, 1973–83, now Emeritus; *b* 17 July 1928; *s* of Horace and Daisy Lavinia Holmes; *m* 1955, Ella Jean Waddell Scott; one *s* one *d*. *Educ:* Woodhouse Grammar Sch., Sheffield; Pembroke Coll., Oxford (BA 1948; MA, BLitt 1952; DLitt 1978). FRHistS 1968. Served Army, RASC, 1948–50 (Mil. Adviser's Staff, New Delhi, 1949–50). Personnel Dept, Hadfield's Ltd, Sheffield, 1951–52; Asst Lectr, Lectr and Sen. Lectr, Univ. of Glasgow, 1952–69; Reader in History, Univ. of Lancaster, 1969–72. Vis. Fellow, All Souls Coll., Oxford, 1977–78. Raleigh Lectr, British Acad., 1979; James Ford Special Lectr, Oxford, 1981. Vice-Pres., RHistS, 1985– (Mem. Council, 1980–84). *Publications:* British Politics in the Age of Anne, 1967; (with W. A. Speck) The Divided Society, 1967; (ed and jtly) Britain after the Glorious Revolution, 1969; The Trial of Doctor Sacheverell, 1973; The Electorate and the National Will in the First Age of Party, 1976; Augustan England: Professions, State and Society 1680–1730, 1982; (ed with Clyve Jones) The London Diaries of William Nicolson, Bishop of Carlisle, 1702–1718, 1985; Politics, Religion and Society in England 1679–1742, 1986; articles and reviews in learned jls. *Recreations:* music, gardening, cricket. *Address:* Tatham House, Burton-in-Lonsdale, Carnforth, Lancs LA6 3LF. *T:* Bentham 61730.

HOLMES, Dr George Arthur, FBA 1985; Fellow and Tutor, St Catherine's College, Oxford, since 1962; *b* 22 April 1927; *s* of late John Holmes and Margaret Holmes, Aberystwyth; *m* 1953, Evelyn Anne, *d* of late Dr John Klein and Audrey Klein; one *s* two *d* (and one *s* decd). *Educ:* Ardwyn County Sch., Aberystwyth; UC, Aberystwyth; St John's Coll., Cambridge (MA, PhD). Fellow, St John's Coll., Cambridge, 1951–54; Tutor, St Catherine's Society, Oxford, 1954–62; Mem., Inst. for Advanced Study, Princeton, 1967–68; Vice-Master, St Catherine's Coll., 1969–71. Chm., Victoria County Hist. Cttee, Inst. of Hist. Res., 1979–. Jt Editor, English Historical Review, 1974–81; Delegate, Oxford Univ. Press, 1982. *Publications:* The Estates of the Higher Nobility in Fourteenth-Century England, 1957; The Later Middle Ages, 1962; The Florentine Enlightenment 1400–1450, 1969; Europe: hierarchy and revolt 1320–1450, 1975; The Good Parliament, 1975; Dante, 1980; Florence, Rome and the Origins of the Renaissance, 1986; articles in learned jls. *Address:* Highmoor House, Bampton, Oxon. *T:* Bampton Castle 850408.

HOLMES, George Dennis, CB 1979; FRSE; Director-General and Deputy Chairman, Forestry Commission, 1977–86; *b* 9 Nov. 1926; *s* of James Henry Holmes and Florence Holmes (*née* Jones); *m* 1953, Sheila Rosemary Woodger; three *d*. *Educ:* John Bright's Sch., Llandudno; Univ. of Wales (BSc (Hons)); FRSE 1982. Post-grad Research, Univ. of Wales, 1947; appointed Forestry Commission, 1948; Asst Silviculturist, Research Div., 1948; Asst Conservator, N Wales, 1962; Dir of Research, 1968; Comr for Harvesting and Marketing, 1973. Hon. Prof., Univ. of Aberdeen, 1984. FICFor; FIWSc. Hon. DSc Wales, 1985. *Publications:* contribs to Forestry Commission pubns and to Brit. and Internat. forestry jls. *Recreations:* sailing, golf, walking. *Address:* Greskine, 7 Cammo Road, Barnton, Edinburgh EH4 8EF. *T:* 031–339 7474.

HOLMES, Dr John Ernest Raymond; Director, Atomic Energy Establishment, Winfrith, United Kingdom Atomic Energy Authority, since 1986; *b* Birmingham, 13 Aug. 1925; *s* of late Dr John K. Holmes and of Ellen R. Holmes; *m* 1949, Patricia Clitheroe; one *s* one *d*. *Educ:* King Edward's School, Birmingham; University of Birmingham (BSc, PhD). Asst Lectr in Physics, Manchester Univ., 1949–52; Research Scientist, AERE Harwell, 1952–59; Atomic Energy Establishment, Winfrith: Research Scientist, 1959–66; Chief Physicist, 1966–73; Dep. Dir, 1973–86. *Publications:* technical papers on nuclear power. *Address:* Atomic Energy Establishment, Winfrith, Dorchester, Dorset DT2 8DH. *T:* Dorchester 63111.

HOLMES, John Wentworth, MBE 1983; Chief Agent, Liberal Party, and Deputy Head, Party HQ, 1974–86; *b* 14 Jan. 1925; *s* of Arthur and Annie Holmes; *m* 1969, Sonia Pratt; four *d*. *Educ:* Caverswall Church School; Longton School of Commerce; North Staffs Technical College (crash course in war-time). Foxwell Colliery Co., 1941–47, NCB 1947–51; Labour Agent, Rugby and Meriden, 1951–62; Liberal Agent, Leicester, 1963–65; Regional Sec., Liberal Party, Home Counties Region, 1965–74. Mem., North Staffs District and Midland Area Council, NUM, 1947–50; formerly Mem., Warwickshire CC; Dir, Rugby Co-operative Soc. Ltd and its subsidiary interests, 1952–70 (Pres. and Chm., Bd of Dirs, 1964–70). *Recreations:* gardening, cooking. *Address:* Crossways, Parsonage Lane, Icklesham, Winchelsea, Sussex. *T:* Hastings 814415.

HOLMES, Prof. Kenneth Charles, PhD; FRS 1981; Director of the Department of Biophysics, Max-Planck-Institute for Medical Research, Heidelberg, since 1968; Professor of Biophysics, Heidelberg University, since 1972; *b* 19 Nov. 1934; *m* 1957, Mary Scruby;

one *s* three *d*. *Educ:* St John's Coll., Cambridge (MA 1959); London Univ. (PhD 1959). Res. Associate, Childrens' Hosp., Boston, USA, 1960–61; Mem., Scientific Staff, MRC Lab. of Molecular Biology, Cambridge, 1962–68. Mem., European Molecular Biol. Organisation. Scientific mem., Max Planck Gesellschaft, 1972–; Corresp. Mem., Soc. Royale des Scis, Liège. *Publications:* (with D. Blow) The Use of X-ray Diffraction in the Study of Protein and Nucleic Acid Structure, 1965; papers on virus structure and molecular mechanism of muscular contraction. *Recreations:* rowing, singing. *Address:* Biophysics Department, Max-Planck-Institute for Medical Research, Jahnstrasse 29, 6900 Heidelberg 1, Germany. *T:* Heidelberg 4861.

HOLMES, Brig. Kenneth Soar, CB 1963; CBE 1954; Managing Director, Posts, Postal Headquarters, 1971–72 (Senior Director, 1970–71); *b* 1912; *s* of W. J. Holmes, Ellesmere, Chaddesden Park Road, Derby; *m* 1936, Anne, *d* of C. A. Chapman, Leicester; one *s*. *Educ:* Bemrose Sch., Derby, and at Derby Technical Coll. Entered Post Office as Asst Traffic Superintendent (Telephones), 1930; Asst Surveyor, 1936; Principal, 1947; Asst Secretary, 1950. Served War of 1939–45 as Officer Commanding 43rd Division Postal Unit, with 21st Army Group and 2nd Army Headquarters, and as Asst Director of Army Postal Services, British Army of the Rhine. Director of: Army Postal Services, War Office, 1950–59; Mechanisation and Buildings, GPO, 1956–60; Postal Services, GPO, 1960–65; London Postal Region, 1965–70. Chairman Executive Cttee of Universal Postal Union, 1960–64. *Publication:* Operation Overlord: a postal history, 1984. *Address:* 1 Wanderdown Road, Ovingdean, Brighton BN2 7BT. *T:* Brighton 37847.

HOLMES, Sir Maurice (Andrew), Kt 1969; Barrister-at-Law; *b* 28 July 1911; *o s* of Rev. A. T. Holmes and Ellen Holmes; *m* 1935, Joyce Esther, *d* of late E. C. Hicks, JP, CC; no *c*. *Educ:* Felsted Sch., Essex. Served with RASC, 1941–45 (Major, despatches). Called to Bar, Gray's Inn, 1948; Practised at Bar, 1950–55. Director, 1955–60, Chairman, 1960–65, The Tilling Association Ltd; Chairman, London Transport Board, 1965–69. Circuit Administrator, South Eastern Circuit, 1970–74. Governor of Felsted School. *Recreations:* golf, music. *Address:* The Limes, Felsted, near Dunmow, Essex. *T:* Great Dunmow 820352. *Club:* Forty.

HOLMES, Prof. Patrick, PhD; Professor of Hydraulics, Imperial College of Science and Technology, since 1983; *b* 23 Feb. 1939; *s* of Norman Holmes and Irene (*née* Shelbourne); *m* 1963, Olive (*née* Towning); one *s* one *d*. *Educ:* University Coll. of Swansea, Univ. of Wales (BSc 1960, PhD 1963). CEng, MICE. Res. Engr, Harbour and Deep Ocean Engrg, US Navy Civil Engrg Lab., Port Hueneme, Calif, 1963–65; Lectr, Dept of Civil Engrg, Univ. of Liverpool, 1966–72, Sen. Lectr, 1972–74, Prof. of Maritime Civil Engrg, 1974–83. Chm., Environment Cttee, SERC, 1981–. *Publications:* articles on ocean and coastal engineering, wave motion, wave loading, coastal erosion and accretion, and harbour and breakwater design, in Proc. ICE and Proc. Amer. Soc. of Civil Engrs. *Recreations:* squash, sailing, walking, music. *Address:* Department of Civil Engineering, Imperial College of Science and Technology, SW7 2AZ; West Winds, The Green, Steeple Morden, near Royston, Herts SG8 0ND. *T:* Steeple Morden 852582. *Club:* Royal Commonwealth Society.

HOLMES, Peter Fenwick, MC 1952; Managing Director, Royal Dutch/Shell Group, since 1982; Chairman, Shell Transport and Trading Co., since 1985; *b* 27 Sept. 1932; *s* of Gerald Hugh Holmes and Caroline Elizabeth Holmes; *m* 1955, Judith Millicent (*née* Walker); three *d*. *Educ:* Trinity Coll., Cambridge (MA). Various posts in Royal Dutch/Shell Group, 1956–, including: Gen. Man., Shell Markets, ME, 1965–68; Chief Rep., Libya, 1970–72; Man. Dir, Shell-BP, Nigeria, 1977–81; Pres., Shell Internat. Trading, 1981–83. FRGS. *Publications:* Mountains and a Monastery, 1958; Nigeria, Giant of Africa, 1985. *Recreations:* mountaineering, travel to remote areas, scuba-diving, photography, 19th century travel books. *Address:* c/o Shell Centre, SE1 7NA. *T:* 01–934 5611. *Clubs:* Athenæum, Alpine, Himalayan, Climbers, Kandahar.

HOLMES, Sir Stanley, Kt 1974; DL; Chief Executive, Merseyside Metropolitan County Council, 1974–77; *b* 15 Dec. 1912; *s* of Stanley and Ethel Holmes, Liverpool; *m* 1939, Doris Elizabeth Burton; one *d*. *Educ:* Liverpool Collegiate School. Deputy Town Clerk, Liverpool, 1956, Town Clerk 1967; Chief Exec. and Town Clerk, 1969. DL County of Merseyside, 1974. Hon. LLD Liverpool, 1974. Kt 1st class Royal Norwegian Order of St Olaf, 1974. *Recreations:* people, places, paintings. *Address:* 44 Green Lane, Liverpool L18 6HD. *T:* 051–724 5432.

HOLMES, Prof. William; Professor of Agriculture, Wye College, University of London, since 1955; *b* Kilbarchan, Renfrewshire, 16 Aug. 1922; *s* of William John Holmes, Bank Manager; *m* 1949, Jean Ishbel Campbell, BSc; two *d*. *Educ:* John Neilson Sch., Paisley; Glasgow Univ.; West of Scotland Agricultural Coll. BSc (Agric), NDD, 1942; NDA (Hons), 1943; PhD Glasgow, 1947; DSc London, 1966. FIBiol 1974. Asst Executive Officer, S Ayrshire AEC, 1943–44; Hannah Dairy Research Inst.: Asst in Animal Husbandry, 1944–47; Head of Department of Dairy and Grassland Husbandry, 1947–55. Member, Cttee on Milk Composition in the UK, 1958–60; Governor, Grassland Research Inst., 1960–75; Pres., British Grassland Soc., 1968–69 (1st recipient, British Grassland Soc. Award, 1979); Pres., British Soc. of Animal Production, 1969–70; Member technical cttees of ARC, JCO MAFF, MMB and Meat and Livestock Commn, 1960–. Correspondent Étranger, Acad. d'Agric. de France, 1984. *Publications:* (ed) Grass, its production and utilization, 1980; (ed) Grassland Beef Production, 1984; papers in technical agricultural journals. *Recreations:* gardening, beekeeping, travel, study of organizations. *Address:* Amage, Wye, Kent. *T:* Wye 812372.

HOLMES, Prof. William Neil; Professor of Physiology, University of California, since 1964; *b* 2 June 1927; *s* of William Holmes and Minnie Holmes (*née* Lloyd); *m* 1955, Betty M. Brown, Boston, Mass; two *s* two *d*. *Educ:* Adams Grammar Sch., Newport, Salop; Liverpool Univ. (BSc, MSc, PhD, DSc); Harvard Univ., Cambridge, Mass. National Service, 2nd Bn RWF, 1946–48. Visiting Scholar in Biology, Harvard Univ., 1953–55; Post-grad. Research Schol., Liverpool Univ., 1955–56; ICI Fellow, Glasgow Univ., 1956–57; Asst Prof. of Zoology, 1957–63, Associate Prof. of Zoology, 1963–64, Univ. of British Columbia, Canada; John Simon Guggenheim Foundn Fellow, 1961–62; Visiting Professor of Zoology: Univ. of Hull, 1970; Univ. of Hong Kong, 1973 and 1982–83. Scientific Fellow, Zoological Soc. of London, 1967; External examiner: for undergraduate degrees, Univ. of Hong Kong, 1976–79, 1985–; for higher degrees, Univs of Hong Kong and Hull, 1976–; Consultant to: Amer. Petroleum Inst., Washington, DC (environmental conservation), 1972–74; US Nat. Sci. Foundn (Regulatory Biology Prog.), 1980–83; US Bureau of Land Management (petroleum toxicity in seabirds), 1982–. Mem. Editorial Bd, American Journal of Physiology, 1967–70. Member: Endocrine Soc., US, 1957–; Soc. for Endocrinology, UK, 1955–; Amer. Physiological Soc., 1960–; Zoological Soc. of London, 1964–. *Publications:* numerous articles and reviews in Endocrinology, Jl of Endocrinology, Gen. and Comp. Endocrinology, Cell and Tissue Res., Archives of Environmental Contamination and Toxicology, Environmental Res., Jl of Experimental Biology. *Recreations:* travel, old maps and prints, carpentry and building. *Address:* 117 East Junipero Street, Santa Barbara, California 93105, USA. *T:* (805) 6827256. *Club:* Tennis (Santa Barbara).

HOLMES à COURT, family name of **Baron Heytesbury.**

HOLMES à COURT, (Michael) Robert (Hamilton); Chairman: The Bell Group International Ltd, since 1982; The Bell Group Ltd, Australia, since 1970; *b* 27 July 1937; *s* of Peter Worsley Holmes à Court and Ethnée Celia Holmes à Court; *m* 1965, Janet Lee Ranford; three *s* one *d*. *Educ:* Michaelhouse, Natal, S Africa; Univ. of Western Australia (LLB). Barrister and Solicitor of the Supreme Court of Western Australia, 1965. *Recreations:* thoroughbred horse breeding and racing. *Address:* 22 The Esplanade, Peppermint Grove, WA 6011, Australia. *T:* Perth 384 3894.

HOLMES SELLORS, Patrick John; *see* Sellors.

HOLMPATRICK, 3rd Baron *cr* 1897; **James Hans Hamilton;** *b* 29 Nov. 1928; *s* of 2nd Baron HolmPatrick and Lady Edina Ainsworth (*d* 1964), 4th *d* of 4th Marquess Conyngham; *S* father, 1942; *m* 1954, Anne Loys Roche, *o d* of Commander J. E. P. Brass, RN (retired); three *s*. *Heir:* *s* Hon. Hans James David Hamilton, [*b* 15 March 1955; *m* 1984, Mrs G. duFeu, *e d* of K. J. Harding]. *Address:* Tara Beg, Dunsany, Co. Meath, Ireland.
See also Baron Swansea.

HOLROYD, Air Vice-Marshal Frank Martyn, CB 1985; Air Officer Engineering, Strike Command, since 1986; *b* 30 Aug. 1935; *s* of George L. Holroyd and Winifred H. Holroyd (*née* Ford); *m* 1958, Veronica Christine, *d* of Arthur Booth; two *s* one *d*. *Educ:* Southend-on-Sea Grammar Sch.; Cranfield College of Technology (MSc). CEng, MIEE, MIERE. Joined RAF, 1956; Fighter Comd units, 1957–60; Blind Landing Development RAE Bedford, 1960–63; Cranfield Coll. of Tech., 1963–65; HQ Fighter Comd, 1965–67; Far East, 1967–69; Wing Comdr, MoD, 1970–72; RAF Brize Norton, 1972–74; Gp Captain Commandant No 1 Radio School, 1974–76; SO Eng. HQ 38 Gp, 1976–77; Air Cdre Director Aircraft Engrg, MoD, 1977–80; RCDS 1981; Dir Weapons and Support Engrg, MoD, 1982, Air Vice-Marshal 1982; DG Strategic Electronics Systems, MoD (Procurement Exec.), 1982–86. *Recreations:* variety of sports, gardening, photography. *Address:* c/o RAF High Wycombe, Bucks HP14 4UE. *Club:* Royal Air Force.

HOLROYD, John Hepworth; Under Secretary, European Secretariat, Cabinet Office, since 1985; *b* 10 April 1935; *s* of Harry Holroyd and Annie Dodgshun Holroyd; *m* 1963, Judith Mary Hudson; one *s* one *d*. *Educ:* Kingswood Sch., Bath; Worcester Coll., Oxford (Open Schol.; BA(Hist.)). Joined MAFF, 1959; Asst Private Sec. to Minister, 1961–63; Principal, Forestry Commn and MAFF, 1963–69; Regional Controller, MAFF, Yorks and Lancs Region, 1969–71; Head of R&D Div., MAFF, 1971–74; Head of Beef Div., MAFF, 1974–78; Under Secretary 1978; Resident Chm., Civil Service Selection Bd, 1978–80; Dir of Establishments, MAFF, 1981–85. Member: Yorks and Humberside Econ. Planning Bd, 1969–71; NW Econ. Planning Bd, 1969–71. Treas. to Governors, Kingswood Sch., 1985–. Lay Reader; Methodist Local Preacher. *Recreations:* music, carpentry, bee-keeping, the topography of Great Britain. *Address:* 9 Beech Place, St Albans, Herts.
See also W. A. H. Holroyd.

HOLROYD, Margaret, (Mrs Michael Holroyd); *see* Drabble, M.

HOLROYD, Michael (de Courcy Fraser); author; *b* London, 27 Aug. 1935; *s* of Basil Holroyd and Ulla (*née* Hall); *m* 1982, Margaret Drabble, *qv*. *Educ:* Eton Coll.; Maidenhead Public Library. Vis. Fellow, Pennsylvania State Univ., 1979. Chm., Soc. of Authors, 1973–74; Chm., Nat. Book League, 1976–78; Pres., English PEN, 1985–. Member: BBC Archives Adv. Cttee, 1976–79; Vice-Chm., Arts Council Literature Panel, 1982–83. FRSL 1968 (Mem. Council, 1977–); FRHistS; FRSA. *Publications:* Hugh Kingsmill: a critical biography, 1964 (rev. edn 1971); Lytton Strachey, 2 vols, 1967, 1968, rev. edn 1971; A Dog's Life: a novel, 1969; (ed) The Best of Hugh Kingsmill, 1970; (ed) Lytton Strachey By Himself, 1971; Unreceived Opinions, 1973; Augustus John (2 vols), 1974, 1975; (with M. Easton) The Art of Augustus John, 1974; (ed) The Genius of Shaw, 1979; (ed with Paul Levy) The Shorter Strachey, 1980; (ed with Robert Skidelsky) William Gerhardie's God's Fifth Column, 1981; (ed) Essays by Divers Hands, vol. XLII, 1982; various radio and television scripts. *Recreations:* listening to stories, watching people dance, avoiding tame animals, squash rackets with Skidelsky, being polite, music, trying to sleep. *Address:* c/o A. P. Watt Ltd, 26/28 Bedford Row, WC1R 4HL.

HOLROYD, William Arthur Hepworth, FHSM; District General Manager, Durham Health Authority, since 1985; *b* 15 Sept. 1938; *s* of late Rev. Harry Holroyd and Annie Dodgshun Holroyd; *m* 1967, Hilary Gower; three *s*. *Educ:* Kingswood Sch., Bath; Trinity Hall, Cambridge (MA History); Manchester Univ. (DSA). Hospital Secretary: Crewe Memorial Hosp., 1963–65; Wycombe General Hosp., 1965–67; secondment to Dept of Health, 1967–69; Dep. Gp Sec., Blackpool and Fylde HMC, 1969–72; Regional Manpower Officer, Leeds RHB, 1972–74; District Administrator, York Health Dist, 1974–82; Regional Administrator, Yorkshire RHA, 1982–85. Member: National Staff Cttee for Admin. and Clerical Staff in NHS, 1973–82; General Nursing Council for England and Wales, 1978–83; English Nat. Board for Nursing, Midwifery and Health Visiting, 1980–. Director, Methodist Chapel Aid Assoc. Ltd, 1978–. *Publication:* (ed) Hospital Traffic and Supply Problems, 1968. *Recreations:* walking, music, visiting the Shetland Isles. *Address:* 3 Dunelm Court, South Street, Durham. *T:* Durham 44765.
See also J. H. Holroyd.

HOLROYDE, Geoffrey Vernon; Director, Coventry Lanchester Polytechnic, since 1975; *b* 18 Sept. 1928; *s* of Harold and Kathleen Holroyde; *m* 1960, Elizabeth Mary, *d* of Rev. E. O. Connell; two *s* two *d*. *Educ:* Wrekin Coll.; Birmingham Univ.; BSc. ARCO. Royal Navy, 1949–54 and 1956–61; Welbeck Coll., 1954–56; English Electric, becoming Principal of Staff Coll., Dunchurch, 1961–70; British Leyland, Head Office Training Staff, 1970–71; Head, Sidney Stringer Sch. and Community Coll., Coventry, 1971–75. Chm., Industrial Liaison Adv. Gp, Cttee of Dirs of Polytechnics, 1979–. Dir, Coventry Cathedral Chapter House Choir, 1983–. Governor, 1978–, Trustee, 1979–, Chm., Governing Body, 1983–, Brathay Hall Trust; Chm. Trustees, St Mary's Hall, Warwick, 1984–; Governor: Mid-Warwickshire Coll. of Further Educn, 1978–; Kings School, Worcester, 1983–. *Publications:* Managing People, 1968; Delegation, 1969; Communication, 1969; Organs of St Mary, Warwick, 1969. *Recreations:* music (organ and choir), canals, sailing, outdoor pursuits. *Address:* 38 Coten End, Warwick. *T:* Warwick 492329.

HOLT, Arthur Frederick; Chairman, Holt Hosiery Co. Ltd, Bolton, 1971–73; *b* 8 Aug. 1914; *m* 1939, Kathleen Mary, MBE, *d* of A. C. Openshaw, Turton, nr Bolton; one *s* one *d*. *Educ:* Mill Hill Sch.; Manchester Univ. Army Territorial Officer (5th Loyals), 1939–45; taken prisoner, Singapore, 1942–45; despatches twice, 1946. MP (L) Bolton West, 1951–64; Liberal Chief Whip, 1962–63. Pres., Liberal Party, Sept. 1974–Sept. 1975. *Recreation:* golf. *Address:* Trees, High Wray, Ambleside, Cumbria. *T:* Ambleside 2258.

HOLT, Christopher Robert Vesey, CVO 1976; VRD 1952; Member of London Stock Exchange, 1938–82; *b* 17 Oct. 1915; *s* of late Vice-Adm. R. V. Holt, CB, DSO, MVO, and Evelyn Constance Holt; *m* 1945, Margaret Jane Venetia, *d* of late Sir Michael Albert James Malcolm, 10th Bt; one *s* one *d*. *Educ:* Eton. Partner, James Capel & Co., Stockbrokers, 1938, Sen. Partner, 1968–70, Chm. (on firm becoming a company), 1970–75, Dir, 1975–76. Served RNVR, War of 1939–45, mostly in destroyers; retd with rank of Lieut-Comdr, 1957. *Recreations:* painting, wildlife. *Address:* Westbury Manor, West Meon, Petersfield, Hants GU32 1ND. *Clubs:* Boodle's, Lansdowne.

HOLT, Constance, CBE 1975; Area Nursing Officer, Manchester Area Health Authority (Teaching), 1973–77; *b* 5 Jan. 1924; *d* of Ernest Biddulph and of Ada Biddulph (*née* Robley); *m* 1975, Robert Lord Holt, OBE, FRCS. *Educ:* Whalley Range High Sch. for Girls, Manchester; Manchester Royal Infirmary (SRN); Queen Charlotte's Hosp., London; St Mary's Hosp., Manchester (SCM); Royal Coll. of Nursing, London Univ. (Sister Tutor Dipl.); Univ. of Washington (Florence Nightingale Schol., Fulbright Award). Nursing Officer, Min. of Health, 1959–65; Chief Nursing Officer: United Oxford Hosps, 1965–69; United Manchester Hosps, 1969–73. Pres., Assoc. of Nurse Administrators (formerly Assoc. of Hosp. Matrons), 1972–. Reader licensed by Bishop of Sodor and Man. Hon. Lectr, Dept of Nursing, Univ. of Manchester, 1972. Hon. MA Manchester, 1980. *Publications:* articles in British and internat. nursing press. *Recreations:* reading, gardening, music. *Address:* Seabank, Marine Terrace, Port St Mary, Isle of Man.

HOLT, Jack; *see* Holt, John Lapworth.

HOLT, Prof. James Clarke, FBA 1978; Professor of Medieval History, since 1978, and Master of Fitzwilliam College, since 1981, Cambridge University; *b* 26 April 1922; *s* of late Herbert and Eunice Holt; *m* 1950, Alice Catherine Elizabeth Suley; one *s*. *Educ:* Bradford Grammar Sch.; Queen's Coll., Oxford (Hastings Schol.). MA 1947; 1st cl. Modern Hist.; DPhil 1952. Served with RA, 1942–45 (Captain). Harmsworth Sen. Schol., Merton Coll., Oxford, 1947; Univ. of Nottingham: Asst Lectr, 1949; Lectr, 1951; Sen. Lectr, 1961; Prof. of Medieval History, 1962; Reading University: Prof. of History, 1966–78; Dean, Faculty of Letters and Soc. Scis, 1972–76; Professorial Fellow, Emanuel Coll., Cambridge, 1978–81 (Hon. Fellow, 1985). Vis. Prof., Univ. of Calif, Santa Barbara, 1977; Vis. Hinkley Prof., Johns Hopkins Univ., 1983; Vis. JSPS Fellow, Japan, 1986. Raleigh Lectr, British Acad., 1975. Mem., Adv. Council on Public Records, 1974–81. Pres., Royal Historical Soc., 1980–84. Hon. DLitt Reading, 1984. Corres. Fellow, Medieval Acad. of America, 1983. *Publications:* The Northerners: a study in the reign of King John, 1961; Praestita Roll 14–18 John, 1964; Magna Carta, 1965; The Making of Magna Carta, 1966; Magna Carta and the Idea of Liberty, 1972; The University of Reading: the first fifty years, 1977; Robin Hood, 1982; Magna Carta and Medieval Government, 1985; papers in English Historical Review, Past and Present, Economic History Review, Trans Royal Hist. Soc. *Recreations:* mountaineering, cricket, fly-fishing. *Address:* 5 Holben Close, Barton, Cambs. *T:* Comberton 3074. *Clubs:* United Oxford & Cambridge University, National Liberal, MCC; Wayfarers' (Liverpool).

HOLT, Sir James (Richard), KBE 1977 (CBE 1972); Managing Director, Sinobrit Ltd (formerly Sino-British Ltd), since 1957; *b* 24 Dec. 1912; *s* of Albert Edward Holt and Margaret Ann Holt; *m* 1974, Jennifer May Squires (marr. diss. 1985); one adopted *s* one adopted *d*. *Educ:* Bishop Vesey's Grammar Sch. Manager, Meklong Railway Co., Ltd, 1938–41; interned, Bangkok, 1942–45; Dir, Sino-British Ltd, 1946–56. Trustee and Mem. Exec. Cttee, Asian Inst. of Technology, 1977–. *Recreations:* racing, swimming. *Address:* c/o Sinobrit Limited, 2137–2139 New Phetburi Road, Bangkok 10310, Thailand; 11 Soi Pranang, Rajvithi Road, Bangkok, Thailand. *T:* 2454071; 71 Belwell Lane, Four Oaks, Sutton Coldfield, West Midlands B74 4TS. *T:* 021–308 0932. *Clubs:* East India, Devonshire, Sports and Public Schools, Royal Automobile; Royal Bangkok Sports (Bangkok, Thailand).

HOLT, (James) Richard; MP (C) Langbaurgh, since 1983; personnel consultant, since 1981; *b* 2 Aug. 1931; *m* 1959, Mary June Leathers; one *s* one *d*. *Educ:* Wembley County Grammar Sch. FIPM. Served RN, 1949–54. Actor, 1954–57. Personnel trainee, Gen. Motors, 1957–63; various personnel appointments with: Smiths Industries, 1963–65; Rolls Royce, 1965–66; William Hill Orgn, 1966–72; E. Gomme Ltd, 1972–78; Bowater Furniture, 1978–81. Member: Brent BC, 1964–74; High Wycombe BC, 1976–; Bucks CC, 1981–. Mem., Thames Water Authy, 1981–. Contested (C) Brent South, Feb. 1974. MBIM. *Address:* House of Commons, SW1; 3 The Brackens, Warren Wood, High Wycombe, Bucks; 11 Milton Street, Saltburn by the Sea, Cleveland.

HOLT, Sir John Anthony L.; *see* Langford-Holt.

HOLT, Rear-Adm. John Bayley, CB 1969; DL; Director: Premmit Associates Ltd; Premmit Engineering Services Ltd; Elint Engineering Ltd; *b* 1 June 1912; *s* of Arthur Ogden Holt and Gertrude (*née* Bayley); *m* 1940, Olga Esme Creake; three *d*. *Educ:* William Hulme Grammar Sch., Manchester; Manchester Univ. BScTech (hons) 1933. FIEE. Electrical Engineer with various cos and electric power undertakings, 1933–41. Joined RN; engaged on degaussing and minesweeping research and development, later on radar and electrical engineering, for Fleet Air Arm, 1941–48; served in HMS Cumberland on Gunnery Trials, Naval Air Stations, HQ and Staff appointments; comd HMS Ariel, 1961–63; subsequently Director of Naval Officer Appointments (Engineering Officers), and Dir-Gen. Aircraft (Naval), 1967–70, Ministry of Defence. Former Naval ADC to HM The Queen. Commander 1948; Captain 1958; Rear-Admiral 1967. Chm., Surrey Br., SS&AFA; Hon. Treas., Diocese of Guildford Endowment Fund. DL Surrey, 1981. *Recreations:* sailing, gardening, sacred music. *Address:* Rowley Cottage, Thursley, Godalming, Surrey. *T:* Elstead 702140. *Club:* Naval and Military.

HOLT, John Lapworth, (Jack Holt), OBE 1979; Founder and Director of Jack Holt Ltd and Holt group of companies, designers and suppliers of small boats and their fittings (Managing Director, 1946–76); *b* 18 April 1912; *s* of Herbert Holt and Annie (*née* Dawson); *m* 1936, Iris Eileen Thornton; one *s* one *d*. *Educ:* St Peter's Sch., London; Shoreditch Techn. Inst. (Schol.). Joiner, boat builder and designer, 1929–46; formed Jack Holt Ltd, 1946; designed: first British post-war sailing dinghy class, Merlin; first British factory-made do-it-yourself boat building kit to construct Internat. Cadet, for Yachting World magazine; International Enterprise, National Solo and Hornet, Heron, Rambler, Diamond, Lazy E, GP14, Vagabond, Mirror Dinghy, Mirror 16, and Pacer; Pandamaran, for World Wildlife Fund. Techn. Adviser to Royal Yachting Assoc. dinghy cttee, 1950–. Jt winner (with Beecher Moore) of 12ft Nat. Championship, 1946 and Merlin Championships, 1946, 1947 and 1949; Merlin Silver Tiller series winner, 1954–56; won Solo Dutch Nat. Championships, 1962. Yachtsman's Award for service to yachting, RYA, 1977. *Recreation:* small boat sailing. *Address:* Cliveden, The Embankment, Putney, SW15 1LB. *T:* 01–788 0330. *Clubs:* Ranelagh Sailing, Wraysbury Lake Sailing, Chichester Yacht, Aldenham Sailing, Carrum Yacht, Black Rock Sailing.

HOLT, John Michael, MD, FRCP; Consultant Physician, John Radcliffe Hospital, Oxford; Fellow of Linacre College, Oxford, since 1968; *b* 8 March 1935; *s* of late Frank Holt, BSc and of Constance Holt; *m* 1959, Sheila Margaret Morton; one *s* three *d*. *Educ:* St Peter's Sch., York; Univ. of St Andrews. MA Oxon; MD St Andrews; MSc Queen's Univ. Ont. Registrar and Lectr, Nuffield Dept of Medicine, Radcliffe Infirmary, Oxford, 1964–66, Cons. Physician 1968; Med. Tutor, Univ. of Oxford, 1967–73; Dir of Clinical Studies, Univ. of Oxford, 1971–76; Chm., Medical Staff, Oxford Hosps, 1982–84. Examiner in Medicine: Univ. of Oxford; Hong Kong; Glasgow; RCP. Member: Assoc. of Physicians;

Soc. of Apothecaries; Cttee on Safety of Medicines, 1979–; Oxford RHA, 1984–. Editor, Qly Jl of Medicine, 1975–. *Publications:* papers on disorders of blood and various med. topics in BMJ, Lancet, etc. *Recreation:* sailing. *Address:* Old Whitehill, Tackley, Oxon OX5 3AB. *T:* Tackley 241. *Clubs:* United Oxford & Cambridge University; Royal Cornwall Yacht (Falmouth).

HOLT, Prof. John Riley, FRS 1964; Professor of Experimental Physics, University of Liverpool, 1966–83; *b* 15 Feb. 1918; *er s* of Frederick Holt and Annie (*née* Riley); *m* 1949, Joan Silvester Thomas; two *s. Educ:* Runcorn Secondary Sch.; University of Liverpool. PhD 1941. British Atomic Energy Project, Liverpool and Cambridge, 1940–45. University of Liverpool: Lecturer, 1945–53, Senior Lecturer, 1953–56, Reader, 1956–66. *Publications:* papers in scientific journals on nuclear physics and particle physics. *Recreation:* gardening. *Address:* Rydalmere, Stanley Avenue, Higher Bebington, Wirral L63 5QE. *T:* 051-608 2041.

HOLT, Mary; Her Honour Judge Holt; a Circuit Judge, since 1977; *d* of Henry James Holt, solicitor, and of Sarah Holt (*née* Chapman); unmarried. *Educ:* Park Sch., Preston; Girton Coll., Cambridge (MA, LLB, 1st cl. Hons). Called to the Bar, Gray's Inn, 1949. Practised on Northern circuit. Former Vice-Chm., Preston North Conservative Assoc.; Member: Nat. Exec. Council, 1969–72; Woman's Nat. Advisory Cttee, 1969–70; representative, Central Council, 1969–71. MP (C) Preston N, 1970–Feb. 1974. Contested (C) Preston N, Feb. and Oct. 1974. *Publication:* 2nd edn, Benas and Essenhigh's Precedents of Pleadings, 1956. *Recreation:* walking. *Address:* The Sessions House, Preston, Lancs. *Club:* Royal Commonwealth Society.

HOLT, Prof. Peter Malcolm, FBA 1975; FSA; Professor of History of the Near and Middle East, University of London, 1975–82, now Professor Emeritus; *b* 28 Nov. 1918; *s* of Rev. Peter and Elizabeth Holt; *m* 1953, Nancy Bury (*née* Mawle); one *s* one *d. Educ:* Lord Williams's Grammar Sch., Thame; University Coll., Oxford (Schol.) (MA, DLitt). Sudan Civil Service: Min. of Education, 1941–53; Govt Archivist, 1954–55. School of Oriental and African Studies, London, 1955–82; Prof. of Arab History, 1964–75. FRHistS 1973; FSA 1980. Hon. Fellow, SOAS, 1985. Gold Medal of Science, Letters and Arts, Repub. of Sudan, 1980. *Publications:* The Mahdist State in the Sudan, 1958, 2nd edn 1970; A Modern History of the Sudan, 1961, 2nd edn 1963; (co-ed with Bernard Lewis) Historians of the Middle East, 1962; Egypt and the Fertile Crescent, 1966; (ed) Political and Social Change in Modern Egypt, 1968; (co-ed with Ann K. S. Lambton and Bernard Lewis) The Cambridge History of Islam, 1970; Studies in the History of the Near East, 1973; (ed) The Eastern Mediterranean Lands in the period of the Crusades, 1977; (with M. W. Daly) The History of the Sudan from the Coming of Islam to the Present Day, 1980; The Memoirs of a Syrian Prince, 1983; The Age of the Crusades, 1986; articles in: Encyclopaedia of Islam, Bulletin of SOAS, Sudan Notes and Records, Der Islam, English Historical Rev., etc. *Address:* Dryden Spinney, Kirtlington, Oxford OX5 3HG. *T:* Bletchington 50477. *Club:* United Oxford & Cambridge University.

HOLT, Richard; *see* Holt, J. R.

HOLT, Richard Anthony Appleby; Managing Director, Hutchinson Ltd, 1978–80 (Chairman, 1959–78); Chairman: Hutchinson Publishing Group, 1965–80; Hutchinson Printing Trust, 1957–80; Director, Constable & Co. Ltd, since 1968; *b* 11 March 1920; *s* of Frederick Appleby Holt and Rae Vera Franz (*née* Hutchinson); *m* 1945, Daphne Vivien Pegram; three *s* two *d. Educ:* Harrow Sch.; King's Coll., Cambridge. Served War of 1939–45, commissioned 60th Rifles, 1941; demobilised, 1946 (Major). Admitted Solicitor, 1949. *Recreation:* lawn tennis. *Address:* 55 Queen's Gate Mews, SW7 5QN. *T:* 01-589 8469. *Clubs:* All England Lawn Tennis, MCC.

HOLT, Victoria; *see* Hibbert, Eleanor.

HOLTBY, Very Rev. Robert Tinsley; Dean of Chichester, since 1977; *b* 25 Feb. 1921; *o s* of William and Elsie Holtby, Thornton-le-Dale, Yorkshire; *m* 1947, Mary, *er d* of late Rt Rev. Eric Graham; one *s* two *d. Educ:* York Minster Choir Sch.; Scarborough Coll. and High School. St Edmund Hall, Oxford, 1939; MA (2nd Class Mod. Hist.), 1946; BD 1957. Choral Scholar, King's Coll., Cambridge, 1944; MA (2nd Class Theol.), 1952. Cuddesdon Theological Coll. and Westcott House, Cambridge, 1943–46. Deacon, 1946; Priest, 1947. Curate of Pocklington, Yorks, 1946–48. Chaplain to the Forces, 1948–52: 14/20th King's Hussars, Catterick; Singapore; Priest-in-charge, Johore Bahru. Acting Chaplain, King's Coll., Cambridge, 1952; Chaplain and Asst Master, Malvern Coll., 1952–54; Chaplain and Assistant Master, St Edward's Sch., Oxford, 1954–58; Canon Residentiary of Carlisle and Diocesan Dir of Educn, 1959–67, Canon Emeritus, 1967–. Gen. Sec., Nat. Soc. for Promoting Religious Education, 1967–77; Sec., Schs Cttee, 1967–74, Gen. Sec., 1974–77, Church of England Bd of Educn. Chm., Cumberland Council of Social Service, 1962–67. Chaplain to High Sheriff of Cumberland, 1964, 1966. *Publications:* Daniel Waterland, A Study in 18th Century Orthodoxy, 1966; Carlisle Cathedral Library and Records, 1966; Eric Graham, 1888–1964, 1967; Carlisle Cathedral, 1969. *Recreations:* music, walking, history. *Address:* The Deanery, Chichester, West Sussex PO19 1PX. *T:* Chichester 783286. *Clubs:* United Oxford & Cambridge University; Sussex (Sussex).

HOLTHAM, Mrs Carmen Gloria, JP; Advice/Information Officer, since 1980, and Legal Executive, since 1985, Earls Court Centre, Royal Borough of Kensington and Chelsea; *b* Kingston, Jamaica, 13 July 1922; *née* Bradshaw. *Educ:* Adventist Girls Sch.; Kingston Technical Coll., Kingston, Jamaica; London Univ. (Extra-Mural Course, Dip. Sociol.); NW London Polytech. (Cert. Office Management); SW London Polytech. (Cert. in Counselling); NE London Polytech. (Post Grad. Dip. Inf. and Advice Studies). Govt of Jamaica, 1942–57; United Jewish Appeal, NY, USA, 1958; Resident, England, 1959–; HM Factory Inspectorate, 1959; ILEA, 1959–64; Inst. of Med. Social Workers, 1964–66; Social Services Dept, London Borough of Camden, 1966; Willesden Citizens' Advice Bureau, London Bor. of Brent, 1967–70; Organiser, Thurrock Citizens' Advice Bureau, Grays, Essex, 1971–79. Member: ILEA Sch. Care Cttee, 1963–67; Brent Community Relns Council, 1968–70; Brent Youth Service, 1969–70; British Caribbean Assoc., 1969–; Magistrates Assoc., 1969–; Grays Probation and After-Care Service, 1971; Thurrock Social Services for Elderly, 1971–; Supplementary Benefits Commn, 1976–78. Mem., Bd of Governors, Treetops Sch., Grays, 1975–. JP Mddx (Highgate Magistrates' Court), 1969–71, Essex (Grays Magistrates' Court), 1972–. *Recreations:* reading, the theatre, ceramics. *Address:* 52 Davall House, Grays, Essex. *T:* Grays Thurrock 70838. *Club:* Friends International.

HOLTON, Michael; Assistant Secretary, Ministry of Defence, since 1976; *b* 30 Sept. 1927; 3rd *s* of late George Arnold Holton and Ethel (*née* Fountain), Hampstead Garden Suburb, London; *m* 1951, Daphne Elizabeth Bache; one *s* two *d. Educ:* Finchley County Grammar Sch.; London Sch. of Economics. National Service, RAF, 1946–48; Min. of Food, 1948–54; Air Ministry, 1955–61; MoD, 1961–68; Sec., Countryside Commn for Scotland, 1968–70; Sec., Carnegie UK Trust, 1971–75. Sec., European Conservation Year Cttee for Scotland, 1970; Member: Consultative Cttee, Family Fund, 1973–75; Bd, Cairngorm Chairlift Co., 1973–; Council, Royal Soc. for Nature Conservation, 1976–.

Hon. Sec., RAF Mountaineering Assoc., 1952–54; Hon. Sec., British Mountaineering Council, 1954–59. *Publication:* Training Handbook for RAF Mountain Rescue Teams, 1953. *Address:* 4 Ludlow Way, N2 0LA. *T:* 01-444 8582. *Clubs:* Athenæum, Alpine; Himalayan (Bombay).

HOLTTUM, Richard Eric, MA; ScD; FLS; Honorary Research Associate: Royal Botanic Gardens, Kew, since 1977; Rijksherbarium, Leiden, Netherlands, since 1955; *b* Linton, Cambs, 20 July 1895; *s* of Richard Holttum; *m* 1927, Ursula, *d* of J. W. Massey, Saffron Walden; two *d. Educ:* Friends' Sch., Saffron Walden; Bootham Sch., York; St John's Coll., Cambridge (Foundation Scholar). Natural Sciences Tripos, Part 2 (Botany) Class 1, and Frank Smart Prize, 1920; Junior Demonstrator in Botany, Cambridge Univ., 1920–22; Assistant Director, Botanic Gardens, Singapore, 1922–25, Director, 1925–49. Professor of Botany, University of Malaya, 1949–54; President: Singapore Gardening Society, 1937–39, 1947–53; Singapore Rotary Club, 1939–41; British Pteridological Society, 1960–63; Section K (Botany), BAAS, 1961; Internat. Assoc. of Pteridologists, 1981. Editor, Series II (Pteridophyta), Flora Malesiana, 1959–. Hon. DSc, University of Malaya, 1949. Linnean gold medal, 1964; VMH 1972; has foreign gold medals, etc., for orchids. *Publications:* Orchids of Malaya, 1953; Gardening in the Lowlands of Malaya, 1953; Plant Life in Malaya, 1954; Ferns of Malaya, 1955; botanical and horticultural papers, especially on ferns and orchids. *Address:* 50 Gloucester Court, Kew Gardens, Richmond, Surrey. *T:* 01-940 6157.

HOLWELL, Peter, FCA; Principal, University of London, since 1985; *b* 28 March 1936; *s* of Frank Holwell and Helen (*née* Howe); *m* 1959, Jean Patricia Ashman; one *s* one *d. Educ:* Palmers Endowed Sch., Grays, Essex; Hendon Grammar Sch.; London Sch. of Econs and Pol Science (BSc Econ). FCA 1972; MBCS 1974. Articled Clerk, 1958–61; Management Consultant, 1961–64; Arthur Andersen and Co.; University of London: Head of Computing, Sch. Exams Bd, 1964–67; Head of University Computing and O & M Unit, 1967–71; Sec. for Accounting and Admin. Computing, 1971–77; Chm., UCCA Computing Gp, 1977–82; Clerk of the Court, 1982–85. *Recreations:* walking, gardening, music, horology. *Address:* University of London, Malet Street, WC1E 7HU. *T:* 01-636 8000. *Club:* Athenæum.

HOMAN, Maj.-Gen. John Vincent, CB 1980; CEng, FIMechE; Facilities Manager, Marconi Space Systems, Portsmouth, since 1982; *b* 30 June 1927; *s* of Charles Frederic William Burton Homan and Dorothy Maud Homan; *m* 1953, Ann Bartlett; one *s* two *d. Educ:* Haileybury; RMA Sandhurst; RMCS Shrivenham. BSc (Eng). Commnd, REME, 1948; Lt-Col 1967; Comdr REME 2nd Div., 1968–70; Col 1970; MoD 1970–72; CO 27 Comd Workshop REME, 1972–74; Brig. 1974; Dep. Dir, Electrical and Mechanical Engineering, 1st British Corps, 1974–76; Dir of Equipment Management, MoD, 1976–77; Dir Gen., Electrical and Mechanical Engrg, MoD, 1978–79; Maj.-Gen. 1978; Sen. Army Mem., RCDS, 1980–82. Col Comdt, REME, 1982–. *Recreations:* hill walking, woodwork. *Address:* Roedean, 25 The Avenue, Andover, Hants. *T:* Andover 51196. *Club:* Army and Navy.

HOMAN, Philip John Lindsay; Director, Metrication Board, 1974–76; *b* 20 July 1916; *e s* of late Arthur Buckhurst Homan and Gertrude Homan; *m* 1940, Elisabeth Clemency Hobson; two *s* one *d. Educ:* Maidstone Grammar Sch.; LSE. Inland Revenue, 1935–49. Served in RN, 1941–46. Board of Trade, 1949–69; Min. of Technology, 1969–70; Under-Sec., 1970; DTI, 1970–74.
See also T. B. Homan.

HOMAN, Rear-Adm. Thomas Buckhurst, CB 1978; *b* 9 April 1921; *s* of late Arthur Buckhurst Homan and Gertrude Homan, West Malling, Kent; *m* 1945, Christine Oliver; one *d. Educ:* Maidstone Grammar Sch. RN Cadet, 1939; served War of 1939–45 at sea; Comdr 1958; Captain 1965; Defence Intell. Staff, 1965; Sec. to Comdr Far East Fleet, 1967; idc 1970; Dir Naval Officer Appts (S), 1971; Captain HMS Pembroke, 1973; Rear-Adm. 1974; Dir Gen., Naval Personal Services, 1974–78. Sub-Treasurer, Inner Temple, 1978–85. *Recreations:* reading, theatre, staying at home, cooking. *Address:* 602 Hood House, Dolphin Suare, SW1V 3NJ. *T:* 01-798 8434. *Clubs:* Army and Navy, Garrick.
See also P. J. L. Homan.

HOMANS, Prof. George Caspar; Professor of Sociology, Harvard University, 1953–81, now Emeritus; *b* 11 Aug. 1910; *s* of Robert Homans and Abigail (*née* Adams); *m* 1941, Nancy Parshall Cooper; one *s* two *d. Educ:* St Paul's Sch., Concord, New Hampshire; Harvard Univ. (AB). Harvard Univ.: Junior Fellow, 1934–39; Instructor in Sociology, 1939–41; Associate Professor of Sociology, 1946–53; Simon Vis. Prof., Univ. of Manchester, 1953; Prof. of Social Theory, Univ. of Cambridge, 1955–56; Vis. Prof., Univ. of Kent, 1967. Overseas Fellow, Churchill Coll., Cambridge, 1972. Pres., American Sociological Assoc., 1963–64; Mem., Nat. Acad. of Sciences, USA, 1972. Officer, US Naval Reserve (Lieut-Commander), 1941–45. *Publications:* Massachusetts on the Sea, 1930; An Introduction to Pareto, 1934; Fatigue of Workers, 1941; English Villagers of the 13th Century, 1941; The Human Group, 1950; Marriage, Authority and Final Causes, 1955; Social Behaviour, 1961, rev. edn 1974; Sentiments and Activities, 1962; The Nature of Social Science, 1967; Coming to my Senses (autobiog.), 1984. *Recreations:* forestry, sailing. *Address:* 11 Francis Avenue, Cambridge, Mass 02138, USA. *T:* 617-547-4737. *Club:* Tavern (Boston, USA).

HOME; *see* Douglas-Home.

HOME; *see* Milne Home.

HOME, 14th Earl of [disclaimed his peerages for life, 23 Oct. 1963]; *see under* Home of the Hirsel, Baron and Douglas-Home, Hon. D. A. C.

HOME OF THE HIRSEL, Baron *cr* 1974 (Life Peer), of Coldstream; **Alexander Frederick Douglas-Home,** KT 1962; PC 1951; DL; Chancellor, Order of the Thistle, since 1973; First Chancellor of Heriot-Watt University, 1966–77; *b* 2 July 1903; *e s* of 13th Earl of Home (*d* 1951), KT, and Lilian (*d* 1966), *d* of 4th Earl of Durham; *S* father, 1951, but disclaimed his peerages for life, 23 Oct. 1963; *m* 1936, Elizabeth Hester, 2nd *d* of late Very Rev. C. A. Alington, DD; one *s* three *d. Educ:* Eton; Christ Church, Oxford. MP (U) South Lanark, 1931–45; MP (C) Lanark Div. of Lanarkshire, 1950–51; Parliamentary Private Sec. to the Prime Minister, 1937–40; Joint Parliamentary Under-Sec., Foreign Office, May-July 1945; Minister of State, Scottish Office, 1951–April 1955; Sec. of State for Commonwealth Relations, 1955–60; Dep. Leader of the House of Lords, 1956–57; Leader of the House of Lords, and Lord Pres. of the Council, 1959–60; Sec. of State for Foreign Affairs, 1960–63; MP (U) Kinross and W Perthshire, Nov. 1963–Sept. 1974; Prime Minister and First Lord of the Treasury, Oct. 1963–64; Leader of the Opposition, Oct. 1964–July 1965; Sec. of State for Foreign and Commonwealth Affairs, 1970–74. Hon. Pres., NATO Council, 1973. Captain, Royal Co. of Archers, Queen's Body Guard for Scotland, 1973. Mem., National Farmers' Union, 1964. DL Lanarkshire, 1960. Hon. DCL Oxon., 1960; Hon. Student of Christ Church, Oxford, 1962; Hon. LLD: Harvard, 1961; Edinburgh, 1962; Aberdeen, 1966; Liverpool, 1967; St Andrews, 1968; Hon. DSc Heriot-Watt, 1966. Hon. Master of the Bench, Inner Temple, 1963; Grand Master, Primrose League, 1966–84; Pres. of MCC, 1966–67. Freedom of Selkirk,

1963; Freedom of Edinburgh, 1969; Freedom of Coldstream, 1972. Hon. Freeman: Skinners' Co., 1968; Grocers' Co., 1977. *Publications:* The Way the Wind Blows (autobiog.), 1976; Border Reflections, 1979; Letters to a Grandson, 1983. *Address:* House of Lords, SW1; The Hirsel, Coldstream, Berwickshire. *T:* Coldstream 2345; Castlemains, Douglas, Lanarkshire. *T:* Douglas, Lanark 851241.

See also Hon. D. A. C. Douglas-Home, Hon. William Douglas-Home, Duke of Sutherland.

HOME, Sir David George, 13th Bt, *cr* 1671; late Temp. Major Argyll and Sutherland Highlanders; *b* 21 Jan. 1904; *o s* of Sir John Home, 12th Bt and Hon. Gwendolina H. R. Mostyn (*d* 1960), *sister* of 7th Baron Vaux of Harrowden; *S* father, 1938; *m* 1933, Sheila, *d* of late Mervyn Campbell Stephen; two *s* one *d* (and one *d* decd). *Educ:* Harrow; Jesus Coll., Cambridge (BA 1925). Member Royal Company of Archers (HM Body Guard for Scotland). FSA (Scotland). *Heir: s* John Home [*b* 1 June 1936; *m* 1966, Nancy Helen, *d* of H. G. Elliott, Perth, Western Australia, and *widow* of Commander Ian Macgregor, RAN; one *s* one *d*]. *Address:* Winterfield, North Berwick, East Lothian. *Clubs:* Brooks's; New (Edinburgh); Royal and Ancient (St Andrews).

See also Sir D. P. M. Malcolm, Bt.

HOME, Prof. George, BL; FIB Scot; Professor of International Banking, Heriot-Watt University, Edinburgh, 1978–85, Professor Emeritus, since 1985; *b* 13 April 1920; *s* of George Home and Leah Home; *m* 1946, Muriel Margaret Birleson; two *s* one *d*. *Educ:* Fort Augustus Village Sch.; Trinity Academy, Edinburgh; George Heriot's Sch., Edinburgh; Edinburgh Univ. (BL 1952). FIB(Scot); FBIM. Joined Royal Bank of Scotland, 1936; served RAF, 1940–46; Dep. Man. Dir, Royal Bank of Scotland Ltd, 1973–80; Dep. Gp Man. Dir, Royal Bank of Scotland Gp Ltd, 1976–80; Director: Williams & Glyn's Bank Ltd, 1975–80; The Wagon Finance Corp. plc, 1980–85. Vice-Pres., Inst. of Bankers in Scotland, 1977–80. *Recreations:* fishing, gardening, reading, travel. *Address:* Bickley, 12 Barnton Park View, Edinburgh EH4 6HJ. *T:* 031–336 7648.

HOME, Hon. William Douglas-; dramatic author; *b* Edinburgh, 3 June 1912; *s* of 13th Earl of Home, KT; *m* 1951, Rachel Brand (*see* Baroness Dacre); one *s* three *d*. *Educ:* Eton; New Coll., Oxford (BA). Studied at Royal Academy of Dramatic Art, and has appeared on the West End stage. Formerly Captain RAC. Contested (Progressive Ind) Cathcart Division of Glasgow, April 1942, Windsor Division of Berks, June 1942, and Clay Cross Division of Derbyshire (Atlantic Charter), April 1944, (Liberal) South Edinburgh, 1957. Author of the following plays: Great Possessions, 1937; Passing By, 1940; Now Barabbas, The Chiltern Hundreds, 1947; Ambassador Extraordinary, 1948; Master of Arts, The Thistle and the Rose, 1949; Caro William, 1952; The Bad Samaritan, 1953; The Manor of Northstead, 1954; The Reluctant Debutante, 1955; The Iron Duchess, 1957; Aunt Edwina, 1959; Up a Gum Tree, 1960; The Bad Soldier Smith, 1961; The Cigarette Girl, 1962; The Drawing Room Tragedy, 1963; The Reluctant Peer, Two Accounts Rendered, 1964; Betzi, A Friend in Need, 1965; A Friend Indeed, 1966; The Secretary Bird, The Queen's Highland Servant, The Grouse Moor Image, The Bishop and the Actress, 1968; The Jockey Club Stakes, Uncle Dick's Surprise, 1970; The Douglas Cause, 1971; Lloyd George Knew My Father, 1972; At the End of the Day, 1973; The Bank Manager, The Dame of Sark, The Lord's Lieutenant, 1974; In The Red, The Kingfisher, Rolls Hyphen Royce, The Perch, The Consulting Room, 1977; The Editor Regrets, 1978; You're All Right: How am I?, 1981; Four Hearts Doubled, Her Mother Came Too, 1982; The Golf Umbrella, 1983; David and Jonathan, 1984; After the Ball is Over, 1985. *Publications:* Mr Home Pronounced Hume: an autobiography, 1979; Sins of Commission, 1985. *Recreations:* golf, politics. *Address:* Derry House, Kilmeston, near Alresford, Hants. *T:* Bramdean 256. *Club:* Travellers'.

See also Baron Home of the Hirsel.

HOME ROBERTSON, John David; MP (Lab) East Lothian, since 1983 (Berwick and East Lothian, Oct. 1978–1983); *b* 5 Dec. 1948; *s* of late Lt-Col J. W. Home Robertson and of Mrs H. M. Home Robertson; *m* 1977, Catherine Jean Brewster; two *s*. *Educ:* Ampleforth Coll.; West of Scotland Coll. of Agriculture. Farmer. Mem., Berwicks DC, 1975–78; Mem., Borders Health Bd, 1976–78. Chm., Eastern Borders CAB, 1977. Chm., Scottish Gp of Labour MPs, 1983; Opposition Scottish Whip, 1983–84; opposition spokesman on agric., 1984–. *Address:* Paxton South Mains, Berwick-on-Tweed; House of Commons, SW1. *T:* 01–219 4135. *Clubs:* East Lothian Labour, Prestonpans Labour.

HOMEWOOD, William Dennis; *b* Bermondsey, March 1920; *m*. *Educ:* Ruskin Coll., Oxford. Full-time trade union officer, ISTC (formerly branch sec. and dist cttee sec.). Rural Dist Councillor, Market Harborough, 1958–65. MP (Lab) Kettering, 1979–83. Contested (Lab) Corby, 1983. Mem., Labour Party, 1946–. *Address:* 8 Gores Lane, Market Harborough, Leics.

HONDROS, Ernest Demetrios, DSc; FRS 1984; Director, Petten Establishments, Commission of European Communities' Joint Research Centre, since 1985; *b* 18 Feb. 1930; *s* of Demetrios Hondros and Athanasia Paleologos; *m* 1968, Sissel Kristine Garder-Olsen; two *s*. *Educ:* Univ. of Melbourne (DSc MSc); Univ. of Paris (Dr d'Univ.). CEng, FIM. Research Officer, CSIRO Tribophysics Laboratory, Melbourne, 1955–59; Research Fellow, Univ. of Paris, Lab. de Chimie Minérale, 1959–62; National Physical Laboratory: Sen. Research Officer, Metallurgy Div., 1962–65; Principal Res. Fellow, 1965–68; Sen. Principal Res. Officer (Special Merit), 1974; Supt, Materials Applications Div., 1979–85. Rosenhain Medallist, Metals Soc., 1976; Howe Medal, Amer. Soc. for Metals, 1978. *Publications:* numerous research papers and reviews in learned jls. *Recreations:* music, literature, walking. *Address:* Petten Establishments, JRC, PO Box 2, 1755 ZG/Petten, The Netherlands. *T:* 31 2246 5401.

HONE, David; landscape and portrait painter; President, Royal Hibernian Academy of Arts, 1978–83; *b* 14 Dec. 1928; *s* of Joseph Hone and Vera Hone (*née* Brewster); *m* 1962, Rosemary D'Arcy; two *s* one *d*. *Educ:* Baymount School; St Columba's College; University College, Dublin. Studied art at National College of Art, Dublin, and later in Italy. Hon. RA, HRSA (ex-officio). *Recreations:* fishing, photography. *Address:* 25 Lower Baggot Street, Dublin 2, Ireland. *T:* Dublin 763746.

HONE, Maj. Gen. Sir (Herbert) Ralph, KCMG 1951; KBE 1946 (CBE Mil. 1943); MC; TD; GCStJ 1973; QC Gibraltar 1934, QC Uganda 1938; barrister-at-law; *b* 3 May 1896; *s* of late Herbert Hone and Miriam Grace (*née* Dracott); *m* 1st, 1918, Elizabeth Daisy, *d* of James Matthews (marr. diss. 1944); one *s* one *d*; 2nd, 1945, Sybil Mary, *widow* of Wing Commander G. Simond; one *s*. *Educ:* Varndean Grammar Sch., Brighton; London Univ. LLB (Hons). Barrister-at-law, Middle Temple. Inns of Court OTC. Gazetted London Irish Rifles, 1915; Lieut, 1916; Captain, 1918; served with BEF, France, 1916 and 1917–18 (wounded, MC), Staff Captain, Ministry of Munitions, 1918–20; Major R of O (TA); Asst Treas., Uganda, 1920; called to Bar; practised and went South Eastern Circuit, 1924–25; Registrar, High Court, Zanzibar, 1925; Resident Magistrate, Zanzibar, 1928; Crown Counsel, Tanganyika Territory, 1930; acted Asst Legal Adviser to the Colonial and Dominions Offices, Jan.-Aug. 1933; Attorney-General, Gibraltar, 1933–36; Commissioner for the Revision of the laws of Gibraltar, 1934; King's Jubilee medal, 1935; Chm., Gibraltar Govt Commn on Slum Clearance and Rent Restriction, 1936; Coronation Medal, 1937; Acting Chief Justice, Gibraltar, on several occasions; Attorney-General, Uganda, 1937–43; Chairman, Uganda Government Cttee on Museum policy, 1938; Commandant, Uganda Defence Force, 1940; Chief Legal Adviser, Political Branch, GHQ, Middle East, 1941; Chief Political Officer, GHQ, Middle East, 1942–43; General Staff, War Office, 1943–45; Chief Civil Affairs Officer, Malaya, 1945–46; Maj.-Gen., 1942–46 (despatches twice, CBE (mil.)); Secretary-General to Governor-General of Malaya, 1946–48; Dep. Commissioner-General in SE Asia, 1948–49; Coronation Medal, 1953, Governor and C-in-C, North Borneo, 1949–54, Head of Legal Division, CRO, 1954–61. Resumed practice at the Bar, 1961. Retd TA with Hon. rank Maj.-Gen., 1956. GCStJ 1973; Mem. Chapter Gen. Order of St John, 1954–. Vice-Pres., Royal Commonwealth Society; Constitutional Adviser, Kenya Govt, Dec. 1961–Jan. 1962; Constitutional Adviser to Mr Butler's Advisers on Central Africa, July-Oct. 1962; Constitutional Adviser to South Arabian Government, Oct. 1965–Jan. 1966, and to Bermuda Government, July-Nov. 1966. Appeal Comr under Civil Aviation Licensing Act, 1961–71; Standing Counsel, Grand Bahama Port Authority, 1962–75. *Publications:* Index to Gibraltar Laws, 1933; revised edn of Laws of Gibraltar, 1935; revised edn of Laws of the Bahamas, 1965; Handbook on Native Courts, etc. *Recreations:* tennis, badminton and philately. *Address:* 1 Paper Buildings, Temple, EC4. *T:* 01–583 7355; 56 Kenilworth Court, Lower Richmond Road, SW15. *T:* 01–788 3367. *Clubs:* Athenæum, Royal Commonwealth Society.

HONE, Robert Monro, MA; Headmaster, Exeter School, 1966–79; *b* 2 March 1923; *s* of late Rt Rev. Campbell R. Hone; *m* 1958, Helen Isobel, *d* of late Col H. M. Cadell of Grange, OBE; three *d*. *Educ:* Winchester Coll. (Scholar); New Coll., Oxford (Scholar). Rifle Brigade, 1942–45. Asst Master, Clifton Coll., 1948–65 (Housemaster, 1958–65). *Address:* St Madron, Throwleigh, Okehampton, Devon.

HONEYCOMBE, Gordon; *see* Honeycombe, R. G.

HONEYCOMBE, Prof. Robert William Kerr, FRS 1981; FEng 1980; Goldsmiths' Professor of Metallurgy, University of Cambridge, 1966–84, now Emeritus; *b* 2 May 1921; *s* of William and Rachel Honeycombe (*née* Kerr); *m* 1947, June Collins; two *d*. *Educ:* Geelong Coll.; Univ. of Melbourne. Research Student, Department of Metallurgy, University of Melbourne, 1941–42; Research Officer, Commonwealth Scientific and Industrial Research Organization, Australia, 1942–47; ICI Research Fellow, Cavendish Laboratory, Cambridge, 1948–49; Royal Society Armourers and Brasiers' Research Fellow, Cavendish Laboratory, Cambridge, 1949–51; Senior Lecturer in Physical Metallurgy, University of Sheffield, 1951–55; Professor, 1955–66. Fellow of Trinity Hall, Cambridge, 1966–73, Hon. Fellow, 1975; Pres. 1973–80, Fellow, 1980–, Clare Hall, Cambridge. Pres., Instn of Metallurgists, 1977; Pres., Metals Soc., 1980–81; Vice-Pres., Royal Institution, 1977–78. Visiting Professor: University of Melbourne, 1962; Stanford Univ., 1965; Monash Univ., 1974; Kyoto Univ., 1979. Hatfield Meml Lectr, 1979. Hon. Member: Iron and Steel Inst. of Japan, 1979; Soc. Française de Métallurgie, 1981; Japan Inst. of Metals, 1983 (Gold Medallist, 1983); Indian Inst. of Metals, 1984. Mem. Ct of Assts, Goldsmiths' Co., 1977– (Prime Warden, 1986–87). Hon. DAppSc Melbourne, 1974; Hon. DMet Sheffield, 1983. Rosenhain Medal of Inst. of Metals, 1959; Sir George Beilby Gold Medal, 1963; Ste-Claire-Deville Medal, 1971; Inst. of Metals Lectr and Mehl Medallist, AIME, 1976. *Publications:* The Plastic Deformation of Metals, 1968; Steels—Microstructure and Properties, 1981; papers in Proc. Royal Soc., Metal Science, etc. *Recreations:* gardening, photography, walking. *Address:* Barrabool, 46 Main Street, Hardwick, Cambridge CB3 7QS. *T:* Madingley 210501.

HONEYCOMBE, (Ronald) Gordon; author, playwright, dramatist, television presenter and narrator; *b* Karachi, British India, 27 Sept. 1936; *s* of Gordon Samuel Honeycombe and Dorothy Louise Reid Fraser. *Educ:* Edinburgh Acad.; University Coll., Oxford (MA English). National Service, RA, mainly in Hong Kong, 1955–57. Announcer: Radio Hong Kong, 1956–57; BBC Scottish Home Service, 1958; actor: with Tomorrow's Audience, 1961–62; with RSC, Stratford-on-Avon and London, 1962–63; acted in BBC TV shows, incl. That Was the Week that Was, Not so Much a Programme, 1964, TV series The Brack Report, 1982, and TV play, CQ, 1984; Newscaster with ITN, 1965–77 (twice chosen as most popular newscaster in national newspaper polls); News presenter, TV-am, 1984–. TV Presenter: (also writer), A Family Tree and Brass Rubbing (documentaries), 1973; children's poems in Stuff and Nonsense, 1975; The Late Late Show (series), and Something Special (series), 1978; Family History (series), 1979; Close, 1981; Narrator: Arthur C. Clarke's Mysterious World (TV series), 1980; A Shred of Evidence (TV), 1984; The Black Museum (Radio 4), 1984; also narrator for indust. documentaries, trng films and cinema shorts; TV commentaries include 50th Anniversary Service of RAF, Westminster Abbey, 1968. Acted in: The Commuter (film), 1968; Play-back 625, Royal Court, 1970; Paradise Lost, York and Old Vic, 1975; Noye's Fludde (Voice of God), Putney, 1978; appeared in various other television plays, series, and films (incl. The Medusa Touch, and Ransom); also appeared in charity and variety shows, Old Vic and Theatre Royal, Stratford, 1970–75; sang at Players' Theatre, 1974. Author of stage productions: The Miracles, Oxford, 1960 and (perf. by RSC), Southwark Cath., 1963 and Consett, 1970; The Princess and the Goblins (musical), Great Ayton, 1976; Paradise Lost, York, Old Vic and Edinburgh Fest., 1975–77; Waltz of my Heart, Bournemouth, 1980; Lancelot and Guinevere, Old Vic, 1980; author of TV plays: The Golden Vision (with Neville Smith), 1968; Time and Again, 1974 (Silver Medal, Film and TV Fest., NY, 1975); The Thirteenth Day of Christmas, 1986; radio dramatisations (all Radio 4): Paradise Lost, 1975; Lancelot and Guinevere, 1976; A King shall have a Kingdom, 1977; devised Royal Gala performances: God save the Queen!, Chichester, 1977; A King shall have a Kingdom, York, 1977. Pres., Bournemouth Operatic Soc., 1979–81. *Publications: non-fiction:* Nagasaki 1945, 1981; Royal Wedding, 1981; The Murders of the Black Museum, 1982; The Year of the Princess, 1982; Selfridges, 1984; TV-am's Official Celebration of the Royal Wedding, 1986; *documentary novels:* Adam's Tale, 1974; Red Watch, 1976; *fiction:* The Redemption (play), 1964; Neither the Sea nor the Sand, 1969; Dragon under the Hill, 1972; The Edge of Heaven, 1981; contrib. Punch, Private Eye, national newspapers and magazines. *Recreations:* brass-rubbing, bridge, crosswords. *Address:* c/o 37 Hill Street, W1X 8JY. *T:* 01–493 0343. *Clubs:* Eccentric, Lord's Taverners.

HONEYMAN, Prof. Alexander Mackie, MA, BLitt, PhD; FRAS; Professor of Oriental Languages in University of St Andrews, 1936–67; *b* 25 Nov. 1907; *s* of late A. M. Honeyman, Cupar, Fife; *m* 1935, Cecilia Mary (*d* 1980), 2nd *d* of late J. Leslie Milne, Edinburgh; one *s* one *d* (and one *d* decd). *Educ:* Universities of St Andrews, Edinburgh, London (School of Oriental Studies), Zürich and Chicago (Oriental Institute). 1st Class Hons Classics, 1929; BLitt in Ancient Languages, 1930; Guthrie Scholar, 1930, University of St Andrews; Commonwealth Fellow, New York and Chicago, 1932–34; PhD Chicago, 1934; Maclean Scholar of University of Glasgow, 1934–35, in Palestine, etc; Interim Lectr in Hebrew and Oriental Languages, Univ. of St Andrews, 1935–36. External Examiner to Univ. of Glasgow, 1941–44, 1946, 1951–54; Univ. of Edinburgh, 1946–48; Queen's Univ., Belfast, 1947–49; Univ. of Leeds, 1954–56, 1959; Univ. of London, 1959; Univ. of Brussels, 1972. Schweich Lecturer of British Academy, 1950; Leverhulme Fellowship, 1954. Travelled and excavated in S Arabia, 1950, 1954 and 1958. Trustee of National Library of Scotland, 1951–56; Mem. Council, Royal Asiatic Soc., 1952–56;

Vice-Pres., British Branch, Hebrew Language Academy, 1954–. *Publications:* The Mission of Burzoe in the Arabic Kalilah wa-Dimnah, 1936; articles and reviews in archæological, philological and historical journals. *Address:* Oldtown, Ardgay, Ross-shire. *T:* Ardgay 423.

HONGLADAROM, Sunthorn; Knight Grand Cordon, Order of Crown of Thailand, and Order of White Elephant; Secretary-General, South-East Asia Treaty Organisation, 1972–77; Hon. Assistant Secretary-General, Thai Red Cross Society, since 1977; *b* 23 Aug. 1912; *m* 1937; five *s* one *d. Educ:* Trinity Coll., Cambridge. Asst Sec.-Gen. to Cabinet, 1946; Sec.-Gen., Nat. Economic Council, 1950; Ambassador to Fedn of Malaya (now Malaysia), 1957; Minister of Economic Affairs, 1959; Minister of Finance, 1960; Chairman of Boards of Governors; IBRD, IMF, IFC, and Internat. Development Assoc., 1961; Minister of Economic Affairs, 1966; Ambassador to UK, 1968–69, to USA, 1969–72. Hon. LLD, St John's Univ., NY, 1970. *Recreations:* golf, motoring. *Address:* Thai Red Cross Society, Chulalongkorn Memorial Hospital, Bangkok, Thailand. *Club:* Roehampton.

HONIG, His Honour Frederick; a Circuit Judge (formerly a County Court Judge), 1968–86; *b* 22 March 1912; 2nd *s* of late Leopold Honig; *m* 1940, Joan, *o d* of late Arthur Burkart. *Educ:* Berlin and Heidelberg Univs. LLD (Hons) Heidelberg, 1934. Barrister, Middle Temple, 1937. War service, 1940–47: Capt., JAG's Dept; Judge Advocate in civilian capacity, 1947–48; subseq. practised at Bar. *Publications:* (jtly) Cartel Law of the European Economic Community, 1963; contribs to Internat. Law Reports (ed. Lauterpacht) and legal jls, incl. Amer. Jl of Internat. Law, Internat. and Comparative Law Quarterly, Law Jl, Propriété Industrielle, etc. *Recreations:* foreign languages, country walking. *Address:* Lamb Building, Temple, EC4. *T:* 01–353 1612; 23 Shilling Street, Lavenham, Suffolk. *T:* Lavenham 247565.

HONORÉ, Prof. Antony Maurice, DCL Oxon; FBA 1972; Regius Professor of Civil Law, University of Oxford, since 1971; Fellow of All Souls College, Oxford, since 1971; *b* 30 March 1921; *o s* of Frédéric Maurice Honoré and Marjorie Erskine (*née* Gilbert); *m* 1st, Martine Marie-Odette Genouville; one *s* one *d*; 2nd, Deborah Mary Cowen (*née* Duncan). *Educ:* Diocesan Coll., Rondebosch; Univ. of Cape Town; New Coll., Oxford. Rhodes Scholar, 1940. Union Defence Forces, 1940–45; Lieut, Rand Light Infantry, 1942. BCL 1948. Advocate, South Africa, 1951; called to Bar, Lincoln's Inn, 1952, Hon. Bencher, 1971. Lectr, Nottingham Univ., 1948; Rhodes Reader in Roman-Dutch Law, 1957–71, Fellow of Queen's Coll., Oxford, 1949–64, of New Coll., 1964–71. Visiting Professor: McGill, 1961; Berkeley, 1968. Hon. DL Edinburgh; Hon. LLD South Africa. *Publications:* (with H. L. A. Hart) Causation in the Law, 1959, 2nd edn 1984; Gaius, 1962; The South African Law of Trusts, 3rd edn 1984; Tribonian, 1978; Sex Law, 1978; (with J. Menner) Concordance to the Digest Jurists, 1980; Emperors and Lawyers, 1981; The Quest for Security, 1982; Ulpian, 1982. *Address:* 126 Freehold Street, Lower Heyford, Oxford. *T:* Steeple Aston 40680.

HONOUR, (Patrick) Hugh, FRSL; writer; *b* 26 Sept. 1927; *s* of late Herbert Percy Honour and Dorothy Margaret Withers. *Educ:* King's Sch., Canterbury; St Catharine's Coll., Cambridge (BA). Asst to Dir, Leeds City Art Gall. and Temple Newsam House, 1953–54. Guest Curator for exhibn, The European Vision of America, National Gall. of Art, Washington, Cleveland Museum of Art, and, as L'Amérique vue par l'Europe, Grand Palais, Paris, 1976. FRSL 1972. Corresp. FBA 1986. *Publications:* Chinoiserie, 1961 (2nd edn 1973); Companion Guide to Venice, 1965 (4th edn 1977); (with Sir Nikolaus Pevsner and John Fleming) The Penguin Dictionary of Architecture, 1966 (3rd rev. edn 1980); Neo-classicism, 1968 (4th edn 1977); The New Golden Land, 1976; (with John Fleming) The Penguin Dictionary of Decorative Arts, 1977; Romanticism, 1979; (with John Fleming) A World History of Art, 1982 (Mitchell Prize, 1982); The Visual Arts: a history (USA). *Recreation:* gardening. *Club:* Travellers'.

HONYWOOD, Sir Filmer (Courtenay William), 11th Bt *cr* 1660; FRICS; Regional Surveyor and Valuer, South Eastern Region, Central Electricity Generating Board, since 1978; *b* 20 May 1930; *s* of Col Sir William Wynne Honywood, 10th Bt, MC, and Maud Naylor (*d* 1953), *d* of William Hodgson Wilson, Hexgreave Park, Southwell, Notts; *S* father, 1982; *m* 1956, Elizabeth Margaret Mary Cynthia, *d* of Sir Alastair George Lionel Joseph Miller of Glenlee, 6th Bt; two *s* two *d. Educ:* Downside; RMA Sandhurst; Royal Agricultural College, Cirencester (MRAC Diploma). Served 3rd Carabiniers (Prince of Wales' Dragoon Guards). Asst Surveyor, Min. of Agriculture, Fisheries and Food, Maidstone, 1966–73; Surveyor, Cockermouth, Cumbria, 1973–74; Senior Lands Officer, CEGB, SE Region, 1974–78. *Heir: s* Rupert Anthony Honywood, *b* 2 March 1957. *Address:* Greenway Forstal Farmhouse, Hollingbourne, Maidstone, Kent ME17 1QA.

HOOD, family name of **Viscounts Bridport** and **Hood.**

HOOD, 7th Viscount *cr* 1796; **Alexander Lambert Hood;** Bt 1778; Baron (Ire.) 1782, (GB) 1795; Chairman, Petrofina (UK) Ltd, since 1982 (Director, since 1958); Director, George Wimpey PLC, since 1957; *b* 11 March 1914; *s* of Rear-Adm. Hon. Sir Horace Hood, KCB, DSO, MVO (*d* 1916) (3rd *s* of 4th Viscount) and Ellen Floyd (*d* 1950), *d* of A. E. Touzalin; *S* brother, 1981; *m* 1957, Diana Maud, CVO 1957, *d* of late Hon. G. W. Lyttelton; three *s. Educ:* RN Coll., Dartmouth; Trinity Coll., Cambridge; Harvard Business Sch. RNVR, 1939–45. Director: J. Henry Schroder Wagg & Co., 1957–75; Tanks Consolidated Investments PLC, 1971–84 (Chm., 1976–83); Benguela Railway Co., 1979–84; Union Minière, 1973–84; Abbott Laboratories Inc., 1971–83; Abbott Laboratories Ltd, 1964–85. Part-time Mem., British Waterways Bd, 1963–73. *Heir: s* Hon. Henry Lyttelton Alexander Hood, *b* 16 March 1958. *Address:* 67 Chelsea Square, SW3. *T:* 01–352 4952; Loders Court, Bridport, Dorset. *T:* Bridport 22983. *Club:* Brooks's.

HOOD, Sir Harold (Joseph), 2nd Bt *cr* 1922, of Wimbledon, Co. Surrey; TD; Circulation Director, Catholic Herald, since 1961; Circulation Director, Universe, 1953–60; *b* 23 Jan. 1916; *e s* of Sir Joseph Hood, 1st Bt, and Marie Josephine (*d* 1956), *e d* of Archibald Robinson, JP, Dublin; *S* father, 1931; *m* 1946, Hon. Ferelith Rosemary Florence Kenworthy, *o d* of 10th Baron Strabolgi and of Doris, Lady Strabolgi, 137 Gloucester Road, SW7; two *s* two *d* (and one *s* decd). *Educ:* Downside Sch. Mem. Editorial Staff, The Universe, 1936–39; Asst Editor, The Catholic Directory, 1950, Managing Ed., 1959–60; Editor, The Catholic Who's Who, 1952 Edition. 2nd Lieutenant 58th Middx Battalion RE (AA) (TA) 1939; Lieut RA, 1941. KSG (Holy See), 1964; KCSG (Holy See), 1978; Kt of Magistral Grace, SMO Malta, 1972. *Heir: s* John Joseph Harold Hood, *b* 27 Aug. 1952. *Address:* 31 Avenue Road, NW8 6BS. *T:* 01–722 9088. *Clubs:* Royal Automobile, MCC, Challoner.

HOOD, Rear-Adm. John, CBE 1981; CEng, FIMechE; Director General Aircraft (Naval), 1978–81; *b* 23 March 1924; *s* of Charles Arthur Hood, architect, and Nellie Ormiston Brown Lamont; *m* 1948, Julia Mary Trevaskis; three *s. Educ:* Plymouth Coll.; RN Engineering Coll., Keyham. Entered Royal Navy, 1945; RNEC, 1945–48; served in Illustrious, 1948; RN Air Stations, Abbotsinch, Anthorn, RAF West Raynham (NAFDU), 1948–51; HQ Min. of Supply, 1951–53; Air Engineer Officer, 1834 Sqdn, 1953–55, Aeroplane and Armament Experimental Estabt, 1955–57; Staff of Dir Aircraft Maintenance and Repair, 1957–59; AEO, HMS Albion, 1959–61; Sen. Air Engr, RNEC, Manadon, 1961–62; Development Project Officer, Sea Vixen 2, Min. of Aviation, 1962–65; AEO, RNAS, Lossiemouth, 1965–67; Staff of Dir of Officer Appointments (E), 1967–70; Defence and Naval Attaché, Argentina and Uruguay, 1970–73; Sen. Officers War Course, 1973; Asst Dir, Naval Manpower Requirements (Ships), 1974–75; Head of Aircraft Dept (Naval), 1975–78. Comdr 1962, Captain 1969, Rear-Adm. 1979. *Recreations:* sailing, gardening. *Club:* RN Sailing Association.

HOOD, (Martin) Sinclair (Frankland), FBA 1983; Archaeologist; *b* 31 Jan. 1917; *s* of late Lt-Comdr Martin Hood, RN, and late Mrs Martin Hood, New York; *m* 1957, Rachel Simmons; one *s* two *d. Educ:* Harrow; Magdalen Coll., Oxford. British Sch. at Athens: student, 1947–48 and 1951–53; Asst Dir, 1949–51; Dir, 1954–62. Student, British Inst. Archaeology, Ankara, 1948–49. Geddes-Harrower Vis. Prof. of Greek Art and Archaeology, Univ. of Aberdeen, 1968. Took part in excavations at: Dorchester, Oxon, 1937; Compton, Berks, 1946–47; Southwark, 1946; Smyrna, 1948–49; Atchana, 1949–50; Sakca-Gozu, 1950; Mycenae, 1950–52; Knossos, 1950–51, 1953–55, 1957–61; Jericho, 1952; Chios, 1952–55. *Publications:* The Home of the Heroes: The Aegean before the Greeks, 1967; The Minoans, 1971; The Arts in Prehistoric Greece, 1978; various excavation reports and articles. *Address:* The Old Vicarage, Great Milton, Oxford OX9 7PB. *T:* Great Milton 202. *Club:* Athenæum.

HOOD, Prof. Neil; Professor of Business Policy, since 1979, Co-Director, Strathclyde International Business Unit, since 1983, and Dean of Strathclyde Business School, since 1985, University of Strathclyde (Associate Dean, 1982–85); *b* 10 Aug. 1943; *s* of Andrew Hood and Elizabeth Taylor Carruthers; *m* 1966, Anna Watson Clark; one *s* one *d. Educ:* Wishaw High Sch.; Univ. of Glasgow. MA, MLitt. Res. Fellow, Scottish Coll. of Textiles, 1966–68; Lectr, later Sen. Lectr, Paisley Coll. of Technol., 1968–78; Economic Advr, Scottish Economic Planning Dept, 1979. Vis. Prof. of Internat. Business, Univ. of Texas, Dallas, 1981; Vis. Prof., Stockholm Sch. of Economics, 1983–. Trade Adviser, UNCTAD-GATT, 1980–85; Economic Consultant to Sec. of State for Scotland, 1980–; Consultant to: Internat. Finance Corp., World Bank, 1982–84; UN Centre on Transnational Corporations, 1982–84. Mem., Irvine Develt Corp., 1985–. Non-executive Director: Euroscot Meat Exports Ltd, 1983–; Scottish Develt Finance Ltd, 1984–; Lanarkshire Industrial Field Executive Ltd, 1984–; Investment Advr, Castleforth Fund Managers Ltd, 1984–. Member: various boards, CNAA, 1971–83; Industry and Employment Cttee, ESRC, 1985–. Pres., European Internat. Business Assoc., 1986. Fellow, European Inst. of Advanced Studies in Management, Brussels, 1985–. *Publications:* (with S. Young): Chrysler UK: Corporation in transition, 1977; Economics of Multinational Enterprise, 1979; European Development Strategies of US-owned Manufacturing Companies Located in Scotland, 1980; Multinationals in Retreat: the Scottish experience, 1982; Multinational Investment Strategies in the British Isles, 1983; (ed) Industrial Policy and the Scottish Economy, 1984; articles on internat. business, marketing and business policy, in various jls. *Recreations:* reading, writing, swimming, golf, gardening. *Address:* Teviot, 12 Carlisle Road, Hamilton ML3 7DB. *T:* Hamilton 424870.

HOOD, Roger Grahame; University Reader in Criminology, Head of the Centre for Criminological Research, and Fellow of All Souls College, Oxford, since 1973; *b* 12 June 1936; 2nd *s* of Ronald and Phyllis Hood; *m* 1963, Barbara Blaine Young (marr. diss. 1985); one *d*; *m* 1985, Nancy Stebbing (*née* Lynah). *Educ:* King Edward's Sch., Five Ways, Birmingham; LSE (BSc Sociology); Downing Coll., Cambridge (PhD). Research Officer, LSE, 1961–63; Lectr in Social Admin, Univ. of Durham, 1963–67; Asst Dir of Research, Inst. of Criminology, Univ. of Cambridge, 1967–73; Fellow of Clare Hall, Cambridge, 1969–73. Vis. Prof., Univ. of Virginia Sch. of Law, 1980–. Member: Parole Bd, 1972–73; SSRC Cttee on Social Sciences and the Law, 1975–79. Mem., Judicial Studies Bd, 1979–85. Mem. Editorial Bd, British Jl of Criminology. *Publications:* Sentencing in Magistrates' Courts, 1962; Borstal Re-assessed, 1965; (with Richard Sparks) Key Issues in Criminology, 1970; Sentencing the Motoring Offender, 1972; (ed) Crime, Criminology and Public Policy: Essays in Honour of Sir Leon Radzinowicz, 1974; (with Sir Leon Radzinowicz) Criminology and the Administration of Criminal Justice: a bibliography, 1976; (with Sir Leon Radzinowicz) A History of English Criminal Law, vol. 5, The Emergence of Penal Policy, 1986. *Address:* 63 Iffley Road, Oxford. *T:* Oxford 246084.

HOOD, Samuel Harold; Director, Defence Operational Analysis Establishment, Ministry of Defence, 1985–86; *b* 21 Aug. 1926; *s* of Samuel N. and Annie Hood; *m* 1959, Frances Eileen Todd; two *s* four *d. Educ:* Larne Grammar Sch., Co. Antrim; Queen's Univ., Belfast (BA Hons Maths). Joined Civil Service, staff of Scientific Advr, Air Min., 1948; Staff of Operational Res. Br., Bomber Comd, 1950; Scientific Officer, BCDU, RAF Wittering, 1954; Operational Res. Br., Bomber Comd, 1959; Staff of Chief Scientist (RAF), 1964; joined DOAE, 1965; Supt, Air Div., DOAE, 1969; Dir, Defence Sci. Divs 1 and 7, MoD, 1974; Head, Systems Assessment Dept, RAE, 1981. *Recreations:* walking, gardening, bird watching. *Address:* Wayside Cottage, Sellack, near Ross-on-Wye, Herefordshire. *T:* Ross-on-Wye 64977.

HOOD, Sinclair; *see* Hood, M. S. F.

HOOD, Col Sir Tom (Fielden), KBE 1967 (OBE 1944); CB 1959; TD 1944; DL; Chairman, Portman Building Society, 1960–82; Director, National Employers' Mutual General Insurance Association Ltd, 1950–76, Chairman, 1970–76, Local Director, since 1976; *b* 16 March 1904; *s* of late Tom Hood, AMICE, AMIMechE, and Emmeline Clayton Hood (*née* Fielden); *m* 1931, Joan, *d* of Richmond P. Hellyar; two *s. Educ:* Clifton Coll. ACA 1930, FCA 1938. Partner, Lawrence, Gardner & Co., Chartered Accountants, Bristol, 1931–57. 2nd Lieut RE (TA), 1923; CRE 61 Div., 1939–42; DCE Scottish Command, 1942–44; DCE Second Army, 1944–45; Col 1945. Chm., Commn of Enquiry into Port of Aden, 1963. Governor of Clifton Coll., 1954–; Mem. of Court of Univ. of Bristol, 1956–. DL Co. Gloucester, 1950–. *Recreation:* reading. *Address:* Penthouse C, Marklands, Julian Road, Sneyd Park, Bristol BS9 1NP. *T:* Bristol 682615. *Clubs:* Army and Navy; Bath and County (Bath).

HOOD, Sir William Acland, 8th Bt *cr* 1806 and 6th Bt *cr* 1809; *b* 5 March 1901; *s* of William Fuller-Acland-Hood (*d* 1933) and Elizabeth (*d* 1966), *d* of M. Kirkpatrick, Salt Lake City, USA; *S* to baronetcies of kinsman, 2nd Baron St Audries, 1971; *m* 1925, Mary, *d* of late Augustus Edward Jessup, Philadelphia; one *d* (one *s* decd). *Educ:* Wellington; RMA Woolwich; Univ. of California (MA). Naturalized American citizen, 1926. Formerly Lieutenant RE. Professor, Los Angeles City College, retired. *Heir:* none. *Address:* SR2, Box 577, 29 Palms, California 92277, USA. *T:* 714 3679345.

HOOK, David Morgan Alfred, FEng 1985; Managing Director, G. Maunsell & Partners, since 1984; Partner, Maunsell Consultants (Melbourne) and Maunsell Consultants Asia (Hong Kong); *b* 16 April 1931; *m* 1957, Winifred (*née* Brown); two *s* one *d. Educ:* Bancroft's School; Queens' College, Cambridge (MA). FICE, FIStructE. Holland & Hannen and Cubitts, 1954–58; Nuclear Civil Constructors, 1958–62; G. Maunsell & Partners (Consulting Engineers), 1962–, Partner, 1968–. *Publications:* papers in Jl of IStructE. *Recreation:* private flying. *Club:* United Oxford & Cambridge University.

HOOK, Rt. Rev. Ross Sydney, MC 1945; an Assistant Bishop, Diocese of Canterbury, since 1981; *b* 19 Feb. 1917; *o s* of late Sydney Frank and Laura Harriet Hook; *m* 1948, Ruth Leslie, *d* of late Rev. Herman Masterman Biddell and Violet Marjorie Biddell; one *s* one *d. Educ:* Christ's Hosp.; Peterhouse, Cambridge (MA); Ridley Hall, Cambridge. Asst Curate, Milton, Hants, 1941–43. Chaplain, RNVR (Royal Marine Commandos), 1943–46. Chaplain, Ridley Hall, Cambridge, 1946–48. Select Preacher, University of Cambridge, 1948; Rector, Chorlton-cum-Hardy, Manchester, 1948–52; Rector and Rural Dean, Chelsea, 1952–61; Chaplain: Chelsea Hosp. for Women, 1954–61; St Luke's Hosp., Chelsea, 1957–61; Residentiary Canon of Rochester and Precentor, 1961–65; Treasurer, 1965; Diocesan Dir of Post Ordination Training, 1961–65; Bishop Suffragan of Grantham, 1965–72; Bishop of Bradford, 1972–80; Chief of Staff to Archbishop of Canterbury, 1980–84. Examining Chaplain to Bishop of Rochester, 1961–65, to Bishop of Lincoln, 1966–72; Prebendary of Brampton (Lincoln Cathedral), 1966–72; Dean of Stamford, 1971–72. Chm., Inspections Cttee, Central Advisory Council for the Ministry, 1966–71 (Sec., 1960–66). Hon. DLitt Bradford, 1981. *Recreation:* cricket. *Address:* Millrock, Newchurch, Romney Marsh, Kent TN29 0DN. *Club:* Army and Navy.

HOOK, Prof. Sidney; Professor, Department of Philosophy, Graduate School of Arts and Science, New York University, 1939–72, now Emeritus Professor; Senior Research Fellow on War, Revolution and Peace, at Hoover Institution, Stanford University, since 1973; Founder of The New York University Institute of Philosophy; *b* 20 Dec. 1902; *s* of Isaac Hook and Jennie Halpern; *m* 1924; one *s*; *m* 1935, Ann Zinken; one *s* one *d. Educ:* College of the City of New York; BS 1923; Columbia Univ. (MA 1926, PhD 1927); Columbia Univ. Fellowship in Philosophy, 1926–27; Guggenheim Research Fellowship in Philosophy for Study Abroad, 1928–29, 1953–; Ford Fellowship for the Study of Asian philosophy and culture, 1958. Teacher, New York City Public Schs, 1923–27; Instr in Philosophy, Washington Square Coll., New York Univ., 1927–32; Asst Prof., 1932–34; Assoc. Prof. and Chm. of Dept of Philosophy, 1933–39; Lectr, New Sch. for Social Research, NYC, 1931–. Vis. Prof., Univ. of California, 1950, Harvard Univ., 1961; Thomas Jefferson Memorial Lectr, Univ. of California at Berkeley, 1961; Regents Prof., Univ. of California at Santa Barbara, 1966; Vis. Prof., Univ. of California at San Diego, 1975. Fellow at Center for Advanced Study in the Behavioral Sciences, Stanford Univ., 1961–62. Butler Silver Medal for distinction in Philosophy, Columbia Univ., 1945. Organiser: conf. on Methods in Philosophy and Sci., conf. on Sci. Spirit and Dem. Faith, and Cttee for Cultural Freedom; Organiser and Co-Chm., Americans for Intellectual Freedom; President: Univ. Centers for Rational Alternatives; John Dewey Foundn (and Treasurer); Mem., American Philosophical Assoc. Vice-Pres., Eastern Div., 1958, Pres., 1959–60, Am. Assoc. Univ. Profs (past Council Mem.); Vice-President: Internat. Cttees for Academic Freedom; Council, Nat. Endowment for the Humanities, 1973–79 (Jefferson Lectr, 1984). Hon. DHL: Univ. of Maine, 1960; Univ. of Utah, 1970; Univ. of Vermont, 1979; Hon LLD: Univ. of California, 1966; Rockford Coll., 1970; Univ. of Florida, 1971. Fellow: American Academy of Arts and Sciences, 1965; Nat. Acad. of Educn, 1968. Presidential Medal of Freedom, 1985. *Publications:* The Metaphysics of Pragmatism, 1927; Towards the Understanding of Karl Marx, 1933; American Philosophy—To-day and To-morrow, 1935; From Hegel to Marx, 1936; Planned Society—Yesterday, To-day, To-morrow, 1937; John Dewey: An Intellectual Portrait, 1939; Reason, Social Myths and Democracy, 1940; The Hero in History, 1943; Education for Modern Man, 1946; Heresy, Yes—Conspiracy No, 1953; The Ambiguous Legacy; Marx and the Marxists, 1955; Common Sense and the Fifth Amendment, 1957; Political Power and Personal Freedom, 1959; The Quest for Being, 1961; The Paradoxes of Freedom, 1962; The Fail-Safe Fallacy, 1963; Religion in a Free Society, 1967; Academic Freedom and Academic Anarchy, 1970; Education and the Taming of Power, 1973; Pragmatism and the Tragic Sense of Life, 1975; Revolution, Reform and Social Justice, 1976; Philosophy and Public Philosophy, 1980; Marxism and Beyond, 1983; Editor of various works; contrib. numerous articles to philosophical journals. *Recreation:* gardening. *Address:* New York University, New York, NY 10003, USA. *T:* 212–598–3262; Hoover Institution, Stanford, Calif 94305, USA. *T:* 415–497–1501.

HOOKER, Michael Ayerst, PhD; Chief Executive Governor, Truman and Knightley Educational Trust, since 1981 (Governor since 1977); *b* 22 Jan. 1923; *s* of Albert Ayerst Hooker, late of Broomsleigh Park, Seal Chart, Kent, and late Marjorie Mitchell Hooker (*née* Gunson). *Educ:* Marlborough; St Edmund Hall, Oxford (MA 1944); Univ. of the Witwatersrand (PhD 1952). Home Guard, Oxford Univ. Sen. Trng Corps and Army Cadet Force (TARO), 1940–48. British Council, 1945–47; Schoolmaster, England and S Africa, 1947–51; London Diocesan Bd of Educn, 1952–66; Visual Aids and Public Relations, 1953–59. Chm., Fedn of Conservative Students, 1944; Parly Candidate (C) Coventry East, 1955; various offices, Conservative Commonwealth Council, 1955–60. Wells Organisation, fund raising in UK and NZ, 1957–58; Man. Dir, Hooker Craigmyle & Co. Ltd (first institutional fund raising consultants in UK), 1959–72; Man. Dir, Michael Hooker and Associates Ltd, 1972–79; Develt Dir, The Look Wide Trust, 1979–80. From 1957, has helped to raise nearly £70 million for various good causes, incl. 13 historic cathedrals, univs, colleges, schools, medical causes, welfare charities, etc. Mem., Adv. Cttee on Charitable Fund Raising, Nat. Council of Social Service, 1971–73. Trustee: Ross McWhirter Foundn, 1976–; Dicey Trust, 1978–; Jerwood Foundn, 1981–; Police Convalescence and Rehabilitation Trust, 1985–; Jt Chm./Founder, Friends of Friends; Hon. Councillor, NSPCC, 1981–; Governor, Oakham Sch., 1971–83. *Publications:* various pamphlets and broadcasts on charities, historic churches, educnl issues, law and taxation, Christian stewardship of money. *Address:* 4 Leinster Square, W2 4PL. *T:* 01–229 5483; 10 Myddelton Gardens, N21 2PA. *T:* 01–360 3206. *Clubs:* Carlton, Royal Commonwealth Society.

HOOKER, Prof. Morna Dorothy; Lady Margaret's Professor of Divinity, University of Cambridge, since 1976; Fellow of Robinson College, Cambridge, since 1976; *b* 19 May 1931; *d* of Percy Francis Hooker, FIA, and Lily (*née* Riley); *m* 1978, Rev. Dr W. David Stacey, MA. *Educ:* Univ. of Bristol (research schol.); Univ. of Manchester (research studentship). MA (Bristol, Oxford and Cambridge); PhD (Manchester). Research Fellow, Univ. of Durham, 1959–61; Lectr in New Testament Studies, King's Coll., London, 1961–70; Visiting Prof., McGill Univ., 1968; Lectr in Theology, Oxford, and Fellow, Linacre Coll., 1970–76 (Hon. Fellow, 1980); Lectr in Theology, Keble Coll., 1972 76; Visiting Fellow, Clare Hall, Cambridge, 1974. FKC 1979. Lectures: T. W. Manson meml, 1977; A. S. Peake meml, 1978; Henton Davies, 1979; Ethel M. Wood, 1984; James A. Gray, Duke Univ., 1984; W. A. Sanderson, Melbourne, 1986. Jt Editor, Jl of Theological Studies, 1986–. *Publications:* Jesus and the Servant, 1959; The Son of Man in Mark, 1967; (ed jtly) What about the New Testament?, 1975; Pauline Pieces, 1979; Studying the New Testament, 1979; (ed jtly) Paul and Paulinism, 1982; The Message of Mark, 1983; contribs to New Testament Studies, Jl of Theological Studies, Theology, etc. *Recreations:* Molinology, music. *Address:* Divinity School, St John's Street, Cambridge.

HOOKER, Ronald George, CBE 1985; FEng; CBIM; FRSA; Chairman: Dubilier plc, since 1978; Management & Business Services Ltd, since 1972; Henry Sykes plc, since 1981; Sarasota Technology Plc, since 1982; Radyne Ltd, since 1982; Thomas Storey Ltd, since 1984; Co-ordinated Land and Estates, since 1985; Melville Technologies Ltd, since 1985; National Radiofone Ltd, since 1986; company directorships; *b* 6 Aug. 1921; *m* 1954, Eve Pigott; one *s* one *d. Educ:* Wimbledon Technical Coll.; London Univ. (external). FEng 1984. CBIM 1972. Apprentice, Philips Electrical Ltd, 1937–41, Develt Engr, 1945–48; FBI, 1948–50; Dir and Gen. Man., Brush Electrical Engineering Co. Ltd, 1950–60; Man. Dir, K & L Steelfounders & Engineers Ltd, 1960–65; Man. Dir, Associated Fire Alarms Ltd, 1965–68; Chm. and Man. Dir, Crane Fruehauf Trailers Ltd, 1968–71; Dir of Manufacture, Rolls Royce (1971) Ltd, 1971 73; Chm. and Man. Dir, John M. Henderson (Holdings) Ltd, 1973–75. Director: GEI Internat. plc, 1974–; Ruberoid plc, 1977–; Hambros Industrial Management Ltd, 1966–; Airship Industries Ltd, 1984–. Pres., Engrg Employers' Fedn, 1986– (Mem. Management Bd, 1977–); Mem., Engrg Council, 1982–. Past Pres., IProdE, 1974–75 (Hon. Life MIProdE 1980). Freeman, City of London. *Publications:* papers on management and prodn engrg to BIM, ICMA, IProdE and IMechE. *Recreations:* gardening, reading, music. *Address:* Loxborough House, Bledlow Ridge, near High Wycombe, Bucks HP14 4AA. *T:* Bledlow Ridge 486; 6 Tufton Court, Tufton Street, SW1P 3QH. *T:* 01–222 6669. *Clubs:* Athenæum, Lansdowne, City of London.

HOOKS, Air Vice-Marshal Robert Keith, CBE 1979; CEng, FRAeS; RAF retired; Projects Director, Helicopter Division, Westland plc, since 1985; *b* 7 Aug. 1929; *s* of late Robert George Hooks and of Phyllis Hooks; *m* 1954, Kathleen (*née* Cooper); one *s* one *d. Educ:* Acklam Hall Sch.; Constantine Coll., Middlesbrough. Bsc(Eng) London. Commissioned RAF, 1951; served at RAF stations West Malling, Fassberg, Sylt, 1952–55; RAF Technical Coll., Henlow, 1956; Fairey Aviation Co., 1957–58; Air Ministry, 1958–60; Skybolt Trials Unit, Eglin, Florida, 1961–63; Bomber Command Armament Sch., Wittering, 1963–65; OC Engrg Wing, RAF Coll., Cranwell, 1967–69; HQ Far East Air Force, 1969–71; Supt of Armament A&AEE, 1971–74; Director Ground Training, 1974–76; Director Air Armament, 1976–80; Vice-Pres. (Air), Ordnance Board, 1980; Dir Gen. Aircraft 2, MoD (Procurement Exec.), 1981–84; Divl Dir (European Business), Westland Helicopters, 1984–85. *Address:* c/o Lloyds Bank, Cox's & King's Branch, 6 Pall Mall, SW1Y 5NH. *Club:* Royal Air Force.

HOOKWAY, Sir Harry (Thurston), Kt 1978; Chairman, Publishers Databases Ltd, since 1984; *b* 23 July 1921; *s* of William and Bertha Hookway; *m* 1956, Barbara Olive, *o d* of late Oliver and Olive Butler; one *s* one *d. Educ:* Trinity Sch. of John Whitgift; London Univ. (BSc, PhD). Various posts in industry, 1941–49; DSIR, 1949–65; Asst Dir, National Chemical Laboratory, 1959; Dir, UK Scientific Mission (North America), Scientific Attaché, Washington, DC, and Scientific Adviser to UK High Comr, Ottawa, 1960–64; Head of Information Div., DSIR, 1964–65; CSO, DES, 1966–69; Asst Under-Sec. of State, DES, 1969–73; Dep. Chm. and Chief Exec., The British Library Bd, 1973–84. Chairman: UNESCO Internat. Adv. Cttee for Documentation, Libraries and Archives, 1975–79; British Council Libraries Adv. Cttee, 1982–86; President: Inst. of Information Scientists, 1973–76; Library Assoc., 1985. Mem., Royal Commn on Historical Monuments (England), 1981–. Governor, British Inst. for Recorded Sound, 1981–86. Dir, Arundel Castle Trustees Ltd, 1976–. Hon. FLA, 1982; Hon. FIInfSc. Hon. LLD Sheffield, 1976; Hon. DLitt Loughborough, 1980. Gold Medal, Internat. Assoc. of Library Assocs, 1985. *Publications:* various contribs to jls of learned societies. *Recreations:* music, travel. *Address:* 35 Goldstone Crescent, Hove, East Sussex. *Club:* Athenæum.

HOOLAHAN, Anthony Terence, QC 1973; a Recorder of the Crown Court, since 1976; a Social Security Commissioner, since 1986; *b* 26 July 1925; *s* of late Gerald Hoolahan and of Val Hoolahan; *m* 1949, Dorothy Veronica Connochie; one *s* one *d. Educ:* Dorset House, Littlehampton, Sussex; Framlingham Coll., Suffolk; Lincoln Coll., Oxford (MA). Served War, RNVR, 1943–46. Oxford Univ., 1946–48. Called to Bar, Inner Temple, 1949, Bencher, 1980; called to the Bar of Northern Ireland, 1980, QC (Northern Ireland) 1980. *Publications:* Guide to Defamation Practice (with Colin Duncan, QC), 2nd edn, 1958; contrib. to Halsbury's Laws of England, Atkin's Court Forms. *Recreations:* squash, swimming. *Address:* 1 Brick Court, Temple, EC4Y 9BY. *T:* 01–353 8845; Fair Lawn, Ormond Avenue, Richmond, Surrey TW10 6TN. *T:* 01–940 1194.

HOOLE, Sir Arthur (Hugh), Kt 1985; Partner, Tuck & Mann, Epsom, since 1951; *b* 14 Jan. 1924; *s* of Hugh Francis and Gladys Emily Hoole; *m* 1945, Eleanor Mary Hobbs; two *s* two *d. Educ:* Sutton County School; Emmanuel College, Cambridge. MA, LLM. Served RAFVR, 1943–46; admitted solicitor, 1951; Mem. Council, Law Society, 1969– (Vice-Pres., 1983–84; Pres., 1984–85); Governor, College of Law, 1976– (Chm., 1983–); Member: Adv. Cttee on Legal Educn, 1977–; Common Professional Examination Bd, 1977–81 (Chm., 1978–81); Criminal Injuries Compensation Bd, 1985–. *Recreations:* cricket, books, music. *Address:* Yew Tree House, St Nicholas Hill, Leatherhead, Surrey. *T:* Leatherhead 373208. *Club:* Royal Automobile.

HOOLEY, Prof. Christopher, FRS 1983; Professor of Pure Mathematics and Head of Department of Pure Mathematics, University College, Cardiff, since 1967; *b* 7 Aug, 1928; *s* of Leonard Joseph Hooley, MA, BSc, and Barbara Hooley; *m* 1954, Birgitta Kniep; two *s. Educ:* Wilmslow Preparatory Sch.; Abbotsholme Sch.; Corpus Christi Coll., Cambridge (MA, PhD, ScD). Captain, RAEC, 1948–49. Fellow, Corpus Christi Coll., Cambridge, 1955–58; Lectr in Mathematics, Univ. of Bristol, 1958–65; Prof. of Pure Mathematics, Univ. of Durham, 1965–67; Dean of Faculty of Science, 1973–76, Dep. Principal, 1979–81, University Coll., Cardiff. Visiting Member: Inst. for Advanced Study, Princeton, 1970–71, and Fall Terms, 1976, 1977, 1982, 1983; IHES, Paris, 1984. Adams Prize, Cambridge, 1973; Sen. Berwick Prize, London Mathematical Soc., 1980. *Publications:* Applications of Sieve Methods to the Theory of Numbers, 1976; (ed with H. Halberstam) Recent Progress in Analytic Number Theory, 1981; memoirs in diverse mathematical jls. *Recreations:* classic cars; antiquities. *Address:* Rushmoor Grange, Backwell, near Bristol. *T:* Flax Bourton 2363.

HOOLEY, Frank Oswald; Research Assistant to John Tomlinson, MEP; *b* 30 Nov. 1923; *m* 1945, Doris Irene Snook; two *d. Educ:* King Edward's High Sch., Birmingham; Birmingham Univ. Admin. Asst, Birmingham Univ., 1948–52; Sheffield Univ.: Asst Registrar, 1952–65; Sen. Asst Registrar, 1965 66; Registrar, Fourah Bay Coll., Sierra Leone, 1960–62 (secondment from Sheffield); Sen. Admin. Asst, Manchester Poly., 1970–71; Chief Admin. Offr, Sheffield City Coll. of Educn, 1971–74. MP (Lab) Sheffield, Heeley, 1966–70 and Feb. 1974–1983. Chm., Parly Liaison Gp for Alternative Energy Strategies, 1978; formerly Member, Select Committees on Sci. and Technol., Overseas Aid, Foreign Affairs, and Procedure. Contested (Lab) Stratford-on-Avon, 1983. Chm., Co-ordinating Cttee, Internat. Anti-Apartheid Year, 1978. *Address:* 6 Mayland Drive, Sutton Coldfield B74 2DG. *T:* 021–353 0982.

HOOLEY, John Rouse; Chief Executive, West Sussex County Council, since 1975; Clerk to the Lieutenancy of West Sussex, since 1976; *b* 25 June 1927; *s* of Harry and Elsie Hooley; *m* 1953, Gloria Patricia Swanston; three *s* one *d. Educ:* William Hulme's Sch., Manchester; Lincoln Coll., Oxford; Manchester Univ. LLB London. Admitted Solicitor (Hons), 1952. Served Lancashire Fusiliers, 1946–48. Asst Solicitor, Chester, Carlisle and Shropshire, 1952–65; Asst Clerk, Cornwall, 1965–67; Dep. Clerk and Dep. Clerk of the Peace, W Sussex, 1967–74; County Sec., W Sussex, 1974–75. FRSA. *Recreations:*

gardening, music. *Address:* County Hall, Chichester PO19 1RQ. *T:* Chichester 777950. *Clubs:* Army and Navy, Royal Over-Seas League.

HOON, Geoffrey William; Member (Lab) Derbyshire, European Parliament, since 1984; *b* 6 Dec. 1953; *s* of Ernest and June Hoon; *m* 1981, Elaine Ann Dumelow; one *s*. *Educ:* Jesus College, Cambridge (MA). Called to the Bar, Gray's Inn, 1978. Labourer at furniture factory, 1972–73; Lectr in Law, Leeds Univ., 1976–82. In practice at Nottingham, 1982–. Vis Prof. of Law, School of Law, Univ. of Louisville, Kentucky, 1979–80. Mem., Legal Affairs Cttee, Eur. Parlt, 1984–. *Recreations:* football, cricket, running, cinema. *Address:* 10 Grosvenor Avenue, Breaston, Derbyshire DE7 3AB. *T:* Draycott 2238. *Clubs:* Long Eaton Labour; Derby Labour.

HOOPER, family name of **Baroness Hooper.**

HOOPER, Baroness *cr* 1985 (Life Peer), of Liverpool and of St James's in the City of Westminster; **Gloria Dorothy Hooper;** Baroness in Waiting, since 1985; *b* 25 May 1939; *d* of late Frances and Frederick Hooper. *Educ:* University of Southampton (BA Hons Law); Universidad Central, Quito, Ecuador (Lic. de Derecho Internacional). Admitted to Law Society, Solicitor, 1973; Partner, Taylor Garrett, 1974–84. MEP (C) Liverpool, 1979–84; Vice-Chm., Environment and Consumer Affairs Cttees, European Parlt, 1979–84; EDG Whip, European Parlt, 1982–84; contested (C) Merseyside West, European Parly elecn, 1984. FRGS 1982; Fellow, Industry and Parlt Trust, 1983. *Publications:* Cases on Company Law, 1967; Law of International Trade, 1968. *Recreations:* theatre and walking. *Address:* 11 Cleveland Row, St James's, SW1. *T:* 01–839 3929.

HOOPER, Sir Anthony (Robin Maurice), 2nd Bt *cr* 1962; *b* 26 Oct. 1918; *o s* of Sir Frederic Collins Hooper, 1st Bt, and Eglantine Irene (Bland); *S* father, 1963; *m* 1970, Cynthia (marr. diss. 1973), *yr d* of Col W. J. H. Howard, DSO. *Educ:* Radley; New Coll., Oxford. Royal Artillery, 1939–41; Asst to Hubert Philips, News Chronicle, 1941–42; Political Research Centre, 1942–44; Actor (Liverpool, Windsor, Birmingham, Oxford, London, BBC), 1944–50; temp. Civil Servant, Cabinet Office, 1950–52. Asst Design Manager, Schweppes Ltd, 1952–64; Director, Couper Gallery, 1964–68. *Recreations:* music, conversation and people. *Club:* Savile.

HOOPER, Ven. Charles German, MA; Archdeacon of Ipswich, 1963–76, now Archdeacon Emeritus; *b* 16 April 1911; 2nd *s* of A. C. Hooper, Solicitor; *m* 1936, Lilian Mary, *d* of late Sir Harold Brakspear, KCVO; one *s* one *d*. *Educ:* Lincoln Coll., Oxford (MA 2nd cl. English). Curacies: Corsham, Wilts, 1934–36; Claremont, CP, South Africa, 1936–39; Rector, Castle Combe, Wilts, 1940; Chaplain, RAFVR, 1942–46 (despatches); Rector, Sandy, Beds, 1946–53; Vicar and Rural Dean, Bishop's Stortford, Herts, 1953–63; Rector of Bildeston, Suffolk, 1963–67; Rector of St Lawrence's and St Stephen's, Ipswich, 1967–74. Chaplain to Cutlers Co., Sheffield, 1964–65, to Drapers Co., 1972–73. *Recreations:* painting in water colours, sailing. *Address:* East Green Cottage, Kelsale, Saxmundham, Suffolk. *T:* Saxmundham 2702.

See also Baron Methuen.

HOOPER, Sir Leonard (James), KCMG 1967 (CMG 1962); CBE 1951; idc; a Deputy Secretary, Cabinet Office, 1973–78, retired; *b* 23 July 1914. *Educ:* Alleyn's, Dulwich; Worcester Coll., Oxford. Joined Air Ministry, 1938, transferred Foreign Office, 1942; Imperial Defence Coll., 1953; Dir, Govt Communications HQ, 1965–73. *Recreation:* sport. *Address:* 9 Vittoria Walk, Cheltenham, Glos GL50 1TL. *T:* Cheltenham 511007. *Club:* New (Cheltenham).

HOOPER, Noel Barrie; Hon. Mr Justice Hooper; Judge of the High Court, Hong Kong, since 1981; *b* 9 Nov. 1931; twin *s* of Alfred Edward Hooper and Constance Violet Hooper; *m* 1959, Pauline Mary (*née* Irwin); two *d*. *Educ:* Prince of Wales Sch., Kenya; St Peter's Hall, Oxford (BA 1954). Called to the Bar, Gray's Inn, 1956. Advocate of High Court, Uganda, 1956–61; Magistrate, Basutoland, 1961–63 and Hong Kong, 1964–68; Sen. Magistrate, Hong Kong, 1968–73; Principal Magistrate, 1973–76; Dist Judge, 1976–81. *Recreations:* tennis, cricket, reading. *Address:* The Courts of Justice, Hong Kong. *Clubs:* MCC; Hong Kong Cricket, Victoria Recreation, Ladies' Recreation (Hong Kong).

HOOPER, Sir Robin (William John), KCMG 1968 (CMG 1954); DSO 1943; DFC 1943; HM Diplomatic Service, retired; *b* 26 July 1914; *s* of late Col John Charles Hooper, DSO, and late Irene Annie Palmer Hooper (*née* Anderson), Harewell, Faversham, Kent; *m* 1941, Constance Mildred Ayshford, *d* of late Lieut-Col Gilbert Ayshford Sanford, DSO, DL, Triley Court, Abergavenny, Mon; three *s*. *Educ:* Charterhouse; The Queen's Coll., Oxford. 3rd Sec., Foreign Office, 1938–40. Served War of 1939–45; on active service with RAF, 1940–44 (Wing-Comdr). Second Sec., HM Embassy, Paris, 1944–47; First Sec., HM Embassy, Lisbon, 1947–49; transferred to FO, 1949; Counsellor, 1950; Head of Personnel Dept, 1950–53; Counsellor, HM Embassy, Bagdad, 1953–56; Head of Perm. Under-Sec.'s Dept, FO, 1956–60; Asst Sec.-Gen. (Political), NATO, 1960–66; Ambassador to Tunisia, 1966–67; Ambassador to Southern Yemen, 1967–68; Dep. Sec., Cabinet Office, 1968–71; Ambassador to Greece, 1971–74. Chm., Anglo-Hellenic League, 1975–78. Dir, Benguela Railway Co., 1976–84. Mem., NATO Appeals Bd, 1977–85. Chevalier, Legion of Honour, 1945. Croix de Guerre, 1939–45 (2 Palms), 1945. *Address:* F3, Albany, Piccadilly, W1; Brook House, Egerton, near Ashford, Kent TN27 9AP. *Club:* Travellers'.

HOOSON, family name of **Baron Hooson.**

HOOSON, Baron *cr* 1979 (Life Peer), of Montgomery in the County of Powys and of Colomendy in the County of Clwyd; **Hugh Emlyn Hooson;** QC 1960; a Recorder of the Crown Court, since 1972 (Recorder of Swansea, 1971); *b* 26 March 1925; *s* of late Hugh and Elsie Hooson, Colomendy, Denbigh; *m* 1950, Shirley Margaret Wynne, *d* of late Sir George Hamer, CBE; two *d*. *Educ:* Denbigh Gram. Sch.; University Coll. of Wales; Gray's Inn (Bencher, 1968; Vice-Treasurer, 1985; Treasurer, 1986). Called to Bar, 1949; Wales and Chester Circuit (Leader, 1971–74); Dep. Chm., Flint QS, 1960–71; Dep. Chm., Merioneth QS, 1960–67, Chm., 1967–71; Recorder of Merthyr Tydfil, 1971. MP (L) Montgomery, 1962–79. Leader, 1966–79, Pres., 1983–86, Welsh Liberal Party. Vice-Chm. Political Cttee, North Atlantic Assembly, 1975–79. Dir (non-exec.), Laura Ashley (Holdings) Ltd, 1985–. Hon. Professorial Fellow, University Coll. of Wales, 1971. Farms Pen-y-banc farm, Llanidloes. *Address:* 1 Dr Johnson's Buildings, Temple, EC4. *T:* 01–353 9328; Summerfield, Llanidloes, Powys. *T:* Llanidloes 2298.

HOOVER, Herbert William, Jr; President, 1954–66, and Chairman of the Board, 1959–66, The Hoover Company, North Canton, Ohio; *b* 23 April 1918; *s* of late Herbert William Hoover and Grace Hoover (*née* Steele); *m* 1941, Carl Maitland Good; one *s* one *d*. *Educ:* Choate Sch., Wallingford, Conn.; Rollins Coll. (AB). Served in US Army, 1943–45. Offices held with Hoover Co.: Exec. Sales, 1941; Dir Public Relations, 1945; Asst Vice-Pres., 1948; Vice-Pres. Field Sales, 1952; Exec. Vice-Pres., 1953. The Hoover Co. Ltd, Canada: Pres., 1954; Dir, 1952; Hoover Ltd, England: Dir 1954, Chm. 1956. Hoover Inc., Panama: Dir and Pres., 1955; Hoover (America Latina) SA, Panama: Dir and Pres., 1955; Hoover Mexicana, Mexico: Dir and Pres., 1955; Hoover Industrial y Comercial SA, Colombia: Dir and Pres., 1960; Hoover Worldwide Corp., NY City: Pres. and Chm., 1960; Dir, S. A. Hoover, France, 1965. Past Regional Vice-Chm., US Cttee for the UN. Dir, Miami Heart Inst.; Mem., Bd of Trustees, Univ. of Miami. Hon. LLD, Mount Union Coll., 1959. Chevalier Légion d'Honneur, France, 1965. *Address:* 70 Park Drive, Bal Harbour, Fla 33154, USA.

HOPCROFT, George William; HM Diplomatic Service, retired; consultant on international relations; *b* 30 Sept. 1927; *s* of late Frederick Hopcroft and Dorothy Gertrude (*née* Bourne); *m* 1951, Audrey Joan Rodd; three *s* one *d*. *Educ:* Chiswick Grammar Sch.; London Univ. (BCom); Brasenose Coll., Oxford; INSEAD, Fontainebleau. Auditor with Wm R. Warner, 1946; entered Export Credits Guarantee Dept, 1946; Asst Trade Comr, Madras, 1953–57; Sen. Underwriter, ECGD, 1957–65; joined FO, 1965; First Sec. (Commercial), Amman, 1965–69; First Sec. (Econ.), Bonn, 1969–71; First Sec. (Comm.), Kuala Lumpur, 1971–75; FCO, 1975–78; Counsellor (Comm. and Econ.), Bangkok, 1978–81; FCO 1981. Lloyd's Underwriter, 1981–. Founder Mem., Export and Overseas Trade Adv. Panel (EOTAP), 1982–; operational expert in for. affairs, attached to Govt of Belize, 1982–83. *Recreations:* leisure and circumnavigation; athletics (Civil Service 880 yds champion, 1947). *Address:* Ffrogs, Pond Road, Hook Heath, Woking, Surrey GU22 0JT. *T:* Woking 5121. *Clubs:* Royal Commonwealth Society; Yvonne Arnaud Theatre; Thames Valley Harriers (Vice-Pres., 1965–); British (Bangkok).

HOPE, family name of **Baron Glendevon, Marquess of Linlithgow** and **Baron Rankeillour.**

HOPE, Maj.-Gen. Adrian Price Webley, CB 1961; CBE 1952; *b* 21 Jan. 1911; *s* of late Adm. H. W. W. Hope, CB, CVO, DSO; *m* 1958, Mary Elizabeth, *e d* of Graham Partridge, Cotham Lodge, Newport, Pembrokeshire; no *c*. *Educ:* Winchester Coll.; RMC, Sandhurst. 2/Lt KOSB, 1931; Adjt, 1/KOSB, 1937–38; Staff Capt. A, Palestine, Egypt, 1938–40; DAQMG (Plans) Egypt, 1940–41; Instructor, Staff Coll., 1941; AQMG, Egypt, Sicily, Italy, 1941–44; Col Asst Quartermaster, Plans, India, 1945; Brig., Quartermaster, SE Asia, 1946; Comdt Sch. of Military Admin., 1947–48; Instructor, jssc, 1948–50; DQMG, GHQ, MELF, 1951–53; Student, idc, 1954; Brig. Quartermaster (ops), War Office, 1955–57; BGS, HQ, BAOR, 1958–59; MGA, GHQ, FARELF, 1959–61; Dir of Equipment Policy, War Office, 1961–64; Dep. Master-Gen. of the Ordnance, Ministry of Defence, 1964–66; retd 1966. *Address:* Monks Place, Charlton Horethorne, Sherborne, Dorset. *Club:* Army and Navy.

HOPE, Alan, JP; Leader, West Midlands County Council Opposition Group (C), since 1981; *b* 5 Jan. 1933; *s* of George Edward Thomas Hope and Vera Hope; *m* 1960, Marilyn Dawson; one *s* one *d*. *Educ:* George Dixon Grammar Sch., Birmingham. Councillor, Birmingham CC, 1964–73; West Midlands County Council: Councillor, 1973; Leader, 1980–81; Chairman: Trading Standards, 1977–79; Finance, 1979–80. JP Birmingham 1974. *Address:* Whitehaven, Rosemary Drive, Little Aston Park, Sutton Coldfield, West Midlands B74 3AG. *T:* 021–353 3011. *Club:* Royal Commonwealth Society; Birmingham (Birmingham).

HOPE, Sir Archibald (Philip), 17th Bt of Craighall, *cr* 1628; OBE 1945; DFC 1940; AE 1943; retired 1977; *b* 27 March 1912; *s* of 16th Bt and Hon. Mary Bruce, OBE, JP Midlothian, *e d* of 10th Lord Balfour of Burleigh; *S* father, 1924; *m* 1938, Ruth, *y d* of Carl Davis, Fryern, Storrington, Sussex; two *s*. *Educ:* Eton; Balliol Coll., Oxford. BA 1934; ACA 1939; FCA 1960; Mem. of Queen's Body Guard for Scotland (Royal Company of Archers). Served, RAFO, 1931–35; 601 (County of London) Sqdn AAF, 1935–39. Served War of 1939–45 (despatches twice, DFC, OBE). Wing Comdr (acting Group Capt.), AAF. Joined Airwork, 1945; Dir, 1951; resigned, June 1956; Dir, D. Napier & Son Ltd, 1956–61; Dir, Napier Aero Engines Ltd, 1961–68; Chief Exec., Napier Aero Engines Ltd, 1962–68; English Electric Co., 1968–70; Gp Treasurer, GEC Ltd, 1970–77. Mem., Air Transport Users Cttee, CAA, 1973–79, Dep. Chm. 1974–77, Chm. 1977–79. Chm., The Air League, 1965–68. FRAeS 1968. *Heir:* *s* John Carl Alexander Hope [*b* 10 June 1939; *m* 1968, Merle Pringle, *d* of Robert Douglas, Southside, Holbrook, Ipswich; one *s* one *d*]. *Address:* The Manor House, Somerford Keynes, near Cirencester, Glos GL7 6DL. *T:* Cirencester 861250. *Clubs:* Royal Air Force; New (Edinburgh); Nairobi (Nairobi).

HOPE, Bob, (Leslie Townes Hope), CBE (Hon.) 1976; Congressional Gold Medal, US, 1963; film, stage, radio, TV actor; *b* England, 29 May 1903; family migrated to US, 1907; *m* 1934, Dolores Reade; two adopted *s* two adopted *d*. *Educ:* Fairmont Gram. Sch. and High Sch., Cleveland, O. Started career as dance instructor, clerk, amateur boxer; formed dancing act for Fatty Arbuckle review. After Mid-West tours formed own Company in Chicago; toured New York and joined RKO Vaudeville and Keith Circuit; first important stage parts include: Ballyhoo, 1932; Roberta, 1933; Ziegfield Follies, 1935; first radio part, 1934. Entered films, 1938. *Films include:* Big Broadcast of 1938; Some Like It Hot; The Cat and the Canary; Road to Singapore; The Ghost Breakers; Road to Zanzibar; Star Spangled Rhythm; Nothing but the Truth; Louisiana Purchase; My Favorite Blonde; Road to Morocco; Let's Face It; Road to Utopia; Monsieur Beaucaire; My Favorite Brunette; They Got Me Covered; The Princess and the Pirate; Road to Rio; Where There's Life; The Great Lover; My Favorite Spy; Road to Bali; Son of Paleface; Here Come the Girls; Casanova's Big Night; The Seven Little Foys; The Iron Petticoat; That Certain Feeling; Beau James; The Facts of Life; Bachelor in Paradise; The Road to Hong Kong; Call Me Bwana; A Global Affair; Boy, Did I Get a Wrong Number!; Eight on the Run; How to Commit Marriage; Cancel My Reservation. *TV Series:* The Bob Hope Show, 1950–; numerous guest appearances. Five Royal Command Performances. Awarded 44 honorary degrees; more than a thousand awards and citations for humanitarian and professional services. *Publications:* They've Got Me Covered, 1941; I Never Left Home, 1944; So This is Peace, 1946; This One's on Me, 1954; I Owe Russia $1200, 1963; Five Women I Love, 1966; The Last Christmas Show, 1974; Road to Hollywood, 1977; Confessions of a Hooker, 1985. *Address:* Hope Enterprises, Inc., 3808 Riverside Drive, Burbank, Calif 91505, USA.

HOPE, Sir (Charles) Peter, KCMG 1972 (CMG 1956); TD 1945; Ambassador to Mexico, 1968–72; *b* 29 May 1912; *s* of G. L. N. Hope and H. M. V. Riddell, Weetwood, Mayfield, Sussex; *m* 1936, H. M. Turner, *d* of late G. L. Turner, company director; three *s*. *Educ:* Oratory Sch., Reading; London and Cambridge Univs. BSc (Hons), ACGI. Asst War Office, 1938; RA, TA, 1939; served until 1946 (TD). Transferred to Foreign Office and posted HM Embassy, Paris, as Temp. First Sec., 1946; transferred to United Nations Dept, Foreign Office, 1950; to HM Embassy, Bonn, as Counsellor, 1953; Foreign Office Spokesman (Head of News Dept Foreign Office), 1956–59; Minister, HM Embassy, Madrid, 1959–62; Consul-General, Houston, USA, 1963–64; Minister and Alternate UK Rep. to UN, 1965–68. Mem., Acad. of International Law. Pres., British Assoc. of Sovereign Military Order of Malta, 1983–; KStJ 1984. Grand Cross: Order of the Aztec Eagle, 1972; Constantine Order of St George, 1981; Grand Cross, Order of Malta, 1984; Grand Officer, Order of Merito Militense, 1975. *Recreations:* shooting and fishing. *Address:* North End House, Heyshott, Midhurst, Sussex. *Club:* White's.

HOPE, Rt. Rev. David Michael; *see* Wakefield, Bishop of.

HOPE, James Arthur David, QC (Scotland) 1978; *b* 27 June 1938; *s* of Arthur Henry Cecil Hope, OBE, WS, Edinburgh and Muriel Ann Neilson Hope (*née* Collie); *m* 1966, Katharine Mary Kerr, *d* of W. Mark Kerr, WS, Edinburgh; twin *s* one *d*. *Educ:* Edinburgh Acad.; Rugby Sch.; St John's Coll., Cambridge (Scholarship 1956, BA 1962, MA 1978); Edinburgh Univ. (LLB 1965). National Service, Seaforth Highlanders, 1957–59 (Lieutenant 1959). Admitted Faculty of Advocates, 1965; Standing Junior Counsel in Scotland to Board of Inland Revenue, 1974–78; Advocate-Depute, 1978–82. Chm., Med. Appeal Tribunal, 1985–; Legal Chm., Pensions Appeal Tribunal, 1985–. *Publications:* (ed jtly) Gloag & Henderson's Introduction to the Law of Scotland, 7th edn, 1968, asst editor, 8th edn, 1980; (ed jtly) Armour on Valuation for Rating, 4th edn 1971, 5th edn 1985. *Recreations:* walking, ornithology, music. *Address:* 34 India Street, Edinburgh EH3 6HB. *T:* 031–225 8245. *Club:* New (Edinburgh).

HOPE, Laurence Frank, OBE 1968; HM Diplomatic Service, retired; HM Consul General, Seattle, 1975–76; *b* 18 May 1918; *y s* of late Samuel Vaughan Trevylian Hope and late Ellen Edith Hope (*née* Cooler); *m* 1940, Doris Phyllis Rosa Hulbert; one *s* one *d*. *Educ:* County Grammar Sch., Lewes, Sussex. Served War, reaching rank of Major, in British Army (12th (2nd City of London Regt) Royal Fusiliers, TA and York and Lancaster Regt); Indian Army (7th Rajput Regt); Mil. Govt of Germany (Economic Div.), 1939–46. Bd of Trade, London, 1946–47; Asst Brit. Trade Comr, Pretoria, 1947–51; Cape Town, 1951–53; Bd of Trade, London, 1953–56; British Trade Comr, Sydney, 1956–60; Canberra, 1960–61; Lahore, 1961–63; Singapore, 1964; transferred to HM Diplomatic Service; Head of Commercial Section, High Commn, Singapore, 1965–68; Counsellor (Economic and Commercial), Lagos, 1969–72; HM Consul-Gen., Gothenburg, 1972–75. *Recreations:* oil painting, reading. *Address:* 22 Cranford Avenue, Exmouth, Devon EX8 2HU. *Club:* Oriental.
See also M. L. H. Hope.

HOPE, Marcus Laurence Hulbert; HM Diplomatic Service; Counsellor and Head of Chancery, Berne, since 1985; *b* 2 Feb. 1942; *s* of Laurence Frank Hope, *qv*; *m* 1980, Uta Maria Luise Müller-Unverfehrt; one *s*. *Educ:* City of London Sch.; Sydney C of E Grammar Sch.; Univ. of Sydney (BA); Univ. of London (BA Hons). Joined HM Diplomatic Service, 1965; Third Sec., CRO, 1965; MECAS, 1966; Second Sec., Tripoli, 1968; FCO, 1970; First Sec., 1972; Head of Chancery, Dubai, 1974; First Sec. (Commercial), Bonn, 1976; FCO, 1980; NATO Defence Coll., Rome, 1984; Counsellor, Beirut, 1984–85. *Recreation:* classical guitar. *Address:* c/o Foreign and Commonwealth Office, King Charles Street, SW1. *Club:* Carlton.

HOPE, Sir Peter; *see* Hope, Sir C. P.

HOPE, Sir Robert Holms-Kerr, 3rd Bt *cr* 1932; *b* 12 April 1900; *s* of Sir Harry Hope, 1st Bt and Margaret Binnie Holms-Kerr; *S* brother, 1979; *m* 1928, Eleanor (*d* 1967), *d* of late Very Rev. Marshall Lang, DD, Whittingehame, East Lothian. *Heir:* none. *Address:* Old Bridge House, Broxmouth, Dunbar, East Lothian.

HOPE-DUNBAR, Sir David, 8th Bt *cr* 1664; *b* 13 July 1941; *o s* of Sir Basil Douglas Hope-Dunbar, 7th Bt, and of his 2nd wife, Edith Maude Maclaren, *d* of late Malcolm Cross; *S* father, 1961; *m* 1971, Kathleen, *yr d* of late J. T. Kenrick; one *s* two *d*. *Educ:* Eton; Royal Agricultural College, Cirencester. Qualified: ARICS 1966. *Recreations:* fishing, shooting. *Heir:* *s* Charles Hope-Dunbar, *b* 11 March 1975. *Address:* Banks Farm, Kirkcudbright. *T:* Kirkcudbright 30424.

HOPE JOHNSTONE, family name of **Earl of Annandale and Hartfell.**

HOPE-JONES, Ronald Christopher, CMG 1969; HM Diplomatic Service, retired; *b* 5 July 1920; *s* of William Hope-Jones and Winifred Coggin; *m* 1944, Pamela Hawker; two *s* one *d*. *Educ:* Eton (scholar); King's Coll., Cambridge (scholar). Served with HM Forces, 1940–45. 3rd Sec., Foreign Office, 1946, Paris, 1947; 2nd Sec., Beirut, 1949; 1st Sec., FO, 1952; Head of Chancery and Consul, Quito, 1955; Commercial Sec., Budapest, 1959; Head of Chancery, 1960; FO, 1961, Counsellor, 1963; UK Rep. to Internat. Atomic Energy Agency, Vienna, 1964–67; FCO 1967; Head of Disarmament Dept, 1967–70; Head of N African Dept, 1970–71; Counsellor, Brasilia, 1972–73; Ambassador in La Paz, 1973–77. *Address:* Wellfield House, Mill Lane, Headley, Bordon, Hants. *T:* Bordon 2793.

HOPE-MORLEY, family name of **Baron Hollenden.**

HOPE-WALLACE, (Dorothy) Jaqueline, CBE 1958; *b* 1909; 2nd *d* of Charles Nugent Hope-Wallace and Mabel Chaplin. *Educ:* Lady Margaret Hall, Oxford. Entered Ministry of Labour, 1932; transferred to National Assistance Board, 1934; Under-Sec., 1958–65; Under-Sec., Min. of Housing and Local Govt, 1965–69, retired. Commonwealth Fellow, 1952–53. Comr, Public Works Loan Bd, 1974–78; Member Board: Corby Develt Corp., 1969–80; Governors, UCH, 1970–74; Inst. for Recorded Sound, 1971–74, 1979–83 (Chm. 1975–76); Nat. Corp. for Care of Old People (now Centre for Policy on Ageing), 1973–81 (Chm., 1978–80); Mem., Nat. Sound Archive Adv. Cttee, 1983–84; Chm., Friends of UCH, 1973–85. *Recreations:* arts, travel, gardening. *Address:* 17 Ashley Court, Morpeth Terrace, SW1; Whitegate, Alciston, East Sussex.

HOPETOUN, Earl of; Adrian John Charles Hope; Stockbroker; *b* 1 July 1946; *s* and *heir* of Marquess of Linlithgow, *qv*; *m* 1968, Anne (marr. diss. 1978), *e d* of A. Leveson, Hall Place, Hants; two *s*; *m* 1980, Peta C. Binding; one *s* one *d*. *Educ:* Eton. Joined HM Navy, 1965. *Heir:* *s* Viscount Aithrie, *qv*. *Address:* Hopetoun House, South Queensferry, West Lothian. *Clubs:* Turf, White's.

HOPEWELL, John Prince; Consultant Surgeon (Urology), Royal Free Hospital, since 1957; *b* 1 Dec. 1920; *s* of Samuel Prince and Wilhelmina Hopewell; *m* 1st, 1959, Dr Natalie Bogdan (*d* 1975); one *s* one *d*; 2nd, 1984, Dr Rosemary Radley-Smith. *Educ:* Bradfield Coll., Berks; King's Coll. Hosp., London. RAMC, 1945–48. Postgrad. education at King's Coll. Hosp. and Brighton, Sussex, and Hosp. for Sick Children, Gt Ormond Street. Formerly Cnslt Surgeon, Putney Hosp. and Frimley Hosp., Surrey. Mem., Hampstead DHA, 1982–85; Chm., Camden Div., BMA, 1985–; Past Chairman: Med. Cttee Royal Free Hosp.; N Camden Dist Med. Cttee. Founder Mem., British Transplantation Soc., 1972; Member: Internat. Soc. of Urology; British Assoc. Urol. Surgeons; Pres., Chelsea Clinical Soc., 1986–; Past President: Section of Urology, RSM, 1982–83; Fellowship of Postgrad. Medicine. Founder Mem., Assoc. of Univ. Hospitals. Hon. Mem., NY Section, AUA. Hunterian Prof., RCS, 1958. *Publications:* contribs to Surgical Aspects of Medicine, Modern Treatment Year Book, and various medical journals. *Recreations:* photography, travel. *Address:* 11 Harley House, Upper Harley Street, NW1. *T:* 01–935 5291.

HOPKIN, Sir Bryan; *see* Hopkin, Sir W. A. B.

HOPKIN, David Armand; Chief Metropolitan Stipendiary Magistrate, since 1982; *b* 10 Jan. 1922; *s* of Daniel and Edmée Hopkin; *m* 1948, Doris Evelyn (*née* Whitaker); one *s* three *d*. *Educ:* St Paul's Sch., W Kensington; University Coll., Aberystwyth; Corpus Christi Coll., Cambridge (BA). Called to the Bar, Gray's Inn, 1949. Served in Army, 1942–47, Hon. Major, 1947. Member of Staff of Director of Public Prosecutions, 1950–70; Metropolitan Stipendiary Magistrate, 1970–. Vice-Pres., British Boxing Board of Control, 1986–. *Recreations:* fencing, tennis. *Address:* 8 Crane Grove, N7. *T:* 01–607 0349.

HOPKIN, John Raymond; His Honour Judge Hopkin; a Circuit Judge, since 1979; *b* 23 June 1935; *s* of George Raymond Buxton Hopkin and Muriel Hopkin; *m* 1965, Susan Mary Limb; one *s* one *d*. *Educ:* King's Sch., Worcester. Called to Bar, Middle Temple, 1958; in practice at the Bar, 1959–. A Recorder of the Crown Court, 1978–79. *Recreations:* showing and judging pedigree dogs, fell walking and climbing, gardening. *Address:* c/o The Crown Court, Canal Street, Nottingham NG1 7EJ. *Clubs:* Kennel; Nottingham and Notts Services.

HOPKIN, Sir (William Aylsham) Bryan, Kt 1971; CBE 1961; Regional Representative for Wales, Charter for Jobs, since 1985; *b* 7 Dec. 1914; *s* of late William Hopkin and Lilian Hopkin (*née* Cottelle); *m* 1938, Renée Ricour; two *s*. *Educ:* Barry (Glam.) County Sch.; St John's Coll., Cambridge (Hon. Fellow, 1982); Manchester Univ. Ministry of Health, 1938–41; Prime Minister's Statistical Branch, 1941–45; Royal Commn on Population, 1945–48; Econ. Sect., Cabinet Office, 1948–50; Central Statistical Office, 1950–52; Dir, Nat. Inst. of Econ. and Soc. Research, 1952–57; Sec., Council on Prices, Productivity, and Incomes, 1957–58; Dep. Dir, Econ. Sect., HM Treasury, 1958–65; Econ. Planning Unit, Mauritius, 1965; Min. of Overseas Devlt, 1966–67; Dir-Gen. of Economic Planning, ODM, 1967–69; Dir-Gen., DEA, 1969; Dep. Chief Econ. Adviser, HM Treasury, 1970–72; Prof. of Econs, UC Cardiff, 1972–82 (on leave of absence, Head of Govt Economic Service and Chief Economic Advr, HM Treasury, 1974–77). Mem., Commonwealth Develt Corp., 1972–74. Chm., Manpower Services Cttee for Wales, 1978–79. *Address:* Aberthin House, Aberthin, near Cowbridge, South Glamorgan CF7 7HB. *T:* Cowbridge 2303.

HOPKINS, Alan Cripps Nind, MA Cantab, LLB Yale; Chairman, Wellman Engineering Corporation, 1972–83 (Director, 1968); *b* 27 Oct. 1926; *s* of late Rt Hon. Sir Richard V. N. Hopkins, GCB and Lady Hopkins; *m* 1st, 1954, Margaret Cameron (from whom divorced, 1962), *d* of E. C. Bolton, Waco, Texas, USA; one *s*; 2nd, 1962, Venetia, *d* of Sir Edward Wills, 4th Bt; twin *s*. *Educ:* Winchester Coll.; King's Coll., Cambridge; Yale University Law Sch., USA. BA Cantab 1947, MA 1950; LLB Yale 1952. Barrister, Inner Temple, 1948. MP (C and Nat L) Bristol North-East, 1959–66; PPS to Financial Sec. to Treasury, 1960–62. Dir, Dexion-Comino Internat. Ltd, 1973–85. *Recreation:* travelling. *Address:* Chalet Topaze, 1972 Anzere, Valais, Switzerland. *T:* 027–38–16–51. *Club:* Brooks's.

HOPKINS, Anthony; actor since 1961; *b* Port Talbot, S Wales, 31 Dec. 1937; *s* of Richard and Muriel Hopkins; *m* 1st, 1968, Petronella (marr. diss. 1972); one *d*; 2nd, 1973, Jennifer, *d* of Ronald Lynton. *Educ:* Cowbridge, S Wales; RADA; Cardiff Coll. of Drama. London debut as Metellus Cimber in Julius Caesar, Royal Court, 1964; National Theatre: Juno and the Paycock, A Flea in Her Ear, 1966; The Dance of Death, The Three Sisters, As You Like It (all male cast), 1967; The Architect and the Emperor of Assyria, A Woman Killed with Kindness, Coriolanus, 1971; Macbeth, 1972; Pravda, 1985 (Observer Award, Lawrence Olivier Awards, 1985; (jtly) Best Actor, British Theatre Assoc. and Drama Magazine Awards, 1985; Royal Variety Club Award, 1985). Other stage appearances include: The Taming of the Shrew, Chichester, 1972; Equus, USA, 1974–75, 1977; The Tempest, LA, 1979; Old Times, New York, 1984; The Lonely Road, Old Vic, 1985. *Films:* The Lion in Winter, 1967; The Looking Glass War, 1968; Hamlet, 1969; When Eight Bells Toll, 1971; Young Winston, 1972; A Doll's House, 1973; The Girl from Petrovka, 1973; All Creatures Great and Small, 1974; Dark Victory, 1975; Audrey Rose, 1976; A Bridge Too Far, 1976; International Velvet, 1977; Magic, 1978; The Elephant Man, 1980; A Change of Seasons, 1980; The Bounty, 1984; The Good Father, 1986; 84 Charing Cross Road, 1986. *American television films:* QB VII, 1973; Bruno Hauptmann in The Lindbergh Kidnapping Case, 1976; The Voyage of the Mayflower, 1979; The Bunker, The Acts of Peter and Paul, 1980; The Hunchback of Notre Dame, 1981; The Arch of Triumph, 1984; Hollywood Wives, 1984; Guilty Conscience, 1984; *BBC television:* Pierre Bezuhov in serial, War and Peace, 1972; Kean, 1978; Othello, 1981; Little Eyolf, 1982; Guy Burgess in Blunt (film), 1986; Indep. TV performances incl. A Married Man (series), 1983. Best TV Actor Award, SFTA, 1973; Best Actor Award, NY Drama Desk, 1975; Outer Critics Circle Award, 1975; American Authors and Celebrities Forum Award, 1975; Emmy award, 1976 and 1981; LA Drama Critics' Award, 1977. *Recreations:* reading, walking, piano. *Address:* c/o Peggy Thompson, 7 High Park Road, Kew, Surrey TW9 4BL.

HOPKINS, Anthony Strother, BSc(Econ); FCA; Under Secretary, Department of Economic Development, Northern Ireland, since 1982; *b* 17 July 1940; *s* of Strother Smith Hopkins, OBE, and Alice Roberta Hopkins; *m* 1965, Dorothy Moira (*née* McDonough); one *s* two *d*. *Educ:* Campbell Coll., Belfast; Queen's University of Belfast (BScEcon). Manager, Thomson McLintock & Co., Chartered Accountants, London, 1966–70; Principal, Dept of Commerce, N Ireland, 1970–74; Northern Ireland Development Agency, 1975–82, Chief Executive, 1979–82; Dep. Chief Executive, Industrial Development Board for N Ireland, 1982–, and Under Secretary, Dept of Economic Development for N Ireland, 1982–. *Recreations:* golf, tennis, sailing. *Club:* Royal Belfast Golf (Co. Down).

HOPKINS, Antony, CBE 1976; composer and conductor; *b* 21 March 1921; *s* of late Hugh and of Marjorie Reynolds; adopted *c* of Major and Mrs T. H. C. Hopkins since 1925; *m* 1947, Alison Purves. *Educ:* Berkhamsted Sch.; Royal Coll. of Music. Won Chappell Gold Medal and Cobbett Prize at RCM, 1942; shortly became known as composer of incidental music for radio; numerous scores composed for BBC (2 for programmes winning Italia prize for best European programme of the year, 1952 and 1957). Composed music for many productions at Stratford and in West End. Dir, Intimate Opera Co., 1952–, and has written a number of chamber operas for this group; *ballets:* Etude and Café des Sports, for Sadler's Wells; *films* (*music*) *include:* Pickwick Papers, Decameron Nights, Cast a Dark Shadow, Billy Budd; John and the Magic Music Man (narr. and orch.; Grand Prix, Besançon Film Festival, 1976). Regular broadcaster with a series of programmes entitled Talking about Music. Formerly Gresham Prof. of Music, City Univ. Hon. FRCM 1964; Hon. RAM 1979; Hon. Fellow, Robinson Coll., Cambridge, 1980. DUniv. Stirling, 1980. *Publications:* Talking about Symphonies, 1961; Talking about Concertos, 1964; Music All Around Me, 1968; Lucy and Peterkin, 1968; Talking about Sonatas, 1971; Downbeat Guide, 1977; Understanding Music, 1979; The Nine Symphonies of Beethoven, 1980; Songs for Swinging Golfers, 1981; Sounds of Music, 1982; Beating Time (autobiog.), 1982; Pathway to Music, 1983; Musicamusings, 1983; The Concertgoer's Companion: Vol. I, 1984; Vol. II, 1985. *Recreations:* motoring, golf. *Address:* Woodyard Cottage, Ashridge, Berkhamsted, Herts. *T:* Little Gaddesden 2257.

HOPKINS, David Rex Eugène; Director of Quality Assurance/Administration, Ministry of Defence, since 1983; *b* 29 June 1930; *s* of Frank Hopkins and Vera (*née* Wimhurst); *m* 1955, Brenda Joyce Phillips; two *s* one *d* (one *d* decd). *Educ:* Worthing High Sch.; Christ

Church, Oxford (MA 1950; Dip. in Econs and Pol. Science, 1951). National Service Commn, RA, 1952; service in Korea. Asst Principal, WO, 1953; Principal, WO, 1957, MoD 1964; Asst Sec., 1967; Home Office, 1969–70; RCDS, 1971; Defence Equipment Secretariat, 1972; Dir, Headquarters Security, 1975; Financial Counsellor, UK Delegn to NATO, 1981–83. *Recreations:* church work, archaeological digging, fell-walking, military history. *Address:* 16 Hitherwood Drive, SE19 1XB. *T:* 01–670 7504.

HOPKINS, Douglas Edward, DMus (London); FRAM, FRCO, FGSM; Examiner, Royal Schools of Music, since 1937; Conductor, Stock Exchange Male Voice Choir, since 1956; *b* 23 Dec. 1902; *s* of Edward and Alice Hopkins; unmarried. *Educ:* St Paul's Cathedral Choir Sch.; Dulwich Coll.; Guildhall Sch. of Music (Ernest Palmer and Corporation Scholarships); Royal Academy of Music. Organist, Christ Church, Greyfriars, EC, 1921; Sub-Organist, St Paul's Cathedral, 1927; Prof., Royal Acad. of Music, 1937–78; Master of the Music, Peterborough Cathedral, 1946; Organist, Canterbury Cathedral, 1953–55; Musical Dir, St Felix Sch., Southwold, 1956–65; Organist, St Marylebone Parish Church, 1965–71; Founder, and Dir 1962–74, Holiday Course for Organists; Organist, Royal Meml Chapel, RMA Sandhurst, 1971–76. Since 1957 has done many overseas tours, inc. NZ, Africa, Malaysia, W Indies, Singapore and Hong Kong. Conductor of Handel Soc., 1928–33, and, since that, of various other musical societies. Liveryman, Worshipful Co. of Musicians. *Address:* 244 Mytchett Road, Mytchett, Camberley, Surrey GU16 6AF.

HOPKINS, Admiral Sir Frank (Henry Edward), KCB 1964 (CB 1961); DSO 1942; DSC 1941; DL; Commander-in-Chief, Portsmouth, 1966–67; retired, 1967; *b* 23 June 1910; *s* of late E. F. L. Hopkins and Sybil Mary Walrond; *m* 1939, Lois Barbara, *d* of J. R. Cook, Cheam, Surrey. *Educ:* Stubbington House; Nautical Coll., Pangbourne. Joined Navy as Cadet, 1927; served in HM Ships: London, Tiger, Whitehall, Vortigern, Winchester, Courageous, Furious, 1928–38; War of 1939–45 (despatches, 1941), in No 826 Fleet Air Arm Squadron (Formidable), 1940–41, and comd No 830 Sqdn, 1941–42, based on Malta; USS Hancock and USS Intrepid, American Pacific Fleet, 1944–45; took part in following operations: Dunkirk, air operations over Europe, Battle of Matapan, evacuation of Crete, bombardment of Tripoli, Malta, Battle of Leyte Gulf; Korean War, Theseus, 1950 (despatches); Capt., 1950; Dir of Air Warfare, Admiralty, comd Myngs, Tyrian, Grenville, and Ark Royal, 1954–58; comd RNC Dartmouth, 1958–60; Rear-Adm. 1960; Flag Officer: Flying Training, 1960–62; Aircraft Carriers, 1962–63; Vice-Adm. 1962; a Lord Comr of the Admiralty, Deputy Chief of Naval Staff and Fifth Sea Lord, 1963–64; Dep. Chief of Naval Staff, MoD, 1964–66; Adm. 1966. DL Devon, 1982. American Legion of Merit, 1948; Comdr, Order of Sword, Sweden, 1954. *Recreations:* sailing, golf. *Address:* Kingswear Court Lodge, Kingswear, S Devon. *Clubs:* Naval and Military, Royal Yacht Squadron; Royal Naval Sailing Assoc.; Britannia Yacht.

HOPKINS, Prof. Harold Horace, FRS 1973; Emeritus Professor, University of Reading, since 1984 (Professor of Applied Optics, 1967–84 and Head of Department of Physics, 1977–80); *b* 6 Dec. 1918; *s* of William Ernest and Teresa Ellen Hopkins; *m* 1950, Christine Dove Ridsdale; three *s* one *d. Educ:* Gateway Sch., Leicester; Univs of Leicester and London. BSc, PhD, DSc, FInstP. Physicist, Taylor, Taylor & Hobson, 1939–42; Royal Engrs, 1942; Physicist: MAP, 1942–45; W. Watson & Sons, 1945–47; Research Fellow, then Reader in Optics, Imperial Coll., 1947–67. Hon. Papers Sec. and Mem. Council, Physical Soc., 1947–59; President: Internat. Commn for Optics, 1969–72; Maths and Phys Sect., British Assoc., 1977. Thomas Young Orator, Inst. of Physics, 1960. Fellow: Optical Soc. of Amer., 1972; Soc. for Photo-Instrumentation Engrs, 1975; Hon. Member: Amer. Assoc. of Gynæcologic Laparoscopy, 1977; Brit. Assoc. of Urological Surgeons, 1977; Brit. Soc. for Gastroenterology, 1980; Hon. FRCS, 1979; Hon. FRCP, 1983. Hon. DrèsSc Besançon, 1960; Hon. DSc: Bristol, 1980; Liverpool, 1982; Reading, 1986; Hon. Dr Med. Munich, 1980. Ives Medal, Optical Soc. of Amer., 1978; St Peter's Medal, Brit. Assoc. of Urological Surgeons, 1979; First Distinguished Service Award, Amer. Soc. for Gastrointestinal Endoscopy, 1980; Gold Medal, Internat. Soc. for Optical Engineering, 1982; Pro-Meritate Medal, Internat. Soc. of Urologic Endoscopy, 1984; Rumford Medal, Royal Soc., 1984. Inventions incl. zoom lenses, fibre optics and medical endoscopes. *Publications:* Wave Theory of Aberrations, 1951; (with J. G. Gow) Handbook of Urological Endoscopy, 1978; papers in Proc. Royal Soc., Proc. Phys. Soc., Optica Acta, Jl Optical Soc. Amer. *Recreations:* keyboard music, sailing, languages, woodwork. *Address:* 26 Cintra Avenue, Reading, Berks. *T:* Reading 871913.

HOPKINS, Sir James S. R. S.; *see* Scott-Hopkins.

HOPKINS, John; writer; *b* 27 Jan. 1931. *Plays:* This Story of Yours, Royal Court, 1968, Long Wharf Theatre, 1981; Find Your Way Home, Open Space, 1970, NY, 1974; Economic Necessity, Haymarket Theatre, Leicester, 1973; Next of Kin, Nat. Theatre, 1974; Losing Time, Manhattan Theatre Club, 1979, Deutsches Schauspielhaus, 1984; Valedictorian, Williston-Northampton Sch., 1982; *TV:* includes: Talking to a Stranger (quartet), 1968; That Quiet Earth; Walk into the Dark; Some Distant Shadow; The Greeks and their Gifts, 1966; A Story to Frighten the Children, 1976; Fathers and Families (sextet), 1977; scripts for Z-Cars (series); (with John Le Carré) Smiley's People (series), 1982; adaptations of classic novels; *film scripts:* The Offence, 1973; Murder by Decree, 1979. *Publications:* Talking to a Stranger, 1967; This Story of Yours, 1969; Find Your Way Home, 1971; Losing Time, 1982. *Address:* Hazelnut Farm, RFD1, Fairfield, Conn 06430, USA.

HOPKINS, Julian; *see* Hopkins, R. J.

HOPKINS, Keith; *see* Hopkins, M. K.

HOPKINS, Rev. Canon Leslie Freeman; Canon Residentiary and Treasurer, Liverpool Cathedral, 1964–79, now Canon Emeritus; *b* 1914; *o s* of Joseph Freeman and Mabel Hopkins, London; *m* 1940, Violet, *d* of Edgar Crick, Crayford; three *s* one *d. Educ:* City of London Sch. (Abbott Schol.); Exeter Coll., Oxford (Squire Schol. and Exhib.); Wells Theological Coll. BA 1937, 2nd Cl. Hon. Mods, 2nd Cl. Hons Theology; MA 1940; BD Oxon 1953. Deacon 1938, priest 1939; Curate of Crayford 1938, Nympsfield 1942; Priest-in-Charge, Holy Trinity, Charlton, 1942–45; Vicar of St Chrysostom's, Peckham, 1945–56; Surrogate, 1946–62; Vicar of All Saints, Battersea Park, 1956–62; Chief Inspector of Schools, Dio. of Southwark, 1954–62; Dir of Religious Education, Dio. of Liverpool, 1962–72; Chaplain of Josephine Butler Coll., 1962–72; Governor of Chester Coll., St Elphin's, Darley Dale and of Grammar Schs; Visiting Lectr in Religious Education; Mem. of Council: Guild of St Raphael, 1944–; USPG. Liveryman, Glass Sellers Co.; Freeman, City of London. FRSA 1982. *Publications:* contribs to press and Syllabuses of Religious Education. *Recreations:* architecture and music. *Address:* Laurel Cottage, Peasmarsh, Rye, Sussex. *T:* Peasmarsh 559.

HOPKINS, Prof. (Morris) Keith, FBA 1984; Professor of Ancient History, University of Cambridge, and Fellow of King's College, since 1985; *b* 20 June 1934; *s* of late Albert Thomas Hopkins and Hélène Dorothy Pratt; *m* 1963, Juliet, *d* of Sir Henry Phelps Brown, *qv*; two *s* one *d. Educ:* Brentwood School; King's College, Cambridge. BA 1958; MA 1961. Asst Lectr in Sociology, Leicester Univ., 1961–63; Research Fellow, King's College, Cambridge, 1963–67; Lectr and Senior Lectr in Sociology, LSE, 1963–67, 1970–72; Prof.

of Sociology: Univ. of Hong Kong, 1967–69; Brunel Univ., 1972–85 (Dean, Faculty of Social Sciences, 1981–85). Mem., Inst. for Advanced Study, Princeton, 1969–70, 1974–75, 1983. *Publications:* Hong Kong: The Industrial Colony (ed), 1971; Conquerors and Slaves, 1978; Death and Renewal, 1983. *Recreation:* drinking wine. *Address:* King's College, Cambridge CB2 1ST. *T:* Cambridge 350411.

HOPKINS, (Richard) Julian; Finance Officer, War on Want, since 1984; *b* 12 Oct. 1940; *s* of Richard Robert Hopkins and late Grace Hilda (*née* Hatfield); *m* 1971, Maureen Mary (*née* Hoye); two *s* one *d. Educ:* Bedford School. Asst Manager, London Palladium, 1963; Central Services Manager, BBC, 1965; joined RSPCA as Accounts Manager, 1972, appointed Admin. and Finance Officer, 1976; Exec. Dir, 1978–82. Dir, and Mem. Exec. Cttee, World Soc. for Protection of Animals, 1980–82; Gen. Manager, Charity Christmas Card Council, 1982–83. Mem., Farm Animal Welfare Council, 1980–83. FBIM. *Recreation:* all theatre, but especially opera, concert-going. *Address:* 22 Falmouth Road, SE1.

HOPKINS, Maj.-Gen. Ronald Nicholas Lamond, CBE 1943; Legion of Merit (US) 1944; psc; Australian Regular Army, retired; *b* 24 May 1897; *s* of Dr Wm F. Hopkins and Rosa M. B. Lamond; *m* 1926, Nora Frances Riceman; one *s. Educ:* Melbourne Grammar Sch.; RMC, Duntroon. Lieut Aust. Permt Forces, 1 Jan. 1918 and seconded 1st AIF; served with 6th Australian Light Horse Regt, Palestine, 1918; Staff Capt. 3rd Australian Light Horse Bde, 1919; Staff Coll., Quetta, 1927–28; attached Royal Tank Corps, England, 1937–38; 2nd AIF 1940; service in Middle East and New Guinea; Hon. ADC to Governor-Gen., 1943–45; late Dep. Chief of Gen. Staff (Australia). Chief Exec. Officer, Adelaide Festival of Arts, 1959–60. Hon. Fellow, St Mark's Coll., Univ. of Adelaide, 1977. *Publication:* Australian Armour, 1978. *Address:* 24 Wilsden Street, Walkerville, SA 5081, Australia. *Club:* Adelaide (Adelaide).

HOPKINSON, family name of **Baron Colyton.**

HOPKINSON, Albert Cyril, CBE 1970; FRIBA; consultant architect; *b* 2 Aug. 1911; *s* of Albert Hopkinson and Isaline Pollard (*née* Cox); *m* 1943, Lesley Evelyn Hill; one *s* one *d. Educ:* Univs of Sheffield and London. BA 1933; MA 1934. FRIBA 1949 (ARIBA 1934); Dipl. Town Planning and Civic Architecture, London, 1938. Min. of Public Building and Works, 1937–64; Dir of Works and Chief Architect, Home Office, 1964–75. *Recreations:* reading, walking. *Address:* Frangate, Frenchlands Hatch, Ockham Road South, East Horsley, Surrey. *T:* East Horsley 4030. *Club:* Wig and Pen.

HOPKINSON, Ven. Barnabas John; Archdeacon of Sarum, since 1986; *b* 11 May 1939; *s* of Prebendary Stephan Hopkinson and Mrs Anne Hopkinson; *m* 1968, Esmé Faith (*née* Gibbons); three *d. Educ:* Emmanuel School; Trinity Coll., Cambridge (MA); Lincoln Theological Coll. Curate: All Saints and Martyrs, Langley, Manchester, 1965–67; Great St Mary's, Cambridge, 1967–70; Chaplain, Charterhouse School, 1970–75; Team Vicar of Preshute, Wilts, 1975–81; RD of Marlborough, 1977–81; Rector of Wimborne Minster, Dorset, 1981–86; RD of Wimborne, 1985–86. Canon of Salisbury Cathedral, 1983–. *Recreations:* mountaineering, camping. *Address:* 121 Harnham Road, Salisbury, Wilts SP2 8JT. *T:* Salisbury 28756.

HOPKINSON, David Hugh; Chief Night Editor of The Times, since 1982; *b* 9 June 1930; *er s* of late C. G. Hopkinson. *Educ:* Sowerby Bridge Grammar Sch. Entered journalism on Huddersfield Examiner, 1950; Yorkshire Observer, 1954; Yorkshire Evening News, 1954; Evening Chronicle, Manchester, 1956; Chief Sub-Editor, Sunday Graphic, London, 1957; Asst Editor, Evening Chronicle, Newcastle upon Tyne, 1959; Chief Asst Editor, Sunday Graphic, 1960; Dep. Editor, Sheffield Telegraph, 1961, Editor, 1962–64; Editor, The Birmingham Post, 1964–73; Dir, Birmingham Post & Mail Ltd, 1967–80; Editor, Birmingham Evening Mail, 1974–79; Editor-in-Chief, Evening Mail series, 1975–79, Birmingham Post and Evening Mail, 1979–80; Asst to Editor of The Times, 1981. Member: Lord Justice Phillimore's Cttee inquiring into law of contempt; International Press Institute; Associate Mem., Justice (British br. of Internat. Commn of Jurists). National Press Award, Journalist of the Year, 1963. *Address:* 39 Watling Street, St Albans, Herts.

HOPKINSON, David Hugh Laing, CBE 1986; RD 1965; Deputy Chairman and Chief Executive, M&G Group PLC, since 1979; Chairman: United States Debenture Corporation, since 1983; Romney and Raeburn Investment Trusts, since 1986; a Deputy Chairman, English China Clays, since 1986 (Director, since 1975); *b* 14 Aug. 1926; *s* of late Cecil Hopkinson and Leila Hopkinson; *m* 1951, Prudence Margaret Holmes; two *s* two *d. Educ:* Wellington Coll.; Merton Coll., Oxford (BA 1949). RNVR and RNR, 1944–65. A Clerk of the House of Commons, 1948–59; Robert Fleming, 1959–62; M&G Investment Management, 1963–: Chm., 1975–; Director: Lloyds Bank Southern Regional Board, 1977–; BR (Southern) Bd, 1978– (Chm., 1979–86); Mem., Adv. Gp of Governor of Bank of England, 1984. Mem., Housing Corp., 1986–. Dir, English Chamber Orchestra and Music Soc., 1970–. Member: General Synod of C of E, 1970–; Central Bd of Finance, 1970–; a Church Comr, 1973–82, 1984–; Chm., Chichester Dio. Bd of Finance, 1977–. Trustee: Chichester Cathedral Development Trust; Pallant House Museum, Chichester; RAM Foundn; St Paul's Choir Sch. Foundn. Governor: Sherborne Sch., 1970–; Wellington Coll., 1978–. Hon. Fellow, St Anne's Coll., Oxford, 1984–. *Recreations:* travelling, walking, opera. *Address:* St John's Priory, Poling, Arundel, W Sussex. *T:* Arundel 882393. *Club:* Brooks's.

HOPKINSON, Maj.-Gen. Gerald Charles, CB 1960; DSO 1945; OBE 1953; MC 1938; retired; *b* Wellington, Som, 27 May 1910; *s* of Capt. Charles Reginald Hopkinson (killed in action, 1914); *m* 1938, Rhona Marion (*d* 1979), *d* of Henry Turner, Farnham, Surrey; one *d. Educ:* Imperial Service Coll.; RMC Sandhurst. Second Lieut, Royal Tank Corps, 1930; served War of 1939–45 (India, Middle East, Italy and Europe); comd 1st RTR, Korea, 1952–53; 33rd Armoured Bde, BAOR, 1953–57; GOC 4th Div., BAOR, 1958–59; Dir, RAC, War Office, Oct. 1959–62. Lieut-Col 1952; Col 1953; Maj.-Gen. 1958. Order of the Crown and Croix de Guerre (Belgium).

HOPKINSON, Giles; Director, London Region Property Services Agency, Department of Environment, since 1983; *b* 20 Nov. 1931; *s* of late Arthur John Hopkinson, CIE, ICS, and of Eleanor (*née* Richardson); *m* 1956, Eleanor Jean Riddell; three *d. Educ:* Marlborough Coll.; Leeds Univ. (BSc). E. & J. Richardson Ltd, 1956–57; Forestal Land, Timber and Rly Co. Ltd, 1957–58; DSIR: Scientific Officer, 1958–61; Sen. Scientific Officer, 1961–64; Private Sec. to Perm. Sec., 1963–64; Principal, MoT, 1964–71; Asst Sec., DoE, 1971; Under-Secretary, DoE, 1976; Dept of Transport (Ports and Freight Directorate), 1979. *Recreations:* music, landscape gardening. *Address:* Digswell Water Mill, Digswell Lane, Welwyn Garden City, Herts AL7 1SW. *Club:* Royal Commonwealth Society.

HOPKINSON, Col (Henry) Somerset (Parnell), OBE 1944; DL; *b* 16 Oct. 1899; *s* of Col H. C. B. Hopkinson, CMG, CBE, and Hon. M. F. L. Parnell, *d* of 3rd Baron Congleton; *m* 1928, Marie Josephine de Gilibert Addison, *d* of Lieut-Col A. J. B. Addison, Royal Irish Rifles; one *d* (and one *d* decd). *Educ:* Winchester and RMC. 2nd Lt Rifle Brigade, 1919; Major, 1938; Staff Coll., 1933–34; Brig. 1945; served War of 1939–45, Palestine, Burma, India; retd 1948. County Councillor Monmouthshire, 1958–64; JP

1950, DL 1951, High Sheriff 1964, Gwent, formerly Monmouthshire. FSA, FSG. *Recreations:* shooting, foreign travel. *Address:* Llanfihangel Court, Abergavenny, Gwent. *T:* Crucorney 217. *Club:* Army and Navy.

See also D. B. Johnson.

HOPKINSON, Sir (Henry) Thomas, Kt 1978; CBE 1967; author, journalist; *b* 19 April 1905; 2nd *s* of late Archdeacon J. H. Hopkinson; *m* 1st, Antonia White; one *d* (and one step *d*); 2nd, Gerti Deutsch; two *d*; 3rd, 1953, Dorothy, *widow of* Hugh Kingsmill. *Educ:* St Edward's Sch., Oxford; Pembroke Coll., Oxford (Scholar). BA, 1927; MA, 1932; Hon. Fellow, 1978. After working as a freelance journalist and in advertising and publicity, was appointed Asst Editor of the Clarion, 1934; Asst Editor, Weekly Illustrated, 1934–38; helped in preparation and launching of Picture Post; Editor, 1940–50; also edited Lilliput, 1941–46; Features Editor, News Chronicle, 1954–56; Editor, Drum Magazine, 1958–61. Dir for Africa of Internat. Press Inst., 1963–66. Senior Fellow in Press Studies, Univ. of Sussex, 1967–69; Vis. Prof. of Journalism, University of Minnesota, 1968–69; Dir, Course in Journalism Studies, UC Cardiff, 1971–75, Hon. Professorial Fellow, 1978. Hon. FRPS 1976; Silver Progress Medal, RPS, 1984. *Publications:* A Wise Man Foolish, 1930; A Strong Hand at the Helm, 1933; The Man Below, 1939; Mist in the Tagus, 1946; The Transitory Venus (short stories), 1948; Down the Long Slide, 1949; Love's Apprentice, 1953; short life of George Orwell, 1953, in British Council series Writers and Their Work; The Lady and the Cut-Throat (short stories), 1958; In the Fiery Continent, 1962; South Africa, 1964 (New York); (ed) Picture Post, 1938–1950, 1970; (with D. Hopkinson) Much Silence: the life and work of Meher Baba, 1974; Treasures of the Royal Photographic Society, 1980; Of This Our Time (autobiog.), 1982; Under the Tropic (autobiog.), 1984; stories in English and American magazines, and for radio. *Address:* 26 Boulter Street, St Clement's, Oxford OX4 1AX. *T:* Oxford 240466.

HOPKINSON, Maj.-Gen. John Charles Oswald Rooke, CB 1984; Director, British Field Sports Society, since 1984; *b* 31 July 1931; *s* of Lt-Col John Oliver Hopkinson and Aileen Disney Hopkinson (*née* Rooke); *m* 1956, Sarah Elizabeth, *d* of Maj.-Gen. M. H. P. Sayers, *qv*; three *s* one *d*. *Educ:* Stonyhurst Coll.; RMA, Sandhurst. sc 1963, jssc 1968, rcds 1979. Commanding Officer, 1st Bn Queen's Own Highlanders, 1972–74 (despatches); Dep. Comdr 2nd Armoured Division, and Comdr Osnabrück Garrison, 1977–78; Director Operational Requirements 3 (Army), 1980–82; Chief-of-Staff, HQ Allied Forces Northern Europe, 1982–84. Colonel, Queen's Own Highlanders, 1983–. *Recreations:* shooting, fishing, sailing. *Address:* Bigsweir, Gloucestershire. *Club:* Army and Navy.

HOPKINSON, Prof. Ralph Galbraith; Haden-Pilkington Professor of Environmental Design and Engineering, University College London, 1965–76, now Emeritus; *b* 13 Aug. 1913; *s* of late Ralph Galbraith Hopkinson and Beatrice Frances (*née* Wright); *m* 1938, Dora Beryl (*née* Churchill); two *s* (and one *s* decd). *Educ:* Erith Grammar Sch.; Faraday House. BSc (Eng), PhD, CEng, FIEE, FRPS. Research Engr, GEC, 1934–47, lighting and radar; Principal Scientific Officer, DSIR Building Research Stn, 1947–64 (Special Merit appointment, 1960); Dean, Faculty of Environmental Studies, UCL, 1972–74. Work on: human response to buildings, leading to concept of environmental design by engr-physicists and architects in collab.; schools with Min. of Educn Develt Gp and on hosps with Nuffield Foundn, 1949–65; lighting design of new Tate Gallery extension and Stock Exchange Market Hall (Design Award of Distinction, Illum. Engrg Soc. of USA, 1974); visual and noise intrusion (urban motorways) for DoE, 1970; consultant, DoE Road Construction Unit. Pres., Illuminating Engrg Soc., 1965–66 (Gold Medallist, 1972; Hon. Mem., 1976); Mem., Royal Soc. Study Gp on Human Biology in the Urban Environment, 1972–74. Trustee, British Institution Fund, 1972–77. Hon. FRIBA 1969, Hon. FCIBS 1977. *Publications:* Architectural Physics: Lighting, 1963; Hospital Lighting, 1964; Daylighting, 1966; (with J. D. Kay) The Lighting of Buildings, 1969; Lighting and Seeing, 1969; The Ergonomics of Lighting, 1970; Visual Intrusion (RTPI), 1972; papers in Nature, Jl Optical Soc. of America, Jl Psychol., Illum. Eng, etc. *Recreations:* music, human sciences, boating, walking. *Address:* Bartlett School of Architecture and Planning, University College London, Wates House, 22 Gordon Street, WC1H 0QB.

HOPKINSON, Col Somerset; *see* Hopkinson, Col H. S. P.

HOPKINSON, Sir Thomas; *see* Hopkinson, Sir H. T.

HOPPE, Iver; Kt of Danish Dannebrog; Kt of Icelandic Falcon; Chairman and Chief Executive, Navalicon Ltd A/S, Denmark, 1975–84; *b* Denmark, 25 July 1920; *s* of Arthur Hans Knudsen Hoppe and Gerda (*née* Raun Byberg); *m* 1943, Ingeborg Lassen; one *d*. *Educ:* Aarhus Katedralskole; Copenhagen Univ. (Law Faculty), 1944. Acting Lecturer, Copenhagen Univ., 1946; Advocate to High Court and Court of Appeal, 1948; Jurisprudential Lecturer, Copenhagen Univ., 1952–58; study sojourn in Switzerland, 1949. A. P. Møller Concern, Copenhagen, 1955–71: Asst Dir, 1960; Man. Dir of Odense Steel Shipyard, Ltd, Odense and Lindø, 1964–71. Chm. A/S Svendborg Skibsvaerft, 1968–71; Mem. Bd of Dansk Boreselskab A/S and other cos until 1971; Man. Dir and Chief Exec., Harland and Wolff Ltd, Belfast, 1971–74; Member: Bd of Den Danske Landmandsbank A/S, 1970–72; Council of Danish National Bank, 1967–71; Bd of Danish Ship Credit Fund, 1965–71; Assoc. of Danish Shipyards, 1964–71; Assoc. of Employers within the Iron and Metal Industry in Denmark, 1967–71; Assoc. of Danish Industries, 1965–72; West of England Steam Ship Owners Protection and Indemnity Assoc., Ltd, 1960–66; Danish Acad. of Technical Sciences; Shipbuilders and Repairers Nat. Assoc. Exec. Council and Management Bd, 1971–74; British Iron and Steel Consumers' Council, 1971–74; Gen. Cttee, Lloyd's Register of Shipping; British Cttee, Det Norske Veritas; Amer. Bureau of Shipping, and other Danish and foreign instns. *Recreations:* reading, swimming, mountain walking, farming. *Address:* Malmmosegaard, Dyreborgvej 7, DK-5600 Faaborg, Denmark. *Club:* Travellers'.

HOPPER, Prof. Frederick Ernest, MDS, FDSRCS; FFDRCSI; Professor of Dental Surgery and Dean of the School of Dentistry, University of Leeds, 1959–85, now Professor Emeritus; Consultant Dental Surgeon, Leeds Area Health Authority, 1959–85; Chairman, Board of Faculty of Medicine, University of Leeds, 1975–78; *b* 22 Nov. 1919; *s* of Frederick Ernest Hopper, MPS and Margaret Ann Carlyle; *m* 1949, Gudrun Eik-Nes, LDSRCS, *d* of Prost Knut Eik-Nes and Nina Eik-Nes, Trondheim, Norway; three *s*. *Educ:* Dame Allan's Sch., Newcastle upon Tyne; King's Coll., University of Durham. BDS (with dist.) 1943; FDSRCS 1948; MDS 1958. House Surg., Newcastle upon Tyne Dental Hosp. and Royal Dental Hospital, 1943–44; served in EMS in Maxillo-Facial Centres at E Grinstead and Shotley Bridge, 1944–46; successively Lecturer, 1946, and Sen. Lecturer, 1956, in Periodontal Diseases, King's Coll., University of Durham; Lecturer in Dental Pharmacology and Therapeutics, 1947–59; Examiner in Dental subjects, Univs of Durham, Edinburgh, St Andrews, Bristol, Liverpool; Dental Surgeon in charge Parodontal Dept, Newcastle upon Tyne Dental Hosp., and Sen. Dental Surg., Plastic and Jaw Unit, Shotley Bridge, 1946–59; Cons. Dent. Surg., United Newcastle Hosps, 1955–59. Hon. Treas., Brit. Soc. of Periodontology, 1949–53, Pres. 1954. Member: General Dental Council, 1959–85 (Chm., Educn Cttee, 1980–85); Brit. Dental Assoc., 1943–; Internat. Dental Fedn, 1948–; Pres., British Soc. for Oral Medicine, 1986. *Publications:* contribs to med. and dental jls. *Recreations:* photography (still and ciné); golf. *Address:* 23 Ancaster Road, Leeds LS16 5HH. *Clubs:* Savage; Alwoodley Golf (Leeds).

HOPPER, Prof. Robert John; Professor of Ancient History, University of Sheffield, 1955–75, now Emeritus; *b* 13 Aug. 1910; *s* of Robert and Alice Hopper, Cardiff, Glamorgan; *m* 1939, Henriette, *d* of Edward and Ella Kiernan, Timperley, Cheshire; no *c*. *Educ:* Mount Radford Sch., Exeter; University of Wales; Gonville and Caius Coll., Cambridge. Served Royal Welch Fusiliers and Intelligence Corps, 1941–45. Macmillan Student of British Sch. at Athens, 1935–37; Fellow of Univ. of Wales (in Athens and Rome), 1936–38; Lectr in Classics, UCW Aberystwyth, 1938–41 and 1945–47; Senior Lecturer in Ancient History, Univ. of Sheffield, 1947–55, Dean of Faculty of Arts, 1967–70. FRNS 1949; FSA 1951. *Publications:* The Acropolis, 1971; The Early Greeks, 1976; Greek Trade and Industry, 1978; articles in classical and archæological periodicals. *Recreations:* numismatics; foreign travel. *Address:* 41 Barholm Road, Sheffield S10 5RR. *T:* Sheffield 302587. *Club:* National Liberal.

HOPPER, William Joseph; Chairman, Shire Trust, since 1986; Adviser, Morgan Grenfell & Co. Ltd, since 1979 (Director, 1974–79); *b* 9 Aug. 1929; *s* of I. Vance Hopper and Jennie Josephine Hopper; *m* 1959, Melisa Carmen Humphreys (marr. diss.); one *d*. *Educ:* Langside Elementary Sch., Glasgow; Queen's Park Secondary Sch., Glasgow; Glasgow Univ. (MA Hons (Mod. Langs) 1953). Financial Analyst, W. R. Grace & Co., NY, 1956–59; London Office Manager, H. Hentz & Co., Members, NY Stock Exchange, 1960–66; Gen. Manager, S. G. Warburg & Co. Ltd, 1966–69; Hill Samuel & Co. Ltd, 1969–74. Director: Wharf Resources Ltd, Calgary, 1984–; Manchester Ship Canal Co., 1985–. MEP (C), Greater Manchester West, 1979–84. Co-founder (1969) and first Chm. (now Mem., Exec. Cttee), Inst. for Fiscal Studies, London; Treasurer, Action Resource Centre. *Publication:* A Turntable for Capital, 1969. *Recreations:* listening to music, gardening. *Address:* 23 Great Winchester Street, EC2P 2AX. *T:* 01–588 4545. *Club:* St James's (Manchester).

HOPTHROW, Brig. Harry Ewart, CBE 1946 (OBE 1940); Hon. Life Member, Solent Protection Society; *b* 13 Nov. 1896; *s* of Frederick Hopthrow; *m* 1925, Audrey Kassel (*d* 1975), *d* of J. Lewer; one *s* one *d*. *Educ:* Queen Elizabeth's Grammar Sch., Gainsborough; City Sch., Lincoln; Loughborough Coll. Served European War 1915–1918, RE, France and Flanders. Civil and Mechanical Engineer, ICI Ltd, 1925–39; Commanded 107 Co. RE, 1931–35, Major; Asst Dir of Works, GHQ, BEF, 1939–40, Lt-Col; served France and Flanders, 1939–40 and 1944; Dep. Chief Engineer: Home Forces, 1940–41, and Western Comd, 1941; Dep. Controller Mil. Works Services, War Office, 1941–43; Dir of Fortifications and Works, WO, 1943–45; Asst Sec., ICI Ltd, 1945–58; Hon. Secretary and a Vice-Pres., Royal Institution, 1960–68. AMIMechE 1924, FIMechE 1933. Mem. Central Advisory Water Cttee (Min. of Housing and Local Govt), 1951–69; Mem. Cttee of Inquiry into Inland Waterways (Bowes Cttee), 1956–58; Vice-Chm. IoW River and Water Authority, 1964–73; UK Rep. to Council of European Industrial Fedns; Vice-Pres., Round Tables on Pollution, 1965–73. Officer of American Legion of Merit, 1946. *Recreations:* yachting, historical research. *Address:* Surrey House, Cowes, Isle of Wight. *T:* Isle of Wight 292430. *Clubs:* Army and Navy; Royal Engineer Yacht; Royal London Yacht, Island Sailing (Cowes).

HOPWOOD, family name of **Baron Southborough.**

HOPWOOD, Prof. David Alan, FRS 1979; John Innes Professor of Genetics, University of East Anglia, Norwich, and Head of the Genetics Department, John Innes Institute, since 1968; *b* 19 Aug. 1933; *s* of Herbert Hopwood and Dora Hopwood (*née* Grant); *m* 1962, Joyce Lilian Bloom; two *s* one *d*. *Educ:* Purbrook Park County High Sch., Hants; Lymm Grammar Sch., Cheshire; St John's Coll., Cambridge (MA, PhD). DSc (Glasgow). Whytehead Major Scholar, St John's Coll., Cambridge, 1951–54; John Stothert Bye-Fellow, Magdalene Coll., Cambridge, 1956–58; Res. Fellow, St John's Coll., 1958–61; Univ. Demonstrator, Univ. of Cambridge, 1957–61; Lectr in Genetics, Univ. of Glasgow, 1961–68. Pres., Genetical Soc. of GB, 1985–. *Publications:* numerous articles and chapters in scientific jls and books. *Address:* John Innes Institute, Colney Lane, Norwich NR4 7UH. *T:* Norwich 52571.

HOPWOOD, Brig. John Adam, CBE 1958; DSO 1943 (and Bar 1944); *b* 26 Jan. 1910; *s* of Ernest Hopwood and Constance Marion Adam; *m* Cressida Mona Browning, *d* of R. Campbell Browning, Armsworth, Alresford, Hants; no *c*. *Educ:* St David's, Reigate; Eton; RMC Sandhurst. Commissioned Black Watch, 1930; served with 1st Bn in India, 1931–35; ADC to Governor of Bengal, 1935–37; with 1st Bn Black Watch, and BEF in France, 1939–40; Staff Coll., 1940; Bde Major, 154 Inf. Bde, 1941; Second in Comd, 7th Bn Black Watch, N Africa and Sicily, 1942; comd 1st Bn Black Watch, Sicily and NW Europe, 1943–45; comd 154 and 156 Inf. Bdes, Germany, 1946; Mem. Training Mission to Iraq Army, Baghdad, 1946–48; attended jssc, Latimer, 1948; Liaison Appt, RAF Fighter Comd, 1949; comd 44 Parachute Bde (TA) London, 1950–53; Col i/c Admin., Hong Kong, 1953–55; comd 3 Inf. Bde, Canal Zone, UK, Cyprus, 1955–58; Vice-Pres., Regular Commissions Board, 1958–60, retd. Chm., Honiton Div. Cons. Assoc., 1977–80. Awarded Bronze Lion of Netherlands. *Recreations:* ornithology (MBOU), field sports, travel. *Address:* Gilletts Farm, Yarcombe, Honiton, Devon. *T:* Chard 3121. *Club:* Naval and Military.

HORAM, John Rhodes; Managing Director, Commodities Research Unit Ltd, 1968–70 and since 1983; *b* 7 March 1939; *s* of Sydney Horam, Preston. *Educ:* Silcoates Sch., Wakefield; Univ. of Cambridge. Market research officer, Rowntree & Co., 1960–62; leader and feature writer: Financial Times, 1962–65; The Economist, 1965–68. Contested (Lab) Folkestone and Hythe, 1966; MP Gateshead West, 1970–83 (Lab, 1970–81, SDP, 1981–83). Parly Under-Sec. of State, Dept of Transport, 1976–79; Labour spokesman on econ. affairs, 1979–81; Parly spokesman on econ. affairs, SDP, 1981–83. Contested (SDP) Newcastle upon Tyne Central, 1983. Member: SDP Nat. Steering Cttee, 1981–83; SDP Economic Policy Cttee. *Address:* 6 Bovingdon Road, SW6 2AP; Commodities Research Unit Ltd, 31 Mount Pleasant, WC1X 0AD. *T:* 01–278 0414.

HORAN, Rt. Rev. Forbes Trevor; *b* 22 May 1905; *s* of Rev. Frederick Seymour Horan and Mary Katherine Horan; *m* 1939, Veronica (*d* 1983), *d* of late Rt Rev. J. N. Bateman-Champain, sometime Bishop of Knaresborough; two *s* two *d*. *Educ:* Sherborne and Trinity Hall, Cambridge. RMC Sandhurst, 1924–25; Oxford and Bucks Lt Infantry, Lieutenant, 1925–29; Trinity Hall, Cambridge, 1929–32; Westcott House, Cambridge, 1932–33; Curate, St Luke's, Newcastle upon Tyne, 1933–35; Curate, St George's, Jesmond, Newcastle upon Tyne, 1935–37; Priest-in-charge, St Peter's, Balkwell, 1937–40; RNVR, 1940–45; Vicar of St Chad's, Shrewsbury, 1945–52; Vicar of Huddersfield Parish Church, 1952–60; Bishop Suffragan of Tewkesbury, 1960–73. *Recreations:* listening to the Third Programme on the radio, bicycling in order to maintain some semblance of independence, cooking and housekeeping. *Address:* 79 Naunton Lane, Leckhampton, Cheltenham, Gloucestershire. *T:* Cheltenham 527313.

HORD, Brian Howard; Director, Mountford Investments, since 1985; Chairman, Bexley Health Authority, since 1986; *b* 20 June 1934; *s* of Edwin Charles and Winifred Hannah

Hord; *m* 1960, Christine Marian Lucas; two *s*. *Educ:* Reedham Sch.; Purley Grammar Sch. FRICS. County Planning Dept, Mddx CC, 1950–51; Surveyor, private practice, 1951–57; National Service, RAF, 1957–59; Estates Surveyor, United Drapery Stores, 1959–66; Richard Costain Ltd, 1966–70; Director, Capcount UK Ltd, principal subsid. of Capital & Counties Property Co. Ltd, 1970–75; Partner, Howard Hord & Palmer, Chartered Surveyors, 1975–84. Mem., London Rent Assessment Panel, 1985–. MEP (C) London West, 1979–84; Whip of European Democratic Gp, 1982–83. *Publication:* (jtly) Rates-Realism or Rebellion. *Recreations:* photography, top-fruit growing, bee-keeping. *Club:* Carlton.

HORDEN, Prof. John Robert Backhouse, FSA; FRSL; Professor of Bibliographical Studies, and Director, Centre for Bibliographical Studies, University of Stirling, since 1982; Editor, Dictionary of Scottish Biography, since 1982; *o s* of late Henry Robert Horden and Ethel Edith Horden (*née* Backhouse), Warwicks; *m* 1948, Aileen Mary (*d* 1984), *o d* of late Lt Col and Mrs W. J. Douglas, Warwicks and S Wales; one *s*. *Educ:* Oxford, Cambridge, Heidelberg, Sorbonne, Lincoln's Inn. Previously Director, Inst. of Bibliography and Textual Criticism, Univ. of Leeds; sometime Tutor and Lectr in English Literature, Christ Church, Oxford. Vis. professorial appts, Univs of Pennsylvania State, Saskatchewan, Erlangen-Nürnberg, Texas at Austin, Münster; Cecil Oldman Meml Lectr in Bibliography and Textual Criticism, 1971. Hon. Life Mem., Modern Humanities Res. Assoc., 1976. DHL (*hc*) Indiana State Univ., 1974. Marc Fitch Prize for Bibliography, 1979. Devised new academic discipline of Publishing Studies and designed degree course at Univ. of Leeds, 1972 (MA). Founded Stirling Univ. Press, 1985. *Publications:* The Isis (revived and ed), 1945; Francis Quarles: a bibliography of his works to 1800, 1953; (ed) Francis Quarles' Hosanna and Threnodes, 1960, 3rd edn 1965; (ed) Annual Bibliography of English Language and Literature, 1967–75; (ed) English and Continental Emblem Books (22 vols), 1968–74; (ed) Dictionary of Concealed Authorship, vol. 1, 1980 (1st vol. of rev. Halkett and Laing); (initiator and first editor) Index of English Literary Manuscripts, vol. 1, 1980, vol. 4, 1982; John Freeth: political ballad writer and inn keeper, 1985; numerous contribs to learned jls. *Recreations:* golf (representative honours), music, painting. *Address:* Centre for Bibliographical Studies, University of Stirling, Stirling FK9 4LA. *T:* Stirling 73171. *Clubs:* Athenæum; Vincent's (Oxford); Hawks (Cambridge).

HORDER, family name of **Baron Horder.**

HORDER, 2nd Baron *cr* 1933, of Ashford in the County of Southampton; **Thomas Mervyn Horder;** Bt, of Shaston, 1923; *b* 8 Dec. 1910; *s* of 1st Baron Horder, GCVO, MD, FRCP, and Geraldine Rose (*d* 1954), *o d* of Arthur Doggett, Newnham Manor, Herts; *S* father, 1955. *Educ:* Winchester; Trinity Coll., Cambridge. BA 1932; MA 1937. Served War of 1939–45: HQ, RAF Fighter Comd, 1940–42 (despatches); Air HQ, India, 1942–44; Headquarters, South-East Asia Command, 1944–45; United Kingdom Liaison Mission, Tokyo, 1945–46; Chairman, Gerald Duckworth & Co. Ltd, 1948–70. *Publications:* The Little Genius, 1966; (ed) Ronald Firbank: memoirs and critiques, 1977; *music:* (ed) The Orange Carol Book, 1962; Norfolk Dances for string orchestra, 1965; Six Betjeman Songs, 1967; A Shropshire Lad (songs), 1980; (ed) The Easter Carol Book, 1982. *Recreations:* music, idling. *Address:* c/o Gerald Duckworth & Co. Ltd, 43 Gloucester Crescent, NW1 7DY.

HORDER, Dr John Plaistowe, CBE 1981 (OBE 1971); FRCP, FRCPE, FRCGP, FRCPsych; general practitioner of medicine, 1951–81, retired; President, Royal College of General Practitioners, 1979–82; Visiting Professor, Royal Free Hospital Medical School, since 1982; *b* 9 Dec. 1919; *s* of Gerald Morley Horder and Emma Ruth Horder; *m* 1940, Elizabeth June Wilson; two *s* two *d*. *Educ:* Lancing Coll.; University Coll., Oxford (BA 1945); London Hosp. (BM BCh 1948). FRCP 1972 (MRCP 1951); FRCGP 1970 (MRCGP 1957); FRCPsych 1980 (MRCPsych 1975); FRCPE 1982. Consultant, 1959, Travelling Fellow, 1964, WHO; Lectr, London School of Economics and Pol. Sci., 1964–69; Sir Harry Jeffcott Vis. Professor, Univ. of Nottingham, 1975; John Hunt Fellow, 1974–77, Wolfson Travelling Prof., 1978, Royal Coll. of Gen. Practitioners. Consultant Adviser, DHSS, 1978–84. Hon. Fellow, RSM, 1983 (Pres., Sect. of Gen. Practice, 1970). Hon. MD Free Univ. Amsterdam, 1985. Hon. Mem., Coll. of Family Physicians of Canada, 1982. *Publications:* ed and co-author, The Future General Practitioner—learning and teaching, 1972; articles on general practice—training for and psychiatry in. . . ., 1953–81. *Recreations:* painting, music. *Address:* 98 Regent's Park Road, NW1. *T:* 01–722 3804.

HORDERN, (Alfred) Christopher (Willoughby); QC 1979; **His Honour Judge Hordern;** a Circuit Judge, since 1983. *Educ:* Oxford Univ. (MA). Called to the Bar, Middle Temple, 1961; a Recorder of the Crown Court, 1974–83. *Address:* 4 King's Bench Walk, Temple, EC4Y 7DL.

HORDERN, Sir Michael (Murray), Kt 1983; CBE 1972; actor; *b* 3 Oct. 1911; *s* of Capt. Edward Joseph Calverly Hordern, CIE, RIN, and Margaret Emily (*née* Murray); *m* 1943, Grace Eveline Mortimer (*d* 1986); one *d*. *Educ:* Brighton Coll. Formerly in business with The Educational Supply Assoc., playing meanwhile as an amateur at St Pancras People's Theatre. First professional appearance as Lodovico in Othello, People's Palace, 1937. Two seasons of repertory at Little Theatre, Bristol, 1937–39; War service in Navy, 1940–46; demobilised as Lieut-Comdr, RNVR. Parts include: Mr Toad in Toad of Toad Hall, at Stratford, 1948 and 1949; Ivanov in Ivanov, Arts Theatre, 1950. Stratford Season, 1952: Jacques, Menenius, Caliban. Old Vic Season, 1953–54: Polonius, King John, Malvolio, Prospero. "BB" in The Doctor's Dilemma, Saville, 1956; Old Vic Season, 1958–59: Cassius, Macbeth. Ulysses (Troilus and Cressida), Edinburgh Fest., 1962; Herbert Georg Beutler in The Physicists, Aldwych, 1963; Southman in Saint's Day, St Martin's, 1965; Relatively Speaking, Duke of York's, 1967; A Delicate Balance, Aldwych, 1969; King Lear, Nottingham Playhouse, 1969; Flint, Criterion, 1970; National Theatre: Jumpers, 1972 and 1976, Gaunt in Richard II, 1972, The Cherry Orchard, 1973, The Rivals, 1983; The Ordeal of Gilbert Pinfold, Manchester, 1977, Round House, 1979; RSC Stratford: Prospero in The Tempest, Armado in Love's Labour's Lost, 1978; also many leading parts in films, radio and television. Hon. DLitt Exeter, 1985. *Recreation:* fishing. *Address:* Flat Y, Rectory Chambers, Old Church Street, SW3 5DA. *Clubs:* Garrick; Flyfishers'.

HORDERN, Sir Peter (Maudslay), Kt 1985; MP (C) Horsham, 1964–74 and since 1983 (Horsham and Crawley, 1974–83); *b* 18 April 1929; British; *s* of C. H. Hordern, MBE; *m* 1964, Susan Chataway; two *s* one *d*. *Educ:* Geelong Grammar Sch., Australia; Christ Church, Oxford, 1949–52 (MA). Mem. of Stock Exchange, London, 1957–74. Chm., F. & C. Alliance Investment, 1986– (Dir, 1976–); Director: Petrofina (UK) Ltd, 1973–; TR Technology, 1975–. Chm., Cons. Parly Finance Cttee, 1970–72; Member: Exec., 1922 Cttee, 1968–; Public Accts Cttee, 1970–; Public Accounts Commn, 1984–. *Recreations:* golf, reading and travel. *Address:* 55 Cadogan Street, SW3.

HORE-RUTHVEN, family name of **Earl of Gowrie.**

HORLICK, Vice-Adm. Sir Edwin John, (Sir Ted Horlick), KBE 1981; FEng, FIMechE, MIMarE; part-time consultant; *b* 1925; *m*; four *s*. *Educ:* Bedford Modern Sch. Joined RN, 1943; Sqdn Eng. Officer, 2nd Frigate Sqdn, 1960–63; Ship Dept, MoD, 1963–66; First Asst to Chief Engineer, HM Dockyard, Singapore, 1966–68; Asst Dir Submarines, 1969–72; SOWC 1973; Fleet Marine Engineering Officer, Staff of C-in-C Fleet, 1973–75; RCDS 1976; Dir Project Team Submarine/Polaris, 1977–79; Dir Gen. Ships, 1979–83; Chief Naval Engineer Officer, 1981–83. *Recreations:* golf, Rugby administration, DIY. *Address:* 33 Church Street, Weston, Bath BA1 4BU. *Club:* Army and Navy.

HORLICK, Sir John (James Macdonald), 5th Bt *cr* 1914; Director, Highland Fish Farmers, since 1978 (Chairman 1978–84); Partner, Tournaig Farming Company, since 1973; *b* 9 April 1922; *s* of Lt-Col Sir James Horlick, 4th Bt, OBE, MC, and Flora Macdonald (*d* 1955), *d* of late Col Cunliffe Martin, CB; *S* father, 1972; *m* 1948, June, *d* of Douglas Cory-Wright, CBE; one *s* two *d*. *Educ:* Eton; Babson Institute of Business Admin, Wellesley Hills, Mass, USA. Served War as Captain, Coldstream Guards. Dep. Chairman, Horlicks Ltd, retired 1971. CStJ 1977. *Recreations:* shooting, model soldier collecting. *Heir:* *s* James Cunliffe William Horlick [*b* 19 Nov. 1956; *m* 1985, Fiona Rosalie, *e d* of Andrew McLaren, Alcester]. *Address:* Tournaig, Poolewe, Achnasheen, Ross-shire. *T:* Poolewe 250; Howberry Lane Cottage, Nuffield, near Nettlebed, Oxon. *T:* Nettlebed 641454. *Clubs:* Beefsteak; Highland.

HORLICK, Sir Ted; *see* Horlick, Sir Edwin John.

HORLOCK, Henry Wimburn Sudell; Underwriting Member of Lloyd's, since 1957; Director, Stepping Stone School, since 1962; *b* 19 July 1915; *s* of Rev. Henry Darrell Sudell Horlock, DD, and Mary Haliburton Laurie; *m* 1960, Jeannetta Robin, *d* of F. W. Tanner, JP. *Educ:* Pembroke Coll., Oxford (MA). Army, 1939–42. Civil Service, 1942–60. Court of Common Council, City of London, 1969–; Deputy, Ward of Farringdon Within, 1978–; Sheriff, City of London, 1972–73; Chm., City of London Sheriffs' Soc., 1985–; Liveryman: Saddlers Co., 1937–, Master, 1976–77; Plaisterers' Co. (Hon.), 1975–; Fletchers' Co., 1977–; Gardeners' Co., 1980–; Member: Parish Clerks' Co., 1966–, Master, 1981–82; Guild of Freemen, 1972–, Master, 1986–87; Farringdon Ward Club, 1970–, Pres., 1978–79; United Wards Club, 1972–, Pres., 1980–81; City Livery Club, 1969–, Pres., 1981–82; Royal Soc. of St George, 1972–. Commander, Order of Merit, Federal Republic of Germany, 1972; Commander, National Order of the Aztec Eagle of Mexico, 1973. *Recreations:* gardening, travel. *Address:* 33 Fitzjohn's Avenue, NW3 5JY. *T:* 01–435 9641/2. *Clubs:* Athenæum, Guildhall, City Livery.

HORLOCK, Dr John Harold, FRS 1976; FEng 1977; Vice-Chancellor, Open University, since 1981; *b* 19 April 1928; *s* of Harold Edgar and Olive Margaret Horlock; *m* 1953, Sheila Joy Stutely; one *s* two *d*. *Educ:* Edmonton Latymer Sch.; (Scholar) St John's Coll., Cambridge. 1st Class Hons Mech. Sci. Tripos, Pt I, 1948, Rex Moir Prize; Pt II, 1949; MA 1952; PhD 1955; ScD 1975. Design and Development Engineer, Rolls Royce Ltd, Derby, 1949–51; Fellow, St John's Coll., Cambridge, 1954–57 and 1967–74; Univ. Demonstrator, 1952–56; University Lecturer, 1956–58, at Cambridge Univ. Engineering Lab.; Harrison Prof. of Mechanical Engineering, Liverpool Univ., 1958–66; Prof. of Engineering, Cambridge Univ., 1967–74; Vice-Chancellor, 1974–80, Prof. of Engineering, 1976–80, Univ. of Salford. Visiting Asst Prof. in Mech. Engineering, Massachusetts Inst. of Technology, USA, 1956–57; Vis. Prof. of Aero-Space Engineering, Pennsylvania State Univ., USA, 1966. Chairman: ARC, 1979–80 (Mem., 1960–63, 1969–72); Adv. Cttee on Safety in Nuclear Installations, 1984–; Member: SRC, 1974–77; Cttee of Inquiry into Engineering Profession, 1977–80; Engineering Council, 1981–83. Director: BICERA Ltd, 1964–65; Cambridge Water Co., 1971–74; British Engine Insurance Ltd, 1979–84; BL (Technol.) Ltd, 1979–; Open University Educational Enterprises Ltd, 1981–; Co-ax Cable Communications Ltd, 1983– (Chm.). A Vice-Pres., Royal Soc., 1982–. FIMechE, FRAeS; Fellow ASME. Hon. DSc: Heriot-Watt, 1980; Salford, 1981. Thomas Hawksley Gold Medal, IMechE, 1969. *Publications:* The Fluid Mechanics and Thermodynamics of Axial Flow Compressors, 1958; The Fluid Mechanics and Thermodynamics of Axial Flow Turbines, 1966; Actuator Disc Theory, 1978; (ed) Thermodynamics and Gas Dynamics of Internal Combustion Engines, vol. I, 1982, vol. II, 1986; contribs to mech. and aero. engineering jls and to Proc. Royal Society. *Recreations:* music, golf. *Address:* The Open University, Walton Hall, Milton Keynes MK7 6AA. *T:* Milton Keynes 653214; Wednesden House, Aspley Guise, Milton Keynes MK17 8DQ. *Clubs:* Athenæum, MCC.

HORN, Alan Bowes, CVO 1971; HM Diplomatic Service, retired; *b* 6 June 1917; *m* 1946, Peggy Boocock; one *s* one *d*. *Educ:* London Sch. of Economics. Served in Army, 1940–46. Joined Foreign Service, 1946; Vice-Consul, Marseilles, 1948–49; 2nd Sec., HM Embassy, Tel Aviv, 1949; promoted 1st Sec. and later apptd: London, 1951–53; New York, 1953–56; Helsinki, 1957–60; FO, 1960–63; Ambassador to the Malagasy Republic, 1963–67; Counsellor, Warsaw, 1967–70; Consul-General, Istanbul, 1970–73. *Address:* Oak Trees, Shere Road, Ewhurst, Cranleigh, Surrey.

HORN, Prof. Gabriel, MA, MD, ScD; FRS 1986; Professor of Zoology, since 1978, and Head of Department, since 1980, University of Cambridge; Fellow of King's College, Cambridge, since 1978; *b* 9 Dec. 1927; *s* of late A. Horn and Mrs Horn; *m* 1st, 1952, Ann Loveday Dean Soper (marr. diss. 1979); two *s* two *d*; 2nd, 1980, Edith Priscilla Barrett. *Educ:* Handsworth Technical Sch. and Coll., Birmingham (Nat. Cert. in Mech. Engrg); Univ. of Birmingham (BSc Anatomy and Physiology; MD, ChB). MA, ScD Cantab. Served in RAF (Educn Br.), 1947–49. House appts, Birmingham Children's and Birmingham and Midland Eye Hosps, 1955–56; Univ. of Cambridge: Univ. Demonstrator in Anat., 1956–62; Lectr in Anat., 1962–72; Reader in Neurobiology, 1972–74; Fellow of King's Coll., 1962–74; Prof. and Head of Dept of Anat., Univ. of Bristol, 1974–77. Sen. Res. Fellow in Neurophysiol., Montreal Neurol Inst., McGill Univ., 1957–58; Vis. Prof. of Physiol Optics, Univ. of Calif, Berkeley, 1963; Vis. Res. Prof., Ohio State Univ., 1965; Vis. Prof. of Zool., Makerere University Coll., Uganda, 1966; Leverhulme Res. Fellow, Laboratoire de Neurophysiologie Cellulaire, France, 1970–71. Member: Biol Sciences Cttee, SRC, 1973–75; Jt MRC and SRC Adv. Panel on Neurobiol., 1971–72; Res. Cttee, Mental Health Foundn, 1973–78; Council, Anatomical Soc., 1976–78; Adv. Gp, ARC Inst. of Animal Physiology, Babraham, 1981–. Dir, Co. of Biologists, 1980–. FIBiol 1978. Kenneth Craik Award in Physiol Psychol., 1962. *Publications:* (ed with R. A. Hinde) Short-Term Changes in Neural Activity and Behaviour, 1970; Memory, Imprinting and the Brain, 1985; contrib. scientific jls, mainly on topics in neurosciences. *Recreations:* walking, cycling, music, riding. *Address:* King's College, Cambridge. *T:* Cambridge 350411.

HORNBY, Sir Antony; *see* Hornby, Sir R. A.

HORNBY, Derrick Richard; *b* 11 Jan. 1926; *s* of late Richard W. Hornby and Dora M. Hornby; *m* 1948, June Steele; two *s* one *d*. *Educ:* University Coll., Southampton (DipEcon). Early career in accountancy; Marketing Dir, Tetley Tea Co. Ltd, 1964–69; Man. Dir, Eden Vale, 1969–74; Chm., Spillers Foods Ltd, 1974–77; Divisional Managing Director: Spillers Internat., 1977–80; Spillers Grocery Products Div., 1979–80. Pres., Food Manufrs Fedn Incorp., 1977–79; Mem., Food and Drinks EDC. Member Council: CBI, to 1979; Food and Drinks Industry Council, to 1979. Chairman: Appeal Fund, Nat.

Grocers Benefit Fund, 1973–74; London Animal Trust, 1978–80. FBIM, FIGD, ACommA. *Recreation:* golf. *Address:* Hillcrest, Dover Road, Branksome Park, Poole, Dorset.

HORNBY, Frank Robert, CBE 1972 (MBE 1944); Chief Officer and Vice-Chairman, Council for National Academic Awards, 1964–72, retired; *b* 20 Aug. 1911; *yr s* of late Robert Wilson Hornby and Jane Hornby; *m* 1939, Kathleen Margaret, *yr d* of late Dr Sidney Berry and Helen Berry. *Educ:* Heversham Sch., Westmorland, Magdalene Coll., Cambridge. 1st Class Natural Sciences Tripos Pts 1 and 2. Schoolmaster, 1933–41. RAOC, 1941–46 (Lieut-Col). Asst Educn Officer, Nottingham Co. Borough, 1946–56; Sec., Nat. Coun. for Technological Awards, 1956–64. Hon. LLD CNAA, 1972. *Address:* 35 High Firs, Gills Hill, Radlett, Herts WD7 8BH. *T:* Radlett 5083.

HORNBY, Prof. James Angus; Professor of Law in the University of Bristol, 1961–85, now Emeritus; *b* 15 Aug. 1922; twin *s* of James Hornby and Evelyn Gladys (*née* Grant). *Educ:* Bolton County Grammar Sch.; Christ's Coll., Cambridge. BA 1944, LLB 1945, MA 1948 Cantab. Called to Bar, Lincoln's Inn, 1947. Lecturer, Manchester Univ., 1947–61. *Publications:* An Introduction to Company Law, 1957, 5th edn 1975; contribs to legal journals. *Recreation:* hill walking. *Address:* 6 Henbury Gardens, Henbury Road, Bristol BS10 7AJ. *Club:* United Oxford & Cambridge University.

HORNBY, Lesley; *see* Twiggy.

HORNBY, Michael Charles St John; retired as Vice-Chairman, W. H. Smith & Son Ltd (1944–65); *b* 2 Jan. 1899; *e s* of C. H. St J. Hornby and Cicely Hornby; *m* 1928, Nicolette Joan, *d* of Hon. Cyril Ward, MVO; two *s* one *d*. *Educ:* Winchester; RMC Sandhurst; New Coll., Oxford. Joined Grenadier Guards, 1918; served in France and Germany. New Coll., Oxford, 1919–21. Entered W. H. Smith & Son, 1921. Prime Warden, Goldsmiths' Company, 1954–55. Chm., National Book League, 1959. *Recreations:* fox-hunting, shooting, cricket, gardening. *Address:* Pusey House, Faringdon, Oxon. *T:* Buckland 222. *Clubs:* White's, MCC.

See also R. M. Holland-Martin, Sir R. A. Hornby, S. M. Hornby.

HORNBY, Richard Phipps, MA; Chairman, Halifax Building Society, since 1983 (Director, 1976; Vice-Chairman, 1981–83); Director: Cadbury Schweppes plc, since 1982; McCorquodale plc, since 1982; *b* 20 June 1922; *e s* of late Rt Rev. Hugh Leycester Hornby, MC; *m* 1951, Stella Hichens; three *s* one *d*. *Educ:* Winchester Coll.; Trinity Coll., Oxford (Scholar). Served in King's Royal Rifle Corps, 1941–45. 2nd Cl. Hons in Modern History, Oxford, 1948 (Soccer Blue). History Master, Eton Coll., 1948–50; with Unilever, 1951–52; with J. Walter Thompson Co., 1952–63, 1964–81 (Dir, 1974–81). Contested (C) West Walthamstow: May 1955 (gen. election) and March 1956 (by-election); MP (C) Tonbridge, Kent, June 1956–Feb. 1974. PPS to Rt Hon. Duncan Sandys, MP, 1959–63; Parly Under-Sec. of State, CRO and CO, Oct. 1963–Oct. 1964. Member: BBC Gen. Adv. Council, 1969–74; Cttee of Inquiry into Intrusions into Privacy, 1970–72; British Council Exec. Cttee, 1971–74. *Recreations:* shooting, fishing, walking, riding. *Address:* 32 Wetherby Mansions, Earl's Court Square, SW5.

HORNBY, Sir (Roger) Antony, Kt 1960; President, Savoy Hotel Ltd, 1977–81 (Vice-Chairman to Dec. 1976); *b* 5 Feb. 1904; *s* of late C. H. St J. Hornby, Shelley House, Chelsea; *m* 1st, 1931, Lady Veronica Blackwood (marr. diss. 1940); one *d*; 2nd, 1949, Lily Ernst (*d* 1985). *Educ:* Winchester Coll.; New Coll., Oxford. MA Oxon. Vice-Chm. King's Coll. Hosp., 1959–74. Served War of 1939–45, Grenadier Guards. A Trustee of the Wallace Collection, 1963–77; Chm., Nat. Art Collections Fund, 1970–75. *Recreation:* collecting pictures. *Address:* Claridge's Hotel, W1. *Clubs:* Garrick, MCC.

See also R. M. Holland-Martin, M. C. St J. Hornby.

HORNBY, Simon Michael; Director, since 1974, Chairman, since 1982, W. H. Smith & Son (Holdings) Ltd; Director, S. Pearson & Son Ltd, since 1978; *b* 29 Dec. 1934; *s* of Michael Hornby, *qv*; *m* 1968, Sheran Cazalet. *Educ:* Eton; New Coll., Oxford; Harvard Business Sch. 2nd Lieut, Grenadier Guards, 1953–55. Entered W. H. Smith & Son, 1958, Dir, 1965; Gp Chief Exec., W. H. Smith & Son (Holdings), 1978–82. Mem. Exec. Cttee, 1966–, Property Cttee, 1979–, Council 1976–, National Trust; Mem. Adv. Council, Victoria and Albert Museum, 1971–75; Council, RSA, 1985–; Trustee, British Museum, 1975–85; Chm., Nat. Book League, 1978–80 (Dep. Chm., 1976–78). Chm., Design Council, 1986–. *Recreations:* gardening, golf. *Address:* 8 Ennismore Gardens, SW7 1LN. *T:* 01–584 1597; Lake House, Pusey, Faringdon, Oxon SN7 8QB. *T:* Buckland 659. *Club:* Garrick.

HORNE, Sir (Alan) Gray (Antony), 3rd Bt *cr* 1929; *b* 11 July 1948; *s* of Antony Edgar Alan Horne (*d* 1954) (*o s* of 2nd Bt), and of Valentine Antonia, *d* of Valentine Dudensing; *S* grandfather, 1984; *m* 1981. *Heir:* none. *Address:* Château du Basty, Thenon, Dordogne, France.

HORNE, Alistair Allan; author, journalist, lecturer; *b* 9 Nov. 1925; *s* of late Sir (James) Allan Horne and Lady (Auriol Camilla) Horne (*née* Hay); *m* 1953, Renira Margaret (marr. diss. 1982), *d* of Adm. Sir Geoffrey Hawkins, KBE, CB, MVO, DSC; three *d*. *Educ:* Le Rosey, Switzerland; Millbrook, USA; Jesus Coll., Cambridge (MA). Served War of 1939–45: RAF, 1943–44; Coldstream Gds, 1944–47; Captain, attached Intelligence Service (ME). Dir, Ropley Trust Ltd, 1948–77; Foreign Correspondent, Daily Telegraph, 1952–55. Founded Alistair Horne Res. Fellowship in Mod. History, St Antony's Coll., Oxford, 1969, Supernumerary Fellow, 1978–. Fellow, Woodrow Wilson Center, Washington, DC, USA, 1980–81. Lectures: Lees Knowles, Cambridge, 1982; Goodman, Univ. of West Ontario, 1983. Member: Management Cttee, Royal Literary Fund, 1969–; Franco-British Council, 1979–; Cttee of Management, Soc. of Authors, 1979–82; Trustee, Imperial War Museum, 1975–82. FRSL. *Publications:* Back into Power, 1955; The Land is Bright, 1958; Canada and the Canadians, 1961; The Price of Glory: Verdun 1916, 1962 (Hawthornden Prize, 1963); The Fall of Paris: The Siege and The Commune 1870–71, 1965; To Lose a Battle: France 1940, 1969; Death of a Generation, 1970; The Terrible Year: The Paris Commune, 1971; Small Earthquake in Chile, 1972; A Savage War of Peace: Algeria 1954–62, 1977 (Yorkshire Post Book of Year Prize, 1978; Wolfson Literary Award, 1978); Napoleon, Master of Europe 1805–1807, 1979; The French Army and Politics 1870–1970, 1984 (Enid Macleod Prize, 1985); contribs to books: Combat: World War I, ed Don Congdon, 1964; Impressions of America, ed R. A. Brown, 1966; Marshal V. I. Chuikov, The End of the Third Reich, 1967; Sports and Games in Canadian Life, ed N. and M. L. Howell, 1969; Decisive Battles of the Twentieth Century, ed N. Frankland and C. Dowling, 1976; The War Lords: Military Commanders of the Twentieth Century, ed Field Marshal Sir M. Carver, 1976; Regular Armies and Insurgency, ed R. Haycock, 1979; Macmillan: a life in pictures, 1983; contribs various periodicals. *Recreations:* skiing, painting, gardening, travel. *Address:* 21 St Petersburgh Place, W2. *Clubs:* Garrick, Beefsteak, Groucho.

HORNE, Frederic Thomas; Chief Taxing Master of the Supreme Court, since 1983 (Master, 1967–83); *b* 21 March 1917; *y s* of Lionel Edward Horne, JP, Moreton-in-Marsh, Glos; *m* 1944, Madeline Hatton; two *s* two *d*. *Educ:* Chipping Campden Grammar Sch. Admitted a Solicitor (Hons), 1938. Served with RAFVR in General Duties Branch (Pilot), 1939–56. Partner in Iliffe Sweet & Co., 1956–67. Mem., Lord Chancellor's Adv. Cttee on Legal Aid, 1983–. *Publications:* (jtly) Cordery's Law Relating to Solicitors, 7th edn, 1981; (contrib.) Atkins Encyclopaedia of Court Forms, 2nd edn, 1983; (ed jtly) The Supreme Court Practice, 1985. *Recreations:* cricket, music, archaeology. *Address:* Dunstall, Quickley Lane, Chorleywood, Herts. *Club:* MCC.

HORNE, Sir Gray; *see* Horne, Sir A. G. A.

HORNE, Prof. Michael Rex, OBE 1981; MA, PhD, ScD Cantab; MSc (Manchester); FRS 1981; FEng, FICE; FIStructE; Professor of Civil Engineering, University of Manchester, 1960–83 (Beyer Professor, 1978–83); *b* 29 Dec. 1921; *s* of late Rev. Ernest Horne, Leicester; *m* 1947, Molly, *d* of late Mark Hewett, Royston, Herts; two *s* two *d*. *Educ:* Boston (Lincs) Grammar Sch.; Leeds Grammar Sch.; St John's Coll., Cambridge. MA Cantab 1945; PhD Cantab 1950, ScD Cantab 1956. John Winbolt Prize for Research, Cambridge Univ., 1944. Asst Engineer, River Great Ouse Catchment Bd, 1941–45; Scientific Officer, British Welding Research Assoc., 1945–51; Asst Dir of Research in Engineering, 1951–56, Lectr in Engineering, 1957–60, Fellow of St John's Coll., 1957–60, Univ. of Cambridge. Instn of Civil Engineers, Telford Premiums, 1956, 1966, 1978. Chm., NW Branch, 1969–70, Pres., 1980–81, IStructE; Pres., Section G, BAAS, 1981–82; Mem., Merrison Cttee on Box Girders, 1970–73; Chm., Review for Govt of Public Utility Streetworks Act, 1984. Hon. DSc Salford, 1981. Diploma, 1971, Bronze Medal, IStructE, 1973; Baker Medal, ICE, 1977. *Publications:* (with J. F. Baker and J. Heyman) The Steel Skeleton, 1956; (with W. F. Merchant) The Stability of Frames, 1965; The Plastic Theory of Structures, 1971; (with L. J. Morris) Plastic Design of Low Rise Frames, 1981; contribs on structures, strength of materials and particulate theory of soils to learned journals. *Recreations:* photography, wine-making, music. *Address:* 19 Park Road, Hale, Altrincham, Cheshire WA15 9NW.

HORNER, Arthur William, CMG 1964; TD and clasp 1946; *b* 22 June 1909; *s* of Francis Moore and Edith Horner; *m* 1938, Patricia Denise (*née* Campbell); two *s* one *d*. *Educ:* Hardenwick; Felsted. Marine Insurance, 1926–39. Served War, 1939–46, Rifle Brigade; Lieut-Col; psc. Farming in Kenya, 1948–50. Colonial Administrative Service (later HM Overseas Civil Service), Kenya, 1950–64; Commissioner of Lands, 1955–61; Permanent Sec., 1961–64; Dir of Independence Celebrations, 1963; Principal, ODM, 1964–73; seconded Diplomatic Service, 1968–70, retired 1973. *Recreations:* music, gardening. *Address:* St Margaret's Cottage, Northiam, Rye, East Sussex.

HORNER, Douglas George, FIB; Chairman, Mercantile Credit Company, 1980–84; Vice Chairman, 1979–81, Director, 1975–85, Barclays Bank UK Limited; *b* Dec. 1917; *s* of Albert and Louise Horner; *m* 1941, Gwendoline Phyllis Wall; one *s*. *Educ:* Enfield Grammar Sch. Commissioned, Royal Norfolk Regt, 1940. Asst Manager/Manager at various bank branches, 1954–71; Local Dir, Lombard Street, 1971; Regional Gen. Manager, London, 1973; Gen. Man., 1975; Senior Gen. Man., 1977; Dir Barclays Bank plc, 1977–83. *Recreations:* golf, gardening. *Address:* Barclays Bank plc, 54 Lombard Street, EC3P 3AH.

HORNER, Frederick, DSc; CEng, FIEE; Director, Appleton Laboratory, Science Research Council, 1977–79; *b* 28 Aug. 1918; *s* of late Frederick and Mary Horner; *m* 1946, Elizabeth Bonsey; one *s* one *d*. *Educ:* Bolton Sch.; Univ. of Manchester (Ashbury Scholar, 1937; Fairbairn Engrg Prize, 1939; BSc 1st Cl. Hons 1939; MSc 1941; DSc 1968). CEng, FIEE 1959. On staff of DSIR, NPL, 1941–52; UK Scientific Mission, Washington DC, 1947; Radio Research Station, later Appleton Lab. of SRC, 1952–79, Dep. Dir, 1969–77; Admin. Staff Coll., Henley, 1959. Delegate: Internat. Union of Radio Science, 1950– (Chm., Commn VIII, 1966–69); Internat. Radio Consultative Cttee, 1953– (Internat. Chm., Study Group 2, 1980–). Member: Inter-Union Commn on Frequency Allocations for Radio Astronomy and Space Science, 1965– (Sec., 1975–82); Electronics Divl Bd, IEE, 1970–76. Mem. Council: RHC, 1979–85 (Vice-Chm., 1982–85); RHBNC, 1985–; Hon. Associate, Physics: RHC, 1975–85; RHBNC, 1985–. *Publications:* more than 50 scientific papers. *Recreations:* tennis, gardening. *Address:* Gralyn, Clarence Drive, Egham, Surrey TW20 0NL. *T:* Egham 33127.

HORNER, Hallam; *see* Horner, L. J. H.

HORNER, John; *b* 5 Nov. 1911; *s* of Ernest Charles and Emily Horner; *m* 1936, Patricia, *d* of Geoffrey and Alice Palmer; two *d*. *Educ:* elementary sch. and Sir George Monoux Grammar Sch., Walthamstow. Apprenticed Merchant Navy, 1927; Second Mate's Certificate, 1932. Joined London Fire Brigade, 1933; Gen. Sec. Fire Brigades Union, 1939–64; MP (Lab) Oldbury and Halesowen, 1964–70. Mem. Select Cttee on Nationalised Industries. *Publication:* Studies in Industrial Democracy, 1974. *Recreations:* gardening, reading history. *Address:* c/o Barclays Bank, Ross-on-Wye, Herefordshire.

HORNER, (Lawrence John) Hallam, CBE 1973 (OBE 1959); Director, Chamber of Shipping of UK, 1966–72; *b* 14 June 1907; *o s* of late David Aitken Horner and Louise Stuart Black; *m* 1935, Kathleen Joan (*d* 1976), *o d* of late Charles D. Taite, Bowdon, Cheshire; two *d*. *Educ:* Malvern Coll.; Corpus Christi Coll., Oxford (MA). Served War of 1939–45, RSF and 52nd Recce Regt, RAC (despatches). Admitted Solicitor (hons), 1931; Asst Solicitor, Cheshire CC, 1932–34; Rees & Freres, parly agents, 1934–51 (Partner, 1936); Sec., Canal Assoc., 1945–48; Parly Solicitor (later also Sec.), Dock and Harbour Authorities' Assoc., 1946–51; Asst Gen. Man. and Solicitor and Parly Agent, Chamber of Shipping of UK, 1951, Gen. Man., 1959. Sec. Adv. Cttee on New Lighthouse Works, etc, 1951–66; Mem. Adv. Cttee on Oil Pollution of the Sea, 1952–66; Mem., City of London Coll. Shipping Adv. Cttee, 1966–72; Mem., Cttee of Management, British Ship Adoption Soc., 1968–72. Hon. FICS, 1972. Netherlands Bronze Cross, 1945. *Recreation:* watching birds. *Address:* 2 Hamstone Court, Great Gates, Salcombe, South Devon TQ8 8JY. *T:* Salcombe 3420. *Club:* Reform.

HORNSBY, Timothy Richard, FRSA; Director of Ancient Monuments and Historic Buildings, since 1983, and Director of Rural Affairs, since 1984, Department of the Environment; *b* 22 Sept. 1940; *s* of late Harker William Hornsby and Agnes Nora French; *m* 1971, Dr Charmian Rosemary Newton; one *s* one *d*. *Educ:* Bradfield Coll.; Christ Church, Oxford Univ. (MA 1st Cl. Hons Modern History). Harkness Fellow, USA, at Harvard, Columbia, Henry E. Huntington Research Inst., 1961–63; Asst Prof., Birmingham Southern Coll., Alabama, 1963–64; Research Lectr, Christ Church, Oxford, 1964–65; Asst Principal, Min. of Public Building and Works, 1965–67; Private Sec. to Controller General, 1968–69; HM Treasury, 1971–73; Principal, Asst Sec., 1975, Dept of Environment. FRSA 1985. *Recreations:* history, skiing, talking. *Address:* Department of the Environment, 2 Marsham Street, SW1P 3EB. *T:* 01–212 4025. *Club:* Athenæum.

HOROWITZ, Myer, EdD; President, University of Alberta, Canada, since 1979; *b* 27 Dec. 1932; *s* of Philip Horowitz and Fanny Cotler; *m* 1956, Barbara, *d* of Samuel Rosen and Grace Midvidy, Montreal; two *d*. *Educ:* High Sch., Montreal; Sch. for Teachers, Macdonald Coll.; Sir George Williams Univ. (BA); Univ. of Alberta (MEd); Stanford Univ. (EdD). Teacher, Schs in Montreal, Sch. Bd, Greater Montreal, 1952–60. McGill University: Lectr in Educn, 1960–63; Asst Prof., 1963–65; Associate Prof., 1965–67; Asst to Dir, 1964–65; Prof. of Educn, 1967–69 and Asst Dean, 1965–69. Univ. of Alberta:

Prof. and Chm., Dept Elem. Educn, 1969; Dean, Faculty of Educn, 1972–75; Vice-Pres. (Academic), 1975–79. *Address:* University of Alberta, Edmonton, Alberta T6G 2J9, Canada; 14319, 60 Avenue, Edmonton, Alberta T6H 1J8.

HOROWITZ, Vladimir; pianist; *b* Kieff, Russia, 1 Oct. 1904; *s* of Samuel Horowitz and Sophie Bodik; *m* 1933, Wanda Toscanini; one *d*. *Educ:* Kieff Conservatory; studied under Sergi Tarnowsky and Felix Blumenfeld. European Début, 1925; début with New York Philharmonic Orchestra, 1928. Soloist, New York Symphony Orchestra and other American orchestras. Winner 18 Grammy Awards. Royal Philharmonic Soc. Gold Medal, 1972. US Medal of Freedom, 1986. *Address:* c/o Columbia Artists Management, Inc., 165 West 57th Street, New York, NY 10019, USA.

HORRELL, John Ray, CBE 1979; TD; DL; farmer; Chairman, East of England Agricultural Society, since 1984; *b* 8 March 1929; *er s* of late Harry Ray Horrell and of Phyllis Mary Horrell (*née* Whittome); *m* 1951, Mary Elizabeth Noëlle Dickinson; one *s* one *d*. Director: Horrell's Farmers Ltd; Horrell's Dairies Ltd. Mem., Board, Peterborough New Town Develt Corp., 1970–; formerly Mem. Oakes and Taylor Cttees of Enquiry. Mem., Cambs (formerly Huntingdon and Peterborough) CC, 1965– (Chm., 1973–77; Chm., Educn Cttee); Chairman: Council of Local Educn Authorities, 1976–79; ACC, 1981–83 (Vice-Chm., 1979–81). Major, TA; a Vice-Chm., 1977–, Chm., 1986, E Anglia TA&VRA. FRSA. High Sheriff, Cambs, 1981–82; DL Cambs, 1973. *Address:* The Grove, Longthorpe, Peterborough. *T:* Peterborough 262618.

HORRELL, Roger William, OBE 1974; HM Diplomatic Service; Counsellor, Foreign and Commonwealth Office, since 1980; *b* 9 July 1935; *s* of William John Horrell and Dorice Enid (*née* Young); *m* 1970, Patricia Mildred Eileen Smith (*née* Binns) (marr. diss. 1975); one *s* one *d*. *Educ:* Shebbear College; Exeter College, Oxford. MA. Served in Devonshire Regt, 1953–55; Colonial Administrative Service, Kenya, 1959–64; joined Foreign Office, 1964; Economic Officer, Dubai, 1965–67; FCO, 1967–70; First Sec., Kampala, 1970–73; FCO, 1973–76; First Sec., Lusaka, 1976–80. *Recreations:* cricket, reading, walking, bridge. *Address:* c/o Foreign and Commonwealth Office, SW1. *Clubs:* Reform; Frederick Pickersgill Memorial Cricket.

HORRIDGE, Prof. (George) Adrian, FRS 1969; FAA 1971; Professor of Neurobiology, Research School of Biological Sciences, Australian National University, ACT 2601, since 1969; *b* Sheffield, England, 12 Dec. 1927; *s* of George William Horridge and Olive Stray; *m* 1954, Audrey Anne Lightburne; one *s* three *d*. *Educ:* King Edward VII Sch., Sheffield. Fellow, St John's Coll., Cambridge, 1953–56; on staff, St Andrews Univ., 1956–69; Dir, Gatty Marine Laboratory, St Andrews, 1960–69. *Publications:* Structure and Function of the Nervous Systems of Invertebrates (with T. H. Bullock), 1965; Interneurons, 1968; (ed) The Compound Eye and Vision of Insects, 1975; Monographs of the Maritime Museum at Greenwich nos 38, 39, 40, 54, 1979–; The Prahu: traditional sailing boat of Indonesia, 1982 (Oxford in Asia); Sailing Craft of Indonesia, 1985 (Oxford in Asia); Outrigger Canoes of Bali & Madura, Indonesia, 1986; contribs numerous scientific papers on behaviour and nervous systems of lower animals, to jls, etc. *Recreations:* optics, mathematics, marine biology; sailing, language, arts, boat construction in Indonesia. *Address:* PO Box 475, Canberra City, ACT 2601, Australia. *T:* Canberra 062–494532, Telex 62219.

HORROCKS, Raymond, CBE 1983; Non-executive Director, Chloride Group, since 1986; Executive Director and Board Member, BL plc, 1981–86; Group Chief Executive, Cars, 1982–86; Chairman and Chief Executive, Austin Rover Group Holdings Ltd, 1981–86; *b* 9 Jan. 1930; *s* of Elsie and Cecil Horrocks; *m* 1953, Pamela Florence Russell; three *d*. *Educ:* Bolton Municipal Secondary School. Textile Industry, 1944–48 and 1950–51; HM Forces, Army Intelligence Corps, 1948–50; Sales Rep., Proctor & Gamble, 1951–52; Merchandiser, Marks & Spencer, 1953–58; Sub Gp Buying Controller, Littlewoods Mail Order Stores, 1958–63; various plant, departmental and divisional management positions, Ford Motor Co., 1963–72; Regional Dir, Europe and Middle East, Materials Handling Gp, Eaton Corp., 1972–77; Chm. and Man. Dir, Austin Morris Ltd, 1978–80; Man. Dir, BL Cars, 1980–81; Chm. and Chief Exec., BL Cars Gp, 1981–82; Chairman: Unipart Group Ltd, 1981–86; Jaguar Cars Holdings Ltd, 1982–84; non-executive Director: Jaguar plc, 1984–85; The Caravan Club, 1983–; Dir, Nuffield Services Ltd, 1982–86. Member: Council, CBI, 1981–86; Europe Cttee, CBI, 1985–86. FIMI; CBIM; FRSA. *Recreations:* fly fishing, gardening, walking. *Address:* Far End, Riverview Road, Pangbourne, Reading, Berks RG8 7AU.

HORSBRUGH-PORTER, Sir John (Simon), 4th Bt *cr* 1902; *b* 18 Dec. 1938; *s* of Col Sir Andrew Marshall Horsbrugh-Porter, 3rd Bt, DSO and Bar, and of Annette Mary, *d* of Brig.-Gen. R. C. Browne-Clayton, DSO; *S* father, 1986; *m* 1964, Lavinia Rose, *d* of Ralph Turton; one *s* two *d*. *Educ:* Winchester College; Trinity Coll., Cambridge (BA Hons History). School Master. *Recreations:* gliding, literature, music. *Heir: s* Andrew Alexander Marshall Horsbrugh-Porter, *b* 19 Jan. 1971. *Address:* Bowers Croft, Coleshill, Amersham, Bucks. *T:* Amersham 4596.

HORSBURGH, John Millar Stewart, QC (Scot.) 1980; *b* 15 May 1938; *s* of late Alexander Horsburgh and Helen Margaret Watson Millar or Horsburgh; *m* 1966, Johann Catriona Gardner, MB, ChB, DObst RCOG; one *s* one *d*. *Educ:* Hutchesons' Boys' Grammar Sch., Glasgow; Univ. of Glasgow (MA Hons, LLB). Admitted to Scots Bar, 1965. Part-time Mem., Lands Tribunal for Scotland, 1985. *Address:* 8 Laverockbank Road, Edinburgh EH5 3DG. *T:* 031–552 5328.

HORSEFIELD, John Keith, CB 1957; Historian, International Monetary Fund, 1966–69; *b* 14 Oct. 1901; *s* of Rev. Canon F. J. Horsefield, Bristol; *m* 1934, Lucy G. G. Florance. *Educ:* Monkton Combe Sch.; University of Bristol; MA 1948, DSc 1971; London Sch. of Economics. Lecturer, LSE, 1939; Min. of Aircraft Production, 1940; International Monetary Fund, 1947; Under-Sec., Min. of Supply, 1951; Dep. Asst Sec.-Gen. for Economics and Finance, NATO, 1952; Supply and Development Officer, Iron and Steel Bd, 1954; Dir of Finance and Accounts, Gen. Post Office, 1955–60; Chief Editor, International Monetary Fund, 1960–66. *Publications:* The Real Cost of the War, 1940; British Monetary Experiments, 1650–1710, 1960; The International Monetary Fund, 1945–1965, 1970; articles in Economica, etc. *Address:* 60 Clatterford Road, Carisbrooke, Newport, Isle of Wight PO30 1PA. *T:* Isle of Wight 523675.

HORSEY, Gordon, JP; *b* 20 July 1926; *s* of late E. W. Horsey, MBE, and of H. V. Horsey; *m* 1951, Jean Mary (*née* Favill); one *d*. *Educ:* Magnus Grammar Sch., Newark, Notts; St Catharine's Coll., Cambridge. BA, LLB. Served RN, 1944–45, RE, 1945–48 (Captain). Admitted solicitor, 1953; private practice in Nottingham, 1953–71; Registrar: Coventry County Court, 1971; Leicester County Court, 1973; a Recorder, 1978–84. JP Leics, 1975. *Recreation:* fly-fishing. *Address:* Scarsdale House, Old Woodhouse, Leics. *T:* Woodhouse Eaves 890948.

HORSFALL, Sir John (Musgrave), 3rd Bt *cr* 1909; MC 1946; TD 1949 and clasp 1951; JP; *b* 26 Aug. 1915; *s* of Sir (John) Donald Horsfall, 2nd Bt, and Henrietta (*d* 1936), *d* of William Musgrave; *S* father, 1975; *m* 1940, Cassandra Nora Bernardine, *d* of late G. E. Wright; two *s* one *d*. *Educ:* Uppingham. Major, Duke of Wellington's Regt. Dir, Skipton Building Society, 1960–85. Mem. Skipton RDC, 1952–74; Pres. Skipton Divl Conservative Assoc., 1966–79. JP North Yorks, 1959. *Recreation:* shooting. *Heir: s* Edward John Wright Horsfall [*b* 17 Dec. 1940; *m* 1965, Rosemary, *d* of Frank N. King; three *s*]. *Address:* Greenfield House, Embsay, Skipton, North Yorkshire. *T:* Skipton 4560.

HORSFIELD, Maj.-Gen. David Ralph, OBE 1962; FIEE; Associate Consultant, PA Management Consultants Ltd, since 1972; *b* 17 Dec. 1916; *s* of late Major Ralph B. and Morah Horsfield (*née* Baynes); *m* 1948, Sheelah Patricia Royal Eagan; two *s* two *d*. *Educ:* Oundle Sch.; RMA Woolwich; Cambridge Univ. (MA). Commnd in Royal Signals, 1936; comd Burma Corps Signals, 1942; Instr, Staff Coll., 1944–45; comd 2 Indian Airborne Signals, 1946–47; Instr, RMA Sandhurst, 1950–53 (Company Comdr to HM King Hussein of Jordan); comd 2 Signal Regt, 1956–59; Principal Army Staff Officer, MoD, Malaya, 1959–61; Dir of Telecommunications (Army), 1966–68; ADC to the Queen, 1968–69; Deputy Communications and Electronics, Supreme HQ Allied Powers, Europe, 1968–69; Maj.-Gen. 1969; Chief Signal Officer, BAOR, 1969–72; Col Comdt, Royal Signals, 1972–78. Vice Pres., Nat. Ski Fedn, 1978–81. *Recreations:* ski-ing (British Ski Champion, 1949), the visual arts. *Address:* Southill House, Cranmore, Shepton Mallet, Somerset. *T:* Cranmore 395. *Club:* Ski Club of Great Britain.

HORSFIELD, Peter Muir Francis, QC 1978; *b* 15 Feb. 1932; *s* of Henry Taylor Horsfield, AFC, and Florence Lily (*née* Muir); *m* 1962, Anne Charlotte, *d* of late Sir Piers Debenham, 2nd Bt, and Lady (Angela) Debenham; three *s*. *Educ:* Beaumont; Trinity Coll., Oxford (BA 1st Cl. Hons Mods and Greats). Served RNR, 1955–57; Lieut RNR, 1960. Called to the Bar, Middle Temple, 1958, Bencher, 1984; in practice at Chancery Bar, 1958–. *Recreation:* observational astronomy. *Address:* (chambers) 8 Stone Buildings, Lincoln's Inn, WC2A 3TA. *Club:* Garrick.

HORSFORD, Alan Arthur; Chief Executive, Royal Insurance plc, since 1985; *b* 31 May 1927; *s* of Arthur Henry Horsford and Winifred Horsford; *m* 1957, Enid Maureen Baker; one *s* one *d*. *Educ:* Holt School; Liverpool University. BA; FCII. Secretary, Royal Insurance Co. Ltd, 1970–72; Dep. General Manager, 1972–74, General Manager, 1974–79, Royal Insurance Canada; General Manager and Director, 1979–83, Dep. Chief Gen. Manager, 1983–84, Royal Insurance plc. Dep. Chm., Assoc. of British Insurers, 1985–. *Recreations:* theatre, music, cycling, golf. *Address:* Royal Insurance plc, 1 Cornhill, EC3V 3QR.

HORSFORD, Maj.-Gen. Derek Gordon Thomond, CBE 1962 (MBE 1953); DSO 1944 and Bar 1945; *b* 7 Feb. 1917; *s* of late Captain H. T. Horsford, The Gloucestershire Regt, and Mrs V. E. Horsford, Bexhill-on-Sea; *m* 1948, Sheila Louise Russell Crawford; one *s* (and one step *s* two step *d*). *Educ:* Clifton Coll.; RMC, Sandhurst. Commissioned into 8th Gurkha Rifles, 1937; despatches 1943 and 1945; comd 4/1 Gurkha Rifles, Burma, 1944–45; transf. to RA, 1948; Instructor Staff Coll., 1950–52; transf. to King's Regt, 1950; GSO1, 2nd Infantry Div., 1955–56; comd 1st Bn, The King's Regt, 1957–59; AAG, AG2, War Office, 1959–60; Comdr 24th Infantry Brigade Group, Dec. 1960–Dec. 1962; Imperial Defence Coll., 1963; Brig., Gen. Staff, HQ, BAOR, 1964–66. Maj.-Gen. 1966; GOC 50 (Northumbrian) Div./Dist, 1966–67; GOC Yorks Dist, 1967–68; GOC 17 Div./Malaya District, 1969–70; Maj.-Gen., Brigade of Gurkhas, 1969–71; Dep. Comdr Land Forces, Hong Kong, 1970–71, retired. Col, The King's Regt, 1965–70; Col, The Gurkha Transport Regt, 1973–78. *Recreations:* travel, outdoor life. *Address:* St Mary's Cottage, Semley, Shaftesbury, Dorset. *Club:* Army and Navy.

HORSHAM, Bishop Suffragan of, since 1975; **Rt. Rev. Ivor Colin Docker;** *b* 3 Dec. 1925; *s* of Colonel Philip Docker, OBE, TD, DL, and Doris Gwendoline Docker (*née* Whitehill); *m* 1950, Thelma Mary, *d* of John William and Gladys Upton; one *s* one *d*. *Educ:* King Edward's High Sch., Birmingham; Univ. of Birmingham (BA); St Catherine's Coll., Oxford (MA). Curate of Normanton, Yorks, 1949–52; Lecturer of Halifax Parish Church, 1952–54; CMS Area Sec., 1954–59; Vicar of Midhurst, Sussex, 1959–64; RD of Midhurst, 1961–64; Vicar and RD of Seaford, 1964–71; Canon and Prebendary of Colworth in Chichester Cathedral, 1966–81; Vicar and RD of Eastbourne, 1971–75; Proctor in Convocation, 1970–75. *Recreations:* photography, travel, reading. *Address:* Bishop's Lodge, Worth, Crawley, Sussex RH10 4RT. *T:* Crawley 883051.

HORSHAM, Archdeacon of; *see* Filby, Ven. W. C. L.

HORSHAM, Jean, CBE 1979; Deputy Parliamentary Commissioner for Administration, 1981–82, retired; Chairman, Solicitors' Complaints Bureau, since 1986; *b* 25 June 1922; *d* of Albert John James Horsham and Janet Horsham (*née* Henderson). *Educ:* Keith Grammar Sch. Forestry Commn, 1939–64, seconded to Min. of Supply, 1940–45; Min. of Land and Natural Resources, 1964–66; Min. of Housing and Local Govt, 1966; Office of Parly Comr for Administration, 1967–82. Member: Subsidence Compensation Review Cttee, 1983–84; Law Soc. Professional Purposes Cttee, 1984–; Council on Tribunals, 1986–. *Address:* 14 Cotelands, Chichester Road, Croydon, Surrey CRO 5UD.

HORSLEY, Air Marshal Sir (Beresford) Peter (Torrington), KCB 1974; CBE 1964; LVO 1956; AFC 1945; idc; psc; pfc; Chairman: Horsley Wood & Co. Ltd, since 1975; Horsley Wood Printing Ltd, since 1975; Development Sharing Ltd, since 1984; Twyford Moors Engineering Ltd, since 1984; Forecourt Services Southern Ltd, since 1984; director of other companies; *b* 26 March 1921; *s* of late Capt. Arthur Beresford Horsley, CBE; *m* 1st, 1943, Phyllis Conrad Phinney (marr. diss. 1976); one *s* one *d*; 2nd, 1976, Ann MacKinnon, *d* of Gareth and Frances Crwys-Williams; two step *s* two step *d*. *Educ:* Wellington Coll. Joined Royal Air Force, 1940; served in 2nd TAF and Fighter Command. Adjt Oxford Univ. Air Sqdn, 1948; Commands: No 9 and No 29 Sqdns, RAF Wattisham, RAF Akrotiri. Equerry to Princess Elizabeth and to the Duke of Edinburgh, 1949–52; Equerry to the Queen, 1952–53; Equerry to the Duke of Edinburgh, 1953–56. Dep. Comdt, Jt Warfare Establishment, RAF Old Sarum, 1966–68; Asst CAS (Operations), 1968–70; AOC No 1 (Bomber) Gp, 1971–73; Dep. C-in-C, Strike Comd, 1973–75. Retired RAF, 1975. Director: M. L. Holdings, 1976–; M. L. Aviation, 1976–; I.D.S. Aircraft, 1983–; Yorkshire Skiing, 1984–; RCR Internat., 1984–; Stanley Gibbons Holdings, 1985–; Twyford Moors (Aircraft & Engrg) Ltd; Forecourt Services Ltd; Horsley Holdings Ltd; Dahlgren Internat. UK Ltd; Mem., Honeywell Adv. Council, 1978–. Croix de Guerre, 1944. Holds Orders of Christ (Portugal), North Star (Sweden), and Menelik (Ethiopia). *Publication:* (as Peter Beresford) Journal of a Stamp Collector, 1972. *Recreations:* ski-ing, philately. *Address:* c/o Barclays Bank, High Street, Newmarket.

HORSLEY, Colin, OBE 1963; FRCM 1973; Hon. RAM 1977; Pianist; Professor, Royal College of Music, London; *b* Wanganui, New Zealand, 23 April 1920. *Educ:* Royal College of Music. Debut at invitation of Sir John Barbirolli at Hallé Concerts, Manchester, 1943. Soloist with all leading orchestras of Great Britain, the Royal Philharmonic Soc. (1953, 1959), Promenade Concerts, etc. Toured Belgium, Holland, Spain, France, Scandinavia, Malta, Ceylon, Malaya, Australia and New Zealand. Festival appearances include Aix-en-Provence, International Contemporary Music Festival, Palermo, British Music Festivals in Belgium, Holland and Finland. Broadcasts frequently, and records for His Master's Voice and Meridian Records. *Recreation:* gardening. *Address:* Tawsden Manor, Brenchley, Kent. *T:* Brenchley 2323.

HORSLEY, (George) Nicholas (Seward); Chairman: Northern Foods plc, 1970–86; News on Sunday Publishing, since 1986; *b* 21 April 1934; *s* of Alec Stewart Horsley and Ida Seward Horsley; *m* 1st, 1958, Valerie Anne Edwards (marr. diss. 1975); two *s* one *d*; 2nd, 1975, Sabita Sarkar (separated 1984). *Educ:* Keswick Grammar Sch.; Bootham Sch., York; Worcester Coll., Oxford (BA). Freelance journalist, 1957–58. Northern Dairies Ltd: Trainee Manager, 1958; Director, 1963; Vice-Chairman, 1968–70 (Northern Dairies Ltd changed its name to Northern Foods Ltd in 1972). Pres., Dairy Trade Fedn, 1975–77 and 1980–85. Chm., BBC Consultative Group on Industrial and Business Affairs, 1980–83; Mem., BBC Gen. Adv. Council, 1980–83. *Recreations:* music, bridge, local pub, watching cricket, reading. *Address:* Welton Lodge, Dale Road, Welton, near Brough, East Yorkshire HU15 1PE. *T:* Hull 668341. *Club:* Groucho.

HORSLEY, Sir Peter; *see* Horsley, Sir B. P. T.

HORSMAN, Dame Dorothea (Jean), DBE 1986; JP; President, National Council of Women of New Zealand, 1982–86; *b* 17 April 1918; *d* of Samuel Morrell and Jean (*née* Morris); *m* 1943, Ernest Alan Horsman; one *s* two *d*. *Educ:* Univ. of New Zealand (MA History); Univ. of Otago (MA Russian); Trained Teacher's Cert. President: NZ Fedn of University Women, 1973–76; Arthritis and Rheumatism Foundn of NZ, 1980–83; Mem., Bd of Management, 1976, Vice-Pres. 1980, Nat. Council of Women of NZ. JP 1979. Silver Jubilee Medal, 1977. *Publications:* What Price Equality? (with J. J. Herd) (for Nat. Council of Women, NZ), 1974; Women at Home (with J. J. Herd) (for NZ Fedn of Univ. Women), 1976; (contrib. and ed) Women in Council—a History (NCW), 1982. *Recreations:* reading, listening to music. *Address:* 10 Balmoral Street, Opoho, Dunedin, New Zealand. *T:* (024) 737–119.

HORSMAN, Malcolm; *b* 28 June 1933; Director, Slater Walker Securities Ltd, 1967–70; Chairman: Ralli International Ltd, 1969–73; Pennine Resources PLC, since 1983; Director: The Bowater Corporation Ltd, 1972–77; Tozer Kemsley & Millbourn (Holdings) Ltd, 1975–82. Member: Study Group on Local Authority Management Structures, 1971–72; South East Economic Planning Council, 1972–74; Royal Commission on the Press, 1974–77; Institute of Contemporary Arts Ltd, 1975–78; Council, Oxford Centre for Management Studies, 1973–84; Chm., British Centre, Internat. Theatre Inst., 1982–84 (Mem. Exec. Council, 1980–). Visiting Fellow, Cranfield Institute of Technology/The School of Management, 1977–. Vis. Lectr, Univ. of Transkei, 1977. Chm., Nat. Youth Theatre, 1982– (Dep. Chm. 1971–82); Member: Court, RCA, 1977–80; Editorial Bd, DRAMA, 1978–81; Council, Birthright, 1974–85. *Address:* 46 Cumberland Terrace, Regent's Park, NW1.

HORSTEAD, Rt. Rev. James Lawrence Cecil, CMG 1962; CBE 1956; DD (Hon.) 1956; Canon Emeritus of Leicester Cathedral; *b* 16 Feb. 1898; *s* of James William and Mary Leah Horstead; *m* 1926, Olive Davidson; no *c*. *Educ:* Christ's Hosp.; University and St John's Coll., Durham (Mathematical Scholar, Lightfoot Scholar). BA 2nd Cl. Maths Hons 1921; Theol. Hons 1923; MA 1924; Deacon, 1923; Priest, 1924; Curate St Margaret's Church, Durham, 1923–26; Sec. for Durham Student Christian Movement, 1923–26; Principal Fourah Bay Coll., 1926–36; Canon Missioner Diocese of Sierra Leone, 1928–36; Sec. Church Missionary Soc., Sierra Leone, 1926–36; Bishop of Sierra Leone, 1936–61; Archbishop of West Africa, 1955–61; Rector of Appleby Magna, 1962–68; Asst Bp, Diocese of Leicester, 1962–76. *Publication:* Co-operation with Africans, International Review of Missions, April 1935.

HORT, Sir James Fenton, 8th Bt *cr* 1767; *b* 6 Sept. 1926; *s* of Sir Fenton George Hort, 7th Bt, and Gwendolene (*d* 1982), *d* of late Sir Walter Alcock, MVO; *S* father 1960; *m* 1951, Joan, *d* of late Edwin Peat, Swallownest, Sheffield; two *s* two *d*. *Educ:* Marlborough; Trinity Coll., Cambridge. MA, MB, BChir, Cambridge, 1950. *Recreation:* fishing. *Heir:* *s* Andrew Edwin Fenton Hort, *b* 15 Nov. 1954. *Address:* Poundgate Lodge, Uckfield Road, Crowborough, Sussex.

HORTON, Dr Eric William; grassland and livestock farmer; Director of Regulatory Affairs, Glaxo Group Research Ltd, 1980–83, Member Board, 1982–83; *b* 20 June 1929; *e s* of late Harold and Agnes Horton; *m* 1956, Thalia Helen, *er d* of late Sir George Lowe; two *s* one *d*. *Educ:* Sedbergh Sch.; Edinburgh Univ. BSc, MB, ChB, PhD, DSc, MD, FRCPE. Mem. Scientific Staff, MRC, Nat. Inst. for Med. Res., London, 1958–60; Dir of Therapeutic Res. and Head of Pharmacology, Miles Labs Ltd, Stoke Poges, 1960–63; Sen. Lectr in Physiology, St Bartholomew's Hosp., London, 1963–66; Wellcome Prof. of Pharmacology, Sch. of Pharmacy, Univ. of London, 1966–69; Prof. of Pharmacology, Univ. of Edinburgh, 1969–80. Hon. Sen. Res. Fellow, Med. Coll. of St Bartholomew's Hosp., London, 1980–; Hon. Lectr in Pharmacol., Royal Free Hosp. Med. Sch., London, 1960–63. Member, Governing Body, Inveresk Res. Foundn (formerly International), 1971–80; Non-executive Director: Inveresk Res. Internat. Ltd, 1977–80; GLP Systems Ltd, 1978–80. Member: Adv. Cttee on Pesticides, MAFF, 1970–73; Biological Research and Cell Boards, MRC, 1973–75; Pharmacy Panel, SRC, 1980–81; Editorial Bd, British Jl of Pharmacology, 1960–66; Editorial Bd, Pharmacological Reviews, 1968–74. Hon. Treasurer, Brit. Pharmacological Soc., 1976–80. Baly Medal, RCP, 1973. *Publications:* Prostaglandins, 1972; papers in learned jls on peptides and prostaglandins. *Recreation:* listening to music and books on cassette. *Address:* Froghole Farm, Gore Common, Shaftesbury, Dorset SP7 0PZ.

HORTON, Maj.-Gen. Frank Cyril, CB 1957; OBE 1953; RM; *b* 31 May 1907; *s* of late Lieut-Comdr F. Horton, Royal Navy, and late Emma M. Hopper; *m* 1934, Jennie Ellaline Hammond: one *d*. *Educ:* Sir Roger Manwood's Sch. 2nd Lieut RM 1925; Lieut RM 1928; HMS Cumberland, China Station, 1928–29; HMS Royal Oak, Mediterranean Station, 1929–31; Captain RM, 1936; HMS Ajax, America and West Indies Station, 1936–37; Brevet Major, 1940; psc 1941; Actg Lieut-Col 1942; GSO1, Staff of Chief of Combined Operations, 1942–43; Comdg Officer, 44 (RM) Commando, SE Asia, 1943–44; Directing Staff, Army Staff Coll., 1945–46; Plans Div., Admiralty, 1946–48; Directing Staff, Jt Services Staff Coll., 1948–51; Comdt, Amphibious Sch., RM, 1951–52; idc 1953; Col GS, Staff of Comdt Gen., RM, 1954; Chief of Staff to Commandant Gen. Royal Marines, 1955–58; Maj. 1946; Lieut-Col 1949, Col 1953; Maj.-Gen. 1955; retired, 1958. County Civil Defence Officer, Essex, 1959; Regional Dir of Civil Defence, S Eastern Region, 1961–68. *Address:* Southland, Florance Lane, Groombridge, Sussex. *T:* Groombridge 355. *Club:* Royal Naval and Royal Albert Yacht (Portsmouth).

HORTON, Robert Baynes; Chairman and Chief Executive Officer, Standard Oil Co., since 1986 (Director, since 1983); *b* 18 Aug. 1939; *s* of late William Harold Horton and of Dorothy Joan Horton (*née* Baynes); *m* 1962, Sally Doreen (*née* Wells); one *s* one *d*. *Educ:* King's School, Canterbury; University of St Andrews (BSc); Massachusetts Inst. of Technology (SM; Sloan Fellow, 1970–71). British Petroleum, 1957–86: General Manager, BP Tankers, 1975–76; General Manager, Corporate Planning, 1976–79; Managing Dir and Chief Exec. Officer, BP Chemicals, 1980–83; Man. Dir, BP Co. plc, 1983–86. Director: ICL plc, 1982–84; BP Canada Inc., 1984–86; Pilkington Bros plc, 1985–. Pres., Chemicals Industry Assoc., 1982–84; Vice-Chm., BIM, 1985– (CBIM 1982); Member: SERC, 1985–86; US/China Cttee, 1986–; Bd and Management Cttee, Amer. Petroleum Inst., 1986–; Business Roundtable, 1986–; Nat. Petroleum Council, USA, 1986–; MIT (Sloan) Vis. Cttee, 1977–80, 1985–; Trustee, CED, 1986–. Gov., King's Sch., Canterbury, 1984–. *Recreations:* music, shooting. *Address:* The Standard Oil Company, 200 Public Square, Cleveland, Ohio 44114-2375, USA. *Clubs:* Carlton; Leander; Union (Cleveland).

HORWOOD, Hon. Owen Pieter Faure, DMS; President, Council of Governors, Development Bank of Southern Africa, since 1983; Chancellor, University of Durban-Westville, since 1973; *b* 6 Dec. 1916; *e s* of late Stanley Ebden Horwood and of Anna Johanna Horwood (*née* Faure), *m* 1946, Helen Mary Watt; one *s* one *d*. *Educ:* Boys' High Sch., Paarl, CP; University of Cape Town (BCom). South African Air Force, 1940–42. Associate Prof. of Commerce, University of Cape Town, 1954–55; Prof. of Economics, University Coll. of Rhodesia and Nyasaland, 1956–57; Univ. of Natal: William Hudson Prof. of Economics, 1957–65; Dir of University's Natal Regional Survey; Principal and Vice-Chancellor, 1966–70. Mem., 1970–80, Leader, 1978–80, South African Senate; Minister of Indian Affairs and Tourism, 1972–74; Minister of Economic Affairs, 1974–75; Minister of Finance, 1975–84. Financial Adviser to Govt of Lesotho, 1966–72. Chairman: Nedbank Gp, 1984– (Dir, 1984–); Cape Wine and Distillers Ltd, 1984–; Nedbank Ltd, 1986–; Director: South African Mutual Life Assurance Soc., 1984–; South African Permanent Building Soc., 1984–; Macsteel (Pty) Ltd, 1984–. Hon. DCom: Port Elizabeth, 1980; Stellenbosch, 1983; Hon. Scriptural degree, Israel Torah Res. Inst. and Adelphi Univ., 1980; Hon. DEcon Rand Afrikaans, 1981. *Publications:* (jtly) Economic Systems of the Commonwealth, 1962; contribs to SA Jl of Economics, SA Bankers' Jl, Economica (London), Optima, etc. *Recreations:* cricket, gardening, sailing. *Address:* PO Box 1144, Johannesburg, South Africa. *Clubs:* Durban (Durban); Durban Country (Natal); Western Province Cricket; Cape Town Cricket (Captain 1943–48).

HOSE, John Horsley; Member, General Executive Council, Transport and General Workers' Union, since 1986 (President, National Union of Agricultural and Allied Workers, 1978–82); Forest Craftsman, Forestry Commission, since 1975 (Forest Worker, 1949, Skilled Forest Worker, 1950); *b* 21 March 1928; *s* of Harry and Margaret Eleanor Hose; *m* 1967, Margaret Winifred Gaskin. *Educ:* Sneinton Boulevard Council Sch.; Nottingham Bluecoat Sch. Architects' Junior Asst, 1943–46. National Service, with Royal Engineers, 1946–48. Chm., Nat. Trade Gp, Agricultural and Allied Workers/TGWU, 1982–86 (Mem., 1982–). *Recreations:* walking, reading, drinking real ale. *Address:* 11 Sandringham Road, Sneinton Dale, Nottingham NG2 4HH. *T:* Nottingham 580494.

HOSEGOOD, Philip James; Under-Secretary, Welsh Office, 1976–80, retired; *b* 9 Sept. 1920; *s* of late George Frank and Madeleine Clarisse Hosegood; *m* 1948, Heather (*née* Roriston); two *d*. *Educ:* Heanor Grammar Sch.; correspondence courses. Joined Civil Service as Tax Officer, 1937; Exec. Officer, India Office, 1939. Served War, Army, 1941–46. Asst Principal, Min. of Civil Aviation, 1948; Principal, Min. of Civil Aviation, 1951 (later Min. of Transport); Asst Sec., Welsh Office, 1965. Chm., Lower Machen Festival, 1977–86. *Recreations:* music, outdoor activities. *Address:* 16 Rheidol Close, Llanishen, Cardiff CF4 5NQ. *T:* Cardiff 756445.

HOSFORD, John Percival, MS, FRCS; retired; Surgeon, Lecturer on Surgery, St Bartholomew's Hospital (1936–60); Surgeon, King Edward VII Hospital for Officers and Florence Nightingale Hospital; Consulting Surgeon to Hospitals at Watford, Leatherhead, Hitchin, St Albans and to the Foundling Hospital and Reedham Orphanage; *b* 24 July 1900; 2nd *s* of Dr B. Hosford, Highgate; *m* 1932, Millicent Sacheverell Violet Sybil Claud, *d* of late Brig.-Gen. C. Vaughan Edwards, CMG, DSO; one *s* one *d*. *Educ:* Highgate Sch.; St Bartholomew's Hosp. MB, BS (London) 1922; FRCS Eng. 1925; MS (London); University Gold Medal, 1925. Formerly Registrar St Bartholomew's Hosp. and of Royal National Orthopædic Hosp. Hunterian Prof., Royal College of Surgeons, 1932. Retired, Oct. 1960. Formerly: Mem. of Court of Examiners of Royal College of Surgeons; Examiner in Surgery at Universities of Oxford, London, Sheffield, Belfast; Fellow Assoc. of Surgeons (on Council) and Royal Society Med. *Publications:* numerous articles in medical and surgical journals and encyclopædias. *Recreation:* gardening. *Address:* 16 Pelham Road, Clavering, Saffron Walden, Essex CB11 4PQ.

HOSIE, James Findlay, CBE 1972 (OBE 1955; MBE 1946); a Director, Science Research Council, 1965–74; *b* 22 Aug. 1913; *m* 1951, Barbara Mary Mansell. *Educ:* Glasgow Univ. (MA Hons); St John's Coll., Cambridge (BA). Indian Civil Service, 1938–47; Principal, 1947–56, Asst Sec., 1956–58, Min. of Defence, London; Asst Sec. QMGF, War Office, 1958–61; Office of Minister for Science, later Dept of Educn. and Science, 1961–65. *Recreations:* bird-watching, gardening. *Address:* The Mansion, Apt 29, Albury Park, near Guildford, Surrey GU5 9BB. *T:* Shere 3296.

HOSIER, John, CBE 1984; Principal, Guildhall School of Music and Drama, since 1978; *b* 18 Nov. 1928; *s* of Harry J. W. Hosier and Constance (*née* Richmond). *Educ:* Preston Manor Sch.; St John's Coll., Cambridge. MA 1954. Taught in Ankara, Turkey, 1951–53; Music Producer, BBC Radio for schools, 1953–59; seconded to ABC, Sydney, to advise on educational music programmes, 1959–60; Music Producer, subseq. Sen. and Exec. Producer, BBC TV, pioneering first regular music broadcasts to schools, 1960–73; ILEA Staff Inspector for music, and Dir of Centre for Young Musicians, 1973–76. Vice-Chm., Kent Opera, 1985–; Founder Mem. and Vice-Chm., UK Council for Music Educn and Training, 1975–81; Member: Gulbenkian Enquiry into training musicians, 1978; Music Panel, British Council, 1984–; Music Panel, GLAA, 1984–; Council of Management, Royal Philharmonic Soc., 1982–; Member Governing Body: NYO, 1979; Chetham's Sch., 1983. FRSA 1976; FGSM 1978; Hon. RAM 1980; FRCM 1981; FRNCM 1985. Hon. DMus City Univ., 1986. *Compositions:* music for: Cambridge revivals of Parnassus, 1949, and Humorous Lovers, 1951; Something's Burning, Mermaid, 1974; many radio and TV productions. *Publications:* The Orchestra, 1961, revd edn 1977; various books, songs and arrangements for children; contribs on music to educnl jls. *Address:* Guildhall School of Music and Drama, Barbican, EC2Y 8DT. *T:* 01–628 2571. *Club:* City Livery.

HOSKER, Gerald Albery; Deputy Treasury Solicitor, since 1984; *b* 28 July 1933; *s* of Leslie Reece Hosker and Constance Alice Rose Hosker (*née* Hubbard); *m* 1956, Rachel Victoria Beatrice Middleton; one *s* one *d*. *Educ:* Berkhamsted Sch., Berkhamsted, Herts. Admitted Solicitor, 1956; Corporate Secretary 1964; Associate of the Faculty of Secretaries and Administrators 1964. Articled to Derrick Bridges & Co., 1951–56; with Clifford-Turner & Co., 1957–59; entered Treasury Solicitor's Dept as Legal Asst, 1960; Sen. Legal Asst, 1966; Asst Solicitor, 1973; Under Sec. (Legal), 1982. FRSA 1964. *Recreations:* the study of biblical prophecy, herbalism. *Address:* Cedar House, Granville Road, Barnet, Herts EN5 4DS. *T:* 01–449 1148.

HOSKING, Barbara Nancy, OBE 1985; Controller of Information Services, Independent Broadcasting Authority, since 1977; *b* 4 Nov. 1926; *d* of late William Henry Hosking and Ada Kathleen Murrish. *Educ:* West Cornwall School for Girls, Penzance; Hillcroft College, Surbiton; and by friends. Secretary to Town Clerk, Council of Isles of Scilly, and local corresp. for BBC and Western Morning News, 1945–47; Editl Asst, The Circle, Odeon and Gaumont cinemas, 1947–50; Asst to Inf. Officer, Labour Party, 1952–55; Asst to Gen. Manager, Uruwira Minerals Ltd, Tanzania, 1955–57; Res. Officer, Broadcasting Section, Labour Party, 1958–65; Science Press Officer, DES, 1965; Press Officer, Min. of Technology, 1967; Press and Publicity Officer, Metrication Board, 1970; Senior Inf.

Officer, 10 Downing Street, 1970; Principal Inf. Officer, DoE, 1972; Private Sec. to Parly Secs, Cabinet Office, 1973; Chief Inf. Officer, DoE, 1974–77. Mem. Council, London Cornish Assoc.; Vice-Pres., Media Soc. FRSA. Special citation, American Women's Forum, NY, 1983. *Publications:* contribs to Punch, New Scientist, Spectator, BBC Radio 4. *Recreations:* opera, lieder, watching politics, watching sport. *Address:* 9 Highgate Spinney, Crescent Road, N8. *T:* 01–340 1853. *Club:* Reform (Cttee Mem., 1984–86).

HOSKING, Eric (John), OBE 1977; photographer, ornithologist, broadcaster; *b* 2 Oct. 1909; 3rd *s* of late Albert Hosking and Margaret Helen, *d* of William Steggall; *m* 1939, Dorothy, *d* of late Harry Sleigh; two *s* one *d*. *Educ:* Stationers' Company's Sch. London, N8. Hon. Fellow, Royal Photographic Society; a Vice-Pres., Royal Society for the Protection of Birds; Hon. Vice-Pres., London Natural History Soc.; a Vice-Pres., British Naturalists' Assoc.; Pres., Nature Photographic Society; Scientific Fellow of Zoological Society; Fellow, British Inst. of Professional Photographers. Exhibited at Royal Photographic Society, 1932– (Council, 1950–56; Fellowship & Associateship Admissions Cttee, 1951–56, 1960–65 and 1967–); Member: BOU, 1935–; Brit. Trust for Ornithology, 1938–; Cornell Laboratory of Ornithology, America, 1961–. Dir of Photography to Coto Doñana Expedn, Spain, 1956 and 1957; Leader of Cazoria Valley Expedition, Spain, 1959; Dir of Photography, British Ornithologists' Expedition to Bulgaria, 1960, to Hungary, 1961; other expeditions: Mountfort-Jordan, 1963; British-Jordan, 1965; Pakistan, 1966; World Wildlife Fund, Pakistan, 1967; Lindblad Galapagos Islands, 1970; Kenya and Rhodesia, 1972; Tanzania and Kenya, 1974 and 1977; Seychelles, 1978; India and Nepal, 1979; Falklands and Antarctic, 1979; circumnavigation of Antarctic, and New Zealand and Australia, 1981; Spitzbergen and Arctic, 1982; Greenland and Canadian Arctic, 1984; Alaska, 1984; Sri Lanka and Israel, 1985; Madagascar, Comoros, Aldabra and Seychelles, 1986. Photographic Editor: of New Naturalist, 1942–; of British Birds, 1960–76. RGS Cherry Kearton Award, 1968; RSPB Gold Medal, 1974; Zoological Soc. Silver Medal, 1975. *Publications:* Intimate Sketches from Bird Life, 1940; The Art of Bird Photography, 1944; Birds of the Day, 1944; Birds of the Night, 1945; More Birds of the Day, 1946; The Swallow, 1946; Masterpieces of Bird Photography, 1947; Birds in Action, 1949; Birds Fighting, 1955; Bird Photography as a Hobby, 1961; Nesting Birds, Eggs and Fledglings, 1967; (with Frank Lane) An Eye for a Bird (autobiog.), 1970; Wildlife Photography, 1973; Birds of Britain, 1978; Eric Hosking's Birds, 1979; (with J. Flegg) Eric Hosking's Owls, 1982; Antarctic Wildlife, 1982; (with W. G. Hale) Eric Hosking's Waders, 1983; (with R. M. Lockley) Eric Hosking's Seabirds, 1983; Just a Lark, 1984; (with Janet Kear) Eric Hosking's Wildfowl, 1985; (with Peter France) The Encyclopaedia of Bible Animals, 1985; (with J. Flegg and David Hosking) Which Bird, 1986. Illustrator of many books on natural history, by photographs. *Address:* 20 Crouch Hall Road, N8 8XH. *T:* 01–340 7703.

HOSKING, Prof. Geoffrey Alan; Professor of Russian History, University of London, since 1984; *b* 28 April 1942; *s* of Stuart William Steggall Hosking and Jean Ross Hosking; *m* 1970, Anne Lloyd Hirst; two *d*. *Educ:* Maidstone Grammar Sch.; King's Coll., Cambridge (MA, PhD); St Antony's Coll., Oxford. Asst Lectr in Government, 1966–68, Lectr in Government, 1968–71, Univ. of Essex; Vis. Lectr in Political Science, Univ. of Wisconsin, Madison, 1971–72; Lectr in History, Univ. of Essex, 1972–76; Sen. Research Fellow, Russian Inst., Columbia Univ., New York, 1976; Sen. Lectr and Reader in Russian History, Univ. of Essex, 1976–84; Vis. Professor, Slavisches Inst., Univ. of Cologne, 1980–81. Mem. Council, Writers and Scholars Educnl Trust. *Publications:* The Russian Constitutional Experiment: Government and Duma 1907–14, 1973; Beyond Socialist Realism: Soviet fiction since Ivan Denisovich, 1980; A History of the Soviet Union, 1985. *Recreations:* squash, chess, walking. *Address:* School of Slavonic Studies, University of London, Senate House, Malet Street, WC1E 7HU. *T:* 01–637 4934.

HOSKINS, Robert William; actor; *b* 26 Oct. 1942; *s* of Robert Hoskins and Elsie Lilian Hoskins; *m* 1st, 1970, Jane Livesey; two *s* two *d*; 2nd, 1984, Linda Banwell. *Educ:* Stroud Green School. *Stage:* Intimate Theatre, Palmers Green, 1966; Victoria, Stoke on Trent, 1967; Century Travelling Theatre, 1969; Royal Court, 1972; Doolittle in Pygmalion, Albery, 1974; RSC season, Aldwych, 1976; The World Turned Upside Down, NT, 1978; Has Washington Legs?, NT, 1978; True West, NT, 1981; Guys and Dolls, NT, 1981; *television:* On the Move, 1976; Pennies from Heaven, 1978; Flickers, 1980; The Dunera Boys, 1985; *films:* Zulu Dawn, 1980; The Long Good Friday, 1981; The Honorary Consul, 1982; Lassiter, 1984; Cotton Club, 1984; Sweet Liberty, 1986; Mona Lisa, 1986 (Best Actor award, Cannes Fest.). *Recreations:* photography, gardening, playgoing. *Address:* 22 Penn Road, N7 9RD. *T:* 01–607 7282.

HOSKINS, Prof. William George, CBE 1971; FBA 1969; MA, PhD; *b* Exeter, 22 May 1908; *e s* of late William George Hoskins and Alice Beatrice Dymond; *m* 1933, Frances Jackson; one *s* one *d*. *Educ:* Hele's Sch., Exeter; University Coll., Exeter. Lectr in Economics, University Coll., Leicester, 1931–41; 1946–48; Central Price Regulation Cttee, 1941–45; Reader in English Local History, University Coll. (now Univ.) of Leicester, 1948–51; Reader in Econ. Hist., University of Oxford, 1951–65; Hatton Prof. of English History, University of Leicester, 1965–68, retired in despair, 1968; Emeritus Professor, 1968. BBC TV Series, Landscapes of England, 1976, 1977, 1978. Mem. Royal Commission on Common Land, 1955–58; Adv. Cttee on Bldgs of Special Architectural and Historical Interest (Min. of Housing and Local Govt), 1955–64; Vice-Pres. Leicestershire Archæol and Hist. Soc., 1952; President: Dartmoor Preserv. Assoc., 1962–76; Devonshire Assoc., 1978–79; British Agricultural History Soc., 1972–74; Leverhulme Res. Fellow, 1961–63; Leverhulme Emeritus Fellowship, 1970–71. Murchison Award, RGS, 1976. Hon. FRIBA, 1973. Hon. DLitt: Exon, 1974; CNAA, 1976; DUniv Open, 1981. *Publications:* Industry, Trade and People in Exeter, 1935; Heritage of Leicestershire, 1946; Midland England, 1949; Essays in Leicestershire History, 1950; Chilterns to Black Country, 1951; East Midlands and the Peak, 1951; Devonshire Studies, (with H. P. R. Finberg), 1952; Devon (New Survey of England), 1954; The Making of the English Landscape, 1955; The Midland Peasant, 1957; The Leicestershire Landscape, 1957; Exeter in the Seventeenth Century, 1957; Local History in England, 1959; Devon and its People, 1959; Two Thousand Years in Exeter, 1960; The Westward Expansion of Wessex, 1960; Shell Guide to Rutland, 1963; The Common Lands of England and Wales (with L. Dudley Stamp), 1963; Provincial England, 1963; Old Devon, 1966; Fieldwork in Local History, 1967; Shell Guide to Leicestershire, 1970; History from the Farm, 1970; English Landscapes, 1973; The Age of Plunder, 1976; One Man's England, 1978. *Recreations:* remembering, quietly reading. *Address:* 19 Howell Road, Exeter.

HOSKYNS, Sir Benedict (Leigh), 16th Bt, *cr* 1676; *b* 27 May 1928; *s* of Rev. Sir Edwyn Clement Hoskyns, 13th Bt, MC, DD and Mary Trym, *d* of Edwin Budden, Macclesfield; *S* brother 1956; *m* 1953, Ann Wilkinson; two *s* two *d*. *Educ:* Haileybury; Corpus Christi Coll., Cambridge; London Hospital. BA Cantab 1949; MB, BChir Cantab 1952. House Officer at the London Hospital, 1953. RAMC, 1953–56. House Officer at Royal Surrey County Hospital and General Lying-In Hospital, York Road, SE1, 1957–58; DObstRCOG 1958; in general practice, 1958–. *Heir:* *s* Edwyn Wren Hoskyns [*b* 4 Feb. 1956; *m* 1981, Jane, *d* of John Sellars. *Educ:* Nottingham Univ. Medical School (BM, BS 1979; MRCP 1984)]. *Address:* Harewood, Great Oakley, near Harwich, Essex. *T:* Ramsey (Essex) 880341.

HOSKYNS, Sir John (Austin Hungerford Leigh), Kt 1982; Director-General, Institute of Directors, since 1984; Director: AGB Research Plc; Clerical Medical & General Life Assurance Society; Ferranti Plc; McKechnie Brothers plc; *b* 23 Aug. 1927; *s* of Lt-Colonel Chandos Benedict Arden Hoskyns and Joyce Austin Hoskyns; *m* 1956, Miranda Jane Marie Mott; two *s* one *d*. *Educ:* Winchester College. Served in The Rifle Brigade, 1945–57 (Captain); IBM United Kingdom Ltd, 1957–64; founded John Hoskyns & Co. Ltd, later part of Hoskyns Group Ltd (Chm. and Man. Dir), 1964–75. Hd of PM's Policy Unit, 1979–82. Hon. DSc Salford, 1985. *Recreations:* opera, shooting. *Address:* 83 Clapham Common West Side, SW4. *T:* 01–228 9505. *Club:* Travellers'.

HOTHAM, family name of **Baron Hotham.**

HOTHAM, 8th Baron, *cr* 1797; **Henry Durand Hotham;** Bt 1621; DL; *b* 3 May 1940; *s* of 7th Baron Hotham, CBE, and Lady Letitia Sibell Winifred Cecil, *er d* of 5th Marquess of Exeter, KG; *S* father, 1967; *m* 1972, Alexandra Stirling Home, *d* of late Maj. Andrew S. H. Drummond Moray; two *s* one *d*. *Educ:* Eton; Cirencester Agricultural Coll. Late Lieut, Grenadier Guards; ADC to Governor of Tasmania, 1963–66. DL Humberside, 1981. *Heir:* *s* Hon. William Beaumont Hotham, *b* 13 Oct. 1972. *Address:* Dalton Hall, Dalton Holme, Beverley, Yorks; Scorborough Hall, Driffield, Yorks.

HOTHFIELD, 5th Baron *cr* 1881; **George William Anthony Tufton,** TD 1949 (and Bar); DL; Bt 1851; *b* 28 Oct. 1904; *s* of Hon. Charles Henry Tufton, CMG (*d* 1923) (3rd *s* of 1st Baron) and Stella Josephine Faudel, OBE (*d* 1958), *d* of Sir George Faudel Faudel-Phillips, 1st Bt, GCIE; *S* cousin, 1986; *m* 1936, Evelyn Margarette, *e d* of late Eustace Charles Mordaunt; two *s* one *d*. *Educ:* Eton; Hertford College, Oxford. Insurance Broker and Underwriting Member of Lloyd's. DL Herts, 1962. *Recreations:* lawn tennis, shooting. *Heir:* *s* Hon. Anthony Charles Sackville Tufton [*b* 21 Oct. 1939; *m* 1975, Lucinda Marjorie, *d* of Captain Timothy John Gurney; one *s* one *d*]. *Address:* 11A High Street, Barkway, Royston, Herts. *T:* Barkway 266. *Club:* Leander (Henley-on-Thames).

HOTSON, Leslie, LittD (Cambridge); FRSL; Shakespearean scholar and writer; *b* Delhi, Ont, Canada, 16 Aug. 1897; *s* of John H. and Lillie S. Hotson; *m* 1919, Mary May, *d* of Frederick W. Peabody. *Educ:* Harvard Univ. Sheldon Travelling Fellow, Harvard, 1923–24; Sterling Research Fellow, Yale, 1926–27; Associate Prof. of English, New York Univ., 1927–29; Guggenheim Memorial Fellow, 1929–31; Prof. of English, Haverford Coll., Pa, 1931–41; served War of 1939–45, 1st Lieut and Capt. Signal Corps, US Army, 1943–46; Fulbright Exchange Scholar, Bedford Coll., London, 1949–50; Research Associate, Yale, 1953; Fellow, King's Coll., Cambridge, 1954–60. *Publications:* The Death of Christopher Marlowe, 1925; The Commonwealth and Restoration Stage, 1928; Shelley's Lost Letters to Harriet, 1930; Shakespeare versus Shallow, 1931; I, William Shakespeare, 1937; Shakespeare's Sonnets Dated, 1949; Shakespeare's Motley, 1952; Queen Elizabeth's Entertainment at Mitcham, 1953; The First Night of Twelfth Night, 1954; Shakespeare's Wooden O, 1959; Mr W. H., 1964; Shakespeare by Hilliard, 1977. *Recreation:* boating. *Address:* Northford, Conn 06472, USA.

HOTTER, Hans; opera and concert singer; producer; Professor at Vienna Musik-Hochschule; teaches masterclasses in Austria, Great Britain, Holland, USA, and Australia, and private students in Munich; *b* Offenbach, Germany; *m* 1936, Helga Fischer; one *s* one *d*. *Educ:* Munich. Concert career began in 1929 and opera career in 1930. Mem. of Munich, Vienna and Hamburg State Operas; guest singer in opera and concerts in all major cities of Europe and USA; concert tours in Australia; for the past 10 years, connected with Columbia Gramophone Co., England; guest singer, Covent Garden Opera, London, 1947–. Festivals: Salzburg, Edinburgh and Bayreuth. *Relevant publication:* Hans Hotter: man and artist, by Penelope Turing, 1984. *Address:* Emil Dittlerstrasse 26, 8000 München 71, West Germany.

HOUGH, George Hubert, CBE 1965; PhD; FRAeS; Chairman: Forthstar Ltd, since 1980; Magnetic Components Ltd, since 1986; *b* 21 Oct. 1921; *m* Hazel Ayrton (*née* Russel); one *s* two *d*. *Educ:* Winsford Grammar Sch.; King's Coll., London. BSc (Hons Physics), PhD; FIEE. Admiralty Signals Estabt, 1940–46. Standard Telecommunication Laboratories Ltd (ITT), 1946–51 (as external student at London Univ. prepared thesis on gaseous discharge tubes); de Havilland Propellers Ltd: early mem. Firestreak team in charge of develt of guidance systems, 1951–59; Chief Engr (Guided Weapons), 1959; Chief Executive (Engrg), 1961; Dir, de Havilland Aircraft Co., 1962; Hawker Siddeley Dynamics Ltd: Technical Dir, 1963; Dep. Managing Dir, 1968; Man. Dir, 1977; Dep. Chief Exec., Dynamics Group British Aerospace, 1977. Dep. Chm., 1977, Chief Exec., 1977–80, Chm., 1978–80, British Smelter Constructions Ltd; Director: Sheepbridge Engrg Ltd, 1977–79; Scientific Finance Ltd, 1979–84; Programmed Neuro Cybernetics (UK) Ltd, 1979–85; Landis & Gyr Ltd, 1980–85. *Recreations:* sailing, golf. *Address:* Trelyon, Rock, near Wadebridge, Cornwall. *T:* Trebetherick 3454. *Club:* St James's.

HOUGH, Prof. Graham Goulder; Praelector and Fellow of Darwin College, Cambridge, 1964–75, now Emeritus Fellow; Professor of English, 1966–75, now Emeritus, University Reader in English, 1965–66; *b* 14 Feb. 1908; *s* of Joseph and Clara Hough; *m* 1st, 1942, Rosamund Oswell; one *s* one *d*; 2nd, 1952, Ingeborg Neumann. *Educ:* Prescot Grammar Sch.; University of Liverpool; Queens' Coll., Cambridge. Lecturer in English, Raffles Coll., Singapore, 1930. Served War of 1939–45, with Singapore Royal Artillery (Volunteer), 1942–45. Professor of English, University of Malaya, 1946; Visiting Lecturer, Johns Hopkins Univ., 1950; Fellow of Christ's Coll., Cambridge, 1950 (Tutor, 1955–60); Visiting Prof. Cornell University, 1958. Hon. DLitt, Malaya, 1955; LittD, Cambridge, 1961. *Publications:* The Last Romantics, 1949; The Romantic Poets, 1953; The Dark Sun, 1957; Image and Experience, 1960; Legends and Pastorals, 1961; A Preface to the Faerie Queene, 1962; The Dream and the Task, 1963; An Essay on Criticism, 1966; Style and Stylistics, 1969; Selected Essays, 1978; The Mystery Religion of W.B. Yeats, 1984. *Recreation:* travel. *Address:* The White Cottage, Grantchester, Cambridge. *T:* Cambridge 840227.

HOUGH, John Patrick; Secretary, Institute of Chartered Accountants in England and Wales, 1972–82; *b* 6 July 1928; *s* of William Patrick Hough, MBE, Lt-Comdr RN and Eva Harriet Hough; *m* 1956, Dorothy Nadine Akerman; four *s* one *d*. *Educ:* Purbrook High School. FCA, MIMC, FBCS. Articled M. R. Cobbett & Co., Portsmouth, 1950–53; Derbyshire & Co., 1953–54; Turquand Youngs & Co., 1954–57; Computer Specialist, IBM United Kingdom Ltd, 1957–61; Consultant 1961–62, Partner 1962–69, Robson Morrow & Co.; Dep. Sec., Inst. of Chartered Accountants in England and Wales, 1969–71. *Recreations:* music, food. *Address:* 5 South Row, Blackheath, SE3; Coastguard Cottage, Newtown, Newport, Isle of Wight. *Clubs:* Travellers'; London Rowing.

HOUGH, Julia Marie, (Judy); *see* Taylor, Judy.

HOUGH, Richard Alexander; writer; *b* 15 May 1922; *s* of late George and Margaret May Hough; *m* 1st, 1943, Helen Charlotte (marr. diss.) *o d* of Dr Henry Woodyatt; four *d*; 2nd, 1980, Judy Taylor, *qv*. *Educ:* Fensham Heights. Served War, RAF Pilot, Fighter

Command, home and overseas, 1941–46. Publisher, 1947–70: Bodley Head until 1955; Hamish Hamilton as Dir and Man. Dir, Hamish Hamilton Children's Books Ltd, 1955–70. Contrib. to: Guardian; Observer; Washington Post; NY Times; Encounter; History Today; New Yorker. Mem. Council, 1970–73, 1975–84, Vice-Pres., 1977–82, Navy Records Society. Chm., Auxiliary Hospitals Cttee, King Edward's Hospital Fund, 1975–80 (Mem. Council, 1975–86). *Publications:* The Fleet that had to Die, 1958; Admirals in Collision, 1959; The Potemkin Mutiny, 1960; The Hunting of Force Z, 1963; Dreadnought, 1964; The Big Battleship, 1966; First Sea Lord: an authorised life of Admiral Lord Fisher, 1969; The Pursuit of Admiral von Spee, 1969; The Blind Horn's Hate, 1971; Captain Bligh and Mr Christian, 1972 (Daily Express Best Book of the Sea Award) (filmed as The Bounty, 1984); Louis and Victoria: the first Mountbattens, 1974; One Boy's War: per astra ad ardua, 1975; (ed) Advice to a Grand-daughter (Queen Victoria's letters), 1975; The Great Admirals, 1977; The Murder of Captain James Cook, 1979; Man o' War, 1979; Nelson, 1980; Mountbatten: Hero of Our Time, 1980; Edwina: Countess Mountbatten of Burma, 1983; The Great War at Sea 1914–1918, 1983; Former Naval Person: Churchill and the Wars at Sea, 1985; *novels:* Angels One Five, 1978; The Fight of the Few, 1979; The Fight to the Finish, 1979; Buller's Guns, 1981; Razor Eyes, 1981; Buller's Dreadnought, 1982; Buller's Victory, 1984; numerous books on motoring history and books for children under *pseudonym* Bruce Carter. *Address:* Denfurlong, Lower Chedworth, near Cheltenham, Glos GL54 4AP. *T:* Fossebridge 422; Flat 7, 217 Sussex Gardens, W2 2RJ. *T:* 01–723 7327. *Clubs:* Garrick, Beefsteak, MCC.

HOUGHTON, family name of **Baron Houghton of Sowerby.**

HOUGHTON OF SOWERBY, Baron *cr* 1974 (Life Peer), of Sowerby, W Yorks; **Arthur Leslie Noel Douglas Houghton,** PC 1964; CH 1967; *b* 11 Aug. 1898; *s* of John and Martha Houghton, Long Eaton, Derbyshire; *m* 1939, Vera Travis (CBE 1986); no *c*. Sec., Inland Revenue Staff Fedn, 1922–60. Broadcaster in "Can I Help You?" Programme, BBC, 1941–64. Alderman LCC, 1947–49; Mem. Gen. Council, TUC, 1952–60. Chm., Staff Side, Civil Service National Whitley Council, 1956–58. MP (Lab) Sowerby, WR Yorks, March 1949–Feb. 1974; Chm. Public Accounts Cttee, 1963–64; Chancellor of the Duchy of Lancaster, 1964–66; Minister Without Portfolio, 1966–67. Chm., Parly Lab. Party, 1967–70, Nov. 1970–1974. Chairman: British Parly Gp, Population and Develt, 1978–84; House of Lords Industry Study Gp, 1979–85. Member: Commn on the Constitution, 1969–73; Royal Commn on Standards of Conduct in Public Life, 1974–75. Chairman: Commonwealth Scholarships Commn, 1967–68; Young Volunteer Force Foundation, 1967–70 (Jt Vice-Chm. 1970–71); Teachers' Pay Inquiry, 1974; Cttee on aid to Political Parties, 1975–76; Cttee on Security of Cabinet Papers, 1976; Cttee for Reform of Animal Experimentation, 1977–; Vice-Pres., RSPCA, 1978–82. *Publication:* Paying for the Social Services, 2nd edn, 1968. *Address:* 110 Marsham Court, SW1. *T:* 01–834 0602; Becks Cottage, Whitehill Lane, Bletchingley, Surrey. *T:* Godstone 3340. *Club:* Reform.

HOUGHTON, Albert Morley; retired 1972 as Under-Secretary, Department of Trade and Industry; *b* 26 June 1914; *m* 1939, Lallie Whittington Hughes; no *c*. Entered Civil Service, Administrative class, 1946; Civil Service Selection Board, 1946–49; Ministry of Transport, 1949–65; UK Delegn to NATO 1954–56; Shipping Attaché to Comr Gen. for SE Asia, 1956–60; Under-Sec., and Hd of Electronics and Telecommunications Div., Min. of Technology, 1965–70. *Recreations:* reading, music, gardening. *Address:* High Beeches, North Pickenham, Swaffham, Norfolk. *T:* Holme Hale 440489.

HOUGHTON, Rev. Alfred Thomas, MA, LTh; General Secretary Bible Churchmen's Missionary Society, 1945–66, Vice-President 1968; Hon. Canon, Diocese of Morogoro, Central Tanganyika, 1965; *b* Stafford, 11 April 1896; *s* of Rev. Thomas Houghton (Editor of the Gospel Magazine and Vicar of Whitington, Stoke Ferry, Norfolk) and Elizabeth Ann Houghton; *m* 1924, Coralie Mary, *d* of H. W. Green, and *g d* of Maj.-Gen. Green, Indian Army; two *s* four *d*. *Educ:* Clarence Sch. (now Canford Sch.); Durham Univ. (University Coll.); London Coll. of Divinity. BA Durham, 1923; MA Durham, 1929. Commissioned 2/5th PA Som LI, Burma, 1917; Staff Officer to Inspector of Infantry, South, AHQ India, 1918; Staff Capt., QMG's Br, AHQ India, 1919; demobilised, 1919; Deacon, 1921; Priest, 1922; Missionary Sch. of Medicine, 1923–24; Supt of BCMS Mission in Burma, 1924–40; Asst Bishop-Designate of Rangoon, 1940–44 (cancelled owing to Japanese occupation of Burma); Travelling Sec., Inter-Varsity Fellowship of Evangelical Unions, 1941–44, and Asst Sec., Graduates' Fellowship, 1944–45. Pres. Missionary Sch. of Medicine, 1948–77; Trustee Keswick Convention Council, 1948, and Chm., 1951–69; Chairman: Conference of British Missionary Socs, 1960; Church of England Evangelical Council, 1960–66; Pres. Mt Hermon Missionary Training Coll., 1960–71; Vice-President: Evangelical Alliance; Lord's Day Observance Soc. *Publications:* Tailum Jan, 1930; Dense Jungle Green, 1937; Preparing to be a Missionary, 1956. *Address:* 14 Alston Court, St Albans Road, Barnet, Herts EN5 4LJ. *T:* 01–449 1741.

HOUGHTON, Arthur Amory, Jr; corporation official; Chairman, Steuben Glass, 1972–78 (President, 1933–72); *b* Corning, New York, USA, 12 Dec. 1906; *s* of Arthur Amory and Mabel Hollister Houghton; *m* 1973, Nina Rodale; one *s* three *d* of a previous marriage. *Educ:* St Paul's Sch., Concord; Harvard Univ. Served War of 1942–45, Capt. to Lt-Col, USAAF. Corning Glass Works: manufg dept, 1929; treasury dept, 1929–30; Asst to Pres., 1930–32; Vice-Pres., 1935–42; now Life Dir. Former Director: NY Life Insce Co.; US Steel Corp.; US Trust Co. of NY. Curator of Rare Books, Library of Congress, 1940–42; Chm., Wye Inst.; Mem. Council on Foreign Relations. Formerly: Dir, Amer. Council of Learned Socs; Chairman: Inst. of Internat. Educn; Metropolitan Mus. of Art; Philharmonic Symphony Soc., NY; Parsons Sch. of Design; Vice-Chairman: Fund for Advancement of Educn (Ford Foundn); Lincoln Center for the Performing Arts; President: E-SU of US; Keats-Shelley Soc. of Amer.; Shakespeare Assoc. of Amer.; Vice-Pres., Pierpont Morgan Liby; Trustee: St John's Coll., Annapolis; Rockefeller Foundn. Hon. Trustee: ICA, Boston; Baltimore Mus. of Art; Hon. Curator, Keats Collection, Harvard Univ. Sen. Fellow, RCA; Sen. FRSA. KStJ. Hon. Phi Beta Kappa, Harvard; 20 hon. doctorates. Michael Friedsam Medal in Industrial Art; Gertrude Vanderbilt Whitney award, Skowhegan Sch. Officier, Légion d'Honneur; Comdr, Ordre des Arts et des Lettres. *Address:* Wye Plantation, Queenstown, Maryland 21658, USA. *Clubs:* Century, Union, Knickerbocker, Harvard, Grolier (New York).

HOUGHTON, Brian Thomas; Under Secretary, Inland Revenue, since 1977; *b* 22 Aug. 1931; *s* of Bernard Charles Houghton and Sadie Houghton; *m* 1953, Joyce Beryl (*née* Williams); three *s* one *d*. *Educ:* City Boys' Sch., Leicester; Christ's Coll., Cambridge. BA (Mod. Langs), MA 1957. Inland Revenue, 1957; Private Sec. to Chief Sec., HM Treasury, 1966–68; Assistant Secretary: Inland Revenue, 1968–75; HM Treasury, 1975–77. *Address:* 1 Barns Dene, Harpenden, Herts AL5 2HH. *T:* Harpenden 5905.

HOUGHTON, Herbert; Director: Stenhouse Holdings Ltd, 1979–83; Reed Stenhouse Cos Ltd, 1977–86; Chancellor Insurance Co. Ltd, since 1984; *b* 4 Oct. 1920; *s* of Herbert Edward and Emily Houghton; *m* 1939, Dorothy Ballantyne; one *s* one *d*. *Educ:* William Hulmes' Grammar School. Director, Cockshoots Ltd, 1955; Man. Dir, Stenhouse Northern Ltd, 1968; Chairman: Sir Wm Garthwaite (Holdings) Ltd, 1973; Sten-Re Ltd, 1973; Director and Chief Executive, A. R. Stenhouse & Partners Ltd, 1977; Dir, British Vita Co. Ltd, 1969–84. *Recreations:* overseas travel, golf, reading, gardening. *Address:* 2 Orchard Court, Grindleford, Sheffield S30 1JH. *T:* Hope Valley 31142.

HOUGHTON, Dr John, JP; Director, Teesside Polytechnic, 1971–79, retired (Principal, Constantine College of Technology, 1961–70); *b* 12 June 1922; *s* of George Stanley Houghton and Hilda (*née* Simpson); *m* 1951, Kathleen Lamb; one *s* one *d*. *Educ:* King Henry VIII Sch., Coventry; Hanley High Sch., Coventry Techn. Coll.; King's Coll., Cambridge; Queen Mary Coll., London Univ. BSc (hons) Engrg 1949; PhD 1952. CEng, MIMechE, FRAeS. Aircraft Apprentice, Sir W. G. Armstrong-Whitworth Aircraft Ltd, 1938–43; design and stress engr, 1943–46; student at univ. (Clayton Fellow), 1946–51; Lectr, Queen Mary Coll., London Univ., 1950–52; Sen. Lectr and Head of Aero-Engrg, Coventry Techn. Coll., 1952–57; Head of Dept of Mech. Engrg, Brunel Coll. Advanced Technology, 1957–61. Freeman, City of Coventry, 1943. JP Middlesbrough, 1962. *Publications:* (with D. R. L. Smith) Mechanics of Fluids by Worked Examples, 1959; various research reports, reviews and articles in professional and learned jls. *Recreations:* keen sportsman (triple Blue), do-it-yourself activities, gardening, pottery, oil painting. *Address:* 14 Marton Moor Road, Nunthorpe, Middlesbrough, Cleveland. *T:* Middlesbrough 35263. *Club:* Middlesbrough Rotary.

HOUGHTON, Dr John Theodore, CBE 1983; FRS 1972; Director General of the Meteorological Office, since 1983; *b* 30 Dec. 1931; *s* of Sidney M. Houghton, schoolmaster, and Miriam Houghton; *m* Margaret Edith Houghton (*née* Broughton) (*d* 1986), MB, BS, DPH; one *s* one *d*. *Educ:* Rhyl Grammar Sch.; Jesus Coll., Oxford (Scholar). BA hons Physics 1951, MA, DPhil 1955. Research Fellow, RAE Farnborough, 1954–57; Lectr in Atmospheric Physics, Oxford Univ., 1958–62; Reader, 1962–76; Professor, 1976–83; Fellow, Jesus Coll., Oxford, 1960–83, Hon. Fellow 1983; on secondment as Dir (Appleton), 1979–83, and Dep. Dir, 1981–83, Rutherford Appleton Laboratory, SERC. Member: Astronomy, Space and Radio Bd, SERC (formerly SRC), 1970–73 and 1976–81; Meteorological Cttee, 1975–80; Jt Organising Cttee, Global Atmospheric Res. Programme, 1976–79; Exec. Cttee, WMO, 1983–; Management Bd, British Nat. Space Centre, 1986–; Chairman: Jt Scientific Cttee, World Climate Research Programme, 1981–84; Earth Observation Adv. Cttee, ESA, 1982–. Pres., RMetS, 1976–78. Cherwell-Simon Meml Lectr, Oxford Univ., 1983–84. Buchan Prize, RMetS, 1966; Charles Chree medal and prize, Inst. of Physics, 1979. FInstP; Fellow, Optical Soc. of America. *Publications:* (with S. D. Smith) Infra-Red Physics, 1966; The Physics of Atmospheres, 1977; (with F. W. Taylor and C. D. Rodgers) Remote Sounding of Atmospheres, 1984; papers in learned jls on atmospheric radiation, spectroscopy and remote sounding from satellites. *Recreations:* sailing, walking, gardening. *Address:* Lindfield, 1 Begbroke Lane, Begbroke, Oxford.

HOUGHTON, Maj.-Gen. Robert Dyer, CB 1963; OBE 1947; MC 1942; DL; *b* 7 March 1912; *s* of late J. M. Houghton, Dawlish, Devon; *m* 1940, Dorothy Uladh, *y d* of late Maj.-Gen. R. W. S. Lyons, IMS; two *s* one *d*. *Educ:* Haileybury Coll. Royal Marines Officer, 1930–64; Col Comdt, Royal Marines, 1973–76. Gen. Sec., Royal UK Beneficent Assoc., 1968–78. DL East Sussex, 1977. *Recreations:* gardening, sailing, model engineering. *Address:* Vert House, Whitesmith, near Lewes, East Sussex. *Club:* Army and Navy.

HOUGHTON, Rev. Canon William Reginald; Canon Residentiary of Gloucester Cathedral, 1969–78, now Emeritus; *b* 28 Sept. 1910; *s* of late William Houghton and late Elizabeth Houghton; unmarried. *Educ:* St John's Coll., Durham; Westcott House, Cambridge. BA (Durham) 1940; Dipl. in Th. (Durham) 1941; MA (Durham) 1943. Curate, St Clement, Leeds, 1941–43, Leeds Parish Church, 1943–47 (Senior Curate, 1945–47); Vicar of Beeston, Leeds, 1947–54. Surrogate, 1949–54. Public Preacher, Dio. Southwark, 1954–62; Asst Sec. South London Church Fund and Southwark Diocesan Board of Finance, 1954–56, Dep. Sec., 1956–60, Sec., 1960–61; Sec. Southwark Dio. Bd of Dilapidations, 1956–60; Canon Residentiary (Treas.) of Southwark Cathedral, 1959–62. Rector of St Mary de Crypt with St John the Baptist, Gloucester, 1962–69. *Recreations:* travel and reading. *Address:* Church Cottage, Diddlebury, Craven Arms, Shropshire SY7 9DH. *T:* Munslow 208.

HOULDEN, Rev. Canon James Leslie; Senior Lecturer in New Testament Studies and Dean, Faculty of Theology and Religious Studies, King's College, London (KQC), since 1986 (Lecturer 1977); *b* 1 March 1929; *s* of James and Lily Alice Houlden. *Educ:* Altrincham Grammar Sch.; Queen's Coll., Oxford. Asst Curate, St Mary's, Hunslet, Leeds, 1955–58; Chaplain, Chichester Theological Coll., 1958–60; Chaplain Fellow, Trinity Coll., Oxford, 1960–70; Principal, Cuddesdon Theol Coll., later Ripon Coll., Cuddesdon, 1970–77. Hon. Canon of Christ Church Oxford, 1976–77. Member: Liturgical Commn, 1969–76; Doctrine Commn of C of E, 1969–76; Gen. Synod of C of E, 1980–. Editor, Theology, 1983–. *Publications:* Paul's Letters from Prison, 1970; (ed) A Celebration of Faith, 1970; Ethics and the New Testament, 1973; The Johannine Epistles, 1974; The Pastoral Epistles, 1976; Patterns of Faith, 1977; (contrib.) The Myth of God Incarnate, 1977; Explorations in Theology 3, 1978; (contrib.) Incarnation and Myth, 1979; What Did the First Christians Believe?, 1982; (contrib.) Alternative Approaches to New Testament Study, 1985; Connections, 1986; reviews and articles in learned jls. *Address:* 33 Raleigh Court, Lymer Avenue, SE19 1LS. *T:* 01–670 6648. *Club:* Athenæum.

HOULDER, John Maurice, CBE 1977 (MBE (mil.) 1941); Chairman, Houlder Offshore Ltd, since 1961; *b* 20 Feb. 1916; *m* 1981, Rody, *d* of late Major Luke White. Licensed Aircraft Engineer. Member: Exec. Board, Technical Cttee and Gen. Cttee, Lloyds Register of Shipping, 1970–; Light Aircraft Requirements Cttee, CAA, 1955–84. Council, RINA. Chm., Comex Houlder Diving Ltd and Chm. or Dir of 23 shipping, offshore drilling, diving, engineering and aviation Cos. Chm., London Ocean Shipowners Joint Dock Labour Piecework Cttee, 1950–60; first Chm., River Plate Europe Freight Conf., 1961–70; Chm., Bulk Cargo Cttee, Continental River Plate Conf., 1954–70. Mem. Council, RSPB, 1974–79; Pres. Soc for Underwater Technology, 1978–80. Vis. Prof., Dept of Ship & Marine Technology, Univ. of Strathclyde. Hon. DSc Univ. of Strathclyde, 1986. Stanley Gray Award, Inst. of Marine Engrs, 1982. *Recreations:* ski-ing, flying, bird-watching, computer programming. *Address:* 53 Leadenhall Street, EC3A 2BR. *T:* 01–481 2963. *Clubs:* Air Squadron; Kandahar Ski, B & B Ski, 1001.

HOULDSWORTH, Sir (Harold) Basil, 2nd Bt, *cr* 1956; Consultant Anæsthetist, Barnsley and District Hospitals, since 1954; *b* 21 July 1922; *s* of Sir Hubert Stanley Houldsworth, 1st Bt, QC and (Hilda Frances) Lady Houldsworth (*née* Clegg) (*d* 1978); *S* father 1956; *m* 1946, Norah Clifford Halmshaw; one *d*. *Educ:* Heckmondwike Grammar Sch.; Leeds Sch. of Medicine, MRCS, LRCP 1946; FFA RCS 1954; DA Eng. 1951. Junior Registrar Anæsthetist, Leeds Gen. Infirmary, 1946–48; Graded Specialist Anæsthetist, RAMC, 1948–50; Registrar Anæsthetist, Leeds General Infirmary and St James Hospital, Leeds, 1950–53; Senior Registrar, Sheffield City General Hospital, 1953–54. *Recreations:* theatre, ballet and gardening. *Heir:* none. *Address:* Shadwell House, Lundhill Road, Wombwell, near Barnsley, South Yorks. *T:* Barnsley 753191.

HOULDSWORTH, Sir Reginald (Douglas Henry), 4th Bt, *cr* 1887, OBE 1945; TD 1944; DL; landowner; *b* 9 July 1903; *s* of Sir Thomas Houldsworth, 3rd Bt, CBE; *S* father 1961; *m* 1934, Margaret May, *d* of late Cecil Emilius Laurie; one *s* two *d*. *Educ:* Shrewsbury Sch.; Cambridge Univ. Hon. Col Ayrshire ECO Yeomanry, 1960–67; Commanded: Ayrshire Yeomanry, 1940–42; 4 Pack Mule Group, 1943–45. DL Ayrshire, 1970–. *Heir:* *s* Richard Thomas Reginald Houldsworth [*b* 2 Aug. 1947; *m* 1970, Jane (marr. diss. 1983), *o d* of Alistair Orr, Sydehead, Beith; two *s*]. *Address:* Kirkbride, Maybole, Ayrshire. *T:* Crosshill 202. *Clubs:* Cavalry and Guards; Western Meeting (Ayr); Prestwick (Prestwick).

See also P. N. C. Howard.

HOUNSFIELD, Sir Godfrey (Newbold), Kt 1981; CBE 1976; FRS 1975; Senior Staff Scientist, THORN EMI Central Research Laboratories (formerly Central Research Laboratories of EMI), Hayes, Mddx, since 1977 (Head of Medical Systems section, 1972–76; Chief Staff Scientist, 1976–77); *b* 28 Aug. 1919; *s* of Thomas Hounsfield, Newark, Notts. *Educ:* Magnus Grammar Sch., Newark; City and Guilds Coll., London (Radio Communications qualif.); Faraday House Electrical Engineering Coll. (Diploma); grad. for IEE. Volunteered for RAF, 1939; served 1939–46 (incl. period as Lectr at Cranwell Radar Sch.); awarded Certificate of Merit (for work done in RAF), 1945. Attended Faraday House, where he studied elec. and mech. engrg, 1947–51. Joined EMI Ltd, 1951, working initially on radar systems and, later, on computers; led design team for the first large, all transistor computer to be built in Great Britain, the EMIDEC 1100, 1958–59; invented the EMI-scanner computerised transverse axial tomography system for X-ray examination, 1969–72 (now used at Atkinson Morley's Hosp., Wimbledon, and leading hosps in the USA and European continent, which are buying the invention); the technique can be applied to cranial examinations and the whole of the body; the system has overcome obstacles to the diagnosis of disease in the brain which have continued since Röntgen's day (1895); it includes a patient-scanning unit; developer of a new X-ray technique (the EMI-scanner system) which won the 1972 MacRobert Award of £25,000 for the invention, and a Gold Medal for EMI Ltd; working on Nuclear Magnetic Resonance Imaging, 1976–. Professorial Fellow in imaging sciences, Manchester Univ., 1978–. Dr Medicine (*hc*) Universität Basel, 1975; Hon. DSc: City, 1976; London, 1976; Hon. DTech Loughborough, 1976. Hon. FRCP 1976; Hon. FRCR 1976. Wilhelm-Exner Medal, Austrian Industrial Assoc., 1974; Ziedses des Plantes Medal, Physikalisch Medizinische Gesellschaft, Würzburg, 1974; Prince Philip Medal Award, CGLI, 1975; ANS Radiation Industry Award, Georgia Inst. of Technology, 1975; Lasker Award, Lasker Foundn, 1975; Duddell Bronze Medal, Inst. Physics, 1976; Golden Plate Award, Amer. Acad. of Achievement, 1976; Reginald Mitchell Gold Medal, Stoke-on-Trent Assoc. of Engrs, 1976; Churchill Gold Medal, 1976; Gairdner Foundn Award, 1976; (jtly) Nobel Prize for Physiology or Medicine, 1979; Ambrogino d'Oro Award, City of Milan, 1980; Deutsche Roentgen Plakette, Deutsche Roentgen Museum, 1980. *Publications:* contribs: New Scientist; Brit. Jl of Radiology; Amer. Jl of Röntgenology. *Recreation:* mountain walking. *Address:* THORN EMI Central Research Laboratories, Dawley Road, Hayes, Mddx UB3 1HH. *T:* 01–848 6404; 15 Crane Park Road, Twickenham TW2 6DF. *T:* 01–984 1746. *Club:* Athenæum.

HOUSDEN, Rt. Rev. James Alan George, BA; *b* Birmingham, England, 16 Sept. 1904; *s* of William James and Jane Housden; *m* 1935, Elfreda Moira Hennessey; two *s* one *d*. *Educ:* Essendon High School; University of Queensland; St Francis College. BA 1st class, Mental and Moral Philosophy, 1928; ThL 1st Class, 1929. Deacon, 1928; Priest, 1929. Curate, St Paul's Ipswich, Qld, 1928–30; Chaplain, Mitchell River Mission, 1930–32; Curate, All Souls' Cathedral, Thursday Island, 1932–33; Rector of Darwin, NT, 1933–37; Vicar of Coolangatta, Qld, 1936–40; Rector and Rural Dean, Warwick, 1940–46; Vicar of Christ Church, S Yarra, Melbourne, 1946–47; Bishop of Rockhampton, 1947–58; Bishop of Newcastle, NSW, 1958–72. *Recreation:* bowls. *Address:* 38 Maltman Street, Caloundra, Qld 4551, Australia. *Club:* Australian (Sydney, NSW).

HOUSE, Lt-Gen. Sir David (George), GCB 1977 (KCB 1975); KCVO 1985; CBE 1967; MC 1944; Gentleman Usher of the Black Rod, House of Lords, 1978–85; Serjeant-at-Arms, House of Lords, and Secretary to the Lord Great Chamberlain, 1978–85; *b* 8 Aug. 1922; *s* of A. G. House; *m* 1947, Sheila Betty Darwin; two *d*. *Educ:* Regents Park Sch., London. War service in Italy; and thereafter in variety of regimental (KRRC and 1st Bn The Royal Green Jackets) and staff appts. Comd 51 Gurkha Bde in Borneo, 1965–67; Chief BRIXMIS, 1967–69; Dep. Mil. Sec., 1969–71; Chief of Staff, HQ BAOR, 1971–73; Dir of Infantry, 1973–75; GOC Northern Ireland, 1975–77. Colonel Commandant: The Light Division, 1974–77; Small Arms School Corps, 1974–77. Dir, Yorks and Humberside, Lloyds Bank, 1985–. *Address:* Dormer Lodge, Aldborough, near Boroughbridge, N Yorks YO5 9EP. *Club:* Army and Navy.

HOUSE, Donald Victor; Lay Member, Restrictive Practices Court, 1962–70, retired; *b* 31 Jan. 1900; *s* of Dr S. H. House, Liverpool; *m* 1925, Cicely May Cox-Moore (*d* 1980); one *s* two *d*. *Educ:* Liverpool Coll. Lieut, Royal Garrison Artillery, 1918. Mem. (Fellow) Inst. of Chartered Accountants in England and Wales, 1922– (Mem. Council, 1942–62; Pres. 1954–55). Senior Partner, Harmood Banner & Co., 1946–62. Mem. Board of Governors, Guy's Hosp., 1955–74, and Chm. of Finance Cttee, 1957–74; Director: National Film Finance Corporation, 1954–70; Finance Cttee, Friends of the Poor and Gentlefolks Help, 1946–70; Mem., London Rent Assessment Panel, 1967–75. Hon. Sec., Herts Golf Union, 1964–75, Pres., 1976–78; Mem. Council, English Golf Union. Dir of several public and other companies (to 1962); Chm., House Cttee enquiring into Northern Ireland shipping facilities. Special Constabulary Long Service Medal, 1943. *Recreations:* golf, amateur dramatics. *Address:* 8 Greyfell Close, Stanmore, Middx HA7 3DQ. *T:* 01–954 0525. *Clubs:* Royal Commonwealth Society; Sandy Lodge Golf (Hon. Mem.), Porters Park Golf (Hon. Mem.).

HOUSE, Ven. Francis Harry, OBE 1955; MA; Officer Royal (Hellenic) Order of Phoenix, 1947; Archdeacon of Macclesfield, 1967–78, now Archdeacon Emeritus; Rector of St James, Gawsworth, 1967–78; *b* 9 Aug. 1908; *s* of late Canon William Joseph House, DD; *m* 1938, Margaret Neave; two *d*. *Educ:* St George's Sch., Harpenden; Wadham Coll., Oxford; Cuddesdon Theological Coll. Sec. of Student Christian Movement of Gt Britain and Ireland, 1931–34; Deacon, 1936; Priest, 1937. Asst Missioner, Pembroke Coll. (Cambridge) Mission, Walworth, 1936–37; Travelling sec. of World's Student Christian Federation, Geneva, 1938–40; Curate of Leeds Parish Church, 1940–42; Overseas Asst, Religious Broadcasting Dept, BBC, London, 1942–44; representative of World Student Relief in Greece, 1944–46; Sec. Youth Dept World Council of Churches, Geneva, and World Conference of Christian Youth, Oslo, 1946–47; Head of Religious Broadcasting BBC, London, 1947–55; Associate Gen. Sec. of the World Council of Churches, Geneva, 1955–62; Vicar of St Giles, Pontefract, 1962–67. Select Preacher, Cambridge Univ., 1949. Member: Gen. Synod of Church of England, 1970–78; Gen. Synod's Commn on Broadcasting, 1971–73; Bd for Mission and Unity, 1971–80 (Vice-Chm., 1971–75). *Publications:* articles contributed to: The Student Movement, The Student World, East and West, the Ecumenical Review, Theology, Crucible, One in Christ, etc. *Address:* 11 Drummond Court, Far Headingley, Leeds LS16 5QE. *T:* Leeds 783646.

HOUSE, Harry Wilfred, DSO 1918; MC; MA; Master of Wellington College, 1941–56; *b* Malvern, 26 Sept. 1895; 2nd *s* of late H. H. House, Acre End, Eynsham, Oxon; *m* 1926, Marjorie Stracey, *yr d* of late Arthur Gibbs, of Bramley, Surrey; two *s* one *d*. *Educ:* Lockers Park, Hemel Hempstead; Rugby Sch.; Queen's Coll., Oxford. Served in HM Forces on leaving Rugby in 1914; temp. 2nd Lieut 7th East Lancs Regt, Sept. 1914; served in France from July 1915 (wounded July 1916; MC; DSO); relinquished commission with rank of Temp. Major, March, 1919; total service in France 3 years 5 months; temp. appointment Colonial Office, March to Dec. 1919; matriculated Oxford Univ., Jan. 1920; 2nd Class Hon. Mods, March 1921; studied at the University of Paris, 1921–23; Fellow and Lecturer Queen's Coll., Oxford, 1923–41; Laming Resident Fellow, Queen's Coll., Oxford, 1924–41; Junior Proctor, Oxford Univ., 1931–32; Major, Oxford and Bucks Light Infantry, 1939–41; Military Asst to Quarter Master Gen., 1940–41. Supernumerary Fellow, Queen's Coll., Oxford, 1953. *Address:* The Old Rectory, Stutton, near Ipswich, Suffolk. *T:* Holbrook 328205.

HOUSE, Dr John Peter Humphry; Lecturer, Courtauld Institute of Art, University of London, since 1980; *b* 19 April 1945; *s* of Madeline Edith Church and Arthur Humphry House; *m* 1968, Jill Elaine Turner; two *s*. *Educ:* Westminster Sch.; New Coll., Oxford (BA); Courtauld Inst. of Art (MA, PhD). Lecturer: UEA, 1969–76; UCL, 1976–80. Slade Prof. of Fine Art, Univ. of Oxford, 1986–87. Organiser of Impressionism Exhibn, RA, 1974; Co-organiser: Post Impressionism exhibn, RA, 1979–80; Renoir exhibn, Arts Council, 1985. *Publications:* Monet, 1977, 2nd edn 1981; Monet: nature into art, 1986; author/co-author, exhibition catalogues; articles in Burlington Magazine, Art History, Art in America. *Recreation:* second hand bookshops. *Address:* Courtauld Institute of Art, University of London, 20 Portman Square, W1H 0BE. *T:* 01–935 9292.

HOUSEHOLD, Geoffrey Edward West, TD; Author; *b* 30 Nov. 1900; *s* of H. W. Household, MA, Barrister-at-Law; *m* 1942, Ilona M. J. Zsoldos-Gutmán; one *s* two *d*. *Educ:* Clifton Coll.; Magdalen Coll., Oxford. Mostly commerce in foreign capitals. *Publications: novels:* The Third Hour, 1937; Rogue Male, 1939; Arabesque, 1948; The High Place, 1950; A Rough Shoot, 1951; A Time to Kill, 1952; Fellow Passenger, 1955; Watcher in the Shadows, 1960; Thing to Love, 1963; Olura, 1965; The Courtesy of Death, 1967; Dance of the Dwarfs, 1968; Doom's Caravan, 1971; The Three Sentinels, 1972; The Lives and Times of Bernardo Brown, 1973; Red Anger, 1975; Hostage: London, 1977; The Last Two Weeks of Georges Rivac, 1978; The Sending, 1980; Summon the Bright Water, 1981; Rogue Justice, 1982; Arrows of Desire, 1985; *autobiography:* Against the Wind, 1958; *short stories:* The Salvation of Pisco Gabar, 1938; Tales of Adventurers, 1952; The Brides of Solomon, 1958; Sabres on the Sand, 1966; The Cats To Come, 1975; The Europe That Was, 1979; Capricorn and Cancer, 1981; *for children:* The Spanish Cave, 1940; Xenophon's Adventure, 1955; Prisoner of the Indies, 1967; Escape into Daylight, 1976. *Recreation:* Atlantic Spain. *Address:* Chatterwell, Charlton, Banbury, Oxon.

HOUSEMAN, Alexander Randolph, CBE 1984; FEng, FIMechE, FIProdE; Deputy Chairman, British Rail Engineering Ltd, since 1985 (Director, since 1979); *b* 9 May 1920; *e s* of Captain Alexander William Houseman and Elizabeth Maud (*née* Randolph); *m* 1942, Betty Edith Norrington; one *d*. *Educ:* Stockport Grammar School and College. FIMC, CBIM, FRSA. Apprenticed Crossley Motors, 1936–40; Production Engineer: Ford Motor Co. (Aero Engines) Ltd, 1940–43; Saunders-Roe Ltd, 1943–48, General Works Manager, 1948–54; Consultant, Director, Man. Dir and Dep. Chm., P-E International Ltd, 1954–81; Dir, P-E Consulting Gp Ltd, 1968–85; Chm., W. Canning Ltd, 1975–80; Dir, Record Ridgway Ltd, 1978–81. Chm., NEDO EDC for Gauge and Tool Industry, 1979–; Institution of Production Engineers: Chm., Technical Policy Bd, 1978–82; Vice-Pres., 1982–83; Pres., 1983–84. Member: Industrial Adv. Panels of Fellowship of Engineering, 1980–; Council, Inst. of Management Consultants, 1968–83; Inst. of Directors; Life Member: Soc. of Manufg Engrs, USA, 1985; Inst. of Industrial Engrs, USA, 1985. Distinguished Engrg Management Award, Nat. Soc. of Professional Engrs, USA, 1983; Distinguished Achievements Award, LA Council of Engrs and Scientists, 1984. *Publications:* articles to learned jls and technical and management press on manufacturing technology and management. *Recreations:* DIY, sailing, photography, walking. *Address:* 11 Kings Avenue, Ealing, W5 2SJ. *T:* 01–997 3936. *Clubs:* Caledonian; Royal Anglesey Yacht (Beaumaris).

HOUSSEMAYNE du BOULAY, (Edward Philip) George, CBE 1985; FRCR, FRCP; Professor of Neuroradiology, University of London at Institute of Neurology, 1975–85, now Emeritus; Head, X-Ray Department, Nuffield Laboratories, Institute of Zoology, Zoological Society of London, since 1965; Director, Radiological Research Trust; *b* 28 Jan. 1922; *yr s* of Philip Houssemayne du Boulay and Mercy Tyrrell (*née* Friend); *m* 1944, Vivien M. Glasson (marr. diss.); four *s* (and two *s* decd); *m* 1968, Pamela Mary Verity; two *d*. *Educ:* Christ's Hospital; King's Coll., London; Charing Cross Hosp. (Entrance Schol. 1940; MB, BS, DMRD). Served RAF (Medical), 1946–48; Army Emergency Reserve, 1952–57. House appts, Charing Cross Hosp. and Derby City Hosp., 1945–46; Registrar (Radiology), Middlesex Hosp., 1948–49; Sen. Registrar (Radiology): St Bartholomew's Hosp., 1949–54; St George's Hosp., 1951–52; Consultant Radiologist: Nat. Hosp. for Nervous Diseases, Maida Vale, 1954–68 (Head, Lysholm Radiol Dept, 1975–84); St Bartholomew's Hosp., 1954–71; Nat. Hosp. for Nervous Diseases, Queen Square, 1968–75. Editor, Neuroradiology. Pres., Brit. Inst. of Radiology, 1976–77, Appeal Co-ordinator 1976–84; Hon. Mem., Société Française de Neuroradiologie; Corresp. Mem., Amer. Soc. of Neuroradiology; Hon. Mem., Swedish Soc. of Neuroradiology; Hon. Mem., German Soc. Neuroradiology. Trustee, Nat. Hosp. Develt Foundn. Glyn Evans Meml Lectr, RCR, 1970; Ernestine Henry Lectr, RCP, 1976. Hon. FACR. Barclay Medal, BIR, 1968. *Publications:* Principles of X-Ray Diagnosis of the Skull, 1965, 2nd edn 1979; (jtly) 4th edn of A Text Book of X-Ray Diagnosis by British Authors: Neuroradiology Vol. 1, 5th edn 1984; (jtly) The Cranial Arteries of Mammals, 1973; (jtly) An Atlas of Normal Vertebral Angiograms, 1976; works in specialist jls. *Recreation:* gardening. *Address:* Old Manor House, Brington, Huntingdon, Cambs PE18 0PX. *T:* Bythorn 353.

HOUSSEMAYNE du BOULAY, Sir Roger (William), KCVO 1982 (CVO 1972); CMG 1975; HM Diplomatic Service, retired; Vice Marshal of the Diplomatic Corps, 1975–82; *b* 30 March 1922; *s* of Charles John Houssemayne du Boulay, Captain, RN, and Mary Alice Veronica, *née* Morgan; *m* 1957, Elizabeth, *d* of late Brig. Home, late RM, and of Molly, Lady Pile; one *d*, and two step *s*. *Educ:* Winchester; Oxford. Served RAFVR, 1941–46 (Pilot). HM Colonial Service, Nigeria, 1949–58; HM Foreign, later Diplomatic, Service, 1959; FO, 1959; Washington, 1960–64; FCO 1964–67; Manila, 1967–71; Alternate Director, Asian Development Bank, Manila, 1967–69, and Director, 1969–71; Counsellor and Head of Chancery, Paris, 1971–73; Resident Comr, New Hebrides, 1973–75. Advr, Solomon Is Govt, 1986. *Address:* Anstey House, near Buntingford, Herts.

HOUŠTECKÝ, Dr Miroslav; Ambassador of Czechoslovak Socialist Republic in the United Kingdom, 1983–86; *b* 10 June 1926; *s* of Josef Houštecký and Blažena Houštecká; *m* 1953, Marie Houštecká (*née* Sedlaková); one *s* two *d*. *Educ:* School of Political and Economic Sciences, Prague, 1946–50; doctorate in Social Sciences (RSDr), 1953; candidate of Historical Sciences, 1958. Lecturer and Reader, Charles Univ., Prague, and School of Political and Economic Sciences, Prague, 1950–64; Correspondent of Czechoslovak News

Agency/CTK, India, 1964–69; Editor and Dep. Director General of CTK, Prague, 1969–77; Senior Official of the Central Committee of the Communist Party of Czechoslovakia, 1977–83; joined Min. of Foreign Affairs, and appointed Ambassador in UK, 1983. State distinction for reconstruction services. *Publications:* (jtly) History of Czechoslovak Foreign Policy (Prague), 1958; (jtly) Survey of the Modern World History, I-II (Prague), 1963. *Address:* 70 Redington Road, NW3. *T:* 01–435 4948.

HOUSTON, Aubrey Claud D.; *see* Davidson-Houston.

HOUSTON, Maj.-Gen. David, CBE 1975 (OBE 1972); *b* 24 Feb. 1929; *s* of late David Houston and late Christina Charleson Houston (*née* Dunnett); *m* 1959, Jancis Veronica Burn; two *s. Educ:* Latymer Upper Sch. Commissioned, Royal Irish Fusiliers, 1949; served Korea, Kenya, BAOR, N Africa; Staff Coll., Camberley, 1961; commanded 1 Loyals and newly amalgamated 1st QLR, 1969–71; in comd 8th Inf. Bde, Londonderry, N Ireland, 1974–75; Mem. RCDS, 1976; Military Attaché and Commander, British Army Staff, Washington, 1977–79; HQ UKLF, 1979–80; Pres., Regular Commissions Bd, 1980–83; retd 1984. Col, The Queen's Lancashire Regt, 1983–; Hon. Col, Manchester and Salford Univs OTC (TA), 1985–. *Recreations:* fishing, shooting, bird watching (feathered). *Address:* c/o Bank of Scotland, Bonar Bridge, Sutherland IV24 3EB.

HOUSTON, James Caldwell, CBE 1982; MD, FRCP; Physician to Guy's Hospital, 1953–82, now Emeritus Physician; Dean, United Medical and Dental Schools, Guys and St Thomas's Hospitals, 1982–84 (Dean, Medical and Dental Schools, Guy's Hospital, 1965–82); *b* 18 Feb. 1917; *yr s* of late David Houston and Minnie Walker Houston; *m* 1946, Thelma Cromarty Cruickshank, MB, ChB, 2nd *d* of late John Cruickshank, CBE; four *s. Educ:* Mill Hill Sch.; Guy's Hosp. Medical Sch. MRCS, LRCP 1939; MB, BS (London) 1940; MRCP 1944; MD 1946; FRCP 1956. Late Major RAMC; Medical Registrar, Guy's Hospital, 1946; Asst Ed., 1954, Jt Ed., 1958–67, Guy's Hosp. Reports; Member: Bd of Governors, Guy's Hosp., 1965–74; SE Metropolitan Regional Hosp. Bd, 1966–71; Lambeth, Lewisham and Southwark AHA (Teaching), 1974–78; Court of Governors, London Sch. of Hygiene and Tropical Med., 1969–84; Senate, Univ. of London, 1970–84; Bd of Faculty of Clinical Medicine, Cambridge Univ., 1975–81; Cttee of Vice-Chancellors and Principals, 1977–80; Special Trustee, Guy's Hosp., 1974–82; Trustee, Hayward Foundn, 1978–. Dir, Clerical, Medical & Gen. Life Assurance Soc., 1965; Vice-Pres., Medical Defence Union, 1970–. *Publications:* Principles of Medicine and Medical Nursing (jtly), 1956, 5th edn 1978; A Short Text-book of Medicine (jtly), 1962, 8th edn 1984; articles in Quart. Jl Med., Brit. Med. Bull., Lancet, etc. *Recreations:* golf, gardening. *Address:* Keats House, Guy's Hospital, St Thomas Street, SE1 9RT. *T:* 01–407 7600; Cockhill Farm, Detling, Maidstone, Kent ME14 3HG. *T:* Medway 31395.

HOUSTON, Prof. William John Ballantyne, PhD, FDSRCS, FDSRCS Edin; Professor of Orthodontics, London University, since 1974; Head of Orthodontic and Children's Department, United Medical and Dental Schools (Guy's), since 1984; *b* 6 June 1938; *s* of George and Mary Houston; *m* 1962, Turid Herdis Böe; one *s* one *d. Educ:* Edinburgh Univ. (BDS); London Univ. (PhD). FDSRCS Edin 1964. Lectr, Edinburgh Univ., 1962–64; Lectr, London Univ., at Royal Dental Hosp. Sch. of Dental Surg., 1964–66, Sen. Lectr 1966–74, Dean of Sch., 1978–85. *Publications:* Orthodontic Diagnosis, 1976; Orthodontic Notes, 1976; papers in Brit. Jl of Orthodontics and Eur. Jl of Orthodontics. *Recreations:* sailing, skiing, music. *Address:* 4 Oaken Coppice, Ashtead, Surrey.

HOUSTOUN-BOSWALL, Sir (Thomas) Alford, 8th Bt *cr* 1836; international economics and business consultant; *b* 23 May 1947; *s* of Sir Thomas Houstoun-Boswall, 7th Bt, and of Margaret Jean, *d* of George Bullen-Smith; *S* father, 1982; *m* 1971, Eliana Michele, *d* of Dr John Pearse, New York; one *s* one *d. Educ:* Lindisfarne College. Chairman, Metropolitan Car Parks and Excelsior Properties Ltd, UK; Partner, Rosedale-Engel, Houstoun-Boswall Partnership, Bermuda; Director, Stair & Co., New York (specialising in fine 18th century English furniture and works of art); Pres., Houstoun-Boswall Inc. (Fine Arts), New York. Lecturer, New York Univ. and Metropolitan Museum of Art, New York. *Heir: s* Alexander Alford Houstoun-Boswall, *b* 16 Sept. 1972. *Address:* 22 Edwardes Square, W8. *T:* 01–602 6763; 15 East 77 Street, New York, NY 10021, USA.

HOVELL-THURLOW-CUMMING-BRUCE, family name of **Baron Thurlow,** and *see* Cumming-Bruce.

HOVEN, Helmert Frans van den; Knight, Order of Netherlands Lion, 1978; Commander, Order of Orange Nassau; Hon. KBE 1980; President, International Chamber of Commerce, Paris, 1985–86; Chairman, Unilever NV, 1975–84; Vice-Chairman, Unilever Ltd, 1975–84; *b* 25 April 1923; *m* 1st, 1950, Dorothy Ida Bevan (marr. diss. 1981); one *s*; 2nd, 1981, Cornelia Maria van As. *Educ:* Grammar and Trade schs in The Netherlands. Joined Unilever N. V., Rotterdam, 1938; transf. to Unilever Ltd, London, 1948, then to Turkey, 1951, becoming Chm. of Unilever's business there, 1958; Chm., Unilever's Dutch margarine business, Van den Bergh en Jurgens B. V., 1962; sen. marketing post, product gp, Margarine, Edible Fats and Oils, 1966; Mem. Bds of Unilever, and responsible for product gp, Sundry Foods and Drinks, 1970; Mem. Supervisory Bds of Shell, Deutsche Bank, Amro Bank and various other cos. *Recreations:* summer and winter sports in general. *Address:* c/o International Chamber of Commerce, 38 Cours Albert 1er, 75008 Paris, France.

HOVING, Thomas; President, Hoving Associates, Inc., since 1977; Editor-in-Chief, The Connoisseur, since 1981; *b* 15 Jan. 1931; *s* of Walter Hoving and Mary Osgood (*née* Field); *m* 1953, Nancy Melissa Bell; one *d. Educ:* Princeton Univ. BA Highest Hons, 1953; Nat. Council of the Humanities Fellowship, 1955; Kienbusch and Haring Fellowship, 1957; MFA 1958; PhD 1959. Dept of Medieval Art and The Cloisters, Metropolitan Museum of Art: Curatorial Asst, 1959; Asst Curator, 1960; Associate Curator, 1963; Curator, 1965; Commissioner of Parks, New York City, 1966; Administrator of Recreation and Cultural Affairs, New York City, 1967; Dir, Metropolitan Museum of Art, 1967–77. Board Member: IBM World Trade Corporation/Americas-Far East; Manhattan Industries Inc. Distinguished Citizen's Award, Citizen's Budget Cttee, 1967. Hon. Mem. AIA, 1967. Hon. LLD, Pratt Inst., 1967; Dr *hc:* Princeton; New York Univ. Middlebury and Woodrow Wilson Awards, Princeton. *Publications:* The Sources of the Ada Group Ivories (PhD thesis), 1959; Guide to The Cloisters, 1962; Metropolitan Museum of Art Calendar, 1966; The Chase and The Capture, 1976; Wyeth Catalogue, 1977; Tutankhamun, the Untold Story, 1978; King of the Confessors, 1981; articles in Apollo magazine and Metropolitan Museum of Art Bulletin. *Recreations:* sailing, ski-ing, bicycling, flying. *Address:* 150 East 73rd Street, New York, NY 10021, USA.

HOW, Sir Friston (Charles), Kt 1958; CB 1948; *b* 17 Sept. 1897; *o c* of Charles Friston and Jane Ethel How, Leytonstone; *m* 1932, Ann Stewart (*d* 1985), *e d* of late Alexander Chisholm Hunter, Aberdeen; no *c. Educ:* County High Sch. for Boys, Leyton; London Univ. Joined HAC, 1916; commissioned RM, 1917; served in France, 1917–18; demobilised 1919. Exchequer and Audit Dept, 1920; HM Inspector of Taxes, 1920–37; Air Ministry, 1937–40; MAP, 1940–45; Ministry of Supply, 1946–53; Sec., Atomic Energy Office, 1954–59; retired, 1959; Member: Air Transport Advisory Council, 1960–61; Air Transport Licensing Bd, 1960–70. BSc (War) (London), 1917. Called to Bar, Middle Temple, 1927. *Address:* Craigard House, Abergeldie Road, Ballater, Aberdeenshire AB3 5RR. *T:* Ballater 55891.

HOWARD; *see* Fitzalan-Howard.

HOWARD, family name of **Earls of Carlisle, Effingham,** and **Suffolk,** and of **Barons Howard of Penrith** and **Strathcona.**

HOWARD DE WALDEN, 9th Baron *cr* 1597; **John Osmael Scott-Ellis,** TD; Baron Seaford, 1826; *b* 27 Nov. 1912; *s* of 8th Baron and Margherita, CBE 1920 (*d* 1974), *d* of late Charles van Raalte of Brownsea Island, Dorset; *S* father, 1946; *m* 1st, 1934, Countess Irene Harrach (*d* 1975), *y d* of Count Hans Albrecht Harrach; four *d*; 2nd, 1978, Gillian Viscountess Mountgarret. *Educ:* Eton; Magdalene Coll., Cambridge (BA 1934, MA). Dir, Howard de Walden Estates Ltd (Chm.). Member of the Jockey Club (Senior Steward, 1957, 1964, 1976). *Heir:* (to Barony of Howard de Walden) four co-heiresses; (to Barony of Seaford) Colin Humphrey Felton Ellis [*b* 19 April 1946; *m* 1971, Susan Magill; one *s* two *d*]. *Address:* Avington Manor, Hungerford, Berks. *T:* Kintbury 58229; Flat K, 90 Eaton Square, SW1. *T:* 01–235 7127. *Clubs:* Turf, White's.

See also Capt. D. W. S. Buchan of Auchmacoy.

HOWARD OF PENRITH, 2nd Baron, *cr* 1930; **Francis Philip Howard,** DL; Captain late RA; *b* 5 Oct. 1905; *s* of 1st Baron and Lady Isabella Giustiniani-Bandini (*d* 1963) (*d* of Prince Giustiniani-Bandini, 8th Earl of Newburgh); *S* father, 1939; *m* 1944, Anne, *widow* of Anthony Bazley; four *s. Educ:* Downside; Trinity Coll., Cambridge (BA); Harvard Univ. Called to Bar, Middle Temple, 1931; served in War, 1939–42 (wounded). DL County of Glos, 1960. *Heir: s* Hon. Philip Esme Howard [*b* 1 May 1945; *m* 1969, Sarah, *d* of late Barclay Walker and of Mrs Walker, Perthshire; two *s* two *d*]. *Address:* Dean Farm, Coln St Aldwyns, Glos.

See also Hon. Edmund B. C. Howard.

HOWARD, Alan (Mackenzie); actor; Associate Artist, Royal Shakespeare Company, since 1967; *b* 5 Aug. 1937; *s* of Arthur John Howard and Jean Compton Mackenzie; *m* 1st, Stephanie Hinchcliffe Davies (marr. diss. 1976); 2nd, Sally Beauman; one *s. Educ:* Ardingly Coll. Belgrade Theatre, Coventry, 1958–60, parts incl. Frankie Bryant in Roots (also at Royal Court and Duke of York's); Wesker Trilogy, Royal Court, 1960; A Loss of Roses, Pembroke, Croydon, 1961; The Changeling, Royal Court, 1961; The Chances, and The Broken Heart, inaugural season, Chichester Festival, 1962; Virtue in Danger, Mermaid and Strand, 1963; Bassanio in The Merchant of Venice, Lysander in A Midsummer Night's Dream, in tour of S America and Europe, 1964; Simon in A Heritage and its History, Phoenix, 1965; Angelo in Measure for Measure, Bolingbroke in Richard II, Nottingham, 1965–66; Cyril Jackson in The Black and White Minstrels, Traverse, Edinburgh, 1972, Hampstead, 1973; A Ride Across Lake Constance, Hampstead and Mayfair, 1973. *Royal Shakespeare Company:* joined company, 1966, playing Orsino in Twelfth Night, Lussurioso in The Revenger's Tragedy; 1967: Jaques in As You Like It (also LA, 1968), Young Fashion in The Relapse; 1968: Edgar in King Lear, Achilles in Troilus and Cressida, Benedick in Much Ado about Nothing; 1969: Benedick (also in LA and San Francisco), Achilles, Lussurioso, and Bartholomew Cokes in Bartholomew Fair; 1970: Mephistophilis in Dr Faustus, Hamlet, Theseus/Oberon in A Midsummer Night's Dream, Ceres in The Tempest; 1971: Theseus/Oberon (NY debut); 1971–72: Theseus/Oberon, Nikolai in Enemies, Dorimant in The Man of Mode, The Envoy in The Balcony; 1972–73: Theseus/Oberon, in tour of E and W Europe, USA, Japan, Australia; 1974: Carlos II in The Bewitched; 1975: Henry V, Prince Hal in Henry IV parts I and II; 1976: Prince Hal (SWET Award for Best Actor in revival), Henry V in tour of Europe and USA, Jack Rover in Wild Oats (also Piccadilly); 1977: Henry V, Henry VI parts I, II and III, Coriolanus (Plays and Players London Critics Award, SWET Award for Best Actor in revival, Evening Standard Best Actor Award, 1978); 1978: Antony in Antony and Cleopatra; 1979: Coriolanus in tour of Europe, The Children of the Sun; 1980: title rôles in Richard II and Richard III (Variety Club Best Actor Award); 1981–82: Neschastlivsev in The Forest; Good (Standard Best Actor Award, 1981); 1985: Nikolai in Breaking the Silence. Best Actor (jt), 1981, Drama (British Theatre Assoc.) awards for Richard II, Good and The Forest. *Films include:* The Heroes of Telemark; Works is a Four Letter Word. *Television appearances include:* The Way of the World; Comet Among the Stars; Coriolanus; The Holy Experiment; Poppyland. *Address:* c/o Julian Belfrage Associates, 60 St James's Street, SW1. *T:* 01–491 4400.

HOWARD, Alexander Edward, CBE 1972; Lecturer in Education, London University Centre for Teachers, 1977–81; *b* 2 Aug. 1909; *o s* of Alexander Watson Howard and Gertrude Nellie Howard; *m* 1937, Phyllis Ada Adams; no *c. Educ:* Swindon Coll.; University Coll. and Westminster Coll., London Univ. BSc (London) 1930; Pt I, BSc (Econ.) 1934. Flt-Lieut, RAF, 1940–46. Asst Master, Sanford Boys' Sch., Swindon, 1931–34; Lectr in Maths, Wandsworth Techn. Coll., 1935–40; Maths Master, Wilson's Grammar Sch., 1946–48; Headmaster: Northfleet Sch. for Boys, Kent, 1948–51; Borough-Beaufoy Sch., London, 1951–54; Forest Hill Sch., London, 1955–63; Wandsworth Sch., 1963–74. Co-ordinating Officer Teaching Practice Organisation, London Univ. Inst. of Educn, 1975–77. Member: Naval Educn Adv. Cttee, 1966–80; Army Educational Adv. Bd, 1957–74. Academic Council, RMA, 1970–75. FRSA 1970. Hon. Mem., CGLI, 1979. *Publications:* The Secondary Technical School in England, 1955; Longman Mathematics Stages 1–5, 1962–67, new Metric edns, 1970–71; Teaching Mathematics, 1968; articles in Times Educational Supplement, The Teacher, Technology, Inside the Comprehensive Sch. *Recreations:* amateur theatre, old-time dancing, music, cricket, travel, rotary. *Address:* 19 Downsway, Sanderstead, Surrey CR2 0JB. *T:* 01–657 3399. *Club:* Surrey County Cricket.

HOWARD, Anthony Michell; Deputy Editor, The Observer, since 1981; *b* 12 Feb. 1934; *s* of late Canon Guy Howard and Janet Rymer Howard; *m* 1965, Carol Anne Gaynor. *Educ:* Westminster Sch.; Christ Church, Oxford. Chm., Oxford Univ. Labour Club, 1954; Pres., Oxford Union, 1955. Called to Bar, Inner Temple, 1956. Nat. Service, 2nd Lieut, Royal Fusiliers, 1956–58; Political Corresp., Reynolds News, 1958–59; Editorial Staff, Manchester Guardian, 1959–61 (Harkness Fellowship in USA, 1960); Political Corresp., New Statesman, 1961–64; Whitehall Corresp., Sunday Times, 1965; Washington Corresp., Observer, 1966–69 and Political Columnist, 1971–72; Asst Editor, 1970–72, Editor, 1972–78, New Statesman; Editor, The Listener, 1979–81; Presenter, Face the Press, Channel Four, 1982–85. *Publications:* (contrib.) The Baldwin Age, 1960; (contrib.) Age of Austerity, 1963; (with Richard West) The Making of the Prime Minister, 1965; (ed) The Crossman Diaries: selections from the Diaries of a Cabinet Minister, 1979; Rab: the life of R. A. Butler, 1987. *Address:* 17 Addison Avenue, W11 4QS. *T:* 01–603 3749.

HOWARD, Dame Christian; *see* Howard, Dame R. C.

HOWARD, Very Rev. Donald; Provost, St Andrew's Cathedral, Aberdeen, since 1978; *b* 21 Jan. 1927; *s* of William Howard and Alexandra Eadie (*née* Buchanan); unmarried.

Educ: Hull Coll. of Technology; London Univ. (BD, AKC). AFRAeS, 1954–58. Design Engineer, Blackburn Aircraft, 1948–52; Hunting Percival Aircraft, 1952–54; English Electric Co., 1954–55. Assistant Minister, Emmanuel Church, Saltburn-by-the-Sea, Yorks, 1959–62; Rector and Mission Director, Dio. Kimberley and Kuruman, S Africa, 1962–65; Rector of St John the Evangelist, East London, S Africa, 1965–72; Rector of Holy Trinity Episcopal Church, Haddington, Scotland, 1972–78. Hon. Canon, Christ Church Cathedral, Hartford, Conn, USA, 1978. *Address:* 15 Morningfield Road, Aberdeen, Scotland AB2 4AP. *T:* Aberdeen 314765.

HOWARD, Sir Douglas Frederick, KCMG 1953 (CMG 1944); MC; *b* 15 Feb. 1897; *s* of late John Howard Howard and of late Mrs Howard, Biddenham House, Bedford. *Educ:* Harrow. Served European War, 1915–18, France 1916 and 1918. Entered Diplomatic Service as 3rd Sec. Christiania, 1922; Bucharest, 1924; 2nd Sec., 1925; Rome, 1926; FO 1929. BA 1932. 1st Sec., 1934; Sofia, 1935; FO 1936; Madrid, 1939; Counsellor, FO, 1941; Madrid, 1945, where he was Chargé d'Affaires, Dec. 1946–Nov. 1949; Ambassador to Uruguay, 1949–53; HM Minister to the Holy See, 1953–57, retired. *Address:* Clophill House, Clophill, Bedford. *T:* Silsoe 60285.

HOWARD, Hon. Edmund Bernard Carlo, CMG 1969; LVO 1961; HM Diplomatic Service, retired; *b* 8 Sept. 1909; *s* of 1st Baron Howard of Penrith, PC, GCB, GCMG, CVO, and Lady Isabella Giustiniani-Bandini (*d* of Prince Giustiniani-Bandini, 8th Earl of Newburgh); *m* 1936, Cécile Geoffroy-Dechaume; three *s* one *d* (and one *d* decd). *Educ:* Downside Sch.; Newman Sch., Lakewood, NJ; New Coll., Oxford. Called to the Bar, 1932; Sec., Trustees and Managers, Stock Exchange, 1937. Served in HM Forces, KRRC, 1939–45. Joined HM Diplomatic Service, 1947; served in: Rome, 1947–51; Foreign Office, 1951–53; Madrid, 1953–57; Bogotá, 1957–59; Florence, 1960–61; Rome, 1961–65; Consul-Gen., Genoa, 1965–69. Comdr, Order of Merit, Italy, 1973. *Publications:* Genoa: history and art in an old seaport, 1971 (Duchi di Galliera prize, 1973); trans. The Aryan Myth, 1974. *Recreations:* travel, gardening, walking. *Address:* Jerome Cottage, Marlow Common, Bucks. *T:* Marlow 2129.

HOWARD, Sir Edward; *see* Howard, Sir H. E. de C.

HOWARD, Elizabeth Jane; novelist; *b* 26 March 1923; *d* of David Liddon and Katharine M. Howard; *m* 1st, 1942, Peter M. Scott; one *d*; 2nd, 1959, James Douglas-Henry; 3rd, 1965, Kingsley Amis, *qv* (marr. diss. 1983). *Educ:* home. Trained at London Mask Theatre Sch. Played at Stratford-on-Avon, and in repertory theatre in Devon; BBC, Television, modelling, 1939–46; Sec. to Inland Waterways Assoc., 1947; subsequently writing, editing, reviewing, journalism and writing plays for television, incl. serials of After Julius in three plays and Something in Disguise in six plays. John Llewellyn Rhys Memorial Prize for The Beautiful Visit, 1950. Hon. Artistic Dir, Cheltenham Literary Festival, 1962; Artistic co-Dir, Salisbury Festival of Arts, 1973. *Publications:* The Beautiful Visit, 1950; The Long View, 1956; The Sea Change, 1959; After Julius, 1965; Something in Disguise, 1969 (TV series, 1982); Odd Girl Out, 1972; Mr Wrong, 1975; (ed) A Companion for Lovers, 1978; Getting It Right, 1982 (Yorkshire Post Prize). *Recreations:* music, gardening, enjoying all the arts, travelling, natural history. *Address:* c/o Jonathan Clowes, 22 Prince Albert Road, NW1 7ST.

HOWARD, Francis Alex, (Frankie Howerd), OBE 1977; *b* 6 March 1922. *Educ:* Shooters Hill Sch., Woolwich, London. *Revues:* Out of this World, 1950; Pardon my French, 1953; Way Out in Piccadilly, 1966. *Plays:* Charlie's Aunt, 1955; Hotel Paradiso, 1957; A Midsummer Night's Dream (playing Bottom), 1958; Alice in Wonderland, 1960; A Funny Thing Happened on the Way to the Forum, 1963 (Critics' Award for Best Musical Actor, 1964); The Wind in the Sassafras Trees, Broadway, 1968; Simple Simon in Jack and the Beanstalk, Palladium, 1973; numerous pantomimes, 1947–83; *opera:* Frosch in Die Fledermaus, Coliseum, 1982; *films:* The Ladykillers, 1956; Runaway Bus, 1956; Touch of the Sun, 1956; Jumping for Joy, 1956; Further up the Creek, 1958; Carry On, Doctor, 1968; Carry on Up the Jungle, 1970; Up Pompeii, 1971; Up the Chastity Belt, 1972; Up the Front, 1972; The House in Nightmare Park, 1973; Sergeant Pepper's Lonely Hearts Club Band, 1978. *TV Series:* Fine Goings On, 1959; Up Pompeii, 1970–71; Up the Convicts (Australia), 1975; The Frankie Howerd Show (Canada), 1976; Frankie Howerd Strikes Again, 1981; in Gilbert and Sullivan series: HMS Pinafore, 1982; Trial by Jury, 1982. Roving reporter for TV-am, 1983–. Royal Variety Performances, 1950, 1954, 1961, 1966, 1968, 1969, 1978, 1982 Variety Club of GB Award (Show Business Personality of the Year), 1966, 1971; Radio and TV Industries Award (Show Business Personality of the Year), 1971. *Publication:* Trumps, 1982. *Recreations:* tennis, swimming, music, reading. *Address:* c/o Tessa Le Bars Management, 18 Queen Anne Street, W1M 9LB. *T:* 01–636 3191.

HOWARD, Lt Comdr Hon. Greville (Reginald), VRD; RNR; *b* 7 Sept. 1909; 3rd *s* of 19th Earl of Suffolk and Berkshire; *m* 1945, Mary Ridehalgh; one *d*. *Educ:* Eton; RMC Sandhurst. Commissioned in King's Shropshire LI, 1930–35. London Manager of G. W. Joynson, Cotton Merchants and Brokers, 1935–39. Councillor Westminster City Council, 1937; Naval Service, War of 1939–45; destroyers commanded: HMS Viscount (temp.), 1943; HMS Sabre, 1943–44; HMS Nith, 1944. Rejoined Westminster City Council, 1945; Mayor of Westminster, 1946–47; Chm. Public Cleansing, Transport, Baths and Contracts Cttee, 1945 and 1947–49; Vice-Chm. Establishments Cttee, 1949; Vice-Chm. Refuse Sub-Cttee, Metropolitan Boroughs Standing Joint Cttee, 1947–49. MP (Nat L and C) St Ives Division of Cornwall 1950–66; retired, 1966. Hon. Overseas Director and European Consultant, Colour Processing Laboratories Ltd, 1969–. Overseas Mem. Cttee of Management and Hon. Vice-Pres., RNLI, 1969–; Pres., Lizard Br., RNLI, 1984–; Vice-President: Kensington and Chelsea Scouts Assoc., 1985–; Sea Rangers Assoc., 1984–; Cdre of the Races, Sail Training Assoc., 1984–; Patron, Discovery Dockland Trust, 1984–. *Recreations:* photography, sailing, bicycling, riding, fishing. *Address:* Redlynch, 14 Mandelbach, 7415 Brouch (Mersch), Grand Duché de Luxembourg. *T:* 63560. *Clubs:* (supernumerary or overseas member of all) White's, Pratt's, Naval, Norwegian; Royal Yacht Squadron, Royal Norwegian Yacht, Royal Naval Sailing Assoc., Royal Cornwall Yacht.

HOWARD, Sir (Hamilton) Edward (de Coucey), 2nd Bt *cr* 1955; GBE 1972; Partner of Stockbroking Firm of Charles Stanley and Company; Chairman, LRC International Ltd, 1971–82; *b* 29 Oct. 1915; *s* of Sir (Harold Walter) Seymour Howard, 1st Bt, and Edith M. (*d* 1962), *d* of Edward Turner; *S* father 1967; *m* 1943, Elizabeth Howarth Ludlow; two *s*. *Educ:* Le Rosey, Rolle, Switzerland; Radley Coll., Abingdon; Worcester Coll., Oxford. Mem. of the Stock Exchange, London, 1946. Sheriff of the City of London, 1966 (Common Councilman, 1951; Alderman, 1963); Lord Mayor of London, 1971–72; one of HM Lieutenants, City of London, 1976–. Master of the Gardeners' Company, 1961. DSc City Univ., 1971. KStJ 1972. *Recreation:* gardening. *Heir:* *s* David Howarth Seymour Howard [*b* 29 Dec. 1945; *m* 1968, Valerie Picton, *o d* of Derek W. Crosse; two *s* two *d*]. *Address:* Courtlands, Bishops Walk, Shirley Hills, Surrey. *T:* 01–656 4444. *Clubs:* Guildhall, City Livery, United Wards.

HOWARD, James Boag, CB 1972; Assistant Under-Secretary of State, Home Office, 1963–75; *b* 10 Jan. 1915; *yr s* of William and Jean Howard, Greenock; *m* 1943, Dorothy Jean Crawshaw; two *d*. *Educ:* Greenock High Sch.; Glasgow Univ. (MA, BSc; 1st cl. Hons Mathematics and Natural Philosophy). Asst Principal, Home Office, 1937; Private Sec. to Permanent Sec., Ministry of Home Security, 1940–41; Principal, 1941; Asst Sec., 1948. *Address:* 12 Windhill, Bishop's Stortford, Herts. *T:* Bishop's Stortford 51728.

HOWARD, Dr James Griffiths, FRS 1984; FIBiol; Assistant Director, The Wellcome Trust, since 1986; *b* 25 Sept. 1927; *s* of late Joseph Griffiths Howard and Kathleen Mildred Howard; *m* 1951, Opal St Clair (*née* Echalaz); two *d* (one *s* decd). *Educ:* Middlesex Hosp. Med. Sch., Univ. of London (MB, BS 1950; PhD 1957; MD 1960). FIBiol 1978. Public Health Lab. Service, 1951–53; Jun. Specialist in Pathology, RAMC, 1953–55; Res. Fellow, Wright-Fleming Inst., St Mary's Hosp., 1955–58; Edinburgh University: Immunologist (Lectr, Sen. Lectr and Reader), Dept of Surgical Science, 1958–66; Reader and Head of Immunobiology Section, Dept of Zoology, 1966–69; Wellcome Research Laboratories: Head, Experimental Immunobiology Dept, 1969–74; Head, Exp. Biology Div., 1974–83; Dir, Biomedical Res., 1984–85. *Publications:* some 130 scientific articles, reviews and chapters in books, pre-dominantly on immunology. *Recreations:* fine arts, music, cinema, cooking, hill walking. *Address:* The Wellcome Trust, 1 Park Square West, NW1 4LJ. *T:* 01–486 4902.

HOWARD, (James) Kenneth, ARA 1983; painter; *b* 26 Dec. 1932; *s* of Frank and Elizabeth Howard; *m* Ann Howard (*née* Popham), dress designer (marr. diss. 1974). *Educ:* Kilburn Grammar School; Hornsey School of Art; Royal College of Art. ARCA. NEAC 1962, ROI 1966, RWA 1981, RWS 1983. British Council scholarship to Florence, 1958–59; taught various London Art Schools, 1959–73; Official Artist for Imperial War Museum in N Ireland, 1973, 1978; painted for the British Army in N Ireland, Germany, Cyprus, Hong Kong, Brunei, Nepal, Belize, Norway, Lebanon, Canada, Oman, 1973–; one man exhibitions: Plymouth Art Centre, 1955; John Whibley Gallery, 1966, 1968; New Grafton Gallery, 1971–; Jersey, 1978, 1980, 1983; Hong Kong, 1979; Nicosia, 1982; Delhi, 1983. Works purchased by Plymouth Art Gall., Imperial War Mus., Guildhall Art Gall., Ulster Mus., Nat. Army Mus., Hove Mus., Sheffield Art Gall., Southend Mus.; commissions for UN, BAOR, Drapers' Co., Stock Exchange, States of Jersey, Banque Paribas, Royal Hosp. Chelsea. First Prize: Hunting Group Award, 1982; Sparkasse Karlsruhe, 1985. *Recreations:* cinema, music. *Address:* 8 South Bolton Gardens, SW5 0DH. *T:* 01–373 2912 (studio); St Clements Hall, Mousehole, Cornwall. *T:* Penzance 731596. *Club:* Chelsea Arts.

HOWARD, Mrs John E.; *see* Laski, Marghanita.

HOWARD, John James, CBE 1985; Chief General Manager, Royal Insurance plc, 1980–84; *b* 9 March 1923; *s* of late Sir Henry Howard, KCIE, CSI, and Lady Howard; *m* 1949, Julia Tupholme Mann; one *s* one *d* (and one *d* decd). *Educ:* Rugby Sch.; Trinity Hall, Cambridge (MA). Pilot, RAFVR, 1942–46 (Flt Lieut). Royal Insurance Company Ltd: Financial Secretary, 1964–69; General Manager, 1970–80, Director, 1970–84. Chm., British Insurance Assoc., 1983–84 (Dep. Chm., 1981–83). Advr, Surrey Business Enterprise, 1986–. Chm., YWCA Central Club, 1986–. *Recreations:* golf, bridge, gardening. *Address:* Highfields, High Barn Road, Effingham, Surrey KT24 5PX.

HOWARD, Hon. John Winston; MP(Lib) for Bennelong, NSW, since 1974; Leader of the Opposition, Australia, since 1985 (Deputy Leader, 1983–85); *b* 26 July 1939; *m* 1971, Alison Janette Parker; two *s* one *d*. *Educ:* Canterbury Boys' High Sch.; Sydney Univ. Solicitor of NSW Supreme Court. Minister for Business and Consumer Affairs, Australia, 1975; Minister assisting Prime Minister, May 1977; Minister for Special Trade Negotiations, July 1977; Federal Treasurer, 1977–83; Leader, Parly Liberal Party, Australia, 1985– (Dep. Leader, 1982–85). *Recreations:* reading, tennis, cricket. *Address:* 19 Milner Crescent, Wollstonecraft, NSW 2065, Australia. *T:* 02–4394360. *Clubs:* Australian (Sydney), Commonwealth (Canberra).

HOWARD, Kenneth; *see* Howard, J. K.

HOWARD, Leonard Henry, RD 1941; retired; *b* 5 Aug. 1904; *m* 1st, 1938, Betty Scourse; one *s* one *d*; 2nd, 1960, Barbara Davies-Colley. *Educ:* Stubbington House Sch.; Nautical Coll., Pangbourne. Sea career in Royal Navy and P&O-Orient Lines (Merchant Navy), 1922–64; commanded several RN units, War of 1939–45; Comdr, troop ship Empire Fowey, and passenger ships Strathmore, Himalaya and Arcadia, P&O Co.; Commodore, P&O-Orient Lines, 1963–64 (now P&O Steam Navigation Co.), retired. *Recreations:* golf, gardening. *Address:* Port, Heyshott, Midhurst, W Sussex. *T:* Midhurst 2560. *Club:* Cowdray Park Golf.

HOWARD, Margaret; freelance broadcaster, since 1969; Presenter, Pick of the Week, BBC Radio 4, since 1974; *b* 29 March 1938; *d* of John Bernard Howard and Ellen Corwena Roberts. *Educ:* St Mary's Convent, Rhyl, N Wales; St Teresa's Convent, Sunbury; Guildhall Sch. of Music and Drama; Indiana Univ., Bloomington, USA. LGSM; LRAM 1960. BBC World Service Announcer, 1967–69; Reporter: The World This Weekend, BBC Radio 4, 1970–74; Edition, BBC TV, 1971; Tomorrow's World, BBC TV, 1972; Presenter, It's Your World, BBC World Service, 1981–; Interviewer/Presenter, Strictly Instrumental, occasional series, 1980–. Female UK Radio Personality of the Year, Sony Awards, 1984. *Publications:* Margaret Howard's Pick of the Week, 1984; Court Jesting, 1986. *Recreations:* riding, tasting wine, walking the Jack Russell. *Address:* c/o London Management, 235/241 Regent Street, W1A 2JT. *T:* 01–493 1610.

HOWARD, Michael, QC 1982; MP(C) Folkestone and Hythe, since 1983; Parliamentary Under-Secretary of State, Department of Trade and Industry, since 1985; a Recorder, since 1986; *b* 7 July 1941; *s* of late Bernard Howard and of Hilda Howard; *m* 1975, Sandra Clare, *d* of Wing-Comdr Saville Paul; one *s* one *d* (and one step *s*). *Educ:* Llanelli Grammar School; Peterhouse, Cambridge. MA, LLB; President of the Union, 1962. Major Scholar, Inner Temple, 1962; called to the Bar, Inner Temple, 1964. Junior Counsel to the Crown (Common Law), 1980–82. Contested (C) Liverpool, Edge Hill, 1966 and 1970; Chm., Bow Group, 1970–71. PPS to Solicitor-General, 1984–85. Jt Sec., Cons. Legal Cttee, 1983–84; Jt Vice-Chm., Cons. Employment Cttee, 1983–84; Vice-Chm., Soc. of Cons. Lawyers, 1985. *Recreations:* watching football (Swansea, Liverpool) and baseball (New York Mets). *Address:* House of Commons, SW1A 0AA. *T:* 01–219 5493. *Clubs:* Carlton, Coningsby (Chm., 1972–73).

HOWARD, Sir Michael Eliot, Kt 1986; CBE 1977; MC 1943; DLitt; FBA 1970; FRHistS; FRSL; Regius Professor of Modern History and Fellow of Oriel College, Oxford, since 1980; *b* 29 Nov. 1922; *y s* of late Geoffrey Eliot Howard, Ashmore, near Salisbury, and of Edith Julia Emma, *o d* of Otto Edinger. *Educ:* Wellington; Christ Church, Oxford. BA 1946, MA 1948. Served War, Coldstream Guards, 1942–45. Asst Lecturer in History, University of London, King's Coll., 1947; Lecturer, 1950; Lecturer in War Studies, 1953–61; Prof. of War Studies, 1963–68; Fellow of All Souls Coll., Oxford, 1968–80; Chichele Prof. of History of War, Univ. of Oxford, 1977–80. Vis. Prof. of European History, Stanford Univ., 1967. Ford's Lectr in English History, Oxford, 1971; Radcliffe Lectr, Univ. of Warwick, 1975; Trevelyan Lectr, Cambridge, 1977; FKC. Vice-Pres. and co-Founder, Internat. Institute for Strategic Studies; Mem., Adv. Council on Public Records. Governor, Wellington Coll. For. Hon. Mem., Amer. Acad. of Arts and

Scis, 1983. Hon. LittD Leeds, 1979. Chesney Meml Gold Medal, RUSI, 1973. *Publications:* The Coldstream Guards, 1920–46 (with John Sparrow), 1951; Disengagement in Europe, 1958; Wellingtonian Studies, 1959; The Franco-Prussian War, 1961 (Duff Cooper Memorial Prize, 1962); The Theory and Practice of War, 1965; The Mediterranean Strategy in the Second World War, 1967; Studies in War and Peace, 1970; Grand Strategy, vol IV (in UK History of 2nd World War, Military series), 1971 (Wolfson Foundn History Award, 1972); The Continental Commitment, 1972; War in European History, 1976; (with P. Paret) Clausewitz On War, 1977; War and the Liberal Conscience, 1978; (ed) Restraints on War, 1979; The Causes of Wars, 1983; Clausewitz, 1983; contributions to The New Cambridge Modern History. *Recreations:* music, weeding. *Address:* Oriel College, Oxford OX1 4EW. *Clubs:* Athenæum, Garrick.

HOWARD, Michael Newman; QC 1986; *b* 10 June 1947; *s* of Henry Ian Howard and Tilly Celia Howard. *Educ:* Clifton College; Magdalen College, Oxford (MA, BCL). Lecturer in Law, LSE, 1970–74; called to the Bar, Gray's Inn, 1971. *Publications:* (ed jtly) Phipson on Evidence, 12th edn 1976, 13th edn 1982; articles in legal periodicals. *Recreations:* books, music, sport. *Address:* Queen Elizabeth Building, Temple, EC4Y 9BS. *T:* 01–353 9153. *Clubs:* United Oxford & Cambridge University, Royal Automobile.

HOWARD, Michael Stockwin; Director, Cantores in Ecclesia, since 1964; Co-founder and Artistic Director, Rye Spring Music, 1976; *b* London, 14 Sept. 1922; *er s* of late Frank Henry Howard (viola, Internat. String Quartet, Foundn principal, Beecham's Philharmonic) and Florence Mabel Howard. *Educ:* Ellesmere; Royal Acad. of Music; privately. Organist, Tewkesbury Abbey, 1943–44; Dir of Music, Ludgrove Sch.; Founder, Renaissance Society, and conductor, Renaissance Singers, 1944–64; Organist and Master of the Choristers, Ely Cath., 1953–58; Dir of Music, St George's Sch., Harpenden, 1959–61; Asst, Music Presentation, BBC, 1968–78; Dir of Music, St Marylebone Parish Church, 1971–79, Dir Emeritus, 1979; Organist to the Franciscans of Rye, 1979–83; Organist and Rector Chori, St Michael's Abbey, Farnborough, 1984–86. Freelance organist, harpsichordist, conductor, broadcaster and writer. Hon. ARAM 1976. Prix Musicale de Radio Brno, 1967; Gustave Charpentier Grand Prix du Disque, 1975. Recordings with essays include: Tallis/Byrd 1575 Cantiones Sacrae, 1969; Tallis at Waltham Abbey, 1974; Palestrina, The Garden of Love, 1974. *Principal compositions include:* Mass, Sonnet VIII, 1961; Scaena Dramatis for Antoinette Michael, 1978; Dances for a Mountain Goat, 1979; opera, The Lion's Mouth, 1980; Sequentia de Insomnia, 1981; Diptych (Arnold and St Ambrose), 1981; Discourse on Chorale by Judith Earley, 1982; Cautiones Iudithae, 1983; In Memoriam Duncan Thomson, 1983; Missa de Ecclesia Christi, 1984; *organ:* Cantique d'un Oiseau matinal, 1982; Carillon des Larmes, 1982. *Publications:* The Private Inferno (autobiog.), 1974; Tribute to Aristide Cavaillé-Coll, 1985; contrib. Musical Times, Monthly Musical Record, Dublin Review, Listener, EMG Monthly Letter. *Recreations:* steam railway traction, village fairgrounds. *Address:* 40 Chapel Park Road, St Leonards-on-Sea, E Sussex.

HOWARD, Air Vice-Marshal Peter, OBE 1957; QHP 1982; FRCP, FRAeS; Commandant, RAF Institute of Aviation Medicine, since 1975 and Dean of Air Force Medicine, since 1985; *b* 15 Dec. 1925; *s* of late Edward Charles Howard and Doris Mary Howard (*née* Cure); *m* 1950, Norma Lockhart (Fletcher); one *s* one *d*. *Educ:* Farnborough Grammar Sch.; St Thomas's Hosp. Med. Sch. (MB BS 1949, PhD 1964); FRCP 1977; FFOM 1981; FRAeS 1973. House Physician, 1950, Registrar, 1951. St Thomas' Hosp.; RAF Medical Branch, 1951–; RAF Consultant in Aviation Physiology, 1964; RAF Consultant Adviser in Occupational Medicine, 1983–85. Chm., Defence Med. Services Postgraduate Council, 1986–; Registrar, Faculty of Occupational Medicine, RCP, 1986–. *Publications:* papers and chapters in books on aviation physiology, medicine, occupational medicine. *Recreations:* fly fishing, computing. *Address:* 135 Aldershot Road, Church Crookham, Hants GU13 0JU. *T:* Fleet 617309. *Club:* Royal Air Force.

HOWARD, Philip Nicholas Charles; Literary Editor of The Times, since 1978; *b* 2 Nov. 1933; *s* of Peter Dunsmore Howard and Doris Emily Metaxa; *m* 1959, Myrtle, *d* of Sir Reginald Houldsworth, *qv*; two *s* one *d*. *Educ:* Eton Coll. (King's Scholar); Trinity Coll., Oxford (MA). Glasgow Herald, 1959–64; The Times, 1964–: reporter, writer, columnist. Liveryman, Wheelwrights' Co. London Editor, Verbatim, 1977–. *Publications:* The Black Watch, 1968; The Royal Palaces, 1970; London's River, 1975; New Words for Old, 1977; The British Monarchy, 1977; Weasel Words, 1978; Words Fail Me, 1980; A Word in Your Ear, 1983; The State of the Language, English Observed, 1984; (jtly) The Times Bicentenary Stamp Book, 1985; We Thundered Out, 200 Years of The Times 1785–1985, 1985. *Recreations:* walking, talking, music, the classics, beagles not beagling. *Address:* Flat 1, 47 Ladbroke Grove, W11 3AR. *T:* 01–727 1077. *Clubs:* Classical Association, Horatian Society, Garrick; Ad Eundem (Oxford and Cambridge).

HOWARD, Robert, (Bob); Northern Regional Secretary, Trades Union Congress, since 1980; *b* 4 April 1939; *s* of Robert and Lily Howard; *m* 1984, Valerie Stewart; one *s* one *d*. *Educ:* Gregson Lane County Primary Sch.; Deepdale Secondary Modern Sch.; Queen Elizabeth's Grammar Sch., Blackburn, Lancs; Cliff Training Coll., Calver via Sheffield, Derbyshire. British Leyland, Lancs, 1961–68: Member, Clerical and Admin. Workers' Union Br. Exec.; Councillor, Walton le Dale UDC, 1962–65; GPO, Preston, Lancs, 1969–80: Telephone Area UPW Telecomms Representative Member: Jt Consultative Council, Jt Productivity Council, Council of PO Unions Area Cttee, Delegate to Preston Trades Council; Secretary, Lancashire Assoc. of Trades Councils, 1977–79; created 14 specialist cttees for LATC; appointment as N Reg. Sec., Trades Union Congress, 1980–, by Gen. Sec., TUC, first full-time secretary to a TUC region. Dir, Washington Youth Training Ltd, 1983–86. Member: Industrial Tribunals, 1979–80; Nat. Trust, 1983–; Northern Regional Bd, GCSE, 1986–. Northern Region Coordinator, Jobs March, 1983. JP Duchy of Lancaster, 1969–74. *Publications:* North-East Lancashire Structure Plan—The Trades Councils' View (with Peter Stock), 1979; Organisation and Functions of TUC Northern Regional Council, 1980. *Recreations:* fell walking, classical music, camping, outdoor sports, reading, chess. *Address:* 8 Caxton Way, North Lodge, Chester le Street, County Durham DH3 4BW. *Club:* Newcastle Press.

HOWARD, Robin Jared Stanley, CBE 1976, Director-General, Contemporary Dance Trust Ltd, since 1966; *b* 17 May 1924; *s* of Hon. Sir Arthur Howard, KBE, CVO, DL, and of Lady Lorna Howard. *Educ:* Eton; Trinity Coll., Cambridge (MA). Served War, 1942–45, Lieut, Scots Guards. Called to Bar, Inner Temple. Hon. Dir, Internat. Service Dept, United Nations Assoc., 1956–64. *Recreation:* sleep. *Address:* 7 Sandwich Street, WC1H 9AB. *Clubs:* Garrick, MCC.

HOWARD, Rev. Canon Ronald Claude; Headmaster, Hurstpierpoint College, 1945–64; *b* 15 Feb. 1902; 2nd *s* of Henry H. and Florence Howard, The Durrant, Sevenoaks. *Educ:* Sidney Sussex Coll., Cambridge; Westcott House, Cambridge. Ordained, 1926; Curate of Eastbourne, 1926–28; Chaplain, Bradfield Coll., 1928–30; Asst Master, Tonbridge Sch., 1930–37; Asst Master, Marlborough Coll., 1937, Chaplain there, 1938–43; Chaplain and Asst Master, Radley Coll., 1943–45. Canon of Chichester, 1957; Communar of Chichester Cathedral, 1964–67. Canon Emeritus, 1967. *Recreations:* painting, collecting water-colours. *Address:* 3 Adelaide Crescent, Hove, East Sussex.

HOWARD, Dame (Rosemary) Christian, DBE 1986; *b* 5 Sept. 1916; *d* of Hon. Geoffrey Howard, *s* of 9th Earl of Carlisle, and Hon. Christian, *d* of 3rd Baron Methuen. *Educ:* Westbourne House, Folkestone; Villa Malatesta, Florence; Ozannes, Paris; and privately. STh Lambeth 1943; MA Lambeth 1979. Divinity Teacher, Chichester High Sch. for Girls, 1943–45; Licensed Lay Worker, Dio. York, 1947–; Sec., Bd of Women's Work, 1947–72; Sec., Lay Ministry, 1972–79; retired 1980. Deleg. to WCC Assemblies, 1961 and 1968; Member: Faith and Order Commn, WCC, 1961–75; BCC, 1974–; Church Assembly, 1960–70, General Synod, 1970–85; Churches' Council for Covenanting, 1978–82. Governor, Malton School. *Publications:* The Ordination of Women to Priesthood, 1972, Supplement 1978, Further Report 1984; Praise and Thanksgiving, 1972; contribs to Ecumenical Review, Year Book of Social Policy, Crucible, New Directions, Chrysalis. *Recreations:* woodwork, gardening, foreign travel. *Address:* Coneysthorpe, York YO6 7DD. *T:* Coneysthorpe 264.

HOWARD, Trevor Wallace; actor; *b* 29 Sept. 1916; father English, mother Canadian; *m* 1944, Helen Mary Cherry. *Educ:* Clifton Coll. Shakespeare Festival, Stratford-on-Avon, 1936 and 1939; French Without Tears, Criterion, 1936–38. Served War in Army, 1940–43, 1st Airborne Division. Played in the Recruiting Officer and Anna Christie, 1944; Old Vic Season, 1947–48, Petruchio in the Taming of the Shrew. *Films include:* Brief Encounter, 1945; The Third Man, 1949; An Outcast of the Islands, 1951; The Heart of the Matter, 1953 (Acad. award); Lovers of Lisbon (French); Cockleshell Heroes, 1955; Run for the Sun, 1956; The Key, Roots of Heaven, 1958; Sons and Lovers, 1960 (Acad. nomination); Mutiny on the Bounty, 1962; Von Ryan's Express, 1965; Father Goose, 1965; The Liquidator, 1966; The Charge of the Light Brigade, 1968; Pretty Polly, 1968; Ryan's Daughter, 1970; Mary Queen of Scots, 1971; Ludwig, 1972; The Offence, 1973; A Doll's House, 1973; The Visitor, 1974; 11 Harrowhouse, 1974; Hennessy, 1975; Conduct Unbecoming, 1975; Count of Monte Cristo, 1976 (Acad. nomination); The Last Remake of Beau Geste, 1977; Slavers, 1978; Stevie, 1978; Superman, 1978; Hurricane, 1980; The Sea Wolves, 1980; Sir Henry at Rawlinson End, 1980; Windwalker, (Cheyenne), 1980; Light Years Away, 1981 (Standard award, 1982); The Missionary, 1983; Gandhi, 1983; Dust, 1985; *Plays include:* The Devil's General, 1953; Lopahin in The Cherry Orchard, Lyric, 1954; Two Stars for Comfort, Garrick, 1962; The Father, Piccadilly, 1964; Waltz of the Toreadors, Haymarket, 1974; Scenario, Toronto, 1977. *Television:* Hedda Gabler, 1962; The Invincible Mr Disraeli, 1963 (Acad. Award); Napoleon at St Helena, 1966 (Acad. nom.); Catholics, 1974; Staying On, 1980; Jonathan Swift, 1981; The Deadly Game, 1983; In Search of the Third Reich, 1983; George Washington, 1984; Handel, in God Rot Tunbridge Wells!, 1985; Time after Time, 1985; This Lightning always Strikes Twice, 1985; Shaka Zulu, 1986; Sir Isaac Newton, in Peter the Great, 1986. *Recreations:* cricket, travel. *Address:* Rowley Green, Arkley, Herts. *Club:* MCC.

HOWARD, Sir Walter Stewart, Kt 1963; MBE 1944; DL; *b* 25 Nov. 1888; *y s* of late Henry Blunt Howard; *m* 1917, Alison Mary Wall (*d* 1985), *e d* of late Herbert F. Waring, Farningham Hill, Kent. *Educ:* Wellington; Trinity Coll., Cambridge. Vice-Chm., Warwicks CC, 1955 (Chm., 1956–60); Chm. Whiteley Village Trust, 1952–62; Governor: King Edward VI Sch., Birmingham; Warwick Sch.; Pres., Association of Education Cttees, 1962–63. Trustee of Shakespeare's birthplace. JP 1931, CC 1939, CA 1948, DL 1952, Warwicks. *Recreation:* foreign travel. *Address:* Barford, Warwick. *T:* Barford 624208. *Club:* United Oxford & Cambridge University.

HOWARD, William Brian; Deputy Chairman, 1984–March 1987, Joint Managing Director, 1976–86, Marks & Spencer plc; *b* 16 July 1926; *s* of William James and Annie Howard; *m* 1952, Audrey Elizabeth (*née* Jenney); one *s* one *d*. *Educ:* Revoe Junior Sch., Blackpool; Blackpool Grammar Sch.; Manchester Univ. (BA (Hons) Mod. Hist., Economics and Politics); Harvard Graduate Business Sch., 1973. Royal Signals, 1944–47. Marks & Spencer Ltd, 1951–87; Dir, 1973–87. A Church Comr, 1977–. *Address:* c/o 57 Baker Street, W1A 1DN.

HOWARD, William McLaren, QC 1964; a Recorder, since 1972; *b* 27 Jan. 1921; 3rd *s* of William George Howard and Frances Jane (*née* McLaren). *Educ:* Merchant Taylors' Sch. Entered RN as Cadet, 1938. Served at sea throughout War of 1939–45; Lieut 1942; resigned commission, 1946. Called to the Bar, Lincoln's Inn, 1947, Bencher, 1972; joined Inner Temple (*ad eundem*), 1960; called to Hong Kong Bar, 1986; Dep. Chm., Norfolk QS, 1967–71; Recorder of Ipswich, 1968–71; Judge Advocate of the Fleet, 1973–86. Mem., Bar Council, 1965–69 (also Mem., Bar Council Special Cttee on Sentencing and Penology). Vice-Pres., Norfolk Assoc. for Care and Resettlement of Offenders. Mem., British Acad. Forensic Sci. Hon. Judge Advocate of US Navy, 1984; Hon. Mem. of the Bar, US Court of Mil. Appeals, 1984. *Address:* The Red House, Holkham, Wells-next-the-Sea, Norfolk; 1201 Prince's Building, Chater Road, Hong Kong. *T:* Hong Kong 5–263585. *Clubs:* Garrick; Norfolk (Norwich).

HOWARD-DOBSON, Gen. Sir Patrick John, GCB 1979 (KCB 1974; CB 1973); National President, Royal British Legion, since 1981; *b* 12 Aug. 1921; *s* of late Canon Howard Dobson, MA; *m* 1946, Barbara Mary Mills; two *s* one *d*. *Educ:* King's Coll. Choir Sch., Cambridge; Framlingham College. Joined 7th Queen's Own Hussars, Egypt, Dec. 1941; served in: Burma, 1942; Middle East, 1943; Italy, 1944–45; Germany, 1946; psc 1950; jssc 1958; comd The Queen's Own Hussars, 1963–65 and 20 Armoured Bde, 1965–67; idc 1968; Chief of Staff, Far East Comd, 1969–71; Comdt, Staff Coll., Camberley, 1972–74; Military Secretary, 1974–76; Quartermaster General, 1977–79; Vice-Chief of Defence Staff (Personnel and Logistics), 1979–81; ADC Gen. to the Queen, 1978–81. Col Comdt, ACC, 1976–82. Virtuti Militari (Poland), 1945; Silver Star (US), 1945. *Recreations:* sailing, golf. *Address:* The Cottage, Benington, near Stevenage, Herts. *Club:* Cavalry and Guards.

HOWARD-DRAKE, Jack Thomas Arthur; Assistant Under-Secretary of State, Home Office, 1974–78; *b* 7 Jan. 1919; *o s* of Arthur Howard and Ruby (*née* Cherry); *m* 1947, Joan Mary, *o d* of Hubert and Winifred Crook; one *s* two *d*. *Educ:* Hele's Sch., Exeter. Asst Inspector, Ministry of Health Insurance Dept, 1937–39 and 1946–47. Served War, RA, 1939–46 (Major, despatches). Colonial Office: Asst Principal, 1947; Principal, 1949; Private Sec. to Sec. of State, 1956–62; Asst Sec., 1962; Asst Sec., Cabinet Office, 1963–65; Asst Sec., Home Office, 1965–72; Asst Under-Sec. of State, NI Office, 1972–74. Chairman: Oxfordshire Local History Assoc., 1984–; Wychwoods Local History Soc., 1984–. *Recreations:* gardening, local history, golf. *Address:* 26 Sinnels Field, Shipton-under-Wychwood, Oxon OX7 6EJ. *T:* Shipton-under-Wychwood 830792.

HOWARD-JOHNSTON, Rear-Admiral Clarence Dinsmore, CB 1955; DSO 1942; DSC 1940; *b* 13 Oct. 1903; *m* 1955, Paulette, *d* of late Paul Helleu. *Educ:* Royal Naval Colls Osborne and Dartmouth. Midshipman, 1921; Commander, 1937; Dir of Studies, Greek Naval War Coll., Athens, 1938–40; Naval staff, anti-submarine Warfare Div., Admlty, 1940; detached to set up anti-sub. trng, Quiberon, 1940; i/c ops for destruction port facilities St Malo, evacuation British troops St Malo and Jersey (despatches); anti-sub. ops, Norwegian fjords, evacuation troops and wounded, Molde and Andalsnes (DSC); in comd anti-sub. escort group, N Atlantic, 1941–42; escorted 1,229 ships (DSO for sinking

U651); staff, Battle of Atlantic Comd, Liverpool, 1942–43; Captain, 1943; Dir, Anti-U-boat Div., Admlty, 1943–45, anti-sub. specialist, PM's Cabinet U-boat meetings; in Comd, HMS Bermuda, British Pacific Fleet and occupation of Japan forces, 1946–47; Naval Attaché, Paris, 1947–50; Naval ADC to the Queen, 1952; Rear-Adm., 1953; Chief of Staff to Flag Officer, Central Europe, 1953–55, retired, 1955. Inventor of simple hydraulic mechanisms; commended by Lords Comrs of the Admiralty for invention and develt of anti-submarine training devices including Johnston Mobile A/S target, 1937. Participated in and prepared maritime historical programmes on French TV, 1967–81. Order of Phœnix (Greece), 1940; Legion of Merit (USA), 1945. *Recreations:* fishing, pisiculture, hill-walking, gardening. *Address:* 45 Rue Emile Ménier, 75116 Paris, France; Le Coteau, Chambre d'Amour, 64600 Anglet, France. *Clubs:* White's, Naval and Military, (Naval Member) Royal Yacht Squadron; Jockey (Paris).

HOWARD-JONES, Maj.-Gen. Leonard Hamilton, CB 1959; CBE 1945 (OBE 1942); *b* 4 April 1905; *s* of late Hubert Stanley Howard-Jones, Maindee Park, Newport, Mon; *m* 1st, 1934, Irene Lucy Gillespie (*d* 1944); 2nd, 1945, Violet, *d* of Sidney Alfred Butler, and *widow* of Lieut-Col Francis John Leland; one *s* one *d*. *Educ:* Imperial Service Coll.; Cardiff Univ. (BSc Eng). Served War of 1939–45 (despatches; OBE; CBE). Commandant REME Training Centre, 1953–57; Inspector, Royal Electrical and Mechanical Engineers, War Office, 1957–60. MIMechE; AMIEE. *Address:* Rifle Range Farm, Fleet Road, Hartley Wintney, Hants RG27 8ED. *T:* Hartley Wintney 2358.

HOWARD-VYSE, Lt-Gen. Sir Edward (Dacre), KBE 1962 (CBE 1955); CB 1958; MC 1941; DL; *b* 27 Nov. 1905; *s* of late Lieut-Col Cecil Howard-Vyse, JP, Langton Hall, Malton, Yorks; *m* 1940, Mary Bridget, *er d* of late Col Hon. Claude Henry Comaraich Willoughby, CVO; two *s* one *d*. *Educ:* Wellington Coll., Berks; RMA. 2nd Lieut, Royal Artillery, 1925; served War of 1939–45: British Expeditionary Force, France, 1939–40; Lieut-Col, 1941; Mediterranean Expeditionary Force, 1941–44; In command 1st Royal Horse Artillery, Central Mediterranean Force, 1944–45. Brigadier, 1949; CRA 7th Armoured Division, BAOR, 1951–53; Commandant, Sch. of Artillery, 1953; Maj.-Gen., 1957; Maj.-Gen., Artillery, Northern Army Group, 1956–59; Dir, Royal Artillery, War Office, 1959–61; GOC-in-C, Western Command, 1961–64; retired, 1964. Lieut-Gen., 1961. Col Comdt: RA 1962–70; RHA 1968–70. Vice-Pres., Army Cadet Force Assoc., 1974–, Chm., 1964–74; Vice-Pres., Nat. Artillery Assoc., 1965–. DL E Riding of Yorks and Kingston upon Hull, 1964, Vice-Lieut, 1968–74; DL N Yorkshire, 1974–. *Recreations:* country pursuits. *Address:* Langton House, Malton, North Yorks. *Club:* Army and Navy.

HOWARTH, Alan Thomas, CBE 1982; MP (C) Stratford-on-Avon, since 1983; *b* 11 June 1944; *e s* of T. E. B. Howarth, *qv*; *m* 1967, Gillian Martha, *d* of Mr and Mrs Arthur Chance, Dublin; two *s* two *d*. *Educ:* Rugby Sch. (scholar); King's Coll., Cambridge (major scholar in History; BA 1965). Sen. Res. Asst to Field-Marshal Montgomery on A History of Warfare, 1965–67; Asst Master, Westminster Sch., 1968–74; Private Sec. to Chm. of Conservative Party, 1975–79; Dir, Cons. Res. Dept, 1979–81; Vice-Chm., Conservative Party, 1980–81. PPS to Dr Rhodes Boyson, MP, Minister of State for NI, 1985–. Sec., Cons. Arts and Heritage Cttee, 1984–85. Public Affairs Adviser, Baring Brothers & Co. Ltd, 1982–. Governor, Royal Shakespeare Theatre, 1984–. *Publications:* (jtly) Changing Charity, 1984; (jtly) Monty at Close Quarters, 1985. *Recreations:* books, travel, the arts, running. *Address:* House of Commons, SW1. *Club:* Beefsteak.

HOWARTH, David Armine, FRSL 1982; author; *b* 18 July 1912; *s* of Dr O. J. R. Howarth and Mrs E. K. Howarth. *Educ:* Tonbridge Sch.; Trinity Coll., Cambridge. BBC Talks Asst etc, 1934–39. War Correspondent, 1939–40; RNVR, 1940–45. Knight 1st class, Order of St Olav (Norway), 1955; Cross of Freedom (Norway) 1945. *Publications:* The Shetland Bus, 1951; We Die Alone (also under title Escape Alone), 1955; The Sledge Patrol, 1957; Dawn of D-Day, 1959; The Shadow of the Dam, 1961; The Desert King, A Biography of Ibn Saud, 1964; The Golden Isthmus, 1966; A Near Run Thing: the Day of Waterloo, 1968; Trafalgar: The Nelson Touch, 1969; Sovereign of the Seas, 1974; The Greek Adventure, 1976; 1066, The Year of the Conquest, 1977; The Voyage of the Armada: the Spanish story, 1981; Tahiti, 1983; Pursued by a Bear (autobiog.), 1986; (with S. Howarth) The Story of P&O; *fiction:* Group Flashing Two, 1952; One Night in Styria, 1953; *for children:* Heroes of Nowadays, 1957; Great Escapes, 1969. As Editor: My Land and My People (by HH The Dalai Lama), 1962. *Address:* Wildlings Wood, Blackboys, Sussex. *T:* Hadlow Down 233.

HOWARTH, Elgar; freelance musician; *b* 4 Nov. 1935; *s* of Oliver and Emma Howarth; *m* 1958, Mary Bridget Neary; one *s* two *d*. *Educ:* Manchester Univ. (MusB); Royal Manchester Coll. of Music (ARMCM 1956; FRMCM 1970). Royal Opera House, Covent Garden (Orchestra), 1958–63; Royal Philharmonic Orchestra, 1963–69; Mem., London Sinfonietta, 1968–71; Mem., Philip Jones Brass Ensemble, 1965–76; freelance conductor, 1970–; Musical Advisor, Grimethorpe Colliery Brass Band, 1972–. *Publications:* various compositions mostly for brass instruments. *Address:* 27 Cromwell Avenue, N6.

HOWARTH, (James) Gerald (Douglas); MP (C) Cannock and Burntwood, since 1983; *b* 12 Sept. 1947; *s* of late James Howarth and of Mary Howarth, Hurley, Berks; *m* 1973, Elizabeth Jane, *d* of Michael and Muriel Squibb, Crowborough, Sussex; two *s* one *d*. *Educ:* Haileybury and ISC Jun. Sch.; Bloxham Sch.; Southampton Univ. (BA Hons). Commnd RAFVR, 1968. Gen. Sec., Soc. for Individual Freedom, 1969–71; entered internat. banking, 1971; Bank of America Internat., 1971–77; European Arab Bank, 1977–81 (Manager, 1979–81); Syndication Manager, Standard Chartered Bank, 1981–83. Dir, Richard Unwin Internat., 1983–. Dir, Freedom Under Law, 1973–77; estabd Dicey Trust, 1976. Mem., Hounslow BC, 1982–83. Jt Sec., Cons. Parly Aviation Cttee, 1983–. *Recreations:* flying (private pilot's licence, 1965), squash, walking up hills, normal family pursuits. *Address:* House of Commons, SW1. *T:* 01–219 3580.

HOWARTH, Prof. Leslie, OBE 1955; FRS 1950; FRAeS; BSc, MA, PhD; Henry Overton Wills Professor of Mathematics, University of Bristol, 1964–76, now Emeritus; *b* 23 May 1911; *s* of late Fred and Elizabeth Ellen Howarth; *m* 1934, Eva Priestley; two *s*. *Educ:* Accrington Grammar Sch.; Manchester Univ.; Gonville and Caius Coll., Cambridge. Mathematical tripos, 1933; Smith's Prize, 1935; PhD, 1936. Berry-Ramsey Research Fellow, King's Coll., Cambridge, 1936–45; Lecturer in Mathematics in the University of Cambridge, 1936–49; Fellow of St John's Coll., Cambridge, 1945–49; Prof. of Applied Mathematics, University of Bristol, 1949–64; Adams Prize, 1951. Worked at External Ballistics Dept, Ordnance Board, 1939–42, and at Armament Research Dept, 1942–45. *Publications:* (ed) Modern Developments in Fluid Dynamics: High Speed Flow; papers on aerodynamics. *Address:* 10 The Crescent, Henleaze, Bristol BS9 4RW. *T:* Bristol 629621.

HOWARTH, Robert Lever; Senior Lecturer in General Studies, Wigan College of Technology, since 1977; Leader, Labour Group, Bolton Metropolitan Borough, since 1975; Leader, Bolton Metropolitan Borough Council, since 1980; Deputy Chairman, Manchester Airport plc; *b* 31 July 1927; *s* of James Howarth and Bessie (*née* Pearson); *m* 1952, Josephine Mary Doyle; one *s* one *d*. *Educ:* Bolton County Grammar Sch.; Bolton Technical Coll. Draughtsman with Hawker Siddeley Dynamics. MP (Lab) Bolton East, 1964–70. Lectr in Liberal Studies, Leigh Technical Coll., 1970–76. *Recreations:* gardening, reading, walking, films. *Address:* 93 Markland Hill, Bolton, Lancs BL1 5EQ. *T:* Bolton 44121.

HOWARTH, Thomas Edward Brodie, MC 1945; TD; *b* 21 Oct. 1914; *e s* of Frank Fielding Howarth; *m* 1943, Margaret Teakle; two *s* one *d* (and one *s* decd). *Educ:* Rugby Sch.; Clare Coll., Cambridge (Scholar, MA, 1st cl. Hons Parts I and II, History Tripos). Asst Master, Winchester Coll., 1938–39, 1946–48; Headmaster King Edward's Sch., Birmingham, 1948–52; Second Master, Winchester Coll., 1952–62; High Master, St Paul's School, 1962–73; Fellow and Sen. Tutor, Magdalene Coll., Cambridge, 1973–80; Headmaster, Campion Sch., Athens, 1980–82. Served War of 1939–45, King's (Liverpool) Regt; Brigade Major, HQ Mersey Garrison; Brigade Major 207 Infantry Bde; NW Europe, June 1944; Personal Liaison Officer to C-in-C 21st Army Group. Trustee, Imperial War Museum, 1964–79. Governor: St John's Sch., Leatherhead; British Sch. of Paris. Mem., Public Schs Commission, 1966. Chm., Headmasters' Conference, 1969. *Publications:* Citizen-King, 1961; Culture, Anarchy and the Public Schools, 1969; Cambridge Between Two Wars, 1978; Prospect and Reality: Great Britain 1945–55, 1985; (ed and contrib.) Monty at Close Quarters, 1985. *Recreation:* golf. *Address:* 112A Elgin Crescent, W11. *T:* 01–221 7549. *Clubs:* Savile, Garrick, Beefsteak, East India.

See also A. T. Howarth.

HOWAT, Prof. Henry Taylor, CBE 1971; MSc (Manch.); MD, FRCP, FRCPE; Professor of Gastroenterology, University of Manchester, 1972–76, now Emeritus; Physician, Manchester Royal Infirmary, 1948–76; *b* 16 May 1911; *s* of late Adam Howat, MA, and late Henrietta Howat, Pittenweem, Fife; *m* 1940, Rosaline, *o d* of late Miles Green, Auckland, NZ; two *s* one *d*. *Educ:* Cameron Public Sch. and Madras Coll., St Andrews; Univ. of St Andrews. MB, ChB (St And) 1933; MD with Hons and Univ. Gold Medal (St And), 1960; MRCP 1937, FRCP 1948; MRCPE 1961, FRCPE 1965. Resident MO, Manchester Royal Infirmary, 1938–40. Served War, MEF and BLA; RMO, Physician Specialist, Officer in charge of Med. Div., Mil. Hosps, 1940–45; temp. Lt-Col, RAMC. Univ. of Manchester: Asst Lectr in Applied Physiology, 1946–48; Lectr in Med., 1948–69 (Chm., Faculty of Med., 1968–72); Reader, 1969–72; Physician, Ancoats Hosp., Manchester, 1946–62. United Manchester Hospitals, 1948–76: Chm., Med. Exec. Cttee, 1968–73; Mem., Bd of Governors, 1966–74. President: European Pancreatic Club, 1965; British Soc. of Gastroenterology, 1968–69; Assoc. of Physicians of GB and Ireland, 1975–76; Manchester Med. Soc., 1975–76; Pancreatic Soc. of GB and Ireland, 1978–79. Hon. MD, Univ. of Louvain, Belgium, 1945. Manchester Man of the Year, 1973. Medallist, J. E. Purkyně Czechoslovak Med. Soc., 1968. *Publications:* (ed) The Exocrine Pancreas, 1979; articles on gastrointestinal physiology and disease. *Recreation:* golf. *Address:* 3 Brookdale Rise, Hilton Road, Bramhall, Cheshire SK7 3AG. *T:* 061–439 2853; 40 High Street, Pittenweem, Fife KY10 2PL. *T:* Anstruther 311325. *Clubs:* Athenæum; Royal and Ancient Golf (St Andrews).

HOWD, Mrs Isobel; Regional Nursing Officer, Yorkshire Regional Health Authority, 1973–83; *b* 24 Oct. 1928 (*née* Young); *m* 1951, Ralph Howd. SRN, RMN, BTA Cert. Matron, Naburn Hosp., York, 1960–63; Asst Regional Nursing Officer, Leeds Regional Hosp. Bd, 1963–70; Chief Nursing Officer, South Teesside Hosp. Management Cttee, 1970–73. Mem., Mental Health Act Commn, 1983–. *Address:* Yew Tree Cottage, Upper Dunsforth, York YO5 9RU. *T:* Boroughbridge 2534. *Club:* Naval and Military.

HOWE, 7th Earl *cr* 1821; **Frederick Richard Penn Curzon;** Baron Howe, 1788; Baron Curzon, 1794; Viscount Curzon, 1802; farmer; Senior Manager, Barclays Bank PLC, since 1984; *b* 29 Jan. 1951; *s* of Chambré George William Penn Curzon (*d* 1976) (*g s* of 3rd Earl) and of Enid Jane Victoria Curzon (*née* Fergusson); *S* cousin, 1984; *m* 1983, Elizabeth Helen Stuart. *Educ:* Rugby School; Christ Church, Oxford (MA Hons Lit. Hum.; Chancellor's Prize for Latin Verse, 1973). AIB. Entered Barclays Bank Ltd, 1973; Manager, 1982. Governor: King William IV Naval Foundation, 1984–; Trident Trust, 1985–; Vice-Pres., Nat. Soc. for Epilepsy, 1984–; President: S Bucks Assoc. for the Disabled, 1984–; Chilterns Br., RNLI, 1985–. *Recreation:* the harpsichord. *Heir: cousin* Charles Mark Penn Curzon, *b* 1967. *Address:* Penn House, Amersham, Bucks HP7 0PS. *T:* High Wycombe 713366. *Club:* Royal Automobile.

HOWE, Allen; Circuit Administrator, Wales and Chester Circuit, 1974–82; Chairman, Medical Appeals Tribunal for Wales, since 1982; *b* 6 June 1918; *s* of late Frank Howe and Dora Howe, Monk Bretton, Yorks; *m* 1952, Katherine, *d* of late Mr and Mrs Griff Davies, Pontypridd; two *d*. *Educ:* Holgate Grammar Sch., Barnsley. Served with E Yorks Regt and RWAFF, 1939–46, France, Africa, India and Burma (Major). HM Colonial Admin. Service, Gold Coast, 1946–55 (Sen. Dist Comr). Called to Bar, Middle Temple, 1953; Judicial Adviser, Ashanti, 1954–55; practised Wales and Chester Circuit, 1955–59; Legal Dept, Welsh Bd of Health, 1959–65; Legal Dept, Welsh Office, 1965–74. *Recreations:* golf, gardening, walking. *Address:* 2 Orchard Drive, Whitchurch, Cardiff CF4 2AE. *T:* Cardiff 626626. *Clubs:* Cardiff and County; Radyr Golf.

HOWE, Prof. Christopher Barry, PhD; Professor of Economics with reference to Asia, University of London, since 1979; *b* 3 Nov. 1937; *s* of Charles Roderick Howe and Patricia (*née* Creeden); *m* 1967, Patricia Anne Giles; one *s* one *d*. *Educ:* William Ellis Sch., London; St Catharine's Coll., Cambridge (MA). PhD London. Economic Secretariat, FBI, 1961–63; Sch. of Oriental and African Studies, London Univ., 1963–: Head, Contemp. China Inst., 1972–78. Member: Hong Kong Univ. and Polytechnic Grants Cttee, 1974–; UGC, 1979–84. Chm., Japan and SE Asia Business Gp, 1983–. *Publications:* Employment and Economic Growth in Urban China 1949–57, 1971; Industrial Relations and Rapid Industrialisation, 1972; Wage Patterns and Wage Policy in Modern China 1919–1972, 1973; China's Economy: a basic guide, 1978; (ed) Studying China, 1979; (ed) Shanghai: revolution and development, 1980; (ed) The Readjustment in the Chinese Economy, 1984. *Recreations:* music, Burmese cats. *Address:* 12 Highgate Avenue, N6 5RX. *T:* 01–340 8104.

HOWE, Derek Andrew; public affairs and political consultant; company director; *b* 31 Aug. 1934; *o s* of late Harold and Elsie Howe; *m* 1st, 1958, Barbara (*née* Estill); two *d*; 2nd, 1975, Sheila (*née* Digger); one *s*. *Educ:* City of Leeds Sch.; Cockburn High Sch., Leeds. Journalist, Yorkshire Evening News, 1951–61; Conservative Central Office, 1962–70; Parliamentary Liaison Officer, 1970–73; Special Adviser, 1973–75; Press Officer, Leader of HM Opposition, 1975–79; special adviser to: Paymaster Gen., 1979–81; Chancellor of Duchy of Lancaster, 1981; Political Secretary, 10 Downing Street, 1981–83 and Special Adviser to Leader of the House of Commons, 1982–83. Trustee, W. H. Smith Meml Inst. Freeman of the City of London. *Recreations:* gardening, reading, philately. *Address:* The Vines, Kimpton, near Andover, Hampshire. *Club:* St Stephen's Constitutional.

HOWE, Elspeth Rosamund Morton, (Lady Howe), JP; Deputy Chairman, Equal Opportunities Commission, 1975–79; Chairman of an Inner London Juvenile Court, since 1970; *b* 8 Feb. 1932; *d* of late Philip Morton Shand and Sybil Mary (*née* Sissons); *m* 1953, Rt Hon. Sir Geoffrey Howe, *qv*; one *s* two *d*. *Educ:* Bath High Sch.; Wycombe Abbey; London Sch. of Econs and Pol Science (BSc 1985). Vice-Chm., Conservative London Area Women's Adv. Cttee, 1966–67, also Pres. of the Cttee's Contact Gp, 1973–77; Mem., Conservative Women's Nat. Adv. Cttee, 1966–71. Member: Lord

Chancellor's Adv. Cttee on appointment of Magistrates for Inner London Area, 1965–75; Lord Chancellor's Adv. Cttee on Legal Aid, 1971–75; Parole Board, 1972–75. Co-opted Mem., ILEA, 1967–70; Mem., Briggs Cttee on Nursing Profession, 1970–72. Governor: Wycombe Abbey, 1968–; Froebel Educn Inst., 1968–75; Cumberlow Lodge Remand Home, 1967–70. Has served as Chm. or Member of several sch. governing bodies in Tower Hamlets; Vice-Pres., Pre-School Playgroups Assoc., 1979–83; President: Women's Gas Fedn, 1979–; Fedn of Recruitment and Employment Services (formerly Fedn of Personnel Services), 1980–; Peckham Settlement, 1976–; Member Council: NACRO, 1974–; PSI, 1983– Gov., LSE, 1985 . JP Inner London Juvenile Court Panel, 1964. *Publication:* Under Five (a report on pre-school education), 1966. *Address:* c/o Barclays Bank, 4 Vere Street, W1.

See also B. M. H. Shand.

HOWE, Eric James; Data Protection Registrar, since 1984; *b* 4 Oct. 1931; *s* of Albert Henry Howe and Florence Beatrice (*née* Hale); *m* 1967, Patricia Enid (*née* Schollick); two *d. Educ:* Stretford Grammar Sch.; Univ. of Liverpool (BA Econs 1954). MIDPM 1981; FBCS 1972. NCB, 1954–59; British Cotton Industry Res. Assoc., 1959–61; English Electric Computer Co., 1961–66; National Computing Centre, 1966–84: Dep. Dir, 1975–84; Mem. Bd of Dirs, 1976–84. Chairman: National Computer Users Forum, 1977–84; Focus Cttee for Private Sector Users, DoI, 1982–84; Member: User Panel, NEDO, 1983–84; Council, British Computer Soc., 1971–74 and 1980–83; NW Regional Council, CBI, 1977–83. Rep. UK, Confedn of Eur. Computer Users Assocs, 1980–83. *Recreations:* gardening, piano, local community work. *Address:* Springfield House, Water Lane, Wilmslow, Cheshire SK9 5AX. *T:* Wilmslow 535711. *Clubs:* Reform, Wig and Pen.

HOWE, Rt. Hon. Sir Geoffrey; *see* Howe, Rt Hon. Sir R. E. G.

HOWE, Prof. Geoffrey Leslie, TD 1962 (Bars 1969 and 1974); Professor of Oral Surgery and Oral Medicine, and Dean of Dental Studies, University of Hong Kong, 1978–83; Director, The Prince Philip Dental Hospital, 1981–83; *b* 22 April 1924; *e s* of late Leo Leslie John Howe, Maidenhead, Berks; *m* 1948, Heather Patricia Joan Hambly; one *s. Educ:* Royal Dental and Middlesex Hospitals. LDS RCS 1946; LRCP, MRCS 1954; FDS RCS 1955; MDS Dunelm, 1961; FFD RCSI 1964; FICD 1981. Dental and Medical Sch. Prizeman; Begley Prize, RCS, 1951; Cartwright Prize, RCS, 1961. Dental Officer, Royal Army Dental Corps, 1946–49. House appointments, etc., Royal Dental and Middlesex Hospitals, 1949–55. Registrar in Oral Surgery, Eastman Dental Hosp. (Institute of Dental Surgery), 1955–56; Senior Registrar in Oral Surgery, Plastic and Oral Surgery Centre, Chepstow, Mon, 1956; Senior Registrar in Oral Surgery, Eastman Dental Hospital, 1956–59; Professor of Oral Surgery, University of Newcastle upon Tyne (formerly King's Coll., University of Durham), 1959–67; Prof. of Oral Surgery, Royal Dental Hosp., London Sch. of Dental Surgery, 1967–78 (Dean of School, 1974–78). Cons. Oral Surgeon, United Newcastle upon Tyne Hosps, 1959–67; Chm., Central Cttee for Hosp. Dental Services, 1971–73; Vice-Pres., BDA, 1979– (Vice-Chm., 1971–73; Chm., 1973–78); Pres., Internat. Assoc. of Oral Surgeons, 1980–83. Hon. Col Comdt, RADC, 1975–. OStJ. *Publications:* The Extraction of Teeth, 1961, 2nd edn 1970; Minor Oral Surgery, 1966, 3rd edn 1985; (with F. I. H. Whitehead) Local Anaesthesia in Dentistry, 1972, 2nd edn 1981; contribs to: Medical Treatment Yearbook, 1959; Modern Trends in Dental Surgery, 1962, and to numerous medical and dental journals. *Recreations:* sailing; Territorial Army Volunteer Reserve (lately Col, OC 217 (L) Gen. Hosp. RAMC (V), graded Cons. Dental Surgeon RADC, TAVR). *Address:* 70 Croham Manor Road, South Croydon, Surrey CR2 7BF. *Clubs:* Savage, Oral Surgery; Hong Kong; Royal Hong Kong Yacht.

HOWE, George Edward; HM Diplomatic Service, retired; Counsellor, Foreign and Commonwealth Office, 1977–82; *b* 18 June 1925; *s* of late George Cuthbert Howe and Florence May (*née* Baston); *m* 1949, Florence Elizabeth Corrish; one *s. Educ:* Highbury Grammar Sch.; Westminster Coll. Served British Army, 1943; Indian Army, 2nd Bn The Burma Rifles, 1945–48 (Major). HMOCS, Malaya, 1949; joined Foreign Service, later Diplomatic Service, 1957; served Pnomn Penh, Hong Kong, Singapore, Paris, Milan and FCO. Mem., RUSI. *Recreations:* fishing, military history. *Address:* c/o Lloyds Bank, 6 Pall Mall, SW1Y 5NH. *Club:* Travellers'.

HOWE, Prof. G(eorge) Melvyn; Professor of Geography, University of Strathclyde, 1967–85, now Emeritus; *b* Abercynon, 7 April 1920; *s* of Reuben and Edith Howe, Abercynon; *m* 1947, Patricia Graham Fennell, *d* of Edgar and Miriam Fennell, Pontypridd; three *d. Educ:* Caerphilly Grammar Sch.; UCW Aberystwyth. BSc 1940; BSc 1st cl. hons Geog. and Anthrop., 1947; MSc 1949; PhD 1957; DSc 1974. FRSE, FRGS, FRSGS, FRMetS. Served with RAF, 1940–46: Meteorological Br., 1940–42; Intell. (Air Photographic Interpretation) Br., 1942–46, in Middle East; commnd. Lectr, later Sen. Lectr, in Geography, UCW Aberystwyth, 1948; Reader in Geog., Univ. of Wales, 1964. Vis. Prof. (Health and Welfare, Canada), 1977. Mem. Council, Inst. of British Geographers (Pres., 1985); Mem. Medical Geography Cttee, RGS, 1960–; British Rep. on Medical Geog. Commn of IGU, 1970–. Gill Memorial Award, RGS, 1964. *Publications:* Wales from the Air, 1957, 2nd edn 1966; (with P. Thomas) Welsh Landforms and Scenery, 1963; National Atlas of Disease Mortality in the United Kingdom, 1963, 2nd edn 1970; The Soviet Union, 1968, 2nd edn 1983; The USSR, 1971; Man, Environment and Disease in Britain, 1972, 2nd edn 1976; (ed and contrib.) Atlas of Glasgow and the West of Scotland, 1972; (contrib.) Wales (ed E. G. Bowen), 1958; (contrib.) Modern Methods in the History of Medicine (ed E. Clarke), 1970; (ed with J. A. Loraine, and contrib.) Environmental Medicine, 1973, 2nd edn 1980; (contrib.) Environment and Man (ed J. Lenihan and W. W. Fletcher), 1976; (ed and contrib.) A World Geography of Human Diseases, 1977; (ed and contrib.) Global Geocancerology, 1986; articles in geographical, meteorological, hydrological and medical jls. *Recreation:* travel. *Address:* Hendre, 50 Heol Croes Faen, Nottage, Porthcawl CF36 3SW. *T:* Porthcawl 772377.

HOWE, Jack, RDI 1961; FRIBA 1953; FSIAD 1955; Architect and Industrial Designer; *b* 24 Feb. 1911; *s* of Charles Henry and Florence Eleanor Howe; *m* 1960, Margaret Crosbie Corrie (*d* 1979); one *s* one *d* (by former marriage); *m* 1981, Jennifer Mary Dixon (*née* Hughes D'Aeth). *Educ:* Enfield Grammar Sch.; Polytechnic Sch. of Architecture. Asst to E. Maxwell Fry, 1933–37; Chief Asst to Walter Gropius and Maxwell Fry, 1937–39; Drawing Office Manager to Holland, Hannan & Cubitts Ltd for Royal Ordnance Factories at Wrexham and Ranskill, 1939–43; Associate Partner, Arcon, 1944–48; private practice, 1949; Partnership with Andrew Bain, 1959–76. Architectural work includes: Highbury Quadrant Primary School, (LCC); Windmill House, Lambeth (LCC Housing Scheme); Television Research Lab. for AEI Ltd; Kodak Pavilion, Brussels Exhibn, 1958; Official Architects for British Trade Fair, Moscow, 1961; Industrial Designs include: Diesel Electric Locomotives and Express Pullman Trains; also Rly equipment. Industrial Design Consultant to various large firms and to BR Board. Mem. Design Index Cttee and Street Furniture Cttee, Design Council (formerly CoID), 1956–; Member: Cttee on Traffic Signs, Min. of Transport, 1962, 1963; Nat. Council for Diplomas in Art and Design. FSIAD (Pres. 1963–64); Master of Faculty, RDI, 1975–77. Duke of Edinburgh's design prize, 1969. *Publications:* articles for various architectural and design jls. *Recreations:* music, theatre. *Address:* 4 Leopold Avenue, Wimbledon, SW19. *T:* 01–946 7116.

HOWE, John Francis, OBE 1974; Private Secretary to Secretary of State for Defence, since 1986; *b* 29 Jan. 1944; *s* of Frank and Marjorie Howe; *m* 1981, Angela Ephrosini (*née* Nicolaides); one *d* one step *d. Educ:* Shrewsbury Sch.; Balliol Coll., Oxford (Scholar; MA). Pirelli General Cable Works, 1964; joined MoD as Asst Principal, 1967; Principal, 1972; Civil Adviser to GOC NI, 1972–73; Private Sec. to Perm. Under-Sec. of State, 1975–78; Asst Sec., 1979; seconded to FCO as Defence Counsellor, UK Delegn to NATO, 1981–84; Head, Arms Control Unit, MoD, 1985–86. *Recreation:* travel. *Address:* 24 Ashcombe Avenue, Southborough, Surbiton, Surrey.

HOWE, Air Vice-Marshal John Frederick George, CB 1985; CBE 1980; AFC 1961; Commandant-General, RAF Regiment and Director General of Security (RAF), 1983–85, retired; *b* 26 March 1930; *m* 1961, Annabelle Gowing; three *d. Educ:* St Andrew's Coll., Grahamstown, SA. SAAF, 1950–54 (served in Korea, 2nd Sqdn SAAF and 19 Inf. Regt, US Army, 1951); 222 Sqdn, Fighter Comd, 1956; 40 Commando RM, Suez Campaign, 1956; Fighter Command: Flt Comdr, 222 Sqdn, 1957; Flt Comdr, 43 Sqdn, 1957–59; Sqdn Comdr, 74 Sqdn, 1960–61; Air Staff, HQ Fighter Command, 1961–63; RAF Staff Coll., 1964; USAF Exchange Tour at Air Defence Comd HQ, Colorado Springs, 1965–67; 229 Operational Conversion Unit, RAF Chivenor, 1967–68; OC 228 OCU, Coningsby, 1968–69; Central Tactics and Trials Org., HQ Air Support Comd, 1969–70; MoD, 1970–72; Station Comdr, RAF Gutersloh, 1973–74; RCDS, 1975; Gp Capt. Ops, HQ No 11 Gp, 1975–77; Comdt, ROC, 1977–80; Comdr, Southern Maritime Air Region, 1980–83. American DFC 1951; Air Medal 1951. *Recreations:* country pursuits, skiing, sailing. *Address:* c/o Barclays Bank International, Oceanic House, 1 Cockspur Street, SW1. *Club:* Royal Air Force.

HOWE, Rt. Rev. John William Alexander; Assistant Bishop, diocese of Ripon, since 1985; *b* 1920. *Educ:* Westcliff High Sch.; St Chad's Coll., Durham Univ. BA 1943; MA, BD 1948. Ordained, 1943; Curate, All Saints, Scarborough, 1943–46; Chaplain, Adisadel Coll., Gold Coast, 1946–50; Vice-Principal, Edinburgh Theological Coll., 1950–55; Hon. Chaplain, St Mary's Cathedral, Edinburgh, 1951–55; Bishop of St Andrews, Dunkeld and Dunblane, 1955–69. Hon. Canon, St Mary's Cath., Glasgow, 1969; Exec. Officer of the Anglican Communion, 1969–71; Secretary General, Anglican Consultative Council, 1971–82; Research Fellow of the Research Project, ACC, 1983–85. Hon. DD: General Theological Seminary, NY, 1974; Lambeth, 1978. *Publication:* Highways and Hedges: Anglicanism and the Universal Church, 1985. *Address:* 31 Scotton Drive, Knaresborough, North Yorks HG5 9HG. *T:* Harrogate 866224.

HOWE, Josephine Mary O'C.; *see* O'Connor Howe.

HOWE, Martin, PhD; Director, Competition Policy Division, Office of Fair Trading, since 1984; *b* 9 Dec. 1936; *s* of late Leslie Wistow Howe and of Dorothy Vernon Howe (*née* Taylor Farrell); *m* 1959, Anne Cicely Lawrenson; three *s. Educ:* Leeds Univ. (BCom (Accountancy), PhD). Asst Lectr, Lectr, Sen. Lectr, in Economics, Univ. of Sheffield, 1959–73; Senior Economic Adviser: Monopolies Commn, 1973–77; Office of Fair Trading, 1977–80; Asst Secretary, OFT and DTI, 1980–84. *Publications:* Equity Issues and the London Capital Market (with A. J. Merrett and G. D. Newbould), 1967; articles on variety of topics in learned and professional jls. *Recreations:* theatre (including amateur dramatics), cricket, gardening. *Address:* 6 Mansdale Road, Redbourn, Herts AL3 7DN. *T:* Redbourn 2074; Office of Fair Trading, Field House, Breams Buildings, EC4A 1PR. *T:* 01–242 2858.

HOWE, Rt. Hon. Sir (Richard Edward) Geoffrey, PC 1972; Kt 1970; QC 1965; MP (C) Surrey East, since 1974 (Reigate, 1970–74); Secretary of State for Foreign and Commonwealth Affairs, since 1983; *b* 20 Dec. 1926; *er s* of late B. E. Howe and Mrs E. F. Howe, JP (*née* Thomson), Port Talbot, Glamorgan; *m* 1953, Elspeth Rosamund Morton Shand (*see* Lady Howe); one *s* two *d. Educ:* Winchester Coll. (Exhibitioner); Trinity Hall, Cambridge (Scholar, MA, LLB); Pres., Trinity Hall Assoc., 1977–78. Lieut Royal Signals 1945–48. Chm. Cambridge Univ. Conservative Assoc., 1951; Chm. Bow Group, 1955; Managing Dir, Crossbow, 1957–60, Editor 1960–62. Called to the Bar, Middle Temple, 1952; Bencher, 1969; Mem. General Council of the Bar, 1957–61; Mem. Council of Justice, 1963–70. Dep. Chm., Glamorgan QS, 1966–70. Contested (C) Aberavon, 1955, 1959; MP (C) Bebington, 1964–66. Sec. Conservative Parliamentary Health and Social Security Cttee, 1964–65; an Opposition Front Bench spokesman on labour and social services, 1965–66; Solicitor-General, 1970–72; Minister for Trade and Consumer Affairs, DTI, 1972–74; opposition front bench spokesman on social services, 1974–75, on Treasury and economic affairs, 1975–79; Chancellor of the Exchequer, 1979–83; Chm., Interim Cttee, IMF, 1982–83. Director: Sun Alliance & London Insce Co. Ltd, 1974–79; AGB Research Ltd, 1974–79; EMI Ltd, 1976–79. Member: (Latey) Interdeptl Cttee on Age of Majority, 1965–67; (Street) Cttee on Racial Discrimination, 1967; (Cripps) Cons. Cttee on Discrimination against Women, 1968–69; Chm. Ely Hospital, Cardiff, Inquiry, 1969. President: Cons. Political Centre Nat. Adv. Cttee, 1977–79; Nat. Union of Cons. and Unionist Assocs, 1983–84. Mem. Council of Management, Private Patients' Plan, 1969–70; an Hon. Vice-Pres., Consumers Assoc., 1974–. *Publications:* various political pamphlets for Bow Group and Conservative Political Centre. *Address:* c/o Barclays Bank, Cavendish Square Branch, 4 Vere Street, W1.

HOWELL, Rt. Hon. David Arthur Russell; PC 1979; MP (C) Guildford since 1966; Director, Savory Milln Ltd; journalist and economic consultant; *b* 18 Jan. 1936; *s* of late Colonel A. H. E. Howell, DSO, TD, DL and of Beryl Howell, 5 Headfort Place, SW1; *m* 1967, Davina Wallace; one *s* two *d. Educ:* Eton; King's Coll., Cambridge. BA 1st class hons Cantab, 1959. Lieut Coldstream Guards, 1954–56. Joined Economic Section of Treasury, 1959; resigned, 1960. Leader-Writer and Special Correspondent, The Daily Telegraph, 1960; Chm. of Bow Gp, 1961–62; Editor of Crossbow, 1962–64; contested (C) Dudley, 1964; a Lord Comr of Treasury, 1970–71; Parly Sec., CSD, 1970–72; Parly Under-Sec.: Dept of Employment, 1971–72; NI Office, March-Nov. 1972; Minister of State: NI Office, 1972–74; Dept of Energy, 1974; Secretary of State: for Energy, 1979–81; for Transport, 1981–83. Sen. Vis. Fellow, PSI, 1983–85. Dir of Conservative Political Centre, 1964–66. Trustee, Federal Trust for Educn and Research. Jt Hon. Sec., UK Council of European Movement, 1968–70. *Publications:* (co-author) Principles in Practice, 1960; The Conservative Opportunity, 1965; Freedom and Capital, 1981; Blind Victory: a study in income, wealth and power, 1986; various pamphlets and articles. *Recreations:* writing, golf. *Address:* House of Commons, SW1. *Clubs:* Carlton, Buck's.

HOWELL, Rt. Hon. Denis Herbert, PC 1976; MP (Lab) Birmingham, Small Heath since March 1961; *b* 4 Sept. 1923; *s* of Herbert and Bertha A. Howell; *m* 1955, Brenda Marjorie, *d* of Stephen and Ruth Willson, Birmingham; two *s* one *d* (and one *s* decd). *Educ:* Gower Street Sch.; Handsworth Grammar Sch., Birmingham. Mem., Birmingham City Council, 1946–56; Hon. Sec. Birmingham City Council Labour Group, 1950–55 (served Catering Establishment, General Purposes, Health and Watch Cttees); Chm. Catering Cttee, 1952–55; Health (Gen. Purposes) Sub-Cttee for setting up of first smokeless zones. MP (Lab) All Saints Div., Birmingham, 1955–Sept. 1959; Jt Parly

Under-Sec. of State, Dept of Educn and Science (with responsibility for sport), 1964–69; Minister of State, Min. of Housing and Local Govt (with responsibility for sport), 1969–70; Opposition Spokesman for Local Govt and Sport, 1970–74; Minister of State, DoE (responsible for environment, water resources and sport), 1974–79; Opposition Spokesman on Environment (Environment and Services, Water Resources, Sport, Recreation and Countryside), 1979–83, on Home Affairs, 1983–84; Opposition front bench spokesman on the Environment (specializing in Sport), 1984–. Mem., Labour Party NEC, 1982–83. Member: Dudley Road Hosp. Group Management Cttee, 1948–64; the Albemarle Cttee on the Youth Service; Management Cttee, City of Birmingham Symphony Orchestra, 1950–55; President: Canoldir Choir, 1979–; Canoldir Male Voice Choir. Governor, Handsworth Grammar Sch. Chairman: Birmingham Assoc. of Youth Clubs, 1963–64; Birmingham Settlement, 1963–64; Sports Council, 1965–70; Youth Service Develt Council, 1964–69 (report: Youth and Community Work in the 70's); Central Council of Physical Recreation, 1973–74 (Vice Pres., 1985); Cttee of Enquiry into Sponsorship of Sport, 1981–83 (report: The Howell Report on Sports Sponsorship); St Peter's Urban Village Trust, 1985–; Pres., Birmingham Olympic Council, 1985–86; Vice-Pres., Warwicks CCC, 1986. Pres., Assoc. of Professional, Exec. Clerical and Computer Staffs (APEX) (formerly CAWU), 1971–83. MIPR 1961. Football League Referee, 1956–70. Silver Medal, Olympic Order, 1981. *Publication:* Soccer Refereeing, 1968. *Recreations:* sport, theatre, music. *Address:* 33 Moor Green Lane, Moseley, Birmingham B13 8NE. *Clubs:* Reform; Warwickshire County Cricket (Birmingham); Birmingham Press.

HOWELL, Air Vice-Marshal Evelyn Michael Thomas, CBE 1961; CEng, FRAeS; *b* 11 Sept. 1913; *s* of Sir Evelyn Berkeley Howell, KCIE, CSI; *m* 1st, 1937, Helen Joan, *o d* of late Brig. W. M. Hayes, CBE, FRICS (marr. diss. 1972); one *s* three *d*; 2nd, 1972, Rosemary, *e d* of I. A. Cram, CEng, MICE; one *s* one *d*. *Educ:* Downside Sch.; RAF Coll., Cranwell. Commissioned, 1934; Dir of Air Armament Research and Devt, Min. of Aviation, 1960–62; Comdt, RAF Techn. Coll., 1963–65; SASO, HQ Technical Training Command RAF, 1966–67; retired, 1967. Gen. Manager, Van Dusen Aircraft Supplies, Oxford, Minneapolis, St Louis, Helsingborg, 1967–79. Mem. Livery of Clothworkers' Co., 1938. *Recreations:* swimming, rifle shooting, tennis, boating. *Address:* Bank Farm, Lorton, Cockermouth, Cumbria CA13 0RQ. *Club:* Royal Air Force.

HOWELL, Gareth, PhD; CChem; Controller, Science, Technology and Education Division, British Council, since 1983; *b* 22 April 1935; *s* of Amwel John and Sarah Blodwen Howell; *m* 1957, Margaret Patricia Ashelford; one *s* two *d*. *Educ:* Ferndale Grammar Sch., Rhondda; University College London; Inst. of Education, Univ. of London. BSc, PhD; PGCE London. MRSC. Asst Master, Canford Sch., Wimborne, Dorset, 1957–61; Lectr, Norwich City Coll., 1961–65; British Council: Science Educn Officer, London, 1965–66; Science Educn Officer, Nigeria, 1966–70; Head, Science Educn Section, 1970–74; Director, Science and Technology Dept, 1974; Representative, Malawi, 1974–76; on secondment to Min. of Overseas Development as Educn Adviser, 1976–79; Counsellor and Dep. Educn Adviser, British Council Div., British High Commn, India, 1979–83. *Recreations:* photography, philately, gardening, tennis, running, travel. *Address:* 13 South Court, Kersfield Road, Putney, SW15 3HQ. *T:* 01–788 7811.

HOWELL, Gwynne Richard; Principal Bass, Royal Opera House, since 1971; *b* Gorseinon, S Wales, 13 June 1938; *s* of Gilbert and Ellaline Howell; *m* 1968, Mary Edwina Morris; two *s*. *Educ:* Pontardawe Grammar Sch.; Univ. of Wales, Swansea (BSc; Hon. Fellow 1986); Manchester Univ. (DipTP); MRTPI 1966. Studied singing with Redvers Llewellyn while at UCW; pt-time student, Manchester RCM, with Gwilym Jones, during DipTP trng at Manchester Univ.; studied with Otakar Kraus, 1968–72. Planning Asst, Kent CC, 1961–63; Sen. Planning Officer, Manchester Corp., 1965–68, meanwhile continuing to study music pt-time and giving public operatic performances which incl. the rôle of Pogner, in Die Meistersinger; as a result of this rôle, apptd Principal Bass at Sadler's Wells, 1968; also reached final of BBC Opera Singers competition for N of Eng., 1967. In first season at Sadler's Wells, sang 8 rôles, incl. Monterone and the Commendatore; appearances with Hallé Orch., 1968 and 1969; Arkel in Pelleas and Melisande, Glyndebourne and Covent Garden, 1969; Goffredo, in Il Pirato, 1969. *Royal Opera House, Covent Garden:* début as First Nazarene, Salome, 1969–70 season; the King, in Aida; Timur, in Turandot; Mephisto, in Damnation of Faust; Prince Gremin, in Eugene Onegin; High Priest, in Nabucco; Reinmar, in Tannhauser, 1973–74 (later rôle, Landgraf); Colline, in La Boheme; Pimen, in Boris Godunov; Ribbing, Un ballo in maschera; Padre Guardiano, in La forza del destino; Hobson, in Peter Grimes, 1975; Sparafucile, in Rigoletto, 1975–76 season; Ramfis in Aida, 1977; Tristan und Isolde, 1978, 1982; Luisa Miller, 1978; Samson et Delilah, 1981; Fiesco in Simon Boccanegra, 1981; Pogner in Die Meistersinger, 1982; Arkell in Pelléas et Mélisande, 1982; Dossifei in Khovanshchina, 1982; Semele, 1982; Die Zauberflöte, 1983; Raimondo, in Lucia di Lammermoor, 1985; Rocco in Fidelio, 1986; *English National Opera:* Don Carlos, Die Meistersinger, 1974–75; The Magic Flute, Don Carlos, 1975–76; Duke Bluebeard's Castle, 1978; The Barber of Seville, 1980; Tristan and Isolde, 1981; Hans Sachs in Die Meistersinger, 1984; Parsifal, 1986; *Metropolitan Opera House, New York:* début as Lódovico in Otello, and Pogner in Die Meistersinger, 1985; *sacred music:* Verdi and Mozart Requiems, Missa Solemnis, St Matthew and St John Passions; sings in Europe and USA; records for BBC and for major recording companies. *Recreations:* tennis, squash, Rugby enthusiast, gardening. *Address:* 197 Fox Lane, N13 4BB. *T:* 01–886 1981.

HOWELL, Prof. John Bernard Lloyd; Foundation Professor of Medicine, University of Southampton, since 1969 (Dean of the Faculty of Medicine, 1978–83); Hon. Consultant Physician, Southampton General Hospital, since 1969; *s* of late David John Howells and Hilda Mary Hill, Ynystawe, Swansea; *m* 1952, Heather Joan Rolfe; two *s* one *d*. *Educ:* Swansea Grammar Sch.; Middx Hosp. Med. Sch. (Meyerstein Scholar 1946). BSc, MB, BS, PhD; FRCP. House Officer posts, Middx and Brompton Hosps; MO RAMC, 1952–54; Lectr in Physiol Medicine, 1954–56, in Pharmacol Medicine, 1958–60, Middlesex Hosp. Med. Sch.; Manchester Royal Infirmary: Sen. Lectr in Medicine and Hon. Consultant Physician, 1960–66; Consultant Physician, 1966–69. Eli Lilly Travelling Fellow, Johns Hopkins Hospital, 1957–58; Goulstonian Lectr, RCP, 1966. Member: Physiol Soc., 1956–; Med. Res. Soc., 1956; Thoracic Soc., 1959; Assoc. of Physicians of GB and Ire., 1964–; GMC, 1978–83. Chm., Southampton and SW Hampshire DHA, 1983–. Hon. Life Mem., Canadian Thoracic Soc., 1978; Hon. FACP 1982. *Publications:* (ed jtly) Breathlessness, 1966; chapters in: Cecil and Loeb's Textbook of Medicine, 13th edn 1970, 14th edn 1974; Recent Advances in Chest Medicine, 1976; Thoracic Medicine, 1981; Oxford Textbook of Medicine, 1982; scientific papers on respiratory physiology and medicine. *Recreations:* DIY, wine. *Address:* The Coach House, Bassett Wood Drive, Southampton SO2 3PT. *T:* Southampton 768878.

HOWELL, Rt. Rev. Kenneth Walter, MA; *b* 4 Feb. 1909; *s* of Frederick John and Florence Sarah Howell; *m* 1st, 1937, Beryl Mary Hope (*d* 1972), *d* of late Capt. Alfred and Mrs Hope, Bedford; two *s* one *d*; 2nd, 1978, Mrs Siri Colvin. *Educ:* St Olave's; St Peter's Hall, Oxford; Wycliffe Hall, Oxford. Curate of St Mary Magdalene, Peckham, 1933–37; Chaplain of Paraguayan Chaco Mission, 1937–38; Chaplain Quepe Mission, Chile, 1938–40; Superintendent of South American Missionary Society's Mission to Araucanian Indians in S Chile, 1940–47; Vicar of Wandsworth, 1948–63, Rural Dean, 1957–63; Chaplain, Royal Hosp. and Home for Incurables, Putney, 1957–63; Hon. Canon of Southwark, 1962–63; Bishop in Chile, Bolivia and Peru, 1963–71; Minister of St John's, Downshire Hill, Hampstead, 1972–79; an Asst Bishop, Diocese of London, 1976–79. *Address:* 96 Colney Hatch Lane, Muswell Hill, N10 1EA.

HOWELL, Maj.-Gen. Lloyd, CBE 1972; Consultant, Technical Education Development, University College, Cardiff, 1980–86 (Fellow, 1982); Director (non-executive), Building Trades Exhibitions Ltd, since 1980; *b* 28 Dec. 1923; *s* of Thomas Idris Howell and Anne Howell; *m* 1st, 1945, Hazel Barker (*d* 1974); five *s* three *d*; 2nd, 1975, Elizabeth June Buchanan Husband (*née* Atkinson); two step *s*. *Educ:* Barry Grammar Sch.; University Coll. of S Wales and Monmouthshire (BSc); Royal Military Coll. of Science. CEng, MRAeS. Commissioned RA, 1944; Field Regt, RA, E Africa, 1945–46; Staff, Divl HQ, Palestine, 1946–47; RAEC 1949; Instr, RMA Sandhurst, 1949–53; TSO II Trials Estabt, 1954–57; SO II (Educn), Divl HQ, BAOR, 1957–59; DS, Royal Mil. Coll. of Science, 1960–64; SEO, Army Apprentices Coll., 1964–67; Headmaster/Comdg, Duke of York's Royal Mil. Sch., 1967–72; Col (Ed), MoD (Army), 1972–74; Chief Educn Officer, HQ UKLF, 1974–76; Dir, Army Educn, 1976–80. Col Comdt, RAEC, 1982–86. Mem. Council, CGLI, 1977–; Mem., Ct of Governors, University Coll., Cardiff, 1980–. Hon. MA Open Univ., 1980. *Recreations:* gardening, golf, reading. *Address:* c/o Midland Bank, 1 Wood Street, Swindon, Wilts. *Club:* Army and Navy.

HOWELL, Michael Edward, OBE 1980; HM Diplomatic Service; High Commissioner to Papua New Guinea, since 1986; *b* 2 May 1933; *s* of Edward and Fanny Howell; *m* 1958; Joan Little; one *s* one *d*. *Educ:* Newport High Sch. Served RAF, 1951–53. Colonial Office, 1953; CRO, 1958; Karachi, 1959; 2nd Secretary: Bombay, 1962; UK Delegn to Disarmament Cttee, Geneva, 1966; 1st Sec. (Parly Clerk), FCO, 1969; Consul (Comm.), New York, 1973; ndc 1975; FCO, 1976; Hd of Chancery and Consul, Kabul, 1978; Consul-General: Berlin, 1981; Frankfurt, 1983. *Recreation:* tennis. *Address:* c/o Foreign and Commonwealth Office, SW1A 2AH.

HOWELL, Paul Frederic; Member (C) Norfolk, European Parliament, since 1979; farmer; *b* 17 Jan. 1951; *s* of Ralph Frederic Howell, *qv*. *Educ:* Gresham's Sch., Holt, Norfolk; St Edmund Hall, Oxford (BA Agric. and Econ.). Conservative Research Dept, 1973–75. Prospective Parly candidate (C) Normanton, 1976–79. Mem., Agricl, Budget and Overseas Develt Cttees, European Parlt, 1979–; spokesman on youth, culture, educn, information and sport, Eur. Democratic Gp, 1984–; Vice-Chm., EEC/Comecon Delegn, 1984; Pres., Council of Centre for Eur. Educn, 1985–. *Recreations:* all sports. *Address:* The White House Farm, Bradenham Road, Scarning, East Dereham, Norfolk NR20 3EY. *T:* Wendling 239.

HOWELL, Paul Philip, CMG 1964; OBE 1955; *b* 13 Feb. 1917; *s* of Brig.-Gen. Philip Howell, CMG (killed in action, 1916) and Mrs Rosalind Upcher Howell (*née* Buxton); *m* 1949, Bridgit Mary Radclyffe Luard; two *s* two *d*. *Educ:* Westminster Sch.; Trinity Coll., Cambridge (Sen. Schol., MA, PhD); Christ Church, Oxford (MA, DPhil). Sudan Polit. Service, 1938; commnd in Sudan Defence Force, ADC to Gov.-Gen., 1940; Overseas Enemy Territory Administration, Eritrea, 1941; District Comr, Central Nuer, 1942; District Comr, Baggara, Western Kordofan, 1946; Chm., Jonglei Investigation, 1948; Chm. (Dep. Gov.), Southern Development Investigation, 1953; Asst Chief Sec., Uganda Protectorate, 1955; Min. of Natural Resources, 1955; Perm. Sec., Min. of Corporations and Regional Communications, 1957; Perm. Sec. Min. of Commerce and Industry, 1959; Chm., E African Nile Waters Co-ordinating Cttee, 1956–61; seconded to FO and Min. of Overseas Development; Head of Middle East Develt Div., Beirut, 1961–69. University of Cambridge: Dir of Develt Studies Courses, 1969–82; Chm., Faculty of Archaeology and Anthropology, 1977–82; Fellow of Wolfson Coll., 1969–83, Emeritus Fellow, 1983. Member: Bd of Governors, Inst. of Development Studies, 1971–85; Council, Overseas Development Inst., 1972–. *Publications:* Nuer Law, 1954; (ed) The Equatorial Nile Project and its Effects in the Anglo-Egyptian Sudan, 1954; (ed) Natural Resources and Development Potential in the Southern Sudan, 1955; contribs to jls on social anthropology and development. *Recreations:* fishing and country pursuits. *Address:* Wolfson College, Cambridge. *T:* Cambridge 64811; Burfield Hall, Wymondham, Norfolk. *T:* Wymondham 603389. *Club:* Royal Commonwealth Society.

HOWELL, Ralph Frederic; MP (C) North Norfolk since 1970; *b* 25 May 1923; *m* 1950, Margaret (*née* Bone); two *s* one *d*. *Educ:* Diss Grammar Sch., Norfolk. Navigator/Bomb-aimer, RAF, 1941–46; farmer, 1946–. Mem., European Parlt, 1974–79. Vice-Chm., Cons. Parly Finance Cttee, 1979–84; Mem., Treasury and Civil Service Select Cttee, 1981–; Chm., Cons. Parly Employment Cttee, 1984–; Sec., Cons. Parly Agriculture Cttee, 1985; Mem. Exec., 1922 Cttee, 1984–. *Publication:* Why Work, 1976, 2nd edn 1981. *Address:* Wendling Grange, Dereham, Norfolk. *T:* Wendling 247. *Clubs:* Carlton, Farmers'.
See also P. F. Howell.

HOWELLS, Anne, (Mrs Stafford Dean), FRMCM (ARMCM); opera, concert and recital singer; *b* 12 Jan. 1941; *d* of Trevor William Howells and Mona Hewart; *m* 1st, 1966, Ryland Davies, *qv* (marr. diss. 1981); 2nd, 1981, Stafford Dean; one *s* one *d*. *Educ:* Sale County Grammar Sch.; Royal Manchester Coll. of Music. Three seasons (Chorus), with Glyndebourne, 1964–66; at short notice, given star rôle there, in Cavalli's L'Ormindo, 1967; rôles, there, also include: Dorabella in Cosi fan Tutte; Cathleen in (world première of) Nicholas Maw's Rising of the Moon, 1970; also the Composer in Ariadne; Diana in Calisto; Unitel Film of Salzburg prodn of Mozart's Clemenza di Tito. Royal Opera House, Covent Garden: under contract for three years, 1969–71, where rôles included: Lena in (world première of) Richard Rodney Bennett's Victory; Rosina in Barber of Seville; Cherubino in Marriage of Figaro. Currently, 1973–, Guest artist with Royal Opera House. Recitals in Brussels and Vienna; operatic guest performances in Chicago, Metropolitan (NY), San Francisco, Geneva, Brussels, Salzburg, Amsterdam, Hamburg (W German début), W Berlin, Paris; sings with Scottish Opera, English Nat. Opera, major orchestras in UK. *Recreations:* cinema, tennis, reading. *Address:* c/o Harrison Parrott, 12 Penzance Place, W11 4PA.

HOWELLS, Derek William; His Honour Judge Howells; a Circuit Judge, since 1980; *b* 8 Oct. 1928; *s* of William Howells and Dinnie Maud (*née* Weeks); *m* 1965, Anne Griffiths. *Educ:* Cardiff High Sch.; Univ. of London. Called to the Bar, Lincoln's Inn, 1955. *Recreations:* golf, gardening. *Address:* 63 Owl's Lodge Lane, Mayals, Swansea SA3 5DP. *T:* Swansea 403845. *Club:* Bristol Channel Yacht.

HOWELLS, Geraint Wyn; MP (L) Ceredigion and Pembroke North, since 1983 (Cardigan, Feb. 1974–1983); *b* 15 April 1925; *s* of David John Howells and Mary Blodwen Howells; *m* 1957, Mary Olwen Hughes Griffiths; two *d*. *Educ:* Ponterwyd Primary Sch.; Ardwyn Grammar School. Farmer; Mem., British Wool Marketing Bd (Vice-Chm., 1971–83); Chm., Wool Producers of Wales Ltd. Sec., Ponterwyd Eisteddfod, 1944–. *Recreations:* walking, sport. *Address:* Glennydd, Ponterwyd, Ceredigion, Dyfed. *T:* Ponterwyd 258.

HOWELLS, Dr Gwyn, CB 1979; MD; FRCP, FRACP; Director-General and Permanent Head, Federal Department of Health, Canberra, Australia, 1973–83; Chairman, Cochlear Pty Ltd, Sydney, since 1984; Director, Nucleus Ltd, Sydney, since 1984; *b* 13 May 1918; *s* of Albert Henry and Ruth Winifred Howells; *m* 1942, Simone Maufe; two *s* two *d*. *Educ:* University College Sch., London; St Bartholomew's Hosp., Univ. of London (MB BS 1942, MD 1950). MRCS 1941; FRCP 1974 (MRCP 1950, LRCP 1941); FRACP 1971 (MRACP 1967). Cons. Phys., Thoracic Annexe, Toowoomba, Qld, Aust.; Chest Phys., Toowoomba Gen. Hosp., Qld, 1957–66; Federal Dept of Health, Canberra: First Asst Director General, 1966–73, Dep. Dir-Gen., Feb.-Sept. 1973. Chairman, Nat. Health and Med. Res. Council, 1973–83; Director of Quarantine for Australia, 1973–83. *Publications:* several articles in Lancet, BMJ, Aust. Med. Jl and other specialist jls. *Recreations:* squash, tennis, reading. *Address:* 23 Beauchamp Street, Deakin, ACT 2600, Australia. *T:* Canberra 812575. *Clubs:* Commonwealth, National Press, National Tennis and Squash Centre (Canberra).

HOWERD, Frankie; *see* Howard, F. A.

HOWES, Christopher Kingston; Director, Land and Property Division, Department of the Environment, since 1985; *b* 30 Jan. 1942; *yr s* of Leonard Howes, OBE and Marion Howes (*née* Bussey); *m* 1967, Clare Cunliffe; two *s* one *d* (and one *d* decd). *Educ:* Gresham's Sch.; LSE; Coll. of Estate Management (BSc 1965); Univ. of Reading (MPhil 1976). ARICS 1967, FRICS 1977. Valuation and Planning Depts, GLC, 1965–67; Partner and Sen. Partner, Chartered Surveyors, Norwich, 1967–79; Dep. Dir, Land Economy, DoE, 1979–81, Chief Estates Officer, 1981. Sen. Vis. Fellow, Sch. of Envtl Scis, UEA, 1975; Vis. Lectr, Univs of Reading, 1976, Aberdeen 1980–; Vis. Prof., Bartlett Sch. of Architecture and Planning, UCL, 1984–. Member: CNAA Surveying Bd, 1978–82; Planning and Develt Divl Council, RICS, 1983–; Policy Review Cttee, RICS, 1984–; Norfolk Archaeological Trust, 1979–. Founder Mem., Norwich Third World Centre, 1970; dir of various housing assocs; Dir, Theatre Royal Trust, 1969–79; Steward and Hon Surveyor to Dean and Chapter, Norwich Cathedral, 1973–79; Mem., Court of Advisers, St Paul's Cathedral, 1980–. Norwich CC, 1969–73; JP Norfolk 1973–80. *Publications:* Acquiring Office Space (jtly), 1975; Value Maps: aspects of land and property values, 1979; papers on land and property policy in learned jls. *Recreations:* music, esp. opera; art, esp. English water colours; sport, esp. sailing. *Address:* Highfield House, Woldingham, Surrey CR3 7BE; Roudham Lodge, Roudham, Norfolk. *Clubs:* Athenæum; Norfolk (Norwich).

HOWES, Sally Ann; actress (stage, film and television); *b* 20 July; *d* of late Bobby Howes; *m* 1958, Richard Adler (marr. diss.); *m* 1969, Andrew Maree (marr. diss.). *Educ:* Glendower, London; Queenswood, Herts; privately. *Films include:* Thursday's Child; Halfway House; Dead of Night; Nicholas Nickleby; Anna Karenina; My Sister and I; Fools Rush In; History of Mr Polly; Stop Press Girl; Honeymoon Deferred; The Admirable Crichton; Chitty, Chitty Bang Bang. First appeared West End stage in (revue) Fancy Free, at Prince of Wales's, and at Royal Variety Performance, 1950. *Stage Shows include:* Caprice (musical debut); Paint Your Wagon; Babes in the Wood; Romance by Candlelight; Summer Song; Hatful of Rain; My Fair Lady; Kwamina, NY; What Makes Sammy Run?, NY; Brigadoon (revival), NY City Center, 1962; Sound of Music, Los Angeles and San Francisco, 1972; Lover, St Martin's; The King and I, Adelphi, 1973, Los Angeles and San Francisco, 1974; Hans Andersen, Palladium, 1977; Hamlet (tour), 1983. Has appeared on television: in England from 1949 (Short and Sweet Series, Sally Ann Howes Show, etc); in USA from 1958 (Dean Martin Show, Ed Sullivan Show, Mission Impossible, Marcus Welby MD); Play of the Week; Panel Shows: Hollywood Squares; Password; Bell Telephone Hour; US Steel Hour, etc. *Recreations:* reading, riding, theatre. *Address:* c/o Kramer and Reiss, 9100 Sunset Boulevard, Los Angeles, Calif 90069, USA.

HOWICK OF GLENDALE, 2nd Baron *cr* 1960; **Charles Evelyn Baring;** a Managing Director, Baring Brothers & Co. Ltd, 1969–82; *b* 30 Dec. 1937; *s* of 1st Baron Howick of Glendale, KG, GCMG, KCVO, and of Lady Mary Cecil Grey, *er d* of 5th Earl Grey; *S* father, 1973; *m* 1964, Clare Nicolette, *y d* of Col Cyril Darby; one *s* three *d*. *Educ:* Eton; New Coll., Oxford. Director: The London Life Association Ltd, 1972–82; Swan Hunter Group Ltd, 1972–79. Member: Exec. Cttee, Nat. Art Collections Fund, 1973–; Council, Friends of Tate Gall., 1973–78. *Heir: s* Hon. David Evelyn Charles Baring, *b* 26 March 1975. *Address:* Howick, Alnwick, Northumberland. *T:* Longhoughton 624; 42 Bedford Gardens, W8. *T:* 01-221 0880.

See also Sir E. H. T. Wakefield.

HOWIE, family name of **Baron Howie of Troon.**

HOWIE OF TROON, Baron *cr* 1978 (Life Peer), of Troon in the District of Kyle and Carrick; **William Howie;** civil engineer, publisher, journalist; General Manager, Thomas Telford Ltd, since 1976; Professional Conduct Liaison Officer, Institution of Civil Engineers, since 1980; *b* Troon, Ayrshire, 2 March 1924; *er s* of late Peter and Annie Howie, Troon; *m* 1951, Mairi Margaret, *o d* of Martha and late John Sanderson, Troon; two *s* two *d*. *Educ:* Marr Coll., Troon; Royal Technical Coll., Glasgow (BSc, Diploma). MP (Lab) Luton, Nov. 1963–70; Asst Whip, 1964–66; Lord Comr of the Treasury, 1966–67; Comptroller, HM Household, 1967–68. A Vice-Chm., Parly Labour Party, 1968–70. MICE 1951, FICE 1984; Member: Council, Instn of Civil Engineers, 1964–67; Cttee of Inquiry into the Engineering Profession, 1977–80; President: Assoc. of Supervisory and Exec. Engrs, 1980–85; Assoc. for Educnl and Trng Technol., 1982–. Member: Governing Body, Imperial Coll. of Science and Technology, 1965–67; Pro-Chancellor, City Univ., 1984–(Mem. Council 1968–). MSocIS (France), 1978; FRSA 1981. *Publications:* (jtly) Public Sector Purchasing, 1968; Trade Unions and the Professional Engineer, 1977; Trade Unions in Construction, 1981. *Recreation:* opera. *Address:* 34 Temple Fortune Lane, NW11 7UL. *T:* 01–455 0492. *Clubs:* Seretse, Luton Labour, Lighthouse, Architecture.

HOWIE, Archibald, PhD; FRS 1978; Professor of Physics, since 1986, and Head of Microstructural (formerly Metal) Physics Research Group, since 1967, Cavendish Laboratory, University of Cambridge; Fellow of Churchill College, Cambridge, since 1960; *b* 8 March 1934; *s* of Robert Howie and Margaret Marshall McDonald; *m* 1964, Melva Jean Scott; one *s* one *d*. *Educ:* Kirkcaldy High Sch.; Univ. of Edinburgh (BSc); California Inst. of Technology (MS); Univ. of Cambridge (PhD). English Speaking Union, King George VI Memorial Fellow (at Calif. Inst. of Technology), 1956–57; Cambridge University: Research Scholar, Trinity Coll., 1957–60; Research Fellow, Churchill Coll., 1960–61; Cavendish Laboratory: ICI Research Fellow, 1960–61; Demonstrator in Physics, 1961–65; Lecturer, 1965–79; Reader, 1979–86. Visiting Scientist, Nat. Research Council, Canada, 1966–67; Vis. Prof. of Physics, Univ. of Aarhus, Denmark, 1974. C. V. Boys Prize, Inst. of Physics (jtly with M. J. Whelan), 1965. Hon. Fellow Royal Microscopical Soc., 1978 (Pres. 1984–86). *Publications:* (co-author) Electron Microscopy of Thin Crystals, 1965, 2nd edn 1977; papers on electron microscopy and diffraction in scientific jls. *Recreations:* gardening, wine-making. *Address:* 194 Huntingdon Road, Cambridge CB3 0LB. *T:* Cambridge 276131.

HOWIE, Sir James (William), Kt 1969; MD (Aberdeen); FRCP, FRCPGlas; FRCPEd; FRCPath; Director of the Public Health Laboratory Service, 1963–73; *b* 31 Dec. 1907; *s* of late James Milne Howie and Jessie Mowat Robertson; *m* 1935, Isabella Winifred Mitchell, BSc; two *s* one *d*. *Educ:* Robert Gordon's Coll., Aberdeen; University of Aberdeen. University lectureships in Aberdeen and Glasgow, 1932–40; Pathologist, RAMC, 1941–45 (served Nigeria and War Office); Head of Dept of Pathology and Bacteriology, Rowett Research Institute, Aberdeen, 1946–51; Prof. of Bacteriology, University of Glasgow, 1951–63. Mem. Agricultural Research Council, 1957–63. Convener, Medical Research Council Working Party on Sterilisers, 1957–64; Pres., Royal College of Pathologists, 1966–69 (Vice-Pres., 1962–66); President: BMA, 1969–70; Assoc. of Clinical Pathologists, 1972–73; Inst. of Sterile Services Management, 1983–. QHP, 1965–68. Hon. ARCVS 1977; Honorary Member: Pathological Soc. of GB and Ireland, 1977; ACP, 1977. Hon. FRCPath, 1983; Hon. LLD Aberdeen, 1969. Gold Medal, BMA, 1984. *Publications:* various publications in medical and scientific periodicals, particularly on bacteriology and nutrition. *Recreations:* golf, music. *Address:* 34 Redford Avenue, Edinburgh EH13 0BU. *T:* 031–441 3910.

See also J. G. R. Howie.

HOWIE, Prof. John Garvie Robertson, FRCGP; Professor of General Practice, University of Edinburgh, since 1980; *b* 23 Jan. 1937; *s* of Sir James Howie, *qv*; *m* 1962, Elizabeth Margaret Donald; two *s* one *d*. *Educ:* High School of Glasgow; Univ. of Glasgow (MD); PhD Aberdeen; MRCPE. House officer, 1961–62; Laboratory medicine, 1962–66; General practitioner, Glasgow, 1966–70; Lectr/Sen. Lectr in General Practice, Univ. of Aberdeen, 1970–80. *Publications:* Research in General Practice, 1979; articles on appendicitis, prescribing and general medical practice and education, in various jls. *Recreations:* golf, gardening, music. *Address:* 4 Ravelrig Park, Balerno, Midlothian EH14 7DL. *T:* 031–449 6305.

HOWIE, Prof. John Mackintosh; Regius Professor of Mathematics, University of St Andrews, since 1970; Dean, Faculty of Science, 1976–79; *b* 23 May 1936; *s* of Rev. David Y. Howie and Janet McD. Howie (*née* Mackintosh); *m* 1960, Dorothy Joyce Mitchell Miller; two *d*. *Educ:* Robert Gordon's Coll., Aberdeen; Univ. of Aberdeen; Balliol Coll., Oxford. MA, DPhil, DSc; FRSE 1971. Asst in Mathematics: Aberdeen Univ., 1958–59; Glasgow Univ., 1961–63; Lectr in Mathematics, Glasgow Univ., 1963–67; Visiting Asst Prof., Tulane Univ., 1964–65; Sen. Lectr in Mathematics, Stirling Univ., 1967–70; Vis. Prof., Monash Univ., 1979. Mem., Cttee to Review Examination Arrangements (Dunning Cttee), 1975–77; Chm., Scottish Central Cttee on Mathematics, 1975–82. Vice-Pres., London Mathematical Soc., 1984–86. Chm., Bd of Governors, Dundee Coll. of Educn, 1983–. Keith Prize for 1979–81, RSE, 1982. *Publications:* An Introduction to Semigroup Theory, 1976; articles in British and foreign mathematical jls. *Recreations:* music, gardening. *Address:* Mathematical Institute, North Haugh, St Andrews, Fife KY16 9SS. *T:* St Andrews 76161.

HOWIE, Prof. Robert Andrew, PhD, ScD; FGS; FKC; Lyell Professor of Geology, Royal Holloway and Bedford New College, University of London, since 1985; *b* 4 June 1923; *s* of Robert Howie; *m* 1952, Honor Eugenie, *d* of Robert Taylor; two *s*. *Educ:* Bedford Sch.; Trinity Coll., Cambridge (MA, PhD, ScD). FGS 1950. Served War, RAF, 1941–46. Research, Dept of Mineralogy and Petrology, Univ. of Cambridge, 1950–53; Lectr in Geology, Manchester Univ., 1953–62; King's College, London: Reader in Geol., 1962–72; Prof. of Mineralogy, 1972–85; Fellow 1980; Dean, Faculty of Science, Univ. of London, 1979–83; Chm., Academic Council, Univ. of London, 1983–86. Geological Society: Mem. Council, 1968–71, 1972–76; Vice-Pres., 1973–75. Mineralogical Society: Mem. Council, 1958–61, 1963–; Gen. Sec., 1965; Vice-Pres., 1975–77; Pres., 1978–80; Managing Trustee, 1978–. Fellow, Mineral Soc. of America, 1962. Member: Council, Internat. Mineral Assoc., 1974–82; Senate, Univ. of London, 1974–78, 1980–; Court, Univ. of London, 1984–. Murchison Medal, Geol Soc., 1976. Editor, Mineralogical Abstracts, 1966–. *Publications:* Rock-forming Minerals (with Prof. W. A. Deer and Prof. J. Zussman), 5 vols, 1962–63 (2nd edn, 1978–); An Introduction to the Rock-forming Minerals, 1966; scientific papers dealing with charnockites and with silicate mineralogy. *Recreations:* mineral collecting, writing abstracts. *Address:* Royal Holloway and Bedford New College, Egham Hill, Egham, Surrey TW20 0EX. *T:* Egham 34455; Gayhurst, Woodland Drive, East Horsley, Surrey. *Club:* Geological.

HOWIE, Thomas McIntyre; Principal, Paisley College of Technology, since 1972; *b* 21 April 1926; *m* 1951, Catherine Elizabeth Logan; three *s*. *Educ:* Paisley Coll. of Technology; Strathclyde Univ. BSc (Eng); CEng, FICE. Civil Engrg Asst, Clyde Navigation Trust, 1947–50; Paisley Coll. of Technology: Lectr in Civil Engrg, 1950–55; Sen. Lectr in Civil Engrg, 1955–58; Head, Dept of Civil Engrg, 1958–72; Vice-Principal, 1970–72. *Recreations:* golf, curling. *Address:* Dunscore, 38 Main Road, Castlehead, Paisley PA2 6AW. *T:* 041–889 5723. *Club:* Caledonian.

HOWITT, Anthony Wentworth; Senior Consultancy Partner, Peat, Marwick, Mitchell & Co., Management Consultants, 1957–84; *b* 7 Feb. 1920; *o s* of late Sir Harold Gibson Howitt, GBE, DSO, MC, and late Dorothy Radford; *m* 1951, June Mary Brent. *Educ:* Uppingham; Trinity Coll., Cambridge (MA). FCA, FCMA, JDipMA, CBIM, FIMC, FBCS. Commissioned RA; served in UK, ME and Italy, 1940–46 (Major). With Peat, Marwick, Mitchell & Co., Chartered Accountants, 1946–57. British Consultants Bureau: Vice-Chm., 1981–83; Mem. Council, 1968–75 and 1979–84; led mission to Far East, 1969. Member Council: Inst. of Management Consultants, 1964–77 (Pres., 1967–68); Inst. of Cost and Management Accountants, 1966–76 (Pres., 1972–73); Management Consultants Assoc., 1966–84 (Chm., 1976); Mem., Devlin Commn of Inquiry into Industrial Representation, 1971–72. Member: Bd of Fellows of BIM, 1973–76; Adv. Panel to Overseas Projects Gp, 1973–76; Price Commn, 1973–77; Domestic Promotions Cttee, British Invisible Exports Council, 1984. Mem., Court of Assistants, Merchant Taylors' Co., 1971– (Master 1980–81). *Publications:* papers and addresses on professional and management subjects. *Recreations:* fox-hunting, tennis, golf. *Address:* 17 Basing Hill, Golders Green, NW11 8TE. *Clubs:* Army and Navy; MCC; Harlequins.

HOWITT, W(illiam) Fowler, DA (Dundee), FRIBA; Partner in Firm of Cusdin Burden and Howitt, Architects, since 1965; *b* Perth, Scotland, May 1924; *s* of late Frederick Howitt, Head Postmaster, Forfar; *m* 1951, Ann Elizabeth, *o d* of late A. J. Hedges, Radipole, Dorset; three *s* one *d*. *Educ:* Perth Academy. Royal Marines, 1943–46. Sch. of Architecture, Dundee, 1948; RIBA Victory Scholar, 1949. Asst Louis de Soissons, London (housing and flats), 1949–52; Prin. Asst to Vincent Kelly, Dublin (hosps & offices), 1952–55; Architect to St Thomas' Hosp. (Hosp. rebuilding schemes, flats, offices), 1955–64. Present projects include: design and supervision of Coll. of Medicine and King Khalid Hosp., King Saud Univ., Riyadh, Saudi Arabia; design of teaching hospitals: Abuja city and Niger State, Nigeria; children's hospitals, Anambra and Imo States, Nigeria; planning consultancy: gen. hosps, Sharjah and Fujairah, UAE; King Fahad Medical City, Riyadh, Saudi Arabia. *Recreations:* reading, golf, childish pursuits. *Address:* Greencoat House, Francis Street, SW1P 1DB. *T:* 01–828 4051; (home) 32 Gloucester Road, Teddington, Mddx TW11 0NU. *T:* 01–977 5772.

HOWKINS, John, MD, FRCS; Gynæcological Surgeon to St Bartholomew's Hospital, 1946–69 (Hon. Consultant Gynæcologist since 1969), to Hampstead General Hospital

1946–67 (Hon. Consultant Gynæcologist, since 1968), and to Royal Masonic Hospital, 1948–73; *b* 17 Dec. 1907; *m* 1940, Lena Brown; one *s* two *d*. *Educ:* Shrewsbury Sch.; London Univ. Arts Scholar, Middlesex Hospital, 1926; MRCS, LRCP, 1932; MB, BS, London, 1933; FRCS, 1936; MS London, 1936; MD (Gold Medal) London, 1937; MRCOG 1937, FRCOG 1947. House Surgeon and Casualty Surgeon, Middlesex Hosp., 1932–34; RMO Chelsea Hosp. for Women, 1936; Gynæcological Registrar, Middlesex Hosp., 1937–38; Resident Obstetric Surg., St Bartholomew's Hosp., 1938 and 1945; Temp. Wing-Comdr, RAFVR Med. Br., 1939–45. Hunterian Prof., RCS 1947. William Meredith Fletcher Shaw Lectr, RCOG, 1975. Sometime Examiner in Midwifery to Univs of Cambridge and London, RCOG, Conjoint Bd of England. Chm., Council Ski Club of Great Britain, 1964–67 (Hon. Life Member, 1968, Trustee, 1969–); Mem., Gynaecological Travellers' Club. *Publications:* Shaw's Textbook of Gynæcology, 7th edn 1956 to 9th edn 1971; Shaw's Textbook of Operative Gynaecology, 2nd edn 1960 to 5th edn 1983 (jtly, 4th edn–); (jtly) Bonney's Textbook of Gynæcological Surgery, 7th edn 1964, 8th edn 1974. *Recreations:* ski-ing, salmon fishing and sheep farming. *Address:* Caen Hen, Abercegir, Machynlleth, Powys, Wales. *Clubs:* Ski Club of Great Britain; Wilks XV (Hon. Mem.).

HOWKINS, John Anthony; Executive Director, International Institute of Communications, since 1984; *b* 3 Aug. 1945; *s* of Col Ashby Howkins and Lesley (*née* Stops); *m* 1st, 1971, Jill Liddington; 2nd, 1977, Annabel Whittet. *Educ:* Rugby Sch.; Keele Univ.; Architectural Association's Sch. of Architecture. Marketing Manager, Lever Bros, 1968–70; jt founder, TV4 Conf., 1971: TV/Radio Editor, Books Editor, Time Out, 1971–74; Sec., Standing Conf. on Broadcasting, 1975–76; Editor, InterMedia, Journal of IIC, 1975–84. Chm., London Internat. Film Sch., 1979–84; Member: Interim Action Cttee on the Film Industry, DTI, 1980–84; British Screen Adv. Council, DTI, 1985–; Vice-Chm. (New Media), Assoc. of Independent Producers, 1984–85. Exec. Editor, National Electronics Review, 1981–; TV Columnist, Illustrated London News, 1981–83. Specialist Advr, Select Cttee on European Communities, House of Lords, 1985–. *Publications:* Understanding Television, 1977; Mass Communications in China, 1982; New Technologies, New Policies, 1982. *Address:* 14 Balliol Road, W10 6LX.

HOWLAND, Lord; Andrew Ian Henry Russell; *b* 30 March 1962; *s* and *heir* of Marquess of Tavistock, *qv*. *Educ:* Heatherdown; Harrow; Harvard. *Recreations:* shooting, racing. *Address:* Woburn Abbey, Bedfordshire MK43 0TP.

HOWLAND, Hon. Chief Justice William Goldwin Carrington; Chief Justice of Ontario, since 1977; *b* 7 March 1915; *s* of Goldwin William Howland and Margaret Christian Carrington; *m* 1966, Margaret Patricia Greene. *Educ:* Upper Canada Coll.; Univ. of Toronto (BA 1936, LLB 1939); Osgoode Hall Law Sch. Barrister-at-law. Practised law, McMillan Binch, 1936–75; Justice of Appeal, Court of Appeal, Supreme Court of Ontario, 1975–77. Law Society of Upper Canada: Bencher, 1960, 1965; Life Bencher, 1969; (Head) Treasurer, 1968–70. President: Fedn of Law Socs of Canada, 1973–74; UN Assoc. in Canada, 1959–60. Hon. lectr, Osgoode Hall Law Sch., 1951–67. Hon. LLD: Queen's Univ., Kingston, Ont., 1972; Univ. of Toronto, 1981; York Univ., 1984; Law Soc. of Upper Canada, 1985; Hon. DSL Wycliffe Coll., 1985. CStJ 1984. *Publications:* special Lectures, Law Soc. of Upper Canada, 1951, 1960. *Recreation:* travel. *Address:* 2 Bayview Wood, Toronto, Ontario M4N 1R7, Canada. *T:* 483–4696. *Clubs:* Toronto, Toronto Hunt, York, National (Toronto).

HOWLETT, Anthony Douglas, RD 1971; Remembrancer of the City of London, 1981–86; *b* 30 Dec. 1924; *s* of late Ernest Robert Howlett and Catherine (*née* Broughton), Grantham, Lincs; *m* 1952, Alfreda Dorothy Pearce, *yr d* of Arthur W. Pearce, Hove, Sussex. *Educ:* King's Sch., Rochester; Wellingborough; King's Sch., Grantham; Trinity Coll., Cambridge. BA Hons 1948, LLB 1949, MA 1950. Served War, 1939–46, RNVR; RNVSR, 1951–60; RNR, 1960–75 (Lt Comdr 1968). Called to the Bar, Gray's Inn, 1950; joined Legal Br., BoT, 1951; Sen. Legal Assistant, 1960; Asst Solicitor, 1972, i/c Export Credit Guarantees Br., 1972–75, i/c Merchant Shipping Br., 1975–81. UK delegate: London Diplomatic Conf. on Limitation of Liability for Maritime Claims, 1976; Geneva Diplomatic Conf. on Multi-Modal Transport, 1980, and other internat. maritime confs. Founder Mem., Sherlock Holmes Soc. of London, 1951 (Chm., 1960–63). Freedom of City of London, 1981; Liveryman, Scriveners' Co., 1981–. Order of King Abdul Aziz (II) (Saudi Arabia), 1981; Order of Oman (III), 1982; Comdr, Order of Orange-Nassau (Netherlands), 1982; Officier, Légion d'Honneur (France), 1984; Comdr, Order of the Lion of Malaŵi, 1985. *Publications:* articles on Conan Doyle and Holmesiana. *Recreations:* book browsing, Sherlock Holmes, opera, photography, foreign travel. *Address:* Rivendell, 37 Links Side, Enfield, Middlesex EN2 7QZ. *T:* 01-363 5802. *Clubs:* Naval, City Livery.

HOWLETT, Gen. Sir Geoffrey (Hugh Whitby), KBE 1984 (OBE 1972); MC 1952; Commander-in-Chief, Allied Forces Northern Europe, since 1986; *b* 5 Feb. 1930; *s* of Brig. B. Howlett, DSO, and Mrs Joan Howlett (later Latham); *m* 1955, Elizabeth Anne Aspinal; one *s* two *d*. *Educ:* Wellington Coll.; RMA, Sandhurst. Commnd Queen's Own Royal W Kent Regt, 1950; served, 1951–69: Malaya, Berlin, Cyprus and Suez; 3 and 2 Para, 16 Parachute Bde and 15 Para (TA); RAF Staff Coll. and Jt Services Staff Coll.; Mil. Asst to CINCNORTH, Oslo, 1969–71; CO 2 Para, 1971–73; RCDS, 1973–75; Comd 16 Parachute Bde, 1975–77; Dir, Army Recruiting, 1977–79; GOC 1st Armoured Div., 1979–82; Comdt, RMA, Sandhurst, 1982–83; GOC SE District, 1983–85. Colonel Commandant: ACC, 1981–, Parachute Regt, 1983–. President: Army Cricket Assoc., 1984–85; Combined Services Cricket Assoc., 1985. Cross of Merit, 1st cl. (Lower Saxony), 1982. *Recreations:* cricket, shooting. *Address:* c/o Lloyds Bank, Tonbridge, Kent. *Clubs:* Naval and Military, MCC.

HOWLETT, Jack, CBE 1969; MA Oxon, PhD Manchester; MIEE, FSS, FBCS, FIMA; Consultant to International Computers Ltd, since 1975 and Editor, ICL Technical Journal, since 1978; Managing Editor, Journal of Information Technology for Development, since 1985; *b* 30 Aug. 1912; *s* of William Howlett and Lydia Ellen Howlett; *m* 1939, Joan Marjorie Simmons; four *s* one *d*. *Educ:* Stand Grammar Sch., Manchester; Manchester Univ. Mathematician, LMS Railway, 1935–40 and 1946–48; mathematical work in various wartime research estabts, 1940–46; Head of Computer Group, Atomic Energy Research Estabt, Harwell, 1948–61; Dir, Atlas Computer Lab., Chilton Didcot, Berks, 1961–75 (under SRC, 1965–75). Chm., Nat. Cttee on Computer Networks, 1976–78. Fellow by special election, St Cross Coll., Oxford, 1966. Hon. Sec., British Cttee of Honour for Celebration of 1300th Anniversary of Foundn of Bulgarian State, 1980–82; 1300th Anniversary Medal of Bulgarian State, 1982. *Publications:* reviews and gen. papers on numerical mathematics and computation; trans of French books on computational subjects. *Recreations:* hill walking, music. *Address:* 20B Bradmore Road, Oxford OX2 6QP. *T:* Oxford 52893. *Clubs:* New Arts, Savile.

HOWLETT, Air Vice-Marshal Neville Stanley, CB 1982; RAF retired, 1982; Member, Panel of Independent Inquiry Inspectors, since 1982; *b* 17 April 1927; *s* of Stanley Herbert Howlett and Ethel Shirley Howlett (*née* Pritchard); *m* 1952, Sylvia, *d* of J. F. Foster; one *s* one *d*. *Educ:* Liverpool Inst. High Sch.; Peterhouse, Cambridge. RAF pilot training, 1945–47; 32 and 64 (Fighter) Squadrons, 1948–56; RAF Staff Coll. Course, 1957; Squadron Comdr, 229 (Fighter) OCU, 1958–59; OC Flying Wing, RAF Coltishall, 1961–63; Directing Staff, RAF Staff Coll., 1967–69; Station Comdr, RAF Leuchars, 1970–72; RCDS, 1972; Dir of Operations (Air Defence and Overseas), 1973–74; Air Attaché, Washington DC, 1975–77; Dir, Management Support of Intelligence, MoD, 1978–80; Dir Gen. of Personal Services (RAF), MoD, 1980–82. Vice-Pres., RAFA, 1984–. *Recreations:* golf, fishing. *Address:* Milverton, Bolney Trevor Drive, Lower Shiplake, Oxon RG9 3PG. *Clubs:* Royal Air Force; Phyllis Court (Henley); Huntercombe Golf.

HOWLETT, Ronald William, OBE 1986; Managing Director, Cwmbran Development Corporation, since 1978; *b* 18 Aug. 1928; *s* of Percy Edward Howlett and Lucy Caroline Howlett; *m* 1954, Margaret Megan Searl; two *s*. *Educ:* University Coll. London. BSc Eng.(Hons); CEng; FICE. Crawley Develt Corp., 1953–56; Exec. Engr, Roads and Water Supply, Northern Nigeria, 1956–61; Bor. of Colchester, 1961–64; Cwmbran Develt Corp., 1964–65; Bor. of Slough, 1965–69; Dep. Chief Engr and Chief Admin. Officer, Cwmbran Develt Corp., 1969–78. *Recreations:* fishing, music. *Address:* Cwmbran Development Corporation, Gwent House, Town Centre, Cwmbran, Gwent NP44 1XZ. *T:* Cwmbran 67777.

HOWSAM, Air Vice-Marshal George Roberts, CB 1945; MC 1918; RCAF, retired: also retired from Federal Emergency Measures Organization, 1962 (Coordinator, Alberta Civil Defence, 1950–57) and from business; *b* 29 Jan. 1895; *s* of Mary Ida and George Roberts Howsam, Port Perry, Ont; *m* 1st, 1918, Lillian Isobel (*d* 1970), *d* of Mary and William Somerville, Toronto; one *s*; 2nd, 1972, Marion Isobel Garrett, *d* of Clarence Albert Mitchell and Mary Blanche McCurdy, New Brunswick and Nova Scotia. *Educ:* Port Perry and Toronto. Joined Canadian Expeditionary Force, March 1916 and RFC 70 Sqdn and 43 Sqdn, 1917–18; served as fighter pilot France and Belgium, 1917–18 (wounded twice, MC); with Army of Occupation in Germany; returned to Canada, 1921; RCAF photographic survey, NW Canada; RAF Staff Coll., England, 1930 (psa); Senior Mem., RCAF 1st Aerobatic Team (Siskin) Display, Cleveland, USA, 1929; Staff Mem. CGAO Operations at AFHQ, 1931–32; SASO MD2 Toronto, 1933–36; OC 2 Army Co-operation Sqdn, Ottawa, 1937; Dir of Training for RCAF, Ottawa, 1938–40; England and France, 1940; later in 1940, SASO, No 4 Training Command, Regina; commanded No 11 Service Flying Training Sch., Yorkton, 1941; AOC No 4 Training Command, Calgary, 1942–44, also AOC Air Staging Route to Alaska, 1942–43 (thereby holding double command for two years); Chm. Organisation Cttee, Air Force HQ, Ottawa, 1945; retired 1946. Dominion Dir The Air Cadet League of Canada, 1946–47; Alberta Chm. RCAF Assoc., 1958–59. Canadian Deleg. to Emergency Measures NATO Assembly, Paris, Oct. 1960. Legion of Merit in Degree of Comdr (US), 1945; Order of White Lion (Czecho-Slovakia), 1946; Commandeur de l'ordre de la Couronne (Belgium), 1948. *Publications:* Rocky Mountain Foothills Offer Great Chance to Gliders (Calgary Daily Herald), 1923; Industrial and Mechanical Development: War (Canadian Defence Qtly Prize Essay), 1931. *Recreations:* gardening, writing, shooting. *Address:* (home) 2040 Pauls Terrace, Victoria, BC V8N 2Z3, Canada; Bank of Montreal, Government Street, Victoria, BC. *Clubs:* Union, Canadian, Victoria Golf (Victoria, BC); Empire (Toronto); Ranchmen's (Calgary).

HOWSE, Lt-Comdr Humphrey Derek, MBE 1954; DSC 1945; FSA, FRIN, FRAS; RN retired; Caird Research Fellow, National Maritime Museum, 1982–86; *b* Weymouth, 10 Oct. 1919; *s* of late Captain Humphrey F. Howse, RN and late Rose Chicheliana (*née* Thornton); *m* 1946, Elizabeth de Warrenne Waller; three *s* one *d*. *Educ:* RN Coll., Dartmouth. FRIN 1976; FRAS 1967; FSA 1986. Midshipman, RN, 1937–39; Sub-Lt, 1939, Lieut 1941; First Lieut of Destroyers, 1940–43; specialized in navigation, 1944, in aircraft direction, 1947 (despatches 3 times 1943–45); Lt-Comdr 1949; HMS Newcastle, Korean War, 1952–54, Inshore Flotilla, 1954–56; retd 1958. Atomic Energy Div., Gen. Electric Co., 1958–61; Associated Industrial Consultants, 1961–62; Continental Oil Co., 1962–63; Asst Keeper, Dept of Navigation and Astronomy, National Maritime Museum, 1963; Head of Astronomy, 1969; Dep. Keeper and Head of Navigation and Astronomy, 1976; Keeper, 1979–82. Clark Library Vis. Prof., UCLA, 1983–84. Member Council: IUHPS (Pres., Scientific Instrument Commn, 1977–82); British Astronomical Assoc., 1980– (Pres., 1980–82); Antiquarian Horological Soc., 1976–82; Royal Astronomical Soc., 1982–83; Royal Inst. of Navigation, 1982–83; Soc. for Nautical Research, 1982–86; Hakluyt Soc., 1984–. Liveryman, Clockmakers' Co., 1981. *Publications:* Clocks and Watches of Captain James Cook, 1969; The Tompion Clocks at Greenwich, 1970; (with M. Sanderson) The Sea Chart, 1973; Greenwich Observatory: the buildings and instruments, 1975; Francis Place and the Early History of Greenwich Observatory, 1975; Greenwich Time and the Discovery of the Longitude, 1980; papers to Mariners' Mirror, L'Astronomie, Antiquarian Horology, Jl of Navigation and Jl of British Astronomical Assoc. *Recreations:* reading, writing, sticking in photos, pottering in the vegetable beds. *Address:* 12 Barnfield Road, Riverhead, Sevenoaks, Kent TN13 2AY. *T:* Sevenoaks 454366. *Club:* Royal Over-Seas League.

HOWSON, Rear-Adm. John, CB 1963; DSC 1944; *b* 30 Aug. 1908; *s* of late George Howson and Mary Howson, Glasgow; *m* 1937, Evangeline Collins; one *s* one *d*. *Educ:* Kelvinside Academy, Glasgow; Royal Naval College, Dartmouth, 1922–25; Lieut, 1930; specialised in gunnery, 1934; Gunnery Officer, HMS Furious, 1936–38; served War of 1939–45 (despatches, DSC); HMS Newcastle, 1939–41; HMS Nelson, 1943–44; Comdr 1945; Fleet Gunnery Officer, British Pacific Fleet, 1947–48; Staff of C-in-C, Far East Stn, 1948–49; Exec. Officer, HMS Superb, 1949–50; Capt. 1951; served on Ordnance Bd, 1950–52; Comdg Officer, HMS Tamar, 1952–54; at SHAPE, 1955–57; UK Nat. Mil. Rep., RN, 1955–58; Chief of Staff to C-in-C, Plymouth, 1958–61; Rear-Adm. 1961; Comdr, Allied Naval Forces, Northern Europe, 1961–62; Naval Dep. to C-in-C Allied Forces, Northern Europe, 1963–64. Regional Officer, N Midlands, British Productivity Council, 1964–71. FRSA. *Address:* 11 Rookery Close, Gillingham, Dorset SP8 4LH. *T:* Gillingham 3129. *Club:* Naval and Military.

HOY, Rev. David, SJ; Superior, St John's, Beaumont, since 1984; *b* 1 March 1913; *s* of Augustine Hilary Hoy and Caroline Lovelace. *Educ:* Mount St Mary's Coll. Entered Society of Jesus, 1931. Senior English Master, Wimbledon Coll., 1947, Asst Head Master, 1957–59. Rector of St Robert Bellarmine, Heythrop, Chipping Norton, 1959–64; Rector of Stonyhurst College, 1964–71 and 1980–84; Superior of Farm St Church, 1972–75. *Recreation:* walking. *Address:* St John's, Beaumont, Old Windsor, Berks.

HOYLAND, John, ARA 1983; *b* 12 Oct. 1934; *s* of John Kenneth and Kathleen Hoyland; *m* 1957, Airi Karkkainen (marr. diss. 1968); one *s*. *Educ:* Sheffield Coll. of Art (NDD 1956); Royal Academy Schs (RA Cert. 1960). Taught at: Hornsey Coll. of Art, 1960–62; Chelsea Sch. of Art, 1962–69, Principal Lectr, 1965–69; St Martin's Sch. of Art, 1974–77; Slade Sch. of Art, 1974–77, 1980, 1983; Charles A. Dana Prof. of Fine Arts, Colgate Univ., NY, 1972. Artist in residence: Studio Sch., NY, 1978; Melbourne Univ., 1979. Selector: Hayward Annual, 1979; RA Silver Jubilee exhibn, 1979. *One-man exhibitions* include: Marlborough New London Gall., 1964; Whitechapel Gall., 1967; Waddington Galls, 1967, annually 1969–71 and 1973–76, 1978, 1978, 1981, 1983, 1985; retrospective: Serpentine Gall., 1979; and in Canada, USA, Brazil, Italy, Portugal, W Germany and Australia. *Group exhibitions* include: Tate Gall., 1964; Hayward Gall., 1974; Walker Art Gall., Liverpool (in every John Moores exhibn, 1963–); also in Belgium, France, Japan and Norway. Work in public collections incl. RA, Tate Gall., V&A Mus. and other galls and instns in UK, Europe, USA and Australia. *Film:* 6 Days in September, BBC TV, 1979. Designs for Zansa, Ballet Rambert, 1986. Gulbenkian Foundn purchase award, 1963; Peter Stuyvesant travel bursary, 1964, 1964; John Moores Liverpool exhibn prize, 1965, 1st prize, 1983; Open Paintings exhibn prize, Belfast, 1966; (jtly) 1st prize, Edinburgh Open 100 exhibn, 1969; 1st prize, Chichester Nat. Art exhibn, 1975; Arts Council purchase award, 1979. *Recreation:* eating chocolate. *Address:* c/o Waddington Galleries, 2 Cork Street, W1X 1PA.

HOYLE, (Eric) Douglas (Harvey); MP (Lab) Warrington North, since 1983 (Warrington, July 1981–1983); consultant; *b* 17 Feb. 1930; *s* of late William Hoyle and Leah Ellen Hoyle; *m* 1953, Pauline Spencer; one *s*. *Educ:* Adlington C of E Sch.; Horwich and Bolton Techn. Colls. Engrg apprentice, British Rail, Horwich, 1946–51; Sales Engr, AEI, Manchester, 1951–53; Sales Engr and Marketing Executive, Charles Weston Ltd, Salford, 1951–74. Mem., Manchester Regional Hosp. Bd, 1968–74; Mem., NW Regional Health Authority, 1974–75. Contested (Lab): Clitheroe, 1964; Nelson and Colne, 1970 and Feb. 1974; MP (Lab) Nelson and Colne, Oct. 1974–1979; Mem., Select Cttee on Trade and Industry, 1984–. Mem. Nat. Exec., Labour Party, 1978–82, 1983–85. Pres., ASTMS, 1977–81, 1985– (Vice-Pres., 1981–85); Chm., ASTMS Parly Cttee, 1975–76. Pres., Adlington Cricket Club, 1974–. JP 1958. *Recreations:* sport, cricket, theatre-going, reading. *Address:* 30 Ashfield Road, Anderton, Chorley, Lancs.

HOYLE, Prof. Sir Fred, Kt 1972; FRS 1957; MA Cantab; Hon. Research Professor: Manchester University, since 1972; University College, Cardiff, since 1975; Visiting Associate in Physics, California Institute of Technology, since 1963; *b* 24 June 1915; *s* of Ben Hoyle, Bingley, Yorks; *m* 1939, Barbara Clark; one *s* one *d*. *Educ:* Bingley Grammar Sch.; Emmanuel Coll., Cambridge (Hon. Fellow, 1983). Mayhew Prizeman, Mathematical Tripos, 1936; Smith's Prizeman, Goldsmith Exhibnr, Senior Exhibnr of Royal Commn for Exhibn of 1851, 1938. War Service for British Admiralty, 1939–45. Fellow, St John's Coll., Cambridge, 1939–72; University Lecturer in Mathematics, Cambridge, 1945–58; Plumian Prof. of Astronomy and Exptl Philosophy, Cambridge Univ., 1958–72; Dir, Inst. of Theoretical Astronomy, Cambridge, 1967–73; Prof. of Astronomy, Royal Instn of GB, 1969–72; Staff Mem., Mount Wilson and Palomar Observatories, 1957–62. California Institute of Technology: Vis. Prof. of Astrophysics, 1953, 1954; Vis. Prof. of Astronomy, 1956; Sherman Fairchild Scholar, 1974–75; Addison White Greenaway Vis. Prof. of Astronomy; Andrew D. White Prof.-at-Large, Cornell Univ., 1972–78. Mem. SRC, 1967–72. Vice-Pres., Royal Society, 1970–71; Pres., Royal Astronomical Soc., 1971–73. Hon. MRIA (Section of Science), 1977; Mem., Amer. Philos. Soc., 1980; Hon. Member: Amer. Acad. of Arts and Sciences, 1964; Mark Twain Soc., 1978; Foreign Associate, US Nat. Acad. of Sciences, 1969. Hon. Fellow, St John's Coll., Cambridge, 1973. Hon. ScD E Anglia, 1967; Hon DSc: Leeds 1969; Bradford 1975; Newcastle 1976. Royal Astronomical Soc. Gold Medal, 1968; UN Kalinga Prize, 1968; Bruce Gold Medal, Astronomical Soc. of Pacific, 1970; Royal Medal, Royal Soc., 1974. *Publications: astronomy:* Some Recent Researches in Solar Physics, 1949; The Nature of the Universe, 1951; A Decade of Decision, 1953; Frontiers of Astronomy, 1955; Man and Materialism, 1956; Astronomy, 1962; Star Formation, 1963; Of Men and Galaxies, 1964; Encounter with the Future, 1965; Galaxies, Nuclei and Quasars, 1965; Man in the Universe, 1966; From Stonehenge to Modern Cosmology, 1972; Nicolaus Copernicus, 1973; The Relation of Physics and Cosmology, 1973; (with J. V. Narlikar) Action-at-a-Distance in Physics and Cosmology, 1974; Astronomy and Cosmology, 1975; Highlights in Astronomy, 1975 (in England, Astronomy Today, 1975); Ten Faces of the Universe, 1977; On Stonehenge, 1977; Energy or Extinction, 1977; (with N. C. Wickramasinghe) Lifecloud, 1978; The Cosmogony of the Solar System, 1978; (with N. C. Wickramasinghe) Diseases From Space, 1979; (with G. Hoyle) Commonsense and Nuclear Energy, 1979; (with J. V. Narlikar) The Physics-Astronomy Frontier, 1980; (with N. C. Wickramasinghe) Space Travellers: the Bringers of Life, 1981; Ice, 1981; (with N. C. Wickramasinghe) Evolution from Space, 1981; The Intelligent Universe, 1983; *novels:* The Black Cloud, 1957; Ossian's Ride, 1959; (with J. Elliot) A for Andromeda, 1962; (with G. Hoyle) Fifth Planet, 1963; (with J. Elliot) Andromeda Breakthrough, 1964; October the First is Too Late, 1966; Element 79, 1967; (with G. Hoyle) Rockets in Ursa Major, 1969; (with G. Hoyle) Seven Steps to the Sun, 1970; (with G. Hoyle) The Molecule Men, 1971; (with G. Hoyle) The Inferno, 1973; (with G. Hoyle) Into Deepest Space, 1974; (with G. Hoyle) The Incandescent Ones, 1977; (with G. Hoyle) The Westminster Disaster, 1978; *children's stories with G. Hoyle:* The Energy Pirate, 1982; The Giants of Universal Park, 1982; The Frozen Planet of Azuron, 1982; The Planet of Death, 1982; Comet Halley, 1985; *autobiography:* The Small World of Fred Hoyle, 1986; *play:* Rockets in Ursa Major, 1962; *libretto:* The Alchemy of Love; space serials for television; scientific papers. *Address:* c/o The Royal Society, 6 Carlton House Terrace, SW1Y 5AG.

HOYLE, Ven. Frederick James; Archdeacon of Bolton, 1982–85, Archdeacon Emeritus, since 1985; *b* 14 Dec. 1918; *s* of Henry and Annie Hoyle; *m* 1939, Lillian Greenlees; two *d*. *Educ:* S John's College, Univ. of Durham (BA 1947, DiplTh 1949, MA 1957). Served War of 1939–45; Imphal, 1944 (despatches). Asst Curate, S Paul, Withington, 1949; Curate in charge, S Martin, Wythenshawe, 1952; Vicar 1960; Vice-Chm. and Exec. Officer, Diocesan Pastoral Cttee (full-time), 1965; Hon. Canon of Manchester, 1967; Vicar of Rochdale, and Rural Dean, 1971; Rector of Rochdale Team Ministry, 1978; Team Vicar, East Farnworth and Kearsley, 1982–85. *Recreations:* rowing, sailing, boat building. *Address:* 37 Toll Bar Crescent, Scotforth, Lancaster LA1 4NR. *T:* Lancaster 37883.

HOYOS, Hon. Sir (Fabriciano) Alexander, Kt 1979; former Lecturer, Cave Hill, University of the West Indies; retired History Teacher, Lodge School, St John; *b* Brazil, 5 July 1912; *s* of Emigdio and Adelina Hoyos, Peru; *m* 1st, 1940, Kathleen Carmen (*d* 1970); three *s* one *d*; 2nd, 1973, Gladys Louise. *Educ:* Wesley Hall Boys' School; Harrison Coll.; Codrington Coll., Durham Univ. (Sen. Island Schol.). BA 1936; MA 1943; Hon. MEd 1963; DLitt UWI, 1982. Taught at: Combermere Sch., Barbados; St Benedict's Coll., Trinidad; Lodge Sch., 1943–72; Moderator, Caribbean History Survey Course, Cave Hill, UWI, 1963–70. Leader-writer of Daily Advocate, 1937–43; Correspondent, London Times, 1938–65. Chm., Nat. Adv. Commn on Educn, 1983–86; Member: Barbados Christian Council, 1976–; Privy Council for Barbados, 1977–; Constitution Review Commn, 1977–78. Queen's Jubilee Medal, 1977. *Publications:* Some Eminent Contemporaries, 1944; Two Hundred Years, 1945; Story of Progressive Movement, 1948; Our Common Heritage, 1953; Memories of Princess Margaret and Our Past, 1955; Road to Responsible Government, 1960; Barbados, Our Island Home, 1960; Rise of West Indian Democracy, 1963; Background to Independence, 1967; Builders of Barbados, 1972; Grantley Adams and the Social Revolution, 1974; Barbados: From the Amerindians to Independence, 1978; Visitor's Guide to Barbados, 1982; The Quiet Revolutionary (autobiog.), 1984. *Recreations:* gardening, swimming. *Address:* Beachy Crest, Belair Cross Road, St Philip, Barbados, WI. *T:* 36323.

HSIUNG, Shih I; author; Founder, 1963, President, 1963–81, Tsing Hua College, Hong Kong; Hon. Secretary of China Society, London, since 1936 (Secretary 1934–36); Member of Universities China Committee, London, since 1935; *b* Nanchang, China, 14 Oct. 1902; *s* of Hsiung, Yuen-Yui and Chou, Ti-Ping; *m* 1923, Tsai, Dymia, (author of Flowering Exile, 1952); three *s* three *d*. *Educ:* Teachers' Coll., National Univ., Peking. Associate Manager of Chen Kwang Theatre, Peking, 1920–23; Managing Director of Pantheon Theatre, Shanghai, 1927–29; Special Editor of Commercial Press, Shanghai; Prof. at Agriculture Coll., Nanchang; Prof. at Min-Kuo Univ., Peking, till 1932. Chinese Delegate to International PEN Congress at Edinburgh, 1934; at Barcelona, 1935; at Prague, 1938; at London, 1941; at Zürich, 1947; Chinese Delegate to First Congress of International Theatre Institute at Prague, 1948; lectured on Modern Chinese and Classical Chinese Drama, University of Cambridge, 1950–53; Visiting Prof., University of Hawaii, Honolulu. Dean, College of Arts, Nanyang Univ., 1954–55; Man.-Dir, Pacific Films Co. Ltd, Hong Kong, 1955–; Dir, Konin Co. Ltd, Hong Kong, 1956–62; Dir, Success Co. Ltd, Hong Kong, 1956–62; Chm., Bd of Dirs Standard Publishers, Ltd (now Cathay Press), Hong Kong, 1961–63. *Publications:* various Chinese books including translations of Bernard Shaw, James Barrie, Thomas Hardy, Benjamin Franklin, etc; English Publications: The Money-God, 1934; Lady Precious Stream, 1934; The Western Chamber, 1935; Mencius Was A Bad Boy, 1936; The Professor From Peking, 1939; The Bridge of Heaven, 1941; The Life of Chiang Kai-Shek, 1943; The Gate of Peace, 1945; Changing China: History of China from 1840 to 1911, 1946; The Story of Lady Precious Stream, 1949; Chinese Proverbs, 1952; Lady on the Roof, 1959. *Recreation:* theatre-going. *Address:* 4000 Tunlaw Road NW, Washington, DC 20007, USA.

HU DINGYI; Ambassador of the People's Republic of China to the Court of St James's, since 1985; *b* Dec. 1922; *m* Xie Heng; one *s* one *d*. *Educ:* Central Univ., Sichuan Province, China (graduate). 3rd Secretary, Embassy of People's Republic of China in India, 1950–54; 2nd Sec., Office of the Chargé d'Affaires of People's Republic of China, 1954–58; Section Chief, Dept of Western European Affairs, Min. of Foreign Affairs, 1958–60; 1st Sec., Ghana, 1960–66; Division Chief, Dept of African Affairs, 1966–71; 1st Sec., then Counsellor, UK, 1972–79; Consul General, San Francisco, 1979–83; Minister, US, 1983–85. *Recreation:* reading. *Address:* Embassy of the People's Republic of China, 31 Portland Place, W1N 3AG. *T:* 01–636 5726.

HUANG, Rayson Lisung, Hon. CBE 1976; DSc, DPhil; FRCPE; Vice-Chancellor, University of Hong Kong, 1972–86; *b* 1 Sept. 1920; *s* of Rufus Huang; *m* 1949, Grace Wei Li; two *s*. *Educ:* Munsang Coll., Hong Kong; Univ. of Hong Kong (BSc); Univ. of Oxford (DPhil, DSc); Univ. of Chicago. DSc (Malaya) 1956. FRCPE 1984. Demonstrator in Chemistry, Nat. Kwangsi Univ., Kweilin, China, 1943; Post-doctoral Fellow and Research Associate, Univ. of Chicago, 1947–50; Univ. of Malaya, Singapore: Lecturer in Chemistry, 1951–54; Reader, 1955–59; Univ. of Malaya, Kuala Lumpur: Prof. of Chemistry, 1959–69, and Dean of Science, 1962–65. Vice-Chancellor, Nanyang Univ., Singapore, 1969–72. Chm. Council, ACU, 1980–81; Pres., Assoc. of SE Asian Instns of Higher Learning, 1970–72, 1981–83. MLC Hong Kong, 1977–83. JP. Hon. DSc Hong Kong, 1968. *Publications:* Organic Chemistry of Free Radicals, 1974 (London); about 50 research papers on chemistry of free radicals, molecular rearrangements, etc, mainly in Jl of Chem. Soc. (London). *Recreation:* music. *Address:* A7 Bellevue Court, 41 Stubbs Road, Hong Kong. *T:* 5–738854. *Club:* Hong Kong

HUBBACK, David Francis, CB 1970; Chairman, Simon Population Trust, since 1983; Clerk of the Financial Committees of the House of Commons, 1979–81 (Special Advisor to the Expenditure Committee, 1976–79); *b* 2 March 1916; *s* of late Francis William and Eva Hubback; *m* 1939, Elais Judith, *d* of late Sir John Fischer Williams; one *s* two *d*. *Educ:* Westminster Sch.; King's Coll., Cambridge. Mines Dept, Bd of Trade, 1939. War of 1939–45: Army, 1940–44; Capt., Royal Signals; Western Desert, Sicily, Normandy; Cabinet Office, 1944. UK Delegn to OEEC, 1948; Treasury, 1950; Principal Private Sec. to Chancellor of the Exchequer, 1960–62; Under-Sec., Treasury, 1962–68, Board of Trade, 1969, DTI, 1970–71; Dep. Sec., DTI, later Dept of Trade, 1971–76. Mem., London Library Cttee, 1971–78. *Publications:* Population Trends in Great Britain: their policy implications, 1983; No Ordinary Press Baron: a life of Walter Layton, 1984. *Recreations:* mountain walking, reading. *Address:* 4 Provost Road, NW3 4ST. *T:* 01–586 4341. *Club:* Reform.

HUBBARD, family name of **Baron Addington.**

HUBBARD, David; see Hubbard, R. D. C.

HUBBARD, Michael Joseph; QC 1985; a Recorder of the Crown Court, since 1984; *b* 16 June 1942; *s* of Joseph Thomas Hubbard and late Gwendoline Hubbard; *m* 1967, Ruth Ann; five *s*. *Educ:* Lancing College. Articled with Morris Bew & Baily, 1961; admitted Solicitor, 1966, Partner in Hubbard & Co., Chichester, 1966–71; called to the Bar, Gray's Inn, 1972, practising Western Circuit: Prosecuting Counsel to Inland Revenue, on Western Circuit, 1983–85. *Recreations:* messing about in boats and living on Herm Island. *Address:* (chambers) 1 Paper Buildings, Temple, EC4; Bartons, Stoughton, Chichester, West Sussex PO18 9JQ. *T:* Compton 315. *Club:* Chichester Sailing.

HUBBARD, Richard David Cairns; Chairman, Powell Duffryn, since 1986; *b* 14 May 1936; *s* of John Cairns Hubbard and Gertrude Emilie Hubbard; *m* 1964, Hannah Neale (*née* Dennison); three *d*. *Educ:* Tonbridge. FCA. Commissioned, Royal Artillery, 1955–57; Peat Marwick Mitchell & Co., 1957–64; Cape Asbestos Co., 1965–74; Bache & Co., 1974–76; Powell Duffryn, 1976–; non-exec. Dir, Blue Circle Industries, 1986–. Mem., Board of Crown Agents for Oversea Govts and Admins, 1986–. Liveryman, Skinners' Co.; Freeman, City of London. *Recreations:* golf, real tennis. *Address:* Meadowcroft, Windlesham, Surrey GU20 6BJ. *T:* Bagshot 72198. *Clubs:* MCC; Berkshire Golf, Lucifer Golfing Society.

HUBBARD-MILES, Peter Charles, CBE 1981; MP (C) Bridgend, since 1983; self-employed small businessman, since 1948; *b* 9 May 1927; *s* of Charles Hubbard and Agnes (*née* Lewis); *m* 1948, Pamela Wilkins; two *s* three *d*. *Educ:* Lewis' Sch., Pengam. Served RAF, 1945–48. County Councillor, Mid Glamorgan CC (formerly Glamorgan CC), 1967– (Leader, Conservative Group, 1974–83); Leader, Cons. Gp, Ogwr Borough Council, 1974–83, first Cons. Mayor 1979–80. Chm., Wales Cons. Local Govt Adv. Council, 1979–83. PPS to Sec. of State for Wales, 1985–. Chm. Governors, Bridgend Tech. Coll., 1977–81. *Recreations:* theatre, showbusiness. *Address:* 18 Lougher Gardens, Porthcawl CF36 3BJ.

HUBEL, Prof. David Hunter, MD; John Franklin Enders University Professor, Harvard Medical School, since 1982; *b* Canada, 27 Feb. 1926; US citizen; *s* of Jesse H. Hubel and Elsie M. Hunter; *m* 1953, S. Ruth Izzard; three *s*. *Educ:* McGill Univ. (BSc Hons Maths and Physics, 1947); McGill Univ. Med. Sch. (MD 1951). Rotating Intern, Montreal Gen. Hosp., 1951–52; Asst Resident in Neurology, Montreal Neurol Inst., 1952–53, and Fellow in Electroencephalography, 1953–54; Asst Resident in Neurol., Johns Hopkins Hosp., 1954–55; Res. Fellow, Walter Reed Army Inst. of Res., 1955–58; Res. Fellow, Wilmer Inst., Johns Hopkins Univ. Med. Sch., 1958–59; Harvard Medical School: Associate in Neurophysiology and Neuropharmacology, 1959–60; Asst Prof. of Neurophys. and Neuropharm., 1960–62; Associate Prof. of Neurophys. and Neuropharm., 1962–65; Prof.

of Neurophys., 1965–67; George Packer Berry Prof. of Physiol. and Chm., Dept of Physiol., 1967–68; George Packer Berry Prof. of Neurobiol., 1968–82. Sen. Fellow, Harvard Soc. of Fellows, 1971–; Mem., Bd of Syndics, Harvard Univ. Press, 1979–83. Associate, Neurosciences Res. Program, 1974. Fellow, Amer. Acad. of Arts and Sciences, 1965; Member: Amer. Physiol Soc., 1959–; National Acad. of Sciences, USA, 1971; Deutsche Akademie der Naturforscher Leopoldina, DDR, 1971; Soc. for Neuroscience, 1970; Assoc. for Res. in Vision and Ophthalmology, 1970; Amer. Philosophical Soc., 1982; Foreign Mem., Royal Soc., 1982; Hon. Member: Physiology. Soc., 1983; Amer. Neurol Assoc. Lectures: George H. Bishop, Washington Univ., St Louis, 1964; Bowditch, Amer. Physiol Soc., 1966; Jessup, Columbia Univ., 1970; Ferrier, Royal Soc., 1972; James Arthur, Amer. Mus. of Nat. Hist., 1972; Harvey, Rockefeller Univ., 1976; Grass Foundn, Soc. for Neuroscience, 1976; Weizmann Meml, Weizmann Inst. of Science, Israel, 1979; Vanuxem, Princeton Univ., 1981; Hughlings Jackson, Montreal Neurol Inst., 1982; first David Marr, Cambridge Univ., 1982; first James S. McDonnell, Washington Univ. Sch. of Medicine, 1982; James A. F. Stevenson Meml, Univ. of W Ont, 1982; Keys Meml, Trinity Coll., Toronto, 1983; Nelson, Univ. of Calif. Davis, 1983; Deane, Wellesley Coll., 1983; first James M. Sprague, Univ. of Pa, 1984; Vancouver Inst., Univ. of BC, 1985. Hon. DSc: McGill, 1978; Manitoba, 1983. Awards: Res. to Prevent Blindness Trustees, 1971; Lewis S. Rosenstiel for Basic Med. Res., Brandeis Univ., 1972; Friedenwald, Assoc. for Res. in Vision and Ophthalmol., 1975; New England Ophthalmol Soc. Annual Award, 1983. Prizes: Karl Spencer Lashley, Amer. Phil Soc., 1977; Louisa Gross Horwitz, Columbia Univ., 1978; Dickson in Medicine, Univ. of Pittsburgh, 1979; Ledlie, Harvard Univ., 1980; Nobel Prize in Medicine or Physiol., 1981. *Publications:* articles in scientific jls. *Recreations:* music, photography, astronomy, Japanese. *Address:* Harvard Medical School, 25 Shattuck Street, Boston, Mass 02115, USA. *T:* (617) 732–1655.

HUCKFIELD, Leslie (John); Member (Lab) Merseyside East, European Parliament, since 1984; *b* 7 April 1942; *s* of Ernest Leslie and Suvla Huckfield. *Educ:* Prince Henry's Grammar Sch., Evesham; Keble Coll., Oxford; Univ. of Birmingham. Lectr in Economics, City of Birmingham Coll. of Commerce, 1963–67. Advertising Manager, Tribune, 1983; Co-ordinator, CAPITAL (transport campaign against London Transport Bill), 1983–84. Contested (Lab) Warwick and Leamington, 1966; MP (Lab) Nuneaton, March 1967–83. PPS to Minister of Public Building and Works, 1969–70; Parly Under-Secretary of State, Dept of Industry, 1976–79. Member: Nat. Exec. Cttee, Labour Party, 1978–82; W Midlands Reg. Exec. Cttee, Labour Party, 1978–82; Political Sec., Nat. Union Lab. and Socialist Clubs, 1979–81. Chairman: Lab. Party Transport Gp, 1974–76; Independent Adv. Commn on Transport, 1975–76; Pres., Worcs Fedn of Young Socialists, 1962–64; Member: Birmingham Regional Hosp. Bd, 1970–72; Political Cttee, Co-op. Retail Soc. (London Regional), 1981–. *Publications:* various newspaper and periodical articles. *Recreation:* running marathons. *Address:* PO Box 200, Wigan, Lancs WN5 0LU.

HUCKLE, Sir (Henry) George, Kt 1977; OBE 1969; Chairman: Agricultural Training Board, 1970–80; Home-Grown Cereals Authority, 1977–83; Deputy Chairman, Extrans Technical Services Ltd, since 1980; *b* 9 Jan. 1914; *s* of George Henry and Lucy Huckle; *m* 1st, 1935, L. Steel (*d* 1947); one *s*; 2nd, 1949, Mrs Millicent Mary Hunter; one *d* and one step *d*. *Educ:*Latymer Sch.; Oxford Univ. (by courtesy of BRCS via Stalag Luft III, Germany). Accountant trng, 1929–33; sales management, 1933–39; RAF bomber pilot, 1940–41; POW, Germany, 1941–45; Shell Group, 1945–70: Man. Dir, Shellstar Ltd, 1965–70, retd. *Recreations:* competition bridge, gardening, golf, following daughter's interest in horse eventing. *Address:* Icknield House, Saxonhurst, Downton, Wilts. *T:* Downton 22754. *Club:* Farmers'.

HUCKSTEP, Prof. Ronald Lawrie, CMG 1971; MD, FRCS, FRCSE, FRACS, FTS; Professor of Traumatic and Orthopaedic Surgery, since 1972, and Chairman, School of Surgery, since 1975, University of New South Wales: Chairman of Departments of Orthopaedic Surgery and Director of Accident Services, Prince of Wales and Prince Henry Hospitals, Sydney, Australia, since 1972; Consultant Orthopaedic Surgeon, Royal South Sydney and Sutherland Hospitals, since 1974; *b* 22 July 1926; *er s* of late Herbert George Huckstep and Agnes Huckstep (*née* Lawrie-Smith); *m* 1960, Margaret Ann, *e d* of Ronald Græme Macbeth, DM, FRCS; two *s* one *d*. *Educ:* Cathedral Sch., Shanghai, China; Queens' Coll., Cambridge; Mddx Hosp. Med. Sch., London. MA, MB, BChir (Cantab) 1952; MD (Cantab) 1957; FRCS (Edinburgh) 1957; FRCS 1958; FRACS (by election) 1973. Registrar and Chief Asst, Orthpaedic Dept, St Bartholomew's Hosp., and various surgical appts Middx and Royal Nat. Orthopaedic Hosps, London, 1952–60; Hunterian Prof., RCS of Eng., 1959–60. Makerere Univ. Coll., Kampala, Uganda: Lectr, 1960–62, Sen. Lectr, 1962–65 and Reader, 1965–67, in Orthopaedic Surgery, with responsibility for starting orthopaedic dept in Uganda; Prof. of Orthopaedic Surgery, Makerere Univ., Kampala, 1967–72. Became Hon. Cons. Orthopaedic Surgeon, Mulago and Mengo Hosps, and Round Table Polio Clinic, Kampala; Adviser on Orthopaedic Surgery, Ministry of Health, Uganda, 1960–72. Corresp. Editor: Brit. and Amer. jls of Bone and Joint Surgery, 1965–72; Jl Western Pacific Orthopædic Assoc.; British Jl of Accident Surgery. Fellow, British Orthopaedic Assoc., 1967; Hon. Fellow, Western Pacific Orthopaedic Assoc., 1968. Commonwealth Foundn Travelling Lectr, 1970, 1978–79 and 1982. FRSM; FTS 1982. Patron Med. Soc., Univ. of NSW; Founder, World Orthopaedic Concern, 1973 (Hon. Mem. 1978); Vice-Pres., Australian Orthopaedic Assoc., 1982–83 (Betts Medal, 1983); Pres., Coast Med. Assoc., Sydney, 1985–86; Chairman, Fellow or Mem. various med. socs and of assocs, councils and cttees concerned with orthopaedic and traumatic surgery, accident services and rehabilitation of physically disabled. Inventions incl. Huckstep femoral fracture nail, hip, knee, shoulder and circlip. Irving Geist Award, 11th World Congress, Internat. Soc. for Rehabilitation of the Disabled, 1969; James Cook Medal, Royal Soc. of NSW, 1984. Hon. Mem., Mark Twain Soc., 1978. *Publications:* Typhoid Fever and Other Salmonella Infections, 1962; A Simple Guide to Trauma, 1970, 4th edn 1986 (trans. Italian 1978, Japanese 1982); Poliomyelitis A Guide for Developing Countries, Including Appliances and Rehabilitation, 1975 (ELBS and repr. edns 1979, 1983, French edn 1983); various booklets, chapters in books, papers and films on injuries, orthopaedic diseases, typhoid fever, appliances and implants. *Recreations:* photography, designing orthopaedic appliances and implants for cripples in developing and developed countries, swimming, travel. *Address:* Department of Traumatic and Orthopaedic Surgery, University of New South Wales, PO Box 1, Kensington, Sydney, NSW 2033, Australia. *T:* Sydney 3990111.

HUDD, Roy; actor; *b* 16 May 1936; *s* of Harold Hudd and Evelyn Barham; *m* 1963, Ann Lambert (marr. diss. 1983); one *s*. *Educ:* Croydon Secondary Technical School. Entered show business, 1957, as half of double act Hudd & Kay; Butlin Redcoats; started as a solo comedian, 1959; first pantomine, Empire Theatre, Leeds, 1959; 4 years' concert party Out of the Blue, 1960–63; first radio broadcast Workers Playtime, 1960; *stage includes:* The Merchant of Venice, 1960; The Give Away, 1969; At the Palace, 1970; Young Vic Co. seasons, 1973, 1976, 1977; Oliver!, 1977; Underneath the Arches, 1982 (SWET Actor of the Year); Run For Your Life, 1986; *films include:* Blood Beast Terror, 1967; Up Pompeii; The Seven Magnificent Deadly Sins; Up the Chastity Belt; The Garnet Saga; An Acre of Seats in a Garden of Dreams, 1973; What'll You Have, 1974; Up Marketing, 1975; *television series include:* Not So much a Programme, More a Way of Life, 1964; Illustrated Weekly Hudd, 1966–68; Roy Hudd Show, 1971; Comedy Tonight, 1970–71; Up Sunday, 1973; Pebble Mill, 1974–75; Hold the Front Page, 1974–75; The 60 70 80 show, 1974–77; Movie Memories, 1981–85; Halls of Fame, 1985; The Puppet Man, 1985; *radio series:* The News Huddlines, 1975–; *author of stage shows:* Victorian Christmas, 1978; Just a Verse and Chorus, 1979; Roy Hudd's Very Own Music Hall, 1980; Beautiful Dreamer, 1980; Underneath the Arches, 1982; While London Sleeps, 1983. Chm., Entertainment Artistes Benevolent Fund, 1980–. Gold Badge of Merit, British Acad. of Songwriters and Composers, 1981. *Publication:* Music Hall, 1976. *Recreations:*collecting old songs and sleeping. *Address:* 652 Finchley Road, NW11. *T:* 01–458 7288. *Club:* Green Room.

HUDDIE, Sir David (Patrick), Kt 1968; FEng 1981; retired; *b* 12 March 1916; *s* of James and Catherine Huddie; *m* 1941, Wilhelmina Betty Booth; three *s*. *Educ:* Mountjoy Sch., Dublin; Trinity Coll., Dublin. FIQA 1980; FIMechE 1974. Aero Engine Division, Rolls-Royce Ltd: Asst Chief Designer, 1947; Chief Development Engineer, 1953; Commercial Dir, 1959; General Manager, 1962; Dir, Rolls-Royce Ltd, 1961; Man. Dir, Aero Engine Div., 1965; Chm. Rolls-Royce Aero Engines Inc., 1969–70; Senior Res. Fellow, Imperial Coll., London, 1971–80, Hon. Fellow, 1981. Hon. DSc Dublin, 1968. *Recreations:* gardening, music, archaeology. *Address:*The Croft, Butts Road, Bakewell, Derbyshire DE4 1EB. *T:* Bakewell 3330. *Club:* Athenæum.

HUDDLESTON, Most Rev. (Ernest Urban) Trevor, CR; DD; Chairman, International Defence and Aid Fund for Southern Africa, since 1983; *b* 15 June 1913; *s* of late Capt. Sir Ernest Huddleston, CIE, CBE; unmarried. *Educ:* Lancing; Christ Church, Oxford; Wells Theological College, 2nd class Hon. Mod. Hist., Oxford, 1934 (BA), MA 1937. Deacon, 1936; Priest, 1937. Joined Community of the Resurrection; Professed, 1941. Apptd Priest-in-charge Sophiatown and Orlando Anglican Missions, diocese Johannesburg, Nov. 1943; Provincial in S Africa, CR, 1949–55; Guardian of Novices, CR, Mirfield, 1956–58; Prior of the London House, Community of the Resurrection, 1958–60; Bishop of Masasi, 1960–68; Bishop Suffragan of Stepney, 1968–78; Bishop of Mauritius, 1978–83; Archbishop of the Indian Ocean, 1978–83. Provost, Selly Oak Colls, 1983–. President: Anti-Apartheid Movement, 1981– (Vice-Pres., 1969–81); Nat. Peace Council, 1983–; IVS, 1984–; Chm., Internat. Defence and Aid Fund, 1983–. Trustee, Runnymede Trust, 1972–. Hon. DD (Aberdeen Univ.), 1956; Hon. DLitt Lancaster, 1972. *Publications:* Naught for Your Comfort, 1956; The True and Living God, 1964; God's World, 1966; I Believe: reflections on the Apostles Creed, 1986. *Recreations:* walking and listening to music. *Address:* House of the Resurrection, Mirfield, W Yorks WF14 0BN.

HUDLESTON, Air Chief Marshal Sir Edmund C., GCB 1963 (KCB 1958; CB 1945); CBE 1943; Air ADC to the Queen, 1962–67, retired 1967; *b* 30 Dec. 1908; *s* of late Ven. C. Hudleston; *m* 1st, 1936, Nancye Davis (*d* 1980); one *s* one *d*; 2nd, 1981, Mrs Brenda Withrington, *d* of A. Whalley, Darwen. *Educ:* Guildford Sch., W Australia; Royal Air Force Coll., Cranwell. Entered Royal Air Force 1927; served in UK until 1933; India, NWFP, 1933–37 (despatches); RAF Staff Coll., 1938; lent to Turkish Govt 1939–40; served Middle East and N Africa, Sicily, Italy, 1941–43 (despatches thrice); AOC No 84 Group, 2 TAF, Western Front, 1944; Imperial Defence Coll., 1946; Head of UK's military delegation to the Western Union Military Staff Cttee, 1948–50; AOC No 1 Group, Bomber Command, 1950–51; Deputy Chief of Staff, Supreme Headquarters, Allied Command, Europe, 1951–53; AOC No 3 Group, Bomber Command, 1953–56; RAF Instructor, Imperial Defence Coll., 1956–57; Vice-Chief of the Air Staff, 1957–62; Air Officer Commanding-in-Chief, Transport Command, 1962–63; Comdr Allied Air Forces, Central Europe, 1964–67, and C-in-C Allied Forces Central Europe, 1964–65. Dir, Pilkington Bros (Optical Div.), 1971–79. Comdr Legion of Merit (USA), 1944; Knight Commander Order of Orange-Nassau (Netherlands), 1945; Commander Order of Couronne, Croix de Guerre (Belgium), 1945; Officer, Legion of Honour, 1956, Croix de Guerre (France), 1957. *Recreations:* cricket, squash, tennis, shooting, etc. *Address:* 156 Marine Court, St Leonards-on-Sea, East Sussex TN38 0DZ. *Club:* Royal Air Force.

HUDSON, Prof. Anthony Hugh, PhD; Professor of Common Law, since 1977 and Dean of Faculty of Law, 1971–78 and since 1984, Liverpool University; *b* 21 Jan. 1928; *s* of late Dr Thomas A. G. Hudson and Bridget Hudson; *m* 1962, Joan O'Malley; one *s* three *d*. *Educ:* St Joseph's Coll., Blackpool; Pembroke Coll., Cambridge (LLB 1950, MA 1953); PhD Manchester 1966. Called to Bar, Lincoln's Inn, 1954. Lecturer in Law: Hull Univ., 1951–57; Birmingham Univ., 1957–62; Manchester Univ., 1962–64; Liverpool Univ.: Sen. Lectr, 1964–71; Professor of Law, 1971–77. *Publications:* (with Prof. O. Hood Phillips) Hood Phillips: A First Book of English Law, 7th edn 1977; (with Prof. R. R. Pennington) Commercial Banking Law, 1978; (with Prof. J. K. Macleod) Stevens and Borrie Mercantile Law, 17th edn 1978; contribs to various legal periodicals. *Recreations:* gardening, walking, history. *Address:* 18 Dowhills Road, Blundellsands, Crosby, Liverpool L23 8SW. *T:* 051–924 5830.

HUDSON, (Eleanor) Erlund, RE 1946 (ARE 1938); RWS 1949 (ARWS 1939); ARCA (London) 1937; Artist; *b* 18 Feb. 1912; *d* of Helen Ingeborg Olsen, Brookline, Boston, USA, and Harold Hudson. *Educ:* Torquay; Dorking; Royal College of Art (Diploma 1937, Travelling Scholarship 1938). Mem. Chicago Print Soc. and Soc. of Artist Print-Makers. Studied and travelled in Italy summer 1939. Interrupted by war. Exhibited in London, Provinces, Scandinavia, Canada, USA, etc.; works purchased by War Artists Advisory Council, 1942–43. Artistic Dir and designer, Brooking Ballet Sch., W1, 1966–. *Recreations:* music, country life. *Address:* 6 Hammersmith Terrace, W6. *T:* 01–748 3778; Meadow House, Old Bosham, W Sussex. *T:* Bosham 573558.

HUDSON, Eric Hamilton, FRCP; Hon. Consulting Physician: West London Hospital; London Chest Hospital; King Edward VII Hospital, Midhurst; Papworth Village Settlement; retired as: Consultant Physician, Manor House Hospital; Senior Medical Officer, Prudential Assurance Co.; *b* 11 July 1902; *s* of James Arthur and Edith Hudson; *m* 1st, 1940, Jessie Marian MacKenzie (*d* 1968); two *s* one *d*; 2nd, 1972, Nora Joan Pitman. *Educ:* Radley Coll.; Emmanuel Coll., Cambridge; Guy's Hosp., London. MRCS, LRCP, 1927; MA, MB, BCh Cantab, 1931; MRCP 1933, FRCP 1941. Late Wing Commander RAF, Officer in charge Medical Div., 1941–45. Late Examr in Medicine, RCP; Past Pres., W London Medico-Chirurgical Soc., 1959. *Publications:* Section on diagnosis and treatment of respiratory Tuberculosis, Heaf's Symposium of Tuberculosis, 1957; contrib. to Perry and Holmes Sellors Diseases of the Chest, 1964; contrib. to medical jls on diseases of the lungs. *Recreation:* fishing. *Address:* The Shieling, Highclere, near Newbury, Berks. *T:* Highclere 253574.

HUDSON, Erlund; *see* Hudson, E. E.

HUDSON, Frank Michael Stanislaus; barrister; a Recorder of the Crown Court, since 1981; *b* 28 Sept. 1916; *s* of Frederick Francis Hudson and Elizabeth Frances (*née* O'Herlihy); *m* 1947, Jean Colburn (*née* Gordon); one *d*. *Educ:* Wimbledon Coll.; London Univ. (BA). Called to the Bar, Middle Temple, 1961; practised Northern Circuit, 1969–. Served War: 77th Field Regt RA, 1939–42; Glider Pilot Regt, 1942–45. Post-war employment in local govt and in trade assocs; Dep. Circuit Judge, 1977–80. *Recreations:* bee-keeping, history of English monasticism. *Address:* 33 Sherwood Avenue, Radcliffe,

Manchester M26 0LE. *T:* 061–764 3807; (chambers) 67 Princess Street, Manchester M2 4EG. *T:* 061–228 1764.

HUDSON, Prof. George, FRCPath; Postgraduate Dean, University of Sheffield, since 1984; Head of Department of Haematology, since 1981; *b* 10 Aug. 1924; *s* of George Hudson, blacksmith, and Edith Hannah (*née* Bennett); *m* 1955, Mary Patricia Hibbert (decd); one *d. Educ:* Edenfield C of E Sch.; Bury Grammar Sch.; Manchester Univ. (MSc, MB, ChB); MD, DSc Bristol. MRCP. House Officer, Manchester Royal Inf., 1949–50; Demonstr in Anatomy, Univ. of Bristol, 1950–51; RAMC, 1951–53; University of Bristol: Lectr, later Reader, in Anatomy, 1953–68; Preclinical Dean, 1963–68; Vis. Prof., Univ. of Minnesota (Fulbright Award), 1959–60; Sheffield University: Admin. Dean, 1968–83; Hon. Clinical Lectr in Haematology, 1968; Prof. of Experimental Haematology, 1975; Hon. Cons. Haematologist, United Sheffield Hosps, 1969. Chm., Conf. of Deans of Provincial Med. Schs, 1980–82; Member: Sheffield RHB, 1970–74; Sheffield HA, 1974–84; DHSS Working Party on NHS Adv. and Representative Machinery, 1980–81; Council for Postgraduate Med. Educn for England and Wales, 1980–83. *Publications:* papers in medical and scientific jls on haematological subjects. *Recreations:* lay reader since 1953, badminton, gardening. *Address:* The Medical School, Beech Hill Road, Sheffield S10 2RX. *T:* Sheffield 21747.

HUDSON, Sir Havelock (Henry Trevor), Kt 1977; Lloyd's Underwriter since 1952; Chairman of Lloyd's, 1975, 1976 and 1977 (Deputy Chairman, 1968, 1971, 1973); *b* 4 Jan. 1919; *er s* of late Savile E. Hudson and Dorothy Hudson (*née* Cheetham); *m* 1st, 1944, Elizabeth (marr. diss., 1956), *d* of Brig. W. Home; two *s*; 2nd, 1957, Cathleen Blanche Lily, *d* of 6th Earl of St Germans; one *s* one *d. Educ:* Rugby. Merchant Service, 1937–38. Served War of 1939–45: Royal Hampshire Regt (Major), 1939–42; 9 Parachute Bn, 1942–44. Member: Cttee Lloyd's Underwriters Assoc., 1963; Cttee of Lloyd's, 1965–68, 1970–73, 1975–78; Exec. Bd, Lloyd's Register of Shipping, 1967–78. Dir, Ellerman Lines Ltd, 1979–84. Vice-Pres., Chartered Insurance Inst., 1973–76, Dep. Pres., 1976–; Chairman: Arvon Foundn, 1973–85; Oxford Artificial Kidney and Transplant Unit, 1976–; Pres., City of London Outward Bound Assoc., 1979–; Member, Board of Governors: Pangbourne Coll., 1976–; Bradfield Coll., 1978–. Lloyd's Gold Medal, 1977. *Recreation:* shooting. *Address:* The Old Rectory, Stanford Dingley, Berkshire. *T:* Bradfield 744346. *Club:* Boodle's.

HUDSON, Ian Francis, CB 1976; Deputy Secretary, Department of Employment, 1976–80; *b* 29 May 1925; *s* of Francis Reginald Hudson and Dorothy Mary Hudson (*née* Crabbe); *m* 1952, Gisela Elisabeth Grettka; one *s* one *d. Educ:* City of London Sch.; New Coll., Oxford. Royal Navy, 1943–47. Customs and Excise, 1947–53; Min. of Labour, 1953–56, 1959–61, 1963–64; Treasury, 1957–58; Dept of Labour, Australia, 1961–63; Asst Sec., 1963; DEA, 1964–68; Under-Sec., 1967; Dept of Employment, 1968–73; Dep. Sec. 1973; Sec., Pay Board, 1973–74; Sec., Royal Commn on Distribution of Income and Wealth, 1974–76.

See also J. A. Hudson.

HUDSON, James Ralph, CBE 1976; FRCS; Surgeon, Moorfields Eye Hospital, 1956–81, now Honorary Consulting Surgeon; Ophthalmic Surgeon, Guy's Hospital, 1963–76; Hon. Ophthalmic Surgeon: Hospital of St John and St Elizabeth, since 1953; King Edward VII Hospital for Officers, 1970–86; Teacher of Ophthalmology, Guy's Hospital, 1964–76, Institute of Ophthalmology, University of London, 1961–81; Consultant Adviser in Ophthalmology, Department of Health and Social Security, 1969–82; *b* 15 Feb. 1916; *o s* of late William Shand Hudson and Ethel Summerskill; *m* 1946, Margaret May Oulpé; two *s* two *d. Educ:* The King's Sch., Canterbury; Middlesex Hosp. (Edmund Davis Exhibnr), Univ. of London, MRCS, LRCP 1939; MB, BS London 1940; DOMS (England) 1948; FRCS 1949. Res. Med. Appts, Tindal House Emergency Hosp. (Mddx Hosp. Sector), 1939–42. RAFVR Med. Service, 1942–46; Sqdn Ldr, 1944–46. Moorfields Eye Hosp., Clin. Asst, 1947, Ho. Surg., 1947–49; Sen. Resident Officer, 1949, Chief Clin. Asst, 1950–56; Middlesex Hosp., Clin. Asst Ophth. Outpatients, 1950–51; Ophth. Surg., W Middlesex Hosp., 1950–56, Mount Vernon Hosp., 1953–59. Civil Consultant in Ophthalmology to RAF, 1970–82. Examr in Ophthalmology (Dipl. Ophth. of Examg Bd of Eng., RCP and RCS, 1960–65; Mem. Court of Examrs, RCS, 1966–72). FRSocMed 1947 (Vice-Pres. Sect. of Ophthalmology, 1965); Member: Ophthal. Soc. UK, 1948– (Hon. Sec. 1956–58, Vice-Pres., 1969–71, Pres., 1982–84); Faculty of Ophthalmologists, 1950– (Mem. Council, 1960–82; Hon. Sec. 1960–70; Vice-Pres., 1970–74; Pres., 1974–77; Rep on Council of RCS, 1968–73; Hon. Mem., 1982–); Soc. Française d'Ophtal., 1950– (membre délégue étranger, 1970–); Cttee d'Honneur Les Entretiens Annuels d'Ophtalmologie, 1970–; Internat. Council of Ophthalmology, 1978–; UK Rep., Union Européenne des Médecins Spécialistes (Ophthalmology Section), 1973– (Pres., 1982–86); Hon. Fellow, Royal Aust. Coll. Ophthalmologists; Pilgrims of Gt Britain; Hon. Steward, Westminster Abbey, 1972–. Liveryman, Soc. of Apothecaries, and Freeman of City of London. *Publications:* (with T. Keith Lyle) chapters in Matthews's Recent Advances in the Surgery of Trauma; contrib. to chapters in Rob and Rodney Smith's Operative Surgery, 1969; articles in: Brit. Jl of Ophthalmology; Trans Ophth. Soc. UK; Proc. Royal Soc. Med. *Recreations:* motoring, travel. *Address:* 8 Upper Wimpole Street, W1M 7TD. *T:* 01–935 5038; 1A Montagu Mews South, W1H 1TE. *T:* 01–402 6511. *Club:* Garrick.

HUDSON, John Arthur, CB 1970; Deputy Under-Secretary of State, Department of Education and Science, 1969–80; *b* 24 Aug. 1920; *s* of Francis Reginald Hudson and Dorothy Mary (*née* Crabbe); *m* 1960, Dwynwen Davies; one *s* one *d. Educ:* City of London Sch.; Jesus Coll., Oxford. Served Royal Corps of Signals, 1941–45 (despatches). Entered Ministry of Education, 1946. Mem., South Bank Theatre Bd, 1967–. *Recreations:* gardening, microscopy. *Address:* The Rosary, Green Lane, Leominster, Herefordshire HR6 8QN. *T:* Leominster 4413.

See also I. F. Hudson.

HUDSON, Prof. John Pilkington, CBE 1975 (MBE 1943); GM 1944 and Bar 1945; BSc, MSc, PhD; NDH; FIBiol; now Emeritus Professor; former Director, Long Ashton Research Station, and Professor of Horticultural Science, University of Bristol, 1967–75; *b* 24 July 1910; *o s* of W. A. Hudson and Bertha (*née* Pilkington); *m* 1936, Mary Gretta, *d* of late W. N. and Mary Heath, Westfields, Market Bosworth, Leics; two *s. Educ:* New Mills Grammar Sch.; Midland Agricultural Coll.; University Coll., Nottingham. Hort. Adviser, E Sussex CC, 1935–39. Served War of 1939–45, Royal Engineers Bomb Disposal (Major). Horticulturist, Dept of Agric., Wellington, NZ, 1945–48; Lecturer in Horticulture, University of Nottingham Sch. of Agric., 1948–50; Head of Dept of Horticulture, University of Nottingham, 1950–67 (as Prof. of Horticulture, 1958–67, Dean, Faculty of Agriculture and Horticulture, 1965–67); seconded part-time to Univ. of Khartoum, Sudan, to found Dept of Horticulture, 1961–63. Associate of Honour, Royal New Zealand Institute of Horticulture, 1948. Chm., Jt Advisory Cttee on Agricultural Education (HMSO report published, 1973); Mem., RHS Exam. Bd; PP and Hon. Mem., Hort. Educn Assoc. Hon. Fellow: RASE, 1977; Inst. of Hort., 1985. VMH, 1977. Editor, Experimental Agriculture, 1965–82; Mem. Editorial Bds, Jl Hort. Sci, SPAN. *Publications:* (ed) Control of the Plant Environment, 1957; many contribs on effects of environment on plant growth and productivity to scientific jls. *Recreations:* music, gardening. *Address:* The Spinney, Wrington, Bristol.

HUDSON, Keith William, FRICS; Director of Construction and Cost Intelligence, and Chief Surveyor, Department of Health and Social Security, 1979–86, retired; *b* 2 June 1928; *s* of William Walter Hudson and Jessie Sarah Hudson; *m* 1952, Ailsa White; two *s* two *d. Educ:* Sir Charles Elliott Sch.; Coll. of Estate Management. FRICS 1945. Served Army, 1948–50 (Lieut). Private practice, 1945–48 and 1950–57; Min. of Works, Basic Grade, 1957–64; Min. of Health (later DHSS), 1964–: Main Grade, 1964–66; Sen. Grade, 1966–74; Superintending, 1974–76; Dir B, 1976–79; Under Sec., 1979. *Publications:* articles in Chartered Surveyor and in Building. *Recreations:* Rugby coaching, athletics coaching. *Address:* Silver Birch, Mill Lane, Felbridge, East Grinstead, West Sussex RH19 2PE. *T:* East Grinstead 25817. *Club:* Felbridge Rugby Football Union (East Grinstead).

HUDSON, Prof. Liam, MA, PhD; Professor of Psychology, Brunel University, since 1977; *b* 20 July 1933; *er s* of Cyril and Kathleen Hudson; *m* 1st, 1955, Elizabeth Ward; 2nd 1965, Bernadine Jacot de Boinod; three *s* one *d. Educ:* Whitgift Sch.; Exeter Coll., Oxford. Post-graduate and post-doctoral research, Psychological Laboratory, Cambridge, 1957–65, and King's Coll., Cambridge, 1965–68; Fellow, King's Coll., Cambridge, 1966–68; Prof. of Educnl Scis, Univ. of Edinburgh, 1968–77, and Dir, Res. Unit on Intellectual Develt, 1964–77. Mem., Inst. for Advanced Study, Princeton, 1974–75. *Publications:* Contrary Imaginations, 1966; Frames of Mind, 1968; (ed) The Ecology of Human Intelligence, 1970; The Cult of the Fact, 1972; Human Beings, 1975; The Nympholepts, 1978; Bodies of Knowledge, 1982; Night Life, 1985. *Recreations:* painting and photography, making things, otherwise largely domestic. *Address:* 34 North Park, Gerrards Cross, Bucks.

HUDSON, Maurice William Petre; Hon. Consulting Anæsthetist: National Dental Hospital (University College Hospital); Westminster Hospital; St Mary's Hospital; Emeritus Consultant Anæsthetist, Princess Beatrice Hospital; Part-time Consultant Anæsthetist, Queen Mary's Hospital, Roehampton; *b* 8 Nov. 1901; *s* of late Henry Hudson, ARCA, and Anna Martha Rosa (*née* Petre); *m* 1922, Fredrica Helen de Pont; one *s* one *d* (and two *s* decd). *Educ:* Sherborne Sch.; St Thomas' Hosp. MB, BS London, 1925; MRCS, LRCP, 1924; DA England, 1936; FFARCS, 1948. Formerly: Resident House Surg., Resident Anæsthetist, and Clin. Asst, Nose and Throat Dept, St Thomas' Hosp. Fellow Assoc. Anæsthetists of Gt Brit. Mem. Royal Soc. Med. *Publications:* contrib. to med. jls. *Recreation:* swimming. *Address:* 10 Devonshire Mews South, W1N 1LA. *T:* 01–580 3977, 01–935 9665.

HUDSON, Norman Barrie; Under Secretary for Africa, Overseas Development Administration, since 1986; *b* 21 June 1937; *s* of William and Mary Hudson; *m* 1963, Hazel (*née* Cotterill); two *s* one *d. Educ:* King Henry VIII Sch., Coventry; Univ. of Sheffield (BA Hons 1958); University Coll., London (MScEcon 1960). Economist, Tube Investments Ltd, 1960; Economist, Economist Intell. Unit, 1962; National Accounts Statistician (UK Technical Assistance to Govt of Jordan), 1963; Statistician, ODM, 1966; Econ. Adviser, ME Develt Div., Beirut, 1967; Econ. Adviser, ODA, 1972, Sen. Econ. Adviser, 1973; Head, SE Asia Develt Div., Bangkok, 1974; Asst Sec., 1977; Under Sec. (Principal Establishments Officer), ODA, 1981. *Recreations:* theatre, reading, music, watching football and cricket. *Address:* The Galleons, Sallows Shaw, Sole Street, Cobham, Kent DA13 9BP. *T:* Meopham 814419.

HUDSON, Pamela May, JP; Regional Nursing Director, North West Thames Regional Health Authority, since 1985, *b* 1 June 1931; *d* of late Leonard Joshua Hudson and of Mabel Ellen Hudson (now Baker). *Educ:* South West Essex High School. SRN. Nursing Officer, Charing Cross Hospital, 1966–67; Matron, Fulham Hosp., 1967–70; Principal Regional Nursing Officer, South East Thames RHB, 1970–73; Area Nursing Officer, Lambeth, Southwark and Lewisham AHA(T), 1973–82; Regional Nursing Officer, NW Thames RHA, 1982–85. Member, Alcohol Education and Research Council, 1982–, JP Inner London SE Div, 1983. *Publications:* contribs to nursing profession jls. *Recreations:* embroidery, theatre. *Address:* 3 Dunstable Court, St John's Park, Blackheath, SE3 7TN. *T:* 01–723 0016.

HUDSON, Lt-Gen. Sir Peter, KCB 1977; CBE 1970 (MBE 1965); DL; Secretary-General of the Order of St John, since 1981; Lieutenant of the Tower of London, since 1986; *b* 14 Sept. 1923; *s* of Captain William Hudson, late The Rifle Bde, and Ivy (*née* Brown); *m* 1949, Susan Anne Knollys; one adopted *s* one *d* and one adopted *d. Educ:* Wellingborough; Jesus Coll., Cambridge. Commnd into The Rifle Bde, 1944; psc 1954; comd company in Mau Mau and Malayan campaigns, 1955–57; jssc 1963; comd 3rd Bn The Royal Green Jackets, 1966–67; Regimental Col The Royal Green Jackets, 1968; Comdr 39 Infantry Bde, 1968–70; IDC 1971; GOC Eastern Dist, 1973–74; Chief of Staff, Allied Forces Northern Europe, 1975–77; Dep. C-in-C, UKLF, 1977–80; Inspector-Gen., T&AVR, 1978–80. Col Comdt, The Light Div., 1977–80; Hon. Colonel: Southampton Univ. OTC, 1980–85; 5 (Volunteer) Bn, The Royal Green Jackets, TA, 1985–. Mem., Gen. Adv. Council, BBC, 1981–85. Mem., Rifle Bde Club and Assoc. (Chm., 1979–85); Trustee, Rifle Bde Museum (Chm., Trustees, 1979–85); Chairman: Green Jacket Club, 1979–85; Council, TA&VRA, 1981–; Pres., Reserve Forces Assoc., 1985–. Chm. Governors, Royal Sch. Bath, 1981–; Governor, Bradfield Coll., 1983–. Freeman of City of London, 1965. DL Berks, 1984. FBIM. KStJ. *Recreations:* travel, fishing, most games. *Address:* Little Orchard, Frilsham, Newbury, Berks. *Clubs:* Naval and Military, MCC; I Zingari; Green Jackets; Free Foresters.

HUDSON, Peter Geoffrey; Director of Resources, British Tourist Authority and English Tourist Board, 1984–86; *b* 26 July 1926; *s* of late Thomas Albert Hudson and late Gertrude Hudson; *m* 1954, Valerie Mary, *yr d* of late Lewis Alfred Hart and late Eva Mary Hart; two *s* one *d. Educ:* King Edward VII Sch., Sheffield; Queen's Coll., Oxford (Hastings Scholar, MA). Gold Medallist, Royal Schs of Music, 1940. Sub-Lt RNVR, 1944–46. Min. of Transport, 1949; Private Sec. to Minister of Transport and Civil Aviation, 1951–53; Principal, Min. of Transport and Civil Aviation, 1953–57; Admin. Staff Coll., Henley, 1957; British Civil Air Attaché, SE Asia and Far East, 1958–61; Asst Sec., Overseas Policy Div. and Estabt Div., Min. of Aviation and BoT, 1963–68; Counsellor (Civil Aviation), British Embassy, Washington, 1968–71; Under-Secretary: DTI, 1971–84. Governor, Coll. of Air Trng, Hamble, 1974–75. *Recreations:* music, travel. *Address:* Candle Hill, Raggleswood, Chislehurst, Kent. *T:* 01–467 1761.

HUDSON, Peter John, CB 1978; Deputy Under-Secretary of State (Finance and Budget), Ministry of Defence, 1976–79; *b* 29 Sept. 1919; *o s* of late A. J. Hudson; *m* 1954, Joan Howard FitzGerald; one *s* one *d. Educ:* Tollington Sch.; Birkbeck Coll., London. Exchequer and Audit Dept, 1938; RNVR, 1940–46 (Lieut); Asst Principal, Air Min., 1947; Private Sec. to Perm. Under Sec. of State for Air, 1948–51; Asst Sec., 1958; Head of Air Staff Secretariat, 1958–61; Imperial Defence Coll., 1962; Head of Programme and Budget Div., MoD, 1966–69; Under-Sec., Cabinet Office, 1969–72; Asst Under-Sec. of State, MoD, 1972–75; Dep. Under-Sec. of State (Air), MoD, 1975–76. *Address:* Folly Hill, Haslemere, Surrey GU27 2EY. *T:* Haslemere 2078. *Club:* Royal Air Force.

HUDSON, Prof. Robert Francis, PhD; FRS 1982; Professor of Organic Chemistry, University of Kent at Canterbury, 1967–85 (part-time, 1981–85), now Emeritus; Consultant, British Petroleum, since 1983; b 15 Dec. 1922; s of late John Frederick Hudson and Ethel Hudson; m 1945, Monica Ashton Stray; one s twin d. Educ: Brigg Grammar Sch.; Imperial Coll. of Science and Technol., London (BSc, ARCS, PhD, DIC). Asst Lectr, Imperial Coll., London, 1945–47; Consultant, Wolsey Ltd, Leicester, 1945–50; Lectr, Queen Mary Coll., London, 1947–59; Res. Fellow, Purdue Univ., 1954; Gp Dir, Cyanamid European Res. Inst., Geneva, 1960–66. Vis. Professor: Rochester, USA, 1970; Bergen, 1971; CNRS, Thiais, Paris, 1973; Calgary, 1975; Mainz, 1979; Queen's, Kingston, Ont., 1983. Lectures: Frontiers, Case-Western Reserve Univ., USA, 1970; Nuffield, Canada, 1975; Quest, Queen's, Ont. 1983. Vice-Pres., Inst. of Science Technol., 1970–76; Member: Council, Chemical Soc., 1967–75 (Foundn Chm., Organic Reaction Mechanism Gp, 1973); Dalton Council, 1973–76; Perkin Council, 1980–83. Publications: (with P. Alexander) Wool—its physics and chemistry, 1954, 2nd edn 1960; Structure and Mechanism in Organophosphorus Chemistry, 1965; papers mainly in Jl of Chem. Soc., Helvetica Chemica Acta and Angewandte Chemie. Address: The Chemical Laboratory, University of Kent at Canterbury, Canterbury, Kent CT2 7NH. T: Canterbury 66822; 37 Puckle Lane, Canterbury CT1 3LA. T: Canterbury 61340. Club: Athenæum.

HUDSON, Thomas Charles, CBE 1975; Chairman: Access Software Ltd, since 1984; ICL Ltd, 1972–80; INFA Communications Ltd, since 1985; Chartered Accountant (Canadian); b Sidcup, Kent, 23 Jan. 1915; British parents; m 1944, Lois Alma Hudson (marr. diss. 1973); two s one d; m 1986, Susan Gillian van Kan. Educ: Middleton High Sch., Nova Scotia. With Nightingale, Hayman & Co, Chartered Accountants, 1935–40. Served War, Royal Canadian Navy, Lieut, 1940–45. IBM Canada, as Sales Rep., 1946–51 (transf. to IBM, UK, as Sales Manager, 1951, and Managing Dir, 1954–65). Plessey Company: Financial Dir, 1967; Dir, 1969–76; Dir, ICL, 1968. Councillor for Enfield, GLC, 1970–73. Recreations: tennis, ski-ing, gardening. Address: Hele Farm, North Bovey, Devon TQ13 8RW. T: Moretonhampstead 40249. Clubs: Carlton, American, Inst. of Directors.

HUDSON, William Meredith Fisher, QC 1967; Barrister-at-law; b 17 Nov. 1916; o s of late Lt-Comdr William Henry Fisher Hudson, RN (killed in action, Jutland, 1916); m 1st, 1938, Elizabeth Sophie (marr. diss., 1948), d of late Reginald Pritchard, Bloemfontein, SA; one s one d; 2nd, 1949, Pamela Helen, d of late William Cecil Edwards, Indian Police; two d. Educ: Imperial Service Coll.; Trinity Hall, Cambridge. BA 1938; Harmsworth Law Scholar, 1939; MA 1940. Called to the Bar, Middle Temple, 1943, Bencher, 1972; South Eastern Circuit, 1945; Mem. of Central Criminal Court Bar Mess. Commissioned Royal Artillery (TA), 1939; served War of 1939–45, Eritrea and Sudan. Chm., Blackfriars Settlement, 1970–. Recreations: trains, travel, theatre; formerly athletics (Cambridge Blue, Cross Country half Blue; rep. England and Wales, European Student Games, 1938). Address: 5 King's Bench Walk, Temple, EC4. T: 01–353 4713; (home) 3 Rivercourt Road, W6. T: 01–741 3125; The Park House, Berkeley, Glos. Clubs: Achilles; Hawks (Cambridge).

HUDSON DAVIES, (Gwilym) Ednyfed; see Davies, G. E. H.

HUDSON-WILLIAMS, Prof. Harri Llwyd, MA; Professor of Greek in the University of Newcastle upon Tyne (formerly King's College, Newcastle upon Tyne, University of Durham), 1952–76 and Head of Department of Classics, 1969–76; now Emeritus Professor; b 16 Feb. 1911; yr s of late Prof. T. Hudson-Williams; m 1946, Joan, er d of late Lieut-Col H. F. T. Fisher; two d. Educ: University College of North Wales; King's Coll., Cambridge (Browne Medallist; Charles Oldham Scholar); Munich University. Asst Lectr in Greek, Liverpool Univ., 1937–40; Intelligence Corps, 1940–41; Foreign Office, 1941–45; Lectr in Greek, Liverpool Univ., 1945–50; Reader in Greek, King's Coll., Newcastle upon Tyne, 1950–52; Dean of the Faculty of Arts, 1963–66. Publications: contribs to various classical jls, etc. Recreation: gardening. Address: The Pound, Mill Street, Islip, Oxford OX5 2SZ. T: Kidlington 5893.

HUEBNER, Michael Denis; Under Secretary, Lord Chancellor's Department, Circuit Administrator, North Eastern Circuit, since 1985; b 3 Sept. 1941; s of Dr Denis William Huebner and late Rene Huebner (née Jackson); m 1965, Wendy Ann Crosthwaite, d of Brig. Peter Crosthwaite; one s one d. Educ: Rugby Sch.; St John's Coll., Oxford (BA Modern History). Called to the Bar, Gray's Inn, 1965. Lord Chancellor's Department: Legal Asst, 1966–68, 1970–71; seconded to Law Officers' Dept, 1968–70; Sen. Legal Asst, 1971; Asst Solicitor, 1978. Secretary: Law Reform Cttee, 1979–82; Judicial Studies Bd, 1982–83. Publications: brief guide to Ormesby Hall (Nat. Trust); contrib. (jtly) Courts, Halsbury's Laws of England, 4th edn 1975; legal articles in New Law Jl. Recreations: looking at pictures, architecture. Address: 26 East Mount Road, York YO2 2BD. T: York 39416.

HUFFINLEY, Beryl; Secretary: Leeds Trades Council, since 1966; Yorkshire and Humberside TUC Regional Council, since 1974; b 22 Aug. 1926; d of Wilfred and Ivey Sharpe; m 1948, Ronald Brown Huffinley. Chairman: Leeds and York Dist Cttee, T&GWU, 1974–; Regional Cttee, T&GWU No 9 Region, 1972–. Member: Regional Econ. Planning Council (Yorkshire and Humberside), 1975–79; Leeds AHA, 1977–; Press Council, 1978–84. Address: Cornerways, South View, Menston, Ilkley, Yorks. T: Menston 75115. Club: Trades Council (Leeds).

HUFTON, Prof. Olwen, (Mrs B. T. Murphy), PhD; Professor of Modern History, University of Reading, since 1975; d of Joseph Hufton and Caroline Hufton; m 1965, Brian Taunton Murphy; two d. Educ: Hulme Grammar Sch., Oldham; Univ. of London (BA 1959, PhD 1962). Lectr, Univ. of Leicester, 1963–66; Lectr, then Reader, Univ. of Reading, 1966–75. Publications: Bayeux in the Late Eighteenth Century, 1967; The Poor of Eighteenth Century France, 1974; Europe, Privilege and Protest, 1730–1789, 1980; articles in Past and Present, Eur. Studies Rev., and French Hist. Studies. Address: 40 Shinfield Road, Reading, Berks. T: Reading 871514.

HUGGETT, Mrs Helen K.; see Porter, Prof. H. K.

HUGGINS, family name of Viscount Malvern.

HUGGINS, Hon. Sir Alan (Armstrong), Kt 1980; Hon. Mr Justice Huggins; Vice-President, Court of Appeal, Hong Kong, since 1980; b 15 May 1921; yr s of late William Armstrong Huggins and Dare (née Copping); m 1st, 1950, Catherine Davidson (marr. diss.), d of late David Dick; two s one d; 2nd, 1985, Elizabeth Low (née Dodd). Educ: Radley Coll.; Sidney Sussex Coll., Cambridge (MA). TARO (Special List), 1940–48 (Actg Major); Admiralty, 1941–46. Called to Bar, Lincoln's Inn, 1947. Legal Associate Mem., TPI, 1949–70. Resident Magistrate, Uganda, 1951–53; Stipendiary Magistrate, Hong Kong, 1953–58; Diocesan Reader, Dio. of Hong Kong and Macao, 1954; District Judge, Hong Kong, 1958–65. Chm., Justice (Hong Kong Br.), 1965–68; Judicial Comr, State of Brunei, 1966–; Judge of Supreme Court, Hong Kong, 1965–76; Justice of Appeal, Hong Kong, 1976–80. Hon. Lectr, Hong Kong Univ., 1979–. Chm., Adv. Cttee on Legal Educn, 1972–. Past Pres., YMCAs of Hong Kong. Hon. Life Governor, Brit. and For. Bible Soc; Hon. Life Mem., Amer. Bible Soc. Liveryman, Leathersellers' Company.

Recreations: boating, archery, amateur theatre, tapestry. Address: Courts of Justice, Queensway, Hong Kong. Club: Royal Over-Seas League.

HUGGINS, Prof. Charles B.; Professor of Surgery, University of Chicago, since 1936; William B. Ogden Distinguished Service Professor since 1962; b Halifax, Canada, 22 Sept. 1901; s of Charles Edward Huggins and Bessie Huggins (née Spencer); citizen of USA by naturalization, 1933; m 1927, Margaret Wellman; one s one d. Educ: Acadia (BA 1920; DSc 1946); Harvard (MD 1924). University of Michigan: Interne in Surgery, 1924–26; Instructor in Surgery, 1926–27; Univ. of Chicago, 1927–: Instructor in Surgery, 1927–29; Asst Prof., 1929–33; Assoc. Prof., 1933–36; Prof., 1936–; Dir, Ben May Laboratory for Cancer Research, 1951–69. Chancellor, Acadia Univ., 1972–79. Alpha Omega Alpha, 1942; Mem. Nat. Acad. of Sciences, 1949; Mem. Amer. Philosophical Soc., 1962. Sigillum Magnum, Bologna Univ., 1964; Hon. Prof., Madrid Univ., 1956; Hon. FRSocMed (London), 1956; Hon. FRCSE 1958; Hon. FRCS 1959; Hon. FACS 1963; Hon. FRSE 1983. Hon. MSc, Yale, 1947; Hon. DSc: Washington Univ., St Louis, 1950; Leeds Univ., 1953; Turin Univ., 1957; Trinity Coll., Hartford, Conn., 1965; Wales, 1967; Univ. of California, Berkeley, 1968; Univ. of Michigan, 1968; Medical Coll. of Ohio, 1973; Gustavus Adolphus Coll., 1975; Wilmington Coll. of Ohio, 1980; Univ. of Louisville, 1980; Hon. LLD: Aberdeen Univ., 1966; York Univ., Toronto, 1968; Hon. DPS, George Washington Univ., 1967. Has given many memorial lectures and has won numerous gold medals, prizes and awards for his work on urology and cancer research, including Nobel Prize for Medicine (jtly), 1966. Holds foreign orders. Publications: Experimental Leukemia and Mammary Cancer: Induction, Prevention, Cure, 1979; over 275 articles. Address: Ben May Laboratory for Cancer Research, University of Chicago, 950 East 59th Street, Chicago, Ill 60637, USA.

HUGGINS, Kenneth Herbert, CMG 1960; b 4 Dec. 1908; m 1934, Gladys E. Walker; one s one d. Educ: Hitchin Grammar Sch.; Tollington Sch.; University Coll., London. BSc London 1930; PhD Glasgow, 1940. Asst and Lecturer in Geography, Glasgow Univ., 1930–41; Ministry of Supply, 1941; Staff of Combined Raw Materials Board, Washington, 1942–46; Board of Trade, 1947; Staff of Administrative Staff Coll., Henley, 1954–55; Commercial Counsellor, British Embassy, Washington, 1957–60; UK Trade Commissioner, subsequently Consul-General, Johannesburg, 1960–62. Dir, British Industrial Develt Office, NY, 1962–68. Publications: atlases and articles in geographical journals. Recreation: computing. Address: 3 Skeyne Mews, Pulborough, W Sussex. T: Pulborough 2365.

HUGGINS, Peter Jeremy William; see Brett, Jeremy.

HUGH-JONES, Sir Wynn (Normington), (Sir Hugh Jones), Kt 1984; LVO 1961; Joint Hon. Treasurer, Liberal Party, since 1984; b 1 Nov. 1923; s of Huw Hugh-Jones and May Normington; m 1958, Ann (née Purkiss); one s two d. Educ: Ludlow; Selwyn Coll., Cambridge (Scholar; MA) Served in RAF, 1943–46. Entered Foreign Service (now Diplomatic Service), 1947; Foreign Office, 1947–49; Jedda, 1949–52; Paris, 1952–56; FO, 1956–59; Chargé d'Affaires, Conakry, 1959–60; Head of Chancery, Rome, 1960–64; FO, 1964–66, Counsellor, 1964; Consul, Elizabethville (later Lubumbashi), 1966–68; Counsellor and Head of Chancery, Ottawa, 1968–70; FCO, 1971, attached Lord President's Office; Cabinet Office, 1972–73; Director-Gen., E-SU, 1973–77; Sec.-Gen., Liberal Party, 1977–83. A Vice-Chm., European-Atlantic Gp, 1985–. President: S Salop Lib. Assoc., 1984–; Westminster S Lib. Assoc., 1985–. Gov., Queen Elizabeth Foundn for the Disabled, 1985–. FBIM. Recreations: golf, gardening. Address: 203 Duncan House, Dolphin Square, SW1. Clubs: National Liberal, Royal Automobile, English-Speaking Union.

HUGH SMITH, Lt-Col Henry Owen, LVO 1976; General Staff Officer Grade 1, Ministry of Defence, since 1980; b 19 June 1937; s of Lt-Comdr Colin Hugh Smith and late Hon. Mrs C. Hugh Smith. Educ: Ampleforth; Magdalene Coll., Cambridge. BA Hons 1961. Commnd Royal Horse Guards, 1957; Blues and Royals, 1969; psc 1969; served Cyprus and Northern Ireland (wounded); Equerry in Waiting to The Duke of Edinburgh, 1974–76; CO The Blues and Royals, 1978–80. Recreations: riding, sailing. Address: c/o National Westminster Bank, 1 Princes Street, EC2P 2AH. Clubs: Boodle's, Pratt's, Cavalry and Guards; Royal Yacht Squadron.

HUGHES, family name of Barons Hughes and Cledwyn of Penrhos.

HUGHES, Baron, cr 1961, of Hawkhill (Life Peer); William Hughes, PC 1970; CBE 1956 (OBE 1942); DL; President: Scottish Federation of Housing Associations, since 1975; Scottish Association for Mental Health, since 1975; Member, Council of Europe and Western European Union, since 1976; company director; b 22 Jan. 1911; e s of late Joseph and Margaret Hughes; m 1951, Christian Clacher, o c of late James and Sophia Gordon; two d. Educ: Balfour Street Public Sch., Dundee; Dundee Technical Coll. ARP Controller Dundee, 1939–43; Armed Forces, 1943–46; Commissioned RAOC, 1944; demobilised as Capt., 1946. Hon. City Treasurer, Dundee, 1946–47; Chairman, Eastern Regional Hospital Board, Scotland, 1948–60; Lord Provost of Dundee and HM Lieut of County of City of Dundee, 1954–60; Member: Dundee Town Council, 1933–36 and 1937–61; Court of St Andrews Univ., 1954–63; Council of Queen's Coll., Dundee, 1954–63; Cttee on Civil Juries, 1958–59; Cttee to Enquire into Registration of Title to Land in Scotland, 1960–62; North of Scotland Hydro-Electric Bd, 1957–64; Scottish Transport Council, 1960–64; Chairman: Glenrothes Develt Corp., 1960–64; East Kilbride Develt Corp., 1975–82; Royal Commn on Legal Services in Scotland, 1976–80. Jt Parly Under-Sec. of State for Scotland, 1964–69; Minister of State for Scotland, 1969–70, 1974–75. Contested (Lab) E Perthshire, 1945 and 1950. Fellow, Inst. of Dirs. Hon. LLD St Andrews, 1960. JP County and City of Dundee, 1943–76; DL Dundee 1960. Chevalier, Légion d'Honneur, 1958. Recreation: gardening. Address: The Stables, Ross, Comrie, Perthshire PH6 2JU. T: Comrie 70557.

HUGHES, Andrew Anderson, MA; Director, Gilmour and Dean Holdings plc, since 1980; b 27 Dec. 1915; s of Alexander and Euphemia Hughes; m 1st, 1944, Dorothy Murdoch (marr. diss. 1946); 2nd, 1946, Margaret Dorothy Aikman; no c. Educ: Waid Academy; St Andrews Univ.; Marburg Univ.; Emmanuel Coll., Cambridge. Colonial Administrative Service, 1939; Private Sec. to Governor, Gold Coast, 1940–42; Colonial Office, 1946; Dept of Health for Scotland, 1947; Asst Sec., 1956; Under-Sec., 1964; Under-Sec., Scottish Development Dept, 1966–69; Man. Dir, Crudens Ltd, 1969–71; Chm., Grampian Construction Ltd, 1971; Director: Grampian Hldgs, 1973–84; Highland Craftpoint Ltd, 1979–85; Cairngorm Chairlift Co., 1981–83. Member: Scottish Tourist Bd, 1969–81; Scottish Council, CBI, 1976–82; Central Arbitration Cttee, 1977–85; Chm., Scottish Crafts Consultative Cttee, 1979–85; Mem., Crafts Council, 1981–85; Chm., Building and Estates Cttee, 1981–. Mem. Ct, Heriot-Watt Univ., 1981–. Recreation: golf. Address: 9 Palmerston Road, Edinburgh EH9 1TL. T: 031–667 2353. Clubs: Royal Commonwealth Society; New (Edinburgh).

HUGHES, Aneurin Rhys; Adviser to Director General for Information, Commission of the European Communities, 1977–80 and since 1985; b 11 Feb. 1937; s of William and Hilda Hughes; m 1964, Jill (née Salisbury); two s. Educ: University College of Wales,

Aberystwyth (BA). President, National Union of Students, 1962–64. Research in S America, 1964–66; HM Diplomatic Service, 1967–73: served, Singapore and Rome; Commission of the European Communities, Brussels, 1973–: Head of Division for Internal Coordination in Secretariat-General, 1973–77; Chef de Cabinet to Mr Ivor Richard, Comr responsible for Employment, Social Affairs and Educn, 1981–85. *Recreations:* squash, golf, music, hashing. *Address:* 200 rue de la Loi, 1040 Brussels, Belgium. *Clubs:* Travellers'; Cercle Gaulois (Belgium).

HUGHES, Maj.-Gen. Basil Perronet, CB 1955; CBE 1944; *b* 13 Jan. 1903; *s of late Rev.* E. B. A. Hughes; *m* 1932, Joan Marion Worthington, two *s*. *Educ:* Eton Coll.; RMA, Woolwich. Commissioned RFA 1923; Staff Coll., 1935–36; Directing Staff, Staff Coll., 1940. Served NW Frontier of India, 1930–31 (medal and clasp); Mohmand, 1933 (clasp); War of 1939–45 (star and despatches). Formerly: Hon. Col 2nd (London) Bn, Mobile Defence Corps; Hon. Colonel 571 LAA Regt (9th Battalion The Middx Regt DCO) RA, TA. ADC to the Queen, 1952–54; GOC 4 Anti-Aircraft Group, 1954; Maj.-Gen. RA (AA), War Office, 1955–58; retired, 1958. Controller, Royal Artillery Instn, 1958–75. Col Comdt RA 1961–68; Hon. Colonel: 5th Bn, The Middx Regt (DCO), TA, 1964–69; 10th Bn, The Queen's Regt (Mddx), T&AVR, 1970–71. *Publications:* British Smooth-Bore Artillery, 1969; The Bengal Horse Artillery 1800–1861, 1971; Firepower, 1974; Honour Titles of the Royal Artillery, 1978; Open Fire, 1983. *Address:* St Nicholas Close, Stour Row, near Shaftesbury, Dorset. *Club:* Leander.

HUGHES, Brodie; *see* Hughes, E. B. C.

HUGHES, Sir David (Collingwood), 14th Bt *cr* 1773; heraldic sculptor; Managing Director, Louis Lejeune Ltd, since 1978; *b* 29 Dec. 1936; *s* of Sir Richard Edgar Hughes, 13th Bt and Angela Lilian Adelaide Pell (*d* 1967); *S* father, 1970; *m* 1964, Rosemary Ann Pain, MA, LLB (Cantab), *d* of Rev. John Pain; four *s*. *Educ:* Oundle and Magdalene College, Cambridge (MA). National Service, RN, 1955–57. United Steel Cos Ltd, 1960–65; Unicam Instruments Ltd (subsequently Pye Unicam Ltd), export executive, 1965–70, E Europe manager, 1970–73. Builder, 1974–76. *Recreations:* shooting, fishing. *Heir:* *s* Thomas Collingwood Hughes, *b* 16 Feb. 1966. *Address:* The Berristead, Wilburton, Ely, Cambs. *T:* Ely 740770.

HUGHES, (David Evan) Peter, MA; Head of Science, Westminster School, since 1984; *b* 27 April 1932; *s* of late Evan Gwilliam Forrest-Hughes, OBE; *m* 1956, Iris (*née* Jenkins); one *s* two *d*. *Educ:* St Paul's Sch.; St John's Coll., Oxford (Gibbs Schol. in Chemistry; MA). National Service, 5 RHA, 1954. Assistant Master, Shrewsbury School, 1956; Head of Chemistry, 1958, Science, 1965; Nuffield Foundation, 1967–68; Second Master, Shrewsbury Sch., 1972; Headmaster, St Peter's Sch., York, 1980–84. *Publications:* Advanced Theoretical Chemistry (with M. J. Maloney), 1964; Chemical Energetics, 1967. *Recreations:* music, bridge, hill-walking. *Address:* 14 Barton Street, SW1P 3NE.

HUGHES, David Glyn; National Agent of the Labour Party, since 1979; *b* 1 March 1928; *s* of Richard and Miriam Hughes; *m* 1958, Mary Atkinson; one *d*. *Educ:* Darwin St Secondary Modern Sch. Apprentice, later fitter and turner, 1944–52; Labour Party Agent: Northwich, Bolton, Tonbridge, Portsmouth, 1952–69; Asst Regional Organiser, 1969–75, Regional Organiser, 1975–79, Northern Region. *Recreations:* gardening, walking. *Address:* 42 Langroyd Road, SW17. *T:* 01–672 2959. *Clubs:* Stella Maris Social (Life-Mem.), Usworth and District Workmen's (Washington, Tyne and Wear).

HUGHES, David John; writer; *b* 27 July 1930; *o s* of Gwilym Fielden Hughes and Edna Frances Hughes; *m* 1st, 1957, Mai Zetterling; 2nd, 1980, Elizabeth Westoll; one *s* one *d*. *Educ:* Eggar's Grammar Sch., Alton; King's College Sch., Wimbledon; Christ Church, Oxford (MA). Editorial Asst, London Magazine, 1953–55; Reader with Rupert Hart-Davis, 1956–60; Editor, Town magazine, 1960–61; script-writer and stills photographer of BBC documentaries and Scandinavian feature-films directed by Mai Zetterling, 1960–72; Editor, New Fiction Society, 1975–78, 1981–82. Asst Visiting Professor: Writers' Workshop, Univ. of Iowa, 1978–79; Univ. of Alabama, 1979; Vis. Assoc. Prof., Univ. of Houston, 1986. Film Critic, Sunday Times, 1982–83; Fiction Critic, Mail on Sunday, 1982–. *Publications: fiction:* A Feeling in the Air, 1957; Sealed with a Loving Kiss, 1958; The Horsehair Sofa, 1961; The Major, 1964; The Man Who Invented Tomorrow, 1968; Memories of Dying, 1976; A Genoese Fancy, 1979; The Imperial German Dinner Service, 1983; The Pork Butcher, 1984 (Welsh Arts Council Fiction Prize, 1984; W. H. Smith Literary Award, 1985); But for Bunter, 1985; (ed) Winter's Tales: New Series I, 1985; (ed with Giles Gordon) Best Short Stories, 1986; *non-fiction:* J. B. Priestley, an informal study, 1958; The Road to Stockholm (travel), 1964; The Seven Ages of England (cultural history), 1967; The Rosewater Revolution, 1971; Evergreens, 1976. *Address:* c/o Anthony Sheil Associates, 43 Doughty Street, WC1N 2LF. *Club:* Savile.

HUGHES, Prof. David Leslie, CBE 1977; PhD, FRCVS, DipBact; Professor of Veterinary Pathology, University of Liverpool, 1955–78, now Emeritus Professor; *b* 26 Oct. 1912; *s* of John and Eva Hughes; *m* 1st, 1938, Ann Marjorie Sparks (*d* 1971) 2nd, 1974, Jean Mavis, *yr d* of C. B. Saul. *Educ:* Wycliffe Coll., Stonehouse; Royal Veterinary Coll., London (MRCVS). PhD Nottingham, 1959. Agricultural Research Council Studentship in Animal Health, 1934–37 (DipBact London, 1936); Research Officer, Veterinary Laboratory, Min. of Agriculture, 1937–38; Lecturer in Bacteriology, Royal Veterinary College, 1938–40; Second Scientific Asst, Agricultural Research Council's Field Station, Compton, 1940–46; Head of Veterinary Science Div., Research Dept, Boots Pure Drug Co. Ltd, 1948–55; Dean of Faculty of Veterinary Science, University of Liverpool, 1965–68; Warden, Roscoe Hall, Univ. of Liverpool, 1965–72; Pro-Vice-Chancellor, Univ. of Liverpool, 1975–78. Mem., ARC, 1973–83. FRCVS 1952; Mem. Council, RCVS, 1964–76 (Pres. 1974–75; Sen. Vice Pres., 1975–76); Pres., British Veterinary Assoc., 1963–64. Governor, Howells Sch., Denbigh, 1974–84. *Publications:* scientific articles in Veterinary Record, British Veterinary Journal, Journal of Comparative Pathology, Journal of Hygiene, etc. *Recreations:* gardening, painting and travel. *Address:* Ty Maen, Llwyn-y-Rhos, Llanrhaeadr, Denbigh, Clwyd LL16 4NH. *T:* Llanynys 364.

HUGHES, David Morgan; His Honour Judge Morgan Hughes; a Circuit Judge, since Nov. 1972; *b* 20 Jan. 1926; *s* of late Rev. John Edward Hughes and Mrs Margaret Ellen Hughes; *m* 1956, Elizabeth Jane Roberts; one *s* two *d*. *Educ:* Beaumaris Grammar Sch.; LSE (LLB). Army, 1944–48: Captain, Royal Welch Fusiliers; attached 2nd Bn The Welch Regt; Burma, 1945–47. London Univ., 1948–51; Rockefeller Foundn Fellowship in Internat. Air Law, McGill Univ., 1951–52; called to Bar, Middle Temple, 1953; practised Wales and Chester Circuit; Dep. Chm., Caernarvonshire QS, 1970–71; a Recorder, Jan.-Nov. 1972; Dep. Chm., Agricultural Lands Tribunal, 1972. *Recreations:* tennis, cricket, gardening. *Address:* Bryn, Kelsall, Cheshire. *T:* Kelsall 51349.

HUGHES, Hon. Sir Davis, Kt 1975; Agent-General for New South Wales, in London, 1973–78; *b* 24 Nov. 1910; *m* 1940, Joan Philip Johnson; one *s* two *d*. *Educ:* Launceston High Sch., Tasmania; Phillip Smith Teachers' Coll., Hobart, Tas. Teacher, Tasmania, incl. Friends' Sch., Hobart, 1930–35; Master, Caulfield Grammar Sch., Melbourne, 1935–40. Served War, Sqdn Ldr, RAAF, Australia and overseas, 1940–45. Dep. Headmaster, Armidale Sch., Armidale, NSW, 1946–49; Mayor of Armidale, 1953–56. MLA, NSW,

1950–53 and 1956–65; Minister for Public Works, NSW, 1965–73. Rep., Derek Crouch Aust. Ltd, 1979–; Dir, Société Générale Australia Ltd, 1980–. Freeman: City of Armidale, NSW, 1965; City of London, 1975. *Recreations:* tennis, golf, fishing, racing. *Address:* 25 Bligh Street, Sydney, NSW 2000, Australia. *Clubs:* Union, Australasian Pioneers (Sydney)

HUGHES, Desmond; *see* Hughes, F. D.

HUGHES, Rev. Edward Marshall, MTh, PhD (London), Vicar of St Mary's, Dover, 1971–84; Chaplain to the Queen, 1973–83; *b* London, 11 Nov. 1913; *o s* of late Edward William Hughes, Newhouse, Mersham, Ashford, Kent, and Mabel Frances (*née* Faggetter); descendant of Edward Hughes, *b* 1719, of Little Swanton, Mersham; unmarried. *Educ:* City of London Sch.; King's Coll., London; Cuddesdon Coll., Oxford. Deacon, 1936, Priest, 1937, Canterbury; Curate, St Martin's, Canterbury, 1936–41; Chaplain RAFVR 1941 (invalided Oct. 1941); Curate Bearsted, Kent, 1941–46; Vicar of Woodnesborough, Kent, 1946–52; Chap. St Bartholomew's Hosp., Sandwich, 1947–52; Off. Chap. RAF Station, Sandwich, 1948–52; Warden of St Peter's Theological Coll., Jamaica, 1952–61; Canon Missioner of Jamaica, 1955–61; Examining Chap. to the Bp of Jamaica, 1953–61; Hon. Chap. Jamaica, RAFA, 1954–61; Mem. Board of Governors Nuttall Memorial Hospital, Kingston, 1956–61, and St Jago High Sch., Spanish Town, 1957–61; Visiting Lecturer, McGill Univ., Canada, 1957; Hon. Lecturer, Union Theological Seminary, Jamaica, 1957–58; Visiting Lecturer, Séminaire de Théologie, Haiti, 1959; Acting Rector, St Matthew's Church, Kingston, and Chap. Kingston Public Hospital, 1959–60; JP (St Andrew, Jamaica), 1959–63; Commissary to Bishop of Jamaica, 1968–. Fellow (Librarian, 1962–65), St Augustine's Coll., Canterbury (Central Coll. of the Anglican Communion), 1961–65; Hon. helper, RAF Benevolent Fund, for Kent, 1961–65, for London (Croydon), 1965–71, for Kent, 1971–; Divinity Master, VI Forms, The King's Sch., Canterbury, 1962–63; Officiating Chap., Canterbury Garrison, 1963–64; Vicar of St Augustine's, S Croydon, 1965–71. Proctor in Convocation, Dio. Canterbury, 1966–75. Examining Chaplain to Archbishop of Canterbury, 1967–76; Rural Dean of Dover, 1974–80; Hon. Chaplain: East and South Goodwin Lightships, 1979–85; Assoc. of Men of Kent and Kentish Men (of which his father was founder-member, 1897), 1979–. *Publications:* various papers on theological education overseas. *Recreations:* gardening, exercising the dogs, computering. *Address:* Woodlands, Sandwich Road, Woodnesborough, Sandwich, Kent CT13 0LZ. *T:* Sandwich 617098.

HUGHES, Prof. Sir Edward (Stuart Reginald), Kt 1977; CBE 1971; Chairman and Professor, Department of Surgery, Monash University, Alfred Hospital, 1973–84, now Emeritus Professor of Surgery; *b* 4 July 1919; *s* of Reginald Hawkins Hughes and Annie Grace Langford; *m* 1944, Alison Clare Lelean; two *s* two *d*. *Educ:* Melbourne C of E Grammar Sch.; Univ. of Melbourne. MB, BS 1943; MD 1945; MS 1946; FRCS 1946 (Hon. FRCS 1985); FRACS 1950. Resident Medical Officer, Royal Melbourne Hosp., 1943–45, Asst Surgeon 1950–53, Surgeon 1954–74; Surgeon, Alfred Hosp., 1973–84. Consultant Surgeon to Australian Army, 1976–82. Royal Australasian College of Surgeons: Mem. Council, 1967–78; Chm. Exec. Cttee, 1971–78; Sen. Vice-Pres., 1974–84; Pres., 1975–78. First Dir, Menzies Foundn for Health, Fitness and Physical Achievement, 1979–. Hon. FACS, Hon. FRCS(C), Hon. FRCSE, Hon. FRCSI; Hon. FPCS 1977. Sir Hugh Devine Medal, RACS, 1977. *Publications:* Surgery of the Anal Canal and Rectum, 1957; All about an Ileostomy, 1966, 3rd edn 1971; All about a Colostomy, 1970, 2nd edn 1977; Ano-Rectal Surgery, 1972; Colo-Rectal Surgery, 1983. *Recreations:* tennis, racing. *Address:* 24 Somers Avenue, Malvern, Victoria 3144, Australia. *T:* 20.7688. *Clubs:* Melbourne, Melbourne Cricket, Victoria Racing, Victoria Amateur Turf (Melbourne).

HUGHES, (Ernest) Brodie (Cobbett), FRCS; Professor of Neurosurgery, 1948–78, and Dean of the Faculty of Medicine and Dentistry, 1974–78, University of Birmingham; *b* 21 Sept. 1913; *o s* of E. T. C. Hughes, surgeon, and D. K. Cobbett, Richmond, Surrey; *m* 1971, Frances Wendy Alexander. *Educ:* Eastbourne Coll.; University Coll. and Hospital, London. MB, BS London 1937, FRCS 1939, ChM Birmingham 1949; resident appointments, UC Hospital, and at National Hospital for Nervous Diseases, Queen Square, London. After various appointments in neurosurgery was appointed Neurosurgeon, Birmingham United Hospitals, 1947. *Publications:* The Visual Fields, 1955; various publications in medical journals on neurosurgery and on perimetry and visual fields in particular. *Recreations:* playing the oboe, fly-fishing for trout; unsuccessful attempts to paint and draw in oils, water-colour, pen-and-ink and other media. *Address:* Fairfield House South, Saxmundham, Suffolk IP17 1AX. *T:* Saxmundham 2060. *Club:* Athenæum.

HUGHES, Air Vice-Marshal (Frederick) Desmond, CB 1972; CBE 1961; DSO 1945; DFC and 2 bars, 1941–43; AFC 1954; DL; *b* Belfast, 6 June 1919; *s* of late Fred C. Hughes, company dir, Donaghadee, Co. Down, and late Hilda (*née* Hunter), Ballymore, Co. Donegal; *m* 1941, Pamela, *d* of late Julius Harrison, composer and conductor; two *s* (and one *s* decd). *Educ:* Campbell Coll., Belfast; Pembroke Coll., Cambridge (MA). Joined RAF from Cambridge Univ. Air Sqdn, 1939; Battle of Britain, No. 264 Sqdn, 1940; night fighting ops in Britain and Mediterranean theatre, 1941–43; comd No. 604 Sqdn in Britain and France, 1944–45; granted perm. commn, 1946; served in Fighter Comd, 1946–53; Directing Staff, RAF Staff Coll., 1954–56; Personal Staff Off. to Chief of Air Staff, 1956–58; comd. RAF Stn Geilenkirchen, 1959–61; Dir of Air Staff Plans, Min. of Def., 1962–64; ADC to the Queen, 1963; Air Officer i/c Administration, HQ Flying Training Command, RAF, 1966–68; AOC, No 18 Group, RAF Coastal Command, and Air Officer, Scotland and N Ireland, 1968–70; Comdt, RAF Coll., Cranwell, 1970–72; SASO Near East Air Force, 1972–74, retired. Hon. Air Cdre, No 2503 RAuxAF Regt Sqdn, 1982–. Dir, Trident Trust, 1976–78. DL Lincoln 1983. *Recreations:* fishing, shooting, music. *Address:* c/o Midland Bank, Sleaford, Lincs. *Club:* Royal Air Force.

HUGHES, George; Chairman and Chief Executive: Hughes International Ltd, since 1970; Willowbrook World Wide Ltd, since 1971; Hampton Court Farms Ltd (formerly Castle Hughes Group), since 1975; Chairman, Hughes Technology Ltd, 1985; *b* 4 May 1937; *s* of Peter and Ann Hughes; *m* 1963, Janet; two *s*. *Educ:* Liverpool Collegiate (Sen. City Scholar; Open State Schol. with 3 distinctions); Gonville and Caius Coll., Cambridge (Open Scholar; MA Hons 1st Cl. German Mod. Lang. Tripos); Harvard Business Sch. (MBA 1968). Ski instructor, 1959; Banking, Paris, 1960; IBM, London, 1960–69 (Strategy Develt Man., 1968–69); Merchant Banking, London, 1969–70; Gp Man. Dir, Duple Gp Ltd, 1970–71. Mem., Mensa, 1961. Chm., Derbys CCC, 1976–77; Mem., TCCB, 1976–77. *Publications:* The Effective Use of Computers, 1968; Military and Business Strategy, 1968; papers on mobility: a basic human need; traffic congestion in capital cities; development as strategic choice; getting action and making things happen; integrated cattle development program; choosing the best way; scenario for the president; new towns; control; spare parts management; road to recovery; strategy for survival; all the milk and meat China needs. *Recreations:* cattle farming, historic buildings, shooting, soccer, tennis, squash. *Address:* Hampton Court Castle, Herefordshire HR6 0PN; Château de Beauchamps, Sarthe, France. *Clubs:* MCC, Carlton, Annabel's.

HUGHES, Prof. George Morgan; Professor of Zoology, Bristol University, 1965–85, now Emeritus; Head of Research Unit for Comparative Animal Respiration, since 1970;

b 17 March 1925; *s* of James Williams Hughes and Edith May Hughes; *m* 1954, Jean Rosemary, *d* of Rowland Wynne Frazier and Jessie Frazier; two *s* one *d*. *Educ*: Liverpool Collegiate Sch.; King's Coll., Cambridge (Scholar). Martin Thackeray Studentship, 1946–48, MA, PhD, ScD (Cantab); Frank Smart Prize, 1946. Cambridge Univ. Demonstrator, 1950–55, Lectr, 1955–65; successively Bye-Fellow, Research Fellow and Fellow of Magdalene Coll., Cambridge, 1949–65. Univ. of Bristol: Head of Dept of Zoology, 1965–70. Research Fellow, California Inst. of Technology, 1958–59; Visiting Lectr in Physiology, State Univ. of New York, at Buffalo, 1964; Visiting Professor: Duke Univ., 1969; Japan Society for the Promotion of Science, Kochi, Kyoto, Kyushu and Hokkaido Univs, 1974; Univ. of Regensburg, 1977; Univs of Bhagalpur and Bretagne Occidentale, 1979; Kuwait, 1983; Nairobi, 1985. Invited Prof., Nat. Inst. of Physiolog. Sciences, Okazaki, 1980. Mem., Internat. Cœlacanth Expdn, 1972. *Publications*: Comparative Physiology of Vertebrate Respiration, 1963; Physiology of Mammals and other Vertebrates (jt), 1965; (ed) several symposium vols; papers in Jl of Experimental Biology and other scientific jls, mainly on respiration of fishes. *Recreations*: travel, golf, photography; hockey for Cambridge Univ., 1945, and Wales, 1952–53. *Address*: 11 Lodge Drive, Long Ashton, Bristol BS18 9JF. *T*: Bristol 393402.

HUGHES, Glyn Tegai, MA, PhD; Warden of Gregynog, University of Wales, since 1964; *b* 18 Jan. 1923; *s* of Rev. John Hughes and Keturah Hughes; *m* 1957, Margaret Vera Herbert, Brisbane, Qld; two *s*. *Educ*: Newtown and Towyn County Sch.; Liverpool Institute; Manchester Grammar Sch.; Corpus Christi Coll., Cambridge (Schol., MA, PhD). Served War, Royal Welch Fusiliers, 1942–46 (Major). Lector in English, Univ. of Basel, 1951–53; Lectr in Comparative Literary Studies, Univ. of Manchester, 1953–64, and Tutor to Faculty of Arts, 1961–64. Contested (L) Denbigh Div., elections 1950, 1955 and 1959. Mem., Welsh Arts Council, 1967–76; Nat. Governor for Wales, BBC, and Chm., Broadcasting Council for Wales, 1971–79; Member: Bd, Channel Four Television Co., 1980–87; Welsh Fourth TV Channel Auth., 1981–87; Vice-Pres., N Wales Arts Assoc.; Chm., Undeb Cymru Fydd, 1968–70. *Publications*: Eichendorffs Taugenichts, 1961; Romantic German Literature, 1979; (ed) Life of Thomas Olivers, 1979; Williams Pantycelyn, 1983; articles in learned journals and Welsh language periodicals. *Recreation*: book-collecting. *Address*: Gregynog, Newtown, Powys. *T*: Tregynon 295.

HUGHES, (Harold) Paul; Pension Fund Consultant British Broadcasting Corporation, since 1984; Director: Kleinwort Benson Farmland Trust (Managers) Ltd, since 1976; *b* 16 Oct. 1926; *o s* of Edmund and Mabel Hughes; *m* 1955, Beryl Winifred Runacres; one *s* one *d*. *Educ*: Stand Grammar Sch., Whitefield, near Manchester. Certified Accountant. Westminster Bank Ltd, 1942–45; Royal Marines and Royal Navy, 1945–49; Arthur Guinness Son & Co. Ltd, 1950–58; British Broadcasting Corporation: Sen. Accountant, 1958–61; Asst Chief Accountant, Finance, 1961–69; Chief Accountant, Television, 1969–71; Dir of Finance, 1971–84; Chm., BBC Enterprises Ltd, 1979–82; Chm., Visnews, 1984–85. *Recreations*: opera, gardening. *Address*: 26 Downside Road, Guildford, Surrey. *T*: Guildford 69166.

HUGHES, Harold Victor; Principal, Royal Agricultural College, Cirencester, since 1978; *b* 2 Feb. 1926; *s* of Thomas Brindley Hughes and Hilda Hughes (*née* Williams). *Educ*: Tenby County Grammar Sch.; UCW, Aberystwyth. Lectr, Glamorgan Training Centre, Pencoed, 1947–49; Crop Husbandry Adv. Officer, W Midland Province, Nat. Agricultural Adv. Service, 1950; Lectr in Agric., RAC, 1950–54; Vice Principal, Brooksby Agricultural Coll., Leics, 1954–60; Royal Agricultural College: Farms Dir and Principal Lectr in Farm Management, 1960–76; Vice Principal and Farms Dir, 1976–78. *Publications*: articles in learned jls and agric. press. *Recreations*: shooting, rugby. *Address*: Royal Agricultural College, Cirencester, Glos. *T*: Cirencester 2531. *Club*: Farmers'.

HUGHES, Rev. Henry Trevor, MA; *b* 27 Feb. 1910; *s* of late Rev. Dr H. Maldwyn Hughes; *m* 1946, Elizabeth Catherine Williams; one *s* one *d*. *Educ*: Perse Sch., Cambridge. National Provincial Bank, 1926–31; Wesley House, Cambridge, 1932–35 (2nd Class Hons Theol Tripos, 1935); Chaplain, Culford Sch., Bury St Edmunds, 1935–41; Chaplain, Royal Air Force, 1941–45 (despatches). Asst Minister, Central Hall, Westminster, 1945–46; Vice-Principal and Chaplain, Westminster College of Education, 1946–53, Principal, 1953–69; Minister, Attleborough Methodist Church, 1969–75. Incorporated MA, Oxford Univ. through Lincoln Coll., 1959. First Methodist Select Preacher, University of Oxford, 1965; Methodist representative, British Council of Churches Preachers' Exchange with the USA, 1964. *Publications*: Prophetic Prayer, 1947; Teaching the Bible to Seniors, 1948; Teaching the Bible to Juniors, 1949; Why We Believe, 1950; The Piety of Jeremy Taylor, 1960; Faith and Life, 1962; Life Worth Living, 1965; A Progress of Pilgrims, 1979; pamphlets: Letters to a Christian, 1947; Teaching the Bible Today, 1957; contributor to London Quarterly Review. *Recreation*: painting. *Address*: 10 Park Close, Hethersett, Norfolk NR9 3EW. *T*: Norwich 811038.

HUGHES, Herbert Delauney, MA; Principal of Ruskin College, Oxford, 1950–79; *b* 7 Sept. 1914; *s* of late Arthur Percy Hughes, BSc, and late Maggie Ellen Hughes; *m* 1937, Beryl Parker. *Educ*: Cheadle Hulme Sch.; Balliol Coll., Oxford (State and County Major Scholar). BA (Hons) in Modern History, 1936. Served War of 1939–45, with 6 Field Regt Royal Artillery. Asst Sec., New Fabian Research Bureau, 1937–39; Organising Sec., Fabian Soc., 1939–46; Mem. Exec. Fabian Soc., 1946– (Vice-Chm. 1950–52, 1958–59, Chm. 1959–60, Vice-Pres., 1971–); MP (Lab) Wolverhampton (West), 1945–50; Parliamentary Private Sec. to Minister of Education, 1945–47; to Financial Sec. to War Office, 1948–50; Mem. Lambeth Borough Council, 1937–42. Governor of Educational Foundation for Visual Aids, 1948–56. Member: Civil Service Arbitration Tribunal, 1955–81; Commonwealth Scholarship Commn, 1968–74; Cttee on Adult Educn, 1969–73. Vice-Pres., Workers' Educational Assoc., 1958–67, Dep. Pres., 1968–71, Pres., 1971–81, Hon. Treasurer, 1981–; Chm. Management Cttee, Adult Literacy Resource Agency, 1975–78; Mem., Adv. Council on Adult and Continuing Educn, 1978–83. Hon. Fellow Sheffield Polytechnic, 1979. *Publications*: (part author) Democratic Sweden, 1937, Anderson's Prisoners, 1940, Six Studies in Czechoslovakia, 1947. Advance in Education, 1947; Towards a Classless Society, 1947; A Socialist Education Policy, 1955; The Settlement of Disputes in The Public Service, 1968; (jt author) Planning for Education in 1980, 1970; (part author) Education Beyond School, 1980. *Recreations*: walking and foreign travel. *Address*: Crossways, Mill Street, Islip, Oxford. *T*: Kidlington 6935.

HUGHES, Howard; Managing Partner, Price Waterhouse UK, since 1985; *b* 4 March 1938; *s* of Charles William Hughes and Ethel May Hughes (*née* Howard); *m* 1964, Joy Margaret Pilmore-Bedford (*d* 1984); two *s* one *d*. *Educ*: Rydal School. FCA. Articled Bryce Hanmer & Co., Liverpool, 1955; joined Price Waterhouse, London, 1960: Partner, 1970; Mem., Policy Cttee, 1979; Dir. London Office, 1982. Auditor, Duchy of Cornwall, 1983–. *Recreations*: golf, music. *Address*: Witham, Woodland Rise, Seal, near Sevenoaks, Kent. *T*: Sevenoaks 61161. *Clubs*: Carlton; Wildernesse Golf (Sevenoaks).

HUGHES, Sir Jack (William), Kt 1980; chartered surveyor; Director: South Bank Estates, since 1960; Brighton Marina Co. (Representative, Brighton Corporation), since 1974; TR Property Investment Trust, since 1982; Property and Reversionary Investment, since 1982; *b* 26 Sept. 1916; 2nd *s* of George William Hughes and Isabel Hughes,

Maidstone, Kent; *m* 1939, Marie-Theresa (Slade School scholar), *d* of Graham Parmley Thompson. *Educ*: Maidstone Grammar Sch.; Univ. of London. BSc (Est. Man.); FRICS. Served with Special Duties Br., RAF, 1940–46; demobilised Squadron Leader. A Sen. Partner, Jones, Lang, Wootton, 1949–76, Consultant, 1976–86. Chairman: Bracknell Develt Corp., 1971–82; Property Adv. Gp, DoE, 1978–82; Director: URPT, 1961–86; MEPC, 1971–86; Housing Corporation (1974) Ltd, 1974–78; BR Property Bd, 1976–86; BR Investment Co., 1981–84; Mem. Cttee, Mercantile Credit Gp Property Div.; Mem. Cttee of Management, Charities Property Unit Trust, 1967–74; Chm., South Hill Park Arts Centre Trust, 1972–79; Member: Adv. Gp to DoE on Commercial Property Develt, 1974–78; DoE Working Party on Housing Tenure, 1976–77. Trustee, New Towns Pension Fund, 1975–82. Freeman, City of London, 1959–; Liveryman, Painter Stainers Guild, 1960–. FRSA. *Publications*: (jtly) Town and Country Planning Act 1949 (RICS); (Chm. of RICS Cttee) The Land Problem: a fresh approach; techn. articles on property investment, develt and finance. *Recreations*: golf, travel, reading. *Address*: Flat 11, 102 Rochester Row, SW1. *Clubs*: Carlton, Royal Air Force, Buck's.

HUGHES, James Ernest, PhD; FEng 1981; Director, Johnson Matthey PLC, retired; *b* 3 Nov. 1927; *s* of Herbert Thomas Hughes and Bessie Beatrice Hughes; *m* 1950, Hazel Aveline (*née* Louguet-Layton); three *d*. *Educ*: Spring Grove Sch.; Imperial Coll., London Univ., (BSc, ARSM (Bessemer Medalist); DIC); PhD London 1952. FIM, MIMM. Associated Electrical Industries, 1952–63; Johnson Matthey PLC, 1963–85, Man. Dir and Chief Exec., 1983–84. Vis. Professor, Univ. of Sussex, 1974–80. President: Inst. of Metals, 1972–73; Metals Soc., 1981–82; Instn of Metallurgists, 1982–83. FRSA 1978. *Publications*: scientific papers in learned jls. *Recreations*: antiques, music, gardening. *Address*: Old Allens, Allens Lane, Plaxtol, near Sevenoaks, Kent.

HUGHES, John; *see* Hughes, R. J.

HUGHES, Prof. John, PhD; Director, Parke-Davis Research Unit, Addenbrooke's, Cambridge, since 1983; Senior Research Fellow, Wolfson College, University of Cambridge, since 1983; Professor of Pharmacological Biochemistry, Department of Biochemistry, Imperial College of Science and Technology, University of London, 1979–82, Visiting Professor since 1983; *b* 6 Jan. 1942; *s* of Joseph and Edith Hughes; *m* 1967, Madelaine Carol Jennings (marr. diss. 1981); one *d*; and one *d* by Julie Pinnington-Hughes. *Educ*: Mitcham County Grammar Sch. for Boys; Chelsea Coll., London (BSc); Inst. of Basic Med. Sciences, London (PhD). Res. Fellow, Yale Univ. Med. Sch., 1967–69; Univ. of Aberdeen: Lectr in Pharmacology, 1969–77; Dep.-Dir, Drug Res. Unit, 1973–77; Reader in Pharmacol Biochemistry, Imperial Coll. of Science and Technol., 1977–79. Gaddum Lectr and Medal, British Parmacol Soc., 1982. Mem., Royal Acad. of Medicine, Belgium, 1983. Dr *hc* Univ. of Liège, 1978. Lasker Prize, Albert and Mary Lasker Foundn, NY, 1978; W. Feldberg Foundn Award, 1981; Lucien Dautrebande Prize, Fondation de Pathophysiologie, Belgium, 1983. *Publications*: Centrally Acting Peptides, 1978; Opioids Past, Present and Future, 1984; articles in Nature, Science, Brit. Jl Pharmacol., and Brain Res. *Recreations*: dogs, gardening. *Address*: Parke-Davis Research Unit, Addenbrooke's Hospital, Hills Road, Cambridge CB2 2QB. *T*: Cambridge 210929.

HUGHES, Very Rev. John Chester; Vicar of Bringhurst with Great Easton and Drayton, since 1978; *b* 20 Feb. 1924; *m* 1950, Sybil Lewis McClelland; three *s* two *d* (and one *s* decd). *Educ*: Dulwich Coll.; St John's Coll., Durham. Curate of Westcliffe-on-Sea, Essex, 1950–53; Succentor of Chelmsford Cathedral, 1953–55; Vicar of St Barnabas, Leicester, 1955–61; Vicar of Croxton Kerrial with Branston-by-Belvoir, 1961–63; Provost of Leicester, 1963–78. ChStJ 1974. *Address*: The Vicarage, Great Easton, Market Harborough, Leics LE16 8SX. *T*: Rockingham 770279.

HUGHES, John Dennis; Principal, Ruskin College, Oxford, since 1979 (Tutor in Economics and Industrial Relations, 1957–70, and Vice Principal, 1970–79); *b* 28 Jan. 1927; *s* of John (Ben) Hughes and Gwendoline Hughes; *m* 1949, Violet (*née* Henderson); four *d*. *Educ*: Westminster City Sch.; Lincoln Coll., Oxford (MA). Lieut, RAEC, 1949–50. Extramural Tutor, Univs of Hull and Sheffield, 1950–57. Dir, Trade Union Res. Unit, 1970–; Dep. Chm., Price Commn, 1977–79. Member: Industrial Develt Adv. Bd, 1975–79; Nat. Consumer Council, 1982–. Governor, London Business School. Mem. Council, St George's House, 1978–83; Trustee, Merchant Navy and Airline Officers Assoc., 1981–. *Publications*: Trade Union Structure and Government, 1968; (with R. Moore) A Special Case? Social Justice and the Miners, 1972; (with H. Pollins) Trade Unions in Great Britain, 1973; Industrial Restructuring: some manpower aspects, 1976; Britain in Crisis, 1981; Fabian Soc. pamphlets. *Recreation*: cycling. *Address*: Rookery Cottage, Stoke Place, Old Headington, Oxford. *T*: Oxford 63076.

HUGHES, John Richard Poulton; DL; County Clerk and Chief Executive, Staffordshire County Council, and Clerk to the Lieutenancy, 1978–83; *b* 21 Oct. 1920; *s* of Rev. John Evan Hughes and Mary Grace Hughes; *m* 1943, Mary Margaret, *e d* of Thomas Francis Thomas; one *s*. *Educ*: Bromsgrove Sch.; LLB Hons London; DPA; LMRTPI. Solicitor. Served War, RN and RNVR, 1940–46; discharged with rank of Lieut, RNVR. Articled in private practice, 1937–40; Asst Solicitor: West Bromwich County Borough Council, 1947–48; Surrey CC, 1948–50; Staffs County Council: Sen. Asst Solicitor, subseq. Chief Asst Solicitor, and Dep. Clerk, 1950–74; Dir of Admin, 1974–78; Sec., Staffs Probation and After Care Cttee, 1978–. Sec., Staffs Historic Bldgs Trust, 1983–. DL Staffs, 1979. *Recreations*: forestry, antiques restoration, sailing, fishing. *Address*: Brookside, Milford, near Stafford. *T*: Stafford 661005; Tyn Siglen, Cynwyd, Clwyd.
See also Sir T. P. Hughes.

HUGHES, Rt. Rev. John Richard Worthington P.; *see* Poole Hughes.

HUGHES, Rt. Rev. John Taylor, CBE 1975; an Assistant Bishop, Diocese of Southwark, since 1986; *b* 12 April 1908; *s* of Robert Edward and Annie Hughes. *Educ*: Castle Hill Sch., Ealing; Uxbridge County Sch.; Bede Coll., University of Durham (BA 1931, MA 1935). Ordained 1931; Asst Chaplain and Tutor, Bede Coll., Durham, 1931–34; Lecturer, Bede Coll., 1934–35; Curate, St John's, Shildon, Co. Durham, 1934–37; Vicar, St James, West Hartlepool, 1937–48; Canon Residentiary and Missioner of Southwark Cathedral and Warden of Diocesan Retreat House, Southwark, 1948–56; Bishop Suffragan of Croydon, 1956–77; Archdeacon of Croydon, 1967–77; Bishop to the Forces, 1966–75; an Asst Bishop, Diocese of Canterbury, 1977–86. *Recreations*: music, reading. *Address*: The Hospital of the Holy Trinity, North End, Croydon CR0 1UB. *T*: 01-686 8313.

HUGHES, Prof. Leslie Ernest, FRCS, FRACS; Professor of Surgery, University of Wales College of Medicine (formerly Welsh National School of Medicine), since 1971; *b* 12 Aug. 1932; *s* of Charles Joseph and Vera Hughes; *m* 1955, Marian Castle; two *s* two *d*. *Educ*: Parramatta High Sch.; Sydney Univ. MB, BS (Sydney); DS (Queensland), 1975; FRCS, 1959; FRACS, 1959. Reader in Surgery, Univ. of Queensland, 1965–71. Hunterian Prof., RCS, 1986. Eleanor Roosevelt Internat. Cancer Fellow, 1970. Audio-visual Aid Merit Award, Assoc. of Surgeons of GB and Ireland, 1983, 1986. *Publications*: numerous papers in medical jls, chiefly on immune aspects of cancer, and diseases of the colon. *Recreation*: music. *Address*: Department of Surgery, University Hospital of Wales, Heath Park, Cardiff CF4 4XW. *T*: Cardiff 755944.

HUGHES, Mark; *see* Hughes, W. M.

HUGHES, Nigel Howard; Director, Royal Signals and Radar Establishment, Malvern, since 1986; *b* 11 Aug. 1937; *s* of late William Howard Hughes and of Florence Hughes (*née* Crawshaw); *m* 1962, Margaret Ann Fairmaner; three *d*. *Educ:* St Paul's Sch.; Queen's Coll., Oxford (MA). CEng, FIMechE. Pilot Officer, RAF, 1956–58. RAE, Bedford, 1961–73; Head of Radio and Navigation Div., 1973–77, Head of Flight Systems Dept, 1977–80, RAE, Farnborough; MoD Central Staffs, 1980–82; Asst Chief Scientific Advr (Projects), MoD, 1982–84; Dep. Chief Scientific Advr, MoD, 1985–86. *Recreations:* Rolls Royce enthusiast; model engineering, amateur radio. *Address:* Royal Signals and Radar Establishment, St Andrews Road, Great Malvern, Worcs WR14 3PS; Landford, 2 Dunmow Hill, Fleet, Aldershot, Hants GU13 9AN.

HUGHES, Paul; *see* Hughes, H. P.

HUGHES, Peter; *see* Hughes, D. E. P.

HUGHES, Philip Arthur Booley, CBE 1982; artist; Chairman, Logica plc, since 1972; *s* of Leslie Booley Hughes and Elizabeth Alice Hughes (*née* Whyte); *m* 1964, Psiche Maria Anna Claudia Bertini; two *d* and two step-*d*. *Educ:* Bedford Sch.; Clare Coll., Cambridge (BA). Engineer, Shell Internat. Petroleum Co., 1957–61; Computer Consultant, SCICON Ltd (formerly CEIR), 1961–69; Co-Founder, Logica, 1969; Man. Dir, Logica Ltd, 1969–72. Vis. Prof., UCL, 1981–. Member: SERC, 1981–85; Nat. Electronics Council, 1981–. Governor, Technical Change Centre, 1980–. Exhibn of paintings with Beryl Bainbridge, Monks Gall., Sussex, 1972; exhibited: Contemp. British Painting, Madrid, 1983; Contemp. Painters, Ridgeway Exhibn Museum and Art Gall., Swindon, 1986; one-man exhibitions: Parkway Focus Gall., London, 1976; Angela Flowers Gall., London, 1977; Gal. Cance Manguin, Vaucluse, 1979, 1985; Francis Kyle Gall., London, 1979, 1982, 1984. Companion of Operational Research, 1985. DUniv Stirling, 1985. *Publications:* articles in nat. press and learned jls on management scis and computing.

HUGHES, Major Richard Charles, MBE 1951; TD 1945; Director, Federation of Commodity Associations, 1973–78; *b* 24 Dec. 1915; *s* of late Frank Pemberton Hughes and Minnie Hughes, Northwich. *Educ:* Wrekin Coll., Wellington, Telford. TA commn, 4/5th (E of C) Cheshire Regt, 1935; regular commn, 22nd (Cheshire) Regt, 1939. Served War of 1939–45: 2 i/c 5th, 2nd and 1st Bns 22nd (Cheshire) Regt. Palestine, 1945–47; S/Captain MS and DAAG Western Comd, 1948–51; Korea, 1954; GSO2 Sch. of Infantry, 1955–56; Sec. of Sch. of Inf. Beagles, 1955–56; retd pay, 1958. Apptd Sec. to Sugar Assoc. of London, British Sugar Refiners Assoc. and Refined Sugar Assoc., 1958; formed British Sugar Bureau and apptd Sec., 1964–66. Hon. Treas., W Kensington Environment Cttee, 1974–75; Mem. Barons Keep Management Cttee, 1975. Member: City Liaison Cttee, Bank of England and City EEC Cttee, 1975; City Adv. Panel to City Univ., and Adviser to City of London Polytechnic, 1975; City Communications Consultative Gp, 1976. *Recreations:* travel, sailing, antiques. *Address:* 8 Barons Keep, Barons Court, W14 9AT. *T:* 01–603 0429. *Club:* Hurlingham.

HUGHES, Robert; MP (Lab) Aberdeen North since 1970; *b* Pittenweem, Fife, 3 Jan. 1932; *m* 1957, Ina Margaret Miller; two *s* three *d*. *Educ:* Robert Gordon's Coll., Aberdeen; Benoni High Sch., Transvaal; Pietermaritzburg Techn. Coll., Natal. Emigrated S Africa, 1947, returned UK, 1954. Engrg apprentice, S African Rubber Co., Natal; Chief Draughtsman, C. F. Wilson & Co. (1932) Ltd, Aberdeen, until 1970. Mem., Aberdeen Town Council, 1962–70; Convener: Health and Welfare Cttee, 1963–68; Social Work Cttee, 1969–70. Mem., AEU, 1952–. Contested (Lab) North Angus and Mearns, 1959. Member: Standing Cttee on Immigration Bill, 1971; Select Cttee, Scottish Affairs, 1971; introd. Divorce (Scotland) Bill 1971 (failed owing to lack of time); Parly Under-Sec. of State, Scottish Office, 1974–75; sponsored (as Private Member's Bill) Rating (Disabled Persons) Act 1978; Principal Opposition Spokesman: on agriculture, 1983–; on transport, 1985– (Jun. Opp. Spokesman, 1981–83); Mem., PLP Shadow Cabinet, 1985–. Chm., Aberdeen City Labour Party, 1961–69. Vice-Chm., Tribune Gp, 1984–. Founder Mem. and Aberdeen Chm., Campaign for Nuclear Disarmament; Vice-Chm., 1975–76, Chm., 1976–, Anti-Apartheid Movement; Member: Gen. Med. Council, 1976–79; Movement for Colonial Freedom, 1955– (Chm. Southern Africa Cttee); Scottish Poverty Action Group; Aberdeen Trades Council and Exec. Cttee, 1957–69; Labour Party League of Youth, 1954–57. *Recreation:* golf.

HUGHES, (Robert) John; journalist; syndicated colomnist and television commentator; *b* Neath, S Wales, 28 April 1930; *s* of Evan John Hughes and Dellis May Hughes (*née* Williams); *m* 1955, Vera Elizabeth Pockman; one *s* one *d*. *Educ:* Stationers' Company's Sch., London. Reporter, sub-editor, corresp. for miscellaneous London and S African newspapers and news agencies (Natal Mercury, Durban; Daily Mirror, Daily Express, Reuter, London News Agency), 1946–54; joined The Christian Science Monitor, Boston, USA, 1954: Africa Corresp., 1955–61; Asst Foreign Editor, 1962–64; Far East Corresp., 1964–70; Man. Editor, 1970; Editor, 1970–76; Editor and Manager, 1976–79; Pres. and Publisher, Hughes Newspapers Inc., USA, 1979–81, 1984–85; Associate Dir, US Information Agency, 1981–82; Dir, Voice of America, 1982; Asst Sec. of State for Public Affairs, USA, 1982–84. Nieman Fellow, Harvard Univ., 1961–62. Pres., Amer. Soc. of Newspaper Editors, 1978–79. Pulitzer Prize for Internat. Reporting, 1967; Overseas Press Club of America award for best daily newspaper or wire service reporting from abroad, 1970; Sigma Delta Chi's Yankee Quill Award, 1977. Hon. LLD Colby Coll., 1978. *Publications:* The New Face of Africa, 1961; Indonesian Upheaval (UK as The End of Sukarno), 1967; articles in magazines and encyclopaedias. *Recreations:* reading, walking, raising Labrador retrievers. *Address:* Box 1053, Orleans, Mass 02653, USA. *T:* (617) 255–3133. *Clubs:* Foreign Correspondents', Hong Kong Country (Hong Kong); Overseas Press (New York); Harvard (Boston); Army and Navy (Washington).

HUGHES, Robert Studley Forrest; Senior Writer (Art Critic), Time Magazine, New York, since 1970; *b* Sydney, Aust., 28 July 1938; *s* of Geoffrey E. F. Hughes and Margaret Sealey Vidal; *m* (marr. diss. 1981); one *s*; *m* 1981, Victoria Whistler. *Educ:* St Ignatius' Coll., Riverview, Sydney; Sydney Univ. (architecture course, unfinished). Contributed articles on art to The Nation and The Observer, Sydney, 1958–62; to Europe, 1964, living in Italy until 1966, when moved to London; freelancing for Sunday Times, BBC and other publications/instns, 1966–70. TV credits include: Landscape with Figures, ten-part series on Australian art for ABC, Australia; Caravaggio, Rubens and Bernini, for BBC, 1976–77; The Shock of the New, eight-part series for BBC, 1980. Hon. Dr Fine Arts, Sch. of Visual Arts, NY, 1982. *Publications:* The Art of Australia, 1966; Heaven and Hell in Western Art, 1969; The Shock of the New (BBC publication), 1980. *Recreations:* gardening, shooting, river and sea fishing, cooking. *Address:* 143 Prince Street, New York, NY 10012, USA.

HUGHES, Air Marshal Sir Rochford; *see* Hughes, Air Marshal Sir S. W. R.

HUGHES, Ronald Frederick, CEng, FICE; Director of Civil Engineering Services, Property Services Agency, since 1983; *b* 21 Oct. 1927; *s* of Harry Frederick and Kate Hughes; *m* 1957, Cecilia Patricia, *d* of Maurice Nunis, MCS, State Treasurer, Malaya, and Scholastica Nunis; two *s* one *d*. *Educ:* Birmingham Central Technical College; Bradford College of Technology. Articled pupil, Cyril Boucher and Partners, 1943; Royal Engineers Engineering Cadet, 1946; commissioned RE, 1950; service in Malaya, 1950–53. Res. Asst, BISRA, 1954; Civil Engineer, H. W. Evans & Co. Ltd, Malaya, 1955, Man. Dir, 1958; War Office, 1959; Head of War Office Works Group, Singapore, 1963; Works Adviser to C-in-C, FARELF, 1964; District Civil Engineer, Malaya, 1966; Regional Site Control Officer, Midland Region, PSA, 1969; Principal Engineer, Post Office Services, 1970; Area Works Officer, PSA Birmingham, 1977; Asst Dir of Civil Engineering Services, 1979. Dir, Construction Industry Computing Assoc., 1982–; Member: Standing Cttee for Structural Safety, 1985–; Maritime Bd, ICE, 1985–; Nat. Jt Consultative Cttee for Building, 1986–; Member Council: Construction Industry Res. and Inf. Assoc., 1984–; BSI, 1985. *Recreations:* squash, photography, music. *Address:* 9A The Street, West Horsley, Surrey. *T:* East Horsley 2182. *Club:* Effingham (Surrey).

HUGHES, Royston John; MP (Lab) Newport East, since 1983 (Newport, Gwent, 1966–83); *b* 9 June 1925; *s* of John Hughes, Coal Miner; *m* 1957, Florence Marion Appleyard; three *d*. *Educ:* Ruskin Coll., Oxford. Mem. Coventry City Council, 1962–66; various offices in Transport and General Workers' Union, 1959–66. PPS to Minister of Transport, 1974–75; Mem., Speaker's panel, 1982–84; opposition frontbench spokesman on Welsh affairs, 1984–. Chairman: PLP Sports Gp, 1974–83; PLP Steel Group, 1978–; Parly Gp, TGWU, 1979–82. Chm., Welsh Grand Cttee, 1982–84. *Recreations:* gardening, watching rugby and soccer. *Address:* 34 St Kingsmark Avenue, Chepstow, Gwent. *T:* 3266. *Clubs:* United Services Mess (Cardiff); Pontllanfraith Workingmen's Social.

HUGHES, Sean Francis; MP (Lab) Knowsley South, since 1983; *b* 8 May 1946; *s* of Francis and Mary Hughes; *m* 1985, Patricia Cunliffe, Rainhill, Merseyside. *Educ:* local primary and grammar schs; Liverpool Univ. (BA); Manchester Univ. (MA). Trainee Personnel Manager, Unilever, 1969; History Teacher, 1970–83, and Head of History Dept, 1972–83, Ruffwood Comprehensive Sch., Kirkby, Merseyside. An Opposition Whip, 1984–. *Recreations:* soccer, running, reading. *Address:* 150 Tarbock Road, Huyton, Merseyside L36 5TJ.

HUGHES, Prof. Sean Patrick Francis, MS; FRCS, FRCSEd, FRCSI, FRCSEd (Orth); George Harrison Law Professor of Orthopaedic Surgery, University of Edinburgh, since 1979; *b* 2 Dec. 1941; *s* of Patrick Joseph Hughes and Kathleen Ethel Hughes (*née* Bigg); *m* 1972, Felicity Mary (*née* Anderson); one *s* two *d*. *Educ:* Downside Sch.; St Mary's Hospital, Univ. of London (MB BS, MS). Senior Registrar in Orthopaedics, Middlesex and Royal National Orthopaedic Hosp., 1974–76; Research Fellow in Orthopaedics, Mayo Clinic, USA, 1975; Sen. Lectr, and Director Orthopaedic Unit, Royal Postgraduate Medical Sch., Hammersmith Hosp., 1977–79. Mem. Council, RCSE, 1984–. Fellow: Brit. Orthopaedic Assoc.; Royal Soc. Med.; Member: Orthopaedic Research Soc.; British Orth. Res. Soc.; Soc. Internat. de Chirurgie Orth. et de Traumatologie; World Orth. Concern. *Publications:* Astons Short Text Book of Orthopaedics, 2nd edn 1976, 3rd edn 1982; Basis and Practice of Orthopaedics, 1981; Basis and Practice of Traumatology, 1983; papers on blood flow and mineral exchange, bone scanning, antibiotics in bone, external fixation of fractures. *Recreations:* sailing, golf. *Address:* 9 Corrennie Gardens, Edinburgh EH10 6DG. *T:* 031–447 1443.

HUGHES, Shirley, (Mrs J. S. P. Vulliamy); free-lance author/illustrator; *b* 16 July 1927; *d* of Thomas James Hughes and Kathleen Dowling; *m* 1952, John Sebastian Papendiek Vulliamy; two *s* one *d*. *Educ:* West Kirby High Sch. for Girls; Liverpool Art Sch.; Ruskin Sch. of Art, Oxford. Illustrator/author; overseas edns or distribn in France, Spain, W Germany, Denmark, Holland, Sweden, Aust., NZ, Japan, USA, China and Canada. Lectures to Teacher Trng Colls, Colls of Further Educn, confs on children's lit. and to children in schs and libraries; overseas lectures incl. tours to Aust. and USA. Member: Cttee of Management, Soc. of Authors, 1983–; Public Lending Right Registrar's Adv. Cttee, 1984–; judges panel, Mother Goose Award (for new illustrators), 1981–85. Children's Rights Other Award, 1976; Kate Greenaway Award, 1978; Silver Pencil Award, Holland, 1980; Eleanor Farjeon Award for services to children's lit., 1984. *Publications:* illustrated about 200 books for children of all ages; written and illustrated: Lucy and Tom's Day, 1960, 2nd edn 1979; The Trouble with Jack, 1970, 2nd edn 1981; Sally's Secret, 1973, 3rd edn 1976; Lucy and Tom go to School, 1973, 4th edn 1983; Helpers, 1975, 2nd edn 1978; Lucy and Tom at the Seaside, 1976, 3rd edn 1982; Dogger, 1977, 4th edn 1980; It's Too Frightening for Me, 1977, 4th edn 1982; Moving Molly, 1978, 3rd edn 1981; Up and Up, 1979, 3rd edn 1983; Here Comes Charlie Moon, 1980, 3rd edn 1984; Lucy and Tom's Christmas, 1981; Alfie Gets in First, 1981, 2nd edn 1982; Charlie Moon and the Big Bonanza Bust-up, 1982, 2nd edn 1983; Alfie's Feet, 1982, 2nd edn 1984; Alfie Gives a Hand, 1983; An Evening at Alfie's, 1984; Lucy and Tom's abc, 1984; A Nursery Collection, 6 vols, 1985–86; Chips and Jessie, 1985. *Recreations:* looking at paintings, dressmaking, writing books for children.

HUGHES, Air Marshal Sir (Sidney Weetman) Rochford, KCB 1967 (CB 1964); CBE 1955 (OBE 1942); AFC 1947; Chairman, Mazda Motors (NZ); Director, First City Finance; *b* 25 Oct. 1914; *s* of late Capt. H. R. Hughes, Master Mariner, and late Mrs Hughes (*née* Brigham), Auckland, NZ; *m* 1942, Elizabeth, *d* of A. Duncum, Colombo, Ceylon; one *d*. *Educ:* Waitaki High School; Oamaru, NZ. Editorial Staff, NZ Herald, 1933–36; RNZ Air Force, 1937–38; RAF, Far East and Middle East, 1939–44 (despatches; Greek DFC); Chief Ops, USAF All Weather Centre, 1948–49; Air Min. and CO Farnborough, 1950–54; Imperial Defence Coll., 1955; CO RAF Jever, Germany, 1956–59; Air Mem. and Chm., Defence Res. Policy Staff, MoD, 1959–61; Air Officer Commanding No 19 Group, 1962–64; Dep. Controller Aircraft (RAF), Ministry of Aviation, 1964–66; Air Comdr, Far East Air Force, 1966–69, retd 1969. Air Adviser, Civil and Military, to Govt of Singapore, 1969–72; Comr, Northland Harbour Bd, 1974. Pres., NZ Nat. Children's Health Res. Foundn; Chm., Salvation Army Adv, Bd, Auckland. Livery Guild of Air Pilots and Air Navigators; FRAeS. *Recreations:* yachting, motoring, fishing. *Address:* Tirimoana, 14 Cliff Road, Torbay, Auckland, New Zealand. *Club:* Royal NZ Yacht Squadron.

HUGHES, Simon Henry Ward; MP (L) Southwark and Bermondsey, since Feb. 1983; Liberal Party Spokesman on the Environment, since 1983; barrister; *b* 17 May 1951, *s* of James Henry Annesley Hughes and Sylvia (Paddy) Hughes (*née* Ward). *Educ:* Llandaff Cathedral Sch., Cardiff; Christ Coll., Brecon; Selwyn Coll., Cambridge (BA 1973, MA 1978); Inns of Court Sch. of Law; Coll. of Europe, Bruges (Cert. in Higher European Studies, 1975). Trainee, EEC, Brussels, 1976; Trainee and Mem. Secretariat, Directorate and Commn on Human Rights, Council of Europe, Strasbourg, 1976–77. Called to the Bar, Inner Temple, 1974; in practice, 1978–. Jun. Counsel, Lib. Party application to European Commn on Human Rights, 1978–79; Chm., Lib. Party Adv. Panel on Home Affairs, 1981–83; Vice-Chm., Southwark Bermondsey Lib. Assoc., 1981–83. Jt Pres., British Youth Council, 1983–84. Pres., Nat. League of Young Liberals, 1986– (Vice-Pres., 1983–86, Mem. 1973–78); Vice-Pres., Union of Liberal Students, 1983– (Mem., 1970–73); Vice-Chm., Parly Youth Affairs Lobby, 1984–. Member: the Christian Church; Gen. Synod of Church of England, 1984–85; Assoc. of Liberal Lawyers, 1977–85; Steering Cttee, Campaign for Fair Votes, 1983–; Southwark Area Youth Cttee; Council of Management, Cambridge Univ. Mission, Bermondsey; Amnesty Internat.; NCCL.

Publications: (jtly) Human Rights in Western Europe; the next 30 years, 1981; (jtly) The Prosecutorial Process in England and Wales, 1981. *Recreations:* music, discotheques and good parties, history, sport, theatre, the countryside and open air, travel, spending time with family and friends. *Address:* House of Commons, SW1A 0AA. *T:* 01–219 6256; 6 Lynton Road, Bermondsey, SE1 5QR. *T:* 01–231 3745.

HUGHES, Stephen Skipsey; Member (Lab) Durham, European Parliament, since 1984; *b* 19 Aug. 1952; *m;* one *s* twin *d. Educ:* St Bede's School, Lanchester; Newcastle Polytechnic. Mem., GMBATU; local govt officer. *Address:* 4 Lime Street, Waldridge, Chester le Street, Co. Durham DH2 3SG.

HUGHES, Ted, OBE 1977; author; Poet Laureate, since 1984; *b* 1930; *s* of William Henry Hughes and Edith Farrar Hughes; *m* 1956, Sylvia Plath (*d* 1963); one *s* one *d; m* 1970, Carol Orchard. *Educ:* Pembroke Coll., Cambridge Univ. (Hon. Fellow, 1986). Author of Orghast (performed at 5th Festival of Arts of Shiraz, Persepolis, 1971). Awards: first prize, Guinness Poetry Awards, 1958; John Simon Guggenheim Fellow, 1959–60; Somerset Maugham Award, 1960; Premio Internazionale Taormina, 1973; The Queen's Medal for Poetry, 1974. *Publications:* The Hawk in the Rain, 1957 (First Publication Award, NY, 1957); Lupercal, 1960 (Hawthornden Prize, 1961); Meet My Folks! (children's verse), 1961; The Earth-Owl and Other Moon People (children's verse), 1963 (US as Moon Whales, 1976); How the Whale Became (children's stories), 1963; (ed, jtly) Five American Poets, 1963; Selected Poems of Keith Douglas (ed, with Introduction), 1964; Nessie, The Mannerless Monster (children's verse story), 1964 (US as Nessie the Monster, 1974); Recklings, 1966; The Burning of the Brothel, 1966; Scapegoats and Rabies, 1967; Animal Poems, 1967; Wodwo, 1967 (City of Florence Internat. Poetry Prize, 1969); Poetry in the Making, 1967 (US as Poetry Is, 1970); The Iron Man (children's story) (US as The Iron Giant, 1968); (ed) A Choice of Emily Dickinson's Verse, 1968; Five Autumn Songs for Children's Voices, 1968; Adaptation of Seneca's Oedipus, 1969 (play, National Theatre, 1968); (libretto) The Demon of Adachigahara, 1969; The Coming of the Kings (4 plays for children), 1970 (US as The Tiger's Bones, 1974); Crow, 1970; A Few Crows, 1970; Crow Wakes, 1970; (ed) A Choice of Shakespeare's Verse, 1971 (US as With Fairest Flowers while Summer Lasts); Shakespeare's Poem, 1971; (with R. Fainlight and Alan Sillitoe) Poems, 1971; Eat Crow, 1971; Prometheus on His Crag, 1973; Spring Summer Autumn Winter, 1974; (libretto) The Story of Vasco, 1974; Cave Birds (limited edn with illustrations by Leonard Baskin), 1975; Season Songs, 1976; Earth-Moon, 1976; (introd. and trans. jtly) János Pilinsky, Selected Poems, 1976; Gaudete, 1977; (ed and introd.) Johnny Panic and the Bible of Dreams, by Sylvia Plath, 1977; Orts, 1978; Moortown Elegies, 1978; Cave Birds, 1978; Moon-Bells and other poems (verse for children), 1978 (Signal Award); (introd. and trans. jtly) Yehuda Amichai's Amen, 1978; Adam and the Sacred Nine, 1979; Remains of Elmet, 1979; Moortown, 1979 (Heinemann Bequest, RSL, 1980); 12 poems in Michael Morpurgo's All Around the Year, 1979; Henry Williamson—A Tribute, 1979; (ed) Sylvia Plath: Collected Poems, 1981; Under the North Star (poems for children), 1981 (Signal Award); Selected Poems 1957–1981, 1982; (ed with Seamus Heaney) The Rattle Bag, 1982; River, 1983; What is the Truth (for children), 1984 (Guardian Children's Fiction Award, 1985). *Address:* c/o Faber and Faber Ltd, 3 Queen Square, WC1.

HUGHES, Thomas Lowe; President and Trustee, Carnegie Endowment for International Peace, Washington, since 1971; *b* 11 Dec. 1925; *s* of Evan Raymond Hughes and Alice (*née* Lowe); *m* 1955, Jean Hurlburt Reiman; two *s. Educ:* Carleton Coll., Minn (BA); Balliol Coll., Oxford (Rhodes Schol., BPhil); Yale Law Sch. (LLB, JD). USAF, 1952–54 (Major). Member of Bar: Supreme Court of Minnesota; US District Court of DC; Supreme Court of US. Professional Staff Mem., US Senate Sub-cttee on Labour-Management Relations, 1951; part-time Prof. of Polit. Sci. and Internat. Relations, Univ. of Southern California, Los Angeles, 1953–54, and George Washington Univ., DC, 1957–58; Exec. Sec. to Governor of Connecticut, 1954–55; Legislative Counsel to Senator Hubert H. Humphrey, 1955–58; Admin. Asst to US Rep. Chester Bowles, 1959–60; Staff Dir of Platform Cttee, Democratic Nat. Convention, 1960; Special Asst to Under-Sec. of State, Dept of State, 1961; Dep. Dir of Intelligence and Research, Dept of State, 1961–63; Dir of Intell. and Res. (Asst Sec. of State), 1963–69; Minister and Dep. Chief of Mission, Amer. Embassy, London, 1969–70; Mem., Planning and Coordination Staff, Dept of State, 1970–71. Chm., Nuclear Proliferation and Safeguards Adv. Panel, Office of Technology Assessment, US Congress; Chm., Bd of Editors, Foreign Policy Magazine; Sec., Bd of Dirs, German Marshall Fund of US; Dir, Arms Control Assoc. Chairman: Oxford-Cambridge Assoc. of Washington; US-UK Bicentennial Fellowships Cttee on the Arts. Member Bds of Visitors: Harvard Univ. (Center for Internat. Studies); Princeton Univ. (Woodrow Wilson Sch. of Public and Internat. Affairs); Georgetown Univ. (Sch. of Foreign Service); Bryn Mawr Coll. (Internat. Adv. Bd.); Univ. of Denver (Soc. Sci. Foundn). Member Bds of Advisers: Center for Internat. Journalism, Univ. of S Calif; Coll. of Public and Internat. Affairs, Amer. Univ., Washington, DC. Member Bds of Trustees: Civilian Military Inst.; Amer. Acad. of Political and Social Sci.; Amer. Cttee, IISS; Hubert H. Humphrey Inst. of Public Affairs; Amer. Inst. of Contemp. German Studies, Washington, DC. Mem. Adv. Bd, Fundacion Luis Munoz Marin, Puerto Rico. Member: Internat. Inst. of Strategic Studies; Amer. Assoc. of Rhodes Scholars; Amer. Political Sci. Assoc.; Amer. Bar Assoc.; Amer. Assoc. of Internat. Law; Amer. For. Service Assoc.; Internat. Studies Assoc.; Washington Inst. of Foreign Affairs; Trilateral Commn; Assoc. for Restoration of Old San Juan, Puerto Rico. Arthur S. Flemming Award, 1965. Hon. LLD Washington Coll., 1973; Denison Univ., 1979; Florida Internat. Univ., 1986; Hon. HLD: Carleton Coll., 1974; Washington and Jefferson Coll., 1979. KStJ 1984. *Publications:* occasional contribs to professional jls, etc. *Recreations:* swimming, tennis, music, 18th century engravings. *Address:* 5636 Western Avenue, Chevy Chase, Md 20815, USA. *T:* (301)6561420; 11 Dupont Circle NW, Washington, DC 20036. *T:* (office) (202)797–6411. *Clubs:* Yale, Century Association, Council on Foreign Relations (New York); Cosmos (Washington).

HUGHES, Sir Trevor Denby L.; *see* Lloyd-Hughes.

HUGHES, Sir Trevor (Poulton), KCB 1982 (CB 1974); CEng, FICE, FIWES; Permanent Secretary, Welsh Office, 1980–85; Member, British Waterways Board, since 1985; *b* 28 Sept. 1925; *y s* of late Rev. John Evan and Mary Grace Hughes; *m* 1st, 1950, Mary Ruth Walwyn (marr. diss.); two *s;* 2nd, 1978, Barbara June Davison. *Educ:* Ruthin Sch. RE, 1945–48, Captain 13 Fd Svy Co. Municipal engineering, 1948–61; Min. of Transport, 1961–62; Min. of Housing and Local Govt: Engineering Inspectorate, 1962–70; Dep. Chief Engineer, 1970–71; Dir, 1971–72 and Dir-Gen., 1972–74, Water Engineering, DoE; Dep. Sec., DoE, 1974–77; Dep. Sec., Dept of Transport, 1977–80. Vice-Chm., Public Works and Municipal Services Congress Council, 1975–; Chief British Deleg., Perm. Internat. Assoc. of Navigation Congresses, 1985–. A Vice-Pres., ICE, 1984–86. Hon. Fellow, Polytechnic of Wales, 1986. Hon. FInstWPC; Hon. FIPHE. *Recreations:* music, gardening, golf. *Address:* Clearwell, 13 Brambleton Avenue, Farnham, Surrey GU9 8RA. *T:* Farnham 714246.
See also J. R. P. Hughes.

HUGHES, William, CB 1953; Chairman, Tooting Youth Project, since 1981; *b* 21 Aug. 1910; *o s* of late William Hughes, Bishop's Stortford, Herts, and of Daisy Constance, *y d* of Charles Henry Davis; *m* 1941, Ilse Erna, *o d* of late E. F. Plohs; one *s* one *d. Educ:* Bishop's Stortford Coll.; Magdalen Coll., Oxford (demy). Board of Trade, 1933; Asst Sec., 1942; Under-Sec., 1948–63 (Sec., Monopolies and Restrictive Practices Commission, 1952–55); Second Sec., 1963–71. Consultant to British Overseas Trade Bd, 1972–73; Under-Sec., Prices Commn, 1973–75; Dep. Sec., DTI, 1970–71. *Recreation:* music. *Address:* 250 Trinity Road, SW18. *T:* 01–870 3652; Page's, Widdington, Essex. *Clubs:* Reform; Leander.

HUGHES, Maj.-Gen. (Retd) William Dillon, CB 1960; CBE 1953; MD; FRCP(I); DTM&H; Commandant, Royal Army Medical College, 1957–60; *b* 23 Dec. 1900; *s* of R. Hughes, JP; *m* 1929, Kathleen Linda Thomas; one *s. Educ:* Campbell Coll., Belfast; Queen's Univ., Belfast. MB, BCh, BAO, 1923; Lieut, RAMC, 1928; Officer i/c Medical Div. 64 and 42 Gen. Hosps, MEF, 1940–42; Officer i/c Medical Div. 105 Gen. Hosp., BAOR, 1944–46; Sen. MO, Belsen, 1945; consulting Physician, Far East Land Forces, 1950–53; ADMS, Aldershot Dist, 1954. Prof. in Tropical Medicine and Consulting Physician, RAM Coll., 1955–56; Vice-Pres., Royal Society of Tropical Medicine and Hygiene, 1959–60; Col Comdt RAMC, 1961–65. QHP 1957; Mitchiner Medal, RCS, 1960. *Address:* Vine House, Summer Court, Tilford Road, Farnham GU9 8DS.

HUGHES, His Honour William Henry; a Circuit Judge, 1972–83; *b* 6 Jan. 1915; *s* of late William Howard Hamilton Hughes; *m* 1961, Jenny, *d* of late Theodore Francis Turner, QC; one *d. Educ:* privately; Keble Coll., Oxford. Served War of 1939–45; AA & QMG, BEF, France and Belgium, N Africa, Italy (despatches, Croix de Guerre (France)); Staff Coll.; Lieut-Col 1944. Called to the Bar, Inner Temple, 1949. Deputy Chairman: Isle of Ely QS, 1959–63; Essex QS, 1961–63; London Sessions, 1962–63, 1968–71; a Metropolitan Magistrate, 1963–71. Formerly a Mem., General Council of the Bar. Chm., Cttee of Inquiry into Children's Homes and Hostels, apptd by Sec. of State for NI, 1984–85. Governor: Camden Sch. for Girls, 1977–86; NLCS. *Recreations:* books, wine, shooting, travel. *Address:* Old Wardour House, Tisbury, Wilts. *T:* Tisbury 870431; 112 Bedford Court Mansions, Bedford Avenue, WC1B 3AG. *Clubs:* Beefsteak, Garrick, PEN.
See also C. G. Turner, Hon. Sir M. J. Turner.

HUGHES, (William) Mark, MA, PhD; MP (Lab) City of Durham, since 1983 (Durham, 1970–83); *b* 18 Dec. 1932; *s* of late Edward Hughes, sometime Prof. of History at Durham, and Sarah (*née* Hughes), Shincliffe, Durham; *m* 1958, Jennifer Mary, *d* of Dr G. H. Boobyer; one *s* two *d. Educ:* Durham Sch.; Balliol Coll., Oxford (MA). BA Oxon 1956; PhD Newcastle 1963. Sir James Knott Research Fellow, Newcastle-upon-Tyne, 1958–60; Staff Tutor, Manchester Univ. Extra-Mural Dept, 1960–64; Lectr, Durham Univ., 1964–70. PPS to Chief Sec. of Treasury, 1974–75; opposition spokesman on agriculture, 1980–; Member: Select Cttee on Expenditure (Trade and Industry Sub-Cttee), 1970–74; Select Cttee on Parly Comr, 1970–75; Delegn to Consultative Assembly of Council of Europe and WEU, 1974–75; European Parlt, 1975–79 (Vice-Chm., Agric. Cttee and Chm., Fisheries Sub-Cttee, 1977–79); Exec. Cttee, British Council, 1974– (Vice-Chm., 1978–85); Gen. Adv. Council, BBC, 1976–84; Adv. Council on Public Records, 1984–. An Hon. Vice-Pres., BVA, 1976–. Fellow, Industry and Parliament Trust. *Recreations:* gardening, fishing, birdwatching. *Address:* Grimsdyke, Vicarage Road, Potten End, Berkhamsted, Herts.

HUGHES, William Reginald Noel, FRINA, RCNC; *b* 14 Dec. 1913; *s* of Frank George Hughes and Annie May Hughes (*née* Lock); *m* 1936, Doris Margaret (*née* Attwool); two *s* two *d. Educ:* Prince Edward Sch., Salisbury, Rhodesia; Esplanade House Sch., Southsea, Hants; Royal Dockyard Sch., Portsmouth; RN Coll., Greenwich. Constr Sub Lieut, Chatham, 1933; Constr Sub Lieut and Lieut, RN Coll., Greenwich, 1934; Admty, London, 1937; HM Dockyard, Chatham, 1938; Admty, Bath, 1940; Constr Comdr, Staff of C-in-C Home Fleet, 1944; HM Dockyard, Hong Kong, 1947; Admty, Bath, 1951; Chief Constr, HM Dockyard, Devonport, 1954; Admty, Bath, 1958; Admty Repair Manager, Malta, 1961; Manager, Constructive Dept, Portsmouth, 1964; Dep. Dir of Dockyards, Bath, 1967–70; Gen. Manager, HM Dockyard, Chatham, 1970–73. *Recreations:* sailing, foreign travel, photography. *Address:* Capstan House, Tower Street, Old Portsmouth, Hants. *T:* Portsmouth 812997. *Clubs:* Little Ship; Royal Naval and Royal Albert Yacht; Royal Naval Sailing Association.

HUGHES JONES, Dr Nevin Campbell, FRS 1985; on scientific staff, Medical Research Council, since 1954; *b* 10 Feb. 1923; *s* of William and Millicent Hughes Jones; *m* 1952, Elizabeth Helen Dufty; two *s* one *d. Educ:* Berkhampsted Sch., Herts; Oriel Coll., Univ. of Oxford; St Mary's Hosp. Med. School. MA, DM, PhD; FRCP. Medical posts held at St Mary's Hosp., Paddington, Radcliffe Infirmary, Oxford, and Postgrad. Med. Sch., Hammersmith, 1947–52; Member: MRC's Blood Transfusion Unit, Hammersmith, 1952–79 (Unit transferred to St Mary's Hosp. Med. Sch., Paddington, as MRC's Experimental Haematology Unit, 1960); MRC's Mechanisms in Tumour Immunity Unit, Cambridge, 1979–. *Publication:* Lecture Notes on Haematology, 1970, 4th edn 1984. *Recreations:* making chairs, walking the Horseshoe Path on Snowdon. *Address:* 65 Orchard Road, Melbourn, Royston, Herts SG8 6BB. *T:* Royston 60471.

HUGHES-MORGAN, Maj.-Gen. Sir David (John), 3rd Bt *cr* 1925; CB 1983; CBE 1973 (MBE 1959); **His Honour Judge Hughes-Morgan;** a Circuit Judge, since 1986; *b* 11 Oct. 1925; *s* of Sir John Hughes-Morgan, 2nd Bt and of Lucie Margaret, *d* of late Thomas Parry Jones-Parry; *S* father, 1969; *m* 1959, Isabel Jean, *d* of J. M. Lindsay; three *s. Educ:* RNC, Dartmouth. Royal Navy, 1943–46. Admitted solicitor, 1950. Commissioned, Army Legal Services, 1955; Brig., Legal Staff, HQ UKLF, 1976–78; Dir, Army Legal Services, BAOR, 1978–80, MoD, 1980–84; a Recorder, 1983–86. *Heir: s* Ian Parry David Hughes-Morgan, *b* 22 Feb. 1960. *Address:* c/o National Westminster Bank, 1 High Street, Bromley BR1 1LL.

HUGHES-YOUNG, family name of **Baron St Helens.**

HUGHESDON, Charles Frederick, AFC 1944; FRAeS; *b* 10 Dec. 1909; *m* 1937, Florence Elizabeth, *widow* of Captain Tom Campbell Black (actress, as Florence Desmond); one *s. Educ:* Raine's Foundation School. Entered insurance industry, 1927; learned to fly, 1932; Flying Instructor's Licence, 1934; commnd RAFO, 1934; Commercial Pilot's Licence, 1936. Joined Stewart, Smith & Co. Ltd, 1936; RAF Instructor at outbreak of war; seconded to General Aircraft as Chief Test Pilot, 1939–43; rejoined RAF, 1943–45 (AFC). Rejoined Stewart, Smith & Co. Ltd, 1946; retired as Chm. of Stewart Wrightson 1976. Dir, Aeronautical Trusts Ltd; Chairman: Tradewinds Helicopters Ltd; The Charles Street Co. Hon. Treas., RAeS, 1969–85. Order of the Cedar, Lebanon, 1972. *Recreations:* flying (helicopter; holds helicopter licence), shooting, horseracing, riding (dressage), yachting, water ski-ing, farming. *Address:* Dunsborough Park, Ripley, Surrey. *T:* Guildford 225366; Flat 12, 5 Grosvenor Square, W1. *T:* 01–493 1494. *Clubs:* Royal Air Force, Royal Thames Yacht, Lloyd's Yacht.

HUGHFF, Victor William, FIA, FSS, CBIM; Chief General Manager, Norwich Union Insurance Group, since 1984; *b* 30 May 1931; *s* of William Scott Hughff and Alice Doris (*née* Kerry); *m* 1955, Grace Margaret (*née* Lambert) one *s* one *d. Educ:* City of Norwich School. Joined Norwich Union Life Insce Soc., 1949; Assistant Actuary, 1966; General

Manager and Actuary, 1975; Main Board Director, 1981. Served in RAF, 1951–53; commnd in Secretarial Br., National Service List. Elder of United Reformed Church. *Recreations:* tennis, badminton. *Address:* 18 Hilly Plantation, Thorpe St Andrew, Norwich NR7 0JN. *T:* Norwich 34517.

HUGILL, John, QC 1976; a Recorder of the Crown Court, since 1972; *b* 11 Aug. 1930; *s* of late John A. and Alice Hugill; *m* 1956, Patricia Elizabeth Hugill (*née* Welton); two *d. Educ:* Sydney C of E Grammar Sch., NSW; Fettes Coll.; Trinity Hall, Cambridge (MA). RA, 1948–49. Called to the Bar, Middle Temple, 1954 (Bencher, 1984); Northern Circuit, 1954; Assistant Recorder, Bolton, 1971. Chairman: Darryn Clare Inquiry, 1979; Stanley Royd Inquiry, 1985. Mem., Senate of the Inns of Court and the Bar, 1984–. *Recreation:* yachting. *Address:* The Boundary House, Lower Withington, Cheshire; Flat 2, 63 Nevern Square, SW5. *Club:* Royal Lymington Yacht.

HUGILL, Michael James; Assistant Master, Westminster School, 1972–86; *b* 13 July 1918; 2nd *s* of late Rear-Adm. R. C. Hugill, CB, MVO, OBE. *Educ:* Oundle; King's Coll., Cambridge, Exhibitioner, King's Coll., 1936–39; MA 1943. War Service in the RN; Mediterranean, Home and Pacific Fleets, 1939–46; rank on demobilisation, Lieut-Comdr. Mathematics Master, Stratford Grammar Sch., 1947–51; Senior Mathematics Master, Bedford Modern Sch., 1951–57; Headmaster, Preston Grammar Sch., 1957–61; Headmaster, Whitgift School, Croydon, 1961–70; Lectr, Inst. of Education, Keele Univ., 1971–72. *Publication:* Advanced Statistics, 1985. *Address:* 42 Kersfield House, Kersfield Road, SW15. *Club:* Army and Navy.

HUGO, Lt-Col Sir John (Mandeville), KCVO 1969 (CVO 1959); OBE 1947; Gentleman Usher to the Queen, 1952–69, an Extra Gentleman Usher since 1969; *b* 1 July 1899; *s* of R. M. Hugo; *m* 1952, Joan Winifred, *d* of late D. W. Hill; two *d. Educ:* Marlborough Coll.; RMA, Woolwich, Commissioned RA, 1917; transf. to Indian Cavalry, 1925; Military Sec. to Governor of Bengal, 1938–40; rejoined 7th Light Cavalry, 1940; Military Sec. to Governor of Bengal 1946–47; Asst Ceremonial Sec., Commonwealth Relations Office, 1948–52; Ceremonial and Protocol Secretary, 1952–69. *Address:* The Cottages, Nizels, Hildenborough, Kent. *T:* Hildenborough 832359. *Club:* Army and Navy.

HUIJSMAN, Nicolaas Basil Jacques, CMG 1973; *b* 6 March 1915; *s* of Nikolaas Kornelis Huijsman, Amsterdam and Hendrika Huijsman (*née* Vorkink). *Educ:* Selborne Coll., E London, S Africa; Univ. of Witwatersrand (BCom); Gonville and Caius Coll., Cambridge (Econ. Tripos). Commnd Royal Scots Fusiliers, 1940; HQ 17 Inf. Bde, 1940; GS03, WO, 1941–42; psc 1942; GSO2, HQ of Chief of Staff to Supreme Cmdr (Des) and SHAEF, 1943–45 (despatches 1944); Controller of Press and Publications, Control Commn for Germany, 1945–48; Colonial Office, 1948–62; Principal Private Sec. to Sec. of State for Commonwealth Relations and Colonies, 1962–64; Asst Sec., Min. of Overseas Develt, 1964–70, and 1974–75, Overseas Develt Admin/FCO, 1970–74. Bronze Star, US, 1945. *Recreations:* Byzantine history, music, opera, painting. *Address:* 13 Regent Square, Penzance TR18 4BG. *Club:* Reform.

HULL, Bishop Suffragan of, since 1981; **Rt. Rev. Donald George Snelgrove,** TD 1972; *b* 21 April 1925; *s* of William Henry Snelgrove and Beatrice Snelgrove (*née* Upshell); *m* 1949, Sylvia May Lowe; one *s* one *d. Educ:* Queens' Coll. and Ridley Hall, Cambridge (MA). Served War, commn (Exec. Br.) RNVR, 1943–46. Cambridge, 1946–50; ordained, 1950; Curate: St Thomas, Oakwood, 1950–53; St Anselm's, Hatch End, 1953–56; Vicar of: Dronfield with Unstone, Dio. Derby, 1956–62; Hessle, Dio. York, 1963–70; Archdeacon of the East Riding, 1970–81. Rural Dean of Hull, 1966–70; Canon of York, 1969. Chaplain T&AVR, 1960–73. *Recreation:* travel. *Address:* Hullen House, Woodfield Lane, Hessle, N Humberside HU13 0ES. *T:* Hull 649019.

HULL, Prof. Derek, FEng, FIM, FPRI; Goldsmiths' Professor of Metallurgy, University of Cambridge, since 1984; Fellow, Magdalene College, Cambridge, since 1984; *b* 8 Aug. 1931; *s* of late William and Nellie Hull (*née* Hayes); *m* 1953, Pauline Scott; one *s* four *d. Educ:* Baines Grammar School, Poulton-le-Fylde; Univ. of Wales. PhD, DSc. AERE, Harwell and Clarendon Lab., Oxford, 1956–60; University of Liverpool: Senior Lectr, 1960–64; Henry Bell Wortley Prof. of Materials Engineering, 1964–84; Dean of Engineering,1971–74; Pro-Vice Chancellor, 1983–84. Dist. Vis. Prof. and Senior Vis. NSF Fellow, Univ. of Delaware, 1968–69; Monash Vis. Prof., Univ. of Monash, 1981; Hon. Fellow, University Coll. Cardiff, 1985. Rosenhain Medal, 1973, A. A. Griffith Silver Medal, 1985, Inst. of Metals. *Publications:* Introduction to Dislocations, 1966, 3rd edn 1984; An Introduction to Composite Materials, 1981; numerous contribs to Proc. Roy. Soc., Acta Met., Phil. Mag., Jl Mat. Sci., MetalScience, Composites. *Recreations:* golf, music, fell-walking. *Address:* Department of Materials Science and Metallurgy, Pembroke Street, Cambridge CB2 3QZ. *T:* Cambridge 334305. *Clubs:* Heswall Golf, Gog Magog Golf.

HULL, John Folliott Charles; Deputy Chairman, Schroders plc, 1977–85; *b* 21 Oct. 1925; *er s* of Sir Hubert Hull, CBE, and of Judith, *e d* of P. F. S. Stokes; *m* 1951, Rosemarie Waring; one *s* three *d. Educ:* Downside; Jesus Coll., Cambridge (Titular Schol.; 1st cl. hons Law; MA). Captain, RA, 1944–48; served with Royal Indian Artillery, 1945–48. Called to Bar, Inner Temple, 1952. J. Henry Schroder Wagg & Co. Ltd, 1957–72, 1974–: a Man. Dir, 1961–72; Dep. Chm., 1974–77; Chm., 1977–83; Dir, 1984–85; Dir, Schroders plc, 1969–72, 1974–; Dep. Chm., Land Securities plc, 1976–; Director: Lucas Industries plc, 1975–; Legal and General Assurance Soc., 1976–79; Legal & General Group plc, 1979–. Dir-Gen., City Panel on Take-overs and Mergers, 1972–74; Chm., City Company Law Cttee, 1976–79. Lay Mem., Stock Exchange, 1983–84. Mem., Council, Manchester Business Sch. *Recreation:* reading political history and 19th century novelists. *Address:* 33 Edwardes Square, W8 6HH. *T:* 01–603 0715. *Club:* MCC.

See also Duke of Somerset.

HULL, John Grove, QC 1983; a Recorder, since 1984; *b* 21 Aug. 1931; *s* of Tom Edward Orridge Hull and Marjorie Ethel Hull; *m* 1961, Gillian Ann, *d* of Leslie Fawcett Stemp; two *d. Educ:* Rugby School; King's College, Cambridge. BA (1st cl. in Mech. Scis Tripos) 1953, MA 1957; LLB 1954. National Service, commissioned RE, 1954–56; called to the Bar, Middle Temple, 1958 (Cert. of Honour, Bar Final); in practice, common law Bar, 1958–. *Recreations:* gardening, English literature. *Address:* Ravenshoe, 16 High Trees Road, Reigate, Surrey. *T:* Reigate 45181.

HULL, Field Marshal Sir Richard (Amyatt), KG 1980; GCB 1961 (KCB 1956; CB 1945); DSO 1943; Lord-Lieutenant of Devon, 1978–82; *b* 7 May 1907; *s* of Maj.-Gen. Sir Charles Patrick Amyatt Hull, KCB; *m* 1934, Antoinette Mary Labouchère de Rougemont; one *s* two *d. Educ:* Charterhouse; Trinity Coll., Cambridge (MA). Joined 17th/21st Lancers, 1928; Commanded 17/21st Lancers, 1941; Commanded 12th Infantry Bde, 1943; Commanded 26 Armd Bde, 1943; Comd 1st Armd Div., 1944; Cmd 5th Infantry Div., 1945; Commandant Staff Coll. Camberley, 1946–48; Dir of Staff Duties, War Office, 1948–50; Chief Army Instructor, Imperial Defence Coll., 1950–52; Chief of Staff, GHQ, MELF, 1953–54; General Officer Commanding, British Troops in Egypt, 1954–56; Dep. Chief of the Imperial Gen. Staff, 1956–58; Comdr-in-Chief, Far East Land Forces, 1958–61; Chief of the Imperial Gen. Staff, 1961–64; ADC Gen. to the Queen, 1961–64; Chief of the Gen. Staff, Ministry of Defence, 1964–65; Chief of the Defence Staff, 1965–67. Constable of the Tower of London, 1970–75. Pres., Army Benevolent Fund, 1968–71; Dir, Whitbread & Co. Ltd, 1967–76. Col Comdt, RAC, 1968–71. DL Devon 1973; High Sheriff, Devon, 1975. Hon. LLD Exeter, 1965. *Address:* Beacon Downe, Pinhoe, Exeter. *Club:* Cavalry and Guards.

HULME, Bishop Suffragan of, since 1984; **Rt. Rev. Colin John Fraser Scott;** *b* 14 May 1933; *s* of Kenneth Miller Scott and Marion Edith Scott; *m* 1958, Margaret Jean MacKay; one *s* two *d. Educ:* Berkhamsted School; Queens' College, Cambridge; Ridley Hall, Cambridge. MA Cantab. Curate: St Barnabas, Clapham Common, 1958–61; St James, Hatcham, 1961–64; Vicar, St Mark, Kennington, 1964–71; Vice-Chm., Southwark Diocesan Pastoral Cttee, 1971–77; Team Rector, Sanderstead Team Ministry, 1977–84. *Address:* 1 Raynham Avenue, Didsbury, Manchester M20 0BW. *T:* 061–445 5922.

HULME, Hon. Sir Alan (Shallcross), KBE 1971; FCA; grazier; *b* 14 Feb. 1907; *s* of Thomas Shallcross Hulme and Emily Clara (*née* Hynes); *m* 1938, Jean Archibald; two *s* one *d. Educ:* North Sydney Boys' High School. Pres., Qld Div. of Liberal Party of Aust., 1946–49, 1962–63. Director: Chandlers (Aust.) Ltd, 1952–58; J. B. Chandler Investment Co. Ltd, 1962–63. Hon. Treas., King's Univ. Coll., 1944–49. Former Vice-Consul for Portugal in Brisbane. Mem., Commonwealth Parlt, Australia, 1949–72; Minister for Supply, 1958–61; acted as Minister: for Army, May-July 1959; for Air, Dec. 1960; Postmaster-General, 1963–72; Minister for Defence, 1965–66 and on subseq. occasions; Vice-Pres., Exec. Council, 1966–72. Member: House Cttee, 1950–58; Jt Cttee of Public Accounts, 1952–58; Chairman: Commonwealth Cttee on Rates of Depreciation, 1954–55; Commonwealth Immigration Planning Council, 1956–58. *Recreations:* gardening, bowls. *Address:* Alcheringa Droughtmaster Stud, Eudlo, Qld 4554, Australia. *T:* Palmwoods 459267. *Club:* Brisbane (Brisbane).

HULME, Geoffrey Gordon, CB 1984; Deputy Secretary, Department of Health and Social Security, since 1981; *b* 8 March 1931; *s* of Alfred and Jessie Hulme; *m* 1956, Shirley Leigh Cumberlidge; one *s* one *d. Educ:* Daybrook Street Elem. Sch.; King's Sch., Macclesfield; Corpus Christi Coll., Oxford (MA, 1st Cl Hons Mod. Langs). Nat. Service, Intelligence Corps, 1949–50; Oxford, 1950–53; Asst Principal, Min. of Health, 1953–59; Principal, 1959–64; Principal Regional Officer, W Midlands, 1964–67; Asst Sec., 1967–74; Under-Sec., 1974–81. *Recreations:* the usual things and collecting edible fungi. *Address:* Stone Farm, Little Cornard, Sudbury, Suffolk; 163A Kennington Park Road, SE11. *T:* 01–735 4461. *Club:* Royal Automobile.

HULME, Dr Henry Rainsford; Chief of Nuclear Research, Atomic Weapons Research Establishment, 1959–73, retired; *b* 9 Aug. 1908; *s* of James Rainsford Hulme and Alice Jane Smith; *m* 1955, Margery Alice Ducker, *d* of late Sir James A. Cooper, KBE, and of Lady Cooper. *Educ:* Manchester Grammar Sch.; Gonville and Caius Coll., Cambridge; University of Leipzig. BA (Math. Tripos) 1929; Smiths' Prizeman, 1931; PhD (Cambridge) 1932; ScD (Cambridge) 1948. Fellow of Gonville and Caius Coll., Cambridge, 1933–38; Chief Asst Royal Observatory, Greenwich, 1938–45; on loan to Admiralty during war. Scientific Adviser Air Ministry, 1946–48. *Publications:* on Mathematical Physics and Astronomy in learned jls. *Recreations:* various. *Address:* Cathay, West End, Sherborne St John, near Basingstoke, Hants RG24 9LE. *T:* Basingstoke 850422.

HULSE, Sir (Hamilton) Westrow, 9th Bt, *cr* 1739; Barrister-at-Law, Inner Temple; *b* 20 June 1909; *o s* of Sir Hamilton Hulse, 8th Bt, and Estelle (*d* 1933) *d* of late William Lorillard Campbell, of New York, USA; *S* father, 1931; *m* 1st, 1932, Philippa Mabel (marr. diss. 1937), *y d* of late A. J. Taylor, Strensham Court, Worcs; two *s*; 2nd, 1938, Amber (*d* 1940), *o d* of late Captain Herbert Stanley Orr Wilson, RHA, Rockfield Park, Mon; 3rd, 1945 (marr. diss.); 4th, 1954, Elizabeth, *d* of late Col George Redesdale Brooker Spain, CMG, TD, FSA. *Educ:* Eton; Christ Church, Oxford. Wing Comdr RAFVR, served 1940–45 (despatches). *Heir: s* Edward Jeremy Westrow Hulse [*b* 22 Nov. 1932; *m* 1957, Verity Ann, *d* of William Pilkington, Ivy Well, St John, Jersey; one *s* one *d*]. *Address:* Breamore, Hants. *TA:* Breamore. *T:* Downton 22773. *Clubs:* Carlton; Leander.

HULSE, Sir Westrow; *see* Hulse, Sir H. W.

HULTON, Sir Edward (George Warris), Kt 1957; Magazine publisher; writer; *b* 29 Nov. 1906; *s* of late Sir Edward Hulton, former proprietor of Evening Standard; *m* 1st, Kira (marr. diss.), *d* of General Goudime-Levkovitsch, Imperial Russian Army; no *c*; 2nd, 1941, Princess Nika Yourievitch (marr. diss., 1966), 2nd *d* of Prince Serge Yourievitch, Russian sculptor, and Helene de Lipovatz, *d* of Gen. de Lipovatz; two *s* one *d. Educ:* Harrow; Brasenose Coll., Oxford (open scholarship. Contested Leek Div. Staffs, as Unionist, 1929; Harwich Div., 1931. Called to Bar, Inner Temple; practised on South-Eastern Circuit; Chm., Hulton Publications Ltd. Pres., European Atlantic Group, 1969–70; Mem., British Atlantic Cttee; Vice-Pres., European League for Economic Co-operation; Mem. Nat. Council, British Council of the European Movement. FRSA. Liveryman and Freeman of Company of Stationers; Freeman of City of London. NATO Peace Medal, 1969. *Publications:* The New Age, 1943; When I Was a Child, 1952; Conflicts, 1966; contrib. various newspapers and books. *Recreation:* reading. *Address:* 5 Carlton Gardens, SW1. *Clubs:* Athenæum, Beefsteak, Carlton, Garrick, Travellers', Buck's.

HULTON, Sir Geoffrey (Alan), 4th Bt, *cr* 1905; JP; DL; *b* 21 Jan. 1920; *s* of Sir Roger Braddyll Hulton, 3rd Bt and Hon. Marjorie Evelyn Louise (*d* 1970), *o c* of 6th Viscount Mountmorres; *S* father 1956; *m* 1945, Mary Patricia Reynolds. *Educ:* Marlborough. Entered Royal Marines, Sept. 1938; Lieut, 1940; sunk in HMS Repulse, Dec. 1941; prisoner-of-war, Far East, Feb. 1942–Aug. 1945; Captain, 1948; retired (ill-health), 1949. Owner of Hulton Park estate. Pres., Bolton West Conservative Association; Life Patron, Bolton and District Agricultural Discussion Soc.; Life Vice-Pres., Royal Lancs Agricultural Soc. (Pres., 1974–80). Chief Scout's Comr, 1964–85; President: Greater Manchester North Scout County; Bolton Scout Trust; Vice-President: Greater Manchester West Scout County; CLA (Lancashire); Lancashire County Cricket Club; Bolton Cricket League; St Ann's Hospice Ltd; Hon. Life Vice-Pres., Westhoughton Cricket Club. JP Lancs, 1955; DL Lancs, later Greater Manchester, 1974. KCSG 1966. *Recreations:* country pursuits. *Heir:* none. *Address:* The Cottage, Hulton Park, Over Hulton, Bolton BL5 1BE. *T:* Bolton 651324. *Clubs:* Lansdowne, Royal Over-Seas League, Spanish, Victory.

HULTON, John, MA; *b* 28 Dec. 1915; *e s* of late Rev. Samuel Hulton, Knaresborough; *m* 1940, Helen Christian McFarlan; two *d. Educ:* Kingswood Sch., Bath; Hertford Coll., Oxford. DipLA; graduate of Landscape Inst. Leeds City Art Gallery and Temple Newsam House (Hon. Asst), 1937–38. Served War, RA, 1939–46. Keeper at Brighton Art Gall., Museum and Royal Pavilion, 1946–48; British Council Fine Arts Dept, 1948; Dir, 1970–75; resigned to study landscape design; now in private practice. Organised many art exhibns abroad. *Recreations:* looking at painting and sculpture; landscape and gardens. *Address:* 70 Gloucester Crescent, NW1 7EG. *T:* 01–485 6906. *Club:* Athenæum.

HUMBLE, James Kenneth; Chief Executive, Local Authorities Coordinating Body on Trading Standards, since 1982; Director; National Metrological Co-ordinating Unit, since 1980; *b* 8 May 1936; *s* of Joseph Humble and Alice (*née* Rhodes); *m* 1962, Freda (*née*

Holden); three *d*. Fellow, Inst. of Trading Standards. Served RN, 1954–56. Weights and Measures, Oldham, 1956–62; Fed. Min. of Commerce and Industry, Nigeria, 1962–66; Chief Trading Standards Officer, Croydon, 1966–74; Asst Dir of Consumer Affairs, Office of Fair Trading, 1974–79; Dir of Metrication Bd, 1979–80. Sec., Trade Descriptions Cttee, Inst. of Trading Standards, 1968–73; Examr, Dip. in Trading Standards, 1978–; Vice Chm., Council of Europe Cttee of Experts on Consumer Protection, 1976–79. Member: Council for Vehicle Servicing and Repair, 1972–75; Methven Cttee, 1974–76; OECD Cttee, Air Package Tours, 1978–79; BSI Divl Council, 1976–79; Eden Cttee on Metrology, 1984–. Sport, Devonport Services, 1954–56; Captain, Oldham Rugby Union, 1957–59; Professional Rugby, Leigh RFC, 1959–65. *Publications:* (contrib.) Marketing and the Consumer Movement, 1978; contrib. to various jls. *Recreations:* theatre, golf, bridge. *Address:* PO Box 6, Fell Road, Croydon. *T:* 01–688 1996. *Club:* Royal Commonwealth.

HUME, Sir Alan (Blyth), Kt 1973; CB 1963; *b* 5 Jan. 1913; *s* of late W. Alan Hume; *m* 1943, Marion Morton Garrett; one *s* one *d*. *Educ:* George Heriot's Sch.; Edinburgh Univ. Entered Scottish Office, 1936. Under-Sec., Scottish Home Department, 1957–59; Asst Under-Sec. of State, Scottish Office, 1959–62; Under-Sec., Min. of Public Bldg and Works, 1963–64; Secretary, Scottish Develt Dept, 1965–73. Chairman: Ancient Monuments Bd, Scotland, 1973–81; Edinburgh New Town Conservation Cttee, 1975–. *Recreations:* golf, fishing. *Address:* 12 Oswald Road, Edinburgh EH9 2HJ. *T:* 031–667 2440. *Clubs:* English-Speaking Union; New (Edinburgh).

HUME, His Eminence Cardinal (George) Basil; *see* Westminster, Archbishop of, (RC).

HUME, James Bell; Under-Secretary, Scottish Home and Health Department, 1977–83; *b* 16 June 1923; *s* of late Francis John Hume and Jean McLellan Hume; *m* 1950, Elizabeth Margaret Nicolson. *Educ:* George Heriot's Sch., Edinburgh; Edinburgh Univ. (MA Hons History, 1st Cl.). RAF, 1942–45. Asst Principal, Dept of Health for Scotland, 1947; Principal 1951; Jt Sec., Royal Commn on Doctors' and Dentists' Remuneration, 1958–59; Asst Sec. 1959; Nuffield Trav. Fellowship, 1963–64; Head of Edinburgh Centre, Civil Service Coll., 1969–73; Under-Sec., Scottish Education Dept, 1973–77. *Recreations:* dance music, gardening, enjoying silence. *Address:* 24 Cherry Tree Gardens, Balerno, Edinburgh EH14 5SP. *T:* 031–449 3781. *Club:* New (Edinburgh).

HUME, John; MP (SDLP) Foyle, since 1983; Member (SDLP) Northern Ireland, European Parliament, since 1979; Leader, Social Democratic and Labour Party, since 1979; *b* 18 Jan. 1937; *s* of Samuel Hume; *m* 1960, Patricia Hone; two *s* three *d*. *Educ:* St Columb's Coll., Derry; St Patrick's Coll., Maynooth, NUI (MA). Res. Fellow in European Studies, TCD; Associate Fellow, Centre for Internat. Affairs, Harvard, 1976. Pres., Credit Union League of Ireland, 1964–68; MP for Foyle, NI Parlt, 1969–73; Member (SDLP), Londonderry: NI Assembly, 1973–75; NI Constitutional Convention, 1975–76; NI Assembly, 1982–86; Minister of Commerce, NI, 1974. Mem. (SDLP) New Ireland Forum, 1983–84. Contested (SDLP) Londonderry, UK elections, Oct. 1974. Member: Cttee on Regl Policy and Regl Planning, European Parlt, 1979–; ACP-EEC Jt Cttee, 1979–; Bureau of European Socialist Gp, 1979–. Mem., Irish T&GWU. Hon. Dr of Letters Massachusetts, 1985. *Address:* 6 West End Park, Derry, N Ireland. *T:* Londonderry 265340.

HUME, Thomas Andrew, CBE 1977; FSA, FMA; Director, Museum of London, 1972–77; *b* 21 June 1917; *o s* of late Thomas Hume, Burnfoot, Oxton, and late Lillias Dodds; *m* 1942, Joyce Margaret Macdonald; two *s* one *d*. *Educ:* Heaton Grammar Sch.; King's Coll., Univ. of Durham (BA Hons Hist.). Gladstone Prizeman, Joseph Cowen Prizeman. Curator: Kirkstall Abbey House Museum, Leeds, 1949–52; Buckinghamshire County Museum, Aylesbury, 1952–60; Dir, City of Liverpool Museums, 1960–72. Member: Museums and Galleries Commn (formerly Standing Commn on Museums and Galleries), 1977–86; Adv. Cttee, London Transport Museum, 1983–. Past Pres., NW Fedn of Museums; Past Vice-Pres., Internat. Assoc. of Transport Museums; Past Chm., ICOM British Nat. Cttee; Museum Consultant, Unesco; Dir Mus. Exchange Programme, ICOM, Unesco, 1978–79. Mem. Finance Cttee, Soc. of Antiquaries. Hon. Mem., ICOM, 1983. *Publications:* contribs Thoresby Soc., Records of Bucks; excavation reports and historical articles. *Recreations:* travel, gardening. *Address:* Home Garth, Church Lane, Whittington, King's Lynn, Norfolk.

HUMMEL, Frederick Cornelius, MA, DPhil, BSc; Head of Forestry Division, Commission of the European Communities, 1973–80, retired; *b* 28 April 1915; *s* of Cornelius Hummel, OBE, and Caroline Hummel (*née* Riefler); *m* 1st, 1941, Agnes Kathleen Rushforth (marr. diss., 1961); one *s* (and one *s* decd); 2nd, 1961, Floriana Rosemary Hollyer; three *d*. *Educ:* St Stephan, Augsburg, Germany; Wadham Coll., Oxford. District Forest Officer, Uganda Forest Service, 1938–46; Forestry Commn, 1946–73; Mensuration Officer, 1946; Chief, Management Sect., 1956; released for service with FAO as Co-Dir, Mexican Nat. Forest Inventory, 1961–66; Controller, Management Services, Forestry Commn, 1966–68, Comr for Harvesting and Marketing, 1968–73. Dr *hc* Munich, 1978. *Publication:* Forest Policy, 1984. *Recreations:* walking, ski-ing. *Address:* Ridgemount, 8 The Ridgeway, Guildford, Surrey GU1 2DG. *T:* Guildford 572383. *Club:* United Oxford & Cambridge University.

HUMPHREY, Arthur Hugh Peters, CMG 1959; OBE 1952; Hon. PMN (Malaya), 1958; Controller of Special Projects, Overseas Development Administration, Foreign and Commonwealth Office, 1961–71; Malayan Civil Service, 1934–60, retired; *b* 18 June 1911; *s* of late Arthur George Humphrey, Bank Manager; *m* 1948, Mary Valentine, *d* of late Lieut-Col J. E. Macpherson; three *d*. *Educ:* Eastbourne Coll.; Merton Coll., Oxford (Open Exhbr 1930, 1st class Maths, 1933; MA 1948). Appointed Malayan Civil Service, 1934; Private Sec. to Governor of Straits Settlements and High Comr for Malay States, 1936–38; Resident, Labuan, 1940–42; interned by Japanese in Borneo, 1942–45; idc 1948; Sec. for Defence and Internal Security, Fedn of Malaya, 1953–57; Mem. of Federal Legislative and Executive Councils, 1953–56; Sec. to the Treasury, Federation of Malaya, 1957–59; Director of Technical Assistance, Commonwealth Relations Office, 1960–61; Controller of Special Projects, ODM, 1961. Official Leader, United Kingdom delegations at Colombo Plan conferences: Tokyo, 1960, and Kuala Lumpur, 1961. Coronation Medal, 1953. *Recreations:* music, tennis. *Address:* 14 Ambrose Place, Worthing, Sussex. *T:* Worthing 33339. *Club:* East India, Devonshire, Sports and Public Schools.

HUMPHREY, Frank Basil, CB 1975; Parliamentary Counsel, 1967–80; *b* 21 Sept. 1918; *s* of late John Hartley Humphrey and Alice Maud Humphrey (*née* Broadbent); *m* 1947, Ol'ga Černá, *y d* of late Františck Černý, Trenčín, Czechoslovakia; two *s*. *Educ:* Brentwood Sch.; St Catharine's Coll., Cambridge (Schol.). 2nd cl. hons Pt I. Mod. Langs Tripos, 1st cl. hons Pt II Law Tripos. Served RA, 1939–45: Adjt 23rd Mountain Regt and DAAG 4 Corps, India and Burma. Called to Bar, Middle Temple, 1946 (Harmsworth Schol.). Seconded as First Parly Counsel, Fedn of Nigeria, 1961–64, and as Counsel-in-charge at Law Commn, 1971–72. *Recreations:* gardening, mountain walking, music. *Address:* 1a The Avenue, Summersdale, Chichester, W Sussex PO19 4PZ. *T:* Chichester 778783.

HUMPHREY, Prof. John Herbert, CBE 1970; BA; MD; FRS 1963; FRCP 1971; Professor of Immunology, Royal Postgraduate Medical School, London University, 1976–81, now Emeritus Professor; *b* 16 Dec. 1915; *s* of Herbert Alfred Humphrey and Mary Elizabeth Humphrey (*née* Horniblow); *m* 1939, Janet Rumney, *d* of Prof. Archibald Vivian Hill, CH, OBE, FRS, ScD, and late Margaret Neville, *d* of late Dr J. N. Keynes; two *s* three *d*. *Educ:* Winchester Coll.; Trinity Coll., Cambridge (Hon. Fellow, 1986); UCH Med. Sch. Jenner Research Student, Lister Inst., 1941–42; Asst Pathologist, Central Middx Hosp., 1942–46; External Staff, Med. Research Council, 1946–49; Member: Scientific Staff, Nat. Inst. for Med. Research, 1949–76, Dep. Dir, 1961–76, Head of Div. of Immunology and Experimental Biology, 1957–76; Expert Cttee on Biological Standardization, WHO, 1955–70; Expert Cttee on Immunology, WHO, 1962–; Nat. Biol. Standards Bd, 1977–85. Editor, Advances in Immunology, 1960–67; Asst Editor, Immunology, 1958–68. Mem. Council, Royal Society, 1967–69. Past Pres., Internat. Union of Immunological Socs. Pres., Medical Campaign against Nuclear Weapons; Chm., Soc. for the Protection of Science and Learning Ltd. Foreign Associate, Nat. Acad. of Scis, 1986. Hon. DSc Brunel, 1979. *Publications:* Immunology for Students of Medicine (with Prof. R. G. White), 1963; (with J. Zimian and P. Sieghart) The World of Science and the Rule of Law, 1986; contribs to Jls of immunology, biochemistry, physiology, etc. *Address:* 30 St James Mansions, Hilltop Road, NW6 2AA. *T:* 01–624 9376; Ducklake House, Ashwell, Baldock, Herts SG7 5LL. *T:* Ashwell 2491.

HUMPHREY, William Gerald, MA Oxon and Cantab, DPhil Oxon; Assistant Secretary, University of Cambridge Appointments Board, 1962–72; Headmaster of The Leys School, Cambridge, 1934–58; Group personnel officer, Fisons Ltd, 1958–62; *b* 2 Aug. 1904; *e s* of late Rev. William Humphrey and Helen Lusher; *m* 1936, Margaret, *er d* of late William E. Swift, Cornwall, Conn., USA; one *s*. *Educ:* King Edward VII Sch., Sheffield; Queen's Coll., Oxford (Hastings Scholar, Taberdar, University Sen. Research Student); 1st Class Final Honour Sch. of Natural Science, 1926; DPhil, 1928; Commonwealth Fund Fellow, Harvard Univ., 1929–31; Senior Science Master, Uppingham Sch., 1932–34. Mem. Ministry of Agriculture Cttee on demand for Agricultural Graduates. *Publications:* The Christian and Education, 1940; Papers in Journal of the Chemical Soc. *Recreation:* painting. *Address:* 15310 Pine Orchard Drive, Silver Spring, Maryland 20906, USA. *T:* 301 598 8368.

HUMPHREYS, Arthur Leslie Charles, CBE 1970; Director: Computer Associated Systems Ltd, since 1982; Upgradeable Systems Ltd, since 1984; Director, Charles Babbage Institute, since 1978; *b* 8 Jan. 1917; *s* of late Percy Stewart Humphreys and late Louise (*née* Weston); *m* 1st, 1943, Marjorie Irene Murphy-Jones (decd); two *s* one *d*; 2nd, 1975, Audrey Norah Urquhart (*née* Dunningham) (decd). *Educ:* Catford Grammar Sch.; Administrative Staff Coll., Henley. International Computers & Tabulators Ltd: Dir 1963–84; Dep. Man. Dir 1964; Man. Dir 1967; ICL Ltd: Dir, 1968–82; Man. Dir, 1968–72; Dep. Chm., 1972–77; Dir, Data Recording Instrument Co. Ltd, 1957–84. *Recreations:* table tennis, bridge, music. *Address:* 24 Middle Street, Thriplow, Royston, Herts SG8 7RD. *T:* Fowlmere 594.

HUMPHREYS, Prof. Arthur Raleigh; Professor of English, University of Leicester, 1947–76; *b* 28 March 1911; *s* of William Ernest Humphreys and Lois (*née* Rainforth); *m* 1947, Kathryn Jane, *d* of James and Jessie Currie, Drumadoon, Isle of Arran. *Educ:* Grammar Sch., Wallasey, Ches; St Catharine's Coll., Cambridge; Harvard Univ., USA. Charles Oldham Shakespeare Schol., Cambridge, 1932; BA (Cambridge), 1933, MA 1936; Commonwealth Fund Fellow, Harvard, 1933–35; AM (Harvard), 1935. Supervisor in English, Cambridge Univ., 1935–37; Lectr in English, Liverpool Univ., 1937–46. Served War of 1939–45, RAF Intelligence, 1940–42 (Flying Officer); British Council Lecturer in English, Istanbul Univ., 1942–45. Fellow Folger Shakespeare Library, Washington, DC, 1960, 1961, 1964; Visiting Fellow: All Souls Coll., Oxford, 1966; Huntington Library, Calif, 1978–79; Visiting Professor: Bogaziçi Univ., Istanbul, 1979–80, 1981–82, 1984; Singapore Univ., 1982–83. *Publications:* William Shenstone, 1937; The Augustan World, 1954; Steele, Addison, and their Periodical Essays, 1959; (ed) Henry IV, Part I, 1960, Part II, 1966; Melville, 1962; (ed) Joseph Andrews, 1962; (ed) Tom Jones, 1962; (ed) Amelia, 1963; (ed) Jonathan Wild, 1964; (ed) Melville's White-Jacket, 1966; Shakespeare, Richard II, 1967; (ed) Henry V, 1968; (ed) Henry VIII, 1971; Shakespeare, Merchant of Venice, 1973; Defoe, Robinson Crusoe, 1980; (ed) Much Ado About Nothing, 1981; (ed) Julius Caesar, 1984; contrib: From Dryden to Johnson (ed B. Ford), 1957; Alexander Pope (ed P. Dixon), 1972; Shakespeare's Art (ed M. Crane), 1973; Shakespeare: Select Bibliographical Guides (ed S. Wells), 1973, and to learned journals. *Recreations:* music, architecture, hill walking. *Address:* Springfield Apts 7, 2 St Mary's Road, Leicester LE2 1XA. *T:* Leicester 705118.

HUMPHREYS, (David) Colin, CMG 1977; *b* 23 April 1925; *s* of late Charles Roland Lloyd Humphreys and Bethia Joan (*née* Bowie); *m* 1952, Jill Allison (*née* Cranmer); two *s* one *d*. *Educ:* Eton Coll. (King's Scholar); King's Coll., Cambridge (MA). Served Army, 1943–46. Air Min., 1949; Private Sec. to Sec. of State for Air, 1959–60; Counsellor, UK Delegn to NATO, 1960–63; Air Force Dept, 1963–69; IDC 1970; Dir, Defence Policy Staff, 1971–72; Asst Sec. Gen. (Defence Planning and Policy), NATO, 1972–76; Asst Under Sec. of State (Naval Staff), MoD, 1977–79; Dep. Under Sec. of State (Air), MoD, 1979–85. Dir of Develt, RIIA, 1985–86. *Address:* Rivendell, North Drive, Virginia Water, Surrey. *T:* Wentworth 2130. *Clubs:* Royal Air Force; Wentworth.

HUMPHREYS, Emyr Owen; Author; *b* 15 April 1919; *s* of William and Sarah Rosina Humphreys, Prestatyn, Flints; *m* 1946, Elinor Myfanwy, *d* of Rev. Griffith Jones, Bontnewydd, Caerns; three *s* one *d*. *Educ:* University Coll., Aberystwyth; University Coll., Bangor. Gregynog Arts Fellow, 1974–75. *Publications:* The Little Kingdom, 1946; The Voice of a Stranger, 1949; A Change of Heart, 1951; Hear and Forgive, 1952 (Somerset Maugham Award, 1953); A Man's Estate, 1955; The Italian Wife, 1957; Y Tri Llais, 1958; A Toy Epic, 1958 (Hawthornden Prize, 1959); The Gift, 1963; Outside the House of Baal, 1965; Natives, 1968; Ancestor Worship, 1970; National Winner, 1971 (Welsh Arts Council Prize, 1972); Flesh and Blood, 1974; Landscapes, 1976; The Best of Friends, 1978; Penguin Modern Poets No 27, 1978 (Soc. of Authors Travelling Award, 1979); The Kingdom of Brân, 1979; The Anchor Tree, 1980; Pwyll a Riannon, 1980; Miscellany Two, 1981; The Taliesin Tradition, 1983 (Welsh Arts Council Non-Fiction Prize, 1984); Jones: a novel, 1984; Salt of the Earth, 1985; An Absolute Hero, 1986. *Recreations:* rural pursuits. *Address:* Llinon, Penyberth, Llanfairpwll, Ynys Môn, Gwynedd LL61 5YT.

HUMPHREYS, Maj.-Gen. George Charles, CB 1952; CBE 1948 (OBE 1945); *b* 5 Oct. 1899; *s* of late George Humphreys, formerly of Croft House, Croft-on-Tees, Co. Durham, and Caroline Huddart; *m* 1931, Doris Isabelle, *d* of late A. B. Baines, Shanghai; no *c*. *Educ:* Giggleswick Sch., Yorks; RMC Sandhurst. 2nd Lieut Royal Northumberland Fusiliers, 1918; Lieut 1920; Capt. 1930; Bt-Major, Major 1938; Lieut-Col 1946; Col 1947; Brig. 1951; Maj.-Gen, 1952. Served with 2nd Bn Royal Northumberland Fusiliers, Iraq, India and China, 1919–31, Adjt 1925–28 (Iraq medal and clasp, 1920); Bde Major, E Lancs and Border TA Bde, 1935–37; GSO2 Public Relations, War Office, 1938–39; War of 1939–45, in UK and Italy; GSO1 War Office, 1939–40; successively (Jan. 1941–May

1946), AA and QMG 55th Inf. Div., 1st and 3rd Armd Gps, 79th Armd Div., Col (Q) ops War Office, Col A/Q (BUCO) 21 Army Gp, Col A/Q, 1944–46; Allied Commn for Austria, took Advance Party into Vienna, 19 July 1945; Dep. Chief Mil. Div. (Brig.), 1946; Brig. i/c Admin Burma Comd, 1946–48; BGS, HQ Scottish Comd, 1948–51; Maj.-Gen. Adminstration, GHQ Middle East Land Forces, 1951–54; Chairman: PAO and PPO Cttees, Middle East, 1951–54; Military Adviser to Contractors for Canal Base (War Office, July 1954–31 May 1955); retired from Army, June 1955, and appointed General Manager, Suez Contractors Management Co. Ltd; appointed Chief Executive to Governing Body of Suez Contractors (Services) Ltd, Jan. 1956 until Liquidation of Suez enterprise, July 1957; Chief Organizer, Dollar Exports Council Conference, 1958. *Recreations:* reading, travel and shooting. *Address:* Lauriston Cottage, Old Green Lane, Camberley, Surrey. *T:* Camberley 21078.

HUMPHREYS, John Henry; Chairman, Industrial Tribunals (Ashford, Kent), since 1976; Legal Officer, Law Commission, since 1973; *b* 28 Feb. 1917; British; *m* 1939, Helen Mary Markbreiter; one *s* one *d*. *Educ:* Cranleigh School. Solicitor. Served with Co. of London Yeomanry, and Northampton Yeomanry, 1939–47; Treasury Solicitor Dept, 1947–73. *Recreations:* sailing, golf, gardening. *Address:* Gate House Cottage, Sandown Road, Sandwich, Kent. *T:* Sandwich 612961. *Club:* Prince's (Sandwich).
See also Q. J. Thomas.

HUMPHREYS, Kenneth William, BLitt, MA, PhD; FLA; Librarian, European University Institute, Florence, 1975–81; *b* 4 Dec. 1916; *s* of Joseph Maxmillian Humphreys and Bessie Benfield; *m* 1939, Margaret, *d* of Reginald F. Hill and Dorothy Lucas; two *s*. *Educ:* Southfield Sch., Oxford; St Catherine's Coll., Oxford. Library Asst, All Souls Coll., Oxford, 1933–36; Asst, Bodleian Library, 1936–50; Dep. Librarian, Brotherton Library, University of Leeds, 1950–52; Librarian, Univ. of Birmingham, 1952–75. Prof. of Library Studies, Haifa Univ., 1982. Hon. Lecturer in Palaeography: University of Leeds, 1950–52; University of Birmingham, 1952–75. Hon. Sec., Standing Conf. of Nat. and University Libraries, 1954–69, Vice-Chm., 1969–71, Chm. 1971–73; Mem. Library Adv. Council for England, 1966–71; Mem. Council, Library Assoc., 1964–75, Chm. Council 1973; Chm. Exec. Cttee, West Midlands Regional Library Bureau, 1963–75; Chairman: Jt Standing Conf. and Cttee on Library Cooperation, 1965–75; Nat. Cttee on Regional Library Cooperation, 1970–75; Mem. Comité International de Paléographie, and Colloque International de Paléographie, 1955–; President: Nat. and University Libraries Section, Internat. Fedn of Library Assocs, 1968–69, Pres., University Libraries Sub-Section, 1967–73; Ligue des Bibliothèques Européennes de Recherche, 1974–80; Round Table on Library History, 1978–. Sec. Cttee, British Acad. Corpus of British Medieval Library Catalogues, 1983–. Editor, Studies in the History of Libraries and Librarianship; Associate Editor, Libri; Jt Editor, Series of Reproductions of Medieval and Renaissance Texts. Hon. LittD Dublin (Trinity Coll.), 1967. Hon. FLA 1980; Socio d'onore, Italian Library Assoc., 1982. *Publications:* The Book Provisions of the Medieval Friars, 1964; The Medieval Library of the Carmelites at Florence, 1964; The Library of the Franciscans of the Convent of St Antony, Padua at the Beginning of the fifteenth century, 1966; The Library of the Franciscans of Siena in the Fifteenth Century, 1977; articles in library periodicals. *Recreation:* collection of manuscripts. *Address:* 94 Metchley Lane, Harborne, Birmingham B17 0HS. *T:* 021–427 2785. *Clubs:* Athenæum; Kildare Street and University (Dublin).

HUMPHREYS, Sir Myles; see Humphreys, Sir R. E. M.

HUMPHREYS, Sir Olliver (William), Kt 1968; CBE 1957; BSc, FInstP, CEng, FIEE, FRAeS; *b* 4 Sept. 1902; *s* of late Rev. J. Willis Humphreys, Bath; *m* 1933, Muriel Mary Hawkins (*d* 1985). *Educ:* Caterham Sch.; University Coll., London. Joined staff GEC Research Labs, 1925, Dir, 1949–61; Director 1953, Vice-Chm., 1963–67, GEC Ltd; Chm. all GEC Electronics and Telecommunications subsidiaries, 1961–66 and GEC (Research) Ltd, 1961–67. Mem. Bd, Inst. Physics, 1951–60 (Pres., 1956–58); Mem. Coun., IEE, 1952–55 (Vice-Pres., 1959–63; Pres., 1964–65); Faraday Lectr, 1953–54. Mem., BoT Cttee on Organisation and Constitution of BSI, 1949–50; Chm., BSI Telecommunications Industry Standards Cttee, 1951–63 (Mem. Gen. Coun., 1953–56; Mem. Exec. Cttee, 1953–60); Chm., Internat. Special Cttee on Radio Interference (CISPR), 1953–61; Chm., Electrical Res. Assoc., 1958–61; Chm., DSIR Radio Res. Bd, 1954–62; Pres., Electronic Engrg Assoc., 1962–64; Founder Chm., Conf. of Electronics Industry, 1963–67; Mem., Nat. ERC, 1963–67. Fellow UCL, 1963. Liveryman, Worshipful Co. of Makers of Playing Cards. *Publications:* various technical and scientific papers in proceedings of learned societies. *Recreations:* travel, walking, reading. *Address:* The Victoria Hotel, Sidmouth, Devon.

HUMPHREYS, Sir (Raymond Evelyn) Myles, Kt 1977; JP; DL; Chairman: Northern Ireland Railways Co. Ltd, since 1967; Northern Ireland Police Authority, Royal Ulster Constabulary, since 1976; company director; *b* 24 March 1925; *s* of Raymond and May Humphreys; *m* 1963, Joan Tate (*d* 1979); two *s*. *Educ:* Skegoniel Primary Sch.; Londonderry High Sch.; Belfast Royal Acad. Research Engineer: NI Road Transport Bd, 1946–48; Ulster Transport Authy, 1948–55; Transport Manager, Nestlé's Food Products (NI) Ltd, 1955–59; Director: Walter Alexander (Belfast) Ltd, 1959–; Quick Service Stations Ltd, 1971–; Bowring Martin Ltd, 1978–; Abbey National Bldg Soc., 1981– (Chm., NI Adv. Bd, 1981–); Chm., Belfast Marathon Ltd, 1981–85. Member of Board: Ulster Transport Authority, 1966–69; NI Transport Holding Co. Ltd, 1968–74. Mem., Belfast City Council, 1964–81; Chairman: Belfast Corp. Housing Cttee, 1966–69; City Council Planning Cttee, 1973–75; Town Planning and Environmental Hlth Cttee, 1973–75; Finance and Gen. Purposes Cttee, 1978–80; High Sheriff of Belfast, 1969; Dep. Lord Mayor, 1970; Lord Mayor, 1975–77. Member: Nat. Planning and Town Planning Council, 1970–81 (Chm., 1976–77); NI Tourist Bd, 1973–80; NI Housing Exec., 1975–78; Chm., Ulster Tourist Develt Assoc., 1968–78; Belfast Harbour Comr, 1979–. Mem., May Cttee of Inquiry into UK Prison Services, 1978–79. Past Chairman: Bd of Visitors, HM Prison, Belfast; Bd of Management, Dunlambert Secondary Sch. Past-Pres., Belfast Junior Chamber of Commerce; Mem. Exec., NI Chamber of Commerce and Industry (Pres., 1982–83); NI Rep., Mobility Internat.; Senator, Junior Chamber Internat.; Pres., Belfast Br., BIM, 1983–. Member: TA&VRA for NI, 1980; Council, Queen's Silver Jubilee Appeal. Pres., NI Polio Fellowship, 1977–. Pres., City of Belfast Youth Orch., 1980; Dir, Ulster Orch. Soc., 1980; Trustee, Ulster Folk & Transport Mus., 1976–81. Mem. Senate, QUB, 1975–77. District Transport Officer, St John Ambulance Brigade, 1946–66. Freeman of City of London, 1976. DL Belfast 1983. FCIT; OStJ. *Address:* Mylestone, Chichester Park, Belfast BT15 5DR. *T:* Belfast 771518. *Club:* Lansdowne.

HUMPHREYS, Prof. Robert Arthur, OBE 1946; MA, PhD Cantab; Director, Institute of Latin-American Studies, University of London, 1965–74; Professor of Latin-American History in University of London, 1948–74, now Emeritus; *b* 6 June 1907; *s* of late Robert Humphreys and Helen Marion Bavin, Lincoln; *m* 1946, Elisabeth, *er d* of late Sir Bernard Pares, KBE, DCL. *Educ:* Lincoln Sch.; Peterhouse, Cambridge (Scholar). Commonwealth Fund Fellow, Univ. of Michigan, 1930–32. Asst Lectr in American History, UCL, 1932, Lectr 1935; Reader in American History in Univ. of London, 1942–48; Prof. of Latin-American History, UCL, 1948–70. Research Dept, FO, 1939–45. Mem., UGC Cttee on Latin American Studies, 1962–64; Chairman: Cttee on Library Resources, Univ. of London, 1969–71; Management Cttee, Inst of Archæology, 1975–80; Mem. Adv. Cttee, British Library Reference Div., 1975–79. Governor, SOAS, 1965–80, Hon. Fellow 1981. Pres., RHistS, 1964–68 (Hon. Vice-Pres., 1968). Lectures: Enid Muir Meml, Univ. of Newcastle upon Tyne, 1962; Creighton, Univ. of London, 1964; Raleigh, Brit. Acad., 1965. Corresp. Member: Hispanic Soc. of America; Argentine Acad. of History; Instituto Histórico e Geográfico Brasileiro; Academia Chilena de la Historia; Sociedad Chilena de Historia y Geografía; Instituto Ecuatoriano de Ciencias Naturales; Sociedad Peruana de Historia; Instituto Histórico y Geográfico del Uruguay; Academia Nacional de la Historia, Venezuela. Hon. DLitt: Newcastle, 1966; Nottingham, 1972; Hon. LittD Liverpool, 1972; DUniv Essex, 1973. Comdr, Order of Rio Branco, Brazil, 1972. Machado de Assis Medal, Academia Brasileira de Letras, 1974. *Publications:* British Consular Reports on the Trade and Politics of Latin America, 1940; The Evolution of Modern Latin America, 1946; Liberation in South America, 1806–1827, 1952; Latin American History: A Guide to the Literature in English, 1958; The Diplomatic History of British Honduras, 1638–1901, 1961; (with G. S. Graham), The Navy and South America, 1807–1823 (Navy Records Soc.), 1962; (with J. Lynch) The Origins of the Latin American Revolutions, 1808–1826, 1965; Tradition and Revolt in Latin America and other Essays, 1969; The Detached Recollections of General D. F. O'Leary, 1969; The Royal Historical Society, 1868–1968, 1969; Robert Southey and his History of Brazil, 1978; Latin American Studies in Great Britain (autobiog.), 1978; Latin America and the Second World War, vol. I, 1939–1942, 1981, vol. II, 1942–1945, 1982; Co-edited: (with A. D. Momigliano) Byzantine Studies and Other Essays by N. H. Baynes, 1955; (with Elisabeth Humphreys) The Historian's Business and Other Essays by Richard Pares, 1961; contrib. to The New Cambridge Modern History, vols VIII, IX and X. *Address:* 5 St James's Close, Prince Albert Road, NW8 7LG. *T:* 01–722 3628.

HUMPHRIES, Barry; *see* Humphries, J. B.

HUMPHRIES, David Ernest; Assistant Chief Scientific Adviser (Projects and Research), Ministry of Defence, since 1986; *b* 3 Feb. 1937; *er s* of late Ernest Augustus Humphries and of Kathleen Humphries; *m* 1959, Wendy Rosemary Cook; one *s* one *d*. *Educ:* Brighton Coll.; Corpus Christi Coll., Oxford (Scholar; MA). RAE Farnborough: Materials Dept, 1961; Avionics Dept, 1966; Head of Inertial Navigation Div., 1974; Head of Bombing and Navigation Div., 1975; Head of Systems Assessment Dept, 1978; Dir Gen. Future Projects, MoD PE, 1981–83; Chief Scientist (RAF) and Dir Gen. of Res. (C), MoD, 1983–84; Dir Gen. Res. Technol., MoD (PE), 1984–86. *Recreations:* music, pipe organ building and playing. *Address:* 18 The Mount, Malton, N Yorks YO17 0ND.

HUMPHRIES, Gerard William; His Honour Judge Humphries; a Circuit Judge since 1980; *b* 13 Dec. 1928; *s* of late John Alfred Humphries and Marie Frances Humphries (*née* Whitwell), Barrow-in-Furness; *m* 1957, Margaret Valerie, *o d* of late W. W. Gelderd and Margaret Gelderd (*née* Bell), Ulverston; four *s* one *d*. *Educ:* St Bede's Coll., Manchester; Manchester Univ. (LLB Hons). Called to Bar, Middle Temple, 1952; admitted to Northern Circuit, 1954; Asst Recorder of Salford, 1969–71; a Recorder of the Crown Court, 1974–80. Chairman: Medical Appeals Tribunal, 1976–80; Vaccine Damage Tribunals, 1979–80. Charter Mem., Serra Club, N Cheshire, 1963– (Pres. 1968, 1973). Chm., SBC Educnl Trust, 1979–. Foundn Governor, St Bede's Coll., Manchester, 1978–. *Recreations:* tennis, golf, music, caravanning. *Address:* 1 Deans Court, Crown Square, Manchester M3 3JL. *Clubs:* Lansdowne; Northern Lawn Tennis, Northenden Golf (Manchester).

HUMPHRIES, John Anthony Charles, OBE 1980; Member, Thames Water Authority, since 1983; *b* 15 June 1925; *s* of Charles Humphries; *m* 1951, Olga June, *d* of Dr Geoffrey Duckworth, MRCP; four *d*. *Educ:* Fettes; Peterhouse, Cambridge (1st Law). Served War, RNVR, 1943–46. Solicitor (Hons), 1951. Chm., Water Space Amenity Commn, 1973–83; Vice-Pres., Inland Waterways Assoc., 1973– (Chm., 1970–73); Mem. Inland Waterways Amenity Adv. Council, 1971–; Adviser to HM Govt on amenity use of water space, 1972; Mem. Nat. Water Council, 1973–83; Chm., Evans of Leeds plc, 1982–; Mem., London Bd, Halifax Building Soc., 1985–; Dep. Chm., CoEnCo, 1985–. *Recreations:* inland waters, gardening. *Address:* 21 Parkside, Wimbledon, SW19. *T:* 01–946 3764. *Clubs:* RNVR, City.

HUMPHRIES, (John) Barry, AO 1982; music-hall artiste and author; *b* 17 Feb. 1934; *s* of J. A. E. Humphries and L. A. Brown; *m* 1st, 1959, Rosalind Tong; two *d*; 2nd, 1979, Diane Millstead; two *s*. *Educ:* Melbourne Grammar Sch.; Univ. of Melbourne. Repertory seasons, Union Theatre, Melbourne, 1953–54; Phillip Street Revue Theatre, Sydney, 1956; Demon Barber, Lyric, Hammersmith, 1959; Oliver, New Theatre, 1960. One-man shows (author and performer): A Nice Night's Entertainment, 1962; Excuse I, 1965; Just a Show, 1968; A Load of Olde Stuffe, 1971; At Least You Can Say That You've Seen It, 1974; Housewife Superstar, 1976; Isn't It Pathetic at His Age, 1979; A Night with Dame Edna, 1979; An Evening's Intercourse with Barry Humphries, 1981–82; Tears Before Bedtime, 1986. Numerous plays, films and broadcasts. *Publications:* Bizarre, 1964; Innocent Austral Verse, 1968; (with Nicholas Garland) The Wonderful World of Barry McKenzie, 1970; (with Nicholas Garland) Bazza Holds His Own, 1972; Dame Edna's Coffee Table Book, 1976; Les Patterson's Australia, 1979; Treasury of Australian Kitsch, 1980; A Nice Night's Entertainment, 1981; Dame Edna's Bedside Companion, 1982; The Traveller's Tool, 1985. *Recreations:* reading secondhand booksellers' catalogues in bed, inventing Australia. *Address:* c/o Allen, Allen and Hemsley, PO Box 50, Sydney, NSW 2001, Australia. *Clubs:* Athenæum, Garrick.

HUMPIDGE, Kenneth Palmer, CMG 1957; *b* 18 Nov. 1902; *s* of James Dickerson Humpidge, Stroud; *m* 1938, Jill Mary Russell, *d* of Russell Pountney, Bristol; two *d*. *Educ:* Wycliffe Coll.; Univ. of Bristol. BSc (Engineering). Public Works Dept, Nigeria, 1926; Director of Public Works, Northern Region, Nigeria, 1948–54; Director of Federal Public Works, 1954–57; Min. of Transport, Nottingham and Cheltenham, 1958–69. FICE. *Address:* Corner Walls, Amberley, Stroud, Glos. *T:* Amberley 3212.

HUNN, Sir Jack (Kent), Kt 1976; CMG 1964; LLM; Retired as Secretary of Defence, New Zealand (1963–66); *b* 24 Aug. 1906; *m* 1932, Dorothy Murray; two *s*; *m* 1985, Mabel Duncan. *Educ:* Wairarapa Coll.; Auckland Univ. Public Trust Office, 1924–46; Actg Sec. of Justice, 1950; Public Service Comr, 1954–61; Actg Sec. of Internal Affairs and Dir of Civil Defence, 1959; Sec. for Maori Affairs and Maori Trustee, 1960–63. Reviewed Cook Islands Public Service, 1949 and 1954; Mem. NZ delegn to Duke of Edinburgh's Conf, 1956; Mem. UN Salary Review Cttee, 1956; reviewed organisation of South Pacific Commn, Noumea and Sydney, 1957, and of SEATO, Bangkok, 1959. Chairman: Wildlife Commission of Inquiry, 1968; Fire Safety Inquiry, 1969; Fire Service Council, 1973; Fire Service Commn, 1974. *Publications:* Hunn Report on Maori Affairs, 1960; Not Only Affairs Of State, 1982. *Address:* 17 Kereru Street, Waikanae, Wellington, New Zealand. *T:* (058) 35033.

HUNNISETT, Dr Roy Frank, FSA, FRHistS; on staff of Public Record Office, since 1953; *b* 26 Feb. 1928; *s* of Frank Hunnisett and Alice (*née* Budden); *m* 1954, Edith Margaret Evans. *Educ:* Bexhill Grammar Sch.; New Coll., Oxford (1st Cl. Hons Mod.

Hist., 1952; Amy Mary Preston Read Scholar, 1952–53; MA, DPhil 1956). FRHistS 1961; FSA 1975. Lectr, New Coll., Oxford, 1957–63. Royal Historical Society: Alexander Prize, 1957; Mem. Council, 1974–77; Vice-Pres., 1979–82; Selden Society: Mem. Council, 1975–84; Vice-Pres., 1984–; Treasurer, Pipe Roll Soc., 1973–. *Publications:* Calendar of Inquisitions Miscellaneous: (ed jtly) vol. IV, 1957 and vol. V, 1962; (ed) vol. VI, 1963 and vol. VII, 1968; The Medieval Coroners' Rolls, 1960; The Medieval Coroner, 1961; (ed) Bedfordshire Coroners' Rolls, 1961; (ed) Calendar of Nottinghamshire Coroners' Inquests 1485–1558, 1969; (contrib.) The Study of Medieval Records: essays in honour of Kathleen Major, 1971; Indexing for Editors, 1972; Editing Records for Publication, 1977; (ed jtly and contrib.) Medieval Legal Records edited in memory of C.A.F. Meekings, 1978; (ed) Wiltshire Coroners' Bills, 1752–1796, 1981; (ed) Sussex Coroners' Inquests 1485–1558, 1985; articles and revs in historical and legal jls. *Recreations:* Sussex, music, cricket. *Address:* 23 Byron Gardens, Sutton, Surrey SM1 3QG. *T:* 01–661 2618.

HUNSDON OF HUNSDON, Baron; *see* Aldenham, Baron.

HUNSWORTH, John Alfred; Director, Banking Information Service, 1954–81; *b* 23 Dec. 1921; *s* of late Fred Sheard Hunsworth and Lillian Margaret (*née* Wetmon); *m* 1972, Phyllis Sparshatt. *Educ:* Selhurst Grammar Sch.; LSE (BCom). Served War, 1941–46: commnd E Surrey Regt; served 2nd Punjab Regt, Indian Army, 1942–45. Dep. Editor, Bankers' Magazine, 1948–54. Freeman, City of London. *Publications:* contrib. prof. jls. *Recreations:* gardening, world travel, philately; formerly lawn tennis and Rugby football. *Address:* 29 West Hill, Sanderstead, Surrey. *T:* 01–657 2585. *Clubs:* Reform, Royal Over-Seas League; Surrey County Cricket.

HUNT; *see* Crowther-Hunt.

HUNT, family name of **Barons Hunt, Hunt of Fawley** and **Hunt of Tanworth.**

HUNT, Baron, *cr* 1966, of Llanfair Waterdine (Life Peer); **(Henry Cecil) John Hunt;** KG 1979; Kt 1953; CBE 1945; DSO 1944; *b* 22 June 1910; *s* of late Capt. C. E. Hunt, MC, IA, and E. H. Hunt (*née* Crookshank); *m* 1936, Joy Mowbray-Green; four *d*. *Educ:* Marlborough Coll.; RMC, Sandhurst. Commissioned King's Royal Rifle Corps, 1930; seconded to Indian Police, 1934–35 and 1938–40 (Indian Police Medal, 1940). War of 1939–45: Comd 11th Bn KRRC, 1944; Comd 11th Indian Inf. Bde, 1944–46. Staff Coll., 1946; Joint Services Staff Coll., 1949; GSO 1, Jt Planning Staffs, MELF, 1946–48; Western Europe C's-in-C Cttee, 1950–51; Allied Land Forces, Central Europe, 1951–52; Col, Gen. Staff, HQ I (British) Corps, 1952; Asst Comdt, The Staff Coll., 1953–55; Comdr 168 Inf. Bde, TA, 1955–56; retired, 1956; Hon. Brigadier. Dir, Duke of Edinburgh's Award Scheme, 1956–66. Rector, Aberdeen Univ., 1963–66. Personal Adviser to Prime Minister during Nigerian Civil War, 1968–70. Chairman: Parole Bd for England and Wales, 1967–74; Adv. Cttee on Police in N Ireland, 1969; President: Nat. Assoc. of Youth Clubs, 1954–70; Council for Volunteers Overseas, 1968–74; Nat. Assoc. of Probation Officers, 1974–80; Rainer Foundn, 1971–85; Council for Nat. Parks, 1980–86; Mem., Royal Commn on the Press, 1974–77; Pres., Britain and Nepal Soc., 1960–75. Joined Social Democratic Party, 1981. Leader, British Expedition to Mount Everest, 1952–53. President: The Alpine Club, 1956–58; Climbers' Club, 1963–66; British Mountaineering Council, 1965–68; The National Ski Fedn, 1968–72; RGS, 1977–80 (Hon. Mem., 1984). Order 1st Class Gurkha Right Hand, 1953; Indian Everest Medal, 1953; Hubbard Medal (US), 1954; Founder's Medal, RGS, 1954; Lawrence Memorial Medal, RCAS, 1954; Hon. DCL Durham 1954; Hon. LLD: Aberdeen 1954; London 1954; City 1976; Leeds 1979. *Publications:* The Ascent of Everest, 1953; Our Everest Adventure, 1954; (with C. Brasher) The Red Snows, 1959; Life is Meeting, 1978; (ed) My Favourite Mountaineering Stories, 1978. *Recreations:* mountaineering, ski-ing. *Address:* Highway Cottage, Aston, Henley-on-Thames. *Clubs:* Alpine, Ski Club of Great Britain.
See also Hugh Hunt.

HUNT OF FAWLEY, Baron *cr* 1973 (Life Peer), of Fawley in the County of Buckingham; **John Henderson Hunt,** CBE 1970; MA, DM Oxon, FRCP, FRCS, FRCGP; Hon. Fellow, Green College, Oxford, since 1980; President, Royal College of General Practitioners, 1967–70; Consulting Physician, St Dunstan's, 1948–66; Governor: Charterhouse School; Sutton's Hospital, Old Charterhouse; Royal Marsden Hospital; *b* 3 July 1905; *s* of late Edmund Henderson Hunt, MCh, FRCS, and Laura Mary Buckingham; *m* 1941, Elisabeth Ernestine, *d* of Norman Evill, FRIBA; two *s* two *d*. (and one *s* decd). *Educ:* Charterhouse School; Balliol College, Oxford; St Bartholomew's Hospital. Theodore Williams Scholar in Physiology, Oxford Univ., 1926; Radcliffe Scholar in Pharmacology, Oxford, 1928. RAF Medical Service, 1940–45 (Wing Comdr). PMO, Provident Mutual Life Assce Assoc., 1947–80. Hon. Cons. in Gen. Practice, RAF. President: Hunterian Soc., 1953; Gen. Practice Section, Royal Soc. Med., 1956; Harveian Soc., 1970; Chelsea Clinical Soc., 1971; Med. Soc. London, 1973; Soc. of Chiropodists, 1974; Carthusian Soc., 1980; Vice-Pres. Brit. Med. Students' Assoc., 1956; Hon. Sec. Council, Coll. of Gen. Practitioners, 1952–67; Med. Soc. of London, 1964–65; Mem. Council: RCS (co-opted), 1957–61; Med. Protection Soc., 1948–69; St Dunstan's, 1966–83. Member: General Advisory Council, BBC, 1958–66; Med. Services Review Cttee, 1958–61; Med. Commn on Accident Prevention, 1967. Fellow and Gold Medallist, BMA, 1980; Honorary Fellow: RSM; Aust. Coll. Gen. Practitioners; Singapore Coll. of Gen. Practitioners; Hon. Mem. and Victor Johnston Medallist, Coll. of Family Physicians of Canada; Hon. Mem., Amer. Acad. of Family Physicians. Lloyd Roberts Lecturer (Manchester), 1956; Albert Wander Lectr (RSM), 1968; Paul Hopkins Memorial Orator (Brisbane), 1969; James MacKenzie Lectr, 1972. Late House Surgeon, and Chief Assistant Medical Professorial Unit, St Bart's. Hosp. and House Physician National Hosp. Queen Square. *Publications:* (ed) Accident Prevention and Life Saving, 1965; various papers in medical journals; chapter on Raynaud's Phenomenon, in British Encyclopædia of Medical Practice, 1938 and 1948; chapter on Peripheral Vascular Disease, in Early Diagnosis, by Henry Miller, 1959; (ed) History of the Royal College of General Practitioners, 1983. *Recreation:* gardening. *Address:* Seven Steep, Fawley, near Henley-on-Thames, Oxon RG9 6JA. *T:* Henley-on-Thames 575853. *Club:* Royal Air Force.

HUNT OF TANWORTH, Baron *cr* 1980 (Life Peer), of Stratford-upon-Avon in the county of Warwickshire; **John Joseph Benedict Hunt,** GCB 1977 (KCB 1973; CB 1968); Secretary of the Cabinet, 1973–79; Chairman: Banque Nationale de Paris plc, since 1980; Prudential Corporation plc, since 1985 (Deputy Chairman, 1982–85); Director, IBM (UK) Ltd; Advisory Director, Unilever plc; Chairman, Disasters Emergency Committee, since 1981; *b* 23 Oct. 1919; *er s* of Major Arthur L. Hunt and Daphne Hunt; *m* 1st, 1941, Hon. Magdalen Mary Lister Robinson (*d* 1971), *yr d* of 1st Baron Robinson; two *s* one *d*; 2nd, 1973, Madeleine Frances, *d* of Sir William Hume, CMG, FRCP, and *widow* of Sir John Charles, KCB, FRCP. *Educ:* Downside; Magdalene College, Cambridge (Hon. Fellow, 1977). Served Royal Naval Volunteer Reserve, 1940–46, Lieut; Convoy escort, Western Approaches and in Far East. Home Civil Service, Admin. Class, 1946; Dominions Office, 1946; Priv. Sec. to Parly Under-Sec., 1947; 2nd Sec., Office of UK High Comr in Ceylon, 1948–50; Principal, 1949; Directing Staff, IDC, 1951–52; 1st Sec., Office of UK High Comr in Canada, 1953–56; Private Secretary to: Sec. of Cabinet and Perm. Sec. to Treasury and Head of Civil Service, 1956–58; Asst Secretary: CRO 1958; Cabinet Office, 1960; HM Treasury, 1962–67, Under-Sec., 1965; Dep. Sec., 1968 and First Civil Service Comr, Civil Service Dept, 1968–71; Third Sec., Treasury, 1971–72; Second Permanent Sec., Cabinet Office, 1972–73. Dep. Chm., Prudential Assurance Co. Ltd, 1982–85. Chm., Inquiry into Cable Expansion and Broadcasting Policy, 1982. Chm., Ditchley Foundn, 1983–. Chm., The Tablet Publishing Co. Ltd, 1984–. *Recreation:* gardening. *Address:* 8 Wool Road, Wimbledon, SW20 0HW. *T:* 01–947 7640.

HUNT, Alan Charles; HM Diplomatic Service; Counsellor (Economic and Commercial), Oslo, since 1983; *b* 5 March 1941; *s* of John Henry Hunt and Nelly Elizabeth Hunt (*née* Hunter); *m* 1978, Meredith Margaret Claydon; two *d*. *Educ:* Latymer Upper School, Hammersmith; Univ. of East Anglia. First Cl. Hons BA in European Studies. Clerical Officer, Min. of Power, 1958–59; FO, 1959–62; Vice-Consul, Tehran, 1962–64; Third Sec., Jedda, 1964–65; floating duties, Latin America, 1965–67; University, 1967–70; Second, later First Sec., FCO, 1970–73; First Sec., Panama, 1973–76; FCO 1976–77; First Sec. (Commercial), Madrid, 1977–81; FCO, 1981–83. *Recreations:* tennis, sailing, skiing, travel, reading, music. *Address:* c/o Foreign and Commonwealth Office, SW1.

HUNT, Arthur James, OBE 1971; FRTPI, FRICS; Chief Reporter for Public Inquiries, Scottish Office, 1974–79; *b* 18 Nov. 1915; *s* of Edward Henry and Norah Hunt; *m* 1946, Fanny Betty Bacon; one *s* three *d*. *Educ:* Tauntons Sch., Southampton. Ordnance Survey, 1938–44; Planning Officer with West Sussex, Kent and Bucks County Councils, 1944–48; Asst County Planning Officer, East Sussex CC, 1948–52; Town Planning Officer, City of Durban, SA, 1953–61; Sen. and Principal Planning Inspector, Min. of Housing and Local Govt, 1961–68; Mem., Roskill Commn on the Third London Airport, 1968–70; Superintending Inspector, Dept of the Environment, 1971–74. *Recreations:* sailing, gardening, caravan touring. *Address:* Pentlands, 4 West Avenue, Middleton-on-Sea, West Sussex PO22 6EF.

HUNT, David James Fletcher, MBE 1973; MP (C) Wirral West, since 1983 (Wirral, March 1976–1983); Parliamentary Under-Secretary of State, Department of Energy, since 1984; *b* 21 May 1942; *s* of Alan Nathaniel Hunt, OBE and Jessie Edna Ellis Northrop Hunt; *m* 1973, Patricia Margery (*née* Orchard); two *s* two *d*. *Educ:* Liverpool Coll.; Montpellier Univ.; Bristol Univ. (LLB); Guildford Coll. of Law. Solicitor of Supreme Court of Judicature, admitted 1968; Partner, Stanleys & Simpson North, 1977–; Consultant, Stanley Wasbrough & Co., 1965–85; Dir, BET Omnibus Services Ltd, 1980–81. Chm., Cons. Shipping and Shipbuilding Cttee, 1977–79; Vice-Chm., Parly Youth Lobby, 1978–80; Vice-Pres., Cons. Group for Europe, 1984– (Vice-Chm., 1978–81; Chm., 1981–82); a Vice-Chm., Cons. Party, 1983–85. PPS to Sec. of State for Trade, 1979–81, to Sec. of State for Defence, 1981; an Asst Govt Whip, 1981–83; a Lord Comr of HM Treasury, 1983–84. Chm., Bristol Univ. Conservatives, 1964–65; winner of Observer Mace for British Universities Debating Competition, 1965–66; Nat. Vice-Chm., FUCUA, 1965–66; Chm., Bristol City CPC, 1965–68; Nat. Vice-Chm., YCNAC, 1967–69; Chm., Bristol Fedn of YCs, 1970–71; Chm., British Youth Council, 1971–74 (Pres., 1978–80); Vice-Pres., Nat. YCs, 1986– (Chm., 1972–73); Vice-Chm., Nat. Union of Cons. and Unionist Assocs, 1974–76. Vice-Pres., Nat. Playbus Assoc., 1981–. Contested (C) Bristol South, 1970, Kingswood, 1974. Member: South Western Economic Planning Council, 1972–76; Adv. Cttee on Pop Festivals, 1972–75. *Publications:* Europe Right Ahead, 1978; A Time for Youth, 1978. *Recreations:* cricket, walking. *Address:* 2 St Margaret's Road, Hoylake, Wirral L47 1HX. *T:* 051–632 4033; 14 Cowley Street, Westminster, SW1P 3LZ. *T:* 01–222 7149. *Club:* Hurlingham.

HUNT, Sir David (Wathen Stather), KCMG 1963 (CMG 1959); OBE 1943; HM Diplomatic Service, retired; Director, Observer Newspapers, since 1982; *b* 25 Sept. 1913; *s* of late Canon B. P. W. Stather Hunt, DD, and late Elizabeth Milner; *m* 1st, 1948, Pamela Muriel Medawar; two *s*; 2nd, 1968, Iro Myrianthousi. *Educ:* St Lawrence Coll.; Wadham Coll., Oxford. 1st Class Hon. Mods. 1934; 1st Class Lit. Hum. 1936; Thomas Whitcombe Greene Prize, 1936; Diploma in Classical Archæology, 1937; Fellow of Magdalen Coll., 1937. Served 1st Bn Welch Regt and General Staff in Middle East, Balkans, North Africa, Sicily, Italy, 1940–46 (despatches 3 times, OBE, US Bronze Star); GSO1 18th Army Group, 1943; 15th Army Group, 1943–45; Col General Staff, Allied Force HQ, 1945–46; attached staff Governor-General Canada, 1946–47; released and granted hon. rank of Colonel, 1947. Principal, Dominions Office, 1947; 1st Secretary, Pretoria, 1948–49; Private Secretary to Prime Minister (Mr Attlee), 1950–51, (Mr Churchill) 1951–52; Asst Secretary, 1952; Deputy High Commissioner for UK, Lahore, 1954–56; Head of Central African Dept, Commonwealth Relations Office, 1956–59; Asst Under Secretary of State, Commonwealth Relations Office, 1959–60; accompanied the Prime Minister as an Adviser, on African tour, Jan.-Feb. 1960; Dep. High Comr for the UK in Lagos, Fedn of Nigeria, Oct. 1960–62; High Comr in Uganda, 1962–65; in Cyprus, 1965–67; in Nigeria, 1967–69; Ambassador to Brazil, 1969–73. Dep. Chm., Exim Credit Management and Consultants, 1974–77, Consultant, 1978–82. Chm., Bd of Governors, Commonwealth Inst., 1974–84. Mem. Appts Commn, Press Council, 1977–82. Montague Burton Vis. Prof. of Internat. Relations, Univ. of Edinburgh, 1980. President: Classical Assoc., 1981–82; Soc. for Promotion of Hellenic Studies, 1986–. FSA 1984. Corresp. Mem., Brazilian Acad. of Arts, 1972. BBC TV Mastermind, 1977 and winner, Tenth Anniversary Mastermind Championship, 1982. US Bronze Star 1945; Grand Cross, Order of the Southern Cross, Brazil, 1985. *Publications:* A Don at War, 1966; On the Spot, 1975; Footprints in Cyprus, 1982; articles in Annual of British School of Archæology at Athens and Journal of Hellenic Studies; Editor, The Times Yearbook of World Affairs, 1978–81. *Recreations:* reading, writing and gardening. *Address:* Old Place, Lindfield, West Sussex RH16 2HU. *T:* Lindfield 2298. *Clubs:* Athenæum, Beefsteak; Pen Clube do Brasil.

HUNT, Rt. Rev. Desmond Charles; a Suffragan Bishop of Toronto, since 1981; *b* 14 Sept. 1918; *s* of George P. and Kathleen Hunt; *m* 1944, Naomi F. Naylor; two *s* two *d*. *Educ:* Univ. of Toronto (BA). Rector: Trinity Church, Quebec City, 1943; St John's, Johnstown, USA, 1949; St James, Kingston, Ont., 1953; Church of the Messiah, Toronto, 1969. Hon. DD, Wycliffe Coll., Toronto, 1980. *Address:* Bishopslodge, Box 1150, Lakefield, Ontario, Canada. *T:* 705–652–7372.

HUNT, Gilbert Adams, CBE 1967; Chairman, Hedin Ltd, since 1978; Deputy Chairman, Thurgar Bardex PLC, since 1985 (Chairman, 1977–85); Director: Technology Transfer Associates Ltd, since 1980; Emray PLC, since 1982; *b* Wolverhampton, 29 Dec. 1914; *s* of late Harold William Hunt, MBE, St Helen's, IoW; *m* 1938, Sarah (marr. diss. 1946), *d* of Captain Wadman-Taylor; *m* 1946, Olive Doreen, *d* of late Maurice Martin O'Brien; no *c*; *m* 1975, Diane Rosemary, *d* of Eric O. Cook; one *d*. *Educ:* Old Hall, Wellington; Malvern Coll., Worcester. Director, High Duty Alloys, Slough, 1950–54; Dir and Gen. Man., High Duty Alloys (Dir, HDA, Canada, Northern Steel Scaffold & Engrg Co., all subsids Hawker Siddeley Gp), 1954–60; Man. Dir, Massey-Ferguson (UK) Ltd; Jt Man. Dir, Massey-Ferguson-Perkins; Dir, Massey-Ferguson Holdings Ltd; Chm. and Man. Dir, Massey-Ferguson (Eire) Ltd; Chairman: Massey-Ferguson (Farm Services Ltd), 1960–67; Managing Dir, 1967–73, Chief Exec. Officer, 1967–76, Chm., 1973–79, Rootes Motors Ltd, later Chrysler UK Ltd (Pres., April-June 1979). Chm., Cttee for Industrial

Technologies, DTI, 1972–78. President: Agricultural Engrs Association Ltd, 1965; The Society of Motor Manufacturers and Traders Ltd, 1972–74. Freeman, City of London, 1968. CEng, CIMechE, FIProdE, MIBF. Hon. DSc Cranfield, 1973. *Recreations:* golfing, sailing. *Address:* The Dutch House, Sheepstreet Lane, Etchingham, E Sussex TN19 7AZ.

HUNT, (Henry) Holman; Member, since 1980, a Deputy Chairman, since 1985, Monopolies and Mergers Commission; *b* 13 May 1924; *s* of Henry Hunt and Jessie Brenda Beale; *m* 1954, Sonja Blom; one *s* two *d. Educ:* Queens Park Sch., Glasgow; Glasgow Univ. (MA). FCMA, FIMC, FBCS, FInstAM. Caledonian Insce Co., 1940–43; RAF, 1943–46; Glasgow Univ., 1946–50; Cadbury Bros, 1950–51; PA Management Consultants: Consultant, 1952–57; Manager, Office Organisation, 1958–63; Dir, Computer Div., 1964–69; Bd Dir, 1970–83; Man. Dir, PA Computers and Telecommunications, 1976–83. Pres., Inst. of Management Consultants, 1974–75. *Recreations:* music, reading, walking, travel, photography, vegetable gardening. *Address:* 28 The Ridings, Epsom, Surrey KT18 5JJ. *T:* Epsom 20974. *Club:* Caledonian.

HUNT, Hugh (Sydney), CBE 1977; MA; Professor of Drama, University of Manchester, 1961–73, now Emeritus; *b* 25 Sept. 1911; *s* of Captain C. E. Hunt, MC, and late Ethel Helen (née Crookshank); *m* 1940, Janet Mary (*née* Gordon); one *s* one *d. Educ:* Marlborough Coll.; Magdalen Coll., Oxford. BA Oxon 1934, MA Oxon 1961. Hon. MA Manchester 1965. Pres. of OUDS, 1933–34; Producer: Maddermarket Theatre, Norwich, 1934; Croydon Repertory and Westminster Theatres, 1934–35; Producer, Abbey Theatre, Dublin, 1935–38; produced The White Steed, Cort Theatre, NY. Entered HM Forces, 1939; served War of 1939–45, with Scots Guards, King's Royal Rifle Corps, and Intelligence Service; demobilised, 1945. Director of Bristol Old Vic Company, 1945–49; Director Old Vic Company, London, 1949–53; Adjudicator Canadian Drama Festival Finals, 1954; Executive Officer, Elizabethan Theatre Trust, Australia, 1955–60; Artistic Dir, Abbey Theatre, Dublin, 1969–71. Mem., Welsh Arts Council, 1979–85 (Chm., Drama Cttee, 1982–85). *Produced:* The Cherry Orchard, 1948, Love's Labour's Lost, 1949, Hamlet, 1950, New Theatre; Old Vic Seasons, 1951–53: Twelfth Night, Merry Wives of Windsor, Romeo and Juliet, Merchant of Venice, Julius Caesar; The Living Room, New York, 1954; in Australia, Medea, 1955, Twelfth Night, 1956, Hamlet, 1957, Julius Caesar, 1959; The Shaughaun, World Theatre Season, Dublin, 1968; Abbey Theatre Productions include: The Well of the Saints, 1969; The Hostage, 1970; The Morning after Optimism, 1971; Arrah-na-Pogue, 1972; The Silver Tassie, 1972; The Three Sisters, 1973; The Vicar of Wakefield, 1974; Red Roses for Me, 1980; Sydney Opera House: Peer Gynt, 1975; The Plough and the Stars, 1977. *Publications:* Old Vic Prefaces, 1954; The Director in the Theatre, 1954; The Making of Australian Theatre, 1960; The Live Theatre, 1962; The Revels History of Drama in the English Language, vol. VII, sections 1 and 2, 1978; The Abbey, Ireland's National Theatre, 1979; Sean O'Casey, 1980; author or co-author of several Irish plays including The Invincibles and In The Train. *Address:* Cae Terfyn, Criccieth, Gwynedd LL52 0SA.

See also Baron Hunt.

HUNT, James; *see* Hunt, P. J.

HUNT, John Leonard; MP (C) Ravensbourne, since 1974 (Bromley, 1964–74); *b* 27 Oct. 1929; *s* of late William John Hunt and of Dora Maud Hunt, Keston, Kent; unmarried. *Educ:* Dulwich Coll. Councillor, Bromley Borough Council, 1953–65; Alderman, Bromley Borough Council, 1961–65; Mayor of Bromley, 1963–64. Contested (C) S Lewisham, Gen. Election, 1959. Member: Select Cttee on Home Affairs (and Mem., Sub-Cttee on Race Relations and Immigration); Speaker's Panel of Chairmen, 1980–. Jt-Chm., British-Caribbean Assoc., 1968–77 and 1984–; Chm., Indo-British Parly Gp, 1979–; UK Rep. at Council of Europe and WEU, 1973–77. Mem., BBC Gen. Adv. Council, 1975–. Mem. of London Stock Exchange, 1958–70. *Recreations:* foreign travel, gardening, good food. *Address:* House of Commons, SW1. *T:* 01–219 4530.

HUNT, John Maitland, MA, BLitt; Headmaster of Roedean Jan. 1971–April 1984; *b* 4 March 1932; *s* of Richard Herbert Alexander Hunt and Eileen Mary Isabelle Hunt (*née* Witt); *m* 1969, Sarah, *d* of Lt-Gen. Sir Derek Lang, *qv*; two *s. Educ:* Radley College; Wadham College, Oxford. BA 1956; BLitt 1959; MA 1960. Assistant Master, Stowe School, 1958–70 (Sixth Form tutor in Geography). Chm., Bd of Managers, Common Entrance Exam. for Girls' Schs, 1974–81. *Publications:* various articles on fine arts and architecture. *Recreations:* estate management, fine arts, writing, travel. *Address:* Logie, Dunfermline, Fife KY12 8QN. *Club:* Royal Commonwealth Society.

HUNT, Brig. Kenneth, OBE 1955; MC 1943; Director, British Atlantic Committee, 1978–81; *b* 26 May 1914; *s* of late John Hunt and Elizabeth Hunt; *m* 1939, Mary Mabel Crickett; two *s* (and one *d* decd). *Educ:* Chatham House Sch., Ramsgate; sc Camberley; idc. Commissioned into Royal Artillery, 1940; served, Africa, Italy, Austria, with HAC, 1 RHA and 2 RHA, 1942–46 (despatches thrice); Bt Lt-Col 1955; CO 40 Fd Regt RA, 1958–60; CRA 51 Highland Div., 1961–63; IDC 1963; Dep. Standing Gp Rep. to N Atlantic Council, 1964–66; resigned commission, 1967. Dep. Dir, Internat. Inst. for Strategic Studies, 1967–77; Specialist Adviser to House of Commons Defence Cttee, 1971–84. Visiting Professor: Fletcher Sch. of Law, Cambridge, Mass, 1975; Univ. of S California, 1978–79; Univ. of Surrey, 1978–. Mem. Council, RUSI, 1977; Fellow: IISS, 1977; Inst. of Security, Tokyo, 1979–. Freeman, City of London, 1977. Hon. Dr (PolSci), Korea Univ., 1977. Order of Rising Sun, 3rd cl. (Japan), 1984. *Publications:* NATO without France, 1967; The Requirements of Military Technology, 1967; Defence with Fewer Men, 1973; (ed) The Military Balance, 1967–77; (jtly) The Third World War, 1978; (jtly) Asian Security, annually, 1979–; contribs to learned jls, and chapters in many books, in UK, USA, E Asia. *Recreations:* fly-fishing, listening to music. *Address:* 22 The Green, Ewell, Surrey KT17 3JN. *T:* 01–393 7906. *Clubs:* Army and Navy; International House of Japan (Tokyo).

HUNT, Martin Robert, RDI 1981; Head of Glass School, Royal College of Art, since 1974; Partner, Queensberry Hunt, design consultancy, since 1966; *b* 4 Sept. 1942; *s* of Frederick and Frances Hunt; *m* 1st, 1963, Pauline Hunt; one *s* one *d;* 2nd, 1980, Glenys Barton; one *s. Educ:* Monmouth. DesRCA, FSIAD. Graduated RCA 1966; formed Queensberry Hunt Partnership, 1966; part time Tutor, RCA, 1968. *Recreation:* sailing. *Address:* 24 Brook Mews North, W2. *T:* 01–724 3701. *Club:* Little Ship.

HUNT, Adm. Sir Nicholas (John Streynsham), KCB 1985; LVO 1961; Commander-in-Chief, Fleet, and Allied Comander-in-Chief, Channel and Eastern Atlantic, since 1985; *b* 7 Nov. 1930; *s* of Brig. and Mrs J. M. Hunt; *m* 1966, Meriel Eve Givan; two *s* one *d. Educ:* BRNC, Dartmouth. CO HMS Burnaston, HMS Palliser, HMS Troubridge, HMS Intrepid, and BRNC, Dartmouth; Asst Private Sec. to late Princess Marina, Duchess of Kent; Executive Officer, HMS Ark Royal, 1969–71; RCDS 1974; Dir of Naval Plans, 1976–78; Flag Officer, Second Flotilla, 1980–81; Dir-Gen., Naval Manpower and Training, 1981–83; Flag Officer, Scotland and NI, and Port Admiral Rosyth, 1983–85. *Recreation:* family. *Address:* c/o Fleet Headquarters, Northwood, Middx. *Club:* Boodle's.

HUNT, Prof. Norman Charles, CBE 1975; Professor of Business Studies, 1967–84, Vice-Principal, 1980–84, University of Edinburgh, now Emeritus Professor; *b* 6 April 1918; *s* of Charles Hunt and Charlotte (*née* Jackson), Swindon, Wilts; *m* 1942, Lorna Mary, 2nd *d* of Mary and William Arthur Mann, Swindon, Wilts; two *s. Educ:* Commonweal Sch.; Swindon Coll.; University of London (Sir Edward Stern Schol., BCom 1st cl. hons); PhD (Edinburgh). On Staff (Research Dept and Personal Staff of Chief Mechanical Engineer); former GWR Co., 1934–45. Lectr in Organisation of Industry and Commerce, University of Edinburgh, 1946–53; Dir of Studies in Commerce, 1948–53; Prof. of Organisation of Industry and Commerce, 1953–66; Dean of Faculty of Social Sciences, 1962–64. Member: Departmental Cttee on Fire Service, 1967–70; Rubber Industry NEDC, 1968–71; UGC, 1969–78 (Vice-Chm., 1974–76); ODM Working Party on Management Educn and Training in Developing Countries, 1968–69; Bd of Governors (and Chm., Management Develt Cttee), Council for Technical Educn and Training in Overseas Countries, 1971–75; Police Adv. Bd for Scotland, 1971–75; Council for Tertiary Educn in Scotland, 1979–84; CNAA, 1979–84. Consultant, UNIDO, 1973–. Chairman: R. and R. Clark Ltd, 1967–70; William Thyne Ltd, 1967–70; Director: William Thyne (Holdings) Ltd, 1963–70; William Thyne (Plastics) Ltd, 1967–70; INMAP Ltd, 1984–; UnivEd Technologies Ltd (Chm. 1984–86). Hon. DLitt Loughborough, 1975. *Publications:* Methods of Wage Payment in British Industry, 1951; (with W. D. Reekie) Management in the Social and Safety Services, 1974; articles in economic and management jls on industrial organisation, industrial relations, and management problems. *Recreations:* photography, motoring, foreign travel. *Address:* 65 Ravelston Dykes Road, Edinburgh EH4 3NU.

HUNT, (Patrick) James; a Recorder of the Crown Court, since 1982; *b* 26 Jan. 1943; *s* of Thomas Ronald Clifford Hunt and Doreen Gwyneth Katarina Hunt; *m* 1969, Susan Jennifer Goodhead; one *s* three *d. Educ:* Ashby de la Zouch Boys' Grammar Sch.; Keble Coll., Oxford (MA Mod. History). Called to the Bar, Gray's Inn, 1968; in practice on Midland and Oxford Circuit, from London chambers. *Recreations:* singing, gardening, stonework. *Address:* Easton Hall, Easton on the Hill, Stamford, Lincs. *T:* Stamford 52266; (chambers) 1 King's Bench Walk, Temple, EC4.

HUNT, Gen. Sir Peter (Mervyn), GCB 1973 (KCB 1969; CB 1965); DSO 1945; OBE 1947; DL; Chief of the General Staff, 1973–76; ADC (General) to the Queen, 1973–76; retired; *b* 11 March 1916; *s* of H. V. Hunt, Barrister-at-law; *m* 1st, 1940, Anne Stopford (*d* 1966), *d* of Vice-Adm. Hon. Arthur Stopford, CMG; one *s* one *d;* 2nd, 1978, Susan, *d* of Captain D. G. Davidson, late Queen's Own Cameron Highlanders. *Educ:* Wellington Coll.; RMC Sandhurst. Commissioned QO Cameron Highlanders, 1936; commanded 7 Seaforth Highlanders, 1944–45; graduated Command and Gen. Staff Coll., Ft Leavenworth, USA. 1948; Instructor, Staff Coll., Camberley, 1952–55; Instructor, Imperial Defence Coll., 1956–57; commanded 1 Camerons, 1957–60; Comdr 152 (H) Infantry Brigade, TA, 1960–62; Chief of Staff, Scottish Command, 1962–64; GOC, 17 Div., also Comdr, Land Forces, Borneo, and Major-Gen., Bde of Gurkhas, 1964–65; Comdt, Royal Military Academy, Sandhurst, 1966–68; Comdr, FARELF, 1968–70; Comdr Northern Army Gp and C-in-C, BAOR, 1970–73. Col Queen's Own Highlanders (Seaforth and Camerons), 1966–75; Col 10th Princess Mary's Own Gurkha Rifles, 1966–75. Constable of the Tower of London, 1980–85. Pres., 1940 Dunkirk Veterans' Assoc., 1976–; Vice-Pres., NRA, 1976–; Pres., NSRA, 1978–; HM Special Comr, Duke of York's Royal Mil. Sch., Dover, 1977–; Chm. Council, King Edward VII Hosp., 1978–. Chm., StJ Council for Cornwall, 1978–. Hon. Liveryman, Haberdashers' Co., 1981. DL Cornwall, 1982. CBIM (FBIM 1975). Chevalier of the Order of Leopold II and Croix de Guerre (Belgium), 1940 (awarded 1945); OStJ 1978. *Address:* Rose Cottage, Portloe, Truro, Cornwall TR2 5RA. *Club:* Naval and Military.

HUNT, Philip Bodley; Director, Welsh Office Industry Department, 1975–76; *b* 28 July 1916; *s* of Bernard and Janet Hunt; *m* 1940, Eleanor Margaret Parnell; three *s* one *d. Educ:* Sedbergh Sch.; Christ Church, Oxford (MA). Joined Board of Trade, 1946; Trade Commissioner, Montreal, 1952; Principal Trade Commissioner, Vancouver, 1955; Commercial Counsellor, Canberra, 1957; returned Board of Trade, 1962; Dept of Economic Affairs, 1964–65; Director, London & SE Region, BoT, 1968; Dir, DTI Office for Wales, 1972–75. Chm., S Wales Marriage Guidance Council, 1974–83; Mem. Nat. Exec., Nat. Marriage Guidance Council, 1977–83; Dept Mem. of Panel, County Structure Plans of S and W Glamorgan, 1978, of Gwent and Mid Glamorgan, 1979; Vice-Pres., Develt Corporation for Wales, 1980–83. Silver Jubilee Medal, 1977. *Recreations:* gardening, music. *Address:* 93 Station Road, Llanishen, Cardiff CF4 5UU. *T:* Cardiff 750480.

HUNT, Ralph Holmes V.; *see* Vernon-Hunt.

HUNT, Sir Rex (Masterman), Kt 1982; CMG 1980; HM Diplomatic Service, retired; Civil Commissioner, Falkland Islands, 1982–Sept. 1985, and High Commissioner, British Antarctic Territory, 1980–85 (Governor and Commander-in-Chief, Falkland Islands, 1980–82; Governor, Oct. 1985); *b* 29 June 1926; *s* of H. W. Hunt and Ivy Masterman; *m* 1951, Mavis Amanda Buckland; one *s* one *d. Educ:* Coatham Sch.; St Peter's Coll., Oxford (BA). Served with RAF, 1944–48; Flt Lt RAFO. Entered HM Overseas Civil Service, 1951; District Comr, Uganda, 1962; CRO, 1963–64; 1st Sec., Kuching, 1964–65; Jesselton, 1965–67; Brunei, 1967; 1st Sec. (Econ.), Ankara, 1968–70; 1st Sec. and Head of Chancery, Jakarta, 1970–72; Asst ME Dept, FCO, 1972–74; Counsellor, Saigon, 1974–75, Kuala Lumpur, 1976–77; Dep. High Comr, Kuala Lumpur, 1977–79. Hon. Freeman, City of London, 1981. *Recreations:* golf, gardening. *Address:* Old Woodside, Broomfield Park, Sunningdale, Berks SL5 0JS. *T:* Ascot 25563. *Club:* Athenæum.

HUNT, Richard Bruce; Chairman, R. B. Hunt and Partners Ltd, since 1966; *b* 15 Dec. 1927; *s* of Percy Thompson Hunt and Thelma Constance Hunt; *m* 1972, Ulrike Dorothea Schmidt; two *d. Educ:* Christ's Hospital. FICS. Served Royal Signals, 1946–48; joined Merchant Bankers Ralli Brothers, 1949–66; formed own company, R. B. Hunt and Partners, 1966. Chm., Baltic Exchange Ltd, 1985–87 (Dir, 1977–80, re-elected, 1981–87). Liveryman, Shipwrights' Co. *Recreations:* golf, ski-ing. *Address:* R. B. Hunt & Partners, Cotts House, Camomile Street, EC3A 7BR. *T:* 01–626 3488. *Clubs:* MCC, Hurlingham, Wimbledon Golf; Royal Lymington Yacht.

HUNT, Richard Henry; Chief Registrar of the High Court of Justice in Bankruptcy, 1980–84; *b* 19 Jan. 1912; *s* of late Francis John and Lucy Edwyna Louise Hunt; *m* 1947, Peggy Ashworth Richardson; two *s. Educ:* Marlborough Coll.; Queen's Coll., Oxford. Called to Bar, 1936. Served with RA, 1939–45: Western Desert, Greece and Crete campaigns (PoW, Crete, 1941). Elected Bencher, Middle Temple, 1964. Registrar of the High Court of Justice in Bankruptcy, 1966–80. *Recreations:* foreign travel, languages. *Club:* Royal Ocean Racing.

HUNT, Sir Robert (Frederick), Kt 1979; CBE 1974; DL; Chairman, Dowty Group PLC, 1975–86; Deputy Chairman, Rover (formerly BL plc), since 1982 (Director, since 1980); Director: Eagle Star Holdings plc, since 1980; Charter Consolidated, since 1983; Dellfield Digital Ltd, since 1983; *b* 11 May 1918; *s* of late Arthur Hunt, Cheltenham and Kathleen Alice Cotton; *m* 1947, Joy Patricia Molly (*d* 1984), *d* of late Charles Leslie Harding, Cheltenham; four *d. Educ:* Pates Grammar Sch., Cheltenham; N Glos Techn. Coll. Apprenticed Dowty Equipment Ltd, 1935; Chief Instructor to Co.'s Sch. of Hydraulics, 1940; RAF Trng Comd, 1940; Export Man., Dowty Equipment Ltd, 1946;

Vice-Pres. and Gen. Man., 1949, Pres., 1954, Dowty Equipment of Canada Ltd; Dir, Dowty Gp Ltd, 1956, Dep. Chm., 1959–75, Chief Exec., 1975–83. Chm., Bd of Trustees, Improvement District of Ajax, Ont., 1954; Dir, Ajax and Pickering Gen. Hosp., 1954; Chm., Cheltenham Hosp. Gp Man. Cttee, 1959; Chm., Glos AHA, 1974–81; Pres., 1967–68, Treas., 1973, Vice-Pres., 1976, Pres., 1977–78, SBAC. FEng 1982; FCASI 1976; FRAeS 1968, Hon. FRAeS 1981. Hon. DSc Bath, 1979. DL Glos, 1977; Hon. Freeman of Cheltenham, 1980. *Recreations:* family interests, golf, gardening. *Address:* Greenacre, 5 Charlton Park Gate, Cheltenham, Glos GL53 7DJ. *T:* Cheltenham 515554. *Club:* New (Cheltenham).

HUNT, Roger; His Honour Judge Hunt; a Circuit Judge, since 1986; *b* 15 Jan. 1935; *s* of late Richard Henry Hunt and Monica Hunt; *m* 1963, Barbara Ann Eccles; two *d*. *Educ:* Giggleswick Sch.; Pembroke Coll., Oxford (MA). Commnd Royal Signals, 1955; served Germany, HQ 4th Guards Bde, 1956; TA 49th Inf. Div., Signal Regt, 1956–63. Called to the Bar, Lincoln's Inn, 1960; joined NE Circuit, 1961; a Recorder, 1978–86. *Recreations:* golf, gardening. *Club:* Moortown Golf.

HUNT, Roland Charles Colin, CMG 1965; HM Diplomatic Service, retired; Director, British National Committee, International Chamber of Commerce, 1973–76; *b* 19 March 1916; *s* of Colin and Dorothea Hunt, Oxford; *m* 1939, Pauline, 2nd *d* of late Dr J. C. Maxwell Garnett, CBE; three *s* two *d*. *Educ:* Rugby Sch. (scholar); The Queen's Coll., Oxford (scholar). Entered Indian Civil Service, 1938. Served in various districts in Madras as Sub-Collector, 1941–45; Joint Sec. and Sec., Board of Revenue (Civil Supplies), Madras, 1946–47; joined Commonwealth Relations Office, 1948; served on staff of United Kingdom High Commissioner in Pakistan (Karachi), 1948–50; Mem. UK Delegation to African Defence Facilities Conference, Nairobi, 1951; served in Office of UK High Comr in S Africa, 1952–55; Asst Sec., 1955; attached to Office of High Comr for Fedn of Malaya, Kuala Lumpur, 1956; Dep. High Commisioner for the UK in the Federation of Malaya, Kuala Lumpur, 1957–59; Imperial Defence Coll., 1960; Asst Sec., Commonwealth Relations Office, 1961; British Dep. High Comr in Pakistan, 1962–65; British High Commissioner in Uganda, 1965–67; Asst Under-Sec. of State, CO and FCO, 1967–70; High Comr, Trinidad and Tobago, 1970–73. *Publication:* (ed jtly) The District Officer in India, 1930–1947, 1980. *Recreations:* ball-games, piano-playing. *Address:* Spindlewood, Whitchurch Hill, Reading, Berks.

See also Baron Hacking.

HUNT, Terence; Regional General Manager, North East Thames Regional Health Authority, since 1984; *b* 8 Aug. 1943; *s* of Thomas John Hunt and Marie Louise Hunt (*née* Potter); *m* 1967, Wendy Graeme George; one *s* one *d*. *Educ:* Huish's Grammar Sch., Taunton. Associate Mem. Inst. of Health Service Management. Tone Vale Group HMC, 1963–65; NE Somerset HMC, 1965–67; Winchester Gp HMC, 1967–69; Lincoln No 1 HMC, 1969–70; Hosp. Sec., Wycombe General Hosp., 1970–73; Dep. Gp Sec., Hillingdon Hosp., 1973–74; Area General Administrator, Kensington and Chelsea and Westminster AHA(T), 1974–77; District Administrator: NW Dist of KCW AHA(T), 1977–82; Paddington and N Kensington, 1982–84. *Recreations:* sculling, cycling, Reading Town Regatta (Treasurer), all things practical with metal and wood. *Address:* 36 Old Bath Road, Charvil, Reading, Berks RG10 9QR. *T:* Reading 341062.

HUNT, Rt. Rev. Warren; *see* Hunt, Rt Rev. W. W.

HUNT, Rt. Rev. (William) Warren, MA; Hon. Assistant Bishop to the Dioceses of Chichester and Portsmouth, since 1978; *b* 22 Jan. 1909; *s* of Harry Hunt, Carlisle; *m* 1939, Mollie, *d* of Edwin Green, Heswall, Cheshire; four *d*. *Educ:* Carlisle Grammar School; Keble College, Oxford; Cuddesdon Theological College, Oxford. Deacon 1932; Priest 1933; Curate: Kendal Parish Church, 1932–35; St Martin-in-the-Fields, London, 1935–40. Chaplain to the Forces, 1940–44. Vicar, St Nicholas, Radford, Coventry, 1944–48; Vicar, Holy Trinity, Leamington Spa, 1948–57, and Rural Dean of Leamington; Vicar and Rural Dean of Croydon, 1957–65; Bishop Suffragan of Repton, 1965–Jan. 1977. Hon. Canon Canterbury Cathedral, 1957. *Recreations:* golf, vicarage lawn croquet (own rules); travel, reading. *Address:* 15 Lynch Down, Funtington, Chichester, West Sussex PO18 9LR. *T:* Bosham 575536.

HUNTE, Joseph Alexander; Senior Community Relations Officer, Tower Hamlets, 1968–82, retired; *b* 18 Dec. 1917; *s* of Clement and Eunice Hunte; *m* 1967, Margaret Ann (formerly Jones); three *d* (and one *d* decd). *Educ:* Swansea University Coll., 1962–65 (BA Politics, Economics, Philosophy); PRO, 1964–65. West Indian Standing Conference: PRO, Sec., Chairman 1958–80; Executive Member: Jt Council for Welfare of Immigrants, 1968–74; CARD, 1969–70 (Grievance Officer); Anne Frank Foundn, 1965–70; Chm., Presentation Housing Assoc., 1981–; Governor, St Martin-in-the-Fields Girls' Sch., SW2, 1982–. Silver Jubilee Medal (for services in community relations), 1977. *Publication:* Nigger Hunting in England, 1965. *Recreations:* reading, watching television. *Address:* 43 Cambria Road, SE5 9AS. *T:* 01–733 5436.

HUNTER, family name of **Baron Hunter of Newington.**

HUNTER, Hon. Lord; John Oswald Mair Hunter, VRD; a Senator of the College of Justice in Scotland, 1961–86; *b* 21 Feb. 1913; *s* of John Mair Hunter, QC(Scot) and Jessie Donald Frew; *m* 1939, Doris Mary Simpson; one *s* one *d*. *Educ:* Edinburgh Acad.; Rugby; New Coll., Oxford (BA 1934, MA 1961); Edinburgh Univ. (LLB 1936, LLD 1975). Entered RNVR, 1933; served War 1939–45 (despatches); Lt-Comdr RNVR; retired list 1949. Called to Bar, Inner Temple, 1937; admitted to Faculty of Advocates, 1937; QC(Scot) 1951. Advocate Depute (Home), 1954–57; Sheriff of Ayr and Bute, 1957–61. Chairman: Deptl Cttee on Scottish Salmon and Trout Fisheries, 1961–64; Lands Valuation Appeal Court, 1966–71; Scottish Law Commn, 1971–81; Scottish Council on Crime, 1972–75; Dep. Chm., Boundary Commn for Scotland, 1971–76. Pres., Scottish Univs Law Inst., 1972–77; Member: Scottish Records Adv. Council, 1966–81; Statute Law Cttee, 1971–81; Chm., later Hon. Pres., Cttee, RNLI (Dunbar), 1969–80 and 1981–; Hon. Pres., Scottish Assoc. for Study of Delinquency, 1971–. *Recreation:* angling.

HUNTER OF NEWINGTON, Baron *cr* 1978 (Life Peer), of Newington in the District of the City of Edinburgh; **Robert Brockie Hunter,** Kt 1977; MBE 1945; FRCP; DL; Vice-Chancellor and Principal, University of Birmingham, 1968–81; *b* 14 July 1915; *s* of Robert Marshall Hunter and Margaret Thorburn Brockie; *m* 1940, Kathleen Margaret Douglas; three *s* one *d*. *Educ:* George Watson's Coll. MB, ChB Edinburgh, 1938; FRCPE 1950; FACP 1963; FRSEd 1964; FInstBiol 1968; FFCM 1975. Personal Physician, Field-Marshal Montgomery, NW Europe, 1944–45. Asst Dir, Edinburgh Post-Graduate Bd for Medicine, 1947; Lectr in Therapeutics, University of Edinburgh, 1947; Commonwealth (Harkness) Fellow in Medicine, 1948; Lectr in Clinical Medicine, University of St Andrews, 1948; Dean of the Faculty of Medicine, 1958–62; Prof. of Materia Medica, Pharmacology and Therapeutics, University of St Andrews, 1948–67, and in University of Dundee, 1967–68; late Consultant Physician to Dundee General Hosps and Dir, Post-graduate Medical Education. Hon. Lectr in Physiology, Boston Univ. Sch. of Medicine, USA, 1950. Member: Clinical Res. Bd, MRC, 1960–64; GMC, 1962–68; Ministry of Health Cttee on Safety of Drugs, 1963–68 (Chm., Clinical Trials Sub-Cttee); UGC, 1964–68 (Chm., Medical Sub-Cttee, 1966–68); West Midlands RHA, 1974–78; Nuffield Cttee of Inquiry into Dental Educn, 1977–80; DHSS Working Party on Medical Administrators in Health Service, 1970–72 (Chm.); DHSS Independent Scientific Cttee on Smoking and Health, 1973–80; Med. Adv. Cttee of Cttee of Vice-Chancellors and Principals, 1976–81; Management Cttee, King Edward's Hospital Fund, 1980–84; House of Lords Select Cttee on Science and Technology, 1980–; Chm., Review Cttee of Medical and Public Health Res. Progs, EEC, 1984–85. Malthe Foundation Lecturer, Oslo, 1958. Editor, Quarterly Journal of Medicine, 1957–67. Fellow (ex-President) Royal Medical Society. Major, Royal Army Medical Corps. Gained Purdue Frederick Medical Achievement Award, 1958. Senior Commonwealth Travelling Fellowship, 1960; Vis. Professor of Medicine: Post-Graduate school, University of Adelaide, 1965; McGill Univ., 1968. Christie Gordon Lectr, Birmingham, 1978; Raymond Priestley Lectr, Birmingham Univ., Goodman Lectr, Royal Soc., 1981; Wade Lectr, Keele Univ., 1982. Hon. FCP. DL West Midlands, 1975. Hon. LLD: Dundee, 1969; Birmingham, 1974; Liverpool, 1984; Hon. DSc Aston, 1981. *Publications:* Clinical Science; contrib. to Br. Med. Jl, Lancet, Edinburgh Med. Jl, Quarterly Jl of Medicine. *Recreation:* fishing. *Address:* 3 Oakdene Drive, Barnt Green, Birmingham. *Club:* Oriental.

HUNTER, Adam; miner; *b* 11 Nov. 1908; *m*; one *s* one *d*. *Educ:* Kelty Public Elem. Sch. Joined Labour Party, 1933; Member: Exec. Cttee NUM (Scot. Area); Lochgelly Dist Council, 1948–52; Sec., Fife Co-op. Assoc. and Dist Council, 1947–64. MP (Lab) Dunfermline Burghs, 1964–74, Dunfermline, 1974–79. Mem. Fife CC, 1961–64. Voluntary Tutor, Nat. Council of Labour Colls. *Recreation:* reading. *Address:* Whitegates Terrace, Kelty, Fife, Scotland.

HUNTER, (Adam) Kenneth (Fisher); Sheriff of North Strathclyde at Paisley; *b* 1920; *o s* of late Thomas C. Hunter, MBE, AMIEE, and Elizabeth Hunter; *m* 1949, Joan Stella Hiscock, MB, ChB; one *s* two *d*. *Educ:* Dunfermline High Sch.; St Andrews Univ. (MA Hons); Edinburgh Univ. (LLB). Called to Bar, 1946; Chm. of the Supreme Court Legal Aid Cttee of the Law Society of Scotland, 1949–53; Standing Junior Counsel to HM Commissioners of Customs and Excise, 1950–53; Sheriff-Substitute, later Sheriff, of Renfrew and Argyll (subseq. N Strathclyde) at Paisley, 1953–. *Recreations:* photography, music, motor boating. *Address:* Ravenswood, Bridge of Weir, Renfrewshire. *T:* 612017.

HUNTER, Dr Alan, CBE 1975; Director, Royal Greenwich Observatory, 1973–75; *b* 9 Sept. 1912; *s* of late George Hunter and Mary Edwards; *m* 1937, W. Joan Portnell (*d* 1985); four *s*. *Educ:* Imperial Coll. of Science and Technology. PhD, DIC; FRAS. Research Asst, Applied Mech. Dept, RNC, 1940–46; Royal Observatory, Greenwich: Asst, 1937–61; Chief Asst, 1961–67; Dep. Dir, 1967–73. Editor, The Observatory, 1943–49. Treas., Royal Astronomical Soc., 1967–76 (Sec. 1949–56, Vice-Pres. 1957, 1965, 1976); Pres., British Astronomical Assoc., 1957–59; Chm., Large Telescope Users' Panel, 1974–75 (sec. 1969–73). Liveryman, Worshipful Co. of Clockmakers, 1975. *Recreation:* gardening. *Address:* Thatched Cottage, Frettenham Road, Hainford, Norwich NR10 3BW. *T:* Norwich 890179.

See also Prof. Louis Hunter.

HUNTER, Sir Alexander (Albert), KBE 1976; Speaker of the House of Representatives of Belize, 1974–79; *b* Belize, British Honduras, 21 May 1920; *s* of Alexander J. Hunter, KSG, and Laura Hunter (*née* Reyes); *m* 1947, Araceli Cayetana Marin S., Alajuela, Costa Rica; one *s* two *d*. *Educ:* St John's Coll. (Jesuit), Belize City; Regis Coll. (Jesuit), Denver, Colo; Queen's Univ., Kingston, Ont. In Accounting Dept, United Fruit Co., Costa Rica, 1940–41 and 1945–47. Served War, NCO, Radar Br., RCAF, 1942–45: active service in UK, Azores, Gibraltar, with 220 Sqdn Coastal Comd, RAF. Joined staff of James Brodie & Co. Ltd, as Accountant, 1947; Company Sec., 1948; Dir 1952–61; Consultant: James Brodie & Co. Ltd, 1975–83; Anschutz Overseas Corp., Denver, Colo, 1975–82; Chm., Belize Airways Ltd, 1979–. MLA (PUP), Fort George Div., 1961; Minister of Natural Resources, Commerce and Industry, March 1961; MHR (PUP), Fort George, under new Constitution, 1965; Minister of Natural Resources and Trade, 1965–69; Minister of Trade and Industry, 1969–74; Mem., Constitutional Ministerial External Affairs Cttee, 1965–74. Represented Belize: Bd of Governors, Caribbean Develt Bank, 1969–74; Council of Ministers, CARIFTA, 1971–73; Council of Ministers, Caribbean Economic Community, 1973–74. Acted as Dep. Governor, Aug. 1975. Pres., Belize Br., CPA; Chairman: Standing Orders Cttee; Regulations Cttee; House Cttee. People's United Party: Treasurer and Mem. Central Party Council, 1961–74; Mem. Exec. Cttee, 1961–74; Chm. Fort George Div., 1961–74. Former Vice-Pres., Belize Chamber of Commerce; Member: Property Valuation Appeal Bd, 1960; Citrus Industry Investigation Cttee, 1960. Member: West India Cttee; Internat. Game Fish Assoc.; Belize Rifle Club; Nat. Geographic Soc. *Recreations:* pistol-shooting, hunting, light and heavy tackle salt-water fishing. *Address:* 6 St Matthew Street, Caribbean Shores, Belize City, Belize. *T:* 44482.

HUNTER, Alistair John, CMG 1985; HM Diplomatic Service; on loan to Department of Trade and Industry as Under Secretary, Overseas Trade, since 1985; *b* 9 Aug. 1936; *s* of Kenneth Clarke Hunter and Joan Tunks; *m* 1st, 1963; one *s* two *d*; 2nd, 1978, Helge Milton (*née* Kahle). *Educ:* Felsted; Magdalen Coll., Oxford. Royal Air Force, 1955–57; CRO, 1961–65; Private Sec. to Permanent Under-Sec., 1961–63; 2nd Sec., Kuala Lumpur, 1963–65; 1st Sec. (Commercial), Peking, 1965–68; seconded to Cabinet Office, 1969–70; FCO, 1970–73; 1st Sec., Rome, 1973–75; FCO, 1975–80; Hd of Chancery, Bonn, 1980–85. *Address:* c/o Department of Trade and Industry, 1–19 Victoria Street, SW1.

HUNTER, Andrew Robert Frederick; MP (C) Basingstoke, since 1983; *b* 8 Jan. 1943; *s* of Sqdn Leader Roger Edward Hunter, DFC and Winifred Mary Hunter (*née* Nelson); *m* 1972, Janet Bourne; one *s* one *d*. *Educ:* St George's Sch., Harpenden; Durham Univ.; Jesus Coll., Cambridge. In industry, 1970; Asst Master, Harrow Sch., 1971–83. Contested (C) Southampton, Itchen, 1979. PPS to Lord Elton, Minister of State, DoE, 1985–86. Sec., Cons. Environment Cttee, 1984–85; Mem., Agriculture Select Cttee, 1985. Commnd Major, TAVR, 1973 (resigned commn, 1984). Order of Merit (Govt of Poland in exile), 1980. *Recreations:* field sports, cricket, model soldiers. *Address:* Farleigh Mortimer, Farleigh Wallop, near Basingstoke, Hants. *T:* Basingstoke 474900. *Clubs:* Carlton, MCC.

HUNTER, Rt. Rev. Anthony George Weaver; *b* 3 June 1916; *s* of Herbert George Hunter and Ethel Frances Weaver; *m* 1st, 1948, Joan Isobel Marshall (*d* 1981); 2nd, 1982, Emlyn Marianne Garton (*née* Dent). *Educ:* Wanstead; Leeds Univ. (BA); Coll. of the Resurrection, Mirfield. Deacon, 1941; Priest, 1942; Curate of St George's, Jesmond, 1941–43; Orlando Mission Dist, 1943–47; Johannesburg Coloured Mission, 1947–48; Curate of St George's, Jesmond, 1948–49; Vicar of Ashington, 1949–60; Proctor in Convocation, 1959–60; Vicar of Huddersfield, 1960–68; Rural Dean of Huddersfield, 1960–68; Hon. Canon of Wakefield, 1962–68; Proctor in Convocation, 1962–68; Bishop of Swaziland, 1968–75; Rector of Hexham, Dio. Newcastle, 1975–79; Asst Bishop, Dio. Newcastle, 1976–80; Supernumerary Bishop, 1980–81; Acting Archdeacon of Lindisfarne, 1981; retd Oct. 1981. OStJ. *Recreations:* walking, gardening, travel. *Address:* Hillside, Sheriff Hutton, N Yorks. *T:* Sheriff Hutton 226.

HUNTER, Prof. Archibald Macbride, MA, BD, PhD Glasgow, Hon. DD Glasgow, DPhil Oxon; Professor of New Testament Exegesis (formerly Biblical Criticism) in

Aberdeen University, 1945–71; Master of Christ's College, Aberdeen, 1957–71; *b* 16 Jan. 1906; *s* of late Rev. Archibald Hunter, Kilwinning, and Crissie Swan MacNeish; *m* 1934, Margaret Wylie Swanson; one *s* one *d*. *Educ:* Hutchesons' Grammar Sch., Glasgow; Universities of Glasgow, Marburg and Oxford. Minister in Comrie, Perthshire, 1934–37; Prof. of New Testament, in Mansfield Coll., Oxford, 1937–42; Minister in Kinnoull, Perth, 1942–45. Hastie Lecturer, Glasgow Univ., 1938; Lee Lecturer, 1950; Sprunt Lecturer (Richmond, Va), 1954. *Publications:* Paul and His Predecessors, 1940; The Unity of the New Testament, 1943; Introducing the New Testament, 1945; The Gospel according to St Mark, 1949; The Work and Words of Jesus, 1950; Interpreting the New Testament, 1951, Design for Life, 1953; Interpreting Paul's Gospel, 1954; The Epistle to the Romans, 1955; Introducing New Testament Theology, 1957; The Layman's Bible Commentary, Vol. 22, 1959; Interpreting The Parables, 1960; Teaching and Preaching the New Testament, 1963; The Gospel according to John, 1965; The Gospel according to St Paul, 1966; According to John, 1968; Bible and Gospel, 1969; Exploring the New Testament, 1971; The Parables Then and Now, 1971; Taking the Christian View, 1974; On P. T. Forsyth, 1974; The New Testament Today, 1974; Gospel and Apostle, 1975; Jesus Lord and Saviour, 1976; The Gospel Then and Now, 1978; Christ and the Kingdom, 1980; The Fifth Evangelist, 1980; Preaching the New Testament, 1981; The Parables for Today, 1983; Introducing the Christian Faith, 1984; articles and reviews in theological journals. *Recreation:* fishing. *Address:* 32 Gartconnell Road, Bearsden, Glasgow.

HUNTER, Rt. Rev. Barry Russell; *see* Riverina, Bishop of.

HUNTER, Dr Colin Graeme, DSC 1939; physician, National Health Service, 1973–82; *b* 31 Jan. 1913; *s* of Robert Hunter and Evelyn Harrison; *m* 1944, Betty Louise Riley; one *s* one *d*. *Educ:* Scots Coll., Univ. of Otago, New Zealand. MD 1958, DSc 1970. Christchurch Hosp. NZ, 1937–38; Royal Naval Medical Service, 1938–55; Univ. of Toronto, Canada, 1955–58; Shell Research Ltd, 1958–73. Fellow: RCP (Lond.); Roy. Coll. of Pathologists, etc. Freeman of City of London. *Publications:* scientific papers in many jls devoted to chemical and radiation toxicology. *Recreations:* sailing, squash. *Address:* 52 Fort Picklecombe, Maker, Torpoint, Cornwall. *T:* Plymouth 823419. *Club:* Royal Naval Sailing Association.

HUNTER, Hon. David Stronach; Hon. Mr Justice Hunter; a Judge of the Supreme Court of Hong Kong, since 1982; *b* 5 Oct. 1926; *s* of late Robert John Hunter and late Jayne Evelyn Hunter; *m* 1959, Janet Muriel Faulkner; one *s* two *d*. *Educ:* Harrow Sch., Hertford Coll., Oxford (Baring Scholar); MA Jurisprudence. Called to Bar, Middle Temple, 1951, Bencher, 1979; QC 1971; a Recorder of the Crown Court, 1975–81. *Recreations:* golf, gardening, painting. *Address:* Supreme Court, Hong Kong; 6E Barnton Court, Harbour City, Tsim Sha Tsui, Kowloon. *Clubs:* MCC; Hong Kong.

HUNTER, Evan; writer; *b* New York, 15 Oct. 1926; *s* of Charles F. Lombino and Marie Lombino; *m* 1st, 1949, Anita Melnick (marr. diss.); three *s*; 2nd, 1973, Mary Vann Finley; one step *d*. *Educ:* Cooper Union; Hunter Coll. (BA 1950). Served USNR. Literary Father of the Year, 1961; Phi Beta Kappa. Grand Master Award, Mystery Writers of America, 1986. *Publications include: as Evan Hunter:* The Blackboard Jungle, 1954; Second Ending, 1956; Strangers When We Meet, 1958; A Matter of Conviction, 1959; The Remarkable Harry, 1960; The Wonderful Button, 1961; Mothers and Daughters, 1961; Happy New Year, Herbie, 1963; Buddwing, 1964; The Paper Dragon, 1966; A Horse's Head, 1967; Last Summer, 1968; Sons, 1969; Nobody Knew They Were There, 1971; Every Little Crook and Nanny, 1972; The Easter Man, 1972; Seven, 1972; Come Winter, 1973; Streets of Gold, 1974; The Chisholms, 1976; Me and Mr Stenner, 1977; Walk Proud, 1978; Love, Dad, 1981; Far From the Sea, 1983; Lizzie, 1984; *as Ed McBain:* Cop Hater, 1956; The Mugger, 1956; The Pusher, 1956; The Con Man, 1957; Killer's Choice, 1958; Killer's Payoff, 1958; Lady Killer, 1958; Killer's Wedge, 1959; 'Til Death, 1959; King's Ransom, 1959; Give the Boys a Great Big Hand, 1960; The Heckler, 1960; See Them Die, 1960; Lady, Lady, I Did It, 1961; The Empty Hours, 1962; Like Love, 1962; Ten Plus One, 1963; Ax, 1964; The Sentries, 1965; He Who Hesitates, 1965; Doll, 1965; Eighty Million Eyes, 1966; Fuzz, 1968; Shotgun, 1969; Jigsaw, 1970; Hail, Hail, the Gang's All Here!, 1971; Sadie When She Died, 1972; Let's Hear It for the Deaf Man, 1972; Death of a Nurse, 1972; Hail to the Chief, 1973; Bread, 1974; Where There's Smoke, 1975; Blood Relatives, 1975; So Long as You Both Shall Live, 1976; Guns, 1976; Long Time No See, 1977; Goldilocks, 1978; Calypso, 1979; Ghosts, 1980; Even the Wicked, 1980; Rumpelstiltskin, 1981; Heat, 1981; Beauty and the Beast, 1982; Ice, 1983; Jack and the Beanstalk, 1984; Lightning, 1984; Snow White and Rose Red, 1985; Eight Black Horses, 1985; Cinderella, 1986; Another Part of the City, 1986; Poison, 1986; *screenplays:* Strangers When We Meet, 1959; The Birds, 1962; Fuzz, 1972; Walk Proud, 1979; Dream West (TV mini-series), 1986; *plays:* The Easter Man, 1964; The Conjuror, 1969. *Recreation:* travelling. *Address:* John Farquharson Ltd, 162–168 Regent Street, W1R 5TB.

HUNTER, Guy, CMG 1973; author and consultant; Overseas Development Institute since 1967; *b* 7 Nov. 1911; *s* of Lt-Col C. F. Hunter, DSO, and Mrs A. W. Hunter (*née* Cobbett); *m* 1941, Agnes Louisa Merrylees. *Educ:* Winchester Coll.; Trinity Coll., Cambridge. 1st cl. hons Classics, MA. Called to Bar, Middle Temple, 1935. Civil Defence, Regional Officer, Edinburgh and Principal Officer, Glasgow and W Scotland, 1939–43; Dir (Admin), Middle East Supply Centre, GHQ, Cairo, 1943–45; Dir, PEP, 1945–46; Warden, Urchfont Manor, Wilts, and Grantley Hall, Yorks, Adult Colleges, 1946–55; Dir of Studies, 1st Duke of Edinburgh's Conf., 1955–56; from 1957, research and consultancy for developing countries overseas, mainly E, W and Central Africa, India, Pakistan, SE Asia, Fiji. Launching and 1st Dir, East African Staff Coll., 1966; Inst. of Race Relations, 1959–66. Visiting Prof., Univ. of Reading, 1969–75. Member: Economic and Social Cttee, EEC, 1975–78; Council for Internat. Develt (ODM), 1977–. Bd of Governors, Inst. of Develt Studies, Sussex Univ. *Publications:* Studies in Management, 1961; The New Societies of Tropical Africa, 1962; Education for a Developing Region, 1963; (ed) Industrialization and Race Relations, 1965; South East Asia: Race, Culture and Nation, 1966; The Best of Both Worlds, 1967; Modernising Peasant Societies, 1969; The Administration of Agricultural Development, 1970; (ed jtly) Serving the Small Farmer, 1974; (ed jtly) Policy and Practice in Rural Development, 1976. *Recreations:* gardening, nature, travel. *Address:* The Miller's Cottage, Hartest, Bury St Edmunds, Suffolk. *T:* Hartest 830334. *Club:* Travellers'.

HUNTER, Sir Ian (Bruce Hope), Kt 1983; MBE 1945; Impresario; Chairman: Harold Holt Ltd; Tempo Video Ltd; *b* 2 April 1919; *s* of late W. O. Hunter; *m* 1st, 1949, Susan (*d* 1977), *d* of late Brig. A. G. Russell; four *d*; 2nd, 1984, Lady Showering, *widow* of Sir Keith Showering. *Educ:* Fettes Coll., Edinburgh; abroad as pupil of Dr Fritz Busch and at Glyndebourne. Served War of 1939–45, Lieut-Col. Asst to Artistic Dir, Edinburgh Festival, 1946–48; Artistic Administrator, Edinburgh Festival, 1949–50; Artistic Dir, Edinburgh Festival, 1951–55. Director, Bath Festivals, 1948, 1955, 1958–68; Adviser, Adelaide Festivals, 1960–64; Dir-Gen., Commonwealth Arts Festival, 1965; Artistic Director: Festivals of the City of London, 1962–80; Brighton Festivals, 1967–83; (with Yehudi Menuhin) Windsor Festivals, 1969–72; Hong Kong Arts Festivals, 1973–75; Malvern Festival, 1977–82; Dir, American Festival, 1984. Dir, British Nat. Day Entertainment, Expo' 67. Dir, Live Music Now, 1983–. Member: Opera/Ballet Enquiry for Arts Council, 1967–69; Arts Administration Course Enquiry for Arts Council, 1970–71; Arts Council Trng Cttee, 1974–76; Exec. Cttee, Musicians' Benevolent Fund; Centenary Appeal Cttee, RCM, 1982–; Adv. Cttee, Britain Salutes New York, 1983; Chm., Entertainments Cttee, Queen's Silver Jubilee Appeal; Pres., British Arts Festivals Assoc., 1978–81; Dep. Chm., Stravinsky Festival Trust; Trustee, Chichester Festival Theatre Trust; Founder and Trustee, Young Concert Artists Trust, 1984–; Chm. of Governors, London Festival Ballet, 1984–; Governor, Yehudi Menuhin Sch. R. B. Bennett Commonwealth Prize for 1966. Hon. Member: Guildhall Sch. of Music and Drama, 1975; RCM 1984. FRSA (Mem. Council, 1968–73, 1976–; Chm. Council, 1981–83; a Vice-Pres., 1981–). Mem. Ct of Assistants, Musicians' Co., 1981–84. *Recreation:* gardening. *Address:* Harold Holt Ltd, 31 Sinclair Road, W14 0NS. *T:* 01–603 4600. *Club:* Garrick.

HUNTER, Ian Gerald Adamson, QC 1980; a Recorder, since 1986; *b* 3 Oct. 1944; *s* of Gerald Oliver Hunter and late Jessie Hunter; *m* 1975, Maggie (*née* Reed); two *s*. *Educ:* Reading Sch.; Pembroke Coll., Cambridge (Open Scholar, Squire Univ. Law Scholar, Trevelyan Scholar, BA (double first in Law), MA, LLB); Harvard Law Sch. (Kennedy Memorial Scholar, LLM). Called to the Bar, Inner Temple, 1967 (Duke of Edinburgh Entrance Scholar, Major Scholar). Mem. and Rapporteur, Internat. Law Assoc. Anti-Trust Cttee, 1968–72; UK Vice-Pres., Union Internat. des Avocats, 1983. *Publications:* articles on public international law. *Recreations:* bebop, other good music, French cooking. *Address:* 4 Essex Court, Temple, EC4. *T:* 01–583 9191. *Club:* Piltdown Golf.

HUNTER, Brig. Ian Murray, CVO 1954; MBE 1943; psc 1943; fsc (US) 1955; FAIM 1964; Chairman and Managing Director, Allied Rubber Products (Qld) Pty Ltd; *b* Sydney, Aust., 10 July 1917; *s* of late Dr James Hunter, Stranraer, Scotland; *m* 1947, Rosemary Jane Batchelor; two *s* two *d*. *Educ:* Cranbrook Sch., Sydney; RMC, Duntroon. Lieut Aust. Staff Corps, and AIF 1939; 2/1 MG Bn, 1939–40; T/Capt. 1940; Staff Capt., 25 Inf. Bde, 1940–41; Middle East Staff Coll., Haifa, 1941; DA QMG (1), HQ 6 Div., 1941–42; T/Major 1942; AQMG, NT Force (MBE), 1942–43; Staff Sch. (Aust.), 1943; Gen. Staff 3 Corps and Advanced HQ Allied Land Forces, 1943–44; Lieut-Col 1945; Instructor, Staff Sch., 1945; AQMG, and Col BCOF, 1946–47; AQMG, AHQ and JCOSA, 1947; AA & QMG, HQ, 3 Div., 1948–50; Royal Visit, 1949; Exec. Commonwealth Jubilee Celebrations, 1950–51; CO 2 Recruit Trg Bn, 1952; CO 4 RAR, 1953; Executive and Commonwealth Marshal, Royal Visit, 1952, and 1954; Command and Gen. Staff Coll., Fort Leavenworth, USA, 1954–55; Military Mission, Washington, 1955–56; Officer i/c Admin., N Comd, 1956–59; Comd 11 Inf. Bde, 1959–60; Command 2nd RQR 1960–62; Chief of Staff 1st Div., 1963; Commandant, Australian Staff Coll., 1963–65; Comdr, Papua New Guinea Comd, 1966–69; DQMG, Army HQ, 1969. Indep. Mem., Presbyterian Church Property Commn, 1974–84. *Recreations:* golf, squash, swimming, riding. *Address:* PO Box 53, Stafford, Qld 4053, Australia; Garthland, 42 Charlton Street, Ascot, Brisbane, Queensland 4007, Australia; Finchley, Hargreaves Street, Blackheath, NSW 2785, Australia. *Clubs:* Australian (Sydney); Queensland (Brisbane); Royal Sydney Golf.

HUNTER, Surg. Rear-Adm. (D) John, CB 1973; OBE 1963; Director of Naval Dental Services, Ministry of Defence, 1971–74; *b* 21 Aug. 1915; *s* of Hugh Hunter and Evelyn Marian Hunter (*née* Jessop), Hale, Cheshire; *m* 1947, Anne Madelaine Hardwicke, Friarmayne, Dorset; three *s* two *d*. *Educ:* Bowdon Coll., Cheshire; Manchester Univ. LDS 1939. Surg. Lieut (D) RNVR 1940; HMS Kenya and 10th Cruiser Sqdn, 1941–42; HMS Newcastle and HMS Howe, British Pacific Fleet, 1944–47; transf. to RN; HMS Forth on Staff of Rear-Adm. Destroyers, Mediterranean (Surg. Lt-Comdr), 1948–50; Dartmouth, Royal Marines; Surg. Comdr, Staff of Flag Officer Flotillas Mediterranean, 1956; service ashore in Admty, 1960–63; Surg. Captain (D), Staff of C-in-C Mediterranean, 1965–66; Staff of C-in-C Plymouth Comd, 1967–68; Fleet Dental Surgeon on Staff of C-in-C Western Fleet, 1969–70. QHDS 1971–74. FRSocMed. Mem., South Hams DC, 1979–83. *Recreations:* ocean racing, cruising, shooting. *Address:* Horsewells, Newton Ferrers, Plymouth PL8 1AT. *T:* Plymouth 872254. *Clubs:* Royal Ocean Racing; Royal Western Yacht.

HUNTER, John; His Honour Judge Hunter; a Circuit Judge, since 1980; *b* 12 April 1921; *s* of Charles and Mary Hunter; *m* 1956, Margaret Cynthia Webb; one *s* two *d*. *Educ:* Fitzwilliam House, Cambridge (MA). Called to the Bar, Lincoln's Inn, 1952. Served War, Army, 1939–46. Industry, 1952–62; practised at the Bar, 1962–80. *Recreations:* sailing, gardening. *Address:* 6 Pump Court, Temple, EC4Y 7AP. *Clubs:* London Rowing; Sussex Yacht.

HUNTER, John Murray, CB 1980; MC 1943; Scottish Tourist Guide; *b* 10 Nov. 1920; *s* of Rev. Dr John Hunter and Frances Hunter (*née* Martin); *m* 1948, Margaret, *d* of late Stanley Cursiter, CBE, RSW, RSA, and Phyllis Eda (*née* Hourston); two *s* three *d*. *Educ:* Fettes Coll.; Clare Coll., Cambridge. Served Army, 1941–45: Captain, The Rifle Bde. Served in Diplomatic Service at Canberra, Bogotá, Baghdad, Prague, Buenos Aires and in FCO (Head of Consular Dept, 1966, and of Latin America Dept, 1971–73); idc 1961, sowc 1965, jssc (Senior Directing Staff), 1967–69. Sec., 1973–75, Comr for Admin and Finance, 1976–81, Forestry Commn. Vice- Chm., 1981–83, Chm., 1983–86, Edinburgh West End Community Council. *Recreations:* music, curling; formerly Rugby football (Cambridge 1946, Scotland 1947). *Address:* 21 Glencairn Crescent, Edinburgh EH12 5BT.

HUNTER, John Oswald Mair; *see* Hunter, Hon. Lord.

HUNTER, Keith Robert, OBE 1981; Controller, Arts Division, British Council, since 1985; *b* 29 May 1936; *s* of Robert Ernest Williamson and Winifred Mary Hunter; *m* 1959, Ann Patricia Fuller; one *s* two *d*. *Educ:* Hymers Coll., Hull; Magdalen Coll., Oxford (MA). Joined British Council, 1962; Lectr, Royal Sch. of Admin, Phnom Penh, 1960–64; Schs Recruitment Dept, 1964–66; SOAS, 1966–67; Asst Rep., Hong Kong, 1967–69; Dir, Penang, 1970–72; Dep. Rep., Kuala Lumpur, 1972–74; London Univ. Inst. of Educn, 1974–75; Rep., Algeria, 1975–78; First Sec. (Cultural), subseq. Cultural Counsellor (British Council Rep.), China, 1979–82; Sec. of Bd, and Hd of Dir-Gen.'s Dept, 1982–85. *Recreation:* music. *Address:* British Council, 10 Spring Gardens, SW1A 2BN.

HUNTER, Kenneth; *see* Hunter, A. K. F.

HUNTER, Prof. Laurence Colvin, FRSE 1986; Professor of Applied Economics, since 1970, Vice-Principal, since 1982, University of Glasgow; Chairman, Post Office Arbitration Tribunal, since 1974; *b* 8 Aug. 1934; *s* of Laurence O. and Jessie P. Hunter; *m* 1958, Evelyn Margaret (*née* Green); three *s* one *d*. *Educ:* Hillhead High Sch., Glasgow; Univ. of Glasgow (MA); University Coll., Oxford (DPhil). Asst, Manchester Univ., 1958–59; National Service, 1959–61; Post-Doctoral Fellow, Univ. of Chicago, 1961–62; Univ. of Glasgow: Lectr, 1962; Sen. Lectr, 1967; Titular Prof., 1969. Member: Ct of Inquiry into miners' strike, 1972; Council, Advisory, Conciliation and Arbitration Service, 1974–; Royal Commn on Legal Services in Scotland, 1976–80; Dep. Chm., Police Negotiating Bd, 1980–. *Publications:* (with G. L. Reid) Urban Worker Mobility, 1968; (with D. J. Robertson) Economics of Wages and Labour, 1969, 2nd edn (with C.

Mulvey), 1981; (with G. L. Reid and D. Boddy) Labour Problems of Technological Change, 1970; (with A. W. J. Thomson) The Nationalised Transport Industries, 1973; (with R. B. McKersie) Pay, Productivity and Collective Bargaining, 1973; several articles in economic jls. *Recreations:* golf, painting. *Address:* 23 Boclair Road, Bearsden, Glasgow. *T:* 041-942 0793. *Club:* Royal Commonwealth Society.

HUNTER, Prof. Louis, PhD, DSc (London); FRSC; retired as Professor of Chemistry and Head of Department of Chemistry, University of Leicester (previously University College) (1946–65); Professor Emeritus, 1966; *b* 4 Dec. 1899; *s* of late George Hunter and Mary Edwards; *m* 1926, Laura Thorpe (decd). *Educ:* East London College (subsequently Queen Mary College), University of London. Assistant Lecturer, University Coll. of North Wales, Bangor, 1920–25; Lecturer and Head of Dept of Chemistry, University Coll., Leicester, 1925, Prof. of Chemistry, 1946, and Vice-Principal, 1952–57, Pro-Vice-Chancellor, University of Leicester, 1957–60. Visiting Professor: Univ. of Ibadan, Nigeria, 1963, and Ahmadu Bello Univ., 1966. Mem. of Council: Chemical Soc., 1944–47, 1950–53, 1956–59; Royal Institute of Chemistry, 1947–50, 1961–64 (Vice-Pres., 1964–66; Chm. E Midlands Section, 1938–40); Sec. Section B (Chemistry), British Assoc. for the Advancement of Science, 1939–51, Recorder, 1951–56, mem. of Council, 1956–60. Hon. Fire Observer, Home Office, 1942–54; Scientific Adviser for Civil Defence, N Midlands, 1951–75; Dep. Chm., 1939, Chm., 1952, Leicester Jt Recruiting Bd. *Publications:* mainly in Jl Chem. Soc. *Address:* Thatched Cottage, Frettenham Road, Hainford, Norwich NR10 3BW.
See also A. Hunter.

HUNTER, Muir Vane Skerrett, QC 1965; Lt-Col (Hon.); MA Oxon; MRI; Barrister-at-Law; *b* 19 Aug. 1913; *s* of late H. S. Hunter, Home Civil Service; *m* 1st, 1939, Dorothea Eason, JP (*d* 1986), *e d* of late P. E. Verstone; one *d*; 2nd, 1986, Gillian Victoria Joyce Petrie, *d* of late Dr Alexander A. W. Petrie, CBE, MD, FRCS, FRCP. *Educ:* Westminster Sch.; Christ Church, Oxford (Scholar). Called, Gray's Inn, 1938 (*ad eundem* Inner Temple, 1965); Holker Senior Scholar; Bencher, Gray's Inn, 1976. Served 1940–46: Royal Armoured Corps; GS Intelligence, GHQ (India), GSO 1 attd War and Legislative Depts, Govt of India; returned to the Bar, 1946; standing counsel (bankruptcy) to Bd of Trade, 1949–65; Dep. Chm., Advisory Cttee on Service Candidates, HO; Member: EEC Bankruptcy Adv. Cttee, Dept of Trade, 1973–76; Insolvency Law Review Cttee, Dept of Trade, 1977–82; Founder-Chairman, N Kensington Neighbourhood Law Centre, 1969–71; Mem. Exec. Cttee and Council of "Justice". Amnesty International Observer: Burundi, 1962; Rhodesia, 1969; Turkey, 1972. Governor, Royal Shakespeare Theatre, 1978–. Member: Council, Royal Shakespeare Theatre Trust; Royal Shakespeare Theatre Centenary Appeal Cttee. Mem. Editl Board, Insolvency Law & Practice, 1985–. *Publications:* Senior Editor, Williams on Bankruptcy, 1958–78, Williams and Muir Hunter on Bankruptcy, 1979–84, Muir Hunter on Personal Insolvency, 1986–; Emergent Africa and the Rule of Law, 1963; Jt editor: Halsbury's Laws, 4th edn, Vol 3; Atkins' Forms, Vol 7; Part Editor, Kerr on Receivers, 16th edn 1983; Butterworth's County Court Precedents and Pleadings, 1984–. *Recreations:* theatre, travel. *Address:* (chambers) 3 Paper Buildings, Temple, EC4Y 7EU; 43 Church Road, Barnes, SW13 9HQ. *T:* 01–748 6693; Los Arcos 2/4, San Agustin, Palma de Mallorca, Spain. *T:* Palma 400246. *Club:* Hurlingham.

HUNTER, Dame Pamela, DBE 1981; Vice-President, National Union of Conservative and Unionist Associations, since 1985 (Vice-Chairman, 1981–84; Chairman, 1984–85); President, Northern Area Conservative Council, since 1986; *b* 3 Oct. 1919; *d* of late Col T. G. Greenwell, TD, JP, DL, and M. W. Greenwell; *m* 1942, Gordon Lovegrove Hunter; one *s* one *d*. *Educ:* Westonbirt Sch., Tetbury; Eastbourne Sch. of Domestic Economy. Served WRNS, 1942–45. Mem., Conservative Nat. Union Exec. Cttee, 1972–; Chairman: Northern Area Cons. Women's Adv. Cttee, 1972–75; Cons. Women's Nat. Adv. Cttee, 1978–81. Pres., Berwick-upon-Tweed Cons. Assoc., 1986–. Mem., Northumbrian Water Authority, 1973–76. Mem., Berwick-upon-Tweed Borough Council, 1973–83. *Recreations:* charity work for NSPCC, SCF and RNLI, antiques. *Address:* The Coach House, Chatton, Alnwick, Northumberland NE66 5PY. *T:* Chatton 259. *Club:* Lansdowne.

HUNTER, Philip Brown, TD; Chairman, John Holt & Co. (Liverpool) Ltd, 1967–71; *b* 30 May 1909; *s* of Charles Edward Hunter and Marion (*née* Harper); *m* 1937, Joyce Mary (*née* Holt); two *s* two *d*. *Educ:* Birkenhead Sch.; London University. Practised as Solicitor, 1933–80. Chm., Guardian Royal Exchange Assurance (Sierra Leone) Ltd, 1972–79; Director: Cammell Laird & Co. Ltd, 1949–70 (Chm. 1966–70); John Holt & Co. (Liverpool) Ltd, 1951–71 (Exec. Dir, 1960); Guardian Royal Exchange, 1969–79; Guardian Assurance Co. Ltd, 1967–79; Royal Exchange (Nigeria) Ltd, 1972–79; Lion of Africa Insurance Co. Ltd, 1972–79; Enterprise Insurance Co. Ltd, Ghana, 1972–79. *Recreations:* sailing, gardening. *Address:* Bryn Hyfryd, Lixwm, Holywell, Clwyd. *T:* Halkyn 780059. *Club:* Caledonian.

HUNTER, Rita, CBE 1980; prima donna; leading soprano, Sadler's Wells, since 1958, and Australian Opera, since 1981; *b* 15 Aug. 1933; *d* of Charles Newton Hunter and Lucy Hunter; *m* 1960, John Darnley-Thomas; one *d*. *Educ:* Wallasey. Joined Carl Rosa, 1950. Debut: Berlin, 1970; Covent Garden, 1972; Metropolitan, NY, 1972; Munich, 1973; Australia, 1978 (returned 1980 and 1981); Seattle Wagner Fest., 1980. Sang Brünnhilde in first complete Ring cycle with Sadler's Wells, 1973; first perf. of Norma, NY Metropolitan, 1975. Has sung leading roles in Aida, Trovatore, Masked Ball, Cavalleria Rusticana, Lohengrin, Flying Dutchman, Idomeneo, Don Carlos, Turandot, Nabucco, Macbeth, Tristan and Isolde, Electra. Many recordings, including complete Ring, complete Euryanthe, and several recital discs. Hon. DLitt Warwick, 1978; Hon. DMus Liverpool, 1983. RAM 1978. *Publication:* Wait till the Sun Shines Nellie (autobiog.), 1986. *Recreations:* sewing, oil painting, reading, gardening (Mem. Royal Nat. Rose Soc.), caravanning (Mem. Caravan Club), swimming. *Address:* 305 Bobbin Head Road, North Turramurra, NSW 2074, Australia. *T:* Sydney 445062; (UK rep.) Arthur Martin, Feock House, 8 The Path, Wimbledon, SW19. *T:* 01–540 9648. *Club:* White Elephant.

HUNTER, William Hill, CBE 1971; CA; JP; Partner in McLay, McAlister & McGibbon, Chartered Accountants, since 1946; *b* 5 Nov. 1916; *s* of Robert Dalglish Hunter and Mrs Margaret Walker Hill or Hunter; *m* 1947, Kathleen, *d* of William Alfred Cole; two *s*. *Educ:* Cumnock Academy. Chartered Accountant, 1940. Served War: enlisted as private, RASC, 1940; commissioned RA, 1941; Staff Capt., Middle East, 1944–46. Director: Abbey National Building Soc. (Scottish Adv. Bd); City of Glasgow Friendly Soc.; J. & G. Grant Glenfarclas Distillery. President: Renfrew W and Inverclyde Conservative and Unionist Assoc., 1972–; Scottish Young Unionist Assoc., 1958–60; Scottish Unionist Assoc., 1964–65. Contested (U) South Ayrshire, 1959 and 1964. Chairman: Salvation Army Adv. Bd in Strathclyde, 1982– (Vice-Chm., 1972–82); Salvation Army Housing Assoc. (Scotland) Ltd, 1986–. Hon. Treasurer, Quarrier's Homes, 1979–; Pres., City of Glasgow Friendly Soc., 1980–. Deacon Convener, Trades House of Glasgow, 1986–. JP Renfrewshire, 1970. *Recreations:* gardening, golf, swimming. *Address:* Armitage, Kilmacolm, Renfrewshire PA13 4PH. *T:* Kilmacolm 2444. *Club:* Royal Scottish Automobile.

HUNTER-BLAIR, Sir Edward (Thomas), 8th Bt *cr* 1786, of Dunskey; landowner and forester since 1964; *b* 15 Dec. 1920; *s* of Sir James Hunter Blair, 7th Bt and Jean Galloway (*d* 1953), *d* of T. W. McIntyre, Sorn Castle, Ayrshire; *S* father, 1985; *m* 1956, Norma (*d* 1972), *d* of late W. S. Harris; one adopted *s* one adopted *d*. *Educ:* Balliol Coll., Oxford (BA); Univ. of Paris (Diploma, French Lang. and Lit.). Temp. Civil Servant, 1941–43; journalist (Asst Foreign Editor), 1944–49; in business in Yorkshire, manager and director of own company, 1950–63. Mem., Kirkcudbright CC, 1970–71; former Pres., Dumfries and Galloway Mountaineering Club. 1939–45 Star, Gen. Service Medal, 1946. *Publications:* Scotland Sings, and A Story of Me, 1981; A Future Time (With an Earlier Life), 1984; articles on learned and other subjects. *Recreations:* gardening, hill-walking. *Heir:* *b* James Hunter Blair, *b* 18 March 1926. *Address:* Parton House, Castle Douglas, Scotland DG7 3NB. *T:* Parton 234. *Clubs:* Royal Over-Seas League; Western Meeting (Ayr).

HUNTER JOHNSTON, David Alan; Director, Trans-Oceanic Trust; *b* 16 Jan. 1915; *s* of James Ernest Johnston and Florence Edith Johnston (*née* Hunter); *m* 1949, Philippa Frances Ray; three *s* one *d*. *Educ:* Christ's Hospital; King's Coll., London. FKC 1970. Royal Ordnance Factories, Woolwich, 1936–39; S Metropolitan Gas Co., 1939–44; Min. of Economic Warfare (Economic and Industrial Planning Staff), 1944–45; Control Office for Germany and Austria, 1945–47; Sec. to Scientific Cttee for Germany, 1946; FO (German Section), Asst Head, German Gen. Economic Dept, 1947–49; HM Treasury, Supply, Estabt and Home Finance Divs, 1949–53. Central Bd of Finance of Church of England: Sec. (and Fin. Sec. to Church Assembly), 1953–59, and Investment Manager, 1959–65; concurrently, Dir, Local Authorities Mutual Investment Trust, 1961–65, and Investment Man. to Charities Official Investment Fund, 1963–65; a Man. Dir, J. Henry Schroder Wagg & Co. Ltd, 1965–74; Chairman: Schroder Executor & Trustee Co. Ltd, 1966–74; Reserve Pension Bd, 1974–75; Assoc. of Investment Trust Cos, 1975–77; Director: Clerical, Medical & General Life Assurance Soc., 1970–74; Lindustries Ltd, 1970–79. Mem., Monopolies Commn, 1969–73. A Reader, 1959–, licensed in dio. of Bath and Wells. *Address:* Eastfield House, North Perrott, Crewkerne, Somerset TA18 7SW. *T:* Crewkerne 75156. *Clubs:* Farmers', City of London.

HUNTER SMART, Norman; *see* Hunter Smart, W. N.

HUNTER SMART, (William) Norman, CA; Senior Partner, Hays Allan, Chartered Accountants, 1983–86 (Partner, 1950–83); Member, Gaming Board for Great Britain, since 1985; *b* 25 May 1921; *s* of William Hunter Smart, CA, and Margaret Thorburn Inglis; *m* 1st, 1948, Bridget Beryl Andreae (*d* 1974); four *s*; 2nd, 1977, Sheila Smith Stewart (*née* Speirs). *Educ:* George Watson's Coll., Edinburgh. Served War, 1939–45; commnd 1st Lothians & Border Horse, 1941; Warwickshire Yeomanry, 1942; served Middle East and Italy; Adjutant-Captain, 1945, mentioned in despatches. Qualified as Chartered Accountant, 1948. Joined Hays, Akers & Hays, 1948. Chm., Assoc. of Scottish Chartered Accountants in London, 1972–73; Institute of Chartered Accountants of Scotland: Council Mem., 1970–75; Vice-Pres., 1976–78; Pres., 1978–79. Dir, C. J. Sims & Co. Ltd. *Recreations:* shooting, gardening. *Address:* West Farmhouse, Bemersyde, Melrose, Roxburghshire TD6 9DP. *T:* St Boswells 23384; Flat 116, Pier House, Oakley Street, Chelsea, SW3 5HN. *T:* 01–351 5416. *Clubs:* Gresham, Caledonian.

HUNTER-TOD, Air Marshal Sir John (Hunter), KBE 1971 (OBE 1957); CB 1969; Head of Engineer Branch and Director-General of Engineering (RAF), 1970–73, retired; *b* 21 April 1917; *s* of late Hunter Finlay Tod, FRCS; *m* 1959, Anne, *d* of late Thomas Chaffer Howard; one *s*. *Educ:* Marlborough; Trinity Coll., Cambridge (MA). DCAe 1948. Commissioned, 1940; Fighter Command and Middle East, 1939–45. Group Capt. 1958; Air Cdre 1963. Dir, Guided Weapons (Air), Min. of Aviation, 1962–65; AOEng, RAF Germany, 1965–67; AOC No 24 Group, RAF, 1967–70; Air Vice-Marshal, 1968; Air Marshal, 1971. CEng. Hon. DSc Cranfield Inst. of Technol., 1974. *Address:* 21 Ridge Hill, Dartmouth, S Devon TQ6 9PE. *T:* Dartmouth 3130. *Club:* Royal Air Force.

HUNTING, (Charles) Patrick (Maule), CBE 1975; TD 1952; FCA; Chairman of Hunting Group, 1962–74; *b* 16 Dec. 1910; *s* of late Sir Percy Hunting; *m* 1941, Diana, *d* of late Brig. A. B. P. Pereira, DSO, of Tavistock, Devon; two *s* two *d*. *Educ:* Rugby Sch.; Trinity Coll., Cambridge. BA (Hons) Mod. and Mediaeval Langs; MA 1975; ACA 1936, FCA 1960. Served Royal Sussex Regt, 1939–45: France and Belgium, 1940; 8th Army, Western Desert, 1942; also in Palestine and Persia; Staff Coll., Camberley (psc), 1945. Entered Hunting Group 1936, Dir, 1946, Vice-Chm., 1961; Director: Hunting Associated Industries Ltd (Chm., 1965–74); Hunting Gibson Ltd (Chm., 1970–74); Hunting Gp Ltd (Chm., 1972–74). Mem. Council, Chamber of Shipping of UK, 1960 (Chm. Tramp Tanker Section, 1962); Master, Ironmongers' Company, 1978 (Mem. Court, 1970–). *Recreations:* golf, fishing. *Address:* The Old House, Birch Grove, Horsted Keynes, Sussex RH17 7BT. *T:* Chelwood Gate 254. *Clubs:* Naval and Military, MCC; Royal Ashdown Forest (Golf).

HUNTING, (Lindsay) Clive; Chairman, Hunting Group of Companies, since 1975; *b* 22 Dec. 1925; *s* of late Gerald Lindsay Hunting and Ruth (*née* Pyman); *m* 1952, Shelagh (*née* Hill Lowe); one *s* one *d*. *Educ:* Loretto; Trinity Hall, Cambridge (MA). Royal Navy, 1944–47; Cambridge, 1947–50; joined Hunting Group, 1950, Dir 1952, Vice-Chm. 1962; Group comprises Hunting Group plc, Hunting Associated Industries plc and Hunting Petroleum Services plc (Chm., 1975–85). Chm., Donkin & Co. PLC, 1952–84. President: British Independent Air Transport Assoc., 1960–62; Fedn Internationale de Transporte Aerien Privée, 1961–63; Air Educn and Recreation Organisation, 1970–; SBAC, 1985–86; Chm., Air League, 1968–71; Mem. Ct, Cranfield Inst. of Technol., 1980–. Master, Coachmakers' and Coach Harness Makers' Co., 1983–84. CBIM 1980; CRAeS 1983. Nile Gold Medal for Aerospace Educn, 1982. *Recreations:* yachting, fishing. *Address:* 14 Conduit Mews, W2 3RE. *T:* 01–402 7914. *Clubs:* City Livery; Royal Yacht Squadron, Royal London Yacht (Cowes).
See also R. H. Hunting.

HUNTING, Patrick; *see* Hunting, C. P. M.

HUNTING, Richard Haigh; Chairman, Hunting Petroleum Services plc, since 1985 (Director, since 1978); *b* 12 Oct. 1927; *s* of late Gerald Lindsay Hunting and Ruth (*née* Pyman); *m* 1955, Isobel, *yr d* of late Cecil and Marjorie Hannay Meredith; one *s* three *d*. *Educ:* Loretto; Trinity Hall, Cambridge. Royal Engineers, 1945–48, commissioned 1947. E. A. Gibson: joined 1952; Dir, 1957; Man. Dir, 1959; Chm., 1961–; Gibson Petroleum Co., Canada: Dir, 1960; Chm., 1984–; Dir, Hunting Group plc, 1985–; Fretoil S. N. Petrole et Affretements, France: Dir, 1957, Chm., 1981–; Mem., Exec. Cttee, Baltic and Internat. Maritime Conf., 1969–85 (Vice-Chm., 1981–85). *Recreations:* field sports, fine arts. *Address:* Westby Lodge, 90 Old Woking Road, West Byfleet, Weybridge, Surrey. *T:* Weybridge 46463. *Clubs:* City Livery, Arts.
See also L. C. Hunting.

HUNTINGDON, 15th Earl of, *cr* 1529; **Francis John Clarence Westenra Plantagenet Hastings,** MA; artist; *b* 30 Jan. 1901; *s* of 14th Earl and Maud Margaret (*d* 1953), 2nd *d* of Sir Samuel Wilson, sometime MP for Portsmouth; *S* father, 1939; *m* 1st, 1925, Cristina (who obtained a divorce, 1943 and *m* 2nd, 1944, Hon. Wogan Philipps, who *S*, 1962, as

2nd Baron Milford, *qv*; she died 1953), *d* of the Marchese Casati, Rome; one *d*; 2nd, 1944, Margaret Lane, *qv*; two *d*. *Educ*: Eton; Christ Church, Oxford. MA Hons, History; Slade School, London Univ. Played Oxford Univ. Polo team. Prof., Sch. of Arts & Crafts, Camberwell, 1938. ARP Officer and Dep. Controller Andover Rural district, 1941–45. Jt Parly Sec., Min. of Agriculture and Fisheries, 1945–50. Prof., Central Sch. of Arts & Crafts, London, 1950. A pupil of Diego Rivera. *Exhibitions*: Paris, London, Chicago, San Francisco; Mural paintings, Evanston, Ill; Monterey, Calif; Hall of Science, World's Fair, Chicago, 1933; Marx House; Buscot Park, Faringdon; Birmingham Univ.; Women's Press Club, London; Casa dello Strozzato, Tuscany; The Priory, Reading; Vineyards, Beaulieu, etc. Chm. of Cttee Soc. of Mural Painters, 1953–57. Pres., Solent Protection Soc., 1958–68. Mem., Wine Trade Art Soc. *Publications*: Commonsense about India; The Golden Octopus. *Heir: cousin* Lt-Col Robin Hood William Stewart Hastings, *qv*. *Address*: Blackbridge House, Beaulieu, Hants.
See also Sir W. L. Wyatt.

HUNTINGDON, Bishop Suffragan of, since 1980; **Rt. Rev. William Gordon Roe;** *b* 5 Jan. 1932; *s* of William Henry and Dorothy Myrtle Roe; *m* 1953, Mary Andreen; two *s* two *d*. *Educ*: Bournemouth School; Jesus Coll., Oxford (MA, DipTh (with distinction), DPhil); St Stephen's House, Oxford. Curate of Bournemouth, 1958–61; Priest-in-charge of St Michael's, Abingdon, 1961–69; Vice-Principal of St Chad's Coll., Durham, 1969–74; Vicar of St Oswald's, Durham, 1974–80; RD of Durham, 1974–80; Chaplain of Collingwood Coll., Durham, 1974–80; Hon. Canon of Durham Cathedral, 1979–80. *Publications*: Lamennais and England, 1966; (with A. Hutchings) J. B. Dykes, Priest and Musician, 1976. *Recreations*: French literature, and camping. *Address*: Powcher's Hall, Ely, Cambs CB7 4DL. *T*: Ely 2137.

HUNTINGDON, Archdeacon of; *see* Sledge, Ven. R. K.

HUNTINGFIELD, 6th Baron *cr* 1796; **Gerard Charles Arcedeckne Vanneck;** Bt 1751; international civil servant with United Nations Secretariat, 1946–75; *b* 29 May 1915; *er s* of 5th Baron Huntingfield, KCMG, and Margaret Eleanor (*d* 1943) *o d* of late Judge Ernest Crosby, Grasmere, Rhinebeck, NY; *S* father, 1969; *m* 1941, Janetta Lois, *er d* of Capt. R. H. Errington, RN, Tostock Old Hall, Bury St Edmunds, Suffolk; one *s* two *d* (and one *d* decd). *Educ*: Stowe; Trinity College, Cambridge. *Heir: s* Hon. Joshua Charles Vanneck [*b* 10 Aug. 1954; *m* 1983, Arabella, *d* of A. H. J. Fraser, MC, Moniack Castle; one *d*]. *Address*: Rue du Sacré du Printemps 4, 1815 Clarens, Switzerland.
See also Hon. Sir Peter Vanneck.

HUNTINGTON-WHITELEY, Sir Hugo (Baldwin), 3rd Bt *cr* 1918; DL; *b* 31 March 1924; *e surv. s* of Captain Sir Maurice Huntington-Whiteley, 2nd Bt, RN, and Lady (Pamela) Margaret Huntington-Whiteley (*d* 1976), 3rd *d* of 1st Earl Baldwin of Bewdley, KG, PC; *S* father, 1975; *m* 1959, Jean Marie Ramsay, JP 1973, DStJ; two *d*. *Educ*: Eton. Served in Royal Navy, 1942–47. Chartered Accountant; Partner, Price Waterhouse, 1963–83. Worcs: High Sheriff 1971; DL 1972. *Recreations*: music, travel. *Heir: b* (John) Miles Huntington-Whiteley, VRD, Lieut-Comdr RNR [*b* 18 July 1929; *m* 1960, Countess Victoria Adelheid Clementine Louise, *d* of late Count Friedrich Wolfgang zu Castell-Rudenhausen; one *s* two *d*]. *Address*: Ripple Hall, Tewkesbury, Glos. *T*: Upton-on-Severn 2431. *Club*: Brooks's.

HUNTLY, 12th Marquess of, *cr* 1599, Earl of, *cr* 1450; **Douglas Charles Lindsey Gordon;** Lord of Gordon before 1408; Earl of Enzie, Lord of Badenoch, 1599; Bt 1625; Baron Aboyne, 1627; Earl of Aboyne, Lord Strathavon and Glenlivet, 1660; Baron Meldrum, 1815; sits under creation of 1815; Premier Marquess of Scotland; Chief of House of Gordon; Gordon Highlanders; *b* 3 Feb. 1908; *s* of late Lieut-Col Douglas Gordon, CVO, DSO, and Violet Ida, *d* of Gerard Streatfeild; *S* great-uncle, 1937; *m* 1st, 1941, Hon. Mary Pamela Berry (marr. diss. 1965), *o d* of 1st Viscount Kemsley; one *s* one *d*; 2nd, 1977, Elizabeth Haworth Leigh, *d* of Lt Cdr F. H. Leigh. *Heir: s* Earl of Aboyne, *qv*. *Address*: Hollybrook, Ewhurst Road, Cranleigh, Surrey. *T*: Cranleigh 71500. *Club*: Army and Navy.

HUNTSMAN, Peter William, FRICS; CAAV; Principal, College of Estate Management, since 1981; *b* 11 Aug. 1935; *s* of late William and Lydia Irene Huntsman (*née* Clegg); *m* 1st, 1961, Janet Mary Bell (marr. diss.); one *s* one *d*; 2nd, 1984, Cicely Eleanor (*née* Tamblin). *Educ*: Hymers Coll., Hull; Coll. of Estate Management, Univ. of London (BSc Estate Man.). Agricultural Land Service: Dorset and Northumberland, 1961–69; Kellogg Foundn Fellowship, USA, 1969–70; Principal Surveyor, London, ADAS, 1971–76; Divl Surveyor, Surrey, Middx and Sussex, 1976–81. Liveryman, Chartered Surveyors' Co., 1985; Freeman, City of London, 1985. *Publications*: (contrib.) Walmsley's Rural Estate Management, 6th edn 1978; contribs to professional jls. *Recreations*: sport, Dorset countryside, reading. *Address*: College of Estate Management, Whiteknights, Reading RG6 2AW. *T*: Reading 861101. *Clubs*: Athenæum, Farmers'; Phyllis Court (Henley).

HURD, Derrick Guy Edmund, JP; Head of the European School, 1978–Aug. 1987; *b* 22 June 1928; *s* of Clifford Rowland Hurd and Viola Beatrice Hurd; *m* 1962, Janet Barton; one *s* two *d*. *Educ*: Peter Symonds' Sch., Winchester; Culham Coll. (Teacher's Cert., 1948); Birkbeck Coll., Univ. of London (BA Hons History 1952, MA (thesis) 1961). Assistant, Hugh Myddelton Sec. Sch., London EC1, 1948–52; Lecteur, Lycée Chaptal, Paris, 1952–53; Head of History Dept, Librarian, Hatfield School, 1953–60 (Exchange, Helmholtz Gymnasium, Bielefeld, 1956); Headmaster, John Mason High Sch., Abingdon, 1960–70; Headmaster, Blandford Upper Sch., Dorset, 1970–72; Principal, Easthampstead Park Educational Centre, Wokingham, 1972–78. Vice-Pres., Nat. Soc. of Non-smokers. JP Berkshire, 1967, now Oxfordshire. *Publication*: Sir John Mason (1503–1566), 1975. *Recreations*: walking, philately, music, ecclesiastical architecture, travel. *Address*: Ody Wharf, Wilsham Road, Abingdon, Oxon OX14 5HP.

HURD, Rt. Hon. Douglas (Richard), CBE 1974; PC 1982; MP (C) Witney, since 1983 (Mid-Oxon, Feb. 1974–1983); Secretary of State for the Home Department, since 1985; *b* 8 March 1930; *e s* of Baron Hurd (*d* 1966) and Stephanie Corner (*d* 1985); *m* 1st, 1960, Tatiana Elizabeth Michelle (marr. diss. 1982), *d* of A. C. Benedict Eyre, Westburton House, Bury, Sussex; three *s*; 2nd, 1982, Judy, *d* of Sidney and Pamela Smart; one *s* one *d*. *Educ*: Eton (King's Scholar and Newcastle Scholar); Trinity Coll., Cambridge (Major Scholar) Pres., Cambridge Union, 1952. HM Diplomatic Service, 1952–66; served in: Peking, 1954–56; UK Mission to UN, 1956–60; Private Sec. to Perm. Under-Sec. of State, FO, 1960–63; Rome, 1963–66. Joined Conservative Research Dept, 1966; Head of Foreign Affairs Section, 1968; Private Sec. to Leader of the Opposition, 1968–70; Political Sec. to Prime Minister, 1970–74; Opposition Spokesman on European Affairs, 1976–79; Minister of State, FCO, 1979–83; Minister of State, Home Office, 1983–84; Sec. of State for NI, 1984–85. Vis. Fellow, Nuffield Coll., Oxford, 1978. *Publications*: The Arrow War, 1967; Truth Game, 1972; Vote to Kill, 1975; An End to Promises, 1979; with Andrew Osmond: Send Him Victorious, 1968; The Smile on the Face of the Tiger, 1969, repr. 1982; Scotch on the Rocks, 1971; War Without Frontiers, 1982; (with Stephen Lamport) Palace of Enchantments, 1985. *Recreation*: writing thrillers. *Address*: House of Commons, SW1. *Club*: Beefsteak.

HURFORD, Peter (John), OBE 1984; organist; *b* 22 Nov. 1930; *e c* of H. J. Hurford, Minehead; *m* 1955, Patricia Mary Matthews; two *s* one *d*. *Educ*: Blundells Sch.; Royal Coll. of Music; Jesus Coll., Cambridge. MA, MusB Cantab, FRCO, FRSCM, ARCM. Director of Music, Bablake Sch., Coventry and Conductor, Leamington Spa Bach Choir, 1956–57; Master of the Music, Cathedral and Abbey Church of St Alban, 1958–78, Conductor, St Albans Bach Choir, 1958–78; Founder, Internat. Organ Festival Soc., 1963. Artist-in-Residence: Univ. of Cincinnati, 1967–68; Sydney Opera Ho., 1980, 1981, 1982; Acting Organist, St John's Coll., Cambridge, 1979–80; recital and lecture tours throughout Europe, USA, Canada, Japan, Philippines, Australia and NZ from 1960. Vis. Prof. of Organ, Univ. of Western Ontario, 1976–77; Prof., RAM, 1982–. Mem. Council, 1963–, Pres., 1980–82, RCO; Mem., Hon. Council of Management, Royal Philharmonic Soc., 1983–85. Has made numerous LP records, incl. complete organ works of J. S. Bach (Gramophone Award, 1979; Silver Disc, 1983), F. Couperin, G. F. Handel, P. Hindemith. Hon. Dr, Baldwin-Wallace Coll., Ohio, 1981. Hon. Mem., RAM, 1981. *Publications*: Suite: Laudate Dominum; sundry other works for organ; Masses for Series III and Rite II of Amer. Episcopal Church; sundry church anthems. *Recreations*: walking and silence. *Address*: Broom House, St Bernard's Road, St Albans, Herts AL3 5RA.

HURLEY, Sir John Garling, Kt 1967; CBE 1959; FAIM; FIDCA; JP; Managing Director, Berlei United Ltd, Sydney, 1948–69; *b* Bondi, NSW, 2 Oct. 1906; *s* of late John Hurley, MLA, and late Annie Elizabeth (*née* Garling); *g g g s* of Frederick Garling (1775–1848), free settler, 1815 and senior of first two solicitors admitted to practice in original Supreme Court of Civil Judicature in NSW; *m* 1st 1929, Alice Edith Saunders (*d* 1975); three *d*; 2nd, 1976, Desolie M. Richardson. *Educ*: Sydney Techn. High Sch. FAIM 1949; FIDCA 1980. With Berlei group of cos, 1922–69, incl. Berlei (UK) Ltd, London, 1931–36; Chm., William Adams Ltd, 1963–74 (Dep. Chm. 1974–76); Director: Manufacturers' Mutual Insurance Ltd, Sydney, 1954–82; Develt Finance Corporation Ltd, 1967–79; Australian Fixed Trusts Ltd, 1970–79; Royal North Shore Hosp. of Sydney, 1969–76. President: Associated Chambers of Manufactures of Austr. 1955–56; Chamber of Manufactures of NSW, 1955–57 (Life Mem.); Member: Inst. of Directors in Australia; Techn. and Further Educn Adv. Council of NSW, 1958–76; Industrial Design Council of Australia, 1958–76 (Dep. Chm., 1970–76); Council, Abbotsleigh Sch., 1960–66; Australian Advertising Standards Adv. Authority, 1974–82; Councillor, Nat. Heart Foundn of Australia (NSW Div.), 1969–. Mem., St Andrew's Cathedral Restoration Appeal Cttee; Patron, St Andrew's Cathedral Sch. Building Fund Appeal, 1977–. Chm., Standing Cttee on Productivity, Ministry of Labour Adv. Coun., 1957; Leader of Austr. Trade Mission to India and Ceylon, 1957. Chm. and Trustee, Museum of Applied Arts and Sciences, NSW, 1958–76. Member: Royal Agricultural Soc.; Sydney Cricket Ground; Australian-American Assoc.; Nat. Trust of Australia; Mem. Council, Australia–Britain Soc. Knighted for distinguished service to Government, industry and the community. *Recreations*: swimming, bowls. *Address*: 12 Locksley Street, Killara, NSW 2071, Australia. *Clubs*: Australian (Sydney); Royal Sydney Yacht Squadron; Australasian Pioneers' (NSW); Warrawee Bowling.

HURLEY, Prof. Rosalinde, (Mrs Peter Gortvai), LLB, MD; FRCPath; Professor of Microbiology, University of London, at Institute of Obstetrics and Gynaecology, Royal Postgraduate Medical School, since 1975; Consultant Microbiologist, Queen Charlotte's Maternity Hospital, since 1963; *b* 30 Dec. 1929; *o d* of late William Hurley and Rose Clancey; *m* 1964, Peter Gortvai, FRCS. *Educ*: Academy of the Assumption, Wellesley Hills, Mass, USA; Queen's Coll., Harley St, London; Univ. of London; Inns of Court. Called to the Bar, Inner Temple, 1958. House Surg., Wembley Hosp., 1955; Ho. Phys., W London Hosp., 1956; Sen. Ho. Officer, 1956–57; Registrar, 1957–58, Lectr and Asst Clin. Pathologist, 1958–62, Charing Cross Hosp. and Med. Sch. Chm., Medicines Commn, 1982–; Mem., Public Health Lab. Service Bd, 1982–. Examiner, RCPath, and univs at home and abroad; Founder Mem., Mem. Council, 1977–, Asst Registrar, 1978–, and Vice-Pres., 1984–, RCPath; Royal Society of Medicine: Pres., Section of Pathology, and Vice-Pres., 1979–; Mem. Council, 1980–; Hon. Sec., 1984–; Chm., 1980–, formerly Vice-Chm., Cttee on Dental and Surgical Materials; Pres., Assoc. of Clinical Pathologists, 1984– (Pres.-elect, 1983–84). DUniv Surrey, 1984. *Publications*: (jtly) Candida albicans, 1964; (jtly) Symposium on Candida Infections, 1966; (jtly) Neonatal and Perinatal Infections, 1979; chapters in med. books; papers in med. and sci. jls. *Recreations*: gardening, reading. *Address*: 2 Temple Gardens, Temple, EC4Y 9AY. *T*: 01–353 0577.

HURLL, Alfred William, CVO 1970; CBE 1955; Member of Council, The Scout Association, since 1948 (Chief Executive Commissioner, 1948–70); *b* 10 Sept. 1905; *s* of Charles Alfred Hurll; *m* 1933, Elsie Margaret, *d* of Frederick Sullivan; one *s* one *d*. *Educ*: Grammar Sch., Acton. Joined staff, The Scout Assoc. HQ, 1921; Sec., Home Dept, 1935; Asst Gen. Sec., 1938; Gen. Sec., 1941. *Publication*: (co-author) BP's Scouts, 1961. *Recreations*: cricket, theatre. *Address*: 106 Montrose Avenue, Twickenham TW2 6HD. *T*: 01–894 1957.

HURON, Bishop of, since 1984; **Rt. Rev. Derwyn Dixon Jones,** DD; *b* 5 Aug. 1925; *s* of Rev. Walter Jones, DD, and Mary Rosalie Jones (*née* Dixon); *m* 1960, Arline Carole Dilamarter; one *s* one *d*. *Educ*: Univ. of Western Ontario (BA); Huron College (LTh, DD). Deacon 1946, priest 1947; Curate: Holy Trinity, Winnipeg, 1946–48; All Saints', Windsor, 1948–49; Rector, St Andrew's, Kitchener, 1949–52; Asst Rector, St Paul's Cathedral, London, Ont, 1952–55; Rector: Canon Davis Memorial Church, Sarnia, 1955–58; St Barnabas, Windsor, 1958–66; St Peter's, Brockville, 1966–69; St James, Westminster, London, Ont, 1969–82; Archdeacon of Middlesex, 1978–82; Suffragan Bishop of Huron, 1982; Coadjutor Bishop, 1983. *Recreation*: music. *Address*: 25 Cherokee Road, London, Ontario, Canada. *T*: (519) 673–0146. *Club*: London (London, Ont).

HURRELL, Sir Anthony (Gerald), KCVO 1986; CMG 1984; HM Diplomatic Service; Ambassador to Nepal, since 1983; *b* 18 Feb. 1927; *s* of late William Hurrell and Florence Hurrell; *m* 1951, Jean Wyatt; two *d*. *Educ*: Norwich Sch.; St Catharine's Coll., Cambridge. RAEC, 1948–50; Min. of Labour, 1950–53; Min. of Educn, 1953–64; joined Min. of Overseas Develt, 1964; Fellow, Center for International Affairs, Harvard, 1969–70; Head of SE Asia Develt Div., Bangkok, 1972–74; Under Secretary: Internat. Div. ODM, 1974–75; Central Policy Rev. Staff, Cabinet Office, 1976; Duchy of Lancaster, 1977; Asia and Oceans Div, ODA, 1978–83; Internat. Div., ODA, 1983. *Recreations*: bird-ringing, bird-watching, digging ponds, music. *Address*: c/o Foreign and Commonwealth Office, SW1A 2AH.

HURRELL, Air Vice-Marshal Frederick Charles, CB 1986; OBE 1968; QHP 1984; Director General, Royal Air Force Medical Services and Deputy Surgeon General (Operations), since 1986; *b* 24 April 1928; *s* of Alexander John Hurrell and Maria Del Carmen Hurrell (*née* De Biedma); *m* 1950, Jay Jarvis; five *d*. *Educ*: Royal Masonic School, Bushey; St Mary's Hosp., Paddington (MB BS 1952). MRCS, LRCP 1952; Dip Av Med (RCP) 1970; MFOM 1981. Joined RAF 1953; served UK, Australia and Singapore; Dep. Dir, Aviation Medicine, RAF, 1974–77; British Defence Staff, Washington DC, 1977–80; CO Princess Alexandra Hosp., RAF Wroughton, 1980–82; Dir, Health and Research, RAF, 1982–84; PMO Strike Command, 1984–86. Chadwick Gold Medal, 1970; CStJ 1986. *Recreations*: walking, climbing, painting, photography. *Address*: Hale House, 4

Upper Hale Road, Farnham, Surrey GU9 0NJ. *T:* Farnham 714190. *Club:* Royal Air Force.

HURRELL, Col Geoffrey Taylor, OBE 1944; Lord-Lieutenant of Cambridgeshire, 1974–75 (of Cambridgeshire and Isle of Ely, 1965–74); *b* 12 March 1900; *s* of Arthur Hurrell and Emily Taylor; *m* 1934, Mary Crossman; one *s* one *d. Educ:* Rugby; Sandhurst. Gazetted 17th Lancers, 1918; Lieut-Col comdg 17th/21st Lancers, 1940; Col 1944. High Sheriff, Cambridgeshire and Huntingdonshire, 1963; JP Cambs 1952, DL 1958. KStJ 1972. *Recreations:* hunting, shooting. *Address:* Park House, Harston, near Cambridge. *Club:* Cavalry and Guards.

HURRELL, Ian Murray, LVO 1961; HM Diplomatic Service, retired; *b* 14 June 1914; *s* of Capt. L. H. M. Hurrell and Mrs Eva Hurrell; *m* 1939, Helen Marjorie Darwin; no *c. Educ:* Dover Coll. Anglo-Iranian Oil Co., 1932–34; Indian Police (United Provinces), 1934–48; entered HM Foreign (subseq. Diplomatic) Service, 1948; Vice-Consul, Shiraz, 1948–51; Consul, Benghazi, 1952; FO, 1952–53; 1st Sec., Quito, 1954 (Chargé d'Affaires, 1955); Bangkok, 1956–60; Tehran, 1960–64; Ankara (UK Delegn to CENTO), 1964–67; Ambassador, Costa Rica, 1968–72. Life FRSA, 1979; Fellow, British Interplanetary Soc., 1981. Imperial Order of the Crown (Iran). *Recreations:* rambling, photography, skin-diving, gardening, chess, etc. *Address:* Quarr House, Sway, Hants. *Club:* Royal Over-Seas League.

HURST, George; Staff Conductor, Western Orchestral Society (Bournemouth Symphony Orchestra and Bournemouth Sinfonietta), since 1973; *b* 20 May 1926; Rumanian father and Russian mother. *Educ:* various preparatory and public schs. in the UK and Canada; Royal Conservatory, Toronto, Canada. First prize for Composition, Canadian Assoc. of Publishers, Authors and Composers, 1945. Asst Conductor, Opera Dept, Royal Conservatory of Music, of Toronto, 1946; Lectr in Harmony, Counterpoint, Composition etc, Peabody Conservatory of Music, Baltimore, Md, 1947; Conductor of York, Pa, Symph. Orch., 1950–55, and concurrently of Peabody Conservatory Orch., 1952–55; Asst Conductor, LPO, 1955–57, with which toured USSR 1956; Associate conductor, BBC Northern Symphony Orchestra, 1957; Principal Conductor, BBC Northern Symphony Orchestra (previously BBC Northern Orchestra), 1958–68; Artistic Adviser, Western Orchestral Soc., 1968–73; Consultant, Nat. Centre of Orchestral Studies, 1980–; Principal Guest Conductor, BBC Scottish Symphony Orchestra, 1986–. Vice-Pres., Western Orch. Soc., 1979. Since 1956 frequent guest conductor in Europe, Israel, Canada. *Publications:* piano and vocal music (Canada). *Recreations:* yachting, horse-riding. *Address:* 21 Oslo Court, NW8. *T:* 01–722 3088.

HURST, Henry Ronald Grimshaw; Overseas Labour Adviser, Foreign and Commonwealth Office, 1976–81, retired; *b* 24 April 1919; *s* of Frederick George Hurst and Elizabeth Ellen (*née* Grimshaw); *m* 1942, Norah Joyce (*d* 1984), *d* of John Stanley Rothwell; one *s* one *d*; *m* 1986, Joy Oldroyde. *Educ:* Darwen and Blackpool Grammar Schs; St Catharine's Coll., Cambridge (MA). Served War, Army, 1940–46. Colonial Service, 1946–70: Permanent Sec., Min. of Labour, Tanzania, 1962–64; Labour Adviser, Tanzania, 1965–68, and Malaŵi, 1969–70; Dep. Overseas Labour Adviser, FCO, 1970–76. *Recreations:* tennis, cricket, gardening. *Address:* Flat 1, Meriden, Weston Road, Bath, Avon BA1 2XZ. *T:* Bath 334429. *Club:* Civil Service.

HURST, Margery, OBE 1976; Chairman, Brook Street Bureau PLC (Managing Director, 1947–76); *b* 23 May 1913; *d* of late Samuel and Deborah Berney; *m* 1948, Eric Hurst, Barrister-at-law; two *d. Educ:* Brondesbury and Kilburn High Sch.; Minerva Coll. RADA. Joined ATS on Direct Commission, 1943 (1939–45 war medal); invalided out of the service, 1944. Commenced business of Brook St Bureau of Mayfair Ltd, 1946; founded Margery Hurst Schs and Colls for administrative and secretarial studies. Co-opted Mem. of LCC Children's Cttee, 1956. Started non-profit making social clubs for secretaries, called Society for International Secretaries, in London, 1960; now in New York; awarded Pimm's Cup for Anglo-American friendship in the business world, 1962. Member: American Cttee, BNEC, 1967–70; Exec. Cttee, Mental Health Research Fund, 1967–72. One of first women elected Underwriting Mem. of Lloyds, 1970. First Lady Mem., Worshipful Co. of Marketors, 1981–; Freeman, City of London, 1981. *Publication:* No Glass Slipper (autobiog.), 1967. *Recreations:* tennis, swimming, drama, opera. *Address:* 125 Edgware Road, W2 2HX. *Clubs:* Royal Corinthian Yacht; Royal Southern Yacht.

HURST, Peter Thomas; Master of the Supreme Court Taxing Office, since 1981; *b* Troutbeck, Westmorland, 27 Oct. 1942; *s* of Thomas Lyon Hurst and Nora Mary Hurst; *m* 1968, Diane Dulcie Irvine, BA; one *s* two *d. Educ:* Stonyhurst College. LLB London. Admitted as Solicitor of the Supreme Court, 1967; Partner: Hurst and Walker, Solicitors, Liverpool, 1967–77; Gair Roberts Hurst and Walker, Solicitors, Liverpool, 1977–81. Chairman: Liverpool Young Solicitors Gp, 1979; NW Young Solicitors Conf., 1980. *Publication:* Butterworth's Costs Service, vol. 2, 1986. *Recreations:* gardening, music, French food and wine. *Address:* Ivy Lodge, Hitchen Hatch Lane, Sevenoaks, Kent. *T:* Sevenoaks 456783. *Club:* Athenæum (Liverpool).

HURST, Dr Robert, CBE 1973; GM 1944; FRSC; retired; *b* Nelson, NZ, 3 Jan. 1915; *s* of late Percy Cecil Hurst and late Margery Hurst; *m* 1946, Rachael Jeanette (*née* Marsh); three *s. Educ:* Nelson Coll.; Canterbury Coll., NZ (MSc); Cambridge Univ. (PhD). FRIC 1977. Experimental Officer, Min. of Supply, engaged in research in bomb disposal and mine detection, 1940–45. Group Leader Transuranic Elements Group, AERE, Harwell, 1948–55; Project Leader, Homogeneous Aqueous Reactor Project, AERE, Harwell, 1956–57; Chief Chemist, Research and Development Branch, Industrial Group UKAEA, 1957–58; Director, Dounreay Experimental Reactor Establishment, UKAEA, 1958–63; Dir of Res., British Ship Res. Assoc., 1963–76. *Publication:* Editor, Progress in Nuclear Engineering, Series IV (Technology and Engineering), 1957. *Recreations:* gardening, sailing. *Address:* 15 Elms Avenue, Parkstone, Poole, Dorset. *Club:* Athenæum.

HURT, John; actor; stage, films and television; Director, United British Artists, since 1982; *b* 22 Jan. 1940; *s* of Rev. Arnould Herbert Hurt and Phyllis Massey; *m* 1984, Donna Peacock. *Educ:* The Lincoln Sch., Lincoln; RADA. Started as a painter. *Stage:* début, Arts Theatre, London, 1962; Chips With Everything, Vaudeville, 1962; The Dwarfs, Arts, 1963; Hamp (title role), Edin. Fest., 1964; Inadmissible Evidence, Wyndhams, 1965; Little Malcolm and his Struggle Against the Eunuchs, Garrick, 1966; Belcher's Luck, Aldwych (RSC), 1966; Man and Superman, Gaiety, Dublin, 1969; The Caretaker, Mermaid, 1972; The Only Street, Dublin Fest. and Islington, 1973; Travesties, Aldwych (RSC), 1974; The Arrest, Bristol Old Vic, 1974; The Shadow of a Gunman, Nottingham Playhouse, 1978; The Seagull, Lyric, Hammersmith, 1985. *Films and Television:* began films with The Wild and the Willing, 1962; A Man for All Seasons, 1966; Sinful Davey, 1967, film 1968; The Waste Places (ATV), 1968; later films and TV include: Before Winter Comes, 1969; In Search of Gregory, 1970; Mr Forbush and the Penguins, 1971; (Evans in) 10 Rillington Place, 1971; The Ghoul, 1974; Little Malcolm, 1974; The Naked Civil Servant (ITV), 1975 (Emmy Award, 1976); Caligula, in I Claudius (series BBC TV) 1976; East of Elephant Rock, 1977; Treats (TV), 1977; The Disappearance, The Shout, Spectre, The Alien, and Midnight Express (BAFTA award, 1978), all 1978; Heaven's Gate, 1979; Crime and Punishment (BBC TV series), 1979; The Elephant Man, 1980 (BAFTA award, 1981); History of the World Part 1, 1981; Partners, 1982; Champions, 1984; Nineteen Eighty-Four, 1984; The Osterman Weekend, 1984; The Hit, 1984; Jake Speed, 1986. *Address:* c/o Julian Belfrage, 60 St James's Street, SW1. *T:* 01–491 4400.

HURWITZ, Vivian Ronald; His Honour Judge Hurwitz; a Circuit Judge, since 1974; *b* 7 Sept. 1926; *s* of Alter Max and Dora Rebecca Hurwitz; *m* 1963, Dr Ruth Cohen, Middlesbrough; one *s* two *d. Educ:* Roundhay Sch., Leeds; Hertford Coll., Oxford (MA). Served RNVR: Univ. Naval Short Course, Oct. 1944–March 1945, followed by service until March 1947. Called to Bar, Lincoln's Inn, 1952, practised NE Circuit. A Recorder of Crown Court, 1972–74. *Recreations:* tennis, bridge, music (listening), art (looking at), sport—various (watching).

HUSAIN, Abul Basher M.; *see* Mahmud Husain.

HUSBAND, Prof. Thomas Mutrie, PhD; CEng, FIProdE, FIMechE; Professor of Engineering Manufacture, since 1981, Director of Centre for Robotics, since 1982, and Head of Department of Mechanical Engineering, since 1983, Imperial College, University of London; *b* 7 July 1936; *s* of Thomas Mutrie Husband and Janet Clark; *m* 1962, Pat Caldwell; two *s. Educ:* Shawlands Acad., Glasgow; Univ. of Strathclyde. BSc(Eng), MA, PhD; CEng, FIProdE. Weir Ltd, Glasgow: Apprentice Fitter, 1953–58; Engr/Jun. Manager, 1958–62; sandwich degree student (mech. engrg), 1958–61; various engrg and management positions with ASEA Ltd in Denmark, UK and S Africa, 1962–65; postgrad. student, Strathclyde Univ., 1965–66; Teaching Fellow, Univ. of Chicago, 1966–67; Lectr, Univ. of Strathclyde, 1967–70; Sen. Lectr, Univ. of Glasgow, 1970–73; Prof. of Manufacturing Organisation, Loughborough Univ., 1973–81. Member: ACARD Working Gp on Advanced Manufg Technology, 1982–83; DTI/SERC Cttee on Advanced Manufg Technology, 1983–; Chm., Manufg Processes Cttee, SERC, 1984–. *Publications:* Work Analysis and Pay Structure, 1976; Maintenance and Terotechnology, 1977; Education and Training in Robotics, 1986; articles in Terotechnica, Industrial Relations Jl, Microelectronics and Reliability, etc. *Recreations:* watching Arsenal FC, music, theatre. *Address:* 33 Featherstone Road, NW7 2BL. *T:* 01–959 5976.

HUSKISSON, Robert Andrews, CBE 1979; Chairman, Lloyd's Register of Shipping, 1973–83 (Deputy Chairman, 1972–73); *b* 2 April 1923; *y s* of Edward Huskisson and Mary Huskisson (*née* Downing); *m* 1969, Alice Marian Swaffin. *Educ:* Merchant Taylors' Sch.; St Edmund Hall, Oxford. Served Royal Corps of Signals, 1941–47 (Major). Joined Shaw Savill & Albion Co. Ltd 1947; Dir 1966–72; Dep. Chief Exec., 1971–72; Director: Overseas Containers Ltd, 1967–72; Container Fleets Ltd, 1967–72; Cairn Line of Steamships Ltd, 1969–72. President: British Shipping Fedn, 1971–72 (Chm. 1968–71); International Shipping Fedn, 1969–73; Chairman: Hotels and Catering EDC, 1975–79; Marine Technology Management Cttee, SRC, 1977–81. *Recreations:* golf, gardening, music. *Address:* Lanterns, Luppitt Close, Hutton Mount, Brentwood, Essex. *Clubs:* Vincent's (Oxford); Thorndon Park Golf.

HUSSAIN, Karamat; Councillor (Lab) Mapesbury Ward, London Borough of Brent, 1971–86; Chairman, National Standing Conference of Afro-Caribbean and Asian Councillors, 1980–86 (Founder Member); *b* Rawalpindi, 1926; *m*; one *d. Educ:* Aligarh Muslim Univ., India (BA Hons Humanities, MPhil). Formerly Mem., Housing, Develt and Finance Cttees, Brent Council; Mayor of Brent, 1981–82 (Dep. Mayor, 1980–81); formerly Mem. and Vice-Chm., Brent Community Relations Council. Sitara-i-Quaid-i-Azam 1982. *Address:* 12 Buckingham Court, Watford Way, NW4.

HUSSEIN bin Onn, Datuk, SPMJ 1972; SPDK 1974; SIMP 1975; PIS 1968; MP for Sri Gading, 1974–81; Prime Minister of Malaysia, 1976–81; *b* Johore Bharu, 12 Feb. 1922; *s* of late Dato' Onn bin Jaafar and of Datin Hajjah Halimah binte Hussein; *m* Datin Suhailah; two *s* four *d. Educ:* English Coll., Johore Bharu; Military Acad., Dehra Dun, India. Called to the Bar, Gray's Inn. Cadet, Johore Mil. Forces, 1940; commnd Indian Army; served Egypt, Syria, Palestine, Persia, Iraq, and GHQ, New Delhi; seconded to Malayan Police Recruiting and Trng Centre, Rawalpindi; returned to Malaya with liberation forces, 1945; Comdt, Police Depot, Johore Bharu; demobilised. Joined Malay Admin. Service; served in Selangor State; Officer i/c Kampong (village) guards, Johore, in Communist emergency, 1948. Entered politics; National Youth Leader and Sec.-Gen., United Malays Nat. Org. (UMNO), 1950; Member: Fed. Legislative Council; Johore Council of State; Johore State Exec. Council; left UMNO when his father Dato' Onn bin Jaafar resigned from the organisation in 1951. Studied law in England; in practice, Kuala Lumpur, 1963. Rejoined UMNO, 1968; MP for Johore Bharu Timor, 1969; Minister of Educn, 1970–73; Dep. Prime Minister, 1973–76; Minister of Trade and Industry, 1973–74; Minister of Finance, and Minister of Coordination and Public Corporations, 1974–76. Chairman: Commonwealth Parly Assoc., Malaysia, 1975–76; Inter Parly Union Malaysia Gp. President: Malayan Assoc. for the Blind; Kelab Golf Negara, Subang. *Recreation:* golf. *Address:* 3 Jalan Kenny, Kuala Lumpur, Malaysia.

HUSSEY, Prof. Joan Mervyn, MA, BLitt, PhD; FSA; FRHistS; Professor of History in the University of London, at Royal Holloway College, 1950–74, now Emeritus. *Educ:* privately; Trowbridge High Sch.; Lycée Victor Duruy, Versailles; St Hugh's Coll., Oxford. Research Student, Westfield Coll., London, 1932–34; Internat. Travelling Fellow (FUW), 1934–35; Pfeiffer Research Fellow, Girton, 1934–37; Gamble Prize, 1935. Asst Lectr in Hist., Univ. of Manchester, 1937–43; Lectr in Hist., 1943–47, Reader in Hist., 1947–50, at Bedford Coll., Univ. of London. Visiting Prof. at Amer. Univ. of Beirut, 1966; Pres., Brit. Nat. Cttee for Byzantine Studies, 1961–71; Hon. Vice-Pres., Internat. Cttee for Byzantine Studies, 1976. Governor, Girton Coll., Cambridge, 1935–37; Mem. Council, St Hugh's Coll., Oxford, 1940–46; Mem. Council, Royal Holloway Coll., 1966–; Hon. Fellow, St Hugh's Coll., Oxford, 1968. Hon. Fellow, Instituto Siciliano de Studi Bizantini, 1975. *Publications:* Church and Learning in the Byzantine Empire 867–1185, 1937 (repr. 1961); The Byzantine World, 1957, 3rd edn 1966; Cambridge Medieval History IV, Pts I and II: ed and contributor, 1966–67; The Finlay Papers, 1973; The Orthodox Church in the Byzantine Empire, 1986; reviews and articles in Byzantinische Zeitschrift, Byzantinoslavica, Trans Roy. Hist. Soc., Jl of Theological Studies, Enc. Britannica, Chambers's Enc., New Catholic Enc., etc. *Address:* 16 Clarence Drive, Englefield Green, Egham, Surrey TW20 0NL.

HUSSEY, Marmaduke James; Chairman, Board of Governors of the BBC, since 1986; Director: MK Electric Group, since 1982; Colonial Mutual Life Assurance Society, since 1982; William Collins PLC, since 1985; *b* 1923; *s* of late E. R. J. Hussey, CMG and Mrs Christine Hussey; *m* 1959, Lady Susan Katharine Waldegrave (*see* Lady Susan Hussey); one *s* one *d. Educ:* Rugby Sch.; Trinity Coll., Oxford (Scholar, MA). Served War of 1939–45, Grenadier Guards, Italy. Joined Associated Newspapers, 1949, Dir 1964; Man. Dir, Harmsworth Publications, 1967–70; joined Thomson Organisation Exec. Bd, 1971; Chief Exec. and Man. Dir, 1971–80, Dir, 1982–86, Times Newspapers Ltd; Jt Chm., Great Western Radio, 1985–86. A Rhodes Trustee, 1972–; Mem. Bd, British Council, 1983–. Chm., Nat. Adv. Council on Employment of Disabled People, 1986–. Chm. Bd of Governors, Royal Marsden Hosp., 1985–. *Address:* Flat 15, 45/47 Courtfield Road, SW7 4DA. *T:* 01–370 1414. *Club:* Brooks's.

HUSSEY, Lady Susan Katharine, DCVO 1984 (CVO 1971); Woman of the Bedchamber to the Queen, since 1960; *b* 1 May 1939; 5th *d* of 12th Earl Waldegrave, KG, *qv*; *m* 1959, Marmaduke James Hussey, *qv*; one *s* one *d*. *Address*: Flat 15, 45/47 Courtfield Road, SW7 4DA. *T*: 01-370 1414.

HUSTON, John; film director and writer; *b* Nevada, Missouri, 5 Aug. 1906; *s* of Walter Huston and Rhea Gore; *m* 1st, Dorothy Harvey (marr. diss.); 2nd, Lesley Black (marr. diss.); 3rd, 1946, Evelyn Keyes (marr. diss. 1950); 4th 1950, Enrica Soma (*d* 1969); one *s* one *d*; 5th, 1972, Celeste Shane (marr. diss. 1975). Became an Irish Citizen, 1964. At beginning of career was reporter, artist, writer and actor at various times. Formerly: Writer for Warner Bros Studios, 1938; Director for Warner Bros 1941; Writer and Dir, Metro-Goldwyn-Mayer, 1949. Dir of several Broadway plays. Films directed or produced include: The Maltese Falcon; Key Largo; The Treasure of Sierra Madre; The Asphalt Jungle; The African Queen; Moulin Rouge; Beat the Devil; Moby Dick; Heaven Knows, Mr Allison; The Barbarian and the Geisha; The Roots of Heaven; The Unforgiven; The Misfits; Freud; The Night of the Iguana; The Bible . . . In the Beginning; Reflections in a Golden Eye; Sinful Davey; A Walk with Love and Death; The Kremlin Letter; Fat City; The Life and Times of Judge Roy Bean; The Mackintosh Man; The Man who would be King; Wise Blood; Phobia; Escape to Victory; Annie; Under the Volcano; Prizzi's Honor (Special Gold Lion, Venice Film Fest., 1985); acted in Lovesick, Young Giants; Winter Kills. Served US Army 1942–45, Major; filmed documentaries of the War. Fellow, BAFTA, 1980. Hon. LittD Trinity Coll., Dublin, 1970. Special Award, Cannes Fest., 1984. *Publication*: (autobiog.) An Open Book, 1981. *Recreation*: foxhunting. *Address*: c/o Jess S. Morgan & Co. Inc., 6420 Wilshire Boulevard, 19th Floor, Los Angeles, Calif 90048, USA.

HUTCHINGS, Andrew William Seymour, CBE 1973; General Secretary, Assistant Masters Association, 1939–78, Joint General Secretary, Assistant Masters and Mistresses Association, Sept-Dec. 1978; Vice-President, National Foundation for Educational Research in England and Wales, since 1983 (Chairman, 1973–83); *b* 3 Dec. 1907; *o s* of William Percy and Mellony Elizabeth Louisa Hutchings; unmarried. *Educ*: Cotham Sch., Bristol; St Catharine's Coll., Cambridge (MA). Asst Master: Downside Sch., 1929–30; Methodist Coll., Belfast, 1930–34; Holt Sch., Liverpool, 1934–36; Asst Sec., Asst Masters Assoc., 1936–39; Hon. Sec., Jt Cttee of Four Secondary Assocs, 1939–78; Sec.-Gen. 1954–65, Pres. 1965–71 and 1972–73, Internat. Fedn of Secondary Teachers; Member: Exec. Cttee, World Confedn of Organisations of Teaching Profession, 1954–80; Secondary Schs Examination Council, and subseq. of Schools Council, 1939–78; Norwood Cttee on Curriculum and Examinations in Secondary Schs, 1941–43; Chm., Teachers' Panel, Burnham Primary and Secondary Cttee, 1965–78; Vice-Chm., Associated Examining Bd, 1982– (Chm., Exec. Cttee, 1979–). FEIS 1963; FCP 1975. *Publications*: educnl and professional articles and memoranda for Asst Masters Assoc. *Recreation*: breeding and showing Great Danes (Mem. Kennel Club). *Address*: Lower Eastacott House, Umberleigh, North Devon EX37 9AJ. *T*: Chittlehamholt 486.

HUTCHINGS, Arthur James Bramwell; Professor of Music, University of Exeter, 1968–71, now Emeritus; *b* Sunbury on Thames, 14 July 1906; *s* of William Thomas Hutchings, Bideford, N Devon, and Annie Bramwell, Freckleton, Lytham, Lancs; *m* 1940, Marie Constance Haverson; one *d*. Formerly schoolmaster and organist; contributor to musical periodicals, critic and reviewer; served with RAF in SEAC; Prof. of Music, University of Durham, 1947–68, now Emeritus. Mem., Editorial Cttee, The English Hymnal, 1954–. Mem. Bd of Governors of Trinity Coll. of Music, 1947–. BA, BMus, PhD London; Hon. FTCL, FRSCM, Hon. RAM. Compositions include: works for strings, comic operas and church music. *Publications*: Schubert (Master Musicians Series), 1941, 5th edn 1978; Edmund Rubbra (contribution to Penguin Special, Music of Our Time), 1941; Delius (in French, Paris), 1946; A Companion to Mozart's Concertos, 1947; Delius, 1947; The Invention and Composition of Music, 1954; The Baroque Concerto, 1960, 4th edn 1978; Pelican History of Music, Vol 3 (The 19th Century), 1962; Church Music in the Nineteenth Century, 1967; Mozart (2 vols), 1976. Contributions to: Die Musik in Geschichte und Gegenwart, 1956; The Mozart Companion, 1956; New Oxford History of Music, 1962; The Beethoven Companion, 1970; Grove's Dictionary of Music and Musicians, 6th edn, 1975; Purcell (BBC Music Guides), 1982. *Address*: 8 Rosemary Lane, Colyton, Devon EX13 6NJ. *T*: Colyton 52542.

HUTCHINS, Frank Ernest, CEng, FIEE, FIMarE; RCNC; retired 1981; consultant engineer, since 1982; *b* 27 Sept. 1922; *s* of Sidney William Hutchins and Eleanor Seager; *m* 1946, Patricia Mary Wakeford-Fullagar; one *d*. *Educ*: Sir Joseph Williamson's Mathematical Sch., Rochester, Kent; Royal Dockyard Sch., Chatham; Royal Naval Coll., Greenwich. BSc(Eng) 1st cl. Hons London. Asst Electrical Engr, Admiralty, Bath, 1945–49; Asst Staff Electrical Officer, BJSM, Washington DC, USA, 1949–51; Electrical Engr, Admiralty, Bath, 1951–63; Suptg Elec. Engr, Weapon Development and Ship Design, MoD (Navy), Bath, 1963–65; HM Dockyard, Devonport: Dep. Elec. Engrg Manager, 1965–68; Dep. Production Manager, 1968–69; Productivity Manager, 1969–70; attended Senior Officers' War Course, RN War Coll., Greenwich, 1970–71; Asst Director Naval Ship Production (Procurement Executive), MoD (Navy), Bath, 1971–73, Dep. Dir of Electrical Engrng, 1973–78; Chief Electrical Engr, Ship Dept, MoD (Navy), 1978–81. Panel Mem., CS Comr's Interview Selection Bd, 1981–. FBIM. *Recreations*: sketching, carpentry, gardening. *Address*: Bonnie Banks, Ralph Allen Drive, Bath BA2 5AE. *Club*: Civil Service.

HUTCHINS, Captain Ronald Edward, CBE 1961; DSC 1943; RN; *b* 7 Jan. 1912; *s* of Edward Albert Hutchins and Florence Ada (*née* Sharman); *m* 1937, Irene (*née* Wood); two *s*. *Educ*: St John's (elem. sch.), Hammersmith; TS Mercury, Hamble, Hants (C. B. Fry); RN Coll., Greenwich. Royal Navy, 1928–61, service in submarines, then Exec. Br. specialising in gunnery; Computer Industry, 1961–79: Manager and Company Dir, ICL and some of its UK subsids, and associated engrg cos. *Recreations*: walking, gardening. *Address*: 11 Virginia Beeches, Callow Hill, Virginia Water, Surrey GU25 4LT.

HUTCHINSON; *see* Hely-Hutchinson.

HUTCHINSON, family name of **Baron Hutchinson of Lullington.**

HUTCHINSON OF LULLINGTON, Baron *cr* 1978 (Life Peer), of Lullington in the County of E Sussex; **Jeremy Nicolas Hutchinson,** QC 1961; *b* 28 March 1915; *o s* of late St John Hutchinson, KC; *m* 1st, 1940, Dame Peggy Ashcroft (marr. diss. 1966); one *s* one *d*; 2nd, 1966, June Osborn. *Educ*: Stowe Sch.; Magdalen Coll., Oxford. Called to Bar, Middle Temple, 1939, Bencher 1963. RNVR, 1939–46. Practised on Western Circuit, N London Sessions and Central Criminal Court. Recorder of Bath, 1962–72; a Recorder of the Crown Court, 1972–76. Member: Cttee on Immigration Appeals, 1966–68; Cttee on Identification Procedures, 1974–76. Mem., Arts Council of GB, 1974–79 (Vice-Chm., 1977–79); Trustee, Tate Gallery, 1977–84 (Chm., 1980–84). *Address*: House of Lords, Westminster, SW1A 0PW. *Club*: MCC.

HUTCHINSON, Arthur Edward; QC 1979; **His Honour Judge Arthur Hutchinson;** a Circuit Judge, since 1984; *b* 31 Aug. 1934; *s* of late George Edward Hutchinson and Kathleen Hutchinson; *m* 1967, Wendy Pauline Cordingley, one *s* two *d*. *Educ*: Silcoates Sch.; Emmanuel Coll., Cambridge (MA). Commissioned, West Yorkshire Regt, 1953; served in Kenya with 5th Fusiliers, 1953–54. Called to Bar, Middle Temple, 1958; joined NE Circuit, 1959; a Recorder, 1974–84. *Recreations*: cricket, gardening, music. *Address*: c/o The Court House, Oxford Row, Leeds LS1 3BE. *T*: Leeds 451616.

HUTCHINSON, Rear-Adm. Christopher Haynes, CB 1961; DSO 1940; OBE 1946; RN retired; *b* 13 March 1906; 2nd *s* of late Rev. Canon Frederick William Hutchinson; *m* 1941, Nancy Marguerite Coppinger. *Educ*: Lydgate House Prep. Sch., Hunstanton; Royal Naval Colleges, Osborne and Dartmouth. Naval Cadet RNC Osborne, Sept. 1919; served largely in submarines; served War of 1939–45, commanding submarine Truant which sank German cruiser Karlsruhe, 9 April 1940 (DSO); submarine base, Malta, 1942 (despatches); Staff Officer, British Pacific Fleet 1945 (OBE); Qualified RN Staff Coll. (1946) and Joint Services Staff Coll. (Directing Staff); Commanding 3rd Submarine Flotilla, 1950–52; Senior Naval Adviser to UK High Commissioner, Australia, 1952–54; Captain, RN Coll., Greenwich, 1954–56; Commodore, 1st Class, Chief of Staff Far East Station, 1956–59; Director-General of Personal Services and Officer Appointments, 1959–61; retired, 1962. *Address*: Pipits Hill, Avington, near Winchester, Hants. *T*: Itchen Abbas 363.

HUTCHINSON, Prof. George William, MA, PhD, Cantab; Professor of Physics, Southampton University, 1960–85, now Emeritus; *b* Feb. 1921; *s* of George Hutchinson, farmer, and Louisa Ethel (*née* Saul), Farnsfield, Notts; *m* 1943, Christine Anne (marr. diss. 1970), *d* of Matthew Rymer and Mary (*née* Proctor), York; two *s*. *Educ*: Abergele Grammar Sch.; Cambridge. MA 1946, PhD 1952, Cantab. State Schol. and Schol. of St John's Coll., Cambridge, 1939–42. Research worker and factory manager in cotton textile industry, 1942–47; Cavendish Lab., Cambridge, 1947–52; Clerk-Maxwell Schol. of Cambridge Univ., 1949–52; Nuffield Fellow, 1952–53, and Lecturer, 1953–55, in Natural Philosophy, University of Glasgow; Research Assoc. of Stanford Univ., Calif, 1954. Lecturer, 1955, Sen. Lectr, 1957, in Physics, University of Birmingham. Member: Nat. Exec. Cttee, AUT, 1978–84; Nat. Council, CND, 1981–84; Nat. Co-ordinating Cttee, Scientists Against Nuclear Arms, 1985– (Internat. Sec., SANA). Duddell Medal, Physical Soc., 1959. FRAS; FRSA. *Publications*: papers on nuclear and elementary particle physics, nuclear instrumentation and cosmic rays. *Recreations*: music, travel. *Address*: Physical Laboratory, University of Southampton, Southampton SO9 5NH. *T*: Southampton 559122.

HUTCHINSON, Sir Joseph (Burtt), Kt 1956; CMG 1944; ScD Cantab; FRS 1951; Drapers' Professor of Agriculture, Cambridge, 1957–69, now Emeritus; Fellow, St John's College; *b* 21 March 1902; *s* of L. M. and Edmund Hutchinson; *m* 1930, Martha Leonora Johnson; one *s* one *d*. *Educ*: Ackworth and Bootham Schs; St John's Coll., Cambridge. Asst Geneticist, Empire Cotton Growing Corporation's Cotton Research Station, Trinidad, 1926–33; Geneticist and Botanist, Institute of Plant Industry, Indore, Central India, 1933–37; Geneticist, Empire Growing Corporation's Cotton Research Station, Trinidad, and Cotton Adviser to the Inspector-General of Agriculture, BWI, 1937–44. Chief Geneticist, Empire Cotton Growing Corp., 1944–49; Dir of its Cotton Research Station, Namulonge, Uganda, 1949–57. Chm. of Council of Makerere Coll., University Coll. of East Africa, 1953–57; Hon. Fellow, Makerere Coll., 1957. Pres., British Assoc., 1965–66; Foreign Fellow, Indian Nat. Science Acad., 1974. Royal Medal, Royal Society, 1967. Hon. DSc: Nottingham, 1966; East Anglia, 1972. *Publications*: The Genetics of Gossypium, 1947; Genetics and the Improvement of Tropical Crops, 1958; Application of Genetics to Cotton Improvement, 1959; Farming and Food Supply, 1972; (ed) Evolutionary Studies in World Crops, 1974; The Challenge of the Third World, 1975; Change and Innovation in Norfolk Farming, 1980; numerous papers on the genetics, taxonomy, and economic botany of cotton. *Address*: Huntingfield, Huntingdon Road, Cambridge CB3 0LH. *T*: Cambridge 276272.

HUTCHINSON, Patricia Margaret, CMG 1981; CBE 1982; HM Diplomatic Service, retired; *b* 18 June 1926; *d* of late Francis Hutchinson and Margaret Peat. *Educ*: abroad; St Paul's Girls' Sch.; Somerville Coll., Oxford (PPE, MA, Hon Fellow, 1980). ECE, Geneva, 1947; Bd of Trade, 1947–48; HM Diplomatic Service, 1948: 3rd Sec., Bucharest, 1950–52; Foreign Office, 1952–55; 2nd (later 1st) Sec., Berne, 1955–58; 1st Sec. (Commercial), Washington, 1958–61; FO, 1961–64; 1st Sec., Lima, 1964–67 (acted as Chargé d'Affaires); Dep. UK Permanent Rep. to Council of Europe, 1967–69; Counsellor: Stockholm, 1969–72; UK Delegn to OECD, 1973–75; Consul-Gen., Geneva, 1975–80; Ambassador to Uruguay, 1980–83; Consul-Gen., Barcelona, 1983–86. *Recreations*: music, reading. *Address*: c/o National Westminster Bank, 6 Tothill Street, SW1. *Club*: United Oxford & Cambridge University.

HUTCHINSON, Richard Hampson; His Honour Judge Hutchinson; a Circuit Judge, since 1974; *b* 31 Aug. 1927; *s* of late John Riley Hutchinson and May Hutchinson; *m* 1954, Nancy Mary (*née* Jones); two *s* three *d*. *Educ*: St Bede's Grammar Sch., Bradford; UC Hull. LLB London. National Service, RAF, 1949–51. Called to Bar, Gray's Inn, 1949; practised on NE Circuit, 1951–74. Recorder: Rotherham, 1971–72; Crown Court, 1972–74. *Recreations*: reading, conversation. *Address*: c/o Crown Court, Holborn House, 10A Newport, Lincoln.

HUTCHINSON, Hon. Sir Ross, Kt 1977; DFC 1944; Speaker, Legislative Assembly, Western Australia, 1974–77, retired; MLA (L) Cottesloe, 1950–77; *b* 10 Sept. 1914; *s* of Albert H. Hutchinson and Agnes L. M. Hutchinson; *m* 1939, Amy Goodall Strang; one *s* one *d*. *Educ*: Wesley Coll. RAAF, 1942–45. School teacher, 1935–49. Chief Sec., Minister for Health and Fisheries, 1959–65; Minister for Works and Water Supplies, 1965–71. Australian Rules Football, former Captain Coach; East Fremantle, West Perth and South Fremantle; Captain Coach, WA, 1939. *Recreations*: tennis, reading. *Address*: 42 Griver Street, Cottesloe, WA 6011, Australia. *T*: 312680. *Club*: Royal King's Park Tennis (Perth, WA).

HUTCHISON, A(lan) Michael Clark; *b* 26 Feb. 1914; *y s* of late Sir George A. Clark Hutchison, KC, MP, of Eriska, Argyll; *m* 1937, Anne, *yr d* of Rev. A. R. Taylor, DD, of Aberdeen; one *s* one *d*. *Educ*: Eton; Trinity Coll., Cambridge. Called to Bar, Gray's Inn, 1937. War of 1939–45 (despatches); served AIF, Middle East and Pacific theatres, psc (Major). Mem. Australian Mil. Mission, Washington, USA, 1945–46. Entered Colonial Admin. Service, 1946, and served as Asst Dist Comr in Palestine till 1948; thereafter as Political Officer and Asst Sec. in Protectorate and Colony of Aden; resigned, 1955. Contested (C) Motherwell Div. of Lanarks, 1955; MP (C) Edinburgh South, May 1957–79; Parliamentary Private Secretary to: Parliamentary and Financial Sec. to the Admiralty, and to the Civil Lord, 1959; the Lord Advocate, 1959–60; Sec. of State for Scotland, 1960–62. Scottish Conservative Members' Committee: Vice-Chm., 1965–66, 1967–68; Chm., 1970–71. Introduced as Private Mem.'s Bills: Solicitors (Scotland) Act; Wills Act; Intestate Succession (Scotland) Act; Confirmation to Small Estates (Scotland) Act. *Recreations*: reading, Disraeliana. *Address*: Wellcroft End, Bucklebury, Reading RG7 6PB. *T*: Woolhampton 713462. *Club*: New (Edinburgh).

See also Lieut-Comdr Sir G. I. C. Hutchison.

HUTCHISON, Bruce; *see* Hutchison, W. B.

HUTCHISON, Hon. Sir Douglas; *see* Hutchison, Hon. Sir J. D.

HUTCHISON, Geordie Oliphant; Managing Director, Calders & Grandidge Ltd, timber importers and manufacturers, since 1974; *b* 11 June 1934; *s* of late Col Ronald Gordon Oliphant Hutchison and of Ruth Gordon Hutchison-Bradburne; *m* 1964, Virginia Barbezat; two *s* one *d*. *Educ:* Eton Coll. Served RN, 1952–54: commnd as aircraft pilot, 1953. Calders Ltd, 1954–59; Calders & Grandidge Ltd, 1959–: Dir, 1969. Comr, Forestry Commn, 1981–. *Recreations:* golf, shooting. *Address:* Swallowfield House, Welby, Grantham, Lincs NG32 3LR. *T:* Loveden 30510. *Club:* Royal and Ancient Golf (St Andrews).

HUTCHISON, Lt-Comdr Sir (George) Ian Clark, Kt 1954; Royal Navy, retired; Member of the Queen's Body Guard for Scotland, Royal Company of Archers; *b* 4 Jan. 1903; *e s* of late Sir George Clark Hutchison, KC, MP, Eriska, Argyllshire; *m* 1926, Sheena (*d* 1966), *o d* of late A. B. Campbell, WS; one *d*. *Educ:* Edinburgh Academy; RN Colleges, Osborne and Dartmouth. Joined Navy as Cadet, 1916; Lieut, 1926; Lieut-Comdr 1934; specialised in torpedoes, 1929; emergency list, 1931; Mem., Edinburgh Town Council, 1935–41; Chm., Public Assistance Cttee, 1937–39; contested Maryhill Div. of Glasgow, 1935; rejoined Navy Sept. 1939; served in Naval Ordnance Inspection Dept, 1939–43; MP (U) for West Div. of Edinburgh, 1941–59. Mem. National Executive Council of British Legion (Scotland), 1943–51; Governor of Donaldson's Sch. for the Deaf, Edinburgh, 1937–75; Mem. Cttee on Electoral Registration, 1945–46; Mem. Scottish Leases Cttee, 1951–52. DL County of City of Edinburgh, 1958–84. *Recreations:* golf, fishing, walking, philately. *Address:* 16 Wester Coates Gardens, Edinburgh EH12 5LT. *T:* 031–337 4888. *Club:* New (Edinburgh).
See also A. M. C. Hutchison, J. V. Paterson.

HUTCHISON, Lt-Comdr Sir Ian Clark; *see* Hutchison, Sir G. I. C.

HUTCHISON, Prof. James Holmes, CBE 1971 (OBE 1945); FRCP 1947; FRCPE 1960; FRCPGlas 1962; MD (Hons) 1939 (Glasgow); FRSE 1965; Professor of Paediatrics, University of Hong Kong, 1977–80; *b* 16 April 1912; *s* of Alexander Hutchison and Catherine Holmes; *m* 1940, Agnes T. A. Goodall; one *s* one *d*. *Educ:* High Sch. of Glasgow; University of Glasgow. Qualified MB, ChB (Glasgow) 1934; Resident Hosp. Posts, 1934–36; Royal Hosp. for Sick Children, Glasgow: McCunn Research Schol., 1936–38; Asst Vis. Phys., 1938–39; Physician in charge of Wards, 1947–61; also Consulting Pædiatrician, Queen Mother's Hospital, Glasgow; Leonard Gow Lectr on Med. Diseases of Infancy and Childhood, 1947–61, Samson Gemmell Prof. of Child Health, 1961–77, Univ. of Glasgow. Dean, Fac. of Medicine, Univ. of Glasgow, 1970–73. President: Royal College of Physicians and Surgeons of Glasgow, Nov. 1966–Nov. 1968. British Paediatric Assoc., 1969–70; Assoc. of Physicians of GB and Ireland, 1973–74; Hong Kong Paediatric Soc., 1979–80. Hon. FACP 1968. RAMC, Major and Lieut-Col, 1939–45. *Publications:* Practical Pædiatric Problems, 1964, 6th edn 1986; Rickets, in British Encyclopædia of Medical Practice, 2nd edn, 1952; Disorders of Storage, Obesity and Endocrine Diseases; chapters 50–57, in Pædiatrics for the Practitioner, 1953 (ed Gaisford and Lightwood); Hypothyroidism, in Recent Advances in Pædiatrics, 1958 (ed Gairdner), 2nd edn 1975; chapter jn Emergencies in Medical Practice (ed C. Allan Birch); chapter in Textbook of Medical Treatment (ed Davidson, Dunlop and Alstead); chapter in Endocrine and Genetic Diseases of Childhood (ed L. I. Gardner), 1969, 2nd edn 1976; Thyroid section in Paediatric Endrocrinology (ed D.Hubble), 1969; chapter in Textbook of Pædiatrics (ed J. O. Forfar and G. C. Arneil), 1973, 3rd edn 1984; many contributions to medical journals. *Recreations:* golf, country dancing (Scottish), motoring. *Address:* 3 Kelvin Court, Glasgow G12 0AB. *T:* 041–334 7545. *Club:* Royal Scottish Automobile.

HUTCHISON, (Joseph) Douglas, CBE 1972; MC 1944; TD 1952; Director, Ranks Hovis McDougall Ltd, 1956–83; *b* 3 April 1918; *s* of late John K. Hutchison, Kinloch, Collessie, Fife and late Ethel Rank, OBE; unmarried. *Educ:* Loretto; Clare Coll., Cambridge. BA Agric. 1939. Served Fife and Forfar Yeomanry, 1939–46 (Major); comd Regt, 1951–53. Director: R. Hutchison & Co. Ltd, 1951–73; Ranks Ltd (later RHM), 1956. Mem., ARC, 1973–78. Pres., Nat. Assoc. British and Irish Millers, 1963–64 and 1974–75; Pres., Research Assoc. Flour Millers and Bakers, 1967–72; Chm., Game Conservancy, 1970–75. *Recreations:* shooting, gardening, music. *Address:* Bolfracks, Aberfeldy, Perthshire. *Club:* New (Edinburgh).

HUTCHISON, Sir Kenneth; *see* Hutchison, Sir W. K.

HUTCHISON, Hon. Sir Michael, Kt 1983; **Hon. Mr Justice Hutchison;** a Judge of the High Court of Justice, Queen's Bench Division, since 1983; Judge, Employment Appeal Tribunal, since 1984; *b* 13 Oct. 1933; *s* of Ernest and Frances Hutchison; *m* 1957, Mary Spettigue; two *s* three *d*. *Educ:* Lancing; Clare College, Cambridge (MA). Called to Bar, Gray's Inn, 1958, Bencher, 1983; a Recorder, 1975–83; QC 1976. *Address:* Royal Courts of Justice, Strand, WC2.

HUTCHISON, Sir Peter, 2nd Bt, *cr* 1939; *b* 27 Sept. 1907; *er s* of Sir Robert Hutchison, 1st Bt, MD, CM, and Lady Hutchison; *S* father 1960; *m* 1949, Mary-Grace (*née* Seymour); two *s* two *d*. *Educ:* Marlborough; Lincoln Coll., Oxford. Admitted as a Solicitor, 1933. Dep.-Clerk of the Peace and of the CC, E Suffolk, 1947–71, Clerk of the Peace, 1971. Mem., Suffolk Coastal DC, 1973–83. Chm. of Governors, Orwell Park Prep. Sch., 1975–85. *Recreations:* gardening, reading. *Heir:* *s* Robert Hutchison, *b* 25 May 1954. *Address:* Melton Mead, near Woodbridge, Suffolk. *T:* Woodbridge 2746. *Club:* Ipswich and Suffolk (Ipswich).

HUTCHISON, Sir Peter Craft, 2nd Bt *cr* 1956; *b* 5 June 1935; *s* of Sir James Riley Holt Hutchison, 1st Bt, DSO, TD, and of Winefryde Eleanor Mary, *d* of late Rev. R. H. Craft; *S* father, 1979; *m* 1966, Virginia, *er d* of late John Millar Colville, Gribloch, Kippen, Stirlingshire; one *s*. *Educ:* Eton; Magdalene Coll., Cambridge. Chm., Hutchison & Craft Ltd, Insurance Brokers, Glasgow, 1979–; Dir, Stakis plc and other cos; Mem., Scottish Tourist Bd, 1981–. Chm. of Trustees, Royal Botanic Gdn, Edinburgh, 1985–. Deacon, Incorporation of Hammermen, 1984–85. *Heir:* *s* James Colville Hutchison, *b* 7 Oct. 1967. *Address:* Milton House, Milton, by Dumbarton G82 2TU.

HUTCHISON, Robert Edward; Keeper, Scottish National Portrait Gallery, 1953–82; *b* 4 Aug. 1922; *y s* of late Sir William Hutchison; *m* 1946, Heather, *d* of late Major A. G. Bird; one *s* one *d*. *Educ:* Gresham's Sch., Holt. Served War, 1940–46, Infantry and RA; Asst Keeper, Scottish National Portrait Gallery, 1949. Hon. MA Edinburgh, 1972. *Publication:* (with Stuart Maxwell) Scottish Costume 1550–1850, 1958. *Address:* North House, Firth Home Farm, Roslin, Midlothian. *T:* Penicuik 75118.

HUTCHISON, Sidney Charles, CVO 1977 (LVO 1967); Hon. Archivist, Royal Academy of Arts, since 1982; *b* 26 March 1912; *s* of late Henry Hutchison; *m* 1937, Nancy Arnold Brindley (*d* 1985); no *c*. *Educ:* Holloway Sch., London; London Univ. (Dip. in Hist. of Art, with Dist.). Joined staff of Royal Academy, 1929. Served War of 1939–45: Royal Navy, rising to Lieut-Comdr (S), RNVR. Librarian of Royal Academy, 1949–68, also Sec. of Loan Exhibitions, 1955–68; Sec., Royal Academy, 1968–82. Secretary: E. A. Abbey Meml Trust Fund for Mural Painting, 1960–; Incorporated E. A. Abbey Scholarships Fund, 1965–; E. Vincent Harris Fund for Mural Decoration, 1970–; British Institution Fund, 1968–82; Chantrey Trustees, 1968–82; Richard Ford Award Fund, 1977–82. Lectr in the History of Art, for Extra-Mural Dept of Univ. of London, 1957–67. Gen. Comr of Taxes, 1972–. Governor, Holloway Sch., 1969–81. Trustee, Chantrey Bequest, 1982–; Pres., Southgate Soc. of Arts, 1983–. Organist and Choirmaster of St Matthew's, Westminster, 1933–37. Associate Mem., ICOM, 1964. FRSA 1950; FSA 1955; FMA 1962; Fellow, Assoc. of Art Historians, 1974. Officer, Polonia Restituta, 1971; Chevalier, Belgian Order of the Crown, 1972; Grand Decoration of Honour (silver), Austria, 1972; Cavaliere Ufficiale, Al Merito della Repubblica Italiana, 1980. *Publications:* The Homes of the Royal Academy, 1956; The History of the Royal Academy, 1768–1968, 1968, enl. and updated, 1768–1986, 1986; articles for Walpole Society, Museums Jl, Encyclopædia Britannica, DNB, Apollo, etc. *Recreations:* music, travel. *Address:* 60 Belmont Close, Mount Pleasant, Cockfosters, Herts EN4 9LT. *T:* 01–449 9821. *Clubs:* Athenæum, Arts.

HUTCHISON, Prof. Terence Wilmot; Professor of Economics, University of Birmingham, 1956–78, now Emeritus Professor; Dean of the Faculty of Commerce and Social Science, 1959–61; *b* 13 Aug. 1912; *m* 1st, 1935, Loretta Hack (*d* 1981); one *s* two *d*; 2nd, 1983, Christine Donaldson. *Educ:* Tonbridge Sch.; Peterhouse, Cambridge. Lector, Univ. of Bonn, 1935–38; Prof., Teachers' Training Coll., Bagdad, 1938–41. Served Indian Army, in intelligence, in Middle East and India, 1941–46; attached to Govt of India, 1945–46. Lecturer, University Coll., Hull, 1946–47; Lecturer, 1947–51 and Reader, 1951–56, London Sch. of Economics. Visiting Professor: Columbia Univ., 1954–55; Univ. of Saarbrücken, 1962, 1980; Yale Univ., 1963–64; Dalhousie Univ., 1970; Keio Univ., Tokyo, 1973; Univ. of WA, 1975; Univ. of California, Davis, 1978; Visiting Fellow: Univ. of Virginia, 1960; Aust. Nat. Univ., Canberra, 1967. Mem. Council, Royal Economic Soc., 1967–72. *Publications:* The Significance and Basic Postulates of Economic Theory, 1938 (2nd edn 1960); A Review of Economic Doctrines 1870–1929, 1953; Positive Economics and Policy Objectives, 1964; Economics and Economic Policy 1946–66, 1968; Knowledge and Ignorance in Economics, 1977; Keynes *v* the Keynesians, 1977; Revolutions and Progress in Economic Knowledge, 1978; The Politics and Philosophy of Economics, 1981; articles, reviews in jls. *Address:* 75 Oakfield Road, Birmingham B29 7HL. *T:* 021–472 2020.

HUTCHISON, Thomas Oliver; Director, Imperial Chemical Industries PLC, since 1985; *b* 3 Jan. 1931; *s* of late James Hutchison and Thomasina Oliver; *m* 1955, Frances Mary Ada Butterworth; three *s*. *Educ:* Hawick High Sch.; Univ. of St Andrews (BSc Hons First Cl. Natural Philosophy). Joined ICI General Chemicals Division, 1954; key prodn, technical and commercial appts on general chemicals side of the Company's business until apptd Head of ICI's Policy Groups Dept, London, 1974; Dep. Chm., ICI Plastics Div., 1977–79; Chairman: ICI Petrochemicals and Plastics Div., 1981–85; Phillips-Imperial Petroleum, 1982–85; Director: Océ Finance Ltd, 1977–79; ICI Australia, 1985–; ICI Impkemix Investments Pty, 1985–; Bank of Scotland, 1985–; Cadbury Schweppes, 1986–. Mem. Council, British Plastics Fedn, 1977–80; Pres., Assoc. of Plastics Manufacturers in Europe, 1980–82; Mem., petrochemicals adv. gp, Conseil Européen des Fédns de l'Industrie Chimique (CEFIC), 1982–85. *Recreations:* fishing, tennis, music. *Address:* Imperial Chemical House, Millbank, SW1P 3JF. *T:* 01–834 4444.

HUTCHISON, (William) Bruce, OC 1967; formerly Editorial Director, Vancouver Sun, now Editor Emeritus; *b* 5 June 1901; *s* of John and Constance Hutchison; *m* 1925, Dorothy Kidd McDiarmid; one *s* one *d*. *Educ:* Public and high schs, Victoria, BC. Political writer: Victoria Times, 1918; Vancouver Province, 1925; Vancouver Sun, 1938; editor, Victoria Times, 1950–63; associate editor, Winnipeg Free Press, 1944. Hon. LLD University of British Columbia, 1951. *Publications:* The Unknown Country, 1943; The Hollow Men, 1944; The Fraser, 1950; The Incredible Canadian, 1952; The Struggle for the Border, 1955; Canada: Tomorrow's Giant, 1957; Mr Prime Minister, 1964; Western Windows, 1967; The Far Side of the Street, 1976; Uncle Percy's Wonderful Town, 1981; The Unfinished Country, 1985. *Recreations:* fishing, gardening. *Address:* 810 Rogers Avenue, Victoria, BC, Canada. *T:* 479–2269. *Club:* Union (Victoria).

HUTCHISON, Sir (William) Kenneth, Kt 1962; CBE 1954; FRS 1966; FEng 1976; FIChemE; Hon. FIGasE; *b* 30 Oct. 1903; *s* of late William Hutchison; *m* 1929, Dorothea Marion Eva (*d* 1985), *d* of late Commander Bertie W. Bluett, Royal Navy; one *d*. *Educ:* Edinburgh Academy; Corpus Christi Coll., Oxford. Joined staff of Gas, Light and Coke Co. as Research Chemist, 1926; seconded to Air Ministry as Asst Dir of Hydrogen Production, 1940, Dir, 1942; Dir of Compressed Gases, 1943; Controller of By-Products, Gas, Light and Coke Co., 1945, and a Managing Dir of the Company from 1947; Chm., South Eastern Gas Board, 1948–59; Deputy Chm., Gas Council, 1960–66; Chm., International Management and Engineering Group, 1967–69; Dir, Newton Chambers & Co. Ltd, 1967–73. President: Institution of Gas Engineers, 1955–56; British Road Tar Assoc., 1953–55; Inst. of Chem. Engineers, 1959–61; Soc. of British Gas Industries, 1967–68; Nat. Soc. for Clean Air, 1969–71. *Publications:* papers in Proc. Royal Society and other jls, 1926–. *Recreations:* garden, golf. *Address:* 2 Arlington Road, Twickenham, Mddx TW1 2BG. *T:* 01–892 1685. *Clubs:* Athenæum, Royal Cruising.

HUTCHISON, Prof. William McPhee; Personal Professor in Parasitology, University of Strathclyde, since 1971; *b* 2 July 1924; *s* of William Hutchison and Ann McPhee; *m* 1963, Ella Duncan McLaughland; two *s*. *Educ:* Eastwood Secondary Sch.; Glasgow Univ. BSc, PhD, DSc; FLS, FIBiol, CBiol; FRSE. Glasgow Univ. Fencing Blue, 1949; Ford Epée Cup; Glasgow Univ. Fencing Champion, 1950. Strathclyde Univ.: Asst Lectr, 1952; Lectr, 1953; Sen. Lectr, 1969. Engaged in res. on Toxoplasma and toxoplasmosis. Robert Koch Medal, 1970. *Publications:* contrib. Trans Royal Soc. Trop. Med. and Hygiene, Ann. Tropical Med. Parasitology, BMJ. *Recreations:* general microscopy, academic heraldry, collection of zoological specimens. *Address:* 597 Kilmarnock Road, Newlands, Glasgow G43 2TH. *T:* 041–637 4882.

HUTSON, Sir Francis (Challenor), Kt 1963; CBE 1960; Senior Partner, D. M. Simpson & Co., Consulting Engineers, Barbados, 1943–70, retired; *b* 13 Sept. 1895; *s* of Francis and Alice Sarah Hutson; *m* 1st, 1925, Muriel Allen Simpkin (*d* 1945); two *s* one *d*; 2nd, 1947, Edith Doris Howell. *Educ:* Harrison Coll., Barbados; Derby Technical Coll., Derby. Resident Engineer, Booker Bros, McConnell & Co. Ltd, British Guiana, 1920–30; Consulting Engineer, Barbados, 1930–35; D. M. Simpson & Co., 1935–70. MLC, 1947–62, MEC, 1958–61, Barbados; PC (Barbados), 1961–70. FIMechE. *Recreation:* bridge. *Address:* Fleetwood, Erdiston Hill, St Michael, Barbados. *T:* 429 3905. *Clubs:* Bridgetown, Royal Barbados Yacht, Savannah (all in Barbados).

HUTSON, Maj.-Gen. Henry Porter Wolseley, CB 1945; DSO 1917; OBE 1919; MC 1915; *b* 22 March 1893; *s* of late Henry Wolseley Hutson, Wimbledon, SW19; *m* 1922, Rowena, *d* of Surg.-Gen. Percy Hugh Benson, IA; two *s* one *d*. *Educ:* King's Coll. Sch.; RMA; 2nd Lieut RE, 1913; Capt. 1917; Major, 1929; Lieut-Col 1937; Col 1939; Temp. Brig. 1940; Maj.-Gen. 1944. Employed with Egyptian Army, 1920–24; under Colonial

Office (Road Engineer Nigeria), 1926–28; Chief Instructor, Field Works and Bridging, Sch. of Military Engineering, 1934–36; Chief Engineer, Forestry Commn, 1947–58. Served European War, 1914–18, France, Belgium, Egypt and Mesopotamia (wounded, despatches thrice, DSO, OBE, MC); War of 1939–45 (despatches, CB); retired pay, 1947. *Publications*: The Birds about Delhi, 1954; (ed) The Ornithologist's Guide, 1956; Majority Rule—Why?, 1973; Rhodesia: ending an era, 1978. *Address*: 23 Hoskins Road, Oxted, Surrey. *T*: Oxted 2354.

HUTSON, John Whiteford, OBE 1966; HM Diplomatic Service, retired; Consul-General, Casablanca, 1984–April 1987; *b* 21 Oct. 1927; *s* of John Hutson and Jean Greenlees Laird; *m* 1954, Doris Kemp; one *s* two *d*. *Educ*: Hamilton Academy; Glasgow Univ. (MA (Hons)). HM Forces, 1949–51; Foreign Office, 1951; Third Secretary, Prague, 1953; FO, 1955; Second Sec., Berlin, 1956; Saigon, 1959; First Sec., 1961; Consul (Commercial) San Francisco, 1963–67; First Sec. and Head of Chancery, Sofia, 1967–69; FCO, 1969; Counsellor, 1970; Baghdad, 1971–72; Inspector, FCO, 1972–74; Head, Communications Operations Dept, FCO, 1974–76; Counsellor (Commercial), Moscow, 1976–79; Consul-Gen., Frankfurt, 1979–83.

HUTT, Rev. David Handley; Vicar of All Saints', Margaret Street, W1, since 1986; *b* 24 Aug. 1938; *s* of Frank and Evelyn Hutt. *Educ*: Brentwood; RMA Sandhurst; King's College London (AKC). Regular Army, 1957–64. KCL, 1964–68. Deacon 1969, priest 1970; Curate: Bedford Park, W4, 1969–70; St Matthew, Westminster, 1970–73; Priest Vicar and Succentor, Southwark Cathedral, 1973–78; Sen. Chaplain, King's Coll., Taunton, 1978–82; Vicar, St Alban and St Patrick, Birmingham, 1982–86. *Recreations*: gardening, cooking, music, theatre. *Address*: All Saints' Vicarage, 7 Margaret Street, W1N 8JQ. *T*: 01–636 1788/9961. *Club*: Athenæum.

HUTT, Prof. William Harold; Distinguished Professor of Economics, University of Dallas, Texas, 1971–77; Professor of Commerce and Dean of the Faculty of Commerce, University of Cape Town, 1931–64; Professor Emeritus since 1965; *b* 3 Aug. 1899; *s* of William Hutt and Louisa (*née* Fricker); *m* 1946, Margarethe Louise Schonken. *Educ*: LCC Schs; Hackney Downs Sch.; London Sch. of Economics, University of London. Personal Asst to Chm., Benn Bros Ltd, and Manager, Individualist Bookshop Ltd, 1924–28; Senior Lecturer, University of Cape Town, 1928–30. Visiting Professor of Economics at various Univs and Colls in USA, 1966–69; Vis. Research Fellow, Hoover Instn, Stanford Univ., Calif., 1969–71; Distinguished Vis. Prof. of Economics, Calif. State Coll., 1970–71. LLD (*hc*) Cape Town, 1977. *Publications*: The Theory of Collective Bargaining, 1930, 2nd edn, 1975; Economists and the Public, 1936; The Theory of Idle Resources, 1939, 2nd edn 1977; Plan for Reconstruction, 1943; Keynesianism-Retrospect and Prospect, 1963; The Economics of the Colour Bar, 1964; Politically Impossible?, 1971; The Strike-Threat System, 1973; A Rehabilitation of Say's Law, 1975; Individual Freedom: a symposium of articles 1934–75 selected and ed by Klingaman and Pejovich, 1976; The Keynesian Episode, 1980; numerous articles in economic jls and symposia. *Recreations*: travel, listening to symphonies, watching football, ballet and opera. *Address*: c/o Standard Bank Ltd, ABC Branch, Adderley Street, Cape Town, South Africa. *Club*: Civil Service and City (Cape Town).

HUTTER, Prof. Otto Fred, PhD; Regius Professor of Physiology, University of Glasgow, since 1971; *b* 29 Feb. 1924; *s* of Isak and Elisabeth Hutter; *m* 1948, Yvonne T. Brown; two *s* two *d*. *Educ*: Chajes Real Gymnasium, Vienna; Bishops Stortford Coll., Herts; University Coll., London (BSc, PhD). Univ. of London Postgrad. Student in Physiology, 1948; Sharpey Scholar, UCL, 1949–52; Rockefeller Travelling Fellow and Fellow in Residence, Johns Hopkins Hosp., Baltimore, 1953–55; Lectr, Dept of Physiology, UCL, 1953–61; Hon. Lectr, 1961–70. Visiting Prof., Tel-Aviv Univ., 1968, 1970; Scientific Staff, Nat. Inst. for Medical Research, Mill Hill, London, 1961–70. *Publications*: papers on neuromuscular and synaptic transmission, cardiac and skeletal muscle, in physiological jls. *Address*: Institute of Physiology, University of Glasgow, Glasgow G12 8QQ. *T*: 041–339 8855.

HUTTON, Alasdair Henry, TD 1977; Member (C) South Scotland, European Parliament, since 1979; *b* 19 May 1940; *s* of Alexander Hutton and Margaret Elizabeth (*née* Henderson); *m* 1975, Deirdre Mary Cassels; two *s*. *Educ*: Dollar Academy; Brisbane State High Sch., Australia. Radio Station 4BH, Brisbane, 1956; John Clemenger Advertising, Melbourne, 1957–59; Journalist: The Age, Melb., 1959–61; Press and Journal, Aberdeen, Scotland, 1962–64; Broadcaster, BBC: Scotland, N Ireland, London, Shetland, 1964–79. European Democratic Gp spokesman on regional policy, European Parlt, 1983–. Mem., Scots Lang. Soc. Trustee, Community Service Volunteers, 1985–. Elder, Kelso N, Church of Scotland. *Recreation*: TA: Watchkeepers and Liaison Officers Pool. *Address*: 34 Woodmarket, Kelso, Roxburghshire TD5 7AX. *T*: Kelso 24369.

HUTTON, Anthony Charles; Under Secretary, Overseas Trade Division 2, Department of Trade and Industry, since 1984; *b* 4 April 1941; *s* of Charles James Hutton and Athene Mary (*née* Hastie); *m* 1963, Sara Flemming; two *s* one *d*. *Educ*: Brentwood School; Trinity College Oxford (MA). HM Inspector of Taxes, 1962; Joined Board of Trade, 1964; Private Sec. to 2nd Perm. Sec., 1967–68; Private Sec. to Sec. of State for Trade, 1974–77; Asst Sec., DoT, 1977, DTI, 1983. *Recreations*: music, reading, 20th century history. *Address*: Department of Trade and Industry, 1 Victoria Street, SW1H 0ET. *T*: 01–215 7877.

HUTTON, Brian Gerald; Deputy Librarian, National Library of Scotland, since 1983 (Assistant Keeper, since 1974, Secretary, since 1976); *b* Barrow-in-Furness, 1 Nov. 1933; *s* of Jjames and Nora Hutton; *m* 1958, Serena Quartermaine May; one *s* one *d*. *Educ*: Barrow Grammar Sch.; Nottingham Univ. (BA Hons Hist.); University Coll. London (Dip. Archive Admin.). National Service as Russian Linguist, RN, 1955–57; London Univ., 1958–59 (Churchill-Jenkinson prizeman). Asst Archivist, Herts County Record Office, 1959–60; Asst Keeper and Dep. Dir, Public Record Office, N Ireland, also Administrator, Ulter Hist. Foundn and Lectr in Archive Admin., Queen's Univ., Belfast, 1960–74. Commissioned, Kentucky Colonel, 1982. *Publications*: contribs to library and archive jls. *Recreations*: walking in Lake District, visiting art galleries, litening to music. *Address*: 9 Wilton Road, Edinburgh EH16 5NX. *T*: 031–667 2145. *Clubs*: Royal Commonwealth Society; New (Edinburgh).

HUTTON, (David) Graham, OBE 1945; economist, author; *b* 13 April 1904; *er s* of late David James and Lavinia Hutton; *m* 1st, Magdalene Ruth Rudolph, Zürich (marr. diss. 1934); 2nd, Joyce Muriel Green (marr. diss. 1958); three *d*; 3rd, Marjorie, *d* of late Dr and Mrs David Bremner, Chicago. *Educ*: Christ's Hospital; London Sch. of Economics; French and German Univs. Gladstone Meml Prizeman, London Univ., 1929; Barrister-at-Law, Gray's Inn, 1932; Research Fellowship and teaching staff, LSE, 1929–33, Hon. Fellow 1971; Asst Editor, The Economist, 1933–38; FO and Min. of Information, 1939–45. *Publications*: Nations and the Economic Crisis, 1932; The Burden of Plenty (as ed. and contributor, 1935); Is it Peace?, 1936; Danubian Destiny, 1939; Midwest at Noon, 1946; English Parish Churches, 1952; We Too Can Prosper, 1953; All Capitalists Now, 1960; Inflation and Society, 1960; Mexican Images, 1963; Planning and Enterprise, 1964; Politics and Economic Growth, 1968; (with Olive Cook) English Parish Churches, 1976; Whatever Happened to Productivity? (Wincott Lecture), 1980. *Recreations*: ecclesiology, music, travel. *Address*: 38 Connaught Square, W2 2HL. *T*: 01–723 4067. *Clubs*: Reform, English-Speaking Union.

HUTTON, Gabriel Bruce; His Honour Judge Hutton; a Circuit Judge, since 1978; *b* 27 Aug. 1932; *y s* of late Robert Crompton Hutton, and Elfreda Bruce; *m* 1st, 1963, Frances Henrietta Cooke (*d* 1963); 2nd, 1965, Deborah Leigh Windus; one *s* two *d*. *Educ*: Marlborough; Trinity Coll., Cambridge (BA). Called to Bar, Inner Temple, 1956; Dep. Chm., Glos QS, 1971. A Recorder of the Crown Court, 1972–77. *Recreations*: hunting (Chm., Berkeley Hunt), shooting, fishing. *Address*: Chestal, Dursley, Glos. *T*: Dursley 3285. *Club*: Beaufort (Bristol).

HUTTON, Graham; *see* Hutton, D. G.

HUTTON, (Hubert) Robin; Director-General: Accepting Houses Committee, since 1982; Issuing Houses Association, since 1983; *b* 22 April 1933; *e s* of Kenneth Douglas and Dorothy Hutton; *m* 1st, 1956, Valerie Riseborough (marr. diss. 1967); one *s* one *d*; 2nd, 1969, Deborah Berkeley; two step *d*. *Educ*: Merchant Taylors' Sch.; Peterhouse, Cambridge (Scholar). MA Cantab 1960. Royal Tank Regt, 1952–53 (commnd). Economic Adviser to Finance Corp. for Industry Ltd, 1956–62; economic journalist and consultant; Dir, Hambros Bank Ltd, 1966–70; Special Adviser: to HM Govt, 1970–72; to Min. of Posts and Telecommunications, 1972–73. Chm., Cttee of Inquiry into Public Trustee Office, 1971; Dir of Banking, Insurance and Financial Instns in EEC, Brussels, 1973–78; Exec. Dir, S. G. Warburg & Co. Ltd, 1978–82. Chm., Soc. des Banques S. G. Warburg et Leu SA, Luxembourg, 1979–82. Director: Ariel Exchange Ltd, 1982–; Associated Book Publishers PLC, 1982–; Northern Rock Building Soc, 1986– (Mem. London Bd, 1978–); Investment Management Regulatory Organisation Ltd, 1986–. Member: Exec. Cttee, BBA, 1982–; Council of Foreign Bondholders, 1983–; Chm., Adv. Cttee on Telecommunications for England, 1985–. *Recreations*: cricket, ski-ing, gardening, travel. *Address*: c/o Accepting Houses Committee, 101 Cannon Street, EC4N 5BA; Church Farm, Athelington, Suffolk. *T*: Worlingworth 361. *Club*: MCC.

HUTTON, Hon. James Brian Edward; Hon. Mr Justice Hutton; a Judge of the High Court of Justice in Northern Ireland, since 1979; *b* 29 June 1931; *s* of late James and Mabel Hutton, Belfast; *m* 1975, Mary Gillian, *o d* of J. R. W. Murland, Saintfield, Co. Down; two *d*. *Educ*: Shrewsbury Sch.; Balliol Coll., Oxford (1st Cl. final sch. of Jurisprudence); Queen's Univ. of Belfast. Called to Northern Ireland Bar, 1954; QC (NI) 1970; Bencher, Inn of Court of Northern Ireland, 1974; called to English Bar, 1972. Junior Counsel to Attorney-General for NI, 1969; Legal Adviser to Min. of Home Affairs, NI, 1973; Sen. Crown Counsel in NI, 1973–79. Mem., Jt Law Enforcement Commn, 1974; Dep. Chm., Boundary Commn for NI, 1986–. *Publications*: articles in Modern Law Review. *Address*: Royal Courts of Justice (Ulster), Belfast. *Club*: Ulster (Belfast).

HUTTON, Janet; Regional Nursing Officer, Yorkshire Regional Health Authority, since 1983; *b* 15 Feb. 1938; *d* of Ronald James and Marion Hutton. *Educ*: Gen. Infirmary at Leeds Sch. of Nursing. SRN 1959. Ward Sister, Leeds Gen. Infirmary, 1962–64, 1966–68; Nursing Sister, Australia, 1964–66; Commng Nurse, Lister Hosp., Stevenage, 1968–71; Planning and Develts Nurse, N London, 1971–73; Divl Nursing Officer, Colchester, 1973–79; Dist Nursing officer, E Dorset, 1979–83. *Recreations*: music, needlework, tennis (spectator and participant).

HUTTON, Prof. John Philip, MA; Professor of Economics and Econometrics, University of York, since 1982; *b* 26 May 1940; *s* of Philip Ernest Michelson Hutton and Hester Mary Black Hutton; *m* 1964, Sandra Smith Reid; one *s* one *d*. *Educ*: Daniel Stewart's Coll., Edinburgh; Edinburgh Univ. (MA 1st Cl.). York University: Junior Research Fellow, 1962; Lecturer, 1963; Sen. Lectr, 1973; Reader, 1976. Economic Adviser, HM Treasury, 1970, 1971; Adviser to Malaysian Treasury, for Internat. Monetary Fund, 1977; Consultant to: NEDO, 1963; Home Office, 1966; Royal Commission on Local Govt in England and Wales, 1967; NIESR, 1980. Chairman, HM Treasury Academic Panel, 1980, 1981; Mem. Council, Royal Economic Soc., 1981–. Jt Managing Editor, Economic Journal, 1980–86; Jt Editor, Bulletin of Economic Research, 1986–; Associate Editor, Applied Economics, 1986–. *Publications*: contribs to learned jls, incl. Economic Jl, Rev. of Economic Studies, Oxford Economic Papers. *Recreations*: family; golf, badminton. *Address*: 1 The Old Orchard, Fulford, York Y01 4LT. *T*: York 38363.

HUTTON, Kenneth; General Manager, Peterborough Development Corporation, since 1984; *b* 11 May 1931; *s* of Wilks and Gertrude Hutton; *m* 1981, Georgia (*née* Hutchinson); one *s*, and two step *s* one step *d*. *Educ*: Bradford Belle Vue Grammar School; Liverpool University (Thomas Bartlett Scholar; BEng). FICE; FIHT. Graduate Asst, Halifax CBC, 1952–54; Royal Engineers, 1954–56; Sen Engineer, Halifax CBC, 1956–59; Sen. Asst Engineer, Huddersfield CBC, 1959–63; Asst Chief Engineer, Skelmersdale Develt Corp., 1963–66; Dep. Chief Engineer, Telford Develt Corp., 1966–68; Chief Engineer, 1968–84, Dep. Gen. Manager, 1984, Peterborough Develt Corp. *Recreations*: swimming, badminton, golf. *Address*: 3 Alwalton Hall, Alwalton, Peterborough, Cambs. *T*: Peterborough 233719.

HUTTON, Sir Leonard, Kt 1956; professional cricketer, retired 1956; Director, Fenner International (Power Transmission) Ltd; retired from business 1984; *b* Fulneck, near Pudsey, Yorks, 23 June 1916; *s* of Henry Hutton; *m* 1939, Dorothy Mary Dennis, *d* of late G. Dennis, Scarborough; two *s*. First played for Yorks, 1934. First played for England *v* New Zealand, 1937; *v* Australia, 1938 (century on first appearance); *v* South Africa, 1938; *v* West Indies, 1939; *v* India, 1946. Captained England *v* India, 1952; *v* Australia, 1953; *v* Pakistan, 1954; *v* Australia, 1954. Captained MCC *v* West Indies, 1953–54. Made record Test score, 364, *v* Australia at the Oval, 1938; record total in a single month, 1294, in June 1949; has made over 100 centuries in first-class cricket. Hon. Mem. of MCC, 1955 (first Professional to be elected). A selector, MCC, 1975–77. Served War of 1939–45: in RA and APTC. Hon. MA Bradford, 1982. *Publications*: Cricket is my Life, 1950; Just my Story, 1956; Fifty Years in Cricket, 1984. *Recreation*: golf. *Address*: 1 Coombe Neville, Warren Road, Kingston-on-Thames, Surrey KT2 7HW. *T*: 01–942 0604.

HUTTON, Robin; *see* Hutton, H. R.

HUTTON, Thomas Edward; Managing Director and Chief Executive, Total Oil GB Ltd, since 1967; Chairman, Eastern Region Advisory Board, British Rail, since 1981 (Director, since 1975); *b* 10 Jan. 1921; *s* of Thomas Oswald Powell Hutton and Doris Hutton; *m* 1946, Margaret June Ward; four *s*. *Educ*: Shrewsbury; St John's Coll., Cambridge. Commnd RNVR (MTBs), 1940–46. Joined Shell as Industrial Rep., 1946; Asphalt Manager, Shell, W of England, 1949; Shell Canada: Asst to Div. Manager, Ont, 1951; Fuel Oil and Asphalt Manager, Ont, 1953; Area Manager, E Ont, 1955; Retail Manager: Ontario, 1957; Shell Canada, 1959; Shell International, 1962; Co-Ordinator, Anglo Saxon subsids, Co. Française des Pétroles (Total), 1965. Director: Renwick Gp Ltd, 1973–81; Wilmot Breeden (Hldgs) Ltd, 1974–81; Berkeley Exploration and Production Ltd, 1981–82. *Recreations*: fishing, walking, golf. *Address*: (office) 33 Cavendish Square, W1M 0JE. *Club*: Oriental.

HUTTON, Maj.-Gen. Walter Morland, CB 1964; CBE 1960; DSO 1943; MC 1936 and bar, 1942; MA (by decree, 1967); FIL (Arabic); Fellow, 1967–72 and Home Bursar, 1966–72, Jesus College, Oxford; *b* 5 May 1912; *s* of Walter Charles Stritch Hutton and Amy Mary Newton; *m* 1945, Peronelle Marie Stella Luxmoore-Ball; two *s* one *d. Educ:* Parkstone Sch.; Allhallows Sch.; RMC Sandhurst. Commissioned into Royal Tank Corps, 1932; served in Palestine, 1936 (MC); 1st Class Army Interpreter in Arabic, 1937; War of 1939–45: Western Desert, Alamein and N Africa (comdg 5 RTR); Italy (comdg 40 RTR); Comdt, Sandhurst, 1944–45; Instructor, Staff Coll., Camberley, 1949–51; BGS, Arab Legion, 1953–56; Imperial Defence Coll., 1957; Deputy Comd (Land), BFAP (Aden), 1957–59; Dir of Administrative Plans, War Office, 1959–60, Dir-Gen. of Fighting Vehicles, 1961–64; Chief Army Instructor, Imperial Defence Coll., 1964–66. Mem., Bd of Governors, United Oxford Hosps, 1969–72. *Address:* c/o Royal Bank of Scotland, Kirkland House, Whitehall, SW1.

HUTTON-WILLIAMS, Derek Alfred, MBE 1947; BSc, ACGI; CEng, FIMechE, MIEE; Director-General, Royal Ordnance Factories, 1969–75, retired; *b* 26 April 1914; *s* of William Hutton-Williams and Violet Woodfall Hutton-Williams; *m* 1936, Albrée Freeman; two *d*; *m* 1948, Yvonne Irene Anthony; one *s* one *d. Educ:* Oundle Sch.; London Univ. (Kitchener Scholar); grad. NATO Defence Coll., Paris. Pupil, Winget Ltd, Rochester, 1935; Techn. Asst, Royal Arsenal, Woolwich, 1938; Asst to Director, Small Arms and Fuzes, Ordance Factories, in charge of UK production of Sten carbine, 1939; Manager, Royal Ordnance Factory, Theale, Berks, 1942; Dep.-Dir, Housing Supplies, Ministry of Supply, 1945; Partner, Hutton-Williams and Partners (Industrial Consultant), 1946; Supt, Royal Ordnance Factory, Maltby, Yorks, 1949; NATO Defence Coll., 1957; Asst Dir, Guided Weapons Production, Min. of Aviation, 1958; Dir, Inspectorate of Armaments, 1959; Dir, Royal Small Arms Factory, Enfield, 1964. *Recreations:* gardening, building, clock repair, music; recognising and accepting the inevitable; admiring craftsmanship. *Address:* The School House, Palgrave, near Diss, Norfolk.

HUWS JONES, Robin; *see* Jones.

HUXLEY, Sir Andrew Fielding, OM 1983; Kt 1974; FRS 1955; MA Cantab; Royal Society Research Professor, in Department of Physiology, University College London, 1969–83, Hon. Research Fellow, since 1983 (Jodrell Professor 1960–69; Hon. Fellow, 1980); Master of Trinity College, Cambridge, since 1984; *b* 22 Nov. 1917; *s* of late Leonard Huxley and Rosalind Bruce; *m* 1947, Jocelyn Richenda Gammell Pease; one *s* five *d. Educ:* University College Sch.; Westminster Sch.; Trinity Coll., Cambridge (MA). Operational research for Anti-Aircraft Command, 1940–42, for Admiralty, 1942–45. Fellow, 1941–60, and Dir of Studies, 1952–60, Trinity Coll., Cambridge; Hon. Fellow, Trinity Coll., 1967; Demonstrator, 1946–50, Asst Dir of Research, 1951–59, and Reader in Experimental Biophysics, 1959–60, in Dept of Physiology, Cambridge Univ. Lectures: Herter, Johns Hopkins Univ., 1959; Jesup, Columbia Univ., 1964; Alexander Forbes, Grass Foundation, 1966; Croonian, Royal Society, 1967; Review Lectr on Muscular Contraction, Physiological Soc., 1973; Hans Hecht, Univ. of Chicago, 1975; Sherrington, Liverpool, 1977; Florey, ANU, 1982; John C. Krantz Jr, Maryland Univ. Sch. of Medicine, 1982; Darwin, Darwin Coll., Cambridge, 1982; Romanes, Oxford, 1983; Fenn, IUPS XXIV Internat. Congress, Sydney, 1983; Green Coll., Oxford, 1986. Fullerian Prof. of Physiology and Comparative Anatomy, Royal Institution, 1967–73; Cecil H. and Ida Green Vis. Prof., Univ. of British Columbia, 1980. President: BAAS, 1976–77; Royal Soc., 1980–85 (Mem. Council, 1960–62, 1977–79, 1980–85); Vice-Pres., Muscular Dystrophy Gp of GB, 1980–; Chm., British Nat. Cttee for Physiological Scis, 1979–80. Member: ARC, 1977–81; Nature Conservancy Council, 1985–. Trustee: BM (Nat. Hist.), 1981–; Science Museum, 1984–. Hon. Member: Physiolog. Soc., 1979; Amer. Soc. of Zoologists, 1985; Hon. MRIA, 1986; Foreign Associate: Nat. Acad. of Scis, USA, 1979; Amer. Philosophical Soc., 1975; Foreign Hon. Member: Amer. Acad. of Arts and Sciences, 1961; Royal Acad. of Medicine, Belgium, 1978; Foreign Fellow, Indian Nat. Science Acad., 1985; Hon. MRI, 1981; Associate Mem., Royal Acad. of Scis, Letters and Fine Arts, Belgium, 1978; Mem., Leopoldina Academy, 1964; Foreign Member: Danish Acad. of Sciences, 1964; Dutch Soc. of Sciences, 1984. Hon. Fellow: Imperial Coll., London, 1980; Darwin Coll., Cambridge, 1981. Hon. FIBiol 1981; Hon. FRSC (Canada) 1982; Hon. FRSE 1983. Hon. MD University of the Saar, 1964; Hon. DSc: Sheffield, 1964; Leicester, 1967; London, 1973; St Andrews, 1974; Aston, 1977; Western Australia, 1982; Oxford, 1983; Pennsylvania, 1984; Harvard, 1984; Keele, 1985; East Anglia, 1985; Humboldt, E Berlin, 1985; Hon. ScD Cambridge, 1978; Hon. LLD: Birmingham, 1979; Dundee, 1984; DUniv York, 1981; Hon. DHL New York, 1982; Hon. Dr Marseille Fac. of Medicine, 1979. Nobel Prize for Physiology or Medicine (jtly), 1963; Copley Medal, Royal Soc., 1973. *Publications:* Reflections on Muscle (Sherrington Lectures XIV), 1980; (contrib.) The Pursuit of Nature, 1977; papers in the Journal of Physiology, etc. *Recreations:* walking, shooting, designing scientific instruments. *Address:* Master's Lodge, Trinity College, Cambridge. *T:* Cambridge 338412.

HUXLEY, Anthony Julian; author, free-lance writer and photographer; *b* 2 Dec. 1920; *s* of Sir Julian Huxley, FRS; *m* 1st, 1943, Priscilla Ann Taylor; three *d*; 2nd, 1974, Alyson Ellen Vivian, *d* of late Beavan Archibald; one *d. Educ:* Dauntsey's Sch.; Trinity Coll., Cambridge (MA). Operational Research in RAF and Min. of Aircraft Production, 1941–47; Economic Research in BOAC, 1947–48; with Amateur Gardening, 1949–71 (editor, 1967–71). Mem. Council, RHS, 1979–. Veitch Meml Medal, RHS, 1979; VMH 1980. *Publications:* (trans.) Exotic Plants of the World, 1955; (gen. editor) Standard Encyclopedia of the World's Mountains, 1962; (gen. editor) Standard Encyclopedia of Oceans and Islands, 1962; Garden Terms Simplified, 1962, 1971; Flowers in Greece: an outline of the Flora, 1964; (with O. Polunin) Flowers of the Mediterranean, 1965; (gen. ed.) Standard Encyclopedia of Rivers and Lakes, 1965; Mountain Flowers, 1967; (ed) Garden Perennials and Water Plants, 1971; (ed) Garden Annuals and Bulbs, 1971; House Plants, Cacti and Succulents, 1972; (ed) Deciduous Garden Trees and Shrubs, 1973; (ed) Evergreen Garden Trees and Shrubs, 1973; Plant and Planet, 1978; (ed) The Financial Times Book of Garden Design, 1975; (with W. Taylor) Flowers of Greece and the Aegean, 1977; (ed) The Encyclopedia of the Plant Kingdom, 1977; (with Alyson Huxley) Huxley's House of Plants, 1978; An Illustrated History of Gardening, 1978; (gen. editor) Success with House Plants, 1979; Penguin Encyclopedia of Gardening, 1981; (with P. and J. Davies) Wild Orchids of Britain and Europe, 1983; (ed) The Macmillan World Guide to House Plants, 1983; Green Inheritance, 1984. *Recreations:* photography, wild flowers, travel, gardening. *Address:* 50 Villiers Avenue, Surbiton, Surrey KT5 8BD. *T:* 01–399 1479.

HUXLEY, Air Vice-Marshal Brian, CB 1986; CBE 1981; Deputy Controller, National Air Traffic Services, since 1985; *b* 14 Sept. 1931; *s* of Ernest and Winifred Huxley; *m* 1955, Frances (*née* Franklin); two *s. Educ:* St Paul's Sch.; RAF College, Cranwell. Commissioned 1952; No 28 Sqdn, Hong Kong, 1953–55; qual. Flying Instructor, 1956; Cranwell, Central Flying Sch. and No 213 Sqdn, 1956–65; MoD, 1966–68; Chief Flying Instr, Cranwell, 1969–71; Commanding RAF Valley, 1971–73; RAF Staff Coll., 1973–74; RCDS 1975; Defence Intelligence Staff, 1976–77; AOC Mil. Air Traffic Ops, 1978–80; Dir of Control (Airspace Policy), and Chm., Nat. Air Traffic Management Adv. Cttee,

1981–84. *Publications:* contribs to Children's Encyclopaedia Britannica, 1970–72, and to Railway Modeller, 1974–. *Recreation:* making models. *Address:* CAA House, Kingsway, WC2. *Club:* Royal Air Force.

HUXLEY, Elspeth Josceline, (Mrs Gervas Huxley), CBE 1962; JP; *b* 23 July 1907; *d* of Major Josceline Grant, Njoro, Kenya; *m* 1931, Gervas Huxley (*d* 1971); one *s. Educ:* European Sch., Nairobi, Kenya; Reading Univ. (Diploma in Agriculture); Cornell Univ., USA. Asst Press Officer to Empire Marketing Board, London, 1929–32; subsequently travelled in America, Africa and elsewhere; Mem. BBC Gen. Advisory Council, 1952–59; UK Independent Mem., Monckton Advisory Commission on Central Africa, 1959. *Publications:* White Man's Country; Lord Delamere and the Making of Kenya, 2 vols, 1935; Murder at Government House (detective story), 1937; Murder on Safari (detective story), 1938, repr. 1982; Death of an Aryan (detective story), 1939, repr. as The African Poison Murders, 1985; Red Strangers (novel), 1939; Atlantic Ordeal, 1943; (with Margery Perham) Race and Politics in Kenya, 1944; The Walled City (novel), 1948; The Sorcerer's Apprentice (travel), 1948; I Don't Mind If I Do (light novel), 1951; Four Guineas (travel), A Thing to Love, 1954; The Red Rock Wilderness, 1957; The Flame Trees of Thika, 1959 (filmed, 1981); A New Earth, 1960; The Mottled Lizard, 1962; The Merry Hippo, 1963; Forks and Hope, 1964; A Man from Nowhere, 1964; Back Street New Worlds, 1965; Brave New Victuals, 1965; Their Shining Eldorado: A Journey through Australia, 1967; Love Among the Daughters, 1968; The Challenge of Africa, 1971; Livingstone and his African Journeys, 1974; Florence Nightingale, 1975; Gallipot Eyes, 1976; Scott of the Antarctic, 1977; Nellie: letters from Africa, 1980; Whipsnade: captive breeding for survival, 1981; The Prince Buys the Manor, 1982; (with Hugo van Lawick) Last Days in Eden, 1984; Out in the Midday Sun: My Kenya, 1985. *Recreations:* resting, gossip. *Address:* Green End, Oaksey, near Malmesbury, Wilts SN16 9TL. *TA:* Oaksey, Malmesbury. *T:* Crudwell 252.

HUXLEY, George Leonard; FSA; MRIA; Research Associate, Trinity College Dublin, since 1983; Director, Gennadius Library, American School of Classical Studies, Athens, since 1986; *b* Leicester, 23 Sept. 1932; *s* of Sir Leonard Huxley, *qv*; *m* 1957, Davina Best; three *d. Educ:* Blundell's Sch.; Magdalen Coll., Oxford. 2nd Mods, 1st Greats, Derby Scholar 1955. Commnd in RE, 1951. Fellow of All Souls Coll., Oxford, 1955–61; Asst Dir, British School at Athens, 1956–58; Prof. of Greek, QUB, 1962–83. Harvard University: Vis. Lectr, 1958 and 1961; Loeb Lectr, 1986; Leverhulme Fellow, European Sci. Foundn, 1980–81; Vis. Lectr, St Patrick's Coll., Maynooth, 1984–85. Mem. of Exec., NI Civil Rights Assoc., 1971–72. Member: Managing Cttee, British Sch. at Athens, 1967–79; Irish Nat. Cttee Greek and Latin Studies, 1972–86 (Chm., 1976–79); Irish Mem., Standing Cttee on Humanities, European Science Foundn, Strasbourg, 1978–86. Royal Irish Academy: Sec., Polite Literature and Antiquities Cttee, 1979–86; Sen. Vice-Pres., 1984–85; Mem. Bureau, Fédn Internat. d'Etudes Classiques, 1981– (Senior Vice-Pres. 1984–). Mem. Edtl Adv. Bd, Greek, Roman and Byzantine Studies, 1986–. Hon. LittD TCD, 1984. Cromer Greek Prize, British Acad., 1963. *Publications:* Achaeans and Hittites, 1960; Early Sparta, 1962; The Early Ionians, 1966; Greek Epic Poetry from Eumelos to Panyassis, 1969; (ed with J. N. Coldstream) Kythera, 1972; Pindar's Vision of the Past, 1975; On Aristotle and Greek Society, 1979; articles on Hellenic and Byzantine subjects. *Recreation:* siderodromophilia. *Address:* American School of Classical Studies, Souedias 54, Athens, GR 106–76, Greece; Forge Cottage, Church Enstone, Oxfordshire OX7 4NN. *Club:* Athenæum.

HUXLEY, Mrs Gervas; *see* Huxley, Elspeth J.

HUXLEY, Hugh Esmor, MBE 1948; MA, PhD, ScD; FRS 1960; Deputy Director, Medical Research Council Laboratory of Molecular Biology, Cambridge, since 1977; Fellow, Churchill College, Cambridge, since 1967; *b* 25 Feb. 1924; *s* of late Thomas Hugh Huxley and Olwen Roberts, Birkenhead, Cheshire; *m* 1966, Frances Fripp, *d* of G. Maxon, Milwaukee; one *d*, and two step-*s* one step-*d. Educ:* Park High Sch., Birkenhead; Christ's Coll., Cambridge (Exhibitioner and Scholar; Hon. Fellow 1981). Natural Science Tripos, Cambridge, 1941–43 and 1947–48 (Pt II Physics); BA 1948, MA 1950, PhD 1952, ScD 1964. Served War of 1939–45, Radar Officer, RAF Bomber Command and Telecommunications Research Establishment, Malvern, 1943–47; Mem. Empire Air Armaments Sch. Mission to Australia and NZ, 1946. Research Student, MRC Unit for Molecular Biology, Cavendish Lab., Cambridge, 1948–52; Commonwealth Fund Fellow, Biology Dept, MIT, 1952–54; Research Fellow, Christ's Coll., Cambridge, 1953–56; Mem. of External Staff of MRC, and Hon. Res. Associate, Biophysics Dept, UCL, 1956–61; Fellow, King's Coll., Cambridge, 1961–67; Scientific Staff, MRC Lab. of Molecular Biol., 1961–. Ziskind Vis. Prof., Brandeis Univ., 1971; Lectures: Harvey Soc., New York, 1964–65; Hooke, Univ. of Texas, 1968; Dunham, Harvard Med. Sch., 1969; Croonian, Royal Soc., 1970; Mayer, MIT, 1971; Penn, Pennsylvania Univ., 1971; Carter-Wallace, Princeton Univ., 1973; Adam Muller, State Univ. of NY, 1973; Pauling, Stanford, 1980; Jesse Beams, Virginia, 1980; Ida Beam, Iowa, 1981. Member: Council, Royal Soc., 1973–75, 1984–85; President's Adv. Bd, Rosentiel Basic Med. Scis Center, Brandeis Univ., 1971–77; Scientific Adv. Council, European Molecular Biol. Lab., 1976–81. Mem., German Acad. of Sci., Leopoldina, 1964; Hon. Member: Amer. Soc. of Biol Chem., 1976; Amer. Assoc. of Anatomy, 1981; Amer. Physiol. Soc., 1981; Amer. Soc. of Zoologists, 1986; Foreign Hon. Member: Amer. Acad. of Arts and Scis, 1965; Danish Acad. of Scis, 1971; Foreign Associate, US Nat. Acad. of Scis, 1978. Hon. ScD Harvard, 1969; Hon. DSc: Chicago, 1974; Pennsylvania, 1976. Feldberg Foundation Award for Experimental Medical Research, 1963; William Bate Hardy Prize (Camb. Phil. Soc.) 1965; Louisa Gross Horwitz Prize, 1971; Internat. Feltrinelli Prize, 1974; Gairdner Foundn Award, 1975; Baly Medal, RCP, 1975; Royal Medal, Royal Soc., 1977; E. B. Wilson Award, Amer. Soc. Cell Biology, 1983. *Publications:* contrib. to learned jls. *Recreations:* ski-ing, sailing. *Address:* Churchill College, Cambridge. *T:* Cambridge 61200; 7 Chaucer Road, Cambridge. *T:* Cambridge 356117.

HUXLEY, Rev. Keith; Rector of Gateshead, Diocese of Durham, since 1983; Chaplain to the Queen, since 1981; *b* 17 Sept. 1933; *s* of George and Eluned Huxley. *Educ:* Birkenhead Sch.; Christ's Coll., Cambridge (MA); Cuddesdon Theol Coll. Curate: St Mary's, Bowdon, 1959–61; Christ Church, Crewe, 1961–62; Chester Diocesan Youth Chaplain, 1962–68; Leader, Runcorn Ecumenical Team Ministry, 1968–75; Vicar, St Andrew's, Runcorn, 1968–73; Rector, East Runcorn Team Ministry, 1973–77; Home Secretary, Bd for Mission and Unity, C of E, 1977–83. Sec., NE Ecumenical Gp, 1983–. *Recreation:* ornithology. *Address:* Gateshead Rectory, 91 Old Durham Road, Gateshead, Tyne and Wear NE8 4BS. *T:* Gateshead 4773990.

HUXLEY, Sir Leonard (George Holden), KBE 1964; MA, DPhil Oxon; PhD Adelaide; FAA; Emeritus Professor, University of Adelaide; Vice-Chancellor, The Australian National University, 1960–67; *b* London, UK, 29 May 1902; *s* of George H. and Lilian S. Huxley; *m* 1929, Ella M. C. (*d* 1981), *d* of F. G. and E. Copeland; one *s* one *d. Educ:* The Hutchins Sch., Hobart; University of Tasmania; New Coll., Oxford. Rhodes Scholar, Tas., 1923; Jessie Theresa Rowden Scholar, New Coll., 1927; Scott Scholar, University of Oxford, 1929. Scientific staff, CSIR, Sydney, 1929–31; Head of Dept of Physics, University Coll. Leicester, 1932–40; Principal Scientific Officer, Telecommunications

Research Estabt, MAP, 1940–46; Reader in Electromagnetism, University of Birmingham, 1946–49; Elder Prof. of Physics, University Adelaide, 1949–60; Mem. Executive, CSIRO, 1960; Mem. Council, University of Adelaide, 1953–60; Mem. Council, Aust. Nat. Univ., 1956–59; Foundation FAA, 1954 (Sec., Physical Sciences, 1959–62); Chm. Australian Radio Research Board, 1958–64; Chm. National Standards Commission, 1953–65; Chm. Radio Frequency Allocation Cttee, 1960–64; Mem. Nat. Library Council, 1961–72; Mem. Bd, US Educnl Foundn in Austr., 1960–65; Australian Deleg. on Cttee on Space Research, (COSPAR), 1959–60. First President Aust. Inst. of Physics, 1962–65. Mem., Queen Elizabeth II Fellowships Cttee, 1963–66; Chm., Gen. Coun. Encyclopædia Britannica Australia Awards, 1964–74; Chm. Bd, Aust./Amer. Educl Foundn, 1965–69; Trustee, Aust. Humanities Res. Council, 1968–70; Mem. Council, Canberra Coll. of Advanced Educn, 1968–74. Hon DSc: Tasmania, 1962; ANU, 1980. *Publications:* Wave Guides, 1949; (with R. W. Crompton) The Diffusion and Drift of Electrons in Gases, 1974; numerous scientific papers on gaseous Electronics, the ionosphere, upper atmosphere and related subjects. *Address:* 19 Glasgow Place, Hughes, Canberra, ACT 2605, Australia. *Club:* Commonwealth (Canberra).

See also Prof. G. L. Huxley.

HUXLEY, Dr Peter Arthur, PhD; FIBiol; Head of Research Development Division, International Council for Research in Agroforestry, Nairobi, since 1979; *b* 26 Sept. 1926; *s* of Ernest Henry Huxley and Florence Agnes (*née* King); *m* 1st, 1954, Betty Grace Anne Foot (marr. diss. 1980); three *s* one *d*; 2nd, 1980, Jennifer Margaret Bell (*née* Pollard); one *s* one *d*. *Educ:* Alleyn's Sch.; Edinburgh Univ.; Reading Univ. (BSc, PhD). FIBiol 1970. RNVR, 1944–46. Asst Lectr to Sen. Lectr, Makerere University Coll., Uganda, 1954–64; Dir of Res., Coffee Res. Foundn, Kenya, 1965–69; Prof. of Horticulture, Univ. of Reading, 1969–74; Prof. of Crop Science, Univ. of Dar es Salaam/FAO, 1974–76; Agric. Res. Adviser/FAO, Agric. Res. Centre, Tripoli, 1977–78. Member: E African Nat. Hist. Soc.; Nairobi Music Soc.; Nairobi Orchestra; Nairobi City Players. FRSA. *Publications:* (ed jtly) Soils Research in Agroforestry, 1980; (ed) Plant Research and Agroforestry, 1983; (ed) Manual of Research Methodology for the Exploration and Assessment of Multipurpose Trees, 1983; approx. 120 pubns in agric., horticult., agroforestry, meteorol and agricl botany jls. *Recreation:* music (double bass) and music-making. *Address:* c/o National Westminster Bank, 49 South Street, Dorchester, Dorset. *Club:* Nairobi (Nairobi).

HUXSTEP, Emily Mary, CBE 1964; BA London: Headmistress of Chislehurst and Sidcup Girls' Grammar School, Kent, 1944–66; *b* 15 Sept. 1906; *d* of George T. and Nellie M. Huxstep (*née* Wood). *Educ:* Chatham Girls' Grammar Sch.; Queen Mary Coll. Headmistress, Hanson Girls' Grammar Sch., Bradford, Yorks, 1938–44. Hon. DCL Kent, 1974. *Address:* 35 Mandeville Court, Union Street, Maidstone, Kent.

HUXTABLE, Lt-Gen. Sir Charles Richard, KCB 1984 (CB 1982); CBE 1976 (OBE 1972; MBE 1961); Quarter Master General, Ministry of Defence, since 1986; *b* 22 July 1931; *m* 1959, Mary, *d* of late Brig. J. H. C. Lawlor; three *d*. *Educ:* Wellington Coll.; RMA Sandhurst; Staff College, Camberley; psc, jssc. Commissioned, Duke of Wellington's Regt, 1952; Captain, 1958, Major, 1965; GS02 (Ops), BAOR, 1964–65; GS01 Staff College, 1968–70; CO 1 DWR, 1970–72; Col, 1973; MoD, 1974; Brig., Comd Dhofar Bde, 1976–78; Maj.-Gen., 1980; Dir, Army Staff Duties, 1982–83; Comdr, Training Estabts, 1983–85; Comdr, Trng and Arms Dirs, 1985–86. Colonel, DWR, 1982–; Col Comdt, The King's Div., 1983–. *Address:* c/o Lloyds Bank, 23 High Street, Teddington, Middlesex TW11 8EX.

HUXTABLE, Rev. (William) John (Fairchild), DD; Executive Officer, Churches' Unity Commission, 1975–78; *b* 25 July 1912; *s* of Rev. John Huxtable and Florence Huxtable (*née* Watts); *m* 1939, Joan Lorimer Snow; one *s* two *d*. *Educ:* Barnstaple Gram. Sch.; Western Coll., Bristol; Mansfield and St Catherine's Colls, Oxford. BA Bristol 1933; BA Oxon 1937, MA 1940. Minister: Newton Abbot Congreg. Church, 1937–42; Palmers Green Congreg. Church, 1942–54; Princ., New Coll., University of London, 1953–64. Chm., 1962–63, Sec., 1964–66, Minister Sec., 1966–72, Congregational Union of England and Wales; Jt Gen. Sec., United Reformed Church, 1972–74; Moderator, United Reformed Church, 1972–73. Vice-President: British Coun. of Churches, 1967–71; World Alliance of Reformed Churches, 1970–77; Vice-Moderator, Free Church Federal Council, 1975–76, Moderator, 1976–77; Member: Central Cttee, World Council of Churches, 1968–75; Jt Cttee of Translation of New English Bible, 1948–74. Vice-Pres. Council, St Dunstan's, 1973–84. Hon. DD: Lambeth, 1973; Aberdeen, 1973. *Publications:* The Ministry, 1943; (ed) John Owen's True Nature of a Gospel Church, 1947; (ed jtly) A Book of Public Worship, 1948; The Faith that is in Us, 1953; The Promise of the Father, 1959; Like a Strange People, 1961; Church and State in Education (C. J. Cadoux Meml Lect.), 1962; The Bible Says (Maynard Chapman Lects), 1962; Preaching the Law, (Joseph Smith Meml Lect.), 1964; The Preacher's Integrity (A. S. Peake Meml Lect.), 1966; Christian Unity: some of the issues (Congreg. Lects), 1966; contribs to symposia: The Churches and Christian Unity, 1962; From Uniformity to Unity, 1962; A Companion to the Bible, 1963; Renewal of Worship, 1965; Outlook for Christianity, 1967; contrib. to Christian Confidence, 1970; A New Hope for Christian Unity, 1977; also contribs to Congreg. Quarterly, Theology, Epworth Review, London Quarterly and Holborn Review, Proc. Internat. Congreg. Council and Theologische Realenzyklopädie. *Recreation:* reading. *Address:* Manor Cottage, East Ogwell, South Devon.

HUYDECOPER, Jonkheer (Jan Louis) Reinier, Hon. GCVO 1982 (Hon. KCVO 1972); Commander, Order of Orange Nassau, 1986 (Officer, 1966); Chevalier, Order of Netherlands Lion, 1980; Ambassador of the Netherlands to the Court of St James's, and concurrently to Iceland, since 1982; *b* 23 Feb. 1922; *s* of Jonkheer Louis Huydecoper and Jonkvrouwe Laurence B. W. Ram; *m* 1944, Baroness Constance C. van Wassenaer; one *s* two *d*. *Educ:* Univ. of Utrecht (LLM). Banking, 1942–44; Legal Dept, Min. of Finance, The Hague, 1945–46; entered Min. of For. Affairs, 1946; UN, NY, 1946; Ottawa, 1947–48; Mil. Mission, Berlin, 1949–50; Bonn, 1950–52; London, 1952–56; Djakarta, 1956–59; Washington, 1959–62; Rome, 1962–66; Min. of For. Affairs, 1966–70; London, 1970–73; Ambassador, Hd of Delegn to Conf. on Security and Co-operation in Europe, Helsinki and Geneva, 1973–74; Ambassador: Moscow, 1974–77; Lisbon, 1978–80; Inspector of For. Service, Min. of For. Affairs, 1981–82. Holds various foreign orders. *Address:* 8 Palace Green, W8. *T:* 01–584 5040. *Clubs:* Boodle's, Dutch, Special Forces, Royal Automobile, Travellers', Hurlingham, Haagsche (The Hague).

HUYGHE, René; Grand Officier de la Légion d'Honneur; Member of the Académie Française since 1960; Hon. Professor of Psychology of Plastic Arts, Collège de France (Professor, 1950–76); Hon. Head Keeper, Musée du Louvre; Director, Museum Jacquemart-André, Paris, since 1974; *b* Arras, Pas-de-Calais, France, 3 May 1906; *s* of Louis Huyghe and Marie (*née* Delvoye); *m* 1950, Lydie Bouthet; one *s* one *d*. *Educ:* Sorbonne; École du Louvre, Paris. Attached to Musée du Louvre, 1927; Asst Keeper, 1930; Head Keeper, Départment des Peintures, Dessins, Chalcographie, 1937. Mem., Conseil Artistique de la Réunion des Musées Nationaux, 1952 (Vice-Pres. 1964, Pres. 1975–); Pres. Assoc. internationale du Film d'Art, 1958. Holds foreign decorations. Praemium Erasmianum, The Hague, 1966. *Publications:* Histoire de l'Art contemporain: La Peinture, 1935; Cézanne 1936 and 1961; Les Contemporains, 1939 (2nd edn, 1949); Vermeer, 1948; Watteau, 1950; various works on Gauguin, 1951, 1952, 1959; Dialogue avec le visible, 1955 (trans. Eng.); L'Art et l'homme, Vol. I, 1957, Vol. II, 1958, Vol. III, 1961 (trans. Eng.); Van Gogh, 1959; Merveilles de la France, 1960; L'Art et l'Ame, 1960 (trans. Eng.); La peinture française aux XVIIe et XVIIIe Siècles, 1962; Delacroix ou le combat solitaire, 1963 (trans. Eng.); Puissances de l'Image, 1965; Sens et Destin de l'Art, 1967; L'Art et le monde moderne, Vol. I, 1970, Vol. II, 1971; Formes et Forces, 1971; La Relève du réel, 1974; La Relève de l'imaginaire, 1976; Ce que je crois, 1976; De l'Art à la Philosophie, 1980; (with D. Ikeda) La Nuit appelle l'Aurore, 1980; Les Signes du Temps et l'Art moderne, 1985. *Address:* 3 rue Corneille, Paris 75006, France. *Club:* Union interalliée (Paris).

HYAM, Michael Joshua; His Honour Judge Hyam; a Circuit Judge, since 1984; *b* 18 April 1938; *s* of Isaac J. Hyam and Rachel Hyam; *m* 1968, Diana Mortimer; three *s*. *Educ:* Westminster Sch.; St Catharine's Coll., Cambridge (MA). Called to Bar, Gray's Inn, 1962; a Recorder, 1983–84; practised on SE Circuit, 1962–84. Member: Council of Legal Education, 1980–; Ethical Cttee, Cromwell Hosp., 1983–. *Recreations:* book collecting, cricket, gardening. *Address:* 5 Essex Court, Temple, EC4. *T:* 01–353 2825. *Clubs:* Garrick, MCC.

HYAMS, Daisy Deborah, (Mrs C. Guderley), OBE 1974; Consultant, Tesco Stores PLC; *b* 25 Nov. 1912; *d* of Hyman Hyams and Annie Burnett; *m* 1936, Sidney Hart; no *c*; *m* 1975, C. Guderley. *Educ:* Coborn Grammar Sch. for Girls, Bow. FGI. Joined Tesco, 1931; Man. Dir, Tesco (Wholesale) Ltd, 1965–82; Dir, Tesco Stores PLC, 1969–82. *Recreations:* travel, reading. *Address:* 10 Noblefield Heights, Great North Road, Highgate, N2 0NX. *T:* 01–348 1591.

HYATALI, Hon. Sir Isaac (Emanuel), Kt 1973; TC 1974; legal consultant; Justice of Appeal, Seychelles Republic, since 1973; Chairman: Elections and Boundaries Commission, Republic of Trinidad and Tobago, since 1983; American Life and General Insurance Co. (Trinidad) Ltd, since 1983; *b* 21 Nov. 1917; *s* of late Joseph Hyatali and Esther Hyatali; *m* 1943, Audrey Monica Joseph; two *s* one *d*. *Educ:* Naparima Coll., San Fernando; Gray's Inn and Council of Legal Education, London. Called to Bar, Gray's Inn, 1947. Private practice at the Bar, 1947–59; Judge, Supreme Court, 1959–62; Justice of Appeal, 1962–72; Pres., Industrial Court, 1965–72; Chief Justice and Pres., Court of Appeal, Trinidad and Tobago, 1972–83. Chm., Arima Rent Assessment Bd, 1953–59; Chm., Agricultural Rent Bd (Eastern Counties), 1953–59. Chairman: Agricultural Wages Council, 1958–59; Oil and Water Bd, 1959–62. Arbitrator and Umpire, ICAO, 1981–. Trinidad and Tobago Editor of West Indian Law Reports, 1961–65. Member: World Assoc. of Judges; Council of Management, British Inst. of Internat. and Comparative Law; Hon. Mem., World Peace through Law Center. *Recreations:* gardening, tennis, cricket, reading, social work. *Address:* (chambers) 3B Empire Building, 78 Edward Street, Port of Spain, Trinidad and Tobago. *T:* (62) 34007; Election and Boundaries Commission, Salvatori Building, Port of Spain. *T:* (62) 38320; (home) 8 Pomme Rose Avenue, Cascade, St Anns, Republic of Trinidad and Tobago. *Clubs:* Royal Commonwealth Society; (Hon. Mem.) Union Park Turf (Trinidad); Rotary (Port of Spain).

HYATT KING, Alexander; *see* King.

HYDE, Lord; George Edward Laurence Villiers; *b* 12 Feb. 1976; *s* and *heir* of 7th Earl of Clarendon, *qv*.

HYDE, H(arford) Montgomery, MA Oxon, DLit Belfast, FRHistS; FRSL; MRIA; author and barrister; *b* Belfast, 14 Aug. 1907; *o s* of late James J. Hyde, JP, Belfast, and Isobel Greenfield Montgomery; *m* 1st, 1939, Dorothy Mabel Brayshaw (from whom he obtained a divorce, 1952), *e d* of Dr J. Murray Crofts, CBE, Disley, Cheshire; 2nd, 1955, Mary Eleanor (marr. diss., 1966), *d* of Col L. G. Fischer, IMS; 3rd, 1966, Rosalind Roberts, *y d* of Comdr J. F. W. Dimond, RN. *Educ:* Sedbergh (Scholar); Queen's Univ. Belfast (Emily Lady Pakenham Scholar); 1st Class Hons Modern History, 1928; Magdalen Coll., Oxford (Open History Exhibitioner); 2nd Class Hons Jurisprudence, 1930; Harmsworth Law Scholar, Middle Temple, 1932. Called to Bar, Middle Temple, 1934; joined NE Circuit; Extension Lecturer in History, Oxford Univ., 1934; Private Sec. to Marquess of Londonderry, 1935–39; Asst Censor, Gibraltar, 1940; commissioned in Intelligence Corps, 1940; Military Liaison and Censorship Security Officer, Bermuda, 1940–41; Asst Passport Control Officer, New York, 1941–42; with British Army Staff, USA, 1942–44; Major, 1942; attached Supreme HQ Allied Expeditionary Force, 1944; Allied Commission for Austria, 1944–45; Lt-Col 1945; Asst Editor, Law Reports, 1946–47; Legal Adviser, British Lion Film Corp. Ltd, 1947–49; MP (U) North Belfast, 1950–59; UK Delegate to Council of Europe Consultative Assembly, Strasbourg, 1952–55; Hon. Col Intelligence Corps (TA), NI, 1958–61; Professor of Hist. and Polit. Sci., University of the Punjab, Lahore, 1959–61; RAF Museum Leverhulme Research Fellowship, 1971–75. Active in campaign for abolition of capital punishment; has travelled extensively in Russia, The Far East, West Indies, Mexico, and South America. Hon. DLit QUB, 1984. *Publications:* The Rise of Castlereagh, 1933; The Russian Journals of Martha and Catherine Wilmot (with the Marchioness of Londonderry), 1934; More Letters from Martha Wilmot, Impressions of Vienna (with the Marchioness of Londonderry), 1935; The Empress Catherine and Princess Dashkhov, 1935; Air Defence and the Civil Population (with G. R. Falkiner Nuttall), 1937; Londonderry House and Its Pictures, 1937; Princess Lieven, 1938; Judge Jeffreys, 1940, new edn, 1948; Mexican Empire, 1946; A Victorian Historian, 1947; Privacy and the Press, 1947; John Law, 1948, new edn 1969; The Trials of Oscar Wilde, 1948, 3rd edn 1973; Mr and Mrs Beeton, 1951; Cases that changed the Law, 1951; Carson, 1953; The Trial of Craig and Bentley, 1954; United in Crime, 1955; Mr and Mrs Daventry, a play by Frank Harris, 1957; The Strange Death of Lord Castlereagh, 1959; The Trial of Roger Casement, 1960, 2nd edn 1964; The Life and Cases of Sir Patrick Hastings, 1960; Recent Developments in Historical Method and Interpretation, 1960; Simla and the Simla Hill States under British Protection, 1961; An International Crime Case Book, 1962; The Quiet Canadian, 1962; Oscar Wilde: the Aftermath, 1963; Room 3603, 1964; A History of Pornography, 1964; Norman Birkett, 1964; Cynthia, 1965; The Story of Lamb House, 1966, 2nd edn 1975; Lord Reading, 1967; Strong for Service: The Life of Lord Nathan of Churt, 1968; Henry James At Home, 1969; The Other Love, 1970; Their Good Names, 1970; Stalin, 1971; Baldwin: the unexpected Prime Minister, 1973; Oscar Wilde, 1975; The Cleveland Street Scandal, 1976; British Air Policy between the Wars, 1976; Neville Chamberlain, 1976; Crime has its Heroes, 1976; Solitary in the Ranks, 1977; The Londonderrys, 1979; The Atom Bomb Spies, 1980; (ed) Oscar Wilde: Three Plays, 1981; Secret Intelligence Agent, 1982; (ed) The Annotated Oscar Wilde, 1982; Lord Alfred Douglas, 1984; A Tangled Web, 1986; (ed) J. F. Bloxam: the priest and the acolyte, 1986; chapter 12 (The Congress of Vienna) in the Cambridge History of Poland, etc. *Recreations:* criminology, music. *Address:* Westwell House, Tenterden, Kent. *T:* Tenterden 3189. *Clubs:* Garrick, Beefsteak; Dormy House (Rye); Grolier (New York).

HYDE, W(illiam) Leonard, FCBSI; Director, Leeds Permanent Building Society, since 1972 (Chief General Manager, 1973–78; Vice-President, 1978–81; President, 1981–83); Local Director, Royal Insurance Co. Ltd, since 1973. Joined Leeds Permanent Building

Soc., 1936. Member Council: Building Socs Assoc., 1973–78; Nat. House Builders, 1973–78; Chm., Yorkshire County Assoc. of Building Socs, 1978–80. *Recreations:* golf, walking. *Address:* 5 Burn Bridge Road, Harrogate, Yorks. *T:* Harrogate 871748. *Clubs:* Lansdowne; Pannal Golf.

HYDE-PARKER, Sir Richard William; *see* Parker.

HYDE-SMITH, Marisa; *see* Robles, Marisa.

HYDE WHITE, Wilfrid; *b* 12 May 1903; *s* of William Edward White, Canon of Gloucester and Ethel Adelaide (*née* Drought); *m* 1927, Blanche Hope Aitken; one *s*; *m* 1957, Ethel Korenman (stage name Ethel Drew); one *s* one *d. Educ:* Marlborough. First appeared in London in Beggar on Horseback, Queen's Theatre, 1925; successful appearances include: Rise Above It, Comedy; It Depends What You Mean, Westminster; Britannus in Cæsar and Cleopatra, St James's, London, and Ziegfeld, New York; Affairs of State, Cambridge; Hippo Dancing, Lyric; The Reluctant Debutante, Cambridge, and Henry Miller's Theatre, New York (nominated for Tony award, 1956); Not in the Book, Criterion; Miss Pell is Missing, Criterion; The Doctor's Dilemma, Haymarket; Lady Windermere's Fan, Phoenix; Meeting at Night, Duke of York's; The Jockey Club Stakes, Duke of York's, and Cort Theatre, NYC (nominated for Tony award for best actor, 1973); The Pleasure of his Company, Phoenix; Rolls Hyphen Royce, Shaftesbury. *Films include:* The 3rd Man, The Browning Version, Golden Salamander, The Million Pound Note, Libel, Two Way Stretch, North West Frontier, Let's Make Love, His and Hers, On the Double, Ada, The Castaways, Crooks Anonymous, On the Fiddle, Aliki, My Fair Lady, 10 Little Indians, The Liquidator, In God We Trust. *Address:* c/o Chatto and Linnit Ltd, Prince of Wales Theatre, Coventry Street, W1V 7FE. *Clubs:* Green Room, Buck's.

HYLTON, 5th Baron, *cr* 1866; **Raymond Hervey Jolliffe,** MA; ARICS; DL; *b* 13 June 1932; *er s* of 4th Baron Hylton and of the Dowager Lady Hylton, *d* of late Raymond Asquith and *sister* of 2nd Earl of Oxford and Asquith, *qv*; *S* father, 1967; *m* 1966, Joanna Ida Elizabeth, *d* of late Andrew de Bertodano; four *s* one *d. Educ:* Eton (King's Scholar); Trinity Coll., Oxford (MA). Lieut R of O, Coldstream Guards. Asst Private Sec. to Governor-General of Canada, 1960–62; Trustee, Shelter Housing Aid Centre 1970–76; Chairman: Catholic Housing Aid Soc., 1972–73; Nat. Fedn of Housing Assocs, 1973–76; Housing Assoc. Charitable Trust; Help the Aged Housing Trust, 1976–82; Hugh of Witham Foundn, 1978–; Vice-Pres., Age Concern (Nat. Old People's Welfare Council), 1971–77; Pres., SW Reg. Nat. Soc. for Mentally Handicapped Children, 1976–79; Founder and Mem., Mendip and Wansdyke Local Enterprise Gp, 1979–85. Trustee: Christian Internat. Peace Service, 1977–82; Acorn Christian Healing Trust, 1983; Governor, Christian Coll. for Adult Educn, 1972–. Mem., Frome RDC, 1968–72. DL Somerset, 1975. *Heir:* s Hon. William Henry Martin Jolliffe, *b* April 1967. *Address:* Ammerdown, Radstock, Bath.

HYLTON-FOSTER, family name of **Baroness Hylton-Foster.**

HYLTON-FOSTER, Baroness, *cr* 1965, of the City of Westminster (Life Peer); **Audrey Pellew Hylton-Foster;** British Red Cross Society: President and Chairman, London Branch, 1960–83, Patron, since 1984; Member, National Headquarters Consultative Panel, since 1984; Convenor, Cross Bench Peers, since 1974; *b* 19 May 1908; *d* of 1st Viscount Ruffside, PC, DL (*d* 1958), and Viscountess Ruffside (*d* 1969); *m* 1931, Rt Hon. Sir Harry Hylton-Foster, QC (*d* 1965); no *c. Educ:* St George's, Ascot; Ivy House, Wimbledon. *Recreations:* gardening, trout fishing. *Address:* The Coach House, Tanhurst, Leith Hill, Holmbury St Mary, Dorking, Surrey RH5 6LU. *T:* Dorking 711975; 54 Cranmer Court, Whiteheads Grove, SW3 3HW. *T:* 01–584 2889.

HYMAN, Joe; Chairman, John Crowther Group Ltd, 1971–81; Underwriting member of Lloyd's; *b* 14 Oct. 1921; *yr s* of late Solomon Hyman and Hannah Hyman; *m* 1st, 1948, Corinne I. Abrahams (marriage dissolved); one *s* one *d*; 2nd, 1963, Simone Duke; one *s* one *d. Educ:* North Manchester Grammar Sch. In textiles, 1939–80; Founder, Viyella International, and Chm., 1961–69. Trustee, Pestalozzi Children's Village Trust, 1967–; Governor, LSE. FRSA 1968; FBIM. Comp. TI. *Recreations:* music, golf, gardening.

Address: Lukyns, Ewhurst, Surrey; 24 Kingston House North, Prince's Gate, SW7. *Clubs:* Royal Automobile, MCC.

HYMAN, Robin Philip; Managing Director, Unwin Hyman Ltd, since 1986; Chairman: Bell & Hyman Ltd, Book Publishers, since 1977; Allen & Unwin (Publishers) Ltd, since 1986; *b* 9 Sept. 1931; *s* of late Leonard Hyman and of Helen Hyman (*née* Mautner); *m* 1966, Inge Neufeld; two *s* one *d. Educ:* Henley Grammar Sch.; Christ's Coll., Finchley; Univ. of Birmingham (BA (Hons) 1955). National Service, RAF, 1949–51. Editor, Mermaid, 1953–54; Bookselling and Publishing: joined Evans Brothers Ltd, Educnl Publishers, 1955; Dir, 1964; Dep. Man. Dir, 1967; Man. Dir, 1972–77; Dir, Rivingtons (Publishers) Ltd, 1967–77; Mem. Editorial Bd, World Year Book of Education, 1969–73. Member: Council, Publishers' Assoc., 1975– (Treasurer, 1982–84); Exec. Cttee, Educnl Publishers' Council, 1971–76 (Treas., 1972–75). Mem., First British Publishers' Delegn to China, 1978. *Publications:* A Dictionary of Famous Quotations, 1962; Bell & Hyman First Colour Dictionary, 1985; Universal Primary Dictionary (for Africa), 1976; (with Inge Hyman) 11 children's books, incl. Barnabas Ball at the Circus, 1967; Runaway James and the Night Owl, 1968; The Hippo who Wanted to Fly, 1973; The Magical Fish, 1974; The Greatest Explorers in the World, 1978; The Treasure Box, 1980; Peter's Magic Hide-and-Seek, 1982. *Recreations:* theatre, reading, cricket. *Address:* 101 Hampstead Way, NW11 7LR. *T:* 01–455 7055. *Clubs:* Garrick, MCC, Samuel Pepys.

HYND, Ronald; choreographer; Ballet Director, National Theater, Munich, 1970–73 and 1984–86; *b* 22 April 1931; *s* of William John and Alice Louisa Hens; *m* 1957, Annette Page, *qv*; one *d. Educ:* erratically throughout England due to multiple wartime evacuation. Joined Rambert School, 1946; Ballet Rambert, 1949; Royal Ballet (then Sadlers Well's Ballet), 1952, rising from Corps de Ballet to Principal Dancer, 1959; danced Siegfried (Swan Lake), Florimund (Sleeping Beauty), Albrecht (Giselle), Poet (Sylphides), Tsarevitch (Firebird), Prince of Pagodas, Moondog (Lady and Fool), Tybalt (Romeo), etc; produced first choreography for Royal Ballet Choreographic Group followed by works for London Festival Ballet, Royal Ballet, Dutch National Ballet and Munich Ballet. *Ballets include:* Le Baiser de la Fée, 1968, new production 1974; Pasiphaë, 1969; Dvorak Variations, 1970; Wendekreise, 1972; In a Summer Garden, 1972; Das Telefon, 1972; Mozartiana, 1973; Charlotte Brontë, 1974; Mozart Adagio, 1974; Galileo (film), 1974; Orient/Occident, 1975; La Valse, 1975; Valses Nobles et Sentimentales, 1975; The Merry Widow, 1975; L'Eventail, 1976; The Nutcracker (new version for Festival Ballet), 1976; ice ballets for John Curry, 1977; Rosalinda, 1978; La Chatte, 1978; Papillon, 1979; The Seasons, 1980; Alceste, 1981; Scherzo Capriccioso, 1982; Le Diable a Quatre, 1984; Fanfare fur Tänzer, 1985; Coppelia (new prodn for Festival Ballet), 1985; Ludwig-Fragmente Eines Rätsels, 1986; *musical:* Sound of Music, 1981. *Recreation:* the gramophone. *Address:* 51 Sutherland Place, W2 5BY.

HYND, Mrs Ronald; *see* Page, Annette.

HYSLOP, James Telfer, OBE 1968; HM Diplomatic Service, retired; Consul General, Detroit, 1971–76; *b* 21 Sept. 1916; *s* of Mr and Mrs John J. Hyslop; *m* 1942, Jane Elizabeth Owers; one *s* one *d. Educ:* Queen Elizabeth's Grammar Sch., Hexham. Royal Navy, 1939–46. Entered Diplomatic Service, 1948; served at: Baltimore, 1948; Valparaiso, 1951; Amman, 1954; Tegucigalpa, 1958; San Francisco, 1961; Johannesburg, 1964; Bogota, 1968. *Recreations:* reading, music. *Address:* 12 Quay Walls, Berwick-on-Tweed.

HYSLOP, Robert John M.; *see* Maxwell-Hyslop.

HYTNER, Benet Alan, QC 1970; a Recorder of the Crown Court, since 1972; Judge of Appeal, Isle of Man, since 1980; *b* 29 Dec. 1927; *s* of late Maurice and of Sarah Hytner, Manchester; *m* 1954, Joyce Myers (marr. diss. 1980); three *s* one *d. Educ:* Manchester Grammar Sch.; Trinity Hall, Cambridge (Exhibr). MA. National Service, RASC, 1949–51 (commnd). Called to Bar, Middle Temple, 1952; Bencher, 1977; Leader, Northern Circuit, 1984–. Member: Gen. Council of Bar, 1969–73; Senate of Inns of Court and Bar, 1977–81, 1984–. *Recreations:* fell walking, music, theatre, reading. *Address:* 5 Essex Court, Temple, EC4.

I

IBBOTSON, Lancelot William Cripps, CBE 1971 (MBE 1948); General Manager of Southern Region, British Railways, and Chairman, Southern Railway Board, 1968–72; *b* 10 Feb. 1909; *s* of William Ibbotson, FRCS and Mrs Dora Ibbotson (*née* Chapman), London; *m* 1931, Joan Marguerite Jeffcock; one *s* one *d*. *Educ:* Radley Coll. Traffic Apprentice, LNER, 1927; Chief Clerk to Dist. Supt, Newcastle, 1939; Asst Dist Supt, York, 1942; Dist Supt, Darlington, 1945; Asst to Operating Supt, Western Region, 1950; Asst Gen. Man., Western Region, 1959; Chief Operating Officer, British Railways, 1963; Gen. Man., Western Region, BR, and Chm., Western Railway Board, 1966–68. Gen. Man., A. Pearce, Partners & Assoc., 1975–79; Dir, Flameless Furnaces Ltd, 1976–84. *Recreations:* foreign travel, photography. *Address:* Monks' Well House, 1 Monks' Well, Waverley, Farnham, Surrey. *T:* Runfold 2328. *Club:* Naval and Military.

IBBOTT, Alec; Counsellor, HM Diplomatic Service; Ambassador to Liberia, since 1985; *b* 14 Oct. 1930; *s* of Francis Joseph Ibbott and Madge Winifred Ibbott (*née* Graham); *m* 1964, Margaret Elizabeth Brown; one *s* one *d*. Joined Foreign (subseq. Diplomatic) Service, 1949; served in HM Forces, 1949–51; FCO, 1951–54; ME Centre for Arab Studies, 1955–56; Second Secretary and Vice Consul, Rabat, 1956–60; Second Secretary, FO, 1960–61; Second Sec. (Information), Tripoli, 1961; Second Sec., Benghazi, 1961–65; First Sec. (Information), Khartoum, 1965–67; First Sec., FO (later FCO), 1967–71; Asst Political Agent, Dubai, 1971; First Secretary, Head of Chancery and Consul: Dubai, 1971–72; Abu Dhabi, 1972–73; First Secretary and Head of Chancery: Nicosia, 1973–74; FCO, 1975–77; Carácas, 1977–79; Counsellor, Khartoum, 1979–82; seconded to IMS Ltd, 1982–85. *Address:* c/o Foreign and Commonwealth Office, SW1. *Club:* Royal Commonwealth Society.

IBBS, Sir (John) Robin, Kt 1982; Director: Imperial Chemical Industries PLC, 1976–80 and since 1982; Lloyds Bank PLC, since 1986; Lloyds Bank UK Management, since 1985; Adviser to the Prime Minister on Efficiency and Effectiveness in Government, since 1983; *b* 21 April 1926; *o s* of late Prof. T. L. Ibbs, MC, DSc, FInstP and of Marjorie Ibbs (*née* Bell); *m* 1952, Iris Barbara, *d* of late S. Hall; one *d*. *Educ:* Univ. of Toronto; Trinity Coll., Cambridge (MA Mech. Scis). Instr Lieut, RN, 1947–49. Called to the Bar, Lincoln's Inn. C. A. Parsons & Co. Ltd, 1949–51; joined ICI, 1952; on secondment as Head, Central Policy Review Staff, Cabinet Office, 1980–82. Member: Governing Body and Council, British Nat. Cttee of ICC, 1976–80; Industrial Develt Adv. Bd, DoI, 1978–80; Council, CBI, 1982– (Mem. Companies Cttee, 1978–80); Council, CIA, 1976–79, 1982– (Vice Pres., 1983–); Chemicals EDC, NEDO, 1982–; Council, RIIA, Chatham House, 1983–; Top Salaries Review Body, 1983–. Mem. Court, Cranfield Inst. of Technology, 1983–. *Address:* Imperial Chemical House, Millbank, SW1P 3JF. *Club:* United Oxford & Cambridge University.

IBIAM, Sir (Francis) Akanu, GCON 1963; LLD, DLit; medical missionary; Eze Ogo Isiala I: Unwana, and the Osuji of Uburu; Chairman, Imo State Council of Traditional Rulers; *b* Unwana, Afikpo Division, Nigeria, 29 Nov. 1906; *s* of late Ibiam Aka Ibiam and late Alu Owora; *m* 1939, Eudora Olayinka Sasegbon (*d* 1974); one *s* two *d*. *Educ:* Hope Waddell Training Instn Calabar; King's Coll., Lagos; University of St Andrews, Scotland. FMCP (GP) Nigeria. Medical Missionary with the Church of Scotland Mission, Calabar, Nigeria, 1936; started and built up new Hosp. in Abiriba, Bende Div., under Calabar Mission, 1936–45; Medical Supt, CSM Hosp., Itu, 1945–48; CSM Hosp., Uburu, 1952–57. MLC, Nigeria, 1947–52; MEC, 1949–52; retd from Politics, 1953; Principal, Hope Waddell Training Instn, Calabar, 1957–60; (on leave) Governor, Eastern Nigeria, 1960–66; Adviser to Military Governor of Eastern Provinces, 1966. Founder (1937) and former Pres., Student Christian Movement of Nigeria, now Hon. President; Trustee: Presbyterian Church of Nigeria, 1945–; Queen Elizabeth Hosp., Umuahia-Ibeku, 1953–; Scout Movement of Eastern Nigeria, 1957–; Mem. Bd of Governors: Hope Waddell Trng Instn, Calabar, 1945–60; Queen Elizabeth Hosp., 1950–60; Mem. Provl Council of University Coll., Ibadan, 1948–54; Mem. Privy Council, Eastern Nigeria, 1954–60; Pres., Christian Council of Nigeria, 1955–58; Mem. Calabar Mission Council, 1940–60 (now integrated with Church); Mem. Admin. Cttee of Internat. Missionary Council, 1957–61; Chm. Provisional Cttee of All Africa Churches Conf., 1958–62; Chairman: Council of University of Ibadan, Nigeria, 1958–60; Governing Council of Univ. of Nigeria, Nsukka, 1966; a Pres. of World Council of Churches, 1961; a Pres. of All Africa Church Conf., 1963; Pres., World Council of Christian Educn and Sunday Sch. Assoc.; Chm. Council, United Bible Socs, 1966–72, Vice-Pres. 1972–; Founder and Pres., Bible Soc. of Nigeria, 1963–74, Patron 1974; Founder and former Pres., All Africa Council of Churches; Founder, Nigerian SPCC; President: Soc. for Promotion of Ibo Lang. and Culture; Cancer Soc. of Nigeria. Patron, Akanu Ibiam Nat. Ambulance; Grand Patron, World Women Christian Temperance Union. Presbyterian Church of Nigeria: Mem. Educ. Authority, 1940–; Mem. Missionaries' Cttee, Med. Bd, and Standing Cttee of Synod; Advanced Training Fund Management Cttee of Synod; Elder, 1940–. Appointed OBE 1949, KBE 1951, KCMG 1962, and renounced these honours 1967 in protest at British Govt policy on Biafra. Upper Room Citation, 1966. Hon. LLD Ibadan; Hon. DSc Ife, 1966. Kt of Mark Twain. Humanitarian of Rosicrucian Order. Golden Cross with crown, Order of Orthodox Knights of Holy Sepulchre, Jerusalem, 1965; Golden Star Medal (1st degree), Order of Russian Orthodox Church, 1965. *Recreation:* reading. *Address:* Ganymede, Unwana, Afikpo Local Government Area, PO Box 240, Imo State, Nigeria.

IBRAHIM, Sir Kashim, GCON 1963; KCMG 1962; CBE 1960 (MBE 1952); Governor of Northern Nigeria, 1962–66; Chancellor, Lagos University, 1976–84; *b* 10 June 1910; *s* of Mallam Ibrahim Lakkani; *m* 1st, 1943, Halima; 2nd, 1944, Khadija; 3rd, 1957, Zainaba; four *s* three *d* (and two *d* decd). *Educ:* Bornu Provincial Sch.; Katsina Teachers' Trng Coll. Teacher, 1929–32; Visiting Teacher, 1933–49; Educ. Officer, 1949–52. Federal Minister of Social Services, 1952–55; Northern Regional Minister of Social Develt and Surveys, 1955–56; Waziri of Bornu, 1956–62. Advr to Military Governor, N Nigeria, 1966. Chm. Nigerian Coll. of Arts, Science and Technology, 1958–62; Chancellor, Ibadan Univ., 1967–75; Chm. Provisional Council of Ahmadu Bello Univ. Hon. LLD: Ahmadu Bello, 1963; Univ. of Ibadan; Univ. of Nigeria (Nsukka); University of Lagos. *Publications:* Kanuri Reader Elementary, I-IV; Kanuri Arithmetic Books, I-IV, for Elementary Schs and Teachers' Guide for above. *Recreations:* walking, riding, polo playing. *Address:* PO Box 285, Maiduguri, Bornu State, Nigeria.

IDALIE, Mme Heinric; *see* Oldenbourg-Idalie, Zoë.

IDDESLEIGH, 4th Earl of, *cr* 1885; **Stafford Henry Northcote,** DL; Bt 1641; Viscount St Cyres, 1885; Chairman, South West Region England and Wales, Trustee Savings Bank, since 1983 (Chairman, South West Trustee Savings Bank, 1981–83); Director: TSB Group, since 1985; Television South West, since 1982; United Dominions Trust, since 1983; *b* 14 July 1932; *er s* of 3rd Earl of Iddesleigh and of Elizabeth, *er d* of late F. S. A. Lowndes and late Marie Belloc; *S* father, 1970; *m* 1955, Maria Luisa Alvarez-Builla y Urquijo (Condesa del Real Agrado in Spain), *d* of late Don Gonzalo Alvarez-Builla y Alvera and of Viscountess Exmouth, *widow* of 9th Viscount Exmouth; one *s* one *d*. *Educ:* Downside. 2nd Lieut, Irish Guards, 1951–52. DL Devon, 1979. Kt SMO Malta. *Heir: s* Viscount St Cyres, *qv*. *Address:* Shillands House, Upton Pyne Hill, Exeter, Devon EX5 5EB. *T:* Exeter 58916. *Club:* Army and Navy.

IDIENS, Dale; Keeper, Department of History and Applied Art, National Museum of Scotland (formerly Department of Art and Archaeology, Royal Scottish Museum), since 1983; *b* 13 May 1942; *d* of Richard Idiens and Ruth Christine Idiens (*née* Hattersley). *Educ:* High Wycombe High Sch.; Univ. of Leicester. BA (Hons); DipEd. Royal Scottish Museum, Department of Art and Archaeology: Asst Keeper in charge of Ethnography, 1964; Dep. Keeper, 1979. *Publications:* African Textiles (ed with K. G. Ponting), 1980; museum publications: Traditional African Sculpture, 1969; Ancient American Art, 1971; The Hausa of Northern Nigeria, 1981; Pacific Art, 1982; articles and papers in Jl of the Polynesian Soc., African Arts, Textile History; reviews and lectures. *Recreations:* travel, film, claret. *Address:* Sylvan House, 13 Sylvan Place, Edinburgh EH9 1LH. *T:* 031–667 2399. *Clubs:* Naval and Military; University Staff (Edinburgh).

IEVERS, Frank George Eyre, CMG 1964; Postmaster-General, East Africa, 1962–65, retired; *b* 8 May 1910; *s* of Eyre Francis and Catherine Ievers; *m* 1936, Phyllis Robinson; two *s*. *Educ:* Dover Coll. Asst Traffic Supt, Post Office, 1933; Traffic Supt, East Africa, 1946; Telecommunications Controller, 1951; Regional Dir, 1959. *Recreations:* golf, photography. *Address:* 20 Heron Close, Worcester WR2 4BW. *T:* Worcester 427121. *Clubs:* Nairobi (Kenya); Sudan (Khartoum).

IEVERS, Rear-Adm. John Augustine, CB 1962; OBE 1944; *b* 2 Dec. 1912; *s* of Eyre Francis Ievers, Tonbridge, Kent; *m* 1937, Peggy G. Marshall; one *s* two *d*. *Educ:* RN Coll., Dartmouth. CO Naval Test Squadron, Boscombe Down, 1945–47; RN Staff Coll., 1948–49; HMS Ocean, 1949; HMS Glory, 1949–50; HMS Burghead Bay, 1951–52; CO, RN Air Station, Lossiemouth, 1952–54; Dep. Dir Naval Air Warfare Div., 1954–57; Captain Air, Mediterranean, 1957–60; Deputy Controller Aircraft, Min. of Aviation, 1960–63; retd, 1964. *Recreation:* golf. *Address:* 3 Hollywood Court, Hollywood Lane, Lymington, Hants. *T:* Lymington 77268.

IGGO, Prof. Ainsley, PhD, DSc; FRCPE; FRS 1978; FRSE; Professor of Veterinary Physiology, University of Edinburgh, since 1962; *b* 2 Aug. 1924; *s* of late Lancelot George Iggo and late Catherine Josefine Fraser; *m* 1952, Betty Joan McCurdy, PhD, *d* of late Donald A. McCurdy, OBE; three *s*. *Educ:* Gladstone Sch., NZ; Southland Technical High Sch., NZ; Lincoln Coll., NZ (Sen. Scholar; MAgrSc 1947); Univ. of Otago (BSc 1949). PhD Aberdeen, 1954; DSc Edinburgh, 1962. FRSE 1962; FRCPE 1985. Asst Lectr in Physiology, Otago Univ. Med. Sch., 1948–50; NZ McMillan Brown Trav. Fellow, Rowett Inst., 1950–51; Lectr in Physiol., Univ. of Edinburgh Med. Sch., 1952–60; Nuffield Royal Soc. Commonwealth Fellow, ANU, 1959; Royal Soc. Locke Res. Fellow, 1960–62; Dean, Faculty of Veterinary Med., Univ. of Edinburgh, 1974–77 and 1985–. Vis. Professor: Univ. of Ibadan, Nigeria, 1968; (also Leverhulme Res. Fellow) Univ. of Kyoto, 1970; Univ. of Heidelberg, 1972. Chm., IUPS Somatosensory Commn, 1974–. Mem. Council: RCVS, 1975–78 and 1985–; Royal Soc., 1982–83; Pres., Internat. Assoc. for Study of Pain, 1980–83. Governor, E of Scotland Coll. of Agriculture, 1968–77. Hon. DSc Pennsylvania. *Publications:* (ed) Sensory Physiology: Vol. II, Somatosensory System, 1973; articles on neurophysiol topics in Jl Physiol., etc. *Recreations:* bee-keeping, gardening. *Address:* 5 Relugas Road, Edinburgh EH9 2NE. *T:* 031–667 4879.

IGNATIEFF, George, CC 1973; Chancellor, University of Toronto, since 1980; Hon. Professor, University of Trinity College, Toronto (Vice-Chancellor and Provost, 1972–79); *b* 16 Dec. 1913; *s* of Count Paul N. Ignatieff and Princess Natalie Mestchersky; *m* 1945, Alison Grant, MVO; two *s*. *Educ:* St Paul's, London; Lower Canada Coll., Montreal; Jarvis Coll., Toronto; Univs of Toronto and Oxford. Rhodes Schol., Ont, 1935; BA Toronto 1935; BA Oxon 1938, MA 1960. Dept of External Affairs, Ottawa, 1940; 3rd Sec., London, 1940–44; Ottawa, 1944–45; Adviser, Canadian Delegn, UN Atomic Energy Commn, 1946; UN Assembly, 1946–47; Alt. Rep., UN Security Council, 1948–49; Councillor, Canadian Embassy, Washington, DC, 1948–53; Imp. Def. Coll., London, 1953–54; Head of Defence Liaison Div., External Affairs, Ottawa, 1954–55; Canadian Ambassador to Yugoslavia, 1956–58; Dep. High Comr, London, 1959–60; Asst Under-Sec. of State for External Affairs, Ottawa, 1960–62; Perm. Rep. and Canadian Ambassador to NATO, 1962–65; Canadian Perm. Rep. and Ambassador to UN: NY, 1965–68; to Cttee on Disarmament, Geneva, 1968–71; to UN and other Internat.

Organisations, Geneva, 1970–71. Advr to Govt on Disarmament, 1984–. Pres., UNA Canada, 1979–. Chm., Bd of Trustees, Nat. Museums of Canada Corp., 1973–79. Hon. Fellow, St John's Coll., Winnipeg, 1973. Hon. LLD: Toronto, 1969; Brock, 1969; Guelph 1970; Saskatchewan, 1973; York, 1975; Hon. DCL Bishop's, 1973; Hon. DLitt, Victoria Coll., Toronto, 1977. Pearson Peace Medal, 1984. *Publication:* The Making of a Peacemonger (memoirs), 1985. *Address:* 18 Palmerston Gardens, Toronto, Ont M6G 1V9, Canada; Chancellor's Office, University of Toronto, Ontario M5S 1A1, Canada.

IKERRIN, Viscount; David James Theobald Somerset Butler; *b* 9 Jan. 1953; *s* and *heir* of 9th Earl of Carrick, *qv*; *m* 1975, Philippa V. J., *yr d* of Wing Commander L. V. Craxton; three *s* (including twin *s*). *Educ:* Downside. *Heir: e s* Hon. Arion Thomas Piers Hamilton Butler, *b* 1 Sept. 1975.

IKIN, Rutherford Graham; Headmaster of Trent College, 1936–68; *b* 22 Jan. 1903; *s* of late Dr A. E. Ikin, formerly Dir of Education, Blackpool; *m* 1936, Elizabeth Mary Mason; two *d. Educ:* King Edward VI Sch., Norwich; King's Coll., Cambridge (Choral Scholar). BA 1925; MA 1928; Asst Master at King's Sch., Ely, 1926–29; History Master and House Master, St Bees Sch., 1929–36. *Publications:* A Pageant of World History; The Modern Age; The History of the King's School, Ely. *Address:* Green Eaves, Whatstandwell, Matlock, Derbyshire. *T:* Ambergate 2315. *Club:* East India, Devonshire, Sports and Public Schools.

ILCHESTER, 9th Earl of, *cr* 1756; **Maurice Vivian de Touffreville Fox-Strangways;** Baron Ilchester of Ilchester, Somerset, and Baron Strangways of Woodsford Strangways, Dorset, 1741; Baron Ilchester and Stavordale of Redlynch, Somerset, 1747; Group Captain, Royal Air Force (rtd); Director, Nottingham Building Society, since 1982 (Vice Chairman, 1985–86); Executive Director, County Border Newspapers Ltd, since 1984; Deputy Chairman, H. N. Barnes Holdings, since 1984; *b* 1 April 1920; *s* of 8th Earl of Ilchester and Laure Georgine Emilie (*d* 1970), *d* of late Evanghelos Georgios Mazaraki, sometime Treasurer of Suez Canal Company; *S* father, 1970; *m* 1941, Diana Mary Elizabeth, *e d* of late George Frederick Simpson, Cassington, Oxfordshire. *Educ:* Kingsbridge Sch. CEng; MRAeS; FINucE (Pres., 1982–84); FBIM; FRSA; FInstD. Pres., Soc. of Engineers, 1974. Mem., H of L Select Cttee on Science and Technology, 1984–. Pres., SE Area, RAF Assoc., 1978–. Chm. of Governors, Cannock Sch., 1978–. *Recreations:* outdoor activities, enjoyment of the arts. *Heir: b* Hon. Raymond George Fox-Strangways [*b* 11 Nov. 1921; *m* 1941, Margaret Vera, *d* of late James Force, North Surrey, BC; two *s*]. *Address:* Farley Mill, Westerham, Kent TN16 1UB. *T:* Westerham 62314. *Clubs:* Brooks's, Royal Air Force.

ILERSIC, Prof. Alfred Roman; Emeritus Professor of Social Studies, Bedford College, University of London, since 1984 (Professor, 1965–84); *b* 14 Jan. 1920; *s* of late Roman Ilersic and Mary (*née* Moss); *m* 1st, 1944, Patricia Florence Bertram Liddle (marr. diss. 1976); one *s* one *d*; 2nd, 1976, June Elaine Browning. *Educ:* Polytechnic Sec. Sch., London; London Sch. of Economics, Lectr in Econs, University Coll. of S West, Exeter, 1947–53; Lectr in Social Statistics, Beford Coll., 1953; Reader in Economic and Social Statistics, Bedford Coll., London, 1963. Vis. Prof., Univ. of Bath, 1983–. Mem., Cost of Living Adv. Cttee, 1970–. Chm., Inst. of Statisticians, 1968–70. Hon. Mem., Rating and Valuation Assoc., 1968. *Publications:* Statistics, 1953; Government Finance and Fiscal Policy in Post-War Britain, 1956; (with P. F. B. Liddle) Parliament of Commerce 1860–1960, 1960; Taxation of Capital Gains, 1962; Rate Equalisation in London, 1968; Local Government Finance in Northern Ireland, 1969. *Recreations:* listening to music, walking. *Address:* 4 Dewhurst House, Winnett Street, W1. *Club:* Reform.

ILIFFE, family name of **Baron Iliffe.**

ILIFFE, 2nd Baron, *cr* 1933, of Yattendon; **Edward Langton Iliffe;** Vice-Chairman of the Birmingham Post and Mail Ltd, 1957–74; formerly Chairman of the Coventry Evening Telegraph and of the Cambridge News; *b* 25 Jan. 1908; *er s* of 1st Baron Iliffe, GBE, and Charlotte Gilding (*d* 1972); *S* father 1960; *m* 1938, Renée, *er d* of René Merandon du Plessis, Mauritius. *Educ:* Sherborne; France; Clare Coll., Cambridge. Served, 1940–46, with RAFVR (despatches). Trustee, Shakespeare's Birthplace; Mem. Council, Univ. of Warwick, 1965–71; Past Pres., Internat. Lawn Tennis Club of Gt Britain. High Sheriff of Berks, 1957. Hon. Freeman, City of Coventry. *Heir: n* Robert Peter Richard Iliffe, *qv. Address:* 38 St James's Place, SW1. *T:* 01–493 1938; Basildon Park, Lower Basildon, near Reading, Berks. *T:* Pangbourne 4409. *Clubs:* Brooks's, Carlton; Royal Yacht Squadron.

ILIFFE, Barrie John; Secretary, William and Mary Tercentenary Trust Ltd, 1985–86; *b* 9 Jan. 1925; *s* of Edward Roy Iliffe; *m* 1959, Caroline Fairfax-Jones; three *d. Educ:* Westcliff High Sch.; University College London. Concerts Manager, Liverpool Philharmonic Orchestra, 1951–55; Orchestral Manager, Philharmonia Orch., 1955–56; Manager, Cape Town Orch., 1956–58; Concerts Manager, Philharmonia Orch., 1958–60; Manager, London Mozart Players, 1961–63; General Manager, New Philharmonia Orch., 1964–65; British Council: Head of Music, 1966–77; Director, Music Dept, 1977–83; Dep. Controller, Arts Div., 1981–83, Controller, 1983–85. *Recreation:* inland waterways. *Address:* 29 Murray Mews, NW1 9RH. *T:* 01–485 5154.

ILIFFE, Robert Peter Richard; Chairman, BPM Holdings plc, since 1982 (Deputy Chairman, 1980, Director, subsidiary companies); *b* Oxford, 22 Nov. 1944; *s* of late Hon. W. H. R. Iliffe and Mrs Iliffe; *m* 1966, Rosemary Anne Skipwith; three *s* one *d. Educ:* Eton; Christ Church, Oxford. Chairman: Coventry Newspapers Ltd; British Transfer Printing Co. Ltd; Cambridge Newspapers Ltd; The Birmingham Post & Mail Ltd, 1978–81; Director: T. Dillon & Co. Ltd; Birmingham Boat Shows Ltd. Member of Council, Royal Agricultural Soc. of England. High Sheriff of Warwicks, 1983–84. *Recreations:* yachting, shooting, fishing and old cars. *Address:* The Old Rectory, Ashow, Kenilworth, Warwickshire CV8 2LE.

ILLINGWORTH, Sir Charles (Frederick William), Kt 1961; CBE 1946; Regius Professor of Surgery, University of Glasgow, 1939, Emeritus, 1964; Hon. Surgeon to the Queen, in Scotland, 1961–65; Extra Surgeon since 1965; *b* 8 May 1899; *s* of John and Edith Illingworth; *m* 1928, Eleanor Mary Bennett (*d* 1971); four *s. Educ:* Heath Grammar Sch., Halifax; Univ. of Edinburgh. Graduated Medicine, 1922. 2nd Lieut, RFC 1917. FRCSE 1925; FRCSGlas, 1963. Hon. FACS, 1954; Hon. FRCS, 1958; Hon. FRCSI, 1964; Hon. FRCS (Canada), 1965; Hon. Fellow, Coll. Surg. S Africa, 1965. DSc (Hon.): University of Sheffield, 1962; University of Belfast, 1963; Hon. LLD (Glasgow, Leeds) 1965. *Publications:* (jtly) Text Book of Surgical Pathology, 1932; Short Text Book of Surgery, 1938; Text Book of Surgical Treatment, 1942; Monograph on Peptic Ulcer, 1953; The Story of William Hunter, 1967; The Sanguine Mystery, 1970; University Statesman: Sir Hector Hetherington, 1971; various contributions to surgical literature, mainly on digestive disorders. *Address:* 57 Winton Drive, Glasgow G12 0QB. *T:* 041–339 3759.

ILLINGWORTH, David Gordon, LVO 1980; MD, FRCPE; Surgeon Apothecary to HM Household at Holyrood Palace, Edinburgh, 1970–86; *b* 22 Dec. 1921; *yr s* of Sir Gordon Illingworth; *m* 1946, Lesley Beagrie, Peterhead; two *s* one *d. Educ:* George Watson's Coll.; Edinburgh University. MB, ChB Edinburgh, 1943; MRCPE 1949; MD (with commendation) 1963; FRCPE 1965; FRCGP 1970. Nuffield Foundn Travelling Fellow, 1966. RN Medical Service, 1944–46 (2nd Escort Gp); medical appts, Edinburgh Northern Hosps Group, 1946–82. Dep. CMO, Scottish Life Assurance Co., 1973–. Hon. Sen. Lectr in Rehabilitation Studies, Dept of Orthopaedic Surgery, Edinburgh Univ., 1977–82; Lectr in Gen. Practice Teaching Unit, Edinburgh Univ., 1965–82. Member: Cancer Planning Group, Scottish Health Service Planning Council, 1976–81; Tenovus, Edinburgh, 1978–; ASH, Royal Colleges Jt Cttee, 1978–82; Specialty Sub-Cttee on Gen. Practice, 1980–82; Nat. Med. Cons. Cttee, 1980–82. AFOM, RCP, 1980. Mem., Harveian Soc. Life Governor, Imperial Cancer Res. Fund, 1978. *Publications:* Practice (jtly), 1978; contribs to BMJ, Jl of Clinical Pathology, Gut, Lancet, Medicine. *Recreations:* golf, gardening. *Address:* 19 Napier Road, Edinburgh EH10 5AZ. *T:* 031–229 8102. *Clubs:* University (Edinburgh); Bruntsfield Links Golfing Soc.

ILLINGWORTH, Rear-Adm. Philip Holden Crothers, CB 1969; *b* 29 Nov. 1916; *s* of late Norman Holden Illingworth, Woking; *m* 1944, Dorothy Jean, *d* of George Wells, Southbourne; three *s* three *d. Educ:* RN Coll., Dartmouth, RNEC. Joined RN 1930, Rear-Adm. 1967. Dep. Controller of Aircraft, Min. of Technology, 1969, MoD, 1971–72; retd 1973; Vice-Chm., EPS (Western) Ltd, 1980–82. *Address:* Manor House, Marston Magna, Somerset. *T:* Marston Magna 850294.

ILLINGWORTH, Raymond, CBE 1973; cricketer; Manager, Yorkshire County Cricket Club, 1979–84; *b* 8 June 1932; *s* of late Frederick Spencer Illingworth and Ida Illingworth; *m* 1958, Shirley Milnes; two *d. Educ:* Wesley Street Sch., Farsley, Pudsey. Yorkshire County cricketer; capped, 1955. Captain: MCC, 1969; Leics CCC, 1969–78; Yorks CCC, 1982–83. Toured: West Indies, 1959–60; Australia twice (once as Captain), 1962–63 and 1970–71. Played in 66 Test Matches (36 as Captain). Hon. MA Hull, 1983. *Publications:* Spinners Wicket, 1969; The Young Cricketer, 1972; Spin Bowling, 1979; Captaincy, 1980; Yorkshire and Back, 1980; (with Kenneth Gregory) The Ashes, 1982. *Recreations:* golf, bridge. *Address:* 386 Bradford Road, Stanningley, Pudsey, West Yorkshire LS28 7TQ. *T:* Pudsey 578137.

ILLINGWORTH, Ronald Stanley; Professor of Child Health, University of Sheffield, 1947–75; *b* 7 Oct. 1909; *s* of late H. E. Illingworth, ARIBA, ARPS, Fairleigh, Skipton Road, Ilkley; *m* Dr Cynthia Illingworth, MB, BS, FRCP, Consultant in Paediatric Accident and Emergency, Children's Hosp., Sheffield; one *s* two *d. Educ:* Clifton House Sch., Harrogate; Bradford Grammar Sch. MB, ChB Leeds, 1934; MRCS, LRCP, 1934; MD Leeds, 1937; MRCP, 1937; DPH Leeds (distinction), 1938; DCH (RCP and S), 1938; FRCP 1947; FRPS, Fellow, Royal Society Medicine; Mem. BMA; Hon. Member: British Paediatric Assoc.; Swedish Pædiatric Assoc.; Finnish Pædiatric Assoc.; Amer. Acad. of Pediatrics; Academy of Pædiatricians of the USSR. West Riding County Major Scholar, 1928; Nuffield Research Studentship, Oxford, 1939–41; Rockefeller Research Fellowship, 1939 and 1946. Formerly Resident Asst, Hospital for Sick Children, Great Ormond Street, London, 1938–39; Medical Specialist and officer in charge of Medical Division (Lt-Col), RAMC, 1941–46. Asst to Prof. of Child Health, Univ. of London, 1946. Freedom, City of Sheffield, 1982. Hon. DSc: Univ. of Baghdad, Iraq, 1975; Leeds, 1982; Hon. MD Sheffield, 1976. Medal, Univ. of Turku, Finland, 1974; Aldrich Award, Amer. Acad. of Pediatrics, 1978; Spence Medal, BPA, 1979; Dawson Williams Prize, BMA, 1981. *Publications:* The Normal Child, 1953, 9th edn 1986 (trans. Greek 1966, 1978, Spanish 1969, 1979, 1985, Japanese 1970, 1975, Farsi 1979, French, 1981); (with C. M. Illingworth) Babies and Young Children: Feeding, Management and Care, 1954, 7th edn 1984 (trans. Polish, 1982); (ed) Recent Advances in Cerebral Palsy, 1958; Development of Infant and Young Child, Normal and Abnormal, 1960, 8th edn 1983 (trans. Japanese 1968, French and Polish 1978, Spanish 1983, Italian 1985); An Introduction to Developmental Assessment in the First Year, 1962; The Normal Schoolchild: His Problems, Physical and Emotional, 1964; (with C. M. Illingworth) Lessons from Childhood: some aspects of the early life of unusual men and women, 1966 (Japanese trans., 1969); Common Symptoms of Disease in Children, 1967, 8th edn 1984 (trans. Greek 1968, Spanish 1968, 1983, Italian 1974, 1980, German, 1979); Treatment of the Child at Home: a guide for family doctors, 1971 (Greek trans., 1975); Basic Developmental Screening, 1973, 3rd edn 1982 (trans. Greek 1978, 1984, Italian 1978, Japanese, 1984); The Child at School: a Paediatrician's Manual for Teachers, 1974 (trans. Italian 1983); Your Child's Development in the First Five Years, 1981; Infections and Immunisation of your Child, 1981; various medical and photographic papers. *Recreations:* photography, philately, travel. *Address:* 8 Harley Road, Sheffield S11 9SD. *T:* 362774.

ILLSLEY, Prof. Raymond, CBE 1979; PhD; Professorial Fellow in Social Policy, University of Bath, since 1984; *b* 6 July 1919; *s* of James and Harriet Illsley; *m* 1948, Jean Mary Harrison; two *s* one *d. Educ:* St Edmund Hall, Oxford (BA 1948). PhD Aberdeen 1956. Served War, 1939–45: active service in GB and ME, 1939–42; PoW, Italy and Germany, 1942–45. Econ. Asst, Commonwealth Econ. Cttee, London, 1948; Social Res. Officer, New Town Develt Corp., Crawley, Sussex, 1948–50; Sociologist, MRC, working with Dept of Midwifery, Univ. of Aberdeen, as Mem., Social Med. Res. Unit and later Mem., Obstetric Med. Res. Unit, 1951–64; Prof. of Sociology, Univ. of Aberdeen, 1964–75, Prof. of Medical Sociology, 1975–84. Dir, MRC Medical Sociology Unit, 1965–83. Vis. Prof., Cornell Univ., NY, 1963–64; Vis. Scientist, Harvard Univ., 1968; Sen. Foreign Scientist, National Sci. Foundn, Boston Univ., 1971–72; Vis. Prof., Dept of Sociology, Boston Univ., 1971–72, Adjunct Prof., 1972–76. Chairman: Scottish TUC Inquiry on Upper Clyde Shipbuilders Ltd, 1971; Social Sciences Adv. Panel, Action for the Crippled Child, 1971–76; Health Services Res. Cttee, Chief Scientist's Org., SHHD, 1976–84. Member: Sec. of State's Scottish Council on Crime, 1972–76; Exec. Cttee, Nat. Fund for Res. into Crippling Diseases, 1972–76; Chief Scientist's Cttee, SHHD, 1973–85; EEC Cttee on Med. Res., 1974–77; SSRC, 1976–78 (Chairman: Sociol. and Soc. Admin Cttee, 1976–79; Social Affairs Cttee, 1982–85); Chief Scientist's Adv. Cttee, DHSS, 1980–81; European Adv. Cttee for Med. Res., WHO, 1981–85. Rock Carling Fellow, Nuffield Prov. Hosps Trust, 1980. Hon. DSc Univ. of Hull. *Publications:* Mental Subnormality in the Community: a clinical and epidemiological study (with H. Birch, S. Richardson, D. Baird et al), 1970; Professional or Public Health, 1980; (with R. G. Mitchell) Low Birth Weight, 1984; articles in learned jls on reproduction, migration, social mobility, mental subnormality. *Recreation:* rough husbandry. *Address:* University of Bath, Claverton Down, Bath BA2 7AY; *T:* (office) Bath 61244; Tisbut House, Box Hill, Wilts SN14 9HG. *T:* Bath 742313. *Club:* National Liberal.

ILLSTON, Dr John Michael, CEng, FICE; Director of the Hatfield Polytechnic, since 1982; *b* 17 June 1928; *s* of Alfred Charles Illston and Ethel Marian Illston; *m* 1951, Olga Elizabeth Poulter; one *s* two *d. Educ:* Wallington County Grammar Sch.; King's Coll., Univ. of London (BScEng, PhD, DScEng; FKC 1985). CEng, FICE 1975. Water engr, then schoolmaster, 1949–59; Lectr, Sen. Lectr and Reader in Civil Engrg, King's Coll., London, 1959–77; Dir of Studies in Civil Engrg, Dean of Engrg, and Dep. Dir, Hatfield Polytechnic, 1977–82. Member: Commonwealth Scholarships Commn, 1983–; Engrg Bd, Sci. and Engrg Council, 1983–; Engrg Council, 1984–. *Publications:* (with J. M. Dinwoodie and A. A. Smith) Concrete, Timber and Metals, 1979; contrib. Cement and

Concrete Res. and Magazine of Concrete Res. *Address:* Hatfield Polytechnic, PO Box 109, Hatfield, Herts AL10 9AB. *T:* Hatfield 79030.

IMBERT, Peter Michael, QPM 1980; Deputy Commissioner, Metropolitan Police, since 1985; *b* 27 April 1933; *s* of late William Henry Imbert and of Frances May (*née* Hodge); *m* 1956, Iris Rosina (*née* Dove); one *s* two *d*. *Educ:* Harvey Grammar Sch., Folkestone, Kent; Holborn College of Law, Languages and Commerce. Joined Metropolitan Police, 1953; Asst Chief Constable, Surrey Constabulary, 1976, Dep. Chief Constable, 1977; Chief Constable, Thames Valley Police, 1979–85. Dep. operational head, Metropolitan Police Anti-Terrorist Squad, 1973–75; Police negotiator at Balcome Street siege, Dec. 1975; visited Holland following Moluccan sieges, and Vienna following siege of OPEC building by terrorists, Dec. 1975. Lectures in UK to police and military on terrorism and siege situations; also in Europe (incl. Berlin, 1978); lecture tours to Australia, 1977 and 1980 to advise on terrorism/sieges, and to Canada, 1981 re practical effects on police forces of recommendations of Royal Commn on Criminal Procedure. Sec., Nat. Crime Cttee-ACPO Council, 1980–83 (Chm., 1983–85). Member: Gen. Advisory Council, BBC, 1980–; Academic Consultative Cttee, King George VI and Queen Elizabeth Foundn of St Catharine's, Cumberland Lodge, Windsor, 1983–. CBIM 1982. *Publications:* book reviews re terrorism/security/sieges police negotiating. *Recreations:* golf, gardening. *Address:* New Scotland Yard, Broadway, SW1H 0BG. *T:* 01–230 1212.

IMBERT-TERRY, Sir Michael Edward Stanley, 5th Bt *cr* 1917, of Strete Ralegh, Whimple, Co. Devon; *b* 18 April 1950; *s* of Major Sir Edward Henry Bouhier Imbert-Terry, 3rd Bt, MC, and of Jean (who *m* 1983, Baron Sackville, *qv*), *d* of late Arthur Stanley Garton; *S* brother, 1985; *m* 1975, Frances Dorothy, *d* of late Peter Scott, Ealing; one *s* two *d*. *Educ:* Cranleigh. *Heir:* *s* Brychan Edward Imbert-Terry, *b* 1975.

IMESON, Kenneth Robert, MA; Headmaster, Nottingham High School, 1954–70; *b* 8 July 1908; *s* of R. W. Imeson; *m* 1st, 1934, Peggy (*d* 1967), *d* of late A. H. Mann, Dulwich; two *d*; 2nd, Peggy (*d* 1979), *widow* of Duncan MacArthur, *d* of late Harold Pow; 3rd, 1982, Barbara Thorpe (*see* Barbara Reynolds). *Educ:* St Olave's; Sidney Sussex Coll., Cambridge (Schol.). Mathematical Tripos, Part 1 1928; Part II 1930. Asst Master, Llandovery Coll., 1930–33; Sen. Mathematical Master, Watford Grammar Sch., 1933–44; Headmaster, Sir Joseph Williamson's Mathematical Sch., 1944–53; Member: Council SCM in Schools, 1948–58; Council of Friends of Rochester Cathedral, 1947–53; Board of Visitors, Nottingham Prison, 1956–57; Teaching Cttee, Mathematical Association, 1950–58; Trustee, Nottingham Mechanics Institution, 1955–70; Court of Nottingham Univ., 1955–64, 1968–70; Lectr, Univ. of Third Age, 1983–. Member: Oxford and Cambridge Examinations Board, 1957–61, 1962–70; Council Christian Education Movement, 1965–69; Council, Arts Educational Schools, 1971–; Cttee, Notts CCC, 1969–72; London Diocesan Bd of Educn, 1971–76; Central Council of Physical Recreation, 1971–. Governor: Lady Margaret Sch., Parson's Green; Purcell Sch. of Music, 1975–78. *Publications:* articles in Journal of Education. *Recreations:* cricket and other games; music. *Address:* 220 Milton Road, Cambridge CB4 1LQ. *T:* Cambridge 357894; 16 Chesterton Towers, Cambridge CB4 1DZ. *T:* Cambridge 358008. *Clubs:* MCC, Yellowhammers Cricket, Forty; Cambridge Society.

IMMS, George, CB 1964; Commissioner and Director of Establishments and Organisation, HM Customs and Excise, 1965–71; *b* 10 April 1911; *o s* of late George Imms; *m* 1938, Joan Sylvia Lance; two *s*. *Educ:* Grange High Sch., Bradford; Emmanuel Coll., Cambridge (Scholar). Joined HM Customs and Excise, 1933; Asst Sec., 1946; Commissioner, 1957–65. Mem. Civil Service Appeals Bd, 1971–79. *Address:* 26 Lynceley Grange, Epping, Essex.

IMRAY, Colin Henry, CMG 1983; HM Diplomatic Service; High Commissioner to Tanzania, since 1986; *b* 21 Sept. 1933; *s* of late Henry Gibbon Imray and of Frances Olive Imray; *m* 1957, Shirley Margaret Matthews; one *s* three *d*. *Educ:* Highgate Sch.; Hotchkiss Sch., Conn; Balliol Coll., Oxford (2nd cl. Hons PPE). Served in Seaforth Highlanders and RWAFF, Sierra Leone, 1952–54. CRO, 1957; Canberra, 1958–61; CRO, 1961–63; Nairobi, 1963–66; FCO, 1966–70; British Trade Comr, Montreal, 1970–73; Counsellor, Head of Chancery and Consul-Gen., Islamabad, 1973–77; RCDS, 1977; Commercial Counsellor, Tel Aviv, 1977–80; Rayner Project Officer, 1980; Dep. High Comr, Bombay, 1980–84; Asst Under-Sec. of State (Dep. Chief Clerk and Chief Inspector), FCO, 1984–85. *Recreations:* travel, walking. *Address:* c/o Foreign and Commonwealth Office, SW1A 2AH. *Clubs:* Royal Commonwealth Society, Travellers'.

INCE, Dr Basil André; High Commissioner for Republic of Trinidad and Tobago in London, since 1986; *b* 1 May 1933; *s* of Mrs Leonora Brown and Arthur J. Ince; *m* 1961, Laurel Barnwell; two *s*. *Educ:* Queen's Royal Coll., Trinidad; Tufts Univ., USA (BA Pol. Sci. and Hist.); New York Univ. (PhD Internat Relations, Comparative Politics, Internat. Law, Amer. Dip. Hist.). Min. of External Affairs Mission to UN, NY, 1963–66; Asst Prof., City Univ., NY, 1966–68; Associate Prof., State Univ., Puerto Rico, 1968–70, State Univ., NY, 1970–73; Sen. Lectr, Inst. of Internat. Relations, Univ. of WI, Trinidad, 1973–81 (Acting Dir, 1978–81); Minister of External Affairs, Trinidad and Tobago, 1981–85; Minister of Sport, Culture and Youth Affairs, 1985–86. *Publications:* Decolonization and Conflict in the United Nations: Guyana's struggle for independence, 1972; (ed) Essays on Race, Economics and Politics in the Caribbean, 1972; (ed) Contemporary International Relations of the Caribbean, 1979; (ed and contrib.) Issues in Caribbean International Relations, 1983. *Recreations:* reading, sports—tennis, track, boxing. *Address:* 42 Belgrave Square, SW1X 8NT. *T:* 01–245 9351. *Club:* Colonial Tennis (Port-of-Spain).

INCE, Brigadier Cecil Edward Ronald, CB 1950; CBE 1946 (OBE 1941); *b* 5 March 1897; 3rd *s* of late C. H. B. Ince, Barrister-at-Law; *m* 1924, Leslie, *o d* of late Robert Badham, Secretary of Midland & GW Rly, Ireland; two *d*. *Educ:* Sevenoaks. Regular Army; RA 1915, RASC 1919–49. Deputy Dir (Supplies), Middle East, 1940–42; War Office, 1943–47; Commandant RASC Trng Centre, 1947–49. Dir of Enforcement, subseq. Dir of Warehousing, Min. of Food and Agric., 1949–55. *Publications:* various military pamphlets and articles in Service publications. *Recreation:* progressive gardening. *Address:* 76 West Grove, Walton-on-Thames, Surrey. *T:* Walton-on-Thames 225035.

INCE, Wesley Armstrong, CMG 1968; Solicitor and Company Director; *b* 27 Nov. 1893; *s* of John and Christina Ince, Melbourne; *m* 1919, Elsie Maud Ince, *d* of Wm H. Smith, Melbourne; two *d*. *Educ:* Wesley Coll., Melbourne; Melbourne Univ. Admitted practice Barrister and Solicitor, 1917; Partner, Arthur Robinson & Co., 1919–67. Chm., Claude Neon Industries Ltd, 1932–70; Chm., Rheem Australia Ltd, 1937–67; Foundn Mem. Coun., Inst. of Public Affairs, 1942–; Foundn Mem., Australian-American Assoc., 1941– (Federal Pres., 1962–63, 1965–67); Chm., Petroleum Refineries (Aust.) Ltd, 1952–61; Director: International Harvester Co. of Australia Pty Ltd, 1945–74; Hoyts Theatres Ltd, 1934–76; Dulux Australia Ltd, 1945–74. *Recreations:* golf, bowls, swimming. *Address:* 372 Glenferrie Road, Malvern, Vic 3144, Australia. *T:* 20 9516. *Clubs:* Athenæum (Melbourne); Royal Melbourne Golf, Melbourne Cricket.

INCH, Sir John Ritchie, Kt 1972; CVO 1969; CBE 1958; QPM 1961; Chief Constable, Edinburgh City Police, 1955–75; *b* 14 May 1911; *s* of James Inch, Lesmahagow, Lanarkshire; *m* 1941, Anne Ferguson Shaw; one *s* two *d*. *Educ:* Hamilton Academy; Glasgow Univ. (MA, LLB). Joined Lanarkshire Constabulary, 1931; apptd Chief Constable, Dunfermline City Police, 1943, and of combined Fife Constabulary, 1949. OStJ 1964. Comdr, Royal Order of St Olav (Norway), 1962; Comdr, Order of Al-Kawkal Al Urdini (Jordan), 1966; Cavaliere Ufficiale, Order of Merit (Italy), 1969; Comdr, Order of Orange-Nassau (Netherlands), 1971; Order of the Oak Crown Class III (Luxembourg), 1972. *Recreations:* shooting, fishing, golf. *Address:* Fairways, 192 Whitehouse Road, Barnton, Edinburgh EH4 6DA. *T:* 031–339 3558. *Club:* Royal Scots (Edinburgh).

INCHBALD, Michael John Chantrey, FSIAD; designer; Director, Michael Inchbald Ltd, since 1953; *b* 8 March 1920; *s* of late Geoffrey H. E. Inchbald and Rosemary Evelyn (*née* Ilbert); *m* 1955, Jacqueline Anne Bromley (marr. diss. 1964; *see* J. A. Thwaites); one *s* one *d*. *Educ:* Sherborne; Architect. Assoc. Sch. of Architecture. FSIAD 1970. Work exhibited: Triennale, Milan; Design Centres London, New York, Helsinki. Design projects for: Bank of America; Crown Estate Comrs; Cunard; Dunhill-Worldwide; Ferragamo; Hanover Trust; Imperial Group; Justerini & Brooks; Law Soc.; John Player; Plessey Co.; Savoy Group; Trust House Forte; ships, QE2, Carmania, Franconia and Windsor Castle; royal and private yachts and houses. Inchbald schs founded under his auspices, 1960. Winner of nat. design competitions: Shapes of Things to Come, 1946; Nat. Chair Design Competition, 1955. Freeman, Clockmakers' Co., 1985. *Publications:* contrib. Arch. Rev., Arch. Digest, Connaissance des Arts, Connoisseur, Country Life, Harpers/Queen, House & Garden, Internat. Lighting Rev., and Vogue. *Recreations:* arts, travel, antiques. *Address:* Stanley House, 10 Milner Street, SW3 2PU. *T:* 01–584 8832.

INCHCAPE, 3rd Earl of, *cr* 1929; **Kenneth James William Mackay;** Viscount Glenapp of Strathnaver, *cr* 1929; Viscount Inchcape, *cr* 1924; Baron Inchcape, *cr* 1911; Chairman and Chief Executive, Inchcape PLC, 1958–82, now Life President; Chairman, P & O Steam Navigation Co., 1973–83, now President (Chief Executive, 1978–81; Director, 1951–83); Director: Standard Chartered PLC; Guardian Royal Exchange Assurance; BAII PLC; International Swiss Bank Corporation; President, Commonwealth Society for the Deaf; *b* 27 Dec. 1917; *e s* of 2nd Earl and Joan (*d* 1933), *d* of late Lord Justice Moriarty; *S* father 1939; *m* 1st, 1941, Mrs Aline Thorn Hannay (marr. diss. 1954), *widow* of Flying Officer P. C. Hannay, AAF, and *d* of Sir Richard Pease, 2nd Bt; two *s* one *d*; 2nd, 1965, Caroline Cholmeley, *e d* of Cholmeley Dering Harrison, Emo Court, Co. Leix, Eire, and Mrs Corisande Harrison, Stradbally, Co. Waterford; two *s* and one adopted *s*. *Educ:* Eton; Trinity Coll., Cambridge (MA). Served War of 1939–45: 12th Royal Lancers BEF France; Major 27th Lancers MEF and Italy. Director: Burmah Oil Co., 1960–75; BP Co., 1965–83. Chm., Council for Middle East Trade, 1963–65; Pres., Gen. Council of British Shipping, 1976–77. Pres., Royal Soc. for India, Pakistan and Ceylon, 1970–76. Prime Warden: Shipwrights' Co., 1967; Fishmongers' Co., 1977–78. One of HM Comrs of Lieutenancy for the City of London, 1980–. Freeman, City of London. *Recreations:* all field sports. *Heir:* *s* Viscount Glenapp, *qv*. *Address:* Addington Manor, Addington, Bucks; Forneth House, Forneth, Blairgowrie, Perthshire PH10 6SH. *Clubs:* White's, Brooks's, Buck's, City, Oriental.

See also Baron Craigmyle, Baron Tanlaw.

INCHIQUIN, 18th Baron of, *cr* 1543; **Conor Myles John O'Brien;** Bt 1686; *b* 17 July 1943; *s* of Hon. Fionn Myles Maryons O'Brien (*d* 1977) (*y s* of 15th Baron) and of Josephine Reine, *d* of late Joseph Eugene Bembaron; *S* uncle, 1982. *Educ:* Eton. Served as Captain, 14th/20th King's Hussars. *Heir:* *cousin* Murrough Richard O'Brien [*b* 25 May 1910; *m* 1st, 1942, Irene Clarice (marr. diss. 1951), *o d* of H. W. Richards; 2nd, 1952, Joan, *d* of Charles Pierre Jenkinson and *widow* of Captain Woolf Barnato; one *s* one *d*]. *Address:* Thomond House, Dromoland, Newmarket on Fergus, Co. Clare, Ireland.

INCHYRA, 1st Baron *cr* 1961; **Frederick Robert Hoyer Millar,** GCMG 1956 (KCMG 1949; CMG 1939); CVO 1938; *b* 6 June 1900; *s* of late R. Hoyer Millar; *m* 1931, Elizabeth de Marees van Swinderen; two *s* two *d*. *Educ:* Wellington Coll.; New Coll., Oxford. Hon. Attaché, HM Embassy, Brussels, 1922; entered HM Diplomatic Service, 1923; served as Third Sec. at Berlin and Paris, and as Second Sec. at Cairo; Asst Private Sec. to Sec. of State for Foreign Affairs, 1934–38; First Sec. at Washington, 1939; Counsellor, 1941–42; Sec., British Civil Secretariat, Washington, 1943; Counsellor, FO, 1944; Asst Under-Sec. 1947; Minister, British Embassy, Washington, 1948; UK Deputy, North Atlantic Treaty Organisation, 1950; UK Permanent Representative on NATO Council, 1952; UK High Commissioner in Germany, 1953–55; British Ambassador to Bonn, 1955–57; Permanent Under-Sec. of State, Foreign Office, 1957–61. *Recreation:* shooting. *Heir:* *s* Hon. Robert Charles Reneke Hoyer Millar [*b* 4 April 1935; *m* 1961, Fiona Sheffield; one *s* two *d*]. *Address:* Inchyra House, Glencarse, Perthshire. *Clubs:* Boodle's, Turf; New (Edinburgh); Metropolitan (Washington).

IND, Jack Kenneth; Headmaster of Dover College, since 1981; *b* 20 Jan. 1935; *s* of Rev. William Price Ind and Mrs Doris Maud Ind (*née* Cavell); *m* 1964, Elizabeth Olive Toombs; two *s* two *d*. *Educ:* Marlborough Coll.; St John's Coll., Oxford (BA Hons Mods, 2nd Cl. Class. Lit. and Lit. Hum.). Asst Master: Wellingborough Sch., 1960–63; Tonbridge Sch., 1963–81 (Housemaster, 1970–81). *Recreations:* tennis, Rugby football, music, reading. *Address:* Headmaster's House, Dover College, Dover, Kent CT17 9RH. *T:* Dover 205905.

INDIAN OCEAN, Archbishop of the, since 1984; **Most Rev. French Kitchener Chang-Him;** Bishop of Seychelles since 1979; *m* 1975, Susan Talma; twin *d*. *Educ:* Lichfield Theolog. Coll.; St Augustine's Coll., Canterbury; Trinity Coll., Univ. of Toronto (LTh 1975). Deacon, Sheffield, 1962; priest, Seychelles,1963; Curate of Goole, 1962–63; Rector of Praslin, Seychelles, 1963–66 and 1969–71; Asst Priest, St Leonard's, Norwood, Sheffield, 1967–68; Vicar General, Seychelles, 1972–73; Rector, S Mahé Parish, 1973–74; Archdeacon of Seychelles, 1973–79; Priest-in-charge, St Paul's Cathedral, Mahé, 1977–79; Dean, Province of the Indian Ocean, 1983–84. *Address:* Box 44, Victoria, Mahé, Seychelles. *T:* 24242.

INGAMELLS, John Anderson Stuart; Director of the Wallace Collection, since 1978; *b* 12 Nov. 1934; *s* of George Harry Ingamells and late Gladys Lucy (*née* Rollett); *m* 1964, Hazel Wilson; two *d*. *Educ:* Hastings Grammar School; Eastbourne Grammar School; Fitzwilliam House, Cambridge. National Service, Army (Cyprus), 1956–58; Art Asst, York Art Gallery, 1959–63; Asst Keeper, Dept of Art, National Museum of Wales, 1963–67; Curator, York Art Gallery, 1967–77; Asst to the Director, Wallace Collection, 1977–78. *Publications:* The Davies Collection of French Art, 1967; The English Episcopal Portrait, 1981; numerous catalogues, including Philip Mercier (with Robert Raines), 1969; Portraits at Bishopthorpe Palace, 1972; museum catalogues at York, Cardiff and the Wallace Collection; articles in Apollo, Connoisseur, Burlington Magazine, Walpole Soc., etc. *Address:* 39 Benson Road, SE23 3RL.

INGE, Maj.-Gen. Peter Anthony; Director General of Logistic Policy (Army), Ministry of Defence, 1986–Aug. 1987; *b* 5 Aug. 1935; *s* of Raymond Albert Inge and late Grace

Maud Caroline Inge (née Du Rose); m 1960, Letitia Marion Beryl, yr d of late Trevor and Sylvia Thornton-Berry; two d. Educ: Summer Fields; Wrekin College; RMA Sandhurst. Commissioned Green Howards, 1956; served Hong Kong, Malaya, Germany, Libya and UK; ADC to GOC 4 Div., 1960–61; Adjutant, 1 Green Howards, 1963–64; student, Staff Coll., 1966; MoD, 1967–69; Coy Comdr, 1 Green Howards, 1969–70; student, JSSC, 1971; BM 11 Armd Bde, 1972; Instructor, Staff Coll., 1973–74; CO 1 Green Howards, 1974–76; Comdt, Junior Div., Staff Coll., 1977–79; Comdr Task Force C/4 Armd Bde, 1980–81; Chief of Staff, HQ 1 (BR) Corps, 1982–83; GOC NE District and Comdr 2nd Inf. Div., 1984–86. Colonel, The Green Howards, 1982–. Recreations: cricket, walking, music and reading, especially military history. Address: c/o Barclays Bank, Leyburn, North Yorks. Clubs: Army and Navy, MCC.

INGE-INNES-LILLINGSTON, George David, CBE 1986; MA, DL; a Crown Estates Commissioner, since 1974; b 13 Nov. 1923; s of late Comdr H. W. Innes-Lillingston, RN, and Mrs Innes-Lillingston, formerly of Lochalsh House, Balmacara, Kyle, Ross-shire; m 1st, 1946, Alison Mary (d 1947), er d of late Canon F. W. Green, MA, BD, Norwich; one d; 2nd, 1955, Elizabeth Violet Grizel Thomson-Inge, yr d of late Lt-Gen. Sir William Thomson, KCMG, CB, MC; two s one d. Educ: Stowe, Buckingham; Merton Coll., Oxford (MA Hons Agric.). Served War as Lieut RNVR, 1942–45, Lt-Comdr RNR, 1966. Member: Agricultural Land Tribunal, 1962–72; Minister's Agricultural Panel for W Midlands, 1972–76; Council for Charitable Support, 1985–; Chairman: N Birmingham and District Hosps, 1968–72; Staffordshire Br., Country Landowners' Assoc., 1968–71 (Pres. 1983–), and Headquarters Exec. Cttee, 1977–79; Agr. and Hort. Cttee, BSI, 1980–; Dep. Pres., CLA, 1977–79, Pres., 1979–81; Pres., Staffs Agricultural Soc., 1970–71. Dir, Lands Improvement Gp Ltd, and associated cos, 1983–. JP 1967–74, DL 1969–, Staffs; High Sheriff, Staffs, 1966. Recreations: growing trees, yachting. Address: Thorpe Hall, Tamworth, Staffs B79 0LH. T: Tamworth 830224. Clubs: Boodle's, Farmers', Royal Thames Yacht; Royal Highland Yacht (Oban).

INGESTRE, Viscount; James Richard Charles John Chetwynd-Talbot; b 11 Jan. 1978; s and heir of 22nd Earl of Shrewsbury and Waterford, qv.

INGHAM, Bernard; Chief Press Secretary to the Prime Minister, since 1979; b 21 June 1932; s of Garnet and Alice Ingham; m 1956, Nancy Hilda Hoyle; one s. Educ: Hebden Bridge Grammar Sch., Yorks. Reporter: Hebden Bridge Times, 1948–52; Yorkshire Post and Yorkshire Evening Post, Halifax, 1952–59; Yorkshire Post, Leeds, 1959–61; Northern Industrial Correspondent, Yorkshire Post, 1961; Reporter, The Guardian, 1962–65; Labour Staff, The Guardian, London, 1965–67. Press and Public Relns Adviser, NBPI, 1967–68; Chief Inf. Officer, DEP, 1968–73; Dir of Information: Dept of Employment, 1973; Dept of Energy, 1974–77; Under Sec., Energy Conservation Div., Dept of Energy, 1978–79. Recreations: walking, gardening, reading. Address: 9 Monahan Avenue, Purley, Surrey CR2 3BB. T: 01–660 8970. Club: Reform.

INGHAM, John Henry, CMG 1956; MBE 1947; retired; b 1910. Educ: Plumtree School, S Rhodesia; Rhodes University College, S Africa; Brasenose College, Oxford. Administrative Officer, Nyasaland, 1936; Secretary for Agricultural and Natural Resources, Kenya, 1947; Administrative Secretary, 1952; Senior Secretary, East African Royal Commission, 1953–55; Secretary for African Affairs, Nyasaland, 1956–60; MEC, Nyasaland, 1961. Minister of Urban Development, Malawi, 1961. Representative of Beit Trust and Dulverton Trust in Central Africa, 1962–81. Hon. MA Rhodesia, 1979. Address: 25 Canterbury Road, Avondale, Harare, Zimbabwe.

INGHAM, Prof. Kenneth, OBE 1961; MC 1946; Professor of History, 1967–84, Part-time Professor of History, 1984–86, now Emeritus Professor, and Head of History Department, 1970–84, University of Bristol; b 9 Aug. 1921; s of Gladson and Frances Lily Ingham; m 1949, Elizabeth Mary Southall; one s one d. Educ: Bingley Grammar Sch.; Keble Coll., Oxford (Exhibitioner). Served with West Yorks Regt, 1941–46 (despatches, 1945). Frere Exhibitioner in Indian Studies, University of Oxford, 1947; DPhil 1950. Lecturer in Modern History, Makerere Coll., Uganda, 1950–56, Prof., 1956–62; Dir of Studies, RMA, Sandhurst, 1962–67. MLC, Uganda, 1954–61. Publications: Reformers in India, 1956; The Making of Modern Uganda, 1958; A History of East Africa, 1962; The Kingdom of Toro in Uganda, 1975; Jan Christian Smuts: the conscience of a South African, 1986; contrib. to Encyclopædia Britannica, Britannica Book of the Year. Address: The Woodlands, 94 West Town Lane, Bristol BS4 5DZ.

INGHAM, Stanley Ainsworth; Deputy Director (Under Secretary), Department for National Savings, 1979–82; b 21 Feb. 1920; s of David Ingham and Ann (née Walshaw); m 1944, Ethel Clara (née Jordan); one s. Educ: King's School, Pontefract, Yorkshire. Clerical Officer, Post Office Savings Bank, 1937; served Royal Artillery, 1940–46; Post Office Savings Bank: Executive Officer, 1946; Higher Executive Officer, 1956; Sen. Executive Officer, 1960; Principal, 1964; Asst Sec., Dept for National Savings, 1972. Recreations: Church affairs, gardening. Address: 2 Manor Crescent, Surbiton, Surrey KT5 8LQ. T: 01–399 1078.

INGILBY, Sir Thomas (Colvin William), 6th Bt cr 1866; MRAC; ARICS; CAAV; managing own estate; b 17 July 1955; s of Sir Joslan William Vivian Ingilby, 5th Bt, DL, JP, and of Diana, d of late Sir George Colvin, CB, CMG, DSO; S father, 1974; m 1984, Emma Clare Roebuck, d of Major R. R. Thompson, Whinfield, Strensall, York; one s. Educ: Aysgarth Sch., Bedale; Eton Coll. Student Teacher, Springvale School, Marandellas, Rhodesia, Sept. 1973–April 1974. Joined Army, May 1974, but discharged on death of father; student at Royal Agricultural Coll., Cirencester, until 1978. Assistant: Stephenson & Son, York, 1978–80; Strutt & Parker, Harrogate, 1981–83. Lecture tours, USA, speaking on castles and historic houses, 1978, 1979. Internat. Hon. Citizen, New Orleans, 1979. Recreations: cricket, tennis, squash. Heir: s James William Francis Ingilby, b 15 June 1985. Address: Ripley Castle, Ripley, near Harrogate, North Yorkshire HG3 3AY. T: Harrogate 770053.

INGLEBY, 2nd Viscount, cr 1955, of Snilesworth; **Martin Raymond Peake;** Landowner; Director, Hargreaves Group Ltd, 1960–80; b 31 May 1926; s of 1st Viscount Ingleby, and Joan, Viscountess Ingleby (d 1979); S father, 1966; m 1952, Susan, d of late Henderson Russell Landale; four d (one s decd). Educ: Eton; Trinity Coll., Oxford (MA). Called to the Bar, Inner Temple, 1956. Sec., Hargreaves Group Ltd, 1958–61. Administrative Staff Coll., 1961. CC Yorks (North Riding), 1964–67. Mem., N Yorks Moors Nat. Park Planning Cttee, 1968–78. Heir: none. Address: Snilesworth, Northallerton, North Yorks DL6 3QD. T: Osmotherley 214.

INGLEDOW, Anthony Brian, OBE 1969; HM Diplomatic Service; Counsellor, Foreign and Commonwealth Office, since 1982; b 25 July 1928; s of Cedric Francis Ingledow and Doris Evelyn Ingledow (née Worrall); m 1956, Margaret Monica, d of Sir Reginald Watson-Jones, FRCS; one s one d. Educ: St Bees School; London Univ. Served HM Forces, 1947–49. Joined Colonial Administrative Service, Nigeria, 1950; District Officer: Auchi, 1954; Oyo, 1956; Secretariat, Ibadan, 1958, retired 1960; joined HM Diplomatic Service, 1961; 2nd Secretary, Khartoum, 1962; FO, 1964; 1st Secretary, Aden, 1966; Lagos, 1967; FCO, 1970; Dakar, 1972; FCO, 1975. Recreations: reading, travel. Address: c/o Foreign

and Commonwealth Office, SW1; Wychwood, 2 Castle Road, Camberley, Surrey GU15 2DS. T: Camberley 65723. Club: Athenæum, Royal Commonwealth Society.

INGLEFIELD, Sir Gilbert (Samuel), GBE 1968; Kt 1965; TD; MA, ARIBA, AADip; b 13 March 1909; 2nd s of late Adm. Sir F. S. Inglefield, KCB; m 1933, Laura Barbara Frances, e d of late Captain Gilbert Thompson, Connaught Rangers; two s one d. Educ: Eton; Trinity Coll., Cambridge. Architect; served War of 1939–45 with Sherwood Foresters, France, Far East. British Council Asst Rep. in Egypt, 1946–49 and in London, 1949–56. Alderman, City of London (Aldersgate Ward), 1959–79; Sheriff, 1963–64; Chm., Barbican Cttee, 1963–66; Lord Mayor of London, 1967–68; one of HM Lieutenants for City of London; Church Commissioner for England, 1962–78; Governor: Thomas Coram Foundation; Royal Shakespeare Theatre; Fedn of British Artists, 1972–; Trustee, London Symphony Orchestra; Chm., City Arts Trust, 1968–76; Member: Royal Fine Art Commission, 1968–75; Redundant Churches Fund, 1972–76. Dep. Kt Principal, Imp. Soc. of Knights Bachelor, 1972–86, now Hon. Master, Haberdashers' Co., 1972; Master, Musicians Co., 1974; Assistant, Painter Stainers Co. Chancellor of the Order of St John of Jerusalem, 1969–78; GCStJ. FRSA; Hon. RBA; Hon. GSM; Hon. FLCM. Hon. DSc City Univ., 1967. Comdr Order of the Falcon (Iceland), 1963; Order of the Two Niles, Class III (Sudan), 1964. Recreations: music, travel. Address: 6 Rutland House, Marloes Road, W8 5LE. T: 01–937 3458. Clubs: Athenæum, City Livery.

INGLEFIELD, Col Sir John (Frederick) C.; see Crompton-Inglefield.

INGLEFIELD-WATSON, Captain Sir Derrick William Inglefield; see Watson.

INGLEWOOD, 1st Baron, cr 1964; **William Morgan Fletcher-Vane,** TD; DL; b 12 April 1909; s of late Col Hon. W. L. Vane and Lady Katharine Vane; assumed name of Fletcher-Vane by deed poll, 1931; m 1949, Mary (d 1982) (late Sen. Comdr ATS (despatches), JP, Mem. LCC, 1949–52, Cumberland CC, 1961–74), e d of Major Sir Richard G. Proby, 1st Bt, MC; two s. Educ: Charterhouse; Trinity Coll., Cambridge (MA). ARICS. 2nd Lt 6 Bn Durham Light Infantry, 1928; served Overseas: 1940, France, with 50 (N) Div. (despatches); 1941–44, Middle East with Durham LI and on the Staff, Lt-Col, 1943. MP (C) for Westmorland, 1945–64; Parliamentary Private Sec. to Minister of Agriculture, 1951–54, to Joint Under-Sec. of State, Foreign Office, 1954–55, and to Minister of Health, Dec. 1955–July 1956; Joint Parliamentary Secretary: Min. of Pensions and National Insurance, 1958–60; Min. of Agriculture, Oct. 1960–July 1962. DL Westmorland 1946, Cumbria 1974–85; Landowner; Mem. Chartered Surveyors Institution; formerly Mem. of Historic Buildings Council for England; Leader of UK Delegation to World Food Congress (FAO) Washington, June 1963. Chm., Anglo-German Assoc., 1973–84 (Vice-Chm., 1966–73). Order of the Phoenix, Greece; Order of the Cedar, Lebanon; Commander, German Order of Merit, 1977. Heir: s Hon. William Richard Fletcher-Vane, MA (Cantab) [b 31 July 1951; m 1986, Cressida, y d of late Desmond Pemberton-Pigott and of Mrs Pemberton-Pigott. Called to the Bar, Lincoln's Inn, 1975; ARICS]. Address: Hutton-in-the-Forest, Penrith, Cumbria CA11 9TH. T: Skelton 207; 21 Stack House, Cundy Street, Ebury Street, SW1W 9JS. T: 01–730 1559. Club: Travellers'.

INGLIS, Brian (St John), PhD; FRSL; journalist; b 31 July 1916; s of late Sir Claude Inglis, CIE, FRS, and late Vera St John Blood; m 1958, Ruth Langdon; one s one d. Educ: Shrewsbury Sch.; Magdalen Coll., Oxford. BA 1939. Served in RAF (Coastal Command), 1940–46; Flight Comdr 202 Squadron, 1944–45; Squadron Ldr, 1944–46 (despatches). Irish Times Columnist, 1946–48; Parliamentary Corr., 1950–53. Trinity Coll., Dublin: PhD 1950; Asst to Prof. of Modern History, 1949–53; Lectr in Economics, 1951–53; Spectator: Asst Editor, 1954–59; Editor, 1959–62; Dir, 1962–63. TV Commentator: What the Papers Say, 1956–; All Our Yesterdays, 1962–73. Trustee, Koestler (formerly KIB) Foundn, 1983–. Publications: The Freedom of the Press in Ireland, 1954; The Story of Ireland 1956; Revolution in Medicine, 1958; West Briton, 1962; Fringe Medicine, 1964; Private Conscience: Public Morality, 1964; Drugs, Doctors and Disease, 1965; A History of Medicine, 1965; Abdication, 1966; Poverty and the Industrial Revolution, 1971; Roger Casement, 1973; The Forbidden Game: the social history of drugs, 1975; The Opium War, 1976; Natural and Supernatural, 1977; The Book of the Back, 1978; Natural Medicine, 1979; The Diseases of Civilisation, 1981; (with Ruth West) The Alternative Health Guide, 1983; Science and Parascience, 1984; The Paranormal: an encyclopedia of Psychic Phenomena, 1985; The Hidden Power, 1986. Address: Garden Flat, 23 Lambolle Road, NW3 4HS. T: 01–794 0297.

INGLIS, Sir Brian Scott, Kt 1977; FTS; Chairman: Ford Motor Co. of Australia Ltd, 1981–85; Salzo Automotive Research Ltd, 1986; b Adelaide, 3 Jan. 1924; s of late E. S. Inglis, Albany, WA; m 1953, Leila, d of E. V. Butler; three d. Educ: Geelong Church of England Grammar School; Trinity Coll., Univ. of Melbourne (BSc; Mem. Council, 1985). Served War of 1939–45; Flying Officer, RAAF, 453 Sqdn, 1942–45. Director and Gen. Manufacturing Manager, 1963–70, first Australian Man. Dir, Ford Motor Co. of Australia Ltd, 1970–81, Vice-Pres., 1981–83, Chm. 1981–85; Chm., Ford Asia-Pacific Inc., 1983–84. Director: Amcor Ltd (formerly APM), 1984; Newmont Holdings, 1984. Chm., Defence Industry Cttee, 1984– (Mem., 1982–). Chm., Centre for Molecular Biology and Medicine, Monash Univ. James N. Kirby Medal, IProdE, 1979; Kernot Medal, Faculty of Engrg, Univ. of Melbourne, 1979. Address: 10 Bowley Avenue, Balwyn, Victoria 3103, Australia. Clubs: Australian (Melbourne); Geelong (Geelong); Barwon Heads Golf.

INGLIS, George Bruton; Senior Partner, Slaughter and May, since 1986; b 19 April 1933; s of Cecil George Inglis and Ethel Mabel Inglis; m 1968, Patricia Mary Forbes; three s. Educ: Winchester College; Pembroke College, Oxford (MA). Solicitor. Partner, Slaughter and May, 1966–. A Governor, Royal Marsden Hosp., 1984–. Recreation: gardening. Address: c/o Slaughter and May, 35 Basinghall Street, EC2V 5DB. T: 01–600 1200.

INGLIS, Ian Grahame, CB 1983; State Under Treasurer for Tasmania, since 1977; b 2 April 1929; s of late William and Ellen Jean Inglis; m 1952, Elaine Arlene Connors; three s one d. Educ: Hutchins Sch., Hobart; Univ. of Tasmania (BComm). Agricl Economist, Tasmanian Dept. of Agric., 1951–58; Economist, State Treasury, 1958–69; Chairman: Rivers and Water Supply Commn, and Metropolitan Water Bd, 1969–77; NW Regl Water Authority, 1977. Member: Ambulance Commn of Tasmania, 1959–65; Tasmanian Grain Elevators Bd, 1962–65; Clarence Municipal Commn, 1965–69. Dir, Comalco Aluminium (Bell Bay) Ltd, 1980–. Recreation: yachting. Address: 5 Sayer Crescent, Sandy Bay, Hobart, Tas 7005, Australia. T: (002) 231928. Clubs: Tasmanian; Royal Yacht of Tasmania (Hobart).

INGLIS, James Craufuird Roger, WS; Partner, Shepherd & Wedderburn, WS, since 1976; Chairman, British Assets Trust plc, since 1978; Director: Edinburgh American Assets Trust plc, since 1957; Atlantic Assets Trust plc, since 1957; Royal Bank of Scotland Group plc, since 1985 (Royal Bank of Scotland plc, 1967–85); Scottish Provident Institution, since 1962; b 21 June 1925; s of Lt-Col John Inglis and Helen Jean Inglis; m 1952, Phoebe Aeonie Murray-Buchanan; two s four d. Educ: Winchester Coll.; Cambridge

Univ. (BA); Edinburgh Univ. (LLB). *Recreation:* golf. *Address:* Inglisfield, Gifford, East Lothian, Scotland. *T:* Gifford 339. *Clubs:* Army and Navy; New (Edinburgh), Royal and Ancient Golf (St Andrews), Hon. Company of Edinburgh Golfers.

INGLIS, Maj.-Gen. Sir (John) Drummond; *see* Inglis, Maj.-Gen. Sir Drummond.

INGLIS, Prof. Kenneth Stanley, DPhil; Professor of History, Australian National University, since 1977; *b* 7 Oct. 1929; *s* of S. W. Inglis; *m* 1st, 1952, Judy Betheras (*d* 1962); one *s* two *d*; 2nd, 1965, Amirah Gust, *Educ:* Univ. of Melbourne (MA), Univ. of Oxford (DPhil). Sen. Lectr in History, Univ. of Adelaide, 1956–60; Reader in History, 1960–62; Associate Prof. of History, Australian National Univ., 1962–65; Prof., 1965–66; Prof. of History, Univ. of Papua New Guinea, 1966–72, Vice-Chancellor, 1972–75; Professorial Fellow in Hist., ANU, 1975–77. Vis. Prof. of Australian Studies, Harvard, 1982; Vis. Prof., Univ. of Hawaii, 1985. *Publications:* Hospital and Community, 1958; The Stuart Case, 1961; Churches and the Working Classes in Victorian England, 1963; The Australian Colonists, 1974; This is the ABC: the Australian Broadcasting Commission, 1932–1983, 1983; The Rehearsal: Australians at War in the Sudan 1885, 1985. *Address:* History Department, Research School of Social Sciences, Australian National University, Canberra, ACT 2600, Australia.

INGLIS, Sheriff Robert Alexander; Sheriff of North Strathclyde (formerly Renfrew and Argyll) at Paisley, 1972–84, now Temporary Sheriff; *b* 29 June 1918; *m* 1950, Shelagh Constance St Clair Boyd (marriage dissolved, 1956); one *s* one *d. Educ:* Malsis Hall, Daniel Stewart's Coll.; Rugby Sch.; Christ Church, Oxford (MA); Glasgow Univ. (LLB). Army, 1940–46; Glasgow Univ., 1946–48; called to Bar, 1948. Interim Sheriff-Sub., Dundee, 1955; perm. appt, 1956; Sheriff of Inverness, Moray, Nairn and Ross and Cromarty, 1968–72. *Recreations:* golf, fishing, bridge. *Address:* 1 Cayzer Court, Ralston, Paisley, Renfrewshire. *T:* 041–883 6498.

INGLIS of Glencorse, Sir Roderick (John), 10th Bt *cr* 1703 (then Mackenzie of Gairloch); MB, ChB; *b* 25 Jan. 1936; *s* of Sir Maxwell Ian Hector Inglis of Glencorse, 9th Bt and Dorothy Evelyn (*d* 1970), MD, JP, *d* of Dr John Stewart, Tasmania; *S* father, 1974; *m* 1960, Rachel (marr. diss. 1975), *d* of Lt-Col N. M. Morris, Dowdstown, Ardee, Co. Louth; twin *s* one *d* (and *e s* decd); *m* Marilyn, *d* of A. L. Irwin, Glasgow. *Educ:* Winchester; Edinburgh Univ. (MB, ChB 1960). *Heir: s* Ian Richard Inglis, *b* 9 Aug. 1965. *Address:* 18 Cordwalles Road, Pietermaritzburg, S Africa.

INGLIS-JONES, Nigel John, QC 1982; Barrister-at-Law; a Recorder of the Crown Court, since 1976; *b* 7 May 1935; 2nd *s* of Major John Alfred Inglis-Jones and Hermione Inglis-Jones; *m* 1965, Lenette Bromley-Davenport (*d* 1986); two *s* two *d. Educ:* Eton; Trinity Coll., Oxford (BA). Nat. Service with Grenadier Guards (ensign). Called to the Bar, Inner Temple, 1959, Bencher, 1981. *Recreations:* gardening, fishing. *Address:* 4 Sheen Common Drive, Richmond, Surrey. *T:* 01–878 1320. *Club:* MCC.

INGOLD, Cecil Terence, CMG 1970; DSc 1940; FLS; Professor of Botany in University of London, Birkbeck College, 1944–72; Vice-Master, Birkbeck College, 1965–70, Fellow, 1973; *b* 3 July 1905; *s* of late E. G. Ingold; *m* 1933, Leonora Mary Kemp; one *s* three *d. Educ:* Bangor (Co. Down) Grammar Sch.; Queen's Univ., Belfast. Graduated BSc, QUB, 1925; Asst in Botany, QUB, 1929; Lectr in Botany, University of Reading, 1930–37; Lecturer-in-charge of Dept of Botany, University Coll., Leicester, 1937–44; Dean of Faculty of Science, London Univ., 1956–60. Dep. Vice-Chancellor, London Univ., 1966–68, Chm. Academic Council, 1969–72. Chm., University Entrance and School Examinations Council, 1958–64; Vice-Chm., Inter-Univ. Council for Higher Educn Overseas, 1969–74. Chm., Council Freshwater Biolog. Assoc., 1965–74; Pres., Internat. Mycological Congress, 1971. Hooker Lectr, Linnean Soc., 1974. Linnean Medal (Botany), 1983. Hon. DLitt Ibadan, 1969; Hon. DSc Exeter, 1972; Hon. DCL Kent, 1978. *Publications:* Spore Discharge in Land Plants, 1939; Dispersal in Fungi, 1953; The Biology of Fungi, 1961; Spore Liberation, 1965; Fungal Spores: their liberation and dispersal, 1971. *Address:* 11 Buckner's Close, Benson, Oxford OX9 6LR.

INGOLD, Dr Keith Usherwood, FRS 1979; FRSC 1969; Associate Director, Division of Chemistry, National Research Council of Canada, since 1977; *b* Leeds, 31 May 1929; *s* of Christopher Kelk Ingold and Edith Hilda (*née* Usherwood); *m* 1956, Carmen Cairine Hodgkin; two *s* one *d. Educ:* University Coll. London (BSc Hons Chem., 1949); Univ. of Oxford (DPhil 1951). Emigrated to Canada, 1951; Post-doctorate Fellow (under Dr F. P. Lossing), Div. of Pure Chem., Nat. Res. Council of Canada, 1951–53; Def. Res. Bd Post-doctorate Fellow (under Prof. W. A. Bryce), Chem. Dept, Univ. of BC, 1953–55; National Research Council of Canada: joined Div. of Appl. Chem., 1955; Head, Hydrocarbon Chem. Section of Div. of Chem., 1965. Hon. DSc Univ. of Guelph, 1985. Amer. Chemical Soc. Award in Petroleum Chem., 1968; Award in Kinetics and Mechanism, Chem. Soc., 1978; Medal of Chem. Inst. of Canada, 1981, Syntex Award for Physical Organic Chemistry, CIC, 1983; Centennial Medal, RSC, 1982; Henry Marshall Tory Medal, RSC, 1985. Silver Jubilee Medal, 1977. *Publications:* over 300 scientific papers in field of physical organic chemistry, partic. free-radical chemistry. *Recreation:* skiing. *Address:* PO Box 712, RR No 5, Ottawa, Ont K1G 3N3, Canada. *T:* (613) 822–1123; (office) (613) 990–0938.

INGRAM; *see* Winnington-Ingram.

INGRAM, Dr David John Edward, MA, DPhil; DSc Oxon 1960; CPhys, FInstP; Vice-Chancellor, University of Kent at Canterbury, since 1980; *b* 6 April 1927; *s* of late J. E. Ingram and late Marie Florence (*née* Weller); *m* 1952, Ruth Geraldine Grace McNair; two *s* one *d. Educ:* King's Coll. Sch., Wimbledon; New Coll., Oxford. Postgraduate research at Oxford Univ., 1948–52; Research Fellow and Lectr, University of Southampton, 1952–57; Reader in Electronics, University of Southampton, 1957–59; Prof. and Head of Dept of Physics, Univ. of Keele, 1959–73; Dep. Vice-Chancellor, University of Keele, 1964–65, 1968–71; Principal, Chelsea Coll., London Univ., 1973–80 (Fellow, 1984). Mem., UGC, Physical Sciences Cttee, 1971–74. Member, Governing Body: Wye Coll., London Univ., 1975–; King's Sch., Canterbury, 1983–; St Lawrence Coll., 1980–; King's Coll. Hosp. Medical Sch., 1982–; Roehampton Inst., 1978–; London Sch. of Contemporary Dance, 1983–85. Chairman: London Univ. Cttee for Non-Teaching Staff, 1979–80; London Univ. Central Coordinating Cttee for Computers, 1978–80; Standing Conf. on Univ. Admissions, 1982–; Sub-Cttee on Staff and Student Affairs, CUCP, 1986–; Kent County Consultative Cttee Industry Year, 1986. Member: Carnegie UK Trust, 1980–; Camberwell DHA, 1982–85; Esso Trust for Tertiary Educn, 1978–; Member Council: SPCK, 1980–; CNAA, 1983–; CET, 1983–85; UCCA, 1984–. Hon. DSc: Clermont-Ferrand, 1965; Keele, 1983. *Publications:* Spectroscopy at Radio and Microwave Frequencies, 1955, 2nd edn, 1967; Free Radicals as Studied by Electron Spin Resonance, 1958; Biological and Biochemical Applications of Electron Spin Resonance, 1969; Radiation and Quantum Physics, 1973; Radio and Microwave Spectroscopy, 1976; various papers in Proc. Royal Soc., Proc. Phys. Soc., etc. *Recreations:* sailing, debating. *Address:* The University, Canterbury, Kent CT2 7NZ; 22 Ethelbert Road, Canterbury, Kent CT1 3NE. *Club:* Athenæum (Mem., Gen. Cttee, 1985–).

INGRAM, Sir James (Herbert Charles), 4th Bt *cr* 1893; *b* 6 May 1966; *s* of (Herbert) Robin Ingram (*d* 1979) and of Shiela, *d* of late Charles Peczenik; *S* grandfather, 1980. *Educ:* Eton. *Recreations:* golf and shooting. *Heir: half b* Nicholas David Ingram, *b* 1975. *Address:* 8 Pitt Street, W8. *T:* 01–937 0727.

INGRAM, Dame Kathleen Annie; *see* Raven, Dame Kathleen.

INGRAM, Paul; Chief Agricultural Officer, Agricultural Development and Advisory Service, Ministry of Agriculture, Fisheries and Food, since 1985; *b* 20 Sept. 1934; *s* of John Granville Ingram and Sybil Ingram (*née* Johnson); *m* 1957, Jennifer (*née* Morgan); one *s* one *d. Educ:* Manchester Central High School; University of Nottingham (BSc 1956). Dept of Conservation and Extension, Fedn of Rhodesia and Nyasaland, 1956–63; Nat. Agricl Adv. Service, later ADAS, MAFF, 1965–; County Livestock Officer, Lancs, 1969–70; Policy Planning Unit, MAFF, 1970–72; Farm Management Adviser, Devon, 1972–76; Regional Farm Management Adviser, Wales, 1976–77; Dep. Sen. Livestock Advr, 1977–79, Sen. Agricl Officer, 1979–85, ADAS. *Address:* Ministry of Agriculture, Fisheries and Food, Great Westminster House, Horseferry Road, SW1P 2AE. *T:* 01–216 6054.

INGRAM, Stanley Edward; solicitor; *b* 5 Dec. 1922; *o s* of late Ernest Alfred Stanley Ingram and Ethel Ann Ingram; *m* 1948, Vera (*née* Brown); one *s* one *d. Educ:* Charlton Central School. Articled clerk with Wright & Bull, Solicitors; admitted Solicitor, 1950. Served RAF, 1942–46. Legal Asst, Min. of Nat. Insurance, 1953; Sen. Legal Asst, Min. of Pensions and Nat. Insurance, 1958; Asst Solicitor, 1971, Under Sec. (Legal), 1978–83, DHSS. Member Council: Civil Service Legal Soc. and of Legal Section of First Division Assoc., 1971–82; Mem., Salaried Solicitors' Cttee of Law Society, 1978–81. *Recreations:* gardening, country walking, cycling. *Address:* 8 Park Road, Beckenham, Kent BR3 1QD. *Club:* Law Society.

INGRAM, Prof. Vernon Martin, FRS 1970; Professor of Biochemistry, Massachusetts Institute of Technology, since 1961; *b* Breslau, 19 May 1924; *s* of Kurt and Johanna Immerwahr; *m* 1st, 1950, Margaret Young; one *s* one *d*; 2nd, 1984, Elizabeth Hendee. *Educ:* Birkbeck Coll., Univ. of London. PhD Organic Chemistry, 1949; DSc Biochemistry, 1961. Analytical and Res. Chemist, Thos Morson & Son, Mddx, 1941–45; Lecture Demonstrator in Chem., Birkbeck Coll., 1945–47; Asst Lectr in Chem., Birkbeck Coll., 1947–50; Rockefeller Foundn Fellow, Rockefeller Inst., NY, 1950–51; Coxe Fellow, Yale, 1951–52; Mem. Sci. Staff, MRC Unit for Molecular Biology, Cavendish Lab., Cambridge, 1952–58; Assoc. Prof. 1958–61, MIT; Lectr (part-time) in Medicine, Columbia, 1961–73; Guggenheim Fellow, UCL, 1967–68. Jesup Lectr, Columbia, 1962; Harvey Soc. Lectr, 1965. Member: Amer. Acad. of Arts and Sciences, 1964; Amer. Chem. Soc.; Chemical Soc.; Biochemical Soc.; Genetical Society. William Allen Award, Amer. Soc. for Human Genetics, 1967. *Publications:* Haemoglobin and Its Abnormalities, 1961; The Hemoglobins in Genetics and Evolution, 1963; The Biosynthesis of Macromolecules, 1965, new edn, 1971; articles on human genetics, nucleic acids, differentiation and molecular biology and neurobiology, in Nature, Jl Mol. Biol., Jl Cell Biol., Develt Biol., Jl Biol Chem., etc. *Recreations:* music; photographer of abstract images. *Address:* Massachusetts Institute of Technology, Massachusetts Avenue, Cambridge, Mass 02139, USA. *T:* 617–253–3706.

INGRAMS, family name of **Baroness Darcy de Knayth.**

INGRAMS, Richard Reid; journalist; Editor, Private Eye, 1963–86, Chairman, since 1974; *b* 19 Aug. 1937; *s* of Leonard St Clair Ingrams and Victoria (*née* Reid); *m* 1962; one *s* one *d* (and one *s* decd). *Educ:* Shrewsbury; University Coll., Oxford. Joined Private Eye, 1962. *Publications:* (with Christopher Booker and William Rushton) Private Eye on London, 1962; Private Eye's Romantic England, 1963; (with John Wells) Mrs Wilson's Diary, 1965; Mrs Wilson's 2nd Diary, 1966; The Tale of Driver Grope, 1968; (with Barry Fantoni) The Bible for Motorists, 1970; (ed) The Life and Times of Private Eye, 1971; (as Philip Reid, with Andrew Osmond) Harris in Wonderland, 1973; (ed) Cobbett's Country Book, 1974; (ed) Beachcomber: the works of J. B. Morton, 1974; The Best of Private Eye, 1974; God's Apology, 1977; Goldenballs, 1979; (with Fay Godwin) Romney Marsh and the Royal Military Canal, 1980; (with John Wells) Dear Bill: the collected letters of Denis Thatcher, 1980; (with John Wells) The Other Half: further letters of Denis Thatcher, 1981; (with John Wells) One for the Road, 1982; (with John Piper) Piper's Places, 1983; (ed) The Penguin Book of Private Eye Cartoons, 1983; (with John Wells) My Round!, 1983; (ed) Dr Johnson by Mrs Thrale, 1984; (with John Wells) Down the Hatch, 1985; (with John Wells) Just the One, 1986; John Stewart Collis: a memoir, 1986; (with John Wells) The Best of Dear Bill, 1986. *Recreation:* litigation. *Address:* c/o Private Eye, 6 Carlisle Street, W1. *T:* 01–437 4017.

INGRESS BELL, Philip; *see* Bell.

INGROW, Baron *cr* 1982 (Life Peer), of Keighley in the County of West Yorkshire; **John Aked Taylor;** Kt 1972; OBE 1960; TD 1951; DL; JP; Chairman and Managing Director, Timothy Taylor & Co. Ltd; Lord-Lieutenant of West Yorkshire, since 1985 (Vice Lord-Lieutenant, 1976–85); *b* 15 Aug. 1917; *s* of Percy Taylor, Knowle Spring House, Keighley, and Gladys Broster (who *m* 2nd, 1953, Sir (John) Donald Horsfall, 2nd Bt); *m* 1949, Barbara Mary, *d* of Percy Wright Stirk, Keighley; two *d. Educ:* Shrewsbury Sch. Served War of 1939–45: Duke of Wellington's Regt and Royal Signals, Major; Norway, Middle East, Sicily, NW Europe and Far East. Mem., Keighley Town Council, 1946–67 (Mayor, 1956–57; Chm., Educn Cttee, 1949–61; Chm., Finance Cttee, 1961–67); Mem. Council, Magistrates' Assoc., 1957–86 (Vice-Chm., Exec. Cttee, 1975–76; Chm., Licensing Cttee, 1969–76; Hon. Treasurer, 1976–86; Vice-Pres., 1986; Past Pres. and Chm., WR Br.; Life Vice-Pres., W Yorks Br.); Chm., Keighley Conservative Assoc., 1952–56 and 1957–67 (Pres., 1971–76, Jt Hon. Treas., 1947–52, and Chm., Young Conservatives, 1946–47); Chm., Yorkshire West Conservative European Constituency Council, 1978–84 (Pres., 1984–85); Chm., Yorkshire Area, Nat. Union of Conservative and Unionist Assocs, 1966–71 (Vice-Chm., 1965–66); Chm., Exec. Cttee of Nat. Union of Conservative and Unionist Assocs 1971–76 (Mem. 1964–83); Pres., Nat. Union of Conservative and Unionist Assocs 1982–83 (Hon. Vice-Pres., 1976–), Gen. Comr of Income Tax, 1965. Vice-Pres., Yorks and Humberside TAVR Assoc., 1985–. Mem. Court, Univ. of Leeds, 1986–. Pres., Council of Order of St John, S and W Yorks, 1985–; KStJ 1986. JP Borough of Keighley 1949; DL West (formerly WR) Yorks, 1971. *Address:* Fieldhead, Keighley, West Yorkshire. *T:* Keighley 603895. *Club:* Carlton.

INKIN, Geoffrey David, OBE 1974 (MBE 1971); DL; Chairman, Cwmbran Development Corporation, since 1983, Member of Board since 1980; Chairman, Land Authority for Wales, since 1986; *b* 2 Oct. 1934; *e s* of late Noel D. Inkin and of Evelyn Margaret Inkin; *m* 1961, Susan Elizabeth, *d* of Col L. S. Sheldon and late Margaret Sheldon, and step *d* of Mrs Rosemary Sheldon; three *s. Educ:* Dean Close Sch.; RMA, Sandhurst; Staff Coll., Camberley; Royal Agricl Coll., Cirencester. Commnd The Royal Welch Fusiliers, 1955; served Malaya, 1955–57 and Cyprus, 1958–59 (despatches); MoD, 1965–67; Bde Major, Strategic Reserve, 1969–71; commanded 1st Bn The Royal Welch Fusiliers, 1972–74. Member: Gwent CC, 1977–83; Gwent Police Authority, 1979–83.

Mem. Bd, Welsh Devlt Agency, 1984–. Chm., Governing Body, Usk Agricl Coll., 1979–81; Mem., Bd of Governors, Monmouth Schs, 1977–. Parly Cand. (C) Ebbw Vale, 1977–79. FRSA. DL Gwent, 1983. *Address:* Court St Lawrence, Llangovan, Monmouth NP5 4BT. *T:* Raglan 690279. *Clubs:* Carlton, Army and Navy; Cardiff and County (Cardiff); Ebbw Vale Conservative.

INMAN, Herbert, CBE 1977; Regional Administrator, Yorkshire Regional Health Authority, 1973–77; Hon. Adviser to the Sue Ryder Foundation, since 1977, and Member of Council, since 1986; Chairman, Sue Ryder Homes Executive Committee, since 1983; *b* 8 Jan. 1917; *s* of Matthew Herbert Inman and Rose Mary Earle; *m* 1939, Beatrice, *d* of Thomas Edward Lee and Florence Lee; twin *s*. *Educ:* Wheelwright Grammar Sch., Dewsbury; Univ. of Leeds. FHSM (Nat. Pres. 1968–69); DPA. Various hosp. appts, Dewsbury, Wakefield and Aylesbury, 1933–48; Dep. Gp Sec., Leeds (A) Gp HMC and Dep. Chief Admin. Officer, 1948–62; Gp Sec. and Chief Admin. Officer, Leeds (A) Gp HMC, 1962–70; Gp Sec. and Chief Admin. Officer, Leeds (St James's) Univ. HMC, 1970–73. *Publications:* occasional articles in Hospital and Health Services jls. *Recreations:* travel, gardening, Rugby football, cricket, swimming. *Address:* 7 Potterton Close, Barwick in Elmet, Leeds LS15 4DY. *T:* Leeds 812538.

INMAN, Peter Donald, CBE 1977; TD 1946; DL; Chief Executive/Clerk, Lancashire County Council, 1974–76; *b* 21 Oct. 1916; *s* of Robert and Sarah Inman, Bradford; *m* 1947, Beatrice Dallas (*d* 1983); one *s* one *d*. *Educ:* Bradford Grammar Sch.; Leeds Univ. (LLB). Solicitor. Served War, 1939–45: KOYLI; France, India and Germany (Major). Asst Solicitor, Dewsbury, 1946; Lancashire County Council: Asst Solicitor, 1948; Dep. Clerk, 1951; Clerk, 1973–74. DL Lancs 1974; Clerk of Lieutenancy, Lancs, 1974. Hon. Treasurer, Lancs Youth Clubs Assoc., 1948–68, Vice-Pres. 1968. *Recreations:* golf, gardening. *Address:* 1 Beech Drive, Fulwood, Preston PR2 3NB. *T:* Preston 862361.

INMAN, Col Roger, OBE (mil.) 1945 (MBE (mil.) 1944); TD 1945; Vice Lord-Lieutenant of South Yorkshire, since 1981; Joint Managing Director, Harrison Fisher Group, since 1951; *b* 18 April 1915; *y s* of S. M. Inman, Sheffield; *m* 1939, Christine Lucas, *e d* of Lt-Col J. Rodgers, Sheffield; two *s*. *Educ:* King Edward VII Sch., Sheffield. Commissioned into 71st (WR) Field Bde, RA TA, 1935; served War, with RA and General Staff, Western Desert, Middle East, Italy, 1939–46; released, 1946, with rank of Lt-Col; reformed and commanded 271 (WR) Fd Regt, RA TA, 1947–51; Brevet Col 1953; Hon. Col, Sheffield Artillery Volunteers, 1964–70; Member, W Riding T&AFA, 1947–; Vice-Chm., Yorkshire and Humberside TA&VRA, 1973–80. JP 1954 (Chm. Sheffield City Bench, 1974–80), DL 1967, West Riding. General Commissioner of Income Tax, 1969–; Chm. of Comrs, Don Div. of Sheffield, 1975–. *Recreation:* golf. *Address:* Flat 1, 15 Whitworth Road, Sheffield S10 3HD. *Clubs:* Army and Navy; Sheffield, Hallamshire Golf (Sheffield).

INMAN, Rt. Rev. Thomas George Vernon; *b* 1904; *s* of late Capt. William James Inman, RE, Durban; *m* 1st, 1935, Alma Coker (*d* 1970), *d* of late Advocate Duncan Stuart Campbell, Bulawayo, Rhodesia; three *s* (one *d* decd); 2nd, 1971, Gladys Marjory Hannah, MB, ChB (she *m* 1st, 1947, Charles William Lysaght, who *d* 1969), *d* of late David Rees Roberts, Cape Town. *Educ:* Selwyn Coll., Cambridge; St Augustine's Coll., Canterbury, MA 1932. Deacon, 1930; priest, 1931; Asst Missioner, Wellington Coll. Mission, Walworth, 1930–33; Curate of Estcourt, Natal, 1933; Curate of St Paul, Durban, 1933–37, Vicar, 1937–51; Canon of Natal, 1944–51; Archdeacon of Durban, 1950–51; Bishop of Natal, 1951–74; retired, 1974. Dean, Province of S Africa, 1966–74. Chaplain and Sub-prelate, Order of St John of Jerusalem, 1953. Hon. DD Univ. of the South, Tenn., USA, 1958. *Address:* PO Box 6190, Coffs Harbour, NSW 2450, Australia. *T:* Coffs Harbour (066) 52-7275.

INNES, Sir Berowald; *see* Innes, Sir R. G. B.

INNES of Coxton, Sir Charles (Kenneth Gordon), 11th Bt *cr* 1686; *b* 28 Jan. 1910; *s* of Major Charles Gordon Deverell Innes (*d* 1953), and Ethel Hilda, *d* of George Earle; *S* 1973 to baronetcy of Innes of Coxton, dormant since the death of Sir George Innes, 8th Bt, 1886; *m* 1936, Margaret Colquhoun Lockhart, *d* of F. C. L. Robertson and *g d* of Sir James Colquhoun of Luss, 5th Bt; one *s* one *d*. *Educ:* Haileybury Coll., Herts. War Service, 1939–45, Royal Artillery; Captain, Ayrshire Yeomanry. *Recreations:* photography, music, art, gardening. *Heir: s* David Charles Kenneth Gordon Innes [*b* 17 April 1940; *m* 1969, Marjorie Alison, *d* of E. W. Parker; one *s* one *d*. *Educ:* Haileybury; London Univ. BScEng; ACGI]. *Address:* October Cottage, Haslemere, Surrey GU27 2LF.

INNES, Fergus Munro, CIE 1946; CBE 1951; Indian Civil Service, retired; *b* 12 May 1903; *s* of late Sir Charles Innes; *m* 1st, Evangeline, *d* of A. H. Chaworth-Musters (marriage dissolved); two *d*; 2nd, Vera, *d* of T. Mahoney; one *s* one *d*. *Educ:* Charterhouse; Brasenose Coll., Oxford. Joined Indian Civil Service, 1926; various posts in Punjab up to 1937; Joint Sec., Commerce Dept, Govt of India, 1944; Mem., Central Board of Revenue, 1947; retired, 1947; Adviser in Pakistan to Central Commercial Cttee, 1947–53; Sec., The West Africa Cttee, 1956–61; Chm., India Gen. Navigation and Railway Co. Ltd, 1973–78. Company director. *Address:* The Hippins, Hook Heath Road, Woking, Surrey GU22 0DP. *T:* Woking 4626. *Club:* Oriental.

INNES, Hammond; *see* Hammond Innes, Ralph.

INNES of Edingight, Malcolm Rognvald, CVO 1981; Baron of Yeochrie; Lord Lyon King of Arms, since 1981; Secretary to the Order of the Thistle, since 1981; *b* 25 May 1938; 3rd *s* of late Sir Thomas Innes of Learney, GCVO, LLD, and Lady Lucy Buchan, 3rd *d* of 18th Earl of Caithness; *m* 1963, Joan, *o d* of Thomas D. Hay, CA, Edinburgh; three *s*. *Educ:* Edinburgh Acad.; Univ. of Edinburgh (MA, LLB). WS 1964. Falkland Pursuivant Extraordinary, 1957; Carrick Pursuivant, 1958; Lyon Clerk and Keeper of the Records, 1966; Marchmont Herald, 1971. Mem., Queen's Body Guard for Scotland (Royal Company of Archers), 1971. Pres., Heraldry Soc. of Scotland. Trustee, Sir William Fraser's Foundn. FSA (Scot.); KStJ. Grand Officer of Merit, SMO Malta. *Recreations:* archery, fishing, shooting, visiting places of historic interest. *Address:* 35 Inverleith Row, Edinburgh EH3 5QH. *T:* 031–552 4924; Edingight House, Banffshire. *T:* Knock 270. *Clubs:* New, Puffins (Edinburgh).

INNES, Maughan William; Controller Finance, National Research Development Corporation, 1965–77; *b* 18 Nov. 1922; *s* of Leslie W. Innes and Bridget Maud (*née* Humble-Crofts); *m* 1950, Helen Mary, *d* of Roper Spyers; one *s* (and one *s* decd). *Educ:* Marlborough College. FCA; FBIM. RAF, 1941–46. Chartered Accountant, 1949; in Canada, 1953–60; retired 1977. *Recreations:* music, theatre. *Address:* Brook Cottage, Four Elms, Edenbridge, Kent TN8 6PA. *T:* Four Elms 232. *Club:* MCC.

INNES, Michael; *see* Stewart, John I. M.

INNES, Lt-Col Sir (Ronald Gordon) Berowald, 16th Bt *cr* 1628, of Balvenie; OBE 1943; *b* 24 July 1907; *s* of Captain J. W. G. Innes, CBE, RN (*d* 1939) and Sheila (*d* 1949), *d* of Col J. F. Forbes of Rothiemay; *S* kinsman, Sir Walter James Innes, 15th Bt, 1978; *m* 1st, 1933, Elizabeth Haughton (*d* 1958), *e d* of late Alfred Fayle; two *s* one *d*; 2nd, 1961, Elizabeth Christian, *e d* of late Lt-Col C. H. Watson, DSO, IMS. *Educ:* Harrow; RMC Camberley. Commissioned Seaforth Highlanders, 1927; PSC; served War of 1939–45; France, 1939–40; Middle East, 1941–43 (wounded); Sicily, 1943; Holland and Germany, 1944–45; GSO1 50 (Northumbrian) Div., 1942–43; GSO1 Directing Staff, Staff Coll., 1943–44; in comd 7th Bn, Seaforth Highlanders, 1945; GSO1 (Infantry), War Office, 1946–48; in comd 4th (Uganda) Bn, KAR, and OC Troops, Uganda, 1948–49; retired as Lt-Col, 1949. *Recreation:* needlepoint embroidery. *Heir: s* Peter Alexander Berowald Innes, MICE [*b* 6 Jan. 1937; *m* 1959, Julia Mary, *d* of A. S. Levesley; two *s* one *d*]. *Address:* The Loom House, Aultgowrie, by Muir of Ord, Ross and Cromarty. *T:* Urray 216. *Club:* Naval and Military.

See also Lt-Col W. A. D. Innes.

INNES, Sheila Miriam; Controller, BBC Educational Broadcasting, since 1984; *b* 25 Jan. 1931; *d* of Dr James Innes, MB, ChB, MA and Nora Innes. *Educ:* Talbot Heath School, Bournemouth; Lady Margaret Hall, Oxford (Exhibnr; BA Hons Mod. Langs; MA). BBC Radio Producer, World Service, 1955–61; BBC TV producer: family programmes, 1961–65; further education, 1965–73; exec. producer, further education, 1973–77; Head, BBC Continuing Educn, TV, 1977–84; Dir, BBC Enterprises Ltd. Chm. Cross-Sector Cttee for Development and Review, BTEC, 1986–; Member: Gen. Board, Alcoholics Anonymous, 1980–; Board of Governors, Centre for Information on Language Teaching and Research, 1981–; Council, Open Univ., 1984–; Council for Educational Technology, 1984–; EBU Educational Working Party, 1984; RTS 1984. FRSA 1986. *Publications:* BBC publications; articles for language jls and EBU Review. *Recreations:* music (classical and jazz), country pursuits, swimming, sketching, photography, travel, languages. *Address:* The Knowle, Seer Green Lane, Jordans, Bucks. *T:* Chalfont St Giles 4575. *Club:* Reform.

INNES, Lt-Col William Alexander Disney, JP; Vice Lord-Lieutenant of Banffshire, since 1971; *b* 19 April 1910; 2nd *s* of late Captain James William Guy Innes, CBE, DL, JP, RN, of Maryculter, Kincardineshire; *m* 1939, Mary Alison, *d* of late Francis Burnett-Stuart, Howe Green, Hertford; two *s*. *Educ:* Marlborough Coll., RMC, Sandhurst. Gordon Highlanders: 2nd Lieut, 1930; Captain 1938; Temp. Major 1941; Major, 1946; Temp. Lt-Col, 1951; retd, 1952. Served War of 1939–45: Far East (PoW Malaya and Siam, 1942–45). Chm., Banffshire T&AFA, 1959. DL 1959, JP 1964, Banffshire. *Recreations:* shooting, gardening. *Address:* Heath Cottage, Aberlour, Banffshire AB3 9QD. *T:* Aberlour 266.

See also Sir Berowald Innes, Bt.

INNES-KER, family name of **Duke of Roxburghe.**

INNISS, Hon. Sir Clifford (de Lisle), Kt 1961; Judge of the Court of Appeal of Belize, 1974–81; Chairman, Integrity Commission of Belize, since 1981; Member, Belize Advisory Council, Feb.–Oct. 1985; *b* Barbados, 26 Oct. 1910; *e s* of late Archibald de Lisle Inniss and Lelia Emmaline, *e d* of Elverton Richard Springer. *Educ:* Harrison Coll., Barbados; Queen's Coll., Oxford. BA (hons jurisprudence), BCL. Called to bar, Middle Temple, 1935. QC (Tanganyika) 1950, (Trinidad and Tobago) 1953; Practised at bar, Barbados; subseq. Legal Draughtsman and Clerk to Attorney-Gen., Barbados, 1938; Asst to Attorney General and Legal Draughtsman, 1941; Judge of Bridgetown Petty Debt Court, 1946; Legal Draughtsman, Tanganyika, 1947; Solicitor Gen., Tanganyika, 1949; Attorney-Gen., Trinidad and Tobago, 1953; Chief Justice, British Honduras, later Belize, 1957–72; Judge of the Courts of Appeal of Bermuda, the Bahamas, and the Turks and Caicos Is, 1974–75. *Recreations:* cricket, tennis, swimming. *Address:* 11/13 Oriole Avenue, Belmopan, Belize. *Clubs:* Barbados Yacht; Kenya Kongonis (hon. mem.).

INSALL, Donald William, OBE 1981; FSA, RWA, FRIBA, FRTPI; architect and planning consultant; Principal, Donald W. Insall & Associates, since 1958; *b* 7 Feb. 1926; *o s* of late William R. Insall and Phyllis Insall, Henleaze, Bristol; *m* 1964, Amy Elizabeth, MA, *er d* of Malcolm H. Moss, Nanpantan, Leics; two *s* one *d*. *Educ:* private prep; Bristol Grammar Sch.; Bristol Univ.; RA; Sch. of Planning, London (Dip. (Hons)); SPAB Lethaby Schol. 1951. FRIBA 1968, FRTPI 1973. Coldstream Guards, 1944–47. Architectural and Town-Planning Consultancy has included town-centre studies, civic and univ., church, domestic and other buildings, notably in conservation of historic towns and buildings; Medal (Min. of Housing and Local Govt), Good Design in Housing, 1962. Visiting Lecturer: RCA, 1964–69; Internat. Centre for Conservation, Rome, 1969–; Coll. d'Europe, Bruges, 1976–81; Catholic Univ. of Leuven, 1982–; Adjunct Prof., Univ. of Syracuse, 1971–81. Mem., Council of Europe Working Party, 1969–70; Nat. Pilot Study, Chester: A Study in Conservation, 1968; Consultant, Chester Conservation Programme (EAHY Exemplar; European Prize for Preservation of Historic Monuments, 1981; Europa Nostra Medal, 1983). Member: Historic Buildings Council for England, 1971–84; Grants Panel, EAHY, 1974; Nat. Cttee, ICOMOS; Council, RSA, 1976–80 (FRSA, 1948); Council, SPAB, 1979–; Ancient Monuments Bd for England, 1980–84; Comr, Historic Blgs and Monuments Commn, 1984–. Hon. Sec., Conf. on Trng Architects in Conservation, 1959–. RIBA: Banister Fletcher Medallist, 1949; Neale Bursar, 1955; Examnr, 1957; Competition Assessor, 1971. Conferences: White House (on Natural Beauty), 1965; IUA (on Architectural Trng), Pistoia, 1968; UNESCO, 1969. Lecture Tours: USA, 1964, 1972 (US Internat. Reg. Conf. on Conservation); Mexico, 1972; Yugoslavia, 1973; Canada, 1974; Argentina, 1976; India, 1979; Portugal, 1982. European Architectural Heritage Year Medal (for Restoration of Chevening), 1973; Queen's Silver Jubilee Medal, 1977. *Publications:* (jtly) Railway Station Architecture, 1966; (jtly) Conservation Areas 1967; The Care of Old Buildings Today, 1973; Historic Buildings: action to maintain the expertise for their care and repair, 1974; Conservation in Action: Chester's Bridgegate, 1982; contrib. to Encyclopædia Britannica, professional, environmental and internat. jls. *Recreations:* visiting, photographing and enjoying places; appreciating craftsmanship; Post-Vintage Thoroughbred Cars (Mem., Rolls Royce Enthusiasts' Club). *Address:* 73 Kew Green, Richmond, Surrey TW9 3AH; (office) 19 West Eaton Place, Eaton Square, SW1X 8LT. *T:* 01–245 9888. *Club:* Athenæum.

INSCH, James Ferguson, CBE 1974; CA; Director, Guest Keen & Nettlefolds plc, 1964–82, Deputy Chairman, 1980–82; Chairman, Birmid-Qualcast Ltd, 1977–84 (Deputy Chairman, 1975–77); *b* 10 Sept. 1911; *s* of John Insch and Edina (*née* Hogg); *m* 1937, Jean Baikie Cunningham; one *s* two *d*. *Educ:* Leith Academy. Chartered Accountant (Scot.). Director, number of GKN companies, 1945–66; Guest Keen & Nettlefolds Ltd: Group Man. Dir, 1967; Gp Dep. Chm. and Man. Dir, 1968–74; Jt Dep. Chm., 1979. Pres., Nat. Assoc. of Drop Forgers and Stampers, 1962–63 and 1963–64. *Recreations:* golf, fishing. *Address:* 1 Denehurst Close, Barnt Green, Birmingham. *T:* 021–445 2517.

INSKIP, family name of **Viscount Caldecote.**

INSKIP, John Hampden, QC 1966; **His Honour Judge Inskip;** a Circuit Judge, since 1982; *b* 1 Feb. 1924; *s* of Sir John Hampden Inskip, KBE, and Hon. Janet, *d* of 1st Baron Maclay, PC; *m* 1947, Ann Howell Davies; one *s* one *d*. *Educ:* Clifton Coll.; King's Coll., Cambridge. BA 1948. Called to the Bar, Inner Temple, 1949; Master of the Bench, 1975. Mem. of Western Circuit; Dep. Chm., Hants QS, 1967–71; Recorder of Bournemouth, later of the Crown Court, 1970–82. Mem., Criminal Law Revision Cttee, 1973–82; Pres., Transport Tribunal, 1982–. *Address:* Clerks, Bramshott, Liphook, Hants.

INSOLE, Douglas John, CBE 1979; Marketing Director, Trollope & Colls Holdings Ltd, since 1975; *b* 18 April 1926; *s* of John Herbert Insole and Margaret Rose Insole; *m* 1948, Barbara Hazel Ridgway (*d* 1982); two *d* (and one *d* decd). *Educ:* Sir George Monoux Grammar Sch.; St Catharine's Coll., Cambridge. MA Cantab. Cricket: Cambridge Univ., 1947–49 (Captain, 1949); Essex CCC, 1947–63 (Captain, 1950–60); played 9 times for England; Vice-Captain, MCC tour of S Africa, 1956–57. Chairman: Test Selectors, 1965–68; Test and County Cricket Bd, 1975–78; Mem., MCC Cttee, 1955–; Manager, England cricket team, Australian tours, 1978–79 and 1982–83. Soccer: Cambridge Univ., 1946–48; Pegasus, and Corinthian Casuals; Amateur Cup Final medal, 1956. Member: Sports Council, 1971–74; FA Council, 1979–. JP Chingford, 1962–74. *Publication:* Cricket from the Middle, 1960. *Recreations:* cricket, soccer. *Address:* 8 Hadleigh Court, Crescent Road, Chingford, E4 6AX. *T:* 01–529 6546. *Clubs:* Carlton, MCC.

INVERFORTH, 4th Baron *cr* 1919, of Southgate; **Andrew Peter Weir;** *b* 16 Nov. 1966; *s* of 3rd Baron Inverforth and of Jill Elizabeth, *o d* of John W. Thornycroft, *qv*; *S* father, 1982. *Educ:* Marlborough College. *Heir: uncle* Hon. John Vincent Weir, *b* 8 Feb. 1935. *Address:* 27 Hyde Park Street, W2 2JS. *T:* 01–283 1266.

INVERNESS (St Andrew's Cathedral), Provost of; *see* Reid, Very Rev. W.G.

INVERURIE, Lord; Michael Canning William John Keith; Master of Kintore; *b* 22 Feb. 1939; *s* and *heir* of 12th Earl of Kintore, *qv*; assumed surname of Keith in lieu of Baird; *m* 1972, Mary Plum, *d* of late Sqdn Leader E. G. Plum, Rumson, NJ, and of Mrs Roy Hudson; one *s* one *d*. *Educ:* Eton; RMA Sandhurst. Lately Lieutenant, Coldstream Guards. ACII. *Heir: s* Master of Inverurie, *qv*. *Address:* The Stables, Keith Hall, Inverurie, Aberdeenshire. *T:* Inverurie 20495.

INVERURIE, Master of; Hon. James William Falconer Keith; *b* 15 April 1976; *s* and *heir* of Lord Inverurie, *qv*.

IONESCO, Eugène; Chevalier de la Légion d'Honneur, 1970; Officier des Arts et lettres, 1961; homme de lettres; Membre de l'Académie française, since 1970; *b* 13 Nov. 1912; *m* 1936, Rodica; one *d*. *Educ:* Bucharest and Paris. French citizen living in Paris. Ballet: The Triumph of Death, Copenhagen, 1972. *Publications:* (most of which appear in English and American editions) Théâtre I; La Cantatrice chauve, La Leçon, Jacques ou La Soumission, Les Chaises, Victimes du devoir, Amédée ou Comment s'en débarrasser, Paris, 1956; Théâtre II: L'Impromptu de l'Alma, Tueur sans gages, Le Nouveau Locataire, L'Avenir est dans les œufs, Le Maître, La Jeune Fille à marier, Paris, 1958. Rhinocéros (play) in Collection Manteau d'Arlequin, Paris, 1959, Le Piéton de l'air, 1962, Chemises de Nuit, 1962; Le Roi se meurt, 1962; Notes et Contre-Notes, 1962; Journal en Miettes, 1967; Présent passé passé présent, 1968; Découvertes (Essays), 1969; Jeux de Massacre (play), 1970; Macbett (play), 1972; Ce formidable bordel (play), 1974; The Hermit (novel), 1975; The Man with the Suitcase, 1975; (with Claude Bonnefoy) Entre la vie et le rêve, 1977; Antidotes (essays), 1977; L'homme en question (essays), 1979; Variations sur un même thème, 1979; Voyages chez les Morts ou Thème et Variations (play), 1980; Noir et Blanc, 1980; contrib. to: Avant-Garde (The experimental theatre in France) by L. C. Pronko, 1962; Modern French Theatre, from J. Giraudoux to Beckett, by Jean Guicharnaud, 1962; author essays and tales. *Relevant publications:* The Theatre of the Absurd, by Martin Esslin, 1961; Ionesco, by Richard N. Coe, 1961; Eugène Ionesco, by Ronald Hayman, 1972. *Address:* c/o Editions Gallimard, 5 rue Sébastien Bottin, 75007 Paris, France.

IONESCU, Prof. George Ghita; Professor of Government, University of Manchester, 1970–80, now Emeritus; Editor, Government and Opposition, since 1965; Chairman, Research Committee, International Political Science Association, since 1975; *b* 21 March 1913; *s* of Alexandre Ionescu and Hélène Sipsom; *m* 1950, Valence Ramsay de Bois Maclaren. *Educ:* Univ. of Bucharest (Lic. in Law and Polit. Sci.). Gen. Sec., Romanian Commn of Armistice with Allied Forces, 1944–45; Counsellor, Romanian Embassy, Ankara, 1945–47; Gen. Sec., Romanian Nat. Cttee, NY, 1955–58; Dir, Radio Free Europe, 1958–63; Nuffield Fellow, LSE, 1963–68. Hon. MA(Econ) Manchester. *Publications:* Communism in Romania, 1965; The Politics of the Eastern European Communist States, 1966; (jtly) Opposition, 1967; (jtly) Populism, 1970; (ed) Between Sovereignty and Integration, 1973; Centripetal Politics, 1975; The Political Thought of Saint-Simon, 1976; (ed) The European Alternatives, 1979; Politics and the Pursuit of Happiness, 1984. *Recreations:* music, bridge, racing. *Address:* 36 Sandileigh Avenue, Manchester M20 9LW. *T:* 061–445 7726. *Club:* Athenæum.

IPSWICH, Viscount; Henry Oliver Charles FitzRoy; *b* 6 April 1978; *s* and *heir* of Earl of Euston, *qv*.

IPSWICH, Bishop of; *see* St Edmundsbury.

IRBY, family name of **Baron Boston.**

IREDALE, Roger Oliver, PhD; Chief Education Adviser, Overseas Development Administration, Foreign and Commonwealth Office, since 1983; *b* 13 Aug. 1934; *s* of Fred Iredale and Elsie Florence (*née* Hills); *m* 1968, Mavis Potter; one *s* one *d*. *Educ:* Harrow County Grammar Sch.; Univ. of Reading (BA 1956, MA 1959, PhD 1971; Hurry Medal for Poetry; Early English Text Soc's Prize; Seymour-Sharman Prize for Literature; Graham Robertson Travel Award); Peterhouse Coll., Univ. of Cambridge (Cert. Ed. 1957). Teacher, Hele's Sch., Exeter, 1959–61; Lectr and Senior Lectr, Bishop Otter Coll., Chichester, 1962–70; British Council Officer and Maître de Conférences, Univ. of Algiers, 1970–72; Lectr, Chichester Coll. of Further Educn, 1972–73; British Council Officer, Madras, 1973–75; Dir of Studies, Educl Admin., Univ. of Leeds, 1975–79; Educn Adviser, ODA, 1979–83. Mem., Commonwealth Scholarship Commn, 1984–; Comr, Sino-British Friendship Scholarship Scheme Commn, 1986–. Governor, Sch. of Oriental and African Studies, 1983–. Poetry Society's Greenwood Prize, 1974. *Publications:* Turning Bronzes (poems), 1974; Out Towards the Dark (poems), 1978; articles in Comparative Education and other jls; poems for BBC Radio 3 and in anthologies and jls. *Recreations:* poetry writing, restoring the discarded. *Address:* 8 Orchard Drive, Blackheath, SE3 0QP. *T:* 01–852 4073.

IRELAND; *see* de Courcy-Ireland.

IRELAND, Frank Edward, BSc, CChem; FRSC; FEng; FIChemE; SFInstE; consultant in air pollution control; HM Chief Alkali and Clean Air Inspector, 1964–78; *b* 7 Oct. 1913; *s* of William Edward Ireland and Bertha Naylor; *m* 1941, Edna Clare Meredith; one *s* three *d*. *Educ:* Liverpool Univ. (BSc). CChem, FRSC (FRIC 1945); CEng, FIChemE 1950; SFInstF 1956. Plant Superintendent, Orrs Zinc White Works, Widnes, Imperial Smelting Corp. Ltd, 1935–51; Prodn Man., Durham Chemicals Ltd, Birtley, Co. Durham, 1951–53; Alkali Inspector based on Sheffield, 1953–58; Dep. Chief Alkali Inspector, 1958–64. Pres., Inst. of Fuel, 1974–75; Vice Pres., Instn of Chem. Engrs, 1969–72. George E. Davis Gold Medal, Instn of Chem. Engrs, 1969. Founder Fellow, Fellowship of Engineering, 1976. *Publications:* Annual Alkali Reports, 1964–77; papers to nat. and internat. organisations. *Recreations:* golf, gardening. *Address:* 59 Lanchester Road, Highgate, N6. *T:* 01–883 6060.

IRELAND, Ronald David, QC (Scotland) 1964; Sheriff of Lothian and Borders (formerly Lothians and Peebles) at Edinburgh, since 1972; *b* 13 March 1925; *o s* of William Alexander Ireland and Agnes Victoria Brown. *Educ:* George Watson's Coll., Edinburgh; Balliol Coll., Oxford (Scholar); Edinburgh Univ. Served Royal Signals, 1943–46. BA Oxford, 1950, MA 1958; LLB Edinburgh, 1952. Passed Advocate, 1952; Clerk of the Faculty of Advocates, 1957–58; Prof. of Scots Law, 1958–71, Dean of Faculty of Law, 1964–67, Aberdeen Univ. Governor, Aberdeen Coll. of Education, 1959–64 (Vice-Chm., 1962–64). Comr, under NI (Emergency Provisions) Act, 1974–75. Member: Bd of Management, Aberdeen Gen. Hosps, 1961–71 (Chm., 1964–71); Departmental Cttee on Children and Young Persons, 1961–64; Cttee on the Working of the Abortion Act, 1971–74; Hon. Sheriff for Aberdeenshire, 1963–. Member: North Eastern Regional Hosp. Bd, 1964–71 (Vice-Chm. 1966–71); After Care Council, 1962–65; Nat. Staff Advisory Cttee for the Scottish Hosp. Service, 1964–65; Chm., Scottish Hosps Administrative Staffs Cttee, 1965–72. Dir, Scottish Courts Admin, 1975–78. *Recreations:* music, bird-watching. *Address:* 6a Greenhill Gardens, Edinburgh EH10 4BW. *Clubs:* New (Edinburgh); Royal Northern and University (Aberdeen).

IREMONGER, Thomas Lascelles; *o s* of Lt-Col H. E. W. Iremonger, DSO, Royal Marine Artillery, and Julia St Mary Shandon, *d* of Col John Quarry, Royal Berks Regiment; *m* Lucille Iremonger, MA (Oxon), FRSL, author and broadcaster; one *d*. *Educ:* Oriel Coll., Oxford (MA). HM Overseas Service (Western Pacific), 1938–46. RNVR (Lt), 1942–46. MP (C) Ilford North, Feb. 1954–Feb. 1974, Redbridge, Ilford North, Feb.-Sept. 1974; PPS to Sir Fitzroy Maclean, Bt, CBE, MP, when Under-Sec. of State for War, 1954–57. Contested (C Ind. Democrat) Redbridge, Ilford N, March 1978 and (C, independently), 1979. Member: Royal Commn on the Penal System, 1964–66; Home Sec.'s Adv. Council on the Employment of Prisoners; Gen. Council, Institute for Study and Treatment of Delinquency. Underwriting Mem. of Lloyd's. *Publications:* Disturbers of the Peace, 1962; Money, Politics and You, 1963. *Address:* 34 Cheyne Row, SW3; La Voûte, Montignac-le-Coq, 16390 St Séverin, France.

IRENS, Alfred Norman, CBE 1969; Chairman: British Electrotechnical Approvals Board for Household Equipment, 1974–84; British Approvals Board for Telecommunications, 1982–84; *b* 28 Feb. 1911; *s* of Max Henry and Guinevere Emily Irens; *m* 1934, Joan Elizabeth, *d* of John Knight, FRIBA, Worsley, Manchester; two *s*. *Educ:* Blundell's Sch., Tiverton; Faraday House, London. College apprentice, Metropolitan Vickers, Ltd, Manchester. Subsequently with General Electric Co., Ltd, until joining Bristol Aeroplane Co., Ltd, 1939, becoming Chief Electrical Engineer, 1943; Consulting Engineer to Govt and other organisations, 1945–56. Part-time mem., SW Electricity Bd, 1948–56, Chm., 1956–73. Past Chm. IEE Utilization Section and IEE Western Sub-Centre; Chairman: British Electrical Development Assoc., 1962–63; SW Economic Planning Council, 1968–71. Chm., Bristol Waterworks Co., 1975–81 (Dir, 1967–81); Dir, Avon Rubber Co. Ltd, 1973–81. JP Long Ashton, Som, 1960–66. Hon. MSc Bristol, 1957. *Recreations:* general outdoor activities. *Address:* Crete Hill House, Cote House Lane, Bristol BS9 3UW. *T:* Bristol 622419.

IRESON, Rev. Canon Gordon Worley; *b* 16 April 1906; *s* of Francis Robert and Julia Letitia Ireson; *m* 1939, Dorothy Elizabeth Walker; two *s* one *d*. *Educ:* Edinburgh Theological Coll.; Hatfield Coll., Durham. Asst Curate of Sheringham, 1933–36; Senior Chaplain of St Mary's Cathedral, Edinburgh, with charge of Holy Trinity, Dean Bridge, 1936–37; Priest-Lecturer to National Soc., 1937–39; Diocesan Missioner of Exeter Diocese, 1939–46; Hon. Chaplain to Bishop of Exeter, 1941–46; Canon Residentiary of Newcastle Cathedral, 1946–58; Canon-Missioner of St Albans, 1958–73; Warden, Community of the Holy Name, 1974–82. Examining Chaplain to Bishop of Newcastle, 1949–59. *Publications:* Church Worship and the Non-Churchgoer, 1945; Think Again, 1949; How Shall They Hear?, 1957; Strange Victory, 1970; Handbook of Parish Preaching, 1982. *Recreation:* making and mending in the workshop. *Address:* St Barnabas College, Blackberry Lane, Lingfield, Surrey RH7 6NJ.

IRISH, Sir Ronald (Arthur), Kt 1970; OBE 1963; Partner, Irish Young & Outhwaite, Chartered Accountants, retired; Chairman, Rothmans of Pall Mall (Australia) Ltd, 1955–81, retired; *b* 26 March 1913; *s* of late Arthur Edward Irish; *m* 1960, Noella Jean Austin Fraser; three *s*. *Educ:* Fort Street High School. Chm., Manufacturing Industries Adv. Council, 1966–72. Pres., Inst. of Chartered Accountants in Australia, 1956–58; Pres., Tenth Internat. Congress of Accountants, 1972; Life Member: Australian Soc. of Accountants, 1972; Inst. of Chartered Accountants in Australia, 1974. Hon. Fellow, Univ. of Sydney, 1986. *Publications:* Practical Auditing, 1935; Auditing, 1947, new edn 1972. *Recreations:* walking, swimming. *Address:* 3/110 Elizabeth Bay Road, Elizabeth Bay, NSW 2011, Australia. *Clubs:* Australian, Union (Sydney).

IRONSIDE, family name of **Baron Ironside.**

IRONSIDE, 2nd Baron, *cr* 1941, of Archangel and of Ironside; **Edmund Oslac Ironside;** Market Co-ordinator (Defence), NEI plc, since 1985; *b* 21 Sept. 1924; *o s* of 1st Baron Ironside, Field Marshal, GCB, CMG, DSO, and Mariot Ysabel Cheyne (*d* 1984); *S* father, 1959; *m* 1950, Audrey Marigold, *y d* of late Lt-Col Hon. Thomas Morgan-Grenville, DSO, OBE, MC; one *s* one *d*. *Educ:* Tonbridge Sch. Joined Royal Navy, 1943; retd as Lt, 1952. English Electric Gp, 1952–63; Cryosystems Ltd, 1963–68; International Research and Development Co., 1968–84. Vice-Pres., Parly and Scientific Cttee, 1984– (Dep. Chm., 1974–77). Mem., Organising Cttee, British Library, 1971–72. President: Electric Vehicle Assoc., 1976–83; European Electric Road Vehicle Assoc., 1980–82; Vice-Pres., Inst. of Patentees and Inventors, 1977; Chm., Adv. Cttee, Science Reference Lib., 1976–84. Governor, Tonbridge Sch. and others; Mem. Ct: City Univ., 1971–; Essex Univ., 1982–. Master, Skinners' Co., 1981–82. *Publication:* (ed) High Road to Command: the diaries of Major-General Sir Edmund Ironside, 1920–22, 1972. *Heir: s* Hon. Charles Edmund Grenville Ironside [*b* 1 July 1956; *m* 1985, Hon. Elizabeth Law, *e d* of Lord Coleraine, *qv*]. *Address:* Broomwood Manor, Chignal St James, Chelmsford, Essex. *T:* Chelmsford 440231. *Club:* Royal Ocean Racing.

IRONSIDE, Christopher, OBE 1971; FRBS; Artist and Designer; *b* 11 July 1913; *s* of Dr R. W. Ironside and Mrs P. L. Williamson (2nd *m*; *née* Cunliffe); *m* 1st, 1939, Janey (*née* Acheson) (marriage dissolved, 1961); one *d*; 2nd, 1961, Jean (*née* Marsden); one *s* two *d*. *Educ:* Central Sch. of Arts and Crafts. Served War of 1939–45, Dep. Sen. Design Off., Directorate of Camouflage, Min. of Home Security. In charge of Educn Sect., Coun. of Industrial Design, 1946–48; part-time Teacher, Royal College of Art, 1953–63. Paintings in public and private collections. *One-man shows:* Redfern Gall., 1941; Arthur Jeffries Gall., 1960. *Design work includes:* Royal Coat of Arms, Whitehall and decorations in Pall Mall, Coronation, 1953; coinages for Tanzania, Brunei, Qatar, Dubai and Singapore (reverses, 1985); reverses for Decimal Coinage, UK and Jamaican; many medals, coins and awards; theatrical work (with brother, late R. C. Ironside); various clocks, coats of arms and tapestries; firegrate for Goldsmiths' Co.; brass and marble meml to 16th Duke of Norfolk, Arundel; meml to Earl and Countess Mountbatten of Burma, Westminster

Abbey. FSIA 1970; FRBS 1977. *Recreation:* trying to keep abreast of modern scientific development. *Address:* 22 Abingdon Villas, W8. *T:* 01–937 9418; Church Farm House, Smannell, near Andover, Hants. *T:* Andover 2309.

IRVINE, Alan Montgomery, RDI; DesRCA, ARIBA; architect in private practice; *b* 14 Sept. 1926; *s* of Douglas Irvine and Ellen Marler; *m* 1st, 1955; one *s*; 2nd, 1966, Katherine Mary Buzas; two *s*. *Educ:* Regent Street Polytechnic, Secondary Sch. and Sch. of Architecture; Royal College of Art. RAF (Aircrew), 1944–47. Worked in Milan with BBPR Gp, 1954–55. In private practice since 1956, specialising in design of interiors, museums and exhibitions; formed partnership Buzas and Irvine in 1965. Work has included interior design for Schroder Wagg & Co., Lazards, Bovis, S Australian Govt, Nat. Enterprise Bd; Mem. of design team for QE2, 1966. Various exhibns for V&A Museum, Tate Gallery, Royal Academy, Imperial War Museum, RIBA, British Council, Olivetti etc. including: Treasures of Cambridge, 1959; Book of Kells, 1961; Architecture of Power, 1963; Mellon Collection, 1969; Age of Charles I, 1972; Pompeii AD79, 1976; Gold of El Dorado, 1978; Horses of San Marco (London, NY, Milan, Berlin), 1979–82; Great Japan Exhibition, 1981; Art and Industry, 1982; Cimabue Crucifix (London, Madrid, Munich), 1982–83; Treasures of Ancient Nigeria, 1983; The Genius of Venice, 1983; Leonardo da Vinci: studies for the Last Supper (Milan, Sydney, Toronto, Barcelona, Tokyo), 1984; Art of the Architect, 1984; Re dei Confessori (Milan, Venice), 1985; C. S. Jagger: War and Peace Sculpture, 1985; New Architecture, 1986; Queen Elizabeth II: portraits of 60 years, 1986; Eye for Industry, 1986. Museum work includes: Old Master Drawings Gallery, Windsor Castle, 1965; New Galleries for Royal Scottish Museum, 1968; Crown Jewels display, Tower of London, 1968; Treasuries at Winchester Cathedral, 1968, Christ Church, Oxford, 1975, and Winchester College, 1982; Heinz Gallery for Architectural Drawings, RIBA, London, 1972; Museum and Art Gallery for Harrow School, 1975; Heralds' Museum, London, 1980; Al Shaheed Museum, Baghdad, 1983; Cabinet War Rooms, London, 1984; West Wing Galls, Nat. Maritime Mus., Greenwich, 1986. Consultant designer to Olivetti, Italy; Consultant architect to British Museum, 1981–84. Mem., Crafts Council, 1984–. Liveryman, Worshipful Co. of Goldsmiths. Hon. Fellow, RCA. *Recreations:* travel, photography. *Address:* 2 Aubrey Place, St John's Wood, NW8 9BH. *T:* 01–328 2229.

IRVINE, Alexander Andrew Mackay; QC 1978; a Recorder, since 1985; *b* 23 June 1940; *s* of Alexander Irvine and Margaret Christina Irvine; *m* 1974, Alison Mary, *y d* of Dr James Shaw McNair, MD, and Agnes McNair, MA; two *s*. *Educ:* Inverness Acad.; Hutchesons' Boys' Grammar Sch., Glasgow; Glasgow Univ. (MA, LLB); Christ's Coll., Cambridge (Scholar; BA 1st Cl. Hons with distinction; LLB 1st Cl. Hons; George Long Prize in Jurisprudence). Called to the Bar, Inner Temple, 1967, Bencher, 1985; Univ. Lectr, LSE, 1965–69. Contested (Lab) Hendon North, Gen. Election, 1970. *Recreation:* collecting paintings. *Address:* 11 King's Bench Walk, Temple, EC4Y 7EQ. *T:* 01–583 0610. *Club:* Garrick.

IRVINE, Rt. Hon. Sir Bryant Godman, Kt 1986; PC 1982; Barrister-at-Law; Farmer; *b* Toronto, 25 July 1909; *s* of late W. Henry Irvine and late Ada Mary Bryant Irvine, formerly of St Agnes, Cornwall; *m* 1945, Valborg Cecilie, *d* of late P. F. Carslund; two *d*. *Educ:* Upper Canada Coll.; St Paul's Sch.; Magdalen Coll., Oxford (MA). Sec. Oxford Union Soc., 1931. Called to Bar. Inner Temple, 1932. Chm. Agricultural Land Tribunal, SE Province, 1954–56. Mem. Executive Cttee, East Sussex NFU, 1947–84; Branch Chm., 1956–58. Chm. Young Conservative Union, 1946–47; Prospective Candidate, Bewdley Div. of Worcs, 1947–49; contested Wood Green and Lower Tottenham, 1951. MP (C) Rye Div., E Sussex, 1955–83; PPS to Minister of Education and to Parly Sec., Ministry of Education, 1957–59, to the Financial Sec. to the Treasury, 1959–60. Mem., Speaker's Panel of Chairmen, House of Commons, 1965–76; a Dep. Chm. of Ways and Means, and a Deputy Speaker, 1976–82; Jt Sec., Exec. Cttee, 1922 Cttee, 1965–68, Hon. Treasurer, 1974–76; Vice-Chm., Cons. Agric. Cttee, and spoke on Agriculture from Opposition Front Bench, 1964–70; Mem., House of Commons Select Cttee on Agriculture, 1967–69; Commonwealth Parliamentary Association: Hon. Treasurer, 1970–73; Mem., General Council, 1970–73; Mem., Exec. Cttee, UK Branch, 1964–76; Jt Sec. or Vice-Chm., Cons. Commonwealth Affairs Cttee, 1957–66; Jt Sec., Foreign and Commonwealth Affairs Cttee, 1967–73 (Vice-Chm., 1973–76); Chm., Cons. Horticulture Sub-Cttee, 1960–62; All Party Tourist and Resort Cttee, 1964–66. President: British Resorts Assoc., 1962–80; Southern Counties Agricl Trading Soc., 1983–. Served War of 1939–45, Lt-Comdr RNVR, afloat and on staff of C-in-C Western Approaches and Commander US Naval Forces in Europe. Comp. InstCE, 1936–74. *Recreations:* ski-ing, travel by sea. *Address:* Great Ote Hall, Burgess Hill, West Sussex. *T:* Burgess Hill 2179; 91 Millbank Court, 24 John Islip Street, SW1. *T:* 01–834 9221; 2 Dr Johnson's Buildings, Temple, EC4. *Clubs:* Carlton, Pratt's, Naval.

IRVINE, Dr Donald Hamilton, OBE 1979; FRCGP; Principal in General Practice, Ashington, since 1960; Regional Adviser in General Practice, University of Newcastle, since 1973; *b* 2 June 1935; *s* of Dr Andrew Bell Hamilton Irvine and Dorothy Mary Irvine; *m* 1960; two *s* one *d*; *m* 1986, Sally Fountain. *Educ:* King Edward Sixth Grammar Sch., Morpeth; Medical Sch., King's Coll., Univ. of Durham (MB BS); DObstRCOG 1960; MD Newcastle 1964; FRCGP 1972 (MRCGP 1965). Ho. Phys. to Dr C. N. Armstrong and Dr Henry Miller, 1958–59. Chm. Council, RCGP, 1982–85 (Vice-Chm., 1981–82); Hon. Sec. of the College, 1972–78; Jt Hon. Sec., Jt Cttee on Postgraduate Trng for General Practice, 1976–82; Fellow, BMA, 1976; Mem., Gen. Medical Council, 1979– (Chm., Cttee on Standards and Medical Ethics); Governor, MSD Foundn, 1982– (Chm., Bd of Governors, 1983). Vice-Pres., Medical Defence Union, 1974–78; Vis. Professor in Family Practice, Univ. of Iowa, USA, 1973; (first) Vis. Prof. to Royal Australian Coll. of General Practitioners, 1977; Vis. Cons. on Postgrad. Educn for Family Medicine to Virginia Commonwealth Univ., 1971, Univ. of Wisconsin-Madison, 1973, Medical Univ. of S Carolina, 1974. *Publications:* The Future General Practitioner: learning and teaching, (jtly), 1972 (RCGP); chapters to several books on gen. practice; papers on clinical and educnl studies in medicine, in BMJ, Lancet, Jl of RCGP. *Recreations:* bird watching, motor cars, politics, watching television. *Address:* Mole End, Fairmoor, Morpeth NE61 3JL; 25 Finchley Park, N12 9JS.

IRVINE, Surg. Captain Gerard Sutherland, CBE 1970; RN retired; Medical Officer, Department of Health and Social Security, 1971–78; *b* 19 June 1913; *s* of Major Gerard Byrom Corrie Irvine and Maud Andrée (*née* Wylde); *m* 1939, Phyllis Lucy Lawrie; one *s*. *Educ:* Imperial Service Coll., Windsor; Epsom Coll.; University Coll. and Hosp., London. MRCS, LRCP, MB, BS 1937; DLO 1940; FRCS 1967. Jenks Meml Schol. 1932; Liston Gold Medal for Surgery 1936. Surg. Sub-Lt RNVR 1935, Surg. Lt RNVR 1937; Surg Lt RN 1939; Surg. Lt-Comdr 1944; Surg. Comdr 1953; Surg. Capt. 1963. Served War of 1939–45 (1939–45 Star, Atlantic Star with Bar for France and Germany, Burma Star, Defence Medal, Victory Medal); subseq. service: Ceylon, 1946; Haslar, 1947–49 and 1957–60; Malta, 1953–56; HMS: Maidstone (Submarine Depot Ship), 1949–51; Osprey (T&A/S Trng Sch.), 1951–53; Collingwood, 1956–57; Lion, 1960–62; Vernon (Torpedo Sch.), 1962–63; Sen. Cons. in ENT, 1953–70; Adviser in ENT to Med. Dir-Gen. (Navy), 1966–70; Sen. MO i/c Surgical Div., RN Hosp. Haslar, 1966–70; QHS 1969–70; retd 1970. Member: BMA 1938; Sections of Otology and Laryngology, RSM, 1948–77 (FRSM 1948–77); British Assoc. of Otolaryngologists, 1945–71 (Council, 1958–70); S Western Laryngological Assoc., 1951–71; Hearing Sub-Cttee of RN Personnel Res. Cttee, 1947–70; Otological Sub-Cttee of RAF Flying Personnel Res. Cttee, 1963–70. OStJ 1969. *Publications:* numerous articles in various medical jls. *Recreations:* gardening, philately, do-it-yourself. *Address:* 9 Alvara Road, Alverstoke, Gosport PO12 2HY. *T:* Gosport 580342.

IRVINE, James Eccles Malise; His Honour Judge Irvine; a Circuit Judge, since 1972 (Leicester County and Crown Courts, 1972–82; Oxford and Northampton County and Crown Courts, since 1982); *b* 10 July 1925; *y s* of late Brig.-Gen. A. E. Irvine, CB, CMG, DSO, Wotton-under-Edge; *m* 1954, Anne, *e d* of late Col G. Egerton-Warburton, DSO, TD, JP, DL, Grafton Hall, Malpas; one *s* one *d*. *Educ:* Stowe Sch. (Scholar); Merton Coll., Oxford (Postmaster). MA Oxon. Served Grenadier Guards, 1943–46 (France and Germany Star); Hon. Captain Grenadier Guards, 1946. Called to Bar, Inner Temple, 1949 (Poland Prizeman in Criminal Law, 1949); practised Oxford Circuit, 1949–71; Prosecuting Counsel for Inland Revenue on Oxford Circuit, 1965–71; Dep. Chm., Glos QS, 1967–71. Lay Judge of Court of Arches of Canterbury and Chancery Court of York, 1981–. *Publication:* Parties and Pleasures: the Diaries of Helen Graham 1823–26, 1957. *Address:* 2 Harcourt Buildings, Temple, EC4; c/o Oxford County Court, St Aldate's, Oxford OX1 1TL.

IRVINE, Maj.-Gen. John, OBE 1955; Director of Medical Services, British Army of the Rhine, 1973–75; *b* 31 May 1914; *s* of late John Irvine and late Jessie Irvine (*née* McKinnon); *m* 1941, Mary McNicol, *d* of late Andrew Brown Cossar, Glasgow; one *d*. *Educ:* Glasgow High Sch.; Glasgow Univ. MB, ChB 1940. MFCM 1973. Commnd into RAMC, 1940; served War of 1939–45 (despatches and Act of Gallantry, 1944): Egypt, Greece, Crete, Western Desert, 1941–43; Sicily, Italy and Yugoslavia, 1943–45; served with British Troops, Austria, 1947–49; Korea, 1953–54 (OBE); Malaya, 1954–56 (despatches); Germany, 1958–61; Ghana, 1961; Germany, 1962–64; DDMS, HQ BAOR, 1968–69; DDMS, 1st British Corps, 1969–71; Dep. Dir-Gen., AMS, 1971–73. QHS 1972–75. OStJ 1971. *Recreations:* tennis, ski-ing. *Address:* Greenlawns, 11 Manor Road, Aldershot, Hants GU11 3DG. *T:* Aldershot 311524.

IRVINE, John Ferguson, CB 1983; Chief Executive, Industrial Therapy Organisation (Ulster), since 1984; *b* 13 Nov. 1920; *s* of Joseph Ferguson Irvine and Helen Gardner; *m* 1st, 1945, Doris Partridge (*d* 1973); one *s* one *d*; 2nd, 1980, Christine Margot Tudor; two *s* and two step *s*. *Educ:* Ardrossan Acad.; Glasgow Univ. (MA). RAF, 1941–46; Scottish Home Dept, 1946–48; NI Civil Service, 1948–66; Chief Exec., Ulster Transport Authority, 1966–68; Chief Exec., NI Transport Holding Co., 1968; NI Civil Service, 1969–83; Dep. Sec., DoE, NI, 1971–76; Permanent Secretary: attached NI Office, 1977–80; Dept of Manpower Services, 1980–81; DoE for NI, 1981–83. Chm. Management Cttee, 1974–75, and Vice-Chm. General Council, 1975, Action Cancer; Member: NI Marriage Guidance Council (Chm., 1976–78); Council, PHAB (NI), 1984–; Council, PHAB (UK), 1984–. Mem., Select Vestry, Down Parish Church, Downpatrick. *Recreations:* distance running, yoga, Majorca, football. *Address:* c/o Allied Irish Banks, 12/16 Donegall Square East, Belfast BT1 5HE.

IRVINE, Very Rev. (John) Murray; Provost and Rector of Southwell Minster, since 1978; *b* 19 Aug. 1924; *s* of Andrew Leicester Irvine and Eleanor Mildred (*née* Lloyd); *m* 1961, Pamela Shirley Brain; one *s* three *d*. *Educ:* Charterhouse; Magdalene Coll., Cambridge; Ely Theological Coll. BA 1946, MA 1949. Deacon, 1948; Priest, 1949; Curate of All Saints, Poplar, 1948–53; Chaplain of Sidney Sussex Coll., Cambridge, 1953–60; Selection Sec. of CACTM, 1960–65; Canon Residentiary, Prebendary of Hunderton, Chancellor and Librarian of Hereford Cathedral, and Dir of Ordination Training, Diocese of Hereford, 1965–78; Warden of Readers, 1976–78. *Address:* The Residence, Vicars Court, Southwell, Notts NG25 0HP. *T:* Southwell 812593.

IRVINE, Norman Forrest, QC 1973; a Recorder of the Crown Court, since 1974; *b* 29 Sept. 1922; *s* of William Allan Irvine and Dorcas Forrest; *m* 1964, Mary Lilian Patricia Edmunds (*née* Constable); one *s*. *Educ:* High Sch. of Glasgow; Glasgow Univ. BL 1941. Solicitor (Scotland), 1943. Served War, 1942–45: Lieut Royal Signals, Staff Captain. HM Claims Commn, 1945–46; London Claims Supt, Provincial Insurance Co. Ltd, 1950–52. Called to Bar, Gray's Inn, 1955. *Recreations:* reading, piano, walking, swimming. *Address:* (chambers) 2 Garden Court, Temple, EC4Y 9BL.

IRVINE, Dr Robin Orlando Hamilton, FRCP, FRACP; Vice-Chancellor, University of Otago, Dunedin, New Zealand, since 1973; *b* 15 Sept. 1929; *s* of late Claude Turner Irvine; *m* 1957, Elizabeth Mary, *d* of late Herbert Gray Corbett; one *s* two *d*. *Educ:* Wanganui Collegiate Sch.; Univ. of Otago. Otago University Med. Sch., 1948–53; MB, ChB, 1953; MD (NZ), 1958; FRCP, FRACP. House Phys., Auckland Hosp., 1954; Dept of Medicine, Univ. of Otago: Research Asst (Emily Johnston Res. Schol.), 1955; Asst Lectr and Registrar, 1956–57. Leverhulme Research Scholar, Middlesex Hosp., London, 1958; Registrar, Postgraduate Medical Sch., London, 1959–60; Isaacs Medical Research Fellow, Auckland Hosp., 1960–61; Med. Tutor and Med. Specialist, Auckland Hosp., 1962–63; Lectr, Sen. Lectr in Med., Univ. of Otago, 1963–67; Associate Prof., 1968; Clinical Dean and Personal Professor, Univ. of Otago Medical Sch., 1969–72. Consultant, Asian Development Bank, 1974–. Member: Selwyn Coll. Bd, 1966–; Pharmacology and Therapeutic Cttee, Min. of Health, 1967–73; Otago Hosp. Bd, 1969–; Med. Educn Cttee of Med. Council of NZ, 1969–73; Cent. Educn Cttee, NZ Med. Assoc., 1970–73; Social Council of Nat. Develt Council of NZ, 1971–74; Cttee on Nursing Educn, Min. of Educn, 1972; Social Develt Council, 1974–79; Commn for the Future, 1976–80; NZ Planning Council, 1977–82; Council, Assoc. of Commonwealth Univs, 1979–80; Otago Polytech. Council, 1973–; Dunedin Teachers Coll. Council, 1973–; NZ Adv. Cttee, Nuffield Foundn, 1973–81; NZ Rhodes Scholarships Selection Cttee, 1976–81; Chairman: Otago Med. Res. Foundn, 1975–81; Ministerial working party on novel genetic techniques, 1977; NZ Vice-Chancellors' Cttee, 1979–80; Convenor, Med. Educn Mission to Univ. of S Pacific, 1971; Dir, Otago Develt Corp., 1982–85; Trustee: McMillan Trust, 1973– (Chm., 1977–); Rowheath Trust, 1973–. Hon. ADC 1969, and Hon. Physician 1970, to the Governor-General, Sir Arthur Porritt. Hon. Mem., Australian Soc. of Nephrology. Dr *hc* Edinburgh, 1976. FRSA 1980; FNZIM 1984. Queen's Silver Jubilee Medal, 1977. Mem. Editorial Bd, Jl of Molecular Medicine. *Publications:* various papers on high blood pressure, renal med. and medical educn. *Recreations:* walking, reading, music. *Address:* University Lodge, St Leonards, Dunedin, New Zealand. *T:* 710.541. *Club:* Fernhill (Dunedin).

IRVING, family name of **Baron Irving of Dartford.**

IRVING OF DARTFORD, Baron *cr* 1979 (Life Peer), of Dartford in the County of Kent; **Sydney Irving;** PC 1969; DL; *b* 1 July 1918; *s* of Sydney Irving, Newcastle upon Tyne; *m* 1942, Mildred, *d* of Charlton Weedy, Morpeth, Northumberland; one *s* one *d* (and one *s* decd). *Educ:* Pendower Sch., Newcastle upon Tyne; London School of Economics, University of London. BSc (Econ.); DipEd. War Service, 1939–46: West Yorks Regt, Major. Chairman Southern Regional Council of Labour Party, 1965–67. Alderman, Dartford Borough Council; Mem. North-West Kent Divisional Executive, Kent

Education Cttee, 1952–74. MP (Lab and Co-op) Dartford, 1955–70 and Feb. 1974–1979; Opposition Whip (S and S Western), 1959–64; Treasurer of the Household and Deputy Chief Government Whip, 1964–66; Dep. Chm. of Ways and Means, 1966–68; Chm. of Ways and Means, and Deputy Speaker, 1968–70; Chairman Select Committees: on Procedure, 1974–79; on Direct Elections to EEC, 1976–77; Chm., Manifesto Gp, 1976–77; Member: Cttee of Privileges, 1974–79; Select Cttee on Members' Interests, 1974–79; Select Cttee on the Member for Walsall, 1975; Liaison Cttee, Parly Lab Party, 1976–79. Mem. CPA delegations: to Hong Kong and Ceylon, 1958; to Council of Europe and WEU, 1963–64; to Canada, 1974; Leader All Party Delegn: to Malta, 1965; to Israel, 1975; to Australia, 1978. Mem. Exec. Cttee, Council European Municipalities 1972–77. Chairman: Dartford Dist Council, 1973–74; Dartford and Darenth Hosp. Management Cttee, 1972–74; Kent County Jt Cttee Chairman, 1967–77. Vice-Chm., Nat. Assoc. of CAB, 1979–. Pres., Thames-side Assoc. of Teachers, NUT, 1955; Mem. Min. of Education's Adv. Cttee on Handicapped Children, 1957–67; a Dep. Pro-Chancellor, Univ. of Kent, 1968–71; Dir, Foundn Fund, Univ. of Kent, 1971–74. Chm., Industry and Parlt Trust, 1982–. DL Kent, 1976. *Address:* 10 Tynedale Close, Dartford, Kent. *T:* 25105.

IRVING, Charles Graham; MP (C) Cheltenham, since Oct. 1974; Consultant on Public Affairs, Dowty Group PLC; County and District Councillor. *Educ:* Glengarth Sch., Cheltenham; Lucton Sch., Hereford. Mem. Cheltenham Borough Council, 1947–74 (Alderman 1959–May 1967, and Sept. 1967–74); Mem., Cheltenham DC, 1974–; Mem. Gloucestershire CC, 1948– (Chm., Social Services Cttee, 1974–); Mayor of Cheltenham, 1958–60 and 1971–72; Dep. Mayor, 1959–63; Alderman of Gloucestershire County, 1965–74; Contested (C): Bilston, Staffs, 1970; Kingswood, Glos, Feb. 1974; Member Cons. Parly Cttees: Aviation; Social Services; Mem., Select Cttee on Administration; Chairman: Select Cttee on Catering, 1979–; All Party Mental Health Cttee, 1979–; All Party Cttee CHAR. Pres., Cheltenham Young Conservatives. Dir, Cheltenham Art and Literary Festival Co. (responsible for the only contemp. Festival of Music in England); Founder Mem., Univ. Cttee for Gloucestershire; Pres., Cheltenham and Dist Hotels' Assoc. Member: Bridgehead Housing Assoc. Ltd; Nat. Council for the Care and Resettlement of Offenders (Nat. Dep. Chm., 1974); (Chm.) NACRO Regional Council for South West; Nat. Council of St Leonard's Housing Assoc. Ltd; (Chm.) SW Midlands Housing Assoc. Ltd; SW Regional Hosp. Bd, 1971–72; Glos AHA, 1974–; (Chm.) Cheltenham and Dist Housing Assoc. Ltd, 1972; (Chm.) Cheltenham Dist Local Govt Re-Organisation Cttee, 1972; Founder and Chm., Nat. Victims Assoc., 1973; Chm., Stonham Housing Assoc., 1976–. Chairman: Irving Hotels Ltd; Irving Engineering Co. Mem. NUJ; MIPR 1964. Freedom, Borough of Cheltenham, 1977. *Publications:* pamphlets (as Chm. SW Region of NACRO and SW Midlands Housing Assoc. Ltd, 1970–73) include: Prisoner and Industry; After-care in the Community; Penal Budgeting; What about the Victim; Dosser's Dream—Planner's Nightmare. Pioneered Frontsheet (1st prison newspaper); reported in national papers, Quest, Social Services, Glos. Life, etc. *Recreations:* antiques, social work. *Address:* 10 Montpellier Grove, Cheltenham, Glos. *T:* Cheltenham 523083. *Club:* St Stephen's Constitutional.

IRVING, Clifford; *see* Irving, E. C.

IRVING, Rear-Adm. Sir Edmund (George), KBE 1966 (OBE 1944); CB 1962; Hydrographer of the Navy, 1960–66, retired; *b* 5 April 1910; *s* of George Clerk Irving, British North Borneo, and Ethel Mary Frances (*née* Poole), Kimberley, SA; *m* 1st, 1936, Margaret Scudamore Edwards (*d* 1974); one *s* one *d*; 2nd, 1979, Esther Rebecca Ellison. *Educ:* St Anthony's, Eastbourne; RN College, Dartmouth. Joined HMS Royal Oak, as Cadet and Midshipman, 1927; Sub-Lieut's Courses, 1930–31; HMS Kellett Surveying Service, Dec. 1931 (various surveying ships); HMS Franklin, in command, 1944; Hydrographic Dept, 1946; HMS Sharpshooter, in command, 1948; Hydrographic Dept, 1949; HMS Dalrymple, in command, 1950; HMS Vidal, in command, 1953; Hydrographic Dept, Asst Hydrographer, 1954; HMS Vidal, in command, Oct. 1956; Hydrographic Dept, Asst Hydrographer, 1959. Acting Conservator of the River Mersey, 1975–85. ADC, 1960. Trustee, Nat. Maritime Museum, 1972–81. FRGS; FRICS; FRSA. Patron's Medal, RGS, 1976. *Recreation:* golf. *Address:* Camer Green, Meopham, Kent DA13 0XR. *T:* Meopham 813253. *Club:* Army and Navy.

IRVING, Edward, ScD; FRS 1979; FRSC 1973; FRAS; Research Scientist, Pacific Geoscience Centre, Sidney, BC, since 1981; *b* 27 May 1927; *s* of George Edward and Nellie Irving; *m* 1957, Sheila Ann Irwin; two *s* two *d*. *Educ:* Colne Grammar Sch.; Cambridge Univ., 1948–54 (BA, MA, MSc, ScD). Served Army, 1945–48. Research Fellow, Fellow and Sen. Fellow, ANU, 1954–64; Dominion Observatory, Canada, 1964–66; Prof. of Geophysics, Univ. of Leeds, 1966–67; Res. Scientist, Dominion Observatory, later Earth Physics Br., Dept of Energy, Mines and Resources, Ottawa, 1967–81; Adjunct Professor: Carleton Univ., Ottawa, 1975–81; Univ. of Victoria, 1985–. FRAS 1958; Fellow: Amer. Geophysical Union, 1976 (Walter H. Bucher Medal, 1979); Geological Soc. of America, 1979. Hon. DSc Carleton, 1979. Gondwanaland Medal, Mining, Geological and Metallurgical Soc. of India, 1962; Logan Medal, Geol Assoc. of Canada, 1975; J. T. Wilson Medal, Canadian Geophys. Union, 1984. *Publications:* Paleomagnetism, 1964; numerous contribs to learned jls. *Recreations:* gardening, carpentry, choral singing. *Address:* Pacific Geoscience Centre, 9860 West Saanich Road, Box 6000, Sidney, BC V8L 4B2, Canada. *T:* (604) 656–8208; 9363 Carnoustie Crescent, Sidney, BC V8L 3S1. *T:* (604) 656–9645.

IRVING, (Edward) Clifford, CBE 1981; Chairman, Executive Council, Isle of Man Government 1977–81 (Member, 1968–81); Member, House of Keys, 1955–61, 1966–81 and since 1984; Acting Speaker, 1971–81; *b* 24 May 1914; *s* of late William Radcliffe Irving and Mabel Henrietta (*née* Cottier); *m* 1941, Nora, *d* of Harold Page, Luton; one *s* one *d*. *Educ:* Isle of Man; Canada. Member, IOM Government Boards: Airports, 1955–58; Assessment, 1955–56; Social Security, 1956; Local Govt, 1956–62; Tourist, 1956–62; Finance, 1966–71; Member: Industrial Adv. Council, 1961–62, 1971–81; CS Commn, 1976–81. Chairman: IOM Tourist Bd, 1971–81; IOM Sports Council, 1971–81; IOM Harbours Bd, 1985–. Chm., Commercial Bank of Wales (IOM), 1985–. President: IOM Assoc. of Veteran Athletes; Wanderers Male Voice Choir; Manx Nat. Powerboat Club. Patron: Manx Variety Club; IOM TT Races. *Recreations:* powerboating, angling. *Address:* Highfield, Belmont Hill, Douglas, Isle of Man. *T:* Douglas 3652.

IRVING, Prof. Harry Munroe Napier Hetherington; Professor of Inorganic and Structural Chemistry, University of Leeds, 1961–71, Professor Emeritus, since 1972; Professor of Analytical Science, University of Cape Town, 1979–85 (of Theoretical Chemistry, 1978); retired; *b* 19 Nov. 1905; *s* of John and Clara Irving; *m* 1st, 1934, Monica Mary Wildsmith (*d* 1972); no *c*; 2nd, 1975, Dr Anne Mawby. *Educ:* St Bees Sch., Cumberland; The Queen's Coll., Oxford. BA 1927; First Class in Final Honour Sch. (Chemistry), 1928; MA, DPhil 1930; DSc 1958 (all Oxon); LRAM 1930. Univ. Demonstrator in Chemistry, Oxford, 1934–61; Lectr in Organic Chemistry, The Queen's Coll., 1930–34; Fellow and Tutor, St Edmund Hall, 1938–51; Vice-Principal, 1951–61; Emeritus-Fellow, 1961–. Member: Chem. Soc. 1935– (Council, 1954, Perkin Elmer Award, 1974); Soc. Chm. Ind., 1935– (Gold Medal, 1980); Soc. for Analytical Chemists, 1950– (Council, 1952–57, 1965–67; Vice-Pres. 1955–57; Gold Medal, 1971); Fellow Royal Inst. of Chemistry, 1948– (Council, 1950–52, 1962–65; Vice-Pres. 1965–67); Mem., S African Chem. Inst., 1979. Has lectured extensively in America, Africa and Europe; broadcasts on scientific subjects. FRSSAf. Hon. DTech Brunel Univ., 1970. *Publications:* (trans.) Schwarzenbach and Flaschka's Complexometric Titrations; Short History of Analytical Chemistry, 1974; Dithizone, 1977; numerous papers in various learned jls. *Recreations:* music, foreign travel, ice-skating. *Address:* 1 North Grange Mount, Leeds LS6 2BY.

IRVING, James Tutin, MA Oxon and Cantab, MD, PhD Cantab; Professor of Physiology in the School of Dental Medicine at Harvard University and the Forsyth Dental Center, 1961–68, Professor Emeritus, 1968, Visiting Lecturer in Oral Biology, 1973–77; Emeritus Professor, National Institute on Aging, Baltimore, 1978–81; *b* Christchurch, New Zealand, 3 May 1902; *m* 1937, Janet, *d* of Hon. Nicholas O'Connor, New York. *Educ:* Christ's Coll., New Zealand; Caius Coll., Cambridge; Trinity Coll., Oxford; Guy's Hospital. Double First Class Hons, Nat. Sci. Tripos, Cambridge, 1923–24; Scholar and Prizeman, Caius Coll., 1923; Benn. W. Levy and Frank Smart Student, 1924–26; Beit Memorial Fellow, 1926–28; Lecturer in Physiology, Bristol Univ., 1931, and Leeds Univ., 1934; Head of Physiology Dept, Rowett Research Inst., and part-time lecturer, Aberdeen Univ., 1936; Prof. of Physiology, Cape Town Univ., 1939–53, Fellow 1948; Professor of Experimental Odontology, and Dir of the Joint CSIR and Univ. of Witwatersrand Dental Research Unit, 1953–59; Prof. of Anatomy, Harvard Sch. of Dental Med., 1959–61. Visiting Professor: Univ. of Illinois Dental Sch. 1947 and 1956; Univ. of Pennsylvania, 1951; Univ. of California, 1956. Chm., Gordon Conference on Bone and Teeth, 1969. Editor, Archives of Oral Biology, 1962–. AM (Hon.) Harvard. Late Hon. Physiologist to Groote Schuur Hosp.; Fellow Odont. Soc. S Africa. Hon. Life Mem. of New York Academy of Sciences. Mem. of Soc. of Sigma Xi. Hon. Mem. of Soc. of Omicron Kappa Upsilon. S African Medal for war services (non-military), 1948. Isaac Schour Meml Award for Res. in Anatomical Scis, 1972. *Publications:* Calcium Metabolism, 1957; Calcium and Phosphorus Metabolism, 1973; many papers in physiological and medical journals, chiefly on nutrition, and bone and tooth formation; also publications on nautical history. *Recreations:* music, gardening, nautical research. *Address:* (home) 5 Peele House Square, Manchester, Mass 01944, USA; (office) 140 The Fenway, Boston, Mass 02115, USA. *Club:* Inanda (Johannesburg).

IRVING, Prof. John; Freeland Professor of Natural Philosophy (Theoretical Physics), University of Strathclyde, Glasgow, 1961–84; retired; *b* 22 Dec. 1920; *s* of John Irving and Margaret Kent Aird; *m* 1948, Monica Cecilia Clarke; two *s*. *Educ:* St John's Grammar Sch.; Hamilton Academy; Glasgow Univ. MA (1st Class Hons in Maths and Nat. Phil.), Glasgow Univ., 1940; PhD (Mathematical Physics), Birmingham Univ., 1951. FInstP 1980. Lectr, Stow Coll., Glasgow, 1944–45; Lectr in Maths, Univ. of St Andrews 1945–46; Lectr in Mathematical Physics, University of Birmingham, 1946–49; Nuffield Research Fellow (Nat. Phil.), University of Glasgow, 1949–51; Sen. Lectr in Applied Maths, University of Southampton, 1951–59; Prof. of Theoretical Physics and Head of Dept of Applied Mathematics and Theor. Physics University of Cape Town, 1959–61. Dean of Sch. of Mathematics and Physics, Strathclyde Univ., 1964–69. *Publications:* Mathematics in Physics and Engineering, 1959 (New York); contrib. to: Proc. Physical Soc.; Philosophical Magazine, Physical Review. *Recreations:* gardening, motoring. *Address:* 15 Leeburn Avenue, Houston, Renfrewshire PA6 7DN. *T:* Bridge of Weir 614549.

IRVING, Laurence Henry Forster, OBE; RDI 1939; *b* 11 April 1897; *s* of late H. B. Irving, actor and author; *m* 1920, Rosalind Woolner (*d* 1978); one *s* one *d*. *Educ:* by Thomas Pellatt; Royal Academy Schools. Served in RNAS and RAF, 1914–19 (Croix de Guerre, France); rejoined RAF Oct. 1939; served on Staff of British Air Forces in France, 1940 (despatches), and in 2nd Tactical Air Force, France, Belgium, 1943–44. Dir of the Times Publishing Co., 1946–62. Exhibited pictures at Royal Academy; held four exhibitions at the Fine Art Soc., 1925, 1928, 1936, 1950, and at Agnew and Sons, 1957; Art Dir to Douglas Fairbanks, 1928 and 1929, for film productions of The Iron Mask and The Taming of the Shrew; has designed a number of stage and film productions, including Pygmalion, Lean Harvest, The Good Companions, Punchinello, The First Gentleman, Marriage à la Mode, Hamlet (Old Vic), 1950, Man and Superman, 1951; The Happy Marriage, 1952; Pygmalion, 1953; The Wild Duck, 1955; produced and designed film production of Lefanu's Uncle Silas. Master of Faculty, RDI, 1963–65. *Publications:* Windmills and Waterways, 1927; Henry Irving: The Actor and his World, 1951; The Successors, 1967; The Precarious Crust, 1971; Great Interruption, 1983; edited and illustrated: The Maid of Athens; Bligh's narrative of The Mutiny of the Bounty; A Selection of Hakluyt's Voyages; illustrated: Masefield's Philip the King; Conrad's The Mirror of the Sea; St Exupéry's Flight to Arras. *Address:* The Lea, Wittersham, Kent. *Club:* Garrick.

IRVING, Robert Augustine, DFC and Bar, 1943; Musical Director, New York City Ballet, New York, 1958; *b* 28 Aug. 1913; *s* of late R. L. G. Irving; unmarried. *Educ:* Winchester; New Coll., Oxford; Royal College of Music. Répétiteur, Royal Opera House, 1936; Music master, Winchester Coll., 1936–40. RA, 1940–41; RAF (Coastal Command), 1941–45. Associate Conductor, BBC Scottish Orchestra, 1945–48; Conductor, Royal Opera House (The Royal Ballet), 1949–58. Many recordings for HMV and Decca, with Philharmonia and Royal Philharmonic Orchestras, also public concerts with these orchestras, London Philharmonic Orchestra and leading Amer. symphony orchestras. Wrote music for film, Floodtide, 1948; for New York production of As You Like It, 1949. Capezio Award, 1975; Dance Magazine Award, 1984. *Recreations:* racing, bridge, mountaineering. *Address:* c/o New York City Ballet, New York State Theatre, Columbus Avenue and 62nd Street, New York, NY 10023, USA. *Club:* Brooks's.

IRWIN, Lord; James Charles Wood; *b* 24 Aug. 1977; *s* and *heir* of 3rd Earl of Halifax, *qv*.

IRWIN, Maj.-Gen. Brian St George, CB 1975; Director General, Ordnance Survey, 1969–77, retired; *b* 16 Sept. 1917; *s* of late Lt-Col Alfred Percy Bulteel Irwin, DSO, and late Eileen Irwin (*née* Holberton); *m* 1939, Audrey Lilla, *d* of late Lt-Col H. B. Steen, IMS; two *s*. *Educ:* Rugby Sch.; RMA Woolwich; Trinity Hall, Cambridge (MA). Commnd in RE, 1937; war service in Western Desert, 1941–43 (despatches); Sicily and Italy, 1943–44 (despatches); Greece, 1944–45; subseq. in Cyprus, 1956–59 (despatches) and 1961–63; Dir of Military Survey, MoD, 1965–69. Col Comdt, RE, 1977–82. FRICS (Council 1969–70, 1972–76); FRGS (Council 1966–70; Vice-Pres., 1974–77). *Recreations:* sailing, gardening, genealogy. *Address:* 16 Northerwood House, Swan Green, Lyndhurst, Hants SO43 7DT. *T:* Lyndhurst 3499. *Club:* Army and Navy.

IRWIN, Francis (Charles), QC 1974; a Recorder (formerly Recorder of Folkestone), since 1971; *b* 5 June 1928; *s* of late R. Stanley Irwin; *m* 1955, Rosalind Derry Wykes, *d* of late Canon W. M. Wykes, Sedgefield, Co. Durham; four *s* one *d*. *Educ:* Glasgow Academy; Queen's Coll., Oxford (Scholar, BA). Served in Army, 1946–48. Called to Bar, Middle Temple, 1953, Bencher, 1984; SE Circuit. Prosecuting Counsel, GPO (SE Circuit), 1964–69; Dep. Chm., W Suffolk QS, 1967–71. Contested (C): Bridgeton Div. of

Glasgow, 1950; Small Heath Div. of Birmingham, 1951. *Address*: 8 New Square, Lincoln's Inn, WC2A 3QP. *T*: 01–242 4986.

IRWIN, Ian Sutherland, CBE 1982; Deputy Chairman and Managing Director, Scottish Transport Group, since 1975; *b* Glasgow, 20 Feb. 1933; *s* of Andrew Campbell Irwin and Elizabeth Ritchie Arnott; *m* 1959, Margaret Miller Maureen Irvine; two *s*. *Educ*: Whitehill Sen. Secondary Sch., Glasgow; Glasgow Univ. BL; CA, IPFA, FCIT, CBIM, FInstD. Commercial Man., Scottish Omnibuses Ltd, 1960–64; Gp Accountant, Scottish Bus Gp, 1964–69; Gp Sec., Scottish Transport Gp, 1969–75; Scottish Bus Gp Ltd (and all subsids) and Caledonian MacBrayne Ltd (and all subsids): Exec. Dir, 1972–; Chm., 1975–; Director: Nat. Bus Co., Nat. Bus Management Ltd, 1975–; British Transport Advertising Ltd, 1985–; Scottish Mortgage & Trust plc, 1986–. Pres., Bus and Coach Council, 1979–80; Vice-Pres., Internat. Union of Public Transport, 1981–; Mem. Council, CIT, 1978– (Vice Pres., 1984–). Hon. Col, 154 Regt RCT (V), 1986–. *Publications*: various papers. *Recreations*: reading, gardening. *Address*: Kilrymont, 6A Easter Belmont Road, Edinburgh EH12 6EX. *T*: 031–443 2108. *Clubs*: Caledonian, MCC.

IRWIN, Sir James (Campbell), Kt 1971; OBE 1945; ED 1947; psc; FRIBA, LFRAIA; Partner in Woods, Bagot, Laybourne-Smith & Irwin, Architects, Adelaide, 1930–74; *b* 23 June 1906; *s* of Francis James and Margaret Irwin; *m* 1933, Kathleen Agnes, *d* of G. W. Orr, Sydney; one *s* one *d*. *Educ*: Queen's Sch., N Adelaide; St Peter's Coll., Adelaide; St Mark's Coll., Univ. of Adelaide (Hon. Fellow, 1973). Served War, AIF, on active service in Middle East, New Guinea, Philippine Islands, 1940–46; Lt-Col RAA. Col Comdt, RAA, 1966–71. Mem. Adelaide City Council, 1935–72 (except for war years); Lord Mayor of Adelaide, 1963–66; Mem. Nat. Capital Planning Cttee, Canberra, 1964–70. President: RAIA, 1962–63; Adelaide Festival of Arts, 1964–66 (Chm. 1969–73); SA Sch. of Art, 1966–72; Home for Incurables, 1966–82; Pioneers Assoc. of S Australia, 1968–73. Chm., Co-op. Foundn, 1979–. *Publication*: The Irwin Family: Junior South Australian Branch, 1977. *Address*: 124 Brougham Place, North Adelaide, SA 5006, Australia. *T*: 2672839. *Clubs*: Adelaide, Naval Military and Air Force of SA (Adelaide).

IRWIN, John Conran; Keeper, Indian Section, Victoria and Albert Museum, 1959–78, with extended responsibility for new Oriental Department, 1970–78; *b* 5 Aug. 1917; *s* of late John Williamson Irwin; *m* 1947, Helen Hermione Scott (*née* Fletcher) (separated 1982), *d* of late Herbert Bristowe Fletcher; three *s*. *Educ*: Canford Sch., Wimborne, Dorset. Temp. commission, Gordon Highlanders, 1939. Private Sec. to Gov. of Bengal, 1942–45; Asst Keeper, Victoria and Albert Museum, 1946; Exec. Sec., Royal Academy Winter Exhibition of Indian Art, 1947–48; UNESCO Expert on museum planning: on mission to Indonesia, 1956; to Malaya, 1962. British Acad. Travelling Fellowship, 1974–75; Leverhulme Res. Fellow, 1978–80; Sen. Fellow, Center for Advanced Study in the Visual Arts, Nat. Gall. of Art, Washington, DC, 1983–84; Vis. Prof., Univ. of Michigan, 1986. Working with research grants from Leverhulme Trust and British Acad., 1978–84. Lectures: Birdwood Meml, 1972; Tagore Meml, 1973; Lowell Inst., Boston, Mass, 1974; guest lectr, Collège de France, 1976. FRSA 1972; FRAS 1946; FRAI 1977; FSA 1978. *Publications*: Jamini Roy, 1944; Indian art (section on sculpture), 1947; The Art of India and Pakistan (sections on bronzes and textiles), 1951, Shawls, 1955; Origins of Chintz, 1970; (with M. Hall) Indian Painted and Printed Fabrics, 1972; Indian Embroideries, 1974; articles in Encyclopædia Britannica, Chambers's Encyclopædia, Jl of Royal Asiatic Soc., Burlington Magazine, Artibus Asiae etc. *Recreations*: music, walking. *Address*: Ashford Chace, Steep, Petersfield, Hants GU32 1AB. *T*: Petersfield 66357.

IRWIN, Dr Michael Henry Knox; Medical Director, United Nations, UNICEF and UN Development Programme, since 1982; *b* 5 June 1931; *s* of late William Knox Irwin, FRCS and of Edith Isabel Mary Irwin; *m* 1st, 1958, Elizabeth Miriam (marr. diss. 1982), *d* of late John and Nancie Naumann; three *d*; 2nd, 1983, Frederica Todd Harlow, *d* of Frederick and Sarah Harlow. *Educ*: St Bartholomew's Hosp. Med. Coll., London (MB, BS 1955); Columbia Univ., New York (MPH 1960). House Phys. and House Surg., Prince of Wales' Hosp., London, 1955–56; MO, UN, 1957–61; Dep. Resident Rep., UN Technical Assistance Bd, Pakistan, 1961–63; MO, 1963–66, SMO, 1966–69, and Med. Dir, 1969–73, United Nations; Dir, Div. of Personnel, UNDP, 1973–76; UNICEF Rep., Bangladesh, 1977–80; Sen. Advr (Childhood Disabilities), UNICEF, 1980–82; Sen. Consultant, UN Internat. Year of Disabled Persons, 1981. Pres., Assistance for Blind Children Internat., 1978–84. Consultant, Amer. Assoc. of Blood Banks, 1984–. Mem. Editl Adv. Panel, Medicine and War. FRSM. Officer Cross, Internat. Fedn of Blood Donor Organizations, 1984. *Publications*: Check-ups: safeguarding your health, 1961; Overweight: a problem for millions, 1964; Travelling without Tears, 1964; Viruses, Colds and Flu, 1966; Blood: new uses for saving lives, 1967; The Truth About Cancer, 1969; What Do We Know about Allergies?, 1972; A Child's Horizon, 1982; Aspirin: current knowledge about an old medication, 1983; Can We Survive Nuclear War?, 1984; Nuclear Energy: good or bad?, 1985. *Recreations*: travelling, bicycling. *Address*: One West 89th Street, New York, NY 10024, USA. *T*: (212) 595–7714.

ISAAC, Alfred James; Chairman, Recruitment Boards, Civil Service Commission (part-time), since 1978; *b* 1 Aug. 1919; *s* of Alfred Jabez Isaac and Alice Marie Isaac (both British); *m* 1943, Beryl Marjorie Rist; one *s* two *d*. *Educ*: Maidenhead Grammar Sch. Post Office Engineering Dept, 1936–49. Served War, RAFVR, Flt Lt (pilot), Coastal Command, 1941–46. Min. of Works, Asst Principal, 1949; Regional Dir, Southern Region, 1960–67; Dir of Professional Staff Management, 1967; Dir of Home Regional Services, DoE, 1971–75. Business Coordinator, Danbury Drilling Ltd, 1977–78. Part-time Clerk, Bigbury Parish Council, 1981–83. *Recreations*: amateur radio, cycling, fishing. *Address*: Wave Crest, Marine Drive, Bigbury on Sea, Kingsbridge, Devon TQ7 4AS. *T*: Bigbury on Sea 810387. *Clubs*: Civil Service; Victoria.

ISAAC, Anthony John Gower, CB 1985; a Deputy Chairman, Board of Inland Revenue, since 1982 (a Commissioner of Inland Revenue, 1973–77 and since 1979); *b* 21 Dec. 1931; *s* of Ronald and Kathleen Mary Gower Isaac; *m* 1963, Olga Elizabeth Sibley; one *s* two *d* (and two *d* decd). *Educ*: Malvern Coll.; King's Coll., Cambridge (BA). HM Treasury, 1953–70: Private Sec. to Chief Sec. to Treasury, 1964–66; Inland Revenue, 1971; on secondment to HM Treasury, 1976–78. *Recreations*: gardening, fishing. *Address*: Moonsfield, Brenchley, Kent. *T*: Brenchley 2810.

ISAAC, James Keith, CBE 1985; FCIT; Managing Director and Chief Executive, West Midlands Travel Ltd, since 1986; *b* 28 Jan. 1932; *s* of late Arthur Burton Isaac and of Doreen (*née* Davies); *m* 1957, Elizabeth Mary Roskell; two *d*. *Educ*: Leeds Grammar Sch. Mem., Inst. of Traffic Admin; FCIT 1978. Asst to Traffic Manager, Aldershot and Dist Traction Co. Ltd, 1958–59; Asst Traffic Man., Jamaica Omnibus Services Ltd, Kingston, Jamaica, 1959–64; Dep. Traffic Man., Midland Red (Birmingham and Midland Motor Omnibus Co. Ltd), Birmingham, 1965–67; Traffic Manager: North Western Road Car Co. Ltd, Stockport, Cheshire, 1967–69; Midland Red, Birmingham, 1969–73; Dir of Ops, 1973–77, Dir Gen., 1977–86, W Midlands Passenger Transp. Exec., Birmingham. Chm., Internat. Commn on Transport Economics, Internat. Union of Public Transport, 1981–; President: Omnibus Soc., 1982; Bus and Coach Council, 1985–86; Mem. Council, CIT, 1982–85. *Recreations*: golf, gardening, travel. *Address*: 24B Middlefield Lane, Hagley,

Stourbridge, West Midlands DY9 0PX. *T*: Hagley 884757. *Clubs*: Rotary of Hagley (Hereford/Worcester); Churchill and Blakedown Golf (near Kidderminster).

ISAAC, Maurice Laurence Reginald, MA; Headmaster, Latymer Upper School, Hammersmith, W6, since 1971; *b* 26 April 1928; *s* of late Frank and Lilian Isaac; *m* 1954, Anne Fielden; three *d*. *Educ*: Selhurst Grammar Sch., Croydon; Magdalene Coll., Cambridge. BA Hist. Tripos, 1950; MA 1955, Cambridge; Certif. in Educn, 1952. Asst Master: Liverpool Collegiate Sch., 1952–56; Bristol Grammar Sch., 1956–62; Head of History, Colchester Royal Grammar Sch., 1962–65; Headmaster, Yeovil Sch., 1966–71. Mem., Francis Holland Schools Council, 1982–. *Publications*: A History of Europe, 1870–1950, 1960; contributor to The Teaching of History, 1965. *Address*: Latymer Upper School, Hammersmith, W6 9LR. *T*: 01–741 1851.

ISAAC, Sir Neil, Kt 1986; QSO 1982; JP; Managing Director, Isaac Group of Companies; *b* 29 Dec. 1915; *s* of Ernest Rupert Isaac and Louisa Isaac; *m* 1946, Jun. Comdr Diana Gilbert, ATS. *Educ*: Prep. Sch.; Timaru Boys' High Sch. Served, 2NZEF, 1941; commnd British Army, 1944; served in Greece, Italy and India, until 1947 (Major). Formed Isaac Construction Group, 1950. Works Comr, Rolleston (New Town), 1972. JP 1970. *Recreation*: salmon farming. *Address*: Clifton, McArthurs Road, Harewood, Christchurch, New Zealand. *T*: (03) 599–145. *Club*: Canterbury (Christchurch, NZ).

ISAAC, Prof. Peter Charles Gerald; Professor of Civil and Public Health Engineering, 1964–81, now Emeritus, and Head of Department of Civil Engineering, 1970–81, University of Newcastle upon Tyne; Partner, Watson Hawksley (consulting engineers), 1973–83; *b* 21 Jan. 1921; *s* of late Herbert George Isaac and Julienne Geneviève (*née* Hattenberger); *m* 1950, Marjorie Eleanor White; one *s* one *d*. *Educ*: Felsted Sch.; London and Harvard Universities. BSc(Eng), SM. Asst Engineer, GWR, 1940–45; Lecturer in Civil Engineering, 1946; Senior Lecturer in Public Health Engineering, 1953, Reader, 1960, Univ. of Durham; Dean of Faculty of Applied Science, Univ. of Newcastle upon Tyne, 1969–73; Sandars Reader in Bibliography, Univ. of Cambridge, 1983–84. Member: Working Party on Sewage Disposal, 1969–70; WHO Expert Adv. Panel on Environmental Health, 1976–; specialist advr, House of Lords Select Cttee on Sci. and Technol. II (Hazardous Waste), 1980–81 and House of Lords Select Cttee on Sci. and Technol. I (Water), 1982; DoE Long-Term Water-Research Requirements Cttee. Chairman: History of the Book Trade in the North, 1965–; British Book Trade Index. Member of Council: ICE, 1968–71, 1972–75, 1977–80; Bibliographical Soc., 1970–74, 1979–83 (Hon. Editor of Monographs, 1982–; Vice-Pres., 1984–); IPHE, 1973– (Pres., 1977–78); Pres., British Occupational Hygiene Soc., 1962–63; Mem. Bd, CEI, 1978–79. Trustee, Asian Inst. Technology, Bangkok, 1968–82 (Vice-Chm., 1979–82). Hon. Mem., Lit. and Phil. Soc., Newcastle upon Tyne. Director: Thorne's Students' Bookshop Ltd, 1969–74; Environmental Resources Ltd, 1972–74. Freeman, Worshipful Co. of Stationers and Newspaper Makers, 1984, Liveryman, 1986. FICE, MIWM; Hon. FIPHE 1986. Clemens Herschel Prize in Applied Hydraulics, 1952; Telford Premium, 1957; Thomas Bedford Award, 1978. *Publications*: Electric Resistance Strain Gauges (with W. B. Dobie), 1948; Public Health Engineering, 1953; Trade Wastes, 1957; Waste Treatment, 1960; River Management, 1967; William Davison of Alnwick: pharmacist and printer, 1968; Farm Wastes, 1970; Civil Engineering-The University Contribution, 1970; Management in Civil Engineering, 1971; Davison's Halfpenny Chapbooks, 1971; (ed) The Burman Alnwick Collection, 1973; contribs to various learned and technical jls. *Recreations*: bibliography, printing, Roman engineering. *Address*: 10 Woodcroft Road, Wylam, Northumberland NE41 8DJ. *T*: Wylam 3174. *Clubs*: Royal Commonwealth Society; Royal Scottish Automobile (Glasgow); Northern Counties (Newcastle).

ISAACS, family name of **Marquess of Reading.**

ISAACS, Dame Albertha Madeline, DBE 1974; former Senator, now worker for the community, in the Bahamas; *b* Nassau, Bahamas, 18 April 1900; *d* of late Robert Hanna and Lilla (*née* Minns); *m*; three *s* one *d*. *Educ*: Cosmopolitan High Sch. and Victoria High Sch., Nassau. Member: Progressive Liberal Party, Senator, 1968–72; also of PLP's Nat. Gen. Council, and of Council of Women. Has joined a Good Samaritan Group. *Address*: c/o Progressive Liberal Party, Head Office, Nassau Court, Nassau, Bahamas.

ISAACS, Jeremy Israel; Chief Executive, Channel Four Television Company, since 1981; *b* 28 Sept. 1932; *s* of Isidore Isaacs and Sara Jacobs; *m* 1958, Tamara (*née* Weinreich) (*d* 1986), Cape Town; one *s* one *d*. *Educ*: Glasgow Acad.; Merton Coll., Oxford (MA). Pres. of the Union, Hilary, 1955. Television Producer, Granada TV (What the Papers Say, All Our Yesterdays), 1958; Associated-Rediffusion (This Week), 1963; BBC TV (Panorama), 1965; Controller of Features, Associated Rediffusion, 1967; with Thames Television, 1968–78: Controller of Features, 1968–74; Producer, The World at War, 1974; Director of Programmes, 1974–78; TV series: A Sense of Freedom, ITV; Ireland, a Television History, BBC. Governor, BFI, 1979– (Chm., BFI Production Bd, 1979–81); Mem., Internat. Council, Nat. Acad. of Television Arts and Scis, NY, 1983–; Mem. Bd of Dirs, Royal Opera House, 1985–. James MacTaggart Meml Lectr, Edinburgh TV Fest., 1979. FRSA 1983; Fellow, BAFTA, 1985. Hon. DLitt Strathclyde, 1983. Desmond Davis Award for outstanding creative contrib. to television, 1972; George Polk Meml Award, 1973; Cyril Bennett Award for outstanding contrib. to television programming, RTS, 1982; Lord Willis Award for Distinguished Service to Television, 1985. *Recreations*: books, walks, opera, sleep. *Address*: (office) 60 Charlotte Street, W1P 2AX.

ISAACS, Mrs Nathan; see Lawrence, E. M.

ISAAMAN, Gerald Michael; journalist; Editor, Hampstead and Highgate Express, since 1968; *b* 22 Dec. 1933; *s* of Asher Isaaman and Lily Finklestein; *m* 1962, Delphine Walker, *e d* of Cecile and Arnold Walker; one *s*. *Educ*: Dame Alice Owens Grammar School. Reporter, North London Observer Series, 1950, Hampstead and Highgate Express, 1955. Founder Trustee, Arkwright Arts Trust, 1971; Chairman: Camden Arts Trust Management Board, 1970–82; Exhibns Cttee, Camden Arts Centre, 1971–82; Russell Housing Soc., 1976–82; Mem., Camden Festival Trust, 1982–. *Recreations*: cooking breakfast, listening to jazz, work. *Address*: 9 Lyndhurst Road, NW3. *T*: 01–794 3950.

ISEPP, Martin Johannes Sebastian; Head of Music Studies, National Opera Studio, since 1979; Head of Music Staff, Glyndebourne Festival Opera, since 1973; Head of Academy of Singing, Banff School of Fine Arts, Alberta, Canada, since 1982; *b* Vienna, 30 Sept. 1930; *s* of Sebastian and Helene Isepp; *m* 1966, Rose Henrietta Harris; two *s*. *Educ*: St Paul's Sch.; Lincoln Coll., Oxford; Royal Coll. of Music, London (ARCM 1952). Studied piano with Prof. Leonie Gombrich, 1939–52. English Opera Gp, 1954–57; Glyndebourne Fest. Opera, 1957–; Head of Opera Trng Dept, Juilliard Sch. of Music, New York, 1973–78. As accompanist, began career accompanying mother, Helene Isepp (the singer and voice teacher); has accompanied many of the world's leading singers and instrumentalists, notably Elisabeth Schwarzkopf, Elisabeth Söderström, Janet Baker and John Shirley-Quirk; harpsichordist with Handel Opera Soc. of New York in most of their Handel Festivals, 1966–; master classes in opera and song at Amer. univs, incl. Southern Calif, Ann Arbor and Colorado, 1975–; coached Peking Opera and Peking Conservatory in Mozart operas, 1983. Carroll Donner Stuchell Medal for Accompanists, Harriet Cohen

Internat. Musical Foundn, 1965. *Recreations:* photography, walking. *Address:* 37A Steele's Road, NW3 4RG. *T:* 01-722 3085.

ISHAM, Sir Ian (Vere Gyles), 13th Bt *cr* 1627; *b* 17 July 1923; *s* of Lt-Col Vere Arthur Richard Isham, MC (*d* 1968) and Edith Irene (*d* 1973), *d* of Harry Brown; *S* cousin, Sir Gyles Isham, 12th Bt, 1976. Served War of 1939–45, Captain RAC. *Heir: b* Norman Murray Crawford Isham [*b* 28 Jan. 1930; *m* 1956, Joan, *d* of late Leonard James Genet; two *s* one *d*]. *Address:* 40 Turnpike Link, Croydon, Surrey CR0 5NX.

ISHERWOOD, Rt. Rev. Harold, LVO 1955; OBE 1959; Auxiliary Bishop, Diocese of Gibraltar in Europe, since 1977; an Assistant Bishop, Diocese of Canterbury, since 1978; *b* 23 June 1907; *s* of James and Margaret Ellen Isherwood; *m* 1940, Hannah Mary Walters. *Educ:* Selwyn Coll., Cambridge; Ely Theol Coll. BA 1938, MA 1946. Deacon 1939; priest 1940; Curate of Beeston, Notts, 1939–43; Chaplain: Nat. Nautical Sch., Portishead, 1943–51; Helsinki and Moscow, 1951–54; Oslo, 1954–59; Brussels, 1959–70; Vicar General, Dio. Gibraltar and Jurisdiction of North and Central Europe, 1970–75; Canon of Gibraltar, 1971–74; Asst Bishop, Dio. Gibraltar, 1974–77. *Recreations:* music, cricket, Rugby and Association football, tennis. *Address:* 16A Burgate, Canterbury, Kent CT1 2HG. *T:* Canterbury 452790. *Club:* Royal Commonwealth Society.

ISHIHARA, Takashi; Chairman: Nissan Motor Co., Ltd, since 1985; Nissan Motor Manufacturing Corporation, USA, since 1980; *b* 3 March 1912; *s* of Ichiji and Shigeyo Ishihara; *m* 1943, Shizuko Nakajo; one *s*. *Educ:* Law Dept, Tohoku Univ. (grad 1937). Joined Nissan Motor Co., Ltd, 1937; promoted to Gen. Man. of Planning and Accounting Depts respectively; Dir of Finance and Accounting, 1954; Man. Dir, 1963; Exec. Man. Dir, 1969; Exec. Vice Pres., 1973; Pres., 1977; Pres., Nissan Motor Corpn in USA, 1960–65. Exec. Dir, Keidanren (Fedn of Econ. Orgns), 1977–; Chm., Keizai Doyukai (Japan Cttee for Econ. Develt), 1985–; Dir, Nikkeiren (Japan Fedn of Employers Assocs), 1978–; President: Japan Automobile Manufacturers Assoc., Inc., 1980–86; Japan Motor Industrial Fedn, Inc., 1980–86. Blue Ribbon Medal (Japan), 1974; First Order of Sacred Treasure (Japan), 1983; Grand Cross (Spain), 1985. *Recreations:* reading, golf, ocean cruising. *Address:* Nissan Motor Co., 17–1 Ginza 6-chome, Chuo-ku, Tokyo 104, Japan; 20–3, 2-chome, Shiroganedai, Minato-ku, Tokyo 108, Japan.

ISLE OF WIGHT, Archdeacon of; *see* Turner, Ven. A. H. M.

ISLES, Maj.-Gen. Donald Edward, CB 1978; OBE 1968; Director (Deputy Managing), British Manufacture & Research Co. Ltd, since 1979; *b* 19 July 1924; *s* of Harold and Kathleen Isles; *m* 1948, Sheila Mary Stephens (formerly Thorpe); three *s* one *d*. *Educ:* Roundhay; Leeds Univ.; RMCS. MRAeS, FBIM. Italian campaign, with 1st Bn, Duke of Wellington's Regt, 1944–45; Palestine, Egypt, Sudan, Syria, with 1DWR, 1945–47; GSO2, HQ BAOR, 1955–58; Asst Mil. Attaché, Paris, 1963–65; CO, 1DWR, BAOR and UN Forces in Cyprus, 1965–67; AMS, MoD, 1968; Col GS, MoD, 1968–71; Col GS, Royal Armament Res. and Develt Estab., 1971–72; Dir of Munitions, Brit. Defence Staff Washington, 1972–75; Dir-Gen. Weapons (Army), 1975–78, retired. Col, The Duke of Wellington's Regt, 1975–82; Col Comdt, The King's Div., 1975–79; Vice-Chm., Yorks and Humberside TA&VRA, 1984–. Hon. Col: 3rd Bn, The Yorkshire Volunteers, 1977–83; Leeds Univ. OTC, 1985–. *Recreations:* tennis, squash. *Address:* c/o Lloyds Bank, 6 Pall Mall, SW1. *Clubs:* Army and Navy, Institute of Directors.

ISMAY, Walter Nicholas; Managing Director, Worcester Parsons Ltd, 1975–82, retired; *b* 20 June 1921; *s* of late John Ismay, Maryport, Cumberland. *Educ:* Taunton's Sch., Southampton; King's Coll., University of London (BSc). Royal Aircraft Establishment, 1939–40; Ministry of Supply, 1940–43; Served Army (Capt., General List), 1943–46; Imperial Chemical Industries, Metals Division, 1948–58 (Technical Dir, 1957–58); Dir, Yorkshire Imperial Metals, 1958–67; Dep. Chm. Yorkshire Imperial Plastics, 1966–67; Dep. Chm. and Man. Dir, Milton Keynes Develt Corp., 1967–71; McKechnie Britain Ltd, 1972–75. FIMechE. *Recreation:* sailing. *Address:* Pitlundie, Monument Lane, Walhampton, Lymington, Hampshire SO4 15SE. *T:* Lymington 73032. *Club:* Royal Lymington Yacht.

ISOLANI, Casimiro Peter Hugh Tomasi, CBE 1975 (OBE 1960; MBE 1945); LVO 1961; *b* 2 Sept. 1917; *s* of late Umberto Tomasi Isolani, Bologna, and late Georgiana Eleanor Lyle-Smyth, Great Barrow, Ches; *m* 1943, Karin Gunni Signe Zetterström, *d* of Henry Zetterström, Gothenburg; one *s*. *Educ:* Aldenham Sch.; Clare Coll., Cambridge; Major open schol., 1936, 1st cl. Mod. and Med. Lang. Tripos 1; Senior Foundn schol., 1937; BA 1939. Commnd RA 1940, Intell. Corps 1941; attached 1st Canadian Div., 1943 (Sicily, Italy landings); Psychol Warfare Br., 1944; GS1 (Civil Liaison, Liaison Italian Resistance), 1945; FO 1946; Vice-Consul, Bologna, 1946; Attaché, later 1st Sec. (Information), British Embassy, Rome, 1947–61; resigned Foreign Service; Dep. Dir, Inst. for Strategic Studies, 1961–63; rejoined Foreign Service; Regional Information Officer, Paris, 1963–72; Counsellor (Information), British Embassy (and UK delegn NATO and UK Representation, EEC), Brussels, 1972–77. United Nations University: Rep. (Europe), 1978–85; Sen. Consultant, 1985–86. *Address:* 44 Pont Street, SW1X 0AD. *T:* 01-584 1543. *Club:* Anglo-Belgian.

ISRAEL, Rev. Dr Martin Spencer, FRCPath; Priest-in-Charge, Holy Trinity with All Saints Church, South Kensington, since 1983; *b* 30 April 1927; *s* of Elie Benjamin Israel, ophthalmic surgeon, and Minnie Israel. *Educ:* Parktown Boys' High Sch.; Johannesburg; Univ. of the Witwatersrand (MB ChB). MRCP 1952, FRCPath 1972. Ho. Phys., Hammersmith Hosp., 1952; Registrar in Pathology, Royal Hosp., Wolverhampton, 1953–55; service in RAMC, 1955–57; Lectr and Sen. Lectr in Pathology, 1958–82, Hon. Sen. Lectr 1982–, RCS. Ordained priest in C of E, 1975. Pres., Guild of Health and Churches' Fellowship for Psychical and Spiritual Studies. *Publications: medical:* General Pathology (with J. B. Walter), 1963, 6th edn 1986; *spiritual matters:* Summons to Life, 1974; Precarious Living, 1976; Smouldering Fire, 1978; The Pain that Heals, 1981; Living Alone, 1982; The Spirit of Counsel, 1983; Healing as Sacrament, 1984; The Discipline of Love, 1985; Coming in Glory, 1986. *Recreations:* music, conversation. *Address:* Flat 2, 26 Tregunter Road, SW10 9LH. *T:* 01-370 5160.

ISRAEL, Prof. Werner, FRS 1986; Professor of Physics, since 1972, and University Professor, University of Alberta; *b* 4 Oct. 1931; *s* of Arthur Israel and Marie Kappauf; *m* 1958, Inge Margulies; one *s* one *d*. *Educ:* Cape Town High Sch.; Univ. of Cape Town (BSc 1951, MSc 1954); Dublin Inst. for Advanced Studies; Trinity Coll., Dublin (PhD 1960). Lectr in Applied Maths, Univ. of Cape Town, 1954–56; Asst Prof., 1958, Associate Prof., 1964, Prof. of Maths, 1968–71, Univ. of Alberta. Sherman Fairchild Dist. Schol., CIT, 1974–75; Vis. Prof., Dublin Inst. for Advanced Studies, 1966–68; Sen. Visitor, Dept of Applied Maths and Theoretical Physics, Univ. of Cambridge, 1975–76; Maître de Recherche Associé, Inst. Henri Poincaré, Paris, 1976–77; Vis. Prof., Berne, 1980, Kyoto, 1986; Vis. Fellow, Gonville and Caius Coll., Cambridge, 1985. Fellow, Canadian Inst. for Advanced Research, 1986–. *Publications:* (ed) Relativity, Astrophysics and Cosmology, 1973; (ed with S. W. Hawking) General Relativity: and Einstein centenary survey, 1979; (ed with S. W. Hawking) 300 Years of Gravitation, 1987; numerous papers on black hole physics, general relativity, relativistic statistical mechanics. *Recreation:* music. *Address:* Avadh Bhatia Physics Laboratory, University of Alberta, Edmonton, Alberta T6G 2J1, Canada. *T:* (403) 432–3552.

ISSERLIS, Alexander Reginald; Burford Branch Chairman, West Oxfordshire Conservative Association; *b* 18 May 1922; *y s* of Isaak Isserlis, Ilford, Essex; *m* 1949, Eleanor Mary Ord, *d* of Prof. R. D. Laurie, Aberystwyth; two *d*. *Educ:* Ilford High Sch.; Keble Coll., Oxford. British and Indian Army, 1942–46. Entered Civil Service, 1947. Principal, Min. of Health, 1950; Principal Private Secretary: to Lord President of the Council and Minister for Science, 1960–61; to Minister of Housing and Local Govt, 1962; Asst Sec., Min. of Housing and Local Govt, 1963; Under-Secretary: Cabinet Office, 1969; Min. of Housing and Local Government, 1969–70; Principal Private Secretary to the Prime Minister, 1970; Asst Under-Sec. of State, Home Office, 1970–72; Dir, Centre for Studies in Social Policy, 1972–77; Dir of Investigations, Office of Parly Comr for Administration, 1977–80; Sen. Res. Fellow, Policy Studies Inst., 1980–82. *Publications:* Conversations on Policy, 1984; occasional articles in Policy Studies. *Recreations:* walking, gardening. *Address:* Rose and Crown Cottage, Upton, Burford, Oxon. *T:* Burford 3434. *Club:* Farmers'.

ISSIGONIS, Sir Alec (Arnold Constantine), Kt 1969; CBE 1964; RDI 1964; FRS 1967; Advanced Design Consultant, British Leyland (Austin-Morris) Ltd, since 1972; *b* Smyrna, 1906; British citizen. *Educ:* Battersea Polytechnic, London (Engrg Dip.). Draughtsman, Rootes Motors Ltd, 1933–36; Suspension Engineer, Morris Motors Ltd, 1936, subsequently Chief Engineer; Deputy Engineering Co-ordinator and Chief Engineer, British Motor Corporation, 1957–61; Technical Director, 1961; Dir of R&D, BMC later British Leyland (Austin-Morris) Ltd, 1961–72; designs include: Morris Minor, 1948; Mini-Minor and Austin Seven, 1959; Morris 1100, 1962. Leverhulme Medal, Royal Society, 1966.

IVAMY, Prof. Edward Richard Hardy; Professor of Law, University of London, since 1960; *b* 1 Dec. 1920; *o s* of late Edward Wadham Ivamy and late Florence Ivamy; *m* 1965, Christine Ann Frances, *o d* of William and Frances Culver; one *s*. *Educ:* Malvern Coll.; University Coll., London. Served War of 1939–45, RA: 67 Field Regt, N Africa, Italy and Middle East; 2nd Lieut 1942; Temp. Capt. 1945; Staff Capt., GHQ, Cairo, 1946. LLB (1st cl. hons) 1947; PhD 1953; LLD 1967. Barrister, Middle Temple, 1949. University Coll., London: Asst Lectr in Laws, 1947–50; Lectr, 1950–56; Reader in Law, 1956–60; Dean of Faculty of Laws, 1964 and 1965; Fellow, 1969. Hon. Sec., Soc. of Public Teachers of Law, 1960–63; Hon. Sec., Bentham Club, 1953–58; Governor, Malvern Coll., 1982–; Mem. Editorial Board: Jl of Business Law; Business Law Review; Lloyd's Maritime and Commercial Law Quarterly. *Publications:* Show Business and the Law, 1955; (ed) Payne and Ivamy's Carriage of Goods by Sea, 7th edn 1963–12th edn, 1985; Hire-Purchase Legislation in England and Wales, 1965; Casebook on Carriage of Goods by Sea, 1965 (6th edn, 1985); Casebook on Sale of Goods, 1966 (4th edn, 1980); (ed) Chalmers's Marine Insurance Act 1906, 6th edn, 1966–9th edn, 1983; General Principles of Insurance Law, 1966 (5th edn, 1985); (ed) Topham and Ivamy's Company Law, 13th edn, 1967–16th edn, 1978; Casebook on Commercial Law, 1967 (3rd edn, 1979); Fire and Motor Insurance, 1968 (4th edn, 1984); Casebook on Insurance Law, 1969 (4th edn, 1984); Marine Insurance, 1969 (4th edn, 1985); Casebook on Shipping Law, 1970 (3rd edn, 1982); Casebook on Partnership, 1970 (2nd edn, 1982); Casebook on Agency, 1971 (2nd edn, 1980); Personal Accident, Life and Other Insurances, 1973 (2nd edn, 1980); (ed) Underhill's Partnership, 10th edn, 1975, 12th edn, 1985; (ed) Halsbury's Laws of England, 4th edn, 1978, vol. 25 (Insurance), 1977, vol. 43 (Shipping and Navigation), 1983; Dictionary of Insurance Law, 1981; Dictionary of Company Law, 1983, 2nd edn, 1985; Insurance Law Handbook, 1983; Dictionary of Shipping Law, 1984; Encyclopaedia of Shipping Law Sources (UK), 1985; Encyclopedia of Oil and Natural Gas Law, 1986; Encyclopedia of the Law of Carriage, 1986; contrib. to Encyclopædia Britannica, Chambers's Encyclopædia, Current Legal Problems, Jl of Business Law; Annual Survey of Commonwealth Law, 1967–77. *Recreations:* railways, cricket, tennis. *Address:* 7 Egliston Mews, SW15 1AP. *T:* 01-785 6718.

IVEAGH, 3rd Earl of, *cr* 1919; **Arthur Francis Benjamin Guinness;** Bt 1885; Baron Iveagh 1891; Viscount Iveagh 1905; Viscount Elveden 1919; Member, Seanad Eireann, 1973–77; President, Guinness PLC; *b* 20 May 1937; *o s* of Viscount Elveden (killed in action, 1945) and Lady Elizabeth Hare, *yr d* of 4th Earl of Listowel; *S* grandfather, 1967; *m* 1963, Miranda Daphne Jane (marr. diss. 1984), *d* of Major Michael Smiley, Castle Fraser, Aberdeenshire; two *s* two *d*. *Educ:* Eton; Trinity Coll., Cambridge; Univ. of Grenoble. *Heir: s* Viscount Elveden, *qv*. *Address:* St James's Gate, Dublin 8. *Clubs:* White's; Royal Yacht Squadron (Cowes); Kildare Street and University (Dublin).

IVENS, Michael William, CBE 1983; Director, Aims of Industry, since 1971; Director of the Foundation for Business Responsibilities, since 1967; *b* 15 March 1924; *s* of Harry Guest Ivens and Nina Ailion; *m* 1st, 1950, Rosalie Turnbull (marr. diss. 1971); three *s* one *d*; 2nd, 1971, Katherine Laurence; two *s*. Dir, Foundn for Business Responsibilities, 1967; Jt Editor, Twentieth Century, 1967; Vice-Pres., Junior Hosp. Doctors Assoc., 1969; Director: Standard Telephone, 1970; Working Together Campaign, 1972–73. Jt Founder and Mem. Council, Freedom Assoc.; Member: Council, Efficiency in Local Govt, 1983–; Adv. Bd, US Industrial Council Educn Foundn, 1980–. *Publications:* Practice of Industrial Communication, 1963; Case Studies in Management, 1964; Case Studies in Human Relations, 1966; Case for Capitalism, 1967; Industry and Values, 1970; Which Way?, 1970; Prophets of Freedom and Enterprise, 1975; (ed jtly) Bachman's Book of Freedom Quotes, 1978; *poetry:* Another Sky, 1963; Last Waltz, 1964; Private and Public, 1968; Born Early, 1975; No Woman is an Island, 1983. *Recreation:* campaigning. *Address:* 40 Doughty Street, WC1N 2LF. *T:* 01-405 5195. *Clubs:* Carlton, Beefsteak, Wig and Pen.

IVERSEN, Leslie Lars, PhD; FRS 1980; Executive Director, Merck, Sharp & Dohme Neuroscience Research Centre, Harlow, Essex, since 1982; *b* 31 Oct. 1937; *s* of Svend Iversen and Anna Caia Iversen; *m* 1961, Susan Diana (*née* Kibble); one *s* one *d* (and one *d* decd). *Educ:* Trinity Coll., Cambridge (BA Biochem, PhD Pharmacol). Harkness Fellow, United States: with Dr J. Axelrod, Nat. Inst. of Mental Health, and Dr E. Kravitz, Dept of Neurobiology, Harvard Med. Sch., 1964–66; Fellow, Trinity Coll., Cambridge, 1964–84; Locke Research Fellow of Royal Society, Dept of Pharmacology, Univ. of Cambridge, 1967–71; Dir, MRC Neurochemical Pharmacology Unit, Cambridge, 1971–82. Foreign Associate, Nat. Acad. of Scis (USA), 1986. *Publications:* The Uptake and Storage of Noradrenaline in Sympathetic Nerves, 1967; (with S. D. Iversen) Behavioural Pharmacology, 1975, 2nd edn 1981. *Recreations:* reading, gardening. *Address:* Merck, Sharp & Dohme Neuroscience Research Centre, Terlings Park, Eastwick Road, near Harlow, Essex CM20 2QR.

IVES, Arthur Glendinning Loveless, CVO 1954 (MVO 1945); *b* 19 Aug. 1904; *s* of late Rev. E. J. Ives, Wesleyan Minister; *m* 1929, Doris Marion, *d* of Thomas Coke Boden; three *s* one *d*. *Educ:* Kingswood Sch.; Queen's Coll., Oxford (classical scholar); MA. George Webb Medley Junior Scholarship for Economics, Oxford Univ., 1926. London Chamber of Commerce, 1928–29; joined staff of King Edward's Hosp. Fund for London,

1929; Sec., 1938–60; retired 1960. Seriously injured in railway accident at Lewisham, Dec. 1957. A Governor of Kingswood Sch., 1954–72. *Publications:* British Hospitals (Britain in Pictures), 1948; Kingswood School in Wesley's Day and Since, 1970; contrib. to The Times, Lancet, etc, on hospital administration and allied topics. *Address:* The Cedars, Bordyke, Tonbridge, Kent. *Club:* Athenæum.

    See also Rev. A. K. Lloyd.

IVISON, David Malcolm; Chief Executive, Institute of Road Transport Engineers, since 1985; *b* 22 March 1936; *s* of John and Ruth Ellen Ivison; *m* 1961, Lieselotte Ivison; one *s* one *d*. *Educ:* King Edward VI School, Lichfield; RMA Sandhurst; Staff College, Camberley. Army, Gurkha Transport Regt, 1955–83 (Lt-Col). Tate & Lyle, 1984–85. *Recreations:* learning languages, tennis, reading. *Address:* 1 Dundaff Close, Camberley, Surrey GU15 1AF. *T:* Camberley 27778; Cromwell Place, SW7 2JF. *T:* 01–589 3744.

IVORY, James Francis; film director; Partner in Merchant Ivory Productions, since 1961; *b* 7 June 1928; *s* of Edward Patrick Ivory and Hallie Millicent De Loney. *Educ:* Univ. of Oregon (BA Fine Arts); Univ. of Southern California (MFA Cinema). Guggenheim Fellow, 1974. Collaborator with Ruth Prawer Jhabvala and Ismail Merchant on the following films: The Householder, 1963; Shakespeare Wallah, 1965; The Guru, 1969; Bombay Talkie, 1970; Autobiography of a Princess, 1975; Roseland, 1977; Hullabaloo over Georgie and Bonnie's Pictures, 1978; The Europeans, 1979; Jane Austen in Manhattan, 1980; Quartet, 1981; Heat and Dust, 1983; The Bostonians, 1984; A Room With a view, 1986. Other films: (with Nirad Chaudhuri) Adventures of a Brown Man in Search of Civilization, 1971; (with George W. S. Trow and Michael O'Donoghue) Savages, 1972; (with Walter Marks) The Wild Party, 1975; (with Terence McNally) The Five Forty Eight, 1979. Documentaries: Venice, Theme and Variations, 1957; The Sword and the Flute, 1959; The Delhi Way, 1964. *Publication:* Autobiography of a Princess (Also Being the Adventures of an American Film Director in the Land of the Maharajas), 1975. *Recreation:* looking at pictures. *Address:* 400 East 52nd Street, New York, NY 10022, USA. *T:* 212 759 3694; (country) Patroon Street, Claverack, New York 12513, USA. *T:* 518 851 7808.

J

JACK, Hon. Sir Alieu (Sulayman), Grand Commander and Chancellor, National Order of The Gambia, 1972; Kt 1970; Speaker, House of Representatives of the Republic of The Gambia, 1962–72, and since 1977; *b* 14 July 1922; *m* 1946, Yai Marie Cham; four *s* four *d* (and one *d* decd). *Educ:* St Augustine's School. Entered Gambia Civil Service, 1939; resigned and took up local appt with NAAFI, 1940–44; Civil Service, 1945–48; entered commerce, 1948; Man. Dir, Gambia National Trading Co. Ltd, 1948–72. Mem., Bathurst City Council, 1949–62. Minister for Works and Communications, The Gambia, 1972–77. Represented The Gambia Parlt at various internat. gatherings; Pres., CPA Gambia Branch. Comdr, National Order of Senegal, 1967; Comdr, Order of Merit of Mauritania, 1967; Commander, Order of Fed. Republic of Nigeria, 1970; Kt Grand Band, Liberia, 1977. *Recreation:* golf. *Address:* PO Box 376, Banjul, The Gambia; House of Representatives, The Republic of The Gambia. *T:* (home) 93.2204, (office) 241. *Club:* Bathurst (Banjul).

JACK, David M.; *see* Morton Jack.

JACK, Prof. Ian Robert James, FBA 1986; Professor of English Literature, University of Cambridge, since 1976; Fellow of Pembroke College, Cambridge, since 1961; *b* 5 Dec. 1923; *s* of John McGregor Bruce Jack, WS, and Helena Colburn Buchanan; *m* 1st, 1948, Jane Henderson MacDonald; two *s* one *d*; 2nd, 1972, Margaret Elizabeth Crone; one *s*. *Educ:* George Watson's Coll. (John Welsh Classical Schol., 1942); Univ. of Edinburgh (James Boswell Fellow, 1946; MA 1947); Merton Coll., Oxford (DPhil 1950); LittD Cantab 1973. Brasenose College, Oxford: Lectr in Eng. Lit., 1950–55; Sen. Res. Fellow, 1955–61; Cambridge University: Lectr in English, 1961–73; Reader in English Poetry, 1973–76; Librarian, Pembroke Coll., 1965–75. Vis. Professor: Alexandria, 1960; Chicago (Carpenter Prof.), 1968–69; California at Berkeley, 1968–69; British Columbia, 1975; Virginia, 1980–81; Tsuda Coll., Tokyo, 1981; de Carle Lectr, Univ. of Otago, 1964; Warton Lectr in English Poetry, British Acad., 1967; Guest Speaker, Nichol Smith Seminar, ANU, 1976; Guest Speaker, 50th anniversary meeting of English Literary Soc. of Japan, 1978; numerous lecture-tours for British Council and other bodies. President: Charles Lamb Soc., 1970–80; Browning Soc., 1980–83; Johnson Soc., Lichfield, 1986–87; Vice-Pres., Brontë Soc., 1973–. *Publications:* Augustan Satire, 1952; English Literature 1815–1832 (Vol. X, Oxf. Hist. of Eng. Lit.), 1963; Keats and the Mirror of Art, 1967; Browning's Major Poetry, 1973; The Poet and his Audience, 1984; *edited:* Sterne: A Sentimental Journey, etc, 1968; Browning: Poetical Works 1833–1864, 1970; (with Hilda Marsden) Emily Brontë: Wuthering Heights, 1976; general editor: Brontë novels (Clarendon edn); The Poetical Works of Browning, vols 1–2, 1983–84; contrib. TLS, RES, etc. *Recreations:* collecting books, travelling hopefully. *Address:* Highfield House, High Street, Fen Ditton, Cambridgeshire CB5 8ST. *T:* Teversham 2697. *Club:* MCC.

JACK, James, CBE 1967; JP; General Secretary, Scottish Trades Union Congress, 1963–75; retired; Member: Scottish Postal Board, 1972–79; Board of the Crown Agents, 1975–77; *b* 6 Dec. 1910; *s* of late Andrew M. Jack and late Margaret Reid; *m* 1936; one *s*. *Educ:* Auchinraith Primary Sch., Blantyre; St John's Gram. Sch., Hamilton. Chm., Glasgow N and E Cttee, Manpower Services Commn, 1975–79; Member: Scottish Economic Council, 1964–76; Scottish Oil Develt Council, 1974–76; Scottish Develt Agency, 1975–78; Lanarkshire Health Bd, 1975–83; Employment Appeal Tribunal, 1976–83. JP Lanark. *Address:* 7 Stonefield Place, Blantyre, Glasgow G72 9TH. *T:* Blantyre 823304.

JACK, Prof. Kenneth Henderson, PhD, ScD; FRS 1980; CChem, FRSC; Professor of Applied Crystal Chemistry, University of Newcastle upon Tyne, 1964–84, and Director of Wolfson Research Group for High-Strength Materials, 1970–84; Leverhulme Emeritus Fellow, 1985–86; *b* 12 Oct. 1918; *e s* of late John Henderson Jack, DSC, and Emily (*née* Cozens), North Shields, Northumberland; *m* 1942, Alfreda Hughes (*d* 1974); two *s*. *Educ:* Tynemouth Municipal High Sch.; King's Coll., Univ. of Durham, Newcastle upon Tyne (BSc 1939, DThPT 1940, MSc 1944); Fitzwilliam Coll., Univ. of Cambridge (PhD 1950, ScD 1978). Experimental Officer, Min. of Supply, 1940–41; Lectr in Chemistry, King's Coll., Univ. of Durham, 1941–45, 1949–52, 1953–57; Sen. Scientific Officer, Brit. Iron and Steel Res. Assoc., 1945–49; research at Crystallographic Lab., Cavendish Laboratory, Cambridge, 1947–49; Research Engr, Westinghouse Elec. Corp., Pittsburgh, Pa, 1952–53; Research Dir, Thermal Syndicate Ltd, Wallsend, 1957–64. Lectures: J.W. Mellor Meml, Brit. Ceramic Soc., 1973; Harold Moore Meml, Metals Soc., 1984; W. Hume-Rothery Meml, Oxford Metallurgical Soc., 1986. Fellow, Amer. Ceramic Soc., 1984; Membre d'Honneur, Société Française de Métallurgie, 1984. Saville-Shaw Medal, Soc. of Chem. Industry, 1944; Sir George Beilby Meml Award, Inst. of Metals, RIC and Soc. of Chem. Industry, 1951; Kroll Medal and Prize, Metals Soc., 1979; (with Dr R.J. Lumby) Prince of Wales Award for Industrial Innovation and Production, 1984. *Publications:* papers in scientific jls and conf. proc. *Address:* 147 Broadway, Cullercoats, Tyne and Wear NE30 3TA. *T:* Tyneside 2573664.

JACK, Raymond Evan; QC 1982; *b* 13 Nov. 1942; *s* of Evan and Charlotte Jack; *m* 1976, Elizabeth Alison, *d* of Rev. Canon James Seymour Denis Mansel, *qv*; two *d*. *Educ:* Rugby; Trinity Coll., Cambridge (MA). Called to Bar, Inner Temple, 1966. *Recreations:* gardening and wood. *Address:* 1 Hare Court, Temple, EC4.

JACK, Prof. Robert Barr; Partner, McGrigor, Donald & Moncrieffs, Solicitors, Glasgow (formerly McGrigor, Donald & Co.), since 1957; Professor of Mercantile Law, Glasgow University, since 1978; *b* 18 March 1928; *s* of Robert Hendry Jack and Christina Alexandra Jack; *m* 1958, Anna Thorburn Thomson; two *s*. *Educ:* Kilsyth Acad.; High Sch., Glasgow; Glasgow Univ. MA 1948, LLB 1951. Admitted a solicitor in Scotland, 1951. Member: Company Law Cttee of Law Society of Scotland, 1971– (Convener,

1978–85); Scottish Law Commn, 1974–77. Scottish observer on Dept of Trade's Insolvency Law Review Cttee, 1977–82; Mem., DoT Adv. Panel on Company Law, 1980–83; Lay Member: Council for the Securities Industry, 1983–85; Stock Exchange Council, 1984–. Chairman: Brownlee plc, Timber Merchants, Glasgow, 1984– (Dir, 1974–); Joseph Dunn (Bottlers) Ltd, Soft Drink Manufacturers, Glasgow, 1983–; Director: Scottish Metropolitan Property plc, 1980–; Clyde Football Club Ltd, 1980–; Bank of Scotland, 1985–. Chm., Scottish Nat. Council of YMCAs, 1966–73; Pres., Scottish Nat. Union of YMCAs, 1983–. Chm., The Turnberry Trust; Governor, Hutchesons' Educational Trust, Glasgow, 1978– (Chm. 1980–). *Publications:* lectures on various aspects of company law, and articles on the legal implications of current cost accounting and recent company legislation. *Recreations:* golf, hopeful support of one of Glasgow's less fashionable football teams; a dedicated lover of Isle of Arran which serves as a retreat and restorative. *Address:* (home) 39 Mansewood Road, Glasgow G43 1TN. *T:* 041–632 1659; (office) Pacific House, 70 Wellington Street, Glasgow G2 6SB. *Clubs:* Caledonian; Western (Glasgow); Pollok Golf; Shiskine Golf and Tennis (Isle of Arran) (Captain 1973–75).

JACKLIN, Anthony, OBE 1970; professional golfer, 1962–85, retired; Commissioner of Golf, Las Aves Golf Club, Sotogrande, since 1983; *b* 7 July 1944; *s* of Arthur David Jacklin; *m* 1966, Vivien; two *s* one *d*. Successes include: British Assistant Pro Championship, 1965; Pringle Tournament, 1967; Dunlop Masters, 1967; Greater Jacksonville Open, USA, 1968; British Open Championship, 1969; US Open Championship, 1970; Benson & Hedges, 1971; British Professional Golfers Assoc., 1972, 1982; Gtr Jacksonville Open, 1972; Bogota Open, 1973 and 1974; Italian Open, 1973; Dunlop Masters, 1973; Scandinavian Open, 1975; Kerrygold International, 1976; English National PGA Championship, 1977; German Open, 1979; Jersey Open, 1981; PGA Champion, 1982; Ryder Cup: player, 1967–80, team captain, 1983–. Professional Golfers' Association: Life Vice-Pres., 1970; Hon. Life Mem., European Tournament Players Div. *Publications:* Golf with Tony Jacklin, 1969; The Price of Success, 1979; (with Peter Dobereiner) Jacklin's Golfing Secrets, 1983; Tony Jacklin: the first forty years, 1985. *Recreations:* shooting, flying. *Address:* Las Aves Golf Club, Sotogrande, Costa del Sol, Spain. *Clubs:* Potters Bar Golf; Hon. Mem. of others.

JACKLING, Sir Roger William, GCMG 1976 (KCMG 1965; CMG 1955); HM Diplomatic Service, retired; *b* 10 May 1913; *s* of P. Jackling, OBE, and Lucy Jackling; *m* 1938, Joan Tustin; two *s* (and one *s* decd). *Educ:* Felsted. DPA, London Univ., 1932; Solicitor, Supreme Court, 1935; Actg Vice-Consul, New York, 1940; Commercial Sec., Quito, 1942; 2nd Sec., Washington, 1943; 1st Sec., 1945; transf. Foreign Office, 1947; seconded to Cabinet Office, 1950 (Asst Sec.); Counsellor (commercial), The Hague, 1951; Economic and Financial Adviser to UK High Commr, Bonn; and UK commercial rep. in Germany, 1953; Minister (Economic), British Embassy, Bonn, 1955; Counsellor, British Embassy, Washington, 1957–59; Asst Under-Sec. of State, FO, 1959–63; Dep. Permanent UK Rep. to United Nations, 1963–67 (with personal rank of Ambassador from 1965); Dep. Under-Sec. of State, FO, 1967–68; Ambassador to Federal Republic of Germany, 1968–72; Leader, UK Delegn to UN Conf. on Law of the Sea, 1973–75. Chm., Bd of Trustees, Anglo-German Foundn for Study of Industrial Society, 1973–77; Mem., Chairmen's Panel, CS Selection Bd, 1974–84. *Recreations:* gardening, golf. *Address:* 37 Boundary Road, St John's Wood, NW8. *Club:* Travellers'.

JACKMAN, Air Marshal Sir Douglas, KBE 1959 (CBE 1943); CB 1946; RAF; idc 1948; Air Officer Commanding-in-Chief, Royal Air Force Maintenance Command, 1958–61, retired; *b* 26 Oct. 1902; twin *s* of late A. J. Jackman; *m* 1931, Marjorie Leonore, *d* of late A. Hyland, Kingsdown, Kent. *Educ:* HMS Worcester. Officer Royal Mail Line until 1926; joined RAF, 1926; served in Iraq, 1928–30, in No 55 Squadron; in UK with Wessex Bombing Area and at Cranwell until 1934; to Middle East Command in 1934 and served at Aboukir until 1938, when posted to HQ Middle East until 1943; with Mediterranean Air Command and Mediterranean Allied Air Forces HQ until 1944; HQ Balkan Air Force, 1944–45 (despatches five times, CB, CBE, Comdr Order George 1st of Greece with Swords, AFC [Greek]); Dir of Movements Air Ministry, 1946–47; Dir of Organization (forecasting and planning), Air Ministry, 1949–52; AOC No 40 Group, 1952–55; Dir-Gen. of Equipment, Air Ministry, 1955–58; Co-ordinator, Anglo-American Relations, Air Ministry, 1961–64. Chm., Lady Jackman Trust to Assist the Blind. *Publication:* technical, on planning, 1942. *Recreations:* golf (Member: RAF Golfing Soc.; Seniors Golfing Soc., Natal); woodworking. *Address:* 7 Poynton Place, Durban, South Africa. *Clubs:* Royal Over-Seas League; Durban Country.

JACKS, Hector Beaumont, MA; Headmaster of Bedales School, 1946–July 1962; *b* 25 June 1903; *s* of late Dr L. P. Jacks; *m* 1st, Mary (*d* 1959), *d* of Rev. G. N. Nuttall Smith; one *s* one *d*; 2nd, Nancy, *d* of F. E. Strudwick. *Educ:* Magdalen Coll. Sch. and Wadham Coll., Oxford. Asst master, Wellington Coll., Berks, 1925–32; Headmaster of Willaston Sch., Nantwich, 1932–37; Second Master, Cheltenham Coll. Junior Sch., 1940–46. *Recreation:* gardening. *Address:* Applegarth, Spotted Cow Lane, Buxted, Sussex. *T:* Buxted 2296.

JACKSON, family name of **Baron Allerton.**

JACKSON, Albert Leslie Samuel, JP; Member, Birmingham City Council, since 1952; Chairman, Birmingham Technology Ltd (Aston Science Park), since 1984; Director and Committee Chairman, National Exhibition Centre, since 1984; *b* 20 Jan. 1918; *s* of Bert Jackson and Olive Powell; *m* Gladys Burley; one *s* one *d*. *Educ:* Handsworth New Road Council Sch. War service, Radio Mechanic, RAF. Lord Mayor, 1975–76, Dep. Lord Mayor, 1978–79, Birmingham. JP 1968. *Recreations:* chess, sailing. *Address:* 10 St Helier

House, Manor Close, Melville Road, Birmingham B16 9NG. *T:* 021–454 0849 and Tewkesbury 72541.

JACKSON, Brig. Alexander Cosby Fishburn, CVO 1957; CBE 1954 (OBE 1943); *b* 4 Dec. 1903; *s* of late Col S. C. F. Jackson, CMG, DSO, and Lucy B. Jackson (*née* Drake); *m* 1934, Margaret Hastings Hervey (*d* 1984), Montclair, NJ, USA; one *s* (and one *s* decd). *Educ:* Yardley Court, Tonbridge; Haileybury Coll.; RMC Sandhurst. 2nd Lt, R Hants Regt, 1923; Brig. 1952; employed RWAFF, 1927–33; served in Middle East, 1940–45 (despatches twice, OBE); Dep. Dir of Quartering, War Office, 1945–48; Comdr Northern Area, Kenya, 1948–51; Comdr Caribbean Area, 1951–54; HBM Military Attaché, Paris, 1954–58. ADC to the Queen, 1955–58. Order of Kutuzov 2nd Class, USSR, 1944; Comdr Legion of Honour, France, 1957. *Publication:* Rose Croix: a history of the Ancient and Accepted Rite for England and Wales, 1981. *Recreation:* bowls. *Address:* Glenwhern, Grouville, Jersey.

JACKSON, Maj.-Gen. Arthur James, BSc; CEng; FIEE; independent consultant; *b* Barrow-upon-Humber, Lincs, 31 March 1923; *e s* of late Comdr A. J. Jackson, RD, RNR, Barrow-upon-Humber; *m* 1948, Joan Marguerite, *d* of late Trevor Lyons Relton, MBE, Whyteleafe, Surrey; two *s* two *d*. *Educ:* Barton Sch.; RMCS. BSc London, 1951. Joined Royal Signals, 1944; commnd 1946; served Italy and British Embassy, Belgrade, 1946–47; Austria, WO, Staff Coll., Far East, RMCS, BAOR, 1948–64; GSO1, Defence Ops Requirements Staff, MoD, 1965–66; CO 4th Div. Signal Regt, BAOR, 1967–68; psc, ptsc, psc†; Comdr (Brigadier), 12 Signal Bde, 1969–71; Dir of Telecommunications (Army), 1972–73; Dep. Comdt and Sen. Military Dir of Studies, RMCS, 1974–75; Mil. Dep., Head of Defence Sales, MoD, 1975–78, retired. Col Comdt, Royal Signals, 1978–84; Chm., Royal Signals Instn, 1979–84. *Recreations:* golf, shooting, gardening, organ music. *Address:* Roughwood House, Fleet, Hampshire; Tower Lodge, Brampford Speke, Devon. *Club:* Army and Navy.

JACKSON, Mrs (Audrey) Muriel W.; *see* Ward-Jackson.

JACKSON, Barry Trevor, MS, FRCS; Surgeon to the Royal Household, since 1983; Consultant Surgeon: St Thomas' Hospital, since 1973; Queen Victoria Hospital, East Grinstead, since 1977; King Edward VII Hospital for Officers, since 1983; *b* 7 July 1936; *er s* of Arthur Stanley Jackson and Violet May (*née* Fry); *m* 1962, Sheila May, *d* of late Bert and Lilian Wood; two *s* one *d*. *Educ:* Sir George Monoux Grammar Sch.; King's College London; Westminster Med. Sch. (Entrance Scholar). MB, BS 1963; MRCS, LRCP 1963; MS 1972; FRCS 1967. Down Bros Ltd, 1952–54; RAF 1954–56; junior surgical appts, Gordon Hosp., St James' Hosp., Balham, St Peter's Hosp., Chertsey, St Helier Hosp., Carshalton, St Thomas' Hosp.; Royal College of Surgeons: Arris & Gale Lectr, 1973; Examr Primary FRCS, 1977–83; Mem. Court of Examrs, 1983–; Asst Editor Annals RCS, 1984–; Hon. Sec., Assoc. of Surgeons of GB and Ireland, 1986– (Mem. Council, 1982–85); ext. examr in surgery: Khartoum, 1981; Ibadan, 1982; Colombo, 1984; Mem., W Lambeth Health Authy, 1982–83; Special Trustee, St Thomas' Hosp., 1982–84; Chm., SE Thames Regional Med. Adv. Cttee, 1983–. *Publications:* contribs to surgical jls and textbooks (surgery of gastro-intestinal tract). *Recreations:* book collecting, reading, medical history, music, especially opera. *Address:* 53 Harley Street, W1N 1DD. *T:* 01–935 2884; 7 St Matthew's Avenue, Surbiton, Surrey KT6 6JJ *T:* 01–399 3157. *Club:* Athenæum.

JACKSON, Very Rev. Brandon Donald; Provost of Bradford Cathedral, since 1977; *b* 11 Aug. 1934; *s* of Herbert and Millicent Jackson; *m* 1958, Mary Lindsay, 2nd *d* of John and Helen Philip; two *s* one *d*. *Educ:* Stockport School; Liverpool Univ.; St Catherine's Coll. and Wycliffe Hall, Oxford (LLB, DipTh). Curate: Christ Church, New Malden, Surrey, 1958–61; St George, Leeds, 1961–65; Vicar, St Peter, Shipley, Yorks, 1965–77. Religious Adviser to Yorkshire Television, 1969–79; Church Commissioner, 1971–73; Mem., Marriage Commn, 1975–78; Examining Chaplain to Bishop of Bradford, 1974–80; Mem. Council, Wycliffe Hall, Oxford, 1971–85. Governor: Harrogate College, 1974–; Bradford Grammar Sch., 1977–. *Recreations:* sport (cricket, squash), fell-walking, fishing. *Address:* Provost's House, Cathedral Close, Bradford BD1 4EG. *T:* Bradford 732023.

JACKSON, Caroline Frances, DPhil; Member (C) Wiltshire, European Parliament, since 1984; *b* 5 Nov. 1946; *d* of G. H. Harvey; *m* 1975, Robert Victor Jackson, *qv*; one *s* decd. *Educ:* School of St Clare, Penzance; St Hugh's and Nuffield Colleges, Oxford. MA, DPhil. Elizabeth Wordsworth Research Fellow, St Hugh's College, Oxford, 1972. Oxford City Councillor, 1970–73; contested (C) Birmingham, Erdington, 1974. Secretariat of Cons. Group, European Parlt, Luxembourg, 1974–76, Brussels, 1976–78; Head, London Office, European Democratic Group, 1979–84. Mem., Nat. Consumer Council, 1982–84. *Publications:* articles in historical jls. *Recreations:* walking, painting, tennis, golf. *Address:* 74 Carlisle Mansions, Carlisle Place, SW1P 1HZ. *T:* (office) 01–222 2160, (home) 01–828 6113; New House, Southmoor, Oxon. *T:* Oxford 821243.

JACKSON, Christopher Murray; Member (C) Kent East, European Parliament, since 1979; European Democratic Group spokesman on development and co-operation, since 1981; *b* 24 May 1935; *s* of Rev. Howard Murray Jackson and Doris Bessie Jackson (*née* Grainger); *m* 1971, Carlie Elizabeth Keeling; one *s* one *d*. *Educ:* Kingswood Sch., Bath; Magdalen Coll., Oxford (Open Exhibnr, BA Hons (Physics) 1959, MA 1964); Goethe Univ., Frankfurt; London Sch. of Economics. National Service, commnd RAF, Pilot, 1954–56. Management Trainee, Unilever, 1959; Sen. Man., Unilever Ltd, 1967; Gen. Marketing Man., Save and Prosper Gp, 1969; Head of Corporate Planning, D. MacPherson Gp, 1971–74; Dir, Corporate Development Spillers Ltd, 1974–80. Contested (C): East Ham South, 1970; Northampton North, Feb. 1974. Member, Gen. Council, Cons. Gp for Europe, 1974–76. Rapporteur-General, ACP-EEC Jt Assembly, 1985–86. Treas. and Council Mem., St Martin-in-the-Fields, 1975–77; Member: Exec. Cttee, Soc. for Long Range Planning, 1976–79; Council, Centre for European Agricl Studies, 1981–. *Publications:* UK Apple Industry, European Democratic Group, 1980; EDG Briefs: Cars and the Uncommon Market, 1983; The EEC and the Third World, 1983; World Hunger, 1984. *Recreations:* music, gardening, ski-ing. *Address:* 8 Wellmeade Drive, Sevenoaks, Kent TN13 1QA. *T:* Sevenoaks (0732) 456688.

JACKSON, Daphne Diana; Personnel and Central Services Officer, Borough Engineer and Surveyor's Department, Borough of Hounslow, since 1978; *b* 8 Oct. 1933; *d* of Major Thomas Casey, MC, South Lancs Regt, and Agnes Nora Casey (*née* Gradden); *m* 1953, John Hudleston Jackson. *Educ:* Folkestone County Grammar School for Girls; South West London College. ACIS. Westminster Bank, 1951–53; Kent Educn Cttee, 1953–57; Pfizer Ltd, Sandwich, 1957–67; Southern Transformer Products, 1967–68; Borough of Hounslow, 1968–. Mem., NACRO Employment Adv. Cttee, 1984–; Chm., Gen. Adv. Council to IBA, 1985– (Mem., 1980). Mem., Soroptimists International. Freeman, City of London, 1980; Liveryman, Chartered Secretaries and Administrators Co., 1980. *Recreations:* bereavement counselling, learning about antiques, reading. *Address:* 9 Abbottsmede Close, Twickenham, Middx. *T:* 01–892 0766.

JACKSON, Prof. Daphne Frances, FIEE; FInstP; Professor and Head of Department of Physics, since 1971, and Dean of Faculty of Science, since 1984, University of Surrey; *b* 23 Sept. 1936; *d* of Albert Henry Jackson and Frances Ethel Elliott. *Educ:* Peterborough County Grammar Sch.; Imperial Coll. of Sci. and Tech., Univ. of London (BSc Phys 1958; ARCS 1958; DSc 1970); Battersea Coll. of Sci and Technol. (PhD 1962). FInstP 1976; MIEEE 1982, FIEE 1984. Lectr in Physics, Battersea Coll. of Technol., 1962–66; Reader in Nuclear Physics, Surrey Univ., 1966–71. Res. Asst Prof., Univ. of Washington, 1963–64; Visiting Professor: Univ. of Maryland, 1970; Univ. de Louvain, 1972; Univ. of Lund, 1980–82. Member: Nuclear Phys. Bd, SERC, 1973–76 (Mem., Phys. Cttee, Sci. Bd, 1974–76, 1985–); Metrology and Standards Req. Bd, DTI, 1973–75; NRPB, 1980–85; W Surrey and NE Hants DHA, 1981– (Vice-Chm., 1983–84); Regional Sci. Cttee, 1976–85, Regional Res. Cttee, 1983–, SW Thames RHA; Ind./Educn Adv. Cttee, DTI, 1983–; Coordinating Gp for Develt of Training for Women, MSC, 1983–; Phys. Scis Sub-Cttee, UGC, 1985–; Chm., Bd of Dirs, Surrey Univ. Press, 1984–. Pres., Women's Engineering Soc., 1983–85 (Vice-Pres., 1981–83); Vice-Pres., Inst. of Physics, 1974–78. FRSA 1984. Liveryman, Co. of Engineers, 1986–. *Publications:* Nuclear Reactions, 1970; Concept of Atomic Physics, 1971; (with R. C. Barrett) Nuclear Sizes and Structure, 1977; (with K. Kouris and N. M. Spyrou) Imaging with Ionising Radiations, 1982; (ed) Imaging with Non Ionising Radiations, 1983; papers and articles on nuclear physics, med. physics, educn, sci. policy in learned jls. *Recreations:* travel, writing, encouraging women in science and engineering. *Address:* 5 St Omer Road, Guildford, Surrey. *T:* Guildford 573996. *Club:* National Liberal.

JACKSON, Prof. David Cooper; Vice-President, Immigration Appeal Tribunal, since 1984; Professor of Law, University of Southampton (part time), since 1984; *b* 3 Dec. 1931; *s* of late Rev. James Jackson and of Mary Emma Jackson; *m* 1967, Roma Lilian (*née* Pendergast). *Educ:* Ashville Coll., Harrogate; Brasenose Coll., Oxford. MA, BCL; Senior Hulme Scholar, 1954. Called to the Bar, Inner Temple, 1957, and Victoria, Australia, 1967. Bigelow Fellow, Univ. of Chicago, 1955; Fellow, Assoc. of Bar of City of New York, 1956; National Service, 1957–59; Senior Lectr, Univ. of Singapore, 1963–64; Sir John Latham Prof. of Law, Monash Univ., 1965–70 (Carnegie Travelling Fellow, 1969); Prof. of Law, Southampton Univ., 1970–83 (Dean of Law, 1972–75, 1978–81; Dep. Vice-Chancellor, 1982–83); Consultant, UNCTAD, 1980, 1983; Dir, Inst. of Maritime Law, 1982–83, Consultant, 1984–. Visiting Professor: Queen Mary Coll., London, 1969; Arizona State Univ., 1976; Melbourne Univ., 1976. JP Hants 1980–84. Editor, World Shipping Laws, 1979– (and contrib.). *Publications:* Principles of Property Law, 1967; The Conflicts Process, 1975; Enforcement of Maritime Claims, 1985; articles in legal jls, Australia, UK, USA. *Recreations:* walking, travel, theatre. *Address:* Fleet House, 9A Captains Row, Lymington, Hants SO4 9RP. *T:* Lymington 72008.

JACKSON, Sir Edward; *see* Jackson, Sir J. E.

JACKSON, Edward Francis, MA; Director, Oxford University Institute of Economics and Statistics, and Professorial Fellow of St Antony's College, Oxford, 1959–82; *b* 11 July 1915; *o s* of F. E. Jackson, schoolmaster, and Miriam Eveline (*née* Jevon); *m* 1st, 1942, Anne Katherine Cloake (marr. diss.); 2nd, 1954, Mrs Marion Marianne Marris (*d* 1972), *o c* of late Arthur Ellinger; two *s*. *Educ:* West Bromwich Grammar Sch.; Univ. of Birmingham; Magdalen Coll., Oxford. BCom Birmingham with 1st cl. hons, 1934; Magdalen Coll., Oxford (Demy): 1st in PPE, 1937; Jun. G. W. Medley Schol., 1935–36; Sen. Demy, 1937; Lecturer in Economics: New Coll., 1938; Magdalen Coll., 1939. Temp. Civil Servant in War Cabinet Offices, 1941–45; established Civil Servant (Central Statistical Office), 1945; Dep. Dir, Res. and Planning Div., UN Econ. Commn for Europe, 1951–56. University Lectr in Economic Statistics, Oxford, and Research Fellow of St Antony's Coll., Oxford, 1956–59. Mem. Transport Adv. Council, 1965. *Publications:* The Nigerian National Accounts, 1950–57 (with P. N. C. Obigbo), 1960; articles in economic journals. *Address:* 62 Park Town, Oxford. *Club:* Reform.

JACKSON, Eric Stead, CB 1954; *b* 22 Aug. 1909; *yr s* of Stead Jackson, Shipley Glen, Yorks; *m* 1938, Yvonne Renée (*d* 1982), *o d* of Devereaux Doria De Brétigny, Victoria, BC; one *s* one *d*. *Educ:* Bradford Grammar Sch.; Corpus Christi Coll., Oxford (Scholar). 1st Class Hons Math. Mods, Math. Finals and Nat. Sci. Finals, Jun. Math. schol., 1930; MA. Asst Principal, Air Ministry, 1932; Sec., British Air Mission to Australia and NZ, 1939; Private Sec. to Minister of Aircraft Production, 1942, and to Resident Minister in Washington, 1943; Sec., British Supply Council in N America, 1944; Dir-Gen. Aircraft Branch, Control Commission, Berlin, 1945; Dep. Pres. Economic Sub-Commission, 1947; British Head of Bizonal Delegation to OEEC, Paris, 1948; Under Sec., Ministry of Supply, 1950–56; Dir-Gen., Atomic Weapons, Ministry of Supply, 1956–59; Under-Secretary: Min. of Aviation, 1959–67; Min. of Technology, 1967–70; Dept of Trade and Industry, 1970–71. *Address:* 10 Ditchley Road, Charlbury, Oxfordshire. *T:* Charlbury 810682.

JACKSON, Francis Alan, OBE 1978; Organist and Master of the Music, York Minster, 1946–82; *b* 2 Oct. 1917; *s* of W. A. Jackson; *m* 1950, Priscilla, *d* of Tyndale Procter; two *s* one *d*. *Educ:* York Minster Choir Sch.; Sir Edward Bairstow. Chorister, York Minster, 1929–33; ARCO, 1936; BMus Dunelm 1937; FRCO (Limpus Prize), 1937; DMus Dunelm 1957. Organist Malton Parish Church, 1933–40. Served War of 1939–45, with 9th Lancers in Egypt, N Africa and Italy, 1940–46. Asst Organist, York Minster, 1946; Conductor York Musical Soc., 1947–82; Conductor York Symphony Orchestra, 1947–80. Pres. Incorp. Assoc. of Organists, 1960–62; Pres., RCO, 1972–74. Hon. FRSCM 1963; Hon. Fellow, Westminster Choir Coll., Princeton, NJ, 1970; Hon. FRNCM, 1982. DUniv York, 1983. Order of St William of York, 1983. *Publications:* organ music, including 4 sonatas, church music, songs, monodramas. *Recreation:* gardening. *Address:* Nethergarth, Acklam, Malton, N Yorks YO17 9RG. *T:* Burythorpe 395.

JACKSON, Frederick Hume, CMG 1978; OBE 1966; HM Diplomatic Service, retired; Consul-General, Düsseldorf, 1975–78; *b* 8 Sept. 1918; *o s* of late Maj.-Gen. G. H. N. Jackson, CB, CMG, DSO, Rathmore, Winchcombe, Glos and Eileen, *d* of J. Hume Dudgeon, Merville, Booterstown, Co. Dublin; *m* 1950, Anne Gibson; two *s* one *d* (and one *s* decd). *Educ:* Winchester; Clare Coll., Cambridge (MA). Military service, 1939–46: GSO3 (Intelligence), HQ 1 Corps District; Colonial Service (Tanganyika), 1946–57; FO, 1957–60; Head of Chancery, Saigon, 1960–62; 1st Sec., Washington, 1962–67; Counsellor and Dep. Head, UK Delegn to European Communities, Brussels, 1967–69; UK Resident Representative, Internat. Atomic Energy Agency, 1969–75; UK Perm. Representative to UNIDO, 1971–75. Chm., Sevenoaks Cons. Assoc., 1982–85, Vice-Pres., 1985–86, Pres., 1986–. *Recreations:* fishing, sailing, shooting, riding. *Address:* The Old Vicarage, Leigh, Tonbridge, Kent TN11 8QJ. *T:* Hildenborough 833495; c/o Barclays Bank, St Nicholas Street, Scarborough, North Yorks YO11 2HS. *Club:* Flyfishers'.

JACKSON, Sir Geoffrey (Holt Seymour), KCMG 1971 (CMG 1963); HM Diplomatic Service, retired; Member, BBC General Advisory Council, 1976–80; *b* 4 March 1915; *s* of Samuel Seymour Jackson and Marie Cecile Dudley Ryder; *m* 1939, Patricia Mary Evelyn Delany; one *s*. *Educ:* Bolton Sch.; Emmanuel Coll., Cambridge. Entered Foreign Service, 1937; Vice-Consul, Beirut, Cairo, Bagdad; Acting Consul-Gen., Basra, 1946; 1st

Sec., Bogotá, 1946–50; Berne, 1954–56; Minister, Honduras, 1956, HM Ambassador to Honduras, 1957–60; Consul-Gen., Seattle, 1960–64; Senior British Trade Commissioner in Ontario, Canada, 1964; Minister (Commercial), Toronto, 1965–69; Ambassador to Uruguay, 1969–72; kidnapped by terrorists and held prisoner for 8 months, Jan.-Sept. 1971; Dep. Under-Sec. of State, FCO, 1973. Mem. London Bd, Nat. and Provincial Building Soc. (formerly Burnley Building Soc.), 1976–86. Chm., BBC Adv. Gp on Social Effects of TV, 1975–77. Pres., Assoc. of Lancastrians, 1974. Freeman, City of London, 1976. *Publications:* The Oven-Bird, 1972; People's Prison, 1973; Surviving the Long Night, 1974; Concorde Diplomacy, 1981. *Recreations:* remembering ski-ing, golf, Latin-Americana. *Address:* 63B Cadogan Square, SW1. *Club:* Canning.

JACKSON, Most Rev. George Frederic Clarence; Priest-in-charge, All Saints, Katepwe, since 1984; *b* 5 July 1907; *s* of James Sandiford Jackson; *m* 1939, Eileen de Montfort Wellborne; two *s* two *d*. *Educ:* University of Toronto. Deacon, 1934; Priest, 1935, Diocese of Niagara. Diocese of: Toronto, 1937–38; Chester, 1938–46; Niagara, 1946–58; Qu'Appelle, 1958–77. Hon. Canon, Christ Church Cathedral, Hamilton, Ontario, 1952; Dean of Qu'Appelle, 1958; Bishop of Qu'Appelle, 1960; Archbishop of Qu'Appelle and Metropolitan of Rupert's Land, 1970–77; Bishop-Ordinary to the Canadian Armed Forces, 1977–80. Priest-in-charge, Abernethy-Balcarres, 1980–84. Mayor, Katepwe Beach Village, 1980–85. DD (*hc*) 1959. *Recreations:* cross-country skiing, gardening. *Address:* Box 519, Fort Qu'Appelle, Saskatchewan S0G 1S0, Canada.

JACKSON, Gerald Breck; *b* 28 June 1916; *o s* of Gerald Breck Jackson and Mary Jackson, Paterson, NJ; *m* 1940, Brenda Mary, *o d* of William and Mary Titshall; one *s*. *Educ:* various schs in USA; Canford Sch., Dorset; Faraday House Engrg Coll. Graduate Trainee, Central Electricity Bd, 1938. HM Forces, RE, 1939–43. Various appts in HV transmission with CEB and BEA, 1943–55; Overhead Line Design Engr, BEA, 1955–61; Asst Regional Dir, CEGB, 1961–64; Chief Ops Engr, CEGB, 1964–66; Regional Dir, NW Region, CEGB, 1966–68; Dir Engineering, English Electric Co. Ltd, 1968–69; Sen. Exec., Thomas Tilling Ltd, and Dir subsid. cos, 1969–71; Man. Dir, John Mowlem & Co. Ltd, 1971–72; Man. Dir, NCB (Ancillaries) Ltd, 1972–78. DFH, CEng, FIEE. *Publications:* Network for the Nation, 1960; Power Controlled, 1966. *Recreations:* photography, pen-and-ink drawing. *Address:* Larchwood, 1A Lansdowne Square, Tunbridge Wells, Kent TN1 2NF.

JACKSON, Glenda, CBE 1978; actress; Director, United British Artists, since 1983; *b* Birkenhead, 9 May 1936; *d* of Harry and Joan Jackson; *m* 1958, Roy Hodges (marr. diss. 1976); one *s*. *Educ:* West Kirby Co. Grammar Sch. for Girls; RADA. Actress with various repertory cos, 1957–63, stage manager, Crewe Rep.; joined Royal Shakespeare Co., 1963. Pres., Play Matters (formerly Toy Libraries Assoc.), 1976–. *Plays:* All Kinds of Men, Arts, 1957; The Idiot, Lyric, 1962; Alfie, Mermaid and Duchess, 1963; Royal Shakespeare Co.: Theatre of Cruelty Season, LAMDA, 1964; The Jew of Malta, 1964; Marat/Sade, 1965, NY and Paris, 1965; Love's Labour's Lost, Squire Puntila and his Servant Matti, The Investigation, Hamlet, 1965; US, Aldwych, 1966; Three Sisters, Royal Ct, 1967; Fanghorn, Fortune, 1967; Collaborators, Duchess, 1973; The Maids, Greenwich, 1974; Hedda Gabler, Australia, USA, London, 1975; The White Devil, Old Vic, 1976; Stevie, Vaudeville, 1977; Antony and Cleopatra, Stratford, 1978; Rose, Duke of York's, 1980; Summit Conference, Lyric, 1982; Great and Small, Vaudeville, 1983; Strange Interlude, Duke of York's, 1984; Phedra, Old Vic, 1984, Aldwych, 1985; Across from the Garden of Allah, Comedy, 1986; *films:* This Sporting Life, 1963; Marat/Sade, 1967; Negatives, 1968; Women in Love (Oscar Award, 1971), 1970; The Music Lovers, 1971; Sunday, Bloody Sunday, 1971; The Boyfriend, 1972; Mary, Queen of Scots, 1972; Triple Echo, 1972; Il Sorviso de Grande Tentatore (The Tempter), 1973; Bequest to the Nation, 1973; A Touch of Class (Oscar Award, 1974), 1973; The Maids, 1974; The Romantic Englishwoman, 1974; Hedda Gabler, 1975; The Incredible Sarah, 1976; House Calls, 1978; Stevie, 1978; The Class of Miss MacMichael, 1978; Lost and Found, 1979; Hopscotch, 1980; Return of the Soldier, 1982; Health, 1982; Giro City, 1982; Sacharov, 1983; Turtle Diary, 1985; *TV:* Elizabeth in Elizabeth R, 1971; The Patricia Neal Story (Amer.). Best film actress awards: Variety Club of GB, 1971, 1975, 1978; NY Film Critics, 1971; Nat. Soc. of Film Critics, US, 1971. *Recreations:* cooking, gardening, reading Jane Austen. *Address:* c/o Crouch Associates, 59 Frith Street, W1.

JACKSON, Gordon Cameron, OBE 1979; actor since 1941; *b* 19 Dec. 1923; *m* 1951, Rona Anderson; two *s*. *Educ:* Hillhead High Sch., Glasgow. Originally an engrg draughtsman. First film, Foreman went to France, 1941; since then has appeared in over 60 films, including: Whisky Galore, 1948; Tunes of Glory, 1960; Mutiny on the Bounty, 1961; The Great Escape, 1962; The Ipcress File, 1964; The Prime of Miss Jean Brodie, 1968; The Shooting Party, 1984; The Whistle Blower, 1985. Theatre work includes: Seagulls over Sorrento, 1951; Moby Dick, 1955; Banquo in Macbeth, 1966; Wise Child, 1967; Horatio in Hamlet, 1969 (Clarence Derwent Award); Tesman in Hedda Gabler, 1970; Veterans, 1972; title role, Noah, and Malvolio in Twelfth Night, 1976; Death Trap, 1981; Cards on the Table, and Mass Appeal, 1982. Television series include: Upstairs, Downstairs, 1970–75 (Royal Television Soc. Award and Variety Club Award, 1975; Emmy Award, USA, 1976); The Professionals, 1977–81; A Town Like Alice, 1980 (Logie Award, Australia, 1982); Shaka Zulu, 1985; My Brother Tom, 1986. *Recreations:* listening to Mozart, gardening. *Address:* c/o ICM Ltd, 388 Oxford Street, W1N 9HE. *T:* 01–629 8080. *Club:* Garrick.

JACKSON, Gordon Noel, CMG 1962; MBE; HM Ambassador to Ecuador, 1967–70, retired; *b* 25 Dec. 1913; *m* 1959, Mary April Nettlefold, *er d* of late Frederick John Nettlefold and of Mrs Albert Coates; one *s* two *d*. Indian Political Service until 1947; then HM Foreign Service; Political Officer, Sharjah, 1947; transf. to Kuwait, Persian Gulf, 1949; transf. to Foreign Office, 1950; Consul, St Louis, USA, 1953; Foreign Service Officer, Grade 6, 1955; Consul-General: Basra, 1955–57; Lourenço Marques, 1957–60; Benghazi, 1960–63; HM Ambassador to Kuwait, 1963–67. *Publications:* Effective Horsemanship (for Dressage, Hunting, Three-day Events, Polo), 1967; (with W. Steinkraus) The Encyclopædia of the Horse, 1973. *Address:* Lowbarrow House, Leafield, Oxfordshire. *Club:* Travellers'.

JACKSON, Herbert, FRIBA; FRTPI; architect and planning consultant; in private practice since 1931; *b* 25 June 1909; *s* of John Herbert Jackson; *m* 1930, Margaret Elizabeth Pearson. *Educ:* Handsworth Grammar Sch.; Birmingham Sch. of Architecture. RIBA Bronze Medal, 1928; RIBA Saxon Snell Prizeman, 1930. Mem. RIBA Council, 1956–58; Vice-Pres. RIBA 1960–62; Chm., RIBA Allied Socs Conf., 1960–62. Gov., Birmingham Coll. of Art; Chm. Birmingham Civic Soc., 1960–65; Pres. Birmingham and Five Counties Architectural Assoc., 1956–58; Pres. Royal Birmingham Society of Artists, 1960–62 (Prof. of Architecture, 1961). *Publications:* (jt) Plans (for Minister of Town and Country Planning): S Wales, 1947; W Midlands and N Staffs, 1948. *Recreations:* travelling, reading. *Address:* 14 Clarendon Square, Leamington Spa, Warwicks. *T:* Leamington 24078.

JACKSON, Ian (Macgilchrist), BA Cantab, MB, BChir, FRCS, FRCOG; Obstetric and Gynæcological Surgeon, Middlesex Hospital, 1948–79, retired; Gynæcological Surgeon: Chelsea Hospital for Women, 1948–79; King Edward VII Hospital for Officers, 1961–84; Royal Masonic Hospital, 1963–79; Consulting Gynæcologist, King Edward VII Hospital, Midhurst, 1959; Consultant Obstetrician and Gynæcologist, RAF, 1964–83; *b* Shanghai, 11 Nov. 1914; *s* of Dr Ernest David Jackson; *m* 1943 (marr. diss., 1967); two *s* one *d*; *m* 1970, Deirdre Ruth Heitz. *Educ:* Marlborough Coll.; Trinity Hall, Cambridge (scholar; double 1st cl. hons, Nat. Sci. tripos pts I, II). London Hospital: open scholarship, 1936; house appointments, 1939; First Asst, Surgical and Obstetric and Gynæcol Depts, 1940–43. Served as Surgical Specialist, RAMC, 1943–47 (Major); Parachute Surgical Team, 224 Para. Field Amb.; Mobile Surgical Unit, 3 Commando Brigade. Royal College of Obstetricians and Gynæcologists: Council, 1951–61, 1962–70; Hon. Sec., 1954–61; Chm., Examination Cttee, 1962–65, Hon. Treas., 1966–70; Hon. Librarian, RSM, 1969–75. Examiner for Univs of Cambridge, Oxford, and London, Conjoint Bd and RCOG. Mem., Court of Assts, Worshipful Soc. of Apothecaries, 1966, Senior Warden 1977, Master 1978, Hon. Treas., 1985–; Pres., Chelsea Clinical Soc., 1979. Order of the Star of Africa (Liberia), 1969; Grand Officer of Order of Istiqlal, Jordan, 1970. *Publications:* British Obstetric and Gynæcological Practice (jtly), 1963; Obstetrics by Ten Teachers (jtly), 1966, 2nd edn 1972; Gynæcology by Ten Teachers (jtly), 1971; numerous contribs to medical literature. *Recreations:* fishing, golf, photography. *Address:* 23 Springfield Road, NW8. *T:* 01–624 3580; The Portland Hospital, 209 Great Portland Street, W1N. *T:* 01–580 4400.

JACKSON, James Barry; *see* Barry, Michael.

JACKSON, Sir (John) Edward, KCMG 1984 (CMG 1977); HM Diplomatic Service, retired; Chairman, Brecon Beacons-Comidel Ltd, since 1985; *b* 24 June 1925; *s* of Edward Harry and Margaret Jackson; *m* 1952, Eve Stainton Harris, *d* of late George James Harris, MC and of Mrs Friede Rowntree Harris, York; two *s* one *d*. *Educ:* Ardingly; Corpus Christi Coll., Cambridge. RNVR (Sub-Lt), 1943–46; joined Foreign (now Diplomatic) Service, 1947; FO, 1947–49; 3rd Sec., Paris, 1949–52; 2nd Sec., FO, 1952–56; Bonn, 1956–57; 1st Sec., Bonn, 1957–59; Guatemala City, 1959–62; FO, 1963–68; Counsellor, 1968; NATO Defence Coll., Rome, 1969; Counsellor (Political Adviser), British Mil. Govt, Berlin, 1969–73; Head of Defence Dept, FCO, 1973–75; Ambassador to Cuba, 1975–79; Head of UK Delegn to Negotiations on Mutual Reduction of Forces and Armaments and Associated Measures in Central Europe, with personal rank of Ambassador, 1980–82; Ambassador to Belgium, 1982–85. Dir, Armistice Festival, 1986–. Trustee, Imperial War Museum, 1986–. *Recreations:* pictures, antiques, tennis, golf. *Address:* 17 Paultons Square, SW3 5AP. *Clubs:* Travellers', Anglo-Belgian, Hurlingham.

JACKSON, John Wharton, JP; *b* 25 May 1902; *s* of John Jackson and Mary Wharton; *m* 1928, Mary Rigg; two *d*. *Educ:* Shrewsbury. Formerly Chm., Jackson's (Hurstead) Ltd, Rochdale. High Sheriff of Radnorshire, 1944–45; JP County of Lancaster, 1952. *Recreation:* golf. *Address:* Brackens, Mottram St Andrew, near Macclesfield, Cheshire. *T:* Prestbury 89277.

JACKSON, Joseph, QC 1967; *b* 21 Aug. 1924; *s* of late Samuel Jackson and of Hetty Jackson; *m* 1st, 1952, Marjorie Henrietta (*née* Lyons) (marr. diss. 1982); three *d*; 2nd, 1982, Hon. Dame Margaret Myfanwy Wood Booth, *qv*. *Educ:* Queens' Coll., Cambridge; University Coll., London. MA, LLB Cantab, LLM London. Barrister, 1947, Gibraltar Bar; Bencher, Middle Temple, 1980. Chairman: Probate and Divorce Bar Assoc., 1968–69; Family Law Bar Assoc., 1980–84. Member: General Council of the Bar, 1969–73; Senate of the Inns of Court, 1975–78; Bar Cttee, 1980–81. Mem., Matrimonial Causes Rules Cttee, 1969–73 and 1977–81; Special Divorce Comr, 1969–70. Dept of Trade Inspector, Dowgate and General Investments Ltd, 1975–78. Mem. legal aid cttees including: Law Soc. Legal Aid Cttee, 1975–78; Lord Chancellor's Working Party to review legal aid legislation; Council of Law Reporting, 1982–. Lectures: Weir Meml, Alberta, 1981; Opas Meml, NSW, 1982. *Publications:* English Legal History, 1951 (2nd edn 1955); Formation and Annulment of Marriage, 1951, 2nd edn, 1969; Rayden on Divorce, 5th edn (supp.) 1951 to 14th edn 1983; Matrimonial Finance and Taxation, 1972, 4th edn, 1986; (consulting editor) Clarke Hall and Morrison on Children, 9th edn, 1977; contrib. to Halsbury's Laws of England, Encyclopædia Britannica, Atkin's Encyclopædia of Court Forms, Law Quarterly Review, Modern Law Review, Canadian Bar Review, Alberta Law Review, etc. *Recreations:* gardening, painting, ceramics. *Address:* 1 Mitre Court Buildings, Temple, EC4. *T:* 01–353 0434/2277.

JACKSON, Prof. Kenneth Hurlstone, CBE 1985; FBA 1957; FSAScot 1951; FRSE 1977; Professor of Celtic Languages, Literatures, History and Antiquities, Edinburgh University, 1950–79; *b* 1 Nov. 1909; *s* of Alan Stuart Jackson and Lucy Hurlstone; *m* 1936, Janet Dall Galloway, of Hillside, Kinross-shire; one *s* one *d*. *Educ:* Whitgift Sch., Croydon; St John's Coll., Cambridge (Exhibitioner and Scholar). First Cl. Hons with Distinction, Classical Tripos, 1930 and 1931 (Senior Classic, 1931); BA 1931; First Cl. Hons with Distinction, Archaeology and Anthropology Tripos, 1932; Sir William Brown medals for Greek and Latin verse, 1930 (two), 1931; Allen Research Studentship, 1932–34; research in Celtic at University Colls of North Wales and Dublin. Fellowship at St John's Coll., and Faculty Lectr in Celtic, Cambridge Univ., 1934–39; MA 1935; LittD 1954; Hon. Fellow, St John's Coll., 1979; Lectureship, 1939, Assoc. Professorship, 1940–49, Professorship, 1949–50, Celtic Languages and Literatures, Harvard Univ. Hon. AM Harvard, 1940. Editor of the Journal of Celtic Studies, 1949–57. Corr. Fellow of Mediæval Acad. of America, 1951; President: Scottish Anthropological and Folklore Soc., 1952–60; English Place-Name Soc., 1979–84 (Vice Pres., 1973–79; Hon. Pres., 1985); Internat. Congress of Celtic Studies, 1975–; Vice-Pres. of Soc. of Antiquaries of Scotland, 1960–63; Mem., Comité Internat. des Sciences Onomastiques, 1955–69, Hon. Mem., 1981; Mem. Council for Name Studies in Great Britain and Ireland, 1961–85; one of HM Commissioners for Ancient Monuments (Scotland), 1963–85. War service in the British Imperial Censorship, Bermuda (Uncommon Languages), 1942–44; in the US censorship, 1944. Hon. DLitt Celt. Ireland, 1958; Hon. DLitt Wales, 1963; Hon. DUniv Haute-Bretagne, 1971. Hon. Mem. Mod. Language Assoc. of America, 1958; Hon. Mem. Royal Irish Academy, 1965; Assoc. Mem., Royal Belgian Acad. for Scis, Letters and Fine Arts, 1975. Derek Allen Prize, British Acad., 1979. *Publications:* Early Welsh Gnomic Poems, 1935; Studies in Early Celtic Nature Poetry, 1935; Cath Maighe Léna, 1938; Scéalta ón mBlascaod, 1939; A Celtic Miscellany, 1951, rev. 1971; Language and History in Early Britain, 1953; Contribs to the Study of Manx Phonology, 1955; The International Popular Tale and Early Welsh Tradition, 1961; The Oldest Irish Tradition, 1964; A Historical Phonology of Breton, 1967; The Gododdin, 1969; The Gaelic Notes in the Book of Deer, 1972; articles on Celtic Languages, literature, history, folklore and archaeology in Zeitschrift für Celtische Philologie, Etudes Celtiques, Bulletin of the Bd of Celtic Studies, Antiquity, Journal of Roman Studies, Folklore, Journal of Celtic Studies, Scottish Gaelic Studies, Speculum, Modern Philology, etc. *Recreation:* walking. *Address:* 34 Cluny Drive, Edinburgh EH10 6DX. *Club:* Edinburgh University Staff.

JACKSON, Laura (Riding), (Mrs Schuyler B. Jackson); *see* Riding, Laura.

JACKSON, Very Rev. Lawrence, AKC; Provost of Blackburn, since 1973; *b* Hessle, Yorks, 22 March 1926; *s* of Walter and Edith Jackson; *m* 1955, Faith Anne, *d* of Philip and Marjorie Seymour; four *d*. *Educ:* Alderman Newton's Sch.; Leicester Coll. of Technology; King's Coll., Univ. of London (AKC 1950); St Boniface Coll., Warminster.

Asst Curate, St Margaret, Leicester, and Asst Chaplain, Leicester Royal Infirmary, 1951–54; Vicar of: Wymeswold, Leicester, 1954–59; St James the Greater, Leicester, 1959–65; Coventry (Holy Trinity), 1965–73. Canon of Coventry Cath., 1967–73; Rural Dean of Coventry N, 1969–73. Senior Chaplain: Leicester and Rutland ACF, 1955–65; Warwickshire ACF, 1965–73; Chaplain, Coventry Guild of Freemen, 1968–73; Dio. Chaplain, CEMS, 1969–71. Mem., Gen. Synod of C of E, 1975–; a Church Comr, 1981–. Dir, The Samaritans of Leicester, 1960–65; Pres., Coventry Round Table, 1968; Governor: Queen Elizabeth Grammar Sch., Blackburn. *Publication*: Services for Special Occasions, 1982. *Recreations*: music, archæology, architecture, countryside, after dinner speaking. *Address*: The Provost's House, Preston New Road, Blackburn BB2 6PS. *T*: Blackburn 52502. *Clubs*: East India, Eccentric, Forty, Lighthouse; Lord's Taverners'.

JACKSON, Hon. Sir Lawrence (Walter), KCMG 1970; Kt 1964; BA, LLB; Judge, 1949–77, and Chief Justice, 1969–77, Supreme Court of Western Australia; Chancellor, University of Western Australia, 1968–81; *b* Dulwich, South Australia, 27 Sept. 1913; *s* of L. S. Jackson; *m* 1937, Mary, *d* of T. H. Donaldson; one *s* two *d*. *Educ*: Fort Street High Sch., Sydney; University of Sydney. *Recreations*: swimming, golf. *Address*: 13 Cliff Way, Claremont, WA 6010, Australia. *Club*: Weld (Perth, WA).

JACKSON, Hon. Dame Margaret Myfanwy Wood; *see* Booth, Hon. Dame Margaret.

JACKSON, (Michael) Rodney; a Recorder, since 1985; Partner, Andrew M. Jackson & Co., Solicitors, since 1964; *b* 16 April 1935; *s* of John William Jackson and Nora Jackson (*née* Phipps); *m* 1968, Anne Margaret, *d* of Prof. E. W. Hawkins, *qv*; two *s*. *Educ*: Queen Elizabeth Grammar Sch., Wakefield; Queens' Coll., Cambridge (MA, LLM). Admitted Solicitor of the Supreme Court, 1962; Notary Public, 1967. *Recreation*: fell walking. *Address*: Andrew M. Jackson & Co., PO Box 47, Victoria Chambers, Bowlalley Lane, Hull HU1 1XY. *T*: Hull 25242. *Club*: National Liberal.

JACKSON, Sir Michael (Roland), 5th Bt, *cr* 1902; MA; MIEE; FIQA; *b* 20 April 1919; *s* of Sir W. D. Russell Jackson, 4th Bt, and Kathleen (*d* 1975), *d* of Summers Hunter, CBE, Tynemouth; *S* father 1956; *m* 1st, 1942, Hilda Margaret (marr. diss. 1969), *d* of late Cecil George Herbert Richardson, CBE, Newark; one *s* one *d*; 2nd, 1969, Hazel Mary, *d* of late Ernest Harold Edwards. *Educ*: Stowe; Clare Coll., Cambridge. Served War of 1939–45; Flight-Lt, Royal Air Force Volunteer Reserve. *Heir*: *s* Thomas St Felix Jackson [*b* 27 Sept. 1946; *m* 1980, Victoria, *d* of George Scatliff, Wineham, Sussex; two *d*]. *Address*: Dragon Cottage, Dragon's Green, Horsham, West Sussex RH13 7JG.

JACKSON, Mrs Muriel W.; *see* Ward-Jackson.

JACKSON, Sir Nicholas (Fane St George), 3rd Bt *cr* 1913; organist, harpsichordist and composer; Organist and Master of the Choristers, St David's Cathedral, 1977–85; *b* 4 Sept. 1934; *s* of Sir Hugh Jackson, 2nd Bt, and of Violet Marguerite Loftus, *y d* of Loftus St George; *S* father, 1979; *m* 1972, Nadia Françoise Genevieve (*née* Michard); one *s*. *Educ*: Radley Coll.; Wadham Coll., Oxford; RAM. LRAM; ARCM. Organist: St Anne's, Soho, 1963–68; St James's, Piccadilly, 1971–74; St Lawrence, Jewry, 1974–77. Musical Dir, St David's Cathedral Bach Fest., 1979. Member of The London Virtuosi. Organ recitals and broadcasts: Berlin, 1967; Paris, 1972, 1975; USA (tour), 1975, 1978; Minorca, 1977; Spain, 1979; Madrid Bach Festival, 1980. Début as harpsichordist, Wigmore Hall, 1963; appeared frequently with Soho Concertante, Queen Elizabeth Hall, 1964–72. Mem. Music Cttee, Welsh Arts Council, 1981–. Recordings: Mass for a Saint's Day, 1971; organ and harpsichord music, incl. works by Arnell, Bach, Couperin, Langlais, Mozart, Vierne and Walther. Liveryman, Drapers' Co., 1965. *Publications*: *compositions*: Mass for a Saint's Day, 1966; 20th Century Merbecke, 1967; 4 Images (for organ), 1971; Solemn Mass, 1977. *Recreations*: sketching, riding. *Heir*: *s* Thomas Graham St George Jackson, *b* 5 Oct. 1980. *Address*: 42 Hereford Road, E2. *T*: 01–727 9669.

JACKSON, Oliver James V.; *see* Vaughan-Jackson.

JACKSON, Patrick; *see* Jackson, W. P.

JACKSON, Peter John Edward; barrister; a Recorder of the Crown Court, since 1983; *b* 14 May 1944; *s* of late David Charles Jackson and of Sarah Ann (*née* Manester); *m* 1967, Ursula, *y d* of late Paul and Henny Schubert, Hamburg, W Germany; two *d*. *Educ*: Brockley County Grammar Sch.; Sprachen und Dolmetscher Inst., Hamburg; London Univ. (LLB Hons 1967); Tübingen Univ., W Germany. Called to the Bar, Middle Temple, 1968 (Blackstone Scholar; Churchill Prize); called to the Bar of NI, 1982. Dep. Circuit Judge, 1979–81; Asst Recorder, 1982–83. ACIArb 1983. *Recreations*: horse riding, the German language. *Address*: 2 Pump Court, Temple, EC4Y 7AH. *T*: 01–353 5597.

JACKSON, Peter (Michael); Senior Lecturer, in Industrial Studies, Institute of Extra-mural Studies, National University of Lesotho, since 1980; *b* 14 Oct. 1928; *s* of Leonard Patterson Jackson; *m* 1961, Christine Thomas. *Educ*: Durham Univ.; University Coll., Leicester. Lecturer, Dept of Sociology, University of Hull, 1964–66; Fellow, Univ. of Hull, 1970–72; Tutor, Open Univ., 1972–74; Senior Planning Officer, S Yorks CC, 1974–77. MP (Lab) High Peak, 1966–70; contested (Lab) Birmingham North, European Parly elecns, 1979. Member: Peak Park Jt Planning Bd, 1973–77, 1979–82; Derby CC, 1973–77. *Recreations*: numismatics, book collecting, ski-ing. *Address*: PO Box 1585, Maseru 100, Lesotho, Southern Africa. *Club*: Maseru (Lesotho).

JACKSON, Air Vice-Marshal Sir Ralph (Coburn), KBE 1973; CB 1963; Adviser in Insurance and Company Medicine; Honorary Civil Consultant in Medicine to RAF; Honorary Consultant (Medicine) to RAF Benevolent Fund; Consultant Medical Referee, Confederation Life Insurance Co.; and Victory Re-insurance Co.; Medical Adviser and Director, French Hospital (La Providence), Rochester; *b* 22 June 1914; *s* of Ralph Coburn Jackson and Phillis Jackson (*née* Dodds); *m* 1939, Joan Lucy Crowley; two *s* two *d*. *Educ*: Oakmount Sch., Arnside; Guy's Hosp., London. MRCS 1937; FRCPE 1960 (MRCPE 1950); FRCP 1972 (MRCP 1968, LRCP 1937). Qualified in Medicine Guy's Hosp., 1937; House Officer appts, Guy's Hosp., 1937–38; commnd in RAF as MO, Nov. 1938; served in France, 1939–40; Russia, 1941; W Africa, 1942–43 (despatches); Sen. MO, 46 Gp for Brit. Casualty Air Evac., 1944–45 (despatches). Med. Specialist, RAF Hosps Wroughton, Aden and Halton, 1946–52 (Consultant in Med., Princess Mary's RAF Hosp. Halton, 1952–63; RAF Hosp., Wegberg, Germany, 1964–66); Consultant Advr in Medicine, 1966–74; Sen. Consultant to RAF, 1971–75; Advr in Medicine to CAA, 1966–75; Chm., Defence Med. Services, Postgrad. Council, 1973–75. QHP 1969–75. MacArthur Lectr, Univ. Edinburgh, 1959. Member: Assurance Med. Soc.; Wild Fowl Trust, 1982; Soc. of Genealogists; Fellow RSPB, 1981; FRSM; Fellow, Huguenot Soc. Liveryman, Worshipful Soc. of Apothecaries; Freeman, City of London. Lady Cade Medal, RCS, 1960. *Publications*: papers on acute renal failure, the artificial kidney and routine electrocardiography in various medical books and journals, 1959–1974. *Recreations*: birdwatching, ancient buildings, history of City of London. *Address*: Piper's Hill, Marwell, Westerham, Kent TN16 1SB. *T*: Westerham 64436; (office) Room 502/6, New Lloyds Building, 51 Lime Street, EC3. *T*: 01–626 6732. *Club*: Royal Air Force.

JACKSON, Col Richard John Laurence, CBE 1971; DL, JP; FRIBA, DipArch; Architect; *b* 17 Oct. 1908; *s* of John Robert and Kathleen Emma Jackson; *m* 1936, Sara Alexander Wilson; one *s*. *Educ*: Scarborough Coll.; Liverpool Univ. Served War of 1939–45, Green Howards; Middle East, Western Desert, Libya, Tunisia, Sicily and Normandy invasions. Member: North Riding of Yorkshire CC, 1949–74 (Alderman, 1961–74); North Yorks CC, 1974–85 (Chm. 1977–81; Hon. Alderman, 1986). JP 1951; DL North Riding, 1967. *Recreation*: angling. *Address*: Bridgeholme, Egton Bridge, Whitby, North Yorks. *T*: Whitby 85221.

JACKSON, Richard Michael, CVO 1983; HM Diplomatic Service; Counsellor (Commercial), Seoul, since 1987; *b* 12 July 1940; *s* of Richard William Jackson and Charlotte (*née* Wrightson); *m* 1961, Mary Elizabeth Kitchin; one *s* one *d*. *Educ*: Queen Elizabeth Grammar Sch., Darlington; Paisley Grammar Sch.; Glasgow Univ. (MA Hons 1961). Joined Home Civil Service, 1961; Scottish Office, 1961–70; seconded to MAFF, 1971–72; seconded to FCO and served in The Hague, 1973–74; trans. to HM Diplomatic Service, 1974; European Integration Dept (External), FCO, 1975–76; Panama City, 1976–79; Arms Control and Disarmament Dept, FCO, 1979–81; Buenos Aires, 1981–82; Falklands Islands Dept, FCO, 1982; Counsellor, Stockholm, 1982–87. *Address*: c/o Foreign and Commonwealth Office, King Charles Street, SW1.

JACKSON, Sir Robert, 7th Bt *cr* 1815; *b* 16 March 1910; *s* of Major Francis Gorham Jackson (*d* 1942) (2nd *s* of 4th Bt) and Ana Maria Biscar Brennan; *S* kinsman, Sir John Montrésor Jackson, 6th Bt, 1980; *m* 1943, Maria E. Casamayou; two *d*. *Educ*: St George's College. Career on estancia. *Heir*: *kinsman* Keith Arnold Jackson [*b* 1921; *m* Pauline Mona, *d* of B. P. Climo, Wellington, NZ; four *s* one *d*]. *Address*: Santiago de Chile 1243, Montevideo, Uruguay. *T*: 905487. *Club*: English (Montevideo).

JACKSON, Comdr Sir Robert (Gillman Allen), KCVO 1962; AC 1986; Kt 1956; CMG 1944; OBE (mil.) 1941; Under Secretary General and Senior Adviser to Secretary General, United Nations, since 1984; Consultant to Volta River Authority, Ghana, since 1962 (Member of Board 1965–76); Senior Consultant to McKinsey & Company since 1970; Counsellor to Interim Mekong Committee, since 1978; *b* 1911; *m* 1950, Barbara Ward (Baroness Jackson of Lodsworth, DBE, FRS) (*d* 1981); one *s*. RAN, 1929–37; transf. to Malta and RN, 1937; Chief Staff Officer to Gov. and C-in-C, Malta GC, 1940; planned Malta Comd Defence Scheme; re-armament of the Fortress; develt Co-ordinated Supply Scheme, 1940 (OBE); transf. by Cabinet decision from Navy and Army Principal Asst to UK Cabinet Minister of State in ME and Dir-Gen., ME Supply Centre (Anglo-American para-mil. orgn for co-ordn civilian and mil. supply ops), 1942–45; develt Aid to Russia Supply route; estab. anti-locust campaign, 1942 (still continuing) (CMG); assisted Bengal famine op., 1943; AFHQ for special duties in Greece, 1944–45; transf. to HM Treasury, 1945; Sen. Dep. Dir-Gen. of UNRRA, 1945–47, and, in 1945, i/c of UNRRA's ops in Europe (inc. 8,500,000 displaced persons); supervised transfer of UNRRA's residual functions to UN, UNESCO, WHO, FAO, and assisted in establishment of IRO (now UNHCR), and International Children's Emergency Fund, 1947 (UNICEF); services recognised by various governments in Europe and Asia; Asst Sec.-Gen. for Co-ordination in the UN, 1948; HM Treasury, for duties with Lord Pres. of Council, 1949; Perm. Sec., Min. of Nat. Development, Australia, 1950–52 (Snowy Mountains Scheme); Adviser to Govt of India on Development Plans, 1952, 1957 and 1962–63, and to Govt of Pakistan, 1952; Chm. of Preparatory Commission for Volta River multi-purpose project, Gold Coast, 1953–56; Chm., Development Commission, Ghana, 1956–61 (Kt); Organisation of Royal Tours in Ghana, 1959 and 1961 (KCVO); Mem. Adv. Bd, Mekong Project, SE Asia, 1962–76; Adviser to President of Liberia, 1962–79; Special Consultant in about 50 countries, including to Administrator, UNDP, 1963–72, Special Adviser, 1978–80; Chm., UN gp reporting on Zambia's security, 1963; Comr i/c, Survey of UN Develt System, 1968–71; Under Sec.-Gen. i/c UN Relief Ops in Bangladesh, 1972–74; Under Sec.-Gen. i/c UN assistance to Zambia, 1973–78, to Indo-China, 1975–78, to Cape Verde Is, 1975–78, to São Tomé and Príncipe, 1977–78, to Kampuchea and Thailand, 1979–85. Member: Cttee, Fédération Mondiale des Villes Jumelées Cités Unies, 1972–; IUCN Commn on Environmental Policy, 1972–; Overseas Service Bureau, Australia, 1976–; ABC (Assistance to Blind Children in Bangladesh), 1980–; Dag Hammarskjöld Foundn, Stockholm, 1981–; Adv. Bd, Foundation for Global Broadcasting, 1985–. Trustee, Inter-Action (UK), 1986–; Patron, PACE-UK Internat. Affairs, 1983–. Mem. Internat. Jury, Prize of Institut de la Vie, 1972–. Freeman, City of Prague, 1946. Hon. DL Syracuse. *Publications*: An International Development Authority, 1955; Report of the Volta River Preparatory Commission, 1956; A Study of the United Nations Development System, 1969; Report on Sen. Volunteers in UN System, 1978; Report on reinforcement of UN Indust. Develt Orgn, 1979; various articles on development, multi-purpose projects and disaster operations. *Recreations*: reading, deepsea fishing, cricket, welfare of tigers. *Address*: United Nations, New York City, NY 10017, USA; Palais des Nations, Geneva, Switzerland. *Clubs*: Brooks's, Royal Over-Seas League; Victoria (Jersey); Melbourne (Victoria).

JACKSON, Robert Victor; MP (C) Wantage, since 1983; *b* 24 Sept. 1946; *m* 1975, Caroline Frances Harvey (*see* C. F. Jackson); one *s* decd. *Educ*: Falcon Coll., S Rhodesia; St Edmund Hall, Oxford (H. W. C. Davis Prize, 1966; 1st Cl. Hons Mod. Hist. 1968); President Oxford Union, 1967. Prize Fellowship, All Souls Coll., 1968 (Fellow, 1968–86). Councillor, Oxford CC, 1969–71; Political Adviser to Sec. of State for Employment, 1973–74; Member, Cabinet of Sir Christopher (now Baron) Soames, EEC Commn, Brussels, 1974–76; Chef de Cabinet, President of EEC Economic and Social Cttee, Brussels, 1976–78; Mem. (C) Upper Thames, European Parlt, 1979–84; Special Adviser to Governor of Rhodesia (Lord Soames), 1979–80; European Parlt's Rapporteur-Gen. on 1983 European Community Budget. Contested (C) Manchester Central Div., general election, Oct. 1974. Editor: The Round Table: Commonwealth Jl of Internat. Relations, 1970–74; International Affairs (Chatham House), 1979–80. *Publications*: South Asian Crisis: India, Pakistan, Bangladesh 1972, 1975; The Powers of the European Parliament, 1977; The European Parliament: Penguin Guide to Direct Elections, 1979; Reforming the European Budget, 1981; Tradition and Reality: Conservative philosophy and European integration 1982; From Boom to Bust?—British farming and CAP reform, 1983; Political Ideas in Western Europe Today, 1984. *Recreations*: reading music, walking. *Address*: House of Commons, SW1A 0AA. *Club*: Beefsteak.

JACKSON, Rodney; *see* Jackson, M. R.

JACKSON, Sir (Ronald) Gordon, AK 1983 (AC 1976); Chairman: Australian Industry Development Corporation, since 1983; Interscan International Ltd, since 1984; Austek Microsystems Ltd, since 1984; Hampton Australia Ltd, since 1984; Member of Board, Reserve Bank of Australia, since 1975; *b* 5 May 1924; *s* of late R. V. Jackson; *m* 1948, Margaret Pratley; one *s* one *d*. *Educ*: Brisbane Grammar Sch.; Queensland Univ. (BCom). FASA; FAIM. Served AIF, 1942–46. Joined CSR Ltd, 1941; Gen. Man., 1972–82; Dir, 1972–85; Dep. Chm., 1983–85. Director: Rothmans Holdings Ltd, 1983–; Rockwell Internat. Pty Ltd, 1985–; Mem., Pacific Adv. Council, United Technologies Corp., 1984–. Chm., Bd of Management, Aust. Graduate Sch. of Management, 1976–82; Pres., Order of Australia Assoc., 1983–86 (Foundn Chm., 1980–83); Vice-Pres., Australia/Japan Business

Co-operation Cttee, 1977–; Hon. Mem., German–Australian Chamber of Industry and Commerce (Foundn Pres., 1977–80; Chm. to 1985); Member: Police Bd of NSW, 1983–; Salvation Army Adv. Bd, 1983– (Chm., Red Shield Appeal, 1981–85, Pres. 1986–). James N. Kirby Meml Award, 1976; John Storey Medal, 1978. Comdr, Order of Merit (FRG), 1980. *Address:* 24th Floor, Qantas International Centre, 18–30 Jamison Street, Sydney, NSW 2000, Australia.

JACKSON, Roy Arthur; Assistant General Secretary, Trades Union Congress, since 1984; *b* 18 June 1928; *s* of Charles Frederick Jackson and Harriet Betsy (*née* Ridewood); *m* 1956, Lilian May Ley; three *d. Educ:* North Paddington Central Sch.; London Univ. Extension Classes; Ruskin Coll., Oxford (DipEcon Pol Sci (Distinction); Worcester Coll., Oxford (BA Hons, PPE). Post Office Savings Bank, 1942; RN, Ord. Signalman, 1946–48; POSB, 1948–52; posts held at branch and Nat. level, CSCA, 1943–52; TUC: Educn Dept, 1956; Dir of Studies, 1964; Head of Educn, 1974–84. Member: Albemarle Cttee of Youth Service, 1958–60; Open Univ. Cttee on Continuing Educn, 1975–76; Adv. Cttee for Continuing and Adult Educn, 1977–83; Schools Council Convocation, 1978–82; Further Educn Unit, DES, 1980–; Special Programmes Bd, MSC, 1978–82; Youth Task Gp on YTS, MSC, 1982; Youth Training Bd, MSC, 1982–85; Tech. Educn Vocational Initiative Steering Cttee, MSC, 1982–85; Holland Working Gp on Funding and Develt of 2 year YTS, MSC, 1985–. *Publications:* contribs to DES Trends in Education and Joint Studies in Econ. Performance. *Recreations:* walking, reading, gardening. *Address:* 27 The Ryde, Hatfield, Herts. *T:* Hatfield 63790.

JACKSON, Sir Thomas; *see* Jackson, Sir W. T.

JACKSON, Thomas; General Secretary, Union of Communication Workers (formerly Post Office Workers), 1967–82; bookseller; *b* 9 April 1925; *s* of George Frederick Jackson and Ethel Hargreaves; *m* 1st, 1947, Norma Burrow (marr. diss. 1982); one *d*; 2nd, 1982, Kathleen Maria Tognarelli; one *d. Educ:* Jack Lane Elementary Sch. Boy Messenger, GPO, 1939; Royal Navy, 1943; Postman, 1946; Executive Mem., Union of Post Office Workers, 1955; Asst Sec., Union of Post Office Workers, 1964. HM Government Dir, British Petroleum, 1975–83. Member: Gen. Council of TUC, 1967–82 (Chm., 1978–79; Chm., Internat. Cttee, 1978–82); Press Council, 1973–76; Annan Cttee on the Future of Broadcasting, 1974–77; CRE, 1977–78; Broadcasting Complaints Commn, 1982–; Yorks Water Authority, 1983–. Mem. Court and Council, Sussex Univ., 1974–78. Vice-Pres., WEA, 1977–; Chm., Ilkley Literature Fest., 1984–. A Governor: BBC, 1968–73; NIESR, 1974–. *Recreations:* cooking, photography. *Address:* 22 Parish Ghyll Road, Ilkley, West Yorks LS29 9NE.

JACKSON, (Walter) Patrick; Under-Secretary, Department of Transport, since 1981; *b* 10 Feb. 1929; *m* 1952, Kathleen Roper; one *s* one *d. Educ:* University Coll., Oxford. John Lewis Partnership, 1952–66; Principal, Min. of Transport and DoE, 1966–72; Asst Sec., DoE, 1972–78; Under Sec. and Regional Dir (E Midlands), DoE and Dept of Transport, 1978–81. *Recreation:* concert- and theatre-going. *Address:* c/o Department of Transport, 2 Marsham Street, SW1.

JACKSON, Gen. Sir William (Godfrey Fothergill), GBE 1975 (OBE 1958); KCB 1971; MC 1940, and Bar, 1943; Military Historian, Cabinet Office, 1977–78, and since 1982; Governor and Commander-in-Chief, Gibraltar, 1978–82; *b* 28 Aug. 1917; *s* of late Col A. Jackson, RAMC, Yanwath, Cumberland, and E. M. Jackson (*née* Fothergill), Brownber, Westmorland; *m* 1946, Joan Mary Buesden; one *s* one *d. Educ:* Shrewsbury; RMA, Woolwich; King's Coll. Cambridge, King's medal, RMA Woolwich, 1937. Commnd into Royal Engineers, 1937; served War of 1939–45: Norwegian Campaign, 1940; Tunisia, 1942–43; Sicily and Italy, 1943–44; Far East, 1945; GSO1, HQ Allied Land Forces SE Asia, 1945–48; Instructor, Staff Coll., Camberley, 1948–50; Instructor, RMA, Sandhurst, 1951–53; AA & QMG (War Plans), War Office, during Suez ops, 1956; Comdr, Gurkha Engrs, 1958–60; Col GS, Minley Div. of Staff Coll., Camberley, 1961–62; Dep. Dir of Staff Duties, War Office, 1962–64; Imp. Def. Coll., 1965; Dir, Chief of Defence Staff's Unison Planning Staff, 1966–68; Asst Chief of General Staff (Operational Requirements), MoD, 1968–70; GOC-in-C, Northern Command, 1970–72; QMG, 1973–76. Colonel Commandant: RE, 1971–81; Gurkha Engrs, 1971–76; RAOC, 1973–78; Hon. Col, Engineer and Rly Staff Corps, RE, TAVR, 1977–83; ADC (Gen.) to the Queen, 1974–76. *Publications:* Attack in the West, 1953; Seven Roads to Moscow, 1957; The Battle for Italy, 1967; Battle for Rome, 1969; Alexander of Tunis as Military Commander, 1971; The North African Campaigns, 1975; Overlord: Normandy 1944, 1978; (ed jtly) The Mediterranean and the Middle East (British Official History, vol. VI), Pt 1, 1984; The Rock of the Gibraltarians, 1986; Withdrawal From Empire, 1986; contribs to Royal United Service Instn Jl (gold medals for prize essays, 1950 and 1966). *Recreations:* fishing, writing, gardening. *Address:* West Stowell Place, Oare, Marlborough, Wilts. *Club:* Army and Navy.

JACKSON, William Theodore, CBE 1967 (MBE 1946); ARIBA; MRTPI; Director of Post Office Services, Ministry of Public Building and Works, 1969–71, retired; *b* 18 July 1906; *y s* of Rev. Oliver Miles Jackson and Emily Jackson; *m* 1932, Marjorie Campbell; one *s* two *d. Educ:* Cheltenham Gram. Sch. Chief Architect, Iraq Govt, 1936–38; Dir, Special Repair Service, Min. of Works, 1939–45; Min. of Public Building and Works, 1946–69; Dir, Mobile Labour Force; Dir of Maintenance; seconded to World Bank as Advr to Iran Technical Bureau of Development Plan organisation, 1956–57; Regional Dir; Dir, Regional Services; Dir, Headquarters Services, 1957–69. *Recreations:* gardening, painting. *Address:* Old Farm, Bull's Head Green, Main Street, Ewhurst, Surrey GU6 7PB. *T:* Cranleigh 277376.

JACKSON, Sir (William) Thomas, 8th Bt *cr* 1869; farmer, since 1969; *b* 12 Oct. 1927; *s* of Sir William Jackson, 7th Bt, and Lady Ankaret Jackson (*d* 1945), 2nd *d* of 10th Earl of Carlisle; *S* father, 1985; *m* 1951, Gilian Malise, *d* of John William Stobart, MBE; three *s. Educ:* Mill Hill School; Royal Agricultural Coll., Cirencester. Qualified Associate Chartered Land Agents Soc., later ARICS; resigned, 1969. Nat. Service, 1947–49, 2/Lt Border Regt; Gen. Reserve as Lieut. Land Agent in various firms and on private estates till 1969, when he left the profession and started farming. Chairman: Cumberland Branch, CLA, 1984–86; Whitehaven Branch, NFU, 1983–85. *Recreations:* pottering around farm, painting. *Heir: e s* (William) Roland Cedric Jackson, PhD [*b* 9 Jan. 1954; *m* 1977, Nicola Mary, *yr d* of Prof. Peter Reginald Davis, PhD, FRCS; two *s*]. *Address:* Routen, Ennerdale, Cleator, Cumbria CA23 3AU.

JACKSON, William Unsworth, CBE 1985; Chief Executive, Kent County Council, 1974–86; *b* 9 Feb. 1926; *s* of William Jackson and Margaret Esplen Jackson (*née* Sunderland); *m* 1952, Valerie Annette (*née* Llewellyn); one *s* one *d. Educ:* Alsop High Sch., Liverpool. Solicitor. Entered local govt service, Town Clerk's Office, Liverpool, 1942; Dep. County Clerk, Kent, 1970. Pres., Soc. of Local Authority Chief Execs, 1985–86 (Hon. Sec., 1980–84). *Address:* 34 Yardley Park Road, Tonbridge, Kent. *T:* Tonbridge 351078. *Club:* Royal Over-Seas League.

JACKSON, Yvonne Brenda, OBE 1985; DL; Chairman, West Yorkshire Metropolitan County Council, 1980–81; *b* 23 July 1920; *d* of Charles and Margaret Wilson; *m* 1946,

Edward Grosvenor Jackson; twin *s* one *d. Educ:* Edgbaston C of E Coll., Birmingham; Manchester Teachers' Trng Coll. (Dip. Domestic Science and qualified teacher). School Meals Organizer, West Bromwich, Staffs, 1942–45. Mem., W Riding CC, 1967–73 (local govt reorganisation); Mem. W Yorks CC, 1973–86; Chm., Fire and Public Protection Cttee, 1977–80; Deputy Leader and Shadow Chairman: Fire Cttee, 1981–86; Trading Standards Cttee, 1981–86; Police Cttee, 1982–86. Chm., Yorks Electricity Consultative Council, 1982–; Mem., Yorks RHA, 1982–. Mem. Exec. Cttee, Nat. Union of Cons. Assocs, 1981– (Dep. Chm., Yorks Area Finance and Gen. Purposes Cttee, 1982–; Divl Chm., Elmet, 1983–). Mem. Council and Court, Leeds Univ. DL W Yorks, 1983, High Sheriff, 1986–87. *Recreations:* badminton, fishing; formerly County hockey and tennis player; former motor rally driver (competed in nat. and internat. events inc. Monte Carlo, Alpine and Tulip rallies). *Address:* The Field House, East Rigton, East Keswick, West Yorkshire LS17 9AR. *T:* Collingham Bridge 73452.

JACKSON-LIPKIN, Miles Henry; Hon. Mr Justice Jackson-Lipkin; armiger; a Judge of the High Court of Hong Kong, since 1981; Commissioner, Supreme Court of Negara Brunei Darussalam, 1984–July 1987; *b* Liverpool; *s* of late I. J. Jackson-Lipkin, MD and F.A. Patley; *m* Lucille Yun-Shim Fung, DLJ, barrister; one *s. Educ:* Harrow; Trinity Coll., Oxford. FCIArb. Called to the Bar, Middle Temple, 1951; admitted Hong Kong Bar, 1963, NSW Bar, 1980; QC Hong Kong, 1974. Panel Mem., Inland Revenue Bd of Review, Hong Kong, 1975; Chm. Exec. Cttee, and Man. Dir, Hong Kong Children and Youth Services, 1978–. Member: Medico-Legal Soc., 1952; Justice, 1956; Council of Honour, Monarchist League; Founder Member: Hong Kong Br., Justice, 1963; Hong Kong Medico-Legal Soc., 1974 (Mem. Cttee, 1976–). Vice-Chm., Hong Kong Island Br., Internat. Wine and Food Soc. Liveryman: Meadmakers' Co. (Edinburgh), 1984; Arbitrators' Co., 1986; Freeman, City of London, 1986. JP Hong Kong, 1977–81. KCLJ 1983 (Grand Priory of Lochore) (KLJ 1977; CLJ 1973). Hon. Mem., Officers' Mess, HQBF, Hong Kong; Associate Mem., Volunteer Officers' Mess, Hong Kong. *Publications:* The Beaufort Legitimation, 1957; Scales of Justice, 1958; Israel Naval Forces, 1959. *Recreations:* gardening, heraldry, classical music, philately, walking. *Address:* 53 Manderly Garden, 48 Deep Water Bay Road, Hong Kong; 62 Eaton Terrace, SW1. *Clubs:* Naval and Military, MCC; Hong Kong, Hong Kong Cricket, Royal Hong Kong Golf, Royal Hong Kong Jockey, American, Arts, China Fleet, Shanghai Fraternity Assoc. (Hon.) (Hong Kong).

JACOB, Ven. Bernard Victor; Archdeacon of Reigate (title changed from Kingston-upon-Thames, 1986), since 1977; *b* 20 Nov. 1921; *m* 1946, Dorothy Joan Carey; one *s* two *d. Educ:* Liverpool Institute; St Peter's College (MA) and Wycliffe Hall, Oxford. Curate, Middleton, Lancs, 1950–54; Vicar, Ulverston, Lancs, 1954–59; Vicar, Bilston, Staffs, 1959–64; Warden of Scargill House, Yorks, 1964–68; Rector of Mortlake, 1968–77. *Recreations:* travel, reading, enjoying life. *Address:* 29 Cornwall Road, Cheam, Sutton SM2 6DU. *T:* (office) 01–681 5496; (home) 01–661 9038.

JACOB, David Oliver Ll.; *see* Lloyd Jacob, D. O.

JACOB, Lt-Gen. Sir (Edward) Ian (Claud), GBE 1960 (KBE 1946; CBE 1942); CB 1944; DL; late RE, Colonel, retired and Hon. Lieutenant-General; Chairman, Matthews Holdings Ltd, 1970–76; *b* 27 Sept. 1899; *s* of late Field Marshal Sir Claud Jacob, GCB, GCSI, KCMG; *m* 1924, Cecil Bisset Treherne; two *s. Educ:* Wellington Coll.; RMA, Woolwich; King's Coll., Cambridge (BA). 2nd Lieut. Royal Engineers, 1918; Capt. 1929; Bt Major, 1935; Major, 1938; Bt Lt-Col, 1939; Col, 1943. Waziristan, 1922–23. Staff Coll., 1931–32; GSO3 War Office, 1934–36; Bde-Maj., Canal Bde, Egypt, 1936–38; Military Asst Sec., Cttee of Imperial Defence, 1938; Military Asst Sec. to the War Cabinet, 1939–46; retired pay, 1946. Controller of European Services, BBC, 1946; Dir of Overseas Services, BBC, 1947 (on leave of absence during 1952); Chief Staff Officer to Minister of Defence and Deputy Sec. (Mil.) of the Cabinet during 1952; Dir-Gen. of the BBC, 1952–60; Director: Fisons, 1960–70; EMI, 1960–73; Chm., Covent Garden Market Authority, 1961–66; a Trustee, Imperial War Museum, 1966–73. CC, E Suffolk, 1960–70, Alderman, 1970–74; CC Suffolk, 1974–77. JP Suffolk, 1961–69; DL Suffolk, 1964–84. US Legion of Merit (Comdr). *Address:* The Red House, Woodbridge, Suffolk. *T:* Woodbridge 2001. *Club:* Army and Navy.

JACOB, Prof. François; Croix de la Libération; Grand-Croix de la Légion d'Honneur; President, Pasteur Institute; Professor of Cellular Genetics, at the College of France, since 1964; *b* Nancy (Meurthe & Moselle), 17 June 1920; *m* 1947, Lysiane Bloch (*d* 1984); three *s* one *d. Educ:* Lycée Carnot, France. DenM 1947; DèsS 1954. Pasteur Institute: Asst, 1950; Head of Laboratory, 1956. Mem., Acad. of Scis, Paris, 1977. Charles Léopold Mayer Prize, Acad. des Sciences, Paris, 1962; Nobel Prize for Medicine, 1965. Foreign Member: Royal Danish Acad. of Letters and Sciences, 1962; Amer. Acad. of Arts and Sciences, 1964; Nat. Acad. of Scis, USA, 1969; Royal Soc., 1973; Acad. Royale de Médecine, Belgique, 1973. Dr *hc* University of Chicago, 1965. *Publications:* The Logic of Life, 1970; The Possible and the Actual, 1981; various scientific. *Recreation:* painting. *Address:* 25 rue du Dr Roux, 75724 Paris, Cedex 15, France.

JACOB, Frederick Henry; CBiol; retired; Director, Ministry of Agriculture, Fisheries and Food's Pest Infestation Control Laboratory, 1968–77; *b* 12 March 1915; *s* of Henry Theodore and Elizabeth Jacob; *m* 1941, Winifred Edith Sloman; one *s* one *d. Educ:* Friars Sch., Bangor; UC North Wales. BSc, MSc; CBiol, FIBiol. Asst Entomologist: King's Coll., Newcastle upon Tyne, 1942–44; Sch. of Agriculture, Cambridge, 1944–45; Adviser in Agric. Zoology, UC North Wales, 1945–46; Adv. Entomologist, Min. of Agriculture and Fisheries, Nat. Agric. Adv. Service, N Wales, 1946–50; Head of Entomology Dept, MAFF, Plant Pathology Lab., 1950–68. Pres., Assoc. of Applied Biologists, 1976–77. *Publications:* papers mainly on systematics of Aphididae in learned jls. *Recreations:* hill walking, fishing, gardening. *Address:* Llys y Gwynt, Llandegai, Bangor, Gwynedd LL57 4BG. *T:* Bangor 353863. *Clubs:* Farmers', Climbers; Wayfarers (Liverpool).

JACOB, Lieut-Gen. Sir Ian; *see* Jacob, Lieut-Gen. Sir E. I. C.

JACOB, Sir Isaac Hai, (Sir Jack Jacob), Kt 1979; QC 1976; Senior Master of the Supreme Court, Queen's Bench Division, and Queen's Remembrancer, 1975–80; Director, Institute of Advanced Legal Studies, University of London, since 1986; Fellow of University College, London, 1966; *b* 5 June 1908; 3rd *s* of late Jacob Isaiah and Aziza Jacob; *m* 1940, Rose Mary Jenkins (*née* Samwell); two *s. Educ:* Shanghai Public Sch. for Boys; London Sch. of Economics; University Coll., London. LLB (1st class Hons), London; Joseph Hume Scholar in Jurisprudence, University Coll., London, 1928 and 1930; Arden Scholar, Gray's Inn, 1930; Cecil Peace Prizeman, 1930. Called to the Bar, Gray's Inn, Nov. 1930; Hon. Bencher, 1978; Mem., Senate of Inns of Court and the Bar, 1975–78. Served in ranks from 1940 until commissioned in RAOC 1942; Staff Capt., War Office (Ord. I), 1943–45. Master, Supreme Court, Queen's Bench Div., 1957–80. Prescribed Officer for Election Petitions, 1975–80. Hon. Lectr in Law, University Coll., London, 1959–74; Hon. Lectr in Legal Ethics, Birmingam Univ., 1969–72; Hon. Visiting Lecturer: Imperial Coll. of Science and Technology, 1963–64; Birmingham Univ., 1964–65; Bedford Coll., 1969–71; European Univ. Institute, Florence, 1978; Vis. Professor: Sydney Univ., 1971; Osgoode Hall Law Sch., York Univ., Toronto, 1971; of

English Law, UCL, 1974–; Central London Polytechnic, 1981–. Member: Lord Chancellor's (Pearson) Cttee on Funds in Court, 1958–59; Working Party on the Revision of the Rules of the Supreme Court, 1960–65; (Payne) Cttee on Enforcement of Judgment Debts, 1965–69; (Winn) Cttee on Personal Injuries Litigation, 1966–68; (Kerr) Working Party on Foreign Judgments, 1976–80. Pres., Assoc. of Law Teachers, 1978–85 (Vice Pres., 1965–78); Vice-President: Industrial Law Soc.; Selden Soc., 1978–84 (Mem. Council, 1976–78, 1985–); Inst. of Legal Executives, 1978–; Mansfield Law Club, City of London Polytechnic, 1965–; Governor, Central London Polytechnic, 1968–; Member, Cttee of Management: Inst. of Judicial Admin, 1968–; Brit. Inst. of Internat. and Comparative Law, 1965–; Law Adv. Cttee of Associated Examining Bd, 1964–84; Friends of Hebrew Univ., Jerusalem, 1965–85; Mem. Council, Justice; Mem. Gen. Cttee, Bar Assoc. of Commerce, Finance and Industry, 1981–85. Chm., Bentham Club, UCL, 1964–84, Pres. 1985, Vice Pres. 1986–. Hon. Member: SPTL, 1981–; Internat. Assoc. of Experts, 1984–; Internat. Assoc. of Procedural Law, 1985–. Hon. Freeman, City of London, 1976. Mem., Broderers' Co. Hon. LLD: Birmingham, 1978; London, 1981; Dr Jur. hc Würzburg, Bavaria, 1982. FCIArb. Adv. Editor, 1962–83, Chief Adv. Editor, 1984–, Court Forms; Editor, Annual Practice, 1961–66; General Editor: Supreme Court Practice, 1967–; Civil Justice Quarterly, 1982–; Adv. Editor, Internat. Encyclopedia of Comparative Law (Civil Procedure vol.), 1968–. Publications: Law relating to Rent Restrictions, 1933, 1938; Law relating to Hire Purchase, 1938; Chitty and Jacob's Queen's Bench Forms (19th, 20th and 21st edns); Bullen, Leake and Jacob's Precedents of Pleadings (12th edn); chapter on Civil Procedure including Courts and Evidence, in Annual Survey of Commonwealth Law, 1965–77; The Reform of Civil Procedural Law and Other Essays in Civil Procedure, 1982; contributed titles: Discovery, Execution (jtly), Practice and Procedure, to Halsbury's Laws of England, 4th edn; Compromise and Settlement, Default Judgments, Discontinuance and Withdrawal, Discovery, Interlocutory Proceedings, Interim Orders, Issues, Judgments and Orders (part), Order 14 Proceedings, Pleadings, Service of Proceedings, Stay of Proceedings, Third Party Procedure, Writs of Summons to Court Forms. Recreations: walking, painting. Address: 16 The Park, Golders Green, NW11 7SU. T: 01–458 3832. Clubs: City Livery, Reform, Royal Automobile; Hendon Golf.

See also R. R. H Jacob.

JACOB, Robert Raphael Hayim, (Robin Jacob), QC 1981; b 26 April 1941; s of Sir Jack I. H. Jacob, qv; m 1967, Wendy Jones; three s. Educ: King Alfred Sch., Hampstead; Mountgrace Secondary Comprehensive Sch., Potter's Bar; St Paul's Sch.; Trinity Coll., Cambridge (BA, MA); LSE (LLB). Called to the Bar, Gray's Inn, 1965 (Atkin Scholar); teacher of law, 1965–66; pupillage with Nigel (now Lord) Bridge, 1966–67, with A. M. Walton, 1967; entered chambers of Thomas Blanco White, 1967. Junior Counsel to Treasury in Patent Matters, 1976–81. Publications: Kerly's Law of Trade Marks (ed jtly) 1972, 1983 and 1986 edns; Patents, Trade Marks, Copyright and Designs (ed jtly), 1970, 1978, 1986; Encyclopedia of UK and European Patent Law (ed jtly), 1977; Editor, Court Forms Sections on Copyright (1978–), Designs and Trade Marks (1975–); section on Trade Marks (ed jtly), 4th edn, Halsbury's Laws of England, 1984. Recreations: photography, country garden. Address: Francis Taylor Building, Temple, EC4Y 7BY. T: 01–353 5657.

JACOB, Rev. Canon William Mungo, PhD; Warden of Lincoln Theological College, since 1986; Canon of Lincoln, since 1986; b 15 Nov. 1944; s of John William Carey Jacob and Mary Marsters Dewar. Educ: King Edward VII School, King's Lynn; Hull Univ. (LLB); Linacre Coll., Oxford (MA); Exeter Univ. (PhD). Deacon 1970, priest 1971; Curate of Wymondham, Norfolk, 1970–73; Asst Chaplain, Exeter Univ., 1973–75; Lecturer, Salisbury and Wells Theological Coll., 1975–80, Vice-Principal, 1977–80; Sec. to Cttee for Theological Education, ACCM, 1980–86. Address: The Warden's House, Drury Lane, Lincoln LN1 3BP. T: Lincoln 38885.

JACOB, Very Rev. William Ungoed; Dean of Brecon Cathedral, 1967–78; Vicar of St Mary's, Brecon with Battle, 1967–78; b 6 Oct. 1910; s of Wm and L. M. M. Jacob; m 1935, Ivy Matilda Hall; one d. Educ: Llanelly Gram. Sch.; Llandovery Coll.; Jesus Coll., Oxford; Wycliffe Hall, Oxford. BA 2nd cl. History, 1932; 2nd cl. Theology, 1933; MA 1937. Ordained deacon, 1934; priest, 1935; Curate of Holy Trinity, Aberystwyth, 1934–36; Lampeter, 1936–40; Vicar of Blaenau Ffestiniog 1940–51; Rector of Hubberston, 1951–55; Vicar of St Peter's, Carmarthen, 1955–67; Canon of St David's Cathedral, 1957–67. Rural Dean of Carmarthen, 1958–60; Archdeacon of Carmarthen, 1960–67. Pres., Council of Churches for Wales 1971–76 (Sec., 1960–65). Mem., Coun. for Wales and Mon, 1963–66. Church in Wales: Gen. Sec., Prov. Council for Mission and Unity, 1967–73; Mem., Standing Liturgical Commn, 1951–71; Chm., Provincial Selection Panel, 1974–78. Publications: Meditations on the Seven Words, 1960; Three Hours' Devotions, 1965; A Guide to the Parish Eucharist, 1969. Address: 110 Sketty Road, Swansea SA2 0JX. T: Swansea 203475.

JACOBI, Derek George, CBE 1985; actor; b 22 Oct. 1938; s of Alfred George Jacobi and Daisy Gertrude Masters. Educ: Leyton County High Sch.; St John's Coll., Cambridge (MA Hons). Artistic Associate, Old Vic Co. (formerly Prospect Theatre Co.), 1976–81; associate actor, RSC. Vice-Pres., Nat. Youth Theatre, 1982–. Stage: Birmingham Repertory Theatre, 1960–63 (first appearance in One Way Pendulum, 1961); National Theatre, 1963–71; Prospect Theatre Co., 1972, 1974, 1976, 1977, 1978; Hamlet (for reformation of Old Vic Co., and at Elsinore), 1979; Royal Shakespeare Co.: Benedick in Much Ado About Nothing (Tony Award, 1985), title rôle in Peer Gynt, Prospero in The Tempest, 1982; title rôle in Cyrano de Bergerac, 1983 (SWET Award; Play and Players Award); appearances include: TV: She Stoops to Conquer, Man of Straw, The Pallisers, I Claudius, Philby, Burgess and Maclean, Richard II, Hamlet, Inside the Third Reich; Mr Pye; films: 1971–: Odessa File; Day of the Jackal; The Medusa Touch; Othello; Three Sisters; Interlude; The Human Factor; Charlotte; The Man Who Went Up in Smoke; Enigma. Awards: BAFTA Best Actor, 1976–77; Variety Club TV Personality, 1976; Standard Best Actor, 1983. Address: Duncan Heath Associates, Paramount House, 162–170 Wardour Street, W1.

JACOBS, Prof. Arthur David; musicologist and critic; Member of Editorial Board, Opera, since 1962; Critic, Audio and Record Review, now Hi-Fi News & Record Review, since 1964; record reviewer, Sunday Times, since 1968; b 14 June 1922; s of late Alexander S. and Estelle Jacobs; m 1953, Betty Upton Hughes; two s. Educ: Manchester Grammar Sch.; Merton Coll., Oxford (MA). Music Critic: Daily Express, 1947–52; Jewish Chronicle, 1963–75; Professor, RAM, 1964–79; Hd of Music Dept, Huddersfield Polytechnic, 1979–84, created Prof. 1984. Founder and Editor, British Music Yearbook (formerly Music Yearbook), 1971–79; Adv. Editor, 1979–83. Leverhulme Res. Fellow in Music, 1977–78. Vis. Fellow, Wolfson Coll., Oxford, 1979, 1984–85; Centennial Lectr, Univ. of Illinois, 1967; Vis. Professor: Univ. of Victoria, BC, 1968; Univ. of California at Santa Barbara, 1969; Temple Univ., Philadelphia, 1970, 1971; UCLA, 1973; Univ. of Western Ontario, 1974; McMaster Univ., 1975, 1983; Univ. of Queensland, 1985. Hon. RAM 1969. Publications: Music Lover's Anthology, 1948; Gilbert and Sullivan, 1951; A New Dictionary of Music, 1958 (also Spanish, Portuguese, Danish and Swedish edns), new

edn, as The New Penguin Dictionary of Music, 1978; Choral Music, 1963 (also Japanese edn); Libretto of opera One Man Show by Nicholas Maw, 1964; (with Stanley Sadie) Pan Book of Opera, 1966, expanded edn 1984 (US edn, Great Operas in Synopsis); A Short History of Western Music, 1972 (also Italian edn); (ed) Music Education Handbook, 1976; Arthur Sullivan: a Victorian musician, 1984; many opera translations incl. Berg's Lulu (first US perf. of complete work, Santa Fe, New Mexico, 1979); contrib. TLS, Musical Times, foreign jls, etc. Recreations: puns, swimming, walking, theatre. Address: 10 Oldbury Close, Sevenoaks, Kent TN15 9DJ. T: Sevenoaks 884006.

JACOBS, David Lewis; DL; radio and television broadcaster; b 19 May 1926; s of David Jacobs and Jeanette Victoria Jacobs; m 1st, 1949, Patricia Bradlaw (marr. diss. 1972); three d (one s decd); 2nd, 1975, Caroline Munro (d 1975); 3rd, 1979, Mrs Lindsay Stuart-Hutcheson. Educ: Belmont Coll.; Strand Sch. RN, 1944–47. First broadcast, Navy Mixture, 1944; Announcer, Forces Broadcasting Service, 1944–45; Chief Announcer, Radio SEAC, Ceylon, 1945–47; Asst Stn Dir, Radio SEAC, 1947; News Reader, BBC Gen. Overseas Service, 1947, subseq. freelance. Major radio credits include: Book of Verse, Housewives' Choice, Journey into Space, Dateline London, Grande Gingold, Curioser and Curioser, Puffney Post Office, Follow that Man, Man about Town, Jazz Club, Midday Spin, Music Through Midnight, Scarlet Pimpernel, Radio 2 DJ Show, Pick of the Pops, Saturday Show Band Show, Melodies for You (12 years), Saturday Star Sounds, Any Questions (Chm. for 17 years), Any Answers; Internat. Fest. of Light. TV credits incl.: Focus on Hocus, Vera Lynn Show, Make up your Mind, Tell the Truth, Juke Box Jury, Top of the Pops, Hot Line, Miss World, Top Town, David Jacobs' Words and Music, Sunday Night with David Jacobs, Little Women, There Goes that Song Again, Make a Note, Where are they Now, What's My Line, Who What or Where, Frank Sinatra Show, Mario Lanza Show, Walt Disney Christmas Show, Wednesday Show, Wednesday Magazine, Eurovision Song Contest, TV Ice Time, Twist, A Song for Europe, Ivor Novello Awards, Aladdin, Airs and Graces, There Goes That Song Again, Tell Me Another, Those Wonderful TV Times, Blankety Blank, Come Dancing, Questions (TVS). Numerous film performances incl. Golden Disc, You Must Be Joking, It's Trad Dad, Stardust; former commentator, British Movietone News. 6 Royal Command Performances; 6 yrs Britain's Top Disc Jockey on both BBC and Radio Luxembourg; Variety Club of Gt Brit., BBC TV Personality of Year, 1960, and BBC Radio Personality of the Year, 1975; Sony Gold Award for Outstanding Contribution to Radio over the Years, 1984; RSPCA Richard Martin Award, 1978. Dir, Duke of York's Theatre. Vice-Pres., Stars Organisation for Spastics (Past Chm.); Mem. Council, RSPCA, 1969–77, Vice-Chm. 1975–76; Pres., Nat. Children's Orch.; Vice-Pres., Wimbledon Girls Choir. Chm., Think British Council, 1985– (Dep. Chm., 1983–85). Pres., Kingston upon Thames Royal British Legion, 1984–. DL Greater London, 1983, Kingston upon Thames, 1984. Publications: (autobiog.) Jacobs' Ladder, 1963; Caroline, 1978; (with Michael Bowen) Any Questions?, 1981. Recreations: talking and listening, hotels. Address: 203 Pavilion Road, SW1X 0BJ; Whiteshill, Chiddingfold, Surrey GU8 4TA. Clubs: Garrick, St James'.

JACOBS, Francis Geoffrey; QC 1984; Professor of European Law, University of London, since 1974; Director, Centre of European Law, King's College London, since 1981; b 8 June 1939; s of late Cecil Sigismund Jacobs and of Louise Jacobs (née Fischhof); m 1st, 1964, Ruth (née Freeman); one s; 2nd, 1975, Susan Felicity Gordon (née Cox); one s three d. Educ: City of London Sch.; Christ Church, Oxford; Nuffield Coll., Oxford. MA, DPhil. Called to the Bar, Middle Temple, 1964; Lectr in Jurisprudence, Univ. of Glasgow, 1963–65; Lectr in Law, LSE, 1965–69; Secretariat, European Commn of Human Rights, and Legal Directorate, Council of Europe, Strasbourg, 1969–72; Legal Sec., Court of Justice of European Communities, Luxembourg, 1972–74. Hon. Sec. UK Assoc. for European Law, 1974–81; UK Deleg., Conf. of Supreme Administrative Courts, EEC, 1984–; Mem., Admin. Tribunal, Internat. Inst. for Unification of Private Law, Rome. Cooley Lectr, Univ. of Mich, 1983. Commandeur de l'Ordre de Mérite, Luxembourg, 1983. Editor, Yearbook of European Law, 1981–; Mem. Editorial Board: Common Market Law Review; European Law Review; Jl of Common Market Studies. Publications: Criminal Responsibility, 1971; The European Convention on Human Rights, 1975; (jtly) References to the European Court, 1975; (ed) European Law and the Individual, 1976; (jtly) The Court of Justice of the European Communities, 1977, 2nd edn 1983; (jtly) The European Union Treaty, 1986. Recreations: family life, books, music, nature, travel. Address: 132 Kingston Road, Teddington, Mddx TW11 9JA. T: 01–943 0503; Fountain Court, Temple, EC4Y 9DH. T: 01–353 7356.

JACOBS, Prof. John Arthur; Professor of Geophysics, 1974–83, and Fellow, Darwin College, since 1976 (Vice Master, 1978–82), University of Cambridge; b 13 April 1916; m 1st, 1941, Daisy Sarah Ann Montgomerie (d 1974); two d; 2nd, 1974, Margaret Jones (marr. diss. 1981); 3rd, 1982, Ann Grace Wintle. Educ: Univ. of London. BA 1937, MA 1939, PhD 1949, DSc 1961. Instr Lieut RN, 1941–46; Lectr, Royal Holloway Coll., Univ. of London, 1946–51; Assoc. Prof., Univ. of Toronto, 1951–57; Prof., Univ. of British Columbia, 1957–67; Dir, Inst. of Earth Sciences, Univ. of British Columbia, 1961–67; Killam Meml Prof. of Science, Univ. of Alberta, 1967–74; Dir, Inst. of Earth and Planetary Physics, Univ. of Alberta, 1970–74. Sec., Royal Astronomical Soc., 1977–82; Harold Jeffreys Lectr, RAS, 1983. FRSC 1958; Centennial Medal of Canada, 1967; Medal of Canadian Assoc. of Physicists, 1975; J. Tuzo Wilson Medal, Canadian Geophys. Union, 1982. Publications: (with R. D. Russell and J. T. Wilson) Physics and Geology, 1959, 2nd edn 1974; The Earth's Core and Geomagnetism, 1963; Geomagnetic Micropulsations, 1970; A Textbook on Geonomy, 1974; The Earth's Core, 1975; Reversals of the Earth's Magnetic Field, 1984. Recreations: walking, music. Address: Department of Earth Sciences, Bullard Laboratories, Madingley Rise, Madingley Road, Cambridge CB3 0EZ. T: Cambridge 337733.

JACOBS, Brig. John Conrad S.; see Saunders-Jacobs.

JACOBS, John Robert Maurice; Golf Commentator, Independent Television, since 1967; Golf Adviser, Golf World Magazine, since 1962; Golf Instructor: Golf Digest Magazine Schools, 1971–76; Golf Magazine Schools, US, 1977; b 14 March 1925; s of Robert and Gertrude Vivian Jacobs; m 1949, Rita Wragg; one s one d. Educ: Maltby Grammar School. Asst Professional Golfer, Hallamshire Golf Club, 1947–49; Golf Professional: Gezira Sporting Club, Cairo, 1949–52; Sandy Lodge Golf Club, 1952–64; Man. Dir, Athlon Golf, 1967–75; Professional Golfers' Association: Tournament Dir-Gen., 1971–76, Advr to Tournament Div., 1977; European Ryder Cup Captain, 1979–81. Adviser to: Walker Cup Team; Curtis Cup Team; English Golf Union team; Scottish Golf Union team; German, Spanish and French nat. teams. Currently associated with John Jacobs' Practical Golf Schools, based in USA. Publications: Golf, 1961; Play Better Golf, 1969; Practical Golf, 1973; John Jacobs Analyses the Superstars, 1974; Golf Doctor, 1979; contrib.: Golf World Magazine; Golf Magazine (US). Recreations: shooting, fishing. Address: Stable Cottage, Chapel Lane, Lyndhurst, Hants SO4 7FG. T: Lyndhurst 2743. Clubs: Lucayan Country (Grand Bahamas); Sandy Lodge Golf, New Forest Golf, Brockenhurst Golf, Bramshaw Golf; Lake Nona Golf and Country (Florida).

JACOBS, Hon. Sir Kenneth (Sydney), KBE 1976; Justice of High Court of Australia, 1974–79; b 5 Oct. 1917; s of Albert Sydney Jacobs and Sarah Grace Jacobs (née Aggs); m

1952, Eleanor Mary Neal; one *d*. *Educ*: Knox Grammar Sch., NSW; Univ. of Sydney (BA, LLB). Admitted to NSW Bar, 1947; QC 1958; Supreme Court of NSW: Judge, 1960; Judge of Appeal, 1966; Pres., Court of Appeal, 1972. *Publication*: Law of Trusts, 1958. *Recreations*: printing and bookbinding; gardening. *Address*: Crooks Lane Corner, Axford, Marlborough, Wilts SN8 2HA.

JACOBS, Sir Wilfred (Ebenezer), GCMG 1981; GCVO 1985 (KCVO 1977); Kt 1967; OBE 1959; QC 1959; Governor-General of Antigua and Barbuda, since 1981; *b* 19 Oct. 1919; 2nd *s* of late William Henry Jacobs and Henrietta Jacobs (*née* Du Bois); *m* 1947, Carmen Sylva, 2nd *d* of late Walter A. Knight and Flora Knight (*née* Fleming); one *s* two *d*. *Educ*: Grenada Boys' Secondary Sch.; Gray's Inn, London. Called to Bar, Gray's Inn, 1946; Registrar and Additional Magistrate, St Vincent, 1946; Magistrate, Dominica, 1947, and St Kitts, 1949; Crown Attorney, St Kitts, 1952; Attorney-Gen., Leeward Is, 1957–59, and Antigua, 1960. Acted Administrator, Dominica, St Kitts, Antigua, various periods, 1947–60. MEC and MLC, St Vincent, Dominica, St Kitts, Antigua, 1947–60; Legal Draftsman and Acting Solicitor-Gen., Trinidad and Tobago, 1960. Barbados: Solicitor-Gen., and Actg Attorney-Gen., 1961–63; PC and MLC, 1962–63; Dir of Public Prosecutions, 1964; Judge of Supreme Court of Judicature, 1967; Governor of Antigua, 1967–81. KStJ. *Recreations*: swimming, gardening, golf. *Address*: Governor-General's Residence, Antigua, West Indies. *Club*: Royal Commonwealth Society.

JACOBSEN, Frithjof Halfdan; Norwegian Ambassador, retired; *b* 14 Jan. 1914; *m* 1941, Elsa Tidemand Anderson; one *s* two *d*. *Educ*: Univ. of Oslo (Law). Entered Norwegian Foreign Service, 1938; Legation, Paris, 1938–40; Norwegian Foreign Ministry, London, 1940–45; held posts in Moscow, London, Oslo, 1945–55; Director-Gen., Political Affairs, Oslo, 1955–59; Norwegian Ambassador to: Canada, 1959–61; Moscow, 1961–66; Under-Sec. of State, Oslo, 1966–70; Ambassador to Moscow, 1970–75; Ambassador to the Court of St James's and to Ireland, 1975–82. *Address*: Schwachsgate 4, Oslo 3, Norway.

JACOBSON, family name of **Baron Jacobson.**

JACOBSON, Baron *cr* 1975 (Life Peer), of St Albans; **Sydney Jacobson,** MC 1944; Editorial Director, International Publishing Corporation Newspapers, 1968–74, Deputy Chairman, 1973–74; *b* 26 Oct. 1908; *m* 1938, Phyllis June Buck; two *s* one *d*. *Educ*: Strand Sch., London; King's Coll., London. Asst Editor: Statesman, India, 1934–36; Lilliput Magazine, 1936–39. Served in Army, 1939–45. Special Correspondent, Picture Post, 1945–48; Editor, Leader Magazine, 1948–50; Political Editor, Daily Mirror, 1952–62; Editor, Daily Herald, 1962–64; Editor, Sun, 1964–65; Chairman, Odhams Newspapers, 1968. Member Press Council, 1969–75. *Recreations*: tennis, walking, reading. *Address*: 6 Avenue Road, St Albans, Herts. *T*: St Albans 53873.

JACOMB, Sir Martin (Wakefield), Kt 1985; Deputy Chairman, Barclays Bank PLC, since 1985; Chairman, Barclays de Zoete Wedd, since 1986; a Director, Bank of England, since 1986; *b* 11 Nov. 1929; *s* of Hilary W. Jacomb and Félise Jacomb; *m* 1960, Evelyn Heathcoat Amory; two *s* one *d*. *Educ*: Eton Coll.; Worcester Coll., Oxford (MA Law 1953). Called to the Bar, Inner Temple, 1955. 2nd Lieut RA, 1948–49. Practised at the Bar, 1955–68; Kleinwort, Benson Ltd, 1968–85, Vice-Chm., 1976–85; Dir, Kleinwort, Benson, Lonsdale Ltd, 1974–85; Chairman: Merchants Trust Ltd, 1974–85; Transatlantic Fund Inc., 1978–85. Director: Christian Salvesen Ltd, 1974–; Mercantile Credit Co., 1973–84; Hudson's Bay Co., Canada, 1971–; Commercial Union Assurance Co. PLC, 1984–; Daily Telegraph, 1986–; Mem., European Adv. Bd, Touche Remnant & Co., 1982–. Deputy Chairman: Council for the Securities Industry, 1983–85; Panel on Take-overs and Mergers, 1983–85; Securities and Investments Board, 1985–. Part-time mem., British Gas Corp., 1981–. Chm., City Capital Markets Cttee, 1980–83; External Mem., Finance Cttee, Delegacy of the OUP, 1971–; Mem., Greenwich Hosp. Cttee, 1976–83. Trustee, Nat. Heritage Meml Fund, 1982–. *Recreations*: theatre, family bridge, tennis. *Address*: 54 Lombard Street, EC3P 3AH. *T*: 01–626 1567; Barclays de Zoete Wedd, PO Box 188, Ebbgate House, 2 Swan Lane, EC4R 3TS. *T*: 01–623 2323.

JACQUES, family name of **Baron Jacques.**

JACQUES, Baron *cr* 1968 (Life Peer), of Portsea Island; **John Henry Jacques;** Chairman of the Co-operative Union Ltd, 1964–70; *b* 11 Jan. 1905; *s* of Thomas Dobson Jacques and Annie Bircham; *m* 1929, Constance White; two *s* one *d*. *Educ*: Victoria Univ., Manchester; (BA(Com)); Co-operative Coll. Sec-Man., Moorsley Co-operative Society Ltd, 1925–29; Tutor, Co-operative Coll., 1929–42; Accountant, Plymouth Co-operative Soc. Ltd, 1942–45; Chief Executive, Portsea Island Co-operative Soc. Ltd, Portsmouth, 1945–65; Pres., Co-operative Congress, 1961. Pres., Retail Trades Education Council, 1971–75. A Lord in Waiting (Govt Whip), 1974–77 and 1979; a Dep. Chm. of Cttees, 1977–. JP Portsmouth, 1951–75. *Publications*: Book-Keeping I, II and III, 1940; Management Accounting, 1966; Manual on Co-operative Management, 1969. *Recreations*: walking, snooker, gardening, West-Highland terriers. *Address*: 23 Hilltop Crescent, Cosham, Portsmouth, Hants PO6 1BB. *T*: Cosham 375511. *Club*: Co-operative (Portsmouth).

JACQUES, Peter Roy Albert; Secretary, TUC Social Insurance and Industrial Welfare Department, since 1971; *b* 12 Aug. 1939; *s* of George Henry Jacques and Ivy Mary Jacques (*née* Farr); *m* 1965, Jacqueline Anne Sears; one *s* one *d*. *Educ*: Archbishop Temple's Secondary Sch.; Newcastle upon Tyne Polytechnic (BSc Sociology); Univ. of Leicester. Building labourer, 1955–58; market porter, 1958–62; Asst, TUC Social Insce and Industrial Welfare Dept, 1968–71. Member: Industrial Injuries Adv. Council, 1972; Nat. Insce Adv. Cttee, 1972–78; Health and Safety Commn, 1974; Royal Commn on the Nat. Health Service, 1976–79; EEC Cttee on Health-Safety, 1976; NHS London Adv. Cttee, 1979–; Social Security Adv. Cttee, 1980–; Health Educn Council, 1984–; Civil Justice Review Adv. Cttee, 1985–. Jt Sec., BMA/TUC Cttee, 1972–; Sec., TUC Health Services Cttee, 1979–; Mem. Exec. Cttee, Royal Assoc. for Disability and Rehabilitation, 1975–. *Publications*: responsible for TUC pubns Health-Safety Handbook; Occupational Pension Schemes. *Recreations*: reading, yoga, walking, camping, vegetable growing. *Address*: TUC, Congress House, Great Russell Street, WC1B 3LS. *T*: 01–636 4030.

JAEGER, Prof. Leslie Gordon; FRSE 1966; Vice President (Research) and Professor of Civil Engineering and Applied Mathematics, Technical University of Nova Scotia, since 1985; *b* 28 Jan. 1926; *s* of Henry Jaeger; *m* 1st, 1948, Annie Sylvia Dyson; two *d*; 2nd, 1981, Kathleen Grant. *Educ*: King George V Sch., Southport; Gonville and Caius Coll., Cambridge. Royal Corps of Naval Constructors, 1945–48; Industry, 1948–52; University College, Khartoum, 1952–56; Univ. Lectr, Cambridge, 1956–62; Fellow and Dir of Studies, Magdalene Coll., Cambridge, 1959–62; Prof. of Applied Mechanics, McGill Univ., Montreal, 1962–65; Regius Prof. of Engineering, Edinburgh Univ., 1965–66; Prof. of Civil Engineering, McGill Univ., 1966–70; Dean, Faculty of Engineering, Univ. of New Brunswick, 1970–75; Academic Vice-President: Acadia Univ., NS, 1975–80; Technical Univ. of NS, 1980–85. A. B. Sanderson Award, Canadian Soc. for Civil Engrg, 1983; Gzowski Medal, Engrg Inst. of Canada, 1985. *Publications*: The Analysis of Grid Frameworks and Related Structures (with A. W. Hendry), 1958; Elementary Theory of Elastic Plates, 1964; Cartesian Tensors in Engineering Science, 1965; (with B. Bakht) Bridge Analysis Simplified, 1985; various papers on grillage analysis in British, European and American Journals. *Recreations*: golf, curling, contract bridge. *Address*: PO Box 1000, Halifax, NS B3J 2X4, Canada. *T*: 429–8300. *Club*: Halifax (Halifax, Canada).

JAFFÉ, (Andrew) Michael, LittD; Director, Fitzwilliam Museum, Cambridge, since 1973; Professor of the History of Western Art, since 1973; Fellow of King's College, Cambridge, since 1952; *b* 3 June 1923; *s* of Arthur Daniel Jaffé, OBE, and Marie Marguerite Strauss; *m* 1964, Patricia Ann Milne-Henderson; two *s* two *d*. *Educ*: Eton Coll.; King's Coll., Cambridge (MA, LittD 1980); Courtauld Inst. of Art. Lt-Comdr, RNVR, retd. Commonwealth Fund Fellow, Harvard and New York Univ., 1951–53; Asst Lectr in Fine Arts, Cambridge, 1956; Prof. of Renaissance Art, Washington Univ., St Louis, 1960–61; Vis. Prof., Harvard Univ., Summer 1961; Lectr in Fine Arts, Cambridge, 1961; Reader in History of Western Art, Cambridge, 1968; Head of Dept of History of Art, Cambridge, 1970–73; a Syndic, Fitzwilliam Museum, 1971–73. Mem., Adv. Council, V&A Museum, 1971–76. Organiser (for Nat. Gall. of Canada) of Jordaens Exhibn, Ottawa, 1968–69; Vis. Prof., Harvard Univ., Fall 1968–69. FRSA 1969. Officier, Ordre de Léopold (Belgium), 1980. *Publications*: Van Dyck's Antwerp Sketchbook, 1966; Rubens, 1967; Jordaens, 1968; Rubens and Italy, 1977; articles and reviews (art historical) in European and N American jls, etc. *Recreation*: viticulture. *Address*: Grove Lodge, Trumpington Street, Cambridge. *Clubs*: Brooks's, Turf, Beefsteak.

JAFFRAY, Alistair Robert Morton, CB 1978; Deputy Under-Secretary of State, Ministry of Defence, 1975–84; *b* 28 Oct. 1925; *s* of late Alexander George and Janet Jaffray; *m* 1st, 1953, Margaret Betty Newman (decd); two *s* one *d*; 2nd, 1980, Edna Mary, *e d* of late S. J. Tasker, Brasted Chart. *Educ*: Clifton Coll.; Corpus Christi Coll., Cambridge. BA First Cl. Hons., Mod. Langs. Served War, RNVR, 1943–46. Apptd Home Civil Service (Admty), 1948; Private Sec. to First Lord of Admty, 1960–62; Private Sec. to successive Secretaries of State for Defence, 1969–70; Asst Under-Sec. of State, MoD, 1971, Dep. Sec. 1975; Sec. to Admty Bd, 1981–84. Governor, Clifton Coll., 1980–; Chm. Management Cttee, Royal Hospital Sch., Holbrook, 1985–. *Address*: Okeford, Lynch Road, Farnham, Surrey.

JAFFRAY, Sir William Otho, 5th Bt, *cr* 1892; *b* 1 Nov. 1951; *s* of Sir William Edmund Jaffray, 4th Bt, TD, JP, DL; *S* father, 1953; *m* 1981, Cynthia Ross Corrington, Montreal, Canada; one *s* one *d*. *Educ*: Eton. *Heir*: *s* Nicholas Gordon Alexander Jaffray, *b* 18 Oct. 1982. *Address*: The Manor House, Priors Dean, Petersfield, Hants. *T*: Hawkley 483.

JAGAN, Cheddi, DDS; Guyanese Politician; Leader of Opposition in National Assembly; *b* March 1918; *m* 1943; one *s* one *d*. *Educ*: Howard Univ.; YMCA Coll., Chicago (BSc); Northwestern Univ. (DDS). Member of Legislative Council, British Guiana, 1947–53; Minister of Agriculture, Lands and Mines, May-Oct. 1953; Minister of Trade and Industry, 1957–61; (first) Premier, British Guiana, and Minister of Development and Planning, 1961–64. Hon. Pres., Guyana Agricl and General Workers' Union; Pres., Guyana Peace Council; Mem. Presidential Cttee, World Peace Council. Order of Friendship, USSR, 1978. *Publications*: Forbidden Freedom, 1954; Anatomy of Poverty, 1964; The West on Trial, 1966; Caribbean Revolution, 1979; The Caribbean—Whose Backyard?, 1984. *Recreations*: swimming, tennis. *Address*: Freedom House, 41 Robb Street, Georgetown, Guyana.

JAGATSINGH, Hon. Sir Kher, Kt 1981; Officier, Ordre National Malgache, 1969; MLA (Lab) Montagne Blanche and Grand River South East, Mauritius, since 1976; President, Conseil d'Administration, Institut Africain et Mauricien de Bilinguisme, since 1977; Managing Director, Century Investments Ltd, since 1982; *b* Amritsar, 23 July 1931; *m* Radhika; two *s* two *d*. *Educ*: Beau Bassin Primary Sch.; privately. Civil servant in Dept of Health, 1950–54; co-founded Mauritius Times, weekly newspaper, 1954; trainee journalist on Times of India, 1956–57; on attachment to Slough Observer and Paddington Times, 1957; joined Labour Party, 1958, Sec.-Gen., 1961–; Chairman: Govt and non-Govt Gen. Workers' Union, 1961–67; Central Housing Auth., 1963–67. MLC for Beau Bassin-Petite Rivière, 1959, for Montagne Blanche and Grand River SE, 1967; Minister: of Health, 1967–71; of Economic Planning and Develt, 1971–76; of Education and Cultural Affairs, 1977–82. Mem. Exec. Bd, UNESCO, 1977–80. Co-founder, The Nation, 1970, now Vice-Chm. Governor for Mauritius, IBRD, Washington; Chairman: Giants Internat. Mauritius Br.; Mauritius Nat. Peace Council. Port Louis correspondent, Bombay Commerce, 1982–. *Publication*: Petals of Dust, 1981. *Address*: c/o Ministry of Education and Cultural Affairs, Port Louis, Mauritius. *T*: (office) 083205; (home) 542215.

JAGO, David Edgar John; Under Secretary, Cabinet Office, since 1984; *b* 2 Dec. 1937; *s* of late Edgar George Jago and of Violet Jago; *m* 1963, Judith (*née* Lissenden); one *s* one *d*. *Educ*: King Edward's Sch., Bath; Pembroke Coll., Oxford (MA). National Service, RA, 1956–58. Asst Principal, Admiralty, 1961; Private Sec. to Permanent Under Sec. of State (RN), 1964–65; Principal 1965; Directing Staff, IDC, 1968–70; Private Sec. to Parly Under Sec. of State for Defence (RN), 1971–73; Ministry of Defence: Asst Sec., 1973; Asst Under Sec. of State: Aircraft, 1979–82; Naval Staff, 1982–84. *Recreations*: theatre, opera, military history, supporting Arsenal FC. *Address*: Cabinet Office, 70 Whitehall, SW1A 2AS. *Club*: United Oxford & Cambridge University.

JAHN, Dr Wolfgang; Chairman, Board of International Commercial Bank plc, since 1984; *b* 27 Sept. 1918; *s* of Dr Georg Jahn and Ella (*née* Schick); *m* 1949, Gabriele (*née* Beck); two *s* one *d*. *Educ*: Zürich Univ.; Berlin Univ.; Heidelberg Univ. (DrEcon). Industrial Credit Bank, Düsseldorf, 1949–54; IBRD, Washington, 1954–57; Commerzbank AG, Düsseldorf, 1957–84 (to Managing Dir). *Address*: International Commercial Bank, 9–10 Angel Court, EC2.

JAHODA, Prof. Marie, (Mrs A. H. Albu), CBE 1974; DPhil; Professor Emeritus, University of Sussex; Senior Research Consultant to Science Policy Research Unit, University of Sussex, since 1971; *b* 26 Jan. 1907; *d* of Carl Jahoda and Betty Jahoda; *m* 1st, 1927, Paul F. Lazarsfeld; one *d*; 2nd, 1958, Austen Albu, *qv*. *Educ*: Univ. of Vienna (DPhil). Prof. of Social Psychology, NY Univ., 1949–58; Res. Fellow and Prof. of Psychol., Brunel Univ., 1958–65; Prof. of Social Psychol., Sussex Univ., 1965–73. Hon. DLit: Sussex, 1973; Leicester, 1973; Bremen, 1984. *Publications*: Die Arbeitslosen von Marienthal, 1933 (Eng. trans. 1971); Research Methods in Human Relations, 1953; Current Concepts of Positive Mental Health, 1958; Freud and the Dilemmas of Psychology, 1977; (ed) World Futures: the great debate, 1977; Employment and Unemployment, 1982. *Recreations*: cooking, cello, chess. *Address*: 17 The Crescent, Keymer, Sussex BN6 8RB. *T*: Hassocks 2267.

JAKEWAY, Sir (Francis) Derek, KCMG 1963 (CMG 1956); OBE 1948; *b* 6 June 1915; *s* of Francis Edward and Adeline Jakeway; *m* 1941, Phyllis Lindsay Watson, CStJ; three *s*. *Educ*: Hele's Sch., Exeter; Exeter Coll., Oxford (BA Hons Mod. Hist.). Colonial Administrative Service, Nigeria, 1937–54, seconded to Seychelles, 1946–49, to Colonial Office, 1949–51; Chief Sec., British Guiana, 1954–59; Chief Sec., Sarawak, 1959–63; Governor and C-in-C, Fiji, 1964–68. Chm., Devon AHA, 1974–82. KStJ 1964. *Address*: 78 Douglas Avenue, Exmouth, Devon. *T*: Exmouth 271342.

JAKOBOVITS, Rabbi Sir Immanuel, Kt 1981; Chief Rabbi of the United Hebrew Congregations of the British Commonwealth of Nations, since 1967; *b* 8 Feb. 1921; *s* of Rabbi Dr Julius Jakobovits and Paula (*née* Wreschner); *m* 1949, Amelie Munk; two *s* four *d*. *Educ:* London Univ. (BA; PhD 1955; Fellow, UCL, 1984–); Jews' Coll. and Yeshivah Etz Chaim, London. Diploma, 1944; Associate of Jews' Coll. Minister: Brondesbury Synagogue, 1941–44; SE London Synagogue, 1944–47; Great Synagogue, London, 1947–49; Chief Rabbi of Ireland, 1949–58; Rabbi of Fifth Avenue Synagogue, New York, 1958–67. Hon. DD Yeshiva Univ., NY, 1975. *Publications:* Jewish Medical Ethics, 1959 (NY; 4th edn 1975); Jewish Law Faces Modern Problems, 1965 (NY); Journal of a Rabbi, 1966 (NY), 1967 (GB); The Timely and the Timeless, 1977; If Only My People . . . Zionism in My Life, 1984; contrib. learned and popular jls in America, England and Israel. *Address:* Adler House, Tavistock Square, WC1. *T:* 01–387 1066.

JALLAND, William Herbert Wainwright, JP; **His Honour Judge Jalland;** a Circuit Judge, Manchester, since 1975 (now sitting in Crown Court, Manchester, and County Courts, Manchester and Salford); *b* 1922; *o s* of Arthur Edgar Jalland, QC, JP and Elizabeth Hewitt Jalland; *m* 1945, Helen Monica, BEM 1984, *o d* of John and Edith Wyatt; one *s* one *d*. *Educ:* Manchester Grammar Sch.; Manchester Univ. LLB 1949. Served War of 1939–45, HM Forces at home and abroad, 1941–46: Captain, King's Own Royal Regt, attached 8th Bn Durham LI. Called to Bar, Gray's Inn, 1950; practised Northern Circuit; part-time Dep. Coroner, City of Salford, 1955–65; part-time Dep. Recorder, Burnley, 1962–70; part-time Dep. Chm., Lancs County Sessions, 1970–71; Recorder, 1972; a Circuit Judge, Liverpool and Merseyside, 1972–75. JP Lancs, 1970; Liaison Judge at Magistrates' Courts, Rochdale, Middleton and Heywood, 1974–. Vice-Pres., Old Mancunians' Assoc., 1979–; Pres., Styal Sports and Social Club, 1979–. *Recreations:* rambling, gardening, photography. *Club:* Manchester (Manchester).

JAMES, family name of **Barons James of Rusholme, Northbourne** and **Saint Brides.**

JAMES OF RUSHOLME, Baron *cr* 1959, of Fallowfield (Life Peer); **Eric John Francis James,** Kt 1956; Chairman, Royal Fine Art Commission, 1976–79 (Member, 1973–79); *b* 1909; *yr s* of F. W. James; *m* 1939, Cordelia, *d* of late Maj.-Gen. F. Wintour, CB, CBE; one *s*. *Educ:* Taunton's School, Southampton; Queen's Coll., Oxford (Exhibitioner and Hon. Scholar, 1927. Hon. Fellow, 1959). Goldsmiths' Exhibitioner, 1929; BA, BSc 1931; MA, DPhil 1933; Asst Master at Winchester Coll., 1933–45; High Master of Manchester Grammar Sch., 1945–62; Vice-Chancellor, Univ. of York, 1962–73. Mem. of University Grants Cttee, 1949–59; Chm. of Headmasters' Conference, 1953–54; Mem. Central Advisory Council on Education, 1957–61; Member: Standing Commission on Museums and Galleries, 1958–61; Press Council, 1963–67; SSRC, 1965–68; Chairman: Personal Social Services Council, 1973–76; Cttee to Inquire into the Training of Teachers, 1970–71. Hon. FRIBA 1979. Hon. LLD: McGill, 1957; York, (Toronto) 1970; Hon. DLitt New Brunswick, 1974; DUniv York, 1974. Fellow, Winchester Coll., 1963–69. *Publications:* (in part) Elements of Physical Chemistry; (in part) Science and Education; An Essay on the Content of Education; Education and Leadership; articles in scientific and educational journals. *Address:* Penhill Cottage, West Witton, Leyburn, N Yorks.

JAMES, Anne Eleanor S.; *see* Scott-James.

JAMES, Anthony Trafford, CBE 1979; PhD; FRS 1983; Non-Executive Director, The Wellcome Foundation, since 1985; Member of Executive Committee of Unilever Research Colworth Laboratory, also Head of Division of Biosciences, 1972–85; *b* Cardiff, Wales, 6 March 1922; *s* of J. M. and I. James; *m* 1st, 1945, O. I. A. Clayton (*d* 1980); two *s* one *d*; 2nd, 1983, L. J. Beare; one *s*. *Educ:* University College Sch.; Northern Polytechnic; University Coll. London (BSc, PhD), Fellow 1975; Harvard Business Sch. (AMP). MRC Junior Fellowship at Bedford Coll., Univ. of London (with Prof. E. E. Turner, subject: Antimalarials), 1945–47; Jun. Mem. staff, Lister Inst. for Preventive Med., London (with Dr R. L. M. Synge, Nobel Laureate, subject: Structure of Gramicidin S), 1947–50; Mem. scientific staff, Nat. Inst. for Med. Res., London (special appt awarded, 1961), 1950–62 (with Dr A. J. P. Martin, FRS, Nobel Laureate, 1950–56); Unilever Research Lab., Sharnbrook: Div. Manager and Head of Biosynthesis Unit, 1962–67; Head of Div. of Plant Products and Biochemistry, 1967–69; Gp Manager, Biosciences Gp, 1969–72. Industrial Prof. of Chemistry, Loughborough Univ. of Technology, 1966–71. Member: SRC, 1973–77; Food Sci. and Technol. Bd, MAFF, 1975–80; Manpower Cttee, SERC, 1981–84; ABRC, 1983–; Chairman: Food Composition, Quality and Safety Cttee, MAFF, 1975–80; Biotechnol. Management Cttee, SERC, 1981–85. Hon. Dr Dijon, 1981; Hon. DSc Cranfield Inst. of Technology, 1985. Has had various awards incl. some from abroad. *Publications:* New Biochemical Separations (ed A. T. James and L. J. Morris), 1964; Lipid Biochemistry—an introduction (M. I. Gurr and A. T. James), 1972. *Recreations:* glass engraving, antique collecting, gardening. *Address:* The Wellcome Foundation Ltd, Wellcome Building, 183 Euston Road, NW1.

JAMES, (Arthur) Walter; Principal, St Catharine's, Windsor, 1974–82; *b* 30 June 1912; *s* of late W. J. James, OBE; *m* 1st, 1939, Elisabeth (marr. diss. 1956), *e d* of Richard Rylands Howroyd; one *d*; 2nd, 1957, Ann Jocelyn, *y d* of late C. A. Leavy Burton; one *d* and one adopted *s* two adopted *d*. *Educ:* Uckfield Grammar Sch.; Keble Coll., Oxford (Scholar); 1st Cl. Mod. Hist.; Liddon Student; Arnold Essay Prizeman. Senior Demy of Magdalen Coll., 1935; Scholar in Mediæval Studies, British School at Rome, 1935; Editorial staff, Manchester Guardian, 1937–46. NFS 1939–45. Contested (L) Bury, Lancs, 1945. Dep. Editor, The Times Educational Supplement, 1947–51, Editor, 1952–69; Special Advisor on Educn, Times Newspapers, 1969–71; also Editor, Technology, 1957–60. Reader in Journalism, Univ. of Canterbury, NZ, 1971–74. Member: BBC Gen. Advisory Council, 1956–64; Council of Industrial Design, 1961–66; Council, Royal Society of Arts, 1964; Cttee, British-American Associates, 1964; Governor, Central School of Art and Design, 1966. Woodard Lecturer, 1965. *Publications:* (Ed.) Temples and Faiths 1958; The Christian in Politics, 1962; The Teacher and his World, 1962; A Middle-class Parent's Guide to Education, 1964; (contrib.) Looking Forward to the Seventies, 1967. *Recreation:* gardening. *Address:* 1 Cumberland Mews, The Great Park, Windsor, Berks. *T:* Egham 31377. *Club:* National Liberal.

JAMES, Aubrey Graham Wallen; Deputy Chief Land Registrar, 1975–81; *b* 5 Jan. 1918; *s* of Reginald Aubrey James and Amelia Martha James; *m* 1952, Audrey Elizabeth, *er d* of Dr and Mrs A. W. F. Edmonds; two *s*. *Educ:* Nantgyle Grammar Sch.; London Univ. (LLB 1939). Solicitor, 1940. Served Second World War, 1940–46, Major, Cheshire Regt. Legal Asst, HM Land Registry, 1948; Asst Land Registrar, 1954; Land Registrar, 1963; Dist Land Registrar, Nottingham, 1963. Chm., E Midlands Region, CS Sports Council, 1970–75. *Recreations:* gardening, motoring, golf; has played Rugby, cricket and tennis with enthusiasm and in latter years, has turned to admin of these and other sports. *Address:* 10 Thameside, Teddington, Mddx TW11 9PW.

JAMES, Basil; Special Commissioner, 1963–82, Presiding Special Commissioner, 1982–83; *b* 25 May 1918; *s* of late John Elwyn James, MA (Oxon.), Cardiff, and Mary Janet (*née* Lewis), Gwaelodygarth, Glam; *m* 1943, Moira Houlding Rayner, MA (Cantab.), *d* of late Capt. Benjamin Harold Rayner, North Staffs Regt, and Elizabeth (*née* Houlding), Preston, Lancs; one *s* twin *d*. *Educ:* Llandovery Coll.; Canton High Sch., Cardiff; Christ's Coll., Cambridge (Exhibnr). Tancred Law Student, Lincoln's Inn, 1936; Squire Law Scholar, Cambridge, 1936. BA 1939; MA 1942. Called to Bar, Lincoln's Inn, 1940. Continuous sea service as RNVR officer in small ships on anti-submarine and convoy duties in Atlantic, Arctic and Mediterranean, 1940–45. King George V Coronation Scholar, Lincoln's Inn, 1946. Practised at Chancery Bar, 1946–63. Admitted to Federal Supreme Court of Nigeria, 1962. *Publications:* contrib. to Atkin's Court Forms and Halsbury's Laws of England. *Recreations:* music, gardening.

JAMES, Cecil; *see* James, T. C. G.

JAMES, Charles Edwin Frederic; a Recorder of the Crown Court since 1982; *b* 17 April 1943; *s* of Frederic Crockett Gwilym James and Marjorie Peggy James (*née* Peace); *m* 1968, Diana Mary Francis (*née* Thornton); two *s*. *Educ:* Trent College, Long Eaton, Derbyshire; Selwyn College, Cambridge. MA 1968. Called to the Bar, Inner Temple, 1965; practising on Northern Circuit. *Recreations:* cricket, golf. *Address:* (home) Broomlands, 38 Vyner Road South, Bidston, Birkenhead, Merseyside L43 7PR. *T:* 051–652 1951; (chambers) Refuge Assurance House, Derby Square, Liverpool L2 1TS. *T:* 051–709 4222. *Clubs:* Cambridge University Cricket; Royal Liverpool Golf, Royal Mersey Yacht.

JAMES, Christopher Philip; His Honour Judge James; a Circuit Judge, since 1980; *b* 27 May 1934; *yr s* of late Herbert Edgar James, CBE, and late Elizabeth Margaret James. *Educ:* Felsted School; Magdalene Coll., Cambridge (MA). Commnd RASC, 1953. Called to the Bar, Gray's Inn, 1959; a Recorder of the Crown Court, 1979. *Address:* Flat 10, 93 Elm Park Gardens, SW10 9QE. *Club:* United Oxford & Cambridge University.

JAMES, Clive Vivian Leopold; writer and broadcaster; feature writer for The Observer, since 1972 (also television critic, 1972–82); *b* 7 Oct. 1939; *s* of Albert Arthur James and Minora May (*née* Darke). *Educ:* Sydney Technical High Sch.; Sydney Univ.; Pembroke Coll., Cambridge. President of Footlights when at Cambridge. Record albums as lyricist for Pete Atkin: Beware of the Beautiful Stranger; Driving through Mythical America; A King at Nightfall; The Road of Silk; Secret Drinker; Live Libel; The Master of the Revels. Song-book with Pete Atkin: A First Folio. *Television series:* Cinema, Up Sunday, So It Goes, A Question of Sex, Saturday Night People, Clive James on Television, The Late Clive James; *television documentaries:* Shakespeare in Perspective: Hamlet, 1980; The Clive James Paris Fashion Show, Clive James and the Calendar Girls, 1981; The Return of the Flash of lightning, 1982; Clive James Live in Las Vegas,1982; Clive James meets Roman Polanski, 1984; The Clive James Great American Beauty Pageant, 1984; Clive James in Dallas, 1985; Clive James on Safari, 1986. *Publications: non-fiction:* The Metropolitan Critic, 1974; The Fate of Felicity Fark in the Land of the Media, 1975; Peregrine Prykke's Pilgrimage through the London Literary World, 1976; Britannia Bright's Bewilderment in the Wilderness of Westminster, 1976; Visions Before Midnight, 1977; At the Pillars of Hercules, 1979; First Reactions, 1980; The Crystal Bucket, 1981; Charles Charming's Challenges on the Pathway to the Throne, 1981; From the Land of Shadows, 1982; Glued to the Box, 1982; Flying Visits, 1984; *fiction:* Brilliant Creatures, 1983; *verse:* Fan-Mail, 1977; Poem of the Year, 1983; Other Passports: poems 1958–85, 1986; *autobiography:* Unreliable Memoirs, 1980; Falling Towards England: Unreliable Memoirs II, 1985. *Address:* c/o The Observer, 8 St Andrew's Hill, EC4.

JAMES, Rt. Rev. Colin Clement Walter; *see* Winchester, Bishop of.

JAMES, Sir Cynlais (Morgan), (Sir Kenneth), KCMG 1985 (CMG 1976); HM Diplomatic Service, retired; Director, Thomas Cook; Consultant: British Rail Engineering; Darwin Instruments Ltd; *b* 29 April 1926; *s* of Thomas James and Lydia Ann James (*née* Morgan); *m* 1953, Mary Teresa, *d* of R. D. Girouard and Lady Blanche Girouard; two *d*. *Educ:* Trinity Coll., Cambridge. Service in RAF, 1944–47. Cambridge 1948–51. Entered Senior Branch of Foreign Service, 1951; Foreign Office, 1951–53; Third Sec., Tokyo, 1953–56; Second Sec., Rio de Janeiro, 1956–59; First Sec. and Cultural Attaché, Moscow, 1959–62; FO, 1962–65; Paris, 1965–69; promoted Counsellor, 1968; Counsellor and Consul-General, Saigon, 1969–71; Head of W European Dept, FCO, 1971–75; NATO Defence Coll., Rome, 1975–76; Minister, Paris, 1976–81; Ambassador to Poland, 1981–83; Asst Under Sec. of State, FCO, 1983; Ambassador to Mexico, 1983–86. Chm., Anglo-Mexican Soc.; Mem., Franco-British Council. Hon. Dr Mexican Acad. of Internat. Law. Order of the Aztec, 1st cl. (Mexico). *Recreation:* tennis. *Address:* 20 Greville Road, NW6; The Old Forge, Lower Oddington, Glos. *Clubs:* Brooks's, Beefsteak, Pratt's, MCC; Travellers' (Paris).

JAMES, Prof. David Edward; Head of Department of Educational Studies, University of Surrey, since 1982; *b* 31 July 1937; *s* of Charles Edward James and Dorothy Hilda (*née* Reeves); *m* 1963, Penelope Jane Murray; two *s* one *d*. *Educ:* Universities of Reading, Oxford, Durham, London (Bsc Hons Gen., BSc Hons Special, MEd, DipEd, DipFE); FRSH. Lectr in Biology, City of Bath Tech. Coll. 1961–63; Lectr in Sci. and Educn, St Mary's Coll. of Educn, Newcastle upon Tyne, 1963–64; University of Surrey: Lectr in Educnl Psych., 1964–69; Dir of Adult Educn and later Prof., 1969–. FRSA. *Publications:* A Student's Guide to Efficient Study, 1966, Amer. edn 1967; Introduction to Psychology, 1968, Italian edn 1972. *Recreation:* farming. *Address:* Flitchings Farm, Plaistow, West Sussex RH14 0NT. *T:* Plaistow 294.

JAMES, Dr (David) Geraint, FRCP; Consultant Physician since 1959, and Dean since 1968, Royal Northern Hospital, London; Consultant Ophthalmic Physician, St Thomas Hospital, London, since 1973; Teacher, University of London, since 1979; *b* 2 Jan. 1922; *s* of David James and Sarah (*née* Davies); *m* 1951, Sheila Sherlock, *qv*; two *d*. *Educ:* Jesus Coll., Cambridge (MA 1945); Mddx Hosp. Med. Sch., London (MD 1953); Columbia Univ., NYC. FRCP 1964. Adjunct Prof. of Medicine, Univ. of Miami, Fla, 1973–, and Prof. of Epidemiology, 1981–; Consulting Phys. to RN, 1972–; Hon. Consultant Phys., US Veterans' Admin, 1978–; Hon. Consulting Phys., Sydney Hosp., Australia, 1969–; World Exec. Sec., Internat. Cttee on Sarcoidosis, 1980–. Pres., Italian Congress on Sarcoidosis, 1983; Past President: Med. Soc. of London; Harveian Soc.; Osler Club (Hon. Fellow); London Glamorgan Soc. Mem. Council: Cymmrodorion Soc.; RCP, 1982–. Lectures: Tudor Edwards, RCP and RCS, 1983; George Wise Meml, New York City, 1983. Hon. LLD Wales, 1982. Carlo Forlanini Gold Medal, Italian Thoracic Soc., 1983. Editor, Internat. Review of Sarcoidosis, 1984–; Mem. Editorial Board: French Thoracic Jl; Postgraduate Medical Jl; British Jl of Antimicrobial Chemotherapy; On Call; Medical Ophthalmology. *Publications:* Diagnosis and Treatment of Infections, 1957; Sarcoidosis, 1970; Circulation of the Blood, 1978; Atlas of Respiratory Diseases, 1981; Sarcoidosis and other Granulomatous Disorders, 1985. *Recreations:* history of medicine, international Welshness, Rugby football. *Address:* 149 Harley Street, W1N 1HG. *T:* 01–935 4444. *Club:* Athenæum.

JAMES, David G.; *see* Guthrie-James.

JAMES, Dr David Gwynfor; Head of Meteorological Research Flight, Royal Aircraft Establishment, Farnborough, 1971–82; *b* 16 April 1925; *s* of William James and Margaret May Jones; *m* 1953, Margaret Vida Gower; two *d*. *Educ:* Univ. of Wales, Cardiff (BSc, PhD). Joined Meteorological Office, 1950; Met. Res. Flight, Farnborough, 1951;

Forecasting Res., Dunstable, 1953; Christmas Island, Pacific, 1958; Satellite Lab., US Weather Bureau, 1961; Cloud Physics Res., Bracknell, 1966; Met. Res. Flight, RAE, 1971. *Publications:* papers in Qly Jl Royal Met. Soc., Jl Atmospheric Sciences, Met. Res. Papers, and Nature. *Recreations:* golf, choral singing. *Address:* Tŷ'r Onnen, 56 Port Lion, Llangwm, Haverfordwest, Dyfed.

JAMES, David Pelham; *see* Guthrie-James, D.

JAMES, Dr David William Francis; Chief Executive, British Ceramic Research Ltd (formerly British Ceramic Research Association), since 1982 (Director of Research, 1978–82); *b* 29 March 1929; *s* of Thomas M. and Margaret A. James, Merthyr Tydfil; *m* 1953, Elaine Maureen, *d* of Thomas and Gladys Hewett, Swansea; two *d*. *Educ:* Cyfarthfa Castle Sch., Merthyr Tydfil; Univ. of Wales (BSc); Univ. of London (PhD). FICeram. Research Asst, Inst. of Cancer Research, Royal Marsden Hosp., 1950–54; Flying Officer, RAF, 1954–56; Research Officer, Imperial Chemical Industries (now Mond Div.), 1956–60; Lectr and Sen. Lectr, UC North Wales, Bangor, 1960–71; Dep. Principal, Glamorgan Polytechnic, 1971–72; Principal and Director, Polytechnic of Wales, 1972–78. Council for National Academic Awards: Mem., 1976–82; Mem., Cttee for Research, 1976–83; Mem., Cttee on Entry Qualifications, 1976–79; Mem., Cttee for Academic Policy, 1979–80; Mem., Gen. Cttee, 1979–83; Chm., Sub-Cttee on College Research Degrees, 1981–85 (Mem., Working Party on Res. Policy, 1982–84); Mem., Cttee for Instns, 1982–86; Mem., Research Adv. Cttee, 1985–; Mem., CATS Adv. Bd, 1986–. Member: WJEC Techn. Educn Cttee, 1972–78, Techn. Examns Cttee and Management Adv. Cttee, 1972–75; SRC Polytechnics Cttee, 1975–78; Mid-Glamorgan Further Educn Cttee, 1974–78; F and GP Cttee, CDRA, 1983–86 (Vice-Chm., 1985–86); Steering Cttee, AIRTO, 1986–; Court, Univ. of Wales; Court, UWIST, 1972–78; Court, Univ. of Surrey, 1978–; Governor, Westminster Coll., 1983–. FRSA. Mem. Editorial Bd, Inst. of Ceramics, 1985–. *Publications:* research papers in various jls; several patents. *Recreations:* photography, reading, church work. *Address:* Fairways, Birchall, Leek, Staffs. *T:* Leek 373311.

JAMES, Derek Claude; Director of Social Services, Leeds, since 1978; *b* 9 March 1929; *s* of Cecil Claude James and Violet (*née* Rudge); *m* 1954, Evelyn (*née* Thomas); one *s* one *d*. *Educ:* King Edward's Grammar Sch., Camp Hill, Birmingham; Open Univ. (BA). Dip. in Municipal Admin. Local Government: Birmingham, 1946–60; Coventry, 1960–63; Bradford, 1963–69; Leeds, 1969–. Mem., Yorks and Humberside RHA, 1976–82; Chm., Leeds Area Review Cttee (Child Abuse), 1978–; Mem., Nat. Adv. Council on Employment of Disabled People, 1984–; Adviser: AMA Social Services Cttee, 1983–; Physical Disablement Res. Liaison Gp, 1986–. *Recreations:* watching sport, garden pottering. *Address:* Hill House, Woodhall Hills, Calverley, Pudsey, West Yorks LS28 5QY. *T:* Pudsey 578044.

JAMES, Air Vice-Marshal Edgar, CBE 1966; DFC 1945; AFC 1948 (Bar 1959); Aviation Consultant; *b* 19 Oct. 1915; *s* of Richard George James and Gertrude (*née* Barnes); *m* 1941, Josephine M. Steel; two *s*. *Educ:* Neath Grammar School. Joined RAF, 1939; commnd; flying instr duties, Canada, until 1944; opl service with Nos 305 and 107 Sqdns, 1944–45. Queen's Commendation for Valuable Service in the Air (1943, 1944, 1956). Empire Flying Sch. and Fighter Comd Ops Staff, until Staff Coll., 1950. Ops Requirements, Air Min., 1951–53; 2nd TAF Germany, 1953–56; comd No 68 Night Fighter Squadron, 1954–56; CFE, 1956–58; HQ Fighter Comd Staff, 1958–59; Asst Comdt, CFS, 1959–61; CO, RAF Leeming, 1961–62; Dir Ops Requirements 1, Min. of Def. (Air Force Dept), 1962–66; Comdr British Forces, Zambia, Feb.-Sept. 1966. Dep. Controller of Equipment, Min. of Technology, 1966–69. Wing Comdr 1953; Gp Capt. 1959; Air Cdre 1963; Air Vice-Marshal 1967. FRAeS 1971. *Recreations:* sailing, golf. *Address:* Lowmead, Traine Paddock, Modbury, Devon PL21 ORN. *T:* Modbury 830492. *Clubs:* Royal Air Force; Royal Western Yacht (Plymouth).

JAMES, Edmund Purcell S.; *see* Skone James.

JAMES, Edward Foster, CMG 1968; OBE 1946; Director, Tace Plc, since 1984; *b* 18 Jan. 1917; *s* of late Arthur Foster James; *m* 1985, Janet Mary Walls; one *s* two *d* by a previous marriage. Served HM Forces, 1939–46, India, Burma, Malaya, Indonesia; Lieut-Colonel (GSO1) (OBE, despatches twice). Joined HM Diplomatic Service, 1947; Rangoon, 1948; Hong Kong, 1951; Foreign Office, 1953; Rome, 1955; Foreign Office, 1958; Berlin, 1960; FO (later FCO), 1961–74. Exec. Dir, Inst. of Directors, 1975–76; Dep. Dir-Gen., CBI, 1976–83. *Address:* Flat 19, Swinton House, 95 Gloucester Terrace, W2 3HB. *T:* 01–262 0139. *Club:* Boodle's.

JAMES, Edwin Kenneth George; Chairman, PAG Ltd, since 1984; Chief Scientific Officer, Civil Service Department, 1970–76; *b* 27 Dec. 1916; *s* of late Edwin and Jessie Marion James; *m* 1941, Dorothy Margaret Pratt; one *d*. *Educ:* Latymer Upper Sch.; Northern Polytechnic. BSc London; FRSC. Joined War Office, 1938; Chem. Defence Exper. Stn, 1942; Aust. Field Exper. Stn, 1944–46; Operational Research Gp, US Army, Md, 1950–54; Dir, Biol and Chem. Defence, WO, 1961; Army (later Defence) Op. Res. Estab., Byfleet, 1965; HM Treasury (later Civil Service Dept), 1968. Silver Medal, Op. Res. Soc., 1979. *Address:* 5 Watersmeet Road, East Harnham, Salisbury, Wilts. *T:* Salisbury 334099. *Club:* Athenæum.

JAMES, Rev. Canon Eric Arthur; Chaplain to HM the Queen, since 1984; Director of Christian Action since 1979; *b* 14 April 1925; *s* of John Morgan James and Alice Amelia James. *Educ:* Dagenham County High School; King's Coll. London (MA, BD; FKC 1986). Asst Curate, St Stephen with St John, Westminster, 1951–55; Chaplain Trinity Coll., Cambridge, 1955–59; Select Preacher to Univ. of Cambridge, 1959–60; Vicar of St George, Camberwell and Warden of Trinity College Mission, 1959–64; Director of Parish and People, 1964–69; Proctor in Convocation, 1964–72; Canon Precentor of Southwark Cathedral, 1964–73; Canon Residentiary and Missioner, Diocese of St Albans, 1973–83; Hon. Canon, 1983–. Preacher to Gray's Inn, 1978–. Commissary to Bishop of Kimberley, 1965–67, to Archbishop of Melanesia, 1969–. Examining Chaplain to Bishop of St Albans, 1973–83, to Bishop of Truro, 1983–. *Publications:* The Double Cure, 1957, 2nd edn 1980; Odd Man Out, 1962; (ed) Spirituality for Today, 1968; (ed) Stewards of the Mysteries of God, 1979. *Address:* 11 Denny Crescent, SE11 4UY. *T:* 01–582 3068. *Clubs:* Reform, Royal Commonwealth Society.

JAMES, (Ernest) Gethin, FRICS; Director, Estate Surveying Services, Property Services Agency, 1977–84, retired; *b* 20 March 1925; *s* of Ernest Bertram James and Gwladys James; *m* 1st, 1949 (marr. diss.); 2nd, 1981, Mrs Margaret Hollis. *Educ:* Christ Coll., Brecon; Coll. of Estate Management. FRICS 1954. Defence Land Agent: Colchester, 1968–69; Aldershot, 1969–72; Dep. Chief Land Agent, MoD, 1972–74, Chief Land Agent and Valuer, 1974–75; Asst Dir (Estates), PSA, London Reg., 1975–77. *Recreations:* living each day, golf, shooting. *Address:* Heath Cottage, Church Lane, Ewshot, Farnham, Surrey. *T:* Aldershot 850548. *Club:* Officers' (Aldershot).

JAMES, Evan Maitland; *b* 14 Jan. 1911; *er s* of late A. G. James, CBE, and late Helen James (*née* Maitland); *m* 1939, Joan Goodnow, *d* of late Hon. J. V. A. MacMurray, State Dept, Washington, DC; one *s* two *d*. *Educ:* Durnford; Eton (Oppidan Scholar); Trinity Coll., Oxford (MA). Served War of 1939–45: War Reserve Police (Metropolitan), 1939; BBC Overseas (Propaganda Research) Dept, 1940–41; Ordinary Seaman, to Lieut, RNVR, 1941–46. Clerk of the Merchant Taylors' Company, 1947–62; Steward of Christ Church, Oxford, 1962–78. *Address:* Upwood Park, Besselsleigh, Abingdon, Oxon OX13 5QE. *T:* Frilford Heath 390535. *Club:* Travellers'.

JAMES, Geraint; *see* James, D. G.

JAMES, Gethin; *see* James, E. G.

JAMES, Henry Leonard, CB 1980; Director-General, European Federation for Retirement Provision, since 1982; *b* 12 Dec. 1919; *o s* of late Leonard Mark James and late Alice Esther James; *m* 1949, Sylvia Mary Bickell. *Educ:* King Edward VI Sch., Birmingham. Entered Civil Service in Min. of Health, 1938; Founder Editor, The Window, Min. of Nat. Insce, 1948–51; Dramatic Critic and London Corresp. of Birmingham News, 1947–51; Press Officer, Min. of Pensions and Nat. Insce, 1951–55; Head of Films, Radio and Television, Admty, 1955–61; Head of Publicity, Min. of Educn, 1961–63; Chief Press Officer, Min. of Educn, 1963–64; Dep. Public Relations Adviser to Prime Minister, 1964; Dep. Press Sec. to Prime Minister, 1964–68; Chief Information Officer, Min. of Housing and Local Govt, 1969–70; Press Sec. to Prime Minister, 1970–71; Dir of Information, DoE, 1971–74; Dir-Gen., COI, 1974–78; Chief Press Sec. to the Prime Minister, 1979; Public Relations Advr to Main Bd, Vickers Ltd, 1978–80; Dir-Gen., Nat. Assoc. of Pension Funds, 1981–86. Member: Pub. Cttee, Internat. Year of the Child, 1979; Council, RSPCA, 1980–84; BOTB, 1980–83. Alumni Guest Lectr, Gustavus Adolphus Coll., Minnesota, 1977. FCAM 1980 (Dep. Chm., 1979–84; Vice-Pres., 1984–). FRSA. FIPR (Pres., 1979; President's Medal, 1976). *Recreation:* visual arts. *Address:* 53 Beaufort Road, W5 3EB. *T:* 01–997 3021.

JAMES, Prof. Ioan Mackenzie, FRS 1968; MA, DPhil; Savilian Professor of Geometry, Oxford University, since 1970; Fellow of New College, Oxford, since 1970; Editor, Topology, since 1962; *b* 23 May 1928; *o s* of Reginald Douglas and Jessie Agnes James; *m* 1961, Rosemary Gordon Stewart, Fellow of Oxford Centre for Management Studies; no *c*. *Educ:* St Paul's Sch. (Foundn Schol.); Queen's Coll., Oxford (Open Schol.). Commonwealth Fund Fellow, Princeton, Berkeley and Inst. for Advanced Study, 1954–55; Tapp Res. Fellow, Gonville and Caius Coll., Cambridge, 1956; Reader in Pure Mathematics, Oxford, 1957–69, and Senior Research Fellow, St John's Coll., 1959–69. London Mathematical Society: Treasurer, 1969–79; Pres., 1985–; Whitehead Prize and Lectr, 1978. Mem. Council, Royal Soc., 1982–83. Gov., St Paul's Schs, 1970–. *Publications:* The Mathematical Works of J. H. C. Whitehead, 1963; The Topology of Stiefel Manifolds, 1976; Topological Topics, 1983; General Topology and Homotopy Theory, 1984; Aspects of Topology, 1984; sundry papers in mathematical jls. *Address:* Mathematical Institute, 24–29 St Giles, Oxford. *T:* Oxford 54295.

JAMES, John, CBE 1981; Founder and Chairman: John James Group of Companies Ltd, Bristol, 1961–79; Broadmead Group of Companies, 1946–60; Dawn Estates Ltd, since 1945; *b* 25 July 1906; *m* 1st (marr. diss.); one *s* two *d* (and one *d* decd); 2nd, Margaret Theodosia Parkes. *Educ:* Merchant Venturers, Bristol. Chm. Bd of Trustees: Dawn James Charitable Foundn, 1965–; John James (Bristol) Charitable Foundn, 1983–. Hon. LLD Bristol, 1983. *Recreations:* chess, swimming. *Address:* Tower Court, Ascot, Berks. *T:* Ascot 21094.

JAMES, John A.; *see* Angell-James.

JAMES, John Anthony, CMG 1973; FRACS; Visiting Neurosurgeon, Wellington Hospital Board, Wellington, NZ, 1965–77; retired 1978; *b* 2 April 1913; *s* of Herbert L. James and Gladys E. Paton; *m* 1941, Millicent Ward, Australia; three *s* one *d*. *Educ:* Melbourne Grammar Sch. (Church of England); Melbourne Univ. (MB, BS). Served War: Surgeon-Lieut, RANR, 1940–43. Neurosurgeon, Neurosurgical Unit, Dunedin Hosp., 1947–52; Dir, Neurosurgical Unit, Otago Univ.; Sen. Lectr in Neurosurgery, Otago Univ., 1951–64. *Publications:* contribs to surgical jls. *Address:* 136 Vipond Road, Whangaparaoa, New Zealand. *Club:* Wellington (Wellington, NZ).

JAMES, John Christopher Urmston; Secretary, Lawn Tennis Association, since 1981 (Assistant Secretary, 1973–81); *b* 22 June 1937; *s* of John Urmston James and Ellen Irene James; *m* 1st, 1959, Gillian Mary Davies (marr. diss. 1982); two *s*; 2nd, 1982, Patricia Mary, *d* of late Arthur Leslie Walter White. *Educ:* Hereford Cathedral Sch. Harrods, 1954; Jaeger, 1961; Pringle, 1972. *Recreations:* lawn tennis, Rugby football, walking, architecture, the countryside. *Address:* c/o Lawn Tennis Association, Barons Court, West Kensington, W14 9EG. *T:* 01–385 2366. *Clubs:* Queen's, London Welsh, International of GB; West Hants (Bournemouth).

JAMES, Prof. John Ivor Pulsford, MB, MS London; FRCS; FRCSE; George Harrison Law Professor of Orthopædic Surgery, Edinburgh University, 1958–79, now Emeritus Professor; Consultant in Orthopædic Surgery to the Navy, 1956–84; Head of Orthopaedic Services, Kuwait, 1980–84; *b* 19 Oct. 1913; *s* of late Stanley B. James and Jessica Heley; *m* 1968, Margaret Eiriol Samuel, MB, ChB; one *s* one *d*. *Educ:* Eggars Grammar Sch., Alton, Hants; University Coll. and Hosp., London, Hampshire County Schol., 1932–38; Ferrière Schol., University Coll., 1935; Goldsmid Schol., University Coll. Hosp., 1935; Magrath Schol., University Coll. Hosp., 1937; Rockefeller Fellowship, 1947–48; Consultant Orthopædic Surgeon, Royal National Orthopædic Hospital, 1946–58; Asst Dir of Studies, Institute of Orthopædics, University of London, 1948–58. Fellow Univ. Coll., London. Hunterian Prof., RCS, 1957; Past Pres., British Orthopædic Assoc. (Fellow); Past Pres., British Soc. for Surgery of the Hand; Mem. Société Internationale de Chirurgie Orthopédique et de Traumatologie; Corresp. Member: Amer. Orthopædic Assoc.; Austr. Orthopædic Assoc.; Scandinavian Orthopædic Assoc.; Hon. Member: Amer. Acad. of Orthopædic Surgeons; Dutch Orthopædic Assoc.; Assoc. for Orthopædic Surgery and Traumatology of Yugoslavia; Canadian Orthopædic Assoc.; New Zealand Orthopædic Assoc.; Hellenic Assoc. of Orthopædics and Traumatology; Société Française d'Orthopédie et de Traumatologie. Hon. FRACS. Late Temp. Lieut-Col RAMC. Golden Star, Order of Service to the Yugoslav People, 1970. *Publications:* Scoliosis, 1967, 2nd edn 1976; Poliomyelitis, 1986; articles relating to curvature of the spine and surgery of the hand in medical journals, etc. *Recreations:* sailing, beekeeping, gardening. *Address:* Abbey Farm, The Vatch, Slad, Glos GL6 7LE.

JAMES, John Jocelyn S.; *see* Streatfeild-James.

JAMES, John Nigel Courtenay, FRICS; Trustee of the Grosvenor Estate, since 1971; a Crown Estate Commissioner, since 1984; *b* 31 March 1935; *s* of Frank Courtenay James and Beryl May Wilford; *m* 1961, Elizabeth Jane St Clair-Ford; one *s* one *d*. *Educ:* Sherborne Sch., Dorset. Chief Agent and Estate Surveyor, Grosvenor Estate, 1968–71. Director: Sun Alliance & London Insurance Gp, 1972–; Woolwich Equitable Building Soc., 1982–; Williams & Glyn's Bank plc, 1983–85; Royal Bank of Scotland, 1985–. Member: Commn for the New Towns, 1978–86; Cttee of Management, RNLI, 1980–; Prince of Wales' Council, 1984–. Pres., RICS, 1980–81. *Recreation:* sailing. *Club:* Brooks's.

JAMES, John Wynford George, OBE 1950; FRAeS 1963; FCIT (MInstT 1954); Member of Board, BEA, 1964–74; Chairman: BEA Airtours, 1972–74; British Airways Helicopters, 1967–74; Gulf Helicopters Ltd, 1970–76; Deputy Chairman, International Aeradio Ltd, 1971–74 (Board Member, 1956); British Airways Group Air Safety Adviser, 1973–74; retired 1976; *b* 13 Feb. 1911; *s* of William George and Elizabeth James; *m* 1934, Bertha Mildred Joyce Everard; one *s* two *d*. *Educ:* Royal Grammar School, Worcester. Joined Imperial Airways as a pilot, 1933; Capt., Imperial Airways/BOAC, 1935–46; BEA Chief Pilot, 1946; Operations Dir, BEA, 1954–68. Chm. BALPA, 1943–48. Mem. Bd, International Helicopters Ltd, 1965. Governor, College of Air Training, 1959– (Chm. 1959–61, 1963–66, 1968–70). Liveryman, GAPAN, 1960. *Recreations:* golf, gardening, fishing, shooting. *Address:* Wynsfield, Mill Lane, Gerrards Cross, Bucks SL9 8AZ. *T:* Gerrards Cross 884038.

JAMES, Sir Kenneth; *see* James, Sir C. M.

JAMES, Lionel Frederic Edward, CBE 1977 (MBE (mil.) 1944); Comptroller, Forces Help Society and Lord Roberts Workshops, 1970–82; *b* 22 Feb. 1912; *s* of late Frederic James, Westmount, Exeter; *m* 1933, Harriet French-Harley; one *s* one *d*. *Educ:* Royal Grammar Sch., Worcester. Investment Co., 1933–39. Served War with Royal Engineers, 1939–46: BEF; Planning Staff, Sicilian Invasion; N Africa, Sicily, Greece and Italy (Major). Dep. Dir, Overseas Service, Forces Help Soc., 1946, Dir, 1948; Asst Sec. of Society, 1953, Company Sec., 1963. *Recreation:* restoration of antiques.

JAMES, Michael; *see* James, R. M.

JAMES, Michael; *see* Jayston, M.

JAMES, Michael Leonard; Chairman, The Hartland Press Ltd, since 1985; writer; Adviser on International Relations and Nuclear Energy, Commission of the European Communities, Brussels, since 1983; *b* 7 Feb. 1941; *s* of Leonard and Marjorie James, Portreath, Cornwall; *m* 1975, Jill Elizabeth, *d* of late George Tarján, OBE and Etelka Tarján, formerly of Budapest; two *d*. *Educ:* Latymer Upper Sch.; Christ's Coll., Cambridge (Holland Rose and Wren Prizes). Entered British govt service, 1963; Private Sec. to Rt Hon. Jennie Lee, MP, Minister for the Arts, 1966–68; Planning Unit of Rt Hon. Margaret Thatcher, MP, Sec. of State for Educn and Science, 1971–73; Consultant to OECD, 1973–75; UK Governor, IIMT, Milan, 1973–75; Asst Sec., Dept of Energy, 1975–78; Director, IAEA, Vienna, 1978–83. Governor: East Devon Coll. of Further Educn, Tiverton, 1985–; Axe Vale Further Educn Unit, Seaton, 1985–; Colyton Grammar Sch., 1985–. FRSA 1982. Hon. Fellow, Univ. of Exeter, 1985. South West Arts Literary Award, 1984. *Publications:* (jtly) Internationalization to Prevent the Spread of Nuclear Weapons, 1980; articles on internat. relations and nuclear energy; three novels under a pseudonym. *Address:* Cotte Barton, Branscombe, Devon. *Clubs:* Athenæum, United Oxford & Cambridge University, International PEN; Honiton Working Men's (Devon).

JAMES, Dame Naomi (Christine), DBE 1979; author and yachtswoman; *b* 2 March 1949; *d* of Charles Robert Power and Joan Power; *m* 1976, Robert Alan James (*d* 1983); one *d*. *Educ:* Rotorua Girls' High Sch., NZ. Hair stylist, 1966–71; language teacher, 1972–74; yacht charter crew, 1975–77. Sailed single handed round the world via the three great Capes, incl. first woman solo round Cape Horn, on 53 ft yacht, Express Crusader, Sept. 1977–June 1978; sailed in 1980 Observer Transatlantic Race, winning Ladies Prize and achieving women's record for single-handed Atlantic crossing, on 53 ft yacht Kriter Lady; won 1982 Round Britain Race with Rob James, on multihull Colt Cars GB. Trustee, Nat. Maritime Museum, 1986–. Royal Yacht Sqdn Chichester Trophy, 1978; NZ Yachtsman of the Year, 1978. *Publications:* Woman Alone, 1978; At One with the Sea, 1979; At Sea on Land, 1981. *Recreations:* tennis, riding, skiing, antiques. *Address:* Woodland Cottages, South Woodchester, Stroud, Glos. *Clubs:* Royal Dart Yacht (Dartmouth); Royal Lymington Yacht (Lymington); Royal Western Yacht (Plymouth).

JAMES, Noel David Glaves, OBE 1964; MC 1945; TD 1946; *b* 16 Sept. 1911; *o s* of late Rev. D. T. R. James, and Gertrude James; *m* 1949, Laura Cecilia (*d* 1970), *yr d* of late Sir Richard Winn Livingstone; two *s* (and one *s* decd). *Educ:* Haileybury Coll.; Royal Agricultural Coll., Cirencester (Gold Medal and Estate Management Prize). In general practice as a land agent, 1933–39. Served War, 1939–46 (MC, despatches); 68 Field Regt RA (TA), France, Middle East, Italy. Bursar, Corpus Christi Coll., Oxford, 1946–51; MA (Oxon.) 1946. Fellow, Corpus Christi Coll., Oxford, 1950–51; Land Agent for Oxford Univ., 1951–61; Estates Bursar and Agent for Brasenose Coll., 1959–61; Fellow, Brasenose Coll., Oxford, 1951–61; Agent for Clinton Devon Estates, 1961–76. President: Land Agents Soc., 1957–58; Royal Forestry Soc. of England and Wales and N Ireland, 1962–64; Member: Central Forestry Examination Bd of UK, 1951–75; Regional Advisory Cttee, Eastern Conservancy, Forestry Commn, 1951–61; Regional Advisory Cttee, SW Conservancy, Forestry Commission, 1962–75; Departmental Cttee on Hedgerow and Farm Timber, 1953; UK Forestry Cttee, 1954–59; Governor Wye Coll., Kent, 1955–61; Governor Westonbirt Sch., 1959–68. FLAS; FRICS (Diploma in Forestry and Watney Gold Medal). Gold Medal for Distinguished Service to Forestry, 1967; Royal Agricultural Coll. Bledisloe Medal for services to agriculture and forestry, 1970. *Publications:* Artillery Observation Posts, 1941; Working Plans for Estate Woodlands, 1948; Notes on Estate Forestry, 1949; An Experiment in Forestry, 1951; The Forester's Companion, 1955 (3rd edn, 1982); The Trees of Bicton, 1969; The Arboriculturalist's Companion, 1972; A Book of Trees (anthology), 1973; Before the Echoes Die Away, 1980; A History of English Forestry, 1981; A Forestry Centenary, 1982; Gunners at Larkhill, 1983. *Recreations:* forestry, shooting. *Address:* Blakemore House, Kersbrook, Budleigh Salterton, Devon. *T:* Budleigh Salterton 3886. *Club:* Army and Navy.

JAMES, Patrick Leonard, FRCS, FDS RCS; Senior Consultant Oral and Maxillo-facial Surgeon, London Hospital, Whitechapel, since 1965; Consultant Oral and Maxillo-facial Surgeon, North East Thames Regional Hospital Board Hospitals, since 1963; Recognized Teacher in Oral Surgery, London University, since 1965; Civilian Consultant in Oral Surgery to RAF, since 1979; *b* 7 Jan. 1926; *s* of late John Vincent James and Priscilla Elsie (*née* Hill), Cuffley, Herts; *m* 1951, Jean Margaret, *er d* of Leslie and Ruth Hatcher, Woking, Surrey; one *s* two *d*. *Educ:* Hertford and Cheshunt Grammar Schs; King's Coll., London; Royal Dental Hosp.; London Hosp. FDSRCS 1958 (LDSRCS 1948); FRCS 1985 (MRCS 1956); LRCP 1956. Served RAF, Flt Lieut, ME Comd, 1949–51. Resident Ho. Surg., Ho. Phys., Cas. Officer, King George Hosp., 1956–57; Sen. Registrar, Queen Victoria Hosp., E Grinstead, 1959–63; Consultant Oral and Maxillo-facial Surgeon: to London Hosp., Honey Lane Hosp., Waltham Abbey, Herts and Essex Hosp., Bishop's Stortford, 1963–; to King George Hosp., 1967–; St Margaret's Hosp., Epping, 1966–; Black Notley Hosp., 1969–. Exchange Fellow, Henry Ford Hosp., Detroit, Mich., 1962; Hunterian Prof., RCS, 1970–71. Member: Academic Bd, London Hosp. Med. Coll., 1968–71; Adv. Cttee in Plastic Surgery, NE Met. Reg. Hosp. Bd, 1969–77; NE Thames Reg. Manpower Cttee, 1975–; Chairman: NE Met. BDA Hosps Gp, 1970–71; NE Thames Reg. Adv. Cttee in hosp. dental surgery, 1982–. Fellow: BAOS, 1963– (Mem. Council, 1971–74); Internat. Assoc. of Oral Surgs (BAOS Rep. on Council, 1974–78); Chm., Sci. Session, 6th Internat. Congress of Oral Surgs, Sydney, 1977; Associate Mem., Brit. Assoc. of Plastic Surgs, 1958–77. FRSM; Member: Council, Chelsea Clin. Soc; Bd of Governors, Eastman Hosp., 1983–84. Mem. of Lloyd's, 1984. Liveryman, Soc. of Apothecaries, 1969; Freeman, City of London, 1978. *Publications:* (chapter in Oral Surgery) Malignancies in Odontogenic Cysts, 1967; (chapter in Oral Surgery) Correction of Apertognathia with Osteotomies and Bone Graft, 1970; (chapter in Oral Surgery, vol. 7) Surgical Treatment of Mandibular Joint Disorders, 1978; numerous articles on surgical treatment of mandibular joint disorders, surgery of salivary glands and maxillo facial surgery in med. and surg. jls. *Recreations:* shooting, fishing, sailing (Cdre, United Hosps Sailing Club, 1968–75), skiing. *Address:* Meesden Hall, Meesden, Buntingford, Herts SG9 0AZ; 19 Harcourt House, 19 Cavendish Square, W1. *T:* 01–580 5123. *Club:* Naval and Military.

JAMES, Prof. Peter Maunde Coram, VRD 1964; John Humphreys Professor of Dental Health, 1966–Sept. 1987, and Postgraduate Advisor in Dentistry, 1983–86, University of Birmingham (Director, Dental School, 1978–82); *b* 2 April 1922; *s* of Vincent Coram James, MRCS, LRCP, and Mildred Ivy (*née* Gooch); *m* 1945, Denise Mary Bond, LDS; four *s*. *Educ:* Westminster Sch.; Royal Dental Hosp., Univ. of London (MDS); Univ. of St Andrews (DPD). LDSRCS. House Surgeon, then Sen. House Surg., Royal Dental Hosp., 1945; Surg. Lieut (D) RNVR, 1945–48; Registrar, Res. Asst and Hon. Lectr, Inst. of Dental Surgery (Eastman Dental Hosp.), 1949–55; Gibbs Travelling Scholar, 1952; Royal Dental Hosp. Sch. of Dental Surgery, Univ. of London: Sen. Lectr, 1955–65; Asst Dean, 1958–66; Dir, Dept of Children's Dentistry, 1962–66; Hon. Cons. Dental Surg., 1961–; Reader in Preventive Dentistry, Univ. of London, 1965; Head, Dept of Dental Health, Univ. of Birmingham, 1966–87. Consultant, Internat. Dental Fedn Commn on Dental Res., 1976–; Cons. Advisor in Community Dentistry to DHSS, 1977–83; Reg. Advisor (W Midlands), Faculty of Dental Surgery, RCS, 1976–83. President: Brit. Paedodontic Soc., 1962; Central Counties Br., BDA, 1981–82; Founding Pres., Brit. Assoc. for Study of Community Dentistry, 1973. Chm., Specialist Adv. Cttee in Community Dental Health, 1981–; Vice-Chm., BDA Central Cttee for Univ. Teachers and Res. Workers, 1984–; Member: Dental Working Party, Cttee on Child Health Services, 1974–77; Standing Panel of Experts in Dentistry, Univ. of London, 1976–; Birmingham AHA (Teaching), 1979–82, Birmingham Central DHA, 1982–; Jt Cttee for Higher Training in Dentistry, 1981–. Ext. Assessor, Univ. of Malaya, 1977–; ext. examr in dental subjects, univs and colls, 1955–. Editor, Community Dental Health, 1983–. *Publications:* contrib. to dental and scientific jls. *Recreations:* music, photography, camping. *Address:* The Pump House, Bishopton Spa, Stratford-upon-Avon, Warwicks. *T:* Stratford-upon-Avon 204330. *Club:* Royal Society of Medicine.

JAMES, Philip; *see* James, W. P. T.

JAMES, Prof. Philip Seaforth; Professor of English Law and Head of the Department of Law, University College at Buckingham, 1975–81; *b* 28 May 1914; *s* of Dr Philip William James, MC, and Muriel Lindley James; *m* 1954. Wybetty, *d* of Claas P. Gerth, Enschede, Holland; two *s*. *Educ:* Charterhouse; Trinity Coll., Oxford (MA), Research Fellow, Yale Univ., USA, 1937–38; Hon. LLD 1986. Called to the Bar, Inner Temple, 1939. Served War of 1939–45, in Royal Artillery, India, Burma (despatches). Fellow of Exeter Coll., Oxford, 1946–49; Prof. and Hd of Dept of Law, Leeds Univ., 1952–75. Visiting Professor: Univs of Yale and of Louisville, Kentucky, USA, 1960–61; Univ. of South Carolina, 1972–73; NY Law Sch., 1981–83. Chairman: Yorks Rent Assessment Panel, 1966–75; Thames Valley Rent Assessment Panel, 1976–; Assessor to County Court under Race Relations Acts. Pres., Soc. of Public Teachers of Law, 1971–72. Governor, Swinton Conservative College, 1970–. Hon. Mem., Mark Twain Soc., 1979. *Publications:* An Introduction to English Law, 1950 (trans. Japanese, 1985); General Principles of the Law of Torts, 1959; Shorter Introduction to English Law, 1969; Six Lectures on the Law of Torts, 1980 (trans. Spanish); various articles, notes and reviews on legal and biographical subjects. *Recreations:* golf and gardening. *Address:* Chestnut View, Mill Road, Whitfield, near Brackley, Northants NN13 5TQ. *Club:* National Liberal.

JAMES, Phyllis Dorothy, (Mrs C. B. White), OBE 1983; JP; author (as P. D. James); *b* 3 Aug. 1920; *d* of Sidney Victor James and Dorothy Amelia James (*née* Hone); *m* 1941, Connor Bantry White (decd); two *d*. *Educ:* Cambridge Girls' High Sch. Administrator, National Health Service, 1949–68; Civil Service: apptd Principal, Home Office, 1968; Police Dept, 1968–72; Criminal Policy Dept, 1972–79. Associate Fellow, Downing Coll., Cambridge, 1986. Chm., Soc. of Authors, 1984–86; Member: Crime Writers' Assoc.; Detection Club. JP: Willesden, 1979–82; Inner London, 1984. *Publications:* Cover Her Face, 1962 (televised 1985); A Mind to Murder, 1963; Unnatural Causes, 1967; Shroud for a Nightingale, 1971 (televised 1984); (with T. A. Critchley) The Maul and the Pear Tree, 1971; An Unsuitable Job for a Woman, 1972 (filmed 1982); The Black Tower, 1975 (televised 1986); Death of an Expert Witness, 1977 (televised 1983); Innocent Blood, 1980; The Skull beneath the Skin, 1982; A Taste for Death, 1986. *Recreations:* exploring churches, walking by the sea. *Address:* c/o Elaine Greene Ltd, 31 Newington Green, N16 9PU.

JAMES, Richard Austin, CB 1980; MC 1945; Receiver for Metropolitan Police District, 1977–80; *b* 26 May 1920; *s* of late Thomas Morris James, Headmaster of Sutton Valence Sch., and Hilda Joan James; *m* 1948, Joan Boorer; two *s* one *d*. *Educ:* Clifton Coll.; Emmanuel Coll., Cambridge. British American Tobacco Co., 1938; Royal Engrs, 1939–41; Queen's Own Royal W Kent Regt, 1941–46; Home Office, 1948; Private Sec. to Chancellor of Duchy of Lancaster, 1960; Asst Sec., 1961; Dep. Receiver for Metropolitan Police District, 1970–73; Asst Under-Sec. of State, Police Dept, Home Office, 1974–76; Dep. Under-Sec. of State, 1980. Member: Council of Management, Distressed Gentlefolk's Aid Assoc., 1982– (Gen. Sec., 1981–82); Cttee of Management, Sussex Housing Assoc. for the Aged, 1985–. Freeman, City of London, 1980. *Recreation:* cricket. *Address:* Cedarwood, Redbrook Lane, Buxted, Sussex. *T:* Buxted 2364. *Clubs:* Athenæum, MCC.

JAMES, (Robert) Michael; HM Diplomatic Service; Deputy High Commissioner, Singapore, since 1984; *b* 2 Oct. 1934; *s* of late Rev. B. V. James and Mrs D. M. James; *m* 1959, Sarah Helen (*née* Bell); two *s* one *d*. *Educ:* St John's, Leatherhead; Trinity Coll., Cambridge (BA Hons History). Schoolmaster: Harrow Sch., 1958–60; Cranleigh Sch., 1960–62; joined CRO, 1962; 3rd Sec., Wellington, NZ, 1963–65; 1st Sec., Colombo, Sri Lanka, 1966–69; FCO, 1969–71; Dep. High Comr and Head of Chancery, Georgetown, Guyana, 1971–73; Econ. Sec., Ankara, Turkey, 1974–76; FCO, 1976–80; Commercial Counsellor and Dep. High Comr, Accra, 1980–83. *Recreations:* sport (cricket Blue, 1956–58), drawing, travel. *Address:* c/o Foreign and Commonwealth Office, King Charles Street, SW1. *T:* 01–233 3000; No 1, 17 North Grove, Highgate, N6 4SH. *T:* 01–348 8689. *Club:* MCC.

JAMES, Robert Vidal R.; *see* Rhodes James.

JAMES, Prof. Dame Sheila (Patricia Violet); *see* Sherlock, Prof. Dame S. P. V.

JAMES, Stanley Francis; Head of Statistics Division 1, Department of Trade and Industry, 1981–84; *b* 12 Feb. 1927; *s* of H. F. James; unmarried. *Educ:* Sutton County Sch.; Trinity Coll., Cambridge. Maths Tripos Pt II; Dip. Math. Statistics. Research Lectr, Econs Dept, Nottingham Univ., 1951; Statistician, Bd of Inland Revenue, 1956; Chief Statistician: Bd of Inland Revenue, 1966; Central Statistical Office, 1968; Asst Dir, Central Statistical

Office, 1970–72; Dir, Stats Div., Bd of Inland Revenue, 1972–77; Head, Econs and Stats Div. 6, Depts of Industry and Trade, 1977–81. Hon. Treasurer, Royal Statistical Soc., 1978–83. *Recreations:* travel, theatre, gardening. *Address:* 23 Hayward Road, Oxford. *Club:* Royal Automobile.

JAMES, Steven Wynne Lloyd; Circuit Administrator, Wales and Chester Circuit, Lord Chancellor's Department, since 1982; *b* 9 June 1934; *s* of late Trevor Lloyd James and of Olwen Ellis; *m* 1962, Carolyn Ann Rowlands, *d* of late James Morgan Rowlands and of Mercia Rowlands; three *s. Educ:* Queen Elizabeth Grammar Sch., Carmarthen; LSE. LLB 1956. Admitted solicitor, 1959. Asst Solicitor in private practice, 1959–61; Legal Asst, HM Land Registry, 1961; Asst Solicitor, Glamorgan CC, 1962–70; Asst Clerk of the Peace, 1970–71; Lord Chancellor's Dept, 1971–: Sen. Principal Courts Administrator, Chester/Mold gp of courts, Wales and Chester Circuit, 1971–76; Asst Sec., 1976; Dep. Circuit Administrator, Wales and Chester Circuit, 1976–82; Under Sec., 1982. *Recreations:* walking, gardening, reading. *Address:* Wales and Chester Circuit Office, 3rd Floor, Churchill House, Churchill Way, Cardiff. *T:* Cardiff 396925. *Club:* Civil Service.

JAMES, (Thomas) Cecil (Garside), CMG 1966; Assistant Under-Secretary of State, Ministry of Defence, 1968–77; *b* 8 Jan. 1918; *s* of Joshua James, MBE, Ashton-under-Lyne; *m* 1941, Elsie Williams, Ashton-under-Lyne; one *s* two *d. Educ:* Manchester Grammar Sch.; St John's Coll., Cambridge. Prin. Priv. Sec. to Sec. of State for Air, 1951–55; Asst Sec., Air Min., 1955; Civil Sec., FEAF, 1963–66; Chief of Public Relations, MoD, 1966–68. *Recreation:* golf. *Address:* 9 Knoll House, Uxbridge Road, Pinner, Middx HA5 3LR. *T:* 01-868 3602.

JAMES, Thomas Garnet Henry, CBE 1984; FBA 1976; Keeper of Egyptian Antiquities, British Museum, since 1974; *b* 8 May 1923; *s* of late Thomas Garnet James and Edith (*née* Griffiths); *m* 1956, Diana Margaret, *y d* of H. L. Vavasseur-Durell; one *s. Educ:* Neath Grammar Sch.; Exeter Coll., Oxford. 2nd Cl. Lit. Hum. 1947; 1st Cl. Oriental Studies 1950, MA 1948. Served War of 1939–45, RA; NW Europe; 2nd Lieut 1943; Captain 1945. Asst Keeper, Dept of Egyptian and Assyrian Antiquities, 1951; Dep. Keeper (Egyptian Antiquities), 1974. Laycock Student of Egyptology, Worcester Coll., Oxford, 1954–60; Wilbour Fellow, Brooklyn Museum, 1964; Vis. Prof., Collège de France, 1983. Editor, Jl of Egyptian Archæology, 1960–70; Editor, Egyptological pubns of Egypt Exploration Soc., 1960–. Chm., Egypt Exploration Soc., 1983–; Mem., German Archæological Inst., 1974. *Publications:* The Mastaba of Khentika called Ikhekhi, 1953; Hieroglyphic Texts in the British Museum I, 1961; The Hekanakhte Papers and other Early Middle Kingdom Documents, 1962; (with R. A. Caminos) Gebel es-Silsilah I, 1963; Egyptian Sculptures, 1966; Myths and Legends of Ancient Egypt, 1969; Hieroglyphic Texts in the British Museum, 9, 1970; Archæology of Ancient Egypt, 1972; Corpus of Hieroglyphic Inscriptions in the Brooklyn Museum, I, 1974; (ed) An Introduction to Ancient Egypt, 1979; (ed) Excavating in Egypt, 1982; (with W. V. Davies) Egyptian Sculpture, 1983; Pharaoh's People, 1984; Egyptian Painting, 1985; (contrib.) W. B. Emery: Great Tombs of the First Dynasty II, 1954; (contrib.) T. J. Dunbabin: Perachora II, 1962; (contrib.) Cambridge Ancient History, 3rd edn, 1973; (contrib.) Encyclop. Britannica, 15th edn, 1974; (ed English trans.) H. Kees: Ancient Egypt, 1961; articles in Jl Egyptian Arch., etc; reviews in learned jls. *Recreations:* music, cooking. *Address:* 14 Turner Close, NW11 6TU. *T:* 01-455 9221.

JAMES, Thomas Geraint Illtyd, FRCS; Hon. Surgeon, Central Middlesex Hospital; Late Teacher of Surgery, Middlesex Hospital, and Hon. Surgical Tutor, Royal College of Surgeons of England; *b* 12 July 1900; *s* of late Evan Thomas and Elizabeth James, Barry; *m* 1932, Dorothy Marguerite, *o d* of late David John, Cardiff; two *s. Educ:* Barry, Glam; University Coll., Cardiff; Welsh National Sch. of Medicine; St Mary's Hosp., London; Guy's Hosp., London. BSc Wales, 1921, Alfred Sheen Prize in Anat. and Physiol.; MRCS, LRCP, 1924; MB, ChB, 1925, Maclean Medal and Prize in Obst. and Gynæcol.; FRCSE, 1927; FRCS, 1928; MCh Wales, 1932; FRSocMed; Fellow Association of Surgeons of Great Britain and Ireland; Erasmus Wilson Lectr, RCS, 1972. Mem., Internat. Soc. for Surgery; Corr. Mem. Spanish-Portuguese Soc. of Neurosurgery. Mem. Soc. of Apothecaries; Freeman of City of London. Formerly: Assoc. Examr University of London; Mem. and Chm., Court of Examiners RCS of England; Examr in Surgery, University of Liverpool; Ho. phys., Ho. surg. and Resident Surgical Officer, Cardiff Royal Infirmary; Clinical Asst St Mark's, St Peter's and Guy's Hosps, London; Asst to Neurosurg. Dept, London Hosp.; Mem., Management Cttee, Leavesden Gp of Hosps. *Publications:* in various jls on surg. and neurosurg. subjects. *Recreations:* literature, travelling. *Address:* 1 Freeland Road, W5. *T:* 01-992 2430.

JAMES, Prof. Vivian Hector Thomas; Professor and Head of Department of Chemical Pathology, St Mary's Hospital Medical School, London University, since 1973; Hon. Chemical Pathologist, Paddington and North Kensington Health Authority, since 1973; *b* 29 Dec. 1924; *s* of William and Alice James; *m* 1958, Betty Irene Pike. *Educ:* Latymer Sch.; London Univ. BSc, PhD, DSc; FRCPath 1977. Flying duties, RAF, 1942–46. Scientific Staff, Nat. Inst. for Med. Res., 1952–56; St Mary's Hospital Medical School, London: Lectr, Dept of Chemical Pathol., 1956; Reader, 1962; Prof. of Chem. Endocrinol., 1967; Chm., Div. of Pathology, St Mary's Hosp., 1981–. Mem., Herts AHA, 1974–77. Secretary: Clin. Endocrinol. Cttee, MRC, 1967–72; Cttee for Human Pituitary Collection, MRC, 1972–76 (Chm., 1976–82); Endocrine Sect., RSocMed, 1972–76 (Pres., 1976–78); Gen. Sec., Soc. for Endocrinology, 1979–85 (Treas., 1986–). Editor, Clinical Endocrinology, 1972–74. Freeman, Haverfordwest, 1946. Fiorino d'oro, City of Florence, 1977. *Publications:* (ed jtly) Current Topics in Experimental Endocrinology, 1971, 5th edn 1983; (ed) The Adrenal Gland, 1979; (ed jtly) Hormones in Blood, 1961, 3rd edn 1983; contribs to various endocrine and other jls. *Address:* Department of Chemical Pathology, St Mary's Hospital Medical School, W2 1PG. *T:* 01-723 1252. *Club:* Royal Society of Medicine.

JAMES, Walter; *see* James, Arthur Walter.

JAMES, Prof. Walter, CBE 1977; Professor of Educational Studies, Open University, 1969–84; *b* 8 Dec. 1924; *s* of late George Herbert James and Mary Kathleen (*née* Crutch); *m* 1948, Joyce Dorothy Woollaston; two *s. Educ:* Royal Grammar Sch., Worcester; St Luke's Coll., Exeter; Univ. of Nottingham. BA 1955. School teacher, 1948–52; Univ. of Nottingham: Resident Tutor, Dept of Extra-Mural Studies, 1958–65; Lectr in Adult Educn, Dept of Adult Educn, 1965–69; Dean and Dir of Studies, Faculty of Educnl Studies, Open Univ., 1969–77. Consultant on Adult Educn and Community Develt to Govt of Seychelles and ODA of FCO, 1973; Adviser: to Office of Educn, WCC, 1974–76; on Social Planning, to State of Bahrain, 1975; Council of Europe: UK Rep., Working Party on Develt of Adult Education, 1973–81; UK Rep., Chm. of Project Gp and Project Adviser, Adult Educn for Community Develt, 1982–; Chairman: Nat. Council for Voluntary Youth Services, 1970–76; Review of Training of part-time Youth and Community Workers, 1975–77; Religious Adv. Bd, Scout Assoc., 1977–82; Inservice Training and Educn Panel for Youth and Community Service, 1978–82; Council for Educn and Trng in Youth and Community Work, 1982–85; Nat. Adv. Council for the Youth Service, 1985–. Member: DES Cttee on Youth and Community Work in 70s, 1967–69; ILO Working Party on Use of Radio and TV for Workers' Educn, 1968; Gen. Synod, C of E, 1970–75; Exec. Cttee, Nat. Council of Social Service, 1970–75; Univs' Council for Educn of Teachers, 1970–84; Univs Council for Adult Educn, 1971–76; BBC Further Educn Adv. Council, 1971–75; Exec. Cttee and Council, Nat. Inst. of Adult Educn, 1971–77; Library Adv. Council for England, 1974–76; Adv. Council, HM Queen's Silver Jubilee Appeal, 1976–78; Trustee: Young Volunteer Force Foundn, 1972–77; Community Projects Foundn, 1977–; Trident Educnl Trust, 1972–; President: Inst. of Playleadership, 1972–74; Fair Play for Children, 1979–82. *Publications:* (with F. J. Bayliss) The Standard of Living, 1964; (ed) Virginia Woolf, Selections from her essays, 1966; (contrib.) Encyclopaedia of Education, 1968; (contrib.) Teaching Techniques in Adult Education, 1971; (contrib.) Mass Media and Adult Education, 1971; (with H. Janne and P. Dominice) The Development of Adult Education, 1980; numerous TV programmes, articles and reviews on youth, adult and higher educn. *Recreation:* living. *Address:* 40 Brecon Way, Bedford MK41 8DD. *T:* Bedford 54819.

JAMES, William Henry E.; *see* Ewart James.

JAMES, Prof. (William) Philip (Trehearne), MD, DSc, FRCP, FRCPEd, FRSE; Director, Rowett Research Institute, Aberdeen, since 1982; Research Professor, Aberdeen University, since 1983; *b* 27 June 1938; *s* of Jenkin William James and Lilian Mary James; *m* 1961, Jean Hamilton (*née* Moorhouse); one *s* one *d. Educ:* Ackworth Sch., Pontefract, Yorks; University Coll. London (BSc Hons 1959; DSc 1983); University Coll. Hosp. (MB, BS 1962; MD 1968). FRCP 1978; FRCPEd 1983; FRSE 1986. Sen. House Physician, Whittington Hosp., London, 1963–65; Clin. Res. Scientist, MRC Tropical Metabolism Res. Unit, Kingston, Jamaica, 1965–68; Harvard Res. Fellow, Mass Gen. Hosp., 1968–69; Wellcome Trust Res. Fellow, MRC Gastroenterology Unit, London, 1969–70; Sen. Lectr, Dept of Human Nutrition, London Sch. of Hygiene and Trop. Medicine, and Hon. Consultant Physician, UCH, 1970–74; Asst Dir, MRC Dunn Nutrition Unit, and Hon. Consultant Physician, Addenbrooke's Hosp., Cambridge, 1974–82. Hon. MA Cantab, 1977. *Publications:* The Analysis of Dietary Fibre in Food, 1981; The Body Weight Regulatory System: normal and disturbed mechanisms, 1981; documents on European national nutrition policy and energy needs for DHSS, FAO and WHO; scientific pubns in Lancet, Nature, Clin. Science. *Recreations:* talking, writing government reports, living in France. *Address:* Wardenhill, Bucksburn, Aberdeen AB2 9SA. *T:* Aberdeen 712623. *Clubs:* Athenæum, Penn.

JAMESON, Derek; news, TV and radio commentator; Presenter, Radio 2 Jameson Show, since 1986; *b* 29 Nov. 1929; *e s* of Mrs Elsie Jameson; *m* 1st, 1948, Jacqueline Sinclair (marr. diss. 1966); one *s* one *d*; 2nd, 1971, Pauline Tomlin (marr. diss. 1978); two *s. Educ:* elementary schools, Hackney. Office boy rising to Chief Sub-editor, Reuters, 1944–60; Editor, London American, 1960–61; features staff, Daily Express, 1961–63; Picture Editor, Sunday Mirror, 1963–65; Asst Editor, Sunday Mirror, 1965–72; Northern Editor, Sunday and Daily Mirror, 1972–76; Managing Editor, Daily Mirror, 1976–77; Editor, Daily Express, 1977–79; Editor-in-Chief, The Daily Star, 1978–80; Editor, News of the World, 1981–84. *Recreations:* opera, music, reading. *Address:* 134 Elgin Avenue, W9 2NS. *T:* 01-286 5861. *Clubs:* Press, Macreadys.

JAMESON, Air Cdre Patrick Geraint, CB 1959; DSO 1943; DFC 1940 (and Bar 1942), psa; Royal Air Force, retired, 1960; *b* Wellington, NZ, 10 Nov. 1912; *s* of Robert Delvin Jameson, Balbriggan, Ireland, and Katherine Lenora Jameson (*née* Dick), Dunedin, NZ; *m* 1941, Hilda Nellie Haiselden Webster, *d* of B. F. Webster, Lower Hutt, NZ; one *s* one *d. Educ:* Hutt Valley High Sch., New Zealand. Commissioned in RAF, 1936. War of 1939–45 (despatches 5 times, DFC and Bar, DSO): 46 Squadron, 1936–40, 266 Sqaudron, 1940–41; Wing Commander Flying, Wittering, 1941–42; Wing Commander (Flying), North Weald, 1942–43; Group Capt. Plans, HQ No 11 Group, 1943–44; 122 Wing in France, Belgium, Holland, Germany and Denmark, 1944–46; Staff Coll., Haifa, 1946; Air Ministry, 1946–48; CFE, West Raynham, 1949–52; Wunsdorf (2nd TAF), 1952–54; SASO, HQ No II Group, 1954–56; SASO HQ RAF Germany (2nd TAF) 1956–59. Norwegian War Cross, 1943; Netherlands Order of Orange Nassau, 1945; American Silver Star, 1945. *Recreations:* fishing, shooting, sailing, golf. *Address:* 70 Wai-Iti Crescent, Lower Hutt, New Zealand. *Clubs:* Royal Air Force; Hutt Golf; Hutt.

JAMIESON, Major David Auldjo, VC 1944; Member of HM Body Guard, Hon. Corps of Gentlemen at Arms, since 1968, Clerk of the Cheque and Adjutant, since 1981; *b* 1 Oct. 1920; *s* of late Sir Archibald Auldjo Jamieson, KBE, MC; *m* 1st, 1948, Nancy Elwes (*d* 1963), *y d* of Robert H. A. Elwes, Congham, King's Lynn; one *s* two *d*; 2nd, 1969, Joanna, *e d* of Edward Woodall. *Educ:* Eton Coll. Commissioned Royal Norfolk Regt May 1939; served War of 1939–45, incl. Normandy, 1944 (VC); retired, 1948. Director: Australian Agricultural Co., 1949–78 (Governor, 1952–76); UK Branch, Australian Mutual Provident Society, 1963– (Dep. Chm., 1973–); National Westminster Bank PLC, 1983–; Steetley plc, 1976–86 (Dep. Chm., 1983–86). High Sheriff of Norfolk, 1980. *Recreations:* shooting, golf. *Address:* The Drove House, Thornham, Hunstanton, Norfolk. *T:* Thornham 206.

JAMIESON, Air Marshal Sir (David) Ewan, KBE 1986 (OBE 1967); CB 1981; Chief of Defence Staff, New Zealand, since 1983; *b* Christchurch, 19 April 1930; *s* of R. D. Jamieson; *m* 1957, Margaret Elaine, *d* of L. J. Bridge; three *s* one *d. Educ:* Christchurch and New Plymouth Boys' High Sch. Joined RNZAF, 1949; OC Flying, Ohakea, 1964; CO Malaysia, 1965–66; Jt Services Staff Coll., 1969; CO Auckland, 1971–72; AOC Ops Group, 1974–76; RCDS 1977; Chief of Air Staff, RNZAF, 1979–83. *Address:* c/o Ministry of Defence, Wellington, New Zealand.

JAMIESON, Hon. Donald Campbell, PC (Can.) 1968; Canadian High Commissioner to the United Kingdom, 1983–85; *b* St John's, Newfoundland, 30 April 1921; *s* of Charles Jamieson and Isabelle Bennett; *m* 1946, Barbara Elizabeth Oakley; one *s* three *d. Educ:* Prince of Wales Coll.; St John's, Newfoundland. Served War with Canadian Naval Special Services and United Service Org. Camp Shows. Regular broadcasts, 1941–46; news broadcasting nightly, 1946; Attaché, Parly Press Gallery, Ottawa, 1948; former Pres., Newfoundland Broadcasting Co. Ltd; also Dir of Broadcast News; Past Chm., Affiliates Sect. Network Advt Cttee, CBC. Pres., Canadian Assoc. of Broadcasters, 1961–65. With Dept of Rural Reconstruction; then Crosbie & Co. Ltd, fishery; Sales Manager, Coca Cola, Newfoundland. MP (Liberal) Burin-Burgeo, St John's, Newfoundland, 1966–79; Minister: of Supply and Services, 1968–69; of Transport, 1969–72; of Regional Economic Expansion, 1972–75; of Industry, Trade and Commerce, Sept. 1975–76; Sec. of State for External Affairs, Canada, 1976–79; MHA (L) Bellevue, Newfoundland, 1979–81; Leader of the Opposition, 1979–80. Past Chm., financial campaign of Canadian Cancer Soc.; Past Director: Canadian Centennial Council; Nat. Theatre School. Hon. LLD: Memorial, 1970; Acadia; St Francis Xavier. *Publication:* The Troubled Air, 1966. *Recreations:* fishing, hunting, boating. *Address:* Over Kilmory, Swift Current, Newfoundland, Canada.

JAMIESON, Air Marshal Sir Ewan; *see* Jamieson, Air Marshal Sir D. E.

JAMIESON, Rt. Rev. Hamish Thomas Umphelby; *see* Bunbury, Bishop of.

JAMIESON, Lt-Col Harvey Morro H.; *see* Harvey-Jamieson.

JAMIESON, Rear-Adm. Ian Wyndham, CB 1970; DSC 1945; Emeritus Fellow, Jesus College, Oxford, 1986 (Home Bursar and Fellow, 1972–86); *b* 13 March 1920; *s* of late S. W. Jamieson, CBE; *m* 1949, Patricia Wheeler, Knowle, Warwickshire; two *s* one *d. Educ:* RNC, Dartmouth. Served War of 1939–45: Anti Submarine Warfare Specialist, 1943. Comdr, 1953; Staff of RN Tactical Sch., 1953–56; HMS Maidstone, 1956–58; Dir, Jt Tactical Sch., Malta, 1958; Capt. 1959; Asst Dir, Naval Intelligence, 1959–61; Comd HMS Nubian and 6th Frigate Sqdn, 1961–64; Dir, Seaman Officers Appts, 1964–66; Comd Britannia RN Coll., Dartmouth, 1966–68; Rear-Adm. 1968; Flag Officer, Gibraltar, and Admiral Superintendent, HM Dockyard, Gibraltar; also NATO Comdr, Gibraltar (Mediterranean Area), 1968–69; C of S to C-in-C Western Fleet, 1969–71; retired. Mem., Southern Arts Council, 1985–. Hon. MA Oxon, 1973. *Recreations:* hockey (Scotland and Combined Services), cricket, golf, tennis. *Address:* Buckels, East Hagbourne, near Didcot, Oxfordshire. *Clubs:* Army and Navy, MCC.

JAMIESON, John Kenneth; Chairman of Board and Chief Executive Officer, Exxon Corporation (formerly Standard Oil Co. (NJ)), 1969–75; *b* Canada, 28 Aug. 1910; *s* of John Locke and Kate Herron Jamieson; US citizen; *m* 1937, Ethel May Burns; one *s* one *d. Educ:* Univ. of Alberta; Massachusetts Inst. of Technology (BS). Northwest Stellarene Co. of Alberta, 1932; British American Oil Co., 1934; Manager, Moose Jaw Refinery; served War of 1939–45 in Oil Controller's Dept of Canadian Govt; subseq. Manager, Manufrg Dept, British American Oil Co.; joined Imperial Oil Co., 1948: Head of Engrg and Develt Div., Sarnia Refinery, 1949; Asst Gen. Man. of Manufrg Dept, 1950; on loan to Canadian Dept of Defence Production, 1951; Dir, Imperial Oil, 1952, Vice-Pres. 1953; Pres. and Dir International Petroleum Co., 1959; Vice-Pres., Dir and Mem. Exec. Cttee Exxon Co., USA (formerly Humble Oil & Refining Co.), 1961, Exec. Vice-Pres. 1962, Pres. 1963–64; Exec. Vice-Pres. and Dir 1964, Pres. 1965–69, Jersey Standard. Dir, Raychem Corp.*Address:* 1100 Milam Building, Suite 4601, Houston, Texas 77002, USA. *Clubs:* Augusta National Golf (Augusta); Ramada, Houston Country (Houston).

JAMIESON, Kenneth Douglas, CMG 1968; HM Diplomatic Service, retired; *b* 9 Jan. 1921; *s* of late Rt Hon. Lord Jamieson, PC, KC, Senator of College of Justice in Scotland and Violet Rhodes; *m* 1946, Pamela Hall; two *s* one *d. Educ:* Rugby; Balliol Coll., Oxford. War Service: 5th Regt RHA, 1941–45; HQ, RA 7th Armoured Div., 1945–46. Joined Foreign Service, 1946; served in: Washington, 1948; FO, 1952; Lima, 1954; Brussels, 1959; FO, 1961; Caracas, 1963; Dir of Commercial Training, DSAO, 1968; Head of Export Promotion Dept, FCO, 1968–70; Minister and UK Dep. Permanent Representative, UN, NY, 1970–74; Ambassador to Peru, 1974–77; Sen. Directing Staff, RCDS, 1977–80. *Address:* Mill Hill House, Bucks Green, Rudgwick, W Sussex.

JAMIL RAIS, Tan Sri Dato' Abdul; *see* Abdul Jamil Rais.

JAMISON, James Hardie, OBE 1974; chartered accountant; Partner, Coopers & Lybrand, Chartered Accountants, 1939–78, retired; *b* 29 Nov. 1913; *s* of late W. I. Jamison; *m* 1940, Mary Louise, *d* of late W. R. Richardson; two *s* one *d. Educ:* Sydney Church of England Grammar Sch. Chm., Commn of Inquiry into Efficiency and Admin of Hosps, 1979–80. Mem., Nat. Council, Aust. Inst. of Chartered Accountants, 1969–77, Vice-Pres., 1973–75, Pres., 1975–76. *Recreation:* sailing. *Address:* 8 McLeod Street, Mosman, NSW 2088, Australia. *Clubs:* Australasian Pioneers' (Pres. 1970–72), Australian, Royal Sydney Yacht Squadron (Sydney).

JAMISON, James Kenneth, OBE 1978; Director, Arts Council of Northern Ireland, since 1969; *b* 9 May 1931; *s* of William Jamison and Alicia Rea Jamison; *m* 1964, Joan Young Boyd; one *s* one *d. Educ:* Belfast College of Art (DA). Secondary school teacher, 1953–61; Art Critic, Belfast Telegraph, 1956–61; Art Organiser, Arts Council of Northern Ireland, 1962–64, Dep. Director, 1964–69. *Publications:* miscellaneous on the arts in the North of Ireland. *Recreations:* the arts, travel. *Address:* 64 Rugby Road, Belfast BT7 1PT. *T:* Belfast 23063. *Club:* Queen's University Common Room (Belfast).

JAMISON, Dr Robin Ralph, FRS 1969, FEng, FRAeS, CChem, MRSC; Chief Technical Executive (Research), Rolls Royce (1971) Ltd (formerly Rolls Royce Ltd), Bristol Engine Division, 1971–75, retired; *b* 12 July 1912; *s* of Reginald Jamison, MD, FRCS, and Eanswyth Heyworth; *m* 1937, Hilda Watney Wilson, Cape Town; two *s* two *d. Educ:* South African Coll.; Univ. of Cape Town. BSc, PhD. S African Govt research grant, 1936–37; research and development of aero engines, Rolls Royce Ltd, 1937–50; Head of Ramjet Dept, Bristol Siddeley Engines Ltd, 1950–62 (Asst Chief Engr, 1956); advanced propulsion res., 1962–65; Chief Engr, Res., 1965–71. Vis. Prof., Bath Univ. of Technology, 1969–73. FEng 1976. Herbert Ackroyd-Stuart Prize, RAeS, 1958; Thulin Bronze Medal, Swedish Aero. Soc., 1960; Silver Medal of RAeS, 1965. *Publications:* papers in aeronautical and scientific jls. *Recreations:* sailing, gardening, music. *Address:* 2 The Crescent, Henleaze, Bristol BS9 4RN. *T:* Bristol 620328.

JANES, (John) Douglas (Webster), CB 1975; Secretary, The Bach Choir, since 1981; Deputy Secretary, Northern Ireland Office, 1974–79; *b* 17 Aug. 1918; *s* of late John Arnold Janes and Maud Mackinnon (*née* Webster); *m* 1943, Margaret Isabel Smith (*d* 1978); one *s* two *d. Educ:* Southgate County Sch., Mddx; Imperial Coll. of Science and Technology. 1st cl. BSc (Eng) London, ACGI, DIC. Entered Post Office Engineering Dept, Research Branch, 1939. Served Royal Signals, RAOC, REME, 1939–45: War Office, 1941–45; Major. Min. of Town and Country Planning, 1947; Min. of Housing and Local Govt, 1951; seconded to Min. of Power, 1956–58; HM Treasury, 1960–63; Min. of Land and Natural Resources, 1964–66; Prin. Finance Officer and Accountant Gen., Min. of Housing and Local Govt, 1968–70; Prin. Finance Officer (Local Govt and Develt), DoE, 1970–73, Dep. Sec., 1973; Chief Executive, Maplin Develt Authority, 1973–74. Chm., Home Grown Timber Adv. Cttee, 1981– (Mem., 1979–); various management and organisation reviews, 1979–81. *Recreations:* singing, do-it-yourself. *Address:* 136 Waterfall Road, N14 7JN. *T:* 01–886 2133.

JANES, Maj.-Gen. Mervyn, CB 1973; MBE 1944; *b* 1 Oct. 1920; *o s* of W. G. Janes; *m* 1946, Elizabeth Kathleen McIntyre; two *d. Educ:* Sir Walter St John's Sch., London. Commnd 1942; served with Essex Yeo. (104 Regt RHA), 1942–46, Middle East and Italy; psc 1951; served with 3 RHA, 1952–53; 2 Div., BMRA, 1954–55; Chief Instructor, New Coll., RMAS, 1956–57; Batt. Comd, 3 RHA, 1958–60; Asst Army Instructor (GSO1), Imperial Defence Coll., 1961–62; comd 1st Regt RHA, 1963–65; Comdr, RA, in BAOR, 1965–67; DMS2 (MoD(A)), 1967–70; GOC 5th Division, 1970–71; Dir, Royal Artillery, 1971–73. Col Comdt, RA, 1973–81. Chm. Cttee, SSAFA Royal Homes for Officers' Widows and Daughters, 1983–. *Recreations:* music, Egyptology, ornithology. *Address:* 115 Wardo Avenue, SW6. *Club:* Army and Navy.

JANION, Rear-Adm. Sir Hugh (Penderel), KCVO 1981; Flag Officer, Royal Yachts, 1975–81; *b* 28 Sept. 1923; *s* of late Engr Captain Ralph Penderel Janion, RN, and late Mrs Winifred Derwent Janion; *m* 1956, Elizabeth Monica Ferard; one *s* one *d. Educ:* Malvern Link Sch., Worcs; RNC Dartmouth. Served War of 1939–45, Russian convoys, invasions of Sicily and Italy; Korean War, 1950–52, Inchon landing. Specialised in navigation; Comdr, 1958, i/c HMS Jewel, and Exec. Officer HMS Ark Royal; Captain, 1966, i/c HMS Aurora and HMS Bristol; Rear-Adm. 1975. Extra Equerry to the Queen, 1975–

Younger Brother, Trinity House, 1976–. *Recreations:* sailing, golf. *Address:* King's Hayes, Batcombe, Shepton Mallet, Somerset BA4 6HF. *T:* Upton Noble 300. *Clubs:* Naval and Military; Royal Yacht Squadron (Cowes); Royal Naval and Royal Albert Yacht (Portsmouth); Imperial Poona Yacht.

JANNEH, Bocar Ousman S.; *see* Semega-Janneh.

JANNER, Lady; Elsie Sybil Janner, CBE 1968; JP; *b* Newcastle upon Tyne; *d* of Joseph and Henrietta Cohen; *m* 1927, Barnett Janner (later Baron Janner) (*d* 1982); one *s* one *d. Educ:* Central Newcastle High Sch.; South Hampstead High Sch.; Switzerland. Founder and first Hon. Club Leader, Brady Girls' Club, Whitechapel, 1925 (now Pres., Brady Clubs and Settlement); Jt Pres., Brady/Maccabi Youth and Community Centre, Edgware, 1980–. War of 1939–45: Captain, Mechanised Transp. Corps (Def. Medal). Chm., Bridgehead Housing Assoc., to acquire property for residential purposes for homeless ex-offenders, 1967–75; Stonham Housing Assoc. (amalgamation of S Western Housing Assoc., St Leonards Housing Assoc., and Bridgehead): Chm. Adv. Bd, 1975–83; Pres., 1984–; Chm., Stonham Meml Trust. Mem., Finance and Develt Cttees; Magistrates Assoc.: Vice-Pres.; Hon. Treasurer, 1971–76; formerly Dep. Chm., Road Traffic Cttee, and Mem., Exec. Cttee; Vice Pres., Inner London Br. (former Chm.); former Mem., Jt Standing Cttee, Magistrates Assoc. and Justices' Clerks Soc. JP, Inner London, 1936; contested (Lab), Mile End, LCC, 1947; a Visiting Magistrate to Holloway Women's Prison, 1950–62; Chm., Thames Bench of Magistrates, 1975; Member: Juvenile Courts Panel, 1944–70 (Chm. 1960–70); SDP Appeals Panel; Former Member: Inner London and NE London Licensing Planning Cttees; Inner London Licensing Compensation Cttee; Inner London Mem., Cttee of Magistrates. Vice-Pres., Assoc. for Jewish Youth; Hon. Vice-Pres., Fedn of Women Zionists of Gt Brit. and Ire.; Mem., Bd of Deputies, British Jews Educn and Youth Cttee (Chm., 1943–66); Chm., United Jewish Educnl and Cultural Org. (internat. body to re-construct Jewish educn in countries of Europe which had been occupied by Germans), 1947–50; Mem., Central Council of Jewish Religious Educn, 1945–; Dep. Chm., Mitchell City of London Charity and Educnl Foundn, 1984– (Trustee, 1950–); Trustee, Barnett Janner Charitable Trust; Member: former Nat. Road Safety Adv. Council, 1965–68; Exec., Inst. Advanced Motorists, 1984– (Vice-Chm., 1980–84). Freeman, City of London, 1975. *Publication:* Barnett Janner—A Personal Portrait, 1984. *Recreation:* grandchildren. *Address:* 45 Morpeth Mansions, Morpeth Terrace, SW1P 1ET. *See also* Hon. G. E. Janner, Lord Morris of Kenwood.

JANNER, Hon. Greville Ewan, MA Cantab; QC 1971; MP (Lab) Leicester West, since 1974 (Leicester North West, 1970–74); barrister, author, lecturer, journalist and broadcaster; *b* 11 July 1928; *s* of late Baron Janner and of Lady Janner, qv; *m* 1955, Myra Louise Sheink, Melbourne; one *s* two *d. Educ:* Bishop's Coll. Sch., Canada; St Paul's Sch. (Foundn Schol.); Trinity Hall, Cambridge (Exhbnr); Harvard Post Graduate Law School (Fulbright and Smith-Mundt Schol.); Harmsworth Scholar, Middle Temple, 1955. Nat. Service: Sgt RA, BAOR, War Crimes Investigator. Pres., Cambridge Union, 1952; Chm., Cambridge Univ. Labour Club, 1952; Internat. Sec., Nat. Assoc. of Labour Students, 1952; Pres., Trinity Hall Athletic Club, 1952. Contested (Lab) Wimbledon, 1955. Mem., Select Cttee on Employment, 1982–; Chm., All-Party Industrial Safety Gp, 1975–; Founder, Trustee and former Chm., All-Party Cttee for Homeless and Rootless People; Vice-Chm., All-Party Parly Cttee for Release of Soviet Jewry, 1971–; Jt Vice-Chm., British-Israel Parly Gp, 1983–; Sec., British-Spanish Parly Gp, 1986–. Vis. Law Fellow, Lancaster Univ., 1985. President: National Council for Soviet Jewry, 1979–85; Bd of Deputies of British Jews, 1979–85; Commonwealth Jewish Council, 1983–; World Jewish Congress, Europe, 1984–86; Vice-President: Assoc. for Jewish Youth, 1970–; Assoc. of Jewish Ex-Servicemen; IVS, 1983–; Mem. World Executive, World Jewish Congress, 1986– (European Vice-Pres., 1984–86); Member: Nat. Union of Journalists; Soc. of Labour Lawyers; Magic Circle; Pres., Retired Executives, Action Clearing House, 1982–; Pres., Jewish Museum, 1985–; Bd of Dirs, Jt Israel Appeal, 1985–; Vice-Pres., Guideposts Trust, 1983–; Founder Mem., Internat. Cttee for Human Rights in USSR; Chm., Slepak Charitable Trust. Former Dir, Jewish Chronicle Newspaper Ltd. Fellow, Inst. of Personnel Management, 1976. Hon. PhD Haifa Univ., 1984. Sternberg Award, CCJ, 1985. *Publications:* 52 books, mainly on employment and industrial relations law, and on public speaking, including: Employment Letters; Complete Speechmaker; Complete Letterwriter; Janner on Presentation. *Address:* House of Commons, SW1. *T:* 01–219 3000.

JANSEN, Elly, (Mrs Elly Whitehouse-Jansen), OBE 1980; Founder and Director, The Richmond Fellowship for mental welfare and rehabilitation, since 1959; *b* 5 Oct. 1929; *d* of Jacobus Gerrit Jansen and Petronella Suzanna Vellekoop; *m* 1969, Alan Brian Stewart Whitehouse (known as George); three *d. Educ:* Paedologisch Inst. of Free Univ., Amsterdam; Boerhave Kliniek (SRN); London Univ. Founded: Richmond Fellowship of America, 1968, of Australia, 1973, of New Zealand, 1978, of Austria, 1979, of Canada, 1981, of Hong Kong, of India, and of Israel, 1984. Richmond Fellowship Internat., 1981. Organised internat. confs on therapeutic communities, 1973, 1975, 1976, 1979, and 1984; has acted as consultant to several govts on issues of community care. Fellowship, German Marshall Meml Fund, 1977–78. *Publications:* (ed) The Therapeutic Community Outside the Hospital, 1980; (contrib.) Mental Health and the Community, 1983; (contrib.) Towards a Whole Society: collected papers on aspects of mental health, 1985; contribs to Amer. Jl of Psychiatry, L'Inf. Psychiatrique, and other jls. *Recreations:* literature, photography, interior design. *Address:* 8 Addison Road, Kensington, W14 8DL. *T:* 01–603 6373.

JANVRIN, Vice-Adm. Sir (Hugh) Richard Benest, KCB 1969 (CB 1965); DSC 1940; *b* 9 May 1915; *s* of late Rev. Canon C. W. Janvrin, Fairford, Glos.; *m* 1938, Nancy Fielding; two *s. Educ:* RNC, Dartmouth. Naval Cadet, 1929; Midshipman, 1933; Sub-Lt, 1936; Lt, 1937; Qualified Fleet Air Arm Observer, 1938. Served War of 1939–45 (took part in Taranto attack, 1940). In Command: HMS Broadsword, 1951–53; HMS Grenville, 1957–58; RNAS Brawdy, 1958; HMS Victorious, 1959–60. Imperial Defence Coll., 1961; Dir, Tactics and Weapons Policy, Admiralty, 1962–63; Flag Officer, Aircraft Carriers, 1964–66; Dep. Chief of Naval Staff, MoD, 1966–68; Flag Officer, Naval Air Comd, 1968–70; retired 1971. Lieut-Comdr, 1945; Comdr, 1948; Capt., 1954; Rear-Adm., 1964; Vice-Adm. 1967. *Recreation:* gardening. *Address:* Allen's Close, Chalford Hill, near Stroud, Glos. *T:* Brimscombe 882336.

JANZON, Mrs Bengt; *see* Dobbs, Mattiwilda.

JAQUES, Prof. Elliott; Director of Institute of Organisation and Social Studies, Brunel University, 1970–85 (Professor of Sociology, 1970–82); *b* 18 Jan. 1917; *m* 1953, Kathleen (*née* Walsh); one *d. Educ:* Univ. of Toronto (BA, MA); Johns Hopkins Med. Sch. (MD); Harvard Univ. (PhD). Qual. Psycho-analyst (Brit. Psycho-An. Soc.) 1951. Rantoul Fellow in Psychology, Harvard, 1940–41; Major, Royal Can. Army Med. Corps, 1941–45; Founder Mem., Tavistock Inst. of Human Relations, 1946–51; private practice as psycho-analyst and industrial consultant, 1952–65; Head of Sch. of Social Sciences, Brunel Univ., 1965–70. Adviser to BoT on organisation for overseas marketing, 1965–69; Mem. Management Study Steering Cttee on NHS Reorganisation, 1972. *Publications:* The

Changing Culture of a Factory, 1951; Measurement of Responsibility, 1956; Equitable Payment, 1961; (with Wilfred Brown) Product Analysis Pricing, 1964; Time-Span Handbook, 1964; (with Wilfred Brown) Glacier Project Papers, 1965; Progression Handbook, 1968; Work, Creativity and Social Justice, 1970; A General Theory of Bureaucracy, 1976; Health Services, 1978; Levels of Abstraction and Logic in Human Action, 1978; The Form of Time, 1982; Free Enterprise, Fair Employment, 1982; articles in Human Relations, New Society, Internat. Jl of Psycho-Analysis, etc. *Recreations:* art, music, ski-ing. *Address:* c/o Brunel University, Uxbridge, Mddx. *T:* Uxbridge 56461.

JARDINE, Sir Andrew (Colin Douglas), 5th Bt *cr* 1916; with Henderson Administration Group plc, since 1981; *b* 30 Nov. 1955; *s* of Brigadier Sir Ian Liddell Jardine, 4th Bt, OBE, MC, and of Priscilla Daphne, *d* of Douglas Middleton Parnham Scott-Phillips; *S* father, 1982. *Educ:* Charterhouse. Commissioned Royal Green Jackets, 1975–78. *Heir: b* Michael Ian Christopher Jardine [*b* 4 Oct. 1958; *m* 1982, Maria Milky Pineda; one *s*]. *Address:* 99 Addison Road, W14 8DD. *T:* 01-603 6434. *Club:* Boodle's.

See also Sir J. R. G. Baird, Bt.

JARDINE, Sir (Andrew) Rupert (John) Buchanan-, 4th Bt *cr* 1885; MC 1944; DL; landowner and farmer; *b* 2 Feb. 1923; *s* of Sir John William Buchanan-Jardine, 3rd Bt and of Jean Barbara, *d* of late Lord Ernest Hamilton; *S* father, 1969; *m* 1950, Jane Fiona (marr. diss. 1975), 2nd *d* of Sir Charles Edmonstone, 6th Bt; one *s* one *d*. *Educ:* Harrow; Royal Agricultural College. Joined Royal Horse Guards, 1941; served in France, Holland and Germany; Major 1948; retired, 1949. Joint-Master, Dumfriesshire Foxhounds, 1950. JP Dumfriesshire, 1957; DL Dumfriesshire, 1978. Bronze Lion of the Netherlands, 1945. *Recreations:* country pursuits. *Heir: s* John Christopher Rupert Buchanan-Jardine [*b* 20 March 1952; *m* 1975, Pandora Lavinia, *d* of Peter Murray Lee; three *d*]. *Address:* Dixons, Lockerbie, Dumfriesshire. *T:* Lockerbie 2508. *Club:* MCC.

JARDINE, James Christopher Macnaughton; Sheriff of Glasgow and Strathkelvin, since 1979; *b* 18 Jan. 1930; *s* of James Jardine; *m* 1955, Vena Gordon Kight; one *d*. *Educ:* Glasgow Academy; Gresham House, Ayrshire; Glasgow Univ. (BL). National Service (Lieut RASC), 1950–52. Admitted as Solicitor, in Scotland, 1953. Practice as principal (from 1955) of Nelson & Mackay, and as partner of McClure, Naismith, Brodie & Co., Solicitors, Glasgow, 1956–69; Sheriff of Stirling, Dunbarton and Clackmannan, later N Strathclyde, at Dumbarton, 1969–79. A Vice-Pres., Sheriffs' Assoc., 1976–79. Sec., Glasgow Univ. Graduates Assoc., 1956–66; Mem., Business Cttee of Glasgow Univ. Gen. Council, 1964–67. Mem. Professional Advisory Cttee, Scottish Council on Alcoholism, 1982–85. *Recreations:* boating, enjoyment of music and theatre. *Address:* Sheriff's Chambers, Sheriff Court House, 1 Carlton Place, Glasgow.

JARDINE, John Frederick James; Under Secretary, Department of Employment, since 1985; *b* 22 Dec. 1926; *s* of late James Jardine; *m* 1957, Pamela Joyce; four *s* two *d*. *Educ:* Rock Ferry High Sch., Birkenhead. RAF, 1945–48; Inland Revenue, 1948–55; BoT, 1955–58; British Trade Comr, Karachi, 1958–63; BoT, 1963–66; Midland Regional Controller, 1966–71; DTI, 1971–73; seconded to HM Diplomatic Service (Under-Sec.), 1973; HM Consul-General, Johannesburg, 1973–78; Dept of Trade, 1978–80; Dept of Industry, 1980–83; DTI, 1983–85. *Recreations:* tennis, golf, bridge. *Address:* 7 Lynwood Avenue, Epsom, Surrey KT17 4LQ. *T:* Epsom 29156. *Club:* Royal Automobile.

JARDINE, Michael James, CB 1976; Deputy Director of Public Prosecutions, 1974–79; *b* 20 Nov. 1915; *s* of Judge James Willoughby Jardine, KC; *m* 1939; two *s* one *d*. *Educ:* Eton; King's Coll., Cambridge (BA). Called to Bar, Middle Temple, 1937. Served War with Scots Guards, 1940–46: active service in North Africa and Italy. Legal Asst to Director of Public Prosecutions, 1946; Asst Solicitor, 1965; Asst Director of Public Prosecutions, 1969. *Recreation:* bridge.

JARDINE, Sir Rupert Buchanan-; *see* Jardine, Sir A. R. J. B.

JARDINE OF APPLEGIRTH, Sir Alexander Maule, (Sir Alec), 12th Bt *cr* 1672 (NS); Chief of the Clan Jardine; *b* 24 Aug. 1947; *s* of Col Sir William Edward Jardine of Applegirth, 11th Bt, OBE, TD, JP, DL, and of Ann Graham, *yr d* of late Lt-Col Claud Archibald Scott Maitland, DSO; *S* father, 1986; *m* 1982, Mary Beatrice, *d* of late Hon. John Michael Inigo Cross and of Mrs James Parker-Jervis; one *s* one *d*. *Educ:* Gordonstoun. Member of Queen's Body Guard for Scotland, Royal Co. of Archers. *Heir: s* William Murray Jardine, yr of Applegirth, *b* 4 July 1984. *Address:* Little Dyke, Dalton, Lockerbie, Dumfriesshire DG11 1DU.

JARDINE PATERSON, Lt-Col Arthur James, OBE 1958; TD 1945; Lord Lieutenant of Dumfries, since 1982; *b* 14 July 1918; *s* of late R. Jardine Paterson; *m* 1948, Mary Fearne Balfour-Kinnear; one *d*. *Educ:* Eton; Jesus Coll., Cambridge. TA, 1939; served War of 1939–45, KOSB, NW Europe; comd 5th Bn KOSB, 1955–58. CC Dumfriesshire, 1960; Reg. Council, Dumfries and Galloway, 1974–82. DL 1964, JP 1965, Dumfriesshire. *Recreation:* shooting. *Address:* Skairfield, Lockerbie, Dumfriesshire DG11 1JL. *T:* Lochmaben 201. *Club:* Army and Navy.

See also Sir J. Jardine Paterson.

JARDINE PATERSON, Sir John (Valentine), Kt 1967; *b* 14 Feb. 1920; *y s* of late Robert Jardine Paterson, Balgray, Lockerbie, Dumfriesshire; *m* 1953, Priscilla Mignon, *d* of late Sir Kenneth Nicolson, MC; one *s* three *d*. *Educ:* Eton Coll.; Jesus Coll., Cambridge. Emergency commn, The Black Watch, RHR, 1939. Director: Jardine Henderson Ltd, Calcutta, 1952–67 (Chm. 1963–67); McLeod Russel PLC, 1967–84 (Chm., 1979–83). Chm., Indian Jute Mills Assoc., 1963; Pres., Bengal Chamber of Commerce and Industry and Associated Chambers of Commerce of India, 1966. *Recreations:* golf, shooting. *Address:* Norton Bavant Manor, Warminster, Wilts. *T:* Warminster 40378. *Clubs:* Oriental; Bengal, Royal Calcutta Turf (Calcutta).

See also A. J. Jardine Paterson.

JARMAN, Air Cdre Lance Michael E.; *see* Elworthy-Jarman.

JARMAN, Nicholas Francis Barnaby; QC 1985; barrister; a Recorder of the Crown Court, since 1982; *b* 19 June 1938; *s* of late A. S. Jarman and Helene Jarman; *m* 1973, Jennifer Michelle Lawrence-Smith (marr. diss. 1978); one *d*. *Educ:* Harrow; Christ Church, Oxford (MA Jurisprudence). Commnd RA, 1956–58 (JUO Mons, 1957). Called to the Bar, Inner Temple, 1965 (Duke of Edinburgh Scholar). *Recreations:* France, fishing, food. *Address:* 13 Blithfield Street, W8; 4 King's Bench Walk, Temple, EC4Y 7DL. *T:* 01-353 3581.

JARMAN, Roger Whitney; Under Secretary, Transport, Highways and Planning Group, Welsh Office, since 1983; *b* 16 Feb. 1935; *s* of Reginald Cecil Jarman and Marjorie Dix Jarman; *m* 1959, Patricia Dorothy Odwell; one *s*. *Educ:* Cathays High Sch., Cardiff; Univ. of Birmingham (BSocSc Hons; Cert. in Educn). Recruitment and Selection Officer, Vauxhall Motors Ltd, 1960–64; Asst Sec., Univ. of Bristol Appts Bd, 1964–68; Asst Dir of Recruitment, CSD, 1968–72; Welsh Office: Principal, European Div., 1972–74; Asst Sec., Devolution Div., 1974–78; Asst Sec., Perm. Sec.'s Div., 1978–80; Under Sec., Land Use Planning Gp, 1980–83. *Recreations:* walking, reading, cooking. *Address:* Coopers Lea, 72 Mill Road, Lisvane, Cardiff CF4 5XJ. *T:* Cardiff 756405. *Club:* Civil Service.

JARRATT, Sir Alexander Anthony, (Sir Alex), Kt 1979; CB 1968; Chairman, Smiths Industries PLC, since 1985 (Director, since 1984); a Deputy Chairman, Midland Bank, since 1980; Chancellor, University of Birmingham, since 1983; *b* 19 Jan. 1924; *o s* of Alexander and Mary Jarratt; *m* 1946, Mary Philomena Keogh; one *s* two *d*. *Educ:* Royal Liberty Gram. Sch., Essex; University of Birmingham. War Service, Fleet Air Arm, 1942–46. University of Birmingham, BCom, 1946–49. Asst Principal, Min. of Power, 1949, Principal, 1953, and seconded to Treas., 1954–55; Min. of Power: Prin. Priv. Sec. to Minister, 1955–59; Asst Sec., Oil Div., 1959–63; Under-Sec., Gas Div., 1963–64; seconded to Cabinet Office, 1964–65; Secretary to the National Board for Prices and Incomes, 1965–68; Dep. Sec., 1967; Dep. Under Sec. of State, Dept of Employment and Productivity, 1968–70; Dep. Sec., Min. of Agriculture, 1970. Man. Dir, IPC, 1970–73; Chm. and Chief Executive, IPC and IPC Newspapers, 1974; Chm., Reed Internat., 1974–85 (Dir, 1970–85); Director: ICI; Prudential Corp.; Thyssen-Bornemisza Group; Mem., Ford European Adv. Council, 1983–. Mem., President's Cttee, and Chm., Employment Policy Cttee, CBI, 1983–; Mem., NEDC, 1976–80. Pres., Advertising Assoc., 1979–83. Mem., Industrial Soc. (Chm., 1975–79); Chm., Henley: The Management Coll.; Governor: London Business Sch.; Ashridge Management Coll. Pres., Periodical Publishers Assoc., 1983–85; Vice-Pres., Inst. of Marketing; Chm., Adv. Bd, Inst. of Occup. Health; Panel Mem., Internat. Centre for Settlement of Investment Disputes. FRSA. Hon. DSc Cranfield, 1973; DUniv Brunel, 1979; Hon. LLD Birmingham, 1982. *Recreations:* the countryside, reading. *Address:* c/o Smiths Industries PLC, 765 Finchley Road, Childs Hill, NW11 8DS. *T:* 01-458 3232. *Club:* Savile.

JARRETT, Sir Clifford (George), KBE 1956 (CBE 1945); CB 1949; Chairman: Tobacco Research Council, 1971–78; Dover Harbour Board, 1971–80; *b* 1909; *s* of George Henry Jarrett; *m* 1st, 1933, Hilda Alice Goodchild (*d* 1975); one *s* two *d*; 2nd, 1978, Mary, *d* of C. S. Beacock. *Educ:* Dover County Sch.; Sidney Sussex Coll., Cambridge. BA 1931. Entered Civil Service, 1932; Asst Principal, Home Office, 1932–34, Admiralty, 1934–38; Private Sec. to Parl. Sec., 1936–38; Principal Private Sec. to First Lord, 1940–44; Principal Establishments Officer, 1946–50; a Dep. Sec., Admiralty, 1950–61; Permanent Sec., Admiralty, 1961–64; Permanent Under-Sec., Min. of Pensions and Nat. Insurance, later Min. of Social Security, later Dept of Health and Social Security, 1964–70. A Trustee, Nat. Maritime Museum, 1969–81. *Address:* The Coach House, Derry Hill, Menston, Ilkley, W Yorks. *Club:* United Oxford & Cambridge University.

JARRETT, Prof. William Fleming Hoggan, FRS 1980; FRSE 1965; Professor of Veterinary Pathology, University of Glasgow, since 1968; *b* 2 Jan. 1928; *s* of James and Jessie Jarrett; *m* 1952, Anna Fraser Sharp; two *d*. *Educ:* Lenzie Academy; Glasgow Veterinary Coll.; Univ. of Glasgow; PhD, MRCVS, FRCPath. Gold Medal, 1949; John Henry Steele Meml Medal, 1961; Steele Bodger Meml Schol. 1955. ARC Research Student, 1949–52; Lectr, Dept of Veterinary Pathology, Univ. of Glasgow Vet. Sch., 1952–53; Head of Hospital Path. Dept of Vet. Hosp., Univ. of Glasgow, 1953–61; Reader in Pathology, Univ. of Glasgow, 1962–65; seconded to Univ. of E Africa, 1963–64; Titular Prof. of Experimental Vet. Medicine, Univ. of Glasgow, 1965. Leeuwenhoek Lectr, Royal Soc., 1986. Makdougall Brisbane Prize, RSE, 1984; J.T. Edwards Meml Medal, RCVS, 1984. *Publications:* various, on tumour viruses, Leukaemia and immunology. *Recreations:* sailing, skiing, mountaineering, music. *Address:* 60 Netherblane, High Pines, Blanefield, Glasgow G63 9JP. *T:* Blanefield 70332. *Clubs:* Clyde Cruising, West Highland Yacht, Glencoe Ski, Scottish Ski.

JARRING, Gunnar, PhD; Grand Cross, Order of the North Star, Sweden; Swedish Ambassador and Special Representative of the Secretary-General of the United Nations on the Middle East question since Nov. 1967; *b* S Sweden, 12 Oct. 1907; *s* of Gottfrid Jönsson and Betty Svensson; *m* 1932, Agnes, *d* of Prof. Carl Charlier, Lund; one *d*. *Educ:* Lund; Univ. of Lund (PhD). Family surname changed to Jarring, 1931. Associate Prof. of Turkish Langs, Lund Univ., 1933–40; Attaché, Ankara, 1940–41; Chief, Section B, Teheran, 1941; Chargé d'Affaires *ad interim:* Teheran and Baghdad, 1945; Addis Ababa, 1946–48; Minister: to India, 1948–51, concurrently to Ceylon, 1950–51; to Persia, Iraq and Pakistan, 1951–52; Dir, Polit. Div., Min. of Foreign Affairs, 1953–56; Permanent Rep. to UN, 1956–58; Rep. on Security Council, 1957–58; Ambassador to USA, 1958–64, to USSR, 1964–73, and to Mongolia, 1965–73. *Publications:* Studien zu einer osttürkischen Lautlehre, 1933; The Contest of the Fruits - An Eastern Turki Allegory, 1936; The Uzbek Dialect of Quilich, Russian Turkestan, 1937; Uzbek Texts from Afghan Turkestan, 1938; The Distribution of Turk Tribes in Afghanistan, 1939; Materials to the Knowledge of Eastern Turki (vols 1–4), 1947–51; An Eastern Turki-English Dialect Dictionary, 1964; Literary Texts from Kashghar, 1980. *Address:* Karlavägen 85, 114 59 Stockholm, Sweden.

JARROW, Bishop Suffragan of, since 1980; **Rt. Rev. Michael Thomas Ball,** CGA; *b* 14 Feb. 1932; *s* of Thomas James Ball and Kathleen Bradley Ball. *Educ:* Lancing Coll., Sussex; Queens' Coll., Cambridge (BA 1955, MA 1959). Schoolmastering, 1955–76; Co-Founder, Community of the Glorious Ascension, 1960; Prior at Stroud Priory, 1963–76; Curate, Whiteshill, Stroud, Glos, 1971–76; Priest-in-charge of Stanmer with Falmer, and Senior Anglican Chaplain to Higher Education in Brighton, including Sussex Univ., 1976–80. *Recreations:* music, sport. *Address:* Melkridge House, Gilesgate, Durham. *T:* Durham 43797.

See also Bishop of Lewes.

JÄRVI, Neeme; Musical Director and Principal Conductor, Scottish National Orchestra, since 1984; Chief Conductor, Gothenburg Symphony Orchestra, Sweden, since 1982; *b* 7 June 1937; *s* of August and Elss Järvi; *m* 1961, Liilia Järvi; two *s* one *d*. *Educ:* Estonia-Tallinn Conservatory of Music; Leningrad State Conservatory. Chief Conductor: Estonian Radio Symphony Orch., 1963–77 (Conductor, 1960–63); theatre, opera and ballet companies, Estonia-Tallinn, 1963–77; toured USA with Leningrad Phil. Orch., 1973 and 1977; Chief Conductor, Estonian State Symph. Orch., 1977–80; since emigration to USA in 1980 has appeared as Guest Conductor with New York Phil. Orch., Philadelphia Orch., Boston Symph., Chicago Symph., Los Angeles Phil., Met. Opera (New York) and in San Francisco, Cincinnati, Indianapolis, Minneapolis and Detroit; has also given concerts in Vienna, London, Canada, Sweden, Finland, Norway, Denmark, Holland, Switzerland and W Germany; Principal Guest Conductor, City of Birmingham Symph. Orch., 1981–84. 1st Prize, Internat. Conductors Competition, Accademia Santa Cecilia, Rome, 1971. Many recordings; current projects incl. complete symphonies of Prokofiev, Sibelius, Glazunov, Wilhelm Stenhammar, Eduard Tubin. *Recreation:* traveller. *Address:* c/o Scottish National Orchestra, 3 La Belle Place, Glasgow G3 7LH; c/o Columbia Artists Management Inc., 165 West 57th Street, New York, NY 10019, USA.

JARVIS, Hon. Eric William George, CMG 1961; Judge of the High Court, Rhodesia, 1963–77; *b* 22 Nov. 1907; *s* of late William Stokes Jarvis and Edith Mary Jarvis (*née* Langley), both of Essex, England; *m* 1937, Eveline Mavis Smith; one *s* one *d*. *Educ:* Salisbury Boys High Sch. (now Prince Edward Sch.), Salisbury, R; Rhodes Univ.,

Grahamstown, SA. BA; LLB; admitted as Advocate High Court of Southern Rhodesia, 1929; appointed Law Officer of Crown, 1934; KC (1949); Solicitor-Gen. for Southern Rhodesia, 1949–55; Attorney-Gen. for Southern Rhodesia, 1955–62. *Recreations:* tennis, golf, bowls. *Address:* c/o S. M. J. Young, 64 Drama Street, Somerset West, 7130, South Africa.

JARVIS, Frederick Frank, (Fred Jarvis); General Secretary, National Union of Teachers, since 1975; Member of General Council, since 1974, Chairman, Sept. 1986–87, Trades Union Congress; *b* 8 Sept. 1924; *s* of Alfred and Emily Ann Jarvis; *m* 1954, Elizabeth Anne Colegrove, Stanton Harcourt, Oxfordshire; one *s* one *d*. *Educ:* Plaistow Secondary Sch., West Ham; Oldershaw Grammar Sch., Wallasey; Liverpool Univ.; St Catherine's Society, Oxford. Dip. in Social Science with dist. (Liverpool Univ.); BA (Hons) in Politics, Philosophy and Economics (Oxon), MA (Oxon). Contested (Lab) Wallasey, Gen. Elec., 1951; Chm., Nat. Assoc. of Labour Student Organisations, 1951; Pres., Nat. Union of Students, 1952–54 (Dep. Pres., 1951–52); Asst Sec., Nat. Union of Teachers, 1955–59; Head of Publicity and Public Relations, 1959–70; Dep. Gen. Sec., NUT, 1970–74 (apptd Gen. Sec. Designate, March 1974). Pres., Eur. Trade Union Cttee for Educn, 1983–84, 1985–86 (Vice-Pres., 1981–83); Chairman, TUC Cttees: Local Govt, 1983–; Educn Training, 1985–. Mem. Council, Nat. Youth Theatre. Hon. FEIS 1980; Hon. FCP 1982. *Publications:* The Educational Implications of UK Membership of the EEC, 1972. Ed, various jls incl.: 'Youth Review', NUT Guide to Careers; NUT Univ. and Coll. Entrance Guide. *Recreations:* swimming, golf, tennis, gardening, cinema, theatre, photography. *Address:* 92 Hadley Road, New Barnet, Herts EN5 5QR. *Club:* Ronnie Scott's.

JARVIS, Patrick William, CB 1985; CEng, FIEE, FIMarE; FRINA; RCNC; Deputy Controller (Warships), Ministry of Defence (PE), and Head of Royal Corps of Naval Constructors, 1983–86; *b* 27 Aug. 1926; *s* of Frederick Arthur and Marjorie Winifred Jarvis; *m* 1951, Amy (*née* Ryley); two *s*. *Educ:* Royal Naval Coll., Greenwich; Royal Naval Engrg Coll., Keyham, Devonport. BScEng. Trade apprentice, HM Dockyard, Chatham, 1942–46; Design Engineer, Admiralty, Bath, 1946–62; Warship Electrical Supt, Belfast, 1962–63; Suptg Engr, MoD(N), Bath, 1963–72; Ship Department, MoD (PE), Bath: Asst Dir and Dep. Dir, 1972–78; Under Sec., 1978; Dir of Naval Ship Production, 1979–81; Dir of Ship Design and Engrg, and Dep. Head of Royal Corps of Naval Constructors, 1981–83; Dep. Sec., 1983. *Recreations:* indoor sports, chess. *Address:* Ranworth, Bathampton Lane, Bath BA2 6ST.

JASPER, Cyril Charles; County Treasurer, Hertfordshire County Council, 1972–81; *b* 16 Oct. 1923; *s* of James Edward Jasper and Daisy (*née* Brown); *m* 1949, Vera Newington; three *s* two *d*. *Educ:* Brockley County Grammar Sch. DPA London 1950; CIPFA (double Hons) 1959; FBIM. Comptroller's Dept, LCC, 1941–60; Asst County Treas., W Sussex CC, 1961–69; Dep. Co. Treas., Herts CC, 1970–72. Consultant to: Mercury Warburg Investment Management Ltd (formerly Rowan Investment Managers Ltd), 1982–; Lazard Securities Ltd, 1980–; Dist Treasurer and Mem. Central Finance Bd, Methodist Church, 1983–. Financial Adviser to Educn Cttee, Assoc. of County Councils, 1972–81. Pres., Soc. of County Treasurers, 1978–79. Collins Gold Medal, CIPFA, 1959. *Publications:* contrib. local govt papers. *Recreations:* amateur dramatics, youth work. *Address:* Dovedale, 47 Walton Road, Ware, Herts SG12 9PF.

JASPER, Robin Leslie Darlow, CMG 1963; HM Diplomatic Service, retired; *b* 22 Feb. 1914; *s* of T. D. Jasper, Beckenham; *m* 1st, 1940, Jean (marr. diss.), *d* of late Brig.-Gen. J. K. Cochrane, CMG; one *d*; 2nd, 1966, Diana Speed (*née* West), two step *d*. *Educ:* Dulwich; Clare Coll., Cambridge. Apprentice, LNER Hotels Dept, 1936–39; Bursar, Dominion Students Hall Trust (London House), 1939–40; RAFVR (Wing Comdr), 1940–45; Principal, India Office (later Commonwealth Relations Office), 1945; concerned with resettlement of the Sec. of State's Services in India, 1947–48; British Dep. High Commissioner, Lahore, Pakistan, 1949–52; Adviser to London Conferences on Central African Federation, and visited Central Africa in this connection, 1952–53; Counsellor, HM Embassy, Lisbon, 1953–55; visited Portuguese Africa, 1954; Commonwealth Relations Office, 1955–60 (Head of Information Policy Dept, 1958–60); attached to the United Kingdom delegation to the United Nations, 1955 and 1956; British Dep. High Commissioner, Ibadan, Nigeria, 1960–64; Counsellor, Commonwealth Office, 1965–67; Consul-Gen., Naples, 1967–71, retired 1972. *Recreations:* tennis, Rugby fives, wind music, 17th Century Church Sculpture, claret. *Address:* c/o Royal Bank of Scotland (Drummonds Branch), 49 Charing Cross, SW1. *Clubs:* MCC, Jesters.

JASPER, Very Rev. Ronald Claud Dudley, CBE 1981; DD; Dean of York, 1975–84, Dean Emeritus, since 1984; *b* 17 Aug. 1917; *o s* of late Claud Albert and late Florence Lily Jasper; *m* 1943, Ethel, *o d* of David and Edith Wiggins; one *s* one *d*. *Educ:* Plymouth Coll.; University of Leeds; College of the Resurrection, Mirfield. MA (with distinction), 1940; DD 1961. FRHistS 1954. Curate of Ryhope, 1940–42; St Oswald's, Durham, 1942–43; Esh, 1943–46; Chaplain of University Coll., Durham, 1946–48; Vicar of Stillington, 1948–55; Succentor of Exeter Cathedral, 1955–60; Lecturer in Liturgical Studies: King's Coll., London, 1960–67, Reader, 1967–68; RSCM, 1965–69; Canon of Westminster, 1968–75; Archdeacon, 1974–75. Chm., Church of England Liturgical Commn, 1964–81. Hon. DLitt Susquehanna, 1976. *Publications:* Prayer Book Revision in England, 1800–1900, 1954; Walter Howard Frere: Correspondence and Memoranda on Liturgical Revision and Construction, 1954; Arthur Cayley Headlam, 1960; George Bell: Bishop of Chichester, 1967; A Christian's Prayer Book, 1972; (ed) The Renewal of Worship, 1965; (ed) The Calendar and Lectionary, 1967; (ed) The Daily Office, 1968; (ed) Holy Week Services, 1971; (ed) Initiation and Eucharist, 1972; (ed) The Eucharist Today, 1974; Prayers of the Eucharist, 1975; Pray Every Day, 1976; The Daily Office Revised, 1978; contribs to: A New Dictionary of Christian Theology, 1983; A New Dictionary of Liturgy and Worship, 1986; A Companion to the Alternative Service Book, 1986; Church Quarterly Review, Jl of Ecclesiastical History, Church Quarterly, London Quarterly, Expository Times, Ecumenica, Heythrop Jl. *Recreations:* reading, writing, television. *Address:* 3 Westmount Close, Ripon HG4 2HU.

JAUNCEY, Hon. Lord; Charles Eliot Jauncey; a Senator of the College of Justice in Scotland, since 1979; *b* 8 May 1925; *s* of late Captain John Henry Jauncey, DSO, RN, Tullichettle, Comrie, and Muriel Charlie, *d* of late Adm. Sir Charles Dundas of Dundas, KCMG; *m* 1st, 1948, Jean (marr. diss. 1969), *d* of Adm. Sir Angus Cunninghame Graham of Gartmore, KBE, CB; two *s* one *d*; 2nd, 1973, Elizabeth (marr. diss. 1977), *widow* of Major John Ballingal, MC; 3rd, 1977, Camilla, *d* of late Lt-Col Charles Cathcart, DSO, Pitcairlie; one *d*. *Educ:* Radley; Christ Church, Oxford; Glasgow Univ. BA 1947, Oxford; LLB 1949, Glasgow. Served in War, 1943–46, Sub-Lt RNVR. Advocate, Scottish Bar, 1949; Standing Junior Counsel to Admiralty, 1954; QC (Scotland) 1963; Kintyre Pursuivant of Arms, 1955–71; Sheriff Principal of Fife and Kinross, 1971–74; Judge of the Courts of Appeal of Jersey and Guernsey, 1972–79. Hon. Sheriff-Substitute of Perthshire, 1962. Mem. of Royal Co. of Archers (Queen's Body Guard for Scotland), 1951. Mem., Historic Buildings Council for Scotland, 1971–. *Recreations:* shooting, fishing, genealogy. *Address:* Tullichettle, Comrie, Perthshire. *T:* 70349; 47 William Street, Edinburgh. *T:* 031–225 4612. *Club:* Royal (Perth).

JAUNCEY, Charles Eliot; *see* Jauncey, Hon. Lord.

JAWARA, Alhaji Sir Dawda Kairaba, Kt 1966; Hon. GCMG 1974; Grand Master, Order of the Republic of The Gambia, 1972; President of the Republic of The Gambia, since 1970; Vice-President of the Senegambian Confederation, since 1982; *b* Barajally, MacCarthy Island Div., 16 May 1924. *Educ:* Muslim Primary Sch. and Methodist Boys' Grammar Sch., Bathurst; Achimota Coll. (Vet. School); Glasgow Univ. MRCVS 1953; Dipl. in Trop. Vet. Med., Edinburgh, 1957. Veterinary Officer for The Gambia Govt, 1954–57, Principal Vet. Officer, 1957–60. Leader of People's Progressive Party (formerly Protectorate People's Party), The Gambia, 1960; MP 1960; Minister of Education, 1960–61; Premier, 1962–63; Prime Minister, 1963–70. Chm., Permanent Inter State Cttee for Drought in the Sahel, 1977–79. Patron, Commonwealth Vet. Assoc., 1967–. Hon. LLD Ife, 1978. Peutinger Gold Medal, Peutinger-Collegium, Munich, 1979; Agricola Medal, FAO, Rome, 1980. Grand Cross: Order of Cedar of Lebanon, 1966; Nat. Order of Republic of Senegal, 1967; Order of Propitious Clouds of China (Taiwan), 1968; Nat. Order of Republic of Guinea, 1973; Grand Officer, Order of Islamic Republic of Mauritania, 1967; Grand Cordon of Most Venerable Order of Knighthood, Pioneers of Republic of Liberia, 1968; Grand Comdr, Nat. Order of Federal Republic of Nigeria, 1970; Comdr of Golden Ark (Netherlands), 1979; Grand Gwanghwa Medal of Order of Diplomatic Service (Republic of Korea), 1984; Nishan-i-Pakistan (Pakistan), 1984. *Recreations:* golf, gardening, sailing. *Address:* State House, Banjul, The Gambia.

JAY, Prof. Barrie Samuel, MD, FRCS; Professor of Clinical Ophthalmology, University of London, since 1985; Consultant Surgeon, Moorfields Eye Hospital, since 1969; Consultant Adviser in Ophthalmology, Department of Health and Social Security, since 1982; *b* 7 May 1929; *er s* of late Dr M. B. Jay and Julia Sterling; *m* 1954, Marcelle Ruby Byre; two *s*. *Educ:* Perse Sch., Cambridge; Gonville and Caius Coll., Cambridge (MA, MD); University Coll. Hosp., London. FRCS 1962. House Surgeon and Sen. Resident Officer, Moorfields Eye Hosp., 1959–62; Sen. Registrar, Ophthalmic Dept, London Hosp., 1962–65; Inst. of Ophthalmology, Univ. of London: Shepherd Res. Scholar, 1963–64; Mem., Cttee of Management, 1972–77, 1979–; Clinical Sub-Dean, 1973–77; Dean, 1980–85; Ophthalmic Surgeon, The London Hosp., 1965–79. Examiner: Dip. in Ophthal., 1970–75; British Orthoptic Council, 1970–; Ophthalmic Nursing Bd, 1971–; Mem. Ct of Examrs, RCS, 1975–80. Brit. Rep., Monospecialist Section of Ophthal., Eur. Union of Med. Specialists, 1973–85. Mem. Council: Section of Ophthal., RSM, 1965–77 (Editorial Rep., 1966–77); Faculty of Ophthalmologists, 1970– (Asst Hon. Sec., 1976–78; Hon. Sec., 1978; Representative on RSC Council, 1983–; Pres., 1986–); Nat. Ophthalmic Treatment Bd Assoc., 1971–75; Internat. Pediatric Ophthal. Soc., 1975–; Ophthal. Soc. UK, 1985–; Member: Ophthal. Nursing Bd, 1974–; Orthoptists Bd, Council for Professions Supplementary to Medicine, 1977– (Vice Chm., 1982–); Specialist Adv. Cttee in Ophthalmology, 1979– (Chm., 1982–); Standing Med. Adv. Cttee, DHSS, 1980–84; Transplant Adv. Panel, DHSS, 1983–. Fellow, Eugenics Soc., 1973; Hon. Mem., Canadian Ophthalmol Soc. Mem., Ct of Assts, Soc. of Apothecaries; Liveryman, Co. of Barbers. Mem., Bd of Governors, Moorfields Eye Hosp., 1971–85. Mem. Editorial Board: Ophthalmic Literature, 1962– (Asst Editor, 1977–78; Editor, 1978–85); British Jl of Ophthalmology, 1965–; Jl of Medical Genetics, 1971–76; Metabolic Ophthalmology, 1975–78; Survey of Ophthalmology, 1976–; Ophthalmic Paediatrics and Genetics, 1981–. *Publications:* contrib. on ophthalmology and genetics to med. jls. *Recreations:* postal history, gardening. *Address:* 10, Beltane Drive, SW19 5JR. *T:* 01–947 1771. *Club:* Athenæum.

JAY, Rt. Hon. Douglas Patrick Thomas, PC 1951; *b* 23 March 1907; *s* of Edward Aubrey Hastings Jay and Isobel Violet Jay; *m* 1st, 1933, Margaret Christian (marr. diss. 1972), *e d* of late J. C. Maxwell Garnett, CBE, ScD; two *s* two *d*; 2nd, 1972, Mary Lavinia Thomas, *d* of Hugh Lewis Thomas. *Educ:* Winchester Coll.; New Coll., Oxford (Scholar). First Class, Litteræ Humaniores; Fellow of All Souls' Coll., Oxford, 1930–37, and 1968–; on the staff of The Times, 1929–33, and The Economist, 1933–37; City Editor of the Daily Herald, 1937–41; Asst Sec., Ministry of Supply, 1941–43; Principal Asst Sec., BoT, 1943–45; Personal Asst to Prime Minister, 1945–46. MP (Lab) Battersea N, July 1946–1974, Wandsworth, Battersea N, 1974–83; Economic Sec. to Treasury, 1947–50; Financial Sec. to Treasury, 1950–51; President, BoT, 1964–67. Chairman: Common Market Safeguards Campaign, 1970–77; London Motorway Action Group, 1968–80. Director: Courtaulds Ltd, 1967–70; Trades Union Unit Trust, 1967–79; Flag Investment Co., 1968–71. *Publications:* The Socialist Case, 1937; Who is to Pay for the War and the Peace, 1941; Socialism in the New Society, 1962; After the Common Market, 1968; Change and Fortune, 1980; Sterling: a plea for moderation, 1985. *Address:* Causeway Cottage, Minster Lovell, Oxon. *T:* Witney 75235.

See also Peter Jay.

JAY, Rev. Canon Eric George; Professor of Historical Theology, Faculty of Divinity, McGill University, 1958–75, Emeritus, 1977; *b* 1 March 1907; *s* of Henry Jay, Colchester, Essex; *m* 1937, Margaret Hilda, *d* of Rev. Alfred W. Webb; one *s* two *d*. *Educ:* Colchester High Sch.; Leeds Univ. BA 1st Cl. Hons Classics, 1929; MA 1930; BD (London) 1937; MTh 1940; PhD 1951. Deacon, 1931; priest, 1932; Curate, St Augustine, Stockport, 1931–34; Lecturer in Theology, King's Coll., London, 1934–47; Curate, St Andrew Undershaft, City of London, 1935–40. Served War as Chaplain in RAFVR 1940–45. Rector, St Mary-le-Strand, 1945–47; Dean of Nassau, Bahamas, 1948–51; Senior Chaplain to the Archbishop of Canterbury, 1951–58; Principal, Montreal Diocesan Theological Coll., 1958–64; Dean, Faculty of Divinity, McGill Univ., 1963–70. Fellow of King's Coll., London, 1948; Canon of Montreal, 1960. Hon. DD: Montreal Diocesan Theolog. Coll., 1964; Trinity Coll., Toronto, 1975; United Theol Coll., Montreal, 1976. *Publications:* The Existence of God, 1946; Origen's Treatise on Prayer, 1954; New Testament Greek; an Introductory Grammar, 1958; Son of Man, Son of God, 1965; The Church: its changing image through twenty centuries, 1977. *Recreations:* reading "thrillers"; crossword puzzles, watching ice hockey, cricket and Rugby football. *Address:* 3421 Durocher Street, Apt 406, Montreal PQ, H2X 2C6, Canada.

JAY, Peter; writer and broadcaster; Chief of Staff to Robert Maxwell, since 1986; Director: BPCC plc, since 1986; Mirror Holdings Ltd, since 1986; Pergamon Holdings Ltd, since 1986; *b* 7 Feb. 1937; *s* of Rt Hon. Douglas Patrick Thomas Jay, *qv*; *m* 1961, Margaret Ann (marr. diss. 1986), *d* of Rt Hon. James Callaghan, *qv*; one *s* two *d*; one *s*. *Educ:* Winchester Coll.; Christ Church, Oxford. MA 1st cl. hons PPE, 1960. President of the Union, 1960. Nuffield Coll., 1960. Midshipman and Sub-Lt RNVR, 1956–57. Asst Principal 1961–64, Private Sec. to Jt Perm. Sec. 1964, Principal 1964–67, HM Treasury; Economics Editor, The Times, 1967–77, and Associate Editor, Times Business News, 1969–77; Presenter, Weekend World (ITV Sunday morning series), 1972–77; The Jay Interview (ITV series), 1975–76; Ambassador to US, 1977–79; Dir Economist Intelligence Unit, 1979–83. Vis. Scholar, Brookings Instn, Washington, 1979–80; Wincott Meml Lectr, 1975; Copland Meml Lectr, Australia, 1980; Shell Lectr, Glasgow, 1985. Consultant, Economist Gp, 1979–81; Chm. and Chief Exec., TV-am Ltd, 1980–83 and TV-am News, 1982–83, Pres., TV-am, 1983–; Presenter, A Week in Politics, Channel 4, 1983–86; Supervising Editor, Banking World, 1986– (Editor, 1984–86). Chm., NACRO Working

Party on Children and Young Persons in Custody, 1976–77; Chairman: NCVO, 1981–86; United Way (UK) Ltd, 1982–83; United Way Feasibility Studies Steering Cttee, 1982–83; United Funds Ltd, 1983–85; United Funds Adv. Cttee, 1983–85; Mem. Council, Cinema and TV Benevolent Fund, 1982–83; Trustee, Charities Aid Foundn, 1981–; Chm., Charities Effectiveness Review Trust, 1986–. Governor, Ditchley Foundn, 1982–; Mem. Council, St George's House, Windsor, 1982–. Dir, New Nat. Theater, Washington, DC, 1979–81. Political Broadcaster of Year, 1973; Harold Wincott Financial and Economic Journalist of Year, 1973; Royal TV Soc.'s Male Personality of Year (Pye Award), 1974; SFTA Shell Internat. TV Award, 1974. FRSA 1975; FRGS 1977. Hon. DH Ohio State Univ., 1978; Hon. DLitt Wake Forest Univ., 1979; Berkeley Citation, Univ. of Calif. 1979. Publications: The Budget, 1972; (contrib.) America and the World 1979, 1980; The Crisis for Western Political Economy and other Essays, 1984. contrib. Foreign Affairs jl. Recreation: sailing. Address: 39 Castlebar Road, W5 2DJ. T: 01–998 3570. Clubs: Garrick; Royal Naval Sailing Association, Royal Cork Yacht.

JAYAWARDANA, Brig. Christopher Allan Hector Perera, CMG 1956; CVO 1954; OBE 1944 (MBE 1941); ED 1936; JP; FLS; KStJ; *b* 29 March 1898; 4th *s* of Gate Muhandiram Herat Perera Jayawardana; *m* 1924, Sylvia Dorothy Samarasinhe, *e d* of late Mudaliyar Soloman Dias Samarasinhe; (one *s* one *d* decd). *Educ:* Trinity Coll., Kandy, Ceylon; Keble Coll., Oxford (MA). Sen. Asst Conservator of Forests, Ceylon (retd); Dep. Warden of Wild Life, Ceylon (retd), 1924–29; served War of 1939–45; OC 1st Bn the Ceylon LI, 1938–43; Chief Comr, Ceylon Boy Scouts' Association, 1949–54; Extra Aide de Camp to HE the Governor Gen. of Ceylon, 1949–; Equerry to HM the Queen, during Royal Visit to Ceylon, 1954; Hon. ADC to the Queen, 1954–. Awarded Silver Wolf, 1949. FLS, 1924. Carnegie Schol., 1931; Smith-Mundt Schol., 1951; KStJ, 1959 (CStJ, 1954). Diploma of Forestry. *Recreations:* rifle shooting, big game hunting, deep sea fishing, golf, tennis, riding, painting, camping, photography. *Clubs:* Corona; Sea Anglers' (Sri Lanka).

JAYES, Percy Harris, MB, BS, FRCS; Plastic Surgeon: St Bartholomew's Hospital, London, 1952–73; Queen Victoria Hospital, East Grinstead, 1948–73; Consultant in Plastic Surgery to the Royal Air Force, since 1960; Consultant Plastic Surgeon, King Edward VII Hospital for Officers since 1966; *b* 26 June 1915; *s* of Thomas Harris Jayes; *m* 1945, Kathleen Mary Harrington (*d* 1963); two *s* one *d*; *m* 1964, Aileen Mary McLaughlin; one *s* one *d*. *Educ:* Merchant Taylors' Sch.; St Bartholomew's Hosp. Resid. Plastic Surg., EMS Plastic Unit, East Grinstead, 1940–48; Surgeon in Charge, UNRRA Plastic Unit, Belgrade, 1946; Mem. Council, Brit. Assoc. Plastic Surgeons, 1954–64 (Pres., Assoc., 1960). *Publications:* contrib. British Journal of Plastic Surgery, Annals of Royal College of Surgeons and other journals. *Recreation:* tennis. *Address:* Barton St Mary, Lewes Road, East Grinstead. *T:* East Grinstead 23461; 149 Harley Street, W1N 2DE. *T:* 01–935 4444.

JAYEWARDENE, Junius Richard, President of Sri Lanka, since 1978; Minister of Defence, and of Plan Implementation, since 1977; Minister of Power and of Energy, since 1981; *b* Colombo, 17 Sept. 1906; *s* of Mr Justice E. W. Jayewardene, KC and A. H. Jayewardene; *m* 1935, Elina B. Rupesinghe; one *s*. *Educ:* Royal Coll., Colombo; Ceylon University Coll.; Ceylon Law Coll. Sworn Advocate of Supreme Court of Ceylon, 1932. Joined Ceylon Nat. Congress, later United Nat. Party, 1938; Hon. Sec., 1940–47; Hon. Treasurer, 1946–48, 1957–58; Vice-Pres., 1954–56, 1958–72; Sec., 1972–73; Pres., 1973–. Member: Colombo Municipal Council, 1940–43; State Council, 1943–47; House of Representatives, 1947–56, 1960–77 (Leader, 1953–56); Minister of: Agriculture and Food, 1953–56; Finance, 1947–52, 1952–53, 1960; Chief Opposition Whip, 1960–65; Minister of State and Parly Sec. to Prime Minister, Minister of Defence and External Affairs, and Chief Govt Whip, 1965–70; Leader of the Opposition, House of Representatives, 1970–72, Nat. State Assembly, 1972–77; Prime Minister, and Minister of Planning and Economic Affairs, 1977. Was a co-author of Colombo Plan, 1950; has been leader of delegations to many UN and Commonwealth conferences; Governor, World Bank and IMF, 1947–52. *Publications:* Some Sermons of Buddha, 1940; Buddhist Essays; In Council, 1946; Buddhism and Marxism, 1950, 3rd edn 1957; Selected Speeches. *Address:* President's House, Colombo, Sri Lanka.

JAYSTON, Michael, (Michael James); actor; *b* 29 Oct. 1935; *s* of Aubrey Vincent James and Edna Myfanwy Llewelyn; *m* 1st, 1965, Lynn Farleigh (marr. diss 1970); 2nd, Heather Mary Sneddon (marr. diss. 1977); 3rd, 1978, Elizabeth Ann Smithson; three *s* one *d*. *Educ:* Becket Grammar School, Nottingham; Guildhall Sch. of Music and Drama (FGSM). *Stage:* Salisbury Playhouse, 1962–63 (parts incl. Henry II, in Becket); Bristol Old Vic, 1963–65; RSC, 1965–69 (incl. Ghosts, All's Well That Ends Well, Hamlet, The Homecoming (NY), The Relapse); Equus, NT, 1973, Albery, 1977; Private Lives, Duchess, 1980; The Sound of Music, Apollo, 1981; The Way of the World, Chichester, 1984, Haymarket, 1985; *films include:* Midsummer Night's Dream, 1968; Cromwell, 1969; Nicholas and Alexandra, 1970; *television includes:* Beethoven, 1969; Mad Jack, 1970; Wilfred Owen, 1971; The Power Game, 1978; Tinker, Tailor, Soldier, Spy, 1979. Life Mem., Battersea Dogs Home. *Recreations:* cricket, darts, chess. *Address:* c/o Michael Whitehall, 125 Gloucester Road, SW7. *Clubs:* MCC, Lord's Taverners', Eccentric, Cricketers'; Gedling Colliery CC (Vice-Pres.); Rottingdean CC.

JEAFFRESON, David Gregory, CBE 1981; Secretary for Security, Hong Kong Government, since 1982; *b* 21 Nov. 1931; *s* of Bryan Leslie Jeaffreson, MD, FRCS, MRCOG and Margaret Jeaffreson; *m* 1959, Elisabeth Marie Jausions; two *s* two *d* (and one *d* decd). *Educ:* Bootham Sch., York; Clare Coll., Cambridge (MA). 2nd Lieut, RA, 1950. Dist Officer, Tanganyika, 1955–58; Asst Man., Henricot Steel Foundry, 1959–60; Admin. Officer, Hong Kong Govt, 1961; Dep. Financial Sec., 1972–76; Sec. for Economic Services, 1976–82. *Recreations:* French and Chinese history, music, sailing and walking. *Address:* 64 Mount Nicholson, Hong Kong. *T:* 5–730551. *Club:* Royal Hong Kong Yacht.

JEANES, Leslie Edwin Elloway, CBE 1982; Chief of Public Relations, Ministry of Defence, 1978–81, retired; *b* 17 Dec. 1920; *er s* of late Edwin Eli Jubilee Jeanes and of Mary Eunice Jeanes; *m* 1942, Valerie Ruth, *d* of Ernest and Ethel Vidler; one *d*. *Educ:* Westcliff High Sch. Entered Civil Service, 1939; Inf. Officer, DSIR, 1948–65; Chief Press Officer, Min. of Technol., 1965–68; Dep. Head of Inf., MoT, 1968–70; Head of News, DoE, 1970–73; Chief Inf. Officer, MAFF, 1973–78. *Recreations:* bowls, gardening, motoring, DIY. *Address:* 14 Whistley Close, Bracknell, Berks. *T:* Bracknell 429429. *Club:* Hurst Bowling.
See also R. E. Jeanes.

JEANES, Ronald Eric; Deputy Director, Building Research Establishment, 1981–86; *b* 23 Sept. 1926; *s* of Edwin and Eunice Jeanes; *m* 1951, Helen Field (née Entwistle); one *s* one *d*. *Educ:* University Coll., Exeter (BSc 1951). Served HM Forces, 1945–48. Royal Naval Scientific Service, 1951–62; BRE, 1962–86. *Publications:* DoE and BRE reports. *Recreation:* amateur theatre. *Address:* 1 Wrensfield, Hemel Hempstead, Herts HP1 1RN. *T:* Hemel Hempstead 58713.
See also L. E. E. Jeanes.

JEAPES, Maj.-Gen. Anthony Showan, OBE 1977; MC 1960; Commander, Land Forces Northern Ireland, since 1985; *b* 6 March 1935; *s* of Stanley Arthur Jeapes; *m* 1959, Jennifer Clare White; one *s* one *d*. *Educ:* Grammar Sch.; RMA Sandhurst. Commissioned Dorset Regt, 1955; joined 22 SAS Regt, 1958; attached US Special Forces, 1961; Staff College, 1966; Brigade Major, 39 Inf. Bde, NI, 1967; Sqn Comdr, 22 SAS Regt, 1968; Nat. Defence Coll., 1971; Directing Staff, Staff Coll., Camberley, 1972; CO 22 SAS Regt, 1974; Mem., British Mil. Adv. Team, Bangladesh, 1977; Dep. Comdr, Sch. of Infantry, 1979; Comdr, 5 Airborne Brigade, 1982. *Publication:* SAS Operation, Oman, 1980. *Recreations:* offshore sailing, deer stalking. *Address:* HQ Northern Ireland, British Forces Post Office 825.

JEBB, family name of **Baron Gladwyn.**

JEBB, Dom Anthony Philip, MA; Head Master, Downside School, since 1980; *b* 14 Aug. 1932; 2nd *s* of late Reginald Jebb and Eleanor, *d* of Hilaire Belloc. *Educ:* Downside; Christ's Coll., Cambridge, 1957–60 (MA Classics). Professed at Downside, 1951; priest, 1956; Curate, Midsomer Norton, 1960–62; teaching at Downside, 1960–; House master, 1962–75; Dep. Head Master, 1975–80. Archivist and Annalist, English Benedictine Congregation, 1972–; Mem., EBC Theological Commn, 1969–82 (Chm., 1979–82); Delegate to General Chapter, EBC, 1981–; Member: Council, Somerset Records Soc., 1975–; Cttee, Area 7, SHA, 1984–; Court, Bath Univ., 1983–. Vice-Pres., SW Amateur Fencing Assoc., 1970–. Chaplain of Magistral Obedience, British Assoc., Sovereign Mil. Order of Malta, 1978–. *Publications:* Missale de Lesnes, 1964; Religious Education, 1968; Widowed, 1973, 2nd edn 1976; contrib. Consider Your Call, 1978, 2nd edn 1979; A Touch of God, 1982; contribs to Downside Review, The Way, The Sword. *Recreations:* fencing, archaeology, astronomy, canoeing. *Address:* Downside School, Stratton-on-the-Fosse, Bath BA3 4RJ. *T:* Stratton-on-the-Fosse 232206.

JEDDERE-FISHER, Arthur; Solicitor, Customs and Excise, 1982–85; *b* 15 July 1924; *s* of late Major Harry and Sarah Jeddere-Fisher; *m* 1947, Marcia Vincent, *d* of Kenneth Clarence Smith; three *s* one *d*. *Educ:* Harrow Sch.; Christ Church, Oxford (MA). Served War of 1939–45, Air Engineer, Royal Navy, 1942–46 (despatches). Called to Bar, Inner Temple, 1949; Magistrate, Senior Magistrate and Chairman Land Tribunal, Fiji, 1953–69; joined Solicitor's Office, HM Customs and Excise, 1970, Principal Asst Solicitor, 1977–82. *Recreations:* the collection and use of historic machinery, cricket, bird photography. *Address:* Apsley Cottage, Kingston Blount, Oxford. *T:* Kingston Blount 51300. *Clubs:* MCC, Vintage Sports Car.

JEELOF, Gerrit, CBE (Hon.) 1981; Vice Chairman, Philips Lamps, Eindhoven, since 1986; *b* 13 May 1927; *m* 1951, Jantje Aleida Plinsinga; two *d*. *Educ:* Dutch Trng Inst. for Foreign Trade, Nijenrode. Philips Industries: Eindhoven, Holland, 1950–53; Spain and S America, 1953–65; Eindhoven, Holland, 1965–70; Varese, Italy, 1970–76; Chm. and Man. Dir, Philips Industries UK, 1976–80. Commendatore nel Ordine al Merito della Repubblica Italiana, 1974; Officer, Order of Oranje-Nassau (Netherlands), 1985. *Recreations:* sailing, golf. *Address:* NV Philips' Gloeilampenfabrieken, Eindhoven, Netherlands. *T:* Eindhoven 79 11 11. *Clubs:* Royal Thames Yacht, Royal Ocean Racing; Royal Yacht Squadron.

JEEPS, Richard Eric Gautrey, CBE 1977; Chairman, Sports Council, 1978–85; Director, Roger Shackleton Associates; *b* 25 Nov. 1931; *s* of Francis Herbert and Mildred Mary Jeeps; *m* 1954, Jean Margaret Levitt (marr. diss.); three *d*. *Educ:* Bedford Modern Sch. Rugby career: Cambridge City, 1948–49; Northampton, 1949–62 and 1964; Eastern Counties, 1950–62; England, 1956–62 (24 caps); Barbarians, 1958–62; British Lions: SA, 1955; NZ, 1959; SA 1962; 13 Tests. Rugby Football Union: Mem. Cttee, 1962–; Pres., 1976–77. Mem., English Tourist Bd, 1984–. Cttee Mem., Sparks (Charity); Trustee, Sports Aid Trust; Governor, Sports Aid Foundn. *Recreations:* Rugby Union football, sport. *Address:* St Mark, Snailwell Road, Newmarket, Suffolk. *Club:* Lord's Taverners.

JEEVES, Prof. Malcolm Alexander, FBPsS; FRSE; Professor of Psychology, University of St Andrews, since 1969; *b* 16 Nov. 1926; *s* of Alderman Alexander Frederic Thomas Jeeves and Helena May Jeeves (née Hammond); *m* 1955, Ruth Elisabeth Hartridge; two *d*. *Educ:* Stamford Sch.; St John's Coll., Cambridge (MA, PhD). Commissioned Royal Lincs Regt, served 1st Bn Sherwood Foresters, BAOR, 1945–48. Cambridge University: Exhibnr, St John's Coll., 1948, Res. Exhibnr, 1952; Burney Student, 1952; Gregg Bury Prizeman, 1954; Kenneth Craik Res. Award, St John's Coll., 1955. Rotary Foundn Fellow, Harvard, 1953; Lectr, Leeds Univ., 1956; Prof. of Psychology, Adelaide Univ., 1959–69, and Dean, Faculty of Arts, 1962–64; Vice-Principal, St Andrews Univ., 1981–85; Dir, MRC Cognitive Neuroscience Res. Gp, St Andrews, 1984–. Lectures: Abbie Meml, Adelaide Univ., 1981; Cairns Meml, Aust., 1986. Member: SSRC Psych. Cttee, 1972–76; Biol. Cttee, 1980–84, Science Bd, 1985–, Council, 1985–, SERC; MRC Neuroscience and Mental Health Bd, 1985–; Council, 1984–, Exec., 1985–, RSE. Hon. Sheriff, Fife, 1986–. *Publications:* (with Z. P. Dienes) Thinking in Structures, 1965 (trans. French, German, Spanish, Italian, Japanese); (with Z. P. Dienes) The Effects of Structural Relations upon Transfer, 1968; The Scientific Enterprise and Christian Faith, 1969; Experimental Psychology: an introduction for Biologists, 1974; Psychology and Christianity: the view both ways, 1976 (trans. Chinese); (with G. B. Greer) Analysis of Structural Learning, 1983; (with R. J. Berry and D. Atkinson) Free to be Different, 1984; Behavioural Sciences: a Christian perspective, 1984; papers in sci. jls, mainly on neuropsycology and cognition. *Recreations:* music, fly fishing, walking. *Address:* Psychology Laboratory, The University, St Andrews KY16 9JU. *T:* St Andrews 76161.

JEEWOOLALL, Sir Ramesh, Kt 1979; *b* 20 Dec. 1940; *s* of Shivprasad Jeewoolall; *m* 1971, Usweenee (née Reetoo); two *s*. *Educ:* in Mauritius; Inns of Court Sch. of Law. Called to the Bar, Middle Temple, 1968; practising at the Bar, 1969–71; Magistrate, 1971–72; practising at the Bar and Chm., Mauritius Tea Develt Authority, 1972–76. Mem., Mauritius Parlt, 1976–82; Dep. Speaker, 1977–79; Speaker, 1979–82. *Recreations:* reading, conversation, chess. *Address:* Q1, Farquhar Avenue, Quatre Bornes, Mauritius. *T:* 4–5918.

JEFFARES, Prof. Alexander Norman, (Derry Jeffares); MA, PhD, DPhil; Docteur de l'Université (hc) Lille, 1977; FRSA 1963; FRSL 1965; FRSE 1981; Professor of English Studies, Stirling University, 1974–86, Hon. Professor, since 1986; *b* 11 Aug. 1920; *s* of late C. Norman Jeffares, Dublin; *m* 1947, Jeanne Agnès, *d* of late E. Calembert, Brussels; one *d*. *Educ:* The High Sch., Dublin; Trinity Coll., Dublin (Hon. Fellow, 1978); Oriel Coll., Oxford. Lectr in Classics, Univ. of Dublin, 1943–44; Lector in English, Univ. of Groningen, 1946–48; Lectr in English, Univ. of Edinburgh, 1949–51; Jury Prof. of English Language and Literature, Univ. of Adelaide, 1951–56; Prof. of English Lit., Leeds Univ., 1957–74. Sec., Australian Humanities Res. Council, 1954–57; Corresp. Mem. for Great Britain and Ireland, 1958–70; Hon. Fellow, Aust. Acad. of the Humanities, 1970–. Mem. Council, RSE, 1985–; Scottish Arts Council: Mem., 1979–84; Vice Chm., 1980–84; Chm., Literature Cttee, 1979–83; Chm., Touring Cttee, 1983–84; Chm., Housing the Arts, 1980–84; Mem., Arts Council of GB, 1980–84. Chm., NBL (Scotland), 1984–; Mem. Ecec. Cttee, NBL, 1984–. Vice-Pres., Film and Television Council of S Aust., 1951–56; Chairman: Assoc. for Commonwealth Literature and Language Studies,

1966–68, Hon. Fellow, 1971; Internat. Assoc. for Study of Anglo-Irish Literature, 1968–70, Co-Chm., 1971–73, Hon. Life Pres., 1973–; Dir, Yeats Internat. Summer Sch., Sligo, 1969–71. Editor, A Review of English Literature, 1960–67; General Editor: Writers and Critics, 1960–73; New Oxford English Series, 1963–; Joint Editor, Biography and Criticism, 1963–73; Literary Editor, Fountainwell Drama Texts, 1968–75; Co-Editor, York Notes, 1980–; Editor: Ariel, A Review of Internat. English Literature, 1970–72; York Handbooks, 1984–. *Publications*: Trinity College, Dublin: drawings and descriptions, 1944; W. B. Yeats: man and poet, 1949, rev. edn 1962; Seven Centuries of Poetry, 1955, rev. edn 1960; (with M. Bryn Davies) The Scientific Background, 1958; The Poetry of W. B. Yeats, 1961; (ed with G. F. Cross) In Excited Reverie: centenary tribute to W. B. Yeats, 1965; Fair Liberty was All His Cry: a tercentenary tribute to Jonathan Swift 1667–1743, 1967; A Commentary on the Collected Poems of W. B. Yeats, 1968; (ed) Restoration Comedy, 4 vols, 1974; (with A. S. Knowland) A Commentary on the Collected Plays of W. B. Yeats, 1975; (ed) Yeats: the critical heritage, 1977; A History of Anglo-Irish Literature, 1982; A New Commentary on the Poems of W. B. Yeats, 1984; also: edns of works by Congreve, Farquhar, Goldsmith, Sheridan, Cowper, Maria Edgeworth, Disraeli, Whitman and Yeats; edns of criticisms of Swift, Scott and Yeats; various monographs on Swift, Goldsmith, George Moore, Yeats, Oliver St John Gogarty; contribs to learned jls. *Recreations*: drawing, motoring. *Address*: Wester Moss, Rumbling Bridge, Kinross. *Clubs*: Athenæum, Royal Commonwealth Society.

JEFFCOATE, Sir (Thomas) Norman (Arthur), Kt 1970; Professor of Obstetrics and Gynæcology, University of Liverpool, 1945–72, now Emeritus; Hon. Consultant Obstetrical and Gynæcological Surgeon, Liverpool Area Health Authority (Teaching); *b* 25 March 1907; *s* of Arthur Jeffcoate and Mary Ann Oakey; *m* 1937, Josephine Lindsay (*d* 1981); four *s*. *Educ*: King Edward VI Sch., Nuneaton; University of Liverpool. MB, ChB (Liverpool) 1st class Hons 1929; MD (Liverpool) 1932; FRCS (Edinburgh) 1932; MRCOG 1932; FRCOG 1939 (Vice-Pres., 1967–69; Pres. 1969–72). Hon. Asst Surgeon: Liverpool Maternity Hosp., 1932–45; Women's Hosp., Liverpool, 1935–45. Lectures: Blair-Bell Memorial, Royal College of Obst. and Gynaec. 1938; Sir Arcot Mudalier, Univ. of Madras, 1955; Margaret Orford, S African Coll. of Physicians, Surgeons and Gynaecologists, 1969; J. Y. Simpson, RCSE, 1976. Joseph Price Orator, Amer. Assoc. of Obstetricians and Gynaecologists, 1966. Sims Black Travelling Commonwealth Prof., 1958; Visiting Professor: New York State Univ., 1955; University of Qld, 1964; Univ. of Melbourne, 1964; Univ. of Texas, 1965; Hon. Visiting Obstetrician and Gynæcologist, Royal Prince Alfred Hospital, Sydney, Australia, 1955–. Chairman, Med. Advisory Council of Liverpool Regional Hosp. Bd, 1962–69; President: N of England Obst. and Gynaec. Soc., 1960; Sect. of Obst. and Gynaec., RSM, 1965–66; Liverpool Med. Inst., 1966–67; Vice-Pres. Family Planning Assoc., 1962–79; Member: Gen. Med. Council, 1951–61; Clinical Research Bd, MRC, 1961–65; Clinical Trials Sub-Cttee of Safety of Drugs Cttee, 1963–69; Bd of Science and Educn, BMA, 1968–69; Standing Maternity and Midwifery Adv. Cttee, Dept of Health and Social Security (formerly Min. of Health), 1963–72 (Chm., 1970–72); Standing Med. Adv. Cttee and Central Health Services Council, Dept of Health and Social Security, 1969–72; Jt Sub-Cttee on Prevention of Haemolytic Disease of the Newborn, 1968–72 (Chm., 1969–72). Hon. FCOG(SA), 1972; Hon. FACOG, 1972; Hon. FRCS (C), 1973; Hon. Member: Amer. Gynec. Club; Amer. Gynec. Soc.; Amer. Assoc. Obst. and Gynec.; Central Assoc. Obst. and Gynec.; Assoc. Surg., Ceylon; Obst. and Gynaec. Socs of: Canada, Finland, Honolulu, Malta, Montreal, Panama, S Africa, Uruguay, Venezuela. Hon. LLD, TCD, 1971. Eardley Holland Gold Medal, RCOG, 1975; Simpson Gold Medal, RCSE, 1976. *Publications*: Principles of Gynæcology, 1957, 4th edn, 1975, 5th edn (rev. V. R. Tindall) as Jeffcoate's Principles of Gynaecology, 1986; communications to medical journals. *Address*: 6 Riversdale Road, Liverpool L19 3QW. *T*: 051–427 1448.

JEFFERIES, David George; Deputy Chairman, Electricity Council, since 1986 (Member since 1981); *b* 26 Dec. 1933; *s* of Rose and George Jefferies; *m* 1959, Jeanette Ann Hanson. *Educ*: SE Coll. of Technology. CEng, FIEE, CBIM, FInstE. Southern Electricity Board: Area Manager, Portsmouth, 1967–72; Staff Coll., Henley, 1970; Chief Engr, 1972–74; Dir, NW Region, CEGB, 1974–77; Dir Personnel, CEGB, 1977–81; Chm., London Electricity Bd, 1981–86. Member: Council, IEE, 1984–; Bd of Governors, London Business Sch., 1980–84. Liveryman, Wax Chandlers' Co., 1984–. *Recreations*: golf, gardening. *Address*: Wychenwood, Gorse Hill Lane, Virginia Water, Surrey. *T*: Wentworth 3623.

JEFFERIES, Roger David; Chief Executive, London Borough of Hounslow, since 1975; *b* 13 Oct. 1939; *s* of George Edward Jefferies and Freda Rose Jefferies (*née* Marshall); *m* 1st, 1962, Jennifer Anne Southgate (marr. diss.); one *s* two *d*; 2nd, 1974, Margaret Sealy (marr. diss.); 3rd, 1984, Pamela Mary Elsey (*née* Holden); one *s*. *Educ*: Whitgift School; Balliol College, Oxford. BA, BCL; solicitor. Mem., Law Society,1965–. Asst Solicitor, Coventry Corporation, 1965–68; Asst Town Clerk, Southend-on-Sea County Borough Council, 1968–70; Director of Operations, London Borough of Hammersmith, 1970–75; Under Secretary, DoE, 1983–85 (on secondment). *Publication*: Tackling the Town Hall, 1982. *Recreations*: the novel, theatre, travel. *Address*: c/o Civic Centre, Lampton Road, Hounslow, Middx. *T*: 01–570 7728.

JEFFERIES, Sheelagh; Deputy Director General, Central Office of Information, since 1983; *b* 25 Aug. 1926; *d* of late Norman and Vera Jefferies. *Educ*: Harrogate Grammar Sch.; Girton Coll., Cambridge (MA); Smith Coll., Northampton, Mass, USA (MA). FIPR. Archivist, RIIA, 1947–50, 1951–52; COI, 1953–60; Office of Chancellor of Duchy of Lancaster, 1960–61; Press Officer, Prime Minister's Office, 1961–67; Principal Inf. Officer, Privy Council Office, 1967–69; Chief Press Officer, Min. of Housing and Local Govt, 1969–71; Head of Parly Liaison Unit and later Head of News, DoE, 1971–74; Chief Inf. Officer, Dept of Prices and Consumer Protection, 1974–77; Dir, Overseas Press and Radio, COI, 1977–78; Controller (Home), COI, 1978–83. *Recreations*: reading, conversation. *Address*: 6 Eversfield Road, Richmond, Surrey TW9 2AP. *T*: 01–940 9229.

JEFFERIES, Stephen; Senior Principal Dancer, Royal Ballet, since 1979 (Principal Dancer, 1973–76 and 1977–79); *b* 24 June 1951; *s* of George and Barbara Jefferies; *m* 1972, Rashna Homji; one *s* one *d*. *Educ*: Turves Green Sch., Birmingham; Royal Ballet Sch. ARAD (Advanced Hons). Joined Sadler's Wells Royal Ballet, 1969; created 10 leading roles whilst with Sadler's Wells; joined National Ballet of Canada as Principal Dancer, 1976; created role of Morris, in Washington Square, 1977; returned to Royal Ballet at Covent Garden, 1977; *major roles include*: Prince in Sleeping Beauty, Swan Lake and Giselle, Prince Rudolf in Mayerling, Petruchio in Taming of the Shrew, Romeo and Mercutio in Romeo and Juliet, Lescaut in Manon; lead, in Song and Dance, 1982; *roles created*: Yukinojo (mime role), in world première of Minoru Miki's opera An Actor's Revenge, 1979; male lead in Bolero, Japan, 1980 (choreographed by Yashiro Okamoto); Antonio in The Duenna, S Africa (choreographed by Ashley Killar), 1980; lead, in Dances of Albion (choreographed by Glen Tetley), 1980; Esenin in Kenneth Macmillan's ballet, Isadora, Covent Garden, 1981; lead, in L'Invitation au Voyage, Covent Garden, 1982. Choreographed ballets: Bits and Pieces, in Canada, 1977; Mes Souvenirs, in London, 1978. Dances in Europe, USA, S America and Far East. Organiser of charity galas, 1982–. *Recreations*: golf, football, sleeping, gardening, swimming and various other sports. *Address*: c/o Royal Ballet, Royal Opera House, Covent Garden, WC2.

JEFFERS, John Norman Richard, FIS, FIBiol, FICFor; consultant; Visiting Professor, Department of Statistics, University of Newcastle; *b* 10 Sept. 1926; *s* of late Lt-Col John Harold Jeffers, OBE, and Emily Matilda Alice (*née* Robinson); *m* 1951, Edna May (*née* Parratt); one *d*. *Educ*: Portsmouth Grammar Sch.; Forestry Commission Forester Trng Sch., 1944–46. Forester in Forestry Commn Research Br., 1946–55; joined Min. of Agriculture, 1955, as Asst Statistician, after succeeding in limited competition to Statistician Class; rejoined Forestry Commn as Head of Statistics Section of Forestry Commn Research Br., 1956; Dir, Nature Conservancy's Merlewood Research Station, 1968; Dep. Dir, Inst. of Terrestrial Ecology, NERC, 1973, Dir, 1976–86. *Publications*: Experimental Design and Analysis in Forest Research, 1959; Mathematical Models in Ecology, 1972; Introduction to Systems Analysis: with ecological applications, 1978; Modelling, 1982; numerous papers in stat., forestry and ecolog. jls. *Recreations*: military history and wargaming, amateur dramatics. *Address*: Ellerhow, Lindale, Grange-over-Sands, Cumbria LA11 6NA. *T*: Grange-over-Sands 3731. *Club*: Athenæum.

JEFFERSON, Bryan; *see* Jefferson, J. B.

JEFFERSON, Sir George Rowland, Kt 1981; CBE 1969; BSc Hons (London); FEng, Hon. FIMechE, FIEE, FRAeS; FRSA; CBIM; FCGI; Chairman, British Telecommunications plc, since 1981 (Chief Executive, 1981–86; Deputy Chairman of the Post Office, 1980); *b* 26 March 1921; *s* of Harold Jefferson and Eva Elizabeth Ellen; *m* 1943, Irene Watson-Browne; three *s*. *Educ*: Grammar Sch., Dartford, Kent. Engrg Apprentice, Royal Ordnance Factory, Woolwich, 1937–42; commnd RAOC, 1942; transf. REME, 1942; served 1942–45, Anti-Aircraft Comd on heavy anti-aircraft power control systems and later Armament Design Dept, Fort Halstead, on anti-aircraft gun mounting development; subseq. Mem. Min. of Supply staff, Fort Halstead, until 1952; joined Guided Weapons Div., English Electric Co. Ltd, 1952; Chief Research Engr, 1953; Dep. Chief Engr, 1958; Dir, English Electric Aviation Ltd, 1961 (on formation of co.); British Aircraft Corporation: Dir and Chief Exec., BAC (Guided Weapons) Ltd, 1963 (on formation of Corp.), Dep. Man. Dir, 1964, Mem. Board, 1965–77, Man. Dir, 1966–68, Chm. and Man. Dir, 1968–77; a Dir, British Aerospace, and Chm. and Chief Exec., Dynamics Gp, British Aerospace, 1977–80 (Mem., Organizing Cttee, 1976–77); Chm., Stevenage/Bristol and Hatfield/Lostock Divs, Dynamics Gp, 1978–80; Chm., BAC (Anti-Tank), 1968–78; Director: British Aerospace (Australia) Ltd, 1968–80; British Scandinavian Aviation AB, 1968–80; Hawker Siddeley Dynamics, 1977–80; Engineering Sciences Data Unit Ltd, 1975–80; Babcock International, 1980–; Lloyds Bank, 1986–. Member: NEB, 1979–80; NEDC, 1981–84; NICG, 1980–84; Member Council: SBAC, 1965–80; Electronic Engineering Assoc., 1968–72; RAeS, 1977–79 (Vice-Pres., 1979). Hon. DSc Bristol, 1984; DUniv Essex, 1985. Freeman of the City of London; Liveryman, Worshipful Co. of Painter-Stainers.

JEFFERSON, Joan Ena; Headmistress, St Swithun's School, Winchester, since 1986; *b* 15 Aug. 1946; *d* of William Jefferson and Ruth Ena Leake. *Educ*: Univ. of Newcastle (BA Hons History); Westminster Coll., Oxford (Dip Ed). Asst Mistress, 1968–70, Head of History, 1970–73, Scarborough Girls' High Sch.; Head of Humanities, Graham Sch., Scarborough, 1973–75; Dep. Head, 1975–79, Headmistress, 1979–86, Hunmanby Hall Sch., Filey. *Recreations*: drama, theatre, reading, cooking, photography; Soroptimist. *Address*: St Swithun's School, Winchester, Hants. *T*: Winchester 61316. *Club*: Royal Commonwealth Society.

JEFFERSON, (John) Bryan, CBE 1983; PPRIBA; Director-General of Design Services, Property Services Agency, Department of the Environment, since 1984; *b* 26 April 1928; *s* of John Jefferson and Marjorie Jefferson (*née* Oxley); *m* 1954, Alison Gray (marr. diss. 1965); three *s*. *Educ*: Lady Manners Sch., Bakewell; Sheffield Univ. DipArch 1954. ARIBA 1954. Morrison and Partners, Derby, 1955–57; established practice in Sheffield and London with Gerald F. Sheard, 1957; Sen. Partner, Jefferson Sheard and Partners, 1957–84. President: Sheffield Soc. of Architects, 1973–74; Concrete Soc., 1977–78; RIBA, 1979–81; Chm., RIBA Yorks Region, 1974–75. Hon. FRAIC, 1980. Hon. DEng Bradford, 1986. *Publications*: broadcasts; articles in lay and professional jls. *Recreations*: music, sailing offshore. *Address*: 6 St Andrews Mansions, Dorset Street, W1H 3FD. *Clubs*: Savile; Royal Western Yacht.

JEFFERSON, Sir Mervyn Stewart D.; *see* Dunnington-Jefferson.

JEFFERY, George Henry Padget, CMG 1965; FASA; Auditor General for South Australia, 1959–72; Chairman, Board of Trustees, Savings Bank of South Australia, 1972–76 (Trustee, 1965–76); *b* 6 June 1907; *s* of late George Frederick Jeffery and late Adelaide Jeffery (*née* Padget), Victor Harbour, S Aust.; *m* 1934, Jean Loudon Watt, *d* of late Thomas Watt, Adelaide; two *s*. *Educ*: Adelaide High Sch.; Victor Harbour High Sch.; University of Adelaide. Associate, University of Adelaide, 1933; Auditor, SA Public Service, 1936–40, Chief Inspector, 1940–51; Sec., Public Buildings Dept, 1951–53; Chief Executive, Radium Hill Uranium Project, 1953–59; Mem., SA Public Service Board, 1956–59. Pres., SA Div., Aust. Soc. of Accountants, 1965–67. Chm., Royal Commission of Enquiry into Grape Growing Industry, 1965. Member: Parly. Salaries Tribunal, 1966–79; Royal Commn on State Transport Services, 1966–67; Cttee of Inquiry into S Australian Racing Industry, 1974–75. Dep. Chm., S Australian Egg Bd, 1973–79. Mem., Bd of Management, Queen Victoria Hosp., 1972–76. FASA 1958. *Recreations*: bowls, cricket. *Address*: 49 Anglesey Avenue, St Georges, SA 5064, Australia. *T*: 79–2929. *Clubs*: Commonwealth, SA Cricket Association, Glenunga Bowling (Adelaide).

JEFFERY, Ven. Robert Martin Colquhoun; Archdeacon of Salop, since 1980; *b* 30 April 1935; *s* of Norman Clare Jeffery and Gwenyth Isabel Jeffery; *m* 1968, Ruth Margaret Tinling; three *s* one *d*. *Educ*: St Paul's School; King's Coll., London (BD, AKC). Assistant Curate: St Aidan, Grangetown, 1959–61; St Mary, Barnes, 1961–63; Asst Sec., Missionary and Ecumenical Council of Church Assembly, 1964–68; Sec., Dept of Mission and Unity, BCC, 1968–71; Vicar, St Andrew, Headington, Oxford, 1971–78; RD of Cowley, 1973–78; Lichfield Diocesan Missioner, 1978–79. Mem., Gen. Synod of C of E, 1982–. *Publications*: (with D. M. Paton) Christian Unity and the Anglican Communion, 1965, 3rd edn 1968; (with T. S. Garret) Unity in Nigeria, 1964; (ed) Lambeth Conference 1968 Preparatory Information; Areas of Ecumenical Experiment, 1968; Ecumenical Experiments: A Handbook, 1971; Case Studies in Unity, 1972. *Recreations*: local history, cooking. *Address*: Tong Vicarage, Tong, Shifnal, Salop TF11 8PW. *T*: Albrighton 2622.

JEFFORD, Barbara Mary, OBE 1965; Actress; *b* Plymstock, Devon, 26 July 1930; *d* of late Percival Francis Jefford and Elizabeth Mary Ellen (*née* Laity); *m* 1953, Terence Longdon (marr. diss., 1961); *m* 1967, John Arnold Turner. *Educ*: Weirfield Sch., Taunton, Som. Studied for stage, Bristol and Royal Academy of Dramatic Art (Bancroft Gold Medal). *Stratford-on-Avon*: (1950–54) Isabella in Measure for Measure; Desdemona in Othello; Rosalind in As You Like It; Katharina in The Taming of the Shrew; toured NZ with NZ Players' Company in The Lady's Not for Burning, 1954–55; Andromache in Tiger at the Gates, London and USA, 1955 and 1956; *Old Vic Company*: (1956–62)

Imogen in Cymbeline; Beatrice in Much Ado About Nothing; Portia in The Merchant of Venice; Queen Margaret in Henry VI; Ophelia in Hamlet; Lady Macbeth; Beatrice in The Cenci; Gwendolen Fairfax in The Importance of Being Earnest; Saint Joan; Lavinia in Mourning Becomes Electra; *for Prospect, at Old Vic:* (1977–79) Gertrude in Hamlet; Cleopatra in All for Love; Cleopatra in Antony and Cleopatra; Nurse in Romeo and Juliet; Anna in The Government Inspector; RSC Nat. Tour, 1980, Mistress Quickly in Henry IV pts 1 and 2. *Other London stage appearances include:* Lina in Misalliance, Royal Court and Criterion, 1963; step-daughter in Six Characters in Search of an Author, Mayfair, 1963; Nan in Ride a Cock Horse, Piccadilly, 1965; Patsy Newquist in Little Murders, Aldwych, 1967; Mother Vauzou in Mistress of Novices, Piccadilly, 1973; Gertrude in Hamlet and Zabina in Tamburlaine the Great, Nat. Theatre, 1976; Filumena, Lyric, 1979; Grace Winslow in The Winslow Boy, Lyric, 1983; On the Edge (world première), Hampstead, 1985. *Other stage appearances include:* Pearl in Our Betters, Nottingham Playhouse, Malvern Fest. and national tour, 1982; Last Summer in Chulimsk (British Première), Birmingham Rep., 1984; Chance Visitor (British première), Palace, Watford, 1984; Veronica's Room, national tour, 1986; has appeared regularly since 1962 at Oxford Playhouse, (plays include The Dance of Death, 1984), Nottingham Playhouse, and Bristol Old Vic, at festivals in Aldenburgh, Bath Chichester and Edinburgh; has toured extensively in UK, Europe, USA, Near East, Far East, Africa, Australia, Russia, Poland and Yugoslavia. *Films:* Ulysses, 1967; A Midsummer Night's Dream, 1967; The Shoes of the Fisherman, 1968; To Love a Vampire, 1970; Hitler: the last ten days, 1973; And the Ship Sails On, 1983. Has appeared in numerous television and radio plays. Silver Jubilee Medal, 1977. *Recreations:* music, swimming, gardening. *Address:* c/o Fraser and Dunlop Ltd, 91 Regent Street, W1R 8RU.

JEFFREYS, family name of **Baron Jeffreys.**

JEFFREYS, 3rd Baron *cr* 1952, of Burkham; **Christopher Henry Mark Jeffreys;** Futures Broker, GNI Ltd, since 1985; *b* 22 May 1957; *s* of 2nd Baron Jeffreys and of Sarah Annabelle Mary, *d* of Major Henry Garnett; *S* father, 1986; *m* 1985, Anne Elisabeth Johnson. *Educ:* Eton. *Recreations:* country sports. *Heir: b* Hon. Alexander Charles Darell Jeffreys, *b* 14 May 1959. *Address:* 23 Alderville Road, SW6. *Clubs:* White's, Annabel's.

JEFFREYS, Dr Alec John, FRS 1986; Reader in Genetics, University of Leicester, since 1984; Lister Institute Research Fellow, since 1982; *b* 9 Jan. 1950; *s* of Sidney Victor Jeffreys and Joan (*née* Knight); *m* 1971, Susan Miles; two *d. Educ:* Luton Grammar School; Luton VIth Form College; Merton College, Oxford (Postmaster; Christopher Welch Schol.; BA, MA, DPhil 1975). EMBO Research Fellow, Univ. of Amsterdam, 1975–77; Lectr, Dept of Genetics, Univ. of Leicester, 1977–84. Mem., EMBO, 1983. Editor, Jl of Molecular Evolution, 1985. Colworth Medal for Biochemistry, Biochem. Soc., 1985; UK Patent application on genetic fingerprints. *Publications:* research articles on molecular genetics and evolution in Nature, Cell, etc. *Recreations:* philately, postal history, swimming, auctioneering.

JEFFREYS, David Alfred, QC 1981; a Recorder of the Crown Court, since 1979; *b* 1 July 1934; *s* of Coleman and Ruby Jeffreys; *m* 1964, Mary Ann Elizabeth Long; one *s* one *d. Educ:* Harrow; Trinity Coll., Cambridge (BA Hons). Served, Royal Signals, 1952–54; City, 1958. Called to the Bar, Gray's Inn, 1958; Junior Prosecuting Counsel to the Crown: Inner London Crown Court, 1974; Central Criminal Court, 1975; Sen. Prosecuting Counsel to the Crown, CCC, 1979–81. Member, Bar Council and Senate of the Inns of Court and Bar, 1977–80. *Address:* (chambers) Queen Elizabeth Building, Temple, EC4Y 9BS.

JEFFREYS, Sir Harold, Kt 1953; MA Cambridge; DSc Durham; FRS 1925; Fellow of St John's College, Cambridge, since 1914; Plumian Professor of Astronomy and Experimental Philosophy, 1946–58; *b* 22 April 1891; *o s* of R. H. and E. M. Jeffreys, Birtley, Durham; *m* 1940, Bertha, *d* of late W. A. Swirles and H. Swirles, Northampton. *Educ:* Armstrong Coll., Newcastle upon Tyne; St John's Coll., Cambridge. University Reader in Geophysics, 1931–46. Mathematical Tripos, 1913; Isaac Newton Student, 1914; Smith's Prize, 1915; Adams Prize, 1927; commended, 1923; Buchan Prize of Royal Meteorological Society, 1929. Gold Medal of Royal Astronomical Society, 1937; Murchison Medal of Geological Soc., 1939; Victoria Medal of RGS, 1942; Royal Medal of Royal Society, 1948; Ch. Lagrange Prize, Acad. Royal Sci., Belg., 1948; Bowie Medal, Amer. Geophys. Union, 1952; Copley Medal, Royal Society, 1960; Vetlesen Prize, 1962; Guy Medal, Royal Statistical Society, 1963; Wollaston Medal, Geological Soc., 1964; Medal of Seismological Soc. of Amer., 1979. President: Royal Astronomical Soc., 1955–57; Internat. Seism. Assoc., 1957–60; For. Associate, US Nat. Acad. of Sciences; Accad. dei Lincei, Rome, Acad. Sci. Stockholm, New York Acad. Sci., Amer. Acad. of Arts and Sciences, Acad. Roy. de Belgique; Hon. FRSE; Hon. FRSNZ; Corresp. Member: Amer. Geophys. Union; Geolog. Soc. America; RIA; Hon. Member: Inst. of Mathematics; Seismological Soc. of Amer.; RMetS; Hon. Corresponding-Astronomer, Royal Observatory of Belgium, 1984. Hon. LLD Liverpool, 1953; Hon. ScD Dublin, 1956; Hon. DCL Durham, 1960; Hon. DSc, Southern Methodist Univ., Dallas, 1967; Hon. DPhil Uppsala, 1977. *Publications:* The Earth: Its Origin, History, and Physical Constitution, 1924, 1929, 1952, 1959, 1962, 1970, 1976; Operational Methods in Mathematical Physics, 1927, 1931; The Future of the Earth, 1929; Scientific Inference, 1931, 1937, 1957, 1973; Cartesian Tensors, 1931, 1952, 1969; Earthquakes and Mountains, 1935, 1950; Theory of Probability, 1939, 1948, 1962, 1967, 1983; Methods of Mathematical Physics (with B. Jeffreys), 1946, 1950, 1956, 1962, 1972; Asymptotic Approximations, 1962, 1968; papers on Astronomy, Geophysics, Theory of Scientific Method, and Plant Ecology, republished in Collected Papers of Sir Harold Jeffreys, vols 1–6, 1971–77. *Address:* 160 Huntingdon Road, Cambridge CB3 0LB.

JEFFREYS, Mrs Judith Diana; Assistant Director (Keeper), the Tate Gallery, 1975–83; *b* 22 Sept. 1927; *d* of Prof. Philip Cloake, FRCP and Letitia Blanche (*née* MacDonald); *m* 1968, William John Jeffreys. *Educ:* Bedales; Courtauld Inst. of Art, Univ. of London (BA Hons History of Art). Tate Gallery: Asst Keeper, 1951–64; Publications Manager, 1960–65; Dep. Keeper, 1964–75. *Recreations:* reading, music, gardening. *Address:* Dairy Farm Cottage, North Houghton, Stockbridge, Hants.

JEFFRIES, Lionel Charles; actor since 1949, screen writer since 1959, and film director since 1970; *b* 10 June 1926; *s* of Bernard Jeffries and Elsie Jackson; *m* 1951, Eileen Mary Walsh; one *s* two *d. Educ:* Queen Elizabeth's Grammar Sch., Wimborne, Dorset; Royal Academy of Dramatic Art (Dip., Kendal Award, 1947). War of 1939–45: commissioned, Oxf. and Bucks LI, 1945; served in Burma (Burma Star, 1945); Captain, Royal West African Frontier Force. Stage: (West End) *plays:* Carrington VC; The Enchanted; Blood Wedding; Brouhaha; Hello Dolly; See How They Run; Two Into One; *films:* Colditz Story; Bhowani Junction; Lust for Life; The Baby and The Battleship; Doctor at Large; Law and Disorder; The Nun's Story; Idle on Parade; Two Way Stretch; The Trials of Oscar Wilde; Fanny; The Notorious Landlady (Hollywood); The Wrong Arm of the Law; The First Men in the Moon; The Truth about Spring; Arrivederci Baby; The Spy with a Cold Nose; Camelot (Hollywood); Chitty, Chitty, Bang Bang; Eyewitness; Baxter (also dir. 1971; Golden Bear Award for Best Film, Europe); The Prisoner of Zenda;

Ménage à Trois. Wrote and directed: The Railway Children, 1970 (St Christopher Gold Medal, Hollywood, for Best Film); The Amazing Mr Blunden, 1972 (Gold Medal for Best Screen Play, Internat. Sci. Fiction and Fantasy Film Fest., Paris, 1974); Wombling Free, 1977; co-wrote and directed: The Water Babies, 1979; *television:* Cream in my Coffee, 1980; Shillingbury Tales, 1981; Father Charlie; Tom, Dick, and Harriet, 1982; Minder, 1983. *Recreations:* swimming, painting. *Address:* c/o John Redway, 16 Berners Street, W1P 3DD. *Club:* St James'.

JEFFS, Group Captain (George) James (Horatio), CVO 1960 (LVO 1943); OBE 1950; *b* 27 Jan. 1900; *s* of late James Thomas Jeffs, Chilvers Coton, Warwicks; *m* 1921, Phyllis Rosina (*née* Bell); two *s* one *d. Educ:* Kedleston Sch., Derby. Served European War: RNAS, 1916–18; RAF, 1918–19. Air Ministry, 1919–23; Croydon Airport, 1923–34; Heston Airport, 1934–37; Air Ministry, 1937–39. Served War of 1939–45, RAF: Aircrew Mem. of all flights of HM King George VI and Sir Winston Churchill; Fighter, Ferry, and Transport Commands, Group Captain. Ministry of Transport and Civil Aviation, 1945. Nat. Air Traffic Control Officers' Licence No 1; Airport Commandant, Prestwick, 1950–57; Airport Commandant, London Airport, 1957–60. Legion of Merit, USA, 1944. Liveryman, GAPAN. *Address:* Pixham Firs Cottage, Pixham Lane, Dorking, Surrey. *T:* Dorking 884084. *Club:* Naval and Military.

JEFFS, Julian, QC 1975; Barrister; a Recorder of the Crown Court since 1975; *b* 5 April 1931; *s* of Alfred Wright Jeffs, Wolverhampton, and Janet Honor Irene (*née* Davies); *m* 1966, Deborah, *d* of Peter James Stuart Bevan; three *s. Educ:* Mostyn House Sch.; Wrekin Coll.; Downing Coll., Cambridge (MA; Associate Fellow, 1986). Royal Navy (nat. service), 1949–50. Sherry Shipper's Asst, Spain, 1956. Barrister, Gray's Inn, 1958 (Bencher 1981), Inner Temple, 1971; Midland and Oxford Circuit. Chm., Patent Bar Assoc., 1980–; Mem., Senate of Inns of Court and Bar, 1984–85. Editor, Wine and Food, 1965–67; Mem., Cttee of Management, International Wine & Food Soc., 1965–67, 1971–82; Chm., 1970–72, Vice-Pres., 1975–, Circle of Wine Writers. Dep. Gauger, City of London, 1979. Lauréat de l'Office International de la Vigne et du Vin, 1962; Glenfiddich wine writer awards, 1974 and 1978. General Editor, Faber's Wine Series. *Publications:* Sherry, 1961, 3rd edn 1982; (an editor) Clerk and Lindsell on Torts, 13th edn 1969, 15th edn 1982; The Wines of Europe, 1971; Little Dictionary of Drink, 1973; (jtly) Encyclopedia of United Kingdom and European Patent Law, 1977. *Recreations:* writing, wine, walking, old cars, musical boxes, follies, Iberian things. *Address:* Francis Taylor Building, Temple, EC4. *T:* 01–353 5657, telex 25182; Church Farm House, East Ilsley, Newbury, Berks. *T:* East Ilsley 216. *Clubs:* Beefsteak, Garrick, Reform, Saintsbury.

JEFFS, Kenneth Peter, CMG 1983; Executive Vice-President (Military Affairs), British Aerospace Inc., since 1984; *b* 30 Jan. 1931; *s* of Albert Jeffs and Theresa Eleanor Jeffs; *m* Iris Woolsey; one *s* two *d. Educ:* Richmond and East Sheen County Sch. jssc. National Service, RAF, 1949–51. Entered CS as Clerical Officer, Bd of Control, 1947; Air Min., 1952; Principal, 1964; JSSC, 1966–67; Private Secretary: to Under-Sec. of State (RN), MoD, 1969–71; to Minister of Defence, 1971–72; Asst Sec., Dir Defence Sales, MoD, 1972–75; Counsellor, Defence Supply, Washington, DC, 1976–79; Dir Gen. (Marketing), MoD, 1979–83. *Recreations:* rowing, tennis. *Address:* 6604 Madison McLean Drive, McLean, Va 22101, USA.

JEGER, Baroness *cr* 1979 (Life Peer), of St Pancras in Greater London; **Lena May Jeger;** *b* 19 Nov. 1915; *e d* of Charles and Alice Chivers, Yorkley, Glos; *m* 1948, Dr Santo Wayburn Jeger (*d* 1953); no *c. Educ:* Southgate County Sch., Middx; Birkbeck Coll., London University (BA). Civil Service: Customs and Excise, Ministry of Information, Foreign Office, 1936–49; British Embassy Moscow, 1947; Manchester Guardian London Staff, 1951–54, 1961–; Mem. St Pancras Borough Council, 1945–59; Mem. LCC for Holborn and St Pancras South, 1952–55. Mem., Nat. Exec. Cttee, Labour Party, 1968–80 (Vice-Chm., 1978–79; Chm., 1980). MP (Lab) Holborn and St Pancras South, Nov. 1953–1959 and 1964–74, Camden, Holborn and St Pancras South, 1974–79. Mem., Chairmen's Panel, House of Commons, 1971–79. Chm., Govt Working Party on Sewage Disposal, 1969–70. Member, Consultative Assembly: Council of Europe, 1969–71; WEU, 1969–71; UK delegate, Status of Women Commn, UN, 1967. *Address:* 9 Cumberland Terrace, Regent's Park, NW1.

JEHANGIR, Sir Hirji, 3rd Bt, *cr* 1908; *b* 1 Nov. 1915; 2nd *s* of Sir Cowasjee Jehangir, 2nd Bt, GBE, KCIE, and Hilla, MBE, *d* of late Hormarji Wadia, Lowji Castle, Bombay; *S* father, 1962; *m* 1952, Jinoo, *d* of K. H. Cama; two *s. Educ:* St Xavier Sch., Bombay; Magdalene Coll., Cambridge. Chm., Jehangir Art Gallery, Bombay. *Heir: s* Jehangir, *b* 23 Nov. 1953. *Address:* Readymoney House, 49 L. Jagmohandas Marg, Bombay 36, India; 24 Kensington Court Gardens, Kensington Court Place, W8. *Clubs:* Brooks's; Willingdon (Bombay).

JEJEEBHOY, Sir Jamsetjee, 7th Bt *cr* 1857; *b* 19 April 1913; *s* of Rustamjee J. C. Jamsetjee (*d* 1947), and Soonabai Rustomjee Byramjee Jejeebhoy (*d* 1968); *S* cousin, Sir Jamsetjee Jejeebhoy, 6th Bt, 1968, and assumed name of Jamsetjee Jejeebhoy in lieu of Maneckjee Rustomjee Jamsetjee Jejeebhoy; *m* 1943, Shirin Jehangir H. Cama; one *s* one *d. Educ:* St Xavier's Coll., Bombay (BA). Chairman: Sir Jamsetjee Jejeebhoy Charity Funds; Sir J. J. Parsee Benevolent Instn; Wadiaji's Atash-behram; M. F. Cama Athornan Instn; Iran League; Parsi Charity Orgn Soc.; Rustomjee Jamsetjee Jejeebhoy Gujrat Schools' Fund; Swabal Stores; Trustee: Sir J. J. Sch. of Arts; Byramjee Jejeebhoy Parsee Charitable Instn; A. H. Wadia Charity Trust; Zoroastrian Bldg Fund; Exec. Cttee, B. D. Petit Parsee Gen. Hosp.; K. R. Cama Oriental Instn (Vice Chm.). Created Special Executive Magistrate, 1977. *Heir: s* Rustom Jejeebhoy, *b* 16 Nov. 1957. *Address:* (residence) Beaulieu, 95 Worli Sea Face, Bombay 25, India. *T:* 4930955; (office) Maneckjee Wadia Building, Mahatma Gandhi Road, Fort, Bombay 1. *T:* 273843. *Clubs:* Willingdon Sports, Royal Western India, Turf (Bombay).

JELF, Maj.-Gen. Richard William, CBE 1948 (OBE 1944); *b* 16 June 1904; *s* of late Sir Ernest Jelf, King's Remembrancer and Master of the Supreme Court; *m* 1928, Nowell, *d* of Major Sampson-Way, RM, Manor House, Henbury; three *s* one *d. Educ:* Cheltenham Coll.; RMA Woolwich. Commissioned Royal Artillery, 1924; Staff Coll., Quetta, 1936; Dep. Dir Staff Duties, War Office, 1946; Imperial Defence Coll., 1948; CRA 2nd Division, 1949; Dep. Chief, Organization and Training Div., SHAPE, 1951; Comdr 99 AA Bde (TA), 1953; Chief of Staff, Eastern Command, 1956; Maj.-Gen., 1957; Commandant, Police Coll., Bramshill, 1957–63; Dir of Civil Defence, Southern Region, 1963–68. ADC to the Queen, 1954. Served North-West Frontier, India (Loe Agra), 1934; NW Europe, 1939–45. Hon. Sec., Lyme Regis RNLI, 1972–84. *Recreation:* yachting. *Address:* 1 Library Cottage, Marine Parade, Lyme Regis, Dorset. *T:* 3284.

JELLICOE, family name of **Earl Jellicoe.**

JELLICOE, 2nd Earl, *cr* 1925; **George Patrick John Rushworth Jellicoe,** KBE 1986; DSO 1942; MC 1944; PC 1963; Viscount Brocas of Southampton, *cr* 1925; Viscount Jellicoe of Scapa, *cr* 1918; Chairman: Medical Research Council, since 1982; Davy Corporation PLC, since 1985; Director: S. G. Warburg & Co., since 1973; Sotheby & Co., since 1973; Morgan Crucible, since 1974; Tate & Lyle, since 1974 (Chairman,

1978–82); Chancellor, Southampton University, since 1984; *b* 4 April 1918; *o s* of Admiral of the Fleet 1st Earl Jellicoe and late Florence Gwendoline, *d* of Sir Charles Cayzer, 1st Bt; godson of King George V; *S* father, 1935; *m* 1st, 1944, Patricia Christine (marr. diss., 1966), *o d* of Jeremiah O'Kane, Vancouver, Canada; two *s* two *d*; 2nd, 1966, Philippa, *o d* of late Philip Dunne; one *s* two *d*. *Educ:* Winchester; Trinity Coll., Cambridge (Exhibnr). Hon. Page to King George VI; served War of 1939–45, Coldstream Guards, 1 SAS Regt (despatches, DSO, MC, Légion d'Honneur, Croix de Guerre, Greek Military Cross). Entered HM Foreign Service, 1947; served as 1st Sec. in Washington, Brussels, Baghdad (Deputy Sec. General Baghdad Pact). Lord-in-Waiting, Jan.-June 1961; Jt Parly. Sec., Min. of Housing and Local Govt, 1961–62; Minister of State, Home Office, 1962–63; First Lord of the Admiralty, 1963–64; Minister of Defence for the Royal Navy, April-Oct. 1964; Deputy Leader of the Opposition, House of Lords, 1967–70; Lord Privy Seal and Minister in Charge, Civil Service Dept, 1970–73; Leader of the House of Lords, 1970–73. Chairman: Brit. Adv. Cttee on Oil Pollution of the Sea, 1968–70; 3rd Int. Conf. on Oil Pollution of the Sea, 1968. Dir, Smiths Industries, 1973–86; Chm., Pres., London Chamber of Commerce and Industry, 1979–82; Mem., BOTB, 1982–86 (Chm., 1983–86). Chm., Anglo-Hellenic League, 1978–86. A Governor, Centre for Environmental Studies, 1967–70; President: National Federation of Housing Societies, 1965–70; Parly and Scientific Cttee, 1980–83. Chm. of Council, KCL, 1977–86. FKC 1979. *Recreation:* ski-ing. *Heir: s* Viscount Brocas, *qv*. *Address:* Tidcombe Manor, Tidcombe, near Marlborough, Wilts. *T:* Oxenwood 225; 97 Onslow Square, SW7. *T:* 01–584 1551. *Club:* Brooks's.

See also Adm. Sir Charles Madden, Bt.

JELLICOE, Ann; *see* Jellicoe, P. A.

JELLICOE, Sir Geoffrey (Alan), Kt 1979; CBE 1961; FRIBA (Dist TP); PPILA; FRTPI; formerly Senior Partner of Jellicoe & Coleridge, Architects; *b* London, 8 Oct. 1900; *s* of George Edward Jellicoe; *m* 1936, Ursula (*d* 1986), *d* of late Sir Bernard Pares, KBE, DCL. *Educ:* Cheltenham Coll.; Architectural Association. Bernard Webb Student at British School at Rome; RIBA Neale Bursar. Principal, Arch. Assoc. Schs, 1939–41. Pres., Inst. of Landscape Architects, 1939–49; Hon. Pres. Internat. Fed. of Landscape Architects; Mem. Royal Fine Art Commission, 1954–68; former Trustee of the Tate Gallery; Hon. Corr. Mem. American and Venezuelan Societies of Landscape Architects. Gardens for: Sandringham; Royal Lodge (Windsor); Ditchley Park; RHS central area, Wisley; Chequers; Horsted Place (Sussex); Hartwell House (Aylesbury); Shute House (Wilts); Delta Works (W Bromwich); Hilton Hotel (Stratford-upon-Avon); Dewlish House, Dorchester; The Grange, Winchester; Sutton Place, Surrey; Barnwell Manor, Northants; botanical gardens for Moody Foundn, Galveston, Texas,USA, 1984; Town Plans for: Guildford, Wellington (Salop), Hemel Hempstead New Town. Arch. Cons. to N Rhodesian Govt, 1947–52. Housing for Basildon, Scunthorpe, LCC; Plymouth Civic Centre; Chertsey Civic Centre; Cheltenham Sports Centre; GLC Comprehensive Sch., Dalston; Durley Park, Keynsham; Grantham Crematorium and Swimming Pool; comprehensive plans for central area, Gloucester, and for Tollcross, Edinburgh; civic landscapes for Modena and Brescia, Italy; Kennedy Memorial, Runnymede; Plans for Sark, Isles of Scilly, and Bridgefoot, Stratford-upon-Avon. Medal of Amer. Soc. of Landscape Architects, 1981; Medal of Landscape Inst., 1985. *Publications:* Italian Gardens of the Renaissance (joint), 1925, rev. edn 1986; (with J. C. Shepherd) Gardens and Design, 1927; Baroque Gardens of Austria, 1931; Studies in Landscape Design, Vol. I 1959, Vol. II 1966, Vol. III 1970; Motopia, 1961; (with Susan Jellicoe) Water, 1971; The Landscape of Man, 1975, rev. edn 1987; The Guelph Lectures on Landscape Design, 1983. *Address:* 14 Highpoint, North Hill, Highgate, N6 4BA. *T:* 01–348 0123.

JELLICOE, (Patricia) Ann, (Mrs Roger Mayne), OBE 1984; playwright and director; *b* 15 July 1927; *d* of John Andrea Jellicoe and Frances Jackson Henderson; *m* 1st, 1950, C. E. Knight-Clarke (marr. diss., 1961); 2nd, 1962, Roger Mayne; one *s* one *d*. *Educ:* Polam Hall, Darlington; Queen Margaret's, York; Central Sch. of Speech and Drama (Elsie Fogarty Prize, 1947). Actress, stage manager and dir, London and provinces, 1947–51; privately commnd to study relationship between theatre architecture and theatre practice, 1949; founded and ran Cockpit Theatre Club to experiment with open stage, 1952–54; taught acting and directed plays, Central Sch., 1954–56; Literary Manager, Royal Court Theatre, 1973–75; Founder, 1979, and Director, 1979–85, Colway Theatre Trust to produce community plays. *Plays:* The Sport of My Mad Mother, Royal Court, 1958; The Knack, Arts (Cambridge), 1961, Royal Court, 1962, New York, 1964, Paris, 1967 (filmed, 1965); Shelley, Royal Court, 1965; The Rising Generation, Royal Court, 1967; The Giveaway, Garrick, 1969; Flora and the Bandits, Dartington Coll. of Arts, 1976; The Bargain, SW Music Theatre, 1979; *community plays:* The Reckoning, Lyme Regis, 1978; The Tide, Seaton, 1980; (with Fay Weldon and John Fowles) The Western Women, Lyme Regis, 1984; *plays for children:* You'll Never Guess!, Arts, 1973; Clever Elsie, Smiling John, Silent Peter, Royal Court, 1974; A Good Thing or a Bad Thing, Royal Court, 1974; *translations include:* Rosmersholm, Royal Court, 1960; The Lady from the Sea, Queen's, 1961; The Seagull (with Ariadne Nicolaeff), Queen's, 1963; Der Freischütz, Sadlers Wells, 1964. *Principal productions include:* The Sport of My Mad Mother (with George Devine), 1958; For Children, 1959; The Knack (with Keith Johnstone), 1962; Skyvers, 1963; Shelley, 1965; A Worthy Guest, 1974; The Reckoning, 1978; The Tide, 1980; The Poor Man's Friend, 1981; The Garden, 1982; The Western Women, 1984; Entertaining Strangers, 1985. *Publications:* (apart from plays) Some Unconscious Influences in the Theatre, 1967; (with Roger Mayne) Shell Guide to Devon, 1975. *Address:* c/o Margaret Ramsay Ltd, 14a Goodwin's Court, St Martin's Lane, WC2.

JENCKS, Charles Alexander, PhD; Lecturer in Architecture, Architectural Association, since 1970; Professor, University of California at Los Angeles School of Architecture, since 1985 (Lecturer in Architecture, 1974–85); *b* 21 June 1939; *s* of Gardner Platt Jencks and Ruth Pearl Jencks; *m* 1st, 1960, Pamela Balding (marr. diss. 1973); two *s*; 2nd, 1978, Margaret Keswick; one *s* one *d*. *Educ:* Harvard University (BA Eng. Lit. 1961; BA, MA Arch. 1965); London University (PhD Arch. Hist., 1970). Architectural Association, 1968; writer on Post-Modern architecture, 1975–, Late-Modern architecture, 1978–; designer of furniture, and Alessi Tea and Coffee Set, 1983; numerous Univ. lectures, incl. Peking, Warsaw, Tokyo, USA, Paris; house designs incl. The Garagia Rotunda, 1976–77, The Elemental House, 1983, The Thematic House, 1984. Fulbright Schol., Univ. of London, 1965–67; Melbourne Oration, Australia, 1974; Bossom Lectr, RSA, 1980; Mem., Cttee for selection of architects, Venice Biennale, 1980; Editor at Academy Editions, 1979–; Member: Architectural Assoc.; RSA. *TV films:* (wrote) Le Corbusier, BBC, 1974; (wrote and presented) Kings of Infinite Space (Frank Lloyd Wright and Michael Graves), 1983. *Publications:* Meaning in Architecture, 1969; Architecture 2000, 1971; Adhocism, 1972; Modern Movements in Architecture, 1973; Le Corbusier and the Tragic View of Architecture, 1974; The Language of Post-Modern Architecture, 1977, 4th edn 1984; Late-Modern Architecture, 1980; Post-Modern Classicism, 1980; Free-Style Classicism, 1982; Architecture Today (Current Architecture), 1982; Abstract Representation, 1983; Kings of Infinite Space, 1983; Towards a Symbolic Architecture, 1985; articles in Encounter, Connoisseur, l'Oeil, TLS. *Recreations:* travel, collecting Chinese (bullet-hole) rocks. *Address:* 19 Lansdowne Walk, W11; 519 Latimer Road, Santa Monica, Calif 90402, USA.

JENKIN, Rt. Hon. (Charles) Patrick (Fleeming), PC 1973; MA; MP (C) Wanstead and Woodford, since 1964; *b* 7 Sept. 1926; *s* of late Mr and Mrs C. O. F. Jenkin; *m* 1952, Alison Monica Graham; two *s* two *d*. *Educ:* Dragon Sch., Oxford; Clifton Coll.; Jesus Coll., Cambridge. MA (Cantab.) 1951. Served with QO Cameron Highlanders, 1945–48; 1st Class Hons in Law, Cambridge, 1951; Harmsworth Scholar, Middle Temple, 1951; called to the Bar, 1952. Distillers Co. Ltd, 1957–70. Member: Hornsey Borough Council, 1960–63; London Coun. of Social Service, 1963–67. An Opposition front bench spokesman on Treasury, Trade and Economics, 1965–70; Jt Vice-Chm., Cons. Parly Trade and Power Cttee, 1966–67; Chm., All Party Parly Group on Chemical Industry, 1968–70; Financial Sec. to the Treasury, 1970–72; Chief Sec. to Treasury, 1972–74; Minister for Energy, 1974; Opposition front bench spokesman: on Energy, 1974–76; on Soc. Services, 1976–79; Secretary of State: for Social Services, 1979–81; for Industry, 1981–83; for the Environment, 1983–85. Pres., National CPC Cttee, 1983–86. Director: Tilbury Contracting Gp Ltd, 1974–79; Royal Worcester Ltd, 1975–79; Continental and Industrial Trust Ltd, 1975–79; Dir and Chm. Designate, Friends' Provident Life Office, 1986–; UK Co-Chm., UK-Japan 2000 Gp, 1986–. Adviser, Arthur Andersen & Co., Management Consultants, 1985–; Mem., UK Adv. Bd, Nat. Economic Res. Associates Inc., 1985–. Governor: Westfield Coll., 1964–70; Clifton Coll., 1969– (Mem. Council, 1972–79). *Recreations:* music, gardening, sailing, bricklaying. *Address:* House of Commons, SW1; Home Farm, Matching Road, Hatfield Heath, Bishop's Stortford, Herts CM22 7AS; 59 Cardigan Street, SE11 5PF. *Club:* West Essex Conservative (Wanstead).

See also Rear-Adm. D. C. Jenkin.

JENKIN, Rear Adm. David Conrad, CB 1983; Commandant, Joint Service Defence College (formerly National Defence College), 1981–84, retired; *b* 25 Oct. 1928; *s* of Mr and Mrs C. O. F. Jenkin; *m* 1958, Jennifer Margaret Nowell; three *s* one *d*. *Educ:* Dragon Sch., Oxford; RNC, Dartmouth. Entered RN at age of 13½, 1942; qual. in Gunnery, 1953; commanded: HMS Palliser, 1961–63; HMS Cambrian, 1964–66; HMS Galatea, 1974–75; HMS Hermes (aircraft carrier), 1978–79; Flag Officer, First Flotilla, 1980–81. *Recreations:* sailing, skiing, do-it-yourself. *Address:* Knapsyard House, West Meon, Hants GU32 1LF. *T:* West Meon 227.

See also Rt Hon. C. P. F. Jenkin.

JENKIN, Rt. Hon. Patrick; *see* Jenkin, Rt Hon. C. P. F.

JENKINS; *see* Martin-Jenkins.

JENKINS, family name of **Baron Jenkins of Putney.**

JENKINS OF PUTNEY, Baron *cr* 1981 (Life Peer), of Wandsworth in Greater London; **Hugh Gater Jenkins;** *b* 27 July 1908; *s* of Joseph Walter Jenkins and Florence Emily (*née* Gater), Enfield, Middlesex; *m* 1936, Marie (*née* Crosbie), *d* of Sqdn Ldr Ernest Crosbie and Ethel (*née* Hawkins). *Educ:* Enfield Grammar Sch. Personal exploration of employment and unemployment, and political and economic research, 1925–30; Prudential Assce Co., 1930–40. ROC, 1938; RAF: Fighter Comd, 1941; became GCI Controller (Flt Lt); seconded to Govt of Burma, 1945, as Dir Engl. Programmes, Rangoon Radio. Nat. Union of Bank Employees: Greater London Organiser, 1947; Res. and Publicity Officer; Ed., The Bank Officer, 1948; British Actors' Equity Assoc.: Asst Sec., 1950; Asst Gen. Sec., 1957–64. LCC: Mem. for Stoke Newington and Hackney N, 1958–65 (Public Control and Town Planning Cttees). Fabian Soc. lectr and Dir of Summer Schools in early post-war years; Chairman: H Bomb Campaign Cttee, 1954; Campaign for Nuclear Disarmament, 1979–81 (Vice-Pres., 1981–); CND, Aldermaston Marcher, 1957–63; Chm. Victory for Socialism, 1956–60; Mem. Exec. Cttee Greater London Labour Party. Contested (Lab): Enfield W, 1950; Mitcham, 1955; MP (Lab) Wandsworth, Putney, 1964–79; Minister for the Arts, 1974–76. Former Mem., Public Accounts Cttee. Member: Arts Council, 1968–71; Drama Panel, 1972–74; Nat. Theatre Bd, 1976–80; Dep. Chm., Theatres Trust, 1977–79, Dir, 1979–. Vice-Pres., Theatres' Adv. Council, 1986– (former Chm.); President: Battersea Arts Centre; Soc. for Cultural Relations with USSR, 1985–. Occasional broadcasts and lectures on communications, theatrical and disarmament subjects. *Publications:* Essays in Local Government Enterprise (with others), 1964; The Culture Gap, 1979; Rank and File, 1980; A Day in September (semi-autobiog.), 1986; In Time of War, 1986; radio plays (BBC Radio 4): Solo Boy, 1983; When You and I Were Seventeen, 1985; various pamphlets; contrib. to Tribune, New Statesman, Guardian, etc. *Recreations:* reading, writing, talking, walking, viewing, listening, avoiding retirement. *Address:* House of Lords, SW1A 0PW. *T:* 01–219 6706, (office) 01–836 8591.

JENKINS, Alan Roberts; Editorial executive, The Times, since 1981; *b* 8 June 1926; *s* of Leslie Roberts Jenkins and Marjorie Kate Cawston; *m* 1st, 1949, Kathleen Mary Baker (*d* 1969); four *s*; 2nd, 1971, Helen Mary Speed; one *s*. *Educ:* Aylesbury Grammar Sch. Commnd Royal Berks Regt, 1945; Captain, W African Liaison Service, GHQ India; Staff Captain Public Relations, Royal W African Frontier Force, Lagos; DADPR W Africa Comd (Major). Reporter, Reading Mercury and Berkshire Chronicle, 1948; Sub-editor, Daily Herald; Daily Mail: Sub-editor; Night Editor, 1962–69; Northern Editor, 1969–71; Asst Editor, Evening Standard, 1971; Dep. Editor, Sunday People, 1971–72; Asst Editor, Sunday Mirror, 1972–77; Editor, Glasgow Herald, 1978–80. *Recreations:* golf, travel, moving house. *Address:* 21 The Heights, 97 Frognal, Hampstead, NW3.

JENKINS, Arthur Robert, CBE 1972; JP; Director: Robert Jenkins & Co. Ltd, Rotherham, since 1934 (Chairman, 1958–83); Robert Jenkins (Holdings) Ltd, since 1968 (Chairman, 1968–83); *b* 20 June 1908; *s* of Edgar Jackson Jenkins and Ethel Mary Bescoby; *m* 1933, Margaret Fitton Jones; one *s* three *d*. *Educ:* Rotherham Grammar Sch.; Sheffield Univ. CEng, FIMechE. Chairman: British Welding Res. Assoc., 1956–68; Tank and Industrial Plant Assoc., 1958–61; of Council, Welding Inst., 1968–71; of Council, Process Plant Assoc., 1971–75 (Vice-Pres., 1975); Pres., Welding Inst., 1951–53 and 1973–75; Vice-Pres., British Mechanical Engrg Confedn, 1972–. Mem. Exec. Bd, BSI, 1974. Hon. FWeldI 1982. JP 1948. *Recreation:* gardening. *Address:* Orchard End, Sunderland Street, Tickhill, Doncaster DN11 9QJ.

JENKINS, Prof. Aubrey Dennis; Professor of Polymer Science, University of Sussex, since 1971; *b* 6 Sept. 1927; *s* of Arthur William Jenkins and Mabel Emily (*née* Street); *m* 1950, Audrey Doreen Middleton; two *s* one *d*. *Educ:* Dartford Grammar Sch.; Sir John Cass Technical Inst.; King's Coll., Univ. of London. BSc 1948, PhD 1951; DSc 1961. FRIC 1957. Research Chemist, Courtaulds Ltd, Fundamental Research Laboratory, Maidenhead, 1950–60; Head of Chemistry Research, Gillette Industries Ltd, Reading, 1960–64 (Harris Research Labs, Washington, DC, 1963–64); University of Sussex, 1964–: Sen. Lectr in Chemistry, 1964–68; Reader, 1968–71; Dean, Sch. of Molecular Scis, 1973–78. Visiting Professor: Inst. of Macromolecular Chemistry, Prague, 1978; Univ. of Massachusetts, Amherst, 1979. Member: Internat. Union of Pure and Applied Chemistry, Commn on Macromolecular Nomenclature, 1974– (Chm., 1977–); UNESCO European Expert Cttee on Polymer Chemistry, Industry and Environment, 1977–. Mem., GB/East Europe Centre. Mem., Brighton HA, 1983–. Examining chaplain to Bishop of Chichester, 1980–. *Publications:* Kinetics of Vinyl Polymerization by Radical Mechanisms (with C. H. Bamford, W. G. Barb and P. F. Onyon), 1958; Polymer Science, 1972; (with A. Ledwith) Reactivity, Mechanism and Structure in Polymer Chemistry, 1974; (with J.

F. Kennedy) Macromolecular Chemistry, Vol. I 1980, Vol. II 1982, Vol. III 1984; Progress in Polymer Science (11 vols),1967–; papers in learned jls. *Recreations:* music, travel (esp. Czechoslovakia), photography. *Address:* 32 Silverdale Road, Burgess Hill, Sussex RH15 0EF. *T:* Burgess Hill 3332.

JENKINS, Brian Garton, FCA; Partner, Coopers & Lybrand, Chartered Accountants, since 1969; *b* 3 Dec. 1935; *s* of late Owen Garton Jenkins and Doris Enid (*née* Webber); *m* 1967, Elizabeth Ann, *d* of John Philip Manning Prentice, MSc, FRAS and Elizabeth Mason (*née* Harwood); one *s* one *d. Educ:* Tonbridge; Trinity Coll., Oxford (State Scholar, MA). ACA Hons 1963; FCA 1974. Served RA, Gibraltar, 1955–57 (2nd Lieut). Joined Cooper Brothers & Co. (now Coopers & Lybrand), 1960; Mem., Exec. Cttee, 1979–85 and 1986–; Head of Audit, 1986–; Dir, Royal Ordnance Factories, 1976–83. Institute of Chartered Accountants in England and Wales: Mem. Council, 1976–; Vice-Pres., 1983; Dep. Pres. 1983–85; Pres., 1985–86; Chm., Courses Cttee, 1979–80; Chm., Educn and Trng Directorate, 1980–83. Chm., London and Dist Soc. of Chartered Accountants, 1975–76; Vice-Pres., Chartered Accountants Students' Soc. of London, 1978–. Alderman, City of London (Ward of Cordwainer),1980–; Liveryman: Co. of Chartered Accountants in England and Wales, 1980– (Mem. Court, 1980–); Merchant Taylors Co., 1984–; Mem., Court of Assts, Corp. of Sons of the Clergy. 1983–. Governor, Royal Shakespeare Theatre, 1981–. Mem., Bd of Green Cloth Verge of the Palaces, 1984–. FRSA. *Publications:* An Audit Approach to Computers, 1978, 3rd edn 1986; contrib. accountancy magazines. *Recreations:* garden construction, old books, large jigsaw puzzles, ephemera. *Address:* Plumtree Court, EC4A 4HT. *T:* 01–583 5000. *Clubs:* Brooks's, City of London, City Livery.

JENKINS, Lt-Col Charles Peter de Brisay, MBE 1960; MC 1945; Clerk, Worshipful Company of Goldsmiths, since 1975; *b* 19 Aug. 1925; *s* of late Brig. A. de B. Jenkins and of Mrs Elizabeth Susan Jenkins; *m* 1949, Joan Mary, *e d* of late Col and Mrs C. N. Littleboy, Thirsk; one *s. Educ:* Cheltenham Coll.; Selwyn Coll., Cambridge. Commnd RE, 1944; served in Italy, 1944–45; subseq. Hong Kong, Kenya and Germany; jssc 1960; Instructor, Staff Coll., Camberley, 1961–63; Comdr, RE 1st Div., 1965–67; retd 1967. Asst Clerk, Goldsmiths' Co., 1968. Mem., Hallmarking Council, 1977–; Vice-Chm., Goldsmiths' Coll. (Univ. of London) Delegacy, 1983–. Trustee Nat. Centre for Orchestral Studies, 1980–. *Recreations:* swimming, gardening, Wagner. *Address:* Goldsmiths' Hall, Foster Lane, EC2.

JENKINS, Christopher; *see* Jenkins, J. C.

JENKINS, Clive; *see* Jenkins, D. C.

JENKINS, David, CBE 1977; MA; Librarian, National Library of Wales, 1969–79; *b* 29 May 1912; *s* of late Evan Jenkins and Mary (*née* James), Blaenclydach, Rhondda; *m* 1948, Menna Rhys, *o d* of late Rev. Owen Evans Williams, Penrhyn-coch, Aberystwyth; one *s* one *d. Educ:* Ardwyn Grammar Sch., Aberystwyth; UCW, Aberystwyth. BA Hons Welsh Lit. 1936, MA 1948; W. P. Thomas (Rhondda) Schol. 1936; Sir John Williams Research Student, 1937–38. Served War of 1939–45, Army; Major, 1943; NW Europe. National Library of Wales: Asst, Dept MSS, 1939–48; Asst Keeper, Dept of Printed Books, 1949, Keeper, 1957, Sen. Keeper, 1962. Professorial Fellow, UCW Aberystwyth, 1971–79. Gen. Comr of Income Tax, 1968–; Chairman: Mid-Wales HMC, 1969–70; Welsh Books Council, 1974–80 (Vice-Chm. 1971–74); Library Adv. Council (Wales), 1979–82; Member: Court of Governors, Univ. of Wales; Ct and Council, UC Aberystwyth; Adv. Council, British Library, 1975–82; BBC Archives Adv. Cttee, 1976–79; Hon. Soc. of Cymmrodorion; Pantyfedwen Trust, 1969–; Coll. of Librarianship Wales; Governor: Ardwyn Grammar Sch., 1963–72; Penweddig Compreh. Sch., 1973–77. Editor: NLW Jl, 1968–79; Jl Welsh Bibliog. Soc., 1964–79; Ceredigion, Trans Cards Antiq. Soc., 1973–84. JP Aberystwyth 1959–82: Chm. Llanbadarn Bench 1965–69; Vice-Chm., Aberystwyth Bench, 1980; Member: Dyfed Magistrates' Courts Cttee, 1975–79; Dyfed-Powys Police Authority, 1977–81. Hon. DLitt Wales, 1979. Sir Ellis Griffith Meml Prize, Univ. of Wales, 1975. *Publications:* Cofiant Thomas Gwynn Jones, 1973 (biog.; Welsh Arts Council Prize, 1974); (ed) Erthyglau ac Ysgrifau Kate Roberts, 1978; Bardd a Bro: T. Gwynn Jones, Cyngor y Celfyddydau, 1984; articles in NLW Jl, Bull. Bd of Celtic Studies and many other jls; contrib. Dictionary of Welsh Biography. *Recreation:* walking. *Address:* Maesaleg, Penrhyn-coch, Aberystwyth, Dyfed. *T:* Aberystwyth 828 766.

JENKINS, (David) Clive; General Secretary, Association of Scientific, Technical and Managerial Staffs, since 1970 (Joint General Secretary, 1968–70); Member of the General Council of the TUC, since 1974 (Chairman, Education Committee, since 1979); *b* 2 May 1926; *s* of David Samuel Jenkins and Miriam Harris Jenkins (*née* Hughes); *m* 1963, Moira McGregor Hilley; one *s* one *d. Educ:* Port Talbot Central Boys' Sch.; Port Talbot County Sch.; Swansea Techn. Coll. (evenings). Started work in metallurgical test house, 1940; furnace shift supervisor, 1942; i/c of laboratory, 1943; tinplate night shift foreman, 1945; Mem., Port Talbot Cooperative Soc. Educn. Cttee, 1945; Branch Sec. and Area Treas., AScW, 1946; Asst Midlands Divisional Officer, ASSET, 1947; Transport Industrial Officer, 1949; Nat. Officer, 1954; Gen. Sec., ASSET, 1961–68. Metrop. Borough Councillor, 1954–60 (Chm. Staff Cttee, St Pancras Borough Coun.); Chm., Nat. Jt Coun. for Civil Air Transport, 1967–68; Member: NRDC, 1974–80; Bullock Cttee on Industrial Democracy, 1975–; Wilson Cttee to Review the Functioning of Financial Institutions, 1977–80; BNOC, 1979–82; BOTB, 1980–83; NEDC, 1983–; Commn of Inquiry into Labour Party, 1979 (Chm., Finance Panel, 1979); TUC-Labour Party Liaison Cttee, 1980–; Council, ACAS, 1986–; Chairman: TUC Educnl Trust, 1979–; Roosevelt Meml Trust, 1979–; Friends of the Earth Trust, 1984–86; Trustee, Nat. Heritage Meml Fund, 1980–; Governor, Sadler's Wells Foundn, 1985–. Editor, Trade Union Affairs, 1961–63. Sometime columnist, Tribune, Daily Mirror, Daily Record. *Publications:* Power at the Top, 1959; Power Behind the Screen, 1961; (with J. E. Mortimer) British Trade Unions Today, 1965; (with J. E. Mortimer) The Kind of Laws the Unions Ought to Want, 1968; with B. D. Sherman: Computers and the Unions, 1977; Collective Bargaining: what you always wanted to know about trade unions and never dared ask, 1977; The Collapse of Work, 1979; The Rebellious Salariat: white collar unionism, 1979; The Leisure Shock, 1981. *Recreations:* not much. *Address:* (home) 16 St Marks Crescent, NW1. *T:* 01–485 4509; (office) 79 Camden Road, NW1. *T:* 01–267 4422.
See also T. H. Jenkins.

JENKINS, Rt. Rev. David Edward; *see* Durham, Bishop of.

JENKINS, David Edward Stewart; Research Fellow, Policy Studies Institute, since 1986; Morris Ginsberg Fellow in Sociology, London School of Economics and Political Science, Oct. 1986–Sept. 1987; *b* 9 May 1949; *s* of William Stephen Jenkins and Jean Nicol Downie; *m* 1972, Maggie Lack, *d* of Dr C. H. and Mrs J. D. Lack; two *s* one *d. Educ:* Univ. of London Goldsmiths' College (BA(Soc) 1977); LSE. Warden, Ellison Hse Adult Probation Hostel, SE17, 1973–74; Lecturer: (part-time) in Sociology, Brunel Univ., 1980–81; (part-time) in Social Administration, LSE and Goldsmiths' Coll., 1980–81; in Criminology, Univ. of Edinburgh, 1981; Dir, Howard League, 1982–86. *Recreations:*

music, swimming, cycling. *Address:* 99 Woodwarde Road, Dulwich Village, SE22 8UP. *T:* 01–693 2080.

JENKINS, David John; General Secretary, Wales Trades Union Congress, since 1983; *b* 21 Sept. 1948; *s* of William and Dorothy Jenkins; *m* 1976, Felicity Anne (*née* Wood); two *s* one *d. Educ:* Canton High Sch., Cardiff; Liverpool Univ. (BA Hons); Garnett Coll., London (CertEd). Industrial Sales Organiser, ITT (Distributors), 1970–74; steel worker, GKN, 1974; Lectr, Peterborough Tech. Coll., 1975–78; Research and Admin. Officer, Wales TUC, 1978–83. *Recreation:* finding time to spend with family. *Address:* 1 Cathedral Road, Cardiff. *T:* Cardiff 372345.

JENKINS, Elizabeth, OBE 1981. *Educ:* St Christopher School, Letchworth; Newnham College, Cambridge. *Publications:* The Winters, 1931; Lady Caroline Lamb, a Biography, 1932; Harriet (awarded the Femina Vie Heureuse Prize), 1934; The Phoenix' Nest, 1936; Jane Austen, a Biography, 1938; Robert and Helen, 1944; Young Enthusiasts, 1946; Henry Fielding (The English Novelists Series), 1947; Six Criminal Women, 1949; The Tortoise and the Hare, 1954; Ten Fascinating Women, 1955; Elizabeth the Great (biography), 1958; Elizabeth and Leicester, 1961; Brightness, 1963; Honey, 1968; Dr Gully, 1972; The Mystery of King Arthur, 1975; The Princes in the Tower, 1978; The Shadow and the Light, 1983. *Address:* 8 Downshire Hill, Hampstead, NW3. *T:* 01–435 4642.

JENKINS, Very Rev. Frank Graham; Dean of Monmouth and Vicar of St Woolos, since 1976; *b* 24 Feb. 1923; *s* of Edward and Miriam M. Jenkins; *m* 1950, Ena Doraine Parry; two *s* one *d. Educ:* Cyfarthfa Sec. Sch., Merthyr Tydfil; Port Talbot Sec. Sch.; St David's Coll., Lampeter (BA Hist); Jesus Coll., Oxford (BA Theol., MA); St Michael's Coll., Llandaff. HM Forces, 1942–46. Deacon 1950, priest 1951, Llandaff; Asst Curate, Llangeinor, 1950–53; Minor Canon, Llandaff Cathedral, 1953–60; CF (TA), 1956–61; Vicar of Abertillery, 1960–64; Vicar of Risca, 1964–75; Canon of Monmouth, 1967–76; Vicar of Caerleon, 1975–76. *Address:* The Deanery, Stow Hill, Newport, Gwent NP9 4ED. *T:* Newport 63338.

JENKINS, Garth John; Deputy Secretary and Legal Adviser and Solicitor to Ministry of Agriculture, Fisheries and Food, Forestry Commission, and Intervention Board for Agricultural Produce, since 1983; *b* 7 Dec. 1933; *s* of John Ernest Jenkins and Amy Elizabeth Jenkins; *m* 1965, Patricia Margaret Lindsay; one *d. Educ:* Birmingham Royal Inst. for the Blind; Royal National College for the Blind; Birmingham Univ. (LLB). Called to Bar, Gray's Inn, 1963. Birmingham Corporation, 1954; South Shields Corporation, 1964; The Land Commission, 1967; MAFF, 1971–; Under Sec., 1981. *Recreations:* literature, theatre, music, chess; food, drink and conversation. *Address:* 98 Dora Road, Wimbledon, SW19. *T:* 01–947 4598.

JENKINS, Prof. George Charles, MB, BS, PhD; FRCPath; Consultant Haematologist, The London Hospital, since 1965; Hon. Consultant, St Peter's Hospitals, since 1972; Professor of Haematology in the University of London, since 1974; Consultant to the Royal Navy; *b* 2 Aug. 1927; *s* of late John R. Jenkins and Mabel Rebecca (*née* Smith); *m* 1956, Elizabeth, *d* of late Cecil J. Welch, London; one *s* two *d. Educ:* Wyggeston, Leicester; St Bartholomew's Hosp. Med. Coll. MB, BS, PhD; MRCS, LRCP 1951; FRCPath 1975 (MRCPath 1964). House Phys. and Ho. Surg., St Bart's Hosp., 1951–52. Sqdn Ldr, RAF Med. Br., 1952–54. Registrar in Pathology, St Bart's Hosp., 1954–57; MRC Research Fellow, Royal Postgraduate Med. Sch., 1957–60; Sen. Registrar, Haematology, London Hosp., 1960–63; Cons. Haematologist, N Middlesex Hosp., 1963–65. Examiner: Univ. of London, 1971–; Univ. of Cambridge, 1984–; Sen. Examiner, RCPath, 1971–, Mem. Council, 1979–, Vice-Pres., 1981–84. Mem. subcttee on biologicals, Cttee on Safety of Medicines, 1976–. Member: British Soc. for Haematology (formerly Hon. Sec.), 1962–; Internat. Soc. of Haematology, 1975–; Assoc. of Clinical Pathologists, 1958–; British Acad. of Forensic Scis, 1977– (Chm. Exec. Council, 1985–). *Publications:* Advanced Haematology (jtly), 1974; papers and contribs to med. and sci. books and jls. *Recreations:* theatre, music. *Address:* The London Hospital, Whitechapel, E1 1BB. *T:* 01–247 5454. *Club:* Royal Navy Medical.

JENKINS, Gilbert Kenneth; Keeper, Department of Coins and Medals, British Museum, 1965–78; *b* 2 July 1918; *s* of late Kenneth Gordon Jenkins and of Julia Louisa Jenkins (*née* Colbourne); *m* 1939, Cynthia Mary, *d* of late Dr Hugh Scott, FRS; one *s* two *d. Educ:* All Saints Sch., Bloxham; Corpus Christi Coll., Oxford. Open Classical Scholar (Corpus Christi Coll.), 1936; First Class Honour Mods, 1938. War Service in Royal Artillery, 1940–46 (SE Asia, 1944–46). BA, 1946. Asst Keeper, British Museum, 1947; Dep. Keeper, 1956. An Editor of Numismatic Chronicle, 1964–. Mem., German Archaeological Inst., 1967; Corresp. Mem., Amer. Numismatic Soc., 1958; Hon. Mem., Swiss Numismatic Soc., 1979; Hon. FRNS, 1980. Akbar Medal, Numismatic Soc. of India, 1966; Royal Numismatic Soc. Medal, 1975; Archer Huntington Medal, Amer. Numismatic Soc., 1976. *Publications:* Carthaginian Gold and Electrum Coins (with R. B. Lewis), 1963; Coins of Greek Sicily, 1966; Sylloge Nummorum Graecorum (Danish Nat. Museum), part 42, N Africa (ed), 1969, part 43, Spain-Gaul (ed), 1979; The Coinage of Gela, 1970; Ancient Greek Coins, 1972; (with U. Westermark) The Coinage of Kamarina, 1980; articles in numismatic periodicals. *Recreations:* music, cycling. *Address:* 3 Beechwood Avenue, Kew Gardens, Surrey.

JENKINS, Prof. Harold, MA, DLitt; Professor Emeritus, University of Edinburgh; *b* 19 July 1909; *s* of late Henry and Mildred Jenkins, Shenley, Bucks; *m* 1939, Gladys Puddifoot (*d* 1984); no *c. Educ:* Wolverton Grammar Sch.; University Coll., London. George Smith Studentship, 1930. Quain Student, University Coll., London, 1930–35; William Noble Fellow, University of Liverpool, 1935–36; Lecturer in English, University of the Witwatersrand, South Africa, 1936–45; Lecturer in English, University Coll., London, 1945–46, then Reader in English, 1946–54; Prof. of English, University of London (Westfield Coll.), 1954–67; Regius Prof. of Rhetoric and English Lit., Edinburgh Univ., 1967–71. Visiting Prof., Duke Univ., USA, 1957–58, Univ. of Oslo, 1974. Hon. LittD Iona Coll., New Rochelle, NY, 1983. Shakespeare Prize, FVS Foundn, Hamburg, 1986. Jt Gen. Editor, Arden Shakespeare, 1958–82. *Publications:* The Life and Work of Henry Chettle, 1934; Edward Benlowes, 1952; The Structural Problem in Shakespeare's Henry IV, 1956; The Catastrophe in Shakespearean Tragedy, 1968; John Dover Wilson (British Acad. memoir), 1973; (ed) Hamlet (Arden edn), 1982; articles in Modern Language Review, Review of English Studies, The Library, Shakespeare Survey, Studies in Bibliography, etc. *Address:* 22 North Crescent, Finchley, N3 3LL. *Club:* Athenæum.

JENKINS, Hon. Dr Henry Alfred; Australian Ambassador to Spain; *b* 24 Sept. 1925; *s* of Henry Alfred Jenkins and Eileen Clare Jenkins (*née* McCormack); *m* 1951, Hazel Eileen Winter; three *s* one *d. Educ:* Ormond, Eltham and Heidelberg State Schools; Ivanhoe Grammar Sch.; Univ. of Melbourne (MSc, MB BS); Deakin Univ. (BA). Tutor, Univ. of Melbourne, 1946–52; RMO Alfred Hosp., 1953; Medical Practitioner, 1953–61; MLA (Lab) Reservoir Parliament of Victoria, 1961–69; MP (Lab) Scullin, Federal Parliament of Australia, 1969–85; Chm. of Committees and Dep. Speaker, House of Representatives, 1975–76, Speaker, 1983–85. *Recreations:* reading, hobby farming, community service. *Address:* 164 Casey Drive, Lalor, Vic 3075, Australia. *T:* (03)

465.6038. *Clubs:* Royal Automobile of Victoria, Melbourne Cricket, Preston FCS, Macedonian Social.

JENKINS, Hugh Royston, FRICS, FPMI; Director, Allied Dunbar Assurance PLC, since 1986; Group Investment Director, Heron International, since 1985; *b* 9 Nov. 1933. *Educ:* Llanelli Grammar Sch.; National Service, Royal Artillery, 1954–56. Valuer, London County Council, 1956–62; Assistant Controller, 1962–68, Managing Director, 1968–72, Coal Industry (Nominees) Ltd; Dir Gen. of Investments, NCB, 1972–84. Vice Chm., National Assoc. of Pension Funds, 1979–80; Chief Exec. Officer, Heron Financial Corp., 1985–86; Member: Property Adv. Gp, DoE, 1976–85; The City Capital Markets Cttee, 1982; Lay Mem. of the Stock Exchange, 1984–85. *Recreation:* golf. *Address:* (office) 9–15 Sackville Street, W1X 1DE. *Club:* Garrick.

JENKINS, Dr Ivor, CBE 1970; FEng 1979; freelance Consultant, since 1979; Group Director of Research, Delta Metal Co. Ltd, 1973–78; Managing Director, 1973–77, Deputy Chairman, 1977–78, Delta Materials Research Ltd; *b* 25 July 1913; *m* 1941, Carolina Wijnanda James; two *s*. *Educ:* Gowerton Grammar Sch.; Univ. of Wales, Swansea. BSc, MSc, DSc; Hon. Fellow, UC Swansea, 1986. Bursar, GEC Research Labs, Wembley, 1934; Mem. Scientific Staff, GEC, 1935; Dep. Chief Metallurgist, Whitehead Iron & Steel Co., Newport, Mon, 1944; Head of Metallurgy Dept, 1946, Chief Metallurgist, 1952, GEC, Wembley; Dir of Research, Manganese Bronze Holdings Ltd, and Dir, Manganese Bronze Ltd, 1961–69; Dir of Research, Delta Metal Co., and Dir, Delta Metal (BW) Ltd, 1969–73. Vis. Prof., Univ. of Surrey, 1978–. FIM 1948 (Pres. 1965–66); Fellow, Amer. Soc. of Metals, 1974; Pres., Inst. of Metals, 1968–69; Mem., Iron and Steel Inst., 1937– (Williams Prize, 1946). Platinum medallist, Metals Soc., 1978. *Publications:* Controlled Atmospheres for the Heat Treatment of Metals, 1946; contribs to learned jls at home and abroad on metallurgical and related subjects. *Recreations:* music, gardening, swimming. *Address:* Drift Cottage, Worthing, Dereham, Norfolk NR20 5HF. *T:* Elmham 601. *Clubs:* Athenæum, Anglo-Belgian.

JENKINS, (James) Christopher; Parliamentary Counsel, since 1978; *b* 20 May 1939; *s* of Percival Si Phillips Jenkins and Dela (*née* Griffiths); *m* 1962, Margaret Elaine Edwards, *yr d* of Rt Hon. L. John Edwards and Dorothy (*née* Watson); two *s* one *d*. *Educ:* Lewes County Grammar Sch.; Magdalen Coll., Oxford. Solicitor, 1965. Joined Office of Parly Counsel, 1967; at Law Comm, 1970–72 and 1983–86. *Address:* 36 Whitehall, SW1. *Club:* United Oxford & Cambridge University.

JENKINS, Dame Jennifer; *see* Jenkins, Dame M. J.

JENKINS, John George, CBE 1971; farmer; Chairman, United Oilseeds Ltd, since 1984; *b* 26 Aug. 1919; *s* of George John Jenkins, OBE, FRCS and Alice Maud Jenkins, MBE; *m* 1948, Chloe Evelyn (*née* Kenward); one *s* three *d*. *Educ:* Winchester; Edinburgh University. Farmed in Scotland, 1939–62; farmed in England (Cambs and Lincs), 1957–. Pres., NFU of Scotland, 1960–61; Chm., Agricultural Marketing Development Exec. Cttee, 1967–73. Director: Agricultural Mortgage Corporation Ltd; Childerley Estates Ltd. Compère, Anglia Television programme Farming Diary, 1963–80. *Publications:* contrib. Proc. Royal Soc., RSA Jl, etc. *Recreations:* tennis, bridge, music and the arts generally. *Address:* Childerley Hall, Dry Drayton, Cambridge CB3 8BB. *T:* Madingley 210271. *Club:* Farmers'.

JENKINS, Ven. (John) Owen; *b* 13 June 1906; *m* 1939, Gwladys Margaret Clark Jones, *d* of Ven. D. M. Jones, sometime Archdeacon of Carmarthen. *Educ:* St David's Coll., Lampeter; Jesus Coll., Oxford. Deacon 1929, priest 1930; Curate of: Cwmamman, 1929–33; Llanelly, 1933–39; Vicar of Spittal with Trefgarn, 1939–48; TCF, 1943–46; Vicar of Llangadock, 1948–60; Canon of St David's, 1957–62; Rector of Newport, Pembs, 1960–67; Archdeacon of Cardigan, 1962–67; Archdeacon of Carmarthen and Vicar of Llanfihangel Aberbythick, 1967–74. Editor, St David's Dio. Year Book, 1954–63. *Address:* Morfa Gwyn, Aberporth, Cardigan SA43 2EN. *T:* Aberporth 810060.

JENKINS, John Owen, MBE 1978; Chartered Physiotherapist; Senior Lecturer, St Mary's Hospital School of Physiotherapy, W2, since 1975 (Lecturer, 1959); *b* 4 Nov. 1922; *s* of late J. O. Jenkins, JP, and M. E. Jenkins, Great House, Dilwyn, Hereford; *m* 1953, Catherine MacFarlane Baird, MCSP; three *d*. *Educ:* Worcester College for the Blind; NIB School of Physiotherapy, London. MCSP, TMMG, TET. Chartered Society of Physiotherapy: Mem. Council, 1952–81; Chm., Finance and Gen. Purposes Cttee, 1955–79; Member: Education Cttee, 1953–71; Executive Cttee, 1955–79; Trustee, Members' Benevolent Fund, 1955–. CSP Examiner, 1954–; Pres., Orgn of Chartered Physiotherapists in Private Practice, 1980–. Physiotherapy Representative: Min. of Health Working Party on Statutory Registration, 1954; Council for Professions Supplementary to Medicine, 1961–76; Chm., Physiotherapists' Board, 1962–76. Director, LAMPS, 1969–, Chm., 1980–; Trustee, Moira Pakenham-Walsh Foundn, 1978–. Churchwarden, St James the Great, N20, 1974–81. *Publications:* contribs to Physiotherapy and Rehabilitation. *Recreations:* chess, rowing. *Address:* Fintray, 8 Ravensdale Avenue, N12 9HS. *T:* 01–445 6072.

JENKINS, John Robin; *b* Cambuslang, Lanarks, 11 Sept. 1912; *s* of late James Jenkins and of Annie Robin; *m* 1937, Mary McIntyre Wyllie; one *s* two *d*. *Educ:* Hamilton Academy; Glasgow Univ. (MA Hons). *Publications:* (as Robin Jenkins) Happy for the Child, 1953; The Thistle and the Grail, 1954; The Cone-Gatherers, 1955; Guests of War, 1956; The Missionaries, 1957; The Changeling, 1958; Some Kind of Grace, 1960; Dust on the Paw, 1961; The Tiger of Gold, 1962; A Love of Innocence, 1963; The Sardana Dancers, 1964; A Very Scotch Affair, 1968; The Holy Tree, 1969; The Expatriates, 1971; A Toast to the Lord, 1972; A Far Cry from Bowmore, 1973; A Figure of Fun, 1974; A Would-be Saint, 1978; Fergus Lamont, 1979; The Awakening of George Darroch, 1985; Poverty Castle, 1986. *Recreations:* travel, golf. *Address:* Fairhaven, Toward, by Dunoon, Argyll, Scotland. *T:* Toward 288.

JENKINS, Katherine Mary; Under Secretary, Cabinet Office, and Head of Prime Minister's Efficiency Unit, since 1986; *b* 1945; *d* of Daniel Jenkins and Nell Jenkins; *m* 1967, Euan Sutherland; one *s* one *d*. *Educ:* South Hampstead High Sch.; St Anne's Coll., Oxford (BA Hons); London School of Economics (MScEcon). Called to Bar, Inner Temple, 1971. Asst Principal, 1968, Principal, 1973, Dept of Employment; Central Policy Review Staff, 1976; Asst Sec., Dept of Employment, 1979; Dep. Head of Efficiency Unit, 1984. *Address:* 70 Whitehall, SW1. *T:* 01–233 7359.

JENKINS, Dame (Mary) Jennifer, DBE 1985; Chairman, National Trust, since 1986 (Member Executive Committee, since 1984); *b* 18 Jan. 1921; *d* of late Sir Parker Morris; *m* 1945, Rt Hon. Roy Harris Jenkins, *qv*; two *s* one *d*. *Educ:* St Mary's Sch., Calne; Girton Coll., Cambridge. Chm., Cambridge Univ. Labour Club. With Hoover Ltd, 1942–43; Min. of Labour, 1943–46; Political and Economic Planning (PEP), 1946–48; part-time extra-mural lectr, 1949–61; part-time teacher, Kingsway Day Coll., 1961–67. Chm., Consumers' Assoc., 1965–76; Historic Buildings Council for England, 1975–84; Member: Exec. Bd, British Standards Instn, 1970–73; Design Council, 1971–74; Cttee of Management, Courtauld Inst., 1981–84; Ancient Monuments Bd, 1982–84; Historic Buildings and Monuments Commn, 1984–85 (Chm., Historic Buildings Adv. Cttee, 1984–85); Pres., Ancient Monuments Soc., 1985– (Sec., 1972–75). Chm., N Kensington Amenity Trust, 1974–77. Trustee, Wallace Collection, 1977–83. Director: J. Sainsbury Ltd, 1981–86; Abbey National Building Soc., 1984–. JP London Juvenile Courts, 1964–74. Hon. FRIBA, Hon. RICS. *Address:* 2 Kensington Park Gardens, W11; St Amand's House, East Hendred, Oxon; 12 Kirklee Terrace, Glasgow G12 0TH.

JENKINS, Michael Romilly Heald, CMG 1984; HM Diplomatic Service; Minister, British Embassy Washington, since 1985; *b* 9 Jan. 1936; *s* of Prof. Romilly Jenkins and Celine Juliette Haeglar; *m* 1968, Maxine Louise Hodson; one *s* one *d*. *Educ:* privately; King's Coll., Cambridge (Exhibr, BA). Entered Foreign (subseq. Diplomatic) Service, 1959; served in Paris, Moscow and Bonn; Deputy Chef de Cabinet, 1973–75, Chef de Cabinet, 1975–76, to Rt Hon. George Thomson, EEC; Principal Advr to Mr Roy Jenkins, Pres. EEC, Jan–Aug. 1977; Head of European Integration Dept (External), FCO, 1977–79; Hd of Central Adv. Gp, EEC, 1979–81; Dep. Sec. Gen., Commn of the Eur. Communities, 1981–83; Asst Under Sec. of State (Europe), FCO, 1983–85. *Publications:* Arakcheev, Grand Vizier of the Russian Empire, 1969; contrib. History Today. *Address:* c/o Foreign and Commonwealth Office, SW1. *Club:* MCC.

JENKINS, Sir Owain (Trevor), Kt 1958; *b* 1907; 5th *s* of late Sir John Lewis Jenkins, KCSI, ICS; *m* 1940, Sybil Léonie, *y d* of late Maj.-Gen. Lionel Herbert, CB, CVO. *Educ:* Charterhouse; Balliol Coll., Oxford. Employed by Balmer Lawrie & Co. Ltd, Calcutta, 1929; Indian Army, 1940–44; Man. Dir, Balmer Lawrie, 1948–58. Pres. of the Bengal Chamber of Commerce and Industry and Pres. of the Associated Chambers of Commerce of India, 1956–57. Formerly Director: Singapore Traction Co.; Calcutta Electric Supply Corp.; Macleod Russel PLC; retd 1982. Mem., Econ. Survey Mission to Basutoland, Bechuanaland Protectorate and Swaziland, 1959. *Address:* Boles House, East Street, Petworth, West Sussex GU28 0AB. *Club:* Oriental.

JENKINS, Ven. Owen; *see* Jenkins, Ven. J. O.

JENKINS, Peter; Political Columnist, The Sunday Times, since 1985; *b* 11 May 1934; *s* of Kenneth E. Jenkins and Joan E. Jenkins (*née* Croger); *m* 1st, 1960, Charlotte Strachey (decd); one *d*; 2nd, 1970, Polly Toynbee, *qv*; one *s* two *d*. *Educ:* Culford Sch.; Trinity Hall, Cambridge (BA Hist., MA). Journalist, Financial Times, 1958–60; The Guardian: Journalist, 1960; Labour Correspondent, 1963–67; Washington Correspondent, 1972–74; Political Commentator and Policy Editor, 1974–85. Theatre Critic, The Spectator, 1978–81. First stage play, Illuminations, performed at Lyric, Hammersmith, 1980; TV series, Struggle, 1983. Vis. Fellow, Nuffield Coll., Oxford, 1980–. Awards include: Granada TV Journalist of the Year, 1978. *Publication:* The Battle of Downing Street, 1970. *Address:* 1 Crescent Grove, SW4 7AF. *T:* 01–622 6492. *Club:* Garrick.

JENKINS, Peter White; Director of Finance, Welsh Water Authority, since 1984; *b* 12 Oct. 1937; *s* of John White Jenkins, OBE, and Dorothy Jenkins; *m* 1961, Joyce Christine Muter; one *s* one *d*. *Educ:* Queen Mary's Grammar Sch., Walsall; King Edward VI Grammar Sch., Nuneaton. CIPFA. Local govt service in Finance Depts at Coventry, Preston, Chester, Wolverhampton; Dep. Treasurer, Birkenhead, 1969–73; County Treasurer, Merseyside CC, 1973–84. *Recreations:* walking, gardening, reading. *Address:* Welsh Water Authority, Cambrian Way, Brecon, Powys LD3 7HP.

JENKINS, Robin; *see* Jenkins, J. R.

JENKINS, Rt. Hon. Roy Harris, PC 1964; MP (SDP) Glasgow, Hillhead, since March 1982; First Leader, Social Democratic Party, 1982–83 (Member of Joint Leadership, 1981–82); *b* 11 Nov. 1920; *o s* of late Arthur Jenkins, MP, and of Hattie Jenkins; *m* 1945, Jennifer Morris (*see* Dame Jennifer Jenkins); two *s* one *d*. *Educ:* Abersychan Grammar Sch.; University Coll., Cardiff (Hon. Fellow 1982); Balliol Coll., Oxford (Hon. Fellow 1969). Sec. and Librarian, Oxford Union Society; Chairman, Oxford Univ. Democratic Socialist Club; First Class in Hon. Sch. of Philosophy, Politics and Economics, 1941. Served War of 1939–45, in RA, 1942–46; Captain, 1944–46. Contested (Lab) Solihull Div. of Warwicks, at Gen. Election, 1945. Mem. of Staff of Industrial and Commercial Finance Corp. Ltd, 1946–48. Mem. Exec. Cttee of Fabian Soc., 1949–61; Chm., Fabian Soc., 1957–58; Mem. Cttee of Management, Soc. of Authors, 1956–60; Governor, British Film Institute, 1955–58; Adviser to John Lewis Partnership, 1954–62, Dir of Financial Operations, 1962–64. Dir, Morgan Grenfell Hldgs Ltd, 1981–82. MP (Lab): Central Southwark, 1948–50; Stechford, Birmingham, 1950–76; PPS to Sec. of State for Commonwealth Relations, 1949–50; Minister of Aviation, 1964–65; Home Sec., 1965–67, 1974–76; Chancellor of the Exchequer, 1967–70; Dep. Leader, Labour Party, 1970–72. Pres., European Commn, 1977–81; contested Warrington by-election as first Social Democratic candidate, July 1981. UK Deleg. to Council of Europe, 1955–57. Vice-Pres., Inst. of Fiscal Studies, 1970–. Formerly: Dep. Chm. Federal Union; Pres., Britain in Europe, Referendum Campaign, 1975; Chm., Labour European Cttee. A President of United Kingdom Council of the European Movement. Pres., UWIST, 1975–81. Trustee, Pilgrim Trust, 1973–. Dimbleby Lecture, 1979. Liveryman, Goldsmiths' Co.; Freeman, City of London, 1965. Freeman, City of Brussels, 1980. Hon. Foreign Mem., Amer. Acad. Arts and Scis, 1973. Hon. Fellow, Berkeley Coll., Yale, 1972. Hon. LLD: Leeds, 1971; Harvard, 1972; Pennsylvania, 1973; Dundee, 1973; Loughborough, 1975; Bath, 1978; Michigan, 1978; Wales, 1979; Bristol, 1980; Hon. DLitt: Glasgow, 1972; City, 1976; Warwick, 1978; Reading, 1979; Hon. DCL Oxford, 1973; Hon. DSc Aston, 1977; DUniv: Keele, 1977; Essex, 1978; Open, 1979; Hon. DPhil Katholieke Univ., Leuven, 1979; Hon. doctorates: Urbino, 1979; TCD, 1979. Charlemagne Prize, 1972; Robert Schuman Prize, 1972; Prix Bentinck, 1978. Order of European Merit (Luxemburg), 1976; Grand Cross: Legion of Honour of Senegal, 1979; Legion of Honour of Mali, 1979; Order of Charles III (Spain), 1980. *Publications:* (ed) Purpose and Policy (a vol. of the Prime Minister's Speeches), 1947; Mr Attlee: An Interim Biography, 1948; Pursuit of Progress, 1953; Mr Balfour's Poodle, 1954; Sir Charles Dilke: A Victorian Tragedy, 1958; The Labour Case (Penguin Special), 1959; Asquith, 1964; Essays and Speeches, 1967; Afternoon on the Potomac?, 1972; What Matters Now, 1972; Nine Men of Power, 1975; Partnership of Principle, 1985; Truman, 1986; Baldwin, 1987; contrib. to New Fabian Essays, 1952; contrib. to Hugh Gaitskell, A Memoir, 1964. *Address:* 2 Kensington Park Gardens, W11; St Amand's House, East Hendred, Oxon; 12 Kirklee Terrace, Glasgow. *Clubs:* Athenæum, Brooks's, Pratt's, Reform.

JENKINS, Simon David; Political Editor, The Economist, since 1979; *b* 10 June 1943; *s* of Dr Daniel Jenkins and Nell Jenkins; *m* 1978, Gayle Hunnicutt; one *s* and one step *s*. *Educ:* Mill Hill Sch.; St John's Coll., Oxford (BA Hons); Research Student, Univ. of Sussex, 1964–65. Country Life magazine, 1965; Research Asst, Univ. of London Inst. of Educn, 1966; News Editor, Times Educational Supplement, 1966–68; Evening Standard, 1968–74; Insight Editor, Sunday Times, 1974–75; Dep. Editor, Evening Standard, 1976, Editor, 1976–78. Member: British Railways Bd, 1979– (Chm., BR Environment Panel, 1984–); LRT Bd, 1984–86; South Bank Bd, 1985–. Director: Municipal Journal Ltd, 1980–; Faber & Faber, 1980–. Mem. Council, Bow Group, and Editor of Crossbow, 1968–70; Member: Cttee Save Britain's Heritage, 1976–85; Historic Buildings and Monuments Commn, 1985– (Chm., Historic Areas Cttee); Mem. Council: Inst. of Contemporary Arts, 1976–85; Old Vic Co., 1979–81; Dep. Chm., Thirties Soc., 1979–85.

Governor, Mus. of London, 1985–. *Publications:* A City at Risk, 1971; Landlords to London, 1974; (ed) Insight on Portugal, 1975; Newspapers: the power and the money, 1979; The Companion Guide to Outer London, 1981; (with Max Hastings) The Battle for the Falklands, 1983; Images of Hampstead, 1983; (with Anne Sloman) With Respect Ambassador, 1985; The Market for Glory, 1986; various pamphlets and articles in political and architectural jls. *Recreation:* living in London. *Address:* 174 Regent's Park Road, NW1. *Club:* Garrick.

JENKINS, Stanley Kenneth; HM Diplomatic Service, retired; *b* 25 Nov. 1920; *s* of Benjamin and Ethel Jane Jenkins; *m* 1957, Barbara Mary Marshall Webb; four *d*. *Educ:* Brecon; Cardiff Tech. Coll. President, Nat. Union of Students, 1949–51. LIOB 1950. Served War, Royal Artillery and Royal Engineers, 1942–46, retiring as Major. Joined Foreign (later Diplomatic) Service, 1951; Singapore, 1953; Kuala Lumpur, 1955; FO, 1957; Singapore, 1959; Rangoon, 1959; FO, 1964; Nicosia, 1967; FO, 1970–78, Counsellor. *Recreations:* gardening, tennis. *Address:* Willow Cottage, 1 Beehive Lane, Ferring, Worthing, Sussex BN12 5NL. *T:* Worthing 47356. *Club:* Royal Commonwealth Society.

JENKINS, Very Rev. Thomas Edward; *b* 14 Aug. 1902; *s* of late David Jenkins, Canon of St David's Cathedral and Vicar of Abergwili, and of Florence Helena Jenkins; *m* 1928, Annie Laura, *d* of late David Henry, Penygroes, Carms; one *s*. *Educ:* Llandyssul Grammar Sch.; St David's Coll., Lampeter; Wycliffe Hall, Oxford. St David's Coll., Lampeter, BA 1922, BD 1932, Powys Exhibitioner, 1924; Welsh Church Scholar, 1921. Ordained, 1925; Curate of Llanelly, 1925–34; Rector of Begelly, 1934–38; Vicar: Christ Church, Llanelly, 1938–46; Lampeter, 1946–55 (Rural Dean, 1949–54); Canon, St David's Cathedral, 1951–57; Vicar of Cardigan, 1955–57; Dean of St David's, 1957–72. *Address:* 18 North Road, Cardigan, Dyfed SA43 1AA.

JENKINS, Thomas Harris, (Tom), CBE 1981; General Secretary, Transport Salaried Staffs' Association, 1977–82; *b* 29 Aug. 1920; *s* of David Samuel Jenkins and Miriam Hughes (*née* Harris); *m* 1946, Joyce Smith; two *d*. *Educ:* Port Talbot Central Boys' Sch.; Port Talbot County Sch.; Shrewsbury Technical Coll. (evenings); Pitmans Coll., London (evenings). MCIT 1980. Served War, RAMC, 1941–46 (Certif. for Good Service, Army, Western Comd, 1946). Railway clerk, 1937–41; railway/docks clerk, 1946–49. Full-time service with Railway Clerks' Assoc., subseq. re-named Transport Salaried Staffs' Assoc., 1949–82: Southern Reg. Divl Sec., 1959; Western Reg. Divl Sec., 1963; LMR Divl Sec., 1966; Sen. Asst Sec., 1968; Asst Gen. Sec., 1970, also Dep. to Gen. Sec., 1973. Member: Cttee of Transport Workers in European Community, 1976–82; Transport Industry, Nationalised Industries, and Hotel and Catering Industry Cttees of TUC, 1977–82; Management and Indus. Relns Cttee, SSRC, 1979–81; Air Transport and Travel Industry Trng Bd, 1976–82; Hotel and Catering Industry Trng Bd, 1978–82; Employment Appeal Tribunal, 1982–; British Railways Midland and NW Reg. Bd, 1982–86; Police Complaints Bd, 1983–85; Central Arbitration Cttee, 1983–; ACAS Arbitration Bd, 1983–. Mem. Labour Party, 1946–; Mem., Lab. Party Transport Sub-Cttee, 1970–82. *Recreations:* watching cricket, athletics and Rugby football. *Address:* 23 The Chase, Edgware, Mddx. *T:* 01–952 5314. *Clubs:* MCC, Middlesex County Cricket.
See also D. C. Jenkins.

JENKINS, Vivian Evan, MBE 1945; Director of Social Services, Cardiff City Council, 1971–74, retired; *b* 12 Sept. 1918; *s* of late Arthur Evan Jenkins and late Mrs Blodwen Jenkins; *m* 1946, Megan Myfanwy Evans; one *s* one *d*. *Educ:* UC Cardiff (BA). Dipl. Social Science. Army, 1940; commnd Royal Signals, 1943; served with 6th Airborne Div. as parachutist, Europe, Far East and Middle East, 1943–46 (Lieut). Child Care Officer, Glamorgan CC, 1949; Asst Children's Officer, 1951; Mem. Home Office Children's Dept Inspectorate, 1952. *Recreations:* Rugby football (former Captain of Univ. XV and Pontypridd RFC; awarded two Wales Rugby caps as schoolboy, 1933 and 1937); cricket, golf. *Address:* 24 Windsor Road, Radyr, Cardiff. *T:* Radyr 842485. *Club:* Radyr Golf.

JENKINSON, Sir Anthony Banks, 13th Bt, *cr* 1661; *b* 3 July 1912; *S* grandfather, 1915; *s* of Captain John Banks Jenkinson (killed European War, Sept. 1914) and Joan, *o d* of late Col Joseph Hill, CB (she *m* 2nd, 1920, Maj.-Gen. Algernon Langhorne, CB, DSO, who died 1945); *m* 1943, Frances, *d* of Harry Stremmel; one *s* two *d*. *Educ:* Eton; Balliol Coll., Oxford (Editor, The Isis, 1933–34). Foreign Correspondent, 1935–40: first British reporter to interview Mao Tse-tung in Yenan, NW China, Daily Sketch, 1938; Mediterranean Snoop Cruise Series, Daily Express, 1939; Caribbean Snoop Cruise, N American Newspaper Alliance & Reader's Digest, 1940; Editor, Allied Labour News Service, London and New York, 1940–46. Managing Director: Cayman Boats Ltd, Cayman Is, 1947–52; Morgan's Harbour Ltd, Port Royal, Jamaica, 1953–73; Director: Port Royal Co. of Merchants Ltd, 1965–72; Spanish Main Investments Ltd, Grand Cayman, 1962–; Caribbean Bank (Cayman) Ltd, 1973–80; Cayman Free Press Ltd, 1974–; Cayman Corporate Services Ltd, 1982–. *Publications:* America Came My Way, 1935; Where Seldom a Gun is Heard, 1937. *Recreations:* sailing, travel. *Heir:* *s* John Banks Jenkinson, *b* 16 Feb. 1945. *Address:* 491 South Church Street, Grand Cayman, British West Indies. *Clubs:* United Oxford & Cambridge University; MCC; Bembridge Sailing; Cayman Islands Yacht.

JENKS, Sir Richard Atherley, 2nd Bt, *cr* 1932; *b* 26 July 1906; *er s* of Sir Maurice Jenks, 1st Bt, and Martha Louise Christabel, *d* of late George Calley Smith; *S* father 1946; *m* 1932, Marjorie Suzanne Arlette, *d* of late Sir Arthur du Cros, 1st Bt; two *s*. *Educ:* Charterhouse. Chartered Accountant, retired. *Heir:* *s* Maurice Arthur Brian Jenks [*b* 28 Oct. 1933; *m* 1962, Susan, *e d* of Leslie Allen, Surrey; one *d*]. *Address:* 42 Sussex Square, W2 2SP. *T:* 01–262 8356.

JENKYNS, Henry Leigh; Under-Secretary, Department of the Environment, 1969–75; *b* 20 Jan. 1917; *y s* of H. H. Jenkyns, Indian Civil Service; *m* 1947, Rosalind Mary Home; two *s* one *d*. *Educ:* Eton and Balliol Coll., Oxford. War Service in Royal Signals; Lt-Col, East Africa Command, 1944. Treasury, 1945–66; Private Sec. to Chancellor, 1951–53. Treasury Representative in Australia and New Zealand, 1953–56; UK Delegation to OECD, Paris, 1961–63; Asst Under-Sec. of State, DEA, 1966–69; Chm., SE Economic Planning Bd, 1968–71. Mem., Southwark Diocesan Adv. Cttee for Care of Churches, 1977–78. Mem., Exmoor Study Team, 1977. *Recreations:* music, garden, sailing, mending things. *Address:* Westcroft, Priors Hill Road, Aldeburgh, Suffolk. *T:* Aldeburgh 2357. *Club:* United Oxford & Cambridge University.

JENNER, Ann Maureen; Ballerina, Australian Ballet, 1978–80; Guest Ballet Teacher, since 1980: Victorian College of the Arts, and National Ballet School, Melbourne; Australian Ballet; Queensland Ballet; and many other schools in Sydney and Melbourne; *b* 8 March 1944; *d* of Kenneth George Jenner and Margaret Rosetta (*née* Wilson); *m* 1980, Dale Robert Baker; one *s*. *Educ:* Royal Ballet Junior and Senior Schools. Royal Ballet Co., 1961–78: Soloist 1964; Principal Dancer 1970. Roles include: Lise, Fille Mal Gardée, 1966; Swanhilda, Coppelia, 1968; Cinderella, 1969; Princess Aurora, Sleeping Beauty, 1972; Giselle, 1973; Gypsy, Deux Pigeons, 1974; White Girl, Deux Pigeons, 1976; Juliet, Romeo and Juliet, 1977; Countess Larisch, Mayerling, 1978; Flavia, Spartacus, 1979; Kitri, Don Quixote, 1979; Anna, Anna Karenina, 1980; Poll, Pineapple Poll, 1980; one-act roles include: Symphonic Variations, 1967; Firebird, 1972; Triad, 1973; Les Sylphides; Serenade; Les Patineurs; Elite Syncopations, Concert, Flower Festival Pas de Deux, etc. Guest Teacher, San Francisco Ballet Co. and San Francisco Ballet Sch., 1985. *Address:* c/o Australian Ballet, 11 Mount Alexander Road, Flemington, Vic. 3031, Australia.

JENNETT, Frederick Stuart, CBE 1985; Chairman and Senior Partner, Percy Thomas Partnership, since 1971; *b* 22 April 1924; *s* of Horace Frederick Jennett and Jenny Sophia Jennett; *m* 1948, Nada Eusebia Phillips; two *d*. *Educ:* Whitchurch Grammar School; Welsh School of Architecture, UWIST (Dip. in Architecture (dist.)). FRIBA, MRTPI, FRSA. T. Alwyn Lloyd & Gordon, Architects, Cardiff, 1949; Cwmbran Develt Corp., 1951; Louis de Soissons Peacock Hodges & Robinson, Welwyn Garden City, 1955; S. Colwyn Foukes & Partners, Colwyn Bay, 1956; Associate, 1962, Partner, 1964, Sir Percy Thomas & Son, Bristol. *Publications:* papers on hospital planning. *Recreations:* running, water colour painting. *Address:* Portland Lodge, Lower Almondsbury, Bristol BS12 4EJ. *T:* Almondsbury 615175. *Club:* Reform.

JENNETT, Prof. (William) Bryan, FRCS, FRCSGlas; Professor of Neurosurgery, since 1968, Dean of the Faculty of Medicine, since 1981, University of Glasgow; *b* 1 March 1926; *s* of Robert William Jennett and Jessie Pate Loudon; *m* 1950, Sheila Mary Pope; three *s* one *d*. *Educ:* Univ. of Liverpool (MB ChB 1949, MD 1960). House Physician to Lord Cohen of Birkenhead, 1949; Ho. Surg. to Sir Hugh Cairns, 1950; Surgical Specialist, RAMC, 1951–53; Registrar in Neurosurgery, Oxford and Cardiff, 1954–56; Lectr in Neurosurgery, Univ. of Manchester, 1957–62; Rockefeller Travelling Fellow, Univ. of California, LA, 1958–59; Cons. Neurosurgeon, Glasgow, 1963–68. Member: MRC, 1979–83; GMC, 1984–; Chief Scientists' Cttee, 1983–. Rock Carling Fellow, London, 1983. *Publications:* Epilepsy after Blunt Head Injury, 1962, 2nd edn 1975; Introduction to Neurosurgery, 1964, 4th edn 1983; (with G. Teasdale) Management of Head Injuries, 1981; High Technology Medicine: benefits and burdens, 1984, 2nd edn 1986; many papers in Lancet, BMJ and elsewhere. *Recreations:* cruising under sail, writing. *Address:* 4 Cleveden Drive, Glasgow G12 0SE. *T:* 041–334 5148. *Club:* Royal Society of Medicine.

JENNINGS, Sir Albert (Victor), Kt 1969; Founder and Past Chairman, Jennings Industries Ltd, 1932, retired 1972; *b* 12 Oct. 1896; *s* of John Thomas Jennings; *m* 1922, Ethel Sarah, *d* of George Herbert Johnson; two *s*. *Educ:* Eastern Road Sch., Melbourne. Served First World War, AIF. Council Mem., Master Builders Assoc., 1943–; Vice Pres. Housing, Master Builders Fedn of Aust., 1970–71; Member: Commonwealth Building Research and Advisory Cttee, 1948–72; Manufacturing Industries Adv. Council to Australian Govt, 1962–; Decentralisation and Develt Adv. Cttee to Victorian State Govt, 1965–; Commonwealth of Aust. Metric Conversion Bd, 1970–72; Trustee, Cttee for Economic Develt of Australia. Fellow: Aust. Inst. of Building (Federal Pres., 1964–65 and 1965–66); UK Inst. of Building, 1971. Aust. Inst. of Building Medal 1970; Urban Land Inst. Total Community Develt Award, 1973; Sir Charles McGrath Award for Services to Marketing, 1976. *Recreations:* swimming, golf. *Address:* Ranelagh House, Rosserdale Crescent, Mount Eliza, Victoria 3930, Australia. *T:* 7871350. *Clubs:* Commonwealth (Canberra); Melbourne, Savage (Melbourne).

JENNINGS, Arnold Harry, CBE 1977; MA; Headmaster, Ecclesfield School, Sheffield, 1959–79 (formerly, 1959–67, Ecclesfield Grammar School); *b* 24 May 1915; *s* of Harry Jennings and Alice Mary (*née* Northrop); *m* 1939, Elizabeth Redman; one *s* one *d*. *Educ:* Bradford Grammar Sch.; Corpus Christi Coll., Oxford (Classical Schol.; MA). Tutor, Knutsford Ordination Test Sch., Hawarden, 1939–40. Served War, Captain RA, England, N Ireland, France, Belgium, Holland and Germany, 1940–46. Sen. Classical Master, Chesterfield Grammar Sch., 1946–53; Headmaster, Tapton House Sch., Chesterfield, 1953–58; part-time extra-mural Lectr, Sheffield Univ., 1946–54. Mem., NUT Executive, 1958–59 and 1960–72 (Chm., Secondary Adv. Cttee, 1968–72); Secondary Heads Association: Hon Sec., 1978–79; Membership Sec., 1979–81; Hon. Mem., 1981–; President: Head Masters' Assoc., 1977; Jt Assoc. of Classical Teachers, 1975–77; Mem., Secondary Schs Examinations Council, 1961–64; Schools Council: Mem., 1964–84; Dep. Chm. and Acting Chm., 1982–84; Chm., Steering Cttee 'C', 1975–78; Chm., Second Examinations Cttee, 1968–76; Jt Chm., Jt Examinations Sub-Cttee, 1971–76; Chm., Exams Cttee, 1978–83; Chm., Classics Cttee; Convenor, A-level Classics Scrutiny Panel, Secondary Examinations Council, 1984. Mem. Court, Sheffield Univ., 1959–78. Sheffield City Councillor, 1949–58; contested (Lab) Heeley, Sheffield, 1950 and 1951. *Publications:* (ed) Management and Headship in the Secondary School, 1977; (ed) Discipline in Primary and Secondary Schools Today, 1979; articles on educn *passim*. *Recreations:* work, wine, opera, photography, travel. *Address:* 74 Clarkegrove Road, Sheffield S10 2NJ. *T:* Sheffield 662520.

JENNINGS, Audrey Mary; Metropolitan Stipendiary Magistrate, since 1972; *b* 22 June 1928; *d* of Hugh and late Olive Jennings, Ashbrook Range, Sunderland; *m* 1961, Roger Harry Kilbourne Frisby, *qv* (marr. diss. 1980); two *s* one *d*. *Educ:* Durham High Sch.; Durham Univ. (BA); Oxford Univ. (DPA). Children's Officer, City and County of Cambridge, 1952–56. Called to Bar, Middle Temple, 1956 (Harmsworth Schol.); practised at Criminal Bar, London, 1956–61 and 1967–72. Mem., Criminal Law Revision Cttee, 1977–. *Recreations:* theatre, music, gardening.

JENNINGS, Bernard Antony; Legal Adviser, BBC, since 1977; Director: BBC Enterprises Ltd, since 1979; Video Copyright Protection Society Ltd, since 1981; *b* 29 May 1939; *s* of Bernard Joseph Francis Jennings and Constance Nora Jennings (*née* O'Shea). *Educ:* St Bede's Coll., Manchester; Christ's Coll., Cambridge (MA). Articled Clerk, John Gorna & Co., Manchester; admitted Solicitor, 1964; BBC Solicitor's Dept, 1964–74; BBC Head of Copyright, 1974–77. Chm., Legal Cttee, EBU, 1982–. *Publication:* (jtly) Satellite Broadcasting, 1985. *Address:* Broadcasting House, W1A 1AA. *T:* 01–580 4468.

JENNINGS, Elizabeth (Joan); author; *b* 18 July 1926; *d* of Dr H. C. Jennings, Oxon. *Educ:* Oxford High Sch.; St Anne's Coll., Oxford. Asst at Oxford City Library, 1950–58; Reader for Chatto & Windus Ltd, 1958–60. *Publications: poetry:* Poems (Arts Council Prize), 1953; A Way of Looking, 1955 (Somerset Maugham Award, 1956); A Sense of the World, 1958; (ed) The Batsford Book of Children's Verse, 1958; Song for a Birth or a Death, 1961; a translation of Michelangelo's sonnets, 1961; Recoveries, 1964; The Mind Has Mountains, 1966 (Richard Hillary Prize, 1966); The Secret Brother (for children), 1966; Collected Poems, 1967; The Animals' Arrival, 1969 (Arts Council Bursary, 1969); (ed) A Choice of Christina Rossetti's Verse, 1970; Lucidities, 1970; Relationships, 1972; Growing Points, 1975; Consequently I Rejoice, 1977; After the Ark (for children), 1978; Selected Poems, 1980; Moments of Grace, 1980; (ed) The Batsford Book of Religious Verse, 1981; Celebrations and Elegies, 1982; In Praise of Our Lady (anthology), 1982; Extending the Territory, 1985; (contrib.) A Quintet (for children), 1985; Collected Poems, 1953–86, 1986; *prose:* Let's Have Some Poetry, 1960; Every Changing Shape, 1961; Robert Frost, 1964; Christianity and Poetry, 1965; Seven Men of Vision, 1976; also poems and articles in: New Statesman, New Yorker, Botteghe Oscure, Observer, Spectator, Listener, Vogue, The Scotsman, etc. *Recreations:* travel, looking at pictures, the theatre, the cinema, music, collecting, conversation. *Address:* c/o David Higham Associates Ltd, 5–8 Lower John Street, W1R 4HA. *Club:* Society of Authors.

JENNINGS, John Charles; *b* 10 Feb. 1903; *m* 1927, Berta Nicholson (*d* 1979); one *s* decd. *Educ:* Bede Coll., Durham; King's Coll., Durham Univ. Headmaster. Contested (C), SE Derbyshire, 1950 and 1951. MP (C) Burton-on-Trent, Staffs, 1955–Feb. 1974; Chm., Cttees of House of Commons, 1964–74. *Recreation:* politics. *Address:* Two Trees, Meadowfield Road, Stocksfield, Northumberland. *T:* Stocksfield 843565.

JENNINGS, Very Rev. Kenneth Neal; Dean of Gloucester, since 1983; *b* 8 Nov. 1930; *s* of Reginald Tinsley and Edith Dora Jennings; *m* 1972, Wendy Margaret Stallworthy; one *s* one *d. Educ:* Hertford Grammar School; Corpus Christi College, Cambridge (MA); Cuddesdon College, Oxford. Asst Curate, Holy Trinity, Ramsgate, 1956–59; Lecturer 1959–61, Vice-Principal 1961–66, Bishop's College, Calcutta; Vice-Principal, Cuddesdon Theological Coll., 1967–73; Vicar of Hitchin, 1973–76; Team Rector of Hitchin, 1977–82. *Recreations:* music, fell-walking. *Address:* The Deanery, Miller's Green, Gloucester GL1 2BP. *T:* Gloucester 24167.

JENNINGS, Paul (Francis), FRSL; writer; *b* 20 June 1918; *s* of William Benedict and Mary Gertrude Jennings; *m* 1952, Celia Blom; three *s* three *d. Educ:* King Henry VIII, Coventry, and Douai. Freelance work in Punch and Spectator began while still in Army (Lt Royal Signals); Script-writer at Central Office of Information, 1946–47; Copy writer at Colman Prentis Varley (advertising), 1947–49; on staff of The Observer, 1949–66. Trustee, Philharmonia Trust. *Publications:* Oddly Enough, 1951; Even Oddlier, 1952; Oddly Bodlikins, 1953; Next to Oddliness, 1955; Model Oddlies, 1956; Gladly Oddly, 1957; Idly Oddly, 1959; I Said Oddly, Diddle I?, 1961; Oodles of Oddlies, 1963; The Jenguin Pennings, 1963; Oddly Ad Lib, 1965; I Was Joking, of Course, 1968; The Living Village, 1968; Just a Few Lines, 1969; It's An Odd Thing, But..., 1971; (ed) The English Difference, 1974; Britain As She Is Visit, 1976; The Book of Nonsense, 1977; I Must Have Imagined It, 1977; Companion to Britain, 1980; (ed) A Feast of Days, 1982; (ed) My Favourite Railway Stories, 1982; Golden Oddlies, 1983; East Anglia, 1986; *novel:* And Now for Something Exactly the Same, 1977; *for children:* The Hopping Basket, 1965; The Great Jelly of London, 1967; The Train to Yesterday, 1974. *Recreations:* madrigal singing and thinking about writing another vast serious book. *Address:* 25 High Street, Orford, Woodbridge, Suffolk.

JENNINGS, Percival Henry, CBE 1953; *b* 8 Dec. 1903; *s* of late Rev. Canon H. R. Jennings; *m* 1934, Margaret Katharine Musgrave, *d* of late Brig.-Gen. H. S. Rogers, CMG, DSO; three *d. Educ:* Christ's Hospital. Asst Auditor, N Rhodesia, 1927; Asst Auditor, Mauritius, 1931; Auditor, British Honduras, 1934; Dep. Dir of Audit, Gold Coast, 1938; Dep. Dir of Audit, Nigeria, 1945; Dir of Audit, Hong Kong, 1948; Dep. Dir-Gen. of the Overseas Audit Service, 1955; Dir-Gen. of the Overseas Audit Service, 1960–63, retd. *Recreation:* golf. *Address:* Littlewood, Lelant, St Ives, Cornwall. *T:* Hayle 753407. *Clubs:* Royal Commonwealth Society; West Cornwall Golf.

JENNINGS, Rev. Peter; Superintendent Minister, Whitechapel Mission, since 1982; *b* 9 Oct. 1937; *s* of Robert William Jennings and Margaret Irene Jennings; *m* 1963, Cynthia Margaret Leicester; two *s. Educ:* Manchester Grammar Sch.; Keble Coll., Oxford (MA); Hartley Victoria Methodist Theological Coll.; Manchester Univ. (MA). Ordained 1965. Minister: Swansea Methodist Circuit, 1963–67; London Mission (East) Circuit, 1967–78, and Tutor Warden, Social Studies Centre, 1967–74; Gen. Sec., Council of Christians and Jews, 1974–81; Associate Minister, Wesley's Chapel, 1978–81; Asst Minister, Walthamstow and Chingford Methodist Circuit, 1981–82. Hon. Treasurer, London Rainbow Group; Mem., Exec. Cttee, London Soc. of Jews and Christians. *Publications:* papers and articles on aspects of Christian-Jewish relations. *Recreations:* photography, being educated by Tim and Nick. *Address:* The Whitechapel Mission, 212 Whitechapel Road, E1 1BJ. *T:* 01-247 8280.

JENNINGS, Sir Raymond (Winter), Kt 1968; QC 1945; Master, Court of Protection, 1956–70; *b* 12 Dec. 1897; *o s* of late Sir Arthur Oldham Jennings and Mabel Winter; *m* 1930, Sheila (*d* 1972), *d* of Selwyn S. Grant, OBE; one *s* one *d. Educ:* Rugby; RMC, Sandhurst; Oriel Coll., Oxford (MA, BCL). Served 1916–19 in Royal Fusiliers. Called to Bar, 1922; Bencher of Lincoln's Inn, 1951. *Recreation:* fishing. *Address:* 14C Upper Drive, Hove, East Sussex BN3 6GN. *T:* Brighton 773361. *Club:* Athenæum.

JENNINGS, Sir Robert (Yewdall), Kt 1982; QC 1969; MA, LLB Cantab; a Judge of the International Court of Justice, since 1982; *b* 19 Oct. 1913; *o s* of Arthur Jennings; *m* 1955, Christine, *yr d* of Bernard Bennett; one *s* two *d. Educ:* Belle Vue Grammar Sch., Bradford; Downing Coll., Cambridge (scholar; 1st cl. pts I & II Law Tripos; LLB; Hon. Fellow, 1982). Served War, Intelligence Corps, 1940–46; Hon. Major, Officers' AER. Called to the Bar, Lincoln's Inn, 1943 (Hon. Bencher, 1970). Whewell Scholar in Internat. Law, Cambridge, 1936; Joseph Hodges Choate Fellow, Harvard Univ., 1936–37; Asst Lectr in Law, LSE, 1938–39; Jesus College, Cambridge: Fellow, 1939, Hon. Fellow, 1982; Sen. Tutor, 1949–55; Sometime Pres. Whewell Prof. of Internat. Law, Cambridge Univ., 1955–81; Reader in Internat. Law, Council of Legal Educn, 1959–70. Member: Permanent Court of Arbitration, 1982–; Inst. of Internat. Law, 1967– (Vice-Pres., 1979; Pres., 1981–83; Hon. Mem., 1985–); Hon. Life Mem., Amer. Soc. of Internat. Law, 1986–. Joint Editor: International and Comparative Law Quarterly, 1956–61; British Year Book of International Law, 1960–82. *Publications:* The Acquisition of Territory, 1963; General Course on International Law, 1967; articles in legal periodicals. *Address:* Jesus College, Cambridge.

JENOUR, Sir (Arthur) Maynard (Chesterfield), Kt 1959; TD 1950; JP; Director: Aberthaw & Bristol Channel Portland Cement Co. Ltd, 1929–83 (Chairman and Joint Managing Director, 1946–83); T. Beynon & Co. Ltd, 1938–83 (Chairman and Joint Managing Director, 1946–83); Ruthin Quarries (Bridgend) Ltd, 1947–83 (Chairman, 1947–83); Associated Portland Cement Manufacturers Ltd, 1963–75; Blue Jacket Motel (Pty) Ltd, Australia, 1964; *b* 7 Jan. 1905; *s* of Brig.-Gen. A. S. Jenour, CB, CMG, DSO, Crossways, Chepstow and Emily Anna (*née* Beynon); *m* 1948, Margaret Sophie (who *m* 1927, W. O. Ellis Fielding-Jones, *d* 1935; three *d*), *d* of H. Stuart Osborne, Sydney, NSW. *Educ:* Eton. Entered business, 1924. Served War of 1939–45, in England and Middle East, Royal Artillery, Major. High Sheriff of Monmouthshire, 1951–52; Pres., Cardiff Chamber of Commerce, 1953–54; Chm. Wales & Mon. Industrial Estates Ltd, 1954–60; Mem. Board, Development Corporation for Wales, 1958–81. JP Mon 1946; DL Mon, 1960; Vice-Lieut of Mon, 1965–74, Vice Lord-Lieut of Gwent, 1974–79. KStJ 1969. *Recreations:* walking, gardening, shooting. *Address:* Stonycroft, 13 Ridgeway, Newport, Gwent. *T:* Newport 63802. *Clubs:* Army and Navy; Cardiff and County (Cardiff); Union (Sydney, NSW).

JEPHCOTT, Hon. Sir Bruce (Reginald), Kt 1983; CBE 1976; company director; Owner/Manager, Dumpu Pty Ltd, since 1961; Chairman: Livestock Development Corporation, Papua New Guinea, since 1983; Kiunga & Telefomin Transport Co., since 1985; *b* 19 March 1929; *s* of Reginald Francis Jephcott and Thelma Mary (*née* Rogers); *m* 1956, Barbara Aileen Harpham; one *s* two *d. Educ:* King's Coll., Adelaide; Prince Alfred Coll., Adelaide; Adelaide Univ. (BSc 1948). ARACI 1951; MRIC, CChem 1953. Bacteriologist, F. H. Faulding, 1949–50; Chief Vet. Bio-chemist, NT Admin, 1950–59; Manager, Ainora Coffee Plantation, 1959–61; Res. Scholar, Rowett Res. Inst., Scotland, 1953; Minister for Transport, PNG, 1972–78; Dir, Pagini Transport Co., 1985–. Alternate Chm., National Airline Commn, PNG, 1982–. Pres., Polocrosse Assoc., PNG, 1982; Vice-Pres., Polocrosse Internat., 1982–. Independence Medal, PNG, 1975; Silver Jubilee Medal, 1977. *Publications:* contrib. veterinary and chemical jls. *Recreations:* tennis, golf, polocrosse. *Address:* Dumpu, Box 1299, Lae, Papua New Guinea. *T:* 722574. *Clubs:* Papua (Port Moresby, PNG); Warwick (Qld).

JEPHCOTT, Sir (John) Anthony, 2nd Bt *cr* 1962; *b* 21 May 1924; *s* of Sir Harry Jephcott, 1st Bt, and Doris (*d* 1985), *d* of Henry Gregory; *S* father, 1978; *m* 1st, 1949, Sylvia Mary, *d* of Thorsten Frederick Relling, Wellington, NZ; two *d*; 2nd, 1978, Josephine Agnes Sheridan. *Educ:* Aldenham; St John's Coll., Oxford; London School of Economics (BCom). Served with REME and RAEC, 1944–47. Director, Longworth Scientific Instrument Co. Ltd, 1946; Managing Director and Chairman, 1952–73; Managing Director and Chairman, Pen Medic Ltd (NZ), 1973–78. *Publications:* correspondence in Anaesthesia (UK), and Anaesthesia and Intensive Care (Australia). *Recreations:* gardening, photography. *Heir: b* Neil Welbourn Jephcott [*b* 3 June 1929; *m* 1st, 1951, Mary Denise (*d* 1977), *d* of Arthur Muddiman; two *s* one *d*; 2nd, 1978, Mary Florence Daly]. *Address:* 144 Puriri Park Road, Whangarei, New Zealand.

JEPSON, Selwyn; author and occasional soldier; *o s* of late Edgar Jepson. *Educ:* St Paul's Sch. War of 1939–45, Major, The Buffs, Military Intelligence and SOE (recruiting secret agents). *Publications: novels:* The Qualified Adventurer, 1921; That Fellow MacArthur, 1922; The King's Red-Haired Girl, 1923; Golden Eyes, 1924; Rogues and Diamonds, 1925; Snaggletooth, 1926; The Death Gong, 1928; Tiger Dawn, 1929; I Met Murder, 1930; Rabbit's Paw, 1932; Keep Murder Quiet, 1940; Man Running, 1948; The Golden Dart, 1949; The Hungry Spider, 1950; Man Dead, 1951; The Black Italian, 1954; The Assassin, 1956; Noise in the Night, 1957; The Laughing Fish, 1960; Fear in the Wind, 1964; The Third Possibility, 1965; Angry Millionaire, 1968; Dead Letters, 1970; Letter to a Dead Girl, 1971; The Gill Interrogators, 1974; *short stories:* (with Michael Joseph) Heads or Tails, 1933; *stage play:* (with Lesley Storm) Dark Horizon, 1933; *screen plays:* Going Gay, 1932; For the Love of You, 1932; Irresistible Marmaduke, 1933; Monday at Ten, 1933; The Love Test, 1934; The Riverside Murders, 1934; White Lilac, Hyde Park Corner (Hackett), 1935; Well Done, Henry, 1936; The Scarab Murder, 1936; Toilers of the Sea (adapted and directed), 1936; Sailing Along, 1937; Carnet de Bal: Double Crime on the Maginot Line (English Version), 1938; *television plays:* Thought to Kill, 1952; Dialogue for Two Faces, 1952; My Name is Jones, 1952; Little Brother, 1953; Last Moment, 1953; Forever my Heart, 1953; Leave it to Eve (serial), 1954; The Interloper, 1955; Noise in the Night (USA), 1958; The Hungry Spider, 1964; The Peppermint Child, 1976; The Angry Millionaire (Tom McFadden), 1984; *radio serial:* The Hungry Spider, 1957; *radio plays:* The Bath that Sang, 1958; Noise in the Night, 1958; Art for Art's Sake, 1959; Small Brother, 1960; Call it Greymail, 1961; Dark Corners, 1963. *Recreations:* book collecting, painting. *Address:* The Far House, Liss, Hants. *Club:* Savile.

JEREMIAH, Melvyn Gwynne; Principal Finance Officer (Under Secretary), Welsh Office, since 1979; *b* 10 March 1939; *s* of Bryn Jeremiah and Evelyn (*née* Rogers); *m* 1960, Lilian Clare (*née* Bailey) (marr. diss. 1966). *Educ:* Abertillery County Sch. Apptd to Home Office, 1958; HM Customs and Excise, 1963–75; Cabinet Office, 1975–76; Treasury, 1976–79. Sec., Assoc. of First Div. Civil Servants, 1967–70. *Recreations:* work, people. *Address:* 110 Ashley Gardens, Thirleby Road, SW1P 1HJ. *T:* (office) Cardiff 825220. *Club:* Reform.

JERNE, Prof. Niels Kaj, MD; FRS 1980; *b* London, 23 Dec. 1911; *s* of Hans Jessen Jerne and Else Marie (*née* Lindberg); *m* 1964, Ursula Alexandra (*née* Kohl); two *s. Educ:* Univ. of Leiden, Holland; Univ. of Copenhagen, Denmark (MD). Res. worker, Danish State Serum Inst., 1943–56; Res. Fellow, Calif Inst. of Technol., Pasadena, 1954–55; CMO for Immunology, WHO, Geneva, 1956–62; Prof. of Biophysics, Univ. of Geneva, 1960–62; Chm., Dept of Microbiology, Univ. of Pittsburgh, 1962–66; Prof. of Experimental Therapy, Johann Wolfgang Goethe Univ., Frankfurt, 1966–69; Director: Paul-Ehrlich-Institut, Frankfurt, 1966–69; Basel Inst. for Immunology, 1969–80. Prof., Pasteur Inst., Paris, 1981–82. Member: Amer. Acad. of Arts and Sciences, 1967; Royal Danish Acad. of Sciences, 1968; National Acad. of Sciences, USA, 1975; Amer. Philosophical Soc., 1979; Acad. des Scis de l'Institut de France, 1981. DSc *hc*: Chicago, 1972; Columbia, 1978; Copenhagen, 1979; PhD *hc*: Basel, 1981; Weizmann Inst., Israel, 1985; MD *hc* Rotterdam, 1983. Nobel Prize for Physiology or Medicine, 1984. *Publications:* scientific papers on immunology in learned jls. *Address:* Château de Bellevue, Castillon-du-Gard, Gard 30210, France. *T:* 66/370075.

JEROME, Hon. James Alexander; PC (Can.) 1981; QC (Can.) 1976; **Hon. Mr Justice Jerome;** Associate Chief Justice, Federal Court of Canada, since 1980; lawyer, since 1958; *b* Kingston, Ont., 4 March 1933; *s* of Joseph Leonard Jerome and Phyllis Devlin; *m* 1958, Barry Karen Hodgins; three *s* two *d. Educ:* Our Lady of Perpetual Help Sch., Toronto; St Michael's Coll. High Sch., Toronto; Univ. of Toronto; Osgoode Hall. Alderman, Sudbury, Ont., 1966–67. MP, Sudbury, 1968–80; Parly Sec. to President of Privy Council, 1970–74; Speaker of the House of Commons, 1974–80. Pres., Commonwealth Parly Assoc., 1976. *Recreations:* golf, piano. *Address:* 12 Claret Court, Ottawa, Ontario K1V 9C4, Canada. *T:* 737–2118.

JERRAM, Maj.-Gen. Richard Martyn, CB 1984; MBE 1960; retired 1984; *b* Bangalore, India, 14 Aug. 1928; *e s* of late Brig. R. M. Jerram, DSO, MC, and late Monica (*née* Gillies). *Educ:* Stubbington House; Marlborough Coll.; RMA, Sandhurst. Commissioned into Royal Tank Regt, 1948; served in 2, 3 or 4 RTRs, or in Staff appts in Hong Kong, Malaya (twice) (MBE), Libya, N Ireland, USA, Germany (four times), MoD (three times). Instr, Staff Coll., Camberley, 1964–67; CO 3 RTR, 1969–71; DRAC, 1981–84. Col Comdt, RTR, 1982–. *Recreations:* travel, countryside, literature, chess. *Address:* Trehane, Trevanson, Wadebridge, Cornwall. *T:* Wadebridge 2523. *Clubs:* MCC, Army and Navy.

JERSEY, 9th Earl of, *cr* 1697; **George Francis Child-Villiers;** Viscount Grandison (of Limerick), 1620; Viscount Villiers (of Dartford), and Baron Villiers (of Hoo), 1691; Chairman: Jersey Island Semen Exports Ltd; Associated Hotels (Jersey) Ltd; Hotel L'Horizon Ltd; *b* 15 Feb. 1910; *e s* of 8th Earl and Lady Cynthia Almina Constance Mary Needham (who *m* 2nd, 1925, W. R. Slessor (*d* 1945); she died 1947), *o d* of 3rd Earl of Kilmorey; *S* father, 1923; *m* 1st, 1932, Patricia Kenneth (who obtained a divorce, 1937; she *m* 2nd, 1937, Robin Filmer Wilson, who *d* 1944; 3rd, 1953, Col Peter Laycock, who *d* 1977), *o d* of Kenneth Richards, Cootamundra, NSW, and of late Eileen Mary (who *m* later Sir Stephenson Kent, KCB); one *d*; 2nd, 1937, Virginia (who obtained a divorce, 1946), *d* of James Cherrill, USA; 3rd, 1947, Bianca Maria Adriana Luciana, *er d* of late Enrico Mottironi, Turin, Italy; two *s* one *d.* Director: Jersey General Investment Trust Ltd; Jersey General Executor and Trustee Co. Ltd. *Heir: s* Viscount Villiers, *qv. Address:* Radier Manor, Longueville, Jersey, Channel Islands. *T:* Jersey 53102.

JERSEY, Dean of; *see* O'Ferrall, Very Rev. B. A.

JERVIS, family name of **Viscount St Vincent.**

JERVIS, Charles Elliott, OBE 1966; Editor-in-Chief, Press Association, 1954–65; *b* Liverpool, 7 Nov. 1907; *y s* of late J. H. Jervis, Liverpool; *m* 1931, Ethel Braithwaite (*d* 1979), Kendal, Westmorland; one *d*. Editorial Asst, Liverpool Express, 1921–23; Reporter, Westmorland Gazette, 1923–28; Dramatic Critic and Asst Editor, Croydon Times, 1928–37; Sub-Editor, Press Assoc., 1937–47; Asst Editor, 1947–54. Pres., Guild of British Newspaper Editors, 1964–65; Mem. of the Press Council, 1960–65. *Address:* The Old Vicarage, Allithwaite, Grange over Sands, Cumbria. *T:* Grange-over-Sands 3703.

JERVIS, Charles Walter Lionel; a Recorder of the Crown Court, 1978–86; Senior Partner, 1962–80, Consultant, since 1980, Vivian Thomas & Jervis, Solicitors, Penzance; *b* 9 Dec. 1914; *s* of Henry Jervis, MA Oxon, and Elsie Jervis; *m* 1939, Mary Aileen Clarke; two *s* one *d*. *Educ:* Exeter Sch., Exeter. Solicitor of the Supreme Court. Served War, 1942–46; RNVR, in Asdic Ships (Atlantic Star 1944); demobilized, Lieut RNVR, 1946. Articled in IoW; Asst Solicitor, Penzance, 1939; practised as country solicitor, 1946; Dep. Coroner, Penzance Bor., 1948; Dep. Circuit Judge, 1975–86. Pres., Cornwall Law Soc., 1965–66. Mem., Legal Aid Area Cttee, 1967–78. Dir, Tregarthens Hotel (Scilly) Ltd. Mem., W of England Steam Engine Soc., Redruth. *Publications:* contrib. Justice of Peace, Law Jl, and Criminal Law Rev. *Recreations:* gardening, steam locomotion, wearing old clothes. *Address:* 62 Park Road, Kingskerswell, Newton Abbot, Devon TQ12 5BG.

JERVIS, Roger P.; *see* Parker-Jervis.

JESSEL, family name of **Baron Jessel.**

JESSEL, 2nd Baron, *cr* 1924, of Westminster; **Edward Herbert Jessel,** Bt, *cr* 1917; CBE 1963; a Deputy Speaker, House of Lords, 1963–77; *b* 25 March 1904; *o s* of 1st Baron, CB, CMG, and Maud (*d* 1965), 5th *d* of late Rt Hon. Sir Julian Goldsmid, Bt, MP; *S* father 1950; *m* 1st, 1935, Lady Helen Maglona Vane-Tempest-Stewart (from whom he obtained a divorce, 1960; she *d* 1986), 3rd *d* of 7th Marquess of Londonderry, KG, PC, MVO; one *d* (and one *s* one *d* decd); 2nd, 1960, Jessica, *d* of late William De Wet and Mrs H. W. Taylor, Cape Town. *Educ:* Eton; Christ Church, Oxford (MA). Called to Bar, Inner Temple, 1926. Formerly Chairman, Associated Leisure Ltd; formerly Director: Textile Machinery Makers Ltd; Truscon Ltd; Westminster Trust. Chm., Assoc. of Indep. Unionist Peers, 1959–64. *Address:* 4 Sloane Terrace Mansions, SW1. *T:* 01–730 7843. *Clubs:* Garrick, White's.
See also Sir G. W. G. Agnew.

JESSEL, Sir Charles (John), 3rd Bt *cr* 1883; farmer; *b* 29 Dec. 1924; *s* of Sir George Jessel, 2nd Bt, MC, and Muriel (*d* 1948), *d* of Col J. W. Chaplin, VC; *S* father, 1977; *m* 1st, 1956, Shirley Cornelia (*d* 1977), *o d* of John Waters, Northampton; two *s* one *d*; 2nd, 1979, Gwendolyn Mary (marr. diss. 1983), *d* of late Laurance Devereux, OBE, and of Mrs Devereux, and *widow* of Charles Langer, MA. *Educ:* Eton; Balliol College, Oxford. Served War of 1939–45, Lieut 15/19th Hussars (despatches). Hon. Fellow, Psionic Med. Soc., 1977. JP Kent 1960–78. *Recreation:* gardening. *Heir: s* George Elphinstone Jessel, *b* 15 Dec. 1957. *Address:* South Hill Farm, Hastingleigh, near Ashford, Kent. *T:* Elmsted 325. *Club:* Cavalry and Guards.

JESSEL, Oliver Richard; Chairman, Jessel Group plc, since 1955; *b* 24 Aug. 1929; *s* of Comdr R. F. Jessel, DSO, OBE, DSC, RN; *m* 1950, Gloria Rosalie Teresa (*née* Holden); one *s* five *d*. *Educ:* Rugby. Founded group of companies, 1954; opened office in City of London, 1960; Chm., London, Australian and General Exploration Co. Ltd., 1960–75; formed New Issue Unit Trust and other trusts, 1962–68; responsible for numerous mergers, incl. Johnson & Firth Brown Ltd, and Maple Macowards Ltd; Chm., Charles Clifford Industries Ltd, 1978–81. *Address:* The Grange, Marden, Kent. *T:* Maidstone 831264. *Club:* Garrick.
See also T. F. H. Jessel.

JESSEL, Toby Francis Henry; MP (C) Twickenham since 1970; *b* 11 July 1934; *y s* of Comdr R. F. Jessel, DSO, OBE, DSC, RN, Grange Cottage, Marden, Kent; *m* 1st, 1967 (marr. diss. 1973); one *d* decd; 2nd, 1980, Eira Gwen, *y d* of late Horace and Marigwen Heath. *Educ:* Royal Naval Coll., Dartmouth; Balliol Coll., Oxford (MA). Sub-Lt, RNVR, 1954. Conservative Candidate: Peckham, 1964; Hull (North), 1966. Parly deleg. to India and Pakistan, 1971; Member: Council of Europe, 1976–; WEU, 1976–. Chm., South Area Bd GLC Planning and Transportation Cttee, 1968–70. (Co-opted) LCC Housing Cttee, 1961–65; Councillor, London Borough of Southwark, 1964–66; Mem. for Richmond-upon-Thames, GLC, 1967–73; Hon. Sec. Assoc. of Adopted Conservative Candidates, 1961–66; Jt Sec., Indo-British Parly Gp; Chairman: Cons. Parly Arts and Heritage Cttee, 1983 (Vice-Chm., 1979); Anglo-Belgian Parly Gp, 1983. Hon. Sec., Katyn Meml Fund, 1972–75. Mem. Metropolitan Water Bd, 1967–70; Mem., London Airport Consultative Cttee, 1967–70. Mem. Council, Fluoridation Soc., 1976. Mem., Exec. Cttee and Organizing Cttee, European Music Year, 1985. Liveryman, Worshipful Co. of Musicians. Chevalier, Ordre de la Couronne (Belgium), 1980; Order of Polonia Restituta (Polish Govt in Exile); Order of Merit (Liechtenstein), 1979. *Recreations:* music (has performed Mozart and Schumann piano concertos), gardening, croquet (Longworth Cup, Hurlingham, 1961), ski-ing. *Address:* Old Court House, Hampton Court, East Molesey, Surrey. *Clubs:* Garrick, Hurlingham.
See also O. R. Jessel, A. Panufnik, J. H. Walford.

JESSUP, Frank William, CBE 1972; Director, Department for External Studies, Oxford University, 1952–76; Librarian of Wolfson College, Oxford, since 1974 (Fellow, 1965–80, Honorary Fellow, 1980); *b* 26 April 1909; *s* of Frederick William Jessup and Alice Sarah (*née* Cheeseman); *m* 1935, Dorothy Hilda Harris; two *s* one *d*. *Educ:* Gravesend Boys' Grammar Sch.; Univ. of London (BA, LLB); Univ. of Oxford (MA). Called to Bar, Gray's Inn, 1935. Dep. County Educn Officer, Kent, until 1952. Chairman: Library Adv. Council (England), 1965–73; British Library Adv. Council, 1976–81; Oxon Rural Community Council, 1976–82; Vice-Chm., Universities Council for Adult Educn, 1973–76. Pres., Kent Archaeol Soc., 1976–82. Chm. of Governors, Rose Bruford Coll. of Speech and Drama, 1960–72. FSA; Hon. FLA. Hon. DCL Kent 1976. *Publications:* Problems of Local Government, 1949; Introduction to Kent Feet of Fines, 1956; A History of Kent, 1958, repr. 1974; Sir Roger Twysden, 1597–1672, 1965, etc; contrib. to Archæologia Cantiana, Studies in Adult Educn, Möbius. *Recreations:* reading, music, gardening. *Address:* Striblehills, Thame, Oxon. *T:* Thame 2027.

JEVONS, Prof. Frederic Raphael, AO 1986; Vice-Chancellor, Deakin University, Australia, 1976–85, now Emeritus Professor; *b* 19 Sept. 1929; *s* of Fritz and Hedwig Bettelheim; *m* 1956, Grete Bradel; two *s*. *Educ:* Langley Sch., Norwich; King's Coll., Cambridge (Major Schol.). 1st Cl. Hons Nat. Scis Pt II (Biochem) Cantab 1950; PhD Cantab 1953; DSc Manchester 1966. Postdoctoral Fellow, Univ. of Washington, Seattle, 1953–54; Fellow, King's Coll., Cambridge, 1953–59; Univ. Demonstrator in Biochem., Cambridge, 1956–59; Lectr in Biol Chem., Manchester Univ., 1959–66; Prof. of Liberal Studies in Science, Manchester Univ., 1966–75. Chairman: Gen. Studies Cttee, Schools Council, 1974–75; Grad. Careers Council of Aust., 1976–80; Policy Cttee, Victorian Technical and Further Educn Off-Campus Network, 1985–; Member: Jt Matriculation Bd, Manchester, 1969–75; Jt Cttee, SRC and SSRC, 1974–75; Educn Res. and Develt Cttee, Aust., 1980–81; Council, Sci. Mus. of Vic., 1980–83; Council, Mus. of Vic., 1983–; Aust. Vice-Chancellors' Exec. Cttee, 1981–82; Standing Cttee on External Studies, Commonwealth Tertiary Educn Commn, Canberra, 1985–; Aust. Sci. and Technol. Council, 1986– (Mem., Technolog. Change Cttee, 1986–). Interviewer for Civil Service Commn on Final Selection Bds, 1970–75; Adviser to Leverhulme project on educnl objectives in applied science, Strathclyde Univ., 1972–75; British Council tours in India, E Africa, Nigeria, 1972–75. Mem., Editorial Advisory Boards: R and D Management, 1972–76; Studies in Science Educn, 1974–; Scientometrics, 1978–; Australasian Studies in History and Philosophy of Science, 1980–. Life Gov., Geelong Hosp., 1986. DUniv Open, 1985; Hon. DLitt Deakin, 1986; Hon. DSc Manchester, 1986. *Publications:* The Biochemical Approach to Life, 1964, 2nd edn 1968 (trans. Italian, Spanish, Japanese, German); The Teaching of Science: education, science and society, 1969; (ed jtly) University Perspectives, 1970; (jtly) Wealth from Knowledge: studies of innovation in industry, 1972; (ed jtly) What Kinds of Graduates do we Need?, 1972; Science Observed: science as a social and intellectual activity, 1973; Knowledge and Power, 1976; numerous papers on biochem., history of science, science educn and science policy. *Recreations:* music, theatre, reading. *Address:* Deakin University, Vic 3217, Australia.

JEWELL, David John, MA, MSc; Headmaster of Repton School, 1979–March 1987; Master of Haileybury and Imperial Service College, from April 1987; *b* 24 March 1934; *s* of late Wing Comdr John Jewell, OBE, FRAeS, and Rachel Jewell, Porthleven, Cornwall; *m* 1958, Katharine Frida Heller; one *s* three *d*. *Educ:* Blundell's Sch., Tiverton; St John's Coll., Oxford. Honours Sch. of Natural Science (Chemistry), BA 1957, MA 1961; BSc Physical Sciences, 1959, MSc 1981. National Service with RAF, 1952–54. Head of Science Dept, Eastbourne Coll., 1958–62; Winchester Coll., 1962–67; Dep. Head, Lawrence Weston Comprehensive Sch., Bristol, 1967–70; Head Master, Bristol Cathedral Sch., 1970–78. Chairman: Choir Schools' Assoc., 1976–77; Direct Grant Sub-Cttee of Headmasters' Conference, 1977–78. FRSA 1981. *Publications:* papers and articles in various scientific and educnl jls. *Recreations:* music, cricket, cooking, Cornwall. *Address:* The Hall, Repton, Derby DE6 6FH. *T:* Burton-on-Trent 702375; (from April 1987) The Master's Lodge, Haileybury, Hertford SG13 7NU. *T:* Hoddesdon 462352; Chapel Downs Cottage, Breageside, Porthleven, Cornwall. *T:* Helston 563152. *Clubs:* East India, Devonshire, Sports and Public Schools, MCC; Bristol Savages.

JEWELL, Prof. Peter Arundel, PhD; CBiol, FIBiol; Mary Marshall and Arthur Walton Professor of Physiology of Reproduction and Fellow of St John's College, University of Cambridge, since 1977; *b* 16 June 1925; *s* of Percy Arundel Jewell and Ivy Dorothea Enness; *m* 1958, Juliet Clutton-Brock; three *d*. *Educ:* Wandsworth Sch.; Reading Univ. (BSc Agric.); Cambridge Univ. (BA, MA, PhD). Lectr, Royal Veterinary Coll., 1950–60; Research Fellow, Zoological Soc. of London, 1960–66; Prof. of Biological Sciences, Univ. of Nigeria, 1966–67; Sen. Lectr and Dir of Conservation Course, University Coll. London, 1967–72; Prof. of Zoology, Royal Holloway Coll., 1972–77. *Publications:* The Experimental Earthwork on Overton Down, Wiltshire, 1960; Island Survivors: the Ecology of the Soay Sheep of St Kilda, 1974; Management of Locally Abundant Wild Mammals, 1981; scientific papers in Jl Animal Ecology, Jl Physiology, Jl Zoology, Ark, etc. *Recreations:* emulating Cornish ancestors, watching wild animals, saving rare breeds, painting and pottery, archaeology. *Address:* St John's College, Cambridge CB2 1TP.

JEWERS, William George, CBE 1982 (OBE 1976); Managing Director, Finance, and Member, British Gas plc (formerly British Gas Corporation), 1976–86; *b* 18 Oct. 1921; *s* of late William Jewers and Hilda Jewers (*née* Ellison); *m* 1955, Helena Florence Rimmer; one *s* one *d*. *Educ:* Liverpool Inst. High Sch. for Boys. Liverpool Gas Co., 1938–41. Served War: RAFVR Observer (Flying Officer), 1941–46: Indian Ocean, 265 Sqdn (Catalinas), 1943–44; Burma 194 Sqdn (Dakotas), 1945. Liverpool Gas Co./NW Gas Bd, Sen. Accountancy Asst, 1946–52; W Midlands Gas Bd: Cost Acct, Birmingham and Dist Div., 1953–62; Cost Acct, Area HQ, 1962–65; Asst Chief Acct, 1965–66; Chief Acct, 1967; Dir of Finance, 1968; Gas Council, Dir of Finance, 1969–73; British Gas Corp., Dir of Finance, 1973–76. FCMA, FCCA, JDipMA, CompIGasE, CBIM. *Publications:* papers and articles to gas industry jls. *Recreations:* music, reading, golf. *Address:* 17 South Park View, Gerrards Cross, Bucks SL9 8HN. *T:* Gerrards Cross 886169.

JEWKES, Gordon Wesley, CMG 1980; HM Diplomatic Service; Governor, Falkland Islands and High Commissioner, British Antarctic Territory, since 1985; *b* 18 Nov. 1931; *er s* of late Jesse Jewkes; *m* 1954, Joyce Lyons; two *s*. *Educ:* Barrow Grammar Sch.; Magnus Grammar Sch., Newark-on-Trent, and elsewhere. Colonial Office, 1948; served HM Forces, Army, 1950–52; Gen. Register Office, 1950–63; CS Pay Res. Unit, 1963–65; Gen. Register Office, 1965–68; transf. to HM Diplomatic Service, 1968; CO, later FCO, 1968–69; Consul (Commercial), Chicago, 1969–72; Dep. High Comr, Port of Spain, 1972–75; Head of Finance Dept, FCO, and Finance Officer of Diplomatic Service, 1975–79; Consul-General: Cleveland, 1979–82; Chicago, 1982–85. *Recreations:* music, travel, walking, boating. *Address:* c/o Foreign and Commonwealth Office, SW1A 2AH. *Club:* Travellers'.

JEWKES, John, CBE 1943; MA (Oxon); MCom; *b* June 1902; *m* 1929, Sylvia Butterworth; one *d*. *Educ:* Barrow Grammar Sch.; Manchester Univ. MCom. Asst Sec., Manchester Chamber of Commerce, 1925–26; Lecturer in Economics, University of Manchester, 1926–29; Rockefeller Foundation Fellow, 1929–30; Professor of Social Economics, Manchester 1936–46; Stanley Jevons Prof. of Political Economy, Manchester, 1946–48; Prof. of Economic Organisation, Oxford, and Fellow of Merton College, 1948–69, Emeritus Fellow 1969. Visiting Prof., University of Chicago, 1953–54; Visiting Prof., Princeton Univ., 1961. Dir, Economic Section, War Cabinet Secretariat, 1941; Dir-Gen. of Statistics and Programmes, Ministry of Aircraft Production, 1943; Principal Asst Sec., Office of Minister of Reconstruction, 1944; Mem. of Fuel Advisory Cttee, 1945; Independent Mem. of Cotton Industry Working Party, 1946; Mem. of Royal Commission on Gambling, Betting and Lotteries, 1949. Mem. of Royal Commission on Doctors' and Dentists' Remuneration, 1957–60; Dir, Industrial Policy Gp, 1969–74. Hon. DSc Hull, 1973. *Publications:* An Industrial Survey of Cumberland and Furness (with A. Winterbottom), 1931; Juvenile Unemployment (with A. Winterbottom), 1933; Wages and Labour in the Cotton Spinning Industry (with E. M. Gray), 1935; The Juvenile Labour Market (with Sylvia Jewkes) 1938; Ordeal by Planning, 1948; The Sources of Invention (with David Sawers and Richard Stillerman), 1958; The Genesis of the British National Health Service (with Sylvia Jewkes), 1961; Value for Money in Medicine (with Sylvia Jewkes), 1962; Public and Private Enterprise, 1965; New Ordeal by Planning, 1968; A Return to Free Market Economics?, 1978. *Recreation:* gardening. *Address:* Entwood, Red Copse Lane, Boars Hill, Oxford.
See also B. C. Clarke.

JHABVALA, Mrs Ruth Prawer; author; *b* in Germany, of Polish parents, 7 May 1927; *d* of Marcus Prawer and Eleonora Prawer (*née* Cohn); came to England as refugee, 1939; *m* 1951, C. S. H. Jhabvala; three *d*. *Educ:* Hendon County Sch.; Queen Mary Coll., London Univ. Started writing after graduation and marriage, alternating between novels and short stories; occasional original film-scripts (with James Ivory and Ismail Merchant), including: Shakespeare-wallah, 1965; The Guru, 1969; Bombay Talkie, 1971; Autobiography of a Princess, 1975; Roseland, 1977; Hullabaloo over Georgie and Bonnie's Pictures, 1978; The Europeans (based on Henry James' novel), 1979; Jane Austen in Manhattan, 1980; Quartet (based on Jean Rhys' novel), 1981; Heat and Dust (based on own novel), 1983; The Bostonians (based on Henry James' novel), 1984; A Room with a View (based on E. M. Forster's novel), 1986. *Publications: novels:* To Whom She Will, 1955; The Nature of Passion, 1956; Esmond in India, 1958; The Householder, 1960; Get Ready for Battle, 1962; A Backward Place, 1965; A New Dominion, 1973; Heat and Dust, 1975 (Booker Prize, 1975); In Search of Love and Beauty, 1983; *short story collections:* Like Birds, like Fishes, 1964; A Stronger Climate, 1968; An Experience of India, 1971; How I became a Holy Mother and other Stories, 1976; Out of India: selected stories, 1986. *Recreation:* writing film-scripts. *Address:* c/o John Murray, 50 Albemarle Street, W1.

See also Prof. S. S. Prawer.

JILANI, Asaf; with the Eastern Service of the BBC; *b* 24 Sept. 1934; *s* of Abdul Wahid Sindhi and Noor Fatima Jilani; *m* 1961, Mohsina Jilani; two *s* one *d*. *Educ:* Jamia Millia, Delhi; Sindh Madvasa, Karachi; Karachi Univ. (BA, Economics and Persian). Sub-Editor, Daily Imroze, Karachi (Progressive Papers Ltd), 1952; Political Corresp., Daily Imroze, 1954; Special Corresp., Daily Jang, Karachi (posted in India), 1959–65; London Editor: Daily Jang (Karachi, Rawalpindi, Quetta); Daily News, Karachi, and Akhbar-Jehan, Karachi, 1965–73; Editor, Daily Jang, London (first Urdu Daily in UK), 1973–82. *Recreations:* cricket, swimming, painting. *Address:* BBC, Eastern Service, Bush House, WC2. *T:* 01-257 2142; (home) 23 Horsham Avenue, N12. *T:* 01-368 5697.

JIMENEZ DE ARECHAGA, Eduardo, DrJur; President, World Bank Administrative Tribunal, since 1981; Professor of International Law, Montevideo Law School, since 1946; *b* Montevideo, 8 June 1918; *s* of E. Jiménez de Aréchaga and Ester Sienra; *m* 1943, Marta Ferreira; three *s* two *d*. *Educ:* Sch. of Law, Univ. of Montevideo. Under-Sec., Foreign Relations, 1950–52; Sec., Council of Govt of Uruguay, 1952–55; Mem., Internat. Law Commn of UN, 1961–69 (Pres., 1963); Cttee *Rapporteur*, Vienna Conf. on Law Treaties, 1968–69; Minister of the Interior, Uruguay, 1968; Pres. of the International Ct of Justice, The Hague, 1976–79 (Judge of the Ct, 1970–79). Inter-Amer. Bar Assoc. Book Award, 1961. *Publications:* Reconocimiento de Gobiernos, 1946; Voting and Handling of Disputes in the Security Council, 1951; Treaty Stipulations in Favour of Third States, 1956; Derecho Constitucional de las Naciónes Unidas, 1958; Curso de Derecho Internacional Público, 2 vols, 1959–61; International Law in the Past Third of a Century, vol. I, 1978; Derecho Internacional Contemporáneo, 1980. *Address:* Casilla de Correo 539, Montevideo, Uruguay.

JINKS, Prof. John Leonard, CBE 1984; FRS 1970; Professor of Genetics, Birmingham University, since 1985; Secretary and Deputy Chairman, Agricultural and Food Research Council, since 1985; *b* 21 Oct. 1929; *s* of Jack and Beatrice May Jinks; *m* 1955, Diana Mary Williams; one *s* one *d*. *Educ:* Longton High Sch., Stoke-on-Trent; Univ. of Birmingham. BSc Botany 1950, PhD Genetics 1952, DSc Genetics 1964, Birmingham. ARC Research Student: Univ. of Birmingham, 1950–52; Carlsberg Labs, Copenhagen; Istituto Sieroterapico, Milan, 1952–53; Scientific Officer, ARC Unit of Biometrical Genetics, Univ. of Birmingham, 1953–59; Harkness Fellow, California Inst. of Technology, 1959–60; Principal Scientific Officer, ARC Unit of Biometrical Genetics, 1960–65; Birmingham University: Hon. Lectr, 1960–62; Reader, 1962–65; Head of Dept of Genetics, 1965–85; Dean, Faculty of Sci. and Engrg, 1972–75; Pro-Vice-Chancellor, 1981–85; Vice-Principal, 1984–85. Member: SRC, 1975–79; AFRC (formerly ARC), 1979–85; Chm., Governing Body, Nat. Veg. Research Station, 1979–85. Pres., Genetical Soc. of GB, 1981–84. FIBiol 1968. Editor of Heredity, 1960–75, Acting Editor, 1976–77; Editor, Jl of Agricl Scis, 1981–. *Publications:* Extrachromosomal Inheritance, 1964; (jtly) Biometrical Genetics, 1971, 1981; Cytoplasmic Inheritance, 1976; (jtly) Introduction to Biometrical Genetics, 1977; numerous papers and chapters in books on microbial genetics, biometrical genetics and behavioral genetics. *Recreations:* piano, gardening. *Address:* 81 Witherford Way, Selly Oak, Birmingham B29 4AN. *T:* 021-472 2008.

JOB, Rev. Canon (Evan) Roger (Gould); Canon Residentiary, Precentor and Sacrist of Winchester Cathedral, since 1979; *b* 15 May 1936; 2nd *s* of late Thomas Brian Job and of Elsie Maud Job (*née* Gould), Ipswich; *m* 1964, Rose Constance Mary, *o d* of late Stanley E. and Audrey H. Gordon, Hooton, Wirral; two *s*. *Educ:* Cathedral Choir School and King's Sch., Canterbury; Magdalen Coll., Oxford; Cuddesdon Theol Coll. BA 1960, MA 1964; ARCM 1955. Deacon 1962, priest 1963. Asst Curate, Liverpool Parish Church, 1962–65; Vicar of St John, New Springs, Wigan, 1965–70; Precentor of Manchester Cath., 1970–74; Precentor and Sacrist of Westminster Abbey, 1974–79; Chaplain of The Dorchester, 1976–79. *Recreations:* gardening, piano. *Address:* 8 The Close, Winchester SO23 9LS. *T:* Winchester 54771.

JOBERT, Michel; Officier de la Légion d'Honneur; Croix de Guerre (1939–45); Founder, Mouvement des Démocrates, 1974; *b* Meknès, Morocco, 11 Sept. 1921; *s* of Jules Jobert and Yvonne Babule; *m* Muriel Frances Green; one *s*. *Educ:* Lycées of Rabat and Meknès; Dip. de l'Ecole libre des sciences politiques; Ecole nationale d'Administration. Cour des comptes: Auditor, 1949; Conseiller Référendaire, 1953. Member of Ministerial Cabinets: Finance, Labour and Social Security, President of the Council, 1952–56; Director of the Cabinet of the High Commission of the Republic in French West Africa, 1956–58; Dir of Cabinet of Minister of State, 1959–61; Jt Dir, 1963–66, then Director, 1966–68, of the Prime Minister's Cabinet (Georges Pompidou); Pres., Council of Admin of Nat. Office of Forests, 1966–73; Administrator of Havas, 1968–73; Secretary-Gen., Presidency of the Republic, 1969–73; Minister for Foreign Affairs, 1973–74; Minister of State and Minister for Overseas Trade, 1981–83. Conseiller-maitre, Cour des comptes, 1971. Editor, La Lettre de Michel Jobert, 1974–84. *Publications:* Mémoires d'avenir, 1974; L'autre regard, 1975; Lettre ouverte aux femmes politiques, 1976; Parler aux Français, 1977; La vie d'Hella Schuster (novel), 1977; Maroc: extrême Maghreb du soleil couchant, 1978; La rivière aux grenades, 1982; Chroniques du Midi Libre, 1982; Vive l'Europe Libre, 1984; Par Trente-six chemins, 1984; Naghreb, à l'ombre de ses mains, 1985. *Address:* (home) 21 quai Alphonse-Le Gallo, 92100 Boulogne-sur-Seine, France; (office) 108 quai Louis Blériot, 75016 Paris, France.

JOBLING, Captain James Hobson, RN; Metropolitan Stipendiary Magistrate, since 1973; *b* 29 Sept. 1921; *s* of late Captain and Mrs J. S. Jobling, North Shields, Northumberland; *m* 1946, Cynthia, *o d* of late F. E. V. Lean, Beacon Park, Plymouth; one *s* one *d*. *Educ:* Tynemouth High Sch.; London Univ. (LLB Hons, 1971). Entered Royal Navy, 1940; awarded Gedge Medal and Prize, 1946; called to Bar, Inner Temple, 1955; Comdr, 1960; JSSC course, 1961–62; Dir, Nat. Liaison, SACLANT HQ, USA, 1962–65; Chief Naval Judge Advocate, in rank of Captain, 1969–72; retd, 1973. Planning Inspector, DoE, 1973; a Dep. Circuit Judge, 1976–82. *Recreations:* gardening, walking. *Address:* Pinewell Lodge, Wood Road, Hindhead, Surrey. *T:* Hindhead 4426.

JOCELYN, family name of **Earl of Roden.**

JOCELYN, Dr Henry David, FBA 1982; Hulme Professor of Latin, University of Manchester, since 1973; *b* 22 Aug. 1933; *s* of late John Daniel Jocelyn and Phyllis Irene Burton; *m* 1958, Margaret Jill, *d* of Bert James Morton and Dulcie Marie Adams; two *s*. *Educ:* Canterbury Boys' High Sch.; Univ. of Sydney (BA); St John's Coll., Univ. of Cambridge (BA, PhD). Teaching Fellow in Latin, Univ. of Sydney, 1955; Cooper Travelling Scholar in Classics, 1955–57; Scholar in Classics, British Sch. at Rome, 1957–59; Univ. of Sydney: Lectr in Latin, 1960–64; Sen. Lectr in Latin, 1964–66; Reader in Latin, 1966–70; Prof. of Latin, 1970–73. Visiting Lectr in Classics, Yale Univ., 1967; Vis. Fellow, ANU, 1979; British Acad. Leverhulme Vis. Prof., *Thesaurus Linguae Latinae*, Munich, 1983; Vis. Lectr in Classics, Univ. of Cape Town, 1985. Corresp. Fellow, Accademia Properziana del Subasio, 1985. FAHA 1970. Mem., Editorial Bd, Cambridge Classical Texts and Commentaries, 1982–. *Publications:* The Tragedies of Ennius, 1967 (corr. reprint 1969); (with B. P. Setchell) Regnier de Graaf on the Human Reproductive Organs, 1972; papers on Greek and Latin subjects in various periodicals. *Address:* 4 Clayton Avenue, Manchester M20 0BN. *T:* 061–434 1526.

JOEL, Hon. Sir Asher (Alexander), KBE 1974 (OBE 1956); AO 1986; Kt 1971; Member of Legislative Council of New South Wales, 1957–78; Company Director and Public Relations Consultant; *b* 4 May 1912; *s* of Harry and Phoebe Joel, London and Sydney; *m* 1st, 1937 (marr. diss. 1948); two *s*; 2nd, 1949, Sybil, *d* of Frederick Mitchell Jacobs; one *s* one *d*. *Educ:* Enmore Public Sch.; Cleveland Street High Sch., Sydney. Served War of 1939–45: AIF, 1942, transf. RAN; Lieut RANVR, 1943; RAN PRO staff Gen. MacArthur, 1944–45, New Guinea, Halmaheras, Philippines. Chairman: Asher Joel Media Gp; Carpentaria Newspapers Pty Ltd; Mount Isa TV Pty Ltd; Nat. Pres., Anzac Mem. Forest in Israel; Dir, Royal North Shore Hosp. of Sydney, 1959–81. Mem., Sydney Cttee (Hon. Dir, 1956–64); Hon. Dir and Organiser, Pageant of Nationhood (State welcome to the Queen), 1963; Exec. Mem., Citizens Welcoming Cttee visit Pres. Johnson, 1966; Chm., Citizens Cttee Captain Cook Bi-Centenary Celebrations, 1970; Dep. Chm., Citizens Welcoming Cttee visit Pope Paul VI to Australia, 1970; Chm., Sydney Opera Hse Official Opening Citizens Cttee, 1972; Dep. Chm., Aust. Govt Adv. Commn on US Bi-Centenary Celebrations, 1976; Mem., Nat. Australia Day Cttee. Mem., Sydney Opera Hse Trust, 1969–79; Chm., Sydney Entertainment Centre, 1979–84. Chm. Emeritus, Organising Cttee 1988 Public Relations World Congress, 1985–; Mem., Adv. Council 31st IAA World Advertising Congress, 1984–. Fellow: Advertising Inst. of Austr. (Federal Patron); Public Relations Inst. of Austr.; Austr. Inst. Management; FInstD; FRSA; Mem., Public Relations Soc. of America; Hon. Mem., Royal Australian Historical Soc., 1970. Hon. Fellow, Internat. Coll. of Dentists, 1975. US Bronze Star, 1943; Ancient Order of Sikatuna (Philippines), 1975; Kt Comdr, Order of Rizal (Philippines), 1978. *Publications:* Without Chains Free (novel), 1977; Australian Protocol and Procedures, 1982. *Recreations:* fishing, gardening. *Address:* GPO Box 3780, Sydney, NSW 2001, Australia. *T:* 20249. *Clubs:* American, Journalists, (Hon. Mem.) Australian Pioneers, Royal Agricultural Society (Sydney); Royal Sydney Yacht Squadron.

JOEL, Harry Joel; *b* 4 Sept. 1894; *o s* of Jack Barnato Joel, JP. *Educ:* Malvern Coll. Served European War 1914–18 with 15th Hussars. *Recreation:* racing. *Address:* The Stud House, Childwick Bury, St Albans, Herts. *Clubs:* Buck's; Jockey (Newmarket).

JOHANNESBURG, Assistant Bishop of; *see* Pickard, Rt Rev. S. C.

JOHANSEN-BERG, Rev. John; Founder/Leader, Community for Reconciliation, since 1986; Moderator, Free Church Federal Council, March 1987–88; *b* 4 Nov. 1935; *s* of John Alfred and Caroline Johansen-Berg, Middlesbrough; *m* 1971, Joan, *d* of James and Sally Ann Parnham, Leeds; two *s* one *d*. *Educ:* Acklam Hall Grammar Sch., Middlesbrough; Leeds Univ. (BA Hons Eng. Lit., BD); Fitzwilliam Coll., Cambridge Univ. (BA Theol Tripos, MA); Westminster Theol Coll. (Dip. Theol.). Tutor, Westminster Coll., Cambridge, 1961; ordained, 1962; pastoral charges: St Ninian's Presbyterian Church, Luton, 1962–70 (Sec., Luton Council of Churches); Founder Minister, St Katherine of Genoa Church, Dunstable (dedicated 1968); The Rock Church Centre, Liverpool (Presbyterian, then United Reformed), 1970–77, work begun in old public house, converted into Queens Road Youth Club, new Church Centre dedicated 1972, a building designed for youth, community and church use; Minister, St Andrew's URC, Ealing, 1977–86. Convener, Church and Community Cttee of Presbyterian C of E, 1970–72; Chm. Church and Society Dept, URC, 1972–79; Moderator of the Gen. Assembly of the URC, 1980–81. British Council of Churches: Mem., Div. of Internat. Affairs; formerly Mem., Div. of Community Affairs. Chm. Gp on Violence, Non-violence and Social Change (for Britain Today and Tomorrow Programme, 1977); Convener, Commission on Non-Violent Action (report published 1973). Chm., Christian Fellowship Trust; Founder Mem. and Sponsor, Christian Concern for Southern Africa; Founder Mem., The Community for Reconciliation, 1984–; Jt Leader, Ecumenical Festivals of Faith in Putney and Roehampton, Stroud, and in Banstead, etc. Jt Editor, Jl of Presbyterian Historical Soc. of England, 1964–70. *Publication:* Arian or Arminian? Presbyterian Continuity in the Eighteenth Century, 1969. *Recreations:* mountain walking, badminton, drama. *Address:* Barnes Close, Chadwick Manor Estate, Bromsgrove, Worcs B61 0RA. *T:* 710231.

JOHANSON, Rev. Dr Brian; Director of Ministerial Training, Presbyterian Church of Southern Africa, Johannesburg, since 1985; *b* 8 March 1929; *s* of Bernard Johanson and Petra Johanson; *m* 1955, Marion Shirley Giles; one *s* two *d*. *Educ:* Univ. of South Africa (BA, DD); Univ. of London (BD). Parish Minister, S Africa, 1956–63; Sen. Lectr in Theology, 1964–69, Prof. of Theol., 1970–76, Univ. of SA; Minister of the City Temple, London, 1976–85. Vis. Res. Fellow: Princeton Theol Seminary, 1970; Univ. of Aberdeen, 1976. *Publications:* univ. pubns in S Africa; booklets; essays in collections; articles in theol jls. *Address:* Box 72057, Parkview, 2122, South Africa. *T:* 011 643 3151.

JOHN, Arthur Walwyn, CBE 1967 (OBE 1945); FCA; company director and financial consultant; Chairman, Property Holding and Investment Trust Ltd, since 1977 (Director, since 1976); Underwriting Member of Lloyds, since 1977; *s* of Oliver Walwyn and Elsie Maud John; *m* 1949, Elizabeth Rosabelle (*d* 1979), *yr d* of Ernest David and Elsie Winifred Williams; one *s* two *d*. *Educ:* Marlborough Coll. Mem. Institute of Chartered Accountants, 1934 (Mem. Council, 1965–81). Asst to Commercial Manager (Collieries), Powell Duffryn Associated Collieries Ltd, 1936. Joined Army, 1939; served War of 1939–45: commissioned, 1940; War Office, 1941; DAQMG First Army, 1942, and HQ Allied Armies in Italy; AQMG Allied Forces HQ, 1944 (despatches, 1943, 1945). Chief Accountant, John Lewis & Co Ltd, 1945; Dep. Dir-Gen. of Finance, National Coal Board, 1946; Dir-Gen. of Finance, 1955; Member, NCB, 1961–68; Chm., NCB Coal Products Div., 1962–68. Director: Unigate Ltd, 1969–75; Stenhouse Holdings Ltd, 1976–84 (Chm., 1982–84); Reed Stenhouse Companies Ltd, Canada, 1977–84; J. H. Sankey & Son Ltd, 1965–86; Schroder Property Fund, 1971–; Teamdale Distribution Ltd, 1982– (Chm., 1982–); Chartered Accountants Trustees Ltd, 1982–; Wincanton Contracts Finance Ltd, 1983–85. Mem., Price Commn, 1976–77. Mem. and Court, Worshipful Co. of Chartered Accts in England and Wales, 1977– (Master, 1981–82). *Recreations:* golf, gardening. *Address:* Limber, Top Park, Gerrards Cross, Bucks SL9 7PW. *T:* Gerrards Cross 84811. *Club:* Army and Navy.

JOHN, Brynmor Thomas; MP (Lab) Pontypridd since 1970; *b* 18 April 1934; *s* of William Henry and Sarah Jane John; *m* 1960, Anne Pryce Hughes; one *s* one *d*. *Educ:* Pontypridd Boys' Grammar Sch.; University Coll., London. LLB Hons 1954. Articled, 1954; admitted Solicitor, 1957; National Service (Officer, Educn Br., RAF), 1958–60; practising Solicitor, Pontypridd, 1960–70. Parly Under-Sec. of State for Defence (RAF), MoD, 1974–76; Minister of State, Home Office, 1976–79; Opposition spokesman on NI, 1979, on defence, 1980–81, on social security, 1981–83, on agriculture, 1984–. *Recreation:* watching Rugby football. *Address:* House of Commons, SW1A 0AA.

JOHN, David Dilwyn, CBE 1961; TD; DSc; Director, National Museum of Wales, Cardiff, 1948–68; *b* 20 Nov. 1901; *e s* of Thomas John, St Bride's Major, Glam; *m* 1929, Marjorie, *d* of J. W. Page, HMI, Wellington, Salop; one *s* one *d*. *Educ:* Bridgend County Sch.; University Coll. of Wales, Aberystwyth. Zoologist on scientific staff, Discovery Investigations, engaged in oceanographical research in Antarctic waters, 1925–35; awarded Polar Medal. Appointed Asst Keeper in charge of Echinoderms at British Museum (Natural History), 1935; Deputy Keeper, 1948. Joined Territorial Army, 1936; promoted Major, RA, 1942. Hon. LLD Univ. of Wales, 1969; Hon. Fellow, UC Cardiff, 1982. *Publications:* papers, chiefly on Echinoderms, in scientific journals. *Address:* 7 Cyncoed Avenue, Cardiff CF2 6ST. *T:* Cardiff 752499.

JOHN, Elton Hercules, (Reginald Kenneth Dwight); musician, composer; *b* 25 March 1947; *s* of Stanley Dwight and Sheila (now Farebrother); *m* 1984, Renate Blauel. *Educ:* Pinner County Grammar Sch.; Royal Acad. of Music, London. Played piano in Northwood Hills Hotel, 1964; joined local group, Bluesology, 1965; signed to Dick James Music as writer and singer, 1967; visited America for concert and was overnight success, 1970; formed Elton John Band, 1970; regularly tours America, Europe, Australia and Japan; first internat. pop singer to perform in Russia, 1979. Vice-Pres. and Mem. Council, National Youth Theatre of GB, 1975–; Chm., Watford Football Club, 1976– (Dir, 1974–); toured China with Watford Football Club, 1983. *Hit Records include: albums:* Empty Sky, 1969; Elton John, Tumbleweed Connection, 1970; Friends, 11.17.70, Madman Across the Water, 1971; Honky Chateau, 1972; Don't Shoot Me, Goodbye Yellow Brick Road, 1973; Caribou, Greatest Hits, 1974; Captain Fantastic, Rock of the Westies, 1975; Here and There, Blue Moves, 1976; Greatest Hits vol. II, 1977; A Single Man, 1978; Victim of Love, 1979; 21 at 33, Lady Samantha, 1980; The Fox, 1981; Jump Up, 1982; Too Low for Zero, 1983; Breaking Hearts, 1984; *singles:* Your Song, 1971; Rocket Man, Crocodile Rock, 1972; Daniel, Goodbye Yellow Brick Road, 1973; Candle in the Wind, Don't Let the Sun Go Down On Me, The Bitch is Back, Lucy in the Sky with Diamonds, 1974; Philadelphia Freedom, Someone Saved My Life Tonight, 1975; Don't Go Breaking My Heart, Sorry Seems to be the Hardest Word, 1976; Ego, Part Time Love, Song for Guy, 1978; Little Jeannie, 1980; Nobody Wins, 1981; Blue Eyes, Empty Garden, Princess, 1982; I Guess that's Why They Call It the Blues, 1983; Sad Songs (Say So Much), 1984. *Films:* Goodbye to Norma Jean, 1973; To Russia with Elton, 1980; played Pinball Wizard, in Tommy, 1973. Recipient of gold discs for all albums; Ivor Novello Award, Best Pop Song, 1976–77, Best Instrumental, 1978–79. *Recreations:* include playing tennis. *Address:* c/o John Reid Enterprises, Niddry House, 51 Holland Street, W8 7SB. *T:* 01–938 1741.

JOHN, Maldwyn Noel, FEng 1979, FIEE, FIEEE; Partner, Kennedy & Donkin, since 1972; *b* 25 Dec. 1929; *s* of Thomas Daniel John and Beatrice May John; *m* 1953, Margaret Cannell; two *s*. *Educ:* University College Cardiff. BSc 1st Cl. Hons, Elec. Eng. Metropolitan Vickers Elec. Co. Ltd, Manchester, 1950–59; Atomic Energy Authy, Winfrith, 1959–63; AEI/GEC, Manchester, as Chief Engineer, Systems Dept, Chief Engineer, Transformer Div., and Manager, AC Transmission Div., 1963–69; Chief Elec. Engineer, Kennedy & Donkin, 1969–72. President: IEE, 1983–84; Convention of Nat. Socs of Engineering of Western Europe, 1983–84. *Publications:* (jtly) Practical Diakoptics for Electrical Networks, 1969; (jtly) Power Circuit Breaker Theory and Design, 1st edn 1975, 2nd edn 1982; papers in IEE Procs. *Recreation:* golf. *Address:* 65 Orchard Drive, Horsell, Woking, Surrey GU21 4BS. *T:* Woking 73995.

JOHN, Michael M.; *see* Morley-John, M.

JOHN, Sir Rupert (Godfrey), Kt 1971; Governor of St Vincent, 1970–76; Member, Barclays Bank International Ltd Policy Advisory Committe (St Vincent), since 1977; Director, St Vincent Building and Loan Association, since 1977; Consultant to UNITAR, since 1978; *b* 19 May 1916; 2nd *s* of late Donelley John; *m* 1937, Hepsy, *d* of late Samuel Norris; three *s* one *d* (and one *s* decd). *Educ:* St Vincent Grammar Sch.; Univ. of London (BA, DipEd); Gray's Inn; New York University. First Asst Master, St Kitts/Nevis Grammar Sch., 1944; Asst Master, St Vincent Grammar Sch., 1944–52; private practice at Bar of St Vincent, 1952–58; Magistrate, Grenada, 1958–60; Actg Attorney-General, Grenada, 1960–62; Human Rights Officer, UN, 1962–69; Mem. Internat. Team of Observers, Nigeria, 1969–70; Senior Human Rights Officer, 1970. Has attended numerous internat. seminars and confs as officer of UN. Pres., Assoc. of Sen. Citizens of St Vincent and the Grenadines, 1981–; Mem. Editorial Adv. Bd, Jl of Third World Legal Studies, 1981–. KStJ 1971. *Publications:* St Vincent and its Constitution, 1971; Pioneers in Nation-Building in a Caribbean Mini-State, 1979; Racism and its Elimination, 1980; papers in various jls. *Recreations:* cricket, walking, swimming. *Address:* PO Box 677, Cane Garden, St Vincent, West Indies. *T:* 61500. *Club:* Royal Commonwealth Society.

JOHN CHARLES, Rt. Rev. Brother; *see* Vockler, Rt. Rev. J. C.

JOHN-MACKIE, Baron *cr* 1981 (Life Peer), of Nazeing in the County of Essex; **John John-Mackie;** Chairman, Forestry Commission, 1976–79; *b* 24 Nov. 1909; *s* of late Maitland Mackie, OBE, Farmer, and Mary Ann Mackie (*née* Yull); *m* 1934, Jeannie Inglis Milne; three *s* two *d*. *Educ:* Aberdeen Gram. Sch.; North of Scotland Coll. of Agriculture. Managing director of family farming company at Harold's Park Farm, Nazeing, Waltham Abbey, Essex, 1953–; Vicarage and Plumridge Farms, Hadley Wood, Enfield, 1968–79. MP (Lab) Enfield East, 1959–Feb. 1974; Jt Parly Sec., Min. of Agriculture, 1964–70. Mem., Aberdeen and Kincardine Agricl Exec. Cttee, 1939–47; Governor, North of Scotland Coll. of Agriculture, 1942–64, Vice Chm. 1956–64; Chm., Aberdeen and Kincardine Health Exec. Cttee, 1948–51; Governor, Nat. Inst. of Agricl Engrg, 1949–61; Member: Secretary of State for Scotland's Adv. Council, 1944–54; Plant Cttee on Poultry Diseases, 1963–64. Chm., Glentworth Scottish Farms Ltd, 1947–68. *Publication:* (for Fabian Soc.) Land Nationalisation. *Recreation:* tree planting. *Address:* Harold's Park, Nazeing, Waltham Abbey, Essex. *T:* Nazeing 2202. *Club:* Farmers'.

See also I. L. Aitken, Baron Mackie of Benshie, Sir Maitland Mackie.

JOHN PAUL II, His Holiness Pope, (Karol Jozef Wojtyla); *b* Wadowice, Poland, 18 May 1920; *s* of Karol Wojtyla. *Educ:* Jagiellonian Univ., Cracow; Pontificio Ateneo 'Angelicum' (Dr in Theology). Ordained Priest, 1946; Prof. of Moral Theology, Univs of Lublin and Cracow, 1954–58; titular Bishop of Ombi, and Auxiliary Bishop of Cracow, 1958; Vicar Capitular, 1962; Archbishop and Metropolitan of Cracow, 1964–78. Cardinal, 1967; elected Pope, 16 Oct. 1978. Formerly Member, Congregations Pro Institutione Catholica, Pro Sacramentis et Cultu Divino, and Pro Clero. *Publications:* The Goldsmith Shop (play), 1960; Love and Responsibility, 1962; Person and Act, 1969; The Foundations of Renewal, 1972; Sign of Contradiction, 1976; The Future of the Church, 1979; Easter Vigil and other poems, 1979; Collected Poems (trans. Jerzy Peterkiewicz), 1982. *Address:* Apostolic Palace, 00120 Vatican City.

JOHNS, Alun Morris, MD, FRCOG; Hon. Consulting Gynæcological and Obstetric Surgeon, Queen Charlotte's Hospital, London; *m* 1927, Joyce, *d* of T. Willoughby, Carlton-in-Coverdale, Yorks; one *s* two *d*. *Educ:* Manchester Univ. MB, ChB 1923, MD Manchester (Commend) 1925; FRCOG 1947. Late Consulting Surgeon, Surbiton Hospital and Erith and Dartford Hospitals. Examiner Central Midwives Board; Fellow Royal Society of Medicine; Fellow Manchester Med. Soc.; Fellow Manchester Path. Soc. *Address:* Loosley Row, near Princes Risborough, Bucks HP17 0PE. *T:* Princes Risborough 5298.

JOHNS, Glynis; actress; *b* Pretoria, South Africa; *d* of Mervyn Johns and Alice Maude (*née* Steel-Payne); *m* 1st, Anthony Forwood (marr. diss.); one *s*; 2nd, David Foster, DSO, DSC and Bar (marr. diss.); 3rd, Cecil Peter Lamont Henderson; 4th, Elliott Arnold. *Educ:* Clifton and Hampstead High Schs. First stage appearance in Buckie's Bears as a child ballerina, Garrick Theatre, London, 1935. Parts include: Sonia in Judgement Day, Embassy and Strand, 1937; Miranda in Quiet Wedding, Wyndham's, 1938 and in Quiet Weekend, Wyndham's, 1941; Peter in Peter Pan, Cambridge Theatre, 1943; Fools Rush In, Fortune; The Way Things Go, Phœnix, 1950; Gertie (title role), NY, 1952; Major Barbara (title role), NY, 1957; The Patient in Too True to Be Good, NY, 1962; The King's Mare, Garrick, 1966; Come as You Are, New, 1970; A Little Night Music, New York, 1973 (Tony award for best musical actress); Ring Round the Moon, Los Angeles, 1975; 13 Rue de l'Amour, Phœnix, 1976; Cause Célèbre, Her Majesty's, 1977 (Best Actress Award, Variety Club); Hayfever, UK; The Boy Friend, Toronto. Entered films as a child. *Films include:* South Riding, 49th Parallel, Frieda, An Ideal Husband, Miranda (the Mermaid), State Secret, No Highway, The Magic Box, Appointment with Venus, Encore, The Card, Sword and the Rose, Personal Affair, Rob Roy, The Weak and the Wicked, The Beachcomber, The Seekers, Poppa's Delicate Condition, Cabinet of Dr Caligari, Mad About Men, Josephine and Men, The Court Jester, Loser Takes All, The Chapman Report, Dear Bridget, Mary Poppins. Also broadcasts; television programmes include: Star Quality; The Parkinson Show (singing Send in the Clowns); Mrs Amworth (USA); All You Need is Love; Across a Crowded Room; Little Gloria, Happy at Last; Sprague; Love Boat; Murder She Wrote. *Address:* c/o Gottlieb, Schiff, Ticktin and Schachter, 555 5th Avenue, New York, NY 10017, USA.

JOHNS, Patricia Holly, MA; Headmistress, St Mary's School, Wantage, Oxon, since 1980; *b* 13 Nov. 1933; *d* of William and Violet Harris; *m* 1958, Michael Charles Bedford Johns (*d* 1965), MA; one *s* one *d*. *Educ:* Blackheath High Sch.; Girton Coll., Cambridge (BA 1956, MA 1959, CertEd with distinction 1957). Asst Maths Mistress; Cheltenham Ladies' Coll., 1957–58; Macclesfield Girls' High Sch., 1958–60; Asst Maths Mistress, then Head of Maths and Dir of Studies, St Albans High Sch., 1966–75; Sen. Mistress, and Housemistress of Hopeman House, Gordonstoun, 1975–80. *Recreations:* choral singing, walking, camping, dogs (corgis). *Address:* St Mary's School, Newbury Street, Wantage, Oxon OX12 8BZ; 8 Garden Close, Salisbury Avenue, St Albans, Herts AL1 4TX. *T:* St Albans 52185.

JOHNS, Paul; Chairperson, Campaign for Nuclear Disarmament, since 1985; Director, Profile Consulting Ltd, since 1983; *b* 13 March 1934; *s* of Alfred Thomas Johns and Margherita Johns; *m* 1st, 1956, Ruth Thomas (marr. diss. 1973); two *s* one *d*; 2nd, 1984, Margaret Perry. *Educ:* Kingswood School, Bath; Oriel College, Oxford (BA Hons Modern Hist.). MIPM. Personnel Management, Dunlop Rubber Co., 1958–63 and Northern Foods Ltd, 1963–68; Senior Partner, Urwick Orr & Partners, 1968–83. *Publications:* contribs to jls on management and on nuclear issue. *Recreations:* photography, listening to music, watching football (keen supporter of Nottingham Forest). *Address:* The Covers, Fox Road, West Bridgford, Nottingham NG2 6AS. *T:* Nottingham 816944.

JOHNSON; *see* Croom-Johnson.

JOHNSON, Alan Campbell; *see* Campbell-Johnson.

JOHNSON, Anne Montgomrey; Matron, The Royal Star and Garter Home for Disabled Sailors, Soldiers and Airmen, 1975–82; *b* 12 June 1922; *y c* of late Frederick Harold Johnson and late Gertrude Le Quesne (*née* Martin). *Educ:* St John's, Bexhill-on-Sea; Queen Elizabeth Hosp. (SRN); Brompton Hosp. (BTA Hons); Simpson Memorial Maternity Pavilion, Edinburgh (SCM). Asst Matron, Harefield Hosp., 1956–59; Dep. Matron, St Mary's Hosp., Paddington, 1959–62; Matron, Guy's Hosp., 1962–68; Mem. Directing and Tutorial Staff, King Edward's Hosp. Fund for London, 1968–71; Regional Dir, Help the Aged, 1971–73. Member: King's Fund Working Party, 'The Shape of Hospital Management 1980', 1966–67 (report publd 1967); Jt Cttee of Gen. Synod Working Party 'The Hospital Chaplain' (report publd 1974); Hosp. Chaplaincies Council, 1963–81; Nursing Cttee, Assoc. of Indep. Hosps, 1978–83. *Recreations:* straight theatre, travel. *Address:* Flat 5, 6 Cardigan Road, Richmond-on-Thames, Surrey TW10 6BJ.

JOHNSON, Prof. Barry Edward, PhD; FRS 1978; Professor of Pure Mathematics, since 1969, and Dean of Faculty of Science since 1986, University of Newcastle upon Tyne; *b* 1 Aug. 1937; *s* of Edward Johnson and Evelyn May (*née* Bailey); *m* (marr. diss. 1979); two *s* one *d*. *Educ:* Epsom County Grammar Sch.; Hobart State High Sch.; Univ. of Tasmania (BSc 1956); Cambridge Univ. (PhD 1961). Instr, Univ. of Calif, Berkeley, 1961–62; Vis. Lectr, Yale Univ., 1962–63; Lectr, Exeter Univ., 1963–65; University of Newcastle upon Tyne: Lectr, 1965–68; Reader, 1968–69; Head of Dept of Pure Maths, 1976–83; Head of Sch. of Maths, 1983–86. Vis. Prof., Yale Univ., 1970–71. Mem., London Math. Soc. (Mem. Council, 1975–78; Pres., 1980–82). *Publications:* Cohomology of Banach Algebras, 1972; papers in Jl of London Math. Soc. and Amer. Jl of Maths. *Recreations:* reading, travel. *Address:* 12 Roseworth Crescent, Gosforth, Newcastle upon Tyne NE3 1NR. *T:* Tyneside 2845363.

JOHNSON, Brian; *see* Johnson, R. B.

JOHNSON, Bruce Joseph F.; *see* Forsyth-Johnson.

JOHNSON, Carol Alfred, CBE 1951; *b* 1903. Admitted a Solicitor, 1933 (Hons); practised City of London; Hon. Solicitor to Housing Assocs in Southwark and Fulham; Asst Town Clerk, Borough of Southall, 1940–43; Secretary of the Parliamentary Labour Party, 1943–59. Alderman, Lambeth Borough Council, 1937–49 (sometime Leader). MP (Lab) Lewisham S, Sept. 1959–Feb. 1974; served on Chairman's Panel, presiding over cttees and occasionally the House; sometime Chm., History of Parliament Trust and Anglo-Italian Parly Cttee; Mem., Parly delegations to Nigeria, Persia (now Iran), the Cameroons and India. Served on Council of Europe; many years Jt Hon. Sec., British Council of European Movement, now Vice-Pres., Lab. Cttee for Europe. Sometime Hon. Sec., Friends of Africa and later Treasurer, Fabian Colonial Bureau; original Mem., Local Govt Adv. Panel, Colonial Office; Member: Fabian delegn to Czechoslovakia, 1946; British Council Lecture Tour to Finland. Exec. Mem., Commons (now Open Spaces) Soc. (formerly Chm.); Mem., Standing Cttee on Nat. Parks (now Council on Nat. Parks).

Trustee, William Morris Soc.; Mem. Exec. Cttee, British-Italian Soc.; Governor, British Inst., Florence, 1965–86. Comdr, Italian Order of Merit. *Address:* 11 Cliffe House, Radnor Cliff, Folkestone, Kent CT20 2TY.

JOHNSON, Charles Ernest, JP; Chairman, Greater Manchester County Council, 1982–83 (Councillor, 1974–86); *b* 2 Jan. 1918; adopted *s* of Henry and Mary Johnson; *m* 1942, Betty, *d* of William Nelson Hesford, farmer; one *s. Educ:* elementary school. Commenced work as apprentice coppersmith, 1932; called up to Royal Navy, 1940, demobilised, 1946. Councillor and Alderman, Eccles Town Council, 1952–73; Mayor, 1964–65; Chm. of various cttees, incl. Housing, for 14 years, and of Local Employment Cttee, for ten years; Mem., Assoc. of Municipal Councils, 1958–. JP Eccles, 1965. 1939–45 Medal, Atlantic Medal, Africa Star, Victory Medal; Imperial Service Medal, 1978. *Recreations:* gardening, watching football, swimming. *Address:* 17 Dartford Avenue, Winton, Eccles, Manchester M30 8NF. *T:* 061–789 4229.

JOHNSON, David Burnham, QC 1978; a Recorder, since 1984; *b* 6 Aug. 1930; *s* of late Thomas Burnham Johnson and of Elsie May Johnson; *m* 1968, Julia Clare Addison Hopkinson, *o d* of Col H. S. P. Hopkinson, *qv*; one *s* three *d. Educ:* Truro Sch.; Univ. of Wales. Solicitor and Notary Public, Oct. 1952. Commissioned, National Service, with Royal Artillery, 1952–54. Private practice as solicitor, Cardiff and Plymouth, 1954–67; called to Bar, Inner Temple, 1967, Bencher, 1985. *Recreations:* sailing, walking, shooting, reading, music. *Address:* 25 Murray Road, Wimbledon, SW19. *T:* 01–947 9188; (chambers) 3 Essex Court, Temple, EC4Y 9AL. *T:* 01–583 9294. *Clubs:* Army and Navy; Royal Western Yacht (Plymouth).

JOHNSON, Prof. David Hugh Nevil; Professor of International Law, Sydney University, 1976–85, now Emeritus; *b* 4 Jan. 1920; 2nd *s* of James Johnson and Gladys Mary (*née* Knight); *m* 1952, Evelyn Joan Fletcher. *Educ:* Winchester Coll.; Trinity Coll., Cambridge; Columbia Univ., New York. MA, LLM Cantab. Served Royal Corps of Signals, 1940–46. Called to Bar, Lincoln's Inn, 1950. Asst Legal Adviser, Foreign Office, 1950–53; Reader in Internat. Law, 1953–59, in Internat. and Air Law, 1959–60, Prof., 1960–Dec. 1975, Dean of Faculty of Laws, 1968–72, Univ. of London. Sen. Legal Officer, Office of Legal Affairs, UN, 1956–57. Registrar, the Court of Arbitration, Argentine-Chile Frontier Case, 1965–68. *Publications:* Rights in Air Space, 1965; articles in legal jls. *Address:* 91 Eastwood Avenue, Epping, NSW 2121, Australia.

JOHNSON, David Robert W.; *see* Wilson-Johnson.

JOHNSON, (Denis) Gordon, CBE 1969; Chairman, Geo. Bassett Holdings Ltd, 1955–78 (Managing Director, 1955–71); Chairman: W. R. Wilkinson & Co. Ltd, Pontefract, 1961–78; Drakes Sweets Marketing Ltd, 1961–78; B. V. de Faam, Holland, 1964–78; Barratt & Co. Ltd, London, 1968–78; *b* 8 Oct. 1911; *s* of late Percy Johnson; unmarried. *Educ:* Harrow; Hertford Coll., Oxford (MA). President: Cocoa, Chocolate and Confectionery Alliance, 1964–66 (Hon. Treas., 1972–77); Confectioners' Benevolent Fund, 1967–68; Member: Yorks Electricity Bd, 1965–75; Food Manufacturing Economic Develt Cttee, 1967–70; Council of CBI, 1968–78; Council, Sheffield Univ., 1972–81; Chm., S Yorks Industrialists' Council, 1976–78. Chm., Hallam Conservative Assoc., 1966–69, and 1973–76; Hon. Treas., City of Sheffield Conservative Fedn, 1969–73; Chm., City of Sheffield Cons. Assocs, 1976–78. Pres., Sheffield and Hallamshire Lawn Tennis Club. Vis. Fellow, Yorks and Humberside Regional Management Centre. CBIM; MInstD. *Publications:* address to British Assoc. (Economics Section), 1964; contributor to: Business Growth (ed Edwards and Townsend), 1966; Pricing Strategy (ed Taylor and Wills), 1969. *Recreations:* walking, travel, philosophy. *Address:* 7 Broadbent Street, W1X 9HJ. *T:* 01–629 1642.

JOHNSON, Donald Edwin, RIBA, FRTPI; Under Secretary, 1978–80, and Deputy Chief Planner, 1975–80, Department of the Environment; *b* 4 July 1920; *s* of Henry William Johnson and Ann Catherine (*née* Lake); *m* 1947, Thérèse Andrée Simone Marquant; two *s* one *d. Educ:* Haberdashers' Aske's, Hatcham; School of Architecture, Regent Polytechnic; APRR School of Planning. Served War, Royal Artillery and Royal Engineers, 1940–45. Planning Officer, Min. of Town and Country Planning, 1947; Sen. Planning Officer, 1950, Principal Planner, 1965, Asst Chief Planner, 1972. *Publications: fiction:* Project 38, 1963; Crooked Cross, 1964; Flashing Mountain, 1965; Devil of Bruges, 1966. *Address:* Flat D, 1 Morpeth Terrace, SW1P 1EW. *T:* 01–834 7300.

JOHNSON, Prof. Douglas William John; Professor of French History, University College London, since 1968; *b* Edinburgh, 1 Feb. 1925; *o s* of John Thornburn Johnson and Christine Mair; *m* 1950, Madeleine Rébillard; one *d. Educ:* Royal Grammar Sch., Lancaster; Worcester Coll., Oxford (BA, BLitt); Ecole Normale Supérieure, Paris. Birmingham Univ.: Lectr in Modern History, 1949; Prof. of Modern History and Chm. of Sch. of History, 1963–68; Head of Dept of History, 1979–83, Dean, Faculty of Arts, 1979–82, UCL. Vis. Prof., Univs of Aix-en-Provence, Nancy, Paris, British Columbia, Toronto. Chm. Bd of Examrs in History, Univ. of London, 1973–75; Member: CNAA; Franco-British Council. FRHistS. Ordre Nat. du Mérite (France), 1980. *Publications:* Guizot: Aspects of French History 1787–1874, 1963; France and the Dreyfus Affair, 1966; France, 1969; Concise History of France, 1970; The French Revolution, 1970; (ed jtly) Britain and France: Ten Centuries, 1980; (General Editor) The Making of the Modern World; (General Editor) The Fontana History of Modern France. *Recreations:* music, French politics. *Address:* University College, Gower Street, WC1E 6BT; 29 Rudall Crescent, NW3 1RR; 4 rue de la Cité, Saint-Servan-sur-Mer, 35400 Saint-Malo, France.

JOHNSON, Eric Alfred George, CBE 1953; retired chartered engineer; specialist in flood control, sea defences and land drainage engineering; *b* 3 Sept. 1911; *s* of Ernest George Johnson and Amelia Rhoda Johnson; *m* 1936, Barbara Mary Robin; one *d. Educ:* Taunton's Sch., Southampton; UC Southampton. Grad. Engrg, 1931; served for periods with Great Ouse and Trent Catchment Boards, 1933–37; joined Min. of Agriculture, 1937; Chief Engr, 1949–72. Has been associated with most major flood alleviation schemes carried out 1931–81, incl. Thames Barrier; Consultant, Sir Murdoch MacDonald & Partners, 1972–82; Vice-Pres., Internat. Commn of Irrigation and Drainage, 1958–61; former chm. of several internat. and nat. cttees. *Publications:* papers in ICE and other professional jls. *Recreation:* visiting the countryside and sea coast to see some of the areas with which he has been associated through floods and protection schemes. *Address:* 94 Park Avenue, Orpington, Kent. *T:* Orpington 23802.

JOHNSON, Prof. Francis Rea; Professor of Anatomy, London Hospital Medical College, 1968–86; Pre-clinical Sub-Dean, 1979–86; *b* 8 July 1921; *s* of Marcus Jervis Johnson and Elizabeth Johnson; *m* 1951, Ena Patricia Laverty; one *s* one *d. Educ:* Omagh Academy, N Ire.; Queen's Univ., Belfast. MB, BCh, BAO 1945, MD 1949. House appts, Belfast City Hosp., 1946; Demonstrator in Anatomy and Physiology, QUB, 1947–50; Lectr in Anatomy, Sheffield Univ., 1950–57; Reader in Anatomy, London Hosp. Med. Coll., 1957–64; Prof. of Histology, London Hosp. Med. Coll., 1964–68. *Publications:* papers on histochemistry and ultrastructure of tissues and organs in various jls. *Recreations:* motoring, camping, gardening. *Address:* 11 Beacon Rise, Sevenoaks, Kent. *T:* Sevenoaks 53343.

JOHNSON, Air Vice-Marshal Frank Sidney Roland, CB 1973; OBE 1963; CBIM; Base Manager, British Aircraft Corporation RSAF, Dhahran, Saudi Arabia, 1977–82, retired; *b* 4 Aug. 1917; *s* of Major Harry Johnson, IA, and Georgina Marklew; *m* 1943, Evelyn Hunt; two *s. Educ:* Trinity County Secondary Sch., Wood Green. Enlisted, 1935; served in UK and India; commnd, 1943; Germany (Berlin Airlift), 1948; Western Union Defence Organisation, 1955–57; Directing Staff, RAF Staff Coll., 1958–60; comd 113 MU, RAF Nicosia, 1960–63; Chief Instructor Equipment and Secretarial Wing, RAF Coll. Cranwell, 1963–64; Dep. Dir MoD, 1965–66; idc 1967; Chief Supply Officer, Fighter and Strike Comds, 1968–70; Dir-Gen. of Supply, RAF, 1971–73; Supply Manager, BAC, Saudi Arabia, 1974–76; Base Manager, BAC RSAF, Khamis Mushayt, Saudi Arabia, 1976–77. *Recreations:* golf, squash, hockey, cricket. *Address:* 9 Hazely, Tring, Herts. *T:* Tring 6535. *Club:* Royal Air Force.

JOHNSON, Frederick Alistair, PhD; FInstP; Director, Marconi Maritime Applied Research Laboratory, and Chief Scientist, Marconi Underwater Systems Ltd, since 1985; *b* Christchurch, NZ, 9 April 1928; *s* of Archibald Frederick Johnson and Minnie, *d* of William Frederick Pellew; *m* 1952, Isobel Beth, *d* of Horace George Wilson; two *d. Educ:* Christchurch Boys' High Sch.; Univ. of Canterbury, New Zealand (MSc, PhD). Rutherford Meml Fellow, 1952; Lectr, Univ. of Otago, 1952; post graduate research, Bristol Univ., 1953–55. Royal Radar Establishment, 1956–75: Individual Merit Promotion, 1964; Head of Physics Dept, 1968–73; Dep. Director, 1973–75; Dep. Dir, Royal Armament Research & Development Estabt, 1975–77; Dir of Scientific and Technical Intell., MoD, 1977–79; Chief Scientist (Royal Navy) and Dir Gen. Research A, MoD, 1980–84. Visiting Professor, Massachusetts Inst. of Technology, 1967–68; Hon. Prof. of Physics, Birmingham Univ., 1969–75. *Publications:* numerous papers on spectroscopy, optics and lattice dynamics in Proc. Physical Soc. and Proc. Royal Soc. *Recreation:* sailing. *Address:* Otia Tuta, Grassy Lane, Sevenoaks, Kent TN13 1PL.

JOHNSON, Maj.-Gen. Garry Dene, OBE 1977 (MBE 1971); MC 1965; Assistant Chief of Defence Staff (NATO/UK), 1985–June 1987; Commander, British Forces Hong Kong, and Major General, Brigade of Gurkhas, from June 1987; *b* 20 Sept. 1937; *s* of James Hill Johnson and Doreen Johnson; *m* 1962, Caroline Sarah Frearson; two *s. Educ:* Christ's Hospital. psc, ndc, rcds. Commissioned 10th Princess Mary's Own Gurkha Rifles, 1956; Malaya and Borneo campaigns, 1956–67; Royal Green Jackets, 1970; command, 1st Bn RGJ, 1976–79; Comdr, 11 Armoured Brigade, 1981–82; Dep. Chief of Staff, HQ BAOR, 1983; Colonel, 10th PMO Gurkha Rifles, 1985–. *Publication:* Brightly Shone the Dawn, 1979. *Recreations:* travel, study of history, enjoyment of food and wine, preferably in combination. *Address:* Ministry of Defence, Main Building, Whitehall, SW1; (from June 1987) BFPO 1. *Clubs:* Army and Navy; Tanglin (Singapore).

JOHNSON, Gordon; *see* Johnson, D. G.

JOHNSON, Graham Rhodes; concert accompanist; *b* 10 July 1950; *s* of John Edward Donald Johnson and Violet May Johnson (*née* Johnson). *Educ:* Hamilton High Sch., Bulawayo, Rhodesia; Royal Acad. of Music, London. FRAM 1984. Concert début, Wigmore Hall, 1972; has since accompanied Elisabeth Schwarzkopf, Jessye Norman, Victoria de los Angeles (USA Tour 1977), Dame Janet Baker, Sir Peter Pears, Felicity Lott, Margaret Price (USA Tour 1985), Peter Schreier, John Shirley Quirk, Valerie Masterson, Dame Kiri Te Kanawa. Work with contemporaries led to formation of The Songmakers' Almanac (Artistic Director); has devised and accompanied more than 90 London recitals for this group since Oct. 1976. Tours of US with Sarah Walker, Richard Jackson, and of Australia and NZ with The Songmakers' Almanac, 1981. Writer and presenter of major BBC Radio 3 series on Poulenc songs, and BBC TV programmes on Schubert songs (1978) and the songs of Liszt (1986). Lectr at song courses in Savonlinna (Finland), US and at Pears-Britten Sch., Snape; Artistic advr and accompanist, Alte Oper Festival, Frankfurt, 1981–82; Festival appearances in Aldeburgh, Edinburgh, Bath, Hong Kong, Bermuda. Many recordings incl. those with Songmakers' Almanac and Martyn Hill. *Publications:* (contrib.) The Britten Companion, ed Christopher Palmer, 1984; (contrib.) Gerald Moore, The Unashamed Accompanist, rev. edn 1984; reviews in TLS, articles for music jls. *Recreation:* eating in good restaurants with friends and fine wine. *Address:* 83 Fordwych Road, NW2 3TL. *T:* 01–452 5193.

JOHNSON, Ven. Hayman; Archdeacon of Sheffield, 1963–78, Archdeacon Emeritus 1978; a Canon Residentiary of Sheffield Cathedral, 1975–78; Chaplain to HM The Queen, 1969–82; *b* 29 June 1912; *s* of late W. G. Johnson, Exeter; *m* 1943, Margaret Louise Price; one *d. Educ:* Exeter Sch.; New Coll., Oxon. Chaplain, RAFVR, 1941–46; Chaplain and Vicar Temporal, Hornchurch, 1953–61; Examining Chaplain to Bishop of Sheffield, 1962–78. *Address:* Flat 1, Parklands, 56 Kibbles Lane, Southborough, Tunbridge Wells, Kent TN4 0LQ.

JOHNSON, Sir Henry (Cecil), KBE 1972 (CBE 1962); Kt 1968; FCIT; Chairman: MEPC Ltd, 1971–76; Development and Property Associates Ltd, since 1984; *b* 11 Sept. 1906; *s* of William Longland and Alice Mary Johnson, Lavendon, Bucks; *m* 1932, Evelyn Mary Morton; two *d. Educ:* Bedford Modern Sch. Traffic Apprentice L & NER, 1923–26; series of posts in Operating Dept; Asst Supt, Southern Area, L & NER, 1942; Chief Operating Supt of Eastern Region, BR, 1955; Asst Gen. Man., Eastern Region, Dec. 1955, Gen. Man., 1958; Gen. Man., London Midland Region, BR, 1962, Chm. and Gen. Man., 1963–67; Chm., BR Bd, 1968–71 (Vice-Chm., 1967). Mem., GB Adv. Bd, Imperial Life of Canada, 1976–; Member: Greater London Regional Bd, Lloyds Bank, 1971–76; Imperial Life (UK) Ltd, 1985–; Trident Life Assurance Co. Ltd, 1985–; Trident Investors Life Assurance Co. Ltd, 1985. *Recreations:* golf, continuing interest in farming. *Address:* Rowans, Harewood Road, Chalfont St Giles, Bucks. *T:* Little Chalfont 2409. *Clubs:* MCC; Royal and Ancient (St Andrews).

JOHNSON, Henry Leslie, FTI; farmer; *b* 4 March 1904; *s* of Henry and Annie Letitia Johnson, formerly of Macclesfield, Cheshire and Coventry; *m* 1939, Mabel Caroline Hawkins, Woking, Surrey; one *s* two *d. Educ:* Rugby. Joined Courtaulds Ltd, 1922; Dir, 1933–68; Managing Dir, 1935–47. Vice-Chm., Warwicks CC, 1974–75. Pres., Textile Institute, 1942 and 1943. Liveryman, Worshipful Co. of Farmers; Freeman, City of London, 1959. *Address:* Offchurch Bury, near Leamington Spa, Warwicks CV33 9AR. *TA* and *T:* Leamington Spa 24293.

JOHNSON, Howard Sydney; solicitor; Senior Partner, Howard Johnson & McQue, 1933–83; Director, Alliance Building Society, since 1970; *b* 25 Dec. 1911; *s* of Sydney Thomas Johnson; *m* 1939, Betty Frankiss, actress. *Educ:* Brighton; Highgate. Served War of 1939–45, Africa; invalided out as Major. Joined TA before the war. Mem. of Brighton Town Council, 1945–50. MP (C) Kemptown Div. of Brighton, 1950–Sept. 1959. *Publication:* (contrib.) P. Moore: Against Hunting, 1965. *Address:* Ballakinnag Cottage, Smeale, Andreas, Isle of Man. *T:* Kirk Andreas 712.

JOHNSON, Hugh Eric Allan; author and editor; *b* 10 March 1939; *s* of late Guy Francis Johnson, CBE and Grace Kittel; *m* 1965, Judith Eve Grinling; one *s* two *d. Educ:* Rugby Sch.; King's Coll., Cambridge (MA). Staff writer, Condé Nast publications, 1960–63; Editor, Wine & Food, and Sec., Wine and Food Soc., 1963–65; Wine Corresp., 1962–67, and Travel Editor, 1967, Sunday Times; Editor, Queen, 1968–70. Pres., Direct Sunday Times Wine Club, 1973–; Vice-Pres., British Acad. of Gastronomes, 1984–. Chairman: Conservation Cttee, Internat. Dendrology Soc., 1979–; Winestar Productions Ltd, 1984–; The Hugh Johnson Collection Ltd, 1985–. Dir, Château Latour, 1987–. Editorial Director: Jl of RHS, 1975–; The Plantsman, 1979–. Wine Editor, Cuisine, New York, 1983–84; Video Consultant to Jardine Matheson Ltd, Hong Kong, 1985–. Gardening Correspondent, New York Times, 1986–. Video, How to Handle a Wine, 1984 (Glenfiddich Trophy, 1984); TV series, Wine—a user's guide (KQED, San Francisco), 1986, *Publications:* Wine, 1966, rev. edn 1974, The World Atlas of Wine, 1971, 3rd edn 1985; The International Book of Trees, 1973, rev. edn 1984; (with Bob Thompson) The California Wine Book, 1976; Hugh Johnson's Pocket Wine Book, annually 1977–; The Principles of Gardening, 1979, rev. edn 1984; Understanding Wine, 1980; (with Paul Miles) The Pocket Encyclopedia of Garden Plants, 1981; Hugh Johnson's Wine Companion, 1983; How to Enjoy Your Wine, 1985; The Hugh Johnson Cellar Book, 1986; The Atlas of German Wines, 1986; Hugh Johnson's Wine Cellar, (US) 1986; articles on gastronomy, travel and gardening. *Recreations:* travelling, staying at home. *Address:* Saling Hall, Great Saling, Essex; 73 St James's Street, SW1. *Clubs:* Garrick, Saintsbury.

JOHNSON, James, BA, DPA; *b* 16 Sept. 1908; *s* of James and Mary Elizabeth Johnson; *m* 1937, Gladys Evelyn Green; one *d. Educ:* Duke's Sch., Alnwick; Leeds Univ. BA 1st Cl. Hons Geography, 1931; Diploma in Education, 1932; Diploma in Public Administration (London), 1944. FRGS. Schoolmaster: Queen Elizabeth Grammar Sch., Atherstone, 1931; Scarborough High Sch., 1934; Bablake Sch., Coventry, 1944. Lecturer, Coventry Tech. Coll., 1948–50. MP (Lab): Rugby Div. of Warwicks, 1950–59; Kingston upon Hull West, 1964–83. Trade Union Advr, Kenya Local Govt Workers, 1959–60; Student Adviser, Republic of Liberia, 1960–64. Treasurer, Commonwealth Parly Assoc., 1979–82; Chm., Anglo-Somali Soc., 1980–. Dir, Hull City Football Club, 1982–. Freeman, City of Kingston-upon-Hull, 1982. Played soccer for British Univs and Corinthians. Grand Comdr Order of Star of Africa (Liberia), 1967; Commander's Cross 2nd Class (Austria), 1985. *Recreation:* watching soccer and snooker. *Address:* 70 Home Park Road, SW19. *T:* 01–946 6224. *Clubs:* Royal Over-Seas League; Humber St Andrews Engineering Social and Recreation.

JOHNSON, Air Vice-Marshal James Edgar, (Johnnie Johnson), CB 1965; CBE 1960; DSO 1943 and Bars, 1943, 1944; DFC 1941 and Bar, 1942; DL; Chief Executive, Johnnie Johnson Housing Trust, Ltd; Director of Companies in Canada, South Africa and UK; *m* Pauline Ingate; two *s. Educ:* Loughborough Sch.; Nottingham Univ. Civil Engr and Mem. of RAFVR until 1939; served with 616 Sqdn AAF, 1940–42; 610 Sqdn AAF, 1943; Wing Comdr Flying: Kenley, 1943; 127 Wing, 1944; Officer Comdg: 125 Wing (2nd TAF), 1944–45; 124 Wing (2nd TAF), 1945–46; RCAF Staff Coll., 1947–48; USAF (Exchange Officer), 1948–50; served Korea (with USAF), 1950–51; OC, RAF Wildenrath (2nd TAF), 1952–54; Air Ministry, 1954–57; Officer Commanding, RAF Cottesmore, Bomber Command, 1957–60; idc 1960; Senior Air Staff Officer, No 3 Group, Bomber Command, Mildenhall, Suffolk, 1960–63; AOC, Air Forces Middle East, Aden, 1963–65; retired. DL Leicester, 1967. Order of Leopold, 1945, Croix de Guerre, 1945 (Belgium); Legion of Merit, 1950, DFC 1943, Air Medal, 1950 (USA). *Publications:* Wing Leader, 1956; Full Circle, 1964; The Story of Air Fighting, 1985. *Recreations:* shooting, golf. *Address:* The Stables, Hargate, Buxton, Derbyshire SK17 8TA. *Club:* Royal Air Force.

JOHNSON, Rt. Rev. James Nathaniel; see St Helena, Bishop of.

JOHNSON, John Robin; His Honour Judge Johnson; a Circuit Judge, since 1973; *b* 27 Nov. 1927; *s* of Sir Philip Bulmer Johnson, Hexham, Northumberland; *m* 1958, Meriel Jean, *d* of H. B. Speke, Aydon, Corbridge; one *s* one *d. Educ:* Winchester; Trinity Coll., Cambridge. Called to Bar, Middle Temple, 1950. Dep. Chm., Northumberland QS, 1966–71; a Recorder of the Crown Court, 1972–73. *Address:* c/o Crown Court, Kenton Bar, Newcastle-upon-Tyne.

JOHNSON, John Rodney, CMG 1981; HM Diplomatic Service; High Commissioner in Kenya, since 1986; *b* 6 Sept. 1930; *s* of Edwin Done Johnson, OBE and Florence Mary (*née* Clough); *m* 1956, Jean Mary Lewis; three *s* one *d. Educ:* Manchester Grammar Sch.; Oxford Univ. (MA). HM Colonial Service, Kenya, 1955–64; Dist Comr, Thika, 1962–64; Administrator, Cttee of Vice-Chancellors and Principals of UK Univs, 1965; First Sec., FCO, 1966–69; Head of Chancery, British Embassy, Algiers, 1969–72; Dep. High Comr, British High Commn, Barbados, 1972–74; Counsellor, British High Commn, Lagos, 1975–78; Head of W African Dept, FCO, and Ambassador (non-resident) to Chad, 1978–80; High Comr in Zambia, 1980–84; Assist Under Sec. of State (Africa), FCO, 1984–86. *Recreations:* climbing, reaching remote places, gardening. *Address:* c/o Foreign and Commonwealth Office, SW1. *Clubs:* Travellers'; Climbers; Bridgetown (Barbados).

JOHNSON, Air Vice-Marshal Johnnie; see Johnson, James Edgar.

JOHNSON, Kenneth James, OBE 1966; industrial consultant; Member Board of Crown Agents for Oversea Governments and Administrations, since 1980; Crown Agents Holding and Realisation Board, since 1980; Chairman: Crown Agents Pensions Trust, since 1984; Black and Edgington Industries Ltd, since 1984; Mark Wong & Associates (UK) Ltd, since 1986; *b* 8 Feb. 1926; *s* of Albert Percy Johnson and Winifred Florence (*née* Coole); *m* 1951, Margaret Teresa Bontoft Jenkins; three *s* two *d. Educ:* Rishworth School, near Halifax; Wadham Coll., Oxford; LSE; SOAS. Indian Army (14 Punjab Regt), 1945–47. Colonial Admin. Service, Nigeria, 1949–61, senior appts in Min. of Finance and Min. of Commerce and Industry; Head of Economic Dept, later Dir of Industrial Affairs, CBI, 1961–70; Courtaulds Ltd, 1970–73: Chm. and Man. Dir, various subsidiary cos; Dep. Chm., Pay Board, 1973–74. Dunlop Group: 1974–85: Personnel Dir, 1974–79; Overseas Dir, Dunlop Holdings plc, 1979–84; Chm., Dunlop International AG, 1984/5; Group Overseas Consultant, 1985. FRSA 1972; FIPM 1976. *Recreations:* family pursuits, travel. *Address:* Woodgetters, Shipley, Horsham, West Sussex. *T:* Southwater 730481. *Clubs:* Oriental, Royal Commonwealth Society.

JOHNSON, Prof. Kenneth Langstreth, PhD; FRS 1982; Professor of Engineering, Cambridge University, since 1977; Fellow of Jesus College, Cambridge, since 1957; *b* 19 March 1925; *s* of Frank Herbert Johnson and Ellen Howorth Langstreth; *m* 1954, Dorothy Rosemary Watkins; one *s* two *d. Educ:* Barrow Grammar Sch.; Manchester Univ. (MScTech, MA, PhD). FIMechE. Engr, Messrs Rotol Ltd, Gloucester, 1944–49; Asst Lectr, Coll. of Technology, Manchester, 1949–54; Lectr, then Reader in Engrg, Cambridge Univ., 1954–77. *Publications:* Contact Mechanics, 1985; contrib. scientific and engrg jls, and Proc. IMechE. *Recreations:* mountain walking, swimming. *Address:* 13 Park Terrace, Cambridge. *T:* Cambridge 355287.

JOHNSON, Merwyn; see Johnson, W. M.

JOHNSON, Michael Howard; a Recorder of the Crown Court, since 1980; a Social Security Commissioner, since 1986; *b* 9 May 1930; *m*; two *d. Educ:* Charterhouse; Chelsea School of Art. ACIArb 1984. Called to the Bar, Gray's Inn, 1964. Asst Parliamentary

Boundary Commissioner, 1976–84. Chm., Hertfordshire FPC, 1985–86. *Address:* Office of the Social Security Commissioners, 6 Grosvenor Gardens, SW1W 0DH. *T:* 01–370 9236.

JOHNSON, Michael York-; see York, M.

JOHNSON, Dame Monica; see Golding, Dame (Cecilie) Monica.

JOHNSON, Nevil; Nuffield Reader in the Comparative Study of Institutions, University of Oxford, and Professorial Fellow, Nuffield College, since 1969; *b* 6 Feb. 1929; *s* of G. E. Johnson and Doris Johnson, MBE, Darlington; *m* 1957, Ulla van Aubel; two *s. Educ:* Queen Elizabeth Grammar Sch., Darlington; University Coll., Oxford (BA PPE 1952, MA 1962). Army service, 1947–49. Admin. Cl. of Home Civil Service: Min. of Supply, 1952–57; Min. of Housing and Local Govt, 1957–62; Lectr in Politics, Univ. of Nottingham, 1962–66; Sen. Lectr in Politics, Univ. of Warwick, 1966–69. Chm. Board, Faculty of Social Studies, Oxford, 1976–78. Visiting Professor: Ruhr Univ. of Bochum, 1968–69; Univ. of Munich, 1980. Mem., ESRC (formerly SSRC), 1981– (Chm., Govt and Law Cttee, 1982–86). Civil Service Comr (pt-time), 1982–85. Mem. Exec. Council, Royal Inst. of Public Admin, 1965–; Chm., Study of Parlt Gp, 1984–. Hon. Editor, Public Administration, 1967–81. *Publications:* Parliament and Administration: The Estimates Committee 1945–65, 1967; Government in the Federal Republic of Germany, 1973; In Search of the Constitution, 1977 (trans. German, 1977); (with A. Cochrane) Economic Policy-Making by Local Authorities in Britain and Western Germany, 1981; State and Government in the Federal Republic of Germany, 1983; articles in Public Admin, Political Studies, Parly Affairs, Ztschr. für Politik, Die Verwaltung, and Der Staat. *Recreations:* jogging, swimming, gardening. *Address:* 50 Norman Avenue, Abingdon, Oxon OX14 2HL. *T:* Abingdon 20078. *Club:* United Oxford & Cambridge University.

JOHNSON, Prof. Newell Walter, MDSc, PhD; FDSRCS, FRACDS, FRCPath; Nuffield Research Professor of Dental Science, Royal College of Surgeons of England, and Hon. Director, Medical Research Council, Dental Research Unit, London Hospital Medical College, since 1984; Hon. Consultant Dental Surgeon, London Hospital, since 1968; *b* 5 Aug. 1938; *s* of Otto Johnson and Lorna (*née* Guy); *m* 1965, Pauline Margaret Trafford (marr. diss. 1984); two *d. Educ:* University High Sch., Melbourne; Univ. of Melbourne (BDSc Hons 1960; MDSc 1963); Univ. of Bristol (PhD 1967). FDSRCS 1964; FRACDS 1966; FRCPath 1982. Res. Fellow in Pathology, Univ. of Melbourne, 1961–63; Lectr in Dental Surgery, UCL, 1963–64; Scientific Officer, MRC Dental Res. Unit, Bristol, 1964–67; London Hosp. Medical College: Reader in Experimental Oral Path., 1968–76; Prof. of Oral Path., 1976–83; Governor, 1983 (Chm., Academic Div. of Dentistry, 1983); Chm., London Hosp. Div. of Dentistry, 1981–83. Consultant in Oral Health, WHO, 1984–; Consultant, Fédération Dentaire Internationale, 1984–. Chm., UK Cttee, Royal Australasian Coll. of Dental Surgeons, 1981–83; FRSM; Mem. Council, Section of Odontology, RSM, 1972–. Mem. Editorial Bd, Jl of Oral Pathology, 1982–. *Publications:* (jtly) The Oral Mucosa in Health and Disease, 1975; (jtly) The Human Oral Mucosa: structure, metabolism and function, 1976; (jtly) Dental Caries: aetiology, pathology and prevention, 1979; articles in scientific jls. *Recreations:* choral singing, music, theatre, squash, the environment, the Third World. *Club:* Blizard.

JOHNSON, Patrick, OBE 1945; MA; *b* 24 May 1904; 2nd *s* of A. F. W. Johnson, JP, and F. E. L. Cocking; unmarried. *Educ:* RN Colls, Osborne and Dartmouth; Tonbridge Sch.; Magdalen Coll., Oxford. Fellow and Lecturer in Natural Science, Magdalen Coll., 1928–47, Dean, 1934–38, Vice-Pres., 1946–47. Flying Officer, RAFO, 1929–34; commissioned in RA (TA), 1938; served War of 1939–45, in Middle East and NW Europe, Lt-Col, Asst Dir of Scientific Research, 21st Army Group and comdg No. 2 operational research section. Dir of Studies, RAF Coll., Cranwell, 1947–52; Dean of Inst. of Armament Studies, India, 1952–55; Scientific Adviser to the Army Council, 1955–58; Asst Scientific Adviser, SHAPE, 1958–62; Head of Experimental Develt Unit, Educnl Foundn for Visual Aids, 1962–70. *Recreations:* rowing (rowed against Cambridge, 1927), sailing, shooting. *Address:* 5 Linley Court, Rouse Gardens, SE21 8AQ. *Club:* Leander (Henley-on-Thames).

JOHNSON, Paul (Bede); author; *b* 2 Nov. 1928; *s* of William Aloysius and Anne Johnson; *m* 1957, Marigold Hunt; three *s* one *d. Educ:* Stonyhurst; Magdalen Coll., Oxford. Asst Exec. Editor, Réalités, 1952–55; Editorial Staff, New Statesman, 1955, Dir, Statesman and Nation Publishing Co., 1965, Editor of the New Statesman, 1965–70. Member: Royal Commn on the Press, 1974–77; Cable Authority, 1984–. *Publications:* The Suez War, 1957; Journey into Chaos, 1958; Left of Centre, 1960; Merrie England, 1964; Statesmen and Nations, 1971; The Offshore Islanders, 1972; (with G. Gale) The Highland Jaunt, 1973; Elizabeth I, 1974; A Place in History, 1974; Pope John XXIII, 1975 (Yorkshire Post Book of the Year Award, 1975); A History of Christianity, 1976; Enemies of Society, 1977; The National Trust Book of British Castles, 1978; The Recovery of Freedom, 1980; British Cathedrals, 1980; Ireland: Land of Troubles, 1980; Pope John Paul II and the Catholic Restoration, 1982; A History of the Modern World from 1917 to the 1980s, 1983; The Pick of Paul Johnson, 1985. *Recreations:* mountaineering, painting. *Address:* Copthall, Iver, Bucks. *T:* Iver 653350.

JOHNSON, Sir Peter (Colpoys Paley), 7th Bt *cr* 1755; Publishing Director, Nautical Books, London, since 1981; *b* 26 March 1930; *s* of Sir John Paley Johnson, 6th Bt, MBE, and of Carol, *d* of late Edmund Haas; *S* father, 1975; *m* 1st, 1956, Clare (marr. diss. 1973), *d* of Dr Nigel Bruce; one *s* two *d*; 2nd, 1973, Caroline Elisabeth, *d* of late Sir John Hodsoll, CB; one *s. Educ:* Wellington Coll.; Royal Military Coll. of Science. Served RA, 1949; retired 1961, Captain. Dir, Sea Sure Ltd, 1965–73; Dir and Editor, Nautical Publishing Co. Ltd, 1970–81. British Delegate, Internat. Offshore (Yachting) Council, 1970–79 (Chm. Internat. Technical Cttee, 1973–76); Ocean Racing Correspondent, Yachting World, London, 1971–81. *Publications:* Ocean Racing and Offshore Yachts, 1970, 2nd edn 1972; Boating Britain, 1973; Guinness Book of Yachting Facts and Feats, 1975; Guinness Guide to Sailing, 1981; This is Fast Cruising, 1985. *Recreation:* sailing. *Heir: s* Colpoys Guy Johnson, *b* 13 Nov. 1965. *Address:* Dene End, Buckland Dene, Lymington, Hants SO4 9DT. *T:* Lymington 75921 *Clubs:* Royal Ocean Racing; Royal Yacht Squadron.

JOHNSON, Philip Cortelyou; architect, with own firm, 1953–67, with Johnson/Burgee Architects, since 1967; *b* Cleveland, Ohio, 8 July 1906; *s* of Homer H. Johnson and Louise Pope Johnson. *Educ:* Harvard (AB 1927, *cum laude*). Dir, Dept of Architecture, The Museum of Modern Art, New York, 1932–54, Trustee, 1958–; Graduate Sch. of Design, Harvard, 1940–43 (BArch). Has taught and lectured at: Yale Univ.; Cornell Univ.; Pratt Inst. (Dr Fine Arts, 1962). Mem. AIA (New York Chapter); Architectural League, NY. Hon. Dr Fine Arts Yale, 1978. Gold Medal, AIA, 1978; Pritzker Architecture Prize, 1979. *Publications:* Machine Art, 1934; Mies van der Rohe, 1st edn 1947, 2nd edn 1953; (with Henry-Russell Hitchcock) The International Style, Architecture since 1922, 1932, new edn 1966; (with others) Modern Architects, 1932; Architecture 1949–65, 1966; Philip Johnson Writings, 1979; contributor to Architectural Review. *Address:* (business) Philip Johnson, 375 Park Avenue, New York, NY 10152, USA. *T:* 751–7440; (home) Ponus Ridge Road, New Canaan, Conn. *T:* 966–0565. *Clubs:* Athenæum, Century.

JOHNSON, (Reginald) Stuart, CBE 1985; Director of Education, Leeds City Council, since 1973; *b* 12 April 1933; *s* of late Reginald Johnson and Sarah Anne Johnson; *m* 1960, Dr Jennifer Johnson (*née* Craig); one *s* one *d*. *Educ:* Durham Univ. (BSc Hons); London Univ. (PGCE, DipEd). Deputy Education Officer, Leeds CC, 1968–73. Member: UGC, 1979–; Advisory Cttee on Supply and Educn of Teachers, 1980– (Chm., Teacher Trng Sub-Cttee, 1981–); PPITB, 1977–80 (Chm., Trng Cttee, 1978–80). Mem., BBC Schools and Further Educn Broadcasting Council, 1976–82. Adviser to Burnham Cttee, 1984–. Administrator, Leeds International Pianoforte Competition, 1978–81. *Publications:* frequent articles in educnl press. *Recreations:* golf, cricket, fishing. *Address:* Green Mead, Foxhill Crescent, Leeds LS16 5PD. *T:* Leeds 756705. *Clubs:* Lansdowne; Leeds (Leeds).

JOHNSON, Rex; Director of Social Services, Lancashire County Council, 1978–June 1986; *b* 19 Aug. 1921; *s* of Samuel and Ellen Johnson; *m* 1946, Mary Elizabeth Whitney; two *d*. *Educ:* Accrington Grammar Sch.; St Paul's Trng Coll., Cheltenham (qual. teacher); Leeds Univ. (MA). Served War, RAF, 1942–46; radar mechanic, educn instr; served Ireland, India, Singapore (Burma Star). Asst Master, Darwen, 1946–49; Dep. Supt, Boys' Remand Home, Lincoln, 1949–52; Head of Springfield Reception Centre, Bradford, 1953–64; Home Office Inspector, Children's Dept, 1964–65; Educnl Psychologist, Bradford, 1965–67; Univ. Lectr, Leeds, 1967–69; Social Work Service Officer, DHSS (formerly Home Office Inspector), 1969–72; Dep. Dir of Social Services, Lancs, 1972–78. Mem., Personal Social Services Council, 1977–80. *Publications:* (ed) ABC of Behaviour Problems, 1962 (2nd edn 1969); (ed) ABC of Social Problems and Therapy, 1963; (ed) ABC of Social Services, 1964; articles in Soc. Work Today, Residential Soc. Work, Community Care, Hosp. and Soc. Services Jl, and Jl RSH. *Address:* Ebor, 5 Links Road, St Annes-on-Sea, Lancs. *T:* St Annes 724014.

JOHNSON, Richard Keith; actor and producer; Founder Chairman and Joint Chief Executive, United British Artists, since 1983; *b* 30 July 1927; *s* of Keith Holcombe and Frances Louisa Olive Johnson; *m* 1st, 1957, Sheila Sweet (marr. diss); one *s* one *d*; 2nd, 1965, Kim Novak (marr. diss.); 3rd, 1982, Marie-Louise Norlund; one *s*. *Educ:* Parkfield School; Felsted School; RADA. RN, 1945–48. 1st stage appearance, Opera House, Manchester, 1944; repertory, Haymarket, 1944–45; *stage:* contract, Royal Shakespeare Theatre, 1957–62; Antony in Antony and Cleopatra, RSC, 1972–73; NT, 1976–78; *films:* MGM contract, 1959–65; The Haunting; Moll Flanders; Operation Crossbow; Khartoum; The Pumpkin Eater; Danger Route; Deadlier than the Male; Oedipus the King; Hennessy (also wrote original story); Aces High; The Four Feathers; Turtle Diary (also prod); Castaway (Exec. Producer). Mem. Council, BAFTA, 1977–79. *Recreations:* reading, gardening, travelling. *Address:* United British Artists, Russell Chambers, Covent Garden, WC2E 8AA. *T:* 01-240 9891/6.

JOHNSON, (Robert) Brian, QPM 1981; Chief Constable, Lancashire Constabulary, since 1983; *b* 28 July 1932; *s* of Robert and Hilda Johnson; *m* 1954, Jean Thew; two *d*. *Educ:* Stephenson Memorial Boys' Sch.; College of Commerce, Newcastle. Newcastle City Police: Police Cadet, 1948; Police Constable, 1952; Detective Constable, 1955; Detective Sergeant, 1962; Detective Inspector, 1966; Detective Chief Inspector, 1969; Detective Supt, Northumbria Police, 1971; Chief Supt, Northumbria Police, Home Office, 1976; Asst Chief Constable, Northumbria, 1977; Dep. Chief Constable, Lancashire, 1981. President: NW Area, National Assoc. of Retired Police Officers (also Pres., Blackpool Br.), 1983–; Lancs Assoc. of Boys Clubs, 1983–; Lancs Outward Bound Assoc., 1983–; Vice-Pres., Lancs Council for Voluntary Youth Services, 1985; Patron: NW Counties Schools ABA, 1983–; Blackburn Area, Road Safety Assoc., 1983–. *Recreations:* reading, gardening. *Address:* Police Headquarters, Hutton, Preston, Lancs PR4 5SB. *Club:* Special Forces.

JOHNSON, Robert Lionel; QC 1978; a Recorder of the Crown Court, since 1977; barrister-at-law; *b* 9 Feb. 1933; *er s* of late Edward Harold Johnson, MSc, FRIC, and of Ellen Lydiate Johnson, Cranleigh; *m* 1957, Linda Mary, *er d* of late Charles William Bennie and Ena Ethel Bennie, Egglescliffe; one *s* two *d*. *Educ:* Watford Grammar Sch. (1940–51); London Sch. of Econs and Polit. Science. 5th Royal Inniskilling Dragoon Guards, 1955–57, Captain; ADC to GOC-in-C Northern Comd, 1956–57; Inns of Court Regt, 1957–64. Called to the Bar, Gray's Inn, 1957; Mem., Bar Council, 1981–. Jun. Counsel to Treasury in Probate Matters, 1975–78; Legal Assessor, GNC, 1977–82. Chairman: Bar Fees and Legal Aid Cttee, 1984–86 (Vice-Chm., 1982–84); Family Law Bar Assoc., 1984–; Member: Supreme Court Procedure Cttee, 1982–; Law Soc. Legal Aid Cttee, 1981–. Internat. Sec., Internat. Cystic Fibrosis Assoc., 1984–; Trustee: (and Founder Mem.) Council, Cystic Fibrosis Res. Trust, 1964–; Robert Luff Charitable Foundn, 1977–. *Publications:* (with James Comyn) Wills & Intestacies, 1970; Contract, 1975; (with Malcolm Stitcher) Atkin's Trade, Labour and Employment, 1975. *Recreations:* charitable work, gardening. *Address:* Queen Elizabeth Building, Temple, EC4Y 9BS. *T:* 01-583 7837.

JOHNSON, Robert White, CBE 1962; Director, Cammell Laird & Co. Ltd, 1946–70; Chairman: Cammell Laird & Co. (Shipbuilders and Engineers) Ltd, 1957–68; Cammell Laird (Shiprepairers) Ltd, 1963–68; retired; *b* 16 May 1912; *s* of late Sir Robert (Stewart) Johnson, OBE; *m* 1950, Jill Margaret Preston; two *s* one *d*. *Educ:* Rossall Sch. Robt Bradford & Co. Ltd (Insurance Brokers), 1931–35. Served War of 1939–45, Provost Marshal's Dept, RAF, becoming Wing Comdr. Director: Patent Shaft & Axletree Co. Ltd, Wednesbury, Staffs, 1946–51; Metropolitan-Cammell Carriage and Wagon Co. Ltd, Birmingham, 1946–64; North Western Line (Mersey) Ltd, 1964–70; Bradley Shipping Ltd, 1964–70; formerly Dir, Scottish Aviation Ltd; Coast Lines Ltd; English Steel Corp. Ltd; Chm. of North West Tugs Ltd, Liverpool, 1951–66; Mem. Mersey Docks and Harbour Board, 1948–70; Pt-time Mem. Merseyside and North Wales Electricity Board, 1956–66; Chm., Merseyside Chamber of Commerce and Industry, 1972–74. Underwriting Mem., Lloyd's, 1937–. Pres., Shipbuilding Employers' Federation, 1958–59. *Recreations:* fishing, shooting, golf. *Address:* The Oaks, Well Lane, Heswall, Wirral, Merseyside L60 8NE. *T:* 051-342 3304.

JOHNSON, Sir Ronald (Ernest Charles), Kt 1970; CB 1962; JP; *b* 3 May 1913; *o c* of Ernest and Amelia Johnson; *m* 1938, Elizabeth Gladys Nuttall; two *s* (and one *s* decd). *Educ:* Portsmouth Grammar Sch.; St John's Coll., Cambridge. Entered Scottish Office, 1935; Sec., Scottish Home and Health Dept, 1963–72. Chm., Civil Service Savings Cttee for Scotland, 1963–78. Sec. of Commissions for Scotland, 1972–78. Chm., Scottish Hosp. Centre, 1964–72. Member: Scottish Records Adv. Council, 1975–81; Cttee on Admin of Sheriffdoms, 1981–82; Chm., Fire Service Res. and Training Trust. Served RNVR on intelligence staff of C-in-C, Eastern Fleet, 1944–45. President: Edinburgh Bach Soc., 1973–86; Edinburgh Soc. of Organists, 1980–82. JP Edinburgh, 1972. *Publications:* articles in religious and musical jls. *Recreation:* church organ. *Address:* 14 Eglinton Crescent, Edinburgh EH12 5DD. *T:* 031-337 7733.

JOHNSON, Stanley, CBE 1970; FCA; FCIT; Managing Director, British Transport Docks Board, 1967–75; European Agent, Northland Harbour Board, New Zealand, since 1980; *b* 10 Nov. 1912; *s* of late Robert and Janet Mary Johnson; *m* 1940, Sheila McLean Bald; two *s* two *d*. *Educ:* King George V Sch., Southport. Served as Lieut (S) RINVR, 1942–45. Joined Singapore Harbour Board, 1939; Asst Gen. Man. 1952; Chm. and Gen. Man. 1958–59; Chief Docks Man., Hull Docks, 1962; Asst Gen. Man. 1963, Mem. and Dep. Man. Dir 1966, British Transport Docks Board. Chm. Major Ports Cttee, Dock and Harbour Authorities Assoc., 1971–72. Mem., Exec. Council, British Ports Assoc., 1973–75; Vice-Pres., Internat. Assoc. of Ports and Harbours, 1975–77. Vice-Pres., CIT, 1973–75. *Recreations:* walking, reading, travel. *Address:* 4 Berry Hill Court, Taplow, Bucks. *Club:* Naval and Military.

JOHNSON, Stanley Patrick; Adviser on Environmental Protection, Commission of the European Communities, since 1984; *b* 18 Aug. 1940; *s* of Wilfred Johnson and Irène (*née* Williams); *m* 1st, 1963, Charlotte Offlow Fawcett (marr. diss.); three *s* one *d*; 2nd, 1981, Mrs Jennifer Kidd; one *s* one *d*. *Educ:* Sherborne Sch.; Exeter Coll., Oxford (Trevelyan Schol., Sen. Classics Schol.); Harkness Fellow, USA, 1963–64. MA Oxon 1963; Dip. Agric. Econs Oxon 1965. World Bank, Washington, 1966–68; Project Dir, UNA-USA Nat. Policy Panel on World Population, 1968–69; Mem. Conservative Research Dept, 1969–70; Staff of Internat. Planned Parenthood Fedn, London, 1971–73; Consultant to UN Fund for Population Activities, 1971–73; Mem. Countryside Commn, 1971–73; Head of Prevention of Pollution and Nuisances Div., EEC, 1973–77; Adviser to Head of Environment and Consumer Protection Service, EEC, 1977–79; Member (C) Wight and Hants E, Eur. Parlt, 1979–84. Newdigate Prize for Poetry, 1962; Richard Martin Award, RSPCA, 1982; Greenpeace Award, 1984. *Publications:* Life Without Birth, 1970; The Green Revolution, 1972; The Politics of the Environment, 1973; (ed) The Population Problem, 1973; The Pollution Control Policy of the EEC, 1979, 2nd edn 1984; Antarctica—the last great wilderness, 1985; *novels:* Gold Drain, 1967; Panther Jones for President, 1968; God Bless America, 1974; The Doomsday Deposit, 1980; The Marburg Virus, 1982; Tunnel, 1984; The Commissioner, 1987. *Recreations:* writing, travel. *Address:* Nethercote, Winsford, Minehead, Somerset. *Club:* Savile.

JOHNSON, Stuart; *see* Johnson, R. S.

JOHNSON, Sir Victor Philipse Hill, 6th Bt, *cr* 1818; *b* 7 May 1905; *s* of late Hugh Walters Beaumont Johnson, Kingsmead, Windsor Forest, and Winifred Mena Johnson (*née* Hill, later W. M. Livingstone), Fern Lea, Southampton; *S* cousin, Sir Henry Allen Beaumont Johnson, 5th Bt, 1965; unmarried. *Educ:* Cheltenham Coll. Ranched in BC, Canada, 1926–38. Served with RAF, 1939–45. *Recreations:* gardening, playing at golf. *Heir: kinsman* Robin Eliot Johnson [*b* 1929; *m* 1954, Barbara Alfreda, *d* of late Alfred T. Brown; one *s* two *d*]. *Address:* Beach House, 64 Sea Lane, Goring-by-Sea, Worthing, West Sussex. *T:* Worthing 43630.

JOHNSON, Walter Hamlet; *b* Hertford, 21 Nov. 1917; *s* of John Johnson; *m* 1945. *Educ:* Devon House Sch., Margate. Councillor, Brentford and Chiswick for 6 years. Nat. Treasurer, 1965–77, Pres., 1977–81, Transport Salaried Staffs' Assoc. Joined Labour Party, 1945. Contested (Lab) Bristol West, 1955 and South Bedfordshire, 1959, in General Elections; also Acton (Lab), 1968, in by-election. MP (Lab) Derby South, 1970–83; an Assistant Govt Whip, 1974–75. Is particularly interested in welfare services, transport, labour relations and aviation matters; Chm., PLP Aviation Cttee, 1979–83. Principal Executive Assistant, London Transport, 1980–83 (formerly a Sen. Exec., Staff Trng). Governor, Ruskin Coll., Oxford, 1966–85. *Recreation:* sport. *Address:* 9 Milton Court, Haywards Heath RH16 1EY. *T:* Haywards Heath 412629.

JOHNSON, Prof. William, DSc Manchester, MA Cantab; FRS 1982; FEng, FIMechE; Emeritus Professor, Cambridge University; *b* 20 April 1922; *er s* of James and Elizabeth Johnson; *m* 1946, Heather Marie (*née* Thornber); three *s* two *d*. *Educ:* Central Grammar Sch., Manchester; Manchester Coll. of Science and Technology (BScTech). BSc London; FEng 1983. Served War, Lt REME, UK and Italy, 1943–47. Asst Principal, Administrative Grade, Home Civil Service, 1948–50; Lecturer, Northampton Polytechnic, London, 1950–52; Lectr in Engineering, Sheffield Univ., 1952–56; Senior Lectr in Mechanical Engineering, Manchester Univ., 1956–60; Prof. of Mechanical Engrg, 1960–75, Chm. of Dept of Mechanical Engrg, 1960–69, 1971–73, Dir of Medical Engrg, 1973–75, UMIST; Prof. of Mechanics, Engrg Dept, CambridgeUniv., 1975–82; Professorial Fellow, Fitzwilliam Coll., 1975–82. Visiting Professor: McMaster Univ., Canada, 1969; Springer Prof., Univ. of Calif, Berkeley, 1980; Singapore, 1982; Allied Irish Banks Prof., Univ. of Belfast, 1983; Industrial Engrg Dept, Purdue Univ., Indiana, 1984 and 1985. Hon. Sec., Yorks Br. of IMechE, 1953–56, and Chm., NW Br., 1974–75; Pres., Manchester Assoc. of Engrs, 1983–84. Founder, and Editor-in-Chief: Internat. Jl Mech. Sciences, 1960–; Internat. Jl Impact Engineering, 1983–; Chm., Internat. Jl Mech. Engrg Educn, 1960–84. Fellow UCL, 1982. For. Fellow, Nat. Acad. of Athens, 1982. Hon. DTech Bradford, 1976; Hon. DEng Sheffield, 1986. Premium Award, Jl RAeS, 1956; T. Constantine Medal, Manchester Soc. of Engrs, 1962; Bernard Hall Prize (jt), IMechE, 1965–66 and 1966–67; James Clayton Fund Prize (jt), IMechE, 1972 and 1978. *Publications:* Plasticity for Mechanical Engineers (with P. B. Mellor), 1962; Mechanics of Metal Extrusion (with H. Kudo), 1962; Slip Line Fields: Theory and Bibliography (with R. Sowerby and J. B. Haddow), 1970; Impact Strength of Materials, 1972; Engineering Plasticity (with P. B. Mellor), 1973; Lectures in Engineering Plasticity (with A. G. Mamalis), 1978; Crashworthiness of Vehicles (with A. G. Mamalis), 1978; Plane-Strain Slip-Line Fields for Metal-Deformation Processes (with R. Sowerby and R. Venter), 1982; papers in mechanics of metal forming, impact engineering, mechanics of sports and games, solids, bioengineering and history of engineering mechanics. *Recreation:* landscape gardening. *Address:* Ridge Hall, Chapel-en-le-Frith, Derbyshire.

JOHNSON, His Honour William; QC (NI); County Court Judge for County Tyrone, 1947–78; *b* 1 April 1903; *s* of late William Johnson, CBE, and Ellen Johnson. *Educ:* Newry Intermediate Sch.; Portora Royal Sch., Enniskillen; Trinity Coll., Dublin (BA; Sen. Moderator Legal and Polit. Sci.; LLB (1st cl.)); King's Inns, Dublin (Certif. of Honour at Final Examinations for Call to Bar). Called to Irish Bar and Bar of N Ireland, 1924; Hon. Bencher, Inn of Court of N Ireland. Served War of 1939–45, France, Germany, Holland, Belgium (despatches); ADJAG, Actg Lt-Col. Lectr in Law, QUB, 1933–36; Chm. Court of Referees 1928–30, Dep. Umpire 1930–35, Umpire 1935–47, NI Unemployment Insce and Pensions Acts; KC (Northern Ireland) 1946; Sen. Crown Prosecutor, Co. Antrim, 1947. Chairman: Cttee on Law of Intestate Succession in NI, 1951; Cttee on Law of Family Provision in NI, 1953; Cttee on Examns for Secondary Intermediate Schs in NI, 1958; Vice-Chm., Jt Cttee on Civil and Criminal Jurisdictions in NI, 1971; Chm., Council of HM's County Ct Judges in NI, 1975–78. Has held various positions as Leader and Comr in Scout Assoc., 1923–70; Mem., NI Youth Cttee, 1939; Mem. Council, Scout Assoc., 1958–; Chief Comr for NI, Boy Scouts Assocs, 1955–65; Vice-Pres., NI Scout Council; Pres., Belfast County Scout Council. *Publications:* History and Customs of the Bar and Circuit of Northern Ireland; contrib. NI Legal Qly. *Address:* Bar Library, Royal Courts of Justice, Belfast BT1 3JX.

JOHNSON, William Harold Barrett; Commissioner of Inland Revenue, 1965–76; *b* 16 May 1916; *s* of late William Harold Johnson and Mary Ellen (*née* Barrett); *m* 1940, Susan Gwendolen, *d* of Rev. H. H. Symonds; one *s* one *d*. *Educ:* Charterhouse; Magdalene Coll., Cambridge. Served in Royal Artillery, 1939–45. Entered Inland Revenue Dept, 1945.

Vice-Pres., Cruising Assoc., 1974–77. *Recreations:* cruising under sail, gardening. *Address:* 45 Granville Park, SE13 7DY; Barrow Cottage, Ravenglass, Cumbria CA18 1ST.

JOHNSON, (Willis) Merwyn; Agent General for Saskatchewan in the United Kingdom, 1977–83; *b* 9 May 1923; *s* of Robert Arthur Johnson and Gudborg Kolbinson; *m* 1946, Laura Elaine Aseltine; two *s* two *d.* *Educ:* McKenzie High Sch., Kindersley; Univ. of Saskatchewan. BSA, BA. MP for Kindersley, Parliament of Canada, 1953–57 and 1957–58. *Recreations:* fishing, golf. *Address:* 4044 Hollydene Place, Victoria, BC V8N 3Z7, Canada. *Clubs:* Wig and Pen, Farmers', Royal Automobile, Canada.

JOHNSON-FERGUSON, Sir Neil (Edward), 3rd Bt, *cr* 1906; TD; Lt-Col Royal Corps of Signals; Vice-Lieutenant, Dumfriesshire, since 1965; *b* 2 May 1905; *s* of Sir Edward Alexander James Johnson-Ferguson, 2nd Bt, and Hon. Elsie Dorothea McLaren (*d* 1973), *d* of 1st Baron Aberconway; *S* father 1953; *m* 1931, Sheila Marion (*d* 1985), *er d* of late Col H. S. Jervis, MC; four *s.* *Educ:* Winchester; Trinity Coll., Cambridge (BA). Capt. Lanarks Yeomanry, TA, 1928; Major 1937; Major, Royal Signals, 1939; Lt-Col 1945. JP 1954, DL 1957, Dumfriesshire. American Legion of Merit. *Heir: s* Ian Edward Johnson-Ferguson [*b* 1 Feb. 1932; *m* 1964, Rosemary Teresa, *d* of C. J. Whitehead, The Old House, Crockham Hill, Kent; three *s*]. *Address:* Fairyknowe, Eaglesfield, Dumfriesshire.

JOHNSON-GILBERT, Ronald Stuart, OBE 1976; Secretary, Royal College of Surgeons of England, since 1962; *b* 14 July 1925; *s* of late Sir Ian A. Johnson-Gilbert, CBE and late Rosalind Bell-Hughes; *m* 1951, Ann Weir Drummond; three *d.* *Educ:* Edinburgh Acad.; Rugby; Brasenose Coll., Oxford (Classical Exhbnr and Open Schol., 1943; MA). Intelligence Corps, 1943–46. Trainee, John Lewis Partnership, 1950–51; Admin. Staff, RCS, 1951–; Secretary: Faculties of Dental Surgery and of Anaesthetists, 1958; Jt Conf. of Surgical Colls, 1963–; Internat. Fedn of Surgical Colls, 1967–74; Hon. Sec., Med. Commn on Accident Prevention, 1984–. Hon. FFARCS 1983. John Tomes Medal, BDA, 1980; McNeill Love Medal, RCS, 1981; Royal Australasian Coll. of Surgeons Medal, 1982. *Recreations:* music, painting, literature, golf. *Address:* Potters Wheel, Ruxley Crescent, Claygate, Surrey KT10 0TX. *Club:* Confrères.

JOHNSON-LAIRD, Dr Philip Nicholas, FBA 1986; Fellow of Darwin College, Cambridge, since 1984; Assistant Director, MRC Applied Psychology Unit, Cambridge, since 1983 (special appointment, 1982); *b* 12 Oct. 1936; *s* of Eric Johnson-Laird and Dorothy (*née* Blackett); *m* 1959, Maureen Mary Sullivan; one *s* one *d.* *Educ:* Culford Sch.; University Coll. London (Rosa Morison Medal, 1964; James Sully Schol., 1964–66; BA (Hons) 1964; PhD 1967). MBPsS 1962. 10 years of misc. jobs, as surveyor, musician, hosp. porter (alternative to Nat. Service), librarian, before going to university. Asst Lectr, then Lectr, in Psychol., UCL, 1966–73; Reader, 1973, Prof., 1978, in Exptl Psychol., Univ. of Sussex. Vis. Mem., Princeton Inst. for Advanced Study, 1971–72; Vis. Fellow, Stanford Univ., 1980; Visiting Professor: Stanford Univ., 1985; Princeton Univ., 1986. Member: Psychol. Cttee, SSRC, 1975–79; Linguistics Panel, SSRC, 1980–82; Adv. Council, Internat. Assoc. for Study of Attention and Performance, 1984. Member: Linguistics Assoc., 1967; Exptl Psychol. Soc., 1968; Cognitive Sci. Soc., 1980; Assoc. for Computational Linguistics, 1981. Hon. DPhil Göteborg, 1983. Spearman Medal, 1974, President's Award, 1985, BPsS. *Publications:* (ed jtly) Thinking and Reasoning, 1968; (with P. C. Wason) Psychology and Reasoning, 1972; (with G. A. Miller) Language and Perception, 1976; (ed jtly) Thinking, 1977; Mental Models, 1983; contribs to psychol, linguistic and cognitive sci. jls, reviews in lit. jls. *Recreations:* talking, arguing, laughing, playing modern jazz. *Address:* MRC Applied Psychology Unit, 15 Chaucer Road, Cambridge CB2 2EF. *T:* Cambridge 355294.

JOHNSON-MARSHALL, Percy Edwin Alan, CMG 1975; RIBA; FRTPI; Professor of Urban Design and Regional Planning, University of Edinburgh, 1964–85; Head of Department of Urban Design and Regional Planning, 1967–84; in practice as planning consultant since 1960; *b* 20 Jan. 1915; *s* of Felix William Norman Johnson-Marshall and Kate Jane Little; *m* 1944, April Bridger; three *s* four *d.* *Educ:* Liverpool Univ. Sch. of Architecture; Dip. in Arch.(Dist); (RIBA) RTPI; (RIBA) DisTP; MA (Edin). Planning Architect, Coventry, 1938–41; Served War: with Royal Engrs (India and Burma), 1942–46. Asst Regional Planner, Min. of Town and Country Planning, 1946–49; Gp Planning Officer, in charge of reconstr. areas gp, LCC, 1949–59 (Projects incl.: Lansbury and Stepney/Poplar South Bank, (jtly with City Corp.) Barbican Area, Tower Hill area, etc). Apptd Sen. Lectr, Dept of Architecture, Univ. of Edinburgh, 1959. Director: Architectural Research Unit, 1961–64; Planning Research Unit, 1962. Consultant on Human Settlements for UN Stockholm Conf. on Environment, 1972. Partner of Architectural and Planning Consultancy, Percy Johnson-Marshall & Partners (Projects incl. Edin. Univ. Plan, Kilmarnock and Bathgate Town Centres, Porto Regional Plan, etc). *Publications:* Rebuilding Cities, 1966; contribs to technical jls. *Address:* Bella Vista, Duddingston Village, Edinburgh EH15 3PZ. *T:* 031-661 2019.

JOHNSON SMITH, Sir Geoffrey, Kt 1982; MP (C) Wealden, since 1983 (East Grinstead, Feb. 1965–1983); *b* 16 April 1924; *s* of late J. Johnson Smith; *m* Jeanne Pomeroy, MD; two *s* one *d.* *Educ:* Charterhouse; Lincoln Coll., Oxford. Served War of 1939–45: Royal Artillery, 1942–47; Temp. Capt. RA, 1946. BA Hons, Politics, Philosophy and Economics, Oxford, 1949. Mem., Oxford Union Soc. Debating Team, USA, 1949. Information Officer, British Information Services, San Francisco, 1950–52; Mem. Production Staff, Current Affairs Unit, BBC TV, 1953–54; London County Councillor, 1955–58; Interviewer, Reporter, BBC TV, 1955–59. MP (C) Holborn and St Pancras South, 1959–64; PPS, Board of Trade and Min. of Pensions, 1960–63; Opposition Whip, 1965; Parly Under-Sec. of State for Defence for the Army, MoD, 1971–72; Parly Sec., CSD, 1972–74; Vice-Chm., Cons. Back-bench Defence Cttee, 1980–. Mem. Exec., 1922 Cttee, 1979–. A Vice-Chm., Conservative Party, 1965–71. Member: IBA Gen. Adv. Council, 1975–80; N Atlantic Assembly, 1980– (Chm., Military Cttee, 1985–). Governor, BFI, 1980–. *Address:* House of Commons, SW1. *Club:* Travellers'.

JOHNSTON; *see* Lawson Johnston.

JOHNSTON, Alan Charles Macpherson, QC (Scot.) 1980; Treasurer, Faculty of Advocates, since 1977; *m* 1966, Anthea Jean Blackburn; three *s.* *Educ:* Edinburgh Academy; Loretto School; Jesus Coll., Cambridge (BA Hons); Edinburgh Univ. (LLB). Called to the Bar, 1967; Advocate Depute, 1979–82. *Publication:* (asst editor) Gloag and Henderson, Introduction to Scots Law, 7th edn 1968. *Recreations:* shooting, fishing, golf, walking. *Address:* 3 Circus Gardens, Edinburgh. *Clubs:* University Pitt (Cambridge); New (Edinburgh).

JOHNSTON, Alastair McPherson; *see* Dunpark, Hon. Lord.

JOHNSTON, Sir Alexander, GCB 1962 (CB 1946); KBE 1953; Chairman, Board of Inland Revenue, 1958–68; *b* 27 Aug. 1905; *s* of Alexander Simpson Johnston and Joan Macdiarmid; *m* 1947, Betty Joan Harris (*see* Lady Johnston); one *s* one *d.* *Educ:* George Heriot's Sch.; University of Edinburgh. Entered Home Office, 1928; Principal Asst Sec., Office of the Minister of Reconstruction, 1943–45; Under-Sec., Office of Lord Pres. of the Council, 1946–48; Dep. Sec. of the Cabinet, 1948–51; Third Sec., HM Treasury, 1951–58. Deputy Chairman: Monopolies and Mergers Commn, 1969–76; Panel on Take-overs and Mergers, 1970–83; Council for the Securities Industry, 1978–83. Hon. DSc(Econ) London, 1977; Hon. LLD Leicester, 1986. *Address:* 18 Mallord Street, SW3. *T:* 01–352 6840. *Club:* Reform.

JOHNSTON, Alexander Graham; Sheriff of Strathkelvin at Glasgow, since 1985; *b* 16 July 1944; *s* of Hon. Lord Kincraig, *qv*; *m* 1st, 1972, Susan (marr. diss. 1982); two *s*; 2nd, 1982, Angela; two step *d.* *Educ:* Edinburgh Acad.; Strathallan Sch.; Univ. of Edinburgh (LLB); University Coll., Oxford (BA). Admitted as Solicitor and Writer to the Signet, 1971; Partner, Hagart and Burn-Murdoch, Solicitors, Edinburgh, 1972–82. Sheriff of Grampian, Highland and Isles, 1982–85. Hon. Fellow, Inst. of Professional Investigators, 1980. *Recreations:* golf, piping, curling, bridge, puzzles. *Address:* 3 North Dean Park Avenue, Bothwell, Lanarkshire. *T:* Bothwell 852177. *Clubs:* Oxford and Cambridge Golfing Society; Vincent's (Oxford).

JOHNSTON, Most Rev. Allen Howard, CMG 1978; LTh; *b* Auckland, NZ, 1912; *s* of Joseph Howard Johnston; *m* 1937, Joyce Rhoda, *d* of John A. Grantley, Auckland; four *d.* *Educ:* Seddon Memorial Technical College; St John's College, Auckland; Auckland Univ. College. Deacon, 1935; Priest, 1936. Assistant Curate of St Mark's, Remuera, 1935–37; Vicar of Dargaville, 1937–42; Vicar of Northern Wairoa, 1942–44; Vicar of Otahuhu, 1944–49; Vicar of Whangarei, 1949–53; Archdeacon of Waimate, 1949–53; Bishop of Dunedin, 1953–69; Bishop of Waikato, 1969–80; Primate and Archbishop of New Zealand, 1972–80. Fellow, St John's Coll., Auckland, 1970. Hon. LLD Otago, 1969. ChStJ 1974. *Address:* 3 Wymer Terrace, Hamilton, New Zealand.

JOHNSTON, Betty Joan, (Lady Johnston), JP; Standing Counsel to General Synod of Church of England, since 1983; Chairman: Girls' Public Day School Trust, since 1975; Association of Governing Bodies of Girls' Schools, since 1979; *d* of Edward and Catherine Anne Harris; *m* 1947, Sir Alexander Johnston, *qv*; one *s* one *d.* *Educ:* Cheltenham Ladies' Coll.; St Hugh's Coll., Oxford (1st cl. Hons Jurisprudence; MA; BCL). Called to Bar, Gray's Inn, 1940 (1st cl., Bar Final exams; Arden and Lord Justice Holker Sen. schols). Asst Parly Counsel, 1942–52; Dep. Parly Counsel, Law Commn, 1975–83. Vice-Chm., Direct Grant Schs Jt Cttee, 1975–81; Chm., Francis Holland (Church of England) Schs Trust, 1978–. Dep. Chm., ISJC, 1986– (Mem., 1974–; Chm., 1983–86; Chm., Assisted Places Cttee, 1981–); Mem., Council, Queen's Coll., London. JP Inner London, 1966. *Address:* 18 Mallord Street, SW3. *T:* 01–352 6840.

JOHNSTON, Brian (Alexander), OBE 1983; MC 1945; freelance broadcaster and commentator; *b* 24 June 1912; *s* of Lt-Col C. E. Johnston, DSO, MC; *m* 1948, Pauline, *d* of late Col William Tozer, CBE, TD; three *s* two *d.* *Educ:* Eton; New Coll., Oxford (BA). Family coffee business, 1934–39. Served War of 1939–45: in Grenadier Guards; in 2nd Bn throughout, taking part in Normandy Campaign, advance into Brussels, Nijmegen Bridge and Crossing of Rhine into Germany. Joined BBC, 1945, retired 1972; specialises in cricket commentary for TV and radio (BBC Cricket Corresp., 1963–72), interviews, ceremonial commentary (*eg* Funeral of King George VI, 1952; Coronation of Queen Elizabeth II, 1953; Weddings of Princess Margaret, 1960, Princess Anne, 1973, Prince of Wales, 1981; Queen's Silver Jubilee, 1977); Let's Go Somewhere feature in In Town Tonight, Down Your Way, Twenty Questions, etc. Radio Sports Personality Award, Soc. of Authors/Pye Radio, 1981; Radio Personality of the Year Award, Sony, 1983. *Publications:* Let's Go Somewhere, 1952; Armchair Cricket, 1957; Stumped for a Tale, 1965; The Wit of Cricket, 1968; All About Cricket, 1972; It's Been a Lot of Fun, 1974; It's a Funny Game . . ., 1978; Rain Stops Play, 1979; Chatterboxes, 1983; Now Here's a Funny Thing, 1984; Guide to Cricket, 1986. *Recreations:* cricket, golf, theatre and reading newspapers. *Address:* 43 Boundary Road, NW8. *T:* 01–286 2991. *Club:* MCC.

JOHNSTON, Sir Charles (Collier), Kt 1973; TD; Joint Hon. Treasurer, Conservative Party, since 1984; President, National Union of Conservative and Unionist Associations, since 1986; *b* 4 March 1915; *e s* of late Captain Charles Moore Johnston and Muriel Florence Mellon; *m*; two *s*; *m* 1981, Mrs Yvonne Shearman. *Educ:* Tonbridge Sch., Kent. Served War: HM Forces, Territorial, commissioned 1938; served throughout war, in RA, retd, 1946, rank Major. Managing Dir, 1948–76, Chm., 1951–77, of Standex International Ltd (formerly Roehlen-Martin Ltd), Engravers and Engineers, Ashton Road, Bredbury, Cheshire; Chairman: Thames & Kennet Marina Ltd, 1982–; James Burn International, 1986–; Dir, Standex Holdings Ltd, 1983–. Chm., Macclesfield Constituency Conservative Assoc., 1961–65; Hon. Treas., NW Conservatives and Mem. Conservative Bd of Finance, 1965–71; Chm., NW Area Conservatives, 1971–76; a Vice Pres., Nat. Union of Conservative and Unionist Assocs (Mem. Exec. Cttee, 1965–, Chm. 1976–81). Nat. Chm., Cons. Friends of Israel, 1983–. Mem., Boyd Commn, as official observers of elecns held in Zimbabwe/Rhodesia, April 1980. *Recreations:* spectator sports, travelling, gardening. *Address:* 5A Burton Mews, South Eaton Place, SW1. *Club:* Royal Corinthian Yacht (Cowes).

JOHNSTON, Rear-Adm. Clarence Dinsmore H.; *see* Howard-Johnston.

JOHNSTON, Prof. David, MD, ChM; FRCS, FRCSE, FRCSGlas; Professor of Surgery and Head of Department, University of Leeds at Leeds General Infirmary, since 1977; *b* Glasgow, 4 Sept. 1936; *s* of Robert E. and Jean Johnston; *m*; three *s* one *d.* *Educ:* Hamilton Acad.; Glasgow Univ. (MB, ChB Hons; MD Hons, ChM). FRCSE 1963; FRCSGlas 1964; FRCS 1979. House Surgeon, Western Infirmary, Glasgow, 1961–62; Res. Asst and Registrar, Univ. Dept of Surg., Leeds Gen. Infirm., 1962–64; Lectr in Surg., Univ. of Sheffield, 1965–68; Sen. Lectr and Consultant, Univ. Dept of Surg., Leeds Gen. Infirm., 1968–75; Prof. of Surg. and Head of Dept, Univ. of Bristol (Bristol Royal Infirm.), 1975–77. *Publications:* papers on physiology and surgery of the stomach and colon. *Recreations:* reading, running, tennis, fishing. *Address:* 23 St Helens Gardens, Adel, Leeds 16. *T:* Leeds 678046.

JOHNSTON, David Alan H.; *see* Hunter Johnston.

JOHNSTON, David Lawrence, CEng, FIEE; RCNC; Assistant Under Secretary of State, Ministry of Defence, and Managing Director, HM Dockyard, Devonport, since 1984; *b* 12 April 1936; *s* of late Herbert David Johnston and of Hilda Eleanor Wood; *m* 1959, Beatrice Ann Witten; three *d.* *Educ:* Lancastrian Sch., Chichester; King's Coll., Durham (BSc). Short Service Commn (Lieut), RN, 1959–62. Joined MoD, 1962; Overseeing, Wallsend, 1962–63; Design, Bath, 1963–66; Production and Project Management, Devonport Dockyard, 1966–73; Dockyard Policy, Bath, 1973–76; Design, Bath, 1976–79; Production and Planning, Portsmouth Dockyard, 1979–81; Planning and Production, Devonport Dockyard, 1981–84. Chm. and Man. Dir, Devonport Dockyard Ltd, management buy-out co., 1985–. FBIM. *Recreations:* gardening, modernizing houses. *Address:* The Old Orchard, Harrowbeer Lane, Yelverton, Devon. *T:* Yelverton 854310; HM Dockyard, Devonport, Plymouth. *T:* Plymouth 553987. *Club:* Civil Service.

JOHNSTON, Prof. David Lloyd; Principal and Vice-Chancellor, and Professor of Law, McGill University, since 1979; *b* 28 June 1941; *s* of Lloyd Johnston and Dorothy Stonehouse Johnston; *m* 1963, Sharon Downey; five *d.* *Educ:* Harvard Univ., Cambridge, Mass; Cambridge Univ.; Queen's Univ. at Kingston, Ont. Asst Prof., Faculty of Law, Queen's Univ., Kingston, 1966–68; Faculty of Law, Univ. of Toronto: Asst Prof.,

1968–69; Associate Prof., 1969–72; Prof., 1972–74; Dean and Prof., Faculty of Law, Univ. of Western Ont, 1974–79. LLD *hc* Law Soc. of Upper Canada, 1980. *Publications:* Computers and the Law (ed), 1968; Canadian Securities Regulation, 1977; (jtly) The Law of Business Associations, 1979; (with R. Forbes) Canadian Companies and the Stock Exchange, 1979; articles and reports. *Recreations:* jogging, skiing, tennis. *Address:* McGill University, 845 Sherbrooke Street West, Montreal, Que H3A 2T5, Canada. *T:* 514–392–5347; 18 Sunnyside Avenue, Montreal, Que H3Y 1C2. *T:* 514–485–2166. *Clubs:* University, Faculty (Montreal).

JOHNSTON, Sir (David) Russell, Kt 1985; MP (L) Inverness, Nairn and Lochaber, since 1983 (Inverness, 1964–83); *b* 28 July 1932; *s* of late David Knox Johnston and Georgina Margaret Gerrie Russell; *m* 1967, Joan Graham Menzies; three *s. Educ:* Carbost Public Sch.; Portree High Sch.; Edinburgh Univ. (MA). Commissioned into Intelligence Corps (Nat. Service), 1958; subseq., Moray House Coll. of Educn until 1961; taught in Liberton Secondary Sch., 1961–63. Research Asst, Scottish Liberal Party, 1963–64. Chm., Scottish Liberal Party, 1970– (Vice-Chm., 1965–70), Leader, 1974–; Mem., UK Delegn to European Parlt, 1973–75 and 1976–79, Vice Pres., Political Cttee, 1976–79. Contested (L) Highlands and Islands, European Parly elecn, 1979, 1984. Chairman: All Party Scottish Gaelic Parly Gp; All Party Crofting Gp; Sec., UK-Falkland Is Parly Gp; Treasurer, British-Gibraltar Parly Gp. Mem., Royal Commission on Local Govt in Scotland, 1966–69. *Publications:* (pamphlet) Highland Development, 1964; (pamphlet) To Be a Liberal, 1972; Scottish Liberal Party Conf. Speeches, 1979. *Recreations:* reading, photography. *Address:* House of Commons, SW1A 0AA. *Club:* Scottish Liberal (Edinburgh).

JOHNSTON, Edward Alexander, CB 1975; Government Actuary, since 1973; *b* 19 March 1929; 2nd *s* of Edward Hamilton Johnston, DLitt, and Iris Olivia Helena May; *m* 1st, Veronica Mary Bernays (marr. diss.); two *s* two *d*; 2nd, Christine Elizabeth Nash (*née* Shepherd). *Educ:* Groton Sch., USA; Marlborough Coll.; New Coll., Oxford. BA 1952; FIA 1957; FPMI 1976. Equity & Law Life Assce Soc., 1952–58; Govt Actuary's Dept, 1958. Mem. Council: Inst. of Actuaries, 1973–; Pensions Management Inst., 1983– (Pres., 1985–86). *Address:* c/o Government Actuary's Department, 22 Kingsway, WC2. *Club:* Reform.

JOHNSTON, Very Rev. Frederick Mervyn Kieran; Dean of Cork, 1967–71, retired; *b* 22 Oct. 1911; *s* of Robert Mills Johnston and Florence Harriet O'Hanlon; *m* 1938, Catherine Alice Ruth FitzSimons; two *s. Educ:* Grammar Sch., Galway; Bishop Foy Sch., Waterford; Trinity Coll., Dublin. BA 1933. Deacon, 1934; Priest, 1936; Curate, Castlecomer, 1934–36; Curate, St Luke, Cork, 1936–38; Incumbent of Kilmeen, 1938–40; Drimoleague, 1940–45; Blackrock, Cork, 1945–58; Bandon, 1958–67; Rector of St Fin Barre's Cathedral and Dean of Cork, 1967; Examng Chaplain to Bishop of Cork, 1960–78. *Address:* 1 Pembroke Wood, Passage West, Co. Cork, Republic of Ireland.

JOHNSTON, Frederick Patrick Mair; Chairman, Johnston Newspaper Group, since 1973; Member of the Press Council, since 1973; *b* Edinburgh, 15 Sept. 1935; *e s* of late Frederick M. Johnston and of Mrs M. K. Johnston, Falkirk; *m* 1961, Elizabeth Ann Jones; two *s. Educ:* Morrison's Acad., Crieff; Lancing Coll., Sussex; New Coll., Oxford (MA, Mod. Hist.). Commissioned in Royal Scots Fusiliers, 1955; served in E Africa with 4th (Uganda) Bn, KAR, 1955–56. Joined Editorial Dept of Liverpool Daily Post & Echo, 1959; joined The Times Publishing Co. Ltd, as Asst Sec., 1960; Company Sec., F. Johnston & Co. Ltd, 1969–73; Managing Dir, F. Johnston & Co. Ltd, 1973–80; Chm., Dunn & Wilson Gp Ltd, 1976–. President: Young Newspapermen's Assoc., 1968–69; Forth Valley Chamber of Commerce, 1972–73; Scottish Newspaper Proprietors' Assoc., 1976–78; Chm., Central Scotland Manpower Cttee, 1976–83; Treasurer, Soc. of Master Printers of Scotland, 1981–86. *Recreations:* reading, travelling. *Address:* 1 Grange Terrace, Edinburgh EH9 2LD. *Clubs:* Royal Commonwealth Society; New (Edinburgh).

JOHNSTON, Henry Butler M.; *see* McKenzie Johnston.

JOHNSTON, Hugh Philip, CB 1977; Deputy Secretary, Property Services Agency, Department of the Environment, since 1974; *b* 17 May 1927; *s* of late Philip Rose-Johnston and Dora Ellen Johnston; *m* 1949, Barbara Frances Theodoridi; one *s* three *d. Educ:* Wimbledon Coll.; Faraday House. DFH (Hons). Air Ministry Works Dept: Asst Engr, 1951; Engr, 1956; Ministry of Public Buildings and Works: Prin. Engr, 1964; Asst Dir, 1969; Dir (Under-Sec.), Dept of Environment and Property Services Agency, Engrg Services Directorate, 1970. *Recreations:* motoring, music. *Address:* 9 Devas Road, Wimbledon, SW20 8PD. *T:* 01–946 2021.

JOHNSTON, Ian Alistair, PhD; Chief Executive, Training Division, Manpower Services Commission, since 1985; *b* 2 May 1944; *s* of late Donald Dalrymple Johnston and of Muriel Joyce Johnston (*née* Hill); *m* 1973, Mary Bridget Lube; one *s* one *d. Educ:* Royal Grammar Sch., High Wycombe; Birmingham Univ. (BSc, PhD). Joined Dept of Employment as Assistant Principal, 1969; Private Sec. to Permanent Secretary, Sir Denis Barnes, 1972–73; Principal, 1973; First Sec. (Labour Attaché), British Embassy, Brussels, 1976–77; Asst Sec. (Director, ACAS), 1978; Under-Sec. (Dir of Planning and Resources, MSC), 1984. *Publications:* contribs to learned jls on atomic structure of metals, 1966–69. *Recreations:* birding, gardening, skiing. *Address:* c/o Manpower Services Commission, Moorfoot, Sheffield S1 4PQ. *T:* Sheffield 704108.

JOHNSTON, Ian Henderson, CB 1981; Deputy Controller Aircraft, Procurement Executive, Ministry of Defence, 1982–84; *b* 29 April 1925; *s* of late Peter Johnston and Barbara Johnston (*née* Gifford); *m* 1949, Irene Blackburn; two *d. Educ:* George Heriot's Sch., Edinburgh; Edinburgh Univ. (BSc Eng); Imperial Coll., London (DIC Aeronautics). D. Napier & Sons, 1945–46; National Gas Turbine Estabt, 1947–64; Ramjet Project Officer, Min. of Aviation, 1964–66; Exchange Officer to Wright Patterson Air Force Base, Ohio, 1966–68; Asst Dir (Engine Develt), Min. of Technology, 1968–70; Dep. Dir, National Gas Turbine Estabt, 1970–73; Ministry of Defence: Dir-Gen., Multi-Role Combat Aircraft, (PE), 1973–76; Dir, Mil. Vehicles and Engrg Estabt, 1976–78; Dep. Controller, Estabts and Res. B, and Chief Scientist (Army), 1978–80; Dep. Controller, Estabt Resources and Personnel, MoD, 1980–82. *Publications:* papers on turbine research in Aeronautical Research Council Reports and Memoranda Series. *Recreations:* golf, bridge. *Address:* 49 Salisbury Road, Farnborough, Hants. *T:* Farnborough 41971.

JOHNSTON, Maj.-Gen. James Alexander Deans, OBE 1945; MC 1937; Director of Medical Services, BAOR, 1969–70, retired; *b* 28 Feb. 1911; *s* of Walter Johnston and I. C. Gilchrist; *m* 1940, Enid O. Eldridge; one *s* two *d. Educ:* Glasgow Univ. MB, ChB Glasgow, 1933. House Surgeon, Taunton and Somerset Hosp., 1933–34. Commnd into RAMC, 1934; served in India, 1935–40 (Quetta Earthquake, 1935; Mohmand Ops, 1935; Waziristan Ops, 1936–37); served in NW Europe, 1944–45; SMO during and after liberation of Belsen Concentration Camp, April 1945; ADMS HQ Malaya Comd, 19 Ind. Div. and 2 Br. Inf. Div. in Far East, 1945–47; ADMS Southern Comd, UK, 1947–49; DDMS HQ MELF, 1949–52; ADMS 2 Div., and DDMS HQ BAOR, 1952–57; OC British Military Hosp., Dhekelia, Cyprus, 1957–61; ADG WO, 1961–64; Comdt, Depot and Training Establishment and HQ AER, RAMC, 1964–66; DMS, FARELF, 1966–69.

Major 1943; Lt-Col 1948; Col 1957; Brig. 1964; Maj.-Gen. 1966. QHP 1967–70. *Recreations:* swimming, tennis, country pursuits. *Address:* Park Cottage, Ewhurst Lane, Northiam, East Sussex.

JOHNSTON, James Campbell, CBE 1972; Chairman: Capel Court Corporation Ltd, 1969–84; Australian Foundation Investment Co., 1967–84; Director, National Mutual T&G Life Association of Australasia Ltd (formerly of T&G Mutual Life Society), 1976–84; *b* 7 July 1912; *s* of late Edwin and Estelle Johnston; *m* 1938, Agnes Emily, *yr d* of late Richard Thomas; two *s* one *d. Educ:* Prince Alfred Coll., Adelaide; Scotch Coll., Melbourne; University of Melbourne. Admitted to Inst. Chartered Accountants, Australia, 1933; joined J. B. Were & Son, Stock and Share Brokers, 1935, Sen. Partner, 1967–78; Stock Exchange of Melbourne: Mem., 1947; Chm., 1972–77. Comr, State Electricity Commn of Victoria, 1978–83. Chartered Accountant of the Year, 1984. *Address:* 13 Monaro Road, Kooyong, Victoria 3144, Australia. *T:* 20 2842. *Clubs:* Melbourne, Australian, Athenæum, Victoria Racing, Royal Melbourne Golf (Melbourne).

JOHNSTON, Jennifer, (Mrs David Gilliland), FRSL; author; *b* 12 Jan. 1930; *d* of late (William) Denis Johnston, OBE; *m* 1st, 1951, Ian Smyth; two *s* two *d*; 2nd, 1976, David Gilliland, *qv. Educ:* Park House Sch., Dublin; Trinity Coll., Dublin. FRSL 1979. Plays: Indian Summer, performed Belfast, 1983; The Punch, prod Dublin, 1986. Hon. DLitt NUU, 1984. *Publications:* The Captains and the Kings, 1972; The Gates, 1973; How Many Miles to Babylon?, 1974; Shadows on Our Skin, 1978 (dramatised for TV, 1979); The Old Jest, 1979; (play) The Nightingale and not the Lark, 1980; The Christmas Tree, 1981; The Railway Station Man, 1984. *Recreations:* theatre, cinema, gardening, travelling. *Address:* Brook Hall, Culmore Road, Derry, N Ireland BT48 8JE. *T:* Londonderry 51297.

JOHNSTON, Sir John (Baines), GCMG 1978 (KCMG 1966; CMG 1962); KCVO 1972; HM Diplomatic Service, retired; *b* 13 May 1918; *e s* of late Rev. A. S. Johnston, Banbury, Oxon; *m* 1969, Elizabeth Mary, *d* of late J. F. Crace; one *s. Educ:* Banbury Grammar Sch.; Queen's Coll., Oxford (Eglesfield Scholar). Served War, 1940–46: Adjt 1st Bn Gordon Highlanders, 1944; DAQMG HQ 30 Corps District, 1945. Asst Principal, Colonial Office, 1947; Principal, 1948; Asst Sec., West African Council, Accra, 1950–51; UK Liaison Officer with Commission for Technical Co-operation in Africa South of the Sahara, 1952; Principal Private Sec. to Sec. of State for the Colonies, 1953; Asst Sec., 1956; Head of Far Eastern Dept, Colonial Office, 1956; transferred to Commonwealth Relations Office, 1957; Dep. High Commissioner in S Africa, 1959–61; British High Commissioner: in Sierra Leone, 1961–63; in the Federation of Rhodesia and Nyasaland, 1963, Rhodesia, 1964–65; Asst, later Dep. Under-Secretary of State, FCO, 1968–71; British High Commissioner: in Malaysia, 1971–74; in Canada, 1974–78. A Governor, BBC, 1978–85. Chm., ARELS Exams Trust, 1982–. Mem., Disasters Emergency Cttee, 1985–. *Address:* 5 Victoria Road, Oxford OX2 7QF.

JOHNSTON, Lt-Col Sir John (Frederick Dame), KCVO 1981 (CVO 1977; MVO 1971); MC 1945; Comptroller, Lord Chamberlain's Office, since 1981 (Assistant Comptroller, 1964–81); *b* 24 Aug. 1922; *m* 1949, Hon. Elizabeth Hardinge, JP Windsor 1971, *d* of late 2nd Baron Hardinge of Penshurst, PC, GCB, GCVO, MC, and late Lady Hardinge of Penshurst; one *s* one *d. Educ:* Ampleforth. Served in Grenadier Guards, 1941–64. Extra Equerry to the Queen, 1965–. *Address:* Adelaide Cottage, Windsor Home Park, Berks. *T:* Windsor 868286; Stone Hill, Newport, Dyfed. *Clubs:* Boodle's, Pratt's, MCC; Swinley Forest Golf.

JOHNSTON, Kenneth Robert Hope; QC 1953; *b* 18 June 1905; *e s* of Dr J. A. H. Johnston, Headmaster of Highgate Sch., 1908–36, and Kate Winsome Gammon; *m* 1937, Dr Priscilla Bright Clark, *d* of Roger and Sarah Clark, Street, Somerset; one *s* three *d. Educ:* Rugby Sch.; Sidney Sussex Coll., Cambridge Univ.; Harvard Univ., USA. Called to the Bar, Gray's Inn, 1933; Bencher, 1958. RAFVR, 1939–45. *Address:* 28 Leigh Road, Street, Somerset. *T:* Street 43559. *Club:* MCC.

JOHNSTON, Margaret; *see* Parker, Margaret Annette McCrie J.

JOHNSTON, Lt-Gen. Sir Maurice (Robert), KCB 1982; OBE 1971; Deputy Chief of Defence Staff, 1982–83, retired 1984; Director: Multilift Ltd, since 1984; Unit Security Ltd, since 1985; *b* 27 Oct. 1929; *s* of late Brig. Allen Leigh Johnston, OBE, and Gertrude Geraldine Johnston (*née* Templer); *m* 1960, Belinda Mary Sladen; one *s* one *d. Educ:* Wellington College; RMA Sandhurst. rcds, psc. Commissioned RA, 1949; transf. The Queen's Bays, 1954; served in Germany, Egypt, Jordan, Libya, N Ireland, Borneo. Instr, Army Staff Coll., 1965–67; MA to CGS, 1968–71; CO 1st The Queen's Dragoon Guards, 1971–73; Comdr 20th Armoured Brigade, 1973–75; BGS, HQ UKLF, 1977–78; Senior Directing Staff, RCDS, 1979; Asst Chief of Gen. Staff, 1980; Dep. Chief of Defence Staff (Op. Reqs), 1981–82. Col, 1st The Queen's Dragoon Guards, 1986–. Man. Dir, Freshglen Ltd, Wraxall Gp, 1984–85. *Recreations:* fishing, shooting, gardening, music. *Address:* Ivy House, Worton, Devizes, Wilts. *T:* Devizes 3727. *Club:* Army and Navy.

JOHNSTON, Michael Errington; Under-Secretary, Ministry of Agriculture, Fisheries and Food, 1970–76; *b* 22 Jan. 1916; *s* of late Lt-Col C. E. L. Johnston, RA, and late Beatrix Johnston; *m* 1938, Ida Brown; two *d. Educ:* Wellington; Peterhouse, Cambridge (Scholar). BA, 1st cl. Hist. Tripos, 1937; MA 1947. Served War of 1939–45, Rifle Bde (Capt., despatches), Asst Principal, Board of Education, 1938; Principal, 1946; Asst Sec., HM Treasury, 1952, Under-Sec., 1962–68; Under-Sec., Civil Service Dept, 1968–70. *Recreations:* painting and birdwatching. *Address:* 3 The Terrace, Barnes, SW13 0NP. *T:* 01–876 5265.

JOHNSTON, Ninian Rutherford Jamieson, RSA 1965; architect and town planner in private practice since 1946; *b* 6 March 1912; *s* of John Neill Johnston and Agnes Johnston; *m* 1937, Helen, *d* of Robert Henry Jackson and Jean Patrick Jackson; one *s* two *d. Educ:* Allan Glen's Sch.; Glasgow Sch. of Architecture. Served with Army, 1939–45. BArch 1934; FRIAS 1935; FRTPI (MTPI 1946); FRIBA 1951. *Principal Works:* Pollokshaws Central Redevelopment Area; Woodside Central Redevelopment Area, Glasgow; Central Hospitals at Dumfries, Greenock and Rutherglen. Mem. Roy. Fine Art Commission for Scotland, 1969–76. Pres., Glasgow Inst. of Architects, 1955–58. *Recreations:* music (former leader, Glasgow Sch. of Architecture penny whistle band), painting second rate pictures, gardening (mostly weeds). *Address:* Tithe Barn, Compton Abdale, Cheltenham, Glos. *T:* 041–332 9184. *Club:* Art (Glasgow).

JOHNSTON, Robert Alan, AC 1986; Governor, Reserve Bank of Australia, since 1982; *b* 19 July 1924; *m* 1948, Verna, *d* of H. I. Mullin; two *s* two *d. Educ:* Essendon High School; University of Melbourne. BComm. Commonwealth Bank of Australia, 1940–60; RAAF, 1943–46; Reserve Bank of Australia, 1960–: Dep. Manager and Manager, Investment Dept, 1964–70; Chief Manager, Internat. Dept, 1970–76; Adviser to Governor, 1973; Chief Representative, London, 1976–77; Exec. Dir, World Bank Group, Washington, 1977–79; Secretary, 1980–82. *Address:* (office) Reserve Bank of Australia, 65 Martin Place, GPO Box 3947, Sydney, NSW 2000, Australia. *T:* (02) 234 9333.

JOHNSTON, Robert Gordon Scott; Under Secretary, Department of the Environment, and Director of Civil Accommodation, Property Services Agency, since 1979; *b* 27 Aug.

1933; *s* of Robert William Fairfield Johnston, *qv*; *m* 1960, Jill Maureen Campbell; one *s* one *d*. *Educ:* Clifton; Clare Coll., Cambridge (1st Cl. Hons Classical Tripos, MA). 2/Lieut Scots Guards (National Service), 1955–57. Entered Air Min. as Asst Principal, 1957; Private Sec. to Parly Under Sec. of State for Air, 1959–62; transf. to MPBW, Def. Works Secretariat, 1963; Sec., Bldg Regulation Adv. Cttee, 1964; Principal Private Sec. to successive Ministers of Public Bldg and Works, 1965–68; seconded to Shell Internat. Chemical Co., Finance Div., 1968–70; Asst Dir of Home Estate Management, Property Services Agency, 1970–73; seconded to Cabinet Office, 1973–75; Asst Sec., Railways Directorate, Dept of Transport, 1975–79; Under Sec., seconded to Price Commn, 1979. *Address:* 184 Beckenham Hill Road, Beckenham, Kent BR3 1SZ.

JOHNSTON, Robert Smith; *see* Kincraig, Hon. Lord.

JOHNSTON, Robert William Fairfield, CMG 1960; CBE 1954; MC 1917; TD 1936 (and three Bars, 1947); Assistant Secretary, Ministry of Defence, 1946–62; retired from the Civil Service, 1962; *b* 1 May 1895; *e s* of late Capt. Robert Johnston, Army Pay Dept and Royal Scots; *m* 1922, Agnes Scott (*d* 1980), *o c* of late Peter Justice, Edinburgh; one *s*. Entered Civil Service, Dec. 1910: served in War Office, Bd of Trade, Min. of Labour, Home Office, Office of Minister without Portfolio, Min. of Defence, and seconded to FO, as Counsellor in UK Delegation in Paris to NATO and OEEC, 1953–61. Territorial Army, 1910–47; served European War, 1914–18, The Royal Scots (1st, 9th and 16th Battalions) in France, Flanders, Macedonia and Egypt; commissioned 1917; War of 1939–45, Lieut-Col, Comdg 8th Bn Gordon Highlanders, 1940–42, and 100th (Gordons) Anti-Tank Regt, RA, 1942–44, in 51st (Highland) and 2nd (British) Inf. Divs respectively; retired as Lieut-Col TA, Sept. 1947. *Address:* 8 Broad Avenue, Queen's Park, Bournemouth, Dorset.

See also R. G. S. Johnston.

JOHNSTON, Prof. Ronald Carlyle; Professor of Romance Philology and Medieval French Literature, Westfield College, London, 1961–74, now Emeritus; *b* 19 May 1907; *m*; one *s* three *d*. *Educ:* Ackworth Sch., Yorks; Bootham Sch., York; Merton Coll., Oxford. Travel in France, Germany and Spain, 1929–30. MA Oxon; 1st Cl. Hons Mediaeval and Modern Languages, French, 1929; Docteur de l'Université de Strasbourg, 1935. Asst Master Uppingham Sch., 1930–35; Lectr in French Philology and Old Fr. Lit., Oxford, 1935–45; Fellow of Jesus Coll., Oxford, 1945–48; Professor of French Language and Literature, University of St Andrews, 1948–61. Examiner, awarder etc in modern langs for Oxford Local Exams Delegacy, 1937–; sometime external examiner in French, Universities of Oxford, Cambridge, Edinburgh, Aberdeen, and Manchester. Pres., Anglo-Norman Text Soc., 1982– (Hon. Treasurer, 1969–82). Officier d'Académie. Chevalier de la Légion d'Honneur. *Publications:* Les Poésies lyriques du troubadour Arnaut de Mareuil (Paris), 1935; The Crusade and Death of Richard I (Anglo-Norman Text Soc.), 1961; The Versification of Jordan Fantosme, 1974; Jordan Fantosme's Chronicle, 1981; (with A. Ewert) Selected Fables of Marie de France, 1942; (with D. D. R. Owen) Fabliaux, 1957; (with D. D. R. Owen) Two Old French Gauvain Romances, part 1, 1972; *translations:* (with Ana Cartianu): Creangă's Poveşti şi Povestiri, 1973; Amintiri din copilărie, etc, 1978; articles and reviews in various journals and festschriften. *Recreations:* rough gardening, travel. *Address:* 5 Rawlinson Road, Oxford OX2 6UE. *T:* Oxford 55481.

JOHNSTON, Sir Russell; *see* Johnston, Sir D. R.

JOHNSTON, Sir Thomas Alexander, 14th Bt *cr* 1626, of Caskieben; *b* 1 Feb. 1956; *s* of Sir Thomas Alexander Johnston, 13th Bt, and of Helen Torry, *d* of Benjamin Franklin Du Bois; *S* father, 1984. *Heir: cousin* William Norville Johnston [*b* 11 July 1922; *m* 1952, Kathrine Pauline, *d* of Herbert Sigfred Solberg; three *s* one *d*].

JOHNSTON, Thomas Lothian; Principal and Vice-Chancellor of Heriot-Watt University, since 1981; *b* 9 March 1927; *s* of late T. B. Johnston and Janet Johnston; *m* 1956, Joan, *d* of late E. C. Fahmy, surgeon; two *s* three *d*. *Educ:* Hawick High Sch.; Univs of Edinburgh and Stockholm. MA 1951, PhD 1955, Edinburgh. FRSE 1979; FRSA 1981; CBIM 1983. Served RNVR, 1944–47 (Sub-Lt). Asst Lectr in Polit. Economy, Univ. of Edinburgh, 1953–55, Lectr 1955–65; Res. Fellow, Queen's Univ., Canada, 1965; Prof. and Hd of Dept of Econs, Heriot-Watt Univ., 1966–76. Visiting Professor: Univ. of Illinois, 1962–63; Internat. Inst. for Labour Studies, Geneva, 1973; Western Australia Inst. of Technol., 1979. Sec., Scottish Econ. Soc., 1958–65 (Pres., 1978–81); Member: Scottish Milk Marketing Bd, 1967–72; Nat. Industrial Relations Court, 1971–74; Scottish Cttee on Licensing Laws, 1971–73; Nat. Youth Employment Council, 1968–71; Scottish Telecommunications Bd, 1977–84; Scottish Economic Council, 1977–; Council for Tertiary Educn in Scotland, 1979–83; Chm., Manpower Services Cttee for Scotland, 1977–80; Economic Consultant to Sec. of State for Scotland, 1977–81. Director: First Charlotte Assets Trust, 1981–; Universities Superannuation Scheme, 1985–. Chairman: Council, Fraser of Allander Inst., Univ. of Strathclyde, 1975–78; Council for Applied Sci. in Scotland, 1984–; Scottish Cttee, Industry Year 1986; Univ. Authorities Panel, 1985–. Chm. of Wages Councils; Chairman: Enquiry into staff representation, London Clearing Banks, 1978–79; Water Workers' Enquiry, 1983; consultant, UN Human Resources Develt Project, Suez Canal region, 1980; Arbitrator; Overseas Corresp., Nat. Acad. of Arbitrators, USA. For. Mem., Swedish Royal Acad. of Engrg Scis, 1985. Comdr, Royal Swedish Order of the Polar Star, 1985. DUniv Edinburgh, 1986. *Publications:* Collective Bargaining in Sweden, 1962; (ed and trans.) Economic Expansion and Structural Change, 1963; (jtly) The Structure and Growth of the Scottish Economy, 1971; Introduction to Industrial Relations, 1981; articles in learned jls. *Recreations:* camping, gardening, walking. *Address:* 14 Mansionhouse Road, Edinburgh EH9 1TZ. *T:* 031-667 1439.

JOHNSTON, Very Rev. William Bryce; Minister of Colinton Parish Church, Edinburgh, since 1964; Chaplain to the Queen in Scotland, since 1981; *b* 16 Sept. 1921; *s* of William Bryce Johnston and Isabel Winifred Highley; *m* 1947, Ruth Margaret, *d* of Rev. James Arthur Cowley; one *s* two *d*. *Educ:* George Watson's Coll., Edinburgh; Edinburgh Univ. (MA Hons Classics 1942); New Coll., Edinburgh (BD (Dist.) 1945). Ordained as Chaplain to HM Forces, 1945; served in Germany and as Staff Chaplain, PoW Directorate, War Office, 1945–48; Minister: St Andrew's, Bo'ness, 1949; St George's, Greenock, 1955. Moderator of General Assembly of Church of Scotland, 1980–81. Convener: Board of St Colm's Coll., 1966–70; General Assembly Cttee on Adult Educn, 1970; Church and Nation Cttee, 1972; Inter-Church Relations Cttee, 1978; Cttee on Role of Men and Women, 1976. Mem., British Council of Churches, 1970– (Chm., Exec. Cttee, 1981–84); Delegate to 5th Assembly of World Council of Churches, 1975; Cunningham Lectr, New Coll., 1968–71; Vis. Lectr in Social Ethics, Heriot-Watt Univ., 1966–. Mem., Broadcasting Council for Scotland, 1983–. President, Edinburgh Rotary Club, 1975–76. Hon. DD Aberdeen, 1980. *Publications:* translations: K. Barth, Church Dogmatics, vol. 2, 1955; Calvin, Commentaries on Hebrews, 1 Peter, 1960; (jtly) Devolution and the British Churches, 1978; various Bible study pamphlets and theological articles for SCM, Scottish Jl of Theology. *Recreations:* organ-playing, bowls. *Address:* The Manse of Colinton, Edinburgh EH13 0JR. *T:* 031-441 2315. *Clubs:* New, University Staff (Edinburgh).

JOHNSTON, Ven. William Francis, CB 1983; Chaplain-General to the Forces, 1980–86; *b* 29 June 1930; *m*; two *s* one *d*. *Educ:* Trinity Coll., Dublin (BA 1955). Ordained 1955; Curate of Orangefield, Co. Down, 1955–59. Commissioned into Royal Army Chaplains Dept, 1959; served, UK, Germany, Aden, Cyprus; ACG South East District, 1977–80.

JOHNSTON, William James; Secretary, Association of Local Authorities of Northern Ireland, 1979–82; Director, Northern Ireland Advisory Board, Abbey National Building Society, since 1982; *b* 3 April 1919; *s* of late Thomas Hamilton Johnston and of Mary Kathleen Johnston; *m* 1943, Joan Elizabeth Nancye (*née* Young); two *d*. *Educ:* Portora Royal Sch., Enniskillen. FCA(Ire.). Professional accountancy, 1937–44; Antrim CC, 1944–68, Dep. Sec., 1951–68; Dep. Town Clerk, Belfast, 1968–73, Town Clerk, 1973–79. Member: NI Tourist Bd, 1980–85; Local Govt Staff Commn, 1974–85; Public Service Trng Council (formerly Public Service Trng Cttee), 1974–83 (Chm., 1974–83); Arts Council of NI, 1974–81. *Recreations:* golf, live theatre. *Address:* 47 Layde Road, Cushendall, Co. Antrim. *T:* Cushendall 71211; 1 Dell View, Chepstow, Gwent. *T:* Chepstow 71632.

JOHNSTON, William Robert Patrick K.; *see* Knox-Johnston, Robin.

JOHNSTONE; *see* Hope Johnstone, family name of Earl of Annandale and Hartfell.

JOHNSTONE, VANDEN-BEMPDE-, family name of **Baron Derwent.**

JOHNSTONE, Lord; David Patrick Wentworth Hope Johnstone; Master of Annandale and Hartfell; *b* 13 Oct. 1971; *s* and *heir* of Earl of Annandale and Hartfell, *qv*. *Educ:* Stowe.

JOHNSTONE, Prof. Alan Stewart; Professor of Radiodiagnosis, University of Leeds, 1948–68, now Emeritus; Director of Radiodiagnosis (General Infirmary, Leeds), United Leeds Hospitals, 1939–68; *b* 12 May 1905; *s* of Dr David A. and Margaret E. Johnstone, The Biggin, Waterbeck, Dumfriesshire; *m* 1934, Elizabeth Rowlett; one *s* one *d*. *Educ:* St Bees Sch.; Edinburgh Univ. Radiologist, Hammersmith Post-Graduate Hospital, 1935; Radiologist, Leicester Royal Infirmary, 1936–39. Baker Travelling Prof. in Radiology, Coll. of Radiologists of Australasia, 1959. Pres. Radiology Sect., Royal Society of Med., 1959–60; Pres. Thoracic Soc. of Great Britain, 1961–62. *Publications:* contributor to A Text Book of X-ray Diagnosis by British Authors; many in Br. Jl of Radiology, Jl of Faculty of Radiologists, Post Graduate Med. Jl, Edinburgh Med. Jl, Jl of Anatomy. *Recreations:* golf, fly fishing, chess. *Address:* 46 Stanford Road, Rondebosch, Cape Province, South Africa. *T:* Cape Town 657404.

JOHNSTONE, Air Vice-Marshal Alexander Vallance Riddell, CB 1966; DFC 1940; AE; DL; Chairman, Climax Cleaning Co., since 1983 (Director, since 1981); *b* 2 June 1916; *s* of late Alex. Lang Johnstone and Daisy Riddell; *m* 1940, Margaret Croll; one *s* two *d*. *Educ:* Kelvinside Academy, Glasgow. 602 (City of Glasgow) Sqdn, AAF, 1934–41; CO RAF Haifa, 1942; Spitfire Wing, Malta, 1942–43 (despatches, 1942); RAF Staff Coll., 1943; OC Fairwood Common, 1943–44; HQ AEAF, 1944; Air Attaché Dublin, 1946–48; OC RAF Ballykelly, 1951–52; OC Air/Sea Warfare Devel. Unit, 1952–54; SASO HQ No 12 Gp, 1954–55; Founder and First CAS Royal Malayan Air Force, 1957; OC Middleton St George, 1958–60; idc, 1961; Dir of Personnel, Air Min., 1962–64; Comdr, Air Forces, Borneo, 1964–65; AO Scotland and N Ireland, AOC No 18 Group, and Maritime Air Comdr N Atlantic (NATO), 1965–68. Vice-Chm. Council, TA&VRA, 1969–79. DL Glasgow, 1971. Johan Mengku Negara (Malaya), 1958. *Publications:* Television Series, One Man's War, 1964; Where No Angels Dwell, 1969; Enemy in the Sky, 1976; Adventure in the Sky, 1978; Spitfire into War, 1986. *Recreations:* golf, sailing. *Address:* 36 Greystoke Lodge, Hanger Lane, W5. *Club:* Royal Air Force.

JOHNSTONE, David Kirkpatrick; Director of Programmes, Scottish Television plc, 1977–86; *b* 4 July 1926; *s* of John and Isabel Johnstone; *m* 1950, Kay. *Educ:* Ayr Academy; Scottish Radio College. Reporter, Ayrshire Post; Radio Officer, Blue Funnel Line; Reporter, Glasgow Herald; Night News Editor, Scottish Daily Mail; Scottish Feature Writer, News Chronicle; Scottish TV, 1958–: News Editor; Producer/Director; Head of News and Current Affairs; Asst Controller of Programmes; Controller of Programmes. Chm., Regional Programme Controllers Gp, ITV contractors Assoc., 1984–85. Member, British Academy of Film and Television Arts (BAFTA), 1978. Elder, Church of Scotland. *Recreations:* golf, travel, television. *Club:* Eastwood Golf (Glasgow).

JOHNSTONE, Sir Frederic (Allan George), 10th Bt of Westerhall, Dumfriesshire, *cr* 1700; *b* 23 Feb. 1906; *o s* of Sir George Johnstone, 9th Bt and Ernestine (*d* 1955), *d* of Col Porcelli-Cust; *S* father, 1952; *m* 1946, Doris, *d* of late W. L. Shortridge; two *s*. *Educ:* Imperial Service Coll. *Heir: s* George Richard Douglas Johnstone, *b* 21 Aug. 1948.

JOHNSTONE, James Arthur; Commissioner of Inland Revenue, 1964–73; *b* 29 July 1913; *o s* of Arthur James Johnstone, solicitor, Ayr, and Euphemia Tennant (*née* Fullarton); *m* 1946, Dorothy C. L. Hacket, CBE (*d* 1981), *d* of William Hacket; one *s*. *Educ:* Ayr Academy; Glasgow Univ.; St John's Coll., Cambridge. Entered Inland Revenue Dept, 1936. Sec., Royal Commission on Taxation of Profits and Income, 1952–55; Chm., Hong Kong Inland Revenue Ordinance Rev. Cttee, 1976. *Address:* 63 Cottesmore Court, Stanford Road, W8 5QW. *T:* 01-937 8726. *Club:* Reform.

JOHNSTONE, John Raymond; Chairman, since 1984, and Managing Director, since 1968, Murray Johnstone Ltd; *b* 27 Oct. 1929; *s* of Henry James Johnstone of Alva, Captain RN and Margaret Alison McIntyre; *m* 1979, Susan Sara Gore; five step *s* two step *d*. *Educ:* Eton Coll.; Trinity Coll., Cambridge (BA Maths). CA. Apprenticed Chiene & Tait, Chartered Accts, Edinburgh, 1951–54; Robert Fleming & Co. Ltd, London, 1955–59; Partner in charge of investment management, Brown Fleming & Murray CA (becoming Whinney Murray CA, 1965), Glasgow, 1959–68; Murray Johnstone Ltd, Glasgow, formed to take over investment management dept of Whinney Murray, 1968–. Chairman: Kemper–Murray Johnstone Internat. Inc., 1980–; Murray Technology Investments PLC, 1981–; Murray Electronics PLC, 1983–; Director: Shipping Industrial Holdings, 1964–75; Scottish Amicable Life Assc Soc., 1971– (Chm., 1983–85); Dominion Insurance Co. Ltd, 1973– (Chm., 1978–); Dir, Scottish Opera, 1978– (Chm., 1983–85). *Recreations:* fishing, music, farming. *Address:* Wards, Gartocharn, Dunbartonshire G83 8SB. *T:* Gartocharn 321. *Club:* Western (Glasgow).

JOHNSTONE, Michael Anthony; Metropolitan Stipendiary Magistrate, since 1980; *b* 12 June 1936; *s* of late Thomas Johnstone and Violet Johnstone. *Educ:* St Edmund's College, Ware. Called to the Bar, Inner Temple, 1968; formerly Solicitor of the Supreme Court, admitted 1960; former Dep. Circuit Judge. Member: Soc. for Nautical Res.; Navy Records Soc.; Army Records Soc. Mem., Campaign for Real Ale. *Recreations:* real ale (weight permitting), the study and collection of books on military and naval history. *Address:* Wells Street Magistrates' Court, 59/65 Wells Street, W1A 3AE.

JOHNSTONE, Maj.-Gen. Ralph E.; *see* Edgeworth-Johnstone.

JOHNSTONE, R(obert) Edgeworth, BScTech (Manchester); MSc, DSc (London); FIChemE; FIMechE; FRSC; Lady Trent Professor of Chemical Engineering, University of Nottingham, 1960–67; *b* 4 Feb. 1900; *e s* of Lieut-Col Sir Walter Edgeworth-Johnstone,

KBE, CB; *m* 1931, Jessie Marjorie (*d* 1981), *d* of late R. M. T. Greig; two *s* one *d*. *Educ:* Wellington; RMA Woolwich; Manchester Coll. of Technology; University Coll., London. Fellow Salters' Inst. of Industrial Chem., 1926–27. Held various posts at home and abroad with Magadi Soda Co., Trinidad Leaseholds, Petrocarbon, Min. of Supply and UK Atomic Energy Authority. Vice-Pres., IChemE, 1951; Liveryman, Worshipful Co. of Salters, 1956. Council Medal, IChemE, 1969, Hon. Fellow, 1981. *Publications:* Continuing Education in Engineering, 1969; (with Prof. M. W. Thring) Pilot Plants, Models and Scale-up Methods in Chemical Engineering, 1957; papers in scientific and engineering jls, especially on distillation, process development and engineering education; *as Robert Johnstone:* The Lost World, 1978; (ed) Samuel Butler on the Resurrection, 1980. *Recreations:* music, philosophy. *Address:* 7 Clarendon Mansions, East Street, Brighton BN1 1NF. *Club:* Athenæum.

JOHNSTONE, Maj.-Gen. Robert Maxwell, MBE 1954; MC 1942; MA, MD, FRCPE; Assistant Director (Overseas), British Postgraduate Medical Federation, 1970–76; *b* 9 March 1914; *s* of late Prof. Emer. R. W. Johnstone, CBE; *m* 1958, Marjorie Jordan Beattie (*d* 1960). *Educ:* Edinburgh Acad.; Craigflower; Fettes Coll.; Christ's Coll., Cambridge; Univ. of Edinburgh (MD 1954); AM Singapore, 1965; MRCPE 1940; FRCPE 1944; MRCP 1966. Resident House Phys. and Surg., Royal Infirmary, Edinburgh, 1938–39. Sen. Pres., Royal Med. Soc., 1938–39. RMO, 129 Fd Regt RA, 1938–41; Company Comdr, 167 Fd Amb., RAMC, 1941–43; Staff Coll., Haifa, 1943; CO, 3 Fd Amb., 1945–46. Adviser in Medicine: HQ, E Africa Comd, 1950–51; Commonwealth Forces Korea, 1954–55; Officer i/c Med. Division: Cambridge Mil. Hosp., 1955–57; QAMH, Millbank, 1957–59; Prof. of Med., Univ. of Baghdad and Hon. Cons. Phys., Iraqi Army, 1959–63; CO, BMH, Iserlohn, 1963–65; Cons. Phys., HQ, FARELF, 1965–67; Dep. Director of Med. Services: Southern Comd, 1967–68; Army Strategic Comd, 1968–69; retd; Postgrad. Med. Dean, SW Metropolitan Region, 1969–70. CStJ 1969. *Recreation:* music. *Address:* c/o Royal Bank of Scotland, West End Office, 142/144 Princes Street, Edinburgh; 76 Central Road, Rossmoyne, WA 6155, Australia.

JOHNSTONE, William, CBE 1981; *b* 26 Dec. 1915; *s* of late David Grierson Johnstone and Janet Lang Johnstone (*née* Malcolm); *m* 1942, Mary Rosamund Rowden; one *s* two *d*. *Educ:* Dalry High Sch.; Glasgow Univ. (BSc (Agric)). NDA, NDD. Technical Officer, Overseas Dept of Deutches Kalisyndikat, Berlin, 1938–39; joined ICI Ltd, 1940; seconded to County War Agricl Exec. Cttees in SE England on food prodn campaigns, 1940–45; Reg. Sales Management, ICI, 1950–61; Commercial Dir, Plant Protection Ltd, 1961–63, Man. Dir, 1963–73; Dir, ICI Billingham/Agricl Div., 1961–73; Dep. Chm., ICI Plant Protection Div., 1974–77. Chm. Subsid. Cos: Solplant (Italy), 1967–73; Sopra (France), 1971–75; Zeltia Agraria (Spain), 1976–77; Vis. Dir, ICI (United States) Inc., 1974–77; retd from ICI, 1977. Chairman: Meat and Livestock Commn, 1977–80; British Agricl Export Council, 1977–84; Member: European Trade Cttee, BOTB, 1982–85; Sino-British Trade Council, 1983–85. FRSA. *Recreations:* free-range egg production, gardening. *Address:* Oxenbourne Farm, East Meon, Petersfield, Hants GU32 1QL. *T:* East Meon 216. *Clubs:* Caledonian, Farmers'.

JOHNSTONE, Rev. Prof. William; Professor of Hebrew and Semitic Languages, University of Aberdeen, since 1980; *b* 6 May 1936; *s* of Rev. T. K. Johnstone and Evelyn Hope Johnstone (*née* Murray); *m* 1964, Elizabeth Mary Ward; one *s* one *d*. *Educ:* Hamilton Academy; Glasgow Univ. (MA 1st Cl. Hons Semitic Langs, BD Distinction in New Testament and Old Testament); Univ. of Marburg. Lectr 1962, Sen. Lectr 1972, in Hebrew and Semitic Languages, Univ. of Aberdeen. Member, Mission archéologique française: Ras Shamra, 1963, 1964, 1966; Enkomi, 1963, 1965, 1971; Member, Marsala Punic Ship Excavation, 1973–79. *Publications:* trans. Fohrer: Hebrew and Aramaic Dictionary of the Old Testament, 1973; contributions to: Ugaritica VI, 1969, VII, 1978, Alasia I, 1972; Festschrift for W. McKane, 1986; articles in Aberdeen Univ. Review, Atti del I Congresso Internazionale di Studi Fenici e Punici, Expository Times, Kadmos, Notizie degli Scavi, Palestine Exploration Qly, Trans. Glasgow Univ. Oriental Soc., Scottish Jl of Theology, Theology. *Recreation:* alternative work. *Address:* 37 Rubislaw Den South, Aberdeen AB2 6BD. *T:* Aberdeen 316022; Makkevet Bor, New Galloway, Castle Douglas DG7 3RN.

JOICEY, family name of **Baron Joicey.**

JOICEY, 4th Baron, *cr* 1906; **Michael Edward Joicey;** Bt 1893; DL; *b* 28 Feb. 1925; *s* of 3rd Baron Joicey and Joan (*d* 1967), *y d* of 4th Earl of Durham; *S* father, 1966; *m* 1952, Elisabeth Marion, *y d* of late Lieut-Col Hon. Ian Leslie Melville; two *s* one *d*. *Educ:* Eton; Christ Church, Oxford. DL Northumberland, 1985. *Heir:* *s* Hon. James Michael Joicey, [*b* 28 June 1953; *m* 1984, Harriet, *yr d* of Rev. William Thompson, Oxnam Manse, Jedburgh]. *Address:* Etal Manor, Berwick-upon-Tweed, Northumberland. *T:* Crookham 205. *Clubs:* Lansdowne, Kennel; Northern Counties (Newcastle upon Tyne).

JOLL, Prof. James Bysse, MA; FBA 1977; Stevenson Professor of International History, University of London, 1967–81, now Professor Emeritus; *b* 21 June 1918; *e s* of Lieut-Col H. H. Joll and Alice Muriel Edwards. *Educ:* Winchester; University of Bordeaux; New Coll., Oxford. War Service, Devonshire Regt and Special Ops Exec., 1939–45. Fellow and Tutor in Politics, New Coll., Oxford, 1946–50; Fellow, 1951–67, now Emeritus, and Sub-Warden, 1951–67, St Antony's Coll., Oxford. Vis. Mem., Inst. for Advanced Study, Princeton, 1954 and 1971; Visiting Professor of History: Stanford Univ., Calif., 1958; Sydney Univ., 1979; Univ. of Iowa, 1980; Vis. Lectr in History, Harvard University, 1962; Benjamin Meaker Vis. Prof., Bristol Univ., 1985. Hon. Prof. of History, Warwick Univ., 1981. Hon. Fellow, LSE, 1985. *Publications:* The Second International, 1955, rev. edn 1974; Intellectuals in Politics, 1960; The Anarchists, 1964, rev. edn 1979; Europe since 1870, 1973, rev. edn 1983; Gramsci, 1977; The Origins of the First World War, 1984. *Recreation:* music. *Address:* 24 Ashchurch Park Villas, W12 9SP. *T:* 01–749 5221.

JOLLIFFE, family name of **Baron Hylton.**

JOLLIFFE, Sir Anthony (Stuart), GBE 1982; FCA; Chairman, Walker Greenbank plc, since 1986; Consultant, Grant Thornton & Co.; Chairman, since 1986, and Member of Governing Council, since 1983, Business in the Community; President, London Chamber of Commerce, since 1985; *b* Weymouth, Dorset, 12 Aug. 1938; *s* of Robert and Vi Dorothea Jolliffe. *Educ:* Porchester Sch., Bournemouth. Qualified chartered accountant, 1964; articled to Morison Rutherford & Co.; commenced practice on own account in name of Kingston Jolliffe & Co., 1965, later, Jolliffe Cork & Co., Sen. Partner, 1976. ATII. Director: Rivlin plc; Nikko Trading UK Ltd; JCT Internat. (UK) Ltd; Paccar UK Ltd; Chairman: Causeway Capital Develt Fund; City Merchant Developers. Member: Council, ODI; City and Industrial Liaison Cttee; Trustee, Understanding Industry. Alderman, Ward of Candlewick, 1975–84; Sheriff, City of London, 1980–81; Lord Mayor of London, 1982–83. Chm., Police Dependants' Trust, Trustee, Police Foundn; Governor, Mencap City Foundn; President: British Home and Hosp. for Incurables; Soc. of Dorset Men. Member: Guild of Freemen; Ct, Worshipful Co. of Painter Stainers; Ct, Worshipful Co. of Chartered Accountants in England and Wales; Worshipful Co. of Wheelwrights. FRSA; KStJ 1983. *Clubs:* Royal Automobile, City Livery (Pres., 1979–80), Saints and Sinners.

JOLLIFFE, Christopher, CBE 1971; Chairman, Abbeyfield Richmond Society, since 1980; Director, Science Division, Science Research Council, 1969–72 (Director for University Science and Technology, 1965–69); *b* 14 March 1912; *s* of William Edwin Jolliffe and Annie Etheldreda Thompson; *m* 1936, Miriam Mabel Ash. *Educ:* Gresham's Sch., Holt; University Coll., London. Asst Master, Stowe Sch., 1935–37; Dept of Scientific and Industrial Research, 1937–65. Vice-Chm., Council for Science and Society, 1978–82; Dir, Leverhulme Trust Fund, 1976–77. *Address:* 8 Broomfield Road, Kew, Richmond, Surrey TW9 3HR. *T:* 01–940 4265.

JOLLIFFE, William Orlando, IPFA, FCA; County Treasurer of Lancashire, 1973–85; *b* 16 Oct. 1925; *s* of late William Dibble Jolliffe and Laura Beatrice Jolliffe; *m* 1st (marr. diss.); one *s* one *d*; 2nd, 1975, Audrey (*née* Dale); one step *d*. *Educ:* Bude County Grammar Sch. Institute of Public Finance Accountant. Chartered Accountant (first place in final exam. of (former) Soc. of Incorporated Accountants, 1956). Joined Barclays Bank Ltd, 1941. Served War of 1939–45 (HM Forces, 1944–48). Subseq. held various appts in Treasurers' depts of Devon CC, Winchester City Council, Doncaster CB Council, Bury CB Council (Dep. Borough Treas.), and Blackpool CB Council (Dep. 1959, Borough Treas., 1962). Mem. Council, Chartered Inst. of Public Finance and Accountancy, 1969–85 (Pres., 1979–80); Financial Adviser, ACC, 1976–85; Mem. Council (Pres. 1974–75), Assoc. of Public Service Finance Officers, 1963–76; Chm., Officers' Side, JNC for Chief Officers of Local Authorities in England and Wales, 1971–76; Mem. Exec. Cttee (Pres. 1970–71), NW Soc. of Chartered Accountants, 1966–76; Chm., NW and N Wales Region of CIPFA, 1974–76; Mem., Soc. of County Treasurers (Mem. Exec. Cttee, 1977–85); Hon. Treas., Lancashire Playing Fields Assoc. Financial Adviser to Assoc. of Municipal Corporations, 1969–74; Mem. (Govt) Working Party on Collab. between Local Authorities and the National Health Service, 1971–74. *Publications:* articles for Public Finance and Accountancy and other local govt jls. *Address:* 4 Whitewood Close, Lytham, Lancs FY8 4RN. *T:* Lytham 736201. *Club:* Royal Over-Seas League.

JOLLY, Anthony Charles; His Honour Judge Jolly; a Circuit Judge since 1980; *b* 25 May 1932; *s* of Leonard and Emily Jolly; *m* 1962, Rosemary Christine Kernan; two *s* one *d*. *Educ:* Royal Naval Coll., Dartmouth; Balliol Coll., Oxford (Exhibnr history; 1st Hon. Sch. Jurisprudence; MA). Called to Bar, Inner Temple, 1954; a Recorder of the Crown Court, 1975–80. *Recreations:* sailing, reading, stern sculling. *Address:* (home) Naze House, Freckleton, Lancs PR4 1UN. *T:* Freckleton 632285.

JOLLY, (Arthur) Richard, PhD; development economist; Deputy Executive Director, UNICEF, New York, since 1982; *b* 30 June 1934; *s* of late Arthur Jolly and Flora Doris Jolly (*née* Leaver); *m* 1963, Alison Bishop, PhD; two *s* two *d*. *Educ:* Brighton Coll.; Magdalene Coll., Cambridge (BA 1956, MA 1959); Yale Univ. (MA 1960, PhD 1966). Community Develt Officer, Baringo Dist, Kenya, 1957–59; Associate Chubb Fellow, Yale Univ., 1961–62; Res. Fellow, E Africa Inst. of Social Res., Makerere Coll., Uganda, 1963–64; Res. Officer, Dept of Applied Econs, Cambridge Univ., 1964–68 (seconded as Advr on Manpower to Govt of Zambia, 1964–66); Fellow, 1968–, Dir, 1972–81, Inst. of Develt Studies; Professorial Fellow, Univ. of Sussex, 1971–. Advr on Manpower Aid, ODM, 1968; Sen. Economist, Min. of Develt and Finance, Zambia, 1970; Advr to Parly Select Cttee on Overseas Aid and Develt, 1974–75; ILO Advr on Planning, Madagascar, 1975; Member: Triennial Rev. Gp, Commonwealth Fund for Tech. Co-operation, 1975–76; UK Council on Internat. Develt, 1974–78; UN Cttee for Develt Planning, 1978–81; Special Consultant on N-S Issues to Sec.-Gen., OECD, 1978; sometime member and chief of ILO and UN missions, and consultant to various governments and international organisations. Sec., British Alpine Hannibal Expedn, 1959. Member: Founding Cttee, European Assoc. of Develt Insts, 1972–75; Governing Council, 1976–85, and N-S Round Table, SID, 1976– (Vice-Pres., 1982–85). Mem., Editorial Bd, World Development, 1973–. Master, Curriers' Co., 1977–78. *Publications:* (jtly) Cuba: the economic and social revolution, 1964; Planning Education for African Development, 1969; (ed) Education in Africa: research and action, 1969; (ed jtly) Third World Employment, 1973; (jtly) Redistribution with Growth, 1974 (trans. French 1977); (ed) Disarmament and World Development, 1978, 3rd edn 1986; (ed jtly) Recent Issues in World Development, 1981; (ed jtly) Rich Country Interests in Third World Development, 1982; (ed jtly) The Impact of World Recession on Children, 1984; contributions to: Development in a Divided World, 1971; Employment, Income Distribution and Development Strategy, 1976; The Poverty of Progress, 1982; articles in professional and develt jls. *Recreations:* billiards, croquet, nearly missing trains and planes. *Address:* Institute of Development Studies, University of Sussex, Brighton, Sussex BN1 9RE. *T:* Brighton 606261; UNICEF, United Nations, New York 10017, USA. *T:* (212) 415–8300.

JOLLY, Richard; *see* Jolly, A. R.

JOLLY, Air Cdre Robert Malcolm, CBE 1969; General Manager, Diebold Europe SA and Director, Diebold Research Program Europe, 1983–84; *b* 4 Aug. 1920; *s* of Robert Imrie Jolly and Ethel Thompson Jolly; *m* 1946, Josette Jacqueline (*née* Baindeky); no *c*. *Educ:* Skerry's Coll., Newcastle upon Tyne. Commnd in RAF, 1943; Air Cdre 1971; Dir of Personal Services, MoD, 1970–72; Dir of Automatic Data Processing (RAF), 1973–75, retd. Man. Dir, Leonard Griffiths & Associates, 1975–77; Vice-Pres., UWS Consultants Inc., 1978–80. Fellow British Computer Soc., 1972; CBIM (formerly FBIM) 1973. *Address:* 1 Felbridge Close, Streatham, SW16 2RH. *T:* 01–769 4088. *Clubs:* Royal Air Force, Institute of Directors.

JOLOWICZ, Prof. John Anthony; Professor of Comparative Law, University of Cambridge, since 1976; Fellow, Trinity College, Cambridge, since 1952; *b* 11 April 1926; *e s* of late Prof. Herbert Felix Jolowicz and Ruby Victoria Wagner; *m* 1957, Poppy Stanley; one *s* two *d*. *Educ:* Oundle Sch.; Trinity Coll., Cambridge (Scholar; MA; 1st Cl. Hons Law Tripos 1950). Served HM Forces (commnd RASC), 1944–48. Called to the Bar, Inner Temple and Gray's Inn, 1952; Bencher, Gray's Inn, 1978. Univ. of Cambridge: Asst Lectr in Law, 1955, Lectr, 1959; Reader in Common and Comparative Law, 1972. Professeur associé, Université de Paris 2, 1976; Lionel Cohen Lectr, Hebrew Univ. of Jerusalem, 1983. Pres., SPTL, 1986–87 (Vice-Pres., 1985–86). Hon. Dr Universidad Nacional Autónoma de México, 1985. Editor, Jl of Soc. of Public Teachers of Law, 1962–80. *Publications:* (ed) H. F. Jolowicz's Lectures on Jurisprudence, 1963; Winfield and Jolowicz on Tort, 1971, 12th edn (ed W. V. H. Rogers) 1984; (with M. Cappelletti) Public Interest Parties and the Active Role of the Judge, 1975; contrib. to Internat. Encyc. of Comparative Law and to legal jls. *Address:* Trinity College, Cambridge CB1 1TQ. *T:* Cambridge 338400; West Green House, Barrington, Cambridge CB2 5SA. *T:* Cambridge 870495. *Clubs:* Royal Automobile; Leander (Henley-on-Thames).

JOLY de LOTBINIÈRE, Lt-Col Sir Edmond, Kt 1964; Chairman, Eastern Provincial Area Conservative Association, 1961–65, President, 1969–72; Chairman, Bury St Edmunds Division Conservative Association, 1953–72, President, 1972–79; *b* 17 March 1903; *er s* of late Brig.-Gen. H. G. Joly de Lotbinière, DSO; *m* 1st, 1928, Hon. Elizabeth Alice Cecilia Jolliffe (marr. diss. 1937); two *s*; 2nd, 1937, Helen Ruth Mildred Ferrar (*d*

1953); 3rd, 1954, Evelyn Adelaide (*née* Dawnay) (*d* 1985), *widow* of Lt-Col J. A. Innes, DSO. *Educ:* Eton Coll.; Royal Military Academy, Woolwich. 2nd Lieut Royal Engineers, 1923; served in India; RARO, 1928; re-employed, 1939. Served War of 1939–45: in Aden, Abyssinian Campaign and East Africa (despatches); Major 1941; Lieut-Col 1943; retired 1945. Chm. and Managing Dir of several private companies connected with the building trade. *Recreations:* shooting, bridge. *Address:* Horringer Manor, Bury St Edmunds, Suffolk. *T:* Horringer 208. *Club:* Naval and Military.

JOLY de LOTBINIÈRE, S.; *see* de Lotbinière.

JONAS, Peter; Managing Director, English National Opera, since 1985; *b* 14 Oct. 1946; *s* of Walter Adolf Jonas and Hilda May Jonas. *Educ:* Worth School; Univ. of Sussex (BA Hons); Northern Coll. of Music (LRAM); Royal Coll. of Music (CAMS); Eastman Sch. of Music, Univ. of Rochester, USA. Asst to Music Dir, 1974–76, Artistic Administrator, 1976–85, Chicago Symphony Orch.; Dir of Artistic Admin, Orchestral Assoc. of Chicago (Chicago Symph. Orch., Chicago Civic Orch., Chicago Symph. Chorus, Allied Arts Assoc., Orchestra Hall), 1977–85. Mem. Bd of Management, Nat. Opera Studio, 1985–. *Address:* 18 Lonsdale Place, Barnsbury Street, N1 1EL. *T:* 01–609 9427. *Club:* Athenæum.

JONES; *see* Armstrong-Jones, family name of Earl of Snowdon.

JONES; *see* Avery Jones.

JONES; *see* Elwyn-Jones.

JONES; *see* Gwynne Jones, family name of Baron Chalfont.

JONES; *see* Lloyd Jones and Lloyd-Jones.

JONES; *see* Morris-Jones.

JONES, Alan Payan P.; *see* Pryce-Jones.

JONES, (Albert) Arthur; *b* 23 Oct. 1915; *s* of late Frederick Henry Jones and Emma (*née* Shreeves); *m* 1939, Peggy Joyce (*née* Wingate); one *s* one *d*. *Educ:* Bedford Modern Sch. (Harpur Schol.). Territorial, Beds Yeomanry, RA, 1938; Middle East with First Armd Div., 1941; captured at Alamein, 1942; escaped as POW from Italy, 600 miles walk to Allied Territory. Mem. Bedford RDC, 1946–49; Mem. Bedford Borough Council, 1949–74, Alderman, 1957–74; Mayor of Bedford, 1957–58, 1958–59; Member: Beds CC, 1956–67; Central Housing Advisory Cttee, 1959–62; Internat. Union of Local Authorities; Chm., Local Govt Nat. Adv. Cttee, Cons. Central Office, 1963–73; UK Rep., Consultative Assembly, Council of Europe and Assembly of WEU, 1971–73. Contested (C) Wellingborough, 1955; MP (C) Northants S, Nov. 1962–1974, Daventry, 1974–79; Mem., Speaker's panel of Chairmen, 1974–79. Member: Select Cttee on Immigration and Race Relations, 1969–70; Select Cttee on Expenditure, 1974–79; Chm., Environment Sub-Cttee, 1974–79; Vice-Chm., Cons. Back-Bench Cttee for the Environment, 1974–79. Dir of Private Companies. Hon. Treas., Town and Country Planning Assoc., 1975–81; Mem., Cttee of Management, UK Housing Assoc., 1972–81; Vice-Pres., Inland Waterways Assoc., 1970–; Dep. Chm., New Towns Commn, 1982–; Mem., Anglian Water Authority, 1980–82. Governor: Harpur Charity, 1953– (Chm., Finance Cttee, 1984–); Centre for Policy Studies, 1980–83; Vice-Chm., St Andrew's Hosp., Northampton, 1979–. FSVA. *Publications:* Future of Housing Policy, 1960; War on Waste, 1965; Local Governors at Work, 1968; For the Record: Bedford 1945–74: Land Use and Financial Planning, 1981; Britain's Heritage, 1985. *Address:* Moor Farm, Pavenham, Bedford.

JONES, Prof. Albert Stanley, PhD; DSc; Professor of Chemistry, University of Birmingham, since 1969; *b* 30 April 1925; *s* of Albert Ernest Jones and Florence Jones (*née* Rathbone); *m* 1950, Joan Christine Gregg; one *s* one *d*. *Educ:* Waverley Grammar Sch.; Univ. of Birmingham (BSc (1st Cl. Hons) 1944, PhD 1947, DSc 1957). Beit Memorial Fellow for Medical Research, 1949–52; University of Birmingham: Lectr in Chemistry, 1952–61; Sen. Lectr, 1961–63; Reader in Organic Chemistry, 1963–69. Chemical Society London: Birmingham Representative, 1959–62; Mem. Council, 1966–69; Chm., Nucleotide Group, 1967–72. *Publications:* 160 papers, incl. three review articles, in scientific jls, on various aspects of organic chemistry and biological chemistry, particularly concerning nucleic acid derivatives. *Recreations:* church activities, walking, music, reading. *Address:* Waverley, 76 Manor House Lane, Yardley, Birmingham B26 1PR. *T:* 021–743 2030.

JONES, Allen, ARA 1981; artist; *b* 1 Sept. 1937; *s* of William Jones and Madeline Jones (*née* Aveson); *m* 1964, Janet Bowen (marr. diss. 1978); two *d*. *Educ:* Ealing Grammar Sch. for Boys; Hornsey Sch. of Art (NDD; ATD); Royal Coll. of Art. Teacher of Lithography, Croydon Coll. of Art, 1961–63; Teacher of Painting, Chelsea Sch. of Art, 1966–68; now teaches occasionally in N America and Germany; travels frequently. One-man exhibns include: Arthur Tooth and Sons, London, 1963, 1964, 1967, 1970; Richard Feigen Gall., New York, Chicago and LA, 1964, 1965 and 1970; Marlborough Fine Art, London, 1972; Arts Council sponsored exhibn tour, UK, 1974; Seibu, Tokyo, 1974; Waddington Galls, London, 1976, 1980, 1982, 1983 and 1985; ICA Graphic Retrospective, 1978; first Retrospective of Painting, Walker Art Gall., Liverpool, and tour of England and Germany, 1979; first internat. exhibn, Paris Biennale, 1961; numerous museum and group exhibns in UK and abroad; works included in many public and private collections; has designed sets for television and stage in UK and Germany; designs commercial murals and sculpture for public places. Television films have been made on his work. Prix des Jeunes Artists, Paris Biennale, 1963. *Publications:* Allen Jones Figures, 1969; Allen Jones Projects, 1971; Waitress, 1972; Sheer Magic, 1979, UK 1980; articles in various jls. *Recreations:* very private, also gardening. *Address:* c/o Waddington Galleries, 2 Cork Street, W1. *T:* 01–439 1866. *Club:* Zanzibar.

JONES, Rt. Rev. Alwyn Rice; *see* St Asaph, Bishop of.

JONES, Maj.-Gen. Anthony George Clifford, CB 1978; MC 1945; President, Regular Commissions Board, 1975–78; *b* 20 May 1923; *s* of late Col R. C. Jones, OBE, and M. D. Jones; *m* Kathleen Mary, *d* of Comdr J. N. Benbow, OBE, RN; two *d*. *Educ.* St Paul's School; Trinity Hall, Cambridge. Commissioned RE, 1942; service includes: Troop Comdr, Guards Armd Div., Nijmegen, 1945 (MC 1945; despatches, 1947); Indian Sappers and Miners; Staff Coll., 1954; Bde Major, 63 Gurkha Inf. Bde, 1955 (despatches, 1957); jssc; OC 25 Corps Engineer Regt, 1965–67; Comdr, RE Trng Bde, 1968–72; Head of Ops Staff, Northern Army Group, 1972–74; Dep. Comdr SE District, 1974–75. Hon. Col, RE Volunteers (Sponsored Units), 1978–86. *Club:* Army and Navy.

JONES, Arthur; *see* Jones, (Albert) Arthur.

JONES, Rt. Hon. Aubrey, PC 1955; Director: Thomas Tilling Ltd, 1970–82; Cornhill Insurance Company Ltd, 1971–82 (Chairman, 1971–74); *b* 20 Nov. 1911; *s* of Evan and Margaret Aubrey Jones, Merthyr Tydfil; *m* 1948, Joan, *d* of G. Godfrey-Isaacs, Ridgehanger, Hillcrest Road, Hanger Hill, W5; two *s*. *Educ:* Cyfarthfa Castle Secondary Sch., Merthyr Tydfil; London School of Economics. BSc (Econ.) 1st Cl. Hons, Gladstone Memorial Prizewinner, Gerstenberg Post-grad. Schol., LSE. On foreign and editorial staffs of The Times, 1937–39 and 1947–48. Joined British Iron and Steel Federation, 1949; General Dir, June-Dec. 1955. Served War of 1939–45, Army Intelligence Staff, War Office and Mediterranean Theatre, 1940–46. Contested (C) SE Essex in General Election, 1945 and Heywood and Radcliffe (by-election), 1946; MP (U) Birmingham, Hall Green, 1950–65; Parliamentary Private Sec. to Minister of State for Economic Affairs, 1952, and to Min. of Materials, 1953; Minister of Fuel and Power, Dec. 1955–Jan. 1957; Minister of Supply, 1957–Oct. 1959. Mem., Plowden Cttee of Inquiry into Aircraft Industry, 1965–66. Chairman: Staveley Industries Ltd, 1964–65 (Dir 1962–65); Laporte Industries (Holdings) Ltd, 1970–72; Director: Guest, Keen & Nettlefolds Steel Company Limited, 1960–65; Courtaulds Ltd, 1960–63; Black & Decker, 1977–81. Chm., Nat. Bd for Prices and Incomes, 1965–70; Vice-Pres., Consumers' Assoc., 1967–72; leading consultant to: Nigerian Public Service Commn, 1973–74; Iranian Govt, 1974–78; Plessey Ltd, 1978–80; Mem. Panel of Conciliators, Internat. Centre for Settlement of Investment Disputes, 1974–81. Pres., Oxford Energy Policy Club, 1976–. Regent Lectr, Univ. of California at Berkeley, 1968. Vis. Fellow, New Coll., Oxford, 1978; Sen. Res. Associate, St Antony's Coll., Oxford, 1979–82; Guest Scholar, Brookings Instn, Washington, DC, 1982. Fellow Commoner, Churchill Coll., Cambridge, 1972 and 1982–. Hon. Fellow, LSE, 1959, Mem., Court of Governors, 1964. Hon. DSc Bath, 1968. Winston Churchill Meml Trust Award, 1985. *Publications:* The Pendulum of Politics, 1946; Industrial Order, 1950; The New Inflation: the politics of prices and incomes, 1973; (contrib.) My LSE, 1977; Oil: the missed opportunity, 1981; Britain's Economy: the roots of stagnation, 1985. *Address:* 89 Northend House, Fitzjames Avenue, W14 0RX. *T:* 01–937 4247; Arnen, Limmer Lane, Felpham, Bognor Regis, West Sussex. *T:* Middleton-on-Sea 2722. *Club:* Consul.

JONES, Barry; *see* Jones, Stephen B.

JONES, Maj.-Gen. Basil Douglas, CB 1960; CBE 1950; *b* 14 May 1903; *s* of Rev. B. Jones; *m* 1932, Katherine Holberton (*d* 1986), *d* of Col H. W. Man, CBE, DSO; one *s* two *d*. *Educ:* Plymouth Coll.; RMC, Sandhurst. 2nd Lieut, Welch Regt, 1924; transferred to RAOC, 1935; Major 1939; served with Australian Military Forces in Australia and New Guinea, 1941–44; Temp. Brig. 1947; Brig. 1955; Maj.-Gen. 1958. ADC to the Queen, 1956–58; Inspector, RAOC, 1958–60, retired. Col Commandant, RAOC, 1963–67. *Recreation:* golf. *Address:* Churchfield, Sutton Courtenay, Abingdon, Oxon. *T:* Abingdon 848261.

JONES, Benjamin George, CBE 1979; formerly Partner, Linklaters & Paines, Solicitors; *b* 18 Nov. 1914; *s* of Thomas Jones, Llanarth; *m* 1946, Menna, *d* of Rev. Evelyn Wynn-Jones, Holyhead; one *s* one *d*. *Educ:* Aberaeron County Sch.; UCW Aberystwyth. Chairman: Council for the Welsh Language, 1973–78; Hon. Soc. of Cymmrodorion, 1973–78 (Dep. Sec., 1960–63, Sec., 1963–73; Pres., 1982–). Contested (L) Merioneth, 1959. Mem. Gen. Adv. Council, BBC, 1970–78. Vice-Pres., UCW Aberystwyth, 1975–86; Mem. Court, Univ. of Wales; Mem. Council, Nat. Library of Wales. Dep. Chm., Agricultural Land Tribunal (SE Area). Hon. LLD Wales, 1983. *Recreations:* walking, music, visiting art galleries. *Address:* 12 Thornton Way, NW11 6RY. *Club:* Reform.

JONES, Beti, CBE 1980; *b* 23 Jan. 1919; *d* of Isaac Jones and Elizabeth (*née* Rowlands). *Educ:* Rhondda County Sch. for Girls; Univ. of Wales. BA (Hons) History, Teaching Diploma. Grammar Sch. teaching, 1941–43; S Wales Organiser, Nat. Assoc. of Girls' Clubs, 1943–47; Youth Officer, Educn Branch, Control Commission, Germany, 1947–49; Children's Officer, Glamorgan CC, 1949–68; Chief Adviser on Social Work, Scottish Office, 1968–80. Save the Children Fund: Mem., UK Cttee, 1981–; Chm., Scottish Adv. Cttee, 1985–. Fellow, University Coll., Cardiff, 1982 (Hon. Fellow, Dept of Social Administration, 1970). *Address:* 14 Royal Circus, Edinburgh EH3 6SR. *T:* 031–225 1548; Lochside Cottage, Craigie, Blairgowrie, Perthshire. *T:* Essendy 373. *Clubs:* Royal Over-Seas League (London and Edinburgh).

JONES, Hon. Brian Leslie; Hon. Mr Justice Jones; Judge of the High Court of Justice, Hong Kong, since 1981; *b* 19 Oct. 1930; *s* of late William Leslie Jones and Gladys Gertrude Jones; *m* 1966, Yukiko Hirokane; one *s* two *d*. *Educ:* Bromsgrove Sch.; Birmingham Univ. Admitted Solicitor, 1956. Solicitor, private practice, England, 1956–64; Asst Registrar, Supreme Court, Hong Kong, 1964–68; Legal Officer, Attorney General's Dept, Canberra, 1968–69; Asst Registrar, Hong Kong, 1969–74; District Judge, Hong Kong, 1974–81. Comr, Supreme Ct of Brunei, 1982, 1985. *Recreations:* squash, chess, walking, reading. *Address:* 16B Severn Road, The Peak, Hong Kong. *T:* 5–96327. *Clubs:* Hong Kong, Hong Kong Cricket; Anyos (Andorra).

JONES, Sir Brynmor, Kt 1968; PhD Wales and Cantab, ScD Cantab, FRSC; Chairman, Foundation Committee for Engineering Technology, since 1978; Vice-Chancellor, University of Hull, 1956–72; *b* Sept. 1903; *o c* of late W. E. Jones, Rhos, Wrexham; *m* 1933, Dora Jones. *Educ:* The Grammar School, Ruabon; University Coll. of North Wales, Bangor (Exhibitioner and Research Scholar); St John's Coll., Cambridge (Hon. Fellow, 1970); Sorbonne, Paris; Fellow, Univ. of Wales, 1928–31. Asst Demonstrator, Cambridge, 1930; Lecturer in Organic Chemistry, University of Sheffield, 1931–46; Leverhulme Research Fellowship, 1939; Mem. Extra-Mural Research Team, Min. of Supply, University of Sheffield, 1940–45; G. F. Grant Professor of Chemistry, University Coll. and University of Hull, 1947–56; Dean of Faculty of Science and Dep. Principal, 1949–52, Vice-Principal, 1952–54; Pro-Vice-Chancellor, 1954–56; Chm., Univ's Foundn Cttee for Engineering, 1978–. Sometime Examiner for Univs of St Andrews, London, Leeds, Oxford, Manchester, Edinburgh and the Inst. of Civil Engineers. Dir, Yorkshire TV, 1970–72. Chairman: Nat. Council for Educational Technology, 1967–73; UGC and Min. of Educn's sub-cttee on Audio-Visual Aids (Report, HMSO, 1965); Academic Council, BMA; Univs Council for Adult Educn, 1961–65; Pres., Assoc. for Programmed Learning and Educational Technology, 1969–72; Chairman: Vis. Grants Cttee to Univ. of Basutoland, Bechuanaland Protectorate and Swaziland, 1965; Programme Cttee on Higher Educn, BBC Further Educn Adv. Council, 1967–70, Vice-Chm., 1970–72; Member: Kennedy Memorial Trust, 1964–74; GMC, 1964–74; DSIR Postgraduate Trng Awards Cttee, 1963–65; Univ. Science and Technology Bd (SRC), 1965–68; Brit. Cttee of Selection for Frank Knox Fellowships to Harvard Univ., 1962–72; Inter-Univ. Council (and Exec.) for Higher Educn, Overseas; India Cttee of IUC and British Council, 1972–; Adv. Cttee, Planning Cttee and Council of Open Univ., 1967–72; Royal Commn on Higher Educn in Ceylon, 1969–70; University Council, Nairobi; Provisional Council of Univ. of E Africa and of University Coll., Dar es Salaam, 1961–64; Council of University Coll., Dar es Salaam, 1964–68; Provisional Council, Univ. of Mauritius, 1965–67; General Nursing Council, 1960–66; Acad. Adv. Cttee, Welsh Coll. of Advanced Technology 1964–67; East Riding Educn Cttee, 1956–74; Hull Chamber of Commerce and Shipping; Council of Chemical Soc., 1945–48, and 1953–56; Senior Reporter, Annual Reports of Chemical Soc., 1948; Chm., Humberside Br., British Digestive Foundn, 1978–; President: Hull Civic Soc.; Hull Lit. and Philosoph. Soc., 1955–57; Hull Bach Choir; E Riding Local History Soc. Chm., Beverley Minster Restoration Appeal, 1982– (Vice-Chm., 1977–82). Mem., Court of Universities of Nottingham and Sheffield, 1956–72; Governor: Hymers Coll., 1956–84; Pocklington Sch.; E Riding Coll. of Agriculture, 1977–82. Roscoe Lectr, Univ. of Manchester, 1967. Hon. FCP (Sir Philip Magnus Meml

Lectr, 1973). Hon. LLD Wales, 1968, Leeds, 1974; Hon. DLitt Hull, 1972. *Publications:* numerous papers on Physical Organic and on Organic Chemistry, mainly on kinetics and mechanism of organic reactions and on mesomorphism (liquid crystals), in Journal of Chemical Soc. and other scientific periodicals; articles and published addresses on new learning resources and Educational Technology. University of Sheffield Record of War Work, 1939–45. *Recreations:* music, photography and walking. *Address:* 46 Westwood Road, Beverley, North Humberside HU17 8EJ. *T:* Beverley 861125.

JONES, Charles Beynon Lloyd, CMG 1978; Chairman of Directors, David Jones Ltd, 1963–80; Consul General of Finland in Sydney, since 1971; *b* 4 Dec. 1932; *s* of late Sir Charles Lloyd Jones and Lady (Hannah Beynon) Lloyd Jones, OBE. *Educ:* Cranbrook Sch., Sydney; Univ. of Sydney (not completed). Joined David Jones Ltd, 1951; Alternate Director, 1956; Director, 1957; Joint Managing Director, 1961. Pres. Bd of Trustees, Art Gall. of NSW, 1980–83 (Trustee, 1972; Vice-Pres., 1976–80). Governor, London House for Overseas Graduates, 1983–. Officer, Order of Merit, Republic of Italy (Cavaliere Ufficiale); Comdr, Order of the Lion, Finland. *Address:* 4 Trahlee Road, Bellevue Hill, NSW 2023, Australia; Summerlees Farm, Yarramalong, NSW 2259. *Club:* Royal Sydney Golf.

JONES, Maj.-Gen. Charles Edward Webb, CBE 1985; Director General, Territorial Army and Organisation, since 1985; *b* 25 Sept. 1936; *s* of Gen. Sir Charles Phibbs Jones, *qv*; *m* 1965, Suzanne Vere Pige-Leschallas; two *s* one *d*. *Educ:* Portora Royal School, Enniskillen. Commissioned Oxford and Bucks LI, 1956; 1st Bn Royal Green Jackets, 1958; served BAOR, 1968–70; served NI, 1971–72 (despatches 1972); Directing Staff, Staff Coll., 1972; CO 1st Bn RGJ, 1974–76; Comdr 6th Armd Brigade, 1981–83; Comdr, British Mil. Adv. and Training Team, Zimbabwe, 1983–85. *Recreations:* golf, tennis, fishing. *Club:* Army and Navy.

JONES, Charles Ian McMillan; Director of Studies, Britannia Royal Naval College, Dartmouth, since 1986; *b* 11 Oct. 1934; *s* of Wilfred Charles Jones and Bessie Jones (*née* McMillan); *m* 1962, Jennifer Marie Potter; two *s*. *Educ:* Bishop's Stortford Coll.; St John's Coll., Cambridge. Certif. Educn 1959, MA 1962; FBIM, FRSA. 2nd Lieut RA, 1953–55. Head of Geog. Dept, Bishop's Stortford Coll., 1960–70, Asst to Headmaster, 1967–70; Vice-Principal, King William's Coll., IoM, 1971–75; Head Master, Bedford School, 1975–86. Man., England Schoolboy Hockey XI, 1967–74; Man., England Hockey XI, 1968–69; Pres., English Schoolboys Hockey Assoc., 1980–; Mem. IoM Sports Council, 1972–75. *Publications:* articles in Guardian. *Recreations:* hockey (Captain Cambridge Univ. Hockey XI, 1959; England Hockey XI, 1959–64, 17 caps; Gt Britain Hockey XI, 1959–64, 28 caps), cricket (Captain IoM Cricket XI, 1973–75), squash, gardening. *Address:* Ashford House, Britannia Royal Naval College, Dartmouth, Devon TQ6 0HJ. *Clubs:* MCC, East India, Devonshire, Sports and Public Schools; Hawks (Cambridge).

JONES, General Sir Charles (Phibbs), GCB 1965 (KCB 1960; CB 1952); CBE 1945; MC 1940; Governor of Royal Hospital, Chelsea, 1969–75; Chief Royal Engineer, 1967–72; *b* 29 June 1906; *s* of late Hume Riversdale Jones and Elizabeth Anne (*née* Phibbs); *m* 1934, Ouida Margaret Wallace; two *s*. *Educ:* Portora Royal School, Enniskillen, N Ireland; Royal Military Academy, Woolwich; Pembroke Coll., Cambridge. Commissioned in RE, 1925; service with Royal Bombay Sappers and Miners in India, 1928–34; Adjt of 42nd (EL) Divl Engineers (TA), 1934–39; student at Staff Coll., Camberley, 1939. War of 1939–45: service in BEF, France and Belgium, as Bde Major 127 Inf. Bde, 1940; Instructor at Staff Coll., Camberley, 1940–41; GSO1 at GHQ Home Forces, 1941–42; CRE Guards Armoured Div. in UK and in NW Europe, 1943–44; BGS XXX Corps in NW Europe, 1945. Chief of Staff, Malaya Comd, 1945–46; BGS HQ Western Comd, UK, 1946; idc, 1947; Comdr 2nd Inf. Bde, 1948–50; Dir of Plans, War Office, 1950; GOC 7th Armoured Div., BAOR, 1951–53; Comdt, Staff Coll., Camberley, 1954–56; Vice AG, WO, 1957–58; Dir, Combined Military Planning Staff, CENTO, 1959; GOC, 1st Corps 1960–62; GOC-in-C, Northern Comd, 1962–63; Master General of the Ordnance, 1963–66; ADC (General) to the Queen, 1965–67. A Governor, Corps of Commissionaires, 1969–. Nat. Pres., Royal British Legion, 1970–81. Col Comdt, RE, 1961–72; Hon. Col, Engineer and Rly Staffs Corps, RE, T&AVR, 1970–77. Order of Leopold, Croix de Guerre (Belgium), 1945. *Recreations:* golf and fishing. *Address:* 9 Abbey Mews, Amesbury Abbey, Amesbury, Wilts. *Clubs:* Army and Navy; Dormy House (Rye).

See also C. E. W. Jones.

JONES, Rev. Canon Cheslyn Peter Montague, MA; Rector of Lowick with Sudborough and Slipton, and Priest-in-charge of Islip, Northants, since 1981; *b* 4 July 1918; *e s* of late Montague William and Gladys Muriel Jones; unmarried. *Educ:* Winchester Coll.; New Coll., Oxford. BA 1st cl. Hons Theology, 1939; Senior Demy, Magdalen Coll., 1940–41. Deacon 1941; Priest 1942. Curate of St Peter, Wallsend, 1941–43; St Barnabas, Northolt Park, 1943–46; at Nashdom Abbey, 1946–51; Chaplain, Wells Theological Coll., 1951–52; Librarian, Pusey House, Oxford, 1952–56; Chaplain, Christ Church Cathedral, Oxford, 1953–56; Principal, Chichester Theological Coll., and Chancellor, Chichester Cathedral, 1956–69, Canon Emeritus, 1971; Principal of Pusey House, Oxford, 1971–81. Select Preacher: Oxford Univ., 1960, 1977, 1978 and 1981; Cambridge Univ., 1962; Sir Henry Stephenson Fellow, Univ. of Sheffield, 1969–70; Bampton Lectr, Oxford Univ., 1970. *Publications:* (ed) A Manual for Holy Week, 1967; contributions to: Studies in the Gospels, 1955; Studies in Ephesians, 1956; Thirty 20th century hymns, 1960; Christian Believing, 1976; (editor and contributor): For Better For Worse, 1977; The Study of Liturgy, 1978; Pusey, by Leonard Prestige, 1982; The Study of Spirituality, 1986. *Recreations:* travel, music. *Address:* The Rectory, Lowick, Kettering, Northants NN14 3BQ. *T:* Thrapston 3216.

JONES, Sir Christopher L.; *see* Lawrence-Jones.

JONES, Clement; *see* Jones, John C.

JONES, Clive Lawson; Director for Energy Policy, European Commission, since 1982; *b* 16 March 1937; *s* of Celyn John Lawson Jones and Gladys Irene Jones; *m* 1961, Susan Brenda (*née* McLeod); one *s* one *d*. *Educ:* Cranleigh School; University of Wales. BSc (Chemistry). With British Petroleum, 1957–61; Texaco Trinidad, 1961–68; Principal, Min. of Power, 1968–69; Min. of Technology, 1969–70; DTI, 1970–73; Asst Sec., Oil Emergency Group, 1973–74; Department Energy: Asst Sec., 1974–77; Under Sec., Gas Div., 1981–82; Counsellor (Energy), Washington, 1977–81. *Recreations:* art, antiques. *Address:* Rue Mareyde 37, Woluwe St Pierre, 1150 Brussels, Belgium.

JONES, Daniel Gruffydd; Under-Secretary, Departments of the Environment and of Transport, since 1979; *b* 7 Dec. 1933; *o s* of late Ifor Ceredig Jones and Gwendolen Eluned Jones; *m* 1969, Maureen Anne Woodhall; three *d*. *Educ:* Ardwyn Grammar Sch., Aberystwyth; University Coll. of N Wales, Bangor (BA). Min. of Housing and Local Govt, 1960; Private Sec. to Sec. of Cabinet, 1967–69; Asst Sec., 1969; Sec., Water Resources Bd, 1969–73; DoE, 1973; Sec., Prime Minister's Cttee on Local Govt Rules of Conduct, 1973–74; Under Sec. (Principal Finance Officer), Welsh Office, 1975–79. *Address:* c/o Department of the Environment, 2 Marsham Street, SW1P 3EB. *T:* 01–212 3434.

JONES, Sir David A.; *see* Akers-Jones.

JONES, David Evan Alun, CBE 1985; Commissioner for Local Administration in Wales, 1980–85; *b* 9 Aug. 1925; *s* of David Jacob Jones, OBE, Master Mariner, and Margaret Jane Jones; *m* 1952, Joan Margaret Erica (*née* Davies); two *s*. *Educ:* Aberaeron County Sch.; University Coll. of Wales, Aberystwyth (LLB; Sir Samuel Evans Prize, 1949). Solicitor. Served War, RAF, 1943–47 (Flt Lieut). Articled service, Exeter, 1949–52; asst solicitor posts with Ilford Bor., Southampton County Bor., Berks County and Surrey County Councils, 1952–61; Dep. Clerk, Denbighshire CC, subseq. Clerk of CC and Clerk of the Peace, 1961–74; Chief Exec., Gwynedd CC, 1974–80. Chm., All Wales Adv. Panel on Devclt of Services for Mentally Handicapped People, 1985–; Member: Broadcasting Council for Wales, 1980–85; Local Govt Boundary Commn for Wales, 1985–; Gwynedd HA, 1986–. Mem. Council, UCNW, 1982–. *Recreations:* gardening, travel, a little golf. *Address:* Min-y-Don, West End, Beaumaris, Gwynedd LL58 8BG. *T:* Beaumaris 810225; 11 Dunraven House, Westgate Street, Cardiff CF1 1DL. *T:* Cardiff 41574. *Clubs:* National Liberal; Baron Hill Golf (Beaumaris).

JONES, David Hugh; Associate Director, Royal Shakespeare Company, since 1966; *b* 19 Feb. 1934; *s* of John David Jones and Gwendolen Agnes Langworthy (*née* Ricketts); *m* 1964, Sheila Allen; two *s*. *Educ:* Taunton Sch.; Christ's Coll., Cambridge (MA 1st Cl. Hons English). 2nd Lieut RA, 1954–56. Production team of Monitor, BBC TV's 1st arts magazine, 1958–62, Editor, 1962–64; joined RSC, 1964; Aldwych Co. Dir, 1968–72; Artistic Dir, RSC (Aldwych), 1975–77; Producer, Play of the Month, BBC TV, 1977–78; Artistic Dir, Brooklyn Acad. of Music Theatre Co., 1979–81; Adjunct Prof. of Drama, Yale Univ., 1981. Productions for RSC incl. plays by Arden, Brecht, Gorky, Granville Barker, Günter Grass, Graham Greene, Mercer, O'Casey, Shakespeare, and Chekhov; dir. prodns for Chichester and Stratford, Ontario, Festival Theatres; other productions include: Tramway Road, Lyric Th., Hammersmith, 1984; Old Times, Theatre Royal, Haymarket, 1985. Dir, films for BBC TV, including: biography of poet, John Clare, 1969; adaptations of Hardy and Chekhov short stories, 1972 and 1973; Pinter's screenplay, Langrishe, Go Down, 1978, Merry Wives of Windsor, Pericles, 1982–83. Directed first feature film, Pinter's Betrayal, 1982. Obie Awards, NY, for direction of RSC Summerfolk, 1975, for innovative programming at BAM Theatre Co., 1980. *Recreations:* chess, reading modern poetry, exploring mountains and islands. *Address:* 227 Clinton Street, Brooklyn, NY 11201, USA.

JONES, Rev. David Ian Stewart; Director of the Lambeth Charities, since 1985; *b* 3 April 1934; *s* of Rev. John Milton Granville Jones and Evelyn Moyes Stewart Jones (formerly Chedburn); *m* 1967, Susan Rosemary Hardy Smith; twin *s* and *d*. *Educ:* St John's Sch., Leatherhead; Selwyn Coll., Cambridge (MA). Commnd Royal Signals, 1952–54. Curate at Oldham Parish Church, 1959–62; Vicar of All Saints, Elton, Bury, 1963–66; Asst Conduct and Chaplain of Eton Coll., 1966–70; Conduct and Sen. Chaplain of Eton Coll., 1970–74; Headmaster of Bryanston School, 1974–82; Rector-designate of Bristol City, 1982–85. *Recreations:* reading (theology, philosophy, politics), music. *Address:* 127 Kennington Road, SE11 6SF. *T:* 01–735 1925. *Club:* East India, Devonshire, Sports and Public Schools.

JONES, David le Brun, CB 1975; Director, Long Term Office, International Energy Agency, since 1982; *b* 18 Nov. 1923; *s* of Thomas John Jones and Blanche le Brun. *Educ:* City of London Sch.; Trinity Coll., Oxford. Asst Principal, Min. of Power, 1947; Principal, MOP, 1952; Asst Sec., Office of the Minister for Science, 1962; Asst Sec., MOP, 1963; Under-Sec., MOP, later Min. of Technology and DTI, 1968–73; Dep. Sec., DTI, later DoI, 1973–76; Cabinet Office, 1976–77; Dept of Energy, 1978–82. *Recreations:* walking, reading, chess. *Address:* 47 Grove End Road, NW8 9NB. *Club:* United Oxford & Cambridge University.

JONES, David M.; *see* Mansel-Jones.

JONES, Prof. David Morgan, MA; Professor of Classics in the University of London (Westfield College), 1953–80; *b* 9 April 1915; *m* 1965, Irene M. Glanville. *Educ:* Whitgift Sch.; Exeter Coll., Oxford (Scholar). 1st Class, Classical Hon. Mods, 1936; 1st Class, Lit Hum, 1938; Derby Scholar, 1938; Junior Research Fellow, Exeter Coll., Oxford, 1938–40; Oxford Diploma in Comparative Philology, 1940; Lecturer in Classics, University Coll. of North Wales, 1940–48; Reader in Classics in the University of London (Birkbeck Coll.), 1949–53. *Publications:* papers and reviews in classical and linguistic journals. *Address:* Kemyell Vean, 3 Laregan Hill, Penzance TR18 4NY. *T:* Penzance 63389.

JONES, Derek John Claremont, CMG 1979; Minister for Hong Kong Relations with the European Communities and Member States, since 1982; *b* 2 July 1927; *er s* of Albert Claremont Jones and Ethel Lilian Jones (*née* Hazell); *m* 1st, 1951, Jean Cynthia Withams; one *s* two *d*; 2nd, 1970, Kay Cecile Thewlis; one *s*. *Educ:* Colston Sch., Bristol; Bristol Univ.; London Sch. of Economics and Political Science. Economic Asst, Economic Section, Cabinet Office, 1950–53; Second Sec., UK Delegn to OEEC/NATO, Paris, 1953–55; Asst Principal, Colonial Office, 1955–57; Principal, Colonial Office, 1957–66; First Secretary, Commonwealth Office, 1966–67; Counsellor (Hong Kong Affairs), UK Mission, Geneva, 1967–71; Government of Hong Kong: Dep. Economic Sec., 1971–73; Sec. for Economic Services, 1973–76; Sec. for the Environment, 1976–81; Sec. for Transport, 1981–82. *Recreations:* reading, travel, conversation. *Address:* 56 rue Jules Léjeune, 1060 Brussels, Belgium. *Clubs:* Hong Kong, Royal Hong Kong Jockey.

JONES, Derek R.; *see* Rudd-Jones.

JONES, Rt. Rev. Derwyn Dixon; *see* Huron, Bishop of.

JONES, Captain Desmond V.; *see* Vincent-Jones.

JONES, Rev. Prof. Douglas Rawlinson; Lightfoot Professor of Divinity, University of Durham, 1964–85, now Emeritus; Residentiary Canon of Durham Cathedral, 1964–85, now Emeritus; *b* 11 Nov. 1919; *s* of Percival and Charlotte Elizabeth Jones; *m* 1946, Hazel Mary Passmore; three *s* two *d*. *Educ:* Queen Elizabeth's Hosp., Bristol; St Edmund Hall, Oxford; Wycliffe Hall, Oxford. Squire Scholar, 1938; BA 1941; MA 1945; deacon, 1942; priest, 1943. Curate of St Michael and All Angels, Windmill Hill, Bristol, 1942–45; Lectr, Wycliffe Hall, Oxford, 1945–50; Chaplain, Wadham Coll., Oxford, 1945–50; Lectr in Divinity, 1948–50; University of Durham: Lectr, 1951; Sen. Lectr, 1963. Mem., Gen. Synod of C of E, 1970–80 and 1982–85. Chairman of the Liturgical Commn, 1981–86. DD Lambeth, 1985. *Publications:* Haggai, Zechariah and Malachi, 1962; Isaiah, 56–66 and Joel, 1964; Instrument of Peace, 1965; contrib. to: Peake's Commentary on the Bible, 1962; Hastings' Dictionary of the Bible, 1963; The Cambridge History of the Bible, 1963; articles in Jl of Theolog. Studies, Zeitschrift für die Alttestamentliche Wissenschaft, Vetus Testamentum, Theology, Scottish Jl of Theology. *Recreation:*

carpentry. *Address:* Whitefriars, Kings Road, Longniddry, E Lothian EH32 0NN. *T:* Longniddry 52149.

JONES, Prof. Douglas Samuel, MBE 1945; FRS 1968; Ivory Professor of Mathematics, University of Dundee, since 1965; *b* 10 Jan. 1922; *s* of late J. D. Jones and B. Jones (*née* Streather); *m* 1950, Ivy Styles; one *s* one *d*. *Educ:* Wolverhampton Grammar Sch.; Corpus Christi Coll., Oxford (MA 1947; Hon. Fellow, 1980); DSc Manchester 1957. Flt-Lt, RAFVR, 1941–45. Commonwealth Fund Fellow, MIT, 1947–48; Asst Lectr in Maths, University of Manchester, 1948–51; Lectr 1951–54, Research Prof. 1955, New York Univ.; Sen. Lectr in Maths, Univ. of Manchester, 1955–57; Prof. of Maths, Univ. of Keele, 1957–64. Vis. Prof., Courant Inst., 1962–63. Member: UGC, 1976– (Mem., 1971–, Chm., 1976–, Mathematical Scis Sub-Cttee); Computer Bd, 1977–82; Open Univ. Vis. Cttee, 1982–. Member Council: Royal Soc., 1973–74; IMA, 1982–85. FIMA 1964; FRSE 1967. Hon. DSc Strathclyde, 1975. Keith Prize, RSE, 1974; van der Pol Gold Medal, Internat. Union of Radio Sci., 1981. Trustee, Quarterly Jl of Mechanics and Applied Maths; Associate Editor: Jl IMA, 1964–; RSE, 1969–82; SIAM Jl on Applied Maths, 1975–; Applicable Analysis, 1976–; Mathematical Methods, 1977–; Royal Soc., 1978–83. *Publications:* Electrical and Mechanical Oscillations, 1961; Theory of Electromagnetism, 1964; Generalised Functions, 1966; Introductory Analysis, vol. 1, 1969, vol 2, 1970; Methods in Electromagnetic Wave Propagation, 1979; Elementary Information Theory, 1979; The Theory of Generalised Functions, 1982; Differential Equations and Mathematical Biology, 1983; Acoustic and Electromagnetic Waves, 1986; articles in mathematical and physical jls. *Recreations:* golf, walking, photography. *Address:* Department of Mathematical Sciences, The University, Dundee DD1 4HN. *T:* Dundee 23181.

JONES, Edgar Stafford, CBE 1960 (MBE 1953); *b* 11 June 1909; *s* of late Theophilus Jones; *m* 1938, Margaret Aldis, *d* of late Henry Charles Askew; one *s* one *d*. *Educ:* Liverpool Institute High Sch. Mem. of Local Government Service, 1925–34; joined Assistance Board, 1934. Seconded to Air Min., as Hon. Flt-Lt RAFVR, 1943; Hon. Sqdn-Ldr, 1945. Transferred to Foreign Office, 1946; transferred to Washington, 1949; Dep. Finance Officer, Foreign Office, 1953; Head of Finance Dept, Foreign Office, 1957 and Diplomatic Service Administration Office, 1965, retired 1968. *Address:* 30 Wingfield Road, Kingston upon Thames, Surrey KT2 5LR. *T:* 01–546 9812. *Clubs:* London Welsh Rugby Football, Rugby; Glamorgan County Cricket.

JONES, His Honour Judge Edward; *see* Jones, J. E.

JONES, Air Marshal Sir Edward G.; *see* Gordon Jones.

JONES, Sir Edward Martin F.; *see* Furnival Jones.

JONES, Edward W.; *see* Wilson Jones.

JONES, Rt. Hon. Sir Edward (Warburton), PC 1979; PC (N Ireland) 1965; Kt 1973; Lord Justice of Appeal, Supreme Court of Judicature, N Ireland, 1973–84 (Judge of the High Court of Justice in Northern Ireland, 1968–73); *b* 3 July 1912; *s* of late Hume Riversdale Jones and Elizabeth Anne (*née* Phibbs); *m* 1st, 1941, Margaret Anne Crosland Smellie (*d* 1953); three *s*; 2nd, 1953, Ruth Buchan Smellie; one *s*. *Educ:* Portora Royal School, Enniskillen, N Ireland; Trinity Coll., Dublin. BA (TCD), with First Class Moderatorship, Legal Science, and LLB (TCD) 1935; called to Bar of Northern Ireland, 1936; QC (N Ireland), 1948; called to Bar (Middle Temple), 1964. Junior Crown Counsel: County Down, 1939; Belfast, 1945–55. Enlisted, 1939; commissioned Royal Irish Fusiliers, 1940; Staff Coll., Camberley, 1943; AAG, Allied Land Forces, SEA, 1945; released with Hon. rank Lt-Col, 1946. MP (U) Londonderry City, Parliament of Northern Ireland, 1951–68; Attorney-Gen. for Northern Ireland, 1964–68. Chancellor: Dio. Derry and Raphoe, 1945–64; Dio. Connor, 1959–64 and 1978–81; Dio. Clogher, 1973; Lay Mem. Court of Gen. Synod, Church of Ireland. Bencher, Inn of Court of NI, 1961. Hon. Bencher, Middle Temple, 1982. Vice-Pres., College Historical Soc., TCD, 1983–. *Recreations:* golf, sailing. *Address:* The Lodge, Spa, Ballynahinch, Co. Down, N Ireland. *T:* Ballynahinch 562240; Craig-y-Mor, Trearddur Bay, Anglesey. *T:* Trearddur Bay 860406. *Clubs:* Army and Navy; Ulster Reform (Belfast); Dormy House (Rye).

JONES, Eifion, CMG 1964; OBE 1953; Permanent Secretary, Ministry of Works, Northern Nigeria, 1959–66; Member, Northern Nigerian Development Corporation, 1959–66; retired; *b* Llanelly, Carmarthenshire, 10 June 1912; *s* of I. J. Jones and R. A. Jones (*née* Bassett); *m* 1944, Kathleen, *d* of Donald and E. J. MacCalman, Argyllshire. *Educ:* Llanelli Grammar Sch.; University Coll., Swansea. BSc (Wales). Executive Engineer, Nigeria, 1942; Colonial Service 2nd Course, Camb. Univ., 1949–50 (Mem. Christ's Coll.). Senior Executive Engineer, 1951; Chief Engineer, 1954; Dep. Dir of Public Works, Nigeria, 1958. Member: Lagos Exec. Develt Bd, 1954–57; Governing Cttee, King's Coll., Lagos, 1956–59; Cttee for Develt of Tourism and Game Reserves in N Nigeria, 1965. Mem., West African Council, ICE, 1960–65. JP N Nigeria, 1963–66. FICE 1957; FIWES 1957. *Recreations:* golf, gardening, reading. *Address:* c/o Barclays Bank, Llanelli, Dyfed.

JONES, Sir Elwyn; *see* Jones, Sir W. E. E.

JONES, Emlyn Bartley, MBE 1975; Director General, The Sports Council, 1978–83; sport and leisure consultant, since 1983; *b* 9 Dec. 1920; *s* of Ernest Jones and Sarah Bartley; *m* 1944, Constance Inez Jones; one *d*. *Educ:* Alun Grammar School, Mold, Clwyd; Bangor Normal Coll.; Loughborough Coll. of Physical Education. Diploma Loughborough Coll. (Hons). Flight Lieut, RAF, 1941–46; Teacher, Flint Secondary Modern Sch., 1946; Technical Representative, N Wales, 1947–51; Technical Adviser, Central Council of Physical Recreation, 1951–62; Dir, Crystal Palace Nat. Sports Centre, 1962–78. Director: Jones-Hatton Internat. Ltd, 1983–; Athole Still Associates Ltd, 1983–. Television commentator, 1955–, now specializing in winter sports (ski-ing). Pres., British Assoc. of Nat. Sports Administrators, 1984–. FBIM 1984. *Publications:* Learning Lawn Tennis, 1958; Sport in Space: the implications of cable and satellite television, 1984. *Recreations:* golf, ski-ing, travel, conversation. *Address:* Chwarae Teg, 1B Allison Grove, Dulwich Common, SE21 7ER. *T:* 01–693 7528. *Club:* Royal Air Force.

JONES, Emrys; *see* Jones, J. E.

JONES, Sir Emrys; *see* Jones, Sir W. E.

JONES, Prof. Emrys, MSc, PhD (Wales); FRGS; Professor of Geography, University of London, at London School of Economics, 1961–84, now Emeritus; *b* Aberdare, 17 Aug. 1920; *s* of Samuel Garfield and Anne Jones; *m* 1948, Iona Vivien, *d* of R. H. Hughes; one *d* (and one *d* decd). *Educ:* Grammar Sch. for Boys, Aberdare; University Coll. of Wales, Aberystwyth. BSc (1st Class Hons in Geography and Anthropology), 1941; MSc, 1945; PhD, 1947; Fellow of the University of Wales, 1946–47; Asst Lectr at University Coll., London, 1947–50; Fellow, Rockefeller Foundation, 1948–49; Lectr at Queen's Univ., Belfast, 1950–58, Sen. Lectr, 1958; Reader, LSE, 1959–61. O'Donnel Lectr, Univ. of Wales, 1977. Chairman: Regional Studies Assoc., 1967–69; Council, Hon. Soc. of Cymmrodorion, 1984– (Mem., 1977–); Mem. Council, RGS, 1973–77 (Vice-Pres., 1978–81). Mem. Council, University Coll. of Wales, Aberystwyth, 1978–85. Consultant on urbanisation and planning. Victoria Medal, RGS, 1977. Hon. DSc Belfast, 1978. *Publications:* Hon. Editor, Belfast in its Regional Setting, 1952; (jointly) Welsh Rural Communities, 1960; A Social Geography of Belfast, 1961; Human Geography, 1964; Towns and Cities, 1966; Atlas of London, 1968; (ed jtly) Man and his Habitat, 1971; (contrib.) The Future of Planning, 1973; (with E. van Zandt) The City, 1974; Readings in Social Geography, 1975; (with J. Eyles) Introduction to Social Geography, 1977; (Chief Editor) The World and its Peoples, 1979; articles in geographical, sociological and planning jls. *Recreations:* books, music. *Address:* 2 Pine Close, North Road, Berkhamsted, Herts. *T:* Berkhamsted 75422. *Club:* Athenæum.

JONES, Emrys Lloyd, FBA 1982; Goldsmiths' Professor of English Literature, Oxford University, and Fellow, New College, Oxford, since 1984; *b* 30 March 1931; *s* of Peter Jones and Elizabeth Jane (*née* Evans); *m* 1965, Barbara Maud Everett; one *d*. *Educ:* Neath Grammar Sch.; Magdalen Coll., Oxford (BA, MA). Tutor in English, Magdalen Coll., 1955–77; Reader in Eng. Lit., Oxford Univ., 1977–84; Fellow, Magdalen Coll., Oxford, 1955–84. *Publications:* (ed) Poems of Henry Howard, Earl of Surrey, 1964; Pope and Dulness, 1972; Scenic Form in Shakespeare, 1971; The Origins of Shakespeare, 1977; (ed) Antony and Cleopatra, 1977; contribs to jls and books. *Recreations:* looking at buildings; opera. *Address:* New College, Oxford OX1 3BN. *T:* Oxford 248451.

JONES, Sir Eric (Malcolm), KCMG 1957; CB 1953; CBE 1946; Director, Government Communications Headquarters, Foreign Office, 1952–60, retired; *b* 27 April 1907; *m* 1929, Edith Mary Taylor; one *s* one *d*. *Educ:* King's Sch., Macclesfield. Textile Merchant and Agent, 1925–40. RAFVR 1940–46, Civil Servant, 1946–60; Dir, Simon Engineering Ltd, 1966–77. Legion of Merit (US), 1946. *Recreations:* ski-ing, golf.

JONES, Eric S.; *see* Somerset Jones.

JONES, Ernest Edward; Member, Doncaster Metropolitan Borough Council, since 1980; Chairman, Doncaster Community Health Council, since 1981; *b* 15 Oct. 1931; *s* of William Edward Jones and Eileen Gasser; *m* 1955, Mary Armstrong; one *s* one *d*. *Educ:* Bentley Catholic Primary Sch., Doncaster; Sheffield De La Salle Coll.; Hopwood Hall Coll. of Educn, Middleton, Lancs; Manch. Univ. Sch. of Educn; Management Studies Unit, Sheffield Polytech. Min. of Educn Teaching Certif. (CertEd); Univ. Dipl. in Science Studies (DipSc); Dipl. in Educn Management (DEM). School Master, 1953–. Doncaster County Borough: Councillor, 1962–74 (Chm. Health Cttee, 1971–74; Chm. Social Services Cttee, 1972–73; served on 15 other cttees at various times). South Yorkshire CC: Mem. 1973–77; Dep. Chm., 1973–75; Chm., 1975–76; Chm., Rec., Culture and Health Cttee, 1973–75; Doncaster Metropolitan Borough Council: Chairman: Libraries, Museums and Arts Cttee, 1982–; Further Educn Cttee, 1983–85; Vice-Chm., Educn Services Cttee, 1982–. Chairman: Co. and Council of Management, Northern Coll., 1986– (Vice-Chm., 1982–86); Doncaster Inst. of Further and Higher Educn, 1986–. Member: Nat. Health Exec. Council, 1964–74; Doncaster and Dist Water Bd, 1972–74; AMC (Social Services), 1972–74; Peak Park Planning Bd, 1973–77; Yorks and Humberside Museum and Art Gall. Service, 1973–77, 1984–; Yorks and Humberside Jt Libraries Cttee, 1973–75, 1983–; Yorks and Humberside Assoc. of Further and High Educn, 1982–. Hull Univ. Ct, 1983–85; Sheffield Univ. Council, 1983–85; Mem., Bradford Univ. Ct and Council, 1986–. Exec. Mem., Yorks Arts Assoc., 1983–85; Former Member: Yorks Regional Land Drainage Cttee; Univ. of Hull Educn Delegacy; AMA; Yorks and Humberside Museums and Art Galleries Fedn; Yorks and Humberside Regional Sports Council; Yorks, Humberside and Cleveland Tourist Bd; Exec. Mem., Youth Assoc. of South Yorks. Governor, Sheffield Polytechnic, 1982–. MRSH; FRSA 1980. *Recreations:* music and fine arts, general interest in sport, fell-walking, keen caravanner. *Address:* 11 Norborough Road, Doncaster, South Yorks DN2 4AR. *T:* Doncaster 66122.

JONES, Evan David, CBE 1965; FSA 1959; FLA 1973; Librarian of the National Library of Wales, 1958–69; *b* 6 Dec. 1903; *e s* of Evan Jones and Jane (*née* Davies), Llangeitho; *m* 1933, Eleanor Anne, *o d* of John Humphrey Lewis, master mariner, Aberystwyth; one *s*. *Educ:* Llangeitho Primary Sch.; Tregaron County Sch.; University Coll. of Wales, Aberystwyth. BA 1926, Hons Welsh, Class 1, History 2a; Sir John Williams Research Student, 1928–29. Archivist Asst, National Library of Wales, 1929–36; Dep. Keeper of MSS and Records, 1936–38, Keeper, 1938–58. Lecturer in Archive Administration, UCW, 1957–58. President: Cambrian Archæological Assoc., 1962–63; New Wales Union, 1965–67; Welsh Harp Soc., 1965–80; Welsh Bibliographical Soc., 1968–; Cymdeithas Emynau Cymru, 1968–; Cymdeithas Bob Owen, 1976–; Pres., Union of Welsh Independents, 1974–75. Chairman: Governors of Welsh Sch., Aberystwyth, 1946–47; Executive Cttee, Urdd Gobaith Cymru, 1954–57; Cambrian Archæological Assoc., 1954–57; Cardigans. Congregational Quarterly Meeting, 1960; Undeb y Cymdeithasau Llyfrau, 1959–61; Welsh Books Centre, 1966–70; Welsh Books Council, 1968–70; Govs, Coll. of Librarianship, Wales, 1968–74 (Vice-Chm., 1964–68); Three Counties Congregational Assoc., 1972–73; Sec., Welsh Congregational Church, Aberystwyth, 1938–; Treasurer: New Wales Union, 1970–; Interdenominational Cttee on Welsh Lang., 1970–. Mem. Court of Governors: Nat. Museum of Wales, 1958–69; University of Wales, 1958–71; Member: Council of UCW; Congregational Memorial Coll., Swansea; Bala-Bangor Congregational Coll.; Union of Welsh Independents; Bd of Celtic Studies; Hist. and Law Cttee; Ancient Monuments Bd for Wales, 1970–79; Council of Brit. Records Assoc., 1958–69; Pantyfedwen Trust, 1958–69; Council of Hon. Soc. of Cymmrodorion; National Eisteddfod Council; Broadcasting Council for Wales, 1966–71; Library Advisory Council (Wales), 1965–69; Hon. Mem. of the Gorsedd (also Examr). Hon. FLA 1973. Hon LLD Wales, 1972. Editor: NLW Jl, 1958–69; Jl of Merioneth History and Record Soc.; DWB Supplements. *Publications:* Gwaith Lewis Glyn Cothi, 1953; Victorian and Edwardian Wales, 1972; Gwaith Lewis Glyn Cothi 1837–39, 1973; Ystyriaethau ar Undeb Eglwysig, 1974; Trem ar Ganrif, 1978; Beirdd y Bymthegfed ganrif a'u cefndir, 1982; Lewys Glyn Cothi (Detholiad), 1984; articles in Archæologia Cambrensis, Bulletin of Board of Celtic Studies, and many other journals; contrib. Dictionary of Welsh Biography. *Recreations:* colour photography, walking, gardening. *Address:* Penllerneuadd, North Road, Aberystwyth SY23 2EE. *T:* Aberystwyth 612112.

JONES, Ewan Perrins W.; *see* Wallis-Jones.

JONES, Sir Ewart (Ray Herbert), Kt 1963; DSc Victoria, PhD Wales, MA Oxon; FRS 1950, FRSC; Waynflete Professor of Chemistry, University of Oxford, 1955–78, now Emeritus; Fellow of Magdalen College, 1955–78, Hon. Fellow, 1978; *b* Wrexham, Denbighshire, 16 March 1911; *m* 1937, Frances Mary Copp; one *s* two *d*. *Educ:* Grove Park Sch., Wrexham; University Coll. of North Wales, Bangor; Univ. of Manchester. Fellow of Univ. of Wales, 1935–37; Lecturer, Imperial Coll. of Science and Technology, 1938; Reader in Organic Chemistry, Univ. of London, and Asst Prof., 1945; Sir Samuel Hall Prof. of Chemistry, The University, Manchester, 1947–55. Arthur D. Little Visiting Prof. of Chemistry, MIT, 1952; Karl Folkers Lectr at Univs of Illinois and Wisconsin, 1957; Andrews Lectr, Univ. of NSW, 1960. Mem. Council for Scientific and Industrial Research, and Chm., Research Grants Cttee, 1961–65; Mem. SRC and Chm., Univ. Science and Technology Bd, 1965–69; Mem., Science Bd, 1969–72. Chemical Society:

Tilden Lectr, 1949; Pedler Lectr, 1959; Robert Robinson Lectr, 1978; Dalton Lectr, 1985; Award for Service to the Society, 1973; Award in Natural Product Chem., 1974; Meldola Medal, Royal Institute of Chemistry, 1940; Davy Medal, Royal Society, 1966. Fritzsche Award, American Chemical Soc., 1962. President: Chemical Soc., 1964–66; RIC, 1970–72 (Chm., Chem. Soc./RIC Unification Cttee, 1975–80); Royal Soc. of Chemistry, 1980–82. Fellow, Imperial Coll., 1967; Foreign Mem. Amer. Acad. of Arts and Sciences, 1967. Chm., Anchor and Guardian Housing Assocs, 1979–84. Hon. DSc: Birmingham, 1965; Nottingham, 1966; New South Wales, 1967; Sussex, 1969; Salford, 1971; Wales, 1971; East Anglia, 1978; Ulster, 1978; Hon. LLD Manchester, 1972. *Publications:* scientific papers in Jl of the Chem. Soc. *Address:* 6 Sandy Lane, Yarnton, Oxford OX5 1PB. *T:* Kidlington 2581.

JONES, Major Francis, CVO 1969; TD (3 clasps); MA, FSA; DL; Wales Herald Extraordinary since 1963; County Archivist, Carmarthenshire, 1958–74; *b* Trevine, Pembrokeshire, 5 July 1908; *s* of James Jones, Grinston, Pembs, and Martha Jones; *m* Ethel M. S. A., *d* of late J. J. Charles, Trewilym, Pembs; two *s* two *d. Educ:* Fishguard County Sch., Pembs. Temp. Archivist of Pembs, 1934–36; Archivist, Nat. Library of Wales, 1936–39. Lt 4th Bn Welch Regt (TA), 1931–39; trans. Pembroke Yeomanry (RA, TA), 1939, Battery Captain; served War of 1939–45: RA (Field), N Africa (despatches), Middle East, Italy; Battery Comdr, and 2nd-in-comd of regt; GSO2 War Office; Mil. Narrator, Hist. Section, Cabinet Office, 1945–58 (Compiled Official narrative of Sicilian and Italian Campaigns); Battery Comdr, The Surrey Yeomanry, QMR (RA, TA), 1949–56; Mil. Liaison Officer, Coronation, 1953; served on the Earl Marshal's staff, State Funeral of Sir Winston Churchill, 1965; Mem., Prince of Wales Investiture Cttee, 1967–69. Local Sec. and Mem., Cambrian Assoc.; Pres., Cambrian Archaeol Assoc., 1985–86; Vice-Pres., Council, Hon. Soc. of Cymmrodorion; Member: Gorsedd, Royal National Eisteddfod of Wales; Court and Council, Nat. Library of Wales, 1967–77; Council, Nat. Museum of Wales; Historical Soc. of the Church in Wales; Carmarthenshire Local History Soc.; Pembrokeshire Records Soc. (Vice-Pres.); Croeso '69 Nat. Cttee; Academie Internationale d'Heraldique; Heraldry Soc. Trustee, Elvet Lewis Memorial (Gangell), 1967–81. Vice-Pres., Dyfed Local Councils, 1974–81. DL Dyfed, 1965. Broadcaster (TV and sound radio). Hon. MA Univ. of Wales. CStJ. *Publications:* The Holy Wells of Wales, 1954; The History of Llangunnor, 1965; God Bless the Prince of Wales, 1969; The Princes and Principality of Wales, 1969; (jtly) Royal and Princely Heraldry in Wales, 1969; numerous articles on historical, genealogical and heraldic matters to learned jls. *Recreations:* genealogical research and heraldry, fly-fishing, study of ancient ruins. *Address:* Hendre, Springfield Road, Carmarthen. *T:* Carmarthen 237099.

JONES, Francis Edgar, MBE 1945; PhD, DSc; FRS 1967; FEng, FIEE, FRAeS; FInstP; Director: Philips Industries, 1973–76; Unitech Ltd, since 1974; *s* of Edgar Samuel Jones and Annie Maude Lamb; *m* 1942, Jessie Gladys Hazell (*d* 1985); four *s* one *d. Educ:* Royal Liberty Sch., Romford; King's Coll., London. Demonstrator in Physics, King's Coll., London, 1938–39; at Min. of Aircraft Production Research Estab., finishing as Dep. Chief Scientific Officer, 1940–52; Chief Scientific Officer and Dep. Dir, RAE, Farnborough, 1952–56; Technical Dir, Mullard Ltd, 1956–62, Man. Dir, 1962–72; Chm., Associated Semiconductor Manufacturers Ltd, 1962–72. Chairman: Adv. Council on Road Research, 1966–68; Electronic Components Bd, 1967–69; Radio & Electronic Component Manufacturers Fedn, 1967–69; Electronic Valve & Semiconductor Manufacturers Assoc., 1968; Member: Inland Transport Research and Develt Council, 1969; Cttee on Manpower Resources for Sciences and Technology (Chm., Working Group on Migration, 1967); Council for Scientific Policy, 1965–70; Central Adv. Council for Science and Technology, 1966–70; Nat. Defence Industries Council, 1969–76; Council, IEE, 1965–69 (Vice-Pres. 1972); Council, Royal Society, 1968, 1979–81; Cttee of Enquiry into Research Assocs; (part-time) Monopolies and Mergers Commn, 1973–81; Chairman: EDC for Mech. Engrg, 1973–76; Rank Prize Fund for Optoelectronics. Pres., Engineering Industries Assoc., 1977–81. Fellow, King's Coll., London, 1968. Mem. Delegacy, KCL, 1976. Vis. Prof. of Electrical Engineering, University Coll., London, 1968–. Trustee: Anglo-German Foundn for the Study of Industrial Soc., 1973–79; Rank Prize Funds, 1977–. Hon. Fellow, Univ. of Manchester Inst. of Science and Technology, 1970. Hon. DSc: Southampton, 1968; Nottingham, 1968; Cranfield, 1976; Heriot-Watt, 1978; DUniv Surrey, 1968; Hon. DTech Brunel, 1969; Duddell Premium, IEE, 1949; Glazebrook Medal and Prize, Inst. of Physics, 1971. *Publications:* (with R. A. Smith and R. P. Chasmar) The Detection and Measurement of Infrared-Radiation, 1956; articles in Proc. Royal Society, RAeS Jl, Jl IEE, Nature. *Address:* Hornby House, 5 Latchmoor Avenue, Gerrards Cross, Bucks SL9 8LJ. *T:* Gerrards Cross 885319. *Club:* Athenæum.

JONES, Prof. F(rank) Llewellyn-, CBE 1965; MA, DPhil, DSc Oxon; Hon. LLD; Principal, University College of Swansea, 1965–74 (Vice-Principal, 1954–56 and 1960–62; Acting Principal, 1959–60); Professor Emeritus, since 1974; *b* 30 Sept. 1907; *er s* of Alfred Morgan Jones, JP, Penrhiwceiber, Glamorgan; *m* 1st, 1938, Eileen (*d* 1982), *d* of E. T. Davies, Swansea; one *s* (one *d* decd); 2nd, 1983, Mrs Gwendolen Thomas, Rhossili. *Educ:* West Monmouth Sch.; Merton Coll., Oxford. Science Exhibnr 1925; 1st Cl. Nat. Sci. physics, BA 1929; Research Scholar, Merton Coll., 1929, DPhil, MA, 1931; Senior Demy, Magdalen Coll., 1931. DSc 1955. Demonstrator in Wykeham Dept of Physics, Oxford, 1929–32; Lecturer in Physics, University Coll. of Swansea, 1932–40; Senior Scientific Officer, Royal Aircraft Establishment, 1940–45; Prof. of Physics, Univ. of Wales, and Head of Dept of Physics, University Coll. of Swansea, 1945–65. Vice-Chancellor, Univ. of Wales, 1969–71. Member: Radio Research Board, DSIR, 1951–54; Standing Conference on Telecommunications Research, DSIR, 1952–55; Board of Institute of Physics, 1947–50; Council of Physical Society, 1951–58 (Vice-Pres., 1954–59). Visiting Prof. to Univs in Australia, 1956; Supernumerary Fellow, Jesus Coll., Oxford, 1965–66, 1969–70; Hon. Professorial Res. Fellow, Univ. of Wales, 1974–; Leverhulme Emeritus Fellow, 1977–79. Regional Scientific Adviser for Home Defence, Wales, 1952–59, Sen. and Chief Reg. Sci. Adv., 1959–77; Pres., Royal Institution of South Wales, 1957–60; Mem. of Council for Wales and Mon, 1959–63, 1963–66; Dir (Part-time), S Wales Gp, BSC, 1968–70; Chm., Central Adv. Council for Education (Wales), 1961–64. Sen. Consultant in Plasma Physics, Radio and Space Research Station of SRC, 1964–65. Vice-Pres., Hon. Soc. of Cymmrodorian, 1982. Hon. LLD Wales, 1975. C. V. Boys' Prizeman, The Physical Soc., 1960; Inaugural Ragnar Holm Scientific Achievement Award, 6th Internat. Conf. on Electric Contact Phenomena, Chicago, 1972. *Publications:* Fundamental Processes of Electrical Contact Phenomena, 1953; The Physics of Electrical Contacts, 1957; Ionization and Breakdown in Gases, 1957, 2nd edn 1966; The Glow Discharge, 1966; Ionization, Avalanches and Breakdown, 1966; papers in scientific jls on ionization and discharge physics. *Recreation:* industrial archaeology. *Address:* Brynheulog, 24 Sketty Park Road, Swansea SA2 9AS. *T:* Swansea 202344. *Club:* Athenæum.

JONES, Fred, CB 1978; CBE 1966; Deputy Secretary, HM Treasury, 1975–80, retired; *b* 5 May 1920; *s* of late Fred Jones and of Harriet (*née* Nuttall); *m* 1954, Joy (*née* Field); two *s. Educ:* Preston Grammar Sch.; St Catherine's Coll., Oxford. Economist, Trades Union Congress, 1951–59; Tutor in Economics and Industrial Relations, Ruskin Coll., Oxford, 1960–62; Economist, National Economic Development Office, 1962–64; Dept of Economic Affairs: Senior Economic Adviser, 1964–66; Asst Sec., 1966–68; Asst Under-Sec. of State, 1968–69; HM Treasury, Asst Under-Sec. of State, 1969–75. *Recreations:* walking, gardening, reading. *Address:* The Glen, Haighton Green Lane, Haighton, Grimsargh, Preston, Lancs.

JONES, Prof. Gareth (Hywel), QC 1986; FBA 1982; Fellow of Trinity College, Cambridge, since 1961; Downing Professor of the Laws of England, Cambridge University, since 1975; *b* 10 Nov. 1930; *o c* of late B. T. Jones, FRICS, and late Mabel Jones, Tylorstown, Glam; *m* 1959, Vivienne Joy, *o d* of late C. E. Puckridge, FIA, Debden Green, Loughton; two *s* one *d. Educ:* Porth County Sch.; University Coll. London (PhD); St Catharine's Coll., Cambridge (Scholar); Harvard Univ. (LLM). LLB London 1951; MA, LLB 1953, LLD 1972, Cantab. Choate Fellow, Harvard, 1953; Yorke Prize, 1960. Called to Bar, Lincoln's Inn, 1955 (Scholar); Hon. Bencher 1975. Lecturer: Oriel and Exeter Colls, Oxford, 1956–58; KCL, 1958–61; Trinity College, Cambridge: Lectr, 1961–74; Tutor, 1967; Sen. Tutor, 1972; Vice-Master, 1986; Univ. Lectr, Cambridge, 1961–74; Chm., Faculty of Law, 1978–81. Vis. Professor: Harvard, 1966 and 1975; Chicago, 1976–; California at Berkeley, 1967 and 1971; Indiana, 1971, 1975; Michigan, 1983; Georgia, 1983. Lectures: Harris, Indiana, 1981; Wright, Toronto, 1984; Lionel Cohen, Hebrew Univ., 1985. Hon. Mem., American Law Inst. *Publications:* (with Lord Goff of Chieveley) The Law of Restitution, 1966, 2nd edn 1978; The History of the Law of Charity 1532–1827, 1969; The Sovereignty of the Law, 1973; (with W. H. Goodhart QC) Specific Performance, 1986; various articles. *Address:* Trinity College, Cambridge CB2 1TQ. *T:* Cambridge 338473; 9B Cranmer Road, Cambridge CB3 9BL. *T:* Cambridge 63932; 186 Clay Street, Thornham Magna, Eye, Suffolk. *T:* Occold 640. *Club:* Beefsteak.

JONES, Geoffrey; *see* Jones, John G.

JONES, Prof. Geoffrey M.; *see* Melvill Jones.

JONES, Geoffrey Rippon R.; *see* Rees-Jones.

JONES, Air Marshal Sir George, KBE 1953 (CBE 1942); CB 1943; DFC; RAAF; *b* 22 Nov. 1896; *m* 1st, 1919, Muriel Agnes (decd), *d* of F. Stone; one *s* (and one *s* decd); 2nd, 1970, Mrs Gwendoline Claire Bauer. Served Gallipoli and European War, 1914–18 (despatches, DFC); joined RAAF, 1921; Dir Personnel Services, RAAF, 1936–40; Dir of Training, 1940–42; Chief of Air Staff, 1942–52. *Address:* Flat 10, 104 Cromer Road, Beaumaris, Victoria 3193, Australia. *Club:* Naval and Military (Melbourne).

JONES, George Briscoe; Director, Co-operative Development Agency, since 1982; Director, Job Ownership Ltd, since 1983; *b* 1 June 1929; *s* of late Arthur Briscoe Jones and Mary Alexandra Jones (*née* Taylor); *m* 1955, Audrey Patricia Kendrick; two *d. Educ:* Wallasey and Caldy Grammar Schools. Army, 1947–49; Unilever, 1949–84 (on secondment to CDA, 1982–84); Dir, BOCM Silcocks, 1974–82; Chm., Unitrition, 1977–82. Trustee, Plunkett Foundn, 1985–. *Recreations:* painting, sculpture, chess, bridge. *Address:* 3 Beverley Close, Basingstoke, Hants. *T:* Basingstoke 28239. *Club:* Farmers'.

JONES, Prof. George William; Professor of Government, University of London, since 1976; *b* 4 Feb. 1938; *er s* of George William and Grace Annie Jones; *m* 1963, Diana Mary Bedwell; one *s* one *d. Educ:* Wolverhampton Grammar Sch.; Jesus Coll., Oxford; Nuffield Coll., Oxford. Oxf. BA 1960, MA 1965, DPhil 1965. Univ. of Leeds: Asst Lectr in Govt, 1963; Lectr in Govt, 1965; London Sch. of Economics and Political Science: Lectr in Political Science, 1966; Sen. Lectr in Polit. Sci., 1971; Reader in Polit. Sci., 1974. Sec., Polit. Studies Assoc. of the UK, 1965–68; Exec. Cttee of PSA, 1969–75; Exec. Council, Hansard Soc., 1968–70; Mem., Editorial Cttee of The London Journal, 1973–80. Member: Layfield Cttee of Inquiry into Local Govt Finance, 1974–76; Exams Cttee, and Admin. Staff Qualifications Council, Local Govt Trng Bd, 1977–80; Political Science and Internat. Relns Cttee, SSRC, 1977–81; Chm., Central-Local Govt Relations Panel, SSRC, 1978–81. Member: Governing Council, Wolverhampton Polytechnic, 1978–83; Council, RIPA, 1984–. FRHistS 1980. Hon. Fellow, Inst. of Local Govt Studies, Birmingham Univ., 1979. *Publications:* Borough Politics, 1969; (with B. Donoughue) Herbert Morrison: portrait of a politician, 1973; (ed with A. Norton) Political Leadership in Local Authorities, 1978; (ed) New Approaches to the Study of Central-Local Government Relationships, 1980; (with J. Stewart) The Case for Local Government, 1983, 2nd edn 1985; (ed jtly) Between Centre and Locality, 1985; contribs to Political Studies, Public Admin., Political Qly, Parliamentary Affairs, Government and Opposition, Jl of Admin Overseas; Local Govt Chronicle. *Recreations:* cinema, politics. *Address:* Department of Government, London School of Economics, Houghton Street, WC2A 2AE. *T:* 01–405 7686.

JONES, Geraint Iwan; *b* 16 May 1917; *s* of Rev. Evan Jones, Porth, Glam; *m* 1st, 1940, M. A. Kemp; one *d*; 2nd, 1949, Winifred Roberts. *Educ:* Caterham Sch.; Royal Academy of Music (Sterndale Bennett Scholar). National Gallery Concerts, 1940–44; played complete organ works of Bach in 16 recitals in London, 1946. Musical dir of Mermaid Theatre performances of Purcell's Dido and Aeneas with Kirsten Flagstad, 1951–53. Formed Geraint Jones Singers and Orchestra, 1951, with whom many Broadcasts, and series of 12 Bach concerts, Royal Festival Hall, 1955; series of all Mozart's piano concertos, Queen Elizabeth Hall, 1969–70. Frequent European engagements, 1947– and regular US and Canadian tours, 1948–. Musical Director: Lake District Festival, 1960–78; Kirckman Concert Soc., 1963–; Artistic Director: Salisbury Festival, 1973–77; Manchester Internat. Festival, 1977–. As consultant, has designed many organs, incl. RNCM, St Andrew's Univ., RAM, Acad. for Performing Arts, Hong Kong, and Tsim Sha Tsni culture centre, Hong Kong. Recordings as organist and conductor; Promenade Concerts; also concerts and recordings as harpsichordist, including sonatas with violinist wife, Winifred Roberts. Grand Prix du Disque, 1959 and 1966. *Publications:* translations: Clicquot's Théorie Pratique de la facture de l'orgue, 1985; Davy's Les Grandes Orgues de L'Abbatiale St Etienne de Caen, 1985. *Recreations:* motoring, photography, antiques, reading. *Address:* The Long House, Arkley Lane, Barnet Road, Arkley, Herts.

JONES, Geraint Stanley; Director of Public Affairs, BBC, since 1986; *b* 26 April 1936; *s* of Olwen and David Stanley Jones; *m* 1961, Rhiannon Williams; two *d. Educ:* Pontypridd Grammar Sch.; University Coll. of N Wales (BA Hons; Dip. Ed.). BBC-Wales: Studio Manager, 1960–62; Production Asst, Current Affairs (TV), 1962–65; TV Producer: Current Affairs, 1965–69; Features and Documentaries, 1969–73; Asst Head of Programmes, Wales, 1973–74; Head of Programmes, Wales, 1974–81; Controller, BBC Wales, 1981–85. *Recreations:* music, painting. *Address:* c/o BBC, Broadcasting House, W1A 1AA. *Club:* Cardiff and County (Cardiff).

JONES, Dr Gerald, FRCP; Senior Principal Medical Officer, Department of Health and Social Security, since 1984; *b* 25 Jan. 1939; *s* of John Jones and Gladys Jones (*née* Roberts); *m* 1964, Anne Heatley (*née* Morris); one *s* two *d. Educ:* Swansea Grammar School; Merton College, Oxford; London Hosp. Med. Coll. (BA, BM, BCh, PhD). Appointments in hosp. medicine, 1965–69; research with MRC, 1969–73; pharmaceutical industry, 1974–75; medical staff, DHSS, 1975–. *Publications:* papers on cardiopulmonary physiology, respiratory medicine, cellular immunology and drug regulation. *Recreations:* music, gardening, art history, economics, catching dragonflies, wine making. *Address:* Medicines

Division, Department of Health and Social Security, Market Towers, 1 Nine Elms Lane, Vauxhall, SW8 5NQ. *T:* 01–720 2188.

JONES, Gerallt; *see* Jones, R. G.

JONES, Sir Glyn (Smallwood), GCMG 1964 (KCMG 1960, CMG 1957); MBE 1944; *b* 9 Jan. 1908; *s* of late G. I. Jones, Chester; *m* 1942, Nancy Madoc, *d* of J. H. Featherstone, CP, South Africa; one *d* (and one *s* decd). *Educ:* King's Sch., Chester; St Catherine's, Oxford Univ. (MA); Hon. Fellow, 1977. OUAFC 1928, 1929, 1930. HM Colonial Service (now HM Overseas Civil Service) N Rhodesia: Cadet, 1931; District Officer, 1933; Commissioner for Native Development, 1950; Acting Development Sec., 1956; Prov. Comr, 1956; Resident Comr, Barotseland, 1957; Sec. for Native Affairs, 1958; Minister of Native Affairs and Chief Comr, 1959; Chief Sec., Nyasaland, 1960–61, Governor, 1961–64; Governor-Gen of Malawi, 1964–66. Advr on Govt Admin to Prime Minister of Lesotho, 1969–71; Dep. Chm., Lord Pearce Commn on Rhodesian Opinion, 1971–72; British Govt Observer, Zimbabwe Elections, 1980. Founding Chm., Friends of Malawi Assoc, 1968–83; Chairman: Malawi Church Trust, 1970–; Friends of Jairos Jiri Assoc. (Zimbabwe), 1982–; Zimbabwe Trust (London), 1982–; Malaŵi Against Polio Trust, 1984–. Grand Cordon, Order of the Trinity of Ethiopia, 1965; Order of the Epiphany of Central Africa, 1966. KStJ. *Recreations:* shooting, fishing, golf, tennis. *Address:* Little Brandfold, Goudhurst, Kent. *Clubs:* Athenæum, Royal Commonwealth Society, MCC.

JONES, Gordon Frederick; Director, Product Design Review, since 1985; *b* 25 Aug. 1929; *s* of Harold Frederick and Rose Isabel Jones; *m* 1954, Patricia Mary (*née* Rowley); one *s* one *d*. *Educ:* Saltley Grammar Sch.; The School of Architecture, Birmingham (DipArch); RIBA 1950. FRSA. Architect: in local government, 1952; War Office, 1959; Asst City Architect, Sheffield, 1966; private practice, London, 1968; Property Services Agency, DoE: Architect, 1970; Head of Student Training Office, 1976; Head of Architectural Services, 1979–85. *Recreations:* watching cats, listening to music, re-building houses. *Address:* The Building Centre, 26 Store Street, WC1 7BT.

JONES, Graham Julian; His Honour Judge Graham Jones; a Circuit Judge, since 1985; *b* 17 July 1936; *s* of late David John Jones, CBE, and of Edna Lillie Jones; *m* 1961, Dorothy, *o d* of late James Smith and of Doris Irene Tickle, Abergavenny; two *s* one *d*. *Educ:* Porth County Grammar Sch. (state scholarship); St John's Coll., Cambridge. MA, LLM (Cantab). Admitted Solicitor, 1961; Partner, Morgan Bruce and Nicholas, 1961. Pres., Pontypridd Rhondda and Dist Law Soc., 1973–75; Member Council: Cardiff Law Soc., 1975–78, 1984–85; Associated Law Socs of Wales, 1974–85 (Pres., 1982–84); Mem., Lord Chancellor's Legal Aid Adv. Cttee, 1980–85. Sat as Dep. Circuit Judge, 1975–78; a Recorder, 1978–85. *Recreations:* golf, boats. *Address:* 17 Windsor Road, Radyr, Cardiff CF4 8BQ. *T:* Radyr 842669. *Clubs:* Cardiff and County, Radyr Golf (Cardiff).

JONES, Griffith Winston Guthrie, QC 1963; a Recorder, 1972–74 (Recorder of Bolton, 1968–71); *b* 24 Sept. 1914; second *s* of Rowland Guthrie Jones, Dolgellau, Merioneth; *m* 1st, 1959, Anna Maria McCarthy (*d* 1969); 2nd, 1978, Janet, *widow* of Commodore Henry Owen L'Estrange, DSC. *Educ:* Bootham Sch., York; University of Wales; St John's Coll., Cambridge. Called to the Bar, Gray's Inn, 1939. Dep. Chm., Cumberland QS, 1963–71. War service in Royal Artillery, 1940–46. *Recreation:* gardening. *Address:* Culleenamore, Sligo, Ireland. *Club:* Kildare Street and University (Dublin).

JONES, Gwilym Haydn; MP (C) Cardiff North, since 1983; *s* of Evan Haydn Jones and Mary Elizabeth Gwenhwyfar Jones (*née* Moseley); *m* 1974, Linda Margaret (*née* John); one *s* one *d*. *Educ:* London and S Wales. Dir, Bowring Wales Ltd. Councillor, Cardiff CC, 1969–72 and 1973–83. Mem., Select Cttee on Welsh Affairs, 1983–; Sec., Welsh Cons. Members Gp, 1984–. Founder Chm., Friendship Force in Wales, 1978–81. *Recreations:* golf, model railways, watching Wales win at rugby. *Address:* House of Commons, SW1A 0AA. *T:* 01–219 3000. *Clubs:* County Conservative, Cardiff and County, Rhiwbina Rugby, United Services Mess (Cardiff).

JONES, (Gwilym) Wyn, CBE 1977; Member, Gwynedd Health Authority, since 1982; *b* 12 July 1926; *s* of late Rev. John Jones, MA, BD, and Elizabeth (*née* Roberts); *m* 1951, Ruth (*née* Thomas); one *s* one *d*. *Educ:* Llanrwst Grammar Sch.; UCNW, Bangor (BA Hons); London Univ. Served RN, 1944–47. Cadet, Colonial Admin. Service, Gilbert and Ellice Islands, 1950; DO, DC and Secretariat in Tarawa, Line Islands, Phoenix Islands and Ocean Island, 1950–61; Solomon Islands, 1961; Asst Sec., 1961–67; Sen. Asst Sec., 1967–74; Dep. Chief Sec., 1974; Sec. to Chief Minister and Council of Ministers, 1974–77; Governor, Montserrat, 1977–80. Administrator, Cwmni Theatr Cymru (Welsh Nat. Theatre), 1982–85. Mem. Court, UCNW Bangor, 1980–. *Recreation:* walking alone. *Address:* Y Frondeg, Warren Drive, Deganwy, Gwynedd. *T:* Deganwy 83377.

JONES, Prof. Gwyn, CBE 1965; Professor of English Language and Literature, University College of South Wales, Cardiff, 1965–75, Fellow, 1980; *b* 24 May 1907; *s* of George Henry Jones and Lily Florence (*née* Nethercott); *m* 1st, 1928, Alice (*née* Rees) (*d* 1979); 2nd, 1979, Mair (*née* Sivell), *widow* of Thomas Jones. *Educ:* Tredegar Grammar School; University of Wales. Schoolmaster, 1929–35; Lecturer, University Coll., Cardiff, 1935–40; Prof. of Eng. Language and Lit., University Coll. of Wales, Aberystwyth, 1940–64. Ida Beam Vis. Prof., Iowa Univ., 1982. Dir of Penmark Press, 1939–. Mem. of various learned societies; Pres. of Viking Soc. for Northern Research, 1950–52; Mem. of Arts Council and Chm. of Welsh Arts Council, 1957–67. Hon. DLitt: Wales, 1977; Nottingham, 1978; Southampton, 1983. Fellow, Institut Internat. des Arts et des Lettres, 1960. Christian Gauss Award, 1973. Knight, Order of the Falcon (Iceland), 1963. *Publications:* A Prospect of Wales, 1948; Welsh Legends and Folk-Tales, 1955; *novels:* Richard Savage, 1935; Times Like These, 1936, repr. 1979; Garland of Bays, 1938; The Green Island, 1946; The Flowers Beneath the Scythe, 1952; The Walk Home, 1962; *short stories:* The Buttercup Field, 1945; The Still Waters, 1948; Shepherd's Hey, 1953; Selected Short Stories, 1974; *translations:* The Vatnsdalers' Saga, 1942; (with Thomas Jones) The Mabinogion, 1948; Egil's Saga, 1960; Eirik the Red, 1961; The Norse Atlantic Saga, 1964; A History of the Vikings, 1968; Kings, Beasts and Heroes, 1972; (ed) Welsh Review, 1939–48; Welsh Short Stories, 1956; (ed with I. F. Elis) Twenty-Five Welsh Short Stories, 1971; The Oxford Book of Welsh Verse in English, 1977; *non-fiction:* Being and Belonging (BBC Wales Annual Radio Lecture), 1977; (ed) Fountains of Praise, 1983; contrib. to numerous learned journals. *Address:* Castle Cottage, Sea View Place, Aberystwyth, Dyfed.

JONES, Gwyn Idris M.; *see* Meirion-Jones.

JONES, Gwyn Owain, CBE 1978; MA, DSc Oxon; PhD Sheffield; Director, National Museum of Wales, 1968–77; *b* 29 March 1917; *s* of Dr Abel John Jones, OBE, HMI, and Rhoda May Jones, Cardiff and Porthcawl; *m* 1st, 1944, Sheila Heywood (marr. diss.); two *d*; 2nd, 1973, Elizabeth Blandino. *Educ:* Monmouth Sch.; Port Talbot Secondary Sch.; Jesus Coll., Oxford. Glass Delegacy Research Fellow of University of Sheffield, later mem. of academic staff, 1939–41; Mem. UK Government's Atomic Energy project, 1942–46; Nuffield Foundation Research Fellow at Clarendon Laboratory, Oxford, 1946–49; Reader in Experimental Physics in University of London, at Queen Mary Coll., 1949–53; Prof. of Physics in Univ. of London, and Head of Dept of Physics at Queen Mary Coll., 1953–68; Fellow of Queen Mary Coll. Visiting Prof. Univ. of Sussex, 1964. Member: Court and Council, UWIST, 1968–74; Court, University Coll., Swansea, 1981–84; Hon. Professorial Fellow, University Coll., Cardiff, 1969–79. Yr Academi Gymreig (English Language Section) 1971 (Chm., 1978–81); Gorsedd y Beirdd (Aelod er Anrhydedd) 1974; Governor, Commonwealth Institute, 1974–77. FMA 1976. *Publications:* Glass, 1956; (in collab.) Atoms and the Universe, 1956; papers on solid-state, glass, low-temperature physics; *novels:* The Catalyst, 1960; Personal File, 1962; Now, 1965; *story sequence:* The Conjuring Show, 1981. *Address:* Ivy Cottage, Hudnalls Loop, St Briavels Common, near Lydney, Glos GL15 6SG. *T:* Dean 530510.

JONES, Dame Gwyneth, DBE 1986 (CBE 1976); a Principal Dramatic Soprano: Royal Opera House, Covent Garden, since 1963; Vienna State Opera, since 1966; Bavarian State Opera, since 1967; *b* 7 Nov. 1936; *d* of late Edward George Jones and late Violet (*née* Webster); *m* Till Haberfeld; one *d*. *Educ:* Twmpath Sec. Mod. Sch., Pontypool, Mon; Royal College of Music, London; Accademia Chigiana, Siena; Zürich Internat. Opera Studio; Maria Carpi Prof., Geneva. Oratorio and recitals as well as opera. Guest Artiste: La Scala, Milan; Berlin State Opera; Munich State Opera; Bayreuth Festival; Salzburg Festival; Verona; Tokyo; Zürich; Metropolitan Opera, New York; Paris; Geneva; Dallas; San Francisco; Los Angeles; Teatro Colon, Buenos Aires; Edinburgh Festival; Welsh National Opera; Rome; Hamburg; Cologne; Maggio Musicale, Florence; Chicago. Numerous recordings, radio and TV appearances. FRCM. Kammersängerin, Austria and Bavaria. Hon. DMus Wales. *Address:* Box 380, 8040 Zürich, Switzerland.

JONES, G(wyneth) Ceris; Chief Nursing Officer, British Red Cross Society, 1962–70, retired; *b* 15 Nov. 1906; 2nd *d* of late W. R. Jones, OBE, JP, Tre Venal, Bangor, N Wales. *Educ:* Bangor County Sch. for Girls. State Registered Nurse; trained at Nightingale Training Sch., St Thomas' Hosp., 1927–31; Sister Tutor's Certificate, Univ. of London; Diploma in Nursing, Univ. of London. Sister Tutor, St Thomas' Hosp., 1936–39; served with QAIMNS Reserve, 1939–41; Sister-in-charge, Leys School Annexe to Addenbrooke's Hospital, Cambridge, 1941–43; Asst Matron, London Hospital, 1943–47; Matron, Westminster Hospital, 1947–51; London Hospital, 1951–61. Florence Nightingale Medal, Internat. Cttee, Red Cross, 1971. *Address:* 7 Menai View Terrace, Bangor, Gwynedd LL57 2HF.

JONES, Gwynoro Glyndwr; Assistant Education Officer, Development Forward Planning, West Glamorgan County Council, since 1977; *b* 21 Nov. 1942; *s* of J. E. and late A. L. Jones, Minyrafon, Foelgastell, Cefneithin, Carms; *m* 1967, A. Laura Miles; two *s* one *d*. *Educ:* Gwendraeth Grammar Sch.; Cardiff Univ. BSc Econ (Hons) Politics and Economics. Market Research Officer with Ina Needle Bearings Ltd, Llanelli, 1966–67; Economist Section, Wales Gas Bd, 1967–69; Public Relations Officer, Labour Party in Wales, March 1969–June 1970; Dir of Res., West Glam. CC, 1974–77. Member: INLOGOV Working Gp on Res. and Intelligence Units in Local Govt, 1975–77; S Wales Standing Conf. Working Gp, 1975–77; Council of European Municipalities, 1975–77, 1980–; Local Govt Exec. Cttee of European movement, 1975–77, 1980–; MP (Lab) Carmarthen, 1970–Sept. 1974; Member: House of Commons Expenditure Cttee, 1972–74; Standing Orders Cttee, 1972–74; Council of Europe and WEU, 1974; PPS to Home Sec., 1974. Vice-Pres., District Council Assoc., 1974. Pres., Nat. Eisteddfod of Wales, 1974. Political Educn Officer, Swansea Labour Assoc., 1976–77. Mem., Soc. of Educn Officers, 1978–. Co-ordinator, Wales in Europe campaign, 1975; Sponsor, Wales Lab and TU Cttee for Europe, 1975; joined SDP, May 1981; contested (SDP) Gower, Sept. 1982. Chairman: SDP Council for Wales, 1982–85; Alliance Cttee for Wales, 1983–; Member: Council for Social Democracy, 1982–; SDP Nat. Cttee, 1982–. *Publications:* The Record Put Straight (booklet), 1973; SDP and the Alliance in Wales 1981–1986 (booklet), 1986. *Recreations:* sport (played Rugby for both 1st and 2nd class teams). *Address:* Fonthill, 24 Glanmor Park Road, Sketty, Swansea, West Glam. *T:* Swansea 202278.

JONES, Harry, BSc, PhD Leeds, PhD Cantab; FRS 1952; *b* Pudsey, Yorks, 12 April 1905; *m* 1931, Frances Molly O'Neill; one *s* two *d*. *Educ:* University of Leeds; Trinity Coll., Cambridge. Lecturer at Bristol Univ., 1932–37; Imperial College, London: Reader in Mathematics, 1938–46; Prof. of Mathematics, 1946–72, now Professor Emeritus; Head of Dept, 1955–70, Pro-Rector, 1970–72; Sen. Res. Fellow, 1972–81, Fellow, 1975. *Publications:* (with N. F. Mott) The Theory of the Properties of Metals and Alloys, 1936; Theory of Brillouin Zones and Electronic States in Crystals, 1960; various contributions to scientific journals on Theoretical Physics. *Address:* 41 Berwyn Road, Richmond, Surrey. *T:* 01–876 1931.

See also A. C. R. Rumbold.

JONES, Sir Harry (Ernest), Kt 1971; CBE 1955; Agent in Great Britain for Northern Ireland, 1970–76; *b* 1 Aug. 1911; *m* 1935, Phyllis Eva Dixon; one *s* one *d*. *Educ:* Stamford Sch.; St John's Coll., Cambridge. Entered Northern Ireland Civil Service, 1934; Min. of Commerce: Principal Officer 1940; Asst Sec. 1942; Perm. Sec. 1955; Industrial Development Adviser to Ministry of Commerce, 1969. *Recreation:* fishing. *Address:* 51 Station Road, Nassington, Peterborough. *T:* Stamford 782675.

JONES, Rt. Rev. Haydn Harold; *b* 22 Aug. 1920; *s* of Charles Samuel and Blodwen Jones (*née* Williams), Penarth, Glam. *Educ:* Brotherhood of Saint Paul, Barton. RAF, 1941–44. Deacon 1947, priest 1948, Diocese of Bradford. Curate of St Barnabas, Heaton, Bradford, 1947–49; Tor Mohun, Torquay, 1949–51; Chaplain RN, 1951–53; Licence to Officiate, Diocese of London, 1954–62, Diocese of Coventry, 1962–63; Curate of St Peter's, Coventry, 1963–64; Rector of Clutton, Diocese of Bath and Wells, 1964–76, with Cameley, 1975–76; Surrogate, 1972–76. Dean of St Mary's Cathedral, Caracas, 1976–85; Bishop of Venezuela, 1976–86. *Recreations:* formerly tennis (rep. RN 1952), badminton, squash, bridge, films, theatre. *Address:* Apartado 60.008, Chacao 1060, Caracas, Venezuela. *T:* Caracas (02) 572.1437.

JONES, Henry Arthur, CBE 1974; MA; Professor Emeritus, University of Leicester, since 1981 (Vaughan Professor of Education, 1967–81; Head of the Department of Adult Education, 1967–78; Pro-Vice-Chancellor, 1978–81); *b* 7 March 1917; *er s* of Henry Lloyd Jones; *m* 1st, 1942, Molly (*d* 1971), 4th *d* of Richard Shenton; two *s*; 2nd, 1972, Nancy Winifred (*née* Cox), *widow* of Lt R. B. B. Jack, RN. *Educ:* Chorlton Grammar Sch.; Manchester Univ. George Gissing Prizeman, Manchester Univ., 1936; Graduate Research Fellow, Manchester Univ., 1937, MA 1938. Served War of 1939–45 with Lancs Fusiliers and DLI, 1940–42. Sen. English Master, Chorlton Grammar Sch., 1942–47; Resident Staff Tutor, Manchester Univ., 1947–49; Asst Dir of Extra-Mural Studies, Liverpool Univ., 1949–52, Dep. Dir 1953–57; Principal, The City Literary Institute, 1957–67. Chairman: Assoc. for Adult Education, 1964–67; Adult Educn Cttee, IBA, 1973–77; Vice-Pres., Nat. Inst. of Adult Education (Exec. Chm., 1976–84); Hon. Life Mem., Educnl Centres Assoc.; Vice-Pres., Pre-retirement Assoc.; Member: Library Adv. Council, DES, 1965–68; Sec. of State's Cttee on Adult Educn, DES, 1968–72; Adv. Council for Adult and Continuing Educn, DES, 1977–83. Chm., Leics Consultative Cttee for Voluntary Orgns, 1974–77. Editor: Vaughan Papers in Educn, 1967–82; Studies in

Adult Education, 1974–82. *Publications:* Adult Literacy: a study of the impact, 1978; The Concept of Success in Adult Literacy, 1978; Adult Literacy: the UK experience, 1978; Education and Disadvantage, 1978. *Address:* Stokes House, Great Bowden, Market Harborough, Leics. *T:* Market Harborough 62846.

JONES, Sir Henry (Frank Harding), GBE 1972 (KBE 1965; MBE 1943); Kt 1956; MA; FEng, FICE, FIChemE; Hon.FIGasE; Chairman of the Gas Council, 1960–71; Vice-Chairman, International Executive Council, World Energy Conference, 1970–73, Hon. Vice-Chm. since 1973 (Chairman, British National Committee, 1968–71); *b* 13 July 1906; *s* of Frank Harding Jones, Housham Tye, Harlow, Essex; *m* 1934, Elizabeth Angela, *d* of J. Spencer Langton, Little Hadham, Herts; three *s* one *d. Educ:* Harrow; Pembroke Coll., Cambridge (Hon. Fellow 1973). Served War of 1939–45 with Essex Regt and on staff: France and Belgium, 1939–40; India and Burma, 1942–45. Lieut-Col 1943; Col 1945; Brigadier 1945. Before nationalisation of gas industry was: Deputy Chairman, Watford and St Albans Gas Co., Wandsworth and District Gas Co.; Dir of South Metropolitan, South Suburban and other gas companies. Chm. East Midlands Gas Board, 1949–52; Dep. Chm. Gas Council, 1952–60. Chairman: Benzene Marketing Co., 1972–77; Benzole Producers Ltd, 1972–77. Mem., Royal Commn on Standards of Conduct in Public Life, 1974–76. Chm., EDC for Chemical Industry, 1972–75. Liveryman, Clothworkers' Co., 1928, Master 1972–73. Hon. FIGasE (Pres. 1956–57); FEng 1976. FRSA 1964. Hon. LLD Leeds, 1967; Hon. DSc: Leicester, 1970; Salford, 1971. *Recreations:* gardening, reading. *Address:* Pathacres, Weston Turville, Aylesbury, Bucks HP22 5RW. *T:* Stoke Mandeville 2274. *Clubs:* Athenæum, MCC.

JONES, (Henry) John (Franklin); writer; *b* 6 May 1924; *s* of late Lt-Col James Walker Jones, DSO, IMS, and Doris Marjorie (*née* Franklin); *m* 1949, Jean Verity Robinson; one *s* one *d. Educ:* Blundell's Sch.; Colombo Public Library; Merton Coll., Oxford. Served War, Royal Navy: Ordinary Seaman, 1943; Intell. Staff, Eastern Fleet, 1944. Merton Coll., Oxford: Harmsworth Sen. Scholar, 1948; Fellow and Tutor in Jurisprudence, 1949; Univ. Sen. Lectr, 1956; Fellow and Tutor in Eng. Lit., 1962; Prof. of Poetry, Univ. of Oxford, 1979–84. Dill Meml Lectr, QUB, 1983. Football Correspondent, The Observer, 1956–59. *Publications:* The Egotistical Sublime, 1954, 5th edn 1978; (contrib.) The British Imagination, 1961; On Aristotle and Greek Tragedy, 1962, 5th edn 1980; (contrib.) Dickens and the Twentieth Century, 1962; (ed) H. W. Garrod, The Study of Good Letters, 1963; John Keats's Dream of Truth, 1969, 2nd edn 1980; (contrib.) The Morality of Art, 1969; The Same God, 1971; Dostoevsky, 1983, 2nd edn 1985. *Address:* Holywell Cottage, Oxford. *T:* Oxford 247702; Yellands, Brisworthy, Shaugh Prior, Plympton, Devon. *T:* Shaugh Prior 310.

JONES, Rev. Prof. Hubert C.; *see* Cunliffe-Jones.

JONES, Rev. Hugh; *see* Jones, Rev. R. W. H.

JONES, Sir Hugh; *see* Hugh-Jones, Sir W. N.

JONES, Hugh (Hugo) Jarrett H.; *see* Herbert-Jones.

JONES, Ven. Hughie; *see* Jones, Ven. T. H.

JONES, Hywel Glyn; Chairman, H. G. Jones and Associates, Economic Consultants, since 1985; *b* 1 July 1948; *s* of late Thomas Glyndwr Jones and Anne Dorothy Jones (*née* Williams); *m* 1970, Julia Claire (*née* Davies). *Educ:* Trinity College, Cambridge (Open Scholar, Sen. Scholar, Res. Scholar; MA Hons Econ 1st cl; Wrenbury Scholarship in Political Economy). Lectr in Economics, Univ. of Warwick, 1971–73; Univ. Lectr in Economics of the Firm, Fellow of Linacre Coll., and Lectr, Worcester Coll., Oxford, 1973–77; Henley Centre for Forecasting: Dir of Internat. Forecasting, 1977–81; Dir and Chief Exec., 1981–85. *Publications:* Second Abstract of British Historical Statistics (jtly), 1971; An Introduction to Modern Theories of Economic Growth, 1975, trans Spanish and Japanese; Full Circle into the Future?: Britain into the 21st Century, 1984. *Recreations:* conversation, travel, military history. *Address:* 59 Yarnells Hill, North Hinksey, Oxford OX2 9BE. *T:* Oxford 240916.

JONES, Rt. Rev. Hywel James; *b* 4 March 1918; *s* of Ifor James and Ann Jones; *m* 1946, Dorothy Margaret Wilcox; one *s* one *d. Educ:* Emmanuel Coll., Univ. of Saskatchewan (LTh). Deacon, then priest, 1942; Curate, Tofield, 1942; travelling priest, 1942–44; Incumbent of Parksville–Qualicum Beach, 1944–47; Colwood–Langford, 1947–56; Rector, St Mary the Virgin, Oak Bay, 1956–80. Hon. Canon of BC, 1959–68; Archdeacon of Quatsino, 1968–71, of Victoria, 1971–77; Archdeacon Emeritus, 1977–80; Bishop of British Columbia, 1980–84. *Recreations:* reading, music, gardening. *Address:* 2028 Frederick Norris Road, Victoria, BC V8P 2B2, Canada. *T:* 604–592–7658. *Club:* Union (Victoria, BC).

JONES, Prof. Ian C.; *see* Chester Jones.

JONES, Ian E.; *see* Edwards-Jones.

JONES, Ilston Percival Ll.; *see* Llewellyn Jones.

JONES, Ivor R.; *see* Roberts-Jones.

JONES, Jack L.; *see* Jones, James Larkin.

JONES, Sir James (Duncan), KCB 1972 (CB 1964); *b* 28 Oct. 1914; *m* 1943, Jenefer Mary Wade; one *s. Educ:* Glasgow High Sch.; Glasgow Univ.; University Coll., Oxford. Admiralty, 1941; Ministry of Town and Country Planning: joined 1946; Prin. Priv. Sec., 1947–50; Under-Sec., Min. of Housing and Local Govt, 1958–63; Sec., Local Govt Commn for England, 1958–61; Dep. Sec., Min. of Housing and Local Govt, 1963–66; Dep. Sec., Min. of Transport, 1966–70; Sec., Local Govt and Develt, DoE, 1970–72; Permanent Sec., DoE, 1972–75. Hon. FRIBA; Hon. FRTPI. *Recreations:* cooking, reading, looking at buildings. *Address:* The Courtyard, Ewelme, Oxford OX9 6HP. *T:* Wallingford 39270. *Club:* Oxford Union.

JONES, James Larkin, (Jack), CH 1978; MBE 1950; FCIT 1970; General Secretary, Transport and General Workers' Union, 1969–78; Member, TUC General Council, 1968–78; Chairman, TUC International, Transport and Nationalised Industries Committees, 1972–78; Deputy Chairman, National Ports Council, 1967–79; *b* 29 March 1913; *m* 1938, Evelyn Mary Taylor; two *s. Educ:* elementary sch., Liverpool. Worked in engineering and docks industries, 1927–39. Liverpool City Councillor, 1936–39; served in Spanish Civil War; wounded Ebro battle, Aug. 1938; Coventry District Sec., Transport and General Workers' Union, also District Sec., Confedn of Shipbuilding and Engineering Unions, 1939–55; Midlands Regional Sec., Transport and General Workers' Union, 1955–63, Executive Officer, 1963–69. Mem., Midland Regional Bd for Industry, 1942–46, 1954–63; Chm., Midlands TUC Advisory Cttee, 1948–63. Coventry City Magistrate, 1950–63; Executive Chm., Birmingham Productivity Cttee, 1957–63; Member: Labour Party Nat. Exec. Cttee, 1964–67; Nat. Cttee for Commonwealth Immigrants, 1965–69; Council, Advisory, Conciliation and Arbitration Service, 1974–78; Bd, Crown Agents, 1978–80; Royal Commn on Criminal Procedure, 1978–80. Pres., EFTA Trade Union Council, 1972–73; Founder Mem., European TUC, 1973. Vice-President: ITF, 1974–79; Age Concern, England, 1978–; Pres., Retired Members Assocs, 1979–. Vis. Fellow, Nuffield Coll., Oxford, 1970–78; Associate Fellow, LSE, 1978–82. Dimbleby Lecture, BBC, 1977. Hon. DLitt Warwick, 1978. Freeman, City of London, 1979. Award of Merit, City of Coventry, 1978. *Publications:* (with Max Morris) A-Z of Trade Unionism and Industrial Relations, 1982; A Union Man (autobiog.), 1986. *Recreation:* walking. *Address:* 74 Ruskin Park House, Champion Hill, SE5. *T:* 01–274 7067.

JONES, Jeffrey Richard, CBE 1978; Chief Justice, 1980–85, and President of the Court of Appeal, 1982–85, Kiribati; Puisne Judge of the High Court of the Solomon Islands, 1982–85; Acting Puisne Judge of the Supreme Court of Vanuatu, 1982–85; *b* 18 Nov. 1921; *s* of Rev. Thomas Jones and Winifred (*née* Williams); *m* 1955, Anna Rosaleen Carberry; one *s* one *d. Educ:* Grove Park Sch., Wrexham; Denstone Coll., Staffs; Keble Coll., Oxford, 1940, 1946–49 (MA (Hons) PPE); Middle Temple, 1950–52 (Bar Finals, Council of Legal Educn; called, 1954). Served RAFVR, Flt Lieut (Pilot), 1940–46. Schoolmaster, Mountgrace Comprehensive, Potters Bar, 1953–55; private practice, Zaria, Nigeria, 1955–57; Magistrate, 1957, High Court Judge, 1965, Sen. Puisne Judge, 1970, Northern Nigeria; Chief Justice, Kano State, N Nigeria, 1975, Chief Judge (change of title, decree 41 of 1976), 1976–80. President, Rotary Club, Kano, 1977. Editor, Northern Nigeria Law Reports, 1966–74. *Publications:* Some Cases on Criminal Procedure and Evidence in Northern Nigeria 1968, 1968; Some Cases on Criminal Procedure and Evidence in Northern Nigeria 1969, 1969, 2nd edn combining 1968–69, 1970; Criminal Procedure in the Northern States of Nigeria (annotated), 1975, repr. 1978, 2nd edn 1979. *Recreations:* golf, painting, gardening, bridge, duck shooting, sea fishing. *Address:* Bradley Cottage, Bradley Lane, Holt, near Trowbridge, Wilts. *T:* North Trowbridge 782004.

JONES, Jennifer, (Mrs Norton Simon); film actress (US); *b* Tulsa, Okla; *d* of Philip R. Isley and Flora Mae (*née* Suber); *m* 1st, 1939, Robert Walker (marr. diss. 1945); two *s*; 2nd, 1949, David O. Selznick (*d* 1965); one *d* decd; 3rd, 1971, Norton Simon. *Educ:* schools in Okla and Tex; Northwestern Univ., Evanston, Illinois; American Academy of Dramatic Arts, New York City. Films, since 1943, include: The Song of Bernadette; Since You Went Away; Cluny Brown; Love Letters; Duel in the Sun; We Were Strangers; Madame Bovary; Portrait of Jenny; Carrie; Wild Heart; Ruby Gentry; Indiscretion of an American Wife; Beat the Devil; Love is a Many-Splendoured Thing; The Barretts of Wimpole Street; A Farewell to Arms; Tender is the Night; The Idol; The Towering Inferno. Awards include: American Academy of Motion Pictures, Arts and Sciences Award, 1943; 4 other Academy nominations, etc. Medal for Korean War Work.

JONES, John; *see* Jones, H. J. F.

JONES, (John) Clement, CBE 1972; FRSA 1970; writer, broadcaster, technical adviser to developing countries; *b* 22 June 1915; *o s* of Clement Daniel Jones; *m* 1939, Marjorie, *d* of George Gibson, Llandrindod Wells; three *s. Educ:* Ardwyn, Aberystwyth; BA (Hons) Open Univ., 1983. Various journalistic positions; News Editor, Express and Star, Wolverhampton, 1955; Editor, 1960–71; Editorial Director, 1971–74; Exec. Dir, Beacon Broadcasting, Wolverhampton, 1974–83. Pres., Guild of British Newspaper Editors, 1966–67, Hon. Life Vice-Pres., 1972. Member: Press Council, 1965–74; Adv. Bd, Thomson Foundn, 1965–; BBC W Midlands Adv. Council, 1971–75; (part-time) Monopolies and Mergers Commn (Newspaper Panel), 1973–86; W Midlands Arts Assoc., 1973–78; Exec. Cttee, Soc. Internat. Develt, 1974–78; Vice Chm., Lichfield Dio. Media Council, 1976–82; Mem. Council, and Chm. Press Freedom Cttee, Commonwealth Press Union, 1975–80; Chm., Media Panel, Commn for Racial Equality, 1981–84; Vice-Chm., British Human Rights Trust, 1975–78; Governor, British Inst. Human Rights, 1971–82. Mem. Senate, Open Univ., 1983–86. Founder Mem., Circle of Wine Writers, 1966. Pres., Staffordshire Soc., 1971–74. Founder and Hon. Sec., Frinton and Walton Heritage Trust, 1984–. *Publications:* UNESCO World Survey of Media Councils and Codes of Ethics, 1976; Racism and Fascism, 1981; Race and the Media: thirty years on, 1982; pamphlets on local history, NE Anglia. *Recreations:* travel, gardening, bee keeping. *Address:* 7 South View Drive, Walton on the Naze, Essex CO14 8EP. *T:* Frinton 77087. *Club:* Athenæum.

JONES, John Cyril, CBE 1951; BSc; MICE, FIMechE; *b* 30 Oct. 1899; *s* of John Jones, Swindon, Wilts; *m* 1928, Doris Anne, *d* of A. Tanner, Swindon, Wilts; one *d. Educ:* The College, Swindon; Loughborough Coll., Leics. Design and Research asst, GWR Co., 1922–31; Head of Dept, Loughborough Coll., 1931–34; Principal: St Helen's Municipal Coll., 1934–37, Cardiff Tech. Coll., 1937–41, Royal Tech. Coll., Salford, 1941–44; Dir of Educn, The Polytechnic, Regent Street, W1, 1944–56; Adviser for Tech. Educn to Colonial Office, 1956–61, Dept of Tech. Co-operation, 1961–64, and Min. of Overseas Development, 1964–67. Hon. Sec. Assoc. of Tech. Instns, 1944–56; Hon. Treas. Assoc. of Tech. Instns, 1956–67; Pres., Assoc. of Prins of Tech. Instns, 1951; Mem. Central Advisory Council for Education (Eng.), 1947–56; RAF Educ. Advisory Cttee, 1948–56; Advisory Cttee on Educ. in Colonies, 1953–56; Council for Overseas Colls of Art, Science and Technology, and Council for Tech. Educ. and Training in Overseas Countries, 1949–69. Member: Fulton Commn on Education in Sierra Leone, 1954; Keir Commn on Technical Education in N Rhodesia, 1960. Mem. Council for External Students, University London, 1954–66. Mem. of Council, RSA, 1960–66. Dir Asian Study Tour of Vocational Educ. and Training in the USSR, 1961, 1963; Technical Educn Consultant, World Bank, 1962–83; Mem. International Commn on Tech. Educ. in Sudan, 1966. Officier d'Académie (France), 1950; elected Hon. Mem. City and Guilds of London Inst., 1964. *Publications:* papers on higher technological education and reports on development of technical education in various overseas countries. *Recreations:* books, music, and foreign travel. *Address:* 26 Grand Marine Court, Durley Gardens, Bournemouth BH2 5HS.

JONES, (John) Derek A.; *see* Alun-Jones.

JONES, His Honour (John) Edward; a Circuit Judge (formerly County Court Judge), 1969–84; *b* 23 Dec. 1914; *s* of Thomas Robert Jones, Liverpool; *m* 1945, Katherine Elizabeth Edwards, SRN, *d* of Ezekiel Richard Edwards, Liverpool; one *s* one *d. Educ:* Liverpool Institute High School. ACIS 1939–70; BCom London 1942; LLB London 1945. Called to Bar, Gray's Inn, 1945; Member of Northern Circuit, 1946; Dep. Chm., Lancs QS, 1966–69. Dep. Chm., Workmen's Compensation (Supplementation) and Pneumoconiosis and Byssinosis Benefit Boards, 1968–69; Director: Chatham Building Soc., 1955–59; Welsh Calvinistic Methodist Assurance Trust, 1953–59. Vice President: Merseyside Br., Magistrates' Assoc., 1974–; Liverpool Welsh Choral Union, 1973–; Life Mem., Welsh National Eisteddfod Court. Governor: Aigburth Vale Comprehensive Sch., 1976–85; Calderstones Community Comprehensive Sch., 1985–. Pres., Merseyside Branch, British Red Cross Soc., 1980– (Mem. Nat. Council, 1983–). Welsh Presbyterian Church: Deacon, 1947; Liverpool Presbytery Moderator, 1971. JP Lancs, 1966. *Address:* Law Courts, Derby Square, Liverpool L2 1XA. *Club:* Athenæum (Liverpool).

JONES, John Elfed, CEng, MIEE; Chairman, Welsh Water Authority, since 1982; *b* 19 March 1933; *s* of Urien Maelgwyn Jones and Mary Jones; *m* 1957, Mary Sheila (*née* Rosser); two *d. Educ:* Blaenau Ffestiniog Grammar Sch.; Denbighshire Technical Coll., Wrexham; Heriot Watt Coll., Edinburgh. Student apprentice, 1949–53, graduate trainee, 1953–55, CEGB; National Service, RAF, 1955–57 (FO); Rock Climbing Instr, Outward

Bound Sch., Aberdyfi, 1957; Technical Engr with CEGB, 1957–59; Dep. Project Manager, Rheidol Hydro-Electric Project, 1959–61; Sen. Elec. Engr, Trawsfynydd Nuclear Power Station, 1961–63; Deputy Manager: Mid Wales Gp of Power Stations, 1963–67; Connah's Quay Power Station, 1967–69; Anglesey Aluminium Metal Ltd: Engrg Manager, 1969–73; Production Manager, 1973–76; Admin Director, 1976–77; Dep. Man. Dir, 1977–79; Industrial Dir, Welsh Office (Under Sec. rank), 1979–82. Chm., British Water International Ltd, 1983–. Treasurer, Urdd Gobaith Cymru, 1964–67; Mem., Royal National Eisteddfod of Wales, 1981–; Member: BBC Broadcasting Council for Wales, 1979–83; Council, Food from Britain, 1985–. Member: Court and Council: UCNW, Bangor, 1978–; Nat. Lib. of Wales, 1983–; Coleg Harlech, 1983–; Court, Univ. Coll., Aberystwyth, 1984–. Mem., Civic Trust for Wales, 1982–. FRSA 1984. Hon. Col, Commonwealth of Kentucky, 1976. *Recreations:* fishing for salmon and trout, reading, attending Eisteddfodau. *Address:* Ty Mawr, Coity, Bridgend, Mid Glamorgan.

JONES, (John) Emrys, CBE 1979; Regional Organiser and Secretary, Labour Party, Wales, 1965–79, retired; *b* 12 March 1914; *s* of William Jones and Elizabeth Susan Jones; *m* 1935, Stella Davies; one *d. Educ:* Secondary Sch., Mountain Ash, S Wales. Shop assistant, 1928–29; railwayman, 1929–33; Rootes motor factory, 1933–36; railwayman, 1936–49. Regional Organiser, Labour Party: S West, 1949–60; W Midlands, 1960–65. *Recreations:* reading and writing. *Address:* 11 Ael y Bryn, Energlyn, Caerphilly, Mid Glam CF8 2QX. *T:* Caerphilly 882848.

JONES, Air Vice-Marshal John Ernest A.; *see* Allen-Jones.

JONES, John Ernest P.; *see* Powell-Jones.

JONES, John Eryl O.; *see* Owen-Jones.

JONES, (John) Geoffrey; His Honour Judge Geoffrey Jones; a Circuit Judge since 1975; *b* 14 Sept. 1928; *s* of Wyndham and Lilias Jones; *m* 1954, Sheila (*née* Gregory); three *s. Educ:* Brighton and Hove Grammar Sch.; St Michael's Sch., Llanelli; St David's Coll., Lampeter; University Coll., London. LLB London 1955; LLM London 1985. Army service, 1946–48, commnd into RASC, 1947. Electrical wholesale business, 1948–52. Called to Bar, Gray's Inn, 1956; practised Leicester, 1958–70 and London, 1970–75. *Recreation:* golf. *Address:* c/o The County Court, Lower Hill Street, Leicester LE1 3SJ.

JONES, Sir John H.; *see* Hamilton-Jones.

JONES, Sir John Henry H.; *see* Harvey-Jones.

JONES, John Hubert E.; *see* Emlyn Jones.

JONES, Air Marshal Sir John Humphrey E.; *see* Edwardes Jones.

JONES, John Iorwerth, CBE 1977; retired; Lord Mayor of Cardiff, 1976–77; Member, Cardiff City Council, 1958–83; *b* 22 Oct. 1901; *s* of David Nicholls Jones and Minnie Jones (*née* Rees); single. *Educ:* Carmarthen (public and private). Apprenticed Electrical Engineering, 1918–23. Chm., Cardiff Trades Council, 1960–67. Elected to Cardiff City Council, 1958; on reorganisation elected to new City Council and also to South Glamorgan County Council, May 1974; Dep. Lord Mayor, 1974–75; re-elected to City Council, 1976; re-elected to County Council, 1977. Chm., Cardiff Searchlight Tattoo Cttee, 1979–80 and 1980–82. Governor: WNO, to 1983; Nat. Museum of Wales, to 1983. *Recreations:* Rugby fan; interested in opera, music. *Address:* 11 Anderson Place, Cardiff. *T:* Cardiff 494195. *Club:* Cardiff Athletic (Cardiff).

JONES, Sir (John) Kenneth (Trevor), Kt 1965; CBE 1956; QC 1976; Legal Adviser to the Home Office, 1956–77; *b* 11 July 1910; *s* of John Jones and Agnes Morgan; *m* 1940, Menna, *d* of Cyril O. Jones; two *s. Educ:* King Henry VIII Grammar Sch., Abergavenny; University Coll. of Wales, Aberystwyth; St John's Coll., Cambridge. Called to the Bar, Lincoln's Inn, 1937. Served Royal Artillery, 1939–45. Entered the Home Office as a Legal Asst, 1945. Mem. of the Standing Cttee on Criminal Law Revision, 1959–80. *Address:* 54 Westminster Gardens, SW1. *T:* 01–834 4950. *Club:* Athenæum.

JONES, John Knighton C.; *see* Chadwick-Jones.

JONES, Sir John (Lewis), KCB 1983; CMG 1972; *b* 17 Feb. 1923; *m* 1948, Daphne Nora (*née* Redman). *Educ:* Christ's College, Cambridge (MA). Royal Artillery, 1942–46; Sudan Government, 1947–55; Ministry of Defence, 1955–85. *Recreation:* golf. *Club:* United Oxford & Cambridge University.

JONES, Air Vice-Marshal John Maurice, CB 1986; QHDS 1983; Director of Royal Air Force Dental Services, since 1982, and Director of Defence Dental Services, Ministry of Defence, since 1985; *b* 27 Jan. 1931; *s* of E. Morris Jones and Gladys Jones (*née* Foulkes); *m* 1962, Joan (*née* McCallum); one *s* one *d. Educ:* Liverpool Institute High Sch.; Univ. of Liverpool (BDS); LDSRCS. FBIM. Hospital appt, Liverpool Dental Hosp., 1954; RAF Dental Branch: appts UK and abroad, incl. Christmas Island, Malta, Cyprus and Fontainebleau, 1955–73; Dep. Director of RAF Dental Services, 1973; OC RAF Inst. of Dental Health and Training, 1976; Principal Dental Officer: HQ RAF Germany, 1979; HQ RAF Support Command, 1982. SBStJ 1978. *Publications:* contribs to British Dental Jl. *Recreations:* tennis, shooting, fishing, skiing. *Address:* Wyckenhurst, St Michael's Close, Halton Village, Wendover, Bucks HP22 5NW. *T:* Wendover 624184. *Club:* Royal Air Force.

JONES, John Morgan, CB 1964; CBE 1946; Secretary Welsh Department, Ministry of Agriculture, 1944–68; *b* 20 July 1903; *s* of late Richard and Mary Ellen Jones, Pertheirin, Caersws, Montgomeryshire; *m* 1933, Dorothy Morris, *yr d* of late David Morris, and Margaret Anne Wigley, Llanbrynmair, Montgomeryshire; no *c. Educ:* Newtown County Sch.; University Coll. of Wales, Aberystwyth. BA 1922; Hons in Econ. 1923, History 1924; MA 1926. Research Staff Dept of Agric. Economics, University Coll. of Wales, 1924–30; Marketing Officer, Min. of Agric. and Fisheries, 1930–35; Registrar Univ. Coll. of Wales, Aberystwyth, 1936; seconded to Min. of Agric. as Minister's Liaison Officer for mid- and south-west Wales, 1940; Chm. Cardigan War Agric. Exec. Cttee, 1943. Sec./Treas. Aberystwyth and Dist Old People's Housing Soc. Ltd, 1972–76. Life Governor, UCW (Mem. Council, 1950–77). Hon. LLD Wales, 1973. *Publications:* Economeg Amaethyddiaeth, 1930; articles on rural economics, mainly in Welsh Journal of Agriculture. *Address:* Maesnewydd, North Road, Aberystwyth. *T:* Aberystwyth 612507.

JONES, Brig. John Murray R.; *see* Rymer-Jones.

JONES, Sir John Prichard; *see* Prichard-Jones.

JONES, Rev. Prebendary John Stephen Langton; Residentiary Canon and Precentor of Wells Cathedral, 1947–67, Prebendary, since 1967; *b* 21 May 1889; *m* 1921, Jeanne Charlotte Dujardin; three *s* one *d. Educ:* Dover College; Jesus College, Cambridge. Asst Curate of Halifax Parish Church, 1914; Asst Curate, Hambleden, Berks, 1919; Vicar of Yiewsley, Middx, 1921; Rector of W Lydford, Taunton, 1939–47. Proctor in Convocation for Bath and Wells, 1946–50. *Address:* 25 Irnham Road, Minehead, Somerset.

JONES, Prof. Kathleen; Professor of Social Administration, University of York, since 1965; *b* 7 April 1922; *d* of William Robert Savage and Kate Lilian Barnard; *m* 1944, Rev. David Gwyn Jones (*d* 1976); one *s. Educ:* North London Collegiate Sch.; Westfield Coll., Univ. of London (BA, PhD). Research Asst in Social Administration, Univ. of Manchester, 1951–53, Asst Lectr 1953–55, Sen. History Teacher, Victoria Instn, Kuala Lumpur, 1956–58, also Asst Lectr in History, Univ. of Malaya (part-time); Lectr in Social Administration, Univ. of Manchester, 1958–62, Sen. Lectr 1962–65. Chm., Social Scis Cttee, UK Commn for UNESCO, 1966–69. Mem., Gen. Synod of C of E, 1975–80; Member: Archbishop's Commn on Church and State, 1966–71; Lord Gardiner's Ctte on NI, 1974–75; Archbishop's Commn on Marriage, 1976–78; Mental Health Act Commn, 1983– (NE Chm., 1983–85). Pres., Assoc. of Psychiatric Social Workers, 1968–70; Chm., Social Admin Assoc., 1980–83. Hon. FRCPsych, 1976. *Publications:* Lunacy, Law and Conscience, 1955; Mental Health and Social Policy, 1960; Mental Hospitals at Work, 1962; The Compassionate Society, 1965; The Teaching of Social Studies in British Universities, 1965; A History of the Mental Health Services, 1972; Opening the Door: a study of new policies for the mentally handicapped, 1975; Issues in Social Policy, 1978; Ideas on Institutions, 1984; Eileen Younghusband: a biography, 1985; (ed) Year Book of Social Policy in Britain, 1971–76; (ed) Living the Faith: a call to the Church, 1980; (series editor) International Library of Social Policy, 1968–85. *Address:* Woodland View, Barton-le-Willows, York YO6 7PD. *T:* Whitwell-on-the-Hill 526. *Club:* University Women's.

JONES, Keith H.; *see* Hamylton Jones.

JONES, Sir Keith (Stephen), Kt 1980; FRCSE; FRACS; *b* 7 July 1911; *s* of Stephen William and Muriel Elsy Jones; *m* 1936, Kathleen Mary Abbott; three *s. Educ:* Newington Coll.; Univ. of Sydney (MB, BS). General practitioner, Army MO, Surgeon; President, Aust. Medical Assoc., 1973–76; Chief MO, NSW State Emergency Service, 1966–74; Mem., NSW Medical Bd, 1971–81. Mem., Newington Coll. Council, 1951–72; Mem., Nat. Specialist Recognition Appeals Cttee, 1970–83 (Chm., 1980–83; Chm., Nat. Spec. Qualifications Cttee, 1980–83). Chairman: Australasian Medical Publishing Co., 1976–82; Manly Art Gall., 1982–85; President: Medical Benefits Fund of Aust., 1983–85; Blue Cross Assoc. of Aust., 1983–85. Acting Editor, Medical Jl of Aust., 1981. Hon. FRACGP 1975. Gold Medal, AMA, 1976. *Recreation:* swimming. *Address:* 123 Bayview Garden Village, Cabbage Tree Road, Bayview, NSW 2104, Australia. *T:* 997 2876. *Club:* Union (Sydney).

JONES, Sir Kenneth; *see* Jones, Sir J. K. T.

JONES, Hon. Sir Kenneth (George Illtyd), Kt 1974; **Hon. Mr Justice Kenneth Jones;** a Judge of the High Court, Queen's Bench Division, since 1974; *b* 26 May 1921; *s* of late Richard Arthur Jones and Olive Jane Jones, Radyr, Cardiff; *m* 1st, 1947, Dulcie (*d* 1977); one *s* two *d*; 2nd, 1978, June Patricia (prev. marr. diss.), *o d* of late Leslie Arthur and Winifred Doxey, Harrogate. *Educ:* Brigg Gram. Sch.; University Coll., Oxford (1939–41, 1945–46), MA; Treas., Oxford Union Society, 1941; served in Shropshire Yeo. (76th Medium Regt RA), 1942–45; Staff Captain, HQ 13th Corps, 1945 (despatches). Called to Bar, Gray's Inn, 1946; joined Oxford Circuit, 1947; QC 1962; Mem. Gen. Council of the Bar, 1961–65, 1968–69; Bencher, Gray's Inn, 1969–. Recorder of: Shrewsbury, 1964–66; Wolverhampton, 1966–71; the Crown Court, 1972; Dep. Chm., Herefordshire QS, 1961–71; a Circuit Judge, 1972–73. Dep. Chm., Boundary Commn for Wales, 1984–. *Recreations:* theatre, opera, travel, fishing. *Address:* Royal Courts of Justice, Strand, WC2A 2LL.

JONES, Air Vice-Marshal Laurence Alfred, CB 1984; AFC 1971; Assistant Chief of Air Staff, since 1986; *b* 18 Jan. 1933; *s* of Benjamin Howel and Irene Dorothy Jones; *m* 1956, Brenda Ann; two *d. Educ:* Trinity Sch., Croydon; RAF College, Cranwell. Entry to RAF Coll., 1951, graduated 1953; served as Jun. Officer Pilot with 208 Sqdn in Middle East, 1954–57; Fighter Weapons Sch., 74 Sqdn, until 1961; commanded: No 8 Sqdn, Aden, 1961–63; No 19 Sqdn, RAF Germany, 1967–70; Station Comdr, RAF Wittering, 1975–76; RCDS 1977; Director of Operations (Air Support), MoD, 1978–81; SASO, Strike Command, 1982–84; ACAS(Ops), MoD, 1984; ACDS(Progs), 1985–86. *Recreations:* golf, skiing. *Address:* Ministry of Defence, Main Building, Whitehall, SW1A 2HB. *Club:* Royal Air Force.

JONES, Maj.-Gen. Leonard Hamilton H.; *see* Howard-Jones.

JONES, Leslie, MA; JP; Secretary for Welsh Education, Welsh Office and Department of Education and Science, 1970–77; *b* Tumble, Carms, 27 April 1917; *y s* of late William Jones, ME and Joanna (*née* Peregrine); *m* 1948, Glenys, *d* of late D. R. Davies, Swansea; one *s* one *d. Educ:* Gwendraeth Valley Grammar Sch.; Univ. of Wales. Served with RN, 1940–46 (Lieut RNVR). UC Swansea, 1937–40 and 1946–47 (1st cl. hons Econs); Lectr in Econs, Univ. of Liverpool, 1947–51; Lectr and Sen. Lectr in Econs, UC Cardiff, 1952–65; Dir, Dept of Extra-Mural Studies, UC Cardiff, 1965–69. Hon. Lectr, Dept of Educn, UC Cardiff, 1977–. Member: Ancient Monuments Bd for Wales, 1970–77; Court, UWIST, 1978–; Council, St David's University Coll., 1978–; Court, Univ. of Wales, 1979–; Court, Nat. Library of Wales, 1978–; Court, Nat. Mus. of Wales, 1978–; Council, Dr Barnardo's, 1978–. Hon. Fellow, UC Cardiff, 1971. JP Cardiff 1966. *Publications:* The British Shipbuilding Industry, 1958; articles on maritime, coal, iron and steel industries; industrial economics generally. *Recreations:* walking, gardening. *Address:* 43 Cyncoed Road, Cardiff. *Club:* Naval.

JONES, Lewis C.; *see* Carter-Jones.

JONES, Lilian Pauline N.; *see* Neville-Jones.

JONES, Maude Elizabeth, CBE 1973; Deputy Director-General, British Red Cross Society, 1970–77; *b* 14 Jan. 1921; 2nd *d* of late E. W. Jones, Dolben, Ruthin, North Wales. *Educ:* Brynhyfryd Sch. for Girls, Ruthin. Joined Foreign Relations Dept, Jt War Organisation BRCS and OStJ, 1940; Dep. Dir, Jun. Red Cross, BRCS, 1949; Dir, Jun. Red Cross, 1960; Dep. Dir-Gen. for Branch Affairs, BRCS, 1966. Member: Jt Cttee (and Finance and Gen. Purposes Sub-Cttee) OStJ and BRCS, 1966–77; Council of Nat. Council of Social Service; Council of FANY, 1966–77. Governor, St David's Sch., Ashford, Mddx. SSStJ 1959. *Recreations:* music, gardening, reading. *Address:* Dolben, Ruthin, Clwyd, North Wales. *T:* Ruthin 2443. *Club:* New Cavendish.

JONES, Mervyn; *see* Jones, Thomas Mervyn.

JONES, Mervyn; author; *b* 27 Feb. 1922; *s* of Ernest Jones and Katharine (*née* Jokl); *m* 1948, Jeanne Urquhart; one *s* two *d. Educ:* Abbotsholme School; New York University. Assistant Editor: Tribune, 1955–59; New Statesman, 1966–68; Drama Critic, Tribune, 1959–67. *Publications:* No Time to be Young, 1952; The New Town, 1953; The Last Barricade, 1953; Helen Blake, 1955; On the Last Day, 1958; Potbank, 1961; Big Two, 1962; A Set of Wives, 1965; Two Ears of Corn, 1965; John and Mary, 1966; A Survivor, 1968; Joseph, 1970; Mr Armitage Isn't Back Yet, 1971; Life on the Dole, 1972; Holding

On, 1973; The Revolving Door, 1973; Strangers, 1974; Lord Richard's Passion, 1974; The Pursuit of Happiness, 1975; Scenes from Bourgeois Life, 1976; Nobody's Fault, 1977; Today The Struggle, 1978; The Beautiful Words, 1979; A Short Time to Live, 1980; Two Women and their Man, 1982; Joanna's Luck, 1985; Coming Home, 1986; Chances, 1986. *Address:* 10 Waterside Place, NW1. *T:* 01–586 4404.

JONES, Hon. Mrs Miller; *see* Askwith, Hon. B. E.

JONES, Dr Nevin Campbell H.; *see* Hughes Jones.

JONES, Nigel John I.; *see* Inglis-Jones.

JONES, Ven. Noël Debroy, CB 1986; QHC 1983; Chaplain of the Fleet and Archdeacon for the Royal Navy, since 1984; *b* 25 Dec. 1932; *s* of Brinley and Gwendoline Jones; *m* 1969, Joyce Barbara Leelavathy Arulanandam; one *s* one *d. Educ:* Haberdashers' West Monmouth Sch.; St David's Coll., Lampeter (BA); Wells Theological Coll. Diocese of Monmouth, 1955–59; Vicar of Kano, N Nigeria, 1960–62; Chaplain, RN, 1962; GSM Brunei 1962, Borneo 1963; RM Commando Course prior to service in Aden with 42 Cdo, 1967; GSM S Arabia, 1967; Mid Service Clergy Course at St George's House, Windsor Castle, 1974; Staff Chaplain, MoD, 1974–77. *Recreations:* squash, swimming, music, family; formerly Rugby. *Address:* Flat 1, 111 Belgrave Road, SW1. *Club:* Sion College.

JONES, Norman Henry; QC 1985; *b* 12 Dec. 1941; *s* of Henry Robert Jones and Charlotte Isobel Scott Jones; *m* 1970, Trudy Helen Chamberlain; two *s* one *d. Educ:* Bideford Grammar School; North Devon Tech. Coll.; Univ. of Leeds (LLB, LLM). Called to the Bar, Middle Temple, 1968. Contested Leeds NW (SDP), 1983; Mem., Nat. Cttee, SDP, 1982–84. *Recreations:* boating, SDP politics. *Address:* Danehurst, Greenfield Lane, Guiseley, Leeds LS20 8HF. *T:* Guiseley 78192. *Clubs:* Airedale Boat; Bradford Golf.

JONES, Norman Stewart C.; *see* Carey Jones.

JONES, Norman William, CBE 1984; TD 1962; FIB; Director since 1976, and a Deputy Chairman, since 1984, Lloyds Bank plc; *b* 5 Nov. 1923; *s* of late James William Jones and Mabel Jones; *m* 1950, Evelyn June Hall; two *s. Educ:* Gravesend Grammar Sch. FIB 1972. Served War, Army, 1942–47: commnd Beds and Herts Regt, 1943; with Airborne Forces, 1944–47; TA, 1947–64. Entered Lloyds Bank, 1940; Gen. Man., 1973; Asst Chief Gen. Man., 1975; Dep. Group Chief Exec., 1976; Gp Chief Exec., 1978–83. Director: Lloyds Bank California, 1974–83; National Bank of New Zealand, 1978–; Lloyds Bank International, 1984–85; Lloyds Bank NZA Ltd, 1985–; Lloyds Merchant Bank Hldgs, 1985–. Chm., Aust. and NZ Trade Adv. Cttee, 1985–. FRSA. *Recreations:* sailing, photography, DIY. *Address:* Rowans, 21 College Avenue, Grays, Essex. *T:* Grays Thurrock 73101. *Club:* Overseas Bankers.

JONES, Norvela, (Mrs Michael Jones); *see* Forster, N.

JONES, Sir (Owen) Trevor, Kt 1981; Councillor, Liverpool Metropolitan District Council; *b* 1927; *s* of Owen and Ada Jones, Dyserth. Mem., Liverpool City Council, 1968, Liverpool Metropolitan District Council, 1973– (Leader, 1981–83). Pres., Liberal Party, 1972–73; contested (L): Liverpool, Toxteth, Feb. 1974 and Gillingham, Oct. 1974. *Address:* 221 Queen's Drive, Liverpool L15 6YE; Town Hall, Liverpool L2 3SW.

JONES, Penry; Chief Assistant (Television) (formerly Deputy Head of Programme Services), IBA (formerly ITA), 1971–82, retired; *b* 18 Aug. 1922; *s* of Joseph William and Edith Jones; *m* Beryl Joan Priestley; two *d. Educ:* Rock Ferry High Sch.; Liverpool Univ. Gen. Sec., YMCA, Altrincham, 1940; Sec., SCM, Southern Univs, 1945; Industrial Sec., Iona Community, 1948; Religious Programmes Producer, ABC Television, 1958; Religious Programmes Officer of ITA, 1964; Head of Religious Broadcasting, BBC, 1967. *Recreations:* hill-walking, swimming, watching Rugby football. *Address:* Erraid House, Isle of Iona, Argyll PA76 6SJ. *T:* Iona 448. *Club:* Reform.

JONES, Brig. Percival de Courcy, OBE 1953; Chief Secretary, The Royal Life Saving Society, 1965–75; *b* 9 Oct. 1913; *s* of P. de C. Jones, Barnsley; *m* 1st, 1947, Anne Hollins (marr. diss., 1951); one *s;* 2nd, 1962, Elaine Garnett. *Educ:* Oundle; RMC, Sandhurst. Commissioned KSLI 1933; Staff Coll., 1942; comd 1st Northamptons, Burma, 1945; Staff Coll. Instructor, 1949–50; AA & QMG, 11th Armoured Div., 1951–53; comd 1st KSLI, 1953–55; AQMG, War Office, 1955–58; NATO Defence Coll., 1958–59; Bde Comdr, 1959–62; retd 1962. Mem., Aylesbury Vale DC, 1976–79. Commonwealth Chief Sec., RLSS, 1965–72. Silver Medallion, Fedn Internat. de Sauvetage, 1976. *Recreation:* gardening. *Address:* c/o Midland Bank, 33 High Street, Shrewsbury.

JONES, Peter Benjamin Gurner; Under Secretary; Director of Personnel, Board of Inland Revenue, since 1984; *b* 25 Dec. 1932; *s* of Gurner Prince Jones and Irene Louise Jones (*née* Myall); *m* 1962, Diana Margaret Henly; one *s* one *d. Educ:* Bancroft's Sch.; St Catherine's Society, Oxford (BA (Hons) English Language and Literature). Inspector of Taxes, 1957; Inspector (Higher Grade), 1963; Sen. Inspector, 1969; Principal Inspector, 1975; Sen. Principal Inspector, 1980; Dir of Data Processing, Bd of Inland Revenue, 1981–84. *Recreations:* Rugby, books, canal cruising. *Address:* 106 Vale Road, Ash Vale, Aldershot, Hants GU12 5HS. *Clubs:* Hampshire Rugby Union, Swanage and Wareham RFC.

JONES, Peter Derek; Secretary: Council of Civil Service Unions, since 1980; Civil Service National Whitley Council (Trade Union Side), since 1963; *b* 21 May 1932; *s* of Richard Morgan Jones and Phyllis Irene (*née* Lloyd); *m* 1962, Noreen Elizabeth (*née* Kemp). *Educ:* Wembley County Grammar School. National Service and TA, Green Jackets/Parachute Regt, 1950–56; Civil Service, Nat. Assistance Bd, 1952–59; Asst Sec., Civil Service Nat. Whitley Council, 1959–63. Vice Chm., Civil Service Housing Assoc. Ltd, 1981– (Dir, 1963–81); Dir, Civil Service Building Soc., 1963–. Vice-Chm., RIPA, 1986– (Mem. Exec. Council, 1981–85); Mem., Adv. Council, Civil Service Coll., 1982–. Editor: Whitley Bulletin, 1963–83; CCSU Bulletin, 1984–. *Publications:* articles in RIPA and personnel management jls. *Recreations:* relaxing, reading. *Address:* Highlands Farm, Cross in Hand, East Sussex TN21 0SX. *T:* Heathfield 3577. *Clubs:* Wig and Pen, Belfry; Middlesex CCC.

JONES, Peter Eldon, FRIBA, FRTPI, FSIAD, FRSA; Director: Watkins Gray Peter Jones Ltd, architects, planning consultants and building managers, since 1986; Interior Transformation Ltd, since 1985; Lecturer (part-time) in Architectural Design, Kingston Polytechnic, since 1986; *b* 11 Oct. 1927; *s* of Wilfrid Eldon Jones and Jessie Meikle (*née* Buchanan); *m* 1st, 1954, Gisela Marie von Arnswaldt; two *s* one *d;* 2nd, 1985, Claudia Milner-Brown (*née* Laurence). *Educ:* Surbiton County Grammar Sch.; Kingston Polytechnic; University College London. DipTP. Private practice, 1950–54; joined LCC Architects Dept, 1954; Dep. Schools Architect, LCC, 1960–65; Town Development Architect/Planner, 1965–71; Technical Policy Architect, GLC, 1971–74; Education Architect, ILEA, 1974–82; Acting Director of Architecture, 1980–82, Dir of Architecture and Superintending Architect of Metrop. Bldgs, 1982–86, GLC. Pres., Soc. of Chief Architects of Local Authorities, 1984–85; Mem. Council, Chm. Membership Cttee, and

Vice-Pres., RIBA, 1985–. *Publications:* articles and papers on town development, educn building, housing design and planning. *Recreations:* building, photography, travel. *Address:* Pitmore Farm House, Holly Lane, Worplesdon, Surrey GU3 3PB. *T:* Worplesdon 234 367. *Club:* Arts.

JONES, Peter Ferry, MA, MChir, FRCS, FRCSE; Surgeon to the Queen in Scotland, 1977–85; Honorary Consulting Surgeon, Woodend Hospital and Royal Aberdeen Children's Hospital, Aberdeen (Consultant Surgeon, 1958–86); Clinical Professor of Surgery, University of Aberdeen, 1983–86, now Emeritus; *b* 29 Feb. 1920; *s* of Ernest and Winifred Jones; *m* 1950, Margaret Thomson; two *s* two *d. Educ:* Emmanuel Coll., Cambridge (MA); St Bartholomew's Hosp. Med. Sch., London (MB, MChir). FRCS 1948; FRCSE 1964. Served War, RAMC, 1944–46, Captain. House Surgeon, St Bartholomew's Hosp., 1943; Surg. Registrar, N Middlesex Hosp., 1948–51; Surg. Tutor, St Bartholomew's Hosp., 1951–53; Sen. Surg. Registrar, Central Middlesex Hosp. and the Middlesex Hosp., London, 1953–57; Reader in Surg. Paediatrics, Univ. of Aberdeen, 1965–83. *Publications:* Abdominal Access and Exposure (with H. A. F. Dudley), 1965; Emergency Abdominal Surgery in Infancy, Childhood and Adult Life, 1974, 2nd edn 1987; (jtly) Integrated Clinical Science: Gastroenterology, 1984; A Colour Atlas of Colo-Rectal Surgery, 1985; papers on paediatric and gen. surgery in Brit. Jl of Surg., BMJ, Lancet, etc. *Recreation:* hill walking. *Address:* 7 Park Road, Cults, Aberdeen AB1 9HR. *T:* Aberdeen 867702.

JONES, Peter George Edward Fitzgerald, CB 1985; Director, Atomic Weapons Research Establishment, since 1982; *b* 7 June 1925; *s* of John Christopher Jones and Isobel (*née* Howell); *m* 1st; two *s;* 2nd, Jacqueline Angela (*née* Gilbert); two *s* one *d. Educ:* various schs; Dulwich Coll.; London Univ. (BSc (Special) Physics 1st Cl. Hons 1951). FInstP. Served RAF, flying duties, 1943–47. GEC Res. Labs, 1951–54; AWRE and Pacific Test Site, 1955–63; Asst Dir of Res., London Communications Security, 1963; Atomic Weapons Research Establishment: Supt, Electronics Res., 1964; Head, Electronics Div., 1966; Head, Special Projs, 1971; Chief, Warhead Develt, 1974; Principal Dep. Dir, 1980. *Recreations:* flying, motoring. *Address:* 38 Oakley Lane, Basingstoke, Hants RG23 7JY. *T:* Basingstoke 780706.

JONES, Peter Llewellyn G.; *see* Gwynn-Jones.

JONES, Peter Trevor S.; *see* Simpson-Jones.

JONES, Sir Philip; *see* Jones, Sir T. P.

JONES, Philip Graham, CEng, FIChemE, FIExpE; Deputy Director of Technology and Air Pollution Division, Health and Safety Executive, since 1986; *b* 3 June 1937; *s* of Sidney and Olive Jones; *m* 1961, Janet Ann Collins; one *s* three *d. Educ:* Univ. of Aston in Birmingham (BSc). Professional position in UK explosives industry, 1961–68 and 1972–76; service with Australian Public Service, 1969–71, with UK Civil Service, 1976–; HM Chief Inspector of Explosives, HSE, 1981–86. *Publications:* articles in The Chemical Engineer and Explosives Engineer. *Recreations:* bridge, reading, curling. *Address:* HSE Technology and Air Pollution Division, St Anne's House, University Road, Bootle, Merseyside L20 3MF. *T:* 051–951 4695.

JONES, Philip James, DPhil; FBA 1984; FRHistS; Fellow and Tutor, Modern History, since 1963, Librarian, since 1965, Brasenose College, Oxford; *b* 19 Nov. 1921; *s* of John David Jones and Caroline Susan Jones (*née* Davies); *m* 1954, Carla Susini; one *s* one *d. Educ:* St Dunstan's College; Wadham College, Oxford (1st class Hons Mod. Hist. 1945, MA, DPhil). Senior Demy, Magdalen College, Oxford, 1945–49; Amy Mary Preston Road Scholar, 1946; Bryce Research Student, 1947; Asst in History, Glasgow Univ., 1949–50; Leeds University: Lectr in Med. Hist., 1950–61; Reader in Med. Hist., 1961–63; Eileen Power Meml Student, 1956–57. Corresp. Mem., Deputazione Toscana di Storia Patria, 1975–. *Publications:* The Malatesta of Rimini, 1974; Economia e Societa nell'Italia medievale, 1980; contribs to: Cambridge Economic History, Vol. 1, 2nd edn, 1966; Storia d'Italia, vol. 2, 1974; Storia d'Italia, Annali, Vol. 1, 1978; articles and reviews in hist. jls. *Address:* 167 Woodstock Road, Oxford OX2 7NA. *T:* Oxford 57953.

JONES, Philip (Mark), CBE 1986 (OBE 1977); Head of Wind and Percussion Department, Guildhall School of Music and Drama, City of London, since 1983; *b* 12 March 1928; *m* 1956, Ursula Strebi. *Educ:* Royal College of Music (FRCM 1983 (ARCM 1947)). Principal Trumpet with all major orchestras in London, 1949–72; Founder and Dir, 1951–86, Philip Jones Brass Ensemble; Head of Dept of Wind and Percussion, Royal Northern Coll. of Music, Manchester, 1975–77. Member: Arts Council of GB, 1984–; Royal Soc. of Musicians of GB. Over 50 gramophone records. Grand Prix du Disque, 1977; Composers Guild Award, 1979. FRNCM; FGSM 1984. FRSA. *Publications:* Joint Editor, Just Brass series (for Chester Music London). *Recreations:* history, ski-ing, mountain walking. *Address:* 14 Hamilton Terrace, NW8 9UG. *T:* 01–286 9155.

JONES, Mrs Rachel (Marianne); *b* 4 Aug. 1908; *d* of John Powell Jones Powell, solicitor, Brecon, and Kathleen Mamie Powell; *m* 1935, Very Rev. William Edward Jones (*d* 1974); one *s* three *d. Educ:* Princess Helena Coll.; Bedford Coll., University of London. Subwarden, Time and Talents Settlement, Bermondsey, 1931–32; Member: Bd of Governors, Fairbridge Farm Sch., Western Australia, 1945–49; Council for Wales and Mon, 1959–66; Nat. Governor for Wales of BBC and Chm. of Broadcasting Council for Wales, 1960–65. Member: Governing Body of the Church in Wales, 1953–78; Court and Council of Nat. Museum of Wales, 1962–78; St Fagan's Welsh Folk Museum Cttee, 1978–83; Pres., St David's Diocesan Mothers' Union, 1965–70. *Recreations:* music, gardening. *Address:* 59 Sopwell Lane, St Albans, Herts AL1 1RN. *T:* St Albans 69810.

JONES, Raymond Edgar; HM Diplomatic Service, retired; *b* 6 June 1919; *s* of Edgar George Jones, Portsmouth; *m* 1942, Joan Mildred Clark; one *s* two *d. Educ:* Portsmouth Northern Grammar Sch. Entered Admiralty service as Clerical Officer, 1936; joined RAF, 1941; commissioned, 1943; returned to Admty as Exec. Officer, 1946; transf. to Foreign Service, 1948; Singapore, 1949; Second Sec., Rome, 1950; Bahrain, 1952; Rio de Janeiro, 1955; Consul, Philadelphia, 1958; FO, 1961; First Sec., Copenhagen, 1963; Consul, Milan, 1965; Toronto (Dir of British Week), 1966; Dep. High Comr, Adelaide, 1967–71; FCO, 1971–76; Consul-Gen., Genoa, 1976–79. *Recreations:* music, gardening. *Address:* Green Shadows, 61 Tupwood Lane, Caterham, Surrey.

JONES, Reginald Ernest, MBE 1942; Chief Scientific Officer, Ministry of Technology, 1965–69, retired; *b* 16 Jan. 1904; *m* 1933, Edith Ernestine Kressig; one *s* one *d. Educ:* Marylebone Gram. Sch.; Imperial Coll. of Science and Technology. MSc, DIC, FIEE. International Standard Electric Corp., 1926–33; GPO, 1933–65 (Asst Engr-in-Chief, 1957). Bronze Star (US), 1943. *Recreations:* music, gardening, walking. *Address:* 22 Links Road, Epsom, Surrey. *T:* Epsom 23625.

JONES, Reginald Victor, CB 1946; CBE 1942; FRS 1965; Professor of Natural Philosophy, University of Aberdeen, 1946–81, now Emeritus; *b* 29 Sept. 1911; *s* of Harold Victor and Alice Margaret Jones; *m* 1940, Vera, *d* of late Charles and Amelia Cain; one *s* two *d. Educ:* Alleyn's; Wadham Coll., Oxford (Exhibitioner; MA, DPhil,

1934; Hon. Fellow, 1968); Balliol Coll., Oxford (Skynner Senior Student in Astronomy, 1934–36; Hon. Fellow 1981). Air Ministry: Scientific Officer, 1936 (seconded to Admiralty, 1938–39); Air Staff, 1939; Asst Dir of Intelligence, 1941, Dir, 1946; Dir of Scientific Intelligence, MoD, 1952–53; Mem., Carriers Panel, 1962–63; Chm., Air Defence Working Party, 1963–64; Scientific Adv. Council, War Office, 1963–66. Chairman: Infra-Red Cttee, Mins of Supply and Aviation, 1950–64; British Transport Commn Res. Adv. Council, 1954–55; Safety in Mines Res. Advisory Bd, 1956–60 (Mem., 1950–56); Electronics Res. Council, Mins of Aviation and Technol., 1964–70. Royal Society: Chm., Paul Fund Cttee, 1962–84; a Vice-Pres., 1971–72; Chairman: Inst. of Physics Cttee on Univ. Physics, 1961–63; British Nat. Cttee for History of Science, Medicine and Technol., 1970–78 (Chm., Org. Cttee, Internat. Congress, 1977); President: Crabtree Foundation, 1958; Sect. A, British Assoc., 1971. Also a mem., various cttees on electronics, scientific res., measurement, defence and educn. Rapporteur, European Convention on Human Rights, 1970. Companion, Operational Res. Soc., 1983. Governor, Dulwich Coll., 1965–79; Life Governor, Haileybury Coll., 1978. Jt Editor, Notes and Records of the Royal Society, 1969–. Vis. Prof., Univ. of Colorado, 1982; Visitor, RMCS, 1983. Hon. Fellow: College of Preceptors, 1978; IERE, 1982; Inst. of Measurement and Control, 1984; British Horological Inst., 1985. Hon. Freeman, Clockmakers' Co., 1984. Hon. DSc: Strathclyde, 1969; Kent, 1980; DUniv: York, 1976; Open, 1978; Surrey, 1979; Hon. LLD Bristol, 1979. Bailie of Benachie, 1980. US Medal of Freedom with Silver Palm, 1946; US Medal for Merit, 1947; BOIMA Prize, Inst. of Physics, 1934; Duddell Medal, Physical Soc., 1960; Parsons Medal, 1967; Hartley Medal, Inst. of Measurement and Control, 1972; Mexican Min. of Telecommunications Medal, 1973; Rutherford Medal, USSR, 1977; R. G. Mitchell Medal, 1979; Old Crows Medal, 1980. Hon. Mem., US Air Force, 1982; Hon. Mayor, San Antonio, Texas, 1983. *Publications:* Most Secret War (The Wizard War, USA, La Guerre Ultra Secrète, France), 1978; Future Conflict and New Technology, 1981; Some Thoughts on 'Star Wars', 1985; lectures and papers on scientific subjects, defence, educn, engrg, history of science and policy. *Address:* 8 Queens Terrace, Aberdeen AB1 1XL. *T:* Aberdeen 648184. *Clubs:* Athenæum, Special Forces; Royal Northern (Aberdeen).

JONES, Rhona Mary; Chief Nursing Officer, St Bartholomew's Hospital, 1969–74, retired; *b* 7 July 1921; *d* of late Thomas Henry Jones and late Margaret Evelyn King; single. *Educ:* Liverpool; Alder Hey Children's Hosp.; St Mary's Hosp., Paddington. RSCN 1943; SRN 1945; SCM 1948. Post-Registration Training, and Staff Nurse, Queen Charlotte's Hosp., 1946–48; Ward Sister, 1948–50, Departmental Sister, 1950–52, St Mary's Hosp., Paddington; General Duty Nurse, Canada, 1952–53; Asst Matron, Gen. Infirmary, Leeds, 1953–57; Dep. Matron, Royal Free Hosp., London, 1957–59; Matron, Bristol Royal Hosp., 1959–67; Matron and Superintendent of Nursing, St Bartholomew's Hosp., 1968–69. Chm., Bristol Branch, Royal Coll. of Nursing, 1962–65; Member: Standing Nursing Adv. Cttee, Central Health Services Council, 1963–74; Exec. Cttee, Assoc. Nurse Administrators (formerly Assoc. Hosp. Matrons for England and Wales), 1963–74; Area Nurse Trng Cttee, SW Region, 1965–67; NE Metropolitan Area Nurse Training Cttee, 1969–74; E London Group Hosp. Management Cttee, 1969–74. Vice-Pres., Bristol Royal Hosp. Nurses League. *Recreations:* reading, travel. *Address:* 26 Seaton Drive, Bedford MK40 3BG. *T:* Bedford 65868.

JONES, Air Vice-Marshal Richard Ian, CB 1960; AFC 1948; psa; pfc; *m* 1940, Margaret Elizabeth Wright. *Educ:* Berkhamsted Sch.; Cranwell. Group Captain, 1955; Air Commodore, 1960; Air Vice-Marshal, 1965. Senior Air Staff Officer, Royal Air Force, Germany (Second Tactical Air Force), Command Headquarters, 1959–63; Dir of Flying Training, 1963–64; AOC No 25 Group, RAF Flying Training Command, 1964–67; SASO, Fighter Command, 1967–68; AOC No 11 (Fighter) Gp, Strike Command, 1969–70; retired 1970. *Recreations:* golf, ski-ing. *Clubs:* Royal Air Force; Victoria (Jersey).

JONES, Maj.-Gen. Richard K.; *see* Keith-Jones.

JONES, Richard S.; *see* Stanton-Jones.

JONES, Robert Brannock; MP (C) Hertfordshire West, since 1983; *b* 26 Sept. 1950; *s* of Ray Elwin Jones and Iris Pamela Jones. *Educ:* Merchant Taylors' Sch.; Univ. of St Andrews (MA Hons Modern History). Marketing Develt Exec., Tay Textiles Ltd, Dundee, 1974–76; Head of Res., NHBC, 1976–78; Housing Policy Adviser, Conservative Central Office, 1978–79; Parly Adviser, Fedn of Civil Engrg Contractors, 1979–83. Member: St Andrews Burgh Council, 1972–75; Fife CC, 1973–75; Chiltern DC, 1979–83; Vice-Pres., Assoc. of Dist Councils, 1983–. PPS, Dept of Transport, 1986–. Mem., Environment Select Cttee, 1983–86. Sec., Cons. Employment Cttee, 1985–; Chm., Cons. Party Orgn Cttee, 1986–. Mem., Inland Waterways Amenity Adv. Council, 1985–; Pres., Dacorum Sports Council, 1984–. Vice-Pres., Wildlife Hosp. Trust, 1985–. Freeman, City of London. *Publications:* New Approaches to Housing, 1976; Watchdog: guide to the role of the district auditor, 1978; Ratepayers' Defence Manual, 1980; Economy and Local Government, 1981; Roads and the Private Sector, 1982; Town and Country Chaos: critique of the planning system, 1982. *Recreations:* squash, tennis, shove-halfpenny, music. *Address:* Granary Cottage, 7 Grace's Maltings, Akeman Street, Tring, Herts HP23 6DL. *Clubs:* Rugby; Conservative (Tring).

JONES, (Robert) Gerallt; writer; Senior Tutor, Extra-Mural Department, University College of Wales, Aberystwyth, since 1979; *b* 11 Sept. 1934; *s* of Rev. R. E. Jones and Elizabeth Jones, Nefyn, Wales; *m* 1962, Susan Lloyd Griffith; two *s* one *d*. *Educ:* Denstone; University of Wales (University Student Pres., 1956–57). Sen. English Master, Sir Thomas Jones Sch., Amlwch, 1957–60; Lectr in Educn, University Coll., Aberystwyth, 1961–65; Prin., Mandeville Teachers' Coll., Jamaica, 1965–67; Warden and Headmaster, Llandovery Coll., 1967–76; Fellow in Creative Writing, Univ. of Wales, 1976–77. Dir, Sgrîn 82, 1981–. Member: Gov. Body, Church in Wales, 1959–; Welsh Acad. (Yr Academi Gymreig), 1959– (Vice-Chm., 1981; Chm., 1982–); Broadcasting Council for Wales; Welsh Arts Council; Univ. Council, Aberystwyth. FRSA. Editor of Impact (the Church in Wales quarterly). *Publications:* Ymysg Y Drain, 1959; Y Foel Fawr, 1960; Cwlwm, 1962; Yn Frawd I'r Eos, 1962; (ed) Fy Nghymru I, 1962; Nadolig Gwyn, 1963; Gwared Y Gwirion, 1966; The Welsh Literary Revival, 1966; Jamaican Landscape, 1969; Cysgodion, 1973; Jamaica, Y Flwyddyn Gyntaf, 1974; (ed) Poetry of Wales 1930–1970, 1975; Bardsey, 1976; Jamaican Interlude, 1977; Triptych, 1978; Teithiau Gerallt, 1978; Pererindota, 1978; Cafflogion, 1979; Murmur Llawer Man, 1980; Dyfal Gerddwyr y Maes (poems), 1981; T. S. Eliot (criticism), 1981; (ed) Dathlu, 1985. *Recreations:* cricket, journalism. *Address:* Lerry Dale, Dolybont, Borth, Aberystwyth, Wales.

JONES, Robert Gwilym L.; *see* Lewis-Jones.

JONES, Robert Hefin, CVO 1969; PhD; Under Secretary, Education Department, Welsh Office, since 1980; *b* 30 June 1932; *s* of late Owen Henry and Elizabeth Jones, Blaenau Ffestiniog. *Educ:* Ysgol Sir Ffestiniog; University Coll. of Wales, Aberystwyth (BSc); University of London (PhD). Asst Master, Whitgift Sch., 1957–63; HM Inspector of Schools (Wales), 1963; seconded to Welsh Office as Sec., Prince of Wales Investiture Cttee, and Personal Asst to the Earl Marshal, 1967; Principal, Welsh Office, 1969, Asst Sec. 1972. *Recreations:* music, reading, cooking. *Address:* 34 The Grange, Llandaff, Cardiff. *T:* Cardiff 564573.

JONES, Rev. (Robert William) Hugh; Minister, United Reformed Church, Foleshill Road, Coventry, 1978–81, retired; Moderator of the West Midland Province of the United Reformed Church (formerly of the Congregational Church in England and Wales), 1970–78; *b* 6 May 1911; *s* of Evan Hugh Jones and Sarah Elizabeth Salmon; *m* 1st, 1939, Gaynor Eluned Evans (*d* 1974); one *s* one *d*; 2nd, 1979, Mary Charlotte Pulsford, *widow* of H. E. Pulsford, FIEE. *Educ:* Chester Grammar Sch.; Univs of Wales and Manchester; Lancashire Independent College. BA Wales, History and Philosophy. Ordained, 1939; Congregational Church: Welholme, Grimsby, 1939–45; Muswell Hill, London, 1945–49; Warwick Road, Coventry, 1949–61; Petts Wood, Orpington, 1961–69; President, Congregational Church in England and Wales, 1969–70. Broadcaster, radio and TV; Mem., BBC/ITA Central Religious Adv. Cttee, 1971–75. Guest preacher, USA. *Recreations:* painting, photography. *Address:* 36 Almond Avenue, Leamington Spa, Warwicks. *T:* Leamington Spa 30509.

JONES, Robin Francis McN.; *see* McNab Jones.

JONES, R(obin) Huws, CBE 1969; Associate Director, Joseph Rowntree Memorial Trust, 1972–76 (Consultant, 1976–78); *b* 1 May 1909; *m* 1944, Enid Mary Horton; one *s* two *d*. *Educ:* Liverpool Univ. Frances Wood Prizeman, Royal Statistical Society. Lectr, Social Science Dept, Liverpool Univ., 1937–39; Staff Tutor (City of Lincoln) Oxford Univ. Extra-mural Delegacy, 1939–47; Dir of Social Science Courses, University Coll., Swansea, 1948–61; Principal, Nat. Inst. for Social Work Training, 1961–72. Visiting Prof., University of Minnesota, 1964; Heath Clark Lectr, University of London, 1969. Member: Minister of Health's Long Term Study Group, 1965–69; Cttee on Local Authority and Allied Personal Social Services, 1965–68; NE Metropolitan Reg. Hosp. Bd, 1967–72; Cttee, King's Fund Centre, 1970–75; Chief Scientist's Cttee, DHSS, 1971–77; Scientific Advr to DHSS and to Welsh Office, 1977–82. Mem., Ciba Foundn Cttee on Compensation in Biomedical Research, 1979–80. Founder mem., Swansea Valley Project Cttee, 1961–. Pres., Internat. Assoc. of Schools of Social Work, 1976–80 (Hon. Treasurer, 1970–74). Chm., W Cumbria SDP, 1981–83. Vice-Pres., Beacon Hostels. Hon. Fellow, UC Swansea, 1986. Hon. LLD Wales, 1982. *Publications:* The Doctor and the Social Services, 1971; contributions to journals. *Recreation:* gardening. *Address:* Lambfold, High Lorton, Cockermouth, Cumbria. *T:* Lorton 619.

JONES, Ronald Christopher H.; *see* Hope-Jones.

JONES, Brigadier Ronald M.; *see* Montague-Jones.

JONES, Group Captain Royden Anthony; RAF retired; Regional Chairman of Industrial Tribunals, London (Central) Region, since 1975; *b* 11 June 1925; *s* of Daniel Richard Glyndwr Jones and Hilda Margaret Jones (*née* Carruthers); *m* 1st, 1948, Krystyna Emilia Kumor (decd); one *s*; 2nd, 1955, Peggy Elizabeth Martin; one *s*. *Educ:* Torquay Grammar Sch. Trooper, Household Cavalry, 1943; RMC, Sandhurst, 1944; Captain, Arab Legion armoured car squadron, 1945–48. Qualified as solicitor, 1949; joined RAF Legal Services as prosecuting officer, 1950; RAF Staff Coll., 1961; served as Dep. Dir of Legal Services (RAF), in Cyprus and Germany, retiring as Gp Captain, 1975. *Publication:* Manual of Law for Kenya Armed Forces, 1971. *Recreations:* country pursuits, reading, house maintenance, photography. *Address:* The Ferrers, 130 The Avenue, Sunbury-on-Thames, Middx. *T:* Sunbury 83484. *Club:* Royal Air Force.

JONES, Samuel; Chief Executive and County Clerk, Leicestershire County Council, and Clerk of Lieutenancy, since 1976; *b* 27 Dec. 1939; *s* of Samuel Jones and Sarah Johnston Jones (*née* McCulloch); *m* 1964, Jean Ann Broadhurst; two *d*. *Educ:* Morpeth Grammar Sch.; Manchester Univ. (LLB); Kent Univ. (MA). Admitted Solicitor, 1964. Asst Solicitor, Macclesfield Bor. Council, 1964–67; Asst Town Clerk, Bedford Bor. Council, 1967–71; Head of Legal Div., Coventry CBC, 1971–73; Head of Admin and Legal Dept, Sheffield Dist Council, 1973–76. *Recreations:* dog and coastal walking. *Address:* 7 Grey Crescent, Newtown Linford, Leicester LE6 0AA. *T:* Markfield 243822; Chapel Knoll, 26 Hobbs Hill, Croyde EX33 1LZ. *T:* Croyde 890210.

JONES, Sir Samuel (Owen), Kt 1966; FIREE (Aust.), FIE (Aust.); Chairman, Standard Telephones & Cables Pty Ltd, 1968–76 (Managing Director, 1961–69); Chairman: Concrete Industries (Monier) Ltd, 1969–76; Austral Standard Cables Pty Ltd, 1967–69 and 1972–75; Export Finance and Insurance Corporation, 1975–77; Director, Overseas Corporation (Australia) Ltd, 1969–75; *b* 20 Aug. 1905; *s* of late John Henry Jones and Eliza Jones (*née* Davies); *m* 1932, Jean, *d* of late J. W. Sinclair; two *d*. *Educ:* Warracknabeal High Sch.; University of Melbourne. Engineering Branch, PMG's Dept, 1927–39. Lt-Col comdg Divisional Signal Unit, AIF abroad, 1939–41; CSO Aust. Home Forces, 1941–42; Dir, Radio and Signal Supplies, Min. of Munitions, 1942–45. Technical Manager, Philips Electrical Industries Pty Ltd, 1945–50, Tech. Dir, 1950–61; Chairman: Telecommunication Co. of Aust., 1956–61; Australian Telecommunications Develt Assoc., 1967–70 (Mem., 1963–75); Consultative Council, Export Payments Insurance Corp, 1970–75; Director: Television Equipment Pty Ltd, 1960–61; Cannon Electric (Australia) Pty Ltd, 1964–68. National Pres., Aust. Inst. of Management, 1968–70; Councillor, Chamber of Manufactures of NSW, 1968–72; Member: Govt's Electronics and Telecommunications Industry Adv. Cttee, 1955–72; Export Develt Council, 1969–74; Council, Macquarie Univ., 1969–74; Council, Nat. Library of Australia, 1971–74; Australian Univs Commn, 1972–75. *Publications:* several technical articles. *Recreations:* bowls, fishing. *Address:* Apartment 11, 321 Edgecliff Road, Woollahra, NSW 2025, Australia. *Clubs:* Union (Sydney); Naval and Military (Melbourne).

JONES, Schuyler, DPhil; Curator, Pitt Rivers Museum, and Head of Department of Ethnology and Prehistory, Oxford University, since 1985; *b* 7 Feb. 1930; *s* of Schuyler Jones Jr and Ignace Mead Jones; *m* 1955, Lis Margit Søndergaard Rasmussen; one *s* one *d*. *Educ:* Edinburgh Univ. (MA Hons Anthropology); Oxford Univ. (DPhil Anthropology). Anthropological expeditions to: Atlas Mountains, Southern Algeria, French West Africa, Nigeria, 1951; French Equatorial Africa, Belgian Congo, 1952; East and Southern Africa, 1953; Morocco High Atlas, Algeria, Sahara, Niger River, 1954; Turkey, Iran, Afghanistan, Pakistan, India, Nepal, 1958–59; ten expeditions to Nuristan in the Hindu Kush, 1960–70; to Chinese Turkestan, 1985. Asst Curator, Pitt Rivers Mus., 1970–71; Asst Curator and Univ. Lectr in Ethnology, 1971–85. *Publications:* Sous le Soleil Africain, 1955 (Under the African Sun, 1956); Annotated Bibliography of Nuristan (Kafiristan) and The Kalash Kafirs of Chitral, pt 1 1966, pt 2 1969; The Political Organization of the Kam Kafirs, 1967; Men of Influence in Nuristan, 1974; (jtly) Nuristan, 1979; numerous articles. *Recreation:* travel in remote places. *Address:* Old Close Cottage, Chapel Lane, Enstone OX7 4LY. *T:* Enstone 453.

JONES, Air Cdre Shirley Ann; Director, Women's Royal Air Force, since 1986; ADC to the Queen, since 1986; *d* of late Wilfred Esmond Jones, FRICS, and Louise May Betty Jones (*née* Dutton). *Educ:* Micklefield Sch., Seaford, Sussex. Joined Royal Air Force, 1962; commnd 1962; served UK and Libya, 1962–71; Netherlands and UK, 1971–74; sc 1975; served UK, 1975–82; Dep. Dir, 1982–86. *Recreations:* golf, music, gardening, cookery.

Address: c/o Ministry of Defence, Adastral House, Theobalds Road, WC1X 8RU. *Club:* Royal Air Force.

JONES, Sir Simon (Warley Frederick) Benton, 4th Bt *cr* 1919; *b* 11 Sept. 1941; *o s* of Sir Peter Fawcett Benton Jones, 3rd Bt, OBE, and Nancy (*d* 1974), *d* of late Warley Pickering; *S* father, 1972; *m* 1966, Margaret Fiona, *d* of David Rutherford Dickson; three *s* two *d*. *Educ:* Eton; Trinity College, Cambridge (MA). JP for Lincolnshire (parts of Kesteven), 1971; High Sheriff, Lincs, 1977. *Heir: s* James Peter Martin Benton Jones, *b* 1 Jan. 1973. *Address:* Irnham Hall, Grantham, Lincs. *T:* Corby Glen 212; Sopley, Christchurch, Dorset.

JONES, Stephen Barry; MP (Lab) Alyn and Deeside, since 1983 (Flint East, 1970–83); *b* 1938; *s* of Stephen Jones and late Grace Jones, Mancot, Flintshire; *m* Janet Jones (*née* Davies); one *s*. PPS to Rt Hon. Denis Healey, 1972–74; Parly Under-Sec. of State for Wales, 1974–79; Opposition spokesman on employment, 1980–83; Chief Opposition spokesman on Wales, 1983–. Mem., Labour Shadow Cabinet. *Address:* House of Commons, SW1A 0AA. *T:* 01-219 3556. *Clubs:* Connah's Quay Labour Party, Shotton Royal British Legion.

JONES, S(tuart) Lloyd; *b* 26 Aug. 1917; *s* of Hugh and Edna Lloyd Jones, Liverpool; *m* 1942, Pamela Mary Hamilton-Williams, Heswall; one *s* three *d*. *Educ:* Rydal Sch.; Univ. of Liverpool. Solicitor, 1940; Dep. Town Clerk, Nottingham, 1950–53; Town Clerk of Plymouth, 1953–70; Chief Exec. Officer and Town Clerk of Cardiff, 1970–74; Chm., Welsh Health Technical Services Orgn, 1973–76. Chief Counting Officer, Welsh Referendum, 1979. US State Dept Foreign Leader Scholarship, 1962. One of Advisers to Minister of Housing and Local Govt on Amalgamation of London Boroughs, 1962; Indep. Inspector, extension of Stevenage New Town, 1964; Member: Adv. Cttee on Urban Transport Manpower, 1967–69; Cttee on Public Participation in Planning, 1969; PM's Cttee on Local Govt Rules of Conduct, 1973–74. Pres., Soc. of Town Clerks, 1972. Chm. of Governors, Plymouth Polytechnic, 1982–. Distinguished Services Award, Internat. City Management Assoc., 1976. *Recreations:* sailing, bookbinding. *Address:* High Dolphin, Dittisham, near Dartmouth, Devon. *Club:* Royal Western Yacht Club of England (Plymouth).

JONES, Sydney, CBE 1971; PhD; FEng; Chairman, Conformable Wheel Co., since 1981; independent consultant; Member of Board, British Railways, 1965–76, part-time, 1975–76 (Director of Research, BR Board, 1962–65); Chairman, Computer Systems and Electronics Requirement Board, Department of Industry, 1975–78; *b* 18 June 1911; *s* of John Daniel Jones and Margaret Ann (*née* Evans); *m* 1938, Winifred Mary (*née* Boulton); two *s* one *d*. *Educ:* Cyfarthfa Castle Grammar Sch.; Cardiff Technical Coll.; Cardiff Univ. Coll.; Birmingham Univ. BSc 1st cl. hons (London) 1932; PhD (London) 1951. General Electric Co., Witton, 1933–36; teaching in Birmingham, 1936–40; Scientific Civil Service at HQ, RRE, Malvern, and RAE, Farnborough, 1940–58; Dir of Applications Research, Central Electricity Generating Board, 1958–61; Technical Dir, R. B. Pullin, Ltd, 1961–62. Chm., SIRA Inst. Ltd, 1970–78. Chm., Transport Adv. Cttee, Transport and Road Res. Lab., 1972–77; Independent Consultant, Ground Transport Technology, 1978. FIEE 1960; FIMechE 1965; FCIT 1971; Fellow, Fellowship of Engineering, 1977. Hon. DSc City, 1977. *Publications:* Introductory Applied Science, 1942; papers on automatic control and railways. *Recreations:* gardening, wine, photography, house design. *Address:* Cornerstones, Back Lane, Malvern, Worcs WR14 2HJ. *T:* Malvern 2566. *Club:* Athenæum.

JONES, Sydney T.; *see* Tapper-Jones.

JONES, Terence Leavesley; Under-Secretary, Department of the Environment, 1974–84; *b* 24 May 1926; *s* of late Reginald Arthur Jones and Grace Jones; *m* 1966, Barbara Hall; one *s*. *Educ:* Nottingham High Sch.; Jesus Coll., Cambridge (MA). RNVR, 1944–46 (Sub-Lt). Asst Inspector of Ancient Monuments, Min. of Works, 1949; Principal, 1957; Sec., Historic Buildings Council for England, 1961–67; Asst Sec., 1967; on loan to Housing Corp., 1979–81. *Recreations:* music, archæology. *Address:* 6 Broughton Gardens, Highgate, N6 5RS. *T:* 01-348 3144.

JONES, Thomas E.; *see* Elder-Jones.

JONES, Thomas Glanville; a Recorder of the Crown Court, since 1972; *b* 10 May 1931; *s* of late Evan James and Margaret Olive Jones; Welsh; *m* 1964, Valma Shirley Jones; three *s*. *Educ:* St Clement Dane's Grammar Sch.; University Coll., London (LLB). Called to Bar, 1956. Sec., Swansea Law Library Assoc., 1963; Exec. Mem., Swansea Festival of Music and the Arts, 1967; Chm., Guild for Promotion of Welsh Music, 1970; Chm., Jt Professional Cttees of Swansea Local Bar and Swansea Law Soc. and W. Wales Law Soc.; Mem., Grand Theatre Trust. *Recreations:* Welsh culture, Rugby, reading, music, poetry, gardening. *Address:* Angel Chambers, 94 Walter Road, Swansea SA1 5QA. *T:* Swansea 464623; Gelligron, 12 Eastcliff, Southgate, Swansea SA3 2AS. *T:* Bishopston 3118. *Club:* Ffynone (Swansea).

JONES, Ven. (Thomas) Hughie; Archdeacon of Loughborough, since 1986; *b* 15 Aug. 1927; *s* of Edward Teifi Jones and Ellen Jones; *m* 1949, Beryl Joan Henderson; two *d*. *Educ:* William Hulme's Grammar School, Manchester; Univ. of Wales (BA); Univ. of London (BD); Univ. of Leicester (MA). Warden and Lectr, Bible Trng Inst., Glasgow, 1949–54; RE specialist, Leicester and Leics schs, 1955–63; Sen. Lectr in RE, Leicester Coll. of Educn, 1964–70; Vice-Principal, Bosworth Coll., 1970–75; Principal, Hind Leys College, Leics, 1975–81; Rector, The Langtons and Stonton Wyville, 1981–86. Hon. Canon of Leicester Cathedral, 1983. *Publications:* (contrib. OT articles) New Bible Dictionary, 1962, 2nd edn 1980; Old Testament and religious education articles in relevant jls. *Recreations:* entomology, genealogy, Welsh interests. *Address:* c/o Church House, 3–5 St Martin's East, Leicester LE1 5FX. *T:* Leicester 27445. *Club:* Leicestershire (Leicester).

JONES, (Thomas) Mervyn, CBE 1961; Chairman, Civic Trust for Wales, since 1964; *b* 2 March 1910; *s* of late Rev. Dr Richard Jones and Violet Jones, Llandinam; *m* 1st (marr. diss. 1960); one *s* one *d*; 2nd, 1960, Margaret, *d* of Ernest E. Cashmore, Newport; one *s* one *d*. *Educ:* Newtown Co. Sch.; University Coll. of Wales, Aberystwyth (LLB); Trinity Hall, Cambridge (MA, LLM). Pres. Trinity Hall Law Soc., 1950. Asst Solicitor, Newport Corporation, Town Clerk, 1948; Chairman: Wales Gas Bd, 1948–70; Wales Tourist Bd, 1970–76; Wales Cttee, European Architectural Heritage Year (EAHY), 1975; Trustee, Welsh National Opera Company; Member: Ashby Cttee on Adult Education, 1953–54; Tucker Cttee on Proceedings before Examining Justices, 1957–58. Member: Council, University of Wales; Council, UWIST; Bd of Governors, Christ Coll., Brecon. Pres., Industrial Assoc., Wales and Mon, 1959–60. FBIM; Hon. FSIAD. *Publications:* Planning Law and the Use of Property; Requisitioned Land and War Works Act, 1945; various titles and articles in Local Govt books and journals. *Recreations:* playing at golf, helping to keep Wales beautiful. *Address:* Erw Hir, 38 Fairwater Road, Llandaff, Cardiff. *T:* Cardiff 562070. *Clubs:* United Oxford & Cambridge University; Cardiff and County (Cardiff).

JONES, Sir (Thomas) Philip, Kt 1986; CB 1978; Chairman, Electricity Council, since 1983; *b* 13 July 1931; *s* of William Ernest Jones and Mary Elizabeth Jones; *m* 1955, Mary Phillips; two *s*. *Educ:* Cowbridge Grammar Sch.; Jesus Coll., Oxford (BA). 2nd Lieut, Royal Artillery, 1953–55; Asst Principal, Min. of Supply, 1955; Principal Min. of Aviation, 1959; on loan to HM Treasury, 1964–66; Principal Private Sec. to Minister of Aviation, 1966–67; Asst Sec., Min. of Technology, subseq. Min. of Aviation Supply, 1967–71; Under Secretary, DTI, 1971; Under Sec., 1974, Dep. Sec., 1976–83, Dept of Energy. Member: BNOC, 1980–82; BOTB, 1985–. Chm., Nationalized Industries' Chairmen's Gp, 1986–87. CBIM 1983. *Recreations:* squash, reading. *Address:* c/o Electricity Council, 30 Millbank, SW1P 4RD.

JONES, Tom, CBE 1974 (OBE 1962); JP; Regional Secretary for Wales, Transport and General Workers' Union, 1969–73, retired (N Wales and Border Counties, 1953); Chairman, Appeals Tribunal North Wales, NHS Staff Commission, 1974–81; Member of Industrial Tribunal for North Wales and North West England, 1975–81; *b* 13 Oct. 1908; Welsh parents, father coalminer; *m* 1942, Rosa Jones (*née* Thomas); two *s* two *d*. *Educ:* Elem. Sch., Rhos, Wrexham; WEA Studies, Summer Schools. Coalminer, 1922–36 (having left sch. aged 14). Soldier, Spanish Republican Army (Internat. Bde), 1937–38 (captured by Franco Forces, 1938; PoW, 1940; sentenced to death by Franco Authorities, sentence commuted to 30 years imprisonment; released following representations by British Govt which involved a Trade Agreement; Knight of Order of Loyalty, Spanish Republic (Spanish Govt in Exile) 1974). Worked in Chem. Industry, 1941–44; became full-time Union Official of T&GWU, 1945; Hon. Sec., RAC of N Wales (TUC) for 20 years, retired. Member: Welsh Economic Council; Welsh Council, to 1979 (former Vice-Chm.); Merseyside and N Wales Electricity Bd, 1976–80; Court of Governors, Univ. of Wales; Prince of Wales Cttee; Treasurer, N Wales WEA; Governor, Coleg Harlech (Vice-Chm., 1980–); Past Member: Welsh Industrial Estates Corp.; Welsh Bd for Industry. JP Flint, 1955. *Publication:* (autobiog.) A Most Expensive Prisoner, 1985. *Recreations:* reading, do-it-yourself hobbies, extra-mural activities. *Address:* 2 Blackbrook Avenue, Hawarden, Deeside, Clwyd. *T:* Hawarden 532365.

JONES, Sir Trevor; *see* Jones, Sir O. T.

JONES, Trevor David K.; *see* Kent-Jones.

JONES, Vera June, (Mrs Ernest Brynmor Jones); *see* Di Palma, V. J.

JONES, Rt. Rev. Walter Heath; *see* Rupert's Land, Bishop of.

JONES, Wilfred, CMG 1982; HM Diplomatic Service, retired; *b* 29 Nov. 1926; *m* 1952, Millicent Beresford; two *s*. Joined Foreign Office, 1949; served in Tamsui, Jedda, Brussels, Athens and FCO, 1950–66; First Sec. (Admin), Canberra, 1966–68; FCO, 1968–71; Copenhagen, 1971–74, Blantyre, 1974–75; Lilongwe, 1975–77; FCO, 1977–81; High Comr to Botswana, 1981–86. *Recreations:* sailing, golf, tennis. *Address:* Conifers, 16 The Hummicks, Dock Lane, Beaulieu, Hants SO4 7YJ. *Club:* RAF Yacht.

JONES, William Armand Thomas Tristan G.; *see* Garel-Jones.

JONES, Sir (William) Elwyn (Edwards), Kt 1978; *b* 1904; *s* of the Rev. Robert William Jones and Elizabeth Jane Jones, Welsh Methodist Minister; *m* 1936, Dydd, *d* of Rev. E. Tegla Davies; one *s* two *d*. *Educ:* Bootle Secondary Sch.; Festiniog County Sch.; University of Wales. BA (Wales), LLB (London). Admitted Solicitor, 1927; Clerk to the Justices, Bangor Div., Caernarvonshire, 1934. Town Clerk, Bangor, 1939–69. MP (Lab) Conway Div. of Caernarvonshire, 1950–51. Member: Nat. Parks Commn, 1966–68, Countryside Commn, 1968–71. Mem. Council and Court of Governors, 1943–, Treasurer, 1970–, Vice-Pres., 1977–82, University Coll. of N Wales; Mem., Court of Governors, Univ. of Wales. Hon. LLD Wales, 1979. CC Caernarvonshire, 1948–69. *Publications:* Press articles in Welsh and English. *Recreation:* walking. *Address:* 23 Glyngarth Court, Glyngarth, Menai Bridge, Gwynedd, N Wales. *T:* Menai Bridge 713422.

JONES, Sir (William) Emrys, Kt 1971; BSc; Principal, Royal Agricultural College, Cirencester, 1973–78, now Principal Emeritus; *b* 6 July 1915; *s* of late William Jones and Mary Ann (*née* Morgan); *m* 1938, Megan Ann Morgan (marr. diss., 1966); three *s*; *m* 1967, Gwyneth George. *Educ:* Llandovery Gram. Sch.; University Coll. of Wales, Aberystwyth. Agricultural Instr, Gloucester CC, 1940–46; Provincial Grassland Adv. Officer, NAAS, Bristol, 1946–50; County Agricultural Officer, Gloucester, 1950–54; Dep. Dir, 1954–57, Dir 1957–59, NAAS, Wales; Sen. Advisory Officer, NAAS, 1959–61; Dir, 1961–66; Dir-Gen., Agricultural Develt and Adv. Service (formerly Chief Agricl Advr), MAFF, 1967–73. Mem., Adv. Council for Agriculture and Horticulture in England and Wales, 1973–79. Independent Chm., Nat. Cattle Breeders' Assoc., 1976–79. Dir, North and East Midlands Reg. Bd, Lloyds Bank, 1978–86. Hon. LLD Wales, 1973; Hon. DSc Bath, 1975. *Recreations:* golf, shooting. *Address:* The Draey, 18 St Mary's Park, Louth, Lincs. *Club:* Farmers'.

JONES, William George Tilston; Chief Executive, Technology, British Telecom, since 1984; *b* 7 Jan. 1942; *s* of late Thomas Tilston Jones and of Amy Ethel Jones; *m* 1965, Fiona Mary; one *d*. *Educ:* Portsmouth Grammar School; Portsmouth Polytechnic (BSc). CEng, FIEE. Post Office Engineering Dept, 1960; Head, Electronic Switching Gp, 1969; Head, System X Develt Div., 1978; Dir, System Evolution and Standards, 1983. Member: IEE Electronics Divl Bd, 1984–; Parly IT Cttee, 1985–; Chm., IT Adv. Bd, Polytechnic of Central London, 1984–. Governor, Polytechnic of Central London, 1985–. *Publications:* contribs on telecommunications to learned jls. *Recreations:* theatre, tennis, camping, making furniture. *Address:* 2 Powell Close, Edgware, Middx HA8 7QU. *T:* 01-952 3334.

JONES, Sir William Lloyd M.; *see* Mars-Jones.

JONES, William Pearce A.; *see* Andreae-Jones.

JONES, Wyn; *see* Jones, G. W.

JONES, Sir Wynn Normington H.; *see* Hugh-Jones.

JONES-PARRY, Sir Ernest, Kt 1978; *b* 16 July 1908; *o s* of late John Parry and Charlotte Jones, Rhuddlan; *m* 1938, Mary Powell; two *s*. *Educ:* St Asaph; University of Wales; University of London. MA (Wales) 1932; PhD (London) 1934; FRHistS. Lecturer in History, University Coll. of Wales, 1935–40; Ministry of Food, 1941; Treasury, 1946–47; Asst Sec., Ministry of Food, 1948–57; Under Sec., 1957; Dir of Establishments, Ministry of Agriculture, Fisheries and Food, 1957–61. Exec. Director: Internat. Sugar Council, 1965–68; Internat. Sugar Orgn, 1969–78. *Publications:* The Spanish Marriages, 1841–46, 1936; The Correspondence of Lord Aberdeen and Princess Lieven, 1832–1854 (2 vols), 1938–39; articles and reviews in History and English Historical Review. *Recreations:* reading, watching cricket. *Address:* Flat 3, 34 Sussex Square, Brighton, Sussex BN2 5AD. *T:* Brighton 688894. *Club:* Athenæum.

JONES-WILLIAMS, Dafydd Wyn, OBE 1970; MC 1942; TD 1954; DL; Commissioner for Local Administration for Wales (Local Ombudsman), 1974–79; *b* 13 July 1916; *s* of late J. Jones-Williams, Dolgellau; *m* 1945, Rosemary Sally, *e d* of late A. E. Councell, Blaenau Hall, Rhydymain; two *d*. *Educ:* Dolgellau Grammar Sch.; UCW Aberystwyth (LLB). Served 1939–45 with HAC and X Royal Hussars (Western Desert). Formerly comdg 446 (Royal Welch) AB, LAA Regt, RA (TA). Solicitor, 1939. Clerk of County Council, Clerk of Peace, and Clerk to Lieutenancy, Merioneth, 1954–70; Circuit Administrator, Wales and Chester Circuit, 1970–74. Member: Hughes-Parry Cttee on Legal Status of Welsh Language, 1963–65; Lord Chancellor's Adv. Cttee on Trng of Magistrates, 1974–81; Council on Tribunals, 1980–86; BBC Gen. Adv. Council, 1979–85. Formerly: Mem., Nature Conservancy (Chm., Cttee for Wales); Mem., Nat. Broadcasting Council for Wales; Chm., Merioneth and Montgomeryshire T&AFA. DL Merioneth, 1958. *Recreation:* golf. *Address:* Bryncoedifor, Rhydymain, near Dolgellau, Gwynedd. *T:* Rhydymain 635. *Clubs:* Army and Navy; Royal St Davids Golf, Dolgellau Golf.

JONZEN, Mrs Karin, FRBS; sculptor; *b* London (Swedish parents), 22 Dec. 1914; *d* of U. Löwenadler and G. Munck av Fulkila; *m* 1944, Basil Jonzen (*d* 1967); one *s*; *m* 1972, Åke Sucksdorff. Studied Slade Sch., 1933; Slade Dipl. and Scholarship, 1937; studied Royal Academy, Stockholm, 1939. Lectr, Camden Arts Centre, 1968–72; extra mural lectures in art appreciation, London Univ., 1965–71. Mem. Accad. delle Arte e Lavore, Parma, Italy, 1980 (Gold Medal, 1980); Diploma of Merit, Università delle Arti, Parma, 1982; Gold Medal, Internat. Parliament for Safety and Peace, USA, 1983; Silver Medal, RBS, 1983. *Works in municipal museums and art galleries:* Tate Gall., Bradford, Brighton, Glasgow, Southend, Liverpool, Melbourne, Andrew White Museum, Cornell Univ., USA. *Works commissioned by:* Arts Council (reclining figure), 1950; Festival of Britain for sports pavilion (standing figure), 1950; Modern Schs in Leics and Hertford, 1953 and Cardiff, 1954 (animals and figures in terracotta and stone); Selwyn Coll. Chapel, Cambridge (over-life size ascension group, bronze), 1956; St Michael's Church, Golders Green (carving on exterior), 1959; Guildford Cathedral (carving on exterior), 1961; WHO HQ, New Delhi (life size bronze torso), 1963 (gift of British Govt); St Mary le Bow, Cheapside (Madonna and child), 1969; City of London Corp. for London Wall site (life size bronze figure), 1971; Guildhall Forecourt (over-life size bronze group), 1972; Swedish Church, Marylebone (three-quarter life size Pietà, bronze resin), 1975; Action Research (annual trophy), 1979; Cadogan Estate (figure of young girl for Sloane Gardens), 1981; St Mary and St Margaret Church, South Harting, Hants (Madonna and child), 1985; St Saviour's Church, Warwick Ave (Madonna and child), 1986; Sadler's Wells Theatre (bronze of Dame Ninette de Valois). *Works exhibited by invitation:* Battersea Park open air exhibns, 1948–51; Tate Gall., 1957–59; City of London Festival, 1968; (one man exhibn) Fieldbourne Gall., London, 1974; Poole Wills Gall., NY, 1983. *Portrait busts include:* Sir Alan Herbert, Lord Constantine, Dame Ninette de Valois (purchased by V&A Mus., 1980), Sir Hugh Casson, Donald Trelford, Sir Monty Finniston, Samuel Pepys (over-life size bronze, Seething Lane, EC3). *Relevant publication:* Karin Jonzen: sculptor, introd. Carel Weight, foreword by Norman St John-Stevas, 1976, 2nd edn 1986. *Recreation:* music. *Address:* The Studio, 6A Gunter Grove, SW10.

JOOSTE, Gerhardus Petrus; retired; South African Secretary for External Affairs, 1956–66 (Secretary for Foreign Affairs, 1961); retired, 1966; Special Adviser (part-time) on Foreign Affairs to Prime Minister and Minister of Foreign Affairs, 1966–68; Chairman, State Procurement Board, 1968–71; *b* 5 May 1904; *s* of Nicolaas Jooste and Sofie Jooste (*née* Visser); *m* 1st, 1934, Anna van Zyl van der Merwe (*d* 1974); one *s* one *d*; 2nd, 1981, Jemima Neveling (*née* Steyn). *Educ:* Primary and Secondary Schs, Winburg and Kroonstad; Rondebosch Boys High; Grey Coll., Bloemfontein; Pretoria Univ. Entered Union Public Service, 1924; Priv. Sec. to Hon. N. C. Havenga, Minister of Finance, 1929; Dept of External Affairs, 1934; Legation Sec. and Chargé d'Affaires *ad interim*, Brussels, 1937–40; Chargé d'Affaires to Belgian Government-in-Exile, 1940–41; transf. to Dept of External Affairs, Pretoria, as Head of Economic Div., 1941–46; Head of Political and Diplomatic Div. of the Dept, 1946–49; Ambassador to US and Permanent Delegate to UN, 1949–54; High Commissioner of the Union of South Africa in London, 1954–56. Mem., Commn of Enquiry regarding Water Matters, 1966–; Mem. (ex officio), Atomic Energy Bd, 1956–66. Mem., South African Acad. of Science and Arts. *Recreation:* bowls. *Address:* 851 Government Avenue, Arcadia, Pretoria, South Africa.

JOPE, Prof. Edward Martyn, FBA 1965; FSA 1946; MRIA 1973; Professor of Archæology, The Queen's University of Belfast, 1963–81; Visiting Professor in Archaeological Sciences, University of Bradford, 1974–81, Honorary Visiting Professor, since 1982; *b* 28 Dec. 1915; *s* of Edward Mallet Jope and Frances Margaret (*née* Chapman); *m* 1941, Margaret Halliday; no *c*. *Educ:* Kingswood Sch., Bath; Oriel Coll., Oxford. Staff of Royal Commission on Ancient Monuments (Wales), 1938; Biochemist, Nuffield and MRC Grants, 1940; Queen's Univ., Belfast: Lectr in Archæology, 1949; Reader, 1954. Member: Ancient Monuments Adv. Coun. (NI), 1950; Royal Commission on Ancient Monuments (Wales), 1963–; Sci.-based Archaeology Cttee, SRC, 1976–; Ancient Monuments Bd (England), 1980–; Pres. Section H, British Assoc., 1965. Rhys Res. Fellow and Vis. Sen. Res. Fellow, Jesus Coll., Oxford, 1977–78. Hon. DSc Bradford, 1980. *Publications:* Early Celtic Art in the British Isles, 1977; (ed) Studies in Building History, 1961; (ed and contrib.) Archaeological Survey of Co. Down, 1966; papers in Biochem. Jl, Proc. RSocMed, Phil. Trans Royal Soc., Spectrochemica Acta, Trans Faraday Soc., Proc. Prehistoric Soc., Antiquaries' Jl, Medieval Archæology, Oxoniensia, Ulster Jl of Archæology, Proc. Soc. of Antiquaries of Scotland, etc. *Recreations:* music, travel. *Address:* 1 Chalfont Road, Oxford.

JOPLING, Rt. Hon. (Thomas) Michael; PC 1979; MP (C) Westmorland and Lonsdale, since 1983 (Westmorland, 1964–83); Minister of Agriculture, Fisheries and Food, since 1983; farmer; *b* 10 Dec. 1930; *s* of Mark Bellerby Jopling, Masham, Yorks; *m* 1958, Gail, *d* of Ernest Dickinson, Harrogate; two *s*. *Educ:* Cheltenham Coll.; King's Coll., Newcastle upon Tyne (BSc Agric.). Mem., Thirsk Rural District Council, 1958–64; contested Wakefield (C), 1959; Mem. National Council, National Farmers' Union, 1962–64. Jt Sec., Cons. Parly Agric. Cttee, 1966–70; PPS to Minister of Agriculture, 1970–71; an Asst Govt Whip, 1971–73; a Lord Comr, HM Treasury, 1973–74; an Opposition Whip, March-June 1974; an opposition spokesman on agriculture, 1974–75, 1976–79; Shadow Minister of Agriculture, 1975–76; Parly Sec. to HM Treasury, and Chief Whip, 1979–83. Mem., UK Exec., Commonwealth Parly Assoc., 1974–79 (Vice Chm., 1977–79). *Address:* Ainderby Hall, Thirsk, North Yorks. *T:* Thirsk 567224; Clyder Howe, Windermere, Cumbria. *T:* Windermere 2590. *Clubs:* Carlton, St Stephen's Constitutional, Beefsteak, Buck's.

JORDAN, Dr Carole, FInstP; Wolfson Tutorial Fellow in Natural Science, Somerville College, Oxford, and University Lecturer (CUF), Department of Theoretical Physics, Oxford, since 1976; *b* 19 July 1941; *d* of Reginald Sidney Jordan and Ethel May Jordan (*née* Waller). *Educ:* Harrow County Grammar School for Girls; University College London (BSc 1962, PhD 1965). FInstP 1973. Post-Doctoral Research Associate, Jt Inst. for Lab. Astrophysics, Boulder, Colorado, 1966; Asst Lectr, Dept of Astronomy, UCL, attached to Culham Lab., UKAEA, 1966–69; Astrophysics Research Unit, SRC, 1969–76. Mem., SERC, 1985– (Chm., Solar System Cttee, 1983–86; Mem., Astronomy, Space and Radio Bd, 1979–82, 1982–86). Sec., Royal Astronomical Soc., 1981–. *Publications:* scientific papers on astrophysical plasma spectroscopy and structure and energy balance in cool star coronae, in learned jls. *Address:* Department of Theoretical Physics, 1 Keble Road, Oxford OX1 3NP. *T:* Oxford 53281.

JORDAN, David Harold, CMG 1975; MBE 1962; *b* Sunderland, 27 Oct. 1924; *er s* of late H. G. Jordan, OBE, and Gwendolyn (*née* Rees); *m* 1st, 1951, Lorna Mary Holland (marr. diss.), *er d* of late W. R. Harvey; three *s* one *d*; 2nd, 1971, Penelope Amanda, *d* of late Lt-Col D. L. J. Davy, OBE, TD; one *d*. *Educ:* Roundhay Sch., Leeds; Berkhamsted; Magdalen Coll., Oxford (1st Cl. Chinese), MA 1956. 9th Gurkha Rifles, Indian Army, 1943–47. Colonial Administrative Service (Hong Kong), 1951; Asst Sec. for Chinese Affairs, 1952–55; Colonial Secretariat, 1956–68: Asst Sec., 1956–60; jssc 1960; Defence Sec., 1961–66; Dep. Dir, Commerce and Industry, 1968–70; Dep. Economic Sec., 1970–71; Dep. Financial Sec., 1971–72; Dir of Commerce and Industry, later Trade, Industry and Customs, and MLC, Hong Kong, 1972–79. *Address:* The Lower Farm, Drayton Parslow, Milton Keynes, Bucks MK17 0JS. *T:* Mursley 688. *Clubs:* Hong Kong; Royal Hong Kong Jockey.

JORDAN, Douglas Arthur, CMG 1977; Chief Investigation Officer, International Federation of Phonogram and Videogram Producers, since 1985 (Special Anti-Piracy Advisor, SE Asia, 1984); *b* 28 Sept. 1918; *s* of late Arthur Jordan and Elizabeth Jordan; *m* 1st, 1940, Violet Nancy (*née* Houston); one *d*; 2nd, 1970, Constance Dorothy (*née* Wallis). *Educ:* East Ham Grammar Sch., London. HM Customs and Excise: Officer, 1938; Surveyor, 1953; Inspector, 1960; Asst Collector, Manchester and London, 1962–68; Sen. Inspector, 1968–69; Chief Investigation Officer, 1969–77; Dep. Comr, 1977–79, Comr of Customs and Controls, 1979, Trade, Industry and Customs Dept, Hong Kong (Comr of Customs and Excise, Customs and Excise Dept, 1982–84). Freeman, City of London, 1964. *Recreations:* golf, music. *Address:* International Federation of Phonogram and Videogram Producers, 54 Regent Street, W1; 10 Crouchmans Close, Sydenham Hill, SE26. *T:* 01–670 9638. *Clubs:* Wig and Pen; Dulwich and Sydenham Golf.

JORDAN, Francis Leo, (Frank), QPM 1982; Chief Constable of Kent, since 1982; *b* 15 June 1930; *s* of Leo Thomas and Mary Jordan; *m* 1951, Ruth Ashmore; one *s* two *d*. *Educ:* St Joseph's Coll., Trent Vale, Stoke-on-Trent. CBIM. Staffordshire Police to rank of Chief Supt, 1950; seconded to Cyprus Police during EOKA emergency, 1956–58; Sen. Course in Criminology, Cambridge Univ., 1972; Sen. Comd Course, Police Staff Coll., 1973; Staff Officer to Home Office Police Inspectorate, 1975; Asst Chief Constable, West Midlands Police, 1976; Dep. Chief Constable of Kent, 1979. *Recreations:* walking, old buildings, churches, etc, shooting. *Address:* Kent County Constabulary Headquarters, Sutton Road, Maidstone, Kent. *T:* Maidstone 65432. *Club:* Royal Over-Seas League.

JORDAN, Henry; Under-Secretary, Department of Education and Science, 1973–76; *b* 1919; *s* of late Henry Jordan and Mary Ann Jordan (*née* Shields); *m* 1946, Huguette Yvonne Rayée; one *s*. *Educ:* St Patrick's High Sch., Dumbarton. Served War, RA, 1939–46. Home Civil Service, Post Office, 1936; Foreign Office, 1947; Central Land Board and War Damage Commn, 1949; Min. (later Dept) of Educn, 1957. *Address:* 16 Bainfield Road, Cardross, Strathclyde.

JORDAN, Michael Anthony; Senior Partner, Cork Gully, Chartered Accountants, since 1983; Partner. Coopers & Lybrand, Chartered Accountants, since 1980; *b* 20 Aug. 1931; *s* of Charles Thomas Jordan and Florence Emily (*née* Golder); *m* 1956, Brenda Elizabeth Gee; one *s* one *d*. *Educ:* Haileybury. FCA 1956. Joined R. H. March Son & Co., 1958, Partner, 1959–68; Partner: Saker & Langdon Davis, 1963–; W. H. Cork Gully & Co., 1968–80. Jt Inspector for High Court of IoM into the affairs of the Savings & Investment Bank Ltd, 1983. Gov., Royal Shakespeare Theatre, 1979–. *Publication:* (jtly) Insolvency, 1986. *Recreations:* opera, DIY, gardening. *Address:* Ballinger Farm, Ballinger, near Great Missenden, Bucks. *T:* Great Missenden 3298. *Clubs:* Gresham; Cardiff and County.

JORDAN, Air Marshal Sir Richard Bowen, KCB 1956 (CB 1947); DFC 1941; psa; RAF retired; *b* 7 Feb. 1902; *s* of late A. O. Jordan, Besford Ct, Worcestershire; *m* 1932, F. M. M. Haines (*d* 1985); one *d*. *Educ:* Marlborough Coll.; RAF Coll., Cranwell. Joined RAF, 1921. Late AOC the RAF in India and Pakistan; Air Officer Commanding RAF Gibraltar, 1948–49; Commandant of the Royal Observer Corps, 1949–51; ADC to the King, 1949–51; Air Officer Commanding No 25 Group, 1951–53; Dir-Gen. of Organisation, Air Ministry, 1953–55; Air Officer Commanding-in-Chief, Maintenance Command, 1956–58, retd. *Address:* 4 Stonegate Court, Stonegate, Wadhurst, E Sussex.

JORDAN, William Brian; President, Amalgamated Engineering Union, since 1986; *b* 28 Jan. 1936; *s* of Walter and Alice Jordan; *m* 1958, Jean Ann Livesey; three *d*. *Educ:* Secondary Modern Sch., Birmingham. Convenor of Shop Stewards, Guest Keen & Nettlefolds, 1966; full-time AUEW Divl Organiser, 1976; Mem., TUC General Council, 1986–. Member: NEDC, 1986–; Engrg Industry Training Bd, 1986–. President: European Metal-Workers Fedn, 1986–; British Sect., Internat. Metalworkers Fedn, 1986–. *Recreations:* reading; keen supporter, Birmingham City FC. *Address:* 110 Peckham Road, SE15 5EL. *Club:* E57 Social (King's Heath, Birmingham).

JORDAN-MOSS, Norman, CB 1972; CMG 1965; Director: Crown Life Assurance Company Ltd, since 1980; Crown Life Pensions, since 1980; Crown Life Management Services, since 1980; Crown Financial Management, since 1984; *b* 5 Feb. 1920; *o s* of Arthur Moss and Ellen Jordan Round; *m* 1st, 1965, Kathleen Lusmore (*d* 1974); one *s* one *d*; 2nd, 1976, Philippa Rands; one *d*. *Educ:* Manchester Gram. Sch.; St John's Coll., Cambridge (MA). Ministry of Economic Warfare, 1940–44; HM Treasury, 1944–71; Asst Representative of HM Treas. in Middle East, 1945–48; Principal, 1948; First Sec. (Econ.), Belgrade, 1952–55; Financial Counsellor, Washington, 1956–60; Counsellor, UK Permanent Delegation to OECD, Paris, 1963–66; Asst Sec., 1956–68, Under-Sec., 1968–71, HM Treasury; Dep. Under-Sec. of State, DHSS, 1971–76; Dep. Sec., HM Treasury, 1976–80. *Recreations:* music, theatre. *Address:* Milton Way, Westcott, Dorking, Surrey. *Club:* Travellers'.

JORRE DE ST JORRE, Danielle Marie-Madeleine; High Commissioner for Seychelles in UK, since 1983; concurrently Ambassador to Canada, Cuba, France and USSR; *b* 30 Sept. 1941; *d* of Henri Jorre De St Jorre and Alice Corgat; *m* 1965 (marr. diss. 1983); one *s* one *d*. *Educ:* Univ. of Edinburgh (MA 1965); Inst. of Education, Univ. of London (PGCE 1966); Univ. of York (BPhil 1972). Principal, Teacher Training College, Seychelles, 1974–76; Principal Secretary: Min. of Foreign Affairs, Tourism and Aviation, 1977–79; Min. of Education and Information, 1980–82; Dept of External Relations and Co-operation, Min. of Planning and External Relations, 1983. Mem. or Head of delegn at numerous overseas meetings and conferences; Vice-Pres., Comité International des Etudes Créoles; Exec. Sec., Bannzil Kreyol. *Publications:* Apprenons la nouvelle orthographe, 1978; Dictionnaire Créole Seychellois-français, 1982. *Address:* c/o Seychelles High Commission, 50 Conduit Street, W1A 4PE. *T:* 01–439 0405.

JOSCELYNE, Richard Patrick; Controller, Finance Division, British Council, since 1982; *b* 19 June 1934; *s* of Dr Patrick C. Joscelyne and Rosalind Whitcombe; *m* 1961, Vera Lucia Mello; one *s* one *d*. *Educ:* Bryanston; Queens' Coll., Cambridge. Teaching posts in France, Brazil and Britain, 1958–62. British Council: Montevideo, 1962; Moscow,

1967; Madrid, 1969; Director, North and Latin America Dept, 1973; Representative, Sri Lanka, 1977; Controller, Overseas Div. B (America, Pacific and Asia Div.), 1980. *Address:* c/o British Council, 10 Spring Gardens, SW1A 2BN. *T:* 01–930 8466.

JOSEPH, Sir (Herbert) Leslie, Kt 1952; DL; Vice-Chairman, Trust Houses Forte Ltd, 1970–80; *b* 4 Jan. 1908; *s* of David Ernest and Florence Joseph; *m* 1934, Emily Irene, *d* of Dr Patrick Julian Murphy, Cwmbach, Aberdare; two *d. Educ:* The King's Sch. Canterbury. Commissioned RE, 1940–46. Pres., Assoc. Amusement Parks Proprietors of Great Britain; Chairman: National Amusements Council, 1950–51; Amusement Caterers' Assoc., 1953, 1954; Housing Production Board for Wales, 1952–53. Member: Council, Swansea Univ.; Art Cttee, Univ. of Wales. High Sheriff, 1975–76, DL, Mid Glamorgan. Governor, King's Sch., Canterbury, 1968–. *Recreations:* horticulture and ceramics. *Address:* Coedargraig, Newton, Porthcawl, Mid Glamorganshire. *T:* Porthcawl 2610.

JOSEPH, Rt. Hon. Sir Keith (Sinjohn), 2nd Bt, *cr* 1943; CH 1986; PC 1962; MP (C) Leeds North-East since Feb. 1956; *b* 17 Jan. 1918; *o c* of Sir Samuel George Joseph, 1st Baronet, and Edna Cicely (*d* 1981), *yr d* of late P. A. S. Phillips, Portland Place, W1; *S* father 1944; *m* 1951, Hellen Louise (marr. diss. 1985), *yr d* of Sigmar Guggenheimer, NY; one *s* three *d. Educ:* Harrow; Magdalen Coll., Oxford. War of 1939–45, served 1939–46; Captain RA; Italian campaign (wounded, despatches). Fellow All Souls Coll., Oxford, 1946–60, 1972–; barrister, Middle Temple, 1946. Contested (C) Baron's Court, General Election, 1955. PPS to Parly Under-Sec. of State, CRO, 1957–59; Parly Sec., Min. of Housing and Local Govt, 1959–61; Minister of State at Board of Trade, 1961–62; Minister of Housing and Local Govt and Minister for Welsh Affairs, 1962–64; Secretary of State: for Social Services, DHSS, 1970–74; for Industry, 1979–81; for Educn and Science, 1981–86. Co-Founder and first Chm., Foundation for Management Education, 1959; Founder and first Chm., Mulberry Housing Trust, 1965–69; Founder, and Chm. Management Cttee, Centre for Policy Studies Ltd, 1974–79. Chm., Bovis Ltd, 1958–59; Dep. Chm., Bovis Holdings Ltd, 1964–70 (Dir, 1951–59); Director: Gilbert-Ash Ltd, 1949–59; Drayton Premier Investment Trust Ltd, 1975–79. FIOB. Common councilman of City of London for Ward of Portsoken, 1946, Alderman, 1946–49. Liveryman, Vintners' Company. *Publications:* Reversing the Trend: a critical appraisal of Conservative economic and social policies, 1975; (with J. Sumption) Equality, 1979. *Heir: s* James Samuel Joseph, *b* 27 Jan. 1955. *Address:* 63 Limerston Street, Chelsea, SW10 0BL.

JOSEPH, Sir Leslie; *see* Joseph, Sir H. L.

JOSEPH, Leslie, QC 1978; *b* 13 Aug. 1925; *s* of Benjamin Francis Joseph and Sarah Edelman; *m* 1964, Ursula Mary Hamilton; one *s* two *d. Educ:* Haberdashers' Aske's, Hampstead; University Coll. London (LLB Hons). Called to the Bar, Middle Temple, 1953, Bencher, 1986. *Recreations:* wine and water. *Address:* 34 Upper Park Road, NW3 2UT. *T:* 01–722 3390.

JOSEPHS, Wilfred; composer; *b* 24 July 1927; *s* of Philip Josephs and Rachel (*née* Block); *m* 1956, Valerie Wisbey; two *d. Educ:* Rutherford Coll. Boys' Sch.; Univ. of Durham at Newcastle (now Newcastle Univ.) (BDS Dunelm). Qual. dentistry, 1951. Army service, 1951–53. Guildhall Sch. of Music (schol. in composition, prizes), 1954; Leverhulme Schol. to study musical comp. in Paris with Maître Max Deutsch, 1958–59; Harriet Cohen Commonwealth Medal (for 1st quartet) and prizes; First Prize, La Scala, Milan, for Requiem, 1963. Abandoned dentistry completely and has since been a full-time composer, writing many concert works (incl. nine symphonies), many film and television scores and themes, incl. music for: The Great War, I, Claudius, Disraeli, Cider with Rosie, All Creatures Great and Small, Sister Dora, Swallows and Amazons, The Brontë Series, The Somerset Maugham Series, Horizon, Chéri, A Place in Europe, The Inventing of America, The Norman Conquests, The Ghosts of Motley Hall, The House of Bernardo Alba, The Hunchback of Notre Dame, The Voyage of Charles Darwin, Enemy at the Door, People Like Us, Black Sun, The Uncanny, The Atom Spies, Churchill and the Generals, Pride and Prejudice, Strangled, A Walk in the Dark, Gift of Tongues, Miss Morison's Ghosts, The Human Race, Weekend Theatre, The Moles, The Home Front, The Making of Britain, Courts Martial series, A Married Man, The Gay Lord Quex, Pope John Paul II, Martin's Day, Mata Hari, Drummonds, Return of the Antelope, also a television opera, The Appointment; one-act opera, Pathelin; children's operas, Through the Looking-glass and What Alice Found There; Alice in Wonderland; children's musical, King of the Coast (Guardian/Arts Council Prize, 1969); Equus, the ballet (best ballet award, USA, 1980); Rebecca, 3–act opera. Vis. Prof. of Comp. and Composer-in-Residence at Univ. of Wisconsin-Milwaukee, 1970, at Roosevelt Univ., Chicago, 1972. Member: BAFTA; ISM; Council, SPNM; Composer's Guild of GB; Assoc. of Professional Composers; Assoc. of Indep. Producers. Hon. DMus Newcastle, 1978. *Publications:* Requiem, Symphonies 1–9, various sonatas, quartets etc. *Recreations:* writing music, swimming, reading, opera, theatre, films. *Address:* Flat 3, 76 Priory Road, NW6 3NT. *Club:* Napoleon.

JOSEPHSON, Prof. Brian David, FRS 1970; Professor of Physics, Cambridge University, since 1974; Fellow of Trinity College, Cambridge, since 1962; *b* 4 Jan. 1940; *s* of Abraham Josephson and Mimi Josephson; *m* 1976, Carol Anne Olivier; one *d. Educ:* Cardiff High School; Cambridge Univ. BA 1960, MA, PhD 1964, Cantab. FInstP. Asst Dir of Res. in Physics, 1967–72, Reader in Physics, 1972–74, Univ. of Cambridge. Res. Asst Prof., Illinois Univ., 1965–66; Vis., Fellow, Cornell Univ., 1971; Vis. Faculty Mem., Maharishi European Res. Univ., 1975; Visiting Professor: Wayne State Univ., 1983; Indian Inst. of Sci., Bangalore, 1984. Hon. MIEEE, 1982; For. Hon. Mem., Amer. Acad. of Arts and Scis, 1974. Hon. DSc: Wales, 1974; Exeter, 1984. Awards: New Scientist, 1969; Research Corp., 1969; Fritz London, 1970; Nobel Prize for Physics, 1973. Medals: Guthrie, 1972; van der Pol, 1972; Elliott Cresson, 1972; Hughes, 1972; Holweck, 1973; Faraday, 1982; Sir George Thomson, 1984. *Publications:* Consciousness and the Physical World, 1980 (ed jtly); research papers on physics and theory of intelligence, the convergence of science and religion. *Recreations:* mountain walking, ice skating. *Address:* Cavendish Laboratory, Madingley Road, Cambridge CB3 0HE. *T:* Cambridge 66477; telex 81292 CAVLAB G.

JOSLIN, Peter David, QPM 1983; Chief Constable of Warwickshire, since 1983; *b* 26 Oct. 1933; *s* of Frederick William Joslin and Emma Joslin; *m* 1960, Kathleen Josephine Monaghan; two *s* one *d. Educ:* King Edward VI Royal Grammer School, Chelmsford; Essex University. BA hons. Joined Essex Police, 1954–74 (Police Constable to Superintendent); Chief Superintendent, Divl Comdr, Leicestershire Constabulary, 1974–76; Asst Chief Constable (Operations), Leics Constab., 1976–77; Dep. Chief Constable, Warwicks Constabulary, 1977–83. FBIM. *Recreations:* sport (now mainly as a spectator), house renovation, good wines, after dinner speaking. *Address:* Chief Constable's Office, PO Box 4, Leek Wootton, Warwick CV35 7QB. *T:* Warwick 495431.

JOSLING, John Francis; writer on legal subjects; Principal Assistant Solicitor of Inland Revenue, 1965–71; *b* 26 May 1910; *s* of John Richard Josling, Hackney, London, and Florence Alice (*née* Robinson); *m* 1935, Bertha Frearson; two *s* two *d. Educ:* Leyton Co. High Sch. Entered a private Solicitor's office, 1927; articled, 1937; admitted as Solicitor, 1940. Served War of 1939–45 (war stars and medals): RA, 1940–45; JAG's Br, 1945–46. Entered office of Solicitor of Inland Revenue, 1946; Sen. Legal Asst, 1948; Asst Solicitor, 1952. Mem., Law Society. Coronation Medal, 1953. *Publications:* Oyez Practice Notes on Adoption of Children, 1947, (with A. Levy) 10th edn 1985; Execution of a Judgment, 1948, 5th edn 1974; (with C. Caplin) Apportionments for Executors and Trustees, 1948, 3rd edn 1963; Change of Name, 1948, 13th edn 1985; Naturalisation, 1949, 3rd edn 1965; Summary Judgment in the High Court, 1950, 4th edn 1974; Periods of Limitation, 1951, 6th edn 1986; (with L. Alexander) The Law of Clubs, 1964, 5th edn 1984; contribs to: Simon's Income Tax (2nd edn); Halsbury's Laws of England vol. 20 (3rd edn); Pollard's Social Welfare Law, 1977; (ed) Caplin's Powers of Attorney, 1954, 4th edn 1971; (ed) Wilkinson's Affiliation Law and Practice, 1971, 4th edn 1977; (ed) Summary Matrimonial and Guardianship Orders, 3rd edn 1973; many contribs to Solicitors' Jl and some other legal jls. *Recreations:* music and musical history; Victorian novels; Georgian children and Elizabethan grand-children. *Address:* Proton, Farley Way, Fairlight, E Sussex TN35 4AS. *T:* Hastings 812501.

JOSS, William Hay; a Recorder of the Crown Court, since 1982; *b* 20 May 1927; *s* of William Taylor Barron Joss and Elizabeth Lindsay Lillie Joss; *m* 1961, Rosemary Sarah Joss; two *s. Educ:* Worksop Coll., Notts; Exeter Coll., Oxon (BA Jurisprudence). Served Army, commissioned into 14th/20th King's Hussars, 1945–48. Industry, production management, 1950–62; called to the Bar, Gray's Inn, 1957; practising barrister, 1962–. *Recreations:* golf, music, literature. *Address:* 49 Village Road, Clifton Village, Nottingham NG11 8NP. *T:* Nottingham 211894. *Club:* Nottingham and Notts United Services.

JOSSET, Lawrence; RE 1951 (ARE 1936); ARCA; free-lance artist; *b* 2 Aug. 1910; *s* of Leon Antoine Hyppolite and Annie Mary Josset; *m* 1960, Beatrice, *d* of William Alford Taylor. *Educ:* Bromley County Sch. for Boys; Bromley and Beckenham Schs of Art; Royal College of Art (diploma). Engraver's Draughtsman at Waterlow and Son Ltd, Clifton Street, 1930–32; Art Master at Red Hill Sch., East Sutton, near Maidstone, Kent, 1935–36. Mem. of Art Workers' Guild. *Publications:* Mezzotint in colours; Flowers, after Fantin-Latour, 1937; The Trimmed Cock, after Ben Marshall, 1939; Brighton Beach and Spring, after Constable, 1947; Carting Timber and Milking Time, after Shayer, 1948; The Pursuit, and Love Letters, after Fragonard, 1949; Spring and Autumn, after Boucher, 1951; A Family, after Zoffany, 1953; Master James Sayer, 1954; HM The Queen after Annigoni, commissioned by the Times, 1956, and plates privately commissioned after de Lazlo, James Gunn and Oswald Birley. *Recreations:* outdoor sketching, cycling, etc. *Address:* The Cottage, Pilgrims Way, Detling, near Maidstone, Kent.

JOST, H. Peter, CBE 1969; DSc; CEng; FIMechE; Hon. FIProdE; CBIM 1984; Managing Director, since 1955, and Chairman, since 1973, K. S. Paul Products Ltd; Director of overseas companies; Hon. Industrial Professor, Liverpool Polytechnic, since 1983; Hon. Professor of Mechanical Engineering, University of Wales, since 1986; *b* 25 Jan. 1921; *o s* of late Leo and Margot Jost; *m* 1948, Margaret Josephine, *o d* of late Michael and of Mrs Sara Kadesh, Norfolk Is, S Pacific; two *d. Educ:* City of Liverpool Techn. Coll.; Manchester Coll. of Technology. Apprentice, Associated Metal Works, Glasgow and D. Napier & Son Ltd, Liverpool; Methods Engr, K & L Steelfounders and Engrs Ltd, 1943; Chief Planning Engr, Datim Machine Tool Co. Ltd, 1946; Gen. Man. 1949, Dir 1952, Trier Bros Ltd; Lubrication Consultant: Richard Thomas & Baldwins Ltd, 1960–65; August Thyssen Hütte AG 1963–66; Chairman: Bright Brazing Ltd, 1969–76; Peppermill Brass Foundry Ltd, 1970–76; Centralube Ltd, 1974–77 (Man. Dir, 1955–77); Associated Technology Gp Ltd, 1976–; Engineering & General Equipment Ltd, 1977–; Director: Williams Hudson Ltd, 1967–75; Stothert & Pitt, 1971–85. Chairman: Lubrication Educn and Res. Working Gp, DES, 1964–65; Cttee on Tribology, DTI, 1966–74; Industrial Technologies Management Bd, DTI, 1972–74; Dep. Chm., Cttee for Industrial Technologies, DTI, 1972–74; Member: Adv. Council on Technology, 1968–70; Cttee on Terotechnology, 1971–72. Hon. Associate, Manchester Coll. of Science and Technology, 1962; Univ. of Salford: Privy Council's Nominee to Ct, 1970–; Mem. Council, 1974–84. Mem. Council: IProdE, 1973– (Vice-Pres., 1975–77, Pres., 1977–78; Chm., Technical Policy Bd and Mem., Exec. Policy Cttee, 1974; Hon. Fellow, 1980); IMechE, 1974– (Member: Technical Bd, 1975; Finance Bd, 1979–; Disciplinary Bd, 1979–); Council of Engineering Institutions: Mem. Bd, 1977–83; Mem. Exec., 1979–83 (Mem. External Affairs Cttee, 1974–80; Chm. Home Affairs Cttee, 1980–83); Mem., Parly and Scientific Cttee, 1976–; Steering Cttee, 1983–; President: Internat. Tribology Council, 1973–; Manchester Technology Assoc., 1984–85. Fellow, American Soc. Mechanical Engrs, 1970. Chm., Manchester Technology Assoc. in London, 1976–. Hon. MIPlantE, 1969; Hon. Member: Société Française de Tribologie, 1972; Gesellschaft für Tribologie, 1972; Amer. Soc. of Manufacturing Engrs, 1977; Chinese Mech. Engrg Soc., 1986. Rutherford Lectr, Manchester Technology Assoc., 1979; James Clayton Lectr, IMechE, 1981. Freeman, City of London; Liveryman, Engineers' Co., 1984. Hon. DSc Salford, 1970. San Fernando Valley Engineers Council (USA) Internat. Achievement Award, 1978; State of California State Legislature Commendation, 1978; Georg Vagelpohl Insignia, Germany, 1979. Sir John Larking Medal 1944, Derby Medal 1955, Liverpool Engrg Soc.; Hutchinson Meml Medal 1952, Silver Medal for Best Paper 1952–53, 1st Nuffield Award 1981, IProdE; Merit Medal, Hungarian Scientific Soc. of Mech. Engrs, 1983; Gold Medal, Slovak Tech. Univ., 1984; Gold Insignia, Order of Merit (Poland), 1986. *Publications:* Lubrication (Tribology) Report of DES Cttee, 1966 (Jost Report); The Introduction of a New Technology, Report of DTI Cttee, 1973; various papers in Proc. IMechE, Proc.IProdE, technical jls, etc. *Recreations:* music, opera, gardening, riding. *Address:* Hill House, Wills Grove, Mill Hill, NW7 1QL. *T:* 01–959 3355. *Club:* Athenæum.

JOUGHIN, Michael, CBE 1971; JP; Chairman, North of Scotland Hydro-Electric Board, since 1983; farmer since 1952; *b* 26 April 1926; *s* of John Clague Joughin and May Joughin; *m* 1st, 1948, Lesley Roy Petrie; one *s* one *d*; 2nd, 1981, Anne Hutchison. *Educ:* Kelly Coll., Tavistock. Lieut, Royal Marines, 1944–52, RM pilot with Fleet Air Arm, 1946–49. Pres., NFU of Scotland, 1964–66. Chm. of Governors: N of Scotland Coll. of Agriculture, 1969–72; Blairmore Prep. Sch., 1966–72; Chairman: N of Scotland Grassland Soc., 1970–71; Elgin Market Green Auction Co., 1969–70; Scottish Agricl Develt Council, 1971–80; N of Scotland Milk Marketing Bd, 1974–83. Governor: Rowett Research Inst., 1968–74; Scottish Plant Breeding Inst., 1969–74; Animal Diseases Research Assoc., Moredun Inst., 1969–74; Member: Intervention Bd for Agric. Produce, 1972–76; Econ. Develt Council for Agriculture, 1967–70; Agric. Marketing Develt Exec. Cttee, 1965–68; Scottish Constitutional Cttee, 1969–70; British Farm Produce Council, 1965–66. Contested (C) Highland and Islands, European Parly Elections, 1979. FRAgS 1975. FBIM 1979. JP Moray, 1965; DL Moray, 1974–80. *Recreation:* sailing. *Address:* Elderslie, Findhorn, Moray IV30 3TN. *T:* Findhorn 30277. *Clubs:* New (Edinburgh); Royal Naval Sailing Assoc., Royal Marines Sailing, Royal Findhorn Yacht, Goldfish.

JOWELL, Prof. Jeffrey Lionel; Professor of Public Law since 1975, Dean since 1979, and Head of Department since 1982, Faculty of Laws, University College London; barrister-at-law; *b* 4 Nov. 1938; *s* of Jack and Emily Jowell, Cape Town; *m* 1963, Frances Barbara Suzman; one *s* one *d. Educ:* Cape Town Univ. (BA, LLB 1961); Hertford Coll., Oxford (BA 1963, MA 1969), Pres., Oxford Union Soc., 1963; Harvard Univ. Law Sch. (LLM 1966, SJD 1971). Called to Bar, Middle Temple, 1965. Research Asst, Harvard Law Sch., 1966–68; Fellow, Jt Center for Urban Studies of Harvard Univ. and MIT, 1967–68;

Associate Prof. of Law and Admin. Studies, Osgoode Hall Law Sch., York Univ., Toronto, 1968–72; Leverhulme Fellow in Urban Legal Studies, 1972–74, and Lectr in Law, 1974–75, LSE. Chairman, Social Sciences and The Law Cttee, 1981–84, and Vice-Chm., Govt and Law Cttee, 1982–84, Social Science Res. Council; Asst Boundary Comr, 1976–85; Chm., Cttee of Heads of University Law Schools, 1984–86; Member: Cttee of Management, Inst. of Advanced Legal Studies, 1978–; Standing Cttee, Oxford Centre for Socio-Legal Studies, 1980–84; Gp for Study of Comparative European Admin., 1978–86; Nuffield Cttee on Town and Country Planning, 1983–. Member Editorial Bds: Public Law, 1977–; Policy and Politics, 1976–83; Urban Law and Policy, 1978–83; Jt Editor, Current Legal Problems, 1984–. Publications: Law and Bureaucracy, 1975; (ed jtly) Welfare Law and Policy, 1979; (ed jtly) Lord Denning: the Judge and the Law, 1984; (ed jtly) The Changing Constitution, 1985; articles and reviews in various jls, incl. Jl of Planning and Environmental Law, Public Law, The Listener. Address: 7 Hampstead Hill Gardens, NW3. T: 01–794 6645; Hantons, Exford, Somerset. T: Exford 418.

JOWETT, Very Rev. Alfred, CBE 1972; Dean of Manchester, 1964–83; b 29 May 1914; s of Alfred Edmund Jowett; m 1939, Margaret, d of St Clair Benford; one s three d. Educ: High Storrs Grammar Sch., Sheffield; St Catharine's Coll., Cambridge; Lincoln Theological Coll. BA 1935; Certif. Educn 1936; MA 1959. Deacon 1944; Priest 1945. Curate of St John the Evangelist, Goole, 1944–47; Sec., Sheffield Anglican and Free Church Council and Marriage Guidance Council, 1947–51; Vicar of St George with St Stephen, Sheffield, 1951–60; Part-time Lecturer, Sheffield Univ. Dept of Education, 1950–60; Vicar of Doncaster, 1960–64; Hon. Canon of Sheffield Cathedral, 1960–64. Select Preacher, Oxford Univ., 1964 and 1979. Mem., Community Relations Commn, 1968–77 (Dep. Chm., 1972–77). A Church Comr, 1978–80. Hon. Fellow, Manchester Polytechnic, 1972. OStJ 1979. Hon. LittD Sheffield, 1982. Hon. Freeman, City of Manchester, 1984. Publication: (Part-author) The English Church: a New Look, 1966. Recreations: theatre, music, walking. Address: 37 Stone Delf, Sheffield S10 3QX. T: Sheffield 305455.

JOWITT, Edwin Frank, QC 1969; His Honour Judge Jowitt; a Circuit Judge, since 1980; b 1 Oct. 1929; s of Frank and Winifred Jowitt; m 1959, Anne Barbara Dyson; three s two d. Educ: Swanwick Hall Grammar Sch.; London Sch. of Economics. LLB London 1950. Called to Bar, Middle Temple, 1951, Bencher 1977; Member Midland and Oxford Circuit. Dep. Chm. Quarter Sessions: Rutland, 1967–71; Derbyshire, 1970–71; a Recorder of the Crown Court, 1972–80. Recreation: fell walking. Address: Church House, Desborough, Northants NN14 2NP.

JOWITT, Juliet Diana Margaret, (Mrs Thomas Jowitt); JP; Member, Independent Broadcasting Authority, 1981–86; b 24 Aug. 1940; yr d of late Lt-Col Robert Henry Langton Brackenbury, OBE and Eleanor Trewlove (née Springman); m 1963, Frederick Thomas Benson Jowitt; one s one d. Educ: Hatherop Castle; Switzerland and Spain. Associate Shopping Editor, House and Garden and Vogue, 1966–69; Proprietor, Colour Go Round (Interior Design), 1971–. Member: Interior Decorators and Designers Assoc., 1985–, Domestic Coal Consumers' Council, 1985–. JP North Yorkshire, 1973; Mem. Combined Juvenile Court sitting at Thirsk, 1976–. Address: Thorpe Lodge, Littlethorpe, Ripon, N Yorkshire HG4 3LU; 11 St George's Square, SW1.

JOY, David, CBE 1983; HM Diplomatic Service; Head of Mexico and Central America Department, Foreign and Commonwealth Office, since 1984; b 9 Dec. 1932; s of Harold Oliver Joy and late Doris Kate Buxton; m 1957, Montserrat Morancho Saumench, o d of Angel Morancho Garreta and Josefa Saumench Castells, Zaragoza, Spain; one s one d. Educ: Hulme Grammar Sch., Oldham, Lancs; St Catharine's Coll., Cambridge (MA); Member of Gray's Inn. FBIM. HMOCS, Northern Rhodesia, 1956–64 (Principal, Exec. Council Office, 1962–64); Zambia, 1964–70: Cabinet Office, 1964; Asst Sec., 1966, Under Sec. (Cabinet), 1968; seconded as Town Clerk, Lusaka City Council, 1969; Under Sec., Min. of Commerce and Industry, 1970; Ashridge Management Coll., 1970; joined HM Diplomatic Service, 1971; FCO, 1971–73; First Sec. (Inf.), Caracas, 1973–75; Head of Chancery, Caracas, 1975–77; Asst Head, Mexican and Caribbean Dept, FCO, 1977–78; Counsellor and Head of Chancery, Warsaw, 1978–82; Counsellor and Hd of British Interests Section, Buenos Aires, 1982–84. Recreations: family-life, reading, tennis, golf. Address: c/o Foreign and Commonwealth Office, SW1A 2AH; Flat 6, 9 Beaufort Gardens, SW3 1PT. T: 01–589 6170. Club: United Oxford & Cambridge University.

JOY, Michael Gerard Laurie, CMG 1965; MC 1945; HM Diplomatic Service, retired; b 27 Oct. 1916; s of late Frank Douglas Howarth Joy, Bentley, Hants; m 1951, Ann Félise Jacomb; one s three d. Educ: Winchester; New Coll., Oxford. Served RA, 1940–46 (MC, wounded). Foreign Office, 1947; Private Sec. to Permanent Under Sec. of State, 1948–50; Saigon, 1950–53; Washington, 1953–55; IDC, 1956; Foreign Office, 1957–59; Counsellor, 1959; Addis Ababa, 1959–62; Stockholm, 1962–64; seconded to Cabinet Office, 1964–66; Foreign Office, 1966–68. Recreation: shooting. Address: Marelands, Bentley, Hants. T: Bentley 23288.

JOY, Peter, OBE 1969; HM Diplomatic Service, retired; b 16 Jan. 1926; s of late Neville Holt Joy and Marguerite Mary Duff Beith; m 1953, Rosemary Joan Hebden; two s two d. Educ: Downhouse Sch., Pembridge; New Coll., Oxford. Served with RAF, 1944–47. Entered Foreign (subseq. Diplomatic) Service, 1952; 1st Sec., Ankara, 1959; 1st Sec., New Delhi, 1962; FO, 1965; 1st Sec., Beirut, 1968; FCO, 1973; Counsellor, Kuala Lumpur, 1979–80; Counsellor, FCO, 1980–86. Recreations: shooting, fishing. Address: The Old Rectory, Stoke Bliss, near Tenbury, Worcs. T: Kyre 342; Carrick House, Eday, Orkney.

JOY, Thomas Alfred, LVO 1979; President, Hatchards Ltd, since 1985 (Managing Director, 1965–85); b 30 Dec. 1904; s of Alfred Joy and Annie Carpenter; m 1932, Edith Ellis. Educ: privately; Bedford House Sch., Oxford. Jun. Assistant, Bodleian Library, Oxford, 1919; indentured apprentice, 1919–25, buyer and cataloguer, 1925–35, J. Thornton & Son, University Booksellers, Oxford; Manager, Circulating Library, 1935–45, and Manager, Book Dept, 1942–45, Harrods; Army & Navy Stores: Manager, Book Dept, and founder of Library, 1945–56; Merchandise Manager, 1956; Dep. Managing Dir, 1956–65. Began Hatchards Authors of the Year parties, 1966. Employers' rep., Bookselling and Stationery Trade Wages Council, 1946–79, leader of employers' side, 1957; Member: Nat. Chamber of Trade, 1946–51; Wholesale Trades Adv. Cttee, 1946–51; 1948 Book Trade Cttee; Arts Council working party on obscene pubns, 1968–69, and sub-cttee on Public Lending Rights, 1970. President: Booksellers Assoc. of GB and Ire, 1957–58; Book Trade Benevolent Soc., 1974–86 (Patron, 1986). Inaugurated Nat. Book Sale (first Chm. of Cttee, 1954–65). Hon. Life Member: Soc. of Bookmen; Booksellers Assoc. of GB and Ireland, 1983. FRSA 1967. Jubilee Medal, 1977. Publications: The Right Way to Run a Library Business, 1949; Bookselling, 1953; The Truth about Bookselling, 1964; Mostly Joy (autobiog.), 1971; The Bookselling Business, 1974; contribs to Bookseller and other trade jls. Recreations: reading, gardening, walking, motoring. Address: 13 Cole Park Gardens, Twickenham, Middlesex TW1 1JB. T: 01–892 5660.

JOYCE, Eileen Alannah, CMG 1981; concert pianist; b Zeehan, Tasmania; d of Joseph and Alice Joyce, Western Australia. Educ: Loreto Convent, Perth, Western Australia; Leipzig Conservatoire. Studied in Germany under Teichmuller, and later, Schnabel.

Concert début in London at Promenade Concerts under Sir Henry Wood. Numerous concert tours, radio performances and gramophone recordings. During War of 1939–45, played in association with London Philharmonic Orchestra, especially in blitzed towns and cities throughout Great Britain. Concerts with: all principal orchestras of the UK; Berlin Philharmonic Orchestra in Berlin; Conservatoire and National Orchestras, France; Concertgebouw Orchestra, Holland; La Scala Orchestra, Italy; Philadelphia Orchestra, Carnegie Hall, New York. Concert tours in: Australia, 1948; SA, 1950; Scandinavia and Holland, 1951; S Amer., Scandinavia and Finland, 1952; Jugoslavia, 1955; NZ, 1958; USSR, 1961; India, 1962; also performed harpsichord in several concerts Royal Albert Hall and Royal Festival Hall. Has contributed to sound tracks of films including: The Seventh Veil, Brief Encounter, Man of Two Worlds, Quartet, Trent's Last Case; appeared in films: Battle for Music, Girl in a Million, Wherever She Goes (biographical). Hon. DMus: Cantab, 1971; Univ. of Western Australia, 1979; Melbourne, 1982.

JOYCE, William R., Jr; lawyer, since 1951; Director and Secretary-Treasurer, Battle of Britain Museum Foundation (USA), since 1976; b 18 May 1921; s of William R. Joyce and Winifred Lowery; m 1956, Mary-Hoyt Sherman; one s two d. Educ: Loyola Univ. (BA); New York and Harvard Law Schs. JD. Lawyer, in private practice, New York City and Washington, DC; member of firm, Vance Joyce Carbaugh Fields & Crommelin, 1977–; Consul General ad hon., Republic of Bolivia (Washington, DC), 1963–. Pres., Consular Corps of Washington, DC, 1982–. FRGS. Kt 1973, Kt Comdr (pro Merito Melitensi), Order of Malta, 1977; Kt, Equestrian Order of Holy Sepulchre, Jerusalem, 1976; Kt Comdr of Grace, Order of Constantine and S George (Borbon-Two Sicilies), Naples, 1977; Order of Condor of the Andes, Bolivia, 1978. Recreations: sailing, golf. Address: (residence) 4339 Garfield Street NW, Washington, DC 20007, USA. T: 202/244–7648; (office) 1701 Pennsylvania Avenue NW, Washington, DC 20006. T: 202/298–7133. Clubs: Squash Racquets Association, Middlesex CCC; The Brook, India House, Union, New York Yacht (New York City); Metropolitan, Chevy Chase (Washington); Cooperstown Country (New York); Conanicut Yacht (RI).

JOYNSON-HICKS, family name of **Viscount Brentford.**

JOYNT, Evelyn Gertrude, MBE 1967; Major (retired) WRAC; Director, World Bureau of World Association of Girl Guides and Girl Scouts, 1971–79; b 5 Sept. 1919; 2nd d of late Rev. George Joynt, Dublin. Educ: Collegiate Sch., Enniskillen; Banbridge Academy. Joined ATS, 1942; transf. to WRAC, 1952; jsc, WRAC Staff Coll., 1954; served Middle East and Far East; OC Drivers and Clerks Training Wing, WRAC; DAQMG, Eastern Comd; retired 1967; Nat. Gen. Sec., YWCA of GB, 1968–71. Address: Bowden House, West Street, Alresford, Hants.

JUDD, Clifford Harold Alfred; Under Secretary, HM Treasury, since 1981; b 27 June 1927; s of Alfred Ernest and Florence Louisa Judd; m 1951, Elizabeth Margaret Holmes; two d. Educ: Christ's Hospital; Keble Coll., Oxford. National Service, RA, 1946–48 (to 2/Lt). HM Treasury: Executive Officer, 1948, through ranks to Principal, 1964, Sen. Prin., 1969, Asst Sec., 1973. Recreations: cricket, do-it-yourself. Address: 4 Colets Orchard, Otford, Kent TN14 5RA. T: Otford 2398. Clubs: Sevenoaks Vine; Otford Casuals CC.

JUDD, Eric Campbell, CBE 1974; LVO 1956; Chairman, West Africa Committee, 1976–85 (Vice-Chairman, 1963–76); b St Thomas, Ont, 10 Aug. 1918; s of Frederick William Judd, PhmB (Canada), and Marjorie Katherine (née Bell); m 1947, Janet Creswell (née Fish); two s one d. Educ: Wellington, Canada; St Thomas Collegiate; Toronto Univ. Trainee Manager, Cities Service Oil Co., Canada, 1937–40. RCAF and RAF, 1940–45: Canada, N Atlantic Ferry Comd, Europe, Malta, Middle East, Far East, W Indies; retd Sqdn Ldr RCAF Reserve, 1945. Joined Unilever Ltd, 1946; United Africa Co. Ltd, Nigeria, 1946–60, Chm., 1957–60; Dir, UAC Ltd London, 1960, Man. Dir, 1968; Dep. Chm. and Jt Man. Dir, UAC International, 1969–77. Mem. House of Assembly, Western Nigeria, 1955–56; Chm., BNEC Africa, 1969–72; Chm., Adv. Gp Africa BOTB, 1972–74. Mem. Council, 1975–, a Vice-Pres., 1983–, Royal African Soc. Recreations: golf, tennis, theatre, music, reading. Address: Amberway, 23 Townsend Lane, Harpenden, Herts AL5 2PY. T: Harpenden 2617. Clubs: Pathfinder, MCC; Mid-Herts Golf.

JUDD, Frank Ashcroft; Director, Oxfam, since 1985; Chairman, International Council of Voluntary Agencies, since 1985; b 28 March 1935; s of Charles and Helen Judd; m 1961, Christine Elizabeth Willington; two d. Educ: City of London Sch.; London Sch. of Economics. Sec.-Gen., IVS, 1960–66. Contested (Lab): Sutton and Cheam, 1959; Portsmouth West, 1964; MP (Lab) Portsmouth W, 1966–74, Portsmouth N, 1974–79; PPS: to Minister of Housing, 1967–70; to the Leader of the Opposition, 1970–72; Mem., Opposition's Front Bench Defence Team, 1972–74; Parliamentary Under-Secretary of State: for Defence (Navy), MoD, 1974–76; ODM 1976; Minister of State: for Overseas Develt, 1976–77; FCO, 1977–79; Mem., British Parly Delegn to Council of Europe and WEU, 1970–73. Indep. Advr to UK Delegn to UN Special Session on Disarmament, 1982. Associate Dir, Internat. Defence Aid Fund for Southern Africa, 1979–80; Dir, VSO, 1980–85. Chm., Centre for World Development Educn, 1980–85. Member: Council, Overseas Development Inst.; RIIA; ASTMS; Past Chm., Fabian Soc. Governor, LSE, 1982–. Publications: (jtly) Radical Future, 1967; Fabian International Essays, 1970; Purpose in Socialism, 1973; various papers and articles on current affairs. Recreations: walking, family holidays. Address: 21 Mill Lane, Old Marston, Oxford OX3 0PY.

JUDD, Nadine; see Nerina, Nadia.

JUDGE, Edward Thomas, MA Cantab; Director: ETJ Consultancy Services; Spectra-Tek UK Ltd; Weldall Engineering Ltd; Cleveland Scientific Institution; b 20 Nov. 1908; o s of late Thomas Oliver and Florence Judge (née Gravestock); m 1934, Alice Gertrude Matthews; two s. Educ: Worcester Royal Grammar Sch.; St John's Coll., Cambridge. Joined Dorman Long, 1930, and held various appts, becoming Chief Technical Engr, 1937; Special Dir, 1944; Chief Engr, 1945; Dir, 1947; Asst Man. Dir, Dorman Long (Steel) Ltd, 1959; Jt Man. Dir, 1960; Chm. and Gen. Man. Dir, Dorman Long & Co. Ltd, 1961–67; Dir, Dorman Long Vaderbijl (SA), 1959–79. Chairman: Reyrolle Parsons Ltd, 1969–74 (Dep. Chm., 1968); A. Reyrolle & Co. Ltd, 1969–73; C. A. Parsons & Co. Ltd, 1969–73; Director: BPB Industries, 1967–79; Pilkington Bros, 1968–79; Fibreglass, 1968–79. Mem. Exec. and Develt Cttees of Brit. Iron & Steel Fedn; Rep. of Minister of Transport on Tees Conservancy Commn., 1951–66; part-time Mem. N Eastern Electricity Bd, 1952–62; Vice-Pres., Iron & Steel Inst., 1958. President: British Iron & Steel Federation, 1965, 1966, 1967; British Electrical Allied Manufacturers' Assoc. Ltd, 1970–71 (Dep. Pres., 1969–70). Bessemer Gold Medal, Iron and Steel Inst., 1967. Publications: technical papers. Recreation: fishing. Address: Wood Place, Aspley Guise, Milton Keynes MK17 8EP.

JUDGE, Harry George, MA Oxon, PhD London; Director, University of Oxford Department of Educational Studies, since 1973; Fellow of Brasenose College, since 1973 (Tutor for Admissions, 1980–86); b 1 Aug. 1928; s of George Arthur and Winifred Mary Judge; m 1956, Elizabeth Mary Patrick; one s two d. Educ: Cardiff High Sch.; Brasenose Coll., Oxford. Asst Master, Emanuel Sch. and Wallington County Grammar Sch., 1954–59; Dir of Studies, Cumberland Lodge, Windsor, 1959–62; Head Master, Banbury

Grammar Sch., 1962–67; Principal, Banbury Sch., 1967–73. Vis. Professor: MIT, 1977 and 1980–82; Carnegie-Mellon Univ., 1984–; Univ. of Virginia, 1987; Vis. Schol., Harvard Univ., 1985–87. Member: Public Schools Commission, 1966–70; James Cttee of Inquiry into Teacher Training, 1971–72; Educn Sub-Cttee, UGC, 1976–80; Oxon Educn Cttee, 1982–. Chairman: School Broadcasting Council, 1977–81; RCN Commn on Education, 1984–85. Gen. Editor, Oxford Illus. Encyclopedia, 1985–. *Publications:* Louis XIV, 1965; School Is Not Yet Dead, 1974; Graduate Schools of Education in the US, 1982; A Generation of Schooling: English secondary schools since 1944, 1984; contribs on educational and historical subjects to collective works and learned jls. *Recreation:* canals. *Address:* 2 Upland Park Road, Oxford.

JUDGE, Igor, QC 1979; a Recorder of the Crown Court, since 1976; *b* 19 May 1941; *s* of Raymond and Rosa Judge; *m* 1965, Judith Mary Robinson; one *s* two *d*. *Educ:* Oratory Sch., Woodcote; Magdalene Coll., Cambridge (Exhbnr, MA). Harmsworth Exhbnr and Astbury Scholar, Middle Temple. Called to the Bar, Middle Temple, 1963. Prosecuting Counsel to Inland Revenue, Midland and Oxford Circuit, 1977–79. Member: Senate, Inns of Court and the Bar, 1980–83, 1984–; Judicial Studies Bd, 1984–. *Recreations:* history, music, cricket. *Address:* The Homestead, Crick, Northampton.

JUGNAUTH, Aneerood; Prime Minister of Mauritius, since 1982; *b* 1930. *Educ:* Church of England School, Palma, Mauritius. Called to the Bar, Lincoln's Inn, 1954. Mem., Legislative Council, Mauritius, 1963; Minister of Finance, 1983–84. Co-founder, Mouvement Militant Mauricien, 1971–. *Address:* Office of the Prime Minister, Port Louis, Mauritius.

JUKES, Rt. Rev. John, OFMConv; STL; an Auxiliary Bishop in Southwark, (RC), since 1980; Titular Bishop of Strathearn, since 1980; *b* 7 Aug. 1923; *s* of Francis Bernard Jukes and Florence Jukes (*née* Stampton). *Educ:* Blackheath; Rome. Professed in Order of Friars Minor Conventual, 1948; Priest, 1952. Lectr in Canon Law, Franciscan Study Centre, Univ. of Kent at Canterbury; Minister Provincial, English Province, 1979. Episcopal Vicar for Religious, Southwark; Area Bishop with special responsibility for Deaneries of Canterbury, Chatham, Dover, Gravesend, Maidstone, Ramsgate and Tunbridge Wells. *Publications:* contribs to Misc. Francescana, Studia Canonica, New Life, Clergy Rev., etc. *Recreation:* mountain walking and climbing. *Address:* The Hermitage, More Park, West Malling, Kent ME19 6HN.

JUKES, John Andrew, CB 1968; Member, Merton and Sutton District Health Authority, since 1986; *b* 19 May 1917; *s* of Captain A. M. Jukes, MD, IMS, and Mrs Gertrude E. Jukes (*née* King); *m* 1943, Muriel Child; two *s* two *d*. *Educ:* Shrewsbury Sch.; St John's Coll., Cambridge; London Sch. of Economics. MA in physics Cambridge, BSc (Econ.) London. Cavendish Laboratory, Cambridge, 1939; Radar and Operational Research, 1939–46; Research Dept, LMS Railway, 1946–48; Economic Adviser, Cabinet Office and Treasury, 1948–54; British Embassy, Washington, DC, 1949–51; Economic Adviser to UK Atomic Energy Authority, 1954–64 and Principal Economics and Programming Office, UKAEA, 1957–64; Dep. Dir Gen., DEA, 1964; Dep. Under-Sec. of State, Dept of Economic Affairs, 1967; Dir Gen., Research and Economic Planning, MoT, 1969–70; Dir Gen., Economics and Resources, DoE, 1970–72; Dep. Sec. (Environmental Protection), DoE, 1972–74; Chm., Steering Gp on Water Authority Econ. and Financial Objectives, 1973–74; Dir-Gen., Highways, DoE, 1974–76, Dept of Transport, 1976–77. Mem., CEGB, 1977–80. Councillor, London Borough of Sutton, 1986– (Chm., Finance Sub-Cttee, 1986–). Rep. Sutton SDP on Council for Social Democracy, 1982–. *Recreations:* orienteering, travelling, Himalayan trekking, gardening. *Address:* 38 Albion Road, Sutton, Surrey SM2 5TF. *T:* 01-642 5018.

JUKES, Richard Starr, CBE 1969; FCA; Director, BPB Industries Ltd, 1943–76 (Chairman, 1965–73); *b* 6 Dec. 1906; *s* of late Rev. Arthur Starr Jukes and Mrs Annie Florance Jukes; *m* 1935, Ruth Mary Wilmot; one *s* two *d*. *Educ:* St Edmund's, Canterbury. Mem. Inst. of Chartered Accountants, 1929. Gyproc Products Ltd: Sec./Accountant, 1934; Dir, 1939; The British Plaster Board (Holdings) Ltd: Dir, 1943; Jt Man. Dir, 1947; Man. Dir, 1954; Dep. Chm., 1962; Chm., 1965 (since Aug. 1965 the company has been known as BPB Industries). *Recreation:* golf. *Address:* White House, Watford Road, Northwood, Mddx. *T:* Northwood 24125. *Clubs:* Island Sailing; Sandy Lodge Golf; Hillside Golf (Zimbabwe).

JULIAN, Prof. Desmond Gareth, MD, FRCP; Consultant Medical Director, British Heart Foundation, since 1987; *b* 24 April 1926; *s* of Frederick Bennett Julian and Jane Frances Julian (*née* Galbraith); *m* 1956, Mary Ruth Jessup (decd); one *s* one *d*. *Educ:* Leighton Park Sch.; St John's Coll., Cambridge; Middlesex Hosp. MB BChir (Cantab) 1948; MA 1953; MD 1954; FRCPE 1967; FRCP 1970; FRACP 1970. Surgeon Lieut, RNVR, 1949–51. Med. Registrar, Nat. Heart Hosp., 1955–56; Res. Fellow, Peter Bent Brigham Hosp., Boston, 1957–58; Sen. Reg., Royal Inf., Edinburgh, 1958–61; Cons. Cardiologist, Sydney Hosp., 1961–64, Royal Inf., Edinburgh, 1964–74; Prof. of Cardiology, Univ. of Newcastle upon Tyne, 1975–86. Mem., 1986 Systems Bd, 1980–84. Pres., British Cardiac Soc., 1985–87. *Publications:* Cardiology, 1972, 4th edn 1983; (ed) Angina Pectoris, 1975, 2nd edn 1984; Acute Myocardial Infarction, 1967; contribs to med. jls, particularly on coronary disease and arrhythmias. *Recreations:* walking, ski-ing, writing. *Address:* Old Darras Hall, Edge Hill, Ponteland, Newcastle upon Tyne. *T:* Ponteland 22368. *Club:* Athenæum.

JUMA, Sa'ad; *b* Tafila, Jordan, 21 March 1916; *s* of Mohammed Juma; *m* 1959, Salwa Ghanem, Beirut; two *s* one *d*. *Educ:* Damascus Univ. (L'Essence in Law). Chief of Protocol, Min. of For. Affairs, 1949; Dir of Press, 1950; Sec. to Prime Minister's Office, 1950–54; Under-Sec., Min. of Interior, 1954–57; Governor of Amman, 1957–58; Under-Sec., Min. of For. Affairs, 1958–59; Ambassador: to Iran, 1959–61; to Syria, 1961–62; to USA, 1962–65; Minister of the Royal Court, 1965–67; Prime Minister, 1967; Ambassador to United Kingdom, 1969–70; Senator, 1970–75. Orders of El Nahda (1st Class) and Star of Jordan (1st Class); decorations from Syria, Lebanon, China, Italy, Libya, Malaysia and Ethiopia. *Publications:* Conspiracy and the Battle of Destiny, 1968; Hostile Society, 1970; God or Destruction, 1973; Sons of Snakes, 1973. *Recreations:* reading, music, bridge. *Address:* Jebel Amman, 4th Circle, Amman, Jordan. *T:* Amman 44111. *Clubs:* Travellers', Hurlingham.

JUNGIUS, Vice-Adm. Sir James (George), KBE 1977; DL; farmer; Supreme Allied Commander Atlantic's Representative in Europe, 1978–80, retired; *b* 15 Nov. 1923; *s* of Major E. J. T. Jungius, MC; *m* 1949, Rosemary Frances Turquand Matthey; three *s*. *Educ:* RNC, Dartmouth. Served War of 1939–45 in Atlantic and Mediterranean; Commando Ops in Adriatic (despatches). Specialised in Navigation in 1946, followed by series of appts as Navigating Officer at sea and instructing ashore. Comdr, Dec. 1955; CO, HMS Wizard, 1956–57; Admlty, 1958–59; Exec. Officer, HMS Centaur, 1960–61; Captain, 1963; Naval Staff, 1964–65; CO, HMS Lynx, 1966–67; Asst Naval Attaché, Washington, DC, 1968–70; CO, HMS Albion, 1971–72; Rear-Adm., 1972; Asst Chief of Naval Staff (Operational Requirements), 1972–74; Vice-Adm., 1974; Dep. Supreme Allied Comdr Atlantic, 1975–77. CBIM. DL Cornwall, 1982. *Address:* c/o National Westminster Bank, Wadebridge, Cornwall. *Clubs:* Royal Over-Seas League; RN Club of 1765 and 1785; Pilgrims.

JUNOR, Sir John, Kt 1980; Editor, Sunday Express, 1954–86; *b* 15 Jan. 1919; *s* of Alexander Junor, Black Isle, Ross and Cromarty; *m* 1942, Pamela Mary Welsh; one *s* one *d*. *Educ:* Glasgow Univ. (MA Hons English). Lt (A) RNVR, 1939–45. Contested (L) Kincardine and West Aberdeen, 1945, East Edinburgh, 1948, Dundee West, 1951; Asst Editor, Daily Express, 1951–53; Dep. Editor, Evening Standard, 1953–54; Dir, Beaverbrook (later Express) Newspapers, 1960–86. Hon. LLD New Brunswick, 1973. *Publication:* The Best of JJ, 1981. *Recreations:* golf, tennis, sailing. *Address:* c/o United Newspapers plc, 23–27 Tudor Street, EC4Y 0HR. *Clubs:* Royal Southern Yacht; Royal and Ancient; Walton Heath.

JUPE, George Percival; Under Secretary, Ministry of Agriculture, Fisheries and Food, since 1979; *b* 6 April 1930; *s* of Frederick Stuart Jupe and Elizabeth (*née* Clayton); unmarried. *Educ:* Sandown Grammar Sch., IoW; Hertford Coll., Oxford. Ministry of Agriculture, Fisheries and Food: Asst Principal, 1955; Principal, 1960; Asst Sec., 1970–79: Eggs and Poultry, and Potatoes Divs, 1970–74; Internat. Fisheries Div., 1975–78; Emergencies, Food Quality and Pest Controls Gp, 1979–85; Dir, ADAS Admin, 1985–. *Recreations:* hill walking, gardening, music. *Address:* c/o Ministry of Agriculture, Fisheries and Food, Whitehall Place, SW1A 2HH.

JUPP, Clifford Norman, CMG 1966; *b* 24 Sept. 1919; *s* of Albert Leonard Jupp and Marguerite Isabel (*née* Day Winter); *m* 1945, Brenda (*née* Babbs); one *s* two *d*. *Educ:* Perse Sch., Cambridge; Trinity Hall, Cambridge. Armed Forces, 1940–46. Mem. of HM Foreign and Diplomatic Service, 1946–70; served in: Foreign Office, 1946; Beirut, 1947–49; New York, 1949–51; Foreign Office, 1951–53; Cairo, 1953–56; Kabul, 1956–59; Foreign Office, 1959–61; Brussels, 1961–63; Belgrade, 1963–66; seconded to BoT and Min. of Technology, 1967–70. With Burton Gp Ltd, 1970–72; Dir, British Textile Confedn, 1972–76. *Address:* Tigh nan Croitean, Kildalton, Isle of Islay, Argyll, Scotland.

JUPP, Hon. Sir Kenneth Graham, Kt 1975; MC 1943; **Hon. Mr Justice Jupp;** a Judge of the High Court, Queen's Bench Division, since 1975; *b* 2 June 1917; *s* of Albert Leonard and Marguerite Isabel Jupp; *m* 1947, Kathleen Elizabeth (*née* Richards); two *s* two *d*. *Educ:* Perse Sch., Cambridge; University Coll., Oxford (Sen. Class. Schol., 1936; 1st Cl. Hon. Mods 1938; College Prize for Greek, 1939 MA Oxon (War Degree), 1945); Lincoln's Inn (Cholmeley Schol., 1939; Cassel Schol., 1946). Regimental Service in France, Belgium, N Africa and Italy, 1939–43; War Office Selection Board, 1943–46. Called to Bar, Lincoln's Inn, 1945, Bencher, 1973; QC 1966; Dep. Chm., Cambridge and Isle of Ely QS, 1965–71; a Recorder of the Crown Court, 1972–75; Presiding Judge, NE Circuit, 1977–81. Chm., Independent Schs Tribunal, 1964–67; conducted MAFF inquiry into Wool Marketing Scheme, 1965; Chm., Public Inquiry into Fire at Fairfield Home, Nottingham, 1975. *Recreations:* music (DIY), language. *Address:* Royal Courts of Justice, Strand, WC2. *Club:* Garrick.

JURINAC, (Srebrenka) Sena; opera singer; Member of Vienna State Opera, 1944–82, now Honorary; retired from stage, 1982; *b* Travnik, Yugoslavia, 24 Oct. 1921; *d* of Ludwig Jurinac, MD, and Christine Cerv. *Educ:* High Sch.; Musical Academy. Made first appearance on stage as Mimi with Zagreb Opera, 1942. Frequent appearances at Glyndebourne Festivals, 1949–56, as well as at the Salzburg Festivals. Guest appearances at La Scala, Covent Garden, San Francisco, Teatro Colón. Principal parts include: Donna Anna and Donna Elvira in Don Giovanni; Elisabeth in Tannhauser; Tosca; Jenufa; Marie in Wozzeck; Marschallin in Der Rosenkavalier; Composer in Ariadne auf Naxos; Elisabeth in Don Carlos; Desdemona in Othello. *Film:* Der Rosenkavalier, 1962. Singing teacher; frequent appearances as mem. of jury in singing competitions. Kammersängerin award, 1951; Ehrenkreuz für Wissenschaft und Kunst, 1961; Grosses Ehrenzeichen für Verdienste um die Republik Oesterreich, 1967. *Address:* c/o Vienna State Opera, Austria.

JURY, Archibald George, CBE 1961; FRIBA; FRIAS; City Architect, Glasgow, 1951–72, retired; *b* 23 June 1907; *s* of late George John Jury and Mabel Sophie Jury (*née* Fisher); *m* 1931, Amy Beatrice Maw (MBE 1983); one *d*. *Educ:* Mount Radford, Exeter; SW School of Art. Architect to Council, Taunton, 1938–40, and 1945. Served War, 1940–45, with Corps of Royal Engineers (rank of Major). Chief Housing Architect, Liverpool, 1946–49; Dir of Housing, Glasgow, 1949–51; Dir of Planning, Glasgow, 1951–66. Organised the building of 100,000 houses, 100,000 school places and numerous civic buildings; responsible for the Glasgow Devpt Plan, 1960–80, and implementation of urban renewal programme and official architecture. Several Saltire Soc. awards for best-designed flats in Scotland. Chairman: Technical Panel, Scottish Local Authorities Special Housing Group, 1965–72; Technical Panel, Clyde Valley Planning Adv. Cttee, 1960–70; Pres., Glasgow Inst. of Architects, 1970–72. *Publications:* contrib. professional and technical journals. *Recreations:* fishing, gardening, painting. *Address:* West Acres, Lockerbie, Dumfriesshire.

JUSTHAM, David Gwyn; Chairman: Central Independent Television plc, since 1986 (Director, since 1981); National Exhibition Centre Ltd, since 1982 (Director, since 1979); *b* 23 Dec. 1923; *s* of John Farquhar Richard and Margaret Anne Justham; *m* 1950, Isobel Thelma, *d* of G. Gordon Thomson, MC; one *s* one *d*. *Educ:* Bristol Grammar School. Served RAF, Bomber Pilot (Flt Lieut), 1941–46. Admitted Solicitor, 1949; joined ICI, 1955; Asst Secretary, ICI Dyestuffs Div., 1955–59; Secretary: ICI European Council, 1960–61; ICI Nobel Div., 1961–65; Imperial Metal Industries Ltd (subseq. IMI plc), 1965–73 (Dir, 1968–85); various appts with IMI, 1965–81, incl. Chm., C. A. Norgren Co., Littleton, Colo, USA, 1974–81. Chairman: W Midlands Bd of Central Independent Television plc, 1981–85; Midland Regional Bd of National Girobank, 1982–85; Dir, H. Samuel plc, 1981–84; Pres., Birmingham Chamber of Industry and Commerce, 1974–75 (Mem. Council, 1969–); Chm., Birmingham Hippodrome Theatre Trust, 1979–; Member, Council: Welsh National Opera, 1979–84; Univ. of Aston, 1982–86 (Mem. Convocation, 1974–); Univ. of Birmingham, 1983– (Mem., 1976–, Hon. Life Mem., 1986–, Ct of Governors); City of Birmingham Symphony Orch., 1984–; Mem., W Midlands Economic Planning Council, 1970–74. General Comr of Income Tax, 1972–77. High Sheriff of Co. of W Midlands, 1981–82. *Recreations:* opera and theatre. *Address:* 9 Birch Hollow, Edgbaston, Birmingham B15 2QE. *T:* 021-454 0688.

K

KABERRY, family name of **Baron Kaberry of Adel.**

KABERRY OF ADEL, Baron *cr* 1983 (Life Peer), of Adel in the City of Leeds; **Donald Kaberry;** Bt 1960; TD 1946; DL; *b* 18 Aug. 1907; *m* 1940, Lily Margaret Scott; three *s. Educ:* Leeds Grammar Sch. Solicitor (Mem. of Council of The Law Society, 1950–55). Served War of 1939–45, in RA (despatches twice). Mem. Leeds City Council for 20 years, now Hon. Alderman. MP (C) North-West Div. of Leeds, 1950–83; Asst Government Whip, 1951–April 1955; Parliamentary Sec., Board of Trade, April–Oct. 1955; Vice-Chm., Conservative Party, Oct. 1955–61; Mem., Select Cttee Nationalised Industries, 1961–79 (Chm. Sub-Cttee C, 1974–79); Chm., Select Cttee on Industry and Trade, 1979–83; Mem., Speaker's Panel of Chairmen, 1974–83. Chairman: Yorkshire Chemicals Ltd, 1964–77; W. H. Baxter Ltd; Pres., Yorks Area Council of Conservative Party, 1966– (Chm. 1952–56; Dep. Pres. 1956–65); Chm., Assoc. of Conservative Clubs, 1961–; Chairman: Bd of Governors, United Leeds Hosps, 1961–74; Leeds Teaching Hosps Special Trustee, 1974–86; Pres., Headingly Branch, Royal British Legion; Hon. Legal Adviser, Dunkirk Veterans Assoc. (Pres., Leeds Branch (founder Branch), 1973–); Treasurer, Leeds Poppy Day Appeal Fund, 1947–73. Pres., Incorporated Leeds Law Soc., 1952. DL York and West Yorks, 1974–. *Heir* (to baronetcy only): *s* Hon. Christopher Donald Kaberry [*b* 14 March 1943; *m* 1967, Gaenor Elizabeth Vowe, *yr d* of C. V. Peake; two *s* one *d. Educ:* Repton Sch.]. *Address:* 1 Otley Road, Harrogate, N Yorks HG2 0DJ. *T:* Harrogate 503243; 5 Park Square, Leeds LS1 8AX. *T:* Leeds 436601. *Clubs:* Carlton, St Stephen's Constitutional; Leeds.

KADOORIE, family name of **Baron Kadoorie.**

KADOORIE, Baron *cr* 1981 (Life Peer), of Kowloon in Hong Kong and of the City of Westminster; **Lawrence Kadoorie;** Kt 1974; CBE 1970; JP (Hong Kong); Joint Proprietor, Sir Elly Kadoorie & Sons; Chairman: Sir Elly Kadoorie Successors Ltd; St George's Building Ltd; Director, Sir Elly Kadoorie Continuation Ltd; also chairman and director of many other companies; *b* Hong Kong, 2 June 1899; *s* of Sir Elly Kadoorie, KBE, and Laura Kadoorie (*née* Mocatta); *m* 1938, Muriel, *d* of David Gubbay, Hong Kong; one *s* one *d. Educ:* Cathedral Sch., Shanghai; Ascham St Vincents, Eastbourne; Clifton Coll., Bristol; Lincoln's Inn. With his brother, Horace, founded New Territories Benevolent Soc. Is also Chairman: China Light & Power Co., Ltd, Schroders Asia Ltd, Hong Kong Carpet Manufacturers Ltd, Nanyang Cotton Mill Ltd and others. Mem. Council and Court, Univ. of Hong Kong. Fellow, Mem., Patron, Governor, Chm., etc, of numerous other assocs, cttees, etc. JP Hong Kong 1936; MEC 1954, MLC 1950, 1951, 1954, Hong Kong. Hon. LLD Univ. of Hong Kong, 1961; FInstD (London). KStJ (A) (UK) 1972. Solomon Schechter Award (USA), 1959; Ramon Magsaysay Award (Philippines), 1962. Comdr, Légion d'Honneur (France), 1982 (Officier, 1975; Chevalier, 1939); Officier, Ordre de Léopold (Belgium), 1966; Comdr, Ordre de la Couronne (Belgium), 1983. *Recreations:* sports cars (Life Mem. Hong Kong AA), photography, Chinese works of art. *Address:* St George's Building, 24th floor, 2 Ice House Street, Hong Kong. *T:* 5–249221. *Clubs:* Royal Automobile; Hong Kong, Hong Kong Country, Royal Hong Kong Jockey, Jewish Recreation, American (Hong Kong); Travellers' Century (USA).

KADRI, Sibghat Ullah; barrister-at-law; President, Standing Conference of Pakistani Organisations in UK, since 1978 (Secretary General, 1975–78); Member, Race Relations Committee, Senate, since 1983; *b* 23 April 1937; *s* of Haji Maulana Firasat Ullah Kadri and Begum Tanwir Fatima Kadri; *m* 1963, Carita Elisabeth Idman; one *s* one *d. Educ:* S. M. Coll., Karachi; Karachi Univ. Called to the Bar, Inner Temple, 1969. Sec. Gen., Karachi Univ. Students Union, 1957–58; jailed without trial, for opposing military regime of Ayub Khan, 1958–59; triple winner, All Pakistan Students Debates, 1960; Gen. Sec., Pakistan Students' Fedn in Britain, 1961–62, Vice Pres., 1962–63; Pres., Inner Temple Students Assoc., 1969–70. Producer and broadcaster, BBC Ext. Urdu Service, 1965–68, and Presenter, BBC Home Service Asian Prog., 1968–70. In practice at the Bar, 1969– (Head of Chambers, 11 King's Bench Walk). Chm., Soc. of Afro-Asian and Caribbean Lawyers, UK, 1979–83. Vis. Lectr in Urdu, Holborn Coll., London, 1967–70. Org. Pakistani Def. Cttees during wave of 'Paki-bashing', 1970; active in immigrant and race-relations activities, 1970–; led Asian delegn to Prime Minister, June 1976; attended UN Conf., Migrant Workers in Europe, Geneva, 1975; led Pakistan delegn to 3rd Internat. Conf., Migrant Workers in Europe, Turin, 1977. Gen. Sec., Pakistan Action Cttee, 1973; Convenor, Asian Action Cttee, 1976. Vice Chm., All Party Jt Cttee Against Racism, 1978–80. Publisher, Scopo News, London, until 1984. *Publications:* articles in ethnic minority press on immigration and race relations. *Recreations:* family and reading. *Address:* 11 King's Bench Walk, Temple, EC4Y 7EQ. *T:* 01–353 4931/2.

KAGAN, family name of **Baron Kagan.**

KAGAN, Baron *cr* 1976 (Life Peer), of Elland, W Yorks; **Joseph Kagan;** *b* 6 June 1915; *s* of Benjamin and Miriam Kagan; *m* 1943, Margaret Stromas; two *s* one *d. Educ:* High School, Kaunas, Lithuania; Leeds University. BCom hons (Textiles). Founder of 'Gannex'-Kagan Textiles Limited, 1951, thereafter Chairman and Managing Director. *Recreation:* chess. *Address:* Barkisland Hall, Barkisland, near Halifax, West Yorks.

KAHN, family name of **Baron Kahn.**

KAHN, Baron, *cr* 1965 (Life Peer), of Hampstead; **Richard Ferdinand Kahn,** CBE 1946; FBA 1960; MA; Professor of Economics, Cambridge University, 1951–72; Fellow of King's College, Cambridge; *b* 10 Aug. 1905; *s* of late Augustus Kahn. *Educ:* St Paul's Sch.

(Scholar); King's College, Cambridge (Scholar). Temporary Civil Servant in various Govt Depts, 1939–46. *Publications:* Selected Essays on Employment and Growth, 1973; The Making of Keynes' General Theory, 1984; articles on economic subjects. *Address:* King's College, Cambridge CB2 1ST. *T:* Cambridge 350411. *Club:* United Oxford & Cambridge University.

KAHN-ACKERMANN, Georg; Secretary General, Council of Europe, 1974–79; *b* 4 Jan. 1918; *m* 1945, Rosmarie Müller-Diefenbach; one *s* three *d. Educ:* in Germany and Switzerland. Served in Armed Forces, 1939–45. Press Reporter and Editor from 1946; Commentator with Radio Bavaria and wrote for newspaper, Abendzeitung, 1950. Author of several books, a publisher's reader, and mem. Exec. Cttee of Bavarian Assoc. of Journalists. Dir, VG WORT, Munich, 1972–74; Vice-Chm., Bd of Deutschlandfunk (Cologne). Mem., Social Democratic Party (SDP), from 1946, and of the German Federal Parliament, 1953–57, 1962–69 and 1970–74. Previous appts include: Vice-Pres., Western European Union Assembly, 1967–70; Chm., Political Commn of Western European Union, 1971–74; Vice-Pres., Consultative Assembly of Council of Europe until elected Secretary General in 1974. Vice-Pres., Deutsche Welthunger hilfe; Pres., VG WORT. *Recreation:* ski-ing. *Address:* Sterzenweg 3, 8193 Ammerland, Bayern, Germany.

KAHURANANGA, Rt. Rev. Musa; *b* 1921; *s* of Samweli and Mariamu Kahurananga; *m* 1941, Raheli Lutozi; three *s* four *d* (and one *s* decd). *Educ:* Teachers' Training College, Katoke Bukoba. Teacher; Deacon 1952, Priest 1953; Asst Bishop in Diocese of Central Tanganyika, 1962; Archbishop of Tanzania, 1979–83; Bishop of Western Tanganyika, 1966–83. *Recreation:* farming. *Address:* PO Box 234, Kasulu, Tanzania.

KAISER, Philip M.; political and economic consultant; *b* 12 July 1913; *s* of Morris Kaiser and Temma Kaiser (*née* Sloven); *m* 1939, Hannah Greeley; three *s. Educ:* University of Wisconsin; Balliol Coll., Oxford (Rhodes Scholar). Economist, Bd of Governors, Fed. Reserve System, 1939–42; Chief, Project Ops Staff, also Chief, Planning Staff, Bd Economic Warfare and Foreign Econ. Admin., 1942–46; Expert on Internat. Organization Affairs, US State Dept., 1946; Exec. Asst to Asst Sec. of Labor in charge of internat. labor affairs, US Dept of Labor, 1947–49; Asst Sec. of Labor for Internat. Labor Affairs, 1949–53; mem., US Govt Bd of Foreign Service, Dept of State, 1948–53; US Govt mem., Governing Body of ILO, 1948–53; Chief, US delegn to ILO Confs, 1949–53; Special Asst to Governor of New York, 1954–58; Prof. of Internat. Relations and Dir, Program for Overseas Labor and Industrial Relations, Sch. of Internat. Service, American Univ., 1958–61; US Ambassador, Republic of Senegal and Islamic Republic of Mauritania, 1961–64; Minister, Amer. Embassy, London, 1964–69. Chm., Encyclopaedia Britannica International Ltd, 1969–75; Dir, Guinness Mahon Holdings Ltd, 1975–77. US Ambassador to Hungary, 1977–80, to Austria, 1980–81. Member: US Govt Interdepartmental Cttee on Marshall Plan, 1947–48; Interdepartmental Cttee on Greek-Turkish aid and Point 4 Technical Assistance progs, 1947–49. Sen. Consultant, SRI International, 1981–. Professorial Lectr, Johns Hopkins Sch. of Adv. Internat. Studies, 1983–84; Woodrow Wilson Vis. Fellow, 1983. *Recreations:* tennis, swimming, music. *Address:* 2101 Connecticut Avenue NW, Washington, DC 20008, USA.

KAKKAR, Prof. Vijay Vir, FRCS, FRCSE; Professor of Surgical Science and Director of the Thrombosis Research Unit, King's College School of Medicine and Dentistry, University of London, since 1975; *b* 22 March 1937; *s* of Dr H. B. and Mrs L. W. Kakkar; *m* 1962, Dr Savitri Karnani; two *s. Educ:* Vikram Univ., Ujjain, India (MB, BS 1960). FRCS 1964; FRCSE 1964. House Officer, M. A. Med. Coll. and Irwin Hosp., New Delhi, 1960–61; Sen. House Officer: in Thoracic Surgery, Clare Hall Hosp., 1961–62; in Casualty and Orthopaedics, Royal Hosp., Chesterfield, 1962; in Gen. Surgery, Joyce Green Hosp., Dartford, 1962–63; Res. Surg. Officer, Gravesend and N Kent Hosp., Gravesend, 1963–64; Registrar, Medway and Gravesend Hosp. Gp, 1964–65; Lectr, Nuffield Dept of Surgery, Univ. of Oxford, 1964–65; Dept of Surgery, King's Coll. Hosp., London: Pfizer Res. Fellow and Hon. Sen. Registrar, 1965–68; Sen. Registrar, 1968–69; Lectr and Hon. Sen. Registrar, 1969–71; Sen. Lectr and Hon. Consultant Surgeon, 1972–76; Hon. Consultant Surgeon: King's Coll. Hosp. Gp, 1972–; Mayday Hosp., Croydon, 1984–. Vis. Prof., Harvard Univ. Med. Sch., Boston, 1972. Pres., British Soc. for Haemostasis and Thrombosis, 1984– (Founder Mem., 1980, Sec., 1982–83); Member: Eur. Thrombosis Res. Orgn; Concerted Action Cttee on Thrombosis, EEC; Internat. Soc. on Thrombosis and Haemostasis (Chm., Cttee on Venous Thromboembolism); Internat. Surg. Soc.; Assoc. of Surgeons of GB and NI; Vascular Surg. Soc. of GB; Pan-Pacific Surg. Assoc.; Internat. Soc. for Haematology; Internat. Soc. for Angiology; Surg. Res. Soc. of GB; Hon. Mem., Assoc. of Surgeons of India; Hon. Fellow, Acad. of Medicine of Singapore. Hunterian Prof., RCS, 1969; Lectures: Gunnar Bauer Meml, Copenhagen, 1971; James Finlayson Meml, RCPGlas, 1975; Cross Meml, RCS, 1977; Wright-Schulte, Internat. Soc. on Thrombosis and Haemostasis, 1977; Freyer Meml, RCSI, 1981. David Patey Prize, Surg. Soc. of GB and Ireland, 1971. Member Editorial Board: Haemostasis, 1982–; Clinical Findings, 1982–; Internat. Angiology, 1982–. *Publications:* (jtly) Vascular Disease, 1969; (jtly) Thromboembolism: diagnosis and treatment, 1972; (jtly) Heparin: chemistry and clinical usage, 1976; (jtly) Chromogenic Peptide Substrates: chemistry and clinical usage, 1979; Atheroma and Thrombosis, 1983; 300 pubns in jls on thromboembolism and vascular disease. *Recreations:* golf, skiing, cricket. *Address:* 6 Aspen Copse, Bickley, Kent BR1 2NZ. *T:* 01–467 0628. *Clubs:* Athenæum; Sundridge Park Golf (Bromley, Kent).

KALISHER, Michael David Lionel; QC 1984; a Recorder, since 1985; *b* 24 Feb. 1941; *s* of Samuel and Rose Kalisher; *m* 1967, Helen; one *s* two *d. Educ:* Hove County Grammar Sch.; Bristol Univ. (LLB Hons 1962). Articled as solicitor to Gates & Co., Sussex, 1962–64; admitted as solicitor, 1965; practised as solicitor in London with Avery Midgen & Co., 1965–69, Partner from 1966; called to the Bar, Inner Temple, 1970; practised first from 9 King's Bench Walk, until 1976; then in chambers of John Lloyd-Eley, QC, at 1 Hare Court, Temple. *Recreations:* squash, tennis, and recovering from both. *Address:* 102 Christ Church Road, East Sheen, SW14 7AX. *T:* 01–876 5939. *Club:* Roehampton.

KALMS, Stanley; Founder, Chairman, and Chief Executive, Dixons Group plc; *b* 21 Nov. 1931; *s* of Charles and Cissie Kalms; *m* 1953, Pamela Jimack; three *s*. *Educ:* Christ's College, Finchley. Whole career with Dixons Group: started in 1948 in one store owned by father; went public, 1962; Chairman and Chief Exec., 1967. *Recreations:* communal activities, aft decking. *Address:* Dixons Group plc, 18–24 High Street, Edgware, Middx. *T:* 01–952 2345.

KALO, Sir Kwamala, Kt 1983; MBE 1975; High Commissioner for Papua New Guinea in New Zealand, since 1983; *b* 28 Feb. 1929; *s* of Kalo Navu and Navuga Kila; *m* 1951, Gimaralai Samuel; two *s* two *d*. *Educ:* up to secondary level in Papua New Guinea. Govt Primary School teacher, 1949; served in Dept of Education as classroom teacher, Headmaster, Inspector, Supt of Schools, Asst Sec. of Technical Educn, until 1979; represented Papua New Guinea in Trusteeship Council Meeting of UN, 1963; seconded to Public Services Commn as a Comr, 1979. *Address:* Papua New Guinea High Commission, Princess Towers, 180 Molesworth Street, PO Box 197, Wellington, New Zealand; PO Box 6572, Boroko, Papua New Guinea. *T:* 257217.

KAMBA, Prof. Walter Joseph; Vice-Chancellor, since 1981 (Vice-Principal, 1980–81), Professor of Law, since 1980, University of Zimbabwe; *b* 6 Sept. 1931; *s* of Joseph Mafara and Hilda Kamba; *m* 1960, Angeline Saziso Dube; three *s*. *Educ:* University of Cape Town (BA, LLB); Yale Law School (LLM). Attorney of the High Court of Rhodesia (now Zimbabwe), 1963–66; Research Fellow, Institute of Advanced Legal Studies, London Univ., 1967–68; Lecturer, then Sen. Lectr, in Comparative Law and Jurisprudence, 1969–80, Dean of the Faculty of Law, 1977–80, Univ. of Dundee. Chm., Kingstons (booksellers and distributors) (Zimbabwe), 1984–. Vice-Chm., Bd of Governors, Zimbabwe Broadcasting Corp., 1980–; Member: Public Service Professional Qualifications Panel, Harare, 1981–; Council, ACU, 1981–; Standing Cttee on student mobility within Commonwealth, 1982–; Exec. Bd, Assoc. of African Univs, 1984– (Chm., Finance and Admin. Cttee, 1985–); Chm., Assoc. of Eastern and Southern African Univs; Vice-Pres., Internat. Assoc. of Univs, 1985–. Mem., Univ. of Swaziland Commn on Planning, 1986. Legal Adviser, ZANU (Patriotic Front), 1977–80; Chm., Electoral Supervisory Commn, 1983–. Trustee: Zimbabwe Mass Media Trust, 1981–; Conservation Trust of Zimbabwe, 1981–; Legal Resources Foundn, Zimbabwe, 1984–; African-American Inst., NY, 1985–. Mem., Internat. Bd, United World Colls, 1985–; Mem. Council: Univ. for Peace, Costa Rica, 1981–; Univ. of Zambia, 1982–; United Nations Univ., Tokyo, 1983– (Chm., Council, 1985–; Mem., Cttee on Institutional and Programmatic Develt); Governor, Ranche House Coll., Harare, 1980–; Member Board of Governors: Zimbabwe Inst. of Development Studies, 1982–; Internat. Develt Res. Centre, Canada, 1986–. Hon. LLD Dundee, 1982. Officier dans l'Ordre des Palmes Académiques (France). *Publications:* articles in Internat. and Comparative Law Quarterly, Juridical Review. *Recreation:* tennis. *Address:* University of Zimbabwe, PO Box MP 167, Mount Pleasant, Harare, Zimbabwe. *T:* Harare 303211.

KAN, Prof. Yuet Wai, FRCP 1983; FRS 1981; Louis K. Diamond Professor of Hematology, since 1984, Investigator, Howard Hughes Medical Institute Laboratory, since 1976, and Head, Division of Medical Genetics and Molecular Hematology, Department of Medicine, since 1983, University of California, San Francisco; *b* 11 June 1936; *s* of Kan Tong Po and Kan Li Lai Wan; *m* 1964, Alvera L. Limauro; two *d*. *Educ:* Univ. of Hong Kong (MB, BS, DSc). Research Associate, Children's Hosp. Medical Center, Dept of Pediatrics, Harvard Medical Sch., Boston, Mass; Asst Prof. of Pediatrics, Harvard Medical Sch., 1970–72; Associate Prof. of Medicine, Depts of Medicine and Laboratory Medicine, Univ. of California, San Francisco, 1972–77; Chief, Hematology Service, San Francisco General Hospital, 1972–79; Prof. of Medicine, Univ. of California, 1977–84. Mem., Nat. Acad. of Scis, USA, 1986. Hon. MD Univ. of Cagliari, Sardinia, 1981; Hon. DSc Chinese Univ. of Hong Kong, 1981. *Publications:* contribs to: Nature, Proc. of Nat. Academy of Sciences, Jl of Clinical Investigation, Blood, British Jl of Haematology, and others. *Recreations:* tennis, skiing. *Address:* U426, University of California San Francisco, San Francisco, California 94143, USA. *T:* (415) 476–5841.

See also Sir Kan Yuet-Keung.

KAN Yuet-Keung, Sir, GBE 1979 (CBE 1967; OBE 1959); Kt 1972; JP; Chairman, Hong Kong Trade Development Council, 1979–83; Chairman, Bank of East Asia Ltd, 1963–83; *b* 26 July 1913; *s* of late Kan Tong Po, JP; *m* 1940, Ida; two *s* one *d*. *Educ:* Hong Kong Univ.; London Univ. BA Hong Kong 1934. Solicitor and Notary Public. MLC 1968–72, Sen. Unofficial MEC 1974–80, Hong Kong. Pro-Chancellor, Chinese Univ. of Hong Kong, 1983– (Chm., Council, 1973–83). Hon. Fellow, LSE, 1980. Hon. LLD: Chinese Univ. of Hong Kong, 1968; Univ. of Hong Kong, 1973. Order of Sacred Treasure, 3rd Class, Japan; Officier de l'Ordre National du Mérite (France), 1978; Officer's Cross, Order of Merit 1st class (Germany), 1983; Grand Decoration of Honour in Gold with Star (Austria), 1983; Order of Sacred Treasure, 2nd class (Japan), 1983; Knight Grand Cross, Royal Order of Northern Pole Star (Sweden), 1983. *Recreations:* tennis, swimming, golf. *Address:* Swire House, 11th Floor, Chater Road, Hong Kong. *T:* Hong Kong 238181.

See also Yuet Wai Kan.

KANE, Professor George; FBA 1968; William Rand Kenan Jr Professor of English in the University of North Carolina at Chapel Hill, since 1976, Chairman of the Division of the Humanities, 1980–83; *b* 4 July 1916; *o s* of George Michael and Clara Kane; *m* 1946, Katherine Bridget, *o d* of Lt-Col R. V. Montgomery, MC; one *s* one *d*. *Educ:* St Peter's Coll.; British Columbia University; Toronto Univ.; University Coll., London (Fellow 1971). BA (University of BC), 1936; Research Fellow, University of Toronto, 1936–37; MA (Toronto), 1937; Research Fellow, Northwestern Univ., 1937–38; IODE Schol., for BC, 1938–39. Served War of 1939–45: Artists' Rifles, 1939–40; Rifle Bde, 1940–46 (despatches). PhD (London), 1946; Asst Lecturer in English, University Coll., London, 1946, Lecturer, 1948, Reader in English, 1953; Prof. of English Language and Literature and Head of English Dept, Royal Holloway College, London Univ., 1955–65; Prof. of English Language and Medieval Literature, 1965–76 and Head of English Dept, 1968–76, King's College, London, Prof. Emeritus, 1976, Fellow, 1976. Vis. Prof., Medieval Acad. of America, 1970, 1982, Corresp. Fellow, 1975, Fellow, 1978; Fellow, Amer. Acad. of Arts and Scis, 1977; Sen. Fellow, Southeastern Inst. of Medieval and Renaissance Studies, 1978. Member: Council, Early English Text Soc., 1969; Governing Body, SOAS, 1970–76; Council, British Acad., 1974–76; Governing Body, Univ. of N Carolina Press, 1979–84. Sir Israel Gollancz Memorial Prize, British Acad., 1963; Haskins Medallist, Med. Acad. of Amer., 1978. Chambers Meml Lectr, University Coll. London, 1965; British Academy Lectr, Accademia Nazionale dei Lincei, Rome, 1976; John Coffin Meml Lectr, Univ. of London, 1979; Public Orator, Univ. of London, 1962–66; Annual Chaucer Lectr, New Chaucer Soc., 1980. Gen. editor of London Edn of Piers Plowman. *Publications:* Middle English Literature, 1951; Piers Plowman, the A Version, 1960; Piers Plowman: The Evidence for Authorship, 1965; Piers Plowman: the B version, 1975; Geoffrey Chaucer, 1984; articles and reviews. *Recreation:* fishing. *Address:* Greenlaw Hall, Chapel Hill, North Carolina, USA. *Clubs:* Athenæum, Flyfishers'.

KANE, Jack, OBE 1969; DL; JP; Chairman, Age Concern, Scotland, since 1983; Lord Provost of the City of Edinburgh and Lord Lieutenant of the County of the City of Edinburgh, 1972–75; *b* 1 April 1911; *m* 1940, Anne Murphy; one *s* two *d*. *Educ:* Bathgate Academy. Served War, 1940–46. Librarian, 1936–55. Pres., SE of Scotland Dist, Workers' Educnl Assoc., 1983– (Sec., 1955–76). Chm., Board of Trustees for Nat. Galls of Scotland, 1975–80; Mem., South of Scotland Electricity Bd, 1975–81, Chm., Consultative Council, 1977–81. JP Edinburgh, 1945; DL City of Edinburgh, 1976. Dr *hc* Edinburgh, 1976. Grand Officer, Order of the Oaken Crown (Luxembourg), 1972; Grand Cross of Merit (W Germany). *Recreations:* reading, walking. *Address:* 88 Thirlestane Road, Edinburgh EH9 1AS. *T:* 031–447 7757. *Club:* Newcraighall Miners' Welfare Inst.

KANG, Dr Young Hoon; Ambassador of the Republic of Korea to the Holy See, since 1985; *b* 30 May 1922; *m* 1947, Hyo-Soo Kim; two *s* one *d*. *Educ:* Univ. of Manchuria (BAEcon); graduated from US Comd and Gen. Staff Coll., Kansas, 1958; Univ. of Southern California (MA Internat. Relns 1966, PhD Pol. Sci. 1973). Mil. Attaché to Korean Embassy, Washington DC, 1952–53; Korean Army Div. Comdr, 1953; Dir, Jt Staff, Korean Jt Chiefs of Staff, 1954; Asst Minister of Defence, 1955–56; Korean Army Corps Comdr, 1959–60; Supt, Korean Mil. Acad., 1960–61; retired, rank of Lt-Gen., 1961. Staff Mem., Research Inst. on Communist Strategy and Propaganda, Univ. of S California, 1968–69; Dir, Research Inst. on Korean Affairs, Silver Spring, Md, 1970–76; Dean, Graduate Sch., Hankuk Univ. of For. Studies, Korea, 1977–78; Chancellor, Inst. of For. Affairs and Nat. Security, Min. of For. Affairs, Korea, 1978–80; Ambassador to UK, 1981–84. Military service medals include Ulchi with Silver Star, Chungmu with Gold Star. *Address:* Embassy of the Republic of Korea, Via Della Mendola 109, 00135 Rome, Italy.

KANTOROWICH, Prof. Roy Herman, BArch (Witwatersrand), MA (Manchester), RIBA, FRTPI; Professor of Town and Country Planning, 1961–84, Professor Emeritus, since 1984, Dean of the Faculty of Arts, 1975–76 and Director of Wolfson Design Unit, 1981–84, University of Manchester; *b* Johannesburg, 24 Nov. 1916; *s* of George Kantorowich and Deborah (*née* Baranov); *m* 1943, Petronella Sophie Wissema (violinist, as Nella Wissema); one *s* two *d*. *Educ:* King Edward VII Sch., Johannesburg; University of Witwatersrand. BArch 1939; ARIBA 1940; MTPI 1965 (AMTPI 1946). Post-grad. studies in Housing and Planning, MIT and Columbia Univ., 1939–41; Planning Officer: Vanderbijl Park New Town, 1942–45; directing Cape Town Foreshore Scheme, 1945–48; private practice in Cape Town, in architecture and town planning, 1948–61. Pres., S African Inst. Town and Regional Planners, 1960. Formerly Town Planning Consultant to Cape Provincial Admin., and for many cities and towns in S Africa incl. Durban, Pretoria and Port Elizabeth; Cons. for New Town of Ashkelon, Israel, 1950–56. Member: NW Econ. Planning Coun. 1965–79; Council (Chm., Educn Cttee), RTPI, 1965–70; Planning Cttee, SSRC, 1969–73; Construction and Environment Bd, and Chm., Town Planning Panel, CNAA, 1971–75; Natal Building Soc. Fellowship, 1980. Buildings include: Civic Centre, Welkom, OFS; Baxter Hall, University of Cape Town; Sea Point Telephone Exchange (Cape Province Inst. of Architects Bronze Medal Award); Architecture and Planning Building, Univ. of Manchester. FRSA 1972. *Publications:* Cape Town Foreshore Plan, 1948; (with Lord Holford) Durban 1985, a plan for central Durban in its Regional Setting, 1968; Three Perspectives on planning for the 'eighties, 1981; contribs to SAArch. Record, Jl RTPI and other professional jls. *Recreations:* music, tennis. *Address:* 3 Winster Avenue, Manchester M20 8YA. *T:* 061–445 9417. *Club:* Northern Lawn Tennis.

KAPLAN, Prof. Joseph; Professor of Physics, University of California at Los Angeles (UCLA), 1940–70, now Professor Emeritus; *b* 8 Sept. 1902; *s* of Henry and Rosa Kaplan, Tapolcza, Hungary; *m* 1933, Katherine Elizabeth Feraud; no *c*. *Educ:* Johns Hopkins University, Baltimore, Md, PhD 1927; National Research Fellow, Princeton Univ., 1927–28. University of Calif. at Los Angeles: Asst Prof. of Physics, 1928–35; Associate Prof., 1935–40; Prof., 1940–. Chief, Operations Analysis Section, Second Air Force, 1943–45 (Exceptional Civilian Service Medal, US Air Corps, 1947). Chm., US Nat. Cttee for Internat. Geophysical Year, 1953–64. Fellow: Inst. of Aeronautical Sciences, 1957; Amer. Meteorological Soc., 1970 (Pres., 1963–67). Mem. Nat. Acad. of Sciences, 1957; Hon. Mem., Amer. Meteorological Soc., 1967; Vice-Pres., International Union of Geodesy and Geophysics, 1960–63, Pres., 1963–; Hon. Governor, Hebrew Univ. of Jerusalem, 1968. Hon. DSc: Notre Dame, 1957; Carleton Coll., 1957; Hon. LHD: Yeshiva Univ. and Hebrew Union Coll., 1958; Univ. of Judaism, 1959. Exceptional Civilian Service Medal (USAF), 1960; Hodgkins Prize and Medal, 1965. Exceptional Civilian Service Medal, 1969; John A. Fleming Medal, Amer. Geophysical Union, 1970; Commemorative Medal, 50th Anniversary, Amer. Meteorological Soc., 1970; Special Award, UCLA Alumni Assoc., 1970. *Publications:* Across the Space Frontier, 1950; Physics and Medicine of the Upper Atmosphere, 1952; (co-author) Great Men of Physics, 1969; publications in Physical Review, Nature, Proc. Nat. Acad. of Sciences, Jl Chemical Physics. *Recreations:* golf, ice-skating, walking. *Address:* 1565 Kelton Avenue, Los Angeles, Calif 90024, USA. *T:* Granite 38839. *Club:* Cosmos (Washington, DC).

KAPPEL, Frederick R.; retired as Chairman of Boards, American Telephone & Telegraph Company and International Paper Company; Chairman, Board of Governors, US Postal Service; *b* Albert Lea, Minnesota, 14 Jan. 1902; *s* of Fred A. Kappel and Gertrude M. Towle Kappel; *m* 1st, 1927, Ruth Carolyn Ihm (decd); two *d*; 2nd, 1978, Alice McW. Harris. *Educ:* University of Minnesota (BSE). Northwestern Bell Telephone Company: various positions in Minnesota, 1924–33; Plant Engineer, Nebraska, S Dakota, 1934. Plant Operations Supervisor (Exec.) Gen. Staff, Omaha, Nebraska, 1937, Asst Vice-Pres. Operations, 1939, Vice-Pres. Operations and Dir, 1942. Amer. Telephone & Telegraph Co., NY: Asst Vice-Pres. (O & E), Vice-Pres. (Long Lines), Vice Pres. (O & E), 1949. Pres. Western Electric Co., 1954–56; Chm. and Chief Exec. Officer, Amer. Tel. & Tel. Co., 1956–67, Chm. Exec. Cttee, 1967–69; Chm. Bd, International Paper Co., 1969–71, Chm. Exec. Cttee 1971–74. Director: Amer. Telephone & Telegraph Co., 1956–70; Chase Manhattan Bank, 1956–72; Metropolitan Life Insurance Co., 1958–75; General Foods Corporation, 1961–73; Standard Oil Co. (NJ), 1966–70; Whirlpool Corp., 1967–72; Chase Manhattan Corp., 1969–72; Boys' Club of America; Acad. of Polit. Sciences, 1963–71; Member: Business Council (Chm., 1963–64); Advisory Board of Salvation Army, 1957–73; US Chamber of Commerce; various societies. Trustee: Presbyterian Hospital, 1949–74; Grand Central Art Galleries, Inc., 1957–70; Aerospace Corp., 1967–74; Tax Foundation, 1960–72. Trustee, University of Minnesota Foundation. Holds numerous hon. doctorates and awards, including: Cross of Comdr of Postal Award, France, 1962; Presidential Medal of Freedom, 1964. *Publications:* Vitality in a Business Enterprise, 1960; Business Purpose and Performance. *Recreation:* golf. *Address:* Apt 1101, 435 S Gulfstream Avenue, Sarasota, Fla 33577, USA. *Clubs:* Triangle, University, Economic (New York); International (Washington); Bird Key Yacht, Sarabay Country (Sarasota, Fla).

KARACHI, Archbishop of, (RC), since 1958; **His Eminence Cardinal Joseph Cordeiro;** *b* Bombay, India, 19 Jan. 1918. *Educ:* St Patrick's High School; DJ College,

Karachi; Papal Seminary, Kandy, Ceylon. Priest, 1946; Asst Chaplain, St Francis Xavier's, Hyderabad, Sind, 1947; Asst Principal, St Patrick's High School, Karachi, 1948; Student at Oxford, 1948; Asst Principal, St Patrick's High Sch., 1950; Principal, Grammar Sch., and Rector, Diocesan Seminary, Quetta, 1952. Cardinal, 1973. *Address:* St Patrick's Cathedral, Karachi 3, Pakistan. *T:* 515870.

KARAJAN, Herbert von; *see* von Karajan.

KARANJA, Dr Josphat Njuguna; Chairman, General Accident Insurance Co. (Kenya) Ltd, since 1980; *b* 5 Feb. 1931; *s* of Josphat Njuguna; *m* 1966, Beatrice Nyindombi, Fort Portal, Uganda; one *s* two *d*. *Educ:* Alliance High Sch., Kikuyu, Kenya; Makerere Coll., Kampala, Uganda; University of Delhi, India; Princeton Univ., New Jersey, USA (PhD). Lecturer in African Studies, Farleigh Dickinson Univ., New Jersey, 1961–62; Lecturer in African and Modern European History, University College, Nairobi, Kenya, 1962–63; High Comr for Kenya in London, 1963–70; Vice-Chancellor, Univ. of Nairobi, 1970–79. *Recreations:* golf, tennis. *Address:* General Accident Insurance Co. (Kenya) Ltd, Icea Building, Kenyatta Avenue, PO Box 42166, Nairobi, Kenya.

KARIMJEE, Sir Tayabali Hassanali Alibhoy, Kt 1955; Brilliant Star of Zanzibar (3rd Class); Jubilee Medal of Sultan of Zanzibar; *b* 7 Nov. 1897; *s* of Hassanali A. Karimjee and Zenubbai H. A. Karimjee; *m* 1917, Sugrabai Mohamedali Karimjee; one *d*. *Educ:* Zanzibar and Karachi. Pres., Indian National Association, Zanzibar, 1930 and 1942; Pres. Chamber of Commerce, Zanzibar, 1940, 1941, 1942; Mem. Fighter Fund Cttee, 1940–43; Mem. Red Cross Cttee, 1940–45; MLC, Zanzibar, 1933–45. Chm. Board of Directors, Karimjee Jivanjee & Co. Ltd, Karimjee Jivanjee Estates Ltd, Karimjee J. Properties Ltd, International Motor Mart Ltd (Tanganyika); Director, Karimjee Jivanjee & Co. (UK) Ltd, London. King George V Jubilee Medal, 1935; Coronation Medals, 1937 and 1953. *Address:* 60 Clifton, Karachi-0602, Pakistan. *Clubs:* Royal Commonwealth Society, Royal Over-Seas League; Karachi (Karachi); WIAA (Bombay).

KARK, (Arthur) Leslie; MA (Oxon), FRSA; Author, Barrister; Chairman: Lucie Clayton Secretarial College; Lucie Clayton Ltd; *b* 12 July 1910; *s* of Victor and Helena Kark, Johannesburg; *m* 1st, 1935, Joan Tetley (marr. diss., 1956); two *d*; 2nd, 1956, Evelyn Gordine (*see* E. F. Kark); one *s* one *d*. *Educ:* Clayesmore; St John's Coll., Oxford. Called to Bar, Inner Temple, 1932; Features Editor of World's Press News, 1933; Editor of Photography, 1934; Public Relations Officer to Advertising Association, 1935; Features Editor News Review, 1936–39; London Theatre Critic, New York Herald Tribune; News Editor, Ministry of Information, 1940. Served War of 1939–45, RAF, 1940–46; Air-gunner; Wing Commander in Command of Public Relations (Overseas) Unit; author, Air Ministry's official book on Air War, Far East. Short stories and novels translated into French, Swedish, German, Polish, etc. *Publications:* The Fire Was Bright, 1944; Red Rain, 1946; An Owl in the Sun, 1948; Wings of the Phœnix, 1949; On the Haycock, 1957. *Recreations:* fly-fishing, golf. *Address:* 9 Clareville Grove, SW7. *T:* 01–373 2621; Roche House, Sheep Street, Burford, Oxon. *T:* Burford 3007. *Club:* United Oxford & Cambridge University.

KARK, Austen Steven; Managing Director, External Broadcasting, BBC, 1985–86 (Deputy Managing Director, 1981–85); *b* 20 Oct. 1926; *s* of Major Norman Kark and late Ethel Kark, formerly of Eaton Place, London, and Johannesburg; *m* 1st, 1949, Margaret Solomon (marr. diss. 1954); two *d*; 2nd, 1954, Nina Mary Bawden, *qv*; one *d* one step *s* (and one step *s* decd). *Educ:* Upper Canada Coll., Toronto; Nautical Coll., Pangbourne; RNC; Magdalen Coll., Oxford (MA). Served RN and RIN, 1943–46. Directed first prodn in UK of Sartre's The Flies, Oxford, 1948; trained in journalism, Belfast Telegraph, L'Illustré, Zofingen, Switzerland; Courier, Bandwagon, London Mystery Magazine; free-lance journalist and broadcaster, London and New York, 1952–54; joined BBC, 1954; scriptwriter; Producer, External Services; Head of S European Service, 1964; Head of E European (and Russian) Service, 1972; Editor, World Service, 1973; Controller, English Services, and Editor, World Service, 1974; advised Lord Soames on election broadcasting, Rhodesia, and chaired, for Prime Minister Mugabe, enquiry into future of radio and television in Zimbabwe, 1980. *Recreations:* Real tennis, mosaics, garden, croquet. *Address:* 22 Noel Road, N1 8HA. *Clubs:* Oriental, MCC, Royal Tennis Court, Bushmen (ex-Chairman).

KARK, Mrs Evelyn Florence, (*nom de plume* **Lucie Clayton**); Director; *b* 5 Dec. 1928; *d* of Emily and William Gordine; *m* 1956 (Arthur) Leslie Kark, *qv*; one *s* one *d*. *Educ:* privately and inconspicuously. Asst to Editor, Courier Magazine, 1950; became Head of model school and agency (assuming name of Lucie Clayton), 1952; founded Lucie Clayton Sch. of Fashion Design and Dressmaking, 1961, and Lucie Clayton Secretarial College, 1966. *Publications:* The World of Modelling, 1968; Modelling and Beauty Care, 1985. *Recreations:* talking, tapestry, cooking. *Address:* 9 Clareville Grove, SW7. *T:* 01–373 2621; Roche House, Burford, Oxfordshire. *T:* Burford 3007.

KARK, Leslie; *see* Kark, A. L.

KARK, Mrs Nina Mary; *see* Bawden, N. M.

KARMEL, His Honour Alexander D., QC 1954; an Additional Judge, Central Criminal Court, later a Circuit Judge, 1968–79; *b* 16 May 1904; *s* of Elias Karmel and Adeline (*née* Freedman); *m* 1937, Mary, *widow* of Arthur Lee and *d* of Newman Lipton; one *s*. *Educ:* Newcastle upon Tyne Royal Grammar Sch. Barrister-at-law, Middle Temple, 1932; Master of the Bench, 1962; Leader of Northern Circuit, 1966; Comr of Assize, Stafford, summer 1967; Recorder of Bolton, 1962–68. Mem., Bar Council, 1950–53, 1961–64. *Recreations:* croquet, golf. *Address:* 171 Rivermead Court, Ranelagh Gardens, SW6 3SF. *T:* 01–736 4609. *Clubs:* Royal Automobile, Hurlingham.

KARMEL, Emeritus Prof. Peter Henry, AC 1976; CBE 1967; Vice-Chancellor, Australian National University, since 1982; *b* 9 May 1922; *s* of Simeon Karmel; *m* 1946, Lena Garrett; one *s* five *d*. *Educ:* Caulfield Grammar Sch.; Univ. of Melbourne (BA); Trinity Coll., Cambridge (PhD). Research Officer, Commonwealth Bureau of Census and Statistics, 1943–45; Lectr in Econs, Univ. of Melbourne, 1946; Rouse Ball Res. Student, Trinity Coll., Cambridge, 1947–48; Sen. Lectr in Econs, Univ. of Melbourne, 1949; Prof. of Econs, 1950–62, Emeritus, 1965, Univ. of Adelaide; Principal-designate, Univ. of Adelaide at Bedford Park (subseq. Flinders Univ. of SA), 1961–66; Vice-Chancellor, Flinders Univ. of SA, 1966–71; Chancellor, Univ. of Papua and New Guinea, 1969–70 (Chm., Interim Council, 1965–69); Chairman: Univs Commn, 1971–77; Commonwealth Tertiary Educn Commn, 1977–82. Mem., SSRC, 1952–71; Mem. Council, Univ. of Adelaide, 1955–69; Vis. Prof. of Econs, Queen's Univ., Belfast, 1957–58; Mem. Commonwealth Cttee: on Future of Tertiary Educn, 1961–65; of Economic Enquiry, 1963–65; Mem., Australian Council for Educn Research, 1968– (Pres., 1979–); Chairman: Cttee of Enquiry into Educn in SA, 1969–70; Interim Cttee for Aust. Schools Commn, 1972–73; Cttee of Enquiry on Med. Schs, 1972–73; Cttee of Enquiry on Open Univ., 1973–74; Australia Council, 1974–77; Cttee on Post-Secondary Educn in Tasmania, 1975–76; Quality of Educn Review Cttee, 1984–85; Member: Commonwealth Govt Cttee to Review Efficiency and Effectiveness in Higher Educn, 1986; Adv. Cttee of Cities Commn, 1972–74; CSIRO Adv. Council, 1979–82. Leader,

OECD Review of US Educn Policy, 1978–79 and NZ Educn Policy, 1982. FACE 1969; FASSA 1971. Hon. LLD: Univ. of Papua and New Guinea, 1970; Univ. of Melbourne, 1975; Univ. of Queensland, 1985; Hon. LittD Flinders Univ. of SA, 1971; Hon. DLit, Murdoch Univ., 1975; DU Newcastle, NSW, 1978. Mackie Medal, 1975; Aust. Coll. of Educn Medal, 1981. *Publications:* Applied Statistics for Economists, 1957, 1962 (1970 edn with M. Polasek, 4th edn 1977), Portuguese edn, 1972; (with M. Brunt) Structure of the Australian Economy, 1962, repr 1963, 1966; (with G. C. Harcourt and R. H. Wallace) Economic Activity, 1967 (Italian edn 1969); articles in Economic Record, Population Studies, Jl Royal Statistical Assoc., and other learned jls. *Address:* Australian National rsity, GPO Box 4, Canberra, ACT 2601, Australia. *T:* 062–495111.

KARN, Prof. Valerie Ann; Professor of Environmental Health and Housing, University of Salford, since 1984; *b* 17 May 1939; *d* of Arthur and Winnifred Karn; one *d*. *Educ:* Newquay County Grammar School; Lady Margaret Hall, Oxford (BA Geography); Univ. of the Punjab, Lahore (Commonwealth scholar); Graduate Sch. of Design, Harvard Univ.; PhD Birmingham (Urban Studies). Res. Officer, ODI, 1963; Res. Fellow, Inst. of Social and Economic Res., Univ. of York, 1964–66; Res. Associate, Lectr, Sen. Lectr, Centre for Urban and Regional Studies, Univ. of Birmingham, 1966–84. Res. Officer, Central Housing Adv. Cttee, Sub-Cttee on Housing Management, 1967–69; Member: Housing Services Adv. Gp, 1976–79; Inquiry into British Housing, 1984–86; ESRC Social Affairs Cttee, 1985–. BAAS Lister Lectr, 1979; Vis. Fellow, Urban Inst., Washington DC, 1979–80. *Publications:* Retiring to the Seaside, 1977 (Oddfellows Social Concern Book Prize); (jtly) Housing in Retirement, 1973; (ed jtly) The Consumers' Experience of Housing, 1980; (jtly) Home-ownership in the Inner City, Salvation or Despair, 1985; (jtly) Race, Class, and Public Housing, 1986; chapters in: The Future of Council Housing, 1982; Family Matters, 1983; Ethnic Pluralism and Public Policy, 1983; Between Centre and Locality, 1985; Low Cost Home Ownership, 1985; The Housing Crisis, 1986; res. reports and articles in jls. *Recreations:* gardening, walking. *Address:* 71 Barton Road, Worsley M28 4PF. *T:* (home) 061–794 7791; (office) 061–736 5843.

KARP, David; novelist; *b* New York City, 5 May 1922; *s* of Abraham Karp and Rebecca Levin; *m* 1944, Lillian Klass; two *s*. *Educ:* College of The City of New York. US Army, 1943–46, S Pacific, Japan; College, 1946–48; Continuity Dir, Station WNYC, New York, 1948–49; free-lance motion picture-television writer and motion picture producer, 1949–; President: Leda Productions Inc., 1968–; Television-Radio Branch, Writers Guild of America West, 1969–71; Member: Editorial Bd, Television Quarterly, 1966–71, 1972–77; Council, Writers Guild of America, 1966–73; Bd of Trustees, Producer-Writers Guild of America Pension Plan, 1968– (Chm., 1978); Bd of Trustees, Writers Guild-Industry Health Fund, 1973– (Chm., 1980). Guggenheim Fellow, 1956–57. *Publications:* One, 1953; The Day of the Monkey, 1955; All Honorable Men, 1956; Leave Me Alone, 1957; The Sleepwalkers, 1960; Vice-President in Charge of Revolution (with Murray D. Lincoln), 1960; The Last Believers, 1964; short stories in Saturday Eve. Post, Collier's, Esquire, Argosy, The American, etc; articles and reviews in NY Times, Los Angeles Times, Saturday Review, Nation, etc. *Recreations:* photography, reading. *Address:* 1116 Corsica Drive, Pacific Palisades, Calif 90272, USA. *T:* 459–1623. *Club:* PEN (New York).

KARRAN, Graham, QFSM 1985; Chief Fire Officer, West Yorkshire Fire Service, since 1983; *b* 28 Nov. 1939; *s* of Joseph Karran and Muriel Benson; *m* 1960, Thelma Gott; one *s* one *d*. *Educ:* Bootle Grammar Sch.; Liverpool College of Building. Estate Management, 1958–60; Southport Fire Bde, 1960–63; Lancashire County Fire Bde, 1963–74; Greater Manchester Fire Service, 1974–78; Cheshire County Fire Service, 1978–80; Derbyshire Fire Service, 1980–83. *Publications:* articles in English and Amer. Fire jls. *Recreations:* music, sailing, beachcombing. *Address:* Oakroyd Hall, Birkenshaw, West Yorkshire BD11 2DY. *T:* Bradford (West Yorks) 682311. *Club:* St John's.

KARSH, Yousuf, OC 1968; Portrait Photographer since 1932; *b* Mardin, Armenia-in-Turkey, 23 Dec. 1908; parents Armenian; Canadian Citizen; *m* 1939, Solange Gauthier (*d* 1961); *m* 1962, Estrellita Maria Nachbar. *Educ:* Sherbrooke, PQ Canada; studied photography in Boston, Mass., USA. Portrayed Winston Churchill in Canada's Houses of Parliament, 1941; King George VI, 1943; HM Queen (then Princess) Elizabeth and the Duke of Edinburgh, 1951; HH Pope Pius XII, 1951; also portrayed, among many others: Shaw, Wells, Einstein, Sibelius, Somerset Maugham, Picasso, Eden, Eisenhower, Tito, Eleanor Roosevelt, Thomas Mann, Bertrand Russell, Attlee, Nehru, Ingrid Bergmann, Lord Mountbatten of Burma, Augustus John, Pope John Paul II; nine portraits used on postage stamps of eleven countries. One man exhibns: Men Who Make our World, Pav. of Canada, Expo. 67; Montreal Mus. of Fine Arts, 1968; Boston Mus. of Fine Arts, 1968; Corning Mus., 1968; Detroit Inst. of Arts, 1969; Corcoran Gall. of Art, Washington, 1969; Macdonald House, London, 1969; Seattle Art Museum; Japan (country-wide), and Honolulu, 1970; Men Who Make our World, Europe and USA, 1971, 1972, 1973, 1974, 1975, 1976, 1977, 1978, 1979, 1980; exhibn acquired in toto by: Museum of Modern Art, Tokyo; Nat. Gall. of Australia; Province of Alberta, Canada, 1975–76; numerous exhibns throughout US, 1971–75, 1976–77; Ulrich Museum, Wichita, Kansas, 1978; Museum of Science and Industry, Chicago, 1978; Evansville Museum, Ind., 1979; Palm Springs Desert Museum, 1980; inaugural exhibn, Museum of Photography, Film and TV, Bradford, 1983; NY, 1983; Nat. Portrait Gall., 1983; Edinburgh, 1984; Internat. Center of Photography, NY, 1983; Helsinki, 1984; Minneapolis Museum, 1985; Syracuse Museum 1985. Visiting Professor: Ohio Univ., 1967–69; Emerson Coll., Boston, 1972–73, 1973–74; Photographic Advisor, Internat. Exhibn, Expo '70, Osaka, Japan; Judge, UN 40th anniversary internat. poster contest, 1985. Trustee, Photographic Arts and Scis Foundn, 1970. FRPS; Fellow Rochester Sci. Mus. RCA 1975. Holds fifteen hon. degrees. Canada Council Medal, 1965; Centennial Medal, 1967; Master of Photographic Arts, Prof. Photogrs of Canada, 1970; First Gold Medal, Nat. Assoc. Photog. Art, 1974; Life Achievement Award, Encyclopaedia Britannica, 1980; Silver Shingle Award, Law Sch., Boston Univ., 1983. *Publications:* Faces of Destiny, 1947; (co-author) This is the Mass, 1958; Portraits of Greatness, 1959; (co-author) This is Rome, 1960; (co-author) This is the Holy Land, 1961; (autobiog.) In Search of Greatness, 1962; (co-author) These are the Sacraments, 1963; (co-author) The Warren Court; Karsh Portfolio, 1967; Faces of our Time, 1971; Karsh Portraits, 1976; Karsh Canadians, 1979; Karsh: a fifty year retrospective, 1983. *Recreations:* tennis, bird-watching, archæology, music. *Address:* (business) Chateau Laurier Hotel, Suite 660, Ottawa, Canada. *T:* AC 613–236–7181. *Clubs:* Garrick; Rideau (Ottawa); Century, Dutch Treat (NY).

KASER, Michael Charles, MA; Reader in Economics, University of Oxford, and Professorial Fellow of St Antony's College since 1972; *b* 2 May 1926; *er s* of Charles Joseph Kaser and Mabel Blunden; *m* 1954, Elisabeth Anne Mary, *er d* of Cyril Gascoigne Piggford; four *s* one *d*. *Educ:* King's Coll., Cambridge (Exhibr). Foreign Service, London and Moscow, 1947–51; UN Secretariat, Econ. Commn for Europe, Geneva, 1951–63; Faculty Fellow, St Antony's Coll., Oxford, 1963–72; Associate Fellow, Templeton Coll., Oxford. Vis. Prof. of Econs, Univ. of Michigan, 1966; Vis. Lectr, Cambridge Univ., 1967–68, 1977–78 and 1978–79; Vis. Lectr, INSEAD, Fontainebleau, 1959–82. Specialist Advr, Foreign Affairs Cttee, H of C. Oxford Univ. Latin Preacher, 1982. Convenor/Chm.,

Nat. Assoc. for Soviet and East European Studies, 1965–73, Chm., Jt Cttee with BUAS, 1980–84; Dep. Treas., Internat. Econ. Assoc., 1980–83; Vice-Chm., Internat. Activities Cttee (Vice-Chm., Area Studies Panel, SSRC) ESRC, 1980–84; Vice Chm. Co-ordinating Council, Area Studies Assocs, 1984– (Sec., 1980–84); Governor, Plater Coll., Oxford; Acad. Council, Wilton Park (FCO). Member: Council, Royal Econ. Soc.; Council, RIIA, 1979–85; Internat. Soc. Sci. Council, UNESCO; Council, SSEES; Editorial Boards: Soviet Studies, Energy Economics, Oxford Rev. of Educn, CUP East European Monograph Series; Steering Cttee, Königswinter Anglo-German Confs (Chm., Oxford Organizing Cttee, 1975–78). *Publications:* Comecon: Integration Problems of the Planned Economies, 1965, 2nd edn 1967; (ed) Economic Development for Eastern Europe, 1968; (with J. Zieliński) Planning in East Europe, 1970; Soviet Economics, 1970; (ed, with R. Portes) Planning and Market Relations, 1971; (ed, with H. Höhmann and K. Thalheim) The New Economic Systems of Eastern Europe, 1975; (ed, with A. Brown) The Soviet Union since the Fall of Khrushchev, 1975, 2nd edn 1978; Health Care in the Soviet Union and Eastern Europe, 1976; (ed with A. Brown) Soviet Policy for the 1980s, 1982; (ed jtly) The Cambridge Encyclopaedia of Russia and the Soviet Union, 1982; Gen. Ed., The Economic History of Eastern Europe 1919–1975, vols I and II (1919–49), vol. III (1949–75), 1985; papers in economic jls and symposia. *Address:* 7 Chadlington Road, Oxford. *T:* Oxford 55581. *Club:* Reform.

KASSIM bin Mohammed Hussein, Datuk, DPCM, DIMP, JMN 1978; High Commissioner for Malaysia in London, 1983–86; *b* Perak, Malaysia, 14 Feb. 1928; *s* of Mohammed Hussein and Puteh Sapiah; *m* 1962, Koeswardani; one *s* three *d. Educ:* Malay Coll., Kuala Kangsar, Perak; Univ. of Malaya (BA). Malayan Administrative Service, 1955; Min. of Foreign Affairs, Kuala Lumpur, 1958; Jakarta, 1959; Min. of Foreign Affairs, 1962; Karachi, 1964; Min. of Foreign Affairs, 1965; Counsellor: Manila, 1967; Cairo, 1968; Chargé d'Affaires, Addis Ababa, 1969; Counsellor, later Minister, Washington, 1971; Minister, Tokyo, 1971–74; Ambassador to Burma, 1974; Dir Gen. (ASEAN), Min. of Foreign Affairs, 1977; Ambassador to Belgium, Luxembourg and EEC, 1980–83. Hon. Fellow, Ealing Coll. of Higher Educn, 1984. *Recreations:* golf, tennis. *Address:* 1 Jalan Setia Jaya, Damansara Heights, Kuala Lumpur, Malaysia. *T:* Kuala Lumpur 949–434.

KASTNER, Prof. Leslie James, MA, ScD Cantab, FIMechE; Professor of Mechanical Engineering, King's College, University of London, 1955–76, now Emeritus; Dean of Faculty of Engineering, University of London, 1974–76; *b* 10 Dec. 1911; *o s* of late Professor Leon E. Kastner, sometime Prof. of French Language and Literature, University of Manchester, and of Elsie E. Kastner; *m* 1958, Joyce, *o d* of Lt-Col Edward Lillingston, DSO, Belstone, Devon. *Educ:* Dreghorn Castle Sch.; Colinton, Midlothian; Highgate Sch.; Clare Coll., Cambridge (Mechanical Science Tripos). Apprenticeship with Davies and Metcalfe, Ltd, Locomotive Engineers, of Romiley, Stockport, 1930–31 and 1934–36; Development Engineer, 1936–38; Osborne Reynolds Research Fellowship, University of Manchester, 1938; Lectr in Engineering, University of Manchester, 1941–46; Senior Lectr, 1946–48; Prof. of Engineering, University Coll. of Swansea, University of Wales, 1948–55. Mem. of Council, Institution of Mechanical Engineers, 1954. FKC 1974. Graduates' Prize, InstMechE, 1939; Herbert Ackroyd Stuart Prize, 1943; Dugald Clerk Prize, 1956. *Publications:* various research papers in applied thermodynamics and fluid flow. *Address:* 37 St Anne's Road, Eastbourne. *Club:* National Liberal.

KATCHALSKI-KATZIR, Prof. Ephraim; *see* Katzir, Prof. E.

KATENGA-KAUNDA, Reid Willie; Malaŵi Independence Medal, 1964; Malaŵi Republic Medal, 1966; business executive; *b* 20 Aug. 1929; *s* of Gibson Amon Katenga Kaunda and Maggie Talengeske Nyabanda; *m* 1952, Elicy Nyabanda; one *s* three *d* (and one *s* one *d* decd). *Educ:* Ndola Govt Sch., Zambia; Inst. of Public Administration, Malaŵi; Trinity Coll., Oxford Univ.; Administrative Staff Coll., Henley. Sec., Nkhota Kota Rice Co-op. Soc. Ltd, 1952–62; Dist. Comr, Karonga, Malaŵi, 1964–65; Sen. Asst Sec., Min. of External Affairs, Zomba, Malaŵi, 1966; MP and Parly Sec., Office of the President and Cabinet, Malaŵi, 1966–68; Dep. Regional Chm., MCP, Northern Region, 1967–68; Under Sec., Office of the President and Cabinet, 1968–69; High Comr in London, 1969–70; Perm. Sec., Min. of Trade, Industry and Tourism, 1971–72; High Comr in London, 1972–73, and concurrently to the Holy See, Portugal, Belgium, Holland and France. Dep. Chm., Ncheu and Mchinji Inquiry Commn, 1967. *Recreations:* reading, walking, cinema, Association football. *Address:* c/o PO Box 511, Blantyre, Malaŵi.

KATIN, Peter Roy; Concert Pianist; *b* 14 Nov. 1930; *m* 1954, Eva Zweig; two *s. Educ:* Henry Thornton Sch.; Westminster Abbey; Royal Academy of Music. First London appearance at Wigmore Hall, 1948. A leading Chopin interpreter. Performances abroad include most European countries, West and East, S and E Africa, Japan, Canada, USA, Hong Kong, India, New Zealand, Singapore, Malaysia. Recordings, Decca, Everest, Unicorn, HMV, Philips, Lyrita, MFP, Pickwick International, Claudio. Vis. Prof. in piano, Univ. of Western Ontario, 1978–84. Mem. Incorporated Soc. of Musicians (ISM). FRAM, ARCM. Chopin Arts Award, NY, 1977. *Recreations:* reading, writing, fishing, tape recording, photography. *Address:* c/o John Wright, 5 Kintbury Mill, Kintbury, Berks RG15 0UN. *T:* Kintbury 58963; Steorra Enterprises, 243 West End Avenue, Ste. 907, New York 10023, USA. *T:* (212) 799 5783.

KATO, Tadao; Counsellor in Japan to John Swire & Sons, Imperial Chemicals, Sumitomo Metals, Suntory, Long-Term Credit Bank, since 1980; *b* 13 May 1916; *m* 1946, Yoko; two *s. Educ:* Tokyo Univ.; Cambridge Univ. Joined Japanese Diplomatic Service 1939; Singapore, 1952; London, 1953; Counsellor, Economic Affairs Bureau, Min. of Foreign Affairs, 1956–69; Counsellor, Washington, 1959–63 (Vis. Fellow, Harvard, 1959–60); Dep. Dir, Econ. Affairs Bureau, Min. of Foreign Affairs, 1963–66, Dir, 1966–67; Ambassador to OECD, 1967–70, to Mexico, 1970–74, to UK, 1975–79. Mem. Bd, Adv. Council, Texas Instruments, Dallas, 1981–; Comr, Export Import Transaction Council, Min. Internat. Trade and Industry and Econ. Council of Econ. Planning Agency, 1982–; Comr, Cabinet Adv. Council for External Econ. Problems, 1985–; Mem., Admin. Reform Council, 1984–. Advisor: Hotel Okura; Nitto Kogyo Enterprise. Chm., Japan British Soc.; Japanese Chm., UK-Japan 2000 Gp. Pres., Cambridge English Sch. 1st Class Order of Aztec Star, Mexico, 1972. *Recreations:* golf, goh. *Address:* 3–10–22, Shimo-Ochiai, Shinjuku-Ku, Tokyo, Japan. *Clubs:* Tokyo (Tokyo); Koganei Golf, Abiko Golf, Karuizawa Golf, Hamano Golf (Chm., 1984) (Japan); Green Academy Country (Chm., 1985).

KATRITZKY, Prof. Alan Roy, DPhil, PhD, ScD; FRS 1980; FRSC; Kenan Professor of Chemistry, University of Florida, since 1980; *b* 18 Aug. 1928; *s* of Frederick Charles Katritzky and Emily Catherine (*née* Lane); *m* 1952, Agnes Juliane Dietlinde Kilian; one *s* three *d. Educ:* Oxford Univ. (BA, BSc, MA, DPhil); Cambridge Univ. (PhD, ScD). FRIC 1963. Lectr, Cambridge Univ., 1958–63; Fellow of Churchill Coll., Cambridge, 1960–63; Prof. of Chemistry, Univ. of E Anglia, 1963–80, Dean, Sch. of Chem. Sciences, UEA, 1963–70 and 1976–80. Foreign Fellow, RACI, 1983; Hon. Fellow: Italian Chem. Soc., 1978; Polish Chem. Soc., 1985. Dr *hc* Univ. Nacional, Madrid, 1986. Tilden Medal, Chem. Soc., 1975–76. Heterocyclic Award, RSC, 1983. Cavaliere ufficiale, Order Al Merito Della Repubblica Italiana, 1975. *Publications:* (ed) Advances in Heterocyclic Chemistry, Vols 1–36, 1963–84; (ed) Physical Methods in Heterocyclic Chemistry, Vols 1–6, 1963–72; Principles of Heterocyclic Chemistry, 1968 (trans. into French, German, Italian, Japanese, Russian, Polish and Spanish); Chemistry of Heterocyclic N-Oxides (monograph), 1970; Heteroaromatic Tautomerism (monograph), 1975; Handbook of Heterocyclic Chemistry, 1985; Chm. Editorial Bd, Comprehensive Heterocyclic Chemistry (8 vols), 1985; scientific papers in Heterocylic Chem. *Recreations:* walking, travel. *Address:* Department of Chemistry, University of Florida, Gainesville, Fla 32611, USA. *T:* 904–392–0554.

KATZ, Sir Bernard, Kt 1969; FRS 1952; Professor and Head of Biophysics Department, University College, London, 1952–78, now Emeritus, Hon. Research Fellow, 1978; *b* Leipzig, 26 March 1911; *s* of M. N. Katz; *m* 1945, Marguerite, *d* of W. Penly, Sydney, Australia; two *s. Educ:* University of Leipzig (MD 1934). Biophysical research, University Coll., London, 1935–39; PhD London, and Beit Memorial Research Fellow, 1938; Carnegie Research Fellow, Sydney Hospital, Sydney, 1939–42; DSc London, 1943. Served War of 1939–45 in Pacific with RAAF, 1942–45; Flt-Lt, 1943. Asst Dir of Research, Biophysics Research Unit, University Coll., London, and Henry Head Research Fellow (Royal Society), 1946–50; Reader in Physiology, 1950–51. Lectures: Herter, Johns Hopkins Univ., 1958; Dunham, Harvard Coll., 1961; Croonian, Royal Society, 1961; Sherrington, Liverpool Univ., 1967. A Vice-Pres., Royal Society, 1965, Biological Secretary and Vice-President, 1968–76. Mem., Agric. Research Coun., 1967–77. Fellow of University Coll., London. FRCP, 1968. Hon. FIBiol, 1978. Hon. DSc: Southampton, 1971; Melbourne, 1971; Cambridge, 1980; Hon. PhD Weizmann Inst., Israel, 1979. Feldberg Foundation Award, 1965; Baly Medal, RCP, 1967; Copley Medal, Royal Society, 1967; Nobel Prize (jtly) for Physiology and Medicine, 1970. For. Member: Royal Danish Academy Science and Letters, 1968; Accad. Naz. Lincei, 1968; Amer. Acad. of Arts and Sciences, 1969; For. Assoc., Nat. Acad. of Scis, USA, 1976; Hon. Mem., Japanese Pharmacol. Soc., 1977; Assoc. Mem., European Molecular Biol. Orgn, 1978. Foreign Mem., Orden Pour le Mérite für Wissenschaften und Künste, 1982. *Publications:* Electric Excitation of Nerve, 1939; Nerve, Muscle and Synapse, 1966; The Release of Neural Transmitter Substances, 1969; papers on nerve and muscle physiology in Jl of Physiol., Proc. Royal Society, etc. *Address:* University College, WC1E 6BT.

KATZ, Milton; Director, International Legal Studies, and Henry L. Stimson Professor of Law, Harvard University, 1954–78, now Emeritus; Distinguished Professor of Law, Suffolk University Law School, Boston, Mass, since 1978; *b* 29 Nov. 1907; *m* 1933, Vivian Greenberg; three *s. Educ:* Harvard Univ. AB 1927; JD 1931. Anthropological Expedition across Central Africa for Peabody Museum, Harvard, 1927–28; Mem. of Bar since 1932; various official posts, US Government, 1932–39; Prof. of Law, Harvard Univ., 1940–50; served War of 1939–45, with War Production Board and as US Executive Officer, Combined Production and Resources Board, 1941–43, thereafter Lt-Comdr, USNR, until end of war; Dep. US Special Representative in Europe with rank of Ambassador, 1949–50; Chief US Delegation, Economic Commission for Europe, and US Mem., Defense Financial and Economic Cttee under North Atlantic Treaty, 1950–51; Ambassador of the United States and US Special Representative in Europe for ECA, 1950–51; Associate Dir, Ford Foundation, 1951–54, and Consultant, 1954–66. Dir, Internat. Program in Taxation, 1961–63. Consultant, US Office of Technology Assessment, 1972–82; Chm., Energy Adv. Cttee, 1974–82. Mem. Council, Amer. Acad. of Arts and Sciences, 1982– (Pres., 1979–82); Trustee: Carnegie Endowment for Internat. Peace (Chm. Bd, 1970–78); World Peace Foundation (Exec. Cttee); Citizens Research Foundation (Pres., 1969–78); Brandeis Univ.; Case Western Reserve Univ., 1967–80; International Legal Center (Chm. Bd, 1971–78); Director, Internat. Friendship League; Member: Corp., Boston Museum of Science; Cttee on Foreign Affairs Personnel, 1961–63; Case Inst. of Technology Western Reserve Univ. Study Commn, 1966–67; Panel on Technology Assessment, Nat. Acad. of Sciences, 1968–69; Cttee on Life Sciences and Social Policy, Nat. Research Council, 1968–75 (Chm.); Vis. Cttee for Humanities, MIT, 1970–73; Adv. Bd Energy Laboratory, MIT, 1974–85; Cttee on Technology, Internat. Trade and Econ. Issues, Nat. Acad. of Engrg, 1976–; Co-Chm., ABA-AAAS Cttee on Science and Law, 1978–82. Sherman Fairchild Dist. Schol., Cal. Tech., 1974. John Danz Lectr, Univ. of Washington, 1974, Phi Beta Kappa Nat. Vis. Scholar, 1977–78. Hon LLD Brandeis, 1972. Legion of Merit (US Army), 1945; Commendation Ribbon (US Navy), 1945. Order of Merit, Fed. Rep. of Germany, 1968. *Publications:* Cases and Materials on Administrative Law, 1947; (Co-author and ed) Government under Law and the Individual, 1957; (with Kingman Brewster, Jr) The Law of International Transactions and Relations, 1960; The Things That are Caesar's, 1966; The Relevance of International Adjudication, 1968; The Modern Foundation: its dual nature, public and private, 1968; (contrib., jtly) Man's Impact on the Global Environment, 1970; (ed) Federal Regulation of Campaign Finance, 1972; (jtly) Assessing Biomedical Technologies, 1975; (jtly) Technology, Trade and the US Economy, 1978; (jtly) Strengthening Conventional Deterrence in Europe, 1983; (contrib.) The Positive Sum Strategy, 1986; articles in legal, business and other jls. *Address:* (business) Harvard Law Sch., Cambridge, Mass, USA; (home) 6 Berkeley Street, Cambridge, Mass, USA.

KATZIN, Olga; journalist; pen-name Sagittarius; *b* London, 9 July 1896; *d* of John and Mathilde Katzin; *m* 1921, Hugh Miller, actor; two *s* one *d. Educ:* Privately. *Publications:* Troubadours, 1925; A Little Pilgrim's Peeps at Parnassus, 1927; Sagittarius Rhyming, 1940; London Watches, 1941; Targets, 1943; Quiver's Choice, 1945; Let Cowards Flinch, 1947; Pipes of Peace, 1949; Up the Poll, 1950; Strasbourg Geese and Other Verses, 1953; Unaida (with Michael Barsley), play, 1957; The Perpetual Pessimist (with Daniel George), 1963. *Address:* 44 Hamilton Terrace, NW8.

KATZIR, Prof. Ephraim, PhD; Institute Professor, Weizmann Institute of Science, since 1978; Head, Department (formerly Centre) for Biotechnology, Tel Aviv University, since 1980; President, State of Israel, 1973–78; *b* Kiev, Ukraine, 16 May 1916; *s* of Yehuda Katchalski and Tsila Katchalski; *m* 1938, Nina Gotlieb (decd); one *s* one *d. Educ:* Rehavia High Sch., Jerusalem; Hebrew Univ., Jerusalem (chemistry, botany, zool., bacteriol.; MSc *summa cum laude* 1937; PhD 1941). Settled in Israel with parents, 1922; involved in Labour youth movement; Inf. Comdr, Jewish Self-Defence Forces (Hagana). Asst, Dept of Theoretical and Macromolecular Chem., Hebrew Univ., 1941–45; Res. Fellow, Polytechnic Inst., and Columbia Univ., NY, 1946–48; Actg Head, Dept of Biophys., Weizmann Inst. of Science, Rehovot, Israel, 1949–51, Head 1951–73 (mem. founding faculty of Inst.); Chief Scientist, Israel Def. Min., 1966–68. Vis. Prof. of Biophys., Hebrew Univ., 1953–61; Guest Scientist, Harvard Univ., 1957–59; Vis. Prof., Rockefeller Univ., NY, and Univ. of Mich, Ann Arbor, 1961–65; Sen. Foreign Scientist Fellowship, UCLA, 1964; Battelle Seattle Res. Center, Washington, 1971; Regents Prof., Univ. of Calif., San Diego, 1979; First Herman F. Mark Chair in Polymer Sci., Poly. Inst., NY, 1979. Member: Biochem. Soc. of Israel; Israel Acad. of Sciences and Humanities; Israel Chem. Soc.; Council, Internat. Union of Biochem.; AAAS; Assoc. of Harvard Chemists; Leopoldina Acad. of Science, Germany; World Acad. of Art and Science; New York Acad. of Science (Life Mem.). Centennial Foreign Fellow, Amer. Chem. Soc.; For. Associate, Nat. Acad. of Sciences of USA. For. Member: The Royal Soc.; Amer. Philosoph. Soc. Hon. Member: Amer. Acad. of Arts and Sciences; Amer. Soc. of Biol Chemists;

Harvey Soc. Hon. Prof., Polytechnic Inst. of New York, 1975. Hon. Dr: Hebrew Univ., 1973; Brandeis Univ., Univ. of Mich, and Hebrew Union Coll., 1975; Weizmann Inst. of Science, 1976; Northwestern Univ., Evanston, 1978; Harvard, 1978; McGill, 1980; ETH Zurich, 1980; Thomas Jefferson, 1981; Oxford, 1981; Miami, 1983; Technion, Israel Inst. of Technology, 1983. Tchernikhovski Prize, 1948; Weizmann Prize, 1950; Israel Prize in Nat. Sciences, 1959; Rothschild Prize in Nat. Sciences, 1961; Linderstrøm Lang Gold Medal, 1969; Hans Krebs Medal, 1972. Ephraim Katzir Chair of Biophysics, Bar Ilan Univ., Israel, founded 1976; Alpha Omega Achievement Medal, 1979, first Japan Prize, Science and Technol. Foundn of Japan, 1985. Hon. Editor, Jl of Applied Biochem., 1978–; Mem. Adv. Bd, Progress in Surface and Membrane Science (series), 1972–; Mem. Editorial Board: Biopolymers; (series) Applied Biochem. and Bioengrg; (series) Advances in Exper. Medicine and Biol, 1967–. *Address:* Weizmann Institute of Science, PO Box 26, Rehovot, Israel.

KAUFFMANN, Prof. C. Michael, MA, PhD; FMA; Professor of History of Art and Director, Courtauld Institute of Art, University of London, since 1985; *b* 5 Feb. 1931; *s* of late Arthur and late Tamara Kauffmann; *m* 1954, Dorothea (*née* Hill); two *s*. *Educ:* St Paul's Sch.; Merton Coll., Oxford (Postmaster); Warburg Inst., London Univ. (Jun. Research Fellow). Asst Curator, Photographic Collection, Warburg Inst., 1957–58; Keeper, Manchester City Art Gall., 1958–60; Victoria and Albert Museum: Asst Keeper, 1960–75, Keeper, 1975–85, Dept of Prints & Drawings and Paintings; Asst to the Director, 1963–66; Visiting Associate Prof., Univ. of Chicago, 1969. *Publications:* The Baths of Pozzuoli: medieval illuminations of Peter of Eboli's poem, 1959; An Altar-piece of the Apocalypse, 1968; Victoria & Albert Museum: catalogue of foreign paintings, 1973; British Romanesque Manuscripts 1066–1190, 1975; Catalogue of Paintings in the Wellington Museum, 1982; John Varley, 1984; exhibn catalogues; articles in art historical jls.

KAUFMAN, Rt. Hon. Gerald (Bernard); PC 1978; MP (Lab) Manchester, Gorton, since 1983 (Manchester, Ardwick, 1970–83); *b* 21 June 1930; *s* of Louis and Jane Kaufman. *Educ:* Leeds Grammar Sch.; The Queen's Coll., Oxford. Asst Gen.-Sec., Fabian Soc., 1954–55; Political Staff, Daily Mirror, 1955–64; Political Correspondent, New Statesman, 1964–65; Parly Press Liaison Officer, Labour Party, 1965–70. Parly Under-Sec. of State, DoE, 1974–75, Dept of Industry, 1975; Minister of State, Dept of Industry, 1975–79; Parly Cttee of PLP, 1980–; Shadow Home Sec., 1983–. FRSA. *Publications:* (jtly) How to Live Under Labour, 1964; (ed) The Left, 1966; To Build the Promised Land, 1973; How to be a Minister, 1980; (ed) Renewal: Labour's Britain in the 1980s, 1983; My Life in the Silver Screen, 1985; Inside the Promised Land, 1986. *Recreations:* travel, going to the pictures. *Address:* 87 Charlbert Court, Eamont Street, NW8. *T:* 01–722 6264.

KAUL, Mahendra Nath, OBE 1975; Managing Director: Gaylord Restaurants (Midlands) Ltd, since 1982; Gaylord Caterers Ltd, since 1982; Viceroy of India (Restaurants) Ltd, since 1982; Vice Chairman, Harilela (London) Ltd, since 1981; UK correspondent, Daily Jagran, since 1983; *b* 28 July 1922; *s* of Dina Nath Kaul and Gauri Kaul; *m* 1955, Rajni Kapur, MA, MLS; one *d*. *Educ:* Univ. of the Punjab, India (BA). Joined Radio Kashmir of All India Radio, as news reader, actor and producer of dramas, 1949; appeared in two feature films and assisted in producing several documentaries, 1950–52; news reader and actor in three languages, also drama producer, All India Radio, New Delhi, 1952–55; joined Indian service of Voice of America, Washington DC, 1955, later becoming Editor of the service; joined external service of BBC, as newscaster, producer and dir of radio plays; producer/presenter, BBC TV prog. for Asian Viewers in UK, 1966–82. Director: Hotels & Restaurants Suppliers Ltd (formerly SK Giftware), 1985–; Arts and Crafts Emporium Ltd, 1985–; Bokhara Cuisine Ltd, 1985–. OBE awarded for services to race relations in Gt Britain. Received The Green Pennant from HRH The Duke of Edinburgh, awarded by Commonwealth Expedition (COMEX 10), 1980. *Recreations:* golf, cooking, boating, classical and light classical music, reading political works. *Address:* 50 Grove Court, Grove End Road, St John's Wood, NW8. *T:* 01–286 8131.

KAULBACK, Ronald John Henry, OBE 1946; *b* 23 July 1909; *er s* of late Lieutenant-Colonel Henry Albert Kaulback, OBE, and Alice Mary, *d* of late Rev. A. J. Townend, CF; *m* 1st, 1940, Audrey Elizabeth (marr. diss. 1984), 3rd *d* of late Major H. R. M. Howard-Sneyd, OBE; two *s* two *d*; 2nd, 1984, Joyce Norah, *widow* of Capt. H. S. Woolley, MC. *Educ:* Rugby; Pembroke Coll., Cambridge. In 1933 journeyed through Assam and Eastern Tibet with Kingdon Ward; returned to Tibet, 1935, accompanied by John Hanbury-Tracy, spending eighteen months there in an attempt to discover source of Salween River; 1938 spent eighteen months in Upper Burma hunting and collecting zoological specimens for the British Museum (Natural History); Murchison Grant of Royal Geog. Society, 1937. *Publications:* Tibetan Trek, 1934; Salween, 1938. *Recreations:* fishing, schnorkeling. *Address:* Altbough, Hoarwithy, Hereford. *T:* Carey 676. *Club:* Special Forces.

KAUNDA, David Kenneth; President of Zambia, since Oct. 1964 (Prime Minister, N Rhodesia, Jan.-Oct. 1964); Chancellor of the University of Zambia since 1966; *b* 28 April 1924; *s* of late David Julizgia and Hellen Kaunda, Missionaries; *m* 1946, Betty Banda; seven *s* two *d* and one adopted *s*. *Educ:* Lubwa Training Sch.; Munali Secondary Sch. Teacher, Lubwa Training Sch., 1943–44, Headmaster, 1944–47; Boarding Master, Mufulira Upper Sch., 1948–49. African National Congress: District Sec., 1950–52; Provincial Organising Sec., 1952–53; Sec.-Gen., 1953–58; Nat. Pres., Zambia African Nat. Congress, 1958–59; Nat. Pres., United Nat. Independence Party, 1960; Chm., Pan-African Freedom Movement for East, Central and South Africa, 1962; Minister of Local Government and Social Welfare, N Rhodesia, 1962–63. Chairman: Organization of African Unity, 1970; Non-aligned Countries, 1970. Hon. Doctor of Laws: Fordham Univ., USA, 1963; Dublin Univ., 1964; University of Sussex, 1965; Windsor Univ., Canada, 1966; University of Chile, 1966; Univ. of Zambia, 1974; Univ. of Humboldt, 1980; DUniv York, 1966. *Publications:* Black Government, 1961; Zambia Shall Be Free, 1962; Humanist in Africa, 1966; Humanism in Zambia and its implementation, 1967; Letter to My Children; Kaunda on Violence, 1980. *Recreations:* golf, music, table tennis, football, draughts, gardening and reading. *Address:* State House, PO Box 135, Lusaka, Zambia.

KAUNDA, Reid Willie K.; *see* Katenga-Kaunda.

KAUNTZE, Ralph, MBE 1944; MD; FRCP; Physician to Guy's Hospital, 1948–71, Consultant Physician Emeritus since 1971; *b* 5 June 1911; *s* of Charles Kauntze and Edith, *d* of Ralph Bagley; *m* 1935, Katharine Margaret, *yr d* of late Ramsay Moodie; two *s* one *d*. *Educ:* Canford Sch.; Emmanuel Coll., Cambridge; St George's Hosp., London. William Brown Sen. Schol., St George's Hosp. 1932; MRCS, LRCP 1935; MA, MB, BCh Cantab 1937; MRCP 1939; MD Cantab 1946; FRCP 1950. Served, 1939–45, RAMC, chiefly Mediterranean area, Lt-Col O i/c Med. Div. Asst Dir of Dept of Med., Guy's Hosp., 1947–48, Physician to Cardiac Dept, 1956–71; Cons. Phys. to High Wycombe War Memorial Hosp., 1948–50; Dir Asthma Clinic, 1948–52, and of Dept of Student Health, 1950–63, Guy's Hosp.; Physician to Royal Masonic Hospital, 1963–76. Former Senior Cons. Phys. to: Commercial Union Assurance Co. Ltd; British & European Assurance Co.; European Assurance Co. Ltd. Hon. Vis. Phys., Johns Hopkins Hosp., Baltimore, 1958. Examiner in Medicine: RCP; London Univ. Mem. Brit. Cardiac Soc.; Mem. Assoc. of Physicians. *Publications:* contrib. med. jls. *Recreations:* farming, walking. *Address:* Blewbury Manor, near Didcot, Oxon. *T:* Blewbury 850246.

KAVANAGH, P. J., (Patrick Joseph Gregory Kavanagh); writer; *b* 6 Jan. 1931; *s* of H. E. (Ted) Kavanagh and Agnes O'Keefe; *m* 1st, 1956, Sally Philipps (*d* 1958); 2nd, 1965, Catherine Ward; two *s*. *Educ:* Douai Sch.; Lycee Jaccard, Lausanne; Merton Coll., Oxford (MA). British Council, 1957–59. Actor, 1959–70. *Publications: poems:* One and One, 1960; On the Way to the Depot, 1967; About Time, 1970; Edward Thomas in Heaven, 1974; Life before Death, 1979; Selected Poems, 1982; Presences (new and selected poems), 1987; *novels:* A Song and Dance, 1968 (Guardian Fiction Prize, 1968); A Happy Man, 1972; People and Weather, 1979; Only by Mistake, 1986; *autobiog.:* The Perfect Stranger, 1966 (Richard Hillary Prize, 1966); *for children:* Scarf Jack, 1978; Rebel for Good, 1980; *edited:* Collected Poems of Ivor Gurney, 1982; (with James Michie) Oxford Book of Short Poems, 1985; The Bodley Head G. K. Chesterton, 1985. *Recreation:* walking. *Address:* Sparrowthorn, Elkstone, Cheltenham, Glos.

KAVANAGH, Patrick Bernard, CBE 1977; QPM 1974; Deputy Commissioner, Metropolitan Police, 1977–83; *b* 18 March 1923; *s* of late Michael Kavanagh and late Violet Kavanagh (*née* Duncan); *m* Beryl (*d* 1984), *er d* of late Lt-Comdr Richard Owen Williams, RNR and Annie (*née* McShiells); one *s* two *d*. *Educ:* St Aloysius Coll., Glasgow. Rifle Bde, 1941–43; Para. Regt, 1943–46 (Lieut). Manchester City Police (Constable to Supt), 1946–64; Asst Chief Constable, Cardiff City Police, 1964–69; Asst and Dep. Chief Constable, S Wales Constabulary, 1969–73; Asst Comr (Traffic), Metropolitan Police, 1974–77. Attended Administrative Staff Coll., Henley-on-Thames, 1961. Mem., Gaming Bd for GB, 1983–. *Recreations:* cricket, swimming, music, crosswords. *Address:* c/o Barclays Bank, 82/84 High Street, Epsom, Surrey. *Club:* Royal Automobile.

KAY, Sir Andrew Watt, Kt 1973; retired; Regius Professor of Surgery, University of Glasgow, 1964–81; part-time Chief Scientist, Scottish Home and Health Department, 1973–81; *b* 14 Aug. 1916; of Scottish parentage; *m* 1943, Janetta M. Roxburgh; two *s* two *d*. *Educ:* Ayr Academy; Glasgow Univ. MB, ChB (Hons) with Brunton Memorial Prize, 1939; FRCSEd 1942; FRFPSG 1956 (Pres. 1972–); FRCS 1960; FRCSGlas 1967; FRSE 1971; MD (Hons) with Bellahouston Gold Medal, 1944; Major Royal Army Medical Corps i/c Surgical Div., Millbank Military Hospital, 1946–48; ChM (Hons) 1949; Consultant Surgeon in charge of Wards, Western Infirmary, Glasgow, 1956–58; Asst to Regius Prof. of Surgery, Glasgow Univ., 1942–56; Prof. of Surgery, University of Sheffield, 1958–64. Sims Travelling Prof., Australasia, 1969; McLaughlin Foundn Edward Gallie Vis. Prof., Canada, 1970. Rock Carling Fellowship, 1977. Pres., Surgical Research Soc., 1969–71. Member: Royal Commission on Medical Education, 1965–68; MRC, 1967–71; Chm., Scottish Hosps Endowment Research Trust, 1983–; Hon. Mem., The N Pacific Surgical Assoc. FRACS 1970; FRCSCan 1972; FCS(SoAf) 1972; Hon. Fellow: Norwegian Surgical Assoc., Belgian Surgical Soc.; Amer. Surg. Assoc., 1972; Hon. FACS, 1973; Hon. FRCSI, 1979. Hon. DSc: Leicester, 1973; Sheffield, 1975; Manchester, 1981; Nebraska, 1981; Hon. MD Edinburgh, 1981. Cecil Joll Prize, RCS, 1969; Gordon-Taylor Lectureship and Medal, 1970. *Publications:* (with R. A. Jamieson, FRCS) Textbook of Surgical Physiology, 1959 (2nd edn 1964); Research in Medicine: problems and prospects, 1977; several papers in medical and surgical jls on gastroenterological subjects. *Recreation:* gardening. *Address:* 14 North Campbell Avenue, Milngavie, Glasgow G62 7AA.

KAY, Bernard Hubert Gerard; HM Diplomatic Service, retired; *b* 7 July 1925; *s* of William and Alice Kay; *m* 1957, Teresa Jean Dyer; three *d*. *Educ:* St Bede's, Bradford; Wadham Coll., Oxford (MA, MLitt). Royal Navy, 1943–46. Foreign Office, 1955; served: Hong Kong, 1958–62; Singapore, 1964; Manila, 1965; New Delhi, 1967; Vientiane, 1968; Dacca, 1972; Ulan Bator, 1973; FCO, 1973–80. *Recreations:* Asia, books, mountains, the sea. *Address:* 6 Savona Close, Wimbledon, SW19. *Club:* United Oxford & Cambridge University.

KAY, Brian Wilfrid; Senior Research Fellow, Culham College Institute, since 1982; Co-ordinator, Hulme Project, Department of Educational Studies, Oxford University, since 1982; *b* 30 July 1921; *s* of Wilfrid and Jessie Kay; *m* 1947, Dorothea Sheppard Lawson; two *d*. *Educ:* King's Sch., Chester; University Coll., Oxford (exhibnr). Classics Master, Birkenhead Sch., 1947–59; Head of Classics, Liverpool Collegiate Sch., 1959–64; HM Inspector of Schs (Wales), 1964–71; Staff Inspector, Classics, Secondary Educn, 1971–74; Head of Assessment of Performance Unit, DES, 1974–77; Chief Inspector, Res. and Planning, DES, 1977–79; Chief Inspector, Teacher Trng and Res., DES, 1979–81, retired. *Recreations:* gardening, music, architecture. *Address:* Pond Cottage, Botolph Claydon, Buckingham MK18 2NG. *T:* Winslow 3477.

KAY, Air Vice-Marshal Cyril Eyton, CB 1958; CBE 1947; DFC 1940; retired as Chief of Air Staff, with the rank of Air Vice-Marshal, RNZAF (1956–58); *b* 25 June 1902; *s* of David Kay and Mary, *d* of Edward Drury Butts; *m* 1932, Florence, *d* of Frank Armfield; two *d*. *Educ:* Auckland, NZ. Joined RAF, 1926, 5 years Short Service Commn; joined RNZAF, 1935, Permanent Commn. As Flying Officer: flew London-Sydney in Desoutter Light aeroplane, 1930 (with Flying Off. H. L. Piper as Co-pilot); first New Zealanders to accomplish this flight; also, as Flying Off. flew a De Havilland-Dragon Rapide (with Sqdn Ldr J. Hewett) in London-Melbourne Centenary Air Race, 1934; then continued over Tasman Sea to New Zealand (first direct flight England-New Zealand). Comdg Officer No 75 (NZ) Sqdn "Wellington" Bombers stationed Feltwell, Norfolk, England, 1940; IDC, 1946; Air Board Mem. for Supply, RNZAF, 1947; AOC, RNZAF, London HQ, 1950; Air Board Mem. for Personnel, 1953. *Publication:* The Restless Sky, 1964. *Recreation:* golf. *Address:* c/o Lloyds Bank, 6 Pall Mall, SW1. *Clubs:* Royal Air Force; Officers' (Wellington, NZ).

KAY, Ernest, FRGS; Founder and Director-General, International Biographical Centre, Cambridge, since 1967 (Director-General, New York, 1976–85); *b* 21 June 1915; *s* of Harold and Florence Kay; *m* 1941, Marjorie Peover; two *s* one *d*. *Educ:* Spring Bank Central Sch., Darwen, Lancs. Reporter, Darwen News, 1931–34; Ashton-under-Lyne Reporter, 1934–38, Industrial Corresp., Manchester Guardian and Evening News, 1938–41; The Star, London, 1941–47; London Editor, Wolverhampton Express and Star, 1947–52, Managing Editor, 1952–54; Managing Editor, London Evening News, 1954–57; Editor and Publisher, John O'London's, 1957–61; Managing Editor, Time and Tide, 1961–67. Chairman: Kay Sons and Daughter Ltd, 1967–77; Dartmouth Chronicle Group Ltd, 1968–77; Cambridge and Newmarket Radio Ltd, 1981–; Keyboards and Music Player Magazine, 1983–84; Pres., Melrose Press Ltd, 1970–77. Chm., Cambridge Symphony Orchestra Trust, 1979–83. FRSA 1967; FRGS 1975. Hon. DLitt Karachi, 1967; Hon. PhD Hong Kong, 1976. Emperor Haile Selassie Gold Medal, 1971. Key to City of: Las Vegas, 1972; New York, 1975; Miami, 1978; New Orleans (and Hon. Citizen), 1978; Beverly Hills, 1981; LA, 1981. Staff Col and ADC to Governor of Louisiana, 1979. Gold Medal, Ordre Supreme Imperial Orthodoxe Constantinian de Saint-Georges (Greece), 1977. *Publications:* Great Men of Yorkshire, 1956, 2nd edn 1960; Isles of Flowers: the story of the Isles of Scilly, 1956, 3rd edn 1977; Pragmatic Premier:

an intimate portrait of Harold Wilson, 1967; The Wit of Harold Wilson, 1967; Editor, Dictionary of International Biography, 1967–; Dictionary of Caribbean Biography, 1970–; Dictionary of African Biography, 1970–; Dictionary of Scandinavian Biography, 1972–; International Who's Who in Poetry, 1970–; World Who's Who of Women, 1973–; International Who's Who in Music, 1975–; International Authors and Writers Who's Who, 1976–; Women in Education, 1977–; Who's Who in Education, 1978–; International Youth in Achievement, 1981–. *Recreations:* reading, writing, music, watching cricket, travel. *Address:* Westhurst, 418 Milton Road, Cambridge CB4 1ST. *T:* Cambridge 63893. *Clubs:* Surrey CCC; Derbyshire CCC; National Arts (New York City).

KAY, Prof. Harry, CBE 1981; PhD; Vice-Chancellor, University of Exeter, 1973–84 (Hon. Professor, 1984); *b* 22 March 1919; *s* of late Williamson T. Kay; *m* 1941, Gwendolen Diana, *d* of Charles Edward Maude; one *s* one *d. Educ:* Rotherham Grammar Sch.; Trinity Hall, Cambridge (1938–39, 1946–51). Served War of 1939–45 with Royal Artillery. Research with Nuffield Unit into Problems of Ageing, Cambridge, 1948–51; Psychologist of Naval Arctic Expedition, 1949. Lecturer in Experimental Psychology, Univ. of Oxford, 1951–59; Prof. of Psychology, Univ. of Sheffield, 1960–73. Visiting Scientist, National Institutes of Health, Washington, DC, 1957–58. Pro-Vice-Chancellor, University of Sheffield, 1967–71. Pres., British Psychological Soc., 1971–72. Hon. Director: MRC Unit, Dept of Psychology, Sheffield; Nat. Centre of Programmed Instruction for Industry, Sheffield. Member: SSRC, 1970–73; MRC, 1975–77 (Chm., Environmental Medicine Res. Policy Cttee, 1975–77); CNAA, 1974–79; Open Univ. Acad. Adv. Cttee; BBC Continuing Educn Adv. Cttee; Southern Univs Jt Bd (Chm., 1978–80); UCCA (Chm., 1978–84); Oakes Cttee on Management of Higher Educn, 1977–78; NATO Human Factors Panel, 1972–75. Chairman: Central Council for Educn and Trng in Social Work, 1980–84; Bd of Management, Northcott Theatre, 1973–84. Hon. DSc: Sheffield, 1981; Exeter, 1985. Vernon Prize, 1962. *Publication:* (with B. Dodd and M. Sime) Teaching Machines and Programmed Instruction, 1968. *Recreation:* listening. *Address:* Coastguard House, 18 Coastguard Road, Budleigh Salterton EX9 6NU.

KAY, Prof. Humphrey Edward Melville, MD, FRCP, FRCPath; Haematologist, Royal Marsden Hospital, 1956–84; Professor of Haematology, University of London, 1982–84 (Professor Emeritus, since 1984); *b* 10 Oct. 1923; *s* of late Rev. Arnold Innes and Winifred Julia Kay; *m* 1950, April Grace Lavinia Powlett; one *s* two *d. Educ:* Bryanston Sch.; St Thomas's Hospital. MB, BS 1945. RAFVR, 1947–49; junior appts at St Thomas's Hosp., 1950–56. Sec., MRC Cttee on Leukaemia, 1968–84; Dean, Inst. of Cancer Research, 1970–72. Editor, Jl Clinical Pathology, 1972–80. Mem. Council, Wiltshire Trust for Nature Conservation, 1983–. *Publications:* papers and chapters on blood diseases, etc; occasional poetry. *Recreation:* natural history including gardening. *Address:* New Mill Cottage, Pewsey, Wilts.

KAY, John Menzies, MA, PhD; CEng, FIMechE, FIChemE; engineering consultant; Director, GSK Steel Developments Ltd, 1976–83; *b* 4 Sept. 1920; *s* of John Aiton Kay and Isabel Kay (*née* Menzies). *Educ:* Sherborne Sch.; Trinity Hall Cambridge. University Demonstrator in Chemical Engineering, Cambridge University, 1948; Chief Technical Engineer, Division of Atomic Energy Production, Risley, 1952; Prof. of Nuclear Power, Imperial Coll. of Science and Technology, University of London, 1956; Dir of Engineering Development, Tube Investments Ltd, 1961; Chief Engineer, Richard Thomas & Baldwins Ltd, 1965; Dir-in-charge, Planning Div., BSC, 1968–70; Dir of Engrng, Strip Mills Div., BSC, 1970–76. Mem., Nuclear Safety Adv. Cttee, 1960–76; Chm., Radioactive Waste Study Gp, 1974–81; Mem., Adv. Cttee on Safety of Nuclear Installations, 1980–83. *Publications:* Fluid Mechanics and Transfer Processes, 1963; Fluid Mechanics and Transfer Processes, 1985; contribs to Proc. of Institution of Mechanical Engineers. *Recreations:* hill-walking, gardening, music. *Address:* Church Farm, St Briavels, near Lydney, Glos. *Clubs:* Alpine, United Oxford & Cambridge University.

KAY, John William, QC 1984; a Recorder of the Crown Court, since 1982; *b* 13 Sept. 1943; *y s* of late C. Herbert Kay and Ida Kay; *m* 1966, Jeffa Connell; one *s* two *d. Educ:* Denstone; Christ's Coll., Cambridge (MA). Called to Bar, Gray's Inn, 1968. Tutor in Law, Liverpool Univ., 1968–69; in practice on Northern Circuit, 1968–. *Recreations:* gardening, genealogy, horse racing. *Address:* Markhams, 17 Far Moss Road, Blundellsands, Liverpool L23 8TG. *T:* 051–924 5804. *Clubs:* Athenæum, Racquet (Liverpool); Border and County (Carlisle).

KAY, Jolyon Christopher; HM Diplomatic Service; Counsellor and Consul-General, Dubai, since 1985; *b* 19 Sept. 1930; *s* of Colin Mardall Kay and Gertrude Fanny Kay; *m* 1956, Shirley Mary Clarke; two *s* two *d. Educ:* Charterhouse; St John's Coll., Cambridge (BA). Chemical Engr, Albright and Wilson, 1954; UKAEA, Harwell, 1958; Battelle Inst., Geneva, 1961; Foreign Office, London, 1964; MECAS, 1965; British Interests Section, Swiss Embassy, Algiers, 1967; Head of Chancery and Information Adviser, Political Residency, Bahrain, 1968; FCO, 1970; Economic Counsellor, Jedda, 1974–77; Consul-Gen., Casablanca, 1977–80; Science, later Commercial, Counsellor, Paris, 1980–84. *Recreations:* acting, skiing, croquet. *Address:* c/o Foreign and Commonwealth Office, SW1; Little Triton, Blewbury, Oxfordshire. *T:* Blewbury 850010. *Club:* Harwell Croquet.

KAY, Neil Vincent; Director of Social Services, Sheffield, since 1979 (Deputy Director, 1971–79); *b* 24 May 1936; *s* of Charles Vincent Kay and Emma Kay; *m* 1961, Maureen (*née* Flemons); one *s* two *d. Educ:* Woodhouse Grammar Sch.; Downing Coll., Cambridge (MA); Birmingham Univ. (Prof. Social Work Qual.). Social Worker (Child Care), Oxford CC, and Sheffield CC, 1960–66; Lectr and Tutor in Social Work, Extramural Dept, Sheffield Univ., 1966–71. *Address:* 22 Westwood Road, Sheffield S11 7EY. *T:* Sheffield 301934.

KAY, Maj.-Gen. Patrick Richard, CB 1972; MBE 1945; RM retired; *b* 1 Aug. 1921; *y s* of late Dr and Mrs A. R. Kay, Blakeney, Norfolk; *m* 1944, Muriel Austen Smith; three *s* one *d. Educ:* Eastbourne Coll. Commissioned in Royal Marines, 1940; HMS Renown, 1941–43; 4 Commando Bde, 1944–45; Combined Ops HQ, 1945–48; Staff of Commandant-Gen., Royal Marines, 1948–50 and 1952–54; Staff Coll., Camberley, 1951; 40 Commando, RM, 1954–57; Joint Services Amphibious Warfare Centre, 1957–59; Plans Div., Naval Staff, 1959–62; CO, 43 Commando, RM, 1963–65; CO, Amphibious Training Unit, RM, 1965–66; Asst Dir (Jt Warfare) Naval Staff, 1966–67; Asst Chief of Staff to Comdt-Gen. RM, 1968; IDC, 1969; C of S to Comdt-Gen., RM, 1970–74, retired 1974. Dir of Naval Security, 1974–81. Sec., Defence, Press and Broadcasting Cttee, 1984–86. *Recreations:* gardening, golf. *Address:* Sandy Lodge, Avenue Road, Fleet, Hants.

KAY-SHUTTLEWORTH, family name of **Baron Shuttleworth.**

KAYE, Danny, (Daniel Kominski); Actor (Stage, Film, TV, and Radio); Comedian; Baseball Executive; conductor; *b* New York, NY, 18 Jan.; *s* of Jacob Kominski and Clara Nemorovsky; *m* 1940, Sylvia Fine, producer, lyricist and composer; one *d.* Official Permanent Ambassador-at-Large for UNICEF (first award for Internat. Distinguished Service). Scopus Laureate, 1977. Founder, managing limited partner, Seattle Mariners

baseball team, 1976. Jean Hersholt Humanitarian Award, 1982; George Foster Peabody Award, 1982. *Stage:* Straw Hat Review, Ambassador Theatre, New York City, 1939; Lady in the Dark, 1940; Let's Face It, 1941; appeared London Palladium, also provincial tour, Great Britain, 1949; London Palladium, 1955. *Television:* annual 'Look In' for Children, Metropolitan Opera, NYC (founder), 1975–; Pinocchio, 1976; Skokie, 1981. *Films include:* Up In Arms, 1943; Wonder Man, 1944; Kid from Brooklyn, 1945; The Secret Life of Walter Mitty, 1946; That's Life, 1947; A Song is Born, 1949; The Inspector-General, 1950; On the Riviera, 1951; Hans Christian Andersen, 1952; Knock on Wood, 1954; White Christmas, 1954; The Court Jester, 1956; Merry Andrew, 1957; Me And The Colonel, 1958; Five Pennies, 1959; On the Double, 1960; The Man from The Diner's Club, 1963; The Madwoman of Chaillot, 1969; *Play:* Two by Two, NY, 1970; *Television includes:* weekly show (CBS), 1963–67; The Danny Kaye Show (Special Acad. award, 1954; Emmy award, 1963; George Foster Peabody award, 1963; Best Children's Special award, 1975). *Address:* Box 750, Beverly Hills, Calif, USA.

KAYE, Sir David Alexander Gordon, 4th Bt *cr* 1923, of Huddersfield; *b* 26 July 1919; *s* of Sir Henry Gordon Kaye, 2nd Bt and Winifred (*d* 1971), *d* of Walter H. Scales, Verwood, Bradford; *S* brother, 1983; *m* 1st, 1942, Elizabeth (marr. diss. 1950), *o d* of Captain Malcolm Hurtley; 2nd, 1955, Adelle, *d* of Denis Thomas, Brisbane, Queensland; two *s* four *d. Educ:* Stowe; Cambridge Univ. (BA). MRCS Eng., LRCP London 1943. *Heir: s* Paul Henry Gordon Kaye, *b* 19 Feb. 1958. *Address:* Yerinandah, 73 Moggill Road, The Gap, Brisbane, Queensland 4061, Australia.

KAYE, Col Douglas Robert Beaumont, DSO 1942 (Bar 1945); DL; JP; *b* 18 Nov. 1909; *s* of late Robert Walter Kaye, JP, Great Glenn Manor, Leics; *m* 1946, Florence Audrey Emma, *d* of late Henry Archibald Bellville, Tedstone Court, Bromyard, Herefordshire; one *s* one *d. Educ:* Harrow. 2nd Lieut Leicestershire Yeo., 1928; 2nd Lieut 10th Royal Hussars, 1931. Served War of 1939–45: Jerusalem, 1939–41; Cairo and HQ 30 Corps, 1941–42; Lieut-Col comdg 10th Royal Hussars, Africa and Italy, 1943–46 (despatches twice; wounded). Bde Major, 30 Lowland Armd Bde (TA), 1947–49; Lieut-Col comdg 16th/5th Queen's Royal Lancers, 1949–51; AA & QMG 56 London Armd Div. (TA), 1952–54; Col Comdt and Chief Instructor, Gunnery Sch., RAC Centre, 1954–56; retd 1956. Master of Newmarket and Thurlow Foxhounds, 1957–59. DL 1963, JP 1961, High Sheriff 1971, Cambridgeshire and Isle of Ely. Mem., Newmarket RDC, 1958–74 (Chm., 1972–74), E Cambridgeshire DC, 1974–84. *Recreations:* hunting, shooting. *Address:* Brinkley Hall, near Newmarket, Suffolk. *T:* Stetchworth 202. *Club:* Cavalry and Guards.

KAYE, Elaine Hilda; Headmistress, Oxford High School, GPDST, 1972–81; *b* 21 Jan. 1930; *d* of late Rev. Harold Sutcliffe Kaye and Kathleen Mary (*née* White). *Educ:* Bradford Girls' Grammar Sch.; Milton Mount Coll.; St Anne's Coll., Oxford. Assistant Mistress: Leyton County High Sch., 1952–54; Queen's Coll., Harley Street, 1954–59; South Hampstead High Sch., GPDST, 1959–65; Part-time Tutor, Westminster Tutors, 1965–67; Dep. Warden, Missenden Abbey Adult Coll., 1967–72. Vice-Chm., Oxford Project for Peace Studies, 1984–. *Publications:* History of the King's Weigh House Church, 1968; History of Queen's College, Harley St, 1972; Short History of Missenden Abbey, 1973; (contrib.) Biographical Dictionary of Modern Peace Leaders, 1985; (ed) Peace Studies: the hard questions, 1986. *Recreations:* music, walking, conversation. *Address:* 31 Rowland Close, Wolvercote, Oxford OX2 8PW. *T:* Oxford 53917.

KAYE, Sir Emmanuel, Kt 1974; CBE 1967; Founder and Chairman of The Kaye Organisation Ltd, since 1966; Joint Founder and Governing Director (with J. R. Sharp, died 1965), of Lansing Bagnall Ltd, since 1943; *b* 29 Nov. 1914; *m* 1946, Elizabeth Cutler; one *s* two *d. Educ:* Richmond Hill Sch.; Twickenham Technical Coll. Founded J. E. Shay Ltd, Precision Gauge, Tool and Instrument Makers, and took over Lansing Bagnall & Co. of Isleworth, 1943; then founded Lansing Bagnall Ltd (all with late J. R. Sharp). Transf. to Basingstoke, 1949 (from being smallest manufr of electric lift trucks, became largest in Europe). Royal Warrant as supplier of Industrial Trucks to Royal Household, 1971; Queen's Awards for Export Achievement in 1969, 1970, 1971, 1979, 1980 and only co. to win Queen's Awards for both Export Achievement and Technological Innovation, 1972; Design Council Awards, 1974, 1980; winners of Gold and other Continental Awards. Chairmanships include: Lansing Bagnall International Ltd, Switzerland, 1957–; Fork Truck Rentals, 1961–77; Lansing Leasing Ltd, 1962–; Elvetham Hall Ltd, 1965–; Lansing Bagnall AG, Switzerland, 1957–; Lansing GmbH, Germany, 1966–; Pool & Sons (Hartley Wintney) Ltd, 1967–; Hubbard Bros Ltd, 1969–78; Regentruck Ltd, 1969–78; Hawkington Ltd, 1972–; L. B. Components, 1973–77; Wigan Engineering Ltd, 1973–78; Hadley Contract Hire Ltd, 1973–78; Lansing Bagnall (Northern) Ltd, 1982–; Lansing Bagnall Inc., 1974–; Henley Forklift Gp, 1976–79; Lansing Henley Ltd, 1977–; Lansing Ltd, 1977–80; Bonser Engineering Ltd, 1978–81; Kaye Steel Stockholders, 1978–; Lina Loda, 1981–; Industrial Project Consultants AG, Switzerland; Kaye Office Supplies Ltd, 1983–; Robert Royce Ltd, 1984–. Farriers' Co., 1953; Freeman of City of London, 1954. Founded Unquoted Companies' Gp, 1968; Member: CBI Taxation Cttee, 1970–77; Council of Industry for Management Educn, 1970–; Export Credit Guarantees Adv. Council, 1971–74; Inflation Accounting Cttee, 1974–75; CBI Wealth Tax Panel, 1974–77; Queen's Award Review Cttee, 1975; CBI President's Cttee, 1976–; CBI Council, 1976–; Reviewing Cttee on Export of Works of Art, 1977–80. Visiting Fellow, Univ. of Lancaster, 1970–. Governor: Girls' High Sch., Basingstoke, 1955–70; Queen Mary's Coll., Basingstoke, 1971–75. Trustee, Glyndebourne, 1977–84; Vice-Chm., Thrombosis Research Trust, 1981–; Vice Pres., Natural Medicines Soc., 1986–. Fellow, Psionic Medical Soc., 1977–. FBIM 1975; FRSA 1978. *Recreations:* chess, music, ski-ing. *Address:* Hartley Place, Hartley Wintney, Hampshire RG27 8HT; 25 St James's Place, SW1 1NP. *Club:* Brooks's.

KAYE, Geoffrey John; *b* 14 Aug. 1935; *s* of Michael and Golda Kaye; two *d. Educ:* Christ College, Finchley. Started with Pricerite Ltd when business was a small private company controlling six shops, 1951; apptd Manager (aged 18) of one of Pricerite Ltd stores, 1953; Supervisor, Pricerite Ltd, 1955; Controller of all stores in Pricerite Ltd Gp, 1958; Director, 1963; Chairman and Man. Dir, 1966–73. Mem. Cttee, British Assoc. Monte Carlo. *Recreations:* tennis, golf. *Address:* Europa Résidence, Place des Moulins, Monte Carlo, Monaco. *Club:* British Association (Monaco).

KAYE, Sir John Phillip Lister L.; *see* Lister-Kaye.

KAYE, Mary Margaret, (Mrs G. J. Hamilton), FRSL; authoress and illustrator; *d* of late Sir Cecil Kaye, CSI, CIE, CBE, and Lady Kaye; *m* Maj.-Gen. G. J. Hamilton, CB, CBE, DSO (*d* 1985); two *d. Publications: historical novels:* Shadow of the Moon, 1957, rev. edn 1979; Trade Wind, 1963, revd edn 1981; The Far Pavilions, 1978 (televised 1984); *detective novels:* Six Bars at Seven, 1940; Death Walks in Kashmir, 1953 (republished as Death in Kashmir, 1984); Death Walks in Berlin, 1955; Death Walks in Cyprus, 1956 (republished as Death in Cyprus, 1984); Later Than You Think, 1958 (republished as Death in Kenya, 1983); House of Shade, 1959 (republished as Death in Zanzibar, 1983); Night on the Island, 1960 (republished as Death in the Andamans, 1985); Death in Berlin, 1985; *for children:* The Potter Pinner Books (series), 1937–41; The Ordinary Princess,

1980, US 1984 (shown on BBC TV Jackanory, 1983, 1984); Thistledown, 1981; *edited:* The Golden Calm, 1980; *illustrated:* The Story of St Francis; Children of Galilee; Adventures in a Caravan. *Recreation:* painting. *Club:* Army and Navy.

KAYE, Michael; General Administrator, Young Concert Artists Trust, since 1983; Festival Director, City of London Festival, since 1984; *b* 27 Feb. 1925; *s* of Harry Kaye and Annie Steinberg; *m* 1st, 1950, Muriel Greenberg (marr. diss. 1959); one *d*; 2nd, 1962, Fay Bercovitch. *Educ:* Malmesbury Road, Bow; Cave Road, Plaistow; Water Lane, Stratford; West Ham Secondary Sch., E15. Served in Army, REME and Intelligence Corps, 1943–47. Journalism and Public Relations, 1947–53; Marketing and Public Relations in tobacco industry, 1953–61; PR Manager, later PR Director, Carreras-Rothmans, 1961–76; Director, Peter Stuyvesant Foundation, 1963–76; General Administrator, Rupert Foundn, 1972–76; Man. Dir, London Symphony Orchestra, 1976–80. Trustee: Whitechapel Art Gallery, 1964–75; Youth & Music, 1970–78; Arts Dir, GLC, and Gen. Administrator, S Bank Concert Halls, 1980–83. *Recreations:* photography, music (clarinet). *Address:* 3 Coppice Way, E18 2DU. *T:* 01–989 1281.

KAYLL, Wing Commander Joseph Robert, DSO 1940; OBE 1946; DFC 1940; DL; JP; *b* 12 April 1914; *s* of late J. P. Kayll, MBE, The Elms, Sunderland; *m* 1940, Annette Lindsay Nisbet; two *s*. *Educ:* Aysgarth; Stowe. Timber trader; joined 607 Sqdn AAF, 1934; mobilised Sept. 1939; Commanding Officer 615 Squadron, 1940; (prisoner) 1941; OC 607 Sqdn AAF 1946. DL Durham, 1956; JP Sunderland, 1962. Mem., Wear Boating Assoc. *Recreation:* yachting. *Address:* Hillside House, Hillside, Sunderland, Tyne and Wear SR3 1YN. *T:* 283282. *Clubs:* Royal Ocean Racing; Sunderland Yacht; Royal Northumberland Yacht.

KAYSEN, Prof. Carl; David W. Skinner Professor of Political Economy, since 1977, and Director of Program in Science, Technology, and Society, since 1981, Massachusetts Institute of Technology; *b* 5 March 1920; *s* of Samuel and Elizabeth Kaysen; *m* 1940, Annette Neutra; two *d*. *Educ:* Philadelphia Public Schs; Overbrook High Sch., Philadelphia; Pennsylvania, Columbia and Harvard Univs. AB Pa 1940; MA 1947, PhD 1954, Harvard. Nat. Bureau of Economic Research, 1940–42; Office of Strategic Services, Washington, 1942–43; Intelligence Officer, US Army Air Force, 1943–45; State Dept, Washington, 1945. Dep. Special Asst to President, 1961–63. Harvard University, 1947–66: Teaching Fellow in Econs, 1947; Asst Prof. of Economics, 1950–55; Assoc. Prof. of Economics 1955–57; Prof. of Economics, 1957–66; Assoc. Dean, Graduate Sch. of Public Administration, 1960–66; Lucius N. Littauer Prof. of Political Economy, 1964–66; Jr Fellow, Soc. of Fellows, 1947–50, Actg Sen. Fellow, 1957–58, 1964–65; Syndic, Harvard Univ. Press, 1964–66; Dir, Inst. for Advanced Study, Princeton, NJ, 1966–76, Dir Emeritus, 1976; Vice Chm., and Dir of Research, Sloan Commn on Govt and Higher Educn, 1977–79. Sen. Fulbright Res. Schol., LSE, 1955–56. Trustee: Pennsylvania Univ., 1967–; Russell Sage Foundn. *Publications:* United States *v* United Shoe Machinery Corporation, an Economic Analysis of an Anti-Trust Case, 1956; The American Business Creed (with others), 1956; Anti-Trust Policy (with D. F. Turner), 1959; The Demand for Electricity in the United States (with F. M. Fisher), 1962; The Higher Learning, The Universities, and The Public, 1969; (contrib.) Nuclear Energy Issues and Choices, 1979; A Program for Renewed Partnership (Sloan Commn on Govt and Higher Educn Report), 1980; numerous articles on economic theory, applied economics, higher education, military strategy and arms control. *Address:* E51–110D, Massachusetts Institute of Technology, Cambridge, Mass 02139, USA.

KAZAN, Elia; author; independent producer and director of plays and films; *b* Constantinople, 7 Sept. 1909; *s* of George Kazan and Athena Sismanoglou; *m* 1st, 1932, Molly Thacher (*d* 1963); two *s* two *d*; 2nd, 1967, Barbara Loden (*d* 1980); 3rd, 1982, Frances Rudge. *Educ:* Williams Coll. (AB); 2 years postgraduate work in Drama at Yale. Actor, Group Theatre, 1932–39; first London appearance as Eddie Fuseli in Golden Boy, St James, 1938. Directed *plays:* Skin of Our Teeth, 1942; All My Sons, A Streetcar Named Desire, 1947; Death of a Salesman, 1949; Camino Real, Tea and Sympathy, 1953; Cat on a Hot Tin Roof, 1955; Dark at Top of the Stairs, JB, 1958; Sweet Bird of Youth, 1959; After the Fall, 1964; But For Whom Charlie, 1964; The Changeling, 1964; Four times won best stage Director of Year, 1942, 1947, 1948, 1949. Directed *films:* Streetcar named Desire, 1951; Viva Zapata, 1952; Pinky, 1949; Gentleman's Agreement, 1948 (won Oscar, best Dir); Boomerang, 1947; A Tree Grows in Brooklyn, 1945; On the Waterfront, 1954 (won Oscar, best Dir); East of Eden, 1954; Baby Doll, 1956; A Face in the Crowd, 1957; Wild River, 1960; Splendour in the Grass, 1962; America, America, 1964; The Arrangement, 1969; The Visitors, 1972; The Last Tycoon, 1977. Three times won Best Picture of Year from New York Film Critics, 1948, 1952, 1955. *Publications:* America, America (novel), 1963; The Arrangement (novel), 1967; The Assassins, 1972; The Understudy, 1974; Acts of Love, 1978; The Anatolian, 1982; magazine articles in New York Times, Theatre Arts, etc. *Recreation:* tennis.

KEABLE-ELLIOTT, Dr Robert Anthony, FRCGP; general practitioner, since 1948; *b* 14 Nov. 1924; *s* of Robert Keable and Jolie Buck; *m* 1953, Gilian Mary Hutchison; four *s*. *Educ:* Sherborne Sch., Dorset; Guy's Hosp., London, 1943–48 (MB BS London). Founder Mem., Chiltern Medical Soc., 1956, Vice-Pres. 1958, Pres. 1964; Member, Faculty Board of Thames Valley, Faculty of Royal Coll. of General Practitioners, 1960; Upjohn Travelling Fellowship, 1962; Mem., Bucks Local Med. Cttee, 1958– (Chm., 1964–68). British Medical Association: Mem., 1948–; Mem. Council, 1974–; Treasurer, 1981–; Chm., Gen. Med. Services Cttee, 1966–72. Mem., Finance Corp. of General Practice, 1974–79. Asst Editor, Guy's Hospital Gazette, 1947–48. *Recreations:* sailing, golf, gardening. *Address:* Peels, Ibstone, near High Wycombe, Bucks HP14 3XX. *T:* Turville Heath 385. *Club:* Beefsteak.

KEAL, Dr Edwin Ernest Frederick, FRCP; Consultant Physician: Brompton Hospital, London, since 1966; St Mary's Hospital, London, since 1977; Kensington Chest Clinic, since 1963; Consultant in Chest Diseases to the Army, since 1979; Chief Medical Officer, Eagle Star Insurance Co., since 1968; *b* 21 Aug. 1921; *s* of Frederick Archibald Keal and Mabel Orange Keal; *m* 1945, Constance Mary Gilliams; one *s*. *Educ:* Kingston High Sch., Hull; London Hospital Med. Coll. MB BS London 1952, DCH 1954, MD London 1971; FRCP 1973 (MRCP 1957). Service in RNVR (Lieut), 1939–46. Junior hosp. posts, London Hosp., 1952–59; Sen. Medical Registrar, Brompton Hosp., 1959–63; Cons. Physician, St Charles Hosp., London, 1963–77; Cardiothoracic Institute: Sen. Lectr, 1972–77; Hon. Sen. Lectr, 1978–; Dean, 1979–84. Member: Bd of Governors, National Heart and Chest Hosps, 1975–; Cttee of Management, Cardiothoracic Inst., 1978–84. *Publications:* chapters in various books, and articles, mainly related to diseases of the chest. *Address:* 12 Dorchester Drive, Herne Hill, SE24 0DQ. *T:* 01–733 1766.

KEAN, Arnold Wilfred Geoffrey, CBE 1977; FRAeS; Member, since 1980, and Vice-President, since 1982, UN Administrative Tribunal; *b* 29 Sept. 1914; *s* of late Martin Kean; *m* 1939, Sonja Irene, *d* of late Josef Andersson, Copenhagen; two *d*. *Educ:* Blackpool Gram. Sch.; Queens' Coll., Cambridge (Schol.). 1st cl. 1st div. Law Tripos, Pts I and II; Pres., Cambridge Union, 1935; Wallenberg (Scandinavian) Prize; Commonwealth Fund Fellow, Harvard Law Sch.; Yarborough-Anderson Schol., Inner Temple. Called to the Bar (studentship, certif. of honour, 1939). Wartime service on legal staff of British Purchasing Commn and UK Treas. Delegn in N America. HM Treasury Solicitor's Dept, 1945; Princ. Asst Solicitor, 1964–72; Sec. and Legal Adviser, CAA, 1972–79. Member: Legal Cttee, Internat. Civil Aviation Organisation, 1954– (Chm., 1978–83); Air Travel Reserve Fund Agency, 1975–79; UK Deleg. at internat. confs on maritime, railway, atomic energy and air law. Tutor in Law, Civil Service Coll., 1963–; Visiting Lecturer: Univ. of Auckland, NZ, 1980; Univ. of Sydney, NSW, 1982; UCL, 1983– (Hon. Fellow). Air Law Editor, Jl of Business Law, 1970–. King Christian X Liberation Medal (Denmark), 1945. *Publications:* (ed) Essays in Air Law, 1982; articles in legal periodicals. *Recreations:* music, stamps, gardening. *Address:* Tall Trees, South Hill Avenue, Harrow HA1 3NU. *T:* 01–422 5791.

KEANE, Desmond St John, QC 1981; a Recorder of the Crown Court, since 1979; *b* 21 Aug. 1941; *er s* of late Henry Keane, MB, BCh, and of Patricia Keane; *m* 1968, Susan Mary Little; two *s* one *d*. *Educ:* Downside Sch.; Wadham Coll., Oxford (Schol.; MA Mod. Hist.); Harmsworth Law Schol., 1964. Called to the Bar, Middle Temple, 1964, to the Irish Bar, King's Inns, 1975; to Hong Kong Bar, 1982; High Court Comr, Hong Kong, 1983. Legal Assessor to GMC, 1982–. *Recreation:* cricket. *Address:* 2 Stone Buildings, Lincoln's Inn, WC2. *T:* 01–242 7637; 602 Takshing House, 20 Dis Voeux Road Central, Hong Kong. *T:* 5–215544. *Clubs:* United Oxford & Cambridge University; Kildare Street and University (Dublin); Hong Kong (Hong Kong).

KEANE, Francis Joseph; Sheriff of Glasgow and Strathkelvin, since 1984; *b* 5 Jan. 1936; *s* of Thomas and Helen Keane; *m* 1960, Lucia Corio Morrison; two *s* one *d*. *Educ:* Blairs Coll., Aberdeen; Gregorian Univ., Rome (PhL); Univ. of Edinburgh (LLB). Solicitor; Partner, McCluskey, Keane & Co., 1959; Depute Procurator Fiscal, Perth, 1961, Edinburgh, 1963; Senior Depute PF, Edinburgh, 1971; Senior Legal Asst, Crown Office, Edinburgh, 1972; PF, Airdrie, 1976; Regional PF, S Strathclyde, Dumfries and Galloway, 1980. Pres., PF Soc., 1982–84. *Recreations:* music, painting, tennis. *Address:* 24 Marlborough Avenue, Glasgow G11 7BW. *T:* 041–339 7180.

KEANE, Mary Nesta, (Mrs Robert Keane); (*nom de plume:* **M. J. Farrell**); *b* 20 July 1905; *d* of Walter Clarmont Skrine and Agnes Shakespeare Higginson; *m* 1938, Robert Lumley Keane; two *d*. *Educ:* privately. Author of plays: (with John Perry) Spring Meeting (play perf. Ambassadors Theatre and New York, 1938); Ducks and Drakes (play perf. Apollo Theatre, 1941); Guardian Angel (play perf. Gate Theatre, Dublin, 1944); Treasure Hunt (play perf. Apollo Theatre, 1949). *Publications: as M. J. Farrell:* Young Entry; Taking Chances; Mad Puppettstown; Conversation Piece; Devoted Ladies; Full House; The Rising Tide; Two Days in Aragon, 1941; Loving Without Tears (novel), 1951; Treasure Hunt, 1952; *as Molly Keane:* Good Behaviour, 1981 (televised 1983); Time After Time, 1983 (televised 1986); Nursery Cooking, 1985. *Address:* Dysert, Ardmore, Co. Waterford, Ireland. *TA:* Ardmore. *T:* Youghal 4225.

KEANE, Major Sir Richard (Michael), 6th Bt *cr* 1801; farmer; *b* 29 Jan. 1909; *s* of Sir John Keane, 5th Bart, DSO, and Lady Eleanor Hicks-Beach (*d* 1960), *e d* of 1st Earl St Aldwyn; *S* father, 1956; *m* 1939, Olivia Dorothy Hawkshaw; two *s* one *d*. *Educ:* Sherborne Sch.; Christ Church, Oxford. Diplomatic Correspondent to Reuters 1935–37; Diplomatic Corresp. and Asst to Editor, Sunday Times, 1937–39. Served with County of London Yeomanry and 10th Royal Hussars, 1939–44; Liaison Officer (Major) with HQ Vojvodina, Yugoslav Partisans, 1944; attached British Military Mission, Belgrade, 1944–45. Publicity Consultant to Imperial Chemical Industries Ltd, 1950–62. *Publications:* Germany: What Next?, (Penguin Special), 1939; Modern Marvels of Science (editor), 1961. *Recreation:* fishing. *Heir: s* John Charles Keane, *b* 16 Sept. 1941. *Address:* Cappoquin House, Cappoquin, County Waterford, Ireland. *T:* 058–54004.

KEAR, Graham Francis; Assistant Secretary, Abbeyfield Richmond Society, since 1984; *b* 9 Oct. 1928; *s* of Richard Walter Kear and Eva Davies; *m* 1978, Joyce Eileen Parks. *Educ:* Newport (St Julian's) High Sch., Mon; Balliol Coll., Oxford (BA). Min. of Supply, 1951–52 and 1954–57; UK Delegn to ECSC, 1953–54; Min. of Aviation, 1957–59 and 1960–63; NATO Maintenance Supply Agency, Paris, 1959–60; MoD, 1963–65; Cabinet Office, 1968–71; Min. of Aviation Supply/DTI, 1971–72; Fellow, Harvard Univ. Center for Internat. Affairs, 1972–73; Under-Sec., Dept of Energy, 1974–80. *Recreation:* music. *Address:* 28 Eastbourne Road, Brentford, Mddx TW8 9PE. *T:* 01–560 4746.

KEARLEY, family name of **Viscount Devonport.**

KEARNEY, Sheriff Brian; Sheriff of Glasgow and Strathkelvin, since 1977; *b* 25 Aug. 1935; *s* of late James Samuel and Agnes Olive Kearney; *m* 1965, Elizabeth Mary Chambers; three *s* one *d*. *Educ:* Largs Higher Grade; Greenock Academy; Glasgow Univ. (MA, LLB). Qualified solicitor, 1960; Partner, Biggart, Lumsden & Co., Solicitors, Glasgow, 1965. Sheriff of N Strathclyde at Dumbarton, 1974–77. Sometime tutor in Jurisprudence, and external examnr in legal subjects, Glasgow Univ.; Pres., Glasgow Juridical Soc., 1964–65; Chm., Glasgow Marriage Guidance Council, 1977–. *Publications:* An Introduction to Ordinary Civil Procedure in the Sheriff Court, 1982; articles in legal jls. *Recreations:* cutting sandwiches for family picnics, listening to music, reading, writing and resting. *Address:* Sheriff's Chambers, Sheriff Court House, 149 Ingram Street, Glasgow G1 1EJ.

KEARNEY, Hon. Sir William (John Francis), Kt 1982; CBE 1976; Judge of the Supreme Court of the Northern Territory, since 1982; Aboriginal Land Commissioner, since 1982; *b* 8 Jan. 1935; *s* of William John Kilbeg Kearney and Gertrude Ivylene Kearney; *m* 1959, Jessie Alice Elizabeth Yung; three *d*. *Educ:* Univ. of Sydney (BA, LLB); University Coll. London (LLM). Legal Service of Papua New Guinea, 1963–75; Sec. for Law, 1972–75; dormant Commn as Administrator, 1972–73, and as High Comr, 1973–75; Judge, Supreme Ct of PNG, 1976–80; Dep. Chief Justice, 1980–82. *Recreations:* travelling, literature. *Address:* Judges' Chambers, Supreme Court, Darwin, NT 5794, Australia.

KEARNS, David Todd; Chairman since 1985, and Chief Executive since 1982, Xerox Corp.; *b* 11 Aug. 1930; *m* 1954, Shirley Cox; two *s* four *d*. *Educ:* Univ. of Rochester (BA). Served US Navy; IBM, 1954–71; Xerox Corp.: Corporate Vice Pres., 1971; Group Vice Pres. and Board of Dirs, 1976; Pres. and Chief Operating Officer, 1977. Mem. Boards of Directors: Chase Manhattan Corp.; Time Inc.; Junior Achievement. Mem. Council on Foreign Relations; Trustee, Cttee for Economic Develt; Chairman: Nat. Urban League; Health Corp. of Greater Stamford and Univ. of Rochester; Mem., Business Roundtable Policy Cttee. Mem., Bd of Visitors, Fuqua Sch. of Business Administration, Duke Univ. *Address:* Xerox Corporation, PO Box 1600, Stamford, Conn 06904, USA. *T:* (203) 968–3201.

KEARTON, family name of **Baron Kearton.**

KEARTON, Baron *cr* 1970 (Life Peer), of Whitchurch, Bucks; **Christopher Frank Kearton;** Kt 1966; OBE 1945; FRS 1961; Chancellor, University of Bath, since 1980; *b* 17 Feb. 1911; *s* of Christopher John Kearton and Lilian Hancock; *m* 1936, Agnes Kathleen Brander; two *s* two *d*. *Educ:* Hanley High Sch.; St John's Coll., Oxford. Joined ICI,

Billingham Division, 1933. Worked in Atomic Energy Project, UK and USA, 1940–45. Joined Courtaulds Ltd, i/c of Chemical Engineering, 1946; Dir 1952; Dep. Chm., 1961–64; Chm., 1964–75; Chm. and Chief Exec., British Nat. Oil Corp., 1976–79. Part-time Member: UKAEA, 1955–81; CEGB, 1974–80. Dir, Hill Samuel Gp, 1970–81; Chm., British Printing Corp., 1981. Visitor, DSIR, 1955–61, 1963–68. Chairman: Industrial Reorganisation Corp., 1966–68; Electricity Supply Res. Council, 1960–77 (Mem., 1954–77); Tropical Products Inst. Cttee, 1958–79; East European Trade Council, 1975–77. Member: Windscale Accident Cttee, 1957; Special Advisory Group, British Transport Commn, 1960; Adv. Council on Technology, 1964–70; Council, RIIA, 1964–75; NEDC, 1965–71; Adv. Cttee, Industrial Expansion Bill, 1968–70 (Chm.); Central Adv. Council for Science and Technology; Cttee of Enquiry into Structure of Electricity Supply Industry, 1974–75; Offshore Energy Technology Bd, 1976–79; Energy Commn, 1977–79; Council, Royal Soc., 1970; Pres., Soc. of Chemical Industry, 1972–74 (Chm., Heavy Organic Chemical Section, 1961–62). President: RoSPA, 1973–80; BAAS, 1978–79; Aslib, 1980–82; Market Research Soc., 1983–86. Fellow, Imperial Coll. London, 1976; Hon. Fellow: St John's Coll., Oxford, 1965; Manchester Coll. of Sci. and Techn., 1966; Soc. of Dyers and Colourists, 1974. Comp. TI, 1965; Hon. FIChemE 1968; Hon. LLD: Leeds, 1966; Strathclyde, 1981; Hon. DSc: Bath, 1966; Aston in Birmingham, 1970; Reading, 1970; Keele, 1973; Ulster, 1975; Hon. DCL Oxon, 1978; DUniv Heriot-Watt, 1979. FRSA 1970; CBIM 1980. Grande Ufficiale, Order of Merit (Italy), 1977. *Address:* The Old House, Whitchurch, near Aylesbury, Bucks HP22 4JS. *T:* Aylesbury 641232. *Club:* Athenæum.

KEATING, Donald Norman, QC 1972; FCIArb; a Recorder of the Crown Court, since 1972; *b* 24 June 1924; *s* of late Thomas Archer Keating and late Anne Keating; *m* 1st, 1945, Betty Katharine (*d* 1975); two *s* one *d*; 2nd, 1978, Kay Rosamond, *d* of Geoffrey and Avis Blundell Jones and *widow* of Edmund Deighton; one *s* one step *d*. *Educ:* Roan Sch.; King's Coll., London. BA (History), 1948. RAFVR, 1943–46 (Flt Lt). Called to Bar, Lincoln's Inn, 1950; Bencher, 1979. *Publications:* Building Contracts, edns 1955, 1963, 1969, 1978 and supps 1982, 1984; Guide to RIBA Forms, 1959; various articles in legal and other jls. *Recreations:* theatre, music, travel, walking. *Address:* 10 Essex Street, WC2R 3AA. *T:* 01–240 6981.

KEATING, Frank; Sports Columnist, The Guardian, since 1976; *b* 4 Oct. 1937; *s* of Bryan Keating and Monica Marsh; *m* 1975, Sally Head (separated 1981). *Educ:* Belmont Abbey; Douai. Stroud News, 1956–58; Hereford Times, 1958–60; Evening World, Bristol, 1960–62; Editor, Outside Broadcasts, Rediffusion Television, 1963–67; Editor, Features, and Head of Special Projs, Thames Television, 1968–72; The Guardian, 1972–. Astroturf Sportswriter of the Year, 1978; 'What the Papers Say' Sportswriter of the Year, 1979. *Television series:* Maestro, BBC, 1981–85. *Publications:* Caught by Keating, 1979; Bowled Over, 1980; Another Bloody Day in Paradise, 1981; Up and Under, 1983; Long Days, Late Nights, 1984; High, Wide and Handsome, 1986; contrib. Punch, New Statesman, Spectator, BBC. *Recreations:* bad village cricket, worse golf. *Address:* 57 Holland Park, W11. *T:* 01–727 0269; Hyde Cottage, Lower Chute, Wilts SP10 1BD. *T:* Chute Standen 365. *Clubs:* Chelsea Arts; Chute (Wilts); Jolly Rogers Cricket (Home Counties touring).

KEATING, Henry Reymond Fitzwalter; author; *b* 31 Oct. 1926; *s* of John Hervey Keating and Muriel Marguerita Keating (*née* Clews); *m* 1953, Sheila Mary Mitchell; three *s* one *d*. *Educ:* Merchant Taylors' Sch.; Trinity Coll., Dublin. Journalism, 1952–60; Crime Reviewer for The Times, 1967–83. Chairman: Crime Writers' Assoc., 1970–71; Society of Authors, 1983–84; Pres., Detection Club, 1985. *Publications:* Death and the Visiting Firemen, 1959; Zen there was Murder, 1960; A Rush on the Ultimate, 1961; The Dog it was that Died, 1962; Death of a Fat God, 1963; The Perfect Murder, 1964; Is Skin-Deep, Is Fatal, 1965; Inspector Ghote's Good Crusade, 1966; Inspector Ghote Caught in Meshes, 1967; Inspector Ghote Hunts the Peacock, 1968; Inspector Ghote Plays a Joker, 1969; Inspector Ghote Breaks an Egg, 1970; Inspector Ghote goes by Train, 1971; The Strong Man, 1971; (ed) Blood on My Mind, 1972; Inspector Ghote Trusts the Heart, 1972; The Underside, 1974; Bats Fly Up for Inspector Ghote, 1974; A Remarkable Case of Burglary, 1975; Filmi, Filmi, Inspector Ghote, 1976; Murder Must Appetize, 1976; (ed) Agatha Christie: First Lady of Crime, 1977; A Long Walk to Wimbledon, 1978; Inspector Ghote Draws a Line, 1979; Sherlock Holmes: the man and his world, 1979; The Murder of the Maharajah, 1980; Go West, Inspector Ghote, 1981; (ed) Whodunit, 1982; The Lucky Alphonse, 1982; The Sheriff of Bombay, 1984; Mrs Craggs, Crimes Cleaned Up, 1985; Under a Monsoon Cloud, 1986; Writing Crime Fiction, 1986. *Recreation:* popping round to the post. *Address:* 35 Northumberland Place, W2 5AS. *T:* 01–229 1100.

KEATING, Hon. Paul John; Federal Treasurer of Australia, since 1983; MP (Lab) for Blaxland, NSW, since 1969; *b* 18 Jan. 1944; *s* of Matthew and Minnie Keating; *m* 1975, Anita Johanna Maria Van Iersel; one *s* three *d*. *Educ:* De La Salle College, Bankstown, NSW. Research Officer, Federated Municipal and Shire Council Employees Union of Australia, 1967. Minister for Northern Australia, Oct.-Nov. 1975; Shadow Minister for Agriculture, Jan.-March 1976; Shadow Minister for Minerals and Energy, 1976–83; Shadow Treasurer, Jan.-March 1983. *Address:* House of Representatives, Parliament House, Canberra, ACT 2600, Australia. *T:* 062.727060, 731417.

KEATINGE, Sir Edgar (Mayne), Kt 1960; CBE 1954; *b* Bombay, 3 Feb. 1905; *s* of late Gerald Francis Keatinge, CIE; *m* 1930, Katharine Lucile Burrell; one *s* one *d*. *Educ:* Rugby Sch.; School of Agriculture, S Africa. Diploma in Agriculture, 1925. S African Dept of Agriculture, 1926–29. Served War of 1939–45 with RA. Resigned with rank of Lieut-Col. West African Frontier Force, 1941–43; Commandant Sch. of Artillery, West Africa, 1942–43; CC West Suffolk, 1933–45. Parliamentary Candidate, Isle of Ely, 1938–44; MP (C) Bury St Edmunds, 1944–45; JP Wilts 1946; Chm. Wessex Area Nat. Union of Conservative Assocs, 1950–53; Mem. Panel, Land Tribunal, SW Area. Director: St Madeleine Sugar Co., 1944–62; Caromi Ltd, 1962–66. Governor, Sherborne Sch., 1951–74. Mem. Council, Royal African Soc., 1970–80. *Recreations:* travel, shooting. *Address:* Teffont, Salisbury, Wilts SP3 5RG. *T:* Teffont 224. *Clubs:* Carlton, Boodle's.

See also Prof. W. R. Keatinge.

KEATINGE, Prof. William Richard; MA; PhD; Professor of Physiology, London Hospital Medical College, since 1971; *b* 18 May 1931; *s* of Sir Edgar Keatinge, *qv*; *m* 1955, M. E. Annette Hegarty; one *s* two *d*. *Educ:* Upper Canada Coll.; Rugby Sch.; Cambridge Univ.; St Thomas's Hospital. MB BChir; MRCP 1985. House Phys., St Thomas's Hospital, 1955–56; Surg.-Lt RN (Nat. Service), 1956–58; Jun. Research Fellow and Dir of Studies in Medicine, Pembroke Coll., Cambridge, 1958–60; Fellow, Cardiovascular Research Inst., San Francisco, 1960–61; MRC appt Radcliffe Infirmary, Oxford, 1961–68; Fellow of Pembroke Coll., Oxford, 1965–68; Reader in Physiology, London Hosp. Med. Coll., 1968. *Publications:* Survival in Cold Water, 1969; Local Mechanisms Controlling Blood Vessels, 1980; chapters in textbooks of physiology and medicine; papers in physiological and medical jls on temperature regulation and on control of blood vessels. *Recreations:* ski-ing, archaeology. *Address:* London Hospital Medical College, Turner Street, E1 2AD.

KEAY, Ronald William John, CBE 1977 (OBE 1966); DPhil; Executive Secretary, The Royal Society, 1977–85; *b* 20 May 1920; *s* of Harold John Keay and Marion Lucy (*née* Flick); *m* 1944, Joan Mary Walden; one *s* two *d*. *Educ:* King's College Sch., Wimbledon; St John's Coll., Oxford (BSc, MA, DPhil). Colonial Forest Service, Nigeria, 1942–62. Seconded to Royal Botanic Gardens, Kew, 1951–57; Dir, Federal Dept of Forest Research, Nigeria, 1960–62; Dep. Exec. Sec., The Royal Society, 1962–77. Pres., Science Assoc. of Nigeria, 1961–62; Vice-Pres., Linnean Soc., 1965–67, 1971–73, 1974–76; Pres., African Studies Assoc., 1971–72. Chairman: Finance Cttee, Internat. Biological Programme, 1964–74; UK Br., Nigerian Field Soc.; Treasurer, Scientific Cttee for Problems of the Environment, 1976–77; Member: Lawes Agricl Trust Cttee, 1978–; RHS Review Cttee, 1984–85; Council, Roehampton Inst. of Higher Educn. Church Warden, St Martin-in-the-Fields, 1981–. Hon. FIBiol; Hon. FRHS. *Publications:* Flora of West Tropical Africa, Vol. 1, 1954–58; Nigerian Trees, 1960–64; papers on tropical African plant ecology and taxonomy, and science policy. *Recreations:* gardening, walking, natural history. *Address:* 38 Birch Grove, Cobham, Surrey KT11 2HR. *T:* Cobham 65677. *Club:* Athenæum.

KEDOURIE, Prof. Elie, FBA 1975; Professor of Politics in the University of London, since 1965; Editor, Middle Eastern Studies, since 1964; *b* 25 Jan. 1926; *er s* of A. Kedourie and L. Dangour, Baghdad; *m* 1950, Sylvia, *d* of Gourgi Haim, Baghdad; two *s* one *d*. *Educ:* Collège A-D Sasson and Shamash Sch., Baghdad; London Sch. of Economics; St Antony's Coll., Oxford (Sen. Scholar). BSc(Econ). Has taught at the London Sch. of Economics, 1953–. Visiting Lecturer: Univ. of California, Los Angeles, 1959; Univ. of Paris, 1959; Visiting Prof.: Princeton Univ., 1960–61; Monash Univ., Melb., 1967; Harvard Univ., 1968–69; Tel Aviv Univ., 1969; Brandeis Univ., 1985; Scholar-in-Residence, Brandeis Univ., 1982. Fellow: Netherlands Inst. for Advanced Study, 1980–81; Sackler Inst. of Advanced Studies, Tel-Aviv Univ., 1983. Mem., Cttee of Enquiry into Validation of Acad. Degrees in Public Sector Higher Educn, 1984–85. Hist. Advr, Roads to Conflict, BBC TV, 1978. Mem. Editorial Bd, Cambridge Studies in History and Theory of Politics, 1968–82. *Publications:* England and the Middle East, 1956; Nationalism, 1960 (trans. German, 1968); Afghani and 'Abduh, 1966; The Chatham House Version, 1970; Nationalism in Asia and Africa, 1971; Arabic Political Memoirs, 1974; In the Anglo-Arab Labyrinth, 1976; (ed) The Middle Eastern Economy, 1977; (ed) The Jewish World, 1979; (ed jtly) Modern Egypt, 1980; Islam in the Modern World, 1980; (ed jtly) Towards a Modern Iran, 1980; (ed jtly) Palestine and Israel in the Nineteenth and Twentieth Centuries, 1982; (ed jtly) Zionism and Arabism in Palestine and Israel, 1982; The Crossman Confessions, 1984. *Address:* London School of Economics, Houghton Street, Aldwych, WC2A 2AE. *T:* 01–405 7686.

KEE, Robert; author and broadcaster; *b* 5 Oct. 1919; *s* of late Robert and Dorothy Kee; *m* 1st, 1948, Janetta, *d* of Rev. G. H. Woolley, VC; one *d*; 2nd, 1960, Cynthia, *d* of Edward Judah; one *s* one *d* (and one *s* decd). *Educ:* Stowe Sch.; Magdalen Coll., Oxford (Exhibr, MA). RAF, 1940–46. Atlantic Award for Literature, 1946. Picture Post, 1948–51; Picture Editor, WHO, 1953; Special Corresp., Observer, 1956–57; Literary Editor, Spectator, 1957; Special Corresp., Sunday Times, 1957–58; BBC TV (Panorama, etc), 1958–62; Television Reporters International, 1963–64; ITV (Rediffusion, Thames, London Week-End, ITN, Yorkshire), 1964–78; BBC, 1978–82; Presenter: Panorama, BBC1, 1982; TV-am, 1983; ITV, 1984–. *Television series:* Ireland: a television history (13 parts), 1981; The Writing on the Wall, 1985. Alistair Horne Research Fellow, St Antony's Coll., Oxford, 1972–73. BAFTA Richard Dimbleby Award, 1976. *Publications:* A Crowd Is Not Company, 1947, repr. 1982; The Impossible Shore, 1949; A Sign of the Times, 1955; Broadstrop In Season, 1959; Refugee World, 1961; The Green Flag, 1972; Ireland: a history, 1980; The World We Left Behind: a chronicle of 1939, 1984; 1945: the world we fought for, 1985; many translations from German. *Recreations:* swimming, bicycling, listening to music. *Address:* c/o Lloyds Bank, 112 Kensington High Street, W8.

See also William Kee.

KEE, William; His Honour Judge Kee; a Circuit Judge, since 1972; *b* 15 Oct. 1921; *yr s* of Robert and Dorothy Kee; *m* 1953, Helga Wessel Eckhoff; one *s* three *d*. *Educ:* Rottingdean Sch.; Stowe Sch. Served War, Army, 1941–46: attached 9th Gurkha Rifles, Dehra Dun, 1943; Staff Captain, Bde HQ, 1945–46. Called to Bar, Inner Temple, 1948. Jt Chm., Independent Schools' Tribunal, 1971–72. *Publications:* (jt) Divorce Case Book, 1950; contributor to titles in Atkin's Encyclopaedia of Court Forms; Halsbury's Laws of England. *Recreations:* listening to music, walking. *Address:* Oak Hill Cottage, Oak Hill Road, Sevenoaks, Kent TN13 1NP. *T:* 52737.

See also Robert Kee.

KEEBLE, Sir (Herbert Ben) Curtis, GCMG 1982 (KCMG 1978; CMG 1970); HM Diplomatic Service, retired; Ambassador at Moscow, 1978–82; a Governor, BBC, since 1985; *b* 18 Sept. 1922; *s* of Herbert Keeble and Gertrude Keeble, BEM; *m* 1947, Margaret Fraser; three *d*. *Educ:* Clacton County High Sch.; London University. Served HM Forces, 1942–47. Entered HM Foreign (subsequently Diplomatic) Service, 1947; served in Djakarta, 1947–49; Foreign Office, 1949–51; Berlin, 1951–54; Washington, 1954–58; Foreign Office, 1958–63; Counsellor and Head of European Economic Organisations Dept, 1963–65; Counsellor (Commercial), Berne, 1965–68; Minister, Canberra, 1968–71; Asst Under-Sec. of State, FCO, 1971–73; HM Ambassador, German Democratic Republic, 1974–76; Dep. Under Sec. of State (Chief Clerk), FCO, 1976–78. Special Adviser, H of C Foreign Affairs Cttee, 1985–86. Chm., GB-USSR Assoc., 1985–; Member Council: RIIA, 1985–; SSEES, 1985–. *Publication:* (ed) The Soviet State, 1985. *Recreations:* sailing, skiing. *Address:* Dormers, St Leonards Road, Thames Ditton, Surrey. *T:* 01–398 7778.

KEEBLE, Major Robert, DSO 1940; MC 1945; TD 1946; Director: Associated Portland Cement Manufacturers Ltd, 1970–74; Aberthaw & Bristol Channel Portland Cement Co. Ltd, 1970–74; engaged in cement manufacture; *b* 20 Feb. 1911; *s* of late Edwin Percy and Alice Elizabeth Keeble; unmarried. *Educ:* King Henry VIII's Sch., Coventry. Commanded Royal Engineer Field Company; Territorial Army Commission, passed Staff Coll., Camberley, 1939; served in War of 1939–45 (despatches twice, twice wounded, DSO, MC, 1939–45 Star, African Star, France-Germany Star and Defence Medal, TD). Mem., Inst. Quarrying. Governor, Hull Univ. Hon. Brother, Hull Trinity House. Freeman of City of London and Liveryman of Company of Fanmakers; Fellow, Drapers' Co., Coventry. *Recreation:* fishing. *Address:* 15 Fernhill Close, Kenilworth CV8 1AN. *T:* Kenilworth 55668. *Club:* Army and Navy.

KEEBLE, Thomas Whitfield; HM Diplomatic Service, retired 1976; Senior Clerk (Acting), Committee Office, House of Commons, 1976–83; *b* 10 Feb. 1918; *m* 1945, Ursula Scott Morris; two *s*. *Educ:* Sir John Deane's Grammar Sch., Cheshire; St John's Coll., Cambridge (MA); King's Coll., London (PhD). Served, 1940–45, in India, Persia, Iraq and Burma in RA (seconded to Indian Artillery), Captain. Asst Principal, Commonwealth Relations Office, 1948; Private Sec. to Parliamentary Under Sec. of State; Principal, 1949; First Sec., UK High Commn in Pakistan, 1950–53, in Lahore, Peshawar and Karachi; seconded to Foreign Service and posted to UK Mission to the United Nations in New York, 1955–59; Counsellor, 1958; Head of Defence and Western Dept, CRO, 1959–60; British Dep. High Comr in Ghana, 1960–63; Head of Econ. Gen. Dept, CRO, 1963–66; Minister (Commercial), British Embassy, Buenos Aires, 1966–67; Hon.

Research Associate, Inst. of Latin American Studies, Univ. of London, 1967–68; Minister, British Embassy, Madrid, 1969–71; Head of UN (Econ. and Social) Dept, FCO, 1971–72, of UN Dept, 1972–74; Sen. Directing Staff (Civil), Nat. Defence Coll., Latimer, 1974–76. *Publications:* British Overseas Territories and South America, 1806–1914, 1970; articles in Hispanic reviews. *Recreations:* golf, Spanish literature, bird watching. *Address:* 49 Station Road, Oakington, Cambridge CB4 5AH. *T:* Histon 4922. *Club:* United Oxford & Cambridge University.

KEEFFE, Barrie Colin; dramatist; *b* 31 Oct. 1945; *s* of Edward Thomas Keeffe and Constance Beatrice Keeffe (*née* Marsh); *m* 1st, 1969, Dee Sarah Truman (marr. diss. 1979); 2nd, 1981, Verity Eileen Proud (*née* Bargate) (*d* 1981); Guardian of her two *s*; 3rd, 1983, Julia Lindsay. *Educ:* East Ham Grammar School. Formerly actor with Nat. Youth Theatre; began writing career as journalist; Thames Television Award writer-in-residence, Shaw Theatre, 1977; Resident playwright, Royal Shakespeare Co., 1978; Associate Writer, Theatre Royal, Stratford East, 1986–. Mem. Board of Directors, Soho Theatre Co., 1978–. French Critics Prix Revelation, 1978; Giles Cooper Best Radio Plays, 1980; Mystery Writers of America Edgar Allan Poe Award, 1982. *Theatre plays:* Only a Game, 1973; A Sight of Glory, 1975; Scribes, 1975; My Girl, 1975; Here Comes the Sun, 1976; Gimme Shelter, 1977; A Mad World My Masters, 1977, 1984; Barbarians, 1977; Frozen Assets, 1978; Sus, 1979; Bastard Angel, 1980; She's So Modern, 1980; Black Lear, 1980; Chorus Girls, 1981; Better Times, 1985; *television plays:* Substitute, 1972; Not Quite Cricket, 1977; Gotcha, 1977; Nipper, 1977; Champions, 1978; Hanging Around, 1978; Waterloo Sunset, 1979; King, 1984; *television series:* No Excuses, 1983; *film:* The Long Good Friday, 1981; also radio plays. *Publications: novels:* Gadabout, 1969; No Excuses, 1983; *plays:* Gimme Shelter, 1977; A Mad World My Masters, 1977; Barbarians, 1977; Here Comes the Sun, 1978; Frozen Assets, 1978; Sus, 1979; Bastard Angel, 1980; The Long Good Friday, 1984; Better Times, 1985. *Recreation:* origami. *Address:* 110 Annandale Road, SE10 0JZ.

KEEGAN, Denis Michael; Barrister; General Manager, Mercantile Credit Co. Ltd, 1975–83, retired; Chairman, Marn Finance Co. Ltd; *b* 26 Jan. 1924; *o s* of Denis Francis Keegan and Mrs Duncan Campbell; *m* 1st, 1951, Pamela Barbara (marr. diss.), *yr d* of late Percy Bryan, Purley, Surrey; one *s*; 2nd, 1961, Marie Patricia (marr. diss.), *yr d* of late Harold Jennings; one *s*; 3rd, 1972, Ann Irene, *d* of Norman Morris. *Educ:* Oundle Sch.; Queen's University, Kingston, Ontario, Canada (BA). Served RN Fleet Air Arm, 1944–46 (petty officer pilot). Called to Bar, Gray's Inn, 1950. Mem. Nottingham City Council, 1953–55, resigned. MP (C) Nottingham Sth, 1955–Sept. 1959. Dir, HP Information PLC (Chm. 1984). Formerly Dir, Radio and Television Retailers' Assoc. *Recreations:* reading, talking, music. *Address:* Elizabethan House, Great Queen Street, WC2. *T:* 01-242 1234.

KEEGAN, (Joseph) Kevin, OBE 1982; professional footballer; football expert, Thames Television; *b* 14 Feb. 1951; *s* of late Joseph Keegan; *m* 1974, Jean Woodhouse; two *d*. Professional footballer with: Scunthorpe Utd, 1966–71; Liverpool, 1971–77; Hamburg, 1977–80; Southampton, 1980–82; Newcastle Utd, 1982–84. Internat. appearances for England, 1973–82, Captain, 1976–82. Winners' medals: League Championships, 1973, 1976; UEFA Cup, 1973, 1976; FA Cup, 1974; European Cup, 1977. European Footballer of the Year, 1978, 1979. *Publications:* Kevin Keegan, 1978; Against the World: playing for England, 1979. *Address:* c/o Thames Television, 306 Euston Road, NW1.

KEELE, Prof. Cyril Arthur; Emeritus Professor of Pharmacology, University of London; *b* 23 Nov. 1905; 2nd *s* of Dr David and Jessie Keele; *m* 1942, Joan Ainslie, *er d* of Lieut-Col G. A. Kempthorne; three *s*. *Educ:* Epsom Coll.; Middlesex Hospital Medical Sch. MRCS, LRCP 1927; MB, BS (London) 1928; MRCP 1929; MD London 1930; FRCP 1948; FFARCS 1958. Medical Registrar, Middlesex Hosp., 1930–32; Demonstrator and Lectr in Physiology, 1933–38; Lectr in Pharmacology, 1938–49; Reader in Pharmacology and Therapeutics, 1949–52, at Middlesex Hospital Medical Sch.; Prof. of Pharmacology and Therapeutics, Univ. of London, 1952–68; Dir, Rheumatology Res. Dept, Middlesex Hosp. Med. Sch., 1968–73. Hon. Mem., Internat. Assoc. for the Study of Pain, 1975. *Publications:* (with Prof. J. M. Robson) Recent Advances in Pharmacology, 1956; (with Dr D. Armstrong) Substances Producing Pain and Itch, 1964; (with Prof. E. Neil and Prof. N. Joels) Samson Wright's Applied Physiology, 13th edn, 1982; papers in scientific journals on the control of sweating, analgesic drugs and chemical factors producing pain. *Address:* 25 Letchmore Road, Radlett, Herts WD7 8HU.

KEELEY, Thomas Clews, CBE 1944; MA; physicist; Fellow of Wadham College, Oxford, 1924–61, now Emeritus Fellow; Sub-Warden, 1947–61, retired; *b* 16 Feb. 1894; *s* of T. F. Keeley, Erdington, Birmingham. *Educ:* King Edward's School, Birmingham; St John's Coll., Cambridge (Scholar). Royal Aircraft Establishment, 1917–19. Oxford from 1919. Fellow of the Institute of Physics. *Recreations:* photography, travel. *Address:* Wadham College, Oxford. *T:* 42564. *Club:* English-Speaking Union.

KEELING, Surgeon Rear-Adm. John, CBE 1978; retired; Director of Medical Policy and Plans, Ministry of Defence, 1980–83; Chairman, NATO Joint Civil/Military Medical Group, 1981–83; *b* 28 Oct. 1921; *s* of John and Grace Keeling; *m* 1948, Olwen Anne Dix; one *s* (and one *s* decd). *Educ:* Queen Elizabeth's Sch., Hartlebury; Birmingham Univ. MRCS, LRCP; MFOM. Entered RN as Surg. Lieut, 1946; served with Fleet Air Arm, 1947–75: Pres., Central Air Med. Bd, 1954–56 and 1960–63; SMO, HMS Albion, 1956–57, HMS Victorious, 1965–67, and several Royal Naval Air Stns; Staff MO to Flag Officer Sea Trng, 1970–73; Dir of Environmental Medicine and Dep. MO i/c Inst. of Naval Medicine, 1975–77; Dep. Med. Dir-Gen. (Naval), 1977–80. Surg. Captain 1970, Surg. Cdre 1977, Surg. Rear-Adm. 1980. QHP, 1977–83. Mem., Soc. of Occupational Medicine. *Recreations:* music, gardening, micro-computing, caravanning. *Address:* Merlin Cottage, Brockhampton, Hereford HR1 4TQ. *T:* How Caple 649. *Club:* Army and Navy.

KEELING, Robert William Maynard; a Recorder of the Crown Court, since 1980; Consultant with Monier-Williams; *b* 16 Dec. 1917; *s* of Dr George Sydney Keeling, MD, and Florence Amy Keeling (*née* Maynard); *m* 1942, Kathleen Busill Jones; one *s* two *d*. *Educ:* Uppingham; Corpus Christi Coll., Cambridge (BA 1939). Served War, RASC, 1939–46: Western Desert, Italy, Greece (despatches 1944), Berlin. FO, 1946–47. Solicitor 1950; Partner in Monier-Williams & Keeling, 1956–80; Solicitor to Vintners Company, 1953–79. Director, Sherry Producers Committee Ltd, 1957–80, Chairman 1980–. Knight Comdr, Order of Civil Merit (Spain), 1967. Dipl. of Honour, Corp. of St Vincent of Champagne, 1961. *Recreations:* growing English wine, travel, painting, music. *Address:* Hembury Knoll, Hook Heath, Woking, Surrey GU22 0QE.

KEELY, Eric Philipps, CBE 1950; Director, National Sulphuric Acid Association Ltd, 1959–67; *b* 11 Aug. 1899; *s* of late Erasmus Middleton Keely, Nottingham; *m* 1942, Enid Betty Curtis; two *d*. *Educ:* Highgate Sch. Served European War, 1917–18, Lancashire Fusiliers; Ministry of Agriculture and Fisheries, 1930; Food (Defence Plans) Dept, Board of Trade 1937; Ministry of Food, 1939; seconded to Govt of India, 1943–44; Under-Sec., Ministry of Food, 1952; Under-Sec., Ministry of Agriculture, Fisheries and Food, 1955–59. *Address:* Queen's Cottage, Horsham Road, Findon, West Sussex. *T:* Findon 2677.

KEENE, Air Vice-Marshal Allan L. A. P.; *see* Perry-Keene.

KEENE, David Wolfe, QC 1980; *b* 15 April 1941; *s* of Edward Henry Wolfe Keene and Lilian Marjorie Keene; *m* 1965, Gillian Margaret Lawrance; one *s* one *d*. *Educ:* Hampton Grammar Sch.; Balliol Coll., Oxford (Winter Williams Prizewinner, 1962; BA 1st Cl. Hons Law, 1962; BCL 1963). Called to the Bar, Inner Temple, 1964; Eldon Law Scholar, 1965. Chm. of Panel, Cumbria Structure Plan Examination in Public, 1980. Contested (Lab) Taunton, Feb. 1974, and Croydon S, Oct. 1974; founder Mem., SDP, 1981. *Recreations:* walking, opera, jazz. *Address:* 17 Belsize Lane, NW3 5AD. *T:* 01–794 3570; 4 and 5, Gray's Inn Square, Gray's Inn, WC1R 5AY. *T:* 01–404 5252. *Club:* Athenæum.

KEENE, John Robert R.; *see* Ruck Keene.

KEENLEYSIDE, Hugh Llewellyn, CC (Canada) 1969; consultant; *b* 7 July 1898; *s* of Ellis William Keenleyside and Margaret Louise Irvine; *m* 1924, Katherine Hall Pillsbury, BA, BSc; one *s* three *d*. *Educ:* Langara School and Public Schools, Vancouver, BC; University of British Columbia (BA); Clark University (MA, PhD). Holds several hon. degrees in Law, Science. Instructor and Special Lecturer in History, Brown University, Syracuse Univ., and University of British Columbia, 1923–27; Third Sec., Dept of External Affairs, 1928; Second Sec., 1929; First Sec. and First Chargé d'Affaires, Canadian Legation, Tokyo, 1929; Dept of External Affairs and Prime Minister's Office, 1936; Chm, Board of Review to Investigate charges of illegal entry on the Pacific Coast, 1938; Sec., Cttee in charge of Royal Visit to Canada, 1938–39; Counsellor, 1940; Asst Under-Sec. of State for External Affairs, 1941–44; Mem. and Sec., Canadian Section, Canada-United States Permanent Jt Bd on Defence, 1940–44, Acting Chm., 1944–45; Member: North-West Territories Council, 1941–45; Canada-United States Joint Economic Cttees, 1941–44; Special Cttee on Orientals in BC; Canadian Shipping Board, 1939–41; War Scientific and Technical Development Cttee, 1940–45; Canadian Ambassador to Mexico, 1944–47; Deputy Minister of Resources and Development and Comr of Northwest Territories, 1947–50; Head of UN Mission of Technical Assistance to Bolivia, 1950; Dir-Gen., UN Technical Assistance Administration, 1950–58; Under-Sec. Gen. for Public Administration, UN, 1959. Chairman: BC Power Commn, 1959–62; BC Hydro and Power Authy, 1962–69. Vice-Pres. National Council of the YMCAs of Canada, 1941–45; Vice-Chm., Canadian Youth Commission, 1943–45; Head of Canadian Deleg. to UN Scientific Conf. on Conservation and Utilization of Resources, 1949. Life Mem., Asiatic Soc. of Japan; one of founders and mem. of first Board of Governors of Arctic Institute of North America; Vice-Chm., Board of Governors, Carleton Coll., 1943–50; Pres. Assoc. of Canadian Clubs, 1948–50; Mem. Bd of Trustees, Clark Univ., 1953–56; Mem. Senate, University of British Columbia, 1963–69. Hon. Life Mem., Canadian Association for Adult Education; Mem. Board of Governors, Canadian Welfare Council, 1955–69; Member: Canadian National Cttee of World Power Conference; Adv. Bd (BC), Canada Permanent Cos; Hon. Bd of Dirs, Resources for the Future; Dir, Toronto-Dominion Bank, 1960–70. Assoc. Comr General, UN Conf. on Human Settlements, 1975–76 (Hon. Chm. Canadian Nat. Cttee, 1974–77). Chancellor, Notre Dame Univ., Nelson, BC, 1969–76. Dir and Fellow, Royal Canadian Geographic Soc. Haldane Medal, Royal Inst. of Public Administration, 1954; first recipient, Vanier Medal, Inst. of Public Administration of Canada, 1962. *Publications:* Canada and the United States, 1929, revised edn 1952; History of Japanese Education (with A. F. Thomas), 1937; International Aid: a summary, 1966; Memoirs: Vol. 1, Hammer the Golden Day, 1981; Vol. 2, On the Bridge of Time, 1982; various magazine articles. *Recreations:* reading, outdoor sports, cooking, poker. *Address:* 3470 Mayfair Drive, Victoria, BC V8P 1P8, Canada. *T:* 592–9331.

KEENLYSIDE, Francis Hugh; *b* 7 July 1911; *s* of late Capt. Cecil A. H. Keenlyside and Gladys Mary (*née* Milne); *m* 1st, 1935, Margaret Joan, *d* of late E. L. K. Ellis; two *s* two *d*; 2nd, 1962, Joan Winifred (*née* Collins); one *d*. *Educ:* Charterhouse; Trinity Coll., Oxford. 1st class Hons in Philosophy, Politics and Economics, 1933, Whitehead Travelling Student. Entered Administrative Class, Home Civil Service, 1934; Principal Private Sec. to four successive Ministers of Shipping and War Transport, 1939–43; Asst Sec. in charge of Shipping Policy Div., 1943; Asst Manager, Union Castle, 1947; Dep. Leader, British delegation to Danube Conf., Belgrade, 1948; Gen. Manager, Union Castle, 1953; Asst Managing Dir, Union-Castle, 1956–60; Shipping Adviser, Suez Canal Users Assoc., 1957. Mem., Gen. Council of Chamber of Shipping, 1953–60; Editor, Alpine Journal, 1953–62. Chevalier (1st Cl.) of Order of St Olav (Norway), 1948; Officer of Order of George I (Greece), 1950; King Christian X Liberty Medal (Denmark), 1946. *Publications:* Peaks and Pioneers, 1975; contrib. to mountaineering jls, etc. *Recreation:* mountaineering. *Address:* Spring Farm Vineyard, Moorlinch, Bridgwater, Somerset. *Clubs:* Alpine; Salisbury.

KEENS, Philip Francis, CBE 1973 (OBE 1966); Director, TSB Unit Trust Managers (Channel Islands) Ltd, 1972–83; Chairman, TSB Gilt Fund Ltd, 1978–83; *b* 18 June 1903; *s* of Sir Thomas Keens; *m* 1st, 1930, Sylvia Irene Robinson (*d* 1970); one *s* one *d*; 2nd, 1974, Mrs Margaret Faith Warne. *Educ:* Tettenhall Coll., Staffs. Incorporated Accountant, 1925; Chartered Accountant, 1957. Partner, Keens, Shay, Keens & Co., London, 1926–67; Trustee, Luton Trustee Savings Bank, 1934 (Chairman, 1949–64); Dep. Chm., Trustee Savings Bank Assoc., 1966–76 (Chm. Southern Area, 1967–76); Chm., London South Eastern Trustee Savings Bank, 1964–76 (Vice-Chm., 1958–64); Chairman: Trustee Savings Bank Trust Co. Ltd, 1967–79; Central Trustee Savings Bank Ltd, 1972–79; Trustee Savings Bank, South East, 1975–78, Pres., 1978; Mem., Trustee Savings Bank Central Bd, 1976–79. Past Master, Worshipful Co. of Feltmakers. *Recreation:* golf. *Address:* 15 Links Court, Grouville, Jersey, CI. *T:* Jersey 53719. *Club:* Victoria (Jersey).

KEEP, Charles Reuben; Chairman and Managing Director, Bellair Cosmetics Plc, since 1984; *b* 1932; *m*; one *d*. *Educ:* HCS, Hampstead. Joined Lloyds & Scottish Finance Ltd, 1956, Director, 1969; Man. Dir, International Factors Ltd, 1970; Group Man. Dir, Tozer Kemsley & Millbourn (Holdings) Ltd, 1973–77; Chm., Tozer Kemsley & Millbourn Trading Ltd, 1978–80; Director: Tozer Standard & Chartered Ltd; Barclays Tozer Ltd, 1974–77; Manufacturers Hanover Credit Corp., 1977–80; Chm., Export Leasing Ltd, Bermuda 1974–77; Pres., France Motors sa Paris, 1974–81. *Address:* The Oaks, 20 Forest Lane, Chigwell, Essex IG7 5AE. *T:* 01–504 3897. *Clubs:* Gresham; Chigwell Golf.

KEEPING, Charles William James; artist, book designer and Fine Art Lecturer since 1952; Visiting Lecturer in Printmaking, Camberwell School of Arts and Crafts; *b* 22 Sept. 1924; *s* of Charles Keeping and Eliza Ann Trodd; *m* 1952, Renate Meyer; three *s* one *d*. *Educ:* Frank Bryant Sch., Kennington; Polytechnic, Regent Street. Apprenticed to printing trade, 1938; served as telegraphist, RN, 1942–46; studied for Nat. Diploma of Design at Polytechnic, London, 1946–52; Vis. Lectr in Art, Polytechnic, 1956–63. Illustrated over 180 books, drawings for wall murals, television and advertising. Certificate of Merit (for illustrations to The God Beneath the Sea) 1970, Library Assoc.; Certificate, Highly Commended, for Hans Andersen Medal, Rio de Janeiro, Internat. Bd on Books for Young People, 1974. *Publications:* Black Dolly, 1966; Shaun and the Carthorse, 1966; Charley Charlotte and the Golden Canary, 1967 (Kate Greenaway Medal); Alfie and the Ferryboat, 1968; Tinker Tailor, 1968 (a Francis Williams Meml Bequest prize-winner, 1972); Joseph's Yard, 1969 (Honour Book award) (also filmed for TV); Through the

Window, 1970 (also filmed for TV); Spider's Web, 1973 (Bratislava cert.); Richard, 1973; Railway Passage, 1974 (Golden Apple, Bienalle Illustration Bratislava, 1975); Wasteground Circus, 1975; Cockney Ding Dong, 1975; The Wildman, 1976 (a Francis Williams prize-winner, 1977); Inter-City, 1977; River, 1978; Miss Emily and the Bird of Make-believe, 1978; Willie's Fire-Engine, 1980; Sammy Streetsinger, 1984; *Illustrations for:* The Highwayman, by Alfred Noyes, 1981 (Kate Greenaway Medal, 1982); The Folio Society's Complete Dickens, 1981–; Beowulf, 1982; The Wedding Ghost, by Leon Garfield, 1985; The Lady of Shalott, by Tennyson, 1986. *Recreations:* talking, walking. *Address:* 16 Church Road, Shortlands, Bromley BR2 0HP. *T:* 01–460 7679.

KEETON, George Williams, FBA 1964; Barrister-at-law; Principal, London Institute of World Affairs, 1938–52, President, since 1952; Leverhulme Fellow, 1971; *b* 22 May 1902; *o s* of John William and Mary Keeton; *m* 1st, 1924, Gladys Edith Calthorpe; two *s*; 2nd, Kathleen Marian Willard. *Educ:* Gonville and Caius Coll., Cambridge (Foundation Scholar in Law); Gray's Inn (Bacon Scholar). BA, LLB, with first class hons, 1923; MA, LLM, 1927; LLD 1932. Called to Bar, 1928; Editor, The Cambridge Review, 1924; Reader in Law and Politics, Hong Kong Univ., 1924–27; Senior Lecturer in Law, Manchester Univ., 1928–31; University College London: Reader in English Law, 1931–37, Prof. of English Law, 1937–69, Dean, Faculty of Laws, 1939–54, Vice-Provost, 1966–69; Professor of English Law, Univ. of Notre Dame, 1969–71; Professor Associate, Brunel Univ., 1969–77. Distinguished Vis. Prof., Miami Univ., 1971–73. Mem. Exec. Cttee, American Judicature Soc., 1974–77. Hon. LLD: Sheffield 1966; Hong Kong 1972; DUniv Brunel, 1977. *Publications:* The Development of Extraterritoriality in China, 1928; The Austinian Theories of Law and Sovereignty (with R. A. Eastwood, LLD), 1929; The Elementary Principles of Jurisprudence, 1930, 2nd edn 1949; Shakespeare and his Legal Problems, 1930; The Problem of the Moscow Trial, 1933; The Law of Trusts, 1st edn 1934, 10th edn 1974; An Introduction to Equity, 1st edn 1938, 8th edn 1976; National Sovereignty and International Order, 1939; Making International Law Work (with G. Schwarzenberger, PhD), 1st edn 1939, 2nd edn 1946; The Speedy Return (novel), 1938; Mutiny in the Caribbean (novel), 1940; The Case for an International University, 1941; Russia and Her Western Neighbours (with R. Schlesinger), 1942; China, the Far East, and the Future, 1st edn 1942, 2nd edn 1949; A Liberal Attorney-General, 1949; The Passing of Parliament, 1952; Social Change in the Law of Trusts, 1958; Case Book on Equity and Trusts, 1958, 2nd edn 1974; Trial for Treason, 1959; Trial by Tribunal, 1960; Guilty but Insane, 1961; (with L. A. Sheridan) The Modern Law of Charities, 1962, 3rd edn 1983; The Investment and Taxation of Trust Funds, 1964; Lord Chancellor Jeffreys, 1964; The Norman Conquest and the Common Law, 1966; Shakespeare's Legal and Political Background, 1967; (with L. A. Sheridan) Equity, 1970; Government in Action, 1970; Modern Developments in the Law of Trusts, 1971; The Football Revolution, 1972; English Law: the judicial contribution, 1974; (with S. N. Frommel) British Industry and European Law, 1974; Keeping the Peace, 1976; (with L. A. Sheridan) Trusts in the Commonwealth, 1977; Harvey the Hasty, 1978; numerous contributions to periodicals. *Address:* Picts Close, Picts Lane, Princes Risborough, Bucks. *T:* Princes Risborough 5094.

KEEWATIN, Bishop of, since 1974; **Rt. Rev. Hugh James Pearson Allan,** DD; *b* 7 Aug. 1928; *s* of Hugh Blomfield Allan and Agnes Dorothy (*née* Pearson); *m* 1955, Beverley Edith Baker; one *s* three *d*. *Educ:* St John's Coll., Univ. of Manitoba (LTh 1955, BA 1957). Deacon 1954, priest 1955; Assistant: St Aidan's, Winnipeg, 1954; All Saints, Winnipeg, 1955; Missionary, Peguis Indian Reserve, 1956–60; Rector, St Mark's, Winnipeg, 1960–68; Hon. Canon, Diocese of Rupert's Land, 1967; Rector, St Stephen's Swift Current, Sask., 1968–70; Rural Dean of Cypress, 1968–70; Dean of Qu'Appelle and Rector of St Paul's Cathedral, Regina, Sask., 1970–74. Hon. DD, St John's Coll., Univ. of Manitoba, 1974. *Recreations:* ornithology, boating. *Address:* Bishopstowe, 15 Sylvan Street, Kenora, Ont. P9N 3W7. *T:* (home) 468–5655, (office) 468–7011.

KEGGIN, Air Vice-Marshal Harold, CB 1967; CBE 1962; LDS; Director of Dental Services, Royal Air Force, 1964–69, retired; *b* 25 Feb. 1909; *y s* of John and Margaret Keggin, Port Erin, Isle of Man; *m* 1935, Margaret Joy (*née* Campbell); one *s* two *d*. *Educ:* Douglas High Sch.; University of Liverpool. Dental Officer, RAF, commissioned, 1932; Flt Lieut 1934; Sqdn Ldr 1939; Wing Comdr 1942; Gp Capt. 1954; Air Cdre 1958; Air Vice-Marshal 1964. QHDS 1958–69. *Recreations:* golf, fishing. *Address:* Rosecroft, 7 Cotlands, Sidmouth, Devon EX10 8SP. *T:* Sidmouth 4790.

KEIGHLY-PEACH, Captain Charles Lindsey, DSO 1940; OBE 1941; RN retired; *b* 6 April 1902; *s* of late Admiral C. W. Keighly-Peach, DSO; *m* 1st, V. B. Cumbers; one *s* one *d*; *m* 2nd, Beatrice Mary Harrison (*d* 1974). *Educ:* RN Colleges, Osborne and Dartmouth. Midshipman, 1919; Sub-Lieut 1922; Lieut 1924; 3 Squadron, RAF, 1926; HMS Eagle (402 Sqdn), 1927; H/M S/M M2, 1929; HMS Centaur, 1930; Lieut-Cdr 1932; HMS Glorious (802 Sqdn), 1932; RN Staff Coll., Greenwich, 1934; SOO to RA Destroyers, 1935; HMS London, 1937; Commander, 1938; RN Air Station Lee-on-Solent, 1939; HMS Eagle, 1940–41; Naval Assistant (Air) to 2nd Sea Lord, 1941–44; Capt. 1943; RN Air Station, Yeovilton, 1944–45; Comdg HMS Sultan, Singapore, 1945–47; in command HMS Troubridge and 3rd Destroyer Flot. Med., 1947–49; Dir Captain, Senior Officer's War Course, RN, 1949–51; Asst Chief Naval Staff (Air) on loan to Royal Canadian Navy, 1951–53. *Recreations:* golf, gardening. *Address:* Hatteras, Hall Road, Brockdish, Diss, Norfolk IP21 5JY. *T:* Harleston 853136.

KEIGHTLEY, Maj.-Gen. Richard Charles; Commandant, Royal Military Academy, Sandhurst, since 1983; *b* 2 July 1933; *s* of General Sir Charles Keightley, GCB, GBE, DSO, and Lady (Joan) Keightley (*née* Smyth-Osbourne); *m* 1958, Caroline Rosemary Butler, *er d* of Sir Thomas Butler, Bt, *qv*; three *d*. *Educ:* Marlborough Coll.; RMA, Sandhurst. Commissioned into 5th Royal Inniskilling Dragoon Guards, 1953; served Canal Zone, BAOR, N Africa, Singapore, Cyprus; sc Camberley, 1963; comd 5th Royal Inniskilling Dragoon Guards, 1972–75; Task Force Comdr, 3 Armd Div., 1978–79; RCDS 1980; Brigadier General Staff HQ UKLF, 1981; GOC Western Dist, 1982–83. Col, 5th Royal Inniskilling Dragoon Guards, 1986–. *Recreations:* field sports, cricket, polo. *Address:* Government House, RMA Sandhurst, Camberley, Surrey. *Club:* Cavalry and Guards.

KEIR, James Dewar; QC 1980; Director, Open University Educational Enterprises Ltd, since 1983; Chairman: City and East London Family Practitioner Committee, since 1985; Pharmacists Review Panel, since 1986; *b* 30 Nov. 1921; *s* of David Robert Keir and Elizabeth Lunan (*née* Ross); *m* 1948, Jean Mary, *e d* of Rev. and Mrs E. P. Orr; two *s* two *d*. *Educ:* Edinburgh Acad.; Christ Church, Oxford (MA 1948). Served War, 1941–46: ME, Italy; Captain, The Black Watch (RHR). Called to the Bar, Inner Temple, 1949; Yarborough-Anderson Scholar, Inner Temple, 1950. Legal Adviser, United Africa Co. Ltd, 1954–66, Sec., 1966; Dep. Head of Legal Services, Unilever Ltd, 1973; Jt Sec., Unilever plc and Unilever NV, 1976–84; Dir, UAC Internat. Ltd, 1973–77. Chm., Bar Assoc. for Commerce, Finance and Industry, 1969–72; Member: Bar Council, 1971–73; Senate of Inns of Ct and Bar, 1973–78; Pres., Bar Assoc. for Commerce, Finance and Industry, 1980–82. *Recreations:* ski-ing, Rugby, opera, reading. *Address:* Crossways, High Street, Dormansland, Surrey. *T:* Lingfield 834621. *Club:* Caledonian.

KEIR, Thelma C.; *see* Cazalet-Keir.

KEITH, family name of **Barons Keith of Castleacre** and **Keith of Kinkel** and of **Earl of Kintore.**

KEITH OF CASTLEACRE, Baron *cr* 1980 (Life Peer), of Swaffham in the County of Norfolk; **Kenneth Alexander Keith;** Kt 1969; merchant banker and industrialist; Vice-Chairman, Beecham Group Ltd, since 1970 (Director, since 1949); Chairman, Standard Telephones and Cables, since 1985 (Director, since 1977); *b* 30 Aug. 1916; *er s* of late Edward Charles Keith, Swanton Morley House, Norfolk; *m* 1st, 1946, Lady Ariel Olivia Winifred Baird (marr. diss., 1958), 2nd *d* of 1st Viscount Stonehaven, PC, GCMG, DSO, and Countess of Kintore; one *s* one *d*; 2nd, 1962, Mrs Nancy Hayward (marr. diss. 1972), Manhasset, New York; 3rd, 1973, Mrs Marie Hanbury, Burley-on-the-Hill, Rutland. *Educ:* Rugby Sch. Trained as a Chartered Accountant. 2nd Lt Welsh Guards, 1939; Lt-Col 1945; served in North Africa, Italy, France and Germany (despatches, Croix de Guerre with Silver Star). Asst to Dir Gen. Political Intelligence Dept, Foreign Office, 1945–46. Chm., Philip Hill Investment Trust Ltd; Vice-Chm., BEA, 1964–71; Chm., Hill Samuel Group Ltd, 1970–80; Chm. and Chief Exec., Rolls Royce Ltd, 1972–80; Director: British Airways, 1971–72; Times Newspapers Ltd, 1967–81; Bank of Nova Scotia Ltd. Member: NEDC, 1964–71; CBI/NEDC Liaison Cttee, 1974–78. Chairman: Economic Planning Council for East Anglia, 1965–70; Governor, Nat. Inst. of Economic and Social Research. Council Mem. and Dir, Manchester Business Sch. FBIM; Hon. Companion, RAeS. *Recreations:* farming, shooting, golf. *Address:* 9 Eaton Square, SW1 9DB. *T:* 01–730 4000; The Wicken House, Castle Acre, Norfolk. *T:* Castle Acre 225. *Clubs:* White's, Pratt's; Racquet and Tennis (New York).

KEITH OF KINKEL, Baron *cr* 1977 (Life Peer), of Strathtummel; **Henry Shanks Keith,** PC 1976; a Lord of Appeal in Ordinary, since 1977; *b* 7 Feb. 1922; *s* of late Baron Keith of Avonholm, PC (Life Peer); *m* 1955, Alison Hope Alan Brown; four *s* (including twin *s*) one *d*. *Educ:* Edinburgh Academy; Magdalen Coll., Oxford (MA; Hon. Fellow 1977); Edinburgh Univ. (LLB). War of 1939–45 (despatches); commnd Scots Guards, Nov. 1941; served N Africa and Italy, 1943–45; released, 1945 (Capt.). Advocate, Scottish Bar, 1950; Barrister, Gray's Inn, 1951, Bencher 1976; QC (Scotland), 1962. Standing Counsel to Dept of Health for Scotland, 1957–62; Sheriff Principal of Roxburgh, Berwick and Selkirk, 1970–71; Senator of Coll. of Justice in Scotland, 1971–77. Chairman: Scottish Valuation Adv. Coun., 1972–76 (Mem., 1957–70); Cttee on Powers of Revenue Depts, 1980–83; Dep. Chm., Parly Boundary Commn for Scotland, 1976; Member: Law Reform Cttee for Scotland, 1964–70; Cttee on Law of Defamation, 1971–74; Mem. Panel of Arbiters: European Fisheries Convention, 1964–71; Convention for Settlement of Investment Disputes, 1968–71. *Address:* House of Lords, SW1; Strathtummel, by Pitlochry, Perthshire. *T:* Tummel Bridge 255.

KEITH, David; *see* Steegmuller, Francis.

KEITH, John Lucien, CBE 1951 (OBE 1943); *b* 22 May 1895; 2nd *s* of George Keith, Director of Cable Companies and Felicie, *d* of Charles Pierce, stockbroker; unmarried. *Educ:* Ecole Closelet, Lausanne; Hertford Coll., Oxford (MA). British South Africa Co., N Rhodesia, 1918–25; District Officer, Colonial Service, N Rhodesia, 1925–38; Acting Dir of African Education, N Rhodesia, 1930–31; African Research Survey, Chatham House, 1938–39; Colonial Office, 1939; Head of Welfare and Students Dept, Colonial Office, 1941–56; missions to overseas territories, USA and Canada. Adviser on Students' Affairs, W Nigeria Office, London, 1957–62; London Rep. of Univ. of Ife, Nigeria, 1962–72. *Recreations:* travelling, talking books for the blind. *Address:* 49A Sea Road, Bexhill-on-Sea, East Sussex. *T:* Bexhill-on-Sea 215463.

KEITH, Penelope Anne Constance, (Mrs Rodney Timson); *b* 2 April; *d* of Frederick A. W. Hatfield and Constance Mary Keith; *m* 1978, Rodney Timson. *Educ:* Annecy Convent, Seaford, Sussex; Webber Douglas Sch., London. First prof. appearance, Civic Theatre, Chesterfield, 1959; repertory, Lincoln, Salisbury and Manchester, 1960–63; RSC, Stratford, 1963, and Aldwych, 1965; rep., Cheltenham, 1967; Maggie Howard in Suddenly at Home, Fortune Theatre, 1971; Sarah in The Norman Conquests, Greenwich, then Globe Theatre, 1974; Lady Driver in Donkey's Years, 1976; Orinthia in The Apple Cart, Chichester, then Phoenix Theatre, 1977; Epifania in The Millionairess, Haymarket, 1978; Sarah in Moving, Queen's Theatre, 1981; Maggie in Hobson's Choice, Haymarket, 1982; Lady Cicely Waynflete in Captain Brassbound's Conversion, Haymarket, 1982; Judith Bliss in Hay Fever, Queen's, 1983; The Dragon's Tail, Apollo, 1985; *film:* The Priest of Love, 1980. Television series incl.: The Good Life, 1974–77; The Norman Conquests, 1977; To the Manor Born, 1979, 1980 and 1981; Sweet Sixteen, 1983; Moving, 1985; Executive Stress, 1986. *Recreations:* gardening, theatre-going. *Address:* c/o Howes & Prior, 66 Berkeley House, Hay Hill, W1X 7LH. *T:* 01–493 7570.

KEITH, Robert Farquharson, CB 1973; OBE 1948; Chief Registrar of Trade Unions and Employers' Associations from 1971 until repeal of Industrial Relations Act 1971 in 1974; *b* 22 June 1912; *s* of Dr Robert Donald Keith and Mary Lindsay (*née* Duncan), Turriff, Aberdeenshire; *m* 1958, Jean Abernethy (*née* Fisher); one *s*. *Educ:* Fettes; Caius Coll., Cambridge (Classical Scholar). Indian Civil Service, 1937–47; Dep. Comr, Upper Sind Frontier, 1945–47; Home Civil Service, Min. of Labour, later Dept of Employment, 1948; Under-Sec., Employment Services and Estabs Divs, 1965–71. *Address:* Parkhead, Auchattie, Banchory, Kincardineshire. *T:* Banchory 2166. *Club:* Caledonian.

KEITH, Trevor; Charity Commissioner, 1972–81; *b* 3 Sept. 1921. *Educ:* Isleworth County Grammar School. Called to Bar, Lincoln's Inn, 1951. Entered Civil Service, Air Min., 1938; RAF, 1941–45; Air Min., 1946–48; Inland Revenue, Estate Duty Office, 1948–52; Charity Commn, 1952–81. *Recreations:* cricket, travel, gastronomy. *Address:* 7 Lucastes Road, Haywards Heath, Sussex RH16 1JJ.

KEITH-JONES, Maj.-Gen. Richard, CB 1968; MBE 1947; MC 1944; Manager, Management Development, Mardon Packaging International Ltd, 1969–75; *b* 6 Dec. 1913; *o s* of late Brig. Frederick Theodore Jones, CIE, MVO, VD; *m* 1938, Margaret Ridley Harrison; three *d*. *Educ:* Clifton Coll.; Royal Military Academy Woolwich. Commissioned into Royal Artillery, 1934; served in UK, 1934–42; 1st Airborne Div., 1943–44; War Office, 1944–47; Palestine and Egypt, 1st Regt RHA, 1947–49; Instructor Staff Coll., Camberley, 1949–52; Military Asst to F-M Montgomery, 1953–55; CO 4th Regt, RHA, 1955–57; Senior Army Instructor, JSSC, 1957–59; Dep. Comdr 17 Gurkha Div., Malaya, 1959–61; Student, Imperial Defence Coll., 1962–63; Military Adviser, High Comr, Canada, 1963–64; GOC 50 (Northumbrian) Div. (TA), 1964–66; Comdt, Jt Warfare Establishment, 1966–68; retd 1969. Col Comdt RA, 1970–78; Hon. Col, 266 (Glos Vol. Artillery) Batt., RA, T&AVR, 1975–83. *Recreations:* fishing, shooting, golf. *Address:* The White House, Brockley, Backwell, Bristol BS19 3AU. *Clubs:* MCC; Bath and County (Bath).

KEITH-LUCAS, Prof. Bryan, CBE 1983; Professor of Government, University of Kent at Canterbury, 1965–77, now Emeritus (Master of Darwin College, 1970–74); *b* 1 Aug. 1912; *y s* of late Keith Lucas, ScD, FRS, and Alys (*née* Hubbard); *m* 1946, Mary Hardwicke (MBE 1982; Sheriff of Canterbury, 1971); one *s* two *d*. *Educ:* Gresham's Sch., Holt;

Pembroke Coll., Cambridge. MA Cantab 1937, MA Oxon 1948; DLitt Kent, 1980. Solicitor, 1937. Asst Solicitor: Kensington Council, 1938–46; Nottingham, 1946–48. Served 1939–45 in Buffs and Sherwood Foresters, N Africa and Italy (Major, despatches); DAAG Cyprus, 1945–46. Sen. Lectr in Local Govt, Oxford, 1948–65; Faculty Fellow of Nuffield Coll., 1950–65, Domestic Bursar, 1957–65. Leverhulme Emeritus Fellow, 1983. Part-time Asst Master, King's Sch., Canterbury, 1978–83. Chm., Commn on Electoral System, Sierra Leone, 1954; Commn on local govt elections, Mauritius, 1955–56. Member: Roberts Cttee on Public Libraries, 1957–59; Commn on Administration of Lagos, 1963; Mallaby Cttee on Staffing of Local Govt, 1964–67; Local Govt Commn for England, 1965–66; Royal Commn on Elections in Fiji, 1975. Vice-Chm., Hansard Soc., 1976–80. Chairman: Nat. Assoc. of Parish Councils, 1964–70 (Vice-Pres., 1970–; Pres., Kent Assoc., 1972–81); Canterbury Soc., 1972–75, President: Kent Fedn of Amenity Socs, 1976–81; Wye Historical Soc., 1986. City Councillor, Oxford, 1950–65. Hon. Fellow, Inst. of Local Govt Studies, Birmingham Univ., 1973. *Publications:* The English Local Government Franchise, 1952; The Mayor, Aldermen and Councillors, 1961; English Local Government in the 19th and 20th Centuries, 1977; (with P. G. Richards) A History of Local Government in the 20th Century, 1978; The Unreformed Local Government System, 1980; various articles on local govt. *Address:* 7 Church Street, Wye, Kent. *T:* Wye 812621. *Club:* National Liberal.
See also David Keith-Lucas.

KEITH-LUCAS, Prof. David, CBE 1973; MA; FEng, FIMechE, Hon. FRAeS; Chairman, Airworthiness Requirements Board, 1972–82; *b* 25 March 1911; *s* of late Keith Lucas, ScD, FRS, and Alys (*née* Hubbard); *m* 1st, 1942, Dorothy De Bauduy Robertson (*d* 1979); two *s* one *d*; 2nd, 1981, Phyllis Marion Everard (*née* Whurr). *Educ:* Gresham's Sch., Holt; Gonville and Caius Coll., Cambridge. BA (Mech Sci Tripos, 2nd Class Hons) 1933; MA 1956; FRAeS 1948, Hon. FRAeS 1979; FIMechE 1949; FAIAA 1973, Hon. FAIAA 1974; FEng 1978. Apprenticed 1933–35, design team 1935–39, C. A. Parsons & Co. Ltd; Chief Aerodynamicist, Short Bros Ltd, 1940–49; Short Bros & Harland Ltd: Chief Designer, 1949–58; Technical Dir, 1958–64; Dir of Research, 1964–65; Dir, John Brown & Co., 1970–77; Cranfield Inst. of Technology: Prof. of Aircraft Design, 1965–72; Pro-Vice-Chancellor, 1970–73; Prof. of Aeronautics and Chm. College of Aeronautics, 1972–76, now Emeritus Prof. Member: Senate, Queen's Univ., Belfast, 1955–65; Council, Air Registration Board, 1967–82; Commn on Third London Airport, 1968–70; Civil Aviation Authority, 1972–80. President: RAeS, 1968; Engrg Section, British Assoc. for the Advancement of Science, 1972. Hon. DSc: Queen's Univ., Belfast, 1968; Cranfield Inst. of Technology, 1975. Gold Medal, RAeS, 1975. *Publications:* The Shape of Wings to Come, 1952; The Challenge of Vertical Take-Off (lects IMechE), 1961–62; The Role of Jet Lift (lect. RAeS), 1962; Design Council report on design educn; papers on aircraft design, vertical take-off, engrg economics, in engrg jls. *Recreation:* small boats. *Address:* Manor Close, Emberton, Olney, Bucks MK46 5BX. *T:* Bedford 711552.
See also B. Keith-Lucas.

KEKWICK, Prof. Ralph Ambrose, FRS 1966; Professor of Biophysics, University of London, 1966–71, now Emeritus; Member Staff, Lister Institute, 1940–71 (Head, Division of Biophysics, 1943–71); *b* 11 Nov. 1908; 2nd *s* of late Oliver A. and Mary Kekwick; *m* 1st, 1933, Barbara (*d* 1973), 3rd *d* of W. S. Stone, DD, New York; one *d*; 2nd, 1974, Dr Margaret Mackay (*d* 1982), *er d* of J. G. Mackay, MB, BS, Adelaide, Australia. *Educ:* Leyton County High Sch.; University Coll., London (Fellow, 1971). BSc 1928; MSc 1936; DSc 1941. Bayliss-Starling Scholar, University Coll. London, 1930–31. Commonwealth Fund Fellow, New York and Princeton Univs, 1931–33. Lectr in Biochemistry University Coll. London, 1933–37. Rockefeller Fellow, University of Uppsala, Sweden, 1935; MRC Fellow, Lister Inst., 1937–40. Reader in Chemical Biophysics, University of London, 1954–66. Oliver Memorial Award for Blood Transfusion, 1957. *Publications:* MRC Special Report "Separation of protein fractions from human plasma" (with M. E. Mackay), 1954. Papers on physical biochemistry and hæmatology, mostly in Biochemical Jl and Brit. Jl of Hæmatology. *Recreations:* music, gardening and bird watching. *Address:* 31 Woodside Road, Woodford Wells, Essex IG8 0TW. *T:* 01-504 4264.

KELBIE, Sheriff David; Sheriff of Grampian, Highland and Islands, at Aberdeen, since 1986; *b* 28 Feb. 1945; *s* of Robert Kelbie and Monica Eileen Pearn; *m* 1966, Helen Mary Smith; one *s* one *d*. *Educ:* Inverurie Acad.; Aberdeen Univ. (LLB Hons). Advocate; called to the Scottish Bar, 1968; Sheriff of N Strathclyde, 1979–86. Associate Lectr, Heriot-Watt Univ., 1971–75; Hon. Sec., Scottish Congregational Coll., 1975–82. *Publications:* articles in legal jls. *Recreations:* sailing, hill-walking, reading. *Address:* Sheriff's Chambers, Aberdeen.

KELBURN, Viscount of; David Michael Douglas Boyle; *b* 15 Oct. 1978; *s* and *heir* of 10th Earl of Glasgow, *qv*.

KELL, Joseph; *see* Burgess, Anthony.

KELLAS, Arthur Roy Handasyde, CMG 1964; HM Diplomatic Service, retired; High Commissioner in Tanzania, 1972–74; *b* 6 May 1915; *s* of Henry Kellas and Mary Kellas (*née* Brown); *m* 1952, Katharine Bridget, *d* of Sir John Le Rougetel, KCMG, MC; two *s* one *d*. *Educ:* Aberdeen Grammar Sch.; Aberdeen Univ.; Oxford Univ.; Ecole des Sciences Politiques. Passed into Diplomatic Service, Sept. 1939. Commissioned into Border Regt, Nov. 1939. War of 1939–45: Active Service with 1st Bn Parachute Regt and Special Ops, Af. and Gr, 1941–44 (despatches twice). Third Sec. at HM Embassy, Tehran, 1944–47; First Sec. at HM Legation, Helsingfors, 1948–50; First Sec. (press) at HM Embassy, Cairo, 1951–52; First Sec. at HM Embassy, Baghdad, 1954–58; Counsellor, HM Embassy, Tehran, 1958–62; Imperial Defence Coll., 1963–64; Counsellor, HM Embassy and Consul-Gen., Tel Aviv, 1964–65; Ambassador to Nepal, 1966–70, to Democratic Yemen, 1970–72. Pres., Britain-Nepal Soc., 1975–79. *Recreations:* reading, reviewing books. *Address:* Inverockle, Achateny, Ardnamurchan, Argyll PH36 4LG. *T:* Kilchoan 265. *Club:* United Oxford & Cambridge University.

KELLAWAY, (Charles) William; Secretary and Librarian, Institute of Historical Research, University of London, 1971–84; *b* 9 March 1926; *s* of late Charles Halliley Kellaway, FRS; *m* 1952, Deborah, *d* of late Sir Hibbert Alan Stephen Newton; one *s* two *d*. *Educ:* Geelong Grammar Sch.; Lincoln Coll., Oxford. BA Modern History, 1949, MA 1955. FLA, FRHistS, FSA. Asst Librarian, Guildhall Library, 1950–60; Sub-Librarian, Inst. of Historical Research, 1960–71. Hon. General Editor, London Record Society, 1964–83. *Publications:* The New England Company, 1649–1776, 1961; (ed jtly) Studies in London History, 1969; Bibliography of Historical Works Issued in UK, 1957–70, 3 vols, 1962, 1967, 1972; (ed jtly) The London Assize of Nuisance 1301–1431, 1973. *Address:* 18 Canonbury Square, N1. *T:* 01-354 0349.

KELLEHER, Dame Joan, (Joanna), DBE 1965; Hon. ADC to the Queen, 1964–67; Director, Women's Royal Army Corps, 1964–67; *b* 24 Dec. 1915; *d* of late Kenneth George Henderson, Stonehaven; *m* 1970, Brig. M. F. H. Kelleher, OBE, MC, late RAMC. *Educ:* privately at home and abroad. Joined ATS, 1941; commissioned ATS, 1941; WRAC, 1949. *Recreations:* golf and gardening. *Address:* c/o Midland Bank, 123 Chancery Lane, WC2.

KELLER, Prof. Andrew, FRS 1972; Research Professor in Polymer Science, Department of Physics, University of Bristol, since 1969; *b* 22 Aug. 1925; *s* of Imre Keller and Margit Klein; *m* 1951, Eva Bulhack; one *s* one *d*. *Educ:* Budapest Univ. (BSc); Bristol Univ. (PhD). FInstP. Techn. Officer, ICI Ltd, Manchester, 1948–55; Bristol Univ.: Min. of Supply res. appt, 1955–57; Res. Asst, 1957–63; Lectr, 1963–65; Reader, 1965–69. High Polymer Prize, Amer. Phys. Soc., 1964; Swinburne Award, Plastics Inst., 1974; Max Born Medal, Inst. Physics and Deutsche Physik Gesellschaft, 1983. *Publications:* numerous papers in Jl Polymer Science, Progress Reports in Physics, Proc. Royal Soc., Macromol. Chem., etc. *Recreations:* outdoor sports, mountain walking, concerts. *Address:* 41 Westbury Road, Bristol BS9 3AU. *T:* Bristol 629767.

KELLER, René Jacques; Ambassador of Switzerland to Austria, 1976–79, retired; *b* 19 May 1914; *s* of Jacques Keller and Marie (*née* Geiser); *m* 1942, Marion (*née* Werder); one *s* two *d*. *Educ:* Geneva; Trinity Coll., Cambridge. Vice-Consul, Prague, 1941–45; 2nd Sec. of Legation, The Hague, 1947–50; 1st Sec., London, 1950–54; Head of News Dept, Berne, 1954–56; 1st Counsellor, Swiss Embassy, Paris, 1957–60; Ambassador to Ghana, Guinea, Liberia, Mali and Togo, 1960–62; Ambassador to Turkey, 1962–65; Head of Perm. Mission of Switzerland to Office of UN and Internat. Organisations, Geneva, 1966–68; Ambassador of Switzerland to UK, 1968–71; Head of Direction for International Organisation, Foreign Ministry of Switzerland, 1971–75. *Recreations:* golf, sailing. *Address:* 1 Promenade du Pin, CH-1204 Geneva, Switzerland. *Club:* Cercle de la Terrase (Geneva).

KELLER, Prof. Rudolf Ernst, MA Manchester; DrPhil Zürich; Professor of German Language and Medieval German Literature, University of Manchester, 1960–82, now Emeritus; *b* 3 Feb. 1920; *m* 1947, Ivy Sparrow; two *d*. *Educ:* Kantonsschule Winterthur, Switzerland; University of Zürich. Teacher at Kantonsschule Winterthur, 1944–46; Asst, 1946–47, Asst Lecturer, 1947–49, University of Manchester; Lecturer in German, Royal Holloway College, University of London, 1949–52; Sen. Lecturer, 1952–59, Reader in German, 1959–60, Dean of Faculty of Arts, 1968–70, Pro-Vice-Chancellor, 1976–79, University of Manchester. Corresp. Mem., Inst. für deutsche Sprache, 1969; Goethe Medal, 1981. *Publications:* Die Ellipse in der neuenglischen Sprache als semantisch-syntaktisches Problem, 1944; Die Sprachen der Welt, 1955 (trans. Bodmer: The Loom of Language); German Dialects, Phonology and Morphology with Selected Texts, 1961; The German Language, 1978; articles in learned periodicals. *Recreations:* reading, travel. *Address:* 8 Wadham Way, Hale, Altrincham, Cheshire WA15 9LJ. *T:* 061-980 5237.

KELLETT, Alfred Henry, CBE 1965; Chairman, South Western Areas, National Coal Board, 1967–69, retired; *b* 2 Aug. 1904; British; *m* 1934, Astrid Elizabeth (*née* Hunter); one *s* three *d*. *Educ:* Rossall Sch.; Universities of Cambridge and Birmingham. Man. Dir, Washington Coal Co. Ltd, 1940–47; Area Gen. Man., NCB Durham Div., 1950–59; Dep. Chm., Durham Div., 1960; Chm., South Western Div., NCB, 1961–67. CStJ. *Recreation:* travel. *Address:* Pent House, Benenden, Cranbrook, Kent.

KELLETT, Sir Brian (Smith), Kt 1979; Chairman, Port of London Authority, since 1985; Director: Unigate PLC, since 1974; National Westminster Bank PLC, since 1981; Lombard North Central PLC, since 1985; *b* 8 May 1922; *m* 1947, Janet Lesly Street; three *d*. *Educ:* Manchester Grammar Sch.; Trinity Coll., Cambridge (MA). Wrangler and Sen. Scholar, 1942. Exper. Officer, Admty, 1942–46; Asst Principal, Min. of Transport, 1946–48; Sir Robert Watson-Watt & Partners, 1948–49; Pilkington Bros Ltd, 1949–55; joined Tube Investments Ltd, later TI Group plc, 1955, Dir 1965, a Man. Dir, 1968–82, Dep. Chm. and Chief Exec., 1974, Chm., 1976–84; Chm., British Aluminium Co. Ltd, 1972–79. Member: Royal Commn on Standards of Conduct in Public Life, 1974–76; PO Review Cttee, 1976–77; Council, Industrial Soc., 1981–84. A Vice-Pres., Engineering Employers' Fedn, 1976–84. Governor: London Business Sch., 1976–84; Imperial Coll., 1979–. *Address:* The Old Malt House, Deddington, Oxford OX5 4TG. *T:* Deddington 38257. *Club:* United Oxford & Cambridge University.

KELLETT, Sir Stanley Charles, 7th Bt *cr* 1801; *b* 5 March 1940; *s* of Sir Stanley Everard Kellett, 6th Bt, and of Audrey Margaret Phillips; *S* father, 1983; *m* 1st, 1962, Lorraine May (marr. diss. 1968), *d* of F. Winspear; 2nd, 1968, Margaret Ann (marr. diss. 1974), *d* of James W. Bofinger; 3rd, 1982, Catherine Lorna, *d* of W. J. C. Orr; one *d*. *Heir: uncle* Charles Rex Kellett [*b* 1916; *m* 1940, Florence Helen Bellamy; two *s* one *d*]. *Address:* 58 Glad Gunson Drive, Eleebana, Newcastle, NSW 2280, Australia.

KELLETT-BOWMAN, Edward Thomas, JP; business and management consultant in private practice, since 1974; *b* 25 Feb. 1931; *s* of late R. E. Bowman and of M. Bowman (*née* Mathers); *m* 1st, 1960, Margaret Patricia Blakemore (*d* 1970); three *s* one *d*; 2nd, 1971, (Mary) Elaine Kellett (*see* M. E. Kellett-Bowman). *Educ:* Reed's Sch.; Cranfield Inst. of Technol. MBA, DMS, FBIM. Technical and management trng in textiles, 1951–53; textile management, 1953–55; pharmaceutical man., 1955–72. Mem. (C) Lancs East, European Parlt, 1979–84; contested same seat, 1984. Liveryman, Worshipful Co. of Wheelwrights, 1979; Freeman, City of London, 1978; Hon. Citizen, New Orleans, 1960. JP Mddx, 1966. *Recreations:* shooting, tennis, swimming. *Address:* Park Farm, Gressenhall, Norfolk. *T:* Dereham 860245; 42 Schoolhouse Lane, Halton, Lancaster; 33D Curzon Street, W1.

KELLETT-BOWMAN, (Mary) Elaine, MA; MP (C) Lancaster, since 1970; *b* 8 July 1924; *d* of late Walter Kay; *m* 1st, 1945, Charles Norman Kellett (decd); three *s* one *d*; 2nd, 1971, Edward Thomas Kellett-Bowman, *qv*. *Educ:* Queen Mary Sch., Lytham; The Mount, York; St Anne's Coll., Oxford (post-graduate distinction in welfare diploma). Contested (C): Nelson and Colne, 1955; South-West Norfolk, March and Oct. 1959; Buckingham, 1964, 1966. Mem. (C) European Parlt, 1975–84 (Mem. for Cumbria, 1979–84); Mem. Social Affairs and Regional Policy Cttees, Europ. Parlt, 1975–84. Camden Borough Council: Alderman, 1968–74; Vice-Chm., Housing Cttee, 1968; Chm., Welfare Cttee, 1969. Called to Bar, Middle Temple, 1964. Lay Mem., Press Council, 1964–68. Governor, Culford Sch., 1963; Mem. Union European Women, 1956; Delegate to Luxemburg, 1958. No 1 Country Housewife, 1960; Christal MacMillan Law Prize, 1963. *Recreations:* gardening, collecting and repairing antiques. *Address:* House of Commons, SW1; 42 Schoolhouse Lane, Halton, Lancaster. *Club:* English-Speaking Union.

KELLEY, Joan; Under Secretary, 1979–86, Principal Establishment Officer and Principal Finance Officer, 1984–86, HM Treasury; *b* 8 Dec. 1926; *er d* of late George William Kelley and Dora Kelley. *Educ:* Whalley Range High Sch. for Girls, Manchester; London Sch. of Econs and Polit. Science (BScEcon 1947). Europa Publications Ltd, 1948; Pritchard, Wood & Partners Ltd, 1949; joined Civil Service as Econ. Asst in Cabinet Office, 1949; admin. work in Treasury, 1954; Principal, 1956; Asst Sec., 1968; Under Sec., 1979; on secondment to NI Office, 1979–81. *Recreations:* gardening, map reading, drinking wine, foreign travel. *Address:* 21 Langland Gardens, NW3 6QE.

KELLEY, Mrs Joanna Elizabeth, OBE 1973; Assistant Director of Prisons (Women), 1967–74; *b* 23 May 1910; *d* of late Lt-Col William Beadon, 51st Sikhs; *m* 1934, Harper Kelley (*d* 1962); no *c*. *Educ:* Hayes Court; Girton Coll., Cambridge (MA). Souschargé,

Dept of Pre-History, Musée de l'Homme, Paris, 1934–39; Mixed Youth Club Leader, YWCA, 1939–42; Welfare Officer, Admiralty, Bath, 1942–47; Prison Service, 1947–74; Governor of HM Prison, Holloway, 1959–66. Member: Council, St George's House, Windsor, 1971–77; Redundant Churches Cttee, 1974–79; Scott Holland Trust, 1978–86; Sponsor, YWCA of GB, 1979–. FSA. Hon. Fellow Girton Coll., Cambridge, 1968. Hon. LLD Hull Univ., 1960. *Publications:* When the Gates Shut, 1967; Who Casts the First Stone, 1978. *Recreation:* reading. *Address:* c/o Lloyds Bank, 6 Pall Mall, SW1V 4AQ.

KELLEY, Richard; *b* 24 July 1904; *m* 1924; four *s* three *d*. *Educ:* Elementary Sch. Councillor, West Riding of Yorks County Council, 1949–59; a Trade Union Secretary for ten years. MP (Lab) Don Valley, W Yorks, 1959–79. Mem. of the National Union of Mineworkers. *Address:* 23 St Lawrence Road, Dunscroft, Doncaster, S Yorks DN7 4AS.

KELLGREN, Prof. Jonas Henrik, FRCS, FRCP; Professor of Rheumatology, University of Manchester, 1953–76, now Emeritus; Dean, 1970–73; *b* 11 Sept. 1911; *s* of Dr Harry Kellgren and Vera (*née* Dumelunksen); *m* 1942, Thelma Marian Reynolds; four *d*. *Educ:* Bedales Sch.; University Coll., London. MB, BS, 1934; FRCS 1936; FRCP 1951. Junior clinical appointments, University Coll. Hosp., 1934–42 (Beit Memorial Fellow 1938–39); served War, 1942–46, as surgical and orthopædic specialist, RAMC; Mem. Scientific Staff, Med. Research Council, Wingfield Morris Orthopædic Hosp., Oxford, Chronic Rheumatism, University of Manchester, 1947. Pres. Heberden Soc., 1958–59. *Publications:* numerous articles in medical and scientific jls. *Recreation:* landscape painting. *Address:* Beckside Cottage, Rusland, Ulverston, Cumbria LA12 8JY. *T:* Ulverton 84244.

KELLIHER, Sir Henry (Joseph), Kt 1963; Founder, 1929, President, 1982, Dominion Breweries Ltd (Chairman to 1980, Managing Director to 1982); *b* March 1896; *s* of Michael Joseph Kelliher; *m* 1917, Evelyn J., *d* of R. S. Sproule; one *s* four *d*. *Educ:* Clyde Sch. Dir, Bank of New Zealand, 1936–42. Founded League of Health of NZ Youth, 1934 (objective, Free milk scheme for NZ children, in which it succeeded); purchased Puketutu Island, 1938; established Puketutu Ayrshire Stud, 1940, Aberdeen Angus Stud, 1942, Suffolk Stud, 1946; Thoroughbred and Standard Bred Studs, 1969. Founded: Kelliher Art Trust, 1961; Kelliher Charitable Trust, 1963. KStJ 1960. *Publications:* New Zealand at the Cross Roads, 1936; Why your £ buys Less and Less, 1954. *Recreations:* gardening, riding. *Address:* Puketutu Island, Manukau Harbour, Auckland, New Zealand. *T:* 543733.

KELLOCK, Jane Ursula, JP; Member, Police Complaints Board, 1977–85; *b* 21 Oct. 1925; *d* of late Arthur George Symonds and late Gertrude Frances Symonds; *m* 1967, Thomas Oslaf Kellock, *qv*. *Educ:* Priors Field Sch., Godalming. WRNS, 1943–45. Sec., Africa Bureau, London, 1957–67; Editor, Africa Digest, 1957–75; Board Member, Commonwealth Development Corporation, 1965–73. Former Mem., S Metropolitan Conciliation Cttee, Race Relations Bd. JP: Inner London, 1968–77; Nottingham City Bench, 1977. Editor, Commonwealth Judicial Jl, 1985–. *Recreation:* travel. *Address:* 8 Huntingdon Drive, The Park, Nottingham NG7 1BW; 8 King's Bench Walk, EC4Y 7DU.

KELLOCK, Thomas Oslaf; QC 1965; **His Honour Judge Kellock;** a Circuit Judge, since 1976; Deputy Senior Judge (non-resident), Sovereign Base Areas, Cyprus, since 1983; *b* 4 July 1923; *s* of late Thomas Herbert Kellock, MA, MD, MCh Cambridge, FRCS LRCP; *m* 1967, Jane Ursula Kellock, *qv*. *Educ:* Rugby; Clare Coll., Cambridge. Sub-Lieut (Special Branch), RNVR, 1944–46. Called to the Bar, Inner Temple, 1949, Bencher, 1973. Admitted: Gold Coast (Ghana) Roll of Legal Practitioners, 1955; N Rhodesia (Zambia) Bar, 1956; Nigeria Bar, 1957; Ceylon (Sri Lanka) Roll of Advocates, 1960; Sierra Leone Bar, 1960; Malayan Bar, 1967; Fiji Bar, 1975. Has also appeared in courts of Kenya, Malaŵi, Pakistan, Jammu and Kashmir, Sarawak. Dir, Legal Div., Commonwealth Secretariat, 1969–72; a Recorder of the Crown Court, 1974–76. Constitutional Advr to HH Sultan of Brunei, 1975–76. Chm., Anti-Apartheid Movement, 1963–65; Contested (L) Torquay, 1949, S Kensington, 1966 and March 1968, Harwich, Oct. 1974. *Recreation:* travelling. *Address:* 8 Huntingdon Drive, The Park, Nottingham NG7 1BW. *T:* Nottingham 418304; 8 King's Bench Walk, Temple, EC4. *T:* 01–353 6997. *Club:* Reform.

KELLOW, Kathleen; *see* Hibbert, Eleanor.

KELLY, Anthony, FRS 1973; FEng; Vice-Chancellor, University of Surrey, since 1975; *s* of late Group Captain Vincent Gerald French and Mrs Violet Kelly; *m* 1956, Christina Margaret Dunleavie, BA; three *s* one *d*. *Educ:* Presentation Coll., Reading; Univ. of Reading (Schol.); Trinity Coll., Cambridge. BSc Reading 1949; PhD 1953, ScD 1968, Cantab. Research Assoc., Univ. of Illinois, 1953–55; ICI Fellow, Univ. of Birmingham, 1955; Asst, Associate Prof., Northwestern Univ., 1956–59; Univ. Lectr, Cambridge, 1959–67; Founding Fellow, 1960, Extraordinary Fellow, 1985, Churchill Coll.; Dir of Studies, Churchill Coll., 1960–67; Supt, Div. of Inorganic and Metallic Structure, 1967–69, Dep. Dir, 1969–75, Nat. Physical Lab. (seconded to ICI, 1973–75). Director: Teddington Developments Ltd, 1981–; Johnson Wax Ltd, 1981–; QUO-TEC Ltd, 1984–; Chm., Surrey Satellite Technology, 1985–. Vis. Fellow, Univ. of Göttingen, 1960; Vis. Prof., Carnegie Inst. of Technol., 1967; Prof. invité, Ecole Polytechnique Fédérale de Lausanne, 1977. Member: SRC Cttee, 1967–72; Council, Inst. of Metals, 1969–74; Council, British Non-Ferrous Metals Res. Assoc., 1970–73; Engrg Materials Requirements Bd, DoI, 1973–75 (Chm., 1976–80); Adv. Cttee, Community Ref. Bureau of EEC, 1973–75. Foreign Associate, Nat. Acad. of Engrg of USA, 1986. William Hopkins Prize, 1967; Beilby Medal, 1967; A. A. Griffith Medal, 1974; Medal of Excellence, Univ. of Delaware, 1984. *Publications:* Strong Solids, 1966, 3rd edn (with N. H. Macmillan) 1986; (with G. W. Groves) Crystallography and Crystal Defects, 1970; many papers in jls of physical sciences. *Recreations:* science of materials, sailing. *Address:* Yardfield, Church Lane, Worplesdon, Surrey.

KELLY, Rt. Hon. Sir Basil; *see* Kelly, Rt Hon. Sir J. W. B.

KELLY, Brian; *see* Kelly, H. B.

KELLY, Charles Henry, CBE 1986; QPM 1978; DL; Chief Constable of Staffordshire, since 1977; *b* 15 July 1930; *s* of Charles Henry Kelly and Phoebe Jane Kelly; *m* 1952, Doris (*née* Kewley); one *s* one *d*. *Educ:* Douglas High Sch. for Boys, IOM; London Univ. LLB (Hons). Asst Chief Constable of Essex, 1972; Dep. Chief Constable of Staffordshire, 1976. Pres., Staffordshire Small Bore Rifle Assoc.; Chm., Staffordshire Police St John Special Centre. DL Stafford, 1979. CStJ 1983. *Recreations:* cricket, reading, walking. *Address:* Chief Constable's Office, Cannock Road, Stafford ST17 0QG. *T:* Stafford 57717; 55530. *Club:* Special Forces.

KELLY, Edward Ronald; journalist and trout farmer; *b* 14 Oct. 1928; *s* of late William Walter Kelly and of Millicent Kelly; *m* 1954, Storm Massada. *Educ:* Honiton Sch. Journalist: Bath Evening Chronicle, 1952; East African Standard, 1953; Sunday Post, Kenya, 1954; Reuters, 1956; Central Office of Information, 1958–: Editor in Chief, Overseas Press Services Div., 1964; Asst Overseas Controller, 1968; Dir, Publications and Design Services Div., 1970; Home Controller, 1976; Overseas Controller, 1978–84. *Recreations:* fishing, fly-tying, carpentry. *Address:* Duncton Mill, near Petworth, West Sussex GU28 0LF. *T:* Petworth 42294. *Club:* Flyfishers'.

KELLY, Graham; *see* Kelly, R. H. G.

KELLY, Air Vice-Marshal (Herbert) Brian, CB 1983; LVO 1960; MD, FRCP; RAF, retired; Consultant to Civil Aviation Authority, since 1974; Consultant Medical Adviser to PPP Medical Centres, since 1983; *b* 12 Aug. 1921; *s* of late Surg. Captain James Cecil Kelly and of Meta Matheson (*née* Fraser). *Educ:* Epsom Coll.; St Thomas' Hosp. (MB, BS 1943, MD 1948). MRCP 1945, FRCP 1968; DCH 1966; MFOM 1982. House appts, St Thomas' Hosp., and St Luke's Hosp., Guildford, 1943–45; RNVR, Med. Specialist, RNH Hong Kong, 1945–48; Med. Registrar and Lectr in Medicine, St Thomas' Hosp., 1948–53; joined RAF Medical Br., 1953; Consultant in Medicine at RAF Hosps, Aden, Ely, Nocton Hall, Singapore, Cyprus, Germany, 1953–83; Consultant Adviser in Medicine to RAF, 1974, Senior Consultant, 1979–83. QHS 1978–83. FRSocMed; Fellow, Med. Soc. London; Mem., British Cardiac Soc. Liveryman, Worshipful Soc. of Apothecaries, 1978; Freeman, City of London, 1978. *Publications:* papers in BMJ, Lancet, Brit. Heart Jl, and Internat. Jl of Epidemiology. *Recreation:* choir singing. *Address:* 32 Chiswick Quay, Hartington Road, W4. *T:* 01–995 5042. *Club:* Royal Air Force.

KELLY, Rev. Canon John Norman Davidson, DD; FBA 1965; Principal of St Edmund Hall, Oxford, 1951–79, Honorary Fellow 1979; Vice-Chancellor, Oxford University, Sept.–Oct. 1966 (Pro-Vice-Chancellor, 1964–66, 1972–79); *b* 13 April 1909; *s* of John and Ann Davidson Kelly. *Educ:* privately; Glasgow Univ.; The Queen's Coll., Oxford (Ferguson Scholar; Hertford Scholar; 1st Cl. Hon. Mods, Greats and Theology; Hon. Fellow, 1963); St Stephen's House. Deacon, 1934; priest, 1935; Curate, St Lawrence's, Northampton, 1934; Chaplain, St Edmund Hall, Oxford, 1935; Vice-Principal and Trustee, 1937. Select Preacher (Oxford), 1944–46, 1959, 1961, 1962; Speaker's Lectr in Biblical Studies, 1945–48; University Lecturer in Patristic Studies, 1948–76; Select Preacher (Cambridge), 1953; Chm. Cttee of Second Internat. Conf. on Patristic Studies, Oxford, 1955; Proctor in Convocation of Canterbury representing Oxford University, 1958–64; Chm. Archbishop's Commn on Roman Catholic Relations, 1964–68; accompanied Archbishop of Canterbury on his visit to Pope Paul VI, 1966; Mem., Academic Council, Ecumenical Theological Inst., Jerusalem, 1966–. In the War of 1939–45 did part-time work at Chatham House and collaborated in organizing the Oxford Leave Courses for United States, Allied, and Dominions Forces. Canon of Chichester and Prebendary of Wightring, 1948, Highleigh, 1964. Took lead in obtaining Royal Charter, new statutes and full collegiate status for St Edmund Hall, 1957. Mem. Governing Body: Royal Holloway Coll., London, 1959–69; King's Sch., Canterbury. Lectures: Paddock, General Theological Seminary, NY, 1963; Birkbeck, Cambridge, 1973; Hensley Henson, Oxford, 1979–80. Hon. DD: Glasgow, 1958; Wales, 1971. Dean of Degrees, St Edmund Hall, 1982–. *Publications:* Early Christian Creeds, 1950, 3rd edn 1972; Rufinus, a Commentary on the Apostles' Creed, 1955; Early Christian Doctrines, 1958, 5th edn 1977; The Pastoral Epistles, 1963; The Athanasian Creed, 1964; The Epistles of Peter and of Jude, 1969; Aspects of the Passion, 1970; Jerome, 1975; The Oxford Dictionary of Popes, 1986. *Recreations:* motoring, gardening, travel. *Address:* 7 Crick Road, Oxford OX2 6QJ. *T:* Oxford 512907. *Clubs:* Athenæum; Vincent's (Oxford).

KELLY, Rt. Hon. Sir (John William) Basil, Kt 1984; PC 1984; PC (NI) 1969; **Rt. Hon. Lord Justice Kelly;** Lord Justice of Appeal, Supreme Court of Judicature, Northern Ireland, since 1984; a Judge of the High Court of Justice in Northern Ireland, 1973–84; *b* 10 May 1920; *o s* of late Thomas William Kelly and late Emily Frances (*née* Donaldson); *m* 1957, Pamela, *o d* of late Thomas Colmer and Marjorie Colthurst. *Educ:* Methodist Coll., Belfast; Trinity Coll., Dublin. BA (Mod.) Legal Science, 1943; LLB (Hons) 1944. Called to Bar: of Northern Ireland, 1944; Middle Temple, 1970; QC (N Ireland) 1958. Senior Crown Counsel: Co. Fermanagh, 1965–66; Co. Tyrone, 1966–67; Co. Armagh, 1967–68; MP (U) Mid-Down, Parliament of Northern Ireland, 1964–72; Attorney-Gen. for Northern Ireland, 1968–72. Mem., Law Adv. Cttee, British Council, 1982–. *Recreations:* golf, music. *Address:* Royal Courts of Justice, Belfast.

KELLY, Laurence Charles Kevin; Chairman, Helical Bar Ltd, since 1984 (Director, since 1972, Deputy Chairman, 1981–84); Chairman, Queenborough Steel Co., since 1980; Member, Monopolies and Mergers Commission, since 1982; *b* 11 April 1933; *s* of late Sir David Kelly, GCMG, MC, and Lady Kelly (*née* Jourda de Vaux); *m* 1963, Alison Linda McNair Scott; one *s* two *d*. *Educ:* Downside Sch.; New Coll., Oxford (Beresford Hope Schol.; MA Hons); Harvard Business Sch. Lieut, The Life Guards, 1949–52; served (temp.) Foreign Office, 1955–56; Guest, Keen and Nettlefolds, 1956–72; Director: GKN International Trading Ltd, 1972; Morganite International Ltd, 1984–; KAE Ltd. Member, Northern Ireland Development Agency, 1972–78; Chairman, Opera da Camera Ltd (charity), 1981–. Vice-Chm., British Iron and Steel Consumers' Council, 1976–85. Sen. Associate Mem., St Antony's Coll., Oxford, 1985. FRGS 1972. *Publications:* Lermontov, Tragedy in the Caucasus (biog.), 1978 (Cheltenham Literary Prize, 1979); St Petersburg, a Travellers' Anthology, 1981; Moscow, a Travellers' Anthology, 1983; reviews, TLS, etc. *Recreations:* skiing, shooting. *Address:* 44 Ladbroke Grove, W11 2PA. *T:* 01–727 4663. *Clubs:* Beefsteak, Brooks's, Turf; Kildare Street and University (Dublin).

KELLY, Dr Michael, CBE 1983; JP; DL; journalist; Lord Rector, University of Glasgow, since 1983; Public Affairs Consultant: House of Fraser, since 1984; Edinburgh Chamber of Commerce, since 1985; *b* 1 Nov. 1940; *s* of David and Marguerite Kelly; *m* 1965, Zita Harkins; one *s* two *d*. *Educ:* Univ. of Strathclyde (BSc(Econ), PhD). Asst Lectr in Economics, Univ. of Aberdeen, 1965–67; Lectr in Economics, Univ. of Strathclyde, 1967–84. Councillor: Anderston Ward Corp. of Glasgow, 1971–75 (Convener, Schools and Sch. Welfare; Vice-Convener, Transport); Hillington Ward, Glasgow Dist, 1977–84 (Chairman: General Purposes Cttee; Buildings and Property Cttee); Lord Provost of Glasgow, 1980–84 (masterminded "Glasgow's Miles Better" Campaign). Hon. Mem., Clan Donald, USA; Hon. Mayor, Tombstone, Ariz; Hon. Citizen: Illinois; San José; St Petersburg; Kansas City; Dallas; Fort Worth; Winnipeg. JP Glasgow 1973; DL Glasgow 1984. Hon. LLD Glasgow, 1984. Glasgow Herald Scot of the Year, 1983. OStJ 1983. Founding Editor, Jl Economic Studies. *Publication:* Studies in the British Coal Industry, 1970. *Recreations:* photography, football, philately. *Address:* 50 Aytoun Road, Glasgow G41 5HE. *T:* 041–427 1627.

KELLY, Owen; Commissioner of Police for City of London, since 1985; *b* 10 April 1932; *s* of Owen Kelly and Anna Maria (*née* Hamill); *m* 1957, Sheila Ann (*née* McCarthy); five *s*. *Educ:* St Modan's High School, St Ninians, Stirlingshire. National Service, RAF, 1950–52; Metropolitan Police in all ranks from Police Constable to Commander, 1953–82; Asst and Dep. to Comr of Police for City of London, 1982–85; 18th Senior Command Course, Nat. Police Coll., 1981. Chm., City of London Br., Leukaemia Res. Fund, 1985; Vice-Pres., City of London Br., Outward Bound Assoc., 1985. Commendation, Order of Civil Merit, Spain, 1986. *Recreations:* enjoying the society of a large family, do-it-yourself house and car maintenance, dinghy sailing, wind surfing, horse riding. *Address:* 26 Old Jewry, EC2R 8DJ. *T:* 01–601 2222.

KELLY, Rt. Rev. Patrick A.; *see* Salford, Bishop of, (RC).

KELLY, Peter (John); Under-Secretary for Atomic Energy, United Kingdom Department of Energy, 1980–82; *b* 26 Nov. 1922; *s* of Thomas and Lucy Kelly; *m* 1949, Gudrun Kelly (*née* Falck); two *s* three *d* (and one *s* decd). *Educ:* Downside; Oxford Univ. (BA). RNVR, 1942–46. 3rd Secretary, Moscow Embassy, 1948–49; journalism, 1950; rejoined public service, 1956; posts in Foreign Office, Defence Dept, Dept of Trade and Industry; Asst Secretary for Internat. Atomic Affairs, 1969–71; Counsellor, Office of UK Permanent Representative to the European Communities, Brussels, 1972–75; Director, Internat. Energy Agency, 1976–79. *Publication:* Safeguards in Europe, 1985. *Recreations:* walking, music. *Address:* 2 The Crouch, Seaford, Sussex BN25 1PX. *T:* Seaford 896881.

KELLY, Richard Denis Lucien, MC 1944; a Recorder of the Crown Court, 1972–80; *b* 31 Jan. 1916; *e s* of late Richard Cecil Kelly, OBE and Joan Maisie Kelly, Hyde Manor, Kingston, Sussex; *m* 1945, Anne Marie (marr. diss. 1954), *o d* of late James Stuart Anderson, Hinton House, Christchurch; one *d. Educ:* Marlborough Coll.; Balliol Coll., Oxford. Served Surrey and Sussex Yeomanry, 1939–40; Indian Mountain Artillery, India and Burma, 1941–45; Hon. Major, retd. Called to Bar, in absentia, Middle Temple, 1942; Midland and Oxford Circuit; Bencher, 1976. Blackstone Pupillage Prize, 1947; Harmsworth Law Scholar, 1948. Dep. Chm., Kesteven QS, and Dep. Recorder of Bedford, 1968. Alternate Chm., Burnham Cttee, 1973–. *Publications:* (abridgement) The Second World War, by Sir Winston Churchill, 1959; (with R. MacLeod) The Ironside Diaries 1939–40, 1962. *Recreations:* walking, history. *Address:* 3 Temple Gardens, Temple, EC4Y 9AU. *T:* 01–353 4949. *Club:* Garrick.

KELLY, (Robert Henry) Graham, FCIS; Secretary of the Football League, since 1979; *b* 23 Dec. 1945; *s* of Thomas John Kelly and Emmie Kelly; *m* 1970, Elizabeth Anne Wilkinson; one *s* one *d. Educ:* Baines Grammar Sch., Poulton-le-Fylde. FCIS 1973. Barclays Bank, 1964–68; Football League, 1968–. Trustee, Football Grounds Improvement Trust, 1985–. *Address:* The Football League, Lytham St Annes, Lancs FY8 1JG. *T:* St Annes 729421.

KELLY, Rosaline; publishing and industrial relations consultant; Visiting Lecturer in Journalism, London College of Printing, since 1981; *b* 27 Nov. 1922; *d* of Laurence Kelly and Ellen (*née* Fogarty), Drogheda, Co. Louth, Eire. *Educ:* St Louis Convent, Carrickmacross; University Coll., Dublin, NUI. Journalist with Woman magazine, 1958–77; local management, IPC Magazines Ltd, 1977–80. Active for 28 yrs in NUJ: Mem., National Exec. Council, 1972–78; first woman Pres., 1975–77; Membership of Honour, 1979; Member: NUJ Appeals Tribunal, 1978–; NUJ Standing Orders Cttee, 1978–; Trustee, Widow and Orphan Fund, 1977–80, Chairperson Management Cttee, 1980–82. Mem., Press Council, 1977–80 (first woman to represent Press side). Has been rejected as a catalogue holder by Empire Stores. *Recreations:* language and languages, music, compulsive reader. *Address:* 2 Elmar Court, Fulham Road, SW6 5SQ. *T:* 01–736 4290; Arash Areesh, 7 Lakeview Road, Wicklow, Eire. *T:* Wicklow 9596.

KELLY, Sir Theo, (William Theodore), Kt 1966; OBE 1958; JP; Chairman, Woolworths Ltd, Australia, 1963–80, retired (Managing Director, 1945–71), and its subsidiary and associated companies; Chairman: Woolworths (NZ) Ltd, 1963–79 (Director and General Manager, 1934–71); Woolworths Properties Limited, 1963–80; retired 1980; *b* 27 June 1907; *s* of W. T. Kelly; *m* 1944, Nancy Margaret, *d* of W. E. Williams, NZ; two *s* two *d.* War of 1939–45; RAAF, 1942–44, Wing Comdr. Chm., RAAF Canteen Services Bd, 1944–59. General Manager: Woolworths Ltd (NZ), 1932; Woolworths (Australia and NZ), 1945. Mem. Board, Reserve Bank of Australia, 1961–75; Dep. Chm., Australian Mutual Provident Soc., 1972–79 (Dir, 1967–79); Chm., Aust. Mutual Provident Fire and Gen. Insurance Pty Ltd, 1967–79. Life Governor, Royal Life Saving Soc.; Vice-Pres., Royal Hort. Soc., NSW; Trustee, National Parks and Wildlife Foundn, 1969–. Mem. Board, Royal North Shore Hosp., 1969–77. Fellow, Univ. of Sydney Senate, 1968–75. FRSA 1971; FAIM 1967. JP NSW, 1946. *Recreations:* golf, boating. *Address:* 8/73 Yarranabbe Road, Darling Point, Sydney, NSW 2027, Australia. *Clubs:* Sydney Rotary, American National, Royal Sydney Golf, White City Tennis (Sydney).

KELLY, Sir William Theodore; *see* Kelly, Sir Theo.

KELSALL, William, OBE 1971; QPM 1969; DL; Chief Constable of Cheshire, 1974–77; retired; *b* 10 Jan. 1914. DL Cheshire, 1979. CStJ 1983. *Address:* Three Keys Cottage, Quarry Bank, Utkinton, Tarporley, Cheshire.

KELSEY, Mrs Denys E. R.; *see* Grant, Joan.

KELSEY, Maj.-Gen. John, CBE 1968; Director, Wild Heerbrugg (UK) Ltd, since 1978; Director of Military Survey, 1972–77; *b* 1 Nov. 1920; *s* of Benjamin Richard Kelsey and Daisy (*née* Powell); *m* 1944, Phyllis Margaret, *d* of Henry Ernest Smith, Chingford; one *s* one *d. Educ:* Royal Masonic Sch.; Emmanuel Coll., Cambridge; Royal Mil. Coll. of Science. BSc. Commnd in RE, 1940; war service in N Africa and Europe; Lt-Col 1961; Col 1965; Dep. Dir Mil. Survey; Brig. Dir Field Survey, Ordnance Survey, 1968; Dir of Mil. Survey, Brig. 1972; Maj.-Gen. 1974. *Recreations:* Rugby football (played for Cambridge Univ., Richmond, Dorset, Wilts; Mem. RFU, 1965–66); sailing. *Address:* 33 Courtenay Place, Lymington, Hants. *T:* Lymington 73649.

KELSEY, Julian George, CB 1982; consultant to Glengrove Ltd and associated companies, since 1983; Deputy Secretary (Fisheries and Food), Ministry of Agriculture, Fisheries and Food, 1980–82; *b* 1922; *s* of William and Charlotte Kelsey, Dulwich; *m* 1944, Joan (*née* Singerton); one *d.* Lord Chancellor's Dept, 1939; War Service, 1941–46: Captain, Lancs Fusiliers and RAC; SOE and Force 136; Comdg No 11 Searcher Party Team, Burma; Exec. Officer, Central Land Board, 1948; Asst Principal, MAFF, 1951; Under Sec., 1969; Dir of Establishments, 1971–76; Fisheries Sec., 1976–80. *Address:* Shaston House, St James, Shaftesbury, Dorset SP7 8HL. *T:* Shaftesbury 51147. *Club:* Special Forces.

KELSICK, Osmund Randolph, DFC 1944; Chairman and Managing Director of Carib Holdings Ltd (owning and operating The Blue Waters Beach Hotel); Antigua Land Development Co. Ltd; Director: Caribbean Consultants Ltd; Vigie Beach Hotel Ltd (St Lucia); T. H. Kelsick Ltd (Montserrat); Caribbean Hotel Association; *b* 21 July 1922; *s* of T. H. Kelsick; *m* 1950, Doreen Avis Hodge; one *s* (and one *s* decd); two step *d. Educ:* private preparatory sch.; Montserrat Grammar Sch.; Oxford Univ. (Devonshire Course). RAF, Fighter Pilot, 1940–46. ADC and Personal Sec. to Governor of the Leeward Islands, 1946–47; District Commissioner, Carriacou, 1947–51; Asst Chief Sec., Governor's Office, Grenada, 1951–52; Asst Administrator and Administrator, St Vincent, 1952–57. In 1956 seconded for short periods as Asst Trade Commissioner for British West Indies, British Guiana and British Honduras in UK, and Executive Sec. of Regional Economic Cttee in Barbados. Chief Sec., Leeward Islands, 1957–60. Past Pres., Caribbean Hotel Assoc. FRSA 1973. *Recreations:* fishing, gardening, tennis. *Address:* Blue Waters Beach Hotel, Antigua, Leeward Islands, West Indies. *Clubs:* Royal Commonwealth Society (West Indian); New (Antigua); Celebrity (Toronto).

KELWAY, Colonel George Trevor, CBE 1963; TD 1941; DL; JP; District Registrar, HM High Court of Justice in Pembrokeshire and Carmarthenshire, 1940–62; *b* 30 March 1899; *yr s* of late George Stuart Kelway, Milford Haven, Ch. de la Légion d'Honneur, Ch. de l'Ordre de Léopold, &c.; *m* 1931, Gwladys, *d* of late Joseph Rolfe, Goodig, Burry Port, Carm., formerly High Sheriff of Carmarthenshire; one *d. Educ:* Warminster; St Edmund Hall, Oxford. Served European War, 1914–18, and War of 1939–45; Comdg Pembrokeshire Hy. Regt RA (TA), 1927–35; formerly Hon. Col. Pembs Coast Regt. 424 and 425 (Pembs.) Regts RA (TA), and The Pembroke Yeomanry, 1943–58; Chm. Pembs T&AFA, 1945–60. Admitted a Solicitor, 1922. Dep. Chm., Pembs QS, 1960–71. Chm. Pembs Conservative Assoc., 1950–60; Pres. Wales & Mon Cons. Party, 1957 and 1961; Mem. Lloyd's, 1942–; an original Mem. Milford Haven Conservancy Bd, 1958–. DL 1948, JP 1957, Pembrokeshire; High Sheriff, 1958. Provincial Grand Master, S Wales (Western Div.). *Recreation:* golf. *Address:* Cottesmore, near Haverfordwest, Dyfed. *T:* Haverfordwest 66015. *Club:* Pembrokeshire County (Haverfordwest).

KEM, (pseudonym of Kimon Evan Marengo); Political Cartoonist and Journalist; *b* Zifta, Egypt, 4 Feb. 1906; 2nd *s* of Evangelo Tr. Marengo and Aristea, *d* of Capt. John Raftopoulo, Lemnos; *m* 1954, Una O'Connor (*d* 1979); two *s. Educ:* privately, publicly and personally and from time to time attended such seats of learning as the Ecole des Sciences Politiques, Paris, Exeter Coll., Oxford, etc. Edited and Illustrated Maalèsh, a political weekly published simultaneously in Cairo and Alexandria, 1923–31; in summer of 1928 represented a group of Newspapers at International Press Conference, Cologne; has travelled extensively; a fluent linguist, has command of English, French, Greek, Italian, and Arabic and understands a few other languages. *Publications:* In French: Oua Riglak! 1926; Gare les Pattes! 1929; Alexandrie, Reine de la Méditerranée, 1928. In English: Toy Titans, International politics in verse and pictures, 1937; Lines of Attack, 1944. In Arabic: Adolf and his donkey Benito, 1940; now a free-lance, contributing to newspapers and periodicals all over the world. *Recreations:* swimming, riding, drawing, and castigating politicians. *Address:* 46 Redcliffe Gardens, SW10 9HB. *T:* 01-351 3160.

KEMBALL, Prof. Charles, MA, ScD Cantab; FRS 1965; FRSC; MRIA; FRSE; Professor of Chemistry, Edinburgh University, 1966–83, Fellow since 1983 (Dean of the Faculty of Science, 1975–78); *b* 27 March 1923; *s* of late Charles Henry and Janet Kemball; *m* 1956, Kathleen Purvis, *o d* of late Dr and Mrs W. S. Lynd, Alsager, Cheshire; one *s* two *d. Educ:* Edinburgh Academy; Trinity Coll., Cambridge (Sen. Schol.). First Class Hons in Natural Sciences Tripos, Pt I, 1942, Pt II, 1943. Employed by Ministry of Aircraft Production in Dept of Colloid Science, University of Cambridge, 1943–46; Commonwealth Fund Fellow, Princeton Univ., 1946–47; Fellow of Trinity Coll., Cambridge, 1946–54 (Junior Bursar, 1949–51; Asst Lectr, 1951–54); Univ. Demonstrator in Physical Chemistry, 1951–54; Professor of Physical Chemistry, Queen's Univ., Belfast, 1954–66 (Dean of the Faculty of Science, 1957–60, Vice-Pres., 1962–65). President: RIC, 1974–76 (Vice-Pres., 1959–61; Chm., Publications Bd, Chem. Soc./RSC, 1973–81); British Assoc. Section B (Chem.), 1976–77; Vice President: Faraday Soc., 1970–73; RSE, 1971–74, 1982–85; Governor, East of Scotland Coll. of Agriculture, 1977–84. Hon. DSc: Heriot-Watt, 1980; QUB, 1983. Meldola Medal, 1951, Royal Inst. of Chemistry; Corday-Morgan Medal, 1958, Tilden Lectr, 1960, Surface and Colloid Chem. Award, 1972, Chemical Soc.; Ipatieff Prize, American Chemical Soc., 1962; Gunning Victoria Jubilee Prize, RSE, 1981. *Publications:* contributions to various scientific jls. *Recreation:* hill walking. *Address:* 5 Hermitage Drive, Edinburgh EH10 6DE. *Clubs:* New (Edinburgh); English-Speaking Union.

KEMBALL, Brig. Humphrey Gurdon, CBE 1971 (OBE 1966); MC 1940; *b* 6 Nov. 1919; *s* of late Brig.-Gen. Alick Gurdon Kemball (late IA) and late Evelyn Mary (*née* Synge); *m* 1945, Ella Margery Emmeline (*née* Bickham); no *c. Educ:* Trinity Coll., Glenalmond; RMC, Sandhurst. Commissioned 1939, 1st Bn The Prince of Wales's Volunteers. Served War of 1939–45 (MC); Staff Coll., 1943. JSSC, 1956; commanded 1st Bn The Lancashire Regt (PWV), 1961–63; i/c Administration, HQ Federal Regular Army, Aden, 1964–66; Asst Dir, MoD, 1966–68; Mil. Attaché, Moscow, 1968–71; HQ British Forces, Near East, 1971–73; Dep. Comdr, SW District, 1973–74, retired. *Recreations:* fishing, travelling. *Address:* c/o Grindlay's Bank, 13 St James's Square, SW1. *Club:* Naval and Military.

KEMBALL, Air Vice Marshal Richard John, CBE 1981; Commander, British Forces, Falkland Islands, 1985–86; *b* 31 Jan. 1939; *s* of Richard and Margaret Kemball; *m* 1962, Valerie Geraldine Webster; two *d. Educ:* Uppingham. Commissioned RAF, 1957; OC No 54 Squadron, 1977; OC RAF Laarbruch, 1979; Commandant, CFS, 1983–85. ADC to HM The Queen, 1984–85. *Recreations:* shooting, tennis, cricket, gardening. *Address:* c/o Midland Bank plc, 46 Market Hill, Sudbury, Suffolk. *Club:* Royal Air Force.

KEMBALL-COOK, Brian Hartley, MA Oxon; Headmaster, Bedford Modern School, 1965–77; *b* 12 Dec. 1912; *s* of Sir Basil Alfred Kemball-Cook, KCMG, CB, and Lady (Nancy Annie) Kemball-Cook (*née* Pavitt); *m* 1947, Marian, *d* of R. C. R. Richards, OBE; three *s* one *d. Educ:* Shrewsbury Sch. (Sidney Gold Medal for Classics); Balliol Coll., Oxford (Scholar). First Class Classical Honour Mods, 1933; First Class, Litt. Hum., 1935. Sixth Form Classics Master, Repton Sch., 1936–40. Intelligence Corps, 1940–46 (despatches); Regional Intelligence Officer and Political Adviser to Regional Comr, Hanover, 1946; Principal, Min. of Transport, 1946–47. Sen. Classics Master, Repton Sch., 1947–56; Headmaster, Queen Elizabeth's Grammar Sch., Blackburn, 1956–65. Chm., Bedfordshire Musical Festival, 1967–77. Croix de Guerre with Palm, 1946. *Publications:* Ed. Shakespeare's Coriolanus, 1954; (contrib.) Education: Threatened Standards, 1972. *Recreations:* mountaineering, music, translating Homer. *Address:* 23 Grosvenor Road, East Grinstead, West Sussex RH19 1HS. *T:* East Grinstead 23360. *Club:* Climbers.

KEMBER, Anthony Joseph, MA; General Manager, South West Thames Regional Health Authority, since 1984; *b* 1 Nov. 1931; *s* of Thomas Kingsley Kember and May Lena (*née* Pryor); *m* 1957, Drusilla Mary (*née* Boyce); one *s* two *d. Educ:* St Edmund Hall, Oxford (MA). Associate, Inst. of Health Services Management (AHSM). Deputy House Governor and Secretary to Bd of Governors, Westminster Hospital, 1961–69; Gp Secretary, Hillingdon Gp Hospital Management Cttee, 1969–73; Area Administrator, Kensington and Chelsea and Westminster AHA(T), 1973–78; Administrator, SW Thames RHA, 1978–84. Trustee, Disabled Living Foundn, 1981–. *Publications:* various articles for professional jls. *Recreations:* painting, tennis, golf. *Address:* 16 Orchard Rise, Richmond, Surrey TW10 5BX.

KEMBER, William Percy, FCA; FCT; Corporate Financial Controller (formerly Chief Accountant), British Telecommunications, since 1981; *b* 12 May 1932; *s* of late Percy Kember, Purley, and Mrs Q. A. Kember, Oxted, Surrey; *m* 1982, Lynn Kirkham. *Educ:* Uppingham. Chartered Accountant; Corporate Treasurer. Various posts with Royal Dutch/Shell Group in Venezuela, 1958–63; British Oxygen Co., 1963–67; Coopers & Lybrand, 1967–72; Post Office (Telecommunications), 1972–81. Visitor, Royal Institution, 1977, Chm., 1979. *Recreations:* golf, ski-ing. *Address:* 83 Hillway, N6 6AB. *T:* 01–341 2300. *Clubs:* Royal Automobile, Highgate Golf, Ski Club of Great Britain.

KEMMER, Prof. Nicholas, FRS 1956; FRSE 1954; MA Cantab, DrPhil Zürich; Tait Professor of Mathematical Physics, University of Edinburgh, 1953–79, now Professor Emeritus; *b* 7 Dec. 1911; *o s* of late Nicholas P. Kemmer and of late Barbara Kemmer (*née* Stutzer; later Mrs Barbara Classen); *m* 1947, Margaret, *o d* of late George Wragg and late Nellie (who *m* 2nd, C. Rodway); two *s* one *d*. *Educ:* Bismarckschule, Hanover; Universities of Göttingen and Zürich. DrPhil Zürich, 1935; Imperial Coll., London: Beit Scientific Research Fellow, 1936–38; Demonstrator, 1938; Fellow 1971. Mem. of UK Govt Atomic Energy Research teams in Cambridge and Montreal, 1940–46; University Lecturer in Mathematics, Cambridge, 1946–53 (Stokes Lecturer since 1950). Hughes Medal, Royal Society, 1966; J. Robert Oppenheimer Meml Prize (Univ. of Miami), 1975; Max Planck Medal, German Physical Soc., 1983; Gunning Victoria Jubilee Prize, RSE, 1985. *Publications:* The Theory of Space, Time and Gravitation, 1959 (trans. from the Russian of V. Fock, 1955); What is Relativity?, 1960 (trans from the Russian, What is the theory of Relativity?, by Prof. L. D. Landau and Prof. G. B. Rumer, 1959); Vector Analysis, 1977; papers in scientific jls on theory of nuclear forces and elementary particles. *Address:* 35 Salisbury Road, Edinburgh EH16 5AA. *T:* 031–667 2893.

KEMP, family name of **Viscount Rochdale.**

KEMP, Arnold; Editor, Glasgow Herald, since 1981; *b* 15 Feb. 1939; *s* of Robert Kemp and Meta Strachan; *m* 1963, Sandra Elizabeth Shand; two *d*. *Educ:* Edinburgh Academy; Edinburgh Univ. (MA). Sub-Editor, Scotsman, 1959–62, Guardian, 1962–65; Production Editor, Scotsman, 1965–70, London Editor, 1970–72, Dep. Editor, 1972–81. *Recreations:* jazz, reading, theatre. *Address:* 15 Princes Gardens, Glasgow G12 9HR. *T:* 041–334 1576. *Club:* Caledonian.

KEMP, Athole Stephen Horsford, LVO 1983; OBE 1958 (MBE 1950); Secretary, Royal Commonwealth Society Library Trust, since 1984; *b* 21 Oct. 1917; *o s* of late Sir Joseph Horsford Kemp, CBE, KC, LLD, and Mary Stuart; *m* 1940, Alison, *yr d* of late Geoffrey Bostock, FCA; two *s* one *d*. *Educ:* Westminster Sch.; Christ Church, Oxford (MA). War service, RA, 1939–46; POW Far East (Thailand-Burma Railway). Malayan CS, 1940–64 (Sec. to Govt, 1955–57; Dep. Perm. Sec., PM's Dept, 1957–61); Sec. Gen., Royal Commonwealth Soc., 1967–83. JMN 1957. *Recreations:* gardening, public rights of way, wine. *Address:* Lockey House, Langford, Lechlade, Glos GL7 3LF. *T:* Filkins 239. *Club:* Royal Commonwealth Society.

KEMP, Charles Edward; retired as Headmaster of Reading School; *b* 18 Nov. 1901; *e s* of Frederick Kemp, Salford, Lancs; *m* 1927, Catherine Mildred (*d* 1980), *e d* of W. H. Taggart, IOM; two *s*. *Educ:* Manchester Grammar School (Foundation Scholar); Corpus Christi Coll., Oxford (open Scholar), Goldsmith Exhibitioner, 1922; 1st Class Maths, 1923. Master, Manchester Grammar Sch., 1923–30; Master, Royal Naval Coll., Dartmouth, 1930–34; Headmaster: Chesterfield Sch., 1934–39; Reading Sch., 1939–66. *Address:* The Coombe House, Streatley, Reading, Berks RG8 9QL.

KEMP, Rear-Adm. Cuthbert Francis, CB 1967; ADC 1965; Chief Service Manager, Westland Helicopters, 1968–69; *b* 15 Sept. 1913; *s* of A. E. Kemp, Willingdon; *m* 1947, Margaret Law, *d* of L. S. Law, New York; two *s*. *Educ:* Victoria Coll., Jersey. Joined RN, 1931; RN Engrg Coll., 1936. Served in HMS Ajax and Hood; Pilot, 1939. Served War of 1939–45: carriers and air stations at home and abroad; Naval Staff, Washington, 1945–47; Fleet Engr Officer, E Indies, 1950–52; qual. Staff Coll., 1956; Admty, 1957–59; qual. Canadian Nat. Defence Coll., 1962; Supt RN Aircraft Yard, Belfast, 1962–65; Rear-Adm., Engineering, Staff of Flag Officer, Naval Air Command, 1965, retd 1967. *Recreations:* cricket, squash, shooting. *Address:* Beech House, Marston Magna, Som. *T:* Marston Magna 850563. *Clubs:* Army and Navy; Royal Naval and Royal Albert Yacht (Portsmouth).

KEMP, David Ashton McIntyre, QC 1973; a Recorder of the Crown Court, since 1976; *b* 14 Oct. 1921; *s* of late Sir Kenneth McIntyre Kemp and Margaret Caroline Clare Kemp; *m* 1st, 1949, Margaret Sylvia Jones (*d* 1971); 2nd, 1972, Maureen Ann Frances Stevens, *widow*. *Educ:* Winchester Coll.; Corpus Christi Coll., Cambridge. 1st cl. hons Law Cantab. Called to Bar, Inner Temple, 1948, Bencher, 1980. *Publications:* (with M. S. Kemp) The Quantum of Damages, Personal Injuries Claims, 1954 (4th edn 1975); (with M. S. Kemp) The Quantum of Damages, Fatal Accident Claims, 1956 (4th edn 1975). *Recreations:* ski-ing, tennis, gardening. *Address:* 63 Brixton Water Lane, SW2. *T:* 01–733 9735. *Clubs:* Hurlingham, Ski Club of Great Britain; Kandahar Ski.

KEMP, Edward Peter; Deputy Secretary, HM Treasury, since 1983; *b* 10 Oct. 1934; *s* of late Thomas Kemp and Nancie (*née* Sargent); *m* 1961, Enid van Popta; three *s* one *d*. *Educ:* Millfield Sch.; Royal Naval Coll., Dartmouth. FCA (ACA 1959). Professional work in this country and overseas, 1959–67. Principal, later Asst Sec., Min. of Transport, 1967–73; HM Treasury, 1973, Under-Sec., 1978. *Recreations:* reading, sailing. *Address:* 2 Longton Avenue, SE26 6QJ. *T:* 01–778 7310.

KEMP, Rt. Rev. Eric Waldram; *see* Chichester, Bishop of.

KEMP, Air Vice-Marshal George John, CB 1976; *b* 14 July 1921; *m* 1943, Elspeth Beatrice Peacock; one *s* two *d*. Commnd RAF, 1941; served in night fighter sqdns with spell on ferrying aircraft to Middle East; served in Iraq, 1953–54 and Far East, 1960–61; Stn Comdr RAF Upwood, 1968–69; Dir of Manning RAF, 1970–71; Dir of Personnel (Policy and Plans) RAF, 1972; Dir-Gen. of Personnel Management, RAF, 1973–75. *Recreations:* many and various. *Address:* Courts Cottage, Forge Hill, Acrise, Folkestone, Kent CT18 8LJ. *T:* Hawkinge 3188. *Club:* Royal Air Force.

KEMP, Hubert Bond Stafford, MS; FRCS, FRCSE; Consultant Orthopaedic Surgeon: Royal National Orthopaedic Hospital, London and Stanmore, since 1974; The Middlesex Hospital, since 1984; Hon. Consultant Orthopaedic Surgeon, St Luke's Hospital for the Clergy, since 1975; University Teacher in Orthopaedics; *b* 25 March 1925; *s* of John Stafford Kemp and Cecilia Isabel (*née* Bond); *m* 1947, Moyra Ann Margaret Odgers; three *d*. *Educ:* Cardiff High Sch.; Univ. of South Wales; St Thomas' Hosp., Univ. of London (MB, BS 1949; MS 1969); MRCS, LRCP 1947; FRCSE 1960; FRCS 1970. Robert Jones Gold Medal and Assoc. Prize, 1969 (Proxime Accessit, 1964); Hunterian Prof., RCS, 1969; Hon. Consultant, Royal Nat. Orthopaedic Hosp., London and Stanmore, 1965–74; Sen. Lectr, Inst. of Orthopaedics, 1965–74, Hon. Sen. Lectr, 1974–. Vis. Professor, VII Congress of Soc. Latino Amer. de Orthopedia y Traumatologica, 1971. Member: MRC Working Party on Tuberculosis of the Spine, 1974–; MRC Working Party on Osteosarcoma, 1985. Fellow, Brit. Orthopaedic Assoc., 1972–; Member: Brit. Orthopaedic Research Soc., 1967–; Internat. Skeletal Soc., 1977–. *Publications:* (jtly) Orthopaedic Diagnosis, 1984; chapter in A Postgraduate Textbook of Clinical Orthopaedics, 1983; papers on diseases of the spine, the hip, metal sensitivity, bone scanning and haemophilia. *Recreations:* fishing, painting (walls and canvasses). *Address:* 55 Loom Lane, Radlett, Herts WD7 8NX. *T:* Radlett 4265; 107 Harley Street, W1N 1DG. *T:* 01–935 2776.

See also G. D. W. Odgers.

KEMP, Prof. Kenneth Oliver; Emeritus Professor of Civil Engineering and Fellow, University College London, 1984; *b* 19 Oct. 1926; *s* of Eric Austen Kemp; *m* 1952, Josephine Gloria (*née* Donovan); no *c*. *Educ:* University College London. BSc(Eng), PhD, FICE, FIStructE. Surveyor, Directorate of Colonial Surveys, 1947–49; Asst Engr, Collins and Mason, Consulting Engrs, 1949–54. University College London: Lectr, Sen. Lectr, Dept of Civil Engrg, 1954–69; Reader in Structural Engrg, 1969–70; Chadwick Prof. of Civil Engrg and Hd of Civil Engrg Dept, 1970–84. *Publications:* papers in: Proc. Instn of Civil Engrs; The Structural Engr; Magazine of Concrete Research; Internat. Assoc. of Bridge and Structural Engrg. *Recreation:* Norfolk. *Address:* Frenchmans, Duck Street, Wendens Ambo, Essex CB11 4JU. *T:* Saffron Walden 40966.

KEMP, Sir Leslie (Charles), KBE 1957 (CBE 1948); BScEng; FICE, MIEE, ACGI; Vice-Chairman, General Development Corporation, Athens, since 1960; *b* 22 April 1890; *s* of John Charles Kemp, London; *m* 1st, 1918, Millicent Constance (marr. diss., 1959), *d* of late Thomas Maitland; two *s*; 2nd, 1961, Melina Enriquez. *Educ:* Forest Hill House School; London Univ. BScEng 1st Cl. Hons, 1910. Engineer with Fraser and Chalmers, Erith, 1910–14. Served as captain in RGA, France, 1914–19. Contract Engineer, English Electric Co., 1919–23; Technical Adviser, Power and Traction Finance Co., 1923–25; Midlands Branch Manager, English Electric Co., 1924–26; Man. Dir, Athens Piraeus Electricity Co., 1926–41; Manager, Asmara War (land plane repair) base, Asmara, Eritrea, 1942–43; Dep. Regional Dir, Middle East, BOAC, 1943–44; Vice-Chm and Managing Director, Athens Piraeus Electricity Co., 1944–55; Vice-Chm., Société Générale Héllenique, 1957–72. Citizen (Feltmaker) and Freedom of City of London, 1956. Cross of Commander of Royal Order of George I of Greece, 1951. *Recreations:* yachting and golf. *Address:* 4 Herodotou Street, Aghia Varvara, Halandri, Athens, Greece. *Club:* Royal Hellenic Yacht (Greece).

KEMP, Leslie Charles, CBE 1982; FCIArb, FBIM; Chairman, Griffiths McGee Ltd, Demolition Contractors, since 1982; Proprietor, Leslie Kemp Associates, since 1976; *b* 10 Oct. 1920; *s* of Thomas and Violet Kemp. *Educ:* Hawkhurst Moor Boys' School. Apprentice blacksmith, 1934–39; served War, 1939–46: Infantry, N Africa and Italy. Civil Engrg Equipment Operator, 1947–51; District Organiser, 1951–57, Regional Organiser, 1958–63, Nat. Sec. (Construction), TGWU, 1963–76. Jt Registrar, 1975–76, Dep. Chm., 1976–81, Demolition and Dismantling Industry Registration Council. Member, Nat. Jt Council for Building Industry, 1957–76; Operatives Sec., Civil Engrg Construction Conciliation Bd for GB, 1963–76; Mem., 1964–73, Dep. Chm., 1973–76, Chm., 1976–85, Construction Industry Trng Bd (Chm., Civil Engrg Cttee, 1964–76); Member: EDC for Civil Engrg, 1964–76; Construction Ind. Liaison Gp, 1974–76; Construction Ind. Manpower Bd, 1976–; Bragg Adv. Cttee on Falsework, 1973–75; Vice-Pres., Construction Health and Safety Gp. Chm., Corby Develt Corp., 1976–80; Dep. Chm., Peterborough Develt Corp., 1974–82. Member, Outward Bound Trust, 1977–; Pres., W Norfolk Outward Bound Assoc., 1983–. Chm., Syderstone Parish Council, 1983–. Construction News Man of the Year Award, 1973; in recognition of services to trng, Leslie Kemp Europ. Prize for Civil Engrg trainees to study in France, instituted 1973. CompICE. *Recreations:* golf, walking, fishing. *Address:* Lamberts Yard, Syderstone, King's Lynn, Norfolk. *Clubs:* Lighthouse; Fakenham Golf (Pres., 1985).

KEMP, Prof. Martin John; Professor of Fine Arts, Department of Art History, since 1981, Associate Dean of Graduate Studies, Faculty of Arts, since 1983, University of St Andrews; *b* 5 March 1942; *s* of Frederick Maurice Kemp and Violet Anne Tull; *m* 1966, Jill Lightfoot, *d* of Dennis William Lightfoot and Joan Betteridge; one *s* one *d*. *Educ:* Windsor Grammar Sch.; Cambridge Univ. (MA Nat. Scis and Art History); Courtauld Inst. of Art, London Univ. (Academic Dip.). Lectr in History of Art, Dalhousie Univ., Halifax, NS, Canada, 1965–66; Lectr in History of Fine Art, Univ. of Glasgow, 1966–81; Fellow, Inst. for Advanced Study, Princeton, 1984–85. Prof. of History and Hon. Mem., Royal Scottish Acad., 1985–. Trustee: National Gall. of Scotland, 1982–; V&A Museum, 1985–. FRSA 1983. Mitchell Prize for best first book in English on Art History, 1981. *Publications:* Leonardo da Vinci, The Marvellous Works of Nature and Man, 1981; articles in Jl of Warburg and Courtauld Insts, Burlington Magazine, Art History, Art Bull., Connoisseur, Procs of British Acad., JL of RSA, L'Arte, Bibliothèque d'Humanisme et Renaissance, Med. History, TLS, London Rev. of Books, Guardian and Sunday Times. *Recreations:* hockey, cricket, running, gardening, avoiding academics. *Address:* Orillia, 45 Pittenweem Road, Anstruther, Fife KY10 3DT. *T:* Anstruther 310842.

KEMP, Oliver, CMG 1969; OBE 1960; *b* 12 Sept. 1916; *s* of Walter Kemp; *m* 1940, Henrietta Taylor; two *s*. *Educ:* Wakefield Grammar Sch.; Queen's Coll., Oxford. MA Oxon (Lit. Hum.), 1939. Served in HM Forces, 1939–45. Apptd Officer in HM Foreign Service, 1945; served in Moscow, Egypt, Indonesia, Yemen, Laos, Mongolia and Foreign Office. HM Chargé d'Affaires in Yemen, 1957–58; First Secretary and Head of Chancery in Laos, 1958–60. HM Ambassador to Togo (and Consul-General), 1962–65; Deputy Head of the United Kingdom Delegation to the European Communities, Luxembourg, 1965–67; HM Ambassador to Mongolia, 1967–68; FCO, 1968–70 and 1971–73 (European affairs). Dir, BSC Office, Brussels, 1973–81. *Recreations:* music, reading, golf, gardening. *Address:* 37 Cornelian Drive, Scarborough, N Yorks YO11 3AL. *T:* Scarborough 364948.

KEMP, Lt-Comdr Peter Kemp, OBE 1963; RN (retd); FSA, FRHistS; Head of Naval Historical Branch and Naval Librarian, Ministry of Defence, 1950–68; Editor of Journal of Royal United Service Institution, 1957–68; *b* 11 Feb. 1904; *e s* of Henry and Isabel Kemp; *m* 1st, 1930, Joyce, *d* of Fleming Kemp; 2nd, 1949, Eleanore, *d* of Frederick Rothwell; two *d* (and one *s* decd). *Educ:* Royal Naval Colleges, Osborne and Dartmouth. Served in submarines till 1928 (invalided); Naval Intelligence Division, 1939–45. Asst Editor, Sporting and Dramatic, 1933–36; Member: Editorial Staff, The Times, 1936–39 and 1945–50; Council of Navy Records Society; Editorial Adv. Board of Military Affairs (US). *Publications:* Prize Money, 1946; Nine Vanguards, 1951; HM Submarines, 1952; Fleet Air Arm, 1954; Boys' Book of the Navy, 1954; HM Destroyers, 1956; Famous Ships of the World, 1956; Victory at Sea, 1958; Famous Harbours of the World, 1958; (with Prof. C. Lloyd) Brethren of the Coast, 1960; History of the Royal Navy, 1969; The British Sailor: a social history of the lower deck, 1970; Escape of the Scharnhorst and Gneisenau, 1975; A History of Ships, 1978; Merchant Ships, 1982; Seamanship, 1983; (with Richard Ormond) The Great Age of Sail, 1986. Regimental Histories of: Staffordshire Yeomanry; Royal Norfolk Regiment; Middlesex Regiment; King's Shropshire Light Infantry; Royal Welch Fusiliers. Books on sailing. Children's novels. Edited: Hundred Years of Sea Stories; Letters of Admiral Boscawen (NRS); Fisher's First Sea Lord Papers, Vol. I (NRS), 1960, Vol. II (NRS), 1964; Oxford Companion to Ships and the Sea, 1976; Encyclopædia of Ships and Seafaring, 1980. *Recreations:* sailing, golf. *Address:* 53 Market Hill, Maldon, Essex. *T:* Maldon 52609. *Clubs:* West Mersea Yacht, Maldon Golf.

KEMP, Robert Thayer; Director, International Group, Export Credits Guarantee Department, since 1985; *b* 18 June 1928; *s* of Robert Kemp and Ada Kemp (*née* Thayer); *m* 1951, Gwendolyn Mabel Minty; three *s*. *Educ:* Bromley Grammar Sch.; London Univ. (BA (Hons) Medieval and Mod. History). Export Credits Guarantee Department: Asst

Sec., 1970; Under-Sec., 1975; Head of Project Underwriting Gp, 1981–85. *Recreations:* cricket, music, theatre. *Address:* c/o Export Credits Guarantee Department, Aldermanbury House, Aldermanbury, EC2P 2EL. *T:* 01–606 6699. *Club:* Overseas Bankers.

KEMP, Thomas Arthur, MD; FRCP; Physician, St Mary's Hospital, 1947–75, Paddington General Hospital 1950–75; *b* 12 Aug. 1915; *s* of late Fred Kemp and Edith Peters; *m* 1942, Ruth May Scott-Keat; one *s* one *d. Educ:* Denstone Coll.; St Catharine's Coll., Cambridge (Exhibitioner); St Mary's Hospital, London (Scholar). MB, BChir 1940; MRCP 1941; FRCP 1949; MD 1953. Examiner in Medicine, Universities of London and Glasgow. FRSM (Jt Hon. Sec., 1961–67). Served in Middle East, 1944–47; Lt-Col RAMC Officer i/c Medical Division; Hon. Cons. Physician to the Army, 1972–75. Pres. Brit. Student Health Assoc., 1962–63; Chm. Brit. Student Tuberculosis Foundation, 1963–65. Fellow, Midland Div., Woodard Schs, 1962–85; Commonwealth Travelling Fellowship, 1967. *Publications:* papers in medical journals. *Recreations:* games, especially Rugby football (played for Cambridge, 1936, for Barbarians, 1936–49, for St Mary's Hosp., 1937–43, for England, 1937–48 (Captain, 1948, Selector, 1954–61); President: Rugby Football Union, 1971–72; Students' RFU, 1980–). *Address:* 2 Woodside Road, Northwood, Mddx. *T:* Northwood 21068. *Club:* Hawk's (Cambridge).

KEMP-WELCH, John; Joint Senior Partner, Cazenove & Co., since 1980; *b* 31 March 1936; *s* of Peter Wellesbourne Kemp-Welch and Peggy Penelope Kemp-Welch; *m* 1964, Diana Elisabeth Leishman; one *s* three *d. Educ:* Winchester Coll. CBIM 1984. Hoare & Co., 1954–58; Cazenove & Co., 1959–; Dir, Savoy Hotel PLC, 1985–. Governor: Ditchley Foundn, 1980–; North Foreland Lodge Sch., 1980–; Trustee, King's Med. Res. Trust, 1984–. *Recreations:* shooting, farming, the hills of Perthshire. *Address:* Little Hallingbury Place, Bishop's Stortford, Herts CM22 7RE. *T:* Bishop's Stortford 722455. *Clubs:* White's, City of London, MCC.

KEMPE, John William Rolfe, CVO 1980; Headmaster of Gordonstoun, 1968–78; *b* 29 Oct. 1917; *s* of late William Alfred Kempe and Kunigunda Neville-Rolfe; *m* 1957, Barbara Nan Stephen, *d* of late Dr C. R. Huxtable, MC, FRCS and Mrs Huxtable, Sydney, Australia; two *s* one *d. Educ:* Stowe; Clare Coll., Cambridge (Exhibitioner in Mathematics). Served war of 1939–45, RAFVR Training and Fighter Command; CO 153 and 255 Night Fighter Squadrons. Board of Trade, 1945; Firth-Brown (Overseas) Ltd, 1946–47; Head of Maths Dept, Gordonstoun, 1948–51; Principal, Hyderabad Public Sch., Deccan, India, 1951–54; Headmaster, Corby Grammar School, Northants, 1955–67. Chm., Round Square Internat. Service Cttee, 1979–; Vice Chm., The European Atlantic Movement, 1982–. Exploration and mountaineering, Himalayas, Peru, 1952–56; Member: Cttee, Mount Everest Foundation, 1956–62; Cttee, Brathay Exploration Group, 1964–73. FRGS. *Publications:* articles in Alpine Jl, Geographical Jl, Sociological Review. *Address:* Two Gates, Old North Road, Wansford, near Peterborough. *Club:* Alpine.

KEMPFF, Wilhelm Walter Friedrich; pianist and composer; *b* Jüterbog, Berlin, 25 Nov. 1895. *Educ:* Viktoria Gymnasium, Potsdam; Berlin University and Conservatoire (studied under H. Barth and Robert Kahn). Professor and Director of Stuttgart Staatliche Hochschule für Musik, 1924–29, has made concert tours throughout the world since then. Has made numerous recordings. Mem. of Prussian Academy of Arts. Mendelssohn Prize, 1917; Swedish Artibus et Litteris Medal; French Arts et Lettres Medal, 1975; German Maximiliansorden, 1984, etc. Hon. RAM, 1980; Hon. Mem., Bayerische Akad. der schönen Künste, 1980. *Compositions include:* two symphonies; four operas; piano and violin concertos; chamber, vocal and choral works. *Publications:* Unter dem Zimbelstern, Das Werden eines Musikers (autobiog.), 1951; Was ich hörte, was ich sah: Reisebilder eines Pianisten, 1981. *Address:* Wallgraben 14, D-8193 Ammerland-Münsing 2, Germany; c/o Ibbs & Tillett, 450–452 Edgware Road, W2 1EG.

KEMPNER, Prof. Thomas; Principal, Administrative Staff College, Henley-on-Thames, and Professor and Director of Business Studies, Brunel University, since 1972; *b* 28 Feb. 1930; *s* of late Martin and Rosa Kempner; *m* 1st, 1958, June Maton (*d* 1980); three *d*; 2nd, 1981, Mrs Veronica Ann Vere-Sharp. *Educ:* University Coll. London (BSc (Econ)). Asst Administrator, Hyelm Youth Hostels, 1948–49, and part-time, 1951–55; Research Officer, Administrative Staff Coll., Henley, 1954–59; Lectr (later Sen. Tutor) in Business Studies, Sheffield Univ., 1959–63; Prof. of Management Studies, Founder, and Dir of Management Centre, Univ. of Bradford, 1963–72. Member of various cttees, including: Social Studies and Business Management Cttees of University Grants Cttee, 1966–76; Management, Education and Training Cttee of NEDO, 1969– (Chm. of its Student Grants Sub-Cttee); Chm., Food Industry Manpower Cttee of NEDO, 1968–71; Jt Chm., Conf. of Univ. Management Schools, 1973–75. CBIM (FBIM 1971). Hon. DSc Cranfield, 1976; Hon. LLD Birmingham, 1983. Burnham Gold Medal, 1970. *Publications:* editor, author, and contributor to several books, including: Bradford Exercises in Management (with G. Wills), 1966; Is Corporate Planning Necessary? (with J. Hewkin), 1968; A Guide to the Study of Management, 1969; Management Thinkers (with J. Tillet and G. Wills), 1970; Handbook of Management, 1971; (with K. Macmillan and K. H. Hawkins) Business and Society, 1974; Models for Participation, 1976; numerous articles in Management jls. *Recreation:* travel. *Address:* Administrative Staff College, Henley-on-Thames, Oxon. *T:* Henley-on-Thames 571454.

KEMPSON, Rachel, (Lady Redgrave); actress; *b* Devon, 28 May 1910; *d* of Eric William Edward Kempson and Beatrice Hanitton Kempson; *m* 1935, Sir Michael Redgrave, CBE (*d* 1985); one *s* two *d. Educ:* St Agnes Convent, East Grinstead; Colchester County High Sch.; Oaklea, Buckhurst Hill; RADA. First stage appearance in Much Ado About Nothing, Stratford, 1933; first London appearance in The Lady from Alfaqueque, Westminster, 1933. Stratford season, 1934; Liverpool Playhouse, 1935–36; Love's Labour's Lost, Old Vic, 1936; Volpone, Westminster, 1937; Twelfth Night, Oxford, 1937; The School for Scandal, Queen's, 1937; The Shoemaker's Holiday, Playhouse, 1938; Under One Roof, Richmond, 1940; The Wingless Victory, Phoenix, 1943; Uncle Harry, Garrick, 1944; Jacobowsky and the Colonel, Piccadilly, 1945; Fatal Curiosity, Arts, 1946; The Paragon, Fortune, 1948; The Return of the Prodigal, Globe, 1948; Candida, Oxford, 1949; Venus Observed, Top of the Ladder, St James's, 1950; The Happy Time, St James's, 1952; Shakespeare Meml Theatre Co., 1953; English Stage Co., 1956. Recent *stage* appearances include: The Seagull, St Joan of the Stockyards, Queen's, 1964; Samson Agonistes, Lionel and Clarissa, Guildford, 1965; A Sense of Detachment, Royal Court, 1972; The Freeway, National Theatre, 1974; A Family and a Fortune, Apollo, 1975; The Old Country, Queen's, 1977; Savannah Bay, 1983; Chekhov's Women, Queen's, 1986; The Cocktail Party, Phoenix, 1986; World's Beyond, 1986. *Films* include: The Captive Heart, 1945; Georgy Girl; The Jokers; Charge of the Light Brigade; The Virgin Soldiers; Jane Eyre; Out of Africa, 1985; The Understanding, 1985. Frequent *television* appearances include series: Elizabeth R; Jennie; Love for Lydia; The Jewel in the Crown, 1984; The Black Tower, 1985; plays: Winter Ladies, Sweet Wine of Youth, 1979; Kate, the Good Neighbour, Getting On, The Best of Everything, and Jude, 1980; Blunt Instrument, Bosom Friends, The Box wallah, and The Bell, 1981. *Publication:* A Family and its Fortunes (autobiog.), 1986. *Recreations:* gardening, letter writing. *Address:* Hutton Management Ltd, 200 Fulham Road, SW10.

See also Lynn Redgrave, Vanessa Redgrave.

KEMPSTER, Hon. Michael Edmund Ivor; Hon. Mr Justice Kempster; a Justice of Appeal of the Supreme Court of Hong Kong, since 1984 (a Judge of the Supreme Court, 1982–84); Commissioner, Supreme Court of Brunei, since 1983; *b* 21 June 1923; *s* of late Rev. Ivor T. Kempster, DSO; *m* 1949, Sheila, *d* of late Dr T. Chalmers, KiH, Inverness; two *s* two *d. Educ:* Mill Hill Sch.; Brasenose Coll., Oxford (Scholar, MA, BCL). Royal Signals, 1943–46; commissioned in India, served 14th Army. Called to Bar, Inner Temple, 1949; Profumo Prize; Bencher 1977. QC 1969; a Recorder of the Crown Court, 1972–81. Mem., Govt Cttee on Privacy, 1971. Chm., Court of Governors, Mill Hill School, 1979–82. FCIArb, 1982. *Recreations:* fishing, hare-hunting. *Address:* 2801A Tregunter Mansions, Hong Kong. *Clubs:* Travellers'; Hong Kong (Hong Kong).

KEMSLEY, 2nd Viscount *cr* 1945, of Dropmore; **(Geoffrey) Lionel Berry,** DL; Bt 1928; Baron 1936; *b* 29 June 1909; *e s* of 1st Viscount Kemsley, GBE and Mary Lilian (*d* 1928), *d* of Horace George Holmes; *S* father, 1968; *m* 1933, Lady Helen Hay, DStJ, *e d* of 11th Marquess of Tweeddale; four *d. Educ:* Marlborough; Magdalen Coll., Oxford. Served War of 1939–45. Capt. Grenadier Guards; invalided out of Army, 1942. MP (C) Buckingham Div. of Bucks, 1943–45. Dep. Chm., Kemsley Newspapers Ltd, 1938–59. Chm., St Andrew's Hospital, Northampton, 1973–84; Pres., Assoc. of Independent Hospitals, 1976–83. Mem. Chapter General, Order of St John. Master of Spectacle Makers' Co., 1949–51, 1959–61. CC Northants, 1964–70; High Sheriff of Leicestershire, 1967, DL 1972. FRSA; KStJ. *Heir: nephew* Richard Gomer Berry [*b* 17 April 1951; *m* 1981, Tana-Marie, *e d* of Clive Lester]. *Address:* Field House, Thorpe Lubenham, Market Harborough, Leics. *T:* Market Harborough 62816. *Clubs:* Turf, Pratt's, Royal Over-Seas League.

See also Sir G. N. Mobbs.

KEMSLEY, Col Sir Alfred Newcombe, KBE 1980 (CBE 1960); CMG 1973; MSM 1916; ED 1947; FIA; business consultant; *b* Prospect, SA, 29 March 1896; *s* of Alfred Kemsley; *m* 1st, 1921, Glydus Logg (decd); one *s* (killed, RAAF, 1941); 2nd, 1925, Jean Oldfield (decd); one *s* one *d*; 3rd, 1972, Anne Copsey. *Educ:* Adelaide Business Training Academy. Lands Dept, Adelaide, 1911–15; served War, AIF, 1915–18 (Private to Staff Captain; MSM); BHP Co., 1920–23; Sec., Melbourne Metrop. Town Planning Commn, 1923–29; Sec., Liquor Trades Defence Union, 1930–34; Gen. Manager, 3UZ Melbourne, 1934–44; Vice-Pres., Aust. Fedn of Commercial Broadcasting Stations, 1935–36, Trustee, 1938–40; War of 1939–45 (Captain to Colonel): DADOS, 4th Div.; Dir of Organisation and Recruiting, Army HQ, 1941–43; Business Adviser and Army Rep., Bd of Administration, 1943–46; Mem., Mil. Bd, 1946; R of O. Dir, United Services Publicity, later USP Needham Pty Ltd, 1945–65 (Chm., 1960–64), Consultant Dir, 1965–. Director: Fire Fighting Equipment Pty Ltd, 1959–62; Ponsford Newman and Benson, 1964–69; Aust. Inhibitor Paper Pty Ltd, 1965–73; Consultant, TraveLodge Aust. Ltd, 1966–75. Member: Town and Country Planning Bd, 1945–68 (Mem. Aust. Planning Inst.; Sir James Barnett Meml Medal for Town Planning, 1964); Council, Melb. Chamber of Commerce, 1947–76; Inst. of Public Affairs, 1950–69; Aust. Inst. of Management, 1956–64; Aust. Nat. Travel Assoc., 1956–68 (Dep. Chm., 1967–68); Inst. of Directors, 1958–. Trustee, Melb. Nat. War Meml, 1938– (Chm., 1978); Founder Mem., Bd of Governors, Corps of Commissionaires, 1946– (Vice-Chm., 1964); Founder Mem., Field Marshal Sir Thomas Blamey Meml Cttee, 1954– (Chm., 1978); Member: War Nurses Meml Cttee, 1945–; Discharged Servicemen's Employment Bd, 1969–74; Fourth University Cttee, 1970–71; Dep. Chm., Lt-Gen. Sir Edmund Herring Meml Cttee, 1982–. *Address:* 41 Bay Street, Brighton, Victoria 3186, Australia. *Clubs:* Melbourne Legacy (Founder Mem., 1923; Pres., 1932); Australian (Melbourne); Melbourne Cricket.

KENDAL, Felicity, (Mrs Michael Rudman); actress; *d* of Geoffrey and Laura Kendal; *m* (marr. diss.); one *s*; *m* 1983, Michael Rudman, *qv. Educ:* six convents in India. First appeared on stage at age of 9 months, when carried on as the Changeling boy in A Midsummer Night's Dream; grew up touring India and Far East with parents' theatre co., playing pageboys at age of eight and graduating through Puck, at nine, to parts such as Viola in Twelfth Night, Jessica in The Merchant of Venice, and Ophelia in Hamlet; returned to England, 1965; made London debut, Carla in Minor Murder, Savoy, 1967; Katherine in Henry V, and Lika in The Promise, Leicester, 1968; Amaryllis in Back to Methuselah, Nat. Theatre, 1969; Hermia in A Midsummer Night's Dream, and Hero in Much Ado About Nothing, Regent's Park, 1970; Anne Danby in Kean, Oxford, 1970, London, 1971; Romeo and Juliet, 'Tis Pity She's A Whore, and The Three Arrows, 1972; The Norman Conquests, Globe, 1974; Viktosha in Once Upon a Time, Bristol, 1976; Arms and The Man, Greenwich, 1978; Mara in Clouds, Duke of York's, 1978; Constance Mozart in Amadeus, NT, 1979; Desdemona in Othello, NT, 1980; Christopher in On the Razzle, NT, 1981; Paula in The Second Mrs Tanqueray, NT, 1981; The Real Thing, Strand, 1982; Jumpers, Aldwych, 1985; Made in Bangkok, Aldwych, 1986. *Television:* four series of The Good Life, 1975–77; Viola in Twelfth Night, 1979; Solo, 1980, 2nd series 1982; The Mistress, 1985; plays and serials. *Films:* Shakespeare Wallah, 1965; Valentino, 1976. Variety Club Most Promising Newcomer, 1974, Best Actress, 1979; Clarence Derwent Award, 1980; Variety Club Woman of the Year Best Actress Award, 1984. *Recreation:* golf. *Address:* c/o Chatto & Linnit, Prince of Wales Theatre, Coventry Street, W1V 7FE. *T:* 01–930 6677.

KENDALL, Prof. David George, DSc; FRS 1964; Professor of Mathematical Statistics, University of Cambridge, 1962–85 and Fellow of Churchill College, since 1962; *b* 15 Jan. 1918; *s* of Fritz Ernest Kendall and Emmie Taylor, Ripon, Yorks; *m* 1952, Diana Louise Fletcher; two *s* four *d. Educ:* Ripon GS; Queen's Coll., Oxford (MA, DSc; Hon. Fellow 1985). Fellow Magdalen Coll., Oxford, and Lectr in Mathematics, 1946–62. Visiting Lecturer: Princeton Univ., USA, 1952–53 (Wilks Prize, 1980); Zhong-shan Univ., Guangzhou; Xiangtan Univ.; Changsha Inst. Rlwys; Jiaotong Univ., Xi'an, 1983. Larmor Lectr, Cambridge Philos. Soc., 1980; Milne Lectr, Wadham Coll., Oxford, 1983; Hotelling Lectr, Univ. of N Carolina, 1985. Mem. Internat. Statistical Inst.; Mem. Council, Royal Society, 1967–69, 1982–83; President: London Mathematical Soc., 1972–74; Internat. Assoc. Statist. in Phys. Sci., 1973–75; Bernoulli Soc. for Mathematical Stats and Probability, 1975; Section A (Math.) and Section P (Physics), BAAS, 1982. Chm. Parish Reg. Sect., Yorks Archaeol. Soc., 1974–79. Hon. D. de l'U. Paris (René Descartes), 1976; Hon. DSc Bath, 1986. Guy Medal in Silver, Royal Statistical Soc., 1955; Weldon Meml Prize and Medal for Biometric Science, 1974; Sylvester Medal, Royal Soc., 1976; Whitehead Prize, London Math. Soc., 1980; Guy Medal in Gold, Royal Statistical Soc., 1981. *Publications:* (jt ed) Mathematics in the Archaeological and Historical Sciences, 1971; (jt ed) Stochastic Analysis, 1973; (jt ed) Stochastic Geometry, 1974; (ed) Analytic and Geometric Stochastics. *Address:* 37 Barrow Road, Cambridge.

KENDALL, Denis; *see* Kendall, W. D.

KENDALL, Rev. Frank; North West Regional Director, Departments of the Environment and Transport, since 1984; Licensed Preacher, Diocese of Manchester, since 1984; *b* 15 Dec. 1940; *s* of Norman and Violet Kendall; *m* 1965, Brenda Pickin; one *s* one *d. Educ:* Bradford Grammar School; Corpus Christi College, Cambridge (MA Classics); Southwark Ordination Course (London Univ. Dip. in Religious Studies). MPBW, 1962 (Private Sec. to Parly Sec., 1965–67); DEA, 1967–68; MPBW, later DoE (Private Sec. to Perm. Sec.,

1969–70; DVLC, Swansea, 1975–78); Under Secretary 1984. Hon. Curate: Lingfield, dio. Southwark, 1974–75 and 1978–82; Sketty, dio. Swansea and Brecon, 1975–78; Limpsfield, dio. Southwark, 1982–84. *Recreations:* painting: (i) pictures, (ii) decorating. *Address:* 9 Abberton Road, Manchester M20 8HX. *T:* 061-434 5657.

KENDALL, Henry Walter George, OBE 1979; Director, British Printing Industries Federation, 1972–81; *b* 21 Dec. 1916; *s* of Henry Kendall and Beatrice (Kerry) Kendall; *m* 1945, Audrey Alison Woodward; two *s* one *d*. *Educ:* Archbishop Temple's Sch., Lambeth. FCMA. Training with Blades, East & Blades Ltd, 1933–40. War service, RAOC; special duties, War Office, London, 1941; Mil. Coll. of Science, Inspecting Ordnance Officer Western Comd, HQ Allied Land Forces SE Asia, 1940–46. Cost accountant, British Fedn of Master Printers, 1947–55; Chief Cost Accountant, 1955; Head of Management Services, 1967. Mem. Council: CBI, 1972–81; Printing Industry Research Assoc., 1972–81; Inst. of Printing, 1972–81. *Recreations:* theatre, gardening, travel. *Address:* 28 Foxgrove Avenue, Beckenham, Kent BR3 2BA. *Clubs:* Royal Automobile, Wig and Pen.

KENDALL, Raymond Edward, QPM 1984; Secretary General, International Criminal Police Organisation (Interpol), since 1985; *b* 5 Oct. 1933; *m* Antoinette Marie. *Educ:* Simon Langton School, Canterbury; Exeter College, Oxford (MA hons). RAF, 1951–53 (principally Malaya). Asst Supt of Police, Uganda Police, 1957–62; Metropolitan Police, New Scotland Yard, 1962–85 (principally Special Branch). *Recreations:* shooting, golf. *Address:* 26 rue Armengaud, 92 St Cloud, France. *T:* (1) 602-55-50. *Club:* Special Forces.

KENDALL, (William) Denis, PhD; FRSA; FIMechE; MIAE; Chartered Engineer; *b* Halifax, Yorks, 27 May 1903; *yr s* of J. W. Kendall, Marton, Blackpool; *m* 1952, Margaret Hilda Irene Burden. *Educ:* Trinity Sch.; Halifax Technical Coll. MP (Ind.) Grantham Division of Kesteven and Rutland, 1942–50; Mem., War Cabinet Gun Bd, 1941–45 (decorated). Cadet in Royal Fleet Auxiliary; Asst to Chief Inspector, Budd Manufacturing Corp., Philadelphia, Pa, 1923; Dir of Manufacturing, Citroen Motor Car Co., Paris, 1929–38; Managing Director, British Manufacture and Research Co., Grantham, England (manufacturers of aircraft cannon and shells), 1938–45, and Consultant to Pentagon, Washington, on high velocity small arms. Executive Vice-Pres., Brunswick Ordnance Corp., New Brunswick, NJ, 1952–55 (also Dir and Vice-Pres. Ops, Mack Truck Corp.); President and Director: American MARC, Inc., 1955–61 (manufacturers of Diesel Engines, who developed and produced the world's first Diesel outboard engine, and also electric generators, etc), Inglewood, Calif; Dynapower Systems Corp. (Manufacturers of Electro-Medical equipment), Santa Monica, Calif, 1961–73; Pres., Kendall Medical International, Los Angeles, Calif, 1973–82. Mem. President's Council, American Management Assoc. Mem. Worshipful Co. of Clockmakers, Freeman City of London, 1943; Governor of King's Sch., Grantham, 1942–52. Chevalier de l'Ordre du Ouissam Alouite Cherifien. Mason. Religious Society of Friends (Quakers). *Address:* 1319 North Doheny Drive, Los Angeles, Calif 90069, USA. *T:* (213) 5508963. *Clubs:* Riviera Country, United British Services (Los Angeles, Calif).

KENDALL, William Leslie, CBE 1983; Secretary General, Council of Civil Service Unions (formerly Civil Service National Whitley Council, Staff Side), 1976–83; *b* 10 March 1923; *m* 1943, Irene Canham; one *s* one *d*. Clerk Insurance Cttee, 1937–41. RAF 1941–46. Entered Civil Service, 1947; Civil Service Clerical Association: Asst Sec., 1952; Dep. Gen. Sec., 1963; Gen. Sec., CPSA (formerly CSCA), 1967–76. Sec., Civil Service Alliance, 1967; Governor, Ruskin Coll., 1967–76. Member: CS Nat. Whitley Council (Chm. Staff Side, 1973–75); Advisory Council, Civil Service Coll., 1976–83; Civil Service Pay Bd, 1978–81; Vice Pres., Civil Service Council Further Educn, 1978–83. Member: Employment Appeal Tribunal, 1976–; CS Appeal Bd, 1985–; ACAS Indep. Panel on Teachers' Dispute, 1986–. Dir, Civil Service Building Soc., 1980–. *Recreations:* reading, music, pottering. *Address:* 87 Christian Fields, SW16 3JU. *T:* 01-764 7735.

KENDALL-CARPENTER, John MacGregor Kendall; Headmaster, Wellington School, since 1973; *b* 25 Sept. 1925; *s* of late C. E. Kendall-Carpenter and F. F. B. Kendall-Carpenter (*née* Rogers); *m* 1955, Iris Anson; three *s* two *d*. *Educ:* Truro Sch.; Exeter Coll., Oxford. Fleet Air Arm, Pilot RNVR, 1943–46. Oxford, 1947–51; Asst Master, Clifton Coll., 1951–61, and Housemaster, 1957–61; Headmaster: Cranbrook School, Kent, 1961–70; Eastbourne Coll., 1970–73. Member: Air Cadet Council, 1965–70; Air League Council, 1963–70; Chairman: Boarding Schools Assoc., 1981–83; Rugby World Cup Tournament Cttee, 1985–; President: Rugby Football Union, 1980–81 (Member or Captain: Oxford Univ. Rugby XV, 1948–50, England Rugby XV, 1948–54); RFSU, 1985– (Chm., 1981–83); Cornwall RFU, 1984–; Mem., Internat. Rugby Football Bd, 1984–. Hon. Manager Australasian Team, Rugby Football Schools' Union, 1979. Bard of the Gorsedd of Cornwall, 1981–. *Recreations:* outdoor activities, church architecture. *Address:* Headmaster's House, South Street, Wellington, Som; 1 Coulson's Terrace, Penzance, Cornwall. *Clubs:* East India, Devonshire, Sports and Public Schools; Vincent's (Oxford).

KENDELL, Prof. Robert Evan, FRCP; FRCPsych; Professor of Psychiatry since 1974, and Dean of the Faculty of Medicine since 1986, University of Edinburgh; *b* 28 March 1935; *s* of Robert Owen Kendell and Joan Evans; *m* 1961, Ann Whitfield; two *s* two *d*. *Educ:* Mill Hill School; Peterhouse, Cambridge. MA, MD. KCH Med. School, 1956–59; Maudsley Hosp., 1962–68; Vis. Prof., Univ. of Vermont Coll. of Medicine, 1969–70; Reader in Psychiatry, Inst. of Psychiatry, 1970–74. Chm., WHO Expert Cttee on Alcohol Consumption, 1979; Mem., MRC, 1984–. Gaskell Medal, RCPsych, 1967. *Publications:* The Classification of Depressive Illnesses, 1968; The Role of Diagnosis in Psychiatry, 1975; (ed) Companion to Psychiatric Studies, 1983. *Recreations:* overeating and walking up hills. *Address:* 3 West Castle Road, Edinburgh EH10 5AT. *T:* 031-229 4966. *Club:* Climbers'.

KENDREW, Maj.-Gen. Sir Douglas (Anthony), KCMG 1963; CB 1958; CBE 1944; DSO 1943 (Bar 1943, 2nd Bar 1944, 3rd Bar 1953); Governor of Western Australia, 1963–73; *b* 22 July 1910; *er s* of Alexander John Kendrew, MC, MD, Barnstaple, North Devon; *m* 1936, Nora Elizabeth, *d* of John Harvey, Malin Hall, County Donegal; one *s* one *d*. *Educ:* Uppingham Sch. 2nd Lieut Royal Leicestershire Regt, 1931; Capt. 1939; Major 1941; served War of 1939–45: Bde Major, N Africa, 1942; comd 6th Bn York and Lancaster Regt. N Africa and Italy, 1943; Bde Comd. Italy, Middle East and Greece, 1944–46; Commandant, Sch. of Infantry, Rhine Army, 1946–48; Commandant Army Apprentice Sch., Harrogate, 1948–50; Chief of Staff, NID, 1950–52; Bde Comd. 29 Brit. Inf. Bde, Korea, 1952–53; idc 1954; Brig. Administration HQ Northern Comd, 1955; GOC Cyprus Dist, and Dir of Ops, 1956–58; Dir of Infantry, War Office, 1958–60; Head of British Defence Liaison Staff, Australia, 1961–63. Col, Royal Leicestershire Regt, 1963–64. Hon. Col, SAS Regt, RWAR Australia, 1965. Pres., Knights of the Round Table, 1975–83. Comr, Royal Hospital, Chelsea, 1974–80. Hon. LLD Univ. of WA, 1969. KStJ 1964. *Recreations:* Rugby football (played for England 10 times, Capt. 1935; toured NZ and Australia, 1930; Army XV, 1932–36); golf and fishing. *Address:* The Manor House, Islip, Northants. *T:* Thrapston 2325. *Club:* Army and Navy (Chm., 1982).

KENDREW, Sir John (Cowdery), Kt 1974; CBE 1963; ScD; FRS 1960; President of St John's College, Oxford, 1981–July 1987; *b* 24 March 1917; *s* of late Wilfrid George Kendrew, MA, and Evelyn May Graham Sandberg. *Educ:* Dragon Sch., Oxford; Clifton Coll., Bristol; Trinity Coll., Cambridge (Hon. Fellow, 1972). Scholar of Trinity Coll., Cambridge, 1936; BA 1939; MA 1943; PhD 1949; ScD 1962. Min. of Aircraft Production, 1940–45; Hon. Wing Comdr, RAF, 1944. Fellow, Peterhouse, Cambridge, 1947–75 (Hon. Fellow, 1975); Dep. Chm., MRC Lab. for Molecular Biology, Cambridge, 1946–75; Dir Gen., European Molecular Biology Lab., 1975–82. Reader at Davy-Faraday Laboratory at Royal Instn, London, 1954–68. Mem., Council for Scientific Policy, 1965–72 (Dep. Chm., 1970–72); Sec.-Gen., European Molecular Biology Conf., 1970–74. Chm., Defence Scientific Adv. Council, 1971–74; Pres., British Assoc. for Advancement of Science, 1973–74; Trustee, British Museum, 1974–79. President: Internat. Union for Pure and Applied Biophysics, 1969–72; Confedn of Science and Technology Orgns for Develt, 1981–85; Sec. Gen, ICSU, 1974–80, first Vice-Pres., 1982–83, Pres., 1983–; Trustee, Internat. Foundn for Science, 1975–78; Mem. Council, UN Univ., 1980–86, (Chm., 1983–85); Chm., Bd of Governors, Joint Research Centre, EEC, 1985–. Hon. MRIA 1981; Hon. Member: American Soc. of Biological Chemists, 1962; British Biophysical Soc.; Foreign Hon. Mem., Amer. Acad. of Arts and Sciences, 1964; Leopoldina Academy, 1965; Foreign Assoc., Amer. Nat. Acad. of Sciences, 1972; Hon. Fellow: Inst. of Biology, 1966; Weizmann Inst., 1970; Corresp. Mem., Heidelberg Acad. of Scis, 1978; Foreign Mem., Bulgarian Acad. of Scis, 1979. Lectures: Herbert Spencer, Univ. of Oxford, 1965; Crookshank, Faculty of Radiologists, 1967; Procter, Internat. Soc. of Leather Chemists, 1969; Fison Meml, Guy's Hosp., 1971; Mgr de Brún, Univ. Coll. of Galway, 1979; Saha Meml, Univ. of Calcutta, 1980. Hon. Prof., Univ. of Heidelberg, 1982. Hon. DSc: Univ. of Reading, 1968; Univ. of Keele, 1968; Exeter, 1982; Univ. of Buckingham, 1983; DUniv Stirling, 1974; Dr *honoris causa* Pécs, Hungary, 1975. (Jointly) Nobel Prize for Chemistry, 1962; Royal Medal of Royal Society, 1965; Order of Madara Horseman, 1st degree, Bulgaria, 1980. Editor in Chief, Jl of Molecular Biology, 1959–. *Publications:* The Thread of Life, 1966; scientific papers in Proceedings of Royal Society, etc. *Address:* (until July 1987) President's Lodgings, St John's College, Oxford OX1 3JP. *T:* Oxford 247671; The Guildhall, 4 Church Lane, Linton, Cambridge CB1 6JX. *T:* Cambridge 891545. *Club:* Athenæum.

KENDRICK, John Bebbington Bernard; Chief Inspector of Audit, Ministry of Housing and Local Government, 1958–65, retired; *b* 12 March 1905; 3rd *s* of late John Baker Kendrick and Lenora Teague, Leominster, Herefordshire; *m* 1932, Amelia Ruth, 4th *d* of late James Kendall, Grange-over-Sands; two *s*. *Educ:* Leominster Grammar Sch.; King's Sch., Chester; Queen's Coll., Oxford (MA). Called to Bar, Middle Temple. Asst District Auditor, 1926; Deputy District Auditor, 1946; District Auditor, 1953; Deputy Chief Inspector of Audit, 1958. *Recreation:* fell walking. *Address:* Green Acres, Old Hall Road, Troutbeck Bridge, Windermere, Cumbria LA23 1HF. *T:* Windermere 3705.

KENEALLY, Thomas Michael; author; *b* 7 Oct. 1935; *s* of Edmond Thomas Keneally; *m* 1965, Judith Mary Martin; two *d*. Studied for NSW Bar. Schoolteacher until 1965; Commonwealth Literary Fellowship, 1966, 1968, 1972; Lectr in Drama, Univ. of New England, 1968–69. FRSL 1973. Silver City (screenplay, with Sophia Turkiewicz), 1985. *Publications:* The Place at Whitton, 1964; The Fear, 1965, 2nd edn 1973; Bring Larks and Heroes, 1967, 2nd edn 1973; Three Cheers for the Paraclete, 1968; The Survivor, 1969; A Dutiful Daughter, 1971; The Chant of Jimmie Blacksmith, 1972 (filmed 1978); Blood Red, Sister Rose, 1974; Gossip from the Forest, 1975 (TV film, 1979); The Lawgiver, 1975; Season in Purgatory, 1976; A Victim of the Aurora, 1977; Ned Kelly and the City of the Bees, 1978; Passenger, 1979; Confederates, 1979; Schindler's Ark, 1982 (Booker Prize; LA Times Fiction Prize); Outback, 1983; The Cut-Rate Kingdom, 1984; A Family Madness, 1985. *Recreations:* swimming, crosswords, hiking. *Address:* c/o Tessa Sayle Agency, 11 Jubilee Place, SW3 3TE.

KENILOREA, Rt. Hon. Sir Peter (Kauona Keninaraiso'ona), KBE 1982; PC 1979; MP (formerly MLA), East Are-Are, Solomon Islands, since 1976; Prime Minister, 1978–81 and since 1985; *b* Takataka, Malaita, 23 May 1943; *m* 1971, Margaret Kwanairara; two *s* two *d*. *Educ:* Univ. and Teachers' Coll., NZ (Dip. Ed.). Teacher, King George VI Secondary Sch., 1968–70. Asst Sec., Finance, 1971; Admin. Officer, Dist Admin, 1971–73; Lands Officer, 1973–74; Dep. Sec. to Cabinet and to Chief Minister, 1974–75; Dist Comr, Eastern Solomon Is, 1975–76; Chief Minister, 1976–78; Leader of the Opposition, 1981–85. Queen's Silver Jubilee Medal, 1977; Solomon Is Indep. Medal, 1978. *Publications:* political and scientific, numerous articles. *Address:* c/o Legislative Assembly, Honiara, Guadalcanal, Solomon Islands.

KENILWORTH, 4th Baron *cr* 1937, of Kenilworth; **(John) Randle Siddeley;** Managing Director, Siddeley Landscapes, since 1976; Director, John Siddeley International Ltd; *b* 16 June 1954; *s* of John Tennant Davenport Siddeley (3rd Baron Kenilworth) and of Jacqueline Paulette, *d* of late Robert Gelpi; *S* father, 1981; *m* 1983, Kim, *o d* of Danie Serfontein, Newcastle upon Tyne. *Educ:* Northease Manor, near Lewes, Sussex; West Dean College (studied Restoration of Antique Furniture); London College of Furniture. Worked at John Siddeley International as Interior Designer/Draughtsman, 1975; formed own company, Siddeley Landscapes, as Landscape Gardener, 1976. *Recreation:* ski-ing. *Address:* 52 Hartismere Road, Fulham, SW6. *Clubs:* St James's; Annabel's.

KENNABY, Very Rev. Noel Martin; *b* 22 Dec. 1905; *s* of Martin and Margaret Agnes Kennaby; *m* 1st, 1933, Margaret Honess Elliman; 2nd, 1937, Mary Elizabeth Berry. *Educ:* Queens' Coll., Cambridge; Westcott House, Cambridge. BA 1928; MA 1932. Deacon 1929, priest 1930, Diocese of Guildford; Curate of Epsom, 1929–32; in charge of Christ Church, Scarborough, 1932–36; Vicar of St Andrew's, Handsworth, 1936–42; Tynemouth, 1942–47; Surrogate from 1942; Rural Dean of Tynemouth, 1943–47; Provost and Vicar of Newcastle upon Tyne, 1947–61; Rural Dean of Newcastle upon Tyne, 1947–61; Senior Chaplain to the Archbishop of Canterbury, 1962–64; Hon. Canon, Newcastle Cathedral, 1962–64; Dean of St Albans and Rector of the Abbey Church, 1964–73, Dean Emeritus, 1973. Commissary, Jamaica, 1950–67. *Publication:* To Start You Praying, 1951. *Address:* 60 Alexandra Road, Bridport, Dorset.

KENNAN, Prof. George Frost; Professor, Institute for Advanced Study, Princeton, NJ, 1956–74, now Professor Emeritus; *b* 16 Feb. 1904; *m* 1931, Annelise Sorensen; one *s* three *d*. *Educ:* Princeton Univ. (AB); Seminary for Oriental Languages, Berlin. Foreign Service of the USA; many posts from 1926–52; US Ambassador to the USSR, 1952–53; Institute for Advanced Study, Princeton, 1953–61; US Ambassador to Yugoslavia, 1961–63. George Eastman Vis. Prof., Oxford, 1957–58; Reith Lectr, BBC, 1957; Prof., Princeton Univ., 1963 and 1964. Hon. LLD: Dartmouth and Yale, 1950; Colgate, 1951; Notre Dame, 1953; Kenyon Coll., 1954; New School for Social Research, 1955; Princeton, 1956; University of Michigan and Northwestern, 1957; Brandeis, 1958; Wisconsin, 1963; Harvard, 1963; Denison, 1966; Rutgers, 1966; Marquette, 1972; Catholic Univ. of America, 1976; Duke, 1977; Ripon Coll., 1978; Dickinson Coll., 1979; Lake Forest Coll., 1982; Clark Univ., 1983; Oberlin Coll., 1983; Brown Univ., 1983; New York Univ., 1985; William and Mary Coll., and Columbia Univ., 1986; Hon. DCL Oxford, 1969; Dr of Politics *hc* Univ. of Helsinki, 1986. Benjamin Franklin Fellow RSA, 1968.

President: Nat. Inst. of Arts and Letters, 1965–68; Amer. Acad. of Arts and Letters, 1968–72; Corresp. FBA, 1983. Pour le Mérite (Germany), 1976. Albert Einstein Peace Prize, Albert Einstein Peace Prize Foundn of Chicago, 1981; Grenville Clark Prize, Grenville Clark Fund at Dartmouth Coll., Inc., 1981; Börsenverein Peace Prize, Frankfurt, 1982; Gold Medal for History, AAIL, 1984; Creative Arts Award for Nonfiction, Brandeis Univ., 1986. *Publications:* American Diplomacy, 1900–50, 1951 (US); Realities of American Foreign Policy, 1954 (US); Amerikanisch Russische Verhältnis, 1954 (Germany); Soviet-American Relations, 1917–20; Vol. I, Russia Leaves the War, 1956 (National Book Award; Pulitzer Prize 1957); Vol. II, The Decision to Intervene, 1958; Russia, the Atom and the West, 1958; Soviet Foreign Policy, 1917–1941, 1960; Russia and the West under Lenin and Stalin, 1961; On Dealing with the Communist World, 1964; Memoirs, vol. 1, 1925–1950, 1967 (National Book Award 1968; Pulitzer Prize 1968); Memoirs, vol. 2, 1950–1963, 1973; From Prague after Munich: Diplomatic Papers 1938–1940, 1968; Democracy and the Student Left, 1968; The Marquis de Custine and his 'Russie en 1839', 1972; The Cloud of Danger, 1977; (jtly) Encounters with Kennan: the Great Debate, 1979; The Decline of Bismarck's European Order, 1979; The Nuclear Delusion, 1982; The Fateful Alliance: France, Russia and the coming of the First World War, 1985. *Club:* Century (New York City).

KENNARD, Sir George Arnold Ford, 3rd Bt *cr* 1891; *b* 27 April 1915; *s* of Sir Coleridge Kennard, 1st Bt; *S* brother, 1967; *m* 1st, 1940, Cecilia Violet Cokayne Maunsel (marr. diss. 1958); one *d*; 2nd, 1958, Jesse Rudd Miskin (marr. diss. 1974), *d* of Hugh Wyllie; 3rd, 1985, Nichola, *o d* of late Peter Carew, Tiverton. *Educ:* Eton. Commissioned 4th Queen's Own Hussars, 1939; served War of 1939–45 (despatches twice), Egypt, Greece (POW Greece); comd Regt, 1955–58; retired, 1958. Joined Cement Marketing Co., 1967, becoming Midland Representative; retired 1979. *Recreations:* hunting, shooting, fishing. *Heir:* none. *Address:* Gogwell, Tiverton, Devon EX16 4PP. *T:* Tiverton 2154. *Club:* Cavalry and Guards.

KENNAWAY, Prof. Alexander, MA; CEng, FIMechE, FPRI; consulting engineer, since 1966; Chairman, Terrafix Ltd, since 1983; *b* 14 Aug. 1923; *s* of late Dr and Mrs Barou; *m* 1st, 1947, Xenia Rebel (marr. diss. 1970); two *s* one *d*; 2nd, 1973, Jean Simpson. *Educ:* Downsend Sch., Leatherhead; St Paul's Sch., London; Pembroke Coll., Cambridge (MA). CEng, FIMechE 1962; FPRI 1968. Engr Officer, RN: active list, 1942–47; reserve, 1970. Imperial Chemical Industries Ltd, 1947–58; Metal Box Co., 1958–60; Director: BTR Industries, 1960–66; Allied Polymer Gp, 1972–78; Thomas Jourdan, 1976–83; Imperial Polymer Technology, 1984–86. Mem. Bd, CAA, 1979–83. Hon. medical engrg consultant, various hosps and charities, 1950–. Mem., Standing Adv. Cttee on artificial limbs, DHSS, 1964–70. Vis. Prof. of Mech. Engrg, Imp. Coll. of Science and Technology, 1976–. Interim Sec., Nat. Fedn of Zool Gardens of GB and Ireland, 1984–86. *Publications:* (contrib.) Advances in Surgical Materials, 1956; (contrib.) Polythene—technology and uses, 1958, 2nd edn 1960; (contrib.) Engineers in Industry, 1981; (contrib.) The British Malaise, 1982; some 30 papers on biomechanics, technology of use and production of rubbers and plastics, and on design of specific aids for disabled living. *Recreations:* sailing, chess, music, enlarging the limits imposed by an insular and specialist education, avoiding the natural pessimism of old(er) age, applying thought to the solution of useful problems. *Address:* 12 Fairholme Crescent, Ashtead, Surrey KT21 2HN. *T:* Ashtead 77678.

See also L. Archibald.

KENNAWAY, Sir John (Lawrence), 5th Bt, *cr* 1791; *b* 7 Sept. 1933; *s* of Sir John Kennaway, 4th Bt and Mary Felicity, *yr d* of late Rev. Chancellor Ponsonby; *S* father 1956; *m* 1961, Christina Veronica Urszenyi, MB, ChB (Cape Town); one *s* two *d*. *Educ:* Harrow; Trinity Coll., Cambridge. *Heir:* *s* John Michael Kennaway, *b* 17 Feb. 1962. *Address:* Escot, Ottery St Mary, Devon EX11 1LU.

KENNEDY, family name of **Marquess of Ailsa.**

KENNEDY, Sir Albert (Henry), Kt 1965; KPM 1947; Chairman, Securicor (Ulster) Ltd; Director, Securicor Main Board. Held various ranks in Royal Ulster Constabulary, incl. Inspector General, 1961–69. *Club:* Royal Belfast Golf (Ulster).

KENNEDY, A(lfred) James, CBE 1979; DSc (London), PhD (London), FEng, MIEE, FIMM, FIM, FInstP; consultant; *b* 6 Nov. 1921; *m* 1950, Anna Jordan; no *c*. *Educ:* Haberdashers' Aske's Hatcham Sch.; University Coll., London (Fellow 1976). BSc (Physics) 1943. Commissioned R Signals, 1944; Staff Major (Telecommunications) Central Comd, Agra, India, 1945–46 and at Northern Comd, Rawalpindi, 1946–47; Asst Lectr in Physics, UCL 1947–50; Res. Fellow, Davy-Faraday Lab. of Royal Institution, London, 1950–51; Royal Society, Armourers' and Brasiers' Research Fellow in Metallurgy (at Royal Institution), 1951–54; Head of Metal Physics Sect., BISRA, 1954–57; Prof. of Materials and Head of Dept. of Materials, Coll. of Aeronautics, Cranfield, 1957–66; Dir, British Non-Ferrous Metals Res. Assoc., later BNF Metals Technol. Centre, Wantage, 1966–78; Dir of Research, Delta Metal Co., and Man. Dir, Delta Material Research Ltd, 1978–81; Dep. Dir, Technical Change Centre, 1981–86; Dir, BL Technology Ltd, 1979–83. Vis. Prof. in Metallurgy, Imperial Coll. of Science and Technol., London, 1981–86. Institution of Metallurgists: Pres., 1976–77; a Vice Pres., 1971–74, 1975–76; Mem. Council, 1968–76. President: Inst. of Metals, 1970–71 (Mem. Council, 1968–73; Fellow, 1973); Engrg Section, BAAS, 1983; Member: Metallurgy Cttee, CNAA, 1965–71; ARC, 1967–70, 1971–74, 1977–80 (also Mem., ARC cttees); Adv. Council on Materials, 1970–71; Council, The Metals Soc., 1974–84 (Platinum Medallist, 1977); Inst. of Physics, 1968–71; SRC, 1974–78; Metall. and Mat. Cttee, SRC, 1970–75 (Chm. 1973–74); Engrg Bd, 1973–78; Council of Env. Sci. and Eng., 1973–78; Adv. Council for Applied R&D, 1976–80; Mat. and Chem. Res. Requirements Bd, DoI, 1981–83 (Chm., Non-Ferrous Metals Cttee); Chm., Council of Sci. and Tech. Insts, 1983–84. Fellow, Amer. Soc. Met., 1972. Pres., Brit. Soc. of Rheology, 1964–66; a Governor, Nat. Inst. for Agric. Engrg, 1966–74. Hon. DSc Aston, 1980. *Publications:* Processes of Creep and Fatigue in Metals, 1962; The Materials Background to Space Technology, 1964; Creep and Stress Relaxation in Metals (English edn), 1965; (ed) High Temperature Materials, 1968; research papers and articles, mainly on physical aspects of deformation and fracture in crystalline materials, particularly metals. *Recreations:* music, painting. *Address:* Woodhill, Milton under Wychwood, Oxon. *T:* Shipton under Wychwood 830334. *Club:* Athenæum.

KENNEDY, Brig. Archibald Gordon M.; *see* Mackenzie-Kennedy.

KENNEDY, Prof. Arthur Colville, FRCPE, FRCPGlas, FRCP; FRSE 1984; Muirhead Professor of Medicine, Glasgow University, since 1978; *b* 23 Oct. 1922; *s* of Thomas and Johanna Kennedy; *m* 1947, Agnes White Taylor; two *d* (one *s* decd). *Educ:* Whitehill Sch., Glasgow; Univ. of Glasgow. MB ChB 1945, MD 1956. FRCPE 1960, FRCPGlas 1964, FRCP 1977. Hon. Consultant in Medicine, Royal Infirmary, Glasgow, 1959–; Titular Professor, Univ. of Glasgow, 1969–78. Pres., RCPSG, 1986–. *Publications:* various papers on renal disease. *Recreations:* gardening, walking, reading, photography. *Address:* 16 Boclair Crescent, Bearsden, Glasgow G61 2AG. *T:* 041–942 5326. *Club:* Athenæum.

KENNEDY, Charles Peter; MP (SDP) Ross, Cromarty and Skye, since 1983; *b* Inverness, 25 Nov. 1959; *yr s* of Ian Kennedy, crofter, and Mary McVarish MacEachen. *Educ:* Lochaber High Sch., Fort William; Univ. of Glasgow (joint MA Hons Philosophy and Politics). President, Glasgow Univ. Union, 1980–81; winner, British Observer Mace for Univ. Debating, 1982. Journalist, BBC Highland, Inverness, 1982; Fulbright Schol. and Associate Instructor in Dept of Speech Communication, Indiana Univ., Bloomington Campus, 1982–83. SDP spokesman on health, social services, social security and Scottish issues, 1983–; Mem., Select Cttee on Social Services, 1986–. Occasional journalist, broadcaster and lecturer. *Publication:* article to annual US Speech Communication Assoc. Conf., Washington, DC, 1983. *Address:* House of Commons, SW1A 0AA. *T:* 01–219 5090.

KENNEDY, Sir Clyde (David Allen), Kt 1973; Chairman of Sydney (New South Wales) Turf Club, 1972–77 and 1980–83 (Vice-Chairman, 1967–72); company director; *b* 20 Nov. 1912; *s* of late D. H. Kennedy; *m* 1937, Sarah Stacpoole; two *s* one *d*. Member, NSW Totalisator Agency Board, 1965–82; Chairman, Spinal Research Foundation. *Address:* 13A/23 Thornton Street, Darling Point, NSW 2027, Australia. *Clubs:* Australian Jockey, Sydney Turf; Rugby, Tattersalls (all NSW).

KENNEDY, David Matthew; American Banker; Special Representative of the First Presidency of The Church of Jesus Christ of Latter-day Saints; *b* Randolph, Utah, 21 July 1905; *s* of George Kennedy and Katherine Kennedy (*née* Johnson); *m* 1925, Lenora Bingham; four *d*. *Educ:* Weber Coll., Ogden, Utah (AB); George Washington Univ., Washington, DC (MA, LLB); Stonier Grad. Sch. of Banking, Rutgers Univ. (grad.). Special Asst to Chm. of Bd, Federal Reserve System, 1930–46; Vice-Pres. in charge of bond dept, Continental Illinois Bank and Trust Co., Chicago, 1946–53, full Vice-Pres., 1951, Pres., 1956–58, Chm. Bd and Chief Exec. Officer, 1959– (temp. resigned, Oct. 1953–Dec. 1954, to act as special Asst to Sec. of Treas., in Republican Admin.); after return to Continental Illinois Bank, still advised Treasury (also under Democrat Admin). Appointed by President Kennedy as incorporator and dir of Communication Satellite Corp.; Chm. of Commn (apptd by President Johnson) to improve drafting of Federal budget, 1967; Chm of Cttee (apptd by Mayor of Chicago) for Economic and Cultural Develt of Chicago, 1967. Again in Govt, when nominated to Nixon Cabinet, Dec. 1968; Secretary of the Treasury, 1969–70; Ambassador-at-large, USA, and Mem. President Nixon's Cabinet, 1970–73; US Ambassador to NATO, 1972. Director (past or present) of many corporations and companies including: Internat. Harvester Corp.; Abbott Laboratories; Swift & Co.; Pullman Co.; Nauvoo Restoration Inc.; Member of numerous organizations; Trustee: Univ. of Chicago; George Washington Univ.; Brookings Instn, etc. Holds hon. doctorates. *Address:* 3793 Parkview Drive, Salt Lake City, Utah 84124, USA. *Clubs:* Union League, Commercial Executives (Chicago); Old Elm Country (Fort Sheridan, Ill); Glenview Country, etc.

KENNEDY, Douglas Neil, OBE 1952 (MBE); Vice-President, English Folk Dance and Song Society; President, Folk Lore Society, 1964–65; *b* Edinburgh, 1893; *s* of John Henderson Kennedy and Patricia Grieve Thomson, *g s* of David Kennedy the Scottish singer; *m* 1st, 1914, Helen May Karpeles; two *s*; 2nd, 1976, Elizabeth Ann Ogden. *Educ:* George Watson's Coll., Edinburgh; Imperial College of Science. Served London Scottish prior to and during European War, 1914–18, and received his commission in that regiment; MBE for War services, and retired with the rank of Captain; served War of 1939–45, RAF, 1940–45. Demonstrator in the Department of Botany, Imperial Coll., 1919–24; Organising Dir, English Folk Dance Society (on the death of its founder Cecil J. Sharp), 1924–61. *Publications:* England's Dances, 1950; English Folk-dancing Today and Yesterday, 1964; other works relating to traditional dance and song. *Address:* Deck House, Waldringfield, Woodbridge, Suffolk.

KENNEDY, Eamon, MA, BComm, PhD; Irish Ambassador to Italy, Turkey and Libya, since 1983; *b* 13 Dec. 1921; *s* of Luke William Kennedy and Ellen (*née* Stafford); *m* 1960, Barbara Jane Black, New York; one *s* one *d*. *Educ:* O'Connell Schools, Dublin; University Coll., Dublin (MA, BComm); National University of Ireland (PhD 1970). Entered Irish Diplomatic Service, 1943; 2nd Sec., Ottawa, 1947–49; 1st Sec., Washington, 1949–50; 1st Sec., Paris, 1950–54; Chief of Protocol, Dublin, 1954–56; Counsellor, UN Mission, New York, 1956–61; Ambassador to: Nigeria, 1961–64; Federal Republic of Germany, 1964–70; France, OECD and UNESCO, 1970–74; UN, 1974–78; UK, 1978–83. Grand Cross: German Order of Merit, 1970; French Order of Merit, 1974. *Recreations:* golf, theatre, music. *Address:* Irish Embassy, Largo del Nazareno 3, 00187 Rome, Italy. *Club:* Acquasanta Country (Rome).

KENNEDY, Edward Arthur Gilbert; retired; occasional Chairman, Housing Benefit Review Boards; *b* Dublin, 5 May 1920; *s* of Captain Edward H. N. Kennedy, RN, and Frances A. Gosling, Bermuda; *m* 1944, Margarita Dagmara Hofstra; two *s* two *d*. *Educ:* Oundle; Pembroke Coll., Cambridge (BA Mod Langs). Served War, RNVR, 1941–46. Joined Northern Ireland Civil Service, 1947; served mainly in Dept of Commerce until 1970, then in Office of NI Ombudsman (Sen. Dir, 1973–83). Vice-Chm., Music Cttee, N Ireland Arts Council, 1978–83; Hon. Pres., Belfast Ballet Club, 1970–82; Chm., Belfast Picture Borrowing Gp, 1970–84. *Recreation:* interest in the arts. *Address:* 29 Tweskard Park, Belfast BT4 2JZ. *T:* Belfast 63638.

KENNEDY, Edward Moore; US Senator (Democrat) from Massachusetts, since 1963; *b* Boston, Mass, 22 Feb. 1932; *y s* of late Joseph Patrick Kennedy and of Rose Kennedy (*née* Fitzgerald); *m*; two *s* one *d*. *Educ:* Milton Acad.; Harvard Univ. (BA 1954); Internat. Law Inst., The Hague; Univ. of Virginia Law Sch. (LLB 1959). Served US Army, 1951–53. Called to Massachusetts Bar, 1959; Asst Dist Attorney, Suffolk County, Mass, 1961–62. Senate majority whip, 1969–71; Chm., Judiciary Cttee, 1979–81; Ranking Democrat, Labor and Human Resources Cttee, 1981–; Member: Senate Armed Forces Cttee; Senate Jt Economic Cttee; Bd, Office of Technology Assessment. Pres., Joseph P. Kennedy Jr Foundn, 1961–; Trustee: John F. Kennedy Lib.; John F. Kennedy Center for the Performing Arts; Robert F. Kennedy Meml Foundn. Holds numerous hon. degrees and foreign decorations. *Publications:* Decisions for a Decade, 1968; In Critical Condition, 1972; Our Day and Generation, 1979; (with Senator Mark Hatfield) Freeze: how you can help prevent nuclear war, 1982. *Address:* United States Senate, Washington, DC 20510, USA.

KENNEDY, Sir Francis, KCMG 1986; CBE 1977 (MBE 1958); HM Diplomatic Service, retired; Special Adviser to the Chairman and Board, British Airways, since 1986; Adviser to Crown Agents, since 1986; *b* 9 May 1926; *s* of late James and Alice Kennedy; *m* 1957, Anne O'Malley; two *s* two *d*. *Educ:* Univs of Manchester and London. RN, 1944–46. Min. of Supply, 1951–52; HM Colonial Service, Nigeria, 1953–63; Asst Dist Officer, 1953–56; Dist Officer, 1956–59; Principal Asst Sec. to Premier E Nigeria, 1961–62; Provincial Sec., Port Harcourt, 1962–63; HM Diplomatic Service, 1964; First Sec., Commercial and Economic, Dar-es-Salaam, 1965; First Sec. and Head of Post, Kuching, 1967–69; Consul, Commercial, Istanbul, 1970–73; Consul-Gen., Atlanta, 1973–78; Counsellor later Minister Lagos, 1978–81; Ambassador to Angola, 1981–83; Dir-Gen., British Trade Develt Office, and Consul-Gen., NY, 1983–86. Director: Fluor

Daniel, 1986–; Frank B. Hall (Holdings) PLC, 1986–; Leslie & Godwin Ltd, 1986–; Global Analysis Systems, 1986–; Mem. Bd and Council, Inward, 1986–. *Address:* 36 Eaton Place, SW1. *Clubs:* Brooks's; Shaw Hill Golf and Country; Lancashire County Cricket.
See also Rt Rev. Mgr J. Kennedy.

KENNEDY, (George) Michael (Sinclair), OBE 1981; Associate Northern Editor, The Daily Telegraph, since 1986 (Northern Editor, 1960–86), and Staff Music Critic, since 1950; *b* 19 Feb. 1926; *s* of Hew Gilbert Kennedy and Marian Florence Sinclair; *m* 1947, Eslyn Durdle; no *c. Educ:* Berkhamsted School. Joined Daily Telegraph, Manchester, 1941; served Royal Navy (BPF), 1943–46; rejoined Daily Telegraph, Manchester, serving in various capacities on editorial staff; Asst Northern Editor, 1958. Mem. Council, Royal Northern Coll. of Music; Mem. Cttee, Vaughan Williams Trust, 1965– (Chm., 1977–); Trustee: Barbirolli Memorial Foundn, 1971; Elgar Foundn and Birthplace Trust, 1975; Civic Trust for the North West, 1978. Hon. Mem., Royal Manchester Coll. of Music, 1971. Hon. MA Manchester, 1975. FJI 1967; FRNCM 1981. *Publications:* The Hallé Tradition, 1960; The Works of Ralph Vaughan Williams, 1964, 2nd edn 1980; Portrait of Elgar, 1968, 2nd rev. edn, 1982; Portrait of Manchester, 1970; Elgar Orchestral Works, 1970; History of Royal Manchester College of Music, 1971; Barbirolli: Conductor Laureate, 1971; (ed) The Autobiography of Charles Hallé, 1973; Mahler, 1974 (Japanese edn 1978); Richard Strauss, 1976; (ed) Concise Oxford Dictionary of Music, 3rd edn, 1980; Britten, 1981; The Hallé, 1858–1983, 1983; Strauss Tone Poems, 1984; Oxford Dictionary of Music, 1985; Adrian Boult, 1987; scripts for BBC, contrib. musical jls. *Recreations:* listening to music, watching cricket. *Address:* 3 Moorwood Drive, Sale, Cheshire M33 4QA. *T:* 061–973 7225. *Club:* Portico Library (Manchester).

KENNEDY, Lt-Col Sir (George) Ronald (Derrick), 7th Bt *cr* 1836; OBE 1975; Director, Saint Francis Hospice Development Trust; *b* 19 Nov. 1927; *s* of Sir Derrick Edward de Vere Kennedy, 6th Bt, and of Phyllis Victoria Levine, *d* of late Gordon Fowler; *S* father, 1976; *m* 1949, Noelle Mona, *d* of Charles Henry Green; one *s* one *d. Educ:* Clifton College. Regimental service in RA, 1947–58; Staff Coll., Camberley, 1959; staff duties, Aden, 1960–63; regimental duty, 1963–66; staff duties, MoD and HQ BAOR, 1966–71; Defence Attaché, Mexico City, Havana and El Salvador, 1971–74; GSO 1, UK Delegn to Live Oak, SHAPE, 1974–77; HQ Dhekelia Garrison, 1977; retired 1979. *Recreations:* foreign travel, military history. *Heir:* *s* Michael Edward Kennedy [*b* 12 April 1956; *m* 1984, Helen Christine Jennifer, *d* of Patrick Lancelot Rae]. *Address:* Harraton Square, Church Lane, Exning, near Newmarket, Suffolk.

KENNEDY, Horas Tristram, OBE 1966; HM Diplomatic Service, retired; *b* 29 May 1917; *s* of George Lawrence Kennedy and Mary Dow; *m* 1953, Maureen Beatrice Jeanne Holmes (formerly Stevens) (*d* 1976); three *d* (one *s* decd). *Educ:* Oundle; King's Coll., Cambridge. History and Mod Langs, MA. Entered HM Consular Service, 1939; Vice-Consul, Valparaiso, Chile, 1939–46; Foreign Office, 1946–48; 1st Secretary: Belgrade, 1949–52; Buenos Aires, 1952–56; Berne, 1956–61; Santiago de Chile, 1961–67; Commercial Counsellor, Warsaw, 1967–70; Consul-Gen., Barcelona, 1971–73. *Recreations:* country walking, painting, carpentry. *Address:* Borea Farm, Nancledra, Penzance, Cornwall. *T:* Penzance 62722.

KENNEDY, Prof. Ian McColl; Professor of Medical Law and Ethics, King's College London, since 1983, and Director, Centre of Medical Law and Ethics (formerly Centre of Law, Medicine and Ethics), since 1978; *b* 14 Sept. 1941; *s* of Robert Charles Kennedy and Dorothy Elizabeth Kennedy; *m* 1980, Andrea, *d* of Frederick and Barbara Gage, Oceanside, Calif; one *s. Educ:* King Edward VI Sch., Stourbridge; University Coll. London (1st Cl. Hons LLB); Univ. of Calif, Berkeley (LLM). Called to the Bar, Inner Temple, 1974. Fulbright Fellow, 1963–65; Lectr in Law, UCL, 1965–71; Ford Foundn Fellow, Yale Univ. and Univ. of Mexico, 1966–67; Vis. Prof., Univ. of Calif, LA, 1971–72; Lectr in Law, King's Coll., London, 1973–78, Reader in English Law 1978–83; British Acad. Res. Fellow, 1978. Member: Medicines Commn, 1984–; GMC, 1984–. Member: Editorial Bd, Jl of Medical Ethics, 1978–; Council, Open Section, RSM, 1978– (Vice-Pres., 1981–; FRSM 1985). Reith Lectr, 1980. *Publication:* The Unmasking of Medicine, 1981, rev. edn 1983. *Address:* 5 Estelle Road, NW3.

KENNEDY, James; *see* Kennedy, A. J.

KENNEDY, James Cowie; *b* 27 Dec. 1914; *e s* of Robert and Elizabeth Kennedy; *m* 1st, 1939, Eleanor Colman (*d* 1970); one *s* one *d*; 2nd, 1972, Joan G. Cooper, Bristol. *Educ:* Bishops Stortford Coll.; Northern Polytechnic, London. Joined LCC, 1947; Chief Officer, GLC Parks Dept, 1970–79. Mem. Council, SPCK, 1980. *Recreations:* playing with children; enjoying food and drink; working for the Church. *Address:* 174 Clarence Gate Gardens, NW1 6AR.

KENNEDY, Joanna Alicia Gore, CEng; Senior Engineer, Ove Arup and Partners, since 1979; *b* 22 July 1950; *d* of Captain G. A. G. Ormsby, DSO, DSC, RN and late Susan Ormsby; *m* 1979, Richard Paul Kennedy, MA; one *s. Educ:* Queen Anne's School, Caversham; Lady Margaret Hall, Oxford (Scholar, 1969; BA 1st cl. Hons Eng. Sci. 1972; MA 1976; Hon. Mem., Senior Common Room, 1985). MICE 1979, ACIArb 1983. Ove Arup and Partners, consulting civil engineers: Design Engineer, 1972; Asst Resident Engineer (Runnymede Bridge), 1977. Member: Engineering Council, 1984–86; Council, ICE, 1984–; Duke of Edinburgh's Commonwealth Study Conf., Australia, 1986. Governor, Downe House School. *Address:* Ove Arup & Partners, 13 Fitzroy Street, W1P 6BQ. *T:* 01–636 1531.

KENNEDY, Rt. Rev. Mgr John; Rector, Venerable English College, Rome, since 1984; *b* 31 Dec. 1930; *s* of James Kennedy and Alice Kennedy (*née* Bentham). *Educ:* St Joseph's College, Upholland; Gregorian University, Rome (STL); Oxford University (MPhil). Curate: St John's, Wigan, 1956–63; St Austin's, St Helens, 1963–65; St Edmund's, Liverpool, 1965–68; Lectr in Theology, Christ's College, Liverpool, 1968–84 (Head of Dept, 1976–84). *Recreations:* golf, squash. *Address:* Veneràbile Collegio Inglese, Via di Monserrato 45, Roma 00186, Italy. *T:* 656–4185.
See also Sir Francis Kennedy.

KENNEDY, Prof. John (Stodart), FRS 1965; Research Associate, Department of Zoology, University of Oxford, since 1983; Deputy Chief Scientific Officer, Agricultural Research Council, 1967–77, and Professor of Animal Behaviour in the University of London, Imperial College at Silwood Park, Ascot, 1968–77, then Professor Emeritus; *b* 19 May 1912; *s* of James John Stodart Kennedy, MICE, and Edith Roberts Kennedy (*née* Lammers); *m* 1st, 1936, Dorothy Violet Bartholomew (divorced, 1946); one *s*; 2nd, 1950, Claude Jacqueline Bloch (*widow, née* Raphaël); one step *s*, one *s* one *d. Educ:* Westminster Sch.; University Coll., London. BSc (London) 1933; DSc (London) 1956. Locust Investigator for Imperial Inst. of Entomology, University of Birmingham, 1934–36, Anglo-Egyptian Sudan, 1936–37; MSc (London) 1936; London Sch. of Hygiene and Trop. Med., 1937–38; PhD (Birmingham) 1938; Rockefeller Malaria Res. Lab., Tirana, Albania, 1938–39; Wellcome Entomolog. Field Labs, Esher, Surrey, 1939–42; Res. Officer, Middle East Anti-Locust Unit, 1942–44; Chem. Defence Exptl Station, Porton, Wilts, 1944–45; ARC Unit of Insect Physiology, Cambridge, 1946–67. Sen. Res. Fellow, Imperial Coll., 1977–83. Pres. Royal Entomological Society, 1967–69 (Hon. Fellow, 1974; Wigglesworth Medal, 1985). Fellow: University (now Wolfson) Coll., Cambridge, 1966; University Coll., London, 1967; Imperial Coll., London, 1982. Gold Medal, Linnean Soc., 1984. *Publications:* numerous research papers, review articles and essays on the biology of locusts, mosquitos, moths and greenfly, and insect behaviour generally. *Address:* 17 Winchester Road, Oxford OX2 6NA. *T:* Oxford 54484.

KENNEDY, Ludovic Henry Coverley; writer and broadcaster; *b* Edinburgh, 3 Nov. 1919; *o s* of Captain E. C. Kennedy, RN (killed in action, 1939, while commanding HMS Rawalpindi against German battle-cruisers Scharnhorst and Gneisenau), and Rosalind, *d* of Sir Ludovic Grant, 11th Bt of Dalvey; *m* 1950, Moira Shearer King (*see* Moira Shearer); one *s* three *d. Educ:* Eton; Christ Church, Oxford (MA). Served War, 1939–46: Midshipman, Sub-Lieut, Lieut, RNVR. Priv. Sec. and ADC to Gov. of Newfoundland, 1943–44. Librarian, Ashridge (Adult Education) Coll., 1949; Rockefeller Foundation Atlantic Award in Literature, 1950; Winner, Open Finals Contest, English Festival of Spoken Poetry, 1953; Editor, feature, First Reading (BBC Third Prog.), 1953–54; Lecturer for British Council, Sweden, Finland and Denmark, 1955; Belgium and Luxembourg, 1956; Voltaire Meml Lectr, 1985; Mem. Council, Navy Records Soc., 1957–60. Contested (L) Rochdale, by-elec., 1958 and Gen. elec., 1959; Pres., Nat. League of Young Liberals, 1959–61; Mem., Lib. Party Council, 1965–67. Pres., Sir Walter Scott Club, Edinburgh, 1968–69. FRSA 1974–76. Hon. LLD Strathclyde, 1985. Columnist: Newsweek International, 1974–75; Sunday Standard, 1981–82. Chm., Royal Lyceum Theatre Co. of Edinburgh, 1977–84. Cross, First Class, Order of Merit, Fed. Repub. of Germany, 1979. *TV and radio:* Introd. Profile, ATV, 1955–56; Newscaster, Independent Television News, 1956–58; Introducer of AR's feature On Stage, 1957; Introducer of AR's, This Week, 1958–59; Chm. BBC features: Your Verdict, 1962; Your Witness, 1967–70; Commentator: BBC's Panorama, 1960–63; Television Reporters Internat., 1963–64 (also Prod.); Introducer, BBC's Time Out, 1964–65, World at One, 1965–66; Presenter: Lib. Party's Gen. Election Television Broadcasts, 1966; The Middle Years, ABC, 1967; The Nature of Prejudice, ATV, 1968; Face the Press, Tyne-Tees, 1968–69, 1970–72; Against the Tide, Yorkshire TV, 1969; Living and Growing, Grampian TV, 1969–70; 24 Hours, BBC, 1969–72; Ad Lib, BBC, 1970–72; Midweek, BBC, 1973–75; Newsday, BBC, 1975–76; Tonight, BBC, 1976–78; A Life with Crime, BBC, 1979; Change of Direction, BBC, 1979; Lord Mountbatten Remembers, 1980; Did You See?, 1980–; Timewatch, 1984. *Films include:* The Sleeping Ballerina; The Singers and the Songs; Scapa Flow; Battleship Bismarck; Life and Death of the Scharnhorst; U-Boat War; Target Tirpitz; The Rise of the Red Navy; Lord Haw-Haw; Coast to Coast; Who Killed the Lindbergh Baby; Elizabeth: the first thirty years; Happy Birthday, dear Ma'am. *Publications:* Sub-Lieutenant, 1942; Nelson's Band of Brothers, 1951; One Man's Meat, 1953; Murder Story (play, with essay on Capital Punishment), 1956; play: Murder Story (Cambridge Theatre), 1954; Ten Rillington Place, 1961; The Trial of Stephen Ward, 1964; Very Lovely People, 1969; Pursuit: the chase and sinking of the Bismarck, 1974; A Presumption of Innocence: the Amazing Case of Patrick Meehan, 1975; Menace: the life and death of the Tirpitz, 1979; The Portland Spy Case, 1979; Wicked Beyond Belief, 1980; (ed) A Book of Railway Journeys, 1980; (ed) A Book of Sea Journeys, 1981; (ed) A Book of Air Journeys, 1982; The Airman and the Carpenter, 1985; Gen. Editor, The British at War, 1973–77. *Address:* c/o A. D. Peters, 10 Buckingham Street, WC2. *Clubs:* Beefsteak, Brooks's, Army and Navy, MCC.

KENNEDY, Michael; *see* Kennedy, G. M. S.

KENNEDY, Michael Denis; QC 1979; **His Honour Judge Kennedy;** a Circuit Judge, since 1984; *b* 29 April 1937; *s* of Denis George and Clementina Catherine (MacGregor); *m* 1964, Elizabeth June Curtiss; two *s* two *d. Educ:* Downside School; Gonville and Caius College, Cambridge (open Schol., Mod. Langs; MA). 15/19 King's Royal Hussars, 1955–57. Called to the Bar, Inner Temple, 1961; a Recorder, 1979–84. *Address:* Upper Furzefield, Fragbarrow Lane, Ditchling, Sussex BN6 8TP. *T:* Burgess Hill 3871. *Club:* Travellers'.

KENNEDY, Moira, (Mrs L. Kennedy); *see* Shearer, M.

KENNEDY, Nigel Paul; solo concert violinist; *b* 28 Dec. 1956; *s* of John Kennedy and Scylla Stoner; *m* 1980, Joanna Phillips. *Educ:* Yehudi Menuhin School; Juilliard School of Performing Arts, NY. ARCM. Début at Festival Hall with Philharmonia Orch., 1977; regular appearances with London and provincial orchestras, 1978–; Berlin début with Berlin Philharmonic, 1980; Henry Wood Promenade début, 1981; tour of Hong Kong and Australia, with Hallé Orch., 1981; foreign tours, 1978–: India, Japan, S Korea, Turkey, USA; many appearances as jazz violinist with Stephane Grappelli, incl. Edinburgh Fest., 1974 and Carnegie Hall, 1976; many TV and radio appearances, incl. Coming Along Nicely, BBC TV documentary on early life, 1973–78. *Recreations:* golf, football (watching and playing), cricket. *Address:* c/o Harold Holt Ltd, 31 Sinclair Road, W14 0NS. *T:* 01–603 4600.

KENNEDY, Hon. Sir Paul (Joseph Morrow), Kt 1983; **Hon. Mr Justice Kennedy;** a Judge of the High Court of Justice, Queen's Bench Division, since 1983; Presiding Judge, North Eastern Circuit, since 1985; *b* 12 June 1935; *o s* of Dr J. M. Kennedy, Sheffield; *m* 1965 Virginia, twin *d* of Baron Devlin, *qv*; two *s* two *d. Educ:* Ampleforth Coll.; Gonville and Caius Coll., Cambridge (MA, LLB). Called to Bar, Gray's Inn, 1960, Bencher, 1982; a Recorder, 1972–83; QC 1973. *Address:* Royal Courts of Justice, Strand, WC2A 2LL.

KENNEDY, Sir Ronald; *see* Kennedy, Sir G. R. D.

KENNEDY, Thomas Alexander; energy consultant; *b* 11 July 1920; *s* of late Rt Hon. Thomas Kennedy, PC, and Annie S. Kennedy (*née* Michie); *m* 1947, Audrey (*née* Plunkett); one *s* two *d. Educ:* Alleyn's Sch., Dulwich; Durham Univ. (BA). Economist: Bd of Trade, 1950–52; Colonial Office, 1952–55; Lecturer in Economics at Makerere Coll., Uganda, 1955–61; Economist: Treasury, Foreign Office, DEA, 1961–67; Economic Director, NEDO, 1967–70; Under-Sec.: DTI, 1970–74; Dept of Energy, 1974–80, resigned. Chief Tech. Adviser (Economist Planner), Min. of Petroleum and Mineral Resources, Bangladesh, 1980–81. Vis. Fellow, Clare Hall, Cambridge, 1981–82. *Address:* Honeysuckle Cottage, Little Thurlow, Suffolk. *T:* Thurlow 514.

KENNEDY, Air Chief Marshal Sir Thomas (Lawrie), GCB 1985 (KCB 1980; CB 1978); AFC 1953 and Bar 1960; Royal Air Force, retired; Air Member for Personnel, 1983–86; Air ADC to the Queen, 1983–86; *b* 19 May 1928; *s* of James Domoné Kennedy and Margaret Henderson Lawrie; *m* 1959, Margaret Ann Parker; one *s* two *d. Educ:* Hawick High Sch. RAF Coll., Cranwell, 1946–49; commissioned, 1949. Sqdn service, 1949–53; exchange service, RAAF, 1953–55; returned to UK, 1955; 27 Sqdn (Canberra), 1955–57; Radar Research Estabt, 1957–60; RAF Coll. Selection Bd, 1960–62; RN Staff Coll., Greenwich, 1962; HQ Middle East, 1962–64; CO, No 99 (Britannia) Sqdn, 1965–67; HQ Air Support Comd, 1967–69; CO, RAF Brize Norton, 1970–71; Dep. Comdt, RAF Staff Coll., 1971–73; Dir of Ops (AS) MoD, 1973–75; Royal Coll. of Defence Studies, 1976; Comdr, Northern Maritime Air Region, 1977–79; Deputy C-in-

C, RAF Strike Command, 1979–81; C-in-C, RAF Germany, and Comdr, 2nd Allied Tactical Air Force, 1981–83. *Recreations:* golf, sailing. *Club:* Royal Air Force.

KENNEDY-GOOD, Sir John, KBE 1983; QSO 1977; JP; Mayor of Lower Hutt, since 1970; *b* Goulburn, NSW, 8 Aug. 1915; *s* of Charles Kennedy-Good; *m* 1940, June, *d* of Charles Mackay; four *s* three *d*. *Educ:* Southland Boys' High Sch.; Otago Univ. (BDS). Practised as dentist, 1942–72. Mem., Lower Hutt City Council, 1962–. Dir, Hutt Milk Corp., 1970–71, 1974–; Chairman: Hutt Valley Underground Water Authy, 1970–72 (Mem., 1962–72); Wellington Regl Council, 1980– (Dep. Chm., 1980–83); NZ Council of Social Services, 1975–82; Member: Wellington Harbour Bd, 1971–80; Hutt Valley Energy Bd, 1970–. Past Mem., NZ Catchment Authorities' Exec. Pres., NZ Sister Cities Inc. Chm., Dowse Art Mus. Bd, 1971–; Dep. Chm., Nat. Art Gall. and Mus. Trust Bd (Mem., 1971–). Mem., NZ Acad. Fine Arts, 1948. Founder Chm., John Kennedy-Good Human Resources Centre; Chm., Wellington Paraplegic Trust Bd (Vice-Pres., NZ Fed.); past Chm., Council for Dental Health, and past Pres., Wellington Br., NZ Dental Assoc.; Life Patron and Mem. Bd, Hutt Valley Disabled Resources Trust; Pres., Wellington Div., Order of St John; Patron, Wellington Reg. Centre, NZ Red Cross Soc.; patron, pres. or vice-pres. of numerous charity, cultural and sporting orgns. Trustee, Waiwhetu Marae, 1970–; Hon. Elder, Te Atiawa Tribe. JP Lower Hutt, 1970. *Address:* Mayoral Chambers, City Council, Private Bag, Lower Hutt, New Zealand. *T:* 666 959; Greenwood, 64 King's Crescent, Lower Hutt, New Zealand. *T:* 661 227. *Clubs:* Hutt, Hutt Rotary (past Pres.), Hutt Golf.

KENNEDY MARTIN, (Francis) Troy; writer; *b* 15 Feb. 1932; *s* of Frank Martin and Kathleen Flanagan; *m* 1967, Diana Aubrey; one *s* one *d*. *Educ:* Finchley Catholic Grammar Sch.; Trinity Coll., Dublin (BA (Hons) History). Following nat. service with Gordon Highlanders in Cyprus, wrote Incident at Echo Six, a TV play, 1959; *BBC TV:* originated: Storyboard, and The Interrogator, 1961; Z Cars, 1962; Diary of a Young Man, 1964; Man Without Papers, 1965; Edge of Darkness, 1985; *Thames TV:* Reilly, Ace of Spies, 1983; *films:* The Italian Job, 1969; Kelly's Heroes, 1970. Jt Screenwriters' Guild Award, 1962; BAFTA Scriptwriter's Award, 1962. *Publications:* Beat on a Damask Drum, 1961; Edge of Darkness, 1986. *Recreations:* his children, collecting marine models. *Address:* 6 Ladbroke Gardens, W11. *T:* 01–727 2698.

KENNERLEY, Prof. (James) Anthony (Machell), CEng, MIMechE; Chairman, West Surrey and North East Hampshire Health Authority, since 1986; Director, InterMatrix Ltd, Management Consultants, since 1984; *b* 24 Oct. 1933; *s* of William James Kennerley and late Vida May (*née* Machell); *m* 1978, Dorothy Mary (*née* Simpson); one *s* one *d* (twins). *Educ:* Universities of Manchester (BSc; Silver Medallist, 1955) and London (MSc; IMechE James Clayton Fellow). AFIMA, AFRAeS. Engineer, A. V. Roe, Manchester, 1955–58; Aerodynamicist, Pratt & Whitney, Montreal, Canada, 1958–59; Jet Pilot, RCAF, 1959–62; Asst Professor of Mathematics, Univ. of New Brunswick, Canada, 1962–67; Director of Graduate Studies, Manchester Business Sch., 1967–69; Associate Professor of Business Studies, Columbia Univ., New York, 1969–70; Director, Executive Programme, London Business Sch., 1970–73; Prof. of Business Admin, and Dir, Strathclyde Business Sch., 1973–83; Vis. Prof. of Management, Univ. of Surrey, 1984–. Chairman: Management Res. Gp, Scotland, 1981–82; Scottish Milk Marketing Scheme Arbitration Panel, 1981–83. Member: South of Scotland Electricity Bd, 1977–84; Management Studies Bd, CNAA, 1977–84; BIM Educn Cttee, 1982–; Chm., Conf. of Univ. Management Schs, 1981–83; Dir, Business Graduates Assoc., 1983–86. Arbitrator, ACAS, 1976–. Mem., Trans-Turkey Highway World Bank Mission, 1982–83. Founder Mem., Bridgegate Trust, Glasgow, 1982–85. *Publications:* Guide to Business Schools, 1985; articles, papers on business studies and on applied mathematics. *Recreations:* flying, travelling. *Address:* InterMatrix, 4 Cromwell Place, South Kensington, SW7 2JJ. *T:* 01–589 0228; 5 Old Rectory Gardens, Busbridge, Godalming, Surrey GU7 1XB. *T:* Godalming 28108. *Clubs:* Reform, Caledonian.

KENNET, 2nd Baron *cr* 1935; **Wayland Hilton Young;** author and politician; *b* 2 Aug. 1923; *s* of 1st Baron Kennet, PC, GBE, DSO, DSC, and of Kathleen Bruce (who *m* 1st, Captain Robert Falcon Scott, CVO, RN, and died 1947); *S* father 1960; *m* 1948, Elizabeth Ann, *d* of late Captain Bryan Fullerton Adams, DSO, RN; one *s* five *d*. *Educ:* Stowe; Trinity Coll., Cambridge. Served in RN, 1942–45. Foreign Office, 1946–47, and 1949–51. Deleg., Parliamentary Assemblies, WEU and Council of Europe, 1962–65; Parly Sec., Min. of Housing and Local Govt, 1966–70; Opposition Spokesman on Foreign Affairs and Science Policy, 1971–74; SDP Chief Whip in H of L, 1981–83; SDP spokesman on for. affairs and defence, 1981–. Chairman: Adv. Cttee on Oil Pollution of the Sea, 1970–74; CPRE, 1971–72; Internat. Parly Confs on the Environment, 1972–78; Dir, Europe Plus Thirty, 1974–75; Mem., European Parlt, 1978–79. Hon. FRIBA 1970. Editor of Disarmament and Arms Control, 1962–65. *Publications:* (as Wayland Young): The Italian Left, 1949; The Deadweight, 1952; Now or Never, 1953; Old London Churches (with Elizabeth Young), 1956; The Montesi Scandal, 1957; Still Alive Tomorrow, 1958; Strategy for Survival, 1959; The Profumo Affair, 1963; Eros Denied, 1965; Thirty-Four Articles, 1965; (ed) Existing Mechanisms of Arms Control, 1965; (as Wayland Kennet) Preservation, 1972; The Futures of Europe, 1976; The Rebirth of Britain, 1982; Fabian and SDP pamphlets on defence, disarmament, environment, multinational companies, etc. *Heir:* *s* Hon. William Aldus Thoby Young, *b* 24 May 1957. *Address:* 100 Bayswater Road, W2.

KENNETT BROWN, David, JP; a Metropolitan Stipendiary Magistrate, since 1982; a Chairman, Inner London Juvenile Panel, since 1983; an Assistant Recorder, since 1984; *b* 29 Jan. 1938; *s* of late Thomas Kennett Brown, solicitor, and of Vanda Brown; *m* 1966, Wendy Margaret Evans; one *s* two *d*. *Educ:* Monkton Combe Sch.; Lincoln Coll., Oxford. Admitted Solicitor, 1965. FCIArb 1982. Partner, Kennett Brown & Co., 1965–82. Chm., London Rent Assessment Panel, 1979–82; Pres., Central and S Mddx Law Soc., 1982. Churchwarden, St John's Church, W Ealing, 1972–86; Treasurer, Oxford-Kilburn Youth Club, 1961–79. JP Willesden, 1975. *Recreations:* walking, gardening. *Address:* 34 The Mall, Ealing, W5 8BE.

KENNEY, Prof. Edward John, FBA 1968; Kennedy Professor of Latin, University of Cambridge, 1974–82; Fellow of Peterhouse, Cambridge, since 1953; *b* 29 Feb. 1924; *s* of George Kenney and Emmie Carlina Elfrida Schwenke; *m* 1955, Gwyneth Anne, *d* of late Henry Albert Harris. *Educ:* Christ's Hospital; Trinity Coll., Cambridge. BA 1949, MA 1953. Served War of 1939–45: Royal Signals, UK and India, 1943–46; commissioned 1944, Lieut 1945. Porson Schol., 1948; Craven Schol., 1949; Craven Student, 1949; Chancellor's Medallist, 1950. Asst Lectr, Univ. of Leeds, 1951–52; University of Cambridge: Research Fellow, Trinity Coll., 1952–53; Asst Lectr, 1955–60, Lectr, 1966–70; Reader in Latin Literature and Textual Criticism, 1970–74; Peterhouse: Director of Studies in Classics, 1953–74; Librarian, 1953–82; Tutor, 1956–62; Senior Tutor, 1962–65. Jt Editor, Classical Quarterly, 1959–65. James C. Loeb Fellow in Classical Philology, Harvard Univ., 1967–68; Sather Prof. of Classical Literature, Univ. of California, Berkeley, 1968; Carl Newell Jackson Lectr, Harvard Univ., 1980. President: Jt Assoc. of Classical Teachers, 1977–79; Classical Assoc., 1982–83. For. Mem., Royal Netherlands Acad. of Arts and Scis, 1976. Treasurer and Chm., Council of Almoners, Christ's Hosp., 1984–. *Publications:* P. Ouidi Nasonis Amores etc (ed), 1961; (with Mrs P. E. Easterling) Ovidiana Graeca (ed), 1965; (with W. V. Clausen, F. R. D. Goodyear, J. A. Richmond) Appendix Vergiliana (ed), 1966; Lucretius, De Rerum Natura III (ed), 1971; The Classical Text, 1974; (with W. V. Clausen) Latin Literature (ed and contrib.) (Cambridge History of Classical Literature II), 1982; The Ploughman's Lunch (*Moretum*), 1984; articles and reviews in classical jls. *Recreations:* cats and books. *Address:* Peterhouse, Cambridge CB2 1RD. *T:* Cambridge 338200.

KENNEY, Reginald; Principal, Harper Adams Agricultural College, 1962–77; *b* 24 Aug. 1912; *m* 1946, Sheila Fay De Sa; two *d*. *Educ:* King Edward VII School, Lytham St Anne's; Leeds Univ.; West of Scotland Agric. Coll. Warden and Lectr, Staffordshire Farm Inst. (now Staffordshire Coll. of Agriculture), 1937–38; Asst County Agric. Educn Officer, Beds CC, 1938–42 (seconded Beds WAEC, 1939–42); Lectr in Farm Management and Animal Husbandry, University of Reading, 1942–48; Principal, Dorset Farm Inst. (now Dorset Coll. of Agriculture), 1948–62. Hon. FRAgS. *Publication:* Dairy Husbandry, 1957. *Recreations:* travel, golf, mountains. *Address:* 10 Woodridge Close, Edgmond, Newport, Shropshire. *T:* Newport 812514. *Club:* Farmers'.

KENNEY, (William) John; United States lawyer; Partner, Squire, Sanders & Dempsey; *b* Oklahoma, 16 June 1904; *s* of Franklin R. Kenney and Nelle Kenney (*née* Torrence); *m* 1931, Elinor Craig; two *s* two *d*. *Educ:* Lawrenceville Sch., New Jersey; Stanford Univ (AB); Harvard Law Sch. (LLB). Practised law in San Francisco, 1929–36; Head of oil and gas unit, Securities and Exchange Commission, 1936–38; practised law in Los Angeles, 1938–41; Special Asst to Under-Sec. of the Navy; Chm. Navy Price Adjustment Board, General Counsel, 1941–46; Asst Sec. of the Navy, 1946–47; Under-Sec. of the Navy, 1947–49; Minister in charge of Economic Cooperation Administration Mission to the UK, 1949–50; Deputy Dir for Mutual Security, resigned 1952. Chairman: Democratic Central Cttee of DC, 1960–64; DC Chapter, American Red Cross, 1968–71. Director: Riggs National Bank, 1959–81; Merchants Fund Inc., 1954–; Porter International, 1953–; Trustee, George C. Marshall Foundn, Lexington, Va, 1963–. *Address:* 2700 Calvert Street, NW, Washington, DC 20008; (office) 1201 Pennsylvania Avenue, NW, Washington, DC 20004, USA. *Clubs:* California (Los Angeles); Alibi, Metropolitan, Chevy Chase (Washington).

KENNON, Vice-Adm. Sir James (Edward Campbell), KCB 1983; CBE 1974 (OBE 1962); Chief of Fleet Support, 1981–83; *b* 26 Nov. 1925; *s* of late Robert Kennon, MC, FRCS, and Ethel Kennon, OBE; *m* 1950, Anne, *e d* of Captain Sir Stuart Paton, RN retd, *qv*; two *s* one *d*. *Educ:* Stowe School. Special entry to RN, 1943; Military Assistant to CDS, 1959–62; Supply Officer, HMS Kent, 1963–65; Secretary: to VCNS, 1965–67; to C-in-C Fleet, 1968–70; Admiralty Interview Bd, 1970; Sec. to First Sea Lord, 1971–74; NATO Defence Coll., 1974; Captain, HMS Pembroke, 1974–76; Dir, Naval Administrative Planning, 1976–78; Asst Chief of Naval Staff (Policy), 1978–79; Chief Naval Supply Officer, 1979–81, and Port Adm., Rosyth, 1980–81. Pres., RN Benevolent Trust, 1984–. Governor, Stowe Sch. (Chm., 1986–). *Recreations:* walking, languages, photography. *Address:* c/o National Westminster Bank, 26 Haymarket, SW1. *Club:* Army and Navy.

KENNY, Dr Anthony John Patrick, FBA 1974; Master of Balliol College, Oxford, since 1978 (Fellow, 1964–78; Senior Tutor, 1971–72 and 1976–78); *b* Liverpool, 16 March 1931; *s* of John Kenny and Margaret Jones; *m* 1966, Nancy Caroline, *d* of Henry T. Gayley, Jr, Swarthmore, Pa; two *s*. *Educ:* Gregorian Univ., Rome (STL); St Benet's Hall, Oxford; DPhil 1961, DLitt 1980. Ordained priest, Rome, 1955; Curate in Liverpool, 1959–63; returned to lay state, 1963. Asst Lectr, Univ. of Liverpool, 1961–63; University of Oxford: Lectr in Philosophy, Exeter and Trinity Colls, 1963–64; University Lectr, 1965–78; Wilde Lectr in Natural and Comparative Religion, 1969–72; Speaker's Lectureship in Biblical Studies, 1980–83; Pro-Vice-Chancellor, 1984–86; Vice-Chm., Libraries Bd, 1985. Jt Gifford Lectr, Univ. of Edinburgh, 1972–73; Stanton Lectr, Univ. of Cambridge, 1980–83; Bampton Lectr, Columbia Univ., 1983. Visiting Professor: Univs of Chicago, Washington, Michigan, Minnesota and Cornell, Stanford and Rockefeller Univs. Mem. Council, British Acad., 1985. Hon. DLitt Bristol, 1982. Editor, The Oxford Magazine, 1972–73. *Publications:* Action, Emotion and Will, 1963; Responsa Alumnorum of English College, Rome, 2 vols, 1963; Descartes, 1968; The Five Ways, 1969; Wittgenstein, 1973; The Anatomy of the Soul, 1974; Will, Freedom and Power, 1975; The Aristotelian Ethics, 1978; Freewill and Responsibility, 1978; Aristotle's Theory of the Will, 1979; The God of the Philosophers, 1979; Aquinas, 1980; The Computation of Style, 1982; Faith and Reason, 1983; Thomas More, 1983; The Legacy of Wittgenstein, 1984; A Path from Rome (autobiog.), 1985; Wyclif, 1985; The Logic of Deterrence, 1985; The Ivory Tower, 1985; A Stylometric Study of the New Testament, 1986. *Address:* Balliol College, Oxford. *T:* Oxford 249601. *Clubs:* Athenæum, United Oxford & Cambridge University.

KENNY, Anthony Marriott; a Recorder of the Crown Court, since 1980; *b* 24 May 1939; *o s* of late Noel Edgar Edward Marriott Kenny, OBE, and Cynthia Margaret Seton Kenny (*née* Melville); *m* 1969, Monica Grant Mackenzie, *yr d* of H. B. Grant Mackenzie, Pretoria; three *s*. *Educ:* St Andrew's Coll., Grahamstown, Cape Province; Christ's Coll., Cambridge (MA). Called to the Bar, Gray's Inn, 1963; South Eastern Circuit. *Recreations:* music, reading, squash. *Address:* Melbury Place, Wentworth, Surrey GU25 4LB; 12 King's Bench Walk, Temple, EC4. *T:* 01–583 0811.

KENNY, Arthur William, CBE 1977; CChem, FRSC; Director in the Directorate General of Environmental Protection of the Department of the Environment, 1974–79; *b* 31 May 1918; *s* of Ernest James Kenny and Gladys Margaret Kenny; *m* 1947, Olive Edna West; one *s* two *d*. *Educ:* Canton High Sch., Cardiff; Jesus Coll., Oxford (schol.). BA (1st Cl. Hons Natural Sci.), MA, BSc, Oxon. Min. of Supply, 1941; Min. of Health, 1950; Min. of Housing and Local Govt, 1951; DoE, 1971. *Publications:* papers on disposal of radioactive and toxic wastes and on quality of drinking water. *Address:* 134 Manor Green Road, Epsom, Surrey KT19 8LL. *T:* Epsom 24850.

KENNY, Lt-Gen. Sir (Brian) Leslie Graham, KCB 1985; CBE 1979; Commander 1st (British) Corps, British Army of the Rhine, since 1985; *b* 18 June 1934; *s* of late Brig. James Wolfenden Kenny, CBE, and of Aileen Anne Georgina Kenny (*née* Swan); *m* 1958, Diana Catherine Jane Mathew; two *s*. *Educ:* Canford School. Commissioned into 4th Hussars (later Queen's Royal Irish Hussars), 1954; served BAOR, Aden, Malaya and Borneo; Pilot's course, 1961; Comd 16 Recce Flt QRIH; psc 1965; MA/VCGS, MoD, 1966–68; Instructor, Staff Coll., 1971–73; CO QRIH, BAOR and UN Cyprus, 1974–76; Col GS 4 Armd Div., 1977–78; Comd 12 Armd Bde (Task Force D), 1979–80; RCDS 1981; Comdr 1st Armoured Div., 1982–83; Dir, Army Staff Duties, MoD, 1983–85. Col QRIH, 1985; Col Comdt, RAVC, 1983–. Governor, Canford Sch., 1983–. *Recreations:* skiing, cricket, shooting, racing, moving house. *Address:* c/o Lloyds Bank plc, Camberley, Surrey. *Clubs:* Cavalry and Guards, MCC, I Zingari, Free Foresters.

KENNY, David John; Regional General Manager, North West Thames Regional Health Authority, since 1984 (Regional Administrator, 1982–84); *b* 2 Dec. 1940; *s* of late Gerald Henry Kenny and Ellen Veronica (*née* Crosse); *m* 1964, Elisabeth Ann, *d* of late Robert and of Jean Ferris; three *s*. *Educ:* Royal Belfast Academical Instn; Queen's Univ., Belfast (LLB). FHSM. Dep. House Governor, Bd of Governors, London Hosp., 1972; Dist Administrator, Tower Hamlets Health Dist, 1974; Area Administrator, Kensington and Chelsea and Westminster AHA, 1978. Mem. Nat. Council, Inst. of Health Service Administrators, 1975– (Pres. 1981–82); Chm., Data Protection Working Gp, Internat. Med. Informatics Assoc., 1979–. *Publications:* (jtly) Data Protection in Health Information Systems, 1980; articles on management topics and data protection. *Recreations:* theatre, athletics, rugby football. *Address:* 131 Maze Hill, SE3 7UB. *T:* 01–858 1545. *Club:* Athenæum.

KENNY, Douglas Timothy, MA, PhD; President of the University of British Columbia, 1975–84; Professor of Psychology, since 1965; *b* Victoria, BC, 1923; *m*; two *c*. *Educ:* Univ. of British Columbia (BA 1945, MA 1947); Univ. of Washington (PhD). Dept of Psychology, Univ. of British Columbia, 1950, Head of Dept 1965–69; Dean of Faculty of Arts, 1970–75 (Acting Dean, 1969–70). Pres., Faculty Assoc., 1962. Pres., BC Psychological Assoc., 1961. Member: Canada Council, 1975–78; Bd of Trustees, Vancouver Gen. Hosp., 1976–78; Social Scis and Humanities Res. Council, 1978–. *Publications:* articles in Canadian and US jls. *Address:* University of British Columbia, Vancouver, BC V6T 1W5, Canada.

KENNY, Michael, ARA 1976; Sculptor; Head of Fine Art, Goldsmiths' College, University of London, since 1983; *b* 10 June 1941; *s* of James Kenny and Helen (*née* Gordon); *m*; one *s* one *d* and one step *d*; *m* Angela Kenny (*née* Smith); two step *s* one step *d*. *Educ:* St Francis Xavier's Coll., Liverpool; Liverpool Coll. of Art; Slade Sch. of Fine Art (DFA London). Works in public collections of: Arts Council; V&A; British Council; British Museum; Borough of Camden; Contemporary Arts Soc.; Tate Gall.; Leicestershire Education Cttee; North West Arts Assoc.; Wilhelm Lehmbruck Museum, Duisburg; Staatsgalerie, Stuttgart; Unilever Collection, London; Lumsden Village, Aberdeenshire; Hara Mus. of Contemporary Tokyo; Leeds City Art Gall.; private collections in England, Europe, Japan and America. Numerous one-man and mixed exhibitions in GB, Europe, S America, Canada, Japan and Australia. Chairman, Faculty of Sculpture, British School at Rome, 1982–; Mem. Bd of Governors, London Inst. *Relevant publications:* Contemporary Artists, 1977; Contemporary British Artists, 1979; exhibition catalogues. *Recreation:* ornithology. *Address:* c/o Juda Rowan Gallery Ltd, Tottenham Mews, W1. *Club:* Chelsea Arts.

KENNY, Sir Patrick (John), Kt 1976; FRCS, FRACS; Consultant Emeritus Surgeon, St Vincent's Hospital and Lewisham Hospital, Sydney; *b* 12 Jan. 1914; *s* of Patrick John Kenny and Agnes Margaret Carberry; *m* 1942, Beatrice Ella Hammond; two *s*. *Educ:* Marcellin Coll., Sydney; Sydney Univ. (MB, BS 1936, MS 1946). FRCS 1940; FRACS 1944. War Service, AIF, UK, ME and SWPA, 1940–46. Hon. Surgeon: St Vincent's Hosp., 1946–79; Lewisham Hosp., Sydney, 1946–76. Anderson Stuart Memorial Res. Fellow, Sydney Univ., 1938, Lectr in Surg. Anat., 1949–55. Royal Australasian Coll. of Surgeons: Councillor, 1959; Vice Pres., 1967–69; Pres., 1969–71; Mem., Ct of Honour, 1979–. Pres., NSW Med. Bd, 1974–79. FRCPS(Hon.) 1970. *Publications:* surgical treatises. *Recreation:* gardening. *Address:* 13 David Street, Mosman, Sydney, NSW 2088, Australia. *T:* 960–2820. *Club:* Australian.

KENSINGTON, 8th Baron *cr* 1776 (Ire.); **Hugh Ivor Edwardes;** Baron Kensington (UK) 1886; *b* 24 Nov. 1933; *s* of Hon. Hugh Owen Edwardes (*d* 1937) (2nd *s* of 6th Baron) and of Angela Dorothea (who *m* 1951, Lt Comdr John Hamilton, RN retd), *d* of late Lt-Col Eustace Shearman, 10th Hussars; *S* uncle, 1981; *m* 1961, Juliet Elizabeth Massy Anderson; two *s* one *d*. *Educ:* Eton. *Heir:* *s* Hon. William Owen Alexander Edwardes, *b* 21 July 1964. *Address:* Friar Tuck, PO Box 549, Mooi River, Natal, 3300, Republic of S Africa. *Clubs:* Boodle's; Durban (Durban).

KENSINGTON, Area Bishop of, since 1981; **Rt. Rev. Mark Santer,** MA; *b* 29 Dec. 1936; *s* of late Rev. Canon Eric Arthur Robert Santer and Phyllis Clare Barlow; *m* 1964, Henriette Cornelia Weststrate; one *s* two *d*. *Educ:* Marlborough Coll.; Queens' Coll., Cambridge; Westcott House, Cambridge. Deacon, 1963; priest 1964; Asst Curate, Cuddesdon, 1963–67; Tutor, Cuddesdon Theological Coll., 1963–67; Fellow and Dean of Clare Coll., Cambridge, 1967–72 (and Tutor, 1968–72); Univ. Asst Lectr in Divinity, 1968–72; Principal of Westcott House, Cambridge, 1973–81; Hon. Canon of Winchester Cathedral, 1978–81. Co-Chm., Anglican Roman Catholic Internat. Commn, 1983–. *Publications:* (contrib.) The Phenomenon of Christian Belief, 1970; (with M. F. Wiles) Documents in Early Christian Thought, 1975; Their Lord and Ours, 1982; (contrib.) The Church and the State, 1984; (contrib.) Dropping the Bomb, 1985; articles in: Jl of Theological Studies; New Testament Studies; Theology. *Address:* 19 Campden Hill Square, W8 7JY. *T:* 01–727 9818.

KENSWOOD, 2nd Baron, *cr* 1951; **John Michael Howard Whitfield;** *b* 6 April 1930; *o s* of 1st Baron Kenswood; *S* father, 1963; *m* 1951, Deirdre Anna Louise, *d* of Colin Malcolm Methven, Errol, Perthshire; four *s* one *d*. *Educ:* Trinity Coll. Sch., Ontario; Harrow; Grenoble Univ.; Emmanuel Coll., Cambridge (BA). *Heir:* *s* Hon. Michael Christopher Whitfield, *b* 3 July 1955. *Address:* Domaine de la Forêt, 31340 Villemur sur Tarn, France. *T:* (61) 09 22 90.

KENT, Arthur William, CMG 1966; OBE 1950; Chairman, United Transport Overseas Ltd, 1980–82 (Deputy Chairman, 1978–80, Joint Managing Director, 1977–80); Managing Director, United Transport Co., 1980–82; *b* 22 March 1913; *s* of Howard and Eliza Kent; *m* 1st, 1944, Doris Jane (*née* Crowe; marr. diss., 1958); one *s* one *d*; 2nd, 1958, Mary (*née* Martin). Deputy City Treasurer, Nairobi, 1946–48, City Treasurer, 1948–65. Chief Executive: United Transport Overseas Ltd, Nairobi, 1966–69; Transport Holdings of Zambia Ltd, 1969–71; Chief Exec., United Transport Holdings (Pty) Ltd, Johannesburg, 1971–76; Dir of a number of cos owned by United Transport Overseas Ltd and other BET cos. IPFA; FCA; FCIT. *Address:* (home) Muthaiga, Beechwood Road, Combe Down, Bath, Avon.

KENT, Very Rev. Mgr. Bruce; campaigner for nuclear disarmament; Vice-Chairman, Campaign for Nuclear Disarmament since 1985 (General Secretary, 1980–85; Hon. Vice President, 1985); *b* 22 June 1929; *s* of Kenneth Kent and Rosemary Kent (*née* Marion). *Educ:* Lower Canada Coll., Montreal; Stonyhurst Coll.; Brasenose Coll., Univ. of Oxford. LLB. Ordination, Westminster, 1958; Curate, Kensington, North and South, 1958–63; Sec., Archbishop's House, Westminster, 1963–64; Chm., Diocesan Schools Commn, 1964–66; Catholic Chaplain to Univ. of London, 1966–74; Chaplain, Pax Christi, 1974–77; Parish Priest, Somers Town, NW1, 1977–80. Pres., Internat. Peace Bureau, 1985–. *Publications:* essays and pamphlets on disarmament, Christians and peace. *Recreations:* friends, walking. *Address:* c/o Campaign for Nuclear Disarmament, 22–24 Underwood Street, N1 7JG. *T:* 01–250 4010.

KENT, Dorothy Miriam; Under-Secretary, Department of Employment, 1973–80; *d* of Donald Roy Thom, CBE, and Elsie Miriam Thom (*née* Rundell); *m* 1948 Eric Nelson Kent; one *s* two *d*. *Educ:* North London Collegiate Sch.; Somerville Coll., Oxford (Scholar). MA Hons History. Temp. wartime civil service posts, 1941–46; entered Min. of Labour, 1946; Principal, 1950; Asst Sec., 1964; Under-Sec., 1973; retired, 1980. *Address:* 45 Lytton Grove, SW15 2HD. *T:* 01–788 0214.

KENT, Geoffrey Charles; Director, 1975–86, Chairman and Chief Executive, 1981–86, Imperial Group plc; *b* 2 Feb. 1922; *s* of late Percival Whitehead and Madge Kent; *m* 1955, Brenda Georgine Conisbee. *Educ:* Blackpool Grammar Sch. CBIM 1976; FInstM 1977. Served RAF, 1939–46; Flt Lieut Coastal Comd. Advertising and marketing appts with Colman, Prentis & Varley, Mentor, and Johnson & Johnson, 1947–58; John Player & Son: Advertising Manager, 1958; Marketing Dir, 1964; Asst Man. Dir, 1969; Chm. and Man. Dir, 1975; Chm. and Chief Exec., Courage Ltd, 1978–81. Director: Lloyds Bank plc, 1981–; Lloyds Bank International, 1983–85; Lloyds Merchant Bank Holdings Ltd, 1985–; Corah plc, 1986–; John Howitt Group Ltd, 1986–; Brewers' Soc., 1978–86. Mem., Lloyd's of London, 1985–. *Recreations:* flying, ski-ing. *Address:* Hill House, Gonalston, Nottingham NG14 7JA.

KENT, Sir Harold Simcox, GCB 1963 (KCB 1954; CB 1946); QC 1973; Commissary to Dean and Chapter of St Paul's Cathedral, since 1976; *b* 11 Nov. 1903; *s* of late P. H. B. Kent, OBE, MC; *m* 1930, Zillah Lloyd; one *s* (one *d* decd). *Educ:* Rugby School; Merton Coll., Oxford. Barrister-at-law, 1928; Parliamentary Counsel to the Treasury, 1940–53; HM Procurator-General and Treasury Solicitor, 1953–63; Solicitor to Vassall Tribunal, 1963; Mem., Security Commn, 1965–71; Standing Counsel to Church Assembly and General Synod, 1964–72; Vicar-General of the Province of Canterbury, 1971–76; Dean of the Arches Court of Canterbury and Auditor of the Chancery Court of York, 1972–76. Mem., Departmental Cttee to examine operation of Section 2 of Official Secrets Act, 1911, 1971–72. DCL Lambeth, 1977. *Publication:* In On the Act, 1979. *Address:* Alderley, Calf Lane, Chipping Campden, Glos. *T:* Evesham 840421. *Club:* United Oxford & Cambridge University.

KENT, John Philip Cozens, PhD; FSA; FBA 1986; Keeper, Department of Coins and Medals, British Museum, since 1983; *b* 28 Sept. 1928; *s* of John Cozens Kent, DCM and late Lucy Ella Kent; *m* 1961, Patricia Eleanor Bunford; one *s* one *d*. *Educ:* Minchenden County Grammar Sch.; University Coll. London (BA 1949; PhD 1951). FSA 1961. Nat. Service, 1951–53. Asst Keeper, 1953, Dep. Keeper, 1974, Dept of Coins and Medals, BM. President: British Assoc. of Numismatic Socs, 1974–78; Royal Numismatic Soc., 1984–; London and Middlesex Archaeological Soc., 1985–. Mem., Instituto de Sintra, 1986. *Publications:* (jtly) Late Roman Bronze Coinage, 1960; (with K. S. Painter) Wealth of the Roman World, 1977; Roman Coins, 1978; 2000 Years of British Coins and Medals, 1978 (Lhotka Meml Prize, RNS); Roman Imperial Coinage, vol. VIII: the family of Constantine I 337–364, 1981; A Selection of Byzantine Coins in the Barber Institute of Fine Arts, 1985; contribs to Festschriften, congress procs, and Numismatic Chronicle, British Numismatic Jl etc. *Recreations:* local history and archaeology, early (mediaeval) music, railway history and model railways, monumental brasses. *Address:* 16 Newmans Way, Hadley Wood, Barnet, Herts EN4 0LR. *T:* 01–449 8072.

KENT, Paul Welberry, DSc; FRSC; JP; Student Emeritus of Christ Church, Oxford; *b* Doncaster, 19 April 1923; *s* of Thomas William Kent and Marion (*née* Cox); *m* 1952, Rosemary Elizabeth Boutflower, *y d* of Major C. H. B. Shepherd, MC; three *s* one *d*. *Educ:* Doncaster Grammar Sch.; Birmingham Univ. (BSc 1944, PhD 1947); Jesus Coll., Oxford (MA 1952, DPhil 1953, DSc 1966). Asst Lectr, subseq. ICI Fellow, Birmingham Univ., 1946–50; Vis. Fellow, Princeton Univ., 1948–49; Univ. Demonstrator in Biochem., Oxford, 1950–72; Lectr, subseq. Student, Tutor and Dr Lees Reader in Chem., Christ Church, 1955–72; Master of Van Mildert Coll. and Dir, Glycoprotein Res. Unit, Durham Univ., 1972–82. Research Assoc., Harvard, 1967; Vis. Prof., Windsor Univ., Ont, 1971, 1980. Mem., Oxford City Council, 1964–72; Governor, Oxford Coll. of Technology, subseq. Oxford Polytechnic, 1964–72, 1983– (Vice-Chm. 1966–69, Chm. 1969–70); Member: Cttee, Biochemical Soc., 1963–67; Chemical Council, 1965–70; Res. Adv. Cttee, Cystic Fibrosis Res. Trust, 1977–82; Commn on Religious Educn in School. Sec., Foster and Wills Scholarships Bd, 1960–72; Pres., Soc. for Maintenance of the Faith, 1975–; Governor, Pusey House, 1983–. JP Oxford, 1972. Hon. DLitt Drury Coll., 1973. Hon. Fellow, Canterbury Coll., Ont, 1976. Rolleston Prize, 1952; Medal of Société de Chemie Biologique, 1969; Verdienstkreuz (Bundesrepublik), 1970. *Publications:* Biochemistry of Amino-sugars, 1955; (ed) Membrane-Mediated Information, Vols I and II, 1972; (ed) International Aspects of the Provision of Medical Care, 1976; (ed) New Approaches to Genetics, 1978; (ed with W. B. Fisher) Resources, Environment and the Future, 1982; articles in sci. and other jls. *Recreations:* music, travel. *Address:* 18 Arnolds Way, Cumnor Hill, Oxford OX2 9JB. *T:* Oxford 862087; Briscoe Gate, Cotherstone, Barnard Castle, Co. Durham. *Club:* Athenæum.

KENT, Ronald Clive, CB 1965; Deputy Under-Secretary of State, MoD, 1967–76; *b* 3 Aug. 1916; *s* of Dr Hugh Braund Kent and Margaret Mary Kent; *m* 1965, Mary Moyles Havell; one step-*s* one step-*d*. *Educ:* Rugby Sch.; Brasenose Coll., Oxford. Air Ministry, 1939; Royal Artillery, 1940–45; Air Ministry, 1945–58; Asst Under-Sec. of State, Air Min., 1958–63, MoD, 1963–67. Dir (Admin), ICE, 1976–79, Consultant and Council Sec., 1980–85. *Address:* 10 Radnor Court, Linkfield Street, Redhill, Surrey RH1 6BZ.

KENT, Brig. Sidney Harcourt, OBE 1944; *b* 22 April 1915; *s* of Major Geoffrey Harcourt Kent, Hindhead; *m* 1945, Nina Ruth, *d* of Gen. Sir Geoffry Scoones, KCB, KBE, CSI, DSO, MC; one *s* one *d*. *Educ:* Wellington Coll.; RMC Sandhurst. 2nd Lieut KOYLI, 1935; Lt-Col 1944; Brig. 1944; GSO1 Eighth Army, 1944; BGS Allied Land Forces, SE Asia, 1944. Comd 128 Inf. Bde (TA), 1960–63. Manager and Sec., Turf Board, 1965; Gen. Manager, 1969, Chief Executive, 1973–76, The Jockey Club. Racing Adviser, Royal Horse Soc., Iran, 1978; Consultant Steward, Jamaica Racing Commn, 1984–86. *Recreations:* farming, travel. *Address:* The Old Vicarage, Kingsey, Aylesbury, Bucks. *T:* Haddenham 291411.

KENT, Thomas George, CBE 1979; CEng, MIMechE, FRAeS; Group Deputy Chief Executive, British Aerospace Dynamics Group, since 1980; Board Member, British Aerospace, since 1981; Chairman, since 1984, Director, since 1980, British Aerospace Australia Ltd; *b* 13 Aug. 1925. *Educ:* Borden Grammar School; Medway College of Technology. Joined English Electric Co., 1951; Special Director, British Aircraft Corp., 1967; Dep. Managing Director, 1974. Director, Hatfield/Lostock Division and Stevenage/Bristol Div. of Dynamics Group, British Aerospace, 1977–79. Director: Arab British Dynamics, 1980–; BAJ Vickers Ltd, 1982– (non.-exec.). *Address:* Mereworth, 5 Deards Wood, Knebworth, Herts. *T:* Stevenage 812057; British Aerospace, Dynamics Group, Stevenage, Herts. *T:* Stevenage 2422.

KENT-JONES, Trevor David, TD; a Recorder, since 1985; barrister; *b* 31 July 1940; *s* of late David Sandford Kent-Jones and of Madeline Mary Kent-Jones (*née* Russell-Pavier); *m* 1972, Angela Rosalind, *d* of Norman Stead Lodge, JP; one *s* one *d*. *Educ:* Bedford Sch.; Liverpool Univ. (LLB). Called to the Bar, Gray's Inn, 1962. Mem., NE Circuit, 1963–. Commnd KOYLI TA, 1959; served 4th Bn KOYLI, 5th Bn Light Infantry, HQ NE Dist, 1959–; Lt-Col 1977. *Recreations:* rifle shooting, cricket, travel. *Address:* 10 Park Square, Leeds LS1 2LH; 6 Beechwood Crescent, Harrogate, N Yorks HG2 0PA. *Club:* Naval and Military.

KENTNER, Louis Philip, CBE 1978; Concert Pianist and Composer; *b* Silesia, 19 July 1905; *s* of Julius and Gisela Kentner; *m* 1931, Ilona Kabos (marr. diss. 1945); *m* 1946, Griselda Gould, *d* of late Evelyn Suart; no *c. Educ*: Budapest, Royal Academy of Music (at age of 6) under Arnold Szekely, Leo Weiner, Zoltan Kodaly. Concert début Budapest at age of 15; awarded a Chopin prize, Warsaw, a Liszt prize, Budapest. Has given concerts in most European countries; toured South Africa, Far East, New Zealand, Australia, S America: 6 tours of USA; three tours of USSR. First world performance, Bartok 2nd Piano Concerto, Budapest, and first European performance, Bartok 3rd Piano Concerto, London, 1946; many first performances of Kodaly and Weiner's Piano works; first performance: Rawsthorne's First Piano Concerto, London; Tippett's Piano Concerto, London. Came to England, 1935; naturalised British, 1946; since residence in England played much modern British music. Played numerous troop concerts during War of 1939–45. Has made many gramophone recordings. President: Liszt Society, 1965–; European Piano Teachers Assoc., 1978–. Hon. RAM 1970. *Publications*: Three Sonatinas for Piano, 1939; two essays in Liszt Symposium, 1967; The Piano, 1976. *Recreations*: reading, chess playing. *Address*: 1 Mallord Street, Chelsea, SW3.

KENTRIDGE, Sydney; QC 1984; *b* Johannesburg, 5 Nov. 1922; *s* of Morris and May Kentridge; *m* 1952, Felicia Geffen; two *s* two *d. Educ*: King Edward VII Sch., Johannesburg; Univ. of the Witwatersrand (BA); Exeter Coll., Oxford Univ. (MA; Hon. Fellow, 1986). War service with S African forces, 1942–46. Advocate 1949, Senior Counsel 1965, South Africa; called to the English Bar, Lincoln's Inn, 1977, Bencher, 1986. Mem., Ct of Appeal, Botswana, 1981–. Roberts Lectr, Univ. of Pennsylvania, 1979. Hon. LLD Leicester, 1985. Granville Clark Prize, USA, 1978. *Recreation*: opera-going. *Address*: 1 Brick Court, Temple, EC4. *T*: 01–583 0777. *Club*: Athenæum.

KENWARD, Michael; Editor, New Scientist, since 1979; *b* 12 July 1945; *s* of Ronald Kenward and Phyllis Kenward; *m* 1969, Elizabeth Rice. *Educ*: Wolverstone Hall; Sussex Univ. Res. scientist, UKAEA, Culham Laboratory, 1966–68; Technical editor, Scientific Instrument Res. Assoc., 1969; various editorial posts, New Scientist, 1969–79. Mem., Royal Soc. Cttee on Public Understanding of Science. *Publications*: Potential Energy, 1976; articles on science and technology and energy in particular. *Recreations*: photography, collecting 'middle-aged' books. *Address*: Grange Cottage, Staplefield, W Sussex.

KENWORTHY, family name of **Baron Strabolgi.**

KENWORTHY, Cecil; Registrar of Family Division (formerly Probate and Divorce Division), of High Court of Justice, 1968–83; *b* 22 Jan. 1918; *s* of John T. and Lucy Kenworthy; *m* 1944, Beryl Joan Willis, no *c. Educ*: Manchester and Bristol Grammar Schools. Entered Principal Probate Registry, 1936. *Publications*: (co-editor) supplements to Rayden on Divorce, 1967, 1968; (co-editor) Tolstoy on Divorce, 7th edn, 1971. *Address*: 526 Ben Jonson House, Barbican, EC2.

KENWORTHY, Frederick John; Director of Operations, Disablement Services Division, Department of Health and Social Security, since 1986; *b* 6 Dec. 1943; *s* of late Rev. Fred Kenworthy and of Mrs Ethel Kenworthy; *m* 1968, Diana Flintham; one *d. Educ*: William Hulme's Grammar Sch., Manchester; Manchester Univ. (BA Econ Hons, Politics). Entered Admin. Class, Home Civil Service, as Asst Principal, MoD (Navy), 1966; Treasury Centre for Admin. Studies, 1968–69; joined BSC, Sheffield, 1969; Principal, MoD, 1972; Royal Commn on the Press Secretariat, 1974; Asst Sec., Dir, Weapons Resources and Progs (Naval), MoD, 1979–83; Head of Resources and Progs (Navy) (formerly DS4), RN Size and Shape Policy, MoD, 1983–86. *Recreations*: music, sport, photography. *Address*: The Meadows, Skellingthorpe, Lincs LN6 0RH; 108 Dewsbury Road, Dollis Hill, NW10 1EP. *T*: 01–452 5506. *Club*: Lansdown Lawn Tennis and Squash Racquets (Bath).

KENWORTHY, Joan Margaret, BLitt, MA; Principal, St Mary's College, University of Durham, since 1977; *b* Oldham, Lancs, 10 Dec. 1933; *o d* of late Albert Kenworthy and Amy (*née* Cobbold). *Educ*: Girls Grammar Sch., Barrow-in-Furness; St Hilda's Coll., Oxford (BLitt, MA). Henry Oliver Beckit Prize, Oxford, 1955; Leverhulme Overseas Res. Scholar, Makerere Coll., Uganda, and E African Agriculture and Forestry Res. Org., Kenya, 1956–58; Actg Tutor, St Hugh's Coll., Oxford, 1958–59; Tutorial Res. Fellow, Bedford Coll., London, 1959–60; Univ. of Liverpool: Asst Lectr in Geography, 1960–63; Lectr, 1963–73; Sen. Lectr, 1973–77; Warden of Salisbury Hall, 1966–77 and of Morton House, 1974–77. IUC short-term Vis. Lectr, Univ. of Sierra Leone, 1975; Vis. Lectr, Univ. of Fort Hare, Ciskei, 1983. Mem., NE England, Churches Regl Broadcasting Council, 1978–82. Member: Council, African Studies Assoc. of UK, 1969–71; Council, Inst. of Brit. Geographers, 1976–78; Cttee, Merseyside Conf. for Overseas Students Ltd, 1976–77; Council, RMetS, 1980–83; Treasurer, Assoc. of Brit. Climatologists, 1976–79; Northern Chm., Durham Univ. Soc., 1979–82. *Publications*: (contrib.) Geographers and the Tropics, ed R. W. Steel and R. M. Prothero, 1964; (contrib.) Oxford Regional Economic Atlas for Africa, 1965; (contrib.) Studies in East African Geography and Development, ed S. Ominde, 1971; (contrib.) An Advanced Geography of Africa, ed J. I. Clarke, 1975; (contrib.) Rangeland Management and Ecology in East Africa, ed D. J. Pratt and M. D. Gwynne, 1977; (contrib.) The Climatic Scene: essays in honour of Emeritus Prof. Gordon Manley, ed M. J. Tooley and G. Sheail,1985; articles in jls and encycs. *Address*: 1 Elvet Garth, South Road, Durham DH1 3TP. *T*: Durham 43865. *Club*: Royal Commonwealth Society.

KENWORTHY-BROWNE, (Bernard) Peter (Francis); Registrar of the High Court (Family Division), since 1982; *b* 11 May 1930; *s* of late Bernard Elelyn Kenworthy-Browne and Margaret Sibylla Kenworthy-Browne; *m* 1975, Jane Elizabeth Arthur (marr. diss. 1982). *Educ*: Ampleforth; Oriel Coll., Oxford. MA. 2nd Lieut, Irish Guards, 1949–50. Called to the Bar, Lincoln's Inn, 1955; Oxford, and Midland and Oxford Circuit, 1957–82; a Recorder of the Crown Court, 1981–82. *Recreations*: music, hunting, shooting. *Address*: 30 Dewhurst Road, W14 0ES. *T*: 01–603 9580.

KENYA, Archbishop of, since 1980; **Most Rev. Manasses Kuria;** Bishop of Nairobi, since 1980; *b* 22 July 1929; *s* of John Njoroge Kuria; *m* 1947, Mary Kuria; two *s* four *d. Educ*: locally. Teaching, 1944–53; Deacon, 1955; ordained Priest, 1957; Archdeacon of Eldoret, 1965–70; Asst Bishop of Nakuru, 1970–75; Bishop of Nakuru, 1976–79. *Publication*: Uwakili Katika Kristo (Stewardship of Christ), 1969. *Address*: PO Box 40502, Nairobi, Kenya. *T*: 721838/723394/28146.

KENYON, family name of **Baron Kenyon.**

KENYON, 5th Baron, *cr* 1788; **Lloyd Tyrell-Kenyon,** CBE 1972; FSA; DL; Bt 1784; Baron of Gredington, 1788; Captain late Royal Artillery, TA; *b* 13 Sept. 1917; *o s* of 4th Baron and Gwladys Julia (*d* 1965), *d* of late Col H. R. Lloyd Howard, CB; S father, 1927; *m* 1946, Leila Mary, *d* of Comdr John Wyndham Cookson, RN, Strand Hill, Winchelsea, and Mary, *d* of Sir Alan Colquhoun, 6th Bt, KCB, JP, DL, and *widow* of Lt Hugh William Jardine Ethelston Peel, Welsh Guards; two *s* one *d* (and one *s* decd). *Educ*: Eton; Magdalene Coll., Cambridge. BA (Cambridge), 1950. 2nd Lt Shropshire Yeo. 1937; Lt RA, TA, retired (ill-health) 1943 with hon. rank of Captain. Dir, Lloyds Bank Plc, 1962– (Chm. North West Bd); President: University Coll. of N Wales, Bangor, 1947–82; Nat. Museum of Wales, 1952–57. Trustee, Nat. Portrait Gall., 1953–, Chm., 1966–; Chairman:

Wrexham Powys and Mawddach Hosp. Management Cttee, 1960–74; Clwyd AHA, 1974–78; Friends of the Nat. Libraries, 1962–85; Flint Agricultural Exec. Cttee, 1964–73. Member: Standing Commn on Museums and Galleries, 1953–60; Welsh Regional Hosp. Bd, 1958–63; Council for Professions Supplementary to Medicine, 1961–65; Royal Commn on Historical MSS, 1966–; Ancient Monuments Bd for Wales, 1979–; Bd of Governors, Welbeck Coll. Chief Comr for Wales, Boy Scouts' Assoc., 1948–65. DL Co. Flint, 1948; CC Flint, 1946 (Chm., 1954–55). Hon. LLD Wales, 1958. *Heir: s* Hon. Lloyd Tyrell-Kenyon, [*b* 13 July 1947; *m* 1971, Sally Carolyn, *e d* of J. F. P. Matthews; two *s*]. *Address*: Cumbers House, Gredington, Whitchurch, Salop SY13 3DH. *TA*: Hanmer 330. *T*: Hanmer 330. *Clubs*: Brooks's, Cavalry and Guards, Beefsteak.

KENYON, Clifford, CBE 1966; JP; farmer; *b* 11 Aug. 1896; *m* 1922, Doris Muriel Lewis, Herne Hill, London; three *s* two *d. Educ*: Brighton Grove Coll., Manchester; Manchester Univ. Joined Labour Party, 1922; Mem. Rawtenstall Council, 1923; Mayor, 1938–42, resigned from Council, 1945. MP (Lab) Chorley Div. of Lancs, 1945–70. JP Lancs, 1941. *Address*: Scarr Barn Farm, Crawshawbooth, Rossendale, Lancs. *T*: Rossendale 5703.

KENYON, Sir George (Henry), Kt 1976; DL; JP; LLD; *b* 10 July 1912; *s* of George Henry Kenyon and Edith (*née* Hill); *m* 1938, Christine Dorey (*née* Brentnall); two *s* one *d. Educ*: Radley; Manchester Univ. Director: William Kenyon & Sons Ltd, 1942– (Chm., 1961–82); Tootal Ltd, 1971–79 (Chm., 1976–79); Manchester Ship Canal, 1972; Williams & Glyn's Bank, 1972–83 (Chm., 1978–83); Royal Bank of Scotland, 1975–83; Chm., Vuman Ltd, 1982–. Gen. Comr, Inland Revenue, 1957–73. Manchester University: Chm. Bldgs Cttee, 1962–70; Treas., 1970–72, 1980–82; Chm. Council, 1972–80. Hon. Treas., Civic Trust, NW, 1962–78, Vice Pres., 1978; Member: NW Adv. Cttee, Civil Aviation, 1967–72; Manchester Reg. Hosp. Bd, 1962–68; NW Reg. Econ. Planning Council, 1970–73. JP Cheshire, 1959; Chm., S Tameside Bench, 1974–82; DL Chester, 1969, Greater Manchester, 1983. High Sheriff, Cheshire, 1973–74. Hon. LLD Manchester, 1980. *Recreations*: reading, talking, travel. *Address*: Limefield House, Hyde, Cheshire. *T*: 061–368 2012.

KENYON, Ian Roy; HM Diplomatic Service; Overseas Inspectorate, since 1986; *b* 13 June 1939; *s* of late S. R. Kenyon and of Mrs E. M. Kenyon; *m* 1962, Griselda Rintoul; one *s* one *d. Educ*: Lancaster Royal Grammar School; Edinburgh University. BSc Hons. CEng, MIChemE. Lever Bros, 1962–68; Birds Eye Foods, 1968–74; First Secretary, FCO, 1974–76; Geneva, 1976–78; Head of Chancery, Bogota, 1979–81; FCO, 1982–83; Head of Nuclear Energy Dept, FCO, 1983–85. *Recreation*: riding. *Address*: c/o Foreign and Commonwealth Office, SW1A 2AH. *Club*: Travellers'.

KENYON, Prof. John Philipps, FBA 1981; Professor of Modern History, University of St Andrews, since 1981; *b* 18 June 1927; *s* of William Houston Kenyon and Edna Grace Philipps; *m* 1962, Angela Jane Ewert (*née* Venables); one *s* two *d. Educ*: King Edward VII Sch., Sheffield; Univ. of Sheffield (BA; Hon. LittD, 1980); Christ's Coll., Cambridge (PhD). Fellow of Christ's Coll., Cambridge, 1954–62; Lectr in Hist., Cambridge, 1955–62; G. F. Grant Prof. of History, Univ. of Hull, 1962–81. Visiting Prof., Columbia Univ., New York, 1959–60; Junior Proctor, Cambridge, 1961–62; John U. Nef Lectr, Univ. of Chicago, 1972; Ford's Lectr in English Hist., Oxford, 1975–76; Andrew W. Mellon Fellow, Huntington Library, Calif, 1985. *Publications*: Robert Spencer Earl of Sunderland, 1958; The Stuarts, 1958, 2nd edn 1970; The Stuart Constitution, 1966; The Popish Plot, 1972; Revolution Principles, 1977; Stuart England, 1978; The History Men, 1983; contribs to various learned jls. *Recreation*: bridge. *Address*: 82 Hepburn Gardens, St Andrews, Fife KY16 9LN. *T*: St Andrews 73356.

KEOHANE, Desmond John, FBIM; Principal, Oxford College of Further Education, since 1976; *b* 5 July 1928; *s* of William Patrick Keohane and Mabel Margaret Keohane; *m* 1960, Mary Kelliher; two *s* two *d. Educ*: Borden Grammar Sch., Sittingbourne; Univ. of Birmingham (BA and Baxter Prize in History, 1949); London Univ. (Postgrad. Cert. in Educn). FBIM 1981. Postgrad. res., 1949–50; Nat. Service, Educn Officer, RAF, 1950–52; sch. teacher and coll. lectr, 1953–64; Head, Dept of Social and Academic Studies, 1964–68, and Vice-Principal, 1969–71, Havering Technical Coll.; Principal, Northampton Coll. of Further Educn, 1971–76. Member: Council, Southern Regional Council for Further Educn, 1977– (Chm., Adv. Cttee for Health and Social Services, 1983–85); Secondary Exams Council, 1983–86; Berks and Oxon Area Manpower Board, 1985–; Special Employment Measures Adv. Gp, MSC, 1986–. Governor: Oxford Area Arts Council, 1980–85; Thomas Becket Sch., Northampton, 1973– (Chm., 1983–); St Mary's Sch., Northampton, 1972–; Oxford Sch., 1982–86; Oxford Polytechnic, 1983–. *Recreations*: enjoying family and friends, watching cricket. *Address*: 14 Abington Park Crescent, Northampton NN3 3AD. *T*: Northampton 38829; Oxford College of Further Education, Oxpens Road, Oxford OX1 1SA. *T*: Oxford 245871.
See also K. W. Keohane.

KEOHANE, Dr Kevin William, CBE 1976; Rector, Roehampton Institute of Higher Education, since 1976; *b* 28 Feb. 1923; *s* of William Patrick and Mabel Margaret Keohane; *m* 1949, Mary Margaret (Patricia) Ashford; one *s* three *d. Educ*: Borden Grammar Sch., Sittingbourne, Kent; Univ. of Bristol (BSc; PhD). FInstP. War service, RAF, Radar Br. Research appts and Lectr in Anatomy, Univ. of Bristol, 1947–59; Chelsea College, London: Reader in Biophysics, 1959; Prof. of Physics and Head of Dept of Physics, 1965; Prof. of Science Educn and Dir, Centre for Science Educn, 1967–76; Vice-Principal, 1966–76. Royal Society Leverhulme Prof., Fed. Univ. of Bahia, Brazil, 1971; Vis. Prof., Chelsea College, 1977–82. Member: Academic Adv. Cttee, Open Univ., 1970–81 (Chm., 1978–81); Court, Univ. of Bristol, 1968–76; Court, Univ. of Surrey, 1982–; University of London: Member: Academic Council, 1974–76; Extra-Mural Council, 1974–76; School Examinations Council, 1975–76. Dir, Nuffield Foundn Science Projects, 1966–79; Chairman: DES Study Gp on Cert. of Extended Educn, 1978–79; Education Cttee, Commonwealth Inst., 1978–85; Nuffield-Chelsea Curriculum Trust, 1979–; Vice Chm., Internat. Adv. Panel for Provincial Univs in China, 1986–; Member: Nat. Programme Cttee for Computers in Educn, 1974–78; Royal Society/Inst. of Physics Educn Cttee, 1970–73; SSRC Educn Bd, 1971–74; BBC Further Educn Adv. Cttee, 1972–75; TEAC, RAF, 1977–79; Gen. Optical Council, 1979–84; Bd of Educn, Royal Coll. of Nursing, 1980–84; National Adv. Bd for Higher Educn, 1983–. Manager, Royal Instn, 1972–75. Mem. Delegacy, Goldsmiths' Coll., 1974–76; Chm. of Governors, Garnett Coll., 1974–78; Governor: Philippa Fawcett and Digby Stuart Colls, 1973–76; Ursuline Convent Sch., Wimbledon, 1967–; Heythrop Coll., Univ. of London, 1977–; Wimbledon Coll., 1982–; Commonwealth Inst., 1977–85; Chm. of Governors, St Francis Xavier VIth Form Coll., 1985–. Numerous overseas consultancies and visiting professorships; Academic Mem., British Assoc. of Science Writers, 1971–; Editor, Jl of Physics Educn, 1966–69; Mem., Editorial Bd, Jl Curriculum Studies, and Studies in Sci. Educn. KSG 1983. *Recreations*: Rugby (spectator), railways, bee-keeping. *Address*: Roehampton Institute, Grove House, Roehampton Lane, SW15 5PJ. *T*: 01–878 5751; 3 Thetford Road, New Malden, Surrey. *T*: 01–942 6861. *Club*: Athenæum.
See also D. J. Keohane.

KEPA, Sailosi Wai; High Commissioner for Fiji in London, since 1985; *b* 4 Nov. 1938; *m* Adi Teimumu Tuisawau; four *c. Educ*: Draiba Fijian Sch.; Lelean Memorial Sch.;

Nasinu Training Coll.; Sydney Univ. (Dip. in Teaching of English, 1966). Called to the Bar, Middle Temple, 1972; Barrister and Solicitor, Fiji, 1974. Joined Judicial Dept, as Magistrate, 1969; served Suva, Northern Div., Sigatoka, Nadi; Chief Magistrate, July 1980; Dir of Public Prosecutions, Nov. 1980. Rugby player (rep. Fiji, Australia 1961), coach, manager, administrator; Chm., Fiji Rugby Union, 1983–85. *Address:* 34 Hyde Park Gate, SW7 5BN. *T:* 01–584 3661.

KEPPEL, family name of **Earl of Albemarle.**

KEPPEL-COMPTON, Robert Herbert, CMG 1953; *b* 11 Dec. 1900; *s* of late J. H. Keppel-Compton, Southampton; *m* 1930, Marjorie, *yr d* of late Rev. W. B. Preston; one *s* one *d. Educ:* Oakham Sch.; Sidney Sussex Coll., Cambridge. BA, LLB Cantab. Entered Colonial Administrative Service, 1923. Dep. Provincial Commissioner, 1945; Development Sec., 1946; Provincial Commissioner, Nyasaland, 1949–55; retired from Colonial Service, 1955. *Address:* April Cottage, Churchstow, Kingsbridge, Devon.

KER, *see* Innes-Ker, family name of **Duke of Roxburghe.**

KERBY, John Vyvyan; Under Secretary and Principal Establishment Officer, Overseas Development Administration, Foreign and Commonwealth Office, since 1986; *b* 14 Dec. 1942; *s* of Theo Rosser Fred Kerby and Constance Mary (*née* Newell); *m* 1978, Shirley Elizabeth Pope; one step *s* one step *d. Educ:* Eton Coll.; Christ Church, Oxford (MA). Temp. Asst Principal, CO, 1965; Asst Principal, ODM, 1967; Pvte Sec. to Parly Under-Sec. of State, FCO, 1970; Principal, ODA, 1971–74, 1975–77; CSSB, 1974–75; Asst Sec., ODA, 1977; Head of British Develt Div. in Southern Africa, 1983. *Recreations:* gardening, cricket, music, entomology. *Address:* c/o Overseas Development Administration, Eland House, Stag Place, SW1. *T:* 01–213 4849.

KEREMA, Archbishop of, (RC), since 1976; **Most Rev. Virgil Copas,** KBE 1982; DD; Member of Religious Order of Missionaries of Sacred Heart (MSC); *b* 19 March 1915; *s* of Cornelius Copas and Kathleen (*née* Daly). *Educ:* St Mary's Coll. and Downlands Coll., Toowoomba, Queensland. Sec. to Bp L. Scharmach, Rabaul, New Britain, New Guinea, 1945–51; Religious Superior, Dio. of Darwin, Australia, 1954–60; Bishop of Port Moresby, 1960–66; Archbishop of Port Moresby, 1966–76, resigned in favour of a national archbishop. *Address:* Catholic Church, Box 90, PO Kerema, Gulf Province, Papua New Guinea, Oceania. *T:* Kerema 681079.

KERLE, Rt. Rev. Ronald Clive; Rector of St Swithun's Pymble, Diocese of Sydney, since 1976; *b* 28 Dec. 1915; *s* of William Alfred Ronald Kerle and Isabel Ada (*née* Turner); *m* 1940, Helen Marshall Jackson; one *s* one *d. Educ:* Univ. of Sydney (BA); Moore Theological Coll., Sydney. Sydney ACT, ThL 1937; BA 1942. Deacon 1939; Priest, 1940; Curate, St Paul's, Sydney, 1939; St Anne, Ryde, 1939–41; Rector, Kangaroo Valley, 1941–43; St Stephen, Port Kembla, 1943–47; Chaplain, AIF, 1945–47; Gen. Sec., NSW Branch, Church Missionary Society, 1947–54; Rector of Summer Hill, 1954–56; Archdeacon of Cumberland, 1954–60; Bishop Co-adjutor of Sydney, 1956–65; Bishop of Armidale, 1965–76. *Address:* Rectory, 11 Merrivale Road, Pymble, NSW 2073, Australia.

KERMACK, Stuart Ogilvy; Sheriff of Tayside, Central and Fife at Forfar and Arbroath, since 1971; *b* 9 July 1934; *s* of late Stuart Grace Kermack, CBE and of Nell P., *y d* of Thomas White, SSC; *m* 1961, Barbara Mackenzie, BSc; three *s* one *d. Educ:* Glasgow Academy; Jesus Coll., Oxford; Glasgow Univ.; Edinburgh Univ. BA Oxon (Jurisprudence), 1956; LLB Glasgow, 1959. Elected to Scots Bar, 1959. Sheriff Substitute of Inverness, Moray, Nairn and Ross, at Elgin and Nairn, 1965–71. *Publications:* articles in legal journals. *Address:* 7 Little Causeway, Forfar, Angus. *T:* Forfar 64691.

KERMAN, Prof. Joseph Wilfred; Chambers Professor of Music, University of California at Berkeley, since 1986 (Professor of Music, since 1974); *b* 3 April 1924; *m* 1945, Vivian Shaviro; two *s* one *d. Educ:* New York Univ. (AB); Princeton Univ. (PhD). Dir of Graduate Studies, Westminster Choir Coll., Princeton, NJ, USA, 1949–51; Music Faculty, Univ. of California at Berkeley, 1951–72 (Dep. Chm., 1960–63); Heather Prof. of Music, Oxford Univ., and Fellow of Wadham Coll., Oxford, 1972–74. Co-editor, 19th Century Music, 1977–. Guggenheim, Fulbright and NEH Fellowships; Visiting Fellow: All Souls Coll., Oxford, 1966; Society for the Humanities, Cornell Univ., USA, 1970; Clare Hall, Cambridge, 1971; Walker-Ames Vis. Prof., Univ. of Washington, 1986. Fellow, American Academy of Arts and Sciences; Corresp. FBA 1984. Hon. FRAM. Hon. DHL Fairfield Univ., 1970. *Publications:* Opera as Drama, 1956; The Elizabethan Madrigal, 1962; The Beethoven Quartets, 1967; A History of Art and Music (with H. W. Janson), 1968; (ed) Ludwig van Beethoven: Autograph Miscellany, 1786–99 (Kafka Sketchbook), 2 vols, 1970 (Kinkeldey Award); Listen, 1972; The Masses and Motets of William Byrd, 1981 (Kinkeldey Award; Deems Taylor Award); The New Grove Beethoven (with A. Tyson), 1983; (co-ed) Beethoven Studies, vol. 1 1973, vol 2 1977, vol. 3 1982; Musicology, 1985; essays, in music criticism and musicology, in: Hudson Review, New York Review, San Francisco Chronicle, etc. *Address:* Music Department, University of California, Berkeley, Calif 94720, USA; 107 Southampton Avenue, Berkeley, Calif 94707.

KERMODE, Prof. (John) Frank, MA; FBA 1973; Fellow of King's College, Cambridge, since 1974; *b* 29 Nov. 1919; *s* of late John Pritchard Kermode and late Doris Pearl Kermode; *m* 1st, 1947, Maureen Eccles (marr. diss. 1970); twin *s* and *d*; 2nd, 1976, Anita Van Vactor. *Educ:* Douglas High Sch.; Liverpool Univ. BA 1940; War Service (Navy), 1940–46; MA 1947; Lecturer, King's Coll., Newcastle, in the University of Durham, 1947–49; Lecturer in the University of Reading, 1949–58; John Edward Taylor Prof. of English Literature in the University of Manchester, 1958–65; Winterstoke Prof. of English in the University of Bristol, 1965–67; Lord Northcliffe Prof. of Modern English Lit., UCL, 1967–74; King Edward VII Prof. of English Literature, Cambridge Univ., 1974–82. Charles Eliot Norton Prof. of Poetry at Harvard, 1977–78. Co-editor, Encounter, 1966–67. Editor: Fontana Masterguides and Modern Masters series; Oxford Authors. FRSL 1958. Mem. Arts Council, 1968–71; Chm., Poetry Book Soc., 1968–76. For. Hon. Mem., Amer. Acad. of Arts and Scis. Hon. DHL Chicago, 1975; Hon. DLitt Liverpool, 1981. Officier de l'Ordre des Arts et des Sciences. *Publications:* (ed) Shakespeare, The Tempest (Arden Edition), 1954; Romantic Image, 1957; John Donne, 1957; The Living Milton, 1960; Wallace Stevens, 1960; Puzzles & Epiphanies, 1962; The Sense of an Ending, 1967; Continuities, 1968; Shakespeare, Spenser, Donne, 1971; Modern Essays, 1971; Lawrence, 1973; (ed, with John Hollander) Oxford Anthology of English Literature, 1973; The Classic, 1975; (ed) Selected Prose of T. S. Eliot, 1975; The Genesis of Secrecy, 1979; Essays on Fiction, 1971–82, 1983; Forms of Attention, 1985; contrib. Review of Eng. Studies, Partisan Review, New York Review, New Statesman, London Rev. of Books, etc. *Address:* King's College, Cambridge CB2 1ST. *T:* Cambridge 350411; 27 Luard Road, Cambridge. *T:* Cambridge 247398.

KERMODE, Hon. Sir Ronald (Graham Quayle), KBE 1986 (CBE 1975); Judge of the Court of Appeal, Fiji, since 1985; *b* 26 June 1919; *s* of George Graham Kermode and Linda Margaret (*née* McInnis); *m* 1945, Amy Rivett Marr; two *s* two *d. Educ:* Whangarei High Sch., NZ; Auckland University Coll. (LLB). Served with NZ and Fiji Mil. Forces, 1939–45. In private legal practice, 1945–75; Puisne Judge, Supreme Court of Fiji,

1976–86; Judge of the Court of Appeal, Republic of Kiribati, 1983–. Tribunal, Fiji Sugar Industry, 1985–. Elected European MLC, Fiji, 1958, and served for 15 years as Mem. of Council and Parliament; first elected Speaker of the House of Representatives, 1968–73. *Recreations:* golf, contract bridge, reading, gardening, bird watching. *Address:* 12 Hedge Row, Pakuranga, Auckland, New Zealand. *T:* 564393.

KERN, Karl-Heinz; Ambassador of German Democratic Republic to the Court of St James's, 1973–80; *b* 18 Feb. 1930; *m* 1952, Ursula Bennmann; one *s. Educ:* King George Gymnasium, Dresden; Techn. Coll., Dresden (chem. engrg); Acad. for Polit. Science and Law (Dipl. jur., post-grad. History). Leading posts in diff. regional authorities of GDR until 1959; foreign policy, GDR, 1959–62; Head of GDR Mission in Ghana, 1962–66; Head of African Dept, Min. of For. Affairs, 1966–71; Minister and Chargé d'Affaires, Gt Britain, 1973. Holds Order of Merit of the Fatherland, etc. *Recreations:* sport, reading, music. *Address:* Ministry of Foreign Affairs, 102 Berlin, Marx Engels Platz, German Democratic Republic.

KERNOHAN, Thomas Hugh, CBE 1978 (OBE 1955); Parliamentary Commissioner for Administration and Commissioner for Complaints, Northern Ireland, since 1980; *b* 11 May 1922; *s* of Thomas Watson Kernohan and Caroline Kernohan; *m* 1948, Margaret Moore; one *s* one *d. Educ:* Carrickfergus Model Sch.; Carrickfergus Technical Sch. On staff (admin), Harland & Wolff Ltd, Belfast, 1940–44; Engineering Employers' NI Association: Asst Sec., 1945; Sec., 1953; Dir, 1966–80; Founder, 1959, and Chm., 1961–80, family joinery and plastic firm, Kernohans Joinery Works Ltd. *Recreations:* Rugby (management now), boating, fishing. *Address:* Beach House, Island Park, Greenisland, Carrickfergus, N Ireland BT38 8TW. *T:* Whiteabbey 62030.

KERR, family name of **Marquess of Lothian** and **Baron Teviot.**

KERR, Prof. Allen, FRS 1986; FAA; Professor of Plant Pathology, University of Adelaide, since 1980; *b* 21 May 1926; *s* of A. B. Kerr and J. T. Kerr (*née* White); *m* 1951, Rosemary Sheila Strachan; two *s* one *d. Educ:* George Heriot's Sch., Edinburgh; Univ. of Edinburgh. North of Scotland Coll. of Agric., 1947–51; University of Adelaide: Lectr, 1951–59; Sen. Lectr, 1959–67 (seconded to Tea Research Inst., Ceylon, 1963–66); Reader, 1968–80. *Recreation:* golf. *Address:* 5 Kent Avenue, Glenalta, SA 5052, Australia. *T:* 278–2967.

KERR, Andrew Stevenson, CBE 1976; arbitrator in industrial relations disputes; *b* 28 Aug. 1918; *s* of John S. Kerr and Helen L. Kerr; *m* 1946, Helen Reid Bryden; two *s* two *d. Educ:* Spiers' Sch., Beith, Ayrshire; Glasgow Univ. MA (Hons). Served Army, 1940–46. Entered Min. of Labour, 1947; general employment work in the Ministry, in Scotland, 1947–63; Industrial Relns Officer for Scotland, Min. of Labour, 1964–66; Dep. Chief Conciliation Officer, Min. of Labour, 1966–68; Chief Conciliation Officer, Dept of Employment, 1968–71; Controller (Scotland), Dept of Employment, 1972–74; Chief Conciliation Officer, ACAS, 1974–80. *Recreations:* golf, history. *Address:* 11 Forest Way, Tunbridge Wells, Kent TN2 5HA. *T:* Tunbridge Wells 24858.

KERR, Archibald Brown, CBE 1968 (OBE 1945); TD; Hon. Consulting Surgeon, Western Infirmary, Glasgow (Surgeon, 1954–72); *b* 17 Feb. 1907; *s* of late Robert Kerr and Janet Harvey Brown; *m* 1940, Jean Margaret, *d* of late John Cowan, MBE; one *d. Educ:* High Sch. and University of Glasgow. BSc 1927; MB, ChB 1929; Hon. LLD, 1973; FRFPSGlas. 1933; FRCSEd 1934; FRCSGlas. 1962. Asst to Prof. Path. Glasgow Univ., 1931–33; Surg. to Out-Patients, West. Infirm. Glasgow, 1932–39. Served in 156 (Lowland) Field Amb. and as Surgical Specialist, Officer in Charge of Surgical Div. and Col Comdg No. 23 (Scottish) Gen. Hosp., 1939–45. Surg. to Royal Alexandra Infirmary, Paisley, 1946–54; Asst Surg., West. Infirm., Glasgow, 1945–54. Lectr in Clinical Surgery, Univ. of Glasgow, 1946–72. Pres. 1951–52, Hon. Mem. 1971, Royal Medico-Chirurgical Society of Glasgow; Pres., Royal College of Physicians and Surgeons of Glasgow, 1964–66. Mem., Western Regional Hosp. Bd. Mem. Court, Univ. of Glasgow, 1974–82. Periods on Council of RCPS Glasgow and RCS Edinburgh. *Publications:* The Western Infirmary 1874–1974, 1974; contribs to Med. and Surg. Jls. *Recreation:* golf. *Address:* 10 Iain Road, Bearsden, Glasgow G61 4LX. *T:* 041–942 0424. *Clubs:* College (University of Glasgow), Royal Scottish Automobile.

KERR, Clark; educator; *b* 17 May 1911; *s* of Samuel W. and Caroline Clark Kerr; *m* 1934, Catherine Spaulding; two *s* one *d. Educ:* Swarthmore Coll. (AB); Stanford Univ. (MA); Univ. of Calif., Berkeley (PhD). Actg Asst Prof., Stanford Univ., 1939–40; Asst Prof., later Assoc. Prof., Univ. of Washington, 1940–45; Prof., Dir, Inst. of Industrial Relations, Univ. of Calif, Berkeley, 1945–52; Chancellor, Univ. of Calif at Berkeley, 1952–58; Pres., Univ. of Calif, 1958–67, now Emeritus President. Chairman: Carnegie Commn on Higher Educn, 1967–74; Carnegie Council on Policy Studies in Higher Educn, 1974–80; Bd, Work in America Inst., 1975–; Bd, Global Perspectives in Educn, 1976–85, now Chm. Emeritus. Govt service with US War Labor Board, 1942–45. Mem. Pres. Eisenhower's Commn on Nat. Goals, President Kennedy and President Johnson Cttee on Labor-Management Policy; Program Dir, Strengthening Presidential Leadership Project, Assoc. of Governing Bds of Univs and Colls, 1982–85; Contract Arbitrator for: Boeing Aircraft Co. and Internat. Assoc. of Machinists, 1944–45; Armour & Co. and United Packinghouse Workers, 1945–47, 1949–52; Waterfront Employers' Assoc. and Internat. Longshoremen's and Warehousemen's Union, 1946–47, etc. Member: Amer. Acad. of Arts and Sciences; Royal Economic Society; Amer. Econ. Assoc.; Nat. Acad. of Arbitrators, etc. Phi Beta Kappa, Kappa Sigma. Trustee, Rockefeller Foundation, 1960–75; Chm., Armour Automation Cttee, 1959–79. Hon. Fellow, LSE, 1977. Hon. LLD: Swarthmore, 1952; Harvard, 1958; Princeton, 1959; Notre Dame, 1964; Chinese Univ. of Hong Kong, 1964; Rochester, 1967; Hon. DLitt, Strathclyde, 1965; Hon. Dr, Bordeaux, 1962, etc. *Publications:* Unions, Management and the Public (jt), 1948 (rev. edns 1960, 1967); (jtly) Industrialism and Industrial Man, 1960 (rev. edns 1964, 1973); The Uses of the University, 1963 (3rd edn 1982); Labor and Management in Industrial Society, 1964 (rev. edn 1972); Marshall, Marx and Modern Times, 1969; (jtly) Industrialism and Industrial Man Reconsidered, 1975; Labor Markets and Wage Determination, 1977; Education and National Development, 1979; The Future of Industrial Societies, 1983; (jtly) The Many Lives of Academic Presidents, 1986; contribs to American Economic Review, Review of Economics and Statistics, Quarterly Jl of Economics, etc. *Recreation:* gardening. *Address:* 8300 Buckingham Drive, El Cerrito, Calif 94530, USA. *T:* 5291910; (office) Institute of Industrial Relations, University of California, Berkeley, Calif 94720. *T:* (415) 642 8106.

KERR, Dr David Leigh; Chief Executive, Manor House Hospital, London NW11, since 1982; *b* 25 March 1923; *s* of Myer Woolf Kerr and Paula (*née* Horowitz); *m* 1st, 1944, Aileen Saddington (marr. diss. 1969); two *s* one *d*; 2nd, 1970, Margaret Dunlop; one *s* two *d. Educ:* Whitgift Sch., Croydon; Middlesex Hosp. Med. Sch., London. Hon. Sec., Socialist Medical Assoc., 1957–63; Hon. Vice-Pres., 1963–72. LCC (Wandsworth, Central), 1958–65, and Coun., London Borough of Wandsworth, 1964–68. Contested (Lab) Wandsworth, Streatham (for Parlt), 1959; MP (Lab) Wandsworth Central, 1964–70. Vis. Lectr in Medicine, Chelsea Coll., 1972–82. War on Want: Dir, 1970–77; Vice-Chm., 1973–74; Chm., 1974–77. Family Doctor, Tooting, 1946–82. Member: Royal Society of Medicine; Inter-departmental Cttee on Death Certification and Coroners.

Governor, British Film Inst., 1966–71. *Recreations:* gardening, photography, squash. *Address:* 19 Calder Avenue, Brookmans Park, Herts AL9 7AH. *T:* Potters Bar 53954.

KERR, Dr David Nicol Sharp, FRCP, FRCPE; Dean, Royal Postgraduate Medical School, University of London, since 1984; *b* 27 Dec. 1927; *s* of William Kerr and Elsie (Ransted) Kerr; *m* 1960, Eleanor Jones; two *s* one *d*. *Educ:* George Watson's Boys' College; Edinburgh University (MB ChB); University of Wisconsin (MSc); FRCPE 1966; FRCP 1967; House Physician and Surgeon, Royal Infirmary, Edinburgh, 1951–52; Exchange scholar, Univ. of Wisconsin, 1952–53; Surgeon Lieut, RNVR, 1953–55; Asst Lectr, Univ. of Edinburgh, 1956–57; Registrar, Hammersmith Hosp., 1957–59; Lectr, Univ. of Durham, 1959–63; Consultant physician, Royal Victoria Infirmary, Newcastle upon Tyne, 1962–83; Senior Lectr, 1963–68, Prof. of Medicine, 1968–83, Univ. of Newcastle upon Tyne. *Publications:* Short Textbook of Renal Disease, 1968; chapters in numerous books incl. Cecil-Loeb Textbook of Medicine and Oxford Textbook of Medicine; articles on renal disease in med. jls. *Recreations:* fell walking, jogging. *Address:* Royal Postgraduate Medical School, Hammersmith Hospital, Du Cane Road, W12 0HS. *T:* 01–743 2030, ext. 3200; 22 Carbery Avenue, W3 9AL. *T:* 01–992 3231.

KERR, Deborah Jane, (Deborah Kerr Viertel); Actress; *b* 30 Sept. 1921; *d* of Capt. Arthur Kerr-Trimmer; *m* 1st, 1945, Sqdn Ldr A. C. Bartley (marr. diss., 1959); two *d*; 2nd, 1960, Peter Viertel. *Educ:* Northumberland House, Clifton, Bristol. Open Air Theatre, Regent's Park, 1939, Oxford Repertory, 1939–40; after an interval of acting in films, appeared on West End Stage; Ellie Dunn in Heartbreak House, Cambridge Theatre, 1943; went to France, Belgium, and Holland for ENSA, playing in Gaslight, 1945. *Films:* Major Barbara, 1940; Love on the Dole, 1940–41; Penn of Pennsylvania, 1941; Hatter's Castle, 1942; The Day Will Dawn, 1942; Life and Death of Colonel Blimp, 1942–43; Perfect Strangers, 1944; I See a Dark Stranger, 1945; Black Narcissus, 1946; The Hucksters and If Winter Comes, 1947 (MGM, Hollywood); Edward My Son, 1948; Please Believe Me, 1949 (MGM, Hollywood); King Solomon's Mines, 1950; Quo Vadis, 1952; Prisoner of Zenda, Julius Caesar, Dream Wife, Young Bess (MGM), 1952; From Here to Eternity, 1953; The End of the Affair, 1955; The Proud and Profane, The King and I, 1956; Heaven Knows, Mr Allison, An Affair to Remember, Tea and Sympathy, 1957; Bonjour Tristesse, 1958; Separate Tables, The Journey, Count Your Blessings, 1959; The Sundowners, The Grass is Greener, The Naked Edge, The Innocents, 1961; The Chalk Garden, The Night of the Iguana, 1964; Casino Royale, 1967; Eye of the Devil, Prudence and the Pill, 1968; The Arrangement, 1970; The Assam Garden, 1985. *Stage:* Tea and Sympathy, NY, 1953; The Day After the Fair, London, 1972, tour of US, 1973–74; Seascape, NY, 1975; Candida, London, 1977; The Last of Mrs Cheyney, tour of US, 1978–79; The Day After the Fair, Melbourne and Sydney, 1979; Overheard, Haymarket, 1981; The Corn in Green, Old Vic, 1985. *Address:* Klosters, 7250 Grisons, Switzerland.

KERR, Desmond Moore, OBE 1970; HM Diplomatic Service; Head of Claims Department, Foreign and Commonwealth Office, since 1983; *b* 23 Jan. 1930; *s* of late Robert John Kerr and Mary Elizabeth Kerr; *m* 1956, Evelyn Patricia South; one *s* two *d*. *Educ:* Methodist Coll., Belfast; Queen's Univ., Belfast. BA Hons (Classics and Ancient History). CRO, 1952; British High Commn, Karachi, 1956–59, Lagos, 1959–62; Second Sec., 1960; Commonwealth Office, 1962–66; First Sec., 1965; Dep. British Govt Rep., West Indies Associated States, 1966–70; FCO, 1970–76; Dep. High Comr, Dacca, 1976–79; High Comr, Swaziland, 1979–83. *Address:* c/o Foreign and Commonwealth Office, SW1.
See also E. Kerr.

KERR, Donald Frederick, CVO 1961; OBE 1960; Manager, Government Press Centre, Foreign and Commonwealth Office, 1976–77, retired; *b* 20 April 1915; *s* of Dr David Kerr, Cheshire; *m* 1942, Elizabeth Hayward (*d* 1978); two *s* one *d*. *Educ:* Sydney High Sch.; University of Sydney (BEcon). Served RAF (Navigator), SEAC, 1942–46. Deputy Director: British Information Services, New Delhi, 1947–53; UK Information Service, Ottawa, 1953–55; UK Information Service, Toronto, 1955–56; Dir, UK Information Service in Canada, Ottawa, 1956–59; Dir, British Information Services in India, New Delhi, 1959–63; Controller (Overseas), COI, 1963–76; on secondment, Dir of Information, Commonwealth Secretariat, Sept. 1969–Sept. 1970. *Recreation:* golf. *Address:* 4 Southdown House, 11 Lansdowne Road, Wimbledon, SW20. *Club:* Royal Wimbledon Golf.

KERR, Dr Edwin, CBE 1986; Chief Officer, Council for National Academic Awards, 1972–86; *b* 1 July 1926; *e s* of late Robert John Kerr and Mary Elizabeth Kerr (*née* Ferguson); *m* 1949, Gertrude Elizabeth (*née* Turbitt); one *s* two *d*. *Educ:* Royal Belfast Academical Instn; Queen's Univ., Belfast (BSc, PhD). FIMA, FBCS. Asst Lectr in Maths, QUB, 1948–52; Lectr in Maths, Coll. of Technology, Birmingham (now Univ. of Aston in Birmingham), 1952–55; Lectr in Maths, Coll. of Science and Technology, Manchester (now Univ. of Manchester Inst. of Science and Technology), 1956–58; Head of Maths Dept, Royal Coll. of Advanced Technology, Salford (now Univ. of Salford), 1958–66; Principal, Paisley Coll. of Technology, 1966–72. Member: Adv. Cttee on Supply and Training of Teachers, 1973–78; Adv. Cttee on Supply and Educn of Teachers, 1980–85; Bd for Local Authority Higher Educn, 1982–85; Bd for Public Sector Higher Educn, 1985–86; Mem. and Vice-Chm., Continuing Educn Standing Cttee, 1985–. President: Soc. for Res. into Higher Educn, 1974–77; The Mathematical Assoc., 1976–77. Hon. FCP 1984; Hon. Fellow, Coventry Lanchester, Newcastle upon Tyne, Portsmouth and Sheffield Polytechnics. Hon. DUniv Open, 1977; Hon. DSc Ulster. *Publications:* (with R. Butler) An Introduction to Numerical Methods, 1962; various mathematical and educational. *Recreation:* gardening. *Address:* The Coppice, Kingfisher Lure, Loudwater, Chorleywood, Herts. *T:* Rickmansworth 720187.
See also D. M. Kerr.

KERR, Francis Robert Newsam, OBE 1962; MC 1940; JP; farmer since 1949; Vice Lieutenant of Berwickshire since 1970; *b* 12 Sept. 1916; *s* of late Henry Francis Hobart Kerr and Gertrude Mary Kerr (*née* Anthony); *m* 1941, Anne Frederica Kitson; two *s* one *d*. *Educ:* Ampleforth College. Regular Officer, The Royal Scots, 1937–49; TA 1952–63; retired as Lt-Col. Member: Berwickshire County Council, 1964–75; SE Scotland Regional Hosp. Bd, 1971–74; Borders Area Health Bd, 1973–81 (Vice-Chm.); Borders Reg. Council, 1974–78; Post Office Users Nat. Council, 1972–73; Whitley Council, 1970–81; Council, Multiple Sclerosis Soc., 1973–. Sheriff of Berwick upon Tweed, 1974; JP Berwickshire, 1975. *Recreations:* country pursuits. *Address:* The Lodge, Blanerne, Duns, Berwickshire TD11 3PZ. *T:* Chirnside 483.

KERR, James, QPM 1979; Chief Constable, Lincolnshire Police, 1977–83; *b* 19 Nov. 1928; *s* of William and Margaret Jane Kerr; *m* 1952, Jean Coupland; one *d*. *Educ:* Carlisle Grammar School. Cadet and Navigating Officer, Merchant Navy, 1945–52 (Union Castle Line, 1949–52). Carlisle City Police and Cumbria Constabulary, 1952–74; Asst Director of Command Courses, Police Staff Coll., Bramshill, 1974; Asst Chief Constable (Operations), North Yorkshire Police, 1975; Deputy Chief Constable, Lincs, 1976. Officer Brother, OStJ, 1980. *Recreations:* music, squash. *Address:* Laythes, Norfolk Road, Carlisle, Cumbria CA2 5PQ. *Clubs:* Carlisle Edenside Bowls, Cumbria Indoor Bowling.

KERR, Rear-Adm. John Beverley; Flag Officer First Flotilla, since 1986; *b* 27 Oct. 1937; *s* of Wilfred Kerr and Vera Kerr (*née* Sproule); *m* 1964, Elizabeth Anne, *d* of late Dr and Mrs C. R. G. Howard, Burley, Hants; three *s*. *Educ:* Moseley Hall County Grammar Sch., Cheadle; Britannia Royal Naval Coll., Dartmouth. Served in various ships, 1958–65 (specialized in navigation, 1964); Staff, BRNC, Dartmouth, 1965–67; HMS Cleopatra, 1967–69; Staff, US Naval Acad., Annapolis, 1969–71; NDC, Latimer, 1971–72; i/c HMS Achilles, 1972–74; Naval Plans, MoD, 1974–75; Defence Policy Staff, MoD, 1975–77; RCDS, 1978; i/c HMS Birmingham, 1979–81; Dir of Naval Plans, MoD, 1981–83; i/c HMS Illustrious, 1983–84; ACNS (Op. Requirements), 1984; ACDS (Op. Requirements) (Sea Systems), 1985–86. *Recreations:* music, sailing, hill walking, history. *Address:* c/o Lloyds Bank, Dartmouth, Devon.

KERR, John Olav; HM Diplomatic Service; Head of Chancery, Washington, since 1984; *b* 22 Feb. 1942; *s* of Dr and Mrs J. D. O. Kerr; *m* 1965, Elizabeth, *d* of Mr and Mrs W. G. Kalaugher; two *s* three *d*. *Educ:* Glasgow Academy; Pembroke Coll., Oxford. Entered Diplomatic Service, 1966; served FO, Moscow, Rawalpindi, FCO; Private Sec. to Permanent Under Secretary, FCO, 1974–79; Head of DM1 Division, HM Treasury, 1979–81; Principal Private Sec. to Chancellor of the Exchequer, 1981–84. *Address:* c/o Foreign and Commonwealth Office, King Charles Street, SW1.

KERR, Rt. Hon. Sir John (Robert), AK 1976 (AC 1975); GCMG 1976 (KCMG 1974; CMG 1966); GCVO 1977; PC 1977; Governor-General of Australia, 1974–77; *b* 24 Sept. 1914; *s* of late H. Kerr, Sydney; *m* 1st, 1938, Alison (*d* 1974), *d* of F. Worstead, Sydney; one *s* two *d*; 2nd, 1975, Mrs Anne Robson, *d* of J. Taggart. *Educ:* Fort Street Boys' High Sch.; Sydney Univ. LLB First Cl. Hons; Sydney Univ. Medal. Admitted NSW Bar, 1938. Served War of 1939–45: 2nd AIF, 1942–46; Col, 1945–46. First Princ., Australian Sch. of Pacific Admin., 1946–48; Organising Sec., S Pacific Commn, 1946–47, Acting Sec.-Gen., 1948; returned to Bar, 1948; QC (NSW) 1953; Mem. NSW Bar Coun., 1960–64; Vice-Pres., 1962–63, Pres., 1964, NSW Bar Assoc.; Vice-Pres., 1962–64, Pres., 1964–66, Law Coun. of Australia; Judge of Commonwealth Industrial Court and Judge of Supreme Court of ACT, 1966–72; Judge of Courts of Marine Inquiry, 1967–72; Judge of Supreme Court of Northern Territory, 1970–72; Chief Justice, Supreme Court, NSW, 1972–74; Lieutenant Governor, NSW, 1973–74. Chairman: Commonwealth Cttee on Review of Admin. Decisions, 1968–72; Commonwealth Cttee on Review of Pay for Armed Services, 1970; Deputy President: Trades Practices Tribunal, 1966–72; Copyright Tribunal, 1969–72; President: 3rd Commonwealth and Empire Law Conf., Sydney, 1965; Industrial Relations Soc., 1960–63; Industrial Relations Soc. of Aust. (in formation) (*pro tem*), 1964–66; NSW Marriage Guidance Coun., 1961–62; Law Assoc. for Asia and W Pacific, 1966–70; Member: Bd of Coun. on New Guinea Affairs, 1964–71; Med. Bd of NSW, 1963–66; Hon. Life Mem., Law Soc. of England and Wales, 1965; Hon. Mem., Amer. Bar Assoc., 1967–. World Lawyer Award, World Peace Through Law Conf., Philippines, 1977. KStJ 1974. *Publications:* Matters for Judgment, 1979; Uniformity in the Law: trends and techniques (Robert Garran Meml Lectr), 1965; Law in Papua and New Guinea (Roy Milne Meml Lectr), 1968; The Ethics of Public Office (Robert Garran Meml Lectr), 1974; various papers and articles on judicial administration, industrial relations, New Guinea affairs, organisation of legal profession, etc. *Address:* Suite 2404, 56 Pitt Street, Sydney, NSW 2000, Australia. *Club:* Union (Sydney).

KERR, Rt. Hon. Sir Michael (Robert Emanuel), Kt 1972; PC 1981; **Rt. Hon. Lord Justice Kerr;** a Lord Justice of Appeal, since 1981; *b* 1 March 1921; *s* of Alfred Kerr; *m* 1st, 1952, Julia (marr. diss. 1982), *d* of Joseph Braddock; two *s* one *d*; 2nd, 1983, Diana, *yr d* of H. Neville Sneezum; one *d*. *Educ:* Aldenham Sch.; Clare Coll., Cambridge (Hon. Fellow, 1986). Served War, 1941–45 (Pilot; Flt-Lt). BA Cantab (1st cl. Hons Law) 1947, MA 1952; called to Bar, Lincoln's Inn, 1948, Bencher 1968; QC 1961. Member: Bar Council, 1968–72; Senate, 1969–72. Dep. Chm., Hants QS, 1961–71; Mem. Vehicle and General Enquiry Tribunal, 1971–72; a Judge of the High Court of Justice, Queen's Bench Div., and of the Commercial and Admiralty Cts, 1972–78; Chm., Law Commn of England and Wales, 1978–81. Pres., London Court of Internat. Arbitration, 1985–. Mem. Council of Management: British Inst. of Internat. and Comparative Law, 1973–; Inst. of Advanced Legal Studies, 1979–85; Chairman: Lord Chancellor's inter-deptl cttee on Foreign Judgments, 1974–81; Cttee of Management, Centre of Commercial Law Studies, QMC, 1980–; Supreme Court Procedure Cttee, 1982–86; Mem., Internat. Adv. Cttee, British Columbia Internat. Arbitration Centre, 1986–. Vice-Pres., British Maritime Law Assoc., 1977–. Mem., Amer. Law Inst., 1985–. Pres., CIArb., 1983–86. Hon. Life Mem., Amer. and Canadian Bar Assocs, 1976. Chorley Lectr, LSE, 1977; Alexander Lectr, CIArb, 1984. Governor, Aldenham Sch., 1959–. Hon. Fellow, QMC, 1986. *Publications:* McNair's Law of the Air, 1953, 1965; articles and lectures on commercial law and arbitration. *Recreations:* travel, ski-ing, music. *Address:* c/o Royal Courts of Justice, Strand, WC2. *Clubs:* Garrick, Pilgrims.

KERR, Robert Reid, TD; MA, LLB; Sheriff of Tayside, Central and Fife (formerly Stirling, Dumbarton and Clackmannan) at Falkirk, 1969–83; *b* 7 May 1914; *s* of James Reid Kerr, sugar refiner, and Olive Rodger; *m* 1942, Mona Kerr; three *d*. *Educ:* Cargilfield; Trinity Coll., Glenalmond; Oxford Univ.; Glasgow Univ. Sheriff-Substitute: of Inverness, Moray, Nairn and Ross and Cromarty at Fort William, 1952–61; of Aberdeen, Kincardine and Banff at Banff, 1961–69. OStJ. *Address:* Bagatelle, 14 Rennie Street, Falkirk FK1 5QW.

KERR, Thomas Henry, CB 1983; Director, Hunting Engineering plc; Consultant: HEL; Systems Designers Scientific; *b* 18 June 1924; *s* of late Albert Edward Kerr and Mrs Francis Jane Kerr (*née* Simpson); *m* 1946, Myrnie Evelyn Martin Hughes; two *d*. *Educ:* Magnus Grammar, Newark; University Coll., Durham Univ. BSc 1949; CEng, FRAeS; Diplôme Paul Tissendier 1957. RAFVR pilot, 1942–46. Aero Flight, RAE, 1949–55; Head of Supersonic Flight Group, 1955–59; Scientific Adviser to C-in-C Bomber Comd, High Wycombe, 1960–64; Head of Assessment Div., Weapons Dept, RAE, 1964–66; Dep. Dir and Dir of Defence Operational Analysis Estabt, 1966–70; Head of Weapons Research Gp, Weapons Dept, RAE, 1970–72; Dir Gen. Establishments Resources Programmes (C), MoD (PE), 1972–74; Director: Nat. Gas Turbine Estabt, 1974–80; RAE, 1980–84; R&D Dir, Royal Ordnance plc, 1984–86. Mem. Council, RAeS, 1979, Pres., 1985–86. FRSA 1980. *Publications:* reports and memoranda of Aeronautical Research Council, lectures to RAeS and RUSI. *Recreations:* bridge, water ski-ing, tennis, badminton. *Address:* Bundu, 013 Kingsley Avenue, Camberley, Surrey GU15 2NA. *T:* Camberley 25961.

KERR, Sir William Alexander B., (Sir Alastair); *see* Blair-Kerr.

KERR, William Francis Kennedy, OBE 1984; PhD, CEng, FIMechE; Principal, Belfast College of Technology, 1969–84; *b* 1 Aug. 1923; *m* 1953, H. Adams; two *s*. *Educ:* Portadown Technical Coll. and Queen's Univ., Belfast. BSc (Hons) in Mech. Engineering, MSc, PhD. Teacher of Mathematics, Portadown Techn. Coll., 1947–48; Teacher and Sen. Lectr in Mech. Eng, Coll. of Techn., Belfast, 1948–55; Lectr and Adviser of Studies in Mech. Eng, Queen's Univ. of Belfast, 1955–62; Head of Dept of Mech., Civil, and Prod. Eng, Dundee Coll. of Techn., 1962–67; Vice-Principal, Coll. of Techn., Belfast, 1967–69.

Member: Belfast Educn and Library Bd, 1977–81; NI Council for Educnl Develt, 1980–84; NI Manpower Council, 1981–84; Chm., Assoc. of Principals of Colleges (NI Branch), 1982; Governor, Royal Belfast Academical Instn, 1969–84; Mem. Court, Ulster Univ., 1985–. FRSA 1984. *Publications:* contribs on environmental testing of metals, etc. *Recreations:* golf, motoring, reading. *Address:* 27 Maxwell Road, Bangor, Co. Down BT20 3SG, Northern Ireland. *T:* Bangor 465303.

KERR-DINEEN, Rev. Canon Frederick George; Rector of Stopham with Hardham, since 1973; Canon Emeritus of Chichester, since 1983; *b* 26 Aug. 1915; second *s* of late Mr and Mrs Henry John Dineen and adopted *s* of late Prebendary Colin Kerr; added Kerr to family name in 1938; *m* 1951, Hermione Iris, *er d* of late Major John Norman MacDonald (KEH) and Mrs MacDonald; four *s* one *d*. *Educ:* Tyndale Hall, Clifton; St John's Coll., Durham. MA, LTh. Ordained, 1941; Curate: St Paul's, Portman Square, 1941–44; St John's, Weymouth, 1945–46; Vicar: St Michael's, Blackheath Park, 1946–53; Lindfield, 1953–62; Holy Trinity, Eastbourne, 1962–73; Archdeacon of Chichester, and Canon Residentiary of Chichester Cathedral, 1973–75; Proctor in Convocation, 1970–74; Archdeacon of Horsham, 1975–83. *Address:* The Rectory, Stopham, Pulborough, West Sussex. *T:* Fittleworth 333.

KERRIN, Very Rev. Richard Elual, MA; Dean of Aberdeen and Orkney, 1956–69; Rector of St John's Episcopal Church, Aberdeen, 1954–70, retired; *b* 4 July 1898; *s* of Rev. Daniel Kerrin and Margaret Kerrin; *m* 1925, Florence Alexandra, *d* of Captain J. Reid; one *s*. *Educ:* Robert Gordon's Coll., Aberdeen; University of Aberdeen (MA); Edinburgh Theological Coll. (Luscombe Scholar). Ordained deacon, 1922; priest, 1923. Curate, Old St Paul, Edinburgh, 1922–25; Rector, Inverurie, 1925–37; Rector, Holy Trinity, Stirling, 1937–47; Rector, Fraserburgh, 1947–54; Canon of Aberdeen, 1954–56. *Address:* Elora, St Bryde's Road, Kemnay, Aberdeenshire AB5 9NB. *T:* Kemnay 2480.

KERRUISH, Sir (Henry) Charles, Kt 1979; OBE 1964; Speaker of the House of Keys, Isle of Man, since 1962; *b* 23 July 1917; *m* 1st, 1944, Margaret Gell; one *s* three *d*; 2nd, 1975, Kay Warriner. *Educ:* Ramsey Grammar Sch. Farmer. Member, House of Keys, 1946–. Pres., CPA, 1983–84 (Regional Councillor for British Isles and Mediterranean, 1975–77). Mem. Court, Liverpool Univ., 1974–. *Recreations:* light horse breeding, motor cycling. *Address:* Ballafayle, Maughold, Isle of Man. *T:* Ramsey (IOM) 812293. *Club:* Farmers'.

KERRY, Knight of; *see* FitzGerald, Sir G. P. M.

KERRY, Sir Michael (James), KCB 1983 (CB 1976); QC 1984; *b* 5 Aug. 1923; *s* of Russell Kerry and Marjorie (*née* Kensington); *m* 1951, Sidney Rosetta Elizabeth (*née* Foster); one *s* two *d*. *Educ:* Rugby Sch.; St John's Coll., Oxford (MA; Hon. Fellow 1986). Served with RAF, 1942–46. Called to Bar, Lincoln's Inn, 1949, Bencher 1984. Joined BoT as Legal Asst, 1951; Sen. Legal Asst, 1959; Asst Solicitor, 1964; Principal Asst Solicitor, Dept of Trade and Industry, 1972, Solicitor, 1973–80; HM Procurator Gen. and Treasury Solicitor, 1980–84. *Recreations:* golf, tennis, gardening. *Address:* South Bedales, Lewes Road, Haywards Heath, W Sussex. *T:* Scaynes Hill 303. *Club:* Piltdown Golf.

KERSH, Cyril; author and journalist; *b* 24 Feb. 1925; *s* of Hyman and Leah Kersh; *m* 1956, Suzanne Fajner. *Educ:* Westcliff High Sch., Essex. Served War, RN, 1943–47. Worked variously for newsagent, baker, woollen merchant and toy manufr, 1939–43; Reporter, then News and Features Editor, The People, 1943–54; Features Editor, Illustrated, 1954–59; Features staff, London Evening Standard, 1959–60; Editor, Men Only, 1960–63; Daily Express (one day), 1963; Features Editor, then Sen. Features Exec., 1963–76, Sunday Mirror; Editor, Reveille, 1976–79 (Fleet Street's 1st photocomposition editor); Asst Editor (Features), 1979–84, Man. Editor, 1984–86, Sunday Mirror. *Publications:* The Aggravations of Minnie Ashe, 1970; The Diabolical Liberties of Uncle Max, 1973; The Soho Summer of Mr Green, 1974; The Shepherd's Bush Connection, 1975; Minnie Ashe at War, 1979. *Recreations:* talking, walking, reading, writing. *Address:* 14 Ossington Street, W2 4LZ. *T:* 01–229 6582. *Club:* Our Society.

KERSHAW, family name of **Baron Kershaw.**

KERSHAW, 4th Baron, *cr* 1947; **Edward John Kershaw;** JP; Chartered Accountant; Partner in Kidsons, Chartered Accountants, 3 Beaufort Buildings, Spa Road, Gloucester; *b* 12 May 1936; *s* of 3rd Baron and Katharine Dorothea Kershaw (*née* Staines); *S* father, 1962; *m* 1963, Rosalind Lilian Rutherford; one *s* two *d*. *Educ:* Selhurst Grammar Sch., Surrey. Entered RAF Nov. 1955, demobilised Nov. 1957. Admitted to Inst. of Chartered Accountants in England and Wales, Oct. 1964. Lay Governor, The King's Sch., Gloucester, 1986–. JP Gloucester, 1982. *Heir:* *s* Hon. John Charles Edward Kershaw, *b* 23 Dec. 1971.

KERSHAW, Sir Anthony; *see* Kershaw, Sir J. A.

KERSHAW, Henry Aidan; His Honour Judge Kershaw; a Circuit Judge, since 1976; *b* 11 May 1927; *s* of late Rev. H. Kershaw, Bolton; *m* 1960, Daphne Patricia, *widow* of Dr. C. R. Cowan; four *s*. *Educ:* St John's, Leatherhead; Brasenose Coll., Oxford (BA). Served RN, 1946–48. Called to Bar, Inner Temple, 1953. Councillor, Bolton CBC, 1954–57. Asst Recorder of Oldham, 1970–71; a Recorder of the Crown Court, 1972–76. Dep. Chm., Agricultural Land Tribunal, 1972–76. Chm., Lancs Schs Golf Assoc., 1981–84; Vice-Pres., English Schs Golf Assoc., 1984–. *Recreations:* golf, ski-ing, oil-painting. *Address:* Broadhaven, St Andrew's Road, Lostock, Bolton, Lancs. *T:* Bolton 47088. *Club:* Bolton Golf.

KERSHAW, Sir (John) Anthony, Kt 1981; MC 1943; MP (C) Stroud Division of Gloucestershire, since 1955; Barrister-at-Law; *b* 14 Dec. 1915; *s* of Judge J. F. Kershaw, Cairo and London, and of Anne Kershaw, Kentucky, USA; *m* 1939, Barbara, *d* of Harry Crookenden; two *s* two *d*. *Educ:* Eton; Balliol Coll., Oxford (BA). Called to the Bar 1939. Served War, 1940–46: 16th/5th Lancers. Mem. LCC, 1946–49; Westminster City Council, 1947–48. Parly Sec., Min. of Public Building and Works, June-Oct. 1970; Parliamentary Under-Secretary of State: FCO, 1970–73; for Defence (RAF), 1973–74; Chm., H of C Select Cttee on Foreign Affairs, 1979–; Mem. Exec., 1922 Cttee, 1983–. Vice-Chm., British Council, 1974–. *Address:* West Barn, Didmarton, Badminton, Avon EL9 1DT. *Club:* White's.

KERSHAW, Joseph Anthony; independent management consultant, since 1975; Director, Allia (Holdings) Ltd, since 1984; Chairman, Antonian Investments Ltd, since 1985; *b* 26 Nov. 1935; *s* of Henry and Catherine Kershaw, Preston; *m* 1959, Ann Whittle; three *s* two *d*. *Educ:* Ushaw Coll., Durham; Preston Catholic Coll., SJ. Short service commn, RAOC, 1955–58; Unilever Ltd, 1958–67; Gp Marketing Manager, CWS, 1967–69; Managing Director: Underline Ltd, 1969–71; Merchant Div., Reed International Ltd, 1971–73; Head of Marketing, Non-Foods, CWS, 1973–74; (first) Director, Nat. Consumer Council, 1975. Dir, John Stork & Partners Ltd, 1980–85; Associate Director: Foote, Cone & Belding Ltd, 1979–84; Phoenix Advertising, 1984–86; *Recreations:* fishing, gardening, cooking; pilot of hot air balloon; CPRE. *Address:* Westmead, Meins Road, Blackburn, Lancs BB2 6QF. *T:* Blackburn 55915. *Club:* Institute of Directors.

KERSHAW, Michael; *see* Kershaw, P. M.

KERSHAW, (Philip) Michael, QC 1980; a Recorder of the Crown Court, since 1980; *b* 23 April 1941; *s* of His Honour Philip Kershaw; *m* 1980, Anne (*née* Williams); one *s*. *Educ:* Ampleforth Coll.; St John's Coll., Oxford (MA). Called to the Bar, Gray's Inn, 1963; in practice, 1963–. *Address:* 5 Essex Court, Temple, EC4Y 9AH. *Clubs:* Reform; Portico (Manchester).

KERSHAW, Mrs W. J. S.; *see* Paling, Helen Elizabeth.

KERSHAW, Prof. William Edgar, CMG 1971; VRD; Professor of Biology, University of Salford, 1966–76, now Emeritus Professor; Advisor in Tropical Medicine to Manchester Area Health Authority, since 1976. *Educ:* Manchester University. MB, ChB, 1935; MRCS, LRCP, 1936; DTM&H Eng. 1946; MD 1949; DSc 1956. Chalmers Memorial Gold Medal, Royal Society of Tropical Medicine and Hygiene, 1955. Formerly: Surgeon Captain, RNR; Demonstrator in Morbid Anatomy, Manchester Univ.; Leverhulme Senior Lectr in Med. Parasitology, Liverpool Sch. of Trop. Med. and Liverpool Univ.; Walter Myers and Everett Dutton Prof. of Parasitology and Entomology, Liverpool Univ., 1958–66. Hon. Lectr, Dept of Bacteriology, Univ. of Manchester, 1977–. *Address:* Mill Farm, Hesketh Bank, Preston PR4 6RA. *T:* Hesketh Bank 4299.

KERWIN, Prof. Larkin, CC 1980 (OC 1977); FRSC; President, National Research Council of Canada, since 1980; *b* 22 June 1924; *s* of T. J. Kerwin and Catherine Lonergan-Kerwin; *m* 1950, Maria Guadaloupe Turcot; five *s* three *d*. *Educ:* St Francis Xavier Univ. (BSc 1944); MIT (MSc 1946); Université Laval (DSc 1949). Laval University: Dir, Dept of Physics, 1961–67; Vice-Dean, Faculty of Sciences, 1967–68; Vice-Rector, Academic, 1969–72; Rector, 1972–77. Sec.-Gen., IUPAP, 1972–84, First Vice-Pres., 1984–. Pres., Royal Soc. of Canada, 1976–77. Hon. LLD: St Francis Xavier, 1970; Toronto, 1973; Concordia, 1976; Alberta, 1983; Dalhousie, 1983; Hon. DSc: British Columbia, 1973; McGill, 1974; Memorial, 1978; Ottawa, 1981; Royal Military Coll., Canada, 1982; Hon. DCL Bishop's, 1978; DSc (*hc*): Winnipeg, 1983; Windsor, 1984; Moncton, 1985. Médaille du Centenaire, 1967; Médaille de l'Assoc. Canadienne des Physiciens, 1969; Médaille Pariseau, 1965; Medal of Centenary of Roumania, 1977; Jubilee Medal, 1977; Laval Alumni Medal, 1978; Gold Medal, Canadian Council of Professional Engineers, 1982; Rousseau Medal, l'ACFAS, 1983. Kt Comdr with star, Holy Sepulchre of Jerusalem, 1974. *Publications:* Atomic Physics, 1963 (trans. French, 1964, Spanish, 1970); papers in jls. *Recreation:* sailing. *Address:* 2166 Parc Bourbonnière, Sillery, Quebec G1T 1B4, Canada. *T:* (613) 993–2024. *Club:* Cercle Universitaire (Quebec).

KESSEL, Prof. William Ivor Neil, MD; FRCP, FRCPE, FRCPsych; Professor of Psychiatry, since 1965 and Dean of Postgraduate Studies, Faculty of Medicine, since 1982, University of Manchester; *b* 10 Feb. 1925; *s* of Barney Kessel and Rachel Isabel Kessel; *m* 1958, Pamela Veronica Joyce (*née* Boswell); one *s* one *d*. *Educ:* Highgate Sch.; Trinity Coll., Cambridge (MA, MD); UCH Med. Sch.; Inst. of Psychiatry. MSc Manchester. FRCP 1967; FRCPE 1968; FRCPsych 1972. Staff, Inst. of Psych., 1960; scientific staff, MRC Unit for Epidemiol. of Psych. Illness, 1961, Asst Dir 1963; Hon. Sen. Lectr, Edinburgh Univ., 1964; Dean, Faculty of Med., Univ. of Manchester, 1974–76. Member: NW RHA, 1974–77; GMC, 1974–; Adv. Council on Misuse of Drugs, 1972–80; Health Educn Council, 1979–86; Chm., Adv. Cttee on Alcoholism, DHSS, 1975–78; Cons. Adviser on alcoholism to DHSS, 1972–81, 1983–86. *Publications:* Alcoholism (with Prof. H. J. Walton), 1965, 3rd edn 1975; articles on suicide and self-poisoning, alcoholism, psych. in gen. practice, psychosomatic disorders, psych. epidemiol. *Address:* Department of Psychiatry, University Hospital of South Manchester, West Didsbury, Manchester M20 8LR. *T:* 061–447 4361. *Club:* Athenæum.

KESWICK, Henry Neville Lindley; Chairman, Matheson & Co. Ltd, since 1975; Member, London Advisory Committee, Hongkong and Shanghai Banking Corporation, since 1975; *b* 29 Sept. 1938; *e s* of Sir William Keswick, *qv*; *m* 1985, Tessa, Lady Reay, *y d* of 17th Baron Lovat, *qv*. *Educ:* Eton Coll.; Trinity Coll., Cambridge. BA Hons Econs and Law. Commnd Scots Guards, Nat. Service, 1956–58. Dir, Jardine, Matheson & Co. Ltd, Hong Kong, 1967 (Chairman, 1972–75); Director: Sun Alliance and London Insurance, 1975–; Robert Fleming Holdings Ltd; United Race Courses. Proprietor, The Spectator, 1975–81. Trustee, Nat. Portrait Gall., 1982–. *Recreation:* country pursuits. *Address:* 28 Arlington House, St James's, SW1. *Clubs:* White's, Turf; Third Guards.

See also J. C. L. Keswick, S. L. Keswick.

KESWICK, John Chippendale Lindley; Chairman, Hambros Bank Ltd, since 1986; *b* 2 Feb.1940; 2nd *s* of Sir William Keswick, *qv*; *m* 1966, Lady Sarah Ramsay, *d* of 16th Earl of Dalhousie, *qv*; three *s*. *Educ:* Eton; Univ. of Aix/Marseilles. Glyn Mills & Co., 1961–65; joined Hambros Bank, 1965: Dir and Vice-Pres., Hambro America Inc., NY, 1969; Banking Dir, London, 1970; Exec. Dir i/c Banking Div., 1974; Dep. Chm., 1983. Director: Sovereign Oil & Gas; Persimmon; Equipment Leasing Co.; Hambros Leasing; Strauss Turnbull & Co. Mem. Council, Cancer Research Campaign; Hon. Treas., Children's Country Holidays Fund. Mem., Queen's Body Guard for Scotland, Royal Company of Archers. *Recreations:* bridge, field sports. *Address:* Hambros Bank, 41 Bishopsgate, EC2P 2AA. *T:* 01–588 2851. *Clubs:* White's, Portland (Chm.).

KESWICK, Simon Lindley; Chairman: Jardine Matheson Holdings Ltd since 1984; Jardine Matheson & Co. Ltd, Hong Kong, since 1983 (Director since 1972); Hongkong Land Co., since 1983; Hongkong & Shanghai Banking Corp., since 1983; *b* 20 May 1942; *s* of Sir William Keswick, *qv*; *m* 1971, Emma, *d* of Major David Chetwode; two *s* two *d*. *Educ:* Eton Coll.; Trinity Coll., Cambridge. Chm., Jardine Matheson Insurance Brokers Ltd, 1978–82; Man. Dir, Jardine Matheson & Co., Hong Kong, 1982; Director: Fleetways Holdings Ltd, Australia, 1970–72; Greenfriar Investment Co. Ltd, 1979–82; Matheson & Co. Ltd, 1978–82. Mem., the Queen's Body Guard for Scotland, Royal Co. of Archers, 1982–. *Recreations:* country pursuits, Tottenham Hotspurs. *Address:* 35 Mount Kellett Road, Hong Kong. *T:* 5–8496948. *Clubs:* White's, Turf; Union (Sydney).

See also H. N. L. Keswick, J. C. L. Keswick.

KESWICK, Sir William (Johnston), Kt 1972; Director, Matheson & Co. Ltd, 1943–75 (Chairman, 1949–66); *b* 6 Dec. 1903; *s* of late Major Henry Keswick of Cowhill Tower, Dumfries, Scotland; *m* 1937, Mary, *d* of late Rt Hon. Sir Francis Lindley, PC, GCMG; three *s* one *d*. *Educ:* Winchester Coll.; Trinity Coll., Cambridge. Director: Hudson's Bay Co., 1943–72 (Governor 1952–65); Bank of England, 1955–73; British Petroleum Co. Ltd, 1950–73; Jardine, Matheson & Co. Ltd (Hong Kong and Far East); Chm. of various public companies in Far East; Chm., Shanghai Municipal Council of late International Settlement; Mem., Royal Commission on Taxation of Profits and Income; Brigadier Staff Duties 21 Army Gp; Mem., Royal Company of Archers. Trustee, National Gallery 1964–71. *Recreations:* shooting, fishing. *Address:* Theydon Priory, Theydon Bois, Essex. *T:* Theydon Bois 2256; Glenkiln, Shawhead, Dumfries, Scotland. *Club:* White's.

See also H. N. L. Keswick, J. C. L. Keswick, S. L. Keswick.

KETTLE, Captain Alan Stafford Howard, CB 1984; Royal Navy (retired); General Manager, HM Dockyard, Chatham, 1977–84; *b* 6 Aug. 1925; *s* of Arthur Stafford Kettle and Marjorie Constance (*née* Clough); *m* 1952, Patricia Rosemary (*née* Gander); two *s*. *Educ:* Rugby School. CEng, FIMechE. Joined RN, 1943; Comdr, Dec. 1959; Captain,

Dec. 1968; retired, Sept. 1977. Entered Civil Service as Asst Under-Sec., Sept. 1977. *Address:* 3 Leather Tor Close, Grangelands, Yelverton PL20 6EQ. *T:* Yelverton 854249.

KETTLE, Roy Henry Richard; Group Managing Director, Tarmac plc, since 1982; *b* 2 May 1924; *s* of Arthur Charles Edwin and Emily Grace Kettle; *m* 1956, Jean; one *s* three *d*. *Educ:* Wolverhampton Grammar School. Tarmac Roadstone Ltd: Accountancy Asst, 1947; Management Acct, 1960; Chief Management Acct, 1964; Dir of Admin, 1967; Man. Dir, 1976; Tarmac plc: Dir, 1977; Man. Dir, 1982. Chm., Cooper Industries, 1986–; Dir, Evered Holdings, 1986–. *Recreations:* walking, gardening. *Address:* Hilbre, Watling Street South, Church Stretton, Shropshire. *T:* Church Stretton 722445.

KETTLEWELL, Comdt Dame Marion M., DBE 1970 (CBE 1964); General Secretary, Girls' Friendly Society, 1971–78; *b* 20 Feb. 1914; *d* of late George Wildman Kettlewell, Bramling, Virginia Water, Surrey, and of Mildred Frances (*née* Atkinson), Belford, Northumberland. *Educ:* Godolphin Sch., Salisbury; St Christopher's Coll., Blackheath. Worked for Fellowship of Maple Leaf, Alta, Canada, 1935–38; worked for Local Council, 1939–41; joined WRNS as MT driver, 1941; commnd as Third Officer WRNS, 1942; Supt WRNS on Staff of Flag Officer Air (Home), 1961–64; Supt WRNS Training and Drafting, 1964–67; Director, WRNS, 1967–70. Pres., Assoc. of Wrens, 1981–. *Recreations:* needlework, walking, and country life. *Address:* c/o Lloyds Bank, 1 Butler Place, Victoria Street, SW1H 0PR.

See also R. W. Kettlewell.

KETTLEWELL, Richard Wildman, CMG 1955; Colonial Service, retired 1962; *b* 12 Feb. 1910; *s* of late George Wildman Kettlewell and of Mildred Frances Atkinson; *m* 1935, Margaret Jessie Palmer; one *s* one *d*. *Educ:* Clifton Coll.; Reading and Cambridge Univs. BSc 1931; Dip. Agric. Cantab 1932; Associate of Imperial Coll. of Tropical Agriculture (AICTA), 1933. Entered Colonial Agricultural Service, 1934; appointed to Nyasaland. Served War of 1939–45 (despatches) with 2nd Bn King's African Rifles, 1939–43; rank of Major. Recalled to agricultural duties in Nyasaland, 1943; Dir of Agriculture, 1951–59; Sec. for Natural Resources, 1959–61; Minister for Lands and Surveys, 1961–62. Consultant to Hunting Technical Services, 1963–79. *Address:* Orchard Close, Over Norton, Chipping Norton, Oxon OX7 5PH. *T:* Chipping Norton 2407.

See also Comdt Dame M. M. Kettlewell.

KEVILL-DAVIES, Christopher Evelyn, CBE 1973; JP; DL; *b* 12 July 1913; 3rd *s* of William A. S. H. Kevill-Davies, JP, Croft Castle, Herefordshire; *m* 1938, Virginia, *d* of Adm. Ronald A. Hopwood, CB; one *s* one *d*. *Educ:* Radley College. Served with Suffolk Yeomanry, 1939–43 and Grenadier Gds, 1943–45, France, Belgium and Germany. Mem., Gt Yarmouth Borough Council, 1946–53; Chm., Norfolk Mental Deficiency HMC, 1950–69; Mem., East Anglian Regional Hosp. Bd, 1962 (Vice-Chm. 1967); Vice-Chm., E Anglian RHA, 1974–82. JP 1954, DL 1974–83, Norfolk; High Sheriff of Norfolk, 1965. *Address:* 11 Hale House, 34 De Vere Gardens, Kensington, W8. *T:* 01–937 5066. *Clubs:* Cavalry and Guards; Norfolk (Norwich).

KEVILLE, Sir (William) Errington, Kt 1962; CBE 1947; *b* 3 Jan. 1901; *s* of William Edwin Keville; *m* 1928, Ailsa Sherwood, *d* of late Captain John McMillan; three *s* two *d*. *Educ:* Merchant Taylors'. Pres., Chamber of Shipping, 1961 (Vice-Pres. 1960, Mem. of Council, 1940–); Chairman: Gen. Coun. of British Shipping, 1961; International Chamber of Shipping, 1963–68; Cttee of European Shipowners, 1963–65; Member: Executive Council of Shipping Federation Ltd, 1936–68; Board of PLA, 1943–59; National Maritime Board, 1945–68; Mem. of Cttee of Lloyd's Register of Shipping, 1957–68; Director: Shaw Savill & Albion Co. Ltd, 1941–68 (former Dep. Chm.); National Bank of New Zealand Ltd, 1946–75; Economic Insurance Co. Ltd, 1949–68 (Chm., 1962–68); National Mortgage & Agency Co. of NZ Ltd, 1950–68; British Maritime Trust Ltd, 1959–72 (Chm. 1962–68); Furness Withy & Co. Ltd, 1950–68 (Chm., 1962–68); Chm., Air Holdings Ltd, 1968–69. *Recreations:* walking, history. *Address:* Stroud Close, Grayswood, Haslemere, Surrey GU27 2DJ. *T:* Haslemere 3653.

KEWISH, John Douglas, CB 1958; TD 1944; DL; Registrar, Westminster County Court, 1971–73; *b* 4 May 1907; *s* of late John James Kewish, Birkenhead; *m* 1934, Marjorie Phyllis, *d* of late Dr Joseph Harvey, Wimbledon; one *s* one *d*. *Educ:* Birkenhead Sch. Admitted a Solicitor, 1931. Served TA, 1928–45; served 1939–44, with 4th Bn Cheshire Regt (UK, France and Belgium); commanded 4th Bn, 1940–44; commanded depots, The Cheshire Regt and The Manchester Regt and 24 Machine Gun Training Centre, 1944–45. Hon. Col 4th Bn Cheshire Regt, 1947–62. Chm., Cheshire T & AFA, 1951–59. Head of County Courts Branch in Lord Chancellor's Dept, 1960–71; Mem. Civil Judicial Statistics Cttee, 1966–68. Chm., Liverpool Shipwreck and Humane Soc., 1953–60. DL Cheshire, 1952. *Address:* Gargrave House, Gargrave, Skipton, N Yorks BD23 3PH.

KEY, Brian Michael; Member (Lab) Yorkshire South, European Parliament, 1979–84; *b* 20 Sept. 1947; *s* of Leslie Granville Key and Nora Alice (*née* Haylett); *m* 1974, Lynn Joyce Ambler. *Educ:* Darfield County Primary Sch.; Wath upon Dearne Grammar Sch.; Liverpool Univ. (BA Hons). Careers Officer, West Riding County Council, 1970–73; Sen. Administrative Officer, South Yorkshire CC, 1973–79. *Address:* 25 Cliff Road, Darfield, Barnsley S73 9HR. *Clubs:* Darfield Working Men's; Trades and Labour (Doncaster).

KEY, Maj.-Gen. Clement Denis, MBE 1945; late RAOC; *b* 6 June 1915; *s* of late William Clement Key, Harborne, Birmingham; *m* 1941, Molly, *d* of late F. Monk, Kettering, Northants; two *s*. *Educ:* Seaford Coll. Commnd in RAOC, 1940; served in: England, 1940–44; France, Belgium, Burma, Singapore, 1944–48; Staff Coll., Camberley, 1945; England, 1948–51; USA, 1951–54; England, 1954–59; jssc 1954; Belgium, 1959–61; War Office, 1961–64; Dep. Dir of Ordnance Services, War Office, 1964–67; Dep. Dir of Ordnance Services, Southern Comd, 1967; Comdr, UK Base Organisation, RAOC, 1968–70; retd, 1970. Hon. Col, RAOC (T&AVR), 1968–71; Col Comdt, RAOC, 1972–75. Bursar, 1971–76, Clerk to Govrs, 1976–85, Tudor Hall Sch., Banbury. *Recreations:* rowing, gardening, bee-keeping. *Address:* 104 Maidenhead Road, Stratford-upon-Avon, Warwicks. *T:* Stratford-upon-Avon 204345.

KEY, (Simon) Robert; MP (C) Salisbury, since 1983; *b* 22 April 1945; *s* of late Rt Rev. J. M. Key; *m* 1968, Susan Priscilla Bright Irvine, 2nd *d* of late Rev. T. T. Irvine; one *s* two *d* (and one *s* decd). *Educ:* Salisbury Cathedral Sch.; Forres Sch., Swanage; Sherborne Sch.; Clare Coll., Cambridge. MA; CertEd. Assistant Master: Loretto Sch., Edinburgh, 1967; Harrow Sch., 1969–83. Warden, Nanoose Field Studies Centre, Wool, Dorset, 1972–78; Governor: Sir William Collins Sch., NW1, 1976–81; Special Sch. at Gt Ormond Street Hosp. for Sick Children, 1976–81; Roxeth Sch., Harrow, 1979–82. Founder Chm., ALICE Trust for Autistic Children, 1977–; Council Mem., GAP Activity Projects 1975–. Vice-Chm., Wembley Br., ASTMS, 1976–80. Contested (C) Camden, Holborn and St Pancras South, 1979. Political Sec. to Rt Hon. Edward Heath, 1984–85; PPS to Minister of State for Energy, 1985–. Mem., Select Cttee on Educn, Science and the Arts, 1983–; Sec., Cons. Parly Backbench Cttee on Arts and Heritage, 1983–84; Jt Parly Chm., Council for Educn in the Commonwealth, 1984–. Chm., Harrow Central Cons. Assoc., 1980–82; Vice-Chm., Central London Cons. Euro-Constit., 1980–82; Mem., Cons. Party Nat. Union Exec., 1981–83. Mem., UK Nat. Commn for UNESCO, 1984–85. Mem., Chorus of Academy of St Martin-in-the-Fields, 1975–. *Recreations:* singing, cooking, country life. *Address:* House of Commons, SW1A 0AA. *T:* 01–219 3000.

KEYES, family name of **Baron Keyes.**

KEYES, 2nd Baron, *cr* 1943, of Zeebrugge and of Dover; **Roger George Bowlby Keyes;** Bt, *cr* 1919; RN, retired; *b* 14 March 1919; 2nd *s* of Admiral of the Fleet Baron Keyes, GCB, KCVO, CMG, DSO and Eva Mary Salvin Bowlby (*d* 1973), Red Cross Order of Queen Elisabeth of Belgium, *d* of late Edward Salvin Bowlby, DL, of Gilston Park, Herts, and Knoydart, Inverness-shire; *S* father 1945; *m* 1947, Grizelda Mary, 2nd *d* of late Lieut-Col William Packe, DSO; three *s* two *d*. *Educ:* King's Mead Sch., Seaford; RNC, Dartmouth. *Publication:* Outrageous Fortune, 1984. *Heir:* *s* Hon. Charles William Packe Keyes, *b* 8 Dec. 1951. *Address:* Elmscroft, Charlton Lane, West Farleigh, near Maidstone, Kent. *T:* Maidstone 812477.

KEYNES, Prof. Richard Darwin, CBE 1984; MA, PhD, ScD Cantab; FRS 1959; Professor of Physiology, University of Cambridge, 1973–86; Fellow of Churchill College, since 1961; *b* 14 Aug. 1919; *e s* of Sir Geoffrey Keynes, MD, FRCP, FRCS, FRCOG, and late Margaret Elizabeth, *d* of Sir George Darwin, KCB; *m* 1945, Anne Pinsent Adrian, *e d* of 1st Baron Adrian, OM, FRS, and Dame Hester Agnes Adrian, DBE, *o d* of Hume C. and Dame Ellen Pinsent, DBE; three *s* (and one *s* decd). *Educ:* Oundle Sch. (Scholar); Trinity Coll., Cambridge (Scholar). Temporary experimental officer, HM Anti-Submarine Establishment and Admiralty Signals Establishment, 1940–45. 1st Class, Nat. Sci. Tripos Part II, 1946; Michael Foster and G. H. Lewes Studentships, 1946; Research Fellow of Trinity Coll., 1948–52; Gedge Prize, 1948; Rolleston Memorial Prize, 1950. Demonstrator in Physiology, University of Cambridge, 1949–53; Lecturer, 1953–60; Fellow of Peterhouse, 1952–60; Head of Physiology Dept and Dep. Dir, 1960–64, Dir, 1965–73, ARC Inst. of Animal Physiology. Sec.-Gen., Internat. Union for Pure and Applied Biophysics, 1972–78, Vice-Pres., 1978–81, Pres., 1981–84; Chairman: Internat. Cell Research Orgn, 1981–83; ICSU/Unesco Internat. Biosciences Networks, 1982–. A Vice-Pres., Royal Society, 1965–68, Croonian Lectr, 1983. Fellow of Eton, 1963–78. For. Member: Royal Danish Acad., 1971; American Philosophical Soc., 1977; Amer. Acad. of Arts and Scis, 1978. Dr *hc* Univ. of Brazil, 1968. *Publications:* The Beagle Record, 1979; (with D. J. Aidley) Nerve and Muscle, 1981; papers in Journal of Physiology, Proceedings of Royal Soc., etc. *Recreations:* sailing, gardening. *Address:* 4 Herschel Road, Cambridge. *T:* Cambridge 353107; Primrose Farm, Wiveton, Norfolk. *T:* Cley 740317.

See also S. J. Keynes.

KEYNES, Stephen John; Director: The English Trust Group plc (formerly The English Association Group plc) and subsidiaries, since 1980; Sun Life Assurance Society plc; Premier Consolidated Oilfields plc; *b* 19 Oct. 1927; 4th *s* of Sir Geoffrey Keynes, MD, FRCP, FRCS, FRCOG, and late Margaret Elizabeth, *d* of Sir George Darwin, KCB; *m* 1955, Mary, *o d* of late Senator the Hon. Adrian Knatchbull-Hugessen, QC (Canada), and late Margaret, *o d* of G. H. Duggan; three *s* two *d*. *Educ:* Oundle Sch.; King's Coll., Cambridge (Foundn Scholar; MA). Royal Artillery, 1949–51. Partner, J. F. Thomasson & Co., Private Bankers, 1961–65; Director: Charterhouse Japhet Ltd and Charterhouse Finance Corp., 1965–72; Arbuthnot Latham Holdings Ltd, 1973–80. Member: IBA (formerly ITA), 1969–74; Cttee and Treas., Islington and North London Family Service Unit, 1956–68; Adv. Cttee, Geffrye Museum; Trustee: Centerprise Community Project, 1971–75; Needham Research Inst. (E Asian Hist. of Science Trust); Chairman of Trustees: Whitechapel Art Gallery; English Chamber Theatre; William Blake Trust. *Recreations:* medieval manuscripts, painting, gardening, travelling. *Address:* 16 Canonbury Park South, Islington, N1. *T:* 01–226 8170; White Hart Cottage, Brinkley, Newmarket, Suffolk. *T:* Stetchworth 223; Gunnerside, near Richmond, Yorks. *Clubs:* City of London, Cranium, Roxburghe.

See also R. D. Keynes.

KEYS, Sir (Alexander George) William, Kt 1980; OBE 1969; MC 1951; company director; National President, Returned Services League of Australia, since 1978; Deputy Chairman, Canberra Permanent Building Society, since 1980; *b* 2 Feb. 1923; *s* of John Alexander Binnie Keys and Irene Daisy Keys; *m* 1950, Dulcie Beryl (*née* Stinton); three *d*. *Educ:* Hurlstone Agricultural High Sch. National Secretary, RSL, 1961–78 (Life Member); Nat. President, Korea and SE Asia Forces Assoc. of Australia, 1964–; World Pres., Internat. Fedn of Korean War Veterans Assoc., 1978–; Mem. Nat. Exec., Royal Australian Regt Assoc., 1967–; Nat. Chm., Australian Forces Overseas Fund, 1978–, Legatee, 1955–; Mem. Bd of Trustees, Aust. War Memorial, 1975; Pres., ACT, Churchill Fellows Assoc. Korean Order of National Security and Merit, 1980. *Address:* Glenlee, Post Office Box 455, Queanbeyan, NSW 2620, Australia. *T:* (home) 97 5440; (office) 48 7199. *Clubs:* Commonwealth, National Press (Canberra); Returned Services League (Queanbeyan).

KEYS, Prof. Ivor Christopher Banfield, CBE 1976; MA, DMus Oxon; FRCO; FRAM; Hon. RAM; Professor of Music, University of Birmingham, 1968–86; *b* 8 March 1919; *er s* of Christopher Richard Keys, Littlehampton, Sussex; *m* 1944, Margaret Anne Layzell; two *s* two *d*. *Educ:* Christ's Hospital, Horsham; Christ Church, Oxford. FRCO 1935; music scholar and asst organist, Christ Church Cathedral, Oxford, 1938–40 and 1946–47. Served with Royal Pioneer Corps, 1940–46. Lecturer in Music, Queen's University of Belfast, 1947, Reader, 1950, Sir Hamilton Harty Professor of Music, QUB, 1951–54; Prof. of Music, Nottingham Univ., 1954–68. Pres., RCO, 1968–70. Chairman: Nat. Fedn of Music Socs, 1985–; BBC Central Music Adv. Cttee, 1985–. Hon. DMus QUB, 1972. *Publications:* The Texture of Music: Purcell to Brahms, 1961; Brahms Chamber Music, 1974; Mozart, 1980; *compositions:* Sonata for Violoncello and Pianoforte; Completion of Schubert's unfinished song Gretchens Bitte; Concerto for Clarinet and Strings; Prayer for Pentecostal Fire (choir and organ); The Road to the Stable (3 Christmas songs with piano); Magnificat and Nunc Dimittis (choir and organ); editions of music; reviews of music, in Music and Letters, and of books, in Musical Times. *Recreation:* bridge. *Address:* 6 Eastern Road, Birmingham B29 7JP.

KEYS, Sir William; *see* Keys, Sir A. G. W.

KEYS, William Herbert; General Secretary, Society of Graphical and Allied Trades 1982–85; Chairman, Trade Union Co-ordinating Committee, since 1985; *b* 1 Jan. 1923; *s* of George William and Jessie Keys; *m* 1941, Enid Gledhill; two *s*. *Educ:* Grammar Sch., South London. Served Army, 1939–46. National Organiser, Printing, Bookbinding and Paper Workers Union, 1953–61; Secretary, London, 1961–70. Society of Graphical and Allied Trades (SOGAT): General President, 1970–74; Gen. Sec., 1974–82 (on amalgamation with NATSOPA); Gen. Sec., after amalgamation, SOGAT '82, 1982–85. Member, General Council, TUC, 1974–85; Chairman: TUC Printing Industries Committee, 1974–85; TUC Employment Policy and Organisation Cttee (Mem., 1976–85); Member: TUC Media Cttee, 1977–85; Equal Rights Cttee, TUC, 1974–85; Race Relations Cttee, TUC, 1974–85; TUC/Lab Party Liaison Cttee, 1981–85; TUC Economic Cttee, 1982–85; TUC Gen. Purposes Cttee, 1982–85. Member: Central Arbitration Cttee, 1977–; Commission for Racial Equality, 1977–81; Manpower Services

Commn, 1979–85; Joint Chairman, Pulp and Paper Division, Internat. Chemical Federation, 1976–85. Member: Inst. of Manpower Studies, 1979–; European Social Fund, 1979–. *Recreation*: music. *Address*: 242 Maplin Way North, Thorpe Bay, Essex SS1 3NT.

KHORANA, Prof. Har Gobind; Sloan Professor of Chemistry and Biology, Massachusetts Institute of Technology, since 1970; *b* Raipur, India, 9 Jan. 1922; *s* of Shri Ganpat Rai and Shrimata Krishna (Devi); *m* 1952, Esther Elizabeth Sibler; one *s* two *d*. *Educ*: Punjab Univ. (BSc, MSc); Liverpool Univ. (PhD, Govt of India Student). Post-doctoral Fellow of Govt of India, Federal Inst. of Techn., Zurich, 1948–49; Nuffield Fellow, Cambridge Univ., 1950–52; Head, Organic Chemistry Group, BC Research Council, 1952–60. Univ. of Wisconsin: Co-Dir, Inst. for Enzyme Research, 1960–70; Prof., Dept of Chemistry, 1962–70; Conrad A. Elvehjem Prof. in the Life Sciences, 1964–70. Visiting Professor: Rockefeller Inst., NY, 1958–60; Stanford Univ., 1964; Harvard Med. Sch., 1966. Has given special or memorial lectures in USA, Poland, Canada, Switzerland, UK and Japan. Fellow: Chem. Inst. of Canada; Amer. Assoc. for Advancement of Science; Amer. Acad. of Arts and Sciences; Overseas Fellow, Churchill Coll., Cambridge; Member: Nat. Acad. of Sciences; Deutsche Akademie der Naturforscher Leopoldina; Foreign Mem., Royal Society, 1978. Hon. Dr Science, Chicago, 1967. Merck Award, Chem. Inst. Canada, 1958; Gold Medal for 1960, Professional Inst. of Public Service of Canada; Dannie-Heinneman Preiz, Germany, 1967; Remsen Award, Johns Hopkins Univ., ACS Award for Creative Work in Synthetic Organic Chemistry, Louisa Gross Horwitz Award, Lasker Foundn Award for Basic Med. Research, Nobel Prize for Medicine (jtly), 1968. *Publications*: Some Recent Developments in the Chemistry of Phosphate Esters of Biological Interest, 1961; numerous papers in Biochemistry, Jl Amer. Chem. Soc., etc. *Recreations*: hiking, swimming. *Address*: Department of Biology and Chemistry, Massachusetts Institute of Technology, Cambridge, Mass 02139, USA.

KIBBEY, Sidney Basil; Under-Secretary, Department of Health and Social Security, 1971–76; *b* 3 Dec. 1916; *y s* of late Percy Edwin Kibbey and Winifred Kibbey, Mickleover, Derby; *m* 1939, Violet Gertrude Eyre; (twin) *s* and *d*. *Educ*: Derby Sch. Executive Officer, Min. of Health, 1936; Principal, Min. of National Insurance, 1951; Sec., Nat. Insurance Adv. Cttee, 1960–62; Asst Sec., Min. of Pensions and Nat. Insurance, 1962. *Address*: 29 Beaulieu Close, Datchet, Berks. *T*: Slough 49101.

KIBBLE, Prof. Thomas Walter Bannerman, PhD; FRS 1980; Professor of Theoretical Physics, since 1970, and Head of the Department of Physics, since 1983, Imperial College, London; *b* 1932; *s* of Walter Frederick Kibble and Janet Cowan Watson (*née* Bannerman); *m* 1957, Anne Richmond Allan; one *s* two *d*. *Educ*: Doveton-Corrie Sch., Madras; Melville Coll., Edinburgh; Univ. of Edinburgh (MA, BSc, PhD). Commonwealth Fund Fellow, California Inst. of Technology, 1958–59; Imperial College, London: NATO Fellow, 1959–60; Lecturer, 1961; Sen. Lectr, 1965; Reader in Theoretical Physics, 1966. Sen. Visiting Research Associate, Univ. of Rochester, New York, 1967–68. Member: Nuclear Physics Bd, SERC, 1982–; Astronomy, Space and Radio Bd, 1984–; Physical Sciences Sub-cttee, UGC, 1985–. Chairman: Scientists Against Nuclear Arms, 1985– (Vice-Chm., 1981–85); Martin Ryle Trust, 1985–. Hughes Medal, Royal Soc., 1981; (jtly) Rutherford Medal, Inst. of Physics, 1984. *Publications*: Classical Mechanics, 1966, 3rd edn 1985; papers in Phys. Rev., Proc. Royal Soc., Nuclear Physics, Nuovo Cimento, Jl Physics, and others. *Recreations*: cycling, destructive gardening. *Address*: Blackett Laboratory, Imperial College, Prince Consort Road, SW7 2BZ. *T*: 01–589 5111.

KIDD, Prof. Cecil; Regius Professor of Physiology, Marischal College, University of Aberdeen, since 1984; *b* 28 April 1933; *s* of Herbert Cecil and Elizabeth Kidd; *m* 1956, Margaret Winifred Goodwill; three *s*. *Educ*: Queen Elizabeth Grammar School, Darlington; King's College, Newcastle upon Tyne, Univ. of Durham (BSc, PhD). Research Fellow then Demonstrator in Physiology, King's Coll., Univ. of Durham, 1954–58; Asst Lectr then Lectr in Physiol., Univ. of Leeds, 1958–68; Res. Fellow in Physiol., Johns Hopkins Univ., 1962–63; Sen. Lectr then Reader in Physiol., 1968–84, Sen. Res. Associate in Cardiovascular Studies, 1973–84, Univ. of Leeds. *Publications*: scientific papers in physiological jls. *Recreations*: squash, gardening. *Address*: Department of Physiology, Marischal College, University of Aberdeen, Aberdeen AB9 1AS. *T*: Aberdeen 40241.

KIDD, Dame Margaret (Henderson), (Dame Margaret Macdonald), DBE 1975; QC (Scotland), 1948; Sheriff Principal of Perth and Angus, 1966–74 (of Dumfries and Galloway, 1960–66); *b* 14 March 1900; *e d* of James Kidd, Solicitor, Linlithgow (sometime MP (U) for W Lothian), and late J. G. Kidd (*née* Turnbull); *m* 1930, Donald Somerled Macdonald (*d* 1958), WS Edinburgh; one *d*. *Educ*: Linlithgow Acad.; Edinburgh Univ. Admitted to the Scottish Bar, 1923; contested (U) West Lothian, 1928. Keeper of the Advocates' Library, 1956–69; Editor Court of Session Reports in Scots Law Times, 1942–76; Vice-Pres. British Federation of University Women, Ltd. Hon. LLD: Dundee, 1982; Edinburgh, 1984. *Address*: 5 India Street, Edinburgh EH3 6HA. *T*: 031–225 3867.

KIDD, Sir Robert (Hill), KBE 1979; CB 1975; Head of Northern Ireland Civil Service, 1976–79; *b* 3 Feb. 1918; *s* of Andrew Kidd and Florence Hill, Belfast; *m* 1942, Harriet Moore Williamson; three *s* two *d*. *Educ*: Royal Belfast Academical Instn; Trinity Coll., Dublin. BA 1940, BLitt 1941. Army, 1941–46: commnd 1942, Royal Ulster Rifles, later seconded to Intell. Corps. Entered Northern Ireland Civil Service, 1947; Second Sec., Dept of Finance, NI, 1969–76. Chairman: NI Local Board, Allied Irish Banks, 1980–85 (Dir, 1979–85); Ireland Co-operation North (UK) Ltd, 1982–85; Belfast Car Ferries Ltd, 1983–; Dir, Allied Irish Banks, 1979–85 (Mem., NI Adv Bd, 1985–). Governor, Royal Belfast Academical Inst., 1967–76, 1979–83; a Pro-Chancellor and Chm. Council, New Univ. of Ulster, 1980–84; Pres., TCD Assoc. of NI, 1981–83; Trustee: Scotch-Irish Trust of Ulster, 1980–; Ulster Historical Foundn, 1981–. Hon. DLitt Ulster, 1985. *Recreation*: gardening. *Address*: 24 Massey Court, Belfast BT4 3GJ. *T*: Belfast 768693.

KIDD, Ronald Alexander; HM Diplomatic Service, retired; *b* 19 June 1926; *s* of Alexander and Jean Kidd; *m* 1st, 1954, Agnes Japp Harrower (marr. diss. 1985); two *d*; 2nd, 1985, Pamela Dempster. *Educ*: Robert Gordon's College, Aberdeen; Queens' College, Cambridge; BA Hons 1951, MA 1956. Royal Air Force, 1944–48; Foreign Office, 1951; served at Singapore, Djakarta, Osaka and Macau, 1952–56; FO, 1956–60; Second, later First Sec., Seoul, 1961–62; Djakarta, 1962–63; Tokyo, 1964–68; FCO, 1968–71; Dar Es Salaam, 1971–72; Tokyo, 1972–77; Counsellor, FCO, 1977–81. Jubilee Medal, 1977. *Recreation*: golf. *Address*: 41 Princess Road, NW1 8JS. *T*: 01–722 8406. *Clubs*: Royal Air Force; Ecurie Ecosse (Edinburgh).

KIDMAN, Thomas Walter, ERD 1954; Regional Administrator, East Anglian Regional Health Authority, 1973–75, retired; *b* 28 Aug. 1915; *s* of Walter James Kidman and Elizabeth Alice Kidman (*née* Littlejohns); *m* 1939, Lilian Rose Souton; one *s* two *d*. *Educ*: Cambridge Central Sch.; Cambs Techn. Coll. FHSM. War service, 1939–46: Warrant Officer, RAMC, BEF France, 1940; Major, Suffolk Regt, seconded Corps of Mil. Police, MEF Egypt and Palestine, 1943–46; served in TA/AER, 1939–67. Local Govt Officer, Health and Educn, Cambridgeshire CC, 1930–48; East Anglian Regional Hosp. Bd: Admin. Officer, 1948; Asst Sec., 1952; Dep. Sec., 1957; Sec. of Bd, 1972. Mem., NHS Advisory Service, 1976–83; Chm., Cambs Mental Welfare Assoc., 1977–86. *Recreations*: photography, walking, gardening, golf. *Address*: Alwoodley, 225 Arbury Road, Cambridge CB4 2JJ. *T*: Cambridge 357384.

KIDU, Hon. Sir Buri (William), Kt 1980; Chief Justice of Papua New Guinea, since 1980; *b* 8 Aug. 1945; *s* of Kidu Gaudi and Dobi Vagi; *m* 1969, Carol Anne Kidu; three *s* two *d*. *Educ*: Univ. of Queensland, Australia (LLB). Barrister-at-Law of Supreme Courts of Queensland and Papua New Guinea. Legal Officer, Dept of Law, 1971; Crown Prosecutor, 1972; Deputy Crown Solicitor, 1973–74; Crown Solicitor, 1974–77; Secretary for Justice, 1977–79; Secretary of Prime Minister's Dept, 1979–80. Chancellor, Univ. of Papua New Guinea, 1981–. *Recreations*: reading, swimming. *Address*: Supreme Court, PO Box 7018, Boroko, Port Moresby, Papua New Guinea. *T*: 25 7099.

KIDWELL, Raymond Incledon, QC 1968; a Recorder, since 1972; *b* 8 Aug. 1926; *s* of Montague and late Dorothy Kidwell; *m* 1st, 1951, Enid Rowe (marr. diss. 1975); two *s*; 2nd, 1976, Carol Evelyn Beryl Maddison, *d* of late Warren G. Hopkins, Ontario. *Educ*: Whitgift Sch.; Magdalen Coll., Oxford. RAFVR, 1944–48. BA (Law) 1st cl. 1950; MA 1951; BCL 1st cl. 1951; Vinerian Law Schol., 1951; Eldon Law Schol., 1951; Arden Law Schol., Gray's Inn, 1952; Birkenhead Law Schol., Gray's Inn, 1955. Called to Bar, 1951; Bencher, 1978. Lectr in Law, Oriel Coll., Oxford, 1952–55; Mem., Winn Commn on Personal Injuries, 1966–68. Member: Bar Council, 1967–71; Senate, 1981–85. *Address*: Sanderstead House, Rectory Park, Sanderstead, Surrey. *T*: 01–657 4161; 2 Crown Office Row, Temple, EC4. *T*: 01–353 9337. *Club*: United Oxford & Cambridge University.

KIELY, Dr David George; consultant engineer; Group Chief Executive and Director, Chemring PLC, 1984–85; Chairman, R&D Policy Committee of the General Lights Authorities of the UK and Eire, since 1974; *b* 23 July 1925; *o s* of late George Thomas and Susan Kiely, Ballynahinch, Co. Down; *m* 1956, Dr Ann Wilhelmina (*née* Kilpatrick), MB, BCh, BAO, DCH, DPH, MFCM, Hillsborough, Co. Down; one *s* one *d*. *Educ*: Down High Sch., Downpatrick; Queen's Univ., Belfast (BSc, MSc); Sorbonne (DSci). CEng, FIEE; CPhys, FInstP; psc 1961. Appts in RN Scientific Service from 1944; Naval Staff Coll., 1961–62; Head of Electronic Warfare Div., ASWE, 1965–68; Head of Communications and Sensor Dept, ASWE, 1968–72; Dir-Gen., Telecommunications, 1972–74, Dir-Gen., Strategic Electronic Systems, 1974–76, Dir-Gen., Electronics Res., 1976–78, Exec. Officer, Electronics Research Council, 1976–78, Dir, Naval Surface Weapons, ASWE, 1978–83, Chief Naval Weapons Systems Engr, PE, 1983–84, MoD, PE. Gp Chief Exec. and Dir, Chemring PLC, 1984–85. Governor, Portsmouth Coll. of Technology, 1965–69. Mem., 1982–, Chm., 1985–, Council, Chichester Cathedral. *Publications*: Dielectric Aerials, 1953; chapter: in Progress in Dielectrics, 1961; in Fundamentals of Microwave Electronics, 1963; papers in Proc. IEE and other learned jls, etc. *Recreations*: fly fishing, gardening, World Pheasant Assoc. *Address*: Cranleigh, 107 Havant Road, Emsworth, Hants. *T*: Emsworth 372250. *Club*: Naval and Military.

KIERNAN, Prof. Christopher Charles; Professor of Behavioural Studies in Mental Handicap, Director of the Hester Adrian Research Centre, University of Manchester, since 1984; *b* 3 June 1936; *s* of Christopher J. and Mary L. Kiernan; *m* 1962, Diana Elizabeth Maynard; two *s* one *d*. *Educ*: Nottingham Univ. (BA); London Univ. (PhD); ABPsS. Lecturer in Psychology, Birkbeck Coll., London Univ., 1961–70; Sen. Lectr, Child Development, Univ. of London Inst. of Education, 1970–74; Dep. Director, Thomas Coram Research Unit, Univ. of London Inst. of Education, 1975–84. *Publications*: Behaviour Assessment Battery, 1977, 2nd edn 1982; Starting Off, 1978; Behaviour Modification with the Severely Retarded, 1975; Analysis of Programmes for Teaching, 1981; Signs and Symbols, 1982. *Recreation*: road running. *Address*: 6 Parkfield Road South, Didsbury, Manchester M20 0DB.

KIESINGER, Kurt Georg; Member of Bundestag, 1949–58 and 1969–80; Chancellor of the Federal Republic of Germany, 1966–69; *b* 6 April 1904; *m* Marie-Luise Schneider; one *s* one *d*. *Educ*: Tübingen Univ.; Berlin Univ. Lawyer. Minister-Pres., Baden-Württemberg 1958–66; Pres., Bundesrat, 1962–63. Chm., Christian Democratic Group, 1955–58. Member: Consultative Assembly, Council of Europe, 1950–58 (Vice-Pres.); WEU Assembly, 1958; Central Cttee, Christian Democratic Party (Chm., 1967–71). DIuris *hc*: Univ. of Cologne, 1965; New Delhi, 1967; Maryland, 1968; Coimbra, 1968. Grand Cross, Order of Merit, German Federal Republic; Grand Cross, Order of Merit, Italian Republic; Grand Officier de la Légion d'Honneur, Palmes Académiques. *Address*: Tübingen, Engelfriedshalde 48, West Germany.

KIKI, Hon. Sir (Albert) Maori, KBE 1975; Chairman of the Constitutional Commission, since 1976; *b* 21 Sept. 1931; *s* of Erevu Kiki and Eau Ulamare; *m* 1957, Elizabeth Hariai Miro; two *s* three *d*. *Educ*: London Missionary Soc. Sch.; Sogeri Central Sch., Papua New Guinea; Fiji Sch. of Med. (Pathology); Papua New Guinea Admin. Coll. Medical Orderly, Kerema, Gulf Province, 1948; Teacher Trng, Sogeri, CP, 1950; Central Med. Sch., Fiji, 1951; Dept of Public Health, Port Moresby, 1954. Formed first trade union in Papua New Guinea and Pres., Council of Trade Unions; Welfare Officer, CP, Land Claims work amongst Koiari people, 1964; studied at Admin. Coll., 1964–65; Foundn Mem. and first Gen. Sec. of Pangu Pati (PNG's 1st Political League); Mem., Port Moresby CC, 1971. MP for Port Moresby, 1972; Minister for Lands, Papua New Guinea, 1972; Deputy Prime Minister and Minister for Defence, Foreign Affairs and Trade, 1975–77. Chairman of Directors, 1977–: Nat. Shipping Corp.; New Guinea Motors Pty Ltd; Credit Corp. (PNG) Ltd; Kwila Insurance Corp. Ltd; Ovameveo Develts Pty Ltd (Property Developers); Maruka Pty Ltd; On Pty Ltd; Mae Pty Ltd; Maho Investments Ltd; Consultants Pty Ltd. Hon. Dr Laws Kyung Hee Univ., South Korea, 1976. *Publications*: Ten Thousand Years in a Lifetime (autobiog.), 1970; (with Ulli Beier) HoHao: art and culture of the Orokolo people, 1972. *Recreations*: care of farm; formerly Rugby (patron and founder of PNG Rugby Union). *Address*: PO Box 1739, Boroko, Papua New Guinea; (private) Granville Farm, 8 Mile, Port Moresby, PNG.

KILBRACKEN, 3rd Baron, *cr* 1909, of Killegar; **John Raymond Godley**; journalist and author; *b* 17 Oct. 1920; *er s* of 2nd Baron, CB, KC, and Elizabeth Helen Monteith, *d* of Vereker Monteith Hamilton and *widow* of Wing Commander N. F. Usborne, RNAS; *S* father 1950; *m* 1st, 1943, Penelope Anne (marr. diss., 1949), *y d* of Rear-Adm. Sir C. N. Reyne, KBE; one *s* (and one *s* decd); 2nd, 1981, Susan Lee, *yr d* of N. F. Heazlewood, Melbourne, Australia; one *s*. *Educ*: Eton; Balliol Coll., Oxford (MA). Served in RNVR (Fleet Air Arm), as air pilot, 1940–46 (DSC 1945); entered as naval airman, commissioned 1941; Lieut-Comdr 1944; commanded Nos 835 and 714 Naval Air Sqdns. A reporter for: Daily Mirror, 1947–49; Sunday Express, 1949–51; freelancing for many UK, US and foreign journals, 1951–; mainly foreign corresp., 1960–74; cameraman (TV and stills), 1962–84; editl dir, Worldwatch magazine, 1984–85. Joined Parly Liberal Party, 1960; transferred to Labour, 1966. Hon. Sec., Connacht Hereford Breeders' Assoc., 1973–76. Pres., British-Kurdish Friendship Soc., 1975–. *Publications*: Even For An Hour (poems), 1940; Tell Me The Next One, 1950; The Master Forger, 1951; (ed) Letters From Early New Zealand, 1951; Living Like a Lord, 1955; A Peer Behind the Curtain, 1959; Shamrocks and Unicorns, 1962; Van Meegeren, 1967; Bring Back My Stringbag, 1979; The Easy Way to Bird Recognition, 1982; The Easy Way to Tree Recognition, 1983; The Easy Way to Wild Flower Recognition, 1984. TV documentaries: The Yemen,

1964; Morgan's Treasure, 1965; Kurdistan, 1966. *Recreation:* bird-watching. *Heir:* *s* Hon. Christopher John Godley [*b* 1 Jan. 1945; *m* 1969, Gillian Christine, *yr d* of late Lt-Comdr S. W. Birse, RN retd, Alverstoke; one *s* one *d*. *Educ:* Rugby; Reading Univ. (BSc Agric.)]. *Address:* Killegar, Cavan, Ireland. *T:* Cavan 34309.

See also Hon. W. A. H. Godley.

KILBRANDON, Baron *cr* 1971 (Life Peer), of Kilbrandon, Argyll; **Charles James Dalrymple Shaw,** PC 1971; a Lord of Appeal in Ordinary, 1971–76; *b* 15 Aug. 1906, *s* of James Edward Shaw, DL, County Clerk of Ayrshire, and Gladys Elizabeth Lester; *m* 1937, Ruth Caroline Grant; two *s* three *d*. *Educ:* Charterhouse; Balliol Coll., Oxford; Edinburgh Univ. Admitted to Faculty of Advocates, 1932, Dean of Faculty, 1957; KC 1949; Sheriff of Ayr and Bute, 1954–57; Sheriff of Perth and Angus, 1957; Senator of Coll. of Justice in Scotland and Lord of Session, 1959–71. Chairman: Standing Consultative Council on Youth Service in Scotland, 1960–68; Departmental Cttee on Treatment of Children and Young Persons, 1964; Scottish Law Commn, 1965–71; Commn on the Constitution, 1972–73 (Mem., 1969–72); Bd of Management, Royal Infirmary, Edinburgh, 1960–68. Hon. LLD Aberdeen, 1965; Hon. DSc (Soc. Sci.) Edinburgh, 1970. Hon. Fellow, Balliol Coll., Oxford, 1969, Visitor, 1974–86; Hon. Bencher, Gray's Inn, 1971. *Address:* Kilbrandon House, Balvicar, by Oban. *T:* Balvicar 239. *Clubs:* New, Royal Highland Yacht (Oban).

KILBURN, Prof. Tom, CBE 1973; FRS 1965; FEng 1976; Professor of Computer Science, University of Manchester, 1964–81, now Emeritus; *b* 11 Aug. 1921; *o s* of John W. and Ivy Kilburn, Dewsbury; *m* 1943, Irene (*née* Marsden); one *s* one *d*. *Educ:* Wheelwright Grammar Sch., Dewsbury; Sidney Sussex Coll., Cambridge (MA 1944); Manchester Univ. (PhD 1948; DSc 1953). FIEE; FBCS 1970 (Distinguished Fellow, 1974). Telecommunications Research Estab., Malvern, 1942–46. Manchester Univ., 1947–81; Lecturer, 1949; Senior Lecturer, 1951; Reader in Electronics, 1955; Prof. of Computer Engineering, 1960. Foreign Associate, Nat. Acad. of Engrg, USA, 1980. Hon. Fellow, UMIST, 1984; DU Essex, 1968; DUniv Brunel, 1977; Hon. DSc Bath, 1979; Hon. DTech CNAA, 1981. McDowell Award, 1971, Computer Pioneer Award, 1982, IEEE; John Player Award, BCS, 1973; Royal Medal, Royal Society, 1978; Eckert Mauchly Award, ACM-IEEE, 1983. Mancunian of the year, Manchester Junior Chamber of Commerce, 1982. *Publications:* papers in Jl of Instn of Electrical Engineers, etc. *Address:* 11 Carlton Crescent, Urmston, Lancs. *T:* Urmston 3846.

KILBY, Michael Leopold; Member (C) Nottingham, European Parliament, since 1984; *b* 3 Sept. 1924; *s* of Guy and Grace Kilby; *m* 1952, Mary Sanders; three *s*. *Educ:* Luton College of Technology. General Motors, 1942–80: Apprentice; European Planning and Govt and Trade Regulations Manager; European Sales, Marketing and Service Ops Manager; Plant Manager; internat. management consultant, 1980–84. Mayor of Dunstable, 1963–64. Member: SE Economic Planning Council; Industry and Economic Cttee, British Assoc. of Chambers of Commerce. *Publications:* The Man at the Sharp End, 1983; technical and political papers. *Recreations:* all sports; first love cricket; former Minor Counties cricketer. *Address:* Grange Barn, Haversham Village, Milton Keynes, Bucks. *T:* Milton Keynes 313613.

KILDARE, Marquess of; Maurice FitzGerald; landscape and contract gardener; *b* 7 April 1948; *s* and *heir* of 8th Duke of Leinster, *qv*; *m* 1972, Fiona Mary Francesca, *d* of Harry Hollick; one *s* two *d*. *Educ:* Millfield School. Pres., Oxfordshire Dyslexia Assoc. *Heir:* *s* Earl of Offaly, *qv*. *Address:* Stowford Farm, Headington, Oxford.

KILDARE AND LEIGHLIN, Bishop of, (RC), since 1967; **Most Rev. Patrick Lennon,** DD; *b* Borris, Co. Carlow, 1914. *Educ:* Rockwell Coll., Cashel; St Patrick's Coll., Maynooth. BSc 1934; DD 1940. Prof. of Moral Theology, St Patrick's Coll., Carlow, 1940; Pres., St Patrick's Coll., 1956–66; Auxiliary Bishop and Parish Priest of Mountmellick, 1966–67. *Address:* Bishop's House, Carlow, Ireland. *T:* Carlow (0503) 31102.

KILÉNYI, Edward A.; Adjunct Professor of Music, Florida State University, since 1982 (Professor of Music, 1953–82); *b* 7 May 1911; *s* of Edward Kilényi and Ethel Frater; *m* 1945, Kathleen Mary Jones; two *d*. *Educ:* Budapest; since childhood studied piano with Ernö Dohnányi; Theory and conducting Royal Academy of Music. First concert tour with Dohnányi (Schubert Centenary Festivals), 1928; concert tours, recitals, and soloist with Principal Symphony Orchestras, 1930–39, in Holland, Germany, Hungary, Roumania, France, Scandinavia, North Africa, Portugal, Belgium; English debut, 1935, with Sir Thomas Beecham in Liverpool, Manchester, London; tours, 1940–42, and 1946–, US, Canada, Cuba. Columbia and Remington Recordings internationally distributed. Served War of 1939–45, Capt. US Army, European theatre of operations. *Address:* 2206 Ellicott Drive, Tallahassee, Fla 32312, USA.

KILFEDDER, James Alexander; MP North Down since 1970 (UU 1970–80, UPUP since 1980) (resigned seat Dec. 1985 in protest against Anglo-Irish Agreement; re-elected Jan. 1986); Leader, Ulster Popular Unionist Party, since 1980; Barrister-at-law; *b* 16 July 1928; *yr s* of late Robert and Elizabeth Kilfedder; unmarried. *Educ:* Model Sch. and Portora Royal Sch., Enniskillen, NI; Trinity Coll., Dublin (BA); King's Inn, Dublin. Called to English Bar, Gray's Inn, 1958. MP (UU) Belfast West, 1964–66. Mem. (Official Unionist), N Down, NI Assembly, 1973–75; Mem. (UUUC) N Down, NI Constitutional Convention, 1975–76; Mem. (UPUP) N Down and Speaker, NI Assembly, 1982–86. Former Chief Whip and Hon. Sec., Ulster Unionist Parly Party; Mem., Trustee Savings Banks Parly Cttee. *Recreation:* walking in the country. *Address:* 96 Seacliff Road, Bangor, Co. Down B20 5EZ. *T:* Bangor 451690; House of Commons, SW1. *T:* 01–219 3563.

KILFOIL, Geoffrey Everard; a Recorder of the Crown Court, since 1980; *b* 15 March 1939; *s* of Thomas Albert Kilfoil and Hilda Alice Kilfoil; *m* 1962, Llinos Mai Morris; one *s* one *d*. *Educ:* Acrefair Primary Sch.; Ruabon Grammar Sch.; Jesus Coll., Oxford. Called to the Bar, Gray's Inn, 1966; practises on Wales and Chester Circuit; Dep. Circuit Judge, 1976. *Address:* (chambers) 40 King Street, Chester. *T:* Chester 49591; 5 Essex Court, Temple, EC4. *T:* 01–353 2440; (home) Clayton Court, Mold, Clwyd. *T:* Mold 3859.

KILGOUR, Dr John Lowell; Director of Prison Medical Services, Home Office, since 1983; *b* 26 July 1924; *s* of Ormonde John Lowell Kilgour and Catherine (*née* MacInnes); *m* 1955, Daphne (*née* Tully); two *s*. *Educ:* St Christopher's Prep. Sch., Hove; Aberdeen Grammar Sch.; Aberdeen Univ. MB, ChB 1947, MRCGP, FFCM. Joined RAMC, 1948; served in: Korea, 1950–52; Cyprus, 1956; Suez, 1956; Singapore, 1961–64 (Brunei, Sarawak); comd 23 Para. Field Amb., 1954–57; psc 1959; ADMS HQ FARELF, 1961–64; jssc 1964; Comdt, Field Trng Sch., RAMC, 1965–66. Joined Min. of Health, 1968, Med. Manpower and Postgrad. Educn Divs; Head of Internat. Health Div., DHSS, 1971–78; Under-Sec. and Chief Med. Advr, Min. of Overseas Develt, 1973–78; Dir of Co-ordination, WHO, 1978–83. UK Deleg. to WHO and to Council of Europe Public Health Cttees; Chm., European Public Health Cttee, 1976; Mem. WHO Expert Panel on Communicable Diseases, 1972–78, 1983–; Chm., Cttee for Internat. Surveillance of Communicable Diseases, 1976. Vis. Lectr, LSHTM, 1976–. Mem. Governing Council, Liverpool Sch. of Tropical Medicine; Mem. Council, Royal Commonwealth Society for the Blind, 1983–. Mem., Medico-Legal Soc. Mem., RHS, 1984–. Winner, Cons. Constituency Speakers' Competition for London and the SE, 1968. *Publications:* chapter in, Migration of Medical Manpower, 1971; contrib. The Lancet, BMJ, Hospital Medicine, Health Trends and other med. jls. *Recreations:* reading, gardening, travel. *Address:* Medical Directorate, HM Prison Service, Home Office, Cleland House, Page Street, SW1P 4LN; Stoke House, 22 Amersham Road, Chesham Bois, Bucks HP6 5PE. *Clubs:* Athenæum, Hurlingham; Royal Windsor Racing.

KILLALOE, Bishop of, (RC), since 1967; **Most Rev. Michael Harty;** *b* Feb. 1922; *s* of Patrick Harty, Lismore, Toomevara, Co. Tipperary, Ireland. *Educ:* St Flannan's Coll., Ennis, Ire.; St Patrick's Coll., Maynooth, Ire.; University Coll., Galway. Priest, 1946; Prof., St Flannan's Coll., Ennis, 1948; Dean, St Patrick's Coll., Maynooth, 1949, 1955–67; Asst Priest, dio. Los Angeles, 1954. BA, BD, LCL, DD (Hon.); HDiplEduc. *Address:* Westbourne, Ennis, Co. Clare, Ireland. *T:* Ennis 28638.

KILLANIN, 3rd Baron, *cr* 1900; **Michael Morris;** Bt *cr* 1885; MBE 1945; TD 1945; MA; Author, Film Producer; President, International Olympic Committee, 1972–80, now Honorary Life President; *b* 30 July 1914; *o s* of late Lieut-Col Hon. George Henry Morris, Irish Guards, 2nd *s* of 1st Baron, and Dora Maryan (who *m* 2nd, 1918, Lieut-Col Gerard Tharp, Rifle Brigade (*d* 1934)), *d* of late James Wesley Hall, Melbourne, Australia; *S* uncle, 1927; *m* 1945, Mary Sheila Cathcart, MBE 1946, *o d* of late Rev. Canon Douglas L. C. Dunlop, MA, Kilcummin, Galway; three *s* one *d*. *Educ:* Eton; Sorbonne, Paris; Magdalene Coll., Cambridge. BA 1935; MA 1939; formerly on Editorial Staff, Daily Express; Daily Mail, 1935–39; Special Daily Mail War Correspondent Japanese-Chinese War, 1937–38. Political Columnist Sunday Dispatch, 1938–39. Served War of 1939–45 (MBE, TD), KRRC (Queen's Westminsters); Brigade Maj. 30 Armd Bde, 1943–45. Director: Chubb (Ireland) Ltd (Chm.); Northern Telecom (Ireland) Ltd (Chm.); Life Assoc. Ireland Ltd (Chm.); Gallahers (Dublin) Ltd (Chm.); Past Chairman: Ulster Investment Bank; Lombard Ulster Ireland Ltd. Member of Lloyd's. International Olympic Committee: Mem., 1952; Mem., Exec. Bd, 1967; Vice-Pres., 1968–72; President: Olympic Council of Ireland, 1950–73; Incorporated Sales Managers' Association (Ireland), 1955–58; Galway Chamber of Commerce, 1952–53; Chm. of the Dublin Theatre Festival, 1958–70. Chairman: Irish Govt Commn on Film Industry, 1957; Irish Govt Commn on Thoroughbred Breeding, 1982. Member: Council Irish Red Cross Soc., 1947–72; Cttee RNLI (a Vice-Pres.); Cultural Adv. Cttee to Minister for External Affairs, 1947–72; Nat. Monuments of Ireland Advisory Council, 1947– (Chm., 1961–65); RIA, 1952; Irish Nat. Sports Council, 1970–72; Irish Turf Club (Steward 1971–73, 1981–83); National Hunt Steeplechase Cttee; first President, Irish Club, London, 1947–65; Hon. Life Mem., Royal Dublin Soc., 1982–86; Trustee, Irish Sailors and Soldiers Land Trust, 1947–. Hon. LLD NUI, 1975; Hon. DLitt New Univ. of Ulster, 1977. Mem., French Acad. of Sport, 1974. Knight of Honour and Devotion, SMO, Malta, 1943; Comdr, Order of Olympic Merit (Finland), 1952; Star of Solidarity 1st Class (Italy), 1957; Comdr, Order of the Grimaldis, 1961; Medal, Miroslav Tyrš (Czechoslovakia), 1970; Grand Cross, German Federal Republic, 1972 (Commander); Star of the Sacred Treasure, (second class) (Japan), 1972; Order of the Madara Rider (Bulgaria), 1973; Grand Officer, Order of Merit of Rep. of Italy, 1973; Grand Cross, Order of Civil Merit (Spain), 1976; Grand Officer, Order of Republic (Tunis), 1976; Grand Officer, Order of the Phoenix of Greece, 1976; Commander, Order of Sports Merit (Ivory Coast), 1977; Chevalier, Order of Duarte Sanchez y Mella (Dominican Rep.), 1977; Commander's Order of Merit with Star (Poland), 1979; Comdr, Legion of Honour (France), 1980; Olympic Order of Merit (gold), 1980; Yugo Slav Flag with ribbon, 1984; decorations from Africa, Austria, Brazil, China, Columbia, USSR etc. *Films:* (with John Ford) The Rising of the Moon; Gideon's Day; Young Cassidy; Playboy of the Western World; Alfred the Great; Connemara and its Pony (scriptwriter). *Publications:* contributions to British, American and European Press; (ed and contrib.) Four Days; Sir Godfrey Kneller; Shell Guide to Ireland, 1975 (with Prof. M. V. Duignan); (ed with J. Rodda) The Olympic Games, 1976; Olympic Games Moscow-Lake Placid, 1979; My Olympic Years (autobiog.), 1983; (ed with J. Rodda) Olympic Games—Los Angeles and Sarajevo, 1984. *Heir:* *s* Hon. (George) Redmond (Fitzpatrick) Morris, film executive [*b* 26 Jan. 1947; *m* 1972, Pauline, *o d* of late Geoffrey Horton, Dublin; one *s* one *d*. *Educ:* Ampleforth; Trinity Coll., Dublin]. *Address:* 9 Lower Mount Pleasant Avenue, Dublin 6. *T:* Dublin 972214; St Annins, Spiddal, County Galway. *T:* Galway 83103. *Clubs:* Garrick, Beefsteak; Stephen's Green (Dublin); County (Galway).

See also W. C. R. Bryden.

KILLEARN, 2nd Baron, *cr* 1943; **Graham Curtis Lampson;** 4th Bt *cr* 1866; *b* 28 Oct. 1919; *er s* of 1st Baron Killearn, PC, GCMG, CB, MVO, and his 1st wife (*née* Rachel Mary Hele Phipps) (*d* 1930), *d* of W. W. Phipps; *S* father as 2nd Baron, 1964, and kinsman as 4th Bt, 1971; *m* 1946, Nadine Marie Cathryn, *o d* of late Vice-Adm. Cecil Horace Pilcher, DSO; two *d*. *Educ:* Eton Coll.; Magdalen Coll., Oxford (MA). Served war of 1939–45, Scots Guards (Major). US Bronze Star. *Heir:* *half-b* Hon. Victor Miles George Aldous Lampson, Captain RARO, Scots Guards [*b* 9 Sept. 1941; *m* 1971, Melita Amaryllis Pamela Astrid, *d* of Rear-Adm. Sir Morgan Morgan-Giles, *qv*; two *s* two *d*]. *Address:* 6 Trevor Street, SW7. *T:* 01–584 7700.

See also Sir N. C. Bonsor, Bt, Lord Eliot.

KILLEN, Hon. Sir (Denis) James, KCMG 1982; LLB; MP (Lib) for Moreton, Queensland, 1955–83; *b* 23 Nov. 1925; *s* of James W. Killen, Melbourne; *m* 1949, Joyce Claire; two *d*. *Educ:* Brisbane Grammar Sch.; Univ. of Queensland. Barrister-at-Law. Jackaroo; RAAF (Flight Serjeant); Mem. staff, Rheem (Aust.) Pty Ltd. Minister for the Navy, 1969–71; Opposition Spokesman: on Educn, 1973–74; on Defence, 1975; Minister for Defence, 1975–82; Vice-Pres. of Exec. Council and Leader, House of Representatives, Commonwealth of Australia, 1982–83. Foundn Pres., Young Liberals Movement (Qld); Vice-Pres., Lib. Party, Qld Div., 1953–56. *Recreations:* horseracing, golf. *Address:* 253 Chapel Hill Road, Chapel Hill, Qld 4069, Australia. *Clubs:* Johnsonian, Tattersall's, Irish Association, QTC (Brisbane), Brisbane Cricket.

KILLIAN, James Rhyne, Jr; Chairman of Corporation, 1959–71, Hon. Chairman of Corporation, 1971–79, Massachusetts Institute of Technology, USA; *b* 24 July 1904; *s* of James R. and Jeannette R. Killian; *m* 1929, Elizabeth Parks; one *s* one *d*. *Educ:* Trinity Coll. (Duke Univ.), Durham, North Carolina; Mass Institute of Technology, Cambridge, Mass (BS). Asst Managing Editor, The Technology Review, MIT, 1926–27; Managing Editor, 1927–30; Editor, 1930–39; Exec. Asst to Pres., MIT, 1939–43; Exec. Vice-Pres., MIT, 1943–45; Vice-Pres., MIT, 1945–48; 10th Pres. of MIT, 1948–59 (on leave 1957–59). Special Asst to Pres. of United States for Science and Technology, 1957–59; Mem., 1957–61, Chm. 1957–59, Consultant-at-large, 1961–73, President's Science Advisory Cttee; Mem., President's Bd of Consultants on Foreign Intelligence Activities, 1956–59 (Chm., 1956–57); Mem. of President's Commission on National Goals, 1960; Chm., President's Foreign Intelligence Advisory Board, 1961–63. Mem., Bd of Trustees, Mitre Corporation, 1960–82; Pres. Bd of Trustees, Atoms for Peace Awards, Inc., 1959–69; Mem., Bd of Visitors, Tulane Univ., 1960–69; Trustee: Institute for Defense

Analyses, Inc., 1959–69 (Chm., 1956–57, 1959–61); Mount Holyoke Coll., 1962–72; Alfred P. Sloan Foundn, 1954–77; Boston Museum of Science; Boston Museum of Fine Arts, 1966–79; Chairman: Carnegie Commn on Educl TV, 1965–67; Corp. for Public Broadcasting, 1973–74 (Dir, 1968–75); Director: Polaroid Corp.; former Director: Amer. Tel. & Tel. Co.; Cabot Corp.; General Motors Corp.; IBM; Ingersoll-Rand Co. Fellow Amer. Acad. of Arts and Sciences; Hon. Mem., Amer. Soc. for Engrg Educn; Mem., Nat. Acad. of Engineering; Moderator, Amer. Unitarian Assoc., 1960–61; President's Certificate of Merit, 1948; Certificate of Appreciation, 1953, and Exceptional Civilian Service Award, 1957, Dept of the Army; Public Welfare Medal of the Nat. Acad. of Sciences, 1957; Officier Légion d'Honneur (France), 1957. Gold Medal Award, Nat. Inst. of Social Sciences, 1958; World Brotherhood Award, Nat. Conf. of Christians and Jews, 1958; Award of Merit, Amer. Inst. of Cons. Engineers, 1958; Washington Award, Western Soc. of Engineers, 1959; Distinguished Achievement Award, Holland Soc. of NY, 1959; Gold Medal of Internat. Benjamin Franklin Soc., 1960; Good Govt Award, Crosscup-Pishon Post, American Legion, 1960; Hoover Medal, 1963; George Foster Peabody Award, 1968 and 1976; first Marconi Internat. Fellowship, 1975; Sylvanus Thayer Award, 1978; Vannevar Bush Award, Nat. Science Foundn, 1980. Hon. degrees: ScD: Middlebury Coll., 1945; Bates Coll., 1950; University of Havana, 1953; University of Notre Dame, Lowell Technological Inst., 1954; Columbia Univ., Coll. of Wooster, Ohio, Oberlin Coll., 1958; University of Akron, 1959; Worcester Polytechnic Inst., 1960; University of Maine, 1963; DEng: Drexel Inst. of Tech., 1948; University of Ill., 1960; University of Mass., 1961; LLD: Union Coll., 1947; Bowdoin Coll., Northeastern Univ., Duke Univ., 1949; Boston Univ., Harvard Univ., 1950; Williams Coll., Lehigh Univ., University of Pa, 1951; University of Chattanooga, 1954; Tufts Univ., 1955; University of Calif. and Amherst Coll., 1956; College of William and Mary, 1957; Brandeis Univ., 1958; Johns Hopkins Univ., New York Univ., 1959; Providence Coll., Temple Univ. 1960; University of S Carolina, 1961; Meadville Theological Sch., 1962; DAppl Sci., University of Montreal, 1958; EdD, Rhode Island Coll., 1962; HHD, Rollins Coll., 1964; DPS, Detroit Inst. of Technology, 1972. *Publications:* Sputnik, Scientists, and Eisenhower, 1977; Moments of Vision (with Harold E. Edgerton), 1979; The Education of a College President: a memoir, 1985. *Address:* 77 Massachusetts Avenue, Cambridge, Mass 02139, USA. *Clubs:* St Botolph (Boston); The Century, University (New York).

KILLICK, Anthony John, (Tony); Director, Overseas Development Institute, since 1982; *b* 25 June 1934; *s* of William and Edith Killick; *m* 1958, Ingeborg Nitzsche; two *d*. *Educ:* Ruskin and Wadham Colls, Oxford (BA Hons PPE). Lectr in Econs, Univ. of Ghana, 1961–65; Tutor in Econs, Ruskin Coll., Oxford, 1965–67; Sen. Econ. Adviser, Min. of Overseas Develt, 1967–69; Econ. Adviser to Govt of Ghana, 1969–72; Res. Fellow, Harvard Univ., 1972–73; Ford Foundn Vis. Prof., Econs Dept, Univ. of Nairobi, 1973–79; Res. Officer, Overseas Develt Inst., 1979–82. Member: Commn of Inquiry into Fiscal System of Zimbabwe, 1984–86; Council, Develt Studies Assoc.; Council, Books for Develt. Former consultant: Govt of Sierra Leone; Govt of Kenya; Govt of Republic of Dominica; various internat. orgns. Associate, Inst. of Develt Studies, Univ. of Sussex. Hon. Res. Fellow, Dept of Political Economy, UCL. Editorial adviser: Journal of Economic Studies; Eastern Africa Economic Review. *Publications:* The Economies of East Africa, 1976; Development Economics in Action: a study of economic policies in Ghana, 1978; Policy Economics: a textbook of applied economics on developing countries, 1981; (ed) Papers on the Kenyan Economy: structure, problems and policies, 1981; (ed) Adjustment and Financing in the Developing World: the role of the IMF, 1982; The Quest for Economic Stabilisation: the IMF and the Third World, 1984; The IMF and Stabilisation: developing country experiences, 1984; learned articles and contribs to books on Third World develt and economics. *Recreations:* gardening, music. *Address:* Karibu, 64 Thundridge Hill, Cold Christmas Lane, Ware, Herts SG12 0UF. *T:* Ware 5493.

KILLICK, Sir John (Edward), GCMG 1979 (KCMG 1971; CMG 1966); HM Diplomatic Service, retired; President, British Atlantic Committee, since 1985; *b* 18 Nov. 1919; *s* of late Edward William James Killick and Doris Marjorie (*née* Stokes); *m* 1st, 1949, Lynette du Preez (*née* Leach) (*d* 1984); no *c*; 2nd, 1985, I. M. H. Easton, OBE. *Educ:* Latymer Upper Sch.; University Coll., London, Fellow 1973; Bonn Univ. Served with HM Forces, 1939–46: Suffolk Regt, W Africa Force and Airborne Forces. Foreign Office, 1946–48; Control Commn and High Commn for Germany (Berlin, Frankfurt and Bonn), 1948–51; Private Sec. to Parly Under-Sec., Foreign Office, 1951–54; British Embassy, Addis Ababa, 1954–57; Canadian Nat. Def. Coll., 1957–58; Western Dept, Foreign Office, 1958–62; Imp. Def. Coll., 1962; Counsellor and Head of Chancery, British Embassy, Washington, 1963–68; Asst Under-Sec. of State, FCO, 1968–71; Ambassador to USSR, 1971–73; Dep. Under-Sec. of State, FCO and Permanent Rep. on Council of WEU, 1973–75; Ambassador and UK Permanent Rep. to NATO, 1975–79. Dir, Dunlop South Africa, 1980–85. *Recreations:* golf. *Address:* Challoner's Cottage, 2 Birchwood Avenue, Southborough, Kent TN4 0UE. *Clubs:* East India, Devonshire, Sports and Public Schools, Brooks's.

KILLICK, Paul Victor St John, OBE 1969; HM Diplomatic Service, retired; Ambassador to the Dominican Republic, 1972–75; *b* 8 Jan. 1916; *s* of C. St John Killick and Beatrice (*née* Simpson); *m* 1947, Sylva Augusta Leva; one *s* two *d*. *Educ:* St Paul's School. Served with Army, N Africa and Italy, 1939–46 (despatches 1944). Diplomatic Service: Singapore, 1946–47; Tokyo, 1947–49; Katmandu, 1950–53; FO, 1953–55; Oslo, 1955–58; San Francisco, 1958–60; Djakarta, 1960–61; Rome, 1962–66; Pretoria/Cape Town, 1966–70; Tangier, 1971–72. *Recreations:* walking, gardening. *Address:* c/o Barclays Bank, 1 Brompton Road, SW3 1EB.

KILLICK, Tony; see Killick, A. J.

KILMAINE, 7th Baron *cr* 1789; **John David Henry Browne;** Bt 1636; Director of Fusion (Bickenhill) Ltd, since 1969; Director of Whale Tankers Ltd, since 1974; *b* 2 April 1948; *s* of 6th Baron Kilmaine, CBE, and of Wilhelmina Phyllis, *o d* of Scott Arnott, Brasted, Kent; *S* father, 1978; *m* 1982, Linda, *yr d* of Dennis Robinson; one *s* one *d*. *Educ:* Eton. Heir: *s* Hon. John Francis Sandford Browne, *b* 4 April 1983.

KILMARNOCK, 7th Baron *cr* 1831; **Alastair Ivor Gilbert Boyd;** Chief of the Clan Boyd; *b* 11 May 1927; *s* of 6th Baron Kilmarnock, MBE, TD, and Hon. Rosemary Guest (*d* 1971), *er d* of 1st Viscount Wimborne; *S* father, 1975; *m* 1st, 1954, Diana Mary (marr. diss. 1970, she *d* 1975), *o d* of D. Grant Gibson; 2nd, 1977, Hilary Ann, *yr d* of Leonard Sidney and Margery Bardwell; one *s*. *Educ:* Bradfield; King's Coll., Cambridge. Lieutenant, Irish Guards, 1946; served Palestine, 1947–48. Mem. SDP, 1981–; Chief SDP Whip, House of Lords, 1983–. Vice-Pres., Assoc. of Dist Councils. Mem., Delegacy, Goldsmiths' Coll., London. *Publications:* Sabbatical Year, 1958; The Road from Ronda, 1969; The Companion Guide to Madrid and Central Spain, 1974, revised edn 1986. Heir: *b* Dr the Hon. Robin Jordan Boyd, MB BS, MRCP, MRCPEd, DCH, *b* 6 June 1941. *Address:* House of Lords, SW1A 0PW.

KILMARTIN, Terence Kevin; Literary Editor, The Observer, since 1952; *b* 10 Jan. 1922; *s* of Ambrose Joseph Kilmartin and Eve (*née* Hyland); *m* 1952, Joanna (*née* Pearce); one *s* one *d*. *Educ:* Xaverian Coll., Mayfield, Sussex. Private tutor, France, 1938–39;

Special Operations Executive, 1940–45; Asst Editor, World Review, 1946–47; freelance journalist, Middle East, 1947–48; Asst Editor, Observer Foreign News Service, 1949–50; Asst Literary Editor, 1950–52. *Publications:* A Guide to Proust, 1983; translations of Henry de Montherlant: The Bachelors, 1960; The Dream, 1962; Chaos and Night, 1964; The Girls, 1968; The Boys, 1974; André Malraux: Anti-Memoirs, 1968; Lazarus, 1977; Charles de Gaulle: Memoirs of Hope, 1971; Marcel Proust: rev. trans. of Remembrance of Things Past, 1981. *Address:* 44 North Side, Clapham Common, SW4. *T:* 01–622 2697.

KILMISTER, Prof. Clive William; Professor of Mathematics, King's College, London, 1966–July 1984; *b* 3 Jan. 1924; *s* of William and Doris Kilmister: *m* 1955, Peggy Joyce Hutchins; one *s* two *d*. *Educ:* Queen Mary Coll., Univ. of London. BSc 1944, MSc 1948, PhD 1950. King's Coll. London: Asst Lectr, 1950; Lectr, 1953; Reader, 1959; FKC 1983. Gresham Prof. of Geometry, 1972–. President: British Soc. for History of Mathematics, 1973–76; Mathematical Assoc., 1979–80; British Soc. for Philos. of Science, 1981–83. *Publications:* Special Relativity for Physicists (with G. Stephenson), 1958; Eddington's Statistical Theory (with B. O. J. Tupper), 1962; Hamiltonian Dynamics, 1964; The Environment in Modern Physics, 1965; Rational Mechanics (with J. E. Reeve), 1966; Men of Physics: Sir Arthur Eddington, 1966; Language, Logic and Mathematics, 1967; Lagrangian Dynamics, 1967; Special Theory of Relativity, 1970; The Nature of the Universe, 1972; General Theory of Relativity, 1973; Philosophers in Context: Russell, 1984. *Recreation:* opera going. *Address:* 11 Vanbrugh Hill, Blackheath, SE3 7UE. *T:* 01–858 0675.

KILMORE, Bishop of, (RC), since 1972; **Most Rev. Francis J. McKiernan,** DD; *b* 3 Feb. 1926; *s* of Joseph McKiernan and Ellen McTague. *Educ:* Aughawillan National School; St Patrick's Coll., Cavan; University College, Dublin; St Patrick's Coll., Maynooth. BA, BD, HDE. St. Malachy's Coll., Belfast, 1951–52; St Patrick's Coll., Cavan, 1952–53; University Coll., Dublin, 1953–54; St Patrick's Coll., Cavan, 1954–62; Pres., St Felim's Coll., Ballinamore, Co. Leitrim, 1962–72. Editor of Breifne (Journal of Breifne Historical Society), 1958–72. *Address:* Bishop's House, Cullies, Cavan. *T:* 049–31496.

KILMORE, ELPHIN AND ARDAGH, Bishop of, since 1981; **Rt. Rev. William Gilbert Wilson,** PhD; *b* 23 Jan. 1918; *s* of Adam and Rebecca R. Wilson; *m* 1944, Peggy Muriel Busby; three *s* three *d*. *Educ:* Belfast Royal Academy; Trinity Coll., Dublin. BA 1939; MA, BD 1944; PhD 1949. Curate Assistant, St Mary Magdalene, Belfast, 1941–44; St Comgall's, Bangor, 1944–47; Rector of Armoy with Loughguile, 1947–76; Prebendary of Cairncastle in Chapter of St Saviour's, Connor, 1964–76; Dean of Connor, 1976–81; Rector of Lisburn Cathedral, 1976–81; Clerical Hon. Sec. of Connor Synod and Council, 1956–81. *Publications:* A Guild of Youth Handbook, 1944; Church Teaching, A Church of Ireland Handbook, 1954, revised edn 1970; How the Church of Ireland is Governed, 1964; (jtly) Anglican Teaching—An Exposition of the Thirty-nine Articles, 1964; The Church of Ireland after 1970—Advance or Retreat?, 1968; The Church of Ireland— Why Conservative?, 1970; Is there a Life after Death?, 1974; A Critique of 'Authority in the Church', 1977; Irish Churchwardens' Handbook, 1979 (expanded, revised and rewritten edn of 1901 pubn); The Faith of an Anglican, 1980; The Way of the Church, 1983; Should we have Women Deacons?, 1984; contribs to Jl of Theol Studies and The Church Qly Review. *Recreations:* gardening, woodworking. *Address:* The See House, Kilmore, Cavan, Republic of Ireland. *T:* Cavan 31336. *Club:* Dublin University.

KILMOREY, 6th Earl of; see Needham, Richard Francis.

KILMUIR, Countess of; see De La Warr, Countess.

KILNER BROWN, Hon. Sir Ralph; see Brown.

KILPATRICK, Rev. George Dunbar; Dean Ireland's Professor of Exegesis of Holy Scripture, Oxford, 1949–77; Fellow of the Queen's College, Oxford, 1949–77; Fellow of University College, London, since 1967; *b* Coal Creek, Fernie, BC, Canada, 15 Sept. 1910; *o c* of late Wallace Henry and Bessie Kilpatrick; *m* 1943, Marion, *d* of Harold Laver and Dorothy Madeline Woodhouse; one *s* three *d*. *Educ:* Ellis Sch., BC; St Dunstan's Coll.; University Coll., London; Oriel Coll., Oxford (Scholar); University of London, Granville Scholar, 1931; BA Classics (1st Class), 1932; University of Oxford, BA Lit. Hum. (2nd Class), 1934; Theology (2nd Class), 1936; Junior Greek Testament Prize, 1936; Senior Greek Testament Prize, 1937, Junior Denyer and Johnson Scholarship, 1938, BD 1944; Grinfield Lecturer, 1945–49; DD 1948; Schweich Lecturer, 1951. Deacon 1936; Priest 1937; Asst Curate of Horsell, 1936; Tutor, Queen's Coll., Birmingham, 1939; Asst Curate of Selly Oak, 1940; Acting Warden of Coll. of the Ascension, Birmingham, 1941; Rector of Wishaw, Warwicks, and Lecturer at Lichfield Theological Coll., 1942; Head of Dept of Theology and Reader in Christian Theology, University Coll., Nottingham, 1946. Vice-Pres., British and Foreign Bible Soc., 1958. *Publications:* The Origins of the Gospel according to St Matthew, 1946; The Trial of Jesus, 1953; (ed) The New Testament in Greek, British and Foreign Bible Society's 2nd edn, 1958; Remaking the Liturgy, 1967; The Eucharist in Bible and Liturgy, 1984; contributions to periodicals. *Recreation:* reading. *Address:* 27 Lathbury Road, Oxford. *T:* Oxford 58909.

KILPATRICK, Prof. (George) Stewart, OBE 1986; MD; FRCP, FRCPE; David Davies Chair of Tuberculosis and Chest Diseases and Head of Department since 1968, Dean of Clinical Studies since 1970, University of Wales College of Medicine, Cardiff; Senior Hon. Consultant Physician to South Glamorgan Health Authority; *b* 26 June 1925; *s* of Hugh Kilpatrick and Annie Merricks Johnstone Stewart; *m* 1954, Joan Askew. *Educ:* George Watson's Coll., Edinburgh; Edinburgh Univ. Med. Sch. (MB ChB 1947, MD 1954). MRCPE 1952, FRCPE 1966; MRCP 1971, FRCP 1975. Medical posts in Edinburgh; Captain RAMC, 1949–51; Mem., Scientific Staff, MRC Pneumoconiosis Research Unit, 1952–54; med. and res. posts, London, Edinburgh and Cardiff. Chm., Sci. Cttees, Internat. Union Against Tuberculosis (formerly Chm., Treatment Cttee); Chm. Council, Assoc. for Study of Med. Educn, 1981–; Chm., Assoc. of Medical Deans in Europe, 1982–85. Ext. Examr in Medicine, Queen's Univ. Belfast, 1986–. FRSocMed. Silver Jubilee Medal, 1977. *Publications:* numerous papers to med. and sci. jls; chapters in books on chest diseases, tuberculosis, heart disease, anaemia and med. educn. *Recreations:* travel, reading, photography. *Address:* Millfield, 14 Millbrook Road, Dinas Powys, South Glamorgan. *T:* Cardiff 513149.

KILPATRICK, Sir Robert, Kt 1986; CBE 1979; Dean, Faculty of Medicine, since 1975, and Professor of Medicine, University of Leicester, since 1984 (Professor and Head of Department of Clinical Pharmacology and Therapeutics, 1975–83); *b* 29 July 1926; *s* of Robert Kilpatrick and Catherine Sharp Glover; *m* 1950, Elizabeth Gibson Page Forbes; two *s* one *d*. *Educ:* Buckhaven High Sch.; Edinburgh Univ. MB, ChB (Hons) 1949; Ettles Schol.; Leslie Gold Medallist; MD 1960; FRCP(Ed) 1963; FRCP 1975. Med. Registrar, Edinburgh, 1951–54; Lectr, Univ. of Sheffield, 1955–66; Rockefeller Trav. Fellowship, MRC, Harvard Univ., 1961–62; Commonwealth Trav. Fellowship, 1962; Prof. of Clin. Pharmacology and Therapeutics, Univ. of Sheffield, 1966–75; Dean, Faculty of Medicine, Univ. of Sheffield, 1970–73. Chm., Adv. Cttee on Pesticides, 1975–; Chm., Soc. of Endocrinology, 1975–78; Mem., GMC, 1972–76 and 1979–. *Publications:* articles in med.

and sci. jls. *Recreations:* golf, sailing. *Address:* The Barn, Smeeton Westerby, Leics LE8 0QL. *T:* Kibworth 2202. *Club:* Royal and Ancient (St Andrews).

KILPATRICK, Stwart; *see* Kilpatrick, G. S.

KILPATRICK, Sir William (John), AC 1981; KBE 1965 (CBE 1958); Chairman: Mulford Holdings Ltd; Kilpatrick Holdings Ltd; Director, Guardian Assurance Group, 1958–74; *b* 27 Dec. 1906; *s* of late James Park Scott Kilpatrick, Scotland; *m* 1932, Alice Margaret Strachan; one *s* three *d*. *Educ:* Wollongong, NSW. Sqdn Ldr, RAAF, 1942–45. Pastoral interests, Victoria. Mem., Melbourne City Council, 1958–64. Chm. Cancer Service Cttee, Anti-Cancer Coun. of Vic., 1958–79; Dep. Nat. Pres., Nat. Heart Foundn of Aust., 1960–64; Chm., Finance Cttee, Nat. Heart Foundn of Aust., 1960–79; Pres. Aust. Cancer Soc., 1961–64, 1974–80; World Chm., Finance Cttee, Internat. Union Against Cancer, 1961–78; Ldr Aust. Delegn to 8th Internat. Cancer Congr, Moscow, 1962. Nat. Chm. Winston Churchill Mem. Trust, 1965; Chm., Drug Educn Sub-Cttee, Commonwealth Govt, 1970; Chm., Plastic and Reconstructive Surgery Foundn, 1970–79. *Recreations:* golf, swimming. *Address:* 23 Hopetoun Road, Toorak, Victoria 3142, Australia. *T:* 20 5206. *Clubs:* Naval and Military, Victorian Golf, VRC, VATC (all Melbourne); Commonwealth (Canberra).

KILROY, Dame Alix; *see* Meynell, Dame Alix.

KILROY-SILK, Robert; television presenter; *b* 19 May 1942; *m* 1963, Jan Beech; one *s* one *d*. *Educ:* Saltley Grammar Sch., Birmingham; LSE (BScEcon). Lectr, Dept of Political Theory and Institutions, Liverpool Univ., 1966–74. MP (Lab): Ormskirk, Feb. 1974–1983; Knowsley N, 1983–86; PPS to Minister for the Arts, 1974–75; opposition frontbench spokesman on Home Office, 1984–85. Vice-Chairman: Merseyside Gp of MPs, 1974–75; PLP Home Affairs Gp, 1976–86; Chairman: Parly All-Party Penal Affairs Gp, 1979–86; PLP Civil Liberties Gp, 1979–84; Parly Alcohol Policy and Services Group, 1982–83; Mem., Home Affairs Select Cttee, 1979–84. Member: Council, Howard League for Penal Reform, 1979–; Adv. Council, Inst. of Criminology, Cambridge Univ., 1984–; Sponsor, Radical Alternatives to Prison, 1977–; Patron, APEX Trust; Chm., FARE, 1981–84. Governor, National Heart and Chest Hospital, 1974–77. Political columnist: Time Out; Police Review. *Publications:* Socialism since Marx, 1972; (contrib.) The Role of Commissions in Policy Making, 1973; The Ceremony of Innocence: a novel of 1984, 1984; Hard Labour: the political diary of Robert Kilroy-Silk, 1986; articles in Political Studies, Manchester School of Economic and Social Science, Political Quarterly, Industrial and Labor Relations Review, Parliamentary Affairs, etc. *Recreation:* gardening. *Address:* Woodlea House, Wymers Wood Road, Burnham, Bucks.

KILVINGTON, Frank Ian; Headmaster of St Albans School, 1964–84; *b* West Hartlepool, 26 June 1924; *e s* of H. H. Kilvington; *m* 1949, Jane Mary, *d* of late Very Rev. Michael Clarke and of Katharine Beryl (*née* Girling); one *s* one *d*. *Educ:* Repton (entrance and foundn scholar); Corpus Christi, Oxford (open class. scholar). 2nd cl. Lit Hum, 1948; MA 1950. Served War of 1939–45: RNVR, 1943–46 (Lt); West Africa Station, 1943–45; RN Intelligence, Germany, 1945–46. Westminster School: Asst Master, 1949–64; Housemaster of Rigaud's House, 1957–64. Chairman: St Albans Marriage Guidance Council, 1968–74; St Albans CAB, 1981–86; Herts Record Soc., 1985–; Pres., St Albans and Herts Architectural and Archæological Soc., 1974–77. E-SU Page Scholar, 1976–77. *Publication:* A Short History of St Albans School, 1970. *Recreations:* music, local history. *Address:* 122 Marshalswick Lane, St Albans, Herts AL1 4XD.

KIM, Young Choo; Ambassador of the Republic of Korea to the Court of St James's, since 1984, and to Dublin, since 1985; *b* 1 June 1923; *s* of late Chi Whan Kim; *m* 1950, Kwang-Ok (*née* Yoon); one *s* three *d*. *Educ:* College of Law, Seoul University. Korean Ministry of Foreign Affairs, 1950–55; served Tokyo, 1955–57; Dir-Gen. for Political Affairs, Min.of Foreign Affairs, 1957–60; served Paris, 1960–61; Dir-Gen. for Planning and Co-ordination, Min. of Foreign Affairs, 1961–62; served London, 1962–63, Bonn, 1963–64, Kampala, 1964–65; Vice-Minister of Foreign Affairs, 1965–67; Ambassador in Bonn, 1967–74, Ottawa, 1974–77; Vienna, 1977–80; Min. of Foreign Affairs, 1980–84. Korean Order of Service Merit, 1962; Korean Order of Diplomatic Service Merit, 1970. *Address:* Embassy of the Republic of Korea, 4 Palace Gate, W8 5NF. *T:* 01–581 0247.

KIMBALL, family name of **Baron Kimball.**

KIMBALL, Baron *cr* 1985 (Life Peer), of Easton in the County of Leicestershire; **Marcus Richard Kimball,** Kt 1981; DL; Director, Royal Trust Co. of Canada, since 1970; *b* 18 Oct. 1928; *s* of late Major Lawrence Kimball; *m* 1956, June Mary Fenwick; two *d*. *Educ:* Eton; Trinity Coll., Cambridge. Contested (C) Derby South, 1955; MP (C) Lincs, Gainsborough, Feb. 1956–1983. Privy Council Rep., Council of RCVS, 1969–82, Hon. ARCVS 1982. External Mem. Council, Lloyd's, 1982–. Jt Master and Huntsman: Fitzwilliam Hounds, 1950–51 and 1951–52; Cottesmore Hounds, 1952–53, 1953–54, 1955–56 (Jt Master, 1956–58). Chm., British Field Sports Soc., 1966–82. Chm., River Naver Fishing Bd, 1964–. Non-exec. Chm., Maybox plc, 1984–. Lt Leics Yeo. (TA), 1947; Capt., 1951. Mem. Rutland CC, 1955. DL Leics, 1984. *Address:* Great Easton Manor, Market Harborough, Leics LE16 8TB. *T:* Rockingham 770333; Altnaharra, Lairg, Sutherland IV27 4AE. *T:* Altnaharra 224. *Clubs:* White's, Pratt's.

KIMBER, Sir Charles Dixon, 3rd Bt, *cr* 1904; *b* 7 Jan. 1912; *o surv. s* of Sir Henry Dixon Kimber, 2nd Bt, and Lucy Ellen, *y d* of late G. W. Crookes; *S* father 1950; *m* 1st, 1933, Ursula (marr. diss., 1949; she *d* 1981), *er d* of late Ernest Roy Bird, MP; three *s*; 2nd, 1950, Margaret Bonham (marr. diss., 1965), writer; one *d* (and one *s* decd). *Educ:* Eton; Balliol Coll., Oxford (BA). *Heir: s* Timothy Roy Henry Kimber [*b* 3 June 1936; *m* 1960, Antonia Kathleen Brenda (marr. diss. 1974), *d* of Sir Francis Williams, Bt, *qv*; two *s*; *m* 1979, Susan, *widow* of Richard North, Newton Hall, near Carnforth]. *Address:* No 2 Duxford, Hinton Waldrist, near Faringdon, Oxon. *T:* Longworth 820004.

KIMBER, Derek Barton, OBE 1945; FEng; Chairman, London & Overseas Freighters plc, since 1984; Director: Eggar Forrester (Holdings), since 1983; Wilks Shipping Co. Ltd, since 1986; Deputy Chairman, AMARC (T.E.S.) Ltd, since 1986; *b* 2 May 1917; *s* of George Kimber and Marion Kimber (*née* Barton); *m* 1943, Gwendoline Margaret Maude Brotherton; two *s* two *d*. *Educ:* Bedford Sch.; Imperial Coll., London Univ; Royal Naval Coll., Greenwich. MSc(Eng), FCGI, DIC; FRINA, FIMechE, FIMarE, FNECInst, FRSA. Royal Corps of Naval Constructors, 1939–49; Consultant, Urwick, Orr & Partners Ltd, 1950–54; Fairfield Shipbuilding & Engineering Co. Ltd: Manager, 1954; Dir, 1961; Dep. Man. Dir, 1963–65; Dir, Harland & Wolff Ltd, 1966–69; Dir Gen., Chemical Industries Assoc., 1970–73; Chairman: Austin & Pickersgill, 1973–83; Bartram & Sons, 1973–83; Sunderland Shipbuilders, 1980–83; Govan Shipbuilders, 1980–83; Smith's Dock, 1980–83; Director: A. & P. Appledore International Ltd, 1974–77; British Ship Research Assoc. (Trustees) Ltd, 1973–81; R. S. Dalgliesh Ltd, 1978–80; Equity Capital for Industry Ltd, 1977–86. Dir, Glasgow Chamber of Commerce, 1962–65. Chm., C. & G. Jt Adv. Cttee for Shipbuilding, 1968–70; Pres., Clyde Shipbuilders Assoc., 1964–65; Member: Shipbuilding Industry Trng Bd, 1964–69; Scottish Cttee, Lloyds Register of Shipping, 1964–65, Gen. Cttee, 1973–, Technical Cttee, 1976–80, Exec. Bd, 1978–84; Research Council, British Ship Res. Assoc., 1973–81; Brit. Tech. Cttee, Amer. Bureau of Shipping, 1976–; Standing Cttee, Assoc. of W European Shipbuilders, 1976–84 (Chm., 1983–84); Underwriting Mem., Lloyd's, 1985–; Chm., Management Bd, Shipbuilders & Repairers Nat. Assoc., 1974–76, Vice-Pres., 1976–77; Mem., Jt Industry Cons. Cttee, (SRNA/CSEU), 1966–76. Member: EDC for Chem. Industry, 1970–72; Process Plant Working Party (NEDO), 1970–72; CBI Central Council, 1970–72, 1975–84; CBI Northern Reg. Council, 1973–80 (Chm. 1975–77); Steering Cttee, Internat. Maritime Industries Forum, 1981–. Member: Council, RINA, 1961– (Chm., 1973–75, Pres. RINA 1977–81); Council, Welding Inst., 1959–74, 1976–82; Bd, CEI, 1977–81, Exec. Cttee, 1978–80; C. & G. Senior Awards Cttee, 1970–81; Council, NE Coast Inst. of Engrs and Shipbuilders, 1974– (Pres., 1982–84); Vice-Pres., British Maritime League, 1985. Trustee, AMARC Foundn, 12986–. Mem., City of London Br., Royal Soc. of St George, 1985–. Liveryman: Worshipful Co. of Shipwrights, 1967 (Asst to Court 1974–, Prime Warden, 1986–87). Engineers' Co., 1984–. Mem., Smeatonion Soc., 1984–; Pres., Old Centralians, 1985–86. Mem. Court, City Univ., 1984–; Governor, Imperial Coll., London Univ., 1967–. FEng 1976. Hon. FRINA 1981. RINA Gold Medallist, 1977. *Publications:* papers on shipbuilding subjects in learned soc. trans. *Recreations:* DIY, golf, rough gardening. *Address:* Broughton, Monk's Road, Virginia Water, Surrey. *T:* Wentworth 4274. *Clubs:* Brooks's, Caledonian, City Livery, Anchorites, MCC; Den Norske Klub; Yacht Club of Greece.

KIMBER, Herbert Frederick Sidney; Director, Southern Newspapers Ltd, 1975–82 (Chief Executive, 1980–81); *b* 3 April 1917; *s* of H. G. Kimber; *m* Patricia Boulton (*née* Forfar); one *s*. *Educ:* elementary sch., Southampton. Southern Newspapers Ltd, office boy, 1931. Served War, Royal Navy, 1939–46: commissioned Lieut RNVR, 1941. Manager, Dorset Evening Echo, 1960; Advertisement Manager-in-Chief, Southern Newspapers Ltd, 1961; then Dep. Gen. and Advertisement Manager, 1972; Gen. Manager, 1974. Chairman: Bird Bros, Basingstoke, 1976–81; W. H. Hallett, 1981–82; Southtel, 1981–82. Dir, Regl Newspaper Advertising Bureau, 1980–81. Member: Press Council, 1977–81; Council, Newspaper Soc., 1974–81 (Mem., Industrial Relations Cttee, 1975–81). *Recreations:* reading, travel, gardening under protest. *Address:* Cortijo Cabrera, Turre, Almería, Spain; (postal) Apartados Correos 350, Garrucha, Almería, Spain.

KIMBERLEY, 4th Earl of, *cr* 1866; **John Wodehouse;** Bt, 1611; Baron Wodehouse, 1797; Lt Grenadier Guards; Director: Airship Industries (UK) Ltd; R. J. Levitt Group of Companies; Rodney Simpson Racing Stables Ltd, Lambourn; AKS Craft Products Ltd; *b* 12 May 1924; *o s* of 3rd Earl and Margaret (*d* 1950), *d* of late Col Leonard Howard Irby; *S* father 1941; *m* 1st, 1945; 2nd, 1949; one *s*; 3rd, 1953; two *s*; 4th, 1961; one *s*; 5th, 1970; 6th, 1982, Sarah Jane Hope Consett, *e d* of Colonel Christopher D'Arcy Preston Consett, DSO, MC. *Educ:* Eton; Cambridge. Lieut, Grenadier Guards, 1942–45; Active Service NW Europe. Member: House of Lords All Party Defence Study Gp, 1976– (Sec., 1978–); House of Lords All Party UFO Study Gp, 1979–; former Liberal Spokesman on: aviation and aerospace; defence; voluntary community services; left Liberal Party, May 1979, joined Cons. Party. Mem. Exec. Cttee, Assoc. of Cons. Peers, 1981–84; Member: Council, The Air League; Council, British Maritime League; RUSI; IISS; British Atlantic Cttee. Delegate to N Atlantic Assembly, 1981–. Vice-Pres., World Council on Alcoholism; Chm., Nat. Council on Alcoholism, 1982–. Mem., British Bobsleigh Team, 1949–58. ARAeS 1977. *Recreations:* shooting, fishing, all field sports, gardening, bridge. *Heir: s* Lord Wodehouse, *qv*. *Address:* House of Lords, Westminster, SW1; Hailstone House, Cricklade, Swindon, Wilts SN6 6JP. *T:* Swindon 750344. *Clubs:* White's, Naval and Military, MCC; House of Lords' Yacht; Falmouth Shark Angling (Pres.).

KIMBERLEY AND KURUMAN, Bishop of, since 1983; **Rt. Rev. George Alfred Swartz;** *b* 8 Sept. 1928; *s* of Philip and Julia Swartz; *m* 1957, Sylvia Agatha (*née* George); one *s* one *d*. *Educ:* Umbilo Road High Sch., Durban; Univ. of the Witwatersrand, Johannesburg; Coll. of the Resurrection, Mirfield, Yorks; St Augustine's Coll., Canterbury. BA, Primary Lower Teacher's Cert., Central Coll. Dip. (Canterbury). Asst Teacher, Sydenham Primary Sch., 1951–52; Deacon, 1954; Priest, 1955; Asst Curate, St Paul's Church, Cape Town, 1955–56; Priest in Charge, Parochial Dist of St Helena Bay, Cape, 1957–60; St Augustine's Coll., Canterbury, 1960–61; Dir, Cape Town Dio. Mission to Muslims, 1962–63; Dir, Mission to Muslims and Rector St Philip's Church, Cape Town, 1963–70; Regional Dean of Woodstock Deanery, 1966–70; Priest in Charge, Church of the Resurrection, Bonteheuwel, Cape, 1971–72; a Bishop Suffragan of Cape Town, 1972–83; Canon of St George's Cathedral, Cape Town, 1969–72. *Recreations:* cinema, music (traditional jazz; instruments played are guitar and saxophone). *Address:* Bishopsgarth, PO Box 921, Kimberley, 8300, Republic of South Africa. *T:* 0531–29387.

KIMBLE, Dr David (Bryant), OBE 1962; Vice-Chancellor of the University of Malaŵi, 1977–86; *b* 12 May 1921; *s* of John H. and Minnie Jane Kimble; *m* 1st, 1949, Helen Rankin (marr. diss.); four *d*; 2nd, 1977, Margareta Westin. *Educ:* Eastbourne Grammar Sch.; Reading Univ. (BA 1942, DipEd 1943, Pres. Students Union, 1942–43); London Univ. (PhD 1961). Lieut RNVR, 1943–46. Oxford Univ. Staff Tutor in Berks, 1946–48, and Resident Tutor in the Gold Coast, 1948–49; Dir, Inst. of Extra-Mural Studies, Univ. of Ghana, 1949–62, and Master of Akuafo Hall, 1960–62; Prof. of Political Science, Univ. Coll., Dar es Salaam, Univ. of E Africa, and Dir, Inst. of Public Admin, Tanzania, 1962–68; Research Advr in Public Admin and Social Sciences, Centre africain de formation et de recherche administratives pour le développement, Tanger, Morocco, 1968–70, and Dir of Research, 1970–71; Prof. of Govt and Admin, Univ. of Botswana, Lesotho, and Swaziland, 1971–75, and Nat. Univ. of Lesotho, 1975–77; Prof. Emeritus, Nat. Univ. of Lesotho, 1978. Founder and Joint Editor (with Helen Kimble), West African Affairs, 1949–51, Penguin African Series, 1953–61, and Jl of Modern African Studies, 1963–71; Editor, Jl of Modern African Studies, 1972–. Officier, Ordre des Palmes Académiques, 1982. *Publications:* The Machinery of Self-Government, 1953; (with Helen Kimble) Adult Education in a Changing Africa, 1955; A Political History of Ghana, Vol. I, The Rise of Nationalism in the Gold Coast, 1850–1928, 1963. *Recreations:* cricket, editing. *Address:* c/o Barclays Bank, Wimborne, Dorset.

See also G. H. T. Kimble.

KIMBLE, George (Herbert Tinley), PhD; retired; *b* 2 Aug. 1908; *s* of John H. and Minnie Jane Kimble; *m* 1935, Dorothy Stevens Berry; one *s* one *d*. *Educ:* Eastbourne Grammar Sch.; King's Coll., London (MA); University of Montreal (PhD). Asst Lecturer in Geography, University of Hull, 1931–36; Lecturer in Geography, University of Reading, 1936–39. Served War as Lt and Lt-Comdr, British Naval Meteorological Service, 1939–44. Prof. of Geography and Chm. Dept of Geography, McGill Univ., 1945–50; Sec.-Treasurer, Internat. Geographical Union, 1949–56; Chm., Commn on Humid Tropics, Internat. Geog. Union, 1956–61. Dir, Amer. Geog. Soc., 1950–53; Dir, Survey of Tropical Africa, Twentieth Century Fund, NY, 1953–60. Chm., Dept of Geography, Indiana Univ., 1957–62; Prof. of Geography, Indiana Univ., 1957–66; Research Dir, US Geography Project, Twentieth Century Fund, 1962–68. Rushton Lecturer, 1952; Borah Lecturer, University of Idaho, 1956; Haynes Foundn Lectr, University of Redlands, 1966; Visiting Prof., University of Calif. (Berkeley), 1948–49; Stanford Univ., 1961; Stockholm Sch. of Economics, 1961. Governor, Eastbourne Sixth Form Coll., 1980–81. FRGS; FRMetS. Hon. Mem., Inst. British Geographers. Editor, Weather Res. Bulletin, 1957–60. *Publications:* Geography in the Middle Ages, 1938; The

World's Open Spaces, 1939; The Shepherd of Banbury, 1941; (co-author) The Weather, 1943 (Eng.), 1946 (Amer.), (author) 2nd (Eng.) edn, 1951; Military Geography of Canada, 1949; (with Sir Dudley Stamp) An Introduction to Economic Geography, 1949; (with Sir Dudley Stamp) The World: a general geography, 1950; The Way of the World, 1953; Our American Weather, 1955; Le Temps, 1957; Tropical Africa (2 vols), 1960; Ghana, 1960; Tropical Africa (abridged edition), 1962; (with Ronald Steel) Tropical Africa Today, 1966; Hunters and Collectors, 1970; Man and his World, 1972; Herdsmen, 1973; From the Four Winds, 1974; This is our World, 1981; (ed for Hakluyt Soc.) Esmeraldo de Situ Orbis, 1937; (ed for American Geographical Soc. with Dorothy Good) Geography of the Northlands, 1955; articles in: Geog. Jl, Magazine, Review; Canadian Geog. Jl; Bulletin Amer. Meteorological Soc.; The Reporter; Los Angeles Times; The New York Times Magazine. *Recreations*: music, gardening. *Address*: 2 Dymock's Manor, Ditchling, E Sussex BN6 8SX.
See also Dr D. B. Kimble.

KIMMANCE, Peter Frederick, CB 1981; Chief Inspector of Audit, Department of the Environment, 1979–82; Member, Audit Commission for Local Authorities in England and Wales, since 1983; *b* 14 Dec. 1922; *s* of Frederick Edward Kimmance, BEM, and Louisa Kimmance; *m* 1944, Helen Mary Mercer Cooke. *Educ*: Raines Foundation, Stepney; University of London. Post Office Engineering Dept, 1939; served Royal Signals, 1943; District Audit Service, 1949; District Auditor, 1973; Controller (Finance), British Council, 1973–75; Dep. Chief Inspector of Audit, DoE, 1978. Mem. Council, CIPFA, 1979–83; Hon. Mem., British Council, 1975. *Recreations*: sailing, books, music. *Address*: Herons, School Road, Saltwood, Hythe, Kent CT21 4PP. *T*: Hythe 67921. *Clubs*: Royal Over-Seas League; Medway Yacht (Lower Upnor).

KIMMINS, Simon Edward Anthony, VRD 1967; Lt-Comdr RNR; *b* 26 May 1930; *s* of late Captain Anthony Kimmins, OBE, RN, and of Mrs Elizabeth Kimmins; *m* 1976, Jonkvrouwe Irma de Jonge; one *s* one *d*. *Educ*: Horris Hill; Charterhouse. Man. Dir, London American Finance Corpn Ltd (originally BOECC Ltd), 1957–73; Dir (non-exec.), Balfour Williamson, 1971–74; Chief Exec., Thomas Cook Gp, 1973–75; Director: Debenhams Ltd, 1972–; TKM International Trade Finance, 1978–80; Chairman: Ardil SA, Geneva, 1980–; Associated Retail Develt Internat. Ltd, 1981–. Vice-Pres., British Export Houses Assoc., 1974– (Chm., 1970–72). Governor, Royal Shakespeare Theatre, 1975–. *Recreations*: cricket (played for Kent), golf, shooting. *Address*: 37 Chemin de Grange Canal, Geneva 1208, Switzerland. *T*: Geneva 35 6657. *Clubs*: Garrick, MCC, The Pilgrims; Haagseclub.

KINAHAN, Charles Henry Grierson, CBE 1972; JP; DL; retired 1977; Director, Bass Ireland Ltd, Belfast, and subsidiary companies, 1956–77; *b* 10 July 1915; *e s* of Henry Kinahan, Belfast, and Ula, *d* of late Rt Rev. C. T. P. Grierson, Bishop of Down and Connor and Dromore; *m* 1946, Kathleen Blanche McClintock, MB, BS, *e d* of Rev. E. L. L. McClintock; three *s*. *Educ*: Stowe School. Singapore Volunteer Corps, 1939–45, POW Singapore, 1942–45. Commerce, London, 1933–38 and Malaya, 1938–56. Dir, Dunlop Malayan Estates Ltd, 1952–56; Man. Dir, Lyle and Kinahan Ltd, Belfast, 1956–63. Mem. (Alliance) Antrim S, NI Constitutional Convention, 1975–76; contested (Alliance) Antrim S, gen. election 1979. Belfast Harbour Comr, 1966–80; Chm., 1969–73, Pres., 1975–84, NI Marriage Guidance Council; Mem. Senate, QUB, 1968–; Chairman: NI Historic Buildings Council, 1973–; Ulster '71 Exhibn, 1971; NI Mountain Rescue: Working Party, 1976–77; Coordinating Cttee, 1978–85; Trustee, Nat. Heritage Memorial Fund, 1980–. JP 1961, High Sheriff 1971, DL 1977, Co. Antrim; Mem., Antrim District Council (Alliance Party), 1977–81. *Recreations*: mountain trekking, farming, classical music. *Address*: Clady Cottage, Dunadry, Antrim. *T*: Templepatrick 32379. *Club*: Royal Over-Seas League.
See also Sir R. G. C. Kinahan, D. McClintock.

KINAHAN, Maj.-Gen. Oliver John, CB 1981; Paymaster-in-Chief and Inspector of Army Pay Services, 1979–83; *b* 17 Nov. 1923; *m* 1950, Margery Ellis Fisher (*née* Hill); one *s* two *d*. Commissioned Royal Irish Fusiliers, 1942; served with Nigeria Regt, RWAFF, Sierra Leone, Nigeria, India, Burma, 1943–46; Instr, Sch. of Signals, 1947–49, Sch. of Infantry, 1950–51; transf. to RAPC, 1951; Japan and Korea, 1952–53; psc 1957; Comdt, RAPC Trng Centre, 1974–75; Dep. Paymaster-in-Chief (Army), 1977–78. Col Comdt RAPC, 1984–. FBIM. *Recreations*: country pursuits. *Address*: c/o Royal Bank of Scotland, Kirkland House, Whitehall, SW1. *Club*: Army and Navy.

KINAHAN, Sir Robert (George Caldwell), (Sir Robin Kinahan), Kt 1961; ERD 1946; JP; Lord-Lieutenant, County Borough of Belfast, since 1985 (Vice Lord-Lieutenant, 1976–85); Director: Abbey Life (Ireland) Ltd, 1981; Standard Telephones and Cables (Northern Ireland) Ltd, 1974; *b* 24 Sept. 1916; *s* of Henry Kinahan, Lowwood, Belfast; *m* 1950, Coralie I., *d* of late Capt. C. de Burgh, DSO, RN; two *s* three *d*. *Educ*: Stowe Sch., Buckingham. Vintners' Scholar (London), 1937. Served Royal Artillery, 1939–45, Capt. Chairman: Inglis & Co. Ltd, 1962–82; E. T. Green Ltd, 1964–82; Ulster Bank Ltd, 1970–82 (Dir, 1963–85); Director: Bass Ireland, 1958–78; Gallaher Ltd, 1967–82; NI Bd, Eagle Star, 1970–81; Nat. Westminster Bank, 1973–82; Abbeyfield Belfast Soc., 1983–; Cheshire House (NI), 1983–. Mem., NI Adv. Commn, 1972–73. MP (NI) Clifton, 1958–59. Councillor, Belfast Corporation, 1948; Lord Mayor of Belfast, 1959–61. JP Co. Antrim, 1950, DL 1962; High Sheriff: Belfast, 1956; Co. Antrim, 1969. Hon. LLD (Belfast) 1962. *Recreations*: gardening, family life. *Address*: Castle Upton, Templepatrick, Co. Antrim. *T*: Templepatrick 32466. *Club*: Kildare Street and University (Dublin).
See also C. H. G. Kinahan, Sir A. T. C. Neave, Bt.

KINCADE, James, MA, PhD; Headmaster, Methodist College, Belfast, since 1974; National Governor for Northern Ireland, BBC, since 1985; *b* 4 Jan. 1925; *s* of George and Rebecca Jane Kincade; *m* 1952, Elizabeth Fay, 2nd *d* of J. Anderson Piggot, OBE, DL, JP; one *s* one *d*. *Educ*: Foyle Coll.; Magee University Coll.; Trinity Coll. Dublin (Schol. and Gold Medallist, MA, Stein Research Prize); Oriel Coll., Oxford (MA, BLitt); Edinburgh Univ. (PhD). Served RAF, India and Burma, 1943–47 (commnd, 1944). Senior English Master, Merchiston Castle Sch., 1952–61; Vis. Professor of Philosophy, Indiana Univ., 1959; Headmaster, Royal Sch., Dungannon, 1961–74. Chairman, Schools Cttee Ulster Savings, 1973–; President, Ulster Headmasters' Assoc., 1975–77; Chm., Joint Five, 1980–. QUB: Mem. of Senate, 1982–; Mem., Faculty of Theology, 1984–. *Publications*: articles in Mind, Hermathena, Jl of Religion. *Recreations*: reading, writing and arithmetic. *Address*: 23 Adelaide Park, Belfast BT9 6FX.

KINCH, Anthony Alec; Head of Division for Project Operations, European Regional Development Fund operations, Commission of the European Communities, 1982–86; *b* 13 Dec. 1926; *s* of late Edward Alec Kinch, OBE, retd Polit. Adviser, Iraq Petroleum Co. Ltd, and Catherine Teresa Kinch (*née* Cassidy); *m* 1952, Barbara Patricia (*née* Paton Walsh); four *s* two *d*. *Educ*: Ampleforth; Christ Church, Oxford (MA). Practised at Bar, 1951–57; Contracts Man., Electronics Div., Plessey Co. Ltd, 1957–60; Legal Adviser and Insce Consultant, R. & H. Green and Silley Weir Ltd, 1960–66; Dir, Fedn of Bakers, 1966–73; Head of Foodstuffs Div., Commn of EEC, 1973–82. Chm., Brussels Area, SDP, 1981–84; Mem., Council for Social Democracy, 1982–. Contested (SDP) Kent E, European Parly elecn, 1984. Chevalier du Fourquet (Belgium), 1980. KCHS with star, 1985 (KCHS 1981). *Recreation*: living. *Address*: c/o National Westminster Bank, 1 St James's Square, SW1Y 4JX.

KINCHIN SMITH, Michael; Appointments' Secretary to Archbishops of Canterbury and York, and Secretary, Crown Appointments Commission, since 1984; *b* 8 May 1921; *s* of Francis John Kinchin Smith, Lectr in Classics, Inst. of Educn, London, and Dione Jean Elizabeth, *d* of Sir Francis Henry May, GCMG, sometime Governor of Hong Kong; *m* 1947, Rachel Frances, *er d* of Rt Hon. Sir Henry Urmston Willink, Bt, MC, QC, Master of Magdalene Coll., Cambridge; four *s* two *d*. *Educ*: Westminster Sch. (King's Schol.); Christ Church, Oxford (Schol.). 1st cl. hons Mod. History; Pres. Oxford Union, 1941. Served with 2nd and 3rd Bns, Coldstream Guards in Italian Campaign (Captain; despatches). Commercial and Admin. Trainee, ICI Ltd, 1947; admin. posts with BBC, 1950–78: Asst, Staff Admin, 1950; Admin Officer, Talks (Sound), 1954; Asst Estabt Officer, TV, 1955; Estabt Officer, Programmes, TV, 1961; Staff Admin Officer, 1962; Asst Controller, Staff Admin, 1964; Controller, Staff Admin, 1967; Controller, Development, Personnel, 1976. Lay Assistant to Archbishop of Canterbury, 1979–84. Chm. Exec. Council, RIPA, 1975–77; CIPM; Vice Pres. (Pay and Employment Conditions), IPM, 1978–80; Lay Selector, ACCM, 1963–73 (Mem. Candidates Cttee, 1966–69); Lay Chm., Richmond and Barnes Deanery Synod, 1970–76; Mem. General Synod, C of E, 1975–78. 1st Chm., Mortlake with East Sheen Soc., 1969–71; Chm., Assoc. of Amenity Societies in Richmond-upon-Thames, 1973–77. *Publication*: (jtly) Forward from Victory, 1943. *Recreations*: walking, local history. *Address*: The Old Bakery, Epwell, Banbury, Oxon OX15 6LA. *T*: Swalcliffe 773. *Club*: United Oxford & Cambridge University.

KINCRAIG, Hon. Lord; Robert Smith Johnston; a Senator of the College of Justice in Scotland, since 1972; *b* 10 Oct. 1918; *s* of W. T. Johnston, iron merchant, Glasgow; *m* 1943, Joan, *d* of late Col A. G. Graham, Glasgow; one *s* one *d*. *Educ*: Strathallan, Perthshire; St John's Coll., Cambridge; Glasgow Univ. BA (Hons) Cantab, 1939; LLB (with distinction) Glasgow, 1942. Mem. of Faculty of Advocates, 1942; Advocate-Depute, Crown Office, 1953–55; QC (Scotland) 1955; Home Advocate Depute, 1959–62; Sheriff of Roxburgh, Berwick and Selkirk, 1964–70; Dean of the Faculty of Advocates of Scotland, 1970–72. Contested (U) Stirling and Falkirk Burghs General Election, 1959. *Recreations*: golf, curling, gardening. *Address*: Westwood, Longniddry, East Lothian. *T*: Longniddry 52197. *Clubs*: Hon. Company of Edinburgh Golfers (Edinburgh); Royal Scottish Automobile (Glasgow).
See also A. G. Johnston.

KINDERSLEY, family name of **Baron Kindersley.**

KINDERSLEY, 3rd Baron *cr* 1941; **Robert Hugh Molesworth Kindersley,** DL; Chairman, Commonwealth Development Corporation, since 1980; Director, Lazard Bros & Co. Ltd, since 1960 (a Vice-Chairman, 1981–85); *b* 18 Aug. 1929; *s* of 2nd Baron Kindersley, CBE, MC, and Nancy Farnsworth (*d* 1977), *d* of Dr Geoffrey Boyd, Toronto; *S* father, 1976; *m* 1954, Venice Marigold (Rosie), *d* of late Captain Lord (Arthur) Francis Henry Hill; three *s* one *d*. *Educ*: Eton; Trinity Coll., Oxford; Harvard Business Sch., USA. Lt Scots Guards; served Malaya, 1948–49. Director: London Assurance, 1957–; Witan Investment Co. Ltd, 1958–85; Steel Company of Wales, 1959–67; Marconi Co. Ltd, 1963–68; Sun Alliance & London Insurance Gp, 1965–; English Electric Co. Ltd, 1966–68; Gen. Electric Co. Ltd, 1968–70; British Match Corp. Ltd, 1969–73; Swedish Match Co., 1973–85; Aall Trust and Banking Corp., 1980–; Phoenix Assurance, 1985–; Maersk Co. Ltd, 1986–. Financial Adviser to Export Gp for the Constructional Industries, 1961–; Mem., Adv. Panel, Overseas Projects Gp, 1975–77; Dep. Chm., ECGD Adv. Council, 1975–80; Chm., Exec. Cttee, BBA, 1976–78; Pres., Anglo-Taiwan Trade Cttee, 1976–. Hon. Treasurer, YWCA, 1965–76. Member: Institut International d'Etudes Bancaires, 1971–85; Ct, Fishmongers' Co, 1973–, Renter Warden, 1985–86, Second Warden, 1986–87. DL Kent, 1986. *Recreations*: all country pursuits, including tennis and ski-ing. *Heir*: *s* Hon. Rupert John Molesworth Kindersley [*b* 11 March 1955; *m* 1975, Sarah, *d* of late John D. Warde; one *d*]. *Address*: West Green Farm, Shipbourne, Kent TN11 9PU. *T*: Plaxtol 810293. *Clubs*: Pratt's, MCC, All England Lawn Tennis and Croquet, Queen's.

KINDERSLEY, Lt-Col Claude Richard Henry, DSO 1944; MC 1943; DL; Vice Lord-Lieutenant, Isle of Wight, 1980–86; *b* 11 Dec. 1911; *s* of late Lt-Col Archibald Ogilvie Lyttelton Kindersley, CMG, and Edith Mary Kindersley (*née* Craven); *m* 1938, Vivien Mary, *d* of late Charles John Wharton Darwin, Elston Hall, Notts; three *d*. *Educ*: Wellington Coll.; Trinity Coll., Cambridge. MA. Commissioned HLI, 1933; served with 2nd Bn HLI, NW Frontier, Palestine and Middle East, 1936–43, and with 1st Bn HLI, France and Germany, 1944–45; commanded 1st Bn HLI, 1945; comd Infantry Boys' Batt., 1953–54; retd 1955. DL: Hants, 1962–74; Isle of Wight, 1974; High Sheriff, Isle of Wight, 1974–75. President: Country Landowners' Assoc. (IoW Branch), 1978–; Isle of Wight Scout Assoc., 1966–86. *Recreation*: yachting. *Address*: Hamstead Grange, Yarmouth, Isle of Wight. *T*: Yarmouth 760230. *Clubs*: Royal Yacht Squadron; Royal Solent (Yarmouth).

KINDERSLEY, David Guy, MBE 1979; stone-carver and designer of alphabets (self-employed); in partnership with Lida Lopes Cardozo, since 1981; *b* 11 June 1915; *s* of Guy Molesworth Kindersley and Kathleen Elton; *m* 1957, Barbara Pym Eyre Petrie; two *s* one *d*. *Educ*: St Cyprian's, Eastbourne (prep. sch.); Marlborough Coll., Wilts. Apprenticed to Eric Gill, ARA, 1933–36. Taught at Cambridge Coll. of Arts and Technology, 1946–57; one-time adviser to MoT on street-name alphabets; adviser to Shell Film Unit on design of titles, 1949–58; consultant to Letraset Internat., 1964–; Dir, Cambridge Super Vision Ltd, 1983–. Sen. Research Fellow, William Andrews Clark Memorial Library, Univ. of California, Los Angeles, 1967. Chm., Wynkyn de Worde Soc., 1976. *Publications*: Optical Letter Spacing and its Mechanical Application, 1966 (rev. and repub. by Wynkyn de Worde Soc., 1976); Mr Eric Gill, 1967, new edn (Eric Gill—Further Thoughts by an Apprentice), 1982; Graphic Variations, 1979; (with L. L. Cardozo) Letters Slate Cut, 1981; contribs to Printing Technology, Penrose Annual, Visible Language. Limited edns: Variations on the Theme of 26 Letters, edn 50, 1969; Graphic Sayings, edn 130, 1973. *Recreation*: archaeology. *Address*: 152 Victoria Road, Cambridge CB4 3DZ. *T*: Cambridge 62170. *Clubs*: Arts, Double Crown; (Hon. Mem.) Rounce and Coffin (Los Angeles).

KING, family name of **Baron King of Wartnaby** and **Earl of Lovelace.**

KING OF WARTNABY, Baron *cr* 1983 (Life Peer), of Wartnaby in the County of Leicestershire; **John Leonard King;** Kt 1979; Chairman: Babcock International plc (formerly Babcock & Wilcox Ltd), since 1972; British Airways, since 1981; *yr s* of Albert John King and Kathleen King; *m* 1st 1941, Lorna Kathleen Sykes (*d* 1969); three *s* one *d*; 2nd, 1970, Hon. Isabel Monckton, *y d* of 8th Viscount Galway. Founded Ferrybridge Industries Ltd and Whitehouse Industries Ltd, subseq. Pollard Ball & Roller Bearing Co. Ltd, 1945 (Man. Dir 1945, Chm., 1961–69); Chm., Dennis Motor Hldgs Ltd, 1970–72; Dir, David Brown Corp. Ltd, 1971–75. Current chairmanships and directorships include: National Nuclear Corp.; British Nuclear Associates Ltd; Royal Ordnance Factories; SKF

(UK) Ltd; Dick Corp. (USA); First Union Corp. (USA). Member: Engineering Industries Council, 1975; NEDC Cttee on Finance for Investment, 1976–78; Grand Council and Financial Policy Cttee, CBI, 1976–78; Chairman: City and Industrial Liaison Council, 1973–85; Review Bd for Govt Contracts, 1975–78; British Olympic Appeals Cttee, 1975–78; Macmillan Appeal for Continuing Care, 1977–78; NEB, 1980–81 (Dep. Chm., 1979–80); Alexandra Rose Day Foundn, 1980–85; Mem. Cttee, Ranfurly Library Service; Vice-Pres., Nat. Soc. for Cancer Relief. Dir, Royal Opera Trust. MFH: Badsworth Foxhounds, 1949–58, Duke of Rutland's Foxhounds (Belvoir), 1958–72; Chm., Belvoir Hunt, 1972. Freeman, City of London, 1984. Hon. Dr Gardner-Webb Coll., USA, 1980. FBIM 1978; FCIT 1982. Hon. CRAeS, 1986. Comdr, Royal Order of Polar Star (Sweden), 1983. *Recreations:* hunting, field sports, racing. *Address:* Cleveland House, St James's Square, SW1Y 4LN. *T:* 01–930 9766. *Clubs:* White's, Pratts'; Brook (New York).

KING, Sir Albert, Kt 1974; OBE 1958; Leader, Labour Group, Leeds Metropolitan District Council, 1975–78, retired (Leader of the Council with one break, 1958–75); *b* 20 Aug. 1905; *s* of George and Ann King; *m* 1928, Pauline Riley; one *d. Educ:* Primrose Hill, Leeds. Full-time officer, engrg, 1942–70, retd. Hon. Freedom of the City of Leeds, 1976. *Recreations:* walking, reading. *Address:* 25 Brook Hill Avenue, Leeds LS17 8QA. *T:* Leeds 684684. *Clubs:* Beeston Working Men's, East Leeds Labour (Leeds).

KING, Albert Leslie, MBE 1945; *b* 28 Aug. 1911; *s* of late William John King and late Elizabeth Mary Amelia King; *m* 1938, Constance Eileen Stroud; two *d. Educ:* University Coll. Sch., Hampstead. Joined Shell-Mex and BP Statistical Dept, 1928. Joined Territorial Army, 1939; Major, RA, 1944. Manager, Secretariat, Petroleum Board, 1947; Manager, Trade Relations Dept, Shell-Mex and BP Ltd, 1948; Gen. Manager: Administration, 1954; Sales, 1957; Operations, 1961; apptd Dir, 1962, Managing Dir, 1963–66. Dep. Dir-Gen., BIM, 1966–68. FCCA; FSS; CBIM; Hon. JDipMA. Barrister (Called to the Bar 1980). *Address:* Highlands, 50 Waggon Road, Hadley Wood, Barnet, Herts. *T:* 01–449 6424. *Clubs:* MCC; Surrey CCC, Saracens.

KING, Alexander, CMG 1975; CBE 1948; President, since 1984, and Co-Founder, 1968, Club of Rome; *b* Glasgow, 26 Jan. 1909; *s* of J. M. King; *m* 1933, Sarah Maskell Thompson; three *d. Educ:* Highgate Sch.; Royal College of Science, London (DSc); University of Munich. Demonstrator, 1932, and later Senior Lecturer, until 1940, in physical chemistry, Imperial Coll. of Science; Dep. Scientific Adviser, Min. of Production, 1942; Head of UK Scientific Mission, Washington, and Scientific Attaché, British Embassy 1943–47; Head of Lord President's Scientific Secretariat, 1947–50; Chief Scientific Officer, Dept of Scientific and Industrial Research, 1950–56; Dep. Dir, European Productivity Agency, 1956–61; Dir for Scientific Affairs, OECD, 1961–68, Dir-Gen., 1968–74; Chm., Internat. Federation of Insts for Advanced Study, 1974–84. Adviser, Govt of Ontario. Assoc. Fellow, Center for the Study of Democratic Institutions, Santa Barbara, Calif; Vis. Professor: Brandeis Univ., 1978; Univ. of Montréal, 1979. Leader Imperial Coll. Expedition to Jan Mayen, 1938; Harrison Prize of Chemical Soc., 1938; Gill Memorial Prize, Royal Geographical Society, 1938, Mem. Council, 1939–41; Hon. Sec. Chemical Soc., 1948–50; DSc (hc) Ireland, 1974; DUniv Open, 1976; Hon. LLD Strathclyde, 1982. *Publications:* The International Stimulus, 1974; The State of the Planet, 1980; various chemistry textbooks, and papers in Journal of The Chemical Soc., Faraday Soc.; numerous articles on education, science policy and management. *Address:* 168 Rue de Grenelle, Paris 75007, France. *Club:* Athenæum.

KING, Alexander Hyatt; musical scholar; a Deputy Keeper, Department of Printed Books, British Museum, 1959–76, retired; *b* 18 July 1911; *s* of Thomas Hyatt King and Mabel Jessie (*née* Brayne); *m* 1943, Evelyn Mary Davies; two *s. Educ:* Dulwich Coll.; King's Coll., Cambridge (schol.; MA). Entered Dept of Printed Books, British Museum, 1934; Dep. Keeper, 1959–76; Supt of Music Room, 1944–73; Music Librarian, Ref. Div., British Library, 1973–76. Hon. Sec., British Union Catalogue of Early Music, 1948–57; Mem. Council, Royal Musical Assoc., 1949–, Editor, Proc. of the Assoc., 1952–57, Pres., 1974–78; Pres., Internat. Assoc. of Music Libraries, 1955–59 (Hon. Mem., 1968), Pres., UK Br., 1953–68, Vice-Chm. jt cttee, Internat. Musicological Soc. and IAML, for Internat. Inventory of Musical Sources, 1961–76; Chm., exec. cttee, Brit. Inst. of Recorded Sound, 1951–62. Sandars Reader in Bibliography, Univ. of Cambridge, 1962; Vice-Chm., exec. cttee, Grove's Dictionary of Music, 1970–74; Trustee, Hinrichsen Foundn, 1976–82; Hon. Librarian, Royal Philharmonic Soc., 1969–82. Mem., Zentralinst. für Mozartforschung, 1953. DUniv York, 1978; Hon. DMus St Andrews, 1981. *Publications:* Chamber Music, 1948; (jtly) catalogue: Music in the Hirsch Library, 1951; catalogue: Exhibition of Handel's Messiah, 1951; Mozart in Retrospect, 1955, 3rd edn 1976; Mozart in the British Museum, 1956, repr. 1975; exhibn catalogue: Henry Purcell—G. F. Handel, 1959; Some British Collectors of Music, 1963; 400 Years of Music Printing, 1964, 2nd edn 1968; Handel and his Autographs, 1967; Mozart Chamber Music, 1968, 2nd edn 1970; Mozart String and Wind Concertos, 1978; Printed Music in the British Museum: an account of the collections, the catalogues, and their formation, up to 1920, 1979; A Wealth of Music in the various collections of the British Library (Reference Division) and the British Museum, 1983; A Mozart Legacy: aspects of the British Library collections, 1984; *edited:* (jtly) Mozart's Duet Sonata in C K19d, 1953; illustr. edn of Alfred Einstein's Short History of Music, 1953; P. K. Hoffmann's Cadenzas and elaborated slow movements to 6 Mozart piano concertos, 1959; (jtly) 2nd edn of Emily Anderson's Letters of Mozart and his Family, 1966; Concert Goer's Companion series, 1970–; Auction catalogues of Music, 1973–; *contribs to:* Year's Work in Music, 1947–51; Schubert, a symposium, 1947; Music, Libraries and Instruments, 1961; Deutsch Festschrift, 1963; Essays in honour of Victor Scholderer, 1970; Grasberger Festschrift, 1975; Essays in honour of Sir Jack Westrup, 1976; The New Grove, 1980; Rosenthal Festschrift, 1984; various articles; *relevant publication* (ed by Oliver Neighbour) Music and Bibliography: Essays in honour of Alec Hyatt King, 1980. *Recreations:* watching cricket, opera, exploring Suffolk. *Address:* 29 Lauradale Road, N2 9LT. *T:* 01–883 1623. *Club:* MCC.

KING, Alison, OBE 1978; Co-ordinator Properties, Women's Royal Voluntary Service, 1974–78; Director, WRVS Office Premises Ltd, since 1969; Member, WRVS Housing Association Committee, since 1973. Flight-Capt., Operations, Air Transport Auxiliary, 1940–45. Dir, Women's Junior Air Corps, 1952–58; Gen. Sec., NFWI, 1959–69. Chm., British Women Pilots' Assoc., 1956–64. *Publication:* Golden Wings, 1956 (repr. 1975). *Recreations:* writing, painting in oils. *Address:* 4 Chagford House, Chagford Street, NW1. *T:* 01–262 4631. *Club:* University Women's.

KING, Prof. Anthony Stephen; Professor of Government, since 1969, Pro-Vice Chancellor, since 1986, University of Essex; *b* 17 Nov. 1934; *o s* of late Harold and Marjorie King; *m* 1st, 1965, Vera Korte (*d* 1971); 2nd, 1980, Jan Reece. *Educ:* Queen's Univ., Kingston Ont. (1st Cl. Hons, Hist. 1956); Magdalen Coll., Oxford (Rhodes Schol.; 1st Cl. Hons, PPE, 1958). Student, Nuffield Coll., Oxford, 1958–61; DPhil (Oxon) 1962. Fellow of Magdalen Coll., Oxford, 1961–65; Sen. Lectr, 1966–68, Reader, 1968–69, Essex Univ. ACLS Fellow, Columbia Univ., NY, 1962–63; Fellow, Center for Advanced Study in the Behavioral Scis, Stanford, Calif., 1977–78; Visiting Professor: Wisconsin Univ., 1967; Princeton Univ., 1984. Elections Commentator, BBC. Co-Editor, British Jl of Political Science, 1984– (Editor, 1972–77). *Publications:* (with D. E. Butler) The British General Election of 1964, 1965; (with D. E. Butler) The British General Election of 1966, 1966; (ed) British Politics: People, Parties and Parliament, 1966; (ed) The British Prime Minister, 1969, 2nd edn 1985; (with Anne Sloman) Westminster and Beyond, 1973; British Members of Parliament: a self-portrait, 1974; (ed) Why is Britain becoming Harder to Govern?, 1976; Britain Says Yes: the 1975 referendum on the Common Market, 1977; (ed) The New American Political System, 1978; (ed) Both Ends of the Avenue: the Presidency, the Executive Branch and Congress in the 1980s, 1983; frequent contributor to British and American jls and periodicals. *Recreations:* music, theatre, holidays, walking. *Address:* Department of Government, University of Essex, Wivenhoe Park, Colchester, Essex CO4 3SQ. *T:* Colchester 862286; The Mill House, Middle Green, Wakes Colne, Colchester, Essex CO6 2BP. *T:* Earls Colne 2497.

KING, Billie Jean; tennis player; Commissioner, Team Tennis, since 1981; *b* 22 Nov. 1943; *d* of Willard J. Moffitt; *m* 1965, Larry King. *Educ:* Los Cerritos Sch.; Long Beach High Sch.; Los Angeles State Coll. Played first tennis match at age of eleven; won first championship, Southern California, 1958; coached by Clyde Walker, Alice Marble, Frank Brennan and Mervyn Rose; won first All England Championship, 1966, and five times subseq., and in 1979 achieved record of 20 Wimbledon titles (six Singles, ten Doubles, four Mixed Doubles); has won all other major titles inc. US Singles and Doubles Championships on all four surfaces, and 24 US national titles in all. Pres., Women's Tennis Assoc., 1980–81. *Publications:* Tennis to Win, 1970; Billie Jean, 1974; (with Joe Hyams) Secrets of Winning Tennis, 1975; Tennis Love (illus. Charles Schulz), 1978; (with Frank Deford) Billie Jean King, 1982. *Address:* Future, Inc., 1801 Century Park East, Suite 1400, Los Angeles, Calif 90067, USA.

KING, Dr Brian Edmund; Director, since 1967, and Chief Executive, since 1977, Wira Technology Group Ltd (formerly Wool Industries Research Association); *b* 25 May 1928; *s* of Albert Theodore King and Gladys Johnson; *m* 1952 (marr. diss.); two *s*; *m* 1972, Eunice Wolstenholme; one *d. Educ:* Pocklington Sch.; Leeds Univ. TMM (Research) Ltd, 1952–57; British Oxygen, 1957–67. *Recreations:* bridge, swimming, tennis. *Address:* Victoria Villa, Mount Street, Cleckheaton, W Yorks BD19 3QD. *T:* Cleckheaton 861170. *Club:* Royal Commonwealth Society.

KING, Cecil (Harmsworth); *b* 20 Feb. 1901; *e* surv. *s* of Sir Lucas White King, CSI, and Geraldine Adelaide Hamilton, *d* of Alfred Harmsworth, barrister of the Middle Temple; *m* 1st, 1923, Agnes Margaret (*d* 1985), *d* of the Rev. Canon G. A. Cooke, DD, Regius Prof. of Hebrew, Oxford, and Canon of Christ Church; one *s* one *d* (and two *s* decd). 2nd, 1962, Dame Ruth Railton, *qv. Educ:* Winchester; Christ Church, Oxford (2nd class hons history, MA). Dir, Daily Mirror, 1929; Dep. Chm., Sunday Pictorial, 1942; Chairman: Daily Mirror Newspapers Ltd and Sunday Pictorial Newspapers Ltd, 1951–1963; International Publishing Corp., 1963–68; The Reed Paper Group, 1963–68; Wall Paper Manufacturers, 1965–67; British Film Institute, 1948–52; Newspaper Proprietors' Assoc., 1961–68; Nigerian Printing & Publishing Co., 1948–68; Butterworth & Co. Ltd, 1968. Director: Reuters, 1953–59; Bank of England, 1965–68. Part-time Mem., National Coal Board, 1966–69. Mem., National Parks Commn, later Countryside Commn, 1966–69. Gold Badge for services to City of Warsaw; Gold Medal for services to British paper trade. Hon. DLitt Boston, 1974. *Publications:* The Future of the Press, 1967; Strictly Personal, 1969; With Malice Towards None: a war diary, 1970; Without Fear or Favour, 1971; The Cecil King Diary 1965–70, 1972; On Ireland, 1973; The Cecil King Diary 1970–74, 1975; Cecil King's Commonplace Book, 1981. *Recreation:* reading. *Address:* 23 Greenfield Park, Dublin 4, Ireland. *T:* Dublin 695870.

See also Sir G. V. K. Burton.

KING, Charles Andrew Buchanan, CMG 1961; MBE 1944; HM Diplomatic Service, retired; Chairman, Premier Sauna Ltd, 1970–81; *b* 25 July 1915; *s* of late Major Andrew Buchanan King, 7th Argyll and Sutherland Highlanders and of Evelyn Nina (*née* Sharpe). *Educ:* Wellington Coll.; Magdalene Coll., Cambridge (MA). Vice-Consul: Zürich, 1940, Geneva, 1941; Attaché, HM Legation, Berne, 1942; transf. to FO, 1946; 2nd Sec., Vienna, 1950; transf. to FO 1953; to Hong Kong, 1958; to FO 1961; retired, 1967; Head of W European Div., Overseas Dept, London Chamber of Commerce, 1968–70. *Recreation:* travel. *Address:* 19 Archery Close, W2. *Club:* Naval and Military.

KING, Charles Martin M.; *see* Meade-King.

KING, Colin Sainthill W.; *see* Wallis-King.

KING, Prof. David Anthony, FRSC, MInstP; Brunner Professor of Physical Chemistry, University of Liverpool, since 1974; *b* 12 Aug. 1939; *s* of Arnold King and Patricia (*née* Vardy), Durban; *m* Jane Lichtenstein; one *d* (and two *s* by previous marriage). *Educ:* St John's Coll., Johannesburg; Univ. of the Witwatersrand, Johannesburg. BSc, PhD (Rand), ScD (E Anglia). Shell Scholar, Imperial Coll., 1963–66; Lectr in Chemical Physics, Univ. of E Anglia, Norwich, 1966–74. Member: Comité de Direction of Centre de Cinétique Physique et Chimique, Nancy, 1974–81; Nat. Exec., Assoc. of Univ. Teachers, 1970–78 (Nat. Pres., 1976–77); British Vacuum Council, 1978– (Chm., 1982–85); Internat. Union for Vacuum Science and Technology, 1978–86; Faraday Div., Council, Chem. Soc., 1979–82; Scientific Adv. Panel, Daresbury Lab., 1980–82; Res. Adv. Cttee, Leverhulme Trust, 1980–; Beirat, Fritz Haber Inst., West Berlin, 1981–86. Chm., Gallery Cttee, Bluecoat Soc. of Arts. Member Editorial Board: Jl of Physics C, 1977–80; Surface Science Reports, 1983–. Chem. Soc. Award for surface and colloid chemistry, 1978. *Publications:* papers on the physics and chemistry of solid surfaces in: Proc. Royal Soc., Surface Science, Jl Chem. Soc., Jl of Physics, etc. *Recreations:* photography, reading, squash. *Address:* Briarwood, Carnatic Road, Liverpool L18 8BY. *T:* (home) 051–724 1477, (office) 051–709 6022 (ext. 2560).

KING, (Denys) Michael (Gwilym), CEng, FICE, MIMechE; Chairman and Managing Director, Heathrow Airport Ltd, since 1986 (Director, 1977–86); Director, BAA plc, since 1986 (Member, British Airports Authority, 1980–86); *b* 29 May 1929; *s* of William James King, FCIS, and Hilda May King; *m* 1st, 1956, Monica Helen (marr. diss. 1973); three *d*; 2nd, 1985, Ann Elizabeth. *Educ:* St Edmund's Sch., Canterbury; Simon Langton Sch., Canterbury; Battersea Polytechnic, London (BScEng Hons London, 1949). MIMechE 1966; FICE 1977. Engr, J. Laing Construction Ltd, 1961–71, Dir, 1971–74; Engrg Dir, BAA, 1974–77 (also at other cos). *Recreations:* yachting, squash, golf. *Address:* c/o British Airports Authority, D'Albiac House, Heathrow, Hounslow, Mddx. *T:* 01–745 7241. *Clubs:* Foxhills Country (Ottershaw); Mid Surrey Squash (Stoneleigh).

KING, Douglas James Edward, FRICS; Senior Partner, King & Co., Chartered Surveyors, since 1960; Director: Bradford & Bingley Building Society, since 1982; Frogmore Estates plc, since 1982; *b* 12 April 1919; *s* of Herbert James King, OBE, FRICS and Gertrude Carney; *m* 1941, Betty Alice Martin; two *s* one *d. Educ:* Hillcrest Prep. Sch., Frinton-on-Sea; Taunton Sch. FRICS 1952. Served War, TA, 1939–46, Captain RA. Chm., Hearts of Oak & Enfield Bldg Soc., 1975–82. A Vice Pres., London Chamber of Commerce and Industry, 1980– (Chm., 1978–80); Chm., London Court of Internat. Arbitration, 1981–82; Gen. Comr of Income Tax, City of London, 1978–. Master, Wheelwrights' Co., 1985–86. Governor, Queenswood Sch., 1980–. *Recreation:* lives and writings of

Johnson, Boswell and Pepys. *Address:* Monkswood Cottage, 73a Camlet Way, Hadley Wood, Herts EN4 0NL. *T:* 01–236 3000. *Clubs:* Carlton, City Livery.

KING, Prof. Edmund James, MA, PhD, DLit; Professor of Education, University of London King's College, 1975–79, now Emeritus Professor; *b* 19 June 1914; *s* of James and Mary Alice King; *m* 1939, Margaret Mary Breakell; one *s* three *d*. *Educ:* Univ. of Manchester (BA, MA); Univ. of London (PhD, DLit). Taught in grammar schs, 1936–47; Asst, then Sen. Asst to Dir of Extra-Mural Studies, Univ. of London, 1947–53; Lectr, subseq. Reader, Univ. of London King's Coll., 1953–75, also Dir, Comparative Research Unit, King's Coll., 1970–73. Visiting appts at Amer., Can. and Chinese univs; also in Melbourne, Tokyo, Tehran, etc; lecturing and adv. assignments in many countries. Editor, Comparative Education, 1978–. *Publications:* Other Schools and Ours, 1958, 5th edn 1979; World Perspectives in Education, 1962, 2nd edn 1965; (ed) Communist Education, 1963; Society, Schools and Progress in the USA, 1965; Education and Social Change, 1966; Comparative Studies and Educational Decision, 1968; Education and Development in Western Europe, 1969; (ed) The Teacher and the Needs of Society, 1970; The Education of Teachers: a comparative analysis, 1970; (with W. Boyd) A History of Western Education, 1972; Post-compulsory Education, vol. I: a new analysis in Western Europe, 1974; vol. II: the way ahead, 1975 (both with C. H. Moor and J. A. Mundy); (ed) Reorganizing Education, 1977; (ed) Education for Uncertainty, 1979; Technological/occupational Challenge, Social Transformation and Educational Response, 1986. *Recreations:* gardening, music, writing. *Address:* 40 Alexandra Road, Epsom, Surrey.

KING, Very Rev. Edward Laurie; Dean of Cape Town since 1958; *b* 30 Jan. 1920; *s* of William Henry and Norah Alice King; *m* 1950, Helen Stuart Mathers, MB, BCh, MMed; one *s* three *d*. *Educ:* King's Coll., Taunton; University of Wales (BA). Deacon, 1945; priest, 1946, Monmouth; Associate in Theology (S Af.). Curate of Risca, 1945–48; Diocese of Johannesburg, 1948–50; Rector of Robertson, Cape, 1950–53; Rector of Stellenbosch, 1953–58. *Recreations:* cricket, reading. *Address:* The Deanery, Upper Orange Street, Cape Town 8001, South Africa. *T:* 45–2609. *Club:* City and Civil Service.

KING, Evelyn Mansfield, MA; *b* 30 May 1907; *s* of Harry Percy King and Winifred Elizabeth Paulet; *m* 1935, Hermione Edith, *d* of late Arthur Felton Crutchley, DSO; one *s* two *d*. *Educ:* Cheltenham Coll.; King's Coll., Cambridge; Inner Temple. Cambridge Univ. Correspondent to the Sunday Times, 1928–30; Asst Master Bedford Sch., 1930; Headmaster and Warden, Clayesmore Sch., 1935–50; Gloucestershire Regt 1940; Acting Lt-Col 1941. MP (Lab) Penryn and Falmouth Div. of Cornwall, 1945–50; Parly Sec., Min. of Town and Country Planning, 1947–50. Resigned from Labour Party, 1951, and joined Conservative Party; contested (C) Southampton (Itchen), 1959; MP (C) Dorset S, 1964–79. Member of Parly delegations: Bermuda and Washington, 1946; Tokyo, 1947; Cairo and ME, 1967; Jordan and Persian Gulf, 1968; Kenya and Seychelles, 1969; Malta, 1970 (leader); Malawi, 1971 (leader); Mem. Select Cttee on Overseas Aid, 1971; Chm. Food Cttee, 1971–73. *Publications:* (with J. C. Trewin) Printer to the House, Biography of Luke Hansard, 1952. *Recreations:* boats, riding. *Address:* Embley Manor, near Romsey, Hants. *T:* Romsey 512342; 11 Barton Street, SW1. *T:* 01–222 4525. *Clubs:* Carlton, Little Ship.

See also Sir R. G. Cooke.

KING, Francis Henry, CBE 1985 (OBE 1979); FRSL 1948; author; Drama Critic, Sunday Telegraph, since 1978; *b* 4 March 1923; *o s* of Eustace Arthur Cecil King and Faith Mina Read. *Educ:* Shrewsbury; Balliol Coll., Oxford. Chm., Soc. of Authors, 1975–77; Internat. Pres., PEN, 1986– (Pres., English PEN, 1978–86; Vice-Pres., 1977). *Publications: novels:* To the Dark Tower, 1946; Never Again, 1947; An Air That Kills, 1948; The Dividing Stream, 1951 (Somerset Maugham Award, 1952); The Dark Glasses, 1954; The Widow, 1957; The Man on the Rock, 1957; The Custom House, 1961; The Last of the Pleasure Gardens, 1965; The Waves Behind the Boat, 1967; A Domestic Animal, 1970; Flights (two short novels), 1973; A Game of Patience, 1974; The Needle, 1975; Danny Hill, 1977; The Action, 1978; Act of Darkness, 1983; Voices in an Empty Room, 1984; *short stories:* So Hurt and Humiliated, 1959; The Japanese Umbrella, 1964 (Katherine Mansfield Short Story Prize, 1965); The Brighton Belle, 1968; Hard Feelings, 1976; Indirect Method, 1980; One is a Wanderer, 1985; *poetry:* Rod of Incantation, 1952; *biography:* E. M. Forster and His World, 1978; (ed) My Sister and Myself: the diaries of J. R. Ackerley, 1982; *general:* (ed) Introducing Greece, 1956; Japan, 1970; Florence, 1982; (ed) Lafcadio Hearn: Writings from Japan, 1984. *Address:* 19 Gordon Place, W8 4JE. *T:* 01–937 5715. *Club:* PEN.

KING, Gen. Sir Frank (Douglas), GCB 1976 (KCB 1972; CB 1971); MBE 1953; Chairman: John Taylor Trust, since 1978; Assets Protection International Ltd, since 1981; Director, since 1978: John Taylor Ltd; John Taylor (Worksop); Leicester Frozen Foods; Kilton Properties; Springthorpe Property Co.; PLAZA Fish Ltd; Director, Control Risks Ltd, since 1979; *b* 9 March 1919; *s* of Arthur King, Farmer, and Kate Eliza (*née* Sheard), Brightwell, Berks; *m* 1947, Joy Emily Ellen Taylor-Lane; one *s* two *d*. *Educ:* Wallingford Gram. Sch. Joined Army, 1939; commnd into Royal Fusiliers, 1940; Parachute Regt, 1943; dropped Arnhem, Sept. 1944; Royal Military College of Science (ptsc), 1946; Staff Coll., Camberley (psc), 1950; comd 2 Parachute Bn, Middle East, 1960–62; comd 11 Infantry Bde Gp, Germany, 1963–64; Military Adviser (Overseas Equipment), 1965–66; Dir, Land/Air Warfare, MoD, 1967–68; Dir, Military Assistance Overseas, MoD, 1968–69; Comdt, RMCS, 1969–71; GOC-in-C, Army Strategic Comd, 1971–72; Dep. C-in-C UK Land Forces, 1972–73; GOC and Dir of Ops, N Ireland, 1973–75; Comdr, Northern Army Gp, and C-in-C BAOR, 1976–78; ADC Gen. to the Queen, 1977–78. Col Comdt, Army Air Corps, 1974–79. Trustee, Airborne Forces Security Trust, 1981–; Mem. Council, Air League, 1982–. Kermit Roosevelt Lectr, 1977. *Recreations:* golf, gardening, flying. *Address:* c/o Royal Bank of Scotland, Columbia House, 69 Aldwych, WC2. *Clubs:* Army and Navy; Berkshire Golf, Ashridge Golf.

KING, Frank Gordon, QC 1970; *b* 10 March 1915; *s* of late Lt-Col Frank King, DSO, OBE; *m* 1937, Monica Beatrice, *d* of late Arthur Collins; two *s* one *d*. *Educ:* Charterhouse, Godalming; Christ's Coll., Cambridge (BA 1936, LLM 1938). Served War of 1939–45; RA 1939–46, Major 1943. Called to the Bar, Gray's Inn, 1946. A Church Commissioner, 1973–81. *Address:* Red Chimneys, Warren Drive, Kingswood, Surrey. *Club:* Walton Heath Golf.

KING, Frederick Ernest, FRS 1954; MA, DPhil, DSc Oxon; PhD London; Scientific Adviser to British Petroleum Co. Ltd, 1959–71, retired; *er s* of late Frederick and Elizabeth King, Bexhill, Sussex. *Educ:* Bancroft's Sch.; University of London; Oriel Coll., Oxford. Ramsay Memorial Fellow, 1930–31; Demonstrator, Dyson Perrins Laboratory, 1931–34; University Lecturer and Demonstrator in Chemistry, Oxford Univ., 1934–48, and sometime lecturer in Organic Chemistry, Magdalen Coll. and Balliol Coll.; Sir Jesse Boot Prof. of Chemistry, University of Nottingham, 1948–55; Dir in charge of research, British Celanese Ltd, 1955–59. Fellow Queen Mary Coll., 1955. Tilden Lectr, Chem. Soc., 1948. *Publications:* scientific papers mainly in Jl of Chem. Soc. *Recreation:* gardening. *Address:* Glyde's Farm, Ashburnham, East Sussex TN33 9PB; 360 The Water Gardens, W2. *Club:* Athenæum.

KING, Hilary William, CBE 1964; HM Diplomatic Service, retired; *b* 10 March 1919; *s* of Dr W. H. King, Fowey, Cornwall; *m* 1947, Dr Margaret Helen Grierson Borrowman; one *s* three *d*. *Educ:* Sherborne; Corpus Christi Coll. Cambridge. Served War of 1939–45; Signals Officer, mission to Yugoslav Partizan GHQ, 1943–45 (MBE 1944). Apptd Mem. Foreign (subseq. Diplomatic) Service, Nov. 1946. A Vice-Consul in Yugoslavia, 1947–48; transferred to Foreign Office, 1949; promoted 1st Sec., 1950; transf. to Vienna as a Russian Sec., 1951; Washington, 1953; transf. Foreign Office, 1958; Commercial Counsellor, Moscow, 1959; acted as Chargé d'Affaires, 1960; Ambassador (and Consul-Gen.) to Guinea, 1962–65; St Antony's Coll., Oxford, Oct. 1965–June 1966; Counsellor of Embassy, Warsaw, 1966–67; Head of UN (Economic and Social) Dept, FCO, 1968–71; Consul-Gen., Hamburg, 1971–74. *Recreations:* sailing, amateur radio. *Address:* Fuaim an Sruth, South Cuan, Oban, Argyll PA34 4TU.

KING, Prof. Hubert John, CBE 1976; FEng, FIMinE; *b* 5 May 1915; *s* of Hubert and Emmeline Elizabeth King; *m* 1940, Ceridwen Richards; one *s* two *d*. *Educ:* Porth County Sch.; University Coll., Cardiff (PhD London); Glamorgan Polytechnic. Underground worker, S Wales Coalfield, 1931–36; served HM Forces, 1939–45; successively, Lecturer, Reader and Head of Mining and Mineral Sciences Dept, Univ. of Leeds, 1947–67; Univ. of Nottingham: Professor and Head, Mining Engineering Dept, 1967–77, Emeritus Prof., 1977; Dean, Faculty of Applied Science, 1973–76. President, Instn of Mining Engineers, 1974 (Institution Medal, 1980); Member and Chairman, Safety in Mines Research Adv. Cttee, 1967–79; Mem., Internat. Cttee for World Mining Congresses, 1967–77. *Publications:* various research papers in fields of surveying, rock mechanics and mineral economics. *Recreation:* golf. *Address:* 41 Breary Lane East, Leeds LS16 9EU.

KING, Isobel Wilson; see Buchanan, I. W.

KING, Sir James Granville Le Neve, 3rd Bt, *cr* 1888; TD; *b* 17 Sept. 1898; *s* of Sir John Westall King, 2nd Bt, and Frances Rosa (*d* 1942), *d* of John Neve, Oaken, Staffs; *S* father 1940; *m* 1928, Penelope Charlotte, *d* of late Capt. E. Cooper-Key, CB, MVO, RN; one *s* two *d*. *Educ:* Eton; King's Coll., Cambridge. *Heir:* *s* John Christopher King [*b* 31 March 1933; *m* 1st, 1958, Patricia Monica (marr. diss. 1972), *o d* of late Lt-Col Kingsley Foster and of Mrs Foster, Hampton Court Palace; one *s* one *d*; 2nd, 1984, Mrs Aline Jane Holley, *e d* of late Col D. A. Brett, GC, OBE, MC]. *Address:* Church Farm House, Chilbolton, Hants.

KING, Prof. James Lawrence; Regius Professor of Engineering, 1968–83, University Fellow, since 1983, Edinburgh University; *b* 14 Feb. 1922; *s* of Lawrence Aubrey King and Wilhelmina Young McLeish; *m* 1951, Pamela Mary Ward Hitchcock; one *s* one *d*. *Educ:* Latymer Upper Sch.; Jesus Coll., Cambridge; Imperial Coll., London. Min. of Defence (Navy), 1942–68. *Recreation:* walking. *Address:* 16 Lyne Park, West Linton, Peeblesshire EH46 7HP. *T:* West Linton 60038.

KING, Prof. Jeffrey William Hitchen, MSc, CEng, FICE, FIStructE; Professor of Civil Engineering, Queen Mary College, University of London, 1953–72, now Emeritus Professor; *b* 28 Sept. 1906; *s* of George and Edith King, Wigan; *m* 1930, Phyllis Morfydd Harris (*d* 1977), *d* of Rev. W. Harris; one *s* one *d*. *Educ:* Ashton-in-Makerfield Grammar Sch.; Manchester Univ. Engineer and Agent to Cementation Co. Ltd, British Isles, Spain and Egypt, 1927–36; Research Engineer, Michelin Tyre Co. 1936–37; Lecturer in Civil Engineering, University Coll., Nottingham, 1937–47; Reader in Civil Engineering, Queen Mary Coll., London, 1947–53. Governor, Queen Mary Coll., 1962–65; formerly Mem., Academic Board and Vice-Chm., Civil Engineering Cttee of Regional Advisory Council for Higher Technological Education; formerly mem., Research Cttee, formerly Chm., Concrete Specification Cttee and Cttee on Accelerated Testing of Concrete, Instn of Civil Engineers; formerly Mem. BSI Cttees, CEB/4/4, CEB/21. *Publications:* papers in Journals of Instn of Civil Engineers, Instn of Structural Engineers, and Inst. of Mine Surveyors, and in various technical periodicals. *Recreations:* many and varied. *Address:* The Nook, Crayke Road, Easingwold, York YO6 3PN. *T:* Easingwold (0347) 21151.

KING, John Arthur Charles, BSc, FBCS; Corporate Director and Managing Director, Overseas Division, British Telecommunications plc, since 1984; *b* 7 April 1933; *s* of Charles William King and Doris Frances King (*née* Crooks); *m* 1958, Ina Solavici; two *s*. *Educ:* Univ. of Bristol. IBM UK, 1956–70; Managing Director, Telex Computer Products UK Ltd, 1970–73; Dir, DP Div., Metra Consulting Gp, 1974–75; Marketing Dir, UK, later Europe (Brussels), ITT, 1976–81; Commercial Dir, Business Communications Systems, Philips (Hilversum), 1981–83. CBIM 1986; FIOD 1986. *Recreations:* tennis, squash, bridge, music. *Address:* British Telecom Centre, 81 Newgate Street, EC1A 7AJ. *T:* 01–356 5266. *Club:* Reform.

KING, John Edward; Principal Establishment Officer and Under Secretary, Welsh Office, 1977–82; Consultant, Faculty of Education, and Director, China Studies Centre, University College, Cardiff; *b* 30 May 1922; *s* of late Albert Edward and of Margaret King; *m* 1st, 1948, Pamela White (marr. diss.); one *d*; 2nd, 1956, Mary Margaret Beaton; two *d*. *Educ:* Penarth County Sch.; Sch. of Oriental and African Studies, London Univ. Served with Rifle Bde, RWF and Nigeria Regt, 1941–47; Chindit campaign, Burma, with 77 Bde (despatches). Cadet, Colonial Admin. Service, N Nigeria, 1947; Permanent Sec., Fed. Govt of Nigeria, 1960; retired from HMOCS, 1963. Principal, CRO, 1963; Navy Dept, MoD, 1966–69; Private Sec. to Sec. of State for Wales, 1969–71; Asst Sec., Welsh Office, 1971–77. CS Mem., 1977–82, External Mem., 1982–, Final Selection Bd, CS Commn. *Recreations:* books, swimming, tennis. *Address:* Fairfields, Fairwater Road, Llandaff, Cardiff CF5 2LF. *T:* Cardiff 562825. *Clubs:* Civil Service; Cardiff Lawn Tennis.

KING, John George Maydon, CMG 1959; OBE 1953 (MBE 1945); retired from Colonial Agricultural Service; *b* 26 Jan. 1908; 2nd *s* of late Harold Edwin and Elizabeth Lindsay King, Durban, Natal, SA; *m* 1st, 1938, Françoise Charlotte de Rham (*d* 1966), Lausanne; two *s*; 2nd, 1970, Violet, *widow* of Colin MacPherson, late of Tanganyika Administration Service. *Educ:* University Coll. Sch. (Preparatory); Oundle Sch.; London Univ. (Wye Coll.); Cambridge Univ. (Colonial Office Schol., Cambridge Univ. and Imperial Coll. of Tropical Agric.). Appointed to Colonial Agricultural Service as Agricultural Officer, Tanganyika, 1932–46; seconded to Cambridge Univ. as Lecturer in Tropical Agric. to Colonial Services Courses, 1946–48; Dir of livestock and Agricultural Services, Basutoland, 1948–54; Dir of Agriculture, Uganda, 1954–60; Swaziland, 1960–63; Regional Manager, Lower Indus Project, Hyderabad-Sind, 1964–66. *Recreations:* walking, photography. *Address:* Brockley House, Nailsworth, near Stroud, Glos GL6 0AR. *T:* Nailsworth 2407. *Club:* Farmers'.

KING, Prof. John Oliver Letts, FRCVS; FIBiol; Professor of Animal Husbandry, University of Liverpool, 1969–82, now Emeritus; *b* 21 Dec. 1914; *s* of Richard Oliver King and Helen Mary (*née* Letts); *m* 1942, Helen Marion Gudgin; one *s* one *d*. *Educ:* Berkhamsted Grammar Sch.; Royal Veterinary Coll. (MRCVS); Univ. of Reading (BScAgric); Univ. of Liverpool (MVSc, PhD); FRCVS 1969. Assistant in veterinary practice, 1937; Ho. Surg., Royal Veterinary Coll., 1938; Lectr in Animal Husbandry, 1941, Sen. Lectr 1948, Reader 1961, Univ. of Liverpool. Mem. Council, British Veterinary Assoc., 1953–68; Chairman: Council, N of England Zoological Soc., 1972–86; British

Council Agric. and Vet. Adv. Panel, 1978–84; Member: Medicines Commn, 1969–71; Horserace Anti-Doping Cttee, 1973–86, Horserace Scientific Adv. Cttee, 1986–; Farm Animal Welfare Council, 1979–84; President: Assoc. of Veterinary Teachers and Research Workers, 1961; Lancashire Veterinary Assoc., 1967; British Veterinary Zoological Soc., 1971–74; Royal Coll. of Veterinary Surgeons, 1980. Dalrymple-Champneys Cup, 1976; Bledisloe Vet. Award, 1983. *Publications:* Veterinary Dietetics, 1961; An Introduction to Animal Husbandry, 1978; papers on animal husbandry in various scientific pubns. *Recreation:* gardening. *Address:* Arnside, Hooton Road, Willaston, South Wirral L64 1SL. *T:* 051–327 4850. *Club:* Athenæum.

KING, Dr John William Beaufoy; Head of AFRC Animal Breeding Liaison Group; *b* 28 June 1927; *s* of late John Victor Beaufoy and Gwendoleen Freda King; *m* 1951, Pauline Margaret Coldicott; four *s*. *Educ:* Marling Sch., Stroud; St Catharine's Coll., Cambridge; Edinburgh Univ. BA Cantab 1947, MA Cantab 1952; PhD Edinburgh 1951; FIBiol 1974; FRSE 1975. ARC Animal Breeding Res. Organisation, 1951–82. Kellogg Foundn Schol. to USA, 1954; Genetics Cons. to Pig Industry Develt Authority, 1959; David Black Award (services to pig industry), 1966; Nuffield Foundn Fellowship to Canada, 1970; Vis. Lectr, Göttingen Univ., 1973. *Publications:* papers in scientific jls. *Recreations:* gardening, shooting, dog training. *Address:* Cottage Farm, West Linton, Peeblesshire EH46 7AS. *T:* West Linton 60448. *Club:* Farmers'.

KING, Joseph, OBE 1971; JP; Group Industrial Relations Advisor, Smith and Nephew Associated Cos Ltd, 1978–82; *b* 28 Nov. 1914; *s* of John King, coal miner, and Catherine King (*née* Thompson); *m* 1939, Lily King (*née* Pendlebury); one *s* five *d*. *Educ:* St James' RC Sch., Atherton, Lancashire. Left school at age of 14 and commenced work in cotton mill, 1929. Took active part in Union of Textile and Allied Workers from early years in industry. Elected, 1949: Labour Councillor, Tyldesley; Trades Union Organiser; Dist. Sec., NE Lancs. Gen. Sec., Nat. Union of Textile and Allied Workers, 1962–75; Jt Gen. Sec., Amalgamated Textile Workers' Union, 1974; Mem., TUC Gen. Council, 1972–75; Member, many cttees in Textile Industry. Industrial Advr ACAS NW Reg., 1975–78. Created Accrington Pakistan Friendship Association, 1961 (Pres.). Dir, Castle Cards Ltd, Preston, 1984–85. JP Accrington, 1955. *Recreations:* pleasure is in domestic work in the home and family and in trade union and political field. *Address:* 44 Southwood Drive, Baxenden, Accrington, Lancs. *T:* Accrington 394551.

KING, Hon. Leonard James; Hon. Mr Justice King; Chief Justice of South Australia, since 1978; *b* 1 May 1925; *s* of Michael Owen and Mary Ann King; *m* 1953, Sheila Therese (*née* Keane); two *s* three *d*. *Educ:* Marist Brothers Sch., Norwood, S Aust; Univ. of Adelaide, S Aust (LLB). Admitted to Bar, 1950; QC 1967. Member, House of Assembly, Parlt of S Australia, 1970; Attorney-General and Minister of Community Welfare, 1970; additionally, Minister of Prices and Consumer Affairs, 1972. Judge of Supreme Court of S Aust, 1975. *Address:* c/o Chief Justice's Chambers, Supreme Court House, Victoria Square, Adelaide, South Australia 5000, Australia. *T:* 218 6211.

KING, Prof. Mervyn Allister; Professor of Economics, London School of Economics and Political Science, since 1984; *b* 30 March 1948; *s* of Eric Frank King and Kathleen Alice Passingham. *Educ:* Wolverhampton Grammar School; King's College, Cambridge (BA 1st cl. hons 1969, MA 1973). Research Officer, Dept of Applied Economics, Cambridge, 1969–76; Kennedy Schol., Harvard Univ., 1971–72; Fellow, St John's Coll., Cambridge, 1972–77; Lectr, Faculty of Economics, Cambridge, 1976–77; Esmée Fairbairn Prof. of Investment, Univ. of Birmingham, 1977–84. Vis. Professor of Economics: Harvard Univ., 1982; MIT, 1983–84. Member: Meade Cttee, 1978; Council and Exec., Royal Economic Soc., 1981–86; Fellow, Econometric Soc., 1982. Managing Editor, Review of Economic Studies, 1978–83; Associate Editor: Jl of Public Economics, 1983–; Amer. Economic Review, 1985–. Helsinki Univ. Medal, 1982. *Publications:* Public Policy and the Corporation, 1977; (with J. A. Kay) The British Tax System, 1978, 4th edn 1986; (with D. Fullerton) The Taxation of Income from Capital, 1984; numerous articles in economics jls. *Address:* Lionel Robbins Building, London School of Economics, Houghton Street, WC2A 2AE. *T:* 01–405 7686.

KING, Michael; *see* King, D. M. G.

KING, Michael, (Mike); Chief Executive, East Anglian Regional Health Authority, since 1985; *b* 31 Aug. 1934; *s* of Mac and Jessie King; *m* 1960, Teresa Benjamin; one *s* one *d*. *Educ:* Buckhurst Hill School, London Univ. (BA). Buyer, Ford Motor Co., 1958–64; Purchasing Manager, Servicing Manager, Hotpoint, 1964–68; Dir and Div. Man. Dir, Lake & Elliot, 1968–72; Chief Exec., Heatrae-Sadia International, 1972–84; Management Consultant, 1984–85. *Recreations:* tennis, skiing, music, antiques, computers. *Address:* Moat Cottage, Pleshey, Essex. *T:* Chelmsford 37202. *Club:* Institute of Directors.

KING, His Honour Michael Gardner; a Circuit Judge, 1972–87; *b* 4 Dec. 1920; *s* of late David Thomson King and late Winifred Mary King, Bournemouth; *m* 1951, Yvonne Mary Lilian, *d* of late Lt-Col M. J. Ambler; two *s* one *d*. *Educ:* Sherborne Sch.; Wadham Coll., Oxford (MA). Served in RN, Lieut RNVR, 1940–46. Called to Bar, Gray's Inn, 1949. Dep. Chm., IoW QS, 1966–72; Dep. Chm., Hants QS, 1968–72. *Recreations:* sailing, shooting, golf. *Clubs:* Hampshire (Winchester); Royal Naval Sailing Association, Royal Lymington Yacht (Cdre, 1986–), Bar Yacht; Brokenhurst Manor Golf.

KING, Rear-Adm. Norman Ross Dutton; Naval Secretary, since 1987; *b* 19 March 1933; *s* of Sir Norman King, KCMG and Lady (Mona) King (*née* Dutton); *m* 1967, Patricia Rosemary, *d* of Dr L. B. Furber; two *d*. *Educ:* Fonthill School; RNC Dartmouth; graduate, Naval Command College, Newport, USA, 1969; RCDS 1978. RN Cadet, 1946; served HM Ships Indefatigable, Tintagel Castle, Ceylon, Wild Goose, Hickleton, 1951–57, and Corunna, 1957–59; long TAS course, 1960; BRNC Dartmouth, 1961–63; CO HMS Fiskerton, 1963–64; Jun. Seaman Appointer, Naval Sec's Dept, 1965–66; CO HMS Leopard, 1967–68; Staff Officer (TAS) to CBNS (Washington), 1969–71; XO HMS Intrepid, 1972–73; Staff Warfare TAS Officer, to Dir Naval Warfare, 1974–75; Naval Asst to Second Sea Lord, 1975–77; CO HMS Newcastle and Capt. 3rd Destroyer Sqn, 1979–80; CSO to CBNS (Washington), 1981–82; Dir of Naval Officer Appts (Seaman Officers), 1983–84; Comdr, British Navy Staff and British Naval Attaché, Washington, and UK Nat. Liaison Rep. to SACLANT, 1984–86. *Publications:* (jointly) All The Queen's Men, 1967, paperback edn as Strictly Personal, 1972. *Recreations:* tennis, music, chess. *Address:* c/o Lloyd's Bank, Faversham, Kent ME13 7AP. *Club:* Royal Navy Club of 1765 and 1785.

KING, Air Vice-Marshal Peter Francis, OBE (mil.) 1964; QHS 1979; FRCSE; The Senior Consultant, RAF, 1985; Air Vice-Marshal, Princess Mary's RAF Hospital, Halton, 1983; *b* 17 Sept. 1922; *s* of William George King, RAF, and Florence Margaret King (*née* Sell); *m* 1945, Doreen Maxwell Aaröe, 2nd *d* of Jorgen Hansen-Aaröe; one *s* one *d*. *Educ:* Framlingham Coll.; King's Coll. London, 1940–42; Charing Cross Hosp., 1942–45; Univ. of Edinburgh, 1947. DLO; MRCS, LRCP; MFOM. Kitchener Med. Services Schol. for RAF, 1941; Ho. Phys., Ho. Surg., Charing Cross Hosp., 1945; commnd RAF, 1945; specialist in Otorhinolaryngology, employed Cosford, Ely, Fayid, Halton, CME; Cons. in Otorhinolaryngology, 1955; Hunterian Prof., RCS, 1964; Cons. Adviser in Otorhinolaryngology, 1966; Air Cdre 1976; Reader in Aviation Med., Inst. of Aviation Med., 1977; Whittingham Prof. in Aviation Med., IAM and RCP, 1979; Dean of Air Force Medicine, 1983. Cons. to Herts HA, 1963, and CAA, 1973; Examiner for Dip. in Aviation Med., RCP, 1980. Pres., Sect. of Otology, RSocMed, 1977–78 (Sec., 1972–74); Chm., Brit. Soc. of Audiology, 1979–81; Vice-Chm., RNID, 1980–; Member: BMA, 1945–; Scottish Otological Soc., 1955–; Royal Aeronaut. Soc., 1976–; Council, Brit. Assoc. of Otorhinolaryngologists, 1960–; Editorial Bd, British Jl of Audiology, 1980–. Fellow, Inst. of Acoustics, 1977. FRSM. Lady Cade Medal, RCS, 1967. *Publications:* Noise and Vibration in Aviation (with J. C. Guignard), 1972; numerous articles, chapters, lectures and papers, in books and relevant jls on aviation otolaryngology, noise deafness, hearing conservation, tympanoplasty, facial paralysis, otic barotrauma, etc. *Recreations:* sculpture, looking at prints. *Address:* Squirrels Nook, Oak Glade, Northwood, Mddx HA6 2TY. *T:* Northwood 23961. *Club:* Royal Air Force.

KING, Phillip, CBE 1975; ARA 1977; sculptor; Professor of Sculpture, Royal College of Art, since 1980; *b* 1 May 1934; *s* of Thomas John King and of Gabrielle (*née* Liautard); *m* 1957, Lilian Odelle; one *s* decd. *Educ:* Mill Hill Sch.; Christ's Coll., Cambridge Univ. (languages); St Martin's Sch. of Art (sculpture). Teacher at St Martin's Sch. of Art, 1959–78; Asst to Henry Moore, 1959–60. Trustee, Tate Gallery, 1967–69; Mem. Art Panel, Arts Council, 1977–79. Vis. Prof., Berlin Sch. of Art, 1979–81. *One-man Exhibitions include:* British Pavilion, Venice Biennale, 1968; European Mus. Tour, 1974–75 (Kroller-Muller Nat. Mus., Holland; Kunsthalle, Düsseldorf; Kunsthalle, Bern; Musée Galliera, Paris; Ulster Mus., Belfast); UK Touring Exhib., 1975–76 (Sheffield, Cumbria, Aberdeen, Glasgow, Newcastle, Portsmouth); Hayward Gall. (retrospective), 1981. Commission, European Patent Office, Munich, 1978. First Prize, Socha Piestanskych Parkov, Piestany, Czechoslovakia, 1969. *Address:* c/o Juda Rowan Gallery, 11 Tottenham Mews, W1P 9PJ. *T:* 01–637 5517.

KING, Ralph Malcolm MacDonald, OBE 1968; Colonial Service, retired; *b* 8 Feb. 1911; *s* of Dr James Malcolm King and Mrs Norah King; *m* 1948, Rita Elizabeth Herring; two *s* one *d*. *Educ:* Tonbridge Sch. Solicitor (Hons) 1934. Asst to Johnson, Stokes and Master, Solicitors, Hong Kong, 1936–41. Commissioned Middx Regt, 1941; prisoner of war, 1941–45; demobilised, 1946. Colonial Legal Service, 1947; Legal Officer, Somaliland, 1947; Crown Counsel, Somaliland, 1950. Called to Bar, Gray's Inn, 1950. Solicitor-General, Nyasaland, 1953; Attorney-General, Nyasaland, 1957–61. Disbarred at his own request and since restored to Roll of Solicitors, in April 1961. Legal Draftsman to Government of Northern Nigeria, 1963–67, and to Northern States of Nigeria, 1967–73; Dir, Legislative Drafting Courses, Commonwealth Secretariat, Jamaica, 1974–75, Trinidad, 1976, and Barbados, 1977. *Recreations:* watching cricket, walking. *Address:* 36 Mill View Close, Woodbridge, Suffolk. *T:* Woodbridge 5417.

KING, Sir Richard (Brian Meredith), KCB 1976 (CB 1969); MC 1944; Adviser to Mercury International Group plc; Chairman, Books for Development, 1985; Trustee, Simon Population Trust, since 1985; *b* 2 Aug. 1920; *s* of late Bernard and Dorothy King; *m* 1944, Blanche Phyllis Roberts; two *s* one *d*. *Educ:* King's Coll. Sch., Wimbledon. Air Ministry, 1939; Min. of Aircraft Prod., 1940. Army 1940–46: Major, N Irish Horse; N Af. and Ital. campaigns (MC, Cassino). Min. of Supply, 1946; Asst Principal, Ministry of Works, 1948; Principal, 1949; Asst Regional Dir (Leeds), 1949–52; seconded Treas., 1953–54; Prin. Priv. Sec. to Minister of Works, 1956–57; Asst Sec., 1957; seconded Cabinet Off., 1958 (Sec. of Commonwealth Educn. Conf. (Oxford), 1959; Constitutional Confs: Kenya, 1960; N Rhodesia, Nyasaland and Fed. Review, 1960; WI Fedn, 1961); Dept of Tech. Co-op., on its formation, 1961; Min. of Overseas Develt, on its formation, 1964: Under-Sec., 1964; Dep. Sec., 1968; Permanent Sec., 1973–76; Exec. Sec., IMF/World Bank Develt Cttee, 1976–80; Senior Advr to S. G. Warburg & Co. Ltd, 1980–85. *Publications:* The Planning of the British Aid Programme, 1971; Criteria for Europe's Development Policy to the Third World, 1974. *Recreations:* music, lawn tennis, gardening, doing-it-himself. *Address:* Woodlands Farm House, Woodlands Lane, Stoke D'Abernon, Cobham, Surrey. *T:* Oxshott 3491. *Club:* All England Lawn Tennis.

KING, Robert George Cecil; Under Secretary (Legal), HM Customs and Excise, 1985–Apr. 1987; *b* 21 Jan. 1927; *s* of Stanley Cecil and Kathleen Mary King; *m* 1952, Mary Marshall. *Educ:* Nunthorpe Grammar School, York. Called to the Bar, Lincolns Inn, 1965. Army, 1945–48; British Rail, 1948–53; Judicial Dept, Kenya, 1954–61; East African Common Services Organisation, 1962–64; Solicitor's Office, HM Customs and Excise, 1965–87. *Recreations:* golf, watching cricket, watching television. *Address:* 15 Shillibeer Place, W1H 1DQ. *T:* 01–382 5124. *Clubs:* MCC; Royal Nairobi Golf.

KING, Robert Shirley; Secretary, Health Promotion Research Trust, since 1984; *b* 12 July 1920; *s* of Rev. William Henry King, MC, TD, MA, and late Dorothy King (*née* Sharpe); *m* 1st, 1947, Margaret Siddall (*d* 1956); two *d*; 2nd, 1958, Mary Rowell; one *s* two *d*. *Educ:* Alexandra Road Sch., Oldham; Manchester Grammar Sch.; Trinity Coll., Cambridge (Schol., MA). Served War, RAF, 1940–45. Colonial Service, Tanganyika, 1949–62 (Dist Comr, Bukoba, 1956–58, Geita, 1959–62); Home Office: Principal, 1962–69 (seconded to Civil Service Dept, 1968–69); Asst Sec., 1969–70; transf., with Children's Dept, to DHSS, 1971; DHSS, Asst Sec., 1971–76, Under Sec., 1976–80; Sec., Wkg Party on Role and Tasks of Social Workers, Nat. Inst. for Social Work, 1980–82; part-time Asst Sec., Home Office, 1985–86. Member Council: British and Foreign Sch. Soc., 1982–; Shape, 1982–. Governor: Cheshunt Foundn, 1976–83; Bell Educnl Trust, 1984–. *Recreations:* walking, gardening, African affairs. *Address:* 3 Nightingale Avenue, Cambridge. *T:* Cambridge 248965.

KING, Roger Douglas; MP (C) Birmingham, Northfield, since 1983; *b* 26 Oct. 1943; *s* of Douglas and Cecilie King; *m* 1976, Jennifer Susan (*née* Sharpe); twin *s* one *d*. *Educ:* Solihull Sch. Served automobile engrg apprenticeship with British Motor Corp., 1960–66; sales rep., 1966–74; own manufg business, 1974–81; self-employed car product distributor, 1982–83. Mem., H of C Transport Select Cttee, 1984–; Vice-Chm., All Party Motor Industry Gp, 1985–; Jt Sec., Cons. Tourism Cttee. FIMI. *Recreations:* swimming, motoring. *Address:* c/o House of Commons, SW1A 0AA.

KING, Dame Ruth; *see* Railton, Dame R.

KING, Sir Sydney (Percy), Kt 1975; OBE 1965; JP; District Organiser, National Union of Agricultural and Allied Workers, 1946–80; Chairman, Trent Regional Health Authority, 1973–82; *b* 20 Sept. 1916; *s* of James Edwin King and Florence Emily King; *m* 1944, Millicent Angela Prendergast; two *d*. *Educ:* Brockley Central School. Member: N Midland Regional Board for Industry (Vice-Chm. 1949); Sheffield Regional Hosp. Bd, 1963–73 (Chm, 1969–73); E Midland Economic Planning Council, 1965–; E Midlands Gas Board, 1970; MAFF E Midland Regional Panel, 1972– (Chm., 1977). JP 1956, Alderman 1967, Kesteven. Hon. LLD: Leicester, 1980; Nottingham, 1981. *Recreations:* reading, music, talking. *Address:* 49 Robertson Drive, Sleaford, Lincs. *T:* Sleaford 302056.

KING, Prof. Thea, (Mrs T. Thurston), OBE 1985; FRCM; freelance musician; Professor of Clarinet, Royal College of Music, since 1961; *b* 26 Dec. 1925; *m* Jan. 1953, Frederick John Thurston (*d* Dec. 1953). *Educ:* Bedford High Sch.; Royal College of Music (FRCM

1975; ARCM 1944 and 1947). Sadler's Wells Orchestra, 1950–52; Portia Wind Ensemble, 1955–68; London Mozart Players, 1956–84; Member: English Chamber Orchestra, Melos Ensemble of London, Vesuvius Ensemble, Robles Ensemble. Frequent soloist, broadcaster, recitalist; recordings include Mozart, Spohr, Finzi, Bruch, Mendelssohn, Stanford and 20th Century British music. *Publications:* clarinet solos, Chester Woodwind series, 1977; arrangement of J. S. Bach, Duets for 2 Clarinets, 1979. *Recreations:* cows, drawing, painting, travel. *Address:* 16 Milverton Road, NW6 7AS. *T:* 01–459 3453.

KING, Rt. Hon. Thomas Jeremy, (Tom); PC 1979; MP (C) Bridgwater since March 1970; Secretary of State for Northern Ireland, since 1985; *b* 13 June 1933; *s* of late J. H. King, JP; *m* 1960, Jane, *d* of late Brig. Robert Tilney, CBE, DSO, TD; one *s* one *d. Educ:* Rugby; Emmanuel Coll., Cambridge (MA). National service, 1951–53: commnd Somerset Light Inf., 1952; seconded to KAR; served Tanganyika and Kenya; Actg Captain 1953. Cambridge, 1953–56. Joined E.S. & A. Robinson Ltd, Bristol, 1956; various positions up to Divisional Gen. Man., 1964–69; Chm., Sale, Tilney Co Ltd, 1971–79 (Dir 1965–79). PPS to: Minister for Posts and Telecommunications, 1970–72; Minister for Industrial Develt, 1972–74; Front Bench spokesman for: Industry, 1975–76; Energy, 1976–79; Minister for Local Govt and Environmental Services, DoE, 1979–83; Sec. of State for the Environment, Jan.-June 1983, for Transport, June-Oct. 1983, for Employment, 1983–85. Vice-Chm., Cons. Parly Industry Cttee, 1974. *Recreations:* cricket, ski-ing. *Address:* House of Commons, SW1.

KING, Air Vice-Marshal Walter MacIan, CB 1961; CBE 1957; retired, 1967; *b* 10 March 1910; *s* of Alexander King, MB, ChB, DPH, and Hughberta Blannin King (*née* Pearson); *m* 1946, Anne Clare Hicks; two *s. Educ:* St Mary's Coll., Castries, St Lucia, BWI; Blundell's Sch., Tiverton, Devon. Aircraft Engineering (Messers Westland Aircraft Ltd, Handley-Page Ltd, Saunders-Roe Ltd), 1927–33; joined Royal Air Force, 1934; Overseas Service: No 8 Sqdn, Aden, 1935–37; South-east Asia, 1945–47; Middle East (Egypt and Cyprus), 1955–57. Student: RAF Staff Coll., 1944; Joint Services Staff Coll., 1947; IDC, 1954. Directing Staff, RAF Staff Coll., 1957–58; Comdt, No 16 MU, Stafford, 1958–60; Dir of Equipment (B), Air Ministry, 1961–64; Air Cdre Ops (Supply), HQ's Maintenance Command, during 1964; Senior Air Staff Officer, RAF Maintenance Command, 1964–67. Joined Hooker Craigmyle & Co. Ltd, 1967; Gen. Manager, Hooker Craigmyle (Scotland) Ltd, 1969–72; Dir, Craigmyle & Co. (Scotland) Ltd, 1972–76. *Recreations:* swimming (rep. RAF in inter-services competition, 1934); gardening. *Address:* 24 Arthur's Avenue, Harrogate HG2 0DX.

KING, Sir Wayne Alexander, 8th Bt *cr* 1815; *b* 2 Feb. 1962; *s* of Sir Peter Alexander King, 7th Bt, and of Jean Margaret (who *m* 2nd, 1978, Rev. Richard Graham Mackenzie), *d* of Christopher Thomas Cavell, Deal; *S* father, 1973.

KING-HAMILTON, His Honour (Myer) Alan (Barry), QC 1954; an additional Judge of the Central Criminal Court, 1964–79; a Deputy Circuit Judge, 1979–83; *b* 9 Dec. 1904; *o s* of Alfred King-Hamilton; *m* 1935, Rosalind Irene Ellis; two *d. Educ:* Bishop's Stortford Grammar Sch.; Trinity Hall, Cambridge (BA 1927, MA 1929; Pres. Cambridge Union Soc., 1927). Called to Bar, Middle Temple, 1929; served War of 1939–45, RAF, finishing with rank of Squadron Leader; served on Finchley Borough Council, 1938–39 and 1945–50. Recorder of Hereford, 1955–56; Recorder of Gloucester, 1956–61; Recorder of Wolverhampton, 1961–64; Dep. Chm. Oxford County Quarter Sessions, 1955–64, 1966–71; Leader of Oxford Circuit, 1961–64. Elected Bencher, Middle Temple, 1961. Elected to General Council of Bar, 1958. President: West London Reform Synagogue, 1967–75, 1977–83; Westlon Housing Assoc., 1975–; Vice-Pres., World Congress of Faiths, 1967–. Legal Mem., Med. Practices Cttee, Min. of Health, 1961–64; Member: Cttee, Birnbeck Housing Assoc., 1982–; Arts and Library Cttee, MCC, 1985; Chm., Mary Whitehouse Res. and Educn Trust, 1986–. Trustee, Barnet Community Trust, 1986–. Freeman of City of London; Master, Needlemakers Co., 1969. *Publication:* And Nothing But the Truth (autobiog.), 1982. *Recreations:* cricket, gardening, the theatre. *Clubs:* Royal Air Force, MCC.

KING-HELE, Desmond George, FRS 1966; Deputy Chief Scientific Officer, Space Department, Royal Aircraft Establishment, Farnborough, since 1968; *b* 3 Nov. 1927; *s* of late S. G. and of B. King-Hele, Seaford, Sussex; *m* 1954, Marie Thérèse Newman; two *d. Educ:* Epsom Coll.; Trinity Coll., Cambridge. BA (1st cl. hons Mathematics) 1948; MA 1952. At RAE, Farnborough, from 1948, working on space research from 1955. Mem., International Academy of Astronautics, 1961. Chm., British Nat. Cttee for the History of Science, Medicine and Technology, 1985–. FIMA; FRAS. Hon. DSc Aston, 1979. Eddington Medal, RAS, 1971; Charles Chree Medal, Inst. of Physics, 1971; Lagrange Prize, Acad. Royale de Belgique, 1972. Lectures: Symons, RMetS, 1961; Duke of Edinburgh's, Royal Inst. of Navigation, 1964; Jeffreys, RAS, 1971; Halley, Oxford, 1974; Bakerian, Royal Soc., 1974; Sydenham, Soc. of Apothecaries, 1981; H. L. Welsh, Univ. of Toronto, 1982; Milne, Oxford, 1984. *Publications:* Shelley: His Thought and Work, 1960, 3rd edn 1984; Satellites and Scientific Research, 1960; Erasmus Darwin, 1963; Theory of Satellite Orbits in an Atmosphere, 1964; (ed) Space Research V, 1965; Observing Earth Satellites, 1966, 2nd edn 1983; (ed) Essential Writings of Erasmus Darwin, 1968; The End of the Twentieth Century?, 1970; Poems and Trixies, 1972; Doctor of Revolution, 1977; (ed) The Letters of Erasmus Darwin, 1981; (ed) The RAE Table of Earth Satellites, 1981, 2nd edn 1983; Animal Spirits, 1983; Erasmus Darwin and the Romantic Poets, 1986; *radio drama scripts:* A Mind of Universal Sympathy, 1973; The Lunaticks, 1978; numerous papers in Proc. Royal Society, Nature, Keats-Shelley Memor. Bull., New Scientist, Planetary and Space Science, and other scientific and literary jls. *Recreations:* tennis, walking, reading, gardening. *Address:* 3 Tor Road, Farnham, Surrey. *T:* Farnham 714755.

KING-MARTIN, Brig. John Douglas, CBE 1966; DSO 1957; MC 1953; Deputy Commander, HQ Eastern District, 1968–70, retired; *b* 9 March 1915; *s* of late Lewis King-Martin, Indian Forest Service; *m* 1940, Jeannie Jemima Sheffield Hollins, *d* of late S. T. Hollins, CIE; one *s* one *d. Educ:* Allhallows Sch.; RMC Sandhurst. Commnd 1935; 3rd Royal Bn 12 Frontier Force Regt, IA, 1936; Waziristan Ops, 1936–37; Eritrea, Western Desert, 1940–42; Staff Coll., Quetta, 1944; Bde Maj., 1944–46, India, Java; GSO 2, Indian Inf. Div., Malaya, 1946–47; transf. to RA, 1948; Battery Comdr, 1948–50; DAQMG 2 Inf. Div., 1951–54; Korea, 1952–53; CO, 50 Medium Regt, RA, 1956–57; Suez, Cyprus, 1956–57; Coll. Comdr, RMA Sandhurst, 1958–60; Dep. Comdr and CRA, 17 Gurkha Div., 1961–62; Comdr, 17 Gurkha Div., 1962–64; Comdr, Rhine Area, 1964–67. Lieut-Col 1956; Brig. 1961. ADC to The Queen, 1968–70. *Recreations:* golf, painting, photography. *Address:* White House Farm, Polstead, Suffolk. *T:* Boxford 210327. *Club:* East India, Devonshire, Sports and Public Schools.

KING MURRAY, Ronald; *see* Murray.

KING-REYNOLDS, Guy Edwin, JP; Head Master, Dauntsey's School, West Lavington, 1969–85; *b* 9 July 1923; *er s* of late Dr H. E. King Reynolds, York; *m* 1st, 1947, Norma Lansdowne Russell (*d* 1949); 2nd, 1950, Jeanne Nancy Perris Rhodes; one *d. Educ:* St Peter's Sch., York; Emmanuel Coll., Cambridge (1944–47). Served RAF, 1942–44. BA 1946, MA 1951. Asst Master, Glenhow Prep. Sch., 1947–48; Head of Geography Dept, Solihull Sch., Warwickshire, 1948–54; family business, 1954–55; Head of Geography, Portsmouth Grammar Sch., 1955–57; Solihull School: Housemaster, 1957–63, Second Master, 1963–69. Part-time Lecturer in International Affairs, Extra-Mural Dept, Birmingham Univ.; Chm., Solihull WEA. LRAM (speech and drama) 1968. Governor: St Peter's Sch., York, 1984–; Dean Close Sch., Cheltenham, 1985–; La Retraite, Salisbury, 1985–. Mem. Cttee, GBA, 1986. JP Solihull, 1965–69, Wiltshire, 1970–; Vice-Chm., Devizes Bench, 1985– (Chm., 1982–85). *Recreations:* drama (director and actor); travel. *Address:* Denewood House, The Fairway, Devizes, Wilts.

KING-TENISON, family name of **Earl of Kingston.**

KINGDOM, Thomas Doyle, CB 1959; Controller, Government Social Survey Department, 1967–70, retired; *b* 30 Oct. 1910; *er s* of late Thomas Kingdom; *m* 1937, Elsie Margaret, *d* of late L. C. Scott, MBE, Northwood; two *d. Educ:* Rugby; King's Coll., Cambridge (MA). Entered Civil Service as Asst Principal, Inland Revenue, 1933; transferred to Unemployment Assistance Bd, 1934; seconded to HM Treasury as Dep. Dir, Organisation and Methods, 1945–49; Under Sec., 1955. Chm., Exec. Council, Royal Inst. of Public Administration, 1965–66. Chm. West London Suppl. Benefit Appeal Tribunal, 1971–83; Charities' VAT Advr, Nat. Council for Voluntary Orgns, 1972–. *Address:* 2 Grosvenor Road, Northwood, Mddx HA6 3HJ. *T:* Northwood 22006.

KINGHAM, James Frederick; His Honour Judge Kingham; a Circuit Judge, since 1973; *b* 9 Aug. 1925; *s* of late Charles William and Eileen Eda Kingham; *m* 1958, Vivienne Valerie Tyrrell Brown; two *s* two *d. Educ:* Wycliffe Coll.; Queens' Coll., Cambridge (MA); Graz Univ., Austria. Served with RN, 1943–47. Called to Bar, Gray's Inn, 1951; Mem. Gen. Council of Bar, 1954–58; Mem. Bar Council Sub-Cttee on Sentencing and Penology. A Recorder, 1972–73; Liaison Judge, Beds, 1982–. Dep. County Comr, Herts Scouts, 1971–80, formerly Asst County Comr for Venture Scouts; Venture Scout Leader: Harpenden, 1975–86; Kimpton and Wheathampstead, 1986–. *Recreations:* mountain activities, squash, ski-ing, youth work, history, gardening, watching football. *Address:* Stone House, High Street, Kimpton, Hitchin, Herts SG4 8RJ. *T:* Kimpton 832308. *Club:* Union (Cambridge).

KINGHORN, Squadron Leader Ernest; *b* 1 Nov. 1907; *s* of A. Kinghorn, Leeds; *m* 1942, Eileen Mary Lambert Russell (*d* 1980); one *s* (and one *s* one *d* decd). *Educ:* Leeds, Basel and Lille Universities. Languages Master Ashville Coll., Doncaster Grammar Sch. and Roundhay Sch., Leeds. Served in Intelligence Branch, RAF. British Officer for Control of Manpower, SHAEF, and Staff Officer CCG. MP (Lab) Yarmouth Division of Norfolk, 1950–51, Great Yarmouth, 1945–50. *Address:* 59 Queens Avenue, Hanworth, Middx.

KINGHORN, William Oliver; Chief Agricultural Officer, Department of Agriculture and Fisheries for Scotland, 1971–75; *b* 17 May 1913; *s* of Thomas Kinghorn, Duns, and Elizabeth Oliver; *m* 1943, Edith Johnstone; one *s* two *d. Educ:* Berwickshire High Sch.; Edinburgh Univ. BSc (Agr) Hons, BSc Hons. Senior Inspector, 1946; Technical Develt Officer, 1959; Chief Inspector, 1970. SBStJ. *Publication:* contrib. Annals of Applied Biology, 1936. *Address:* 23 Cumlodden Avenue, Edinburgh EH12 6DR. *T:* 031–337 1435.

KINGMAN, Sir John (Frank Charles), Kt 1985; FRS 1971; Vice-Chancellor, University of Bristol, since 1985; *b* 28 Aug. 1939; *er s* of late Dr F. E. T. Kingman, FRSC; *m* 1964, Valerie, *d* of late F. Cromwell, OBE, ISO; one *s* one *d. Educ:* Christ's Coll., Finchley; Pembroke Coll., Cambridge. MA, ScD Cantab; Smith's Prize, 1962. Fellow of Pembroke Coll., Cambridge, 1961–65. Asst Lectr in Mathematics, 1962–64, Lectr, 1964–65, Univ. of Cambridge; Reader in Mathematics and Statistics, 1965–66, Prof. 1966–69, Univ. of Sussex; Prof. of Maths, Univ. of Oxford, 1969–85; Fellow, St Anne's Coll., Oxford, 1978–85, Hon. Fellow, 1985. Visiting appointments: Univ. of Western Australia, 1963, 1974; Stanford Univ., USA, 1968; ANU, 1978. Chairman: Science Bd, SRC, 1979–81; SERC, 1981–85; Vice-Pres., Parly and Scientific Cttee, 1986– (Vice-Chm., 1983–86); Member: Council, British Technology Gp, 1984–; Bd, British Council, 1986–. Director, IBM (UK) Ltd, 1985–. Mem., Brighton Co. Borough Council, 1968–71; Chm., Regency Soc. of Brighton and Hove, 1975–81. Chm., 1973–76, Vice-Pres., 1976–, Inst. of Statisticians; Vice-Pres., Royal Statistical Soc., 1977–79 (Guy Medal in Silver, 1981). Hon. DSc: Sussex, 1983; Southampton, 1985. Royal Medal, Royal Soc., 1983. *Publications:* Introduction to Measure and Probability (with S. J. Taylor), 1966; The Algebra of Queues, 1966; Regenerative Phenomena, 1972; Mathematics of Genetic Diversity, 1980; papers in mathematical and statistical jls. *Address:* Senate House, Tyndall Avenue, Bristol BS8 1TH. *Clubs:* Lansdowne, United Oxford & Cambridge University.

KINGS NORTON, Baron *cr* 1965, of Wotton Underwood (Life Peer); **Harold Roxbee Cox,** Kt 1953; PhD, DIC; FEng 1976; FIMechE, Hon. FRAeS; Chairman: Landspeed Ltd, since 1975; Cotswold Research Ltd, since 1978; Landsaver Ltd, since 1986; President: Campden Food Preservation Research Association, since 1961; British Balloon Museum and Library, since 1980; Chancellor, Cranfield Institute of Technology, since 1969; *b* 6 June 1902; *s* of late William John Roxbee Cox, Birmingham, and Amelia Stern; *m* 1st, 1927, Marjorie (*d* 1980), *e d* of late E. E. Withers, Northwood; two *s*; 2nd, 1982, Joan Ruth Pascoe, *d* of late W. G. Pack, Torquay. *Educ:* Kings Norton Grammar Sch.; Imperial Coll. of Science and Technology (Schol.). Engineer on construction of Airship R101, 1924–29; Chief Technical Officer, Royal Airship Works, 1931; Investigations in wing flutter and stability of structures, RAE, 1931–35; Lectr in Aircraft Structures, Imperial Coll., 1932–38; Principal Scientific Officer. Aerodynamics Dept, RAE, 1935–36; Head of Air Defence Dept, RAE, 1936–38; Chief Technical Officer, Air Registration Board, 1938–39; Supt of Scientific Research, RAE, 1939–40; Dep. Dir of Scientific Research, Ministry of Aircraft Production, 1940–43; Dir of Special Projects Ministry of Aircraft Production, 1943–44; Chm. and Man. Dir Power Jets (Research and Development) Ltd, 1944–46; Dir National Gas Turbine Establishment, 1946–48; Chief Scientist, Min. of Fuel and Power, 1948–54. Chairman: Metal Box Co., 1961–67 (Dir, 1957–67, Dep. Chm., 1959–60); Berger Jenson & Nicholson Ltd, 1967–75; Applied Photophysics, 1974–81; Withers Estates, 1976–81; Submarine Products, 1978–82; Director: Ricardo & Co. (Engrs) 1927 Ltd, 1965–77; Dowty Rotol, 1968–75; British Printing Corp., 1968–77; Hoechst UK, 1970–75. Chm. Gas Turbine Collaboration Cttee, 1941–44, 1946–48; Mem. Aeronautical Research Council, 1944–48, 1958–60; Chairman: Coun. for Scientific and Industrial Research, 1961–65; Council for National Academic Awards, 1964–71; Air Registration Bd, 1966–72; President: Royal Aeronautical Soc., 1947–49; Royal Instn, 1969–76. Fellow of Imperial Coll. of Science and Technology, 1960; FCGI 1976. Membre Correspondant, Faculté Polytechnique de Mons, 1946. R38 Memorial Prize, 1928; Busk Memorial Prize, 1934; Wilbur Wright Lecturer, 1940; Wright Brothers Lecturer (USA), 1945; Hawksley Lecturer, 1951; James Clayton Prize, 1952; Thornton Lectr, 1954; Parsons Memorial Lectr, 1955; Handley Page Memorial Lectr, 1969. Hon. DSc: Birmingham, 1954; Cranfield Inst. of Technology, 1970; Hon. DTech Brunel, 1966; Hon. LLD CNAA, 1969. Bronze Medal, Univ. of Louvain, 1946; Medal of Freedom with Silver Palm, USA, 1947. *Publications:* numerous papers on theory of structures, wing flutter, gas turbines, civil aviation and airships. *Address:* Westcote House, Chipping Campden, Glos. *T:* Evesham 840 440. *Clubs:* Athenæum, Turf.

KINGSALE, 35th Baron *cr* 1223 (by some reckonings 30th Baron); **John de Courcy;** Baron Courcy and Baron of Ringrone; Premier Baron of Ireland; Chairman, Strand Publications Ltd, since 1971; Director, D'Olier, Grantmesnil & Courcy Acquisitions Ltd, since 1970; Chairman, National Association for Service to the Realm; *b* 27 Jan. 1941; *s* of Lieutenant-Commander the Hon. Michael John Rancé de Courcy, RN (killed on active service, 1940), and Joan (*d* 1967), *d* of Robert Reid; *S* grandfather, 1969. *Educ:* Stowe; Universities of Paris and Salzburg. Short service commission, Irish Guards, 1962–65. At various times before and since: law student, property developer, film extra, white hunter, bingo caller, etc. *Recreations:* shooting, food and drink, palaeontology, venery. *Heir:* cousin Nevinson Russell de Courcy [*b* 21 July 1920; *m* 1954, Nora Lydia, *yr d* of James Arnold Plint; one *s* one *d*]. *Address:* Crawley Farm House, South Brewham, Somerset. *Club:* Cavalry and Guards.

KINGSBOROUGH, Viscount; Robert Charles Henry King-Tenison; *b* 20 March 1969; *s* and *heir* of 11th Earl of Kingston, *qv*.

KINGSHOTT, (Albert) Leonard; Director, International Banking Division, Lloyds Bank Plc, since 1985; *b* 16 Sept. 1930; *s* of A. L. Kingshott and Mrs K. Kingshott; *m* 1958, Valerie Simpson; two *s* one *d*. *Educ:* London Sch. of Economics (BSc); ACIS 1958, FCIS 1983. Flying Officer, RAF, 1952–55; Economist, British Petroleum, 1955–60; Economist, British Nylon Spinners, 1960–62; Financial Manager, Iraq Petroleum Co., 1963–65; Chief Economist, Ford of Britain, 1965; Treas., Ford of Britain, 1966–67; Treas., Ford of Europe, 1968–70; Finance Dir, Whitbread & Co., 1972; Man. Dir, Finance, BSC, 1972–77; Dir, Lloyds Bank International, responsible for Merchant Banking activities, 1977–80, for European Div., 1980–82, for Marketing and Planning Div., 1983–84; Dep. Chief Exec., Lloyds Bank International, 1985. Director: Bank of London and South America Ltd; Lloyds Bank California; Lloyds Bank (France) Ltd; Lloyds Bank International. Associate Mem. of Faculty, 1978, Governor, 1980–, Ashridge Management Coll. FCIS. *Publication:* Investment Appraisal, 1967. *Recreations:* golf, chess. *Address:* The White House, Great Warley, Brentwood, Essex. *T:* Brentwood 210671.

KINGSHOTT, Air Vice-Marshal Kenneth, CBE 1972; DFC 1953; Royal Air Force, retired 1980; *b* 8 July 1924; *s* of Walter James Kingshott and Eliza Ann Kingshott; *m* 1948, Dorrie Marie (*née* Dent) (*d* 1978); two *s*. Joined RAF, 1943; served: Singapore and Korea, 1950; Aden, 1960; Malta, 1965; MoD, London, 1968; OC RAF Cottesmore, 1971; HQ 2 Allied Tactical Air Force, 1973; HQ Strike Command, 1975; Dep. Chief of Staff Operations and Intelligence, HQ Allied Air Forces Central Europe, 1977–79. *Recreations:* golf, tennis, music. *Address:* Tall Trees, Manor Road, Penn, Bucks. *Club:* Royal Air Force.

KINGSHOTT, Leonard; *see* Kingshott, A. L.

KINGSLAND, Sir Richard, Kt 1978; CBE 1967; DFC 1940; idc; psa; Secretary to Department of Veterans' Affairs, Canberra, 1976–81; *b* Moree, NSW, 19 Oct. 1916; *m* 1943, Kathleen Jewel, *d* of late R. B. Adams; one *s* two *d*. *Educ:* Sydney High Sch., NSW. Served War: No 10 Sqdn, Eng., 1939–41; commanded: No 11 Sqdn, New Guinea, 1941–42; RAAF Stn, Rathmines, NSW, 1942–43; Gp Captain 1943; Dir, Intell., RAAF, 1944–45. Director: Trng, 1946; Org. RAAF HQ, 1946–48; Manager, Sydney Airport, 1948–49; Airline Pilot, 1949–50; SA Reg. 1950–51, NT Reg. 1951–52, Dept of Civil Aviation; Chief Admin. Asst to CAS, RAAF, 1952–53; IDC 1955. Asst Sec., Dept of Air, Melb., 1954–58; First Asst Sec., Dept of Defence, 1958–63; Secretary: Dept of Interior, 1963–70; Dept of Repatriation, 1970–74; Repatriation and Compensation, 1974–76. Chairman: Repatriation Commn, 1970–81; ACT Arts Develt Bd (first Chm.), 1981–83; Commonwealth Films Bd of Review, 1982–86; Uranium Adv. Council, 1982–84. Hon. Nat. Sec., Nat. Heart Foundn, 1976–. A Dir, Arts Council of Aust., 1970–72; first Chairman Council: Canberra Sch. of Music, 1970–74; Canberra Sch. of Art, 1976–83; Member: Canberra Theatre Trust, 1965–75; Aust. Opera Nat. Council, 1983–; Mem. Bd of Trustees, Aust. War Meml, Canberra, 1966–76; a Dir, Aust. Bicentennial Authority, 1983–. Pres., Bd of Management, Goodwin Retirement Villages, 1984–. *Recreations:* music, looking at paintings. *Address:* 36 Vasey Crescent, Campbell, ACT 2601, Australia. *Clubs:* Commonwealth, National Press (Canberra).

KINGSLEY, Ben; actor; *b* 31 Dec. 1943; *s* of Rahimtulla Harji Bhanji and Anna Leina Mary Bhanji; *m* 1978, Gillian Alison Macaulay Sutcliffe; one *s*. *Educ:* Manchester Grammar Sch. Associate artist, Royal Shakespeare Co.; work with RSC includes, 1970–80: Peter Brook's Midsummer Night's Dream, Stratford, London, Broadway, NY; Gramsci in Occupations; Ariel in The Tempest; title role, Hamlet; Ford in Merry Wives of Windsor; title role, Baal; Squeers and Mr Wagstaff in Nicholas Nickleby; title rôle, Othello, 1985; Melons, 1986; National Theatre, 1977–78: Mosca in Volponë; Trofimov in The Cherry Orchard; Sparkish in The Country Wife; Vukhov in Judgement; additional theatre work includes: Johnny in Hello and Goodbye (Fugard), King's Head, 1973; Errol Philander in Statements After An Arrest (Fugard), Royal Court, 1974; Edmund Kean, Harrogate, 1981, Haymarket, 1983 (also televised); title role, Dr Faustus, Manchester Royal Exchange, 1981; *television* 1974–, includes The Love School (series), 1974; Silas Marner (film), 1985, and several plays; *films:* title role, Gandhi, 1980 (2 Hollywood Golden Globe awards, 1982; NY Film Critics' Award, 2 BAFTA awards, Oscar, LA Film Critics Award, 1983, Variety Club of GB Best Film Actor award, 1983); Betrayal, 1982; Harem, 1985; Turtle Diary, 1985. Best Film Actor, London Standard Award, 1983. Hon. MA Salford, 1984. Padma Shri (India), 1984. *Recreations:* music, gardening. *Address:* c/o ICM Ltd, 388/396 Oxford Street, W1.

KINGSLEY, David John; consultant in management, marketing and communications, since 1975; Director: King Publications Ltd, since 1975; Francis Kyle Gallery Ltd, since 1978; The Consortium Ltd, since 1985; Chairman, Stokecroft Arts Ltd, since 1983; *b* 10 July 1929; *s* of Walter John Kingsley and Margery Kingsley; *m* 1st, 1954, Enid Sophia Jones; two *d*; 2nd, 1968, Gillian Leech; two *s*. *Educ:* Southend High Sch.; London School of Economics (BScEcon). Pres., Students' Union, LSE, 1952; Vice-Pres., Nat. Union of Students, 1953. Served RAF, Personnel Selection, commnd 1948. Prospective Parly Candidate (Lab) E Grinstead, 1952–54; founded Kingsley, Manton and Palmer, advertising agency, 1964; Publicity Advisor to Labour Party and Govt, 1962–70; Publicity and Election advisor to President of Republic of Zambia, 1974–; Election and Broadcasting advisor to Govt of Mauritius, 1976–; Publicity advisor to SDP, 1981–. Mem. Boards, CNAA, 1970–82; Mem., Central Religious Adv. Cttee for BBC and IBA, 1974–82; Governor, LSE, 1966–. Chm., Inter-Action Trust, 1981–; Treas., Centre for World Develt Educn, 1985–; Vice-Chm., Royal Philharmonic Orch., 1972–77. FIPA; FRSA; ASIAD. *Publications:* Albion in China, 1979; contribs to learned jls; various articles. *Recreations:* politics, creating happy national events, music, travel, art and any books. *Address:* 99 Hemingford Road, N1 1BY. *Clubs:* Reform, Royal Automobile.

KINGSLEY, Sir Patrick (Graham Toler), KCVO 1962 (CVO 1950); Secretary and Keeper of the Records of the Duchy of Cornwall, 1954–72 (Assistant Secretary, 1930–54); *b* 1908; *s* of late Gerald Kingsley; *m* 1947, Priscilla Rosemary, *o d* of late Capt. Archibald A. Lovett Cameron, RN; three *s* one *d*. *Educ:* Winchester; New Coll., Oxford. OUCC 1928–30 (Capt. 1930), OUAFC 1927 and 1929. Served War of 1939–45 with Queen's Royal Regt. *Address:* West Hill Farm, West Knoyle, Warminster, Wilts.

KINGSLEY, Roger James, FEng, FIChemE; General Manager, Duolite International Worldwide, since 1981; *b* 2 Feb. 1922; *s* of Felix and Helene Loewenstein; changed name to Kingsley, 1942; *m* 1949, Valerie Marguerite Mary (*née* Hanna); one *s* two *d*. *Educ:* Manchester Grammar Sch.; Faculty of Technol., Manchester Univ. (BScTech); Harvard Business Sch. (Internat. Sen. Managers Program). Served War, Royal Fusiliers, 1940–46; Commando service, 1942–45; Captain; mentioned in despatches, 1946. Chemical Engr, Petrocarbon Ltd, 1949–51; technical appts, ultimately Tech. Dir, Lankro Chemicals Ltd, 1952–62; gen. management appts, Lankro Chemicals Group Ltd, 1962–77; Man. Dir, Lankro Chemicals Group Ltd, 1972–77; Director: ICI-Lankro Plasticisers Ltd, 1972–77; Fallek-Lankro Corp., Tuscaloosa, Ala, 1976–77. Dep. Chm., Diamond Shamrock Europe, 1977–82. Pres., IChemE, 1974–75 (Vice-Pres., 1969–71 and 1973–74). Member: Court of Governors, Univ. of Manchester Inst. of Science and Technol., 1969–79; Adv. Cttee for Chem. Engrg and Fuel Technol., Univ. of Sheffield, 1977–80. *Publications:* contrib. Chem. Engr, and Proc. IMechE. *Recreations:* skiing, riding, music. *Address:* Fallows End, Wicker Lane, Hale Barns, Cheshire WA15 0HQ. *T:* 061–980 6253. *Club:* Anglo-Belgian.

KINGSTON, 11th Earl of, *cr* 1768; **Barclay Robert Edwin King-Tenison,** Bt 1682; Baron Kingston, 1764; Viscount Kingsborough, 1766; Baron Erris, 1800; Viscount Lorton, 1806; formerly Lieutenant, Royal Scots Greys; *b* 23 Sept. 1943; *o s* of 10th Earl of Kingston and Gwyneth, *d* of William Howard Evans (who *m* 1951, Brig. E. M. Tyler, DSO, MC, late RA; she *m* 1963, Robert Woodford); *S* father 1948; *m* 1st, 1965, Patricia Mary (marr. diss. 1974), *o d* of E. C. Killip, Llanfairfechan, N Wales; one *s* one *d*; 2nd, 1974, Victoria (marr. diss. 1979), *d* of D. C. Edmonds. *Educ:* Winchester. *Heir:* *s* Viscount Kingsborough, *qv*. *Address:* c/o Midland Bank, 47 Ludgate Hill, EC4.

KINGSTON (Ontario), Archbishop of, (RC), since 1982; **Most Rev. Francis John Spence;** *b* Perth, Ont., 3 June 1926; *s* of William John Spence and Rose Anna Spence (*née* Jordan). *Educ:* St Michael's Coll., Toronto (BA 1946); St Augustine's Seminary, Toronto; St Thomas Univ., Rome (JCD 1955). Ordained priest, 1950; Bishop, 1967; Mil. Vicar, Canadian Forces, 1967–70; Bishop of Charlottetown, PEI, 1970–82. *Address:* 390 Palace Road, PO Box 997, Kingston, Ont K7L 4X8, Canada.

KINGSTON-UPON-THAMES, Bishop Suffragan of, since 1984; **Rt. Rev. Peter Stephen Maurice Selby,** PhD; *b* 7 Dec. 1941. *Educ:* Merchant Taylors' School; St John's Coll., Oxford (BA 1964, MA 1967); Bishops' Coll., Cheshunt. PhD (London) 1975. Asst Curate, Queensbury, 1966–68; Assoc. Director of Training, Southwark, 1969–73; Asst Curate, Limpsfield with Titsey, 1969–77; Vice-Principal, Southwark Ordination Course, 1970–72; Asst Missioner, Dio. Southwark, 1973–77; Canon Residentiary, Newcastle Cathedral, 1977–84; Diocesan Missioner, Dio. Newcastle, 1977–84. *Address:* 24 Albert Drive, SW19 6LS.

KINGTON, Miles Beresford; humorous columnist; *b* 13 May 1941; *s* of William Beresford Nairn Kington and Jean Anne Kington; *m* 1964, Sarah Paine (separated 1980); one *s* one *d*. *Educ:* Trinity College, Glenalmond; Trinity College, Oxford (BAMod Langs). Plunged into free-lance writing, 1963; took up part-time gardening while starving to death, 1964; jazz reviewer, The Times, 1965; joined staff of Punch, 1967, Literary Editor, 1973, left 1980; free-lance, 1980–; regular Let's Parler Franglais column in Punch and daily Moreover column in The Times, 1981–; member, musical group Instant Sunshine on double bass; jazz player, 1970–; *television:* various programmes incl. Three Miles High (Great Railway Journeys of the World series), 1980, and Steam Days, 1986. *Publications:* World of Alphonse Allais, 1977, repr. as A Wolf in Frog's Clothing, 1983; 4 Franglais books, 1979–82; Moreover, 1982; Miles and Miles, 1982; Nature Made Ridiculously Simple, 1983; Moreover, Too . . ., 1985. *Recreations:* bicycling, jazz, growing parsley, meeting VAT people, trying to find something to beat friend Barlow at. *Address:* Flat 1, 51 Ladbroke Grove, W11 3AX. *T:* 01–727 6606. *Clubs:* Garrick, 100, Ronnie Scott's.

KININMONTH, Sir William (Hardie), Kt 1972; PPRSA, FRIBA, FRIAS; Architectural Consultant, formerly Senior Partner, Sir Rowand Anderson, Kininmonth and Paul, architects, Edinburgh; *b* 8 Nov. 1904; *s* of John Kininmonth and Isabella McLean Hardie; *m* 1934, Caroline Eleanor Newsam Sutherland (*d* 1978); one *d*. *Educ:* George Watson's Coll., Edinburgh. Architectural training in Edinburgh Coll. of Art, and in offices of Sir Edwin Lutyens, Sir Rowand Anderson and Paul, and Wm N. Thomson; entered partnership Rowand Anderson and Paul, 1933; served War of 1939–45: RE 1940, North Africa, Sicily and Italy; resumed architectural practice, 1945; buildings for Edinburgh Univ., Renfrew Air Port and Naval Air Station, Edinburgh Dental Hospital, Town Hall, churches, banks, hospitals, schools, housing, etc. Saltire and Civic Trust Awards. Appointed: 1955, Adviser to City of Edinburgh, for development of Princes Street; 1964, to design new Festival Theatre and Festival Centre. Pres., Royal Scottish Academy, 1969–73 (formerly Treas. and then Sec.); Pres. Edinburgh Architectural Association, 1951–53; Member: Royal Fine Arts Commn for Scotland, 1952–65; Council RIBA, 1951–53; Council Royal Incorp. of Architects in Scot., 1951–53; Board, Edinburgh Coll. of Art, 1951–, Board Merchant Co. of Edinburgh, 1950–52. Edinburgh Dean of Guild Court, 1953–69. Hon. LLD Dundee, 1975; Hon. RA; Hon. RSW. *Address:* The Lane House, 46a Dick Place, Edinburgh EH9 2JB. *T:* 031–667 2724. *Clubs:* Scottish Arts, New (Edinburgh).

KINLOCH, Sir David, 13th Bt *cr* 1686, of Gilmerton; *b* 5 Aug. 1951; *s* of Sir Alexander Davenport Kinloch, 12th Bt and of Anna, *d* of late Thomas Walker, Edinburgh; *S* father, 1982; *m* 1976, Susan Middlewood; one *s* one *d*. *Educ:* Gordonstoun. Career in research into, and recovery and replacement of underground services. *Recreation:* treasure hunting. *Heir:* *s* Alexander Kinloch, *b* 31 May 1978. *Address:* Gilmerton House, North Berwick, East Lothian. *T:* Athelstaneford 207.

KINLOCH, Henry, (Harry); Chairman and Chief Executive, Aetna Montagu Life Insurance Co., since 1984; *b* 7 June 1937; *s* of William Shearer Kinloch and Alexina Alice Quartermaine Kinloch; *m* 1966, Gillian Anne Ashley (marr. diss. 1979); one *s* one *d*. *Educ:* Queen's Park Sch., Glasgow; Univs of Strathclyde, Birmingham and Glasgow. MSc, PhD, ARCST, CEng, FIMechE. Lecturer in Engineering: Univ. of Strathclyde, 1962–65; Univ. of Liverpool, 1966; Vis. Associate Prof. of Engrg, MIT, 1967; Sen. Design Engr, CEGB, 1968–70; PA Management Consultants, 1970–73; Chief Exec., Antony Gibbs (PFP) Ltd, 1973–74; Chm. and Chief Exec., Antony Gibbs Financial Services Ltd, 1975–77; Man. Dir, British Shipbuilders, 1978–80; Dep. Man. Dir and Chief Exec., Liberty Life Assce Co., 1980–83. *Publications:* many publications on theoretical and applied mechanics, financial and business studies. *Recreations:* piano music, opera, political biography. *Address:* 45 Breton House, The Barbican, EC2Y 8DF *T:* 01–628 3870. *Clubs:* Athenæum; Wentworth; Royal Liverpool Golf.

KINLOCH, Sir John, 4th Bt, of Kinloch, *cr* 1873; *b* 1 Nov. 1907; *e s* of Sir George Kinloch, 3rd Bt, OBE, and Ethel May (*d* 1959), *y d* of late Major J. Hawkins; *S* father 1948; *m* 1934, Doris Ellaline, *e d* of C. J. Head, London; one *s* two *d*. *Educ:* Charterhouse;

Magdalene Coll., Cambridge. Served with British Ministry of War Transport as their repr. at Abadan, Persia, and also in London. Employed by Butterfield & Swire in China and Hong Kong, 1931–63, and by John Swire & Sons Ltd, London, 1964–73. *Heir: s* David Oliphant Kinloch, CA [*b* 15 Jan. 1942; *m* 1st, 1968, Susan Minette (marr. diss. 1979), *y d* of Maj.-Gen. R. E. Urquhart, *qv*; three *d*; 2nd, 1983, Sabine, *o d* of Philippe de Loes, Geneva; one *s*]. *Address:* Aldie Cottage, Kinross, Kinross-shire KY13 7QH. *T:* Fossoway 305. *Club:* New (Edinburgh).

KINLOSS, Lady (12th in line, of the Lordship *cr* 1602); **Beatrice Mary Grenville Freeman-Grenville** (surname changed by Lord Lyon King of Arms, 1950); *b* 1922; *e d* of late Rev. Hon. Luis Chandos Francis Temple Morgan-Grenville, Master of Kinloss; *S* grandmother, 1944; *m* 1950, Dr Greville Stewart Parker Freeman-Grenville, FSA, FRAS (name changed from Freeman by Lord Lyon King of Arms, 1950), Capt. late Royal Berks Regt, *er s* of late Rev. E. C. Freeman; one *s* two *d*. *Heir: s* Master of Kinloss, *qv*. *Address:* North View House, Sheriff Hutton, York YO6 1PT. *T:* Sheriff Hutton 447. *Club:* Royal Commonwealth Society.

KINLOSS, Master of; Hon. Bevil David Stewart Chandos Freeman-Grenville; *b* 20 June 1953; *s* of Dr Greville Stewart Parker Freeman-Grenville, FSA, Capt. late Royal Berks Regt, and of Lady Kinloss, *qv*. *Educ:* Redrice Sch. *Address:* North View House, Sheriff Hutton, York YO6 1PT.

KINNAIRD, family name of **Lord Kinnaird.**

KINNAIRD, 13th Lord *cr* 1682, of Inchture; **Graham Charles Kinnaird;** Baron Kinnaird of Rossie (UK), 1860; Flying Officer RAFVR; *b* 15 Sept. 1912; *e s* of 12th Lord Kinnaird, KT, KBE, and Frances Victoria (*d* 1960), *y d* of late T. H. Clifton, Lytham Hall, Lancs; *S* father, 1972; *m* 1st, 1938, Nadia (who obtained a decree of divorce, 1940), *o c* of H. A. Fortington, OBE, Isle of Jethou, Channel Islands; 2nd, 1940, Diana, *yr d* of R. S. Copeman, Roydon Hall, Diss, Norfolk; four *d* (one *s* decd). *Educ:* Eton. Demobilised RAF, 1945. *Address:* Rossie Priory, Inchture, Perthshire. *T:* Inchture 246; Durham House, Durham Place, SW3. *Clubs:* Brooks's, Pratt's.

KINNEAR, Ian Albert Clark, CMG 1974; HM Diplomatic Service, retired; consultant in inward investment; *b* 23 Dec. 1924; *s* of late George Kinnear, CBE and Georgina Lilian (*née* Stephenson), Nairobi; *m* 1966, Rosemary, *d* of Dr K. W. D. Hartley, Cobham; two *d*. *Educ:* Marlborough Coll.; Lincoln Coll., Oxford (MA). HM Forces, 1943–46 (1st E Africa Reconnaissance Regt). Colonial Service (later HMOCS): Malayan Civil Service, 1951–56: District Officer, Bentong, then Alor Gajah, Asst Sec. Econ. Planning Unit; Kenya, 1956–63: Asst Sec., then Sen. Asst Sec., Min. of Commerce and Industry; 1st Sec., CRO, later Commonwealth Office, 1963–66; 1st Sec. (Commercial), British Embassy, Djakarta, 1966–68; 1st Sec. and Head of Chancery, British High Commn, Dar-es-Salaam, 1969–71; Chief Sec., later Dep. Governor, Bermuda, 1971–74; Senior British Trade Comr, Hong Kong, 1974–77; Consul-Gen., San Francisco, 1977–82. *Recreation:* painting. *Address:* Castle Hill Cottages, Castle Hill, Brenchley, Tonbridge, Kent TN12 7BS. *T:* Brenchley 3782.

KINNEAR, Nigel Alexander, FRCSI; Surgeon to Federated Dublin Voluntary Hospitals until 1974, retired; *b* 3 April 1907; *s* of James and Margaret Kinnear; *m* 1947, Frances Gardner; one *d*. *Educ:* Mill Hill Sch.; Trinity Coll., Dublin (MA, MB). Surgeon to Adelaide Hosp., Dublin, 1936; Regius Prof. of Surgery, TCD, 1967–72. President: RCSI, 1961; Royal Academy of Medicine of Ireland, 1968 (Hon. Fellow, 1983); James IV Surgical Assoc. Hon. FRCSGlas. *Publications:* articles in surgical jls. *Recreations:* salmon fishing, gardening. *Address:* Summerseat Cottage, Clonee, Co. Meath. *T:* Dunboyne 255353. *Club:* Kildare Street and University (Dublin).

KINNOCK, Rt. Hon. Neil Gordon; PC 1983; MP (Lab) Islwyn, since 1983 (Bedwellty, 1970–83); Leader of the Labour Party, and Leader of the Opposition, since 1983; *b* 28 March 1942; *s* of Gordon Kinnock, Labourer, and Mary Kinnock (*née* Howells), Nurse; *m* 1967, Glenys Elizabeth Parry; one *s* one *d*. *Educ:* Lewis Sch., Pengam; University Coll., Cardiff. BA in Industrial Relations and History, UC, Cardiff (Chm. Socialist Soc., 1962–65; Pres. Students' Union, 1965–66). Tutor Organiser in Industrial and Trade Union Studies, WEA, 1966–70; Mem., Welsh Hosp. Bd, 1969–71. PPS to Sec. of State for Employment, 1974–75. Member: Nat. Exec. Cttee, Labour Party, 1978–; Parly Cttee of PLP, 1979–; Chief Opposition spokesman on educn, 1979–83. Director (unpaid): Tribune Publications, 1974–82; Fair Play for Children, 1979–; 7:84 Theatre Co. (England) Ltd, 1979–; Mem., Socialist Educational Assoc., 1975–; Pres., Assoc. of Liberal Educn, 1980–82. *Publications:* Wales and the Common Market, 1971; contribs to Tribune, Guardian, New Statesman, etc. *Recreations:* male voice choral music, reading, children; Rugby Union and Association football. *Address:* House of Commons, SW1.

KINNOULL, 15th Earl of, *cr* 1633; **Arthur William George Patrick Hay;** Viscount Dupplin and Lord Hay, 1627, 1633, 1697; Baron Hay (Great Britain), 1711; *b* 26 March 1935; *o surv. s* of 14th Earl and Mary Ethel Isobel Meyrick (*d* 1938); *S* father 1938; *m* 1961, Gay Ann, *er d* of Sir Denys Lowson, 1st Bt; one *s* three *d*. *Educ:* Eton. Chartered Land Agent, 1960; Mem., Agricultural Valuers' Assoc., 1962. Fellow, Chartered Land Agents' Soc., 1964. Pres., National Council on Inland Transport, 1964–76. Mem. of Queen's Body Guard for Scotland (Royal Company of Archers), 1965. Junior Cons. Whip, House of Lords, 1966–68; Cons. Opposition Spokesman on Aviation, House of Lords, 1968–70. Chm., Property Owners' Building Soc., 1976– (Dir, 1971–). Mem., Air League Council, 1972; Council Mem., Deep Sea Fishermen's Mission, 1977. Vice-Pres., Nat. Assoc. of Local Councils (formerly Nat. Assoc. of Parish Councils), 1970–. FRICS 1970. *Heir: s* Viscount Dupplin, *qv*. *Address:* 15 Carlyle Square, SW3; Pier House, Seaview, Isle of Wight. *Clubs:* Turf, Pratt's, White's, MCC.

KINROSS, 5th Baron *cr* 1902; **Christopher Patrick Balfour;** Partner in Shepherd & Wedderburn, WS, Solicitors, since 1977; *b* 1 Oct. 1949; *s* of 4th Baron Kinross, OBE, TD, and Helen Anne (*d* 1969), *d* of A. W. Hog; *S* father, 1985; *m* 1974, Susan Jane, *d* of I. R. Pitman, WS; two *s*. *Educ:* Belhaven Hill School, Dunbar; Eton College; Edinburgh Univ. (LLB). Mem., Law Soc. of Scotland, 1975; WS 1975. UK Treas., James IV Assoc. of Surgeons, 1981– (Hon. Mem., 1985–); Treas., Edinburgh Gastro-intestinal Res. Fund, 1981–. Member, Queen's Body Guard for Scotland, Royal Company of Archers, 1980–. *Recreations:* pistol, rifle and shotgun shooting, stalking, motorsport. *Heir: s* Hon. Alan Ian Balfour, *b* 4 April 1978. *Address:* 11 Belford Place, Edinburgh. *T:* 031-332 9704. *Clubs:* New, Musketeers' Rifle and Pistol (Edinburgh).

KINROSS, John Blythe, CBE 1967 (OBE 1958); *b* 31 Jan. 1904; *s* of late John Kinross, RSA, architect, and late Mary Louisa Margaret Hall; *m* 1st, 1930; one *s* two *d*; 2nd, 1943, Mary Elizabeth Connon; one *s* two *d*. *Educ:* George Watson's Coll., Edinburgh. Manager Issue Dept, Gresham Trust, until 1933 when started business on own account as Cheviot Trust (first Issuing House to undertake small issues). Joined Industrial & Commercial Finance Corp. Ltd at inception, 1945; Gen. Man., 1948; Exec. Dir, 1961; Dep. Chm., 1964–74. Mem. Finance Cttee, Royal College of Surgeons, 1956–79; Hon. Financial Adviser to Royal Scottish Academy, 1950–. Founded Mary Kinross Charitable Trust, 1957 (includes Good Companions Workshops Ltd, Student Homes Ltd and various med. res. projects). Chairman: Imperial Investments (Grosvenor) Ltd; Estate Duties Investment Trust Ltd, 1973–76; Director: Equity Income Trust Ltd, 1962–82; House of Fraser Ltd, 1966–72; London Atlantic Investment Trust Ltd, 1962–83; Scottish Ontario Investment, 1961–79; Investment Trust of Guernsey Ltd and other companies. Hon. RSA, 1957; Hon. FFARCS, 1961. *Publication:* Fifty Years in the City, 1982. *Recreation:* farming. *Address:* 23 Cumberland Terrace, NW1. *T:* 01-935 8979; (office) 01-928 7822. *Club:* Athenæum.

KINSELLA, Thomas; poet; Professor of English, Temple University, Philadelphia, since 1970; *b* 4 May 1928; *m* 1955, Eleanor Walsh; one *s* two *d*. Entered Irish Civil Service, 1946; resigned from Dept of Finance, 1965. Artist-in-residence, 1965–67, Prof. of English, 1967–70, Southern Illinois Univ. Elected to Irish Academy of Letters, 1965. J. S. Guggenheim Meml Fellow, 1968–69, 1971–72. *Publications: poetry:* Poems, 1956; Another September, 1958; Downstream, 1962; Nightwalker and other poems, 1968; Notes from the Land of the Dead, 1972; Butcher's Dozen, 1972; A Selected Life, 1972; Finistère, 1972; New Poems, 1973; Selected Poems 1956 to 1968, 1973; Vertical Man and The Good Fight, 1973; One, 1974; A Technical Supplement, 1976; Song of the Night and Other Poems, 1978; The Messenger, 1978; Fifteen Dead, 1979; One and Other Poems, 1979; Poems 1956–73, 1980; Peppercanister Poems 1956–73, 1980; One Fond Embrace, 1981; Songs of the Psyche, 1985; Her Vertical Smile, 1985; St Catherine's Clock, 1986; Out of Ireland, 1986; (trans.) The Táin, 1969; contrib. essay in Davis, Mangan, Ferguson, 1970; (ed) Selected Poems of Austin Clarke, 1976; An Duanaire—Poems of the Dispossessed (trans. Gaelic poetry, 1600–1900), 1981; (ed) Our Musical Heritage: lectures on Irish traditional music by Seán Ó Riada, 1982; (ed, with translations) The New Oxford Book of Irish Verse, 1986. *Address:* 47 Percy Place, Dublin, Ireland.

KINSEY, Thomas Richard Moseley, FEng 1982; Deputy Chief Executive, Mitchell Cotts plc, since 1982; Chairman, Birmingham Battery & Metal Co. Ltd, since 1984; Director: Gower International plc, since 1984; Telcon Ltd, since 1984; *b* 13 Oct. 1929; *s* of late Richard Moseley Kinsey and Dorothy Elizabeth Kinsey; *m* 1953, Ruth (*née* Owen-Jones); two *s*. *Educ:* Newtown Sch.; Trinity Hall, Cambridge (MA). FIMechE; CBIM. ICI Ltd, 1952–57; Tube Investments,1957–65; joined Delta plc, 1965; Director, 1973–77; Jt Man. Dir, 1977–82. *Recreations:* golf, travel. *Address:* Pinewood, Poolhead Lane, Tanworth-in-Arden, Warwickshire B94 5ED. *T:* Tanworth-in-Arden 2082. *Clubs:* Athenæum, East India, Devonshire, Sports and Public Schools; Edgbaston Golf.

KINSMAN, Surgeon Rear-Adm. Francis Michael, CBE 1982 (OBE 1972); Surgeon Rear Admiral (Ships and Establishments), 1980–82, retired; *b* 5 May 1925; *s* of Oscar Edward Kinsman and Margaret Vera Kinsman; *m* 1st, 1949, Catherine Forsyth Barr; one *s*; 2nd, 1955, Margaret Emily Hillier; two *s*. *Educ:* Rydal Sch., Colwyn Bay; St Bartholomew's Hosp. MRCS, LRCP, MFCM; DA. Joined RN, 1952; served, 1952–66: HMS Comus, HMS Tamar, HMS Centaur; RN Hosp. Malta, RN Air Med. Sch., RNAS Lossiemouth; Pres., Central Air Med. Bd, 1966–69; Jt Services Staff Coll., 1969; Staff, Med. Dir Gen. (Naval), 1970–73; Dir, Naval Med. Staff Trng, 1973–76; Comd MO to C-in-C Naval Home Comd, 1976–79; MO i/c RN Hosp. Gibraltar, 1979–80. QHP 1980–82. OStJ 1977. *Recreations:* music, painting, fishing, woodwork. *Address:* Pound House, Meonstoke, Southampton, Hants.

KINTORE, 12th Earl of, *cr* 1677; **James Ian Keith;** Lord Keith of Inverurie, 1677 (Scot.); Bt 1897; Baron 1925; Viscount Stonehaven 1938; CEng; AIStructE; Major, RM, Royal Marine Engineers; Member Royal Company of Archers; *b* 25 July 1908; *er s* of John Lawrence Baird, 1st Viscount Stonehaven, PC, GCMG, DSO, and Lady Ethel Sydney Keith-Falconer (later Countess of Kintore, 11th in line), *e d* of 9th Earl of Kintore; name changed from Baird to Keith, 1967; *S* to Viscountcy of Stonehaven, 1941, and to Earldom of Kintore, 1974; *m* 1935, Delia Virginia, *d* of William Loyd; two *s* one *d*. *Educ:* Eton; Royal School of Mines, London. UK Delegate to Council of Europe and Western European Union, 1954–64. Councillor, Grampian Region (Chm., Water Services Cttee), 1974–78. DL Kincardineshire, 1959; Vice-Lieut, 1965–76. *Heir: s* Master of Kintore, Lord Inverurie, *qv*. *Address:* Glenton House, Rickarton, near Stonehaven, Kincardineshire. *T:* Stonehaven 63071. *Clubs:* Beefsteak; Rand (Johannesburg).

KIPARSKY, Prof. Valentin Julius Alexander, MA, PhD; Finnish writer and Professor, Helsinki, retired 1974; Member of the Finnish Academy, 1977; *b* St Petersburg, 4 July 1904; *s* of Professor René Kiparsky and Hedwig (*née* Sturtzel); *m* 1940, Aina Dagmar, MagPhil, *d* of Rev. Matti Jaatinen and Olga (née Jungmann); one *s*. *Educ:* St Annen-Schule, St Petersburg; St Alexis Sch., Perkjärvi, Finland; Finnish Commercial Sch., Viipuri, Finland; Helsinki Univ.; Prague Univ.; and research work in different countries. Helsinki University: Junior Lectr, 1933, Sen. Lectr, 1938, actg Prof., 1946, Prof., 1947 and again, 1963. Visiting Prof., Indiana Univ., Bloomington, USA, 1952, Minnesota Univ., USA, 1961–62; Prof. of Russian Language and Literature, University of Birmingham, 1952–55, when he returned to Finland; Prof. of Slavonic Philology, Freie Univ., Berlin, 1958–63. Co-Editor: Slavistische Veröffentlichungen (W Berlin), 1958–; Scando-Slavica (Copenhagen), 1963–. Lt Finnish Army, 1939–40, 1941–42; Translator and Interpreter to Finnish Govt, 1942–44; Director: Finnish Govtl Inst. for studies of USSR, 1948–50; Osteuropa-Institut, W Berlin, 1958–63. Pres., Societas Scientiarum Fennica; Mem., Finn. Acad.; Corresp. Member: Akad. der Wissenschaften und der Literatur, Mainz; Internat. Cttee of Slavists. Dr *hc*: Poznań, 1973; Stockholm 1975. Comdr of the Finnish Lion, 1954; Order Zasługi, Poland, 1974. *Publications:* Die gemeinslavischen Lehnwörter aus dem Germanischen, 1934; Fremdes im Baltendeutsch, 1936; Die Kurenfrage, 1939; Suomi Venäjän Kirjallisuudessa, 1943 and 1945; Venäjän Runotar, 1946; Norden i den Ryska Skönlitteraturen, 1947; Wortakzent der russischen Schriftsprache, 1962; Russische historische Grammatik I, 1963; English and American Characters in Russian Fiction, 1964; Russische historische Grammatik II, 1967, III, 1974; numerous articles in various languages in learned jls. *Recreation:* cycling. *Address:* Maurinkatu 8–12 C 37, Helsinki, Finland.

KIPKULEI, Benjamin Kipkech; High Commissioner for Kenya in London, concurrently Ambassador to Italy and Switzerland, since 1984; *b* 5 Jan. 1946; *s* of Mr and Mrs Kipkulei Chesoro; *m* 1972, Miriam; three *s* two *d*. *Educ:* BAEd Nairobi; DipEd Scotland; MEd London. Local Government, 1964 and 1965; Teacher, 1970; Education Officer, 1974; Under Secretary, 1982. *Recreations:* swimming, photography. *Address:* Kenya High Commission, 45 Portland Place, W1N 4AS. *T:* 01-636 2371.

KIRALFY, Prof. Albert Kenneth Roland; Professor of Law, King's College, London, 1964–81, now Emeritus Professor; *b* Toronto, 5 Dec. 1915; *s* of Bolossy Kiralfy, Theatrical Impresario, and Helen Dawnay; *m* 1960, Roberta Ann Routledge. *Educ:* Streatham Grammar Sch.; King's Coll., London Univ. LLB 1935, LLM 1936, PhD 1949. Served War of 1939–45. Called to the Bar, Gray's Inn, 1947. King's Coll., London: Asst Lectr, 1937–39 and 1947–48; Lectr, 1948–51; Reader, 1951–64; Dean of College Law Faculty, 1974–77; FKC 1971. Chm., Bd of Studies in Laws, London Univ., 1971–74; Dean of Univ. Law Faculty, 1980–81. Vis. Prof., Osgoode Hall Law Sch., Toronto, 1961–62; Exchange Scholar, Leningrad Law Sch., Spring 1964, Moscow Law Sch., April 1970; Prague Acad. of Sciences, April 1975. Dir, Comparative Law Course, Luxembourg, Aug. 1968. Chm., Council of Hughes Parry Hall, London Univ., 1970–82. Editor, Journal of

Legal History, 1980–; Mem. Editorial Bd, Internat. and Comparative Law Quarterly, 1956–; Reviser, English trans., Polish Civil Code, 1981. *Publications:* The Action on the Case, 1951; The English Legal System, 1954 (and later edns; 7th edn 1984); A Source Book of English Law, 1957; Potter's Historical Introduction to English Law, (4th edn) 1958; (with Prof. G. Jones) Guide to Selden Society Publications, 1960; Translation of Russian Civil Codes, 1966; chapter, English Law, in Derrett, Introduction to Legal Systems, 1968; (with Miss R. A. Routledge) Guide to Additional MSS at Gray's Inn Library, 1971; General Editor, Comparative Law of Matrimonial Property, 1972; (ed jtly): New Perspectives in Scottish Legal History, 1984; Custom, Courts and Counsel, 1985; contributed: Encyclopædia of Soviet Law (Leiden), 1973; Contemporary Soviet Law, 1974; East-West Business Transactions, 1974; Common Law, Encyclopædia Britannica, 1974; Codification in the Communist World, 1975, Russian Law: Historical Perspectives, 1977; Le Nuove Frontiere del Diritto, 1979; Jl of Legal History, NY Jl of Internat. and Comparative Law; Review of Socialist Laws; *Rapporteur,* The Child without Family Ties, Congress of Jean Bodin Soc., Strasbourg, 1972. *Recreations:* travel, reading, languages. *Address:* Faculty of Laws, King's College, Strand, WC2; 58 Cheriton Square, SW17.

KIRBY, David Donald; Member, British Railways Board, and Joint Managing Director (Railways), since 1985; *b* 12 May 1933; *s* of Walter Donald Kirby and Margaret Irene (*née* Halstead); *m* 1955, Joan Florence (*née* Dickins); one *s* one *d*. *Educ:* Royal Grammar Sch., High Wycombe; Jesus Coll., Oxford (MA). FCIT. British Rail and its subsidiaries: Divisional Shipping Manager, Dover, 1964; Operations Manager, Shipping and Continental, 1965; Asst Gen. Man., Shipping and International Services, 1966; Continental Traffic Man., BR, 1968; Gen. Man., Shipping and Internat. Services, 1974; Man. Dir, Sealink UK Ltd, 1979; Dir, London and SE, 1982–85. *Recreations:* messing about in boats, choral singing. *Address:* British Railways Board, Rail House, Euston Station, NW1.

KIRBY, Dennis, MVO 1961; MBE 1955; Directeur Associé, European Investment Bank, since 1984 (Conseiller Principal, 1974, Directeur Adjoint, 1976); *b* 5 April 1923; *s* of William Ewart Kirby and Hannah Kirby; *m* 1943, Mary Elizabeth Kilby. *Educ:* Hull Grammar Sch.; Queen's Coll., Cambridge. Lt (A) RNVR (fighter pilot), 1940–46. Colonial Service, Sierra Leone, 1946–62 (District Comr, 1950; Perm. Sec., 1961–62); 1st Sec., UK Diplomatic Service, 1962; General Manager: East Kilbride Development Corp., 1963–68; Irvine Development Corp., 1967–72; Industrial Dir, Scotland, DTI, 1972–74. *Recreations:* shooting, golf. *Address:* European Investment Bank, 100 Boulevard Konrad Adenauer, Luxembourg; 68 Pall Mall, SW1. *Clubs:* United Oxford & Cambridge University; RNVR (Scotland) (Glasgow); Grand-Ducal Golf (Luxembourg).

KIRBY, Prof. Gordon William, ScD, PhD; FRSC; FRSE; Regius Professor of Chemistry, University of Glasgow, since 1972; *b* 20 June 1934; *s* of William Admiral Kirby and Frances Teresa Kirby (*née* Townson); *m* 1964, Audrey Jean Rusbridge (marr. diss. 1983), *d* of Col C. E. Rusbridge; two *s*. *Educ:* Liverpool Inst. High Sch.; Gonville and Caius Coll., Cambridge (Schuldham Plate 1956; MA, PhD, ScD); FRIC 1970; FRSE 1975. 1851 Exhibn Senior Student, 1958–60, Asst Lectr, 1960–61, Lectr, 1961–67, Imperial Coll. of Science and Technology; Prof. of Organic Chemistry, Univ. of Technology, Loughborough, 1967–72; Mem., Chem. Cttee, SRC, 1971–75. Chm., Jls Cttee, Royal Chem. Soc., 1981–84. Corday-Morgan Medal, Chem. Soc., 1969; Tilden Lectr, Chem. Soc., 1974–75. *Publications:* Co-editor: Elucidation of Organic Structures by Physical and Chemical Methods, vol. IV, parts I, II, and III, 1972; Fortschritte der Chemie organischer Naturstoffe, 1971–; contributor to Jl Chem. Soc., etc. *Address:* Chemistry Department, The University, Glasgow G12 8QQ.

KIRBY, Gwendolen Maud, LVO 1969; Matron, The Hospital for Sick Children, Great Ormond Street, 1951–69; *b* 17 Dec. 1911; 3rd *d* of late Frank M. Kirby, Gravesend, Kent. *Educ:* St Mary's Sch., Calne, Wilts. State Registered Nurse: trained at Nightingale Training Sch., St Thomas' Hosp., SE1. 1933–36; The Mothercraft Training Soc., Cromwell House, Highgate, 1936; State Certified Midwife: trained at General Lying-in Hosp., York Road, Lambeth, 1938–39; Registered Sick Children's Nurse: trained at the Hospital for Sick Children, Great Ormond Street, WC1, 1942–44. Awarded Nightingale Fund Travelling Scholarship, 1948–49, and spent 1 year in Canada and United States. Mem. of Gen. Nursing Council, 1955–65. *Address:* Brackenfield, Winsford, Minehead, Som.

KIRBY, Jack Howard, CBE 1972; Chairman, International Tanker Owners Pollution Federation, 1968–73; Chairman, Shell Tankers (UK) Ltd, 1963–72; Managing Director, Shell International Marine Ltd, 1959–72; Director, Shell International Petroleum Co. Ltd, 1969–72; *b* 1 Feb. 1913; *s* of late Group Captain Frank Howard Kirby, VC, CBE and late Kate Kirby; *m* 1940, Emily Colton; one *s*. *Educ:* Sir Roger Manwood's Sch., Sandwich. Joined Shell, 1930, retired 1972; in USA with Shell, 1937–52, incl. secondment to British Shipping Mission and British Petroleum Mission, Washington, DC, 1940–46. Chm., Lights Adv. Cttee, 1958–78. Pres., Chamber of Shipping of the UK, 1971–72. Chevalier 1st Class, Order of St Olav, 1968. *Recreations:* golf, fishing, gardening, bridge. *Address:* 1 Beaufort House, Hillside, Cross Road, Sunningdale, Berks SL5 9RP. *T:* Ascot 21429. *Club:* Berkshire Golf.

KIRBY, Louis; Editorial Director, Associated Newspapers, since 1986; *b* 30 Nov. 1928; 2nd *s* of late William Kirby and Anne Kirby; *m* 1st, 1952, Marcia Teresa Lloyd (marr. diss. 1976); two *s* three *d*; 2nd, 1976, Heather Veronica (*née* Nicholson); one *s* one *d*; 3rd, 1983, Heather McGlone. *Educ:* Our Lady Immaculate, Liverpool; Coalbrookdale High Sch. Daily Mail: Gen. Reporter, subseq. Courts Corresp., and Polit. Corresp., 1953–62; Daily Sketch: Chief Reporter, subseq. Leader Writer and Polit. Editor, Asst Editor, Exec. Editor, and, Actg Editor, 1962–71; Daily Mail (when relaunched): Dep. Editor, 1971–74; Editor, Evening News, 1974–80; Vice-Chm., Evening News Ltd, 1975–80; Editor, The London Standard, 1980–86; Dir, Mail Newspapers plc, 1986–. *Recreations:* theatre, reading. *Address:* Carmelite House, EC4Y 0JA. *Clubs:* National Liberal, St James's.

KIRBY, Michael Donald, CMG 1983; **Hon. Justice Kirby;** President, Court of Appeal, Supreme Court, Sydney, since 1984; *b* 18 March 1939; *s* of Donald Kirby and Jean Langmore Kirby. *Educ:* Fort Street Boys' High Sch.; Univ. of Sydney (BA, LLM, BEc). Admitted Solicitor, 1962; called to the Bar of NSW, 1967; Mem., NSW Bar Council, 1974; Judge, Federal Court of Australia, 1983–84. Dep. Pres., Aust. Conciliation and Arbitration Commn, 1974–83; Chairman: Australian Law Reform Commn, 1975–84; OECD Inter-govtl Gp on Privacy and Internat. Data Flows, 1978–80; Member: Admin. Review Council of Australia, 1976–84; Council of Aust. Acad. of Forensic Scis, 1978–; Aust. National Commn for Unesco, 1980–83; Aust. Inst. of Multi-cultural Affairs, 1981–84; Exec., CSIRO, 1983–. Deleg., Unesco Gen. Conf., Paris, 1983. Member: Internat. Commn of Jurists, 1984–; Internat. Consult. Commn for Transborder Data Flow Develt, Intergovtl Bureau of Information, Rome, 1985–; Bd, Internat. Trustees, Internat. Inst. for Inf. and Communication, Montreal, 1986–; President: Criminology Sect., ANZAAS, 1981–82; Law Sect., ANZAAS, 1984–85. Mem., Library Council of NSW, 1978–85; Pres., Nat. Book Council of Australia, 1980–83. Fellow, Senate, Sydney Univ., 1964–69; Dep. Chancellor, Univ. of Newcastle, NSW, 1978–84; Chancellor, Macquarie Univ., Sydney, 1984–. Mem. Bd of Governors, Internat. Council for Computer Communications, Washington, 1984–. *Publications:* Reform the Law, 1983; Industrial Index to Australian Labour Law, 2nd edn 1983; The Judges (Boyer Lectures), 1983; essays and articles in legal and other jls. *Recreation:* work. *Address:* 4A Dumaresq Road, Rose Bay, NSW 2029, Australia. *T:* (02) 230–8202.

KIRBY, Maj.-Gen. Norman George, OBE 1971; FRCS; Consultant Casualty Surgeon, Guy's Hospital, since 1982; Director, Clinical Services, Orthopaedics, Accidents and Emergencies, since 1985; *b* 19 Dec. 1926; *s* of George William Kirby and Laura Kirby; *m* 1949, Cynthia Bradley; one *s* one *d*. *Educ:* King Henry VIII Sch., Coventry; Univ. of Birmingham (MB, ChB). FRCS 1964, FRCSE 1980; FICS 1980. Surgical Registrar: Plastic Surg. Unit, Stoke Mandeville Hosp., 1950–51; Birmingham Accident Hosp., 1953–55; Postgraduate Med. Sch., Hammersmith, 1964. Regt MO 10 Parachute Regt, 1950–51; OC 5 Parachute Surgical Team, 1956–59 (Suez Landing, 5 Nov. 1956); Officer i/c Surg. Div., BMH Rinteln, 1959–60; OC and Surg. Specialist, BMH Tripoli, 1960–62; OC and Consultant Surgeon, BMH Dhekelia, 1967–70; Chief Cons. Surgeon, Cambridge Mil. Hosp., 1970–72; Cons. Surg. HQ BAOR, 1973–78; Dir of Army Surgery, Cons. Surg. to the Army and Hon. Surgeon to the Queen, 1978–82; Hon. Cons. Surgeon, Westminster Hosp., 1979–. Examnr in Anatomy, RCSE, 1982. Chm., Army Med. Dept Working Party Surgical Support for BAOR, 1978–80; Mem., Med. Cttee, Defence Scientific Adv. Council, 1979–82. Hon. Colonel: 308 (Co. of London) Gen. Hosp. RAMC, TA, 1982–; 144 Field Ambulance RAMC (Volunteers), TA, 1985–. Member: Council Internat. Coll. of Surgeons; Airborne Med. Soc.; Casualty Surgeons Assoc., 1981–; Vice-Pres., British Assoc. of Trauma in Sport, 1982–; Chm., Accidents & Emergencies Cttee, SE Thames Regl Hosp. Authy, 1984. Liveryman, Soc. of Apothecaries of London, 1983–. McCombe Lectr, RCSE, 1979. Mem., Editl Bd, Brit. Jl Surg. and Injury, 1979–82. Mem., Surgical Travellers Club, 1979–. FMS London 1981. OStJ 1977. Mitchener Medal, RCS, 1982. *Publications:* (ed) Field Surgery Pocket Book, 1981; contrib. Brit. Jl Surg. and Proc. RSocMed. *Recreations:* travel, motoring, reading, archaeology. *Address:* 12 Woodsyre, Sydenham Hill, Dulwich, SE26 6SS. *T:* 01–670 5327. *Club:* Athenæum.

KIRBY, Hon. Sir Richard (Clarence), Kt 1961; AC 1985; Chairman, Advertising Standards Council, since 1973; *b* 22 Sept. 1904; *s* of Samuel Enoch Kirby and Agnes Mary Kirby, N Queensland; *m* 1937, Hilda Marie Ryan; two *d*. *Educ:* The King's Sch., Parramatta; University of Sydney (LLB). Solicitor, NSW, 1928; called to Bar, 1933; served AIF, 1942–44; Mem. Adult Adv. Educl Council to NSW Govt, 1944–46; Judge, Dist Court, NSW, 1944–47; Mem. Austr. War Crimes Commn, 1945, visiting New Guinea, Morotai, Singapore, taking evidence on war crimes; Australia Rep. on War Crimes, Lord Mountbatten's HQ, Ceylon, 1945; Royal Commissioner on various occasions for Federal, NSW and Tasmanian Govts, 1945–47; Acting Judge Supreme Court of NSW, 1947; Chief Judge, Commonwealth Court of Conciliation and Arbitration, 1956–73; Austr. Rep., UN Security Council's Cttee on Good Offices on Indonesian Question, 1947–48, participating in Security Council Debates, Lake Success, USA; Chm. Stevedoring Industry Commn, 1947–49; (first) Pres., Commonwealth Conciliation and Arbitration Commn, 1956–73. Chm., Nat. Stevedoring Conf., 1976–77. Pres., H. V. Evatt Meml Foundn, 1979–85. Mem. Council, Wollongong Univ., 1979–84. Hon. DLitt Wollongong Univ., 1984. *Recreation:* encouraging good will in industry. *Address:* The White House, Berrara, NSW 2540, Australia. *T:* Nowra 412171. *Clubs:* Athenæum, Victoria Racing, Victoria Amateur Turf, Moonee Valley Racing and Mornington Racing, Victoria Golf (Melbourne).

KIRCHNER, Peter James, MBE 1970; HM Diplomatic Service, retired; Consul General, Berlin, 1978–79; *b* 17 Sept. 1920; *s* of late William John Kirchner and Winifred Emily Homer (*née* Adams); *m* 1952, Barbro Sarah Margaretha (*née* Klockhoff); one *s* two *d*. *Educ:* St Brendan's Coll., Clifton, Bristol. Served War, RA, 1939–41. Timber production, UK and Germany, 1941–48; FO, Germany, 1948; Home Office Immigration Dept, 1952–64; Head of UK Refugee Missions in Europe, 1960–63; FCO (formerly FO): Barbados, 1965; Nairobi, 1968; Ankara, 1970; Vienna, 1973; Jerusalem, 1976. Freeman, City of London, 1963. *Recreations:* chatty golf, 18th-19th century Europe, discovering European backwaters, trying to write. *Address:* 86 York Mansions, Prince of Wales Drive, SW11 4BN. *T:* 01–622 7068.

KIRK, Prof. Geoffrey Stephen, DSC 1945; LittD; FBA 1959; Regius Professor of Greek, University of Cambridge, 1974–82, now Emeritus; Fellow of Trinity College, Cambridge, 1974–82; *b* 3 Dec. 1921; *s* of Frederic Tilzey Kirk, MC, and Enid Hilda (*née* Pentecost); *m* 1st, 1950, Barbara Helen Traill (marr. diss. 1975); one *d*; 2nd, 1975, Kirsten Jensen (Ricks). *Educ:* Rossall Sch.; Clare Coll., Cambridge. LittD Cambridge, 1965. Served War in Royal Navy, 1941–45; commissioned 1942; Temp. Lt, RNVR, 1945. Took Degree at Cambridge, 1946; Research Fellow, Trinity Hall, 1946–49; Student, Brit. Sch. at Athens, 1947; Commonwealth Fund Fellow, Harvard Univ., 1949–50; Fellow, Trinity Hall, 1950–70; Cambridge University: Asst Lecturer in Classics, 1951; Lecturer in Classics, 1952–61; Reader in Greek, 1961–65; Prof. of Classics, Yale Univ., 1965–70; Prof. of Classics, Bristol Univ., 1971–73. Visiting Lecturer, Harvard Univ., 1958; Sather Prof. of Classical Literature, University of California, Berkeley, 1968–69; Mellon Prof., Tulane Univ., 1979. Pres., Soc. for Promotion of Hellenic Studies, 1977–80. MA (Yale) 1965. *Publications:* Heraclitus, the Cosmic Fragments, 1954; (with J. E. Raven) The Presocratic Philosophers, 1958; The Songs of Homer, 1962 (abbrev., as Homer and the Epic, 1965); Euripides, Bacchae, 1970; Myth, 1970; The Nature of Greek Myths, 1974; Homer and the Oral Tradition, 1977; The Iliad: a commentary, Vol.1, books 1–4, 1985; articles in classical, archæological and philosophical journals. *Recreation:* sailing. *Address:* 10 Sion Hill, Bath, Avon BA1 2UH.

KIRK, Grayson Louis; President Emeritus, Columbia University; *b* 12 Oct. 1903; *s* of Traine Caldwell Kirk and Nora Eichelberger; *m* 1925, Marion Louise Sands; one *s*. *Educ:* Miami Univ. (AB); Clark Univ. (AM); Ecole Libre des Sciences Politiques, Paris, 1928–29. PhD University of Wisconsin, 1930. Prof. of History, Lamar Coll., Beaumont, Tex, 1925–27; Social Science Research Coun. Fellowship (chiefly spent at London Sch. of Economics), 1936–37; Instructor in Political Science, 1929–30, Asst Prof., 1930–36, Associate Prof., 1936–38, Prof., 1938–40, University of Wisconsin; Associate Prof. of Government, Columbia Univ., 1940–43; Head, Security Section, Div. of Political Studies, US Dept of State, 1942–43; Mem. US Delegn Staff, Dumbarton Oaks, 1944; Exec. Officer, Third Commn, San Francisco Conf., 1945. Research Associate, Yale Inst. of Internat. Studies, 1943–44; Prof. of Government, Columbia Univ., 1943–47; Prof. of Internat Relations, Acting Dir of Sch. of Internat. Affairs, and Dir of European Inst., 1947–49. Appointed Provost in Nov. 1949, and also Vice-Pres in July 1950; became acting head of Columbia in President Eisenhower's absence on leave, March 1951; Pres. and Trustee of Columbia Univ., 1953–68; Bryce Prof. of History of Internat. Relations, Columbia, 1959–72, Emeritus Prof., 1972. Trustee Emeritus, The Asia Foundation; Trustee: French Inst.; Lycée Français of NY; Academy of Political Science (Chm. and Dir); American Philosophical Soc.; Pilgrims of the US (Vice-Pres.); Council on Foreign Relations; Amer. Acad. of Arts and Sciences; Amer. Soc. of French Legion of Honour (Chm.). Director: Monthly Income Shares Inc.; Money Shares Inc.; Bullock Fund Ltd;

Bullock Tax-Free Shares Inc.; Dividend Shares Inc.; High Income Shares; Nation-Wide Securities Co. Inc.; France-America Soc.; Mem. Adv. Bd, International Business Machines Corp. Hon. LLD: Miami, 1950; Waynesburg Coll., Brown Univ., Union Coll, 1951; Puerto Rico, Clark, Princeton, New York, Wisconsin, Columbia, Jewish Theol. Seminary of America, 1953; Syracuse, Williams Coll., Pennsylvania, Harvard, Washington, St Louis, Central Univ., Caracas, Univ. of the Andes, Merida, Venezuela, Univ. of Zulia, Maracaibo, Venezuela, Univ. of Delhi, India, Thamasset Univ., Bangkok, 1954; Johns Hopkins Univ., Baltimore, Amherst, 1956; Dartmouth Coll., Northwestern Univ., 1958; Tennessee, 1960; St Lawrence, 1963; Denver, Notre Dame, Bates Coll., 1964; Waseda (Japan), Michigan, 1965; Sussex, 1966; Hon. LHD N Dakota, 1958; Hon. PhD Bologna, 1951; Dr of Civil Law King's Coll., Halifax, Nova Scotia, 1958. Associate KStJ 1959. Comdr, Order of Orange-Nassau, 1952; Hon. KBE, 1955; Grand Officer, Order of Merit, of the Republic, Italy, 1956; Grand Officier Légion d'Honneur, France, 1973. Medal of the Order of Taj, Iran, 1961; Grand Cross, Order of George I (Greece), 1965; Order of the Sacred Treasure, 1st Class (Japan), 1965; Comdr, Ordre des Palmes Académiques (France), 1966. *Publications*: Philippine Independence, 1936; Contemporary International Politics (with W. R. Sharp), 1940; (with R. P. Stebbins) War and National Policy, Syllabus, 1941; The Study of International Relations in American Colleges and Universities, 1947. *Address*: 28 Sunnybrook Road, Bronxville, NY 10708, USA. *T*: 227–3300. *Clubs*: Century, University (New York); Bohemian (San Francisco).

KIRK, Rt. Hon. Herbert Victor, PC (N Ireland) 1962; Member (U) for South Belfast, Northern Ireland Assembly, 1973–75; *b* 5 June 1912; *s* of Alexander and Mary A. Kirk; *m* 1944, Gladys A. Dunn; three *s*. *Educ*: Queen's Univ., Belfast (BComSc). MP Windsor Div. of Belfast, NI Parlt, 1956–72; Minister of Labour and Nat. Insce, Govt of N Ireland, 1962–64; Minister of Education, 1964–65; Minister of Finance, 1965–72, Jan.-May 1974, resigned. FCA 1940. JP Co. Borough Belfast. *Recreation*: golf. *Address*: 38 Massey Avenue, Belfast BT4 2JT, Northern Ireland. *Clubs*: Royal Portrush Golf, Belvoir Park Golf (Pres.).

KIRK, John Henry, CBE 1957; Emeritus Professor of Marketing (with special reference to horticulture), University of London; *b* 11 April 1907; *s* of William Kirk, solicitor; *m* 1946, Wilfrida Margaret Booth; two *s*. *Educ*: Durban High Sch., S Africa; Universities of S Africa, Cambridge, North Carolina and Chicago. Ministry of Agriculture (from 1934, as economist and administrator); Under-Sec., 1959–65; Prof. of Marketing, Wye Coll., 1965–72. *Publications*: Economic Aspects of Native Segregation, 1929; Agriculture and the Trade Cycle, 1933; United Kingdom Agricultural Policy 1870–1970, 1982; contributions to journals of sociology, economics and agricultural economics. *Recreation*: gardening. *Address*: Burrington, Cherry Gardens, Wye, Ashford, Kent. *T*: Wye 812640.

KIRK, Dame (Lucy) Ruth, DBE 1975; Patron, Society for the Protection of the Unborn Child; *m* 1941, Norman Eric Kirk (later, Rt Hon. Norman Kirk, PC, Prime Minister of New Zealand; *d* 1974); three *s* two *d*. Awarded title, Dame of the Order of the British Empire, for public services. *Address*: 7 Rimu Vale Street, Rotorua, New Zealand.

KIRK, Dame Ruth; *see* Kirk, Dame L. R.

KIRKALDY, Prof. John Francis, DSc (London); FGS; Emeritus Professor of Geology, University of London, since 1974; *b* 14 May 1908; *o s* of late James and Rose Edith Kirkaldy, Sutton, Surrey; *m* 1935, Dora Muriel, *e d* of late Grimshaw Heyes Berry, Enfield, Middlesex; four *d*. *Educ*: Felsted Sch.; King's Coll., London. 1st Cl. Special Hons BSc (Geol.) 1929; MSc 1932; DSc 1946. Demonstrator in Geology, King's Coll., 1929–33; Asst Lectr in Geology, University Coll., London, 1933–36; Lectr in Geology, King's Coll., London, 1936–47. War Service with Meteorological Branch, RAF, Sqdn Ldr, 1939–45. Reader in Geology and Head of Dept, Queen Mary Coll., 1947–62; Prof. of Geology and Head of Dept, QMC, 1962–74. FKC 1970; Fellow, Queen Mary College, 1976. Daniel Pidgeon Fund, Geol. Soc., 1935; Foulerton Award, Geologists' Assoc., 1947. *Publications*: Outline of Historical Geology (with A. K. Wells), 1948 (and subseq. edns); General Principles of Geology, 1954 (and subseq. edns); Rocks and Minerals in Colour, 1963. Papers in Quart. Jl Geol. Soc.; Proc. Geol. Assoc., Geol. Mag., etc. *Recreation*: gardening. *Address*: Stone House, Byfield Road, Chipping Warden, Banbury, Oxon. *T*: Chipping Warden 689. *Club*: Geological Society's.

KIRKBY, Emma; free-lance classical concert singer; soprano; *b* 26 Feb. 1949; *d* of Geoffrey and Daphne Kirkby. *Educ*: Hanford School; Sherborne School for Girls; Somerville College, Oxford (BA Classics). Private singing lessons with Jessica Cash. Regular appearances with Taverner Choir and Players, 1972–; Member: Consort of Musicke, 1973–; Academy of Ancient Music, 1975–; numerous radio broadcasts, gramophone recordings, appearances at the Proms, 1977–. Hon. DLitt Salford, 1985.

KIRKE, Rear-Adm. David Walter, CB 1967; CBE 1962 (OBE 1945); Chairman: Trafalgar Operations Ltd, since 1985; Director: Brim Exports Ltd, since 1970; GRP Technical Services Ltd; Mercantile Airship Transportation Ltd; Consultant: Airship Industries Ltd; Coverdale Training Ltd; Wren Skyships Ltd; *b* 13 March 1915; *s* of late Percy St George Kirke and late Alice Gertrude, *d* of Sir James Gibson Craig, 3rd Bt; *m* 1st, 1936, Tessa O'Connor (marr. diss., 1950); one *s*; 2nd, 1956, Marion Margaret Gibb; one *s* one *d*. *Educ*: RN Coll., Dartmouth. China Station, 1933–35; Pilot Training, 1937; served War of 1939–45, Russian Convoys, Fighter Sqdns; loaned RAN, 1949–50; Chief of Naval Aviation, Indian Navy, New Delhi, 1959–62; Rear-Adm. 1965; Flag Officer, Naval Flying Training, 1965–68; retired, 1968. MBIM 1967. *Recreation*: golf. *Address*: Lismore House, Pluckley, Kent. *T*: Pluckley 439. *Club*: Army and Navy.

KIRKHAM, Donald Herbert, FCSI, FCBSI; Chief Executive, Woolwich Equitable Building Society, since 1986; *b* 1 Jan. 1936; *s* of Herbert and Hettie Kirkham; *m* 1960, Kathleen Mary Lond; one *s* one *d*. *Educ*: Grimsby Technical College. Woolwich Equitable Building Society: Representative, 1959; Branch Manager, 1963; Gen. Manager's Asst, 1967; Business Planning Manager, 1970; Asst Gen. Manager, 1972; Gen. Manager, 1976; Mem. Local Board, 1979; Dep. Chief Gen. Manager, 1981; Mem. Board, 1982. Chartered Building Societies Institute: Mem. Council, 1976; Dep. Pres., 1980; Pres., 1981; Vice-Pres., 1986; Institute of Chartered Secretaries and Administrators: Mem. Council, 1979; Vice-Pres., 1984. FBIM. *Recreations*: boating, squash. *Address*: 2 Chaundrye Close, The Court Yard, Eltham, SE9 5QB. *T*: 01–850 6144. *Club*: City Livery.

KIRKHAM, Rt. Rev. John Dudley Galtrey; *see* Sherborne, Area Bishop of.

KIRKHILL, Baron *cr* 1975 (Life Peer), of Kirkhill, Aberdeen; **John Farquharson Smith;** *b* 7 May 1930; *s* of Alexander F. Smith and Ann T. Farquharson; *m* 1965, Frances Mary Walker Reid; one step-*d*. *Educ*: Robert Gordon's Colleges, Aberdeen. Lord Provost of the City and Royal Burgh of Aberdeen, 1971–75. Minister of State, Scottish Office, 1975–78. Chm., N of Scotland Hydro-Electric Bd, 1979–82. Hon. LLD Aberdeen, 1974. *Recreation*: golf. *Address*: 3 Rubislaw Den North, Aberdeen. *T*: Aberdeen 34167.

KIRKLAND, Joseph Lane; President, American Federation of Labor & Congress of Industrial Organizations, since 1979; *b* Camden, SC, 12 March 1922; *s* of Randolph Withers Kirkland and Louise Richardson; *m* Irena Neumann; five *d*. *Educ*: US Merchant Marine Academy, Kings Point, NY (grad. 1942); Georgetown Univ. Sch. of Foreign Service (BS 1948). Deck officer, various merchant ships, 1942–45; Staff Scientist, US Navy Hydrographic Office, 1945–48; Staff Representative, AFL-CIO, 1948–58; Research and Information Dir, Internat. Union of Operating Engrs, 1958–60; Exec. Asst to President, AFL-CIO, 1960–69; Sec.-Treasurer, AFL-CIO, 1969–79. Member: US Delegn, ILO Confs, Geneva, 1958, 1969, 1970, 1975, 1976, 1980, 1981; Blue Ribbon Defense Panel, 1969–70; Commn on CIA Activities Within the US, 1975; Commn on Foundns and Private Philanthropy, 1969–70; Gen. Adv. Cttee on Arms Control and Disarmament, 1974–78; Nat. Commn on Productivity, 1971–74; Presidential Commn on Financial Structure and Regulation, 1970–72; President's Maritime Adv. Cttee, 1964–66; President's Missile Sites Labor Commn (Alternate), 1961–67; Commn on Exec., Legislative and Judicial Salaries; Cttee on Selection of Fed. Judicial Officers; President's Commn on Social Security, 1982–83; Bipartisan Commn on Central America, 1983–84. Director: Amer. Council on Germany; Amer. Arbitration Assoc.; Afr.-Amer. Labor Center; Asian-Amer. Free Labor Inst.; Nat. Urban League; Rockefeller Foundn; Amer. Inst. for Free Labor Develt; Council on For. Relns, Inc.; Nat. Planning Assoc. Mem., Internat. Org. of Masters, Mates and Pilots; FAAAS. *Recreation*: archaeology. *Address*: (office) 815 16th Street NW, Washington, DC 20006, USA. *T*: (202) 637–5000.

KIRKLEY, Sir (Howard) Leslie, Kt 1977; CBE 1966; Chairman, Public Voice Communications Ltd, since 1979; Director: Andrews Group Holdings Ltd, since 1977; Charity Appointments, since 1984; *b* Manchester, 1911; *m* 1st, Elsie May (*née* Rothwell) (*d* 1956); 2nd, Constance Nina Mary (*née* Bannister-Jones); three *s* two *d*. *Educ*: Manchester Central High Sch. Associate of the Chartered Inst. of Secretaries (ACIS). Worked in local government in Manchester until War of 1939–45 (during which he was engaged in relief work in Europe). Founder and Hon. Sec. of the Leeds and District European Relief Cttee; Gen. Sec., Oxford Cttee for Famine Relief, 1951–61; Dir, Oxfam, 1961–74. Mem., Bd of Crown Agents, 1974–80. Chief Exec., Voluntary and Christian Service Trust, 1979–84; Exec. Chm., Action Aid Internat. 1983–84; Exec. Dir, Overseas Develt Action Aid, 1984–85. Pres., Gen. Conf., Internat. Council of Voluntary Agencies, 1968–71, Chm., Governing Board, 1972–76; Vice-Chm., 1974–77, Chm., 1977–81, Disasters Emergency Cttee. Chairman: Standing Conf. on Refugees, 1974–81 (Vice-Chm., 1969–74); UK Standing Conf. on 2nd UN Develt Decade, 1975–76; Chairperson, British Volunteer Programme, 1981–84; Vice-Chairman: Voluntary Cttee for Overseas Aid and Develt, 1973–76; British Refugee Council, 1981–. Chairman: Cala Sona Enterprise, 1972–; Voluntary and Christian Service Housing Assoc., 1981–84; Help the Aged Housing Trust, 1982–85. Hon. MA: Oxford, 1969; Leeds, 1970; Bradford, 1974. Fellow, Manchester Polytechnic, 1971. Knight Comdr of the Order of St Sylvester (conferred by HH the Pope), 1963; holds other foreign decorations. *Address*: 25 Capel Close, Oxford. *T*: Oxford 53167. *Club*: Royal Commonwealth Society.

KIRKMAN, William Patrick; Secretary, University of Cambridge Careers Service, since 1968; Fellow, Wolfson College, Cambridge (formerly University College); *b* 23 Oct. 1932; *s* of late Geoffrey Charles Aylward Kirkman and Bertha Winifred Kirkman; *m* 1959, Anne Teasdale Fawcett; two *s* one *d*. *Educ*: Churcher's Coll., Petersfield, Hants; Oriel Coll., Oxford. 2nd cl. hons, mod. langs, 1955; MA 1959; MA (Cantab) by incorporation, 1968. National Service, 1950–52, RASC (L/Cpl). Editorial staff: Express & Star, Wolverhampton, 1955–57; The Times, 1957–64 (Commonwealth staff, 1960–64, Africa Correspondent, 1962–64). Asst Sec., Oxford Univ. Appointments Cttee, 1964–68. Chm., Standing Conf. of University Appointments Services, 1971–73; Member: Management Cttee, Central Services Unit for Univ. Careers and Appointments Services, 1971–74, 1985–; British Cttee, Journalists in Europe, 1985–. Wolfson Coll: Vice-Pres., 1980–84; Mem. Council, 1969–73, 1976–80; Dir, Press Fellowship Programme, 1982–. Churchwarden, St Mary and All Saints Willingham, 1978–85. Trustee: Sir Halley Stewart Trust, 1970– (Hon. Sec., 1978–82); Willingham British Sch. Trust, 1974–; Homerton Coll., 1980–; Mem. Cttee, Cambridge Soc., 1979–83. *Publications*: Unscrambling an Empire, 1966; contrib.: Policing and Social Policy, 1984; Models of Police/Public Consultation in Europe, 1985; The Gower Recruitment Handbook, 4th edn, 1986; contributor to journals incl.: Commonwealth, International Affairs, Africa Contemporary Record, Financial Times, Cambridge, and to BBC. *Recreations*: broadcasting, gardening, church activities, writing. *Address*: 19 High Street, Willingham, Cambridge CB4 5ES. *T*: Willingham 60393. *Club*: Royal Commonwealth Society.

KIRKNESS, Donald James, CB 1980; Deputy Secretary, Overseas Development Administration, 1977–80; *b* 29 Sept 1919; *s* of Charles Stephen and Elsie Winifred Kirkness; *m* 1947, Monica Mary Douch; one *d*. *Educ*: Harvey Grammar Sch., Folkestone. Exchequer and Audit Dept, 1938. Served War: RA and Royal Berkshire Regt, 1939–46. Colonial Office, 1947 (Asst Principal); Financial and Economic Adviser, Windward I, 1955–57; Dept of Economic Affairs, 1966; Civil Service Dept, 1970–73; ODA/ODM, 1973. UK Governor, Internat. Fund for Agricultural Develt, 1977–81; Mem., Exec. Bd, UNESCO, 1978–83.

KIRKPATRICK, Sir Ivone Elliott, 11th Bt, *cr* 1685; *b* 1 Oct. 1942; *s* of Sir James Alexander Kirkpatrick, 10th Bt and Ellen Gertrude, *o d* of Captain R. P. Elliott, late RNR; *S* father 1954. *Educ*: Wellington Coll., Berks; St Mark's Coll., University of Adelaide. *Heir*: *b* Robin Alexander Kirkpatrick, *b* 19 March 1944. *Address*: c/o ANZ Bank, 81 King William Street, Adelaide, SA 5000, Australia.

KIRKPATRICK, John Lister, CBE 1981; Senior Partner, KMG Thomson McLintock (formerly Thomson McLintock & Co.), Chartered Accountants, Scotland, since 1980; UK Deputy Chairman, KMG Thomson McLintock, since 1983; Partner, Klynveld Main Goerdeler (KMG), since 1979; Chairman, International Accounting Standards Committee, since 1985 (Member, since 1978); *b* 27 June 1927; *s* of late Henry Joseph Rodway Kirkpatrick and Nora (*née* Lister); *m* 1977, Gay Elmslie (*née* Goudielock); one *s* one *d* of former marriage. *Educ*: Inverness Royal Acad. CA. Served RNVR, 1944–47. Thomson McLintock & Co.: apprentice, 1948; qual. CA 1952; Partner, 1958; Joint Senior Partner, Glasgow and Edinburgh, 1974–80; Co-Chm., UK Policy Council, 1974–83; Chm., KMG Region I, Europe, Africa, ME, Pakistan, India, 1979–85. Member: BoT Accountants' Adv. Cttee, 1967–72; Review Body on Doctors' and Dentists' Remuneration, 1983–; Lay Mem., Scottish Solicitors' Discipline Tribunal, 1981–. Vice-Pres., Inst. of Chartered Accountants of Scotland, 1975–77, Pres., 1977–78. *Publications*: various papers. *Recreations*: fishing, gardening. *Address*: 1 Letham Drive, Glasgow G43 2SL. *T*: 041–633 1407. *Clubs*: Caledonian; Western (Glasgow); New (Edinburgh).

KIRKPATRICK, William Brown, JP; investment banker; *b* 27 April 1934; *s* of late Joseph Kirkpatrick and Mary Laidlaw Kirkpatrick (*née* Brown), Thornhill, Dumfriesshire. *Educ*: Morton Acad., Thornhill; George Watson's Coll., Edinburgh; Univ. of Strathclyde (BScEcon); Columbia Business Sch., NY (MS and McKinsey Scholar); Stanford Business Sch. After two years in manufacturing industry in Glasgow, Dundee and London, joined ICFC (now Investors in Industry plc), 1960; retired 1985, having worked in London, Scotland and Australia in develt/venture capital, corporate finance, various fixed interest markets, in govt (on secondment to the Scottish Office) and as a company director. JP Inner London, 1985. *Recreations*: Scottish paintings, porcelain pigs, farming, current affairs. *Address:* 20 Abbotsbury House, Abbotsbury Road, W14 8EN. *T:* 01–603 3087; Kirkpatrick Hill, Closeburn, Dumfriesshire. *Club:* Caledonian.

KIRKUP, James; travel writer, poet, novelist, playwright, translator, broadcaster; *b* 23 April 1923; *o s* of James Harold Kirkup and Mary Johnston. *Educ:* South Shields High Sch.; Durham Univ. (BA). FRSL 1962. Atlantic Award in Literature (Rockefeller Foundation), 1950; Keats Prize for Poetry, 1974; Gregory Fellow in Poetry, University of Leeds, 1950–52. Visiting Poet and Head of English Dept, Bath Academy of Art, Corsham Court, Wilts, 1953–56; Lectr in English, Swedish Ministry of Education, Stockholm, 1956–57; Prof. of Eng. Lang. and Lit., University of Salamanca, 1957–58, of English, Tohoku Univ., Sendai, Japan, 1958–61; Lecturer in English Literature, University of Malaya in Kuala Lumpur, 1961–62; Literary Editor, Orient/West Magazine, Tokyo, 1963–64; Prof., Japan Women's Univ., 1964–; Poet in Residence and Visiting Prof., Amherst Coll., Mass, 1968–; Prof. of English Literature, Nagoya Univ., 1969–72. Arts Council Fellowship in Creative Writing, Univ. of Sheffield, 1974–75; Morton Vis. Prof. of Internat. Literature, Ohio Univ., 1975–76; Playwright in Residence, Sherman Theatre, University Coll., Cardiff, 1976–77; Prof. of English Lit., Kyoto Univ. of Foreign Studies, Kyoto, Japan, 1977–. President: Poets' Soc. of Japan, 1969; Blackmore Soc., 1970; Inst. of Pyschophysical Res., 1970. Mabel Batchelder Award, 1968. *Plays performed:* Upon this Rock (perf. Peterborough Cathedral), 1955; Masque, The Triumph of Harmony (perf. Albert Hall), 1955; The True Mistery of the Nativity, 1957; Dürrenmatt, The Physicists (Eng. trans.), 1963; Dürrenmatt, The Meteor (Eng. trans.); Dürrenmatt, Play Strindberg (Eng. trans.), 1972; The Magic Drum, children's play, 1972, children's musical, 1977; Dürrenmatt, Portrait of a Planet, 1972; Dürrenmatt, The Conformer, 1974; Schiller, Don Carlos, 1975; Cyrano de Bergerac, 1975; *operas:* An Actor's Revenge, 1979; Friends in Arms, 1980; The Damask Drum, 1982; *television plays performed:* The Peach Garden, Two Pigeons Flying High, etc. Contributor to BBC, The Listener, The Spectator, Times Literary Supplement, Time and Tide, New Yorker, Botteghe Oscure, London Magazine, Japan Qly, English Teachers' Magazine (Tokyo), etc. *Publications:* The Drowned Sailor, 1948; The Cosmic Shape, 1947; The Creation, 1950; The Submerged Village, 1951; A Correct Compassion, 1952; A Spring Journey, 1954; Upon This Rock, 1955; Camara Laye, The Dark Child (Eng. trans.), 1955; Ancestral Voices (Eng. trans.), 1956; Camara Laye, The Radiance of the King (Eng. trans.), 1956; The True Mistery of the Nativity, 1957; The Descent into the Cave, 1957; The Only Child (autobiog.), 1957; Simone de Beauvoir, Memoirs of a Dutiful Daughter (Eng. trans.), 1958; The Girl from Nowhere (Eng. trans.), 1958; Sorrows, Passions and Alarms, 1959; The Prodigal Son (poems), 1959; It Began in Babel (Eng. trans.), 1961; The Captive (Eng. trans.), 1962; Sins of the Fathers (Eng. trans.), 1962; The Gates of Paradise (Eng. trans.), 1962; These Horned Islands, A Journal of Japan, 1962; frères Gréban, The True Mistery of the Passion, 1962; The Love of Others (novel), 1962; Refusal to Conform, 1963; Tropic Temper: a Memoir of Malaya, 1963; The Heavenly Mandate (Eng. trans.), 1964; Daily Life of the Etruscans (Eng. trans.), 1964; Erich Kästner, The Little Man (Eng. trans.), 1966; Erich Kästner, The Little Man and The Little Miss (Eng. trans.), 1969; Heinrich von Kleist, The Tales of Hoffmann (Eng. trans.), 1966; Michael Kohlhaas (Eng. trans.), 1966; Japan Industrial, 1964–65 (2 vols); Daily Life in the French Revolution, 1964; Tokyo, 1965; England, Now, 1965; Japan, Now, 1966; Camara Laye, A Dream of Africa (Eng. trans.), 1967; Frankly Speaking, I-II, 1968; Paper Windows: Poems from Japan, 1968; Bangkok, 1968; One Man's Russia, 1968; Filipinescas, 1968; Streets of Asia, 1969; Japan Physical, 1969; Aspects of the Short Story, 1969; Shepherding Winds (anthol.), 1969; Songs and Dreams (anthol.), 1970; White Shadows, Black Shadows: Poems of Peace and War, 1970; Hong Kong, 1970; Japan Behind the Fan, 1970; The Eternal Virgin (Eng. trans of Valéry's La Jeune Parque), 1970; The Body Servant; poems of exile, 1971; Insect Summer (novel for children), 1971; A Bewick Bestiary (poems), 1971; (trans., with C. Fry) The Oxford Ibsen, vol III, Brand and Peer Gynt, 1972; (trans.) Selected Poems of Takagi Kyozo, 1973; The Magic Drum (children's novel), 1973; Heaven, Hell and Hara-Kiri, 1974; (with Birgit Skiöld) Zen Gardens, 1974; Scenes from Sesshu, 1977; Modern Japanese Poetry (anthol.), 1978; Zen Contemplations, 1979; (with Birgit Skiöld) The Tao of Water, 1980; Camara Laye, The Guardian of the Word (trans.), 1980; Eibungaku Saiken (essays), 1980; Dengonban Messages (one-line poems), 1980; Cold Mountain Poems (trans. Han Shan), 1980; To the Unknown God (trans.), 1982; Ecce Homo: My Pasolini (poems and trans.), 1982; No More Hiroshimas (poems and trans.), 1982; Folktales Japanesque, 1982; An African in Greenland (trans.), 1982; The Bush Toads (trans.), 1982; The Damask Drum (opera), 1982; I Am Count Dracula, 1982; I Am Frankenstein's Monster, 1983; Miniature Masterpieces of Kawabata Yasunari, 1983; To the Ancestral North: poems for an autobiography, 1983; When I was a Child: a study of nursery-rhymes, 1983; My Way—USA, 1984; The Glory that was Greece, 1984; The Sense of the Visit: new poems, 1984; The Guitar-Player of Zuiganji (poems), 1985; The Joys of Japan (essays), 1985; Lafcadio Hearn (biog. essays), 1985; James Kirkup's International Movie Theatre (essays), 1985; Fellow Feelings (poems), 1986; Hitorikko (autobiog.), 1986; Trends and Traditions (essays), 1986. *Recreation:* standing in shafts of moonlight. *Address:* BM-Box 2780, London WC1N 3XX.

KIRKWOOD, family name of **Baron Kirkwood.**

KIRKWOOD, 3rd Baron *cr* 1951, of Bearsden; **David Harvie Kirkwood;** Senior Lecturer in Metallurgy, Sheffield University, since 1976; *b* 24 Nov. 1931; *s* of 2nd Baron Kirkwood and of Eileen Grace, *d* of Thomas Henry Boalch; *S* father, 1970; *m* 1965, Judith Rosalie, *d* of late John Hunt; three *d. Educ:* Rugby; Trinity Hall, Cambridge (MA, PhD); CEng. Lectr in Metallurgy, Sheffield Univ., 1962; Warden of Stephenson Hall, Sheffield Univ., 1974–80. *Heir: b* Hon. James Stuart Kirkwood [*b* 19 June 1937; *m* 1965, Alexandra Mary, *d* of late Alec Dyson; two *d*]. *Address:* 56 Endcliffe Hall Avenue, Sheffield S10 3EL. *T:* Sheffield 663107.

KIRKWOOD, Archy, (Archibald Johnstone Kirkwood); MP (L/Alliance), Roxburgh and Berwickshire, since 1983; *b* 22 April 1946; *s* of David Kirkwood and Jessie Barclay Kirkwood; *m* 1972, Rosemary Chester; one *d* one *s. Educ:* Cranhill School; Heriot-Watt University. BSc Pharmacy. Notary Public; Solicitor; Partner, Andrew Haddon & Crowe, WS, Hawick, Roxburghshire. Trustee, Joseph Rowntree Social Service Trust, 1985–. *Address:* House of Commons, SW1A 0AA. *T:* 01–219 3000. *Club:* National Liberal.

KIRKWOOD, Ian Candlish, QC (Scot.) 1970; *b* 8 June 1932; *o s* of late John Brown Kirkwood, OBE, and of Mrs Constance Kirkwood, Edinburgh; *m* 1970, Jill Ingram Scott; two *s. Educ:* George Watson's Boys' Coll., Edinburgh; Edinburgh Univ.; Univ. of Michigan, USA. MA (Edin) 1952; LLB (Edin) 1954; LLM (Mich) 1956. Called to Scottish Bar, 1957; apptd Standing Junior Counsel to Scottish Home and Health Dept, 1963; Mem. Rules Council (Court of Session). Pres., Wireless Telegraphy Appeal Tribunal in Scotland. Chm., Med. Appeal Tribunal in Scotland. Contested (C) Dunfermline Burghs, 1964, 1966, 1970. *Recreations:* fishing, golf, chess. *Address:* 58 Murrayfield Avenue, Edinburgh EH12 6AY. *T:* 031–337 3468; Knockbrex House, near Borgue, Kirkcudbrightshire.

KIRKWOOD, Prof. Kenneth, MA; Rhodes Professor of Race Relations, University of Oxford, 1954–86; Fellow of St Antony's College, since 1954, and Sub-Warden, 1968–71; *b* Benoni, Transvaal, 1919; *s* of late Thomas Dorman Kirkwood and Lily Kirkwood (*née* Bewley); *m* 1942, Deborah Burton, *d* of late Burton Ireland Collings and Emily Frances Collings (*née* Loram); three *s* three *d.* BA; BSc Rand. Captain, South African Engineer Corps, War of 1939–45; served in East Africa, North Africa and Italy (despatches). Lecturer, University of the Witwatersrand, 1947; Lecturer, University of Natal, 1948–51; Fellowship, University of London (Inst. of Commonwealth Studies, 1952); Carnegie Travelling Fellowship, USA, 1953; Senior Research Officer, Inst. of Colonial Studies, Oxford Univ., 1953; Organiser of Institute for Social Research, University of Natal, 1954. Chm. Regional Cttee, S African Inst. of Race Relations in Natal, 1954; UK Rep. SA Inst. of Race Relations, 1955. Investigation on behalf UNESCO into trends in race relations in British Non-Self-Governing Territories of Africa, 1958; Visiting Prof. of Race Relations (UNESCO), University Coll. of Rhodesia and Nyasaland, 1964; composed memorandum on meaning, and procedure for further study of 'racial discrimination,' for UN Div. of Human Rights, 1966–67; Mem., Africa Educational Trust, Oxfam, etc, 1955–. Chm., UK Standing Cttee on University Studies of Africa, 1975–78. UK Official Observer, Rhodesian Elections, March 1980. *Publications:* The Proposed Federation of the Central African Territories, 1952; other booklets and articles on race relations and international affairs; contributions to revision of Lord Hailey's An African Survey, 1957, and 2nd edn, Vol. VIII, Cambridge History of the British Empire, 1963; Britain and Africa, 1965; Editor, St Antony's Papers: African Affairs, number 1, 1961; number 2, 1963; number 3, 1969; (ed, with E. E. Sabben-Clare and D. J. Bradley) Health in Tropical Africa during the Colonial Period, 1980; (ed and contrib.) Biosocial Aspects of Ethnic Minorities, 1983. *Address:* St Antony's College, Oxford. *T:* Oxford 515867.

KIRSOP, Arthur Michael Benjamin; Chairman, Forth Thyme Ltd, since 1976; *b* 28 Jan. 1931; *s* of Arthur Kirsop and Sarah (*née* Cauthery); *m* 1957, Patricia (*née* Cooper); two *s. Educ:* St Paul's Sch., Brazil; Glasgow Academy; Univ. of Oxford (BA). Joined English Sewing Cotton Co. Ltd, 1955; Area Sales Man., 1957; Export Sales Man., 1961; Man. Dir, Thread Div., 1964; Dir, English Sewing Cotton Co. Ltd, 1967 (later English Calico Ltd, then Tootal Ltd); Jt Man. Dir, 1973–76; Chief Exec., 1974–76; Chm., Tootal Ltd, 1975–76; Chm. and Man. Dir, Ollerenshaw Threads Ltd, 1981–86. Hon. Consul for the Netherlands, 1971–80. CBIM (FBIM 1973). *Recreations:* gardening, sport. *Address:* Peel House, 5 Planetree Road, Hale, Cheshire WA15 9JJ. *T:* 061–980 5173. *Clubs:* MCC; St James's (Manchester); Lancs CC.

KIRSTEIN, Lincoln Edward; Director: School of American Ballet; New York City Ballet Company; *b* Rochester, NY, 4 May 1907; *s* of Louis E. Kirstein and Rose Stein; *m* 1941, Fidelma Cadmus; no *c. Educ:* Harvard Coll.; BS 1930. Edited Hound & Horn, 1927–34; founded School of American Ballet, 1934; founded and directed American Ballet Caravan, 1936–41; Third US Army (Arts, Monuments and Archives Section), 1943–45. Editor, The Dance Index, 1941–47. Benjamin Franklin Medal, RSA, 1981; Governor's Arts Award, NY State, 1984; US Presidential Medal of Freedom, 1984; Nat. Medal of Arts, 1985; Municipal Art Soc. Award, 1985. *Publications:* Flesh is Heir, 1932, repr. 1975; Dance, A Short History of Theatrical Dancing, 1935; Blast at Ballet, 1938; Ballet Alphabet, 1940; Drawings of Pavel Tchelitchew, 1947; Elie Nadelman Drawings, 1949; The Dry Points of Elie Nadelman, 1952; What Ballet is About, 1959; Three Pamphlets Collected, 1967; The Hampton Institute Album, 1968; Movement and Metaphor: four centuries of ballet, 1970; Lay This Laurel, 1974; Nijinsky, Dancing, 1975; Ballet: bias and belief, 1983; *verse:* Rhymes of a PFC (Private First Class), 1964; *monographs:* Gaston Lachaise, 1935; Walker Evans, 1938; Latin American Art, 1942; American Battle Art, 1945; Henri Cartier-Bresson, 1946; Dr William Rimmer, 1946; Elie Nadelman, 1948; Pavel Tchelitchew, 1964; W. Eugene Smith, 1970; George Tooker, 1983; Paul Cadmus, 1983; *edited:* The Classic Dance, Technique and Terminology, 1951; William Shakespeare: A Catalogue of the Works of Art in the American Shakespeare Festival Theater, 1964; Elie Nadelman, 1973; New York City Ballet, 1973; Thirty Years: the New York City Ballet, 1978; A. Hyatt Mayor: collected writings, 1983. *Address:* School of American Ballet, 144 West 66th Street, New York, NY 10023, USA. *T:* 877–0600.

KIRTON, Col Hugh, TD 1952; Vice Lord-Lieutenant, County Durham, since 1978; *b* Plawsworth, Co. Durham, 7 Aug. 1910; 2nd *s* of late Hugh Kirton and Margaretta Kirton (*née* Darling). *Educ:* Durham Sch. Chartered Accountant, 1933. Army Service: commnd in Tyne Electrical Engrs (TA), 1937; RE(TA), 1937–40; RA(TA), 1940–45 and 1951–56, Lt Col 1945; Dep. Comdr, 31AA Bde(TA), 1959–61, Col 1959; Hon. Col 439 (Tyne) Lt AD Regt RA(TA), 1961–67. With Procter & Gamble Ltd, Newcastle upon Tyne, 1934–70, Dir, 1963–70; retired 1970. Mem., North Regional Health Authority, 1973–76; General Comr of Taxes (Newcastle upon Tyne), 1965–85. Mem. Council, Inst. of Chartered Accountants in England and Wales, 1966–70; Pres., Northern Soc. of Chartered Accountants, 1968–69. Mem., St John Council for Co. Durham, 1970–, Chm., 1974–86. DL: Northumberland 1961; Durham 1974; High Sheriff Co. Durham 1973–74. KStJ 1983. *Recreations:* golf, gardening. *Address:* Plawsworth House, Plawsworth, Chester-le-Street, Co. Durham DH2 3LD. *T:* Durham 710261. *Clubs:* Army and Navy; Northern Counties (Newcastle upon Tyne), County (Durham); Brancepeth Castle Golf (Captain 1969–71).

KIRTON, Robert James, CBE 1963; MA, FIA; Director, Equity and Law Life Assurance Society, Ltd, 1944–77 (General Manager, 1939–66; Actuary, 1947–66); Chairman, Equity and Law Unit Trust Managers Ltd, 1969–77; *b* 13 July 1901; *er s* of late Albert William Kirton, Ealing, Middlesex; *m* 1931, Isabel Susan, *y d* of late Henry Hosegood, JP, Bristol; two *s* two *d. Educ:* Merchant Taylors' Sch.; Peterhouse, Cambridge. Scottish Widows' Fund and Life Assurance Soc., 1923–32; Scottish Amicable Life Assce Soc., 1932–38; Equity and Law Life Assce Soc. Ltd, 1938–77. Chairman: Life Offices' Assoc., 1945–47; Royal UK Beneficent Assoc., 1958–74 (Vice-Pres., 1981–); Nat. Council of Social Service: Hon. Treas., 1962–72; Vice-Pres., 1972–80; Trustee, Charities Official Investment Fund, 1962–77; Governor, London Sch. of Economics, 1963–; Vice-Chm., St Peter's Hosp., 1967–75; Mem. Council, Bath Univ., 1967–75; Mem., Buitengewoon Lid, Actuarial Genootschap, Holland, 1949. Silver Medal, Institute of Actuaries, 1966. *Publications:* contrib. Jl Inst. Actuaries, Trans. Faculty of Actuaries (with A. T. Haynes). *Recreations:* walking, ski-ing and squash rackets. *Address:* Byron Cottage, North End Avenue, NW3 7HP. *T:* 01–455 0464. *Club:* Athenæum.

KIRWAN, Sir (Archibald) Laurence (Patrick), KCMG 1972 (CMG 1958); TD; MLitt Oxon; Hon. Vice-President, Royal Geographical Society, since 1981 (Director and Secretary, 1945–75); *b* 1907; 2nd *s* of Patrick Kirwan, Cregg, County Galway, Ireland, and Mabel Norton; *m* 1st, 1932, Joan Elizabeth Chetwynd; one *d*; 2nd, 1949, Stella Mary Monck. *Educ:* Wimbledon Sch.; Merton Coll., Oxford. Asst Dir of the Archaeological Survey of Nubia, Egyptian Dept of Antiquities, 1929–34; Field Dir, Oxford Univ. Expeditions to Sudan, 1934–37; Tweedie Fellowship in Archæology and Anthropology, Edinburgh Univ., 1937–39. Boston and Philadelphia Museums, 1937; Exploratory journeys, Eastern Sudan and Aden Protectorate, 1938–39. TARO Capt., General Staff, 1939; Major, 1941; Lieut-Col 1943; Joint Staffs, Offices of Cabinet and Ministry of Defence, 1942–45; Hon. Lt-Col, 1957. Editor, Geographical Journal, 1945–78; Pres., Brit.

Inst. in Eastern Africa, 1961–81, Hon. Life Pres. and Hon. Mem., 1981. Pres. (Section E), British Assoc. for the Advancement of Science, 1961–62; Member: Court of Arbitration, Argentine-Chile Frontier Case, 1965–68 (Leader, Field Mission, 1966); Sec. of State for Transport's Adv. Cttee on Landscape Treatment of Trunk Roads, 1968–81 (Dep. Chm., 1970–80); UN Register of fact-finding experts, 1968–; Court, Exeter Univ., 1969–80; a Governor, Imperial Coll. of Science and Technology, 1962–81; British Academy/Leverhulme Vis. Prof., Cairo, 1976; Mortimer Wheeler Lectr, Brit. Acad., 1977. Fellow: University Coll. London; Imperial College of Science and Technology; Hon. Fellow, SOAS. Hon. Member: Geographical Societies of Paris, Vienna, Washington; Royal Inst. of Navigation; Institut d'Egypte; Hon. Fellow, American Geographical Society. Founder's Medal, RGS, 1975. Knight Cross of the Order of St Olav, Norway; Jubilee Medal, 1977. *Publications:* Excavations and Survey between Wadi-es-Sebua and Adindan, 1935 (with W. B. Emery); Oxford University Excavations at Firka, 1938; The White Road (polar exploration), 1959; papers on archæology, historical and political geography, exploration, in scientific and other publications. *Recreation:* travel. *Address:* c/o Royal Geographical Society, SW7. *Club:* Geographical.

KIRWAN, Sir Laurence; *see* Kirwan, Sir A. L. P.

KISCH, (Alastair) Royalton; Conductor of Symphony Concerts; Artistic Director, Cork Street Art Gallery; *b* London, 20 Jan. 1919; *s* of late E. Royalton Kisch, MC and Pamela Kisch; *m* 1940, Aline, *d* of late Bruce Hylton Stewart and M. F. (Molly) Hylton Stewart; one *s* two *d*. *Educ:* Wellington Coll., Berks; Clare Coll., Cambridge. War service, Captain, KRRC (60th Rifles), 1940–46. Has conducted Royal Festival Hall concerts with London Philharmonic Orchestra, London Symphony Orchestra, Philharmonia Orchestra, Royal Philharmonic Orchestra, etc. Guest conductor to Hallé Orchestra, Birmingham Symphony Orchestra, etc. Has also conducted concerts in Europe with Paris Conservatoire Orchestra, Palestine Symphony Orchestra, Florence Philharmonic Orchestra, Athens State Symphony Orchestra, Pasdeloup Orchestra of Paris, Royal Opera House Orchestra of Rome, San Carlo Symphony Orchestra of Naples, Vienna Symphony Orchestra, etc. Has broadcast on BBC with London Symphony Orchestra, Royal Philharmonic Orchestra, and Philharmonia Orchestra. Gramophone recordings for Decca. Specialist in English and French paintings of 20th century. Mem., Friends of Tate Gallery. *Recreations:* good food and wine. *Address:* 2 Edwardes Square, Kensington, W8. *T:* 01–602 6655. *Clubs:* Athenæum, Hurlingham.

KISCH, John Marcus, CMG 1965; *b* 27 May 1916; *s* of late Sir Cecil Kisch, KCIE, CB, and late Myra Kisch; *m* 1951, Gillian Poyser; four *d*. *Educ:* Rugby Sch.; King's Coll., Cambridge. Asst Principal, Board of Inland Revenue, 1938; Asst Principal, Colonial Office, 1939. Served Royal Corps of Signals, 1939–45. Colonial Office, 1945; seconded E Africa High Commission, 1951; Kenya Govt 1952; Asst Sec., Colonial Office, 1956; seconded CRO, 1964; transferred Min. of Defence, 1965; Asst Sec., MoD (Navy Dept), 1965–68; Asst Sec., ODM, later ODA, 1968–72; Planning Inspector, DoE, 1972–79. *Address:* Westwood, Dunsfold, Surrey. *T:* Dunsfold 252; 21 Pembroke Square, W8. *T:* 01–937 8590.

KISCH, Royalton; *see* Kisch, A. R.

KISSIN, family name of **Baron Kissin.**

KISSIN, Baron *cr* 1974 (Life Peer), of Camden in Greater London; **Harry Kissin;** President, Guinness Peat Group, since 1979; Chairman, Lewis & Peat Holdings Ltd, since 1982 (Chairman, Lewis & Peat Ltd, 1961–72, Guinness Peat Group, 1973–79); Director: Tycon SPA Venice, since 1975, and of other public and private companies in the City of London, since 1934; *b* 23 Aug. 1912; *s* of Israel Kissin and Reusi Kissin (*née* Model), both of Russian nationality; *m* 1935, Ruth Deborah Samuel, London; one *s* one *d*. *Educ:* Danzig and Switzerland. Dr of Law, Basle, Swiss lawyer until 1933. Chairman: Linfood Holdings, 1974–81; Esperanza International Services plc, 1970–83; Dir, Transcontinental Services NV, 1982–86. Dir, Royal Opera Hse, Covent Gdn, 1973–84; Mem., Royal Opera House Trust, 1974– (Chm., 1974–80). Chm. Council, ICA, 1968–75. Governor: Bezalel Acad. of Arts and Design, 1975–; Hebrew Univ. of Jerusalem, 1980. Comdr, Ordem Nacional do Cruzeiro do Sul (Brazil), 1977; Chevalier, Légion d'honneur, 1981. *Address:* c/o House of Lords, SW1. *Clubs:* Reform, East India, Devonshire, Sports and Public Schools.

KISSINGER, Henry Alfred; Bronze Star (US); Chairman, Kissinger Associates Inc., since 1982; University Professor of Diplomacy, School of Foreign Service, Georgetown University, since 1977; Counselor to Center for Strategic and International Studies, Georgetown University, since 1977; Contributing Analyst for ABC News, since 1983; Chairman, National Bipartisan Commission on Central America, 1983; *b* 27 May 1923; *s* of late Louis Kissinger and of Paula (*née* Stern); *m* 1st, 1949, Anne Fleischer (marr. diss. 1964); one *s* one *d*; 2nd, 1974, Nancy Maginnes. *Educ:* George Washington High Sch., NYC; Harvard Univ., Cambridge, Mass (AB, MA, PhD). Teaching Fellow, Harvard Univ., 1950–54; Study Director: Council on Foreign Relations, 1955–56: Rockefeller Bros Fund, 1956–58; Associate Professor of Govt, Harvard Univ., 1958–62, Prof. of Govt, 1962–71, and Faculty Mem., Center for Internat. Affairs, Harvard; Director: Harvard Internat. Seminar, 1951–71; Harvard Defense Studies Program, 1958–71; Asst to US President for Nat. Security Affairs, 1969–75; Secretary of State, USA, 1973–77. Consultant to various government agencies. Mem., Internat. Adv. Cttee, Chase Manhattan Bank, 1977–. Mem., President's Foreign Intelligence Adv. Bd, 1984–; Hon. Gov., Foreign Policy Assoc., 1985–. Trustee: Rockefeller Brothers Fund, 1977–; Metropolitan Mus. of Art, 1977–. Syndicated writer, Los Angeles Times, 1984–. (Jtly) Nobel Peace Prize, 1973; Presidential Medal of Freedom, 1977; Medal of Liberty, 1986. *Publications:* A World Restored: Castlereagh, Metternich and the Restoration of Peace, 1957; Nuclear Weapons and Foreign Policy, 1957 (Woodrow Wilson Prize, 1958; citation, Overseas Press Club, 1958); The Necessity for Choice: Prospects of American Foreign Policy, 1961; The Troubled Partnership: a reappraisal of the Atlantic Alliance, 1965; Problems of National Strategy: A Book of Readings (ed), 1965; American Foreign Policy: three essays, 1969, 3rd edn 1977; White House Years (memoirs), 1979; For the Record, 1981; Years of Upheaval (memoirs), 1982; Observations, 1985; articles in Foreign Affairs, Harper's Magazine, The Reporter, New York Times Sunday Magazine, etc. *Address:* Suite 400, 1800 K Street, NW, Washington, DC 20006, USA; 350 Park Avenue, New York, NY 10022, USA. *Clubs:* Century, River (New York); Federal City, Metropolitan (Washington); Bohemian (San Francisco).

KITAJ, R. B., ARA 1984; artist; *b* Ohio, 29 Oct. 1932; *m* (wife decd); two *c*; *m* 1983, Sandra Fisher; one *s*. *Educ:* Cooper Union Inst., NY; Acad. of Fine Art, Vienna; Ruskin Sch. of Art, Oxford; RCA (ARCA). Part-time teacher: Camberwell Sch. of Art, 1961–63; Slade Sch., 1963–67; Visiting Professor: Univ. of Calif. at Berkeley, 1968; UCLA, 1970. Lives in London. One-man Exhibitions: Marlborough New London Gall., 1963, 1970; Marlborough Gall., NY, 1965, 1974; Los Angeles County Museum of Art, 1965; Stedelijk Mus., Amsterdam, 1967; Mus. of Art, Cleveland, 1967; Univ. of Calif, Berkeley, 1967; Galerie Mikro, Berlin, 1969; Kestner Gesellschaft, Hanover, 1970; Boymans-van-Beuningen Mus., Rotterdam, 1970; (with Jim Dine) Cincinnati Art Mus., Ohio, 1973; Marlborough Fine Art, 1977, 1980, 1985; Retrospective Exhibitions: Hirshhorn Museum, Washington, 1981; Cleveland Museum of Art, Ohio, 1981; Kunsthalle, Düsseldorf, 1982. Member: US Inst. of Arts and Letters, NY, 1982; Nat. Acad. of Design, NY, 1982. Hon. DLit London, 1982. *Relevant publication:* R. B. Kitaj by M. Livingstone, 1985. *Address:* c/o Marlborough Fine Art (London) Ltd, 6 Albemarle Street, W1.

KITCATT, Peter Julian, CB 1986; Under Secretary, HM Treasury, since 1973; *b* 5 Dec. 1927; *s* of late Horace Wilfred Kitcatt and of Ellen Louise Kitcatt (*née* Julian); *m* 1952, Audrey Marian Aylen; three *s* two *d*. *Educ:* Borden Grammar Sch., Sittingbourne; King's Coll., Cambridge. RASC (2nd Lt) 1948. Asst Principal, Colonial Office, 1950–53; Asst Private Sec. to Sec. of State for the Colonies, 1953–54; Principal, Colonial Office, 1954–64; Sec. to HRH The Princess Royal on Caribbean Tour, 1960; Sec., E African Econ. and Fiscal Commn, 1960; HM Treasury: Principal, 1964; Asst Sec., 1966; RCDS, 1972; Under Sec., 1973, seconded to DHSS, 1975–78. *Recreation:* golf. *Address:* 20 Winchelsey Rise, South Croydon, Surrey. *T:* 01–688 7990. *Club:* Croham Hurst Golf (Croydon).

KITCHEN, Frederick Bruford, CBE 1975; *b* Melbourne, 15 July 1912; *o s* of F. W. Kitchen, Malvern, Vic, Australia; *m* 1936, Una Bernice Sloss; two *s* one *d*. *Educ:* Melbourne Grammar Sch.; Melbourne Univ. (BSc). Joined family firm (in Melb.), J. Kitchen and Sons Pty Ltd, which had become a Unilever soap co., 1934. Sales Dir, Lever Bros Ltd, Canada, 1946. Came to England, 1949, as Chm., Crosfields (CWG) Ltd; Chm., Lever Bros Ltd, 1957; Marketing Dir, Lever Bros & Associates Ltd, 1960; Chm., Van den Berghs & Jurgens Ltd, 1962–74; Mem., Price Commn, 1973–75. Past Pres.: Incorp. Soc. of British Advertisers; Internat. Fedn of Margarine Assocs; Margarine and Shortening Manufacturers' Assoc. Associate, Royal Australian Chemical Inst. *Recreation:* gardening. *Address:* Southdown, Yal Yal Road, Merricks, Victoria 3916, Australia. *T:* 059–898411. *Club:* Australian (Melbourne).

KITCHEN, Michael; actor; with Royal Shakespeare Co., since 1986; *b* 31 Oct. 1948; *s* of Arthur and Betty Kitchen. *Educ:* City of Leicester Boys' Grammar School. Entered acting profession, 1970; *stage includes:* seasons at Belgrade Theatre, Coventry, National Youth Theatre; Royal Court, 1971–73; Big Wolf, Magnificence, Skyvers; Young Vic, 1975: Othello, Macbeth, As You Like It, Charley's Aunt; National Theatre: Spring Awakening, 1974; Romeo and Juliet, 1974; State of Revolution, 1977; Bedroom Farce, 1977; No Man's Land, 1977; The Homecoming, 1978; Family Voices, 1981; On the Razzle, 1981; The Provok'd Wife, 1981; Rough Crossing, 1984; *films include:* The Bunker; Breaking Glass; Towards the Morning; Out of Africa; *television series:* Freud, 1983; numerous TV and radio performances. *Recreations:* piano, guitar, flying, writing, tennis. *Address:* 94A Cecile Park, N8. *T:* 01–341 2169.

KITCHEN, Stanley, FCA; Chairman, STEP Management Services Ltd, 1978–85; *b* 23 Aug. 1913; *s* of late Percy Inman Kitchen and Elizabeth Kitchen; *m* 1941, Jean Craig; two *d*. *Educ:* Rugby Sch. ACA 1937, FCA 1953. Army, 1939–46: Major, RASC. Sec., British Rollmakers Corp. Ltd, Wolverhampton, 1946–48; Partner, Foster & Stephens, later Touche Ross & Co., chartered accountants, Birmingham, 1948–81. Birmingham and West Midlands Soc. of Chartered Accountants: Mem. Cttee, 1951–81; Sec., 1953–55; Pres., 1957–58; Inst. of Chartered Accountants in England and Wales: Mem. Council, 1966–81; Vice-Pres., 1974–75; Dep. Pres., 1975–76; Pres., 1976–77. *Publications:* Learning to Live with Taxes on Capital Gains, 1967; Important Aspects of Professional Partnerships, 1974. *Recreations:* gardening, golf. *Address:* 1194 Warwick Road, Knowle, Solihull, West Midlands B93 9LL. *T:* Knowle 2360. *Clubs:* Lansdowne; Birmingham, Chamber of Commerce (Birmingham).

KITCHENER OF KHARTOUM, and of Broome; 3rd Earl, *cr* 1914; **Henry Herbert Kitchener,** TD; DL; Viscount, *cr* 1902, of Khartoum; of the Vaal, Transvaal, and Aspall, Suffolk; Viscount Broome, *cr* 1914, of Broome, Kent; Baron Denton, *cr* 1914, of Denton, Kent; late Major, Royal Corps of Signals; *b* 24 Feb. 1919; *er s* of Viscount Broome (*d* 1928) and Adela Mary Evelyn (*d* 1986), *e d* of late J. H. Monins, Ringwould House, near Dover; *S* grandfather, 1937. *Educ:* Sandroyd Sch.; Winchester Coll.; Trinity Coll., Cambridge. DL Cheshire 1972. *Heir:* none. *Address:* Westergate Wood, Chichester, W Sussex PO20 6SB. *T:* Eastergate 3061. *Club:* Brooks's.

KITCHIN, Prof. Laurence Tyson; university teacher, translator and critic; *b* 21 July 1913; *s* of James Tyson Kitchin, MD Edin, and Eliza Amelia Kitchin (*née* Hopps); *m* 1955, Hilary Owen, artist; one step *s*. *Educ:* Bootham Sch.; King's Coll., London Univ. (BA 1934); Central Sch. of Drama. Served War, RAMC and briefly, RAEC, 1941–46. Mem., univ. debates team, USA, 1933; acted in Housemaster on stage and screen, 1936, and in films, incl. Pimpernel Smith; wrote extensively for BBC Third Prog., 1948–55; The Times corresp. and drama critic, 1956–62; numerous BBC talks on literature and drama, 1962–66; UK rep., Théâtre dans le Monde, UNESCO, 1961–66; Lectr, Bristol Univ. and Tufts, London, 1966–70; Vis. Prof. of Drama, Stanford Univ., Calif, 1970–72; Vis. Prof. of Liberal Arts, City Univ. of NY, 1972–73, Prof., 1973–76; Vis. Prof. of Shakespeare Studies, Simon Fraser Univ., Canada, 1976–77. Renaissance verse translations from Italian, French and Spanish, BBC, 1978–79. Selected as one of Outstanding Educators of America, 1973. *Publications:* Len Hutton, 1953; Three on Trial, 1959; Mid-Century Drama, 1960, 2nd edn 1962; Drama in the Sixties, 1966; radio scripts, incl.: The Trial of Lord Byron, 1948, Canada 1978; The Trial of Machiavelli, 1957; The Court Lady (trans. from Castiglione), 1954; The Elizabethan, Canada 1978; The Flaming Heart (Crashaw), 1981; translations in Confronto Letterario no. 4, 1985; contrib. Shakespeare Survey, Mod. Lang. Rev., TLS, Encounter, Observer, Listener and THES. *Recreations:* tennis, televised soccer. *Address:* c/o National Westminster Bank, 1 St James's Square, SW1Y 4JT. *Club:* Athenæum.

KITCHING, Maj.-Gen. George, CBE 1945; DSO 1943; Canadian Military Forces, retired; President, Duke of Edinburgh's Award in Canada, 1967–70, President, British Columbia and Yukon Division, 1979–82; *b* 1910; *m* 1946, Audrey Calhoun; one *s* one *d*. *Educ:* Cranleigh; Royal Military College. 2nd Lieut Glos Regt, 1930. Served War of 1939–45 with Royal Canadian Regt and Loyal Edmonton Regt, in Sicily, Italy and North-West Europe; commanding Canadian Infantry Brigade, 1943; actg Maj.-Gen. comdg an armoured div., 1944 (despatches, DSO, CBE). Subseq. Vice-Chief of General Staff at Army Headquarters, Ottawa; Chairman of the Canadian Joint Staff in London, 1958–62; GOC Central Command, Canada, 1962–65, retd. Col Comdt of Infantry, 1974–78. Comr, Ont Pavilion, Osaka, Japan, for Expo 1970; Chief Comr, Liquor Control Bd of Ont, 1970–76. Chm. and Patron, Gurkha Welfare Appeal (Canada), 1974–; Patron: United World Colls, 1970 (Exec. Dir, Canadian Nat. Cttee, 1968–70); Sir Edmund Hillary Foundn (Canada), 1976–; Old Fort York, Toronto, 1975–. Commander: Order of Orange Nassau (Netherlands); Military Order of Italy; Order of Merit (US). *Publication:* Mud and Green Fields (autobiog.), 1986. *Address:* 3434 Bonair Place, Victoria, BC V8P 4V4, Canada.

KITCHING, John Alwyne, OBE 1947; FRS 1960; ScD (Cambridge); PhD (London); Professor of Biology, University of East Anglia, 1963–74, now Emeritus Professor; Dean of School of Biological Sciences, 1967–70; Leverhulme Fellowship, 1974; *b* 24 Oct. 1908; *s* of John Nainby Kitching; *m* 1933, Evelyn Mary Oliver; one *s* three *d*. *Educ:* Cheltenham Coll.; Trinity Coll., Cambridge. BA 1930, MA 1934, ScD 1956; PhD London. Lecturer:

Birkbeck Coll., London, 1931; Edinburgh Univ., 1936; Bristol Univ., 1937; Rockefeller Fellow, Princeton Univ., 1938; Research in aviation-medical problems under Canadian Nat. Research Council, 1939–45; Reader in Zoology, University of Bristol, 1948–63. Hon. DSc NUI, 1983. *Publications*: contrib. Jl of Experimental Biol., Jl of Ecology, Jl of Animal Ecology, etc. *Recreations*: travel, gardening. *Address*: University of East Anglia, University Plain, Norwich NR4 7TJ; 29 Newfound Drive, Cringleford, Norwich NR4 7RY.

KITSON, family name of **Baron Airedale.**

KITSON, Alexander Harper, JP; Deputy General Secretary, Transport and General Workers Union, 1980–86; *b* 21 Oct. 1921; *m* 1942, Ann Brown McLeod; two *d. Educ:* Kirknewton Sch., Midlothian, Scotland. Lorry Driver, 1935–45; Trade Union official, 1945–86. Mem., Freight Integration Council, 1969–78. Mem. Nat. Exec. Cttee of Labour Party, 1968–86; Chm., Labour Party, 1980–81. *Address:* c/o Transport and General Workers Union, Transport House, Smith Square, SW1P 3JB.

KITSON, Gen. Sir Frank (Edward), GBE 1985; CBE (mil.) 1972; OBE 1968; MBE 1959; KCB 1980; MC 1955 and Bar 1958; *b* 15 Dec. 1926; *s* of late Vice-Adm. Sir Henry Kitson, KBE, CB and Lady (Marjorie) Kitson (*née* de Pass); *m* 1962, Elizabeth Janet, *d* of Col C. R. Spencer, OBE; three *d. Educ:* Stowe. 2nd Lt Rifle Bde, 1946; served BAOR, 1946–53; Kenya, 1953–55; Malaya, 1957; Cyprus, 1962–64; CO 1st Bn, Royal Green Jackets, 1967–69; Defence Fellow, University Coll., Oxford, 1969–70; Comdr, 39 Inf. Bde, NI, 1970–72 (CBE for gallantry); Comdt, Sch. of Infantry, 1972–74; RCDS, 1975; GOC 2nd Division, later 2nd Armoured Division, 1976–78; Comdt, Staff College, 1978–80; Dep. C-in-C, UKLF, and Inspector-Gen., TA, 1980–82; C-in-C, UKLF, 1982–85. ADC Gen. to the Queen, 1983–85. Col Comdt, 1979–87, Rep. Col Comdt, 1982–85, 2nd Bn, The Royal Green Jackets; Hon. Col, Oxford Univ. OTC, 1982–. *Publications:* Gangs and Counter Gangs, 1960; Low Intensity Operations, 1971; Bunch of Five, 1977. *Recreations:* horses, wildlife, books. *Address:* c/o Lloyds Bank, Farnham, Surrey. *Club:* Boodle's.

KITSON, George McCullough; Principal, Central School of Speech and Drama, London, 1978–May 1987; *b* Castlegore, Ireland, 18 May 1922; *s* of George Kitson and Anna May McCullough-Kitson; *m* 1951, Jean Evelyn Tyte; four *s. Educ:* early educn in Ireland; London Univ. (Dip. in Child Develt, 1947); Trent Park Coll. (Teachers' Cert., 1949). Associate, Cambridge Inst. of Educn, 1956; MEd Leicester, 1960. Served War, RAF, 1940–45; Navigator, Coastal Comd. Asst Master, schs in Herts, 1949–54; Dep. Headmaster, Broadfield Sch., Hemel Hempstead, Herts, 1954–56; Lectr in Educn, Leicester Coll. of Educn, 1956–66; Tutor i/c Annexe for Mature Teachers, Northampton, 1966–71; Dep. Principal, Furzedown Coll., London, 1971–76; Vice-Principal, Philippa Fawcett and Furzedown Coll., 1976–78. Mem., Nat. Council of Drama Trng, 1978–; Chm., Conference of Drama Schs, 1980–. *Publications:* (contrib.) Map of Educational Research, 1969; articles on educn, social psychol., and interprofessionalism in Forum, New Era, Educn for Teaching, and Brit. Jl of Educnl Psychol. *Recreations:* book collecting (first editions), sailing, walking, music, theatre. *Address:* 56 Woodbourne Avenue, SW16 1BU. *T:* 01–769 7621. *Club:* Arts.

KITSON, Sir Timothy (Peter Geoffrey), Kt 1974; Chairman, Provident Financial Group, since 1983; *b* 28 Jan. 1931; *s* of late Geoffrey H. and of Kathleen Kitson; *m* 1959, Diana Mary Fattorini; one *s* two *d. Educ:* Charterhouse; Royal Agricultural College, Cirencester. Farmed in Australia, 1949–51. Member: Thirsk RDC, 1954–57; N Riding CC, 1957–61. MP (C) Richmond, Yorks, 1959–83; PPS to Parly Sec. to Minister of Agriculture, 1960–64; an Opposition Whip, 1967–70; PPS to the Prime Minister, 1970–74, to Leader of the Opposition, 1974–75. Chm., Defence Select Cttee, 1982–83. *Recreations:* shooting, hunting, racing. *Address:* Leases Hall, Leeming Bar, Northallerton, North Yorks. *T:* Bedale 2180.

KITTO, Rt. Hon. Sir Frank (Walters), AC 1983; KBE 1955; PC 1963; Chancellor, University of New England, 1970–81; Chairman, Australian Press Council, 1976–82; *b* 30 July 1903; *s* of late James W. Kitto, OBE, Austinmer, New South Wales; *m* 1928, Eleanor (*d* 1982), *d* of late Rev. W. H. Howard; four *d. Educ:* North Sydney High Sch.; Sydney Univ. BA 1924; Wigram Allen Scholar, G. and M. Harris Scholar and Pitt Cobbett Prizes in Faculty of Law, and LLB first class hons, 1927; called to Bar of NSW, 1927. KC (NSW), 1942. Challis Lecturer in Bankruptcy and Probate, Sydney Univ., 1930–33; Justice of the High Court of Australia, 1950–70. Mem. Council, University of New England, 1967–81, Deputy Chancellor, 1968–70. Hon. DLitt New England, 1982; Hon. LLD Sydney, 1983. *Address:* Unit 18, Autumn Lodge, Armidale, NSW 2350, Australia. *T:* Armidale (067) 72–1189.

KITZINGER, Sheila Helena Elizabeth, MBE 1982; author, social anthropologist and birth educator; *b* 29 March 1929; *d* of Alec and Clare Webster; *m* 1952, Uwe Kitzinger, *qv*; five *d. Educ:* Bishop Fox's Girls' Sch., Taunton; Ruskin Coll., Oxford; St Hugh's Coll., Oxford; motherhood; educn continuing. Res. Asst, Dept of Anthropology, Univ. of Edinburgh, 1952–53 (MLitt 1954; thesis on race relations in Britain). Course Team Chm., Open Univ., 1981–83. Member: Panel of Advisers, National Childbirth Trust of GB; Managing Bd, Midwives Information and Resource Service, 1985–; Chairperson, Foundation for Women's Health Res. and Develt, 1985–; Consultant, Internat. Childbirth Educn Assoc. MRSocMed. Joost de Blank Award, to do research on problems facing West Indian mothers in Britain, 1971–73. *Publications:* The Experience of Childbirth, 1962, 5th edn 1984; Giving Birth, 1971, rev. and expanded edn 1979; Education and Counselling for Childbirth, 1977; Women as Mothers, 1978; (ed with John Davis) The Place of Birth, 1978; The Good Birth Guide, 1979; The Experience of Breastfeeding, 1979; Pregnancy and Childbirth, 1980; Sheila Kitzinger's Birth Book, 1981; (with Rhiannon Walters) Some Women's Experiences of Episiotomy, 1981; Episiotomy: physical and emotional aspects, 1981; Birth over Thirty, 1982; The New Good Birth Guide, 1983; Woman's Experience of Sex, 1983; (ed with Penny Simkin) Episiotomy and the Second Stage of Labor, 1984; Being Born, 1986; (contrib.) Ethnography of Fertility and Birth, 1982; (contrib.) The Management of Labour, 1985. *Recreations:* painting, talking. *Address:* The Manor, Standlake, Oxfordshire OX8 7RH. *T:* Standlake 266.

See also David Webster.

KITZINGER, Uwe, CBE 1980; President, Templeton College, Oxford (formerly Oxford Centre for Management Studies), since 1984 (Director, 1980–84); *b* 12 April 1928; *o s* of late Dr G. Kitzinger and Mrs L. Kitzinger, Abbots Langley, Herts; *m* 1952, Sheila Helena Elizabeth Webster (*see* S. H. E. Kitzinger); five *d. Educ:* Watford Grammar Sch.; Balliol Coll. and New Coll. (Foundn Schol.), Oxford. 1st in Philosophy, Politics and Economics, MA, MLitt; Pres., Oxford Union, 1950. Economic Section, Council of Europe, Strasbourg, 1951–58; Nuffield College, Oxford: Research Fellow, 1956–62, Official Fellow, 1962–76; Emeritus Fellow, 1976; Acting Investment Bursar, 1962–64; Investment Bursar, 1964–76; Mem., Investment Cttee, 1962–. Assessor of Oxford University, 1967–68. Visiting Prof.: of Internat. Relations, Univ. of the West Indies, 1964–65; of Government, at Harvard, 1969–70; at Univ. of Paris (VIII), 1970–73. Leave of absence as Adviser to Sir Christopher (now Lord) Soames, Vice-Pres. of the Commn of the European Communities, Brussels, 1973–75; Dean, INSEAD (European Inst. of Business Admin), Fontainebleau, 1976–80 (Mem. Board, 1976–83). Member: ODM Cttee for University Secondment, 1966–68; British Universities Cttee of Encyclopædia Britannica, 1967–73; Nat. Council of European Movement, 1974–76; RIIA, 1973–85; Court, Cranfield Inst. of Technology, 1984–85. Consultant to various nat. and internat. orgns. Member: Oxfam Council, 1981–84 (Mem., Finance Cttee, 1984–); Major Projects Assoc., 1981– (Chm., 1981–86); Adv. Bd, Pace Univ., NY, 1982–; Berlin Science Centre, 1983. Trustee: European Foundn for Management Educn, Brussels, 1978–80; Oxford Trust for Music and the Arts, 1986–. Hon. LLD, Buena Vista, 1986. *Publications:* German Electoral Politics, 1960, German edn, 1960; The Challenge of the Common Market, 1961 (Amer. edn, The Politics and Economics of European Integration, 1963, et al); Britain, Europe and Beyond, 1964; The Background to Jamaica's Foreign Policy, 1965; The European Common Market and Community, 1967; Commitment and Identity, 1968; The Second Try, 1968; Diplomacy and Persuasion, 1973, French edn, 1974; Europe's Wider Horizons, 1975; (with D. E. Butler) The 1975 Referendum, 1976. Founding Editor, Jl of Common Market Studies, 1962–. *Recreations:* sailing, travel, old buildings. *Address:* Templeton College, Oxford. *T:* Oxford 735422; Standlake Manor, near Witney, Oxon. *T:* Standlake 266; La Rivière, 11100 Bages, France. *T:* (68) 412960. *Clubs:* Reform; Royal Thames Yacht.

KLARE, Hugh John, CBE 1967; *b* Berndorf, Austria, 22 June 1916; *yr s* of F. A. Klare; *m* 1946, Eveline Alice Maria, *d* of Lieut-Col J. D. Rankin, MBE. *Educ:* privately. Came to England, 1932. Served war in Middle East and Europe; Major. Dep. Dir, Economic Organisation Br., Brit. Control Commn for Germany, 1946–48; Sec., Howard League for Penal Reform, 1950–71; seconded to Coun. of Europe as Dep. Head, Div. of Crime Problems, 1959–61; Head of Div., 1971–72; Member of Council: Internat. Soc. of Criminology, 1960–66; Inst. for Study and Treatment of Delinquency, 1964–66; Nat. Assoc. for Care and Resettlement of Offenders, 1966–71. Chm. Planning Cttee, Brit. Congress on Crime, 1966. Member: Bd of Visitors, Long Lartin Prison, 1972–76; Gloucestershire Probation and Aftercare Cttee, 1972–85; Parole Board, 1972–74. A Governor, British Inst. of Human Rights, 1974–80. *Publications:* Anatomy of Prison, 1960; (ed and introd) Changing Concepts of Crime and its Treatment, 1966; (ed jtly) Frontiers of Criminology, 1967; People in Prison, 1972; contribs on crime and penology to Justice of the Peace. *Address:* 28 Pittville Court, Albert Road, Cheltenham GL52 3JA. *T:* Cheltenham 34224.

KLEEMAN, Harry, CBE 1984; Chairman, Kleeman Plastics group of companies, since 1968; *b* 2 Mar. 1928; *s* of Max Kleeman and Lottie Bernstein; *m* 1955, Avril Lees; two *s* two *d. Educ:* Westminster Sch.; Trinity Coll., Cambridge. Director, O. & M. Kleemann Ltd, 1951–65. President, British Plastics Fedn, 1979–80; Chairman: Polymer Engineering Directorate, SERC, 1980–84; Plastics Processing EDC, NEDO, 1980–85; Small Firms Cttee, OFTEL, 1985–; Council, Plastics & Rubber Inst., 1985–; Member: CBI Smaller Firms Council, 1982–; CBI Council, 1984–. FPRI 1980. Member: Zoological Soc., 1950–; Royal Society of Arts, 1978–; Worshipful Co. of Horners, 1954–. *Recreations:* horse riding, amateur radio. *Address:* 41 Frognal, NW3 6YD. *T:* 01–794 3366. *Club:* City Livery.

KLEIN, Bernat, CBE 1973; FSIAD 1974; Chairman and Managing Director, Bernat Klein Ltd, since 1973; *b* 6 Nov. 1922; *s* of Lipot Klein and Serena Weiner; *m* 1951, Margaret Soper; one *s* two *d. Educ:* Senta, Yugoslavia; Bezalel Sch. of Arts and Crafts, Jerusalem; Leeds Univ. Designer to: Tootal, Broadhurst, Lee, 1948–49; Munrospun, Edinburgh, 1949–51; Chm. and Man. Dir, Colourcraft, 1952–62; Man. Dir of Bernat Klein Ltd, 1962–66; Chm. and Man. Dir, Bernat Klein Design Ltd, 1966–81. Member: Council of Industrial Design, Scottish Cttee, 1965–71; Royal Fine Art Commn for Scotland, 1980–. Exhibitions of paintings: E-SU, 1965; Alwyn Gall., 1967; O'Hana Gall., 1969; Assoc. of Arts Gall., Capetown, Goodman Gall., Johannesburg, and O'Hana Gall., 1972; Laing Art Gall., Newcastle upon Tyne, 1977; Manchester Polytechnic, 1977. *Publications:* Eye for Colour, 1965; Design Matters, 1976. *Recreations:* reading, tennis, walking. *Address:* High Sunderland, Galashiels, Selkirkshire. *T:* Selkirk 20730.

KLEIN, Prof. Lawrence Robert; economist; Benjamin Franklin Professor, University of Pennsylvania, since 1968; *b* Omaha, 14 Sept. 1920; *s* of Leo Byron Klein and Blanche Monheit; *m* 1947, Sonia Adelson; one *s* three *d. Educ:* Univ. of Calif at Berkeley (BA); MIT (PhD 1944); Lincoln Coll., Oxford (MA 1957). Chicago Univ., 1944–47; Nat. Bureau of Econ. Res., NY, 1948–50; Michigan Univ., 1949–54; Oxford Inst. of Stats, 1954–58; Prof., 1958, University Prof., 1964, Univ. of Pennsylvania. Consultant: UNCTAD, 1966, 1967, 1975; UNIDO, 1973–75; Congressional Budget Office, 1977–; Council of Econ. Advisers, 1977–80. Mem., Commn on Prices, Fed. Res. Bd, 1968–70. Member: Adv. Bd, Strategic Studies Center, Stanford Res. Inst., 1974–76; Adv. Council, Inst. for Advanced Studies, Vienna, 1977–. Fellow: Econometric Soc. (past Pres.); Amer. Acad. of Arts and Scis; Member: Nat. Acad. of Scis; Amer. Philosophical Soc.; Amer. Economic Assoc. (Past Pres.; J. B. Clark Medal, 1959). William F. Butler Award, NY Assoc. of Business Economists, 1975; Nobel Prize for Economics, 1980. *Publications:* The Keynesian Revolution, 1947; Textbook of Econometrics, 1953; An Econometric Model of the United States 1929–52, 1955; Wharton Econometric Forecasting Model, 1967; Essay on the Theory of Economic Prediction, 1968; (ed) Econometric Model Performance, 1976. *Address:* 1317 Medford Road, Wynnewood, Pa 19096, USA; University of Pennsylvania, Philadelphia, Pa 19104, USA.

KLEIN, Prof. Rudolf Ewald; Professor of Social Policy, University of Bath, since 1978; *b* 26 Aug. 1930; *o s* of Robert and Martha Klein; *m* 1957, Josephine Parfitt; one *d. Educ:* Bristol Grammar Sch.; Merton Coll., Oxford (Postmaster) (Gibbs Schol. 1950; MA). Leader Writer, London Evening Standard, 1952–62; Editor, 'The Week', Leader Writer, Home Affairs Editor, The Observer, 1962–72; Research Associate, Organisation of Medical Care Unit, London Sch. of Hygiene and Tropical Medicine, 1972–73; Sen. Fellow, Centre for Studies in Social Policy, 1973–78. Member: Wiltshire AHA, 1980–82; Bath DHA, 1982–84. Jt Editor, Political Quarterly, 1981–. *Publications:* Complaints Against Doctors, 1973; (ed) Social Policy and Public Expenditure, 1974; (ed) Inflation and Priorities, 1975; (with Janet Lewis) The Politics of Consumer Representation, 1976; The Politics of the NHS, 1983; (ed with Michael O'Higgins) The Future of Welfare, 1985; (with P. Day) Accountabilities, 1987; papers on public policy, health policy and public expenditure in various jls. *Recreations:* opera, cooking, football. *Address:* 3 Macaulay Buildings, Widcombe Hill, Bath BA2 6AS. *T:* Bath 310774.

KLEINDIENST, Richard Gordon; attorney; *b* 5 Aug. 1923; *s* of Alfred R. Kleindienst and late Gladys Love, Massachusetts; *m* 1948, Margaret Dunbar; two *s* two *d. Educ:* Harvard Coll. (*Phi Beta Kappa, magna cum laude*); Harvard Law Sch. Associate and Partner of Jennings, Strouss, Salmon & Trask, Phoenix, Arizona, 1950–57; Sen. Partner of Shimmel, Hill, Kleindienst & Bishop, 1958–Jan. 1969. Dep. Attorney-Gen. of the US, Jan. 1969–Feb. 1972; Actg Attorney-Gen. of the US, Feb. 1972–June 1972; Attorney-Gen. of the US, 1972–73, resigned 1973; private practice of law, Washington DC, 1973–75. Pres., Federal Bar Assoc., US, 1972– (was Pres. elect, Oct. 1971–72). Hon. Dr of Laws, Susquehanna Univ., 1973. *Recreations:* golf, chess, classical music, art. *Address:* (home) 6138 W Miramar, Tucson, Arizona 85715, USA. *T:* 602–885–3150.

KLEINPOPPEN, Prof. Hans Johann Willi; Professor of Experimental Physics, University of Stirling, since 1968 (Head of Physics Department, 1970–73; Director of Institute of Atomic Physics, 1975–81); *b* Duisburg, Germany, 30 Sept. 1928; *m* 1958, Renate Schröder. *Educ:* Univ. of Giessen (Dipl. Physics); Univ. of Tübingen. Dr re.nat. 1961. Habilitation, Tübingen, 1967; Vis. Fellow, Univ. Colorado, 1967–68; Vis. Associate Prof., Columbia Univ., 1968; Fellow, Center for Theoretical Studies, Univ. of Miami, 1972–73; Guest Prof., Bielefeld Univ.; Vis. Fellow, Zentrum für interdisziplinäre Forschung, Bielefeld Univ., 1979–80. Chairman: Internat. Symposium on Physics of One- and Two-Electron Atoms (Arnold Sommerfeld Centennial Meml Meeting, Munich 1968); Internat. Symposium on Electron and Photon Interactions with Atoms, in honour of Ugo Fano, Stirling, 1974; Internat. Workshop on Coherence and Correlation in Atomic Collisions, University Coll., London, 1978; Internat. Symp. on Amplitudes and State Parameters in Atomic Collisions, Kyoto, 1979; Co-Dir, Advanced Study Inst. on Fundamental Processes in Energetic Atomic Collisions, Maratea, Italy, 1982; Dir, Advanced Study Inst. on Fundamental Processes in Atomic Collision Physics, S Flavia, Sicily, 1984. FInstP 1969; Fellow Amer. Physical Soc. 1969; FRAS 1974. *Publications:* edited: (with F. Bopp) Physics of the One- and Two-Electron Atoms, 1969; (with M. R. C. McDowell) Electron and Photon Interactions with Atoms, 1976; (with W. Hanle) Progress in Atomic Spectroscopy, Vol. A 1978, Vol. B 1979, Vol. C (with H.-J. Beyer), 1984; (with J. F. Williams) Coherence and Correlations in Atomic Collisions, 1980; (jtly) Inner-Shell and X-Ray Physics of Atoms and Solids, 1981; (jtly) Fundamental Processes in Energetic Atomic Collisions, 1983; (jtly) Fundamental Processes in Atomic Collision Physics, 1985; (with P. G. Burke) series editor, Physics of Atoms and Molecules; papers in Zeitschr. f. Physik, Z. f. Naturf., Z. f. Angew Physik, Physikalische Blätter, Physical Review, Jl of Physics, Physics Letters, Internat. Jl of Quantum Chemistry; Physics Reports, Advances of Atomic and Molecular Physics, Applied Physics. *Address:* 27 Kenningknowes Road, Stirling.

KLEINWORT, Sir Kenneth (Drake), 3rd Bt *cr* 1909; Director, Kleinwort, Benson, Lonsdale plc, since 1976; *b* 28 May 1935; *s* of Ernest Greverus Kleinwort (*d* 1977) (4th *s* of 1st Bt) and of Joan Nightingale Kleinwort, MBE, JP, DL, *d* of late Prof. Arthur William Crossley, CMG, CBE, FRS; *S* uncle, 1983; *m* 1st, 1959, Lady Davina Pepys (*d* 1973), *d* of 7th Earl of Cottenham; one *s* one *d*; 2nd, 1973, Madeleine Hamilton, *e d* of Ralph Taylor; two *s* one *d*. *Educ:* Eton College; Grenoble Univ. Joined Kleinwort Sons & Co. Ltd, 1955; Director: Kleinwort Benson (Europe) SA, Brussels, 1970–; Banque Kleinwort Benson SA, Geneva, 1971–; Kleinwort Benson Ltd, 1971–76; Exec. Dir, Trebol International Corp., USA, 1978–; Pres., Interalia Leasing SA, Chile, 1980–. Trustee, World Wildlife Fund International, Switzerland, 1978–; Mem. Council, Wildfowl Trust, UK, 1982–. *Recreations:* travel, photography, skiing, tennis. *Heir:* *s* Richard Drake Kleinwort, *b* 4 Nov. 1960. *Address:* La Massellaz, 1111 Vaux-sur-Morbes, Switzerland. *T:* (4121)–72–41–48.

KLEVAN, Rodney Conrad, QC 1984; a Recorder of the Crown Court, since 1980; *b* 23 May 1940; *s* of Sidney Leopold Klevan and late Florence Klevan (*née* Eaton); *m* 1968, Susan Rebecca (*née* Lighthill); two *s* one *d*. *Educ:* Temple Primary School; Manchester Central Grammar School; Birmingham Univ. (LLB Hons 1962). Pres., Birmingham Univ. Guild of Undergraduates, 1962–63. Called to the Bar, Gray's Inn, 1966; Deputy Circuit Judge, 1977. *Recreations:* theatre, television, following the fortunes of Lancashire CCC. *Address:* Beech House, 45 Manor Road, Bramhall, Stockport, Cheshire. *T:* 061–485 1847.

KLIBANSKY, Raymond, MA, PhD; Frothingham Professor of Logic and Metaphysics, McGill University, Montreal, 1946–75, now Emeritus Professor; Extraordinary Fellow of Wolfson College, Oxford, since 1981; *b* Paris, 15 Oct. 1905; *s* of late Hermann Klibansky. *Educ:* Paris; Odenwald Sch.; Univs of Kiel, Hamburg, Heidelberg. PhD, 1928; MA Oxon by decree, 1936. Asst, Heidelberg Acad., 1927–33; Lecturer in Philosophy: Heidelberg Univ., 1931–33; King's Coll., London, 1934–36; Oriel Coll., Oxford, 1936–48; Forwood Lectr in Philosophy of Religion, Univ. of Liverpool, 1938–39. Political Intelligence Dept, FO, 1941–46. Dir of Studies, Warburg Inst., Univ. of London, 1947–48. Vis. Prof. of History of Philosophy, Université de Montréal, 1947–68; Mahlon Powell Prof., Indiana Univ., 1950; Cardinal Mercier Prof. of Philosophy, Univ. of Louvain, 1956; Vis. Prof. of Philosophy, Univ. of Rome, 1961, Univ. of Genoa, 1964, Univ. of Tokyo, 1971; Prof. Emeritus, Heidelberg Univ., 1975–, Hon. Senator, 1986–. President: Inst. Internat. de Philosophie, Paris, 1966–69 (Hon. Pres. 1969–); Société Internationale pour l'étude de la Philos. Médiévale, Louvain, 1968–72 (Hon. Pres., 1972–); Canadian Soc. for History and Philosophy of Science, 1959–72 (Pres. Emeritus, 1972–); Internat. Cttee for Anselm Studies, 1970–. FRSC; FRHistS; Fellow: Accademia Nazionale dei Lincei, Rome; Acad. of Athens; Académie Internationale d'Histoire des Sciences, Paris; Iranian Acad. of Philosophy, Teheran; Accad. Mediterranea delle Scienze, Catania; Corresponding Fellow: Mediaeval Acad. of America; Heidelberg Acad. of Scis. Hon. Member: Allgemeine Gesellsch. für Philosophie in Deutschland; Assoc. des Scientifiques de Roumanie, Bucarest. Hon. Fellow: Oriel Coll., Oxford; Warburg Inst., Univ. of London; Accad. Ligure delle Scienze, Genoa. Guggenheim Foundation Fellow, 1954 and 1965; Vis. Fellow, Wolfson Coll., Oxford, 1976–78. Dir, Canadian Academic Centre in Italy, Rome, 1980. Mem. Exec. Council, Union Académique Internationale, 1978–80. Comité Directeur, Fedn Internat. des Socs de Philosophie, 1958–83. DPhil *hc* Ottawa. Gen. Editor, Corpus Platonicum Medii Aevi, (Plato Latinus and Plato Arabus), Union Académique Internat., 1937–; Joint Editor and contributor to: Magistri Eckardi Opera Latina, 1933–36; Philosophy and History, 1936; Mediaeval and Renaissance Studies, 1941–68; Editor: Philosophical Texts, 1951–62; Philosophy and World Community, 1957–81; Philosophy in the Mid-Century, 1958–59; Contemporary Philosophy, 1968–71. *Publications:* Ein Proklos-Fund und seine Bedeutung, 1929; Heidelberg Acad. edn of Opera Nicolai de Cusa, 5 vols, 1929–82; The Continuity of the Platonic Tradition, 1939, enlarged 3rd edn incl. Plato's Parmenides in the Middle Ages and the Renaissance, 1981; (with E. Panofsky and F. Saxl) Saturn and Melancholy, 1964; articles in Jahresberichte d. Heidelberger Akademie, Proceedings of British Acad., Enciclopedia Italiana, and elsewhere. *Address:* Wolfson College, Oxford OX2 6UD; Leacock Building, McGill University, Montreal H3A 2T7, Canada.

KLIEN, Walter; musician (concert pianist); soloist with leading conductors and orchestras; *b* 27 Nov. 1928. *Educ:* Frankfurt-am-Main; Vienna. Concert tours in: Europe, USA, Canada, South America, Far East. Many recordings, which include complete solo-works by Mozart and Brahms, also the complete Schubert Sonatas. *Address:* c/o Kaye Artists Management Ltd, 250 King's Road, SW3.

KLOOTWIJK, Jaap; Managing Director, Shell UK Oil, since 1983; a Managing Director, Shell UK Ltd, since 1983; Chairman: UK Oil Pipelines Ltd, since 1983; The Flyfishers' Co. Ltd, since 1985; *b* 16 Nov. 1932; *s* of Jacob Leendert Klootwijk and Woutrina Johanna Boer; unmarried. *Educ:* primary educn in Indonesia and Thailand; Rotterdam Grammar Sch.; Delft Univ., Holland (MSc Mech. Eng, 1956). Lieut Royal Netherlands Navy, 1956–58. Joined Shell Research, 1958; Shell Refining and Marketing Co. Ltd, 1964–66; East African Oil Refineries Ltd, 1967–69; Shell Internat. Petroleum Mij., 1970–73; Shell Refining and Marketing Co. Ltd, 1974–76; Shell Internat. Petroleum Co. Ltd, 1976–82; Area Co-ordinator, SE Asia, 1976–79; Man. Dir, Shell Internat. Gas Ltd, 1979–82. Pres., UK Petroleum Industry Assoc., 1985– (Vice-Pres., 1984–85). FinstPet; FRSA. *Recreations:* deer-stalking, shooting, fishing, reading. *Address:* 26 Manor House Court, Warwick Avenue, W9 2PZ. *T:* 01–289 4276. *Club:* Flyfishers' (Pres., 1985–).

KLUG, Aaron, PhD (Cantab); FRS 1969; Joint Head, Division of Structural Studies, Medical Research Council Laboratory of Molecular Biology, Cambridge, since 1978 (member of staff, since 1962); Fellow of Peterhouse, since 1962; *b* 11 Aug. 1926; *s* of Lazar Klug and Bella Silin; *m* 1948, Liebe Bobrow, Cape Town, SA; two *s*. *Educ:* Durban High Sch.; Univ. of the Witwatersrand (BSc); Univ. of Cape Town (MSc). Junior Lecturer, 1947–48; Research Student, Cavendish Laboratory, Cambridge, 1949–52; Rouse-Ball Research Studentship, Trinity Coll., Cambridge, 1949–52; Colloid Science Dept, Cambridge, 1953; Nuffield Research Fellow, Birkbeck Coll., London, 1954–57; Head, Virus Structure Research Group, Birkbeck Coll., 1958–61. Lectures: Leeuwenhoek, Royal Soc., 1973; Dunham, Harvard Medical Sch., 1975; Harvey, NY, 1979; Lane, Stanford Univ., 1983; Silliman, Yale Univ., 1985; Nishina Meml, Tokyo, 1986. For. Associate, Nat. Acad. of Scis, USA, 1984; For. Mem., Max Planck Soc., Germany, 1984; For. Hon. Mem., Amer. Acad. of Arts and Scis, 1969. Hon. Fellow, Trinity Coll., Cambridge, 1983. Hon. DSc: Chicago, 1978; Columbia Univ., 1978; Dr *hc* Strasbourg, 1978; Hon. Dsc: Witwatersrand, 1984; Hull, 1985; Hon. PhD Jerusalem, 1984; Hon. Dr Fil. Stockholm, 1980. Heineken Prize, Royal Netherlands Acad. of Science, 1979; Louisa Gross Horwitz Prize, Columbia Univ., 1981; Nobel Prize in Chemistry, 1982; Gold Medal of Merit, Univ. of Cape Town, 1983; Copley Medal, Royal Soc., 1985; Harden Medal, Biochem. Soc., 1985. *Publications:* papers in scientific jls. *Recreations:* reading, gardening. *Address:* 70 Cavendish Avenue, Cambridge. *T:* 248959.

KLYBERG, Rt. Rev. Charles John; *see* Fulham, Bishop Suffragan of.

KLYNE, Barbara Evelyn, (Mrs William Klyne); *see* Clayton, B. E.

KNAGGS, Kenneth James, CMG 1971; OBE 1959; Consultant, Commonwealth Development Corporation, since 1974; *b* 3 July 1920; *e s* of late James Henry Knaggs and Elsie Knaggs (*née* Walton); *m* 1945, Barbara, *d* of late Ernest James Page; two *s*. *Educ:* St Paul's Sch., London. Served War, 1939–46 (Major). Northern Rhodesia Civil Service, 1946; Sec. to Govt, Seychelles, 1955; Northern Rhodesia: Asst Sec., 1960; Under Sec., 1961; Permanent Sec., Min. of Finance and subseq. the same in Zambia, 1964; retd 1970. European Rep. and Manager, Zambia Airways, 1970–72. *Recreations:* walking, gardening, cooking. *Address:* High House Farm, Earl Soham, near Framlingham, Suffolk IP13 7SN. *T:* Earl Soham 416.

KNAPMAN, Dr Paul Anthony; HM Coroner for Westminster, since 1980 (Jurisdiction of Inner West London); *b* 5 Nov. 1944; *s* of Frederick Ethelbert and Myra Knapman; *m* 1970, Penelope Jane Cox; one *s* three *d*. *Educ:* Epsom Coll.; King's Coll., London; St George's Hosp. Med. Sch. (MB, BS 1968). MRCS, LRCP 1968; DMJ 1975. Called to the Bar, Gray's Inn, 1972. Dep. Coroner for Inner W London, 1975–80. Hon. Lectr in Med. Jurisprudence: St George's Hosp. Med. Sch., 1978–; St Thomas's Hosp. Med. Sch., 1980–; Westminster Hosp. Med. Sch., 1981–; Middlesex Hosp. Med. Sch., 1981–; St Mary's Hosp. Med. Sch., 1981–. Pres., S Eastern England Coroners' Soc., 1980. Gov., London Nautical Sch., 1981–. Liveryman, Worshipful Soc. of Apothecaries. *Publications:* (jtly) Coronership: the law and practice on coroners, 1985; papers on medico-legal subjects. *Recreations:* squash, sailing. *Address:* Westminster Coroner's Court, Horseferry Road, SW1P 2ED. *T:* 01–834 6515. *Clubs:* Athenæum; Royal Torbay Yacht.

KNAPP, David; *see* Knapp, J. D.

KNAPP, Edward Ronald, CBE 1979; Managing Director, Timken Europe, 1973–85; *b* 10 May 1919; *s* of Percy Charles and Elsie Maria Knapp; *m* 1942, Vera Mary Stephenson; two *s* two *d*. *Educ:* Cardiff High Sch.; St Catharine's Coll., Cambridge (MA 1940); Harvard Business Sch. (AMP 1954). Served RNVR, Special Branch, Lt-Comdr, 1940–46: HMS Aurora, 1941–44; US Naval Research, Anacostia, 1944–46. Joined British Timken, 1946, Man. Dir, 1969; Dir, Timken Co., USA, 1976. Technical and Management Educnl Governor, Nene Coll., 1953–; Vice-Chm., Regional Adv. Council for Organisation of Further Educn, 1978–. *Recreations:* gardening, golf; played Rugby for Wales, 1940, Captain of Cambridge Univ. 1940 and Northampton RFC, 1948. *Address:* The Elms, 1 Millway, Duston, Northampton NN5 6ER. *T:* Northampton 584737. *Clubs:* East India, Devonshire, Sports and Public Schools, Naval; Northampton and County; Hawks (Cambridge).

KNAPP, James; General Secretary, National Union of Railwaymen, since 1983; *b* 29 Sept. 1940; *s* of James and Jean Knapp; *m* 1965, Sylvia Florence Yeomans; one *d*. *Educ:* Hurlford Primary Sch.; Kilmarnock Academy. British Rail employee (signalman), 1955–72; Hurlford NUR Branch Secretary, 1961–65; Sec., Amalgamated Kilmarnock and Hurlford NUR Br., 1965–72; Glasgow and W Scotland NUR Dist Council Sec., 1970–72; full time Divisional Officer, NUR, 1972–81; Headquarters Officer, NUR, 1981–82. Dir, Unity Trust, 1984–. *Recreations:* walking, soccer, countryside. *Address:* 2 Midsummer Hill, Kennington, near Ashford, Kent.

KNAPP, (John) David; Director of Conservative Political Centre, since 1975; an Assistant Director, Conservative Research Department, since 1979; *b* 27 Oct. 1926; *s* of late Eldred Arthur Knapp and Elizabeth Jane Knapp; *m* 1st, 1954, Dorothy Ellen May (*née* Squires) (marr. diss.); one *s*; 2nd, 1980, Daphne Monard, OBE, *widow* of Major S. H. Monard. *Educ:* Dauntsey's Sch., Wilts; King's Coll., London (BA Hons). Dir, Knapp and Bates Ltd, 1950–54. Vice-Chm., Fedn of University Conservative and Unionist Assoc., 1948–49; Conservative Publicity and Political Educn Officer, Northern Area, 1952–56; Political Educn Officer, NW Area, 1956–61, and Home Counties N Area, 1961; Dep. Dir, Conservative Political Centre, 1962–75. *Recreations:* philately, listening to classical music. *Address:* 71 Kirby Road, Portsmouth, Hants PO2 0PF. *T:* Portsmouth 663709. *Clubs:* St Stephen's Constitutional; Royal Naval and Royal Albert Yacht (Portsmouth).

KNAPP, Trevor Frederick William Beresford; Director General (Marketing), Ministry of Defence, since 1983; *b* 26 May 1937; *s* of Frederick William Knapp and Linda Knapp (*née* Poffley); *m* 1964, Margaret Fry; one *s* one *d*. *Educ:* Christ's Hospital; King's College London (BSc 1958). ARIC 1960. Ministry of Aviation, 1961; Sec., Downey Cttee, 1965–66; Sec., British Defence Research and Supply Staff, Canberra, 1968–72; Asst Sec., MoD, 1974; GEC Turbine Generators Ltd, 1976; Central Policy Review Staff, 1977–79; Under-Sec., MoD, 1983. *Address:* c/o Ministry of Defence, Main Building, Whitehall, SW1A 2HB.

KNAPP-FISHER, Rt. Rev. Edward George; *b* 8 Jan. 1915; *s* of late Rev. George Edwin Knapp-Fisher and Agatha Knapp-Fisher; *m* 1965, Joan, *d* of late R. V. Bradley. *Educ:* King's School, Worcester; Trinity College, Oxford. Assistant Curate of Brighouse, Yorks, 1939; Chaplain, RNVR, 1942; Chaplain of Cuddesdon College, 1946; Chaplain of St John's College, Cambridge, 1949; Vicar of Cuddesdon and Principal of Cuddesdon Theological College, 1952–60; Bishop of Pretoria, 1960–75; Canon and Archdeacon of

Westminster, 1975–87; Sub-Dean, 1982–87; Asst Bishop, Dio. Southwark 1975–87, Dio. London 1976–87. Member, Anglican Roman-Catholic Preparatory Commission, 1967–68; Member, Anglican-Roman Catholic Internat. Commn, 1969–81. *Publications:* The Churchman's Heritage, 1952; Belief and Prayer, 1964; To be or not to be, 1968; Where the Truth is Found, 1975; (ed jtly and contrib.) Towards Unity in Truth, 1981. *Recreations:* walking, travel. *Address:* 2 Vicars' Close, Canon Lane, Chichester, West Sussex PO19 1PT.

KNARESBOROUGH, Bishop Suffragan of; *no appointment at time of going to press.*

KNATCHBULL, family name of **Baron Brabourne** and **Countess Mountbatten of Burma.**

KNEALE, (Robert) Bryan (Charles), RA 1974 (ARA 1970); sculptor; *b* 19 June 1930; *m* 1956, Doreen Lister; one *s* one *d*. *Educ:* Douglas High Sch.; Douglas Sch. of Art, IOM; Royal Academy Schools: Rome prize, 1949–51; RA diploma. Tutor, RCA Sculpture Sch., 1964–; Head of Sculpture Sch., Hornsey, 1967; Assoc. Lectr, Chelsea Sch. of Art, 1970. Fellow RCA, 1972; Head of Sculpture Dept, RCA, 1985– (Sen. Tutor, 1980–85); Prof. of Sculpture, RA, 1985– (Master of Sculpture, 1982–85). Member: Fine Art Panels, NCAD, 1964–71, Arts Council, 1971–73, CNAA, 1974–82; Chm., Air and Space, 1972–73. *Organised:* Sculpture '72, RA, 1972; Battersea Park Silver Jubilee Sculpture, 1977 (also exhibited); Sade Exhbn, Cork, 1982. *Exhibitions:* at Redfern Gallery, 1954, 1956, 1958, 1960, 1962, 1964, 1967, 1970, 1976, 1978, 1981, 1983; John Moores, 1961; Sixth Congress of Internat. Union of Architects, 1961; Art Aujourd'hui, Paris, 1963; Battersea Park Sculpture, 1963, 1966; Profile III Bochum, 1964; British Sculpture in the Sixties, Tate Gall., 1965; Whitechapel Gall. 1966 (Retrospective), 1981; Structure, Cardiff Metamorphis Coventry, 1966; New British Painting and Sculpture, 1967–68; City of London Festival, 1968; Holland Park, Sculpture in the Cities, Southampton, and British Sculptors, RA, 1972; Holland Park, 1973; Royal Exchange Sculpture Exhibition, 1974; New Art, Hayward Gallery, 1975; Sculpture at Worksop, 1976; Taranman Gall., 1977, 1981; Serpentine Gall., 1978; Monumental Sculpture for Manx Millenium, Ronaldsway, Isle of Man, 1979; Compass Gall., Glasgow, 1981; 51 Gall., Edinburgh, 1981; Bath Art Fair, 1981. Arts Council Tours, 1966–71. *Collections:* Arts Council of Gt Britain; Contemp. Art Soc.; Manx Museum; Leics Educn Authority; Nat. Galls of Victoria, S Australia and New Zealand; City Art Galls, York, Nottingham, Manchester, Bradford and Leicester; Tate Gall.; Beaverbrook Foundn, Fredericton; Museum of Modern Art, Sao Paulo, Brazil; Bahia Museum, Brazil; Oriel Coll., Oxford; Museum of Modern Art, New York; City Galleries, Middlesbrough, Birmingham, Wakefield; Fitzwilliam Museum, Cambridge; W Riding Educn Authority; Unilever House Collection; Walker Art Gallery. *Address:* 7 Winthorpe Road, SW15. *T:* 01–788 0869.

KNEALE, Prof. William Calvert, FBA 1950; White's Professor of Moral Philosophy, University of Oxford, and Fellow of Corpus Christi College, 1960–66; *b* 22 June 1906; *s* of late William Kneale; *m* 1938, Martha Hurst, Fellow of Lady Margaret Hall, Oxford; one *s* one *d*. *Educ:* Liverpool Institute; Brasenose Coll., Oxford (Classical Scholar). Senior Hulme Scholar, Brasenose Coll., 1927, studied in Freiburg and Paris; Asst in Mental Philosophy, University of Aberdeen, 1929; Asst Lecturer in Philosophy, Armstrong Coll., Newcastle upon Tyne, 1931; Lecturer in Philosophy, Exeter Coll., Oxford, 1932; Fellow, 1933–60; Senior Tutor, 1945–50; Emeritus Fellow, 1960. War of 1939–45, temp. Civil Servant, Ministry of Shipping (later War Transport). Vice-Pres., British Acad., 1971–72. Hon. Fellow, Brasenose Coll., Oxford, 1962, and Corpus Christi Coll., Oxford, 1966. Hon. LLD Aberdeen, 1960; Hon. DLitt: Durham, 1966; St Andrews, 1973. *Publications:* Probability and Induction, 1949; (with M. Kneale) The Development of Logic, 1962; On Having a Mind, 1962; articles in Mind, Proceedings of Aristotelian Society, etc. *Address:* 4 Bridge End, Grassington, near Skipton, North Yorks. *T:* Grassington 752710.

KNEIPP, Hon. Sir (Joseph Patrick) George, Kt 1982; a Judge of the Supreme Court of Queensland, since 1969; Chancellor, James Cook University of North Queensland, since 1974; *b* 13 Nov. 1922; *s* of A. G. Kneipp and K. B. McHugh; *m* 1948, Ada Joan Crawford Cattermole; two *s* one *d*. *Educ:* Downlands Coll., Toowoomba; Univ. of Queensland (LLB). Called to the Queensland Bar, 1950; in practice as Barrister-at-Law, 1950–69. *Recreations:* reading, gardening. *Address:* 20 Kenilworth Avenue, Hyde Park, Townsville, Qld 4812, Australia. *T:* 794652. *Clubs:* North Queensland, James Cook University, Townsville Turf, North Queensland Amateur, (Queensland).

KNELL, Rt. Rev. Eric Henry, MA Oxon; *b* 1 April 1903; *s* of Edward Henry and Edith Helen Knell; unmarried. *Educ:* Trinity College, Oxford. Assistant Curate of St Barnabas, Southfields, 1928; Domestic Chaplain to Bishop of Lincoln, 1933; in charge of Trinity College, Oxford, Mission in Stratford, E15, 1936; Vicar of Emmanuel, Forest Gate, 1941; Vicar of Christ Church, Reading, 1945; Archdeacon of Berkshire, 1955–67; Suffragan Bishop of Reading, 1955–72; Assistant Bishop, Diocese of Oxford, 1972–75. *Address:* College of St Barnabas, Lingfield, Surrey.

KNELLER, Alister Arthur; Hon. Mr Justice Kneller; Chief Justice of Gibraltar, since 1986; *b* 11 Nov. 1927; *s* of Arthur Kneller and Hester (*née* Farr). *Educ:* King's Sch., Canterbury; Corpus Christi Coll., Cambridge (MA 1954; LLM 1985). Kenya: Resident Magistrate, 1955; Sen. State Counsel, 1962; Registrar of the High Court, 1965; Puisne Judge, 1969; Judge of the Court of Appeal, 1982. *Recreations:* music, reading. *Address:* 2 Mount Road, Gibraltar. *T:* Gibraltar 75762. *Clubs:* United Oxford & Cambridge University; Mombasa (Kenya).

KNIGHT, Sir Allan Walton, Kt 1970; CMG 1960; Hon. FIE (Aust.); FTS; Commissioner, The Hydro-Electric Commission, Tasmania, 1946–77; Chief Commissioner, Tasman Bridge Restoration Commission, 1975–80; *b* 26 Feb. 1910; *s* of late Mr and Mrs G. W. Knight, Lindisfarne, Tasmania; *m* 1936, Margaret Janet Buchanan; two *s* one *d*. *Educ:* Hobart Technical Coll.; University of Tasmania. Diploma of Applied Science, 1929; BSc 1932; ME 1935; BCom 1946. Chief Engineer, Public Works Dept, Tasmania, 1937–46. Member: Australian Univs Commn, 1966–74; Council, Tasmanian Coll. of Advanced Education, 1968–75. Peter Nicol Russell Medal, Instn of Engrs of Australia, 1963; William Kernot Medal, Univ. of Melbourne, 1963; Wilfred Chapman Award, Inst. of Welding, Australia, 1974; John Storey Medal, Inst. of Management, Australia, 1975. *Recreation:* royal tennis. *Address:* 64 Waimea Avenue, Sandy Bay, Hobart, Tasmania 7005, Australia. *T:* Hobart 251498. *Club:* Tasmanian (Hobart).

KNIGHT, Andrew Stephen Bower; Chief Executive, Daily Telegraph plc, since 1986; *b* 1 Nov. 1939; *s* of M. W. B. Knight and S. E. F. Knight; *m* 1st, 1966, Victoria Catherine Brittain (marr. diss.); one *s* (Casimir); 2nd, 1975, Begum Sabiha Rumani Malik; two *d*. Editor, The Economist, 1974–86. Chm., Ballet Rambert, 1984–. Dir, Tandem Computers Inc., 1984–. Member: Steering Cttee, Bilderberg Meetings, 1980–; Adv. Bd, Center for Economic Policy Research, Stanford Univ., 1981–; Council, Templeton Coll., Oxford, 1984–; Council, Friends of Covent Garden, 1981–. Governor and Mem. Council of Management, Ditchley Foundn, 1982–; Governor: Imperial Coll. of Science and Technology, 1977–; Atlantic Inst., 1985–; Trustee, V & A Museum, 1983–. *Address:* 135 Fleet Street, EC4P 4BL. *Clubs:* Brooks's, Royal Automobile.

KNIGHT, Sir Arthur (William), Kt 1975; Chairman, National Enterprise Board, 1979–80; Chairman, Courtaulds Ltd, 1975–79; *b* 29 March 1917; *s* of Arthur Frederick Knight and Emily Scott; *m* 1st, 1945, Beatrice Joan Osborne (*née* Oppenheim) (*d* 1968); one *s* three *d*; 2nd, 1972, Sheila Elsie Whiteman. *Educ:* Tottenham County Sch.; London Sch. of Economics (evening student) (BCom; Hon. Fellow 1984). J. Sainsbury, Blackfriars, 1933–38; LSE, Dept of Business Admin (Leverhulme Studentship), 1938–39; Courtaulds, 1939. Served War, Army, 1940–46. Courtaulds, 1946–79: apptd Dir, 1958; Finance Dir, 1961. Non-exec. Director: Pye Holdings, 1972–75; Rolls-Royce (1971), 1973–78; Richard Thomas & Baldwin, 1966–67; Dunlop Holdings, 1981–84. Member: Council of Manchester Business Sch., 1964–71; Cttee for Arts and Social Studies of Council for Nat. Academic Awards, 1965–71; Commn of Enquiry into siting of Third London Airport, 1968–70; Council of Industry for Management Educn, 1970–73; Finance Cttee, RIIA, 1971–75; Council, RIIA, 1975–85; Court of Governors, London Sch. of Economics, 1971–; Economic Cttee, CBI, 1965–72; Cairncross (Channel Tunnel) Cttee, 1974–75; NIESR Exec. Cttee, 1976–; BOTB, 1978–79; The Queen's Award Adv. Cttee, 1981–86; Cttee on Fraud Trials, 1984–85. *Publications:* Private Enterprise and Public Intervention: the Courtauld experience, 1974; various papers. *Recreations:* walking, music, reading. *Address:* Charlton End, Singleton, West Sussex PO18 0HX. *Club:* Reform.

KNIGHT, Brian Joseph; QC 1981; practising barrister, since 1966; *b* 5 May 1941; *s* of Joseph Knight and Vera Lorraine Knight (*née* Docksey); *m* 1967, Cristina Karen Wang Nobrega de Lima. *Educ:* Colbayns High Sch., Clacton; University Coll. London. LLB 1962, LLM 1963. Called to the Bar, Gray's Inn, 1964; *ad eundem* Lincoln's Inn, 1979; called to the Bar of Hong Kong, 1978, of Northern Ireland, 1979. *Address:* 22 Old Buildings, Lincoln's Inn, WC2A 3UJ. *T:* 01–405 2072. *Clubs:* Carlton, Garrick.

KNIGHT, Charles, RWS 1935 (VPRWS 1961–64; ARWS 1933); ROI 1933; Landscape Painter and Designer; Vice-Principal, Brighton College of Art and Crafts, 1959–67, retired; *b* 27 Aug. 1901; *s* of Charles and Evelyn Mary Knight; *m* 1934, Leonora Vasey (*d* 1970); one *s*. Art training, Brighton Coll. of Art; Royal Academy Schools, London (Turner Gold Medal); works in permanent collections, London, British Museum, Victoria and Albert Museum, Sheffield, Leeds, Hull, Oxford, Brighton, Hove, Eastbourne, Preston, etc; regular exhibitor RA, 1924–65. Illustrated monograph by Michael Brockway, 1952. *Address:* Chettles, 34 Beacon Road, Ditchling, Sussex. *T:* Hassocks 3998.

KNIGHT, Edmund Alan; consultant on indirect taxation; *b* 17 June 1919; *s* of Arthur Philip and Charlotte Knight; *m* 1953, Annette Ros Grimmitt; one *d*. *Educ:* Drayton Manor Sch.; London Sch. of Economics. Entered Exchequer and Audit Dept, 1938; HM Customs and Excise, 1948; Asst Sec., 1957; Sec. to Cttee on Turnover Taxation, 1963–64; seconded to Inland Revenue, 1969–71; Comr of Customs and Excise, 1971–77; Eur. Affairs Adviser to BAT Co., 1978–85. Member: SITPRO Bd, 1971–76; EDC for Internat. Freight Movement, 1971–76. *Recreation:* gardening. *Address:* 40 Park Avenue North, Harpenden, Herts AL5 2ED. *Club:* Royal Commonwealth Society.

KNIGHT, Eric John Percy Crawford L.; *see* Lombard Knight.

KNIGHT, Esmond Pennington; actor; *b* 4 May 1906; 3rd *s* of Francis and Bertha Knight; *m* 1st, 1929, Frances Clare (marr. diss.); one *d*; 2nd, 1946, Nora Swinburne, *qv*. *Educ:* Willington Prep. Sch.; Westminster. Made first appearance on stage at Pax Robertson's salon in Ibsen's Wild Duck, 1925; Old Vic., 1925–27; Birmingham Repertory Co., 1927–28; Contraband, Prince's Theatre; To What Red Hell, Wyndham's, 1928; The Children's Theatre; Fashion, Kingsway; Maya, Studio des Théâtres des Champs-Elysées, Paris, 1929; Art and Mrs Bottle, Royalty; Hamlet, Queen's, 1930; Salome, Gate; Waltzes from Vienna, Alhambra, 1931; Wild Violets, Drury Lane, 1932; Three Sisters, Drury Lane; Streamline, Palace, 1934; Wise Tomorrow, Lyric; Van Gogh, Arts Theatre Club; Night Must Fall, Cambridge Theatre, 1936; The Insect Play, Little; The King and Mistress Shore, Little, 1937; Crest of the Wave, Tour; Twelfth Night, Phœnix, 1938; in management with Wilson Barrett, King's, Hammersmith and Edinburgh, 1939; Peaceful Inn, Duke of York's; Midsummer Night's Dream, Open Air, 1940. Joined RNVR (HMS King Alfred, Drake, Excellent, Prince of Wales); discharged from Navy as a result of being blinded in HMS Prince of Wales during action with Bismarck, 1941. Returned to stage in Crisis in Heaven, March 1945; shared lead with Evelyn Laye in The Three Waltzes, Princes. Season of plays with travelling Repertory Theatre, King's, Hammersmith, 1946; The Relapse, 1947; Memorial Theatre, Stratford-on-Avon, 1948–49; Caroline (by Maugham), Arts Theatre Club; Old Vic Co., Edinburgh Festival, 1950, in Bartholomew Fair by Ben Jonson; Who is Sylvia, Criterion, 1950; Sir Laurence Olivier's Festival Season, St James's Theatre, 1951; Heloise, Duke of York's; Montserrat, Lyric; Bermuda Festival (Bermuda); Emperor's Clothes (New York); Age of Consent; Bell, Book and Candle, Phœnix, 1955; The Caine Mutiny, Hippodrome, 1956; The Country Wife, Adelphi, 1957; The Russian, Lyric, Hammersmith, 1958; A Piece of Silver (Cheltenham), 1960; The Lady from the Sea, Queen's, 1961; Becket, Taming of the Shrew, Aldwych, 1961; Two Stars for Comfort, Garrick, 1962; last Old Vic Season, 1962–63; Season, Mermaid, 1965; Edinburgh Festival: Winter's Tale, and Trojan Women 1966; Getting Married, Strand, 1967; Greenwich Theatre: Martin Luther King, 1969; Spithead, 1969; The Servants and the Snow, 1970; Mister, Duchess, 1971; Family Reunion, '69 Theatre Co., Manchester, 1973, Vaudeville, 1979; The Cocktail Party, '69 Theatre Co., Manchester, 1975; Loves Old Sweet Song, Greenwich, 1976; Three Sisters, Cambridge, 1976; Henry V and Agincourt, The Archer's Tale, Open Air Theatre, 1976; Crime and Punishment, Royal Exchange, Manchester, and City of Munster Fest., 1978; Family Reunion, Royal Exchange, Manchester, The Round House and Vaudeville, 1979; Hamlet, Young Vic, 1982; Moby Dick, Royal Exchange, Manchester, 1983; The Devils, RSC, 1984. *Films:* Romany Love, 77 Park Lane, The Ringer, Pagliacci, Waltzes from Vienna, Black Roses (Ufa, Berlin), What Men Live By, The Bermondsey Kid, The Blue Squadron, Girls Will Be Boys, Dandy Dick, Someday, Crime Unlimited, Contraband, The Silver Fleet, Half-Way House, King Henry V, A Canterbury Tale, Black Narcissus, Hamlet, Red Shoes, Gone to Earth, The River, 1950, Helen of Troy (Rome), 1954, The Dark Avenger, Ratcliffe in Olivier's Richard III, The Sleeping Prince, On Secret Service, Battle of the V1; Sink the Bismarck; The Spy Who Came in From the Cold; Anne of the Thousand Days; Where's Jack, 1968; The Boy who turned Yellow; The Yellow Dog; Robin and Marian, 1975; The Element of Crime, 1985. Assisted in making several Natural History films. *Television:* has appeared frequently on BBC and Independent Television, notably in Dickens and Ibsen; Dr Finlay's Casebook; Elizabeth I; The Pallisers; Fall of Eagles; History of the English-speaking Peoples; Shades of Greene; Ballet Shoes; Quiller; I Claudius; 1900: Voices from the Past; Kilvert's Diaries; Supernatural; Romeo and Juliet; Rebecca; Nelson; The Borgias; Troilus and Cressida; My Cousin Rachel; Drake's Venture; King Lear; The Grassless Grave; The Invisible Man; Blott on the Landscape; Sleeping Murder. Also tours with his one man show: Agincourt—The Archer's Tale. *Publications:* Seeking the Bubble (Autobiography), 1943; Story in Blackwood's, Jan. 1942; various articles in daily and weekly Press. *Recreation:* painting. *Club:* Savage.

KNIGHT, Geoffrey Cureton, MB, BS London; FRCS; FRCPsych; Consulting Neurological Surgeon in London, since 1935; Hon. Consultant Neurosurgeon: West End Hospital for Neurology and Neurosurgery; SE Metropolitan Regional Neurosurgical

Centre; Royal Postgraduate Medical School of London; formerly Teacher of Surgery, University of London; *b* 4 Oct. 1906; *s* of Cureton Overbeck Knight; *m* 1933, Betty, *d* of Francis Cooper Havell, London; two *s*. *Educ:* Brighton Coll.; St Bartholomew's Hosp. Medical Sch. Brackenbury Surgical Schol. St Bart's Hosp., 1930. Ho. Surg. and Chief Asst, Surgical Professorial Unit at St Bart's Hosp.; Demonstrator in Physiology, St Bart's Hosp. Medical Sch.; Leverhulme Research Scholar, Royal College of Surgeons, 1933–35; Mackenzie Mackinnon Research Scholar, 1936–38; Bernard Baron Research Scholar, 1938; Hunterian Prof., 1935–36 and 1963. FRSocMed; Fellow Soc. Brit. Neurological Surgeons; Fellow Med. Soc. London; Vice-Pres., Internat. Soc. for Psychosurgery. Neurological Surg. Armed Forces of Czecho-Slovakia, 1941; Hon. Fellow, Czecho-Slovak Med. Soc., Prague, 1946; Officer, Order of the White Lion of Czecho-Slovakia, 1946. *Publications:* contrib. med. jls on aetiology and surgical treatment of diseases of the spine and nervous system and the surgical treatment of mental illness. *Recreations:* gardening, swimming. *Address:* 7 Aubrey Road, Campden Hill, W8. *T:* 01–727 7719 (Sec., 01–935 7549). *Club:* Hurlingham.

KNIGHT, Geoffrey Egerton, CBE 1970; Director: Guinness Peat Group plc, since 1976; GPA Group Ltd, since 1977; Chairman, Fenchurch Insurance Holdings Ltd, since 1980; Director, Trafalgar House Public Limited Company, since 1980; *b* 25 Feb. 1921; *s* of Arthur Egerton Knight and Florence Gladys Knight (*née* Clarke); *m* 1947, Evelyn Bugle; two *d*. *Educ:* Stubbington House; Brighton Coll. Royal Marines, 1939–46. Joined Bristol Aeroplane Co. Ltd, 1953; Dir, Bristol Aircraft Ltd, 1956; Dir, BAC Ltd, 1964–77, Vice Chm., 1972–76. *Publication:* Concorde: the inside story, 1976. *Address:* 33 Smith Terrace, SW3. *T:* 01–352 5391. *Clubs:* Boodle's, White's, Turf.

KNIGHT, Dr Geoffrey Wilfred; retired; Regional Medical Officer, North West Thames Regional Health Authority, 1973–76; *b* 10 Jan. 1920; *s* of Wilfred Knight and Ida Knight; *m* 1944, Christina Marion Collins Scott; one *s* one *d*. *Educ:* Leeds Univ. Med. Sch. MB, ChB, MD, DPH (Chadwick Gold Medal). County Med. Officer of Health, Herts, 1962–73. Formerly: Governor, Nat. Inst. of Social Work; Member: Personal Social Services Council; Central Midwives Bd; Exec. Cttee, Child Health Bureau; Adv. Panel, Soc. for Health Educn; formerly Mem., Govt Techn. and Sci. Cttee on Disposal of Toxic Wastes. *Recreations:* painting, golf. *Address:* 4947 197A Street, Langley, BC V3A 6W1, Canada.

KNIGHT, Air Vice-Marshal Glen Albyn Martin, CB 1961; CBE 1956; *b* 10 Sept. 1903; *e s* of Lt-Col G. A. Knight, OBE, VD, Melbourne, Australia; *m* 1933, Janet Elizabeth Warnock (*d* 1982), *o d* of Peter Crawford, Dargavel, Dumfriesshire; two *d*. *Educ:* Scotch Coll., Melbourne, Australia; Melbourne Univ. MB, BS, 1927; Diploma in Laryngology and Otology (RCP & S), 1937. House Surgeon and Physician, Alfred and Children's Hospitals, Melbourne; joined Medical Branch, RAF, 1932. War Service: South Africa, Malta (despatches), Italy; PMO Desert Air Force. Principal Medical Officer, 2nd Tactical Air Force, 1956–57; Dep. Dir-Gen. of Medical Services, Royal Air Force, 1958–61, retired, 1961. QHS, 1959–61. *Recreation:* golf.

KNIGHT, Gregory; MP (C) Derby North, since 1983; *b* 4 April 1949; *s* of George Knight and Isabella Knight (*née* Bell). *Educ:* Alderman Newton's Grammar School, Leicester; College of Law, Guildford. Self employed solicitor, 1973–83. Member: Leicester City Council, 1976–79; Leicestershire County Council, 1977–83 (Chm., Public Protection Cttee). Dir, Leicester Theatre Trust (former Chm., Finance Cttee). *Publications:* pamphlets and articles for law publications. *Recreations:* music, the arts, writing, film comedy. *Address:* House of Commons, SW1A 0AA. *T:* 01–219 5099.

KNIGHT, Sir Harold (Murray), KBE 1980; DSC 1945; Chairman: Mercantile Mutual Holdings, since 1985; IBJ Bank Australia Ltd, since 1985; Director: Western Mining Corporation, since 1982; Techway Ltd, since 1984; *b* 13 Aug. 1919; *s* of W. H. P. Knight, Melbourne; *m* 1951, Gwenyth Catherine Pennington; four *s* one *d*. *Educ:* Scotch Coll., Melbourne; Melbourne Univ. Commonwealth Bank of Australia, 1936–40. AIF (Lieut), 1940–43; RANVR (Lieut), 1943–45. Commonwealth Bank of Australia, 1946–55; Asst Chief, Statistics Div., Internat. Monetary Fund, 1957–59; Reserve Bank of Australia: Research Economist, 1960–62; Asst Manager, Investment Dept, 1962–64, Manager, 1964–68; Dep. Governor and Dep. Chm. of Board, 1968–75; Governor and Chm. of Bd, 1975–82. Pres., Scripture Union, NSW. *Publication:* Introducción al Analisis Monetario (Spanish), 1959. *Address:* 146 Springdale Road, Killara, NSW 2071, Australia.

KNIGHT, Jeffrey Russell, FCA; Chief Executive, The Stock Exchange, since 1982; *b* 1 Oct. 1936; *s* of Thomas Edgar Knight and Ivy Cissie Knight (*née* Russell); *m* 1959, Judith Marion Delver Podger; four *d*. *Educ:* Bristol Cathedral Sch.; St Peter's Hall, Oxford (MA). Chartered Accountant, 1966; The Stock Exchange, 1967–: Head of Quotations Dept, 1973; Dep. Chief Executive, 1975. Member: City Company Law Cttee, 1974–80; Dept of Trade Panel on Company Law Revision, 1980–84; Accounting Standards Cttee, 1982–; Special Adviser to Dept of Trade, 1975–; Adviser to Council for the Securities Industry, 1978–85; UK Delegate: to EEC Working Parties; to Internat. Fedn of Stock Exchanges, 1973–; to Cttee of Stock Exchanges in EEC (Chm., Wking Cttee). *Recreations:* cricket, music. *Address:* Harlyn, Busbridge Lane, Godalming, Surrey. *T:* Godalming 24399. *Clubs:* Brooks's; Dorset Rangers (Cricket).

KNIGHT, Dame Joan Christabel Jill, (Dame Jill Knight), DBE 1985 (MBE 1964); MP (C) Birmingham, Edgbaston since 1966; *m* 1947, Montague Knight (*d* 1986); two *s*. *Educ:* Fairfield Sch., Bristol; King Edward Grammar Sch., Birmingham. Mem., Northampton County Borough Council, 1956–66. Member: Parly Select Cttee on Race Relations and Immigration, 1969–72; Council of Europe, 1977–; WEU, 1977– (Chm., Cttee for Parly and Public Relations, 1984–); Select Cttee for Home Affairs, 1980–83; Chairman: Lords and Commons All-Party Child and Family Protection Gp, 1978–; Cons. Back Bench Health and Social Services Cttee, 1982–; Sec., 1922 Cttee, 1983–. Pres., West Midlands Conservative Political Centre, 1980–83. Kentucky Colonel, USA, 1973; Nebraska Admiral, USA, 1980. *Recreations:* music, reading, tapestry work, theatre-going, antique-hunting. *Address:* House of Commons, SW1.

KNIGHT, Very Rev. Marcus; Dean of Exeter, 1960–72; *b* 11 Sept. 1903; *e s* of late Mark Knight, Insurance Manager; *m* 1931, Claire L. Hewett, MA, *o d* of late Charles H. Hewett, Bank Dir; two *s*. *Educ:* Christ's Hosp.; University of London; Birkbeck Coll. (BA Hons); King's Coll. (BD Hons); Fellow of King's Coll.; Union Theological Seminary, New York; STM 1930. Curacies at Stoke Newington and Ealing; Priest-Vicar of Exeter Cathedral; Vicar of Cockington, 1936–40; Vicar of Nuneaton; RD of Atherstone, 1940–44; Examining Chaplain to Bishop of Coventry, 1944; Canon of St Paul's, 1944–60, Precentor, 1944–54, Chancellor, 1954–60. Hon. Sec. Church of England Council for Education, 1949–58; Chapter Treas., St Paul's, 1950–60; Church Commissioner, 1968–72. Hon. LLD Exeter, 1973. *Publications:* Spiritualism, Reincarnation, and Immortality, 1950; (part author) There's an Answer Somewhere, 1953; many papers and reviews. *Recreations:* reading, TV, walking. *Address:* 1 Execliff, Trefusis Terrace, Exmouth, Devon. *T:* Exmouth 271153.

KNIGHT, Air Chief Marshal Sir Michael (William Patrick), KCB 1983 (CB 1980); AFC 1964; UK Military Representative to NATO, since 1986; Air Aide-de-Camp to the Queen, since 1986; *b* 23 Nov. 1932; *s* of William and Dorothy Knight; *m* 1967, Patricia Ann (*née* Davies); one *s* two *d*. *Educ:* Leek High Sch.; Univ. of Liverpool (BA Hons 1954; Hon. DLitt 1985). MBIM 1977; FRAeS 1984. Univ. of Liverpool Air Sqn, RAFVR, 1951–54; commnd RAF, 1954; served in Transport and Bomber Comds, and in Middle and Near East Air Forces, 1956–63; Comd No 32 Sqn, RAF Akrotiri, 1961–63; RAF Staff Coll., 1964; Min. of Aviation, 1965–66; Comd Far East Strike Wing, RAF Tengah, 1966–69; Head of Secretariat, HQ Strike Comd, 1969–70; Mil. Asst to Chm., NATO Mil. Cttee, 1970–73; Comd RAF Laarbruch, 1973–74; RCDS, 1975; Dir of Ops (Air Support), MoD, 1975–77; SASO, HQ Strike Command, 1977–80; AOC No 1 Gp, 1980–82; Air Mem. for Supply and Organisation, 1983–86. ADC to the Queen, 1973–74. Mem. Council, RUSI, 1984–. Chm., Combined Services RFC, 1977–79; Mem., RFU Cttee, 1977–; President: RAF Rugby Union, 1985– (Chm., 1975–78); RAF Lawn Tennis Assoc., 1984–86. *Recreations:* Rugby football, lesser sports, music, writing, after-dinner speaking. *Address:* UKMILREP, HQ NATO, Brussels, BFPO 49. *Club:* Royal Air Force.

KNIGHT, Dr Peter Clayton; Director, City of Birmingham Polytechnic, since 1985; *b* 8 July 1947; *s* of Norman Clayton Knight and Vera Catherine Knight; *m* 1977, Catherine Mary (*née* Ward); one *s* one *d*. *Educ:* Bishop Vesey's Grammar Sch., Sutton Coldfield; Univ. of York (BA 1st cl. Hons Physics; DPhil). SRC Studentship, 1968; Asst Teacher, Plymstock Comprehensive Sch., 1971; Plymouth Polytechnic: Lectr, 1972; Sen. Lectr, 1974; Head of Combined Studies, 1981; Dep. Dir, Lancashire Polytechnic, 1982–85. Nat. Pres., NATFHE, 1977; Member: Burnham Cttee of Further Educn, 1976–81; Working Party on Management of Higher Educn, 1977; Nat. Adv. Body on Public Sector Higher Educn, 1982–85. *Publications:* articles, chapters and reviews in learned jls on educnl policy, with particular ref. to higher educn. *Recreation:* running. *Address:* Sandy Lodge, Sandy Lane, Brewood, Staffs. *T:* Brewood 851339.

KNIGHT, Richard James, MA; JP; *b* 19 July 1915; *s* of Richard William Knight; *m* 1953, Hilary Marian, *d* of Rev. F. W. Argyle; two *s* one *d*. *Educ:* Dulwich Coll. (Scholar); Trinity Coll., Cambridge (Scholar). 1st class Hons Classical Tripos Pt I, 1936, Part II, 1937. Asst Master, Fettes Coll., Edinburgh, 1938–39. Served War of 1939–45 in Gordon Highlanders, Capt. Asst Master and Housemaster, Marlborough Coll., 1945–56; Headmaster of Oundle Sch., 1956–68, of Monkton Combe Sch., 1968–78. Lay Reader, Dio. Bath and Wells. JP Northants, 1960, Bath, 1970, Avon, 1974. *Recreations:* cricket and other games. *Address:* 123 Midford Road, Bath.

KNIGHT, Warburton Richard; Director of Educational Services, Bradford Metropolitan District Council, since 1974; *b* 2 July 1932; *s* of Warburton Henry Johnston and Alice Gweneth Knight; *m* 1961, Pamela Ann (*née* Hearmon); two *s* one *d*. *Educ:* Trinity Coll., Cambridge (MA). Teaching in Secondary Modern and Grammar Schs in Middlesex and Huddersfield, 1956–62; joined West Riding in junior capacity, 1962; Asst Dir for Secondary Schs, Leics, 1967; Asst Educn Officer for Sec. Schs and later for Special and Social Educn in WR, 1970. *Recreations:* choral music, beekeeping, general cultural interests. *Address:* Thorner Grange, Sandhills, Thorner, Leeds LS14 3DE. *T:* Leeds 892356. *Club:* Royal Over-Seas League.

KNIGHT, William Arnold, CMG 1966; OBE 1954; Controller and Auditor-General of Uganda, 1962–68, retired; *b* 14 June 1915; *e s* of late William Knight, Llanfairfechan, and of Clara Knight; *m* 1939, Bronwen Parry; one *s* one *d*. *Educ:* Friars' Sch., Bangor; University Coll. of North Wales (BA Hons). Entered Colonial Audit Dept as an Asst Auditor, 1938; service in Kenya, 1938–46; Mauritius, 1946–49; Sierra Leone, 1949–52; British Guiana, 1952–57; Uganda, 1957–68; Commissioner, inquiry into economy and efficiency, Uganda, 1969–70. *Recreations:* fishing and gardening. *Address:* Neopardy Mills, near Crediton, Devon. *T:* Crediton 2513. *Club:* East India.

KNIGHTLEY; *see* Finch-Knightley.

KNIGHTON, William Myles, CB 1981; Deputy Secretary, Department of Transport, since 1984; *b* 8 Sept. 1931; *s* of late George Harry Knighton, OBE, and Ella Knighton (*née* Stroud); *m* 1957, Brigid Helen Carrothers; one *s* one *d*. *Educ:* Bedford School; Peterhouse, Cambridge (BA). Asst Principal, Min. of Supply, 1954; Principal, Min. of Aviation, 1959; Cabinet Office, 1962–64; Principal Private Sec. to Minister of Technology, 1966–68; Asst Sec., Min. of Technology, subseq. DTI and Dept of Trade, 1967–74; Under Sec., 1974–78, Dep. Sec., 1978–84, Dept of Trade, subseq. DTI. *Publication:* (with D. E. Rosenthal) National Laws and International Commerce, 1982. *Recreations:* gardening, hill-walking, listening to music. *Address:* 115 Dacre Park, SE13 5BZ. *T:* 01–852 8267. *Club:* United Oxford & Cambridge University.

KNIGHTS, Lionel Charles, MA, PhD; King Edward VII Professor of English Literature, University of Cambridge, 1965–73, now Emeritus Professor; Fellow, Queens' College, Cambridge, 1965–73; *b* 15 May 1906; *s* of C. E. and Lois M. Knights; *m* 1936, Elizabeth M. Barnes; one *s* one *d*. *Educ:* grammar schs; Selwyn Coll. (Hon. Fellow, 1974), and Christ's Coll., Cambridge Univ.; Charles Oldham Shakespeare Scholar, 1928; Members' Prize, 1929. Lecturer in English Literature, Manchester Univ., 1933–34, 1935–47; Prof. of English Lit., Univ. of Sheffield, 1947–52; Winterstoke Prof. of English, Bristol Univ., 1953–64. Fellow, Kenyon Sch. of Letters, 1950; Andrew Mellon Vis. Prof., Univ. of Pittsburgh, 1961–62 and 1966; Mrs W. Beckman Vis. Prof., Berkeley, 1970. Mem. of editorial board of Scrutiny, a Quarterly Review, 1932–53. For. Hon. Mem., Amer. Acad. of Arts and Sciences, 1981. Docteur (*hc*) de l'Univ. de Bordeaux, 1964; Hon. DUniv York, 1969; Hon. DLitt: Manchester, 1974; Sheffield, 1978; Warwick, 1979; Bristol, 1984. *Publications:* Drama and Society in the Age of Jonson, 1937; Explorations: Essays in Literary Criticism, 1946; Shakespeare's Politics, Shakespeare Lecture, British Academy, 1957; Some Shakespearean Themes, 1959; An Approach to Hamlet, 1960; (ed with Basil Cottle), Metaphor and Symbol, 1961; Further Explorations, 1965; Public Voices: literature and politics (Clark Lectures), 1971; Explorations 3, 1976; Hamlet and other Shakespeare Essays, 1979; Selected Essays in Criticism, 1981. *Address:* 57 Jesus Lane, Cambridge. *Club:* Royal Commonwealth Society.

KNIGHTS, Sir Philip (Douglas), Kt 1980; CBE 1976 (OBE 1971); QPM (Dist. Service) 1964; DL; Chief Constable, West Midlands Police, 1975–85; *b* 3 Oct. 1920; *s* of Thomas James Knights and Ethel Knights; *m* 1945, Jean Burman. *Educ:* King's Sch., Grantham. Lincolnshire Constabulary: Police Cadet, 1938–40; Constable, 1940. Served War, RAF, 1943–45. Sergeant, Lincs Constab., 1946; seconded to Home Office, 1946–50; Inspector, Lincs Constab., 1953, Supt 1955, Chief Supt 1957. Asst Chief Constable, Birmingham City Police, 1959; seconded to Home Office, Dep. Comdt, Police Coll., 1962–66; Dep. Chief Constable, Birmingham City Police, 1970; Chief Constable, Sheffield and Rotherham Constab., 1972–74; Chief Constable, South Yorks Police, 1974–75. Winner of Queen's Police Gold Medal Essay Competition, 1965. Mem. Lord Devlin's Cttee on Identification Procedures, 1974–75. Pres., Assoc. of Chief Police Officers, 1978–79. Mem. Council, Univ. of Aston in Birmingham, 1985–. CBIM. DL W Midlands, 1985. *Recreations:* sport, gardening. *Address:* 11 Antringham Gardens, Edgbaston, Birmingham B15 3QL.

KNILL, Sir John Kenelm Stuart, 4th Bt *cr* 1893, of The Grove, Blackheath; *b* 8 April 1913; *s* of Sir John Stuart Knill, 3rd Bt and Lucy Emmeline (*d* 1952), *o d* of Captain Thomas Willis, MN, FRGS; *S* father, 1973; *m* 1950, Violette Maud Florence Martin Barnes (*d* 1983); two *s*. *Educ:* St Gregory's School, Downside. Gas industry apprenticeship, 1932–39. Served as Lieut, RNVR, 1940–45 (Atlantic Star, Italy, France and Germany Stars). Industrial management trainee, 1945–48; canal transport proprietor, 1948–54; pig farmer, 1954–63; civil servant, MoD, 1963–77. Pres., Avon Transport 2000; Vice-Pres., Thames Severn Canal Trust; Founder and Chm., Associated Canal Enterprises, 1982–; Member: Kennet and Avon Canal Trust, Great Western Soc., Inland Waterways Assoc. *Recreations:* canal and railway restoration, scouting. *Heir:* *s* Thomas John Pugin Bartholomew Knill [*b* 24 Aug. 1952; *m* 1977, Kathleen Muszynski]. *Address:* Canal Cottage, Bathampton, Somerset. *T:* Bath 63603. *Club:* Victory Services.

KNILL, Prof. John Lawrence, PhD, DSc; FICE, FIGeol; Professor of Engineering Geology since 1973, and Head of Department of Geology since 1979, Imperial College of Science and Technology, University of London; *b* 22 Nov. 1934; *s* of late William Cuthbert Knill and of Mary (*née* Dempsey); *m* 1957, Diane Constance Judge; one *s* one *d*. *Educ:* Whitgift Sch.; Imperial Coll. of Science and Technol. (BSc, ARCS 1955; PhD, DIC 1957; DSc 1981). FIGeol 1985; FICE 1981. Geologist, Sir Alexander Gibb & Partners, 1957; Asst Lectr 1957, Lectr 1959, Reader in Engrg Geology 1965, Dean of Royal Sch. of Mines 1980–83, Imperial Coll. of Science and Technol. Member: Nature Conservancy Council, 1985–; Radioactive Waste Management Adv. Cttee; Council, Nat. Stone Centre. President: Instn of Geologists, 1981–84; Geologists' Assoc., 1982–84. Membre Correspondant, Société Geologique de Belgique, 1976. Whitaker Medal, IWES, 1969. *Publications:* Industrial Geology, 1978; articles on geology of Scotland and engrg geology. *Recreation:* viticulture. *Address:* Highwood Farm, Shaw-cum-Donnington, Newbury, Berks RG16 9LB. *Clubs:* Athenæum, Chaps.

KNIPE, Sir Leslie Francis, Kt 1980; MBE; farmer; *b* Pontypool, 1913. *Educ:* West Monmouth School, Pontypool. Served War of 1939–45, Burma; RASC, attained rank of Major. President: Conservative Party in Wales (Chairman, 1972–77); Monmouth Conservative and Unionist Assoc. *Address:* Brook Acre, Llanvihangel, Crucorney, Abergavenny, Gwent NP7 8DH.

KNOLLYS, family name of **Viscount Knollys.**

KNOLLYS, 3rd Viscount, of Caversham, *cr* 1911; **David Francis Dudley Knollys;** Baron *cr* 1902; *b* 12 June 1931; *s* of 2nd Viscount Knollys, GCMG, MBE, DFC, and Margaret, *o d* of Sir Stuart Coats, 2nd Bt; *S* father 1966; *m* 1959, Hon. Sheelin Virginia Maxwell (granted, 1959, title, rank and precedence of a baron's *d*, which would have been hers had her father survived to succeed to barony of Farnham), *d* of late Lt-Col Hon. Somerset Maxwell, MP and late Mrs Remington Hobbs; three *s* one *d*. *Educ:* Eton. Lt, Scots Guards, 1951. *Heir:* *s* Hon. Patrick Nicholas Mark Knollys, *b* 11 March 1962. *Address:* Bramerton Grange, Norwich NR14 7HF. *T:* Surlingham 266.

KNORPEL, Henry, CB 1982; Counsel to the Speaker, House of Commons, since 1985; *b* 18 Aug. 1924; 2nd *s* of late Hyman Knorpel and Dora Knorpel; *m* 1953, Brenda Sterling; two *d*. *Educ:* City of London Sch.; Magdalen Coll., Oxford. BA 1945, BCL 1946, MA 1949. Called to Bar, Inner Temple, 1947, Entrance Scholar, 1947–50; practised 1947–52; entered Legal Civil Service as Legal Asst, Min. of Nat. Insce, 1952; Sen. Legal Asst, Min. of Pensions and Nat. Insce, 1958; Law Commn, 1965; Min. of Social Security, 1967; Dept of Health and Social Security: Asst Solicitor, 1968; Principal Asst Solicitor (Under-Sec.), 1971; Solicitor (also to OPCS and Gen. Register Office), 1978–85. Vis. Lecturer: Kennington Coll. of Commerce and Law, 1950–58; Holborn Coll. of Law, Languages and Commerce, 1958–70; Polytechnic of Central London, 1970–. *Publications:* articles on community law. *Recreation:* relaxing. *Address:* Conway, 32 Sunnybank, Epsom, Surrey KT18 7DX. *T:* Epsom 21394.

KNOTT, Sir John Laurence, AC 1981; Kt 1971; CBE 1960; Director, Equity Trustees Co. Ltd; Chairman: ACTA (Australian) Pty; Pratt & Co. Holdings Pty; Pratt & Co. Financial Services Pty; Scandinavian Pacific Holdings Pty Ltd; *b* 6 July 1910; *s* of J. Knott, Kyneton, Victoria; *m* 1935, Jean R., *d* of C. W. Milnes; three *s* one *d*. *Educ:* Cobram State Sch.; Melbourne Univ. (Dip Com). Private Sec. to Minister for Trade Treaties, 1935–38; Sec., Aust. Delegn, Eastern Gp Supply Council, New Delhi, 1940; Exec. Officer, Secondary Industries Commn, 1943–45; Mem. Jt War Production Cttee; Dir, Defence Prod. Planning Br., Dept of Supply, 1950–52; Sec., Dept of Defence Prod., 1957–58; Mem., Aust. Defence Mission to US, 1957; Sec., Dept of Supply, Melb., 1959–65; Leader, Aust. Mission to ELDO Confs: London, 1961; Paris, 1965, 1966; Rome, 1967; Vice-Pres., ELDO Council, 1967–69. Dep. High Comr for Australia, London, 1966–68; Dir-Gen., Australian PO, 1968–72. Mem. Council, Melbourne Univ., 1973–76. Pres., ESU (Victoria); Chairman: Epworth Hosp. Foundn; Salvation Army Red Shield Appeal. Freeman, City of London. AASA, FCIS, AFAIM, LCA; idc. *Recreations:* bowls (Vice-Pres., Royal Victorian Bowling Assoc., 1957–58; Chm., World Bowls (1980) Ltd), golf, gardening. *Address:* 3 Fenwick Street, Kew, Victoria 3101, Australia. *T:* 86 7777. *Clubs:* Melbourne, West Brighton (Melbourne); Union (Sydney).

KNOTT, Air Vice-Marshal Ronald George, CB 1967; DSO 1944; DFC 1943; AFC 1955; retired 1972; *b* 19 Dec. 1917; *s* of late George and Edith Rose Knott; *m* 1941, Hermione Violet (*née* Phayre); three *s* one *d*. *Educ:* Borden Grammar Sch., Sittingbourne, Kent. No 20 Sqdn RAF, 1938–40; No 5 Flight IAFVR, 1940–41; HQ Coast Defence Wing, Bombay, 1942; No 179 Sqdn, 1943–44; No 524 Sqdn, 1944–45; RAF, Gatow (Ops), 1949–50; OC, RAF Eindhoven, 1950–51; HQ 2nd TAF, 1951–52; RAF Staff Coll., 1952; Flying Trng Comd, 1953–55; Chief Flying Instructor, Central Flying Sch., 1956–58; Air Plans, Air Min., 1959; OC, RAF Gutersloh, 1959–61; ACOS Plans, 2 ATAF, 1962–63; Defence Res. Policy Staff Min. of Def. 1963; DOR2 (RAF), Min. of Def., 1963–67; SASO, HQ NEAF Cyprus, 1967–70; AOA, HQ Air Support Comd, RAF, 1970–72. *Recreations:* gardening, wine growing. *Address:* Pilgrims Cottage, Charing, Kent TN27 0DR. *T:* Charing 2723.

KNOWELDEN, Prof. John, CBE 1983; JP; MD, FRCP, FFCM, DPH; Professor of Community Medicine (formerly of Preventive Medicine and Public Health), University of Sheffield, 1960–84, retired; *b* 19 April 1919; *s* of Clarence Arthur Knowelden; *m* 1946, Mary Sweet; two *s*. *Educ:* Colfe's Grammar Sch., Lewisham; St George's Hosp. Med. Sch.; London Sch. of Hygiene and Trop. Med.; Johns Hopkins Sch. of Public Health, Baltimore. Surg. Lt, RNVR, 1942–46. Rockefeller Fellowship in Preventive Med., 1947–49; Lectr in Med. Statistics and Mem., MRC Statistical Research Unit, 1949–60. Academic Registrar, FCM, 1977–83. Civil Consultant in Community Medicine to Royal Navy, 1977–84. Editor, Brit. Jl of Preventive and Social Medicine, 1959–69 and 1973–76. Formerly Hon. Sec., Sect. of Epidemiology, Royal Society Medicine and Chm., Soc. for Social Medicine; Mem., WHO Expert Advisory Panel on Health Statistics. *Publications:* (with Ian Taylor) Principles of Epidemiology, 2nd edn, 1964; papers on clinical and prophylactic trials and epidemiological topics. *Recreations:* photography, gardening. *Address:* 2 St Helen's Croft, Grindleford, Sheffield S30 1JG. *T:* Hope Valley 30014.

KNOWLES, Sir Charles (Francis), 7th Bt *cr* 1765; Senior Partner, Charles Knowles Design; *b* 20 Dec. 1951; *s* of Sir Francis Gerald William Knowles, 6th Bt, FRS, and of Ruth Jessie, *d* of late Rev. Arthur Brooke-Smith; *S* father, 1974; *m* 1979, Amanda Louise Margaret, *d* of Lance Bromley, *qv*; one *s*. *Educ:* Marlborough Coll.; Oxford Sch. of Architecture (DipArch 1977; RIBA 1979). FRSA. *Recreations:* shooting, travel. *Heir:* *s* (Charles) William (Frederick Lance) Knowles, *b* 27 Aug. 1985. *Address:* Silbury Hill House, 2 Vaughan Avenue, W6 0XS.

KNOWLES, Colin George; company director; Director of Development and Public Relations, University of Bophuthatswana, since 1985; Secretary and Trustee, University of Bophuthatswana Foundation, since 1985; *b* 11 April 1939; *s* of late George William Knowles, Tarleton, Lancs; *m* 1st, 1961, Mary B. D. Wickliffe, *e d* of William Wickliffe, Co. Antrim, NI; two *d*; 2nd, 1971 (marr. diss. 1980); 3rd, 1981, Mrs Carla Johannes, *d* of Roland Stansfield Stamp, Blantyre, Malaŵi; one *d*. *Educ:* King George V Grammar Sch., Southport; CEDEP, Fontainebleau. MInstM 1966; MIPR 1970; BAIE 1972; FBIM 1972; MPRISA 1983. Joined John Player & Sons, 1960; sales and marketing management appts; Head of Public Relations, 1971–73; joined Imperial Tobacco Ltd, 1973; Hd of Public Affairs, 1973–80; Company Sec., 1979–80. Chairman: Griffin Associates Ltd, 1980–84; Concept Communications (Pty) Ltd (S Africa), 1983–84; Dir, TWS Public Relations (Pty) Ltd (S Africa), 1984–85. Mem. Council, Tobacco Trade Benevolent Assoc., 1975–80. Director: Nottingham Festival Assoc. Ltd, 1969–71; English Sinfonia Orchestra, 1972–80; Midland Sinfonia Concert Soc. Ltd, 1972–80; (also co-Founder) Assoc. for Business Sponsorship of The Arts Ltd, 1975–84 (Chm., 1975–80); Bristol Hippodrome Trust Ltd, 1977–81; Bath Archaeological Trust Ltd, 1978–81; The Palladian Trust Ltd, 1979–82; Mem., Chancellor of Duchy of Lancaster's Cttee of Honour on Business and the Arts, 1980–81. Arts sponsorship initiatives include responsibility for: Internat. Cello Competition (with Tortelier), Bristol, 1975 and 1977; Internat. Conductors Awards, 1978; Pompeii Exhibn, RA, 1976–77; new prodns at Royal Opera House, Covent Garden, at Glyndebourne, and at National Theatre. Governor: Manning Grammar Sch., Nottingham, 1972–73; Clayesmore Sch., Dorset, 1975–85. Liveryman, Worshipful Co of Tobacco Pipe Makers and Tobacco Blenders; Freeman, City of London. FRSA 1975; FRCSoc 1976. OStJ 1977. *Publications:* papers, articles and documentary film treatments on the arts, sponsorship, and tobacco industry topics. *Recreations:* game watching, fishing, shooting, reading. *Address:* Post Bag X2046, Mafikeng, 8670, Republic of Bophuthatswana, Southern Africa. *Clubs:* Carlton, MCC; Press Club of South Africa, Mafikeng Golf.

KNOWLES, George Peter; Registrar of the Province and Diocese of York, and Archbishop of York's Legal Secretary, since 1968; *b* 30 Dec. 1919; *s* of Geoffrey Knowles and Mabel Bowman; *m* 1948, Elizabeth Margaret Scott; one *s* two *d*. *Educ:* Clifton Coll., Bristol; Queens' Coll., Cambridge. MA, LLM. Served war, Royal Artillery, 1939–46 (Lieut). Admitted a solicitor, 1948; Chm., York Area Rent Tribunal, 1959; Mem., Mental Health Review Tribunal for Yorkshire Regional Health Authority Area, 1960. *Recreations:* fishing, wildlife. *Address:* 11 Lang Road, Bishopthorpe, York YO2 1QJ. *T:* York 706443. *Clubs:* Royal Automobile; Yorkshire (York).

KNOWLES, Prof. Jeremy Randall, FRS 1977; Amory Houghton Professor of Chemistry and Biochemistry (formerly of Chemistry), Harvard University, since 1974; *b* 28 April 1935; *s* of Kenneth Guy Jack Charles Knowles and Dorothy Helen Swingler; *m* 1960, Jane Sheldon Davis; three *s*. *Educ:* Magdalen College Sch.; Balliol Coll. (Hon. Fellow 1984), Merton Coll. and Christ Church, Oxford (MA, DPhil). Sir Louis Stuart Exhibr, Balliol Coll., Oxford, 1955–59; Harmsworth Schol., Merton Coll., Oxford, and Research Lectr, Christ Church, Oxford, 1960–62; Research Associate, Calif. Inst. of Technology, 1961–62; Fellow of Wadham Coll., Oxf., 1962–74; Univ. Lectr, Univ. of Oxford, 1966–74. Visiting Prof., Yale Univ., 1969, 1971; Sloan Vis. Prof., Harvard Univ., 1973; Newton-Abraham Vis. Prof., Oxford Univ., 1983–84. Fellow, Amer. Acad. of Arts and Scis, 1982. Charmian Medal, RSC, 1980. *Publications:* research papers and reviews in learned jls. *Address:* 44 Coolidge Avenue, Cambridge, Mass 02138, USA. *T:* (617) 876–8469.

KNOWLES, Hon. Sir Leonard Joseph, Kt 1974; CBE 1963; Chief Justice of the Bahamas, 1973–78; *b* Nassau, 15 March 1916; *s* of late Samuel Joseph Knowles; *m* 1939, Harriet Hansen, *d* of John Hughes, Liverpool; two *s*. *Educ:* Queen's Coll., Nassau, Bahamas; Faculty of Laws, King's Coll., Univ. of London (LLB); first Bahamian student to take and pass Higher Sch. Certif. in Bahamas, 1934; LLB Hons 1937, Cert. of Honour in Final Bar Examinations. Called to the Bar, Gray's Inn, London, 1939; Lord Justice Holker Scholar, Gray's Inn, 1940; practised law in Liverpool for some years. Served War of 1939–45, Royal Air Force (radar). Returned to Nassau, 1948, and was called to local Bar; Attorney-at-Law and Actg Attorney-Gen. of the Bahamas, 1949; Registrar-Gen., 1949–50. Past Stipendiary and Circuit Magistrate. Chm., Labour Board, Bahamas, 1953–63; MLC (Upper House of Legislature), 1960–63; President, Senate, 1964; re-elected, 1967, 1968, and continued to hold that office until 1972. Has always been an active lay preacher. *Publications:* Elements of Bahamian Law; Financial Relief in Matrimonial Cases. *Recreations:* music, motion photography, swimming. *Address:* PO Box SS 6378, Nassau, Bahamas. *Club:* Royal Commonwealth Society.

KNOWLES, Maurice Baxendale, CBE 1952; late Government Actuary's Department; retired 1953; *b* 6 Nov. 1893; *m* 1919, Lilla Shepherdson (decd); one *s* one *d*. *Educ:* Bridlington Sch. Served European War, 1914–18, in 3 London Regt and RFC. *Address:* Janvier, Moor Road, Langham, Colchester, Essex CO4 5NR.

KNOWLES, Michael; MP (C) Nottingham East, since 1983; *b* 21 May 1942; *s* of Martin Christopher and Anne Knowles; *m* 1965, Margaret Isabel Thorburn; three *d*. *Educ:* Clapham Coll. RC Grammar Sch. Sales Manager, Export & Home Sales. Mem. (C), 1971–83, Leader, 1974–83, Kingston upon Thames Borough Council. PPS to Minister for Planning and Regional Affairs, DoT, 1986–. *Recreations:* walking, history. *Address:* 63 Guilford Avenue, Surbiton, Surrey. *T:* 01–399 6449.

KNOWLES, Wyn; Editor, Woman's Hour, BBC, 1971–83; *b* 30 July 1923; *d* of Frederick Knowles and Dorothy Ellen Knowles (*née* Harrison). *Educ:* St Teresa's Convent, Effingham; Convents of FCJ in Ware and Switzerland; Polytechnic Sch. of Art, London. Cypher Clerk, War Office, 1941–45. Secretarial work, 1948–57; joined BBC, 1951; Asst Producer, Drama Dept, 1957–60; Woman's Hour: Producer, Talks Dept, 1960–65; Asst Editor, 1965–67; Dep. Editor, 1967–71. *Publication:* (ed with Kay Evans) The Woman's Hour Book, 1981. *Recreations:* travel, cooking, writing, painting, being a London Zoo Volunteer. *Address:* 80A Parkway, Regent's Park, NW1 7AN. *T:* 01–485 8258.

KNOWLTON, Richard James, CBE 1983; QFSM 1977; HM Chief Inspector of Fire Services (Scotland), since 1984; *b* 2 Jan. 1928; *s* of Richard John Knowlton and Florence May Humby; *m* 1949, Pamela Vera Horne; one *s*. *Educ:* Bishop Wordsworth's Sch., Salisbury. FIFE; FBIM. Served 42 Commando RM, 1945. Southampton Fire Bde, 1948; Station Officer, Worcester City and County Fire Bde, 1959; London Fire Brigade: Asst Divl Officer, 1963; Divl Officer, 1965; Divl Comdr, 1967; Winston Churchill Travelling Fellowship, 1969; Firemaster: SW Area (Scotland) Fire Bde, 1971; Strathclyde Fire Bde, 1975–84. Mem., later Chm., Bds, Fire Service Coll. Extended Interview, 1970–81; Mem.,

Fire Service Coll. Bd, 1978–82; Mem., later Chm., Scottish Fire Services Examinations Panel, 1971–75; Mem., Scottish Fire Service Examinations Bd, 1974–75; Fire Adviser: to Scottish Assoc. of CCs, 1974; to Convention of Scottish Local Authorities, 1975–81; Sec. to Appliances and Equipment Cttee of Chief and Asst Chief Fire Officers Assoc., 1974–81, Pres. of the Assoc., 1980; Chm., Scottish Dist Chief and Asst Chief Fire Officers Assoc., 1977–81; Zone Fire Comdr (Designate), CD for Scotland, 1975–84; Member: Scottish Central Fire Bdes Adv. Council, 1977–81 (Uniform and Personal Equipment Cttee, 1974–82); Jt Cttee on Design and Develt, 1978–82; England and Wales Central Fire Bdes Adv. Council, 1979–81; Chairman: London Branch, Instn of Fire Engineers, 1969; Scottish Assoc., Winston Churchill Fellows, 1979–81; Hazfile Cttee, 1979–81; Vice-Pres., Fire Services Nat. Benevolent Fund, 1981– (Chm. 1980). Mem., Nat. Jt Council for Chief Fire Officers, 1980–82; Mem., later Chm., Management Structures Working Gp of Nat. Jt Council for Local Authority Fire Bdes, 1980–83; British Mem., Admin. Council of European Assoc. of Professional Fire Bde Officers, 1981–85 (Vice Pres., 1984–85). *Address:* Scottish Home and Health Department, St Andrews House, Edinburgh EH1 3DE. *T:* 031–556 8501.

KNOX, family name of **Earl of Ranfurly.**

KNOX, Bryce Harry, CB 1986; a Deputy Chairman, and Director General, Internal Taxation Group, Board of Customs and Excise, since 1983; *b* 21 Feb. 1929; *e s* of Brice Henry Knox and Rose Hetty Knox; *m* Norma, *d* of late George Thomas and of Rose Thomas; one *s*. *Educ:* Stratford Grammar Sch.; Nottingham Univ. BA(Econ). Asst Principal, HM Customs and Excise, 1953; Principal, 1958; on loan to HM Treasury, 1963–65; Asst Sec., HM Customs and Excise, 1966; seconded to HM Diplomatic Service, Counsellor, Office of UK Perm. Rep. to European Communities, 1972–74; Under-Sec., 1974, Comr, 1975, HM Customs and Excise. *Address:* 9 Manor Way, Blackheath, SE3 9EF. *T:* 01–852 9404. *Clubs:* Reform; MCC.

KNOX, Col Bryce Muir, MC 1944 and Bar, 1944; TD 1947; Lord-Lieutenant of Ayr and Arran (formerly County of Ayr), since 1974 (Vice-Lieutenant, 1970–74); Vice-Chairman, Lindustries Ltd, 1979 (Director, 1953–79); *b* 4 April 1916; *s* of late James Knox, Kilbirnie; *m* 1948, Patricia Mary Dunsmuir; one *s* one *d*. *Educ:* Stowe; Trinity Coll., Cambridge. Served with Ayrshire (ECO) Yeomanry, 1939–45, N Africa and Italy; CO, 1953–56; Hon. Col, 1969–71; Hon. Col, The Ayrshire Yeomanry Sqdn, Queen's Own Yeomanry, T&AVR, 1971–77; Pres., Lowlands TA&VRA, 1978–83. Member, Queen's Body Guard for Scotland, Royal Company of Archers. CStJ. *Recreation:* country sports. *Address:* Martnaham Lodge, By Ayr KA6 6ES. *T:* Dalrymple 204. *Club:* Cavalry and Guards.

KNOX, David Laidlaw; MP (C) Staffordshire Moorlands, since 1983 (Leek Division of Staffordshire, 1970–83); *b* 30 May 1933; *s* of late J. M. Knox, Lockerbie and Mrs C. H. C. Knox (*née* Laidlaw); *m* 1980, Mrs Margaret Eva Maxwell, *d* of late A. McKenzie. *Educ:* Lockerbie Academy; Dumfries Academy; London Univ. (BSc (Econ) Hons). Management Trainee, 1953–56; Printing Executive, 1956–62; O&M Consultant, 1962–70. Contested (C): Stechford, Birmingham, 1964 and 1966; Nuneaton, March 1967. PPS to Ian Gilmour, Minister of State for Defence, 1973, Sec. of State for Defence, 1974. Secretary: Cons. Finance Cttee, 1972–73; Cons. Trade Cttee, 1974; Vice-Chm., Cons. Employment Cttee, 1979–80; Chairman: W Midlands Area Young Conservatives, 1963–64; W Midlands Area Cons. Political Centre, 1966–69; a Vice Chairman: Cons. Party Organisation, 1974–75; Cons. Gp for Europe, 1984–86. Editor, Young Conservatives National Policy Group, 1963–64. *Recreations:* watching association football, reading. *Address:* House of Commons, SW1.

KNOX, Prof. Henry Macdonald; Professor of Education, The Queen's University of Belfast, 1951–82; Assessor in Education, University of Strathclyde, since 1984; *b* 26 Nov. 1916; *e s* of Rev. R. M. Knox, Edinburgh, and J. E. Church; *m* 1945, Marian, *yr d* of N. Starkie, Todmorden; one *s* one *d*. *Educ:* George Watson's Coll., Edinburgh; University of Edinburgh. MA 1938; MEd 1940; PhD 1949. Served as Captain, Intelligence Corps, commanding a wireless intelligence section, Arakan sector of Burma, and as instructor, War Office special wireless training wing, 1940–46. Lecturer in Education, University Coll. of Hull, 1946; Lecturer in Education, University of St Andrews, 1949; former Dean of Faculty of Education, and acting Dir, Inst. of Educn, 1968–69, QUB. Sometime Examiner in Educn, Universities of Durham, Leeds, Sheffield, Aberdeen, Glasgow, Strathclyde, Wales and Ireland (National); occasional Examiner, Universities of Edinburgh, Dublin and Bristol. Chm., N Ireland Council for Educn Research, 1979–82; Member: Advisory Council on Educn for N Ireland, 1955–58, 1961–64; Senior Certificate Examination Cttee for N Ireland, 1962–65; Adv. Bd for Postgraduate Studentships in Arts Subjects, Ministry of Educn for N Ireland, 1962–74; Adv. Cttee on Supply and Training of Teachers for NI, 1976–82; NI Council for Educnl Develt, 1980–82. Mem. Governing Body: Stranmillis Coll. of Educn, Belfast, 1968–82 (Vice-Chm., 1975–82); St Joseph's Coll. of Educn, Belfast, 1968–82. *Publications:* Two Hundred and Fifty Years of Scottish Education, 1696–1946, 1953; John Dury's Reformed School, 1958; Introduction to Educational Method, 1961; Schools in Europe (ed W. Schultze): Northern Ireland, 1969; numerous articles in educational journals. *Address:* 9 Elliot Gardens, Colinton, Edinburgh EH14 1EH. *T:* 031–441 6283; Faculty of Arts and Social Studies, University of Strathclyde, Glasgow G1 1XQ. *T:* 041–552 4400.

KNOX, Henry Murray Owen, OBE 1944; Senior Partner, Oxley, Knox & Co., Stockjobbers, retired, 1965; *b* 5 March 1909; *yr s* of late Brig.-Gen. and Mrs H. O. Knox; *m* 1932, Violet Isabel (*d* 1962), *yr d* of late Mr and Mrs Frank Weare, The Dell, Tunbridge Wells, Kent; two *s*; *m* 1963, Mrs E. M. Davidson. *Educ:* Charterhouse; Trinity Coll., Oxford (MA Hons Law). Joined Oxley, Knox & Co., 1930; Partner, 1931. Served War of 1939–45, Queen's Own Royal West Kent Regt (despatches, wounded, OBE); various appts. Staff, ending in Col "A" Organisation, HQ 21 Army Group. Master, Skinners' Company, 1951–52 and 1972–73. Stock Exchange Council, 1948–64; Dep. Chm., Stock Exchange, 1958–64, Actg Chm., 1963–64. Governor, Tonbridge Sch.; formerly: Governor, Charterhouse Sch.; Chm. of Govs, Sutton's Hosp. in Charterhouse. *Recreations:* golf, gardening. *Address:* Brooklands, Manwood Road, Sandwich, Kent.

KNOX, Mrs Jean M.; *see* Swaythling, Lady.

KNOX, John; Under-Secretary, Department of Trade and Industry, retired, 1974; Head of Research Contractors Division, 1972–74; *b* 11 March 1913; *s* of William Knox and May Ferguson; *m* 1942, Mary Blackwood Johnston, *d* of late Rt Hon. Thomas Johnston, CH; one *s* one *d*. *Educ:* Lenzie Acad.; Glasgow Univ. (Kitchener's Schol.; MA). Business Management Trng, 1935–39; joined RAE, 1939; Op. Research with RAF, 1939–45; Asst Chief Scientific Adviser, Min. of Works, 1945–50; Dep. Dir and Dir, Intelligence Div., DSIR, 1950–58; Dep. Dir (Industry), DSIR, 1958–64; Min. of Technology, later DTI: Asst Controller, 1964–65; CSO, Head of External Research and Materials Div., 1965–68; Head of Materials Div., 1968–71; Head of Res. Div., 1971–73. *Publications:* occasional articles on management of research, development and industrial innovation. *Recreation:* golf. *Address:* 6 Mariners Court, Victoria Road, Aldeburgh, Suffolk IP15 5EH. *T:* Aldeburgh 3657.

KNOX, John, RSA 1979 (ARSA 1972); RGI 1980; Head of Painting Studios, Glasgow School of Art, since 1981; *b* 16 Dec. 1936; *s* of Alexander and Jean Knox; *m* 1960, Margaret Kyle Sutherland; one *s* one *d*. *Educ:* Lenzie Acad.; Glasgow Sch. of Art (DA). On the Drawing and Painting Staff at Duncan of Jordanstone Coll. of Art, Dundee, 1965–81. Work in permanent collections: Scottish Nat. Gallery of Modern Art; Arts Council; Contemporary Arts Soc.; Scottish Arts Council; Otis Art Inst., Los Angeles; Olinda Museum, São Paulo; Aberdeen, Dundee and Manchester art galleries; Hunterian Museum, Glasgow. Retrospective exhibn, Knox 1960–83, Scottish Arts Council, 1983. Member: Scottish Arts Council, 1974–79; Trustees Cttee, Scottish Nat. Gallery of Modern Art, 1975–; Bd of Trustees, Nat. Galls of Scotland, 1982–; Bd of Governors, Duncan of Jordanstone Coll. of Art, Dundee, 1980–82; Bd of Governors, Glasgow Sch. of Art, 1985–. *Address:* 31 North Erskine Park, Bearsden, Glasgow.

KNOX, John Andrew; Under Secretary, since 1979, and Head of Industrial Financial Appraisal Division, since 1985, Department of Trade and Industry; *b* 22 July 1937; *s* of late James Telford Knox and of Mary Knox; *m* 1964, Patricia Mary Martin; one *s* one *d*. *Educ:* Dame Allan's Sch., Newcastle upon Tyne; Merton Coll., Oxford (MA). ACA 1964, FCA 1974. Cooper Brothers & Co. Chartered Accountants, 1961–65; Vickers Ltd, 1966–72; entered CS as a Sen. Accountant, 1972; Chief Accountant, 1973; Asst Sec., 1976; Head of Accountancy Services Div., DTI, 1977–85. Leonard Shaw Award for Management Accountancy, Leonard Shaw Meml Fund, 1973. *Recreation:* tennis. *Address:* c/o Department of Trade and Industry, Victoria Street, SW1.

KNOX, Prof. John Henderson, FRS 1984; FRSE 1971; Emeritus Professor of Physical Chemistry, University of Edinburgh, 1984; *b* 21 Oct. 1927; *s* of John Knox and Elizabeth May Knox (*née* Henderson); *m* 1957, Josephine Anne Wissler; four *s*. *Educ:* George Watson's Boys' Coll.; Univ. of Edinburgh (BSc 1949, DSc 1963); Univ. of Cambridge (PhD 1953). University of Edinburgh: Lectr in Chemistry, 1953–66; Reader in Physical Chemistry, 1966–74; Director of Wolfson Liquid Chromatography Unit, 1972–; Personal Prof. of Phys. Chem., 1974–84. Sen. Vis. Research Scientist Fellow, Univ. of Utah, 1963. *Publications:* Gas Chromatography, 1962; Molecular Thermodynamics, 1971, 2nd edn 1978; Applications of High Speed Liquid Chromatography, 1974; High Performance Liquid Chromatography, 1978, 3rd edn 1983. *Recreations:* skiing, sailing, hill walking. *Address:* 67 Morningside Park, Edinburgh EH10 5EZ. *T:* 031–447 5057.

KNOX, Hon. Sir John (Leonard), Kt 1985; **Hon. Mr Justice Knox;** a Judge of the High Court of Justice, Chancery Division, since 1985; *b* 6 April 1925; *s* of Leonard Needham Knox and Berthe Hélène Knox; *m* 1953, Anne Jacqueline Mackintosh; one *s* three *d*. *Educ:* Radley Coll.; Worcester Coll., Oxford (Hon. Mods, 1st Cl.; Jurisprudence, 1st Cl.). Called to the Bar, Lincoln's Inn, 1953, Bencher, 1977; Member, Senate of the Inns of Court, 1975–78. QC 1979; Junior Treasury Counsel: in *bona vacantia*, 1971–79; in probate, 1978–79; Attorney-Gen., Duchy of Lancaster, 1984–85. Member: Lord Chancellor's Law Reform Cttee, 1978–; Council of Legal Educn, 1975–79; Chm., Chancery Bar Assoc., 1985. *Address:* Royal Courts of Justice, Strand, WC2.

KNOX, Robert, MA, MD, FRCP, FRCPath; Emeritus Professor of Bacteriology, University of London (Professor of Bacteriology, Guy's Hospital Medical School, 1949–69); *b* 29 May 1904; *s* of Dr Robert Knox, radiologist; *m* 1936, Bessie Lynda Crust; three *d*. *Educ:* Highgate; Balliol Coll., Oxford (Classical Scholar); St Bartholomew's Hosp. 1st Class Hon. Mods, 1924, 2nd Class Lit Hum, 1926; BA Oxford, 1927; MB, BS London, 1932; MD 1934; MRCS 1932; LRCP 1932, MRCP 1934, FRCP 1953; FCPath, 1964. House Physician and Chief Asst St Bartholomew's Hosp., 1932–35; MA Cambridge 1935; Demonstrator in Pathology, University of Cambridge, 1935–37; Mem. of Scientific Staff, Imperial Cancer Research Fund, 1937–39; Dir of Public Health Laboratories (Med. Research Council) at Stamford, 1939, Leicester 1940, and Oxford, 1945; MA Oxford, 1945. Fellow Royal Society Medicine; Member: Pathological Soc.; Soc. of Gen. Microbiology; Assoc. of Clinical Pathologists. *Publications:* on bacteriological subjects in medical and scientific journals. *Recreations:* coxed Oxford Univ., 1925; golf. *Address:* Five Pines, The Marld, Ashtead, Surrey KT21 1RQ. *T:* Ashtead 75102. *Club:* Athenæum.

KNOX, Hon. Sir William Edward, Kt 1979; FCIT, FAIM; MLA (Lib), Nundah, since 1957; Leader of Parliamentary Liberal Party, Queensland, since 1983; *b* 14 Dec. 1927; *s* of E. Knox, Turramurra; *m* 1956, Doris Ross; two *s* two *d*. *Educ:* Melbourne High School. State Pres., Qld Young Liberals, 1953–56; Vice-Pres., Qld Div., Liberal Party, 1956–57, Mem. Exec., 1953–58, 1962–65; Sec., Parly Lib. Party, 1960–65. Minister for Transport, Qld, 1965–72; Minister for Justice and Attorney-Gen., Qld, 1971–76; Dep. Premier and Treasurer of Qld, 1976–78; Leader, State Parly Liberal Party, 1976–78; Minister for Health, Qld, 1978–80; Minister for Employment and Labour Relations, Qld, 1980–83. Chm., Qld Road Safety Council and Mem., Aust. Transport Adv. Council, 1965–72. Mem., Nat. Exec. Aust. Jnr Chamber of Commerce, 1961–62; Senator Jnr Chamber Internat., 1962–; State Pres., Father and Son Movement, 1965; Chm., St John Council for Qld, 1983–. *Address:* 1621 Sandgate Road, Nundah, Queensland 4012, Australia.

KNOX-JOHNSTON, Robin, (William Robert Patrick Knox-Johnston), CBE 1969; RD 1983; Marina Consultant since 1974; *b* 17 March 1939; *s* of late David Robert Knox-Johnston and Elizabeth Mary Knox-Johnston (*née* Cree); *m* 1962, Suzanne (*née* Singer); one *d*. *Educ:* Berkhamsted School. Master Mariner; FRGS. Merchant Navy, 1957–67. First person to sail single-handed non-stop Around the World 14 June 1968 to 22 April 1969, in yacht Suhaili; won Sunday Times Golden Globe, 1969; won Round Britain Race, Ocean Spirit, 1970; won round Britain Race, British Oxygen, 1974; set British transatlantic sailing record, from NY to the Lizard, 11 days 7 hours 45 mins, 1981; established new record of 10 days 14 hours 9 mins, 1986; set world sailing record for around Ireland, 76 hours 5 mins 34 secs, May 1986; World Class II Multihull Champion, 1985. Man. Dir, St Katharine's Yacht Haven Ltd, 1975–76; Director: Mercury Yacht Harbours Ltd, 1970–73; Rank Marine International, 1973–75; Troon Marina Ltd, 1976–83; National Yacht Racing Centre Ltd, 1979–; Knox-Johnston Insurance Brokers Ltd, 1983–. Pres., British Olympic Yachting Appeal, 1977–; Mem. Cttee of Management, RNLI, 1983–. Freeman, Borough of Bromley, Kent, 1969; Younger Brother, Trinity House, 1973. Mem., Co. of Master Mariners, 1975. Lt-Comdr RNR 1971. Yachtsman of the Year, 1969. *Publications:* A World of my Own, 1969; Sailing, 1975; Twilight of Sail, 1978; Last but not Least, 1978; Bunkside Companion, 1982. *Recreation:* sailing. *Address:* 26 Sefton Street, Putney, SW15. *Clubs:* Naval, Royal Cruising, Royal Ocean Racing.

KNOX-MAWER, Ronald; retired; *b* 3 Aug. 1925; *s* of George Robert Knox-Mawer and Clare Roberts; *m* 1951, June Ellis; one *s* one *d*. *Educ:* Grove Park Sch.; Emmanuel Coll., Cambridge (MA). Royal Artillery, 1943–47. Called to Bar, Middle Temple; Wales and Chester Circuit, 1947–52; Chief Magistrate and Actg Chief Justice, Aden, 1952–58; Sen. Magistrate, Puisne Judge, Justice of Appeal, Actg Chief Justice, Fiji, and conjointly Chief Justice, Nauru and Tonga, 1958–71; Northern Circuit, 1971–75; Metropolitan Stipendiary Magistrate, 1975–84. *Publications:* Palm Court, 1979 (as Robert Overton); short stories (under different pseudonyms) in Punch, Cornhill, Argosy, The Times, Sunday Express, Blackwoods, Listener etc. *Recreation:* countryside. *Address:* c/o Midland Bank, Ruabon, N Wales. *Club:* Royal Commonwealth Society.

KNUDSEN, Semon Emil; retired; Chairman and Chief Executive, White Motor Corporation, 1971–80; *b* 2 Oct. 1912; *o s* of William S. and Clara Euler Knudsen; *m* 1938, Florence Anne McConnell; one *s* three *d*. *Educ:* Dartmouth Coll.; Mass Inst. of Technology. Joined General Motors, 1939; series of supervisory posts; Gen. Man., Detroit Diesel Div., 1955; Gen. Man., Pontiac Motor Div., 1956; Gen. Man., Chevrolet Motor Div., 1961; Dir of General Motors and Gp Vice-Pres. i/c of all Canadian and overseas activities, 1965; Exec. Vice-Pres. with added responsibility for domestic non-automotive divs, 1966, also defense activities, 1967; resigned from Gen. Motors Corp., 1968; Pres., Ford Motor Co., 1968–69. Director: Michigan National Corp.; First National Bank in Palm Beach. Mem., MIT Corp. Mem. Bd of Dirs, Boys Clubs of Amer.; Trustee, Oakland (Mich) Univ. Foundn and Cleveland Clinic Fund. *Recreations:* golf, tennis, deepsea fishing, hunting. *Address:* 1700 N Woodward, Suite E, Bloomfield Hills, Mich 48013, USA. *Clubs:* Detroit Athletic (Detroit); Bloomfield Hills Country (Mich); Everglades, Seminole (Fla); Augusta National (Ga).

KNUSSEN, (Stuart) Oliver; composer and conductor; Co-Artistic Director, Aldeburgh Festival, since 1983; *b* Glasgow, 12 June 1952; *s* of Stuart Knussen and Ethelyn Jane Alexander; *m* 1972, Susan Freedman; one *d*. *Educ:* Watford Field Sch.; Watford Boys Grammar Sch.; Purcell Sch. Private composition study with John Lambert, 1963–68; Countess of Munster Awards, 1964, 1965, 1967; Peter Stuyvesant Foundn Award, 1965; début conducting Symph. no 1 with LSO, 1968; Watney-Sargent award for Young Conductors, 1969; Fellowships to Berkshire Music Center, Tanglewood, 1970, 1971, 1973; Caird Trav. Schol., 1971; Margaret Grant Composition Prize (Symph. no 2), Tanglewood, 1971; study with Gunther Schuller in USA, 1970–73; Koussevitzky Centennial Commn, 1974; Composer-in-residence: Aspen Fest., 1976; Arnolfini Gall., 1978; Instr in composition, RCM Jun. Dept, 1977–82; BBC commn for Proms 1979 (Symph. no 3); Guest Teacher, Berkshire Music Center, Tanglewood, 1981; Arts Council Bursaries, 1979, 1981; winner, first Park Lane Gp Composer award (suite from Where the Wild Things Are), 1982; BBC commn for Glyndebourne Opera, 1983. Composer-in-residence, Philharmonia Orch., 1984–. Frequent guest conductor: London Sinfonietta, Philharmonia Orch., many other ensembles, UK and abroad, 1981–. Mem. Executive Cttee, Soc. for Promotion of New Music, 1978–85; Member: Leopold Stokowski Soc.; International Alban Berg Soc., New York. Principal publisher, Faber Music Ltd. *Publications:* Symphony no 1 op. 1, 1966–67; Symphony no 2 op. 7, 1970–71; Symphony no 3 op. 18, 1973–79; Where the Wild Things Are—opera (Maurice Sendak), op. 20, 1979–83 (staged, Glyndebourne at NT, 1984); Higglety Pigglety Pop!—opera (Sendak), op. 21, 1983–85 (staged Glyndebourne, 1984 and 1985); numerous orchestral, chamber, vocal works; articles in Tempo, The Listener, etc. *Recreations:* cinema, foreign literature, record collecting, record producing. *Address:* Flat 3, 167 West End Lane, NW6 2LG.

KNUTSFORD, 6th Viscount *cr* 1895; **Michael Holland-Hibbert;** Bt 1853; Baron 1888; DL; *b* 27 Dec. 1926; *s* of Hon. Wilfrid Holland-Hibbert (*d* 1961) (2nd *s* of 3rd Viscount) and of Audrey, *d* of late Mark Fenwick; *S* cousin, 1986; *m* 1951, Hon. Sheila, *d* of 5th Viscount Portman; two *s* one *d*. *Educ:* Eton College; Trinity Coll., Cambridge (BA). SW Regional Director, Barclays Bank, 1956–86. National Trust: Chm. Cttee for Devon and Cornwall, 1973–86; Mem. Exec. Cttee, 1973–86; Mem. Council, 1979–85. DL 1977, High Sheriff 1977–78, Devon. *Heir: er s* Hon. Henry Thurstan Holland-Hibbert, *b* 6 April 1959. *Address:* Broadclyst House, Exeter, Devon EX5 3EW. *T:* Exeter 61244. *Club:* Brooks's.

KNUTTON, Maj.-Gen. Harry, CB 1975; MSc, CEng, FIEE; Director-General, City and Guilds of London Institute, 1976–85; *b* Rawmarsh, Yorks, 26 April 1921; *m* 1958, Pamela Brackley, E Sheen, London; three *s* one *d*. *Educ:* Wath-upon-Dearne Grammar Sch.; RMCS. Commnd RA, 1943; served with 15th Scottish and 1st Airborne Divs, NW Europe, 1944–45; India, 1945–47; Instructor in Gunnery, 1946–49; Project Officer, Min. of Supply, 1949–51; served Middle East, 1953–55; Directing Staff, RMCS, 1955–58; jssc 1958; various staff appts, MoD, 1958–60, 1962–64, 1966–67; Comdr Missile Regt, BAOR, 1964–66; Comdr Air Defence Bde, 1967–69; Fellow, Loughborough Univ. of Technology, 1969–70; Dir-Gen. Weapons (Army), 1970–73; Dir, Royal Ordnance Factories and Dep. Master-Gen. of Ordnance, 1973–75; retd. Col Comdt, RA, 1977–82. Teacher, Whitgift Foundn, 1975–76. Member: Associated Examining Bd, 1976–85; Dep. Chm., Standing Conf. on Schools' Science and Technology, 1983–. Governor, Imperial Coll. of Science and Technology, 1976–. FCollP 1983. Liveryman, Engineers' Co. *Address:* 43 Essendene Road, Caterham, Surrey. *T:* Caterham 47278.

KOCH, Edward Irving; Mayor, City of New York, since 1978; *b* 12 Dec. 1924; *s* of Louis Koch and Joyce Silpe. *Educ:* Southside High School, Newark, NJ; City Coll. of NY; NY Univ. Law Sch. Served US Army, 1943–46, USA, France, Rhineland. Mem., NY State Bar, 1949; private law practice, 1949–64; Senior Partner, Koch, Lankenau, Schwartz & Kovner, 1965–69. Democratic dist. leader, Greenwich Village, 1963–65; Mem., NY City Council, 1967–68; NY Congressman, 1969–77. *Publications:* Mayor, 1983; Politics, 1985. *Address:* (home) 14 Washington Place, New York, NY 10003, USA; (office) City Hall, New York, NY 10007, USA.

KOECHLIN-SMYTHE, Patricia Rosemary, OBE 1956; President, British Show Jumping Association, 1983–86; Member of British Show Jumping Team, 1947–64; *b* 22 Nov. 1928; *d* of late Capt. Eric Hamilton Smythe, MC, Légion d'Honneur, and late Frances Monica Smythe (*née* Curtoys); *m* 1963, Samuel Koechlin (*d* 1985), Switzerland; two *d*. *Educ:* St Michael's Sch., Cirencester; Talbot Heath, Bournemouth. Show Jumping: first went abroad with British Team, 1947; Leading Show Jumper of the Year, 1949, 1958 (with T. Edgar), and 1962; European Ladies' Championship: Spa, 1957; Deauville, 1961; Madrid, 1962; Hickstead, 1963; Harringay: BSJA Spurs, 1949, 1951, 1952, 1954 (Victor Ludorum Championship), 1953 and 1954; Harringay Spurs, 1953; Grand Prix, Brussels, 1949, 1952 and 1956. Ladies' record for high jump (2 m. 10 cm.) Paris, 1950; won in Madrid, 1951. White City: 1951 (Country Life Cup); 1953 (Selby Cup). Was Leading Rider and won Prix du Champion, Paris, 1952; Leading Rider, etc, Marseilles, 1953; Individual Championship, etc, Harrisburg, Penn, USA, 1953; Pres. of Mexico Championship, New York, 1953; Toronto (in team winning Nations Cup), 1953; Lisbon (won 2 events), Grand Prix, Madrid, and Championship, Vichy, 1954; Grand Prix de Paris and 3 other events, 1954; Bruxelles Puissance and new ladies' record for high jump (2m. 20 cm.), Leading Rider of Show, 1954; BHS Medal of Honour, Algiers Puissance and Grand Prix, 4 events in Paris, 4 events at White City including the Championship, 1955; Grand Prix and Leading Rider of Show and 4 other events, Brussels, 1956; Grand Prix Militaire and Puissance, Lucerne; Mem. British Equestrian Olympic Team, Stockholm (Show Jumping Bronze Medal), 1956; IHS National Championship, White City; Leading Rider and other events, Palermo, 1956; won 2 Puissance events, Paris, 1957; BSJA, 1957; Ladies' National Championship in 1954–59 and 1961 and 1962 (8 times); Daily Mail Cup, White City, 1955, 1957, 1960, 1962; Mem. winning British Team, White City: 1952, 1953, 1956, 1957; Amazon Prize, Aachen, 1958; Queen's Cup, Royal Internat. Horse Show, White City, 1958; Preis von Parsenn, Davos, 1957, 1958, 1959; Championship Cup, Brussels Internat. Horse Show, 1958; Lisbon Grand Prix, 1959; Olympic Trial, British Timken Show, and Prix de la Banque de Bruxelles at Brussels, 1959. Lucerne Grand Prix; Prince Hal Stakes, Country Life and Riding Cup, White City; Pembroke Stakes, Horse Show Cttee Cup, and Leading Rider, Dublin (all in 1960). Mem. British Olympic Team in Rome, 1960. Copenhagen Grand Prix; Amazon Prize, Aachen; John Player Trophy, White City; St Gall Ladies Championship (all in 1961); Saddle of Honour and Loriners' Cup, White City, 1962; British Jumping Derby, Hickstead, 1962. Internat. Council Mem., World Wildlife Fund. Hon. Freeman, Worshipful Co. of Farriers, 1955; Freeman of the City of London, 1956; Hon. Freeman, Worshipful Company of Loriners, 1962; Yeoman, Worshipful Company of Saddlers, 1963. *Publications:* (as Pat Smythe): Jump for Joy; Pat Smythe's Story, 1954; Pat Smythe's Book of Horses, 1955; One Jump Ahead, 1956; Jacqueline rides for a Fall, 1957; Three Jays against the Clock, 1957; Three Jays on Holiday, 1958; Three Jays go to Town, 1959; Horses and Places, 1959; Three Jays over the Border, 1960; Three Jays go to Rome, 1960; Three Jays Lend a Hand, 1961; Jumping Round the World, 1962; Florian's Farmyard, 1962; Flanagan My Friend, 1963; Bred to Jump, 1965; Show Jumping, 1967; (with Fiona Hughes) A Pony for Pleasure, 1969; A Swiss Adventure, 1970; (with Fiona Hughes) Pony Problems, 1971; A Spanish Adventure, 1971; A Cotswold Adventure, 1972. *Recreations:* tennis, swimming, music, ski-ing, sailing, all sports, languages. *Address:* Sudgrove House, Miserden, near Stroud, Glos. *T:* Miserden 360; Im Steinacker, 4117 Burg-im-Leimental, BE, Switzerland. *T:* Basle 751411.

KOENIGSBERGER, Prof. Helmut Georg, MA, PhD; Professor of History, King's College London, 1973–84, now Emeritus; *b* 24 Oct. 1918; *s* of late Georg Felix Koenigsberger, chief architect, borough of Treptow, Berlin, Germany, and of late Käthe Koenigsberger (*née* Born); *m* 1961, Dorothy M. Romano; two *d* (twins). *Educ:* Adams' Grammar Sch., Newport, Shropshire; Gonville and Caius Coll., Cambridge. Asst Master: Brentwood Sch., Essex, 1941–42; Bedford Sch., 1942–44. Served War of 1939–45, Royal Navy, 1944–45. Lecturer in Economic History, QUB, 1948–51; Senior Lecturer in Economic History, University of Manchester, 1951–60; Prof. of Modern History, University of Nottingham, 1960–66; Prof. of Early Modern European History, Cornell, 1966–73. Visiting Lecturer: Brooklyn Coll., New York, 1957; University of Wisconsin, 1958; Columbia University, 1962; Cambridge Univ., 1963; Washington Univ., St Louis, 1964; Fellow, Historisches Kolleg, Munich, 1984–85. Sec., 1955–75, Vice-Pres., 1975–80, Pres., 1980–85, Internat. Commn for the History of Representative and Parliamentary Institutions; Vice-Pres., RHistS, 1982–85. *Publications:* The Government of Sicily under Philip II of Spain, 1951, new edn, as The Practice of Empire, 1969; The Empire of Charles V in Europe (in New Cambridge Modern History II), 1958; Western Europe and the Power of Spain (in New Cambridge Modern History III), 1968; Europe in the Sixteenth Century (with G. L. Mosse), 1968; Estates and Revolutions, 1971; The Habsburgs and Europe, 1516–1660, 1971; (ed) Luther: a profile, 1972; Politicians and Virtuosi, 1986; Medieval Europe, 1987; Early Modern Europe, 1987; (ed) Republics and Republicanism in Early Modern Europe, 1987; contrib. to historical journals. *Recreations:* playing chamber music, sailing, travel. *Address:* 41A Lancaster Grove, NW3.

KOGAN, Prof. Maurice; Professor of Government and Social Administration, Brunel University, since 1969; *b* 10 April 1930; *s* of Barnett and Hetty Kogan; *m* 1960, Ulla Svensson; two *s*. *Educ:* Stratford Grammar Sch.; Christ's Coll., Cambridge (MA). Entered Civil Service, admin. cl. (1st in open examinations), 1953. Secretary: Secondary Sch. Exams Council, 1961; Central Advisory Council for Educn (England), 1963–66; Harkness Fellow of Commonwealth Fund, 1960–61. Asst Sec., DES, 1966. Member: Educn Sub-Cttee, Univ. Grants Cttee, 1972–75; SSRC, 1975–77; Davies Cttee on Hosp. Complaints' Procedure, 1971; Houghton Cttee on Teachers' Pay, 1974; Genetic Manipulation Adv. Gp, 1979–; Head of School, Sch. of Social Sciences, Brunel Univ., 1971–74. George A. Miller Vis. Prof., Univ. of Illinois, 1976; Vis. Scholar, Univ. of Calif, Berkeley, 1981. *Publications:* The Organisation of a Social Services Department, 1971; Working Relationships within the British Hospital Service, 1971; The Government of Education, 1971; The Politics of Education, 1971; (ed) The Challenge of Change, 1973; County Hall, 1973; Advisory Councils and Committees in Education, 1974; Educational Policy-Making, 1975; The Politics of Educational Change, 1978; The Working of the National Health Service, 1978; (with T. Becher) Process and Structure in Higher Education, 1980; The Government's Commissioning of Research, 1980; (with T. Bush) Directors of Education, 1982; (with D. Kogan) The Battle for the Labour Party, 1982; (with M. Henkel) Government and Research, 1983; (with D. Kogan) The Attack on Higher Education, 1983; (with T. Husen) Educational Research and Policy: how do they relate?, 1984; (with D. Johnson and others) School Governing Bodies, 1984; Education Accountability, 1986; contribs to TES, THES, Jl of Social Policy. *Recreations:* reading, listening to music. *Address:* 48 Duncan Terrace, Islington, N1 8AL. *T:* 01–226 0038.

KOHL, Helmut; Chancellor, Federal Republic of Germany, since 1982; Chairman, Christian Democratic Union of Germany, since 1973; Member, Bundestag, since 1976; *b* 3 April 1930; *s* of Hans and Cecilie Kohl; *m* 1960, Hannelore Renner; two *s*. *Educ:* Frankfurt Univ.; Heidelberg Univ. (Dr phil 1958 Heidelberg). On staff of a Trade Assoc., 1958–59; Mem., Parlt of Rhineland Palatinate, 1959; Leader, CDU Parly Party in Rhineland Palatinate Parlt, 1963–69; Mem., Federal Exec. Cttee of CDU at federal level, 1964–; Chm., CDU, Rhineland Palatinate, 1966–73; Minister-President, Rhineland Palatinate, 1969–76; Leader of the Opposition, Bundestag, 1976–82. *Publications:* Hausputz hinter den Fassaden, 1971; Zwischen Ideologie und Pragmatismus, 1973. *Address:* Bundeskanzleramt, Adenauerallee 139, 53 Bonn 1, West Germany; 6700 Ludwigshafen/Rhein, Marbacher Strasse 11, W Germany.

KOHLER, Foy David; Associate, Advanced International Studies Institute; consultant, 1978–85; *b* 15 Feb. 1908; *s* of Leander David Kohler and Myrtle McClure; *m* 1935, Phyllis Penn. *Educ:* Toledo and Ohio State Univs, Ohio. US Foreign Service 1932–67: posts include: Amer. Emb., London, 1944; 1st Sec. Amer. Emb., Moscow, 1947; Counselor, 1948; Minister, Oct. 1948; Chief, Internat. Broadcasting Div., Dept of State, 1949; VOA 1949; Asst Administr, Internat. Information Admin, 1952; Policy Planning Staff, Dept of State, 1952; Counselor, Amer. Emb., Ankara, Turkey, 1953–56; detailed ICA, 1956–58; Deputy Asst Sec. of State for European Affairs, 1958–59; Asst Sec. of State, 1959–62; US Ambassador to USSR, 1962–66; Deputy Under-Sec. of State for Political Affairs, United States, 1966–67; Career Ambassador, USA, 1966. Prof., Univ. of Miami, 1968–80. Editor, Soviet World Outlook, 1976–85. Holds honorary doctorates. *Publications:* Understanding the Russians: a citizen's primer, 1970; (jtly) Soviet Strategy for the Seventies: from Cold War to peaceful coexistence, 1973; (jtly) The Role of Nuclear Forces in Current Soviet Strategy, 1974; (jtly) The Soviet Union: yesterday, today, tomorrow, 1975; Custine's Eternal Russia, 1976; Salt II: how not to negotiate with the Russians, 1979. *Recreations:* golf, swimming. *Address:* 215 Golf Club Circle, Tequesta, Fla 33469, USA.

KOHLER, Irene; pianist; Professor, Trinity College of Music, London, 1952–79; *b* London; *m* 1950, Dr Harry Waters, medical practitioner. *Educ:* Royal College of Music. Studied with Arthur Benjamin; Challen Medal, Danreuther Prize, etc; travelling scholarship to Vienna; studied there with Edward Steuermann and Egon Wellesz. BMus; Hon. FTCL, GRSM, LRAM, ARCM. First professional engagement, Bournemouth, 1933, resulting in engagement by BBC; played at first night of 40th Promenade Season, 1934. First foreign tour (recitals and broadcasts), Holland, 1938. During War of 1939–45 gave concerts for the Forces in this country and toured France and Belgium, also India and Burma, under auspices of ENSA; subsequently played in many countries of Europe and made tours. Eugene Goossens selected her for first European performance of his Phantasy Concerto; broadcast 1st performance of Sonata by Gunilla Lowenstein, Stockholm. She gave 3 concerts at the Festival Hall in Festival of Britain Year, 1951. Canadian American Tour, 1953; World Tour, 1955–56; African Tour, 1958; 2nd African Tour, 1959; Bulgarian Tour, 1959; 2nd World Tour, 1962; Czechoslovakian Tour, 1963; Scandinavian Tour, 1970; Far and Middle East Tour, 1972; recitals and master classes, Japan, 1979, 1981; Polish Tour, 1980. Film appearances include: Train of Events, Odette, Secret People, Lease of Life, and a documentary for the Ministry of Information. *Address:* 28 Castelnau, SW13 9RU. *T:* 01–748 5512.

KOHNSTAM, George, PhD; Principal of the Graduate Society, University of Durham, 1981–86 (Deputy Principal, 1972–81); Reader in Physical Chemistry, University of Durham, 1962–86; *b* 25 Dec. 1920; *s* of Emil and Margaret Kohnstam; *m* 1953, Patricia Elizabeth, *d* of Rev. A. W. G. Duffield and Margaret Duffield; one *s* three *d*. *Educ:* Royal Grammar Sch., High Wycombe; University Coll. London (BSc 1940, PhD 1948). Tuffnel Scholar, Univ. of London, 1940 (postponed); applied chemical res., 1941–45; Temp. Asst Lectr in Chemistry, UCL, 1948–50; Lectr in Phys. Chem., Univ. of Durham, 1950–59, Sen. Lectr, 1959–62. *Publications:* papers and review articles in chemical jls. *Recreations:* dinghy sailing, gardening, bridge, travel. *Address:* 67 Hallgarth Street, Durham City DH1 3AY. *T:* Durham 42018.

KOHNSTAMM, Max; Comdr of the Order of Orange-Nassau, 1981; Comdr of the Order of House of Orange, 1949; Secretary-General Action Committee for Europe, since 1985; *b* 22 May 1914; *s* of Dr Philip Abraham Kohnstamm and Johanna Hermana Kessler; *m* 1944, Kathleen Sillem; two *s* three *d*. *Educ:* Univ. of Amsterdam (Hist. Drs); American Univ., Washington. Private Sec. to Queen Wilhelmina, 1945–48; subseq. Head of German Bureau, then Dir of European Affairs, Netherlands FO; Sec. of High Authority, 1952–56; 1st Rep. of High Authority, London, 1956; Sec.-Gen. (later Vice-Pres.), Action Cttee for United States of Europe, 1956–75; Pres., European Community Inst. for Univ. Studies, 1958–75; Principal, Eur. Univ. Inst. of Florence, 1975–81. Co-Chm., Cttee on Soc. Develt and Peace, World Council of Churches and Pontifical Commn for Justice and Peace, 1967–75; European Pres., Trilateral Commn, 1973–75. Grande Ufficiale dell' Ordine Al Merito della Repubblica Italiana, 1981; Grosse Verdienstkreuz, Bundesrepublik Deutschland, 1982. *Publications:* The European Community and its Role in the World, 1963; (ed jtly) A Nation Writ Large?, 1972. *Recreations:* tennis, walking. *Address:* 5560 Ciergnon-Fenffe, Belgium. *T:* (84) 37 71 83.

KOHOBAN-WICKREME, Alfred Silva, CVO 1954; Member Ceylon Civil Service; Secretary to the Cabinet, 1968–70; *b* 2 Nov. 1914; *m* 1941, Mona Estelle Kohoban-Wickreme. *Educ:* Trinity Coll., Kandy; University Coll., Colombo. BA (Hons) London, 1935. Cadet, Ceylon Civil Service, 1938; served as Magistrate, District Judge, Asst Govt Agent etc, until 1948; Chief Admin. Officer, Ceylon Govt Rly, 1948; Asst Sec., Min. of Home Affairs, 1951; attached to Ceylon High Commissioner's Office in UK, May-July, 1953; Dir of Social Services and Commissioner for Workmen's Compensation, Ceylon, 1953; Conservator of Forests, Ceylon, 1958; Port Commissioner, Ceylon, 1959; Postmaster General and Dir of Telecommunications, Dec. 1962; Permanent Sec., Ministry of: Local Govt and Home Affairs, April 1964; Cultural Affairs and Social Services, June 1964; Ministry of Communications, 1965. Organised the Queen's Tour in Ceylon, April 1954 (CVO). *Recreations:* sports activities, particularly Rugby football, tennis and cricket. *Address:* 6 Kalinga Place, Jawatta Road, Colombo 5, Sri Lanka. *T:* (residence) 86385.

KOHT, Paul; Ambassador of Norway to Denmark, 1975–82; *b* 7 Dec. 1913; *s* of Dr Halvdan Koht and Karen Elisabeth (*née* Grude); *m* 1938, Grete Sverdrup; two *s* one *d*. *Educ:* University of Oslo. Law degree, 1937. Entered Norwegian Foreign Service, 1938; held posts in: Bucharest, 1938–39; London, 1940–41; Tokyo, 1941–42; New York, 1942–46; Lisbon, 1950–51; Mem. Norwegian Delegn to OEEC and NATO, Paris, and Perm. Rep. to Coun. of Europe, 1951–53; Dir General of Dept for Econ. Affairs, Min. of For. Affairs, Oslo, 1953–56; Chargé d'Affaires, Copenhagen, 1956–58; Ambassador to USA, 1958–63; Ambassador to Fed. Republic of Germany, 1963–68; Ambassador to the Court of St James's, 1968–75. Comdr, Order of St Olav; Grand Cross, Order of Dannebrog; Grand Cross, Order of Merit (Federal Republic of Germany). *Address:* Lille Frogner Allé 4b, Oslo 2, Norway.

KOLAKOWSKI, Leszek, PhD, FBA 1980; Senior Research Fellow, All Souls College, Oxford, since 1970; *b* 23 Oct. 1927; *s* of Jerzy and Lucyna (*née* Pietrusiewicz); *m* 1949, Dr Tamara Kołakowska (*née* Dynenson); one *d*. *Educ:* Łódź Univ., Poland 1945–50; Warsaw Univ. (PhD 1953). Asst in Philosophy: Łódź Univ., 1947–49; Warsaw Univ., 1950–59; Prof. and Chm., Section of History of Philosophy, Warsaw Univ., 1959–68, expelled by authorities for political reasons; Visiting Professor: McGill Univ., 1968–69; Univ. of California, Berkeley, 1969–70; Yale Univ., Conn, 1975. McArthur Fellowship, 1983. Mem. Internat. Inst. of Philosophy; Foreign Mem., Amer. Academy of Arts and Science; Mem.-correspondent, Bayerische Akademie des Künste. Hon. Dr Lit. Hum Bard Coll., 1984; Hon. LLD Reed Coll., 1985. Friedenpreis des Deutschen Buchhandels, 1977; Jurzykowski Foundn award, 1968; Charles Veillou Prix Européen d'Essai, 1980; (jtly) Erasmus Prize, 1984; Jefferson Award, 1986. *Publications:* about 30 books, some of them only in Polish; trans. of various books in 14 languages; *in English:* Marxism and Beyond, 1968; Conversations with the Devil, 1972; Positivist Philosophy, 1972; Husserl and the Search for Certitude, 1975; Main Currents of Marxism, 3 vols, 1978; Religion, 1982; Bergson, 1985; *in French:* Chrétiens sans Eglise, 1969; *in German:* Traktat über die Sterblichkeit der Vernunft, 1967; Geist und Ungeist christlicher Traditionen, 1971; Die Gegenwärtigkeit des Mythos, 1973; Der revolutionäre Geist, 1972; Leben trotz Geschichte Lesebuch, 1977; Zweifel und die Methode, 1977. *Address:* 77 Hamilton Road, Oxford OX2 7QA. *T:* Oxford 58790.

KOLO, Sule; Chairman, Alheri Enterprises; Executive Director, Rainone-Washik Construction Co.; Consultant, Knight Frank & Rutley (Nigeria); High Commissioner for Nigeria in London, 1970–75; *b* 1926; *m* 1957, Helen Patricia Kolo; two *s* four *d*. BSc (Econ); attended Imperial Defence College. Counsellor, Nigerian High Commn in London, 1962; Perm. Sec., Nigerian Min. of Defence, 1963; Perm. Sec., Nigerian Min. of Trade, 1966; Nigeria's Perm. Representative to European Office of UN and Ambassador to Switzerland, 1966; Chm. of GATT, 1969. Pres., Lions Club Internat. Dist 404, Nigeria. FREconS; FRSA 1973. Franklin Peace Medal, 1969. *Recreations:* swimming, tennis. *Address:* PO Box 1453, Jos, Nigeria. *Clubs:* Travellers'; Island (Lagos).

KOLTAI, Ralph, CBE 1983; freelance stage designer; designer for Drama, Opera and Dance, since 1950; Associate Designer, Royal Shakespeare Company, 1963–66 and since 1976; *b* 31 July 1924; Hungarian-German; *s* of Dr(med) Alfred Koltai and Charlotte Koltai (*née* Weinstein); *m* 1956, Annena Stubbs. *Educ:* Central Sch. of Art and Design (Dip. with Dist.). Early work entirely in field of opera. First production, Angelique, for London Opera Club, Fortune Theatre, 1950. Designs for The Royal Opera House, Sadler's Wells, Scottish Opera, National Welsh Opera, The English Opera Group. First of 7 ballets for Ballet Rambert, Two Brothers, 1958. *Productions:* RSC: The Caucasian Chalk Circle, 1962; The Representative, 1963; The Birthday Party; Endgame; The Jew of Malta, 1964; The Merchant of Venice; Timon of Athens, 1965; Little Murders, 1967; Major Barbara, 1970; Too True To Be Good, 1975; Old World, 1976; Wild Oats, 1977; The Tempest, Love's Labour's Lost, 1978; Hippolytus, Baal, 1979; Romeo and Juliet, Hamlet, 1980; The Love Girl and the Innocent, 1981 (London Drama Critics Award); Much Ado About Nothing, Molière, 1982; Custom of the Country, Cyrano de Bergerac (SWET Award), 1983; Troilus and Cressida, Othello, 1985; for National Theatre: an "all male" As You Like It, 1967; Back to Methuselah, 1969; State of Revolution, 1977; Brand (SWET Award), The Guardsman, 1978; Richard III, The Wild Duck, 1979; Man and Superman, 1981; *other notable productions include:* for Sadler's Wells/English National Opera: The Rise and Fall of the City of Mahagonny, 1963; From the House of the Dead, 1965; Bluebeard's Castle, 1972; Wagner's (complete) Ring Cycle, 1973; Seven Deadly Sins, 1978; Anna Karenina, 1981; for The Royal Opera House: Taverner, 1972; The Ice Break, 1977; for Sydney Opera House: Tannhäuser, 1973; for Netherlands Opera: Wozzeck, 1973; Billy, Drury Lane, 1974; Fidelio, Munich, 1974; Verdi's Macbeth, Edinburgh Festival, 1976; for Aalborg Theatre, Denmark: Threepenny Opera, 1979; The Love Girl and the Innocent, 1980; Terra Nova, 1981; The Carmelites, 1981; Mahagonny, 1984; Les Soldats, Lyon Opera, 1983; Bugsy Malone, Her Majesty's, 1983; Pack of Lies, Lyric, 1983; Dear Anyone, Cambridge, 1983; Italian Girl in Algiers, 1984, Tannhäuser, 1986, Geneva; Across from the Garden of Allah, Comedy, 1986; (also dir.) Flying Dutchman, Hong Kong, 1987; has worked in most countries in Western Europe, also Bulgaria, Argentine, USA, Canada, Australia. London Drama Critics Award, Designer of the Year, 1967 (for Little Murders and As You Like It); (jtly) Gold Medal, Internat. Exhibn of Stage Design, Prague Quadriennale, 1975, 1979. *Recreation:* wildlife photography. *Address:* c/o Macnaughton Lowe Representation Ltd, 200 Fulham Road, SW10. *T:* 01–351 5442.

KOMINSKI, Daniel; *see* Kaye, Danny.

KONSTANT, Rt. Rev. David Every; *see* Leeds, Bishop of, (RC).

KOOTENAY, Bishop of, since 1971; **Rt. Rev. Robert Edward Fraser Berry;** *b* Ottawa, Ont; *s* of Samuel Berry and Claire Hartley; *m* 1951, Margaret Joan Trevorrow Baillie; one *s* one *d*. *Educ:* Sir George Williams Coll., Montreal; McGill Univ., Montreal; Montreal Diocesan Theological Coll. Assistant, Christ Church Cathedral, Victoria, BC, 1953–55; Rector: St Margaret's, Hamilton, Ont, 1955–61; St Mark's, Orangeville, Ont, 1961–63; St Luke's, Winnipeg, Manitoba, 1963–67; St Michael and All Angels, Kelowna, BC, 1967–71. Hon. DD, Montreal Diocesan Theol Coll., 1973. *Address:* (home) 1857 Maple Street, Kelowna, BC V1Y 1H4, Canada. *T:* (604) 762–2923; (office) Box 549, Kelowna, BC V1Y 7P2, Canada. *T:* (604) 762–3306.

KOPAL, Prof. Zdeněk; Professor of Astronomy, University of Manchester, 1951–81, now Emeritus; *b* 4 April 1914; 2nd *s* of Prof. Joseph Kopal, of Charles University, Prague, and Ludmila (*née* Lelek); *m* 1938, Alena, *o d* of late Judge B. Muldner; three *d*. *Educ:* Charles University, Prague; University of Cambridge, England; Harvard Univ., USA. Agassiz Research Fellow, Harvard Observatory, 1938–40; Research Associate in Astronomy, Harvard Univ., 1940–46; Lecturer in Astronomy, Harvard Univ., 1948; Associate Prof., Mass Institute of Technology, 1947–51. Pres., Foundation Internationale du Pic-du-Midi; Mem. Internat. Acad. of Astronautical Sciences, New York Acad. of Sciences; Chm., Cttee for Lunar and Planetary Exploration, Brit. Nat. Cttee for Space Research; Mem. Lunar-Planetary Cttee, US Nat. Space Bd. Editor-in-Chief, Astrophysics and Space Science, 1968–; Founding Editor: Icarus (internat. jl of solar system); The Moon (internat. jl of lunar studies), 1969–. Pahlavi Lectr, Iran, 1977. Gold Medal, Czechoslovak Acad. of Sciences, 1969; Copernicus Medal, Krakow Univ., 1974. For. Mem., Greek Nat. Acad. of Athens, 1976; DSc (*hc*) Krakow, 1974; Hon. Citizen of Delphi, 1978. *Publications:* An Introduction to the Study of Eclipsing Variables, 1946 (US); The Computation of Elements of Eclipsing Binary Systems, 1950 (US); Tables of Supersonic Flow of Air Around Cones, 3 vols, 1947–49 (US); Numerical Analysis (London), 1955; Astronomical Optics (Amsterdam), 1956; Close Binary Systems, 1959; Figures of Equilibrium of Celestial Bodies, 1960; The Moon, 1960; Physics and Astronomy of the Moon, 1962, 2nd edn 1971; Photographic Atlas of the Moon, 1965; An Introduction to the Study of the Moon, 1966; The Measure of the Moon, 1967; (ed) Advances in Astronomy and Astrophysics, 1968; Telescopes in Space, 1968; Exploration of the Moon by Spacecraft, 1968; Widening Horizons, 1970; A New Photographic Atlas of the Moon, 1971; Man and His Universe, 1972; The Solar System, 1973; Mapping of the Moon, 1974; The Moon in the Post-Apollo Stage, 1974; Dynamics of Close Binary Systems, 1978; The Realm of Terrestrial Planets, 1978; Language of the Stars, 1979; Of Stars and Men: reminiscences of an astronomer, 1986; over 350 original papers on astronomy, aerodynamics, and applied mathematics in publications of Harvard Observatory, Astrophysical Journal, Astronomical Journal, Astronomische Nachrichten, Monthly Notices of Royal Astronomical Society, Proc. Amer. Phil. Soc., Proc. Nat. Acad. Sci. (US), Zeitschrift für Astrophysik, etc. *Recreation:* mountaineering. *Address:* Greenfield, Parkway, Wilmslow, Cheshire. *T:* Wilmslow 522470. *Club:* Explorers' (NY).

KOPELOWITZ, Dr (Jacob) Lionel (Garstein), JP; General Medical Practitioner, since 1953; *b* 9 Dec. 1926; *s* of Maurice and Mabel Kopelowitz; *m* 1980, Sylvia Waksman (*née* Galler). *Educ:* Clifton Coll., Bristol; Trinity Coll., Cambridge (MA 1947); University Coll. Hosp. London. MRCS, LRCP 1951; MRCGP 1964. Resident MO, London Jewish Hosp., 1951–52; Flying Officer, RAF Med. Branch, 1952–53. Member: General Medical Council, 1984–; General Optical Council, 1979–; Standing Med. Adv. Cttee, DHSS, 1974–78; British Medical Association: Fellow, 1980; Mem. Council, 1982–; Chm., Newcastle Div., 1968–69; Pres., Northern Regional Council, 1984–; Mem., Gen. Med. Services Cttee, 1971– (Past Chm., Maternity Services Sub-Cttee); Chm., Central Adv. Cttee, Deputising Services, 1980–; Dep. Chm., Private Practice Cttee, 1972–. President: Board of Deputies of British Jews, 1985–; European Jewish Congress, 1986–; Mem., Chm., Pres., numerous med. bodies and Jewish organisations, UK and overseas. Liveryman, Apothecaries' Co., 1969. JP Northumberland, 1964. *Publications:* articles in med. jls; contrib. to Med. Annual. *Recreations:* foreign travel, contract bridge. *Address:* 41 Montagu Court, Montagu Avenue, Newcastle upon Tyne NE3 4JL. *T:* 091–285 3230. *Club:* Athenæum.

KORALEK, Paul George, CBE 1984; Partner in Ahrends Burton and Koralek, architects, since 1961; *b* 7 April 1933; *s* of Ernest and Alice Koralek; *m* 1958, Jennifer Chadwick; one *s* two *d*. *Educ:* Aldenham School; Architectural Assoc. School of Architecture. ARIBA; AA Dip. Hons. 1st prize, internat. competition for design of new library, Trinity Coll., Dublin, 1961; work in educational, library, housing, industrial, commercial and retail buildings, 1961–; exhibns of drawings and works include: Heinz Gall., RIBA, 1980; RIAI, Dublin, 1981; Museum of Finnish Arch. and Alvar Aalto Museum, Finland, 1982; Braunschweig and Hannover Schs of Arch., 1982; RA; part-time teaching, lecturing and ext. examining at schs of arch., 1965–. *Publications:* paper and articles in RIBA and other prof. jls. *Recreations:* drawing, walking, gardening. *Address:* Unit 1, 7 Chalcot Road, NW1. *T:* 01–586 3311.

KORNBERG, Prof. Arthur; Professor of Biochemistry, Stanford University, since 1959; *b* Brooklyn, 3 March 1918; *m*; three *s. Educ:* College of the City of New York (BSc 1937); University of Rochester, NY (MD 1941). Strong Memorial Hospital, Rochester, 1941–42; National Insts of Health, Bethesda, Md, 1942–52; Professor of Microbiology, Washington Univ., and Head of Dept of Microbiology, 1953–59; Head of Dept of Biochemistry, Stanford Univ., 1959–69. MNAS; MAAS; Mem. Amer. Phil Soc. Foreign Mem., Royal Soc., 1970. Many honours and awards, including: Paul Lewis Award in Enzyme Chemistry, 1951; Nobel Prize (joint) in Medicine, 1959; Nat Medal of Science, 1979. *Publications:* DNA Synthesis, 1974; DNA Replication, 1980 (Suppl., 1982); articles in scientific jls. *Address:* Stanford University Medical Center, Palo Alto, Calif 94305, USA.

KORNBERG, Prof. Sir Hans (Leo), Kt 1978; MA, DSc Oxon, ScD Cantab, PhD Sheffield; FRS 1965; FIBiol 1965; Sir William Dunn Professor of Biochemistry, University of Cambridge, and Fellow of Christ's College, since 1975; Master of Christ's College, Cambridge, since 1982; *b* 14 Jan. 1928; *o s* of Max Kornberg and Margarete Kornberg (*née* Silberbach); *m* 1956, Monica Mary (*née* King); twin *s* two *d. Educ:* Queen Elizabeth Grammar Sch., Wakefield; University of Sheffield (BSc). Commonwealth Fund Fellow of Harkness Foundation, at Yale University and Public Health Research Inst., New York, 1953–55; Mem. of scientific staff, MRC Cell Metabolism Res. Unit, University of Oxford, 1955–60; Lectr, Worcester Coll., Oxford, 1958–61 (Hon. Fellow 1980); Prof. of Biochemistry, Univ. of Leicester, 1960–75. Visiting Instructor, Marine Biological Lab., Woods Hole, Mass, 1964–66, 1981–, Trustee, 1982–. Member: SRC, 1967–72 (Chm., Science Bd, 1969–72); UGC Biol. Sci. Cttee, 1967–77; NATO Adv. Study Inst. Panel, 1970–76 (Chm., 1974–75); Kuratorium, Max-Planck Inst., Dortmund, 1979– (Chm., Sci. Adv. Cttee); AFRC (formerly ARC), 1980–84; Priorities Bd for R & D in Agriculture, 1984–; BP Venture Res. Council, 1981–; ACARD, 1982–85; Adv. Council on Public Records, 1984–; UK Cttee on Eur. Year of the Environment, 1986–; Vice-Chm., EMBO, 1978–81; Chairman: Royal Commn on Environmental Pollution, 1976–81; Adv. Cttee on Genetic Manipulation, 1986–; Co-ordinating Cttee on Environmental Res., Res. Councils, 1986–; Pres., BAAS, 1984–85; Vice-Pres., Inst. of Biol., 1971–73. A Managing Trustee, Nuffield Foundn, 1973–; Academic Governor, Hebrew Univ. of Jerusalem, 1976–; Governor, Weizmann Inst., 1980–. Hon. Fellow, Brasenose Coll., Oxford, 1983. FRSA 1972. For Associate, Nat. Acad. of Sciences, USA, 1986; Hon. Member: Amer. Soc. Biol Chem., 1972–; Biochem. Soc. FRG, 1973–; Japanese Biochem. Soc., 1981–. Hon. ScD Cincinnati, 1974; Hon. DSc: Warwick, 1975; Leicester, 1979; Sheffield, 1979; Bath, 1980; Strathclyde, 1985; DUniv Essex, 1979; Dr med Leipzig, 1984. Colworth Medal of Biochemical Soc., 1965; Otto Warburg Medal, Biochem. Soc. of Federal Republic of Germany, 1973. *Publications:* (with Sir Hans Krebs) Energy Transformations in Living Matter, 1957; articles in scientific jls. *Recreations:* cooking and conversation. *Address:* The Master's Lodge, Christ's College, Cambridge CB2 3BU; Department of Biochemistry, Tennis Court Road, Cambridge CB2 1QW.

KÖRNER, Prof. Stephan, JurDr, PhD; FBA 1967; Professor of Philosophy, Bristol University, 1952–79, and Yale University, 1970–84; *b* Ostrava, Czechoslovakia, 26 Sept. 1913; *o s* of Emil Körner and Erna (*née* Maier); *m* 1944, Edith Laner, CBE, BSc, LLD, JP; one *s* one *d. Educ:* Classical Gymnasium; Charles' Univ., Prague; Trinity Hall, Cambridge. Army Service, 1936–39, 1943–46. University of Bristol: Lectr in Philosophy, 1946; Dean, Faculty of Arts, 1965–66; Pro-Vice-Chancellor, 1968–71; Visiting Prof. of Philosophy: Brown Univ., 1957; Yale Univ., 1960; Texas Univ., 1964; Indiana Univ., 1967; Graz Univ., 1980–86 (Hon. Prof., 1982). President: Brit. Soc. for Philosophy of Science, 1965; Aristotelian Soc., 1967; Internat. Union of History and Philosophy of Science, 1969; Mind Assoc., 1973. Editor, Ratio, 1961–80. Hon. DLitt Belfast, 1981; Hon. Phil. Dr Graz, 1984. *Publications:* Kant, 1955; Conceptual Thinking, 1955; (ed) Observation and Interpretation, 1957; The Philosophy of Mathematics, 1960; Experience and Theory, 1966; Kant's Conception of Freedom (British Acad. Lecture), 1967; What is Philosophy?, 1969; Categorial Frameworks, 1970; Abstraction in Science and Morals (Eddington Meml Lecture), 1971; (ed) Practical Reason, 1974; (ed) Explanation, 1976; Experience and Conduct, 1976; Metaphysics: its structure and function, 1984; contribs to philosophical periodicals. *Recreation:* walking. *Address:* 10 Belgrave Road, Bristol BS8 2AB.

KOSINSKI, Jerzy Nikodem; author; *b* Lodz, Poland, 14 June 1933; naturalised US citizen, 1965; *s* of Mieczyslaw and Elzbieta (Liniecka) Kosinski; *m* 1962, Mary H. Weir (*d* 1968). *Educ:* Univ. of Lodz (MA (Polit. Sci.) 1953; MA (Hist.) 1955). Asst Prof., Inst. Sociology and Cultural Hist., Polish Acad. of Scis, Warsaw, 1955–57; Ford Foundn Fellow, Univ. of Columbia, 1958–60, postgrad. student, 1958–65 (PhD); Guggenheim Lit. Fellow, 1967; Fellow, Center for Advanced Studies, Wesleyan Univ., 1968–69; Sen. Fellow, Council of Humanities. Vis. Lectr in English, Princeton, 1969–70; Vis Prof. in English Prose, Sch. of Drama, Yale, also resident Fellow, Davenport Coll., 1970–73. Member: PEN (Pres., 1973–75); Bd, Nat. Writers Club; Bd, Internat. League for Human Rights; Amer. Civil Liberties Union (Chm., Artists and Writers Cttee; Mem., Nat. Adv. Council); Authors Guild. Film début as Zimoviev in Reds, 1982. Literature Award, Amer. Acad. Arts and Letters, 1970; Brith Sholom Humanitarian Freedom Award, 1974; ACLU First Amendment Award, 1980; Polonia Media Perspectives Award, 1980; Spertus Coll. Internat. Award, 1982 (Hebrew Letters). *Publications:* The Future is Ours, Comrade (under pen-name, Joseph Novak), 1960; No Third Path (under pen-name, Joseph Novak), 1962; The Painted Bird, 1965 (Best Foreign Book Award, Paris, 1966); Steps, 1968 (Nat. Book Award, 1969); Being There, 1971 (filmed, 1978; Best Screenplay Awards, Writers Guild of Amer., 1979, and BAFTA, 1980); The Devil Tree, 1973, rev. and enlarged edn 1981; Cockpit, 1975; Blind Date, 1977; Passion Play, 1979; Pinball, 1982; The Hermit, 1986. *Address:* Hemisphere House (18-k), 60 W 57th Street, New York, NY 10019, USA. *Club:* Century Association (NY).

KOSSOFF, David; actor; author; illustrator; *b* 24 Nov. 1919; *s* of Louis and Anne Kossoff, both Russian; *m* 1947, Margaret (Jennie) Jenkins; one *s* (and one *s* decd) *Educ:* elementary sch.; Northern Polytechnic. Commercial Artist, 1937; Draughtsman, 1937–38; Furniture Designer, 1938–39; Technical Illustrator, 1939–45. Began acting, 1943; working as actor and illustrator, 1945–52, as actor and designer, 1952–. BBC Repertory Company, 1945–51. Took over part of Colonel Alexander Ikonenko in the Love of Four Colonels, Wyndham's, 1952; Sam Tager in The Shrike, Prince's, 1953; Morry in The Bespoke Overcoat, and Tobit in Tobias and the Angel, Arts, 1953; Prof. Lodegger in No Sign of the Dove, Savoy, 1953; Nathan in The Boychik, Embassy, 1954 (and again Morry in The Bespoke Overcoat); Mendele in The World of Sholom Aleichem, Embassy, 1955, and Johannesburg, 1957; one-man show, One Eyebrow Up, The Arts, 1957; Man on Trial, Lyric, 1959; Stars in Your Eyes, Palladium, 1960; The Tenth Man, Comedy, 1961; Come Blow Your Horn, Prince of Wales, 1962; one-man show, Kossoff at the Prince Charles, 1963, later called A Funny Kind of Evening (many countries); Enter Solly Gold, Mermaid, 1970; Cinderella, Palladium, 1971; Bunny, Criterion, 1972; own Bible storytelling

programmes on radio and TV, as writer and teller, 1964–66; solo performance (stage), 'As According to Kossoff', 1970–. Has appeared in many films. Won British Acad. Award, 1956. Elected MSIA 1958. FRSA 1969. *Play:* Big Night for Shylock, 1968. *Publications:* Bible Stories retold by David Kossoff, 1968; The Book of Witnesses, 1971; The Three Donkeys, 1972; The Voices of Masada, 1973; The Little Book of Sylvanus, 1975; You Have a Minute, Lord?, 1977; A Small Town is a World, 1979; Sweet Nutcracker, 1985. *Recreations:* conversation, working with the hands. *Address:* 45 Roe Green Close, Hatfield, Herts.

KOSTERLITZ, Hans Walter, MD, PhD, DSc; FRCPE 1981; FRS 1978; FRSE 1951; Director, Unit for Research on Addictive Drugs, University of Aberdeen, since 1973; *b* 27 April 1903; *s* of Bernhard and Selma Kosterlitz; *m* 1937, Johanna Maria Katherina Gresshöner; one *s. Educ:* Univs of Heidelberg, Freiburg and Berlin. MD Berlin 1929; PhD 1936, DSc 1944, Hon. LLD 1979, Aberdeen. Assistant, 1st Medical Dept, Univ. of Berlin, 1928–33; University of Aberdeen: Research Worker in Physiology, 1934–36; Asst and Carnegie Teaching Fellow, 1936–39; Lectr, 1939–45; Sen. Lectr, 1945–55; Reader in Physiology, 1955–68; Prof. of Pharmacology and Chm., 1968–73. Visiting Lecturer: in Pharmacology, Harvard Med. Sch., 1953–54; in Biology, Brown Univ., 1953; Vis. Prof. of Pharmacology, Harvard Med. Sch., 1977; Lectures: J. Y. Dent Meml, 1970; Otto Krayer, 1977; Scheele, 1977; Gen. Session, Fedn Amer. Socs for Experimental Biol., 1978; Sutcliffe Kerr, 1978; Charnock Bradley Meml, 1979; Arnold H. Maloney, 1979; Lister, 1980; Lita Annenberg Hazen, 1980; Lilly, 1980; Sherrington Meml, RSocMed, 1982; N. J. Giarman Meml, Yale Univ. Sch. of Med., 1982; Third Transatlantic, Endocrine Soc., 1982; Lorenzini, Milan, 1982. Foreign Associate, National Acad. of Sciences, USA, 1985. Dr *hc* Liège, 1978; Hon. DSc St Andrews, 1982. Schmiedeberg Plakette, German Pharmacol Soc., 1976; Pacesetter Award, US Nat. Inst. on Drug Abuse, 1977; Nathan B. Eddy Award, US Cttee on Problems of Drug Dependence, 1978; (jtly) Albert Lasker Prize, 1978; Baly Medal, RCP, 1979; Royal Medal, 1979, Wellcome Foundn Prize, 1982, Royal Soc.; Makdougall-Brisbane Medal, RSE, 1980; Thudichum Medal, Biochem. Soc., 1980; Feldberg Foundn Prize, 1981; Harvey Prize, Technion, 1981; Prof. Lucien Dautrebande Prize, 1982. *Publications:* (joint editor) Agonist and Antagonist Actions of Narcotic Analgesic Drugs, 1972; The Opiate Narcotics, 1975; Opiates and Endogenous Opioid Peptides, 1976; Pain and Society, 1980; Neuroactive Peptides, 1980; articles in Nature, Jl of Physiol, Brit. Jl of Pharmacol. *Recreations:* music, walking, travelling. *Address:* Unit for Research on Addictive Drugs, University of Aberdeen, Aberdeen AB9 1AS. *T:* Aberdeen 40241; 16 Glendee Terrace, Cults, Aberdeen AB1 9HX. *T:* Aberdeen 867366. *Club:* Lansdowne.

KOTCH, Laurie, (Mrs J. K. Kotch); see Purden, R. L.

KOTSOKOANE, Hon. Joseph Riffat Larry; Commander, Order of Ramatseatsana, 1982; Minister of Education, Sports and Culture, Lesotho, since 1984; *b* 19 Oct. 1922; *s* of Basotho parents, living in Johannesburg, South Africa; *m* 1947, Elizabeth (*née* Molise); two *s* three *d.* BSc (SA); BSc Hons (Witwatersrand); Cert. Agric. (London). Development Officer, Dept of Agric., Basutoland, 1951–54; Agric. Educn Officer i/c of Agric. Sch. for junior field staff, 1955–62; Agric. Extension Officer i/c of all field staff of Min. of Agric., 1962–63; Prin. Agric. Off. (Dep. Dir), Min. of Agric., 1964–66; High Comr for Lesotho, in London, 1966–69; Ambassador to Germany, Holy See, Rome, France, and Austria, 1968–69; Permanent Sec. and Hd of Diplomatic Service, Lesotho, 1969–70; Permanent Sec. for Health, Educn and Social Welfare, Lesotho, 1970–71; High Comr for Lesotho in East Africa, Nigeria and Ghana, 1972–74; Minister: of Foreign Affairs, Lesotho, 1974–75; of Education, 1975–76; of Agriculture, 1976–78; Perm. Rep. to UN, 1978; Sec. to the Cabinet and Head of CS (Sen. Perm. Sec.), 1978–84. Guest of Min. of Agric., Netherlands, 1955; studied agric. educn, USA (financed by Carnegie Corp. of NY and Ford Foundn), 1960–61; FAO confs in Tunisia, Tanganyika and Uganda, 1962 and 1963; Mem. Lesotho delegn to 24th World Health Assembly, 1971; travelled extensively to study and observe methods of agric. administration, 1964; meetings on nutrition, Berlin and Hamburg, 1966; diplomatic trainee, Brit. Embassy, Bonn, 1966. *Recreations:* swimming, tennis, amateur dramatics, photography, debating, reading, travelling. *Address:* c/o Ministry of Education, PO Box MS 47, Maseru, Lesotho, Southern Africa.

KOVACEVICH, Stephen B.; see Bishop-Kovacevich.

KRAFT, Rt. Rev. Richard Austin; see Pretoria, Bishop of.

KRAMER, Prof. Ivor Robert Horton, OBE 1984; MDS; FDSRCS, FFDRCSI, Hon. FRACDS, FRCPath; Emeritus Professor of Oral Pathology, University of London; Hon. Consultant, Mount Vernon Hospital, Northwood; *b* 20 June 1923; *yr s* of late Alfred Bertie and Agnes Maud Kramer; *m* 1st, 1946, Elisabeth Dalley; one *s*; 2nd, 1979, Mrs Dorothy Toller. *Educ:* Royal Dental Hosp. of London Sch. of Dental Surgery; MDS 1955; FDSRCS 1960 (LDSRCS 1944); FRCPath 1970 (MCRPath 1964); FFDRCSI 1973. Asst to Pathologist, Princess Louise (Kensington) Hosp. for Children, 1944–48; Wright Fleming Inst. of Microbiol., 1948–49; Instr in Dental Histology, Royal Dental Hosp. Sch. of Dental Surgery, 1944–50; Asst Pathologist, Royal Dental Hosp., 1950–56; Institute of Dental Surgery: Lectr in Dental Path., 1949–50, Sen. Lectr, 1950–57; Reader in Oral Path., 1957–62; Prof. of Oral Path., 1962–83; Sub-dean, 1950–70; Dean and Dir of Studies, 1970–83; Head, Dept of Path., Eastman Dental Hosp., 1950–83. Civilian Cons. in Dental Path., RN, 1967–83. Member: WHO Expert Adv. Panel on Dental Health, 1975–; Bd of Faculty of Dental Surgery, RCS, 1964–80, Council, RCS, 1977–80; GDC, 1973–84; Mem., Council for Postgrad. Med. Educn in Eng. and Wales, 1972–77 (Chm., Dental Cttee, 1972–77); Pres., Odontological Section, RSocMed, 1973–74; Pres., British Div., Internat. Assoc. for Dental Res., 1974–77. Hon. Pres. of the Assoc., 1974–75. Editor, Archives of Oral Biology, 1959–69. Lectures: Wilkinson, Manchester, 1962; Charles Tomes, 1969, Webb Johnson, 1981, RCS; Holme, UCH, 1969; Elwood Meml, QUB, 1970; Hutchinson, Edinburgh, 1971. Hon. FRACDS 1978. Howard Mummery Prize, BDA, 1966; Maurice Down Award, Brit. Assoc. of Oral Surgeons, 1974; Colyer Gold Medal, FDS, RCS, 1985. *Publications:* (with J. J. Pindborg and H. Torloni) World Health Organization International Histological Classification of Tumours: Odontogenic Tumours, Jaw Cysts and Allied Lesions, 1972; (with B. Cohen) Scientific Foundations of Dentistry, 1976; numerous papers in med. and dental jls. *Address:* 33 Sandy Lodge Road, Rickmansworth, Herts WD3 1LP. *T:* Northwood 25012.

KRAMER, Prof. Dame Leonie (Judith), DBE 1983 (OBE 1976); DPhil; Professor of Australian Literature, University of Sydney, since 1968; Director: Australia and New Zealand Banking Group, since 1983; Western Mining Corporation Ltd; *b* 1 Oct. 1924; *d* of Alfred and Gertrude Gibson; *m* 1952, Harold Kramer; two *d. Educ:* Presbyterian Ladies Coll., Melbourne; Univ. of Melbourne (BA 1945); Oxford Univ. (DPhil 1953). FAHA; FACE. Tutor and Lectr, Univ. of Melb., 1945–49; Tutor and Postgrad. Student, St Hugh's Coll., Oxford, 1949–52; Lectr, Canberra University Coll., 1954–56; Lectr, subseq. Sen. Lectr and Associate Prof., Univ. of NSW, 1958–68. Chm., ABC, 1982–83. Mem., Univs Council, 1977–. Hon. DLitt Tasmania, 1977; Hon. LLD: Melbourne, 1983; ANU, 1984. Britannica Award, 1986. *Publications:* as L. J. Gibson: Henry Handel Richardson and Some of Her Sources, 1954; as Leonie Kramer: A Companion to Australia Felix, 1962;

Myself when Laura: fact and fiction in Henry Handel Richardson's school career, 1966; Henry Handel Richardson, 1967, repr. as contrib. to Six Australian Writers, 1971; (with Robert D. Eagleson) Language and Literature: a synthesis, 1976; (with Robert D. Eagleson) A Guide to Language and Literature, 1977; A. D. Hope, 1979; (ed and introd) The Oxford History of Australian Literature, 1981; (ed with Adrian Mitchell) The Oxford Anthology of Australian Literature, 1985; (ed and introd) My Country: Australian poetry and short stories—two hundred years, 1985. *Recreations:* gardening, music. *Address:* 12 Vaucluse Road, Vaucluse, NSW 2030, Australia. *T:* 371.9686.

KRAMRISCH, Stella, PhD; Professor of Indian Art, Institute of Fine Arts, New York University, since 1964; Curator Emeritus, Indian Art, Philadelphia Museum of Art, since 1954; *d* of Jacques Kramrisch, scientist, and Berta Kramrisch; *m* 1929, Laszlo Neményi (*d* 1950). *Educ:* Vienna University. Prof. of Indian Art, Univ. of Calcutta, 1923–50; Prof. in the Art of South Asia, Univ. of Pennsylvania, 1950–69; Lectr on Indian Art, Courtauld Inst. of Art, Univ. of London, 1937–41. Public lectures in USA, Canada, India, Nepal, W Germany, including: Aditi Exhibn Seminar, Fest. of India, London, 1982; Fest. of India, Washington, DC, 1985. Mem., Adv. Bd, South Asian Regional Art Studies. Editor: Jl Indian Soc. of Oriental Art, 1932–50; Indian Section, Artibus Asiae, 1959–. Hon. DLit Visva Bharati Univ., 1974; Hon. LLD Pennsylvania, 1981; Hon. DHL: Smith Coll., 1982; Chicago, 1984; Hon. DLit Columbia, NY, 1985. Cross of Honour for Science and Art, Austria, 1979; Padma Bhushan Award, India, 1982; National Women's Caucus for Art Conf. Award, 1983; Prabala Gorkhadakshina Bahu Award, Nepal, 1984; Charles Lang Freer Medal, Washington, DC, 1985. *Publications:* Principles of Indian Art, 1924; Vishnudharmottara, 1924; History of Indian Art, 1929; Indian Sculpture, 1932; Asian Miniature Painting, 1932; A Survey of Painting in the Deccan, 1937; Indian Terracottas, 1939; Kantha, 1939; The Hindu Temple, 1946, repr. 1976; Arts and Crafts of Travancore, 1948; Dravida and Kerala, 1953; Art of India, 1954; Indian Sculpture in the Philadelphia Museum of Art, 1960; The Triple Structure of Creation, 1962; The Art of Nepal, 1964; Unknown India: Ritual Art in Tribe and Village, 1968; The Presence of Siva, 1981; Manifestations of Shiva, 1981; The Antelope, 1982; (contrib.) Discourses on Siva, ed Michael Meister, 1985; Painted Delight (exhibn catalogue), 1986; various articles. *Relevant publication:* Exploring India's Sacred Art: selected writings of Stella Kramrisch, by Barbara Stoler Miller, 1983. *Address:* Philadelphia Museum of Art, PO Box 7646, Philadelphia, Pa 19101, USA.

KREBS, John Richard, DPhil; FRS 1984; University Lecturer in Zoology, Oxford University, since 1976; E. P. Abraham Fellow, Pembroke College, Oxford, since 1981; *b* 11 April 1945; *s* of Sir Hans Adolf Krebs, FRCP, FRS and Margaret Cicely Krebs; *m* 1968, Katherine Anne Fullerton; two *d*. *Educ:* City of Oxford High School; Pembroke College, Oxford. BA 1966; MA 1970; DPhil 1970. Asst Prof., Univ. of British Columbia, 1970–73; Lectr in Zoology, UCNW, 1973–75. Storer Lectr, Univ. of Calif, 1985. Scientific Mem., Max Planck Soc., 1985. Scientific Medal, Zool. Soc., 1981; Bicentenary Medal, Linnaean Soc., 1983. *Publications:* Behavioural Ecology, 1978, 2nd edn 1984; Introduction to Behavioural Ecology, 1981, 2nd edn 1986; Foraging Theory, 1986; articles in Animal Behaviour, Jl of Animal Ecology. *Recreations:* cricket, gardening, squash, violin. *Address:* Edward Grey Institute of Field Ornithology, Department of Zoology, South Parks Road, Oxford OX1 3PS. *T:* Oxford 56789; 11 Brookside, Oxford. *T:* Oxford 63211.

KREISEL, Prof. Georg, FRS 1966; Professor of Logic and the Foundations of Mathematics, Stanford University, Stanford, California, USA; *b* 15 Sept. 1923. *Address:* Department of Philosophy, Stanford University, Stanford, California 94305, USA.

KREMER, Michael, MD; FRCP; Emeritus Neurologist, Middlesex Hospital, W1; Honorary Consulting Neurologist, National Hospital, Queen Square, WC1; Hon. Consultant Neurologist to St Dunstan's, since 1966; Hon. Consultant in Neurology to the Army, since 1969; *b* 27 Nov. 1907; *s* of W. and S. Kremer; *m* 1933, Lilian Frances (*née* Washbourn); one *s* two *d*. *Educ:* Middlesex Hosp. Medical Sch. BSc 1927; MD 1932; FRCP 1943. *Recreations:* music, reading, photography. *Address:* 121 Harley Street, W1. *T:* 01–935 4545.

KRESTIN, David, MD (London), BS, MRCP; retired; formerly: Consulting Physician, London Jewish Hospital; Medical Specialist, Ministries of Pensions and of National Insurance; late Physician with charge of Out-Patients, Dreadnought Hospital; Medical Registrar, Prince of Wales' Hospital; Lecturer in Medicine, N-E London Post-Graduate Medical College; *b* London; *s* of Dr S. Krestin; *m* Ruth Fisher; one *s*. *Educ:* University of London; London Hosp. Medical Coll.; University of Pennsylvania. Anatomy prize, London Hosp.; MRCS, LRCP 1922; MB, BS London 1923, Hons Medicine and Surgery; MD London 1926, MRCP 1926. Clinical Asst, House Surg., House Physician, Medical Registrar and First Asst, London Hosp.; Rockefeller Medical Fellowship, 1928–29; Fellow in Pathology, Henry Phipps Institute, University Penna; Yarrow Research Fellow, London Hosp. *Publications:* Pulsation in Superficial Veins, Lancet, 1927; The Seborrhœic facies in Post-Encephalitic Parkinsonism, Qly Jl Med., 1927; Congenital Dextrocardia and Auric. Fibrillation, BMJ, 1927; Latent Pulmonary Tuberculosis, Qly Jl Med., 1929; Glandular Fever, Clinical Jl, 1931 and other medical papers. *Recreation:* fishing. *Address:* 14 Spaniards End, NW3. *T:* 01–455 1500.

KRETZMER, Herbert; television critic, Daily Mail, since 1979; feature writer and lyric writer; *b* Kroonstad, OFS, S Africa, 5 Oct. 1925; *s* of William and Tilly Kretzmer; *m* 1961, Elisabeth Margaret Wilson (marr. diss., 1973); one *s* one *d*. *Educ:* Kroonstad High Sch.; Rhodes Univ., Grahamstown. Entered journalism, 1946, writing weekly cinema newsreel commentaries and documentary films for African Film Productions, Johannesburg. Reporter and entertainment columnist, Sunday Express, Johannesburg, 1951–54; feature writer and columnist, Daily Sketch, London, 1954–59; Columnist, Sunday Dispatch, London, 1959–61; theatre critic, Daily Express, 1962–78. TV Critic of the Year, Philips Industries Award, 1980; commended in British Press Awards, 1981. As lyric writer, contributed weekly songs to: That Was The Week . ., Not So Much A Programme . ., BBC 3, That's Life. Wrote lyrics for Ivor Novello Award song Goodness Gracious Me, 1960, and ASCAP award song Yesterday When I was Young, 1969; Gold record for She, 1974; Our Man Crichton, Shaftesbury Theatre, 1964 (book and lyrics); The Four Musketeers, Drury Lane, 1967 (lyrics); Les Misérables, RSC, 1985 (lyrics); *film:* Can Heironymus Merkin Ever Forget Mercy Humppe And Find True Happiness?, 1969 (lyrics); has also written lyrics for other films, and for TV programmes. *Publications:* Our Man Crichton, 1965; (jointly) Every Home Should Have One, 1970. *Address:* 55 Lincoln House, Basil Street, SW3. *T:* 01–589 2541. *Club:* Royal Automobile.

KRIKLER, Dennis Michael, MD; FRCP; Consultant Cardiologist, Hammersmith and Ealing Hospitals, and Senior Lecturer in Cardiology, Royal Postgraduate Medical School, since 1973; *b* 10 Dec. 1928; *s* of Barnet and Eva Krikler; *m* 1955, Anne (*née* Winterstein); one *s* one *d*. *Educ:* Muizenberg High Sch.; Univ. of Cape Town, S Africa. Ho. Phys. and Registrar, Groote Schuur Hosp., 1952–55; Fellow, Lahey Clinic, Boston, 1956; C. J. Adams Meml Travelling Fellowship, 1956; Sen. Registrar, Groote Schuur Hosp., 1957–58; Consultant Physician: Salisbury Central Hosp., Rhodesia, 1958–66; Prince of Wales's Hosp., London, 1966–73. Expert Clinicien en Cardiologie, Ministère des Affaires Sociales, Santé, France, 1983. Vis. Prof., Baylor, Indiana and Birmingham Univs, 1985; Internat. Lectr, Amer. Heart Assoc., 1984 (Paul Dudley White Citation for internat. achievement). Member, British Cardiac Soc., 1971– (Treasurer, 1976–81); Hon. Member: Soc. Française de Cardiologie, 1981–; Soc. di Cultura Medica Vercellese, Italy; Soc. de Cardiologia de Levante, Spain. Editor, British Heart Journal, 1981–; Member, Editorial Committee: Cardiovascular Res., 1975–; Archives des Maladies du Coeur et des Vaisseaux, 1980–; Revista Latina de Cardiologia, 1980–; Mem. Scientific Council, Revista Portuguesa de Cardologia, 1982–. FACC 1971. Hon. Fellow, Council on Clin. Cardiol., Amer. Heart Assoc., 1984. McCullough Prize, 1949; Sir William Osler Award, Miami Univ., 1981. *Publications:* Cardiac Arrhythmias (with J. F. Goodwin), 1975; (with A. Zanchetti) Calcium antagonism in cardiovascular therapy, 1981; (with D. A. Chamberlain and W. J. McKenna) Amiodarone and arrhythmias, 1983; (with P. G. Hugenholtz) Workshop on calcium antagonists, 1984; papers on cardiology in British, American and French jls. *Recreations:* reading, especially history; photography. *Address:* 55 Wimpole Street, W1M 7DF. *T:* 01–935 2098.

KRIKLER, Leonard Gideon; His Honour Judge Krikler; a Circuit Judge, since 1984; *b* 23 May 1929; *s* of late Major James Harold Krikler, OBE, ED, and Tilly Krikler; *m* 1st, 1955, Dr Thilla Krikler (*d* 1973); four *s*; 2nd, 1975, Lily Appleson; one *s*, and one step *s* two step *d*. *Educ:* Milton Sch., Bulawayo, S Rhodesia (Zimbabwe). Called to Bar, Middle Temple, 1953. Crown Counsel, Court Martial Appeals Court, 1968; Dep. Circuit Judge, 1974; a Recorder, 1980–84. *Recreations:* cartooning, carpentry, homiletics. *Address:* Lamb Building, Temple, EC4. *T:* 01–353 0774.

KRIKORIAN, Gregory, CB 1973; Solicitor for the Customs and Excise, 1971–78; *b* 23 Sept. 1913; *s* of late Kevork and late Christine Krikorian; *m* 1943, Seta Mary, *d* of Souren Djirdjirian; one *d*. *Educ:* Polytechnic Secondary Sch.; Lincoln Coll., Oxford (BA). Called to Bar, Middle Temple, 1939; practised at Bar, 1939; BBC Overseas Intell. Dept, 1940; served in RAF as Intell. Officer, Fighter Comd, 1940–45 (despatches); practised at Bar, 1945–51, Junior Oxford Circuit, 1947; joined Solicitor's Office, HM Customs and Excise, 1951. *Publication:* (jtly) Customs and Excise, in Halsbury's Laws of England, 1975. *Recreations:* gardening, bird-watching. *Address:* The Coach House, Hawkchurch, Axminster, Devon. *T:* Hawkchurch 414. *Clubs:* Reform, Civil Service, MCC.

KRISH, Tanya, (Mrs Felix Krish); *see* Moiseiwitsch, T.

KRISTENSEN, Prof. Thorkil; Director, Institute for Development Research, Copenhagen, 1969–72; Secretary-General, Organisation for Economic Co-operation and Development, 1960–69; *b* Denmark, 9 Oct. 1899; *m* 1931, Ellen Christine Nielsen; one *s* one *d*. *Educ:* School of Commerce; People's Coll., Askov; University of Copenhagen (Cand. polit.). Dipl. Polit. and Econ. Sciences, 1927. Lectr in High Sch. of Commerce, Aarhus, and in University of Copenhagen, 1927–38; Prof. of Commercial and Industrial Economics: University of Aarhus, 1938–47; Sch. of Advanced Commercial Studies, Copenhagen, 1947–60. Mem., Danish Parliament, 1945–60; Minister of Finance, 1945–47 and 1950–53; Mem. Finance Cttee, 1947–49 and 1953–60; Mem. Consultative Assembly of Council of Europe, 1949–50; Mem. Foreign Affairs Cttee, 1953–60; Mem. Nordic Council, 1953–60; Mem. Acad. of Technical Sciences; Pres. Foreign Policy Soc., 1948–60; Pres. Nat. Anti-Unemployment Fedn, 1956–60; Mem. Assurance Council, 1958–60; Mem. Institute of History and Economics. DrSc Pol *hc* (Ankara), 1962. *Publications:* several, on finance, 1930–39; The Food Problem of Developing Countries, 1968. Editor of: De europaeiske markedsplaner (European Markets-Plans and Prospects), 1958; The Economic World Balance, 1960; Development in Rich and Poor Countries, 1974, 2nd edn 1982; Inflation and Unemployment in the Modern Society, 1981, etc. *Address:* Odinsvej 18, 3460 Birkerłd, Denmark.

KRISTIANSEN, Erling (Engelbrecht), Grand Cross, Order of Dannebrog; Hon. GCVO 1974; Director, East Asiatic Co., since 1978, and other companies; *b* 31 Dec. 1912; *s* of Kristian Engelbrecht Kristiansen, Chartered Surveyor, and Andrea Kirstine (*née* Madsen); *m* 1938, Annemarie Selinko, novelist. *Educ:* Herning Gymnasium; University of Copenhagen (degree awarded equiv. of MA Econ). Postgraduate Studies, Economics and Internat. Relations, Geneva, Paris, London, 1935–37. Sec.-Gen., 1935, Pres. 1936, of the Fédération Universitaire Internationale pour la Société des Nations. Danish Civil Servant, 1941; served with: Free Danish Missions, Stockholm, 1943; Washington, 1944; London, 1945; joined Danish Diplomatic Service and stayed in London until 1947; Danish Foreign Ministry, 1947–48; Head of Denmark's Mission to OEEC, Paris, 1948–50; Sec. to Economic Cttee of Cabinet, 1950–51; Asst Under-Sec. of State, 1951; Dep. Under-Sec. of State (Economic Affairs), Danish For. Min., 1954–64; Ambassador to UK, 1964–77 (concurrently accredited to Republic of Ireland, 1964–73); Doyen of the Diplomatic Corps, 1973–77; retd 1977. Dir, S. G. Warburg & Co. International Holdings Ltd, 1980–84; Mem., Internat. Adv. Bd, S. G. Warburg & Co., 1984–86, Mercury Internat. Gp, 1986–; Nordic Investment Bank: Dir, 1977–86; Vice-Chm., 1977–78; Chm., 1978–80. Grand Officier, Légion d'Honneur; Kt Comdr: Order of St Olav; Order of White Rose of Finland; Star of Ethiopia; Knight Grand Cross, Icelandic Falcon; Comdr, Order of Northern Star of Sweden. *Publication:* Folkeforbundet (The League of Nations), 1938. *Recreations:* ski-ing, fishing and other out-door sports, modern languages. *Address:* 4 Granhøjen, DK-2900, Hellerup, Denmark. *Clubs:* MCC; Special Forces *et al.*

KROHN, Dr Peter Leslie, FRS 1963; Professor of Endocrinology, University of Birmingham, 1962–66; *b* 8 Jan. 1916; *s* of Eric Leslie Krohn and Doris Ellen Krohn (*née* Wade); *m* 1941, Joanna Mary French; two *s*. *Educ:* Sedbergh; Balliol Coll., Oxford. BA 1st Cl. Hons Animal Physiol, 1937; BM, BCh Oxon, 1940. Wartime Research work for Min. of Home Security, 1940–45; Lectr, then Reader in Endocrinology, University of Birmingham, 1946–53; Nuffield Sen. Gerontological Research Fellow and Hon. Prof. in University, 1953–62. *Publications:* contrib. to scientific jls on physiology of reproduction, transplantation immunity and ageing. *Recreations:* ski-ing, mountain walking. *Address:* Coburg House, New St John's Road, St Helier, Jersey, Channel Islands. *T:* Jersey 74870.

KROLL, Natasha, RDI, FSIAD; freelance television and film designer; *b* Moscow, 20 May 1914; *d* of Dr (phil.) Hermann Kroll and Sophie (*née* Rabinovich). *Educ:* Berlin. Teacher of window display, Reimann Sch. of Art, London, 1936–40; Display Manager: Messrs Rowntrees, Scarborough and York, 1940–42; Simpson Piccadilly Ltd, 1942–55; Sen. Designer, BBC TV, 1955–66: programmes include: Monitor, Panorama, science programmes, Lower Depths, Death of Danton, The Duel, Ring Round the Moon, La Traviata, Day by the Sea, The Sponge Room and many others; freelance designer, 1966–; TV designs include: The Seagull, 1966; Family Reunion, 1966; Eugene Onegin, 1967; The Soldier's Tale, 1968; La Vida Breve, 1968; Mary Stuart, 1968; Doll's House, 1969; Three Sisters, Cherry Orchard, Rasputin, Wild Duck, 1971; Summer and Smoke, Hedda Gabler, 1972; The Common, 1973; Lady from the Sea, 1974; Love's Labour's Lost, 1975; Very Like a Whale, 1980; production-designer of: The Music Lovers, 1970; The Hireling, 1973 (FTA Film award for best Art Direction); Summer Rag-time, 1976; Absolution, 1978. RDI 1966. *Publication:* Window Display, 1954. *Recreations:* painting, family, entertaining. *Address:* 5 Ruvigny Gardens, SW15 1JR. *T:* 01–788 9867.

KROLL, Dss Dr Una (Margaret Patricia); Deaconess Doctor; Senior Clinical Medical Officer, Hastings Health District, since 1985 (Clinical Medical Officer, 1981–85); licensed deaconess to St Andrews and St Peters, Fairlight, since 1984; worker deaconess, since 1970; writer and broadcaster, since 1970; *b* 15 Dec. 1925; *d* of George Hill, CBE, DSO, MC, and Hilda Hill; *m* 1957, Leopold Kroll; one *s* three *d. Educ:* St Paul's Girls' Sch.; Malvern Girls' Coll.; Girton Coll., Cambridge; The London Hosp. MB, BChir (Cantab) 1951; MA 1969. MRCGP 1967. House Officer, 1951–53; Overseas service (Africa), 1953–60; General Practice, 1960–81. Theological trng, 1967–70; licensed deaconess to St Clement's and All Saints, Hastings, 1981–84; political work as a feminist, with particular ref. to status of women in the churches in England and internationally, 1970–; Member: Gen. Synod of C of E, 1985–; Churches Council for Health and Healing, 1980–; Burrswood Working Party, 1985–. *Publications:* Transcendental Meditation: a signpost to the world, 1974; Flesh of My Flesh: a Christian view on sexism, 1975; Lament for a Lost Enemy: study of reconciliation, 1976; Sexual Counselling, 1980; The Spiritual Exercise Book, 1985; contrib. Cervical Cytology (BMJ), 1969. *Recreations:* gardening, reading, sitting. *Address:* Datcha, Clinton Way, Fairlight Cove, E Sussex TN35 4DL. *T:* Hastings 3241.

KRUGER, Prudence Margaret; see Leith, P. M.

KRUSIN, Sir Stanley (Marks), Kt 1973; CB 1963; Second Parliamentary Counsel, 1970–73; *b* 8 June 1908; *m* 1st, 1937 (she *d* 1972); one *s* one *d*; 2nd, 1976. *Educ:* St Paul's Sch.; Balliol Coll., Oxford. Called to the Bar, Middle Temple, 1932. Served RAFVR, Wing Comdr, 1944. Dep. Sec., British Tabulating Machine Co. Ltd, 1945–47. Entered Parliamentary Counsel Office, 1947; Parliamentary Counsel, 1953–69. *Address:* 5 Coleridge Walk, NW11. *T:* 01–458 1340. *Club:* Royal Air Force.

KUBELIK, Rafael; conductor and composer; Chief Conductor of Bayerischer Rundfunk, München, 1961–79; *b* Bychory, Bohemia, 29 June 1914; *s* of Jan Kubelik, violinist, and Marianne (*née* Szell); *m* 1942, Ludmila Bertlova (*decd*), violinist; one *s*; *m* 1963, Elsie Morison, singer. *Educ:* Prague Conservatoire. Conductor, Czech Philharmonic Society, Prague, 1936–39; Musical Director of Opera, Brno, Czechoslovakia, 1939–41; Musical Dir, Czech Philharmonic Orchestra, 1941–48; Musical Dir, Chicago Symphony Orchestra, 1950–53; Musical Dir of the Covent Garden Opera Company, 1955–58; Music Dir, Metropolitan Opera, New York, 1973–74. *Compositions* include: 5 operas; 2 symphonies with chorus; a third symphony (in one movement); Orphikon, symphony for orch.; Sequences for orch.; Peripeteia for organ and orch.; 6 string quartets; 1 violin concerto; 1 cello concerto; 1 cantata; cantata without words for chorus and orch.; Requiems: Pro Memoria Uxoris; Libera Nos; Quattro Forme per Archi; songs; piano and violin music. Hon. RAM; Hon. Member: Bavarian Acad. of Fine Arts; Royal Swedish Acad. of Music; Italian Assoc. Anton Bruckner. Hon. Dr Amer. Conservatory of Music, Chicago. Karl Amadeus Hartmann Gold Medal; Gold Medal, City of Munich; Gustav Mahler Gold Medal, Gustav Mahler Soc., Vienna; Carl Nielsen Gold Medal, Copenhagen; Medal of City of Amsterdam; Mahler Medal, Bruckner Soc. of Amer.; Golden Key, City of Cleveland. Grosses Bundesverdienstkreuz (FRG); Bavarian Order of Merit; Chevalier, Order of the Dannebrog (Denmark); Comtur Istrucao Publica (Portugal); Commandeur de l'ordre des Arts et des Lettres (France). *Address:* 6047 Kastanienbaum, Haus im Sand, Switzerland.

KUBRICK, Stanley; producer, director, script writer; *b* 26 July 1928; *s* of Dr Jacques L. Kubrick and Gertrude Kubrick; *m* 1958, Suzanne Christiane Harlan; three *d. Educ:* William Howard Taft High Sch.; City Coll. of City of New York. Joined Look Magazine, 1946. At age of 21 made Documentary, Day of the Fight; made Short for RKO, Flying Padre. *Feature Films:* Fear and Desire, 1953 (at age of 24); Killer's Kiss, 1954; The Killing, 1956; Paths of Glory, 1957; Spartacus, 1960; Lolita, 1962; Dr Strangelove or How I Learned to Stop Worrying and Love the Bomb, 1964; 2001: A Space Odyssey, 1968; A Clockwork Orange, 1971; Barry Lyndon, 1975; The Shining, 1978. *Recreations:* literature, music, public affairs. *Address:* c/o Loeb & Loeb, 10100 Santa Monica Boulevard, Suite 2200, Los Angeles, Calif 90067, USA.

KUENSSBERG, Ekkehard von, CBE 1969; FRCGP, 1967; FRCOG (*ae*) 1981; FRCPEd 1981; President, Royal College of General Practitioners, 1976–79; *b* 1913; *s* of Prof. Eberhard von Kuenssberg; *m* 1941, Dr Constance Ferrar Hardy; two *s* two *d. Educ:* Schloss Schule, Salem; Univs of Innsbruck, Heidelberg and Edinburgh. MB, ChB 1939. Gen. practice throughout (Edin.). RAMC, 1944–46 (Lt-Col, DADMS E Africa Comd). Mem., Safety of Drugs Cttee, 1964–71; Chm., Gen. Med. Services Cttee, Scotland; Mem., GMSC, UK, 1960–68; RCGP: Chm. Council, 1970–73; Hon. Treas., Research Foundn Bd, 1960–77; Mackenzie Lectr, 1970; Wolfson Travelling Prof., 1974. Mem., Lothian Area Health Bd, 1974–80; Member: Council, Queen's Nursing Inst., 1972–76; Court, Edinburgh Univ., 1971–79. Foundation Council Award, RCGP, 1967; Hippocrates Medal, 1974 (SIMG). FRSocMed. *Publications:* The Team in General Practice, 1966; An Opportunity to Learn, 1977. *Recreations:* skiing, forestry. *Address:* Little Letham, Haddington, East Lothian. *T:* Haddington 2529.

See also N. C. D. Kuenssberg.

KUENSSBERG, Nicholas Christopher Dwelly; Director, Coats Viyella Plc, since 1986; *b* 28 Oct. 1942; *s* of Ekkehard von Kuenssberg, *qv*; *m* 1965, Sally Robertson; one *s* two *d. Educ:* Edinburgh Acad.; Wadham Coll., Oxford (BA Hons). FCIS; FBIM. Worked overseas, 1965–78; Dir. J. & P. Coats Ltd, 1978; Dir, 1978, Chm. 1982–86, Textile Mouldings Ltd; Chm., Dynacast Internat. Ltd, 1978; Dir, Coats Patons Plc, 1985. Director: S of Scotland Electricity Bd, 1984; W of Scotland Bd, Bank of Scotland, 1984. Hon. Res. Fellow, Strathclyde Business Sch., 1986. Mem., Council and Exec. Cttee, Scottish Enterprise Foundn, 1986. *Recreations:* sport, travel, opera, printing and publishing. *Address:* Coats Viyella Plc, 155 St Vincent Street, Glasgow G2 5PA. *T:* 041–221 8711.

KUHN, Heinrich Gerhard, FRS 1954; DPhil, MA; Reader in Physics, Oxford University, 1955–71, now Emeritus; Fellow of Balliol College 1950–71, now Emeritus; *b* 10 March 1904; *s* of Wilhelm Felix and Martha Kuhn; *m* 1931, Marie Bertha Nohl; two *s. Educ:* High Sch., Lueben (Silesia); Universities of Greifswald and Göttingen. Lecturer in Physics, Göttingen Univ., 1931; Research at Clarendon Laboratory, Oxford, 1933–71; Lecturer, University Coll., Oxford, 1938; work for atomic energy project, 1941–45; University Demonstrator, Oxford, 1945–55. Prof. a.D, Göttingen Univ., 1957. Dr hc Aix-Marseille, 1958. Holweck Prize, 1967. *Publications:* Atomspektren, 1934 (Akad. Verl. Ges., Leipzig); Atomic Spectra, 1962, 2nd edn 1970; articles on molecular and atomic spectra and on interferometry. *Address:* 25 Victoria Road, Oxford OX2 7QF. *T:* 55308.

KUIPERS, John Melles; Chairman, ATT Ltd, since 1984; Director, Gowrings Ltd, since 1980; *b* 7 July 1918; *s* of late Joh Kuipers and Anna (*née* Knoester); *m* 1947, Joan Lilian Morgan-Edwards; one *s* three *d. Educ:* Royal Masonic Sch., Bushey. Served RA, 1939–46 (Lt-Col). Ford Motor Co. Ltd, 1947–51; Treasurer, Canadian Chemical Co. Ltd, Montreal, 1951–55; Gp Manager, Halewood, and Dir, Stamping and Assembly Gp, Ford Motor Co. Ltd, 1955–67; EMI Ltd, 1967–80: Chief Exec. Electronic and Industrial Ops, 1969–72; Chm. and Chief Exec., EMI (Australia) Ltd, 1974–77; Man. Dir and Vice-Chm., 1977–79; Dir, Thames TV Ltd, 1977–81; Chm., Huntleigh Gp PLC, 1980–83.

CBIM. *Recreations:* golf, home-making. *Address:* Marsh Mills Stable, Wargrave Road, Henley-on-Thames, Oxon. *T:* Henley-on-Thames 574760.

KULUKUNDIS, Eddie, (Elias George); Chairman, Knightsbridge Theatrical Productions Ltd, since 1970; Director: Rethymnis & Kulukundis Ltd, since 1964; London & Overseas Freighters plc, since 1980; Member of Lloyd's, since 1964, elected External Member Council, since 1982; Member, Baltic Exchange, since 1959; *b* 20 April 1932; *s* of late George Elias Kulukundis and of Eugénie (*née* Diacakis); *m* 1981, Susan Hampshire, *qv. Educ:* Collegiate Sch., New York; Salisbury Sch., Connecticut; Yale Univ. Governor: Greenwich Theatre Ltd; The Raymond Mander and Joe Mitchenson Theatre Collection Ltd; Royal Shakespeare Theatre; Sports Aid Foundn Ltd. Director: Apollo Soc. Ltd; Hampstead Theatre Ltd; New Shaw Theatre Co. Ltd; Pioneer Theatres Ltd. Member, Councils of Management: Royal Shakespeare Theatre; Royal Shakespeare Theatre Trust; Traverse Theatre Club. Mem. Exec. Council, SWET. Trustee: Salisbury Sch., Connecticut; Theatres Trust. FRSA. As Theatrical Producer, London prodns incl. (some jtly): Enemy, 1969; The Happy Apple, Poor Horace, The Friends, How the Other Half Loves, Tea Party and The Basement (double bill), The Wild Duck, 1970; After Haggerty, Hamlet, Charley's Aunt, Straight Up, 1971; London Assurance, Journey's End, 1972; Small Craft Warnings, A Private Matter, Dandy Dick, 1973; The Waltz of the Toreadors, Life Class, Pygmalion, Play Mas, The Gentle Hook, 1974; A Little Night Music, Entertaining Mr Sloane, The Gay Lord Quex, What the Butler Saw, Travesties, Lies, The Sea Gull, A Month in the Country, A Room With a view, Too True to Be Good, The Bed Before Yesterday, 1975; Dimetos, Banana Ridge, Wild Oats, 1976; Candida, Man and Superman, Once A Catholic, 1977; Privates on Parade, Gloo Joo, 1978; Bent, Outside Edge, Last of the Red Hot Lovers, 1979; Beecham, Born in the Gardens, 1980; Tonight At 8.30, Steaming, Arms and the Man, 1981; Steafel's Variations, 1982; Messiah, Pack of Lies, 1983; Of Mice and Men, The Secret Diary of Adrian Mole Aged 13¾, 1984; Camille, 1985. New York prodns (jtly): How the Other Half Loves, 1971; Sherlock Holmes, London Assurance, 1974; Travesties, 1975; The Merchant, 1977; Players, 1978; Once a Catholic, 1979. *Address:* c/o Rethymnis & Kulukundis, Ltd, 12/15 Fetter Lane, EC4A 1JJ. *T:* 01–583 2266; c/o Knightsbridge Theatrical Productions, Ltd, 2 Goodwin's Court, St Martin's Lane, WC2N 4LL. *T:* 01–240 2196. *Club:* Garrick.

KUNCEWICZ, Eileen, (Mrs Witold Kuncewicz); see Herlie, E.

KUNERALP, Zeki, Hon. GCVO 1971; *b* Istanbul, 5 Oct. 1914; *s* of Ali Kemal and Sabiha, *d* of Mustafa Zeki Pasha; *m* 1943, Necla Ozdilci (*d* 1978); two *s. Educ:* Univ. of Berne. DrIuris 1938. Entered Diplomatic Service, 1940: served Bucharest, Prague, Paris, Nato Delegn and at Min. of Foreign Affairs, Ankara; Asst Sec.-Gen. 1957; Sec.-Gen. 1960; Ambassador to Berne, 1960, to Court of St James's, 1964–66; Sec.-Gen. at Min. of Foreign Affairs, Ankara, 1966–69; Ambassador to Court of St James's, 1969–72, to Spain, 1972–79, retired. Mem., Hon. Soc. of Knights of the Round Table. Holds German, Greek, Italian, Papal, Jordanian, Iranian and National Chinese orders. *Publication:* Sadece Diplomat (memoirs), 1981. *Recreations:* reading, ballet. *Address:* Fenerbahçe Cad. 85/B, D4, Kiziltoprak, Istanbul, Turkey.

KÜNG, Prof. Dr Hans; Ordinary Professor of Ecumenical Theology, since 1980 and Director of Institute for Ecumenical Research, since 1963, University of Tübingen; *b* Sursee, Lucerne, 19 March 1928. *Educ:* schools in Sursee and Lucerne; Papal Gregorian Univ., Rome (LPhil, LTh); Sorbonne; Inst. Catholique, Paris. DTheol 1957. Further studies in Amsterdam, Berlin, Madrid, London. Ordained priest, 1954. Pastoral work, Hofkirche, Lucerne, 1957–59; Asst for dogmatic theol., Univ. of Münster, 1959–60; Ord. Prof. of fundamental theol., 1960–63, Ord. Prof. of dogmatic and ecumenical theol., 1963–80, Univ. of Tübingen. Official theol. consultant (peritus) to 2nd Vatican Council, 1962–65; Guest Professor: Union Theol. Seminary, NYC, 1968; Univ. of Basle, 1969; Univ. of Chicago Divinity Sch., 1981; Univ. of Michigan, 1983; Toronto Univ., 1985; guest lectures at univs in Europe, America, Asia and Australia; Hon. Pres., Edinburgh Univ. Theol Soc., 1982–83. Editor series, Theologische Meditationen; co-Editor series, Ökumenische Forschungen and Ökumenische Theologie; Associate Editor: Tübingen Theologische Quartalschrift, 1960–80; Jl of Ecum. Studies; Mem. Exec. Editorial Cttee, Concilium. Mem., Amer. and German Pen Clubs. Holds hon. doctorates. *Publications:* (first publication in German) The Council and Reunion, 1961; That the World may Believe, 1963; The Living Church, 1963; The Changing Church, 1965; Justification: the doctrine of Karl Barth and a Catholic reflection, 1965; Structures of the Church, 1965; The Church, 1967; Truthfulness: the future of the Church, 1968; Infallible? an enquiry, 1971 (paperback 1972); Why Priests?, 1972; 20 Thesen zum Christsein, 1975; On Being a Christian, 1977 (abridged as The Christian Challenge, 1979); Was ist Firmung?, 1976; Jesus im Widerstreit: ein jüdisch-christlicher Dialog (with Pinchas Lapide), 1976; Signposts for the Future, 1978; Does God Exist?, 1980; Freud and the Problem of God, 1979; The Church—Maintained in Truth?, 1980; Eternal Life?, 1984; (jtly) Christianity and World Religions, 1986; The Incarnation of God, 1986; contribs to Theologische Meditationen, and to Christian Revelation and World Religions, ed J. Neuner, 1967. American edns of the above books and also of contribs to Theol. Med., etc, the latter under one title, Freedom Today, 1966. *Address:* 7400 Tübingen 1, Waldhäuserstrasse 23, SW Germany.

KURIA, Most Rev. Manasses; see Kenya, Archbishop of.

KURONGKU, Most Rev. Sir Peter; see Port Moresby, Archbishop of, (RC).

KUROSAWA, Akira; Japanese film director; *b* 23 March 1910. *Educ:* Keika Middle School. Assistant Director, Toho Film Co., 1936. Mem. Jury, Internat. Film Fest. of India, 1977. Directed first film, Sanshiro Sugata, 1943. *Films include:* Sanshiro Sugata; The Most Beautiful, 1944; Sanshiro Sugata II, 1945; They Who Step on the Tiger's Tail, 1945; No Regret for our Youth, 1946; One Wonderful Sunday, 1947; Drunken Angel, 1948; The Quiet Duel, 1949; Stray Dog, 1949; Scandal, 1950; Rashomon (1st prize, Venice Film Fest.), 1950; The Idiot, 1951; Ikuru, 1952; Seven Samurai, 1954; Record of a Living Being, 1955; The Throne of Blood, 1957; The Lower Depths, 1957; The Hidden Fortress, 1958; The Bad Sleep Well, 1960; Yojimbo, 1961; Sanjuro, 1962; High and Low, 1963; Red Beard, 1965; Dodes'kaden, 1970; Dersu Uzala (Oscar award), 1975; Kagemusha (Golden Palm Award, Cannes Film Festival), 1980; Ran, 1985. *Publication:* Something like an Autobiography (trans. Audie Bock), 1984.

KURTI, Prof. Nicholas, CBE 1973; FRS 1956; MA Oxon; DrPhil (Berlin); FInstP; Emeritus Professor of Physics, University of Oxford; Vice-President, Royal Society, 1965–67; *b* 14 May 1908; *s* of late Károly Kürti and Margit Pintér, Budapest; *m* 1946, Georgiana, *d* of late Brig.-Gen. and Mrs C. T. Shipley; two *d. Educ:* Minta-Gymnasium, Budapest; University of Paris (Licence ès sci. phys.); University of Berlin (DrPhil). Asst, Techn Hochschule Breslau, 1931–33; Research Position, Clarendon Laboratory, Oxford, 1933–40; UK Atomic Bomb Project, 1940–45; University Demonstrator in Physics, Oxford, 1945–60; Reader in Physics, Oxford, 1960–67; Prof. of Physics, Oxford, 1967–75; Senior Research Fellow, Brasenose Coll., 1947–67; Professorial Fellow, 1967–75, Emeritus Fellow, 1975–. Buell G. Gallagher Visiting Prof., City Coll., New York, 1963; Vis. Prof., Univ. of Calif, Berkeley, 1964; Dist. Vis. Prof., Amherst Coll., 1979. May Lecture, Inst. of Metals, 1963; Kelvin Lecture, IEE, 1971; Larmor Lecture,

Queen's Univ., Belfast, 1975; James Scott Prize and Lecture, RSE, 1976; Cherwell-Simon Lecture, Oxford Univ., 1977; Tyndall Lecture, Inst. of Physics, Royal Dublin Soc., 1980. A Governor, College of Aeronautics, Cranfield, 1953–69. Member: Electricity Supply Research Council, 1960–79; Advisory Cttee for Scientific and Technical Information, 1966–68; Comité de Direction, Service Nat. des Champs Intenses, CNRS, 1973–75; Comité, Problèmes Socio-économique de l'Energie, CNRS, 1975–78; Chairman: Adv. Cttee for Research on Measurement and Standards, DTI, 1969–73; Jt Cttee on Scientific and Technol Records, Royal Soc./Royal Commn on Historical MSS, 1970–76. Member: Council, Royal Soc., 1964–67; Council, Soc. Française de Physique, 1957–60, 1970–73; Council, Inst. of Physics and Physical Soc., 1969–73; Treasurer, CODATA (Cttee on data for sci. and technol., ICSU), 1973–80; Chm., Cttee of Management, Science Policy Foundn, 1970–75. Foreign Hon. Mem., Amer. Acad. Arts and Sciences, 1968; Hon. Member: Hungarian Acad. of Sciences, 1970; Société Française de Physique, 1974; Fachverband deutscher Köche, 1978; Foreign Member: Finnish Acad. of Sciences and Letters, 1974; Akad. der Wissenschaften der DDR, 1976. Holweck Prize (British and French Physical Socs), 1955; Fritz London Award, 1957; Hughes Medal, Royal Soc., 1969. Chevalier de la Légion d'Honneur, 1976. Publications: (jointly) Low Temperature Physics, 1952. Papers on cryophysics, magnetism, energy and culinary physics; articles in the New Chambers's Encyclopædia. Recreations: cooking, enjoying its results and judiciously applying physics to the noble art of cookery. Address: 38 Blandford Avenue, Oxford OX2 8DZ. T: 56176; Department of Engineering Science, Parks Road, Oxford OX1 3PJ. T: 59988. Club: Athenæum.

KUSCH, Prof. Polykarp; Regental Professor Emeritus, Department of Physics, The University of Texas at Dallas, since 1982; b Germany, 26 Jan. 1911; s of John Matthias Kusch and Henrietta van der Haas; m 1935, Edith Starr McRoberts (d 1959); three d; m 1960, Betty Jane Pezzoni; two d. Educ: Case Inst. of Technology, Cleveland, O (BS); Univ. of Illinois, Urbana, Ill. (MS, PhD). Asst, Univ. of Illinois, 1931–36; Research Asst, Univ. of Minnesota, 1936–37; Instr in Physics, Columbia Univ., 1937–41; Engr, Westinghouse Electric Corp., 1941–42; Mem. Tech. Staff, Div. of Govt Aided Research, Columbia Univ., 1942–44; Mem. Tech. Staff, Bell Telephone Laboratories, 1944–46; Columbia University: Associate Prof. of Physics, 1946–49; Prof. of Physics, 1949–72; Exec. Officer, Dept of Physics, 1949–52, Chm. 1960–63; Exec. Dir, Columbia Radiation Laboratory, 1952–60; Vice-Pres. and Dean of Faculties, 1969–70; Exec. Vice-Pres. and Provost, 1970–71; University of Texas at Dallas: Prof. of Physics, 1972–74; Eugene McDermott Prof., 1974–80; U. T. System Chair, 1980–82. Member: Nat. Acad. of Sciences, US; American Philosophical Soc.; Amer. Acad. of Arts and Scis. Phi Beta Kappa. Hon. DSc: Case Inst. of Tech., 1956; Ohio State Univ., 1959; Colby Coll., 1961; Univ. of Illinois, 1961; Gustavus Adolphus Coll., 1963; Yeshiva Univ., 1976; Incarnate Word Coll., 1980; Columbia Univ., 1983. (Jointly) Nobel Prize in Physics, 1955. Publications: technical articles in Physical Review and other jls. Address: University of Texas at Dallas, Department of Physics, PO Box 830688, Richardson, Texas 75080–0688, USA; 7241 Paldao, Dallas, Texas 75240, USA. T: (214)661–1247.

KUSTOW, Michael David; Commissioning Editor for Arts Programmes, Channel Four Television, since 1981; writer, stage director; b 18 Nov. 1939; m 1973, Orna, d of Jacob and Rivka Spector, Haifa, Israel. Educ: Haberdashers' Aske's; Wadham Coll., Oxford (BA Hons English). Festivals Organiser, Centre 42, 1962–63; Royal Shakespeare Theatre Company: Dir, RSC Club, Founder of Theatregoround, Editor of Flourish, 1963–67; Dir, Inst. of Contemporary Arts, 1967–70; Associate Dir, National Theatre, 1973–81. Lectr in Dramatic Arts, Harvard Univ., 1980–82. Productions: Punch and Judas, Trafalgar Square, 1963; I Wonder, ICA, 1968; Nicholas Tomalin Reporting, 1975; Brecht Poetry and Songs, 1976; Larkinland, Groucho Letters, Robert Lowell, Audience, 1977–78; Miss South Africa, Catullus, A Nosegay of Light Verse, The Voice of Babel, Anatol, 1979; Iris Murdoch's Art and Eros, Shakespeare's Sonnets, Stravinsky's Soldier's Tale, 1980; Charles Wood's Has Washington Legs, Harold Pinter's Family Voices, 1981. Exhibitions: Tout Terriblement Guillaume Apollinaire, ICA, 1968; AAARGH! A Celebration of Comics, ICA, 1971. Publications: Punch and Judas, 1964; The Book of US, 1968; Tank: an autobiographical fiction, 1975. Recreations: painting, jazz. Address: c/o Channel Four Television, 60 Charlotte Street, W1.

KUTSCHER, Hans, Dr Jur; President, Court of Justice of the European Communities, 1976–80 (Judge of Court, 1970–80), retired 1980; b Hamburg, 14 Dec. 1911, m 1946, Irmgard Schroeder; two step d. Educ: Univ. of Graz, Austria; Univ. of Freiburg-im-Breisgau, Berlin. Started career as civil servant; Ministry of: Commerce and Industry, Berlin, 1939; Transport, Baden Württemberg, 1946–51; Foreign Affairs, Bonn, 1951; Sec., Legal Cttee and Conf. Cttee of Bundesrat, 1951–55; Judge, Federal Constitutional Court, 1955–70. Hon. Prof., Univ. of Heidelberg, 1965. Hon. Bencher: Middle Temple, 1976; King's Inns, Dublin, 1977. Awarded Grand Cross Verdienstorden of Federal Republic of Germany, 1980. Publications: Die Enteignung, 1938; Bonner Vertrag mit Zusatzvereinbarungen, 1952; various contribs to professional jls. Recreations: literature, history. Address: Viertelstrasse 10, D-7506 Bad Herrenalb 5, W Germany.

KUYPERS, Prof. Henricus Gerardus Jacobus Maria; Professor of Anatomy and Head of the Department of Anatomy, University of Cambridge, since 1984; b 9 Sept. 1925; s of A. Kuypers and C. J. M. Kuypers(née Buys); m 1955, M. F. Schaap (decd); two s four d. Educ: RC Gymnasium, Rotterdam; Univ. of Leiden, faculty of Medicine (MD, PhD). Resident, Clinical Neurology, University, Groningen, 1954–55; Asst Prof./Associate Prof. of Anatomy, Univ. of Maryland Med. Sch., 1955–62; Associate Prof./Full Prof. of Anatomy, Western Reserve Med. Sch., Cleveland, Ohio, 1962–66; Prof. of Anatomy/Head of Dept of Anatomy, Erasmus University Med. Sch., Rotterdam, 1966–84. Publications: Handbook of the American Physiological Society, 1980; Progress in Brain Research, 1982; regular contributor to Brain, Brain Res., Neuroscience Letters, Experimental Brain Res. Recreations: history, pictorial art, swimming, canoeing. Address: 2 Southmead, 21 Chaucer Road, Cambridge CB2 2EB. T: Cambridge 62696.

KWAKYE, Dr Emmanuel Bamfo; Project Coordinator, UNESCO, Nairobi, Kenya, since 1985 (Consultant Project Coordinator, 1982–85); b 19 March 1933; s of Rev. W. H. Kwakye and F. E. A. Kwakye; m 1964, Gloria E. (née Mensah); two d. Educ: a Presbyterian sch., Ghana; Achimota Secondary Sch., Ghana; Technical Univ., Stuttgart, West Germany (DipIng, DrIng). Development Engr, Siemens & Halske, Munich, W Germany, 1960–62; Univ. of Science and Technology, Kumasi: Lectr, 1963; Sen. Lectr, 1964; Associate Prof., 1966; Head of Dept, 1970; Dean of Faculty, 1971; Pro Vice-Chancellor, 1971; Vice-Chancellor, 1974–82. Visiting Prof., Bradley Univ., Peoria, USA, 1981. Publications: design and research reports on digital equipment. Recreations: reading, indoor games, opera and operette. Address: UNESCO-ROSTA, PO Box 30592, Nairobi, Kenya.

KWAPONG, Alexander Adum, MA, PhD Cantab; Vice-Rector for Institutional Planning and Resource Development, United Nations University, since 1976; b Akropong, Akwapim, 8 March 1927; s of E. A. Kwapong and Theophilia Kwapong; m 1956, Evelyn Teiko Caesar, Ada; six d. Educ: Presbyterian junior and middle schools, Akropong; Achimota Coll.; King's Coll., Cambridge (Exhibr, Minor Schol. and Foundn

Schol.). BA 1951, MA 1954, PhD 1957, Cantab. 1st cl. prelims, Pts I and II, Classical Tripos, 1951; Sandys Res. Student, Cambridge Univ.; Richards Prize, Rann Kennedy Travel Fellowship, King's Coll., Cambridge. Lectr in Classics, UC Gold Coast, 1953, Sen. Lectr in Classics 1960; Vis. Prof., Princeton Univ., 1961–62; Prof. of Classics, Univ. of Ghana, 1962; Dean of Arts, Pro-Vice-Chancellor, Univ. of Ghana, 1963–65, Vice-Chancellor 1966–75. Chairman: Educn Review Cttee, Ghana Govt, 1966–67; Smithsonian Instn 3rd Internat. Symposium, 1969; Assoc. of Commonwealth Univs, 1971. Member: Admin. Bd, Internat. Assoc. Univs, Paris; Exec. Bd, Assoc. African Univs, 1967–74; Bd of Trustees, Internat. Council for Educnl Develt, NY; Aspen Inst. for Humanistic Studies; Bd of Dirs, Internat. Assoc. for Cultural Freedom, Paris, 1967–75. Fellow, Ghana Academy of Arts and Sciences. Hon. DLitt: Warwick; Ife; Hon. LLD Princeton. Order of Volta, Ghana. Publications: Higher Education and Development in Africa Today: a reappraisal, 1979; Underdevelopment and the Challenges of the 1980's: the role of knowledge, 1980; The Relevance of the African Universities to the Development Needs of Africa, 1980; The Humanities and National Development: a second look, 1984; The Crisis of Development: education and identity, 1985; contribs to: Grecs et Barbars, 1962; Dawn of African History (ed R. Oliver); Man and Beast: Comparative Social Behaviour (ed J. F. Eisenberg and W. S. Dillon), 1971; various articles in classical jls, especially on Ancient and Greco-Roman Africa; various addresses and lectures on internat. higher educn in ICED pubns. Recreations: tennis, billiards, music and piano-playing. Address: The United Nations University, Toho Seimei Building, 15–1, Shibuya 2–chome, Shibuya-ku, Tokyo 150, Japan. T: 03–499–2811. Club: Athenæum.

KYLE, James, FRCSE; FRCSI; FRCS; Consultant Surgeon, Aberdeen Royal Infirmary, since 1959; Chairman, British Medical Association, since 1984; b 26 March 1925; s of John Kyle and Dorothy Frances Kyle; m 1950, Dorothy Elizabeth Galbraith; two d. Educ: Queen's Univ., Belfast. MB BCh BAO 1947 (Gold Medal in Surgery); MCh 1956 (Gold Medal); DSc 1972. FRCSI 1953; FRCS 1954; FRCSE 1964. Mayo Clinic, USA, 1950; Tutor in Surgery, QUB, 1952; Lectr in Surgery, Univ. of Liverpool, 1957; Aberdeen University: Sen. Lectr, Surgery, 1959; Mem., Univ. Senatus, 1970. Member: GMC, 1979; Grampian Health Bd, 1973; Chairman: Scottish Cttee for Hosp. Med. Services, 1977; Rep. Body, BMA, 1984; Scottish Jt Consultants' Cttee, 1984. FRPSL. Publications: Peptic Ulceration, 1960; Pye's Surgical Handicraft, 21st edn, 1962; Scientific Foundations of Surgery, 3rd edn, 1967; Crohn's Disease, 1973; papers on surgery, history, philately. Recreations: amateur radio (callsign GM4 CHX), philately. Address: Grianan, 74 Rubislaw Den North, Aberdeen AB2 4AN. T: Aberdeen 317966. Club: Royal Northern (Aberdeen).

KYLE, Air Chief Marshal Sir Wallace (Hart), GCB 1966 (KCB 1960; CB 1953); KCVO 1977; CBE 1945; DSO 1944; DFC 1941; Governor of Western Australia, 1975–80, retired; b 22 Jan. 1910; s of A. Kyle, Kalgoorlie, Western Australia; m 1941, Molly Rimington (née Wilkinson); three s one d. Educ: Guildford Sch., WA; RAF Coll., Cranwell. 17 Sqdn, 1930–31; Fleet Air Arm, 1931–34; Flying Instructor, 1934–39; served War of 1939–45; Bomber Command, 1940–45; Staff Coll., 1945–47; Middle East, 1948–50; ADC to King George VI, 1949; Asst Commandant, RAF Coll., Cranwell, 1950–52; Dir of Operational Requirements, Air Ministry, 1952–54; AOC Malaya, 1955–57; ACAS (Op. Req.), 1957–59. AOC-in-C Technical Training Command, 1959–62; VCAS, 1962–65; AOC-in-C, Bomber Command, 1965–68, Strike Command, 1968; retired. ADC to the Queen, 1952–56. Air Marshal, 1961; Air Chief Marshal, 1964; Air ADC to the Queen, 1966–68. Pres., Fairbridge Soc., 1980–. Hon. DTech W Australia Inst. of Technology, 1979; Hon. LLD Univ. of Western Australia, 1980. KStJ 1976. Recreation: golf. Address: Kingswood, Tiptoe, near Lymington, Hants. Club: Royal Air Force.

KYME, Rt. Rev. Brian Robert; an Assistant Bishop of Perth, Western Australia, since 1982; b 22 June 1935; s of John Robert Kyme and Ida Eileen Benson; m 1961, Doreen Muriel Williams; one s one d. Educ: Melbourne High School; Ridley Theological Coll., Melbourne (ThL, DipRE). Deacon, 1958; priest, 1960; Curate: St John's, E Malvern, 1958–60; Glenroy and Broadmeadows, 1960–61; Morwell, 1961–63; Vicar, St Matthew's, Ashburton, 1963–69; Dean, Holy Cross Cathedral, Geraldton, WA, 1969–74; Rector, Christ Church, Claremont, Perth, 1974–82; Archdeacon of Stirling, 1977–82. Recreations: golf, reading. Address: 52 Swan Street, Guildford, Western Australia. T: (office) (09)325.7455, (home) (09)279.7790. Club: Rotary.

KYNASTON, Nicolas; freelance organist, since 1971; Consultant Tutor, Birmingham School of Music, since 1986; b 10 Dec. 1941; s of Roger Tewkesbury Kynaston and late Jessie Dearn Caecilia Kynaston (née Parkes); m 1961, Judith Felicity Heron; two s two d. Educ: Westminster Cathedral Choir Sch.; Downside; Accademia Musicale Chigiana, Siena; Conservatorio San Cecilia, Rome; Royal Coll. of Music. Organist of Westminster Cathedral, 1961–71; concert career, 1971–, travelling throughout Europe, North America, Asia and Africa. Début recital, Royal Festival Hall, 1966; Recording début, 1968. Consultant, J. W. Walker & Sons Ltd, 1982–83 (Artistic Dir, 1978–82). Jury member: Grand Prix de Chartres, 1971; St Albans Internat. Organ Festival, 1975. Pres., Incorp. Assoc. of Organists, 1983–85. Hon. FRCO 1976. Records incl. 5 nominated Critic's Choice; EMI/CFP Sales Award, 1974; MTA nomination Best Solo Instrumental Record of the Year, 1977; Deutscher Schallplattenpreis, 1978. Recreations: walking, church architecture. Address: 28 High Park Road, Kew Gardens, Richmond-upon-Thames, Surrey TW9 4BH. T: 01–878 4455.

KYNCH, Prof. George James, ARCS, DIC, PhD (London); CPhys; FIMA; Professor of Mathematics at the Institute of Science and Technology and in the University of Manchester, 1957–78, now Emeritus; Dean, Faculty of Technology, 1973–75; b 26 Oct. 1915; s of Vincent Kynch; m 1944, Eve, d of Edward A. Robinson; one s two d. Educ: Selhurst Grammar Sch.; Imperial Coll. of Science, London. BSc in physics, 1935, and mathematics, 1936; PhD 1939; Sir John Lubbock Memorial Prize, 1936; Hon. MScTech Manchester, 1960. Demonstrator at Imperial Coll., 1937; Lecturer at Birmingham Univ., 1942–52; Prof. of Applied Mathematics, University Coll. of Wales, Aberystwyth, 1952–57. Founder Mem., Council of Inst. of Mathematics and its Applications, 1963–66; Pres., Northenden Civic Soc., 1966–80; Member: Manchester Literary and Philosophical Soc., 1959– (Pres., 1971–73); Manchester Statistical Soc., 1983–. Publications: Mathematics for the Chemist, 1955; articles in scientific jls. Recreations: lecturing, photography, caravanning, dry stone wall-building. Address: Rectory Cottage, Ford Lane, Northenden, Manchester M22 4NQ.

KYPRIANOU, Spyros; Grand Cross of the Order of George I of Greece, 1962; Grand Cross, Order of the Saviour, Greece, 1983; President of the Republic of Cyprus, since 1977; b Limassol, 1932; s of Achilleas and Maria Kyprianou; m Mimi Kyprianou; two s. Educ: Greek Gymnasium, Limassol; City of London Coll. Called to the Bar, Gray's Inn, 1954 (Hon. Bencher, 1985); Dip. Comparative Law. Founded Cypriot Students' Union in England (first Pres. 1952–54). Sec. of Archbp Makarios, in London, 1952; Sec. of Cyprus Ethnarchy in London, 1954; left Britain for Greece, 1956, to work for world projection of Cyprus case; later in 1956, rep. Cyprus Ethnarchy, New York, until 1957;

resumed London post until signing of Zürich and London Agreements, returning to Cyprus with the Archbp in 1959. On declaration of Independence, 16 Aug. 1960, following brief appt as Minister of Justice, became Foreign Minister, accompanying the Pres. on visits to countries world-wide, 1961–71; rep. Cyprus at UN Security Council and Gen. Assembly sessions, notably during debates on the Cyprus question; signed Agreement in Moscow for Soviet Military Aid to Cyprus, 1964; had several consultations with Greek Govt on Cyprus matter. Mem. Cttee of Ministers of Council of Europe at meetings in Strasburg and Paris (Pres. Cttee, April–Dec. 1967). Resigned post of Foreign Minister, 1972, after dispute with military régime in Athens. Practised law, withdrawing from politics until the coup and Turkish invasion of Cyprus, 1974; travelled between Athens, London and New York, where he led Cyprus delegn during debate on Cyprus in Gen. Assembly of UN, 1974; participated in talks between Greek Govt and Pres. Makarios, 1974; an *ad hoc* member of Cyprus delegn at Security meeting in New York, 1975. Announced estabt of Democratic Party in Cyprus, 1976, becoming Pres. of House of Reps on the party's victory in parly elections. On death of Archbp Makarios, Aug. 1977, became Actg Pres. of Republic, until elected Pres. in same month; re-elected Pres., unopposed, in Feb. 1978 for a full five-year term; re-elected for further five-year term, 1983. Holds numerous foreign decorations. *Recreations:* literature, music, sport. *Address:* The Presidential Palace, Nicosia, Cyprus.

KYRIAZIDES, Nikos Panayis; Comdr, Order of George I of Greece; Greek Ambassador to the Court of St James's, 1982–85; *b* 3 Sept. 1927; *m* 1960, Ellie Kyrou; one *s* one *d*.

Educ: Exeter Coll., Oxford Univ. (BA); Chicago Univ. Min. of Co-ordination, 1949; Head, Monetary Policy Div., 1950–51; Dir, External Payments and Trade, 1951–54; Asst Economic Advr, Bank of Greece, 1956–60; Mem., Greek Delegn, negotiations for EFTA and assoc. of Greece to EEC, 1957–61; seconded to Min. of Co-ordination as Dir Gen., relations with EEC, 1962–64; Economic Advr, Nat. Bank of Greece, 1964–67; Sen. Economist, IMF, 1968–70; Advr to Cyprus Govt, negotiations for assoc. of Cyprus to EEC, 1971–72; Dep. Governor, Bank of Greece, 1974–77; Head of Greek delegn to Accession negotiations to the EEC, 1974–77; Advr to Cyprus Govt on relations with EEC, 1979–82. Knight Commander: Order of Merit (Italy); Order of Leopold II (Belgium); Comdr, Order of Merit (FRG). *Address:* 2 Misthou Street, Athens, Greece. *Clubs:* Athenæum; Athens (Athens).

KYRLE POPE, Rear-Adm. Michael Donald, CB 1969; MBE 1946; DL; *b* 1 Oct. 1916; *e s* of late Comdr R. K. C. Pope, DSO, OBE, RN retd, and of Mrs A. J. Pope (*née* Macdonald); *m* 1947, Angela Suzanne Layton; one *s* one *d*. *Educ:* Wellington Coll., Berks. Joined RN, 1934; Sen. Naval Off., Persian Gulf, 1962–64; MoD (Naval Intell.), 1965–67; Chief of Staff to C-in-C Far East, 1967–69; retd 1970. Comdr 1951; Capt. 1958; Rear-Adm. 1967. Gen. Manager, Middle East Navigation Aids Service, Bahrain, 1971–77. Dean's Administrator, St Alban's Cathedral, 1977–80. DL Herts 1983. *Recreations:* country pursuits, sailing. *Address:* Hopfields, Westmill, Buntingford, Herts. *T:* Royston 71835. *Club:* Army and Navy.
    See also Sir J. E. Pope.

L

LABOUCHERE, Sir George (Peter), GBE 1964; KCMG 1955 (CMG 1951); b 2 Dec. 1905; s of late F. A. Labouchere; m 1943, Rachel Katherine, d of Hon. Eustace Hamilton-Russell. Educ: Charterhouse Sch.; Sorbonne, Paris. Entered Diplomatic Service, 1929. Served in Madrid, Cairo, Rio de Janeiro, Stockholm, Nanking, Buenos Aires. UK Deputy-Commissioner for Austria, 1951–53; HM Minister, Hungary, 1953–55; Ambassador to Belgium, 1955–60; Ambassador to Spain, 1960–66. Retired, 1966. Member of Council, Friends of the Tate Gallery; Pres., Shropshire Br., CPRE; Mem., Dilettanti Society; FRSA. Recreations: shooting, fishing, Chinese ceramics, contemporary painting and sculpture. Address: Dudmaston, Bridgnorth, Salop. Clubs: Brooks's, Pratt's, Beefsteak.

LABOUISSE, Henry (Richardson); consultant on organisation and development matters; lawyer, US; b New Orleans, La., 11 Feb. 1904; s of Henry Richardson Labouisse; m 1935, Elizabeth Scriven Clark (d 1945); one d; m 1954, Eve Curie, qv. Educ: Princeton Univ. (AB); Harvard Univ. (LLB). Attorney-at-Law, NYC, 1929–41. Joined US State Dept, 1941; Minister Economic Affairs, US Embassy, Paris, 1945; Chief, Special Mission to France of Economic Co-operation Administration, 1951–54; Director, UN Relief and Works Agency for Palestine Refugees, 1954–58; Consultant, International Bank for Reconstruction and Development, 1959–61 (Head of IBRD Mission to Venezuela, 1959); Director, International Co-operation Admin., 1961–62; US Ambassador to Greece, 1962–65; Exec. Dir, United Nations Children's Fund (UNICEF), 1965–79. Hon. LLD: University of Bridgeport, 1961; Princeton Univ., 1965; Lafayette Coll., 1966; Tulane Univ., 1967; Hon. LHD: Brandeis Univ., 1983; Hartwick Coll., 1983. Holds several decorations and hon. awards, incl. Woodrow Wilson Award, Princeton Univ., 1978. Recreations: swimming, golf, reading. Address: 1 Sutton Place South, New York, NY 10022, USA. Clubs: Century Association, River, Princeton (NY); Metropolitan, Chevy Chase (Washington).

LABOUISSE, Mrs H. R.; see Curie, Eve.

LABOVITCH, Neville, MBE 1977; Director: Brenta Construction, since 1985; Cadogan Press, since 1979; b Leeds; s of late Mark and Anne Labovitch; m 1958, Sonia Deborah Barney (marr. diss. 1986); two d. Educ: Whittingehame College; Brasenose College, Oxford (MA). Treasurer, Oxford Union, 1945. Dir, 1954–82, Man. Dir, 1966–82, Darley Mills. Chairman: Trafalgar Square Assoc., 1974–; Knightsbridge Assoc., 1978–; Cleaner London Campaign, 1978–; London Environmental Campaign, 1983–; Piccadilly Tourist Trust, 1978–82; Great Children's Party for IYC, 1979; Westminster Quatercentenary Cttee, 1984–; Mem., London Celebrations Cttee for Queen's Silver Jubilee, 1977; Chm., Silver Jubilee Exhibn, Hyde Park; Vice-Chm., Jubilee Walkway Trust, 1978–; Chm., Organizing Cttee, Queen's 60th Birthday Celebrations, 1986. Mem., Vis. Cttee, RCA, 1983–. Dir, Nat. Children's Charities Fund, 1979–. FRSA. Recreations: reading and ruminating. Club: Brooks's.

LACEY, Ven. Clifford George; Archdeacon of Lewisham, since 1985; b 1 April 1921; s of Edward and Annie Elizabeth Lacey; m 1944, Sylvia Lilian George; one s two d. Educ: King's College London (AKC); St Boniface Coll., Warminster. RAFVR, 1941–46. Curate: St Hilda, Crofton Park, 1950–53; Kingston-upon-Thames, 1953–56; Vicar: St James, Merton, 1956–66; Eltham, 1966–79; Borough Dean of Greenwich, 1979–85. Recreation: photography. Address: 8 Shrewsbury Lane, Shooters Hill, SE18 3JF. T: 01–856 3641.

LACEY, Frank; Director, Metrication Board, 1976–79, retired; b 4 Feb. 1919; s of Frank Krauter and Maud Krauter (née Lacey); m 1944, Maggie Tyrrell Boyes, 2nd d of late Sydney Boyes; one s one d. Educ: St Ignatius Coll., N7. Served War, 1939–46, RAFVR. Tax Officer, Inland Revenue, 1936; joined Board of Trade, 1946, Regional Dir, E Region, 1967–70; Counsellor (Commercial), UK Mission, Geneva, 1973–76. Hon. Advr on Metrication to Commonwealth Secretariat, 1979–. Recreation: ski-ing. Address: Alma Cottage, Whistley Green, Hurst, Berks RG10 0EH. T: Twyford 340880.

LACEY, George William Brian; Keeper, Department of Transport, Science Museum, London, since 1971; b 15 Nov. 1926; m 1956, Lynette (née Hogg); two s. Educ: Brighton, Hove and Sussex Grammar Sch., 1938–44; Brighton Technical Coll., 1944–47. BSc(Eng) 2nd Cl. Hons (External, London). National Service, REME, 1947–49. Rolls-Royce Ltd, Derby: Grad. Apprentice, Tech. Asst, Mechanical Develt and Performance Analysis, 1949–54. Asst Keeper, Science Museum, London, SW7, 1954. Chairman: Historical Gp, Royal Aeronautical Soc., 1971–78; Assoc. British Transport Museums, 1973–; Mem. Council, Transport Trust, 1978–. Recreation: golf. Address: Hurst Grange Cottage, Albourne Road, Hurstpierpoint, Hassocks, W Sussex BN6 9ES. T: Hurstpierpoint 833914.

LACEY, Janet, CBE 1960; Director, Christian Aid Department, British Council of Churches, 1952–68, retired; b 25 Oct. 1903; d of Joseph Lacey, Property Agent, and Elizabeth Lacey. Educ: various schools, Sunderland; Drama Sch., Durham. YWCA, Kendal, 1926; General Secretary, YMCA/YWCA Community Centre, Dagenham, 1932; YMCA Education Secretary, BAOR, Germany, 1945; Youth Secretary, British Council of Churches, 1947. Dir, Family Welfare Assoc., 1969–73; Consultant to Churches' Council for Health and Healing, 1973–77. Hon. DD Lambeth, 1975. Publications: A Cup of Water, 1970; series booklets, Refugees, Aid to Developing Countries, Meeting Human Need with Christian Aid, 1956–64. Recreations: theatre, music, reading, crosswords. Club: Nikaean.

LACHMANN, Prof. Peter Julius, FRCP 1973; FRCPath 1981; FRS 1982; Sheila Joan Smith Professor of Tumour Immunology, University of Cambridge, since 1977; Honorary Director of MRC Mechanisms in Tumour Immunity Unit, since 1980 (Head, MRC Group on Mechanisms in Tumour Immunity, 1976–77, Honorary Head, 1977–80); Hon. Clinical Immunologist, Addenbrooke's Hospital, since 1976; Fellow, Christ's College, Cambridge, since 1976; b 23 Dec. 1931; s of late Heinz Lachmann and Thea (née Heller); m 1962, Sylvia Mary, d of Alan Stephenson; two s one d. Educ: Christ's Coll., Finchley; Trinity Coll., Cambridge; University College Hosp. MA, MB BChir, PhD, ScD (Cantab). John Lucas Walker Student, Dept of Pathology, Cambridge, 1958–60; Vis. Investigator, Rockefeller Univ., New York, 1960–61; Empire Rheumatism Council Res. Fellow, Dept of Pathology, Cambridge, 1962–64; Asst Dir of Res. in Pathology, Univ. of Cambridge, 1964–71; Fellow, Christ's Coll., Cambridge, 1962–71; Prof. of Immunology, Royal Postgraduate Med. Sch., 1971–75. Member: Systems Bd, MRC, 1982–86; Med. Adv. Cttee, British Council, 1983–; Council, RCPath, 1982–85. Vis. Investigator, Scripps Clinic and Research Foundn, La Jolla, 1966, 1975, 1980 and 1986; Vis. Scientist, Basel Inst. of Immunology, 1971. Lectures: Foundn, RCPath, 1982; Langdon-Brown, RCP, 1986; first R. R. Porter Meml, 1986; Heberden Oration, 1986. Publications: co-ed, Clinical Aspects of Immunology, 3rd edn 1975, 4th edn 1982; papers in sci. jls on complement and immunopathology. Recreations: walking in mountains, keeping bees. Address: Conduit Head, 36 Conduit Head Road, Cambridge CB3 0EY. T: Cambridge 354433.

LACHS, Henry Lazarus; His Honour Judge Lachs; a Circuit Judge, since 1979; b 31 Dec. 1927; s of Samuel and Mania Lachs; m 1959, Edith Bergel; four d. Educ: Liverpool Institute High Sch.; Pembroke Coll., Cambridge (MA, LLB). Called to Bar, Middle Temple, 1951. A Recorder of the Crown Court, 1972–79. Chm., Merseyside Mental Health Review Tribunal, 1968–79. Chm. of Governors, King David High Sch., Liverpool, 1971–. Address: 41 Menlove Gardens West, Liverpool L18 2ET. T: 051–722 5936.

LACHS, Manfred; Judge, International Court of Justice, since 1967 (President, 1973–76); b 21 April 1914; m Halina Kirst. Educ: Univs of Cracow, Vienna, London and Cambridge; Univ. of Cracow, Poland (LLM 1936, Dr jur 1937); Univ. of Nancy, France (Dr); Univ. of Moscow (DSc Law). Legal Adviser, Polish Ministry Internat. Affairs, 1947–46 (Ambassador, 1960–66). Prof., Acad. Polit. Sci., Warsaw, 1949–52; Prof. Internat. Law, Univ. of Warsaw, 1952; Dir, Inst. Legal Scis, Polish Academy of Sciences, 1961–67. Chm., Legal Cttee, UN Gen. Assemblies, 1949, 1951, 1955; Rep. of Poland, UN Disarmament Cttee, 1962–63; Pres. of Tribunal, Guinea/Guinea-Bissau case, 1983–85. Rapporteur, Gen. Colloque. Internat. Assoc. Juridical Sciences, UNESCO, Rome, 1948; Internat. Law Commn, UN, 1962; Chm., Legal Cttee UN Peaceful Uses of Outer Space, 1962–66; Hon. Sen. Fellow, UNITAR. Member: Inst. of Internat. Law; Ind. Commn on Internat. Humanitarian Issues, 1983–; Curatorium, Hague Acad. of Internat. Law (Vice-Pres.); Acad. of Bologna; Polish Acad. of Sciences. Hon. Mem., Amer. Soc. Internat. Law; Corr. Mem., Institut de France; Foreign Mem., Dutch Soc. of Scis, 1982. LLD (Hon.), Univs of: Budapest 1967; Algiers 1969; Delhi 1969; Nice 1972; Halifax, 1973; Bruxelles, 1973; Bucarest, 1974; New York, 1974; Southampton, 1975; Howard (Washington), 1975; Sofia, 1975; Vancouver, 1976; London, 1976; Helsinki, 1980; Vienna, 1984. Gold medal for outstanding contribs devel. rule of law outer space, 1966; World Jurist Award for enormous contrib. to improvement of justice, Washington, 1975; Netherland's Wateler Peace Prize, 1976; also other awards. Publications: War Crimes, 1945; The Geneva Agreements on Indochina, 1954; Multilateral Treaties, 1958; The Law of Outer Space, 1964; Polish-German Frontier, 1964; The Law of Outer Space—an experience in law making, 1972; Teachings and Teaching of International Law, 1977; The Teacher in International Law, 1982 (Cert. of Merit, Amer. Soc. of Internat. Law); numerous essays and articles in eleven languages. Address: International Court of Justice, Peace Palace, The Hague, Holland. T: 92–44–41.

LACK, Victor John Frederick, FRCP, FRCS; FRCOG; retired; b 29 Sept. 1893. Educ: London Hospital (MB, BS 1934). FRCS 1921; FRCP 1934; FRCOG 1935. Examiner: Universities of Oxford and Cambridge and Central Midwives' Board; Midwifery and Diseases of Women Conjoint Board, London; late Lectr in Midwifery and Diseases of Women, Birmingham Univ.; Asst Obst. Queen Elizabeth Hosp., Birmingham; Obst. Regist., Ho. Surg. and Ho. Phys. London Hosp. Obstetrical and Gynæcological Surgeon, London Hospital; Cons. Obstetrician Greenwich Borough Council Maternity Home; Gynæcologist King George's Hosp., Ilford; Obst. and Gyn. Surgeon, Royal Bucks Hosp., Aylesbury. FRSM (Mem. Obst. Sect.); a Vice-Pres., RCOG, 1955–. Publications: (jointly) Ten Teachers of Midwifery and Diseases of Women. Contrib. to medical jls. Address: 82 Bradwell Road, Loughton, Milton Keynes, Bucks MK8 0AL. T: Milton Keynes 666243.

LACKEY, Rt. Rev. Edwin Keith; see Ottawa, Bishop of.

LACKEY, Mary Josephine, CB 1985; OBE 1966; former Under Secretary, Department of Trade and Industry; b 11 Aug. 1925; d of William and Winifred Lackey. Educ: King Edward VI High Sch., Birmingham; Lady Margaret Hall, Oxford (MA). Board of Trade, 1946; Asst Principal, Central Land Bd, 1947–50; BoT, 1950–61; UK Delegn to EFTA and GATT, 1961–66; BoT, subseq. DTI and Dept of Trade, 1966–85; Asst Sec., 1968; Under Sec., 1974. Club: United Oxford & Cambridge University.

LACOME, Myer; Principal, Duncan of Jordanstone College of Art, Dundee, since 1978; b 13 Nov. 1927; s of Colman Lacome and Sara (née Sholl); m 1954, Jacci Edgar; one s two d. Educ: Regional Coll. of Art, Liverpool. MSIAD, MSTD, MInstPkg; FRSA. National Service, RAF, 1946–48. Post-grad. course, 1948–49; designer, New York, 1949–51; consultant designer, London, 1951–59; Head of Sch. of Design, Duncan of Jordanstone Coll. of Art, Dundee, 1962–77. Vis. Fellow, Royal Melbourne Inst. of Technol., 1979. Chm., Fine Art Cttee, Scottish Arts Council, 1986–; Member: Senate, Univ. of Dundee,

1979–; Council, CNAA, 1979–; Scottish Design Council Higher Educn Cttee, 1984–; Governor, Scottish Film Council, 1982–. *Publications:* papers on crafts in Scotland and on Scandinavian design and crafts. *Recreations:* the Arts, the man-made environment, travel, swimming. *Address:* 14 Tayview Terrace, Newport-on-Tay, Fife DD6 8AT. *T:* Newport-on-Tay 543230.

LACON, Sir Edmund (Vere), 8th Bt *cr* 1818; General Manager, Abdul Aziz Al-Babtain, Kuwait, since 1980; *b* 3 May 1936; *s* of Sir George Vere Francis Lacon, 7th Bt, and of Hilary Blanche (now Mrs J. D. Turner), *d* of late C. J. Scott, Adyar, Walberswick; *S* father, 1980; *m* 1963, Gillian, *d* of J. H. Middleditch, Wrentham, Suffolk; one *s* one *d*. *Educ:* Taverham Hall, Norfolk; Woodbridge School, Suffolk. RAF Regiment, 1955–59. Career in sales management and marketing, 1959–. *Recreations:* golf, water-skiing. *Heir: s* (Edmund) Richard (Vere) Lacon, *b* 2 Oct. 1967. *Address:* c/o Abdul Aziz Al-Babtain, PO Box 599, Kuwait. *T:* Kuwait 2412730; Milbrook, Holton St Peter, Halesworth, Suffolk. *T:* Halesworth 2536.

LACOSTE, Paul, OC 1977; DU Paris; Rector, Université de Montréal, 1975–85; *b* 24 April 1923; *s* of Emile Lacoste and Juliette Boucher Lacoste; *m* 1973, Louise Marcil; one *s* two *d*. *Educ:* Univ. de Montréal (BA, MA, LPh, LLL). DUP 1948. Fellow, Univ. of Chicago, 1946–47; Univ. de Montréal: Prof., Faculty of Philosophy, 1948; Full Prof., 1958; Vice-Rector, 1968–75. Practising lawyer, 1964–66. Pres., Assoc. des universités partiellement ou entièrement de langue française, 1978–81. Hon. LLD: McGill, 1975; Toronto, 1978. Chevalier de la Légion d'Honneur, 1985. *Publications:* (jtly) Justice et paix scolaire, 1962; A Place of Liberty, 1964; Le Canada au seuil du siècle de l'abondance, 1969; Principes de gestion universitaire, 1970; (jtly) Education permanente et potentiel universitaire, 1977. *Address:* Université de Montréal, PO Box 6128, Montréal H3C 3J7, Canada. *T:* 343–7761; 2900 boulevard Edouard-Montpetit, Montréal.

LACY, Sir Hugh Maurice Pierce, 3rd Bt, *cr* 1921; *b* 3 Sept 1943; *s* of Sir Maurice John Pierce Lacy, 2nd Bt, and of his 2nd wife, Nansi Jean, *d* of late Myrddin Evans, Bangor, Caernarvonshire; *S* father, 1965; *m* 1968, Deanna, *d* of Howard Bailey. *Educ:* Aiglon Coll., Switzerland. *Heir: b* Patrick Bryan Finucane Lacy [*b* 18 April 1948; *m* 1971, Phyllis Victoria, *d* of E. P. H. James; one *s* one *d*].

LADAS, Mrs Diana Margaret; *b* 8 Feb. 1913; *er d* of late Bertram Hambro and late Mrs Charles Boyle; *m* 1945, Alexis Christopher Ladas (marr. diss. 1955); one *s*. *Educ:* Downe House Sch.; Girton Coll., Cambridge. Before the war, Sec. in Geneva, Malta and London. During War of 1939–45, worked as temp. asst Principal in Min. of Economic Warfare, Board of Trade and Political Warfare executive in Cairo. Transferred to UNRRA, worked in Athens, Washington and London; on the staff of British Information Services, in New York, 1948–50. Began teaching at Westminster Tutors, 1955; joined staff of Heathfield Sch., 1958; Dep. Head of Moira House Sch., 1959, Head Mistress, 1960; Vice-Principal of Queen's Gate Sch., 1962–65; Head Mistress, Heathfield Sch., 1965–72. *Recreations:* gardening and travelling. *Address:* Prospect Place, 154 Peckham Rye, SE22.

LADDIE, Hugh Ian Lang; QC 1986; *b* 15 April 1946; *s* of Bertie Daniel Laddie and Rachel Laddie; *m* 1970, Stecia Elizabeth (*née* Zamet); two *s* one *d*. *Educ:* Aldenham Sch.; St Catharine's Coll., Cambridge (MA). Called to the Bar, Middle Temple, 1969 (Blackstone Pupillage Award); Jun. Counsel to HM Treasury in Patent Matters, 1981–86. Sec., Patent Bar Assoc., 1971–75. Asst Ed.-in-Chief, Annual of Industrial Property Law, 1975–79; UK Correspondent, European Law Rev., 1978–83. *Publications:* (jtly) Patent Law of Europe and the United Kingdom, 1978; (jtly) The Modern Law of Copyright, 1980. *Recreations:* music, gardening, fishing.

LAFITTE, Prof. François; Professor of Social Policy and Administration, University of Birmingham, 1959–80; *b* 3 Aug. 1913; *s* of John Armistead Collier and Françoise Lafitte and adopted *s* of late Havelock Ellis; *m* 1938, Eileen (*née* Saville); (one *s* decd). *Educ:* Collège Municipal, Maubeuge; George Green's Sch., Poplar; St Olave's Grammar Sch., Southwark; Worcester Coll., Oxford. Research and translating for Miners' Internat. Fed., 1936–37; on research staff, and subseq. Dep. Sec., PEP, 1938–43; on editorial staff of The Times, as special writer on social questions, 1943–59; Chm. of PEP research groups on health services, 1943–46, on housing policy, 1948–51. Dean of Faculty of Commerce and Social Science, Birmingham, Univ., 1965–68. Member: Home Office Advisory Council on the Treatment of Offenders, 1961–64; Adv. Cttees Social Science Research Council, 1966–69; Redditch New Town Corp., 1964–75; Chm., British Pregnancy Adv. Service, 1968–. *Publications:* The Internment of Aliens, 1940; Britain's Way to Social Security, 1945; Family Planning in the Sixties, 1964; (part author) Socially Deprived Families in Britain, 1970; many PEP Planning monographs; many papers on abortion and related issues; contributed to British Journal of Delinquency, Eugenics Review, Chambers's Encyclopædia. etc. *Address:* 77 Oakfield Road, Birmingham B29 7HL. *T:* 021–472 2709. *Clubs:* Royal Society of Medicine (London); University (Birmingham).

LA FRENAIS, Ian; writer, screenwriter and producer; *b* 7 Jan. 1937; *s* of Cyril and Gladys La Frenais; *m* 1984, Doris Vartan; one step *s*. *Educ:* Dame Allan's School, Northumberland. *Television:* writer or co-writer (with Dick Clement): The Likely Lads, 1965–68; The Adventures of Lucky Jim, 1968; Whatever Happened to the Likely Lads, 1971–73; Seven of One, 1973; Thick as Thieves, 1974; Comedy Playhouse, 1975; Porridge, 1974–77; Going Straight, 1978; Further Adventures of Lucky Jim, 1983; Auf Wiedersehen Pet, 1983–84; Mog, 1985; Lovejoy, 1986; *US television:* On The Rocks, 1976–77; Billy, 1979; Sunset Limousine, 1983; *films:* writer or co-writer (with Dick Clement): The Jokers, 1967; The Touchables, 1968; Otley, 1968; Hannibal Brooks, 1969; The Virgin Soldiers, 1969; Villain, 1970; Catch Me a Spy, 1971; The Likely Lads, 1975; Porridge, 1979; To Russia with Elton, 1979; Prisoner of Zenda, 1981; Water, 1984; *stage:* writer, Billy, 1974; co-producer, Anyone for Denis?, 1982. Partner (with Dick Clement and Allan McKeown), Witzend Productions; producer, co-producer, director, numerous productions. Awards from BAFTA, Broadcasting Guild, Evening News, Pye, Screen Writers' Guild, Soc. of TV Critics. *Publications:* novelisations of The Likely Lads, Whatever Happened to the Likely Lads, Porridge, Auf Wiedersehen Pet. *Recreations:* music, films, sports, wine, driving. *Address:* 2557 Hutton Drive, Beverly Hills, Calif 90211, USA.

LAGACOS, Eustace P.; Greek Ambassador to the Court of St James's, 1979–82; retired 1983; *b* 4 June 1921; one *d*. *Educ:* Univ. of Athens (Graduate of Law). Embassy Attaché, 1949; served Athens, Paris, Istanbul, Nicosia, London; Minister, 1969; Foreign Ministry, Athens, 1970; Ambassador to Nicosia, 1972; Dir Gen., Economic Affairs, Foreign Ministry, Athens, 1974; Permanent Representative to NATO, Brussels, 1976. Grand Officer of Order of the Phoenix, Greece; Commander of Order of George I, Greece; Grand Cordon of Order of Manuel Amadoi Guerrero, Panama; Commander of Legion of Honour, France; Kt Commander of Order of Queen Isabella I, Spain; Grand Officer of Order of the Republic, Egypt. *Address:* 7 Kapsali Street, Athens 10674, Greece.

LAGDEN, Godfrey William; *b* 12 April 1906; *s* of Augustine William and Annie Lagden; *m* 1935, Dorothy Blanche Wheeler. *Educ:* Richmond Hill Sch., Richmond, Surrey. Sun Insurance Office, London, 1931–34; IBM (United Kingdom) Ltd, 1934–. MP (C) Hornchurch, 1955–66. Pres., Harold Wood Hosp. League of Friends. *Recreations:* cricket, water polo, boxing, and dog breeding. *Address:* St Austell, 187 Southend Arterial Road, Hornchurch, Essex. *T:* Ingrebourne 42770. *Clubs:* St Stephen's Constitutional, Wig and Pen, Spanish.

LAGESEN, Air Marshal Sir Philip (Jacobus), KCB 1979 (CB 1974); DFC 1945; AFC 1959; FBIM; *b* 25 Aug. 1923; *s* of late Philip J. Lagesen, Johannesburg, South Africa; *m* 1944, Dulcie, *d* of late H. McPherson, Amanzimtoti, Natal, S Africa; one *s* one *d*. *Educ:* Jeppe, Johannesburg. Served War, 1939–45, South African Air Force. Joined RAF, 1951; Flying Instructor, Rhodesia Air Trng Gp, 1952–53; Kenya, 1953–55; No 50 Squadron, 1955–57; Staff, RAF Flying Coll., Manby, 1957–59; PSO, C-in-C Middle East, 1959–61; Comdr, No 12 (B) Sqdn, 1961–64; Wing Comdr Ops, No 1 (B) Group 1964–66; CO, RAF Tengah, Singapore, 1966–69; SPSO, Strike Comd, 1969–70; Dir Ops (S), RAF, MoD, 1970–72; SASO, HQ Strike Comd, 1972–73; Dep. Comdr, RAF Germany, 1973–75; AOC 1 Group, 1975–78; AOC 18 Group, 1978–80. *Recreations:* golf, motoring. *Address:* c/o Lloyds Bank, 6 Pall Mall, SW1. *Club:* Royal Air Force.

LAGHZAOUI, Mohammed; Ouissam El Ouala (1st class) and Commander of the Order of the Crown, Morocco; Moroccan Ambassador to France, 1971–72; *b* Fez, Morocco, 27 Sept. 1906; *m* 1940, Kenza Bouayad; three *s* three *d*. *Educ:* Moulay Idriss Coll., Fez. Founded many commercial and industrial companies; Chm., Société marocaine des Transports Laghzaoui. During French Protectorate over Morocco, he was Mem. Government's Council (many times Chm.); one of principal Signatories to Act of Independence, 1944; Dir-Gen. of Nat. Security (apptd by late Mohammed V), 1956–60. Then, as Dir-Gen. of Office chérifien des Phosphates (first nat. mining concern) he promoted production and export; later, he was responsible for Office marocain des Phosphates, and Coordinator of Nat. Mining and Industrial Cos. In charge of four ministries: Industry, Mining, Tourism and Handicraft, and was Pres. of Afro-Asiatic Assoc. for Economic Development, 1966–69; Moroccan Ambassador to UK, 1969–71. Holds foreign orders. *Recreations:* bridge, football. *Address:* Résidence Laghzaoui, Route de Suissi, Rabat, Morocco.

LAGOS, Archbishop of, (RC), since 1973 (and Metropolitan); **Most Rev. Anthony Olubunmi Okogie,** DD; *b* Lagos, 16 June 1936. *Educ:* St Gregory's Coll., Lagos; St Peter and St Paul's Seminary, Ibadan; Urban Univ., Rome. Priest, 1966; appointments include: Acting Parish Priest, St Patrick's Church, Idumagbo, 1967–71; Asst Priest, and Master of Ceremonies, Holy Cross Cathedral, Lagos, 1967–71; Religious Instructor, King's Coll., Lagos, 1967–71; Director of Vocations, Archdiocese of Lagos, 1968–71; Manager, Holy Cross Group of Schools, Lagos, 1969–71; Auxiliary Bishop of Oyo, 1971–72; Auxiliary Bishop to Apostolic Administrator, Archdiocese of Lagos, 1972–73. Vice-Pres., Catholic Bishops Conf. of Nigeria; Roman Catholic Trustee of Christian Assoc. of Nigeria; Mem., State Community Relns Cttee. *Address:* Holy Cross Cathedral, PO Box 8, Lagos, Nigeria. *T:* 635729 and 633841.

LAHNSTEIN, Manfred; Member of Executive Board, Bertelsmann Corporation, since 1983; President, Bertelsmann printing and manufacturing group, since 1983; *b* 20 Dec. 1937; *s* of Walter and Hertha Lahnstein; one *s* one *d*. *Educ:* Cologne Univ. (Dipl. Kfm). German Trade Union Fedn, Dusseldorf, 1962–64; European Trade Union Office, Brussels, 1965–67; European Commn, 1967–73; German Govt service, 1973–82: served in Finance Min. and as Head of Chancellor's Office; Minister of Finance, April-Oct. 1982. *Publications:* various articles. *Recreation:* classical music. *Address:* c/o 4830 Gütersloh, Carl Bertelsmann Strasse 270, Federal Republic of Germany. *T:* 05241–801.

LAÏDI, Ahmed; Algerian Ambassador to the Court of St James's, since 1984; *b* 20 April 1934; *m* 1964, Aicha Chabbi-Lemsine; one *d* two *s*. *Educ:* Algiers Univ. (BA); Oran Univ. (LLB). Counsellor to Presidency of Council of Algerian Republic, 1963; Head of Cabinet of Presidency, 1963–64; Head of Political and Economic Dept, Min. of Foreign Affairs, 1964–66; Chm., Prep. Cttee, second Afro-Asian Conf., 1964–65; Special Envoy to Heads of States, Senegal, Mali, Ivory Coast and Nigeria, 1966; Ambassador to Spain, 1966–70; Head, Delegn to Geneva Conf. of non-nuclear countries, 1968; Wali (Governor): province Médea, 1970–74; province Tlemcen, 1975–78; Ambassador to Jordan, 1978–84; Special Envoy to Heads of States and govts, Zambia, Malaŵi, Botswana, Zimbabwe, 1985. Foreign Orders: Liberia, 1963; Bulgaria, 1964; Yugoslavia, 1964; Spain, 1970; Jordan, 1984. *Recreations:* theatre, cinema, football. *Address:* 21 Holland Park, W11.

LAIDLAW, Sir Christophor (Charles Fraser), Kt 1982; Chairman, Bridon plc, since 1985; Director: Barclays Bank PLC, since 1981; Barclays Bank International, since 1980; Amerada Hess Corporation, since 1983; Director, Redland PLC, since 1984; Dalgety PLC, since 1984; Barclays Merchant Bank Ltd, since 1984; TWIL Ltd, since 1985; Mercedes Benz (UK) Ltd, since 1986; *b* 9 Aug. 1922; *m* 1952, Nina Mary Prichard; one *s* three *d*. *Educ:* Rugby Sch.; St John's Coll., Cambridge (MA). Served War of 1939–45: Europe and Far East, Major on Gen. Staff. Joined British Petroleum, 1948: BP Rep. in Hamburg, 1959–61; Gen. Manager, Marketing Dept, 1963–67; Dir, BP Trading, 1967; Dir (Ops), 1971–72; a Man. Dir, 1972–81, and Dep. Chm., BP, 1980–81; President, BP: Belgium, 1967–71; Italiana, 1972–73; Deutsche BP, 1972–83; Chairman: BP Oil, 1977–81; BP Oil Internat., 1981; Boving & Co. Ltd, 1984–86; Director: Commercial Union Assurance, 1978–83; Soc. Française BP, 1964–85; Equity Capital for Industry Ltd, 1983–86. Chm., ICL plc, 1981–84; Pres., ICL France, 1983. Pres., German Chamber of Industry and Commerce, 1983–86; Mem., Internat. Council, 1980–, Chm. UK Adv. Bd, 1984–, INSEAD. Warden, Tallow Chandlers' Co., 1982–. *Address:* 49 Chelsea Square, SW3 6LH.

LAIGHT, Barry Pemberton, OBE 1970; FEng, FIMechE, FRAeS; Consultant to: Design Council; VAWT Ltd; *b* 12 July 1920; *s* of Donald Norman Laight and Nora (*née* Pemberton); *m* 1951, Ruth Murton; one *s* one *d*. *Educ:* Johnston Sch., Durham; Birmingham Central Tech. Coll.; Merchant Venturers' Tech. Coll., Bristol; Bristol Univ. MSc. FEng 1981. SBAC Scholar, apprentice, Bristol Aeroplane Co., 1937; Chief Designer, 1952, Technical Dir, 1960, Blackburn & General Aircraft (devel of Beverley and design of Buccaneer, 1953, for RN service, 1960); Chief Engineer Kingston, 1963, Dir for Military Projects, 1968, Hawker Siddeley Aviation (Harrier develt to RAF service; introd. Hawk Trainer); Exec. Dir Engineering, Short Brothers, 1977–82 (develt SD360 and Blowpipe); Sec., RAeS, 1983–85. Mem. Council, RAeS, 1955– (Pres., 1974–75; British Silver Medal in Aeronautics, 1963); Chairman: Educn Cttee, SBAC, 1962–67; Tech. Board, SBAC, 1967–82; Member: Aircraft Res. Assoc. Board, 1972–77 (Chm., Tech. Cttee); ARC, 1973–76; Air Educn and Recreational Organisation Council, 1969–72; CBI: Mem., Res. and Tech. Cttee; Educn Cttee; Chm., Transport Technology Panel, SRC, 1969–73; Hon. Treasurer, Internat. Council of Aero. Scis, 1978–84; AGARD Nat. Delegate, 1968–73; Sec., Bristol Gliding Club, 1949–52; Mem., Mensa, 1945; Mem., Inst. of Directors. *Publications:* papers in RAeS jls. *Recreations:* reading on any subject, house and car maintenance, music. *Address:* 5 Littlemead, Esher, Surrey KT10 9PE. *T:* Esher 63216. *Club:* Athenæum.

LAINE, Cleo, (Mrs Clementina Dinah Dankworth), OBE 1979; vocalist; *b* 28 Oct. 1927; British; *m* 1st, 1947, George Langridge (marr. diss. 1957); one *s*; 2nd, 1958, John Philip William Dankworth, *qv*; one *s* one *d*. Joined Dankworth Orchestra, 1953. Melody Maker and New Musical Express Top Girl Singer Award, 1956; Moscow Arts Theatre Award for acting role in Flesh to a Tiger, 1958; Top place in Internat. Critics Poll by Amer. Jazz magazine, Downbeat, 1965. Lead, in Seven Deadly Sins, Edinburgh Festival and Sadler's Wells, 1961; acting roles in Edin. Fest., 1966, 1967, Cindy-Ella, Garrick, 1968. Many appearances with symphony orchestras performing Façade (Walton), Pierrot Lunaire and other compositions; played Julie in Show Boat, Adelphi, 1971; title role in Colette, Comedy, 1980; Hedda Gabler; Valmouth; A Time to Laugh; The Women of Troy. Frequent TV appearances. Woman of the Year, 9th annual Golden Feather Awards, 1973; Edison Award, 1974; Variety Club of GB Show Business Personality Award (with John Dankworth), 1977; TV Times Viewers Award for Most Exciting Female Singer on TV, 1978; Grammy Award for Best Female Jazz Vocalist, 1985; Theatre World Award, 1986; Gold Discs: Feel the Warm; I'm a Song; Live at Melbourne; Platinum Discs: Best Friends; Sometimes When We Touch. Hon. MA Open, 1975; Hon. DMus Berklee Sch. of Music, 1982. *Recreation:* painting. *Address:* International Artistes Representation, Regent House, 235 Regent Street, WC1. *T:* 01–439 8401.

LAING, Alastair Stuart, CBE 1980; MVO 1959; *b* 17 June 1920; *s* of Captain Arthur Henry Laing and Clare May Laing (*née* Ashworth); *m* 1946 Audrey Stella Hobbs, MCSP, *d* of Dr Frederick Hobbs and Gladys Marion Hobbs (*née* George); one *s* decd. *Educ:* Sedbergh School. Served Indian Army, 10th Gurkha Rifles, 1940–46, Captain; seconded to Civil Administration, Bengal, 1944–46. Commonwealth War Graves Commission, 1947–83 (Dep. Dir Gen., 1975–83). Chm., Vale of Aylesbury Hunt, 1981–. *Publications:* various articles. *Recreations:* gardening, foxhunting, fell walking, history. *Address:* Wagtails, Lower Wood End, Marlow, Bucks SL7 2HN. *T:* Marlow 4481.

LAING, Austen, CBE 1973; Director General, British Fishing Federation Ltd, 1962–80; Chairman, Home-Grown Cereals Authority, since 1983; *b* 27 April 1923; *s* of William and Sarah Ann Laing; *m* 1945, Kathleen Pearson; one *s* one *d*. *Educ:* Bede Grammar Sch., Sunderland; Newcastle Univ. BA (Social Studies) and BA (Econs). Lectr, Univ. of Durham, 1950–56; Administrator, Distant Water Vessels Develt Scheme, 1956–61. Mem. Cttee of Inquiry into Veterinary Profession, 1971–75. *Address:* Boulder Cottage, Swanland, North Ferriby, North Humberside HU14 3PE. *Club:* Army and Navy.

LAING, Sir Hector, Kt 1978; Chairman, United Biscuits (Holdings) plc, since 1972 (Director, 1953; Managing Director, 1964); Director, Court of the Bank of England; *b* 12 May 1923; *s* of Hector Laing and Margaret Norris Grant; *m* 1950, Marian Clare, *d* of Maj.-Gen. Sir John Laurie, 6th Bt, CBE, DSO; three *s*. *Educ:* Loretto Sch., Musselburgh, Scotland; Jesus Coll., Cambridge. Served War, Scots Guards, 1942–47 (American Bronze Star, despatches, 1944); final rank, Captain. McVitie & Price: Dir, 1947; Chm., 1963. Mem. Bd, Royal Insurance Co., 1970–78; Director: Allied-Lyons, 1979–82; Exxon Corp. (USA), 1984–. Chm., Food and Drink Industries Council, 1977–79. Mem. Council, Wycombe Abbey Sch., 1981–. DUniv Stirling, 1985; Hon. DLitt Heriot Watt, 1986. Businessman of the Year Award, 1979; National Free Enterprise Award, 1980. *Recreations:* gardening, walking, flying. *Address:* United Biscuits (UK) Ltd, Grant House, Syon Lane, Isleworth, Middx TW7 5NN. *T:* 01–560 3131. *Club:* White's.

LAING, James Findlay; Under Secretary, Industry Department for Scotland (formerly Scottish Economic Planning Department), since 1979; *b* 7 Nov. 1933; *s* of Alexander Findlay Laing and Jessie Ross; *m* 1969, Christine Joy Canaway; one *s*. *Educ:* Nairn Academy; Edinburgh Univ. MA (Hons History). Nat. Service, Seaforth Highlanders, 1955–57. Asst Principal and Principal, Scottish Office, 1957–68; Principal, HM Treasury, 1968–71; Asst Sec., Scottish Office, 1972–79. *Recreations:* squash, chess. *Address:* 6 Barnton Park Place, Edinburgh EH4 6ET. *T:* 031–336 5951. *Clubs:* Royal Commonwealth Society; Edinburgh Sports.

LAING, Prof. John Archibald, PhD; MRCVS; Professor Emeritus, University of London, since 1984 (Courtauld Professor of Animal Husbandry and Hygiene, at Royal Veterinary College, University of London, 1959–84); *b* 27 April 1919; *s* of late John and Alexandra Laing; *m* 1946, June Margaret Lindsay Smith, *d* of Hugh Lindsay Smith, Downham Market; one *s* two *d*. *Educ:* Johnston Sch.; Royal (Dick) School of Veterinary Studies, Edinburgh University; Christ's Coll. Cambridge. BSc(Edinburgh); MRCVS; PhD Cantab. FIBiol. Aleen Cust Scholar, Royal Coll. of Veterinary Surgeons. Research Officer, 1943–46, Asst Veterinary Investigation Officer, 1946–49, Ministry of Agriculture; Lecturer in Veterinary Science, 1949–51, Senior Lecturer in Veterinary Medicine, 1951–57, Reader in Veterinary Science, 1957–59, Univ. of Bristol. Anglo-Danish Churchill Fellowship, Univ. of Copenhagen, 1954; Visiting Professor, Univs of: Munich, 1967; Mexico, 1967; Queensland, 1970 (and John Thompson Memorial Lectr); Ankara, 1977; Assiut, 1980; Consultant to FAO, UN, 1955–57; Representative of FAO in Dominican Republic, 1957–58; Consultant to UNESCO in Central America, 1963–65; Mem., British Agricultural Mission to Peru, 1970. Member: EEC Veterinary Scientific Cttee, 1981–; Dairy Product Quota Tribunal for England and Wales, 1984–. Pres., Perm. Cttee, Internat. Congress on Animal Reproduction, 1980–84 (Sec., 1961–80); Member: Governing Body, Houghton Poultry Research Station, 1968–74; Council, Royal Veterinary Coll., 1975–84; Vice-Pres., University Fedn for Animal Welfare, 1977–84 (Treasurer, 1969–75; Chm., 1975–77). Hon. Fellow Veterinary Acad., Madrid. Editor, British Veterinary Journal, 1960–84. *Publications:* Fertility and Infertility in the Domestic Animals, 1955, 3rd edn 1979; papers on animal breeding and husbandry in various scientific journals. *Address:* Ayot St Lawrence, Herts. *T:* Stevenage 820413. *Club:* Athenæum.

LAING, (John) Martin (Kirby); Chairman, John Laing, since 1985; *b* 18 Jan. 1942; *s* of Sir (William) Kirby Laing, *qv*; *m* 1965, Stephanie Stearn Worsdell; one *s* one *d*. *Educ:* St Lawrence College, Ramsgate; Emmanuel College, Cambridge (MA). FRICS. Joined Laing Group 1966; Dir, John Laing, 1980. Member: Exec. Cttee, Nat. Contractors' Group, Building Employers' Confedn, 1981– (Vice-Chm., 1986); CBI Council, 1986–; CBI Overseas Cttee, 1983– (Chm., CBI Export Promotion Cttee, 1983–); SE Asia Trade Adv. Group, 1985–. Dir, Herts Groundwork Trust, 1986–. Mem. Board of Governors, Papplewick School, Ascot, 1983–. *Recreations:* gardening, music, travel. *Address:* Hunsdon House, Hunsdon, near Ware, Herts SG12 8PP.

LAING, Sir (John) Maurice, Kt 1965; Director, since 1939, and President, since 1982, John Laing plc (formerly John Laing & Son Ltd) (Deputy Chairman, 1966–76, Chairman, 1976–82); *b* 1 Feb. 1918; *s* of Sir John Laing, CBE, and late Beatrice Harland; *m* 1940, Hilda Violet Richards; one *s*. *Educ:* St Lawrence Coll., Ramsgate. RAF, 1941–45. Dir, Bank of England, 1963–80. Member: UK Trade Missions to Middle East, 1953, and to Egypt, Sudan and Ethiopia, 1955; Economic Planning Bd, 1961; Export Guarantees Adv. Council, 1959–63; Min. of Transport Cttee of Inquiry into Major Ports of Gt Brit. (Rochdale Cttee), 1961–62; NEDC, 1962–66. First Pres., CBI, 1965–66; President: British Employers Confederation, 1964–65; Export Group for the Constructional Industries, 1976–80; Fedn of Civil Engrg Contractors, 1977–80. Visiting Fellow, Nuffield Coll., 1965–70; A Governor: Administrative Staff Coll., 1966–72; Nat. Inst. of Economic and Social Research, 1964–82. Admiral, Royal Ocean Racing Club, 1976–82; Rear-Cdre, Royal Yacht Squadron, 1982–86; Pres., Royal Yachting Assoc., 1983–. Hon. FCIOB 1981. Hon. LLD University of Strathclyde, 1967. City and Guilds of London Insignia Award (*hc*), 1978; winner, Aims of Industry Free Enterprise Award, 1979. Has keen interest in Church activities at home and abroad. *Recreations:* sailing, swimming. *Address:* Reculver, 63 Totteridge Village, N20 8AG. *Clubs:* Royal Yacht Squadron, Royal Ocean Racing, Arts.

See also Sir W. K. Laing.

LAING, Sir Kirby; *see* Laing, Sir W. K.

LAING, Martin; *see* Laing, J. M. K.

LAING, Sir Maurice; *see* Laing, Sir J. M.

LAING, Peter Anthony Neville Pennethorne; *b* 12 March 1922; *s* of late Lt-Col Neville Ogilvie Laing, DSO, 4th QO Hussars, and of Zara Marcella (*née* Pennethorne), Fleet, Hants; *m* 1958, Penelope Lucinda, *d* of Sir William Pennington-Ramsden, 7th Bt; two *d*. *Educ:* Eton; Paris Univ. Served War: volunteer, French Army, 1939–40, Free French Forces, 1942–44; Grenadier Guards, 1944–46. Attaché, British Embassy, Madrid, 1946; internat. marketing consultant in Western Europe, USA, Caribbean and Latin America; UN, 1975–: Dir of ITC proj. for UNDP in the Congo; Dir, Help the Aged internat. charity, 1976–82; Adviser, European Affairs, Internat. Centre Social Gerontology, 1982–. Creator, Mediterranean Retirement Inc. (wardened housing villages for ageing Europeans of ind. means), 1985–. *Recreations:* people, foreign travel, riding any horse, fine arts. *Address:* Northfields House, Turweston, near Brackley, Northants. *T:* Brackley 700049, 703498. *Club:* Turf.

LAING, Ronald David, MB, ChB, DPM; *b* 7 Oct. 1927; *s* of D. P. M. and Amelia Laing. *Educ:* Glasgow Univ. Glasgow and West of Scotland Neurosurgical Unit, 1951; Central Army Psychiatric Unit, Netley, 1951–52; Psychiatric Unit, Mil. Hosp., Catterick, 1952–53; Dept of Psychological Med., Glasgow Univ., 1953–56; Tavistock Clinic, 1956–60; Tavistock Inst. of Human Relations, 1960–; Fellow, Foundns Fund for Research in Psychiatry, 1960–67; Dir, Langham Clinic for Psychotherapy, 1962–65; Fellow, Tavistock Inst. of Med. Psychology, 1963–64; Principal Investigator, Schizophrenia and Family Research Unit, Tavistock Inst. of Human Relations, 1964–67. Chm., Philadelphia Assoc., 1964–82. *Publications:* The Divided Self, 1960 (London and New York) (Pelican edn, 1962, Penguin repr. 1971); The Self and Others, 1961 (London and New York) (rev. edn 1969, Penguin, 1971); (with D. Cooper) Reason and Violence (introd. by J. P. Sartre), 1964 (London and New York) (Pantheon, 1971); (with E. Esterson) Sanity, Madness and the Family, 1965 (London and New York); (with H. Phillipson and A. R. Lee) Interpersonal Perception, 1966 (London and NY); The Politics of Experience and the Bird of Paradise (Penguin), 1967 (London, repr. 1971), (Pantheon, 1967, New York); Knots, 1970 (London), (Pantheon, 1970, New York), (Penguin, 1972); The Politics of the Family, 1971 (London); The Facts of Life, 1976 (Pantheon, New York); Do You Love Me?, 1977 (London); Conversations with Children, 1978 (London); Sonnets, 1979 (London); The Voice of Experience, 1982 (London and NY); Wisdom, Madness and Folly, 1985. *Address:* 2 Eton Road, NW3. *T:* 01–722 9448.

LAING, (William James) Scott; international trade and marketing consultant, New York City; *b* 14 April 1914; *er s* of late William Irvine Laing and Jessie C. M. Laing (*née* Scott); one *s*. *Educ:* George Watson's Coll., Edinburgh Univ. Appointed to Dept of Overseas Trade, 1937; Asst to Commercial Counsellor, British Embassy, Buenos Aires, 1938; Second Sec. (Commercial), Buenos Aires, 1944; First Sec. (Commercial), Helsinki, 1947; Consul, New York, 1950; Consul-Gen. (Commercial), New York, 1954; Counsellor (Commercial), Brussels and Luxembourg, 1955; Consultant to UN Secretariat, Financial Policies and Institutions Section, 1958, African Training Programme, 1960; Editor, UN Jl, 1964; Chief, Publications Sales Section, UN Secretariat, 1969–76. *Publications:* The US Market for Motor Vehicle Parts and Accessories, 1977; Concentration and Diversification of the Self-Propelled Heavy Machinery Industries in USA, 1979; (jtly) Financial Assessment of the US Automotive Industry, 1982; (jtly) Foreign Outsourcing by US Auto Manufacturers, 1983. *Address:* PO Box 384, Grand Central PO, New York, NY 10163, USA. *Club:* Caledonian.

LAING, Sir (William) Kirby, Kt 1968; JP; MA, FEng, FICE; DL; Chairman, Laing Properties plc, 1978–April 1987; *b* 21 July 1916; *s* of late Sir John Laing, CBE, and late Lady Laing (*née* Beatrice Harland); *m* 1939, Joan Dorothy Bratt (*d* 1981); three *s*; *m* 1986, Dr (Mary) Isobel Lewis, *er d* of late Edward C. Wray. *Educ:* St Lawrence Coll., Ramsgate; Emmanuel Coll., Cambridge (Hon. Fellow, 1983). Served with Royal Engineers, 1943–45. Dir John Laing plc (formerly John Laing & Son Ltd), 1939–80 (Chm., 1957–76). President: London Master Builders Assoc., 1957; Reinforced Concrete Assoc., 1960; Nat. Fedn of Building Trades Employers (now Building Employers' Confedn) 1965, 1967 (Hon. Mem., 1975); ICE, 1973–74 (a Vice-Pres., 1970–73); Construction Industry Res. and Inf. Assoc., 1984– (Chm., 1978–81); Chm., Nat. Jt Council for Building Industry, 1968–74. Member, Board of Governors: St Lawrence Coll. (Pres., 1977–); Princess Helena Coll., 1984–; Member: Court of Governors, The Polytechnic of Central London, 1963–82; Council, Royal Albert Hall, 1970– (Pres., 1979–); Trustee, Inter-Varsity Fellowship; Hon. Mem., Amer. Assoc. of Civil Engineers. Master, Paviors' Co., 1987–88. DL Greater London, 1978. *Publications:* papers in Proc. ICE and other jls concerned with construction. *Address:* Laing Properties plc, Watford, Herts WD1 1JL. *Club:* Naval and Military.

See also J. M. K. Laing.

LAINSON, Prof. Ralph, FRS 1982; Director, Wellcome Parasitology Unit, Instituto Evandro Chagas, Belém, Pará, Brazil, since 1965; *b* 21 Feb. 1927; *s* of Charles Harry Lainson and Anne (*née* Woods); *m* 1st, 1957, Anne Patricia Russell; one *s* two *d*; 2nd, 1974, Zeá Constante Lins. *Educ:* Steyning Grammar Sch., Sussex; London Univ. (BSc, PhD, DSc). Lecturer in Medical Protozoology, London Sch. of Hygiene and Tropical Medicine, London Univ., 1955–59; Officer-in-Charge, Dermal Leishmaniasis Unit, Baking-Pot, Cayo Dist, Belize, 1959–62; Attached Investigator, Dept of Medical Protozoology, London Sch. of Hygiene and Tropical Medicine, 1962–65. Career devoted to research in Medical Protozoology in the Tropics. Hon. Fellow, LSHTM, 1982; Hon. Professor, Federal Univ. of Pará, Brazil, 1982; Hon. Mem., British Soc. of Parasitology, 1984. Chalmer's Medal, Royal Soc. of Tropical Medicine and Hygiene, 1971; Oswaldo Cruz Medal, Conselho Estadual de Cultura do Pará, 1973; Manson Medal, Royal Soc. of Tropical Medicine and Hygiene, 1983. *Publications:* author, or co-author, of approximately 170 pubns in current scientific jls, on protozoal parasites of man and animals. *Recreations:* fishing, swimming, collecting South American Lepidoptera, music, philately. *Address:* Avenida Visconde de Souza Franco, 1237 (Edificio 'Visconti'), Apartamento 902, 66.000 Belém, Pará, Brazil. *T:* 223–2382 (Belém).

LAIRD, Edgar Ord, (Michael Laird), CMG 1969; MBE 1958; HM Diplomatic Service, retired; *b* 16 Nov. 1915; *s* of late Edgar Balfour Laird; *m* 1940, Heather Lonsdale Forrest;

four *d. Educ:* Rossall; Emmanuel Coll., Cambridge. Surveyor, Uganda Protectorate, 1939. Served Army, 1939–46 (Major). Appointed to Malayan Civil Service, 1947; Sec. to Government, Federation of Malaya, 1953–55; Sec. for External Defence, Federation of Malaya, 1956; Sec., Federation of Malaya Constitutional Commission, 1956–57; Dep. Sec., Prime Minister's Dept, Federation of Malaya, 1957. Appointed to Commonwealth Relations Office, 1958; First Sec. (Finance), Office of British High Comr, Ottawa, Canada, 1960–63; High Comr in Brunei, 1963–65; Dep. High Comr, Kaduna, 1965–69; RNC Greenwich, 1969–70; Head of Hong Kong and Indian Ocean Dept, FCO, 1970–72; British Govt Rep., West Indies Associated States, 1972–75. *Recreations:* playing the piano, reading. *Address:* St Jude's Cottage, 87 Fore Street, Topsham, Exeter. *Club:* Royal Commonwealth Society.

LAIRD, Gavin Harry; General Secretary, since 1982, Member, Executive Council, since 1975, Amalgamated Engineering Union (formerly Amalgamated Union of Engineering Workers); Director, Bank of England, since 1986; *b* 14 March 1933; *s* of James and Frances Laird; *m* 1956, Catherine Gillies Campbell; one *d. Educ:* Clydebank High School. Convener of Shop Stewards, Singer Manufacturing Co. Ltd, UK, 1964–71; full-time Trade Union Official, 1971–; Mem., TUC Gen. Council, 1979–82. Dir, BNOC, 1976–86; non-exec. Dir, Scottish TV plc, 1986–; Part-time Dir, Highlands and Islands Develt Bd, 1974–75. Mem., Arts Council of GB, 1983–. *Recreations:* hill walking, reading, bowls. *Address:* Flat 9, 270 Camphill Avenue, Langside, Glasgow G41 3AS. *Club:* AUEW Social Club (Clydebank).

LAIRD, John Robert, (Robin Laird), TD 1946; FRICS; chartered surveyor; Member, Lands Tribunal, England and Wales, 1956–76; retired; *b* Marlow, Bucks, 3 Sept. 1909; *o s* of late John Laird, JP, and Mary (*née* Wakelin); *m* 1st, 1940, Barbara Joyce Muir (marr. diss. 1965); one *s* one *d*; 2nd, 1966, Betty Caroline McGregor (widow). *Educ:* Sir William Borlase's Sch., Marlow; Coll. of Estate Management, London. Partner, private practice, Lawrence, Son & Laird, Chartered Surveyors, Marlow, 1938–56. Served war: 2nd Lieut RA (TA), 1939; Staff Captain 35AA Bde, RA, 1941; Acting Lt-Col Eastern Comd, 1945. *Recreations:* hockey (Scottish International; 12 caps; Captain 1935), rowing, sailing, walking. *Address:* 8 Marine Square, Kemp Town, Brighton, E Sussex BN2 1DL. *T:* Brighton 602065.

LAIRD, Hon. Melvin R.; Senior Counsellor for National and International Affairs, Reader's Digest Association, since 1974; *b* 1 Sept. 1922; *s* of Melvin R. Laird and Helen Laird (*née* Connor); *m* 1945, Barbara Masters; two *s* one *d. Educ:* Carleton Coll., Northfield, Minn (BA 1944). Enlisted, US Navy, 1942, commissioned, 1944; served in Third Fleet and Task Force 58 (Purple Heart and other decorations). Elected: to Wisconsin State Senate, 1946 (re-elected, 1948); to US Congress, Nov. 1952 (83rd through 90th; Chm., House Republican Conf., 89th and 90th); Sec. of Defense, 1969–73; Counsellor to President of the US, 1973–74. Director: Chicago Pneumatic Tool Co.; Metropolitan Life Insurance Co.; Northwest Airlines; Communications Satellite Corp.; Investors Gp of Cos; Phillips Petroleum Co.; Science Applications Internat. Corp.; Martin Marietta Corp.; Public Oversight Bd (SEC Practice Sect., AICPA). Member Board of Trustees: George Washington Univ.; Kennedy Center. Various awards from Assocs, etc (for med. research, polit. science, public health, nat. educn); many hon. memberships and hon. degrees. *Publications:* A House Divided: America's Strategy Gap, 1962; Editor: The Conservative Papers, 1964; Republican Papers, 1968. *Recreations:* golf, fishing. *Address:* Suite 212, 1730 Rhode Island Avenue NW, Washington, DC 20036, USA. *Club:* Burning Tree (Washington, DC).

LAIRD, Michael; *see* Laird, E. O.

LAIRD, Robin; *see* Laird, J. R.

LAISTER, Peter; Director, Inchcape PLC, since 1982; *b* 24 Jan. 1929; *s* of late Horace Laister and of Mrs I. L. Bates; *m* 1st, 1951, Barbara Cooke; one *s* one *d*; 2nd, 1958, Eileen Alice Goodchild (*née* Town); one *d. Educ:* King Edward's Sch., Birmingham; Manchester Univ., Coll. of Technology (BSc Tech; AMCT; FUMIST). FInstPet; FIChemE; CBIM. Process Engr to Refining Co-ordinator, then Gen. Manager, Marketing Ops, Esso Petroleum Co. Ltd, 1951–66; British Oxygen Co. Ltd (BOC Intl Ltd): Chief Exec. Chemical Plant Div., 1966; Chief Exec., Gases Div., 1967–69; a Gp Man. Dir, 1969–73; Chm., BOC Financial Corp. (USA), 1974–75; Gp Man. Dir, Ellerman Lines Ltd, 1976–79; Chairman: Tollemache and Cobbold Breweries, 1978–79; London & Hull Insce Co., 1976–79; Group Man. Dir, Thorn Electrical Industries, later THORN EMI, 1979–83, Chm. and Chief Exec., 1984–85. Industrial Society: Council Mem., 1971–; Mem. Exec. Cttee, 1976–83; Mem., Industrial Develt Adv. Bd, 1981–83. BUPA: Governor, Medical Centre, 1977–; Dir, Research Co., 1977–; Governor, 1980–. Chm., British Foundn for Age Res., 1982–. Mem., Council, UCL, 1978–. *Recreations:* private pilot, gardening, boating and angling, photography.

LAIT, Leonard Hugh Cecil, (Josh Lait); a Recorder of the Crown Court, since1985; *b* 15 Nov. 1930; *m* 1967, Cheah Phaik Teen; one *d. Educ:* John Lyon School, Harrow; Trinity Hall, Cambridge (BA). Called to the Bar, Inner Temple, 1959; Mem., SE circuit. *Recreations:* music, gardening. *Address:* Devereux Chambers, Devereux Court, Temple, WC2R 3JJ.

LAITHWAITE, Prof. Eric Roberts; Professor of Heavy Electrical Engineering, Imperial College of Science and Technology, London, 1964–86; *b* 14 June 1921; *s* of Herbert Laithwaite; *m* 1951, Sheila Margaret Gooddie; two *s* two *d. Educ:* Kirkham Gram. Sch.; Regent Street Polytechnic; Manchester Univ. RAF, 1941–46 (at RAE Farnborough, 1943–46). BSc 1949, MSc 1950. Manchester Univ.: Asst Lectr, 1950–53; Lectr, 1953–58; Sen. Lectr, 1958–64; PhD 1957; DSc 1964. Prof. of Royal Instn, 1967–76. Pres., Assoc. for Science Educn, 1970. S. G. Brown Award and Medal of Royal Society, 1966; Nikola Tesla Award, IEEE, 1986. *Publications:* Propulsion without Wheels, 1966; Induction Machines for Special Purposes, 1966; The Engineer in Wonderland, 1967; Linear Electric Motors, 1971; Exciting Electrical Machines, 1974; (with A. Watson and P. E. S. Whalley) The Dictionary of Butterflies and Moths, 1975; (ed) Transport without Wheels, 1977; (with M. W. Thring) How to Invent, 1977; Engineer through the Looking-Glass, 1980; (with L. L. Freris) Electric Energy: its Generation, Transmission and Use, 1980; Invitation to Engineering, 1984; A History of Linear Electric Motors, 1986; many papers in Proc. IEE (7 premiums) and other learned jls. *Recreations:* entomology, gardening. *Address:* Department of Electrical Engineering, Imperial College, SW7 2BT. *T:* 01–589 5111. *Club:* Athenæum.

LAITHWAITE, John, FIMechE, FInstPet; Director, Capper Neill Ltd, 1965–83 (Vice-Chairman, 1972–82); *b* 29 Nov. 1920; *s* of Tom Prescott Laithwaite and Mary Anne Laithwaite; *m* 1943, Jean Chateris; one *s* two *d. Educ:* Manchester Univ. (BSc Hons Mech. Eng). FIMechE 1974; FInstPet 1960; MInstW 1950. Wm Neill & Son (St Helens) Ltd, 1942–43; Dartford Shipbuilding & Engineering Co., 1943–44; Dir, Wm Neill & Son (St Helens) Ltd, 1955–58, Man. Dir, 1958–64; Man. Dir, Capper Neill Ltd, 1968–72. Mem. Council, NW Regional Management Centre. Chm., Process Plant Assoc., 1975–77, Hon. Vice-Pres., 1980–. *Publications:* articles on process plant industry and pressure vessel standardisation. *Recreations:* shooting, golf. *Address:* Gwydd Gwyllt, Malltraeth, Gwynedd LL62 5AW. *T:* 840586. *Clubs:* Royal Automobile; Haydock Park.

LAITHWAITE, Sir (John) Gilbert, GCMG 1953 (KCMG 1948); KCB 1956; KCIE 1941 (CIE 1935); CSI 1938; Deputy Chairman Inchcape & Co. Ltd, 1960–64, Director 1964–69; former Chairman: Bedford Life Assurance Co. Ltd; Bedford General Insurance Co. Ltd; UK Committee of Federation of Commonwealth Chambers of Commerce; *b* 5 July 1894; *e s* of late J. G. Laithwaite, formerly of the Post Office Survey. *Educ:* Clongowes; Trinity Coll., Oxford (Scholar). Hon. Fellow, Trinity Coll., Oxford, 1955. Served in France with 10th Lancs Fusiliers, 1917–18 (wounded); appointed to India Office, 1919; Principal, 1924, specially attached to Prime Minister (Mr Ramsay MacDonald) for 2nd Indian Round Table Conference, Sept.-Dec. 1931; Secretary, Indian Franchise (Lothian) Committee, Jan.-June 1932; Secretary, Indian Delimitation Cttee, Aug. 1935–Feb. 1936; Private Secretary to the Viceroy of India (Marquess of Linlithgow), 1936–43, and a Secretary to the Governor-General 1937–43; Assistant Under-Secretary of State for India, 1943; an Under-Secretary (Civil) of the War Cabinet, 1944–45; Deputy Under-Secretary of State for Burma, 1945–47, for India, 1947, for Commonwealth Relations, 1948–49; Ambassador, 1950–51 (United Kingdom Representative, 1949–50) to the Republic of Ireland; High Commissioner for the UK in Pakistan, 1951–54; Permanent Under-Secretary of State for Commonwealth Relations, 1955–59. Vice-Chm., Commonwealth Inst., 1963–66; Governor, Queen Mary Coll., Univ. of London, 1959–; Trustee, Hakluyt Soc., 1958–84 (Pres., 1964–69); former Vice-Pres., Royal Central Asian Soc., (Chm. Council, 1964–67); Vice-Pres., RGS, 1969 (Pres., 1966–69); Mem. Standing Commn on Museums and Galleries, 1959–72. A Freeman of the City of London, 1960. Master, Tallowchandlers' Co., 1972–73. Hon. LLD Dublin, 1957. Kt of Malta, 1960; Kt Templar, 1986. *Publications:* The Laithwaites, Some Records of a Lancashire Family, 1941, rev. edn 1961; Memories of an Infantry Officer, 1971; etc. *Address:* c/o Grindlay's Bank, 13 St James's Square, SW1. *Clubs:* Travellers', United Oxford & Cambridge University.

LAJTHA, Prof. Laszlo George, CBE 1983; MD, DPhil, FRCPE, FRCPath; Director of Paterson Laboratories, Christie Hospital and Holt Radium Institute, 1962–83; Professor of Experimental Oncology, University of Manchester, 1970–83, now Emeritus Professor; *b* 25 May 1920; *s* of Laszlo John Lajtha and Rose Stephanie Hollos; *m* 1954, Gillian Macpherson Henderson; two *s. Educ:* Presbyterian High School, Budapest; Medical School, Univ. of Budapest (MD 1944); Exeter Coll., Univ. of Oxford (DPhil 1950). FRCPath 1973; FRCPE 1980. Asst Prof., Dept of Physiology, Univ. of Budapest, 1944–47; Research Associate, Dept of Haematology, Radcliffe Infirmary, Oxford, 1947–50; Head, Radiobiology Laboratory, Churchill Hosp., Oxford, 1950–62; subseq. Research Fellow, Pharmacology, Yale Univ., New Haven, Conn., USA. Editor, British Jl of Cancer, 1972–82. President: British Soc. of Cell Biology, 1977–80; European Orgn for Res. on Treatment of Cancer, 1979–82. Hon. Citizen, Texas, USA; Hon. Member: Amer. Cancer Soc.; German, Italian and Hungarian Socs of Haematology; Hungarian Acad. of Sciences, 1983. Dr *hc* Szeged Univ., Hungary, 1981. *Publications:* Isotopes in Haematology, 1961; over 250 articles in scientific (medical) jls. *Recreation:* alpine gardening. *Address:* Brook Cottage, Little Bridge Road, Bloxham, Oxon OX15 4PU. *T:* Banbury 720311. *Club:* Athenæum.

LAKE, Sir (Atwell) Graham, 10th Bt *cr* 1711; Senior Technical Adviser, Ministry of Defence, retired 1983; *b* 6 Oct. 1923; *s* of Captain Sir Atwell Henry Lake, 9th Bt, CB, OBE, RN, and Kathleen Marion, *d* of late Alfred Morrison Turner; *S* father, 1972; *m* 1983, Mrs Katharine Margaret Lister, *d* of late D. W. Last and of Mrs M. M. Last. *Educ:* Eton. British High Commission, Wellington, NZ, 1942; Gilbert and Ellice Military Forces, 1944; Colonial Administrative Service, 1945 (Secretary to Govt of Tonga, 1950–53); Norris Oakley Bros, 1957; Min. of Defence, 1959; British High Commission, New Delhi, 1966; attached Foreign and Commonwealth Office, 1969–72. *Recreations:* golf, bridge, chess, skiing. *Heir:* *b* Edward Geoffrey Lake [*b* 17 July 1928; *m* 1965, Judith Ann, *d* of John Fox; one *s* one *d*]. *Address:* Magdalen Laver Hall, Chipping Ongar, Essex. *Club:* Lansdowne.

LAKEMAN, Miss Enid, OBE 1980; Editorial Consultant and a Vice-President, Electoral Reform Society, since 1979 (Director, 1960–79); Vice-President, Liberal Party, since 1984; *b* 28 Nov. 1903; *d* of Horace B. Lakeman and Evereld Simpson. *Educ:* Tunbridge Wells County Sch.; Bedford Coll., Univ. of London. Posts in chemical industry, 1926–41; WAAF, 1941–45; Electoral Reform Soc., 1945–. Parly candidate (L): St Albans, 1945; Brixton, 1950; Aldershot, 1955 and 1959. *Publications:* When Labour Fails, 1946; (with James D. Lambert) Voting in Democracies, 1955, (2nd edn 1959; 3rd and 4th edns, 1970 and 1974, as sole author, as How Democracies Vote); Nine Democracies, 1973 (3rd edn 1978); Power to Elect, 1982; pamphlets; articles in polit. jls. *Recreations:* travel, gardening. *Address:* 37 Culverden Avenue, Tunbridge Wells, Kent TN4 9RE. *T:* Tunbridge Wells 21674. *Club:* National Liberal.

LAKER, Sir Freddie, (Sir Frederick Alfred Laker), Kt 1978; Director: Sir Freddie Laker Ltd, since 1982; Northeastern International Airlines Inc. (USA), since 1984; *b* 6 Aug. 1922; British. *Educ:* Simon Langton Sch., Canterbury. Short Brothers, Rochester, 1938–40; General Aircraft, 1940–41; Air Transport Auxiliary, 1941–46; Aviation Traders, 1946–65; British United Airways, 1960–65; Chm. and Man. Dir, Laker Airways Ltd, 1966–82; Dir, Freddie Laker's Skytrain Ltd, 1982–83; creator of Skytrain Air Passenger Service to USA. Hon. Fellow Univ. of Manchester Inst. of Science and Technol., 1978; Hon. DSc: City, 1979; Cranfield Inst. of Technol., 1980; Hon. LLD Manchester, 1981. *Recreations:* horse breeding, racing, sailing. *Clubs:* Eccentric, Little Ship, Jockey.

LAKES, Major Gordon Harry, MC 1951; Deputy Director General, Prison Service, since 1985; *b* 27 Aug. 1928; *s* of Harry Lakes and Annie Lakes; *m* 1950, Nancy (*née* Smith); one *d. Educ:* Army Technical School, Arborfield; RMA Sandhurst. Commissioned RA 1948; service in Tripolitania, Korea, Japan, Hong Kong, Gold Coast (RWAFF), Ghana (Major), 1949–60. Prison Service College, 1961–62; HM Borstal Feltham, 1962–65; Officers' Training Sch., Leyhill, 1965–68; Governor, HM Remand Centre, Thorp Arch, 1968–70; Prison Service HQ, 1970–74; HM Prisons: Pentonville, 1974–75; Gartree, 1975–77; Prison Service HQ, 1977–82; HM Dep. Chief Inspector of Prisons, 1982–85. *Recreations:* golf, photography. *Address:* 3 Claverton Close, Bovingdon, Hemel Hempstead, Herts HP3 0QP. *T:* Hemel Hempstead 833696.

LAKEY, Prof. John Richard Angwin, PhD; CEng, FINucE; CPhys, FInstP; Professor of Nuclear Science and Technology, Royal Naval College, Greenwich, since 1980; *b* 28 June 1929; *s* of late William Richard Lakey and Edith Lakey (*née* Hartley); *m* 1955, Dr Pamela Janet, *d* of Eric Clifford Lancey and late Florence Elsie Lancey; three *d. Educ:* Morley Grammar Sch.; Sheffield Univ. BSc (Physics) 1950, PhD (Fuel Technology) 1953. R&D posts with Simon Carves Ltd, secondment to AERE Harwell and GEC, 1953–60; Asst Prof., 1960–80, Dean, 1984–86, RNC Greenwich. Reactor Shielding Consultant, DG Ships, 1967–; Radiation Consultant, WHO, 1973–74; CNAA Physics Board, 1973–82; Publications Dir, Internat. Radiation Protection Assoc., 1979–; External Examr, Univ. of Surrey, 1980–; Medway Health Authy, 1981–; Vis. Lectr, Harvard Univ., 1984–; Chm., UK Liaison Cttee for Scis Allied to Medicine and Biology, 1984–. Vice Pres., Instn of

Nuclear Engrs, 1983–. Mem. Editorial Bd, Physics in Medicine and Biology, 1980–83; News Editor, Health Physics, 1980–. *Publications:* Protection Against Radiation, 1961; Radiation Protection Measurement: philosophy and implementation, 1975; papers on nuclear reactor safety, radiological protection and management of emergencies. *Recreations:* yachting, photography, conversation. *Address:* Royal Naval College, Greenwich, SE10 9NN. *T:* 01–858 2154. *Clubs:* Athenæum; Medway Yacht; Royal Naval Sailing Association.

LAKIN, Sir Michael, 4th Bt *cr* 1909; *b* 28 Oct. 1934; *s* of Sir Henry Lakin, 3rd Bt, and Bessie (*d* 1965), *d* of J. D. Anderson, Durban; *S* father, 1979; *m* 1965, Felicity Ann Murphy; one *s* one *d. Educ:* Stowe. *Heir: s* Richard Anthony Lakin, *b* 26 Nov. 1968. *Address:* Torwood, PO Box 40, Rosetta, Natal, South Africa. *T:* Rosetta 1613.

LAKING, Sir George (Robert), KCMG 1985 (CMG 1969); Chief Ombudsman, New Zealand, 1977–84, retired; *b* Auckland, NZ, 15 Oct. 1912; *s* of R. G. Laking; *m* 1940, Patricia, *d* of H. Hogg; one *s* one *d. Educ:* Auckland Grammar Sch.; Auckland Univ.; Victoria Univ. of Wellington (LLB). Prime Minister's and Ext. Affairs Depts, 1940–49; New Zealand Embassy, Washington: Counsellor, 1949–54; Minister, 1954–56. Dep. Sec. of Ext. Affairs, Wellington, NZ, 1956–58; Acting High Comr for NZ, London, 1958–61, and NZ Ambassador to European Economic Community, 1960–61; New Zealand Ambassador, Washington, 1961–67; Sec. of Foreign Affairs and Permanent Head, Prime Minister's Dept, NZ, 1967–72; Ombudsman, 1975–77; Privacy Comr, 1977–78. Member: Human Rights Commn, 1978–84; Public and Administrative Law Reform Cttee, 1980–85. Chairman: NZ-US Educnl Foundn, 1976–78; NZ Oral History Archive Trust, 1985–; Wellington Civic Trust, 1985–; Legislation Adv. Cttee, 1986–; Pres., NZ Inst. of Internat. Affairs, 1980–84. Mem. Internat. Council, Asia Soc., NY, 1985–. *Address:* 3 Wesley Road, Wellington 1, New Zealand. *T:* 728–454.

LAL, Prof. Devendra, PhD; FRS 1979; Senior Professor, Physical Research Laboratory, India, since 1983 (Director, 1972–83); Professor (half-time), Geological Research Division, Scripps Institution of Oceanography, University of California, La Jolla, since 1967; *b* 14 Feb. 1929; *s* of Radhekrishna Lal and Sita Devi; *m* 1955, Aruna L. Damany. *Educ:* Banaras Hindu Univ. (MSc); Univ. of Bombay (PhD). Fellow, Indian Acad. of Sciences, 1964. Tata Inst. of Fundamental Research, Bombay: Res. Student, 1949–50; Res. Asst, 1950–53; Res. Fellow, 1953–57; Fellow, 1957–60; Associate Prof., 1960–63; Prof., 1963–70; Sen. Prof., 1970–72. Res. Geophysicist, UCLA-IGPP, 1965–66. Vis. Prof., UCLA, 1983–84. Foreign Sec., Indian Nat. Sci. Acad., 1981–84 (Fellow, 1971); Founder mem., Third World Acad. of Scis, Trieste, 1983; President: Internat. Assoc. of Physical Scis of the Ocean, 1979–83; Internat. Union of Geodesy & Geophysics, 1983–87. Foreign Associate, Nat. Acad. of Sciences, USA, 1975; Associate, RAS, 1984; Mem., Internat. Acad. Astronautics, 1985. Mem., Sigma Xi, USA, 1984. *Publications:* (ed) Early Solar System Processes and the Present Solar System, 1980; *contributed:* Earth Science and Meteoritics, 1963; International Dictionary of Geophysics, 1968; The Encyclopedia of Earth Sciences: vol. IV, Geochemistry and Environmental Sciences, 1972; Further Advances in Lunar Research: Luna 16 and 20 samples, 1974; jt author of chapters in books; scientific papers to learned jls; proc. confs. *Recreations:* music, puzzles, painting, photography. *Address:* Physical Research Laboratory, Navrangpura, Ahmedabad 380–009, India. *T:* (office) 462129, (home) 401451; Scripps Institution of Oceanography, La Jolla, Calif 92093, USA. *T:* (office) 619 534–2134, (home) 619 587–1535.

LAL, Shavax Ardeshir, CIE 1941; Advocate, High Court, Bombay; *b* 12 Nov. 1899; *s* of Ardeshir Edulji Lal, Nasik, Bombay Presidency; *m* 1933, Coomi, *d* of N. N. Master; three *d. Educ:* Fergusson College and Law College, Poona. Practised law, 1926–30; joined Bombay Judicial Service, 1930; transferred to Legal Department, Bombay, 1930; Assistant Secretary to Government of Bombay, Legal Department, 1932–36; nominated member and Secretary of Council of State, 1936–46; Secretary to Government of India, Ministry of Law, 1947–48; Secretary to Governor-General of India, 1948–50; Secretary to President of India, 1950–54. *Address:* Windcliffe, Pedder Road, Bombay, India.

LALANDI, Lina, OBE 1975; Festival Director, English Bach Festival, since 1962; *b* Athens; *d* of late Nikolas Kaloyeropoulos (former Dir of Byzantine Museum, Athens, and Dir of Beaux Arts, Min. of Educn, Athens) and Toula Gelekis. *Educ:* Athens Conservatoire (grad. with Hons in Music); privately, in England (harpsichord and singing studies). International career as harpsichordist in Concert, Radio and TV. Founded English Bach Festival Trust, 1962. Officier, l'Ordre des Arts et des Lettres, 1978. *Recreations:* cats, cooking, Flamenco. *Address:* 15 South Eaton Place, SW1W 9ER. *T:* 01–730 5925.

LALANNE, Bernard Michel L.; *see* Loustau-Lalanne.

LALONDE, Hon. Marc; PC (Can.) 1972; QC 1971; Law Partner, Stikeman, Elliott, Montreal, since 1984; *b* 26 July 1929; *s* of late J. Albert Lalonde and Nora (*née* St Aubin); *m* 1955, Claire Tétreau; two *s* two *d. Educ:* St Laurent Coll., Montreal (BA 1950); Univ. of Montreal (LLL 1954; MA Law 1955); Oxford Univ. (Econ. and Pol. Science; MA 1957); Ottawa Univ. (Dip. of Superior Studies in Law, 1960). Prof. of Commercial Law and Econs, Univ. of Montreal, 1957–59; Special Asst to Minister of Justice, Ottawa, 1959–60; Partner, Gelinas, Bourque Lalonde & Benoit, Montreal, 1960–68; Lectr in Admin. Law for Doctorate Students, Univ. of Ottawa and Univ. of Montreal, 1961–62; Policy Advisor to Prime Minister, 1967; Principal Sec. to Prime Minister, 1968–72; MP (L) Montreal-Outremont, 1972–84; Minister of National Health and Welfare, 1972–77; Minister of State for Federal-Provincial Relations, 1977–78; Minister resp. for Status of Women, 1975–78; Minister of Justice and Attorney-Gen., 1978–79; Minister of Energy, Mines and Resources, 1980–82; Minister of Finance, 1982–84. Counsel before several Royal Commns inc. Royal Commn on Great Lakes Shipping and Royal Commn on Pilotage. Mem., Cttee on Broadcasting, 1964; Dir, Canadian Citizenship Council, 1960–65; Member, Bd of Directors: Inst. of Public Law, Univ. of Montréal, 1960–64; Steinberg Inc., 1984–; Citibank Canada, 1985–; Chm. of Bd, Hotel-Dieu Hosp., Montreal, 1985–. Dana Award, Amer. Public Health Assoc., 1978. *Publications:* The Changing Role of the Prime Minister's Office, 1971; New Perspectives on the Health of Canadians (working document), 1974. *Recreations:* tennis, squash, skiing, jogging, sailing, reading. *Address:* 5440 Légaré, Outremont, Québec H3T 1Z4, Canada.

LALOUETTE, Marie Joseph Gerard; retired; *b* 24 Jan. 1912; 3rd *s* of late Henri Lalouette and Mrs H. Lalouette; *m* 1942, Jeanne Marrier d'Unienville; four *s* two *d. Educ:* Royal Coll., Mauritius; Exeter Coll., Oxford; London School of Economics; Middle Temple. District Magistrate, Mauritius, 1944; Electoral Commissioner, 1956; Addl. Subst. Procureur-General, 1956; Master, and Registrar, Supreme Court, 1958; Assistant Attorney-General, 1959; Solicitor-General, 1960; Puisne Judge, 1961; Senior Puisne Judge, Supreme Court, Mauritius, 1967–70; Attorney, Republic of S Africa, 1973–83; Justice of Appeal, Seychelles, 1977–82. *Publications:* Digest of Decisions of Supreme Court of Mauritius, 1926–43; The Mauritius Digest to 1950; A First Supplement to the Mauritius Digest, 1951–55; A Second Supplement to the Mauritius Digest, 1956–60; The Seychelles Digest, 1982; contrib. Internat. Encyclopedia of Comparative Law. *Recreations:* music, gardening. *Address:* 419 Windermere Centre, Windermere Road, Durban, Republic of South Africa. *T:* 031–237598.

LAM, Martin Philip; Associate Consultant to Mackintosh International, EEC, and others; *b* 10 March 1920; *m* 1953, Lisa Lorenz; one *s* one *d. Educ:* University College Sch.; Gonville and Caius Coll., Cambridge (Scholar). Served War of 1939–45, Royal Signals. Asst Principal, Board of Trade, 1947; Nuffield Fellowship (Latin America), 1952–53; Asst Sec., 1960; Counsellor, UK Delegn to OECD, 1963–65, Advr, Commercial Policy, 1970–74, Leader UNCTAD Delegn, 1972; Under-Sec. (Computer Systems and Electronics), DoI, 1974–78. *Address:* 22 The Avenue, Wembley, Middlesex HA9 9QJ. *T:* 01–904 2584.

LAMB, family name of **Baron Rochester.**

LAMB, Sir Albert; *see* Lamb, Sir Larry.

LAMB, Sir Albert Thomas, (Sir Archie), KBE 1979 (MBE 1953); CMG 1974; DFC 1945; Director, Britoil plc, since 1982; *b* 23 Oct. 1921; *s* of R. S. Lamb and Violet Lamb (*née* Haynes); *m* 1944, Christina Betty Wilkinson; one *s* two *d. Educ:* Swansea Grammar Sch. Served RAF 1941–46. FO 1938–41; Embassy, Rome, 1947–50; Consulate-General, Genoa, 1950; Embassy, Bucharest, 1950–53; FO 1953–55; Middle East Centre for Arabic Studies, 1955–57; Political Residency, Bahrain, 1957–61; FO 1961–65; Embassy, Kuwait, 1965; Political Agent in Abu Dhabi, 1965–68; Inspector, 1968–70, Sen. Inspector, 1970–73, Asst Under-Sec. of State and Chief Inspector, FCO, 1973–74; Ambassador to Kuwait, 1974–77; Ambassador to Norway, 1978–80. Member: BNOC, 1981–82; Bd, British Shipbuilders, 1985–; Sen. Associate, Conant and Associates Ltd, Washington DC, 1985–. *Address:* East House, Wyke Hall, Gillingham, Dorset. *T:* Gillingham 3409. *Club:* Royal Air Force.

LAMB, Air Vice-Marshal George Colin, CB 1977; CBE 1966; AFC 1947; Chief Executive, Badminton Association of England, since 1978; *b* 23 July 1923; *s* of late George and Bessie Lamb, Hornby, Lancaster; *m* 1st, 1945, Nancy Mary Godsmark; two *s*; 2nd, 1981, Mrs Maureen Margaret Mepham. *Educ:* Lancaster Royal Grammar School. War of 1939–45: commissioned, RAF, 1942; flying duties, 1942–53; Staff Coll., 1953; Air Ministry, special duties, 1954–58; OC No 87 Sqdn, 1958–61; Dir Admin. Plans, MoD, 1961–64; Asst Comdt, RAF Coll., 1964–65; Dep. Comdr, Air Forces Borneo, 1965–66; Fighter Command, 1966; MoD (Dep. Command Structure Project Officer), 1967; HQ, Strike Command, 1967–69; OC, RAF Lyneham, 1969–71; RCDS, 1971–72; Dir of Control (Operations), NATS, 1972–74; Comdr, Southern Maritime Air Region, RAF Mount Batten, 1974–75; C of S, No 18 Gp Strike Comd, RAF, 1975–78. RAF Vice-Pres., Combined Cadet Forces Assoc., 1978–. Chm., Lilleshall National Sports Centre, 1984–; Member: Sports Council, 1983–; Sports Cttee, Prince's Trust, 1985–; Privilege Mem. of RFU, 1985– (Mem., RFU Cttee, 1973–85). FBIM. *Recreations:* international Rugby football referee, cricket (former Pres., Adastrian Cricket Club). *Address:* Hambledon, 17 Meadway, Berkhamsted HP4 2PN. *T:* Berkhamsted 2583. *Club:* Royal Air Force.

LAMB, Harold Norman, CBE 1978; Regional Administrator, South East Thames Regional Health Authority, 1973–81; *b* 21 July 1922; *s* of Harold Alexander and Amelia Lamb; *m* 1946, Joyce Marian Hawkyard; one *s* one *d. Educ:* Saltley Grammar School. FHA. Served War, RAF, 1941–46. House Governor, Birmingham Gen. Hosp., 1958; Dep. Sec., United Birmingham Hosps, and House Governor, Queen Elizabeth Hosp., 1961; Sec., SE Metrop. RHB, 1968. Mem. Exec. Council, Royal Inst. of Public Admin, 1970–78. *Recreations:* golf, music. *Address:* 40 Windmill Way, Reigate, Surrey RH2 0JA. *T:* Reigate 21846. *Club:* Walton Heath Golf.

LAMB, Prof. John, CBE 1986; FEng; James Watt Professor of Electrical Engineering, since 1961, and Vice-Principal, 1977–80, University of Glasgow; *b* 26 Sept. 1922; *m* 1947, Margaret May Livesey; two *s* one *d. Educ:* Accrington Grammar Sch.; Manchester Univ. BSc (1st class Hons) Manchester Univ. 1943; Fairbairn Prizeman in Engineering; MSc 1944, PhD 1946, DSc 1957, Manchester. Ministry of Supply Extra-Mural Res., 1943–46. Assistant Lecturer, 1946–47, Lecturer, 1947–56, Reader, 1956–61, in Electrical Engineering at Imperial Coll. (London Univ.); Assistant Director, Department of Electrical Engineering, Imperial Coll., 1958–61. Gledden Fellow, Univ. of WA, Perth, 1983. Pres., British Soc. of Rheology, 1970–72. Chm., Scottish Industry Univ. Liaison Cttee in Engrg, 1969–71; Member: Nat. Electronics Council, 1963–78; CNAA, 1964–70. FInstP 1960; Fellow, Acoustical Society of America, 1960; FRSE 1968; FIEE 1983; FEng 1984; Hon. Fellow, Inst. of Acoustics, 1980. *Publications:* numerous in Proc. Royal Society, Trans Faraday Society, Proc. Instn Electrical Engineers, Proc. Physical Society, Journal Acoustical Society of America, Quarterly Reviews of Chem. Society, Nature, Phys. Review, Journal of Polymer Science; contrib.: (The Theory and Practice of Ultrasonic Propagation) to Principles and Practice of Non-destructive Testing (ed J. H. Lamble), 1962; (Dispersion and Absorption of Sound by Molecular Processes) to Proc. International School of Physics "Enrico Fermi" Course XXVII (ed D. Sette), 1963; (Thermal Relaxation in Liquids) to Physical Acoustics, Vol. II (ed W. P. Mason), 1965; (Theory of Rheology) to Interdisciplinary Approach to Liquid Lubricant Technology (ed P. M. Ku), 1973; (Viscoelastic and Ultrasonic Relaxation Studies) to Molecular Motions in Liquids (ed J. Lascombe), 1974; (Motions in Low Molecular Weight Fluids and Glass forming Liquids) to Molecular Basis of Transitions and Relaxations (ed D. J. Meier), 1978; Shear Waves of Variable Frequency for Studying the Viscoelastic Relaxation Processes in Liquids and Polymer Melts (ed A. Kawski and A. Sliwinsky), 1979; (Development of Integrated Optical Circuits) to Integrated Optics (ed S. Martellucci and R. N. Chester), 1983. *Recreations:* walking, wine-making, music. *Address:* 5 Cleveden Crescent, Glasgow G12 0PD. *T:* 041–339 2101.

LAMB, Hon. Kenneth Henry Lowry, CBE 1985; Secretary to the Church Commissioners, 1980–85; *b* 23 Dec. 1923; *y s* of 1st Baron Rochester, CMG; *m* 1952, Elizabeth Anne Saul; one *s* two *d. Educ:* Harrow; Trinity Coll., Oxford (MA). President of the Union, Oxford, 1944. Instructor-Lieut, Royal Navy, 1944–46. Lecturer, then Senior Lecturer in History and English, Royal Naval Coll., Greenwich, 1946–53. Commonwealth Fund Fellow in United States, 1953–55. Joined BBC in 1955 as a Talks Producer (Radio); became a Television Talks Producer, 1957, and then Chief Assistant, Current Affairs, TV talks, 1959–63; Head of Religious Broadcasting, BBC, 1963–66; Secretary to the BBC, 1967–68; Dir, Public Affairs, BBC, 1969–77; Special Adviser (Broadcasting Research), BBC, 1977–80. *Recreations:* cricket, walking, golf. *Address:* 25 South Terrace, Thurloe Square, SW7 2TB. *T:* 01–584 7904. *Clubs:* MCC, National Liberal; Royal Fowey Yacht.

See also Baron Rochester.

LAMB, Sir Larry, Kt 1980; Editor, Daily Express, 1983–86; Chairman, Larry Lamb Associates, since 1986; *b* Fitzwilliam, Yorks, 15 July 1929; *m* Joan Mary Denise Grogan; two *s* one *d. Educ:* Rastrick Grammar Sch. Worked as journalist on Brighouse Echo, Shields Gazette, Newcastle Journal, London Evening Standard; Sub-Editor, Daily Mirror; Editor: (Manchester) Daily Mail, 1968–69; The Sun, 1969–72, 1975–81; Dir, 1970–81, Editorial Dir, 1971–81, News International Ltd; Dep. Chm., News Group, 1979–81; Dir, The News Corporation (Australia) Ltd, 1980–81; Dep. Chm. and Editor-in-Chief, Western Mail Ltd, Perth, Australia, 1981–82; Editor-in-Chief, The Australian, May

1982–Feb. 1983. *Recreations:* fell-walking, cricket, fishing. *Address:* Hoskins Barn, Buckland Road, Bampton, Oxfordshire OX8 2AA.

LAMB, Sir Lionel (Henry), KCMG 1953 (CMG 1948); OBE 1944; HM Diplomatic Service, retired; *b* 9 July 1900; *s* of late Sir Harry Lamb, GBE, KCMG; *m* 1927, Jean Fawcett (*née* MacDonald); one *s*. *Educ:* Winchester; Queen's Coll., Oxford. Appointed HM Consular Service in China, Dec. 1921; Consul (Gr. II), 1935; served Shanghai, 1935–37, Peking, 1937–40; Consul (Gr. I), 1938; Superintending Consul and Assistant Chinese Secretary, Shanghai, 1940; transferred to St Paul-Minneapolis, 1943; Chinese Counsellor, HM Embassy, Chungking, 1945; HM Minister, Nanking, 1947–49; Chargé d'Affaires, Peking, China, 1951–53; Ambassador to Switzerland, 1953–58, retired. *Address.* Roxford Barn, Hertingfordbury, Herts.

LAMB, Captain William John, CVO 1947; OBE 1944; RN retired; *b* 26 Dec. 1906; *s* of late Sir Richard Amphlett Lamb, KCSI, CIE, ICS, and Kathleen Maud Barry; *m* 1948, Bridget, *widow* of Lieut-Commander G. S. Salt, RN; two *d*. *Educ:* St Anthony's, Eastbourne; RNC Osborne and Dartmouth. Commander, 1941; Staff of C-in-C Mediterranean Fleet, 1940–42; Staff of C-in-C, Eastern Fleet, 1942–44; Executive Officer, HMS Vanguard, 1945–47; Deputy Director of Naval Ordnance, 1948–50; Comd HMS Widemouth Bay and Captain (D) 4th Training Flotilla, Rosyth, 1951–52; Commanding Admiralty Signal and Radar Establishment, 1952–54; Commanding HMS Cumberland, 1955–56. Hon. Life Member: BIM, 1974; RNSA, 1985. *Recreation:* sailing. *Address:* Westons, Bank, Lyndhurst, Hampshire. *T:* Lyndhurst 2620. *Clubs:* Naval and Military; Royal Cruising.

LAMB, Prof. Willis E(ugene), Jr; Professor of Physics and Optical Sciences, University of Arizona, since 1974; *b* Los Angeles, California, USA, 12 July 1913; *s* of Willis Eugene Lamb and Marie Helen Metcalf; *m* Ursula Schaefer. *Educ:* Los Angeles High Sch.; University of California (BS, PhD). Columbia Univ.: Instructor in Physics, 1938–43, Associate, 1943–45, Assistant Professor, 1945–47, Associate Professor, 1947–48, Professor of Physics, 1948–52; Professor of Physics, Stanford Univ., California, 1951–56; Wykeham Prof. of Physics and Fellow of New Coll., University of Oxford, 1956–62; Yale University: Ford Prof. of Physics, 1962–72; Gibbs Prof. of Physics, 1972–74. Morris Loeb Lectr, Harvard Univ., 1953–54; Lectr, University of Colorado, Summer, 1959; Shrum Lectr, Simon Fraser Univ., 1972; Visiting Professor, Tata Institute of Fundamental Research, Bombay, 1960; Guggenheim Fellow, 1960–61; Visiting Professor, Columbia Univ., 1961; Fulbright Lecturer, University of Grenoble, Summer, 1964. MNAS, 1954. Hon. DSc: Pennsylvania, 1954; Gustavus Adolphus Coll., 1975; MA (by decree), Oxford, 1956; Hon. MA Yale, 1961; Hon. LHD Yeshiva, 1965; Hon. Fellow: Institute of Physics and Physical Society, 1962; RSE, 1981; Res. Corp Award, 1954; Rumford Medal, American Academy of Arts and Sciences, 1953; (jointly) Nobel Prize in Physics, 1955; Guthrie Award, The Physical Society, 1958; Yeshiva University Award, 1962. *Publications:* (with M. Sargent and M. O. Scully) Laser Physics, 1974; contributions to The Physical Review, Physica, Science, Journal of Applied Physics, etc. *Address:* Department of Physics, University of Arizona, Tucson, Arizona 85721, USA.

LAMBART, family name of **Earl of Cavan.**

LAMBERT, family name of **Viscount Lambert.**

LAMBERT, 2nd Viscount, *cr* 1945, of South Molton; **George Lambert,** TD; *b* 27 Nov. 1909; *e s* of 1st Viscount Lambert, PC; *S* father, 1958; *m* 1939, Patricia Mary, *d* of J. F. Quinn; one *d* (one *s* decd). *Educ:* Harrow Sch.; New Coll., Oxford. War of 1939–45: TA, Lieut-Colonel 1942. MP (L-Nat) South Molton Division, Devon, July 1945–Feb. 1950. (Nat. L-C) Torrington Division, Devon, 1950–58. Chm., Devon and Exeter Savings Bank, 1958–70. Formerly Chm. Governors, Seale-Hayne Agricultural Coll., Newton Abbot, Devon. Pres., Young Farmers' Club, 1968–70; Life Vice-Pres., National Federation of Young Farmers' Clubs, 1970. DL Devon, 1969–70. *Recreation:* golf. *Heir presumptive: b* Hon. Michael John Lambert [*b* 29 Sept. 1912; *m* 1939, Florence Dolores, *d* of N. L. Macaskie; three *d*]. *Address:* Les Fougères, 1806 St-Légier, Switzerland. *T:* (021) 53 10 63. *Clubs:* Carlton, Army and Navy.

See also Hon. Margaret Lambert, P. W. Gibbings.

LAMBERT, Sir Anthony (Edward), KCMG 1964 (CMG 1955); HM Diplomatic Service, retired; *b* 7 March 1911; *o s* of late R. E. Lambert, Pensbury House, Shaftesbury, Dorset; *m* 1948, Ruth Mary, *d* of late Sir Arthur Fleming, CBE; two *d*. *Educ:* Harrow; Balliol Coll., Oxford (scholar). Entered HM Foreign (subseq. Diplomatic) Service, 1934, and served in: Brussels, 1937; Ankara, 1940; Beirut and Damascus, 1942; Brussels, 1944; Stockholm, 1949; Athens, 1952; HM Minister to Bulgaria, 1958–60; HM Ambassador to: Tunisia, 1960–63; Finland, 1963–66; Portugal, 1966–70. *Address:* 16 Kent House, 34 Kensington Court, W8 5BE. *Club:* Brooks's.

LAMBERT, David Arthur Charles; General President, National Union of Hosiery and Knitwear Workers, since 1982 (General Secretary, 1975–82); *b* 2 Sept. 1933; *m*; two *s* one *d*. *Educ:* Hitchin Boys' Grammar Sch., Herts. Employed as production worker for major hosiery manufr; active as lay official within NUHKW; full-time official, NUHKW, 1964–. Member: Employment Appeal Tribunal, 1978–; TUC Gen. Council, 1984–. *Address:* 55 New Walk, Leicester LE1 7EB.

LAMBERT, Sir Edward (Thomas), KBE 1958 (CBE 1953); CVO 1957; retired from Foreign Service, 1960; *b* 19 June 1901; *s* of late Brig. and Mrs T. S. Lambert; *m* 1936, Rhona Patricia Gilmore, *d* of late H. St G. Gilmore and Mrs J. H. Molyneux; one *s* one *d*. *Educ:* Charterhouse and Trinity Coll., Cambridge. Member of HM Diplomatic (formerly Foreign) Service. Entered Far Eastern Consular Service, 1926; served at Bangkok, Batavia, Medan, Curaçao, and The Hague. Consul-General, Geneva, 1949–53, Paris, 1953–59. Commandeur, Légion d'Honneur, 1957. *Recreations:* reading and travel. *Address:* Crag House, Aldeburgh, Suffolk. *T:* 2296.

LAMBERT, Eric Thomas Drummond, CMG 1969; OBE 1946; KPM 1943; retd, 1968; *b* 3 Nov. 1909; *s* of late Septimus Drummond Lambert. *Educ:* Royal Sch., Dungannon; Trinity Coll., Dublin, 1928–29. Indian (Imperial) Police, 1929–47: Political Officer for Brahmaputra-Chindwin Survey, 1935–36, and Tirap Frontier Tract, 1942; District Comr, Naga Hills, 1938. Commnd General, Chinese Armed Forces, to find and evacuate Chinese Vth Army from Burma to Assam, India, June Aug. 1942; Chief Civil Liaison Officer XIVth Army, 1944; FCO, 1947–68, with service in SE Asia, W Africa, S America, Nepal, Afghanistan. Pres., Republic of Ireland Br., Burma Star Assoc. Trustee, Nat. Library of Ireland. Corresp. Mem., Acad. of History, Venezuela. Chinese Armed Forces Distinguished Service, 1st Order, 1st class, 1942; Cruz Militar, Venezuela, 1983. *Publications:* Assam (jointly with Alban Ali), 1943; Carabobo 1821, 1974; Voluntarios Britanicos y Irlandeses en la Gesta Bolivariana, 1982; articles in jls of RGS and Royal Siam Soc.; Man in India; The Irish Sword. *Recreations:* golf, historical research, lecturing. *Address:* Drumkeen, Glenamuck Road, Dublin 18. *T:* 893169. *Club:* Stephen's Green (Dublin).

LAMBERT, Sir Greville Foley, 9th Bt, *cr* 1711; *b* 17 Aug. 1900; *s* of late Lionel Foley Lambert, 4th *s* of 6th Bt; *S* cousin (Sir John Foley Grey), 1938; *m* 1932, Edith Roma, *d* of Richard Batson; three *d*. *Educ:* Rugby Sch. Chartered Accountant. *Heir: kinsman,* Peter John Biddulph Lambert, archaeologist, Min. of Culture and Recreation and Historical Researches Branch, Govt of Ontario [*b* 5 April 1952. *Educ:* Upper Canada Coll.; Trent Univ.; Univ. of Manitoba. BSc(Hons), MA].

LAMBERT, Harold George; *b* 8 April 1910; *s* of late Rev. David Lambert; *m* 1934, Winifred Marthe, *d* of late Rev. H. E. Anderson, Farnham, Surrey; two *s*. *Educ:* King Edward's Sch., Birmingham; Corpus Christi Coll., Cambridge (MA); Imperial College of Science, London. Entered Ministry of Agriculture and Fisheries, 1933; Private Secretary to Parliamentary Secretary, 1938–39; Sec., Agricultural Machinery Develt Bd, 1942–45; Assistant Secretary, 1948; Under-Sec., MAFF, 1964–70, retired. Mem., panel of indep. inspectors for local enquiries, DoE and DoT, 1971–80. *Recreations:* music, art, travel. *Address:* 74 Chichester Drive West, Saltdean, Brighton. *Club:* Royal Commonwealth Society.

LAMBERT, Henry Uvedale Antrobus; Chairman: Sun Alliance and London Insurance Group, since 1985 (Vice-Chairman, 1978–83; Deputy Chairman, 1983–85); Agricultural Mortgage Corporation PLC, since 1985 (Deputy Chairman, 1977–85); Director: Barclays Bank PLC, since 1966; British Airways, since 1985; *b* 9 Oct. 1925; *o s* of late Roger Uvedale Lambert and Muriel, *d* of Sir Reginald Antrobus, KCMG, CB; *m* 1951, Diana, *y d* of Captain H. E. Dumbell, Royal Fusiliers; two *s* one *d*. *Educ:* Winchester College (Scholar); New College, Oxford (Exhibitioner; MA). Served War of 1939–45, Royal Navy, in HM Ships Stockham and St Austell Bay in Western Approaches and Mediterranean, subseq. RNR; Lt-Comdr (retired). Entered Barclays Bank 1948; a Local Dir at Lombard Street, 1957, Southampton, 1959, Birmingham, 1969; Vice-Chm., Barclays Bank UK Ltd, 1972; Chm., Barclays Bank Internat., 1979–83; Dep. Chm., Barclays Bank PLC, 1979–85. Fellow, Winchester Coll., 1979. *Recreations:* fishing, gardening, golf, naval history. *Address:* c/o Agricultural Mortgage Corporation PLC, Bucklersbury House, Queen Victoria Street, EC4N 8DU. *Clubs:* Brooks's, MCC.

LAMBERT, Sir John (Henry), KCVO 1980; CMG 1975; HM Diplomatic Service, retired; Director, Heritage of London Trust, since 1981; Chairman, Channel Tunnel Investments plc, since 1986; *b* 8 Jan. 1921; *s* of Col R. S. Lambert, MC, and Mrs H. J. F. Mills; *m* 1950, Jennifer Ann (*née* Urquhart); one *s* two *d*. *Educ:* Eton Coll.; Sorbonne; Trinity Coll., Cambridge. Grenadier Guards, 1940–45 (Captain). Appointed 3rd Secretary, HM Embassy, The Hague, 1945; Member of HM Foreign Service, 1947; FO, 1948; 2nd Secretary, Damascus, 1951; 1st Secretary, 1953; FO, 1954; Dep. to UK Representative on International Commn for Saar Referendum, 1955; Belgrade, 1956; Head of Chancery, Manila, 1958; UK Delegation to Disarmament Conference, Geneva, 1962; FO, 1963; Counsellor, Head of Chancery, Stockholm, 1964–67; Head of UN (Political) Dept, FCO, 1967–70; Commercial Counsellor and Consul-Gen. Vienna, 1971–74; Minister and Dep. Comdt, Berlin, 1974–77; Ambassador to Tunisia, 1977–81. *Recreations:* the arts, music, tennis, golf. *Address:* 103 Rivermead Court, SW6 3SB. *T:* 01–731 5007. *Clubs:* MCC; Hurlingham, Royal St George's Golf.

LAMBERT, Hon. Margaret (Barbara), CMG 1965; PhD; British Editor-in-Chief, German Foreign Office Documents, 1951–83; *b* 7 Nov. 1906; *yr d* of 1st Viscount Lambert, PC. *Educ:* Lady Margaret Hall, Oxford; London School of Economics. BA 1930, PhD 1936. Served during War of 1939–45 in European Service of BBC. Assistant Editor British Documents on Foreign Policy, 1946–50; Lecturer in Modern History, University College of the South-West, 1950–51; Lecturer in Modern European History, St Andrews University, 1956–60. *Publications:* The Saar, 1934; When Victoria began to Reign, 1937; (with Enid Marx) English Popular and Traditional Art, 1946, and English Popular Art, 1952. *Address:* 39 Thornhill Road, Barnsbury Square, N1. *T:* 01–607 2286; 1 St Germans, Exeter.

LAMBERT, Olaf Francis, CBE 1984; Director General, The Automobile Association, 1977–July 1987; *b* 13 Jan. 1925; *s* of late Walter Lambert and Edith (*née* Gladstone); *m* 1950, Lucy, *d* of late John Adshead, Macclesfield, and Helen Seymour (*née* Ridgway); two *s* two *d*. *Educ:* Caterham Sch.; RMA, Sandhurst (war time). Commnd Royal Tank Regt, 1944; retd with rank of Major, 1959. Joined Automobile Assoc., 1959; Man. Dir, 1973–77. Director: Drive Publications Ltd, 1974–; AA Insurance Services Ltd, 1974–; AA Travel Services Ltd, 1977–; AA Pensions Trustees Ltd, 1977–; AA Executive Pensions Trustees Ltd, 1977–; Mercantile Credit Co. Ltd, 1980–85; AA Re-insurance Ltd, 1982–; AA Underwriting Services Ltd, 1982–; Automobile Association Ltd, 1982–; Fanum Ltd, 1982–; AA Pension Investment Trustees Ltd, 1984–; AA Developments Ltd, 1984–; AA Financial Services Ltd, 1985–. Member: Cttee of Management, AA Friendly Soc., 1982– (Chm., 1986–); AA Exec. Cttee, 1982–; Council, Inst. of Advanced Motorists, 1968–; Exec. Cttee, British Road Fedn, 1977–; Management Cttee, Alliance Internationale de Tourisme, 1976– (Pres., 1983–86); Hampshire Cttee, Army Benevolent Fund, 1980–; Winchester Cathedral Trust Council, 1984–. FIMI 1984 (MIMI 1977); CBIM 1980; FRSA 1984. Freeman, City of London, 1978; Liveryman, Worshipful Co. of Coachmakers and Coach Harness Makers, 1978. Hon. Col, RMP(TA), 1984–. Col, Commonwealth of Kentucky, 1979. *Recreations:* hunting, skiing, mountain walking, travel, music. *Address:* Elm Farm, Baybridge, Owslebury, Hants. *Club:* Army and Navy.

LAMBERT, Patricia, OBE 1981; Chairman, Consumer Standards Advisory Committee, British Standards Institution, since 1981; *b* 16 March 1926; *d* of Frederick and Elsie Burrows; *m* 1949, George Richard Lambert (marr. diss. 1983); one *s* one *d*. *Educ:* Malet Lambert High Sch., Hull; West Bridgford Grammar Sch., Nottingham; Nottingham and Dist Technical Coll. Served Royal Signals, Germany, 1944–46; medical technician, 1946–49. Fedn Chm., Notts WI, 1974–78; Member: BSI, 1972– (Mem. Bd, 1980); National Consumer Council, 1977–82; National House Bldg Council, 1981–; Cttee on Electrical Safety, Dept of Trade, 1981–; Adv. Panel, Unit Trust Assoc., 1981–; Direct Mail Services Standards Bd, 1983–; National Accreditation Council for Certification Bodies, 1985–; Bd, Assoc. of Short Circuit Testing Authorities, 1986–. Mem. Council: British Electrotechnical Approvals Bd, 1981–; British Approvals Bd for Telecoms, 1982–; Vice-Chm., Think British Campaign, 1983–. Local Govt Councillor, 1959–78. *Recreations:* driving (Mem., Inst. of Advanced Motorists), music, theatre, glass engraving. *Address:* 42 Tollerton Lane, Tollerton, Nottingham NG12 4FQ.

LAMBERT, Prof. Thomas Howard; Professor since 1967, Kennedy Professor since 1983, and Head of Department of Mechanical Engineering, since 1977, University College London; *b* 28 Feb. 1926; *s* of Henry Thomas Lambert and Kate Lambert. *Educ:* Emanuel Sch.; Univ. of London (BSc (Eng), PhD). FIMechE; FRINA. D. Napier & Sons: Graduate Apprentice, 1946–48; Develt Engr, 1948–51; University College London: Lectr, 1951–63; Sen. Lectr, 1963–65; Reader, 1965–67. Hon. RCNC. *Publications:* numerous articles in learned jls, principally in Stress Analysis, Medical Engrg and Automatic Control. *Recreations:* gardening, sailing, practical engineering. *Address:* Department of Mechanical Engineering, University College London, Gower Street, WC1. *T:* 01–387 7050.

LAMBERT, Verity Ann, (Mrs C. M. Bucksey); independent film and television producer; Director, Cinema Verity Ltd, since 1985; *b* 27 Nov. 1935; *d* of Stanley Joseph Lambert and Ella Corona Goldburg; *m* 1973, Colin Michael Bucksey. *Educ:* Roedean; La Sorbonne, Paris. Joined BBC Television as drama producer, 1963; first producer of Dr Who; also produced: The Newcomers, Somerset Maugham Short Stories (BAFTA Award, 1969), Adam Adamant, Detective; joined LWT as drama producer, 1970: produced Budgie and Between the Wars; returned to BBC, 1973: produced and co-created Shoulder to Shoulder; joined Thames Television as Controller of Drama Dept, 1974 (Dir of Drama, 1981–82; Dir, Thames Television, 1982–85): resp. for: Rock Follies, Rooms, Rumpole of the Bailey, Edward and Mrs Simpson, The Naked Civil Servant (many awards), Last Summer, The Case of Cruelty to Prawns, No Mama No; made creatively resp. for Euston Films Ltd, 1976 (Chief Executive, 1979–82): developed series which included Out and Danger UXB; resp. for: Minder (three series), Quatermass, Fox, The Flame Trees of Thika, Reilly: ace of spies; single films include: Charlie Muffin, Stainless Steel and the Star Spies, The Sailor's Return, The Knowledge; Dir of Prodn, THORN EMI Screen Entertainment, 1982–85: resp. for: Morons from Outer Space, Dreamchild, Restless Natives, Link, Clockwise. Governor: BFI, 1981– (Chairperson, Prodn Bd, 1981–82); Nat. Film and Television Sch. Veuve-Clicquot Businesswoman of 1982. *Recreations:* reading, eating. *Address:* (office) Elstree Studios, Shenley Road, Borehamwood, Herts WD6 1JG.

LAMBETH, Archdeacon of; *see* Pinder, Ven. C.

LAMBIE, David; MP (Lab) Cunninghame South, since 1983 (Ayrshire Central, 1970–83); *b* 13 July 1925; *m* 1954, Netta May Merrie; one *s* four *d. Educ:* Kyleshill Primary Sch.; Ardrossan Academy; Glasgow University; Geneva University. BSc, DipEd. Teacher, Glasgow Corp., 1950–70. Chm., Glasgow Local Assoc., Educnl Inst. for Scotland, 1958–59; Chm., Scottish Labour Party, 1964; Chief Negotiator on behalf of Scottish Teachers in STSC, 1969–70; Sec., Westminster Branch, Educnl Inst. for Scotland, 1985–. Chm., Select Cttee on Scottish Affairs, 1981–; Sec., Parly All-Party Cttee for Energy Studies, 1980–. FEIS 1970. *Recreation:* watching football. *Address:* 11 Ivanhoe Drive, Saltcoats, Ayrshire, Scotland. *T:* Saltcoats 64843; (constituency office) 17 Townhead, Irvine, Ayrshire. *T:* Irvine 76844. *Club:* Cunninghame North Constituency Labour Social (Saltcoats).

LAMBO, Prof. Thomas Adeoye, NNOM 1979; CON 1979; OBE 1962; MD, DPM; FRCPE, FRCPsych; JP; Deputy Director-General, World Health Organization, since 1973 (Assistant Director-General, 1971–73); *b* 29 March 1923; *s* of Chief D. B. Lambo, The Otunbade of Igbore, Abeokuta, and Madam F. B. Lambo, The Iyalode of Egba Christians; *m* 1945, Dinah Violet Adams; three *s. Educ:* Baptist Boys' High Sch., Abeokuta; Univs of Birmingham and London. From 1949, served as House Surg. and House Phys., Birmingham, England; Med. Officer, Lagos, Zaria and Gusau; Specialist, Western Region Min. of Health, 1957–60; Consultant Psychiatrist, UCH Ibadan, 1956–63; Sen. Specialist, Western Region Min. of Health, Neuro-Psychiatric Centre, 1960–63; Prof. of Psychiatry and Head of Dept of Psychiatry and Neurology, Univ. of Ibadan, 1963–71; Dean, Medical Faculty, Univ. of Ibadan, 1966–68; Vice-Chancellor, Univ. of Ibadan, 1968–71. Member: Scientific Council for Africa (Chm., 1965–70); Expert Adv. Panel on Mental Health, WHO, 1959–71; UN Perm. Adv. Cttee on Prevention of Crime and the Treatment of Offenders (Chm. 1968–71); Exec. Cttee, World Fedn for Mental Health, 1964–; Scientific Adv. Panel, Ciba Foundn, 1966–; WHO Adv. Cttee on Med. Research, 1970–71; Scientific Cttee on Advanced Study in Developmental Sciences, 1967–; Nigeria Medical Council; Scientific Council of the World Future Studies Fedn; World Soc. for Ekistics (Pres., 1979–81); Adv. Bd, Earthscan; Vice-Chm., UN Adv. Cttee on Application of Science and Technology to Development, 1970–71; Co-Chm., Internat. Soc. for Study of Human Development, 1968–; Chairman: West African Examinations Council, 1969–71, co-ordinating Bd, African Chairs of Technology in Food Processing, Biotechnologies and Nutrition and Health, etc. Founding Member: Third World Acad. of Scis; African Acad. of Scis. Mem. Pontifical Acad. of Sciences, 1974–. Hon. Fellow: RCPsych (Founding Fellow); Royal Australian and NZ Coll. of Psychiatrists. JP Western State, 1968. Hon. LLD: Kent State, Ohio, 1969; Birmingham 1971; Pennsylvania, Philadelphia; Hon. DSc: Ahmadu Bello, Nigeria; Long Island, NY, 1975; McGill, Canada, 1978; Jos, Nigeria, 1979; Nigeria, Nsukka, 1979; Hacettepe, Ankara, 1980; Hahnemann, Philadelphia, 1984; Dr *hc*: Benin, 1973; Aix-Marseille, France, 1974; Louvain, Belgium, 1976. Haile Selassie African Res. Award, 1970. *Publications:* (jtly) Psychiatric Disorders Among the Yorubas, 1963; monographs, and contribs to medical and other scientific jls. *Recreation:* tennis. *Address:* World Health Organization, 1211 Geneva 27, Switzerland. *T:* 91 27 16; (home) Chemin des Châtaigniers 27, 1292 Chambésy-Genève, Switzerland. *T:* 58 19 42.

LAMBOLL, Alan Seymour, JP; Underwriting Member of Lloyd's; *b* 12 Oct. 1923; *s* of late Frederick Seymour and Charlotte Emily Lamboll. *Educ:* Ascham St Vincents, Eastbourne (preparatory sch.); Marlborough Coll. BBC Engineering Staff, 1941–43. Served War: Royal Signals, East Africa Command (Captain), 1943–47. Dir, family firm of wine merchants, City of London, Slack & Lamboll, Ltd, 1947–54. Lloyd's Insurance Broker, Alexr Howden, Stewart Smith (Home), 1954–57; Past Director: Anglo-Portuguese Agencies Ltd (Insurance and Reinsurance Agents), 1957–62; Aga Dictating Machine Co. Ltd, 1962–70; Roger Grayson Ltd, Wine Merchants, 1971–74; London Investment Trust Ltd; Ellinger Heath Western (Underwriting Agencies) Ltd, 1974–82; Consultant to Rank Orgn, 1970–72. JP Inner London, 1965; Chm., S Westminster PSD, 1978–80; Dep. Chm., City of London Commn, 1979–82, Supplemental List, 1982. Mem. Council: City and Guilds of London Inst., 1965–79; Toynbee Hall, 1958–81 (Hon. Sec., 1968–79); Drama Centre London Ltd, 1974–82 (Chm. Council, 1975–82). Dir, City Arts Trust Ltd, 1962–77; Member: Royal Gen. Theatrical Fund Assoc., 1963– (Vice-Chm., 1967–); Cttee, Industrial Sponsors, 1974–84; Grand Master's Cttee, 1974–83; Governor: Mermaid Theatre Trust, 1966–77; Christ's Hospital (Donation Governor, 1971–). Secretary: Ross McWhirter Foundation, 1980–82; Dicey Trust, 1980–82. Mem. Court of Assts, Worshipful Co. of Distillers (Master, 1972–73, Tercentenary Year); Hon. Assistant, Worshipful Co. of Parish Clerks (Master, 1975–76); Freedom of City of London, 1947; Common Council, Ward of Langbourn, 1949–70; Alderman, Ward of Castle Baynard, 1970–78; Sheriff, City of London, 1976–77 (Silver Jubilee Year). St John Council for London, 1971–82; CStJ 1973. FRSA 1970. *Recreations:* theatre, music, television, swimming, Tibetan spaniels. *Address:* Little Buckden, Iken, near Woodbridge, Suffolk IP12 2EY. *T:* Snape 530. *Clubs:* Athenæum, Garrick, Pratt's.

LAMBTON, family name of **Earldom of Durham.**

LAMBTON, Viscount; Antony Claud Frederick Lambton; *b* 10 July 1922; *s* of 5th Earl of Durham (*d* 1970) and Diana (*d* 1924), *o d* of Granville Farquhar; disclaimed peerages for life, 1970 but allowed by Mr Speaker Lloyd to continue to sit in Parliament using courtesy title; *m* 1942, Belinda, *d* of Major D. H. Blew-Jones, Westward Ho!, North Devonshire; one *s* five *d.* MP (C) Berwick upon Tweed Div. of Northumberland, 1951–73; Parly Under-Sec. of State, MoD, 1970–May 1973; PPS to the Foreign Secretary, 1955–57. *Publications:* Snow and Other Stories, 1983; Elizabeth and Alexandra, 1985; The Abbey in the Wood, 1986. *Heir to disclaimed peerages:* s Hon. Edward Richard

Lambton (Baron Durham) [*b* 19 Oct. 1961; *m* 1983, Christabel, *y d* of late Rory McEwen and of Mrs McEwen, Bardrochat]. *Address:* Villa Cetinale, Sovicille, Siena, Italy; Biddick Hall, Chester-le-Street, Co. Durham.
    See also Marquess of Abergavenny, Sir Edmund Fairfax-Lucy, Bt, Sir V. E. Naylor-Leyland, Bt.

LAMBTON, Prof. Ann Katharine Swynford, OBE 1942; FBA 1964; Professor of Persian, University of London, 1953–79, now Emeritus; *b* 8 Feb. 1912; *d* of late Hon. George Lambton. PhD London, 1939; DLit London, 1953. Press Attaché, British Embassy (formerly Legation), Tehran, 1939–45; Senior Lecturer in Persian, School of Oriental and African Studies, 1945–48; Reader in Persian, University of London, 1948–53. Hon. Fellow: New Hall, Cambridge, 1973; SOAS, Univ. of London, 1983. Hon. DLit Durham, 1971; Hon. LittD Cambridge, 1973. *Publications:* Three Persian Dialects, 1938; Landlord and Peasant in Persia, 1953; Persian Grammar, 1953; Persian Vocabulary, 1964; The Persian Land Reform 1962–66, 1969; (ed, with others) The Cambridge History of Islam, vols 1–11, 1971; Theory and Practice in Medieval Persian Government, 1980; State and Government in Medieval Islam, 1981. *Address:* Gregory, Kirknewton, Wooler, Northumberland.

LAMBURN, Patricia, (Mrs Donald Derrick), CBE 1985; Editorial Director, IPC Magazines Ltd, since 1981 (Director, since 1968); *er d* of Francis John Lamburn and Nell Winifred (*née* Kennedy); *m* 1949, Donald G. E. Douglas Derrick, DDS, LDSRCS, FACD, FICD; one *s* one *d. Educ:* Queen's Gate Sch., S Kensington. Amalgamated Press, 1943–49; Curtis Publishing Co., USA, 1949–50; joined George Newnes Ltd, 1950; during ensuing yrs. edited, developed and was associated creatively with wide range of women's and teenage magazines; Dir, George Newnes Ltd, 1966–68; IPC, 1968–: Gp Dir, Young Magazines Gp, 1968–71; Publishing Dir, Women's Magazines Gp, 1971–76, Asst Man. Dir (Editorial), 1976–81. MRC Mem., RCOG Voluntary Licensing Authority for In Vitro Fertilisation and Embryology, 1986–. Chm., Gen. Adv. Council, IBA, 1982–85 (Mem., 1980–82); Member: Health Educn Council, 1973–78; Information Cttee, British Nutrition Foundn, 1979–85; Periodical Publishing Trng Cttee, PPITB, 1980–82; Public Relations Cttee, RCP, 1981–; Press Council, 1982–87. Editorial Cttee, Periodical Publishers' Assoc., 1975–. *Recreations:* early mesoamerican civilisation, bird-watching. *Address:* (office) King's Reach Tower, Stamford Street, SE1 9LS; (home) Chelsea, London.

LAMERTON, Leonard Frederick, PhD, DSc, FInstP, FRCPath; Director, Institute of Cancer Research, London, 1977–80; Professor of Biophysics as Applied to Medicine, University of London, 1960–80; *b* 1 July 1915; *s* of Alfred Lamerton and Florence (*née* Mason); *m* 196 Morag MacLeod. *Educ:* King Edward VI Sch., Southampton; University Coll., Southampton (PhD, DSc London). Staff member, Royal Cancer Hosp. and Inst. of Cancer Research, 1938–41 and 1946–80, Dean of the Inst., 1967–77; seconded to United Nations as a Scientific Sec. of First UN Conf. on Peaceful Uses of Atomic Energy, 1955. President: British Inst. of Radiology, 1957–58; Hosp. Physicists Assoc., 1961; Member: Bd of Governors, Royal Marsden Hosp., 1955–80; Bd of Governors, 1978–82, and Cttee of Management, 1978–, Cardiothoracic Hosp. and Inst. Roentgen Award, 1950, Barclay Medal, 1961, British Inst. of Radiology. *Publications:* various papers on medical physics, radiation hazard, cell kinetics, experimental cancer therapy. *Recreations:* music, study of the development of Man. *Address:* 10 Burgh Mount, Banstead, Surrey SM7 1ER. *T:* Burgh Heath 53697.

LAMFORD, (Thomas) Gerald, OBE 1979; ASVU Representative, Cyprus, since 1985; Commandant, Police Staff College, 1976–79; *b* Carmarthen, 3 April 1928; *s* of late Albert and Sarah Lamford; *m* 1952, Eira Hale; one *s* one *d. Educ:* Technical Coll., Swansea; London Univ. (LLB 1969); Police Coll. (Intermed. Comd Course, 1969; Sen. Comd Course, 1973). Radio Officer, Merchant Navy, 1945; Wireless Operator, RAF, 1946–48, Aden. Carmarthenshire Constab. (now Dyfed Powys Police), 1949; reached rank of Chief Inspector, CID, Crime Squad; Force Trng Officer, 1965–69; Supt, Haverfordwest, 1970; Chief Supt, Llanelli, 1971–74; Asst Chief Constable, Greater Manchester Police, 1974–79; Investigating Officer, FCO, 1981–84. Vis. Prof. of Police Science, John Jay Coll. of Criminal Justice, City Univ. of New York, 1972; sometime Vis. Lecturer: Southern Police Inst., Univ. of Louisville, Ky; N Eastern Univ., Boston; NY Univ. Sch. of Law; Rutgers Univ., NJ; Mercy Coll., Detroit. County Comr, St John Amb. Bde, Pembrokeshire, 1970; SBStJ. *Publications:* articles in Police Studies, Internat. Rev. of Police Develt, Police Rev., Bramshill Jl, World Police. *Recreations:* photography, antiques. *Address:* ASVU Representative, BFPO 58.

LAMING, Rev. Canon Frank Fairbairn; *b* 24 Aug. 1908; *s* of William John Laming and Maude Elizabeth (*née* Fairbairn); *m* 1939, Ruth Marion, *d* of Herbert William Pinder and Rose Marion (*née* Price). *Educ:* King Edward VI Sch., Retford; The Theological Coll., Edinburgh. In business, 1925–33; Edinburgh Theological Coll., 1933–36; Luscombe Scholar, 1936; Durham LTh, 1936. Deacon, 1936; Priest, 1937; Assistant Priest, Christ Church, Glasgow, 1936–39; Priest in Charge, St Margaret, Renfrew, 1939–44; Rector, Holy Trinity Church, Motherwell, 1944–53; Rector and Provost of St Mary's Cathedral, Glasgow, 1953–66; Provost of St Andrew's Cathedral, Inverness, 1966–74; Priest-in-Charge, St. Ninian's, Glenurquhart, 1974–84, retired; Hon. Canon, Inverness Cathedral, 1974–. Editor, Year Book and Directory of the Episcopal Church in Scotland, 1976–84. *Recreation:* woodworking. *Address:* 16 South Street, Aberchirder, Huntly, Aberdeenshire AB5 5TR. *T:* Aberchirder 625.

LAMOND, James Alexander, JP; MP (Lab) Oldham Central and Royton, since 1983 (Oldham East, 1970–83); *b* Burrelton, Perthshire, 29 Nov. 1928; *s* of Alexander N. G. Lamond and Christina Lamond (*née* Craig); *m* 1954, June Rose Wellburn; three *d. Educ:* Burrelton Sch.; Coupar Angus Sch. Draughtsman, 1944–70. PPS to Minister of State: for NI, 1974–75; DHSS, 1975–76. Mem., Aberdeen City Council, 1959–71; Lord Provost of Aberdeen, 1970–71; Lord Lieutenant of the County of the City of Aberdeen, 1970–71. Mem., AUEW (TASS), 1944– (Chm., No 1 Divisional Council of DATA, 1965–70); Pres., Aberdeen Trades Council, 1969. Vice-Pres., World Peace Council; Pres., British Peace Assembly. JP Aberdeen. *Recreations:* golf, travel, reading, thinking. *Address:* 59 Trafalgar Street, Oldham, Lancs. *T:* 061–626 1354. *Clubs:* Labour, Irish (Oldham); Trades Council, Boilermaker's (Aberdeen).

LAMONT, Rt. Hon. Norman Stewart Hughson, PC 1986; MP (C) Kingston-upon-Thames since May 1972; Financial Secretary to HM Treasury, since 1986; *b* Lerwick, Shetland, 8 May 1942; *s* of late Daniel Lamont and of Helen Irene; *m* 1971, Alice Rosemary, *d* of Lt-Col Peter White; one *s* one *d. Educ:* Loretto Sch. (scholar); Fitzwilliam Coll., Cambridge (BA). Chm., Cambridge Univ. Conservative Assoc., 1963; Pres., Cambridge Union, 1964. PA to Rt Hon. Duncan Sandys, MP, 1965; Conservative Research Dept, 1966–68; Merchant Banker, N. M. Rothschild & Sons, 1968–79. Contested (C) East Hull, Gen. Election, 1970. PPS to Norman St John-Stevas, MP, Minister for the Arts, 1974; an Opposition Spokesman on: Prices and Consumer Affairs, 1975–76; Industry, 1976–79; Parly Under Sec. of State, Dept of Energy, 1979–81; Minister of State, DTI (formerly DoI), 1981–85; Minister of State for Defence Procurement, 1985–86. Chairman: Coningsby Club, 1970–71; Bow Group, 1971–72. *Publications:* newspaper articles and Bow Group memoranda. *Recreations:* reading, ornithology, following Association football and American politics. *Address:* House of Commons, SW1. *Club:* Carlton.

LAMONTAGNE, Hon. (J.) Gilles, CD 1980; PC (Can.); Lieutenant-Governor of Quebec, since 1984; *b* 17 April 1919; *s* of Trefflé Lamontagne and Anna Kieffer; *m* 1949, Mary Katherine Schaefer; three *s* one *d*. *Educ:* Collège Jean-de-Brébeuf, Montréal, Québec (BA). Served RCAF, 1941–45 (despatches, 1945). Businessman in Québec City, 1946–66. Alderman, Québec City, 1962–64, Mayor, 1965–77. MP (L) Langelier, 1977–84; Parly Sec. to Minister of Energy, Mines and Resources, 1977; Minister without Portfolio, Jan. 1978; Postmaster Gen., Feb. 1978; Actg Minister of Veterans Affairs, 1980–81; Minister of National Defence, 1980–83. Dir, Québec City Chamber of Commerce and Industry; Member: Econ. Council of Canada; Br. 260, Royal Canadian Legion. KStJ 1985. Hon. LLD Kingston Royal Mil. Coll., 1986. Croix du Combattant de l'Europe. *Address:* (office) 1050 St-Augustin Street, Québec, PQ G1A 1A1, Canada; Government House, 1010 St Louis Road, Sillery, PQ G1S 1C7, Canada. *Clubs:* Québec City Rotary (Pres.), Quebec Garrison, Royal Québec Golf.

LAMPARD, Martin Robert; Consultant, Ashurst Morris Crisp & Co., since 1986 (Senior Partner, 1974–86); *b* 21 Feb. 1926; *s* of Austin Hugo Lampard and late Edith Gertrude Lampard (formerly White); *m* 1957, Felice MacLean; three *d*. *Educ:* Radley College, Oxford; Christ Church, Oxford (MA). Served RNVR. Admitted solicitor, 1952; joined Ashurst Morris Crisp & Co., 1954, Partner, 1957. Farming in East Anglia, Simmental beef herd. *Address:* 20 Allingham Road, N1. *T:* 01–247 7666; Theberton House, Theberton, near Leiston, Suffolk. *T:* Leiston 830510. *Clubs:* Royal Ocean Racing; Royal Yacht Squadron.

LAMPSON, family name of **Baron Killearn.**

LANCASTER, Bishop Suffragan of, since 1985; **Rt. Rev. Ian Harland;** *b* 19 Dec. 1932; *s* of late Canon Samuel James Harland and of Brenda Gwendolyn Harland; *m* 1967, Susan Hinman; one *s* three *d*. *Educ:* Dragon School, Oxford; Haileybury; Peterhouse, Cambridge (MA); Wycliffe Hall, Oxford. Teaching at Sunningdale School, 1956–58; Curate, Melton Mowbray, 1960–63; Vicar, Oughtibridge, Sheffield, 1963–72; Member, Wortley RDC, 1969–73; Vicar, St Cuthbert, Fir Vale, Sheffield, 1972–75; Priest-in-charge, All Saints, Brightside, 1973–75; RD of Ecclesfield, 1973–75; Vicar of Rotherham, 1975–79; RD of Rotherham, 1976–79; Archdeacon of Doncaster, 1979–85. Proctor in Convocation, 1975–85. *Recreations:* politics; sport. *Address:* Wheatfield, 7 Dallas Road, Lancaster LA1 1TN. *T:* Lancaster 32897.

LANCASTER, Bishop of, (RC), since 1985; **Rt. Rev. John Brewer;** *b* 24 Nov 1929; *s* of Eric W. Brewer and Laura H. Brewer (*née* Webster). *Educ:* Ushaw College, Durham; Ven. English College, Rome and Gregorian Univ. PhL, STL, JCL. Ordained priest, 1956; Parish Assistant, 1959–64; Vice-Rector, Ven. English Coll., Rome, 1964–71; Parish Priest of St Mary's, Middlewich, 1971–78; Auxiliary Bishop of Shrewsbury, 1971–83; Bishop Coadjutor of Lancaster, 1984. Officiating Chaplain, Royal Navy, 1966–71; Representative of RC Bishops of England and Wales in Rome, 1964–71. Chaplain to HH Pope Paul VI, 1965. *Recreations:* walking, golf. *Address:* Bishop's House, Cannon Hill, Lancaster. *T:* Lancaster 32231.

LANCASTER, Archdeacon of; *see* Gibbons, Ven. K. H.

LANCASTER, Dame Jean, DBE 1963; *b* 11 Aug. 1909; *d* of late Richard C. Davies; *m* 1967, Roy Cavander Lancaster (*d* 1981). *Educ:* Merchant Taylors' Sch., Crosby, Lancashire. Director, Women's Royal Naval Service, 1961–64. *Address:* Greathed Manor, Dormansland, Lingfield, Surrey RH7 6PA.

LANCASTER, Joan Cadogan; *see* Lancaster Lewis, J. C.

LANCASTER, Vice-Admiral Sir John (Strike), KBE 1961; CB 1958; retired 1962; *b* 26 June 1903; *s* of George Henry Lancaster; *m* 1927, Edith Laurie Jacobs (*d* 1980); two *d*. *Educ:* King Edward VI Sch., Southampton. Joined RN, 1921; Commander, 1940; Captain, 1951; Rear-Admiral, 1956; Vice-Admiral, 1959. Served War of 1939–45: HMS Gloucester; RN Barracks, Portsmouth; Persian Gulf; HMS Ocean. Rear-Admiral Personnel, Home Air Command, Lee-on-the-Solent, 1956; Director-General of Manpower, 1959–62; Chief Naval Supply and Secretariat Officer, 1959–62. *Recreation:* gardening. *Address:* Moorings, Western Way, Alverstoke, Hants.
See also P. M. Lancaster.

LANCASTER, Patricia Margaret; Headmistress, Wycombe Abbey School, since 1974; *b* 22 Feb. 1929; *d* of Vice-Adm. Sir John Lancaster, *qv*. *Educ:* Univs of London (BA) and Southampton (Certif. Educn). English Mistress, St Mary's Sch., Calne, 1951–58; Housemistress, St Swithun's Sch., Winchester, 1958–62; Headmistress, St Michael's, Burton Park, Petworth, 1962–73. Pres., Girls' Schools' Assoc., 1979–80. *Recreation:* theatre. *Address:* Wycombe Abbey School, High Wycombe, Bucks. *T:* High Wycombe 20381.

LANCASTER LEWIS, Joan Cadogan, CBE 1978; Director, India Office Library and Records, 1972–78; *b* 2 Aug. 1918; *yr d* of Cyril Cadogan Lancaster and Mary Ann Lancaster; *m* 1983, Rev. Kenneth Lionel Lewis, MA. *Educ:* Charles Edward Brooke Sch., London; Westfield Coll., Univ. of London. BA 1940, MA 1943; ALA 1943; FRHistS 1956; FSA 1960. Asst Librarian, University Coll., Leicester, and Asst Archivist, the Museum, Leicester, 1940–43. Served War, ATS, 1943–46. Archivist, City of Coventry, 1946–48; Asst Librarian, Inst. of Historical Research, Univ. of London, 1948–60; Asst Keeper, India Office Records, 1960–67; Dep. Librarian and Dep. Keeper, India Office Library and Records, 1968–72. Reviews Editor, Archives (Jl of British Records Assoc.), 1951–57, Editor, Archives, 1957–63. *Publications:* Guide to St Mary's Hall, Coventry, 1949, rev. edn 1981; Bibliography of historical works issued in the United Kingdom 1946–56 (Inst. of Historical Research), 1957; Guide to lists and catalogues of the India Office Records, 1966; Godiva of Coventry, 1967; India Office Records: Report for the years 1947–67 (FCO), 1970; contribs on Coventry to: Victoria County History, 1969; Historic Towns, vol. 2, 1974; Medieval Coventry—a city divided?, 1981; articles and reviews in Bulletin of Inst. of Historical Research, Archives, Asian Affairs, etc. *Recreations:* music, photography. *Address:* 109 The Street, Mereworth, Maidstone, Kent ME18 5LY. *T:* Maidstone 813308. *Club:* United Oxford & Cambridge University.

LANCE, Rev. Preb. John Du Boulay, MC 1945; MA; Prebendary of Henstridge in Wells Cathedral, since 1974; Assistant Curate, St Cuthbert, Wells, since 1981; *b* 14 March 1907; *s* of late Rev. Arthur Porcher Lance and Harriet Agatha Lance, Buckland St Mary, Somerset; *m* 1936, Lena Winifred Clifford; one *s*. *Educ:* Marlborough; Jesus Coll., Cambridge; Cuddesdon Theological Coll. Assistant Curate, St Peter, Wolverhampton, 1930–34; Missioner, Trinity Coll., Oxford. Mission, Stratford, 1934–36; Vicar of Bishops Lydeard, 1936–47. Chaplain to the Forces, 1941–46 (despatches). Vicar of St Andrew's, Taunton, 1947–57; Preb. of Wells, 1951–63; Rector of Bathwick, Bath, 1957–63; Archdeacon of Wells and Canon of Wells Cathedral, 1963–73; Diocesan Dir of Ordinands, Wells, 1974–76. Proctor in Convocation, 1959–64; Diocesan Adviser in Christian Stewardship, 1961–67; Warden, Abbey Retreat House, Glastonbury, 1965–82. *Address:* 14 Portway Avenue, Wells, Somerset BA5 2QF. *T:* Wells 72756. *Club:* Hawks (Cambridge).

LANCELOT, James Bennett, FRCO; Master of the Choristers and Organist, Durham Cathedral, since 1985; *b* 2 Dec. 1952; *s* of Rev. Roland Lancelot; *m* 1982, Sylvia Jane (*née* Hoare). *Educ:* St Paul's Cathedral Choir Sch.; Ardingly Coll., Royal College of Music (ARCM); King's Coll., Cambridge (Dr Mann Organ Student; MA; BMus). Asst Organist, St Clement Danes and Hampstead Parish Ch., 1974–75; Sub Organist, Winchester Cath., 1975–85; Asst Conductor, Winchester Music Club, 1983–85. Numerous recordings. *Recreations:* railways, walking. *Address:* 6 The College, Durham. *T:* Durham 3864766.

LANCELYN GREEN, Roger G.; *see* Green, R. G. L.

LANCHBERY, John Arthur, FRAM; Conductor; *b* London, 15 May 1923; *s* of William Lanchbery and Violet (*née* Mewett); *m* 1951, Elaine Fifield (divorced 1960); one *d*. *Educ:* Alleyn's Sch., Dulwich; Royal Academy of Music. Henry Smart Composition Scholarship, 1942. Served, Royal Armoured Corps, 1943–45. Royal Academy of Music, 1945–47; Musical Director, Metropolitan Ballet, 1948–50; Sadler's Wells Theatre Ballet, 1951–57; Royal Ballet, 1957–72 (Principal Conductor, 1959–72); Musical Director: Australian Ballet, 1972–77; American Ballet Theatre, 1978–80. ARAM 1953; Bolshoi Theatre Medal, Moscow, 1961. *Publications:* Arrangements and Compositions of Ballets include: Pleasuredrome, 1949; Eve of St Agnes (BBC commission), 1950; House of Birds, 1955; La Fille Mal Gardée, 1960; The Dream, 1964; Don Quixote, 1966; Giselle, 1968; La Sylphide, 1970; Tales of Beatrix Potter, 1971; Tales of Hoffman, 1972; Merry Widow, 1975; Month in the Country, 1976; Mayerling, 1978; Rosalinda, 1978; Papillon, 1979; La Bayadère, 1980; Peer Gynt, 1980; The Devil to Pay, 1982; The Sentimental Bloke, 1985; Le Chat Botté, 1985; Midsummer Night's Dream, 1985. *Recreations:* walking, reading. *Address:* c/o Roger Stone Management, West Grove, Hammers Lane, NW7 4DY. *Club:* Garrick.

LANCHESTER, Elsa; Actress; *d* of James Sullivan and Edith Lanchester; *m* 1929, Charles Laughton (*d* 1962); became American Citizen, 1950. *Educ:* Privately. Started the Children's Theatre, Charlotte Street, Soho, 1918; first appearance on stage, 1922; afterwards played at Lyric, Hammersmith, in The Way of the World, 1924, in The Duenna, 1924 and in Riverside Nights, 1926; first appearance in New York at Lyceum Theatre, 1931; joined Old Vic-Sadler's Wells company, 1933; was Peter Pan, Palladium, 1936; was in They Walk Alone, New York, 1941; 10 years as star of Turnabout Theatre, Los Angeles, California; Turnabout Theatre, nightly continuously, from 1941. Acted in The Party, London, 1958. Has appeared in films including The Constant Nymph, Potiphar's Wife, The Private Life of Henry VIII, David Copperfield, Bride of Frankenstein, Naughty Marietta, The Ghost Goes West, Rembrandt, Vessel of Wrath, Ladies in Retirement, Son of Fury, Passport to Destiny, Lassie Come Home, Spiral Staircase, Razor's Edge, The Big Clock, The Inspector General, The Secret Garden, Come to the Stable, Buccaneer Girl, The Glass Slipper, Witness for the Prosecution, Bell, Book and Candle, Mary Poppins, That Darn Cat, Blackbeard's Ghost, Me Natalie, Rascal, My Dog, The Thief, Willard, Terror in the Wax Museum, Arnold, Murder by Death. Television series, The John Forsythe Show; talk shows: Jack Paar; David Frost; Dick Cavitt; Johnny Carson; Joey Bishop. *Publications:* Charles Laughton and I, 1938; Elsa Lanchester Herself (autobiog.), 1983. *Recreation:* wild flowers.

LANCHIN, Gerald; consultant; Chairman, Direct Mail Services Standards Board, since 1983; *b* 17 Oct. 1922; *o s* of late Samuel Lanchin, Kensington; *m* 1951, Valerie Sonia Lyons; one *s* two *d*. *Educ:* St Marylebone Grammar Sch.; London Sch. of Economics. BCom 1st cl. hons 1951; Leverhulme Schol. 1950–51. Min. of Labour, 1939–51; served with Army, RAOC and REME, 1942–46; Board of Trade (subseq. DTI and Dept of Trade): Asst Principal, 1952; Principal 1953; 1st Sec., UK Delegn to OEEC, Paris, 1955–59; Principal, Estabt and Commercial Relations and Exports Divs, 1959–66; Asst Sec., Finance and Civil Aviation Divs, 1966–71; Under-Sec., Tariff, Commercial Relations and Export, Shipping Policy, General and Consumer Affairs Divs, 1971–82. Chm., Packaging Council, 1983–84. *Publication:* Government and the Consumer, 1985. *Recreations:* reading, gardening, music. *Address:* 28 Priory Gardens, Berkhamsted, Herts. *T:* Berkhamsted 75283. *Club:* Reform.

LAND, Edwin Herbert; US physicist and inventor; Founder, President and Director of Research, Rowland Institute for Science, since 1981; Founder Chairman of Board and Consulting Director of Basic Research, Polaroid Corporation, retired 1982 (President, 1937–75; Chief Executive Officer and Director of Research, 1937–80); Fellow and Visiting Institute Professor, Massachusetts Institute of Technology, since 1956; *b* Bridgeport, Connecticut, 7 May 1909; *s* of Harry M. and Matha G. Land; *m* 1929, Helen Maislen; two *d*. *Educ:* Norwich Acad.; Harvard. Founded Polaroid Corporation, 1937. War of 1941–45, in charge of research into development of weapons and materials, and cons. on missiles to US Navy. Invented polarizer for light in form of extensive synthetic sheet; also camera which produces complete photograph immediately after exposure, 1947. Member: President's Science Adv. Cttee, 1957–59 (Consultant-at-large, 1960–73); President's Foreign Intelligence Adv. Bd, 1961–77; Nat. Commn on Technology, Automation, and Economic Progress, 1964–66; Carnegie Commn on Educational TV, 1966–67; President's Cttee, Nat. Medal of Science, 1969–72. Harvard University: Mem. Vis. Cttee, Dept of Physics, 1949–66, 1968; William James Lectr on Psychol., 1966–67; Morris Loeb Lectr on Physics, 1974. Trustee, Ford Foundn, 1967–75. Fellow: Photographic Soc. of America, 1950–; Amer. Acad. of Arts and Sciences, 1943– (Pres., 1951–53); Royal Photographic Society, 1958–; Nat. Acad. of Sciences, 1953–, etc; Foreign Mem., Royal Soc., 1986. Hon. MRI, 1975; Hon. Mem., Soc. of Photographic Science and Technology, Japan, 1975; Hon. Fellow: Royal Microscopical Society, and many other American and foreign learned bodies. ScD (Hon.) Harvard Univ., 1957, and holds many other hon. doctorates in science and law. Awards include: Hood Medal and Progress Medal, RPS; Cresson Medal and Potts Medal, Franklin Inst.; Scott Medal, Philadelphia City Trusts; Rumford Medal, Amer. Acad. of Arts and Scis, 1945; Holley Medal, ASME, 1948; Duddell Medal, British Physical Soc., 1949; Nat. Medal of Science, 1967. Presidential Medal of Freedom, 1963. *Publications:* contributions Journal Opt. Soc. America, Amer. Scientist, Proceedings of Nat. Acad. of Science. *Recreations:* music, horseback riding. *Address:* 163 Brattle Street, Cambridge, Mass 02138, USA; (office) 100 Cambridge Parkway, Cambridge, Mass 02142. *T:* 617 497–4632. *Clubs:* Harvard (NY and Boston); Century Association (New York); St Botolph, Harvard Faculty (Boston); Cosmos (Washington, DC).

LAND, Prof. Frank William, MSc, PhD London; Professor of Education, University of Hull, 1961–77; *b* 9 Jan. 1911; *s* of Charles and Mary Land; *m* 1937, Nora Beatrice Channon; two *s* one *d*. *Educ:* King's Coll., University of London. Assistant Master, The Grammar School, Hampton-on-Thames, 1933–37; Mathematics Lecturer: College of St Mark and St John, Chelsea, 1937–39; Birkbeck Coll., London, 1939–40. Instructor Lieut, Royal Navy, 1940–46. Vice-Principal, College of St Mark and St John, Chelsea, 1946–49;

Senior Lecturer, University of Liverpool, 1950–61. Chairman, Association of Teachers in Colleges and Departments of Education, 1956–57. *Publications:* Recruits to Teaching, 1960; The Language of Mathematics, 1961. *Recreation:* gardening. *Address:* Cremel Cwm, Church Lane, Gwernaffield, Mold, Clwyd CH7 5DT.
See also M. F. Land.

LAND, Gillian; *see* Lynne, Gillian.

LAND, Prof. Michael Francis, FRS 1982; PhD; Professor of Neurobiology, University of Sussex, since 1984; *b* 12 April 1942; *s* of Prof. Frank William Land, *qv*; *m* 1980, Rosemary (*née* Clarke); one *s* two *d*. *Educ:* Birkenhead Sch., Cheshire; Jesus Coll., Cambridge (MA); University Coll. London (PhD). Asst Lectr in Physiology, UCL, 1966–67; Miller Fellow, 1967–79, and Asst Prof. of Physiology-Anatomy, 1979–81, Univ. of Calif, Berkeley; Lectr in Biol Sciences, 1971–77, Reader, 1977–84, Univ. of Sussex. Vis. Prof., Univ. of Oregon, 1980; Sen. Res. Fellow, ANU, 1982–84. *Publications:* numerous papers on animal vision in learned jls. *Recreations:* photography, music. *Address:* White House, Cuilfail, Lewes, East Sussex BN7 2BE. *T:* Lewes 476780.

LAND, Dr Roger Burton, FRSE 1985; Director, Animal Breeding Research Organisation, Agricultural Food Research Council, since 1983; *b* 30 April 1940; *s* of Albert Land and Betty Newton Land (*née* Burton); *m* 1968, Moira Helen Murdoch (*née* Mackay); one *s* two *d*. *Educ:* Bradford Grammar School; Nottingham Univ. (BSc 1962); Edinburgh Univ. (PhD 1965). Joined Animal Breeding Research Organisation, 1966. *Publication:* (jtly) Food Chains to Biotechnology, 1983; contribs to Jl of Reproduction and Fertility and Animal Production. *Recreations:* family activities, gardening. *Address:* Eshiels House, Peebles EH45 8NA. *T:* Peebles 21117.

LANDA, Hon. Abram, CMG 1968; LLB; Notary Public; Agent-General for New South Wales in London, 1965–70; *b* 10 Nov. 1902; *s* of late D. Landa, Belfast; *m* 1930, Perla (*d* 1976), *d* of late L. Levy; one *s* one *d*. *Educ:* Christian Brothers' Coll., Waverley, NSW; University of Sydney. Solicitor, 1927–. MLA for Bondi, NSW, 1930–32 and 1941–65; Minister for Labour and Industry, 1953–56; Minister for Housing and Co-operative Societies, 1956–65; Minister for Housing, NSW, 1956–65. Past Member Senate, University of Sydney; Past Trustee, NSW Public Library. *Recreations:* swimming, bowls. *Address:* 22 Coolong Road, Vaucluse, NSW, Australia. *Club:* Tattersall's (Sydney).

LANDA, Lynda, (Mrs Clive Landa); *see* Chalker, L.

LANDAU, Dennis Marcus; Chief Executive, Co-operative Wholesale Society Ltd, since 1980 (Deputy Chief Executive Officer, 1974–80); *b* 18 June 1927; *s* of late Michael Landau, metallurgist. *Educ:* Haberdashers' Aske's Hampstead Sch. Schweppes Ltd, 1952; Man. Dir, Schweppes (East Africa) Ltd, 1958–62; Chivers-Hartley: Prodn Dir, 1963; Man. Dir, 1966–69; Chm., Schweppes Foods Div., 1969; Dep. Chm. and Man. Dir, Cadbury Schweppes Foods, 1970; Controller, Food Div., Co-operative Wholesale Society Ltd, 1971. Director: Co-operative Retail Services Ltd; Sorbie Cheese Ltd; CWS (NZ Hldgs) Ltd; CWS (India) Ltd; Co-operative Bank plc; Co-operative Insce Soc. Ltd. Member: Metrication Bd, 1972–80; Exec. Cttee, Food & Drink Fedn (formerly Food Manufacturers' Fedn Inc.), 1972–. FIGD 1977 (Pres. 1982–85); CBIM 1980. *Recreations:* Rugby, cricket, music. *Address:* 9 Grey Road, Altrincham, Cheshire WA14 4BT. *T:* 061–928 4116. *Club:* Lancashire CC.

LANDELS, William, (Willie); Editor, Departures, since 1986; *b* Venice, 14 June 1928; *s* of late Reynold Landels and Carla Manfredi; *m* 1958, Angela Ogden; two *d*. *Educ:* privately. Apprentice stage designer at La Scala, Milan, 1947; Art Director, J. Walter Thompson, 1950; Art Editor, Queen Magazine, 1965; Editor, Harpers & Queen, 1970–86. *Publication:* (with Alistair Burnet) The Best Years of Our Lives, 1981. *Recreations:* furniture design, cooking. *Address:* 292 South Lamberth Road, SW8.

LANDEN, Dinsdale (James); actor; *b* 4 Sept. 1932; *s* of Edward James Landen and Winifred Alice Landen; *m* 1959, Jennifer Daniel. *Educ:* King's Sch., Rochester; Hove County Grammar Sch. *Stage:* Dead Secret, Piccadilly, 1957; Auntie Mame, Adelphi; Provok'd Wife, Vaudeville; Philanthropist, May Fair, 1970; London Assurance, New, 1972; Alphabetical Order, May Fair, 1975; Bodies, Ambassadors, 1980; Taking Steps, Lyric, 1980; Loot, Lyric, 1984; Sufficient Carbohydrate, Albery, 1984; Wife Begins at Forty, Ambassadors, 1985; *National Theatre:* Plunder; The Philanderer; On the Razzle, 1981; Uncle Vanya, 1982; *television:* Great Expectations, Mickey Dunne, The Spies, Glittering Prizes, Devenish, Two Sundays, Fathers and Families, Pig in the Middle, Radio Pictures, Absent Friends, Events in a Museum. *Recreations:* walking, golf. *Address:* 90 Felsham Road, SW15. *Club:* Stage Golfing Society.

LANDON, Alfred Mossman; Independent Oil Producer; *b* 9 Sept. 1887; *s* of John Manuel Landon and Anne Mossman; *m* 1915, Margaret Fleming (*d* 1918); one *d*; *m* 1930, Theo Cobb; one *s* one *d*. *Educ:* University of Kansas. Republican State Chm., 1928; Governor of Kansas, 1933–37; Republican nominee for Pres. of United States, 1936; Delegate to Eighth International Conference, Lima, Peru, 1938; Chm. Kansas Delegation Republican Nat. Convention, 1940, 1944, and 1948; Mem. Methodist Church; Member, Kansas Bar; Member, Phi Gamma Delta; Mason, Elks, Odd Fellows. Hon. LHD Kansas State, 1968; Hon. LLD Emporia Coll., 1969. Distinguished Citizenship Award: Washburn Univ., 1967; Baker Univ., 1975. *Recreations:* horseback riding, fishing, bridge. *Address:* 521 Westchester Road, Topeka, Kansas 66606, USA. *T:* 233–4136.

LANDON, Howard Chandler Robbins; author and music historian; *b* 6 March 1926; *s* of late William Grinnell Landon and Dorothea LeBaron Robbins; *m* 1957, Else Radant. *Educ:* Aiken Preparatory Sch.; Lenox Sch.; Swarthmore Coll.; Boston Univ., USA (BMus). European rep. of Intercollegiate Broadcasting System, 1947; founded Haydn Soc. (which recorded and printed music of Joseph Haydn), 1949; became a Special Correspondent of The Times, 1957 and contrib. to that newspaper until 1961. Visiting Prof., Queen's Coll., NYC, 1969; Regents Prof. of Music, Univ. of California (Davis), 1970, 1975, 1979; John Bird Prof. of Music, UC Cardiff, 1978–; Christian Johnson Prof. of Music, Middlebury Coll., Vermont, USA, 1980–. Hon. Professorial Fellow, University Coll., Cardiff, 1971–79; Hon. Fellow, Lady Margaret Hall, Oxford, 1979–. Hon. DMus: Boston Univ., 1969; Queen's Univ., Belfast, 1974; Bristol, 1982. Verdienstkreuz für Kunst und Wissenschaft from Austrian Govt, 1972. Co-editor, The Haydn Yearbook, 1962–. *Publications:* The Symphonies of Joseph Haydn, 1955 (London); The Mozart Companion (co-ed with Donald Mitchell), 1956 (London); The Collected Correspondence and London Notebooks of Joseph Haydn, 1959 (London); Essays on Eighteenth-Century Music, 1969 (London); Ludwig van Beethoven: a documentary study, 1970 (London); critical edn of the 107 Haydn Symphonies, (completed) 1968; five-vol. biog. of Haydn: vol. 3, Haydn in England, 1976; vol. 4, Haydn: The Years of The Creation, 1977; vol. 5, Haydn: The Late Years, 1977; vol. 1, Haydn: The Early Years, and vol. 2, Haydn in Eszterhaza, 1978–80; Haydn: a documentary study, 1981; Mozart and the Masons, 1982; Handel and his World, 1984; scholarly edns of eighteenth-century music (various European publishing houses). *Recreations:* swimming, cooking, walking. *Address:* Anton Frankgasse 3, Vienna 1180, Austria. *T:* 314205; Château de Foncoussières, 81800 Rabastens (Tarn), France. *T:* (63) 40.61.45.

LANDRETH, Rev. Canon Derek, TD 1963; Vicar of Icklesham, Diocese of Chichester, since 1983 (Priest-in-charge, 1982–83), also Priest-in-charge of Fairlight, 1984–86); Chaplain to the Queen, since 1980; Rural Dean of Rye, since 1984; *b* 7 June 1920; *s* of Rev. Norman Landreth and Muriel Landreth; *m* 1943, Myra Joan Brown; one *s* three *d*; *m* 1986, Dss Mavis Isabella White. *Educ:* Kingswood School, Bath; King's College, Cambridge (MA); Bishops' College, Cheshunt. Commissioned, Royal Artillery, 1942–46 (service India and Burma); CF (TA), 1951–67, (TAVR) 1967–70; Asst Curate, St George, Camberwell, 1948–53; Vicar, St Mark, Battersea Rise, 1953–59; Deputy Chaplain, HM Prison, Wandsworth, 1954–59; Vicar of Richmond, Surrey, and Chaplain, Star and Garter Home for Disabled Soldiers, Sailors and Airmen, 1959–70; Rector of Sanderstead, Surrey, 1970–77; Hon. Chaplain to Bishop of Southwark, 1962–80; Hon. Canon of Southwark Cathedral, 1968–77; Canon Residentiary and Librarian, Southwark Cathedral, 1977–82; Canon Emeritus, 1982–. Proctor in Convocation, 1980–83. Indep. Mem., Richmond Borough Council, 1961–65. *Recreations:* gardening, fishing. *Address:* Icklesham Vicarage, Winchelsea, East Sussex TN36 6BH. *T:* Hastings 814207.

LANE, family name of **Baron Lane.**

LANE, Baron *cr* 1979 (Life Peer), of St Ippollitts; **Geoffrey Dawson Lane;** PC 1974; Kt 1966; AFC 1943; Lord Chief Justice of England, since 1980; *b* 17 July 1918; *s* of late Percy Albert Lane, Lincoln; *m* 1944, Jan, *d* of Donald Macdonald; one *s*. *Educ:* Shrewsbury; Trinity Coll., Cambridge (Hon. Fellow 1981). Served in RAF, 1939–45; Sqdn-Leader, 1942. Called to Bar, Gray's Inn, 1946; Bencher 1966. QC 1962. Dep. Chm., Beds. QS, 1960–66; Recorder of Bedford, 1963–66; a Judge of the High Court of Justice, Queen's Bench Div., 1966–74; a Lord Justice of Appeal, 1974–79; a Lord of Appeal in Ordinary, 1979–80. Mem., Parole Board, 1970–72 (Vice-Chm., 1972). Hon. Bencher, Inner Temple, 1980. Hon. LLD Cambridge, 1984. *Address:* Royal Courts of Justice, Strand, WC2.

LANE, Dr Anthony John, FRCP, FFCM; Regional Medical Officer, North Western Regional Health Authority, 1974–86; *b* 6 Feb. 1926; *s* of John Gill Lane and Marian (*née* Brumfield); *m* 1948, Hannah Holečková; one *s* two *d*. *Educ:* St Christopher's Sch., Letchworth; Emmanuel Coll., Cambridge. MA, MB, BChir. House posts in surgery, medicine, obstetrics and paediatrics, 1949–51; MO with Methodist Missionary Soc., Andhra State, India, 1951–57; Registrar: Tropical Diseases, UCH, 1958; Gen. Med., St James' Hosp., Balham, 1958–61; Infectious Diseases, Western Hosp., Fulham, 1961–63; MO (Trainee), Leeds RHB, 1963–64; Asst Sen. MO, Leeds RHB, 1964–66; Principal Asst Sen. MO, Leeds RHB, 1966–70; Dep. Sen. Admin. MO, SW Metrop. RHB, 1970–71; Sen. Admin. MO, Manchester RHB, 1971–74. Hon. MD. *Publications:* contrib. Positions, Movements and Directions in Health Services Research, 1974; contrib. Proc. Royal Soc. Med. *Recreations:* music, competitive indoor games, walking, gardening. *Address:* 4 Queens Road, Wilmslow, Cheshire SK9 5HS. *T:* Wilmslow 523889.

LANE, Anthony John; Under Secretary, International Trade Policy Division, Department of Trade and Industry, since 1984; *b* 30 May 1939; *s* of Eric Marshall Lane and Phyllis Mary Lane; *m* 1967, Judith Sheila (*née* Dodson); two *s* one *d*. *Educ:* Caterham Sch.; Balliol Coll., Oxford (BA PPE, MA). Investment Analyst, Joseph Sebag & Co., 1964–65; Asst Principal, Min. of Technology, 1965; Private Sec. to Parly Sec., 1968–69; Principal, 1969; Private Secretary: to Minister for Aerospace and Shipping, 1973–74; to Sec. of State for Prices and Consumer Protection, 1974–75; Asst Sec., Dept of Prices, 1975, Dept of Trade, 1979; Under Sec., Dept of Trade, then Dept of Transport, 1980–84. *Recreations:* music, gardens, travel. *Address:* Foxbury, East Grinstead, Sussex RH19 3SS. *T:* East Grinstead 23293.

LANE, Dr Anthony Milner, FRS 1975; Deputy Chief Scientific Officer, Atomic Energy Research Establishment, Harwell, since 1976; *b* 27 July 1928; *s* of Herbert William Lane and Doris Ruby Lane (*née* Milner); *m* 1952, Anne Sophie Zissman (*d* 1980); two *s* one *d*; *m* 1983, Jill Valerie Parvin; five step *d*. *Educ:* Trowbridge Boys' High Sch.; Selwyn Coll., Cambridge. BA Maths, PhD Theoretical Physics. Joined Harwell, 1953. *Publications:* Nuclear Theory, 1963; numerous research articles in Review of Modern Physics, Phys. Review, Nuclear Physics, etc. *Recreations:* gardening, bird-watching. *Address:* 6 Walton Street, Oxford OX1 2HG. *T:* Oxford 56565.

LANE, David Neil, CMG 1983; HM Diplomatic Service; Ambassador to the Holy See, since 1985; *b* 16 April 1928; *er s* of late Clive and Hilda Lane, Bath; *m* 1968, Sara, *d* of Cecil Nurcombe, MC; two *d*. *Educ:* Abbotsholme Sch.; Merton Coll., Oxford. Army, 1946–48; Foreign (later Foreign and Commonwealth) Office: 1951–53, 1955–58, 1963–68, 1972–74; British Embassy, Oslo, 1953–55; Ankara, 1959–61, 1975–78; Conakry, 1961–63; UK Mission to the United Nations, New York, 1968–72, 1979; High Comr in Trinidad and Tobago, 1980–85. Pres., UN Trusteeship Council, 1971–72; UK Delegate, Internat. Exhibns Bureau, 1973–74. *Recreation:* music. *Address:* British Embassy to the Holy See, Via dei Condotti 91, I-00187 Rome, Italy. *T:* (6) 678 94 62. *Club:* Travellers'.

LANE, Prof. David Stuart, PhD, DPhil; Professor of Sociology, University of Birmingham, since 1981; *b* Monmouthshire (now Gwent), 24 April 1933; *s* of Reginald and Mary Lane; *m* 1962, Christel Noritzsch; one *s* one *d*. *Educ:* Univ. of Birmingham (BSocSc); Univ. of Oxford (DPhil). PhD Cantab. Graduate student, Nuffield Coll., Oxford, 1961–63. Formerly engrg trainee, local authority employee, sch. teacher; univ. teacher, Birmingham, Essex and Cambridge Univs. Official Fellow, Emmanuel Coll., Cambridge, 1974–80. *Publications:* Roots of Russian Communism, 1969, 2nd edn 1975; Politics and Society in the USSR, 1970, 2nd edn 1978; The End of Inequality?, 1971; (with G. Kolankiewicz) Social Groups in Polish Society, 1973; The Socialist Industrialist State, 1976; (with F. O'Dell) The Soviet Industrial Worker, 1978; The Work Needs of Mentally Handicapped Adults, 1980; Leninism: a sociological interpretation, 1981; The End of Social Inequality?: class status and power under state socialism, 1982; State and Politics in the USSR, 1985; Soviet Economy and Society, 1985. *Recreations:* soccer, squash, gardening, films, TV; active in numerous voluntary associations. *Address:* Department of Sociology, University of Birmingham, Birmingham B15 2TT. *T:* 021–472 1301.

LANE, Sir David (William Stennis Stuart), Kt 1983; Chairman, National Association of Youth Clubs, since 1982; *b* 24 Sept. 1922; *s* of Hubert Samuel Lane, MC; *m* 1955, Lesley Anne Mary Clauson; two *s*. *Educ:* Eton; Trinity Coll., Cambridge; Yale Univ. Served War of 1939–45 (Navy). British Iron and Steel Federation, 1948 (Sec., 1956); Shell International Petroleum Co., 1959–67. Called to the Bar, Middle Temple, 1955. Chm., N Kensington Cons. Assoc., 1961–62. Contested (C) Lambeth (Vauxhall), 1964, Cambridge, 1966; MP (C) Cambridge, Sept. 1967–Nov. 1976; PPS to Sec. of State for Employment, 1970–72; Parly Under-Sec. of State, Home Office, 1972–74; Chm., Commn for Racial Equality, 1977–82. *Recreations:* walking, golf, travel. *Address:* 5 Spinney Drive, Great Shelford, Cambridge. *Club:* MCC.

LANE, Dame Elizabeth (Kathleen), DBE 1965; a Judge of the High Court, Family Division (formerly Probate, Divorce and Admiralty Division), 1965–79; *b* 9 Aug. 1905; *o d* of late Edward Alexander Coulborn and late Kate May Coulborn (*née* Wilkinson); *m* 1926, Henry Jerrold Randall Lane, CBE (*d* 1975); one *s* decd. *Educ:* Malvern Girls Coll.

and privately. Barrister, Inner Temple, 1940; Master of the Bench, 1965. Mem. of Home Office Committee on Depositions in Criminal Cases, 1948. An Asst Recorder of Birmingham, 1953–61; Chm. of Birmingham Region Mental Health Review Tribunal, 1960–62; Recorder of Derby, 1961–62; Commissioner of the Crown Court at Manchester, 1961–62; Judge of County Courts, 1962–65; Acting Dep. Chm., London Sessions, 1965. Chm., Cttee on the Working of the Abortion Act, 1971–73. *Publication:* Hear the Other Side, 1985. *Recreations:* gardening, needlework. *Address:* Hillcrest, 60 Chilbolton Avenue, Winchester, Hants SO22 5HQ.

LANE, Frank Laurence, CBE 1961; Chairman, Elder Dempster Lines Ltd, 1963–72; *b* 1912; *s* of late Herbert Allardyce Lane, CIE, and late Hilda Gladys Duckle Lane (*née* Wraith); *m* 1938, Gwendolin Elizabeth Peterkin; one *s*. *Educ:* Wellington Coll., Berks; New Coll., Oxford. Mansfield & Co. Ltd, Singapore and Penang, 1934–42; BOAC, UK and USA, 1942–45; Mansfield & Co. Ltd, Singapore, 1945–61; Elder Dempster Lines Ltd, Liverpool, 1962–72. *Recreations:* golf, fishing. *Address:* Amberwood, Bisterne Close, Burley, Ringwood, Hampshire. *T:* Burley 3249.

LANE, John, CB 1981; Deputy Director, Central Statistical Office, 1978–81; *b* 23 Oct. 1924; *e s* of R. J. I. and M. E. L. Lane; *m* 1954, Ruth Ann Crocker; one *s*. *Educ:* John Lyon Sch., Harrow; HMS Conway; Univ. of London (BSc(Econ)). Merchant Navy, 1943–47. Joined Ministry of Transport, 1950; Statistician, 1954; Asst Sec. to Council on Prices, Productivity and Incomes, 1959–61; Principal, MoT, 1962; Asst Sec., 1966; Under-Sec., DoE, 1972; Regional Dir, SE Region and Chm., SE Economic Planning Bd, 1973–76; Under Sec., Dept of Transport, 1976–78. *Address:* Fern Hill, 67 Mount Ephraim, Tunbridge Wells, Kent TN4 8BG. *T:* Tunbridge Wells 27293.

LANE, Kenneth Frederick; freelance mining consultant; formerly Consultant and Visiting Professor, Royal School of Mines; *b* 22 March 1928; British; *m* 1950, Kathleen Richards; one *s* two *d*. *Educ:* Emanuel Coll., Cambridge. Degree in Maths. Steel Industry in Sheffield, 1951–59; North America, 1959–61; Rio Tinto-Zinc Corp., 1961–65; Man. Dir, RTZ Consultants Ltd, 1965–70; Dir, RTZ Corp., 1970–75. Advisor on Civil Service Reform, 1970–74. *Recreations:* boat building, sailing. *Address:* Down House, Lezant, Launceston, Cornwall PL15 9PR. *T:* Stoke Climsland 70495.

LANE, Margaret; novelist, biographer, journalist; *b* 23 June 1907; *o d* of late H. G. Lane; *m* 1st, 1934, Bryan (marr. diss. 1939), *e s* of Edgar Wallace; 2nd, 1944, 15th Earl of Huntingdon, *qv*; two *d*. *Educ:* St Stephen's, Folkestone; St Hugh's Coll., Oxford (MA). Reporter, Daily Express, 1928–31; special correspondent: in New York and for International News Service, USA, 1931–32; for Daily Mail, 1932–38. President: Women's Press Club, 1958–60; Dickens Fellowship, 1959–61, 1970; Johnson Soc., 1971; Brontë Soc., 1975–79; Jane Austen Soc., 1985–. *Publications:* Faith, Hope, No Charity (awarded Prix Femina-Vie Heureuse), 1935; At Last the Island, 1937; Edgar Wallace: The Biography of a Phenomenon, 1938; Walk Into My Parlour, 1941; Where Helen Lies, 1944; The Tale of Beatrix Potter, 1946, revd edn, 1985; The Brontë Story, 1953; A Crown of Convolvulus, 1954; A Calabash of Diamonds, 1961; Life With Ionides, 1963; A Night at Sea, 1964; A Smell of Burning, 1965; Purely for Pleasure, 1966; The Day of the Feast, 1968; Frances Wright and the Great Experiment, 1971; Samuel Johnson and his World, 1975; Flora Thompson, 1976; The Magic Years of Beatrix Potter, 1978; (ed) Flora Thompson's A Country Calendar and other writings, 1979; The Drug-Like Brontë Dream, 1980; Operation Hedgehog, 1981; series natural history for children: The Fox, The Spider, The Stickleback, The Squirrel, The Frog, The Beaver, 1982. *Address:* Blackbridge House, Beaulieu, Hants.

LANE, Hon. Mrs Miriam; *see* Rothschild, Hon. M. L.

LANE, Sir Peter (Stewart), Kt 1984; JP; FCA; Senior Partner, Binder Hamlyn, Chartered Accountants, since 1979; Chairman, Brent Chemicals International, since 1985; Deputy Chairman, More O'Ferrall, since 1985; *b* 29 Jan. 1925; *s* of late Leonard George Lane; *m* Doris Florence (*née* Botsford) (*d* 1969); two *d*. *Educ:* Sherborne Sch., Dorset. Served RNVR (Sub-Lieut), 1943–46. Qualified as chartered accountant, 1948; Partner, Binder Hamlyn or predecessor firms, 1950–. National Union of Conservative Associations: Vice Chairman, 1981–83; Chairman, 1983–84, 1986–; Vice President, 1984–86. Governor, Nuffield Nursing Homes Trust, 1985–. JP Surrey, 1976–; Freeman, City of London. *Address:* Rossmore, Pond Road, Hook Heath, Woking, Surrey GU22 0JY. *T:* Woking 61858. *Clubs:* Boodle's, City of London, MCC.
See also Baron Trefgarne.

LANE, Ronald Anthony Stuart, CMG 1977; MC 1945; Deputy Chairman, Chartered Trust Ltd, 1979–83; *b* 8 Dec. 1917; 2nd *s* of late Wilmot Ernest Lane and F. E. Lane (*née* Blakey); *m* 1948, Anne Brenda, 2nd *d* of E. Walsh; one *s* one *d*. *Educ:* Lancing College. FIB. Served War, 1940–45, 7th Light Cavalry, Indian Army, India and Burma (Major). Joined Chartered Bank of India, Australia & China, 1937; served in Far East, 1939–60; Gen. Manager, 1961, Chief Gen. Manager, 1972, Man. Dir, 1973–77, Vice-Chm., 1977–83, Standard Chartered Bank Ltd. Mem., Export Guarantees Adv. Council, 1973–78 (Dep. Chm., 1977–78). *Recreations:* sailing, gardening. *Address:* West Hold, By the Church, West Mersea, Essex CO5 8QD. *T:* West Mersea 2563. *Clubs:* East India, MCC; West Mersea Yacht.

LANE, Prof. Ronald Epey, CBE 1957; MD; FRCP; Emeritus Nuffield Professor of Occupational Health, University of Manchester (Professor, 1945–65); *b* 2 July 1897; *s* of E. E. Lane; *m* 1st, 1924, Winifred E. Tickner (*d* 1981); one *s* (one *d* decd); 2nd, 1982, Ida, *widow* of Arnold Bailey. *Educ:* Simon Langton Sch. Canterbury; Guy's Hospital. MRCP 1925, FRCP 1938; MSc Manchester, 1946; MD London, 1947. Served European War, RFC, 1915–19. Guy's Hospital, 1919–24, qualified, 1923; General Medical practice, 1925–27; Medical Officer, Chloride Elec. Storage Co. Ltd, 1928; Physician, Salford Royal Hospital, 1935; Milroy Lecturer (Royal College of Physicians), 1947, McKenzie Lecturer, 1950. Mem. of various Govt Advisory Cttees. *Publications:* original papers on Lead Poisoning, Medical Education, Occupational Health and Universities, in Lancet, BMJ, Brit. Jl of Industrial Med., Jl of Industrial Hygiene and Toxicology, etc. *Recreations:* golf, fishing. *Address:* 3 Daylesford Road, Cheadle, Cheshire. *T:* 061–428 5738. *Club:* Athenæum.

LANE, Rear-Adm. Walter Frederick Boyt, CB 1960; DSC 1941; FIMechE; MIMarE; Director of Marine Engineering, Admiralty, 1958–61; *b* 7 Feb. 1909; *s* of W. H. Lane, Freshwater, IoW; *m* 1931, Anne Littlecott; one *s*. *Educ:* RN Engineering Coll., Devonport. Eng.-in-Chief, Admiralty, Bath, 1957; Rear-Adm., 1957; retired. Formerly Director, Fairfields (Eng.) Co., Glasgow. *Recreations:* tennis, painting. *Address:* Foxleaze, Limpley Stoke, Wilts. *T:* Limpley Stoke 3225.

LANE-FOX, Baroness *cr* 1981 (Life Peer), of Bramham in the County of West Yorkshire; **Felicity Lane-Fox,** OBE 1976; Vice-President, Royal Association for Disability and Rehabilitation, since 1963; Chairman of Patients' Association, Phipps Respiratory Unit, St Thomas' Hospital, since 1979; *b* 22 June 1918; *d* of late Edward Lane Fox and Enid Maud Lane Fox, MBE. Mem. Nat. Union Exec., Cons. and Unionist Assoc., 1963–66. Mem., Nuffield Orthopaedic Centre House Cttee, Oxford, 1958–66; Vice-President: Yorks Assoc. for Disabled, 1958–80; Action for Dysphasic Adults, 1981–; Patron: Handicapped Adventure Playground Assoc., 1978–; Kensington and Chelsea Action for Disabled, 1982–; Third World Gp for Disabled People, 1983–; Design and Manufacture for Disability (DEMAND), 1983. Chairman: IBA's London Local Radio Adv. Cttee, 1976–80; Thames Help Trust (Thames Television's Telethon Trust), 1985–. Member: Prince of Wales' Adv. Gp on Disability, 1982–; Carnegie Council for Arts and Disabled People, 1985–. *Recreations:* drama, documentaries and sport on television, radio; watching racing, cricket and tennis. *Address:* 30 Marlborough Court, Pembroke Road, W8 6DE. *T:* 01–602 3734.

LANE FOX, Col Francis Gordon Ward; Vice-Lieutenant of West Riding of Yorkshire, 1968–74; Royal Horse Guards, 1919–46, retired; *b* 14 Oct. 1899; *s* of late C. Ward Jackson; assumed surname of Lane Fox in lieu of that of Jackson, by deed poll, 1937; *m* 1929, Hon. Marcia Agnes Mary (*d* 1980), *e d* of 1st and last Baron Bingley, PC (*d* 1947); two *s* one *d*. *Educ:* Eton; RMC, Sandhurst. West Riding of Yorkshire: JP 1948; DL 1952; CC 1949, CA 1955. KStJ 1965. Officer Order of the Crown, with Palm, and Croix de Guerre, with Palm (Belgium), 1946. *Address:* The Little House, Bramham Park, Wetherby, W Yorks LS23 6LS. *T:* Boston Spa 843220. *Club:* Yorkshire (York).

LANE FOX, Robin James, FRSL; Fellow, New College, Oxford, since 1977; University Lecturer in Ancient History, Oxford, since 1977; *b* 5 Oct. 1946; *s* of James Henry Lane Fox and Anne (*née* Loyd); *m* 1970, Louisa Caroline Mary, *d* of Charles and Lady Katherine Farrell; one *s* one *d*. *Educ:* Eton; Magdalen Coll., Oxford (Craven and de Paravicini scholarships, 1966; Passmore Edwards and Chancellors' Latin Verse Prize, 1968). FRSL 1974. Fellow by examination, Magdalen Coll., Oxford, 1970–73; Lectr in Classical Lang. and Lit., 1973–76, Res. Fellow, Classical and Islamic Studies, 1976–77, Worcester Coll., Oxford. Weekly gardening correspondent, Financial Times, 1970–. *Publications:* Alexander the Great, 1973, 3rd edn 1978 (James Tait Black, Duff Cooper, W. H. Heinemann Awards, 1973–74); Variations on a Garden, 1974, rev. edn 1986; Search for Alexander, 1980; Better Gardening, 1982; Pagans and Christians, 1986. *Recreations:* gardening, hunting, poetry, rough travel. *Address:* Old Manor House, Beckley, Oxon. *T:* Stanton St John 251. *Club:* Beefsteak.

LANESBOROUGH, 9th Earl of *cr* 1756; **Denis Anthony Brian Butler;** TD; DL; Baron of Newtown-Butler, 1715; Viscount Lanesborough, 1728; Major, Leicestershire Yeomanry (RA); *b* 28 Oct. 1918; *er s* of 8th Earl and Grace Lilian (*d* 1983), *d* of late Sir Anthony Abdy, 3rd Bt; *S* father 1950; *m* 1939, Bettyne Ione (marr. diss. 1950), *d* of late Sir Lindsay Everard; one *d* (and one *d* decd). *Educ:* Stowe. Leicestershire Yeomanry; Lieutenant, 1939; Major, RAC, TA, 1945. Member: Nat. Gas Consumers' Council, 1973–78; Trent RHA, 1974–82 (Vice-Chm., 1978–82). Chm., Loughborough and District Housing Assoc., 1978–85. DL 1962, JP 1967, Leicester. *Heir: kinsman,* Comdr Terence Brinsley John Danvers Butler, RN; *b* 7 March 1913. *Address:* Alton Lodge, Kegworth, Derby. *T:* Kegworth 2243.

LANG, Prof. Andrew Richard, FRS 1975; Professor of Physics, University of Bristol, since 1979; *b* 9 Sept. 1924; *s* of late Ernest F. S. Lang and late Susannah (*née* Gueterbock); unmarried. *Educ:* University College of South-West, Exeter, (BSc Lond. 1944; MSc Lond. 1947); Univ. of Cambridge (PhD 1953). Research Dept, Lever Bros, Port Sunlight, 1945–47; Research Asst, Cavendish Laboratory, 1947–48; North American Philips, Irvington-on-Hudson, NY, 1952–53; Instructor, Harvard Univ., 1953–54; Asst Professor, Harvard Univ., 1954–59; Lectr in Physics, 1960–66, Reader, 1966–79, Univ. of Bristol. MInstP, Mem. Geol Assoc.; Mem. Soc. Sigma Xi. Charles Vernon Boys Prize, Inst. of Physics, 1964. *Publications:* contribs to learned jls. *Address:* 1B Elton Road, Bristol BS8 1SJ. *T:* Bristol 739784.

LANG, Prof. David Marshall, MA, PhD, DLit, LittD; Professor of Caucasian Studies in the University of London, 1964–84, now Emeritus; Warden of Connaught Hall, University of London, 1955–84; Special Assistant (Georgian), Department of Oriental Manuscripts and Printed Books, since 1950; *b* 6 May 1924; *s* of Dr David Marshall Lang, Medical Practitioner, Bath, and Mrs May Rena Lang; *m* 1956, Janet, *d* of late George Sugden, Leeds; one *s* two *d* (and one *s* decd). *Educ:* Monkton Combe Sch.; St John's Coll., Cambridge. Actg Vice-Consul, Tabriz, 1944–46; 3rd Sec., British Embassy, Tehran, 1946; Research Fellow, St John's Coll., Cambridge, 1946–52; Lectr in Georgian, School of Oriental and African Studies, University of London, 1949–58; Senior Fellow, Russian Inst., Columbia Univ., 1952–53; Reader in Caucasian Studies, University of London, 1958–64; Vis. Prof. of Caucasian Languages, University of California, Los Angeles, 1964–65. Hon. Sec., Royal Asiatic Society, 1962–64; Vice-Pres., Holborn Soc., 1973–; Pres., Georgian Cultural Circle, 1974–. Hon. Dr Philological Sciences, Tbilisi State Univ.; Prix Brémond, 1971. *Publications:* Studies in the Numismatic History of Georgia in Transcaucasia, 1955; Lives and Legends of the Georgian Saints, 1956; The Wisdom of Balahvar, 1957; The Last Years of the Georgian Monarchy, 1957; The First Russian Radical: Alexander Radishchev, 1959; A Modern History of Georgia, 1962; Catalogue of the Georgian Books in the British Museum, 1962; The Georgians, 1966; The Balavariani, 1966; Armenia, Cradle of Civilization, 1970, 3rd edn 1980; (with C. Burney) The Peoples of the Hills, 1971; (ed) Guide to Eastern Literatures, 1971; The Bulgarians, 1976; (with C. Walker) The Armenians (Minority Rights Gp report), 1976; The Armenians: a people in exile, 1981; articles in Bulletin of School of Oriental and African Studies, Encyclopædia Britannica, etc. *Recreations:* music, foreign travel. *Address:* (office) School of Oriental and African Studies, University of London, WC1. *T:* 01–637 2388. *Club:* Leander.

LANG, Lt-Gen. Sir Derek (Boileau), KCB 1967 (CB 1964); DSO 1944; MC 1941; DL; Associate Consultant, PA Management Consultants Ltd, since 1975; *b* 7 Oct. 1913; *s* of Lt-Col C. F. G. Lang and Mrs Lumsden Lang (*née* M. J. L. Forbes); *m* 1st, 1942, M. Massy Dawson (*d* 1953); one *s* one *d*; 2nd, 1953, A. L. S. Shields (marr. diss. 1969); 3rd, 1969, Mrs E. H. Balfour (*d* 1982); 4th, 1983, Mrs Maartje McQueen. *Educ:* Wellington Coll.; RMC Sandhurst. Commnd, The Queen's Own Cameron Highlanders, 1933; Adjutant, TA, 1938; Chief Instructor, Sch. of Infantry, 1943–44; Comdr, 5th Camerons, 1944–45; Comdt, Sch. of Infantry, BAOR, 1945–46; Directing Staff, Staff Coll., Camberley, 1947–48; Staff, Australia, 1949–51; GSO1, War Office, 1951–53; Chief Instructor, Sch. of Infantry Tactical Wing, 1953–55; AAG, War Office, 1955–57; NDC, 1957–58; Comd Infty Bde (153–TA), 1958–60; Chief of Staff, Scottish Comd, 1960; Gen. Officer Commanding, 51st Highland Div. and District, Perth, 1962–64; Dir of Army Training, 1964–66; GOC-in-C, Scottish Command, 1966–69; Governor of Edinburgh Castle, 1966–69; Sec., Univ. of Stirling, 1970–73; Hon. Col, 153 (Highland) Regt, RCT (Volunteers), T&AVR, 1970–76; Pres., Army Cadet Force Assoc. (Scotland), 1975–85. DL Edinburgh, 1978. OStJ. *Publication:* Return to St Valéry, 1974. *Recreations:* golf, fishing, shooting. *Address:* The Rowans, 21 Pentland Avenue, Edinburgh EH13 0HY. *T:* 031–441 2235. *Clubs:* Army and Navy; New (Edinburgh); Senior Golfers' Society; Hon. Co. of Edinburgh Golfers (Muirfield).
See also J. M. Hunt.

LANG, Henry George, CB 1977; consultant and company director, since 1977; *b* 3 March 1919; *s* of Robert and Anna Lang; *m* 1942, Octavia Gwendolin (*née* Turton); one *s* four

d. *Educ:* Victoria Univ., Wellington. DPA, BA, BCom. Private enterprise, 1939–44; RNZAF, 1944–46. NZ government service: various economic appointments, 1946–55; Economic Advisor to High Comr in London, 1955–58; Treasury, 1958–77, Sec. to Treasury, 1968–77. Vis. Prof. of Economics, Victoria Univ. of Wellington, 1977–82, consultant, 1982–. Hon. LLD Victoria Univ., Wellington, 1984. *Publications:* (with J. V. T. Baker) Economic Policy and National Income, in, NZ Official Year Book, 1950; articles in learned journals. *Recreations:* skiing, swimming, reading. *Address:* 81 Hatton Street, Wellington, NZ. *T:* 768 788. *Club:* Wellington (Wellington, NZ).

LANG, Hugh Montgomerie, CBE 1978; Chairman, P-E International plc, since 1980 (Director, since 1972; Chief Executive since 1977); *b* Glasgow, 7 Nov. 1932; *s* of John Montgomerie Lang and Janet Allan (*née* Smillie); *m* 1st, 1959, Marjorie Jean Armour (marr. diss. 1981); one *s* one *d*; 2nd, 1981, Susan Lynn Hartley (*née* Russell). *Educ:* Shawlands Acad., Glasgow; Glasgow Univ. (BSc). ARCST 1953; CEng 1967; FIProdE 1976; FIMC 1970; CBIM 1980. Officer, REME, 1953–55 (National Service). Colvilles Ltd, 1955–56; Glacier Metal Co. Ltd, 1956–60; L. Sterne & Co. Ltd, 1960–61; P-E Consulting Group, 1961–: Manager for ME, 1965–68; Scottish Reg. Manager, 1968–72; Man. Dir, 1974–77. Director: Redman Heenan Internat., 1981–86 (Chm., 1982–86); Fairey Holdings Ltd, 1978–82; UKO International, 1985–86. Chairman: Food, Drink and Packaging Machinery Sector Working Party, 1976–81; Technology Transfer Services Adv. Cttee, 1982–85 (Mem., 1978–85); Member: Business Educn Council, 1980–81; CBI Industrial Policy Cttee, 1980–83; Design Council, 1983–; Engrg Council, 1984–86. FRSA 1984. *Recreations:* gardening, golf, reading. *Address:* Mount Hill Farm, Gerrards Cross, Bucks SL9 8SU. *T:* Fulmer 2406. *Clubs:* Army and Navy; Denham Golf.

LANG, Ian Bruce; MP (C) Galloway and Upper Nithsdale, since 1983 (Galloway, 1979–83); Parliamentary Under Secretary of State, Scottish Office, since 1986; Vice-Chairman, Conservative Party in Scotland, since 1983; *b* 27 June 1940; *y s* of James Fulton Lang, DSC, and Maude Margaret (*née* Stewart); *m* 1971, Sandra Caroline *e d* of John Alastair Montgomerie, DSC; two *d*. *Educ:* Lathallan Sch., Kincardineshire; Rugby Sch.; Sidney Sussex Coll., Cambridge (BA 1962). Director: Hutchison & Craft Ltd, 1975–81; Hutchison & Craft (Underwriting Agents) Ltd, Lloyd's, 1976–81; P. MacCallum & Sons Ltd, 1976–81; Rose, Thomson, Young & Co. (Glasgow) Ltd, 1966–75. Member, Queen's Body Guard for Scotland (Royal Company of Archers), 1974–. Dir, Glasgow Chamber of Commerce, 1978–81; Trustee: Savings Bank of Glasgow, 1969–74; West of Scotland Trustee Savings Bank, 1974–83. Contested (C): Central Ayrshire, 1970; Glasgow Pollok, Feb. 1974. An Asst Govt Whip, 1981–83; a Lord Comr of HM Treasury, 1983–86; Parly Under Sec. of State, Dept of Employment, 1986. Mem., Select Cttee on Scottish Affairs, 1979–81. Pres., Scottish Young Conservatives, 1982–84. OStJ 1974. *Recreations:* skiing, sailing, shooting, music. *Address:* House of Commons, SW1A 0AA. *Clubs:* Pratt's; Western (Glasgow); Prestwick Golf.

LANG, Very Rev. John Harley; Dean of Lichfield, since 1980; Chaplain to HM the Queen, 1976–80; *b* 27 Oct. 1927; *e s* of Frederick Henry Lang and Eileen Annie Lang (*née* Harley); *m* 1972, Frances Rosemary Widdowson; three *d*. *Educ:* Merchant Taylors' Sch.; King's Coll., London. MA Cantab, BD London, LRAM. Subaltern, XII Royal Lancers, 1951–52; Asst Curate, St Mary's Portsea, 1952–57; Priest Vicar, Southwark Cathedral, 1957–60; Chaplain, Emmanuel Coll., Cambridge, 1960–64; Asst Head of Religious Broadcasting, BBC, 1964–67; Head of Religious Programmes, Radio, 1967–71; Head of Religious Broadcasting, BBC, 1971–80. Member: Nat. Trust Cttee for Mercia, 1984–; Central Religious Adv. Cttee, BBC and IBA, 1985–. Chairman: Governors, Lichfield Cathedral Sch., 1980–; Council, Abbots Bromley Sch., 1984–. *Recreation:* music. *Address:* The Deanery, Lichfield, Staffs WS13 7LD.

LANG, John Russell, CBE 1963; Deputy Chairman, The Weir Group Ltd, 1968–73; *b* 8 Jan. 1902; *s* of Chas Russell Lang, CBE; *m* 1st, 1934, Jenny (*d* 1970), *d* of Sir John Train, MP, of Cathkin, Lanarkshire; four *d* (one *s* decd); 2nd, 1973, Gay Mackie (*d* 1979); 3rd, 1981, Kay, *widow* of Norman Macfie. *Educ:* Loretto Sch., Musselburgh; France and USA. Dir, G. & J. Weir Ltd, 1930–67. Chairman, Weir Housing Corp., 1946–66. President, Scottish Engineering Employers' Association, 1963–64. Mem., Toothill Cttee and EDC for Mec. Eng. Lt-Col 277 Field Regt, RA (TA), 1937. *Recreations:* hunting, shooting, golf. *Address:* The White House of Milliken, Brookfield, Renfrewshire PA5 8UN. *T:* Johnstone 20898. *Clubs:* Royal Scottish Automobile; Prestwick Golf; Troon Golf.

LANG, Rear-Adm. William Duncan, CB 1981; retired; *b* 1 April 1925; *s* of James Hardie Lang and Elizabeth Foggo Paterson Lang (*née* Storie); *m* 1947, Joyce Rose Weeks; one *s* one *d* *Educ:* Edinburgh Acad. FRAeS. Entered Royal Navy, 1943; trained as Pilot; served in 800, 816 and 825 Sqdns and as Flying Instr and Test Pilot; comd 802 Sqdn, 1958–59; Commander (Air): RNAS Culdrose, 1962–63; HMS Eagle, 1964–65; Fleet Aviation Officer, Far East Fleet, 1966–68; Captain 1969; comd RNAS Lossiemouth, 1970–72; Dep. Comdt, Jt Warfare Estabt, 1973–74; COS to Flag Officer, Naval Air Comd, 1975–76; Mil. Dep. to Hd of Defence Sales, 1978–81; Dir, National Security, MoD, 1981–86. Naval ADC to the Queen, 1978; Rear-Adm. 1978. *Recreation:* golf (Pres., RN Golf Soc., 1979–85). *Address:* c/o Midland Bank, 19 High Street, Haslemere, Surrey GU27 2HQ. *Club:* Army and Navy.

LANG, William Marshall F.; *see* Farquharson-Lang.

LANGAN, Peter St John Hevey, QC 1983; *b* 1 May 1942; *s* of late Frederick Hevey Langan and of Myrrha Langan (*née* Jephson), Mount Hevey, Hill of Down, Co. Meath; *m* 1976, Oonagh May Winifred McCarthy. *Educ:* Downside School; Trinity College, Dublin (MA, LLB); Christ's College, Cambridge (PhD). Called to the Irish Bar, King's Inns, 1964; called to the Bar, Lincoln's Inn, 1967; Lectr in Law, Univ. of Durham, 1966–69; in practice at Chancery Bar, 1970–. Chm., Eton Housing Assoc. Ltd, 1979–83. Mem., Management Cttee, Catholic Fund for Overseas Develt, 1984–. *Publications:* Maxwell on Interpretation of Statutes, 12th edn, 1969; Civil Procedure and Evidence, 1st edn, 1970, 3rd edn (with L. D. J. Henderson) as Civil Procedure, 1983; (with P. V. Baker) Snell's Principles of Equity, 28th edn, 1982. *Address:* 2 New Square, Lincoln's Inn, WC2A 3RU. *T:* 01-242 6201. *Club:* Athenæum.

LANGDALE, Simon John Bartholomew; Headmaster, Shrewsbury School, since 1981; *b* 26 Jan. 1937; *s* of G. R. Langdale and H. J. Langdale (*née* Bartholomew); *m* 1962, Diana Marjory Hall; two *s* one *d*. *Educ:* Tonbridge Sch.; St Catharine's Coll., Cambridge. Taught at Radley Coll., 1959–73 (Housemaster, 1968–73); Headmaster, Eastbourne Coll., 1973–80. *Recreations:* cricket, fives, golf, china fairings. *Address:* Headmaster's House, The Schools, Shrewsbury, Shropshire SY3 7AP. *Clubs:* Hawks (Cambridge); Free Foresters, Jesters.

LANGDON, Alfred Gordon, CMG 1967; CVO 1966; QPM 1961; retired; *b* 3 July 1915; *s* of Wilfred James Langdon and Norah (*née* Nixon); *m* 1947, Phyllis Elizabeth Pengelley; one *s* two *d*. *Educ:* Munro Coll., Jamaica. Berkhampstead Sch., Herts. Bank of Nova Scotia, Kingston, Jamaica, 1933–37; Jamaica Infantry Volunteers, 1937–39; Jamaica Constabulary Force, 1939–70: Asst Comr of Police, 1954–62; Dep. Comr, 1962–64; Comr, 1964–70, retd. Security Advisor, Min. of Home Affairs, Jamaica, 1970–72. *Recreations:* fishing, tennis, swimming. *Address:* 2637 Burntfork Drive, Clearwater, Fla 33519, USA. *Clubs:* Kingston Cricket; Countryside Country (Clearwater).

LANGDON, Anthony James; Under Secretary, Cabinet Office, since 1985; *b* 5 June 1935; *s* of Dr James Norman Langdon and Maud Winifred Langdon; *m* 1969, Helen Josephine Drabble, *y d* of His Honour J. F. Drabble, QC; one *s* one *d*. *Educ:* Kingswood Sch., Bath; Christ's Coll., Cambridge. Entered Home Office, 1958; Office of Minister for Science, 1961–63; Treasury, 1967–69. *Address:* c/o Cabinet Office, SW1.

LANGDON, (Augustus) John; chartered surveyor and land agent; *b* 20 April 1913; *e s* of late Rev. Cecil Langdon, MA and Elizabeth Mercer Langdon, MBE; *m*; two *d*; *m* 1949, Doris Edna Clinkard; one *s*. *Educ:* Berkhamsted Sch.; St John's Coll., Cambridge (Nat. Science Tripos; MA). FRICS (Chartered Land Agent); FRSA. Asst to J. Carter Jonas & Sons, Oxford, 1936–37, Partner 1945–48; Suptg Lands Officer, Admty, 1937–45; Regional Land Comr, Min. of Agriculture, 1948–65; Dep. Dir, Agric. Land Service, Min. of Agriculture, 1965–71; Chief Surveyor, Agricultural Develt and Advisory Service, MAFF, 1971–74; with the National Trust in London, 1974–76. Chm., Statutory Cttee on Agricultural Valuation; RICS: Mem., Gen. Council; Mem., Land Agency and Agricultural Divisional Council, 1971–75. *Publications:* contrib. Rural Estate Management (ed R. C. Walmsley), Fream's Elements of Agriculture, professional and agric. jls. *Recreations:* gardening, walking, collecting. *Address:* Thorn Bank, Long Street, Sherborne, Dorset DT9 3BS. *T:* Sherborne 812910. *Club:* United Oxford & Cambridge University.

LANGDON, David, FRSA; Cartoonist and Illustrator; Member of Punch Table; regular contributor to Punch since 1937, to The New Yorker since 1952; Cartoonist to Sunday Mirror, since 1948; *b* 24 Feb. 1914; *er s* of late Bennett and Bess Langdon; *m* 1955, April Sadler-Phillips; two *s* one *d*. *Educ:* Davenant Gram. Sch., London. Architect's Dept, LCC, 1931–39; Executive Officer, London Rescue Service, 1939–41; served in Royal Air Force, 1941–46; Squadron Leader, 1945. Editor, Royal Air Force Jl, 1945–46. Creator of Billy Brown of London Town for LPTB. Official Artist to Centre International Audio-Visuel d'Etudes et de Recherches, St Ghislain, Belgium. Exhibitions: Oxford, New York, London. *Publications:* Home Front Lines, 1941; All Buttoned Up, 1944; Meet Me Inside, 1946; Slipstream (with R. B. Raymond), 1946; The Way I See It, 1947; Hold Tight There!, 1949; Let's Face It, 1951; Wake Up and Die (with David Clayton), 1952; Look at You, 1952; All in Fun, 1953; Laugh with Me, 1954; More in Fun, 1955; Funnier Still, 1956; A Banger for a Monkey, 1957; Langdon At Large, 1958; I'm Only Joking, 1960; Punch with Wings, 1961; How to Play Golf and Stay Happy, 1964; David Langdon's Casebook, 1969; How To Talk Golf, 1975; Punch in the Air, 1983. *Recreations:* golf, non-League soccer. *Address:* 46 Albert Street, Tring, Herts HP23 6AU. *T:* Tring 3070. *Club:* Royal Air Force.

LANGDON, John; *see* Langdon, A. J.

LANGDON, Michael, CBE 1973; Principal Bass Soloist, Royal Opera House, Covent Garden, since 1951; Consultant, National Opera Studio, since 1986 (Director, 1978–86); *b* 12 Nov. 1920; *s* of Henry Langdon, Wednesfield Road, Wolverhampton; *m* 1947, Vera Duffield, Norwich; two *d*. *Educ:* Bushbury Hill Sch., Wolverhampton. First Principal Contract, Royal Opera House, Covent Garden, 1951; first Gala Performance, before Queen Elizabeth II (Gloriana), 1953; Grand Inquisitor in Visconti Production of Don Carlos, 1958; debut as Baron Ochs (Rosenkavalier), 1960; first International Engagement (Hamburg), 1961; first Glyndebourne Festival, 1961; since then, has appeared in international performances in Paris, Berlin, Aix-en-Provence, San Francisco and Los Angeles, 1962; Lausanne, Geneva, Vienna and Budapest, 1963; Zürich, New York, 1964; Geneva, Marseilles, 1965; Seattle, Buenos Aires; Houston, 1975; Gala Performances, 1967, 1969. *Publication:* (with Richard Fawkes) Notes from a Low Singer, 1982. *Recreations:* swimming, walking and Association football (now only as spectator). *Address:* 34 Warnham Court, Grand Avenue, Hove, East Sussex.

LANGDON, Richard Norman Darbey, FCA; chairman and director of companies; *b* 19 June 1919; *s* of Norman Langdon and Dorothy Langdon; *m* 1944, June Dixon; two *s*. *Educ:* Shrewsbury Sch. Officer, RA, 1939–46. Admitted Mem. Inst. of Chartered Accountants in England and Wales, 1947; joined Spicer and Pegler, 1949, Partner 1953, Managing Partner, 1971–82, Senior Partner, 1978–84. Chairman: First National Finance Corp., 1985–; Finlay Packaging PLC; Hammond and Champness Ltd; Aspinall Hldg PLC; Time Products PLC; Dir, Rockware Group PLC, 1985–; Dep. Chm., Chemring PLC, 1985–. Treasurer, CGLI, 1982–. Liveryman, Co. of Chartered Accountants of England and Wales. *Recreations:* sailing, gardening, bricklaying. *Address:* Rough Hill House, Munstead, near Godalming, Surrey. *T:* Godalming 21507. *Clubs:* City of London; Old Salopian.

LANGDON-DOWN, Antony Turnbull; Part-time Chairman, Social Security Appeals Tribunal, since 1985; Clerk to Merchant Taylors Company, 1980–85; *b* 31 Dec. 1922; *s* of Dr Reginald Langdon-Down and Ruth Langdon-Down (*née* Turnbull); *m* 1954, Jill Elizabeth Style (*née* Caruth); one *s* one *d*. *Educ:* Harrow School. Member of Lincoln's Inn, 1940–60, called to the Bar, 1948; enrolled as a solicitor, 1960; practised as solicitor, 1961–80. Pilot, Royal Air Force, 1942–47 (finally Flt Lieut). Master of Merchant Taylors Company, 1979–80. *Recreations:* sailing, tennis, bridge, music, art. *Address:* Tinley Lodge, Shipbourne, Tonbridge, Kent TN11 9QB. *T:* Plaxtol 810720. *Clubs:* Savile, MCC; Bough Beech Sailing, Law Society Yacht.

LANGDON-DOWN, Barbara; *see* Littlewood, Lady (Barbara).

LANGE, Rt. Hon. David Russell; PC 1984; MP (Lab) Mangere, New Zealand, since 1977; Prime Minister of New Zealand, Minister of Foreign Affairs and Minister in charge of Security Intelligence Service, since 1984; *b* 4 Aug. 1942; *s* of Eric Roy Lange and Phoebe Fysh Lange; *m* 1968, Naomi Joy Crampton; two *s* one *d*. *Educ:* Univ. of Auckland (LLM Hons). Called to the Bar of NZ and admitted Solicitor, 1966. Dep. Leader of the Opposition, 1979–83, Leader 1983–84. *Address:* 282 Massey Road, Mangere, Auckland, New Zealand. *T:* (09) 276–7356; Executive Suite, Parliament Building, Wellington, New Zealand.

LANGFORD, 9th Baron, *cr* 1800; **Colonel Geoffrey Alexander Rowley-Conwy,** OBE 1943; DL; RA, retired; Constable of Rhuddlan Castle and Lord of the Manor of Rhuddlan; *b* 8 March 1912; *s* of late Major Geoffrey Seymour Rowley-Conwy (killed in action, Gallipoli, 1915), Bodrhyddan, Flints, and Bertha Gabrielle Rowley-Conwy, JP (*d* 1984), *d* of late Lieutenant Alexander Cochran, Royal Navy, Ashkirk, Selkirkshire; *S* kinsman 1953; *m* 1st, 1939, Ruth St John (marr. diss. 1956), *d* of late Albert St John Murphy, The Island House, Little Island, County Cork; 2nd, 1957, Grete (*d* 1973), *d* of late Col E. T. C. von Freiesleben, formerly Chief of the King's Adjutants Staff to the King of Denmark; three *s*; 3rd, 1975, Susan Winifred Denham, *d* of C. C. H. Denham, Chester; one *s* one *d*. *Educ:* Marlborough; RMA Woolwich. Served War of 1939–45, with RA; Singapore, (POW escaped) and with Indian Mountain Artillery in Burma, 1941–45 (despatches, OBE); Staff Coll., Quetta, 1945; Berlin Airlift, Fassberg, 1948–49; GSOI 42 Inf. Div., TA, 1949–52; Lt-Col 1945; retired 1957; Colonel (Hon.), 1967. DL Clwyd,

1977. *Heir: s* Hon. Owain Grenville Rowley-Conwy, *b* 27 Dec. 1958. *Address:* Bodrhyddan, Rhuddlan, Clwyd. *Club:* Army and Navy.

LANGFORD-HOLT, Sir John (Anthony), Kt 1962; Lieutenant-Commander RN (Retired); *b* 30 June 1916; *s* of late Ernest Langford-Holt; *m* 1944, Elisabeth Charlotte Marie (marr. diss. 1950), *d* of late Ernst Newstadtl, Vienna; *m* 1953, Flora Evelyn Innes (marr. diss. 1969), *d* of late Ian St Clair Stuart; one *s* one *d*; *m* 1971, Betty Ann (marr. diss. 1981), *d* of H. Maxworthy; *m* 1984, Irene, *d* of late David Alexander Kerr. *Educ:* Shrewsbury Sch. Joined RN and Air Branch (FAA), 1939. MP (C) Shrewsbury, 1945–83. Sec. of Conservative Parly Labour Cttee, 1945–50; Chm., Anglo-Austrian Soc., 1960–63, 1971–82; Member: CPA, 1945–83; IPU, 1945–83, and other Internat. Bodies; Parliamentary and Scientific Cttee, 1945–83; Estimates Cttee, 1964–68; Expenditure Cttee, 1977–79. Chm., Select Cttee on Defence, 1979–81. Formerly Dir, Authority Investments Ltd. Freeman and Liveryman of City of London. Grand Decoration of Honour, in Silver with Star (Austria), 1980. *Address:* 704 Nelson House, Dolphin Square, SW1. *T:* 01–798 8186; Lymington 73094. *Clubs:* White's, Carlton; Royal Yacht Squadron (Cowes).

LANGHAM, Sir James (Michael), 15th Bt *cr* 1660; TD 1965; *b* 24 May 1932; *s* of Sir John Charles Patrick Langham, 14th Bt, and of Rosamond Christabel (MBE 1969), *d* of late Arthur Rashleigh; *S* father, 1972; *m* 1959, Marion Audrey Eleanor, *d* of O. H. Barratt, Gararagua Estate, Tanzania; two *s* one *d*. *Educ:* Rossall School, Fleetwood. Served as Captain, North Irish Horse, 1953–67. *Recreations:* shooting, skin-diving. *Heir: s* John Stephen Langham, *b* 14 Dec. 1960. *Address:* Claranagh, Tempo, Co. Fermanagh. *T:* Tempo 247.

LANGHORNE, Richard Tristan Bailey; FRHistS; Fellow and Junior Bursar, St John's College, Cambridge, since 1974; *b* 6 May 1940; *s* of Eadward John Bailey Langhorne and Rosemary Scott-Foster; *m* 1971, Helen Logue, *o d* of William Donaldson, CB and Mary Donaldson; one *s* one *d*. *Educ:* St Edward's Sch., Oxford; St John's Coll., Cambridge (Exhibr). BA Hist. Tripos, 1962; Certif. in Hist. Studies, 1963; MA 1965. Tutor in History, Univ. of Exeter, 1963–64; Research Student, St John's Coll., Cambridge, 1964–66; Lectr in History, 1966–74 and Master of Rutherford Coll., 1971–74, Univ. of Kent at Canterbury; Steward, St John's Coll., Cambridge, 1974–79. Vis. Prof., Univ. of Southern Calif, 1986. *Publications:* chapters in: The Twentieth Century Mind, 1971; British Foreign Policy under Sir Edward Grey, 1977; The Collapse of the Concert of Europe, 1890–1914, 1980; (ed) Diplomacy and Intelligence during the Second World War, 1985; reviews and articles in Historical Jl and History. *Recreations:* music, railways. *Address:* St John's College, Cambridge; 15 Madingley Road, Cambridge. *Club:* Athenæum.

LANGLANDS, Prof. Robert Phelan, FRS 1981; Professor of Mathematics, Institute for Advanced Study, Princeton, New Jersey, since 1972; *b* 6 Oct. 1936; *s* of Robert Langlands and Kathleen Johanna (*née* Phelan); *m* 1956, Charlotte Lorraine Cheverie; two *s* two *d*. *Educ:* Univ. of British Columbia (BA 1957, MA 1958); Yale Univ. (PhD 1960). FRSC 1972. Princeton University: Instructor, 1960–61; Lectr, 1961–62; Asst Prof., 1962–64; Associate Prof., 1964–67; Prof., Yale Univ., 1967–72. Associate Prof., Ortadoğu Teknik Universitesi, 1967–68; Gast Prof., Universität Bonn, 1980–81. Hon. DSc: Univ. of BC, 1985; McMaster Univ., 1985; City Univ., New York, 1985. Cole Prize, Amer. Math. Sec., 1982; Common Wealth Award, Sigma Xi, 1984. *Publications:* Automorphic Forms on GL(2) (with H. Jacquet), 1970; Euler Products, 1971; On the Functional Equations satisfied by Eisenstein Series, 1976; Base Change for GL(2), 1980; Les débuts d'une formule des traces stable, 1983; contrib. Canadian Jl Maths, Proc. Amer. Math. Soc. Symposia, Springer Lecture Notes. *Address:* Institute for Advanced Study, Princeton, New Jersey, USA. *T:* 609–734–8106.

LANGLEY, Brig. Charles Ardagh, CB 1962; CBE 1945; MC 1916 (Bar, 1918); Consultant, Kennedy & Donkin, 1974–81; *b* 23 Aug. 1897; *s* of late John Langley, CBE, Under Sec. of State, Egyptian Govt, 1922; *m* 1st, 1920, V. V. M. Sharp (*d* 1931); one *s* one *d*; 2nd, 1936, M. J. Scott (*d* 1981); two *d*. *Educ:* Cheltenham Coll.; Royal Military Academy, Woolwich. Served European War: commissioned Royal Engineers, 1915; France, 1916, served in field co. and as Adjutant to divisional engineers (MC and Bar; despatches three times). Subseq. took course of higher military engineer training, including one year at Cambridge Univ.; Railway Training Centre, Longmoor, 1922–27; seconded to Great Indian Peninsular Railway, 1927–33, in connection with electrification of Bombay-Poona main line, including construction of power station at Kalyan; Railway Trg Centre, Longmoor, 1933–38; various appointments, including Chief Instructor of Railways, War Office, 1938–40; War of 1939–45: responsible for initial transportation developments in Middle East; later formed Transportation Trg Centre for raising and training Docks and Inland Water Transport troops of Indian Engineers. Dep. Quartermaster-Gen. (Movements and Transportation), Allied Land Forces, South East Asia Command, 1943–45 (despatches, CBE); Commandant, Transportation Trg Centre, Longmoor, 1946. Inspecting Officer of Railways, 1946–58, Chief Inspecting Officer, 1958–63, Min. of Transport. Consultant: British Railways Bd, 1963–66; Transmark, 1972–73; Projects Manager, UKRAS (Consultants) Ltd, 1966–69, Man. Dir, 1969–72. Pres. Junior Institution of Engineers, 1961–62. FCIT. *Publications:* several military text books on transportation. *Recreation:* gardening. *Address:* Beeches, Little Austins, Farnham, Surrey GU9 8JR. *T:* Farnham 723212.

LANGLEY, Gordon Julian Hugh, QC 1983; a Recorder, since 1986; *b* 11 May 1943; *s* of late Gordon Thompson Langley and of Marjorie Langley; *m* 1968, Beatrice Jayanthi Langley; two *d*. *Educ:* Westminster School; Balliol College, Oxford (BA, BCL). Called to the Bar, Inner Temple, 1966. *Recreations:* music, sport. *Address:* 2 Bridgeman Road, Teddington, Mddx TW11 9AH. *T:* 01–353 1878. *Club:* Travellers'.

LANGLEY, Maj.-Gen. Sir (Henry) Desmond (Allen), KCVO 1983; MBE 1967; Administrator, Sovereign Base Areas and Commander, British Forces, Cyprus, 1983–85; *b* 16 May 1930; *s* of late Col Henry Langley, OBE, and Winsome Langley; *m* 1950, Felicity Joan, *d* of Lt-Col K. J. P. Oliphant, MC; one *s* one *d*. *Educ:* Eton; RMA Sandhurst. Commissioned The Life Guards, 1949; Adjt, Household Cavalry Regt, 1953–54; GSO3 HQ 10th Armoured Div., 1956–57; Regtl Adjt, Household Cavalry, 1959–60; psc 1961; GSO2(Ops) HQ Far East Land Forces, 1963–65; Bde Major, Household Bde, 1965–67; Comdg Officer, The Life Guards, 1969–71; Asst Sec., Chiefs of Staff Secretariat, 1971–72; Lt-Col Comdg Household Cavalry and Silver Stick-in-Waiting, 1972–75; Comdr 4th Guards Armoured Bde, 1976–77; RCDS 1978; BGS HQ UK Land Forces, 1979; GOC London District and Maj.-Gen. Comdg Household Div., 1979–83; retired, 1986. *Address:* c/o Lloyds Bank Ltd, 6 Pall Mall, SW1.

LANGLEY MOORE, D.; *see* Moore, Doris L.

LANGRIDGE, Philip Gordon, FRAM; concert and opera singer (tenor), since 1964; *b* 16 Dec. 1939; *m* 1981, Ann Murray; one *s* two *d* by former marriage. *Educ:* Maidstone Grammar Sch.; Royal Academy of Music, London. ARAM 1977; FRAM 1985. Glyndebourne Festival début, 1964; BBC Promenade Concerts, 1970–; Edinburgh Fest., 1970–; Netherlands Opera, Scottish Opera, Handel Opera etc. Covent Garden: L'Enfant et les Sortilèges, Rossignole, Boris, Jenufa, Alceste; ENO: Turn of the Screw, Osud (Olivier Award, Outstanding Individual Performer in a New Opera Production, 1984), The Mask of Orpheus; Glyndebourne, 1977–: Don Giovanni, Idomeneo, Fidelio; La Scala, 1979–: Rake's Progress, Wozzeck, Boris Godunov, Il Sosia, Idomeneo; Frankfurt Opera: Castor and Pollux, Rigoletto, Die Entführung; Zurich Opera: Poppea, Lucio Silla; La Fenice: Janacek's Diary; Palermo: Otello (Rossini); Pesaro: La Donna del Lago; Aix en Provence: Alcina, Les Boriades; Metropolitan Opera, NY: Così fan Tutte. Concerts with major international orchestras and conductors including: Boston (Previn), Chicago (Solti, Abbado), Los Angeles (Christopher Hogwood), Sydney (Mackerras), Vienna Phil. (Previn), Orchestre de Paris (Barenboim, Mehta), and all major British orchestras. Many first performances of works, some dedicated to and written for him. Has made over 50 records of early, baroque, classical, romantic and modern music (Grammy Award for Schönberg's Moses und Aron, 1985). Mem., Music Panel, Arts Council of GB, 1983–86. *Recreation:* collecting water colour paintings and Victorian postcards. *Address:* c/o Allied Artists Agency, 42 Montpellier Square, SW7 1JZ. *T:* 01–589 6243.

LANGRIDGE, Richard James; HM Diplomatic Service; Deputy High Commissioner and Head of Chancery, Colombo, since 1986; *b* 29 Oct. 1932; *m* 1965, Jeannine Louise Joosen; one *d*. HM Forces, 1951–53; joined FO 1953; served NY, Leopoldville, Athens, Dakar, Paris and FCO; Ambassador to Madagascar, 1979–84; FCO, 1985. *Address:* c/o Foreign and Commonwealth Office, SW1.

LANGRISHE, Sir Hercules (Ralph Hume), 7th Bt *cr* 1777; *b* 17 May 1927; *s* of Sir Terence Hume Langrishe, 6th Bt, and Joan Stuart (*d* 1976), *d* of late Major Ralph Stuart Grigg; *S* father, 1973; *m* 1955, Hon. Grania Sybil Enid Wingfield, *d* of 9th Viscount Powerscourt; one *s* three *d*. *Educ:* Summer Fields, St Leonards; Eton. 2nd Lieut, 9th Queen's Royal Lancers, 1947; Lieut, 1948; retd 1953; *Recreations:* shooting, fishing. *Heir: s* James Hercules Langrishe [*b* 3 March 1957; *m* 1985, Gemma, *d* of Patrick O'Daly; one *d*]. *Address:* Ringlestown House, Kilmessan, Co. Meath. *T:* Navan 25243. *Club:* Kildare Street and University (Dublin).

LANGSTONE, Rt. Rev. John Arthur William; *b* 30 Aug. 1913; *s* of Arthur James Langstone and Coullina Cook; *m* 1944, Alice Patricia Whitby; two *s*. *Educ:* Univ. of Toronto (BA); Trinity Coll., Toronto (LTh); Yale Univ. (MDiv). Asst Curate, St John Baptist, Toronto, 1938; Chaplain, Cdn Army, 1943; Exec. Officer, Dio. Toronto, 1947; Rector: Trinity Church, Port Credit, Toronto, 1950; St George's, Edmonton, 1958; St Faith's, Edmonton, 1969; Canon of All Saints' Cathedral, Edmonton, 1963; Archdeacon of Edmonton, 1965; Exec. Archdeacon, 1971; Bishop of Edmonton, 1976–79. Hon. DD Trinity Coll., Toronto, 1977. *Address:* 5112 109 Avenue, Edmonton, Alberta T6A 1S1, Canada. *T:* 465–4111.

LANGTON; *see* Temple-Gore-Langton, family name of Earl Temple of Stowe.

LANGTON, Sir Henry Algernon; *see under* Calley, Sir H. A.

LANGTRY, Ian; *see* Langtry, J. I.

LANGTRY, (James) Ian; Under Secretary, Department of Education and Science, since 1982; *b* 2 Jan. 1939; *s* of late Rev. H. J. Langtry and I. M. Langtry (*née* Eagleson); *m* 1959, Eileen Roberta Beatrice (*née* Nesbitt); one *s* one *d*. *Educ:* Coleraine Academical Instn; Queen's Univ., Belfast (BSc). Assistant Master, Bangor Grammar Sch., 1960–61; Lectr, Belfast College of Technology, 1961–66; Asst Director of Examinations/Recruitment, Civil Service Commission, 1966–70; Principal, Dept of Educn and Science, 1970–76, Asst Sec., 1976–82. *Recreations:* golf, sailing. *Clubs:* Royal Portrush Golf; West Kent Golf.

LA NIECE, Rear-Adm. Peter George, CB 1973; CBE 1967; *b* 23 July 1920; *s* of late George David Nelson La Niece and Gwynneth Mary (*née* Morgan); *m* 1948, Evelyn Mary Wrixon Babington (*d* 1982); two *s* one *d*. *Educ:* Whitgift Sch., Croydon. Entered RN, 1937; served War of 1939–45 in battleships, cruisers and destroyers; Gunnery Specialist 1945; Comdr 1953; Captain 1961; comd HMS Rame Head, 1962; Senior UK Polaris Rep., Washington, 1963–66; comd HMS Triumph, 1966–68; Cdre Clyde in Comd Clyde Submarine Base, 1969–71; Rear-Adm. 1971; Flag Officer Spithead and Port Admiral, Portsmouth, 1971–73; retired 1973. Dir in Exco Gp of Cos, 1976–85. *Recreation:* gardening. *Address:* Charltons, Yalding, Kent ME18 6DF. *T:* Maidstone 814161. *Club:* Army and Navy.

LANKESTER, Richard Shermer; Clerk of Select Committees, House of Commons, since 1979; Registrar of Members' Interests, since 1976; *b* 8 Feb. 1922; *s* of late Richard Ward Lankester; *m* 1950, Dorothy, *d* of late Raymond Jackson, Worsley; three *s* one *d*. *Educ:* Haberdashers' Aske's Hampstead Sch.; Jesus Coll., Oxford (MA). Served Royal Artillery, 1942–45. Entered Dept of Clerk of House of Commons, 1947; Clerk of Standing Cttees, 1973–75; Clerk of Expenditure Cttee, 1975–79. Co-Editor, The Table, 1962–67. *Address:* The Old Farmhouse, The Green, Boughton Monchelsea, Maidstone, Kent. *T:* Maidstone 43749.

LANKESTER, Timothy Patrick; Economic Minister, Washington, and UK Executive Director, International Monetary Fund and World Bank, since 1985; *s* of Preb. Robin Prior Archibald Lankester and Jean Dorothy (*née* Gilliat); *m* 1968, Patricia Cockcroft; three *d*. *Educ:* Monkton Combe Sch.; St John's Coll., Cambridge (BA); Jonathan Edwards Coll., Yale (Henry Fellow, MA). Teacher (VSO), St Michael's Coll., Belize, 1960–61; Fereday Fellow, St John's Coll., Oxford, 1965–66; Economist, World Bank, Washington DC, 1966–69; New Delhi, 1970–73; Principal 1973, Asst Sec. 1977, HM Treasury; Private Secretary to Rt Hon. James Callaghan, 1978–79; to Rt Hon. Margaret Thatcher, 1979–81; seconded to S. G. Warburg and Co. Ltd, 1981–83; Under Sec., HM Treasury, 1983–85. Dir, Ocean Transport and Trading plc, 1984–85. Trustee, CSV. *Recreations:* tennis, music, sailing. *Address:* c/o Foreign and Commonwealth Office, SW1A 2AH.

LANSBURY, Angela Brigid; actress; *b* London, England, 16 Oct. 1925; *d* of Edgar Lansbury and late Moyna MacGill (who *m* 1st, Reginald Denham); *m* 1st, Richard Cromwell; 2nd, 1949, Peter Shaw; one *s* one *d* and one step *s*; naturalized American citizen, 1951. *Educ:* South Hampstead High Sch. for Girls; Webber Douglas Sch. of Singing and Dramatic Art, Kensington; Feagin Sch. of Drama and Radio, New York. With Metro-Goldwyn-Mayor, 1943–50; *films* included: Gaslight, 1944; National Velvet, 1944; Dorian Gray, 1944; Harvey Girls, 1946; Till the Clouds Roll By, 1946; If Winter Comes, 1947; State of the Union, 1948; Samson and Delilah, 1949. As free lance, 1950–: *films* include: Kind Lady, 1951; The Court Jester, 1956; The Long Hot Summer, 1957; The Reluctant Debutante, 1958; Summer of the 17th Doll, 1959; A Breath of Scandal, 1959; Dark at the Top of the Stairs, 1960; Blue Hawaii, 1962; All Fall Down, 1962; The Manchurian Candidate, 1963; In the Cool of the Day, 1963; The World of Henry Orient, 1964; Out of Towners, 1964; Harlow, 1965; Bedknobs and Broomsticks, 1972; Black Flowers for the Bride, 1972; Death on the Nile, 1978; The Lady Vanishes, 1979; The Mirror Crack'd, 1980; The Pirates of Penzance, 1983; The Company of Wolves, 1984; *plays:* appearances include: Hotel Paradiso (Broadway debut), 1957; Helen, in A Taste of Honey, Lyceum Theatre, New York, 1960; Anyone can Whistle (Broadway musical), 1964; Mame (Tony Award for best actress in a Broadway musical), Winter Garden,

NYC, 1966–68; Dear World (Broadway), 1969 (Tony Award); Gypsy (Broadway Musical), Piccadilly, 1973, US tour, 1974 (Tony Award; Chicago, Sarah Siddons Award, 1974); Gertrude, in Hamlet, Nat. Theatre, 1975; Anna, in The King and I (Broadway), 1978; Mrs Lovett, in Sweeney Todd (Broadway), 1979 (Tony Award). TV series, Murder She Wrote, 1984. NY Drama Desk Award, 1979; Sarah Siddons Award, 1980 and 1983; inducted Theatre Hall of Fame, 1982. *Address:* Suite 501, 1650 Broadway, New York City, NY 10019, USA.

LANSDOWN, Gillian Elizabeth, (Mrs Richard Lansdown); *see* Tindall, G. E.

LANSDOWNE, 8th Marquess of (GB), *cr* 1784; **George John Charles Mercer Nairne Petty-Fitzmaurice;** 29th Baron of Kerry and Lixnaw, 1181; Earl of Kerry, Viscount Clanmaurice, 1723; Viscount FitzMaurice and Baron Dunkeron, 1751; Earl of Shelburne, 1753; Baron Wycombe, 1760; Earl of Wycombe and Viscount Calne, 1784; PC 1964; *b* 27 Nov. 1912; *o s* of Major Lord Charles George Francis Mercer Nairne, MVO (killed in action, 1914; 2nd *s* of 5th Marquess), and Lady Violet Mary Elliot (she *m* 2nd, 1916, 1st Baron Astor of Hever), *d* of 4th Earl of Minto; *S* cousin, 1944; *m* 1st, 1938, Barbara, (*d* 1965), *d* of Harold Stuart Chase, Santa Barbara; two *s* one *d* (and one *d* decd); 2nd, 1969, Mrs Polly Carnegie (marr. diss. 1978), *d* of Viscount Eccles, *qv*; 3rd, 1978, Gillian Ann, (*d* 1982), *d* of Alured Morgan. *Educ:* Eton; Christ Church, Oxford. Sec. Junior Unionist League for E Scotland, 1939. Served War of 1939–45, Capt. Royal Scots Greys 1940, formerly 2nd Lt Scottish Horse (TA); Major 1944; served with Free French Forces (Croix de Guerre, Légion D'Honneur); Private Sec. to HM Ambassador in Paris (Rt Hon. A. Duff Cooper), 1944–45. Lord-in-Waiting to the Queen, 1957–58; Joint Parliamentary Under-Sec. of State, Foreign Office, 1958–62; Minister of State for Colonial Affairs, 1962–64, and for Commonwealth Relations, 1963–64. Mem. Royal Company of Archers (Queen's Body Guard for Scotland); JP, Perthshire, 1950; DL Wilts, 1952–73. Patron of two livings. Chm., Victoria League in Scotland, 1952–56; Inter-Governmental Cttee on Malaysia, 1962. Chm., Franco-British Soc., 1972–83; Pres., Franco-Scottish Soc. Prime Warden, Fishmongers' Company, 1967–68. Comdr, Légion d'Honneur, 1979. *Heir: s* Earl of Shelburne, *qv*. *Address:* Meikleour House, Perthshire. *Clubs:* Turf; New (Edinburgh).
See also Lady Nairne.

LAPOINTE, Col Hon. Hugues, PC (Canada) 1949; QC; Barrister; *b* Rivière-du-Loup, Quebec, 3 March 1911; *s* of Rt Hon. Ernest Lapointe, PC, QC, Minister of Justice at Ottawa, and Emma Pratte; *m* 1938, Lucette, *d* of Dr and Mrs R. E. Valin, Ottawa. *Educ:* University of Ottawa (BA 1932); Laval Univ., Quebec (LLL 1935). Mem. of Quebec Bar, July 1935; KC 1949. Served War of 1939–45, Overseas, with Regt de la Chaudière. Elected (L) to House of Commons, Lotbinière County Constituency, 1940, 1945, 1949, 1953. Delegate to Gen. Assembly, UN: Paris, Sept. 1948; Lake Success, April 1949; Lake Success, Sept. 1950 (Vice-Chm. Canadian Delegation). Parliamentary Asst to Minister of National Defense, 1945, to Sec. of State for External Affairs, 1949; Solicitor-Gen. of Canada, 1949; Minister of Veterans Affairs, Aug. 1950; Postmaster Gen., 1955; Agent-Gen. for Quebec in the United Kingdom, 1961–66; Lieut-Governor of Quebec, 1966–78. Hon. Col, Le Régiment de la Chaudière, 1970. Hon. LLD: University of Ottawa, 1954; Royal Military Coll. of Canada, 1967. Croix de Guerre avec palme. KStJ 1966; Kt Grand Cross, SMO, Malta, 1966. Is a Roman Catholic. *Clubs:* Garrison (Quebec); Royal Quebec Golf (Boischatel).

LAPOINTE, Paul André; Deputy High Commissioner for Canada in the United Kingdom, since 1981; *b* 1 Nov. 1934; *s* of Henri and Regina Lapointe; *m* 1965, Iris Donati; one *d*. *Educ:* Université Laval. BA, LLL. Called to the Bar, Québec, 1958. Journalist, Le Soleil, 1959–60; joined Canadian Foreign Service, 1960; served Vietnam and Laos, 1961–62, NATO, Paris, 1962–64, Geneva, 1968–72, New Delhi, 1975–76, New York, 1976–79; Dep. Perm. Rep. to UN Security Council, 1977–78. *Address:* Canadian High Commission, Macdonald House, 1 Grosvenor Square, W1. *T:* 01–629 9492. *Club:* Travellers'.

LAPOTAIRE, Jane; actress; *b* 26 Dec. 1944; *d* of unknown father and Louise Elise Lapotaire; *m* 1st, 1965, Oliver Wood (marr. diss. 1967); 2nd, 1974, Roland Joffé (marr. diss. 1982); one *s*. *Educ:* Northgate Grammar Sch., Ipswich; Old Vic Theatre Sch., Bristol. Bristol Old Vic Co., 1965–67; Nat. Theatre Co., 1967–71, incl. Measure for Measure, Flea in Her Ear, Dance of Death, Way of the World, Merchant of Venice, Oedipus, The Taming of the Shrew; freelance films and TV, 1971–74; RSC, 1974–75 (roles included Viola in Twelfth Night, and Sonya in Uncle Vanya); Prospect Theatre Co., West End, 1975–76 (Vera in A Month in the Country, Lucy Honeychurch in A Room with a View); freelance films and TV, 1976–78; Rosalind in As You Like It, Edin. Fest., 1977; RSC, 1978–81: Rosaline in Love's Labours Lost, 1978–79; title role in Piaf, The Other Place 1978, Aldwych 1979, Wyndhams 1980, Broadway 1981; National Theatre: Eileen, Kick for Touch, 1983; Belvidera, Venice Preserv'd, Antigone, 1984; Saint Joan (title rôle), Compass Co., 1985; Double Double, Fortune Theatre, 1986; *television:* Marie Curie (serial), 1977; Antony and Cleopatra, 1981; Macbeth, 1983; Seal Morning (series), 1985; *films:* Eureka, 1983; Lady Jane, 1986. SWET Award 1979, London Critics Award and Variety Club Award 1980, and Broadway Tony Award 1981 (all for Piaf). *Recreations:* water colours, cordon bleu cookery. *Address:* c/o William Morris Inc., 147–149 Wardour Street, W1.

LAPPER, Maj.-Gen. John; Medical Director, International Hospitals Group, since 1984; *b* 24 July 1921; *s* of late Col Wilfred Mark Lapper, OBE, Legion of Merit (USA), late RE, and Agnes Lapper (*née* Powner); *m* 1948, Dorothy, *d* of late Roland John and Margaret Simpson (*née* Critchlow); three *s*. *Educ:* Wolverhampton Grammar Sch.; King Edward VI Sch., Birmingham; Birmingham Univ. MB, ChB 1946; DLO 1952. House appts, Queen Elizabeth and Children's Hosp., Birmingham, and Ronkswood Hosp. and Royal Infirm., Worcester; Registrar, Royal Berks Hosp., Reading. Commnd RAMC, 1950; ENT specialist, Mil. Hosps in UK, Libya, Egypt, Germany, Singapore, Malaya; CO 14 Field Amb., BAOR, 1958; CO BMH Rinteln, BAOR, 1964; Asst Comdt, Royal Army Med. Coll., 1965–68; ADMS Hong Kong, 1969–71; CO Queen Alexandra's Mil. Hosp., Millbank, 1971–73; ADMS 3 Div., 1973; DDMS HQ UKLF, 1974–77; Dir, Med. Supply, MoD, 1977; Dir, Med. Policy and Plans, MoD, 1978–80, retired; QHS 1977–80. Hospital and Medical Dir, Nat. Guard Saudi Arabia, 1981–83. Hudson-Evans Lectr, W Kent Medico-Chirurgical Soc., 1980; Mem. Sands Cox Med. Soc., Birmingham Univ. FFCM 1980; FBIM 1980; FRSocMed; FMedSoc London; Mem. BMA; Pres. Med. Soc., Hong Kong, 1970–71; Mem., RUSI; Chm. Council, Yateley Industries for the Disabled. OStJ 1959. *Publications:* articles in professional jls. *Recreations:* travel, militaria. *Address:* Holmbush, Old School Lane, Yateley, Camberley, Surrey GU17 7NG. *T:* Yateley 874180; Rocas Del Mar, Mijas Costa, (Malaga), Spain. *Club:* Army and Navy.

LAPPERT, Prof. Michael Franz, FRS 1979; Professor of Chemistry, University of Sussex, since 1969; *b* 31 Dec. 1928; *s* of Julius Lappert and Kornelie Lappert (*née* Beran); *m* 1980, Lorna McKenzie. *Educ:* Wilson's Grammar School; Northern Polytechnic, London. BSc, PhD, DSc (London). FRSC. Northern Polytechnic, London: Asst Lecturer, 1952–53; Lecturer, 1953–55; Sen. Lectr, 1955–59. UMIST: Lectr, 1959–61; Sen. Lectr, 1961–64; Reader, Univ. of Sussex, 1964–69. SERC Sen. Res. Fellow, 1980–85. First recipient of (London) Chemical Soc. Award in Main Group Metal Chemistry, 1970; Award in Organometallic Chemistry, 1978; Tilden Lectr, 1972–73; F. S. Kipping Award of American Chem. Soc., 1976. *Publications:* (ed jtly) Developments in Inorganic Polymer Chemistry, 1962; (jtly) Metal and Metalloid Amides, 1980; (jtly) Organo-zirconium and -hafnium Compounds, 1986; approx. 450 papers in Jl Chem. Soc., etc. *Recreations:* golf, tennis, walking, theatre, opera. *Address:* 4 Varndean Gardens, Brighton BN1 6WL. *T:* Brighton 503661.

LAPPING, Anne Shirley Lucas; Producer, Channel Four politics programme, since 1982; *b* 10 June 1941; *d* of late Frederick Stone and of Dr Freda Lucas Stone; *m* 1963, Brian Michael Lapping; three *d*. *Educ:* City of London Sch. for Girls; London Sch. of Econs. New Society, 1964–68; London Weekend TV, 1970–73; writer on The Economist, 1974–82. Other writing and broadcasting. Member: SSRC, 1977–79; Nat. Gas Consumers' Council, 1978–79. *Recreations:* literature, housework. *Address:* 94 Highgate Hill, N6 5HE. *T:* 01–341 0523.

LAPSLEY, Air Marshal Sir John (Hugh), KBE 1969 (OBE 1944); CB 1966; DFC 1940; AFC 1950; *b* 24 Sept. 1916; *s* of late Edward John Lapsley, Bank of Bengal, Dacca, and Norah Gladis Lapsley; *m* 1st, 1942, Jean Margaret MacIvor (*d* 1979); one *s* one *d*; 2nd, 1980, Millicent Rees (*née* Beadnell), *widow* of T. A Rees. *Educ:* Wolverhampton Sch.; Royal Air Force Coll., Cranwell. Served in Fighter Squadrons in UK, Egypt and Europe, 1938–45; psc 1946; Air Ministry Directorate of Policy, 1946–48; Commander No 74 Fighter Squadron and Air Fighting Development Squadron, 1949–52; HQ Fighter Command Staff, 1952–54; 2nd TAF Germany, 1954–58; Ministry of Defence Joint Planning Staff, 1958–60; Deputy Chief of Staff Air, 2nd Allied TAF, 1960–62; IDC, 1963; Secretary to Chiefs of Staff Cttee and Director of Defence Operations Staff, Ministry of Defence, 1964–66; No 19 Group, RAF Coastal Comd, 1967–68; AOC-in-C, RAF Coastal Comd, 1968–69; Head of British Defence Staff and Defence Attaché, Washington, 1970–73. Mem. Council, Officers' Pension Soc., 1976–. Dir-Gen., Save the Children Fund, 1974–75. Dir, Falkland Is R&D Assoc. Ltd, 1978–83; Councillor, Suffolk Coastal District Council, 1979–, Chm. 1983. Fellow RSPB. *Recreations:* golf, fishing, ornithology. *Address:* Milcroft, 149 Saxmundham Road, Aldeburgh, Suffolk IP15 5PB. *T:* Aldeburgh 3957. *Clubs:* Royal Air Force; Aldeburgh Golf; Suffolk Fly Fishers.

LAPUN, Sir Paul, Kt 1974; Member for South Bougainville, Papua New Guinea House of Assembly, since 1964; *b* 1923; *m* 1951, Lois, two *s* one *d*. *Educ:* Catholic Mission, Vunapope. Teacher, Catholic Mission, 1947–61. Under-Secretary for Forests, Papua and New Guinea, 1964–67. Founder, Pangu Party, 1967 (Leader, 1967–68; Dep. Parly Leader, 1968–); Minister: for Mines and Energy, 1972–75; for Health, 1975–77. Hon. Mem., Internat. Mark Twain Soc., USA. *Address:* c/o House of Assembly, Port Moresby, Papua New Guinea.

LAQUEUR, Walter; Chairman, Research Council, Center for Strategic and International Studies, Georgetown University, since 1975; Director, Institute of Contemporary History and Wiener Library, London, since 1964; *b* 26 May 1921; *s* of late Fritz Laqueur and late Else Laqueur; *m* 1941, Barbara (*née* Koch), *d* of Prof. Richard Koch and Maria Koch (*née* Rosenthal); two *d*. Agricultural labourer during War, 1939–44. Journalist, free lance author, 1944–55; Editor of Survey, 1955–65; Co-editor of Journal of Contemporary History, 1966–. Prof., History of Ideas, Brandeis Univ., 1967–71; Prof. of Contemporary History, Tel Aviv Univ., 1970–; Vis. Prof.: Chicago Univ.; Johns Hopkins Univ.; Harvard Univ. *Publications:* Communism and Nationalism in the Middle East, 1956; Young Germany, 1961; Russia and Germany, 1965; The Road to War, 1968; Europe Since Hitler, 1970; Out of the Ruins of Europe, 1971; Zionism, a History, 1972; Confrontation: the Middle East War and World Politics, 1974; Weimar: a Cultural History, 1918–33, 1974; Guerrilla, 1976; Terrorism, 1977; The Missing Years, 1980; (ed jtly) A Reader's Guide to Contemporary History, 1972; (ed) Fascism: a reader's guide, 1978; The Terrible Secret, 1980; Farewell to Europe, 1981; Germany Today: a personal report, 1985; World of Secrets: the uses and limits of intelligence, 1986. *Recreations:* swimming, motor-boating. *Address:* 4 Devonshire Street, W1; 1800 K Street NW, Washington, DC, USA.

LARCOM, Sir (Charles) Christopher (Royde), 5th Bt, *cr* 1868; Partner in Grieveson, Grant & Co., Stockbrokers, since 1960; *b* 11 Sept. 1926; *s* of Sir Philip Larcom, 4th Bt, and Aileen Monica Royde (*née* Colbeck); *S* father, 1967; *m* 1956, Barbara Elizabeth, *d* of Balfour Bowen; four *d*. *Educ:* Radley; Clare Coll., Cambridge. (Wrangler, 1947; BA, 1947; MA, 1951). Served RN (Lieutenant), 1947–50. Articled to Messrs Spicer and Pegler (Chartered Accountants), 1950–53; ACA 1954; FCA 1965; joined Grieveson, Grant and Co., 1955; Member, The Stock Exchange, London, 1959 (Mem. Council, 1970–80). *Recreations:* sailing, music. *Address:* 8 The Postern, Barbican, Wood Street, EC2Y 8BJ. *T:* 01–920 0388.

LARDINOIS, Petrus Josephus; Chairman, Executive Board, Rabobank Nederland, since 1977; *b* Noorbeek, 13 Aug. 1924; *m* Maria Hubertina Gerardine Peeters; two *s* three *d*. *Educ:* Wageningen Agricultural Coll. Various agricultural posts until 1960; Agricultural Attaché, Dutch Embassy, London, 1960–63; Mem., Second Chamber, 1963–73 (Catholic People's Party); Mem., European Parliament, 1963–67; Minister of Agriculture and Fisheries, 1967–72; Comr for Agriculture, Commn of the European Communities, 1973–76. Pres., Brabant Farmers' Union, 1965–67. *Address:* Rabobank Nederland, PO Box 17100, 3500 HG Utrecht, The Netherlands.

LARGE, Prof. John Barry; Professor of Applied Acoustics, since 1969, Dean of Faculty of Engineering and Applied Science, since 1982, and Director of Industrial Affairs, University of Southampton; Chairman, Chilworth Centre Ltd, since 1984; *b* 10 Oct. 1930; *s* of Thomas and Ada Large; *m* Barbara Alicia Nelson; two *s*. *Educ:* Queen Mary Coll., London Univ.; Purdue Univ., USA. BScEng (Hons), MS. Group Engr, EMI Ltd, Feltham, Mddx, 1954–56; Sen. Systems Engr, Link Aviation, Binghampton, NY, USA, 1956–58; Chief Aircraft Noise Unit, Boeing Co., Seattle, USA, 1958–69. Dir, Inst. of Sound and Vibration Res., Southampton Univ., 1978–82. Mem., Noise Adv. Council, 1976–80; Pres., Assoc. Noise Consultants. Hon. Dep. Chief Scientific Officer, Royal Aircraft Estabt, 1974–. Corresp. Mem., INCE, USA. *Publications:* contrib. (regarding aircraft noise, etc) to: Commn of European Communities, Eur 5398e, 1975; Proc. 5th Worlds' Airports Conf., Instrn of CE, 1976; RSH Conf., Eastbourne, 1977; Proc. of Internoise 80, Miami, Internoise 81, Amsterdam, Internoise 82, San Francisco; Internoise 83, Edinburgh; Internoise 84, Hawaii; Internoise 85, Munich; Internoise 86, Mass, USA; Polmet 85, Hong Kong; The Development of Criteria for Environmental Noise Control (Proc. Royal Instn, vol. 52), 1979; Internat. Congress of Acoustics, 1983. *Recreations:* skiing, gardening. *Address:* Chinook, Southdown Road, Shawford, Hants. *T:* Twyford 712307.

LARGE, Maj.-Gen. Stanley Eyre, MBE 1945; *b* 11 Aug. 1917; *s* of late Brig. David Torquil Macleod Large and Constance Lucy Houston; *m* 1941, Janet Mary (*née* Brooks); three *s*. *Educ:* Edinburgh; Cheltenham Coll.; Caius Coll., Cambridge (MA, MD); St Thomas' Hosp. FRCP, FRCPE. Commnd in RAMC, 1942; war service in Tunisia, Italy, Austria, Greece, with field ambs and as Regimental MO; psc 1948; spec. medicine; served in hosps at home and overseas as med. specialist, later consultant in medicine, with particular interest in diseases of chest, 1950–65; various sen. admin. appts in Cyprus and BAOR, 1965–75; DMS, UKLF, 1975–78. QHP 1974–78. Dir of Med. Servs, King Edward VIII Hosp., Midhurst, 1978–83. *Publications:* contrib. med. literature. *Recreations:* travel, ski-ing, golf, photography; formerly running (half blue, Cambridge v Oxford, mile, 1937). *Address:* Churt House, Churt, Farnham, Surrey GU10 2PX. *T:* Frensham 2642.

LARKIN, John Cuthbert, MA; Headmaster, Wyggeston School, Leicester, 1947–69, retired; *b* 15 Oct. 1906; *s* of J. W. Larkin; *m* 1933, Sylvia Elizabeth Pilsbury; one *s* three *d.* *Educ:* King Edward VI Sch., Nuneaton, Downing Coll., Cambridge. Assistant Master, Shrewsbury Sch., 1928–45; Headmaster, Chesterfield Grammar Sch., 1946–47. *Recreations:* cricket, gardening. *Address:* Groves Cottage, Summers Lane, Totland Bay, Isle of Wight. *T:* Freshwater 752506.

LARMINIE, (Ferdinand) Geoffrey, OBE 1971; External Affairs Co-ordinator, Health, Safety and Environmental Services, British Petroleum Co. plc, since 1984; *b* 23 June 1929; *s* of late Ferdinand Samuel Larminie and of Mary Larminie (*née* Willis); *m* 1956, Helena Elizabeth Woodside Carson; one *s* one *d.* *Educ:* St Andrews Coll., Dublin; Trinity Coll., Dublin (BA 1954, MA 1972). Asst Lectr in Geology, Univ. of Glasgow, 1954–56; Lectr in Geology, Univ. of Sydney, 1956–60; joined British Petroleum Co. Ltd, 1960: Exploration Dept in Sudan, Greece, Canada, Libya, Kuwait, California, New York, Thailand and Alaska, 1960–74; Scientific Advr, Inf. Dept, London, 1974–75; Gen. Manager, Public Affairs and Inf. Dept, London, 1975–76; Gen. Manager, Environmental Control Centre, London, 1976–84. Member: Royal Commn on Environmental Pollution, 1979–83; NERC, 1983–. Council Mem., RGS, 1984–. Pres., Alaska Geol Soc., 1969; Trustee, Bermuda Biological Station 1978–; Member: Bd of Management, Inst. of Offshore Engrg, Heriot-Watt Univ., 1981–; Polar Res. Bd, Nat. Res. Council, Washington, DC, 1984–. Mem., IBA Gen. Adv. Council, 1980–85. Mem. of numerous scientific and professional socs. *Publications:* papers in scientific and technical jls on oil ind., and occasional reviews. *Recreations:* archaeology, natural history, reading, shooting. *Address:* Lane End, Lanes End, Tring, Herts. *T:* Wendover 624907.

LARMOUR, Sir Edward Noel, (Sir Nick Larmour), KCMG 1977 (CMG 1966); HM Diplomatic Service, retired; *b* 25 Dec. 1916; *s* of Edward and Maud Larmour, Belfast, N Ireland; *m* 1946, Nancy, 2nd *d* of Thomas Bill; one *s* two *d.* *Educ:* Royal Belfast Academical Institution (Kitchener Scholar); Trinity Coll., Dublin (Scholar) (1st Class Hons and University Studentship in Classics, 1939); Sydney Univ., NSW. Royal Inniskilling Fusiliers, 1940; Burma Civil Service, 1942; Indian Army, 1942–46 (Major); Dep. Secretary to Governor of Burma, 1947; Commonwealth Relations Office, 1948; served in New Zealand, Singapore, Australia and Nigeria, 1950–68; Asst Under-Secretary of State, 1964; Dep. Chief of Administration, FCO, 1968–70; High Comr, Jamaica, and non-resident Ambassador, Haiti, 1970–73; Asst Under Sec. of State, FCO, 1973–75; High Comr (non-resident) for New Hebrides, 1973–76; Dep. Under Sec. of State, FCO, 1975–76. Mem., Price Commn, 1977–80; Chm., Bermuda Constituency Boundaries Commn, 1979. *Recreations:* cricket, golf, music. *Address:* 68 Wood Vale, N10. *T:* 01–444 9744. *Clubs:* Royal Commonwealth Society; MCC.

LAROSIÈRE de CHAMPFEU, Jacques Martin Henri Marie de; *see* de Larosière de Champfeu.

LARSEN, Cyril Anthony; Senior Clerk, House of Commons, 1980–86, retired; *b* 29 Dec. 1919; *s* of late Niels Arthur Larsen and Ella Bessie Larsen (*née* Vaughan); *m* 1956, Patricia Sneade; two *s* three *d.* *Educ:* St Francis Xavier's College, Liverpool. Board of Trade, 1936–38; Min. of Labour, 1938–40; Royal Navy, Lieut, 1940–46; entered administrative class, Dept of Employment, 1947; seconded to HM Treasury, 1950–53; Asst Sec., 1963; seconded to Prices and Incomes Board, 1966–69; Under Sec., 1971–79. *Address:* 51 Park Hill Road, Wallington, Surrey SM6 0RJ. *T:* 01–647 9380.

LARSON, Frederick H., DFM 1943; General Manager, Business Development, Alberta Opportunity Co., Edmonton, Alberta (Alberta Crown Corporation), since 1974; *b* 24 Nov. 1913; *s* of Herman B. and Martha C. Larson; *m* 1941, Dorothy A. Layng; one *s.* *Educ:* University of Saskatchewan. Observer, RCAF, 1941–43. Member for Kindersley, Parliament of Canada, 1949–53; Delegate to UN, Paris, 1952. Ten years in oil and gas business, production refining and sales, domestic and offshore; eight years in financial trust business, representing financial interests, Canada amd Jamaica; three years in construction and engineering; agricultural interests, Saskatchewan; Agent-Gen. for Province of Saskatchewan in London, 1967–73. *Recreation:* golf. *Address:* c/o Guaranty Trust Company, 10010 Jasper Avenue, Edmonton, Alberta, Canada. *Clubs:* Ranchmen's (Calgary); Mayfair Golf (Edmonton, Alta).

LARTIGUE, Sir Louis C.; *see* Cools-Lartigue.

LASCELLES, family name of **Earl of Harewood.**

LASCELLES, Viscount; David Henry George Lascelles; *b* 21 Oct. 1950; *s* and *heir* of 7th Earl of Harewood, *qv*; *m* 1979, Margaret Rosalind Messenger; three *s* one *d.* *Educ:* The Hall Sch.; Westminster. *Address:* 2 Orme Square, W2.

LASCELLES, Maj.-Gen. Henry Anthony, CB 1967; CBE 1962 (OBE 1945); DSO 1944; Director-General, Winston Churchill Memorial Trust, 1967–80; *b* 10 Jan. 1912; *s* of Edward Lascelles and Leila Kennett-Barrington; *m* 1941, Ethne Hyde Ussher Charles. *Educ:* Winchester; Oriel Coll., Oxford (MA). Served War of 1939–45: Egypt, North Africa, Sicily and Italy, rising to second in command of an armoured brigade. Instructor, Staff Coll., Camberley, 1947–49; GSO 1, HQ 7th Armoured Div., BAOR, 1949–52; Comdg Officer 6th Royal Tank Regt, BAOR, 1952–55; Instructor NATO Defence Coll., 1955–56; Brigadier Royal Armoured Corps HQ 2nd Infantry Div., BAOR, 1956–57; National Defence Coll., Canada, 1958–59; BGS Military Operations, War Office, 1959–62; Chief of Staff, HQ Northern Ireland Command, 1962–63; Maj.-General, General Staff, Far East Land Forces, 1963–66. Pres., British Water Ski Fedn, 1980–. *Recreations:* squash, tennis, golf, music, gardening. *Address:* Manor Farm Cottage, Hedgerley Green, Bucks. *T:* Gerrards Cross 883582. *Club:* Naval and Military.

LASCELLES, Mary Madge, FBA 1962; Hon. Fellow, Somerville College, 1967; *b* 7 Feb. 1900; *d* of William Horace and Madeline Lascelles. *Educ:* Sherborne School for Girls; Lady Margaret Hall, Oxford. Research Studentship, Westfield Coll., 1923; Assistant Lecturer, Royal Holloway Coll., 1926; Somerville College: Tutor in English Language and Literature, 1931; Fellow, 1932–67; Vice-Principal, 1947–60; University Lecturer in English Literature, 1960–66; Reader, 1966–67. *Publications:* Jane Austen and her Art, 1939; Shakespeare's Measure for Measure, 1953; (ed) The Works of Samuel Johnson, Yale vol. ix, A Journey to the Western Islands of Scotland, 1971; The Adversaries and Other Poems, 1971; Notions and Facts, 1973; The Story-Teller Retrieves the Past, 1980; Further Poems, 1982; contributions to learned journals, etc. *Address:* 3 Stratfield Road, Oxford OX2 7BG. *T:* Oxford 57817. *Club:* University Women's.

LASDUN, Sir Denys (Louis), Kt 1976; CBE 1965; FRIBA; architect in private practice with Peter Softley, since 1960; *b* 8 Sept. 1914; *s* of Norman Lasdun and Julie Abrahams; *m* 1954, Susan Bendit; two *s* one *d.* *Educ:* Rugby Sch.; Architectural Assoc. Served with Royal Engineers, 1939–45 (MBE). Practised with Wells Coates, Tecton and Drake. Hoffman Wood Professor of Architecture, University of Leeds, 1962–63. Assessor, Competitions for Belgrade Opera Hse, 1971, and new Parly Bldg, London, 1971–72. Principal works: housing and schools for Bethnal Green and Paddington; London HQ, NSW Govt; flats at 26 St James's Place; Royal College of Physicians; Fitzwilliam College, and Christ's College extension, Cambridge; new University of East Anglia and work for the Universities of London (SOAS, Inst. of Educn, Law Inst., project for Courtauld Inst.), Leicester and Liverpool; National Theatre and IBM Central London Marketing Centre, South Bank; EEC HQ for European Investment Bank, Luxembourg; design for new Hurva Synagogue, Old City, Jerusalem; Cannock Community Hosp.; Geneo Opera House competition; office building 6–12 Fenchurch St. Trustee, BM, 1975–85; Member: CIAM and MARS Gp, 1935–59; V & A Adv. Cttee, 1973–83; Slade Cttee, 1976–; Arts Panel, Arts Council of GB, 1980–84; Académie d'Architecture, Paris, 1984–; Accademia Nazionale di San Luca, Rome, 1984–. Hon. Fellow: American Institute of Architects, 1966; Bulgarian Inst. of Architects, 1985; Hon. FRCP, 1975. Hon. DA, Manchester, 1966; Hon. DLitt: E Anglia, 1974; Sheffield, 1978; Hon. Diploma, First World Biennale of Architecture, Sofia, 1981. RIBA London Architecture Bronze Medallist, 1960 and 1964; Civic Trust Awards: Class I, 1967; Group A, 1969; Special Award, São Paulo Biennale, Brazil, 1969; Concrete Society Award, 1976; Royal Gold Medal for Architecture, RIBA, 1977; RIBA Architectural, Award for London Region, 1978. *Publications include:* An Architect's Approach to Architecture, 1965 (RIBA Jl); A Language and a Theme, 1976; Architecture in an Age of Scepticism, 1984; contributions to architectural and other papers; lectures in UK, USA, Spain, Portugal, Norway, Denmark, Italy, China and Hong Kong. *Address:* 146 Grosvenor Road, SW1V 3JY. *T:* 01–630 8211.

LASH, Prof. Nicholas Langrishe Alleyne, DD; Norris-Hulse Professor of Divinity, University of Cambridge, since 1978; *b* 6 April 1934; *s* of Henry Alleyne Lash and Joan Mary Lash (*née* Moore); *m* 1976, Janet Angela Chalmers; one *s.* *Educ:* Downside Sch.; Oscott Coll.; St Edmund's House, Cambridge. MA, PhD, BD, DD. Served RE, 1952–57. Oscott Coll., 1957–63; Asst Priest, Slough, 1963–68; Fellow, 1969–85, Dean, 1971–75, St Edmund's House, Cambridge; Univ. Asst Lectr, Cambridge, 1974–78. *Publications:* His Presence in the World, 1968; Change in Focus, 1973; Newman on Development, 1975; Voices of Authority, 1976; Theology on Dover Beach, 1979; A Matter of Hope, 1982; Theology on the Way to Emmaus, 1986. *Address:* Faculty of Divinity, St John's Street, Cambridge CB2 1TW. *T:* Cambridge 358933; 4 Hertford Street, Cambridge CB4 3AG.

LASKEY, Sir Denis (Seward), KCMG 1974 (CMG 1957); CVO 1958; HM Diplomatic Service, retired; *b* 18 Jan. 1916; *s* of F. S. Laskey; *m* 1947, Perronnelle Mary Gemma, *d* of late Col Sir Edward Le Breton, MVO; one *s* three *d.* *Educ:* Marlborough Coll.; Corpus Christi Coll., Oxford. 3rd Secretary, Diplomatic Service, 1939; FO, Sept. 1939–June 1940; served in Army, 1940–41; FO, 1941–46; Berlin, 1946–49; Member UK Delegation to UN, New York, 1949–53; FO, 1953–59; Private Secretary to Secretary of State for Foreign Affairs, 1956–59; Minister, HM Embassy, Rome, 1960–64; Under-Secretary, Cabinet Office, 1964–67; Minister, HM Embassy, Bonn, 1967–68; Ambassador to: Rumania, 1969–71; Austria, 1972–75. *Recreations:* ski-ing, fishing, golf. *Address:* Loders Mill, near Bridport, Dorset. *Club:* Leander (Henley-on-Thames).

LASKEY, Prof. Ronald Alfred, FRS 1984; Charles Darwin Professor of Animal Embryology, since 1983 and Fellow of Darwin College, since 1982, University of Cambridge; *b* 26 Jan. 1945; *s* of Thomas Lesley and Bessie Laskey; *m* 1971, Margaret Ann Page; one *s* one *d.* *Educ:* High Wycombe Royal Grammar Sch.; Queen's Coll., Oxford. MA, DPhil 1970. Scientific Staff: Imperial Cancer Research Fund, 1970–73; MRC Lab. of Molecular Biology, 1973–83; Co-Dir, Molecular Embryology Group, Cancer Research Campaign, 1983–. Colworth Medal, Biochem. Soc., 1979. *Publications:* articles on cell biology in scientific jls. *Recreations:* building, music, theatre. *Address:* CRC Molecular Embryology Group, Department of Zoology, Downing Street, Cambridge CB2 3EJ. *T:* Cambridge 358717.

LASKI, Marghanita; (Mrs J. E. Howard); *b* 24 Oct. 1915; *d* of late Neville J. Laski, QC; *m* 1937, John Eldred Howard; one *s* one *d.* *Educ:* Ladybarn House Sch., Manchester; Somerville Coll., Oxford. MA Oxon. Novelist, critic, journalist. Mem., Annan Cttee of Inquiry into Future of Broadcasting, 1974–77; Arts Council of Great Britain: Mem., 1979–; Vice-Chm., Drama Adv. Panel, 1980–82 (Chm., 1980); Chm., Literature Adv. Panel, 1980–84; Vice-Chm., 1982–86; Vice-Chm., Visiting Arts Unit, 1983–86; Chm., Arts Films Cttees 1984–86. Hon. Fellow, Manchester Polytechnic, 1971. F. D. Maurice Meml Lectures, 1974. Radio and TV programmes. *Publications:* Love on the Supertax (novel), 1944; The Patchwork Book (anthology), 1946; To Bed with Grand Music (pseudonymous novel), 1946; (ed) Stories of Adventure, 1947; (ed) Victorian Tales, 1948; Tory Heaven (novel), 1948; Little Boy Lost (novel), 1949; Mrs Ewing, Mrs Molesworth, Mrs Hodgson Burnett (criticism), 1950; The Village (novel), 1952; The Victorian Chaise-Longue (novel), 1953; The Offshore Island (play), 1959; Ecstasy: A study of some secular and religious experiences, 1961; Domestic Life in Edwardian England, 1964; (ed, with E.G. Battiscombe) A Chaplet for Charlotte Yonge, 1965; The Secular Responsibility (Conway Memorial Lecture), 1967; Jane Austen and her World, 1969; George Eliot and her World, 1973; Kipling's English History, 1974 (radio programmes on Kipling, 1973, 1983); Everyday Ecstasy, 1980; Ferry the Jerusalem Cat (children's novel), 1983; From Palm to Pine, 1987; reviews. *Address:* c/o David Higham Associates, 5–8 Lower John Street, W1R 3PE.

LASKO, Prof. Peter Erik, CBE 1981; FSA; FBA 1978; Professor of the History of Art, Courtauld Institute, University of London, 1974–85; Director, Courtauld Institute, 1974–85; *b* 5 March 1924; *s* of Leo Lasko and Wally Lasko (*née* Seifert); *m* 1948, Gwendoline Joan Norman; three *d.* *Educ:* Courtauld Institute, Univ. of London. BA Hons 1949. Asst Keeper, British Museum, 1950–65; Prof. of the Visual Arts, Univ. of East Anglia, 1965–73. Member: Cathedrals Adv. Commn, 1981–; Royal Commn on Historical Monuments (England), 1984–; Trustee: British Mus., 1981–; Royal Armouries, 1984–. *Publication:* Ars Sacra 800–1200 (Pelican History of Art), 1972.

LASKY, Melvin Jonah, MA; Editor, Encounter Magazine, since 1958; *b* New York City, 15 Jan. 1920; *s* of Samuel Lasky and Esther Lasky (*née* Kantrowitz); *m* 1947, Brigitte Newiger (marr. diss. 1974); one *s* one *d.* *Educ:* City Coll. of New York (BSS); Univ. of Michigan (MA); Columbia Univ. Literary Editor, The New Leader (NY), 1942–43; US Combat Historian in France and Germany, 1944–45; Capt., US Army, 1946; Foreign Correspondent, 1946–48; Editor and Publisher, Der Monat (Berlin), 1948–58 and 1978–; Co-Editor, Encounter Magazine (London), 1958–; Editorial Director, Library Press, NY, 1970–; Publisher, Alcove Press, London, 1972–. Regular television broadcaster, Cologne, Zürich and Vienna, 1955–. Univ. of Michigan, Sesquicentennial Award, 1967; Distinguished Alumnus Award, City Univ., NY, 1978. *Publications:* Reisenotizen und Tagebücher, 1958; Africa for Beginners, 1962; Utopia and Revolution, 1976; contributor to: America and Europe, 1951; New Paths in American History, 1965; Sprache und Politik, 1969; Festschrift for Raymond Aron, 1971; (ed) The Hungarian Revolution, 1957. *Address:* c/o Encounter, 43–44 Great Windmill Street, W1V 7PA. *T:* 01–434 3063. *Club:* Garrick.

LASLETT, (Thomas) Peter (Ruffell), FBA 1979; Reader in Politics and the History of Social Structure, Cambridge University, since 1966; Director, Cambridge Group for the History of Population and Social Structure, since 1964; Fellow of Trinity College, Cambridge, since 1953; *b* 18 Dec. 1915; *s* of Rev. G. H. R. Laslett and E. E. Laslett (*née* Alden); *m* 1947, Janet Crockett Clark; two *s. Educ:* Watford Grammar Sch.; St John's Coll., Cambridge. Served War, Royal Navy, 1940–45: Lieut RNVR, Japanese Naval Intelligence. Producer, BBC, 3rd Programme Talks, 1946–49; Fellow: St John's Coll., Cambridge, 1948–51; Inst. for Advanced Study, Princeton, 1959; Founder (with E. A. Wrigley), Cambridge Gp for the History of Population and Social Structure, 1964; Member, Working Party on Foundn of Open Univ., 1965–. Visiting Professor: Collège de France, Paris, 1976; Yale Univ., 1977. DUniv. Open, 1980. *Publications:* Locke's Two Treatises of Government, 1960, 12th impr. 1978; The World We Have Lost, 1965, 15th Eng. Lang. impr. 1979; (with R. Wall) Household and Family in Past Time, 1972, 3rd impr. 1979; Family Life and Illicit Love in Earlier Generations, 1977, 3rd impr. 1979; (with R. M. Smith and others) Bastardy and its Comparative History, 1980. *Recreations:* book collecting, gardening. *Address:* Trinity College, Cambridge; 27 Trumpington Street, Cambridge. *T:* (Cambridge Group) Cambridge 354298.

LASOK, Prof. Dominik, QC 1982; PhD, LLD; Professor of European Law, 1973–86, and Director of Centre for European Legal Studies, 1972–86, University of Exeter; *b* 4 Jan. 1921; *s* of late Alojzy Lasok and Albina (*née* Przybyla); *m* 1952, Sheila May Corrigan; two *s* three *d. Educ:* secondary educn in Poland and Switzerland; Fribourg Univ. (Lic. en Droit); Univ. of Durham (LLM); Univ. of London (PhD, LLD); Universitas Polonorum in Exteris (Dr Juris). Called to the Bar, Middle Temple, 1954. Served Polish Army, Poland, France and Italy, 1939–46 (British, French and Polish mil. decorations). Industry, 1948–51; commerce, 1954–58; academic career, 1958–: Prof. of Law, Univ. of Exeter, 1968. Visiting Professor: William and Mary, Williamsburg, Va, 1966–67 and 1977; McGill, Montreal, 1976–77; Rennes, 1980–81; Fribourg, 1984; Coll. d'Europe, Bruges, 1984–; Aix-Marseille, 1985; Officier dans l'Ordre des Palmes Académiques, 1983. *Publications:* Polish Family Law, 1968; (jtly, also ed) Polish Civil Law, 4 vols, 1973–75; (with J. W. Bridge) Introduction to the Law and Institutions of the European Communities, 1973, 3rd edn 1982; The Law of the Economy in the European Communities, 1980; (jtly, also ed) Les Communautés Européennes en Fonctionnement, 1981; Customs Law of the European Communities, 1983; over 100 articles in British and foreign legal jls. *Address:* Reed, Barley Lane, Exeter EX4 1TA. *T:* Exeter 72582.

LAST, Maj.-Gen. Christopher Neville, OBE 1976; Vice Master General of the Ordnance, since 1986; *b* 2 Sept. 1935; *s* of Jack Neville Last, MPS, FSMC, FBOA and Lorna (*née* Goodman), MPS; *m* 1961, Pauline Mary Lawton; two *d. Educ:* Culford Sch.; Brighton Tech. Coll. psc†, ndc. Commnd Royal Signals, 1956; Germany, Parachute Bde, Borneo, Singapore, 1956–67; OC 216 Para. Signal Sqdn, 1967; RMCS and Staff Coll., Logistics Staff 1 (BR) Corps, 1968–71; NDC, 1972; Lt-Col, Signal Staff HQ, BAOR, 1973; CO Royal Signals NI, 1974; Staff, MoD Combat Develt, Mil. Ops, 1976; Col, Project Manager MoD (PE) for Army ADP Comd and Control, 1977; CO (Col) 8 Signal Regt Trng, Royal Signals, 1980; Brig., Comd 1 Signal Bde 1 (BR) Corps, 1981; Dir, Mil. Comd and Control Projects, MoD (PE), 1984; Head of Defence Procurement Policy (Studies Team), on Chief of Defence Procurement Personal Staff, MoD (PE), 1985. *Recreations:* travel, theatre, ballet, sailing, ski-ing, shooting, country pursuits, hockey (Corps, BAOR Army and Combined Services). *Address:* c/o National Westminster Bank, 34 North Street, Lancing, Sussex BN15 9AB.

LAST, John William; Special Duties Executive, The Littlewoods Organisation, Liverpool; *b* 22 Jan. 1940; *s* of late Jack Last (sometime Dir of Finance, Metrop. Police) and Freda Last (*née* Evans); *m* 1967, Susan Josephine, *er d* of John and late Josephine Farmer; three *s. Educ:* Sutton Grammar Sch., Surrey; Trinity Coll., Oxford (MA 1965). Joined Littlewoods Organisation, Liverpool, 1969. Mem., Merseyside CC, 1973–86 (Chm., Arts Cttee, 1977–81); contested (C) Liverpool, West Derby, Feb. and Oct. 1974, Stockport N, 1979. Bd Mem., Royal Liverpool Philharmonic Soc., 1973– (Chm., 1977–81); Founder Chairman: Merseyside Maritime Museum, 1977; Empire Theatre (Merseyside) Trust, 1979–81 (Bd Mem., 1986–); Chairman: Walker Art Gall., Liverpool, 1977–81; Library Assoc./Arts Council Wkg Party on Art in Libraries, 1982–84; Nat. Chm., Area Museums Councils of GB, 1979–82; Vice Chairman: NW Museum and Art Gall. Service, 1986– (Chm., 1977–82); Merseyside Arts, 1985–; Member: Museums Assoc. Council, 1978– (Vice-Pres., 1983); Arts Council of GB, 1980–84 (Chm., Housing the Arts Cttee, 1981–84; Chm., Regional Cttee, 1981–84); Museums and Galleries Commn., 1983– (Mem., Scottish Wkg Pty, 1984–85); Bd, Northern Ballet Theatre, 1986–; Merseyside Tourism Bd, 1986–; NW Industrial Council, 1985–; Court, Liverpool Univ., 1973– (Mem. Council, 1977–81); Lay Mem., Press Council, 1980–; Advr on Local Govt to Arts Council, 1984–; Chm., Arts, Initiative and Money Cttee, Gulbenkian Foundn, 1980–83. Trustee: Norton Priory Museum, 1983–; V&A Museum, 1984– (Mem., Adv. Council, 1978–84; Mem., Theatre Museum Cttee, 1983–86); Nat. Museums and Galls on Merseyside, 1986–; Gov., NYO, 1985–. Freedom of City of London, 1985; Freeman, Barber Surgeons' Co., 1985. *Recreations:* swimming, music, Victoriana. *Address:* The Knoll, Meols Drive, Hoylake, Wirral, Merseyside L47 4AF. *T:* 051–632 4027. *Club:* Royal Automobile.

LAST, Prof. Raymond Jack, FRCS, FRACS; Professor of Applied Anatomy, and Warden, Royal College of Surgeons, 1949–70; *b* 26 May 1903; English. *Educ:* Adelaide High Sch., Australia. MB, BS (Adelaide), 1924; Medical practice S. Australia, 1927–38; arrived London, 1939; Surgeon, EMS, Northern Hospital, N21, 1939–40. OC Abyssinian Medical Unit, Hon. Surgeon to Emperor Haile Selassie I, also OC Haile Selassie Hospital, Surgeon to British Legation, Addis Ababa, 1941–44; returned to London, Lieut-Colonel, RAMC, 1945; ADMS, British Borneo, 1945–46. Anatomical Curator and Bland Sutton Scholar, RCS, 1946; FRCS 1947; Adviser to Central Government of Pakistan on organization and conduct of primary FRCS instruction, Colombo Plan, 1961. Vis. Prof. of Anatomy: UCLA, 1970–84; Mt Sinai Sch. of Medicine, NY, 1971–72. *Publications:* Anatomy, Regional and Applied, 7th edn 1984; Wolff's Anatomy of Eye and Orbit, 6th edn, 1968; Aids to Anatomy, 12th edn, 1962; contrib. to Journals of Surgery; various articles. *Address:* 22 Koonga Avenue, Prospect, SA 5082, Australia.

LATEY, Rt. Hon. Sir John (Brinsmead), Kt 1965; MBE 1943; PC 1986; **Rt. Hon. Mr Justice Latey;** Judge of the High Court of Justice, Family Division (formerly Probate, Divorce and Admiralty Division), since 1965; *b* 7 March 1914; *s* of late William Latey, CBE, QC, and Anne Emily, *d* of late Horace G. Brinsmead; *m* 1938, Betty Margaret (*née* Beresford); one *s* one *d. Educ:* Westminster; Christ Church, Oxford. MA (Hon. Sch. Jurispr.). Called to the Bar, 1936; QC 1957. Served in Army during War, 1939–45, mainly in MEF (Lieut–Colonel, 1944–). General Council of the Bar, 1952–56, 1957–61 and 1964– (Hon. Treasurer, 1959–61). Master of the Bench of the Middle Temple, 1964.

Chairman, Lord Chancellor's Cttee on Age of Majority, 1965–67. Dep. Chairman, Oxfordshire QS, 1966. *Publications:* (Asst Ed.) Latey on Divorce, 14th edn, 1952; Halsbury's Laws of England (Conflict of Laws: Husband and Wife), 1956. *Recreations:* golf, bridge, chess. *Address:* 16 Daylesford Avenue, Roehampton, SW15 5QR. *T:* 01–876 6436. *Club:* United Oxford & Cambridge University.

LATHAM, family name of **Baron Latham.**

LATHAM, 2nd Baron *cr* 1942; of Hendon; **Dominic Charles Latham;** Civil Engineer with Electricity Commission of New South Wales, since 1979; *b* 20 Sept. 1954; *s* of Hon. Francis Charles Allman Latham (*d* 1959) and of Gabrielle Monica, *d* of Dr S. M. O'Riordan; *S* grandfather, 1970. *Educ:* Univ. of New South Wales, Australia (BEng (civil), 1977, Hons I; MEngSc 1981). *Recreations:* tennis, squash, snooker, electronics, sailboarding. *Heir: yr* twin *b* Anthony Michael Latham, *b* 20 Sept. 1954. *Address:* PO Box 355, Kensington, NSW 2033, Australia.

LATHAM, Arthur Charles; Member, London Transport Executive, 1983–84 (part-time Member, July-Nov. 1983); *b* Leyton, 14 Aug. 1930; *m* 1951, Margaret Latham; one *s* one *d. Educ:* Romford Royal Liberty Sch.; Garnett Coll. of Educn. Lectr in Further Educn, Southgate Technical Coll., 1967–. Havering Council (formerly Romford Borough Council): Mem., 1952–78 and 1986–; Leader, Labour Gp, 1962–70 and 1986–; Leader of the Opposition, 1986–; Alderman, 1962–78. Mem., NE Regional Metropolitan Hosp. Bd, 1966–72. MP (Lab) Paddington N, Oct. 1969–1974, City of Westminster, Paddington, 1974–79; Jt Chm., All Party Gp for Pensioners, 1971–79; Chm., Tribune Gp, 1975–76 (Treasurer, 1977–79). Contested (Lab): Woodford, 1959; Rushcliffe, Notts, 1964; City of Westminster, Paddington, 1979; Westminster N, 1983. Chm., Greater London Lab. Party, 1977–; Vice-Chm., Nat. Cttee, Labour League of Youth, 1949–53; Vice-President: Labour Action for Peace; AMA; Treasurer, Liberation (Movement for Colonial Freedom), 1969–79; Member: British Campaign for Peace in Vietnam; Campaign for Nuclear Disarmament. Vegetarian. *Recreations:* bridge, chess, cricket. *Address:* 17 Tudor Avenue, Gidea Park, Romford RM2 5LB.

LATHAM, Cecil Thomas, OBE 1976; Stipendiary Magistrate, Greater Manchester (sitting at Salford), since 1976; *b* 11 March 1924; *s* of Cecil Frederick James Latham and Elsie Winifred Latham; *m* 1945, Ivy Frances (*née* Fowle); one *s* one *d. Educ:* Rochester Cathedral Choir Sch.; King's Sch., Rochester. Solicitor. War Service, 1942–45. Asst Clerk, Magistrates' Courts: Chatham, 1939–42; Maidstone, 1945; Leicester, 1948–54; Bromley, 1954–63; Dep. Justices' Clerk, Liverpool, 1963–65; Justices' Clerk, Manchester, 1965–76. Member: Royal Commn on Criminal Procedure, 1978–81; Criminal Law Revision Cttee, 1981–. Hon. MA Manchester, 1984. *Publications:* (ed) Stone's Justices' Manual, 101st-109th edns; How Much?: determining maintenance in magistrates' courts, 1976; (ed) Family Law Reports, 1980–; contrib. Criminal Law Rev., Justice of Peace, Family Law. *Recreation:* music. *Address:* 19 Southdown Crescent, Cheadle Hulme, Cheshire SK8 6EQ. *T:* 061–485 1185.

LATHAM, Christopher George Arnot; Deputy Chairman, James Latham PLC, since 1973; Trustee, Timber Trade Benevolent Society (Past President); *b* 4 June 1933; *s* of late Edward Bryan Latham, and of Anne Arnot Duncan; *m* 1963, Jacqueline Cabourdin; three *s. Educ:* Stowe Sch.; Clare Coll., Cambridge (MA). FCA. Articled Fitzpatrick Graham, chartered accountants, 1955; joined James Latham Ltd, timber importers, 1959, Dir 1963. A Forestry Comr, 1973–78. Pres., Inst. of Wood Sci., 1977–79; Chairman: Timber Res. and Develt Assoc., 1972–74; Commonwealth Forestry Assoc., 1975–77; Psychiatric Rehabilitation Assoc., 1983–; Timber Trade Trng Assoc., 1985–. *Recreations:* tennis, beagling, forestry. *Address:* Place Farm, Doddinghurst, Brentwood, Essex. *T:* Coxtie Green 73293.

LATHAM, David Nicholas Ramsay; QC 1985; a Recorder of the Crown Court, since 1983; *b* 18 Sept. 1942; *s* of Robert Clifford Latham, *qv; m* 1967, Margaret Elizabeth (*née* Forrest); three *d. Educ:* Bryanston Sch.; Queens' Coll., Cambridge (MA). Called to the Bar, Middle Temple, 1964; one of the Junior Counsel to the Crown, Common Law, 1979–85; Junior Counsel to Dept of Trade in export credit matters, 1981–85. *Recreation:* reading. *Address:* 1 Crown Office Row, EC4. *T:* 01–353 1801; (home) The Firs, Church Road, Sunningdale, Berks. *T:* Ascot 22686. *Club:* Leander.

LATHAM, Sir Joseph, Kt 1960; CBE 1950; Director, George Wimpey plc, 1960–84; *b* 1 July 1905; *s* of John and Edith Latham, Prestwich, Lancs; *m* 1932, Phyllis Mary Fitton; one *s* one *d. Educ:* Stand Grammar Sch. Chartered Accountant, 1926; Liaison Officer, Lancashire Associated Collieries, 1935; Director and Secretary, Manchester Collieries Ltd, 1941; Director-General of Finance, National Coal Board, 1946–55; Finance Member, NCB, 1955–56; Deputy Chairman, NCB, 1956–60. Vice-Chm., AEI, 1964–65, Dep. Chm., 1965–68, Man. Dir, 1967–68. Mem., ECGD, Advisory Council, 1964–69; Chm., Economic Development Cttees, Food Processing and Chocolate & Sugar Confectionery Industries, 1965–66. *Publication:* Take-over, 1969. *Address:* 25 Badingham Drive, Leatherhead, Surrey KT22 9EU. *T:* Leatherhead 372433. *Club:* Effingham Golf.

LATHAM, Michael Anthony; MP (C) Rutland and Melton, since 1983 (Melton, Feb. 1974–1983); *b* 20 Nov. 1942; *m* 1969, Caroline Terry; two *s. Educ:* Marlborough Coll.; King's Coll., Cambridge; Dept of Educn, Oxford. BA Cantab 1964, MA Cantab 1968, CertEd Oxon 1965. Housing and Local Govt Officer, Conservative Research Dept, 1965–67; Parly Liaison Officer, Nat. Fedn of Building Trades Employers, 1967–73; Dir, House-builders Fedn, 1971–73. Westminster City Councillor, 1968–71. Contested (C) Liverpool, West Derby, 1970. Vice-Chairman: Cons. Parly Housing Cttee, 1974–76; Cons. Parly Environment Cttee, 1979–83; Member: House of Commons Expenditure Cttee, 1974–79; Jt Cttee on Statutory Instruments, 1974–75; Jt Ecclesiastical Cttee of both Houses of Parliament, 1974–; Select Cttee on Energy, 1979–82; Public Accounts Cttee, 1983–. Sec., British-Gibraltar Parly Gp, 1981–; Chairman: British-Israel Parly Gp, 1981–; Exec. Cttee, Anglo-Israel Assoc., 1986–; Vice Pres., Cons. Friends of Israel, 1985– (Chm., 1982–85). Dir, Lovell Homes Ltd, 1975–85; Housing Adviser, Y. J. Lovell PLC, 1985–. Mem., Adv. Council on Public Records, 1985–; Mem. Bd of Management, Shelter, 1976–82. Vice-Pres., Building Socs Assoc., 1981–. CofE Deleg. to BCC, 1977–81. *Publications:* articles on housing, land, town planning and building. *Recreations:* gardening, fencing, listening to classical music, cricket. *Address:* House of Commons, SW1A 0AA. *Club:* Carlton.

LATHAM, Air Vice-Marshal Peter Anthony, CB 1980; AFC 1960; Senior Air Adviser, Short Bros PLC, since 1985; *b* 18 June 1925; *s* of late Oscar Frederick Latham and Rhoda Latham; *m* 1953, Barbara Mary; two *s* six *d. Educ:* St Phillip's Grammar Sch., Birmingham; St Catharine's Coll., Cambridge. psa 1961. Joined RAF, 1944; 1946–69: served No 26, 263, 614, and 247 Sqdns; CFE; Air Min.; Comd No 111 Sqdn; RAF Formation Aerobatic Team (Leader of Black Arrows, 1959–60); MoD Jt Planning Staff; Comd NEAF Strike and PR Wing; Coll. of Air Warfare; Ops No 38 Gp; Comd RAF Tengah, 1969–71; MoD Central Staff, 1971–73; Comd Officer and Aircrew Selection Centre, Biggin Hill, 1973–74; SASO No 38 Gp, 1974–76; Dir Def. Ops, MoD Central Staff, 1976–77; AOC No 11 Group, 1977–81. Principal, Oxford Air Trng Sch., and Dir,

CSE Aviation Ltd, 1982–85. Cdre, RAF Sailing Assoc., 1974–80; Pres., Assoc. of Service Yacht Clubs, 1978–81. *Recreations:* sailing, horology. *Address:* (office) Short Brothers, Berkeley Square House, Berkeley Square, W1X 5LB. *Club:* Royal Air Force.

LATHAM, Sir Richard Thomas Paul, 3rd Bt, *cr* 1919, of Crow Clump; *b* 15 April 1934; *s* of Sir (Herbert) Paul Latham, 2nd Bt, and Lady Patricia Doreen Moore (*d* 1947), *o d* of 10th Earl of Drogheda; *S* father, 1955; *m* 1958, Marie-Louise Patricia, *d* of Frederick H. Russell, Vancouver, BC; two *d. Educ:* Eton; Trinity Coll., Cambridge. *Address:* 881 Picacho Lane, Santa Barbara, Calif 93108, USA.

LATHAM, Robert Clifford, CBE 1973; FBA 1982; FRSL 1983; Hon. Fellow of Magdalene College, Cambridge, since 1984 (Fellow, 1972–84; Pepys Librarian, 1972–82); *b* 11 March 1912; *s* of Edwin Latham, and Alice Latham, Audley, Staffs; *m* 1st, 1939, Eileen Frances Redding Ramsay (*d* 1969); one *s* one *d*; 2nd, 1973, Rosalind Frances Birley. *Educ:* Wolstanton County Grammar Sch., Staffs; Queens' Coll., Cambridge (scholar). Hist. Tripos Pt I 1932, Pt II 1933; MA 1938. Asst Lectr in History, King's Coll., London, 1935; Lectr, 1939; University Reader in History, Royal Holloway Coll., London, 1947; Visiting Associate Prof., Univ. of Southern California, Los Angeles, 1955; Prof. of History, Univ. of Toronto, 1968–69; Research Fellow, Magdalene Coll., Cambridge, 1970–72. Wheatley Medal, LA, 1983; Marc Fitch prize, Univ. of Leeds, 1984. *Publications:* (ed) Bristol Charters, 1509–1899 (Bristol Rec. Soc., vol. xii), 1947; (ed) The Diary of Samuel Pepys, vols i-ix (with Prof. W. Matthews), 1970–76, vols x and xi, 1983; (ed) The Illustrated Pepys, 1978; gen. editor, Catalogue of the Pepys Library at Magdalene College, Cambridge, 1978– (in progress); (ed) The Shorter Pepys, 1985; articles and reviews in learned and other jls. *Recreations:* music, gossip. *Address:* Magdalene College, Cambridge CB3 0AG. *T:* Cambridge 61545.

　See also D. N. R. Latham.

LATHE, Prof. Grant Henry; Professor of Chemical Pathology, University of Leeds, 1957–77, now Emeritus Professor; *b* 27 July 1913; *s* of Frank Eugene and Annie Smith Lathe; *m* 1st, 1938, Margaret Eleanore Brown; one *s*; 2nd, 1950, Joan Frances Hamlin; one *s* two *d. Educ:* McGill Univ.; Oxford Univ. ICI Research Fellow: Dept. of Biochemistry, Oxford Univ., 1946; Dept. of Chemical Pathology, Post Graduate Medical School of London, 1948; Lecturer in Chemical Pathology, Guy's Hospital Medical School, 1948; Biochemist, The Bernhard Baron Memorial Research Laboratories, Queen Charlotte's Maternity Hospital, London, 1949. John Scott Award (with C. R. J. Ruthven), 1971, for invention of gel filtration. *Publications:* papers in medical and biochemical journals. *Recreation:* campaigning against nuclear weapons. *Address:* 12A The Avenue, Leeds LS8 1EH. *T:* 661507.

LATIMER, Sir (Courtenay) Robert, Kt 1966; CBE 1958 (OBE 1948); *b* 13 July 1911; *er s* of late Sir Courtenay Latimer, KCIE, CSI, *m* 1944, Elizabeth Jane Gordon (*née* Smail); one *s* one *d. Educ:* Rugby; Christ Church, Oxford. ICS, 1934 (Punjab); IPS, 1939; Vice-Consul, Bushire, 1940–41; Sec. Foreign Publicity Office, Delhi, 1941–42; Sec. Indian Agency Gen., Chungking, 1944; in NW Frontier Prov., as Asst Political Agent N Waziristan, Dir of Civil Supplies, Sec. to Governor and District Comr, Bannu, 1942–43 and 1945–47. HM Overseas Service, 1948; served in Swaziland, 1948–49; Bechuanaland Protectorate, 1951–54; Office of High Comr for Basutoland, the Bechuanaland Protectorate and Swaziland, as Asst Sec., 1949–51; Sec. for Finance, 1954–60; Chief Sec., 1960–64; Minister, British Embassy, Pretoria, 1965–66; Registrar, Kingston Polytechnic, 1967–76. *Recreations:* golf, photography. *Address:* Benedicts, Old Avenue, Weybridge, Surrey.

LATIMER, Sir Graham (Stanley), KBE 1980; President, New Zealand Maori Council, since 1972 (Delegate, 1964; Vice-President, 1969–72); *b* Waiharara, N Auckland, 7 Feb. 1926; *s* of Graham Latimer and Lillian Edith Latimer (*née* Kenworth *m* 1948, Emily Patricia Moore; two *s* two *d. Educ:* Pukenui and Kaitaia District High School. Dairy farmer, 1961–. Member: Tai Tokerau Dist Maori Council, 1962– (Sec. 1966–75); Otamatea Maori Exec., 1959– (Sec. Treas. 1962–72, Chm. 1975–); Otamatea Maori Cttee, 1955–62; Arapaoa Maori Cttee, 1962– (Chm. 1962–69 and 1972–); N Auckland Power Bd, 1977–; Waitangi Tribunal, 1976–. Chm., since inception, Northland Community Coll.; Trustee, Maori Education Foundn; Member: Cttee, Nat. Art Gall. Museum and War Memorial; NZ Maori Arts and Crafts Inst., 1980–; Tourist Adv. Council; Northland Regional Develt Council, 1980–; Alcoholic Liquor Adv. Council, 1980–. Lay Canon, Auckland Anglican Cathedral, 1978; Mem. Gen. Synod. *Recreations:* Rugby football, tennis. *Address:* RD1, Taipuha, Northland, New Zealand. *T:* Taipuha 837.

LATIMER, Sir Robert; *see* Latimer, Sir C. R.

LATNER, Prof. Albert Louis; Professor of Clinical Biochemistry, University of Newcastle upon Tyne, 1963–78, now Emeritus Professor, and Director of Cancer Research Unit, 1967–78; Consultant Clinical Biochemist, Royal Victoria Infirmary, Newcastle upon Tyne, 1948–78, Hon. Consultant, since 1978; *b* 5 Dec. 1912; *s* of Harry Latner and Miriam Gordon; *m* 1936, Gertrude Franklin (*d* 1986). *Educ:* Imperial College of Science and University College, London; University of Liverpool. ARCSc, 1931; MSc (London) 1933; DIC, 1934; MB, ChB (Liverpool) 1939; MD (Liverpool) 1948; FRIC 1953; MRCP 1956; DSc (Liverpool) 1958; FRCPath 1964; FRCP 1964. Lectr in Physiology, Univ. of Liverpool, 1933–36 and 1939–41; Pathologist in RAMC, 1941–46; Sen. Registrar, Postgrad. Medical Sch., 1946–47; Lectr in Chem. Pathol., King's Coll., Univ. of Durham, 1947–55; Reader in Medical Biochemistry, Univ. of Durham, 1955–61; Prof. of Clin. Chem., Univ. of Durham, 1961–63. Vis. Lectr, Amer. Assoc. Clinical Chemists, 1972. Hon. Member: Assoc. of Clinical Biochemists, 1984 (Chm., 1958–61; Pres., 1961–63); British Electrophoresis Soc., 1986. Mem., Editorial Bd of Clinica Chimica Acta, 1960–68; Co-editor, Advances in Clinical Chemistry, 1971–84. Titular Member, Section of Clinical Chemistry, International Union of Pure and Applied Chemistry, 1967–73; Hon. Fellow, American Nat. Acad. of Clinical Biochemistry, 1977–. Mem. Editorial Bd, Electrophoresis, 1980–. Wellcome Prize, 1976. *Publications:* Isoenzymes in Biology and Medicine, 1968 (co-author); Cantarow and Trumper Clinical Biochemistry, 7th edn, 1975; Chapter on Metabolic Aspects of Liver Disease in Metabolic Disturbances in Clinical Medicine (ed G. A. Smart), 1958; Chapters on Chemical Pathology and Clinical Biochemistry in British Encyclopædia of Med. Practice, Med. Progress (ed Lord Cohen of Birkenhead), 1961, 1962, 1964, 1966 and 1968; Chapter on Isoenzymes in Recent Advances in Clinical Pathology, Series IV, 1964; Section on Isoenzymes in Advances in Clinical Chemistry (ed C. P. Stewart), 1966; (ed with O. Bodansky and contrib. section on Isoelectric Focusing) Advances in Clinical Chemistry, 1975; contribs to Medical and Scientific Journals dealing with cancer, liver disease, pernicious anæmia, the serum proteins in disease and isoenzymes. *Recreations:* art, photography, gardening. *Address:* Ravenstones, Rectory Road, Gosforth, Newcastle upon Tyne NE3 1XP. *T:* Gosforth 2858020. *Club:* Athenæum.

LATOUR-ADRIEN, Hon. Sir (Jean François) Maurice, Kt 1971; Chief Justice of Mauritius, 1970–77; Chairman, Mauritius Union Assurance Co. Ltd, since 1982 (Director since 1978); Legal Consultant, Mauritius Commercial Bank Ltd, since 1983; *b* 4 March 1915; 2nd *s* of late Louis Constant Emile Adrien and late Maria Ella Latour. *Educ:* Royal Coll., Mauritius; Univ. Coll., London; Middle Temple, London. LLB 1940. Called to the Bar, Middle Temple, 1940. Mauritius: Dist Magistrate, 1947; Crown Counsel, 1950; Additl Subst. Procureur and Advocate-Gen., 1954; Sen. Crown Counsel, 1958; Asst Attorney-Gen., 1960; Solicitor-Gen., 1961; Dir of Public Prosecutions, 1964; Puisne Judge, 1966–70. Pres., Mauritius Red Cross Soc., 1978–; Vice-Pres., Inst. Internat. de Droit d'Expression Française (IDEF). Dir, Mauritius Commercial Bank Ltd, 1980–83, 1984–. Vice-Pres., Mental Health Assoc., 1978–. KLJ 1969. *Address:* Vacoas, Mauritius.

LA TROBE-BATEMAN, Richard George Saumarez, furniture designer/maker; *b* 17 Oct. 1938; *s* of John La Trobe-Bateman and Margaret Schmid; *m* 1969, Mary Elizabeth Jolly; one *s* two *d. Educ:* Westminster Sch.; St Martin's Sch. of Art; Royal Coll. of Art (MDesRCA). Set up workshop, 1968. Mem., Council of Management, British Crafts Centre, 1975–; Crafts Council: Mem., 1984–; Index Selector, 1972–73; Chm., Index Selection Cttee, 1980–82; Work in: V&A Collection, 1979; Crafts Council Collection, 1981 and 1984; Keble Coll., Oxon, 1981; Temple Newsam Collection, 1983; Southern Arts Collection, 1983; Pembroke Coll., Oxon, 1984; Crafts Study Centre Collection, Bath, 1985; work presented by Crafts Council to the Prince of Wales, 1982. *Publication:* article in Crafts. *Recreations:* listening to music, hill-walking. *Address:* Hillclose, Batcombe, Shepton Mallet, Somerset BA4 6AB. *T:* Upton Noble 442. *Club:* British Crafts Centre.

LATTER, Leslie William; Director General, Merseyside Passenger Transport Executive, 1977–86; *b* 4 Nov. 1921; *s* of William Richard and Clara Maud Latter; *m* 1948, Pamela Jean Marsh; one *s. Educ:* Beckenham Grammar Sch., Kent. IPFA, FRVA, FCIT. Served Royal Air Force, 1940–46. London County Council, 1947–62; Chief Asst, Beckenham Borough Council, 1962–64; Asst Borough Treasurer, Bromley, 1964–68; Dep. Borough Treasurer, Greenwich, 1968–74; Dir of Finance and Administration, Merseyside PTE, 1974–77. *Recreations:* gardening, music. *Address:* Clarkston, 66A Freshfield Road, Formby, Liverpool L37 7BQ. *T:* Formby 72036. *Clubs:* Royal Commonwealth Society; Skal (Liverpool).

LATTIMORE, Owen; Professor of Chinese Studies, Leeds University, 1963–70, now Professor Emeritus; Director, Page School of International Relations, 1938–50 and Lecturer in History to 1963, Johns Hopkins University, USA; *b* Washington, DC, 29 July 1900; *s* of David Lattimore and Margaret Barnes; *m* 1926, Eleanor, (*d* 1970), *d* of Dr T. F. Holgate, Evanston, Ill.; one *s. Educ:* St Bees Sch., Cumberland; Collège Classique Cantonal, Lausanne; Research Student at Harvard Univ., 1929. Early childhood in China; returned to China, 1919; engaged in business in Tientsin and Shanghai, 1920; Journalism in Tientsin, 1921; business in Tientsin and Peking with Arnhold and Co., 1922–25; travelled in Mongolia, 1926; in Chinese Turkestan, 1927; studied in America, 1928, 1929; travelled in Manchuria, as Fellow of Social Science Research Council, 1929–30; Research work in Peking, as Fellow of Harvard-Yenching Institute, 1930–31; Research Fellow, Guggenheim Foundation, Peking, 1931–33; travelled in Mongolia, 1932–33; editor, Pacific Affairs, 1934–41; research work in China and Mongolia, 1934–35, 1937; Political Adviser to Generalissimo Chiang Kai-Shek, 1941–42; Director, Pacific Operations, Office of War Information, San Francisco, 1943; accompanied Vice-President Wallace in Siberia and China, 1944; economic consultant, American Reparations Mission in Japan, 1945; UN Technical Aid Mission, Afghanistan, 1950; Visiting Lecturer: Ecole Pratique des Hautes Etudes, Sorbonne, 1958–59; University of Copenhagen, 1961. Travelled in Soviet Central Asia, 1960, Mongolia, 1961, 1964, 1966, 1969, 1970, 1971, 1972, 1973, 1974, 1975, 1976, 1978, 1979, China, 1972. Chichele Lecturer, Oxford, 1965; Vis. Prof., Rutgers Univ., 1979. Awarded Cuthbert Peek Grant by Royal Geographical Society for travels in Central Asia, 1930; gold medallist, Geographical Society of Philadelphia, 1933; Patron's Medal, Royal Geographical Society, 1942; Univ. of Indiana Medal, Perm. Internat. Altaistic Congress, 1974. FRGS; Fellow, Royal Asiatic Society; Member: Royal Soc. for Asian Affairs; American Historical Society; American Philosophical Society; For. Member, Academy of Sciences, Mongolian People's Republic; Hon. Member: American Geographical Society, Soc. Csoma Körösi, Hungary. Hon. DLitt Glasgow, 1964; Hon. PhD: Copenhagen, 1972; Leeds, 1984; Hon. Dr Law Brown Univ., 1974. Order of Golden Nail (Polar Star) (Mongolian People's Republic), 1979. *Publications:* The Desert Road to Turkestan, 1928; High Tartary, 1930; Manchuria: Cradle of Conflict, 1932; The Mongols of Manchuria, 1934; Inner Asian Frontiers of China, 1940; Mongol Journeys, 1941; Solution in Asia, 1945; China, A Short History (with Eleanor Lattimore), 1947; The Situation in Asia, 1949; Sinkiang, Pivot of Asia, 1950; Ordeal by Slander, 1950; Nationalism and Revolution in Mongolia, 1955; Nomads and Commissars, 1962; Studies in Asian Frontier History, 1962; Silks, Spices and Empire (with Eleanor Lattimore), 1968; contributor to periodicals. *Recreation:* cycling. *Address:* 3 Larchfield, Gough Way, Barton Road, Cambridge CB3 9LR; c/o Department of Chinese Studies, The University, Leeds LS2 9JT.

LATTO, Dr Douglas; private medical practice; Chairman, British Safety Council, since 1971 (Vice-Chairman, 1968–71); *b* Dundee, Scotland, 13 Dec. 1913; *s* of late David Latto, Town Clerk of Dundee, and late Christina Latto; *m* 1945, Dr Edith Monica Druitt; one *s* three *d. Educ:* Dundee High Sch.; St Andrews Univ. MB, ChB (St And.) 1939; DObst, RCOG 1944, MRCOG 1949. During War: Ho. Surg., Dundee Royal Infirmary, 1939; Ho. Phys., Cornelia and East Dorset Hosp., Poole, 1940; Resident Obstetrician and Gynaecologist, Derbyshire Hosp. for Women, Derby, 1940; Res. Surgical Officer, Hereford Gen. Hosp., 1941; Res. Obst. and Gynaec., East End Maternity Hosp., London, 1942; Res. Obst. and Gynaec., City of London Maternity Hosp., 1943; Res. Surgical Officer, Birmingham Accident Hosp., 1944; Casualty Officer, Paddington Gen. Hosp., London, 1944; Asst Obst. and Gynaec., Mayday Hosp., Croydon, 1945. Res. Obst. and Gynaec., Southlands Hosp., Shoreham-by-Sea, Sussex, 1946–49; Asst, Nuffield Dept of Obstetrics and Gynaecology, Radcliffe Infirmary, Oxford, 1949–51. Member: BMA; Council, Soil Assoc.; Chm., Plantmilk Soc.; Vice-President: International Vegetarian Union; GB Philatelic Soc., 1986–. Governor, Internat. Inst. of Safety Management. Mem., Order of the Cross. FRSocMed; FRPSL 1975. Silver Jubilee Medal, 1977; Sword of Honour, British Safety Council, 1985. *Publications:* Smoking and Lung Cancer: a report to all Members of Parliament for the British Safety Council, May 1969; contribs to BMJ; Proc. Royal Soc. Med.; Philatelic Jl; etc. *Recreations:* squash, travelling, gardening, philately (Internat. Stamp Exhibns: Large Gold Medal, London, 1970; Gold Medal, Brussels, 1972, Munich, 1973, Basle, 1974; Large Gold Medals: Paris 1975; Copenhagen, 1976 and Prix d'Honneur); London, 1980 (and GB Philatelic Soc. Award); Vienna, 1981. *Address:* Lethnot Lodge, 4 Derby Road, Caversham, Reading, Berks RG4 0EY. *T:* Reading 472282; 59 Harley Street, W1N 1DD. *T:* 01–580 1070. *Clubs:* Royal Automobile, Rolls-Royce Enthusiasts' (Paulersbury).

LATYMER, 7th Baron, *cr* 1431; **Thomas Burdett Money-Coutts;** Member, 1948–80, Chairman, 1948–75, London Committee of Ottoman Bank; *b* 6 Aug. 1901; *e s* of 6th Baron and Hester Frances, 4th *d* of late Maj.-Gen. John Cecil Russell, CVO; *S* father 1949; *m* 1925, Patience (*d* 1982), *d* of late W. Courtenay-Thompson and Mrs Herbert Money; one *s* two *d. Educ:* Radley; Trinity Coll., Oxford. Served War of 1939–45. OStJ. *Heir: s* Hon. Hugo Neville Money-Coutts [*b* 1 March 1926; *m* 1st, 1951, Penelope Ann Clare (marr. diss., 1965), *yr d* of late T. A. Emmet and of Baroness Emmet of Amberley; two *s* one *d*; 2nd, 1965, Jinty, *d* of P. G. Calvert, London; one *s* two *d*]. *Address:* San Rebassa, Moscari, Mallorca. *Club:* MCC.

LAUCKE, Hon. Sir Condor (Louis), KCMG 1979; Lieutenant-Governor, State of South Australia, since 1982; *b* 9 Nov. 1914; *s* of Friedrich Laucke and Marie (*née* Jungfer); *m* 19 Rose Hambour; one *s* one *d*. *Educ:* Immanuel Coll., Adelaide; South Australian School of Mines. Elected to S Australian House of Assembly, 1956, 1959, 1962; Government Whip, 1962–65; Member, Australian Senate for S Australia, 1967–81; Pres. Senate, Parlt of Commonwealth of Australia, 1976–81. Member, Liberal Party Executive, 1972–74. Joint President: CPA, 1976– (also Chm., Exec. Cttee, 1976–); IPU. *Address:* Bunawunda, Greenock, SA 5360, Australia. *T:* 085 628143.

LAUDER, Sir Piers Robert Dick-, 13th Bt *cr* 1688; *b* 3 Oct. 1947; *s* of Sir George Andrew Dick-Lauder, 12th Bt and of Hester Marguerite, *d* of late Lt-Col G. C. M. Sorell-Cameron, CBE, Gorthleck House, Inverness-shire; *S* father, 1981. *Heir: b* Mark Andrew Dick-Lauder [*b* 3 May 1951; *m* 1970, Jeanne Mullineaux (marr. diss. 1981); one *s*]. *Address:* 91 Womerah Avenue, Darlinghurst, Sydney, NSW, Australia.

LAUDERDALE, 17th Earl of, *cr* 1624; **Patrick Francis Maitland;** Baron Maitland, 1590; Viscount Lauderdale, 1616; Viscount Maitland, Baron Thirlestane and Boltoun, 1624; Bt of Nova Scotia, 1680; Hereditary Bearer of the National Flag of Scotland, 1790 and 1952; *b* 17 March 1911; *s* of Reverend Hon. Sydney G. W. Maitland and Ella Frances (*née* Richards); *S* brother, 1968; *m* 1936, Stanka, *d* of Professor Milivoje Lozanitch, Belgrade Univ.; two *s* two *d*. *Educ:* Lancing Coll., Sussex; Brasenose Coll., Oxford. BA Hons Oxon, 1933; Journalist 1933–59. Appts include: Balkans and Danubian Corresp., The Times, 1939–41; Special Corresp. Washington, News Chronicle, 1941; War Corresp., Pacific, Australia, New Zealand, News Chronicle, 1941–43. Foreign Office, 1943–45. MP (U) for Lanark Div. of Lanarks, 1951–Sept. 1959 (except for period May-Dec. 1957 when Ind. C). Founder and Chairman, Expanding Commonwealth Group, House of Commons, 1955–59; re-elected Chairman, Nov. 1959. Chm., Sub-Cttee on Energy, Transport and Res., House of Lords Select Cttee on EEC Affairs, 1974–79. Director: Elf-Aquitaine (UK) Holdings; Harwich International Terminal (Holdings). Editor of The Fleet Street Letter Service, and of The Whitehall Letter, 1945–58. Mem., Coll. of Guardians of National Shrine of Our Lady of Walsingham, Norfolk, 1955–82 (Guardian Emeritus, 1982–). President, The Church Union, 1956–61. FRGS. *Publications:* European Dateline, 1945; Task for Giants, 1957. *Heir: s* The Master of Lauderdale, Viscount Maitland, *qv*. *Address:* 10 Ovington Square, SW3 1LH. *T:* 01–589 7451; 12 St Vincent Street, Edinburgh. *T:* 031–556 5692. *Clubs:* New (Edinburgh); Royal Scottish Automobile (Glasgow).
See also R. W. P. H. Hay.

LAUDERDALE, Master of; *see* Maitland, Viscount.

LAUGHARNE, Albert, CBE 1983; QPM 1978; Deputy Commissioner, Metropolitan Police, 1983–85; *b* 20 Oct. 1931; *s* of Reginald Stanley Laugharne and Jessica Simpson Laugharne; *m* 1954, Barbara Thirlwall; two *d*. *Educ:* Baines' Grammar Sch., Poulton-le-Fylde; Manchester Univ. Detective Inspector, Manchester City Police, 1952–66; Supt, Cumbria Constab., 1966–70; Chief Supt, W Yorks Constab., 1970–73; Asst Chief Constable, Cheshire Constab., 1973–76; Chief Constable: Warwicks, 1977–78; Lancashire, 1978–83. RCDS, 1975. *Publication:* Seaford House Papers, 1975. *Recreations:* gardening, painting.

LAUGHLAND, (Graham Franklyn) Bruce, QC 1977; a Recorder of the Crown Court, since 1972; *b* 18 Aug. 1931; 3rd *s* of late Andrew and late Constance Laughland; *m* 1969, Victoria Nicola Christina Jarman; one *s*. *Educ:* King Edward's Sch., Birmingham; Christ Church, Oxford. Stick of Honour, Mons Officer Cadet Sch., 1954; Lieut 8th RTR, 1954–56. Called to Bar, Inner Temple, 1958, Bencher, 1985; Dep. Chm., Bucks QS, 1971; Standing Counsel to the Queen's Proctor, 1968; First Prosecuting Counsel to the Inland Revenue (Midland and Oxford Circuit), 1973–77; actg Judge of the Supreme Court of the Falkland Is, 1985. Mem., Gen. Council of the Bar, 1970; Treas., Midland and Oxford Circuit, 1986. Chm., Westminster Assoc. for Youth, 1984–. *Address:* 4 King's Bench Walk, Temple, EC4 7DL. *T:* 01–353 3581; 30 Monmouth Road, W2 4UT. *T:* 01–229 5045.

LAUGHTON, Dr Anthony Seymour, FRS 1980; Director, Institute of Oceanographic Sciences, since 1978; *b* 29 April 1927; *s* of Sydney Thomas Laughton and Dorothy Laughton (*née* Chamberlain); m 1st, 1957, Juliet Ann Chapman (marr. diss. 1962); one *s*; 2nd, 1973, Barbara Clare Bosanquet; two *d*. *Educ:* Marlborough Coll.; King's Coll., Cambridge (MA, PhD). RNVR, 1945–48. John Murray Student, Columbia Univ., NY, 1954–55; Nat. Inst. of Oceanography, later Inst. of Oceanographic Sciences, 1955–: research in marine geophysics in Atlantic and Indian Oceans, esp. in underwater photography, submarine morphology, ocean basin evolution, midocean ridge tectonics; Principal Scientist of deep sea expedns. Mem., nat. and internat. cttees on oceanography and geophysics. Member: Governing Body, Charterhouse Sch., 1981–; Council, University Coll. London, 1983–. Silver Medal, RSA, 1958; Cuthbert Peek grant, RGS, 1967; Prince Albert 1er Monaco Gold Medal for Oceanography, 1980. *Publications:* papers on marine geophysics. *Recreations:* music, gardening, sailing. *Address:* Okelands, Pickhurst Road, Chiddingfold, Surrey. *T:* Wormley 3941. *Club:* Naval.

LAUGHTON, Prof. Eric; Firth Professor of Latin in the University of Sheffield, 1952–76, now Emeritus; *b* 4 Sept. 1911; 2nd *s* of Rev. G. W. Laughton; *m* 1938, Elizabeth Gibbons; one *s* one *d*. *Educ:* King Edward VII Sch., Sheffield; St John's Coll., Oxford (open classical scholar). Asst in Humanity Dept, University of Edinburgh, 1934–36; University of Sheffield: Asst Lecturer in Classics, 1936; Lecturer in Classics, 1939; Senior Lecturer, 1946; Public Orator, 1955–68; Pro-Vice-Chancellor, 1968–72. Service in Intelligence Corps, South East Asia, 1943–45. *Publications:* verse translation of Papyrus (17th-century Latin poem by J. Imberdis), 1952; The Participle in Cicero, 1964. Articles and reviews in various classical journals. *Recreations:* walking, music. *Address:* Forelane, Deerhurst, Glos. *T:* Tewkesbury 295437.

LAURENCE, Ven. Christopher; *see* Laurence, Ven. J. H. C.

LAURENCE, Dan Hyman; Literary and Dramatic Advisor, Estate of George Bernard Shaw, since 1973; Literary Advisor, The Shaw Festival, Ontario, since 1982; *b* 28 March 1920. *Educ:* New York City public schs; Hofstra Univ. (BA 1946); New York Univ. (MA 1950). First went on the stage as child actor, 1932; radar specialist with Fifth Air Force, USA, in S Pacific, 1942–45; wrote and performed for Armed Forces Radio Service in New Guinea and the Philippines during World War II, and subseq. for radio and television in USA and Australia; began teaching in 1950 as graduate asst, New York Univ.; Instr of English, Hofstra Univ., 1953–58; Editor, Readex Microprint Corp., 1959–60; Associate Prof. of English, New York Univ., 1962–67, Prof., 1967–70. Vis. Professor: Indiana Univ., 1969; Univ. of Texas at Austin, 1974–75; Tulane Univ., 1981 (Mellon Prof. in the Humanities); Univ. of Guelph, 1983 (Dist. Vis. Prof. of Drama); Univ. of BC, Vancouver, 1984; Vis. Fellow, Inst. for Arts and Humanistic Studies, Pennsylvania State Univ., 1976. John Simon Guggenheim Meml Fellow, 1960, 1961 and 1972; Montgomery Fellow, Dartmouth Coll., 1982. Associate Mem., RADA, 1979. Phi Beta Kappa (hon.), 1967. *Publications:* Henry James: a bibliography (with Leon Edel), 1957 (3rd edn 1981); Robert Nathan: a bibliography, 1960; (ed) Collected Letters of Bernard Shaw, vol. 1, 1874–1897, 1965, vol. 2, 1898–1910, 1972, vol. 3, 1911–1925, 1985; (ed) Bernard Shaw, Collected Plays with their Prefaces, 1970–74; Shaw, Books, and Libraries, 1976; Shaw: an exhibit, 1977; (dramatization) The Black Girl in Search of God, 1977; (ed) Shaw's Music, 1981; Bernard Shaw: a bibliography, 1983; A Portrait of the Author as a Bibliography (Engelhard Lecture on the Book, L of C, 1982), 1983; (Uncollected Writings of Shaw): How to Become a Musical Critic, 1960 (2nd edn 1978); Platform and Pulpit, 1961; (ed with David H. Greene) The Matter with Ireland, 1962; (ed with Daniel J. Leary) Flyleaves, 1977; (Gen. Editor) Bernard Shaw: Early Texts, Play Manuscripts in Facsimile, 12 vols, 1981; (with James Rambeau) Agitations: letters to the Press 1875–1950, 1985; (with Martin Quinn) Shaw on Dickens, 1985. *Recreations:* theatre-going, music, book-collecting, mountain climbing. *Address:* c/o The Society of Authors, 84 Drayton Gardens, SW10 9SD.

LAURENCE, Ven. (John Harvard) Christopher; Archdeacon of Lindsey, Diocese of Lincoln, since 1985; *b* 15 April 1929; *s* of Canon H. P. Laurence and Mrs E. Laurence; *m* 1952, E. Margaret E. Chappell; one *s* one *d*. *Educ:* Christ's Hospital; Trinity Hall, Cambridge (MA); Westcott House, Cambridge. Nat. service commn, Royal Lincolnshire Regt, 1948–50. Asst Curate, St Nicholas, Lincoln, 1955–59; Vicar, Crosby St George, Scunthorpe, 1959–73; St Hugh's Missioner, Lincoln Diocese, 1974–79; Bishops' Director of Clergy Training, London Diocese, 1979–85. *Recreations:* piano, clarinet, sculpture. *Address:* The Archdeaconry, 2 Greenstone Place, Lincoln LN2 1PP. *T:* Lincoln 31444. *Club:* Christ's Hospital.

LAURENCE, Sir Peter (Harold), KCMG 1981 (CMG 1976); MC 1944; HM Diplomatic Service, retired; Chairman of Council, British Institute of Archaelogy, Ankara, since 1984; *b* 18 Feb. 1923; *s* of late Ven. George Laurence, MA, BD and late Alice (*née* Jackson); *m* 1948, Elizabeth Aïda Way; two *s* one *d*. *Educ:* Radley Coll.; Christ Church, Oxford. 60th Rifles, 1941–46 (Major). Entered Foreign Service, 1948; Western Dept, FO, 1948–50; Athens, 1950–53; Asst Political Adviser, Trieste, 1953–55; 1st Sec., Levant Dept, FO, 1955–57; Prague, 1957–60; Cairo, 1960–62; North and East African Dept, FO, 1962–65; Personnel Dept, DSAO, 1965–67; Counsellor, 1965; Political Adviser, Berlin, 1967–69; Visiting Fellow, All Souls Coll., 1969–70; Counsellor (Commercial), Paris, 1970–74; Chief Inspector, HM Diplomatic Service (Asst Under-Sec. of State), 1974–78; Ambassador to Ankara, 1980–83. Chairman: Foreign Anglican Church and Educnl Assoc. Ltd, 1976–; Community Council of Devon, 1986–; Fellow, Woodard Corp. (W Div.), 1985. *Address:* Trevilla, Beaford, Winkleigh, N Devon EX19 8NS. *Club:* Army and Navy.

LAURENS, André; Editor-in-Chief of Le Monde, 1982–84; *b* 7 Dec. 1934; unmarried. Journalist: L'Eclaireur méridional, Montpellier, 1953–55; l'Agence centrale de la presse, Paris, 1958–62; joined Le Monde, 1963; Home Affairs reporter, 1969; Associate Editor, Home Affairs, 1979. Vice-Pres., Société des Rédacteurs. *Publications:* Les nouveaux communistes, 1972; D'une France à l'autre, 1974; Le métier politique, 1980. *Address:* 34 rue de Clichy, 75009 Paris, France.

LAURIE, Sir (Robert) Bayley (Emilius), 7th Bt *cr* 1834; Chairman, Bowring Members Agency Ltd, 1983; *b* 8 March 1931; *s* of Maj.-Gen. Sir John Emilius Laurie, 6th Bt, CBE, DSO, and of Evelyn Clare, *d* of late Lt-Col Lionel James Richardson-Gardner; *S* father, 1983; *m* 1968, Laurelie, *d* of Sir Reginald Lawrence William Williams, 7th Bt, MBE, ED; two *d*. *Educ:* Eton. National Service, 1st Bn Seaforth Highlanders, 1949–51; Captain, 11th Bn Seaforth Highlanders (TA), 1951–67. Member of Lloyd's, 1955. *Heir: cousin* Andrew Ronald Emilius Laurie [*b* 20 Oct. 1944; *m* 1970, Sarah Anne, *e d* of C. D. Patterson; two *s*]. *Address:* The Old Rectory, Little Tey, Colchester, Essex. *T:* Colchester 210410.

LAURIE, Robert Peter; JP; farmer, since 1958; Vice-Lord Lieutenant, Essex, since 1985; *b* 20 Aug. 1925; *s* of Col Vernon Stewart Laurie, CBE, TD, DL, and Mary, *d* of Selwyn Robert Pryor; *m* 1952, Oonagh Margaret Faber Wild, *d* of W. P. Wild, Warcop Hall, Westmorland; three *s* one *d*. *Educ:* Eton College. Served Coldstream Guards, 1943–47, Hon. Captain. Member of Stock Exchange, 1953; Partner, Heseltine, Powell & Co., then Heseltine, Moss & Co., 1953–80, Consultant, 1980–86; Director, British Empire Securites & General Trust Ltd, 1954– (Chm., 1973–84). Governor: Brentwood Sch., 1974–; Alleyn's Sch., 1984–; Chm., 1977–86, Pres., 1986–, Essex Assoc. of Boys' Clubs; Pres., Essex Agricl Soc., 1987; Master, Saddlers' Co., 1981–82. JP 1974, High Sheriff 1978–79, DL 1979, Essex. *Recreations:* foxhunting and field sports, gardening, reading. *Address:* Heatley's, Ingrave, Brentwood, Essex CM13 3QW. *T:* Brentwood 810224. *Club:* Cavalry and Guards.

LAURISTON, Alexander Clifford, QC 1972; **His Honour Judge Lauriston;** a Circuit Judge, since 1976; *b* 2 Oct. 1927; *s* of Alexander Lauriston and Nellie Lauriston (*née* Ainsworth); *m* 1954, Inga Louise Cameron; two *d*. *Educ:* Coatham Sch., Redcar, Yorks; Trinity Coll., Cambridge (MA). National Service: Army, Green Howards and RAPC, 2nd Lieut, 1948–50. Called to Bar, Inner Temple, 1952. A Recorder of the Crown Court, 1972–76. Mem., Loriners' Co., 1969. *Recreations:* outdoor activities, painting, music. *Address:* 2 Harcourt Buildings, Temple, EC4. *Clubs:* United Oxford & Cambridge University; Berkshire Golf.
See also R. B. Lauriston.

LAURISTON, Richard Basil; a Permanent Chairman of Industrial Tribunals, since 1976; formerly Senior Partner, Alex Lauriston & Son, Solicitors, Middlesbrough; *b* 26 Jan. 1917; *s* of Alexander Lauriston, MBE, and Nellie Lauriston; *m* 1944, Monica, *d* of Wilfred Leslie Deacon, BA, Tonbridge, and Dorothy Louise Deacon; three *s*. *Educ:* Sir William Turner's Sch., Redcar; St John's Coll., Cambridge (MA, LLM). Solicitor, 1948; a Recorder of the Crown Court, 1974–82. Commnd and served in War of 1939–45, Royal Corps of Signals. *Recreations:* fishing, travelling. *Address:* 26 Easby Lane, Great Ayton, North Yorks TS9 6JZ. *T:* Great Ayton 722429.
See also A. C. Lauriston.

LAUTERPACHT, Elihu, QC 1970; Fellow of Trinity College, Cambridge, since 1953; Reader in International Law, since 1981, and Director, Research Centre for International Law, since 1983, University of Cambridge; *b* 13 July 1928; *o s* of late Sir Hersch Lauterpacht, QC and Rachel Steinberg; *m* 1955, Judith Maria (*d* 1970), *er d* of Harold Hettinger; one *s* two *d*; *m* 1973, Catherine Daly; one *s*. *Educ:* Phillips Acad., Andover, Mass; Harrow; Trinity Coll., Cambridge (Entrance Schol.). 1st cl. Pt II of Law Tripos and LLB; Whewell Schol. in Internat. Law, 1950; Holt Schol. 1948 and Birkenhead Schol. 1950, Gray's Inn; called to Bar, 1950, Bencher, 1983. Joint Sec., Interdepartmental Cttee on State Immunity, 1950–52; Asst Lectr in Law, Univ. of Cambridge, 1953, Lecturer, 1958–81; Sec., Internat. Law Fund, 1955–85; Dir of Research, Hague Academy of Internat. Law, 1959–60; Vis. Prof. of Internat. Law, Univ. of Delhi, 1960. Chm., East African Common Market Tribunal, 1972–75; Consultant to Central Policy Review Staff, 1972–74, 1978–81; Legal Adviser to Australian Dept of Foreign Affairs, 1975–77;

Consultant on Internat. Law, UN Inst. for Training and Res., 1978–79; mem. arbitration panel, Internat. Centre for Settlement of Investment Disputes; Deputy Leader: Australian Delegn to UN Law of the Sea Conf., 1975–77; Australian Delegn to UN Gen. Assembly, 1975–77. Member: Social Sciences Adv. Cttee, UK Nat. Commn for Unesco, 1980–84; World Bank Administrative Tribunal, 1980–; Panel of Arbitrators, Internat. Energy Agency Dispute Settlement Centre; Associate, Inst. of Internat. Law; Trustee, Internat. Law Fund, 1983. Editor: British Practice in International Law, 1955–68; International Law Reports, 1960–. Comdr, Order of Merit, Chile, 1969; awarded Annual Cert. of Merit, Amer. Soc. Internat. Law, 1972. *Publications:* Jerusalem and the Holy Places, 1968; (ed) International Law: the collected papers of Sir Hersch Lauterpacht, vol I, 1970, vol. II, 1975, vol. III, 1977, vol. IV, 1978; various articles on international law. *Address:* Trinity College, Cambridge. *T:* Cambridge 358201; 3 Essex Court, Temple, EC4. *T:* 01–353 2624; 7 Herschel Road, Cambridge. *T:* Cambridge 354707. *Club:* Athenæum.

LAUTI, Rt. Hon. Toaripi, PC 1979; MP; Leader of the Opposition, Tuvalu Parliament, since 1981; *b* Papua New Guinea, 1928; *m*; three *s* two *d. Educ:* Tuvalu; Fiji; St Andrew's Coll., Christchurch, NZ; Christchurch Teachers' Training Coll., NZ. Taught in Tarawa, Kiribati, 1953–62; engaged in Labour Relations, Nauru, Training Officer, British Phosphate Commn; returned to Tuvalu, 1974, and entered politics; elected unopposed to House of Assembly, May 1975; elected Chief Minister, Tuvalu, upon separation of Ellice Islands (Tuvalu) from Kiribati, Oct. 1975, re-elected Chief Minister in Sept. 1977; First Prime Minister, Tuvalu, 1978–81. Chm. 18th South Pacific Conference, Noumea, Oct. 1978. *Address:* Alapi, Funafuti Island, Tuvalu, South West Pacific.

LAVAN, Hon. Sir John Martin, Kt 1981; Senior Puisne Judge of the Supreme Court of Western Australia; *b* 5 Sept. 1911; *s* of late M. G. Lavan, KC; *m* 1939, Leith Harford; one *s* three *d. Educ:* Aquinas Coll., Perth; Xavier Coll., Melbourne. Barrister in private practice, 1934–69; a Judge of the Supreme Court of WA, 1969–. Chm., Parole Bd, WA, 1969–79. Mem., Barristers' Bd, WA, 1960–69; Pres., Law Soc. of WA, 1964–66. KStJ. *Address:* Supreme Court, Perth, Western Australia 6000; 165 Victoria Avenue, Dalkeith, WA 6009, Australia. *Club:* Weld (Perth).

LAVELLE, Roger Garnett; Deputy Secretary, HM Treasury, since 1985; *b* 23 Aug. 1932; *s* of Henry Allman Lavelle and Evelyn Alice Garnett; *m* 1956, Elsa Gunilla Odeberg; three *s* one *d. Educ:* Leighton Park; Trinity Hall, Cambridge (BA, LLB). Asst Principal, Min. of Health, 1955; Principal, HM Treasury, 1961; Special Assistant (Common Market) to Lord Privy Seal, 1961–63; Private Sec. to Chancellor of the Exchequer, 1965–68; Asst Secretary, 1968, Under Sec., 1975, HM Treasury. *Recreations:* music and gardening. *Address:* 36 Cholmeley Crescent, Highgate, N6. *T:* 01–340 4845.

LAVER, Frederick John Murray, CBE 1971; Member, Post Office Corporation, 1969–73, retired; *b* 11 March 1915; *er s* of late Clifton F. Laver and Elsie Elizabeth Palmer, Bridgwater; *m* 1948, Kathleen Amy Blythe; one *s* two *d. Educ:* Plymouth Coll. BSc London. Entered PO Engrg Dept, 1935; PO Research Stn, 1935–51; Radio Planning, 1951–57; Organization and Efficiency, 1957–63; Asst Sec., HM Treasury, 1963–65; Chief Scientific Officer, Min. of Technology, 1965–68; Director, National Data Processing Service, 1968–70; Mem., NRDC, 1974–80. Vis. Prof., Computing Lab., Univ. of Newcastle upon Tyne, 1975–79. Mem. Council: IEE, 1966–69, 1972–73; British Computer Soc., 1969–72; Nat. Computing Centre, 1966–68, 1970–73; IEE Electronic Divl Bd, 1966–69, 1970–73. Mem. Council, 1979–87, Chm., 1985–87, Pro-Chancellor, 1981–87, Exeter Univ. CEng, FIEE; Hon. FBCS. *Publications:* nine introductory books on physics and computing; several scientific papers. *Recreations:* reading, writing, and watching the sea. *Address:* 2 Park Lane, Budleigh Salterton, Devon EX9 6QT. *T:* Budleigh Salterton 5271.

LAVER, Patrick Martin; HM Diplomatic Service, retired; Director of Research, Foreign and Commonwealth Office, 1980–83; *b* 3 Feb. 1932; *s* of late James Laver, CBE, RE, FRSL, and late Veronica Turleigh; *m* 1st, 1966, Marianne Ford (marr. diss. 1973); one *d*; 2nd, 1979, Dr Elke Maria Schmitz, *d* of Thomas and Anneliese Schmitz. *Educ:* Ampleforth Coll., Yorks; New Coll., Oxford. Third Sec., Foreign Office, 1954; Second Sec., Djakarta, 1956; FO, 1957; Paris, 1958; Yaoundé, 1961; UK Delegn to Brussels Conf., 1962; First Sec., FO, 1963; UK Mission to UN, New York, 1964; Diplomatic Service Admin., 1965; Commercial Sec., Nairobi, 1968; FCO, 1970; Counsellor (Economic), Pretoria, 1973; UK Delegn to Conf. on Security and Co-operation in Europe, Geneva, 1974; Head of Rhodesia Dept, FCO, 1975–78; Counsellor, Paris, 1979–80. *Address:* c/o Department of Political Science, Carleton University, Ottawa, Ontario, K1S 5B6, Canada. *T:* (613) 564–2697. *Club:* Athenæum.

LAVER, William Scott, CBE 1962; HM Diplomatic Service, retired; *b* 7 March 1909; *s* of Robert John Laver, Latchingdon, Essex, and Frances Lucy (*née* Pasmore), Windsor; *m* 1969, Marjorie Joan Hall, Chislehurst, Kent. *Educ:* St Dunstan's Coll., Catford; Downing Coll., Cambridge. Dept of Overseas Trade, 1932; Asst to Commercial Counsellor: Brussels, 1934, Rome, 1936; Commercial Sec., Rio de Janeiro, 1940; Commercial Sec., Cairo, 1946; Foreign Office, 1950–51; Financial Sec., Bahrain, 1951; Political Agent, Bahrain, 1951–52; Counsellor (Economic), Belgrade, 1954; Counsellor (Commercial), Oslo, 1958–62; Ambassador to Congo Republic, Gabon, Republic of Chad, and Central African Republic, 1962–66. *Address:* Flat 30, Mapledene, Kemnal Road, Chislehurst, Kent.

LAVERICK, Elizabeth, PhD, CEng, FIEE, FInstP, FIEEE (US); consultant; *b* 25 Nov. 1925; *d* of William Rayner and Alice Garland; *m* 1946 (marr. diss. 1960); no *c. Educ:* Dr Challoner's Grammar Sch., Amersham; Durham Univ. Research at Durham Univ., 1946–50; Section Leader at GEC, 1950–53; Microwave Engineer at Elliott Bros, 1954; Head of Radar Research Laboratory of Elliott-Automation Radar Systems Ltd, 1959; Jt Gen. Manager, Elliott-Automation Radar Systems Ltd, 1968–69, Technical Dir, 1969–71. IEE: Mem. Electronics Divisional Bd, 1967–70; Mem. Council, 1969–70; Dep. Sec., 1971–85. Electronics CADMAT (Computer Aided Design, Manufacture and Test) Project Dir, 1982–85. President, Women's Engineering Soc., 1967–69; Governor, Hatfield Polytechnic; Member: Council, Inst. of Physics, 1970–73; Council, City and Guilds of London Inst., 1984–; DE Adv. Cttee on Women's Employment, 1970–82; Adv. Cttee for Electronic and Electrical Engrg, Sheffield Univ., 1984–; Court, Brunel Univ., 1985–. Hon. Fellow, UMIST, 1969. *Publications:* contribs to IEE and IEEE Jls. *Recreations:* music, gardening, careers talks, tapestry, sailing. *Address:* Flat 4, Carlton Mansions, 16/17 York Buildings, WC2N 6LS.

LAVERS, Patricia Mae, (Mrs H. J. Lavers); Executive Director, Bond Street Association, 1961–76, and Regent Street Association, 1972–76; *b* 12 April 1919; *d* of Edric Allan Jordan and May Holdcraft; *m* 1st, 1945, Frederick Handel Hayward (*d* 1965); one *s*; 2nd, 1966, John Harold Ellen; 3rd, 1976, Lt-Comdr Herbert James Lavers. *Educ:* Sydenham High School. Clerk, Securities Dept, National Provincial Bank, 1938–45; Export Dir, Perth Radios, 1955–60. Alderman, St Pancras Council, 1960–66 (Libraries/Public Health). Elected to Executive of Westminster Chamber of Commerce, 1971, Chm. City Affairs Cttee, 1971–75. Chm., Sandwich Soc., 1983–. FZS. *Recreations:* swimming, collecting first editions and press books. *Address:* Horse Pond Sluice, Delf Street, Sandwich, Kent. *Clubs:* Arts, Lansdowne, Players Theatre.

LAVIN, Deborah Margaret; Principal, Trevelyan College, University of Durham, since 1980; *b* 22 Sept. 1939. *Educ:* Roedean Sch., Johannesburg, SA; Rhodes Univ., Grahamstown, SA; Lady Margaret Hall, Oxford (MA, DipEd). Asst Lectr, Dept of History, Univ. of the Witwatersrand, 1962–64; Lectr, Dept of Mod. Hist., The Queen's Univ. of Belfast, 1965–78, Sen. Lectr, 1978. Senior Associate, St Antony's Coll., Oxford. *Publications:* South African Memories, 1979; articles in learned jls. *Recreations:* broadcasting; the arts; passionate but unsuccessful tennis player. *Address:* Trevelyan College, Elvet Hill Road, Durham DH1 3LN. *T:* Durham 61133; Hickmans Cottages, Cat Street, East Hendred, Oxon OX12 8JT. *T:* Abingdon 833408. *Club:* Royal Commonwealth Society.

LAVIN, Mary, (Mrs M. MacDonald Scott); Writer; *b* East Walpole, Mass, USA, 11 June 1912; *m* 1st, 1942, William Walsh (*d* 1954), MA, NUI; three *d*; 2nd, 1969, Michael MacDonald Scott, MA, MSc. *Educ:* National Univ. of Ireland, Dublin (Graduate, MA; Hon DLitt, 1968). Mem. of Irish Academy of Letters, President, 1971. Guggenheim Fellow 1959, 1962 and 1972. Katherine Mansfield Prize, 1961; Ella Lynam Cabot Award, 1971; Eire Soc. Gold Medal, Boston, 1974; Arts Award, Royal Meath Assoc., 1975; Gregory Medal, Dublin, 1975; Amer. Irish Foundn Literary Award, 1979; Allied Irish Bank Award, 1981. Personality of the Year, Royal Meath Assoc., 1976. *Publications:* Tales from Bective Bridge (short stories, awarded James Tait Black Memorial Prize), 1942 (London, 1943); The Long Ago (short stories), 1944; The House in Clewe Street (novel), 1945, repr. 1986; At Sally Gap (Boston), 1946; The Becker Wives, 1946; Mary O'Grady (novel), 1950, repr. 1986; Patriot Son (short stories), 1956; A Single Lady (short stories); A Likely Story (short novel), 1957; Selected Stories, 1959 (New York); The Great Wave (short stories), 1961; Stories of Mary Lavin, 1964; In the Middle of the Fields (short stories), 1966; Happiness (short stories), 1969; Collected Stories, 1971; A Memory and other Stories, 1972; The Second Best Children in the World, 1972; The Stories of Mary Lavin, vol. II, 1973; The Shrine and other stories, 1976; A Family Likeness, 1985; The Stories of Mary Lavin, vol. III, 1985. *Address:* The Abbey Farm, Bective, Co. Meath. *T:* 046 21243; Apt 5 Gilford Pines, Gilford Road, Sandymount, Dublin 4.

LAVINGTON, His Honour Cyril Michael, MBE 1946; JP; a Circuit Judge (formerly Judge of County Courts), 1971–83; *b* 21 June 1912; *e s* of Cyril Claude Lavington, MB, BS of Bristol and Nora Vernon Lavington; *m* 1950, Frances Anne (marr. diss. 1968), *d* of Colston Wintle, MD, of Bristol; one *s*. Barrister-at-Law, Middle Temple, 1936; Western Circuit, Wilts QS. Joined Army, 1939; Major, DAA and QMG, 1 GRTD, N Africa, 1943; DAAG 37 Mil. Miss. to Yugoslav Army of Nat. Liberation, 1944; DAAG 3 Corps, Greece, 1945 (despatches twice, MBE). Returned to practice, 1946. Recorder of Barnstaple, 1964–71, Honorary Recorder, 1972–; Dep. Chm., Quarter Sessions: Dorset, 1962–71; Wiltshire, 1970–71; Hampshire, 1971. JP Cornwall, 1974. *Recreations:* sailing, gardening. *Address:* Stockadon Villa, St Mellion, Saltash, Cornwall. *T:* Liskeard 50259. *Clubs:* Royal Yachting Association; Bar Yacht.

LAVOIPIERRE, Jacques Joseph Maurice; Justice of Seychelles Court of Appeal, 1977–83; *b* 4 April 1909; 3rd *s* of Antoine Lavoipierre and Elisa la Hausse de Lalouvière; *m* 1939, Pauline Koenig; two *s* one *d. Educ:* Royal Coll., Mauritius; King's Coll., London (LLB); Middle Temple. Magistrate, Mauritius, 1944; Civil Comr, 1946; Magistrate, Industrial Court, 1949; Master and Registrar, Supreme Court, 1952; Substitute Procureur and Advocate-Gen., 1954. QC (Mauritius), 1961; Judge of Supreme Court, Mauritius, 1956–60; Attorney-Gen., 1960–64; after new constitution, reverted to private practice, 1965–66; Legal Officer, La Trobe Univ., Aust., 1966–74. Coronation Medal, 1953. *Address:* 34 Hillcrest, Sir Winston Churchill Street, Curepipe, Mauritius. *Clubs:* Mauritius Turf, Grand Sable (Mauritius).

LAW, family name of **Barons Coleraine** and **Ellenborough.**

LAW, Alfred Noel, CMG 1947; MC 1918; retired; *b* 1895; *s* of late Frank Law; *m* 1937, Kathleen, *d* of A. Fishkin, Newcastle upon Tyne; one *d. Educ:* Northampton Sch.; Hertford Coll., Oxford. Served European War, 1914–19, with 4th Battalion Northamptonshire Regiment. Entered Colonial Service (Palestine), 1920; District Commissioner, Haifa, Palestine, 1942–48; Chief Sec., British Administration, Somalia, 1948–50; Dep. Dir of Education (Administration), Uganda, 1950–53; Ministry of Education, Labour and Lands, Nairobi, Kenya, 1954–57. *Address:* 23 The Sheraton, Oak Avenue, Kenilworth, 7700, South Africa.

LAW, Sir Eric (John Ewan), Kt 1979; **Hon. Mr Justice Law;** Justice of Appeal, Court of Appeal, Seychelles, since 1983; *b* 10 June 1913; *er s* of late Sir Charles Ewan Law; *m* 1948, Patricia Constance Elizabeth, *d* of C. W. S. Seed, CBE; two *s* one *d. Educ:* Wrekin Coll.; St Catharine's Coll., Cambridge (Exhibitioner), MA (Hons). Called to Bar, Middle Temple, 1936. War Service, 1939–42: E Yorks Regt and KAR, Capt. Asst Judicial Adviser to Govt of Ethiopia, 1942–44; Crown Counsel, Nyasaland, 1944–53; Resident Magistrate, Tanganyika, 1953–55; Senior Resident Magistrate, 1955–56; Asst Judge, Zanzibar, 1956–58; Judge, Tanganyika, 1958–64; Justice of Appeal, Court of Appeal for E Africa, 1965–77 (Vice-Pres., 1975–77) and for Kenya, 1977–83. *Address:* 19 Blackfriars Street, Canterbury, Kent CT1 2AP. *T:* Canterbury 453771. *Clubs:* Mombasa, Muthaiga (Kenya).

LAW, Francis Stephen, (Frank Law), CBE 1981; Chairman: Varta Group UK, since 1971; CEAG Group UK, since 1971; Altana UK Group, since 1978; Deputy Chairman, National Freight Consortium, 1982–85 (Director, Consortium and its predecessors, since 1969); *b* 31 Dec. 1916; *s* of Henry and Ann Law-Lowensberg; *m* 1959, Nicole Vigne (*née* Fesch); one *s* (one *d* by previous *m*). *Educ:* on the Continent. War service, 1939–45. Wills Law & Co., 1947; Truvox Engrg, 1960, subseq. Dir of Controls and Communications; Director: B. Elliott and Co. Ltd, 1968–; BMW (GB) Ltd, 1978–; Siemens, 1984–; Member: Org. Cttee, NFC, 1968; Economic and Social Cttee, EEC, 1978–. *Recreations:* music, reading, theatre, skiing, tennis, riding, swimming. *Address:* 61 Cadogan Square, SW1. *T:* 01–235 7879. *Clubs:* Boodle's; Pilgrims.

LAW, Frank William, MA, MD, BChir Cantab, FRCS, LRCP; KStJ; Consulting Ophthalmic Surgeon, Guy's Hospital; Consulting Surgeon, Moorfields Eye Hospital; Hon. Visiting Ophthalmologist, Johns Hopkins Hospital, Baltimore; Past Pres. Ophth. Soc. of UK; late Master Oxford Ophth. Congress; Mem., Chapter General and Ophth. Hosp. Cttee, Order of St John; Mem. Council, European Ophth. Soc.; Life Mem., Irish Ophth. Soc.; Membre d'Honneur, Soc. Belge d'Ophth.; Hon. Mem., Greek Ophth. Soc., Pan-American Medical Assoc. and American Acad. Ophth.; American Medical Assoc.; Canadian Ophth. Soc.; Past Master, Company of Spectacle Makers, and Freeman of the City of London; *b* Isleworth, 1898; *y s* of late Thomas Law and Emma Janet MacRae; *m* 1929, Brenda, *d* of Edwin Thomas; one *s* one *d. Educ:* St Paul's Sch.; St John's Coll., Cambridge; Middlesex Hosp. Served European War, France and Flanders, 1917–19, Royal Field Artillery; Capt. Lady Margaret Boat Club, 1922; Spare Man for Varsity Boat and Trial Cap, 1922; rowed 2 for Cambridge, 1923; Late Consultant to the Army in Ophthalmology and Surgeon to Queen Alexandra Military Hosp., Millbank; late Consulting Ophthalmic Surgeon, King Edward VII Hospital for Officers; Past Pres. and Councillor, Faculty of Ophthalmologists; Sec. Gen., International Ophth. Congress, 1950;

Past Mem. International Ophthalmological Council. Hon. FBOA 1957. *Publications:* Ultra-Violet Therapy in Eye Disease, 1934; History of Moorfields Eye Hospital, 1975; History of the Worshipful Company of Spectacle Makers, 1979; History of the Ophthalmic Society of the UK, 1980; articles in Brit. Jl of Ophthalmology, Transactions of Ophthalmological Society, and other Med. Jls. *Address:* Baldersby Cottage, Chipperfield, Herts WD4 9DB. *T:* Kings Langley 62905; Flat 14, 59 Weymouth Street, W1N 3LH. *T:* 01-935 7328. *Clubs:* Athenæum, MCC; Leander.

LAW, Harry Davis; President, Portsmouth Polytechnic, since 1982; *b* 10 Nov. 1930; *s* of late Harold and Edna Betina Law; *m* 1956, Hazel M. Harding; one *s* one *d*. *Educ:* King Edward VI Sch., Stafford; Keele Univ. (BA); Manchester Univ. (PhD). FRSC. Demonstrator, Keele Univ., 1957–58; Commonwealth Fund Fellow, Cornell Med. Sch., NY, 1958–59; ICI Research Fellow, Liverpool Univ., 1959–60; Head, Chemistry, Miles Labs, Stoke Poges, subseq. Head, Therapeutic Research Labs, 1960–65; Head Chemistry and Biol., Liverpool Reg. Coll. Technology, 1965–69; Head Chemistry and Chm., Faculty of Science, Liverpool Polytechnic, 1969–71; Dep. Dir, Glasgow Coll. of Technology, 1971–73; Dir, Preston Polytechnic, 1973–82. Cttee of Directors of Polytechnics: Vice-Chm., 1983–84; Chm., 1984–86; Chm., Polytechnics Central Admission System, 1984–. Chm., CNAA Bd of Food, Accommodation and Related Sciences (formerly Instnl and Domestic Science), 1975–81; Member: Lancs Educn Cttee, 1974–82; Hampshire CC Educn Cttee, 1982–; TEC, later BTEC, 1977–84 (Vice-Chm., 1982–83; Chm., Educn Cttee, 1979–83); Cttee for Internat. Co-operation in Higher Educn, British Council, 1981– (Vice-Chm., 1983–86); Sci. Bd, SRC, 1978–81; SERC, 1986–. Hon. Fellow, Lancashire Polytechnic, 1983; Hon. DSc Keele, 1986. *Publications:* The Organic Chemistry of Peptides, 1970; numerous pubns in learned jls. *Recreation:* fishing. *Address:* Town Mount, Hampshire Terrace, Portsmouth PO1 2QG. *T:* Portsmouth 833929.

LAW, Adm. Sir Horace (Rochfort), GCB 1972 (KCB 1967; CB 1963); OBE 1950; DSC 1941; retired 1972; Chairman, R. & W. Hawthorn Leslie & Co., 1973–81; *b* 23 June 1911; *s* of S. Horace Law, MD, FRCSI, and Sybil Mary (*née* Clay); *m* 1941, Heather Valerie Coryton; two *s* two *d*. *Educ:* Sherborne Sch. Entered Royal Navy, 1929; gunnery specialist, 1937. Served War of 1939–45 (DSC): AA Cruisers: Cairo, 1939; Coventry, 1940; Cruiser Nigeria, 1942; Comdr 1946; Capt. 1952; comd HMS Centaur, 1958 and Britannia, RN Coll., 1960; Rear-Adm. 1961; Vice-Adm. 1965; Flag Officer Sea Training, 1961–63; Flag Officer, Submarines, 1963–65; Controller of the Navy, 1965–70; C-in-C, Naval Home Comd, and Flag Officer, Portsmouth Area, 1970–72; First and Principal Naval Aide-de-Camp to the Queen, 1970–72. Mem., Security Commn, 1973–82. President: RINA, 1975–77; Officers' Christian Union, 1976–86; Chm., Church Army Bd, 1980–. *Recreations:* sailing, gardening. *Address:* West Harting, Petersfield, Hants.

LAW, James, QC (Scot.) 1971; *b* 7 June 1926; *s* of late George Law, MA, and Isabella Rebecca Lamb (or Law), MA; *m* 1956, Kathleen Margaret, *d* of late Alexander Gibson; two *s* one *d*. *Educ:* Kilmarnock Academy; Girvan High Sch.; Univ. of Glasgow (MA 1948, LLB 1950). Admitted to Faculty of Advocates, 1951; Advocate-Depute, 1957–64. Mem., Criminal Injuries Compensation Bd, 1970–. *Address:* 7 Gloucester Place, Edinburgh EH3 6EE. *T:* 031-225 2974. *Clubs:* New, Caledonian (Edinburgh).

LAW, Phillip Garth, AO 1975; CBE 1961; MSc, FAIP, FTS, FAA; *b* 21 April 1912; *s* of Arthur James Law and Lillie Lena Chapman; *m* 1941, Nellie Isabel Allan; no *c*. *Educ:* Hamilton High Sch.; Ballarat Teachers' Coll.; Melbourne Univ. Science master, State secondary schs, Vic., 1933–38; Tutor in Physics, Newman Coll., Melbourne Univ., 1940–47; Lectr in Physics, 1943–48. Research Physicist and Asst Sec. of Scientific Instrument and Optical Panel of Austr. Min. of Munitions, 1940–45. Sen. Scientific Officer, ANARE, 1947–48; cosmic ray measurements in Antarctica and Japan, 1948; Dir, Antarctic Div., Dept of External Affairs, Aust., and Leader, ANARE, 1949–66; Expedition relief voyages to Heard I. and Macquarie I., 1949, 1951, 1952, 1954. Australian observer with Norwegian-British-Swedish Antarctic Exped., 1950; Leader of expedition: to establish first permanent Australian station in Antarctica at Mawson, MacRobertson Land, 1954; which established second continental station at Davis, Princess Elizabeth Land, 1957; which took over Wilkes station from USA, 1959; to relieve ANARE stations and to explore coast of Australian Antarctic Territory, annually, 1955–66. Chm., Australian Nat. Cttee for Antarctic Research, 1966–80. Exec. Vice-Pres., Victoria Inst. of Colls, 1966–77; Pres., Victorian Inst. of Marine Scis, 1978–80. Member: Council of Melbourne Univ., 1959–78; Council, La Trobe Univ., 1964–74; President: Royal Soc. of Victoria, 1967, 1968; Aust. and NZ Schs Exploring Soc., 1977–82. Dep. Pres., Science Museum of Victoria, Melbourne, 1979–82 (Trustee, 1968–83). Pres., Grad. Union, Melbourne Univ., 1972–77. Patron, British Schs Exploring Soc. Fellow: Australian Acad. of Technological Sciences; Aust. Acad. of Sci.; Aust. Inst. of Physics; ANZAAS. Hon. Fellow, Royal Melbourne Inst. of Technology. Hon. DAppSc (Melbourne); Hon. DEd (Victoria Inst. of Colls). Founder's Gold Medal, RGS, 1960. *Publications:* (with John Béchervaise) ANARE, 1957; Antarctic Odyssey, 1983; chapters in: It's People that Matter, ed Donald McLean, 1969; Search for Human Understanding, ed M. Merbaum and G. Stricker, 1971; ed series of ANARE scientific reports; numerous papers on Antarctica and education. *Recreations:* tennis, ski-ing, skin diving, music, photography. *Address:* 16 Stanley Grove, Canterbury, Vic 3126, Australia. *Clubs:* Melbourne, Kelvin, Melbourne Cricket, Royal South Yarra Lawn Tennis (Melbourne).

LAW, Sylvia, OBE 1977; Head of Planning Policy Study Group, Greater London Council; *b* 29 March 1931; *d* of late Reginald Howard Law and late Dorothy Margaret Law. *Educ:* Lowther Coll.; Girton Coll., Cambridge (MA); Regent Street Polytechnic (DipTP). MRTPI. Teaching, Benenden Sch., 1952–55; market research, Unilever Ltd, 1955–58; town and country planning and policy studies and research, Kent CC and GLC, 1959–86. Royal Town Planning Institute: Mem. Council, 1965–78; Chm. of Educn Cttee, 1970–73; Vice-Pres., 1972–74; Pres., 1974–75. Mem. Planning Cttee, SSRC, 1977–79. *Publications:* (contrib.) Recreational Economics and Analysis, 1974; (ed) Planning and the Future, 1976; articles in RTPI Jl, Official Architecture and Planning, Planning Outlook, Town Planning Rev., Greater London Intelligence Qly, etc. *Recreations:* music, photography.

LAW-SMITH, Sir (Richard) Robert, Kt 1980; CBE 1965; AFC 1943; Chairman, National Australia Bank Ltd; grazier; *b* Adelaide, 9 July 1914; *s* of W. Law-Smith; *m* 1941, Joan, *d* of Harold Gordon Darling; two *d*. *Educ:* St Edward's Sch., Oxford; Adelaide Univ. Served War, RAAF, 1940–46 (AFC), Sqdn Ldr. Director: Nat. Bank of Australasia, later Nat. Commercial Banking Corp. of Australia, now Nat. Australia Bank, 1959– (Vice-Chm., 1968; Chm., 1978–86); Australian Mutual Provident Soc., 1960–84 (Chm. Victoria Br., 1977–84); Broken Hill Pty Co. Ltd, 1961–84; Commonwealth Aircraft Corp., 1965–84; Blue Circle Southern Cement Ltd, 1974–84. Mem., Australian National Airlines Commn, 1962–84 (Vice-Chm., 1975–79; Chm., 1979–84). Councillor, Royal Flying Doctor Service (Victorian Div.), 1956–. *Address:* Bolobek, Macedon, Vic 3440, Australia. *Clubs:* Australian, Melbourne (Melbourne).

LAWDER, Rear-Adm. Keith Macleod, CB 1948; OBE 1919; Associate of the Chartered Institute of Secretaries; *b* 1893; *s* of F. E. Lawder; *m* 1918, Joyce Katharine Mary Watson (*d* 1980); two *d* (one *s* decd). *Educ:* Fettes Coll., Edinburgh. Joined Royal Navy, 1910; served European War, 1914–18 and War of 1939–45; retired, 1949. *Address:* Brook Cottage, South Zeal, Okehampton, Devon EX20 2QB. *T:* Whiddon Down 308. *Club:* Climbers'.

LAWLER, Geoffrey John; MP (C) Bradford North, since 1983; *b* 30 Oct. 1954; *s* of Major Ernest Lawler (RAEC retd) and Enid Lawler. *Educ:* Richmond Sch., N Yorks; Hull Univ. (BSc (Econ); Pres., Students' Union, 1976–77). Trainee chartered accountant, 1977–78. Community Affairs Dept, 1978–80, Research Dept, 1980–82, Cons. Central Office; Public Relations Exec., 1982–83; Dir, publicity co., 1983. Hon. Pres., British Youth Council, 1983–86. *Recreations:* tennis, cricket, music, travel. *Address:* House of Commons, SW1A 0AA. *T:* 01-219 3000.

LAWLER, Sir Peter (James), Kt 1981; OBE 1965; Australian Ambassador to Ireland and the Holy See, since 1983; *b* 23 March 1921; *m*; five *s* two *d*. *Educ:* Univ. of Sydney (BEc). Prime Minister's Dept, Canberra, 1949–68 (British Cabinet Office, London, 1952–53); Dep. Secretary: Dept of the Cabinet Office, 1968–71; Dept of the Prime Minister and Cabinet, 1972–73; Secretary: Dept of the Special Minister of State, 1973–75; Dept of Admin. Services, Canberra, 1975–83. *Recreation:* farming. *Address:* Australian Embassy, Fitzwilton House, Wilton Terrace, Dublin 2, Ireland. *Clubs:* Melbourne (Melbourne); University House (Canberra); Royal Canberra Golf.

LAWLEY, Dr Leonard Edward; Director of Kingston Polytechnic, 1969–82; *b* 13 March 1922; *yr s* of late Albert Lawley; *m* 1944, Dorothy Beryl Round; one *s* two *d*. *Educ:* King Edward VI Sch., Stourbridge; Univs of Wales and Newcastle upon Tyne. BSc, PhD; FInstP, CPhys. Served with RAF, 1941–46; Lectr, Univ. of Newcastle upon Tyne, 1947–53; Sen. Lectr, The Polytechnic, Regent Street, 1953–57; Kingston Coll. of Technology: Head of Dept of Physics and Maths, 1957–64; Vice-Principal, 1960–64; Principal, 1964–69. *Publications:* various papers in scientific jls on transmission ultrasonic sound waves through gases and liquids and on acoustic methods for gas analysis.

LAWLOR, Prof. John James, MA, DLitt, FSA; Professor of English Language and Literature, University of Keele, 1950–80, now Emeritus; *b* 5 Jan. 1918; *o s* of Albert John Lawlor, Chief Armourer, RN, and Teresa Anne Clare Lawlor, Plymouth; *m* 1st, 1941, Thelma Joan Weeks, singer (marr. diss. 1979); one *s* three *d*; 2nd, 1984, Kimie Imura, Prof. Meisei Univ., Tokyo. *Educ:* Ryder's; Magdalen Coll., Oxford. BA Hons English Cl. I, 1939. Service in Devonshire Regt, 1940–45; Asst Chief Instructor, 163 Artists' Rifles OCTU, 1943–44; CMF, 1944–45; AMG Austria. Sen. Mackinnon Scholar, Magdalen Coll., 1946; Sen. Demy, 1947; Lectr in English, Brasenose and Trinity Colls, 1947–50; University Lectr in Eng. Lit., Oxford, 1949–50. Fellow of Folger Shakespeare Library, Washington, DC, 1962. Toured Australian and NZ Univs and visited Japan, 1964. Ziskind Visiting Prof., Brandeis Univ., Mass, 1966; Vis. Professor: Univ. of Hawaii, 1972; Univ. of Maryland, 1981–82; Univ. of Arizona, 1983–84. Sec.-Gen. and Treasurer, Internat. Assoc. of University Profs. of English; Contrib. Mem. Medieval Academy of America; Gov., Oswestry Sch.; Pres., N Staffs Drama Assoc.; Mem. Western Area Cttee, Brit. Drama League; Vice-Pres., The Navy League. *Publications:* The Tragic Sense in Shakespeare, 1960; Piers Plowman, an Essay in Criticism, 1962; The Chester Mystery Plays (with Rosemary Sisson), perf. Chester, 1962; The Vision of Piers Plowman, commnd, Malvern, 1964; (ed) Patterns of Love and Courtesy, 1966; (with W. H. Auden) To Nevill Coghill from Friends, 1966; Chaucer, 1968; (ed) The New University, 1968; (ed) Higher Education: patterns of change in the seventies, 1972; Elysium Revisited, 1978; (as James Dundonald): Letters to a Vice-Chancellor, 1962; La Vita Nuova, 1976; articles on medieval and modern literature in various journals and symposia. *Recreations:* travel, book-collecting, any sort of sea-faring. *Address:* Penwithian, Higher Fore Street, Marazion, Cornwall TR17 0BQ. *T:* Penzance 711180; 5-19-7 Arai, Nakano-ku, Tokyo 165, Japan. *T:* Tokyo 389–3633. *Clubs:* Athenæum; Royal Fleet (Devonport).

LAWRANCE, John Ernest; Under Secretary, Director, Technical Division 1, Inland Revenue, since 1982; *b* 25 Jan. 1928; *s* of Ernest William and Emily Lewa Lawrance; *m* 1956, Margaret Elsie Ann Dodwell; two *s* one *d*. *Educ:* High School for Boys, Worthing; Southampton Univ. (BA Hons Modern History). Entered Inland Revenue as Inspector of Taxes, 1951; Principal Inspector, 1968; Senior Principal Inspector on specialist technical duties, 1974. *Address:* 71A Alderton Hill, Loughton, Essex IG10 3JD. *T:* 01-508 7562.

LAWRANCE, Mrs June Cynthia; Headmistress of Harrogate College, since 1974; *b* 3 June 1933; *d* of late Albert Isherwood and of Ida Emmett; *m* 1957, Rev. David Lawrance, MA, BD; three *d*. *Educ:* St Anne's Coll., Oxford (MA). Teaching appts: Univ. of Paris, 1954–57; Cyprus, 1957–58; Jordan, 1958–61; Oldham, Lancs, 1962–70; Headmistress, Broughton High Sch., Salford, 1971–73. *Recreations:* music, French literature, chess. *Address:* Harrogate College, Clarence Drive, Harrogate, N Yorks. *T:* Harrogate 504543.

LAWRANCE, Keith Cantwell; Deputy Chairman, Civil Service Appeal Board, since 1981 (Member since 1980); Chairman, Civil Service Retirement Fellowship, since 1982; *b* 1 Feb. 1923; *s* of P. J. Lawrance; *m* 1952, Margaret Joan (*née* Scott); no *c*. *Educ:* Latymer Sch., N9. Clerical Officer, Admiralty, 1939. Served War, RNVR, 1942–46; Sub-Lt (A), 1945. Exec. Officer, Treasury, 1947; Asst Principal, Post Office, 1954; Principal, Post Office, 1959; Asst Sec., Dept of Economic Affairs, Dec. 1966; Under-Sec., Civil Service Dept, 1971–79. Mem. Cttee of Management, Inst. for Cancer Research, 1986. *Recreations:* model engineering, music. *Address:* 8 Clement Road, Wimbledon, SW19. *T:* 01-947 1676.

LAWRENCE, family name of **Baron Lawrence** and of **Baron Trevethin and Oaksey.**

LAWRENCE, 5th Baron *cr* 1869; **David John Downer Lawrence;** Bt 1858; *b* 4 Sept. 1937; *s* of 4th Baron Lawrence and Margaret Jean (*d* 1977), *d* of Arthur Downer, Kirdford, Sussex; *S* father, 1968. *Educ:* Bradfield College. *Address:* c/o Bird & Bird, 2 Gray's Inn Square, WC1.

LAWRENCE, Arnold Walter, MA; FSA; Professor of Archæology, University College of Ghana, and Director, National Museum of Ghana, 1951–57; Secretary and Conservator, Monuments and Relics Commission of Ghana, 1952–57; Laurence Professor of Classical Archæology, Cambridge University, 1944–51, and Fellow of Jesus College; *b* 2 May 1900; *s* of T. R. Lawrence; *m* 1925, Barbara Thompson; one *d*. *Educ:* City of Oxford Sch.; New Coll., Oxford. Student, British Schs of Athens and Rome; Ur excavations, 1923; Craven Fellow, 1924–26; Reader in Classical Archæology, Cambridge Univ., 1930; Corr. Mem., German Archæological Institute; literary executor of T. E. Lawrence, 1935; Military Intelligence, Middle East, 1940; Scientific Officer, Coastal Command, RAF, 1942; Ministry of Economic Warfare, 1943; lectured in Latin America, 1948; Leverhulme Research Fellow, 1951. Hon. FBA 1982. *Publications:* Later Greek Sculpture and its Influence, 1927; Classical Sculpture, 1929; Herodotus, Rawlinson's translation revised and annotated, 1935; (ed) T. E. Lawrence by his Friends, 1937; Greek Architecture (Pelican History of Art), 1957, rev. edns 1967 and 1974, rev. by R. A. Tomlinson, 1984; (ed) Letters to T. E. Lawrence, 1962; Trade Castles and Forts of West Africa, 1963, abr. as Fortified Trade Posts: the English in West Africa, 1968; Greek and Roman Sculpture, 1972; The Castle of Baghras, in The Armenian Kingdom of Cilicia (ed T. S. R. Boase), 1978; Greek Aims in Fortification, 1980. *Recreation:* going to and fro in the earth and walking up and down in it. *Address*: c/o Barclays Bank, High Street, Pateley Bridge, Harrogate HG3 5LA.

LAWRENCE, Bernard Edwin, CBE 1957; Chief Education Officer, County of Essex, 1939–65, retired; Dean of the College of Preceptors, 1958–68, Vice President, 1969–80; *b* 3 Jan. 1901; *s* of late Albert Edward and Emma Lawrence; *m* 1925, Dorothy Rosa Collings; two *s* one *d*. *Educ*: Sir Joseph Williamson's Sch., Rochester; Worcester Coll., Oxford. BA Oxon double first class Hons 1922; MA 1930; PhD, University Coll. London, 1934. Asst Master: George Green's Sch., 1923–25; Skinners' Sch., 1925–28; Lecturer: Goldsmiths' Coll., 1928–35; Birkbeck Coll., 1930–35; Asst Dir of Education, Essex, 1936–39; Chairman: Educational Commission to Uganda and Kenya, 1961; Nat. Inst. of Adult Educn, 1964–69. Pres. Assoc. of Chief Educn. Officers, 1957–58. Chevalier de la Légion d'Honneur, 1958. *Publications*: The Administration of Education in Britain, 1972; occasional contribs to Educational Jls and to Proceedings of London Mathematical Society and Mathematical Gazette. *Recreation*: gardening. *Address*: White Gable, Felsted, Great Dunmow, Essex.

LAWRENCE, Rt. Rev. Caleb James; see Moosonee, Bishop of.

LAWRENCE, Christopher Nigel; silversmith; industrial designer; *b* 23 Dec. 1936; *s* of late Rev. William W. Lawrence and of Millicent Lawrence; *m* 1958, Valerie Betty Bergman; two *s* two *d*. *Educ*: Westborough High Sch.; Central School of Arts and Crafts. Nat. Dip. Design, Full Technol. Cert. (City and Guilds of London). FIPG. Apprenticed, C. J. Vander Ltd; started own workshops, 1968. *One man exhibitions*: Galerie Jean Renet, 1970, 1971; Hamburg, 1972; Goldsmiths' Hall, 1973; Ghent, 1975; Hasselt, 1977. Major commissions from British Govt, City Livery cos, banks, manufacturing cos. Judge and external assessor for leading art colleges; specialist in symbolic presentation pieces and limited edns of decorative pieces, eg silver mushrooms. Chm., Goldsmiths, Silversmiths and Jewellers Art Council, 1976–77; Liveryman, Goldsmiths' Co., 1978–; television and radio broadcaster. Jacques Cartier Meml award for Craftsman of the Year, 1960, 1963, 1967 (unique achievement). *Recreations*: cruising on family's narrow boat, archery, badminton, carpentry, pottery. *Address*: 20 St Vincent's Road, Westcliff-on-Sea, Essex SS0 7PR. *T*: Southend-on-Sea 338443; (workshops and showroom) Quintessence, 172–174 London Road, Southend-on-Sea, Essex SS1 1PH. *T*: Southend-on-Sea 344897.

LAWRENCE, Prof. Clifford Hugh; Professor of Medieval History, since 1970, and Head of the Department of History, Bedford College, University of London, 1981–85; *b* 28 Dec. 1921; *s* of Ernest William Lawrence and Dorothy Estelle; *m* 1953, Helen Maud Curran; one *s* five *d*. *Educ*: Stationers' Co.'s Sch.; Lincoln Coll., Oxford. BA 1st Cl. Hons Mod. Hist. 1948, MA 1953, DPhil 1956. War service in RA and Beds and Herts: 2nd Lieut 1942, Captain 1944, Major 1945. Asst Archivist to Co. of Gloucester, 1949. Bedford Coll., London: Asst Lectr in History, 1951; Lectr, 1953–63; Reader in Med. History, 1963–70. External Examr, Univ. of Newcastle upon Tyne, 1972–74; Univ. of Bristol, 1975–77; Univ. of Reading, 1977–79; Chm., Bd of Examnrs in History, London Univ., 1981–83. Member: Press Council, 1976–80; Governing Body, Heythrop Coll., Univ. of London; Council, Westfield Coll., Univ. of London. FRHistS 1960; FSA 1984. *Publications*: St Edmund of Abingdon, History and Hagiography, 1960; The English Church and the Papacy in the Middle Ages, 1965; Medieval Monasticism, 1984; contribs to: Pre-Reformation English Spirituality, 1967; The Christian Community, 1971; The History of the University of Oxford, Vol. I, 1984; articles and reviews in Eng. Hist. Review, History, Jl Eccles. Hist., Oxoniensia, Encycl. Brit., Lexicon für Theol u Kirche, etc. *Recreations*: gardening, painting. *Address*: 11 Durham Road, SW20 0QH. *T*: 01–946 3820.

See also G. C. Lawrence.

LAWRENCE, Sir David (Roland Walter), 3rd Bt, *cr* 1906; late Captain, Coldstream Guards, 1951; *b* 8 May 1929; *er s* of Sir Roland Lawrence, 2nd Bt, MC, and Susan, 3rd *d* of late Sir Charles Addis, KCMG; *S* father 1950; *m* 1955, Audrey, Duchess of Leeds, *yr d* of Brig. Desmond Young, OBE, MC. *Educ*: Radley; RMC Sandhurst. *Heir*: *b* Clive Wyndham Lawrence [*b* 6 Oct. 1939; *m* 1966, Sophia Annabel Stuart, *d* of late (Ian) Hervey Stuart Black, TD; three *s*]. *Address*: 28 High Town Road, Maidenhead, Berks. *Club*: Cavalry and Guards.

LAWRENCE, Dennis George Charles, OBE 1963; Director, 1978–82, Board Member, 1981–84, Cooperative Development Agency; retired; *b* 15 Aug. 1918; *s* of late George Herbert and Amy Frances Lawrence; *m* 1946, Alida Jantine, *d* of late Willem van den Berg, The Netherlands. *Educ*: Haberdashers' Aske's Hatcham School. Entered Civil Service as Clerical Officer, Min. of Transport, 1936; served RA, 1939–46; Exec. Officer 1946; Asst Principal, Central Land Board, 1947; Principal, 1949; GPO, 1953; Asst Sec. 1960; Sec., Cttee on Broadcasting, 1960–62; Asst Sec., GPO, 1962; Under-Secretary: GPO, 1969; Min. of Posts and Telecommunications, 1969–74; Dept of Industry, 1974–78. Chm., Working Group on a Cooperative Develt Agency, 1977. *Publication*: Democracy and Broadcasting (pamphlet), 1986. *Recreations*: walking, painting, travel. *Address*: Little London Farmhouse, Cann, Shaftesbury, Dorset. *T*: Shaftesbury 2252. *Clubs*: National Liberal; Lanzarote Beach.

LAWRENCE, Evelyn M., (Mrs Nathan Isaacs); BSc (Econ) London, PhD; *b* 31 Dec. 1892; *d* of Samuel and Mary Lawrence, Walton-on-Thames; *m* 1950, Nathan Isaacs, OBE (*d* 1966). *Educ*: Tiffins Sch., Kingston-on-Thames; Stockwell Training Coll.; London Sch. of Economics, University of London. Teacher in LCC schs, 1913–24; BSc Econ. 1st cl. Hons 1923; Ratan Tata and Metcalfe scholar, London Sch. of Economics, 1924–26; on staff of Malting House Sch., Cambridge, 1926–28; Commonwealth Fund scholar, USA, 1929; Chief Social Worker, London Child Guidance Clinic, 1929–30; Lecturer in Education, National Training Coll. of Domestic Subjects, 1931–43. Dir, National Froebel Foundation, and Editor, Froebel Foundation Bulletin, 1943–63. Hon. Sec. British Psychological Soc., Education Section, 1931–34; Mem. of Council of Eugenics Soc., 1949–59. *Publications*: The Relation between Intelligence and Inheritance, 1931; (Ed) Friedrich Froebel and English Education, 1952. *Recreations*: walking, gardening, music. *Address*: Grove Cottage, Owletts Lane, Ashurst Wood, East Grinstead, W Sussex. *T*: Forest Row 2728.

LAWRENCE, Geoffrey Charles, CMG 1963; OBE 1958; *b* 11 Nov. 1915; *s* of Ernest William Lawrence; *m* 1945, Joyce Acland Madge, MBE 1959, *d* of M. H. A. Madge, MC. *Educ*: Stationers' Company's Sch.; Brasenose Coll., Oxford. Served 1939–46, Middlesex Yeo. and Brit. Mil. Administration of Occupied Territories (Major). HM Overseas Civil Service (Colonial Administrative Service). Administrative Officer, Somaliland Protectorate, 1946; Asst Chief Sec., 1955; Financial Sec., 1956; Financial Sec., Zanzibar and Mem. of East African Currency Board, 1960–63; Colonial Office, 1964–66; ODM, later ODA, FCO, 1966–73; ODM, 1973–76. *Address*: c/o Barclays Bank, 42 Coombe Lane, SW20.

See also C. H. Lawrence.

LAWRENCE, Sir Guy Kempton, Kt 1976; DSO 1943; OBE 1945; DFC 1941; Chairman, Eggs Authority, 1978–81; *b* 5 Nov. 1914; *s* of Albert Edward and Bianca

Lawrence; *m* 1947, Marcia Virginia Powell; two *s* one *d*. *Educ*: Marlborough Coll. FBIM, FIGD. RAFO, 1934–45; War of 1939–45: Bomber Pilot (48 sorties), Sqdn Comdr, 78 Sqdn, Gp Captain Trng, HQ Bomber Command (DFC DSO, despatches, OBE). Contested (L) Colne Valley, 1945. Man. Dir, Chartair Ltd-Airtech Ltd, 1945–48; Chairman: Glacier Foods Ltd, 1948–75; Findus (UK) Ltd, 1967–75; Dep. Chairman: J. Lyons & Co. Ltd, 1950–75; Spillers French Holdings Ltd, 1972–75; Vice-Chm., DCA Food Industries Inc., 1973–; Dir, Eagle Aircraft Services, 1977–81. Chm., Food and Drink Industries Council, 1973–77. Member of Stock Exchange, London, 1937–45. British Ski Team, FIS, 1937–38. *Recreations*: farming, carpentry, squash, tennis. *Address*: Courtlands, Kier Park, Ascot, Berks SL5 7DS. *T*: Ascot 21074. *Club*: Royal Air Force.

LAWRENCE, (Henry) Richard (George); Music Director, Arts Council of Great Britain, since 1983; *b* 16 April 1946; *s* of late George Napier Lawrence, OBE, and of Peggy Neave (*née* Breay). *Educ*: Westminster Abbey Choir Sch.; Haileybury Coll. (music schol.) Worcester Coll., Oxford (Hadow Schol.; BA 1967). Overseas Dept, Ginn & Co., educational publishers, 1968–73; Music Officer, Arts Council of GB, 1973–83. Chm., Arts Council Staff Assoc., 1974–76. *Recreation*: travelling in Asia. *Address*: c/o Arts Council of Great Britain, 105 Piccadilly, W1V 0AU. *T*: 01–629 9495.

LAWRENCE, Ivan John, QC 1981; Barrister-at-law; MP (C) Burton, since Feb. 1974; *b* 24 Dec. 1936; *o s* of Leslie Lawrence, Brighton; *m* 1966, Gloria Hélène, *d* of Charles Crankshaw, Newcastle; one *d*. *Educ*: Brighton, Hove and Sussex Grammar Sch.; Christ Church, Oxford (MA). Nat. Service with RAF, 1955–57. Called to Bar, Inner Temple, 1962; S Eastern Circuit; Asst Recorder, 1983–. Contested (C) Peckham (Camberwell), 1966 and 1970. Vice-Chairman: Cons. Parly Legal Cttee, 1979–; Cons. Parly Home Affairs Cttee, 1982–; Chm., All-party Parly Anti-Fluoridation Cttee; Sec., All-Party Parly Cttee for Release of Soviet Jewry; Member: Parly Expenditure Select Sub-Cttee, 1974–79; Jt Parly Cttee on Consolidation of Statutes, 1974–; Foreign Select Cttee, 1983–. Member: Council of Justice and its Working Party on appeals in criminal cases, 1980–; Council, Statute Law Soc., 1985–. Vice-Pres., Fed. of Cons. Students, 1980–82; Mem., W Midlands Cons. Council, 1985–. Chm., Burton Breweries Charitable Trust, 1982–. *Publications*: pamphlets (jointly): Crisis in Crime and Punishment; The Conviction of the Guilty; Towards a New Nationality; Financing Strikes; newspaper articles on law and related topics. *Recreations*: piano, squash, football, travel. *Address*: 1 Essex Court, Temple, EC4Y 9AR. *T*: 01–583 7759; Dunally Cottage, Lower Halliford Green, Shepperton, Mddx. *T*: Walton-on-Thames 224692; Grove Farm, Drakelow, Burton-on-Trent. *T*: Burton-on-Trent 44360.

LAWRENCE, John, OBE 1974; Controller, America, Pacific and South Asia Division, British Council, since 1982; *b* 22 April 1933; *s* of William and Nellie Lawrence. *Educ*: Queens' College, Cambridge (BA 1956, Cert. Ed. 1957, MA 1961); Indiana University (MA 1959). Teaching posts in USA and UK, 1957–60; British Council headquarters appts, 1961; Regional Representative, Sabah, 1965; Representative, Zambia, 1968; Sudan, 1974; Malaysia, 1976; Dir, South Asia Dept, 1980. *Recreations*: walking and talking, simultaneously or otherwise. *Address*: c/o British Council, 10 Spring Gardens, SW1A 2BN. *T*: 01–930 8466.

LAWRENCE, Air Vice-Marshal John Thornett, CB 1975; CBE (mil.) 1967 (OBE (mil.) 1961); AFC 1945; *b* 16 April 1920; *s* of late T. L. Lawrence, JP, and Mrs B. M. Lawrence; *m* 1951, Hilary Jean (*née* Owen); three *s* one *d*. *Educ*: The Crypt School, Gloucester. RAFVR 1938. Served War of 1939–45 in Coastal Command (235, 202 and 86 Squadrons); Directing staff, RAF Flying Coll., 1949–53; CO 14 Squadron, 1953–55; Group Captain Operations, HQ AFME, 1962–64; CO RAF Wittering, 1964–66; AOC, 3 Group, Bomber Command, 1967; Student, IDC, 1968; Dir of Organisation and Admin Plans (RAF), 1969–71; Dir-Gen. Personnel Management (RAF), 1971–73; Comdr N Maritime Air Region and AOC Scotland and NI, 1973–75, retired 1975. Mem. Council, Cheltenham Ladies' Coll., 1977–. Chm., Glos County SS&AFA, 1980. Order of Leopold II, Belgium, 1945; Croix de Guerre, Belgium, 1945. *Recreation*: golf. *Address*: Corinium House, Edge, Stroud, Glos. *Club*: Royal Air Force.

LAWRENCE, Sir John (Waldemar), 6th Bt, *cr* 1858; OBE 1945; Editor of Frontier, 1957–75; *b* 27 May 1907; *s* of Sir Alexander Waldemar Lawrence, 4th Bt, and Anne Elizabeth Le Poer (*née* Wynne); *S* brother, Sir Henry Eustace Waldemar Lawrence, 5th Bt, 1967; *m* 1948, Jacynth Mary (*née* Ellerton); no *c*. *Educ*: Eton; New Coll., Oxford (MA, Lit. Hum.). Personal Asst to Dir of German Jewish Aid Cttee, 1938–39; with BBC as European Intelligence Officer and European Services Organiser, 1939–42; Press Attaché, HM Embassy, USSR, 1942–45; became freelance writer, 1946. Pres., Keston College (formerly Centre for Study of Religion and Communism), 1984— (Chm., 1969–83); Chm., GB USSR Assoc., 1970–85. Officer, Order of Orange Nassau, 1950. *Publications*: Life in Russia, 1947; Russia in the Making, 1957; A History of Russia, 1960; The Hard Facts of Unity, 1961; Russia (Methuen's Outlines), 1965; Soviet Russia, 1967; Russians Observed, 1969; Take Hold of Change, 1976; The Journals of Honoria Lawrence, 1980; The Hammer and the Cross, 1986. *Recreations*: travelling, reading in ten languages. *Heir*: *b* George Alexander Waldemar Lawrence [*b* 22 Sept. 1910; *m* 1949, Olga, *d* of late Peter Schilovsky; one *s* two *d*]. *Address*: 24 St Leonard's Terrace, SW3. *T*: 01–730 8033. *Club*: Athenæum.

LAWRENCE, Michael Hugh, CMG 1972; Head of the Administration Department, House of Commons, 1972–80; retired 1980; *b* 9 July 1920; *s* of late Hugh Moxon Lawrence and Mrs. L. N. Lawrence; *m* 1948, Rachel Mary (MA Cantab), *d* of late Humphrey Gamon, Gt Barrow, Cheshire; one *s* two *d*. *Educ*: Highgate (Scholar); St Catharine's Coll., Cambridge (Exhibnr; MA). Served Indian Army, 1940–45. Indian Civil Service, 1945–46; Asst Clerk, House of Commons, 1947; Senior Clerk, 1948; Deputy Principal Clerk, 1962; Clerk of the Overseas Office, 1967–72; Clerk Administrator, of Services Cttee, 1972–76; Mem., Bd of Management, House of Commons, 1979–80. Sec., History of Parliament Trust, 1959–66. *Recreations*: beagling, sea bathing, looking at churches, gardening. *Address*: 22 Stradbroke Road, Southwold, Suffolk. *T*: Southwold 722794.

LAWRENCE, Murray; see Lawrence, W. N. M.

LAWRENCE, Peter Anthony, PhD; FRS 1983; Staff Scientist, Medical Research Council Laboratory of Molecular Biology, Cambridge, since 1969; *b* 23 June 1941; *s* of Ivor Douglas Lawrence and Joy Lawrence (*née* Liebert); *m* 1971, Birgitta Haraldson. *Educ*: Wennington Sch., Wetherby, Yorks; Cambridge Univ. (MA, PhD). Harkness Fellowship, 1965–67; Dept of Genetics, Univ. of Cambridge, 1967–69. *Publications*: Insect Development (ed), 1976; scientific papers. *Recreations*: gardening, fungi, trees, golf, theatre. *Address*: 9 Temple End, Great Wilbraham, Cambridge CB1 5JF. *T*: Cambridge 880505.

LAWRENCE, Richard; see Lawrence, H. R. G.

LAWRENCE, Air Vice-Marshal Thomas Albert, CB 1945; CD; RCAF, retired; *b* 1895; *s* of K. J. Lawrence; *m* 1921, Claudine Audrey Jamieson. Served War of 1914–18, France; Flight Cadet, RFC, later 24 Fighter Sqdn, RAF. Pilot-Navigator, Canadian Air

Bd; one of original gp of officers commnd into perm. RCAF, 1924; comdr, Hudson Strait Expedn, 1927; Liaison Officer, RCAF, Air Ministry, London, 1932–35; served War of 1939–45: Dir, Plans and Ops, Air Force HQ, 1939; CO Trenton, Ont., 1940; AOC, 2 Training Comd, BCATP, 1942–44; AOC, NW Air Comd, Canada, 1944–47, retd. Comdr, Legion of Merit (USA), 1945. Mem., Canada's Aviation Hall of Fame, 1980. *Address*: 581 Avenue Road, Toronto, Ont M4V 2K4, Canada.

LAWRENCE, Timothy; Senior Partner, Claude Hornby & Cox, Solicitors, since 1977; a Recorder of the Crown Court, since 1983; *b* 29 April 1942; *s* of A. Whiteman Lawrence and Phyllis G. Lawrence (*née* Lloyd-Jones). *Educ*: Bedford School. Admitted Solicitor, 1967; with Solicitor's Dept, New Scotland Yard, 1967–70; Partner with Claude Hornby & Cox, Solicitors, 1970–. An Asst Recorder, 1980. Pres., London Criminal Courts Solicitors' Assoc., 1984–86 (Sec., 1974–84); Chm., No 14 Area, Regional Duty Solicitors Cttee, 1984–; Member: No 13 Area, Legal Aid Cttee, 1983–; Law Society's Criminal Law Cttee, 1980–; Council, Westminster Law Soc., 1979–82; Judicial Studies Bd, 1984–; British Academy of Forensic Sciences, 1972–. Legal Assessor: Professions Supplementary to Medicine, 1976–; Insurance Brokers Registration Council, 1983–. Mem., Chelsea Old Church PCC, 1981–84. *Publications*: various articles in legal jls. *Recreations*: walking, wine, travel. *Address*: 8 Slaidburn Street, SW10 0JP; Hill Cottage, Great Walsingham, Norfolk. *Clubs*: Savile, Hurlingham.

LAWRENCE, (Walter Nicholas) Murray; a Deputy Chairman of Lloyd's, 1982, 1984, 1985, 1986 (Member: Committee of Lloyd's, 1979–82; Council of Lloyd's, 1984, 1985, 1986); Senior Partner, Murray Lawrence & Partners, since 1985; *b* 8 Feb. 1935; *s* of Henry Walter Neville Lawrence and Sarah Schuyler Lawrence (*née* Butler); *m* 1961, Sally Louise O'Dwyer; two *d*. *Educ*: Winchester Coll.; Trinity Coll., Oxford (BA, MA). C. T. Bowring & Co. (Ins.) Ltd, 1957–62; Asst Underwriter, H. Bowring & Others, 1962–70, Underwriter, 1970–84; Director: C. T. Bowring (Underwriting Agencies), 1973–84; C. T. Bowring & Co. Ltd, 1976–84; Chm., Fairway (Underwriting Agencies), 1979–85. Mem., Lloyd's Underwriters Non-Marine Assoc., 1970–84 (Dep. Chm., 1977; Chm., 1978). *Recreations*: golf, opera, travelling. *Clubs*: Boodle's, MCC; Royal & Ancient (St Andrews), Woking, Swinley, Royal St George's (Sandwich), Rye.

LAWRENCE, Sir William, 4th Bt, *cr* 1867; Sales Consultant, Long and Hambly Ltd (retired); Senior Executive, Wilmot Breeden, Ltd (retired); Major East Surrey Regiment; *b* 14 July 1913; *er s* of Sir William Matthew Trevor Lawrence, 3rd Bt, and Iris Eyre (*d* 1955), *y d* of late Brig.-Gen. E. M. S. Crabbe, CB; *S* father, 1934; *m* 1940, Zoë (marr. diss., 1945), *yr d* of H. S. S. Pether, Stowford, Headington, Oxford; *m* 1945, Pamela, *yr d* of J. E. Gordon, Beechbank, Bromborough, Cheshire; one *s* two *d*. *Educ*: Bradfield Coll. FRHS. Pres., W Warwickshire Scout Council; Vice-Pres., Stratford on Avon and S Warwickshire Cons. Assoc. *Recreation*: gardening. *Heir*: *s* William Fettiplace Lawrence, *b* 23 Aug. 1954. *Address*: The Knoll, Walcote, near Alcester, Warwicks. *T*: Great Alne 303.

LAWRENCE-JONES, Sir Christopher, 6th Bt *cr* 1831; Chief Medical Officer, Imperial Chemical Industries Ltd, Millbank, SW1, since 1985; Chairman, Medichem, since 1986; *b* 19 Jan. 1940; *S* uncle, 1969; *m* 1967, Gail Pittar, Auckland, NZ; two *s*. *Educ*: Sherborne; Gonville and Caius Coll., Cambridge; St Thomas' Hospital. MA Cantab 1964; MB, BChir Cantab 1964; DIH Eng. 1968. MFOM 1979. Medical adviser to various orgns, 1967–. *Recreation*: cruising under sail. *Heir*: *s* Mark Christopher Lawrence-Jones, *b* 28 Dec. 1968. *Club*: Royal Cruising.

LAWRENCE-WILSON, Harry Lawrence; Under-Secretary, Procurement Executive, Ministry of Defence, 1971–72; *b* 18 March 1920; *s* of late H. B. Wilson and of Mrs May Wilson, Biddenden, Kent; *m* 1945, Janet Mary Gillespie; two *s* one *d*. *Educ*: Cranbrook Sch.; Worcester Coll., Oxford. Served Indian Army, 1940–46. Colonial Office, 1946–47; MoD, 1947–66; Cabinet Office, 1967–69. Asst Principal, 1947; Principal, 1948; Assistant Secretary, 1956; Under-Secretary, 1961; Under-Secretary: Min. of Technology, 1969–70; DTI, 1970–71; CSD, 1971. *Address*: 22 Marlborough Crescent, Riverhead, Sevenoaks, Kent.

LAWRENSON, Prof. Peter John, DSc; FRS 1982; FEng, FIEE, FIEEE; Professor of Electrical Engineering, Leeds University, since 1966 (Head, Department of Electrical and Electronic Engineering, 1974–84); Director and Chairman, Switched Reluctance Drives Ltd, since 1981; *b* 12 March 1933; *s* of John Lawrenson and Emily (*née* Houghton); *m* 1958, Shirley Hannah Foster; one *s* three *d*. *Educ*: Prescot Grammar Sch.; Manchester Univ. (BSc, MSc; DSc 1971). FEng 1980; FIEE 1974; FIEEE 1975. Duddell Scholar, IEE, 1951–54; Res. Engr, Associated Electrical Industries, 1956–61; Univ. of Leeds: Lectr, 1961–65; Reader, 1965–66; Chm., Jt Faculties of Science and Applied Science, 1978–80; Chm., Shadow Faculty of Engrg, 1981. Science Research Council (now SERC): Mem., Electrical and Systems Cttee, 1971–; Chm., Electrical Engrg Sub-Cttee, 1981–84; Mem., Machines and Power Cttee, 1981–84; Mem., Engrg Bd, 1984–. Instn of Electrical Engineers: Mem. Council, 1966–69 and 1981–; Chm., Accreditation Cttee, 1979–83; Mem., Power Divisional Bd, 1981– (Chm., 1985–86). Mem. of cttees, Engrg Council, 1983–. IEE Awards: Premia-Crompton, 1957 and 1967; John Hopkinson, 1965; The Instn, 1981. James Alfred Ewing Medal, ICE in conjunction with Pres., Royal Soc., 1983; Royal Soc. Esso Energy Award, 1985. *Publications*: (with K. J. Binns) Analysis and Computation of Electromagnetic Field Problems, 1963, 2nd edn 1973; (with M. R. Harris and J. M. Stephenson) Per Unit Systems, 1970; papers and patents in areas of electromagnetism, electromechanics and control. *Recreations*: lawn tennis, squash, chess, bridge, jewelry making. *Address*: Spen Watch, 318 Spen Lane, Leeds LS16 5BA. *T*: Leeds 755849.

LAWREY, Keith, JP; Dean, Faculty of Business and Management, Harrow College of Higher Education, since 1984; *b* 21 Aug. 1940; *s* of George William Bishop Lawrey and Edna Muriel (*née* Gass); *m* 1969, Helen Jane Marriott; two *s* two *d*. *Educ*: Colfe's Sch.; Birkbeck Coll., Univ. of London (MSc Econ; LLB). Barrister-at-Law; called to Bar, Gray's Inn, 1972. Education Officer, Plastics and Rubber Inst., 1960–68; Lectr and Sen. Lectr, Bucks Coll. of Higher Educn, 1968–74; Head of Dept of Business Studies, Mid-Kent Coll. of Higher and Further Educn, 1974–78; Sec.-Gen., Library Assoc., 1978–84. F Coll P; FCIS. Mem., Worshipful Co. of Chartered Secretaries and Administrators. JP Inner London, 1974. *Publications*: papers in Jl, Coll. of Preceptors, Jl Assoc. of Law Teachers, Trans and Jl of Plastics Inst. *Recreations*: preaching, sailing, swimming, theatre, gardening. *Clubs*: Old Colfeians; Dell Quay Sailing.

LAWS, Courtney Alexander, OD 1978; Director, Brixton Neighbourhood Community Association, since 1971; *b* Morant Bay, St Thomas, Jamaica, 16 June 1934; *s* of Ezekiel Laws and Agatha Laws; *m* 1955, Wilhel, (Rubie), Brown, JP; one *s* two *d*. *Educ*: Morant Bay Elem. Sch.; Jones Pen and Rollington Town Elem. Sch.; Lincoln Coll.; Nat. Coll. for Youth Workers, Leicester; Cranfield Coll., Bedford. Rep., Works Cttee, Peak Freans Biscuit Co., 1960–69; Shop Steward, TGWU, 1960–70. Member: Lambeth Council for Community Relations, 1964–; Consortium of Ethnic Minorities, Lambeth, 1978–; W Indian Standing Conf., 1959–; Campaign against Racial Discrimination, 1960–; NCCI, 1960–; Commn for Racial Equality, 1977–80; Central Cttee, British Caribbean Assoc. (Exec. Mem.), 1960–; Assoc. of Jamaicans (Founder Mem.), 1965; Geneva and Somerleyton Community Assoc., 1966–; Consultative Cttee, ILEA, Lambeth, 1975–; Consultative Council, City and E London Coll., 1975–; South Eastern Gas Consumers' Council, 1980–; Governor, Brixton Coll. of Further and Higher Educn, 1970–; Member: W Indian Sen. Citizens' Assoc. (Pres.), 1973–; St John's Interracial Club, 1958–; Brixton United Cricket Club, 1968– (Pres.); Brixton Domino Club (Chm.); Oasis Sports and Social Club, 1969–. Officer, Order of Distinction, Jamaica, 1978. *Recreations*: reading, music. *Address*: 164 Croxted Road, West Dulwich, SE21. *T*: 01-761 2614.

LAWS, Frederick Geoffrey; Vice-Chairman, Commission for Local Administration in England, since 1984; *b* Blackpool, 1 Aug. 1928; *s* of Frederick and Annetta Laws; *m* 1955, Beryl Holt; two *d*. *Educ*: Arnold School; Manchester Univ.; London Univ. (LLB); solicitor 1952. Asst Solicitor, Blackpool Corp., 1952–54, Bournemouth Corp., 1954–59; Southend-on-Sea Corporation: Asst Sol., 1959–62; Dep. Town Clerk and Clerk of the Peace, 1962–71; Town Clerk, 1971–74; Chief Exec., Southend-on-Sea Borough Council, 1974–84. Pres., Southend-on-Sea Law Soc., 1981. Hon. Freeman, Southend-on-Sea Borough Council, 1985. *Recreations*: Rugby football, golf. *Address*: 270 Maplin Way North, Southend-on-Sea, Essex. *T*: Southend 587459. *Clubs*: Athenæum; Thorpe Hall Golf (Captain, 1983); Southend Rugby Football.

LAWS, John Grant McKenzie; First Junior Treasury Counsel, Common Law, since 1984; a Recorder, since 1985; *b* 10 May 1945; *s* of late Dr Frederic Laws and Dr Margaret Ross Laws, *d* of Prof. John Grant McKenzie; *m* 1973, Sophie Susan Sydenham Cole Marshall, BLitt, MA; one *d*. *Educ*: Durham Cathedral Choir Sch.; Durham Sch. (King's Scholar); Exeter Coll., Oxford (Sen. Open Classical Scholar; BA 1967, Hon. Sch. of Lit. Hum. 1st Cl.; MA 1976). Called to the Bar, Inner Temple, 1970, Bencher, 1985; practice at Common Law Bar, 1971–; Asst Recorder, 1983–85. *Publications*: (contrib.) Dict. of Medical Ethics, 1977; reviews for Theology, Law & Justice. *Recreations*: Greece, living in London, gardening, philosophy, painting. *Address*: 2 Garden Court, Temple, EC4Y 9BL; 19 Longmoore Street, SW1. *Club*: United Oxford & Cambridge University.

LAWS, Dr John William, CBE 1982; FRCP; FRCR; consultant diagnostic radiologist; Director of Radiology, King's College Hospital, and Director of Radiological Studies, King's College Hospital Medical School, 1967–86; *b* 25 Oct. 1921; *s* of Robert Montgomery Laws and Lucy Ibbotson; *m* 1945, Pamela King, MRCS, LRCP (*d* 1985); one *s* one *d*; *m* 1986, Dr Diana Brinkley (*née* Rawlence), FRCR. *Educ*: The Leys Sch., Cambridge; Sheffield Univ. Med. Sch. MB ChB 1944; DMRD 1952; MRCP 1951; FRCR (FFR 1955); FRCP 1967. Nat. service, 1947–49 (Captain RAMC). House Physician and House Surg., Royal Hosp., Sheffield, 1944–45; Res. Surgical Officer, Salisbury Gen. Infirmary, 1945–47; Med. Registrar, 1949–51, Radiology Registrar and Sen. Registrar, 1951–55, United Sheffield Hosps; Consultant Radiologist, Dep. Dir, Hammersmith Hosp., and Hon. Lectr, RPMS, 1955–67. Consultant Civilian Advr to Army, 1976–86; Med. Dir, King's Centre for Assessment of Radiol Equipment, 1979–86. Chm., Radiol Equipment Sub-Cttee, DHSS, 1972–81; Member: Central Adv. Cttee on Hosp. Med. Records, DHSS, 1969–74; Radiol Adv. Cttee, DHSS, 1972–86; Consultant Advr in Radiol., DHSS, 1982–86. Chm., British Delegn, XV Internat. Congress of Radiol., 1981. Royal College (formerly Faculty) of Radiologists: Mem. Fellowship Bd, 1966–71; Hon. Sec., 1974–75; Registrar, 1975–76; Warden of Fellowship, 1976–80; Pres., 1980–83; Knox Lectr, 1984. Mem. Council, RCS, 1981–84. Vis Prof. and Lectr at academic instns and congresses worldwide. Member Editorial Board: Clin. Radiol., 1960–63; Gut, 1970–74; Gastrointestinal Radiol., 1975–85; Asst, later Hon., Editor, British Jl of Radiol., 1961–71. Hon. FACR 1973; Hon. FFR RCSI 1975; Hon. FRACR 1979. Barclay Prize, British Inst. of Radiol., 1964. *Publications*: numerous papers and pubns on various aspects of clinical radiology, particularly gastrointestinal and hepatic radiology and the radiology of pulmonary disease, in medical journals and books. *Recreations*: listening to music, golf. *Address*: 5 Frank Dixon Way, Dulwich, SE21 7BB. *T*: 01-693 4815.

LAWS, Richard Maitland, CBE 1983; PhD; FRS 1980; Director, British Antarctic Survey, 1973–April 1987; Master, St Edmund's House, Cambridge, since 1985; *b* 23 April 1926; *s* of Percy Malcolm Laws and Florence May (*née* Heslop); *m* 1954, Maureen Isobel Winifred (*née* Holmes); three *s*. *Educ*: Dame Allan's Sch., Newcastle-on-Tyne; St Catharine's Coll., Cambridge (Open Scholar, 1944; Res. Scholar, 1952–53; Hon. Fellow, 1982). BA Cantab 1947, MA 1952, PhD 1953; FInstBiol 1973. Biologist and Base Leader, Falkland Is Dependencies Survey, 1947–53; Biologist and Whaling Inspector, F/F Balaena, 1953–54; Principal Sci. Officer, Nat. Inst. of Oceanography, 1954–61; Dir, Nuffield Unit of Tropical Animal Ecology, Uganda, 1961–67; Dir, Tsavo Research Project, Kenya, 1967–68; Smuts Meml Fund Fellowship, 1968–69; Leverhulme Research Fellowship, 1969; Head, Life Sciences Div., British Antarctic Survey, 1969–73. Dir, NERC Sea Mammal Res. Unit, 1977–; Scientific Committee for Antarctic Research: Convener, gp of specialists on seals, 1972–; Chm., Biology Working Gp, 1980–86; UK Delegate, 1984–. Zool Soc. of London: Mem. Council, 1982–; Vice-Pres., 1983–84; Sec., 1984–. Vice-Pres., Inst. Biol., 1984–85. 36th annual Lectr, CIBA Foundn, 1984. Bruce Medal, RSE, 1954; Scientific Medal, Zool Soc. London, 1965; Polar Medal, 1976. *Publications*: (with I. S. C. Parker and R. C. B. Johnstone) Elephants and their Habitats, 1975; (ed) Scientific Research in Antarctica, 1977; (ed) Antarctic Ecology, 1984; (co-ed) Antarctic Nutrient Cycles and Food Webs, 1985; papers in biol jls. *Recreations*: walking, photography, painting. *Address*: (until April 1987) British Antarctic Survey, NERC, Madingley Road, Cambridge CB3 0ET. *T*: Cambridge 61188; St Edmund's House, Cambridge CB3 0BN. *T*: Cambridge 350398; 3 The Footpath, Coton, Cambridge CB3 7PX. *T*: Madingley 210567.

LAWSON, family name of **Baron Burnham.**

LAWSON, His Honour Charles, QC 1961; a Circuit Judge, Central Criminal Court, 1972–82; *b* 23 Feb. 1916; 2nd *s* of late Barnet Lawson, London; *m* 1943, Olga Daphne Kay; three *d*. *Educ*: Grocers' Company Sch.; University College, London. LLB 1937. Served War of 1939–45: in Army, 1940–46; Major, Royal Artillery. Recorder: Burton-upon-Trent, 1965–68; Gloucester, 1968–71. Bencher, Inner Temple, 1968. *Recreations*: golf, music. *Address*: Mayes Green Cottage, Ockley, Surrey RH5 5PN.

LAWSON, Sir Christopher (Donald), Kt 1984; management consultant; Director of Special Services, Conservative and Unionist Party; *b* 31 Oct. 1922; *s* of James Lawson and Ellen de Verrine; *m* 1945, Marjorie Bristow; two *s* one *d*. *Educ*: Magdalen Coll., Oxford. Served RAF, 1941–49: Pilot, Sqdn Leader. Thomas Hedley (Proctor and Gamble), 1949–57; Cooper McDougal Robertson, 1958–61; Managing Dir, TMC, 1961–63; Director: Mars Ltd, 1965–81; Mars Inc., USA, 1975–82; Pres., Mars Snackmaster, USA, 1977–82; Chm. and Man. Dir, Goodblue Ltd, 1981–; Chm., Spearhead Ltd, 1983–; Dir, Communications Centre, 1984–. Dir of Marketing, Cons. and Unionist Party, 1982–83. *Recreations*: collecting antiques and new artists' work; all sport, particularly golf, cricket, hockey. *Address*: Church Cottage, Great Witcombe, Glos GL3 4TT. *Clubs*: Royal Air Force, Carlton, MCC; Lillybrook Golf (Cheltenham); Doublegate Country (Ga, USA).

LAWSON, Prof. Donald Douglas; Professor of Veterinary Surgery, University of Glasgow, 1974–86; *b* 25 May 1924; *s* of Alexander Lawson and Jessie Macnaughton; *m* 1949, Barbara Ness; two *s* two *d*. *Educ*: Whitehill Sch., Glasgow; Glasgow Veterinary

Coll. MRCVS, BSc, DVR. Asst in Veterinary Practice, 1946–47; Asst, Surgery Dept, Glasgow Vet. Coll., 1947–49; Glasgow Univ.: Lectr, Vet. Surgery, 1949–57; Sen. Lectr, 1957–66; Reader, 1966–71; Titular Prof., 1971–74. *Publications:* many articles in Veterinary Record and Jl of Small Animal Practice. *Recreations:* gardening, motoring. *Address:* Burnbrae, Balfron, Glasgow G63 0NY. *T:* Balfron 40232.

LAWSON, Rear-Adm. Frederick Charles William, CB 1971; DSC 1942 and Bar, 1945; Chief Executive, Royal Dockyards, Ministry of Defence, 1972–75; *b* 20 April 1917; *s* of M. L. Lawson, formerly of Public Works Dept, Punjab, India; *m* 1945, Dorothy (*née* Norman) (*d* 1986), Eastbourne; one *s* three *d*. *Educ:* Eastbourne Coll.; RNEC. Joined RN, 1935; specialised in engrg: Cmdr 1949; Captain 1960; Cdre Supt Singapore, 1965–69; Rear-Adm. 1969; Flag Officer, Medway and Adm. Supt, HM Dockyard, Chatham, 1969–71, retired. *Recreation:* golf. *Address:* Weaverhoult, Woolley Street, Bradford-on-Avon, Wilts.

LAWSON, Prof. Gerald Hartley; Professor of Business Finance, Manchester Business School, University of Manchester, since 1969; Director (non-executive), Dietsmann (UK) Ltd, since 1984; financial and economic consultant; *b* 6 July 1933; of English parents; *m* 1957, Helga Elisabeth Anna Heine; three *s*. *Educ:* King's Coll., Univ. of Durham. BA (Econ), MA (Econ); MBA Manchester; FCCA. Accountant in industry, 1957–59; Lectr in Accountancy and Applied Economics, Univ. of Sheffield, 1959–66; Prof. of Business Studies, Univ. of Liverpool, 1966–69. Prof., Univ. of Augsburg, Germany, 1971–72; Prof., Univ. of Texas, 1977, 1981; Prof., Ruhr Univ., Bochum, 1980; British Council Scholar, Hochschule für Welthandel, Vienna, 1967, and Univ. of Louvain, 1978. *Publications:* (with D. W. Windle): Tables for Discounted Cash Flow, etc, Calculations, 1965 (5th repr. 1978); Capital Budgeting in the Corporation Tax Regime, 1967; many articles and translations. *Recreations:* cricket, skiing. *Address:* Manchester Business School, Booth Street West, Manchester M15 6PB. *T:* 061–273 8228. *Club:* Manchester Business School.

LAWSON, Hugh McDowall, BScEng London; CEng, FICE; Director of Leisure Services, Nottingham City Council, 1973–76; *b* Leeds, 13 Feb. 1912; *s* of late John Lawson, Pharmaceutical Chemist; *m* 1937, Dorothy (*d* 1982), *d* of late Rev. T. H. Mallinson, BA; two *s*. *Educ:* Nottingham High Sch.; University Coll., Nottingham. Served in Royal Engineers, 1940–44. MP (Common Wealth) Skipton Div. of Yorks, 1944–45. Contested (Common Wealth) Harrow West Div., 1945; (Lab) Rushcliffe Div., 1950; (Lab) King's Lynn Div., 1955; joined SDP, 1981. Dep. City Engr, Nottingham, 1948–73. Mem. Council, ICE, 1972–75. *Address:* 68 Marshall Hill Drive, Mapperley, Nottingham NG3 6FS. *T:* 605241.

LAWSON, Air Vice-Marshal Ian Douglas Napier, CB 1965; CBE 1961; DFC 1941, Bar 1943; AE 1945; RAF, retired; *b* 11 Nov. 1917; *y s* of late J. L. Lawson and Ethel Mary Lawson (*née* Ludgate); *m* 1945, Dorothy Joyce Graham Nash; one *s* one *d*. *Educ:* Brondesbury Coll.; Polytechnic, Regent Street. Aircraft Industry, 1934–39. Joined RAFVR 1938. Served War of 1939–45 (despatches thrice): Bomber Comd, 1940–41; Middle East Comd, 1941–45. Permanent Commission, 1945. Bomber Comd, 1945–46; Staff Coll., 1946; Air Ministry, 1946–49; Transport Comd, 1949–50; Middle East Comd, 1950–52; JSSC, 1953; Ministry of Defence, 1953–56; Flying Coll., Manby, 1956–57; Transport Comd, 1957–62; Air Forces Middle East, 1962–64; Commandant, RAF Coll., Cranwell, 1964–67; Asst Chief Adviser (Personnel and Logistics), MoD, 1967–69. Joined BAC, 1969, Chief Sales Exec., Weybridge, Bristol Div., 1974–79; Gen. Marketing Manager (civil), BAe, 1979–81; non-exec. Dir, Glos Air (Holdings) Ltd, 1981–82. FBIM. US Legion of Merit. *Recreations:* gardening, motor sport. *Address:* Grove House, Lacock, Wilts. *T:* Lacock 307. *Club:* Royal Air Force.

LAWSON, James Robert; Regional Nursing Officer, Mersey, since 1985; *b* 29 Dec. 1939; *s* of James and Grace Lawson; *m* 1962, Jean; two *d*. *Educ:* Keswick High School; Royal Albert Hosp. (Registered Nurse of Mentally Handicapped); Cumberland Infirmary (Registered Gen. Nurse). Chief Nurse, 1972; Area Nurse, Personnel, 1974; Divl Nursing Officer, 1976; District Nursing Officer, 1982–85. *Recreations:* fellwalking, caravaning, active sports. *Address:* Browside Cottage, Tanhouse Lane, Burtonwood, Warrington, Cheshire. *T:* Warrington 32735.

LAWSON, John Alexander Reid, OBE 1979; FRCGP; General Medical Practitioner, since 1948; Regional Adviser in General Practice, Tayside Region, 1972–82; *b* 30 Aug. 1920; *s* of Thomas Reid Lawson and Helen Scrimgour Lawson; *m* 1944, Pat Kirk; two *s* two *d*. *Educ:* High Sch. of Dundee; Univ. of St Andrews (MB, ChB). RAMC, 1944–47 (Major). Surgical Registrar, Royal Infirmary, Dundee, 1947–48. Royal College of General Practitioners: Mem., 1952; Fellow, 1967; Chm. Council, 1973–76; Pres., 1982–85. Mem. Cttee of Enquiry into Competence to Practice, 1974–76; Chairman: Jt Cttee on Postgraduate Training for General Practice, 1975–78; Armed Service Gen. Practice Approval Bd, 1979–. *Recreations:* shooting, fishing, golf, gardening. *Address:* The Ridges, 458 Perth Road, Dundee. *T:* Dundee 67408. *Clubs:* New (Edinburgh); Royal and Ancient Golf (St Andrews).

LAWSON, Col Sir John Charles Arthur Digby, 3rd Bt, *cr* 1900; DSO 1943; MC 1940; Lieutenant-Colonel 11th Hussars, retired; former Chairman, Fairbairn Lawson Ltd, Leeds; *b* 24 Oct. 1912; *e s* of Sir Digby Lawson, Bt, TD, JP, and late Mrs Gerald Wallis (*née* Iris Mary Fitzgerald); *S* father 1959; *m* 1st, 1945, Rose (marr. diss., 1950; she *d* 1972), *widow* of Pilot Officer William Fiske, RAF, and *er d* of late D. C. Bingham and late Lady Rosabelle Brand; 2nd, 1954, Tresilla Ann Elinor (de Pret Roose) (*d* 1985), *d* of late Major E. Buller Leyborne Popham, MC; one *s*. *Educ:* Stowe; RMC, Sandhurst; commissioned 11th Hussars (PAO), 1933; Palestine, 1936–37; Transjordan Frontier Force, 1938; Western Desert, 1940–43 (despatches twice, MC, DSO); Armoured Adviser to Gen. Patton, N Africa, 1943; Staff Coll., 1943; US Marines Staff Course, 1944; Special Liaison Officer to Gen. Montgomery, NW Europe, 1944; Comd Inns of Court Regt, 1945–47; retired, 1947. Colonel, 11th Hussars (PAO), 1965–69; Col, The Royal Hussars (PWO), 1969–73. Legion of Merit (US). *Heir:* *s* Charles John Patrick Lawson [*b* 19 May 1959. *Educ:* Harrow; Royal Agricl Coll., Cirencester]. *Address:* Calle Castilla 2, Sotogrande (Cadiz), Spain. *T:* 956792474. *Clubs:* Army and Navy, MCC.

LAWSON, John David, ScD; FRS 1983; Deputy Chief Scientific Officer, Rutherford Appleton Laboratory, Science and Engineering Research Council, Chilton, Oxon, since 1978; *b* 4 April 1923; *s* of Ronald L. Lawson and Ruth (*née* Houseman); *m* 1949, Kathleen (*née* Wyllie); two *s* one *d*. *Educ:* Wolverhampton Grammar Sch.; St John's Coll., Cambridge (BA, ScD). FInstP. TRE Malvern, Aerials group, 1943; AERE Malvern Br., Accelerator gp, 1947; AERE Harwell, Gen. Physics Div., 1951–62; Microwave Laboratory, Stanford, USA, 1959–60; Rutherford Laboratory (later Rutherford Appleton Laboratory), Applied Phys. Div., and later Technology Div., 1962–, except, Vis. Prof., Dept of Physics and Astronomy, Univ. of Maryland, USA, 1971; Culham Lab., Technology Div., 1975–76. *Publications:* The Physics of Charged Particle Beams, 1977; papers on various topics in applied physics in several jls. *Recreations:* travel, mountain walking, collecting old books. *Address:* 7 Clifton Drive, Abingdon, Oxon OX14 1ET. *T:* Abingdon 21516.

LAWSON, Hon. Sir Neil, Kt 1971; Judge of High Court of Justice, Queen's Bench Division, 1971–83; *b* 8 April 1908; *s* of late Robb Lawson and Edith Marion Lawson (*née* Usherwood); *m* 1933, Gweneth Clare (*née* Wilby); one *s* one *d*. Called to Bar, Inner Temple, 1929; QC 1955; Recorder of Folkestone, 1962–71; a Law Commissioner, 1965–71. RAFVR, 1940–45. Hon. Fellow, LSE, 1974. Foreign decorations: DK (Dato' Peduka Kerubat), 1959, DSN (Dato' Setia Negara), 1962, PSMB (Dato' Sri Mahota), 1969, Brunei. *Recreations:* literature, music, the country. *Address:* 30a Heath Drive, Hampstead, NW3.

LAWSON, Rt. Hon. Nigel, PC 1981; MP (C) Blaby, Leicestershire, since Feb. 1974; Chancellor of the Exchequer, since 1983; *b* 11 March 1932; *o s* of late Ralph Lawson and of Joan Elisabeth Lawson (*née* Davis); *m* 1st, 1955 Vanessa Salmon (marr. diss. 1980; she *d* 1985); one *s* three *d*; 2nd, 1980, Thérèse Mary Maclear; one *s* one *d*. *Educ:* Westminster; Christ Church, Oxford (Scholar). 1st class hons PPE, 1954. Served with Royal Navy (Sub-Lt RNVR), 1954–56. Mem. Editorial Staff, Financial Times, 1956–60; City Editor, Sunday Telegraph, 1961–63; Special Assistant to Prime Minister (Sir Alec Douglas-Home), 1963–64; Financial Times columnist and BBC broadcaster, 1965; Editor of the Spectator, 1966–70; regular contributor to: Sunday Times and Evening Standard, 1970–71; The Times, 1971–72; Fellow, Nuffield Coll., Oxford, 1972–73; Special Pol Advr, Cons. Party HQ, 1973–74. Contested (C) Eton and Slough, 1970. An Opposition Whip, 1976–77; an Opposition Spokesman on Treasury and Economic Affairs, 1977–79; Financial Sec. to the Treasury, 1979–81; Sec. of State for Energy, 1981–83. Chm., Coningsby Club, 1963–64. Vice-Chm., Cons. Political Centre Nat. Adv. Cttee, 1972–75. *Publications:* (jtly) Britain and Canada, 1976; (with Jock Bruce-Gardyne) The Power Game, 1976; (jtly) The Coming Confrontation, 1978; The New Conservatism (pamphlet), 1980. *Address:* The Old Rectory, Stoney Stanton, Leics; 11 Downing Street, SW1. *Clubs:* Garrick, Pratt's, Political Economy.

LAWSON, Gen. Sir Richard (George), KCB 1980; DSO 1962; OBE 1968; Commander-in-Chief, Allied Forces Northern Europe, 1982–86; *b* 24 Nov. 1927; *s* of John Lawson and Florence Rebecca Lawson; *m* 1956, Ingrid Lawson; one *s*. *Educ:* St Alban's Sch.; Birmingham Univ. CO, Independent Squadron, RTR (Berlin), 1963–64; GSO2 MoD, 1965–66; CofS, South Arabian Army, 1967; CO, 5th RTR, 1968–69; Comdr, 20th Armoured Bde, 1972–73; Asst Military Deputy to Head of Defence Sales, 1975–77; GOC 1st Armoured Div., 1977–79; GOC Northern Ireland, 1980–82. Col Comdt, RTR, 1980–82. Leopold Cross (Belgium), 1963; Knight Commander, Order of St Sylvester (Vatican), 1964. *Publications:* Strange Soldiering, 1963; All the Queen's Men, 1967; Strictly Personal, 1972. *Address:* c/o Royal Bank of Scotland, Kirkland House, SW1. *Club:* Army and Navy.

LAWSON, Richard Henry; Deputy Chairman: Greenwell Montagu & Co.; The Stock Exchange, since 1985; *b* 16 Feb. 1932; *s* of Sir Henry Brailsford Lawson, MC, and of Lady (Mona) Lawson; *m* 1958, Janet Elizabeth Govier; three *s* (one *d* decd). *Educ:* Lancing College. ICI, 1952–54; W. Greenwell & Co. (now Greenwell Montagu & Co.), 1954–; Jt Sen. Partner, 1980. *Recreations:* golf, tennis, walking, birdwatching, skiing. *Address:* Cherry Hill, Burrows Lane, Gomshall, Guildford, Surrey GU5 9QE. *Club:* Naval and Military.

LAWSON, Sonia, ARA 1982; ARWS 1985; artist; Visiting Lecturer at Art Colleges in UK, since 1960; *b* 2 June 1934; *d* of Frederick Lawson and Muriel (*née* Metcalfe), artists; *m* 1969, C. W. Congo; one *d*. *Educ:* Southwick Girls' Sch.; Doncaster Sch. of Art; Royal Coll. of Art (ARCA 1st cl.). Travelling Scholarship, France, 1960. 10 Solo exhibns, London and provinces, 1960–79. Retrospective exhibn, Shrines of Life, toured 1982–83, Sheffield (Mappin), Hull (Ferens), Bradford (Cartwright), Leicester Poly, Milton Keynes Art Gallery. Mixed exhibns, 1960–: Arts Council of GB Touring Exhibn; Tolly Cobbold National Exhibn; Hayward Annual; Soho Building, Soho, NY; Fruitmarket Gall., Edinburgh; Royal Acad. Annual; John Moores, Liverpool; London Gp. Work in public collections: Arts Council of GB; Graves Art Gall., Sheffield; Huddersfield Art Gall.; Carlisle, Belfast, Middlesbrough, Dewsbury, and Harrogate Art Galls; Imperial War Mus.; Min. of Educn; Min. of Works; Leeds Univ.; Open Univ.; Cranfield Inst. of Technol.; RCA; St Peter's Hall, Oxford; Nuffield Foundn; private collections in UK, Germany, Australia, USA.BBC TV ,Monitor, 1960, John Schlesinger's doc. "Private View". Rowney Prize, Royal Acad., 1984; Gainsborough House Drawing Prize, Eastern Arts, 1984. *Recreation:* denizen watching. *Address:* c/o Royal Academy of Arts, Burlington House, Piccadilly, W1V 0DS. *T:* 01–734 9052; (studios): Leighton Buzzard 374156; Wensleydale 22520. *Club:* Chelsea Arts.

LAWSON, Sir William (Howard), 5th Bt *cr* 1841; DL; *b* 15 July 1907; *s* of Sir Henry Joseph Lawson, 3rd Bt, and Ursula Mary (*d* 1960), *o c* of Philip John Canning Howard, Corby Castle, Carlisle; *S* brother, 1975; *m* 1933, Joan Eleanor, *d* of late Arthur Cowie Stamer, CBE; three *s* one *d*. *Educ:* Ampleforth College. DL Cumberland, 1963–84. *Recreations:* field sports. *Heir:* *s* John Philip Howard [*b* 6 June 1934; assumed surname and arms of Howard by Royal Licence, 1962; *m* 1960, Jean Veronica, *d* of late Col John Evelyn Marsh, DSO, OBE; two *s* one *d*]. *Address:* Wood House, Warwick Bridge, Carlisle. *T:* Wetheral 60330.

LAWSON DICK, Clare, OBE 1975; BBC Controller Radio 4, 1975–76; *b* 13 Oct. 1913; *d* of late John Lawson Dick, MD, FRCS, and Winifred Lawson Dick (*née* Duke). *Educ:* Channing Sch., Highgate; King's Coll., London (Dip. Journalism). Joined BBC, 1935. *Recreations:* enjoying the amenities of London; escaping from London into the country. *Address:* Flat 8, 92 Elm Park Gardens, SW10. *T:* 01–352 8395.

LAWSON JOHNSTON, family name of **Baron Luke.**

LAWSON JOHNSTON, Hon. Hugh de Beauchamp, TD 1951; DL; *b* 7 April 1914; *yr s* of 1st Baron Luke of Pavenham, KBE, and *b* of 2nd Baron Luke, *qv*; *m* 1946, Audrey Warren, *d* of late Colonel F. Warren Pearl and late Mrs A. L. Pearl; three *d*. *Educ:* Eton; Chillon Coll.; Corpus Christi, Cambridge. BA 1934, MA (Cantab), 1938. With Bovril Ltd, 1935–71, finally as Chm. Territorial Service with 5th Bn Beds and Herts Regt, 1935–; Captain, 1939, and throughout War. Chm., Tribune Investment Trust Ltd, 1951–86; Chm., Pitman Ltd, 1973–81. Chm. of Cttees, United Soc. for Christian Literature, 1949–82. High Sheriff of Bedfordshire, 1961–62; DL Beds, 1964. *Recreations:* walking, gardening, photography. *Address:* Flat 1, 28 Lennox Gardens, SW1. *T:* 01–584 1446; Woodleys Farm House, Melchbourne, Bedfordshire. *T:* Riseley 282.

LAWSON-TANCRED, Sir Henry, 10th Bt, *cr* 1662; JP; *b* 12 Feb. 1924; *e surv. s* of Major Sir Thomas Lawson-Tancred, 9th Bt, and Margery Elinor (*d* 1961), *d* of late A. S. Lawson, Aldborough Manor; *S* father, 1945; *m* 1st, 1950, Jean Veronica (*d* 1970), 4th and *y d* of late G. R. Foster, Stockeld Park, Wetherby, Yorks; five *s* one *d*; 2nd, 1978, Mrs Susan Drummond, *d* of Sir Kenelm Cayley, 10th Bt. *Educ:* Stowe; Jesus Coll., Cambridge. Served as Pilot in RAFVR, 1942–46. JP West Riding, 1967. *Heir:* *s* Andrew Peter Lawson-Tancred, *b* 18 Feb. 1952. *Address:* Aldborough Manor, Boroughbridge, Yorks YO5 9EP. *T:* Boroughbridge 2716.

LAWTHER, Prof. Patrick Joseph, CBE 1978; DSc; FRCP; Professor of Environmental and Preventive Medicine, University of London, at St Bartholomew's Hospital Medical College, 1968–81, also at London Hospital Medical College, 1976–81, now Professor Emeritus; Member, Medical Research Council Scientific Staff, 1955–81; *b* 9 March 1921; *s* of Joseph and Winefride Lawther; *m* 1944, Kathleen May Wilkowski, MB BS; two *s* one *d. Educ:* Carlisle and Morecambe Grammar Schs; King's Coll., London; St Bartholomew's Hosp. Med. Coll. MB BS 1950; DSc London 1971. FRCP 1963 (MRCP 1954); FFOM 1981 (MFOM 1980). St Bartholomew's Hospital: Ho. Phys., Med. Professorial Unit, 1950; Cooper & Coventson Res. Schol., 1951–53; Associate Chief Asst, 1952–62; Hon. Cons. and Phys.-in-Charge, Dept of Envir. and Prev. Med., 1962–81; Consulting Physician, 1981–. Director, MRC Air Pollution Unit (later Envir. Hazards Unit), 1955–77; Head of Clinical Sect., MRC Toxicology Unit, 1977–81. Cons. Expert, WHO, 1960–; Civilian Cons. in Envir. Medicine, RN, 1975–. Chairman: DHSS Cttee on Med. Aspects of Contamination of Air and Soil, 1973–83; DHSS Working Party on Lead and Health, 1978–80; Environmental Dirs Gp, MRC, 1981–85; Cttee on Environmental and Occupational Health, MRC, 1985–; Assessor, Inquiry on Lorries, People and Environment, (Armitage Inquiry), 1979–80. Pres., Nat. Soc. for Clean Air, 1975–77. Sir Arthur Thomson Vis. Prof., Univ. of Birmingham, 1975–76; RCP Marc Daniels Lectr, 1970; Harben Lectr, RIPH&H, 1970; Guymer Meml Lectr, St Thomas' Hosp., 1979. RSA Silver Medal, 1964; Acad. Nat. de Médecine Bronze Medal, 1972; RCP Bissett Hawkins Medal, 1974; RSM Edwin Stevens Gold Medal, 1975. *Publications:* various papers and chapters in books relating to environmental and occupational medicine. *Recreations:* almost everything. *Address:* Apple Trees, Church Road, Purley, Surrey CR2 3QQ. *T:* 01–660 6398. *Club:* Surrey CCC.

LAWTON, Alistair; *see* Lawton, J. A.

LAWTON, Prof. Denis; Director, University of London Institute of Education, since 1983; *b* 5 April 1931; *s* of William Benedict Lawton and Ruby (*née* Evans); *m* 1953, Joan Weston; two *s. Educ:* St Ignatius Coll.; Univ. of London Goldsmiths' Coll. (BA); Univ. of London Inst. of Education (PhD). Asst Master, Erith Grammar Sch., 1958–61; Head of English/Housemaster, Bacon's Sch., SE1, 1961–63; Institute of Education: Research Officer, 1963–64; Lectr in Sociology, 1964–67; Sen. Lectr in Curriculum Studies, 1967–72; Reader in Education, 1972–74; Professor of Education, 1974; Dep. Dir, 1978–83. Hon. Fellow, College of Preceptors, 1983. *Publications:* Social Class, Language and Education, 1968; Social Change, Education Theory and Curriculum Planning, 1973; Class, Culture and the Curriculum, 1975; Social Justice and Education, 1977; The Politics of the School Curriculum, 1980; An Introduction to Teaching and Learning, 1981; Curriculum Studies and Educational Planning, 1983. *Recreations:* walking German Shepherd dogs, photographing bench-ends, sampling real ale, music. *Address:* Laun House, Laundry Lane, Nazeing, Essex.

LAWTON, Prof. Sir Frank (Ewart), Kt 1981; DDS; FDSRCS; Professor of Operative Dental Surgery, University of Liverpool, 1956–80, now Emeritus Professor; *b* 23 Oct. 1915; *s* of Hubert Ralph Lawton and Agnes Elizabeth (*née* Heath); *m* 1943, Muriel Leonora Bacon; one *s* one *d. Educ:* Univ. of Liverpool (BDS 1st Cl. Hons 1937); Northwestern Univ., Chicago (DDS 1948). FDSRCS 1948. Lectr, 1939, and Dir of Dental Educn, 1957–80, Univ. of Liverpool. President: BDA, 1973–74; GDC, 1979–. Editor, Internat. Dental Jl, 1963–81. Hon. DDSc Newcastle, 1981; Hon. DDS Birmingham, 1982; Hon. DSc Manchester, 1984. *Publications:* (ed with Ed Farmer) Stones Oral and Dental Diseases, 1966; contrib. scientific and prof. jls. *Recreation:* music. *Address:* Newcroft, Castle Bolton, Leyburn, N Yorks DL8 4EX. *T:* Wensleydale 22802.

LAWTON, Rt. Hon. Sir Frederick (Horace), PC 1972; Kt 1961; a Lord Justice of Appeal, 1972–86; *b* 21 Dec. 1911; *o s* of William John Lawton, OBE; *m* 1937, Doreen (*née* Wilton) (*d* 1979); two *s. Educ:* Battersea Grammar Sch.; Corpus Christi Coll., Cambridge (Hon. Fellow, 1968). Barrister, Inner Temple, 1935; Bencher, 1961. Served with London Irish Rifles, 1939–41; invalided out of Army, 1941, and returned to practice at the Bar. QC 1957; Judge of the High Court of Justice, Queen's Bench Div., 1961–72. Recorder of City of Cambridge, 1957–61; Dep. Chm., Cornwall QS, 1968–71. Member: Bar Council, 1957–61; Departmental Cttee on Proceedings before Examining Justices, 1957–58; Standing Cttee on Criminal Law Revision, 1959–86 (Chm., 1977–86); Inter-departmental Cttee on Court of Criminal Appeal, 1964–65; Chm., Adv. Cttee on Legal Educn, 1976–86. Presiding Judge, Western Circuit, 1970–72. President, British Academy of Forensic Sciences, 1964. *Address:* 2 Harcourt Buildings, Temple, EC4Y 9DB. *T:* 01–353 3720; Mordryg, Stoptide, Rock, near Wadebridge, Cornwall. *T:* Trebetherick 3375. *Club:* Garrick.

LAWTON, Harold Walter, MA; Docteur de l'Université de Paris; Officier d'Académie; Emeritus Professor, University of Sheffield, since 1964; *b* Stoke-on-Trent, 27 July 1899; *y s* of late William T. C. and Alice Lawton; *m* 1933, Bessie, *y d* of T. C. Pate; two *s* one *d. Educ:* Middle Sch., Newcastle under Lyme; Rhyl Grammar Sch.; Universities of Wales and Paris. BA Hons (Wales) 1921; MA (Wales) 1923; Fellow University of Wales, 1923–26; Docteur de l'Univ. de Paris, 1926. University College, Southampton: Lecturer in French, 1926–37; Professor of French, 1937–50; Dean of Faculty of Arts, 1945–49; first Warden of New, later Connaught, Hall, 1930–33; University of Sheffield: Professor of French, 1950–64; Warden of Ranmoor House, 1957–63; Deputy Pro-Vice-Chancellor, 1958–61; Pro-Vice-Chancellor, 1961–64. Médaille d'Argent de la Reconnaissance Française, 1946; Officier d'Académie, 1948. *Publications:* Térence en France au XVIe Siècle: éditions et traductions (Paris), 1926; repr. 1970; Handbook of French Renaissance Dramatic Theory, 1950, repr. 1972; J. du Bellay, Poems, selected with introduction and notes, 1961; Térence en France au XVIe Siècle: imitation et influence, 1972; articles and reviews to British and French periodicals. *Recreations:* walking, drawing. *Address:* Ranmoor, 4 Timber Bank, Vigo Village, Meopham, Kent DA13 0RZ. *T:* Fairseat 822712.

LAWTON, (John) Alistair, CBE 1981; DL; with Sea Properties Ltd, since 1955; *b* 1 Oct. 1929; *s* of Richard Geoffrey Lawton and Emma Lawton; *m* 1952, Iris Lilian Barthorpe; one *s* two *d. Educ:* Crewkerne Sch., Somerset. Southern Rhodesia Govt, 1946–55. Member: Deal Borough Council, 1956–74 (Mayor, 1966–68); Kent County Council, 1966– (Chm., 1977–79). Comr, Manpower Services Commn, 1983–85. DL Kent, 1983. Hon. DCL Kent, 1982. *Recreations:* Cricket, Rugby (non-participating now). *Address:* 6 Archery Square, Walmer, Deal, Kent CT14 7HP. *T:* Deal 375060.

LAWTON, Rev. Canon John Arthur; Rector of Winwick since 1969; Archdeacon of Warrington, 1970–81; *b* 19 Jan. 1913; *s* of Arthur and Jennie Lawton; unmarried. *Educ:* Rugby; Fitzwilliam House, Cambridge (MA); Cuddesdon Theological College, Oxford. Curate, St Dunstan, Edgehill, Liverpool, 1937–40; Vicar of St Anne, Wigan, 1940–56; Vicar of St Luke, Southport, 1956–60; Vicar of Kirkby, Liverpool, 1960–69; Canon Diocesan of Liverpool, 1963–. *Address:* Winwick Rectory, Golborne Road, Winwick, Warrington WA2 8SZ. *T:* Warrington 32760.

LAWTON, Louis David, QC 1973; Barrister-at-Law; a Recorder of the Crown Court, since 1972; *b* 15 Oct. 1936; *m* 1959, Helen Margaret (*née* Gair); one *s* two *d. Educ:* Repton Sch.; Sidney Sussex Coll., Cambridge (MA). Called to Bar, Lincoln's Inn, 1959; Bencher,

Lincoln's Inn, 1981. Mem. Criminal Injuries Compensation Bd, 1981–83. *Address:* 2 Harcourt Buildings, Temple, EC4. *Club:* United Oxford & Cambridge University.

LAWTON, Philip Charles Fenner, CBE 1967; DFC 1941; Group Director and Chairman, BEA, 1972–73; Member: British Airways Board, 1972–73; Board, BOAC, 1972–73; *b* Highgate, London, 18 Sept. 1912; *o s* of late Charles Studdert Lawton and late Mabel Harriette Lawton; *m* 1941, Emma Letitia Gertrude, *y d* of late Lieut-Colonel Sir Henry Kenyon Stephenson, 1st Bt, DSO, and Frances, Hassop Hall, Bakewell, Derbyshire; one *s* one *d. Educ:* Westminster Sch. Solicitor, 1934–39. Joined AAF, 1935. Served War of 1939–45 (despatches twice, Group Captain): Pilot with 604 Aux. Sqdn (night fighters), 1939–41; Staff Officer HQ, Fighter Command, 1942; Station Commander, RAF Predannock; RAF Portreath; RAF Cranfield and Special Duties for Inspector-General, RAF, 1943–45. Joined BEA, 1946; Commercial and Sales Dir, 1947–71, Mem. Corporation 1964, Exec. Bd Member 1971; Chm., BEA Airtours, 1969–72. LLB Hons Degree, 1933; FCIT (MInstT 1955). *Address:* Fenner House, Glebe Way, Wisborough Green, West Sussex. *T:* Wisborough Green 700606; 17 Pembroke Walk, W8. *T:* 01–937 3091. *Club:* RAF.

LAXNESS, Halldor Kiljan; Icelandic writer; *b* 23 April 1902; *s* of Gudjon Helgason and Sigridur Halldorsdottir, Iceland; *m* 1st, Ingibjörg Einarsdottir; one *s*; 2nd, Audur Sveinsdottir; two *d.* Awarded Nobel literary prize, 1955; Sonning Prize, 1969. *Publications:* (many of which have been translated into English): Undir Helgahnúk (Under the Holy Mountain), 1924; Vefarinn mikli frá Kasmir (The Great Weaver from Kashmir), 1927; Althydubókin (The Book of the People) (essays), 1929; Salka Valka, 1934 (first published as Thu vinvidur hreini, 1931, and Fuglinn i fjorunni, 1932); Sjálfstoett fólk (Independent People), 2 vols, 1934–35; Ljós heimsins, 1937, Holl sumarlandsins, 1938; Hus skaldsins, 1939, Fegurd himinsins, 1940 (these four republished as Heimsljos (The Light of the World), 2 vols, 1955); The Atom Station, 1948; Happy Warriors, 1952; Fish Can Sing, 1957; Paradise Reclaimed, 1960; Skaldatimi, 1963; Sjostafakverid, 1964; Kristnihald undir Jokli, 1968; Innansveitarkronika, 1970; Gudsgjafathula, 1972; I tuninu heima, 1975; Ungur eg var, 1976; Sjomeistarasagan, 1978; Grikklandsarid, 1980; translations into Icelandic include: Farewell to Arms by Ernest Hemingway; Candide by Voltaire. *Address:* PO Box 664, Reykjavik, Iceland.

LAYARD, Prof. Peter Richard Grenville; Professor of Economics, London School of Economics, since 1980, Convenor, Economics Department, since 1984, and Head, Centre for Labour Economics, since 1974; Chairman of Executive Committee, Employment Institute and Charter for Jobs, since 1985; *b* 15 March 1934; *s* of Dr John Layard and Doris Layard. *Educ:* Eton Coll.; King's Coll., Cambridge (BA); London School of Economics (MScEcon). History Master: Woodberry Down Sch., 1959–60; Forest Hill Sch., 1960–61; Senior Research Officer, Robbins Cttee on Higher Educn, 1961–63; London School of Economics: Dep. Director, Higher Educn Research Unit, 1964–74 (part-time from 1968); Lectr in Economics, 1968–75; Reader in the Economics of Labour, 1975–80. Mem., UGC, 1985–. *Publications:* (jtly) The Causes of Educated Unemployment in India, 1969; (jtly) The Impact of Robbins: Expansion in Higher Education, 1969; (jtly) Qualified Manpower and Economic Performance: An Inter-Plant Study in the Electrical Engineering Industry, 1971; (ed) Cost-Benefit Analysis, 1973; (jtly) Microeconomic Theory, 1978; (jtly) The Causes of Poverty, 1978; More Jobs, Less Inflation, 1982; How to Bend Unemployment, 1986. *Recreations:* walking, the clarinet. *Address:* 18 Provost Road, NW3. *T:* 01–722 6347.

LAYCRAFT, Hon. James Herbert; Chief Justice of Alberta, since 1985; *b* 5 Jan. 1924; *s* of George Edward Laycraft and Hattie Cogswell Laycraft; *m* 1948, Helen Elizabeth Bradley; one *s* one *d. Educ:* University of Alberta (BA, LLB 1951). Admitted to Bar, 1952; law practice, 1952–75; Trial Div. Judge, Supreme Court of Alberta, 1975; Court of Appeal, Alberta, 1979–85. Hon. LLD Calgary, 1986. *Publications:* articles in Canadian Bar Review and Alberta Law Review. *Recreations:* outdoor activities. *Address:* 8952 Baybridge Drive SW, Calgary, Alberta, Canada; Court House, 611 4th Street SW, Calgary. *T:* (403) 297 7434. *Club:* Ranchman's (Calgary).

LAYDEN, Councillor John, JP; miner; Councillor Rotherham Metropolitan Borough Council, since 1974, Leader since 1974; *b* 16 Jan. 1926; *m* 1949, Dorothy Brenda McLean; two *s.* Joined Labour Party, 1944. Elected to Maltby UDC, 1953 (Chm., 1959–60 and 1970–71). Chm., Assoc. of Metropolitan Authorities, 1984–; Vice-Chm., British Section, IULA/CEM, 1974–; Mem., Trent RHA, 1974–. JP Rotherham Borough, 1965. *Recreations:* music, sport (particularly football). *Address:* 9 Lilac Grove, Maltby, Rotherham, South Yorkshire S66 8BX. *T:* Rotherham 812481.

LAYE, Evelyn, CBE 1973; actress; singer; *b* London, 10 July 1900; *o d* of Gilbert Laye and Evelyn Froud; *m* 1st, 1926, Sonnie Hale (from whom she obtained a divorce, 1931); 2nd, 1934, Frank Lawton (*d* 1969). *Educ:* Folkestone; Brighton. Made first appearance on stage, Theatre Royal, Brighton, 1915, in Mr Wu. First London appearance in The Beauty Spot, Gaiety, 1918; first big success in title-role of The Merry Widow, Daly's, 1923; subsequently starred in London in Madame Pompadour, Daly's, 1923; The Dollar Princess, Daly's, 1925; Cleopatra, Daly's, 1925; Betty in Mayfair, Adelphi, 1925; Merely Molly, Adelphi, 1926; Princess Charming, Palace, 1927; Lilac Time, Daly's, 1927; Blue Eyes, Piccadilly, 1928; The New Moon, Drury Lane, 1929; Bitter Sweet, His Majesty's, 1930; Helen!, Adelphi, 1932; Give Me A Ring, Hippodrome, 1933; Paganini, Lyceum, 1937; Lights Up, Savoy, 1940; The Belle of New York, Coliseum, 1942; Sunny River, Piccadilly, 1943; Cinderella, His Majesty's, 1943; Three Waltzes, Princes', 1945; Cinderella, Palladium, 1948; Two Dozen Red Roses, Lyric, 1949; Peter Pan, Scala, 1953; Wedding in Paris, Hippodrome, 1954–56; Silver Wedding, Cambridge, 1957; The Amorous Prawn, Saville/Piccadilly, 1959–62; Never Too Late, Prince of Wales, 1964; The Circle, Savoy, 1965; Strike A Light!, Piccadilly, 1966; Let's All Go Down the Strand, Phoenix, 1967; Charlie Girl, Adelphi, 1969; Phil the Fluter, Palace, 1969; No Sex, Please-We're British, Strand, 1971–73; A Little Night Music (revival), Exeter, 1979, 1981, on tour, 1979, Nottingham, 1980–81, 1982; one woman show, 1983; pantomime, Chichester, 1984–85, Richmond, 1986. First New York appearance in Bitter Sweet, Ziegfeld Theatre, 1929; subsequently on Broadway in Sweet Aloes, Booth, 1936; Between the Devil, Majestic, 1937. Film début in silent production, The Luck of the Navy, 1927. Films include: One Heavenly Night (Hollywood), 1932; Waltz Time, 1933; Princess Charming, 1934; Evensong, 1935; The Night is Young (Hollywood), 1936; Make Mine A Million, 1959; Theatre of Death, 1967; Within and Without, 1969; Say Hello to Yesterday, 1971. Numerous broadcasts and television appearances incl. rôles in Dizzy, Tales of the Unexpected, The Gay Lord Quex, 1983. *Publication:* Boo, to my Friends (autobiography), 1958. *Address:* c/o Jeremy Conway Ltd, 109 Jermyn Street, SW1Y 6HB.

LAYFIELD, Sir Frank (Henry Burland Willoughby), Kt 1976; QC 1967; a Recorder of the Crown Court, since 1979; *b* Toronto, 9 Aug. 1921; *s* of late H. D. Layfield; *m* 1965, Irene Patricia, *d* of late Captain J. D. Harvey, RN (retired); one *s* one *d. Educ:* Sevenoaks Sch. Army, 1940–46. Called to the Bar, Gray's Inn, 1954, Bencher, 1974. Chairman: Inquiry into Greater London Development Plan, 1970–73; Cttee of Inquiry into Local Government Finance, 1974–76; Inspector, Inquiry into Sizewell B Nuclear Power Station,

1983–85. Associate, RICS, 1977; Hon. FSVA 1978; Hon. Fellow, Coll. of Estate Management, 1982. Gold Medal, Lincoln Inst. of Land Policy, 1984. *Publications:* (with A. E. Telling) Planning Applications, Appeals and Inquiries, 1953; (with A. E. Telling) Applications for Planning Payments, 1955; Engineering Contracts, 1956. *Recreations:* walking, tennis. *Address:* 2 Mitre Court Buildings, Temple, EC4Y 7BX. *T:* 01–583 1355. *Clubs:* Garrick, United Oxford & Cambridge University.

LAYMAN, Captain Herbert Francis Hope, DSO and Bar, 1940; RN; *b* 23 March 1899; *s* of Major F. H. Layman, 11th Hussars; *m* 1934, Elizabeth, *o d* of Rear-Admiral A. P. Hughes; one *s* one *d. Educ:* Haileybury. Grand Fleet, 1918; Fleet Signal Officer, Home Fleet, 1933–36. Director of Radio Equipment, Admiralty, 1949–51; Commanded HMS Hotspur, 1939–41; HMS Rajah, 1945–46; Royal Naval Air Station, Culham, Oxon, 1947–48; Chief of Staff to Commander-in-Chief, The Nore, 1951–53; retired, 1953. Vice-Pres., Tennis and Rackets Association. *Publications:* articles on Rackets. *Address:* Shortalls, Bridus Way, Blewbury, Didcot, Oxon OX11 9NW.

LAYTON, family name of **Baron Layton.**

LAYTON, 2nd Baron *cr* 1947, of Danehill; **Michael John Layton;** Director: Wolff Steel Holdings Ltd, 1977–83; Economist Newspaper Ltd, 1973–85; *b* 28 Sept. 1912; *s* of Walter Thomas, 1st Baron Layton, and Eleanor Dorothea (*d* 1959), *d* of Francis B. P. Osmaston; *S* father, 1966; *m* 1938, Dorothy, *d* of Albert Luther Cross, Rugby; one *s* one *d. Educ:* St Paul's Sch.; Gonville and Caius Coll., Cambridge. BA Mech. Scis Cantab, 1934; CEng, FIMechE, FIM. Student Apprentice, British Thomson Houston Co. Ltd, Rugby (specialised in Industrial Admin), 1934–37; Student Engr, Goss Printing Co., Chicago, 1937–39; Works Man. and Production Engr, Ibbotson Bros & Co. Ltd, Sheffield, Manufacturing 25–pounder armour piercing shot, 1939–43; Gen. Man., two armoured car production plants, Rootes Ltd, Birmingham, 1943–46; Mem. Control Commn for Germany in Metallurgy Br. and latterly in Econ. Sub-Commn, assisting at formation of OEEC, 1946–48; Head of Internat. Relations Dept of British Iron and Steel Fedn, 1948–55; Sales Controller, 1956, Dir, 1960, Asst Man. Dir, 1965–67, Man. Dir, 1967, The Steel Co. of Wales Ltd; Exec. Board Mem., BSC, 1967–77. President: Court, British Shippers Council, 1977–; European Atlantic Gp, 1984–. *Heir: s* Hon. Geoffrey Michael Layton [*b* 18 July 1947; *m* 1969, Viviane (marr. diss. 1970), *y d* of François Cracco, Belgium]. *Address:* 6 Old Palace Terrace, The Green, Richmond, Surrey.

See also Hon. C. W. Layton.

LAYTON, Hon. Christopher Walter; Research Associate, Federal Trust, since 1984; Editor, Alliance, 1982–83, Associate Editor, New Democrat, since 1983; *b* 31 Dec. 1929; *s* of 1st Baron Layton; *m* 1st, 1952, Anneliese Margaret, *d* of Joachim von Thadden, Hanover (marr. diss. 1957); one *s* one *d*; 2nd, 1961, Margaret Ann, *d* of Leslie Moon, Molesey, Surrey; three *d. Educ:* Oundle; King's Coll., Cambridge. Intelligence Corps, 1948–49; ICI Ltd, 1952; The Economist Intelligence Unit, 1953–54; Editorial writer, European affairs, The Economist, 1954–62; Economic Adviser to Liberal Party, 1962–69; Dir, Centre for European Industrial Studies, Bath Univ., 1968–71; Commission of European Communities: Chef de Cabinet to Commissioner Spinelli, 1971–73; Dir, Computer Electronics, Telecomms and Air Transp. Equipment Manufg, Directorate-Gen. of Internal Market and Industrial Affairs, 1973–81; Hon. Director-General, EEC, and Special Adviser on Technology, 1981–. Contested (SDP) London W, European Parly Elecn, 1984. *Publications:* Transatlantic Investment, 1966; European Advanced Technology, 1968; Cross-frontier Mergers in Europe 1970; (jtly) Industry and Europe, 1971; (jtly) Ten Innovations: International Study on Development Technology and the Use of Qualified Scientists and Engineers in Ten Industries, 1972. *Address:* Orchard House, 3 Grange Road, SW13.

See also Baron Layton.

LAYTON, His Honour Paul Henry; a Circuit Judge (formerly Deputy Chairman, Inner London Quarter Sessions), 1965–79, retired; *b* Walsall, 11 July 1905; *s* of Frank George Layton, MRCS, LRCP, and Dorothea Yonge; *m* 1950, Frances Evelyn Weekes, Ottawa; two *s. Educ:* Epsom Coll.; St John's Coll., Cambridge (MA). Called to Bar, Inner Temple, 1929; Joined Oxford Circuit, 1930; Recorder of Smethwick, 1952–64; Dep. Chm., Staffs QS, 1955–65; Chm., Agricultural Land Tribunal, W Midlands, 1955–65; Mem., Mental Health Review Tribunal, Birmingham Region, 1960–65; Recorder of Walsall, 1964–65. Pres., Medico-Legal Soc., 1983–85. Served War of 1939–45, AAF and RAF. *Recreation:* gardening. *Address:* 70A Leopold Road, SW19 7JQ. *T:* 01–946 0865.

LAYTON, Thomas Arthur; writer on wine and food; editor; wine merchant; *b* 31 Dec. 1910; *s* of late T. B. Layton, DSO, FRCS, and Edney Sampson; *m* 1935, Eleanor de P. Marshall; one *s* (one *d* decd). *Educ:* Bradfield Coll., Berks. Vintners' Co. Travelling Schol., 1929. Public Relations Officer, Wine Trade, 1951. Pres., Circle of Wine Tasters, 1936. Contested (Spare the Earth): Hove, 1983; Chesterfield, Mar. 1984; Portsmouth, June 1984. Chevalier, Order of Civil Merit (Spain), 1971. *Publications:* Choose Your Wine, 1940 (rewritten, 1959); Table for Two, 1942; Restaurant Roundabout, 1944; Five to a Feast, 1948; Wine's my Line, 1955; Choose Your Cheese, 1957; Winecraft, 1959; Wines and Castles of Spain, 1959; Wines of Italy, 1961; Vignes et Vins de France (trans.), 1962; Choose Your Vegetables, 1963; Modern Wines, 1964; A Year at The Peacock, 1964; Cheese and Cheese Cookery, 1967; Wines and Chateaux of the Loire, 1967; Cognac and Other Brandies, 1968; Wines and People of Alsace, 1969; The Way of St James, 1976. Editor: Wine Magazine, 1958–60; Anglo-Spanish Journal (Quarterly), 1960–87; Hispano-British Circle, 1987–. *Recreations:* wine, travelling in Spain. *Address:* c/o Lloyds Bank, 39 Old Bond Street, W1X 4BH.

LAZARUS, Sir Peter (Esmond), KCB 1985 (CB 1975); FCIT; Permanent Secretary, Department of Transport, 1982–85; Member, Civil Aviation Authority, since 1986; *b* 2 April 1926; *er s* of late Kenneth M. Lazarus and Mary R. Lazarus (*née* Halsted); *m* 1950, Elizabeth Anne Marjorie Atwell, *e d* of late Leslie H. Atwell, OBE; three *s. Educ:* Westminster Sch.; Wadham Coll., Oxford (Open Exhibition). Served RA, 1945–48. Entered Ministry of Transport, 1949: Secretary, London and Home Counties Traffic Advisory Cttee, 1953–57; Private Secretary to Minister, 1961–62; Asst Sec., 1962; Under-Sec., 1968–70; Under-Sec., Treasury, 1970–72; Deputy Secretary: DoE, 1973–76; Dept of Transport, 1976–82. Chm., Assoc. of First Div. Civil Servants, 1969–71. Chm., Council, Liberal Jewish Synagogue, St John's Wood, 1972–75. FRSA 1981. *Recreations:* music, reading. *Address:* 28 Woodside Avenue, N6 4SS. *T:* 01–883 3186. *Club:* Athenæum.

LAZARUS, Robert Stephen, QC; Social Security (formerly National Insurance) Commissioner, 1966–81; *b* 29 Oct. 1909; *s* of late Solomon and Mabel Lazarus; *m* 1938, Amelia (*née* Isaacs); two *d. Educ:* Marlborough Coll.; Caius Coll., Cambridge. Called to the Bar, at Lincoln's Inn, 1933; QC 1958. Member: Bar Council, 1960–64; Legal Aid Cttee, 1961–66. Bencher, 1964. Served with RASC, 1940–46. *Recreations:* music, gardening. *Address:* 41 The Cliff, Roedean, Brighton, E Sussex BN2 5RF. *T:* Brighton 691162.

LAZENBY, Prof. Alec, FTS, FIBiol; Vice-Chancellor, University of Tasmania, since 1982; *b* 4 March 1927; *s* of G. and E. Lazenby; *m* 1957, Ann Jennifer, *d* of R. A. Hayward; one *s* two *d. Educ:* Wath on Dearne Grammar Sch.; University Coll. of Wales, Aberystwyth. BSc 1949, MSc 1952, Wales; MA 1954, PhD 1959, ScD 1985, Cantab. Scientific Officer, Welsh Plant Breeding Station, 1949–53; Demonstr in Agricultural Botany, 1953–58, Lectr in Agricultural Botany, 1958–65, Univ. of Cambridge; Fellow and Asst Tutor, Fitzwilliam Coll., Cambridge, 1962–65; Foundation Prof. of Agronomy, Univ. of New England, NSW, 1965–70, now Professor Emeritus; Vice-Chancellor, Univ. of New England, Armidale, NSW, 1970–77; Dir, Grassland Res. Inst., 1977–82. Vis. Prof., Reading Univ., 1978; Hon. Professorial Fellow, Univ. of Wales, 1979. Hon DRurSci New England, NSW, 1981. *Publications:* (jt Editor) Intensive Pasture Production, 1972; (jt Editor) Australian Field Crops, vol. I, 1975, vol. II, 1979; papers on: pasture plant breeding; agronomy; weed ecology, in various scientific jls. *Recreation:* golf. *Address:* University of Tasmania, Box 252C, GPO, Hobart, Tasmania 7001, Australia.

LEA, Christopher Gerald, MC; **His Honour Judge Christopher Lea;** a Circuit Judge, since 1972; *b* 27 Nov. 1917; *y s* of late George Percy Lea, Franche, Kidderminster, Worcs; *m* 1952, Susan Elizabeth Dorrien Smith, *d* of Major Edward Pendarves Dorrien Smith, Greatwood, Restronguet, Falmouth, Cornwall; two *s* one *d* (and one *d* decd). *Educ:* Charterhouse; RMC, Sandhurst. Commissioned into XX The Lancashire Fusiliers, 1937, and served with Regt in UK until 1939. Served War of 1939–45 (despatches, MC): with Lancashire Fusiliers, No 11 Special Air Service Commando, and Parachute Regt in France, Italy and Malaya. Post-war service in Indonesia, Austria and UK; retired, 1948. Called to Bar, Inner Temple, 1948; Oxford Circuit. Mem. Nat. Assistance Bd Appeal Tribunal (Oxford Area), 1961–63; Mem. Mental Health Review Tribunal (Oxford Region), 1962–68, 1983–. A Metropolitan Magistrate, 1968–72; Dep. Chm., Berks QS, 1968–71. *Address:* Simms Farm House, Mortimer, Berks. *T:* Mortimer 332360. *Club:* English-Speaking Union.

See also Sir G. H. Lea.

LEA, David Edward, OBE 1978; Assistant General Secretary of the Trades Union Congress, since 1977; *b* 2 Nov. 1937; *s* of Edward Cunliffe Lea and Lilian May Lea. *Educ:* Farnham Grammar Sch.; Christ's Coll., Cambridge. Economist Intelligence Unit, 1961; Economic Dept, TUC, 1964, Asst Sec., 1967, Sec. 1970. Jt Sec., TUC-Labour Party Liaison Cttee, 1972–. Member: Royal Commn on the Distribution of Income and Wealth, 1974–79; Adv. Gp on Channel Tunnel and Cross-Channel Services, 1974–75; Cttee of Inquiry on Industrial Democracy, 1975–77; Energy Commn, 1977–79; Retail Prices Index Adv. Cttee, 1977–; EEC Expert Group on Economic and Social Concepts in the Community, 1977–79; NEDC Cttee on Finance for Investment, 1978–; Expert Adviser, UN Commn on Transnational Corporations, 1977–; Kreisky Commn on Unemployment in Europe, 1986–; Chairman: TUC Working Group on Employment and Technology, 1978–; Econ. Cttee, ETUC, 1980–. Mem., Franco-British Council, 1982–. Governor, NIESR, 1981–. *Publications:* Trade Unionism, 1966; contrib. The Multinational Enterprise, 1971; Industrial Democracy (TUC), 1974; Keynes Plus: a participatory economy (ETUC), 1979. *Address:* 17 Ormonde Mansions, 106 Southampton Row, WC1B 4BP. *T:* 01–405 6237.

LEA, Lt-Gen. Sir George (Harris), KCB 1967 (CB 1964); DSO 1957; MBE 1950; Lieutenant, HM Tower of London, 1972–75; Chairman, Eagle Star Trust Co., Jersey and Guernsey, since 1983; *b* 28 Dec. 1912; *s* of late George Percy Lea, Franche, Kidderminster, Worcs; *m* 1948, Pamela Elizabeth, *d* of Brig. Guy Lovett-Tayleur; one *s* two *d. Educ:* Charterhouse; RMC, Sandhurst. Commnd into Lancashire Fusiliers, 1933, and served with Regt in UK, China and India until 1940. Served War of 1939–45 with Lancashire Fusiliers and Parachute Regt in India, N Africa, Italy and NW Europe. Post-war service: Regtl duty and on staff with Parachute Regt, Royal Marine Commando Bde and SAS Regt in UK, China and Malaya. Post-war staff appts in Allied Command Europe (SHAPE) and as Dep. Military Secretary (War Office); despatches, 1956; Comd 2nd Inf. Bde Group, 1957–60; GOC 42 (Lancs) Div. and North-West District, 1962–63; Comdr Forces, Northern Rhodesia and Nyasaland, 1963–64; Director of Borneo Operations and Commander Land Forces, Borneo, 1965–66; Head, British Defence Staff, Washington, 1967–70, retired. Col, The Lancashire Fusiliers, 1965–68; Col, The Royal Regt of Fusiliers, 1974–77 (Dep. Col for Lancashire, 1968–73). A Senior Administrator: Spey Investments Ltd, 1972; Brandt's Ltd, 1973–75; Man. Dir, Martin-Scott & Co. Ltd, 1975–82. Dato Seri Setia, Order of Paduka Stia Negara, Brunei, 1965. *Address:* Les Ruisseaux Lodge, St Brelade, Jersey, Channel Islands. *Clubs:* Army and Navy; Victoria, Royal Channel Islands Yacht.

See also C. G. Lea.

LEA, Vice-Adm. Sir John (Stuart Crosbie), KBE 1979; retired; Director, GEC Marine & Industrial Gears Ltd, since 1986 (Chm., 1980–86); *b* 4 June 1923; *m* 1947, Patricia Anne Thoseby; one *s* two *d. Educ:* Boxgrove Sch., Guildford; Shrewsbury Sch.; RNEC, Keyham. Entered RN, 1941; Cruisers Sheffield and Glasgow, 1943; RNEC, 1942–45; HMS Birmingham, 1945; entered Submarines, 1946; HMS/Ms Talent, Tireless, Aurochs, Explorer; Sen. Engr, HMS Forth (Depot Ship), 1952–53; on Staff, RNEC; psc 1958; Sqdn Engr Officer, 2nd Destroyer Sqdn and HMS Daring, 1959–61; Staff of CinC Portsmouth, 1961–62; Naval Staff in Ops Div., 1963–65; Engr Officer, HMS Centaur, 1966; Staff of Flag Officer Submarines; Dep. Supt, Clyde Submarine Base, 1967–68; idc 1969; Dir of Naval Admin. Planning, 1970–71; Cdre HMS Nelson, 1972–75; Asst Chief of Fleet Support, 1976–77; Dir Gen., Naval Manpower and Trng, 1977–80. Comdr 1957; Captain 1966; Rear-Adm. 1976; Vice-Adm. 1978. Chairman: Portsmouth Naval Heritage Trust, 1985; Regular Forces Employment Assoc., 1986; Hayling Island Horticultural Soc., 1983–. *Recreations:* walking, gardening. *Address:* Springfield, Brights Lane, Hayling Island, Hants PO11 0JX.

LEA, Sir (Thomas) Julian, 4th Bt *cr* 1892; *b* 18 Nov. 1934; *s* of Sir Thomas Claude Harris Lea, 3rd Bt and Barbara Katherine (*d* 1945), *d* of Albert Julian Pell, Wilburton Manor, Isle of Ely; *S* father, 1985; *m* 1970, Gerry Valerie, *d* of late Captain Gibson C. Fahnestock, USAF, and of Mrs David Knightly, Brockenhurst, Hants; three *s* two *d.* Lieut RN, retired. *Heir: s* Thomas William Lea, *b* 6 Sept. 1973. *Address:* Bachelors Hall, Hundon, Sudbury, Suffolk.

LEACH, Allan William, FLA; Director-General and Librarian, National Library for the Blind, since 1982; *b* 9 May 1931; *yr s* of Frank Leach, MBE and Margaret Ann Bennett; *m* 1962, Betty, *e d* of William George Gadsby and Doris Cree; one *s* one *d. Educ:* Watford Grammar Sch.; Loughborough Coll. BA Open; DPA London. Various posts with Hertfordshire County Library, 1948–59; Librarian, RAF Sch. of Educn, 1949–51; Regional Librarian, Warwickshire County Libr., 1959–65; County Librarian, Bute County Libr., 1965–71; Librarian and Curator, Ayr Burgh, 1971–74; Dir of Library Services, Kyle and Carrick District, 1974–82. Mem., Standing Cttee, IFLA Section of Libraries for the Blind, 1983–, Chm., 1985–. Editor: Rickmansworth Historian, 1961–66; Ayrshire Collections, 1973–82. *Publications:* Begin Here, 1966; Rothesay Tramways, a brief history, 1969; Round old Ayr (with R. Brash and G. S. Copeland), 1972; Libraries in Ayr, 1975; articles on libraries, local history, literature and educn. *Recreations:* music, the countryside, books, people. *Address:* 4 Windsor Road, Hazel Grove, Stockport, Cheshire SK7 4SW. *T:* 061–483 6418.

LEACH, Archibald A.; *see* Grant, Cary.

LEACH, David; potter, designer, lecturer; *b* 7 May 1911; *e s* of Bernard Leach, CH, CBE, and Edith Muriel, *o d* of Dr William Evans Hoyle; *m* 1938, Mary Elizabeth Facey; three *s. Educ:* Prep. Sch., Bristol; Dauntsey's Sch., Wilts. At age of 19, began to work in his father's pottery at St Ives, Cornwall (tuition from him and associates); Manager and Partner, 1946–55; took Manager's course, N Staffs Technical Coll., Stoke-on-Trent, to 1937; taught pottery at Dartington Hall Progressive Sch., 1933. Served War, DCLI, 1941–45. Taught at Penzance Sch. of Art and St Ives, 1945. Designed and made David Leach Electric Kiln, 1950; helped to start a pottery in Norway, 1951; in charge of Ceramic Dept, and taught, at Loughborough Coll. of Art, 1953 (later Vis. Lectr). Started workshop at Bovey Tracey, 1956; researched into glazes and changed from slipware to stoneware, 1961; now makes a large percentage of porcelain. Late Mem. Council, Craftsmen Potters Assoc. of GB (Past Chm.), late Mem. Grants Cttee of the Crafts Adv. Commn; Mem. Council, Crafts Council, 1977; Chm., Devon Guild of Craftsmen, 1986; Adviser, Dartington Pottery Trng Workshop. Has exhibited in Europe, USA and Far East; first major one-man show, CPA, 1966; Internat. Ceramics Exhibn, 1972, and Craftsmen's Art, 1973, V&A Mus., 1973; major one-man show, NY, 1978; exhibitions in Germany (Darmstadt, Munich, Deidesheim, Sandhausen-bei-Heidelberg, and Hanover), Holland (Amsterdam), Belgium (Brussels), USA (San Francisco), Japan (Osaka) and Norway (Oslo); Joint Exhibitions: New Ashgate Gall., Farnham, 1982, 1983, (3 Generations Leach) 1986; Beaux Arts Gall., Bath, 1984; (with John Leach) Peter Dingley Gall., Stratford, 1985; Solus Exhibitions: NY, and lecture tour, USA, 1978; Washington DC, and 2nd lecture tour, USA, 1979; British Crafts Centre, London, 1979. Galerie St Martin, Cologne, 1982; St Paul's Sch., Barnes, 1982; Robert Welch Gall., Chipping Campden, 1982; Frontroom Gall., Dallas, 1983; Chestnut Gall., Bourton-on-the-Water, 1984; Century Gall., Henley-on-Thames, 1984; Castle Mus., Norwich, 1985. Craft of the Potter, BBC, 1976. Gold Medal, Istanbul, 1967. *Publications:* David Leach: A Potter's Life, with Workshop Notes (introd. by Bernard Leach), 1977. *Address:* Lowerdown Pottery, Bovey Tracey, Devon. *T:* Bovey Tracey 833408.

LEACH, Prof. Sir Edmund Ronald, Kt 1975; FBA 1972; MA Cantab, PhD London; Provost of King's College, Cambridge, 1966–79; Professor of Social Anthropology, 1972–78 (University Reader, 1957–72); *b* 7 Nov. 1910; *s* of late William Edmund Leach; *m* 1940, Celia Joyce, *d* of late Henry Stephen Guy Buckmaster; one *s* one *d. Educ:* Marlborough Coll.; Clare Coll., Cambridge (Exhibnr; Hon. Fellow, 1986). Served War of 1939–45, Burma Army. Commercial Asst, Butterfield & Swire, Shanghai, 1932–37; Graduate Student, LSE, 1938–39, 1946–47; Lectr, later Reader, in Social Anthrop., LSE, 1947–53 (Hon. Fellow, 1974); Lectr, Cambridge, 1953–57. Anthropological Field Research: Formosa, 1937; Kurdistan, 1938; Burma, 1939–45; Borneo, 1947; Ceylon, 1954, 1956. Fellow of King's Coll., Cambridge, 1960–66, 1979–; Fellow, Center for Advanced Study in Behavioral Sciences, Stanford, 1961; Sen. Fellow, Eton Coll., 1966–79; Hon. Fellow, SOAS, 1974; Hinkley Vis. Prof., Johns Hopkins Univ., 1976. Hon. degrees: Chicago 1976, Brandeis 1976. Mem., Social Science Research Council, 1968–72; Trustee, British Museum, 1975–80. Royal Anthrop. Institute: Vice-Pres., 1964–66, 1968–70, Pres., 1971–75 (Curl Essay Prize, 1951, 1957; Rivers Medal, 1958; Henry Myers Lectr, 1966); Chm. Assoc. of Social Anthropologists, 1966–70; Pres. British Humanist Assoc., 1970–72; Lectures: Malinowski, 1959; Munro, 1963, 1977; Myers, 1966; Reith, 1967; Morgan, 1975; Radcliffe-Brown, 1976; Marett, 1977; Huxley, 1980; Frazer, 1982. Foreign Hon. Mem., Amer. Acad. of Arts and Sciences, 1968. *Publications:* Social and Economic Organization of the Rowanduz Kurds, 1940; Social Science Research in Sarawak, 1950; Political Systems of Highland Burma, 1954; Pul Eliya: A Village in Ceylon, 1961; Rethinking Anthropology, 1961; A Runaway World?, 1968; Genesis as Myth, 1970; Lévi-Strauss, 1970; Culture and Communication, 1976; Social Anthropology, 1982; (with D. A. Aycock) Structuralist Interpretations of Biblical Myth, 1983; Editor and contributor to various anthrop. symposia; numerous papers in Man, Journal of the Royal Anthropological Institute, American Anthropologist, South Western Journal of Anthropology, Daedalus, European Archives of Sociology, New Society, Current Anthropology, etc.; various articles in Encyclop. Britannica, Internat. Encyclop. of the Social Sciences. *Recreations:* ski-ing, travel. *Address:* 11 West Green, Barrington, Cambs. *T:* Cambridge 870675. *Club:* United Oxford & Cambridge University.

LEACH, Admiral of the Fleet Sir Henry (Conyers), GCB 1978 (KCB 1977); Chairman, St Dunstan's, since 1983 (Member of Council, since 1982); *b* 18 Nov. 1923; 3rd *s* of Captain John Catterall Leach, MVO, DSO, RN and Evelyn Burrell Leach (*née* Lee), Yarner, Bovey Tracey, Devon; *m* 1958, Mary Jean, *yr d* of Adm. Sir Henry McCall, KCVO, KBE, CB, DSO; two *d. Educ:* St Peter's Court, Broadstairs; RNC Dartmouth. Cadet 1937; served in: cruiser Mauritius, S Atlantic and Indian Ocean, 1941–42; battleship Duke of York, incl. Scharnhorst action, 1943–45; destroyers in Mediterranean, 1945–46; spec. Gunnery, 1947; various gunnery appts, 1948–51; Gunnery Officer, cruiser Newcastle, Far East, 1953–55; staff appts, 1955–59; comd destroyer Dunkirk, 1959–61; comd frigate Galatea as Captain (D) 27th Sqdn and Mediterranean, 1965–67; Dir of Naval Plans, 1968–70; comd Commando Ship Albion, 1970; Asst Chief of Naval Staff (Policy), 1971–73; Flag Officer First Flotilla, 1974–75; Vice-Chief of Defence Staff, 1976–77; C-in-C, Fleet, and Allied C-in-C, Channel and Eastern Atlantic, 1977–79; Chief of Naval Staff and First Sea Lord, 1979–82. First and Principal Naval ADC to the Queen, 1979–82. psc 1952; jssc 1961. President: RN Benevolent Soc., 1983–; Sea Cadets Assoc., 1984–; Naval Pres., Officers' Assoc., 1985–; Chm., Royal Navy Club of 1765 and 1785, 1986–; Patron, British Naval Equipment Assoc., 1983–. *Recreations:* fishing, gardening. *Address:* Wonston Lodge, Wonston, Winchester, Hants.

LEACH, Norman, CMG 1964; Under-Secretary, Foreign and Commonwealth Office (Overseas Development Administration), 1970–72; *b* 8 March 1912; *s* of W. M. Leach. *Educ:* Ermysted's Gram. Sch., Skipton in Craven, Yorks; St Catharine's Coll., Cambridge (Scholar). 1st Class Hons, Pts I and II English Tripos, 1933 and 1934; Charles Oldham Shakespeare Schol., 1933. Asst Principal, Inland Revenue Dept, 1935; Under-Secretary: Ministry of Pensions and National Insurance, 1958–61; Dept of Technical Co-operation, 1961–64; ODM, 1964–70. *Address:* Low Bank, 81 Gargrave Road, Skipton in Craven, North Yorks. *T:* Skipton 3719.

LEACH, Paul Arthur; General Consultant to The Law Society, 1980–81, retired; *b* 10 July 1915; *s* of Rev. Edward Leach and Edith Swannell Leach; *m* 1st, 1949, Daphne Copeland (marr. diss. 1957); one *s* one *d*; 2nd, 1958, Rachel Renée Lachmann. *Educ:* Marlborough Coll.; Keble Coll., Oxford (1st Cl. Hons BA Mod. Hist., 1937; MA 1945); Birmingham Univ. (2nd Cl. Hons LLB 1940). Law Soc. Finals, 1940; admitted Solicitor, 1946. Served War, RA, 1940–45: Staff Captain 1st AA Bde; attached SO II, RAEC, 1945–46. Private practice as solicitor, 1946–48; Talks Producer, BBC Home Talks, 1949; joined Law Soc. staff, 1950; Clerk and later Sec., Professional Purposes Cttee, 1950–71; Secretary: Future of the Profession Cttee, 1971–80; Internat. Relations Cttee, 1975–80; Dep. Sec.-Gen., 1975–80. Secretary: UK Delegn to Commn Consultative des Barreaux de

la Communauté Européenne, 1975–81; Inter-Professional Gp, 1978–81; UK Vice-Pres., Union Internationale des Avocats, 1978–81. *Publications:* (ed) Guide to Professional Conduct of Solicitors, 1974; articles in Law Society's Gazette. *Recreations:* foreign travel, gardening, history, listening to classical music. *Address:* c/o 7 Litchfield Way, NW11 6NN; 5333 Myrtlewood Drive, The Meadows, Sarasota, Fla 33580, USA.

LEACH, Rodney, PhD; FInstM; Chief Executive and Managing Director, Vickers Shipbuilding and Engineering Ltd, since 1985; Chairman, Cammell Laird Shipbuilders Ltd, since 1985; *b* 3 March 1932; *s* of Edward and Alice Leach; *m* 1958, Eira Mary (*née* Tuck); three *s* one *d. Educ:* Baines Grammar Sch., Poulton Le Fylde, Lancs; Birmingham Univ. (BSc, PhD). Radiation Physicist, Nuclear Power Plant Co. Ltd, 1957; Physicist, UKAEA, 1960; Sen. Physicist, South of Scotland Electricity Board, 1963; Associate, McKinsey & Co. Inc., 1965, Partner, 1970; Peninsular & Oriental Steam Navigation Co.: Hd of European and Air Transport Div., 1974; Dir, 1978–85; Chairman: P&O European Transport Services Ltd, 1979–83; P&O Cruises Ltd, 1980–85. Mem., RYA, 1977–. Liveryman, Worshipful Company of Carmen; Freeman, City of London, 1976. *Publications:* (jtly) Containerization: the key to low cost transport, 1965; frequent papers in scientific and technical jls, 1965–72. *Recreations:* sailing, gardening, literature. *Address:* Cleeve Howe, Windermere, Cumbria LA23 1AS. *T:* Windermere 4199. *Club:* Royal Automobile.

LEACH, Sir Ronald (George), GBE 1976 (CBE 1944); Kt 1970; FCA; Chairman, Standard Chartered Bank(CI), since 1980; Director: Samuel Montagu & Co. (Jersey) Ltd, since 1980; International Investment Trust of Jersey, since 1980; Ann Street Brewery Ltd, since 1981; *b* 21 Aug. 1907; *s* of William T. Leach, 14 Furze Croft, Hove; *m* Margaret Alice Binns. *Educ:* Alleyn's. Dep. Financial Sec. to Ministry of Food, Sept. 1939–June 1946. Sen. Partner in firm of Peat, Marwick, Mitchell & Co., Chartered Accountants, 1966–76; Dir, Samuel Montagu & Co., 1977–80. Member: Cttee on Coastal Flooding, 1953; Inquiry into Shipping, 1967–70; National Theatre Board, 1972–79; Chairman: Consumer Cttee for GB (Agricultural Marketing Acts, 1931–49), 1958–67; Accounting Standards Steering Cttee, 1970–76. Pres. Inst. of Chartered Accountants in England and Wales, 1969–70. Hon. LLD Lancaster, 1977. *Publication:* (with Prof. Edward Stamp) British Accounting Standards: the first ten years, 1981. *Address:* La Rosière, Mont de la Rosière, St Saviour, Jersey, CI. *T:* Jersey 77039 or 78427.

LEADBEATER, Howell; Controller of Supplies, 1968–76, and Board Member, Property Services Agency, Department of the Environment, 1972–76, retired 1976; *b* 22 Oct. 1919; *s* of late Thomas and Mary Ann Leadbeater; *m* 1946, Mary Elizabeth Roberts; two *s* one *d. Educ:* Pontardawe Grammar Sch.; University College of Swansea. Army Service, 1940–46: Adjt 11th E African Divl Signals. Min. of Works, later MPBW and Dept of Environment: Asst Principal, 1948; Asst Sec., 1958; Under Sec., 1968; Under/Dep. Sec., 1973. Design Coordinator for Caernarfon Castle, Investiture of Prince of Wales, 1969. Mem., Crafts Adv. Cttee, 1978–80. *Address:* Tides Reach, Llansteffan, Carmarthen, Dyfed SA33 5EY. *T:* Llansteffan 375.

LEADBETTER, David Hulse, CB 1958; Assistant Under-Secretary of State, Department of Education and Science, 1964–68 (Under Secretary, Ministry of Education, 1953–64); *b* 14 Aug. 1908; *s* of late Harold Leadbetter; *m* 1933, Marion, *d* of late Horatio Ballantyne, FRIC, FCS; two *s* two *d* (and one *d* decd.). *Educ:* Whitgift; Merton Coll., Oxford. Entered Board of Education, 1933. *Recreations:* photography, gardening. *Address:* Ryall's Ground, Queen Street, Yetminster, Sherborne, Dorset. *T:* Yetminster 872216.

LEADBITTER, Edward; MP (Lab) The Hartlepools, since 1964; *b* 18 June 1919; *s* of Edward Leadbitter, Easington, Durham; *m* 1940, Phyllis Irene Mellin, Bristol; one *s* one *d. Educ:* State Schs; Teachers' Training Coll. Served War, 1939–45, with RA; commissioned 1943; War Office Instructor in Gunnery. Became a teacher. Joined Labour Party, 1938; Pres., Hartlepools Labour Party, 1958–62; Mem., West Hartlepool Borough Council, 1954–67 (sometime Mem., Town Planning, Finance, Housing, Industrial Develt, and Educn Cttees). Member: Estimates Cttee, 1966–69; Select Cttee on Science and Technology, 1970–80; Select Cttee on Energy, 1980–; Chairmens' Panel, House of Commons, 1980–; Chairman: Industrial Development Cttee; PLP Ports Cttee, 1975–; PLP Transport Gp, 1979–; Anglo-Tunisian Parly Group, 1974–. Sponsored Children's Homes Registration Bill, 1982. Mem. NUPE, 1963–. Organizer of Exhibition on History of Labour Movement, 1956. Pres., Hartlepool Football Club, 1983–. First Hon. Freeman, Co. Borough of Hartlepool, 1981; Freeman of City of London, 1986. *Address:* 8 Warkworth Drive, Hartlepool, Cleveland. *T:* Hartlepool 263404.

LEADBITTER, Jasper Michael, OBE 1960; HM Diplomatic Service, retired 1973; Secretary, Royal Humane Society, 1974–78, Committee Member, 1978–83; *b* 25 Sept. 1912; *s* of late Francis John Graham Leadbitter, Warden, Northumberland, and Teresa del Riego Leadbitter; *m* 1942, Anna Lisa Hahne Johansson, Stockholm, Sweden; one *d. Educ:* Shrewsbury and Dresden. Asst Press Attaché, Stockholm, 1938–45, Press Attaché, 1945–47; established in Diplomatic Service, 1947; Foreign Office, 1947; Panama, 1948; Actg Consul-Gen., Detroit, 1952; First Sec. (Information), Buenos Aires, 1953 and Helsinki, 1956; Foreign Office, 1958; HM Consul and, later, 1st Sec. at Léopoldville, Congo, Dec. 1959 and at Brazzaville, 1961; Dep. Permanent UK Representative to Council of Europe and Consul at Strasbourg, March 1962; HM Consul-Gen., Berlin, Nov. 1963–66; Consul, Palermo, 1966–69; Consul-Gen., Hanover, 1969–73. Committee Member: Anglo-German Assoc.; Anglo-Swedish Soc., 1943–83. *Address:* Oak Lodge, Bayhall Road, Tunbridge Wells, Kent. *Club:* East India, Devonshire, Sports and Public Schools.

LEAHY, Sir John (Henry Gladstone), KCMG 1981 (CMG 1973); HM Diplomatic Service; High Commissioner in Australia, since 1984; *b* 7 Feb. 1928; *s* of late William Henry Gladstone and late Ethel Leahy; *m* 1954, Elizabeth Anne, *d* of J. H. Pitchford, *qv*; two *s* two *d. Educ:* Tonbridge Sch.; Clare Coll., Cambridge; Yale University. RAF, 1950–52; FO, 1952–54 (Asst Private Sec. to Minister of State, 1953–54); 3rd, later 2nd Sec., Singapore, 1955–57; FO, 1957–58; 2nd, later 1st Sec., Paris, 1958–62; FO, 1962–65; Head of Chancery, Tehran, 1965–68; Counsellor, FCO, 1969; Head of Personnel Services Dept, 1969–70; Head of News Dept, FCO, 1971–73; Counsellor and Head of Chancery, Paris, 1973–75; seconded as Under-Sec., NI Office, 1975–76; Asst Under-Sec. of State, FCO, 1977–79; Ambassador to South Africa, 1979–82; Dep. Under- Sec. of State, FCO, 1982–84. Member of Livery, Skinners' Co., 1954. *Recreations:* golf, tennis. *Address:* c/o Foreign and Commonwealth Office, SW1; Manor Stables, Bishopstone, near Seaford, East Sussex BN25 2UD. *T:* Seaford 898898. *Club:* United Oxford & Cambridge University.

LEAKE, Prof. Bernard Elgey, PhD, DSc, FRSE, FGS; Head of Department of Geology, and Keeper of Geological Collections in Hunterian Museum, University of Glasgow, since 1974; *b* 29 July 1932; *s* of late Norman Sidney Leake and Clare Evelyn (*née* Walgate); *m* 1955, Gillian Dorothy Dobinson; five *s. Educ:* Wirral Grammar Sch., Bebington, Cheshire; Liverpool Univ. (1st Cl. Hons BSc, PhD); Bristol Univ. (DSc 1974). Leverhulme post-doctoral Res. Fellow, Liverpool Univ., 1955–57; Asst Lectr, subseq. Lectr in Geology, Bristol Univ., 1957–68, Reader in Geol., 1968–74; Res. Associate, Berkeley, Calif, 1966. Chm., Cttee on amphibole nomenclature, Internat.

Mineral Assoc., 1982– (Sec., 1968–79); Member: NERC, 1978–84 (Chm., Vis. Gp to Brit. Geol Survey, formerly Inst. of Geological Sciences, 1982–84); Council, Mineral Soc., 1965–68, 1978–80 (Vice-Pres., 1979–80); Council, Geol Soc., 1971–74, 1979–85 (Vice-Pres., 1980, Treasurer, 1981–85, Pres., 1986–; Lyell Medal, 1977); publication cttees, Mineral and Geol Socs, 1970–. FRSE 1978. Editor: Mineralogical Magazine, 1970–83; Jl of Geol Soc., 1973 and 1974. *Publications:* A catalogue of analysed calciferous and sub-calciferous amphiboles together with 90 papers in geol, mineral and geochem. jls on geol. of Connemara, study of amphiboles, X-ray fluorescence anal. of rocks and use of geochem. in identifying origins of highly metamorphosed rocks; (map) The geological map of Connemara, 1982. *Recreations:* walking, reading, theatre, gardening, museums, genealogy, study of railway and agricultural development. *Address:* Geology Department, The University, Glasgow G12 8QQ. *T:* 041–339 8855, ext. 7435; 2 Garngaber Avenue, Lenzie, Kirkintilloch, Dunbartonshire. *Club:* Geological Society.

LEAKE, Rt. Rev. David; *see* Northern Argentina, Bishop of.

LEAKEY, Maj.-Gen. Arundell Rea, CB 1967; DSO 1945; MC 1941 (Bar 1942); Director and Secretary, Wolfson Foundation, 1968–80; *b* 30 Dec. 1915; parents British; *m* 1950, Muriel Irene Le Poer Trench; two *s. Educ:* Weymouth Coll.; Royal Military Coll., Sandhurst. Command of 5th Royal Tank Regt, 1944; Instructor at Staff Coll., Camberley, 1951–52; Comdr, 1st Arab Legion Armoured Car Regt, 1954–56; Instructor (Col), Staff Coll., Camberley, 1958–60; Comdr, 7th Armoured Brigade, 1961–63; Dir-Gen. of Fighting Vehicles, 1964–66; GOC Troops in Malta and Libya, 1967–68; retired 1968. Czechoslovakian Military Cross, 1944. *Recreations:* tennis; enjoying retirement. *Address:* Ladymead Cottage, Houghton, Stockbridge, Hants. *Club:* Naval and Military.

LEAKEY, Prof. Felix William; author; *b* 29 June 1922; *s* of Hugh Leakey and Kathleen Leakey (*née* March); *m* 1947, Daphne Joan Sleep (*née* Salter); one *s* two *d. Educ:* St Christopher Sch., Letchworth; Queen Mary Coll., London. BA, PhD (London). Asst Lectr, then Lectr in French, Univ. of Sheffield, 1948–54; Univ. of Glasgow: Lectr in French, 1954–64; Sen. Lectr, 1964–68; Reader, 1968–70; Prof. of French, Univ. of Reading, 1970–73; Prof. of French Lang. and Lit., Bedford Coll., London, 1973–84 (Head of Department, 1973–79 and 1982–84). Carnegie Research Fellow, 1961–62; Leverhulme Research Fellow, 1971–72. Assoc. of University Profs of French: Hon. Sec., 1972–73; Jt Hon. Sec., 1973–75; Vice-Chm., 1975–76; Chm., 1976–77. Public performances as poetry speaker: Baudelaire's Les Fleurs du Mal, French Inst., London, 1984, and Glasgow Univ., 1985; bilingual recital, Chants/Songs, univ. centres in Britain, France and W Germany, 1976–. *Publications:* Baudelaire and Nature, 1969; (ed jtly) The French Renaissance and its Heritage: essays presented to Alan Boase, 1968; Sound and Sense in French Poetry (Inaugural Lecture, with readings on disc), 1975; (ed jtly) Samuel Beckett, Drunken Boat, 1977; contribs to: French Studies; Rev. d'hist. litt. de la France; Rev. de litt. comparée; Rev. des sciences humaines; Etudes baudelairiennes, etc. *Recreations:* foxhunting, beagling, riding, poetry, art, music, especially opera.

LEAKEY, Mary Douglas, FBA 1973; FSA; FRAI; Director, Olduvai Gorge Excavations; *b* 6 Feb. 1913; *d* of Erskine Edward Nicol and Cecilia Marion Frere; *m* 1936, Louis Seymour Bazett Leakey, FBA (*d* 1972); three *s. Educ:* privately. Hon. Mem., American Assoc. for Arts and Sciences, 1979–. Geological Soc. of London, Prestwich Medal and Nat. Geographic Soc. Hubbard Medal (jointly with late L. S. B. Leakey); Gold Medal, Soc. of Women Geographers, USA; Linneus Gold Medal, Roy. Swedish Acad., 1978. Elizabeth Blackwell Award, Mary Washington Coll., 1980; Bradford Washburn Award, Boston, 1980. Hon. DSc: Witwatersrand, 1968; Western Michigan, 1980; Chicago, 1981; Hon. DSSc Yale, 1976; Hon. DLitt Oxford, 1981. *Publications:* Olduvai Gorge, vol. 3, Excavation in Beds I and II, 1971; Africa's Vanishing Art: the rock paintings of Tanzania, 1983; Disclosing the Past (autobiog.), 1984; various papers in Nature and other scientific jls. *Recreations:* reading, game watching. *Address:* c/o National Museum, Box 30239, Nairobi, Kenya.
    See also R. E. F. Leakey.

LEAKEY, Richard Erskine Frere; Director, National Museums of Kenya, since 1974 (Administrative Director, 1968–74); *b* 19 Dec. 1944; *s* of late Louis Seymour Bazett Leakey, FBA, and of Mary Leakey, qv; *m* 1970, Dr Meave (*née* Epps); thre *d. Educ:* Nairobi Primary Sch.; Lenana (formerly Duke of York) Sch., Nairobi. Self employed tour guide and animal trapper, 1961–65; Dir, Photographic Safaris in E Africa, 1965–68. Co-leader, palaeontol expedn to Lake Natron, Tanzania, 1963–64; expedn to Lake Baringo, Kenya, in search of early man, 1966; Co-leader, Internation Omo River Expedn, Ethiopia, in search of early man, 1967; Leader, E Turkana (formerly E Rudolf) Res. Proj. (multi-nat., interdisciplinary sci. consortium investigation of Plio/Pleistocene, Kenya's northern Rift Valley), 1968–. Former Chm., Foundn for Res. into Origin of Man (FROM); Vice-Chm., E African Wild Life Soc.; Trustee: Nat. Fund for the Disabled; Rocklord Coll., Illinois, 1983–; Wildlife Clubs of Kenya, 1985–; Governor, Regents Coll., London, 1985–. Presenter, The Making of Mankind, BBC TV series, 1981. *Publications:* (contrib.) General History of Africa, vol. 1, 1976; (with R. Lewin) Origins, 1978; (with R. Lewin) People of the Lake, 1979; (with M. G. Leakey) Koobi Fora Research Project, vol. I, 1979; The Making of Mankind, 1981; Human Origins, 1982; One Life, 1984; articles on palaeontol. in Nature, Jl of World Hist., Science, Amer. Jl of Phys. and Anthropol. *Address:* PO Box 40658, Nairobi, Kenya.

LEAN, Sir David, Kt 1984; CBE 1953; film director; *b* 25 March 1908; *s* of late Francis William le Blount Lean and Helena Annie Tangye; *m* 1st; one *s*; 2nd, 1949, Ann Todd, qv (marr. diss. 1957); 3rd, 1960, Mrs Leila Matkar (marr. diss. 1978); 4th, 1981, Sandra Hotz (marr. diss. 1985). *Educ:* Leighton Park Sch., Reading. Entered film industry as number board boy, 1928; edited and did commentary for Gaumont Sound News and British Movietone News; then edited Escape Me Never, Pygmalion, 49th Parallel, etc. Co-directed, with Noel Coward, In Which We Serve. *Directed:* This Happy Breed, Blithe Spirit, Brief Encounter, Great Expectations, Oliver Twist, The Passionate Friends, Madeleine, The Sound Barrier (British Film Academy Award, 1952), Hobson's Choice, Summer Madness (Amer. title Summertime), The Bridge on the River Kwai (US Academy Award for Best Picture, 1957), Lawrence of Arabia (US Academy Award, 1963, Italian silver ribbon, 1964), Doctor Zhivago, Ryan's Daughter, Passage to India. Officier de l'Ordre des Arts et des Lettres, France, 1968. Fellow: BAFTA, 1974; BFI, 1983. DLitt 1986.

LEANING, Ven. David; Archdeacon of Newark, since 1980. *Educ:* Keble Coll., Oxford, 1957–58; Lichfield Theological Coll. Deacon 1960, priest 1961, dio. Lincoln; Curate of Gainsborough, 1960–65; Rector of Warsop with Sookholme, 1965–76; Vicar of Kington and Rector of Huntington, Diocese of Hereford, 1976–80; RD of Kington and Weobley, 1976–80. *Address:* St Wilfrid's House, Church Lane, South Muskam, Newark, Notts NG23 6EQ. *T:* Newark 706308.

LEAPER, Prof. Robert Anthony Bernard, CBE 1975; Professor of Social Administration, University of Exeter, since 1970; *b* 7 June 1921; *s* of William Bambrick Leaper and Gertrude Elizabeth (*née* Taylor); *m* 1950, Elizabeth Arno; two *s* one *d. Educ:* Ratcliffe Coll., Leicester; St John's Coll., Cambridge (MA); Balliol Coll., Oxford (MA). Dipl. Public and Social Admin. (Oxon). Coal miner, 1941–44. Warden, St John Bosco Youth Centre, Stepney, 1945–47; Cadet officer, Civil Service, 1949–50; Co-operative Coll., Stanford Hall, 1950–56; Principal, Social Welfare Trng Centre, Zambia, 1956–59; Lectr, then Sen. Lectr, then Acting Dir, Social Admin., UC, Swansea, 1960–70. Exec., later Vice-Chm., Nat. Council of Social Service, 1964–80; Pres., European Region, Internat. Council on Social Welfare, 1971–79; Chairman: Area Bd, MSC, 1975–86; Centre for Policy on Ageing Adv. Council, 1982–. Editor, Social Policy and Administration. Médaille de l'Ecole Nationale de Santé, France, 1975. *Publications:* Communities and Social Change, 1966; Community Work, 1969, 2nd edn 1972; Health, Wealth and Housing, 1980; Change and Continuity, 1981; At Home in Devon, 1986. *Recreations:* walking, railways, wine. *Address:* Birchcote, New North Road, Exeter. *T:* Exeter 72565. *Club:* University Staff (Exeter).

LEAR, Cyril James; Editorial Manager, News Group Newspapers Ltd, 1974–76 (Editor, News of the World, 1970–73); *b* 9 Sept. 1911; *s* of R. H. Lear, Plymouth; *m* Marie Chatterton; five *s* one *d. Educ:* Hoe Grammar Sch., Plymouth. Served War of 1939–45: Rifleman, Queen's Westminsters; Major, Royal Berks Regt. Western Morning News, 1928–32; Torquay Times, 1932–34; Daily Mail, 1934–38; Daily Telegraph, 1938–39; News of the World, 1946–70: Features Editor, Asst Editor, Dep. Editor. *Recreations:* fishing, bridge. *Address:* c/o News International Ltd, 30 Bouverie Street, EC4.

LEARMONT, Maj.-Gen. John Hartley, CBE 1980 (OBE 1975); Commander Artillery, 1 (British) Corps, since 1985; *b* 10 March 1934; *s* of Captain Percy Hewitt Learmont, CIE, RIN and Doris Orynthia Learmont; *m* 1957, Susan (*née* Thornborrow); three *s. Educ:* Fettes College; RMA Sandhurst. Commissioned RA, 1954; Instructor, RMA, 1960–63; student, Staff Coll., 1964; served 14 Field Regt, Staff Coll. and 3 RHA, 1965–70; MA to C-in-C BAOR, 1971–73; CO 1 RHA, 1974–75 (despatches 1974); HQ BAOR, 1976–78; Comdr, 8 Field Force, 1979–81; Dep. Comdr, Commonwealth Monitoring Force, Rhodesia, Nov. 1979–March 1980; student RCDS, 1981; Chief of Mission, British Cs-in-C Mission to Soviet Forces in Germany, 1982–84. *Recreations:* fell walking, golf, theatre. *Address:* HQ Artillery, 1 (BR) Corps, BFPO 39. *Club:* Naval and Military.

LEAROYD, Wing Comdr Roderick Alastair Brook, VC 1940; RAF; *b* 5 Feb. 1913; *s* of late Major Reginald Brook Learoyd and Marjorie Scott Boadle. *Educ:* Wellington Coll. *Address:* 5 Selsey Court, Chanctonbury Road, Rustington, W Sussex.

LEARY, Brian Leonard; QC 1978; *b* 1 Jan. 1929; *o s* of late A. T. Leary; *m* 1965, Myriam Ann Bannister, *d* of Kenneth Bannister, CBE, Mexico City. *Educ:* King's Sch. Canterbury; Wadham Coll., Oxford. MA Oxon. Called to the Bar, Middle Temple, 1953; Harmsworth Scholar. Senior Prosecuting Counsel to the Crown at Central Criminal Court, 1971–78. *Recreations:* travel, sailing, growing herbs. *Address:* The Old Rectory, Ightham, Kent. *T:* Borough Green 882608; 5 Paper Buildings, Temple, EC4. *T:* 01–353 7811.

LEARY, Leonard Poulter, CMG 1973; MC 1917; QC (New Zealand) 1952; retired; *b* 1891; *s* of Richard Leary and Florence Lucy Giesen; *m*; three *s* two *d* (and one *d* decd). *Educ:* Palmerston North High Sch.; Wellington Coll.; Victoria University Coll. and Auckland University Coll. (LLB). Called to the Bar, New Zealand, 1920. Served European War, 1914–18: Samoan Exped. Force (NZR), 1914; Special Reserve RFA Egypt and France, 1914–18 (Captain, MC); served War of 1939–45: NZ Home Forces; Lt-Col RNZA, Actg CRA, 1944. Mem., later Chm., Disciplinary Cttee of NZ Law Soc., 1948–74; Pres., Lake Weed Control Soc. *Publications:* New Zealanders in Samoa, 1918; Tutankhamen (musical play), 1923; Abbess of Whitby (musical play), 1924; Not Entirely Legal (autobiog.), 1977. *Recreations:* music, gardening, fishing. *Address:* RD4 Otaramarae, Rotorua, New Zealand. *T:* Okere Falls 635. *Clubs:* Northern, Officers' (Auckland).

LEASK, Lt-Gen. Sir Henry (Lowther Ewart Clark), KCB 1970 (CB 1967); DSO 1945; OBE 1957 (MBE 1945); GOC Scotland and Governor of Edinburgh Castle, 1969–72, retired; *b* 30 June 1913; *s* of Rev. James Leask, MA; *m* Zoë de Camborne, *d* of Col W. P. Paynter, DSO, RHA; one *s* two *d*. 2nd Lt Royal Scots Fusiliers, 1936. Served War of 1939–45 in Mediterranean and Italy; GSO 1942; Bde Major Inf. Bde 1943; 2nd in Comd and CO, 8 Bn Argyll and Sutherland Highlanders, 1944–45; Comd 1st Bn London Scottish, 1946–47; Gen. Staff Mil. Ops, WO, 1947–49; Instr Staff Coll., 1949–51; Comd 1st Bn The Parachute Regt, 1952–54; Asst Military Sec. to Sec. of State for War, 1955–57; Comdt, Tactical Wing Sch. of Inf., 1957–58; Comd Infantry Bde, 1958–61; idc 1961; Dep. Mil. Sec. to Sec. of State for War, 1962–64; GOC 52 Lowland Div., 1964–66; Dir of Army Training, MoD (Army), 1966–69. Brig. 1961, Maj.-Gen. 1964, Lt-Gen. 1969. Col of the Royal Highland Fusiliers, 1964–69; Col Comdt, Scottish Div. of Infantry, 1968–72. *Recreations:* shooting and fishing. *Address:* 9 Glenalmond House, Manor Fields, SW15. *Clubs:* Carlton, Hurlingham; New (Edinburgh).

LEASOR, (Thomas) James; author; *b* 20 Dec. 1923; *s* of late Richard and Christine Leasor, Erith, Kent; *m* 1951, Joan Margaret Bevan, Barrister-at-law, *o d* of late Roland S. Bevan, Crowcombe, Somerset; three *s. Educ:* City of London Sch.; Oriel Coll., Oxford. Kentish Times, 1941–42. Served in Army in Burma, India, Malaya, 1942–46, Capt. Royal Berks Regt. Oriel Coll., Oxford, 1946–48, BA 1948; MA 1952; edited The Isis. On staff Daily Express, London, 1948–55, as reporter, foreign correspondent, feature writer. Contrib. to many American and British magazines, newspapers and periodicals; scriptwriter for TV series The Michaels in Africa. FRSA. OStJ. *Publications: novels:* Not Such a Bad Day, 1946; The Strong Delusion, 1951; NTR-Nothing to Report, 1955; Passport to Oblivion, 1964; Spylight, 1966; Passport in Suspense, 1967; Passport for a Pilgrim, 1968; They Don't Make Them Like That Any More, 1969; A Week of Love, 1969; Never had a Spanner on Her, 1970; Love-all, 1971; Follow the Drum, 1972; Host of Extras, 1973; Mandarin Gold, 1973; The Chinese Widow, 1974; Jade Gate, 1976; Love and the Land Beyond, 1979; Open Secret, 1982; Ship of Gold, 1984; Tank of Serpents, 1986; *non-fiction:* Author by Profession, The Monday Story, 1951; Wheels to Fortune, The Serjeant Major, 1954; The Red Fort; (with Kendal Burt) The One That Got Away, 1956; The Millionth Chance, 1957; War at the Top, 1959; (with Peter Eton) Conspiracy of Silence, 1959; Bring Out Your Dead, 1961; Rudolf Hess: The Uninvited Envoy, 1961; Singapore: The Battle that Changed the World, 1968; Green Beach, 1975; Boarding Party, 1977; The Unknown Warrior, 1980; Who Killed Sir Harry Oakes?, 1983. *Recreation:* vintage sports cars. *Address:* Swallowcliffe Manor, Salisbury, Wilts; Casa do Zimbro, Praia da Luz, Lagos, Algarve, Portugal. *Club:* Garrick.

LEATHAM, Dr Aubrey (Gerald), FRCP; Consultant Physician: St George's Hospital; National Heart Hospital; Cardiologist, King Edward VII Hospital; Dean, Institute of Cardiology, 1962–69; *b* 23 Aug. 1920; *s* of Dr H. W. Leatham (*d* 1973), Godalming and Kathleen Pelham Burn (*d* 1971), Nosely Hall, Leicester; *m* 1954, Judith Augustine Savile Freer; one *s* three *d. Educ:* Charterhouse; Trinity Hall, Cambridge; St Thomas' Hospital. BA Cambridge 1941; MB, BChir 1944; MRCP 1945; FRCP 1957. House Phys. St Thomas' Hosp., 1944; RMO, Nat. Heart Hosp., 1945; Phys., RAMC, 1946–47. Research Fellow, Cardiac Dept, and Sen. Registrar, London Hosp., 1948– Inst. of Cardiology, 1951–54. Goulstonian Lectr, RCP, 1958. R. T. Hall Tra Australia and NZ, 1963. Member: Brit. Cardiac Soc.; Sociedad Peruana de

1966; Sociedad Colombiana de Cardiologia, 1966. Hon. FACC 1986. Royal Order of Bhutan, 1966. *Publications:* Auscultation of the Heart and Phonocardiography, 1970; articles in Lancet, British Heart Jl, etc, on auscultation of the heart and phonocardiography, artificial pacemakers, coronary artery disease, etc. *Recreations:* ski-ing and ski-touring, mountain walking, tennis, racquets, gardening, photography. *Address:* 75 Albert Drive, SW19 6LB. *T:* 01–788 5759; 45 Wimpole Street, W1M 7D9. *T:* 01–935 5295; Rookwood Lane House, West Wittering, Sussex.

LEATHART, Air Cdre James Anthony, CB 1960; DSO 1940; *b* 5 Jan. 1915; *s* of P. W. Leathart, BSc, MD, Ear, Nose and Throat Specialist, Liverpool; *m* 1939, E. L. Radcliffe, Birkenhead; two *s* one *d. Educ:* St Edward's, Oxford; Liverpool Univ. Joined Auxiliary Air Force (610 County of Chester Squadron), 1936; transferred RAF, 1937; Chief of Staff Headquarters, 12 Group, RAF, 1959–61; Dir of Operational Requirements, Air Ministry, 1961–62, retd. Oct. 1962. *Recreations:* fly-fishing, motoring, ornithology, gardening. *Address:* Wortley Farmhouse, Wotton-under-Edge, Glos. *T:* Dursley 842312.

LEATHER, Sir Edwin (Hartley Cameron), KCMG 1974; KCVO 1975; Kt 1962; Governor and C-in-C of Bermuda, 1973–77; writer and broadcaster; *b* 22 May 1919; *s* of Harold H. Leather, MBE, Hamilton, Canada, and Grace C. Leather (*née* Holmes); *m* 1940, Sheila A. A. (CStJ), *d* of Major A. H. Greenlees, Hamilton; two *d. Educ:* Trinity College Sch., Canada; Royal Military Coll., Kingston, Canada. Served War of 1939–45 with Canadian Army, UK and in Europe, 1940–45. Contested (C) South Bristol, 1945; MP (C) N Somerset, 1950–64. Mem., Exec. Cttee, British Commonwealth Producers Organisation, 1960–63; Chairman: Bath Festival Soc., 1960–65; Horder Centres for Arthritics, 1962–65; Cons. and Unionist Assocs, 1969–70 (Mem. Nat. Exec. Cttee, 1963–70); Mem. Cons. Party Bd of Finance, 1963–67; Mem., Bd of Dirs, Yehudi Menuhin Sch., 1967–; Dir, N. M. Rothschild (Bermuda), and other cos. Canadian Legion rep. on Exec. Cttee of Brit. Commonwealth Ex-Servicemen's League, 1954–63; Pres., Institute of Marketing, 1963–67. Lay reader, in Church of England. Mem. Council, Imp. Soc. of Knights Bachelor, 1969–. FRSA 1969; Hon. LLD Bath, 1975. KStJ 1974. Gold Medal, Nat. Inst. Social Sciences, NY, 1977; Hon. Citizen, Kansas City, USA. Medal of Merit, Royal Canadian Legion. *Publications:* The Vienna Elephant, 1977; The Mozart Score, 1979; The Duveen Letter, 1980. *Address:* PO Box 819, Hamilton, Bermuda. *Clubs:* Hamilton (Ont.); York (Toronto); Canadian (NY); Royal Bermuda Yacht.

LEATHER, Ted; *see* Leather, Sir E. H. C.

LEATHERLAND, Baron, *cr* 1964, of Dunton (Life Peer); **Charles Edward Leatherland,** OBE 1951; Treasurer and Member of Council, University of Essex, from foundation until 1973; *b* 18 April 1898; *e s* of John Edward Leatherland, Churchover, Warwicks; *m* 1922, Mary Elizabeth, *d* of Joseph Henry Morgan, Shareshill, Staffs; one *s* one *d. Educ:* Harborne, Birmingham; University Extension Courses. Asst Editor, Daily Herald, until retirement, 1963. Served European War, 1914–19 (despatches, MSM); enlisted, 1914, aged 16; served in France, Belgium, Germany; Company Sgt Major, Royal Warwicks Regt; Essex TA Assoc., 1946–68, and E Anglian TA Assoc., 1968. Chm., Essex County Council, 1960–61 (Vice-Chm. 1952–55 and 1958–60); CA Essex, 1946–68. Dep. Chm., Epping Magistrates Bench. JP (Essex) 1944–70; DL Essex, 1963. Mem. Bd of Basildon Development Corporation, 1967–71. Additional Mem., Monopolies Commn, to consider newspaper mergers, 1969. Chm., E Counties Regional Council of the Labour Party, 1950–66. DUniv. Essex, 1973. *Publications:* (part author) The Book of the Labour Party, 1925; Labour Party pamphlets; contribs on local govt affairs in Municipal Jl and general press; 4 Prince of Wales Gold Medals 1923 and 1924 for essays on: Measures that may be taken by other countries to promote an improvement in the economic condition of Czecho-Slovakia, 1923; The possibilities of the cinema in the development of commercial education, 1923; Difficulties attending the economic position of Czecho-Slovakia after the Peace Treaty, and the methods adopted to remove them, 1924; Home and foreign trade: their relative importance and interdependence, 1924. *Recreations:* formerly fox hunting, now walking. *Address:* 19 Starling Close, Buckhurst Hill, Essex. *T:* 01–504 3164.

LEATHERS, family name of Viscount Leathers.

LEATHERS, 2nd Viscount, *cr* 1954; **Frederick Alan Leathers;** Baron Leathers, 1941; Director: National Westminster Bank, Outer London Region; *b* 4 April 1908; *er s* of 1st Viscount Leathers, PC, CH, LLD; *S* father, 1965; *m* 1st, 1940, Elspeth Graeme (marr. diss. 1983; she *d* 1985), *yr d* of late Sir Thomas (Alexander) Stewart; two *s* two *d*; 2nd, 1983, Mrs Lorna M. Barnett. *Educ:* Brighton Coll.; Emmanuel Coll., Cambridge (MA (hons) in Economics). Mem. of Baltic Exchange. Director: Wm Cory & Son Ltd, 1929–72 (Chm.); Cory Mann George Ltd, 1941–72 (Chm.); Cory Ship Towage Ltd, 1941–72 (Chm.); Smit & Cory International Port Towage Ltd, 1970–72 (Chm.); Hull Blyth & Co. Ltd, 1949–72 (Chm.); Rea Ltd, 1941–72 (Chm.); St Denis Shipping Co. Ltd, 1957–72 (Chm.); Laporte Industries Ltd, 1959–71; Laporte Industries (Holdings) Ltd, 1959–71; Tunnel Cement Ltd, 1960–74; Guardian Cement Co. Ltd, 1963–71; New Zealand Cement Holdings Ltd, 1963–71. Member: Court of Worshipful Company of Shipwrights; Court of Watermen's and Lightermen's Company; Fellow Institute of Chartered Shipbrokers; FRPSL; FRSA; MInstPet. Heir: *s* Hon. Christopher Graeme Leathers [*b* 31 Aug. 1941; *m* 1964, Maria Philomena, *yr d* of Michael Merriman, Charlestown, Co. Mayo; one *s* one *d*]. *Address:* Park House, Chiddingfold, Surrey GU8 4TS. *T:* Wormley 3222. *Club:* Royal Automobile.

LEATHES, Maj.-Gen. Reginald Carteret de Mussenden, CB 1960; LVO 1947; OBE 1952; *b* 19 Sept. 1909; *s* of late Major Carteret de M. Leathes; *m* 1939, Marjorie Mary Elphinston; three *s* one *d. Educ:* Imperial Service Coll. 2nd Lt, Royal Marines, 1928; HMS Resolution, 1931–33; ADC to Governor of Queensland, 1935–37; 1st Bn Royal Marines, 1940–43; 42 Commando RM, 1943–44; GSO1 HQ, SACSEA, 1944–45; GSO1 HQ, Land Forces Hong Kong, 1945–46; HMS Vanguard, 1947; RN Staff Coll., 1947–49; 45 Commando RM, 1950–52; Comdt Amphibious Sch., RM, 1952–55; Col GS Staff Comdt Gen., RM, 1956; idc 1957, ADC to the Queen, 1957–58. Chief of Staff to Comdt Gen., RM, 1958–60; Maj.-Gen. Commanding Royal Marines, Portsmouth, 1961–62. Retired, 1962. Col Comdt, RM, 1971–74. Ski-ing representative, British Olympic Cttee, 1965–76. Officer Order of Phoenix (Greece), 1933; Chevalier Legion of Honour and Croix de Guerre (France), 1945; Officer Order of Cloud and Banner (China), 1945. *Recreations:* fishing, ski-ing. *Address:* c/o Lloyds Bank PLC, Boltro Road, Haywards Heath, West Sussex RH16 1BY.

LEAVER, Sir Christopher, GBE 1981; JP; Managing Director, Russell & McIver Group of Companies (Wine Merchants); *b* 3 Nov. 1937; *s* of Dr Robert Leaver and Mrs Audrey Kerpen; *m* 1975, Helen Mireille Molyneux Benton; one *s* two *d. Educ:* Eastbourne Coll. Commissioned (Army), RAOC, 1956–58. Member, Retail Foods Trades Wages Council, 1963–64. JP Inner London, 1970–83, City, 1974–; Member: Council, Royal Borough of Kensington and Chelsea, 1970–73; Court of Common Council (Ward of Dowgate), City of London, 1973; Alderman (Ward of Dowgate), City of London, 1974; Sheriff of the City of London, 1979–80; Lord Mayor of London, 1981–82; HM Lieutenant, City of London, 1982. Chm., London Tourist Bd, 1983–; Dep. Chm., Thames Water Authority, 1983–; Dir, Thermal Scientific plc. Member: Ct of Assistants, Carmen's Company, 1973;

Bd of Brixton Prison, 1975–78; Court, City Univ., 1978– (Chancellor, 1981–82); Ct, Mary Rose Trust, 1982–; St Bartholomew's Hosp. Voluntary Bd, 1983–85; Council of the Missions to Seamen, 1983–; Council, Wine and Spirit Benevolent Soc.; Finance Cttee, London Diocesan Fund, 1983–86; Trustee: Chichester Festival Theatre, 1982–; LSO, 1983–; Vice-President: Bridewell Royal Hosp., 1982–; European Academy GB, 1982–; NPFA, 1983–; Governor: Christ's Hospital Sch., 1975; City of London Girls' Sch., 1975–78; City of London Freemen's Sch., 1980–81; Almoner Trustee, St Paul's Cathedral Choir Sch. Foundn. Trustee, Music Therapy Trust, 1981–; Chairman, Young Musicians' Symphony Orch. Trust, 1979–81; Hon. Mem., Guildhall Sch. of Music and Drama, 1982–. Church Warden, St Olave's, Hart Street, 1975–; Church Comr, 1982–. Hon. Liveryman, Farmers' Company; Freedom, Co. of Watermen and Lightermen; Hon. Mem., Co. of Environmental Cleaners, 1983–; Hon. Col, 151 (Greater London) Tpt Regt RCT (V). Hon. DMus City, 1981. KStJ 1982; FCIT 1981; FRSA 1980. Order of Oman Class II. *Recreations:* gardening, music. *Address:* The Rectory, St Mary-at-Hill, EC3R 8EE. *T:* 01–283 3575. *Clubs:* City Livery, Guildhall, Eccentric.

LEAVER, Prof. Christopher John, FRS 1986; Professor of Plant Molecular Biology, University of Edinburgh, since 1986; *b* 31 May 1942; *s* of Douglas Percy Leaver and Elizabeth Constance Leaver; *m* 1971, Anne (*née* Huggins); one *s* one *d. Educ:* Imperial College, University of London (BSc, ARCS, DIC, PhD). Fulbright Scholar, Purdue Univ., 1966–68; Scientific Officer, ARC Plant Physiology Unit, Imperial Coll., 1968–69; University of Edinburgh: Lectr, Dept of Botany, 1969–80; Reader, 1980–86; SERC Sen. Res. Fellow, 1985–. T. H. Huxley Gold Medal, Imperial Coll., 1970; Tate & Lyle Award, Phytochem. Soc. of Europe, 1984. *Publications:* numerous papers in internat. sci. jls. *Recreations:* walking and talking. *Address:* 12 Ross Road, Edinburgh EH16 5QN. *T:* 031–667 8873.

LEAVETT, Alan; Member: Development Commission, since 1982; Woodspring District Council, 1986; Vice-Chairman, Avon Community Council, since 1981; *b* 4 May 1924; *s* of George and Mabel Dorothy Leavett; *m* 1948, Jean Mary, *d* of Arthur Wanford, ISO, Harwich; three *d. Educ:* Gosport County Sch.; UC, Southampton. BA Hons 1943. MAP (RAE), 1943; HM Customs and Excise, 1947; HM Foreign Service, 1949; Rio de Janeiro, 1950–53; Bangkok, 1955–59; UK Perm. Delegate to ECAFE, 1958; Cabinet Office, 1961; Min. of Housing and Local Govt, 1963; Sec., Noise Adv. Council, 1970; Under-Sec., Civil Service Selection Bd, 1973, Dept of Environment, 1974–81. Gen. Sec., Avon Wildlife Trust, 1981–84; Member: Council, World Wildlife Fund UK, 1983–; Exec. Cttee, ECOVAST, 1984–. *Publication:* Historic Sevenoaks, 1969. *Recreations:* book-collecting, music. *Address:* Darenth House, St Martins, Long Ashton, Bristol BS18 9HP. *T:* Long Ashton 392876. *Club:* Royal Commonwealth Society (Bristol).

LEAVEY, John Anthony, BA; Chairman, Edward Barber & Co. Ltd; *b* 3 March 1915; *s* of George Edwin Leavey and Marion Louise Warnock; *m* 1952, Lesley Doreen, *d* of Rt Hon. Sir Benjamin Ormerod. *Educ:* Mill Hill Sch.; Trinity Hall, Cambridge. Served War, 1939–46; 5th Royal Inniskilling Dragoon Guards. MP (C) Heywood and Royton Div. of Lancashire, 1955–64. *Recreation:* fishing. *Address:* 30 Pembroke Gardens Close, W8 6HR. *Club:* Army and Navy.

LE BAILLY, Vice-Adm. Sir Louis (Edward Stewart Holland), KBE 1972 (OBE 1952); CB 1969; DL; Director-General of Intelligence, Ministry of Defence, 1972–75; *b* 18 July 1915; *s* of Robert Francis Le Bailly and Ida Gaskell Le Bailly (*née* Holland); *m* 1946, Pamela Ruth Berthon; three *d. Educ:* RNC Dartmouth. HMS Hood, 1932; RNEC, 1933–37; HMS Hood, 1937–40; HMS Naiad, 1940–42; RNEC, 1942–44; HMS Duke of York, 1944–46; Admiralty, 1946–50; HMS Bermuda, 1950–52; RNEC, 1955–58; Admiralty: Staff Officer to Dartmouth Review Cttee, 1958; Asst Engineer-in-Chief, 1958–60; Naval Asst to Controller of the Navy, 1960–63; IDC, 1963; Dep. Dir of Marine Engineering, 1963–67; Naval Attaché, Washington, DC, and Comdr, British Navy Staff, 1967–69; Min. of Defence, 1970–72; Vice-Adm. 1970, retired 1972. Mem. Council, Inst. for Study of Conflict. DL Cornwall, 1982. FIMechE; FInstPet; MIMarE. *Address:* Garlands House, St Tudy, Bodmin, Cornwall. *Club:* Naval and Military.

LE BAS, Air Vice-Marshal Michael Henry, CB 1969; CBE 1966; DSO 1944; AFC 1954; retired; *b* 28 Sept. 1916; *s* of late R. W. O. Le Bas and Florence Marrs; *m* 1945, Moyra Benitz; one *s* one *d. Educ:* St George's Coll., Buenos Aires; Malvern Coll. Joined RAF, 1940; served in Fighter Command, Malta, Western Desert, and Italy, 1941–44; RAF Staff Coll., 1948–51; HQ 2 TAF and RAF Wildenrath, 1951–54; Sch. of Land Air Warfare, 1954–56; Suez, 1956; OC, RAF Coningsby, 1959–61; HQ Bomber Comd, 1961–63; SASO, Air Forces Middle East, 1963–66; AOC No. 1 Group, Bomber Command, 1966–68; AOC No. 1 (Bomber) Gp, Strike Comd, 1968; Dir Gen. of Personal Services (RAF), MoD, 1969–71. *Recreations:* golf, shooting, photography. *Address:* c/o Midland Bank, Oakham, Leicestershire. *Club:* Royal Air Force.

LEBETER, Fred; Keeper, Department of Transport and Mining, Science Museum, 1953–67; *b* 27 Dec. 1903; *e s* of Arthur Lebeter, Mining Engineer, and Lucy Wilson; *m* 1926, Sybil Leah, *o d* of Henry Ward; one *d* decd. *Educ:* Rotherham and Bridgnorth Gram. Schs; Birmingham Univ. BSc 1925; MSc (Research on Classification of British Coals) 1926. Manager, Magnesite Mines and Works, Salem, S India, 1926–31; Lecturer in Mining, Heanor Mining Sch., 1931–33; Sen. Lectr in Mining, Chesterfield Tech. Coll., 1933–37; Asst Keeper, Science Museum, 1937–39; Dep. Chief Mining Supplies Officer, Min. of Fuel and Power, 1939–47; Asst Keeper, Science Museum, 1947–49, Dep. Keeper, 1949–53. Consultant on Mine Ventilation and Underground Transport, 1931–; Mem. Council Nat. Assoc. of Colliery Managers (Midland Br.), 1935–37; Adviser to Coal Commission, Germany, on Mining Supplies, 1944; UK rep. to European Coal Organisation, 1945–47. United Kingdom delegate to European Coal Organisation, Paris, 1946. Mem., Industrial Cttee, National Museum of Wales, 1959–67. Retired 1967. *Publications:* contributor of many technical articles to Colliery Engineering, Mine and Quarry Engineering, historical articles in Zeitschrift für Kunst und Kultur im Bergbau, etc. *Recreations:* sport and gardening. *Address:* The Lodge, 9a Southdown Road, Seaford, E Sussex BN25 4PA. *T:* Seaford 894751.

LEBLANC, Rt. Rev. Camille André; Chaplain at Caraquet Hospital; *b* Barachois, NB, 25 Aug. 1898. *Educ:* Collège Sainte-Anne, Church Point, NS; Grand Séminaire Halifax, NS. Priest, 1924; Subseq. Curé at Shemogue and the Cathedral of Nôtre Dame de l'Assomption, Moncton; Bishop of Bathurst, 1942–69. *Address:* c/o Caraquet Hospital, Caraquet, NB, Canada.

LEBLOND, Prof. C(harles) P(hilippe), OC 1977; MD, PhD, DSc; FRSC 1951; FRS 1965; Professor of Anatomy, McGill University, Canada, since 1948; *b* 5 Feb. 1910; *s* of Oscar Leblond and Jeanne Desmarchelier; *m* 1936, Gertrude Elinor Sternschuss; three *s* one *d. Educ:* Sch. St Joseph, Lille, France; Univs. of Lille, Nancy, Paris, Montreal. L-ès-S, Nancy 1932; MD Paris 1934; PhD Montreal 1942; DSc Sorbonne 1945. Asst in Histology, Med. School, Univ. of Paris, 1934–35; Rockefeller Fell., Sch. of Med., Yale Univ., 1936–37; Asst, Laboratoire de Synthèse Atomique, Paris, 1938–40; McGill Univ.: Lectr in Histology and Embryology, 1941–42; Asst Prof. of Anatomy, 1942–43; Assoc. Prof. of Anatomy, 1946–48; Prof. of Anatomy, 1948–; Chm. of Dept of Anatomy,

1957–75. Mem. Amer. Assoc. of Anatomists; Fellow, Amer. Acad. of Arts and Scis. Hon. DSc: Acadia, 1972; McGill, 1982; Montreal, 1985. *Publications*: over 300 articles, mainly on radio-autography, in anatomical journals. *Recreation*: country. *Address*: (home) 68 Chesterfield Avenue, Westmount, Montreal, Quebec H3Y 2M5, Canada. *T*: 514-486–4837; (office) Department of Anatomy, McGill University, 3640 University Street, Montreal, Quebec H3A 2B2, Canada. *T*: 514–392–4931.

LE BRETON, David Francis Battye, CBE 1978; HM Diplomatic Service; Head of Nationality and Treaty Department, Foreign and Commonwealth Office, since 1986; *b* 2 March 1931; *e s* of late Lt-Col F. H. Le Breton, MC, and Elisabeth Le Breton (*née* Trevor-Battye), Endebess, Kenya; *m* 1961, Patricia June Byrne; one *s* two *d. Educ*: Winchester; New Coll., Oxford. Colonial Administrative Service, Tanganyika, 1954; Private Sec. to Governor, 1959–60; Magistrate, 1962; Principal, CRO, 1963; HM Diplomatic Service, 1965; First Sec., Zanzibar, 1964; Lusaka, 1964–68; FCO, 1968–71; Head of Chancery, Budapest, 1971–74; HM Comr in Anguilla, 1974–78; Counsellor and Head of Chancery, Nairobi, 1978–81; High Comr in The Gambia, 1981–84; Head of Commonwealth Co-ordination Dept, FCO, 1984–86. *Recreations*: travel, African affairs. *Address*: c/o Foreign and Commonwealth Office, SW1; Brackenwood, French Street, near Westerham, Kent TN16 1PN.

le BROCQUY, Louis, FSIAD 1960; HRHA 1983; painter since 1939; *b* Dublin, 10 Nov. 1916; *s* of late Albert le Brocquy, MA, and late Sybil Staunton; *m* 1st, 1938, Jean Stoney (marr. diss., 1948); one *d*; 2nd, 1958, Anne Madden Simpson; two *s. Educ*: St Gerard's Sch., Wicklow, Ireland. Self-taught. Founder-mem. of Irish Exhibn of Living Art, 1943; Visiting Instructor, Central Sch. of Arts and Crafts, London, 1947–54; Visiting Tutor, Royal Coll. of Art, London, 1955–58. Mem., Irish Council of Design, 1963–65. Adv. Council, Guiness Pete Awards, 1980–. Dir, Kilkenny Design Workshops, 1965–77. Represented Ireland, Venice Biennale (awarded internat. prize), 1956. Work exhibited in "50 Ans d'Art Moderne", Brussels, 1958. One Man Shows: Leicester Galleries, London, 1948; Gimpel Fils, London, 1947, 1949, 1951, 1955, 1956, 1957, 1959, 1961, 1966, 1968, 1971, 1974, 1978, 1983; Waddington, Dublin, 1951; Robles Gallery, Los Angeles, 1960; Gallery Lienhard, Zürich, 1961; Dawson/Taylor Gallery, Dublin, 1962, 1966, 1969, 1971, 1973, 1974, 1975, 1981, 1985; Municipal Gallery of Modern Art, Dublin, 1966, 1978; Ulster Mus., Belfast (retrospective), 1966–67; Gimpel-Hanover, Emmerich Zürich, 1969, 1978 1983; Gimpel, NY, 1971, 1978, 1983; Foundation Maeght, 1973; Bussola, Turin, 1974; Arts Council, Belfast, 1975, 1978; Musée d'Art Moderne, Paris, 1976; Giustiniani, Genoa, 1977; Waddington, Montreal, Toronto, 1978; Maeght, Barcelona, Madrid, Granada, 1978–79; Jeanne Bucher, Paris, 1979, 1982; NY State Mus., 1981; Boston Coll. 1982; Westfield Coll., Mass, 1982; Palais des Beaux Arts, Charleroi, 1982; Chicago Internat. (Brownstone), 1986. Public Collections possessing work include: Albright Museum, Buffalo; Arts Council, London; Carnegie Inst., Pittsburgh; Centre National d'Art Pompidou, Paris; Chicago Arts Club; Columbus Mus., Ohio; Detroit Inst. of Art; Dublin Municipal Gallery; Fort Worth Center, Texas; Gulbenkian Mus., Lisbon; Guggenheim Museum, NY; J. H. Hirshhorn Foundation, Washington; Kunsthaus, Zürich; Fondation Maeght, St Paul; Leeds City Art Gallery; Musée d'Art Moderne, Paris; Musée Picasso, Antibes; Foundation of Brazil Museum, Bahia; San Diego Mus., Calif.; Tate Gallery; Uffizi, Florence; Ulster Museum, Belfast; V&A Museum. RHA 1950–69. Chevalier de la Légion d'Honneur, 1974. Hon. DLitt Dublin, 1962. Commandeur du Bontemps de Médoc et des Graves, 1969. *Illustrated work*: The Táin, trans. Thomas Kinsella, 1969; The Playboy of the Western World, Synge, 1970; The Gododdin, 1978; Dubliners, Joyce, 1986. *Relevant publication*: Louis le Brocquy by D. Walker, introd. John Russell, Ireland 1981, UK 1982. *Address*: c/o Gimpel Fils, 30 Davies Street, W1Y 1LG.

LE CARRÉ, John; *see* Cornwell, David John Moore.

LE CHEMINANT, Peter, CB 1976; Director-General, General Council of British Shipping, since 1985; *b* 29 April 1926; *s* of William Arthur Le Cheminant; *m* 1959, Suzanne Elisabeth Horny; three *s. Educ*: Holloway Sch.; London Sch. of Economics. Sub-Lt, RNVR, 1944–47. Min. of Power, 1949; Cabinet Office, 1950–52 and 1964–65; UK Delegn to ECSC, 1962–63; Private Sec. to Prime Minister, 1965–68; Min. of Power, later Min. of Technology, 1968–71; Under-Sec., DTI, 1971–74; Deputy Secretary: Dept of Energy, 1974–77; Cabinet Office, 1978–81; CSD, subseq. HM Treas., 1981–83; Second Perm. Sec., Cabinet Office (MPO), 1983–84. *Recreations*: reading, walking, history. *Address*: 30–32 St Mary Axe, EC3.

LE CHEMINANT, Air Chief Marshal Sir Peter (de Lacey), GBE 1978; KCB 1972 (CB 1968); DFC 1943, and Bar, 1951; Lieutenant-Governor and Commander-in-Chief of Guernsey, 1980–85; *b* 17 June 1920; *s* of Lieut-Colonel Keith Le Cheminant and Blanche Etheldred Wake Le Cheminant (*née* Clark); *m* 1940, Sylvia, *d* of J. van Bodegom; one *s* two *d. Educ*: Elizabeth Coll., Guernsey; RAF Coll., Cranwell. Flying posts in France, UK, N Africa, Malta, Sicily and Italy, 1940–44; comd No 223 Squadron, 1943–44; Staff and Staff Coll. Instructor, 1945–48; Far East, 1949–53; comd No 209 Sqn, 1949–51; Jt Planning Staff, 1953–55; Wing Comdr, Flying, Kuala Lumpur, 1955–57; jssc 1958; Dep. Dir of Air Staff Plans, 1958–61; comd RAF Geilenkirchen, 1961–63; Dir of Air Staff Briefing, 1964–66; SASO, HQ FEAF, 1966–67, C of S, 1967–68; Comdt Joint Warfare Estabt, MoD, 1968–70; Asst Chief of Air Staff (Policy), MoD, 1971–72; UK Mem., Perm. Mil. Deputies Gp, CENTO, Ankara, 1972–73; Vice-Chief of Defence Staff, 1974–76; Dep. C-in-C, Allied Forces, Central Europe, 1976–79. KStJ 1980. *Recreations*: golf, sailing, reading. *Address*: La Madeleine De Bas, Ruette de la Madeleine, St Pierre du Bois, Guernsey, CI. *Club*: Royal Air Force.

LECHIN-SUAREZ, Brigadier General Juan, Condor de los Andes, Guerrillero José Miguel Lanza, Mérito Aeronautico, Mérito Naval (Bolivia); *b* 8 March 1921; *s* of Juan Alfredo Lechín and Julia Suárez; *m* 1947, Ruth Varela; one *s* three *d. Educ*: Bolivian Military College. Chief of Ops, Bolivian Army HQ, 1960–61; Military and Air Attaché, Bolivian Embassy, Bonn, 1962–63; Comdr, Bolivian Army Fifth Inf. Div., 1964; Pres., Bolivian State Mining Corp. (with rank of Minister of State), 1964–68; Comdr, Bolivian Army Third Inf. Div., 1969; Bolivian Ambassador to the UK and to the Netherlands, 1970–74; Minister for Planning and Co-ordination, 1974–78; Chm., Nat. Adv. and Legislation Council, 1980–81. Das Grosse Verdienstkreuz (Fed. Rep. Germany). *Recreations*: tennis, swimming. *Address*: Casilla 4405, La Paz, Bolivia.

LECHMERE, Sir Berwick (Hungerford), 6th Bt, *cr* 1818; JP; Vice Lord-Lieutenant, Hereford and Worcester, since 1977; Land Agent; *b* 21 Sept. 1917; *s* of Sir Ronald Berwick Hungerford Lechmere, 5th Bt, and Constance Marguerite (*née* Long) (*d* 1981); S father, 1965; *m* 1954, Norah Garrett Elkington; no *c. Educ*: Charterhouse; Magdalene Coll., Cambridge. High Sheriff of Worcs, 1962, JP, 1966, DL 1972. FRICS. CStJ. *Heir: cousin* Reginald Anthony Hungerford Lechmere [*b* 24 Dec. 1920; *m* 1956, Anne Jennifer Dind; three *s* one *d*]. *Address*: Church End House, Hanley Castle, Worcester. *T*: Upton-on-Severn 2130.

LECKIE, John, CB 1955; *b* 2 Sept. 1911; *o s* of late Alexander M. Leckie; *m* 1937, Elizabeth Mary Murray Brown; two *s. Educ*: Hamilton Academy; Glasgow Univ. (MA, BSc). Entered Administrative Class, Home Civil Service, by competitive examination,

1934; Customs and Excise Dept, 1934; transferred to Board of Trade, 1940; Head of Board of Trade Delegation, Washington, USA, 1943–45; Adviser on Commercial Policy, 1950; Under-Sec., 1950–60, Second Sec., 1960–64, BoT; Deputy Secretary: Min. of Technology, 1964–70; DTI, 1970–72, retd 1972. *Address*: 1 The Wedges, West Chiltington Lane, Itchingfield, Horsham, Sussex RH13 7TA.

LECKONBY, William Douglas, CBE 1967; Collector of Customs and Excise, London Port, 1963–67, retired; *b* 23 April 1907; *m* 1933; one *d. Educ*: Hymers Coll., Hull. Entered Customs and Excise, 1928; subsequently held various posts in that department. *Address*: Ebor, Withyham Road, Groombridge, Sussex. *T*: Groombridge 401.

LECKY, Arthur Terence, CMG 1968; HM Diplomatic Service, retired; *b* 10 June 1919; *s* of late Lieut-Colonel M. D. Lecky, DSO, late RA, and late Bertha Lecky (*née* Goss); *m* 1946, Jacqualine (*d* 1974), *d* of late Dr A. G. Element; three *s. Educ*: Winchester Coll.; Clare Coll., Cambridge (1938–39). Served RA, 1939–46. FO (Control Commission for Germany), 1946–49; FO, 1950–54; Vice-Consul, Zürich, 1954–56; FO, 1957–61; First Secretary, The Hague, 1962–64, FCO (formerly FO), 1964–70, retired. Mem., Hants CC, 1981–. *Address*: Springfield, Mill End, Damerham, near Fordingbridge, Hants SP6 3HU. *T*: Rockbourne 595.

LECKY, Maj.-Gen. Samuel Knox, CB 1979; OBE 1967; BSc(Eng), CEng, FIMechE, FIAgrE, CBIM; Director-General, Agricultural Engineers Association, since 1980; *b* 10 Feb. 1926; *s* of late J. D. Lecky, Coleraine; *m* 1947, Sheila Jones; one *s* two *d. Educ*: Coleraine Acad.; Queen's Univ., Belfast (BSc). Commnd REME, 1946; served Egypt, 1951–52; Kenya, 1953–54; jssc 1964; AA&QMG HQ 1(BR) Corps, 1965–66; CREME 4 Div., 1966–68; Sec., Principal Personnel Officers, MoD, 1968–70; RCDS, 1971; Comdt, SEME, 1972–74; DEME, BAOR, 1975; Dir, Military Assistance Office, MoD, 1976–77; Minister (DS), British Embassy, Tehran, 1977–79. Hon. Col, QUB OTC, 1978–83; Col Comdt, REME, 1980–86. *Recreations*: fishing, shooting. *Address*: 6 Buckingham Gate, SW1E 6JU. *Club*: Caledonian.

LECONFIELD, Baron; *see* Egremont.

LECOURT, Robert; Commandeur, Legion of Honour; Croix de Guerre; Rosette de la Résistance; Member, Constitutional Council of the French Republic, since 1979; *b* 19 Sept. 1908; *s* of Léon Lecourt and Angèle Lépron; *m* 1932, Marguerite Chabrerie; one *d. Educ*: Rouen; Univ. de Caen (DenDroit). Advocate, Court of Appeal: Rouen, 1928; Paris, 1932. Served with French Air Force, 1939–40; Mem. Resistance Movt, 1942–44; Deputy for Paris, 1945–58 and for Hautes Alpes, 1958–61, National Assembly; Pres., MRP Party, 1945–48 and 1952–57; Minister of Justice, 1948–49 and 1957–58; Minister of State responsible for co-operation with Africa, 1958–61. Judge, Court of Justice, European Community, 1962, President 1967–76; Hon. Bencher, Gray's Inn, 1972; DUniv Exeter, 1975. Holds numerous foreign decorations. *Publications*: Nature juridique de l'action en réintégrande, 1931; Code pratique du travail, Responsabilité des architectes et entrepreneurs, etc, 1932–39; Le Juge devant le marché commun, 1970; L'Europe des juges, 1976; Concorde sans concordat 1952–57, 1978; contrib. Le Monde, Figaro, Aurore, and other European jls. *Address*: 11 Boulevard Suchet, 75016 Paris, France.

LEDERBERG, Prof. Joshua, PhD; President, Rockefeller University, since 1978; consultant; *b* Montclair, NJ, USA, 23 May 1925; *s* of Zwi H. and Esther Lederberg (*née* Goldenbaum); *m* 1968, Marguerite Stein Kirsch, MD; one *d*, one step *s. Educ*: Stuyvesant High Sch., NYC; Columbia Coll. (BA); Yale Univ. (PhD). Assistant Professor of Genetics, University of Wisconsin, 1947; Associate Professor, 1950; Professor, 1954; Fulbright Vis. Prof. of Bacteriology, Univ. of Melbourne, Aust., 1957; Prof. and Exec. Head, Dept of Genetics, Sch. of Medicine, Stanford Univ., 1959–78. Dir, Procter & Gamble Co., Cincinnati, Ohio, 1984–; Consultant: Cetus Cos, Berkeley, Calif, 1972–; J. D. Wolfensohn Assoc., NY, 1983–. Shared in discoveries concerning genetic re-combination, and organization of genetic material of bacteria, contributing to cancer research; discovered a method of artificially introducing new genes into bacteria in investigation of hereditary substance. Chm., President's Cancer Panel (US), 1980–81. Member: Defense Sci. Bd, USA, 1979–; CNO Exec. Panel, USN, 1981–; Council of Scholars, US Library of Congress, 1985–; Adv. Cttee for Med. Res., WHO, 1971–76; Trustee, Carnegie Corp., NYC, 1985–. Columnist, Science and Man (Washington Post Syndicate), 1966–71. Mem., National Academy of Sciences, United States, 1957. For. Mem., Royal Society, 1979. ScD (*hc*): Yale Univ.; Columbia Univ.; Univ. of Wisconsin; Mt Sinai Sch. of Medicine; Rutgers; New York Univ.; MD (*hc*): Tufts Univ.; Univ. of Turin; LittD (*hc*) Jewish Theol Seminary; LLD (*hc*) Univ. of Pennsylvania. (Jointly) Nobel Prize in Medicine, 1958. *Publications*: contribs to learned journals on genetics, bacteria and general biological problems. *Address*: Rockefeller University, 1230 York Avenue, New York, NY 10021, USA. *T*: 212.570.8080.

LEDGER, Frank, OBE 1985; Board Member, Central Electricity Generating Board, since 1986; *b* 16 June 1929; *s* of Harry and Doris Ledger; *m* 1953, Alma Moverley; two *s. Educ*: Leeds College of Technology (BSc Eng). CEng; FIEE; MIMechE. Student Apprentice, Leeds Corp. Elect. Dept, 1947; appts in power station construction and generation operation in CEA then CEGB, 1955–65; Station Manager, Cottam Power Station, 1965; CEGB: Group Manager, Midlands Region, 1968; System Operation Engineer, 1971; Dir, Resource Planning, Midlands Region, 1975; Dir of Computing, 1980; Dir of Operations, 1981. *Recreations*: music, photography, gardening, walking. *Address*: 3 Barns Dene, Harpenden, Herts AL5 2HH. *T*: Harpenden 62188.

LEDGER, Sir Frank, (Joseph Francis), Kt 1963; retired Company Director (engineering etc); *b* 29 Oct. 1899; *s* of Edson and Annie Frances Ledger; *m* 1923, Gladys Muriel Lyons; one *s* two *d. Educ*: Perth Boys' Sch., Perth, WA. President: J. E. Ledger Cos; Mitchell Cotts Gp; Dir, Mitchell Cotts Australia; Governing Dir, Ledger Investments; Past Chm. of Dirs, S Australian Insurance Co.; Director: Chamber of Manufrs Insurance Co.; ARC Engineering Co.; Winget Moxey (WA) Pty Ltd; Lake View and Star Ltd; Member, Past Chairman: WA Branch of Inst. of Directors (London); WA Govt Industrial Develt Adv. Cttee; Pres., Royal Commonwealth Society (WA Branch); Past President: WA Chamber of Manufacturers; WA Employers Federation; Ironmasters Assoc. (WA); Metal Industries Assoc. (WA); Inst. of Foundrymen (WA); Past Vice-Pres., Associated Chamber of Manufacturers (Canberra). Pres., WA Trotting Assoc.; Vice-Pres., Australian Trotting Council. *Recreations*: golfing, sailing. *Address*: 2 The Esplanade, Peppermint Grove, WA 6011, Australia. *Clubs*: Weld, Perth, Royal Freshwater Bay Yacht, Cottesloe Golf; WA Turf, WA Cricket Association (all in Perth, WA).

LEDGER, Sir Joseph Francis; *see* Ledger, Sir Frank.

LEDGER, Philip (Stevens), CBE 1985; FRCM 1983; Hon. RAM 1984; Principal, Royal Scottish Academy of Music and Drama, since 1982; *b* 12 Dec. 1937; *s* of Walter Stephen Ledger and Winifred Kathleen (*née* Stevens); *m* 1963, Mary Erryl (*née* Wells); one *s* one *d. Educ*: Bexhill Grammar Sch.; King's Coll., Cambridge (Maj. Schol.). John Rannoch Schol. in Sacred Music; 1st Cl. Hons in Pt I and Pt II, of Music Tripos; MusB (Cantab). FRCO (Limpus and Read prizes). Master of the Music, Cathedral, 1962–65; Dir of Music, Univ. of East Anglia, 1965–73 (Dean of S

Arts and Music, 1968–71); Dir of Music and Organist, King's Coll., Cambridge, 1974–82; Conductor, CU Musical Soc., 1973–82. An Artistic Dir, Aldeburgh Festival of Music and the Arts, 1968–. *Publications:* (ed) Anthems for Choirs 2 and 3, 1973; (ed) The Oxford Book of English Madrigals, 1978; other edns of Byrd, Handel and Purcell; carol arrangements. *Recreations:* swimming, theatre, membership of Sette of Odd Volumes. *Address:* 322 Albert Drive, Pollokshields, Glasgow G41 5DZ. *T:* 041–429 0967. *Club:* Athenæum.

LEDGER, Ronald Joseph; Casino Proprietor and Manager; *b* 7 Nov. 1920; *s* of Arthur and Florence Ledger; *m* 1946, Madeleine Odette de Villeneuve; three *s* one *d*. *Educ:* Skinners Grammar Sch., Tunbridge Wells; Nottingham Univ. Toolroom Engineer, 1938–42. Served RAF, 1942–47, fitter, Leading Aircraftsman; India three years. Univ. of Nottingham, 1947–49 (Diploma in Social Science); Staff Training Officer, Enfield Highway Co-op. Society, 1949; Business Partner, 1950, Company Director, 1953, Employment Specialists. Mem. Herts CC, 1952–54. Contested (Lab) Rushcliffe Div. of Nottingham, 1951; MP (Lab and Co-op) Romford, 1955–70. Director: Enfield Electronics (CRT) Ltd, 1958; London Co-operative Society Ltd, 1961. Chairman, Hairdressing Council, 1966–79. *Recreations:* tennis, cricket, golf, snooker. *Address:* Pomona, Shanklin, Isle of Wight. *T:* Shanklin 2398. *Clubs:* Sandown and Shanklin Golf, Enfield Golf.

LEDINGHAM, John Gerard Garvin, DM; FRCP; May Reader in Medicine, University of Oxford, since 1974 (Director of Clinical Studies, 1977–82); Fellow of New College, Oxford, since 1974; *b* 1929; *s* of late John Ledingham, MB BCh, DPH, and late Una Ledingham, MD, FRCP, *d* of J. L. Garvin, CH, Editor of The Observer; *m* 1961, Elaine Mary, *d* of late R. G. Maliphant, MD, FRCOG, and of Dilys Maliphant, Cardiff; four *d*. *Educ:* Rugby Sch.; New Coll., Oxford; Middlesex Hosp. Med. Sch. (1st Cl. Physiol.; BM BCh; DM 1966). FRCP 1971 (MRCP 1959). Junior appts, Middlesex, London Chest, Whittington, and Westminster Hospitals, London, 1957–64; Travelling Fellow, British Postgraduate Med. Fedn, Columbia Univ., New York, 1965–66. Chairman, Medical Staff Council, United Oxford Hosps, 1970–72; Hon. Consultant Physician, Oxfordshire Health Authority, 1982– (Consultant Physician, Oxford AHA (T), 1966–82). Hon. Sec., Assoc. of Physicians of Gt Britain and Ireland 1977–82, Hon. Treas., 1982–; Pro-Censor, RCP, 1983–84, Censor, 1984–85; Governing Trustee, Nuffield Provincial Hosps Trust, 1978–. *Publications:* (ed jtly) Oxford Textbook of Medicine, 1982; contribs to med. books and scientific jls in the field of hypertension and renal diseases. *Recreations:* music, golf. *Address:* 22 Hid's Copse Road, Cumnor Hill, Oxford OX2 9JJ. *T:* Oxford 862023. *Club:* Vincent's (Oxford).

LEDINGHAM, Prof. John Marshall, MD, FRCP; Consultant Physician, The London Hospital, 1954–81, now Consulting Physician; Professor of Medicine, University of London, at London Hospital Medical College, 1971–81, now Emeritus; *b* 1916; *s* of late Prof. Sir John C. G. Ledingham, CMG, FRS, of The Lister Institute, London, and late Lady Barbara Ledingham; *m* 1950, Josephine, *d* of late Matthew and Jane Metcalf, Temple Sowerby, Westmorland; two *s*. *Educ:* Whitgift Sch.; University College, London; The London Hospital. BSc (London) First Class Hons in Physics, 1936; MRCS, LRCP, 1942; MD (London) Gold Medal, 1951, FRCP, 1957. Service in RAMC as Graded Clinical and Experimental Pathologist, in UK, France, Middle and Far East, 1942–47. Lectr in Medicine, London Hosp. Med. Sch., 1948–53; Univ. Reader in Medicine, 1953–64; Prof. of Experimental Medicine, 1964–71, London Hosp. Med. Coll., London Univ. Vis. Prof., Maiduguri Univ., Nigeria, 1982. Mem., Professional and Linguistic Assessment Bd, GMC, 1984–. Past Pres., Section of Exptl Med. and Therapeutics, RSM; Bertram Louis Abrahams Lectr, RCP, 1970; Censor, RCP, 1975. Editor, Dep. Chm. and Chm. Editl Bd, Clinical Science, 1965–70. *Publications:* numerous scientific, mainly in field of hypertension and renal disease, 1938–. *Address:* 11 Montpelier Walk, SW7. *T:* 01–584 7976.

LEDLIE, John Kenneth, OBE 1977; Chief of Public Relations, Ministry of Defence, since 1985; *b* 19 March 1942; *s* of late Reginald Cyril Bell Ledlie and Elspeth Mary Kaye; *m* 1965, Rosemary Julia Allan; three *d*. *Educ:* Westminster School (Hon. Schol.); Brasenose Coll., Oxford (Triplett Exbnr; MA Lit Hum). Solicitor of the High Court; articles with Coward Chance, 1964–67; Min. of Defence, 1967; Asst Private Sec. to Minister of State for Equipment and Sec. of State for Defence, 1969–70; First Sec., UK Delegn to NATO, Brussels, 1973–76; Dep. Chief, Public Relations, 1977–79; NI Office and Cabinet Office, 1979–81; Procurement Exec., MoD, 1981–83; Head, Defence Secretariat 19, MoD, 1983; Regional Marketing Dir, Defence Sales Orgn, 1983–85. *Recreations:* ornithology, cricket, tennis, squash, theatre, opera. *Address:* Ministry of Defence, Main Building, Whitehall, SW1A 2HB. *T:* 01–218 7900. *Club:* Royal Commonwealth Society.

LEDSOME, Neville Frank; Under Secretary, Personnel Management Division, Department of Trade and Industry, since 1983; *b* 29 Nov. 1929; *s* of late Charles Percy Ledsome and Florence Ledsome; *m* 1953, Isabel Mary Lindsay; three *s*. *Educ:* Birkenhead Sch. Exec. Officer, BoT, 1948; Monopolies Commn, 1957; Higher Exec. Officer, BoT, 1961; Principal, 1964; DEA, 1967; HM Treasury, 1969; DTI, 1970; Asst Sec., 1973; Under Sec., 1980. *Recreations:* gardening, theatre. *Address:* 3 Homefield Close, Woodham, Weybridge, Surrey KT15 3QH. *T:* Byfleet 44330.

LEDWIDGE, Sir (William) Bernard (John), KCMG 1974 (CMG 1964); writer; HM Diplomatic Service, retired; Chairman, United Kingdom Committee for UNICEF, since 1976; *b* 9 Nov. 1915; *s* of late Charles Ledwidge and Eileen O'Sullivan; *m* 1st, 1948, Anne Kingsley (marr. diss. 1970); one *s* one *d*; 2nd, 1970, Flora Groult. *Educ:* Cardinal Vaughan Sch.; King's Coll., Cambridge; Princeton Univ., USA. Commonwealth Fund Fellow, 1937–39; served War of 1939–45: RA 1940; Indian Army, 1941–45. Private Secretary to Permanent Under-Secretary, India Office, 1946; Secretary, Frontier Areas Cttee of Enquiry, Burma, 1947; Foreign Office, 1947–49; British Consul, St Louis, USA, 1949–52; First Secretary, British Embassy, Kabul, 1952–56; Political Adviser British Military Govt, Berlin, 1956–61; Foreign Office, 1961–65; Minister, Paris, 1965–69; Ambassador to Finland, 1969–72; Ambassador to Israel, 1972–75. Mem., Police Complaints Bd, 1977–82. *Publications:* Frontiers (novel), 1979; (jtly) Nouvelles de la Famille (short stories), 1980; De Gaulle, 1982; De Gaulle et les Américains, 1984. *Recreations:* drinking, talking. *Address:* 54 rue de Bourgogne, 75007 Paris, France. *T:* 705 8026; 19 Queen's Gate Terrace, SW7. *T:* 01–584 4132. *Clubs:* Travellers', MCC.

LEE OF ASHERIDGE, Baroness *cr* 1970 (Life Peer), of the City of Westminster; **Janet Bevan, (Jennie Lee),** PC 1966; Director of Tribune; Member of Central Advisory Committee on Housing; Member, National Executive Committee, Labour Party, 1958–70 (Chairman, 1967–68); *b* 3 Nov. 1904; *d* of James Lee, Fifeshire miner; *m* 1934, Rt Hon. Aneurin Bevan, PC, MP (*d* 1960). *Educ:* Edinburgh Univ. MA, LLB. MP (Lab) North Lanark, 1929–31, Cannock, 1945–70. Parly Sec., Ministry of Public Building and Works, 1964–65; Parly Under-Sec. of State, Dept of Education and Science, 1965–67, Minister of State, 1967–70. Hon. Fellow, Royal Acad., 1981. Hon. LLD Cambridge, 1974. *Publications:* Tomorrow is a New Day, 1939; Our Ally, Russia, 1941; This Great Journey, 1963; My Life with Nye, 1980. *Address:* 67 Chester Row, SW1.

LEE, Sir Arthur (James), KBE 1966 (CBE 1959); MC and Bar (1939–45); Company Director; National President, Returned Services League, Australia, 1960–74 (State

President, 1954–60); *b* 30 July 1912; *s* of Arthur James and Kathleen Maud Lee; *m* 1945, Valerie Ann Scanlan; three *s* one *d*. *Educ:* Collegiate School of St Peter, Adelaide. Chairman: Regional Cttees Services Canteen Fund, S Australia, 1947–; War Veterans Home, SA, 1967–. *Recreation:* golf. *Address:* 2 Arthur Street, Toorak Gardens, SA 5065, Australia. *T:* 35106. *Clubs:* Adelaide, Naval and Military, Royal Adelaide Golf (Adelaide).

LEE, Arthur James, CBE 1979; DSC (and Bar); Controller of Fisheries Research and Development, Ministry of Agriculture, Fisheries and Food, 1977–80; *b* 17 May 1920; *s* of Arthur Henry and Clara Lee; *m* 1953, Judith Graham; three *d*. *Educ:* City Boys' Sch., Leicester; St Catharine's Coll., Cambridge (MA). Served War of 1939–45 (DSC and Bar). Apptd: Scientific Officer at Fisheries Laboratory, Lowestoft, 1947; Dep. Dir of Fishery Research, 1965, Dir, 1974–77. *Publications:* (ed) Atlas of the Seas around the British Isles, 1981; contribs to various marine science jls. *Recreation:* gardening. *Address:* 191 Normanston Drive, Oulton Broad, Lowestoft, Suffolk NR32 2PY. *T:* Lowestoft 4707.

LEE, Christopher Frank Carandini; actor; entered film industry, 1947; *b* 27 May 1922; *s* of Geoffrey Trollope Lee (Lt-Col 60th KRRC), and Estelle Marie Carandini; *m* 1961, Birgit, *d* of Richard Emil Kroencke; one *d*. *Educ:* Wellington Coll. RAFVR, 1941–46 (Flt Lieut; mentioned in despatches, 1944). Films include: Moulin Rouge; Tale of Two Cities; Dracula; Rasputin; The Devil Rides Out; Private Life of Sherlock Holmes; The Wicker Man; The Three Musketeers; The Four Musketeers; The Man with the Golden Gun; To the Devil, a Daughter; Airport '77; The Passage; Bear Island; 1941; The Serial; The Last Unicorn; Safari 3000, The Salamander; Goliath Awaits; An Eye for an Eye; Charles and Diana; The Return of Captain Invincible; The House of the Long Shadows; The Far Pavilions; The Disputation; Mio My Mio. Officier des Arts et des Lettres, France, 1973. *Publications:* Christopher Lee's 'X' Certificate, 1975 (2nd edn 1976); Christopher Lee's Archives of Evil, USA 1975 (2nd edn 1976); (autobiog.) Tall, Dark and Gruesome, 1977. *Recreations:* travel, opera, golf, cricket. *Address:* c/o Duncan Heath, Paramount House, 162 Wardour Street, W1; c/o ICM, 8899 Beverly Boulevard, Los Angeles, Calif 90049, USA. *Clubs:* Buck's, Special Forces, MCC; Honourable Company of Edinburgh Golfers; Travellers' (Paris).

LEE, David John, FEng 1980; Chairman: G. Maunsell and Partners, Consulting Engineers, since 1984 (Partner since 1966); Maunsell Consultants (Holdings) Ltd; Maunsell Consultants Ltd; Maunsell Consultants (Middle East) Ltd; Maunsell Structural Plastics Ltd; Partner: Maunsell Consultants; Maunsell Consultants Asia; *b* 28 Aug. 1930; *s* of Douglas and Mildred Lee; *m* 1957, Helga Bass; one *s* one *d*. *Educ:* Manchester Univ. (BSc Tech 1950); Imperial Coll. of Science and Technol. (DIC 1954). MICE 1957, FICE 1966; MIStructE 1960, FIStructE 1968. National Service, RE, 1950–52. Engr, Reinforced Concrete Steel Co. Ltd, 1952–53 and 1954–55; G. Maunsell and Partners, Consulting Engineers: Resident Engr, 1955–59; Sen. Engr, 1960–65; Associate, 1965–66. Engr and Transportation Staff Corps, RE (T&AVR), 1977– (Lt-Col). Member: General Cttee, Parly and Scientific Cttee; Standing Cttee on Structural Safety. Mem. Council, IStructE, 1974–77, 1978–, Pres., 1985–86; Mem. Council, Concrete Soc., 1968–71, Vice Pres. 1977–78. George Stephenson Medal, ICE, 1969; Medal, Fedn Internationale de la Précontrainte, 1974. *Publications:* The Theory and Practice of Bearings and Expansion Joints for Bridges, 1971; (contrib. chapter on bridges) The Civil Engineer's Reference Book, 3rd edn 1975; (contrib. chapter on bridges) Developments in Pre-stressed Concrete, vol. 2 1978; papers in Proc. ICE and Proc. IStructE. *Recreations:* art, music, simple barbecuing. *Address:* G. Maunsell and Partners, Yeoman House, 63 Croydon Road, Penge, SE20 7TP. *T:* 01–778 6060. *Club:* East India.

LEE, Air Chief Marshal Sir David (John Pryer), GBE 1969 (KBE 1965; CBE 1947; OBE 1943); CB 1953; retired, 1971; *b* 4 Sept. 1912; *s* of late John Lee, Byron Crescent, Bedford; *m* 1938, Denise, *d* of late Louis Hartoch; one *s* one *d*. *Educ:* Bedford Sch.; RAF Coll., Cranwell. NWFP, India, 1933–36; Central Flying Sch., Upavon, 1937; RAF Examining Officer, Supt. of Reserve, 1938–39; Bomber Command, Hemswell, 1939–40; RAF Staff Coll. (student), 1942; Deputy Director Plans, Air Ministry, 1943–44; OC 904 Fighter Wing, Batavia, Java, 1945–46; Directing Staff, RAF Staff Coll., 1948–50; Deputy Director Policy, Air Ministry, 1951–53; OC RAF Scampton, Lincs, 1953–55; Secretary, Chiefs of Staff Cttee, Ministry of Defence, 1956–59; AOC, AFME (Aden), 1959–61; Comdt, RAF Staff Coll., 1962–65; Air Member for Personnel, MoD, 1965–68; UK Military Rep. to NATO, 1968–71. Chairman: Grants Cttee, RAF Benevolent Fund, 1971–; Exec. Cttee, 1975–; Governing Trustees, 1986, Nuffield Trust for Armed Forces; Dir, Utd Services Trustee, 1971–; Pres., Corps of Commissionaires, 1984–. *Publications:* Flight from the Middle East, 1981; Never Stop the Engine When It's Hot, 1983; Eastward: a history of the Royal Air Force in the Far East 1945–1972, 1984. *Address:* Danemore Cottage, South Godstone, Surrey. *T:* South Godstone 893162. *Club:* Royal Air Force.

LEE, Sir Desmond; *see* Lee, Sir H. D. P.

LEE, Rev. Donald Rathbone, MBE 1945; Methodist Minister, retired; an Ecumenical Chaplain, St Albans Cathedral, since 1983; President of the Methodist Conference, 1973; Moderator, Free Church Federal Council, 1975–76; *b* 28 March 1911; *s* of Thomas and Alice Lee, Stockport, Cheshire; *m* 1940, Nora Olive Fothergill, Greenock, Renfrewshire; two *s* three *d*. *Educ:* Stockport Grammar School; Handsworth College, Birmingham. BD (London). Methodist Circuit appointments in: Greenock, 1935; Runcorn, 1936; Edinburgh, 1937; Perth, 1940; Stockport, 1947; Upminster, 1951; Oxford, Wesley Memorial, 1952; Worcester, 1957; Sutton Coldfield, 1964–68; Chm., Southampton District, 1968–77; Supt, Jersey Methodist Circuit, 1977–82. Religious Adviser (Free Church): Southern Television, 1972–77; Channel Television, 1977–82. Chm., Adv. Cttee, Inter-Church Travel Ltd, 1976–83; Pres., Jersey Council of Churches, 1978–80. Royal Army Chaplains' Dept, 1942–47 (Senior Chaplain, 1st Infantry Div., 1946). *Recreations:* music, gardening, ecumenical travel. *Address:* 12 Marshalswick Lane, St Albans, Herts.

LEE, Edward, MSc, PhD; FInstP; Director, Admiralty Research Laboratory, Teddington, 1971–74, retired; *b* 2 March 1914; *s* of Thomas and Florence Lee; *m* 1942, Joan Pearson; three *d*. *Educ:* Consett Grammar Sch.; Manchester Univ.; Pembroke Coll., Cambridge. Admiralty Research Laboratory, 1939–46; Ministry of Defence, 1946–48; Dept of Physical Research, Admiralty, 1948–51; Admiralty Research Laboratory, 1951–55; Dir of Operational Research, Admty, 1955–58; Dep. Dir, Nat. Physical Laboratory, 1958–60; Director, Stations and Industry Div., DSIR, 1960–65; Dep. Controller (R), Min. of Technology, 1965–70; Head of Res. Services, Dept of Trade and Industry, 1970–71. *Publications:* scientific papers. *Recreations:* golf, gardening. *Address:* 17 Farington Acres, Vale Road, Weybridge, Surrey KT13 9NH. *T:* Weybridge 41114.

LEE, (Edward) Stanley, FRCS; Consulting Surgeon Westminster Hospital; formerly Civilian Consultant in Surgery of Neoplastic Diseases, Queen Alexandra Military Hospital; Surgeon Emeritus, Guildford Radiotherapy Centre; *b* 1907. *Educ:* Westminster Hospital. MB, BS 1931; FRCS, 1933; MS London, 1936. Past Member of Court of Examiners, Royal College of Surgeons, England, 1953–59; Past Member: Grand Council British Empire Cancer Campaign; Internat. Union against Cancer; Assoc. of Head and Neck Oncologists of GB. FRSM; Sen. Fellow, Assoc. of Surgeons. Hon. Mem. Royal

College of Radiologists. *Publications:* contributions to medical literature, etc. *Address:* Westminster Hospital, SW1; Ingram, The Grand, Folkestone, Kent CT20 2LR.

LEE, George Ranson, CVO 1980; CBE 1983; HM Diplomatic Service, retired; *b* 26 Sept. 1925; *s* of late Wilfred Lee and Janet (*née* Ranson); *m* 1955, Anne Christine Black; one *d.* Served Indian Army, 6th Gurkha Rifles, NW Frontier Prov., 1945–47; TA, W Yorks Regt, 1948–53. Employed in Trng Dept, Min. of Food, 1948–53; joined CRO, 1954; Karachi, 1955–58; First Sec., Madras, 1959–63; CRO, 1964; Head of Chancery: Singapore, 1965–69; Santiago, 1969–72; FCO, 1972–74; Dep. UK Perm. Rep. to Council of Europe, Strasbourg, 1974–78; Counsellor, Berne, 1978–83. *Address:* Garthmynd, Trevor Hill, Church Stretton, Shropshire SY6 6JH. *Club:* Royal Commonwealth Society.

LEE, George Russell, CMG 1970; Acting Assistant Director, Ministry of Defence, 1967–78, retired; *b* 11 Nov. 1912; *s* of Ernest Harry Lee and Alice Mary Lee (*née* Russell); *m* 1947, Annabella Evelyn (*née* Dargie); one *s* one *d. Educ:* Birkenhead Sch., Cheshire. WO and MoD, 1940–78. *Address:* 13 Abberbury Road, Iffley, Oxford OX4 4ET.

LEE, Gilbert Henry Clifton; Chairman, European Hotel Corporation NV, 1975–76; *b* 19 April 1911; *s* of Walter Lee and Sybil Townsend; *m* 1938, Kathleen Cooper; two *d. Educ:* Worksop College. FCIT. Joined Imperial Airways, 1931; served overseas India, E Africa, Pakistan; Gen. Man., West African Airways Corp., 1949–52; BOAC: Traffic Manager, 1953; Gen. Sales Man., 1955; Commercial Dir, 1959; Mem. Bd, BOAC, 1961–73; Chm., BOAC Associated Cos Ltd, 1964–75. *Recreation:* golf. *Address:* Dana, Callow Hill, Virginia Water, Surrey. *T:* Wentworth 2195. *Clubs:* Oriental; Wentworth (Virginia Water).

LEE, Brig. Sir Henry; *see* Lee, Brig. Sir L. H.

LEE, Sir (Henry) Desmond (Pritchard), Kt 1961; MA; President, Hughes Hall, Cambridge, 1973–78, Hon. Fellow 1978; *b* 30 Aug. 1908; *s* of Rev. Canon Henry Burgass Lee; *m* 1935, Elizabeth, *d* of late Colonel A. Crookenden, CBE, DSO; one *s* two *d. Educ:* Repton Sch. (George Denman Scholar); Corpus Christi Coll., Cambridge (Entrance Scholar). 1st Class Part 1 Classical Tripos, 1928; Foundation Scholar of the College; 1st Class Part 2 Classical Tripos, 1930; Charles Oldham Scholar; Fellow of Corpus Christi Coll., 1933, Life Fellow, 1948–68, 1978–; Tutor, 1935–48; University Lecturer in Classics, 1937–48; Headmaster of Clifton Coll., 1948–54; Headmaster of Winchester Coll., 1954–68. Fellow, University Coll., later Wolfson Coll., Cambridge, 1968–73, Hon. Fellow, 1974. Regional Comr's Office, Cambridge, 1941–44; Mem. Council of the Senate, 1944–48. Mem. Anderson Cttee on Grants to Students, 1958–59; Chm., Headmasters' Conference, 1959–60, 1967. Hon. DLitt (Nottingham), 1963. *Publications:* Zeno of Elea: a Text and Notes, 1935; Aristotle, Meteorologica, 1952; Plato, Republic, 1955, rev. edn 1974; Plato, Timæus and Critias, 1971; Entry and Performance at Oxford and Cambridge, 1966–71, 1972; (ed) Wittgenstein's Lectures 1930–32, 1980. *Address:* 8 Barton Close, Cambridge.

LEE, Col Tun Sir Henry Hau Shik, SMN 1959 (Federation of Malaya); KBE 1957 (CBE 1948); JP; Chancellor of the Most Exalted Order of the Realm, Malaysia, since 1978; sole Proprietor, H. S. Lee Tin Mines, Malaya; Chairman: China Press Ltd; On Tai Development Sdn Berhad; Development & Commercial Bank Ltd, 1966–85; *b* 19 Nov. 1901; *e s* of late K. L. Lee; *m* 1st, 1922 (wife *d* 1926); one *s*; 2nd, 1929, Choi Lin (*née* Kwan); three *s* one *d* (and two *s* one *d* decd). *Educ:* Queen's Coll., Hongkong; Univ. of Cambridge. BA (Cantab) 1923. FREconS. War of 1939–45; Chief of Passive Defence Forces, Kuala Lumpur, 1941; Col in Allied Armed Forces, 1942–45. Member: Council of State, Selangor, 1946–47; Fed. Finance Cttee, 1946–56 (Chm., 1956–59); Fed. Legislative Council and Fed. Exec. Council, 1948–57; Dir, Ops Cttee, 1948–55; Minister of Transport, 1953–56, of Finance, 1956–59; Member: Merdeka Mission to London, 1956; Financial Mission to London, 1957; Cabinet, 1957–59. Co-founder, Alliance Party, 1949; Mem., Alliance Exec. Cttee and Nat. Council, 1953–59; Chm., MCA Standing Sub-Cttee, 1957–59. Member: KL Sanitary Bd, 1929–32, 1938–41, 1946–48; Council, FMS Chamber of Mines, 1929–55; War Damage Commn, 1946–56; Chinese Tin Mines Rehabilitation Loan Bd, 1946–59; Malayan Union Adv. Council, 1946–47; Tin Adv. Cttee, 1946–55; Malayan Tin Delegn, Internat. Tin Meetings, 1946–60. President: Selangor Chinese Chamber of Commerce, 1936–55; Kuen Cheng Girls' Sch., 1937–41, 1945–52; Miners Assoc. of Negeri Sembilan, Selangor and Pahang, 1938–55; All Malaya Chinese Mining Assoc., 1946–55; Associated Chinese Chambers of Commerce, 1947–55; United Lee's Assoc., 1949–59; Selangor Malaysian Chinese Assoc., 1949–56; Sen. Golfers Soc. of Malaya, 1957–58, 1960–63; Fedn of Malaya Red Cross Soc., 1957–62; Fedn of Malaya Olympic Council, 1957–59; Malaysian Golf Assoc., 1960–75 (Patron, 1975–); Oxford and Cambridge Soc., 1959–64; Royal Commonwealth Soc., 1969–73 (Vice Patron, 1973–); Selangor Miners Club, 1938–; All Malaya Kochow Assoc., 1949–; Fedn of Kwang Tung Assocs, 1962–; Selangor Kwan Tung Assoc., 1962–; Vice-Pres., Malaysian Zoo. Soc., 1965–. Hon. Pres., Wine and Food Soc., KL, 1970–; Hon. Vice-Pres., Selangor Chinese Recreation Club. Hon. Member, Clubs: KL Rotary, 1963–; KL Lake; Royal Selangor Golf; Selangor; Selangor Turf. JP Kuala Lumpur, 1938. *Recreations:* riding, golf, tennis. *Address:* 22 Jalan Langgak Golf, Kuala Lumpur 01–28, Malaysia. *Clubs:* Oriental, United Oxford & Cambridge University; Chinese (Hongkong); Royal and Ancient Golf (St Andrews); Royal Liverpool Golf (Hoylake); Singapore Island Country.

LEE, James Giles; Chairman, Direct Broadcasting by Satellite Consortium, since 1986; *b* 23 Dec. 1942; *s* of John Lee, CBE and Muriel Giles; *m* 1966, Linn Macdonald; one *s* two *d. Educ:* Trinity Coll., Glenalmond; Glasgow Univ.; Harvard Univ., USA. Consultant, McKinsey & Co., 1969–80; Mem., Central Policy Review Staff, 1972. Dep. Chm. and Chief Exec., Pearson Longman, 1980–83; Chairman: Penguin Publishing Co., 1980–84; Longman Gp, 1980–84; Deputy Chairman: Westminster Press, 1980–84; Financial Times, 1980–84; Yorkshire TV, 1982–85; Dir, S. Pearson & Son, 1981–84; Chm., 1981–85, Chief Exec., 1983–85, Goldcrest Films and Television. *Publications:* Planning for the Social Services, 1978; The Investment Challenge, 1979. *Recreations:* photography, travelling, sailing. *Address:* Meadow Wood, Penshurst, Kent. *T:* Penshurst 870309. *Clubs:* Reform; Harvard (New York, USA).

LEE, Hon. James Matthew, PC 1982; MLA; Leader, Progressive Conservative Party, Prince Edward Island, since 1981; *b* Charlottetown, 26 March 1937; *s* of late James Matthew Lee and of Catherine Blanchard Lee; *m* 1960, Patricia, *d* of late Ivan Laurie; one *s* two *d. Educ:* Queen's Square Sch.; St Dunstan's Univ. Architectural draftsman. First elected MLA (PC) for 5th Queens Riding, by-election, 1975; re-elected since; former Minister: of Health and Social Services; of Tourism, Parks and Conservation; Premier and Pres. Exec. Council, PEI, 1981–86. Jaycee Internat. Senator, 1983. *Address:* 41 Centennial Drive, Sherwood, Prince Edward Island, Canada. *T:* 902–892–6653.

LEE, John Michael Hubert; Barrister-at-Law; *b* 13 Aug. 1927; *s* of late Victor Lee, Wentworth, Surrey, and late Renee Lee; *m* 1960, Margaret Ann, *d* of James Russell, ICS, retired, and late Kathleen Russell; one *s* one *d. Educ:* Reading Sch.; Christ's Coll., Cambridge (Open Exhibnr Modern Hist.; 2nd Cl. Hons Pts I and II of Hist. Tripos; MA). Colonial Service: Administrative Officer, Ghana, 1951–58; Principal Assistant Secretary, Min. of Communications, Ghana, 1958. On staff of BBC, 1959–65. Called to the Bar, Middle Temple, 1960; practising, Midland and Oxford Circuit, 1966–; Dep. Circuit Judge, 1978–81; Assistant Recorder, 1981–. MP (Lab) Reading, 1966–70; MP (Lab) Birmingham, Handsworth, Feb. 1974–1979; Chm., W Midland Gp of Labour MPs, 1974–75. *Recreations:* watching tennis, watching cricket, good conversation, walking, studying philosophy. *Address:* 2 Dr Johnson's Buildings, EC4. *Club:* Royal Over-Seas League.

LEE, John Robert Louis; MP (C) Pendle, since 1983 (Nelson and Colne, 1979–83); Parliamentary Under Secretary of State, Department of Employment, since 1986; *b* 21 June 1942; *s* of late Basil and Miriam Lee; *m* 1975, Anne Monique Bakirgian; two *d. Educ:* William Hulme's Grammar Sch., Manchester. FCA. Accountancy Articles, 1959–64; Henry Cooke, Lumsden & Co., Manchester, Stockbrokers, 1964–66; Founding Dir, Chancery Consolidated Ltd, Investment Bankers; Director, Paterson Zochonis (UK) Ltd, 1975–76. Vice-Chm., NW Conciliation Cttee, Race Relations Bd, 1976–77; Chm. Council, Nat. Youth Bureau, 1980–. Political Sec. to Rt Hon. Robert Carr (now Lord Carr of Hadley), 1974; contested (C) Manchester, Moss Side, Oct. 1974; PPS to Minister of State for Industry, 1981–83, to Sec. of State for Trade and Industry, 1983; Parly Under Sec. of State, MoD, 1983–86. Jt Sec., Conservative Back Benchers' Industry Cttee, 1979–80. *Recreations:* fly fishing, collecting. *Address:* House of Commons, SW1A 0AA.

LEE, John (Thomas Cyril); His Honour Judge John Lee; Circuit Judge (attached Midland Oxford Circuit), since Sept. 1972; *b* 14 Jan. 1927; *s* of Cyril and Dorothy Lee; *m* 1956, Beryl Lee (*née* Haden); one *s* three *d. Educ:* Holly Lodge Grammar Sch., Staffs; Emmanuel Coll., Cambridge (MA, LLB). Called to Bar, Gray's Inn, 1952. Practised, Oxford Circuit, 1952–72. Chairman various Tribunals. *Recreation:* golf. *Address:* The Red House, Upper Colwall, Malvern, Worcs. *T:* Colwall 40645. *Clubs:* Union and County (Worcester); Worcester Golf and Country.

LEE KUAN YEW; Prime Minister, Singapore, since 1959; *b* 16 Sept. 1923; *s* of Lee Chin Koon and Chua Jim Neo; *m* 1950, Kwa Geok Choo; two *s* one *d. Educ:* Raffles Coll., Singapore; Fitzwilliam Coll., Cambridge (class 1 both parts of Law Tripos; Hon. Fellow, 1969). Called to Bar, Middle Temple, 1950, Hon. Bencher, 1969. Advocate and Solicitor, Singapore, 1951. Formed People's Action Party, 1954, Sec.-Gen., 1954–; People's Action Party won elections, 1959; became PM, 1959, re-elected 1963, 1968, 1972, 1976, 1980, 1984; MP Fed. Parlt of Malaysia, 1963–65. Hon. Freeman, City of London, 1982. Hon. CH 1970; Hon. GCMG 1972. Bintang Republik Indonesia Adi Pradana, 1973; Order of Sikatuna, The Philippines, 1974; Most Honourable Order of Crown of Johore (1st Cl.), Malaysia, 1984. *Recreations:* jogging, swimming. *Address:* Prime Minister's Office, Istana Annexe, Singapore 0923. *T:* 7375133.

LEE, Laurie, MBE 1952; poet and author; *m* 1950, Catherine Francesca Polge; one *d. Educ:* Slad Village Sch.; Stroud Central Sch. Travelled Mediterranean, 1935–39; GPO Film Unit, 1939–40; Crown Film Unit, 1941–43; Publications Editor, Ministry of Information, 1944–46; Green Park Film Unit, 1946–47; Caption Writer-in-Chief, Festival of Britain, 1950–51. Freeman of City of London, 1982. *Publications:* The Sun My Monument (Poems), 1944; Land at War (HMSO), 1945; (with Ralph Keene) A Film in Cyprus, 1947; The Bloom of Candles (Poems), 1947; The Voyage of Magellan, 1948; My Many-Coated Man (Poems), 1955; A Rose for Winter, 1955; Cider With Rosie (autobiography), 1959; Pocket Poets (Selection), 1960; The Firstborn, 1964; As I Walked Out One Midsummer Morning (autobiography), 1969; I Can't Stay Long, 1975; Selected Poems, 1983; Two Women, 1983. *Recreations:* indoor sports, music, travel. *Address:* 9/40 Elm Park Gardens, SW10. *T:* 01–352 2197. *Clubs:* Chelsea Arts, Garrick.

LEE, Brig. Sir (Leonard) Henry, Kt 1983; CBE 1964 (OBE 1960); Deputy Director, Conservative Board of Finance, since 1970; *b* 21 April 1914; *s* of late Henry Robert Lee and Nellie Lee; *m* 1949, Peggy Metham. *Educ:* Portsmouth Grammar Sch.; Southampton Univ. (Law). Served War, 1939–45; with BEF in France, ME and NW Europe (despatches, 1945); Royal Scots Greys, Major; Staff Lt-Col 1954: Chief of Intelligence to Dir of Ops, Malaya, 1957–60; Mil. and Naval Attaché, Saigon, S Vietnam, 1961–64; Chief of Personnel and Admin, Allied Land Forces Central Europe, France, 1964–66; Chief of Intelligence, Allied Forces Central Europe, Netherlands, 1966–69; retd 1969. *Recreations:* gardening, golf. *Address:* Fairways, Sandy Lane, Kingswood, Surrey. *T:* Mogador 832577. *Club:* Kingswood Golf.

LEE, Malcolm Kenneth, QC 1983; a Recorder of the Crown Court, since 1980; *b* 2 Jan. 1943; 2nd *s* of late Thomas Marston Lee, solicitor, Birmingham, and of Fiona Margaret Lee, JP (*née* Mackenzie); *m* 1970, Phyllis Anne Brunton Speed, *er d* of Andrew Watson Speed, Worcs; three *s* three *d* (and one *d* decd). *Educ:* King Edward's Sch., Birmingham (Foundation Schol.); Worcester Coll., Oxford (Schol.; MA Class. Hon. Mods and Lit.Hum.). Assistant Master: Marlborough Coll., 1965; King Edward's Sch., Birmingham, 1966; Major Schol., Inner Temple, 1967; called to the Bar, Inner Temple, 1967; practised on Midland Circuit, 1968–71, Midland and Oxford Circuit, 1972–. Dep. Chm., Agricl Land Tribunal, E Midland Area, 1979–82, Midland Area, 1982–; Prosecuting Counsel to DHSS, Midland and Oxford Circuit, 1979–83. *Recreations:* squash, tennis, walking, reading. *Address:* (chambers) Francis Taylor Building, Temple, EC4. *T:* 01–353 2182; (chambers) 4 Fountain Court, Steelhouse Lane, Birmingham B4 6DR. *T:* 021–236 3476; (home) 24 Estria Road, Edgbaston, Birmingham B15 2LQ. *T:* 021–440 4481.

LEE, Michael Charles M.; *see* Malone-Lee.

LEE, Maj.-Gen. Patrick Herbert, CB 1982; MBE 1964; CEng, FIMechE; Director, Wincanton Transport Ltd, since 1983; Member, Wessex Water Authority, since 1983; *b* 15 March 1929; *s* of Percy Herbert and Mary Dorothea Lee; *m* 1952, Peggy Eveline Chapman; one *s* one *d. Educ:* King's Sch., Canterbury; London Univ. (BSc (Gen.), BSc (Special Physics)). Commnd RMA Sandhurst, 1948; Staff Coll., 1960; WO Staff Duties, 1961–63; CO, Parachute Workshop, 1964–65; JSSC, 1966; Military Asst to Master General of Ordnance, 1966–67; Directing Staff, Staff Coll., 1968–69; Commander, REME 2nd Div., 1970–71; Col AQ 1 British Corps, 1972–75; Dep. Comdt, Sch. of Electrical and Mechanical Engrg, 1975–77; Comdt, REME Trng Centre, 1977–79; Dir Gen., Electrical and Mechanical Engrg (Army), 1979–83. Col Comdt, REME, 1983–. *Recreations:* gardening, railways, Roman history, industrial archaeology. *Address:* c/o Royal Bank of Scotland, Holts Branch, Farnborough, Hants. *Club:* Army and Navy.

LEE, Rt. Rev. Paul Chun Hwan, CBE 1974; Bishop of Seoul, 1965–83; *b* 5 April 1922; unmarried. *Educ:* St Michael's Theological Seminary, Seoul; St Augustine's College, Canterbury. Deacon, 1952 (Pusan Parish); Priest, 1953 (Sangju and Choungju Parish). Director of Yonsei University, Seoul, 1960–, Chm., Bd of Trustees, 1972–, Hon. DD 1971. Chairman: Christian Council of Korea, 1966–67; Christian Literature Soc. of Korea, 1968–83; Korean Bible Soc., 1972–83 (Vice-Pres., 1969–72); Nat. Council of Churches in Korea, 1976–78. Hon. LLD Korea, 1978. *Recreation:* reading. *Address:* 3 403 Sin Panp'o Apartments, 279–5 Panp'o Dong, Kangnam Ku, Seoul 135, Korea. *T:* 02–599–1123.

LEE, Peter Gavin; Senior Partner, Strutt & Parker, since 1979; *b* 4 July 1934; *s* of Mr and late Mrs J. G. Lee; *m* 1963, Caroline Green; two *s* one *d*. *Educ:* Midhurst Grammar School; College of Estate Management; Wye College. FRICS. Joined Strutt & Parker, 1957; became full partner, 1972. *Recreations:* vintage cars, clocks, flying. *Address:* Fanners, Great Waltham, Chelmsford, Essex. *T:* Chelmsford 360470. *Club:* Boodle's.

LEE, Rowland Thomas Lovell; a Recorder of the Crown Court, since 1979; *b* 7 March 1920; *s* of late Ronald Lovell Lee and of Jessie Maude Lee; *m* 1944, Marjorie Betty, *d* of late William Holmes and Clare Johnston Braid Holmes; two *d*. *Educ:* Bedford Modern School. Served Royal Navy, 1939–48. Bedfordshire Constabulary, 1948–52; Articles with E. A. S. Barnard, Dunstable, 1954; qualified as solicitor, 1957; Principal, Wynter Davies & Lee, Hertford, 1959–. Chairman: Medical Services Cttee, Hertfordshire Family Practitioners Cttee, 1970–77; N Herts HA (formerly Herts AHA), 1977–84. *Address:* Culpepers, 5 Letty Green, Hertford, Herts SG14 2NZ. *T:* Hatfield 61445.

LEE, Stanley; *see* Lee, (Edward) S.

LEE, Tsung-Dao; Enrico Fermi Professor of Physics, since 1964, and University Professor, since 1984, Columbia University, USA; *b* 25 Nov. 1926; 3rd *s* of C. K. and M. C. Lee; *m* 1950, Jeannette H. C. Chin; two *s*. *Educ:* National Chekiang Univ., Kweichow, China; National Southwest Associated Univ., Kunming, China; University of Chicago, USA. Research Associate: University of Chicago, 1950; University of California, 1950–51; Member, Inst. for Advanced Study, Princeton, 1951–53. Columbia University: Asst Professor, 1953–55; Associate Professor, 1955–56; Professor, 1956–60; Member, Institute for Advanced Study, Princeton, 1960–63; Columbia Univ.: Adjunct Professor, 1960–62; Visiting Professor, 1962–63; Professor, 1963–. Hon. Professor: Univ. of Sci and Technol. of China, 1981; Jinan Univ., China, 1982; Fudan Univ., China, 1982; Qinghua Univ., 1984; Peking Univ., 1985; Nanjing Univ., 1985. Member: Acad. Sinica, 1957; Amer. Acad. of Arts and Scis, 1959; Nat. Acad of Scis, 1964; Amer. Philosophical Soc., 1972; Acad. Nazionale dei Lincei, Rome, 1982. Hon. DSc: Princeton, 1958; City Coll., City Univ. of NY, 1978; Bard Coll., 1984; Hon. LLD Chinese Univ. of Hong Kong, 1969; Hon. LittD Drexel Univ., 1986; Dip. di Perfezionamento in Physics, Scuola Normale Superiore, Pisa, 1982. Nobel Prize for the non-conservation of parity (with C. N. Yang), 1957; Albert Einstein Award in Science, 1957. *Publications:* Particle Physics: an introduction to field theory, 1981; papers mostly in Physical Review, and Nuclear Physics. *Address:* Department of Physics, Columbia University, New York, New York 10027, USA.

LEE, Sir William (Allison), Kt 1975; OBE 1945; TD 1948; DL; Chairman, Northern Regional Health Authority, 1973–78; *b* 31 May 1907; *s* of Samuel Percy and Florence Ada Lee, Darlington; *m* 1st, 1933, Elsa Norah (*d* 1966), *d* of late Thomas Hanning, Darlington; 2nd, 1967, Mollie Clifford, *d* of late Sir Cuthbert Whiteside, Knysna, S Africa; no *c*. *Educ:* Queen Elizabeth Grammar Sch., Darlington. Insurance Branch Manager, retd. Served R Signals, 1935–53; Dep. Comdr, 151 Inf. Bde (TA), 1953–58; County Comdt, Durham ACF, 1962–70. Mem., Darlington RDC, 1949–61, Chm. 1957–60. Chairman: Winterton HMC, 1967–70 (Mem., 1954–70); Newcastle Reg. Hosp. Bd, 1973–74 (Mem., 1956–74). President: Darlington Civic Soc.; Darlington Branch, SSAFA. DL County of Durham, 1965; High Sheriff, Durham, 1978. *Recreations:* beagling, fell walking, gardening. *Address:* The Woodlands, Woodland Road, Darlington, Co. Durham. *T:* Darlington 62318; Candle House, Feetham, Richmond, N Yorks. *T:* Richmond 86207.

LEE YONG LENG, Dr; Professor of Geography, National University of Singapore, since 1977; *b* 26 March 1930; *m* Wong Loon Meng; one *d*. *Educ:* Univs of Oxford, Malaya and Singapore. BLitt (Oxon), MA (Malaya), PhD (Singapore). Research Asst, Univ. of Malaya, 1954–56; University Lectr/Sen. Lectr, Univ. of Singapore, 1956–70; Associate Prof., Univ. of Singapore, 1970–71; High Comr for Singapore in London, 1971–75; Ambassador to Denmark, 1974–75, and Ireland, 1975; Min. of Foreign Affairs, Singapore, 1975–76. Chm., Singapore Nat. Library Bd, 1978–80. Dir, Centre for Advanced Studies, National Univ. of Singapore, 1983–85. *Publications:* North Borneo, 1965; Sarawak, 1970; Southeast Asia and the Law of the Sea, 1978; The Razor's Edge: boundaries and boundary disputes in Southeast Asia, 1980; Southeast Asia: essays in political geography, 1982; articles in: Population Studies; Geog. Jl; Erdkunde; Jl Trop. Geog., etc. *Recreations:* swimming, tennis, travelling, reading. *Address:* Department of Geography, National University of Singapore, Kent Ridge, Singapore 0511.

LEE-BARBER, Rear-Adm. John, CB 1959; DSO 1940 and Bar 1941; Admiral Superintendent, HM Dockyard, Malta, 1957–59, retired; *b* 16 April 1905; *s* of Richard Lee-Barber, Herringfleet, near Great Yarmouth; *m* 1939, Suzanne (*d* 1976), *d* of Colonel Le Gallais, ADC, MC, La Moye, Jersey, CI; two *d*. *Educ:* Royal Naval Colleges, Osborne and Dartmouth. Service in destroyers and in Yangtze gunboat until 1937; CO Witch, 1937–38; CO Griffin, 1939–40–41; Commander, 1941; CO Opportune, 1942–44; 2nd in Command, HMS King Alfred, 1945; CO, HMS St James, 1946–47; Captain, 1947; Senior Officer Reserve Fleet, Harwich, 1948–49; Naval Attaché, Chile, 1950–52; CO Agincourt and Captain D4, 1952–54; Commodore, Inshore Flotilla, 1954–56; Rear-Admiral, 1957. Polish Cross of Valour, 1940. *Recreation:* sailing. *Address:* Ferry House, The Quay, Wivenhoe, Essex. *T:* Wivenhoe 2592. *Club:* Royal Ocean Racing.

LEE-STEERE, Sir Ernest (Henry), KBE 1977 (CBE 1963); JP; Lord Mayor of Perth, Western Australia, 1972–78; company director, pastoralist and grazier; *b* Perth, 22 Dec. 1912; *s* of Sir Ernest Lee-Steere, JP, KStJ; *m* 1942, Jessica Margaret, *d* of Frank Venn; two *s* three *d*. *Educ:* Hale Sch., Perth; St Peter's Coll., Adelaide. Served War: Captain Army/Air Liaison Group, AIF; SW Pacific Area, 1944–45. President (for WA): Pastoralists and Graziers Assoc., 1959–72; Boy Scout Assoc., 1957–64; National Trust, 1969–72. Vice-Pres., Council of Royal Flying Doctor Service of WA, 1954–59 and 1962–74. Chairman: State Adv. Cttee, CSIRO, 1962–71 (Councillor, Fed. Adv. Council, 1960–71); WA Soil Conservation Adv. Cttee, 1955–72; Aust. Capital Cities Secretariat, 1975–76; WA Turf Club, 1963– (Vice-Chm., 1959–63). Member: Nat. Council of Aust. Boy Scouts Assoc., 1959–64; Exec. Cttee of WA State Cttee, Freedom from Hunger Campaign; WA State Adv. Cttee, Aust. Broadcasting Commn, 1961–64; Aust. Jubilee Cttee for the Queen's Silver Jubilee Appeal for Young Australians, 1977; Aust. Wool Industry Conf., 1971–74 (also Mem. Exec. Cttee). Councillor: Aust. Wool Growers and Graziers Council (Pres., 1972–73); St George's Coll., Univ. of WA, 1945–81. Chm. and dir of several cos. Leader, Trade Mission to India, 1962. JP Perth, 1965. *Recreation:* polo (played in WA Polo Team in Australasian Gold Cup). *Address:* Dardanup, 26 Odern Crescent, Swanbourne, WA 6010, Australia. *T:* 384–2929. *Club:* Weld (Perth).

LEECH, Air Vice-Marshal David Bruce, CBE 1978 (OBE 1976); Commandant General, RAF Regiment and Director General of Security (RAF), since 1985; *b* 8 Jan. 1934; *s* of Mrs S. A. Leech; *m* 1958, Shirley Anne (*née* Flitcroft); two *d*. *Educ:* Bolton School, Lancs. Joined RAF 1954, and served with Nos 11 and 20 Sqns, 1956–58; Pilot attack instr, APC Sylt, 1958–61; Mem., RAF 2 TAF Air Gunnery Team, Cazaux, 1958; qualified flying instr, RAF Coll., Cranwell, CFS and Church Fenton, 1961–66; Chief Instr, Canadian Tactical Air Ops Sch., Rivers, Manitoba, 1966–69; RAF Staff Coll., 1969–70; HQ 38 Gp, Ops Staff, 1970–72; OC Ops Wing, RAF Wittering, 1973–75; Stn Comdr, RAF Wildenrath, RAF Gutersloh and Comdr RAF Germany Harrier Force, 1975–77; Dir, Dept of Warfare, RAF Coll., 1977–79; Inspector of Flight Safety, 1979–81; RCDS 1982; Comdr, Allied Sector Ops Centre No 1, Brockzetel, 1983–85. *Recreations:* golf, country pursuits. *Address:* National Westminster Bank, 196 Monton Road, Monton, Eccles, Greater Manchester M30 9PY. *Club:* Royal Air Force.

LEECH, Prof. Geoffrey Neil; Professor of Linguistics and Modern English Language, University of Lancaster, since 1974; *b* 16 Jan. 1936; *s* of Charles Richard Leech and Dorothy Eileen Leech; *m* 1961, Frances Anne Berman; one *s* one *d*. *Educ:* Tewkesbury Grammar School; University College London (BA 1959; MA 1963; PhD 1968). Asst Lectr, UCL, 1962–64; Harkness Fellow, MIT, 1964–65; Lectr, UCL, 1965–69; Reader, Univ. of Lancaster, 1969–74. Visiting Professor: Brown Univ., 1972; Kobe Univ., 1984. *Publications:* English in Advertising, 1966; A Linguistic Guide to English Poetry, 1969; Towards a Semantic Description of English, 1969; Meaning and the English Verb, 1971; (with R. Quirk, S. Greenbaum and J. Svartvik) A Grammar of Contemporary English, 1972; Semantics, 1974, 2nd edn 1981; (with J. Svartvik) A Communicative Grammar of English, 1975; Explorations in Semantics and Pragmatics, 1980; (ed with S. Greenbaum and J. Svartvik) Studies in English Linguistics: for Randolph Quirk, 1980; (with M. Short) Style in Fiction, 1981; (with R. Hoogenraad and M. Deuchar) English Grammar for Today, 1982; Principles of Pragmatics, 1983; (with R. Quirk, S. Greenbaum, and J. Svartvik) A Comprehensive Grammar of the English Language, 1985. *Recreations:* music, esp. playing the piano in chamber music groups. *Address:* Department of Linguistics, University of Lancaster, Bailrigg, Lancaster LA1 4YT.

LEECH, John, (Hans-Joachim Freiherr von Reitzenstein); Head of External Relations and Member of Management Board, Commonwealth Development Corporation, 1981–85; Chairman: Rural Investment Overseas Ltd, since 1985; Bioventures Ltd, since 1986; *b* 21 April 1925; *s* of Hans-Joachim and Josefine von Reitzenstein; *m* 1st, 1949, Mair Eiluned Davies (marr. diss. 1958); one *d*; 2nd, 1963, Noretta Conci, concert pianist. *Educ:* Bismarck Gymnasium, Berlin; Whitgift, Croydon. L. G. Mouchel & Partners, Consulting Civil Engineers, 1942–52; Bird & Co. Ltd, Calcutta, 1953–57; Dir, Europe House, London, and Exec. Mem. Council, Britain in Europe Ltd, 1958–63; Pres., Internat. Fedn of Europe Houses, 1961–65; Dir, Joint Industrial Exports Ltd, 1963–65; with Commonwealth Develt Corp., London and overseas, 1965–85; Co-ordinator, Interact Gp of European develt finance instns, 1973–85. Asst Dir, NATO Parliamentarians' Conf., 1959–60. Vice-Chairman: Indian Concrete Soc., 1953–57; Anglo-Ivory Coast Soc., 1981–; Member: National Council, European Movement, 1967–; Council, Federal Trust for Educn and Research, 1985–; Exec. Cttee, London Symphony Orch., 1979–; International Panel, Duke of Edinburgh's Award, 1980–; Council, Royal Commonwealth Soc. for the Blind, 1983–. Liveryman, Worshipful Co. of Paviors, 1968–. FRSA. *Publications:* The NATO Parliamentarians' Conference 1955–59, 1960; Europe and the Commonwealth, 1961; Aid and the Community, 1972; contrib. to jls on aspects of overseas develt, European matters and arts subjects. *Recreations:* music, travel, Italy. *Address:* 8 Chester Square Mews, SW1W 9DS. *T:* 01–730 2307. *Club:* Travellers'.

LEECH, His Honour Robert Radcliffe; a Circuit Judge (formerly Judge of County Courts), 1970–86; Hon. Recorder of Carlisle, since 1986; *b* 5 Dec. 1919; *s* of late Edwin Radcliffe Leech; *m* 1951, Vivienne Ruth, *d* of A. J. Rickerby, Carlisle; two *d*. *Educ:* Monmouth Sch.; Worcester Coll., Oxford (Open Classics Exhibnr 1938). Served War, 1940–44, Border Regt (despatches twice). Called to Bar, Middle Temple, 1949 (Harmsworth Law Scholar); Dep. Chm., Cumberland QS, 1966–71. *Recreations:* sailing, golf. *Address:* Scaur House, Cavendish Terrace, Stanwix, Carlisle, Cumbria CA3 9ND; Goldsmith Building, Temple, EC4. *Clubs:* Oriental; County and Border (Carlisle).

LEECH, William Charles, CBE 1980; Founder, 1932, President (since 1975) and Director (since 1940), William Leech Ltd; *b* 15 July 1900; *s* of Albert William Leech and Lucy Sophia Wright (*née* Slack); *m* 1947, Ellen Richards; two *d*. *Educ:* Westgate Road Council Sch., Newcastle upon Tyne. Apprentice Engineer, 1916–21; served RFC, 1916–19; window cleaning for eleven years; started building in own name, 1932; created limited company, 1940, public company, 1976. Creator and Pres., Northern Home & Estates Ltd; President: William Leech (Investments) Ltd; William Leech Foundation Ltd; William Leech Charity Ltd; William Leech Property Trust Ltd. Hon. DCL Newcastle upon Tyne, 1975; Hon. Freeman, Borough of Wallsend, 1972; Order of Distinguished Auxiliary Service, Salvation Army, 1974. Mason (Doric Lodge). *Recreation:* inside gardening. *Address:* High House, Morpeth NE61 2YU. *T:* Morpeth 513364. *Club:* Heaton Rotary (Founder Mem. 1943).

LEEDALE, Harry Heath, CBE 1972; Controller of Surtax and Inspector of Foreign Dividends, 1968–74; *b* 23 June 1914; *s* of John Leedale and Amy Alice Leedale (*née* Heath), New Malden; *m* 1st, 1940, Audrey Beryl (*née* Platt) (*d* 1970); one *d*; 2nd, 1971, Sheila Tyas Stephen. *Educ:* Henry Thornton Sch., Clapham, London. Served War, RAF, 1941–46. Entered Inland Revenue, 1933; Controller, Assessments Div., 1961; Asst Clerk to Special Commissioners of Income Tax, 1963; Controller, Superannuation Funds Office, 1964. *Recreations:* gardening, foreign travel. *Address:* Lavender Cottage, Rotherfield, Sussex. *T:* Rotherfield 2424.

LEEDS, Bishop of, (RC), since 1985; **Rt. Rev. David Every Konstant;** *b* 16 June 1930; *s* of Antoine Konstant and Dulcie Marion Beresford Konstant (*née* Leggatt). *Educ:* St Edmund's College, Old Hall Green, Ware; Christ's College, Cambridge (MA); Univ. of London Inst. of Education (PGCE). Priest, dio. Westminster, 1954; Cardinal Vaughan School, Kensington, 1959; Diocesan Adviser on Religious Education, 1966; St Michael's School, Stevenage, 1968; Director, Westminster Religious Education Centre, 1970; Auxiliary Bishop of Westminster (Bishop in Central London) and Titular Bishop of Betagbara, 1977–85. Chm., Dept for Christian Doctrine and Formation, Bishops' Conf. of Eng. and Wales, 1984–. *Publications:* various books on religious education and liturgy. *Recreation:* music. *Address:* Bishop's House, Eltofts, Carr Lane, Thorner, Leeds LS14 3HF. *T:* Leeds 892687.

LEEDS, Archdeacon of; *see* Comber, Ven. A. J.

LEEDS, Sir Christopher (Anthony), 8th Bt *cr* 1812; Maître de Conférences Associé, teaching at University of Nancy II, since 1982; *b* 31 Aug. 1935; *s* of Geoffrey Hugh Anthony Leeds (*d* 1962) (*b* of 6th Bt) and Yoland Thérèse Barré (*d* 1944), *d* of James Alexander Mitchell; *S* cousin, 1983; *m* 1974, Elaine Joyce (marr. diss. 1981), *d* of late Sqdn Ldr C. H. A. Mullins. *Educ:* King's School, Bruton; LSE, Univ. of London (BSc Econ. 1958); Univ. of Southern California (Sen. Herman Fellow in Internat. Relations, MA 1966). Assistant Master: Merchant Taylors' School, Northwood, 1966–68; Christ's Hospital, 1972–75; Stowe School, 1978–81. Publisher, 1975–78. *Publications include:* Political Studies, 1968, 3rd edn 1981; European History 1789–1914, 1971, 2nd edn 1980; Italy under Mussolini, 1972; Unification of Italy, 1974; Historical Guide to England, 1976; (with R. S. Stainton and C. Jones) Management and Business Studies, 1974, 3rd edn

1983; Basic Economics Revision, 1982; Politics in Action, 1986. *Recreations:* tennis, modern art, travel. *Heir: cousin* Aubrey Leeds [*b* 4 Aug. 1903; *m* 1933, Barbara, *o c* of J. Travis, Lightcliffe, Yorks; one *s* two *d*]. *Address:* c/o 45A High Street, Wimbledon Village, SW19 5AU. *Clubs:* National Liberal, Lansdowne.

LEELAND, John Roger; HM Diplomatic Service; Counsellor, Foreign and Commonwealth Office, since 1984; *b* 11 April 1930; *s* of H. L. A. Leeland and F. Leeland (*née* Bellamy); *m* 1958, D. M. M. O'Donel; four *d*. *Educ:* Bournemouth School. Army 1949. Board of Trade, 1951; served Karachi, Lahore, Brisbane, Kampala and FCO, 1956–73; First Sec., 1966; Ankara, 1973; Kaduna, 1977; Rangoon, 1981; Inspectorate, 1984. *Recreation:* walking. *Address:* c/o Foreign and Commonwealth Office, SW1A 2AH. *Club:* Travellers'.

LEEMING, John Coates; Director Policy and Programmes, British National Space Centre, since 1985; *b* 3 May 1927; *s* of late James Arthur Leeming and Harriet Leeming; *m* 1st, 1949 (marr. diss. 1974); two *s*; 2nd, 1985, Cheryl Gillan. *Educ:* Chadderton Grammar Sch., Lancs; St John's Coll., Cambridge (Schol.). Teaching, Hyde Grammar Sch., Cheshire, 1948. Asst Principal, HM Customs and Excise, 1950 (Private Sec. to Chm.); Principal: HM Customs and Excise, 1954; HM Treasury, 1956; HM Customs and Excise, 1958; Asst Sec., HM Customs and Excise, 1965; IBRD (World Bank), Washington, DC, 1967; Asst Sec., 1970, Under Sec., 1972, CSD; a Comr of Customs and Excise, 1975–79; Dept of Industry (later DTI), 1979–85. *Recreation:* golf. *Address:* 9 Walnut Close, Epsom, Surrey. *T:* Epsom 25397. *Club:* Royal Automobile.

LEEPER, Richard Kevin; Life President of The Lep Group plc; *b* 14 July 1894; *s* of late William John Leeper of Leeperstown, Welchtown, Co. Donegal; *m* 1916, Elizabeth Mary Fenton (*d* 1975); two *s*. *Educ:* Sligo Gram. Sch.; London Univ. Served in Army, European War, 1914–18; Dir of Transport, MAP, 1940–45. Engaged in shipping and forwarding in Yugoslavia, 1920–32; British Vice Consul: Dubrovnik, 1922–25; Susak, 1926–32; Man. Dir, Lep Transport Ltd, and Chief Exec., Lep Group of Cos, 1932; Chm., The Lep Gp Ltd, 1956–72. FCIT; MIFF; FRSA. KCHS; Order of St Sava (Yugoslavia), 1930. *Address:* Holly Wood House, West Byfleet, Surrey. *T:* Byfleet 42537.

LEES, Prof. Anthony David, FRS 1968; Senior Research Fellow, Imperial College at Silwood Park, since 1982; *b* 27 Feb. 1917; *s* of Alan Henry Lees, MA and Mary Hughes Bomford; *m* 1943, Annzella Pauline Wilson; one *d*. *Educ:* Clifton Coll., Bristol; Trinity Hall, Cambridge (Schol.). BA 1939; PhD (Cantab) 1943; ScD 1966. Mem., ARC Unit of Insect Physiology at Zoology Dept, Cambridge, 1945–67; Lalor Fellow, 1956; Vis. Prof., Adelaide Univ., 1966; Hon. Lectr, London Univ., 1968; DCSO and Prof. of Insect Physiology, ARC at Imperial Coll. Field Station, Ascot, 1969–82, now Prof. Emeritus. Pres., Royal Entomological Soc., 1973–75, Hon. Fellow 1984. *Publications:* scientific papers. *Recreations:* gardening, fossicking. *Address:* Wells Lane Corner, Sunninghill, Ascot, Berks.

LEES, Sir Antony; *see* Lees, Sir W. A. C.

LEES, C(harles) Norman; His Honour Judge Lees; a Circuit Judge since 1980; *b* 4 Oct. 1929; *s* of late Charles Lees, Bramhall, Cheshire; *m* 1961, Stella, *d* of late Hubert Swann, Stockport; one *d*. *Educ:* Stockport Sch.; Univ. of Leeds. LLB 1950. Called to Bar, Lincoln's Inn, 1951. Dep. Chm., Cumberland County QS, 1969–71; a Recorder of the Crown Court, 1972–80; Chm., Mental Health Review Tribunal, Manchester Region, 1977–80 (Mem., 1971–80). *Recreations:* squash rackets, music, history. *Address:* 1 Deans Court, Crown Square, Manchester M3 3JL. *T:* 061–834 4097. *Clubs:* Lansdowne; Manchester (Manchester); Northern Lawn Tennis.

LEES, David Bryan, FCA; Finance Director, GKN plc (formerly Guest Keen and Nettlefolds plc), since 1982; *b* 23 Nov. 1936; *s* of late Rear-Adm. D. M. Lees, CB, DSO, and of C. D. M. Lees; *m* 1961, Edith Mary Bernard; two *s* one *d*. *Educ:* Charterhouse. Qualified as a chartered accountant, 1962. Chief Accountant, Handley Page Ltd, 1964–69; GKN Sankey Ltd: Chief Accountant, 1970–72; Dep. Controller, 1973; Director and Controller, 1974–76; GKN plc: Group Finance Executive, 1977; General Manager Finance, 1978–81. Member, Audit Commission, 1983–. Mem. Governing Body, Shrewsbury Sch., 1986. *Recreations:* walking, golf, opera, music. *Address:* Burnside House, Mill Road, Meole Brace, Shrewsbury, Shropshire SY3 9JT. *T:* Shrewsbury 3278. *Club:* MCC.

LEES, Prof. Dennis Samuel, CBE 1980; Emeritus Professor of Industrial Economics, University of Nottingham, since 1983 (Professor, 1968–82); *b* 20 July 1924; *s* of late Samuel Lees and Evelyn Lees (*née* Withers), Borrowash, Derbyshire; *m* 1950, Elizabeth Bretisch, London; two *s* one *d*. *Educ:* Derby Technical Coll.; Nottingham Univ. BSc(Econ), PhD. Lecturer and Reader in Economics, Keele Univ., 1951–65; Prof. of Economics, University Coll., Swansea, 1965–67. Visiting Prof. of Economics: Univ. of Chicago, 1963–64; Univ. of California, Berkeley, 1971; Univ. of Sydney, 1975. Consultant, Economists Advisory Gp Ltd, 1967–82; Chairman: Nat. Ins. Advisory Committee, 1972–80; Industrial Injuries Advisory Council, 1973–78; Mem., Adv. Council, Inst. of Econ. Affairs, 1974–. Freeman, City of London, 1973. *Publications:* Local Expenditure and Exchequer Grants, 1956; Health Thru Choice, 1961; Economic Consequences of the Professions, 1966; Economics of Advertising, 1967; Financial Facilities for Small Firms, 1971; Impairment, Disability, Handicap, 1974; Economics of Personal Injury, 1976; Solicitors' Remuneration in Ireland, 1977; articles on industrial and social policy in: Economica, Jl of Political Economy, Amer. Econ. Rev., Jl of Law and Econ., Jl Industrial Econ., Jl Public Finance. *Recreations:* cricket and pottering. *Address:* 8 Middleton Crescent, Beeston, Nottingham NG9 2TH. *T:* Nottingham 258730.

LEES, Geoffrey William; Headmaster, St Bees School, 1963–80; *b* 1 July 1920; *o s* of late Mr and Mrs F. T. Lees, Manchester; *m* 1949, Joan Needham, *yr d* of late Mr and Mrs J. Needham, Moseley, Birmingham. *Educ:* King's Sch., Rochester; Downing Coll., Cambridge. Royal Signals, 1940–46 (despatches): commissioned 1941; served in NW Europe and Middle East, Captain. 2nd Class Hons English Tripos, Pt I, 1947; History Tripos, Part II, 1948; Asst Master, Brighton Coll., 1948–63. Leave of absence in Australia, Asst Master, Melbourne Church of England Gram. Sch., 1961–62. *Recreations:* reading, lepidoptera, walking. *Address:* 10 Merlin Close, Upper Drive, Hove, Sussex BN3 6NU. *Clubs:* MCC; Hawks', Union (Cambridge).

LEES, Norman; *see* Lees, C. N.

LEES, Air Vice-Marshal Robin Lowther, CB 1985; MBE 1962; FIPM, FBIM; RAF retired; Chief Executive, British Hotels, Restaurants and Caterers Association, since 1986; Air Officer Administration RAF Support Command, 1982–85, and Head of Administrative Branch, RAF, 1983–85; *b* 27 Feb. 1931; *e s* of late Air Marshal Sir Alan Lees, KCB, CBE, DSO, AFC, and Norah Elizabeth (*née* Thompson); *m* 1966, Alison Mary Benson, *o d* of late Col C. B. Carrick, MC, TD, JP; three *s*. *Educ:* Wellington Coll.; RAF Coll., Cranwell. Commissioned RAF, 1952; served AAFCE Fontainebleau, 1953–56; Waterbeach, 1956–58; UKSLS Ottawa, 1958–61; DGPS(RAF) Staff MoD, 1962–66; Wyton, 1966–68; HQ Far East Comd, 1968–70; Directing Staff RAF Staff Coll., 1971–74; RAF PMC, 1974–76; Dir of Personnel (Ground) MoD, 1976; Dir of Personal Services (2) (RAF) MoD, 1976–80; RCDS 1980; Dir of Personnel Management (Policy and Plans) (RAF) MoD, 1981–82. *Recreations:* real tennis, lawn tennis, squash, golf. *Address:* c/o Barclays Bank, 6 Market Place, Newbury, Berks. *Clubs:* Royal Air Force (Chairman, 1977–82); Jesters', All England Lawn Tennis and Croquet.

LEES, Air Marshal Sir Ronald Beresford, KCB 1961 (CB 1946); CBE 1943; DFC; retired as C-in-C, RAF, Germany, 1963–65; *b* 27 April 1910; *s* of John Thomas and Elizabeth Jane Lees; *m* 1931, Rhoda Lillie Pank; one *s* one *d*. *Educ:* St Peter's Coll., Adelaide, Australia. Joined Royal Australian Air Force, 1930; transferred Royal Air Force, 1931. ADC to the Queen, 1952–53 (to King George VI, 1949–52); AOC No 83 Gp, 2nd TAF in Germany, 1952–55; Asst Chief of Air Staff (Operations), 1955–58; SASO, Fighter Command, 1958–60; Dep. Chief of the Air Staff, 1960–63; Air Marshal, 1961. *Address:* 1 Stonyfell Road, Wattle Park, SA 5066, Australia.

LEES, Sir Thomas (Edward), 4th Bt, *cr* 1897; landowner; *b* 31 Jan. 1925; 2nd *s* of Sir John Victor Elliott Lees, 3rd Bt, DSO, MC, and Madeline A. P. (*d* 1967), *d* of Sir Harold Pelly, 4th Bt; *S* father 1955; *m* 1949, Faith Justin, *d* of G. G. Jessiman, OBE, Great Durnford, Wilts; one *s* three *d*. *Educ:* Eton; Magdalene Coll., Cambridge. Served War in RAF; discharged 1945, after losing eye. Magdalene, Cambridge, 1945–47; BA Cantab 1947 (Agriculture). Since then has farmed at and managed South Lytchett estate. Chm., Post Green Community Trust Ltd. Mem., General Synod of C of E, 1970–. JP 1951, CC 1952–74, High Sheriff 1960, Dorset. *Recreation:* sailing. *Heir: s* Christopher James Lees [*b* 4 Nov. 1952; *m* 1977, Jennifer, *d* of John Wyllie]. *Address:* Post Green, Lytchett Minster, Poole, Dorset. *T:* Lytchett Minster 622048. *Club:* Royal Cruising.

LEES, Sir Thomas Harcourt Ivor, 8th Bt *cr* (UK) 1804, of Black Rock, County Dublin; *b* 6 Nov. 1941; *s* of Sir Charles Archibald Edward Ivor Lees, 7th Bt, and Lily, *d* of Arthur Williams, Manchester; *S* father, 1963. *Heir: kinsman* John Cathcart d'Olier-Lees [*b* 12 Nov. 1927; *m* 1957, Wendy Garrold, *yr d* of late Brian Garrold Groom; two *s*].

LEES, Dr William, CBE 1970; TD 1962; FRCOG; Medical Manpower Consultant to South West Thames Regional Health Authority, since 1981; *b* 18 May 1924; *s* of William Lees and Elizabeth Lees (*née* Massey); *m* 1947, Winifred Elizabeth (*née* Hanford); three *s*. *Educ;* Queen Elizabeth's, Blackburn; Victoria Univ., Manchester. MB ChB; LRCP; MRCS; MRCOG, FRCOG; DPH; MFCM. Obstetrics and Gynaecology, St Mary's Hosps, Manchester, 1947–58; Min. of Health, later DHSS, 1959–81; Under Sec., (SPMO) 1977–81. QHP, 1969–72. Col, 10th, later no 257, Gen. Hosp., TAVR RAMC, 1966–71; Col Comdt, NW London Sector, ACF, 1971–76; Mem. for Greater London, TA&VRA, 1966–. OStJ 1967. *Publications:* numerous contribs on: intensive therapy, progressive patient care, perinatal mortality, day surgery, district general hospital. *Recreations:* music, golf, travel. *Address:* 13 Hall Park Hill, Berkhamsted, Herts. *T:* Berkhamsted 3010. *Clubs:* Athenæum, St John's.

LEES, Sir (William) Antony Clare, 3rd Bt *cr* 1937; *b* 14 June 1935; *s* of Sir (William) Hereward Clare Lees, 2nd Bt, and of Lady (Dorothy Gertrude) Lees, *d* of F. A. Lauder; *S* father, 1976. *Educ:* Eton; Magdalene Coll., Cambridge (MA). *Heir:* none.

LEES-MILNE, James; *b* 6 Aug. 1908; *er s* of George Crompton Lees-Milne, Crompton Hall, Lancs and Wickhamford Manor, Worcs; *m* 1951, Alvilde, formerly wife of 3rd Viscount Chaplin and *d* of late Lt-Gen. Sir Tom Molesworth Bridges, KCB, KCMG, DSO; no *c*. *Educ:* Eton Coll.; Magdalen Coll., Oxford. Private Sec. to 1st Baron Lloyd, 1931–35; on staff, Reuters, 1935–36; on staff, National Trust, 1936–66; Adviser on Historic Buildings to National Trust, 1951–66. 2nd Lieut Irish Guards, 1940–41 (invalided). FRSL 1957; FSA 1974. *Publications:* The National Trust (ed), 1945; The Age of Adam, 1947; National Trust Guide: Buildings, 1948; Tudor Renaissance, 1951; The Age of Inigo Jones, 1953; Roman Mornings, 1956 (Heinemann Award, 1956); Baroque in Italy, 1959; Baroque in Spain and Portugal, 1960; Earls of Creation, 1962; Worcestershire: A Shell Guide, 1964; St Peter's, 1967; English Country Houses: Baroque 1685–1714, 1970; Another Self, 1970; Heretics in Love, 1973; Ancestral Voices, 1975; William Beckford, 1976; Prophesying Peace, 1977; Round the Clock, 1978; Harold Nicolson, vol. I, 1980, vol. II, 1981 (Heinemann Award, RSL, 1982); (with David Ford) Images of Bath, 1982; The Country House (anthology), 1982; Caves of Ice, 1983; The Last Stuarts, 1983; Midway on the Waves, 1985. *Recreation:* work. *Address:* Essex House, Badminton, Avon GL9 1DD. *T:* Badminton 288. *Club:* Brooks's.

LEES-SPALDING, Rear-Adm. Ian Jaffery, (Tim), CB 1973; RN retd; Joint Editor, Macmillan and Silk Cut Nautical Almanac, since 1980; *b* London, 16 June 1920; *s* of Frank Souter Lees-Spalding and Joan (*née* Bodilly); *m* 1946, June Sandys Lyster Sparkes; two *d*. *Educ:* Blundells Sch.; RNEC. Served War of 1939–45 (King's Commendation for Bravery, 1941; Royal Lifesaving Inst. medal, 1942); served in HMS Sirius, HM S/Ms Trespasser, Teredo, Truculent and Andrew, HMS Cleopatra and Tiger; Chief of Staff to C-in-C Naval Home Comd, 1969; CSO (Technical) to C-in-C Fleet, 1971; retd 1974. Administrator, London Internat. Film Sch., 1975–79. *Recreations:* music, travelling. *Address:* St Olaf's, Wonston, Winchester, Hants S021 3LP. *T:* Winchester 760249. *Club:* Army and Navy.

LEESE, John Arthur; Editor, London Standard, since 1986; *b* 4 Jan. 1930; *s* of late Cyril Leese and May Leese; *m* 1959, Maureen Jarvis; one *s* one *d*. *Educ:* Bishop Vesey's School, Warwicks. Editor, Coventry Evening Telegraph, 1964–70; Dep. Editor, Evening News, 1970–76, Editor, 1980; Editor-in-Chief and Publisher, Soho News, NY, 1981–82; Editl Dir, Harmsworth Publishing, 1975–82; Editor, You Magazine and Editor-in-Chief and Man. Dir, Associated Magazines, 1983–86; Dir, Mail Newspapers, 1983–. *Address:* The London Standard, 121 Fleet Street, EC4P 4DD. *T:* 01–353 8000.

LEESE, Sir John Henry Vernon, 5th Bt *cr* 1908; *b* 7 Aug. 1901; *s* of Vernon Francis Leese, OBE (*d* 1927) and Edythe Gwendoline (*d* 1929), *d* of Charles Frederick Stevenson; *g s* of Sir Joseph Francis Leese, 1st Bt; *S* cousin, 1979. *Heir:* none.

LE FANU, (George) Victor (Sheridan); Serjeant at Arms, House of Commons, since 1982; *b* 1925; *s* of late Maj.-Gen. Roland Le Fanu, DSO, MC, and Marguerite (*née* Lumsden); *m* 1956, Elizabeth, *d* of late Major Herbert Hall and Kitty (*née* Gauvain); three *s*. *Educ:* Shrewsbury School. Served Coldstream Guards, 1943–63; Asst-Adjt, Royal Military Academy, Sandhurst, 1949–52; Adjt 2nd Bn Coldstream Guards, 1952–55; sc Camberley, 1959; Staff Captain to Vice-Quartermaster-General to the Forces, War Office, 1960–61; GSO2, Headquarters London District, 1961–63; Dep. Asst Serjeant at Arms, House of Commons, 1963–76; Asst Serjeant at Arms, 1976–81; Deputy Serjeant at Arms, 1981–82. *Address:* Speaker's Court, House of Commons, SW1A 0AA.

LE FANU, Mark; General Secretary, The Society of Authors, since 1982; *b* 14 Nov. 1946; *s* of Admiral of the Fleet Sir Michael Le Fanu, GCB, DSC and Prudence, *d* of Admiral Sir Vaughan Morgan, KBE, CB, MVO, DSC; *m* 1976, Lucy Cowen; two *s* one *d*. *Educ:* Winchester; Univ. of Sussex. Admitted Solicitor, 1976. Served RN, 1964–73; McKenna & Co., 1973–78; The Society of Authors, 1979–. *Recreations:* canals, travel, washing up. *Address:* 25 St James's Gardens, W11 4RE. *T:* 01–603 4119. *Club:* PEN.

LE FANU, Victor; *see* Le Fanu, G. V. S.

LE FANU, Mrs W. R.; *see* Maconchy, Elizabeth.

LEFEBVRE, Prof. Arthur Henry; Distinguished Reilly Professor of Combustion Engineering, School of Mechanical Engineering, Purdue University, since 1979 (Professor and Head of School, 1976–80); *b* 14 March 1923; *s* of Henri and May Lefebvre; *m* 1952, Elizabeth Marcella Betts; two *s* one *d*. *Educ:* Long Eaton Grammar Sch; Nottingham Univ.; Imperial Coll., London. DSc (Eng), DIC, PhD, CEng, FIMechE, FRAeS. Ericssons Telephones Ltd: Engrg apprentice, 1938–41; Prodn Engr, 1941–47; res. work on combustion and heat transfer in gas turbines, Rolls Royce, Derby, 1952–61; Prof. of Aircraft Propulsion, Coll. of Aeronautics, 1961–71; Prof. and Hd of Sch. of Mechanical Engrg, Cranfield Inst. of Technol., 1971–76. Mem., AGARD Combustion and Propulsion Panel, 1957–61; Mem., AGARD Propulsion and Energetics Panel, 1970–76; Chm., Combustion Cttee, Aeronautical Res. Council, 1970–74. Gas Turbine Award, ASME, 1982; R. Tom Sawyer Award, ASME, 1984. *Publications:* Gas Turbine Combustion, 1983; papers on combustion and heat transfer in Proc. Royal Soc., internat. symposium vols on combustion, combustion and flame, combustion science and technology. *Recreations:* music, reading, golf. *Address:* 1741 Redwood Lane, Lafayette, Indiana 47905, USA. *T:* (317) 447–0117.

LEFEVER, Kenneth Ernest, CB 1974; Deputy Chairman, Civil Service Appeal Board, 1978–80 (Official Side Member, 1976–78); *b* 22 Feb. 1915; *s* of E. S. Lefever and Mrs E. E. Lefever; *m* 1939, Margaret Ellen Bowley; one *s* one *d*. *Educ:* County High Sch., Ilford. Board of Customs and Excise: joined Dept as Officer, 1935; War Service, 1942–46 (Captain, RE); Principal Inspector, 1966; Dep. Chief Inspector, 1969; Collector, London Port, 1971; Chief Inspector, 1972; Dir of Organisation and Chief Inspector, 1974; Comr, Bd of Customs and Excise, 1972–75, retd. *Recreations:* gardening, walking, cricket. *Address:* Trebarwith, 37 Surman Crescent, Hutton Burses, Brentwood, Essex. *T:* Brentwood 212110. *Clubs:* MCC, Civil Service.

LEFF, Prof. Gordon; Professor of History, University of York, since 1969; *b* 9 May 1926; *m* 1953, Rosemary Kathleen (*née* Fox) (marr. diss 1980); one *s*. *Educ:* Summerhill Sch.; King's Coll., Cambridge. BA 1st Cl. Hons, PhD, LittD. Fellow, King's Coll., Cambridge, 1955–59; Asst Lectr, Lectr, Sen. Lectr, in History, Manchester Univ., 1956–65; Reader in History, Univ. of York, 1965–69. Carlyle Vis. Lectr, Univ. of Oxford, 1983. *Publications:* Bradwardine and the Pelagians, 1957; Medieval Thought, 1958; Gregory of Rimini, 1961; The Tyranny of Concepts, 1961; Richard Fitzralph, 1963; Heresy in the Later Middle Ages, 2 vols, 1967; Paris and Oxford Universities in 13th and 14th Centuries, 1968; History and Social Theory, 1969; William of Ockham: the metamorphosis of scholastic discourse, 1975; The Dissolution of the Medieval Outlook, 1976. *Recreations:* walking, gardening, watching cricket, listening to music. *Address:* The Sycamores, 12 The Village, Strensall, York Y03 5XS. *T:* York 490358.

le FLEMING, Morris John; Chief Executive, Hertfordshire County Council, and Clerk to the Lieutenancy, Hertfordshire, since 1979; *b* 19 Aug. 1932; *s* of late Morris Ralph le Fleming and Mabel le Fleming; *m* 1960, Jenny Rose Weeks; one *s* three *d*. *Educ:* Tonbridge Sch.; Magdalene Coll., Cambridge (BA). Admitted Solicitor, 1958. Junior Solicitor, Worcester CC, 1958–59; Asst Solicitor: Middlesex CC, 1959; Nottinghamshire CC, 1959–63; Asst Clerk, Lindsey (Lincolnshire) CC, 1963–69; Hertfordshire CC: Second Dep. Clerk, 1969–74; County Secretary, 1974–79; Clerk, Magistrates' Courts Cttee; Sec., Probation and After Care Cttee. *Address:* 14 Swangleys Lane, Knebworth, Herts SG3 6AA. *T:* Stevenage 813152.

LE FLEMING, Peter Henry John; Regional General Manager, South East Thames Regional Health Authority, since 1984; *b* 25 Oct. 1923; *s* of late Edward Ralph Le Fleming and Irene Louise Le Fleming (*née* Adams); *m* 1949, Gudrun Svendsen (marr. diss. 1981); two *s*. *Educ:* Addison Gardens Sch., Hammersmith; Pembroke Coll., Cambridge. MA; FHSM. Served 1942–47, RTR and Parachute Regt, MEF, CMF, Palestine; commnd 1943. Sudan Political Service, Equatoria, Kassala, Blue Nile Provinces, 1949–55; NHS, 1955–: Redevelt Sec., St Thomas's Hosp., London, 1955–57; Hosp. Sec., The London Hosp., 1957–61; Dep. Clerk to the Governors, Guy's Hosp., 1961–69; Gp Sec., Exeter and Mid Devon Hosp. Management Cttee, 1969–74; Area Administrator, Kent AHA, 1974–81; Regional Administrator, SE Thames RHA, 1981–84. Mem., Health Service Supply Council, 1982–86. *Recreations:* long distance fell walking, breeding and showing elkhounds, trad jazz and serious music. *Address:* 15 Hawkhurst Way, Cooden, Bexhill-on-Sea, Sussex TN39 3SD. *T:* Cooden 5190.

le FLEMING, Sir William Kelland, 11th Bt *cr* 1705; *b* 27 April 1922; *s* of Sir Frank Thomas le Fleming, 10th Bt, and of Isabel Annie Fraser, *d* of late James Craig, Manaia, NZ; *S* father, 1971; *m* 1948, Noveen Avis, *d* of C. C. Sharpe, Rukuhia, Hamilton, NZ; three *s* four *d*. *Heir: s* Quentin John le Fleming [*b* 27 June 1949; *m* 1971, Judith Ann, *d* of C. J. Peck, JP; two *s* one *d*]. *Address:* Kopane RD6, Palmerston North, New Zealand.

LE GALLIENNE, Eva; Theatrical Producer, Director and Actress; *b* London, England, 11 Jan. 1899; *d* of Richard Le Gallienne and Julie Norregaard. *Educ:* College Sévigné, Paris, France. Début Prince of Wales Theatre, London, in The Laughter of Fools, 1915; New York Début in The Melody of Youth, 1916; appeared in NY and on tour, in Mr Lazarus, season of 1916–17; with Ethel Barrymore in The Off Chance, 1917–18; Not So Long Ago, 1920–21; Liliom, 1921–22; The Swan, 1923; Hannele in The Assumption of Hannele, by Hauptmann, 1923; Jeanne d'Arc, by Mercedes de Acosta, 1925; The Call of Life, by Schnitzler, 1925; The Master Builder, by Henrik Ibsen, 1925–26. Founder and Director Civic Repertory Theatre, NY, 1926; played in Saturday Night, The Three Sisters, Cradle Song, 2x2–5, The First Stone, Improvisations in June, The Would-Be Gentleman, L'Invitation au Voyage, The Cherry Orchard, Peter Pan, On the High Road, The Lady from Alfaqueque, Katerina, The Open Door, A Sunny Morning, The Master Builder, John Gabriel Borkman, La Locandiera, Twelfth Night, Inheritors, The Good Hope, Hedda Gabler, The Sea Gull, Mlle. Bourrat, The Living Corpse, Women Have Their Way, Romeo and Juliet, The Green Cockatoo, Siegfried, Allison's House, Camille, Liliom (revival), Dear Jane, Alice in Wonderland, L'Aiglon, 1934; Rosmersholm, 1935; Uncle Harry, 1942; Cherry Orchard, 1944; Thérèse, 1945; Elizabeth I in Schiller's Mary Stuart, Phœnix Theatre, NYC, 1958; toured in same, 1959–60; Elizabeth the Queen, 1961–62; The Sea Gull, 1963; Ring Round the Moon, 1963; The Mad Woman of Chaillot, 1964; The Trojan Women, 1964; Exit the King, 1967; All's Well That Ends Well, Amer. Shakespeare Theatre, 1970; Mrs Woodfin in The Dream Watcher, 1975; Fanny Cavendish in The Royal Family, NYC, 1976, tour, 1977; To Grandmother's House We Go, NYC, 1981; White Queen in Alice in Wonderland, NYC, 1983 (also dir); *film:* Resurrection, 1980. Man. Dir of Amer. Repertory Theatre, which did six classic revivals in repertory, NY, 1946 and 1947; Dir The Cherry Orchard, Lyceum Theatre, NY, 1967–68. Hon. MA (Tufts Coll.), 1927, and several honorary doctorates from 1930. Member Actors' Equity Assoc. and Managers' Protective Assoc. Has won various awards; Gold Medal, Soc. Arts and Sciences, 1926; Am. Acad. of Arts and Letters medal for good speech, 1945; Drama League Award, 1976; Handel Medallion, 1976; Anta Award, 1977. Cross of St Olav (Norway), 1961. *Publications:* At 33 (autobiography), 1934; Flossie and Bossy, (NY) 1949, (London) 1950; With A Quiet Heart, 1953; A Preface to Hedda Gabler, 1953; The Master Builder, a new translation with a Prefatory Study, 1955; trans. Six Plays by Henrik Ibsen, 1957 (NYC); trans. The Wild Duck and Other Plays by Henrik Ibsen, 1961 (NYC); The Mystic in the Theatre: Eleonora Duse, 1966 (NYC and London); trans. The Spider and Other Stories by Carl Evald, 1980; articles for New York Times, Theatre Arts Monthly, etc. *Recreations:* gardening, painting. *Address:* Weston, Conn 06880, USA.

LEGARD, Sir Charles Thomas, 15th Bt *cr* 1660; *S* father, 1984. *Heir: s* Christopher John Charles Legard.

LÉGER, His Eminence Cardinal Paul Emile; *b* Valleyfield, Quebec, Canada, 26 April 1904; *s* of Ernest Léger and Alda Beauvais. *Educ:* Ste-Thérèse Seminary; Grand Seminary, Montreal. Seminary of Philosophy, Paris, 1930–31; Seminary of Theology, Paris, 1931–32; Asst Master of Novices, Paris, 1932–33; Superior Seminary of Fukuoka, Japan, 1933–39; Prof., Seminary of Philosophy, Montreal, 1939–40; Vicar-Gen., Diocese of Valleyfield, 1940–47; Rector, Canadian Coll., Rome, 1947–50; consecrated bishop in Rome and apptd to See of Montreal, 1950; elevated to Sacred Coll. of Cardinals and given titular Church of St Mary of the Angels, 1953; Archbishop of Montreal, 1950–67; resigned to work as a missionary in Africa; Parish Priest, St Madeleine Sophie Barat parish, Montreal, 1974–75. Variety Club award, 1976. Has several hon. doctorates both from Canada and abroad. Holds foreign decorations. *Address:* CP1500–Succursale A, Montréal, PQ H3C 2Z9, Canada.

LEGG, Allan Aubrey R.; *see* Rowan-Legg.

LEGG, Keith (Leonard Charles), OBE 1981; PhD, MSc (Eng); CEng, FIMechE, FRAeS, FCIT; FHKIE; JP; Hon. Professor and Advisor to Xian Jiaotung University, Shanghai Polytechnic University and South China Institute of Technology, China; consultant on aerospace engineering and on higher education; *b* 24 Oct. 1924; *s* of E. H. J. Legg; *m* 1947, Joan, *d* of H. E. Green; two *s*. *Educ:* London Univ. (External); Cranfield Inst. of Technology. Engineering apprenticeship, 1940–45; Dep. Chief Research and Test Engr, Asst Chief Designer, Chief Project and Structural Engr, Short Bros & Harland Ltd, Belfast, 1942–56; Chief Designer and Prof., Brazilian Aeronautical Centre, São Paulo, 1956–60; Head of Dept and Prof., Loughborough Univ. of Technology, 1960–72 (Sen. Pro Vice-Chancellor, 1967–70); Dir, Lanchester Polytechnic, 1972–75; Dir, Hong Kong Polytechnic, 1975–84. Chm., Internat. Directing Cttee, CERI/OECD Higher Educn Institutional Management, 1973–75; Member: Road Transport Industrial Trng Bd, 1966–75; Bd of Educn, 1975–84; Adv. Cttee on Environmental Protection, 1977–84; Council, Royal Aeronautical Soc.; Hong Kong Management Assoc. Council, 1982–84; Environmental and Pollution Council of Hong Kong; Indust. Develt Bd, 1982–84; Council of City Polytechnic of Hong Kong, 1984. Adviser to OECD in Paris; Mem. various nat. and professional cttees. Fellow, Hong Kong Management Assoc. Hon. DTech Loughborough, 1982; Hon. LLD Hong Kong, 1984. *Publications:* numerous: on aerospace structures and design, transport systems, higher educn and educnl analytical models. *Recreations:* most sports, especially tennis, badminton and squash; aid to the handicapped. *Address:* 19 Broom Park, Broom Road, Teddington, Middx TW11 9RS. *T:* 01–977 8215.

LEGG, Thomas Stuart, CB 1985; Deputy Secretary, Lord Chancellor's Department, since 1982; Deputy Clerk of the Crown in Chancery, since 1986; *b* 13 Aug. 1935; *e s* of Stuart Legg and Margaret Legg (*née* Amos); *m* 1st, 1961, Patricia Irene Dowie (marr. diss.); two *d*; 2nd, 1983, Marie-Louise Clarke, *e d* of late Humphrey Jennings. *Educ:* Horace Mann-Lincoln Sch., New York; Frensham Heights Sch., Surrey; St John's Coll., Cambridge (MA, LLM). Royal Marines, 1953–55. Called to the Bar, Inner Temple, 1960, Bencher, 1984; joined Lord Chancellor's Dept, 1962; Private Secretary to Lord Chancellor, 1965–68; Asst Solicitor, 1975; Under Sec., 1977–82; SE Circuit Administrator, 1980–82. *Address:* Lord Chancellor's Department, House of Lords, SW1.

LEGGATT, Hon. Sir Andrew (Peter), Kt 1982; **Hon. Mr Justice Leggatt**; a Judge of the High Court of Justice, Queen's Bench Division, since 1982; *b* 8 Nov. 1930; *er s* of late Captain William Ronald Christopher Leggatt, DSO, RN and of Dorothea Joy Leggatt (*née* Dreyer); *m* 1953, Gillian Barbara Newton; one *s* one *d*. *Educ:* Eton; King's Coll., Cambridge (Exhibr). MA 1957. Commn in Rifle Bde, 1949–50; TA, 1950–59. Called to the Bar, Inner Temple, 1954, Bencher, 1976. QC 1972; a Recorder of the Crown Court, 1974–82. Mem., Bar Council, 1971–82; Mem. Senate, 1974–83; Chm. of the Bar, 1981–82. Hon. Member: American Bar Assoc.; Canadian Bar Assoc.; non-resident mem., American Law Inst.; Mem., Top Salaries Review Body, 1979–82. Inspector (for Dept of Trade), London & Counties Securities Group, 1975. *Recreations:* listening to music, personal computers. *Address:* Royal Courts of Justice, Strand, WC2A 2LL. *Clubs:* MCC, Pilgrims.

LEGGATT, Hugh Frank John; Senior Partner, Leggatt Brothers (Fine Art Dealers); *b* 27 Feb. 1925; 2nd *s* of late Henry and Beatrice Leggatt; *m* 1953, Jennifer Mary Hepworth (separated 1984); two *s*. *Educ:* Eton; New Coll., Oxford. RAF, 1943–46. Joined Leggatt Bros, 1946; Partner, 1952; Senior Partner, 1962. Pres., Fine Art Trade Provident Instn, 1960–63; Chm., Soc. of London Art Dealers, 1966–70; Mem., Museums and Galleries Commn, 1983–. Hon. Sec., Heritage in Danger, 1974–. *Publications:* contribs to newspapers and jls. *Address:* 17 Duke Street, St James's, SW1Y 6DB. *T:* 01–930 3772. *Club:* White's.

LEGGE, family name of **Earl of Dartmouth.**

LEGGE, Prof. (Mary) Dominica, FBA 1974; Personal Professor of French (Anglo-Norman Studies), University of Edinburgh, 1968–73, Professor Emeritus, 1973; *b* 26 March 1905; 2nd *d* of late James Granville Legge and Josephine (*née* Makins). *Educ:* Liverpool Coll., Huyton; Somerville Coll., Oxford. BA Hon. Mod. Lang, BLitt, MA, DLitt. Editor, Selden Soc., 1928–34; Mary Somerville Res. Fellow, 1935–37; Asst Lectr, Royal Holloway Coll., 1938–42; Voluntary asst, BoT, 1942; Asst, Dundee Univ. Coll., 1942; Lectr, 1943, Reader, 1953, Univ. of Edinburgh. Hon. Fellow, Somerville Coll., 1968. FSAScot; Corresp. Fellow, Mediaeval Acad. of America. Officier des Palmes Académiques. *Publications:* (with Sir William Holdsworth) Year-Book of 10 Edward II, 1934–35; Anglo-Norman Letters and Petitions, 1941; (with E. Vinaver) Le Roman de Balain, 1942; Anglo-Norman in the Cloisters, 1950; Anglo-Norman Literature and its Background, 1963; (with R. J. Dean) The Rule of St Benedict, 1964; contribs to learned jls and volumes, British and foreign. *Recreations:* music, walking. *Address:* 191a Woodstock Road, Oxford OX2 7AB. *T:* Oxford 56455. *Clubs:* Royal Over-Seas League; University of Edinburgh Staff.

LEGGE, Rt. Rev. William Gordon, DD; *b* 20 Jan. 1913; *s* of Thomas Legge and Jane (*née* Gill); *m* 1941, Hyacinth Florence Richards; one *s* one *d*. *Educ:* Bishop Feild and Queen's Colls, St John's, Newfoundland. Deacon 1938, priest 1939; Curate, Channel, 1938–41; Incumbent of Botwood, 1941–44; Rector, Bell Island, 1944–55; Sec., Diocesan Synod, 1955–68; Archdeacon of Avalon, 1955–68; Canon of Cathedral, 1955–76; Diocesan Registrar, 1957–68; Suffragan Bishop, 1968; Bishop of Western Newfoundland,

1976–78. DD *hc*, Univ. of King's College, Halifax, NS, 1973. *Address:* 52 Glenhaven Boulevard, Corner Brook, Newfoundland A2H 4P6.

LEGGETT, Sir Clarence (Arthur Campbell), Kt 1980; MBE (mil.) 1943; FRACS, FACS; Surgeon; Hon. Consulting Surgeon, Princess Alexandra Hospital, Brisbane, since 1968; *b* 24 July 1911; *s* of late A. J. Leggett; *m* 1939, Avril, *d* of late R. L. Bailey; one *s* two *d*. *Educ:* Sydney Univ. (MA, MB BS; 1st cl. Hons, Univ. Medallist, 1936); Queensland Univ. (MS). RMO, Royal Prince Alfred Hosp., Sydney, 1937–38; Asst Dep. Med. Supt, 1939. Major, AAMC, 1941–46. Asst Surgeon, Royal Brisbane Hosp., 1941–51; Junior Surg., 1951–56; Senior Surg., Princess Alexandra Hosp., Brisbane, 1956–68. University of Queensland: Hon. Demonstrator and Examiner, Anatomy Dept, 1941–47; Chief Asst, Dept of Surgery, 1947–51; Mem. Faculty Bd, 1947–51; Special Lectr, 1951–68. Member of Council: Queensland Inst. for Med. Research, 1948–65; RACS, 1966–75 (Gordon Craig Schol.; Chm. Court of Examiners, 1971–75; Junior Vice-Pres., 1973–75; Mem. Ct of Honour). FAMA 1985; Hon. FRCS 1983. *Publications:* numerous surgical and historical papers, orations and theses. *Recreations:* breeding Arabian horses and Hereford cattle; univ. blue, and mem., Australian hockey team, 1934. *Address:* Craigston, 217 Wickham Terrace, Brisbane, Queensland 4000, Australia. *T:* 07-831-0031. *Club:* Queensland (Brisbane).

LEGGETT, Douglas Malcolm Aufrère, MA, PhD, DSc; FRAeS; FIMA; Vice-Chancellor, University of Surrey, 1966–75; *b* 27 May 1912; *s* of George Malcolm Kent Leggett and Winifred Mabel Horsfall; *m* 1943, Enid Vida Southall; one *s* one *d*. *Educ:* Rugby Sch.; Edinburgh Univ.; Trinity Coll., Cambridge. Wrangler, 1934; Fellow of Trinity Coll., Cambridge, 1937; Queen Mary Coll., London, 1937–39; Royal Aircraft Establishment, 1939–45; Royal Aeronautical Society, 1945–50; King's Coll., London, 1950–60; Principal, Battersea Coll. of Technology, 1960–66. FKC 1974; DUniv Surrey 1975. *Publications:* (with C. M. Waterlow) The War Games that Superpowers Play, 1983; (with M. G. Payne) A Forgotten Truth, 1986; contrib. to scientific and technical jls. *Address:* Southlands, Fairoak Lane, Oxshott, Surrey. *T:* Oxshott 3061.

LEGH, family name of **Baron Newton.**

LEGH, Charles Legh Shuldham Cornwall-, CBE 1977 (OBE 1971); AE; DL; *b* 10 Feb. 1903; *er s* of late Charles Henry George Cornwall Legh, of High Legh Hall, Cheshire, and late Geraldine Maud, *d* of Lt-Col Arthur James Shuldham, Royal Inniskilling Fusiliers; *m* 1930, Dorothy, *er d* of late J. W. Scott, Seal, Sevenoaks; one *s* two *d*. Served 1939–45 with AAF and RAF. JP Cheshire, 1938–73; High Sheriff, 1939; DL, 1949; CC 1949–77. Chm., Cheshire Police Authority, 1957–74; Chm., New Cheshire CC, 1974–76 (Shadow Chm., 1973); Hon. Alderman, 1977. *Address:* High Legh House, Knutsford, Cheshire WA16 0QR. *T:* Lymm 2303. *Clubs:* Carlton, MCC.

LE GOY, Raymond Edgar Michel, FCIT; a Director General, Commission of the European Communities, since 1981; *b* 1919; *e s* of J. A. S. M. N. and May Le Goy; *m* 1960, Ernestine Burnett, Trelawny, Jamaica; two *s*. *Educ:* William Ellis Sch.; Gonville and Caius Coll., Cambridge (MA). 1st cl. hons Hist. Tripos, 1939, 1940. Sec. Cambridge Union; Chm., Union Univ. Liberal Socs. Served Army, 1940–46: Staff Captain, HQ E Africa, 1944; Actg Major, 1945. LPTB, 1947; Min. of Transport, 1947; UK Shipping Adviser, Japan, 1949–51; Far East and SE Asia, 1951; Dir, Goeland Co., 1952; Asst Secretary: MoT, 1958; Min. of Aviation, 1959; BoT, 1966; Under-Sec., 1968, BoT, later DTI; Dir Gen. for Transport, EEC, 1973–81. *Publication:* The Victorian Burletta, 1953. *Recreations:* theatre, music, race relations. *Address:* c/o Société Générale de Banque, 10 Rond Point Schuman, Brussels 1040, Belgium.

LE GRICE, Very Rev. F(rederick) Edwin, MA; Dean Emeritus of Ripon Cathedral, since 1984 (Dean, 1968–84); *b* 14 Dec. 1911; *s* of Frederick and Edith Le Grice; *m* 1940, Joyce Margaret Hildreth; one *s* two *d*. *Educ:* Paston Sch., North Walsham; Queens' Coll., Cambridge; Westcott House, Cambridge. BA (2nd class hons Mathematics, 2nd class hons Theology) 1934; MA 1946. Asst Curate: St Aidan's, Leeds, 1935–38; Paignton, 1938–46; Vicar of Totteridge, N20, 1946–58; Canon Residentiary and Sub-Dean of St Albans Cathedral, 1958–68; Examining Chaplain to the Bishop of St Albans, 1958–68. A Church Comr, 1973–82; Mem., Church Commn on Crown Appts, 1977–82. *Address:* The West Cottage, Markenfield Hall, Ripon, N Yorks.

LEHANE, Maureen, (Mrs Peter Wishart); concert and opera singer; *d* of Christopher Lehane and Honor Millar; *m* 1966, Peter Wishart (*d* 1984), composer. *Educ:* Queen Elizabeth's Girls' Grammar Sch., Barnet; Guildhall Sch. of Music and Drama. Studied under Hermann Weissenborn, Berlin (teacher of Fischer Dieskau); also under John and Aida Dickens (Australian teachers of Joan Sutherland); gained Arts Council award to study in Berlin. Speciality is Handel; has sung numerous leading roles (operas inc. Ezio, Ariadne and Pharamondo) with Handel opera societies of England and America, in London, and in Carnegie Hall, New York, also in Poland, Sweden and Germany; gave a number of master classes on the interpretation of Handel's vocal music (notably at s'Hertogenbosch Festival, Holland, July 1972; invited to repeat them in 1973). Debut at Glyndebourne, 1967. Festival appearances include: Stravinsky Festival, Cologne; City of London; Aldeburgh; Cheltenham; Three Choirs; Bath; Oxford Bach; Göttingen Handel Festival, etc; has toured N America; also 3–month tour of Australia at invitation of ABC and 2–month tour of Far East and ME, 1971; sang in Holland, and for Belgian TV, 1978; visits also to Berlin, Lisbon, Poland and Rome, 1979–80, to Warsaw, 1981. Title rôle in: Handel's Ariodante, Sadler's Wells, 1974; (her husband's 4th opera) Clytemnaestra, London, 1974; Purcell's Dido and Aeneas, Netherlands Opera, 1976; castrato lead in J. C. Bach's Adriano in Siria, London, 1982; female lead in Hugo Cole's The Falcon, Somerset, 1983; Peter Wishart's The Lady of the Inn, Reading Univ., 1984. Cyrus in first complete recording of Handel's Belshazzar. Appears regularly on BBC; also in promenade concerts. Has made numerous recordings (Bach, Haydn, Mozart, Handel, etc). Mem. Jury, Internat. Singing Comp., s'Hertogenbosch Fest., Holland, 1982–. *Publication:* (ed with Peter Wishart) Songs of Purcell. *Recreations:* cooking, gardening, reading. *Address:* Bridge House, Great Elm, Frome, Somerset BA11 3NY.

LEHMAN, Prof. Meir, (Manny), PhD; FIEE, FBCS; Emeritus Professor of Computing Science, Imperial College of Science and Technology, University of London, since 1984 (Professor, 1972–84); *b* 24 Jan. 1925; *s* of late Benno and of Theresa Lehman; *m* 1953, Chava Robinson; three *s* two *d*. *Educ:* Letchworth Grammar Sch.; Imperial Coll. of Science and Technol. (BSc Hons, PhD, ARCS, DIC). FIEE 1947; FBCS 1954; MACM 1955; FIEEE 1957. Murphy Radio, 1941–50; Imperial Coll., 1950–56; London Labs, Ferranti, 1956–57; Scientific Dept, Israeli Defence Min., 1957–64; Res. Div., IBM, 1964–72; Dept of Computing, Imperial Coll., 1972–84 (part-time 1984–), Hd of Dept, 1979–84. Founder, Imperial Software Technology Ltd, 1982 (Chm. 1982–84, Exec. Dir and Consultant 1984–). Vice-Chm. of Exec., Kisharon Day Sch. for Special Educn, 1976–. *Publications:* Software Evolution—Processes of Program Change, 1985; over 100 refereed pubns and some 6 book chapters. *Recreations:* family, Talmudic studies, classical orchestral music, gardening, DIY. *Address:* 5 Elm Close, NW4 2PH. *T:* (office) 01–581 8155; 01–589 5111.

LEHMANN, Prof. Andrew George; Professor of European Studies and Deajn, School of Humanities, University of Buckingham, since 1983; *b* 1922; British; *m* 1942, Alastine Mary, *d* of late K. N. Bell; two *s* one *d*. *Educ:* Dulwich Coll.; The Queen's Coll., Oxford. MA, DPhil Oxon. Served with RCS and Indian Army, 6th Rajputana Rifles. Fenced for England (Sabre), 1939. Asst lecturer and lecturer, Manchester Univ., 1945–51; Prof. of French Studies, 1951–68, Dean of Faculty of Letters and Soc. Scis, Univ. of Reading, 1960–66. Vis. Prof. of Comparative Literature, Univ. of Mainz, 1956; Hon. Prof., Univ. of Warwick, 1968–78. Various industry posts, 1968–78. Dir, Inst. of European Studies, Hull Univ., 1978–83. Mem., Hale Cttee on University Teaching Methods, 1961–63; Chm., Industrial Council for Educnl and Trng Technology, 1974–76 (Pres., 1979–81, Vice-Pres., 1981–85); Mem., Anglo-French Permanent Mixed Cultural Commission, 1963–68. Adviser: Chinese Univ. of Hong Kong, 1964; Haile Selassie I Univ., Ethiopia, 1965. Member: Hong Kong Univ. Grants Cttee, 1966–73; Academic Planning Board, New Univ. of Ulster, 1966; Court and Council, Bedford Coll., London Univ., 1971–78; British Library Adv. Cttee (Reference), 1975–78; Princeton Univ. Academic Adv. Council, 1975–81. Governor, Ealing Tech. Coll., 1974. *Publications:* The Symbolist Aesthetic in France, 1950 and 1967; Sainte-Beuve, a portrait of the Critic, 1962; The European Heritage, 1984; articles in various periodicals and learned reviews. *Recreations:* music, travel, gardening. *Address:* Westway Cottage, West Adderbury, Banbury, Oxon. *T:* Banbury 810272. *Club:* Athenæum.

LEHMANN, John Frederick, CBE 1964; FRSL; Editor of the London Magazine from its foundation to 1961; Managing Director of John Lehmann Ltd from its foundation to 1952; Founder and Editor of New Writing and of Orpheus; *b* 2 June 1907; *s* of late Rudolph Chambers Lehmann and Alice Marie Davis. *Educ:* Eton (King's Scholar); Trinity Coll., Cambridge. Partner and Gen. Manager, The Hogarth Press, 1938–46; Advisory Editor, The Geographical Magazine, 1940–45. Editor, New Soundings (BBC Third Programme), 1952, The London Magazine, 1954. Chm., Editorial Advisory Panel, British Council, 1952–58; Mem., Anglo-Greek Mixed Commission, 1962–68; Pres., Royal Literary Fund, 1966–76. Vis. Professor: Univ. of Texas, and State Univ. of Calif at San Diego, 1970–72; Univ. of Calif at Berkeley, 1974; Emory Univ., Atlanta, 1977. Pres. Alliance Française in Great Britain, 1955–63. Hon. DLitt Birmingham, 1980. Silver Jubilee Medal, 1977; Officer, Gold Cross, Order of George I (Greece), 1954, Comdr, 1961; Officier Légion d'Honneur, 1958; Grand Officier, Etoile Noire, 1960; Officier, Ordre des Arts et des Lettres, 1965. Prix du Rayonnement Français, 1961. *Publications:* A Garden Revisited, 1931; The Noise of History, 1934; Prometheus and the Bolsheviks, 1937; Evil Was Abroad, 1938; Down River, 1939; New Writing in Europe, 1940; Forty Poems, 1942; The Sphere of Glass, 1944; Shelley in Italy, 1947; The Age of the Dragon, 1951; The Open Night, 1952; The Whispering Gallery (Autobiography I), 1955; I Am My Brother (Autobiography II), 1960; Ancestors and Friends, 1962; Collected Poems, 1963; Christ the Hunter, 1965; The Ample Proposition (Autobiography III), 1966; A Nest of Tigers, 1968; In My Own Time (condensed one-volume autobiography), 1969 (USA); Holborn, 1970; The Reader at Night and other poems, 1974; Virginia Woolf and Her World, 1975; In the Purely Pagan Sense, 1976; Edward Lear and His World, 1977; Thrown to the Woolfs, 1978; Rupert Brooke: his life and his legend, 1980; English Poets of the First World War, 1981; Three Literary Friendships, 1983; New and Selected Poems, 1985; Editor: Poems from New Writing, 1946, French Stories from New Writing, 1947, The Year's Work in Literature, 1949 and 1950, English Stories from New Writing, 1950, Pleasures of New Writing, 1952; The Chatto Book of Modern Poetry, 1956 (with C. Day Lewis); The Craft of Letters in England, 1956; Modern French Stories, 1956; Coming to London, 1957; Italian Stories of Today, 1959; Selected Poems of Edith Sitwell, 1965; (with Derek Parker) Edith Sitwell: selected letters, 1970; (with Roy Fuller) The Penguin New Writing 1940–50, 1985. *Recreations:* gardening, swimming, reading. *Address:* 85 Cornwall Gardens, SW7. *Clubs:* Naval and Military, Eton Viking.

LEHMANN, Rosamond Nina, CBE 1982; 2nd *d* of R. C. Lehmann and Alice Davis; *m* 1928, Hon. Wogan Philipps (*see* 2nd Baron Milford); one *s* (and one *d* decd). *Educ:* privately; Girton Coll., Cambridge (scholar; Hon. Fellow, 1986). *Publications:* Dusty Answer, 1927, repr. 1981; A Note in Music, 1930, repr. 1982; Invitation to the Waltz, 1932, repr. 1981; The Weather in the Streets, 1936, repr. 1981 (filmed 1983); The Ballad and the Source, 1944, repr. 1982; The Gypsy's Baby, 1946, repr. 1973; The Echoing Grove, 1953, repr. 1981; The Swan in the Evening, 1967; (with W. Tudor Pole) A Man Seen Afar, 1965; (with Cynthia, Baroness Sandys) Letters from Our Daughters, 2 vols, 1971; A Sea-Grape Tree, 1976, repr. 1982; The Awakening Letters, 1978. *Recreations:* reading, music. *Address:* 30 Clareville Grove, SW7 5AS.

LEHRER, Thomas Andrew; writer of songs since 1943; *b* 9 April 1928; *s* of James Lehrer and Anna Lehrer (*née* Waller). *Educ:* Harvard Univ. (AB 1946, MA 1947); Columbia Univ.; Harvard Univ. Student (mathematics, especially probability and statistics) till 1953. Part-time teaching at Harvard, 1947–51. Theoretical physicist at Baird-Atomic, Inc., Cambridge, Massachusetts, 1953–54. Entertainer, 1953–55, 1957–60. US Army, 1955–57. Lecturer in Business Administration, Harvard Business Sch., 1961; Lecturer: in Education, Harvard Univ., 1963–66; in Psychology, Wellesley Coll., 1966; in Political Science, MIT, 1962–71; Vis. Lectr, Univ. of Calif, Santa Cruz, 1972–. *Publications:* Tom Lehrer Song Book, 1954; Tom Lehrer's Second Song Book, 1968; Too Many Songs by Tom Lehrer, 1981; contrib. to Annals of Mathematical Statistics, Journal of Soc. of Industrial and Applied Maths. *Recreation:* piano. *Address:* PO Box 121, Cambridge, Massachusetts 02138, USA. *T:* (617) 354–7708.

LEICESTER, 6th Earl of, *cr* 1837; **Anthony Louis Lovel Coke;** Viscount Coke 1837; farmer, since 1976; *b* 11 Sept. 1909; *s* of Hon. Arthur George Coke (killed in action, 1915) (2nd *s* of 3rd Earl) and of Phyllis Hermione (Lady Howard-Vyse), *d* of late Francis Saxham Elwes Drury; *S* cousin, 1976; *m* 1st, 1934, Moyra Joan (marr. diss. 1947), *d* of late Douglas Crossley; two *s* one *d*; 2nd, 1947, Vera Haigh (*d* 1984), Harare, Zimbabwe; 3rd, 1985, Elizabeth Hope Johnstone, Addo, Eastern Province, South Africa, *d* of late Clifford Arthur Johnstone. *Educ:* Gresham's School, Holt. Served War of 1939–45 in RAF. Career spent ranching. *Recreations:* general. *Heir:* *s* Viscount Coke, *qv*. *Address:* Cottage No 70, Box 416, Plettenberg Bay, 6600, South Africa. *T:* (04457) 32255.

LEICESTER, Bishop of, since 1979; **Rt. Rev. Cecil Richard Rutt,** CBE 1973; MA; *b* 27 Aug. 1925, *s* of Cecil Rutt and Mary Hare Turner; *m* 1969, Joan Mary Ford. *Educ:* Huntingdon Grammar School; Kelham Theol. Coll.; Pembroke Coll., Cambridge. RNVR, 1943–46. Deacon, 1951; Priest, 1952. Asst Curate, St George's, Cambridge, 1951–54; Dio. of Korea, 1954; Parish Priest of Anjung, 1956–58; Warden of St Bede's House Univ. Centre, Seoul, 1959–64; Rector of St Michael's Seminary, Oryu Dong, Seoul, 1964–66; Archdeacon, West Kyonggi (Dio. Seoul), 1965–66; Asst Bishop of Taejon, 1966–68; Bishop of Taejon, 1968–74; Bishop Suffragan of St Germans, 1974–79; Hon. Canon, St Mary's Cathedral, Truro, 1974–79. Associate Gen. Sec., Korean Bible Soc., 1964–74; Episcopal Sec., Council of the Church of SE Asia, 1968–74; Commissary, Dio. Taejon, 1974–; Pres., Roy. Asiatic Soc., Korea Br., 1974. Chm., Adv. Council for Religious Communities, 1980; Mem., Anglican/Orthodox Jt Doctrinal Discussions, 1983–. Interested in the Cornish language. Bard of the Gorsedd of Cornwall, Cornwhylen,

1976. ChStJ 1978. Tasan Cultural Award (for writings on Korea), 1964; Hon. DLitt, Confucian Univ., Seoul, 1974. Order of Civil Merit, Peony Class (Korea), 1974. *Publications:* (ed) Songgonghoe Songga (Korean Anglican Hymnal), 1961; Korean Works and Days, 1964; P'ungnyu Han'guk (in Korean), 1965; (trans.) An Anthology of Korean Sijo, 1970; The Bamboo Grove, an introduction to Korean Sijo poetry, 1971; James Scarth Gale and his History of the Korean People, 1972; Virtuous Women, three masterpieces of traditional Korean fiction, 1974; contribs on Korean classical poetry and history to Trans. Royal Asiatic Soc. (Korea Br.) and various Korean and liturgiological publications. *Address:* Bishop's Lodge, 10 Springfield Road, Leicester LE2 3BD. *T:* Leicester 708985. *Club:* United Oxford & Cambridge University.

LEICESTER, Provost of; *see* Warren, Very Rev. A. C.

LEICESTER, Archdeacon of; *see* Silk, Ven. R. D.

LEIFLAND, Leif, Hon. GCVO 1983; Ambassador of Sweden to the Court of St James's, since 1982; *b* 30 Dec. 1925; *s* of Sigfrid and Elna Leifland; *m* 1954, Karin Abard; one *s* two *d.* *Educ:* Univ. of Lund (LLB 1950). Joined Ministry of Foreign Affairs, 1952; served: Athens, 1953; Bonn, 1955; Stockholm, 1958; Washington, 1961; Stockholm, 1964; Washington, 1970; Stockholm, 1975. Secretary, Foreign Relations Cttee, Swedish Parliament, 1966–70; Under Secretary for Political Affairs, 1975–77; Permanent Under-Secretary of State for Foreign Affairs, 1977–82. *Publications:* various articles on foreign policy and national security questions. *Address:* 27 Portland Place, W1. *T:* 01–724 2101.

LEIGH, family name of **Baron Leigh.**

LEIGH, 5th Baron *cr* 1839; **John Piers Leigh;** *b* 11 Sept. 1935; *s* of 4th Baron Leigh, TD and Anne (*d* 1977), *d* of Ellis Hicks Beach; *S* father, 1979; *m* 1st, 1957, Cecilia Poppy (marr. diss. 1974), *y d* of late Robert Cecil Jackson; one *s* one *d* (and one *d* decd); 2nd, 1976, Susan (marr. diss. 1982), *d* of John Cleave, Whitnash, Leamington Spa; one *s*; 3rd, 1982, Mrs Lea Hamilton-Russell, *o d* of Col Noel Wild, OBE. *Educ:* Eton; Oxford and London Universities. *Recreations:* horses, hunting, racing, sport, country pursuits. *Heir: s* Hon. Christopher Dudley Piers Leigh, *b* 20 Oct. 1960. *Address:* Stoneleigh Abbey, Kenilworth, Warwickshire. *T:* Kenilworth 52116.

LEIGH, (Archibald) Denis, MD, FRCP; Consultant Physician, Bethlem Royal and Maudsley Hospitals, 1949–80, now Emeritus; Secretary-General, World Psychiatric Association, 1966–78; Hon. Consultant in Psychiatry to the British Army, 1969–80; Lecturer, Institute of Psychiatry; *b* 11 Oct. 1915; *o s* of Archibald Leigh and Rose Rushworth; *m* 1941, Pamela Parish; two *s* three *d.* *Educ:* Hulme Grammar Sch.; Manchester Univ.; University of Budapest. Manchester City Schol. in Medicine, 1932; BSc 1936; MB, ChB (1st class hons) 1939; Dauntesey Med. Sen. Schol., Prof. Tom Jones Exhibitioner in Anatomy; Sidney Renshaw Jun. Prize in Physiol.; Turner Med. Prize; John Henry Agnew Prize; Stephen Lewis Prize; Prize in Midwifery; MRCP 1941; MD (Manchester), 1947; FRCP, 1955. RAMC, 1940–45 (Lt-Col); Adviser in Neurology, Eastern Army, India. 1st Assistant, Dept of Neurology, London Hospital; Nuffield Fellow, 1947–48; Clinical Fellow, Harvard Univ., 1948. Recognised Clinical Teacher, London Univ.; Founder European Society of Psychosomatic Research; Editor-in-Chief and Founder, Journal of Psychosomatic Res.; Editorial Bd, Japanese Journal of Psychosomatic Medicine, Medicina Psychosomatica, Psychosomatic Medicine, Behaviour Therapy; Examiner in Psychological Med., Edinburgh Univ., 1958–65; Beattie Smith Lectr, Melbourne Univ., 1967. Governor, Bethlem Royal and Maudsley Hospitals, 1956–62; President Sect. of Psychiatry, Royal Society Med., 1967–68. Hon. Member: Deutschen Gesellschaft für Psychiatrie und Nervenheilkunde; Italian Psychosomatic Soc.; Assoc. Brasileira de Psiquiatria; Sociedad Argentina de Medicina Psicosomática; Polish Psychiatric Assoc.; Corresp. Mem., Pavlovian Soc. of N America; Hon. Corresp. Mem., Austn Acad. of Forensic Scis; Hon Fellow: Swedish Soc. of Med. Scis; Soc. Colombiana de Psiquiatría; Soviet Soc. of Neurologists and Psychiatrists; Czechoslovak Psychiatric Soc.; Finnish Psychiatric Soc. Distinguished Fellow: Amer. Psychiatric Assoc.; Hong Kong Psychiatric Assoc. *Publications:* (trans. from French) Psychosomatic Methods of Painless Childbirth, 1959; The Historical Development of British Psychiatry, Vol. I, 1961; Bronchial Asthma, 1967; A Concise Encyclopaedia of Psychiatry, 1977; chapters in various books; papers on neurology, psychiatry, history of psychiatry and psychosomatic medicine. *Recreations:* fishing, collecting. *Address:* 152 Harley Street, W1. *T:* 01–935 8868; The Grange, Otford, Kent. *T:* Otford 3427.

LEIGH, Christopher Humphrey de Verd; a Recorder of the Crown Court, since 1985; *b* 12 July 1943; *s* of late Wing Commander Humphrey de Verd Leigh and of Johanna Leigh; *m* 1970, Frances Powell. *Educ:* Harrow. Called to the Bar, Lincoln's Inn, 1967. *Recreations:* fishing, travel. *Address:* 1 Paper Buildings, Temple, EC4Y 7EP. *T:* 01–353 3728. *Club:* Hampshire (Winchester).

LEIGH, Edward Julian Egerton; MP (C) Gainsborough and Horncastle, since 1983; *b* 20 July 1950; *s* of Sir Neville Egerton Leigh, *qv*; *m* 1984, Mary Goodman; one *d.* *Educ:* St Philip's Sch., Kensington; Oratory Sch.; French Lycée, London; UC, Durham Univ. (BA Hons). Called to the Bar, Inner Temple, 1977. Mem., Cons. Res. Dept, seconded to office of Leader of Opposition, GLC, 1973–75; Prin. Correspondence Sec. to Rt Hon. Margaret Thatcher, MP, 1975–76. Member (C): Richmond Borough Council, 1974–78; GLC, 1977–81. Contested (C) Teesside, Middlesbrough, Oct. 1974. Chm., Nat. Council for Civil Defence, 1980–82; Dir, Coalition for Peace Through Security, 1982–83. *Publication:* Right Thinking, 1979. *Recreations:* walking, reading. *Address:* House of Commons, SW1A 0AA. *Club:* Carlton.

LEIGH, Sir John, 2nd Bt, *cr* 1918; *b* 24 March 1909; *s* of Sir John Leigh, 1st Bt, and Norah Marjorie, CBE (*d* 1954); *S* father 1959; *m* 1959, Ariane, *d* of late Joseph Wm Allen, Beverly Hills, California, and *widow* of Harold Wallace Ross, NYC. *Educ:* Eton; Balliol Coll., Oxford. *Heir: nephew* Richard Henry Leigh [*b* 11 Nov. 1936; *m* 1st, 1962, Barbro Anna Elizabeth (marr. diss. 1977), *e d* of late Stig Carl Sebastian Tham, Sweden; 2nd, 1977, Chérie Rosalind, *e d* of D. D. Dale and *widow* of A. Reece, RMS]. *Address:* 23 Quai du Mont Blanc, Geneva, Switzerland. *T:* 31 53 63. *Clubs:* Brooks's; Travellers' (Paris).

LEIGH, Prof. Leonard Herschel; Professor of Criminal Law in the University of London, at the London School of Economics and Political Science, since 1982; *b* 19 Sept. 1935; *s* of Leonard William and Lillian Mavis Leigh; *m* 1960, Jill Diane Gale; one *s* one *d.* *Educ:* Univ. of Alberta (BA, LLB); Univ. of London (PhD 1966). Admitted to Bar: Alberta, 1959; NW Territories, 1961. Private practice, Province of Alberta, 1958–60; Dept of Justice, Canada, 1960–62; London School of Economics: Asst Lectr in Law, 1964–65; Lectr, 1965–71; Reader, 1971–82. Vis. Prof., Queen's Univ., Kingston, Ont, 1973–74; British Council Lecturer: Univ. of Strasbourg, 1978; National Univ. of Mexico, 1980; UN Asia and Far East Inst., Tokyo, 1986. Mem., Canadian Govt Securities Regulation Task Force, 1974–78. *Publications:* The Criminal Liability of Corporations in English Law, 1969; (jtly) Northey and Leigh's Introduction to Company Law, 1970, 2nd edn 1980; Police Powers in England and Wales, 1975, 2nd edn 1986; Economic Crime in Europe, 1980; (jtly) The Companies Act 1981, 1981; (jtly) The Management of the Prosecution Process in Denmark, Sweden and the Netherlands, 1981; The Control of Commercial Fraud, 1982; Strict and Vicarious Liability, 1982; articles in British, European, Amer. and Canadian jls. *Recreations:* music, walking. *Address:* London School of Economics and Political Science, Houghton Street, WC2A 2AE. *T:* 01–405 7686.

LEIGH, Mike; dramatist; theatre, television and film director; *b* 20 Feb. 1943; *s* of late Alfred Abraham Leigh, LRCS, MRCP and of Phyllis Pauline Leigh (*née* Cousin); *m* 1973, Alison Steadman; two *s.* *Educ:* North Grecian Street County Primary Sch.; Salford Grammar Sch.; RADA; Camberwell Sch. of Arts and Crafts; Central Sch. of Art and Design (Theatre Design Dept); London Film Sch. Sometime actor, incl. Victoria Theatre, Stoke-on-Trent, 1966; Assoc. Dir, Midlands Arts Centre for Young People, 1965–66; Asst Dir, RSC, 1967–68; Drama Lectr, Sedgley Park and De La Salle Colls, Manchester, 1968–69; Lectr, London Film Sch., 1970–73. Arts Council of GB: Member: Drama Panel, 1975–77; Dirs' Working Party and Specialist Allocations Bd, 1976–84; Member: Accreditation Panel, Nat. Council for Drama Trng, 1978–; Gen. Adv. Council, IBA, 1980–82. NFT Retrospective, 1979; BBC TV Retrospective (incl. Arena: Mike Leigh Making Plays), 1982; George Devine Award, 1973. Productions of own plays and films evolved from scratch entirely by rehearsal through improvisation; *stage plays:* The Box Play, 1965, My Parents Have Gone To Carlisle, The Last Crusade Of The Five Little Nuns, 1966, Midlands Arts Centre; Nenaa, RSC Studio, Stratford-upon-Avon, 1967; Individual Fruit Pies, E15 Acting Sch., 1968; Down Here And Up There, Royal Ct Th. Upstairs, 1968; Big Basil, 1968, Glum Victoria And The Lad With Specs, Manchester Youth Theatre, 1969; Epilogue, Manchester, 1969; Bleak Moments, Open Space, 1970; A Rancid Pong, Basement, 1971; Wholesome Glory, Dick Whittington and his Cat, Royal Ct Th. Upstairs, 1973; The Jaws of Death, Traverse, Edinburgh Fest., 1973; Babies Grow Old, Other Place, 1974, ICA, 1975; The Silent Majority, Bush, 1974; Abigail's Party, Hampstead, 1977; Ecstasy, Hampstead, 1979; Goose-Pimples, Hampstead, Garrick, 1981 (Standard Best Comedy Award); *BBC radio play:* Too Much Of A Good Thing (banned), 1979; *feature film:* Bleak Moments, 1971 (Golden Hugo, Chicago Film Fest., 1972; Golden Leopard, Locarno Film Fest., 1972); *BBC TV plays and films:* A Mug's Game, 1972; Hard Labour, 1973; The Permissive Society, Afternoon, A Light Snack, Probation, Old Chums, The Birth Of The 2001 FA Cup Final Goalie, 1975; Nuts in May, Knock For Knock, 1976; The Kiss Of Death, Abigail's Party, 1977; Who's Who, 1978; Grown-Ups, 1980; Home Sweet Home, 1982; Four Days In July, 1984. (Channel Four film) Meantime, 1983. Directed and designed orig. prodn of Halliwell's Little Malcolm And His Struggle Against The Eunuchs, Unity, 1965. *Relevant publication:* The Improvised Play: the work of Mike Leigh, by Paul Clements, 1983. *Address:* c/o A. D. Peters & Co. Ltd, 10 Buckingham Street, WC2N 6BU.

LEIGH, Sir Neville (Egerton), KCVO 1980 (CVO 1967); Clerk of the Privy Council, 1974–84; *b* 4 June 1922; *s* of late Cecil Egerton Leigh; *m* 1944, Denise Margaret Yvonne, *d* of late Cyril Denzil Branch, MC; two *s* one *d.* *Educ:* Charterhouse. RAFVR, 1942–47 (Flt-Lt). Called to Bar, Inner Temple, 1948. Legal Asst, Treasury Solicitors Dept, 1949–51; Senior Clerk, Privy Council Office, 1951–65; Deputy Clerk of Privy Council, 1965–74. Mem., Press Council, 1986–. Pres., British Orthoptic Soc., 1984–. Consultant, Royal Coll. of Nursing of UK, 1985–. Trustee, R&D Trust for the Young Disabled, Royal Hosp. and Home for Incurables, 1986–; Gov., Suttons Hosp., Charterhouse, 1986–. Hon. FCIOB 1982. *Address:* 11 The Crescent, Barnes, SW13 0NN. *T:* 01–876 4271. *Club:* Army and Navy.

See also Edward Leigh.

LEIGH, Peter William John, FRICS; Director of Property Services, Royal County of Berkshire, since 1984; *b* 29 June 1929; *s* of John Charles Leigh and Dorothy Grace Leigh; *m* 1956, Mary Frances (*née* Smith); two *s* one *d.* *Educ:* Harrow Weald County Grammar Sch.; Coll. of Estate Management (ext.). National Service, Royal Signals, 1947–49. Private surveying practice, 1949–53; Valuation Asst, Mddx CC, 1953–60; Commercial Estates Officer, Bracknell Develt Corp., 1960–66; sen. appts, Valuation and Estates Dept, GLC, 1966–81; Dir of Valuation and Estates, GLC, 1981–84. Member: Gen. Council, RICS, 1984–; Govt Property Adv. Gp, 1984–. Exec. Mem., Assoc. of Local Authority Valuers and Estate Surveyors, 1981–. *Recreations:* exploring Cornwall, drawing, gardening (therapy). *Address:* 41 Sandy Lane, Wokingham, Berks RG11 4SS. *T:* Wokingham 782732.

LEIGH, Ralph Alexander, CBE 1977; FBA 1969; LittD; Professor of French, University of Cambridge, 1973–82, now Emeritus, and Sandars Reader in Bibliography, 1986–87; Professorial Fellow of Trinity College, Cambridge, since 1973 (Fellow since 1952, Prælector since 1967, Senior Research Fellow, 1969–73); *b* London, 6 Jan. 1915; *m* 1945, Edith Helen Kern (*d* 1972); one *s* one *d.* *Educ:* Raine's Sch. for Boys, London; Queen Mary Coll., Univ. of London (Fellow, 1983); Univ. of Paris (Sorbonne). BA London 1st class hons. 1936; Diplôme de l'Université de Paris, 1938. Served War, 1941–46: RASC and Staff; CCG; Lieut (ERE list) 1942; Major, 1944. Lectr, Dept of French, Univ. of Edinburgh, 1946; Lectr, 1952–69, Reader, 1969–73, Cambridge Univ. Vis. Prof., Sorbonne, 1973. Mem., Inst. for Adv. Studies and Fulbright Scholar, Princeton, 1967; Dir and Mem. Cttee, Voltaire Foundn, Oxford, 1983–. Leverhulme Fellow, 1959–60, 1970, 1982–83. LittD (Cambridge) 1968; DUniv Edinburgh, 1986; Docteur (*hc*): Univ. of Neuchâtel, 1978; Univ. of Geneva, 1983. Médaille d'argent de la Ville de Paris, 1978. Chevalier de la Légion d'Honneur, 1979. *Publications:* Correspondance Complète de Jean Jacques Rousseau, vols I-XLV, 1965–86 (in progress); Rousseau and the Problem of Tolerance in the XVIIIth Century, 1979; (ed) Rousseau after 200 years, 1982; contribs to Revue de littérature comparée; Annales Rousseau; Revue d'Histoire littéraire; Modern Language Review; French Studies; Studies on Voltaire; The Library, etc. *Recreations:* book-collecting, music. *Address:* Trinity College, Cambridge. *Club:* United Oxford & Cambridge University.

LEIGH-PEMBERTON, John, AFC 1945; artist painter; *b* 18 Oct. 1911; *s* of Cyril Leigh-Pemberton and Mary Evelyn Megaw; *m* 1948, Doreen Beatrice Townshend-Webster. *Educ:* Eton. Studied Art, London, 1928–31. Past Member Royal Institute of Painters in Oils and other Societies. Served 1940–45 with RAF as Flying Instructor. Series of pictures for Coldstream Guards, 1950. Festival Almanack, 1951, for Messrs Whitbread; Royal Progress, 1953, for Shell Mex & BP Ltd. Works in public and private collections, UK and America; decorations for ships: City of York, City of Exeter, Britannic, Caledonia, Corfu, Carthage, Kenya, Uganda. Many series of paintings, chiefly of natural history subjects, for Midland Bank Ltd. *Publications:* A Book of Garden Flowers, 1960; A Book of Butterflies, Moths and other Insects, 1963; British Wildlife, Rarities and Introductions, 1966; Garden Birds, 1967; Sea and Estuary Birds, 1967; Heath and Woodland Birds, 1968; Vanishing Wild Animals of the World, 1968; Pond and River Birds, 1969; African Mammals, 1969; Australian Mammals, 1970; North American Mammals, 1970; Birds of Prey, 1970; European Mammals, 1971; Asian Mammals, 1971; South American Mammals, 1972; Sea and Air Mammals, 1972; Wild Life in Britain, 1972; Disappearing Mammals, 1973; Ducks and Swans, 1973; Lions and Tigers, 1974; Baby Animals, 1974; Song Birds, 1974; Leaves, 1974; Big Animals, 1975; Apes and Monkeys, 1975; Reptiles, 1976; Seals and Whales, 1976; Butterflies and Moths, 1978; Hedges, 1979; Birds of Britain and Northern Europe, 1979; Bears and Pandas, 1979. *Address:* 5 Roehampton Gate, Roehampton, SW15. *T:* 01–876 3332.

LEIGH-PEMBERTON, Robert, (Robin Leigh-Pemberton); Governor, Bank of England, since 1983; Lord-Lieutenant of Kent, since 1982 (Vice Lord-Lieutenant, 1972–82); *b* 5 Jan. 1927; *e s* of late Robert Douglas Leigh-Pemberton, MBE, MC, Sittingbourne, Kent; *m* 1953, Rosemary Davina, *d* of late Lt-Col D. W. A. W. Forbes, MC, and late Dowager Marchioness of Exeter; five *s*. *Educ:* St Peter's Court, Broadstairs; Eton; Trinity Coll., Oxford (MA; Hon. Fellow, 1984). Grenadier Guards, 1945–48. Called to Bar, Inner Temple, 1954 (Hon. Bencher, 1983); practised in London and SE Circuit until 1960. National Westminster Bank: Dir, 1972–83; Dep. Chm., 1974; Chm., 1977–83. Director: Birmid Qualcast, 1966–83 (Dep. Chm., 1970; Chm., 1975–77); University Life Assce Soc., 1967–78; Redland Ltd, 1972–83; Equitable Life Assce Soc., 1979–83 (Vice-Pres., 1982–83). County Councillor (Chm. Council, 1972–75), 1961–77, CA 1965, Kent. Member: SE Econ. Planning Council, 1972–74; Medway Ports Authority, 1974–76; NEDC, 1982–; Prime Minister's Cttee on Local Govt Rules of Conduct, 1973–74; Cttee of Enquiry into Teachers' Pay, 1974; Cttee on Police Pay, 1977–79. Chm., Cttee of London Clearing Bankers, 1982–83. Trustee: Glyndebourne Arts Trust, 1978–83; RA Trust, 1982–. Pro-Chancellor, Univ. of Kent at Canterbury, 1977–83; Seneschal, Canterbury Cathedral, 1983–. Hon. Colonel: The Kent and County of London Yeomanry (Sharpshooters), 1979–; 71st Yeomanry Signal Regt. Hon. DCL Kent, 1983. FRSA 1977; FBIM 1977. JP 1961–75, DL 1970, Kent. KStJ 1983. *Recreation:* country life. *Address:* Bank of England, EC2R 8AH. *T:* 01-601 4444. *Clubs:* Brooks's, Cavalry and Guards.

LEIGH-WOOD, Roger, DL; *b* 16 Aug. 1906; *s* of Sir James Leigh-Wood, KBE, CB, CMG, and Joanna Elizabeth Turnbull; *m* 1936, Norah Elizabeth Holroyde; four *s*. *Educ:* Winchester Coll.; Trinity Coll., Oxford. Lt-Comdr RNVR, 1939–45. Brown Shipley & Co. Ltd, 1930–42; Eastern Bank Ltd, 1945, Chm. 1967–71; Chartered Bank, 1967–72 (Dep. Chm. 1971); Commercial Union Assce Co. Ltd, 1948–71; Dalgety Ltd, 1948–72; Chm., Scott & Bowne Ltd, 1964–78. High Sheriff of Hampshire, 1964–65; DL Hants, 1970. *Recreations:* yachting, gardening; formerly athletics (Pres. Oxford Univ. Athletic Club, 1929; British Olympic Team, 1928; Empire Games Team, 1930). *Address:* Summerley, Bentworth, Alton, Hants. *T:* Alton 62077. *Club:* Royal Yacht Squadron.

LEIGHTON OF ST MELLONS, 2nd Baron, *cr* 1962; **John Leighton Seager;** Bt 1952; *b* 11 Jan. 1922; *er s* of 1st Baron Leighton of St Mellons, CBE, JP, and of Marjorie, *d* of William Henry Gimson, Breconshire; *S* father, 1963; *m* 1st, 1953, Elizabeth Rosita (*d* 1979), *o d* of late Henry Hopgood, Cardiff; two *s* one *d* (and one *d* decd); 2nd, 1982, Ruth Elizabeth Hopwood. *Educ:* Caldicott Sch.; The Leys Sch., Cambridge. Director: Principality Building Soc.; Watkin Williams & Co; Partner, Property Industrial Maintenance Services. *Heir: s* Hon. Robert William Henry Leighton Seager, *b* 28 Sept. 1955. *Address:* 346 Caerphilly Road, Birchgrove, Cardiff CF4 4NT.

LEIGHTON, Clare, RE 1934; *b* 1899; *d* of late Marie Connor Leighton, and late Robert Leighton. *Educ:* privately; Brighton School of Art; Slade School. Elected Member of Society of Wood Engravers, 1928; First prize International Engraving Exhibition, Art Institute of Chicago, 1930; Fellow National Acad. of Design, New York; Member, Society of American Graphic Arts; Member, National Inst. of Arts and Letters, USA, 1951. Prints purchased for permanent collection of British Museum, Victoria and Albert Museum, National Gallery of Canada, Museums of Boston, Baltimore, New York, etc. Designed: 33 stained glass windows for St Paul's Cathedral, Worcester, Mass; 12 plates for Josiah Wedgwood & Sons Ltd. *Publications:* Illustrated with wood engravings the following books: Thomas Hardy's The Return of the Native, 1929; Thornton Wilder's The Bridge of San Luis Rey, 1930; The Sea and the Jungle, 1930; Wuthering Heights, 1931; E. Madox Roberts's The Time of Man, 1943; North Carolina Folk Lore, 1950; Woodcuts: examples of the Work of Clare Leighton, 1930; The Trumpet in the Dust, 1934; Writer: How to do Wood Engraving and Woodcuts, 1932; Wood Engraving of the 1930's, 1936; Tempestuous Petticoat, 1948; written and illustrated: The Musical Box, 1932; The Farmer's Year, 1933; The Wood That Came Back, 1934; Four Hedges, 1935; Country Matters, 1937; Sometime, Never, 1939; Southern Harvest, 1942; Give us this Day, 1943; Where Land meets Sea, 1954. *Address:* Woodbury, Conn 06798, USA.

LEIGHTON, Prof. Kenneth, MA, DMus; LRAM, FRCM; composer; pianist; Reid Professor of Music, University of Edinburgh, since 1970; *b* 2 Oct. 1929; *s* of Thomas Leighton; *m* 1st, 1953, Lydia Vignapiano; one *s* one *d*; 2nd, 1981, Josephine Ann Prescott. *Educ:* Queen Elizabeth Grammar Sch., Wakefield; Queen's Coll., Oxford (schol.; MA 1955; DMus 1960); Petrassi, Rome. Prof. of Theory, RN Sch. of Music, 1952–53; Gregory Fellow in Music, Leeds Univ., 1953–56; Lectr in Music Composition, Edinburgh Univ., 1956–68; Lectr in Music, Oxford Univ., and Fellow of Worcester Coll., 1968–70. Hon. DMus St Andrews, 1977. *Compositions:* Concertos for: piano (3); violin; cello; viola and two pianos; harpsichord; symphony for string orchestra; three string quartets; piano quintet; sonatas for: violin and piano (2); piano (3); piano duet; partita for cello and piano; clarinet trio; orchestral works; Burlesque, Passacaglia, Chorale and Fugue; three symphonies; The Birds (chorus and strings); The Light Invisible (tenor, chorus and orch.), etc; Fantasia Contrappuntistica (piano); Columba (3 act opera); Columba Mea (chorus, soloists and strings); Veris Gratia (oboe, cello and strings); Laudes Montium (chorus and orch.); incidental music for radio and television drama; church, organ, chamber and piano music. *Recreation:* walking. *Address:* Faculty of Music, University of Edinburgh, Alison House, Nicolson Square, Edinburgh EH8 9BH. *Club:* Edinburgh University Staff.

LEIGHTON, Leonard Horace; Under Secretary, Department of Energy, 1974–80; *b* 7 Oct. 1920; *e s* of Leonard and Pearl Leighton, Bermuda; *m* 1945, Mary Burrowes; two *s*. *Educ:* Rossall Sch.; Magdalen Coll., Oxford (MA). FInstF. Royal Engrs, 1940–46; Nat. Coal Bd, 1950–62; Min. of Power, 1962–67; Min. of Technology, 1967–70; Dept of Trade and Industry, 1970–74. *Publications:* papers in various technical jls. *Address:* 19 McKay Road, Wimbledon, SW20 0HT. *T:* 01-946 4230.

LEIGHTON, Sir Michael (John Bryan), 11th Bt, *cr* 1693; *b* 8 March 1935; *o s* of Colonel Sir Richard Tihel Leighton, 10th Bt, and Kathleen Irene Linda, *o d* of Major A. E. Lees, Rowton Castle, Shrewsbury; *S* father 1957; *m* 1974 (marr. diss. 1980). *Educ:* Stowe; Tabley House Agricultural Sch.; Cirencester Coll. *Address:* Loton Park, Shrewsbury, Salop.

LEIGHTON, Ronald; MP (Lab) Newham North-East, since 1979; *b* 24 Jan. 1930; *s* of Charles Leighton and Edith (*née* Sleet); *m* 1951, Erika Wehking; two *s*. *Educ:* Monteagle and Bifrons Sch., Barking. Newspaper printer. Secretary, Labour Cttee for Safeguards on Common Market, 1967–70; Director, All-Party Common Market Safeguards Campaign, 1970–73; Editor, Resistance News, 1973–74; Secretary, Get Britain Out Campaign, 1974–75; National Organiser, National Referendum Campaign, which campaigned for 'No' vote in Referendum, 1975; Chairman: Labour Common Market Safeguards Cttee, 1975–; Select Cttee on Employment, 1984–. An Opposition Whip on Employment, 1981–84. Sponsored member, Sogat '82. *Publications:* The Labour Case Against Entry to the Common Market; What Labour Should Do About the Common Market; also pamphlets (1963–). *Recreations:* reading, footpath walking. *Address:* c/o House of Comons, SW1.

LEIGHTON-BOYCE, Guy Gilbert; Accountant and Comptroller General, HM Customs and Excise, 1973–80; *b* 23 Oct. 1920; *s* of late Charles Edmund Victor and Eleanor Fannie Leighton-Boyce; *m* 1945, Adrienne Jean Elliott Samms; two *s* two *d*. *Educ:* Dulwich Coll. HM Customs and Excise, 1939. Served War, RAF, 1941–46. Asst Sec., 1960; Under Sec., 1973. *Publications:* Irish Setters, 1973; (with James Iliff) Tephrocactus, 1973; A Survey of Early Setters, 1985; articles in Cactus and Succulent jls. *Recreations:* looking at pictures; dogs, plants. *Address:* 220 Leigham Court Road, Streatham, SW16 2RB. *T:* 01-769 4844. *Club:* Kennel.

LEIGHTON WILLIAMS, John; *see* Williams.

LEINSDORF, Erich; orchestral and operatic conductor; *b* Vienna, 4 Feb. 1912; *s* of Ludwig Julius Leinsdorf and Charlotte (*née* Loebl); *m* 1st, 1939, Anne Frohnknecht (marr. diss. 1968); three *s* two *d*; 2nd, 1968, Vera Graf. *Educ:* University of Vienna; State Academy of Music, Vienna (dipl.). Assistant conductor: Salzburg Festival, 1934–37; Metropolitan Opera, NY, 1937–39; Chief Conductor, German operas, 1939–43; Conductor, Rochester Philharmonic, 1947–56; Director, NYC Opera, 1956; Music Cons. Director, Metropolitan Opera, 1957–62; Music Director, Boston Symphony Orchestra, 1962–69. Director: Berkshire Music Center, Berkshire Music Festival, 1963–69; American Arts Alliance, 1979–; Mem., Nat. Endowment for the Arts, 1980–. Guest appearances with virtually every major orchestra in the USA and Europe, incl. Philadelphia Orchestra, Los Angeles, St Louis, New Orleans, Chicago, Minneapolis, Cleveland, New York, Concertgebouw Amsterdam, Israel Philharmonic, London Symphony, New Philharmonia, San Francisco Opera, Bayreuth, Holland and Prague Festivals, BBC. Records many symphonies and operas. Former Member Executive Cttee, John F. Kennedy Center for Performing Arts. Fellow, American Academy of Arts and Sciences. Holds hon. degrees. *Publications:* Cadenza (autobiog.), 1976; The Composer's Advocate, 1981; transcriptions of Brahms Chorale Preludes; contribs. to Atlantic Monthly, Saturday Review, New York Times, High Fidelity. *Address:* c/o Dodds, 209 East 56th Street, New York, NY 10022, USA.

LEINSTER, 8th Duke of, *cr* 1766; **Gerald FitzGerald;** Baron of Offaly, 1205; Earl of Kildare, 1316; Viscount Leinster (Great Britain), 1747; Marquess of Kildare, 1761; Earl of Offaly, 1761; Baron Kildare, 1870; Premier Duke, Marquess, and Earl, of Ireland; Major late 5th Royal Inniskilling Dragoon Guards; President, CSE Aviation Group of Cos; *b* 27 May 1914; *o s* of 7th Duke of Leinster and May (*d* 1935), *d* of late Jesse Etheridge; *S* father, 1976; *m* 1st, 1936, Joane (who obtained a divorce, 1946), *e d* of late Major McMorrough Kavanagh, MC, Borris House, Co. Carlow; two *d*; 2nd, 1946, Anne Eustace Smith; two *s*. *Educ:* Eton; Sandhurst. *Heir: s* Marquess of Kildare, *qv*. *Recreations:* fishing, shooting. *Address:* Kilkea House, Ramsden, Oxford.

LEISHMAN, Frederick John, CVO 1957; MBE 1944; *b* 21 Jan. 1919; *s* of Alexander Leishman and Freda Mabel (*née* Hood); *m* 1945, Frances Webb, Evanston, Illinois, USA; two *d*. *Educ:* Oundle; Corpus Christi, Cambridge. Served RE, 1940–46, and with Military Government, Germany, 1945–46; Regular Commission, 1945; resigned, 1946. Joined Foreign Service, 1946; FO, 1946–48; Copenhagen, 1948–51; Civil Service Selection Board, 1951; Assistant Private Secretary to the Foreign Secretary, 1951–53; First Secretary, Washington, 1953–58; First Secretary and Head of Chancery, Teheran, 1959–61; Counsellor, 1961; HM Consul-General, Hamburg, 1961–62; Foreign Office, 1962–63. Dir, Hill Samuel & Co. Ltd, 1965–80; Dep. Chm. and Chief Exec., Hill Samuel Gp (SA) Ltd, 1969–72; Partner and Chm., Hill Samuel & Co. oHG, Germany, 1975–77; Dir and Exec. Vice-Pres., Saehan Merchant Banking Corp., Seoul, 1977–80. FRSA. *Recreations:* golf, fishing. *Address:* Saltoun House, Cotherstone, Barnard Castle, Co. Durham DL12 9PF. *T:* Teesdale 50671. *Clubs:* Hawks (Cambridge); Cambridge University Rugby Union Football; London Scottish Football; Royal Ashdown Forest Golf, Brancepeth Castle Golf, Barnard Castle Golf.

LEITCH, David Alexander; Under Secretary, Social Work Services Group, Scottish Education Department, since 1983; *b* 4 April 1931; *s* of Alexander and Eileen Leitch; *m* 1954, Marie (*née* Tain); two *s* one *d*. *Educ:* St Mungo's Acad., Glasgow. Min. of Supply, 1948–58; Dept of Agriculture and Fisheries for Scotland: Asst Principal, 1959; Principal, 1963; Asst Sec., 1971; Asst Sec., Local Govt Finance, Scottish Office (Central Services), 1976–81, Under Sec., 1981–83. *Recreations:* climbing, hill-walking. *Address:* 3 The Glebe, Cramond, Edinburgh EH4 6NW.

LEITCH, Sir George, KCB 1975 (CB 1963); OBE 1945; Chairman, Short Brothers Ltd, 1976–83; *b* 5 June 1915; *er s* of late James Simpson and Margaret Leitch; *m* 1942, Edith Marjorie Maughan; one *d*. *Educ:* Wallsend Grammar Sch.; King's Coll., University of Durham. Research and teaching in mathematics, 1937–39. War Service in Army (from TA), 1939–46 (despatches, OBE): Lieut-Colonel in charge of Operational Research in Eastern, then Fourteenth Army, 1943–45; Brigadier (Dep. Scientific Adviser, War Office), 1945–46; entered Civil Service, as Principal, 1947; Ministry of Supply, 1947–59 (Under-Secretary, 1959); War Office, 1959–64; Ministry of Defence: Asst Under-Secretary of State, 1964–65; Dep. Under-Sec. of State, 1965–72; Procurement Executive, MoD: Controller (Policy), 1971–72; 2nd Permanent Sec., 1972–74; Chief Exec. (Permanent Sec.), 1974–75. Chm., Adv. Cttee on Trunk Rd Assessment, 1977–80. Commonwealth Fund Fellow, 1953–54. Hon. DSc (Durham), 1946. *Recreations:* swimming, gardening. *Address:* 10 Elmfield Road, Gosforth, Newcastle upon Tyne. *T:* Tyneside (091) 2846559; Black Brae, Port Charlotte, Islay, Argyll. *T:* Port Charlotte (049 685) 430.

LEITCH, William Andrew, CB 1963; Law Reform Consultant, Government of Northern Ireland, 1973–78; Examiner of Statutory Rules, Northern Ireland Assembly, 1974–78, retired; *b* 16 July 1915; *e s* of Andrew Leitch, MD, DPH, Castlederg, Co. Tyrone, and May, *d* of W. H. Todd, JP, Fyfin, Strabane, Co. Tyrone; *m* 1939, Edna Margaret, *d* of David McIlvennan, Solicitor, Belfast; one *s* two *d*. *Educ:* Methodist Coll., Belfast; Queen's Univ., Belfast; London Univ. (LLB). Admitted Solicitor, NI, 1937; Asst Solicitors Dept, Ministry of Finance, NI, 1937–43; Asst Parly Draftsman, 1944–56; First Parly Draftsman, 1956–74. Hon. LLM, Queen's Univ., Belfast, 1967. *Publications:* A Handbook on the Administration of Estates Act (NI), 1955, 1957; (jointly) A Commentary on the Interpretation Act (Northern Ireland) 1954, 1955; articles in various legal publications. *Recreations:* fishing, golf, reading. *Address:* 53 Kensington Road, Belfast BT5 6NL. *T:* Belfast 794784.

LEITH, family name of **Baron Burgh.**

LEITH, Sir Andrew George F.; *see* Forbes-Leith.

LEITH, Prudence Margaret, (Mrs Rayne Kruger); Managing Director, Prudence Leith Ltd (parent company of the Leith's Group), since 1972; Cookery Editor, The Guardian, since 1980; *b* 18 Feb. 1940; *d* of late Sam Leith and of Margaret Inglis; *m* Rayne Kruger; one *s* one *d*. *Educ:* Hayward's Heath, Sussex; St Mary's, Johannesburg; Cape Town Univ.; Sorbonne, Paris; Cordon Bleu, London. French studies at Sorbonne, and preliminary cooking apprenticeship with French families; Cordon Bleu sch. course; small outside catering service from bedsitter in London, 1960–65; started Leith's Good Food (commercial catering co.), 1965, and Leith's (restaurant), 1969; Cookery Corresp., Daily

Mail, 1969–73; opened Leith's Sch. of Food and Wine, 1975; added Leith's Farm, 1976; Cookery Corresp., Sunday Express, 1976– mid 1980. Bd Mem., British Transport Hotels, 1977–83; pt-time Mem., BRB, 1980–85. Mem., Food from Britain Council, 1983–. FRSA 1984. *Publications:* Leith's All-Party Cook Book, 1969; Parkinson's Pie (in aid of World Wild Life Fund), 1972; Cooking For Friends, 1978; The Best of Prue Leith, 1979; (with J. B. Reynaud) Leith's Cookery Course (3–part paperback), 1979–80, (comp. hardback with C. Waldegrave), 1980; The Cook's Handbook, 1981; Prue Leith's Pocket Book of Dinner Parties, 1983; (with Caroline Waldegrave) Leith's Cookery School, 1985. *Recreations:* riding, tennis, old cookbooks and kitchen antiques. *Address:* 94 Kensington Park Road, W11. *T:* 01–221 5282.

LEITH-BUCHANAN, Sir Charles (Alexander James), 7th Bt *cr* 1775; President, United Business Machines Inc., Alexandria, Va, since 1978; *b* 1 Sept. 1939; *s* of John Wellesley MacDonald Leith-Buchanan (*g s* of 4th Bt) (*d* 1956) and Jane Elizabeth McNicol (*d* 1955), *d* of Ronald McNicol; *S* cousin, 1973; *m* 1962, Mary Anne Kelly; one *s* one *d. Heir: s* Gordon Leith-Buchanan, *b* 18 Oct. 1974. *Address:* 10504 Adel Road, Oakton, Va 22124, USA.

LEITHEAD, James Douglas; *b* 4 Oct. 1911; *s* of late William Leithead, Berwick-on-Tweed; *m* 1936, Alice, *d* of late Thomas Wylie, Stirling, Scotland; one *s. Educ:* Bradford Grammar Sch. Accountant, 1927–32; ACA 1932; FCA 1960; Chartered Accountant, 1932–39. Lecturer Bradford Technical Coll., 1934–39; Secretarial Assistant, Midland (Amalgamated) District (Coal Mines) Scheme, 1939–42; Ministry of Supply, 1942–45; BoT, 1945–64; HM Diplomatic Service, 1965–68; BoT, later DTI, 1968–72, retired. British Trade Commissioner: Australia, 1950–63; New Zealand, 1963–67. Vice-Pres., W Australian Branch of Royal Commonwealth Soc., 1957–63. *Recreation:* chess. *Address:* 48 Eaton Road, Appleton, Oxon.

LELLO, Walter Barrington, (Barry); Commercial Counsellor, Cairo, since 1984; *b* 29 Sept. 1931; *o s* of Walter Joseph Lello and Louisa (*née* McGarrigle); *m* 1959, Margaret, *o d* of Alexander and Alice McGregor. *Educ:* Liverpool Institute High School. Nat. Service, RN, 1950–52. Open Exec. Comp. to Civil Service, 1949; Min. of Supply, later Aviation, 1952–64; Asst British Civil Aviation Rep., Far East, Hong Kong, 1964–67; BoT, later Dept of Trade, 1967–71; Civil Air Attaché, Middle East, Beirut, 1971–76; DTI, 1976–78; Dir Gen., Saudi–British Economic Co-operation Office, Riyadh, 1978–81; seconded to British Electricity International as Dir, Middle East Ops, 1981–83; DTI, 1983. *Recreations:* mountaineering, reading, theatre. *Address:* c/o Midland Bank, 22 Victoria Street, SW1H 0NJ.

LELOIR, Luis Federico; Director, Institute of Biochemical Research, Campomar, since 1947; Head of Department of Biochemistry, University of Buenos Aires, since 1962; *b* Paris, 6 Sept. 1906; *m* Amelie Zuherbuhler de Leloir; one *d. Educ:* Univ. of Buenos Aires. Engaged in research in Gt Britain, Argentina and USA; subseq. at Inst. of Biology and Experimental Med., Buenos Aires, 1946. Chm., Argentine Assoc. for Advancement of Science, 1958–59; Mem. Directorate, Nat. Research Council, 1958–64; Mem., Nat. Acad. of Med., 1961; Foreign Mem: Royal Society, 1972; Nat. Acad. of Sciences, USA; Amer. Acad. of Arts and Sciences; Amer. Philosophical Soc.; Nat. Acad. of Scis, France, 1978. Holds several hon. doctorates and has won numerous prizes, etc, inc. Nobel Prize for Chemistry, 1970. *Address:* Instituto de Investigaciones Bioquímicas, Fundación Campomar, Antonio Machado 151, 1405 Buenos Aires, Argentina. *T:* 783–2871.

LE MARCHANT, Sir Denis, 5th Bt, *cr* 1841; *b* 28 Feb. 1906; *er s* of Brigadier-General Sir Edward Thomas Le Marchant, 4th Bt, KCB, CBE, JP, DL, and Evelyn Brooks (*d* 1957), *er d* of late Robert Millington Knowles, JP, DL, Colston Bassett Hall, Nottinghamshire; *S* father, 1953; *m* 1933, Elizabeth Rowena, *y d* of late Arthur Hovenden Worth; one *s* one *d* (and one *s* decd). *Educ:* Radley. High Sheriff, Lincolnshire, 1958. *Heir: s* Francis Arthur Le Marchant, *b* 6 Oct. 1939. *Address:* Hungerton Hall, Grantham, Lincolnshire. *T:* Grantham 870244.

LE MASURIER, Sir Robert (Hugh), Kt 1966; DSC 1942; Bailiff of Jersey, 1962–74; *b* 29 Dec. 1913; *s* of William Smythe Le Masurier and Mabel Harriet Briard; *m* 1941, Helen Sophia Sheringham; one *s* two *d. Educ:* Victoria Coll., Jersey. MA 1935; BCL 1936. Sub-Lieut RNVR, 1939; Lieut RNVR, 1943; Lieut-Commander RNVR, 1944. Solicitor-General, Jersey, 1955; Attorney-General, Jersey, 1958. *Recreations:* sailing, carpentry. *Address:* La Ville-à-l'Evêque, Trinity, Jersey. *Clubs:* Royal Ocean Racing; St Helier Yacht, United (Jersey).

LEMIEUX, Most Rev. (M.) Joseph; *b* Quebec City, 10 May 1902; *s* of Joseph E. Lemieux and Eva (*née* Berlinguet). *Educ:* College of St Anne de la Pocatière; Dominican House of Studies, Ottawa; College of Angelico, Rome; Blackfriars, Oxford. Missionary to Japan, 1930; Parish Priest, Miyamaecho, Hakodate, Japan, 1931–36; First Bishop of Sendai, 1936; resigned, 1941; Administrator of Diocese of Gravelbourg, Sask., 1942; Bishop of Gravelbourg, 1944–53; Archbishop of Ottawa, 1953–66; Apostolic Nuncio to Haiti, 1966–69; Apostolic Pro-Nuncio in India, 1969–71; Delegate of St Peter's Basilica in Vatican, 1971–73. *Address:* 143 St Patrick, Ottawa, Ontario K1N 5J9, Canada.

LEMIEUX, Prof. Raymond Urgel, OC (Canada), 1968; FRS 1967; Professor of Organic Chemistry, University of Alberta, 1961–80, University Professor, 1980–85, now Emeritus; *b* 16 June 1920; *s* of Octave Lemieux; *m* 1948, Virginia Marie McConaghie; one *s* five *d* (and one *s* decd). *Educ:* Edmonton, Alberta. BSc Hons (Chem.) Alta, 1943; PhD (Chem.) McGill, 1946. Research Fellow, Ohio State Univ., 1947; Asst Professor, Saskatchewan Univ., 1948–49; Senior Research Officer, National Research Council, Canada, 1949–54, Member, 1976–81; Professor, Ottawa Univ., 1954–61. Pres., Chem. Inst. of Canada, 1984–85. FRSC 1955. Hon. Mem., Canadian Soc. for Chemistry, 1986. Hon. DSc: New Brunswick Univ., 1967; Laval Univ., 1970; Univ. de Provence, 1973; Univ. of Ottawa, 1975; Waterloo Univ., 1980; Meml Univ., Newfoundland, 1981; Quebec, 1982; Queen's Univ., Kingston, Ont, 1983; McGill, 1984; McMaster, 1986; Sherbrooke, 1986; Hon. LLD Calgary, 1979. Chem. Inst. of Canada Medal, 1964; C. S. Hudson Award, Amer. Chem. Soc., 1966; W. N. Haworth Medal, Chem. Soc., 1978; Izaak Walton Killam Award, Canada Council, 1981; Diplôme d'Honneur, Groupe Français des Glucides, 1981; Sir Frederick Haultain Prize, Alberta, 1982; Tischler Award, Harvard Univ., 1983. Medal of Honor, CMA, 1985; Gairdner Foundn Internat. Award in Medical Science, 1985. *Publications:* over 200 research papers mainly in area of carbohydrate chemistry in Canadian Journal of Chemistry, etc. *Recreations:* golf, curling, fishing. *Address:* 7602, 119th Street, Edmonton, Alberta T6G 1N3, Canada. *T:* 436–5167. *Clubs:* University of Alberta Faculty (Edmonton); Lake Edith Golf (Jasper).

LEMKIN, James Anthony, CBE 1986; Senior Partner, Field Fisher & Martineau, Solicitors; *b* 21 Dec. 1926; *s* of William Lemkin, CBE, and Rachel Irene Lemkin; *m* 1960, Joan Dorothy Anne Casserley, FFARCS, MRCPsych; two *s* two *d. Educ:* Charterhouse; Merton Coll., Oxford (MA). Admitted solicitor, 1953; RN, 1945–47. Greater London Council: Additional Mem., 1970–73, Mem. for Hillingdon, Uxbridge, 1973–86; Chm., Legal and Parly Cttee, 1977–78; Chm., Scrutiny Cttee, 1978–81; Cons. spokesman on police, 1981–82; Opposition Chief Whip, 1982–86. Contested: (C and NL) Chesterfield,

1959; (L) Cheltenham, 1964. Chm., Bow Gp, 1952, 1956, 1957 (Founder Chm., Crossbow, 1957–60); Treasurer, Soc. of Cons. Lawyers, 1978–82, 1985–. Member: N London Hosp. Management Cttee, 1971–74; NW Thames RHA, 1980–84; Royal Marsden Hosp. SHA, 1982–; Appeal Cttee, Cancer Res. Campaign, 1967–81; Chm., Barnet FPC, 1985–. Governor: Westfield Coll., London Univ., 1970–83; Commonwealth Inst., 1985–. Trustee, Whitechapel Art Gall., 1983–. Co-founder, Africa Confidential, 1960. *Publication:* (ed) Race and Power, 1956. *Recreation:* umpiring cricket. *Address:* 4 Frognal Close, NW3 6YB. *T:* 01–831 9161. *Club:* Carlton.

LEMMON, Cyril Whitefield, FRIBA, FAIA; Architect, Honolulu, Hawaii (Private Practice), 1946–69; Chairman of the Board, Architects Hawaii Ltd; *b* Kent, 27 Oct. 1901; *s* of T. E. Lemmon and Catherine Whitefield; *m* 1st, 1921, Ethel Belinda Peters, artist (marr. diss., 1936); no *c*; 2nd, 1938, Rebecca Robson Ramsay; two *d. Educ:* University of Pennsylvania, Philadelphia, Pa. Fifth-year Studio Instructor and Lecturer in the School of Architecture, University of Liverpool, 1933–36; Consulting Architect to Government of India for Rebuilding of Quetta, 1936; Consulting Architect to MES for all military buildings in India, 1938. Lieut-Colonel, Royal Indian Engineers, 1941; Director of Civil Camouflage in India, 1943; GSO 1, GHQ, India and 11th Army Group, 1943–44. President, Hawaii Chapter, AIA, 1950; AIA Honour Award, Hawaii State Capitol. Exhibited paintings in Salon des Tuileries, Paris, 1933; travel in United States, Mexico, Europe, N Africa and Asia. Public Lectures on Architecture and Painting. 32° Mason; Potentate, Aloha Temple, AONMS, 1970. *Publications:* contributions to professional journals on Architecture. *Recreations:* golf, swimming. *Address:* Suite 300, 190 South King Street, Honolulu, Hawaii 96813, USA. *T:* 523–9636. *Clubs:* Pacific, Waialae Country, Rotary.

LEMNITZER, General Lyman L., DSM (US Army) (with 3 Oak Leaf Clusters); DSM (US Navy); DSM (US Air Force); Silver Star; Legion of Merit (Officer's Degree); Legion of Merit; Supreme Allied Commander, Europe, 1963–69; Commander-in-Chief, US European Command, 1962–69; *b* Pennsylvania, 29 Aug. 1899; *s* of late William L. Lemnitzer; *m* 1923, Katherine Mead Tryon; one *s* one *d. Educ:* Honesdale High Sch.; US Military Academy. Duty with troops, Instructor at Army Schools, etc., 1920–40; War Plans Division, War Dept General Staff, 1941; Comdg General, 34th Anti-Aircraft Artillery Bde, and Allied Force HQ England, as Asst Chief of Staff for Plans and Ops, 1942 (2nd in Command, Secret Submarine Mission to contact friendly French Officials in N Africa); served in Europe and N Africa, 1942–45; with Joint Chiefs of Staff, 1945–47; Dep. Comdt National War Coll., 1947–49; Asst to Secretary of Defence, 1949–50; Head of US Delegn to Military Cttee of the Five (Brussels Pact) Powers. London; Student, Basic Airborne Course, Fort Benning, 1950; Comdg General 11th Airborne Div., 1951, 7th Infantry Div. (in Korea), 1951–52; DCS (Plans and Research), 1952–55; Comdg General Far East and 8th US Army, 1955; C-in-C, Far East and UN Commands, and Governor of Ryukyu Is, 1955–57; Vice-Chief of Staff, 1957–59, Chief of Staff, 1959–60, US Army; Chairman Joint Chiefs of Staff, 1960–62. Holds several hon. doctorates. Hon. CB and Hon. CBE (Great Britain); Grand Cross, Legion of Honour (France); Grand Cross, Order of Merit (Germany), 1969; and numerous other foreign Orders and decorations. *Recreations:* golf, fishing, photography, interested in baseball, correspondence with his many friends around the world. *Address:* 3286 Worthington Street, NW, Washington, DC 20015, USA.

LEMON, Sir (Richard) Dawnay, Kt 1970; CBE 1958; QPM 1964; Chief Constable of Kent, 1962–74; *b* 1912; *o s* of late Lieut-Colonel F. J. Lemon, CBE, DSO, and of Mrs Laura Lemon; *m* 1939, Sylvia Marie Kentish; one *s* one *d* (and one *d* decd). *Educ:* Uppingham Sch.; RMC, Sandhurst. Joined West Yorks Regt, 1932; retired 1934. Metropolitan Police, 1934–37; Leicestershire Constabulary, 1937–39; Chief Constable of East Riding of Yorkshire, 1939–42; Chief Constable of Hampshire and Isle of Wight, 1942–62. *Recreations:* cricket, golf, shooting. *Address:* Rosecroft, Ringwould, Deal, Kent. *T:* Deal 367554. *Clubs:* Naval and Military; Royal Yacht Squadron (Cowes (hon.)).

LENDRUM, Prof. Alan Chalmers, MA, MD, BSc, ARPS; FRCPath; Professor of Pathology, University of Dundee, 1967–72, Professor Emeritus, 1972, Honorary Research Fellow, 1972; *b* 3 Nov. 1906; *yr s* of late Rev. Dr Robert Alexander Lendrum and Anna, *e d* of late James Guthrie of Pitforthie, Angus; *m* 1st, 1934, Elizabeth Bertram (*d* 1983), *e d* of late Donald Currie, BA, LLB; two *s* one *d*; 2nd, 1984, Dr Ann Brougham Sandison. *Educ:* High Sch., Glasgow; Ardrossan Acad.; University of Glasgow. Asst to Sir Robert Muir, MD, FRS, 1933; Lecturer in Pathology, University of Glasgow; Prof. of Pathology, Univ. of St Andrews, 1947–67. Visiting Prof. of Pathology, Yale, 1960. Kettle Meml Lecture, RCPath, 1973. Hon. For. Mem. Argentine Soc. of Normal and Pathological Anatomy; Hon. Member: Pathol Soc. of GB and Ireland; Nederlandse Patholoog Anatomen Vereniging; Dialectic Soc., Glasgow Univ.; Forfarshire Medical Assoc.; Hon. Fellow, and ex-Pres., Inst. Med. Lab. Sci. Dean of Guildry of Brechin, 1971–73. Capt. RAMC (TA) retd. Sims Woodhead Medal, 1971. Chm. of Governors, Duncan of Jordanstone Coll. of Art, Dundee, 1975–77. *Publications:* (co-author) Recent Advances in Clinical Pathology, 1948; Trends in Clinical Pathology, 1969; publications in medical journals. *Address:* Invergowrie House, Dundee DD2 1UA. *T:* Dundee 66666.

LENG, Gen. Sir Peter (John Hall), KCB 1978 (CB 1975); MBE 1962; MC 1945; Master-General of the Ordnance, 1981–83, retired; *b* 9 May 1925; *s* of J. Leng; *m* 1st, Virginia Rosemary Pearson (marr. diss. 1981); three *s* two *d*; 2nd, 1981, Mrs Flavia Tower, *d* of late Gen. Sir Frederick Browning and of Lady Browning (*see* Dame Daphne du Maurier). *Educ:* Bradfield Coll. Served War of 1939–45: commissioned in Scots Guards, 1944; Guards Armoured Div., Germany (MC). Various post-war appts; Guards Independent Parachute Company, 1949–51; commanded: 3rd Bn Royal Anglian Regt, in Berlin, United Kingdom and Aden, 1964–66; 24th Airportable Bde, 1968–70; Dep. Military Sec., Min. of Defence, 1971–73; Comdr Land Forces, N Ireland, 1973–75; Dir, Mil. Operations, MoD, 1975–78; Comdr 1 (Br) Corps, 1978–80. Colonel Commandant: RAVC, 1976–83; RMP, 1976–83. Fund Raising Dir, Jubilee Sailing Trust, 1984–85. Chm., Racecourse Assoc., 1985–. *Recreations:* fishing, shooting, painting. *Address:* c/o Barclays Bank, 1 Brompton Road, SW3 1EB. *Club:* Naval and Military.

LENIHAN, Brian Joseph; Teachta Dala (TD) for Dublin (West County), Parliament of Ireland, since 1977 (TD for Roscommon/Leitrim, 1961–73); *b* 17 Nov. 1930; *s* of Patrick Lenihan (TD Longford-Westmeath, 1965–70); *m* 1958, Ann Devine; four *s* one *d. Educ:* St Mary's Coll. (Marist Brothers), Athlone; University Coll., Dublin. Member: Roscommon CC, 1955–61; Seanad Eireann (FF), 1957–61 and (as Leader in Seanad, Fianna Fáil), 1973–77; Parly Sec. to Minister for Lands, 1961–64; Minister for: Justice, 1964–68; Educn, 1968–69; Transport and Power, 1969–73; Foreign Affairs, 1973; Fisheries and Forestry, 1977–79; Foreign Affairs, 1979–81; Agriculture, 1982. Mem., European Parlt, 1973–77. Dep. Leader, Fianna Fáil Party, 1983–. *Address:* 24 Park View, Castleknock, Co. Dublin, Ireland.

LENNARD, Rev. Sir Hugh Dacre B.; *see* Barrett-Lennard.

LENNIE, Douglas; *b* 30 March 1910; *e s* of Magnus S. Lennie; *m* 1941, Rhona Young Ponsonby; two *s. Educ:* Berkhamsted Sch.; Guy's Hospital, LDS, RCS, 1934; Northwestern

University, Chicago, DDS, 1938. Served War of 1939–45, Temporary Surg. Lt-Comdr (D) RNVR; formerly Surgeon Dentist to Queen Mary. *Address:* 72 Chiltley Way, Liphook, Hants.

LENNON, Dennis, CBE 1968; MC 1942; Senior Partner, Dennis Lennon & Partners, since 1950; *b* 23 June 1918; British; *m* 1947, Else Bull-Andersen; three *s. Educ:* Merchant Taylors' Sch.; University Coll., London. Served Royal Engineers, 1939–45 (despatches): 1st, 7th, 6th Armd Divs; captured in France 1940, later escaped; 7th Armd Div., N Africa; 6th Armd Div., Italy. Dir, Rayon Industry Design Centre, 1948–50; private practice, 1950–. Main Work: Jaeger shops; London Steak Houses; co-ordinator of interior, RMS Queen Elizabeth II; Chalcot Housing Estate, Hampstead; approved plans for Criterion site, Piccadilly Circus; Central Dining Room, Harrow Sch.; Arts Club; Refurbishment of Ritz Hotel, London. Work for stage: set for Capriccio, Glyndebourne; 9 state galas, Royal Opera House. FRIBA, FSIA, FRSA. *Recreations:* arts and design. *Address:* Hamper Mill, Watford, Herts. *T:* Watford 34445. *Clubs:* Savile; Royal Thames Yacht.

LENNON, Prof. (George) Gordon; retired gynæcologist; Professor Emeritus, University of Western Australia, Perth, 1974; *b* 7 Oct. 1911; *s* of late J. Lennon; *m* 1940, Barbara Brynhild (*née* Buckle); two *s. Educ:* Aberdeen Academy; Aberdeen Univ. MB, ChB Aberdeen, 1934; served in hospital posts in Aberdeen, Glasgow, London, Birmingham; MRCOG 1939; FRCOG 1952; MMSA 1943; ChM (Hons) Aberdeen, 1945. Served War of 1939–45, Sqdn-Ldr in charge of Surgical Div., RAFVR, 1942–46. First Asst, Nuffield Dept of Obstetrics and Gynæcology, Radcliffe Infirmary (University of Oxford), 1946–51; Prof. of Obstetrics and Gynæcology, Univ. of Bristol, 1951–67; Dean, Faculty of Med., Univ. of WA, Perth, 1967–74. Visiting Professor: Iraq and Turkey, 1956; South Africa and Uganda, 1958; Iran, 1965. *Publications:* Diagnosis in Clinical Obstetrics; articles in British Medical Journal, Proceedings of the Royal Society of Medicine, Journal of Obstetrics and Gynæcology of the British Empire, etc. *Recreation:* golf. *Address:* 246 Melksham Road, Holt, Wilts. *T:* North Trowbridge 782935.

LENNON, Most Rev. James Gerard; Auxiliary Bishop of Armagh, (RC), and titular Bishop of Ceannanus Mor, since 1980; *b* 26 Sept. 1923; *s* of Patrick and Catherine Lennon. *Educ:* St Patrick's College, Armagh; St Patrick's College, Maynooth. Studied Celtic Languages and Sociology. Ordained priest, 1948. Hon. DD National University of Ireland. *Address:* St Peters, Fair Street, Drogheda, Co. Louth, Ireland. *T:* Drogheda 38537.

LENNON, Most Rev. Patrick; *see* Kildare and Leighlin, Bishop of, (RC).

LENNOX; *see* Gordon-Lennox and Gordon Lennox.

LENNOX, Robert Smith, CBE 1978; JP; Lord Provost of Aberdeen, 1967–70 and 1975–77; *b* 8 June 1909; *m* 1963, Evelyn Margaret; no *c. Educ:* St Clement Sch., Aberdeen. Hon. LLD Aberdeen, 1970. JP Aberdeen. *Address:* 7 Gillespie Crescent, Ashgrove, Aberdeen. *T:* Aberdeen 43862.

LENNOX-BOYD, family name of **Viscount Boyd of Merton.**

LENNOX-BOYD, Hon. Mark Alexander; MP (C) Morecambe and Lunesdale, since 1983 (Morecambe and Lonsdale, 1979–83); a Lord Commissioner of HM Treasury, since 1986; *b* 4 May 1943; 3rd *s* of 1st Viscount Boyd of Merton, CH, PC and of Lady Patricia Guinness, 2nd *d* of 2nd Earl of Iveagh, KG, CB, CMG, FRS; *m* 1974, Arabella Lacloche; one *d. Educ:* Eton Coll.; Christ Church, Oxford. Called to the Bar, Inner Temple, 1968. Parly Private Secretary: to Sec. of State for Energy, 1981–83; to the Chancellor of the Exchequer, 1983–84; Asst Govt Whip, 1984–86. *Recreation:* travel. *Address:* 3 Bloomfield Terrace, SW1W 8PG. *T:* 01–730 3754; Gresgarth Hall, Caton, Lancashire LA2 9NB. *T:* Caton 770313. *Clubs:* Pratt's, Beefsteak.

LENTON, Aylmer Ingram, PhD; Chairman, since 1984, and Managing Director, since 1981, Bowater Industries plc (formerly Bowater Corporation plc); *b* 19 May 1927; *s* of Albert Lenton and Olive Lenton; *m* 1951, Ursula Kathleen King; one *s* two *d. Educ:* Leeds Grammar Sch.; Magdalen Coll., Oxford (MA); Leeds Univ. (PhD). Richard Haworth & Co. Ltd, 1951; British Nylon Spinners Ltd, 1956; Managing Director, S African Nylon Spinners Ltd, 1964; Director, ICI Fibres Ltd, 1966; Director, John Heathcoat & Co. Ltd, 1967; Man. Dir, 1971; Bowater Corporation Ltd: Chm., Bowater UK Paper Co., 1976; Chm., Bowater UK Ltd, 1979; Director, 1979. *Recreations:* golf, fencing, walking, fishing. *Address:* Bowater House, Knightsbridge, SW1X 7NN. *T:* 01–584 7070.

LEO, Dame Sister Mary, DBE 1973 (MBE 1963), **(Kathleen Agnes Niccol);** of Auckland, New Zealand; Member of the Sisters of Mercy' Auckland. Specialised in vocal training. Entered Order of Sisters of Mercy, 1923. Has been a singing teacher for over 40 years; pupils who have gained international success include Dame Kiri Te Kanawa, DBE, now living in London, Heather Begg, Mina Foley and Malvina Major. Biography in preparation. *Address:* St Mary's Convent, PO Box 47025, Ponsonby, Auckland 1, New Zealand.

LEON, Sir John (Ronald), 4th Bt, *cr* 1911; Actor (stage name, **John Standing**); *b* 16 Aug. 1934; *er s* of 3rd Bt and late Kay Hammond; *S* father, 1964; *m* 1961, Jill (marr. diss. 1972), d of Jack Melford; one *s*; *m* 1984, Sarah, *d* of Bryan Forbes, *qv. Educ:* Eton. Late 2nd Lt, KRRC. *Plays include:* Darling Buds of May, Saville, 1959; leading man, season, Bristol Old Vic, 1960; The Irregular Verb to Love, Criterion, 1961; Norman, Duchess, 1963; So Much to Remember, Vaudeville, 1963; The Three Sisters, Oxford Playhouse, 1964; See How They Run, Vaudeville, 1964; Seasons at Chichester Theatre, 1966, 1967; The Importance of Being Earnest, Haymarket 1968; Ring Round the Moon, Haymarket, 1968; The Alchemist, and Arms and the Man, Chichester, 1970; Popkiss, Globe, 1972; A Sense of Detachment, Royal Court, 1972; Private Lives, Queen's and Globe, 1973, NY and tour of USA, 1974; Jingo, Aldwych, 1975; Plunder, The Philanderer, NT, 1978; Close of Play, NT, 1979; Tonight at 8.30, Lyric, 1981; The Biko Inquest, Riverside, 1984; Rough Crossing, National, 1984. *Films:* The Wild and the Willing, 1962; Iron Maiden, 1962; King Rat, 1964; Walk, Don't Run, 1965; Zee and Co., 1973; The Eagle has Landed, 1976; The Class of Miss MacMichael, 1977; The Legacy, 1977; The Elephant Man, 1979; The Sea Wolves, 1980; (TV film) The Young Visiters, 1984. Television appearances incl. Arms and the Man; The First Churchills; Charley's Aunt; Rogue Male; The Sinking of HMS Victoria; Home and Beauty; Tinker, Tailor, Soldier, Spy; The Other 'Arf. *Recreation:* painting. *Heir: s* Alexander John Leon, *b* 3 May 1965. *Address:* c/o William Morris, 147 Wardour Street, W1.

LEONARD, Dick; *see* Leonard, Richard Lawrence.

LEONARD, Rt. Rev. and Rt. Hon. Graham Douglas; *see* London, Bishop of.

LEONARD, Hon. Sir (Hamilton) John, Kt 1981; **Hon. Mr Justice Leonard;** a Judge of the High Court, Queen's Bench Division, since 1981; Presiding Judge, Wales and Chester Circuit, 1982–86; *b* 28 April 1926; *s* of late Arthur and Jean Leonard, Poole, Dorset; *m* 1948, Doreen Enid, *yr d* of late Lt-Col Sidney James Parker, OBE, and May Florence Parker, Sanderstead, Surrey; one *s* one *d. Educ:* Dean Close Sch., Cheltenham; Brasenose Coll., Oxford (MA). Coldstream Guards (Captain), 1944–47. Called to Bar,

Inner Temple, 1951; Master of the Bench, 1977; practised on South-Eastern Circuit; 2nd Junior Prosecuting Counsel to the Crown at Central Criminal Court, 1964–69; QC 1969; Dep. Chm., Surrey QS, 1969–71; Comr, CCC, 1969–71; a Recorder of the Crown Court, 1972–78; a Circuit Judge, 1978–81; Common Serjeant in the City of London, 1979–81. Member: General Council of the Bar, 1970–74, Senate, 1971–74, Senate of Four Inns and the Bar, 1974–77. Chm., Criminal Bar Assoc., 1975–77. Member: Home Sec.'s Adv. Bd on Restricted Patients, 1973–78; Deptl Cttee to Review Laws on Obscenity, Indecency and Censorship, 1977–79; Judicial Studies Bd, 1979–82. Mem. Council, Hurstpierpoint Coll., 1975–83. Liveryman, Plaisterers' Co.; HM Lieutenant, City of London, 1980–81. *Recreations:* books, music, painting. *Address:* Royal Courts of Justice, WC2A 2LL. *Club:* Garrick.

LEONARD, Hugh, (John Keyes Byrne); playwright since 1959; Programme Director, Dublin Theatre Festival, since 1978; Literary Editor, Abbey Theatre, 1976–77; *b* 9 Nov. 1926; *m* 1955, Paule Jacquet; one *d. Educ:* Presentation College, Dun Laoghaire. Hon. DHL Rhode Island, 1980. *Stage plays:* The Big Birthday, 1956; A Leap in the Dark, 1957; Madigan's Lock, 1958; A Walk on the Water, 1960; The Passion of Peter Ginty, 1961; Stephen D, 1962; The Poker Session, and Dublin 1, 1963; The Saints Go Cycling In, 1965; Mick and Mick, 1966; The Quick and the Dead, 1967; The Au Pair Man, 1968; The Barracks, 1969; The Patrick Pearse Motel, 1971; Da, 1973; Thieves, 1973; Summer, 1974; Times of Wolves and Tigers, 1974; Irishmen, 1975; Time Was, 1976; A Life, 1977; Moving Days, 1981; Kill, 1982; Scorpions (3 stage plays), 1983; The Mask of Moriarty, 1985. *TV plays:* Silent Song (Italia Award, 1967); The Last Campaign, 1978; The Ring and the Rose, 1978; A Life, 1986. *TV serials:* Nicholas Nickleby, 1977; London Belongs to Me, 1977; Wuthering Heights, 1978; Strumpet City, 1979; The Little World of Don Camillo, 1980; Good Behaviour, 1983; O'Neill, 1983; The Irish RM, 1985; Troubles, 1987. *Film:* Herself Surprised, 1977. *Publication:* Home Before Night (autobiog.), 1979. *Recreations:* chess, travel, living. *Address:* 6 Rossaun, Pilot View, Dalkey, Co. Dublin. *T:* Dublin 859856. *Clubs:* Dramatists'; Players' (NY).

LEONARD, His Honour James Charles Beresford Whyte, MA Oxon; a Circuit Judge (formerly Deputy Chairman of Quarter Sessions, Inner London and Middlesex), 1965–79; Judge of the Mayor's and City of London Court, 1972–79; *b* 1905; *s* of Hon. J. W. Leonard, KC; *m* 1939, Barbara Helen, *d* of late Capt. William Incledon-Webber; two *s* one *d. Educ:* Clifton Coll.; Christ Church, Oxford. Called to the Bar, Inner Temple, 1928, Bencher 1961. Served 1940–45, with RAF (Sqdn Ldr). Recorder of Walsall, Staffs, 1951–64; Junior Counsel to Ministry of Agriculture, Fisheries and Food, Forestry Commission and Tithe Redemption Commission, 1959–64; Deputy Chairman of QS: Co. of London, 1964–65; Oxfordshire, 1962–71. Chairman: Disciplinary Cttee, Pharmaceutical Soc. of GB, 1960–64; Adv. Cttee dealing with internment under Civil Authorities (Special Powers) Act (NI) 1962, April-Nov. 1972; Comr under Terrorism (N Ireland) Order 1972, 1972–74; Dep. Chm., Appeal Tribunal, 1974–75. *Address:* Cross Trees, Sutton Courtenay, Oxon. *T:* Abingdon 848230.
See also Earl of Westmeath.

LEONARD, Hon. Sir John; *see* Leonard, Hon. Sir H.J.

LEONARD, Michael William, CVO 1984; BSc(Eng), FEng, FICE, MIMechE, FCIArb; consultant, Secretary, The Fellowship of Engineering, 1976–83; Clerk to the Worshipful Company of Engineers, since 1983; *b* 25 Dec. 1916; *e s* of late Frank Leonard and Marguerite Leonard (*née* Holborow); *m* 1945, Rosalinna Cushnir; thre *s. Educ:* Haberdashers' Aske's; Pupilage in Mechanical Engineering, Messrs Fraser & Chalmers Ltd, Erith; University College London (Pres., Union Society, 1939). Civil Engineer, Mowlem Group of Companies, to 1968; Director: Soil Mechanics Ltd; Engineering Laboratory Equipment Ltd. Mem., BSI Code of Practice Cttee on Site Investigations; Mem., later Chm., Tip Safety Cttee (post Aberfan); Sec., Council of Engineering Institutions, 1969–82; Chm., BSI Code of Practice Cttee on Foundations; Design Council Engineering Design, later Industrial, Adv. Cttee; DoI Cttee for Industrial Technologies; Hon. Treasurer, later Vice-Pres., Parly and Scientific Cttee; Vice Pres., Fédération Européenne d'Associations Nationales d'Ingenieurs; Sec., Commonwealth Engineers' Council; Mem., Executive Cttee, World Fedn of Engineering Organizations. Hon. Prof., Dept of Civil and Structural Engrg, Sheffield Univ. FEng 1983. *Publications:* papers and articles on Foundation and Geotechnical Engineering, and on Professional Engineering, for jls and confs. *Recreations:* touring, golf, fishing. *Address:* 5 Havelock Road, Croydon CR0 6QQ. *T:* 01–654 4493. *Club:* Athenæum.

LEONARD, Richard Lawrence, (Dick Leonard); Syndicated writer on politics and international affairs; *b* 12 Dec. 1930; *s* of late Cyril Leonard, Pinner, Mddx, and Kate Leonard (*née* Whyte); *m* 1963, Irène, *d* of Dr Ernst Heidelberger, Colombes, France, and of Dr Gertrud Heidelberger, Bad Godesberg, Germany; one *s* one *d. Educ:* Ealing Grammar Sch.; Inst. of Education, London Univ.; Essex Univ. (MA). School teacher, 1953–55; Dep. Gen. Sec., Fabian Society, 1955–60; journalist and broadcaster, 1960–68; Sen. Research Fellow (Social Science Research Council), Essex Univ., 1968–70. Mem., Exec. Cttee, Fabian Soc., 1972–80 (Chm., 1977–78); Chm., Library Adv. Council, 1978–81. Trustee, Assoc. of London Housing Estates, 1973–78. Contested (Lab) Harrow W, 1955; MP (Lab) Romford, 1970–Feb. 1974; PPS to Rt Hon. Anthony Crosland, 1970–74; Mem., Speaker's Conf. on Electoral Law, 1972–74. Introduced Council Housing Bill, 1971; Life Peers Bill, 1973. Asst Editor, The Economist, 1974–85. *Publications:* Guide to the General Election, 1964; Elections in Britain, 1968; (ed jtly) The Backbencher and Parliament, 1972; Paying for Party Politics, 1975; BBC Guide to Parliament, 1979; (ed jtly) The Socialist Agenda, 1981; (jtly) World Atlas of Elections, 1986; contrib.: Guardian, Sunday Times, Observer, New Society, Encounter and leading newspapers in USA, Canada, Australia and New Zealand. *Recreations:* walking, gentle cycling, neglecting the garden. *Address:* 22 rue du Gruyer, 1170 Brussels, Belgium.

LEONARD-WILLIAMS, Air Vice-Marshal Harold Guy, CB 1966; CBE 1946; DL; retired; *b* 10 Sept. 1911; *s* of late Rev. B. G. Leonard-Williams; *m* 1937, Catherine Estelle, *d* of late G. A. M. Levett; one *d. Educ:* Lancing Coll.; RAF Coll., Cranwell. 58 Sqdn, 1932–33; 208 Sqdn, Middle East, 1933–36; No 17 Signals Course, 1936–37; Instructor, RAF Coll., 1937–38; Advanced Air Striking Force, France, 1939–40 (despatches, 1940); Air Min. (Signals), 1940–43; Chm., Brit. Jt Communications Bd, 1943–46; RAF Staff Coll., 1947; Dep. CSO, RAF Middle East, 1947–50; Jt Services Staff Coll., 1950–51; CO Radio Engrg Unit, 1951–53; Dep. Dir Signals, Air Min., 1953–56; Sen. Techn. Staff Off., 90 Signals Gp, 1956–57; Dir of Signals, Air Min., 1957–59; Comdt No 1 Radio Sch., 1959–61; Comd. Electronics Off., Fighter Comd., 1961–63; AOA, HQ Far East Air Force, and AOC, HQ Gp, 1963–65; Dir-Gen. of Manning (RAF), Air Force Dept, 1966–68. Warden, St Michael's Cheshire Home, Axbridge, 1968–72. Mem., Somerset CC, 1973–85 (Chm. 1978–83). Chm., Exmoor Nat. Park, 1978–85. DL Somerset 1975. Officer, Legion of Merit (US), 1945. *Recreations:* gardening, do-it-yourself. *Address:* Openbarrow, Barrows Park, Cheddar, Somerset. *T:* Cheddar 742474. *Club:* Royal Air Force.

LEONTIEF, Prof. Wassily; Professor of Economics, since 1975, and Director, Institute for Economic Analysis, since 1978, New York University; *b* Leningrad, Russia, 5 Aug.

1906; *s* of Wassily Leontief and Eugenia Leontief (*née* Bekker); *m* 1932, Estelle Helena Marks; one *d*. *Educ:* Univ. of Leningrad (Learned Economist, 1925; MA); Univ. of Berlin (PhD 1928). Research Associate, Inst. of World Econs, Univ. of Kiel, Germany, 1927–28; Economic Adviser to Chinese Govt, Nanking, 1928–29; Res. Associate, Nat. Bureau of Econ. Res., NY, 1931; Harvard University: Instr Economics, 1932–33; Asst Prof., 1933–39; Associate Prof., 1939–46; Prof. of Econs, 1946–53; Henry Lee Prof. of Pol. Econ., 1953–75; Sen. Fellow, Soc. of Fellows, 1956–75 (Chm., 1965–75); Dir, Harvard Economic Research Project, 1948–72; Guggenheim Fellow, 1940, 1950. Gen. Consultant: US Dept of Labor, 1941–47 and 1961–65; US Dept of Commerce, 1966–82; Office of Technology Assessment, 1980–; Econ. Consultant, Russian Econs Sub-Div., Office of Strategic Services, 1943–45; Consultant: UN Sec.-Gen.'s Consultative Gp of Econ. and Social Consequences of Disarmament, 1961–62; UN Develt Prog., 1980–; Mem., Exec. Bd, Science Adv. Council, Environmental Protection Agency, 1975–80. President: Amer. Econ. Assoc., 1970; Sect. F, BAAS, 1976; Mem., Nat. Acad. of Sciences, 1974; FAAAS 1977; Corr. Mem., Institut de France, 1968; Corr. FBA, 1970; Hon. MRIA, 1976. Dr *hc*: Brussels, 1962; York, 1967; Louvain, 1971; Paris (Sorbonne), 1972; Pennsylvania, 1976; Lancaster, 1976; Toulouse, Louisville, Vermont, Long Island, 1980; Karl Marx Univ., Budapest, 1981. Nobel Prize in Economic Science, 1973. Order of the Cherubim, Univ. of Pisa, 1953. Officier, Légion d'Honneur, 1968; Order of the Rising Sun, Japan, 1984. *Publications:* The Structure of the American Economy 1919–29, 1941, 2nd edn 1953; Studies in the Structure of the American Economy, 1953; Input-Output Economics, 1966, 2nd edn, 1985; Essays in Economics, vol. I 1966, vol. II 1977; The Future of the World Economy, 1977; (with F. Duchin) Military Spending: facts and figures, worldwide implications and future outlook, 1983; (jtly) The Future of Non-Fuel Minerals in the US and World Economy, 1983; (with F. Duchin) The Impact of Automation on Workers, 1985; contribs to learned jls. *Recreation:* fly fishing. *Address:* Institute for Economic Analysis, 269 Mercer Street, 2nd floor, New York, NY 10003, USA.

LEORO-FRANCO, Dr Galo; Gran Cruz, National Order Al Mérito of Ecuador, 1970; Ambassador and Permanent Representative of Ecuador to the Office of the United Nations in Switzerland, since 1984; *s* of José Miguel Leoro and Albertina Franco de Leoro; *m* 1957, Aglae Monroy de Leoro; one *s* two *d*. *Educ:* Central Univ., Quito. Licenciado in Political and Soc. Scis, 1949; Dr in Jurisprudence, Faculty of Law, 1951. Third Sec., Washington, 1955–56, Second Sec., 1956–58; First Sec., Ministry of Foreign Affairs, 1960; Counsellor, Mexico, 1961, Chargé d'Affaires, 1962; Counsellor, Alternate Rep. of Ecuador to OAS, Washington, DC, 1962–64, Minister, 1964–68; Ambassador, 1968–; Chief Legal Advisor to Ministry of Foreign Affairs, 1969–70; Undersec. Gen., Ministry of Foreign Affairs, 1970–71; Ambassador to the Dominican Republic, 1971–72; Perm. Rep. of Ecuador to OAS, 1972–79; Advisor on Internat. Orgns, Ministry of Foreign Affairs, 1979–81; Advisor on Nat. Sovereignty, Ministry of Foreign Affairs, and Rep. of the Ministry in Nat. Congress, 1981–83; Ambassador to UK, 1983–84. Chairman: OAS Permanent Council, 1972–78 (Chm. of several Cttees of OAS Council and Gen. Assembly); Cttee II, Special Commn for Study of Interamerican System, Economic Co-operation problems, Washington, DC, 1973–75; Rapporteur, Interamerican Conf. for Revision of TIAR; elected mem., Interamerican Juridical Cttee, Rio de Janeiro, 1981–84, Vice-Chm., 1982–83, Chm., 1984–85; Representative of Ecuador at over 65 internat. conferences and Chm. of the Delegation at various of them. Gran Cruz: Iron Cross, Fed. Repub. of Germany, 1970; Order of Duarte, Sánchez and Mella, Dominican Repub., 1972; Order of the Sun, Perú, 1976; 1st Class, Order of Francisco de Miranda, Venezuela, 1976. *Publications:* various papers for Ecuadorean Year Book of Internat. Law. *Recreations:* chess, tennis. *Address:* 139 rue de Lausanne, 1202 Geneva, Switzerland. *Club:* Quito Tennis and Golf.

LE POER TRENCH, family name of **Earl of Clancarty.**

LE POER TRENCH, Brinsley; *see* Clancarty, 8th Earl of.

LE PORTZ, Yves; Comdr Légion d'Honneur 1978; Grand Officier de l'Ordre National du Mérite; French financial executive; Inspector-General of Finances, 1971; Chairman, Commission des Opérations de Bourse, Paris, since 1984; *b* Hennebont, 30 Aug. 1920; *m* 1946, Bernadette Champetier de Ribes; five *c*. *Educ:* Univ. de Paris à la Sorbonne; Ecole des Hautes Etudes Commerciales; Ecole Libre des Sciences Politiques. Attached to Inspection Générale des Finances, 1943; Directeur Adjoint du Cabinet, Président du Conseil, 1948–49; Sous-Directeur, then Chef de Service, Min. of Finance and Economic Affairs, 1949–51; Directeur du Cabinet: Sec. of State for Finance and Economic Affairs, 1951–52; Minister for Posts, Telegraphs and Telephones (PTT), 1952–55; Minister for Reconstruction and Housing, 1955–57; French Delegate to UN Economic and Social Council, 1957–58; Dir-Gén., Finance, Algeria, 1958–62; Administrateur-Gén., Development Bank of Algeria, 1959–62. European Investment Bank: Vice-Pres. and Vice-Chm., Bd of Dirs, 1962–70; Pres. and Chm. Bd of Dirs, 1970–84. *Address:* Tour Mirabeau, 39 quai André Citroën, 75015 Paris, France. *T:* (33) 1 578 39 97.

LEPPARD, Captain Keith André, CBE 1977; RN; Secretary, Institute of Brewing, since 1977; Director Public Relations (Royal Navy), 1974–77; *b* 29 July 1924; *s* of Wilfred Ernest Leppard and Dora Gilmore Keith; *m* 1954, Betty Rachel Smith; one *s* one *d*. *Educ:* Purley Grammar Sch. MRAeS 1973; FBIM 1973. Entered RN, FAA pilot duties, 1943; Opnl Wartime Service, Fighter Pilot, N Atlantic/Indian Oceans, 1944–45; Fighter Pilot/Flying Instr, Aircraft Carriers and Air Stns, 1946–57; CO 807 Naval Air Sqdn (Aerobatic Display Team, Farnborough), 1958–59; Air Org./Flying Trng Staff appts, 1959–63; Comdr (Air), HMS Victorious, 1963–64; Jt Services Staff Coll., 1964–65; Dir, Naval Officer Appts (Air), 1965–67; Chief Staff Officer (Air), Flag Officer Naval Air Comd, 1967–69; Chief Staff Officer (Ops/Trng), Comdr Far East Fleet, 1969–71; CO, Royal Naval Air Stn, Yeovilton, and Flag Captain to Flag Officer Naval Air Comd, 1972–74. Naval ADC to the Queen, 1976–77. *Recreations:* country life, tennis, golf. *Address:* Little Holt, Kingsley Green, Haslemere, Surrey. *T:* Haslemere 2797. *Club:* Naval and Military.

LEPPARD, Raymond John, CBE 1983; conductor, harpsichordist, composer; Principal Guest Conductor, St Louis Symphony Orchestra, since 1984; *b* 11 Aug. 1927; *s* of A. V. Leppard. *Educ:* Trinity Coll., Cambridge. Fellow of Trin. Coll., Cambridge, Univ. Lecturer in Music, 1958–68. Hon. Keeper of the Music, Fitzwilliam Museum, 1963–82. Conductor: Covent Garden, Sadler's Wells, Glyndebourne, and abroad; Principal Conductor, BBC Northern Symphony Orchestra, 1972–80. Hon. RAM 1972; Hon. GSM 1983; Hon. FRCM 1984. Hon. DLitt Univ. of Bath, 1972. Commendatore al Merito della Repùbblica Italiana, 1974. *Publications:* realisations of Monteverdi: Il Ballo delle Ingrate, 1958; L'Incoronazione di Poppea, 1962; L'Orfeo, 1965; Il Ritorno d'Ulisse, 1972; realisations of Francesco Cavalli: Messa Concertata, 1966; L'Ormindo, 1967; La Calisto, 1969; Magnificat, 1970; L'Egisto, 1974; L'Orione, 1983; realisation of Rameau's Dardanus, 1980; British Academy Italian Lecture, 1969, Procs Royal Musical Assoc. *Recreations:* music, theatre, books, friends. *Address:* c/o Colbert Artists Management, 111 West 57th Street, New York, NY 10019, USA.

LE QUESNE, Sir (Charles) Martin, KCMG 1974 (CMG 1963); Member of the States of Jersey, since 1978 (Deputy for St Saviour's parish); HM Diplomatic Service, retired; *b* 10 June 1917; *s* of C. T. Le Quesne, QC; *m* 1948; three *s*. *Educ:* Shrewsbury; Exeter Coll., Oxford. Served in Royal Artillery, 1940–45. Apptd HM Foreign Service, 1946; 2nd Sec. at HM Embassy, Baghdad, 1947–48; 1st Secretary: Foreign Office, 1948–51, HM Political Residency, Bahrain, 1951–54; attended course at NATO Defence Coll., Paris, 1954–55; HM Embassy, Rome, 1955–58; Foreign Office, 1958–60; apptd HM Chargé d'Affaires, Republic of Mali, 1960, subsequently Ambassador there, 1961–64; Foreign Office, 1964–68; Ambassador to Algeria, 1968–71; Dep. Under-Sec. of State, FCO, 1971–74; High Comr in Nigeria, 1974–76. Dir and Chm., Barclaytrust International Ltd; Chm., Establishment Trust, 1984–. Mem. Council, Royal African Soc.; Trustee, Southern African Studies Trust, York Univ. *Recreations:* gardening, books. *Address:* Beau Désert, St Saviour's, Jersey, Channel Islands. *T:* Jersey-Central 22076. *Clubs:* Reform (Chairman 1973–74); United (Jersey); Royal Channel Islands Yacht.

See also Sir J. G. Le Quesne, L. P. Le Quesne.

LE QUESNE, Sir (John) Godfray, Kt 1980; QC 1962; Chairman, Monopolies and Mergers Commission, since 1975 (a part-time Member since Oct. 1974); Judge of Courts of Appeal of Jersey and Guernsey, since 1964; a Recorder, since 1972; *b* 1924; 3rd *s* of late C. T. Le Quesne, QC; *m* 1963, Susan Mary Gill; two *s* one *d*. *Educ:* Shrewsbury Sch.; Exeter Coll., Oxford (MA). Pres. of Oxford Union, 1943. Called to bar, Inner Temple, 1947; Master of the Bench, Inner Temple, 1969; admitted to bar of St Helena, 1959. Dep. Chm., Lincs (Kesteven) QS, 1963–71. Chm. of Council, Regent's Park Coll., Oxford, 1958–. *Recreations:* music, walking. *Address:* 1 Crown Office Row, Temple, EC4. *T:* 01–583 9292.

See also Sir C. M. Le Quesne, L. P. Le Quesne.

LE QUESNE, Prof. Leslie Philip, CBE 1984; DM, MCh, FRCS; Medical Administrator, Commonwealth Scholarship Commission, since 1984; *b* 24 Aug. 1919; *s* of late C. T. Le Quesne, QC; *m* 1969, Pamela Margaret, *o d* of late Dr A. Fullerton, Batley, Yorks; two *s*. *Educ:* Rugby; Exeter Coll., Oxford; Middlesex Hosp. Med. Sch. Jun. Demonstrator, Path. and Anat., 1943–45; House Surgeon, Southend Hosp. and St Mark's Hosp., 1945–47; Appointments at Middlesex Hospital: Asst, Surgical Professorial Unit, 1947–52; Asst Dir, Dept of Surgical Studies, 1952–63; Surgeon, 1960–63; Prof. of Surgery, Med. Sch., and Dir, Dept of Surgical Studies, 1963–84; Dep. Vice-Chancellor and Dean, Fac. of Medicine, Univ. of London, 1980–84. Sir Arthur Sims Commonwealth Travelling Prof., 1975. Mem. GMC, 1979–84. Editor, Post Graduate Med. Jl, 1951–52. Arris and Gale Lectr, RCS, 1952; Baxter Lectr, Amer. Coll. Surgs, 1960. Mem., Ct of Examrs, RCS, 1971–77. Formerly Chm., Assoc. of Profs of Surgery; Pres., Surgical Res. Soc. Chm., The British Jl of Surgery. Hon. FRACS, 1975; Hon. FACS, 1982; Hon. Fellow RPMS, 1985. Moynihan Medal, 1953. *Publications:* medical articles and contribs to text books; Fluid Balance in Surgical Practice, 2nd edn, 1957. *Recreations:* sailing, reading. *Address:* 8 Eton Villas, NW3 4SX.

See also Sir C. M. Le Quesne, Sir J. G. Le Quesne.

LE QUESNE, Sir Martin; *see* Le Quesne, Sir C. M.

LERMON, Norman, QC 1966; **His Honour Judge Lermon**; a Circuit Judge (formerly County Court Judge), since 1971; *b* 12 Dec. 1915; *s* of late Morris and Clara Lermon; *m* 1939, Sheila Veronica Gilks; one *d*. *Educ:* Clifton Coll.; Trinity Hall, Cambridge. Joined Royal Fusiliers, 1939; commnd into S Wales Borderers, 1940; served in 53 (W) and 11th Armoured Divs; Staff Officer Ops (Air) 8th Corps, France, Holland and Germany; Major, 1945; NW Europe 1946 (despatches). Called to the Bar, 1943. *Recreations:* golf, reading. *Address:* The Law Courts, Mary Road, Guildford, Surrey.

LERNER, Max; Author; Syndicated newspaper column appears New York Post, Los Angeles Times Syndicate and elsewhere; Professor of American Civilization and World Politics, Brandeis University, USA, 1949–73, now Emeritus; Professor of Human Behavior, Graduate School of Human Behavior, US International University, San Diego, since 1974; *b* 20 Dec. 1902; *s* of Benjamin Lerner and Bessie Podel; *m* 1st; two *d* (and one *d* decd); 2nd, 1941, Edna Albers; three *s*. *Educ:* Yale Univ. (BA); Washington Univ., St Louis (MA); Robert Brookings Graduate Sch. of Economics and Government (PhD). Encyclopædia of Social Sciences, 1927, managing editor; Sarah Lawrence Coll., 1932–36, Prof. of Social Science; Harvard, 1935–36, Prof. of Government; Prof. of Political Science, Williams Coll., 1938–43; Ford Foundation Prof. of Amer. Civilization, Sch. of Internat. Studies, University of Delhi, 1959–60; Ford Foundn res. project on European unity, 1963–64. Welch Prof. of Amer. Studies, Univ. of Notre Dame, 1982–84. Editor of the Nation, 1936–38; Editorial Director PM, 1943–48; Columnist for the New York Star, 1948–49. *Publications:* It is Later Than You Think, 1938, rev. edn, 1943; Ideas are Weapons, 1939; Ideas for the Ice Age, 1941; The Mind and Faith of Justice Holmes, 1943; Public Journal, 1945; The Third Battle for France, 1945; The World of the Great Powers, 1947; The Portable Veblen, 1948; Actions and Passions, 1949; America as a Civilization, 1957; The Unfinished Country, 1959; Education and a Radical Humanism, 1962; The Age of Overkill, 1962; Tocqueville and American Civilization, 1966; (ed) Essential Works of John Stuart Mill, 1961; (ed) Tocqueville, Democracy in America, 1966; Values in Education, 1976; Ted and the Kennedy Legend, 1980. *Address:* 25 East End Avenue, New York, NY 10028, USA; (office) New York Post, 210 South Street, New York, NY 10002, USA.

LeROY-LEWIS, David Henry, FCA; Deputy Chairman, Touche, Remnant & Co., since 1981 (Director, since 1974); Chairman: Henry Ansbacher Holdings plc, since 1982; *b* 14 June 1918; *er s* of late Stuyvesant Henry LeRoy-Lewis and late Bettye LeRoy-Lewis; *m* 1953, Cynthia Madeleine, *er d* of late Comdr John C. Boldero, DSC, RN (Retd); three *d*. *Educ:* Eton. FCA 1947. Chairman: TR North America Trust PLC (formerly Continental Union Trust Ltd) 1974– (Dir, 1948–); R. P. Martin plc, 1981–85; Director: TR Industrial & General Trust PLC, 1967–; Akroyd & Smithers Ltd, 1970–81 (Chm., 1976–81); TR Trustees Corp. PLC, 1973–; TR Energy PLC, 1981–. Mem., 1961–81, a Dep. Chm., 1973–76, Stock Exchange Council. *Recreations:* shooting, fishing. *Address:* Stoke House, Stoke, Andover, Hants SP11 0NP. *T:* St Mary Bourne 548. *Clubs:* Naval and Military, MCC.

LESLIE, family name of **Earl of Rothes.**

LESLIE, Lord; James Malcolm David Leslie; *b* 4 June 1958; *s* and *heir* of 21st Earl of Rothes, *qv*. *Educ:* Eton. *Address:* 8 Kinnoul Road, W6.

LESLIE, Sir Alan; *see* Leslie, Sir C. A. B.

LESLIE, Ann Elizabeth Mary, (Mrs Michael Fletcher); journalist and broadcaster; *b* Pakistan; *d* of Norman Leslie and Theodora (*née* McDonald); *m* 1969 Michael Fletcher; one *d*. *Educ:* Presentation Convent, Matlock, Derbyshire; Convent of the Holy Child, Mayfield, Sussex; Lady Margaret Hall, Oxford (BA). Daily Express, 1962–67; freelance, 1967–: regular contributor to Daily Mail; also contrib. various national newspapers and magazines, incl. Punch, Queen, Nova, Harper's and Playboy. Broadcasting includes Stop the Week, Any Questions, TV-am and Question Time. British Press Awards Commendation, 1980; Variety Club Women of the Year Award for journalism and broadcasting, 1981; British Press Awards Feature Writer of the Year, 1981; British Press

Awards Commendation, 1983, 1985. *Recreations:* family life, photography. *Address:* c/o Daily Mail, Northcliffe House, Tudor Street, EC4Y 0JA. *T:* 01–353 6000.

LESLIE, Sir (Colin) Alan (Bettridge), Kt 1986; President, Law Society, 1985–86; *b* 10 April 1922; *s* of Rupert Colin Leslie and Gladys Hannah Leslie (*née* Bettridge); *m* 1st, 1953, Anne Barbara (*née* Coates) (*d* 1982); two *d*; 2nd, 1983, Jean Margaret (Sally), widow of Dr Alan Cheatle. *Educ:* King Edward VII School, Lytham; Merton College, Oxford (MA Law). Solicitor. Commissioned, The Royal Scots Fusiliers, 1941–46. Legal practice, Stafford Clark & Co., Solicitors, 1948–60; Head of Legal Dept and Company Secretary, British Oxygen Co., later BOC International, then BOC Group, 1960–83. Vice-Pres., Law Society, 1984–85. *Recreation:* fishing. *Address:* Tile Barn Cottage, Alfriston, E Sussex. *T:* Alfriston 870388; 36 Abingdon Road, W8. *T:* 01–937 2874. *Club:* United Oxford & Cambridge University.

LESLIE, Prof. David Clement; consultant engineer; *b* Melbourne, 18 Dec. 1924; *o s* of Clement and Doris Leslie; *m* 1952, Dorothea Ann Wenborn; three *s* two *d*. *Educ:* Westminster; Leighton Park; Wadham Coll., Oxford (MA, DPhil). Royal Navy, 1944–47. Postgrad. research in physics, 1948–50; Sir W. G. Armstrong Whitworth Aircraft, Coventry, 1951–54; Guided Weapons Div., RAE Farnborough, 1954–58; UKAEA Harwell and Winfrith, 1958–68; Prof. of Nuclear Engrg, 1968–84 (Hd of Dept, 1968–80), Dean, Faculty of Engrg, 1980–83, QMC. Member: Scientific and Technical Cttee, EEC, 1980–86 (Chm. 1980–84); Electricity Supply Res. Council, 1981– (Dep. Chm. 1984–); Machines and Power Cttee, SERC, 1985–. Safety Adviser to the Local Authorities for the Sizewell Inquiry, 1981–. *Publications:* Developments in the Theory of Turbulence, 1973; papers in Proc. Royal Soc., Jl of Fluid Mechanics, Nature, Nuclear Science and Engrg, etc. *Address:* 22 Piercing Hill, Theydon Bois, Essex. *T:* Theydon Bois 3249.

LESLIE, Mrs D. G.; *see* Erskine-Lindop, A. B. N.

LESLIE, Rt. Rev. (Ernest) Kenneth, OBE 1972; *b* 14 May 1911; *s* of Rev. Ernest Thomas Leslie and Margaret Jane Leslie; *m* 1941, Isabel Daisy Wilson; two *s* one *d* (and one *s* decd). *Educ:* Trinity Gram. Sch., Kew, Vict.; Trinity Coll., University of Melbourne (BA). Aust. Coll. of Theology. ThL, 2nd Cl. 1933, Th Schol. 1951, 2nd Cl. 1952. Deacon, 1934; Priest, 1935; Asst Curate, Holy Trinity, Coburg, 1934–37; Priest-in-Charge, Tennant Creek, Dio. Carpentaria, 1937–38; Alice Springs with Tennant Creek, 1938–40; Rector of Christ Church, Darwin, 1940–44; Chaplain, AIF, 1942–45; Rector of Alice Springs with Tennant Creek, 1945–46; Vice-Warden, St John's Coll., Morpeth, NSW, 1947–52; Chap. Geelong Church of Eng. Gram. Sch., Timbertop Branch, 1953–58; Bishop of Bathurst, 1959–81. *Recreations:* walking, woodwork, cycling. *Address:* 51 Asca Drive, Green Point, NSW 2250, Australia.

LESLIE, Rear-Adm. George Cunningham, CB 1970; OBE 1944; MA; Domestic Bursar and Fellow of St Edmund Hall, Oxford, since 1970; *b* 27 Oct. 1920; 4th *s* of Col A. S. Leslie, CMG, WS, and Mrs M. I. Leslie (*née* Horne), Kininvie; *m* 1953, Margaret Rose Leslie; one *s* three *d*. *Educ:* Uppingham. Entered RN, 1938; War service in HMS York, Harvester, Volunteer and Cassandra, 1939–45; comd HMS: Wrangler, 1950–51; Wilton, 1951; Surprise, 1954–55; Capt. Fishery Protection Sqdn, 1960–62; Cdre HMS Drake, 1964–65; comd HMS Devonshire, 1966–67; Flag Officer, Admiralty Interview Bd, 1967–68; NATO HQ, Brussels, 1968–70. Comdr 1952; Capt. 1958; Rear-Adm. 1967; retired 1970. *Recreations:* sailing, painting, country pursuits. *Address:* St Edmund Hall, Oxford.

LESLIE, His Honour Gilbert Frank; retired Circuit Judge (formerly Judge of County Courts); *b* 25 Aug. 1909; *e s* of late F. L. J. Leslie, JP and M. A. Leslie (*née* Gilbert), Harrogate; *m* 1947, Mary Braithwaite, MD, JP, *e d* of late Col W. H. Braithwaite, MC, TD, DL and Mrs E. M. Braithwaite, Harrogate; three *d*. *Educ:* St Christopher Sch., Letchworth; King's Coll., Cambridge (MA). Called to the Bar, Inner Temple, 1932; joined North-Eastern Circuit. Served War of 1939–45; Private Sherwood Foresters, 1939; commissioned West Yorkshire Regt, 1940; on Judge-Advocate-General's staff from Nov. 1940; finally ADJAG, HQ BAOR; released Nov. 1945 (Lt-Col). Asst Recorder, Newcastle upon Tyne City Quarter Sessions, 1954–60, Sheffield City Quarter Sessions, 1956–60; Recorder of Pontefract, 1958–60; Recorder of Rotherham, 1960; Dep. Chm., West Riding Quarter Sessions, 1960–63; Judge of County Court Circuit 14, 1960; Circuit 46, 1960–63; Circuit 42 (Bloomsbury and Marylebone), 1963–80; Dep. Chm., Inner London Area Sessions, 1965–71. Dep. Chm., Agricultural Lands Tribunal (Yorkshire Area), 1958–60. Jt Pres., Council of HM Circuit Judges, 1978. Manager, 1974–77, 1980–83, Vice-Pres., 1975–77, 1980–83, Royal Institution. Mem. Board of Faculty of Law and Court of Governors, Sheffield Univ., 1958–61; Governor, 1964–, Chm. of Governors, 1974–84, Parsons Mead Sch. for Girls. Liveryman, Worshipful Co. of Gardeners (Mem. Court, 1978–, Upper Warden, 1986). FRSA. *Recreations:* gardening, horticultural history. *Address:* Ottways, 26 Ottways Lane, Ashtead, Surrey KT21 2NZ. *T:* Ashtead 74191. *Club:* Reform.

LESLIE, Ian (William) Murray, CBE 1971 (OBE 1954); Editor of Building (formerly The Builder), 1948–70; Vice-Chairman, The Builder Ltd, 1970–75; *b* 13 March 1905; 2nd *s* of John Gordon Leslie, MB, CM, Black Isle, Inverness, and Agnes Macrae, Kintail, Wester Ross; *m* 1st, 1929, Josette (marr. diss. 1974), 2nd *d* of late André Délètraz, actor, Paris; one *s*; 2nd, 1974, G. M. Vivian Williams, LLB, barrister, *d* of Evan Hughes, Tintagel, Cornwall. *Educ:* St Paul's (foundation scholar); Crown and Manor Boys' Club, Hoxton. Joined editorial staff of The Builder, 1926; Associate Editor, 1937. Mem. Council, National Assoc. of Boys' Clubs, 1944–54; Chm. London Federation of Boys' Clubs, 1945–50; JP for County of London, 1945–61; Mem., Metropolitan Juvenile Courts Panel, 1947–61 (Chm., Chelsea Children's Court, 1956–61). Founder-Pres., Internat. Assoc. of the Building and Construction Press (UK section), 1970–79; made survey (with J. B. Perks) of Canadian construction industry for The Builder, 1950; organized £1000 house architectural competition for The Builder, 1951; made survey of housing, South Africa and Rhodesia, for The Builder, 1954. Chm., Building Industry Youth Trust, 1975–81. Pres., Invalids Cricket Club, 1974–; Mem., Develt Cttee of MCC, 1974–84; Mem., Medical Sch. Council, St Mary's Hosp., 1974–83. Associate RICS; Hon. Mem. of Art Workers' Guild; Hon. FRIBA; Hon. FCIOB. *Recreations:* watching cricket; sleep. *Address:* 64 Hamilton Terrace, NW8 9UJ. *T:* 01–289 0178. *Clubs:* Savage, Architectural Association (Hon. Mem.), MCC.

LESLIE, James Bolton, AO 1984; MC 1944; Chairman, Qantas Airways Ltd, since 1980; Director: National Mutual Life Association, since 1983; Equity Trustees, since 1980; CIG Ltd, since 1981; Boral Ltd, since 1984; *b* 27 Nov. 1922; *s* of Stuart Deacon Leslie and Dorothy Clare (*née* Murphy); *m* 1955, Alison Baker three *s* one *d*. *Educ:* Trinity Grammar Sch., Melbourne; Harvard Business Sch., Boston, USA. Served war, Australian Infantry, Pacific Theatre, Private to Major, 1941–46. Mobil Oil Australia Ltd: joined, 1946; Manager, Fiji, 1946–50; various postings, Australia, 1950–59; Mobil Corp., New York, 1959–61; Gen. Manager, New South Wales, 1961–66; Director, Mobil Australia, 1966–68; Chm. and Chief Exec., Mobil New Zealand, 1968–72; Chm., Mobil Australia and Pacific, 1972–80. Chairman: Internat. Culture Corp. of Australia, 1980–; Project Australia, 1980–83. Vice-Chm., Inst. of Dirs in Australia, 1982–85. *Recreations:* farming, horse breeding. *Address:* 42 Grey Street, East Melbourne, Victoria 3002, Australia. *T:* 03 4196149. *Clubs:* Melbourne, Australian, Melbourne Cricket, Beefsteak (Melbourne).

LESLIE, Sir John (Norman Ide), 4th Bt *cr* 1876; *b* 6 Dec. 1916; *s* of Sir (John Randolph) Shane Leslie, 3rd Bt and Marjorie (*d* 1951), *y d* of Henry C. Ide, Vermont, USA; *S* father, 1971. *Educ:* Downside; Magdalene College, Cambridge (BA 1938). Captain, Irish Guards; served War of 1939–45 (prisoner-of-war). Kt of Honour and Devotion, SMO Malta, 1947; KCSG 1958. *Recreations:* ornithology, ecology. *Heir:* *b* Desmond Arthur Peter Leslie [*b* 29 June 1921; *m* 1st, 1945, Agnes Elizabeth, *o d* of late Rudolph Bernauer, Budapest; two *s* one *d*; 2nd, 1970, Helen Jennifer, *d* of late Lt-Col E. I. E. Strong; two *d*]. *Address:* 19 Piazza in Piscinula, Trastevere, 00153 Rome, Italy. *Clubs:* Travellers'; Circolo della Caccia (Rome).

LESLIE, Hon. John Wayland; *b* 16 Dec. 1909; 2nd *s* of 19th Earl of Rothes; *m* 1932, Coral Angela, *d* of late G. H. Pinckard, JP, Combe Court, Chiddingfold, Surrey, and 9 Chesterfield Street, Mayfair; one *s* one *d*. *Educ:* Stowe Sch.; Corpus Christi Coll., Cambridge. Formerly Flt-Lieut, RAFVR; invalided 1943. Mem. of Royal Company of Archers (Queen's Body Guard for Scotland). Mem. Clothworkers' Co. *Recreation:* fishing. *Address:* Guildford House, Castle Hill, Farnham, Surrey GU9 7JG. *T:* Farnham 716975. *Club:* Carlton.

LESLIE, Rt. Rev. Kenneth; *see* Leslie, Rt Rev. E. K.

LESLIE, (Percy) Theodore; retired British Aerospace engineer; *b* 19 Nov. 1915; *s* of Frank Harvey Leslie (*d* 1965) (*g g s* of 4th Bt), Christ's Hospital, and Amelia Caroline (*d* 1918), *d* of Alexander Russon; *heir* to the Leslie of Wardis and Findrassie baronetcy (*cr* 1625). *Educ:* London and privately. Freeman, City of London, 1978. Knightly Assoc. of St George, 1983. *Recreations:* chess, gardening and visiting places of historic interest. *Address:* National Westminster Bank, 5 Market Place, Kingston upon Thames, Surrey.

LESLIE, Peter Evelyn; Chief General Manager, Barclays Bank PLC, since 1985 (Director since 1980); *b* 24 March 1931; *s* of late Patrick Holt Leslie, DSc and of Evelyn (*née* de Berry); *m* 1975, Charlotte, former wife of W. N. Wenban-Smith, *qv* and *d* of Sir Edwin Chapman-Andrews, KCMG, OBE and of Lady Chapman-Andrews; two step *s* two step *d*. *Educ:* Dragon Sch., Oxford; Stowe Sch.; New Coll., Oxford (Exhbnr; MA). Commnd Argyll and Sutherland Highlanders, 1951; served 7th Bn (TA), 1952–56. Entered Barclays Bank DCO, 1955; served in Sudan, Algeria, Zaire, Kenya and the Bahamas, 1956–71; Gen. Man., Barclays Bank, 1973–76; Dir 1979, and Sen. Gen. Man., 1980–83, Barclays Bank International. Chm., Exec. Cttee, British Bankers Assoc., 1978–79; Dep. Chm., Export Guarantees Adv. Council, 1986– (Mem., 1978–81); Mem., Matthews Cttee on ECGD, 1983. Governor: National Inst. of Social Work, 1973–83; Stowe Sch., 1983–. *Recreations:* natural history, historical research. *Address:* c/o Barclays Bank PLC, 54 Lombard Street, EC3P 3AH.

LESLIE, Theodore; *see* Leslie, P. T.

LESLIE MELVILLE, family name of **Earl of Leven and Melville.**

LESSER, Sidney Lewis; Vice-President, Royal Automobile Club, since 1979 (Executive Chairman, 1978–79); *b* 23 March 1912; *s* of Joseph and Rachel Lesser; *m* 1938, Nina Lowenthal; two *d*. Solicitor of Supreme Court of Judicature; Comr for Oaths. In sole practice, 1935–82. *Recreations:* golf, travel, reading. *Address:* 37 Fairfax Place, Hampstead, NW6 4EJ. *T:* 01–328 2607. *Clubs:* Royal Automobile; Coombe Hill Golf; Propeller of the United States.

LESSING, Charlotte; Editor of Good Housekeeping, since 1973; *b* 14 May; *m* 1948, Walter B. Lessing; three *d*. *Educ:* Henrietta Barnet Sch.; evening classes. Univ. of London Dipl. Eng. Lit. Journalism and public relations: New Statesman and Nation; Royal Society of Medicine; Lilliput (Hulton Press); Notley Public Relations; Good Housekeeping, 1964–; Editor-in-Chief, Country Living, 1985–86. *Publications:* short stories, travel, wine and feature articles. *Recreations:* travel, wine. *Address:* 1 Stanley Gardens, W11.

LESSING, Mrs Doris (May); author; *b* Persia, 22 Oct. 1919; *d* of Captain Alfred Cook Tayler and Emily Maude McVeagh; lived in Southern Rhodesia, 1924–49; *m* 1st, 1939, Frank Charles Wisdom (marr. diss., 1943); one *s* one *d*; 2nd, 1945, Gottfried Anton Nicholas Lessing (marr. diss., 1949); one *s*. Associate Member: AAAL, 1974; Nat. Inst. of Arts and Letters (US), 1974. Mem., Inst. for Cultural Res., 1974. Hon. Fellow, MLA (Amer.), 1974. Austrian State Prize for European Literature, 1981; Shakespeare Prize, 1982. *Publications:* The Grass is Singing, 1950 (filmed 1981); This Was the Old Chief's Country, 1951; Martha Quest, 1952; Five, 1953 (Somerset Maugham Award, Soc. of Authors, 1954); A Proper Marriage, 1954; Retreat to Innocence, 1956; Going Home, 1957; The Habit of Loving, 1957; A Ripple from the Storm, 1958; Fourteen Poems, 1959; In Pursuit of the English, 1960; The Golden Notebook, 1962 (Prix Médicis 1976 for French trans., Carnet d'or); A Man and Two Women (short stories), 1963; African Stories, 1964; Landlocked, 1965; Particularly Cats, 1966; The Four-Gated City, 1969; Briefing for a Descent into Hell, 1971; The Story of a Non-Marrying Man, 1972; The Summer Before the Dark, 1973; The Memoirs of a Survivor, 1975 (filmed 1981); Collected Stories: Vol. I, To Room Nineteen, 1978; Vol. II, The Temptation of Jack Orkney, 1978; Canopus in Argos: Archives: Re Planet 5, Shikasta, 1979; The Marriages Between Zones Three, Four and Five, 1980; The Sirian Experiments, 1981; The Making of the Representative for Planet 8, 1982; The Sentimental Agents in the Volyen Empire, 1983; The Diaries of Jane Somers, 1984 (Diary of a Good Neighbour, 1983; If the Old Could . . . ., 1984; published under pseudonym Jane Somers); The Good Terrorist, 1985 (W. H. Smith Literary Award, 1986); *play:* play with a Tiger, 1962. *Address:* c/o Jonathan Clowes Ltd, 22 Prince Albert Road, NW1.

LESSOF, Prof. Maurice Hart, FRCP; Professor of Medicine, University of London at Guy's Hospital Medical School, since 1971; *b* 4 June 1924; *s* of Noah and Fanny Lessof; *m* 1960, Leila Liebster; one *s* two *d*. *Educ:* City of London Sch.; King's Coll., Cambridge. Appts on junior staff of Guy's Hosp., Canadian Red Cross Memorial Hosp., Johns Hopkins Hosp., etc.; Clinical Immunologist and Physician, Guy's Hosp., 1967. Past Pres., British Soc. for Allergy. Mem. Senate, London Univ., 1981–85. *Publications:* (ed) Immunological Aspects of Cardiovascular Diseases, 1981; (ed) Immunological and Clinical Aspects of Allergy, 1981; (ed) Clinical Reactions to Food, 1983; (ed) Allergy, 1984. *Recreation:* painting. *Address:* 8 John Spencer Square, Canonbury, N1 2LZ. *T:* 01–226 0919. *Club:* Athenæum.

LESTANG, Sir M. C. E. C. N. de; *see* Nageon de Lestang.

LESTER, Anthony Paul, QC 1975; QC (NI); *b* 3 July 1936; *e s* of Harry and Kate Lester; *m* 1971, Catherine Elizabeth Debora Wassey; one *s* one *d*. *Educ:* City of London Sch.; Trinity Coll., Cambridge (Exhibnr) (BA); Harvard Law Sch. (Harkness Commonwealth Fund Fellowship) (LLM). Served RA, 1955–57. Called to Bar, Lincoln's Inn, 1963 (Mansfield scholar), Bencher, 1985; called to Bar of N Ireland, 1984; jun. mem., Irish Bar, 1983. Special Adviser to: Home Secretary, 1974–76; Standing Adv. Commn on Human

Rights, 1975–77. Hon. Vis. Prof., UCL, 1983–. F.A. Mann Lectr, Lincoln's Inn, 1983. Member: Bd of Overseers, Univ. of Pennsylvania Law Sch., 1978–; Court of Governors, LSE. Chairman: Social Democratic Lawyers Assoc., 1981–; Interights, 1983–. Member: Internat. Law Assoc. Cttee on Human Rights; Amer. Law Inst., 1985–; Trustee, Runnymede Trust. Governor, British Inst. of Human Rights. *Publications:* Justice in the American South, 1964 (Amnesty Internat.); (co-ed.) Shawcross and Beaumont on Air Law, 3rd edn, 1964; (co-author) Race and Law, 1972; contributor to: British Nationality, Immigration and Race Relations, in Halsbury's Laws of England, 4th edn, 1973; The Changing Constitution (ed Jowell and Oliver), 1985. *Address:* 2 Hare Court, Temple, EC4. *T:* 01-583 1770. *Club:* Garrick.

LESTER, James Theodore; MP (C) Broxtowe, since 1983 (Beeston, Feb. 1974–1983); *b* 23 May 1932; *s* of Arthur Ernest and Marjorie Lester; *m*; two *s*. *Educ:* Nottingham High School. Mem. Notts CC, 1967–74. An Opposition Whip, 1976–79; Parly Under-Sec. of State, Dept of Employment, 1979–81. Mem., Select Cttee on Foreign affairs; Vice-Chm., All Party Gp on overseas develt. Deleg. to Council of Europe and WEU, 1975–76. *Recreations:* reading, music, motor racing, travelling. *Address:* Flat 7, 37 Smith Square, SW1.

LESTER, Richard; Film Director; *b* 19 Jan. 1932; *s* of Elliott and Ella Young Lester; *m* 1956, Deirdre Vivian Smith; one *s* one *d*. *Educ:* Wm Penn Charter Sch.; University of Pennsylvania (BSc). Television Director: CBS (USA), 1951–54; AR (Dir TV Goon Shows), 1956. Directed The Running, Jumping and Standing Still Film (Acad. Award nomination; 1st prize San Francisco Festival, 1960). *Feature Films directed:* It's Trad, Dad, 1962; Mouse on the Moon, 1963; A Hard Day's Night, 1964; The Knack, 1964 (Grand Prix, Cannes Film Festival); Help, 1965 (Best Film Award and Best Dir Award, Rio de Janeiro Festival); A Funny Thing Happened on the Way to the Forum, 1966; How I won the War, 1967; Petulia, 1968; The Bed Sitting Room, 1969 (Gandhi Peace Prize, Berlin Film Festival); The Three Musketeers, 1973; Juggernaut, 1974 (Best Dir award, Teheran Film Fest.); The Four Musketeers, 1974; Royal Flash, 1975; Robin and Marian, 1976; The Ritz, 1976; Butch and Sundance: the early days, 1979; Cuba, 1979; Superman II, 1981; Superman III, 1983; Finders Keepers, 1984. *Recreations:* composing, playing popular music. *Address:* Twickenham Film Studios, St Margaret's, Twickenham, Mddx.

LESTER SMITH, Ernest; *see* Smith, E. L.

LESTOR, Joan; freelance lecturer; Director, Trade Unions Child Care Project, since 1986; *b* Vancouver, British Columbia, Canada; one *s* one *d* (both adopted). *Educ:* Blaenavon Secondary Sch., Monmouth; William Morris Secondary Sch., Walthamstow; London Univ. Diploma in Sociology. Nursery Sch. Teacher, 1959–66. Member: Wandsworth Borough Council, 1958–68; LCC, 1962–64; Exec. Cttee of the London Labour Party, 1962–65; Nat. Exec., Labour Party, 1967–82 (Chm., 1977–78); Chm., Internat. Cttee, Labour Party, 1978–. MP (Lab) Eton and Slough, 1966–83; Parliamentary Under-Secretary: Dept of Educn and Science, Oct. 1969–June 1970; FCO, 1974–75; DES, 1975–76; resigned from Labour Govt on cuts policy, 1976. Contested (Lab): Lewisham W, 1964; Slough, 1983; prospective parly cand. (Lab.), Eccles, 1985–. Chm. Council, Nat. Soc. of Children's Nurseries, 1969–70; Co-Chm., Jt Cttee against Racialism, 1978–; Mem., CND Nat. Council, 1983–. *Recreations:* theatre, reading, playing with children.

L'ESTRANGE, Laurence Percy Farrer, OBE 1958; HM Diplomatic Service; retired; company director and consultant; *b* 10 Sept. 1912; *s* of late S. W. L'Estrange and Louie Knights L'Estrange (*née* Farrer); *m* 1933, Anne Catherine (*née* Whiteside) (*d* 1986); two *s*. *Educ:* Shoreham Grammar Sch., Shoreham, Sussex; Univ. of London. Employed at HM Embassy, Caracas, 1939, and Acting Vice-Consul, 1941 and 1942. Resigned and joined RAF, 1943–46. HM Vice-Consul, Malaga, 1946; Second Sec., San Salvador, 1949; Chargé d'Affaires, 1952; Vice-Consul, Chicago, 1953; First Sec. (Commercial): Manila, 1954; Lima, 1958; Chargé d'Affaires, 1961; seconded to Western Hemisphere Exports Council, in charge of Latin American Div., 1962; HM Consul, Denver, 1963; Counsellor (Commercial), Lagos, 1967; Ambassador to Honduras, 1969–72. FRSA 1973. *Recreations:* golf, riding, sailing, fishing and shooting. *Address:* 154 Frog Grove Lane, Wood Street Village, Guildford, Surrey GU3 3HB. *Club:* Royal Automobile.

L'ETANG, Hugh Joseph Charles James; medical editor and writer; *b* 23 Nov. 1917; *s* of late Dr J. G. L'Etang and Frances L'Etang; *m* 1951, Cecily Margaret Tinker, MD, MRCP; one *s* one *d*. *Educ:* Haileybury Coll.; St John's Coll., Oxford; St Bartholomew's Hosp.; Harvard Sch. of Public Health. BA 1939, BM, BCh 1942, DIH 1952. War Service, 1943–46, RMO 5th Bn Royal Berks Regt; TA from 1947, RAMC; Lt-Col 1953–56. Medical Adviser: North Thames Gas Bd, 1948–56; British European Airways, 1956–58; John Wyeth & Brother Ltd, 1958–69; Asst and Dep. Editor, The Practitioner, 1969–72, Editor 1973–82. Mem., Bd of Management, Inst. of Sports Medicine, 1983–. Hira S. Chouké Lectr, Coll. of Physicians of Philadelphia, 1972 (Hon. Fellow, 1985); Henry Cohen Hist. of Medicine Lectr, Univ. of Liverpool, 1986. Member: RUSI; IISS; Military Commentators' Circle; Amer. Civil War Round Table, London; Sherlock Holmes Soc. *Publications:* The Pathology of Leadership, 1969; Fit to Lead?, 1980; articles in Practitioner, Jl RAMC, Army Qtly, Brassey's Annual, Navy Internat., NATO's Fifteen Nations. *Recreation:* medical aspects of military and foreign affairs. *Address:* 27 Sispara Gardens, West Hill Road, SW18 1LG. *T:* 01–870 3836. *Club:* United Oxford & Cambridge University.

LETHBRIDGE, Sir Thomas (Periam Hector Noel), 7th Bt *cr* 1804; *b* 17 July 1950; *s* of Sir Hector Wroth Lethbridge, 6th Bt, and of Evelyn Diana, *d* of late Lt-Col Francis Arthur Gerard Noel, OBE; *S* father, 1978; *m* 1976, Susan Elizabeth Rocke; four *s* two *d*. *Educ:* Milton Abbey. Studied farming, Cirencester Agricultural Coll., 1969–70; Man. Dir, Art Gallery, Dorset and London, 1972–77; Dir, Swaine, Adeney, Brigg & Sons Ltd. Now fine art specialist in sporting paintings and engravings. *Recreations:* shooting, riding. *Heir:* *s* John Francis Buckler Noel Lethbridge, *b* 10 March 1977. *Address:* Lloyds House, Honeymead, Simonsbath, Minehead, Somerset. *Clubs:* Farmers', Naval and Military; Slim Jim's Executive Jymnasium.

LE TOCQ, Eric George, CMG 1975; HM Diplomatic Service, retired; British Government Representative in the West Indies Associated States, 1975–78; *b* 20 April 1918; *s* of Eugene Charles Le Tocq; *m* 1946, Betty Esdaile; two *s* one *d*. *Educ:* Elizabeth Coll., Guernsey; Exeter Coll., Oxford (MA). Served War of 1939–45: commissioned in Royal Engineers, 1939; North Africa, 1942–43; Italy, 1943; Austria and Greece; major. Taught Modern Languages and Mathematics at Monmouth Sch., 1946–48; Assistant Principal, Commonwealth Relations Office, 1948; Karachi, 1948–50; Principal, 1950; Dublin, 1953–55; Accra, 1957–59; Assistant Secretary, 1962; Adviser on Commonwealth and External Affairs, Entebbe, 1962; Deputy High Commissioner, Uganda, 1962–64; Counsellor, British High Commission, Canberra, 1964–67; Head of E African Dept, FCO, 1968–71; High Comr in Swaziland, 1972–75. *Recreations:* golf and gardening. *Address:* Maycroft, Tweed Lane, Boldre, Hants. *Club:* Royal Commonwealth Society.

LETSON, Major-General Harry Farnham Germaine, CB 1946; CBE 1944; MC; ED; CD; *b* Vancouver, BC, 26 Sept. 1896; *e s* of late J. M. K. Letson, Vancouver, BC; *m* 1928, Sally Lang Nichol; no *c*. *Educ:* McGill Univ.; University of British Columbia; University of London. BSc (UBC) 1919; PhD (Eng) London, 1923. Active Service Canadian Army, 1916–19; Associate Professor Mechanical and Electrical Engineering, University of BC, 1923–36; on Active Service Canadian Army, 1939–46; Adjt-General Canadian Army, 1942–44; Commander of Canadian Army Staff in Washington, 1944–46; Secretary to Governor-General of Canada, 1946–52; Adviser on Militia, Canadian Army, 1954–58, retired. Hon. Colonel British Columbia Regt, 1963. LLD (University of BC), 1945. *Recreation:* fishing. *Address:* 474 Lansdowne Road, Ottawa K1M 0X9, Canada. *Clubs:* Rideau (Ottawa); Vancouver (Vancouver, BC).

LETTS, Charles Trevor; Underwriting Member of Lloyd's, since 1944; Deputy Chairman of Lloyd's, 1966 (entered Lloyd's, 1924; Member, 1941; Committee, 1964–67); *b* 2 July 1905; *o s* of late Charles Hubert and Gertrude Letts; *m* 1942, Mary R. (Judy), *o d* of late Sir Stanley and late Lady (Hilda) Woodwark; two *s* one *d*. *Educ:* Marlborough Coll. Served RNVR, Lieut-Commander, 1940–45. Member: Cttee, Lloyd's Underwriters' Assoc., 1960–70 (Chairman, 1963–64); Council, Lloyd's Register of Shipping, 1964–77 (Chairman, Yacht Sub-Cttee, 1967–75); Salvage Association, 1963–70. *Recreations:* sailing, golf. *Address:* Bearwood, Holtye, Edenbridge, Kent. *T:* Cowden 472. *Club:* Royal Ocean Racing.

LETWIN, Prof. William; Professor of Political Science, London School of Economics, since 1976; *b* 14 Dec. 1922; *s* of Lazar and Bessie Letwin; *m* 1944, Shirley Robin; one *s*. *Educ:* Univ. of Chicago (BA 1943, PhD 1951); London Sch. of Economics (1948–50). Served US Army, 1943–46. Postdoctoral Fellow, Economics Dept, Univ. of Chicago, 1951–52; Research Associate, Law Sch., Univ. of Chicago, 1953–55; Asst. Prof. of Industrial History, MIT, 1955–60; Associate Prof. of Economic History, MIT, 1960–67; Reader in Political Science, LSE, 1966–76. Chm., Bd of Studies in Economics, Univ. of London, 1971–73. *Publications:* (ed) Frank Knight, on The History and Method of Economics, 1956; Sir Josiah Child, 1959; Documentary History of American Economic Policy, 1961, 2nd edn 1972; Origins of Scientific Economics 1660–1776, 1963; Law and Economic Policy in America, 1965; (ed) Against Equality, 1983; articles in learned jls. *Address:* 3 Kent Terrace, NW1 4RP. *T:* 01–262 2593.

LEUCHARS, Maj.-Gen. Peter Raymond, CBE 1966; Chief Commander, St John Ambulance, since 1980 (Commissioner-in-Chief, 1978–80 and 1985–86); *b* 29 Oct. 1921; *s* of late Raymond Leuchars and Helen Inez Leuchars (*née* Copland-Griffiths); *m* 1953, Hon. Gillian Wightman Nivison, *d* of 2nd Baron Glendyne; one *s*. *Educ:* Bradfield College. Commnd in Welsh Guards, 1941; served in NW Europe and Italy, 1944–45; Adjt, 1st Bn Welsh Guards, Palestine, 1945–48; Bde Major, 4 Guards Bde, Germany, 1952–54; GSO1 (Instr.), Staff Coll., Camberley, 1956–59; GSO1 HQ 4 Div. BAOR, 1960–63; comd 1st Bn Welsh Guards, 1963–65; Principal Staff Off. to Dir of Ops, Borneo, 1965–66; comd 11 Armd Bde BAOR, 1966–68; comd Jt Operational Computer Projects Team, 1969–71; Dep. Comdt Staff Coll., Camberley, 1972–73; GOC Wales, 1973–76. Col, The Royal Welch Fusiliers, 1974–84. Pres., Guards' Golfing Soc., 1977. KStJ 1978. Order of Istiqlal (Jordan), 1946. *Recreations:* golf, shooting, travel, photography. *Address:* 5 Chelsea Square, SW3 6LF. *T:* 01–352 6187. *Clubs:* Royal and Ancient Golf; Royal Wimbledon Golf; Sunningdale Golf (Captain 1975).

LEUCHARS, Sir William (Douglas), KBE 1984 (MBE (mil.) 1959); ED (2 bars); Dominion President, New Zealand Returned Services Association Inc., since 1974; *b* 8 Aug. 1920; *s* of late James and Isabella Leuchars; *m* 1947, Mary Isbister Walter; three *s* one *d*. *Educ:* Scots College, NZ. New Zealand Army: Territorial Force, 1939–41; NZEF (to Captain), 1941–46; NZ Scottish Regt, Territorial Force (to Lt-Col), 1946–71; Returned Services Association: Pres., Tawa Branch, Wellington RSA, 1949–60, Life Mem., 1981; Mem. Council, Wellington RSA, 1950–57, 1967–71, Life Mem., 1981 (Mem. numerous Cttees, 1955–); Mem., Dominion Exec. Cttee, 1965–68, Dominion Vice-Pres., 1968–74; NZRSA Rep. on numerous bodies and overseas confs; Gold Star and Cert. of Merit, 1966, Gold Badge and Life Mem., 1985, NZRSA. Chm., Scots Coll. Bd of Governors, 1974– (Mem., 1968–); Founder Trustee, Nat. Paraplegic Trust, 1973–; President: Wellington Regional Employers' Assoc., 1975–77, 1983–84 (Mem., 1973–); NZ Employers' Fedn, 1984–86 (Mem. Exec., 1975–; Vice-Pres., 1975–77, 1984); Director: Tolley & Son Ltd, 1957–66 (Chm., 1963–66); Tolley Holdings Ltd, 1963–85; Tolley Industries Ltd, 1966–82; Asea Tolley Electric Co. Ltd, 1985–; Norwich Winterthur Insurance NZ Ltd, 1977–. *Recreation:* bowling (Patron, Tawa Services Bowling). *Address:* 45 Lohia Street, Khandallah, Wellington 4, New Zealand. *T:* 792.391. *Clubs:* various service clubs, NZ.

LEUCKERT, Jean Elizabeth, (Mrs Harry Leuckert); *see* Muir, J. E.

LEUPENA, Sir Tupua, GCMG 1986; MBE 1977; Governor General of Tuvalu, since 1986; *b* 2 Aug. 1922; *s* of Leupena Vaisua, Vaitupu, and Tolotea Vaisua (*née* Tavita), Niutao; *m* 1947, Annie Nitz, Vaitupu; four *s* three *d* (and one *s* decd). *Educ:* Ellice Is Govt Sch., Vaitupu; King George V Secondary Sch., Tarawa, Gilbert Is (now Republic of Kiribati). Clerk, Gilbert and Ellice Is Colony, 1941; Sgt, GEIC Labour Corps, 1944; Clerk 1945, Chief Clerk 1953, Resident Comr's office; transf. to Dist Admin as Asst Admin Officer, 1957, frequently serving in Gilbert Is and Ellice Is Dists, 1958–64 and 1967–69; District Commissioner: Phoenix Is Dist, 1965–66; Ocean Is, 1970–72; Dist Officer, Ellice Is District, 1973–75; acted as Sec. to Govt on Separation of Tuvalu from Kiribati in 1976 and retired from service same year; re-employed on contract as Sec. Reserved Subjects in Queen's Comr's Office, 1977; Speaker of Tuvalu Parlt, 1978; Man., Vaitupu's Private Commercial Enterprise, 1979–81; Chm., Tuvalu's Public Service Commn, 1982–86. *Recreations:* fishing, gardening, cricket, football. *Address:* Vaiaku, Funafuti Island, Tuvalu. *T:* 714.

LEUTWILER, Fritz, PhD; Chairman of the Board of Directors, BBC Brown, Boveri and Co. Ltd, Baden, since 1985; *b* 30 July 1924; *m* 1951, Andrée Cottier; one *s* one *d*. *Educ:* Univ. of Zürich (PhD 1948). Sec., Assoc. for a Sound Currency, 1948–52; Swiss National Bank, Zürich: Econ. Scientist, 1952–59; Manager, 1959–66; Dep. Gen. Man., 1966–68; Mem., Governing Bd, and Head, Dept III, 1968–74; Chm., Governing Bd, and Head, Dept I, 1974–84; Chm. and Pres., BIS, Basle, 1982–84. Hon. Dr: Berne, 1978; Zürich, 1983; Lausanne, 1984. *Recreations:* golf; collector of rare books (Helvetica, Economica). *Address:* Weizenacher 4, CH-8126 Zumikon, Switzerland. *T:* 01/918 03 36. *Club:* Golf and Country (Zumikon).

LEVEN, 14th Earl of, AND MELVILLE, 13th Earl of, *cr* 1641; **Alexander Robert Leslie Melville;** Baron Melville, 1616; Baron Balgonie, 1641; Earl of Melville, Viscount Kirkcaldie, 1690; Lord-Lieutenant of Nairn since 1969; *b* 13 May 1924; *e s* of 13th Earl and Lady Rosamond Sylvia Diana Mary Foljambe (*d* 1974), *d* of 1st Earl of Liverpool; *S* father, 1947; *m* 1953, Susan, *er d* of Lieut-Colonel R. Steuart-Menzies of Culdares, Arndilly House, Craigellachie, Banffshire; two *s* one *d*. *Educ:* Eton. ADC to Governor General of New Zealand, 1951–52. Formerly Capt. Coldstream Guards; retired, 1952. Vice-Pres., Highland Dist TA. Pres., British Ski Fedn, 1981–85. DL, County of Nairn, 1961; Convener, Nairn CC, 1970–74. Chm. Governors, Gordonstoun Sch., 1971–. *Heir:* *s* Lord

Balgonie, *qv. Address:* Glenferness House, Nairn. *T:* Glenferness 202. *Club:* Naval and Military.

LEVENE, Ben, ARA 1975; painter; *b* 23 Dec. 1938; *s* of Mark and Charlotte Levene. *Educ:* Slade School (DFA). Boise Scholarship, 1961; lived in Spain, 1961–62. First one-man show, 1973. *Address:* c/o Royal Academy of Arts, Piccadilly, W1.

LEVENE, Peter Keith; Chief of Defence Procurement, Ministry of Defence, since 1985; *b* 8 Dec. 1941; *s* of late Maurice Levene and Rose Levene; *m* 1966, Wendy Ann (*née* Fraiman); two *s* one *d. Educ:* City of London School; Univ. of Manchester, BA Econ. Joined United Scientific Holdings, 1963; Man. Dir, 1968–85; Chm., 1982–85. Member: SE Asia Trade Adv. Group, 1979–83; Council, Defence Manufacturers' Assoc., 1982– (Vice-Chm., 1983–84; Chm., 1984–85); Personal Adviser to Sec. of State for Defence, 1984. Mem., Bd of Management, London Homes for the Elderly, 1984–. Governor: City of London Sch. for Girls, 1984–85; City of London Sch., 1986–; Sir John Cass Primary Sch., 1985–. Mem. Court, HAC, 1984–; Mem., Court of Common Council, City of London, 1983–84 (Ward of Candlewick); Alderman (Ward of Portsoken), 1984–; Freeman, Carmen's Co., 1984. CBIM, FRSA. *Recreations:* skiing, watching association football, travel. *Address:* c/o Ministry of Defence, Main Building, Whitehall, SW1. *Clubs:* Guildhall, City Livery.

LEVENTHAL, Colin David; Head of Programme Acquisition, Channel Four Television Co. Ltd, since 1981; *b* 2 Nov. 1946; *s* of Morris and Olga Leventhal. *Educ:* Carmel Coll., Wallingford, Berks; King's Coll., Univ. of London (BA Philosophy). Solicitor of Supreme Court of England and Wales. Admitted Solicitor, 1971; BBC, 1974–81: Asst Head of Programme Contracts, 1977; Head of Copyright, 1978. *Recreations:* theatre, film. *Address:* 60 Charlotte Street, W1. *T:* 01–631 4444.

LEVER, family name of **Baron Lever of Manchester** and of **Viscount Leverhulme.**

LEVER OF MANCHESTER, Baron *cr* 1979 (Life Peer), of Cheetham in the City of Manchester; **Harold Lever,** PC 1969; *b* Manchester, 15 Jan. 1914; *s* of late Bernard and Bertha Lever; *m* 1962, Diane, *d* of Saleh Bashi; three *d* (and one *d* from late wife). *Educ:* Manchester Grammar Sch.; Manchester Univ. Called to Bar, Middle Temple, 1935. MP (Lab) Manchester Exchange, 1945–50, Manchester, Cheetham, 1950–74, Manchester Central, 1974–79. Promoted Defamation Act, 1952, as a Private Member's Bill. Joint Parliamentary Under-Secretary, Dept of Economic Affairs, 1967; Financial Sec. to Treasury, Sept. 1967–69; Paymaster General, 1969–70; Chancellor of the Duchy of Lancaster, 1974–79. Chm., Public Accounts Cttee, 1970–73. Chairman: London Interstate Bank (Sparekassen SDS), 1984–; Stormgard, 1985–; Pres., Authority Investments PLC, 1986– (Chm., 1984–86); Mem., Internat. Adv. Bd, Creditanstalt-Bankverein, 1982; Dir, The Guardian and Manchester Evening News, 1979–. Treasurer, Socialist International, 1971–73. Governor: LSE, 1971–; E-SU, 1973–; Trustee, Royal Opera House, 1974–82; Mem. Ct, Manchester Univ., 1975–. Hon. Fellow, and Chm. Trustees, Royal Acad., 1981. Hon. doctorates in Law, Science, Literature and Technology. *Address:* House of Lords, SW1.

LEVER, Sir Christopher; *see* Lever, Sir T. C. A. L.

LEVER, Jeremy Frederick; QC 1972; *b* 23 June 1933; *s* of late A. Lever. *Educ:* Bradfield Coll.; University Coll., Oxford; Nuffield Coll., Oxford. Served RA, 1951–53. 1st cl. Jurisprudence, 1956, MA Oxon; Pres., Oxford Union Soc., 1957, Trustee, 1972–77. Fellow, All Souls Coll., Oxford, 1957– (Sub-Warden, 1982–84). Called to Bar, Gray's Inn, 1957, Bencher, 1985. Director (non-exec.): Dunlop Holdings Ltd, 1973–80; Wellcome plc, 1983–. Governor, Berkhamsted Schs, 1985–. *Publications:* The Law of Restrictive Practices, 1964; other legal works. *Recreations:* walking, music. *Address:* Gray's Inn Chambers, WC1R 5JA. *T:* 01–405 7211. *Club:* Garrick.

LEVER, John Michael, QC 1977; **His Honour Judge Lever;** a Circuit Judge, since 1981; *b* 12 Aug. 1928; *s* of late John Lever and Ida Donaldson Lever; *m* 1964, Elizabeth Marr; two *s. Educ:* Bolton Sch.; Gonville and Caius Coll., Cambridge (Schol.). BA (1st cl. hons Law Tripos), 1949. Flying Officer, RAF, 1950–52. Called to Bar, Middle Temple, 1951 (Blackstone Schol.); practised Northern Circuit from 1952; Asst Recorder, Salford, 1969–71; a Recorder of the Crown Court, 1972–81. Governor, Bolton Sch. *Recreations:* theatre, fell-walking. *Address:* Lakelands, Rivington, near Bolton, Lancs BL6 7RT.

LEVER, Paul; Head of Defence Department, Foreign and Commonwealth Office, since 1986; *b* 31 March 1944; *s* of John Morrison Lever and Doris Grace (*née* Battey). *Educ:* St Paul's Sch.; The Queen's Coll., Oxford (BA). 3rd Secretary, Foreign and Commonwealth Office, 1966–67; 3rd, later 2nd Secretary, Helsinki, 1967–71; 2nd, later 1st Secretary, UK Delegn to NATO, 1971–73; FCO, 1973–81; Asst Private Sec. to Sec. of State for Foreign and Commonwealth Affairs, 1978–81; Chef de Cabinet to Christopher Tugendhat, Vice-Pres. of EEC, 1982–84; Head of UN Dept, FCO, 1985–86. *Recreations:* squash, tennis, walking. *Address:* 20 Lancaster Mews, W2 3QE. *T:* 01–723 2507; Le Village, Oust, Pyrénées Orientales, France.

LEVER, Sir (Tresham) Christopher (Arthur Lindsay), 3rd Bt *cr* 1911; *b* 9 Jan. 1932; *s* of Sir Tresham Joseph Philip Lever, FRSL, 2nd Bt, and Frances Yowart (*d* 1959), *d* of Lindsay Hamilton Goodwin; step *s* of Pamela Lady Lever, *d* of late Lt-Col Hon. Malcolm Bowes-Lyon; *S* father, 1975; *m* 1st, 1970; 2nd, 1975, Linda Weightman McDowell, *d* of late James Jepson Goulden, Tennessee, USA. *Educ:* Eton; Trinity Coll., Cambridge (BA 1954, MA 1957). MBOU; FLS. Commissioned, 17th/21st Lancers, 1950. Dir, John Barran & Sons Ltd, 1956–64. Consultant, Zoo Check, 1984–; Trustee: Internat. Trust for Nature Conservation, 1980– (Vice-Pres. 1986); Migraine Trust, 1983–; Rhino Rescue Appeal, 1986– (Patron 1985–). Mem. Council, Soc. for Protection of Animals in N Africa. *Publications:* Goldsmiths and Silversmiths of England, 1975; The Naturalized Animals of the British Isles, 1977; (contrib.) Evolution of Domesticated Animals, 1984; Naturalized Mammals of the World, 1985; contribs to various fine art, scientific and general publications. *Recreations:* wildlife conservation, golf, fishing. *Heir:* none. *Address:* Newell House, Winkfield, Windsor, Berks SL4 4SE. *T:* Winkfield Row 882604. *Club:* Buck's.

LEVERHULME, 3rd Viscount, *cr* 1922, of the Western Isles; **Philip William Bryce Lever,** TD; Baron, *cr* 1917; Bt, *cr* 1911; Knight of Order of St John of Jerusalem; Major, Cheshire Yeomanry; Lord Lieutenant of City and County of Chester since 1949; Advisory Director of Unilever Ltd; Chancellor of Liverpool University, since 1980; *b* 1 July 1915; *s* of 2nd Viscount and Marion, *d* of late Bryce Smith of Manchester; *S* father, 1949; *m* 1937, Margaret Ann (*d* 1973), *o c* of John Moon, Tiverton; three *d. Educ:* Eton; Trinity Coll., Cambridge. Hon. Air Commodore 663 Air OP Squadron, RAuxAF; Hon. Air Commodore 610 (County of Chester) Squadron, Royal Auxiliary Air Force; Dep. Hon. Col, Cheshire Yeomanry, T&AVR, 1971–72. Hon. Col, 1972–81; Hon. Col, The Queen's Own Yeomanry, 1979–81. Pres. Council, Liverpool Univ., 1957–63, Sen. Pro-Chancellor, 1963–66. Member: National Hunt Cttee, 1961 (Steward, 1965–68); Deputy Senior Steward, Jockey Club, 1970–73, Senior Steward, 1973–76; Council of King George's Jubilee Trust; Chairman, Exec. Cttee Animal Health Trust, 1964. Hon. FRCS 1970; Hon. ARCVS 1975. Hon. LLD Liverpool, 1967. *Recreations:* shooting, hunting,

Heir: none. *Address:* Thornton Manor, Thornton Hough, Wirral, Merseyside; Badanloch, Kinbrace, Sutherland; Flat 6, Kingston House East, Prince's Gate, Kensington, SW7 1LJ. *Clubs:* Boodle's, Jockey.

LEVERSEDGE, Leslie Frank, CMG 1955; MA Cantab; Economic Secretary to Northern Rhodesia Government, 1956–60, retired; *b* 29 May 1904; *s* of F. E. Leversedge, UP, India; *m* 1945, Eileen Melegueta Spencer Payne; two *s* three *d. Educ:* St Paul's Sch., Darjeeling, India; St Peter's Sch., York; St John's Coll., Cambridge; Inner Temple, London. Cadet in Colonial Administrative Service, Northern Rhodesia, Dec. 1926; District Officer, Dec. 1928; Provincial Commissioner, Jan. 1947; Senior Provincial Commissioner, Dec. 1948. Development Secretary to Northern Rhodesia Government, 1951–56. MLC 1951; MEC 1951. British Council Local Correspondent for Kent, 1963–75. FRSA 1973. *Recreations:* walking, overseas travelling. *Address:* 24 Ashley Brake, West Hill, Ottery St Mary, Devon EX11 1TW. *T:* Ottery St Mary 3956.

LEVERTON, Colin Allen H.; *see* Hart-Leverton.

LEVESON, Lord; Granville George Fergus Leveson Gower; *b* 10 Sept. 1959; *s* and heir of 5th Earl Granville, *qv.*

LEVESON, Brian Henry; QC 1986; *b* 22 June 1949; *er s* of late Dr Ivan Leveson and Elaine Leveson, Liverpool; *m* 1981, Lynne Rose, *d* of Aubrey and Regina Fishel, Wallasey; one *s* one *d. Educ:* Liverpool College, Liverpool; Merton College, Oxford (MA). Called to the Bar, Middle Temple, 1970; Harmsworth Scholar, 1970; practised Northern Circuit, 1971; University of Liverpool: Lectr in Law, 1971–81; Mem. Council, 1983–. *Recreation:* golf. *Address:* 5 Essex Court, Temple, EC4Y 9AH. *T:* 01–353 4363; 25 Byrom Street, Manchester M3 4PF. *T:* 061–834 5238. *Clubs:* Athenæum (Liverpool); Woolton Golf.

LEVESON GOWER, family name of **Earl Granville.**

LEVESQUE, Most Rev. Louis, ThD; *b* 27 May 1908; *s* of Philippe Levesque and Catherine Levesque (*née* Beaulieu). *Educ:* Laval Univ. Priest, 1932; Bishop of Hearst, Ontario, 1952–64; Archbishop of Rimouski, 1967–73. Chm., Canadian Cath. Conf., 1965–67; Mem. Congregation Bishops, Rome, 1968–73. *Address:* 300 avenue du Rosaire, Rimouski, PQ G5L 3E3, Canada.

LÉVESQUE, Hon. René; Premier of Province of Québec, Canada, 1976–85; *b* 24 Aug. 1922; *s* of Dominique Lévesque and Diane Dionne; *m* Corinne Cote; two *s* one *d* by previous marriage. *Educ:* schs in New Carlisle and Gaspé; Québec Univ. (BA); Law Sch., Laval, Québec. Overseas duty as reporter with US Forces (attached to Office of War Information, Europe), 1944–45; reporter and commentator, Canadian Broadcasting Corp., 1946–59. Mem., Québec Nat. Assembly, 1960–70; Minister, Public Works, Natural Resources and Social Welfare, 1960–66; Mem. Opposition, 1966–70; Pres., Parti Québécois, 1966–85. Grand Médaille de Vermeil, 1977. Grand Officer, Legion of Honour, 1977. *Publications:* Option-Québec, 1968; La Passion du Québec, 1978; My Quebec, 1979; Oui, 1980. *Recreations:* tennis, swimming, skiing, reading, movies. *Address:* 91b d'Auteuil Street, Quebec City, PQ, Canada. *Club:* Cercle Universitaire (Québec).

LEVEY, Sir Michael (Vincent), Kt 1981; LVO 1965; MA Oxon and Cantab; FRSL; FBA 1983; Director of the National Gallery, 1973–87 (Deputy Director, 1970–73); *b* 8 June 1927; *s* of O. L. H. Levey and Gladys Mary Milestone; *m* 1954, Brigid Brophy, *qv*; one *d. Educ:* Oratory Sch.; Exeter Coll., Oxford, Hon. Fellow, 1973. Served with Army, 1945–48; commissioned, KSLI, 1946, and attached RAEC, Egypt. National Gallery: Asst Keeper, 1951–66, Dep. Keeper, 1966–68, Keeper, 1968–73. Slade Professor of Fine Art, Cambridge, 1963–64; Supernumerary Fellow, King's Coll., Cambridge, 1963–64. *Publications:* Six Great Painters, 1956; National Gallery Catalogues: 18th Century Italian Schools, 1956; The German School, 1959; Painting in 18th Century Venice, 1959, revd edn 1980; From Giotto to Cézanne, 1962; Dürer, 1964; The Later Italian Paintings in the Collection of HM The Queen, 1964; Canaletto Paintings in the Royal Collection, 1964; Tiepolo's Banquet of Cleopatra (Charlton Lecture, 1962), 1966; Rococo to Revolution, 1966; Bronzino (The Masters), 1967; Early Renaissance, 1967 (Hawthornden Prize, 1968); Fifty Works of English Literature We Could Do Without (co-author), 1967; Holbein's Christina of Denmark, Duchess of Milan, 1968; A History of Western Art, 1968; Painting at Court (Wrightsman Lectures), 1971; 17th and 18th Century Italian Schools (Nat. Gall. catalogue), 1971; The Life and Death of Mozart, 1971; The Nude: Themes and Painters in the National Gallery, 1972; (co-author) Art and Architecture in 18th Century France, 1972; The Venetian Scene (Themes and Painters Series), 1973; Botticelli (Themes and Painters Series), 1974; High Renaissance, 1975; The World of Ottoman Art, 1976; Jacob van Ruisdael (Themes and Painters Series), 1977; The Case of Walter Pater, 1978; Sir Thomas Lawrence (Nat. Portrait Gall. exhibn), 1979; The Painter Depicted (Neurath Lect.), 1981; Tempting Fate (fiction), 1982; An Affair on the Appian Way (fiction), 1984; (ed) Pater's Marius the Epicurean, 1985; Giambattista Tiepolo, 1986; contributions Burlington Magazine, etc. *Address:* 185 Old Brompton Road, SW5. *T:* 01–373 9335.

LEVI, Prof. Edward Hirsch; Glen A. Lloyd Distinguished Service Professor, University of Chicago, 1977–84, now Emeritus; *b* 26 June 1911; *s* of Gerson B. Levi and Elsa B. Levi (*née* Hirsch); *m* 1946, Kate Sulzberger; three *s. Educ:* Univ. of Chicago; Yale Univ. Law Sch. Univ. of Chicago: Asst Prof. of Law, 1936–40; Prof. of Law, 1945–75; Dean of the Law School, 1950–62; Provost, 1962–68; President, 1968–75; Pres. emeritus, 1975; Attorney-Gen. of US, 1975–77. Public Dir, Chicago Bd of Trade, 1977–80. Herman Phleger Vis. Prof., Stanford Law Soc., 1978. Special Asst to Attorney-Gen., Washington, DC, 1940–45; 1st Asst, War Div., Dept of Justice, 1943; 1st Asst, Anti-trust Div., 1944–45; Chm., Interdeptl Cttee on Monopolies and Cartels, 1944; Counsel, Subcttee on Monopoly Power Judiciary Cttee, 81st Congress, 1950; Member: White House Task Force on Educn, 1966–67; President's Task Force on Priorities in Higher Educn, 1969–70; White House Central Gp in Domestic Affairs, 1964; Citizens Commn on Graduate Medical Educn, 1963–66; Sloan Commn on Cable Communications, 1970–71; Nat. Commn on Productivity, 1970–75; Commn on Foundations and Private Philanthropy, 1969–70; Martin Luther King, Jr, Federal Holding Commn, 1985–86. Mem. Council, American Law Inst., 1965–; American Bar; Illinois Bar; Chicago Bar; Supreme Court, 1945–; Amer. Judicature Soc.; Council on Legal Educn for Profl. Responsibility, 1968–74; Order of Coif; Phi Beta Kappa; res. adv. bd, Commn Econ. Develt, 1951–54; bd Dirs, SSRC, 1959–62; Nat. Commn on Productivity, 1970–75; Nat. Council on the Humanities, 1974–75. Dir Emeritus, MacArthur Foundn, 1984– (Dir, 1979–84); Trustee: Internat. Legal Center; Museum of Science and Industry, 1971–75; Russell Sage Foundn, 1971–75; Aspen Inst. for Humanist Studies, 1970–75, 1977–79; Univ. Chicago, 1966; Woodrow Wilson Nat. Fellowship Foundn, 1972–75, 1977–79; Inst. Psycho-analysis, Chicago, 1961–75; Member Board of Trustees: Nat. Humanities Center, 1978– (Chm., 1979–83); The Aerospace Corp., 1978–80; William Benton Foundn, 1980–; Mem. Bd of Dirs, Continental Illinois Holding Corp., 1985–. Salzburg Seminar in Amer. Studies, 1980; Mem. Bd of Overseers, Univ. of Pennsylvania Law Sch., 1978–82; Pres., Amer. Acad. of Arts and Scis, 1986–; Hon. Trustee: Inst. of Internat. Educn; Univ. of Chicago,

1975. Fellow: Amer. Bar Foundn; Amer. Acad. Arts and Scis; Amer. Philos. Soc. Chubb Fellow, Yale, 1977. Hon. degrees: LHD: Hebrew Union Coll.; Loyola Univ.; DePaul Univ.; Kenyon Coll.; Univ. of Chicago; Bard Coll.; Beloit Coll.; LLD: Univ. of Michigan; Univ. of California at Santa Cruz; Univ. of Iowa; Jewish Theological Seminary of America; Brandeis Univ.; Lake Forest Coll.; Univ. of Rochester; Univ. of Toronto; Yale Univ.; Notre Dame; Denison Univ., Nebraska Univ. Law Sch.; Univ. of Miami; Boston Coll.; Ben N. Cardozo Sch. of Law, Yeshiva Univ., NYC; Columbia Univ., Dropsie Univ., Pa; Univ. of Pa Law Sch.; Brigham Young Univ.; Duke Univ.; Ripon Coll.; Georgetown Univ.; DCL NY Univ. Legion of Honour (France); Chicago Bar Assoc. Centennial Award, 1975; Distinguished Citizen Award, Ill St Andrews Soc., 1976; Herbert H. Lehman Ethics Medal, Jewish Theol. Seminary, 1976; Learned Hand Medal, Fedn Bar Council, NYC, 1976; Wallace Award, Amer.-Scottish Foundn, 1976; Morris J. Kaplun Meml Prize, Dropsie, 1976; Fed. Bar Assoc. Award, 1977; Louis Stein Award, Fordham, 1977; Citation of Merit, Yale, 1977; Louis Dembitz Brandeis Award, 1978; Illinois Bar Assoc. Award of Honor, 1983. *Publications:* Introduction to Legal Reasoning, 1949; Four Talks on Legal Education, 1952; Point of View, 1969; The Crisis in the Nature of Law, 1969; Elements of the Law (ed, with Roscoe Steffen), 1936; Gilbert's Collier on Bankruptcy (ed, with James W. Moore), 1936; Member, editorial board: Jl Legal Educn, 1956–68; Encyclopaedia Britannica, 1968–75. *Address:* (office) 1116 East 59th Street, Chicago, Illinois 60637, USA. *T:* (312) 962–8588; (home) 4950 Chicago Beach Drive, Chicago, Illinois 60615. *Clubs:* Quadrangle, Columbia Yacht, Mid-America (Chicago); Commercial, Century (New York); Chicago (DC).

LEVI, Peter Chad Tigar, FSA; FRSL; Professor of Poetry, University of Oxford, since 1984; Fellow of St Catherine's College, Oxford, since 1977; *b* 16 May 1931; *s* of Herbert Simon Levi and Edith Mary Tigar; *m* 1977, Deirdre, *o d* of Hon. Dennis Craig, MBE, and *widow* of Cyril Connolly, CBE, CLit. *Educ:* Beaumont; Oxford Univ. (MA). FSA 1976. Society of Jesus, 1948–77: priest, 1964; resigned priesthood, 1977. Tutor and Lectr in Classics, Campion Hall, Oxford, 1965–77; student, Brit. Sch. of Archaeol., Athens, 1965–68; Lectr in Classics, Christ Church, Oxford, 1979–82. The Times Archaeol Correcpondent, 1977–78. Corres. mem., Soc. of Greek Writers, 1983. Television films: Ruined Abbeys, 1966; Foxes have holes, 1967; Seven black years, 1975. *Publications: poetry:* The Gravel Ponds, 1960; Water, Rock and Sand, 1962; The Shearwaters, 1965; Fresh Water, Sea Water, 1966; Ruined Abbeys, 1968; Pancakes for the Queen of Babylon, 1968; Life is a Platform, 1971; Death is a Pulpit, 1971; Collected Poems, 1976; Five Ages, 1978; Private Ground, 1981; The Echoing Green, 1983; (ed) The Penguin Book of English Christian Verse, 1985; Shakespeare's Birthday, 1985; *prose:* Beaumont, 1961; *'Ο τόνος τῆς φωνῆς τοῦ Σεφέρη* (Mr Seferis' Tone of Voice), 1970; The Lightgarden of the Angel King, 1973; The English Bible (1534–1859), 1974; In Memory of David Jones, 1975; John Clare and Thomas Hardy, 1975; The Noise made by Poems, 1976; The Head in the Soup, 1979; The Hill of Kronos, 1980; Atlas of the Greek World, 1980; The Flutes of Autumn, 1983; (ed) Johnson and Boswell, Western Islands, 1984; Grave Witness, 1985; A History of Greek Literature, 1985; *translations:* Yevtushenko, 1962; Pausanias, 1971; Pavlopoulos, The Cellar, 1976; The Psalms, 1976; Marko the Prince (Serbo-Croat heroic verse), 1983; Papadiamantis, The Murderess, 1983; The Holy Gospel of John, a New Translation, 1985. *Recreations:* music, museums, architecture, country pursuits. *Address:* Austin's Farm, Stonesfield, Oxford. *T:* Stonesfield 726. *Club:* Beefsteak.

LÉVI-STRAUSS, Claude; Grand Officier de la Légion d'Honneur; Commandeur, Ordre Nationale du Mérite, 1971; Member of French Academy, since 1973; Professor, Collège de France, 1959–82, Hon. Professor, since 1983; *b* 28 Nov. 1908; *s* of Raymond Lévi-Strauss and Emma Lévy; *m* 1st, 1932, Dina Dreyfus; 2nd, 1946, Rose-Marie Ullmo; one *s*; 3rd, 1954, Monique Roman; one *s*. *Educ:* Lycée Janson-de-Sailly, Paris; Sorbonne. Prof., Univ. of São Paulo, Brazil, 1935–39; Vis. Prof., New School for Social Research, NY, 1941–45; Cultural Counsellor, French Embassy, Washington, 1946–47; Associate Curator, Musée de l'Homme, Paris, 1948–49. Corresp. Member: Royal Acad. of Netherlands; Norwegian Acad.; British Acad.; Nat. Acad. of Sciences, USA; Amer. Acad. and Inst. of Arts and Letters; Amer. Museum of Natural History; Amer. Philos. Soc.; Royal Anthrop. Inst. of Great Britain; London Sch. of African and Oriental Studies. Hon. Dr: Brussels, 1962; Oxford, 1964; Yale, 1965; Chicago, 1967; Columbia, 1971; Stirling, 1972; Univ. Nat. du Zaïre, 1973; Uppsala, 1977; Johns Hopkins, 1978; Laval, 1979; Mexico, 1979; Visva Bharati, India, 1980. *Publications:* La Vie familiale et sociale des Indiens Nambikwara, 1948; Les Structures élémentaires de la parenté, 1949 (The Elementary Structures of Kinship, 1969); Race et histoire, 1952; Tristes Tropiques, 1955, complete edn, 1973 (A World on the Wane, 1961); Anthropologie structurale, Vol. 1, 1958, Vol. 2, 1973 (Structural Anthropology, Vol. 1, 1964, Vol. 2, 1977); Le Totémisme aujourd'hui, 1962 (Totemism, 1963); La Pensée sauvage, 1962 (The Savage Mind, 1966); Le Cru et le cuit, 1964 (The Raw and the Cooked, 1970); Du Miel aux cendres, 1967 (From Honey to Ashes, 1973); L'Origine des manières de table, 1968 (The Origin of Table Manners, 1978); L'Homme nu, 1971 (The Naked Man, 1981); La Voie des masques, 1975 (The Way of the Masks, 1982); Le Regard éloigné, 1983 (The View from Afar, 1985); Paroles Données, 1984; La Potière Jalouse, 1985; *relevant publications:* Conversations with Lévi-Strauss (ed G. Charbonnier), 1969; by Octavio Paz: On Lévi-Strauss, 1970; Claude Lévi-Strauss: an introduction, 1972. *Address:* 2 rue des Marronniers, 75016 Paris, France. *T:* 4288–34–71.

LEVICK, William Russell, FRS 1982; FAA; Professor, John Curtin School of Medical Research, Australian National University, since 1983; *b* 5 Dec. 1931; *s* of Russell L. S. Levick and Elsie E. I. (*née* Nance); *m* 1961, Patricia Jane Lathwell; two *s* one *d*. *Educ:* Univ. of Sydney (BSc 1st Cl. Hons, MSc, MB, BS 1st Cl. Hons). Registered Medical Practitioner, State of NSW. FAA 1973. RMO, Royal Prince Alfred Hosp., Sydney, 1957–58; National Health and Med. Res. Council Fellow, Univ. of Sydney, 1959–62; C. J. Martin Travelling Fellow, Cambridge Univ. and Univ. of Calif, Berkeley, 1963–64; Associate Res. Physiologist, Univ. of Calif, Berkeley, 1965–66; Sen. Lectr in Physiol., Univ. of Sydney, 1967; Professorial Fellow of Physiology, John Curtin Sch. of Medicine, ANU, 1967–83. Fellow, Optical Soc. of America, 1977. *Publications:* articles on neurophysiology of the visual system in internat. scientific jls. *Address:* Department of Physiology, John Curtin School of Medical Research, Australian National University, Canberra, ACT 2601, Australia. *T:* (62)–49–2525.

LEVIN, (Henry) Bernard; journalist and author; *b* 19 Aug. 1928; *s* of late Phillip Levin and Rose (*née* Racklin). *Educ:* Christ's Hospital; LSE, Univ. of London. BSc (Econ.). Has written regularly or irregularly for many newspapers and magazines in Britain and abroad, 1953–, principally The Times, Sunday Times, Observer, Manchester Guardian, Truth, Spectator, Daily Express, Daily Mail, Newsweek, International Herald-Tribune; has written and broadcast for radio and television, 1952–, incl. BBC and most ITV cos. Pres., English Assoc., 1984–85, Vice-Pres., 1985–. Various awards for journalism. Hon. Fellow, LSE, 1977–. Mem., Order of Polonia Restituta (by Polish Government-in-Exile), 1976. *Publications:* The Pendulum Years, 1971; Taking Sides, 1979; Conducted Tour, 1981; Speaking Up, 1982; Enthusiasms, 1983; The Way We Live Now, 1984; A Shakespeare Mystery (English Assoc. Presidential address), 1985; Hannibal's Footsteps, 1985; In These Times, 1986. *Address:* c/o Curtis Brown Ltd, 162–168 Regent Street, W1.

LEVIN, Richard, OBE 1952; RDI 1971; photographer, since 1975; *b* 31 Dec. 1910; *s* of Henry Levin and Margaret Sanders; *m* 1st, 1932, Evelyn Alexander; two *d*; 2nd, 1960, Patricia Foy, Producer, BBC TV. *Educ:* Clayesmore; Slade, UC London. Assistant Art Director, Gaumont British, 1928; private practice; exhibition; graphic and industrial designer working for BBC, C. C. Wakefield Ltd, Bakelite Ltd, LEB, etc, 1931–39; Camouflage Officer, Air Ministry, 1940; MOI Exhibn Div.; Designer, British Army Exhibns, UK and Paris, 1943; private practice, 1946; Designer, Festival of Britain, Land Travelling Exhibn, 1951; Head of Design, BBC Television, 1953–71. FSIAD 1955. Silver Medal, Royal Television Soc., 1972. *Publications:* Television by Design, 1960; Design for Television (BBC lunch-time lecture), 1968. *Recreation:* fishing. *Address:* Sandells House, West Amesbury, Wilts SP4 7BH. *T:* Amesbury 23857.

LEVINE, Sir Montague (Bernard), Kt 1979; general practitioner; Assistant Deputy Coroner, Inner South London; Clinical Tutor in General Practice, St Thomas' Hospital, since 1972; *b* 15 May 1922; *s* of late Philip Levine and of Bessie Levine; *m* 1959, Dr Rose Gold; one *s* one *d*. *Educ:* Royal Coll. of Surgeons in Ireland (LRCSI); Royal Coll. of Physicians in Ireland (MRCPI, LRCPI, LM). DMJ Clin.; MRCGP. Licentiate of Rubber Industry, 1944. Industrial physicist, rubber industry, 1939–45; House Surgeon: Royal Victoria Hosp., Bournemouth, 1955; Meath Hosp., Dublin, 1955; Metrop. Police Surg., 1960–66. Royal Coll. of Surgeons in Ireland: Stoney Meml Gold Medal in Anatomy, 1951; Silver Medallist, Medicine, 1953, Pathology, 1953, and Medical Jurisprudence, 1954; Macnaughton Gold Medal in Obs and Gynae., 1955; Lectr in Anat., 1956. *Publication:* Inter-parental Violence and its Effect on Children, 1975. *Recreations:* fishing, photography, painting. *Address:* Gainsborough House, 120 Ferndene Road, Herne Hill, SE24 0AA. *T:* 01–274 5554. *Club:* Organon.

LEVINE, Sydney; a Recorder, North-Eastern Circuit, since 1975; *b* 4 Sept. 1923; *s* of Rev. Isaac Levine and Mrs Miriam Levine; *m* 1959, Cécile Rona Rubinstein; three *s* one *d*. *Educ:* Bradford Grammar Sch.; Univ. of Leeds (LLB). Called to the Bar, Inner Temple, 1952; Chambers in Bradford, 1953–. *Recreations:* music, gardening, amateur theatre. *Address:* 2A Primley Park Road, Leeds 17. *T:* Leeds 683769.

LEVINGE, Sir Richard (George Robin), 12th Bt *cr* 1704; farming since 1968; *b* 18 Dec. 1946; *s* of Sir Richard Vere Henry Levinge, 11th Bt, MBE, TD, and of Barbara Mary, *d* of late George Jardine Kidston, CMG; *S* father, 1984; *m* 1st, 1969, Hilary (marr. diss. 1978), *d* of Dr Derek Mark; two *s* one *d*; 2nd, 1978, Donna Maria d'Ardia Caracciolo. *Educ:* Brook House, Bray, Co. Wicklow; Hawkhurst Court, West Sussex; Mahwah High School, New York; Craibstone Agricultural Coll. *Heir:* *s* Richard Mark Levinge, *b* 15 May 1970. *Address:* Clohamon House, Bunclody, Co. Wexford, Ireland. *T:* 054–77253.

LEVIS, Maj.-Gen. Derek George, CB 1972; OBE 1951; DL; retired; *b* 24 Dec. 1911; *er s* of late Dr George Levis, Lincoln; *m* 1st, 1938, Doris Constance Tall (*d* 1984); one *d*; 2nd, 1984, Charlotte Anne Nichols, *y d* of late Charles Pratt, Lincoln. *Educ:* Stowe Sch.; Trinity Coll., Cambridge; St Thomas' Hospital, London. BA Cantab 1933; MRCS, LRCP 1936; MB, BChir (Cantab), 1937; DPH 1949. Commnd into RAMC, 1936; house appts, St Thomas' Hospital, 1936–37; served in: China, 1937–39; War of 1939–45 (1939–45 Star, Pacific Star, France and Germany Star, Defence and War Medal): Malaya and Java, 1939–42; Ceylon, 1942–43; NW Europe, 1944–45; qualified as specialist in Army Health, RAM Coll., 1949; Asst Director Army Health, HQ British Troops Egypt, 1949–51; Deputy Asst Dir Army Health, HQ British Commonwealth Forces, Korea, 1952–53 (Korean Co. Medal and UN Medal); Asst Dir Army Health: Malaya Comd, 1953–55 (Gen. Service Medal, Clasp Malaya, despatches); War Office, 1956–58; Deputy Director, Army Health, HQ, BAOR, 1958–62; Comdt Army School of Health, 1962–66; Director of Army Health, Australian Military Forces, Melbourne, 1966–68; Dep. Director Army Health, HQ Army Strategic Comd, 1968; Director of Army Health, MoD (Army), 1968–70; Dep. Dir, Medical Services, Southern Comd, 1970–71. QHP 1969–71. Col Comdt, RAMC, 1973–76. Co. Comr, St John Ambulance Brigade, Lincs, 1972–85. Mem., Faculty of Community Physicians, RCP, 1971. DL Lincs, 1976. KStJ 1983. *Publications:* contribs to Journal RAMC and Proc. Royal Society Med. *Recreations:* fishing, reading. *Address:* 27 The Green, Welbourn, Lincoln LN5 0NJ. *T:* Loveden 72673.

LEVY, Sir Bruce; *see* Levy, Sir E. B.

LEVY, Dennis Martyn; QC 1982; *b* 20 Feb. 1936; *s* of Conrad Levy and Tillie (*née* Swift); *m* 1967, Rachel Jonah; one *s* one *d*. *Educ:* Clifton Coll.; Gonville and Caius Coll., Cambridge (MA). Called to the Bar, Gray's Inn, 1960. Granada Group Ltd, 1960–63; Time Products Ltd, 1963–66; in practice at the Bar, 1966–. *Recreations:* reading, especially tall stories; visiting, especially opera houses, the Barbican and the South Bank; walking, especially on Hampstead Heath. *Address:* 5 Vale Close, W9 1RR. *T:* 01–286 1368.

LEVY, Sir (Enoch) Bruce, Kt 1953; OBE 1950; retired, 1951; *b* 19 Feb. 1892; *s* of William and Esther Ann Levy; *m* 1925, Phyllis R., *d* of G. H. Mason; no *c*. *Educ:* Primary Sch.; Banks Commercial Coll.; Victoria University College (BSc). Brought up on farm to age 18; appointed Dept Agriculture, 1911; agrostologist to 1937; charge seed-testing station. Ecological studies Grasslands and indigenous vegetative cover of NZ; transferred to DSIR, 1937, and appointed Director Grasslands Division; Director Green-keeping Research; Chairman NZ Institute for Turf Culture (Life Mem. 1957); Official Rep. International Grassland Conference, Great Britain, 1937, Netherlands, 1949; Lecture tour, Great Britain, 1949–50; Member: Rotary International; Grassland Assoc. (Life Mem. 1951); NZ Animal Production Society (Life Mem. 1961); Manawatu Catchment Board; Central Standing Cttee, Soil Conservation; Trustee, Grassland Memorial Trust (Chm. 1966–68). Life Member NZ Royal Agric. Society, 1956. Hon. Dr of Science, University of NZ; R. B. Bennett Empire Prize, 1951 (Royal Society of Arts, London). *Publications:* Grasslands of New Zealand, 1943 (revised and enlarged, 1951, 1955 and 1970); Construction, Renovation and Care of the Bowling Green, 1949; Construction, Renovation and Care of the Golf Course, 1950; 150 scientific papers in popular and scientific journals in NZ and overseas. *Recreations:* bowling, gardening. *Address:* Main Waihi Road, RDI, Tauranga, New Zealand. *T:* 64–522.

LEVY, Sir Ewart Maurice, 2nd Bt *cr* 1913; *b* 10 May 1897; *o s* of Sir Maurice Levy, 1st Bt; *S* father, 1933; *m* 1932, Hylda (*d* 1970), *e d* of late Sir Albert Levy; one *d*. *Educ:* Harrow. High Sheriff of Leicestershire, 1937; served, 1940–45, Royal Pioneer Corps, Lieut-Colonel, 1944; BLA, 1944–45 (despatches). JP Co. Leicester. *Heir:* none. *Address:* Welland House, Weston-by-Welland, Market Harborough, Leicestershire. *Club:* Reform.

LEVY, George Joseph; Chairman, H. Blairman & Sons Ltd, since 1965; *b* 21 May 1927; *s* of Percy and Maude Levy; *m* 1952, Wendy Yetta Blairman; one *s* three *d*. *Educ:* Oundle Sch. Joined H. Blairman & Sons Ltd (Antique Dealers), 1950, Dir, 1955. Pres., British Antique Dealers Assoc., 1974–76. Chairman: Grosvenor House Antiques Fair, 1978–79; Somerset Hse Art Treasures Exhibn, 1979; Burlington Hse Fair, 1980–82; Friends of the Iveagh Bequest, Kenwood, 1978–; London Historic House Museums Liaison Gp, English Heritage, 1985–; Mem. Council, Jewish Museum, 1980–. *Recreations:* tennis, photography. *Address:* 27 Oakhill Avenue, NW3 7RD. *T:* 01–435 9528.

LEVY, Prof. John Court, OBE 1984; CEng, FIMechE, FRAeS; FCGI; Director, Engineering Profession, Engineering Council, since 1983; *b* London, 16 Feb. 1926; *s* of Alfred and Lily Levy; *m* 1952, Sheila Frances Krisman; two *s* one *d. Educ:* Owens Sch., London; Imperial Coll., Univ. of London (BScEng, ACGI, PhD); Univ. of Illinois, USA (MS). Stressman, Boulton-Paul Aircraft, 1945–47; Asst to Chief Engr, Fullers Ltd, 1947–51. Asst Lectr, Northampton Polytechnic, London, 1951–53; Fulbright Award to Univ. of Illinois, for research into metal fatigue, 1953–54; Lectr, Sen. Lectr, Reader, Northampton Polytechnic (later City Univ.), 1954–66; also a Recognised Teacher of the Univ. of London, 1958–66; Head of Department of Mechanical Engineering, 1966–83 (now Prof. Emeritus), and Pro-Vice-Chancellor, 1975–81, City Univ. Consultant to Shell International Marine, 1963–85; Chairman, 1st Panel on Marine Technology, SRC, 1971–73; Chm., Chartered Engr Section, Engineers Registration Bd, CEI, 1978–82; non-exec. Dir, City Technology Ltd, 1980–. *Publications:* papers on metal fatigue, marine technology, engrg educn, IMechE, RAeS, etc. *Recreations:* theatre, chess, exploring cities. *Address:* 18 Woodberry Way, Finchley, N12 0HG. *T:* 01–445 5227. *Club:* Island Sailing (Cowes, IoW).

LEVY, Prof. Philip Marcus, PhD, FBPsS; Professor of Psychology, University of Lancaster, since 1972; *b* 4 Feb. 1934; *s* of late Rupert Hyam Levy and of Sarah Beatrice Levy; *m* 1958, Gillian Mary (*née* Harker); two *d. Educ:* Leeds Modern School; Univ. of Leeds (BA 1955); Univ. of Birmingham (PhD 1960). FBPsS. Res. Fellow, Birmingham Univ., 1955–59; Psychologist, RAF, 1959–62; Sen. Res. Fellow, Lectr, Sen. Lectr, Birmingham Univ., 1962–72. Economic and Social Research Council (formerly Social Science Research Council): Mem. Council, 1983–; Mem., Psychol. Cttee, 1976–82 (Chm., 1979–82); Chm., Educn and Human Develt Cttee, 1982–. British Psychological Society: Mem. Council, 1973–80; Pres., 1978–79. Editor, Brit. Jl of Mathematical and Statistical Psychology, 1975–80. *Publications:* (ed with H. Goldstein) Tests in Education: a book of critical reviews, 1984; numerous in psychol jls. *Address:* Department of Psychology, University of Lancaster, Lancaster LA1 4YF. *T:* Lancaster 65201.

LEWANDO, Sir Jan (Alfred), Kt 1974; CBE 1968; *b* 31 May 1909; *s* of Maurice Lewando and Eugenie Lewando (*née* Goldsmid); *m* 1948, Nora Slavouski; three *d. Educ:* Manchester Grammar Sch.; Manchester University. Served War of 1939–45, British Army: British Army Staff, Washington DC and British Min. of Supply Mission, 1941–45 (Lt-Col, 1943). Marks & Spencer Ltd, 1929–70 (Dir 1954–70); Chairman: Carrington Viyella Ltd, 1970–75; Consolidated Textile Mills Ltd, Canada, 1972–75; Pres., Carrington Viyella Inc. (USA), 1971–75; Director: Carrington Tesit (Italy), 1971–75; Heal and Son Holdings, 1975–82 (Dep. Chm., 1977–82); Bunzl PLC (formerly Bunzl Pulp & Paper Ltd), 1976–86; W. A. Baxter & Sons Ltd, 1975–; Johnston Group Inc. (USA) (formerly Johnston Industries Inc.), 1976–85; Edgars Stores Ltd (South Africa), 1976–82; Royal Worcester Spode Ltd, 1978–79; Bunzl and Biach AG (Austria), 1979–80; Johnston Industries Ltd, 1980–85; Chm., Gelvenor Textiles Ltd, S Africa, 1973–75. Vice Chm., Clothing Export Council, 1966–70; Pres., British Textile Confedn, 1972–73; Vice Pres., Comitextil, Brussels, 1972–73; Member: British Overseas Trade Bd, 1972–77 (Mem., European Trade Cttee, 1973–83); British Overseas Trade Adv. Council, 1975–77; BNEC, 1969–71 (Chm., Area Export Cttee for Israel, 1968–71); British Overseas Trade Group for Israel, 1977–; Council, UK-S Africa Trade Assoc., 1973–; Export Council for Europe, 1965–69; European Steering Cttee, CBI, 1968–71; Grand Council, CBI, 1971–75. Vice-Pres., Transport Trust, 1973–. Chm., Appeal Cttee, British Inst. of Radiology, 1979–84. CBIM 1980 (FBIM 1972); FRSA 1973. Companion, Textile Inst., 1972. Order of Legion of Merit (USA), 1946. *Address:* Davidge House, Knotty Green, Beaconsfield, Bucks. *T:* Beaconsfield 4987.

LEWEN, John Henry, CMG 1977; HM Diplomatic Service, retired; Ambassador to the People's Republic of Mozambique, 1975–79; *b* 6 July 1920; *s* of Carl Henry Lewen and Alice (*née* Mundy); *m* 1945, Emilienne Alette Julie Alida Galant; three *s. Educ:* Christ's Hospital; King's Coll., Cambridge. Royal Signals, 1940–45. HM Foreign (subseq. Diplomatic) Service, 1946; HM Embassy: Lisbon, 1947–50; Rangoon, 1950–53; FO, 1953–55; HM Embassy: Rio de Janeiro, 1955–59; Warsaw, 1959–61; FO, 1961–63; Head of Chancery, HM Embassy, Rabat, 1963–67; Consul-General, Jerusalem, 1967–70; Inspector of HM Diplomatic Estabts, 1970–73; Dir, Admin and Budget, Secretariat-Gen. of Council of Ministers of European Communities, 1973–75. OStJ 1969. *Recreations:* singing, sailing. *Address:* 1 Brimley Road, Cambridge CB4 2DQ. *T:* Cambridge 359101.

LEWER, Michael Edward, QC 1983; a Recorder of the Crown Court, since 1983; *b* 1 Dec. 1933; *s* of late Stanley Gordon Lewer and Jeanie Mary Lewer; *m* 1965, Bridget Mary Gill; two *s* two *d. Educ:* Tonbridge Sch.; Oriel Coll., Oxford (MA). Called to Bar, Gray's Inn, 1958. *Address:* Farrar's Building, Temple, EC4. *T:* 01–583 9241.

LEWERS, Very Rev. Benjamin Hugh; Provost of Derby, since 1981; *b* 25 March 1932; *s* of Hugh Bunnett Lewers and Coral Helen Lewers; *m* 1957, Sara Blagden; three *s. Educ:* Sherborne School; Selwyn Coll., Cambridge (MA); Lincoln Theological Coll. Employee, Dunlop Rubber Co., 1953–57. Curate, St Mary, Northampton, 1962–65; Priest-in-charge, Church of the Good Shepherd, Hounslow, 1965–68; Industrial Chaplain, Heathrow Airport, 1968–75; Vicar of Newark, 1975–80, Rector 1980–81. A Church Commissioner, 1985–. *Recreations:* cricket, music, gardening, wine and rug making. *Address:* The Provost's House, 9 Highfield Road, Derby DE3 1GX. *T:* Derby 42971.

LEWES, Suffragan Bishop of, since 1977; **Rt. Rev. Peter John Ball,** CGA; Prebendary of Chichester Cathedral, since 1978; *b* 14 Feb. 1932; *s* of Thomas James and Kathleen Obena Bradley Ball. *Educ:* Lancing; Queens' Coll., Cambridge; Wells Theological College. MA (Nat. Sci.). Ordained, 1956; Curate of Rottingdean, 1956–58; Co-founder and Brother of Monastic Community of the Glorious Ascension, 1960 (Prior, 1960–77). Fellow of Woodard Corporation, 1962–71; Member: Archbishops' Council of Evangelism, 1965–68; Midlands Religious Broadcasting Council of the BBC, 1967–69. Archbishop of Canterbury's Adviser to HMC, 1985–. *Recreations:* squash (Cambridge Blue, 1953) and music. *Address:* The Rectory, Litlington, Polegate, East Sussex BN26 5RB. *T:* Alfriston 870387.

See also Bishop of Jarrow.

LEWES, John Hext, OBE 1944; Lieutenant of Dyfed, 1974–78 (Lord Lieutenant of Cardiganshire, 1956–74); *b* 16 June 1903; *s* of late Colonel John Lewes, RA, and of Mrs Lewes (*née* Hext); *m* 1929, Nesta Cecil, *d* of late Captain H. Fitzroy Talbot, DSO, RN; one *s* two *d. Educ:* RN Colleges Osborne and Dartmouth. Sub-Lieut, 1923, Lieut, 1925; specialised in Torpedoes, 1928; Commander, 1939; commanded: HMS Shikari, Intrepid, 1941–42 (despatches); Ameer, 1944–45 (despatches); retired 1947, with war service rank of Captain, RN. Now farming. FRAgSs 1972. KStJ 1964. *Address:* Llanllyr, near Lampeter, Dyfed. *T:* Aeron 470323.

LEWES AND HASTINGS, Archdeacon of; *see* Godden, Ven. M. L.

LEWIN, family name of **Baron Lewin.**

LEWIN, Baron *cr* 1982 (Life Peer), of Greenwich in Greater London; **Admiral of the Fleet Terence Thornton Lewin,** KG 1983; GCB 1976 (KCB 1973); LVO 1958; DSC 1942; Chief of the Defence Staff, 1979–82; *b* Dover, 19 Nov. 1920; *m* 1944, Jane Branch-Evans; two *s* one *d. Educ:* The Judd Sch., Tonbridge. Joined RN, 1939; War Service in Home and Mediterranean Fleets in HMS Valiant, HMS Ashanti in Malta Convoys, N Russian Convoys, invasion N Africa and Channel (despatches); comd HMS Corunna, 1955–56; Comdr HM Yacht Britannia, 1957–58; Captain (F) Dartmouth Training Squadron and HM Ships Urchin and Tenby, 1961–63; Director, Naval Tactical and Weapons Policy Division, MoD, 1964–65; comd HMS Hermes, 1966–67; Asst Chief of Naval Staff (Policy), 1968–69; Flag Officer, Second-in-Comd, Far East Fleet, 1969–70; Vice-Chief of the Naval Staff, 1971–73; C-in-C Fleet, 1973–75; C-in-C Naval Home Command, 1975–77; Chief of Naval Staff and First Sea Lord, 1977–79. Flag ADC to the Queen, 1975–77; First and Principal ADC to the Queen, 1977–79. Chm., Brooke Marine, 1985–. Chm., White Ensign Assoc. Ltd, 1983–. Trustee, National Maritime Museum, 1981–; Mem., Museums and Galleries Commn, 1983–; President: Shipwrecked Fishermen and Mariners' Royal Benevolent Soc., 1984–; British Schools Exploring Soc., 1985–. Elder Brother of Trinity House, 1975; Hon. Freeman: Skinners' Co., 1976; Shipwrights' Co., 1978. Hon. DSc City, 1978. *Address:* House of Lords, SW1A 0PW.

LEWIS, family name of **Barony of Merthyr.**

LEWIS, Maj.-Gen. Alfred George, CBE 1969; *b* 23 July 1920; *s* of Louis Lewis; *m* 1946, Daye Neville, *d* of Neville Greaves Hunt; two *s* two *d. Educ:* St Dunstan's Coll.; King's Coll., London. Served War of 1939–45, India and Burma. Commanded 15th/19th Hussars, 1961–63; Dir, Defence Operational Requirements Staff, MoD, 1967–68; Dep. Comdt, Royal Mil. Coll. of Science, 1968–70; Dir Gen., Fighting Vehicles and Engineer Equipment, 1970–72, retired 1973. Man. Dir, 1973–80, Dep. Chm., 1980–81, Alvis Ltd; Dep. Chm., Self Changing Gears Ltd, 1976–81; Company Secretary: Leyland Vehicles, 1980–81; Bus Manufacturers (Hldgs), 1980–84; Staff Dir, BL plc, 1981–84. Hon. Col, Queen's Own Mercian Yeomanry, 1977–82. FIIM 1975. *Recreations:* shooting, golf, gardening. *Address:* c/o National Westminster Bank, Sydenham, SE26. *Club:* Cavalry and Guards.

LEWIS, Sir Allen (Montgomery), GCMG 1979; GCVO 1985; Kt 1968; Governor-General of St Lucia, since 1982 (first Governor-General, 1979–80; Governor, 1974–79); *b* 26 Oct. 1909; *s* of George Ferdinand Montgomery Lewis and Ida Louisa (*née* Barton); *m* 1936, Edna Leofrida Theobalds; three *s* two *d. Educ:* St Mary's Coll., St Lucia. LLB Hons (external) London, 1941. Admitted to practice at Bar of Royal Court, St Lucia (later Supreme Court of Windward and Leeward Islands), 1931; called to English Bar, Middle Temple, 1946; in private practice, Windward Islands, 1931–59; Acting Magistrate, St Lucia, 1940–41; Acting Puisne Judge, Windward and Leeward Islands, 1955–56; QC 1956; Judge: of Federal Supreme Court, 1959–62; of British Caribbean Court of Appeal, 1962; of Court of Appeal, Jamaica, 1962–67; Acting President, Court of Appeal, 1966; Acting Chief Justice of Jamaica, 1966; Chief Justice, West Indies Associated States Supreme Court, 1967–72; Chm., Nat. Develt Corp., St Lucia, 1972–74. MLC, St Lucia, 1943–51; Member, Castries Town Council, 1942–56 (Chairman six times); President W Indies Senate, 1958–59. Served on numerous Government and other public cttees; Comr for reform and revision of laws of St Lucia, 1954–58; rep. St Lucia, Windward Islands, and W Indies at various Conferences. Director, St Lucia Branch, British Red Cross Society, 1955–59; President: Grenada Boy Scouts' Assoc., 1967–72; St John Council for St Lucia, 1975–80. Served as President and/or Cttee Member, cricket, football and athletic associations, St Lucia, 1936–59. Chancellor, Univ. of WI, 1975–; Hon. LLD Univ. of WI, 1974. Chief Scout, St Lucia, 1976–80, 1984–. Coronation Medal, 1953; Silver Jubilee Medal, 1977. KStJ. *Publication:* Revised Edition of Laws of St Lucia, 1957. *Recreations:* gardening, swimming. *Address:* Government House, Castries, St Lucia. *T:* 809–45–22481; Beaver Lodge, The Morne, PO Box 1076, Castries, St Lucia. *T:* 809–45–22281. *Clubs:* St Lucia Golf, St Lucia Yacht.

LEWIS, (Alun) Kynric, QC 1978; a Recorder of the Crown Court, since 1979; *b* Harlech, 23 May 1928; 3rd *s* of late Rev. Cadwaladr O. Lewis and Ursula Lewis; *m* 1955, Bethan, *er d* of late Prof. Edgar Thomas, CBE, and Eurwen Thomas; one *s* two *d. Educ:* The Grammar School, Beaumaris; University Coll. of N Wales (BSc); London School of Economics (LLB). Barrister, Middle Temple, 1954; Gray's Inn, 1961. Member: Cttees of Investigation for GB and England and Wales under Agricl Marketing Act, 1979–; Parole Bd, 1982–85; Welsh Arts Council, 1986. *Recreations:* walking, fishing. *Address:* Penrallt, Llys-faen, Caerdydd; Francis Taylor Building, Temple, EC4Y 7BY. *Club:* Reform.

LEWIS, Adm. Sir Andrew (Mackenzie), KCB 1971 (CB 1967); JP; Lord-Lieutenant and Custos Rotulorum of Essex, since 1978; Commander-in-Chief, Naval Home Command, and Flag Officer Portsmouth Area, 1972–74; Flag ADC to The Queen, 1972–74; *b* 24 Jan. 1918; *s* of late Rev. Cyril Lewis; *m* 1943, Rachel Elizabeth Leatham (*d* 1983); two *s. Educ:* Haileybury. Director of Plans, Admiralty, 1961–63; in command of HMS Kent, 1964–65; Director-General, Weapons (Naval), 1965–68; Flag Officer, Flotillas, Western Fleet, 1968–69; Second Sea Lord and Chief of Naval Personnel, 1970–71. DL Essex 1975. KStJ 1978. *Address:* Coleman's Farm, Finchingfield, Braintree, Essex CM7 4PE. *Club:* Brooks's.

See also Sir Clive Rose.

LEWIS, Anthony; *see* Lewis, J. A.

LEWIS, Sir Arthur; *see* Lewis, Sir W. A.

LEWIS, Arthur William John; ex-Trade Union Official (National Union of General and Municipal Workers); *b* 21 Feb. 1917; *s* of late J. Lewis; *m* 1940, Lucy Ethel Clack; one *d. Educ:* Elementary Sch.; Borough Polytechnic. Shop steward of his Dept of City of London Corporation at 17; Vice-Chairman of TU branch (City of London NUGMW) at 18; full-time London district official NUGMW 1938–48; Member of London Trades Council and Holborn City Trades Council, various joint industrial councils, Government cttees, etc; Member: ASTMS; APEX; G&MWU. MP (Lab): West Ham, Upton, 1945–50; W Ham N, 1950–74; Newham NW, 1974–83; contested (Ind. Lab) Newham NW, 1983. Mem., Expenditure Cttee. Formerly Member Exec. Cttee, London Labour Party; Chairman Eastern Regional Group of Labour MPs, 1950–83; Member Eastern Regional Council of Labour Party and Exec. Cttee of that body, 1950–83. Served in the Army. *Recreations:* swimming, motoring, boxing, general athletics.

LEWIS, Prof. Barry, FRCP; FRCPath; Director, Department of Chemical Pathology and Metabolic Disorders, St Thomas' Hospital, and hon. consultant physician and chemical pathologist, since 1976; *b* 16 March 1929; *s* of George Lewis and Pearl Lewis; *m* 1972, Eve Simone Rothschild; three *c. Educ:* Rondebosch School, Cape Town; University of Cape Town. PhD, MD. Training posts, Groote Schuur Hosp., Cape Town, 1953; lectureships and fellowships, St George's Hosp., 1959; MRC, 1963; Consultant Pathologist, St Mark's Hosp., 1967; Sen. Lectr in Chemical Pathology, hon. consultant chem. pathologist and physician, Hammersmith Hosp., 1971. Heinrich Wieland Prize, 1980. *Publications:* The Hyperlipidaemias: clinical and laboratory practice, 1976; (with Eve Lewis) The Heart Book, 1980; (with N. Miller) Lipoproteins, Atherosclerosis and Coronary Heart Disease, 1981; numerous papers on heart disease, nutrition and lipoproteins in med. and sci. jls. *Recreations:* music, travel, reading. *Address:* St Thomas' Hospital, SE1 7EH. *T:* 01–928 9292.

LEWIS, Bernard, BA, PhD; FBA 1963; FRHistS; Cleveland E. Dodge Professor of Near Eastern Studies, Princeton University, and Long-term Member of School of Social Science, Institute for Advanced Study, since 1974; *b* London, 31 May 1916; *s* of H. Lewis, London; *m* 1947, Ruth Hélène (marr. diss. 1974), *d* of late Overretsagflrer M. Oppenhejm, Copenhagen; one *s* one d. *Educ:* Wilson Coll.; The Polytechnic; Universities of London and Paris (Fellow UCL 1976). Derby Student, 1936. Asst Lecturer in Islamic History, Sch. of Oriental Studies, University of London, 1938; Prof. of History of Near and Middle East, SOAS, London Univ., 1949–74. Served RAC and Intelligence Corps, 1940–41; attached to Foreign Office, 1941–45. Visiting Prof. of History, University of Calif, Los Angeles, 1955–56, Columbia Univ., 1960 and Indiana Univ., 1963; Class of 1932 Lectr, Princeton Univ., 1964; Vis. Mem., Inst. for Advanced Study, Princeton, New Jersey, 1969; Gottesman Lectr, Yeshiva Univ., 1974; Vis. Prof., Collège de France, 1980. Mem., Amer. Acad. of Arts and Scis, 1983; Membre Associe, Institut d'Egypte, Cairo, 1969; For. Mem., Amer. Philosophical Soc., 1973. Hon. Fellow, Turkish Historical Soc., Ankara, 1972; Hon. Dr: Hebrew Univ., Jerusalem, 1974; Tel Aviv Univ., 1979. Certificate of Merit for services to Turkish Culture, Turkish Govt, 1973. Harvey Prizewinner, 1978. *Publications:* The Origins of Ismā'īlism, 1940; Turkey Today, 1940; British contributions to Arabic Studies, 1941; Handbook of Diplomatic and Political Arabic, 1947, 1956; (ed) Land of Enchanters, 1948; The Arabs in History, 1950 (5th rev. edn, 1970); Notes and Documents from the Turkish Archives, 1952; The Emergence of Modern Turkey, 1961 (rev. edn, 1968); The Kingly Crown (translated from Ibn Gabirol), 1961; co-ed. with P. M. Holt, Historians of the Middle East, 1962; Istanbul and the Civilization of the Ottoman Empire, 1963; The Middle East and the West, 1964; The Assassins, 1967; Race and Colour in Islam, 1971; Islam in History, 1973; Islam to 1453, 1974; co-ed, Encyclopædia of Islam, 1956–; (ed, with others) The Cambridge History of Islam, vols 1–11, 1971; Islam from the Prophet Muhammad to the Capture of Constantinople, 2 vols, 1974; History, Remembered, Recovered, Invented, 1975; (ed) The World of Islam: Faith, People, Culture, 1976; Studies in Classical and Ottoman Islam, 7th-16th centuries, 1976; (with Amnon Cohen) Population and Revenue in the Towns of Palestine in the Sixteenth Century, 1978; The Muslim Discovery of Europe, 1982; The Jews of Islam, 1984; articles in learned journals. *Address:* Near Eastern Studies Department, Jones Hall, Princeton University, Princeton, NJ 08540, USA. *Club:* Athenæum.

LEWIS, His Honour Bernard; a Circuit Judge (formerly a County Court Judge), 1966–80; *b* 1 Feb. 1905; 3rd *s* of late Solomon and Jeannette Lewis, London; *m* 1934, Harriette, *d* of late I. A. Waine, Dublin, London and Nice; one *s. Educ:* Trinity Hall, Cambridge (MA). Called to the Bar, Lincoln's Inn, 1929. Mem. S-E Circuit. Hon. Mem., Central Criminal Court Bar Mess. *Recreations:* revolver shooting, bricklaying. *Address:* Trevelyan House, Arlington Road, St Margaret's, Middx. *Clubs:* Reform; Cambridge Society; Ham and Petersham Rifle and Pistol.

LEWIS, Cecil Arthur, MC; Author; *b* Birkenhead, 29 March 1898; *m* 1921 (marr. diss. 1940); one *s* one d; *m* 1942 (marr. diss. 1950); no *c*; *m* 1960. *Educ:* Dulwich Coll.; University Coll. Sch.; Oundle. Royal Flying Corps, 1915 (MC, despatches twice); Manager Civil Aviation, Vickers, Ltd, 1919; Flying Instructor to Chinese Government, Peking, 1920, 1921; one of four founders of BBC, Chm. of Programme Board, 1922–26; Varied Literary Activities: stage, screen (first two adaptations of Bernard Shaw's plays to screen, 1930–32), and television plays (Nativity, Crucifixion and Patience of Job, 1956–59) and production connected therewith. RAF, 1939–45. Sheep farming, South Africa, 1947–50. United Nations Secretariat, New York, radio and television, 1953–55. Commercial television, London, 1955–56. Daily Mail, 1956–66; retd. *Publications:* Broadcasting From Within, 1924; The Unknown Warrior, trans. from French of Paul Raynal, 1928; Sagittarius Rising, 1936, repr. 1966 and 1983; The Trumpet is Mine, 1938; Challenge to the Night, 1938; Self Portrait: Letters and Journals of the late Charles Ricketts, RA (Editor), 1939 (filmed for TV, 1979); Pathfinders, 1943, rev. edn 1986; Yesterday's Evening, 1946; Farewell to Wings, 1964; Turn Right for Corfu, 1972; Never Look Back (autobiog.), 1974 (filmed for TV, 1978); A Way to Be, 1977; Gemini to Joburg, 1984. *Address:* c/o National Westminster Bank, 97 Strand, WC2.

LEWIS, Prof. Dan, PhD; DSc; FRS 1955; Quain Professor of Botany, London University, 1957–78, now Emeritus; Hon. Research Fellow, University College, London, since 1978; *b* 30 Dec. 1910; *s* of Ernest Albert and Edith J. Lewis; *m* 1933, Mary Phœbe Eleanor Burry; one d. *Educ:* High Sch., Newcastle-under-Lyme, Staffs; Reading University (BSc); PhD, DSc (London). Research Scholar, Reading Univ., 1935–36; Scientific Officer, Pomology Dept, John Innes Hort. Inst., 1935–48; Head of Genetics Dept, John Innes Horticultural Institution, Bayfordbury, Hertford, Herts, 1948–57. Rockefeller Foundation Special Fellowship, California Inst. of Technology, 1955–56; Visiting Prof. of Genetics, University of Calif, Berkeley, 1961–62; Royal Society Leverhulme Visiting Professor: University of Delhi, 1965–66; Singapore, 1970; Vis. Prof., QMC, 1978–. Pres., Genetical Soc., 1968–71; Mem., UGC, 1969–74. *Publications:* Sexual Incompatibility in Plants, 1979; Editor, Science Progress; scientific papers on Genetics and Plant Physiology. *Recreations:* swimming, gardening, music. *Address:* 56/57 Myddelton Square, EC1R 1YA. *T:* 01–278 6948.

LEWIS, David Courtenay M.; *see* Mansel Lewis.

LEWIS, David Henry L.; *see* LeRoy-Lewis.

LEWIS, David Malcolm, MA, PhD; FBA 1973; Professor of Ancient History, University of Oxford, since 1985; Student of Christ Church, Oxford, since 1956; *b* London, 7 June 1928; *s* of William and Milly Lewis; *m* 1958, Barbara, *d* of Prof. Samson Wright, MD, FRCP; four d. *Educ:* City of London Sch.; Corpus Christi Coll., Oxford (MA); Princeton Univ. (PhD). National Service with RAEC, 1949–51. Mem., Inst. for Advanced Study, Princeton, 1951–52, 1964–65. Student, British Sch. at Athens, 1952–54; Junior Research Fellow, Corpus Christi Coll., Oxford, 1954–55; Tutor in Ancient History, Christ Church, Oxford, 1955–85; Univ. Lectr in Greek Epigraphy, Oxford, 1956–85. Corr. Mem., German Archaeol Inst., 1985. *Publications:* (with John Gould) Pickard-Cambridge: Dramatic Festivals of Athens (2nd edn), 1968; (with Russell Meiggs) Greek Historical Inscriptions, 1969; Sparta and Persia, 1977; Inscriptiones Graecae I, 1981; articles in learned jls. *Recreations:* opera, gardening. *Address:* Christ Church, Oxford. *T:* Oxford 242820.

LEWIS, David Thomas, CB 1963; Hon. Professorial Fellow, Department of Chemistry, University College of Wales, Aberystwyth, 1970–78; *b* 27 March 1909; *s* of Emmanuel Lewis and Mary (née Thomas), Breconshire, Wales; *m* 1st, 1934, Evelyn (née Smetham); one d; 2nd, 1959, Mary (née Sadler). *Educ:* Brynmawr County Sch.; University Coll. of Wales, Aberystwyth. BSc (Wales), 1st Class Hons in Chemistry, 1930; PhD (Wales), 1933; DSc (Wales), 1958. Senior Chemistry Master, Quakers' Yard Secondary Sch., 1934–38; Asst Lecturer, University Coll., Cardiff, 1938–40. Various scientific posts finishing as Principal Scientific Officer, Ministry of Supply, Armaments Research Establishment, 1941–47, and as Senior Superintendent of Chemistry Div., Atomic Weapons Research Establishment, Aldermaston, 1947–60; Govt Chemist, 1960–70. FRIC 1940; FRSH 1964. Dawes Memorial Lectr, 1965. Scientific Governor, British Nutrition Foundn, 1967; Member: British National Cttee for Chemistry (Royal Society), 1961–70; British Pharmacopœia Commission, 1963–73. *Publications:* Ultimate Particles of Matter, 1959; Mountain Harvest (Poems), 1964. Analytical Research Investigations in learned jls; scientific articles in encyclopædias, scientific reviews, etc. *Recreations:* writing, fishing, shooting. *Address:* Green Trees, 24 Highdown Hill Road, Emmer Green, Reading, Berks RG4 8QP. *T:* Reading 471653.

LEWIS, Dr Dennis Aubrey, BSc; FIInfSc; Director, Aslib, the Association for Information Management, since 1981; *b* 1 Oct. 1928; *s* of Joseph and Minnie Lewis; *m* 1956, Gillian Mary Bratby; two *s. Educ:* Latymer Upper Sch.; Univ. of London (BSc 1st Cl. Hons Chemistry, 1953; PhD 1956). FIInfSc 1984. Res. Chemist, 1956–68, Intelligence Manager, 1968–81, ICI Plastics Div. Member: Adv. Council, British Library, 1976–81; Library Adv. Cttee, British Council, 1981–. Member: Welwyn Garden UDC, 1968–74; Welwyn Hatfield DC, 1974– (Chm., 1976–77). *Publications:* Index of Reviews in Organic Chemistry, annually 1963–; pubns on information management in Aslib Procs and other journals. *Recreations:* music, old churches, 'futurology'. *Address:* 11 The Links, Welwyn Garden City, Herts AL8 7DS. *T:* Welwyn Garden 324048.

LEWIS, Donald Gordon; Director, National Exhibition Centre, 1982–84; General Sales Manager, Birmingham Dairies, since 1961; *b* 12 Sept. 1926; *s* of late Albert Francis Lewis and Nellie Elizabeth Lewis; *m* 1950, Doreen Mary (née Gardner); one d. *Educ:* King Edward's Sch., Birmingham; Liverpool Univ. Dairy Industry, 1947–. Councillor (C) Birmingham CC, Selly Oak Ward, 1959, Alderman 1971–74; past Chairman, Transport and Airport Committees; West Midlands County Council: Mem., 1974–81; Chm., 1980–81; Chairman, Airport Cttee, 1974–80; Sec., Conservative Group, 1974–80; City of Birmingham District Council: Mem., 1982–; Chm., Nat. Exhibn Centre Cttee, 1982–84; Chm., Birmingham Housing Cttee, 1983–84. Chm., Selly Oak (Birmingham) Constituency Conservative Assoc., 1975–80, Pres., 1980–; Chairman: Birmingham Cons. Assoc., 1984–; Birmingham S Euro-Constituency Cons. Assoc., 1982–84. Member: West Midlands Passenger Transport Authority, 1984–; Birmingham Internat. Airport Jt Cttee, 1985–. Governor, Dame Elizabeth Cadbury Sch., 1979–; Manager, St Mary's C of E Sch., 1966–. *Recreation:* eating out. *Address:* 8 Pavenham Drive, Edgbaston, Birmingham B5 7TW. *T:* 021–471 3139. *Club:* Selly Oak (Birmingham) Conservative.

LEWIS, Ernest Gordon, (Toby), CMG 1972; OBE 1958; HM Diplomatic Service, retired; Chairman, Marine Chain Ltd, London, since 1977; *b* New Zealand, 26 Sept. 1918; *s* of George Henry Lewis; *m* 1949, Jean Margaret, *d* of late A. H. Smyth. *Educ:* Otago Boys' High Sch.; Otago Univ., NZ. Served War, Army, with 2nd NZ Div., Middle East, 1939–46 (Lt-Col; despatches, MBE). Joined Colonial Service, Nigeria, 1947; Administrator, Turks and Caicos Is, 1955–59; Permanent Sec., to Federal Govt of Nigeria, 1960–62; First Sec., Pakistan, 1963–66; Foreign and Commonwealth Office, 1966–69; Kuching, Sarawak, 1969–70; Governor and C-in-C, Falkland Islands, and High Comr, British Antarctic Territory, 1971–75; Head of Gibraltar and General Dept, FCO, 1975–77. *Recreation:* golf. *Address:* 5 Smith Street, Chelsea, SW3 4EE. *Club:* Army and Navy.

LEWIS, Esyr ap Gwilym; QC 1971; His Honour Judge Esyr Lewis; a Circuit Judge (Official Referee), since 1984; *b* 11 Jan. 1926; *s* of late Rev. T. W. Lewis, BA, and Mary Jane May Lewis (née Selway); *m* 1957, Elizabeth Anne Vidler Hoffmann, 2nd *d* of O. W. Hoffmann, Bassett, Southampton; four d. *Educ:* Salford Grammar Sch.; Mill Hill Sch.; Trinity Hall, Cambridge (MA, LLB). Served in Intelligence Corps, 1944–47. Exhibitioner, 1944, Scholar, 1948, at Trinity Hall (Dr Cooper's Law Studentship, 1950); 1st cl. hons, Law Tripos II, 1949, 1st cl. LLB, 1950, Cambridge. Holker Sen. Schol., Gray's Inn, 1950; Called to Bar, Gray's Inn, 1951; Bencher, 1978. Law Supervisor, Trinity Hall, 1950–55; Law Lectr, Cambridgeshire Technical Coll., 1949–50. A Recorder, 1972–84; Leader, Wales and Chester Circuit, 1978–81. Member: Bar Council, 1965–68; Council of Legal Education, 1967–73; Criminal Injuries Compensation Bd, 1977–84. Contested (L) Llanelli, 1964. *Publication:* contributor to Newnes Family Lawyer, 1963. *Recreations:* reading, gardening, watching Rugby football. *Address:* 2 South Square, Gray's Inn, WC1. *T:* 01–405 5918; Royal Courts of Justice, Strand, WC2A 2LL. *T:* 01–936 6496. *Clubs:* Garrick; Old Millhillians.

See also M. ap G. Lewis.

LEWIS, Dr Geoffrey Lewis, FBA 1979; Senior Lecturer in Turkish, University of Oxford, since 1964; Fellow, since 1961, Senior Tutor, since 1985, St Antony's College, Oxford (Sub-Warden, 1984–85); *b* 19 June 1920; *s* of Ashley Lewis and Jeanne Muriel (née Sintrop); *m* 1941, Raphaela Rhoda Bale Seideman; one *s* (one d decd). *Educ:* University Coll. Sch.; St John's Coll., Oxford (MA 1945, DPhil 1950; James Mew Arabic Scholar, 1947). Lectr in Turkish, 1950–54, and Sen. Lectr in Islamic Studies, 1954–64, Oxford Univ. Vis. Professor: Robert Coll., Istanbul, 1959–68; Princeton Univ., 1970–71, 1974; UCLA, 1975; British Acad. Leverhulme Vis. Prof., Turkey, 1984. Vice-Pres., Anglo-Turkish Soc., 1972–; Mem., British-Turkish Mixed Commn, 1975–; Pres., British Soc. for Middle Eastern Studies, 1981–83. Corresp. Mem., Turkish Language Soc., 1953–. Turkish Govt Cert. of Merit, 1973. DUniv, Univ. of the Bosphorus, Istanbul, 1986. *Publications:* Teach Yourself Turkish, 1953; Modern Turkey, 1955, 4th edn 1974; (trans., with annotations) Katib Chelebi, The Balance of Truth, 1957; Plotiniana Arabica, 1959; (with Barbara Hodge) A Study in Education for International Misunderstanding (Cyprus School History Textbooks), 1966; Turkish Grammar, 1967; (with M. S. Spink) Albucasis on Surgery and Instruments, 1973; The Book of Dede Korkut, 1974; The Atatürk I Knew, 1981; articles on Turkish language, history and politics, and on Arab alchemy. *Recreations:* bodging, etymology. *Address:* Oriental Institute, Pusey Lane, Oxford. *T:* Oxford 59272; 25 Warnborough Road, Oxford. *T:* Oxford 57150; Le Baousset, 06500 Menton, France.

LEWIS, Gillian Marjorie; FIIC; Head of Division of Conservation and Technical Services, National Maritime Museum, since 1978 (Assistant Deputy Director, 1982–86); *b* 10 Oct. 1945; *d* of late William Lewis and of Marjorie Lewis (née Pargeter). *Educ:* Tiffin Sch., Kingston upon Thames; Univ. of Newcastle upon Tyne (BA 1967); DCP, Gateshead Tech. Coll., 1969; FIIC 1977. Shipley Art Gallery, Co. Durham, 1967–69; free-lance conservator, 1969–73; Nat. Maritime Mus., 1973–; Keeper of Conservation, 1978. Vice-Chm., UK Inst. for Conservation, 1983–84 (Mem. Cttee, 1978–80). Member: Cttee, Dulwich Picture Gall., 1983–; Visitor, City and Guilds of London Sch. of Art, 1981–. *Publications:* official publications of the National Maritime Museum. *Address:* c/o National Maritime Museum, SE10 9NF. *T:* 01–858 1167. *Clubs:* Arts; Civil Service Riding.

LEWIS, Prof. Graham Pritchard; Dean, Hunterian Institute (formerly Institute of Basic Medical Sciences), Royal College of Surgeons, since 1982; *b* 5 Aug. 1927; *s* of George Henry and Ruth Lewis; *m* 1973, Averil Myrtle Priscilla; two *s* two d. *Educ:* Monkton House School, Cardiff; University College Cardiff (BPharm, PhD). Mem., Scientific Staff, Nat. Inst. for Med. Research, MRC, 1953–63; Dep. Dir, Research, and Dir, Biological Research, Ciba-Geigy Pharmaceuticals, 1964–73; Vandervell Prof. of Pharmacology,

RCS, 1974–. *Publications:* 5-Hydroxytryptamine, 1958; The Role of Prostaglandins in Inflammation, 1976; Mechanisms of Steroid Action, 1981; Mediators of Inflammation, 1986; numerous contribs to British and overseas sci. jls, esp. Jl Physiol., BJ Pharmacol. *Recreations:* writing unfathomable stories, painting indescribable paintings and cooking excruciating dishes. *Address:* Hunterian Institute, Royal College of Surgeons, Lincoln's Inn Fields, WC2A 3PN. *T:* 01-405 3474.

LEWIS, Gwynedd Margaret; a Recorder of the Crown Court, 1974–81; barrister-at-law; *b* 9 April 1911; *d* of late Samuel David Lewis and Margaret Emma Lewis. *Educ:* King Edward's High Sch., Birmingham; King's Coll., Univ. of London. BA. Called to Bar, Gray's Inn, 1939; Mem., Midland and Oxford Circuit; Dep. Stipendiary Magistrate for City of Birmingham, 1962–74. Legal Mem., Mental Health Review Tribunal for the W Midlands Region, 1972–83. *Recreations:* archaeology, bird-watching. *Address:* Berringtons, Burley Gate, Hereford HR1 3QS; Troutbeck, Leintwardine, Salop.

LEWIS, Henry Nathan; Chairman, J. & J. Fashions Ltd, since 1985; *b* 29 Jan. 1926; *m* 1953, Jenny Cohen; one *s* two *d*. *Educ:* Hollywood Park Council Sch., Stockport; Stockport Sch.; Manchester Univ. (BA Com); LSE. Served RAF (Flt Lt), 1944–48. Joined Marks & Spencer, 1950; Dir, 1965; Jt Man. Dir responsible for textiles, 1973–76, 1983–85, for foods, 1976–83. Mem. Adv. Bd, Bank of Hapoalim BM; Dir, Dixons plc, 1985–. Governor, Jerusalem Inst. of Management; Trustee, Jewish Educational Develt Trust; Member: Bd, Joint Israel Appeal; Bd of Deputies of British Jews; Policy Adv. Gp, Inst. of Jewish Affairs; Council, Anglo-Israel Chamber of Commerce. *Address:* 62 Frognal, NW3.

LEWIS, H(erbert) J(ohn) Whitfield, CB 1968; *b* 9 April 1911; *s* of Herbert and Mary Lewis; *m* 1963, Pamela (*née* Leaford); one *s* three *d*. *Educ:* Monmouth Sch.; Welsh Sch. of Architecture. Associate with Norman & Dawbarn, Architects and Consulting Engineers; in charge of housing work, 1945–50; Principal Housing Architect, Architects Dept, London County Council, 1950–59; County Architect, Middlesex County Council, 1959–64; Chief Architect, Ministry of Housing and Local Govt, 1964–71. FRIBA; FRTPI, DisTP 1957. *Recreations:* music, electronics. *Address:* 8 St John's Wood Road, NW8.

LEWIS, Rt. Rev. Hurtle John; *see* Queensland, North, Bishop of.

LEWIS, Prof. Hywel David, MA, BLitt; Professor of History and Philosophy of Religion, in the University of London, 1955–77; *b* 21 May 1910; *s* of Rev. David John and Rebecca Lewis, Waenfawr, Cærnarvon; *m* 1943, Megan Elias Jones, MA (*d* 1962), *d* of J. Elias Jones, Bangor; *m* 1965, K. A. Megan Pritchard, *d* of T. O. Pritchard, Pentrefoelas. *Educ:* University Coll., Bangor; Jesus Coll., Oxford (Hon. Fellow, 1986). Lecturer in Philosophy, University Coll., Bangor, 1936; Senior Lecturer, 1947; Prof. of Philosophy, 1947–55; Fellow of King's Coll., London, 1963; Dean of the Faculty of Theology in the University of London, 1964–68; Dean of the Faculty of Arts, King's Coll., 1966–68, and Faculty of Theology, 1970–72. President: Mind Association, 1948–49, Aristotelian Soc., 1962–63; Chm. Council, Royal Inst. of Philosophy; Soc. for the Study of Theology, 1964–66; President: Oxford Soc. for Historical Theology, 1970–71; London Soc. for Study of Religion, 1970–72; Inst. of Religion and Theology, 1972–75; International Soc. for Metaphysics, 1974–80. Editor, Muirhead Library of Philosophy, 1947–78; Editor, Religious Studies, 1964–79; Leverhulme Fellow, 1954–55; Visiting Professor: Brynmawr Coll., Pa, USA, 1958–59; Yale, 1964–65; University of Miami, 1968; Boston Univ., 1969; Kyoto Univ., 1976; Santiniketan Univ., 1977; Surrey Univ., 1977–83; Emory Univ., 1977–81; Jadavpur Univ., 1979; Vis. Professorial Fellow, UCW Aberystwyth, 1979–84; Lectures: Robert McCahan, Presbyterian Coll., Belfast, 1960; Wilde, in Natural and Comparative Religion, Oxford, 1960–63; Edward Cadbury, Birmingham, 1962–63; Centre for the Study of World Religions, Harvard, 1963; Ker, McMaster Divinity Coll., Ont, 1964; Owen Evans, University Coll., Aberystwyth, 1964–65; Firth Meml, Nottingham, 1966; Gifford, Edinburgh, 1966–68; L. T. Hobhouse Meml, London, 1966–68; Elton, George Washington Univ., 1969; Otis Meml, Wheaton Coll., 1969; Drew, London, 1973–74; Laidlaw, Toronto, 1979. Commemoration Preacher, University of Southampton, 1958; Commemoration Lectr, Cheshunt Coll., Cambridge, 1960, and Westminster Coll., 1964. Warden, Guild of Graduates, University of Wales, 1974–77; Mem., Advisory Council for Education (Wales), 1964–67. Mem., Gorsedd of Bards. Hon. Vice-Pres., FISP, 1984. Hon. DD St Andrews, 1964; Hon. DLit Emory Univ., USA, 1978. *Publications:* Morals and the New Theology, 1947; Morals and Revelation, 1951; (ed) Contemporary British Philosophy, Vol. III, 1956, Vol. IV, 1976; Our Experience of God, 1959; Freedom and History, 1962; (ed) Clarity is not Enough, 1962; Teach yourself the Philosophy of Religion, 1965; World Religions (with R. L. Slater), 1966; Dreaming and Experience, 1968; The Elusive Mind, 1969; The Self and Immortality, 1973; (ed) Philosophy East and West, 1975; (ed with G. R. Damodaran) The Dynamics of Education, 1975; Persons and Life after Death, 1978; Jesus in the Faith of Christians, 1980; The Elusive Self, 1982; Freedom and Alienation, 1985; Gwerinaeth, 1940; Y Wladwriaeth a'i Hawdurdod (with Dr J. A. Thomas), 1943; Ebyrth, 1943; Diogelu Diwylliant, 1945; Crist a Heddwch, 1947; Dilyn Crist, 1951; Gwybod am Dduw, 1952; Hen a Newydd, 1972; Pwy yw Iesu Grist?, 1979; contributions to Mind, Proc. of Aristotelian Society, Philosophy, Ethics, Hibbert Jl, Philosophical Quarterly, Analysis, Efrydiau Athronyddol, Llenor, Traethodydd, etc. *Address:* 1 Normandy Park, Normandy, near Guildford, Surrey GU3 2AL. *T:* Aldershot 26673.

LEWIS, Sir Ian (Malcolm), Kt 1964; QC (Nigeria) 1961; LLD, MA Cantab, LLM; **His Honour Judge Sir Ian Lewis;** a Circuit Judge, since 1973; *b* 14 Dec. 1925; *s* of late Prof. Malcolm M. Lewis, MC, MA, LLB, and late Eileen (*née* O'Sullivan); *m* 1955, Marjorie, *d* of late W. G. Carrington; one *s*. *Educ:* Clifton Coll. (Governor, 1972–, Mem. Council, 1975–, Chm. Council, 1981–84); Trinity Hall, Cambridge (Scholar, 1st cl. hons Law Tripos Pt 2, and LLM). Served with RAFVR, 1944–47. Called to Bar, Middle Temple, 1951; pupil of R. W. Goff (the late Rt Hon. Lord Justice Goff), 1951. Western Circuit, 1951; Crown Counsel, Nigeria, 1953; Northern Nigeria: Solicitor-Gen., 1958; Dir of Public Prosecutions, 1962; Attorney-Gen. and Minister in the Government of Northern Nigeria, 1962–66; Chancellor, Diocese of Northern Nigeria, 1964–66; a Justice, Supreme Court of Nigeria, 1966–72; Justice of Appeal, Anguilla, 1972–73; Comr in NI dealing with detention of terrorists, 1972–75; Mem., Detention Appeal Tribunal for NI, 1974–75; Adviser to Sec. of State for NI on Detention, 1975–; Liaison Judge for Wiltshire, 1973–81; Mem., Wilts Probation Cttee, 1973–; Pres., Mental Health Review Tribunal, 1983–. Pres., Bristol Medico-Legal Soc., 1983–85; Hon. Vice-Pres., Magistrates Assoc., Wilts, 1973–. Mem. Council, Univ. of Bristol, 1979–. MEC, N Nigeria, 1962–66; Adv. Coun. on the Prerogative of Mercy, House of Assembly, 1962–66. Mem. of Nigerian Bar Council, 1962–66; Mem. of Nigerian Council of Legal Education, 1962–66; Assoc. Mem. Commonwealth Parly Assoc. Hon. LLD, Ahmadu Bello Univ., Nigeria, 1972. *Recreations:* swimming (Capt. Cambridge Univ. Swimming and Water Polo, 1949); bridge; sailing; trying to find chapels in Wales where Grandfather "Elfed" (late Rev. H. Elvet Lewis, CH, DD) had not preached. *Address:* c/o Courts Administrator, Guildhall, Broad Street, Bristol BS1 2HL. *Clubs:* Royal Commonwealth Society; Hawks (Cambridge); Savages, Beaufort (Bristol).

LEWIS, Ian Talbot; Under Secretary (Legal), Treasury Solicitor's Office, since 1982; *b* 7 July 1929; *s* of late Cyril Frederick Lewis, CBE and of Marjorie (*née* Talbot); *m* 1962, Patricia Anne (*née* Hardy) (marr. diss. 1978); two *s*; *m* 1986, Susan Lydia Sargant. *Educ:* Marlborough Coll. Admitted Solicitor, 1951. National Service, 3rd The King's Own Hussars, 1952–53. Solicitor, private practice, London, 1954–57; Treasury Solicitor's Office: Legal Asst, 1957; Sen. Legal Asst, 1963; Asst Treasury Solicitor, 1977. *Recreations:* sport, the countryside, reading, theatre, cinema. *Address:* South Cottage, Fordcombe, near Tunbridge Wells, Kent. *T:* Fordcombe 413. *Clubs:* Cavalry and Guards, MCC; Blackheath Rugby Union Football (Pres.); Piltdown Golf.

LEWIS, Prof. Ioan Myrddin, DPhil; FBA 1986; Professor of Anthropology, London School of Economics and Political Science, since 1969; Hon. Director, International African Institute, since 1981; *b* 30 Jan. 1930; *s* of John Daniel Lewis and Mary Stevenson Scott (*née* Brown); *m* 1954, Ann Elizabeth Keir; one *s* three *d*. *Educ:* Glasgow High Sch.; Glasgow Univ. (BSc 1951); Oxford Univ. (Dip. in Anthrop., 1952; BLitt 1953; DPhil 1957). Res. Asst to Lord Hailey, Chatham House, 1954–55; Colonial SSRC Fellow, 1955–57; Lectr in African Studies, University Coll. of Rhodesia and Nyasaland, 1957–60; Lectr in Social Anthrop., Glasgow Univ., 1960–63; Lectr, then Reader in Anthrop., UCL, 1963–69. Hitchcock Prof., Univ. of Calif at Berkeley, 1977; Vis. Professor: Univ. of Helsinki, Finland, 1982; Univ. of Rome, 1983; Univ. of Malaya, 1986. Malinowski Meml Lectr, London, 1966. Hon. Sec., Assoc. of Social Anthropologists of the Commonwealth, 1964–67; Member: Council and Standing Cttee of Council, Royal Anthropol Inst., 1965–67 and 1981–84; Court of Governors and Standing Cttee, LSE, 1984–; Editor, Man (Jl of RAI), 1969–72. *Publications:* Peoples of the Horn of Africa, 1955, 2nd rev. edn 1969; A Pastoral Democracy: pastoralism and politics among the Northern Somali of the Horn of Africa, 1961, 2nd edn 1982; (with B. W. Andrzejewski) Somali Poetry, 1964, 2nd edn 1968; The Modern History of Somaliland: from nation to state, 1965, 2nd rev. edn 1980; Ecstatic Religion, 1971, 3rd edn 1978 (Dutch Italian, French, Portuguese and Japanese edns); Social Anthropology in Perspective, 1976, 3rd edn 1985; Religion in Context: cults and charisma, 1986; (ed and introd): Islam in Tropical Africa, 1966, 3rd edn 1980; History and Anthropology, 1968 (Spanish edn); Symbols and Sentiments: cross-cultural studies in symbolism, 1977; (co-ed with Fred Eggan and C. von Fürer-Haimendorf), Atlas of Mankind, 1982; Nationalism and Self-Determination in the Horn of Africa, 1983; contrib. learned jls. *Recreations:* travel, fishing. *Address:* 26 Bramshill Gardens, NW5 1JH. *T:* 01-272 1722.

LEWIS, Prof. Sir Jack, Kt 1982; FRS 1973; FRSC; Professor of Chemistry, University of Cambridge, since 1970; Hon. Fellow of Sidney Sussex College (Fellow, 1970–77); (first) Warden of Robinson College, Cambridge, since 1975; *b* 13 Feb. 1928; *m* 1951, Elfreida Mabel (*née* Lamb); one *s* one *d*. *Educ:* Barrow Grammar Sch. BSc London 1949; PhD Nottingham 1951; DSc London 1961; MSc Manchester 1964; MA Cantab 1970; ScD Cantab 1977. Lecturer: Univ. of Sheffield, 1953–56; Imperial Coll., London, 1956–57; Lecturer-Reader, University Coll., London, 1957–62; Prof. of Chemistry: Univ. of Manchester, 1962–67; UCL, 1967–70. Firth Vis. Prof., Univ. of Sheffield, 1969; Lectures: Frontiers of Science, Case/Western Reserve, 1963; Tilden, RIC, 1966; Miller, Univ. of Illinois, 1966; Shell, Stanford Univ., 1968; Venables, Univ. of N Carolina, 1968; A. D. Little, MIT, 1970; Boomer, Univ. of Alberta, 1971; AM, Princeton, 1972; Baker, Cornell, 1974; Nyholm, Chem. Soc., 1974; Chini, Italian Chem. Soc., 1981; Bailar, Illinois Univ., 1982; Dwyer, NSW Inst. of Tech., 1982; Powell, Queensland Univ. 1982; Mond, Chem. Soc., 1984; Leeumaker, Wesleyan Univ., 1984; Pettit May, Texas, 1985; Wheeler, Dublin, 1986. Member: CNAA Cttee, 1964–70; Exec. Cttee, Standing Cttee on Univ. Entry, 1966–76; Schs Council, 1966–76; SERC (formerly SRC): Polytechnics Cttee, 1973–; Chemistry Cttee (Chm., 1975–); Science Bd, 1975–; Council, 1980–; SERC/SSRC Jt Cttee, 1981–; UGC (Phy. Sci.), 1975–81; Council, Royal Soc., 1982–84 (a Vice-Pres., 1984); Vis. Cttee, Cranfield Inst. of Tech., 1983– (Chm., 1985–); Royal Commn on Environmental Pollution, 1985– (Chm., 1986–); Pres., Royal Soc. of Chemistry, 1986. Patron, Student Community Action Develt Unit, 1985–. For. Mem., Amer. Acad. of Arts and Science, 1984. FNA 1980. Dr *hc* Rennes, 1980; DUniv Open, 1982; Hon. DSc: Nottingham, 1983; Keele, 1984; Hon. ScD East Anglia, 1983. American Chem. Soc. Award in Inorganic Chemistry, 1970; Transition Metal Award, Chem. Soc., 1973; Davy Medal, Royal Soc., 1985; Mallinckrodt Award in Inorganic Chemistry, American Chem. Soc., 1986. *Publications:* papers, mainly in Jl of Chem. Soc. *Address:* Chemistry Department, University Chemical Laboratory, Lensfield Road, Cambridge CB2 1EW. *Clubs:* Athenæum, United Oxford & Cambridge University.

LEWIS, John Elliott, MA; Head Master, Geelong Church of England Grammar School, Australia, since 1980; *b* 23 Feb. 1942; *s* of John Derek Lewis and Margaret Helen (*née* Shaw); *m* 1968, Vibeke Lewis (*née* Johansson). *Educ:* King's College, Auckland, NZ; Corpus Christi Coll., Cambridge (Girdlers' Company Schol.; MA Classics). Assistant Master, King's Coll., Auckland, 1964, 1966–70; Jun. Lecturer in Classics, Auckland Univ., 1965; Asst Master, 1971–80, Master in College, 1975–80, Eton College. *Address:* Geelong Church of England Grammar School, Corio, Victoria 3214, Australia. *T:* 052 (Geelong) 739200.

LEWIS, Maj.-Gen. (Retd) John Michael Hardwicke, CBE 1970 (OBE 1955); *b* 5 April 1919; *s* of late Brig. Sir Clinton Lewis, OBE, and Lilian Eyre (*née* Wace); *m* 1942, Barbara Dorothy (*née* Wright); three *s*. *Educ:* Oundle; RMA, Woolwich. Commissioned, 2nd Lieut, RE, 1939. Served War: in 18 Div. and Special Force (Chindits), in Far East, 1940–45. Staff Coll., Camberley, 1949; CRE, Gibraltar, 1959–61; Instr, JSSC, 1961–63; IDC, 1966; Asst Chief of Staff (Ops), HQ Northern Army Gp, 1967–69; Brig. GS (Intell.), MoD, 1970–72; ACOS (Intelligence), SHAPE, 1972–75. *Publications:* Michiel Marieschi: Venetian artist, 1967; J. F. Lewis, RA (1805–1876): a monograph, 1978. *Recreations:* English water-colours, Swiss painters. *Address:* Bedford's Farm, Frimley Green, Surrey. *T:* Deepcut 835188.

LEWIS, (Joseph) Anthony; Chief London Correspondent, New York Times, 1965–72, editorial columnist, since 1969; Lecturer in Law, Harvard Law School, since 1974; *b* 27 March 1927; *s* of Kassel Lewis and Sylvia Lewis (*née* Surut), NYC; *m* 1st, 1951, Linda (marr. diss. 1982), *d* of John Rannells, NYC; one *s* two *d*; 2nd, 1984, Margaret, *d* of Bernard Charles Marshall, Osterville, Mass. *Educ:* Horace Mann Sch., NY; Harvard Coll. (BA). Sunday Dept, New York Times, 1948–52; Reporter, Washington Daily News, 1952–55; Legal Corresp., Washington Bureau, NY Times, 1955–64; Nieman Fellow, Harvard Law Sch., 1956–57. Governor, Ditchley Foundation, 1965–72. Pulitzer Prize for Nat. Correspondence, 1955 and 1963; Heywood Broun Award, 1955; Overseas Press Club Award, 1970. Hon. DLitt: Adelphi Univ. (NY), 1964; Rutgers Univ., NJ, 1973; NY Med. Coll., 1976; Williams Coll., Mass, 1978; Clark Univ., Mass, 1982; Hon. LLD: Syracuse, 1979; Colby Coll., 1983. *Publications:* Gideon's Trumpet, 1964; Portrait of a Decade: The Second American Revolution, 1964; articles in American law reviews. *Recreation:* dinghy sailing. *Address:* 2 Faneuil Hall Marketplace, Boston, Mass 02109, USA. *Clubs:* Garrick; Tavern (Boston).

LEWIS, Keith William, CB 1981; Director General and Engineer in Chief, Engineering and Water Supply Department, South Australia, since 1974; *b* 10 Nov. 1927; *s* of Ernest

John and Alinda Myrtle Lewis; *m* 1958, Alison Bothwell Fleming; two *d*. *Educ*: Adelaide High Sch.; Univ. of Adelaide (BE Civil); Imperial Coll., Univ. of London (DIC); FIE(Aust)/FAIM. Engineer for Water and Sewage Treatment, E and WS Dept, 1968–74. Chairman: S Australian Water Resources Council, 1974–; Australian Water Research Adv. Council, 1985–; Member: Standing Cttee, Australian Water Resources Council, 1974–; Electricity Trust of S Australia, 1974–84; Environmental Protection Council, 1974–84; S Australian Urban Land Trust, 1984–; Pipelines of S Australia Bd, 1984–; Golden Grove Jt Venture Cttee, 1984–. River Murray Commissioner, 1982–. Silver Jubilee Medal, 1977. *Recreations*: golf, skiing, tennis. *Address*: 24 Delamere Avenue, Netherby, SA 5062, Australia. *T*: (home) 338 1507; (office) 227 2022. *Clubs*: Adelaide, Kooyonga Golf (South Australia).

LEWIS, Sir Kenneth, Kt 1983; DL; MP (C) Stamford and Spalding, since 1983 (Rutland and Stamford, 1959–83); *b* 1 July 1916; *s* of William and Agnes Lewis, Jarrow; *m* 1948, Jane, *d* of Samuel Pearson, of Adderstone Mains, Belford, Northumberland; one *s* one *d*. *Educ*: Jarrow; Edinburgh Univ. Served War of 1939–45. RAF, 1941–46; Flt Lt. Chm. Business and Holiday Travel Ltd. Contested (C) Newton-le-Willows, 1945 and 1950, Ashton-under-Lyne, 1951. Chm., Cons. Back Bench Labour Cttee, 1962–64. CC Middx, 1949–51; Mem. NW Metropolitan Hosp. Management Cttee, 1949–62; Trustee: Uppingham Sch.; Oakham Sch. DL Rutland 1973. *Recreations*: music, travel. *Address*: 96 Green Lane, Northwood, Middx. *T*: Northwood 23354; Redlands, Preston, Rutland. *Clubs*: Carlton, Pathfinder, Royal Air Force.

LEWIS, Maj.-Gen. Kenneth Frank Mackay, CB 1951; DSO 1944; MC 1918; retired; *b* 29 Jan. 1897; *s* of Frank Essex Lewis and Anne Florence Mackay; *m* 1930, Pamela Frank Menzies Pyne, *d* of Lt-Col C. E. Menzies Pyne; two *s*. *Educ*: Cathedral Sch., Bristol. Commissioned 2nd Lt RH & RFA, 1916; served with 9th Scottish Div., France and Belgium, 1916–18; ADC to GOC Lowland Div., 1921; ADC to GOC Upper Silesia Force, 1922; Iraq Levies, 1923–25; Adjutant, Portsmouth and IOW, 1926–29; Royal West African Frontier Force, Nigeria Regt, 1929–30; Colchester, 1930–33; India, School of Artillery, 1933–37; Military Coll. of Science, UK, 1938; School of Artillery, Larkhill, 1939–41; CO 7th Survey Regt, 1942; CO 185 Field Regt, 1943; CRA 43 and 49 Divisions, 1944 and 1945 (despatches); CCRA Palestine, 1947 and 1948 (despatches); BRA Western Command, UK, 1948; GOC 4th Anti-Aircraft Group, 1949–50; Dir of Royal Artillery, War Office, Dec. 1950–54; retired, 1954; Col Comdt RA, 1957–62. OStJ 1955. Order of Leopold, Croix de Guerre (Belgium). *Recreations*: books and music. *Address*: 18 Beverley Road, Colchester CO3 3NG. *T*: Colchester 76507.

LEWIS, Kynric; see Lewis, A. K.

LEWIS, Leonard; QC 1969; retired 1982; *b* 11 May 1909; *e s* of Barnet Lewis; *m* 1939, Rita Jeanette Stone; two *s* one *d*. *Educ*: Grocer's Company Sch.; St John's Coll., Cambridge (Major Schol.). Wrangler, Wright's Prizeman, MA Cantab; BSc 1st class Hons London. Called to Bar, 1932 and started to practise. Served War of 1939–45, RAF. *Recreation*: tennis. *Address*: East Park House, Newchapel, near Lingfield, Surrey. *T*: Lingfield 114.

LEWIS, Prof. Leonard John, CMG 1969; BSc; DipEd; Professor of Education, with special reference to Education in Tropical Areas, in the University of London, 1958–73, now Emeritus; *b* 28 Aug. 1909; of Welsh-English parentage; *s* of Thomas James Lewis and Rhoda Lewis (*née* Gardiner); *m* 1940, Nora Brisdon (marr. diss. 1976); one *s* (and one *s* decd); *m* 1982, Gwenda Black. *Educ*: Lewis Sch., Pengam; University Coll., of South Wales and Monmouth (BSc); University of London Institute of Education (DipEd). Lecturer, St Andrew's Coll., Oyo, Nigeria, 1935–36; Headmaster, CMS Gram. Sch., Lagos, Nigeria, 1936–41; Education Sec., CMS Yoruba Mission, 1941–44; Lectr, University of London Institute of Education, 1944–48; Editorial staff, Oxford Univ. Press, 1948–49; Prof. of Educn and Dir of Institute of Educn, University Coll. of Ghana, 1949–58. Principal and Vice-Chancellor, Univ. of Zimbabwe, 1980–81; Vice-Chancellor, PNG Univ. of Technology, 1982–83. Nuffield Visiting Prof., University of Ibadan, 1966. Hon. Professorial Fellow, University Coll., Cardiff, 1973; Hon. FCP 1974. Coronation Medal, 1953; Zimbabwe Independence Medal, 1980. *Publications*: Equipping Africa, 1948; Henry Carr (Memoir), 1948; Education Policy and Practice in British Tropical Areas, 1954; (ed and contrib.) Perspectives in Mass Education and Community Development, 1957; Days of Learning, 1961; Education and Political Independence in Africa, 1962; Schools, Society and Progress in Nigeria, 1965; The Management of Education (with A. J. Loveridge), 1965. *Address*: Flat 1, 6 Stanwell Road, Penarth, S Glamorgan CF6 2EA. *T*: Cardiff 702299.

LEWIS, Michael ap Gwilym; QC 1975; a Recorder of the Crown Court, since 1976; *b* 9 May 1930; *s* of Rev. Thomas William Lewis and Mary Jane May Selway; *m*; three *s* one *d*. *Educ*: Mill Hill; Jesus Coll., Oxford (Scholar). MA (Mod. History). 2nd Royal Tank Regt, 1952–53. Called to Bar, Gray's Inn, 1956; Mem., Senate, 1979–82; South Eastern Circuit. *Address*: 3 Hare Court, Temple, EC4Y 7BJ. *T*: 01–353 7561.
See also E. ap G. Lewis.

LEWIS, Norman; author; *s* of Richard and Louise Lewis. *Educ*: Enfield Grammar Sch. Served War of 1939–45, in Intelligence Corps. *Publications*: Sand and Sea in Arabia, 1938; Samara, 1949; Within the Labyrinth, 1950, new edn 1985; A Dragon Apparent, 1951, new edn 1982; Golden Earth, 1952, repr. 1983; A Single Pilgrim, 1953; The Day of the Fox, 1955, new edn 1985; The Volcanoes Above Us, 1957; The Changing Sky, 1959, repr. 1984; Darkness Visible, 1960; The Tenth Year of the Ship, 1962; The Honoured Society, 1964, rev. edn 1984; A Small War Made to Order, 1966; Every Man's Brother, 1967; Flight from a Dark Equator, 1972; The Sicilian Specialist, 1974, new edn 1985; Naples '44, 1978, repr. 1983; The German Company, 1979; Cuban Passage, 1982; A Suitable Case for Corruption, 1984; Voices of the Old Sea, 1984, new edn 1985; (autobiog.) Jackdaw Cake, 1985; A View of the World, 1986. *Address*: c/o Hamish Hamilton Ltd, Cardon House, Long Acre, WC2.

LEWIS, Prof. Norman Bache, MA, PhD; retired; *b* 8 Nov. 1896; *o s* of G. D. and L. A. Lewis, Newcastle-under-Lyme; *m* 1928, Julia, *o d* of John and Catherine Wood, Riddlesden, Keighley; (one *s* one *d* decd). *Educ*: Boys' High Sch., Newcastle-under-Lyme (foundation scholar); University of Manchester (Jones scholar). Served European War in RFA, 1917–19. Manchester University: Hovell and Shuttleworth Prizes in History, 1919; BA in History Hons Cl. I and graduate scholarship in History, 1921; Research Fellowship in History, 1922. University of Sheffield: Lecturer in Dept of Modern History, 1924; Senior Lecturer in Mediæval History, 1946; Reader in Mediæval History, 1955; Prof. of Mediæval History in the University of Sheffield, 1959–62, Emeritus Prof., 1962. *Publications*: articles in historical journals. *Recreations*: music, reading. *Address*: Sundial House, 79 Old Dover Road, Canterbury CT1 3DB.

LEWIS, Peter Ronald; Director General, Bibliographic Services, British Library, since 1980; *b* 28 Sept. 1926; *s* of Charles Lewis and Florence Mary (née Kirk); *m* 1952, June Ashley; one *s* one *d*. *Educ*: Royal Masonic Sch.; Belfast Univ. (MA). FLA. Brighton, Plymouth, Chester public libraries, 1948–55; Head, Bibliographic Services, BoT Library, 1955–65; Lectr in Library Studies, QUB, 1965–69; Librarian: City Univ., 1969–72;

Univ. of Sussex, 1972–80. Vice-Pres., 1979–85 and Hon. Treasurer, 1980–82, Library Assoc. (Chm., Bd of Fellowship, 1979–86); Chairman: LA Publishing Co., 1983–85; IFLA Bibliographic Control Co-ord. Bd, 1985–. *Publications*: The Literature of the Social Sciences, 1960; The Fall and Rise of National Bibliography (Bangalore), 1982; numerous papers on librarianship and bibliography, 1963–. *Recreation*: walking the South Downs Way. *Address*: 131 Western Road, Hurstpierpoint, W Sussex.

LEWIS, Peter Tyndale; Chairman, John Lewis Partnership, since 1972; *b* 26 Sept. 1929; *s* of Oswald Lewis and Frances Merriman Lewis (*née* Cooper); *m* 1961, Deborah Anne, *d* of late Sir William (Alexander Roy) Collins, CBE and Priscilla Marian, *d* of late S. J. Lloyd; one *s* one *d*. *Educ*: Eton; Christ Church, Oxford. National service, Coldstream Guards, 1948–49; MA (Oxford) 1953; called to Bar (Middle Temple) 1956; joined John Lewis Partnership, 1959. Member: Council, Industrial Soc., 1968–79; Design Council, 1971–74; Chm., Retail Distributors' Assoc., 1972. Trustee, Jt Educnl Trust, 1985–. Governor: NIESR, 1983; Windlesham Hse Sch., 1979–. CBIM; FRSA. *Address*: John Lewis & Co. Ltd, Oxford Street, W1A 1AX.

LEWIS, Richard, CBE 1963; FRAM, FRMCM, LRAM; concert and opera singer, tenor; *b* of Welsh parents; *m* 1963, Elizabeth Robertson; one *s* (and one *s* by a previous *m*). *Educ*: Royal Manchester Coll. of Music (schol.; studied with Norman Allin); RAM. Well known boy soprano in N England. Served in RCS during war. English début in leading rôle of Britten's Opera The Rape of Lucretia at Glyndebourne, where he has sung every year since 1947; début, Teatro Colono, Buenos Aires, 1963; has sung at Edinburgh Fests, Covent Garden, San Francisco, Chicago, Vienna State Opera and Berlin Opera Houses, and toured America, Australia and NZ; has appeared with leading European and American orchs, incl. NY Philharmonic, Chicago Symphony, San Francisco Symphony and Philadelphia. Recitalist and oratorio singer, particularly of Handel, and in name part of Elgar's The Dream of Gerontius; has created parts: Troilus in Sir William Walton's Opera Troilus and Cressida; Mark in The Midsummer Marriage, and Achilles in King Priam, both operas by Michael Tippett; sang in first perf. of Stravinsky's Canticum Sacrum, under composer's direction, Venice Festival; sang Aaron in first British performance of Schoenberg's opera Moses and Aaron at Covent Garden; leading part in first American presentation of Cherubini's Opera, Medea, San Francisco, USA, 1958. Has made numerous recordings and appearances in films and on radio and television. Pres., ISM, 1975–76. Hon. DMus: St Andrews, 1984; Manchester, 1986. *Recreations*: languages, calligraphy, creative photography. *Address*: Combe House, 22 Church Street, Old Willingdon.

LEWIS, Maj.-Gen. (retd) Robert Stedman, CB 1946; OBE 1942; late IA; *b* 20 March 1898; *s* of Sidney Cooke Lewis, MInstCE, and Mary Anne Jane Lewis Lloyd; *m* 1925, Margaret Joan Hart (*d* 1980); one *s* one *d*. *Educ*: Amesbury Sch., Bickley Hall, Kent; Bradfield Coll., Berks; Royal Military Academy, Woolwich. 2nd Lt RFA 1915; Seconded to RFC in 1916 and 1917 and served as a pilot in France in 100 Squadron RFC; served in France with RFA, 1918; proceeded to India with RFA, 1919; Seconded to Indian Army Ordnance Corps, 1922, and permanently transferred to Indian Army, 1925, with promotion to Capt.; Major, 1933; Bt Lt-Col 1937; Lt-Col 1940; Col 1944; employed at General Headquarters, India, 1939; Dir of Ordnance Services (India), 1945; retired, 1948. High Sheriff of Radnorshire, 1951. *Address*: Y Neuadd, Rhayader, Powys. *T*: Rhayader 810227.

LEWIS, Captain Roger Curzon, DSO 1939; OBE 1944; RN retired; *b* 19 July 1909; *s* of late F. W. and K. M. Lewis; *m* 1944, Marguerite Christiane (*d* 1971), *e d* of late Captain A. D. M. Cherry, RN, retd; two *s*. *Educ*: Royal Naval Coll., Dartmouth. HMS Lowestoft, Africa Station, 1927–29; HMS Vivien and HMS Valentine, 6th Flotilla Home Fleet, 1930–32; Qualifying Lt T 1933; HMS Enterprise, East Indies Station, 1935–37; Staff of HMS Vernon, 1938–39; HMS Florentino, 1939–40; HMS Rodney, 1940–42; Staff of Comdr-in-Chief Mediterranean, 1942–45; Superintendent of Torpedo Experimental Establishment, Greenock, 1950–55; Capt. of the Dockyard and Queen's Harbourmaster, Chatham, 1955–58; retired, 1959. *Address*: 3 Albion Street, Shaldon, Teignmouth, Devon TQ14 0DF.

LEWIS, Roland Swaine, FRCS; Honorary Consultant Surgeon to the ENT Department, King's College Hospital, since 1973 (Consultant Surgeon, 1946–65, Senior Consultant Surgeon, 1965–73); Honorary Consultant ENT Surgeon: to Mount Vernon Hospital and The Radium Institute; to Norwood and District Hospital; *b* 23 Nov. 1908; *s* of Dr William James Lewis, MOH, and Constance Mary Lewis, Tyrwaun, Ystalyfera; *m* 1936, Mary Christianna Milne (Christianna Brand); one adopted *d*. *Educ*: Epsom Coll.; St John's Coll., Cambridge; St George's Hospital. BA Cantab 1929; FRCS 1934; MA Cantab 1945; MB BCh Cantab 1945. Surgical Chief Asst, St George's Hospital, 1935. Major, RAMC (ENT Specialist), 1939–45. *Publications*: papers to medical journals. *Recreations*: ornithology, fishing. *Address*: 88 Maida Vale, W9 1PR. *T*: 01–624 6253; Aberdar, Cwrt y Cadno, Llanwrda, Dyfed.

LEWIS, Ronald Howard; MP (Lab) Carlisle since 1964; *b* 16 July 1909; *s* of Oliver Lewis, coal miner; *m* 1937, Edna Cooke (*d* 1976); two *s*. *Educ*: Elementary Sch. and Cliff Methodist Coll. Left school at 14 years of age and worked in coal mines (Somerset; subseq. Derbyshire, 1930–36); then railways (LNER Sheds, Langwith Junction); left that employment on being elected to Parliament. Mem., Blackwell RDC, 1940–73 (twice Chm.); Derbyshire CC, 1949–74; Mem. Bd of Directors, Pleasley Co-operative Soc. Ltd, 1948–70 (Pres. 1952). Mem. NUR. Vice-Chm., House of Commons Trades Union Gp, 1979–82. Methodist Local Preacher. *Recreations*: walking, football, gardening. *Address*: 22 Alandale Avenue, Langwith Junction, Mansfield, Notts. *T*: Mansfield 742460.

LEWIS, Séan D.; see Day-Lewis.

LEWIS, Terence; MP (Lab) Worsley, since 1983; *b* 29 Dec. 1935; *s* of Andrew Lewis; *m* 1958, Audrey, *d* of William Clarke; one *s*. *Educ*: Mt Carmel Sch., Salford. Nat. service, RAMC, 1954–56. Personnel Officer. Member: ASTMS; TGWU. Member: Kearsley UDC, 1971–74; Bolton BC, 1975– (Chm., Educn Cttee, 1982–83). *Address*: House of Commons, SW1; 54 Greenmount Park, Kearsley, Bolton, Lancs. *Labour Clubs*: Astley, Higher Folds, Mosley Common, Little Hulton, Armitage, Walkden, Cadishead.

LEWIS, Sir Terence (Murray), Kt 1986; OBE 1979; GM 1960; QPM 1977; Commissioner of Police, Queensland, since 1976; *b* 29 Feb. 1928; *s* of late George Murray Lewis and of Monica Ellen Lewis (*née* Hanlon); *m* 1952, Hazel Catherine Lewis (*née* Gould); three *s* two *d*. *Educ*: Univ. of Queensland (DPA 1974; BA 1978). Queensland Police Force, 1948; Criminal Investigation Br., 1950–63; Juvenile Aid Bureau, 1963–73; Inspector of Police, 1973. Member: Royal Aust. Inst. of Public Admin., 1964; Internat. Police Assoc., 1968; Internat. Assoc. of Chiefs of Police, 1977. Churchill Fellow, 1968; FAIM 1978. Hon. Correspondent for Royal Humane Soc. of Australasia, 1981. Patron, Vice-Patron, Pres., Trustee, or Mem., numerous Qld organisations. Queensland Father of the Year, 1980. Silver Jubilee Medal, 1977. *Recreation*: reading. *Address*: 30 Makerston Street, Brisbane, Qld 4000, Australia. *T*: (07) 226–6488.

LEWIS, Thomas Loftus Townshend, CBE 1979; FRCS; Consultant Obstetric and Gynæcological Surgeon at Guy's Hospital, Queen Charlotte's Maternity Hospital and

Chelsea Hospital for Women, 1948–83; Hon. Consultant in Obstetrics and Gynaecology, to the Army, 1973–83; *b* 27 May 1918; *e s* of late Neville Lewis and his first wife, Theodosia Townshend; *m* 1946, Kathleen Alexandra Ponsonby Moore; five *s*. *Educ:* Diocesan Coll., Rondebosch, S Africa; St Paul's Sch.; Cambridge Univ.; Guy's Hospital. BA Cantab (hons in Nat. Sci. Tripos), 1939; MB, BChir Cantab, 1942. FRCS 1946; MRCOG 1948; FRCOG 1961. House Appointments Guy's Hospital, 1942–43; Gold Medal and Prize in Obstetrics, Guy's Hospital, 1942. Volunteered to join South African Medical Corps, 1944; seconded to RAMC and served as Capt. in Italy and Greece, 1944–45. Returned to Guy's Hospital; Registrar in Obstetrics and Gynæcology, 1946, Obstetric Surgeon, 1948; Surgeon, Chelsea Hosp. for Women, 1950, Surgeon, Queen Charlotte's Maternity Hosp., 1952. Examiner in Obstetrics and Gynæcology: University of Cambridge, 1950; University of London, 1954; Royal College of Obstetricians and Gynæcologists, 1952; London Soc. of Apothecaries, 1955; University of St Andrews, 1960. Hon. Sec. and Mem. Council, Royal College of Obstetricians and Gynæcologists, 1955–68, 1971–, Vice-Pres., 1976–78; Mem. Council Obstetric Section, Royal Society of Med., 1953– (Pres. 1981); co-opted Mem. Council, RCS, 1978–81. Guest Prof. to Brisbane, Australia, Auckland, New Zealand, 1959, Johns Hopkins Hosp., Baltimore, 1966; Litchfield Lectr, University of Oxford, 1968; Sims-Black Prof. to Australia, NZ and Rhodesia, 1970. *Publications:* Progress in Clinical Obstetrics and Gynæcology, 2nd edn 1964; (ed jtly and contrib.) Obstetrics by Ten Teachers, 11th edn 1966 to 14th edn 1984; (jtly) Queen Charlotte's Textbook of Obstetrics, 12th edn 1970; (ed jtly and contrib.) Gynaecology by Ten Teachers, 12th edn 1970 to 14th edn 1984; (contrib.) French's Index of Differential Diagnosis, 10th edn 1973 to 12th edn 1984; contributions to: Lancet, BMJ, Practitioner, Proc. Roy. Soc. Med., Encyclopædia Britannica Book of the Year (annual contrib.), etc. *Recreations:* ski-ing, sailing, tennis, golf, croquet, wind-surfing, underwater swimming, photography, viniculture on the Isle of Elba. *Address:* Parkside Hospital, Wimbledon, SW19. *T:* 01–946 4202; (home) 13 Copse Hill, Wimbledon, SW20. *T:* 01–946 5089. *Clubs:* Old Pauline; Royal Wimbledon Golf; Guy's Hospital Rugby Football (Pres.).

LEWIS, Trevor Oswin, CBE 1983; JP; *b* 29 Nov. 1935; *s* of 3rd Baron Merthyr, PC, KBE, TD, and of Violet, *y d* of Brig.-Gen. Sir Frederick Charlton Meyrick, 2nd Bt, CB, CMG; *S* father, 1977, as 4th Baron Merthyr, but disclaimed his peerage for life; also as 4th Bt (*cr* 1896) but does not use the title; *m* 1964, Susan Jane, *yr d* of A. J. Birt-Llewellin; one *s* three *d*. *Educ:* Downs Sch.; Eton; Magdalen Coll., Oxford; Magdalene Coll., Cambridge. Mem. Countryside Commn, 1973–83 (Dep. Chm., 1980–83); Chm., Countryside Commn's Cttee for Wales, 1973–80. JP Dyfed, formerly Pembs, 1969. *Heir (to disclaimed peerage):* s David Trevor Lewis, *b* 21 Feb. 1977. *Address:* Hean Castle, Saundersfoot, Dyfed SA69 9AL. *T:* Saundersfoot 812222.

LEWIS, Dame Vera Margaret; *see* Lynn, Dame Vera.

LEWIS, Wilfrid Bennett, CC (Canada) 1967; CBE 1946; FRS 1945; FRSC 1952; MA; PhD; Senior Vice-President, Science, Atomic Energy of Canada Ltd, 1963–73, retired; Distinguished Professor of Science, Queen's University, since 1973; *b* 24 June 1908; *s* of Arthur Wilfrid Lewis and Isoline Maud Steavenson; unmarried. *Educ:* Haileybury Coll., Herts; Gonville and Caius Coll., Cambridge, Hon. Fellow 1971. Cavendish Laboratory, Cambridge, research in Radio-activity and Nuclear Physics, 1930–39; Research Fellowship, Gonville and Caius Coll., 1934–40; University Demonstrator in Physics, 1934; University Lecturer in Physics, 1937; lent to Air Ministry as Senior Scientific Officer, 1939; Chief Superintendent Telecommunications Research Establishment, Ministry of Aircraft Production, 1945–46; Dir of Division of Atomic Energy Research, National Research Council of Canada, 1946–52; Vice-Pres. Research and Development, Atomic Energy of Canada, Ltd, 1952–63. Canadian Representative United Nations Scientific Advisory Cttee, 1955–. Fellow American Nuclear Soc., 1959 (Pres., 1961); For. Associate, Nat. Acad. of Engineering, USA, 1976; Hon. Mem., Alpha Nu Sigma Soc., Iowa State Univ., 1984; Hon. Fellow: IEE, 1974; UMIST, 1974; Silver Jubilee Hon. Fellow, INucE, 1984. Hon. DSc: Queen's Univ., Kingston, Ontario, 1960; Saskatchewan, 1964; McMaster Univ., Hamilton, Ontario, 1965; Dartmouth Coll., New Hampshire, 1967; McGill Univ., Montreal, 1969; Royal Mil. Coll., Kingston, Ont, 1974; Laurentian, 1977; Birmingham, 1977; Univ. of New Brunswick, 1982; Hon. LLD: Dalhousie Univ., Halifax, Nova Scotia, 1960; Carleton Univ., Ottawa, 1962; Trent Univ., Peterborough, Ont, 1969; Toronto, 1972; Victoria, BC, 1975. Amer. Medal of Freedom, with Silver Palms, 1947. First Outstanding Achievement Award, Public Service of Canada, 1966; Atoms for Peace Award (shared), 1967; Can. Assoc. of Physicists 25th anniversary special Gold Medal, 1970; Royal Medal, Royal Soc., 1972; Gen. A. G. L. McNaughton Award and Medal, Canadian Region IEEE, 1981; Enrico Fermi Award and Medal, US Dept of Energy, 1982. *Publications:* Electrical Counting, 1942; (ed jtly) International Arrangements for Nuclear Fuel Reprocessing, 1977; articles in Wireless Engineer, 1929, 1932 and 1936; papers in Proc. Royal Society A. 1931, 1932, 1933, 1934, 1936, 1940; etc. *Recreation:* walking. *Address:* Box 189, 13 Beach Avenue, Deep River, Ontario K0J 1PO. *T:* 613–584–3561.

LEWIS, Sir (William) Arthur, Kt 1963; PhD, BCom (London); MA (Manchester); James S. McDonnell Distinguished University Professor of Economics and International Affairs, Princeton University, 1982–83, Emeritus since 1983; *b* 23 Jan. 1915; 4th *s* of George F. and Ida Lewis, Castries, St Lucia; *m* 1947, Gladys Jacobs; two *d*. *Educ:* St Mary's Coll., St Lucia; London Sch. of Economics. Lecturer at London Sch. of Economics, 1938–47; Reader in Colonial Economics, University of London, 1947; Stanley Jevons Prof. of Political Economy, University of Manchester, 1948–58; Principal, University Coll. of the West Indies, 1959–62; Vice-Chancellor, University of the West Indies, 1962–63; Princeton University: Prof. of Public and International Affairs, 1963–68; James Madison Prof. of Political Economy, 1968–82. Pres., Caribbean Development Bank, 1970–73. Assigned by United Nations as Economic Adviser to the Prime Minister of Ghana, 1957–58; Dep. Man. Dir, UN Special Fund, 1959–60. Temp. Principal, Board of Trade, 1943, Colonial Office, 1944; Consultant to Caribbean Commn, 1949; Mem. UN Group of Experts on Under-developed Countries, 1951; Part-time Mem. Board of Colonial Development Corporation, 1951–53; Mem. Departmental Cttee on National Fuel Policy, 1951–52; Consultant to UN Economic Commission for Asia and the Far East, 1952; to Gold Coast Govt, 1953; to Govt of Western Nigeria, 1955. Mem. Council, Royal Economic Soc., 1949–58; Pres. Manchester Statistical Soc., 1955–56. Chancellor, Univ. of Guyana, 1966–73. Hon. LHD: Columbia, Boston Coll., Wooster Coll., DePaul, Brandeis; Hon. LLD: Toronto, Wales, Williams, Bristol, Dakar, Leicester, Rutgers, Brussels, Open Univ., Atlanta, Hartford, Bard, Harvard, Howard; Hon. LittD: West Indies, Lagos, Northwestern; Hon. DSc, Manchester; Hon. DSc (Econ) London; Hon. DSocSc Yale. Corresp. Fellow, British Acad., 1974; Hon. Fellow, LSE; For. Fellow Amer. Acad. of Arts and Sciences; Mem., Amer. Phil. Soc.; Hon. Fellow Weizmann Inst.; Distinguished Fellow, Amer. Economic Assoc., 1970 (Pres. 1983). (Jtly) Nobel Prize for Economics, 1979. *Publications:* Economic Survey, 1918–1939, 1949; Overhead Costs, 1949; The Principles of Economic Planning, 1949; The Theory of Economic Growth, 1955; Politics in West Africa, 1965; Development Planning, 1966; Reflections on the Economic Growth of Nigeria, 1968; Some Aspects of Economic Development, 1969;

Tropical Development 1880–1913, 1971; The Evolution of the International Economic Order, 1977; Growth and Fluctuations 1870–1913, 1978; Racial Conflict and Economic Development, 1985; articles in technical, economic and law jls. *Address:* Woodrow Wilson School, Princeton University, Princeton, NJ 08540, USA.

LEWIS, William Edmund Ames, OBE 1961; Charity Commissioner, 1962–72; *b* 21 Sept. 1912; *s* of late Ernest W. Lewis, FRCSE, Southport, Lancashire; *m* 1939, Mary Elizabeth, *e d* of late C. R. Ashbee; two *s* one *d*. *Educ:* Merchant Taylors', Great Crosby; Emmanuel Coll., Cambridge. Barrister-at-law, Inner Temple, 1935. Entered Charity Commission, 1939; Asst Commissioner, 1953–61; Sec., 1961–69. Served in RAF, 1941–46. *Recreations:* music, painting. *Address:* Watermans, Ewhurst Green, Robertsbridge, East Sussex. *T:* Staplecross 523. *Club:* United Oxford & Cambridge University.

LEWIS-BOWEN, Thomas Edward Ifor; His Honour Judge Lewis-Bowen; a Circuit Judge, since 1980; *b* 20 June 1933; *s* of Lt-Col J. W. Lewis-Bowen and late Mrs K. M. Lewis-Bowen (*née* Rice); *m* 1965, Gillian, *d* of Reginald Brett, Puckington, Som; one *s* two *d*. *Educ:* Ampleforth; St Edmund Hall, Oxford. Called to Bar, Middle Temple, 1958. A Recorder of the Crown Court, 1974–80. *Address:* Flat 4, Asquith Court, Eaton Crescent, Swansea, West Glamorgan. *T:* Swansea 473736; Clynfyw, Boncath, Dyfed. *T:* Boncath 236.

LEWIS-JONES, Captain (Robert) Gwilym, CBE 1969; RN retired; Chairman, y Dydd Press Ltd, since 1982; *b* 22 Feb. 1922; *s* of Captain David Lewis Jones and Olwen Lewis Jones (*née* Evans), Corris and Dolgellau; *m* 1946, Ann Mary, *d* of David and Margaret Owen, Dolgellau; two *s*. *Educ:* Tywyn Grammar Sch.; Gonville and Caius Coll., Cambridge. CEng, MRAeS, FBIM. FAA Observers Course, 1942–43; 842 Sqdn in HM Ships Indefatigable, Furious and Fencer on Murmansk and Atlantic convoys, 1943–45; Long Air Communications Course, 1945–46; Long Air Electronics/Electrical Course, 1946–47; RRE Malvern, 1947–49; Long Ships Electrical Course, 1950; RAE Farnborough, 1950–53; Sen. Aircraft Engr Off., HMS Albion, 1953–56; Dep. Comd Engr Off., Staff of Flag Officer Naval Air Comd, 1956–58; Head of Air Electrical Comd, RN Air Stn Brawdy, 1958–61; Sqdn Weapons Off., HMS Caesar and 8th Destroyer Sqdn, 1961–63; Exec. Off. and 2nd in Comd, HMS Condor, 1963–65; Gen. Man., RN Aircraft Yard, Belfast, 1965–67; Dir of Aircraft Armament, MoD (N), 1967–68; Jt Services Planning and Co-ordinating Off. responsible for Armed Forces participation in Investiture of Prince of Wales, 1967–69; Sen. Officers War Course, RNC Greenwich, 1969–70; Staff of Dir Gen. Ships (Directorate Naval Ship Production), 1970–72; Dir, Fleet Management Services, 1973–75; Dir, Naval Management and Orgn, 1975–76. ADC to HM the Queen, 1976. Lt-Comdr 1952; Comdr 1958; Captain 1967. Member: (C) for Carshalton, GLC, 1977–81; Dolgellau Town Council (Dep. Mayor). Chm., Merioneth SSAFA, 1984–; Dep. Chm., Gwynedd Valuation Panel, 1984–; Mem., Snowdonia Nat. Park Cttee, 1982–. Deacon, Welsh Presbyterian Church, 1983–. JP SE London, 1979–81. *Recreations:* golf, choral music, Welsh culture. *Address:* Mansiriol, Dolgellau, Gwynedd. *T:* Dolgellau 422526.

LEWISHAM, Viscount; William Legge; Chartered Accountant; *b* 23 Sept. 1949; *e s* and *heir* of 9th Earl of Dartmouth, *qv. Educ:* Eton; Christ Church, Oxford; Harvard Business Sch. Secretary, Oxford Union Soc., 1969. Contested (C): Leigh, Lancs, Feb. 1974; Stockport South, Oct. 1974. *Recreations:* squash, watching American football. *Address:* The Manor House, Chipperfield, King's Langley, Herts. *Clubs:* Turf; Harvard (New York).

LEWISHAM, Archdeacon of; *see* Lacey, Ven. C. G.

LEWISOHN, Anthony Clive Leopold; His Honour Judge Lewisohn; a Circuit Judge, since 1974; *b* 1 Aug. 1925; *s* of John Lewisohn and Gladys (*née* Solomon); *m* 1957, Lone Ruthwen Jurgensen; two *s*. *Educ:* Stowe; Trinity Coll., Oxford (MA). Royal Marines, 1944–45; Lieut, Oxf. and Bucks LI, 1946–47. Called to Bar, Middle Temple, 1951; S Eastern Circuit.

LEWISOHN, Neville Joseph; Director of Dockyard Manpower and Productivity (Under Secretary), Ministry of Defence, 1979–82; *b* 28 May 1922; *s* of Victor and Ruth Lewisohn; *m* 1944, Patricia Zeffertt; two *d* (and one *d* decd). *Educ:* Sutton County Sch., Surrey. Entered Admiralty as Clerical Officer, 1939; promoted through intervening grades to Principal, 1964; Dir of Resources and Progs (Ships), 1972 (Asst Sec.); Head of Civilian Management (Specialists), 2 Div., 1976. *Recreations:* music, drama. *Address:* 46 Middle Stoke, Limpley Stoke, Bath BA3 6JG. *T:* Limpley Stoke 3357.

LEWISON, Peter George Hornby, CBE 1977; Chairman, National Dock Labour Board, 1969–77; Member, National Ports Council, 1972–77; *b* 5 July 1911; *s* of late George and Maud Elizabeth Lewison; *m* 1937, Lyndsay Sutton Rothwell; one *s* one *d*. *Educ:* Dulwich; Magdalen Coll., Oxford. Dunlop Rubber Co., Coventry, 1935–41; Min. of Supply (seconded), 1941–44; RNVR (Special Br.), 1944–46. Min. of Labour, 1946–47; Personnel Manager, British-American Tobacco Co. Ltd, 1947–68, retd. *Recreations:* music, cricket, maintaining a sense of curiosity. *Address:* Court Hill House, East Dean, Chichester, Sussex. *T:* Singleton 200. *Clubs:* MCC; Goodwood Golf.

LE WITT, Jan; painter, poet and designer; *b* 3 April 1907; *s* of Aaron Le Witt and Deborah (*née* Koblenz); *m* 1939, Alina Prusicka; one *s*. *Educ:* autodidact. Began artistic career as self-taught designer in Warsaw, 1927; first one-man exhibn of his graphic work, Soc. of Fine Arts, Warsaw, 1930. Co-author and illustrator of children's books, publ. several European langs. Settled in England, 1937; Brit. subject, 1947–; Member of Le Witt-Him partnership, 1933–54. During War of 1939–45 executed (in partnership) a series of murals for war factory canteens, posters for Min. of Inf., Home Office, GPO, etc. Originator of a range of Britain's World War II anti-invasion defences in 1940 that prevented the Nazis from gaining a foothold on British soil. Co-designer of murals for Festival of Britain, 1951, and Festival Clock, Battersea Park. First one-man exhibn, Zwemmer Gall., London, 1947; subseq. Hanover Gall. London, 1951; in Rome, 1952; Zwemmer Gall., 1953; New York, 1954; Milan, 1957; Paris, 1960; Grosvenor Gall., London, 1961; Paris, 1963; Musée d'Antibes (retrospective), 1965; Salon d'Automne, Paris, 1963; Salon de Mai, Paris, 1964; Warsaw (retrosp.), 1967; Venice (retrosp.) (organised by City of Venice), 1970; Paris, 1972. In 1955 when at top of his profession, he gave up graphic design to devote himself entirely to painting. *Works at:* Musée National d'Art Moderne, Paris; Nat. Museum, Jerusalem; Nat. Museum, Warsaw; Musée d'Antibes; Museum and Art Gall., Halifax; City Art Gall., Middlesbrough; British Council; Contemp. Art Soc., London; and in private collections. Represented in collective exhibns in Tate Gall., London, and many foreign galleries. Other artistic activities: décors and costumes for Sadler's Wells Ballet; glass sculptures Venice (Murano); tapestry designs, Aubusson. Gold Medal, Vienna, 1948; Gold Medal Triennale, Milan, 1954; Member: Alliance Graphique Internationale, 1948–60; Exec. Council, Société Européenne de Culture, Venice, 1961–; Nominated Member Italian Acad. (with Gold Medal), 1980; Fellow, Internat. PEN, 1978. *Publications:* Vegetabull, 1956 (London and New York); A Necklace for Andromeda, 1976; contribs to Poetry Review; Temenos, Adam;

Comprendre, Malahat Review, etc. *Relevant Publication:* Sir Herbert Read, Jean Cassou, Pierre Emmanuel and John Smith (jointly), Jan Le Witt, London 1971, Paris 1972, NY 1973. *Recreations:* music, swimming against the current. *Address:* The Studio, 117 Ladbroke Road, Holland Park, W11 3PR. *T:* 01–229 1570. *Club:* PEN.

LEWITTER, Prof. Lucjan Ryszard; Professor of Slavonic Studies, University of Cambridge, 1968–84; *b* 1922. *Educ:* schools in Poland; Perse Sch., Cambridge; Christ's Coll., Cambridge. PhD 1951. Univ. Asst Lectr in Polish, 1948; Fellow of Christ's Coll., 1951; Dir of Studies in Modern Languages, 1951–64; Tutor, 1960–68; Vice-Master, 1977–80; Univ. Lectr in Slavonic Studies (Polish), 1953–68. *Publications:* articles in learned jls. *Address:* Christ's College, Cambridge CB2 3BU. *T:* Cambridge 334900. *Club:* United Oxford & Cambridge University.

LEWTHWAITE, Brig. Rainald Gilfrid, CVO 1975; OBE 1974; MC 1943; *b* 21 July 1913; 2nd *s* of Sir William Lewthwaite, 2nd Bt of Broadgate, Cumberland, and Beryl Mary Stopford Hickman; *b* of Sir William Anthony Lewthwaite, 3rd Bt, *qv*; *m* 1936, Margaret Elizabeth Edmonds, MBE 1942, 2nd *d* of late Harry Edmonds and Florence Jane Moncrieffe Bolton, High Green, Redding, Conn, USA; two *s* one *d* (and one *d* decd). *Educ:* Rugby Sch.; Trinity Coll., Cambridge. BA (Hons) Law 1934. Joined Scots Guards, 1934. Served War of 1939–45 (MC, despatches twice). Retired as Defence and Military Attaché, British Embassy, Paris, 1968. Dir of Protocol, Hong Kong, 1969–76. French Croix-de-Guerre with Palm, 1945. *Recreation:* country life. *Address:* Broadgate, Millom, Cumbria LA18 5JZ. *T:* Broughton-in-Furness 295; 14 Edwardes Square, W8 6HE. *T:* 01–602 6323. *Clubs:* Cavalry and Guards, The Pilgrims.

LEWTHWAITE, Sir William Anthony, 3rd Bt, *cr* 1927; Solicitor of Supreme Court, 1937–75; *b* 26 Feb. 1912; *e s* of Sir William Lewthwaite, 2nd Bt, JP, and Beryl Mary Stopford (*d* 1970), *o c* of late Major Stopford Cosby Hickman, JP, DL, of Fenloe, Co. Clare; *S* father, 1933; *m* 1936, Lois Mairi, *o c* of late Capt. Robertson Kerr Clark (brother of 1st Baron Inverchapel, PC, GCMG) and Lady Beatrice Minnie Ponsonby, *d* of 9th Earl of Drogheda (who *m* 2nd, 1941, 1st Baron Rankeillour, PC; she *d* 1966); one *d* (and one *d* decd). *Educ:* Rugby; Trinity Coll., Cambridge, BA. Signalman Royal Corps of Signals, 1942–43; Lt, Grenadier Guards, 1943–46. Mem. Council, Country Landowners Association, 1949–64. Mem. Cttee: Westminster Law Society, 1964–73; Brooks's Club, 1953–81. *Heir: b* Brig. Rainald Gilfrid Lewthwaite, *qv*. *Address:* 73 Dovehouse Street, SW3 6JZ. *T:* 01–352 7203.

LEWY, Casimir, FBA 1980; Fellow of Trinity College, Cambridge, since 1959; Reader in Philosophy, University of Cambridge, 1972–82, now Emeritus; *b* 26 Feb. 1919; *o c* of Ludwik Lewy and Izabela Lewy (*née* Rybier); *m* 1945, Eleanor Ford; three *s*. *Educ:* Mikolaj Rej Sch., Warsaw; Fitzwilliam House and Trinity Coll., Cambridge (BA 1939, MA 1943, PhD 1943). Stanton Student, Trinity Coll., Cambridge, 1939–41; Burney Student, Univ. of Cambridge, 1940–42; Sen. Rouse Ball Student, Trinity Coll., Cambridge, 1942–45; Lectr in Philosophy, Univ. of Liverpool, 1945–52; Univ. Lectr in Philosophy, Cambridge, 1952–72, Sidgwick Lectr, 1955–72. Visiting Professor of Philosophy: Univ. of Texas at Austin, 1967; Yale Univ., 1969. *Publications:* Meaning and Modality, 1976; *editor:* G. E. Moore, Commonplace Book 1919–1953, 1962; G. E. Moore, Lectures on Philosophy, 1966; C. D. Broad, Leibniz, 1975; C. D. Broad, Kant, 1978; C. D. Broad, Ethics, 1985; articles in philosophical jls; *relevant publication:* Exercises in Analysis: essays by students of Casimir Lewy, ed Ian Hacking, 1985. *Recreations:* reading, walking. *Address:* Trinity College, Cambridge. *T:* Cambridge 338400.

LEY, Arthur Harris, FRSA; FRIBA, AADip, FIStructE, MRAeS; former Partner, Ley Colbeck & Partners, Architects; *b* 24 Dec. 1903; *s* of late Algernon Sydney Richard Ley, FRIBA, and Esther Eliza Harris; *m* 1935, Ena Constance Riches; one *d*. *Educ:* Westminster City Sch.; AA Coll. of Architecture. Architect for: Principal London Office Barclays Bank DCO; Head Office Nat. Mutual Life Assce Soc.; Palmerston Hse, EC2; Baltic Hse, EC3; Bishops House, Bishopsgate; Broad Street House; Hqrs Marine Soc.; Hqrs SBAC; Hqrs RAeS; Hqrs Instn Struct. Engrs; York Hall, Windsor Gt Park; Aircraft Research Assoc. Estab., Bedford. Factories and Office Blocks for: Vickers Ltd, at Barrow, etc.; British Aircraft Corporation at Weybridge and Hurn; Wallpaper Manufrs Ltd; Sir Isaac Pitman & Sons; Decca Radar Ltd; Ever Ready Co.; also numerous office blocks in the City of London, Leeds, Inverness and Vancouver. Banks for: Hambro; Nat. Provincial; Barclays; Bank of Scandinavia; Head London office, Hongkong and Shanghai Bank. Central area develt, Watford and Ashford, Kent. Hospitals: Watford and Harrow. Schools: London, Hertfordshire, Barrow in Furness and Surrey. Mem. Council: Architects Registr. Coun. of UK, 1958–60; Instn Struct. Engrs, 1951–54; London Chamber of Commerce, 1955–79; Associated Owners of City Properties (Pres., 1971–77). Hosp. Bd, Ravenscourt Pk, 1972–. Consultant, Bishopsgate Foundn; Mem. Court, City Univ.; Liveryman: Worshipful Co. of Paviors (Master, 1962), and of Upholders (Master, 1966); Freeman, City of London; Sheriff 1964–65, and Mem. Court of Common Council, City of London, 1964–80; Churchwarden of St Mary-le-Bow, 1960–83. Grand Officer of the Order of Merit (Chile). *Publications:* contributions to journals and technical press. *Address:* Weston House, 77 St John Street, EC1M 4HP. *T:* 01–253 5555; 14 Fox Close, off Queens Road, Weybridge, Surrey KT13 0AX. *T:* Weybridge 42701. *Clubs:* City Livery (Pres., 1968–69), Guildhall, United Wards (Pres., 1961), Bishopsgate Ward (Pres., 1966).

LEY, Sir Francis (Douglas), 4th Bt *cr* 1905; MBE 1961; TD; DL; JP; *b* 5 April 1907; *yr s* of Major Sir Gordon Ley, 2nd Bt (*d* 1944); *S* brother, 1980; *m* 1931, Violet Geraldine Johnson; one *s* one *d*. *Educ:* Eton; Magdalene Coll., Cambridge (MA). JP 1939, DL 1957, Derbyshire. High Sheriff of Derbyshire, 1956. *Heir: s* Ian Francis Ley [*b* 12 June 1934; *m* 1957, Caroline Margaret, *d* of Major George Henry Errington, MC; one *s* one *d*]. *Address:* Pond House, Shirley, Derby DE6 3AZ. *T:* Ashbourne 60327.

LEYLAND, Sir V. E. N.; *see* Naylor-Leyland.

LEYSER, Prof. Karl Joseph, TD 1963; FBA 1983; Chichele Professor of Medieval History, Oxford University, and Fellow, All Souls College, Oxford, since 1984; *b* 24 Oct. 1920; *s* of late Otto Leyser and of Emmy Leyser; *m* 1962, Henrietta Louise Valerie Bateman; two *s* two *d*. *Educ:* Hindenburg Gymnasium, Düsseldorf; St Paul's School; Magdalen College, Oxford. Gibbs Scholar in History, 1946, Bryce Research Student, 1948. FRHistS 1960, FSA 1980. War service: Pioneer Corps, 1940–43 (Cpl); The Black Watch (RHR), 1943; commissioned 1944; service with 7th Bn, 51 Div., NW Europe, 1944–45 (despatches 1945) (Captain); Territorial, 1949–63, 6/7 The Black Watch and HQ 153 Bde (Major 1961). Official Fellow and Tutor in History, Magdalen Coll., Oxford, 1948–84, Senior Dean of Arts, 1951–55, Vice-Pres., 1971–72; University Lectr, 1950–65, and 1975–84 (CUF); Special Lectr, Medieval European Hist., 1965–75; Chm., Faculty of Modern Hist., 1980–82, Vice-Chm. Bd, 1985–. Lectures: Dark Age, Univ. of Kent, 1981; Raleigh, British Acad., 1983; Collège de France, 1984; Denys Hay Seminar in Medieval and Renaissance Hist., Univ. of Edinburgh, 1986. Governor: Magdalen Coll. Sch., Oxford, 1971–84; St Paul's Schs, 1974–. Mem. Council: Max-Planck-Inst. für Geschichte, Göttingen, 1978–; RHistS, 1985–; German Historical Inst., London, 1985–; corresp. Mem., Zentral-Direktion, Monumenta Germaniae Historica, 1979–; Kuratorium, Historisches Kolleg, 1985–. *Publications:* Rule and Conflict in an Early Medieval Society: Ottonian Saxony, 1979; Medieval Germany and its Neighbours 900–1250, 1982; articles in learned collections. *Address:* All Souls College, Oxford. *T:* Oxford 722251.

LEYTON, Dr (Robert) Nevil (Arthur); Consulting Physician, specialising in Migraine, since 1950; *s* of Prof. A. S. F. Leyton, MD, DSc, FRCP, and Mrs H. G. Leyton, MD; *m* 1943, Wendy (*d* 1960), *er d* of Tom and Dylis Cooper; one *s*. *Educ:* private; Gonville and Caius Coll., Cambridge; Westminster Hospital (entrance Schol.). BA (Cantab) Double Hons Natural Sciences Tripos, 1932; MA 1938. Ho. Phys. and Surg., Westminster Hospital, 1937. Served with RAF, 1943–46, and with 601 Squadron RAuxAF, 1947–57; retired rank Sqdn Leader. Registrar (Med.), St Stephen's Hospital, 1947–50; Hon. Cons. Physician to Migraine Clinic, Putney Health Centre, 1950–68; Hon. Cons. in migraine to Royal Air Forces Assoc., 1947–; Hon. Cons. Physician to Wendy Leyton Memorial Migraine Centre, Harley Street, 1961–; Sen. Medical Adviser, International Migraine Foundn, 1961–; Consulting Physician to Kingdom of Libya, 1968–69; MO, 1971–72, Chief MO, 1972–73, Gath's Mine Hosp., Mashaba, Rhodesia; Specialist Paediatrician, Estate Group Clinics, Lagos, Nigeria, 1975–76; Consultant Physician, County Hosp., Tralee, Eire, 1976–77. Late Medical Adviser, FA. President, 601 Squadron RAuxAF Old Comrades Assoc., 1963–. Air Force Efficiency Medal, 1954. Kt of Mark Twain, 1979. *Publications:* Migraine and Periodic Headache, 1952 (USA, 1954); Headaches, The Reason and the Relief, 1955 (USA); Migraine, 1962; Migraine, Modern Concepts and Preventative Treatment, 1964; contrib.: Lancet, British Medical Journal, Medical World and Journal, Lancet (USA), etc. *Recreations:* travel, riding, horse racing, lawn tennis (Cambridge Univ. Blue, 1933), squash racquets. *Address:* 49 Harrington Gardens, SW7. *Clubs:* All England Lawn Tennis, Lions (Mashaba and British sections); Hawks' (Cambridge).

LI, Choh-Ming, Hon. KBE 1973 (Hon. CBE 1967); Founding Vice-Chancellor, The Chinese University of Hong Kong, 1964–78; Professor Emeritus, University of California (Berkeley), since 1974; *b* 17 Feb. 1912; *s* of Kanchi Li and Mewching Tsu; *m* 1938, Sylvia Chi-wan Lu; two *s* one *d*. *Educ:* Univ. of California at Berkeley (MA, PhD). Prof. of Economics, Nankai and Southwest Associated and Central Univs in China, 1937–43; Mem., China's special mission to USA, Canada and UK, 1943–45; Dep. Dir-Gen., Chinese Nat. Relief and Rehabilitation Admin. (CNRRA), 1945–47; China's chief deleg. to UN Relief and Rehabilitation Confs and to UN Econ. Commn for Asia and Far East, 1947–49; Chm., Board of Trustees for Rehabilitation Affairs, Nat. Govt of China, 1949–50; Expert on UN Population Commn and Statistical Commn, 1952–57; Lectr, Assoc. Prof., and Prof. of Business Admin., and sometime Dir of Center for Chinese Studies, Univ. of California (Berkeley), 1951–63. Mem., Soc. of Berkeley Fellows, Univ. of Calif, 1981–. Hon. Dr of Laws: Hong Kong, 1967; Michigan, 1967; Marquette, 1969; Western Ontario, 1970; Chinese Univ. of Hong Kong, 1978; Hon. Dr Social Science, Pittsburgh, 1969. Hon. Mem., Internat. Mark Twain Soc. Elise and Walter A. Haas Internat. Award, 1974, Clark Kerr Award, 1979, Univ. of Calif; Soong Foundn Hall of Fame Award, 1980. *Publications:* Economic Development of Communist China, 1959; Statistical System of Communist China, 1962; (ed) Industrial Development in Communist China, 1964; (ed) Asian Workshop on Higher Education, 1969; The First Six Years, 1963–69, 1971; The Emerging University, 1970–74, 1975; New Era Begins 1975–78, 1979; C. M. Li's Chinese Dictionary, 1980 (Hong Kong edn 1980, Shanghai edn 1981). *Recreations:* tennis, calligraphy. *Address:* 81 Northampton Avenue, Berkeley, Calif 94707, USA. *Clubs:* American, Country (Hong Kong); Century (New York); International Platform (Cleveland Heights, Ohio).

LI, Fook Kow, CMG 1975; JP; Chairman, Public Service Commission, Hong Kong, since 1980; *b* 15 June 1922; *s* of Tse Fong Li; *m* 1946, Edith Kwong Li; four *c*. *Educ:* Massachusetts Inst. of Technology (BSc,MSc). Mem. Hong Kong Admin. Service; Teacher, 1948–54; various departmental posts and posts in the Government Secretariat, 1955–60; Asst Financial Sec., Asst Estabt Officer, Dep. Financial Sec. and Estabt Officer, 1961–69; Dep. Dir of Commerce and Industry, 1970; Dep. Sec. for Home Affairs, 1971–72; Dir of Social Welfare, 1972; Sec. for Social Services, 1973; Sec. for Home Affairs, 1977–80. JP Hong Kong, 1959. *Address:* Central Government Offices, Lower Albert Road, Hong Kong. *T:* H-95470. *Clubs:* Royal Hong Kong Jockey, Hong Kong Country.

LI, Hon. Simon Fook Sean; Hon. Mr Justice Li; Justice of Appeal, Hong Kong, since 1980; *b* 19 April 1922; 2nd *s* of late Koon Chun Li and late Tam Doy Hing Li; *m* Marie Veronica Lillian Yang; four *s* one *d*. *Educ:* King's Coll., Hong Kong; Hong Kong Univ.; Nat. Kwangsi Univ.; University Coll., London Univ. (LLB 1950). Barrister-at-Law, Lincoln's Inn, 1951. Crown Counsel, Attorney-General's Chambers, Hong Kong, 1953; Senior Crown Counsel, 1962; District Judge, Hong Kong, 1966; Puisne Judge, Hong Kong, 1971–80. *Recreations:* hiking, swimming. *Address:* Appeal Courts Chambers, Courts of Justice, Hong Kong. *T:* 5–233994. *Clubs:* Royal Commonwealth Society; Hong Kong, Chinese (Hong Kong).

LIAO Poon-Huai, Hon. Donald, CBE 1983 (OBE 1972); Secretary for District Administration, Hong Kong, since 1985; Member: Legislative Council, Hong Kong, since 1980; Executive Council, since 1985; *b* 29 Oct. 1929; *s* of late Liao Huk-Koon and Yeo Tsai-Hoon; *m* 1963, Christine Yuen Ching-Me; two *s* one *d*. *Educ:* Univ. of Hong Kong (BArch Hons); Univ. of Durham (Dip. Landscape Design). Architect, Hong Kong Housing Authority, 1960, Housing Architect, 1966; Commissioner for Housing and Member, Town Planning Board, 1968; Director of Housing and Vice-Chm., Hong Kong Housing Authority, 1973; Sec. for Housing and Chm., Hong Kong Housing Authority, 1980. Fellow, Hong Kong Inst. of Architects. Hon. FIH. *Recreations:* golf, skiing, riding. *Address:* (residence) 95A Kadoorie Avenue, Kowloon, Hong Kong. *T:* 3–7155822; (office) City & New Territories Administration, Kowloon, Hong Kong. *T:* 3–660029. *Clubs:* Royal Hong Kong Golf, Royal Hong Kong Jockey (Hong Kong).

LIARDET, Rear-Adm. Guy Francis, CBE 1985; RN; Flag Officer Second Flotilla, since 1986; *b* 6 Dec. 1934; *s* of Maj.-Gen. Henry Maughan Liardet, *qv*; *m* 1962, Jennifer Anne O'Hagan; one *s* two *d*. *Educ:* Royal Naval Coll., Dartmouth. Trng Comdr, BRNC, Dartmouth, 1969–70; comd HMS Aurora, 1970–72; Exec. Officer, HMS Bristol, 1974–76; Defence Policy Staff, MoD, 1978–79; RCDS, 1980; CSO (Trng), C-in-C Naval Home Comd, 1981–82; comd HMS Cleopatra and Seventh Frigate Sqn, 1983–84; Dir of Public Relations (Navy), MoD, 1984–86. *Publications:* contrib. Naval Review. *Recreations:* sailing; student of political history. *Address:* c/o Royal Bank of Scotland, Holt's Branch, Kirkland House, Whitehall, SW1A 2EB.

LIARDET, Maj.-Gen. Henry Maughan, CB 1960; CBE 1945 (OBE 1942); DSO 1945; DL; *b* 27 Oct. 1906; *s* of late Maj.-Gen. Sir Claude Liardet, KBE, CB, DSO, TD, DL; *m* 1933, Joan Sefton, *d* of Major G. S. Constable, MC, JP; three *s*. *Educ:* Bedford School. 1st Commission for Territorial Army, 1924, Royal Artillery; Regular Commission, Royal Tank Corps, 1927; service UK, India, Egypt, 1927–38; Staff Coll., Camberley, 1939; War of 1939–45: War Office, 1939–41; active service in Egypt, N Africa, Italy, 1941–45; General Staff appointments, command of Regiment and Brigade (despatches twice); Dep. Dir, Manpower Planning, War Office, 1950–52; Comdr, 23 Armd Bde, 1953–54; idc,

1955; Chief of Staff, British Joint Services Mission (Army Staff), Washington, DC, 1956–58; ADC to the Queen, 1956–58; Director-General of Fighting Vehicles, WO, 1958–61; Deputy Master-General of the Ordnance, War Office, 1961–64, retired. Colonel Comdt, Royal Tank Regt, 1961–67. Dir, British Sailors' Soc., 1961–78; Chm., SS&AFA W Sussex Cttee, 1966–85. DL, Sussex, 1964–74, W Sussex 1974–. Sussex CC, 1964–74; Alderman, 1970–74. Pres. Sussex Council, Royal British Legion, 1975–81. *Recreations:* shooting, gardening. *Address:* Warningcamp House, Arundel, West Sussex. *T:* Arundel 882533. *Clubs:* Army and Navy; Sussex.
See also G. F. Liardet.

LIBBY, Donald Gerald, PhD, Under Secretary, Department of Education and Science, since 1980; *b* 2 July 1934; *s* of late Herbert Lionel Libby and of Minnie Libby; *m* 1st, 1961, Margaret Elizabeth Dunlop McLatchie (*d* 1979); one *d*; 2nd, 1982, June Belcher. *Educ:* RMA, Sandhurst; London Univ. (BSc, PhD Physics). CEng, MIEE. Dept of Educn and Science: Principal Scientific Officer, 1967–72; Principal, 1972–74; Asst Sec., 1974–80; Under Sec., Planning and Internat. Relations Br., 1980–82, Architects, Bldg and Schs Br., 1982–86, Further and Higher Educn Br. 2, 1986–. *Recreations:* music, rowing, tennis. *Address:* Lygon Cottage, 26 Wayneflete Tower Avenue, Esher, Surrey KT10 8QG.

LICHFIELD, 5th Earl of, *cr* 1831; **Thomas Patrick John Anson;** Viscount Anson and Baron Soberton, 1806; *b* 25 April 1939; *s* of Viscount Anson (Thomas William Arnold) (*d* 1958) and Princess Anne of Denmark (*née* Anne Fenella Ferelith Bowes-Lyon) (*d* 1980); *S* grandfather, 1960; *m* 1975, Lady Leonora Grosvenor (marr. diss. 1986), *d* of 5th Duke of Westminster, TD; one *s* two *d*. *Educ:* Harrow Sch.; RMA, Sandhurst. Joined Regular Army, Sept. 1957, as Officer Cadet; Grenadier Guards, 1959–62 (Lieut). Now Photographer (known professionally as Patrick Lichfield). FBIPP; FRPS. *Publications:* The Most Beautiful Women, 1981; Lichfield on Photography (also video cassettes), 1981; A Royal Album, 1982; Patrick Lichfield's Unipart Calendar Book, 1982; Patrick Lichfield Creating the Unipart Calendar, 1983; Hot Foot to Zabriskie Point, 1985; Lichfield on Travel Photography, 1986; Not the Whole Truth (autobiog.), 1986. *Heir:* *s* Viscount Anson, *qv*. *Address:* 133 Oxford Gardens, W10 6NE. *T:* 01–969 6161; (seat) Shugborough Hall, Stafford. *T:* Little Haywood 881454. *Club:* White's.

LICHFIELD, Bishop of, since 1983; **Rt. Rev. Keith Norman Sutton;** *b* 23 June 1934; *s* of Norman and Irene Sutton; *m* 1963, Edith Mary Jean Geldard; three *s* one *d*. *Educ:* Jesus College, Cambridge (MA 1959). Curate, St Andrew's, Plymouth, 1959–62; Chaplain, St John's Coll., Cambridge, 1962–67; Tutor and Chaplain, Bishop Tucker Coll., Mukono, Uganda, 1968–73; Principal of Ridley Hall, Cambridge, 1973–78; Bishop Suffragan of Kingston-upon-Thames, 1978–83. *Publication:* The People of God, 1983. *Recreations:* Russian literature, third world issues, music. *Address:* Bishop's House, 22 The Close, Lichfield, Staffs WS13 7LG.

LICHFIELD, Dean of; *see* Lang, Very Rev. J. H.

LICHFIELD, Archdeacon of; *see* Ninis, Ven. R. B.

LICHFIELD, Prof. Nathaniel; Emeritus Professor of the Economics of Environmental Planning, University of London, since 1978; Senior Partner, Nathaniel Lichfield & Partners, Planning Development, Transportation and Economic Consultants, since 1962; Research Director, International Centre for Land Policy Studies, since 1980 (Executive Director, 1975–80); *b* 29 Feb. 1916; 2nd *s* of Hyman Lichman and Fanny (*née* Grecht); *m* 1st, 1942, Rachel Goulden (*d* 1969); two *d*; 2nd, 1970, Dalia Kadury; one *s* one *d*. *Educ:* Raines Foundn Sch.; University of London. BSc (EstMan), PhD (Econ), PPRTPI, FRICS, CEng, MIMunE. From 1942 has worked continuously in urban and regional planning, specialising in econs of planning from 1950, with particular reference to social cost-benefit in planning and land policy; worked in local and central govt depts and private offices. Consultant commns in UK and abroad, incl. UN. Special Lectr, UCL, 1950; Prof. of Econs and Environmental Planning, UCL, 1966–79; Vis. Prof., Sch. of Architecture and Planning, UCL, 1979–. Vis. Prof., Univ. of California, Univ. of Tel Aviv, Hebrew Univ. Jerusalem, and Technion, Haifa. Director: Lichfield-Terp, BV, Holland, Consultants, 1978–; Lichfield Internat. Inc., Washington DC, Consultants, 1978–. *Publications:* Economics of Planned Development, 1956; Cost Benefit Analysis in Urban Redevelopment, 1962; Cost Benefit Analysis in Town Planning: A Case Study of Cambridge, 1966; Israel's New Towns: A Development Strategy, 1971; (with Prof. A. Proudlove) Conservation and Traffic: a case study of York, 1975; (with Peter Kettle and Michael Whitbread) Evaluation in the Urban and Regional Planning Process, 1975; (with Haim Darin-Drabkin) Land Policy in Planning, 1980; papers in Urban Studies, Regional Studies, Land Economics, Town Planning Review. *Recreation:* finding out less and less about more and more. *Address:* 13 Chalcot Gardens, Englands Lane, NW3 4YB. *T:* 01–586 0461. *Club:* Reform.

LICHINE, Mme David; *see* Riabouchinska, Tatiana.

LICHTENSTEIN, Roy; American painter and sculptor; *b* 27 Oct. 1923; *s* of Milton Lichtenstein and Beatrice (*née* Werner); *m* 1st, 1949, Isabe Wilson (marr. diss.); two *s*; 2nd, 1968, Dorothy Herzka. *Educ:* Art Students League, NY; Ohio State Univ. Cartographical draughtsman, US Army, 1943–46; Instructor, Fine Arts Dept, Ohio State Univ., 1946–51; product designer for various cos, Cleveland, 1951–57; Asst Prof., Fine Arts Dept, NY State Univ., 1957–60, Rutgers Univ., 1960–63. Works in Pop Art and other themes derived from comic strip techniques. One-man shows include: Carlebach Gall., NY, 1951; Leo Castelli Gall., NY, 1962, 1963, 1965, 1967, 1971–75, 1977, 1979, 1981, 1983, 1985; Galerie Illeana Sonnabend, Paris, 1963, 1965, 1970, 1975; Venice Biennale, 1966; Pasadena Art Museum, 1967; Walker Art Center, Minneapolis, 1967; Stedelijk Museum, Amsterdam, 1967; Tate Gall., London, 1967; Künsthalle, Berne, 1968; Guggenheim Museum, NY, 1969; Nelson Gall., Kansas City, 1969; Museum of Contemporary Art, Chicago, 1970; Galerie Beyeler, Basel, 1973; Centre Nat. d'Art Contemporain, Centre Beaubourg, Paris, 1975; Seattle Art Museum, 1976; Inst. of Contemp. Art, Boston, 1979; Portland Center for Visual Arts, 1980; St Louis Art Museum, 1981; Seattle Art Museum, 1981; Fort Worth Art Museum, 1981; Whitney Museum of Amer. Art, 1981; Musée des Arts Decoratifs, 1982; Mayor Gall., 1986. Group exhibns include: Six Painters and the Object, Guggenheim Museum, 1963; Venice Biennale, 1966; US Pavilion Expo, (Montreal), 1967; São Paulo Biennale, 1968; 36th Biennial Exhibn of Contemp. Amer. Painting, Corcoran Gall., Washington, DC, 1979. Created outside wall for Circarama of NY State Pavilion, NY World's Fair, 1963; billboard for Expo 67; Mural with Blue Brushstroke, for Equitable Life Tower, NY, 1986. *Address:* PO Box 1369, Southampton, New York, NY 11968, USA.

LICKLEY, Sir Robert (Lang), Kt 1984; CBE 1973; BSc; DIC; FRSE; FEng; Hon. FIMechE; FRAeS; FIProdE; consultant; *b* Dundee, 19 Jan. 1912. *Educ:* Dundee High Sch.; Edinburgh Univ. (Hon. DSc 1972); Imperial Coll. (Fellow, 1973); FCGI 1976. Formerly: Professor of Aircraft Design, College of Aeronautics, Cranfield; Managing Director, Fairey Aviation Ltd; Hawker Siddeley Aviation Ltd, 1960–76 (Asst Man. Dir, 1965–76); Head, Rolls Royce Support Staff, NEB, 1976–79. President: IMechE, 1971; IProdE, 1981–82. FRSE 1977. Hon. FIMechE 1982. *Recreation:* golf. *Address:* Foxwood, Silverdale Avenue, Walton-on-Thames, Surrey KT12 1EQ.

LICKORISH, Leonard John, CBE 1975; Director General, British Tourist Authority, 1970–86; Chairman, European Travel Commission, 1984–86; *b* 10 Aug. 1921; *s* of Adrian J. and Josephine Lickorish; *m* 1945, Eileen Maris Wright (*d* 1983); one *s*. *Educ:* St George's Coll., Weybridge; University Coll., London (BA). Served RAF, 1941–46. British Travel Association: Research Officer, 1946; Asst Dir Gen, 1955; Gen. Man., 1963. Officer of Crown of Belgium, 1967. *Publications:* The Travel Trade, 1955; The Statistics of Tourism, 1975; numerous for nat. and internat. organisations on internat. travel. *Recreation:* gardening. *Address:* 46 Hillway, Highgate, N6 6EP. *Clubs:* Royal Over-Seas League, Royal Automobile.

LIDBURY, Sir John (Towersey), Kt 1971; FRAeS; Vice-Chairman, Hawker Siddeley Group PLC, 1974–83 (Director, 1960; Deputy Managing Director, 1970–81; Consultant, 1983–85); *b* 25 Nov. 1912; *m* 1939, Audrey Joyce (*née* Wigzell); one *s* two *d*. *Educ:* Owen's Sch. Joined Hawker Aircraft Ltd, 1940; Dir, 1951, Gen. Manager, 1953, Man. Dir, 1959, Chm., 1961; Jt Man. Dir, Hawker Siddeley Aviation Ltd, 1959, Dir and Chief Exec., 1961, Dep. Chm. and Man. Dir, 1963–77; Chairman: Hawker Siddeley Dynamics Ltd, 1971–77 (Dep. Chm., 1970); High Duty Alloys Ltd, 1978–79 (Dep. Chm., 1971); High Duty Alloys Castings Ltd, 1978–79; High Duty Alloys Extrusions Ltd, 1978–79; High Duty Alloys Forgings Ltd, 1978–79; Carlton Industries PLC, 1981–82 (Dir, 1978–82); Director: Hawker Siddeley International Ltd, 1963–82; Smiths Industries PLC, 1978–85; Invergordon Distillers (Hldgs) PLC, 1978–82. Dir, Hawker Siddeley Pensions Trustees Ltd, 1968–82 (Chm., 1975–82). Pres., 1969–70, Mem. Council, 1959–77, Soc. of British Aerospace Companies Ltd. Trustee, Science Museum, 1984–85. CBIM. JP Kingston-upon-Thames, 1952–62.

LIDDELL, family name of **Baron Ravensworth.**

LIDDELL, Dr Donald Woollven, FRCP 1964; FRCPsych; Head of Department of Psychological Medicine, King's College Hospital, 1961–79; *b* 31 Dec. 1917; *m* 1954, Emily (*née* Horsfall) (marr. diss. 1977); one *s* one *d*. *Educ:* Aldenham Sch.; London Hospital. MRCP 1941; Neurological training as RMO, The National Hospital, Queen Square, 1942–45; Psychiatric training, Edinburgh and Maudsley Hospital. Medical Superintendent, St Francis Hospital, Haywards Heath, 1957–61; retired as Physician to Bethlem and Maudsley Hosps, 1968. Examr to RCP and RCPsych. Founder FRCPsych, 1971. *Publications:* contrib. Journal of Mental Science, Journal of Neurology, Psychiatry and Neuro-surgery, American Journal of Mental Diseases, Journal of Social Psychology. *Address:* 49 Bury Walk, SW3.

LIDDELL, Helen Lawrie; Scottish Secretary of the Labour Party, since 1977; *b* 6 Dec. 1950; *d* of Hugh Reilly and Bridget Lawrie Reilly; *m* 1972, Dr Alistair Henderson Liddell; one *s* one *d*. *Educ:* St Patrick's High Sch., Coatbridge; Strathclyde Univ. Head, Econ. Dept, 1971–75, and Asst Sec., 1975–76, Scottish TUC; Econ. Correspondent, BBC Scotland, 1976–77. *Recreations:* cooking, hill-walking, music. *Address:* Glenisla, Langbank, Renfrewshire, Scotland PA14 6XP. *T:* Langbank 344.

LIDDELL, (John) Robert; author; *b* 13 Oct. 1908; *e s* of late Major J. S. Liddell, CMG, DSO, and Anna Gertrude Morgan. *Educ:* Haileybury Coll.; Corpus Christi Coll., Oxford. Lecturer in Universities of Cairo and Alexandria, 1942–51, and assistant professor of English, Cairo Univ., 1951; Head of English Dept, Athens Univ., 1963–68. FRSL. *Publications:* The Last Enchantments, 1948; The Rivers of Babylon, 1959; An Object for a Walk, 1966; The Deep End, 1968; Stepsons, 1969, and other novels; A Treatise on the Novel, 1947; Aegean Greece, 1954; The Novels of I. Compton-Burnett, 1955; Byzantium and Istanbul, 1956; The Morea, 1958; The Novels of Jane Austen, 1963; Mainland Greece, 1965; Cavafy: a critical biography, 1974; The Novels of George Eliot, 1977; Elizabeth and Ivy, 1986.

LIDDELL, Robert; *see* Liddell, J. R.

LIDDERDALE, Sir David (William Shuckburgh), KCB 1975 (CB 1963); Clerk of the House of Commons, 1974–76; *b* 30 Sept. 1910; *s* of late Edward Wadsworth and Florence Amy Lidderdale; *m* 1943, Lola, *d* of late Rev. Thomas Alexander Beckett, Tubbercurry and Ballinew; one *s*. *Educ:* Winchester; King's Coll., Cambridge (MA). Assistant Clerk, House of Commons, 1934. Served War of 1939–45, The Rifle Brigade (TA); active service, N Africa and Italy. Senior Clerk, 1946, Fourth Clerk at the Table, 1953, Second Clerk Assistant, 1959, Clerk Assistant, 1962, House of Commons. Joint Secretary, Assoc. of Secretaries-General of Parliaments (Inter-Parliamentary Union), 1946–54, Mem., 1954–76, Vice-Pres., 1973–76, Hon. Vice-Pres., 1976. *Publications:* The Parliament of France, 1951; (with Lord Campion) European Parliamentary Procedure, 1953; (ed) Erskine May's Parliamentary Practice, 19th edn, 1976. *Recreation:* walking. *Address:* 46 Cheyne Walk, SW3. *Clubs:* Travellers', MCC.

LIDDIARD, Richard England, CBE 1978; Chairman, Lion Mark Holdings Ltd, since 1983; *b* 21 Sept. 1917; *s* of late E. S. Liddiard, MBE, and M. A. Brooke; *m* 1943, Constance Lily, *d* of late Sir William J. Rook; one *s* three *d*. *Educ:* Oundle; Worcester Coll., Oxford (MA). Lt-Col, Royal Signals, 1939–46. Chairman: C. Czarnikow Ltd, 1958–74; Czarnikow Group Ltd, 1974–83; Sugar Assoc. of London, 1960–78; British Fedn of Commodity Assocs, 1962–70, Vice-Chm., 1970–77; London Commodity Exchange, 1972–76; Mem., Cttee on Invisible Exports, 1966–70. Mem. Ct of Assts, Worshipful Co. of Haberdashers, 1958, Master 1978. FRSA. MC (Poland), 1941. *Recreation:* golf. *Address:* Oxford Lodge, 52 Parkside, Wimbledon, SW19. *T:* 01–946 3434. *Club:* Carlton.

LIDDIARD, Ronald; social work and management consultant, writer and broadcaster; *b* 26 July 1932; *s* of Tom and Gladys Liddiard; *m* 1957, June Alexandra (*née* Ford); two *d*. *Educ:* Canton High Sch., Cardiff; Colleges of Commerce and Technology, Cardiff; Inst. of Local Govt Studies, Birmingham Univ. Dip. Municipal Admin, Certif. Social Work. Health Administrator, 1958–60; Social Worker, 1960–64; Sen. Welfare Administrator, 1964–70; Dir of Social Services: Bath, 1971–74; Birmingham, 1974–85. *Publications:* chapters in: Innovations in the Care of the Elderly, 1984; Self-Care and Health in Old Age, 1986; articles in social work and health jls. *Recreations:* private flying and wines. *Address:* Whitefriars, Portway, Worcs B48 7HP. *T:* Wythall (0564) 826235.

LIDDLE, Sir Donald (Ross), Kt 1971; JP; Chairman, Cumbernauld Development Corporation, 1972–78; Vice-Lord-Lieutenant, City of Glasgow, Strathclyde Region, 1978–80; *b* 11 Oct. 1906; *s* of Thomas Liddle, Bonnington, Edinburgh; *m* 1933, May, *d* of R. Christie, Dennistoun, Glasgow; one *s* two *d*. *Educ:* Allen Glen's School, Glasgow. Served War of 1939–45 with RAOC, Burma and India; Major, 1944. DL, County of Glasgow, 1963; JP 1968; Lord Provost of Glasgow, 1969–72. Chm., Scottish Tourist Consultative Council, 1973–79. CStJ 1970. Hon. LLD Strathclyde, 1971. *Address:* 15 Riddrie Crescent, Riddrie Knowes, Glasgow G33 2QG. *Clubs:* Army and Navy; Conservative (Glasgow).

LIESNER, Hans Hubertus, CB 1980; Chief Economic Adviser, Department of Trade and Industry (formerly Industry, Trade and Prices and Consumer Protection), since 1976; *b* 30 March 1929; *e s* of Curt Liesner, lawyer, and Edith L. (*née* Neumann); *m* 1968, Thelma Seward; one *s* one *d*. *Educ:* German grammar schs; Bristol Univ. (BA); Nuffield Coll., Oxford; MA Cantab. Asst Lectr, later Lectr, in Economics, London Sch. of Economics, 1955–59; Lectr in Economics, Univ. of Cambridge; Fellow, Dir of Studies in Economics and some time Asst Bursar, Emmanuel Coll., Cambridge, 1959–70; Under-Sec. (Economics), HM Treasury, 1970–76. *Publications:* The Import Dependence of Britain and Western Germany, 1957; Case Studies in European Economic Union: the mechanics of integration (with J. E. Meade and S. J. Wells), 1962; Atlantic Harmonisation: making free trade work, 1968; Britain and the Common Market: the effect of entry on the pattern of manufacturing production (with S. S. Han), 1971; articles in jls, etc. *Recreations:* ski-ing, cine-photography. *Address:* 32 The Grove, Brookmans Park, Herts AL9 7RN. *T:* Potters Bar 53269. *Club:* Reform.

LIFAR, Serge; Chevalier de la Légion d'Honneur; Dancer, Choreographer, Writer, Painter; Director, later Rector, Université de Danse, since 1958; Professeur de Chorélogie, Sorbonne; Maître de Ballet, Théâtre National de l'Opéra, Paris, 1929–69 (formerly Professeur); *b* Kieff, South Russia, 2 April 1905; *s* of Michel Lifar. Pupil of Bronislava Nijinska, 1921; joined Diaghileff company, Paris, 1923; studied under Cecchetti. Dir, Institut Chorégraphique, 1947–58. First London appearance, in Cimarosiana and Les Fâcheux, Coliseum, 1924. Choreographer (for first time) of Stravinsky's Renard, 1929; produced Prométhée, Opera House, Paris, 1929. Cochran's Revue, London Pavilion, 1930; returned to Paris, produced and danced in Bacchus and Ariadne, Le Spectre de la Rose, Giselle, and L'Après-midi d'un Faune, 1932; Icare, David Triomphant, Le Roi Nu, 1936; Alexandre le Grand, 1937; arranged season of Ballet at the Cambridge, London, 1946; Choreographer of Noces Fantastiques, Romeo et Juliette (Prokofiev), 1955. Paintings exhibited: Paris, 1972–75; Cannes, 1974; Monte Carlo, Florence, Venice, London. Prix de l'Académie Française; Corres. Mem., Institut de France, 1970. Commandeur des Arts et des Lettres, France; Grand Etoile, Yugoslavia; Gold Medal, Vasa, Sweden, 1965; Medal of City of Paris, 1977. *Publications:* Traditional to Modern Ballet, 1938; Diaghilev, a biography, 1940; A History of Russian Ballet from its Origins to the Present Day (trans. 1954); The Three Graces, 1959; Ma Vie, 1965 (in Eng., 1969). *Address:* Villa de Roc, Glion, Switzerland; Beau-Rivage, Ouchy, Lausanne, France.

LIFFORD, 8th Viscount *cr* 1781; **Alan William Wingfield Hewitt;** *b* 11 Dec. 1900; 2nd but *o* surv. *s* of Hon. George Wyldbore Hewitt (*d* 1924; 7th *s* of 4th Viscount Lifford) and Elizabeth Mary, *e d* of late Charles Rampini, DL, LLD, Advocate; *S kinsman* 1954; *m* 1935, Alison Mary Patricia, *d* of T. W. Ashton, The Cottage, Hursley, nr Winchester; one *s* three *d*. *Educ:* Winchester; RMC, Sandhurst. Lieut late Hampshire Regt. *Heir: s* Hon. Edward James Wingfield Hewitt [*b* 27 Jan. 1949; *m* 1976, Alison, *d* of Robert Law; one *s* one *d*]. *Address:* Field House, Hursley, Hants. *T:* Hursley 75203.

See also Sir Anthony Swann, Bt.

LIGETI, Prof. György Sándor; Member, Order of Merit, Germany, 1975; music composer; Professor for Composition, Hamburg Academy of Music, since 1973; *b* 28 May 1923; *s* of Dr Sándor Ligeti and Dr Ilona Somogyi; *m* 1957, Dr Vera Spitz; one *s*. *Educ:* Budapest Academy of Music (Dipl. in composition). Lecturer for harmony and counterpoint, Budapest Acad. of Music, 1950–56; Guest Prof., Stockholm Acad. of Music, 1961–71; composer in residence, Stanford Univ., Calif, 1972. Member: Swedish Royal Acad. of Music, 1964; Acad. of Arts, Berlin, 1968; Free Acad. of Arts, Hamburg, 1971; Bavarian Acad. of Fine Arts, Munich, 1978. Hon. Mem., Amer. Acad. and Inst. of Arts and Letters, 1984. *Main compositions:* Apparitions, for orch., 1959; Atmosphères, for orch., 1961; Aventures, for 3 singers and 7 instrumentalists, 1962; Requiem, for 2 soli, chorus and orch., 1965; Cello concerto, 1966; Chamber concerto, 1970; Melodien, for orch., 1971; Le Grand Macabre, opera, 1977; Trio, for violin, horn, piano, 1982. *Address:* Himmelhofgasse 34, A-1130 Vienna, Austria; Mövenstrasse 3, D-2000 Hamburg 60, Federal Republic of Germany.

LIGGINS, Sir Edmund (Naylor), Kt 1976; TD 1947; Solicitor; *b* 21 July 1909; *s* of Arthur William and Hannah Louisa Liggins; *m* 1952, Celia Jean Lawrence (OBE 1982), *d* of William Henry and Millicent Lawrence; three *s* one *d*. *Educ:* King Henry VIII Sch., Coventry; Rydal Sch. Joined TA, 1936; commissioned 45th Bn (RWR), RE; served War: comd 399 Battery, RA, subseq. 498 LAA Battery, RA, 1942–45. Subseq. commanded 198 Indep. Battery, RA, 1948–51. Consultant, Liggins & Co., Solicitors, Coventry, Leamington Spa, Balsall Common and Kenilworth. Elected Mem. Council, Law Society, 1963, Vice-Pres., 1974–75, Pres., 1975–76 (Chm., Non-Contentious Business Cttee of Council, 1968–71; Chm., Educn and Trng Cttee, 1973–74); Chm., West Midland Legal Aid Area Cttee, 1963–64; Pres., Warwickshire Law Soc., 1969–70. Mem., Court and Council, Univ. of Warwick. Hon. Mem., Amer. Bar Assoc. *Recreations:* cricket, rugby football, squash rackets; amateur theatre. *Address:* Hareway Cottage, Hareway Lane, Barford, Warwickshire CV35 8DB. *T:* Barford 624246. *Clubs:* Army and Navy, MCC, Forty; Coventry and North Warwickshire Cricket, Drapers' (Coventry).

LIGGINS, Prof. Graham Collingwood, CBE 1983; FRCSE, FRACS, FRCOG; FRS 1980; FRSNZ 1976; Professor of Obstetrics and Gynaecological Endocrinology, University of Auckland, New Zealand, since 1968 (formerly Senior Lecturer); Consultant to National Women's Hospital, Auckland. *Educ:* Univ. of NZ. MB, ChB, Univ. NZ, 1949; PhD, Univ. of Auckland, 1969. MRCOG Lond. 1956; FRCSE 1958; FRACS 1960. Is distinguished for his work on the role of foetal hormones in the control of parturition. Hon. FAGS, 1976; Hon. FACOG, 1978. Hon. MD Lund, 1983. Hector Medal, RSNZ, 1980. *Publications:* over 100 published papers. *Recreations:* forestry, sailing, fishing. *Address:* Postgraduate School of Obstetrics and Gynaecology, National Women's Hospital, Claude Road, Auckland 3, New Zealand. *T:* 775–127; 3/38 Awatea Road, Parnell, Auckland 1, New Zealand.

LIGHT, (Sidney) David; a Civil Service Commissioner, 1978–79; *b* 9 Dec. 1919; *s* of late William Light; *m* Edna Margaret Honey; one *s*. *Educ:* King Edward VI Sch., Southampton. RAF, 1940–46. HM Customs and Excise, 1938; HM Treasury, 1948–68; Asst Sec., CS Commn, 1969–75; Under Sec., CSD, 1975–78. *Recreations:* watching cricket, travel. *Address:* Oakhanger, Vicarage Hill, Farnham, Surrey GU9 8HJ. *T:* Farnham 721522. *Clubs:* Royal Commonwealth Society; Hampshire Cricket.

LIGHTBODY, Ian (Macdonald), CMG 1974; Member, Arun District Council, since 1983; *b* 19 Aug. 1921; *s* of Thomas Paul Lightbody and Dorothy Marie Louise Lightbody (*née* Cooper); *m* 1954, Noreen, *d* of late Captain T. H. Wallace, Dromore, Co. Down; three *s* one *d*. *Educ:* Queens Park Sch., Glasgow; Glasgow Univ. (MA). War service, Indian Army, India and Far East, 1942–46 (Captain); Colonial Admin. Service, Hong Kong, 1945; various admin. posts; District Comr, New Territories, 1967–68; Defence Sec., 1968–69; Coordinator, Festival of Hong Kong, 1969; Comr for Resettlement, 1971; Sec. for Housing and Chm., Hong Kong Housing Authority, 1973–77; Sec. for Admin, Hong Kong, 1977–78; Chm., Public Services Commn, Hong Kong, 1978–80. MLC 1971; MEC 1977; retd from Hong Kong, 1980. *Recreations:* walking, politics, Japanese prints. *Address:* Two Stacks, Lake Lane, Barnham, Sussex. *Clubs:* Hong Kong, Royal Hong Kong Jockey.

LIGHTBOWN, David Lincoln; MP (C) Staffordshire South East, since 1983; an Assistant Government Whip, since 1986; *b* 30 Nov. 1932; *m* Margaret Ann. Engineering Dir (now part-time Consultant), West Midlands PLC. Member: Lichfield Dist Council, 1975– (Leader of Council, 1977–83); Staffs CC, 1977–85 (formerly Chm., Educn and Finance Cttees). *Address:* House of Commons, SW1. *T:* 01–219 6241/4212; The Coach House, Burton Road, Streethay, Lichfield, Staffs. *T:* (office) Lichfield 414636.

LIGHTBOWN, Ronald William, MA, FSA, FRAS; Keeper of the Department of Metalwork, Victoria and Albert Museum, since 1985; *b* Darwen, Lancs, 2 June 1932; *s* of late Vincent Lightbown and of Helen Anderson Lightbown (*née* Burness); *m* 1962, Mary Dorothy Webster; one *s*. *Educ:* St Catharine's Coll., Cambridge (MA). FSA, FRAS. Victoria and Albert Museum: Asst Keeper, Library, 1958–64; Asst Keeper, Dept of Metalwork, 1964–73; Dep. Keeper, 1973–76, Keeper, 1976–85, Library. Fellow, Inst. for Res. in the Humanities, Wisconsin Univ., 1974. A Vice-Pres., Soc. of Antiquaries, 1986– (Sec., 1979–86); Associate Trustee, Soane Mus., 1981–. *Publications:* French Secular Goldsmith's work of the Middle Ages, 1978; Sandro Botticelli, 1978; (with M. Corbett) The Comely Frontispiece, 1978; (ed and trans. with A. Caiger-Smith) Piccolpasso: the art of the potter, 1980; Donatello and Michelozzo, 1980; Andrea Mantegna, 1986; (ed and introd) History of Art in 18th Century England (series of source-books on 18th century British art), 14 vols, 1970–71; V&A Museum Catalogues: (pt author) Italian Sculpture, 1964; Scandinavian and Baltic Silver, 1975; French Silver, 1979; (with M. Archer) India Observed, 1982; many articles in learned jls, incl. Burlington Magazine, Warburg Jl and Art Bulletin. *Recreations:* reading, travel, music, conversation. *Address:* Victoria and Albert Museum, Exhibition Road, SW7 2RL. *T:* 01–589 6371.

LIGHTFOOT, George Michael; a Recorder of the Crown Court, since 1985; *b* 9 March 1936; *s* of Charles Herbert Lightfoot and Mary Lightfoot (*née* Potter); *m* 1963, Dorothy (*née* Miller); two *s* two *d*. *Educ:* St Michael's Catholic College, Leeds; Exeter College, Oxford (MA). Schoolmaster, 1962–66. Called to the Bar, Inner Temple, 1966; practised on NE circuit. Mem., Home Farm Trust, 1980–. *Recreations:* cricket and sport in general, education. *Address:* 6 Park Square, Leeds LS1 2LW. *T:* Leeds 459763. *Club:* Catenian Association (City of Leeds Circle).

LIGHTHILL, Sir (Michael) James, Kt 1971; FRS 1953; FRAeS; Provost of University College London, since 1979, Hon. Fellow, 1982; *b* 23 Jan. 1924; *s* of E. B. Lighthill; *m* 1945, Nancy Alice Dumaresq; one *s* four *d*. *Educ:* Winchester Coll.; Trinity Coll., Cambridge (Hon. Fellow, 1986). Aerodynamics Division, National Physical Laboratory, 1943–45; Fellow, Trinity Coll., Cambridge, 1945–49; Sen. Lectr in Maths, Univ. of Manchester, 1946–50; Beyer Prof. of Applied Mathematics, Univ. of Manchester, 1950–59; Dir, RAE, Farnborough, 1959–64; Royal Soc. Res. Prof., Imperial Coll., 1964–69; Lucasian Prof. of Mathematics, Univ. of Cambridge, 1969–79. Chm., Academic Adv. Cttee, Univ. of Surrey, 1964; Member: Adv. Council on Technology, 1964; NERC, 1965–70; Shipbuilding Inquiry Cttee, 1965; (part-time) Post Office Bd, 1972–74; First Pres., Inst. of Mathematics and its Applications, 1964–66; a Sec. and Vice-Pres., Royal Soc., 1965–69; President: Internat. Commn on Mathematical Instruction, 1971–74; Internat. Union of Theoretical and Applied Mechanics, 1984–. FRAeS 1961. Foreign Member: American Academy of Arts and Sciences, 1958; American Philosophical Soc., 1970; US Nat. Acad. of Sciences, 1976; US Nat. Acad. of Engineering, 1977. Associate Mem., French Acad. of Sciences, 1976. Hon. Fellow American Inst. of Aeronautics and Astronautics, 1961. Hon. DSc: Liverpool, 1961; Leicester, 1965; Strathclyde, 1966; Essex, 1967; Princeton, 1967; East Anglia, 1968; Manchester, 1968; Bath, 1969; St Andrews, 1969; Surrey, 1969; Cranfield, 1974; Paris, 1975; Aachen, 1975; Rensselaer, 1980; Leeds, 1983; Brown, 1984; Southern California, 1984; Ludwig-Prandtl-Ring, 1984. Royal Medal, Royal Society, 1964; Gold Medal, Royal Aeronautical Society, 1965; Harvey Prize for Science and Technol., Israeli Inst. of Technol., 1981; Gold Medal, Inst. of Maths and Its Applications, 1982. Comdr Order of Léopold, 1963. *Publications:* Introduction to Fourier Analysis and Generalised Functions, 1958; Mathematical Biofluiddynamics, 1975; Newer Uses of Mathematics, 1977; Waves in Fluids, 1978; An Informal Introduction to Theoretical Fluid Mechanics, 1986; articles in Royal Soc. Proc. and Trans, Qly Jl of Mechanics and Applied Maths, Philosophical Magazine, Jl of Aeronautical Scis, Qly Jl of Maths, Aeronautical Qly, Communications on Pure and Applied Maths, Proc. Cambridge Philosophical Soc., Jl of Fluid Mechanics, Reports and Memoranda of ARC; contrib. to Modern Developments in Fluid Dynamics: High Speed Flow; High Speed Aerodynamics and Jet Propulsion; Surveys in Mechanics; Laminar Boundary Layers. *Recreations:* music and swimming. *Address:* University College London, Gower Street, WC1. *Club:* Athenæum.

LIGHTMAN, Gavin Anthony, QC 1980; *b* 20 Dec. 1939; *s* of Harold Lightman, *qv*; *m* 1965, Naomi Ann Claff; one *s* two *d*. *Educ:* Univ. of London (LLB); Univ. of Michigan (LLM). Called to the Bar, Lincoln's Inn, 1963. *Publications:* (with G. Battersby) Cases and Statutes on Real Property, 1965; (with G. Moss) The Law Relating to the Receivership of Companies, 1986. *Recreations:* reading, walking, eating. *Address:* 5B Prince Arthur Road, Hampstead, NW3. *T:* 01–794 5180.

LIGHTMAN, Harold, QC 1955; Master of the Bench of Lincoln's Inn; *b* 8 April 1906; *s* of Louis Lightman, Leeds; *m* 1936, Gwendoline Joan, *d* of David Ostrer, London; three *s*. *Educ:* City of Leeds Sch.; privately. Accountant, 1927–29. Barrister, Lincoln's Inn, 1932. Home Guard, 1940–45. Defence Medal, 1946. Liveryman, Company of Glovers, 1960. *Recreation:* reading. *Address:* Stone Buildings, Lincoln's Inn, WC2. *T:* 01–242 3840. *Club:* Royal Automobile.

See also G. A. Lightman.

LIGHTMAN, Ivor Harry, CB 1984; Deputy Secretary, Welsh Office, since 1981; *b* 23 Aug. 1928; *s* of late Abraham Lightman, OBE and Mary (*née* Goldschneider); *m* 1950, Stella Doris Blend; one *s*. *Educ:* Abergele Grammar Sch. Clerical Officer, Min. of Food, 1946; Nat. Service, RAOC (Corp.), 1946–49; Officer of Customs and Excise, 1949–56; Asst Principal, Ministry of Works, 1957; Asst Private Sec. to successive Ministers, 1959–60; Principal, Ministry of Works, 1961–65; Sec., Banwell Cttee on Construction Contracts, 1962–64; Principal, HM Treasury, 1965–67; Asst Sec., MPBW, 1967–70; Asst Sec., CSD, 1970–73; Under Secretary: Price Commn, 1973–76; Dept of Prices and Consumer Protection, 1976–78; Dept of Industry, 1978–81. *Address:* 6 Clos Coedydafarn, Lisvane, Cardiff.

LIGHTMAN, Lionel; Lay Observer attached to Lord Chancellor's Department, since 1986; *b* 26 July 1928; *s* of late Abner Lightman and late Gitli Lightman (*née* Szmul); *m* 1952, Helen, *y d* of late Rev. A. Shechter and late Mrs Shechter; two *d*. *Educ:* City of London Sch.; Wadham Coll., Oxford (MA). Nat. Service, RAEC, 1951–53 (Temp. Captain). Asst Principal, BoT, 1953; Private Sec. to Perm. Sec., 1957; Principal 1958; Trade Comr, Ottawa, 1960–64; Asst Sec. 1967; Asst Dir, Office of Fair Trading, 1973–75; Under Sec., Dept of Trade, 1975–78, DoI, 1978–81; Dir of Competition Policy, OFT, 1981–84. *Address:* 55 The Pryors, East Heath Road, NW3 1BP. *T:* 01–435 3427.

LIGHTON, Sir Christopher Robert, 8th Bt, *cr* 1791; MBE 1945; *b* 30 June 1897; *o s* of 7th Bt and Helen (*d* 1927), *d* of late James Houldsworth, Coltness, Lanarkshire; *S* father, 1929; *m* 1st, 1926, Rachel Gwendoline (marr. diss. 1953), *yr d* of late Rear-Admiral W. S. Goodridge, CIE; two *d*; 2nd, 1953, Horatia Edith (*d* 1981), *d* of A. T. Powlett, Godminster Manor, Bruton, Somerset; one *s*; 3rd, 1985, Eve, *o d* of late Rear-Adm. A. L. Mark-Wardlaw, *widow* of Maj. Stopford Ram. *Educ:* Eton Coll.; RMC. Late The King's Royal Rifle Corps; rejoined the Army in Aug. 1939 and served War of 1939–45. *Heir: s* Thomas Hamilton Lighton, *b* 4 Nov. 1954. *Address:* Heathers, Odiham, Hants.

LIKAKU, Victor Timothy; General Manager, The New Building Society, Blantyre, since 1985; Mayor of City of Blantyre, since 1981; *b* 15 Oct. 1934; *m* 1959, Hilda; one *s* two *d*. Malaŵi Civil Service, Min. of Finance, 1957–62; Malaŵi Govt Schol., St Steven's Coll., Univ. of Delhi, India, 1962 (BA Econ.); Dept of Customs and Excise, 1966; Customs and Admin. Courses, New Zealand, 1967, Vienna 1972; UN Fellowship, GATT, Geneva, 1973; Controller of Customs and Excise, Malaŵi Govt, 1973; High Comr for Malaŵi in London, 1976–78. Mayor, City of Blantyre, 1981–83. *Recreations:* reading, soccer. *Address:* The New Building Society, Building Society House, Victoria Avenue, PO Box 466, Blantyre, Malaŵi. *T:* 634 753. *Clubs:* Hurlingham (Hon. Mem.), International Sporting, Penthouse.

LILFORD, 7th Baron, *cr* 1797; **George Vernon Powys;** *b* 8 Jan. 1931; *s* of late Robert Horace Powys (*g g grandson* of 2nd Baron) and of Vera Grace Bryant, Rosebank, Cape, SA; *S* kinsman, 1949; *m* 1st, 1954, Mrs Eve Bird (marr. diss.); 2nd, 1957, Anuta Merritt (marr. diss., 1958); 3rd, 1958, Norma Yvonne Shell (marr. diss., 1961); 4th, 1961, Mrs Muriel Spottiswoode (marr. diss., 1969); two *d*; 5th, 1969, Margaret Penman; one *s* two *d*. *Educ:* St Aidan's Coll., Grahamstown, SA; Stonyhurst Coll. *Recreations:* golf, cricket. *Heir: s* Hon. Mark Vernon Powys, *b* 16 Nov. 1975. *Address:* Le Grand Câtelet, St John, Jersey, Channel Islands.

LILL, John Richard, OBE 1978; concert pianist; Professor at Royal College of Music; *b* 17 March 1944; *s* of George and Margery Lill. *Educ:* Leyton County High Sch.; Royal College of Music. FRCM; Hon. FTCL; FLCM; Hon. RAM. Gulbenkian Fellowship, 1967. First concert at age of 9; Royal Festival Hall debut, 1963; Promenade Concert debut, 1969. Numerous broadcasts on radio and TV; has appeared as soloist with all leading British orchestras. Recitals and concertos throughout Great Britain, Europe, USA, Canada, Scandinavia, USSR, Japan and Far East, Australia, New Zealand, etc. Overseas tours as soloist with many orchestras including London Symphony Orchestra and London Philharmonic Orchestra. Complete recordings of Beethoven sonatas and concertos; complete Beethoven cycle, London, 1982. Chappell Gold Medal; Pauer Prize; 1st Prize, Royal Over-Seas League Music Competition, 1963; Dinu Lipatti Medal in Harriet Cohen Internat. Awards; 1st Prize, Internat. Tchaikowsky Competition, Moscow, 1970. Hon. DSc Aston, 1978; Hon. DMus Exeter, 1979. *Recreations:* amateur radio, chess, walking. *Address:* c/o Harold Holt Ltd, 31 Sinclair Road, W14 0NS. *T:* 01–603 4600.

LILLEY, Prof. Geoffrey Michael, OBE 1981; CEng, FRSA, FRAeS, MIMechE, FIMA; Professor of Aeronautics and Astronautics, University of Southampton, 1964–82, now Emeritus Professor (Head of Department of Aeronautics and Astronautics, 1963–82); *b* Isleworth, Mddx, 16 Nov. 1919; *m* 1948, Leslie Marion Wheeler; one *s* two *d*. *Educ:* Isleworth Grammar Sch.; Battersea and Northampton Polytechnics; Imperial Coll. BSc(Eng) 1944, MSc(Eng) 1945, DIC 1945. Gen. engrg trg, Benham and Kodak, 1936–40; Drawing Office and Wind Tunnel Dept, Vickers Armstrong Ltd, Weybridge, 1940–46; Coll. of Aeronautics: Lectr, 1946–51; Sen. Lectr, 1951–55; Dep. Head of Dept of Aerodynamics, 1955, and Prof. of Experimental Fluid Mechanics, 1962–64. Vis. Professor: Stanford Univ., 1977–78; ME Technical Univ., Ankara, Turkey, 1983–85. Past Member: Aeronautical Res. Council (past Mem. Council and Chm. Aerodynamics, Applied Aerodynamics, Noise Res., Fluid Motion and Performance Cttees); Noise Advisory Council (Chm., Noise from Air Traffic Working Group); Past Chm., Aerodynamics Cttee, Engrg Sci. Data Unit. Consultant to: Rolls Royce, 1959–61, 1967–84; AGARD, 1959–63; OECD, 1969–71. Gold Medal for Aeronautics, RAeS, 1983; Aerodynamic Noise Medal, AIAA, 1985. *Publications:* (jt editor) Proc. Stanford Conf. on Complex Turbulent Flows; articles in reports and memoranda of: Aeronautical Research Council; Royal Aeronautical Soc., and other jls. *Recreations:* music, chess, walking. *Address:* Highbury, Pine Walk, Chilworth, Southampton SO1 7HQ. *T:* Southampton 769109. *Club:* Athenæum.

LILLEY, Peter Bruce; MP (C) St Albans, since 1983; Director, Greenwell Montagu, since 1986; *b* 23 Aug. 1943; *s* of Arnold Francis Lilley and Lillian (*née* Elliott); *m* 1979, Gail Ansell. *Educ:* Dulwich Coll.; Clare Coll., Cambridge. MA; FInstPet 1978. Economic consultant in underdeveloped countries, 1966–72; investment advisor on energy industries, 1972–84. Chm., London Oil Analysts Gp, 1979–80. Consultant Dir, Cons. Res. Dept, 1979–83. Chm., Bow Group, 1972–75. Contested (C) Tottenham, Oct. 1974. PPS to Ministers for Local Govt, Jan.–Oct. 1984, to Chancellor of the Exchequer, 1984–. *Publications:* Do You Sincerely Want to Win?, 1972, 2nd edn 1973; Lessons for Power, 1974; (with S. Brittan) Delusion of Incomes Policy, 1977; (contrib.) Skidelsky: End of the Keynesian Era, 1980. *Address:* House of Commons, SW1. *T:* 01–219 3000. *Club:* Carlton.

LILLICRAP, Harry George, CBE 1976; Chairman, Cable and Wireless, 1972–76; *b* 29 June 1913; *s* of late Herbert Percy Lillicrap; *m* 1938, Kathleen Mary Charnock; two *s*. *Educ:* Erith County Sch.; University College London. BSc (Eng) 1934. Post Office Telecommunications, 1936–72; Sen. Dir Planning, Sen. Dir Customer Services, 1967–72. Dir, Telephone Rentals Ltd, 1976–84. *Address:* Lower Flat, Leysters, Highfield Road, East Grinstead, West Sussex. *T:* East Grinstead 25811.

LILLIE, Beatrice, (Lady Peel); actress; *b* Toronto, 29 May 1894; *d* of John Lillie, Lisburn, Ireland, and Lucie Shaw; *m* 1920, Sir Robert Peel, 5th Bt (*d* 1934); (one *s*, Sir Robert Peel, 6th and last Bt, killed on active service 1942). *Educ:* St Agnes' Coll., Belleville, Ontario. First appearance, Alhambra, 1914; at the Vaudeville, Prince of Wales's etc., 1915–22; in The Nine O'Clock Revue, Little Theatre, 1922; first New York appearance, Times Square Theatre, in André Charlot's Revue, 1924; in Charlot's Revue at Prince of Wales's, 1925; in New York, 1925–26; at The Globe and The Palladium, 1928; This Year of Grace, New York, 1928; Charlot's Masquerade, at the Cambridge, London, 1930; New York; 1931–32; at the Savoy and London Palladium, 1933–34; New York, 1935; Queen's, London, 1939; Big Top, Adelphi, 1940; Troops: England, 1939–42; Africa, Italy, etc, 1942–45; Seven Lively Arts, Ziegfeld, New York, 1945; Better Late, Garrick, London, 1946; appeared in television and radio programmes, England and America, 1946–47; Inside USA, New York, 1948, subs. on tour for one year, USA; returned to London (cabaret), Café de Paris, 1950 and June 1951. Solo artiste at several Royal performances; appeared in NY television, 1951–52; produced one-woman show, Summer Theatre, 1952; subs. on tour and produced show in Broadway, Oct. 1952–June 1953. Radio and TV, London, July-Aug. 1953. Road tour in US of this production, Sept. 1953–June 1954; London, 1954–55. An Evening with Beatrice Lillie, Globe, AEWBL, Florida, Feb and March, 1956; 2nd one-woman show, Beasop's Fables, USA, June-Sept. 1956; Ziegfeld Follies, New York, 1957–58; Auntie Mame, Adelphi, London, 1958–59; High Spirits, Alvin Theatre, NYC, 1964–65. Appeared in films: Exit Smiling, 1927; Are You There, 1933; Doctor Rhythm, 1938; On Approval, 1944; Around the World in Eighty Days, 1956; Thoroughly Modern Millie, 1967. Free French Liberation Medal, N Africa, 1942, also African Star and George VI Medal, Donaldson Award, USA, 1945, also Antoinette Perry Award, New York, 1953, and many others. *Publication:* (with J. Philip and J. Brough) Every Other Inch a Lady (autobiog.), 1973. *Recreation:* painting. *Address:* Peel Fold, Mill Lane, Henley-on-Thames, Oxon.

LILLINGSTON, George David I. I.; *see* Inge-Innes-Lillingston.

LILLY, Prof. Malcolm Douglas, FEng 1982; Professor of Biochemical Engineering since 1979, and Director, Centre for Biochemical Engineering and Biotechnology since 1982, University College London; *b* 9 Aug. 1936; *s* of Charles Victor Lilly and Amy Gardiner; *m* 1959, Sheila Elizabeth Stuart; two *s*. *Educ:* St Olave's Grammar Sch.; University College London (BSc,PhD,DSc). FIChemE. Lecturer in Biochemical Engrg, UCL, 1963–72, Reader in Enzyme Technology, 1972–79. Director, Whatman Biochemicals, 1968–71; Vis. Prof., Univ. of Pennsylvania, 1969. Chm., 1972–80, Vice-Chm., 1980–, Internat. Orgn for Biotechnology and Bioengineering. Member: Research Cttee, British Gas Corp., 1982–; Bd of Management and Executive Cttee, Inst. for Biotechnological Studies, 1983–. Food, Pharmaceutical and Bioengrg Award, Amer. Inst. of Chem. Engrs, 1976. *Publications:* (jtly) Fermentation and Enzyme Technology, 1979; (jtly) OECD Report, Biotechnology: international trends and perspectives, 1982; numerous papers on biochemical engrg, fermentation and enzyme technology. *Recreations:* sailing, soccer refereeing and coaching. *Address:* 8 Tower Road, Orpington, Kent BR6 0SQ. *T:* Orpington 21762.

LIM, Sir Han-Hoe, Kt 1946; CBE 1941; Hon. LLD (Malaya); MB, ChB (Edinburgh); JP; Pro-Chancellor, University of Malaya, 1949–59; *b* 27 April 1894; 2nd *s* of late Lim Cheng Sah, Singapore; *m* 1920, Chua Seng Neo; two *s* two *d*. *Educ:* St Andrew's Sch. and Raffles Institution; University of Edinburgh. RMO North Devon General Hospital, with charge of Military Auxiliary Hospital, 1919; Municipal Commissioner, Singapore, 1926–31; Member of Legislative Council, Straits Settlements, 1933–42, and its Finance Cttee, 1936–42; Member of Exec. Council, Straits Settlements, 1939–42; Member of Advisory Council, Singapore, 1946–48; Member of Exec. Council, Singapore, 1948–50. Member of Council, King Edward VII College of Medicine, Singapore, 1930–42; Mem. and Chm., Public Services Commission, Singapore, 1952–56. *Recreations:* tennis, chess. *Address:* 758 Mountbatten Road, Singapore 15. *T:* 40655. *Club:* Garden (Singapore).

LIM PIN, Professor, MD; FRCP, FRCPE, FRACP, FACP; Vice-Chancellor, National University of Singapore, since 1981; *b* 12 Jan. 1936; *s* of late Lim Lu Yeh and of Choo Siew Kooi; *m* 1964, Shirley Loo; two *s* one *d*. *Educ:* Univ. of Cambridge (MA; MD 1970). FRCP 1976; FRCPE 1981; FRACP 1978; FACP 1981. MO, Min. of Health, Singapore, 1965–66; Univ. of Singapore: Lectr in Medicine, 1966–70; Sen. Lectr in Medicine, 1971–73; Associate Prof. of Medicine, 1974–77; Prof. and Head, Dept of Medicine, 1978–81; Dep. Vice-Chancellor, 1979–81. Eisenhower Fellow, USA, 1982. Hon. Fellow, Coll. of Gen. Practitioners of Singapore, 1982. Public Administration Medal (Gold), Singapore, 1984. *Publications:* articles in New England Jl of Medicine, Med. Jl of Australia, BMJ, Qly Jl of Medicine, and Tissue Antigens. *Recreations:* swimming, badminton. *Address:* National University of Singapore, Kent Ridge, Singapore 0511, Republic of Singapore. *T:* 7756666. *Clubs:* Singapore Island Country, Pyramid (Singapore).

LIMANN, Dr Hilla, Hon. GCMG 1981; President of Ghana, 1979–81; *b* 1934; *m*; five *c*. *Educ:* Lawra Primary Boarding Sch.; Tamale Middle Boarding Sch.; Govt Teacher Trng Coll.; London Sch. of Economics (Hon. Fellow, 1982); Sorbonne; Univ. of London; Faculty of Law and Econ. Sciences, Univ. of Paris. BSc(Econ.) 1960; BA Hons (Hist.), 1964; PhD (Polit. Sci. and Law), 1965. Teacher, 1952–55; examiner for Civil Service grad. entry, W African Exams Council. Councillor, Tumu Dist Council, 1952 (Chm., 1953–55); contested (Indep.) Constituency, Party Elec., 1954. Head of Chancery and Official Sec., Ghana Embassy, Lomé, Togo, 1968–77; Mem., Constitutional Commn on 1969 Constitution for Ghana; Mem. Govt Delegns for opening of borders of Ghana with the Ivory Coast/Upper Volta; Mem./Sec. to Ghana delegns, OAU and Non-aligned States, Confs of ILO, WHO, Internat. Atomic Energy Agency. Leader, People's National Party.

LIMBU; *see* Rambahadur Limbu.

LIMENTANI, Prof. Uberto; Professor of Italian, University of Cambridge, 1962–81; Fellow of Magdalene College, Cambridge, since 1964; *b* Milan, 15 Dec. 1913; *er s* of Prof. Umberto Limentani and Elisa Levi; *m* 1946, Barbara Hoban (*d* 1984); three *s*. *Educ:* University of Milan (Dr in Giurispr., Dr in Lettere); University of London (PhD); University of Cambridge (MA). Commentator and script-writer Italian Section, BBC European Service, 1939–45. Lector 1945, Assistant Lecturer, 1948, Lecturer, 1952, in Italian, University of Cambridge. Hon. Prof., Dept of Italian, Univ. of Hull, 1981–. Pres., MHRA, 1981. Corresp. Member Accademia Letteraria Ital. dell'Arcadia, 1964. Hon. DLitt Hull, 1985. Commendatore, Ordine al Merito della Repubblica Italiana, 1973. Italian Govt's Gold Medal for services to scholarship, 1982. An Editor, Italian Studies, 1962–82. *Publications:* Stilistica e Metrica, 1936; Poesie e Lettere Inedite di Salvator Rosa, 1950; L'Attività Letteraria di Giuseppe Mazzini, 1950; La Satira nel Seicento, 1961; The Fortunes of Dante in Seventeenth Century Italy, 1964; (ed) The Mind of Dante, 1965; (ed) vol. xii (Scritti vari di critica storica e letteraria) of Edizione Nazionale of Works of U. Foscolo, 1978; (ed) La Fiera, by Michelangelo Buonarroti the Younger (original 1619 version), 1984; Dante's Comedy: introductory readings of selected cantos, 1985; co-editor yearly review, Studi Secenteschi (founded 1960); trans. E. R. Vincent's Ugo Foscolo Esule fra gli Inglesi, 1954; several contrib. on Italian Literature to: Encyclopædia Britannica; Cassell's Encyclopædia of Literature; Italian Studies; La Bibliofilia; Giornale Storico della Letteratura Italiana; Amor di Libro; Studi Secenteschi; Il Pensiero Mazziniano; Bollettino della Domus Mazziniana; Il Ponte; Cambridge Review; Modern Language Review; Times Literary Supplement. *Recreation:* walking in the Alps. *Address:* 19A Victoria Street, Cambridge CB1 1JP. *T:* Cambridge 358198.

LIMERICK, 6th Earl of, *cr* 1803 (Ire.); **Patrick Edmund Pery,** KBE 1983; MA, CA; Baron Glentworth, 1790 (Ire.); Viscount Limerick, 1800 (Ire.); Baron Foxford, 1815 (UK); Deputy Chairman, Kleinwort, Benson Ltd, since 1985 (Director since 1967); Director: Kleinwort, Benson, Lonsdale plc, since 1982; TR Pacific Basin Investment Trust PLC, since 1976; De La Rue Company plc, since 1983; Vice-President, Association of British Chambers of Commerce, since 1977 (President, 1974–77); Chairman, British Invisible Exports Council, since 1984; *b* 12 April 1930; *e s* of 5th Earl of Limerick, GBE, CH, KCB, DSO, TD, and Angela Olivia, Dowager Countess of Limerick, GBE, CH (*d* 1981); *S* father, 1967; *m* 1961, Sylvia Rosalind Lush (*see* Countess of Limerick); two *s* one *d*. *Educ:* Eton; New Coll., Oxford. CA 1957. Commercial Bank of Australia Ltd (London Adv. Bd), 1969–72. Parly Under-Sec. of State for Trade, Dept of Trade and Industry, 1972–74. Dir, Brooke Bond Gp, 1981–84. Chm., BOTB, 1979–83; Pres., Inst. of Export, 1983–. Member: Cttee for ME Trade, 1968–79 (Chm., 1975–79); Council,

London Chamber of Commerce, 1968–79. Chm., Mallinson-Denny Ltd, 1979–81. Trustee, City Parochial Foundn, 1971–; Chm., Bd of Governors, City of London Polytechnic, 1984– (Vice-Chm., 1983–84). Pres., Ski Club of Gt Britain, 1974–81; Pres., Alpine Ski Club, 1985– (Vice-Pres., 1975–77). *Recreations:* skiing, mountaineering. *Heir:* s Viscount Glentworth, *qv. Address:* Chiddinglye, West Hoathly, East Grinstead, West Sussex. *T:* Sharpthorne 810214; 30 Victoria Road, W8 5RG. *T:* 01–937 0573.

LIMERICK, Countess of; Sylvia Rosalind Pery, MA; Chairman, British Red Cross Society, since 1985; President, Health Visitors' Association, since 1984 (a Vice President, 1978–84); Vice-Chairman, Foundation for the Study of Infant Deaths, since 1971; *b* 7 Dec. 1935; *e d* of Maurice Stanley Lush, *qv; m* 1961, Viscount Glentworth (now 6th Earl of Limerick, *qv*); two *s* one *d. Educ:* St Swithun's, Winchester; Lady Margaret Hall, Oxford (MA). Research Asst, Foreign Office, 1959–62. Mem., Bd of Governors, St Bartholomew's Hosp., 1970–74; Vice-Chm., Community Health Council, S District of Kensington, Chelsea, Westminster Area, 1974–77; Mem., Kensington, Chelsea and Westminster AHA, 1977–82. British Red Cross Society: Nat. HQ Staff, 1962–66; Pres., Kensington and Chelsea Div., 1966–72; a Vice-Pres., London Br., 1972–85; Vice President: UK Cttee for UN Children's Fund, 1979– (Pres., 1972–79); Nat. Assoc. for Maternal and Child Welfare, 1985– (Pres., 1973–84). Member: Cttee of Management, Inst. of Child Health, 1976–; Council and Cttee of Management, King Edward's Hospital Fund, 1977–81, 1985–; Maternity Services Adv. Cttee, DHSS, 1981–84. Trustee, Child Accident Prevention Trust, 1979–. Reviewed National Association of Citizens Advice Bureaux, 1983. *Publication:* (jtly) Sudden Infant Death: patterns, puzzles and problems, 1985. *Recreations:* music, mountaineering, ski-ing. *Address:* 30 Victoria Road, W8 5RG. *T:* 01–937 0573; Chiddinglye, West Hoathly, East Grinstead, W Sussex RH19 4QT. *T:* Sharpthorne (0342) 810214.

LIMERICK AND KILLALOE, Bishop of, since 1985; **Rt. Rev. Edward Flewett Darling;** *b* 24 July 1933; *s* of late Ven. Vivian W. Darling and Honor F. G. Darling; *m* 1958, E. E. Patricia Mann; three *s* two *d. Educ:* Cork Grammar School; Midleton Coll., Co. Cork; St John's School, Leatherhead, Surrey; Trinity Coll., Dublin (MA). Curate: St Luke's, Belfast, 1956–59; St John's, Orangefield, Belfast, 1959–62; Incumbent, St Gall's, Carnalea, Co. Down, 1962–72; Chaplain, Bangor Hosp., Co. Down, 1963–72; Rector, St John's, Malone, Belfast, 1972–85; Chaplain, Ulster Independent Clinic, Belfast, 1981–85. *Publication:* Choosing the Hymns, 1984. *Recreations:* music, gardening. *Address:* Bishop's House, North Circular Road, Limerick, Ireland. *T:* Limerick 51532.

LIMON, Donald William; Principal Clerk, Table Office, House of Commons, since 1985; *b* 29 Oct. 1932; *s* of late Arthur and Dora Limon; unmarried. *Educ:* Durham Cathedral Chorister Sch.; Durham Sch.; Lincoln Coll., Oxford (MA). A Clerk in the House of Commons, 1956–; Sec. to House of Commons Commn, 1979–81; Clerk of Financial Cttees, H of C, 1981–84. *Recreations:* cricket, golf, singing. *Address:* Wicket Gate, Churt, Farnham, Surrey GU10 2HY. *T:* Headley Down 714350.

LINACRE, Sir (John) Gordon (Seymour), Kt 1986; CBE 1979; AFC 1943; DFM 1941; CBIM; Deputy Chairman, since 1981, and Chief Executive, since 1983, United Newspapers plc (Director, since 1969; Joint Managing Director, 1981–83); Chairman, Yorkshire Post Newspapers Ltd, since 1983 (Managing Director, 1965–83; Deputy Chairman, 1981–83); Deputy Chairman, Express Newspapers plc, since 1985; *b* 23 Sept. 1920; *s* of John James Linacre and Beatrice Barber Linacre; *m* 1943, Irene Amy (*née* Gordon); two *d. Educ:* Firth Park Grammar Sch., Sheffield. CBIM (FBIM 1973). Served War, RAF, 1939–46, Sqdn Ldr. Journalistic appts, Sheffield Telegraph/Star, 1937–47; Kemsley News Service, 1947–50; Dep. Editor: Newcastle Journal, 1950–56; Newcastle Evening Chronicle, 1956–57; Editor, Sheffield Star, 1958–61; Asst Gen. Man., Sheffield Newspapers Ltd, 1961–63; Exec. Dir, Thomson Regional Newspapers Ltd, London, 1963–65. Chairman: United Provincial Newspapers Ltd, 1983–; Sheffield Newspapers Ltd, 1981–; Lancashire Evening Post Ltd, 1982–; Northampton Mercury Co. Ltd, 1983–; East Yorkshire Printers Ltd, 1965–; Goole Times Printing & Publishing Co. Ltd, 1969–; The Reporter Ltd, 1970–; Blackpool Gazette & Herald Ltd, 1984–; Link House Publications, 1985–86. Director: United Newspapers (Publications) Ltd, 1969–; Trident Television Ltd, 1970–84; Yorkshire Television Ltd, 1967–. Dir, INCA/FIEJ Res. Assoc., Darmstadt, Germany, 1971–79 (Pres., 1974–77); Pres. FIEJ, 1984– (Mem. Bd, 1971–). Member: Newspaper Soc. Council, 1966– (Pres., Newspaper Soc., 1978–79); Newspaper Soc. Indust. Relations Cttee, 1966–80; Press Assoc., 1967–74 (Chm., 1970–71); Reuters Ltd, 1970–74 (Trustee, 1974–); Evening Newspaper Advertising Bureau Ltd, 1966–78 (Chm., 1975–76); English National Opera, 1978–81; Opera North (formerly English National Opera North), 1978– (Chm.); N Eastern Postal Bd, 1974–80; Adv. Bd, Yorks and Lincs, BIM, 1973–75; Health Educn Council, 1973–77. Governor, Harrogate Festival of Arts and Sciences Ltd, 1973–. Trustee, Yorks and Lincs Trustee Savings Bank, 1972–78. Commendatore dell-ordine al Merito della Repubblica Italiana, 1973. *Recreations:* playing cricket, golf, squash; watching County cricket, Leeds United, and Leeds Rugby League Club; country walking, foreign travel. *Address:* White Windows, Staircase Lane, Bramhope, Leeds LS16 9JD. *T:* Arthington 842751. *Clubs:* Alwoodley Golf, Headingley Taverners (Leeds).

LINCOLN, Bishop of, since 1986; **Rt. Rev. Robert Maynard Hardy;** Bishop to HM Prisons, since 1985; *b* 5 Oct. 1936; *s* of Harold and Monica Mavie Hardy; *m* 1970, Isobel Mary, *d* of Charles and Ella Burch; two *s* one *d. Educ:* Queen Elizabeth Grammar School, Wakefield; Clare College, Cambridge (MA). Deacon 1962, priest 1963; Assistant Curate, All Saints and Martyrs, Langley, Manchester, 1962; Fellow and Chaplain, Selwyn College, Cambridge, 1965; Vicar of All Saints, Borehamwood, 1972; Priest-in-charge, Aspley Guise, 1975; Course Director, St Albans Diocese Ministerial Training Scheme, 1975; Incumbent of United Benefice of Aspley Guise with Husborne Crawley and Ridgmont, 1980; Bishop Suffragan of Maidstone, 1980–86. *Recreations:* walking, gardening, reading. *Address:* Bishop's House, Eastgate, Lincoln LN2 1QQ. *T:* Lincoln 34701.

LINCOLN, Dean of; *see* Fiennes, Very Rev. Hon. O. W. T. -W.

LINCOLN, Archdeacon of; *see* Milner, Ven. R. J.

LINCOLN, Sir Anthony (Handley), KCMG 1965 (CMG 1958); CVO 1957; Ambassador to Venezuela, 1964–69; *b* 2 Jan. 1911; *s* of late J. B. Lincoln, OBE; *m* 1948, Lisette Marion Summers; no *c. Educ:* Mill Hill Sch.; Magdalene Coll., Cambridge (BA). Prince Consort and Gladstone Prizes, 1934. Appointed Asst Principal, Home Civil Service, 1934; subsequently transferred to Foreign Service; served in Foreign Office; on UK Delegation to Paris Peace Conf., 1946, and in Buenos Aires. Counsellor, and Head of a Dept of Foreign Office, 1950. Dept. Sec.-Gen., Council of Europe, Strasbourg, France, 1952–55; Counsellor, British Embassy, Copenhagen, 1955–58; British Ambassador to Laos, 1958–60; HM Minister to Bulgaria, 1960–63; Officer Order of Orange Nassau, 1950; Comdr Order of Dannebrog, 1957. *Publication:* Some Political and Social Ideas of English Dissent, 1937. *Recreations:* country pursuits. *Clubs:* Brooks's, Reform.

LINCOLN, Hon. Sir Anthony (Leslie Julian), Kt 1979; **Hon. Mr Justice Lincoln;** a Judge of the High Court of Justice, Family Division, since 1979; a Judge of the Restrictive

Practices Court, since 1980, President, since 1982; Writer and Broadcaster; *b* 7 April 1920; *s* of Samuel and Ruby Lincoln. *Educ:* Highgate; Queen's Coll., Oxford (Schol., MA). Served Somerset Light Inf. and RA, 1941–45. Called to Bar, 1949; QC 1968; Bencher, Lincoln's Inn, 1976; Mem. Senate of Inns of Court and the Bar, 1976–80; Chm., Law Reform Cttee of Senate, 1979–81. A Recorder of the Crown Court, 1974–79. Chm., Justice Cttee on Freedom of Information, 1978; Pres., British Br., Internat. Law Assoc., 1981–. Vice-Princ., Working Men's Coll., 1955–60; Chm., Working Men's Coll. Corp., 1969–79; Chm. and Trustee, Harrison Homes for the Elderly, 1963–80 (Patron, 1980–). *Publications:* Wicked, Wicked Libels, 1972; (ed) Lord Eldon's Anecdote Book, 1960; regular contribs to Observer, Spectator and other jls. *Recreations:* fishing, swimming, walking. *Address:* Royal Courts of Justice, Strand, WC2A 2LL; Woodford, Salisbury, Wilts. *Clubs:* Beefsteak, Lansdowne.

LINCOLN, F(redman) Ashe, QC 1947; MA, BCL; Captain RNVR; a Recorder, 1972–79 (Recorder of Gravesend, 1967–71); Master of the Bench, Inner Temple, since 1955; Master of the Moots, 1955–64, and 1968–70; *s* of Reuben and Fanny Lincoln; *m* 1933, Sybil Eileen Cohen; one *s* one *d. Educ:* Hoe Gram. Sch., Plymouth; Haberdashers' Aske's Sch.; Exeter Coll., Oxford. Called to Bar, Inner Temple, Nov. 1929. Joined RNV(S)R, 1937; served in Royal Navy (RNVR), Sept. 1939–May 1946: Admiralty, 1940–42; in parties to render mines safe, May 1940; rendered safe first type G magnetic mine (King's Commendation for bravery); Mediterranean, 1943, with commandos in Sicily and Italy at Salerno landings, 1943; Seine Bay (D-day) Landings, 1944; assault crossing of Rhine, March 1945 (despatches twice). Dep. World Pres., Internat. Assoc. of Jewish Lawyers and Jurists, 1973–. Renter Warden of Worshipful Company of Plaisterers, 1946–47, Master, 1949–50; Freeman and Liveryman of City of London; fought general election 1945 (C) Harrow East Div. (Middx.); Chm. Administrative Law Cttee of Inns of Court Conservative Association, 1951; Mem. Exec., Gen. Council of the Bar, 1957–61. Associate MNI, 1976; Pres., RNR Officers' Club, 1981–; Dep. Chm., British Maritime League, 1984–; Mem., Exec., London Flotilla, 1984–. Mem., RNSA. Pres., London Devonian Assoc., 1965–. Trustee: British Maritime Charitable Fund; AMARC (TES), 1985–. KStJ 1980. *Publications:* The Starra, 1939; Secret Naval Investigator, 1961. *Recreations:* yachting, tennis. *Address:* 9 King's Bench Walk, Temple, EC4Y 7DX. *T:* 01–353 7202. *Clubs:* Athenæum, Royal Automobile, MCC, Naval; Royal Corinthian Yacht (Burnham-on-Crouch and Cowes); Bar Yacht.

LIND, Per; Swedish Ambassador to the Court of St James's, 1979–82, retired; *b* 8 Jan. 1916; *s* of Erik and Elisabeth Lind; *m* 1942, Eva Sandström; two *s* two *d. Educ:* Univ. of Uppsala. LLB 1939. Entered Swedish Foreign Service as Attaché, 1939; served in Helsinki, 1939–41; Berlin, 1942–44; Second Sec., Stockholm Foreign Ministry, 1944–47; First Sec., Swedish Embassy, Washington, 1947–51; Personal Asst to Sec.-General of UN, 1953–56; re-posted to Swedish Foreign Ministry: Chief of Div. of Internat. Organisations, 1956–59; Dep. Dir Political Affairs, 1959–64; Ambassador with special duties (ie disarmament questions) and actg Chm., Swedish Delegation in Geneva, 1964–66; Ambassador to Canada, 1966–69; Under-Sec. of State for Administration at Foreign Ministry, Stockholm, 1969–75; Chm. Special Political Cttee of 29th Session of Gen. Assembly of UN, 1974; Ambassador to Australia, 1975–79. *Recreation:* golf. *Address:* Gyllenstiernsgatan 7, S-115 26 Stockholm, Sweden.

LINDARS, Rev. Prof. Frederick Chevallier, (Barnabas Lindars), SSF), DD; Rylands Professor of Biblical Criticism and Exegesis, University of Manchester, since 1978 (Dean, Faculty of Theology, 1982–84); *b* 11 June 1923; *s* of Walter St John Lindars and Rose Lindars. *Educ:* Altrincham Grammar Sch.; St John's Coll., Cambridge (Rogerson Scholar, 1941; BA 1945 (1st Cl. Oriental Langs Tripos, Pt I, 1943; 1st Cl. Theol Tripos, Pt I 1946, 2nd Cl. Pt II, 1947); MA 1948, BD 1961, DD 1973). Served War, 1943–45. Westcott House, Cambridge, 1946–48; Deacon 1948, Priest 1949; Curate of St Luke's, Pallion, Sunderland, 1948–52; joined Soc. of St Francis (Anglican religious order), taking the name of Barnabas, 1952; Asst Lectr in Divinity, Cambridge Univ., 1961–66, Lectr, 1966–78; Fellow and Dean, Jesus Coll., Cambridge, 1976–78. Proctor for Northern Univs in Convocation of York and Gen. Synod of C of E, 1980–. Lectures: T. W. Manson Meml, Manchester Univ., 1974; Ethel M. Wood, London Univ., 1983. Canon Theologian (hon.), Leicester Cathedral, 1977–. Member: Studiorum Novi Testamenti Societas; Soc. for Old Testament Study (Pres., 1986). *Publications:* New Testament Apologetic, 1961 (2nd edn 1973); (ed and contrib.) Church without Walls, 1968; (ed with P. R. Ackroyd, and contrib.) Words and Meanings, 1968; Behind the Fourth Gospel, 1971 (also French edn 1974; Italian edn 1978); The Gospel of John, 1972 (2nd edn 1977); (ed with S. S. Smalley, and contrib.) Christ and Spirit in the New Testament, 1973; Jesus Son of Man, 1983; articles in Jl Theol Studies, New Testament Studies, Vetus Testamentum, and Theol. *Recreations:* walking, music. *Address:* Faculty of Theology, The University, Manchester M13 9PL. *T:* 061–273 3333.

LINDBERGH, Anne Spencer Morrow; author, United States; *b* 1906; *d* of Dwight Whitney Morrow and Elizabeth Reeve Morrow (*née* Cutter); *m* 1929, Col Charles Augustus Lindbergh, AFC, DFC (*d* 1974); three *s* two *d* (and one *s* decd). *Educ:* Miss Chapin's Sch., New York City; Smith Coll., Northampton, Mass (two prizes for literature). Received Cross of Honour of United States Flag Association for her part in survey of air route across Atlantic, 1933; received Hubbard Gold Medal of National Geographical Soc. for work as co-pilot and radio operator in flight of 40,000 miles over five continents, 1934. Hon. MA, Smith Coll., Mass., 1935. *Publications:* North to the Orient, 1935; Listen, the Wind, 1938; The Wave of the Future, 1940; The Steep Ascent, 1944; Gift from the Sea, 1955; The Unicorn and other Poems, 1935–55, 1958; Dearly Beloved, 1963; Earth Shine, 1970; Bring Me a Unicorn (autobiog.), 1972; Hour of Gold, Hour of Lead (autobiog.), 1973; Locked Rooms and Open Doors: diaries and letters 1933–35, 1974; The Flower and the Nettle: diaries and letters 1936–39, 1976; War Within and Without: diaries and letters 1939–44, 1980.

LINDEN, Anya, (Lady Sainsbury); Ballerina, Royal Ballet, 1958–65, retired; *b* 3 Jan. 1933; English; *d* of George Charles and Ada Dorothea Eltenton; *m* 1963, Sir John Sainsbury, *qv*; two *s* one *d. Educ:* Berkeley, Calif; Sadler's Wells Sch., 1947. Entered Sadler's Wells Co. at Covent Garden, 1951; promoted Soloist, 1952; Ballerina, 1958. Principal rôles in the ballets: Coppelia; Silvia; Prince of Pagodas; Sleeping Beauty; Swan Lake; Giselle; Cinderella; Agon; Solitaire; Noctambules; Fête Etrange; Symphonic Variations; Invitation; Firebird; Lady and the Fool; Antigone; Ondine; Seven Deadly Sins. Member: Nat. Council for One-Parent Families, 1978– (Hon. Vice-Pres., 1985–; Mem. Appeal Cttee, 1966–); Adv. Council, British Theatre Museum, 1975–83; Drama and Dance Adv. Cttee, British Council, 1981–83; Theatre Museum Assoc., 1984–86. Vice-Chm. and Dep. Dir, Ballet Rambert, 1975–; Governor: Royal Ballet Sch., 1977–; Rambert Sch. of Ballet Charitable Trust Ltd, 1983–; Mem. Council of Management, Benesh Inst. of Notation of Dance, 1986–. *Recreations:* gardening, filming, photography. *Address:* c/o Stamford House, Stamford Street, SE1.

LINDESAY-BETHUNE, family name of **Earl of Lindsay.**

LINDISFARNE, Archdeacon of; *see* Smith, Ven. D. J.

LINDLEY, Sir Arnold (Lewis George), Kt 1964; DSc; CGIA; FEng, FIMechE, FIEE; Chairman, GEC, 1961–64, retired; *b* 13 Nov. 1902; *s* of George Dilnot Lindley; *m* 1927, Winifred May Cowling (*d* 1962); one *s* one *d*; *m* 1963, Mrs Phyllis Rand. *Educ:* Woolwich Polytechnic. Chief Engineer BGEC, South Africa, 1933; Director: East Rand Engineering Co., 1943; BGEC, S Africa, 1945; Gen. Manager Erith Works, GEC, 1949; GEC England, 1953; Vice-Chm. 1959, Managing Dir, 1961–62, GEC. Chairman: BEAMA, 1963–64; Internat. Electrical Assoc., 1962–64; Engineering Industry Trng Bd, 1964–74; Dep. Chm., Motherwell Bridge (Holdings) Ltd, 1965–84. President, Instn of Mechanical Engineers, 1968–69; Chm., Council of Engineering Instns, 1972–73 (Vice-Chm., 1971–72); Member: Council, City Univ., 1969–78; Design Council, 1971– . Appointed by Govt to advise on QE2 propulsion turbines, 1969; Associate Consultant, Thames Barrier, 1970–. *Recreations:* sailing and golf. *Address:* Heathcote House, 18 Nab Lane, Shipley, W Yorks.

LINDLEY, Bryan Charles, CBE 1982; Director: BICC Cables Ltd, since 1985; BICC Research and Engineering Ltd, since 1985; Chairman, Optical Fibres; *b* 30 Aug. 1932; *m* 1956; one *s*. *Educ:* Reading Sch.; University Coll., London (Fellow 1979). BSc (Eng) 1954; PhD 1960; FIMechE 1968; FIEE 1968; FInstP 1968; FInstD 1968; FPRI 1984. National Gas Turbine Establishment, Pyestock, 1954–57; Hawker Siddeley Nuclear Power Co. Ltd, 1957–59; C. A. Parsons & Co. Ltd, Nuclear Research Centre, Newcastle upon Tyne, 1959–61; International Research and Development Co. Ltd, Newcastle upon Tyne, 1962–65; Man., R&D Div., C. A. Parsons & Co. Ltd, Newcastle upon Tyne, 1965–68; Electrical Research Assoc. Ltd: Dir, 1968–73; Chief Exec. and Man. Dir, ERA Technology Ltd, 1973–79; Dir, ERA Patents Ltd, 1968–79; Chm. and Man. Dir, ERA Autotrack Systems Ltd, 1971–79. Director: Dunlop Ltd, 1982–85; Soil-Less Cultivation Systems, 1980–85; Chm. and Dir, Thermal Conversions (UK), 1982–85; Dir of Technology, Dunlop Holdings, 1979–85. Chairman: Materials, Chemicals and Vehicles Requirements Bd, DTI, 1982–85; RAPRA Council, 1984–85; Dir, RAPRA Technology Ltd, 1985–; Member: Nat. Electronics Council, 1969–79; Res. and Technol. Cttee, CBI, 1974–80; Design Council, 1980–86 (Mem., Design Adv. Cttee, 1980–86); Cttee of Inquiry into Engineering Profession, 1977–80; Adv. Council for Applied Research and Develt, 1980–86. Chm., Sci. Educn and Management Div., IEE, 1974–75; Dep. Chm., Watt Cttee on Energy Ltd, 1976–80. Mem., SAE, 1984. *Publications:* articles on plasma physics, electrical and mechanical engineering, management science, impact of technological innovation, etc, in learned jls. *Recreations:* music, ski-ing, walking. *Address:* 1 Edgehill Chase, Wilmslow, Cheshire SK9 2DJ. *Club:* Institute of Directors.

LINDLEY, Prof. Dennis Victor; Professor and Head of Department of Statistics and Computer Science, University College London, 1967–77; *b* 25 July 1923; *s* of Albert Edward and Florence Louisa Lindley; *m* 1947, Joan Armitage; one *s* two *d*. *Educ:* Tiffin Boys' Sch., Kingston-on-Thames; Trinity Coll., Cambridge. MA Cantab 1948. Min. of Supply, 1943–45; Nat. Physical Lab., 1945–46 and 1947–48; Statistical Lab., Cambridge Univ., 1948–60 (Dir, 1957–60); Prof. and Head of Dept of Statistics, UCW, Aberystwyth, 1960–67, Hon. Professorial Fellow, 1978–. Hon. Prof., Univ. of Warwick, 1978–. Vis. Professor: Chicago and Stanford Univs, 1954–55; Harvard Business Sch., 1963; Univ. of Iowa, 1974–75; Univ. of Bath, 1978–81. Guy Medal (Silver), Royal Statistical Soc., 1968. Fellow, Inst. Math. Statistics; Fellow, American Statistical Assoc. *Publications:* (with J. C. P. Miller) Cambridge Elementary Statistical Tables, 1953; Introduction to Probability and Statistics (2 vols), 1965; Making Decisions, 1971, rev. edn 1985; Bayesian Statistics, 1971; (with W. F. Scott) New Cambridge Elementary Statistical Tables, 1985; contribs to Royal Statistical Soc., Biometrika, Annals of Math. Statistics. *Address:* 2 Periton Lane, Minehead, Somerset TA24 8AQ. *T:* Minehead 5189.

LINDNER, Dr Gerhard; Ambassador Extraordinary and Plenipotentiary of the German Democratic Republic to the Court of St James's, since 1984; *b* 26 Feb. 1930; *m*, Edeltraut; two *s*. *Educ:* Leipzig University. Head of Trade Representation of GDR in Denmark, 1971–72; Ambassador in Australia, 1977–81. *Address:* Embassy of the German Democratic Republic, 34 Belgrave Square, SW1. *T:* 01–235 9941.

LINDOP, Audrey Beatrice Noël E.; *see* Erskine-Lindop, A. B. N.

LINDOP, Sir Norman, Kt 1973; MSc, CChem, FRSC; Principal, British School of Osteopathy, since 1982; *b* 9 March 1921; *s* of Thomas Cox Lindop and May Lindop, Stockport, Cheshire; *m* 1974, Jenny C. Quass; one *s*. *Educ:* Northgate Sch., Ipswich; Queen Mary Coll., Univ. of London (BSc, MSc). Various industrial posts, 1942–46; Lectr in Chemistry, Queen Mary Coll., 1946; Asst Dir of Examinations, Civil Service Commn, 1951; Sen. Lectr in Chemistry, Kingston Coll. of Technology, 1953; Head of Dept of Chemistry and Geology, Kingston Coll. of Technology, 1957; Principal: SW Essex Technical Coll. and Sch. of Art, 1963; Hatfield Coll. of Technology, 1966; Dir, Hatfield Polytechnic, 1969–82. Chairman: Cttee of Dirs of Polytechnics, 1972–74; Council for Professions Supplementary to Medicine, 1973–81; Home Office Data Protection Cttee, 1976–78; Cttee of Enquiry into Public Sector Validation, DES, 1984–85; British Library Adv. Council, 1986–; Member: CNAA, 1974–81; US-UK Educn (Fulbright) Commn, 1971–81; SRC, 1974–78; GMC, 1979–84. Chm. Council, Westfield Coll., London Univ., 1983–. Chm., Hatfield Philharmonic Soc., 1970. Fellow, QMC, 1976; FCP 1980; FRSA. Hon. DEd CNAA, 1982. *Recreations:* mountain walking, music (especially opera). *Address:* The British School of Osteopathy, 1–4 Suffolk Street, SW1Y 4HG. *T:* 01–930 9254–8. *Club:* Athenæum.

LINDOP, Prof. Patricia Joyce, (Mrs G. P. R. Esdale); Professor of Radiation Biology, University of London, 1970–84, now Emeritus; *b* 21 June 1930; 2nd *c* of Elliot D. Lindop and Dorothy Jones; *m* 1957, Gerald Paton Rivett Esdale; one *s* one *d*. *Educ:* Malvern Girls' Coll.; St Bartholomew's Hospital Med. Coll.; BSc (1st cl. Hons), MB, BS, PhD; DSc London 1974; MRCP 1956; FRCP 1977. Registered GP, 1954. Research and teaching in physiology and medical radiobiology at Med. Coll. of St Bartholomew's Hosp., 1955–84. UK Mem., Continuing Cttee of Pugwash Confs on Science and World Affairs (Asst Sec. Gen., 1961–71); Mem., Royal Commn on Environmental Pollution, 1974–79; Mem. Council, St Bartholomew's Hospital Med. Coll. Chm. and Trustee, Soc. for Education in the Applications of Science, 1968–; Cttee 10 of ICRU, 1972–79. Member Council: Science and Society, 1975–; Soc. for Protection of Science and Learning, 1974–86; formerly Mem. Council, British Inst. of Radiology; Chairman: Univ. of London Bd of Studies in Radiation Biology, 1979–81; Interdisciplinary Special Cttee for the Environment, 1979–81. Hon. Member: RCR, 1972; ARR, 1984. *Publications:* in field of radiation effects. *Recreation:* watching events. *Address:* 58 Wildwood Road, NW11 6UP. *T:* 01–455 5860. *Club:* Royal Society of Medicine.

LINDSAY, family name of **Earl of Crawford** and **Baron Lindsay of Birker.**

LINDSAY, 15th Earl of, *cr* 1633; **David Lindesay-Bethune;** Lord Lindsay of The Byres, 1445; Lord Parbroath, 1633; Viscount of Garnock, Lord Kilbirny, Kingsburne and Drumry, 1703; *b* 9 Feb. 1926; *er s* of 14th Earl of Lindsay, and of Marjory, DStJ, *d* of late Arthur J. G. Cross and Lady Hawke; *S* father, 1985; *m* 1st, 1953, Hon. Mary Clare Douglas-Scott-Montagu (marr. diss., 1968), *y d* of 2nd Baron Montagu of Beaulieu; one *s* one *d*; 2nd, 1969, Penelope, *er d* of late Anthony Crossley, MP. *Educ:* Eton; Magdalene Coll., Cambridge. Scots Guards, 1943–45. US and Canadian Railroads, 1948–50. Chairman: Severn Valley Railway (Holdings) Ltd, 1972–76 (Pres., 1976–); Romney, Hythe and Dymchurch Light Rly Co., 1976–, Holdings Co., 1976–; Sallingbury Holdings, 1977–83; Sallingbury Ltd, 1977–83; Crossley Karastan Carpet Mills, Canada 1982– (Dir, 1961–); British Property Timeshare Assoc. Ltd, 1981–; Kilconquhar Castle Estate Ltd, 1980–; Edington PLC, 1986–; Tours by Tape PLC; Director: John Crossley & Sons, 1957–74; John Crossley Carpet Trades Hldgs, 1960–70; Festiniog Railway Co. Ltd, 1960–; Abbey Life Insurance Co. of Canada, 1964–81; Carpets Internat. Group Services, 1970–85; Interface Flooring Systems Inc. (formerly Carpets International Georgia Inc.), 1972–; Bank of Montreal, 1975–; Manuge Galleries (Nova Scotia), 1976–; International Harvester Co. of GB Ltd, 1976–85; Bain Dawes Ltd (Northern), 1978–81; Bain Dawes (Canada), 1978–82; Riverside Plantation Co., Inc., 1982–84; Coastal Pollution Controls (formerly Associated Marine Industries Offshore Resources Ltd), 1982–; Debron Investments PLC (formerly Carpets International PLC), 1983–. Mem. International Harvester World Adv. Council, 1980–82; Vice-Chm., N American Adv. Gp, BOTB, 1973–; Chairman: British Carpets Manufrs' Assoc. Export Council, 1976–84; Air Transport Users Cttee, 1983–84; Vice-Pres., Transport Trust, 1973–; Member: BTA, 1976–82; DASA, 1982–. Mem., Queen's Body Guard for Scotland (Royal Company of Archers), 1960. *Recreation:* catching up. *Heir:* *s* Viscount Garnock, *qv*. *Address:* Combermere Abbey, Whitchurch, Salop. *T:* Burleydam 287; Coates House, Upper Largo, Fife. *T:* Upper Largo 249. *Club:* Boodle's.

See also Sir Bourchier Wrey, Bt.

LINDSAY OF BIRKER, 2nd Baron, *cr* 1945; **Michael Francis Morris Lindsay;** Professor Emeritus in School of International Service, The American University, Washington, DC; *b* 24 Feb. 1909; *e s* of 1st Baron Lindsay of Birker, CBE, LLD, and Erica Violet (*née* Storr) (*d* 1962); *S* father 1952; *m* 1941, Li Hsiao-li, *d* of Col Li Wen-chi of Lishih, Shansi; one *s* two *d*. *Educ:* Gresham's Sch., Holt; Balliol Coll., Oxford. Adult education and economic research work in S Wales, 1935–37; Tutor in Economics, Yenching Univ., Peking, 1938–41; Press Attaché, British Embassy, Chungking, 1940. Served War of 1939–45, with Chinese 18th Group Army, 1942–45. Vis. Lectr at Harvard Univ., 1946–47; Lectr in Econs, University Coll., Hull, 1948–51; Sen. Fellow of the Dept of Internat. Relations, ANU, Canberra, 1951–59 (Reader in Internat. Relations, 1959); Prof. of Far Eastern Studies, Amer. Univ., Washington, 1959–74, Chm. of E Asia Programme, 1959–71. Visiting Professor: Yale Univ., 1958; Ball State Univ., Indiana, 1971–72. *Publications:* Educational Problems in Communist China, 1950; The New China, three views, 1950; China and the Cold War, 1955; Is Peaceful Co-existence Possible?, 1960; The Unknown War: North China 1937–45, 1975; Kung-ch'an-chu-i Ts' o-wu ts'ai Na-li, 1976; articles in learned journals. *Recreations:* wireless, tennis. *Heir:* *s* Hon. James Francis Lindsay [*b* 29 Jan. 1945; *m* 1966, Mary Rose, *d* of W. G. Thomas]. *Address:* 6812 Delaware Street, Chevy Chase, Md 20815, USA. *T:* (301)-656–4245.

LINDSAY, Maj.-Gen. Courtenay Traice David, CB 1963; Director-General of Artillery, War Office, 1961–64, retired; *b* 28 Sept. 1910; *s* of late Courtenay Traice Lindsay and Charlotte Editha (*née* Wetenhall); *m* 1934, Margaret Elizabeth, *d* of late William Pease Theakston, Huntingdon; two *s*. *Educ:* Rugby Sch.; RMA Woolwich. 2nd Lt RA, 1930. Mem., Ordnance Board (Col), 1952; Dir of Munitions, British Staff (Brig.), Washington, 1959; Maj.-Gen. 1961. *Address:* Huggits Farm, Stone-in-Oxney, Tenterden, Kent. *Club:* Rye Golf.

LINDSAY, Crawford Callum Douglas; barrister; a Recorder of the Crown Court, since 1982; *b* 5 Feb. 1939; *s* of Douglas Marshall Lindsay, FRCOG and Eileen Mary Lindsay; *m* 1963, Rosemary Gough; one *s* one *d*. *Educ:* Whitgift Sch., Croydon; St John's Coll., Oxford. Called to the Bar, Lincoln's Inn, 1961. *Address:* 6 King's Bench Walk, Temple, EC4Y 7DR. *Club:* MCC.

LINDSAY, Donald Dunrod, CBE 1972; *b* 27 Sept. 1910; *s* of Dr Colin Dunrod Lindsay, Pres. BMA 1938, and Mrs Isabel Baynton Lindsay; *m* 1936, Violet Geraldine Fox; one *s* one *d*. *Educ:* Clifton Coll., Bristol; Trinity Coll., Oxford. Asst Master, Manchester Gram. Sch., 1932; Asst Master, Repton Sch., 1935; temp. seconded to Bristol Univ. Dept of Education as lecturer in History, 1938; Senior History Master, Repton Sch., 1938–42; Headmaster: Portsmouth Gram. Sch., 1942–53; Malvern Coll., 1953–71. Dir, Independent Schs Information Service, 1972–77. Chm., Headmasters' Conference, 1968. Governor, Harrow Sch., 1977–82. *Publications:* A Portrait of Britain Between the Exhibitions, 1952; A Portrait of Britain, 1688–1851, 1954; A Portrait of Britain Before 1066, 1962; Authority and Challenge, Europe 1300–1600, 1975; Europe and the World, 1979; Friends for Life: a portrait of Launcelot Fleming, 1981; Forgotten General, 1986. *Recreations:* walking, theatre, music. *Address:* 34 Belgrave Road, Seaford, East Sussex.

LINDSAY, Maj.-Gen. Edward Stewart, CB 1956; CBE 1952 (OBE 1944); DSO 1945; Assistant Master General of Ordnance, 1961–64; Deputy Controller, Ministry of Supply, 1957–61; *b* 11 July 1905; *s* of Col M. E. Lindsay, DSO, DL, Craigfoodie, Dairsie, Fife; *m* 1933, Margaret, *d* of late Gen. Sir Norman Macmullen, GCB, CMG, CIE, DSO; two *d* (one *s* decd). *Educ:* Harrow Sch.; Edinburgh Univ. (BSc). 2nd Lt, RA 1926; served War of 1939–45, NW Europe (OBE, DSO); despatches, 1946; Col 1949; Brig. 1953; Maj.-Gen. 1955; Prin. Staff Officer to High Comr, Malaya, 1954–56; retired. Comdr Legion of Merit, USA, 1945. *Address:* Hill Cottage, Eversley, Hants. *T:* Eversley 733107. *Club:* Army and Navy.

LINDSAY, Rt. Rev. Hugh; *see* Hexham and Newcastle, Bishop of, (RC).

LINDSAY, Jack, AO 1981; author, *b* Melbourne, Australia, 1900; *s* of late Norman Lindsay; *m* 1958, Meta Waterdrinker; one *s* one *d*. *Educ:* Queensland Univ., BA, DLitt. FRSL. Soviet Badge of Honour, 1968. *Publications:* Fauns and Ladies (Poems); Marino Faliero (Verse Drama); Hereward (Verse drama); Helen Comes of Age (Three verse plays); Passionate Neatherd (Poems); William Blake, Creative Will and the Poetic Image, an Essay; Dionysos; The Romans; The Anatomy of Spirt; Mark Antony; John Bunyan; Short History of Culture; Handbook of Freedom; Song of a Falling World; Byzantium into Europe; Life of Dickens; Meredith; The Romans were Here; Arthur and his Times; A World Ahead; Daily Life in Roman Egypt; Leisure and Pleasure in Roman Egypt; Men and Gods on the Roman Nile; Origins of Alchemy; Origins of Astrology; Cleopatra; The Clashing Rocks; Helen of Troy; The Normans; translations of Lysistrata, Women in Parliament (Aristophanes), complete works of Petronius, Love Poems of Propertius, A Homage to Sappho, Theocritos, Herondas, Catullus, Ausonius, Latin Medieval Poets, I am a Roman; Golden Ass; Edited Metamorphosis of Aiax (Sir John Harington, 1956;) Loving Mad Tom (Bedlamite Verses); Parlement of Pratlers (J. Eliot, 1593); Blake's Poetical Sketches; Into Action (Dieppe), a poem; Russian Poetry, 1917–55 (selections and translations); Memoirs of J. Priestley; Blast-Power and Ballistics; Decay and Renewal: critical essays on twentieth century writing; *novels:* Cressida's First Lover; Rome for Sale; Cæsar is Dead, Storm at Sea; Last Days with Cleopatra; Despoiling Venus; The Wanderings of Wenamen; Come Home at Last; Shadow and Flame; Adam of a New World; Sue Verney; 1649; Lost Birthright; Hannibaal Takes a Hand; Brief Light; Light in Italy; The Stormy Violence; We Shall Return; Beyond Terror; Hullo Stranger; The Barriers are Down; Time to Live; The Subtle Knot; Men of Forty-Eight; Fires in

Smithfield; Betrayed Spring; Rising Tide; Moment of Choice; The Great Oak; Arthur and His Times; The Revolt of the Sons; The Way the Ball Bounces; All on the Never-Never (filmed as Live Now-Pay Later); Masks and Faces; Choice of Times; Thunder Underground; *history:* 1764; The Writing on the Wall; The Crisis in Marxism, 1981; *autobiography;* Life Rarely Tells; The Roaring Twenties; Fanfrolico and After; Meetings with Poets; *art-criticism;* The Death of the Hero; Life of Turner; Cézanne; Courbet; William Morris; The Troubadours; Hogarth; William Blake; Gainsborough. *Address:* 25 Clarendon Street, Cambridge CB1 1JX.

LINDSAY, Sir James Harvey Kincaid Stewart, Kt 1966; President, Institute of Cultural Affairs International, Brussels, since 1982; Chairman, Henley Training Ltd, since 1980; *b* 31 May 1915; *s* of Arthur Harvey Lindsay and Doris Kincaid Lindsay; *m* Marguerite Phyllis Boudville (one *s* one *d* by previous marriage). *Educ:* Highgate Sch. Joined Metal Box Co. Ltd, 1934; joined Metal Box Co. of India Ltd, 1937; Man. Dir, 1961; Chm., 1967–69; Dir of Internat. Programmes, Admin. Staff Coll., Henley-on-Thames, 1970–79. President: Bengal Chamber of Commerce and Industry; Associated Chambers of Commerce and Industry of India, 1965. Director: Indian Oxygen Co., 1966; Westinghouse, Saxon Farmer Ltd, Hindusthan Pilkington, 1966. Pres., Calcutta Management Association, 1964; Pres. (and elected Life Mem.), All India Management Assoc., 1964–69; Mem. of Governing Body: Indian Inst. of Management, Calcutta, 1964; Administrative Staff Coll. of India, 1965; Indian Institutes of Technology, 1966; National Council of Applied Economic Research, 1966; All-India Board of Management Studies, 1964; Indian Inst. of Foreign Trade, 1965; Member: BoT, Central Adv. Council of Industries, Direct Taxes Adv. Cttee, 1966; National Council on Vocational and Allied Trades, 1963. Convener, Internat. Exposition of Rural Develt, 1980–84; Trustee, Inst. of Family and Environmental Research, 1971–. FInstM 1975; CBIM (FBIM 1971). *Recreations:* music, golf, riding, table tennis. *Address:* Christmas Cottage, Lower Shiplake, near Henley-on-Thames, Oxon. *T:* Wargrave 2859. *Club:* East India, Devonshire, Sports and Public Schools.

LINDSAY, Hon. James Louis; *b* 16 Dec. 1906; *yr s* of 27th Earl of Crawford and Balcarres; *m* 1933, Bronwen Mary, *d* of 8th Baron Howard de Walden; three *s* one *d*. *Educ:* Eton; Magdalen Coll., Oxford. Served 1939–45 war, Major KRRC. Contested (C) Bristol South-East, 1950 and 1951; MP (C) N Devon, 1955–Sept. 1959. *Address:* Spring Farm, Coleman's Hatch, Hartfield, East Sussex TN7 4EL. *T:* Forest Row 2414.

LINDSAY, John Edmund Fredric, QC 1981; *b* 16 Oct. 1935; *s* of late George Fredric Lindsay and Constance Mary Lindsay (*née* Wright); *m* 1967, Patricia Anne Bolton; three *d*. *Educ:* Ellesmere Coll.; Sidney Sussex Coll., Cambridge (MA 1959). Fleet Air Arm, 1954–56; Sub-Lt, RNVR. Called to the Bar, Middle Temple, 1961; joined Lincoln's Inn (*ad eundem*); Junior Treasury Counsel, *bona vacantia,* 1979–81. Chm., Employed Barristers' Registration Cttee, 1982–; Member: Senate of Inns of Court and Bar, 1979–82; Legal Panel, Insolvency Law Review Cttee (Cork Report), 1980–82; Insolvency Rules Adv. Cttee, 1985–. *Address:* 7 Stone Buildings, Lincoln's Inn, WC2.

LINDSAY, (John) Maurice, CBE 1979; TD 1946; Consultant, The Scottish Civic Trust, since 1983 (Director, 1967–83); Hon. Secretary-General, Europa Nostra, since 1983; *b* 21 July 1918; *s* of Matthew Lindsay and Eileen Frances Brock; *m* 1946, Aileen Joyce Gordon; one *s* three *d*. *Educ:* Glasgow Acad.; Scottish National Acad. of Music (now Royal Scottish Acad. of Music, Glasgow). Drama Critic, Scottish Daily Mail, Edinburgh, 1946–47; Music Critic, The Bulletin, Glasgow, 1946–60; Prog. Controller, 1961–62, Prodn Controller, 1962–64, and Features Exec. and Chief Interviewer, 1964–67, Border Television, Carlisle. Atlantic-Rockefeller Award, 1946. Editor: Scots Review, 1949–50; The Scottish Review, 1975–85. Mem., Historic Buildings Council for Scotland, 1976–; Trustee, National Heritage Meml Fund, 1980–84. Hon. FRIAS 1985. Hon. DLitt Glasgow, 1982. *Publications: poetry:* The Advancing Day, 1940; Perhaps To-morrow, 1941; Predicament, 1942; No Crown for Laughter: Poems, 1943; The Enemies of Love: Poems 1941–1945, 1946; Selected Poems, 1947; Hurlygush: Poems in Scots, 1948; At the Wood's Edge, 1950; Ode for St Andrews Night and Other Poems, 1951; The Exiled Heart: Poems 1941–1956, 1957; Snow Warning and Other Poems, 1962; One Later Day and Other Poems, 1964; This Business of Living, 1969; Comings and Goings: Poems, 1971; Selected Poems 1942–1972, 1973; The Run from Life, 1975; Walking Without an Overcoat, Poems 1972–76, 1977; Collected Poems, 1979; A Net to Catch the Winds and Other Poems, 1981; The French Mosquitoes' Woman and Other Diversions and Poems, 1985; *prose:* A Pocket Guide to Scottish Culture, 1947; The Scottish Renaissance, 1949; The Lowlands of Scotland: Glasgow and the North, 1953, 3rd edn, 1979; Robert Burns: The Man, His Work, The Legend, 3rd edn, 1980; Dunoon: The Gem of the Clyde Coast, 1954; The Lowlands of Scotland: Edinburgh and the South, 1956, 3rd edn, 1979; Clyde Waters: Variations and Diversions on a Theme of Pleasure, 1958; The Burns Encyclopedia, 1959, 3rd edn, 1980; Killochan Castle, 1960; By Yon Bonnie Banks: A Gallimaufry, 1961; Environment: A Basic Human Right, 1968; Portrait of Glasgow, 1972, rev. edn, 1981; Robin Philipson, 1977; History of Scottish Literature, 1977; Lowland Scottish Villages, 1980; Francis George Scott and the Scottish Renaissance, 1980; (with Anthony F. Kersting) The Buildings of Edinburgh, 1981; Thank You For Having Me: a personal memoir, 1983; (with Dennis Hardley) Unknown Scotland, 1984; The Castles of Scotland, 1986; Count All Men Mortal—The Story of the Scottish Provident Institution, 1987; Victorian and Edwardian Glasgow, 1987; *editor:* Poetry Scotland One, Two, Three, 1943, 1945, 1946; Sailing Tomorrow's Seas: An Anthology of New Poems, 1944; Modern Scottish Poetry: An Anthology of the Scottish Renaissance 1920–1945, 1946, 4th edn, 1986; (with Fred Urquhart) No Scottish Twilight: New Scottish Stories, 1947; Selected Poems of Sir Alexander Gray, 1948; Poems, by Sir David Lyndsay, 1948; (with Hugh MacDiarmid) Poetry Scotland Four, 1949; (with Helen Cruickshank) Selected Poems of Marion Angus, 1950; John Davidson: A Selection of His Poems, 1961; (with Edwin Morgan and George Bruce) Scottish Poetry One to Six 1966–72; (with Alexander Scott and Roderick Watson) Scottish Poetry Seven to Nine, 1974, 1976, 1977; (with R. L. Mackie) A Book of Scottish Verse, 1967, 3rd edn 1983; The Discovery of Scotland: Based on Accounts of Foreign Travellers from the 13th to the 18th centuries, 1964, 2nd edn 1979; The Eye is Delighted: Some Romantic Travellers in Scotland, 1970; Scotland: An Anthology, 1974; As I Remember, 1979; Scottish Comic Verse 1425–1980, 1980. *Recreations:* enjoying and adding to record collection, walking. *Address:* 7 Milton Hill, Milton, Dumbarton G82 2TS. *T:* Dumbarton 61500.

LINDSAY, John Vliet; Mayor of New York City, 1965–73 (elected as Republican-Liberal, Nov. 1965, re-elected as Liberal-Independent, Nov. 1969); *b* 24 Nov. 1921; *s* of George Nelson and Eleanor (Vliet) Lindsay; *m* 1949, Mary Harrison; one *s* three *d*. *Educ:* St Paul's Sch., Concord, NH; Yale Univ. BA 1944; LLB 1948. Lt US Navy, 1943–46. Admitted to: NY Bar, 1949; Fed. Bar, Southern Dist NY, 1950; US Supreme Court, 1955; DC Bar, 1957. Mem., law firm of Webster, Sheffield, NYC, 1949–55, 1957–61, 1974–. Exec. Asst to US Attorney Gen., 1955–57; Mem., 86th-89th Congresses, 17th Dist, NY, 1959–66. Bd Mem., Lincoln Center for Performing Arts; Chm. Bd, Lincoln Center Theatre Co. (the Beaumont), 1985–. Hon. LLD: Williams Coll., 1968; Harvard, 1969. *Publications:* Journey into Politics, 1967; The City, 1970; The Edge, 1976. *Address:* 1 Rockefeller Plaza, New York, NY 10020, USA.

LINDSAY, Kenneth Martin; *b* 16 Sept. 1897; *s* of George Michael Lindsay and Anne Theresa Parmiter; unmarried. *Educ:* St Olave's; Worcester Coll., Oxford. Served European War, HAC, 1916–18; Pres., Oxford Union, 1922–23; Leader, First Debating Visit to Amer. Univs. Barnett Research Fellow, Toynbee Hall, 1923–26; Councillor and Guardian, Stepney, 1923–26; Dir of Voluntary Migration Societies, Dominions Office, 1929–31; First Gen. Sec. Political and Economic Planning, 1931–35; MP (Ind. Nat.) Kilmarnock Burghs, 1933–45; MP (Ind.) Combined English Universities, 1945–50; Civil Lord of the Admiralty, 1935–37; Parliamentary Sec., Board of Education, 1937–40; Founder of Youth Service, and of CEMA (now Arts Council); Mem. Council, National Book League; a Vice-President: Educational Interchange Council (Ex-Chm.), 1968–73; Anglo-Israel Assoc. (Dir, 1962–73); Vis. Prof. at many Amer. Univs. Vice-Pres., Feathers Clubs Assoc. Contested Oxford, Harrow and Worcester. *Publications:* Social Progress and Educational Waste; English Education; Eldorado-An Agricultural Settlement: Towards a European Parliament; European Assemblies. *Recreations:* Association Football, Oxford University, 1921–22; Corinthians; cricket, Authentics. *Club:* Athenæum.

LINDSAY, Maurice; see Lindsay, J. M.

LINDSAY of Dowhill, Sir Ronald Alexander, 2nd Bt *cr* 1962, of Dowhill; 23rd Representer of Baronial House of Dowhill; *b* 6 Dec. 1933; *er s* of Sir Martin Lindsay of Dowhill, 1st Bt, CBE, DSO, and of Joyce Lady Lindsay, *d* of late Major Hon. Robert Lindsay, Royal Scots Greys; *S* father, 1981; *m* 1968, Nicoletta, *yr d* of late Captain Edgar Storich, Royal Italian Navy and late Mrs Storich; three *s* one *d*. *Educ:* Eton College; Worcester Coll., Oxford (MA). National service in Grenadier Guards (Lieut), 1952–54. Insurance executive, 1958–; Dir, AHJ Heath Hogg Robinson Members' Agency, 1985–. Chm., Standing Council of the Baronetage, 1987– (Vice-Chm., 1984–86); Vice-Chm., Anglo-Spanish Soc., 1985–. Member of Queen's Body Guard for Scotland (Royal Company of Archers). FCII 1963. *Heir: s* James Martin Evelyn Lindsay, *b* 11 Oct. 1968. *Address:* Courleigh, Colley Lane, Reigate, Surrey RH2 9JJ. *T:* Reigate 43290.

LINDSAY, Sir William, Kt 1963; CBE 1956; DL; *b* 22 March 1907; *er s* of late James Robertson Lindsay, Tower of Lethendy, Meikleour, Perthshire, and late Barbara Coupar, *d* of late Sir Charles Barrie; *m* 1936, Anne Diana, *d* of late Arthur Morley, OBE, KC; one *s* two *d*. *Educ:* Trinity Coll., Glenalmond; Christ Church, Oxford. BA 1928, MA 1931; Barrister-at-Law, Inner Temple, 1931. Dir, Royal Caledonian Schs, 1934–; Admin Officer, HM Treas., 1940–45. Member: Cuckfield UD Council, 1946–67 (Chm. 1951–54); Mid-Sussex Water Bd, 1946–60 (Chm. 1952–60); E Sussex CC, 1949– (Ald. 1957, Chm. 1961–64); Nat. Health Exec. Coun. for E Sussex, 1954–66; Hailsham Hospital Management Cttee, 1956–68; National Parks Commn, 1961–68, Countryside Commn, 1968–72; Chairman: E Grinstead Conservative Assoc., 1948–51 and 1957–59; Sussex Co. Cons. Org., 1951–53 and 1958–59; Vice-Chm., 1951–54 and 1957–60 and Hon. Treas. 1960–69 of SE Area of Nat. Union of Cons. and Unionist Assocs.; Mem. Nat. Exec. Cttee of Conservative Party, 1952–54 and 1957–69. DL West Sussex, 1970–. Dir, Mid Sussex Water Co., 1961–79. *Address:* Mytten Cedars, Broad Street, Cuckfield, West Sussex. *T:* Haywards Heath 450371.

LINDSAY-FYNN, Sir Basil (Mortimer), Kt 1982; FCA; Director, Ward White Group Ltd (formerly John White Impregnable Boots Ltd, and Ward White Ltd), 1934–83; President and Founder, Friends of Malta GC, since 1962; *b* 22 Dec. 1901; *s* of Newenham Wight Lindsay-Fynn and Annie Cecilia Victoria (*née* Lindsay); *m* 1932, Marion Audrey Ellen Chapman; two *s* one *d*. *Educ:* Wesley Coll., Dublin; Trinity Coll., Dublin, 1929; London Sch. of Econs and Pol. Science, Univ. of London, 1929–31 (BCom). Chartered Accountant, 1924; FCA 1929. Sen. Partner, Smallfield Lindsay-Fynn & Co., 1929–47; Chairman: Gossard Ltd, 1934–60; Lintafoam Industries Ltd, 1946–66; Crown Estate Paving Commn, 1958–81; Dir, Associated Weavers Ltd and Chm. of its successor, AW Securities Ltd, 1936–77. President: Honiton Cons. Assoc., 1969–72; Holborn & St Pancras (S) Cons. Assoc., 1970–73; St Marylebone Cons. Assoc., 1980–84; Westminster N Cons. Assoc., 1984–85 (Patron, 1985–). *Recreations:* walking, swimming, tennis, ballroom dancing; old paintings, silver, glass, objets d'art and old furniture. *Address:* 64 Avenue Road, NW8 6HU. *T:* 01–586 1104. *Club:* Buck's.

LINDSAY-HOGG, Sir William (Lindsay), 3rd Bt *cr* 1905; *b* 12 Aug. 1930; *s* of Sir Anthony Henry Lindsay-Hogg, 2nd Bt and Frances (*née* Doble; she *d* 1969); *S* father, 1968; *m* 1961, Victoria Pares (marr. diss. 1968); one *d*. *Educ:* Stowe. Man. Dir, Roebuck Air Charter Ltd, 1967–70, Chm. 1970–74. Hereditary Cavaliere d'Italia. *Recreations:* riding, skiing. *Heir: uncle* Edward William Lindsay-Hogg [*b* 23 May 1910; *m* 1st, 1936, Geraldine (marr. diss. 1946), *d* of E. M. Fitzgerald; one *s*; 2nd, 1957, Kathleen Mary, *widow* of Captain Maurice Cadell, MC and *d* of James Cooney].

LINDSAY-SMITH, Iain-Mór; Publisher, Lloyd's List, and Executive Director, Lloyd's of London Press, since 1984; Director, Lloyd's of London Press Incorporated, USA, since 1985; *b* 18 Sept. 1934; *s* of Edward Duncanson Lindsay-Smith and Margaret Anderson; *m* 1960, Carol Sara (*née* Paxman); one *s*. *Educ:* High Sch. of Glasgow; London Univ. (diploma course on Internat. Affairs). Scottish Daily Record, 1951–57; Commissioned 1st Bn Cameronians (Scottish Rifles), 1953–55; Daily Mirror, 1957–60; Foreign Editor, subseq. Features Editor, Daily Mail, 1960–71; Dep. Editor, Yorkshire Post, 1971–74; Editor, Glasgow Herald, 1974–77; Exec. Editor, The Observer, 1977–84. *Publication:* article in Electronics and Power. *Recreations:* Highland bagpipes, foreign affairs, outdoors, travel, wine appreciation, shooting, gardening, snooker. *Address:* Lloyd's of London Press, 26–30 Artillery Lane, E1 7LX; Sheepen Place, Colchester, Essex CO3 3LP. *Clubs:* Travellers', Duffers.

LINDSEY, 14th Earl of, *cr* 1626, AND ABINGDON, 9th Earl of, *cr* 1682; Richard Henry Rupert Bertie; Baron Norreys, of Rycote, 1572; *b* 28 June 1931; *o s* of Hon. Arthur Michael Bertie, DSO, MC (*d* 1957) and Aline Rose (*d* 1948), *er d* of George Arbuthnot-Leslie, Warthill, Co. Aberdeen, and *widow* of Hon. Charles Fox Maule Ramsay, MC; *S* cousin, 1963; *m* 1957, Norah Elizabeth Farquhar-Oliver, *yr d* of Mark Oliver, OBE; two *s* one *d*. *Educ:* Ampleforth. Lieut, Royal Norfolk Regt (Supplementary Reserve of Officers), 1951–52. Underwriting Member of Lloyd's, 1958–; company director; Chm., Anglo-Ivory-Coast Soc., 1974–77. High Steward of Abingdon, 1963–. *Heir: s* Lord Norreys, *qv. Address:* Gilmilnscroft, Sorn, Mauchline, Ayrshire; 3 Westgate Terrace, SW10. *Clubs:* White's, Turf, Pratt's.

LINDSEY, Archdeacon of; see Laurence, Ven. J. H. C.

LINDT, Auguste Rudolph, LLD; retired as Swiss Ambassador; *b* Berne, Switzerland, 5 Aug. 1905. Studied law at Universities of Geneva and Berne. Special correspondent of several European newspapers, in Manchuria, Liberia, Palestine, Jordan, the Persian Gulf, Tunisia, Roumania and Finland, 1932–40. Served in Swiss Army, 1940–45. Special delegate of International Cttee of the Red Cross at Berlin, 1945–46. Press Attaché, 1946, Counsellor, 1949, Swiss Legation in London. Switzerland's Permanent Observer to the United Nations (appointed 1953) and subseq. Minister plenipotentiary (1954); appointments connected with work of the United Nations: Chairman Exec. Board of UNICEF, 1953 and 1954; President, UN Opium Conference, 1953; Head of Swiss

Delegation to Conference on Statute of International Atomic Energy Agency, held in New York, 1956. United Nations High Commissioner for Refugees (elected by acclamation), Dec. 1956–60; Swiss Ambassador to USA, 1960–63; Delegate, Swiss Fed. Council for Technical Co-operation, 1963–66; Swiss Amassador to Soviet Union and Mongolia, 1966–69, on leave as International Red Cross Comr-Gen. for Nigeria-Biafra relief operation, 1968–69; Swiss Ambassador to India and Nepal, 1969–70. Adviser to Pres. of Republic of Rwanda, 1973–75. Pres., Internat. Union for Child Welfare, Geneva, 1971–77. Hon. DrUniv Geneva, 1960; Hon. Dr, Coll. of Wilmington, Ohio, 1961. *Publications:* Special Correspondent with Bandits and Generals in Manchuria, 1933; Generäle hungern nie; Geschichte einer Hilfsaktion in Afrika, 1983. *Address:* Jolimontstrasse 2, CH-3001 Berne, Switzerland.

LINE, Maurice Bernard, MA; FRSA; FLA, FIInfSc, FBIM; Director General (Science, Technology and Industry), British Library, since 1985 (Deputy Director General, 1973–74, Director General, 1974–85, Lending Division); *b* 21 June 1928; *s* of Bernard Cyril and Ruth Florence Line; *m* 1954, Joyce Gilchrist; one *s* one *d*. *Educ:* Bedford Sch.; Exeter Coll., Oxford (MA). Library Trainee, Bodleian Library, 1950–51; Library Asst, Glasgow Univ., 1951–53; Sub-Librarian, Southampton Univ., 1954–65; Dep. Librarian, Univ. of Newcastle upon Tyne, 1965–68; Librarian, Univ. of Bath, 1968–71; Librarian, Nat. Central Library, 1971–73; Project Head, DES Nat. Libraries ADP Study, 1970–71. Prof. Associate, Sheffield Univ., 1977–; External Prof., Loughborough Univ. of Technol., 1986–. Member: Library Adv. Council for England, 1972–75; British Library Board, 1974–. Hon. DLitt Heriot Watt, 1980. *Publications:* Bibliography of Russian Literature in English Translation to 1900, 1963; The College Student and the Library, 1965; Library Surveys, 1967, 2nd edn 1982; National Libraries, 1979; Universal Availability of Publications, 1983; National Libraries II, 1987; contribs to: Jl of Documentation; Aslib Proc.; Jl of Librarianship, etc. *Recreations:* music, walking, other people. *Address:* 10 Blackthorn Lane, Burn Bridge, Harrogate, North Yorks HG3 1NZ. *T:* Harrogate 872984.

LINES, (Walter) Moray, CBE 1969; Chairman, Lines Brothers Ltd, 1962–71 (Joint Managing Director, 1962–70); *b* 26 Jan. 1922; *er s* of late Walter Lines; *m* 1955, Fiona Margaret Denton; three *s* one *d*. *Educ:* Gresham Sch. Joined Board of Lines Bros Ltd, 1946; Chm., British Toy Manufacturers Assoc., 1968–70. *Address:* Stable Cottage, Shirwell, near Barnstaple, N Devon. *T:* Shirwell 265.

LINFORD, Alan C.; *see* Carr Linford.

LING, Arthur George, FRIBA; PPRTPI; architect and town planner in practice with Arthur Ling and Associates; *b* 20 Sept. 1913; *s* of George Frederick Ling and Elsie Emily (*née* Wisbey); *m* 1939, Marjorie Tall; one *s* three *d*. *Educ:* Christ's Hospital; University College, London (Bartlett School of Architecture). BA (Architecture), London. Architect in Office of E. Maxwell Fry and Walter Gropius, 1937–39; Structural Engineer with Corporation of City of London (Air raid shelters and War debris clearance), 1939–41; Member town planning team responsible for preparation of County of London Plan, 1943, under direction of J. H. Forshaw and Sir Patrick Abercrombie, 1941–45; Chief Planning Officer, London County Council, 1945–55; Head of Department of Town Planning, University College, London Univ., 1947–48; Sen. Lecturer in Town Planning, 1948–55; City Architect and Planning Officer, Coventry, 1955–64; Prof. and Head of Dept of Architecture and Civic Planning, Univ. of Nottingham, 1964–69, Special Prof. of Environmental Design, 1969–72. Visiting Professor: University of Santiago, Chile, 1963; Univ. of NSW, Australia, 1969; Chancellor Lectures, Univ. of Wellington, NZ, 1969. Joint Architect for Development Plan for University of Warwick. Cons. Architect Planner, Runcorn New Town Corporation. UN (Habitat) Project Manager, Physical Perspective Plan, 1981–2000, Libyan Jamahiriya, 1977–80. Former Chairman, Board of Chief Officers, Midlands Housing Consortium; Past Vice-Pres., RIBA; President: RTPI, 1968–69; Commonwealth Assoc. of Planners, 1968–76. Mem., Sports Council, 1968–71; Vice-Chm., E Midlands Sports Council, 1968–76. Pres., Heckington Village Trust, 1974–84. RIBA Dist. in Town Planning, 1956; Silver Medallist (Essay), 1937; Hunt Bursary, 1939. Fellow University College, London, 1967. *Publications:* Contrib. to professional journals on architecture and town planning. *Address:* The Old Rectory, Howell, Sleaford, Lincolnshire.

LING, Maj.-Gen. (Retd) Fergus Alan Humphrey, CB 1968; CBE 1964; DSO 1944; Defence Services Consultant, Institute for the Study of Conflict, since 1970; *b* 5 Aug. 1914; 3rd *s* of John Richardson and Mabel Ling; *m* 1940, Sheelah Phyllis Sarel; two *s* three *d*. *Educ:* Stowe Sch.; Royal Military Coll., Sandhurst. Comd 2nd/5th Queen's, 1944; GSO 1 (Ops), GHQ, Middle East, 1945–46; British Liaison Officer, US Infantry Centre, 1948–50; Comd Regt Depot, Queen's Royal Regt, 1951; Directing Staff, Staff Coll., Camberley, 1951–53; comd 5th Queen's, 1954–57; Asst Military Secretary, War Office, 1957–58; comd 148 North Midland Brigade (TA), 1958–61; DAG, HQ, BAOR, 1961–65; GOC: 54 (East Anglian) Division/District, 1965–67; East Anglian District, 1967–68; Eastern District, 1968–69. Col, The Queen's Regt, 1973–77 (Dep. Col, 1969–73). Chairman: Surrey T&AVR Cttee, 1973–80; SE T&AVR Assoc., 1978–79. DL Surrey, 1970, Vice Lord-Lieutenant 1975–82. *Recreations:* homes, gardens, grandchildren. *Address:* Mystole Coach House, near Canterbury CT4 7DB. *T:* Canterbury 738496; Shepherd House, Nether Wasdale, Cumbria. *T:* Wasdale 312.

LING, Jeffrey; HM Diplomatic Service; Director of Research, Foreign and Commonwealth Office, since 1986; *b* 9 Sept. 1939; *s* of Frank Cecil Ling and Mary Irene Nixon; *m* 1967, Margaret Anne Tatton; one *s*. *Educ:* Bristol Univ. BSc (Hons); MInstP; FBIM. FCO, 1966–69; Private Sec. to HM Ambassador, Washington, 1969–71; First Sec., Washington, 1971–73; Perm. Delegn to OECD, Paris, 1973–77; FCO, 1977–79; on secondment as Special Adviser to HH the Sultan of Brunei, 1979–82; Counsellor (Technology), Paris, 1982–86. *Recreations:* travel, old cars. *Address:* c/o Foreign and Commonwealth Office, SW1A 2AH.

LING, John de Courcy; *see* de Courcy Ling.

LINGARD, (Peter) Anthony, CBE 1977; TD; *b* 29 Feb. 1916; *s* of late Herbert Arthur Lingard and Kate Augusta Burdett; *m* 1946, Enid Nora Argile; two *d*. *Educ:* Berkhamsted Sch.; London Univ. (BCom). Served RA, 1939–46; Major, 1941 (despatches twice). Co. of London Electric Supply Gp, 1936; Area Manager Lambeth and Camberwell, County Group, 1947; Commercial Officer, S Western Sub-Area, 1948, Chief Commercial Officer, 1959–62, London Electricity Board; Commercial and Development Adviser, Electricity Council, 1962–65; Mem., Electricity Council, 1965–77; Chm., E Midlands Electricity Bd, 1972–77. Member: CEGB, 1972–75; Directing Cttee, Internat. Union of Producers and Distributors of Electrical Energy, 1973–77. St John Ambulance Association: Dir-Gen., 1978–82; County Dir, Suffolk, 1982–85. Member until 1977: Ct of Governors, Admin. Staff Coll.; Council, IEE; Council of Industrial Soc.; E Midlands Econ. Planning Council; Mem. Nottingham Univ. Ct, 1975–77. CompIEE 1967. FBIM 1973. KStJ. *Recreations:* photography, painting, sailing, walking, reading. *Address:* The Dumble, High Street, Orford, Woodbridge, Suffolk IP12 2NW. *T:* Orford 450622. *Clubs:* Army and Navy; Aldeburgh Yacht.

LINGARD, Robin Anthony; Head, Small Firms and Tourism Division, Department of Employment, since 1985; *b* 19 July 1941; *s* of late Cecil Lingard and Lucy Lingard; *m* 1968, Margaret Lucy Virginia Elsden; two *d*. *Educ:* Felsted School; Emmanuel College, Cambridge (Exhibnr, MA). Min. of Aviation, 1963–66; Min. of Technology, 1966–70 (Private Sec. to Jt Parly Sec., 1966–68); DTI, 1971–74; DoI, 1974–83, Asst Sec., 1976; Under Sec., DTI, 1984, Cabinet Office (Enterprise Unit), 1984–85. *Recreations:* reading, walking, watching birds, aviation history. *Address:* Netherfield, Cliddesden, Basingstoke, Hants RG25 2JL. *T:* Basingstoke 25197.

LINGS, Dr Martin; Keeper Emeritus of Oriental Manuscripts and Printed Books, British Library; *b* 24 Jan. 1909; *e s* of late George Herbert Lings and late Gladys Mary Lings (*née* Greenhalgh), Burnage, Lancs; *m* 1944, Lesley, 3rd *d* of late Edgar Smalley. *Educ:* Clifton Coll.; Magdalen Coll., Oxford; Sch. of Oriental and African Studies, Univ. of London. Class. Mods 1930, BA English 1932, MA 1937, Oxon; BA Arabic 1954, PhD 1959, London. Lectr in Anglo-Saxon and Middle English, Univ. of Kaunas, 1935–39; Lectr in English Lit., Univ. of Cairo, 1940–51; Asst Keeper, Dept of Oriental Printed Books and Manuscripts, British Museum, 1955–70; Deputy Keeper, 1970; Keeper, 1971; seconded to the British Library, 1973. FRAS. *Publications:* The Book of Certainty, 1952; (with A. S. Fulton) Second Supplementary Catalogue of Arabic Printed Books in the British Museum, 1959; A Moslem Saint of the Twentieth Century, 1961 (trans. French 1967, Arabic 1972); Ancient Beliefs and Modern Superstitions, 1965 (trans. Turkish, 1982, Portuguese, 1986); Shakespeare in the Light of Sacred Art, 1966; The Elements and Other Poems, 1967; The Heralds and Other Poems, 1970; A Sufi Saint of the Twentieth Century, 1971 (trans. Urdu, 1981, Persian, 1981, Spanish, 1982, Turkish, 1982); What is Sufism?, (trans. French, 1977, Italian, 1978, Spanish, 1981, German, 1985, Portuguese, 1986); (with Y. H. Safadi) Third Supplementary Catalogue of Arabic Printed Books in the British Library, 1976; (with Y. H. Safadi) The Qur'ān, Catalogue of an Exhibition at the British Library, 1976; The Quranic Art of Calligraphy and Illumination, 1977; Muhammad: his life based on the earliest sources, 1983 (trans. French, Urdu and Tamil, 1985); The Secret of Shakespeare, 1984 (trans. Italian, 1986); The Eleventh Hour, 1986; articles in Encycl. Britannica, Encycl. Islam, Studies in Comparative Religion, etc. *Recreations:* walking, gardening, music. *Address:* 3 French Street, Westerham, Kent. *T:* Westerham 62855.

LINKIE, William Sinclair; Controller, Inland Revenue (Scotland), since 1983; *b* 9 March 1931; *s* of late Peter Linkie and of Janet Black Linkie (*née* Sinclair; she *m* 2nd, John McBryde); *m* 1955, Elizabeth Primrose Marion (*née* Reid); one *s* one *d*. *Educ:* George Heriot's Sch., Edinburgh. Dept of Agriculture and Fisheries for Scotland, 1948; Inland Revenue (Scotland), 1952–: HM Inspector of Taxes, 1961; Dist Inspector, Edinburgh 6, 1964; Principal Inspector i/c Centre I, 1975; Dist Inspector, Edinburgh 5, 1982. Pres., Inland Revenue Sports Assoc. (Scotland), 1983–. Elder, Church of Scotland. *Recreations:* golf, badminton, choral singing. *Address:* (office) Lauriston House, 80 Lauriston Place, Edinburgh EH3 9SL.

LINKLATER, Nelson Valdemar, CBE 1974 (OBE 1967); Drama Director, Arts Council of Great Britain, 1970–77; *b* 15 Aug. 1918; *s* of Captain Arthur David Linklater and Elsie May Linklater; *m* 1944, Margaret Lilian Boissard; two *s*. *Educ:* Imperial Service Coll.; RADA. RNVR, 1939–46 (final rank Lieut (S)). Professional theatre as actor and business manager, 1937–39. Documentary Films Manager, Army Kinema Corp., 1946–48; Arts Council of Great Britain: Asst Regional Dir (Nottingham), 1948–52; Asst and Dep. Drama Dir (London), 1952–70. Mem., Southern Arts Gen. Council and Exec. Cttee, 1978–. Chm., CPRE, Wallingford Area Cttee, 1977–80. Member: Bd, Anvil Productions (Oxford Playhouse), 1977–; Trent Polytechnic Theatre Design Adv. Cttee, 1980–83. Mem., London Inst. Formation Cttee, 1985; Governor: Central Sch. of Art and Design, London, 1978–; Wyvern Arts Trust (Swindon), 1978–; Trustee, Arts Council Trust for Special Funds, 1981–. *Publication:* (contrib.) The State and the Arts, 1980. *Recreations:* painting, reading, gardening. *Address:* 1 Church Close, East Hagbourne, Oxon OX11 9LP. *T:* Didcot 813340.

LINKS, Mary, (Mrs J. G. Links); *see* Lutyens, Mary.

LINLEY, Viscount; David Albert Charles Armstrong-Jones; *b* 3 Nov. 1961; *s* and *heir* of 1st Earl of Snowdon, *qv*, and *s* of HRH the Princess Margaret. *Educ:* Bedales; Parnham School for Craftsmen in Wood. Designer and Cabinet maker; Chairman of David Linley Furniture Ltd. Vogue—Sotheby's Cecil Beaton Award for portrait photograph, 1983.

See under Royal Family.

LINLITHGOW, 3rd Marquess of, *cr* 1902; **Charles William Frederick Hope,** MC 1945; TD 1973; MA; Earl of Hopetoun, 1703; Viscount Aithrie, Baron Hope, 1703; Baron Hopetoun (UK) 1809; Baron Niddry (UK), 1814; Bt (Scotland), 1698; Captain (retired), 19th (Lothians and Border Horse) Armoured Car Company, Royal Tank Corps (Territorial Army); Director, Eagle Star Insurance Co. Ltd; *b* 7 April 1912; *er s* of 2nd Marquess of Linlithgow, KG, KT, PC and Doreen Maud, CI 1936, Kaisar-i-Hind Medal 1st Class (*d* 1965), 2nd *d* of Rt Hon. Sir F. Milner, 7th Bt; *S* father 1952; *m* 1st, 1939, Vivien (*d* 1963), *d* of Capt. R. O. R. Kenyon-Slaney, and of Lady Mary Gilmour; one *s* one *d*; 2nd, 1965, Judith, *widow* of Esmond Baring. *Educ:* Eton; Christ Church, Oxford. Lieut, Scots Guards R of O; served War of 1939–45 (prisoner, MC). Lord Lieutenant, West Lothian, 1964–86. *Heir:* *s* Earl of Hopetoun, *qv*. *Address:* Hopetoun House, South Queensferry, West Lothian EH30 9SL. *T:* 031-331 1169. *Club:* White's.

See also Baron Glendevon, Countess of Pembroke.

LINNANE, Prof. Anthony William, FAA; FRS 1980; Professor of Biochemistry, since 1965, Director, Centre for Molecular Biology and Medicine, since 1983, Monash University, Australia; *b* 17 July 1930; *s* of late W. Linnane, Sydney; *m* 1956, Judith Neil (marr. diss. 1980); one *s* one *d*; *m* 1980, Daryl, *d* of A. Skurrie. *Educ:* Sydney Boys' High School; Sydney Univ. (PhD, DSc); Univ. of Wisconsin, USA. Lecturer, then Senior Lectr, Sydney Univ., 1958–62; Reader, Monash Univ., Aust., 1962. Visiting Prof., Univ. of Wisconsin, 1967–68. President: Aust. Biochemical Soc., 1974–76; Fedn of Asian and Oceanic Biochemical Socs, 1975–77; 12th Internat. Congress of Biochemistry, 1982. Work concerned especially with the biogenesis and genetics of mitochondria and molecular biol. of interferons and mucinous cancers. Editor-in-Chief, Biochemistry Internat. *Publications:* Autonomy and Biogenesis of Mitochondria and Chloroplasts, 1971; many contributions to learned journals. *Address:* Department of Biochemistry, Monash University, Clayton, Victoria 3168, Australia. *T:* Melbourne 541-3721; 25 Canterbury Road, Camberwell, Vic 3124, Australia. *Clubs:* Athenæum; Moonee Valley Race; VRC; VATC.

LINNETT, Dr Michael Joseph, OBE 1975; FRCGP; Apothecary to the Prince and Princess of Wales, since 1983; general medical practitioner, since 1957; *b* 14 July 1926; *s* of Joseph Linnett and Dora Alice (*née* Eabry); *m* 1950, Marianne Patricia, *d* of Aubrey Dibdin, CIE; two *d* (and one *s* decd). *Educ:* Wyggeston Grammar School for Boys, Leicester; St Bartholomew's Hosp. Med. Coll., London (MB BS 1949; Wix Prize Essay 1947). FRCGP 1970 (MRCGP 1957). House Physician, 1949, Demonstrator in

Pharmacology, 1954, Jun. Registrar, 1955, St Bartholomew's Hosp., London; Ho. Phys., Evelina Children's Hosp., 1950; RAF Medical Br., Sqdn Ldr, 1950–54. Chm. Council, RCGP, 1976–79; Member: Cttee on Safety of Medicines, 1970–75; Medicines Commn, 1976– (Vice-Chm., 1984–); Med. Adv. Panel, IBA, 1979–; Governor: National Hosp. for Nervous Diseases, 1974–82; Sutton's Hosp., Charterhouse, 1985–. Freeman, City of London, 1980; Chm., Livery Cttee, Worshipful Soc. of Apothecaries, 1982–84, Mem., Ct of Assts, 1985–. Chm., Editorial Bd, Prescribers' Jl, 1973–74. FRSocMed 1958. *Publications:* chapter, People with Epilepsy—the Burden of Epilepsy, in A Textbook of Epilepsy, ed Laidlaw & Richens, 1976; contrib. BMJ (jtly) Drug Treatment of Intractable Pain, 1960. *Recreation:* music. *Address:* 82 Sloane Street, SW1X 9PA. *T:* 01–245 9333; (home) 37 Ashcombe Street, SW6 3AW. *T:* 01–736 2487.

LINSTEAD, Sir Hugh (Nicholas), Kt 1953; OBE 1937; *b* 3 Feb. 1901; *e s* of late Edward Flatman Linstead and Florence Evelyn Hester; *m* 1928, Alice Winifred Freke (*d* 1978); two *d*. *Educ:* City of London Sch.; Pharmaceutical Society's Sch. (Jacob Bell Scholar); Birkbeck Coll. Pharmaceutical chemist; barrister, Middle Temple, 1929. MP (C) Putney Div. of Wandsworth, 1942–64. Chm., Macarthys Pharmaceuticals Ltd, 1964–80. Secretary: Pharmaceutical Society of Great Britain, 1926–64; Central Pharmaceutical War Cttee, 1938–46; Pres., Internat. Pharmaceutical Fedn, 1953–65; Member, Medical Research Council, 1956–64; Chairman and Vice-Chairman, Joint Negotiating Cttee (Hospital Staffs), 1946–48; Member Poisons Board (Home Office), 1935–57; Chairman: Wandsworth Group Hospital Cttee, 1948–53; Parliamentary and Scientific Cttee, 1955–57; Library Cttee, House of Commons, 1963–64; Franco-British Parliamentary Relations Cttee, 1955–60. Member: Central Health Services Council (Min. of Health), 1951–66; Departmental Cttee on Homosexual Offences and Prostitution; Departmental Cttee on Experiments on Animals. Parliamentary Charity Comr for England and Wales, 1956–60. First Chm., Farriers' Registration Council, 1976–79. Comr for Training Scout Officers, Boy Scouts' Assoc., 1932–41; Hon. LLD: British Columbia, 1956; Toronto, 1963; Hon. Member American and Canadian Pharmaceutical Assocs, British Dental Assoc. and other societies; Corresponding Member Académie de Médecine de France and Académie de Pharmacie de Paris; Mem. Court, Farriers Co. (Master 1971–72). Commandeur de la Légion d'Honneur; Officier de la Santé Publique (France); Kt Comdr Al Merito Sanitario (Spain). *Address:* 15 Somerville House, Manor Fields, SW15 3LX. *Club:* Athenæum.

LINTON, Alan Henry Spencer, LVO 1969; HM Diplomatic Service, retired; Consul-General, Detroit, USA, 1976–79; *b* Nottingham, 24 July 1919; *s* of Rt Rev. James Henry Linton, DD and Alicia Pears (*née* Aldous); *m* 1959, Kaethe Krebs; four *d*. *Educ:* St Lawrence, Ramsgate; Magdalen Coll., Oxford (MA). Served War, RA, 1940–46. HM Overseas Civil Service, Tanganyika, 1947–62; FO, 1963–65; First Sec. (Inf.), Vienna, 1965–69; Head of Chancery, Lusaka, Zambia, 1970–73; First Sec. (Commercial), Kingston, Jamaica, 1973–75; Dep. High Comr, Kingston, 1975–76. *Recreations:* skiing, sailing, photography. *Address:* c/o Midland Bank, 47 Ludgate Hill, EC4M 7LA. *Club:* Royal Over-Seas League.

LINTOTT, Sir Henry, KCMG 1957 (CMG 1948); *b* 23 Sept. 1908; *s* of late Henry John Lintott, RSA, and of Edith Lunn; *m* 1949, Margaret Orpen; one *s* one *d*. *Educ:* Edinburgh Acad.; Edinburgh Univ.; King's Coll., Cambridge. Entered Customs and Excise Dept, 1932; Board of Trade, 1935–48; Dep. Secretary-General, OEEC, 1948–56. Dep. Under-Secretary of State, Commonwealth Relations Office, 1956–63; British High Commissioner in Canada, 1963–68. *Address:* 47 Grantchester Street, Cambridge CB3 9HZ. *T:* Cambridge 312410.

LINTOTT, Robert Edward, FInstPet; Director, Esso UK plc, Esso Petroleum, since 1984 (Managing Director, 1984–86); *b* 14 Jan. 1932; *s* of Charles Edward and Doris Mary Lintott; *m* 1958, Mary Alice Scott; three *s*. *Educ:* Cambridgeshire High School; Trinity College, Cambridge. BA Nat. Scis 1955, MA. Served RAF, 1950–52 (Flying Officer); joined Esso Petroleum Co. Ltd, 1955; Manager, Milford Haven Refinery, 1969–72; Manager, Operations Coordination, 1972–75; Corporate Planning Dept, Exxon Corp., 1975–78; Exec. Asst to Chm., Exxon Corp., 1978–79; Director: Esso Petroleum Co. Ltd, 1979–84; Esso Pension Trust, 1979–; Esso Exploration & Production UK, 1984–; Chairman: Irish Refining Co., 1979–82; Esso Teoranta, 1982–84. Vice-Pres., UK Petroleum Industry Assoc., 1985–86; Pres., Oil Industries Club, 1986–. Director, Foundn for Management Educn, 1979–; Mem., Steering Cttee, Oxford Summer Business Sch., 1979–; Mem. Council, Manchester Business Sch., 1985–. *Recreations:* cricket, vintage and modern motoring. *Address:* Esso House, Victoria Street, SW1E 5JW. *T:* 01–834 6677. *Clubs:* MCC; Phyllis Court (Henley).

LION, Jacques Kenneth, OBE 1979; Chairman: Philipp & Lion (Holdings) Ltd; Metal Market & Exchange Co. Ltd, since 1984 (Director since 1972); *b* 18 Dec. 1922; *s* of Felix J. Lion and Ethel (*née* Myers); *m* 1947, Jean Elphinstone (*née* Mackenzie); two *s* one *d*. *Educ:* St Paul's Sch. Pres., Non-Ferrous Div., Bureau Internationale de la Récupération, 1970–74; Mem. Council, British Secondary Metals Assoc., 1956–77 (Pres., 1959 and 1964). *Recreations:* music, gardening, golf. *Address:* c/o Metal Market & Exchange Co. Ltd, Plantation House, Fenchurch Street, EC3M 3AP. *T:* 01–626 3311. *Clubs:* City of London, Royal Automobile.

LIPFRIEND, Alan; His Honour Judge Lipfriend; Circuit Judge since 1974; *b* 6 Oct. 1916; 2nd *s* of I. and S. Lipfriend; *m* 1948, Adèle Burke; one *s*. *Educ:* Central Foundation Sch., London; Queen Mary Coll., London. BSc(Eng) (Hons) 1938. Design Staff, Hawker Aircraft Ltd, 1939–48. Called to Bar, Middle Temple, 1948; Pres., Appeal Tribunal, under Wireless and Telegraphy Act, 1949, 1971–73; Mem. Parole Bd, 1978–81. A Governor, Queen Mary Coll., Univ. of London, 1981–; Trustee and Gov., Central Foundation School for Boys, 1985–. *Recreations:* theatre and all sport. *Address:* 10 Woodside Avenue, N6 4SS. *T:* 01–883 4420. *Club:* Royal Automobile.

LIPKIN, Miles Henry J.; *see* Jackson-Lipkin.

LIPMAN, Maureen Diane, (Mrs J. M. Rosenthal); actress; *b* 10 May 1946; *d* of Maurice and Zelma Lipman; *m* 1973, Jack Morris Rosenthal, *qv*; one *s* one *d*. *Educ:* Newland High Sch. for Girls, Hull; London Acad. of Music and Dramatic Art. Professional début in The Knack, Watford, 1969; Stables Theatre, Manchester, 1970; National Theatre (Old Vic), 1971–73: Molly, in The Front Page; Kathleen, in Long Day's Journey into Night; Miss Richland, in The Good Natur'd Man; Ruth, in Wonderful Tom, Watford Palace, 1986; *West End:* Candida, 1976; Maggie, in Outside Edge, 1978; Meg, in Meg and Mog, 1982; Messiah, 1983; Miss Skillen, in See How They Run, 1984 (Laurence Olivier Award; Variety Club of GB Award); Wonderful Town, Queen's, 1986; other plays include: Celia, in As You Like It, RSC, 1974; Jenny, in Chapter Two, Hammersmith, 1981; Kitty McShane, in On Your Way, Riley, Stratford East, 1983; *television:* plays, series and serials include: The Evacuees; Smiley's People; Couples; Crown Court; The Lovers; Dangerous Davies; The Knowledge; Rolling Home; Outside Edge; Princess of France, in Love's Labour's Lost; Absurd Person Singular; Absent Friends; Jane Lucas, in 3 series of Agony; All at No 20; *films:* Up the Junction, 1969; Educating Rita, 1983; Water, 1984. Founder Mem. and Exec. Mem., Theatre of Comedy, 1983–. Columnist, Options magazine, 1983–85. *Publication:* How Was it for You?, 1985. *Recreations:* the radio, other people's problems, telling jokes, visiting lost property offices for my mislaid chattels, full-time guilt, cartooning.

LIPMAN, Vivian David, CVO 1978; DPhil; FRHistS, FSA; Director of Ancient Monuments and Historic Buildings, Department of the Environment, 1972–78; *b* 27 Feb. 1921; *s* of late Samuel N. Lipman, MBE, and Cecelia (*née* Moses); *m* 1964, Sonia Lynette Senslive; one *s*. *Educ:* St. Paul's Sch.; Magdalen (Classical Demy) and Nuffield Colls, Oxford (MA). Served War, 1942–45, in Royal Signals and Intelligence Corps. Entered Civil Service as Asst Principal, 1947; Principal, 1950; Asst Sec., 1963; Under-Sec., 1972; Crown Estate Paving Commissioner, 1972. Mem., Redundant Churches Fund, 1979–. Hon. Research Fellow, University Coll. London, 1971–. Vice-Pres. (Pres., 1965–67), Jewish Historical Soc. of England, 1967–; Vice-Pres., Ancient Monuments Soc., 1978–. Member Council: Architectural Heritage Fund, 1978–; Textile Conservation Centre, 1978–; SPAB, 1978–. Esher Award, SPAB, 1979. Jt Editor, Littman Library, 1981–; British Editorial Co-ordinator, America Holy Land Proj., 1981–. *Publications:* Local Government Areas, 1949; Social History of the Jews in England, 1954; A Century of Social Service, 1959; (ed) Three Centuries of Anglo-Jewish History, 1961; The Jews of Medieval Norwich, 1967; (ed with S. L. Lipman) Jewish Life in Britain 1962–77, 1981; (ed) Sir Moses Montefiore: a symposium, 1983; (with S. L. Lipman) The Century of Moses Montefiore, 1985. *Recreation:* reading detective stories. *Address:* 9 Rotherwick Road, NW11 7DG. *T:* 01–458 9792. *Club:* Athenæum.

LIPSCOMB, Air Vice-Marshal (retired) Frederick Elvy, CB 1958; CBE 1953; *b* 2 Sept. 1902; *s* of late Arthur Bossley Lipscomb, St Albans; *m* 1931, Dorothy May (*d* 1964), *d* of Frederick Foskett, Berkhamsted, Herts; no *c*. *Educ:* Aldenham Sch.; Middlesex Hospital. MRCS LRCP 1927; DTM&H (Eng.), 1933; DPH (London) 1934. Commnd RAF 1927; psa 1946. Served Aden, Malta, Palestine; War of 1939–45, Mediterranean and West Africa (despatches thrice). Director of Hygiene and Research, Air Ministry, 1950; Principal Medical Officer, Far East Air Force, 1951–54; Dep. Director General RAF Medical Services, 1954–55; Principal Medical Officer, Home Command, 1955–57. KHP 1952; QHP 1952–57. CStJ 1952. *Publications:* Tropical Diseases section, Conybeare's Textbook of Medicine, 6th to 9th edns. Contributions to British Medical Journal, RAF Quarterly, etc. *Address:* 13 Lincoln Court, Charles Street, Berkhamsted, Herts HP4 3EN.

LIPSCOMB, Prof. William Nunn; Abbott and James Lawrence Professor of Chemistry, Harvard University, since 1971; Nobel Laureate in Chemistry, 1976; *b* 9 Dec. 1919; *s* of late William Nunn Lipscomb Sr, and of Edna Patterson Porter; *m* 1983, Jean Craig Evans; one *s* one *d* by previous marriage. *Educ:* Univ. of Kentucky (BS); California Inst. of Technology (PhD). Univ. of Minnesota, Minneapolis: Asst Prof. of Physical Chem., 1946–50; Associate Prof., 1950–54; Actg Chief, Physical Chem. Div., 1952–54; Prof. and Chief of Physical Chem. Div., 1954–59; Harvard Univ.: Prof. of Chemistry, 1959–71 (Chm., Dept of Chem., 1962–65). Member: Bd of Dir's, Dow Chemical Co., USA, 1982–; Scientific Adv. Bd, Robert A. Welch Foundn, 1982–. Member: Amer. Chemical Soc. (Chm., Minneapolis Section, 1949); Amer. Acad. of Arts and Sciences, 1959–; Nat. Acad. of Sciences, USA, 1961–; Internat. Acad. of Quantum Molecular Science, 1980; Académie Européenne des Scis, des Arts et des Lettres, Paris, 1980; Foreign Mem., Netherlands Acad. of Arts and Sciences, 1976; Hon. Member: Internat. Assoc. of Bioinorganic Scientists, 1979; RSC, 1983. MA (hon.) Harvard, 1959; Hon. DSc: Kentucky, 1963; Long Island, 1977; Rutgers, 1979; Gustavos Adolphus, 1980; Marietta, 1981; Miami, 1983; Dr *hc* Munich, 1976. *Publications:* Boron Hydrides, 1963 (New York); (with G. R. Eaton) Nuclear Magnetic Resonance Studies of Boron and Related Compounds, 1969 (New York); chapters in: The Aesthetic Dimensions of Science, ed D. W. Curtin, 1982; Crystallography in North America, ed D. Mchachlan and J. Glusker, 1983; contribs to scientific jls concerning structure and function of enzymes and natural products in inorganic chem. and theoretical chem. *Recreations:* tennis, chamber music. *Address:* Gibbs Chemical Laboratory, Harvard University, 12 Oxford Street, Cambridge, Mass 02138, USA. *T:* 617–495–4098.

LIPSEY, David Lawrence; Editor, New Society, since 1986; *b* 21 April 1948; *s* of Lawrence and Penelope Lipsey; *m* 1982, Margaret Robson; one *d*. *Educ:* Bryanston Sch.; Magdalen Coll., Oxford (1st Cl. Hons PPE). Research Asst, General and Municipal Workers' Union, 1970–72; Political Adviser to Anthony Crosland, MP, 1972–77 (Dept of the Environment, 1974–76; FCO, 1976–77); Prime Minister's Staff, 10 Downing Street, 1977–79; Journalist, New Society, 1979–80; Sunday Times: Political Staff, 1980–82; Economics Editor, 1982–86. Secretary, Streatham Labour Party, 1970–72; Chm., Fabian Soc., 1981–82; Exec. Cttee, Charter for Jobs, 1984–. *Publications:* Labour and Land, 1972; (ed, with Dick Leonard) The Socialist Agenda: Crosland's Legacy, 1981; Making Government Work, 1982. *Recreations:* racing, opera, cooking and washing up. *Address:* 44 Drakefield Road, SW17 8RP. *T:* 01–767 3268.

LIPSEY, Prof. Richard George, FRSC; Sir Edward Peacock Professor of Economics, Queen's University, Kingston, Ontario, since 1970; Senior Economic Advisor, C. D. Howe Institute, Toronto; *b* 28 Aug. 1928; *s* of R. A. Lipsey and F. T. Lipsey (*née* Ledingham); *m* 1960, Diana Louise Smart; one *s* two *d*. *Educ:* Univ. of British Columbia (BA 1st Cl. Hons 1950); Univ. of Toronto (MA 1953); LSE (PhD 1957). Dept of Trade and Industry, British Columbia Provincial Govt, 1950–53; LSE: Asst Lectr, 1955–58; Lectr, 1958–60; Reader, 1960–61; Prof. 1961–63; Univ. of Essex: Prof. of Economics, 1963–70; Dean of School of Social Studies, 1963–67. Vis. Prof., Univ. of California at Berkeley, 1963–64; Simeon Vis. Prof., Univ. of Manchester, 1973; Irving Fisher Vis. Prof., Yale Univ., 1979–80. Economic Consultant, NEDC, 1961–63; Member of Council: SSRC, 1966–69; Royal Economic Soc., 1968–71. Pres., Canadian Economics Assoc., 1980–81. Editor, Review of Economic Studies, 1960–64. Fellow, Econometric Soc., 1972. FRSC 1980. Hon. LLD: McMaster, 1984; Victoria, 1985. *Publications:* An Introduction to Positive Economics, 1963, 7th edn 1987; (with P. O. Steiner) Economics, 1966, 8th edn 1987; (with G. C. Archibald) An Introduction to a Mathematical Treatment of Economics, 1967, 3rd edn 1977; The Theory of Customs Unions: a general equilibrium analysis, 1971; (with G. C. Archibald) An Introduction to Mathematical Economics, 1975; (with C. Harbury) An Introduction to the UK Economy, 1983, 2nd edn 1985; (with F. Flatters) Common Ground for the Canadian Common Market, 1984; (with M. Smith) Canada's Trade Options in a Turbulent World, 1985; articles in learned jls on many branches of theoretical and applied economics. *Recreations:* skiing, sailing, film making. *Address:* C. D. Howe Institute, 125 Adelaide Street E, Toronto, Ont M5C 1L7, Canada.

LIPSON, Prof. Henry Solomon, CBE 1976; FRS 1957; Professor of Physics, University of Manchester Institute of Science and Technology, 1954–77, now Emeritus; *b* 11 March 1910; *s* of Israel Lipson and Sarah (*née* Friedland); *m* 1937, Jane Rosenthal; one *s* two *d*. *Educ:* Hawarden Grammar Sch.; Liverpool Univ. BSc 1930, MSc 1931, DSc 1939 (Liverpool); MA Cambridge, 1942; MSc Tech., Manchester, 1958; Oliver Lodge Scholar, Liverpool, 1933; Senior DSIR Grant, Manchester, 1936. Junior Scientific Officer, National Physical Lab., 1937; Asst in Crystallography, Cambridge, 1938; Head of Physics Dept, Manchester College of Technology, 1945; Dean, Faculty of Technology, Manchester

Univ., 1975. President Manchester Literary and Philosophical Society, 1960–62, 1977–79. Visiting Professor of Physics: University of Calcutta, 1963–64; Technion, Haifa, 1969. *Publications:* The Interpretation of X-ray Diffraction Photographs (with Drs Henry and Wooster), 1951; Determination of Crystal Structures (with Dr Cochran), 1953; Fourier Transforms and X-Ray Diffraction (with Prof. Taylor), 1958; Optical Transforms: Their Preparation and Application to X-ray Diffraction Problems (with Prof. Taylor), 1964; Optical Physics (with Prof. S. G. Lipson), 1968; The Great Experiments in Physics, 1968; Interpretation of X-ray Powder Diffraction Patterns (with Dr Steeple), 1970; Crystals and X-rays (with R. M. Lee), 1970; (ed) Optical Transforms, 1972; papers in Royal Society Proceedings, Acta Crystallographica, etc. *Recreations:* table-tennis, D-I-Y, voluntary hospital work, grandchildren. *Address:* 22 Cranmer Road, Manchester M20 0AW. *T:* 061–445 4517.

LIPSTEIN, Prof. Kurt; Professor of Comparative Law, Cambridge University, 1973–76; Fellow of Clare College, Cambridge, since 1956; *b* 19 March 1909; *e s* of Alfred Lipstein, MD and Hilda (*née* Sulzbach); *m* 1944, Gwyneth Mary Herford; two *d*. *Educ:* Goethe Gymnasium, Frankfurt on Main; Univs of Grenoble and Berlin; Trinity Coll., Cambridge. Gerichtsreferendar 1931; PhD Cantab 1936; LLD 1977. Called to Bar, Middle Temple, 1950, Hon. Bencher, 1966. Univ. Lectr, Cambridge, 1946; Reader in Conflict of Laws, Cambridge Univ., 1962–73. Dir of Research, Internat. Assoc. Legal Science, 1954–59. Vis. Professor: Univ. of Pennsylvania, 1962; Northwestern Univ., Chicago, 1966, 1968; Paris I, 1977. Humboldt Prize, Alexander von Humboldt Stiftung, Bonn, 1981. *Publications:* The Law of the EEC, 1974; Principles of the Conflict of Laws, National and International, 1981; joint editor and contributor: Dicey's Conflict of Laws, 6th edn, 1948—8th edn, 1967; Leske-Loewenfeld, Das Eherecht der europäischen Staaten, 1963; International Encyclopaedia of Comparative Law, vol. Private International Law, 1972; Harmonization of Private International Law by the EEC, 1978; contrib. English and foreign legal periodicals. *Address:* Clare College, Cambridge. *T:* Cambridge 333200; 7 Barton Close, Cambridge. *T:* 357048; 13 Old Square, Lincoln's Inn, WC2A 3UA. *T:* 01–404 4800.

LIPWORTH, Maurice Sydney; Deputy Chairman, Allied Dunbar Assurance plc (formerly Hambro Life Assurance plc), since 1984 (Director, since 1971; Joint Managing Director, 1980–84); Chairman, Allied Dunbar Unit Trusts plc, since 1985 (Managing Director, 1983–85); Director: J. Rothschild Holdings plc, since 1984; BAT Industries plc, since 1985; *b* 13 May 1931; *s* of Isidore and Rae Lipworth; *m* 1957, Rosa Liwarek; two *s*. *Educ:* King Edward VII Sch., Johannesburg; Univ. of the Witwatersrand, Johannesburg (BCom, LLB). Admitted Solicitor, Johannesburg, 1955; called to the South African Bar, 1956. Barrister, Johannesburg, 1956–64; Non-Exec. Dir, Liberty Life Assoc. of Africa Ltd, 1956–64; Director: private trading/financial gps, 1965–67; Abbey Life Assurance Gp, 1968–70. Mem., Monopolies and Mergers Commn, 1981–. Governor, London Contemporary Dance Trust, 1981–; Trustee, Philharmonia Orchestra, 1982–. *Publications:* chapters and articles on investment, taxation, life insurance and pensions. *Recreations:* tennis, music, theatre. *Address:* 9/15 Sackville Street, W1X 1DE. *T:* 01–434 3211.

LISBURNE, 8th Earl of, *cr* 1776; **John David Malet Vaughan**; Viscount Lisburne and Lord Vaughan, 1695; barrister-at-law; *b* 1 Sept. 1918; *o s* of 7th Earl of Lisburne; *S* father, 1965; *m* 1943, Shelagh, *er d* of late T. A. Macauley, 1266 Redpath Crescent, Montreal, Canada; three *s*. *Educ:* Eton; Magdalen Coll., Oxford (BA, MA). Called to Bar, Inner Temple, 1947. Captain, Welsh Guards. Director: British Home Stores Ltd, 1964–; S Wales Regional Bd, Lloyds Bank Ltd, 1978–; Divisional Dir for Wales, Nationwide Building Soc., 1982–. Chm., Wales Council for Voluntary Action (formerly Council of Social Service for Wales), 1976–; Mem. Exec. Cttee, AA, 1981–. *Heir:* *s* Viscount Vaughan, *qv*. *Address:* 22 York House, Kensington Church Street, W8. *T:* 01–937 3043; Cruglas, Ystrad Meurig, Dyfed. *T:* Pontrhydfendigaid 230. *Clubs:* Buck's, Pratt's.

LISLE, 7th Baron, *cr* 1758; **John Nicholas Horace Lysaght**; *s* of late Hon. Horace G. Lysaght and Alice Elizabeth, *d* of Sir John Wrixon Becher, 3rd Bt; *b* 10 Aug. 1903; *S* grandfather, 1919; *m* 1st, 1928, Vivienne Brew (who obtained a divorce, 1939; she *died* 1948); 2nd, 1939, Mary Helen Purgold, Shropshire. *Heir:* *nephew* Patrick James Lysaght [*b* 1 May 1931; *m* 1957, Mrs Mary Louise Shaw-Stewart; two *s* one *d*]. *Address:* The Chestnuts, Barge Farm, Taplow, Bucks.

LISLE, Aubrey Edwin O.; *see* Orchard-Lisle.

LISSMANN, Hans Werner, FRS 1954; Reader, Department of Zoology, Cambridge, 1966–77, now Emeritus, and Director, Sub Department of Animal Behaviour, 1969–77; Fellow of Trinity College, Cambridge, since 1955; *b* 30 April 1909; *s* of Robert and Ebba Lissmann; *m* 1949, Corinne Foster-Barham; one *s*. *Educ:* Kargala and Hamburg. Dr.rer.nat., Hamburg, 1932; MA, Cantab, 1947. Asst Director of Research, Dept of Zoology, Cambridge, 1947–55; Lecturer, 1955–66. *Address:* 9 Bulstrode Gardens, Cambridge. *T:* 356126.

LISTER; *see* Cunliffe-Lister, family name of Earl of Swinton.

LISTER, Geoffrey Richard, FCA; Chief Executive, Bradford & Bingley Building Society, since 1985; *b* 14 May 1937; *s* of Walter and Margaret Lister; *m* 1962, Myrtle Margaret (*née* Cooper); one *s* two *d*. *Educ:* St Bede's Grammar Sch., Bradford. Articled clerk, J. Pearson & Son, 1955–60, qual. chartered accountant, 1960; Computer and Systems Sales, Burroughs Machines Ltd, 1961–63; Audit Man., Thos Gardner & Co., 1963–65; Bradford & Bingley Building Society: Asst Accountant, 1965–67; Computer Man., 1967–70; Chief Accountant, 1970–73; Asst Gen. Man., 1973–75; Dep. Gen. Man., 1975–80; Gen. Man., 1980–84; Dep. Chief Exec., 1984–85. Dir, EFT Ltd, 1984–. Mem. Council, Bldg Socs Assoc., 1984–; Governor: Nab Wood Grammar Sch., Bingley, 1977–; Beckfoot Grammar Sch., Bingley, 1985–. *Recreations:* shooting, boating, fishkeeping, gardening. *Address:* Mandalay, Longwood Hall, Longwood Avenue, Bingley, W Yorks BD16 2RX. *T:* Bradford 562276. *Clubs:* Beckfoot Golf, Bradford and Bingley Rugby Union Football (Bingley).

LISTER, Prof. James, MD, FRCS; Professor of Paediatric Surgery, University of Liverpool, 1974–86, now Emeritus; *b* 1 March 1923; *s* of Thomas and Anna Rebecca Lister; *m* 1946, Greta Redpath; three *d*. *Educ:* St Paul's Sch., London; Edinburgh Univ. (MB, ChB 1945; MD 1972). FRCS 1975, FRCSE 1950, FRCSGlas 1969. Surg. Lieut, RNVR, 1945–48. Surgical training posts, Edinburgh and Dundee, 1948–58; Halstead Res. Fellow, Colorado Univ., 1959; Sen. Lectr in Paediatric Surgery and Consultant Surgeon, Hosp. for Sick Children, Great Ormond St, and Queen Elizabeth Hosp., Hackney Rd, 1960–63; Consultant Paediatric Surgeon, Sheffield Children's Hosp., 1963–74. Civil Consultant in Paediatric Surgery to RN, 1979–86. Examiner, Primary and Final FRCSEd, 1967–; Past Examiner: Univs of Glasgow and Sheffield (in paediatric surgery); DCH London. Mem. Council, RCSEd, 1977– (Convenor of Examinations Cttee, 1986–); Mem., St Helens & Knowsley DHA, 1983–86. Chm., European Union of Paediatric Surgical Assocs, 1983–86; Hon. Member, Paediatric Assocs of Brazil, Chile, Germany, Greece, Hungary, Peru, Poland, Scandinavia, Yugoslavia. Hon. Fellow: Amer. Acad. of Paediatrics, 1976; Assoc. of Surgeons of India, 1985. Member of Editorial Board: Jl of RCSEd; Jl of Paediatric Surgery; Consultant editor, Annals of Tropical Paediatrics, 1985–. *Publications:* Neonatal Surgery, 1969, (ed jtly) 2nd edn 1978; Complications in Paediatric Surgery, 1986; papers on neonatal surgery and myelomeningocele. *Recreations:* gardening, hill walking. *Address:* Kailheugh, Hownam, Kelso, Roxburghshire TD5 8AL. *T:* Morebattle (05734) 224.

LISTER, Very Rev. John Field, MA; *b* 19 Jan. 1916; *s* of Arthur and Florence Lister. *Educ:* King's Sch., Worcester; Keble Coll., Oxford; Cuddesdon Coll., Oxford. Asst Curate, St Nicholas, Radford, Coventry, 1939–44; Asst Curate, St John Baptist, Coventry, 1944–45; Vicar of St John's, Huddersfield, 1945–54; Asst Rural Dean of Halifax, 1955–61; Archdeacon of Halifax, 1961–72; Vicar of Brighouse, 1954–72; Provost of Wakefield, 1972–82. Examng Chaplain to Bishop of Wakefield, 1972–78. Hon. Canon of Wakefield Cathedral, 1961, Canon, 1968; RD of Wakefield, 1972–80. Chaplain to the Queen, 1966–72. *Address:* 5 Larkcliff Court, The Parade, Birchington, Kent CT7 9NB.

LISTER, (Margot) Ruth (Aline); Director, Child Poverty Action Group, since 1979; *b* 3 May 1949; *d* of Dr Werner Bernard Lister and Daphne (*née* Carter). *Educ:* Univ. of Essex (BA Hons Sociology); Univ. of Sussex (MA Multi-Racial Studies). Child Poverty Action Group: Legal Res. Officer, 1971–75; Asst Dir, 1975–77; Dep. Dir, 1977–79. *Publications:* Supplementary Benefit Rights, 1974; Welfare Benefits, 1981; chapters in: Justice, Discretion and Poverty, 1975; Labour and Equality, 1980; The Economics of Prosperity, 1980; Taxation and Social Policy, 1981; Families in Britain, 1982; pamphlets and articles on poverty and social security. *Recreations:* women's group; relaxing—with friends, music, and through walking, meditation and Tai Chi; reading. *Address:* 20 Ambler Road, N4 2QU. *T:* 01–359 9019.

LISTER, Patrick; *see* Lister, R. P.

LISTER, Raymond (George), MA Cantab; President, Royal Society of Miniature Painters, Sculptors and Gravers, 1970–80; Chairman, Board of Governors, Federation of British Artists, 1976–80 (Governor, 1972–80); *b* 28 March 1919; *s* of late Horace Lister and Ellen Maud Mary Lister (*née* Arnold); *m* 1947, Pamela Helen, *d* of late Frank Bishop Brutnell; one *s* one *d*. *Educ:* St John's Coll. Choir Sch., Cambridge; Cambridge and County High Sch. for Boys. Served apprenticeship in family firm (architectural metalworking), 1934–39; specialised war service (engrg), 1939–45; Dir of family firm, 1941–; Man. Editor, Golden Head Press, 1952–72; Dir, John P. Gray and Son, craft bookbinders, 1978–82. Hon. Senior Mem., University Coll., now Wolfson Coll., Cambridge, 1971–75, Fellow, 1975–, Mem. Coll. Council, 1983–85; a Syndic, Fitzwilliam Mus., Cambridge, 1981–. Liveryman, Blacksmiths' Co., 1957, Mem. Ct of Assistants, 1980–. Associate Mem. 1946, Mem. 1948, Royal Soc. of Miniature Painters; Pres., Private Libraries Assoc., 1971–74; Vice-Pres., Architectural Metalwork Assoc., 1970–75, Pres., 1975–77. *Publications:* Decorative Wrought Ironwork in Great Britain, 1957; Decorative Cast Ironwork in Great Britain, 1960; Edward Calvert, 1962; Beulah to Byzantium, 1965; Victorian Narrative Paintings, 1966; William Blake, 1968; Hammer and Hand, 1969; Samuel Palmer and his Etchings, 1969; A Title to Phoebe, 1972; British Romantic Art, 1973; Samuel Palmer: a biography, 1974; (ed) The Letters of Samuel Palmer, 1974; Infernal Methods: a Study of William Blake's art techniques, 1975; Apollo's Bird, 1975; For Love of Leda, 1977; Great Images of British Printmaking, 1978; (jtly) Samuel Palmer: a vision recaptured, 1978; Samuel Palmer in Palmer Country, 1980; George Richmond, 1981; Bergomask, 1982; There was a Star Danced, 1983; Prints and Printmaking, 1984; Samuel Palmer and 'The Ancients', (catalogue of exhibn at Fitzwilliam Mus., Cambridge, also selected by R. Lister), 1984; The Paintings of Samuel Palmer, 1985; The Paintings of William Blake, 1986; contrib. Climbers' Club Jl, The Irish Book, Blake Studies, Blake Quarterly, Gazette des Beaux-arts, Connoisseur, Studies in Romanticism, Book Collector and TLS. *Recreations:* mountaineering in the fens, merels. *Address:* Windmill House, Linton, Cambs CB1 6NS. *T:* Cambridge 891248. *Clubs:* Athenæum, City Livery, Sette of Odd Volumes (Pres. 1960, 1982).

LISTER, (Robert) Patrick; Director and Chief Executive, Engineering Employers West Midlands Association, 1983–84; *b* 6 Jan. 1922; *s* of Robert B. Lister; *m* 1942, Daphne Rosamund, *d* of Prof. C. J. Sisson; three *s* one *d* (and one *s* decd). *Educ:* Marlborough College; Cambridge University (MA); Harvard Business School (MBA). Captain Royal Engineers, 1942–46; Massey Harris, Toronto, 1949–51; joined Coventry Climax Ltd, 1951, Managing Director, 1971–80, Deputy Chairman, 1980–81; Dir, Climax Fork Trucks, 1981–83. President: Fedn Européenne de la Manutention, 1978–80; Coventry and Dist Engineering Employers' Assoc., 1979–80 and 1983; British Indust. Truck Assoc., 1980–81; Vice-Pres., Inst. of Materials Handling, 1982–. Chm., Bd of Governors, Coventry Lanchester Polytechnic, 1986– (Mem., 1984–). *Recreations:* marriage counselling, ex-offenders' hostels, travel, gardening, DIY. *Address:* 35 Warwick Avenue, Coventry CV5 6DJ. *T:* Coventry 73776.

LISTER, Ruth; *see* Lister, M. R. A.

LISTER, Tom, CBE 1978; QFSM 1977; Chief Fire Officer, West Midlands County Council, 1975–81, retired; *b* 14 May 1924; *s* of late T. Lister and of Mrs E. Lister; *m* 1954, Linda, *d* of late T. J. and Mrs H. Dodds; one *d*. *Educ:* Charter House, Hull. Hull Fire Service, 1947–60; divisional officer, Lancs, 1960–62; Asst Chief Fire Officer, Warwicks, 1962–68; Chief Fire Officer, Glos, 1968–71, Bristol and Avon, 1972–75.

LISTER, Dame Unity (Viola), DBE 1972 (OBE 1958); Member of Executive, European Union of Women, since 1971 (Vice-Chairman, 1963–69); Member: European Movement, since 1970; Conservative Group for Europe, since 1970; *b* 19 June 1913; *d* of Dr A. S. Webley; *m* 1940, Samuel William Lister. *Educ:* St Helen's, Blackheath; Sorbonne Univ. of Paris. Member, London County Council, 1949–65 (Dep.-Chm., 1963–64); Chairman: Women's Nat. Advisory Cttee, 1966–69; Nat. Union of Conservative and Unionist Assocs, 1970–71 (Mem. Exec); Mem., Inner London Adv. Cttee on Appt of Magistrates, 1966–. Vice-Chm., Horniman Museums (Chm., 1967–70); Governor: Royal Marsden Hosp., 1952–; various schools and colleges. *Recreations:* languages, travel, music, gardening, theatre, museums, reading, walking. *Address:* 32 The Court Yard, Eltham, SE9 5QE. *T:* 01–850 7038. *Club:* St Stephen's Constitutional.

LISTER-KAYE, Sir John (Phillip Lister), 8th Bt *cr* 1812, of Grange, Yorks; Director of the Aigas Trust, since 1979; *b* 8 May 1946; *s* of Sir John Christopher Lister Lister-Kaye, 7th Bt and Audrey Helen (*d* 1979), *d* of E. J. Carter; *S* father, 1982; *m* 1972, Sorrel Deirdre, *d* of Count Henry Noel Bentinck; one *s* two *d*. *Educ:* Allhallows School. Naturalist, author, farmer, lecturer. Created first field studies centre in Highlands of Scotland, 1970; Founder Director of Scottish conservation charity, the Aigas Trust, 1979. Mem., Internat. Cttee, World Wilderness Foundn, 1983; Chm., Scottish Adv. Cttee, RSPB, 1986. *Publications:* The White Island, 1972; Seal Cull, 1979; The Seeing Eye, 1980. *Recreations:* breeding and showing pedigree highland cattle. *Heir:* *s* John Warwick Noel Lister-Kaye, *b* 10 Dec. 1974. *Address:* Aigas House, Beauly, Inverness-shire IV4 7AD. *T:* Beauly 782729. *Club:* Caledonian.

LISTON, David Joel, OBE 1975 (MBE (mil.) 1944); Development Adviser (Visiting Professor), European Business School, UK, since 1981; Visiting Professor, Polytechnic of

Central London, since 1979 (Pro-Rector, 1972–79); Hon. Education Adviser to British Overseas Trade Board, since 1972; Visiting Fellow, The Management College, Henley, since 1972; Industrial Adviser to Government, 1969–72; *b* 27 March 1914; *s* of Edward Lichtenstein and Hannah Davis, Manchester; *m* Eva Carole Kauffmann; one *s* two *d*. *Educ*: Manchester Grammar Sch.; Wadham Coll., Oxford (Open and Philip Wright Exhibr). MA (Lit. Hum.). FSS; FRSA. Joined Metal Box Co. 1937. TA, 1938; active service, 1939–46; 2nd in comd 8 Corps Sigs (Major, MBE, despatches). Rejoined Metal Box as Head, Information and Statistics Div., 1946; Gen. Man., Plastics Group, 1955; Man. Dir, Shorko-Metal Box, 1961; seconded as Asst Dir Manchester Business Sch., 1966. Member: Council, British Plastics Fedn, 1956–69; CNAA, Cttee for Arts and Social Studies (Vice-Chm.), 1964–71; Econ. Develt Cttees for Food Manufrg and for Chemical Industries, 1969–72; Bd of Governors, English-Speaking Union, 1973–79 (Mem. Nat. Cttee for England and Wales, 1974–80, Current Affairs Cttee, 1981–); Consultative Cttees on Adult Educn for Boroughs of Camden and Westminster, 1976–84; Higher Educn Cttee, Inst. of Export; Mem., Liberal Party Industrial Policy Panel, 1975– (Chm., 1975–85); Chm., International Trade Gp, 1985–86. *Publications*: (editor) Hutchinson's Practical Business Management series, 1971; The Purpose and Practice of Management, 1971; Education and Training for Overseas Trade, BOTB, 1973; Liberal Enterprise: a fresh start for British Industry, 1977; Foreign Languages for Overseas Trade (BOTB Working Party), 1979; mem. editorial bd and contributor, Kluwer International Trade Handbook, 1982; Business Studies, Languages and Overseas Trade, 1985. *Recreations*: travel, walking, current affairs. *Address*: 15 Twyford Court, Northlands Drive, Winchester, Hants SO23 7AL. *T*: Winchester 66087. *Clubs*: National Liberal, English-Speaking Union.

LISTON, James Malcolm, CMG 1958; Chief Medical Adviser, Foreign and Commonwealth Office, Overseas Development Administration, 1970–71; *b* 1909; *m* 1935, Isobel Prentice Meiklem, Edinburgh; one *s* one *d*. *Educ*: Glasgow High Sch.; Glasgow Univ. MB, ChB, Glasgow, 1932; DTM & H Eng., 1939; DPH University of London, 1947; FRCP Glasgow, 1963. Medical Officer, Kenya, 1935; Director of Medical and Health Services, Sarawak, 1947–52; Deputy Director of Medical Services, Hong Kong, 1952–55; Director of Medical Services, Tanganyika, 1955–59; Permanent Secretary to Ministry of Health, Tanganyika, 1959–60; Deputy Chief Medical Officer: Colonial Office, 1960–61; Dept of Tech. Co-op., 1961–62; Chief Medical Adviser, Dept of Tech. Co-op., 1962–64; Medical Adviser, Min. of Overseas Develt, 1964–70. *Address*: 6A Western Terrace, Murrayfield, Edinburgh EH12 5QF. *T*: 031–337 4236.

LISTON FOULIS, Sir Ian P., 13th Bt, *cr* 1634; Language Teacher, Madrid, since 1966; *b* 9 Aug. 1937; *s* of Lieut-Colonel James Alistair Liston-Foulis, Royal Artillery (killed on active service, 1942), and of Mrs Kathleen de la Hogue Moran, 2nd *d* of Countess Olga de la Hogue, Mauritius Island; *S* cousin, Sir Archibald Charles Liston Foulis, 1961. *Educ*: Stonyhurst Coll.; Cannington Farm Inst., Somerset (Dip. Agr.); Madrid (Dip. in Spanish). National Service, 1957–59; Argyll and Sutherland Highlanders, Cyprus, 1958 (Gen. Service Medal). Language Teacher, Estremadura and Madrid, 1959–61; Trainee, Bank of London and South America, 1962; Trainee, Bank of London and Montreal (in Nassau, 1963, Guatemala City, 1963–64; Managua, Nicaragua, 1964–65); Toronto (Sales), 1965–66. Member: Spanish Soc. of the Friends of Castles; Friends of the St James Way. Cert. from Archbishop of Santiago de Compostela for pilgrimage on foot, Somport to Santiago, Jubilee Year, 1971. *Recreations*: long-distance running, swimming, walking, mountaineering, travelling, foreign languages and customs, reading, Spanish medieval history (especially Muslim Spain). *Address*: Urbenova, Calle Soledad II, Portal 5°, Piso 2° Letra C, San Agustin De Guadalix (Madrid), Spain.

LISTOWEL, 5th Earl of, *cr* 1822; **William Francis Hare,** PC 1946; GCMG 1957; Baron Ennismore, 1800; Viscount Ennismore, 1816; Baron Hare (UK), 1869; Chairman of Committees, House of Lords, 1965–76; *b* 28 Sept. 1906; *e* s of 4th Earl and Hon. Freda Vanden-Bempde-Johnstone (*d* 1968), *y* d of 2nd Baron Derwent; *S* father, 1931; *m* 1st, 1933, Judith (marr. diss., 1945), *o* d of R. de Marffy-Mantuano, Budapest; one *d*; 2nd, 1958, Stephanie Sandra Yvonne Wise (marr. diss., 1963), Toronto; one *d*; 3rd, 1963, Mrs Pamela Read; two *s* one *d*. *Educ*: Eton; Balliol Coll., Oxford. PhD London Univ. Lieut, Intelligence Corps; Whip of Labour Party in House of Lords, 1941–44; Parliamentary Under-Secretary of State, India Office, and Deputy Leader, House of Lords, 1944–45; Postmaster-General, 1945–47; Secretary of State for India, April-Aug. 1947; for Burma, 1947–Jan. 1948; Minister of State for Colonial Affairs, 1948–50; Joint Parliamentary Secretary, Ministry of Agriculture and Fisheries, 1950–51; Member (Lab) LCC for East Lewisham, 1937–46, for Battersea North, 1952–57. Governor-General of Ghana, 1957–60. Jt Patron, British Tunisian Soc.; President: British-Cameroon Soc.; Council for Aid to African Students; Jt Pres., Anti-Slavery Soc. for Protection of Human Rights; Vice-Pres., European-Atlantic Gp. *Publications*: The Values of Life, 1931; A Critical History of Modern Æsthetics, 1933 (2nd edn, as Modern Æsthetics: an Historical Introduction, 1967). *Heir*: s Viscount Ennismore, *qv. Address*: 10 Downshire Hill, NW3. *Club*: Reform. *See also* Baron Grantley, Hon. A. V. Hare, Earl of Iveagh.

LITCHFIELD, Jack Watson, FRCP; Consulting Physician, St Mary's Hospital, since 1972 (Physician, 1946–72 and Physician i/c Cardiac Department, 1947–72); *b* 7 May 1909; *s* of H. L. Litchfield, Ipswich; *m* 1941, Nan (*d* 1984), *d* of A. H. Hatherly, Shanghai; two *s* one *d*. *Educ*: Ipswich Sch.; Oriel Coll., Oxford (Scholar); St Mary's Hospital. Theodore Williams Schol. in Physiology, 1929, in Pathology, 1931; Radcliffe Schol. in Pharmacology, 1932; BA (2nd class hons) 1930; BM, BCh 1933; University schol. at St Mary's Hospital Medical Sch., 1931; MRCP 1936; FRCP 1947. Medical Registrar: St Mary's Hospital, 1936; Brompton Hospital, 1938; Physician, King Edward Memorial Hosp., W13, 1947–69. Served in RAMC in N Africa, Italy, etc (despatches), Lt-Col i/c Medical Div. *Publications*: papers on various subjects in medical journals. *Recreations*: gardening, conservation. *Address*: Elm Green, Bradfield St Clare, Bury St Edmunds, Suffolk. *T*: Cockfield Green 828399.

LITCHFIELD, Captain John Shirley Sandys, OBE 1943; RN; *b* 27 Aug. 1903; *e* s of late Rear-Admiral F. S. Litchfield-Speer, CMG, DSO, and late Cecilia Sandys; *m* 1939, Margaret, *d* of late Sir Bertram Portal, KCB, DSO, and late Hon. Lady Portal; one *s* two *d*. *Educ*: St Aubyns, Rottingdean; RN Colleges Osborne and Dartmouth. Midshipman and Lieut in HMS Renown during Royal Cruise to India and Japan, 1921–22 and to Australia and NZ, 1927; Yangtse river gunboat, 1929–31; RN Staff Coll., 1935; comd naval armoured trains and cars, Palestine, 1936 (despatches); Staff Officer (Ops) to C-in-C Mediterranean, 1936–38; comd HMS Walker, 1939, HMS Norfolk 1943, HMS Tyne, 1946–47 and HMS Vanguard, 1951–53; Naval SO, Supreme War Council, 1939, Joint Planning Staff, 1940; SO (O) Western Approaches, 1941; Russian Convoys and N Africa landings, 1941–43; planning staff, Normandy ops, 1944; Combined Chiefs of Staff, Washington, 1945; National War College of US, 1947–48; Dep. Director Naval Intelligence, 1949–50; idc 1951; Director of Ops, Admiralty, 1953–54; retired 1955. CC Kent, 1955–58. MP (C) Chelsea, 1959–66. Mem. Lloyd's. Liveryman, Vintner's Company. *Address*: Snowfield, Bearsted, Kent ME14 4DH. *Clubs*: Naval and Military, Royal Navy Club of 1765 and 1785; Bearsted Cricket.

LITCHFIELD, Dame Ruby (Beatrice), DBE 1981 (OBE 1959); Director, Festival City Broadcasters Ltd, since 1975; Trustee, Adelaide Festival Centre, 1971–82, retired (first

woman to be appointed to these positions); *b* 5 Sept. 1912; *d* of Alfred John Skinner and Eva Hannah Skinner; *m* 1940, Kenneth Lyle Litchfield (decd); one *d*. *Educ*: North Adelaide Primary Sch.; Presbyterian Girls' Coll., Glen Osmond. Bd Mem., Kidney Foundn, 1968–; Chairperson: Carclew Youth Performing Arts Centre, 1972–; Families and Cultural Cttee, S Aust. Jubilee 150th Bd, 1980; Women's Cttee, Nat. Heart Foundn. First woman Mem., Bd of S Aust. Housing Trust, 1962–70; Life Member: Queen Victoria Maternity Hosp., 1972 (Mem., Vice-Pres., 1953–72); Adelaide Rep. Th., 1967 (Mem., 1951–68); Spastic Paralysis Welfare Assoc. Inc. (Mem. Cttee, Miss South Australia Quest, Spastic PWA). Mayoress of Prospect, 1954–57; Pres., Sports Women's Assoc., 1969–74; Mem., Divl Council, Aust. Red Cross, S Aust. Div., 1955–71; Councillor, Royal Dist Bush Nursing Soc., 1956–66; Member: S Aust. Davis Cup Cttee, 1952, 1963, 1968; Aust. Cttee of Royal Acad. of Dancing, 1961–66; Bd, Telethon Channel 9, 1961–85; Bd of Governors, Adelaide Festival of Arts, 1966–; Sponsorship Cttee, Constitutional Mus., 1979–80; Sudden Infant Death Res. Foundn Inc., 1979–; numerous charitable and med. appeal cttees; Bd Mem., Crippled Children's Assoc., 1976–80. Silver Jubilee Medal, 1977. *Recreations*: theatre, radio, tennis (S Aust. Hardcourt Champion, 1932–35, interstate lawn tennis player, 1936–39); charitable work. *Address*: 33 Hallett Road, Burnside, South Australia 5066. *Club*: Royal Commonwealth Society (Adelaide).

LITHERLAND, Prof. Albert Edward, FRS 1974; FRSC 1968; University Professor, since 1979 and Professor of Physics, since 1966, University of Toronto; *b* 12 March 1928; *e* s of Albert Litherland and Ethel Clement; *m* 1956, (Elizabeth) Anne Allen; two *d*. *Educ*: Wallasey Grammar Sch.; Univ. of Liverpool (BSc, PhD). State Scholar to Liverpool Univ., 1946; Rutherford Memorial Scholar to Atomic Energy of Canada, Chalk River, Canada, 1953; Scientific Officer at Atomic Energy of Canada, 1955–66. Guggenheim Fellow, 1986. Canadian Assoc. of Physicists Gold Medal for Achievement in Physics, 1971; Rutherford Medal and Prize of Inst. of Physics (London), 1974; JARI Silver Medal, Pergamon Press, 1981. Izaac Walton Killam Memorial Scholarship, 1980. *Publications*: numerous, in scientific jls. *Address*: 3 Hawthorn Gardens, Toronto, Ontario M4W 1P4, Canada. *T*: 416–923–5616.

LITHERLAND, Robert Kenneth; MP (Lab) Manchester Central, since Sept. 1979; *b* 1930; *s* of Robert Litherland and Mary (*née* Parry); *m* 1953, Edna Litherland; one *s* one *d*. *Educ*: North Manchester High Sch. for Boys. Formerly sales representative for printing firm. Mem., Manchester City Council (Dep. Chm., Housing Cttee; former Chm., Manchester Direct Works Cttee); Dep. Chm., Public Works Cttee, Assoc. of Municipal Authorities. *Address*: House of Commons, SW1; 32 Darley Avenue, Didsbury, Manchester M20 8YD.

LITHGOW, Sir William (James), 2nd Bt of Ormsary, *cr* 1925; DL; CEng; industrialist and farmer; Director, Lithgows Ltd, since 1956 (Chairman, 1959–84); *b* 10 May 1934; *o* s of Colonel Sir James Lithgow, 1st Bt of Ormsary, GBE, CB, MC, TD, DL, JP, LLD, and Gwendolyn Amy, *d* of late John Robinson Harrison of Scalesceugh, Cumberland; *S* father, 1952; *m* 1964, Valerie Helen (*d* 1964), 2nd *d* of late Denis Scott, CBE and Mrs Laura Scott; *m* 1967, Mary Claire, *d* of Colonel F. M. Hill, CBE and Mrs Hill; two *s* one *d*. *Educ*: Winchester Coll. CEng; FRINA; FBIM. Chm., Lithgow Drydocks Ltd, 1967–78; Vice-Chm., Scott Lithgow Ltd, 1968–78; Chm., Western Ferries (Argyll) Ltd, 1972–85; Director: Bank of Scotland, 1962–86; Campbeltown Shipyard Ltd, 1970–; Lithgows Pty Ltd, 1972–; Landcatch, 1981–. Member: British Cttee, Det Norske Veritas, 1966–; Exec. Cttee, Scottish Council Develt and Industry, 1969–85; Scottish Regional Council of CBI, 1969–76; Clyde Port Authority, 1969–71; Bd, National Ports Council, 1971–78; West Central Scotland Plan Steering Cttee, 1970–74; General Board, Nat. Physical Lab., 1963–66; Greenock Dist Hosp. Bd, 1961–66; Scottish Milk Marketing Bd, 1979–83. Chm., Iona Cathedral Trustees Management Bd, 1979–83; Mem. Council, Winston Churchill Meml Trust, 1979–83. Hon. Pres., Students Assoc., and Mem. Court, Univ. of Strathclyde, 1964–69. Member, Queen's Body Guard for Scotland (Royal Company of Archers), 1964. Hon. LLD Strathclyde, 1979. DL Renfrewshire, 1970. *Recreations*: rural life, invention, photography. *Heir*: s James Frank Lithgow, *b* 13 June 1970. *Address*: Ormsary House, by Lochgilphead, Argyllshire PA31 8PE. *T*: Ormsary 252; Drums, Langbank, Renfrewshire. *T*: Langbank 606; (office) PO Box 7, Lochgilphead, Argyllshire PA31 8JH. *Clubs*: Oriental; Western, Royal Scottish Automobile (Glasgow).

LITTLE, Hon. Sir Douglas (Macfarlan), Kt 1973; Justice of Supreme Court of Victoria, Australia, 1959–74; *b* 23 July 1904; *s* of John Little and Agnes Little (*née* Macfarlan); *m* 1931, Ida Margaret Chapple; one *d*. *Educ*: State Sch.; Scotch Coll.; Ormond Coll., Univ. of Melbourne (MA, LLM). QC (Aust.) 1954. Practised profession of the law in Melbourne since admission in 1929. Served War, with RAAF, 1942–45. *Recreations*: golf, lawn bowls. *Clubs*: Australian (Melbourne); Metropolitan Golf; Glenferrie Hill Recreation.

LITTLE, Ian Malcolm David, AFC 1943; FBA 1973; *b* 18 Dec. 1918; *s* of Brig.-Gen. M. O. Little, CB, CBE, and Iris Hermione Little (*née* Brassey); *m* 1946, Doreen Hennessey; one *s* one *d*. *Educ*: Eton; New Coll., Oxford (MA, DPhil). RAF Officer, 1939–46. Fellow: All Souls Coll., Oxford, 1948–50; Trinity Coll., Oxford, 1950–52; Nuffield Coll., Oxford, 1952–76, Emeritus Fellow, 1976. Dep. Dir, Economic Section, Treasury, 1953–55; Mem., MIT Centre for Internat. Studies, India, 1958–59 and 1965; Vice-Pres., OECD Develt Centre, Paris, 1965–67; Prof. of Economics of Underdeveloped Countries, Oxford Univ., 1971–76. Dir, Investing in Success Ltd, 1960–65; Bd Mem., British Airports Authority, 1969–74. Dir, Gen. Funds Investment Trust, 1974–76; Special Adviser, IBRD, 1976–78. Hon. DSc(SocSci) Edinburgh, 1976. *Publications*: A Critique of Welfare Economics, 1950; The Price of Fuel, 1953; (jtly) Concentration in British Industry, 1960; Aid to Africa, 1964; (jtly) International Aid, 1965; (jtly) Higgledy-Piggledy Growth Again, 1966; (jtly) Manual of Industrial Project Analysis in Developing Countries, 1969; (jtly) Industry and Trade in Some Developing Countries, 1970; (jtly) Project Analysis and Planning, 1974; Economic Development: theory, policy and international relations, 1982; many articles in learned jls. *Address*: 7 Ethelred Court, Old Headington, Oxford OX3 9BA.

LITTLE, John Eric Russell, OBE 1961 (MBE 1943); HM Diplomatic Service, retired; *b* 29 Aug. 1913; *s* of William Little and Beatrice Little (*née* Biffen); *m* 1945, Christine Holt; one *s* one *d*. *Educ*: Strand Sch. Served in FO, 1930–40, and in Army, 1940–41. Transferred to Minister of State's Office, Cairo, 1941, and seconded to Treasury. Returned to FO and appointed to British Middle East Office, 1946. Transferred to FO, 1948; Consul, Milan, 1950 (acting Consul-General, 1951, 1952); Bahrain as Asst Political Agent, 1952 (acting Political Agent, 1953, 1954, 1955); 1st Secretary, Paris, 1956; Asst Finance Officer, Foreign Office, 1958; HM Consul-General: Basra, 1962–65; Salonika, 1965–70; Counsellor, British Embassy, Brussels, 1970–72. *Recreations*: walking, reading, music. *Address*: Golna, Stonestile Lane, Hastings, East Sussex.

LITTLE, John Philip Brooke B.; *see* Brooke-Little.

LITTLE, Prof. Kenneth Lindsay; Professor of African Urban Studies, Edinburgh University, 1971–78, now Emeritus; *b* 19 Sept. 1908; *e* s of late H. Muir Little, Liverpool; *m* 1st, 1939, Birte Hoeck (marr. diss.); one *s* one *d*; 2nd, 1957, Iris May Cadogan (marr. diss. 1979). *Educ*: Liverpool Coll.; Selwyn Coll., Cambridge; Trinity Coll., Cambridge

(William Wyse Student). MA Cantab 1944; PhD London 1945. Lectr in Anthropology, LSE, 1946; Reader in Social Anthropology, 1950–65, Professor, 1965–71, Edinburgh Univ. Frazer Lectr, Cambridge Univ., 1965. Leverhulme Res. Fellow, 1974–76. Vis. Prof., 1949–74, at Univs of New York, California, Washington, North Western, Fisk, Ghana and Khartoum. Chm., Adv. Cttee on Race Relations Research (Home Office), 1968–70. Pres., Sociology Section, British Assoc., 1968. Gen. Editor, CUP series Urbanization in Developing Countries, 1973–80. Hon. DCL Univ. of Sierra Leone, 1982. *Publications:* Negroes in Britain, 1948 (rev. edn, 1972); Behind the Colour Bar, 1950 (banned by Malan S African govt); The Mende of Sierra Leone, 1951 (rev. edn, 1967); Race and Society, 1952; West African Urbanization, 1967; African Women in Towns, 1973; Urbanization as a Social Process, 1974; The Sociology of Urban Women's Image in African Literature, 1980. *Recreations:* Mozart piano concertos and West African drumming and dancing. *Address:* 39 Dean Path, Edinburgh EH4 3AY. *Club:* Edinburgh University Staff.

LITTLE, Dr Robert Clement; Head of Chemistry Division, Agricultural Science Service, Ministry of Agriculture, Fisheries and Food, 1979–85; *b* 8 Nov. 1925; *s* of Ernest William Little and Hannah Little; *m* 1950, Margaret Isobel Wilson; two *d. Educ:* Carlisle Grammar Sch.; Manchester Univ. (BScTech); Glasgow Univ. (PhD). W of Scotland Agricultural Coll., 1946–55; Agricultural Develt and Adv. Service (formerly National Agricl Adv. Service), MAFF, 1955–85. *Recreations:* golf, gardening, fell walking. *Address:* 9 Ashcroft Close, Harpenden, Herts AL5 1JJ. *T:* Harpenden 5613.

LITTLE, Most Rev. Thomas Francis; *see* Melbourne, Archbishop of, (RC).

LITTLECHILD, Prof. Stephen Charles; Professor of Commerce and Head of Department of Industrial Economics and Business Studies, University of Birmingham, since 1975; *b* 27 Aug. 1943; *s* of Sidney F. Littlechild and Joyce M. Littlechild (*née* Sharpe); *m* 1974, Kate Crombie (*d* 1982); two *s* one *d. Educ:* Wisbech Grammar Sch.; Univ. of Birmingham (BCom); Univ. of Texas (PhD). Temp. Asst Lectr in Ind. Econs, Univ. of Birmingham, 1964–65; Harkness Fellow, Stanford Univ., 1965–66; Northwestern Univ., 1966–68; Univ. of Texas at Austin, 1968–69; ATT Post-doctoral Fellow, UCLA and Northwestern Univ., 1969; Sen. Res. Lectr in Econs, Graduate Centre for Management Studies, Birmingham, 1970–72; Prof. of Applied Econs and Head of Econs, Econometrics, Statistics and Marketing Subject Gp, Aston Management Centre, 1972–75; Vis. Scholar, Dept of Econs, Univ. of California at Los Angeles, 1975; Vis. Prof., New York, Stanford and Chicago Univs, and Virginia Polytechnic, 1979–80. Mem., Monopolies and Mergers Commn, 1983–. *Publications:* Operational Research for Managers, 1977; The Fallacy of the Mixed Economy, 1978, 2nd edn 1986; Elements of Telecommunications Economics, 1979; Energy Strategies for the UK, 1982; Regulation of British Telecommunications' Profitability, 1983; Economic Regulation of Privatised Water Authorities, 1986; over 50 articles in econs and ops res. jls. *Recreations:* football, genealogy. *Address:* Faculty of Commerce and Social Science, University of Birmingham, Edgbaston, Birmingham B15 2TT. *T:* 021–472 1301 ext. 2669.

LITTLEJOHN, Alan Morrison; Director: Shiprepairers and Shipbuilders Independent Association, since 1977; Association of High Pressure Water Jetting Contractors, since 1980; Secretary General, UK Land and Hydrographic Survey Association Limited, since 1980; Chairman, Catherine Place Personnel Services Ltd, since 1981; *b* 17 Oct. 1925; *s* of Frank Littlejohn and (Ethel) Lucy (*née* Main); *m* 1955, Joy Dorothy Margaret (*née* Till); one *d. Educ:* Dame Allan's Boys' Sch., Newcastle upon Tyne; King's Coll., Durham Univ. (BScAgric); Lincoln Coll. and Agricultural Economics Res. Inst., Oxford Univ. (BLitt, DipAgEcon). Asst Agric. Economist: King's Coll., Durham Univ., 1945–47; Wye Coll., London Univ., 1950–51; Agric. Chemical Div., Shell Internat. Chemical Co., London, 1951–67; Economist, Agric. Engineers Assoc., 1968–73; Dir Gen., Clay Pipe Develt Assoc., 1973–77. Chm., Chorleywood Parish Council, 1985–87 (Mem., 1979–). *Recreations:* current affairs, gardening, photography. *Address:* 5 The Readings, Chorleywood, Herts. *T:* Chorleywood 4420.

LITTLEJOHN, William Hunter, RSA 1973 (ARSA 1966); Head of Fine Art Department, 1982–85, Head of Drawing and Painting Department, 1970–85, Gray's School of Art, Aberdeen, (Lecturer, 1966–70); *b* Arbroath, 16 April 1929; *s* of late William Littlejohn and Alice Morton King. *Educ:* Arbroath High Sch.; Dundee Coll. of Art (DA). National Service, RAF, 1951–53; taught Art at Arbroath High Sch. until 1966. *One man exhibitions:* The Scottish Gallery, Edinburgh, 1962, 1967, 1972, 1977, 1984. Exhibits in RA, RSA, SSA, etc. *Address:* 16 Colvill Place, Arbroath, Angus, Scotland. *T:* Arbroath 74402.

LITTLEJOHN COOK, George Steveni; HM Diplomatic Service, retired; *b* 29 Oct. 1919; *s* of late William Littlejohn Cook, OBE, and Xenia Steveni, BEM; *m* 1st, 1949, Marguerite Teresa Bonnaud; one *d;* 2nd, 1964, Thereza Nunes Campos; one *s. Educ:* Wellington Coll.; Trinity Hall, Cambridge. Served with 2nd Bn Cameronians (Scottish Rifles), 1939–46, rank of Capt.; POW Germany; Political Intelligence Dept, Foreign Office, 1945–46. Entered Foreign Service, 1946; Third Secretary, Foreign Office, 1946–47; Second Secretary, Stockholm, 1947–49; Santiago, Chile, 1949–52; First Secretary, 1950; Foreign Office, 1952–53; Chargé d'Affaires, Phnom-Penh, 1953–55; Berne, 1956–58; Director of British Information Service in Brazil, 1959–64; Head of Information Depts, FO (and FCO), 1964–69; Counsellor and Consul-General, Bangkok, 1969–71. *Recreations:* painting, sailing, ski-ing. *Address:* Quinta da Madrugada, Lagos, Algarve, Portugal. *Clubs:* Brooks's, Royal Automobile.

LITTLER, Sir (James) Geoffrey, KCB 1985 (CB 1981); Second Permanent Secretary (Overseas Finance), HM Treasury, since 1983; *b* 18 May 1930; *s* of late James Edward Littler and Evelyn Mary Littler (*née* Taylor); *m* 1958, Shirley Marsh (*see* Shirley Littler); one *s. Educ:* Manchester Grammar Sch.; Corpus Christi Coll., Cambridge (MA). Asst Principal, Colonial Office, 1952–54; transf. to Treasury, 1954; Principal 1957; Asst Sec. 1966; Under-Sec. 1972; Dep. Sec. 1977. Chm., EEC Monetary Cttee Deputies, 1974–77. Chm., Working Party 3, OECD, 1985–. *Recreation:* music. *Club:* Reform.

LITTLER, Shirley, (Lady Littler); Deputy Director General, Independent Broadcasting Authority, since 1986; *b* 8 June 1932; *d* of late Sir Percy William Marsh, CSI, CIE, and late Joan Mary Beecroft; *m* 1958, Sir (James) Geoffrey Littler, *qv;* one *s. Educ:* Headington Sch., Oxford; Girton Coll., Cambridge (MA). Assistant Principal, HM Treasury 1953; Principal: HM Treasury, 1960; Dept of Trade and Industry, 1964; HM Treasury, 1966; Asst Secretary, National Board for Prices and Incomes, 1969; Secretary, V&G Tribunal, 1971; transf. to Home Office, 1972, Asst Under-Sec. of State, 1978–83. Dir of Admin, IBA, 1983–86. *Recreation:* reading. *Address:* c/o IBA, 70 Brompton Road, SW3 1EY. *T:* 01–584 7011.

LITTLER, William Brian, CB 1959; MSc, PhD; *b* 8 May 1908; *s* of William Littler, Tarporley, Ches; *m* 1937, Pearl Davies, Wrexham; three *d. Educ:* Grove Park, Wrexham; Manchester Univ.; BSc (1st Class), Chemistry, 1929; MSc, 1930; PhD, 1932; Beyer Fellow, 1930–31. Joined Res. Dept, Woolwich, 1933; loaned by Min. of Supply to Defence Res. Bd, Canada; Chief Supt, Cdn Armament Research and Devel. Establishment,

Valcartier, Quebec, 1947–49; Supt of Propellants Research, Explosives Research and Devel. Estab., Waltham Abbey, 1949–50; in industry (Glaxo Laboratories Ltd, Ulverston), 1950–52; Dir of Ordnance Factories (Explosives), Min. of Supply, 1952–55; Principal Dir of Scientific Research (Defence), Ministry of Supply, 1955–56; Dir-Gen. of Scientific Research (Munitions), Ministry of Supply, 1956–60; Dep. Chief Scientist, Min. of Defence (Army), 1960–65; Minister, and Head of Defence R&D Staff, British Embassy, Washington, DC, 1965–69; Chemist-in-Charge, Quality Assurance Directorate (Materials), Royal Ordnance Factory, Bridgwater, 1969–72. *Publications:* Papers on Flame and Combustion in Proc. Royal Society and Jour. Chem. Soc. *Recreations:* golf, swimming. *Address:* 1 Queens Road, High Barnet, Herts. *T:* 01–440 2564.
See also Philip Attenborough.

LITTLETON, family name of **Baron Hatherton.**

LITTLEWOOD, Lady (Barbara); Consultant with Barlows, Solicitors, of Guildford; *b* 7 Feb. 1909; *d* of Dr Percival Langdon-Down, Teddington; *m* 1934, Sir Sydney Littlewood (*d* 1967); one *s. Educ:* Summerleigh Sch., Teddington; King's Coll., London, (BSc). Admitted solicitor, 1936. Pres. West Surrey Law Soc., 1952–53; Mem. Home Office Departmental Committees on: the Summary Trial of Minor Offences, 1954–55; Matrimonial Proceedings in Magistrates' Courts, 1958–59; Financial Limits prescribed for Maintenance Orders made in Magistrates' Courts, 1966–68. Pres., Nat. Fedn of Business and Professional Women's Clubs of Gt Brit. and N Ire., 1958–60; Pres. Internat. Fedn of Business and Professional Women, 1965–68; Lay Member, Press Council, 1968–74. JP Middx, 1950–. *Recreation:* occasional golf. *Address:* 26 St Margarets, London Road, Guildford, Surrey. *T:* Guildford 504348.

LITTLEWOOD, James, CB 1973; Director of Savings, Department for National Savings, 1972–81; *b* Royton, Lancashire, 21 Oct. 1922; *s* of late Thomas and Sarah Littlewood; *m* 1950, Barbara Shaw; two *s* one *d. Educ:* Manchester Grammar Sch.; St John's Coll., Cambridge (Scholar, MA). Army (Captain), 1942–46. HM Treasury, 1947–67; Civil Service Selection Bd, 1951–52; Sec. to Cttee on Administrative Tribunals and Enquiries, 1955–57; Colombo Plan Conf. Secretariat, 1955 and 1959; Dept for Nat. Savings, 1967–81. *Recreations:* golf, bridge. *Address:* 3 Smugglers Lane South, Highcliffe, Christchurch, Dorset BH23 4NF. *Club:* United Oxford & Cambridge University.

LITTLEWOOD, Joan (Maud); theatre artist. *Educ:* London. Dir, Theatre of Action, Manchester (street theatre), 1931–37; founder, Theatre Union, Manchester, introducing individual work system, 1937–39; freelance writer, 1939–45 (banned from BBC and ENSA for political opinions); founded Theatre Workshop with Gerry Raffles, 1945; touring in GB, Germany, Norway, Sweden with original works, 1945–53; moved to Theatre Royal, Stratford, London, with classics, 1953; invited to Theatre of the Nations, Paris, 1955, then yearly (Best Production of the Year three times); Centre Culturel, Hammamet, Tunisia, 1965–67; Image India, Calcutta, 1968; creation of Children's Environments, Bubble Cities linked with Music Hall, around Theatre Royal, Stratford, 1968–75. Left England to work in France, 1975; Seminar Relais Culturel, Aix-en-Provence, 1976. Productions include: Lysistrata, 1958 (Gold Medal, East Berlin, 1958; Olympic Award, Taormina, 1959), transferred to London and Broadway from Stratford, 1960–61; Sparrers Can't Sing (film), 1962; O What a Lovely War (with Gerry Raffles and the Company), 1963. Mem., French Academy of Writers, 1964. SWET Special Award, 1983. Dr *hc,* Univ. of the Air, 1977. *Recreation:* theatre. *Address:* 1 Place Louis Revol, 38200 Vienne, France.

LITTMAN, Mark; QC 1961; resumed practice at Bar, Oct. 1979; Director: Rio Tinto-Zinc Corporation PLC, since 1968; Amerada Hess Corp. (US), since 1973; Granada Group PLC, since 1977; Burton Group plc, since 1983; *b* 4 Sept. 1920; *s* of Jack and Lilian Littman; *m* 1965, Marguerite Lamkin, USA. *Educ:* Owen's Sch.; London Sch. of Economics; The Queen's Coll., Oxford. BScEcon. (first class hons) 1939; MA Oxon 1941. Served RN, Lieut, 1941–46. Called to Bar, Middle Temple, 1947, Bencher, 1970; practised, as Barrister-at-law, 1947–67; Member: General Council of the Bar, 1968–72; Senate of Inns of Court and the Bar, 1968–. Dep. Chm., BSC, 1970–79. Mem. Royal Commn on Legal Services, 1976–79. Director: Commercial Union Assurance Co. Ltd, 1970–81; British Enkalon Ltd, 1976–80; Envirotech Corp. (US), 1974–78. Mem., Internat. Council for Commercial Arbitration, 1978–; Vice-Chm., London Internat. Arbitration Trust, 1980–. Mem., Ct of Governors, LSE, 1980–. *Address:* 79 Chester Square, SW1. *Clubs:* Garrick, Reform; Century Association (New York).

LITTON, Peter Stafford; Under Secretary, Department of Education and Science, 1978–81; a General Commissioner of Income Tax, Epsom Division, since 1983; *b* 26 Oct. 1921; *s* of late Leonard Litton and Louisa (*née* Horn); *m* 1942, Josephine Peggy Bale; one *d. Educ:* Barnstaple Grammar School. Clerical Officer, Board of Education, 1938. Served in Royal Corps of Signals, 1941–46. Min. of Education, 1946; Principal Private Sec. to Secretary of State for Educn and Science, 1965–66. Mem. Council, British and Foreign Schools Soc., 1983–. *Recreations:* gardening, armchair astronomy. *Address:* 14 Guillards Oak, Midhurst, W Sussex GU29 9JZ. *T:* Midhurst 5491.

LIU, Tsz-Ming, Benjamin; Hon. Mr Justice Liu; Judicial Commissioner, State of Brunei, 1978; a Judge of the High Court of Hong Kong, 1980; *b* 17 May 1931; *s* of Dr Y. T. Liu and Dorothy (*née* Kwok); *m* 1954, Annemarie Marent; one *s* one *d. Educ:* Wah Yan College. Called to the Bar, Lincoln's Inn, 1957; QC (Hong Kong) 1973; Judge of the District Court, Hong Kong, 1973. Panel Mem., Inland Revenue Bd of Review, Hong Kong, 1972; Chm., Sub-Cttee on Bail in Criminal Proceedings, Law Reform Commn, 1985. *Address:* Supreme Court, Hong Kong. *T:* 5–238986. *Clubs:* Hong Kong, Chinese, Hong Kong Country (all in Hong Kong).

LIVELY, Penelope Margaret; writer; *b* 17 March 1933; *d* of Roger Low and Vera Greer; *m* 1957, Jack Lively; one *s* one *d. Educ:* St Anne's Coll., Oxford (BA Mod. History). *Publications:* Astercote, 1970; The Whispering Knights, 1971; The Wild Hunt of Hagworthy, 1971; The Driftway, 1972; The Ghost of Thomas Kempe, 1973 (Carnegie Medal); The House in Norham Gardens, 1974; Going Back, 1975; Boy Without a Name, 1975; A Stitch in Time, 1976 (Whitbread Award); The Stained Glass Window, 1976; Fanny's Sister, 1976; The Presence of the Past, 1976; The Road to Lichfield, 1977; The Voyage of QV66, 1978; Nothing Missing but the Samovar and other stories, 1978 (Southern Arts Literature Prize); Treasures of Time, 1979 (National Book Award); Fanny and the Monsters, 1979; Judgement Day, 1980; Fanny and the Battle of Potter's Piece, 1980; The Revenge of Samuel Stokes, 1981; Next to Nature, Art, 1982; Perfect Happiness, 1983; Corruption, 1984; According to Mark, 1984; Uninvited Ghosts, 1984; Pack of Cards, collected short stories, 1986; television and radio scripts. *Recreations:* gardening, landscape history, talking and listening. *Address:* Duck End, Great Rollright, Chipping Norton, Oxfordshire OX7 5SB. *T:* Hook Norton 737565.

LIVERMAN, John Gordon, CB 1973; OBE 1956; Deputy Secretary, Department of Energy, 1974–80; *b* London, 21 Oct. 1920; *s* of late George Gordon Liverman and Hadassah Liverman. *Educ:* St Paul's Sch.; Trinity Coll., Cambridge (BA). Served with RA, 1940–46. Civil servant in various government departments, 1947–80. Mem., British

Nat. Oil Corp., 1976–80. *Address:* 24 Graces Mews, Camberwell, SE5 8JF. *T:* 01–708 5017. *Club:* Royal Commonwealth Society.

LIVERMORE, Sir Harry, Kt 1973; Lord Mayor of Liverpool, 1958–59; *b* 17 Oct. 1908; *m* 1940, Esther Angelman; one *d* (one *s* decd). *Educ:* Royal Grammar Sch., Newcastle upon Tyne; Durham Univ. Solicitor; qualified, 1930; practises in Liverpool. Vice-President: Royal Liverpool Philharmonic Soc.; Liverpool Everyman Theatre, Ltd; Chm., Royal Court Theatre and Arts Trust Ltd. *Recreations:* music, theatre, swimming. *Address:* 18 Burnham Road, Liverpool L18 6JU.

LIVERPOOL, 5th Earl of, *cr* 1905 (2nd creation); **Edward Peter Bertram Savile Foljambe;** Baron Hawkesbury, 1893; Viscount Hawkesbury, 1905; Joint Chairman and Managing Director, Melbourns Brewery Ltd, since 1975; *b* posthumously, 14 Nov. 1944; *s* of Captain Peter George William Savile Foljambe (killed in action, 1944) and of Elizabeth Joan (who *m* 1947, Major Andrew Antony Gibbs, MBE, TD), *d* of late Major Eric Charles Montagu Flint, DSO; *S* great uncle, 1969; *m* 1970, Lady Juliana Noel, *e d* of Earl of Gainsborough, *qv*; two *s*. *Educ:* Shrewsbury School; Univ. for Foreigners, Perugia. Director: Ellangee Holdings Ltd, 1973–; Rutland Properties Ltd; Hart Hambleton Plc. *Heir: s* Viscount Hawkesbury, *qv. Address:* The Grange Farm, Exton, near Oakham, Leics. *Clubs:* Turf, Pratt's.

LIVERPOOL, Archbishop of, (RC), and Metropolitan of Northern Province with Suffragan Sees, Hallam, Hexham, Lancaster, Leeds, Middlesbrough and Salford, since 1976; **Most Rev. Derek John Harford Worlock;** *b* 4 Feb. 1920; 2nd *s* of Captain Harford Worlock and Dora (*née* Hoblyn). *Educ:* St Edmund's Coll., Ware, Herts. Ordained RC Priest, 1944. Curate, Our Lady of Victories, Kensington, 1944–45; Private Secretary to Archbishop of Westminster, 1945–64; Rector and Rural Dean, Church of SS Mary and Michael, London, E1, 1964–65; Bishop of Portsmouth, 1965–76. Privy Chamberlain to Pope Pius XII, 1949–53; Domestic Prelate of the Pope, 1953–65; *Peritus* at Vatican Council II, 1963–65; Consultor to Council of Laity, 1967–76; Episcopal Secretary to RC Bishops' Conference, 1967–76, Vice-Pres., 1979–. Member: Synod Council, 1976–77; Holy See's Laity Council, 1977– (formerly Mem., Cttee for the Family); English delegate to Internat. Synod of Bishops, 1974, 1977, 1980 and 1983. Chm., Nat. Pastoral Congress, 1980. Hon. LLD Liverpool, 1981. Knight Commander of Holy Sepulchre of Jerusalem, 1966. *Publications:* Seek Ye First (compiler), 1949; Take One at Bedtime (anthology), 1962; English Bishops at the Council, 1965; Turn and Turn Again, 1971; Give Me Your Hand, 1977. *Address:* Archbishop's House, 87 Green Lane, Liverpool L18 2EP. *T:* 051–722 2379.

LIVERPOOL, Bishop of, since 1975; **Rt. Rev. David Stuart Sheppard;** *b* 6 March 1929; *s* of late Stuart Morton Winter Sheppard, Solicitor, and Barbara Sheppard; *m* 1957, Grace Isaac; one *d*. *Educ:* Sherborne; Trinity Hall, Cambridge (MA; Hon. Fellow, 1983); Ridley Hall Theological Coll. Asst Curate, St Mary's, Islington, 1955–57; Warden, Mayflower Family Centre, Canning Town, E16, 1957–69; Bishop Suffragan of Woolwich, 1969–75. Cricket: Cambridge Univ., 1950–52 (Captain 1952); Sussex, 1947–62 (Captain 1953); England (played 22 times) 1950–63 (Captain 1954). Hon. LLD Liverpool, 1981. *Publications:* Parson's Pitch, 1964; Built as a City, 1974; Bias to the Poor, 1983; The Other Britain (Richard Dimbleby Lecture), 1984. *Recreations:* family, reading, music, painting, theatre. *Address:* Bishop's Lodge, Woolton Park, Woolton, Liverpool L25 6DT.

LIVERPOOL, Auxiliary Bishops of, (RC); *see* Hitchen, Rt Rev. Anthony; O'Connor, Rt Rev. Kevin; Rawsthorne, Rt Rev. John.

LIVERPOOL, Dean of; *see* Walters, Very Rev. R. D. C.

LIVERPOOL, Archdeacon of; *see* Spiers, Ven. G. H. G.

LIVESAY, Rear-Adm. Michael Howard; Assistant Chief of Naval Staff, since 1986; *b* 5 April 1936; *s* of William Lindsay Livesay and Margaret Eleanor Chapman Steel; *m* 1959, Sara House; two *d*. *Educ:* Acklam Hall Grammar Sch.; Britannia Royal Naval Coll. Joined RN, 1952; training appts, 1954–57; commnd 1957; qual. Aircraft Direction Specialist, 1959; Direction Officer, HMS Hermes, HMS Aisne, Fighter Direction Sch., and 893 Sqdn, 1959–66; i/c HMS Hubberston, 1966–68, HMS Plymouth, 1970–72; Captain Fishery Protection/Captain Mine Counter Measures, 1975–77; 1st CO HMS Invincible, 1979–82; Dir of Naval Warfare, 1982–84; Flag Officer Sea Training, 1984–85. *Recreations:* gliding, sailing, skiing. *Address:* c/o The Naval Secretary, Old Admiralty Building, Ministry of Defence, SW1. *Clubs:* Army and Navy, Royal Navy of 1765 and 1785.

LIVESEY, Ronald John Dearden, QC 1981; a Recorder of the Crown Court, since 1981; *b* 11 Sept. 1935; *s* of John William and Una Florence Livesey; *m* 1965, Elizabeth Jane Coutts; one *s* one *d*. *Educ:* Malvern Coll.; Lincoln Coll., Oxford (BA). Called to the Bar, Lincoln's Inn, 1962. *Recreation:* golf. *Address:* 46A Grosvenor Road, Birkdale, Southport L68 2ET. *T:* Southport 60561. *Clubs:* Athenæum (Liverpool); Union (Southport).

LIVINGS, Henry; *b* 20 Sept. 1929; *m* 1957, Judith Francis Carter; one *s* one *d*. *Educ:* Park View Primary Sch.; Stand Grammar Sch.; Liverpool Univ. Served in RAF. Joined Puritex, Leicester. Theatre Royal Leicester, then many Repertories; Theatre Workshop, 1956. 1st TV play, 1961; 1st stage play, 1961. *Publications:* contribs to Penguin New English Dramatists 5 and 6; Kelly's Eye and Other Plays, 1964; Eh?, 1965; Good Grief!, 1968; The Little Mrs Foster Show, 1969; Honour and Offer, 1969; Pongo Plays 1–6, 1971; This Jockey Drives Late Nights, 1972; The Ffinest Ffamily in the Land, 1973; Jonah, 1974; Six More Pongo Plays, 1975; That the Medals and the Baton be Put on View, 1975; Cinderella, 1976; Pennine Tales, 1983; Flying Eggs and Things, 1986. *Recreations:* dominoes, walking. *Address:* 49 Grains Road, Delph, Oldham, Lancs OL3 5DS. *T:* Saddleworth 70854. *Clubs:* Dobcross Band, Delph Band.

LIVINGSTON, Air Vice-Marshal Graham, QHS 1985; Principal Medical Officer, RAF Support Command, since 1984; *b* 2 Aug. 1928; *s* of late Neil Livingston and Margaret Anderson (*née* Graham); *m* 1970, Carol Judith Palmer; two *s* two *d* (and one *d* decd). *Educ:* Bo'ness Academy; Edinburgh Univ. (MB ChB 1951, DPH 1963); DIH (Conjoint) 1963; MFCM 1974, MFOM 1981. Joined RAF 1952; served N Ireland and Egypt, 1952–55; civilian GP and obst., 1956–57; rejoined RAF 1958; served Lindholme and Honington, 1958–62; post grad. study in public and indust. health, Edinburgh Univ., 1962–63; SMO, RAF Laarbruch, 1963–66; RAF Coll., Cranwell, 1966–70; served Cosford, Halton and Akrotiri, 1970–74; OC RAF Hosps, Cosfod, 1974–76, Wegberg, 1976–79; Dep. Dir. Med. Personnel and Dep. Dir Med. Orgn, MoD, 1979–80; Dep. PMO, Strike Command, 1981–83; PMO, RAF Germany, 1983–84. Consultant in community medicine, 1984. *Recreations:* golf, ski-ing, caravanning. *Address:* c/o Lloyds Bank, Cox's and King's Branch, 6 Pall Mall, SW1Y 5NH. *Club:* Royal Air Force.

LIVINGSTON, James Barrett, CBE 1972; DSC 1942; formerly Consultant, Rockware Group Ltd (Director, retired 1970), Director, Rockware Glass Ltd, 1947–72 (Joint Managing Director, 1951–60; Managing Director, 1960–69; Vice-Chairman, 1967–69);

b 13 Sept. 1906; *yr s* of late Capt. David Liddle Livingston and Ruth Livingston, Bombay and Aberdour; *m* 1933, Joyce Eileen, fourth *d* of late Arthur and Lilian Birkett, Clements Inn and Southwold; one *s* one *d*. *Educ:* HMS Worcester. Served War of 1939–45, RN: Staff Officer (Ops) 10th Cruiser Sqdn, Norwegian Campaign, North Russian and Malta Convoys (despatches 1943); Ops Div. Admiralty, 1943–45 (Comdr). Joined Rockware Group of Cos, 1945; Exec. Director, British Hartford-Fairmont Ltd, 1947–50. Director: Portland Glass Co. Ltd, 1956–69; Jackson Bros (Knottingley) Ltd, 1968–69 (Chm.); Burwell, Reed & Kinghorn Ltd, 1962–71; Blewis & Shaw (Plastics) Ltd, 1960–70; Automotated Inspection Machinery Ltd, 1962–69; Garston Bottle Co. Ltd, 1966–69 (Chm.); Forsters Glass Co. Ltd, 1967–69; also other Glass and Associated Companies. Member: Bd of Govs, Charing Cross Hospital, 1956–73 (Chm., Medical School Council, 1967–73); Council, Glass Manufacturers' Fedn 1967 (Pres. 1970–71); Nat. Cttee, Assoc. of Glass Container Manufacturers, 1959–69 (Vice-Pres.); Nat. Jt Industrial Council 1959–69; Court of Ironmongers' Co., 1946 (Master, 1960–61); Adv. Cttee to Faculty of Materials Technology, Sheffield University, 1969–71; Council CBI, 1970–71; Furniture Develt Council, 1972–; Council, Royal College of Art, 1970–71. *Recreations:* golf, racket re-strings, gardening. *Address:* (home) Ferroners, Beaconsfield, Bucks. *T:* Beaconsfield 3853.

LIVINGSTON BOOTH, John Dick, OBE 1976; charity consultant, since 1981; Chairman, International Standing Conference on Philanthropy, since 1984 (President, 1975–84); Member of Lloyd's, since 1979; *b* 7 July 1918; *o s* of late Julian Livingston Booth and late Grace Marion (*née* Swainson); *m* 1st, 1941, Joan Ashley Tabrum (d 1976), *d* of Ashley Tabrum, OBE, LLM, MA; two *s* one *d*; 2nd, 1979, Audrey Betty Hope Harvey, PhD, AcDipEd, DipHEd, DipSoc, SRN, *d* of Sqdn Leader John James Haslett, RAF. *Educ:* Melbourne Church of England Grammar Sch.; Sidney Sussex Coll., Cambridge (MA). Served War, 1940–43; T/Captain RA; RWAFF; Instructor, 121 HAC OCTU RHA. Nigerian Administrative Service, 1943–57; Perm. Sec., Min. of Local Govt, Eastern Nigeria, 1956–57; Dir, Charities Aid Foundn, 1957–81. Chm., Legislation Monitoring Service for Charities, 1981–; Member: Exec. Cttee, Nat. Council for Voluntary Organisations, 1974–81; Exec. Cttee, Christian Orgs Research and Adv. Trust, 1975–; Develt and Stewardship Cttee, Central Bd of Finance, 1977–80. FRGS. Lay Reader, Church of England, 1955–83. *Publications:* Directory of Grant-Making Trusts, 1968, 7th edn 1981; Trusts and Foundations in Europe, 1971; Report on Foundation Activity, 1977; Charity Statistics (annual), 1978–81; articles and booklets on charity. *Recreations:* home-making, travel, philately. *Address:* Cedar House, Yalding, Maidstone, Kent ME18 6JD. *T:* Maidstone 814431. *Clubs:* Garrick, Royal Commonwealth Society.

LIVINGSTONE, James, CMG 1968; OBE 1951; British Council service, retired; *b* 4 April 1912; *e s* of late Angus Cook Livingstone, sometime Provost of Bo'ness, Scotland, and Mrs Jean Fraser Aitken Wilson Livingstone; *m* 1945, Dr Mair Eleri Morgan Thomas, MB ChB, BSc, DPH, FRCPath, *e d* of late John Thomas, DSc, Harlech and Mrs O. M. Thomas, Llanddewi Brefi and Wilmslow; one *d* (one *s* decd). *Educ:* Bo'ness Acad.; Edinburgh Univ.; Moray House Trng Coll., Edinburgh. Adult Educn and School Posts, Scotland and Egypt, 1936–42; British Coun. Service, Egypt and Iran, 1942–45; Middle East Dept, 1945–46; Asst Rep., Palestine, 1946–48; Dep. Dir, 1949, Dir, 1956, Personnel Dept; Controller: Establishments Div., 1962; Overseas A Div. (Middle East and Africa), 1969–72. Mem. Council, British Inst. of Persian Studies, 1977– (Hon. Treasurer, 1977–82). *Recreations:* photography, exploring the West Highlands and Islands. *Address:* 21 Park Avenue, NW11 7SL. *T:* 01–455 7600; Tan yr Allt, Llangeitho, Dyfed. *Clubs:* Royal Commonwealth Society, Travellers'.

LIVINGSTONE, James Livingstone, MD, FRCP; Retired; Consulting Physician: King's College Hospital; Brompton Hospital; St Dunstan's; *b* 8 May 1900; *m* 1935, Janet Muriel Rocke; two *s* one *d*. *Educ:* Worksop Coll., Notts; King's Coll., University of London; King's Coll. Hospital. MRCS, LRCP, 1922; MB, BS 1923; MRCP 1925; MD London 1925; FRCP 1933. RAF, 1918–19. Fellow of King's Coll., London. Member: Assoc. of Physicians of Gt Britain; Thoracic Soc. *Publications:* Bronchitis and Broncho-pneumonia in Brit. Encyc. of Med. Practice, 2nd edn; Modern Practice in Tuberculosis, 1952; jt editor contributions to medical journals. *Recreations:* golf, fishing. *Address:* 11 Chyngton Road, Seaford, East Sussex. *Club:* Seaford Golf.

LIVINGSTONE, Ken; Member for Paddington, 1981–86, for Hackney North, 1973–81, and Leader, 1981–86, Greater London Council; *b* 17 June 1945; *s* of Robert Moffat Livingstone and Ethel Ada Livingstone; *m* 1973, Christine Pamela Chapman (marr. diss. 1982). *Educ:* Tulse Hill Comprehensive Sch.; Philippa Fawcett Coll. of Educn (Teacher's Cert.). Technician, Chester Beatty Cancer Res. Inst., 1962–70. Joined Labour Party, 1969; Reg. Exec., Greater London Lab. Party, 1974–86; Lambeth Borough Council: Councillor, 1971–78; Vice-Chm., Housing Cttee, 1971–73; Camden Borough Council: Councillor, 1978–82; Chm., Housing Cttee, 1978–80; Greater London Council: Lab. Transport spokesman, 1980–81; Leader, Lab. Gp, 1981–86. Contested (Lab) Hampstead, gen. elec., 1979; prospective parly cand. (Lab) Brent E, 1985–. *Publication:* If voting changed anything they'd abolish it, 1987. *Recreations:* snooker, cinema, science fiction. *Address:* c/o Members' Lobby, ILEA, County Hall, SE1. *Club:* London Lesbian and Gay Centre.

LIVSEY, Richard Arthur Lloyd; MP (L) Brecon and Radnor, since July 1985; *b* 2 May 1935; *s* of Arthur Norman and Lillian Maisie Livsey; *m* 1964, Irene Martin Earsman; two *s* one *d*. *Educ:* Talgarth County Primary Sch.; Bedales Sch.; Seale-Hayne Agricl Coll.; Reading Univ. (MSc Agric.). Develt Officer, Agric. Dir., ICI, 1961–67; Farm Manager, Blairdrummond, 1967–71; farmer at Llanon; Sen. Lectr in Farm Management, Welsh Agricl Coll., Aberystwyth, 1971–85. Joined Liberal party, 1960; contested (L): Perth and E Perth, 1970; Pembroke, 1979; Brecon and Radnor, 1983. Parly spokesman on agric., 1985–. *Recreations:* cricket, fishing. *Address:* House of Commons, SW1.

LLANDAFF, Bishop of, since 1985; **Rt. Rev. Roy Thomas Davies;** *b* 31 Jan. 1934; *s* of Hubert and Dilys Davies; unmarried. *Educ:* St David's Coll., Lampeter (BA); Jesus Coll., Oxford (BLitt); St Stephen's House, Oxford. Asst Curate, St Paul's, Llanelli, 1959–64; Vicar of Llanafan, 1964–67; Chaplain to Anglican Students, University Coll. of Wales, Aberystwyth, 1967–73; Sec., Provincial Council for Mission and Unity of Church in Wales, 1973–79; Vicar of St David's, Carmarthen, 1979–83; Vicar of Llanegwad, 1983–85; Archdeacon of Carmarthen, 1982–85; Clerical Sec., Governing Body of Church in Wales, 1983–85. ChStJ 1986. *Recreations:* walking, reading. *Address:* Llys Esgob, Llandaff, Cardiff. *T:* Cardiff 562400.

LLANDAFF, Dean of; *see* Davies, Very Rev. A. R.

LLEWELLIN, Rt. Rev. John Richard Allan; *see* St Germans, Bishop Suffragan of.

LLEWELLYN, Bryan Henry; Managing Director, The Kitchenware Merchants Ltd; *b* 1 May 1927; *s* of Nora and Charles Llewellyn; *m* 1983, Joanna (*née* Campbell). *Educ:* Charterhouse; Clare Coll., Cambridge (BA). Commissioned, The Queen's, 1946. Research Asst, Dept of Estate Management, Cambridge, 1954; joined Fisons Ltd, 1955; Marketing Manager, Greaves & Thomas Ltd, 1960; Regional Marketing Controller, Thomson Regional Newspapers Ltd, 1962; Marketing Dir, TRN Ltd, 1966; Managing Director:

Thomson Holidays Ltd, 1969; Thomson Travel Ltd, 1972 (Chm., 1977–78); Exec. Dir, Thomson Organisation Ltd, 1972–80; Man. Dir and Chief Exec., Thomson Publications Ltd, 1977–80. Non-Exec. Dir, Orion Insurance Ltd, 1976. *Address:* 18 Stockwell Park Road, SW9.

LLEWELLYN, Prof. David Thomas; Professor of Money and Banking, Head of the Economics Department, and Chairman of the Banking Centre, Loughborough University of Technology, since 1976; *b* 3 March 1943; *s* of Alfred George Llewellyn and Elsie Alexandria Frith; *m* 1970, Wendy Elizabeth James; two *s*. *Educ:* William Ellis Grammar Sch., London; London Sch. of Econs and Pol Science (BSc Econ). Economist: Unilever NV, Rotterdam, 1964; HM Treasury, London, 1965–67; Lectr in Econs, Nottingham Univ., 1967–73; Economist, IMF, Washington, 1973–76. Consultant Economist to Butler Till Ltd and Butler Treasury Services Ltd, 1981–; formerly Consultant to World Bank, Building Societies Assoc., bldg socs and banks. Mem., Bank of England Panel of Academic Consultants. TV and radio broadcasts on financial issues. *Publications:* International Financial Integration, 1980; Framework of UK Monetary Policy, 1984; The Evolution of the British Financial System, 1985; Prudential Regulation and Supervision of Financial Institutions, 1986; articles in academic and professional jls and books on monetary policy and instns, and on internat. finance. *Recreations:* DIY, culinary arts, travels, gardening. *Address:* 8 Landmere Lane, Ruddington, Notts NG11 6ND. *T:* Nottingham 216071.

LLEWELLYN, Sir David (Treharne), Kt 1960; Captain, late Welsh Guards; journalist; *b* Aberdare, 17 Jan. 1916; 3rd *s* of Sir David Richard Llewellyn, 1st Bt, LLD, JP, and of Magdalene Anne (*d* 1966), *yr d* of late Rev. Henry Harries, DD, Porthcawl; *m* Joan Anne Williams, OBE, 2nd *d* of R. H. Williams, Bonvilston House, Bonvilston, near Cardiff; two *s* one *d*. *Educ:* Eton; Trinity Coll., Cambridge. BA 1938; MA 1979. Served War of 1939–45; enlisted Royal Fusiliers, serving in ranks; commissioned Welsh Guards; North-West Europe, 1944–45. Contested (Conservative) Aberavon Div. of Glamorgan, 1945. MP (C) Cardiff, North, 1950–Sept. 1959; Parliamentary Under-Sec. of State, Home Office, 1951–52 (resigned, ill-health). *Publications:* Nye: The Beloved Patrician, 1961; The Adventures of Arthur Artfully, 1974. *Address:* Yattendon, Newbury, Berks.

LLEWELLYN, David Walter, CBE 1983; Managing Director, Walter Llewellyn & Sons Ltd, and other Companies in the Llewellyn Group, since 1953; *b* 13 Jan. 1930; *s* of Eric Gilbert and Florence May Llewellyn; *m* 1st, 1955, Josephine Margaret Buxton (marr. diss. 1985); three *s*; 2nd, 1986, Tessa Caroline Sandwith. *Educ:* Radley College. FCIOB. Commissioned Royal Engineers, 1952. Industrial Adviser to Minister of Housing and Local Govt, 1967–68; Mem., Housing Corp., 1975–77; Pres., Joinery and Timber Contractors' Assoc., 1976–77; Chm., Nat. Contractors' Gp of Nat. Fedn of Building Trades Employers (now Building Employers Confedn), 1977; Chm., Building Regulations Adv. Cttee, 1977–85 (Mem. 1966–74); Dep. Chm., Nat. Building Agency, 1977–82 (Dir. 1968–82). Underwriting Member of Lloyd's, 1978–. Pres., CIOB, 1986–87. Master, Worshipful Co. of Tin Plate Workers alias Wireworkers, 1985. Governor, St Andrew's Sch., Eastbourne, 1966–78; Trustee, Queen Alexandra Cottage Homes, Eastbourne, 1973–. *Recreation:* the use, restoration and preservation of historic vehicles. *Address:* (office) 16/20 South Street, Eastbourne BN21 4XE; (home) Cooper's Cottage, Chiddingly, near Lewes, East Sussex BN21 4XE. *Clubs:* Reform, City Livery; Devonshire (Eastbourne), Eastbourne.

LLEWELLYN, Dr Donald Rees; JP; Vice-Chancellor, University of Waikato, 1964–85; *b* 20 Nov. 1919; *s* of late R. G. Llewellyn, Dursley; *m* 1943, Ruth Marian, *d* of late G. E. Blandford, Dursley; one *s* one *d*. *Educ:* Dursley Grammar Sch.; Univ. of Birmingham, 1939–41, BSc 1st cl. hons Chem. 1941, DSc 1957; Oxford 1941–44, DPhil 1943. Research Fellow, Cambridge Univ., 1944–46; Lectr in Chemistry, UC of N Wales, 1946–49; ICI Research Fellow, UCL, 1949–52; Lectr in Chemistry, UCL, 1952–57; Prof. of Chemistry and Dir of Labs, Univ. of Auckland, 1957–64; Asst Vice-Chancellor, Univ. of Auckland, 1962–64. Mem., NZ Atomic Energy Cttee, 1958–85. Member: Council, Hamilton Teachers Coll., 1965–85; Council, Waikato Tech. Inst., 1968–85; Pres., NZ Nat. Field Days Soc., 1969–75 and 1978–81. JP Waikato, 1971. Freeman, City of Hamilton, 1985. CChem, FRSC (FRIC 1952); FNZIC 1957 (Hon. FNZIC 1985); FRSA 1960. Hon. Dr Waikato, 1985. *Publications:* numerous papers on application of stable isotopes in Jl Chem. Soc. and others. *Recreations:* squash, tennis, showjumping (FEI Judge), photography, travel. *Address:* Hamilton RD4, New Zealand. *T:* 69–172. *Club:* Hamilton (NZ).

See also Sir F. J. Llewellyn.

LLEWELLYN, Sir (Frederick) John, KCMG 1974; Director-General, British Council, 1972–80; *b* 29 April 1915; *er s* of late R. G. Llewellyn, Dursley, Glos.; *m* 1939, Joyce, *d* of late Ernest Barrett, Dursley; one *s* one *d*. *Educ:* Dursley Gram. Sch.; University of Birmingham. BSc, 1st Cl. Hons Chemistry, 1935; PhD, 1938; DSc, 1951 (Birmingham); FRIC, 1944, FNZIC, 1948; FRSA, 1952; FRSNZ, 1964. Lecturer in Chemistry, Birkbeck Coll., 1939–45; Dir, Min. of Supply Research Team, 1941–46; ICI Research Fellow, 1946–47; Prof. of Chemistry, Auckland Univ. Coll., 1947–55; Vice-Chancellor and Rector, University of Canterbury, Christchurch, NZ, 1956–61; Chairman: University Grants Cttee (NZ), 1961–66; N Zealand Broadcasting Corp., 1962–65; Vice-Chancellor, Exeter Univ., 1966–72. Mem. Senate, University of New Zealand, 1956–60; Mem. Council of Scientific and Industrial Research, 1957–61, 1962; Mem. NZ Atomic Energy Cttee, 1958; Mem. NZ Cttee on Technical Education, 1958–66; Chairman: NZ Council of Adult Educn, 1961–66; NZ Commonwealth Scholarships and Fellowships Cttee, 1961–66; Overall Review of Hong Kong Educn System, 1981–82; Member Council: Royal Society of NZ, 1961–63; Assoc. of Commonwealth Univs, 1967–72; Member: Inter-University Council for Higher Education Overseas, 1967–72; British Council Cttee for Commonwealth Univ. Interchange, 1968–72; Representative of UK Universities on Council of Univ. of Ahmado Bello, Nigeria, 1968–72. Chm., Northcott Theatre Bd of Management, 1966–72. Hon. LLD: Canterbury, 1962; Victoria Univ. of Wellington, 1966; Exeter, 1973; Birmingham, 1975; Hon. DSc Salford, 1975; DUniv Open, 1979. *Publications:* Crystallographic papers in Jl of Chemical Soc., London, and in Acta Crystallographica. *Recreations:* photography, computers. *Address:* 30 Lancaster Road, Wimbledon Village, SW19 5DD. *T:* 01–946 2754. *Club:* Arts.

See also D. R. Llewellyn.

LLEWELLYN, Sir Henry Morton, (Sir Harry Llewellyn), 3rd Bt *cr* 1922; Kt 1977; CBE 1953 (OBE 1944); MA; late Warwicks Yeomanry; President, Whitbread Wales Ltd, since 1972 (Chairman, 1958–72); Chairman: Davenco (Engineers) Ltd; Grid Management & Finance Ltd; Director, Chepstow Racecourse Co. Ltd; Vice-Chairman, Civic Trust for Wales, since 1960; *b* 18 July 1911; 2nd *s* of Sir David Llewellyn, 1st Bt, and Magdalene (*d* 1966), *d* of Dr H. Hiley Harries, DD, Porthcawl; *S* brother, 1978; *m* 1944, Hon. Christine Saumarez, 2nd *d* of 5th Baron de Saumarez; two *s* one *d*. *Educ:* Oundle; Trinity Coll., Cambridge (MA). Joined Warwickshire Yeo., Sept. 1939; Iraq-Syria Campaign, 1941; Middle East Staff Coll., Haifa, 1942; 8th Army from El Alamein to Tunis as GSO II Ops (Liaison) (despatches), 1942–43; Sicily, Italy (despatches), 1943; MA Chief of Staff HQ 21 Army Gp, 1943; NW Europe GSO I Ops (Liaison), 1943–44; OBE 1944; US Legion of Merit, 1945; Hon. Lt Col. Riding Ego, came 2nd in Grand National 'chase, 1936, 4th, 1937. Nat. Hunt Cttee, 1946–; The Jockey Club, 1969. Jt Master Monmouthshire Hounds, 1952–57, 1963–65; Captain winning Brit. Olympic Show-Jumping Team, Helsinki (riding Foxhunter), 1952; Chm., Brit. Show Jumping Assoc., 1967–69; Pres./Chm., British Equestrian Fedn, 1976–81. Chm., Welsh Sports Council, 1971–81; Mem., GB Sports Council, 1971–81. President: Inst. of Directors (Wales), 1963–65; Inst. of Marketing, Wales, 1965–67. Chm., C. L. Clay & Co. Ltd (Coal Exporters), 1936–47. Chairman: Wales Bd, Nationwide Building Soc., 1972–86; Eagle Star Assurance Co. (Wales Bd), 1963–81; formerly Director: North's Navigation Colliery Ltd; TWW Ltd; Rhigos Colliery Ltd; S Wales Reg. Bd, Lloyds Bank, 1963–82. Mem., Wales Tourist Board, 1969–75; Pres., Royal Welsh Agricl Show, 1985. Hon. Deleg., FEI, 1983. DL Monmouthshire, 1952, JP 1954–68, High Sheriff 1966. Royal Humane Soc. Medal for Life-saving, 1956; FEI Gold Medal, 1962. *Publications:* Foxhunter in Pictures, 1952; Passports to Life, 1980. *Recreations:* hunting, all sports, wild life photography. *Heir:* *s* David St Vincent Llewellyn [*b* 2 April 1946; *m* 1980, Vanessa Mary Theresa, *y d* of Lieut Comdr Peregrine and Lady Miriam Hubbard; two *d*. *Educ:* Eton]. *Address:* Ty'r Nant, Llanarth, Raglan, Gwent NP5 2AR. *Clubs:* Cavalry and Guards; Shikar.

LLEWELLYN, Rear-Adm. Jack Rowbottom, CB 1974; Assistant Controller of the Navy, 1972–74; retired; *b* 14 Nov. 1919; *s* of Ernest and Harriet Llewellyn, Ashton under Lyne, Lancs; *m* 1944, Joan Isabel, *d* of Charles and Hilda Phillips, Yelverton, Devon; one *s*. *Educ:* Purley County Sch. Entered RN, 1938; RNEC, Keyham, 1939. Served War of 1939–45: HMS Bermuda, 1942; RNC, Greenwich, 1943; HMS Illustrious, 1945. Engr in Chief's Dept, Admlty, 1947; HMS Sluys, 1949; HMS Thunderer, 1951; HMS Diamond, 1953; Comdr, 1953; Asst Engr in Chief, on loan to Royal Canadian Navy, 1954; in charge Admty Fuel Experimental Station, Haslar, 1958; HMS Victorious, 1960; Asst Dir, Marine Engrg, MoD (N), 1963; Captain, 1963; in command, HMS Fisgard, 1966; Dep. Dir, Warship Design, MoD (N), 1969; Rear-Adm., 1972. *Recreations:* travel, gardening. *Address:* 3 Jubilee Terrace, Chichester, W Sussex PO19 1XL. *T:* Chichester 780180.

LLEWELLYN, Sir John; *see* Llewellyn, Sir F. J.

LLEWELLYN, His Honour John Charles, JP; a Circuit Judge (formerly a Judge of County Courts, and a Deputy Chairman, Inner London Area Sessions), 1965–82; *b* 11 Feb. 1908; *o s* of late J. E. Llewellyn, Letchworth, Herts; *m* 1937, Rae Marguerite Cabell Warrens, *d* of Lt-Col E. R. C. Warrens, DSO, Froxfield, Hants; one *s* two *d*. *Educ:* St Christopher Sch., Letchworth; Emmanuel Coll., Cambridge (MA, LLB). Barrister, Inner Temple, 1931; Master of the Bench, Inner Temple, 1963. Common Law Counsel to PO, 1960–65; Recorder of King's Lynn, 1961–65. Mem. Gen. Council of the Bar, 1956–60, and 1961–65; Chm. Jt Advisory Council, Carpet Industry of Gt Brit., 1958–79; Dep. Chm. Agric. Land Tribunal (Eastern Region), 1959–65; JP Greater London, 1965–. *Recreation:* riding. *Address:* Bulford Mill, Braintree, Essex. *T:* Braintree 20616; 2 Temple Gardens, EC4. *T:* 01–353 7907. *Clubs:* Athenæum, Boodle's.

LLEWELLYN, His Honour John Desmond Seys; a Circuit Judge, (formerly a County Court Judge), 1971–85; *b* 3 May 1912; *s* of Charles Ernest Llewellyn, FAI and Hannah Margretta Llewellyn, of Cardiff; *m* 1939, Elaine (*d* 1984), *d* of H. Leonard Porcher, solicitor, and Mrs Hilda Porcher, JP, of Pontypridd; three *s*; *m* 1986, Mrs Joan Banfield James. *Educ:* Cardiff High School; Jesus College, Oxford; Exhibitioner, MA. Joined Inner Temple, 1936. War Service, RTR, 1940–46 (Captain). Called to the Bar, Inner Temple, in absentia OAS, 1945; Profumo Prizeman, 1947; practised on Wales and Chester Circuit, 1947–71; Local Insurance Appeal Tribunal, 1958–71; Dep. Chm., Cheshire QS, 1968–71; joined Gray's Inn, *ad eundem*, same day as youngest son, 1967. Contested Chester Constituency (L), 1955 and 1956. *Recreations:* languages, travel, archaeology, art galleries, music, two English Setters. *Address:* Chetwyn House, Gresford, Clwyd. *T:* Gresford 2419. *Club:* Athenæum (Liverpool).

LLEWELLYN, Rev. John Francis Morgan, LVO 1982; MA; Chaplain at the Chapel Royal of St Peter ad Vincula within HM Tower of London, since 1974; Officiating Chaplain, Order of St John of Jerusalem, since 1974; *b* 4 June 1921; *s* of late Canon D. L. J. Llewellyn; *m* 1955, Audrey Eileen (*née* Binks). *Educ:* King's College Sch., Wimbledon; Pembroke Coll., Cambridge (MA); Ely Theological Coll. Served War, 1941–45, in Royal Welch Fusiliers and in India (Captain). Curate of Eltham, 1949–52; Chaplain and Asst Master, King's College Sch., Wimbledon, 1952–58; Headmaster, Cathedral Choir Sch., and Minor Canon of St Paul's Cathedral, 1958–74; Sacrist and Warden of College of Minor Canons, 1968–74; Dep. Priest-in-Ordinary to the Queen, 1968–70, 1974–, Priest-in-Ordinary, 1970–74; Asst Master, Dulwich Coll. Prep. Sch., 1974–86. Sub-Chaplain, Order of St John of Jerusalem, 1970–74; Chaplain, City Solicitor's Co., 1975–. *Publication:* (contrib.) The Tower of London: Its Buildings and Institutions, 1978. *Recreations:* cricket, golf, fishing. *Address:* Chaplain's Residence, HM Tower of London, EC3N 4AB. *T:* 01–709 0765. *Clubs:* MCC; Hawks (Cambridge).

LLEWELLYN, Lt-Col Sir Michael Rowland Godfrey, 2nd Bt *cr* 1959, of Baglan, Co. Glamorgan; JP; Vice Lord-Lieutenant of West Glamorgan, since 1985; *b* 15 June 1921; *s* of Sir (Robert) Godfrey Llewellyn, 1st Bt, CB, CBE, MC, TD, and Frances Doris (*d* 1969), *d* of Rowland S. Kennard; *S* father, 1986; *m* 1956, Janet Prudence Edmondes; three *d*. *Educ:* Harrow. Commissioned Grenadier Guards, 1941; served Italian campaign, 1943–44; retired from Army, 1949; Comd 1st Bn Glamorgan Army Cadet Force, 1951–59. Director of companies, 1949–; Gen. Comr of Income Tax, 1965–. Pres., Gower Cons. Assoc., 1967–85; Chm., W Wales Gp of Cons Assocs, 1975–78; Chm., 1978–83, Pres., 1983–85, Mid and W Wales Cons. European Assoc. Chm., 1967–79, Vice-Pres., 1979–, St John Council for W Glamorgan; CStJ 1976; High Sheriff of W Glamorgan, 1980–81, DL 1982; JP Swansea, 1984. *Recreations:* shooting, gardening. *Heir:* none. *Address:* Glebe House, Penmaen, Swansea, West Glamorgan SA3 2HH. *T:* Penmaen 232. *Clubs:* Cardiff and County (Cardiff); Bristol Channel Yacht.

LLEWELLYN, Rt. Rev. William Somers; Assistant Curate of Tetbury with Beverston, since 1977; *b* 16 Aug. 1907; *s* of Owen John and Elizabeth Llewellyn; *m* 1947, Innis Mary, *d* of Major Arthur Dorrien Smith, Tresco Abbey, Isles of Scilly; three *s*. *Educ:* Eton; Balliol and Wycliffe Hall, Oxford. BA 1929; diploma in Theology (with dist.) 1934; MA 1937. Priest, 1936; Curate of Chiswick, 1935–37; Vicar of Badminton, with Acton Turville, 1937–49. CF 1940–46; served with Royal Gloucestershire Hussars in Egypt and Western Desert, and as Senior Chaplain with 8th Army HQ, Canal Area and East Africa; Vicar of Tetbury with Beverston, 1949–61; Rural Dean of Tetbury, 1955–61; Archdeacon of Lynn, 1961–72; first Suffragan Bishop of Lynn, 1963–72; Priest-in-charge of Boxwell with Leighterton, 1973–77. *Address:* Glebe House, Leighterton, Tetbury, Glos GL8 8UW. *T:* Leighterton 236.

LLEWELLYN-JONES, Frank; *see* Jones, F. Ll.

LLEWELLYN JONES, Ilston Percival; His Honour Judge Llewellyn Jones; a Circuit Judge, since 1978; *b* 15 June 1916; *s* of Rev. L. Cyril F. Jones and Gertrude Anne Jones; *m* 1963, Mary Evelyn; one *s* (by a former *m*). *Educ:* Baswich House and Fonthill prep. schs; St John's Sch., Leatherhead. Admitted Solicitor, Nov. 1938; practised privately until served Sussex Yeomanry RA and 23rd Field Regt RA (commnd), 1939–42; Solicitors

Dept, Metropolitan Police, New Scotland Yard, 1942–48; private practice, Torquay, 1948–52; Devon County Prosecuting Solicitor, 1952–56; Clerk to N Devon Justices, 1956–62; private practice, 1962–77; a Recorder of the Crown Court, 1972–78. *Recreations:* now mainly golf; formerly Rugby football, tennis, squash, swimming, cross country running. *Address:* Headley House, Badgworth, near Axbridge, Som BS26 2QN.

LLEWELLYN SMITH, Christopher Hubert, DPhil; FRS 1984; Reader in Theoretical Physics, University of Oxford, since 1980; Fellow of St John's College, Oxford, since 1974; *b* 19 Nov. 1942; *s* of J. C. and M. E. F. Llewellyn Smith; *m* 1966, Virginia Grey; one *s* one *d*. *Educ:* Wellington College; New College, Oxford (Scholar). BA 1964, DPhil 1967; full Blue for cross-country running, 1961–63, Captain 1963; full Blue for Athletics, 1963. Royal Society Exchange Fellow, Lebedev Inst., Moscow, 1967; Fellow, CERN, Geneva, 1968; Research Associate, SLAC, Stanford, Calif, 1970; Staff Mem., CERN, 1972; Univ. Lectr, Oxford, 1974. Mem. of various policy and programme cttees for CERN, SLAC, Deutches Elektronen-Synchrotron Hamburg and SERC, 1972–. Maxwell Prize and Medal, Inst. of Physics, 1979; Lectures: Welsh, Toronto, 1979; Wolfson, Oxford, 1980; Larmor, Cambridge, 1983. *Publications:* numerous articles in Nuclear Physics, Physics Letters, Phys. Rev., etc. *Recreations:* books, travel, opera. *Address:* 3 Wellington Place, Oxford OX1 2LD. *T:* Oxford 57145.

See also E. M. Llewellyn-Smith, M. J. Llewellyn Smith.

LLEWELLYN-SMITH, Elizabeth Marion, CB 1985; Deputy Director General, Office of Fair Trading, since 1982; *b* 17 Aug. 1934; *d* of John Clare Llewellyn Smith and Margaret Emily Frances (*née* Crawford). *Educ:* Christ's Hospital, Hertford; Girton Coll., Cambridge (BA). Joined Board of Trade, 1956; various appointments in Board of Trade, Cabinet Office, Dept of Trade and Industry, Dept of Prices and Consumer Protection, 1956–76; Royal Coll. of Defence Studies, 1977; Under Sec., Companies Div., Dept of Trade, later DTI, 1978–82. *Recreations:* travel, books, entertaining. *Address:* 1 Charlwood Road, Putney, SW15 1PJ. *T:* 01–789 1572. *Clubs:* United Oxford & Cambridge University, Players Theatre.

See also C. H. Llewellyn Smith, M. J. Llewellyn Smith.

LLEWELLYN SMITH, Michael John; HM Diplomatic Service; Head of Soviet Department, Foreign and Commonwealth Office, since 1985; *b* 25 April 1939; *s* of J. C. Llewellyn Smith and M. E. F. Crawford; *m* 1967, Colette Gaulier; one *s* one *d*. *Educ:* Wellington Coll.; New Coll., Oxford; St Antony's Coll., Oxford. BA, DPhil. FCO, 1970; Cultural Attaché, Moscow, 1973; Paris, 1976; Royal Coll. of Defence Studies, 1979; Counsellor and Consul Gen., Athens, 1980–83; Hd of Western European Dept, FCO, 1984–85. *Publications:* The Great Island: a study of Crete, 1965, 2nd edn 1973; Ionian Vision: Greece in Asia Minor 1919–22, 1973. *Recreations:* music, walking, wine. *Address:* c/o Foreign and Commonwealth Office, King Charles Street, SW1A 2AH. *Club:* Royal Commonwealth Society.

See also C. H. Llewellyn Smith, E. M. Llewellyn-Smith.

LLEWELYN, Sir John Michael D. V.; *see* Venables-Llewelyn.

LLEWELYN-DAVIES, family name of **Baroness Llewelyn-Davies of Hastoe.**

LLEWELYN-DAVIES OF HASTOE, Baroness *cr* 1967, of Hastoe (Life Peer); **Patricia Llewelyn-Davies,** PC 1975; Principal Deputy Chairman of Committees and Chairman, Select Committee on European Communities, House of Lords, since 1982; *b* 16 July 1915; *d* of Charles Percy Parry and Sarah Gertrude Parry (*née* Hamilton); *m* 1943, Richard Llewelyn-Davies (later Baron Llewelyn-Davies) (*d* 1981); three *d*. *Educ:* Liverpool Coll., Huyton; Girton Coll., Cambridge (Hon. Fellow, 1979). Civil Servant, 1940–51 (Min. of War Transp., FO, Air Min., CRO). Contested (Lab) Wolverhampton S-W, 1951, Wandsworth Cent., 1955, 1959. A Baroness-in-Waiting (Govt Whip), 1969–70; Dep. Opposition Chief Whip, House of Lords, 1972–73; Opposition Chief Whip, 1973–74, 1979–82; Captain of the Gentlemen at Arms (Govt Chief Whip), 1974–79. Hon. Sec., Lab. Parly Assoc., 1960–69. Chm., Women's National Cancer Control Campaign, 1972–75; Member: Bd of Govs, Hosp. for Sick Children, Gt Ormond Street, 1955–67 (Chm. Bd, 1967–69); Court, Univ. of Sussex, 1967–69. Dir, Africa Educnl Trust, 1960–69. Co.-Chm., Women's Nat. Commn, 1976–79. *Address:* Flat 15, 9–11 Belsize Grove, NW3 4UU. *T:* 01–586 4060.

LLOYD, family name of **Barons Lloyd of Hampstead** and **Lloyd of Kilgerran.**

LLOYD OF HAMPSTEAD, Baron *cr* 1965 (Life Peer); **Dennis Lloyd,** QC 1975; Quain Professor of Jurisprudence in the University of London (University College), 1956–82, now Emeritus; Hon. Research Fellow, University College London, since 1982; *b* 22 Oct. 1915; 2nd *s* of Isaac and Betty Lloyd; *m* 1940, Ruth Emma Cecilia Tulla; two *d*. *Educ:* University Coll. Sch.; University Coll., London; Gonville and Caius Coll., Cambridge. LLB (London) 1935; BA 1937, MA 1941, LLD 1956 (Cantab). Called to Bar, 1936; Yorke Prize, 1938; in practice in London, 1937–39 and 1946–82. Served War of 1939–45 in RA and RAOC, Liaison Officer (DADOS) with Free French Forces in Syria and Lebanon, 1944–45. Reader in English Law, University Coll., London, 1947–56; Fellow of University Coll., London; Dean of Faculty of Laws, University of London, 1962–64; Head of Dept of Law, University Coll., 1969–82. Hon. Fellow, Ritsumeikan Univ., Kyoto, Japan, 1978. Member: Law Reform Cttee, 1961–82; Consolidation Bills Cttee, 1965–77; European Communities Cttee, 1973–79, 1984–; Joint Cttee on Theatre Censorship; Joint Cttee on Broadcasting, 1976–81, Select Cttee on Bill of Rights; Interim Action Cttee on Film Industry, 1976–85; Conseil de la Fédération Britannique de l'Alliance Française, 1970–78; Council, BAFTA, 1985–86; British Screen Adv. Council, 1985–; Chairman: Nat. Film Sch. Cttee; Planning for Nat. Film Sch.; Governors, Nat. Film School, 1970–; British Film Inst., 1973–76 (Governor, 1968–76). Pres., Bentham Club (University Coll. London), 1983; Chm. Council, University Coll. Sch., 1971–79. *Publications:* Unincorporated Associations, 1938; Rent Control, 1949, 2nd edition, 1955; Public Policy: A Comparative Study in English and French Law, 1953; United Kingdom: Development of its Laws and Constitution, 1955; Business Lettings, 1956; Introduction to Jurisprudence, 1959, 5th edn 1985; The Idea of Law, 1964, 8 rev. imps, 1968–85, Japanese trans., 1969; Law (Concept Series), 1968; contrib. to periodicals. *Recreations:* painting, listening to music, speaking modern Greek. *Address:* Faculty of Laws, University College London, 4–8 Endsleigh Gardens, WCIH 0EE. *T:* 01–387 7050. *Clubs:* Athenæum, Royal Automobile, PEN (Hon. Life Mem.).

LLOYD OF KILGERRAN, Baron *cr* 1973 (Life Peer), of Llanwenog, Cardigan; **Rhys Gerran Lloyd,** CBE 1953; QC 1961; JP; Barrister-at-law; *s* of late J. G. Lloyd, Kilgerran, Pembrokeshire; *m* Phyllis, *d* of late Ronald Shepherd, JP, Hants; two *d*. *Educ:* Sloane Sch.; Selwyn Coll., Cambridge (science scholar). MA Cantab; BSc London. Wartime service in scientific research Departments of Air Ministry and MAP, 1939–46. Royal Commn on Awards to Inventors, 1946. Contested (L) Anglesey, General Election, 1959. In practice at Patent Bar, 1946–68. Director: Strayfield Ltd; Morgan Marine Ltd. Chairman: Education Trust; Brantwood (John Ruskin) Trust. Mem., Sainsbury Cttee on NHS, 1965–67. Chm., Inst. of Sports Medicine, 1977–81. Vice-Chairman: Victoria League, 1975; Parly and Scientific Cttee, 1978–; House of Lords Select Cttee on Science and Technology, 1980–85; European Communities Cttee, 1975–81; Parly Cttee on Information Technology, 1979–; Dep. Chm., Parly Cttee on Energy, 1980–. Pres., Welsh Liberal Party, 1971–74; Pres., UK Liberal Party, 1973–74, Jt Treas., 1977–83; Liberal Whip, and delegate, Council of Europe and WEU, 1973–75. President: Inst. of Patentees and Inventors, 1975–; Mobile Radio Users Assoc., 1986–; Industrial Copyright Reform Assoc., 1986–; Chm., Foundn of Science and Technology, 1983–. Hon. Fellow, Selwyn Coll., Cambridge, 1967–. JP Surrey, 1954. *Publications:* Kerly on Trade Marks, 8th edn, 1960; Halsbury's Trade Marks and Designs, 3rd edn, 1962. *Address:* 15 Haymeads Drive, Esher, Surrey. *Clubs:* Reform, Royal Commonwealth Society, City Livery, National Liberal.

See also D. G. Robins.

LLOYD, Rev. (Albert) Kingsley; President of the Conference of the Methodist Church, 1964; *b* 1903; *s* of Rev. Albert Lloyd; *m* 1926, Ida Marian (*née* Cartledge) (*d* 1969); one *s* one *d*; 2nd, 1972, Katharine G., *d* of A. G. L. Ives, *qv*. *Educ:* Kingswood Sch., Bath; Richmond Coll., Surrey (University of London). Methodist Circuit Minister: London, Bedford, Cambridge, 1926–52; Chm., London N Dist, 1951–53. Secretary, Dept of Connexional Funds of the Methodist Church, 1952–69. Wesley Historical Soc. Lectr, 1968. *Recreation:* gardening. *Address:* 13 High Street, Orwell, Royston, Herts.

LLOYD, Rt. Hon. Sir Anthony (John Leslie), Kt 1978; PC 1984; DL; **Rt. Hon. Lord Justice Lloyd;** a Lord Justice of Appeal, since 1984; *b* 9 May 1929; *o s* of late Edward John Boydell Lloyd and Leslie Johnston Fleming; *m* 1960, Jane Helen Violet, *er d* of C. W. Shelford, Chailey Place, Lewes, Sussex. *Educ:* Eton (Schol.); Trinity Coll., Cambridge (Maj. Schol.). 1st cl. Classical Tripos Pt I; 1st cl. with distinction Law Tripos Pt II. National Service, 1st Bn Coldstream Guards, 1948. Montague Butler Prize, 1950; Sir William Browne Medal, 1951. Choate Fellow, Harvard, 1952; Fellow of Peterhouse, 1953 (Hon. Fellow, 1981); Fellow of Eton, 1974. Called to Bar, Inner Temple, 1955; QC 1967; Bencher, 1976. Attorney-General to HRH The Prince of Wales, 1969–77; Judge of the High Court of Justice, Queen's Bench Div., 1978–84. Vice-Chairman: Parole Bd, 1984–85 (Mem., 1983–); Security Commn, 1985–; Mem., Criminal Law Revision Cttee, 1981–. Vice-Pres., British Maritime Law Assoc., 1983–. Trustee: Crafts Centre of Great Britain, 1967–72; Smiths Charity, 1971–; Glyndebourne Arts Trust, 1973 (Chm., 1975–); Dir, RAM, 1979– (Hon. FRAM 1985); Mem., Top Salaries Review Body, 1971–77. Chm., Chichester Diocesan Bd of Finance, and Mem., Bishop's Council, 1972–76; Governor: West London Coll., 1970–74; Polytechnic of the South Bank, 1971–73. DL E Sussex, 1983. *Recreations:* music, carpentry; formerly running (ran for Cambridge in Mile, White City, 1950). *Address:* 68 Strand-on-the-Green, Chiswick, W4. *T:* 01–994 7790; Ludlay, Berwick, East Sussex. *T:* Alfriston 870204. *Club:* Brooks's.

LLOYD, Anthony Joseph; MP (Lab) Stretford, since 1983; *b* 25 Feb. 1950; *s* of Sydney and Ciceley Beaumont Lloyd; *m* 1974, Judith Ann Tear; two *d* one *s*. *Educ:* Stretford Grammar Sch.; Nottingham Univ. (BSc Hons); Manchester Business Sch. (DipBA). Lectr, Dept of Business and Administration, Salford Univ., 1979–83. *Address:* 7 Tenby Avenue, Stretford, Manchester M32 0GD. *T:* 061–872 7354.

LLOYD, Prof. Antony Charles; Professor of Philosophy, Liverpool University, 1957–83, now Emeritus; *b* 15 July 1916; *s* of Charles Mostyn Lloyd and Theodosia Harrison-Rowson. *Educ:* Shrewsbury Sch.; Balliol Coll., Oxford. Asst to Prof. of Logic and Metaphysics, Edinburgh Univ., 1938–39 and 1945; served in Army, 1940–45; Lecturer in Philosophy, St Andrews Univ., 1946–57. Visiting Professor: Kansas Univ., 1967; Berkeley, Calif, 1982. *Publications:* Form and Universal in Aristotle, 1981; chapters in Cambridge History of Later Ancient Philosophy, 1967; articles in philosophical journals. *Address:* 11 Palmeira Court, 25–28 Palmeira Square, Hove, E Sussex BN3 2JP.

LLOYD, Bernard Dean, FRVA; IPFA; City Treasurer, Birmingham, 1980–82; *b* 23 March 1923; *s* of Stanley Lloyd and Eva Mary Lloyd; *m* 1955, Margaret Taylor; one *s* one *d*. *Educ:* Cardiff High Sch. CIPFA 1949; FRVA 1977. Served War, RN, 1942–46. City Treasurer's and Controller's Dept, Cardiff, 1940–42 and 1946–48; Accountancy Asst, Borough Treasurer's Dept, Ipswich, 1948–52; Technical Asst, Treasurer's Dept, Birmingham, 1952–72; Dep. Treasurer, Birmingham, 1972–80. Chm., LAMSAC Computer Panel, 1980–. *Publications:* articles in professional jls. *Recreations:* reading, gardening. *Address:* 39 Queens Court, Alderham Close, Solihull, West Midlands B91 2PR. *T:* 021–705 5431.

LLOYD, Dr Brian Beynon, CBE 1983; Chairman of Directors, Oxford Gallery, since 1967; Chairman, Trumedia Study Oxford Ltd, since 1985; *b* 23 Sept. 1920; *s* of David John Lloyd, MA Oxon and Olwen (*née* Beynon); *m* 1949, Reinhild Johanna Engeroff; four *s* three *d* (inc. twin *s* and twin *d*). *Educ:* Newport High Sch.; Winchester Coll. (Schol.); Balliol Coll., Oxford (Domus and Frazer Schol.). Special Certif. for BA (War) Degree in Chem., 1940; took degrees BA and MA, 1946; Theodore Williams Schol. and cl. I in Physiology, 1948; DSc 1969. Joined Oxford Nutrition Survey after registration as conscientious objector, 1941; Pres., Jun. Common Room, Balliol, 1941–42; Chm., Undergraduate Rep. Coun., 1942; Biochemist: SHAEF Nutrition Survey Team, Leiden, 1945; Nutrition Survey Group, Düsseldorf, 1946. Fellow of Magdalen by exam. in Physiology, 1948–52, by special election, 1952–70; Senior Tutor, 1963–64; Vice-Pres., 1967 and 1968; Emeritus Fellow, 1970; Chemist, Laboratory of Human Nutrition, later Univ. Lectr in Physiology, Univ. of Oxford, 1948–70; Senior Proctor, 1960–61; Dir, Oxford Polytechnic, 1970–80. Chairman: CNAA Health and Med. Services Bd, 1975–80; Health Educn Council, 1979–82 (Mem., 1975–82); Mem., Adv. Council on Misuse of Drugs, 1978–81. Vis. Physiologist, New York, 1963. Pres., Section I, 1964–65, Section X, 1980, British Assoc. for the Advancement of Science. Chm. of Govs, Oxford Coll. of Technology, 1963–69. Chairman: Oxford-Bonn Soc., 1973–81; Oxford Management Club, 1979–80; Pres., Oxford Polytechnic Assoc., 1984–. *Publications:* Gas Analysis Apparatus, 1960; (jt ed) The Regulation of Human Respiration, 1962; Cerebrospinal Fluid and the Regulation of Respiration, 1965; articles in physiological and biochemical jls. *Recreations:* Klavarskribo, Correggio, round tables, the analysis of running records, slide rules, ready reckoners. *Address:* High Wall, Pullen's Lane, Oxford OX3 0BX. *T:* Oxford 63353.

See also Sir J. P. D. Lloyd.

LLOYD, Charles William, JP; MA; Master, Dulwich College, 1967–75; *b* 23 Sept. 1915; *s* of late Charles Lloyd and late Frances Ellen Lloyd, London; *m* 1939, Doris Ethel, *d* of late David Baker, Eastbourne; one *s* one *d* (and one *d* decd). *Educ:* St Olave's Sch.; Emmanuel Coll., Cambridge. Asst Master Buckhurst Hill Sch., 1938–40. War Service with RA, 1940–46 (despatches). Asst Master Gresham's Sch., Holt, 1946–51; Headmaster, Hutton Gram. Sch., near Preston, 1951–63; Headmaster, Alleyn's Sch., London, 1963–66. Trustee, Nat. Maritime Museum, 1974–86. JP Inner London, 1970. *Recreations:* golf, gardening. *Address:* Stanhope, 7 Chesterfield Road, Eastbourne, Sussex BN20 7NT. *T:* Eastbourne 20257.

LLOYD, Christopher, VMH 1979; MA, BSc (Hort.); writer on horticulture; regular gardening correspondent, Country Life, since 1963; *b* 2 March 1921; *s* of late Nathaniel Lloyd and Daisy (*née* Field). *Educ:* Wellesley House, Broadstairs, Kent; Rugby Sch.; King's Coll., Cambridge (MA Mod Langs); Wye Coll., Univ of London (BSc Hort.). Asst Lectr in Decorative Horticulture, Wye Coll., 1950–54. Then returned to family home at Great Dixter and started Nursery in clematis and uncommon plants. *Publications:* The Mixed Border, 1957; Clematis, 1965, rev. edn 1977; Shrubs and Trees for Small Gardens, 1965; Hardy Perennials, 1967; Gardening on Chalk and Lime, 1969; The Well-Tempered Garden, 1970, rev. edn 1985; Foliage Plants, 1973, rev. edn 1985; The Adventurous Gardener, 1983; The Well-Chosen Garden, 1984; frequent contributor to gardening magazines, also to Jl of Royal Horticultural Soc. *Recreations:* walking, piano playing (mainly Brahms), canvas embroidery. *Address:* Great Dixter, Northiam, Rye, East Sussex TN31 6PH. *T:* Northiam 3107.

LLOYD, Clive Hubert, AO 1985; Member, since 1968, Captain, 1981–84 and since 1986 Lancashire County Cricket Club; Captain, West Indies cricket team, 1974–78 and 1979–85; Director, Red Rose Radio PLC, since 1981; *b* Georgetown, Guyana, 31 Aug. 1944; *er s* of late Arthur Christopher Lloyd and of Sylvia Thelma Lloyd; *m* 1971, Waveney Benjamin; two *d. Educ:* Chatham High Sch., Georgetown (schol.). Clerk, Georgetown Hosp., 1960–66. Began cricket career, Demarara CC, Georgetown, 1959; début for Guyana, 1963; first Test Match, 1966; played for Haslingden, Lancs League, 1967; capped, Lancashire CCC, 1969; World Series Cricket in Australia, 1977–79. Made first 1st class century, 1966; passed total of 25,000 runs (incl. 69 centuries), 1981; captained WI teams which won World Cup, 1975, 1979. First Pres., WI Players' Assoc., 1973. Hon. MA Manchester. Golden Arrow of Achievement (Guyana), 1975. *Publication:* (with Tony Cozier) Living for Cricket, 1980. *Address:* c/o Lancashire County Cricket Club, Warwick Road, Manchester M16 0PX.

LLOYD, Maj.-Gen. Cyril, CB 1948; CBE 1944 (OBE 1943); TD 1945 (2 bars); psc; Director-General, City and Guilds of London Institute, 1949–67, Consultant, since 1968; President, Associated Examining Board for General Certificate of Education, since 1976 (Chairman, 1970–76); *b* 1906; *s* of late A. H. Lloyd. *Educ:* Brighton Grammar Sch.; London and Cambridge Univs. First Class in Mathematics, Physics, Divinity. Fellow of Institute of Physics; MRST; Lecturer and Teacher; Research Worker in Science; Sussex Territorials (RA), 1929–39; Major, 1939; BEF, 1939–40 (despatches); General Staff, Canadian Army, 1940–42 (despatches, OBE); served various overseas theatres; a Dep Chief of Staff, 21 Army Group, 1943–45; Invasion of Europe (despatches, CBE), 1944–45; Dir-Gen. of Army Education and Training, 1945–49; Member: Council of Boy Scouts Assoc., 1950–70; Council Assoc. of Techn. Institutions, 1961–64; Central Adv. Council for Educn (England) and Adv. Cttee on Educn in Colonies, 1949–53; Adv. Council on Sci. Policy (Jt Enquiry on Technicians, 1962–65; Bd, Internat. Centre for Advanced Technical and Vocational Trg (Turin); Council for Tech. Education and Training for Overseas Countries; Regional Adv. Council for Higher Technological Educn (London), 1950–67; Parly and Scientific Cttee; Nat. Adv. Council for Educn in Industry and Commerce, 1945–68; Southern Regional Council for Further Educn; Council, Instn of Environmental Studies; Vice-Pres. Brit. Assoc. for Commercial and Industrial Educn (Chm. 1955–58); Industrial Trg Council, 1958–64; Central Trg Council and its General Policy Cttee, 1964–68; Chm., Governing Body, National Institute of Agricultural Engineering, 1960–70; Schools Broadcasting Council for the UK, 1962–65; W Sussex Educn Cttee; Council Rural Industries Bureau, 1960–67; Pres., SASLIC, 1970–79; Pres., Soc. for Promotion of Vocational Trng and Educn, 1973; Chm., Cttee on Scientific Library Services; Chm. Governors, Crawley Coll. of Further Educn until 1978; Vice-Pres., Crawley Planning Gp, 1967–; Chief Officer, Commonwealth Tech. Trg Week, 1961; Treas., 1963 Campaign for Educn; Mem. Council for Educl Advance; Trustee: Edward James Foundn; Industrial Trg Foundn; Pres., Roffey Park Management Inst. Governor, Imperial Coll., 1950–70; Mem. Delegacy, City and Guilds Coll., 1950–70; Hon. Exec. Principal, West Dean Coll., 1969–72. Founder Life Mem., Cambridge Soc. Patron, Chalk Pit Museum. Liveryman, Goldsmiths' Co. and Freeman of City of London; FRSA. *Publications:* booklets: British Services Education, 1950; Human Resources and New Systems of Vocational Training and Apprenticeship, 1963; contrib. to jls. *Recreations:* the countryside, sailing, and traditional crafts. *Address:* The Pheasantry, Colgate, Horsham, Sussex RH13 6HU. *Club:* Athenæum.

LLOYD, Air Vice-Marshal Darrell Clive Arthur, CB 1980; Commander, Northern Maritime Air Region, 1981–83; retired; *b* 5 Nov. 1928; *s* of Cecil James Lloyd and Doris Frances Lloyd; *m* 1957, Pamela (*née* Woodside); two *s. Educ:* Stowe; RAF Coll., Cranwell. Commnd 1950; ADC to C-in-C, ME Air Force, 1955–57; Instr, Central Flying Sch., 1958–60; Personal Air Sec. to Sec. of State for Air, 1961–63; CO, RAF Bruggen, 1968–70; RCDS, 1972; Dir of Defence Policy, UK Strategy Div., 1973–75; Dep. Comdr, RAF Germany, 1976–78; ACAS (Ops), 1978–81. *Recreations:* travel, golf (Sec., Tandridge Golf Club), painting. *Address:* c/o Lloyds Bank, 6 Pall Mall, SW1. *Club:* Royal Air Force.

LLOYD, David Bernard; Secretary, Royal College of Physicians, since 1986; *b* 14 Jan. 1938; *s* of George Edwards and Lilian Catherine Lloyd; *m* 1968, Christine Vass; three *d. Educ:* Presteigne Grammar Sch.; Hereford High Sch. FCCA. Early posts in local govt, UCL, UCH Med. Sch.; Royal College of Obstetricians and Gynaecologists: Accountant, 1971–76; Secretary, 1976–82; Secretary, Nat. Inst. of Agricultural Engineering, 1982–86. *Recreations:* school Governor, local charity, garden. *Address:* 29 Bloomfield Road, Harpenden, Herts AL5 4DD. *T:* Harpenden 61292.

LLOYD, Rev. David Richard, (Father Denys Lloyd, CR); Principal, College of the Resurrection, Mirfield, since 1984; *b* 28 June 1939; *s* of Richard Norman Lloyd and Grace Enid Lloyd. *Educ:* Brighton College (George Long Scholar); Trinity Hall, Cambridge (Exhibitioner; BA 1961, MA 1965); Leeds Univ. (MA 1969). Deacon, 1963; Priest, 1964; Asst Curate, St Martin's, Rough Hills, Wolverhampton, 1963–67; professed as Mem. of Community of Resurrection, 1969 (taking name Denys); Tutor, Coll. of Resurrection, 1970–75, Vice-Principal, 1975–84; Associate Lecturer, Dept of Theology and Religious Studies, Univ. of Leeds, 1972–. *Publications:* contribs to theolog. jls. *Recreations:* walking, domestic architecture. *Address:* College of the Resurrection, Mirfield, West Yorks WF14 0BW. *T:* Mirfield 493362.

LLOYD, Denis Thelwall; His Honour Judge Denis Lloyd; a Circuit Judge, since 1972; *b* 3 Jan. 1924; *s* of late Col Glyn Lloyd, DSO, FRCVS, Barrister-at-Law; *m* 1st, 1950, Margaret Sheila (*d* 1976), *d* of Bernard Bushell, Wirral, Ches; one *s* two *d;* 2nd, 1983, Ann, *d* of John and Georgia Cunningham, Montana and Hawaii, USA. *Educ:* Wellington College. Enlisted KRRC, 1942; commnd KRRC Dec. 1942; Central Mediterranean Force, (Italy, S France, Greece) 1943–45; attached 1st York and Lancaster Regt and then joined Parachute Regt, 1944 (wounded); Palestine, 1945–46; GSO3 (ops) HQ British Troops Austria, 1946; Staff Captain British Mil. Mission to Czechoslovakia, 1947. Called to the Bar, Gray's Inn, 1949; joined NE Circuit, 1950; Asst Recorder, Leeds, 1961–67; Recorder of Pontefract, 1971; Dep. Chm., WR Yorks QS, 1968–71. Dep. Chm., Agricultural Land Tribunal, Yorks and Lancs, 1968–71; Legal Mem., Mental Health Review Tribunal, 1983–. Contested (L): York, 1964; Hallam Div. of Sheffield, 1966. Czech War Cross, 1946. *Recreations:* gardening, fishing. *Address:* Deerfield House, Durfold Wood, Plaistow, West Sussex RH14 0PJ; Flat 5, 37 Cadogan Square, SW1X 0H2. *T:* 01–235 7439.

LLOYD, Fr Denys; *see* Lloyd, David Richard.

LLOYD, Major Sir (Ernest) Guy (Richard), 1st Bt *cr* 1960; Kt 1953; DSO 1917; DL; late Administrator J. and P. Coats, Ltd, Glasgow (retired 1938); *b* 7 Aug. 1890; *e s* of late Major E. T. Lloyd, late Bengal Civil Service; *m* 1918, Helen Kynaston (*d* 1984), *yr d* of late Col E. W. Greg, CB; one *s* two *d* (and two *d* decd). *Educ:* Rossall; Keble Coll., Oxford, MA. Served European War, 1914–18 (despatches, DSO); War of 1939–45, 1940. MP (U) East Renfrewshire, Scotland, 1940–Sept. 1959. DL, Dunbartonshire, 1953. *Recreations:* fishing and gardening. *Heir: s* Richard Ernest Butler Lloyd, *qv. Address:* Rhu Cottage, Carrick Castle, Lochgoilhead, Argyll.

See also Sir A. M. A. Denny, Bt, Sir Robert Green-Price, Bt.

LLOYD, Frederick John, CBE 1977; FIA; Chairman, Road Transport Industry Training Board, 1978–83; *b* 22 Jan. 1913; *m* 1942, Catherine Johnson (*née* Parker); one *s* one *d. Educ:* Ackworth Sch., Yorks; Liverpool Univ. (BSc). FIA 1947; FIS 1949; FSS 1953; FCIT 1968. War Service, Operational Research, Bomber Comd, 1942–45. Royal Insurance Co., 1933–47; London Passenger Transport Bd, 1947–69: Staff Admin Officer, 1952; Divl Supt (South), 1957; Chief Operating Manager (Central Buses), 1961; Chief Commercial and Planning Officer, 1965–69; Dir Gen., West Midlands Passenger Transport Exec., 1969–78. *Publications:* contribs to actuarial and transport jls. *Recreations:* golf, gardening. *Address:* 8 Cliveden Coppice, Sutton Coldfield, West Midlands B74 2RG. *T:* 021–308 5683. *Club:* Whittington Barracks Golf (Lichfield, Staffs).

LLOYD, Prof. Geoffrey Ernest Richard, PhD; FBA 1983; Professor of Ancient Philosophy and Science, since 1983, and Fellow of King's College, since 1957, Cambridge University; *b* 25 Jan. 1933; *s* of William Ernest Lloyd and Olive Irene Neville Lloyd; *m* 1956, Janet Elizabeth Lloyd; three *s. Educ:* Charterhouse; King's Coll., Cambridge. BA 1954, MA 1958, PhD 1958. Cambridge University: Asst Lectr in Classics, 1965–67; Lectr, 1967–74; Reader in Ancient Philosophy and Science, 1974–83; Sen. Tutor, King's Coll., 1969–73. Bonsall Prof., Stanford Univ., 1981; Sather Prof., Berkeley, 1983–84. Fellow, Japan Soc. for the Promotion of Science, 1981. *Publications:* Polarity and Analogy, 1966; Aristotle: the growth and structure of his thought, 1968; Early Greek Science: Thales to Aristotle, 1970; Greek Science after Aristotle, 1973; (ed) Hippocratic Writings, 1978; (ed) Aristotle on Mind and the Senses, 1978; Magic, Reason and Experience, 1979; Science, Folklore and Ideology, 1983; Science and Morality in Greco-Roman Antiquity, 1985; contribs to classical and philosophical jls. *Recreation:* travel. *Address:* 2 Prospect Row, Cambridge CB1 1DU.

LLOYD, (George) Peter, CMG 1965; CVO 1983; Governor, Cayman Islands, since 1982; *b* 23 Sept. 1926; *er s* of late Sir Thomas Ingram Kynaston Lloyd, GCMG, KCB; m 1957, Margaret Harvey; two *s* one *d. Educ:* Stowe Sch.; King's Coll., Cambridge. Lieut, KRRC, 1945–48; ADC to Governor of Kenya, 1948; Cambridge, 1948–51 (MA; athletics blue); District Officer, Kenya, 1951–60; Principal, Colonial Office, 1960–61; Colonial Secretary, Seychelles, 1961–66; Chief Sec., Fiji, 1966–70; Defence Sec., Hong Kong, 1971–74; Dep. Governor, Bermuda, 1974–81. *Address:* Government House, Grand Cayman, Cayman Islands. *Clubs:* Royal Commonwealth Society; Royal Bermuda Yacht (Bermuda); Hong Kong (Hong Kong); Muthaiga (Nairobi, Kenya).

LLOYD, George Walter Selwyn; composer and conductor; *b* 28 June 1913; *s* of William Alexander Charles Lloyd and Constance Priestley Rawson; *m* 1937, Nancy Kathleen Juvet. *Educ:* privately, and with Albert Sammons for violin, Harry Farjeon for composition. Works composed and conducted: Symphony No 1, Bournemouth, 1933; Symphony No 2, Eastbourne, 1935; opera Iernin, Lyceum, London, 1935; Symphony No 3, BBC Symph. Orch., 1935; composed 2nd opera The Serf, perf. Convent Garden, 1938; during 1939–45 war served in Royal Marines Band aboard HMS Trinidad, severely shell-shocked 1942, whilst on Arctic convoy; composed opera John Scoman, 1st perf. Bristol, 1951; due to poor health lived in Dorset growing carnations and mushrooms, only composing intermittently; health improved; subseq. composed many more symphonies, concertos (Symphony No 11 commissioned by Albany Symph. Orch, NY, first perf. 1986); numerous recordings. *Publications:* The Vigil of Venus, 1981; A Miniature Tryptich, 1981. *Recreation:* reading. *Address:* 199 Clarence Gate Gardens, Glentworth Street, NW1 6AU. *T:* 01–262 7969.

LLOYD, Glyn, CBE 1979; Executive Member, Union of Construction, Allied Trades and Technicians, 1953–84; *b* 20 June 1919; *s* of William and Elizabeth Lloyd; *m* 1949, Olwen Howel; one *s. Educ:* Melyn Elementary School; Cwrt Sart Central School. Member: Joint Council, Nat. Joint Council, CBI, 1958 (Vice-Chm., 1970; Chm., Conciliation Panel, 1968); Gen. Council, TUC, 1973–83; Health and Safety Commn, 1974–84; Governing Body, ILO, 1977–84. *Recreations:* reading, sport. *Address:* 25 Fuzzeland Drive, Bryncoch, Neath, West Glam. *T:* Neath 2084. *Club:* Brynhyfryd Bowling (Neath).

LLOYD, Major Sir Guy; *see* Lloyd, Major Sir E. G. R.

LLOYD, Very Rev. Henry Morgan, DSO 1941; OBE 1959; MA; *b* 9 June 1911; *y s* of late Rev. David Lloyd, Weston-super-Mare, Somerset; *m* 1962, Rachel Katharine, *d* of late J. R. Wharton, Haffield, nr Ledbury; one *d. Educ:* Canford Sch.; Oriel Coll., Oxford; Cuddesdon Theological Coll. Deacon, 1935; priest, 1936; Curate of Hendon Parish Church, Middlesex, 1935–40. Served War as Chaplain RNVR, 1940–45. Principal of Old Rectory Coll., Hawarden, 1946–48; Secretary of Central Advisory Council of Training for the Ministry, 1948–50; Dean of Gibraltar, 1950–60; Dean of Truro and Rector of St Mary, Truro, 1960–81; Dean Emeritus, 1981. Hon. Burgess of the City of Truro, 1978. *Recreations:* walking and archæology. *Address:* 3 Hill House, The Avenue, Sherborne, Dorset. *T:* Sherborne 2037. *Club:* Royal Commonwealth Society (Fellow).

LLOYD, Humphrey John, QC 1979; *b* 16 Nov. 1939; *s* of Rees Lewis Lloyd of the Inner Temple, barrister-at-law, and Dorothy Margaret Ferry (*née* Gibson); *m* 1969, Ann Findlay; one *s* one *d. Educ:* Westminster; Trinity Coll., Dublin (BA (Mod), LLB; MA). Called to the Bar, Inner Temple, 1963, Bencher, 1985. Pres., Soc. of Construction Law, 1985–. Editor-in-chief, The Internat. Construction Law Rev., 1983–. *Publications:* (ed) The Liability of Contractors, 1986; (ed) Building Law Reports, 1977–. *Address:* 22 Old Buildings, Lincoln's Inn, WC2A 3UJ. *T:* 01–404 0102. *Club:* Reform.

LLOYD, Sir Ian Stewart, Kt 1986; MP (C) Havant, since 1983 (Portsmouth, Langstone, 1964–74, Havant and Waterloo, 1974–83); *b* 30 May 1921; *s* of Walter John Lloyd and late Euphemia Craig Lloyd; *m* 1951, Frances Dorward Addison, *d* of late Hon. W. Addison, CMG, OBE, MC, DCM; three *s. Educ:* Michaelhouse; University of the Witwatersrand; King's Coll., Cambridge. President, Cambridge Union, and Leader, Cambridge tour of USA, 1947; MA 1951; MSc 1952. Econ. Adviser, Central Mining and Investment Corporation, 1949–52; Member, SA Board of Trade and Industries, 1952–55; Director, Acton Soc. Trust, 1956; Dir of Res., 1956–64, Economic Advr, 1956–83, British and Commonwealth Shipping. Chairman, UK Cttee and Vice-Chairman, International Exec., International Cargo Handling Co-ordination Assoc., 1961–64. Chairman: Cons. Parly Shipping and Shipbuilding Cttee, 1974–77; Select Cttee on Sci. Sub-Cttee, 1975–77; Select Cttee on Sci. Sub-Cttee on Technological Innovation, 1977–79; Select Cttee on Energy, 1979–; All-Party Cttee on Information Technology,

1979–; Vice-Pres., Parly and Scientific Cttee, 1983–. Member, UK Delegation, Council of Europe, Western European Union, 1968–72; UK rep., Internat. Parly Conf., Bucharest, 1975; Leader, UK Delegn, OECD Conf. on Energy, 1981. *Publications:* Rolls-Royce, 3 vols, 1978; contribs to various journals on economics, politics and information technology. *Recreations:* yachting, ski-ing, good music. *Address:* Bakers House, Priors Dean, Petersfield, Hants. *Clubs:* Brooks's, Army and Navy, Royal Yacht Squadron.

LLOYD, His Honour Ifor Bowen, QC; a County Court Judge, later a Circuit Judge, 1959–76 (Judge of Wandsworth County Court, 1964–76); *b* 9 Sept. 1902; *er s* of late Rev. Thomas Davies Lloyd and Mrs Margaret Lloyd; *m* 1938, Naomi, *y d* of late George Pleydell Bancroft; one *s* one *d*. *Educ:* Winchester (Exhibitioner); Exeter Coll., Oxford (Scholar). BA Oxford (Mod. Hist.), 1924; called to Bar, Inner Temple, 1925, Bencher 1959, Treasurer 1981; Yarborough Anderson scholar, 1926; Midland Circuit; President, Hardwicke Society, 1929; KC 1951. Liberal Candidate, Burton Division of Staffordshire, 1929, Chertsey Division of Surrey, 1931. Member General Council of the Bar, 1950, 1957. *Address:* 1 Harcourt Buildings, Temple, EC4Y 9DA. *T:* 01–353 1484.

LLOYD, Illtyd Rhys; HM Chief Inspector of Schools (Wales), since 1982; *b* 13 Aug. 1929; *s* of John and Melvina Lloyd; *m* 1955, Julia Lewis; one *s* one *d*. *Educ:* Port Talbot (Glan-Afan) County Grammar Sch.; Swansea UC. BSc, MSc; DipStat, DipEd. Commnd Educn Br., RAF, 1951–54 (Flt Lieut). Second Maths Master, Howardian High Sch. for Boys, Cardiff, 1954–57; Hd of Maths Dept, Pembroke Grammar Sch., 1957–59; Dep. Headmaster, Howardian High Sch., 1959–63; Welsh Office: HM Inspector of Schs, 1964–70; Staff Inspector (Secondary Educn), 1971–82. *Recreation:* walking. *Address:* Welsh Office, Cathays Park, Cardiff CF1 3NQ. *T:* Cardiff 823431; 134 Lake Road East, Roath Park, Cardiff CF2 5NQ. *T:* Cardiff 755296.

LLOYD, James Monteith, CD 1979; CMG 1961; Deputy Chairman, Industrial Disputes Tribunal, Jamaica, 1976–78; *b* 24 Nov. 1911; *s* of late Jethro and Frances Lloyd; *m* 1936, Mavis Anita Frankson; two *s* two *d*. *Educ:* Wolmer's High Sch., Jamaica. Called to Bar, Lincoln's Inn, 1948. Jamaica: entered Public Service as Asst, Registrar-General's Dept, 1931 (2nd Class Clerk, 1939, 1st Class Clerk, 1943, Asst Registrar-General, 1947); Asst Secretary, Secretariat, 1950; Principal Asst Secretary, Secretariat, 1953 (seconded to Grenada on special duty, Dec. 1955–May 1956); Permanent Secretary, Jamaica, 1956; Administrator, Grenada, 1957–62; Permanent Secretary, Jamaica, 1962–72; Chm., Ombudsman Working Party, Jamaica, 1972; retired from Civil Service, 1975. Chief Comr, Scouts, Jamaica, 1973–78. Coronation Medal, 1953; Jamaica Independence Medal, 1962. *Recreations:* cricket, tennis, golf. *Address:* 5 Melwood Avenue, Kingston 8, Jamaica. *Clubs:* Jamaica; Kingston CC; YMCA.

LLOYD, John Graham; Executive Officer/Commercial Surveyor, Commission for the New Towns, Corby, since 1981; *b* Watford, 18 Feb. 1938; *s* of late Richard and Edith Lloyd; *m* 1960, Ann (*née* Plater); three *s*. *Educ:* City of London Sch.; College of Estate Management, London Univ. (BSc Estate Management). FRICS. In private practice, London and Leamington Spa, 1959–75. Commercial and Industrial Manager, Hemel Hempstead, Commission for the New Towns, 1975–78, Manager, 1978–81. *Recreations:* soccer, motor racing, jazz and popular music, gardening. *Address:* 10 Polhill Avenue, Bedford MK41 9DS. *T:* Bedford 56089.

LLOYD, John Nicol Fortune; Editor, New Statesman, since 1986; *b* 15 April 1946; *s* of Joan Adam Fortune and Christopher Lloyd; *m* 1st, 1974, Judith Ferguson (marr. diss. 1979); 2nd, 1983, Marcia Levy. *Educ:* East Fife Comprehensive School; Edinburgh Univ. (MA Hons). Editor, Time Out, 1972–73; Reporter, London Programme, 1974–76; Producer, Weekend World, 1976–77; industrial reporter, labour corresp., industrial and labour editor, Financial Times, 1977–86. Journalist of the Year, Granada Awards, 1984; Specialist Writer of the Year, IPC Awards, 1985. *Publications:* (with Ian Benson) The Politics of Industrial Change, 1982; (with Martin Adeney) The Miners' Strike: loss without limit, 1986. *Recreations:* opera, hill walking, squash. *Address:* New Statesman, 14–16 Farringdon Lane, EC1R 3AU. *T:* (home) 01–737 0941; (office) 01–253 2003.

LLOYD, Sir (John) Peter (Daniel), Kt 1971; Chancellor, University of Tasmania, 1982–85; *b* 30 Aug. 1915; *s* of late David John Lloyd; *m* 1947, Gwendolen, *d* of late William Nassau Molesworth; two *s* four *d*. *Educ:* Rossall Sch.; Brasenose Coll., Oxford (MA). Royal Artillery, 1940–46 (despatches, Order of Leopold, Belgian Croix de Guerre). Joined Cadbury Bros Ltd, Birmingham, 1937; served in UK and Australia; Dir, Cadbury Fry Pascall Australia Ltd, 1949, Chm., 1953–71. Member: Council, Univ. of Tasmania, 1957–85; Council, Australian Admin. Staff Coll., 1959–71; Board, Commonwealth Banking Corp., 1967–82; Board, Goliath Cement Holdings, 1969–; Board, Australian Mutual Provident Society, 1970–. Member: Australian Taxation Review Cttee, 1972–74; Cttee of Inquiry into Educn and Training, 1976–78. *Address:* Stonecrest, Sorell, Tasmania 7172, Australia. *Clubs:* Tasmanian (Hobart); Australian (Sydney).
See also B. B. Lloyd.

LLOYD, Prof. John Raymond; *see under* Lloyd, M. R.

LLOYD, John Wilson; Principal Establishment Officer and Under Secretary, Welsh Office, since 1982; *b* 24 Dec. 1940; *s* of late Dr Ellis Lloyd and of Mrs Dorothy Lloyd; *m* 1967, Buddug Roberts; two *s* one *d*. *Educ:* Swansea Grammar Sch.; Clifton Coll., Bristol; Christ's Coll., Cambridge (MA). Asst Principal, HM Treasury, 1962–67 (Private Sec. to Financial Sec., 1965–67); Principal, successively HM Treasury, CSD and Welsh Office, 1967–75 (Private Sec. to Sec. of State for Wales, 1974–75); Asst Sec., Welsh Office, 1975–82. *Recreations:* golf, squash, swimming. *Address:* 16 Ty Gwyn Road, Penylan, Cardiff CF2 5JE. *T:* Cardiff 496803.

LLOYD, Prof. June Kathleen, FRCP; Nuffield Professor of Child Health, British Postgraduate Medical Federation, London University, since 1985; *b* 1928; *d* of Arthur Cresswell Lloyd and Lucy Bevan Lloyd. *Educ:* Royal School, Bath; Bristol Univ. (MD); Durham Univ. (DPH). Junior Hosp. appts, Bristol, Oxford and Newcastle, 1951–57; Res. Fellow and Lectr in Child Health, Univ. of Birmingham, 1958–65; Sen. Lectr, Reader in Paediatrics, Inst. of Child Health, 1965–73; Prof. of Paediatrics, London Univ., 1973–75; Prof. of Child Health, St George's Hosp. Med. Sch., London Univ., 1975–85. Vis. Examr in Paediatrics in Univs in UK and abroad. Member: Council, RCP, 1982–85, 1986–; MRC, 1984–; DHSS Cttees, incl. Cttee on Med. Aspects Food Policy. *Publications:* research articles, reviews and leading articles in sci. jls. *Recreations:* cooking, gardening, walking. *Address:* Institute of Child Health, 30 Guildford Street, WC1N 1EH.

LLOYD, Rev. Kingsley; *see* Lloyd, Rev. A. K.

LLOYD, Leslie, CBE 1981; FCIT; General Manager, Western Region, British Rail, 1976–82; *b* 10 April 1924; *s* of Henry Lloyd and Lilian Wright; *m* 1953, Marie Snowden; one *s* two *d*. *Educ:* Hawarden Grammar Sch. RAF, 1943–47. British Rail: Management Trainee, Eastern Reg., 1949–52; Chief Controller, Manchester, 1953–56; Freight Officer, Sheffield, 1956–59; Modernisation Asst, King's Cross, 1959–61; Dist Manager, Marylebone, 1961–63; Movements Supt, Great Northern Line, 1963–64; Ops Officer, Eastern Reg., 1964–67; Man., Sundries Div., 1967; Movements Man., Western Reg.,

1967–69; Chief Ops Man., British Rail HQ, 1969–76. *Recreations:* golf, gardening. *Address:* 73 The Fairway, Burnham, Bucks. *Club:* Burnham Beeches Golf (Burnham).

LLOYD, Martin, MA (Cantab); *b* 1908; 2nd *s* of late Thomas Zachary Lloyd, Edgbaston, Birmingham; *m* 1943, Kathleen Rosslyn, *y d* of late Colonel J. J. Robertson, DSO, Wick, Caithness; two *s* two *d*. *Educ:* Marlborough Coll.; Gonville and Caius Coll., Cambridge (1st Class Parts I and II Mod. Languages Tripos). Asst Master, Rugby Sch., 1930–40; on military service, 1940–44. Headmaster of Uppingham Sch., 1944–65; Warden, Missenden Abbey Adult Educn Coll., 1966–74. *Address:* Norton Cottage, Pitchcombe, Stroud, Glos GL6 6LU. *T:* Painswick 812329.

LLOYD, Prof. Michael Raymond; Senior Partner, Sinar Associates, Tunbridge Wells, since 1973; *b* 20 Aug. 1927; *s* of W. R. Lloyd; *m* 1957, Berit Hansen; one *s* two *d*. *Educ:* Wellington Sch., Somerset; AA School of Architecture. AA Dipl. 1953; ARIBA 1954; MNAL 1960. Private practice and Teacher, State School of Arts and Crafts, Oslo, 1955–60 and 1962–63; First Year Master, AA School of Architecture, 1960–62; Dean, Faculty of Arch., and Prof. of Arch., Kumasi Univ. of Science and Technology, 1963–66; Principal, AA Sch. of Architecture, 1966–71; Consultant, Land Use Consultants (Internat.) Lausanne, 1971–72; Consultant Head, Hull Sch. of Architecture, 1974–77. Leverhulme Sen. Res. Fellow, UCL, 1976–78. *Publications:* (as J. R. Lloyd) Tegning og Skissing; ed World Architecture, Vol. I Norway, Vol. III Ghana; Shelter in Society: Norwegian Laftehus. *Recreations:* sailing, ski-ing. *Address:* Studley Cottage, Bishops Down, Park Road, Tunbridge Wells, Kent.

LLOYD, Nicholas Markley, MA; Editor, Daily Express, since 1986; *b* 9 June 1942; *s* of Walter and Sybil Lloyd; *m* 1st, 1968, Patricia Sholliker (marr. diss. 1978); two *s* one *d*; 2nd, 1979, Eve Pollard; one *s*. *Educ:* Bedford Modern Sch.; St Edmund Hall, Oxford (MA Hons History); Harvard Univ., USA. Reporter, Daily Mail, 1964; Educn Correspondent, Sunday Times, 1966; Dep. News Editor, Sunday Times, 1968; News Editor, The Sun, 1970; Asst Editor, News of the World, 1972; Asst Editor, The Sun, 1976; Dep. Editor, Sunday Mirror, 1980; Editor: Sunday People, 1982–83; News of the World, 1984–85. *Recreations:* football, golf, reading, cinema, theatre. *Address:* 121 Fleet Street, EC4P 4JT. *T:* 01–353 8000. *Club:* Reform.

LLOYD, Peter, CBE 1957; Director, Booth International Holdings Ltd, 1973–79 (Consultant, 1980); *b* 26 June 1907; *s* of late Godfrey I. H. Lloyd and late Constance L. A. Lloyd; *m* 1st, 1932, Nora K. E. Patten; one *s* one *d*; 2nd, 1951, Joyce Evelyn Campbell. *Educ:* Gresham's Sch.; Trinity Coll., Cambridge (MA). Industrial Research in Gas Light and Coke Co., London, 1931–41; Royal Aircraft Establishment, 1941–44; Power Jets (Research and Development), 1944–46. National Gas Turbine Establishment, Pyestock, 1946–60, Deputy Director, 1950; Dir-Gen. Engine R&D, Mins of Aviation and Technology, 1961–69; Head of British Defence Research and Supply Staff, Canberra, 1969–72. Chm., Gas Turbine Collaboration Cttee, 1961–68. CEng, FRAeS, SFInstE. Pres., Cambridge Univ. Mountaineering Club, 1928–29; Chm., Mount Everest Foundn, 1982–84 (Vice Chm., 1980–82). Himalayan expeditions: Nanda Devi, 1936; Everest, 1938; Langtang Himal, 1949; Kulu, 1977. *Publications:* various papers in scientific and technical journals. *Recreations:* mountaineering, fishing, gardening. *Address:* Heath Hill, Old Park Lane, Farnham, Surrey. *T:* Farnham 714995. *Clubs:* Athenæum, Alpine (Vice-Pres., 1961–63, Pres., 1977–80).
See also T. A. Evans.

LLOYD, Peter, *see* Lloyd, G. P.

LLOYD, Sir Peter, *see* Lloyd, Sir J. P. D.

LLOYD, Peter Gordon, CBE 1976 (OBE 1965); retired; British Council Representative, Greece, 1976–80; *b* 20 Feb. 1920; *s* of Peter Gleave Lloyd and Ellen Swift; *m* 1952, Edith Florence (*née* Flurey); two *s* one *d*. *Educ:* Royal Grammar Sch., Newcastle upon Tyne; Balliol Coll., Oxford (Horsley Exhibnr, 1939; BA, MA 1948). RA (Light Anti-Aircraft), subseq. DLI, 1940–46, Captain. British Council, 1949–: Brit. Council, Belgium and Hon. Lector in English, Brussels Univ., 1949–52; Reg. Dir, Mbale, Uganda, 1952–56; Dep. Dir Personnel, 1956–60; Representative: Ethiopia, 1960–68; Poland, 1969–72; Nigeria, 1972–76. *Publications:* (introd) Huysmans, A Rebours, 1940; The Story of British Democracy, 1959; critical essays on literature in periodicals. *Recreations:* literature, music, travel. *Address:* 25 Shenley Hill, Radlett, Herts. *T:* Radlett 7310. *Club:* United Oxford & Cambridge University.

LLOYD, Peter Robert Cable; MP (C) Fareham, since 1979; a Lord Commissioner of HM Treasury, since 1986; *b* 12 Nov. 1937; *s* of David and late Stella Lloyd; *m* 1967, Hilary Creighton; one *s* one *d*. *Educ:* Tonbridge Sch.; Pembroke Coll., Cambridge (MA). Formerly Marketing Manager, United Biscuits Ltd. Sec., Cons. Parly Employment Cttee, 1979–81; Vice-Chm., Cons. European Affairs Cttee, 1980–81; PPS to Minister of State, NI Office, 1981–82, to Sec. of State for Educn and Sci., 1983–84; Asst Govt Whip, 1984–86. Chairman, Bow Group, 1972–73; Editor of Crossbow, 1974–76. *Recreations:* theatre, gardening, reading newspapers. *Address:* House of Commons, SW1A 0AA.

LLOYD, Richard Ernest Butler; Deputy Chairman, since 1978, Chief Executive, since 1980, Hill Samuel & Co. Ltd; *b* 6 Dec. 1928; *s* and *heir* of Major Sir (Ernest) Guy Richard Lloyd, Bt, *qv*; *m* 1955, Jennifer Susan Margaret, *e d* of Brigadier Ereld Cardiff, *qv*; three *s*. *Educ:* Wellington Coll.; Hertford Coll., Oxford (MA). Nat. Service (Captain, Black Watch), 1947–49. Joined Glyn, Mills & Co., 1952; Exec. Dir, 1964–70; Chief Executive, Williams & Glyn's Bank Ltd, 1970–78. Director: Legal & Gen. Assce Soc., 1966–; Vickers Ltd, 1978–. Member: CBI Council, 1978–; Industrial Develt Adv. Bd, 1972–77; Nat. Econ. Develt Council, 1973–77; Cttee to Review the Functioning of Financial Institutions, 1977–80; Overseas Projects Bd, 1981–85. Member Council: Inst. of Bankers, 1970–75, 1986–; British Heart Foundn, 1977–; British Bankers' Assoc., 1978–; Ditchley Foundn, 1974–83, 1985–. *Recreations:* walking, fishing, gardening. *Address:* Sundridge Place, Sundridge, Sevenoaks, Kent TN14 6DD. *T:* Westerham 63599. *Club:* Boodle's.

LLOYD, Maj.-Gen. Richard Eyre, CB 1959; CBE 1957 (OBE 1944); DSO 1945; late RE, retired, Sept. 1962; Arms Control and Disarmament Research Unit, Foreign and Commonwealth Office, 1966–73; *b* 7 Dec. 1906; *s* of late Lieut-Colonel W. E. Eyre Lloyd; *m* 1939, Gillian, *d* of late Rear-Adm. J. F. C. Patterson, OBE; one *s* two *d*. *Educ:* Eton; Pembroke Coll. (Cambridge). 2nd Lieut in Royal Engineers, 1927. Served War of 1939–45 on Staff, also with RE in North West Europe; Lieut-Colonel 1942; Colonel, 1951; Brigadier, 1955; Maj.-Gen., 1957. Chief of Staff, Middle East Land Forces, 1957–59; Director of Military Intelligence, 1959–62. Colonel Comdt, Intelligence Corps, 1964–69. *Recreation:* sailing. *Address:* Snooks Farm House, Walhampton, Lymington, Hants SO41 5SF. *T:* Lymington 73569.

LLOYD, Richard Hey; Deputy Headmaster, Salisbury Cathedral Choir School, since 1985; *b* 25 June 1933; *s* of Charles Yates Lloyd and Ann Lloyd; *m* 1962, Teresa Morwenna Willmott; four *d*. *Educ:* Lichfield Cathedral Choir Sch.; Rugby Sch. (Music Scholar); Jesus Coll., Cambridge (Organ Scholar). MA, FRCO, ARCM. Asst Organist, Salisbury Cath., 1957–66; Organist and Master of the Choristers, Hereford Cath., 1966–74;

Conductor, Three Choirs Festival, 1966–74 (Chief Conductor 1967, 1970, 1973); Organist and Master of the Choristers, Durham Cathedral, 1974–85. Examiner, Associated Bd of Royal Schs of Music, 1967–. Mem. Council, RCO, 1974–. *Publications:* church music. *Recreations:* cricket, theatre, travel, reading. *Address:* 5 Millbrook, Salisbury, Wilts SP1 1NH. *T:* Salisbury 23610

LLOYD, Robert Andrew; freelance opera singer, broadcaster and writer; *b* 2 March 1940; *s* of William Edward Lloyd and May (*née* Waples); *m* 1964, Sandra Dorothy (*née* Watkins); one *s* three *d. Educ:* Southend-on-Sea High Sch.; Keble Coll., Oxford (BA Hons Mod. History). Instructor Lieut RN (HMS Collingwood), 1963–66; Civilian Tutor, Police Staff Coll., Bramshill, 1966–68; studied at London Opera Centre, 1968–69; début in Leonore, Collegiate Theatre, 1969; Principal Bass: Sadler's Wells Opera, Coliseum, 1969–72; Royal Opera House, 1972–82. Guest appearances in Amsterdam, Berlin, Hamburg, Aix-en-Provence, Milan (La Scala), San Francisco, Paris, Munich, Nice, Boston, Toronto, Salzburg; soloist with major orchestras; over 50 recordings; associated with rôles of King Philip, Boris Godunov, Gurnemanz, Fiesco, Banquo, King Henry; film, Parsifal. *Publications:* contrib. miscellaneous jls. *Recreations:* sailing barges, straight theatre. *Address:* 33 Etchingham Park Road, N3 2DU. *T:* 01–349 1758. *Club:* Garrick.

LLOYD, Prof. Seton Howard Frederick, CBE 1958 (OBE 1949); FBA 1955; Archæologist; Professor of Western Asiatic Archæology, University of London, 1962–69, now Emeritus; *b* 30 May 1902; *s* of John Eliot Howard Lloyd and Florence Louise Lloyd (*née* Armstrong); *m* 1944, Margery Ulrica Fitzwilliams Hyde; one *s* one *d. Educ:* Uppingham; Architectural Assoc. ARIBA 1926; Asst to Sir Edwin Lutyens, PRA, 1926–28; excavated with Egypt Exploration Society, 1928–30; excavated in Iraq for University of Chicago Oriental Institute, 1930–37; excavated in Turkey for University of Liverpool, 1937–39; FSA 1938 (Vice-Pres., 1965–69); Technical Adviser, Government of Iraq; Directorate-General of Antiquities, 1939–49; Director British Institute of Archæology, Ankara, Turkey, 1949–61. Hon. MA (Edinburgh), 1960. Lawrence of Arabia Meml Medal, RCAS, 1971; Gertrude Bell Meml Medal, British Sch. of Archaeology in Iraq, 1979. *Publications:* Mesopotamia (London), 1936; Sennacherib's Aqueduct at Jerwan (Chicago), 1935; The Gimilsin Temple (Chicago), 1940; Presargonid Temples (Chicago), 1942; Ruined Cities of Iraq (Oxford), 1942; Twin Rivers, (Oxford), 1942; Foundations in the Dust (London), 1947, rev. edn 1980; Early Anatolia (Pelican), 1956; Art of the Ancient Near East (London), 1961; Mounds of the Ancient Near East (Edinburgh) 1963; Highland Peoples of Anatolia (London), 1967; Archaeology of Mesopotamia (London), 1978; Excavation Reports and many articles in journals. *Recreation:* travel. *Address:* Woolstone Lodge, Faringdon, Oxon. *T:* Uffington 248. *Club:* Chelsea Arts.

LLOYD, Timothy Andrew Wigram; QC 1986; *b* 30 Nov. 1946; *s* of late Thomas Wigram Lloyd and of Margo Adela Lloyd (*née* Beasley); *m* 1978, Theresa Sybil Margaret Holloway. *Educ:* Winchester College; Lincoln College, Oxford. MA. Called to the Bar, Middle Temple, 1970; Mem., Middle Temple and Lincoln's Inn. *Address:* 11 Old Square, Lincoln's Inn, WC2A 3TS. *T:* 01–430 0341.

LLOYD DAVIES, John Robert; *see* Davies.

LLOYD-DAVIES, Oswald Vaughan; Surgeon Emeritus: Middlesex Hospital (Surgeon, 1950–81); St Mark's Hospital for diseases of the Colon and Rectum (Surgeon, 1935–81); Former Surgeon: Connaught Hospital; Hampstead General Hospital; *s* of late Rev. Samuel Lloyd-Davies, BA; *m* 1st, 1939, Menna (*d* 1968), *d* of late Canon D. J. Morgan, MA; one *s* one *d*; 2nd, 1970, Rosamund, *d* of late Rev. E. V. Bond, MA. *Educ:* Caterham Sch.; Middlesex Hospital Medical Sch., London Univ. MRCS, LRCP, 1929; MB, BS (London) 1930; FRCS 1932; MS (London) 1932. Fellow Royal Society of Med. (Past Pres. sect. of proctology); Fellow Assoc. of Surgeons of Great Britain and Ireland; Member, Harveian Society; Hon. Fellow, Amer. Soc. of Colon and Rectal Surgeons. *Publications:* various chapters in British Surgical Practice; articles on colon, rectal and liver surgery. *Recreations:* gardening, fishing. *Address:* Townsend Close, Ashwell, Herts. *T:* Ashwell 2386.

LLOYD DAVIES, Trevor Arthur, MD; FRCP; *b* 8 April 1909; *s* of Arthur Lloyd Davies and Grace Margret (*née* Bull); *m* 1936, Joan (*d* 1972), *d* of John Keily, Co. Dublin; one *d*; *m* 1975, Margaret, *d* of Halliday Gracey, Woodford. *Educ:* Woking Grammar Sch.; St Thomas' Hospital, SE1. MRCS, LRCP 1932; MB, BS London (gold medal and hons in surgery, forensic med., obst. and gynæc.); MRCP 1933; MD London 1934; FRCP 1952. Resident Asst Physician, St Thomas' Hospital, 1934–36; MO, Boots Pure Drug Co., 1937–53; Prof. of Social Medicine, University of Malaya, 1953–61; Senior Medical Inspector of Factories, Min. of Labour and Dept of Employment and Productivity, 1961–70; Chief Med. Adviser, Dept of Employment, 1970–73. QHP 1968–71. *Publications:* The Practice of Industrial Medicine, 2nd edn, 1957; Respiratory Diseases in Foundrymen, 1971; Whither Occupational Medicine?, 1973; numerous papers on industrial and social medicine, in Lancet and Medical Journal of Malaya. *Recreations:* gardening, carpentry and bricklaying. *Address:* The Old Bakery, High Street, Elmdon, Saffron Walden, Essex CB11 4NL. *Club:* Athenæum.

LLOYD-EDWARDS, Captain Norman, RD 1971 and Bar 1980, RNR; Vice Lord-Lieutenant for South Glamorgan, since 1986; *b* 13 June 1933; *s* of Evan Stanley Edwards and Mary Leah Edwards. *Educ:* Monmouth School for Boys; Quaker's Yard Grammar School; Univ. of Bristol (LLB). Joined RNVR 1952, RN 1958–60; RNR 1960–86; CO S Wales Div., RNR, 1981–84; Naval ADC to the Queen, 1984. Partner, Cartwrights, Solicitors, Cardiff and Bristol, 1960–. Cardiff City Councillor, 1963–; Dep. Lord Mayor, 1973–74; Lord Mayor, 1985–86. Mem., Welsh Arts Council, 1983–. Chapter Clerk, Llandaff Cathedral, 1975–. Chm. of Wales, Duke of Edinburgh's Award, 1981–. DL S Glamorgan 1978. OStJ 1983. *Recreations:* music, gardening, table talk. *Address:* 169 Pencisely Road, Llandaff, Cardiff CF5 1DP. *T:* Cardiff 566107. *Clubs:* Army and Navy, Cardiff and County.

LLOYD-ELEY, John, QC 1970; a Recorder of the Crown Court, since 1972; *b* 23 April 1923; *s* of Edward John Eley; *m* 1946, Una Fraser Smith; two *s. Educ:* Xaverian Coll., Brighton; Exeter Coll., Oxford (MA). Served War, 1942–46, Lieut 50th Royal Tank Regt and 7th Hussars, N Africa, Sicily and Italy. Barrister, Middle Temple, 1951; South-Eastern Circuit; Mem., Bar Council, 1969. *Recreations:* farming, travel. *Address:* 1 Hare Court, Temple, EC4Y 7BE. *T:* 01–353 5324; Luxfords Farm, East Grinstead. *T:* East Grinstead 21583.

LLOYD GEORGE, family name of **Earl Lloyd George of Dwyfor.**

LLOYD-GEORGE, family name of **Viscount Tenby.**

LLOYD GEORGE OF DWYFOR, 3rd Earl, *cr* 1945; **Owen Lloyd George;** Viscount Gwynedd, 1945; *b* 28 April 1924; *s* of 2nd Earl Lloyd George of Dwyfor, and Roberta Ida Freeman, 5th *d* of Sir Robert McAlpine, 1st Bt; *S* father, 1968; *m* 1st, 1949, Ruth Margaret (marr. diss. 1982), *o d* of Richard Coit; two *s* one *d*; 2nd, 1982, Cecily Josephine, *d* of late Sir Alexander Gordon Cumming, 5th Bt, MC, and of Elizabeth Countess Cawdor, *widow* of 2nd Earl of Woolton and former wife of 3rd Baron Forres. *Educ:* Oundle. Welsh Guards, 1942–47. European War, 1944–45. Formerly Captain Welsh Guards. Director: Sedgwick Construction Services Ltd; Alfred McAlpine plc. An Underwriting Member of Lloyd's. Carried the Sword at Investiture of HRH the Prince of Wales, Caernarvon Castle, 1969. Mem., Historic Buildings Council for Wales, 1971. Mem. Court, Nat. Mus. of Wales, 1978. *Heir: s* Viscount Gwynedd, *qv. Recreation:* shooting. *Address:* The Hall, Freshford, Bath BA3 6EJ; 47 Burton Court, SW3. *Clubs:* White's City of London, Pratt's.

LLOYD-HUGHES, Sir Trevor Denby, Kt 1970; Chairman, Lloyd-Hughes Associates Ltd, International Consultants in Public Affairs; *b* 31 March 1922; *er s* of late Elwyn and Lucy Lloyd-Hughes, Bradford, Yorks; *m* 1st, 1950, Ethel Marguerite Durward (marr. diss., 1971), *o d* of late J. Ritchie, Dundee and Bradford; one *s* one *d*; 2nd, 1971, Marie-Jeanne, *d* of Marcel and late Helene Moreillon, Geneva; one *d* (and one adopted *d*—a Thai girl). *Educ:* Woodhouse Grove Sch., Yorks; Jesus Coll., Oxford (MA). Commissioned RA, 1941; served with 75th (Shropshire Yeomanry) Medium Regt, RA, in Western Desert, Sicily and Italy, 1941–45. Asst Inspector of Taxes, 1948; freelance journalist, 1949; joined staff of Liverpool Daily Post, 1949; Political Corresp., Liverpool Echo, 1950, Liverpool Daily Post, 1951. Press Secretary to the Prime Minister, 1964–69; Chief Information Adviser to Govt, 1969–70. Dir, Trinity International Holdings plc (formerly Liverpool Daily Post and Echo Ltd), 1978–. Member of Circle of Wine Writers, 1961, Chm., 1972–73. FBIM; FInstD. *Recreations:* yoga, playing the Spanish guitar, golf, walking, travel. *Address:* 33 Holly Grove, Peckham, SE15 5DF. *Clubs:* Reform, Belfry, Wellington.

LLOYD-JACOB, David Oliver, CBE 1984; Chairman and Chief Executive Officer, Levinson Steel Co., Pittsburgh, since 1983; *b* 30 March 1938; *s* of Sir George and Lady Lloyd-Jacob; *m* 1st, 1961, Clare Bartlett; two *d*; 2nd, 1982, Carolyn Howard. *Educ:* Westminster; Christ Church, Oxford. Pres., Azcon Corp., USA, 1974–79; Man. Dir, Consolidated Gold Fields plc, 1979–81; Chm., Amcon Group Inc., USA, 1979–82. Chm., Britain Salutes NY, 1981–83. *Recreations:* opera, theatre, restoring old houses. *Address:* 105 East 29th Street, New York, NY 10016, USA. *T:* (212) 684–4749. *Clubs:* Garrick; Leander (Henley-on-Thames); River (New York); Duquesne (Pittsburgh).

LLOYD JONES, Charles Beynon; *see* Jones, C. B. L.

LLOYD JONES, David Elwyn, MC 1946; Under-Secretary, Department of Education and Science, 1969–80; *b* 20 Oct. 1920; *s* of late Daniel and Blodwen Lloyd Jones; *m* 1955, Mrs E. W. Gallie (*widow* of Ian Gallie), *d* of late Prof. Robert Peers, CBE, MC and late Mrs F. D. G. Peers; no *c* (one step *s*). *Educ:* Ardwyn Grammar Sch., Aberystwyth; University College of Wales, Aberystwyth (BA Hons). War Service, 1941–46, Indian Army; with 1st Bn, The Assam Regt, in Burma Campaign (Major, MC). Entered Ministry of Education, 1947. Principal Private Sec. to Chancellor of the Duchy of Lancaster, 1960–61; Asst Sec., Min. (later Dept) of Educn and Science, 1961–69. Mem., councils of Royal Acad. of Dancing, 1980–, Froebel Inst., 1980–, and RCM, 1981–. Hon. Sec., Assam Regt Assoc., 1948–. *Address:* 5 Playfair Mansions, Queen's Club Gardens, W14. *T:* 01–385 0586. *Clubs:* Royal Commonwealth Society, MCC, Roehampton.

LLOYD-JONES, David Mathias; Artistic Director, Opera North, since 1978; *b* 19 Nov. 1934; *s* of late Sir Vincent Lloyd-Jones, and of Margaret Alwena, *d* of late G.H. Mathias; *m* 1964, Anne Carolyn Whitehead; two *s* one *d. Educ:* Westminster Sch.; Magdalen Coll., Oxford (BA). Repetiteur, Royal Opera House, Covent Garden, 1959–60; Chorus Master, New Opera Co., 1961–64; conductor: Bath Fest., 1966; City of London Fest., 1966; Wexford Fest., 1967–70; Scottish Opera, 1968; WNO, 1968; Royal Opera House, 1971; ENO (formerly Sadler's Wells Opera), 1969– (Asst Music Dir, 1972–78); also conductor of BBC broadcasts, TV operas (Eugene Onegin, The Flying Dutchman, Hansel and Gretel), and operas in Amsterdam and Paris; has appeared with most British symph. orchs; recordings with LPO. Hon. DMus Leeds, 1986. *Publications:* (trans.) Boris Godunov (vocal score), 1968; (trans.) Eugene Onegin (vocal score), 1971; Boris Godunov (critical edn of original full score), 1975; The Gondoliers (first ever pubn of a Gilbert and Sullivan full score), 1986; contrib. 5th edn Grove's Dictionary of Music and Musicians, 1980; contrib. Musik in Geschichte und Gegenwart, Music and Letters, and The Listener. *Recreations:* theatre, old shrub roses, French cuisine. *Address:* Opera North, Grand Theatre, Leeds LS1 6NZ. *T:* Leeds 886509; 94 Whitelands House, Cheltenham Terrace, SW3 4RA. *T:* 01–730 8695.

LLOYD-JONES, David Trevor, VRD 1958; **His Honour Judge Lloyd-Jones;** a Circuit Judge, since 1972; *b* 6 March 1917; *s* of Trevor and Anne Lloyd-Jones, Holywell, Flints; *m* 1st, 1942, Mary Violet (*d* 1980), *d* of Frederick Barnardo, MD, London; one *d*; 2nd, 1958, Anstice Elizabeth, MB, BChir (*d* 1981), *d* of William Henry Perkins, Whitchurch; one *s* one *d*; 3rd, 1984, Florence Mary, *d* of William Fairclough, MM, Wallasey. *Educ:* Holywell Grammar School. Banking, 1934–39 and 1946–50. Called to the Bar, Gray's Inn, 1951; practised Wales and Chester Circuit, 1952–71; Prosecuting Counsel to Post Office (Wales and Chester Circuit), 1961–66; Dep. Chm., Caerns QS, 1966–70, Chm, 1970–71; Legal Mem., Mental Health Appeal Tribunal (Wales Area), 1960–72; Dep. Chm., Agricultural Land Tribunal (Wales Area), 1968–72. Served War of 1939–45, RNVR and RNR, Atlantic, Mediterranean and Pacific; Lt-Comdr, RNR, retd. *Recreations:* golf, music. *Address:* 29 Curzon Park North, Chester. *T:* Chester 675144. *Clubs:* Army and Navy; Royal Dornoch Golf.

LLOYD-JONES, Prof. (Peter) Hugh (Jefferd); FBA 1966; Regius Professor of Greek in the University of Oxford and Student of Christ Church since 1960; *b* 21 Sept. 1922; *s* of Major W. Lloyd-Jones, DSO, and Norah Leila, *d* of F. H. Jefferd, Brent, Devon; *m* 1st, 1953, Frances Elisabeth Hedley (marr. diss. 1981); two *s* one *d*; 2nd, 1982, Mary Lefkowitz (Andrew W. Mellon Professor in the Humanities, Wellesley College, Mass), *d* of Harold and Mena Rosenthal, New York. *Educ:* Lycée Français du Royaume Uni, S. Kensington; Westminster Sch.; Christ Church, Oxford. Served War of 1939–45, 2nd Lieut, Intelligence Corps, India, 1942; Temp. Captain, 1944. 1st Cl. Classics (Mods), 1941; MA 1947; 1st Cl., LitHum, 1948; Chancellor's Prize for Latin Prose, 1947; Ireland and Craven Schol., 1947; Fellow of Jesus Coll., Cambridge, 1948–54; Asst Lecturer in Classics, University of Cambridge, 1950–52, Lecturer, 1952–54; Fellow and E. P. Warren Praelector in Classics, Corpus Christi Coll., Oxford, 1954–60; J. H. Gray Lecturer, University of Cambridge, 1961; Visiting Prof., Yale Univ., 1964–65, 1967–68; Sather Prof. of Classical Literature, Univ. of California at Berkeley, 1969–70; Alexander White Vis. Prof., Chicago, 1972; Vis. Prof., Harvard Univ., 1976–77. Fellow, Morse Coll., Yale Univ. Hon. Mem., Greek Humanistic Soc., 1968; Corresponding Member: Acad. of Athens, 1978; Rheinisch-Westfälische Akad. der Wissenschaften, 1983; Accademia di Archeologia Lettere e Belle Arti, Naples, 1984; Hon. Foreign Mem., Amer. Acad. of Arts and Scis, 1978. Hon. DHL Chicago, 1970; Hon. DPhil Tel Aviv, 1984. *Publications:* Appendix to Loeb Classical Library edn of Aeschylus, 1957; Menandri Dyscolus (Oxford Classical Text), 1960; Greek Studies in Modern Oxford, 1961; (trans.) Paul Maas, Greek Metre, 1962; (ed) The Greeks, 1962; Tacitus (in series The Great Historians), 1964; (trans.) Aeschylus: Agamemnon, The Libation-Bearers, and The Eumenides, 1970; The Justice of Zeus, 1971; (ed) Maurice Bowra, 1974; Females of the Species: Semonides of Amorgos on Women, 1975; (with

Marcelle Quinton) Myths of the Zodiac, 1978; (with Marcelle Quinton) Imaginary Animals, 1979; Blood for the Ghosts, 1982; Classical Survivals, 1982; (with P. J. Parsons) Supplementum Hellenisticum, 1983; contribs to periodicals. *Recreations:* cats, watching cricket. *Address:* Christ Church, Oxford. *T:* Oxford 248737; 15 West Riding, Wellesley, Mass 02181, USA. *T:* 617.237.2212.

LLOYD JONES, Richard Anthony, CB 1981; Permanent Secretary, Welsh Office, since 1985; *b* 1 Aug. 1933; *s* of Robert and Anne Lloyd Jones; *m* 1955, Patricia Avril Mary Richmond; two *d. Educ:* Long Dene Sch., Edenbridge; Nottingham High Sch.; Balliol Coll., Oxford (MA). Entered Admiralty, 1957; Asst Private Sec. to First Lord of the Admiralty, 1959–62; Private Sec. to Secretary of the Cabinet, 1969–70; Asst Sec., Min. of Defence, 1970–74; Under Sec., 1974–78, Dep. Sec. 1978–85, Welsh Office. *Recreations:* music, walking. *Address:* c/o Welsh Office, Cathays Park, Cardiff CF1 3NQ. *Club:* United Oxford & Cambridge University.

LLOYD-JONES, Robert; Director-General, Brick Development Association, since 1984; *b* 30 Jan. 1931; *s* of Robert and Edith Lloyd-Jones; *m* 1958, Morny Baggs-Thompson (marr. diss. 1977); two *s* one *d. Educ:* Wrekin Coll.; Queens' Coll., Univ. of Cambridge (MA Hons); Harvard Business School. Short Service Commission, RN, 1956; Shell International, 1959; BTR Industries Ltd, 1962; International Wool Secretariat, 1964; Schachenmayr, Germany, 1971; British Textile Employers Association, 1977–81; Dir-Gen., Retail Consortium, 1981–83. Governor, Coll. for Distributive Trades, 1982–84; Founder Chm., Nat. Retail Trng Council, 1982–84. FRSA. *Recreations:* golf, squash, tennis, music, chess, art, and the general pursuit of pleasure. *Address:* Newell Cottage, Winkfield, Windsor, Berks SL4 4SE. *T:* (office) Winkfield Row 885651. *Clubs:* Lansdowne, Institute of Directors; Royal Birkdale Golf, Rye Golf, Formby Golf, Liphook Golf; Royal Ascot Squash, Royal Ascot Tennis.

LLOYD-MOSTYN, family name of **Baron Mostyn.**

LLOYD OWEN, Maj.-Gen. David Lanyon, CB 1971; DSO 1945; OBE 1954; MC 1942; Chairman, British Association for Shooting and Conservation, 1979–85; *b* 10 Oct. 1917; *s* of late Capt. Reginald Charles Lloyd Owen, OBE, RN; *m* 1947, Ursula Evelyn, *d* of late Evelyn Hugh Barclay and Hon. Mrs Barclay, MBE; three *s. Educ:* Winchester; RMC, Sandhurst. 2nd Lieut, The Queen's Royal Regt, 1938. Comdr, Long Range Desert Group, 1943–45. Military Asst to High Commissioner in Malaya, 1952–53; Comdg 1st Queen's, 1957–59; Comdr 24 Infantry Bde Group, 1962–64; GOC Cyprus District, 1966–68; GOC Near East Land Forces, 1968–69. Pres., Regular Commns Bd, 1969–72, retd. Kt of Cross of Merit, SMO Malta, 1946. *Publications:* The Desert My Dwelling Place, 1957; Providence Their Guide, 1980. *Address:* Violet Bank, Swainsthorpe, Norwich NR14 8PR. *T:* Swainsthorpe 470468. *Club:* Naval and Military.

LLOYD WEBBER, Andrew; composer; *b* 22 March 1948; *s* of late William Southcombe Lloyd Webber, CBE, DMus, FRCM, FRCO, and of Jean Hermione Johnstone; *m* 1st, 1971, Sarah Jane Tudor (née Hugill) (marr. diss. 1983); one *s* one *d;* 2nd, 1984, Sarah Brightman. *Educ:* Westminster Sch. Composer: (with lyrics by Timothy Rice): Joseph and the Amazing Technicolour Dreamcoat, 1968 (rev. 1973); Jesus Christ Superstar, 1970; Evita, 1976 (stage version, 1978); (with lyrics by Alan Ayckbourn) Jeeves, 1975; (with lyrics by Don Black) Tell Me on a Sunday, 1980; Cats, 1981 (based on poems by T. S. Eliot); (with lyrics by Don Black) Song and Dance, 1982; (with lyrics by Richard Stilgoe) Starlight Express, 1984 (with lyrics by Richard Stilgoe and Charles Hart); The Phantom of the Opera, 1986. Producer: Daisy Pulls It Off, 1983; The Hired Man, 1984; Lend Me a Tenor, 1986. Film scores: Gumshoe, 1971; The Odessa File, 1974. Composed "Variations" (based on A minor Caprice No 24 by Paganini), 1977; Requiem Mass, 1985. *Publications:* (with Timothy Rice) Evita, 1978; (with Timothy Rice) Joseph and the Amazing Technicolour Dreamcoat, 1982. *Recreation:* architecture. *Address:* (office) 20 Greek Street, W1V 5LF.
See also J. Lloyd Webber.

LLOYD WEBBER, Julian; 'cellist; *b* 14 April 1951; *s* of late William Southcombe Lloyd Webber, CBE, DMus, FRCM, FRCO, and of Jean Hermione Johnstone; *m* 1974, Celia Mary Ballantyne. *Educ:* University College Sch., London; Royal College of Music. ARCM. Studied 'cello with: Douglas Cameron, 1965–68; Pierre Fournier, Geneva, 1972. Début, Queen Elizabeth Hall, 1972; USA début, Lincoln Center, NY, 1980. Has performed with all major British orchestras; toured: USA, 1980, 1984, 1985, 1986; Germany, Holland, Africa, Bulgaria, S America, Spain, Belgium, France, Scandinavia, Portugal, Denmark, Australasia, Singapore, Japan. Has made first recordings of works by Benjamin Britten, Frank Bridge, Delius, Rodrigo, Holst, Vaughan Williams, Haydn, Sullivan; recorded Elgar Cello Concerto (cond. Menuhin), 1985. Awarded gold and silver discs for Variations, 1978, silver disc for Oasis, 1984. *Publications:* Travels with My Cello, 1984; Song of the Birds, 1985; edited: series, The Romantic 'Cello, 1978, The Classical 'Cello, 1980, The French 'Cello, 1981; Frank Bridge 'Cello Music, 1981; Young Cellist's Repertoire, Books 1, 2, 3, 1984; Holst, Invocation, 1984; Vaughan Williams, Fantasia on Sussex Folk Tunes, 1984; Recital Repertoire for Cellists, 1987; contribs to music jls and national Press in UK, US, Canada and Australia. *Recreations:* topography (especially British), keeping turtles, beer, Orient FC. *Address:* Kaye Artists Management, Kingsmead House, 250 King's Road, SW3 6NR. *T:* 01–352 4494.
See also A. Lloyd Webber.

LO, Kenneth Hsiao Chien; author, Chinese food critic and consultant; *b* 12 Sept. 1913; *s* of Lo Tsung Hsien and Wei Ying; *m* 1954, Anne Phillipe Brown; two *s* two *d. Educ:* Yenching Univ., Peking (BA); Cambridge Univ. (MA). Student-Consul for China, Liverpool, 1942–46; Vice-Consul for China, Manchester, 1946–49. Man. Director, Cathay Arts Ltd (Chinese Fine Art Publishers), 1951–66; Founder Director: Memories of China restaurant, 1980; Ken Lo's Kitchen, chinese cookery sch., 1980. Chm., Chinese Gourmet Club, London, 1975–. *Publications include:* Chinese Food, 1972; Peking Cooking, 1973; Chinese Vegetarian Cooking, 1974; Encyclopedia of Chinese Cookery, 1975; Quick and Easy Chinese Cooking, 1973; Cheap Chow, 1977; Love of Chinese Cooking, 1977; Chinese Provincial Cooking, 1979; Chinese Eating and Cooking for Health, 1979; Wok Cookbook, 1981; Chinese Regional Cooking, 1981. *Recreation:* tennis (Davis cup for China, 1946; Veteran Doubles Champion of Britain, 1976, 1979, 1981, 1982, 1984; Single for UK in Britannia Cup and Crawford Cup, 1981, 1983, 1984, 1985, 1986 (World Super-Veteran Championships). *Address:* 60 Sussex Street, SW1. *Clubs:* Hurlingham, Queen's.

LOACH, Kenneth; television and film director; *b* 17 June 1936. *Educ:* King Edward VI School, Nuneaton; St Peter's Hall, Oxford. BBC Trainee, Drama Dept, 1963. Television: Diary of a Young Man, 1964; 3 Clear Sundays, 1965; The End of Arthur's Marriage, 1965; Up The Junction, 1965; Coming Out Party, 1965; Cathy Come Home, 1966; In Two Minds, 1966; The Golden Vision, 1969; The Big Flame, 1969; After A Lifetime, 1971; The Rank and File, 1972; Days of Hope, 1975; The Price of Coal, 1977; The Gamekeeper, 1979; Auditions, 1980; A Question of Leadership, 1981; Questions of Leadership, 1983 (banned from TV); The Red and the Blue, 1983; Which Side Are You On, 1985. Films: Poor Cow, 1968; Kes, 1970; In Black and White, 1970; Family Life,

1972; Black Jack, 1979; Looks and Smiles, 1981; Fatherland, 1986. *Address:* c/o Central Independent Television, 46 Charlotte Street, W1.

LOADES, David Henry, FIA; Directing Actuary (Under Secretary), Government Actuary's Department, since 1983; *b* 16 Oct. 1937; *s* of John Henry Loades and Evelyn Clara Ralph; *m* 1962, Jennifer Glenys Stevens; one *s* two *d. Educ:* Beckenham and Penge County Grammar Sch. for Boys. FIA 1961. Govt Actuary's Dept, 1956–. Medal of Merit for services to the Scout Assoc., 1986. *Publications:* papers in actuarial jls. *Recreations:* painting, visiting art galleries, supporting the Institute of Actuaries. *Address:* 35 Bushey Way, Beckenham, Kent BR3 2TA. *T:* 01–658 0744.

LOANE, Most Rev. Marcus Lawrence, KBE 1976; DD; *b* 14 Oct. 1911; *s* of K. O. A. Loane; *m* 1937, Patricia Evelyn Jane Simpson Knox; two *s* two *d. Educ:* The King's School, Parramatta, NSW; Sydney University (MA). Moore Theological College, 1932–33; Australian College of Theology (ThL, 1st Class, 1933; Fellow, 1955). Ordained Deacon, 1935, Priest, 1936; Resident Tutor and Chaplain, Moore Theological College, 1935–38; Vice-Principal, 1939–53; Principal, 1954–59. Chaplain AIF, 1942–44. Canon, St Andrew's Cathedral, 1949–58; Bishop-Coadjutor, diocese of Sydney, 1958–66; Archbishop of Sydney and Metropolitan of Province of NSW, 1966–82; Primate of Australia, 1978–82. Hon. DD Wycliffe College, Toronto, 1958. *Publications:* Oxford and the Evangelical Succession, 1950; Cambridge and the Evangelical Succession, 1952; Masters of the English Reformation, 1955; Life of Archbishop Mowll, 1960; Makers of Religious Freedom, 1961; Pioneers of the Reformation in England, 1964; Makers of Our Heritage, 1966; The Hope of Glory, 1968; This Surpassing Excellence, 1969; They Were Pilgrims, 1970; They Overcame, 1971; By Faith We Stand, 1971; The King is Here, 1973; This is My Son, 1977; The God Who Acts, 1978. *Address:* 18 Harrington Avenue, Warrawee, NSW 2074, Australia.

LOBB, Howard Leslie Vicars, CBE 1952; FRIBA, AIStructE, FRSA; architect; *b* 9 March 1909; *e s* of late Hedley Vicars Lobb and Mary Blanche (née Luscombe); *m* 1949, Charmian Isobel (née Reilly); three *s. Educ:* privately; Regent Street Polytechnic School of Architecture. Senior Partner, Howard Lobb Partnership, 1950–74. During War of 1939–45, Architect to various ministries: subseq. built numerous schools for County Authorities; HQ of City and Guilds of London Inst., W1; British Pavilion Brussels International Exhibition, 1958; Cons. Architect for Hunterston Nuclear Power Station, Ayrshire; Dungeness Nuclear Power Station; Newcastle Racecourse; Newmarket Rowley Mile, for Jockey Club; Car park, Savile Row, for City of Westminster; HQ for British Council, SW1; Calgary Exhbn and Stampede, Upper Alberta, Canada. Chairman Architectural Council, Festival of Britain, and later Controller (Constr.) South Bank Exhibition. Member RIBA Council and Executive, 1953–56; Life Vice-Pres. (formerly Chm.), London Group of Building Centres; Chm., Architects' Registr. Council, UK, 1957–60; Vice-Pres., Architects' Benevolent Society, 1980– (Hon. Sec., 1953–80). Freeman of City of London; Master, Worshipful Co. of Masons, 1974–75. Chm., Solent Protection Soc. *Publications:* contrib. various Arch. Journals, Reviews, etc. *Recreations:* sailing, gardening, colour photography, model railways. *Address:* Shallows Cottage, Pilley Hill, Pilley, near Lymington, Hants. *T:* Lymington 77595. *Clubs:* Arts; Royal Corinthian Yacht (Vice-Cdre 1960–63); Island Sailing (Cowes); Tamesis (Teddington) (Cdre, 1954–57); Royal Lymington Yacht.

LOBO, Hon. Sir Rogerio Hyndman, (Hon. Sir Roger Lobo), Kt 1985; CBE 1978 (OBE 1972); JP; Chairman, P. J. Lobo & Co. Ltd, Hong Kong, since 1950; Senior Unofficial Member, Legislative Council, Hong Kong, since 1972; Unofficial Member, Executive Council, since 1978; *b* 15 Sept. 1923; *s* of Dr P. J. Lobo and Branca Helena (née Hyndman); *m* 1947, Margaret Mary (née Choa); five *s* five *d. Educ:* Escola Central, Macao; Seminario de S Jose, Macao; Liceu Nacional Infante Dom Henrique, Macao; La Salle Coll., Hong Kong. Director: Associated Liquor Distributors, 1975–; Danish Fancy Food Group (HK), 1982–; Harper Gilfillan (HK), 1980–; HK Macao Hydrofoil Co., 1970–; HK & Shanghai Hotels, 1985–; dir of 14 other cos. Hon. LLD Univ. of Hong Kong, 1982. JP Hong Kong, 1963. Silver Jubilee Medal, 1977; Civil Aid Services Long Service Medal, 1970; Civil Defence Long Service Clasp, 1982. Comdr, Order of St Gregory the Great, The Vatican, 1969. *Recreation:* golf. *Address:* Woodland Heights, E1, 2 Wongneichong Gap Road, Hong Kong. *T:* 5–740779; (business) 33/F New World Tower, 16–18 Queen's Road, C., Hong Kong. *T:* 5–269418/5–218302. *Clubs:* Les Ambassadeurs; Hong Kong, Rotary, Royal Hong Kong Jockey, Royal Hong Kong Golf, Hong Kong Country, Shek O Country (Hong Kong).

LOCH, family name of **Baron Loch.**

LOCH, 4th Baron *cr* 1895, of Drylaw; **Spencer Douglas Loch,** MC 1945; *b* 12 Aug. 1920; *s* of Maj.-Gen. 2nd Baron Loch, CB, CMG, DSO, MVO, and Lady Margaret Compton (*d* 1970), *o d* of 5th Marquess of Northampton, KG; *S* brother, 1982; *m* 1st, 1948, Hon. Rachel (*d* 1976), *yr d* of Gp Captain H. L. Cooper, AFC, and Baroness Lucas and Dingwall; one *d* (two *s* decd); 2nd, 1979, Davina Julia Boughey, *d* of late Fitzherbert Wright and of Hon. Mrs Wright. *Educ:* Wellington College; Trinity College, Cambridge. Served as Major, Grenadier Guards, 1940–46. Called to the Bar, Lincoln's Inn, 1948. *Heir:* none. *Address:* Bratton House, Westbury, Wilts; Lochluichart, Ross-shire. *Clubs:* Cavalry and Guards, Beefsteak.

LOCK, Air Vice-Marshal Basil Goodhand, CB 1978; CBE 1969; AFC 1954; Security Adviser, Management and Personnel Office (formerly Civil Service Department), since 1979; *b* 25 June 1923; *s* of J. S. Lock; *m* 1944, Mona Rita; one *s.* Entered RAF from Durham Univ. Air Sqdn; commnd RAF, 1943; various operational sqdns, 1944–47; Exchange Sqdn posts, USA, 1947–48; Flying Instructor, RAF Coll., Cranwell, 1950–51; OC, HC Exam. Unit, 1951–54; HQ MEAF, 1954–57; Ops (O), Air Min., 1958–61; OC Flying, RAF Leeming, 1961–63; Plans (Cento), 1964–66; OC, RAF West Raynham, 1967–69; SDS (Air), JSSC, 1969–71; Dir of Ops (AS), MoD, 1971–73; Dir of Personal Services, MoD, 1974–75; Air Vice-Marshal 1975; Air Officer Scotland, 1975–77; Dir Gen. of Security (RAF), 1977–79. CBIM; FRGS. *Recreations:* golf, gardening, music, motoring.

LOCK, (Cecil) Max, FRIBA (Dist. TP), AADip, FRTPI; Head of Max Lock Group; *b* 29 June 1909; *s* of Cecil William Best Lock and Vivian Cecil Hassell. *Educ:* Berkhamsted Sch. Public Schools' Entrance Scholarship to Architectural Assoc., London, 1926. Entered private practice, 1933; (firm established as Max Lock 1933, Max Lock Group 1944, Max Lock & Associates 1950, Max Lock & Partners 1954); retired 1972, remaining Consultant to partnership (now Max Lock, Easton, Perlston & King); formed Max Lock Group of Planning and Development Consultants, in partnership with Michael Theis, 1972; currently Max Lock Group Nigeria, as consultants to Govt of NE State Nigeria, engaged on surveys and master plans for Maiduguri, Nguru, Potiskum, Bauchi, Gombe, Yola-Jimeta and Mubi; retired 1976. Member Watford Borough Council, 1936–40; on staff of AA School of Architecture, 1937–39; Head of Hull School of Architecture, 1939; Leverhulme Research Schol. (carried out a Civic Diagnosis of Hull). Surveys and plans by Max Lock Group for: Middlesbrough, 1946; The Hartlepools, 1948; Portsmouth District, 1949; Bedford, 1951; by Max Lock and Partners, Surveys and Plans for Amman, Aqaba

(Jordan), 1954–55; Town Plans for development of Iraq at Um Qasr, Margil and Basrah, 1954–56; New Towns at El Beida, Libya, 1956, and Sheikh Othman, Aden, 1960. Survey and plan for the Capital City and Territory of Kaduna for Government of Northern Nigeria, 1965–66. British Town Centre redevelopment plans, 1957–71, include: Sevenoaks; Thetford; Sutton Coldfield; Salisbury; Brentford; redevelopment of new central housing communities at Oldham; development of Woodley Airfield, Reading; a plan for Central Area of Beverley, Yorks. Visiting Professor: Dept of City Planning, Harvard Univ., 1957; University of Rio de Janeiro, 1960, 1968; Guest Chairman, 5th Australian National Planning Congress, 1960. Member Council, TPI, 1946–50 and 1961–63. Freeman of the City of London, 1978. *Publications:* The Middlesbrough Survey and Plan, 1946; The Hartlepools Survey and Plan, 1948; The Portsmouth and District Survey and Plan, 1949; Bedford by the River, 1952; The New Basrah, 1956; Kaduna, 1917–1967–2017: A Survey and Plan of the Capital Territory for the Government of Northern Nigeria, 1967; contribs to RIBA Journal, TPI Journal, Town Planning Review, etc. *Recreations:* music, pianist. *Address:* 7 Victoria Square, SW1. *T:* 01–834 7071; Addicroft Mill, Plushabridge, Liskeard, Cornwall. *T:* Liskeard 62510. *Club:* Reform.

LOCK, Lt-Comdr Sir Duncan; *see* Lock, Lt-Comdr Sir J. D.

LOCK, (George) David; Director, New Business Ventures, Frizzell Consumer Services Ltd, since 1986; *b* 24 Sept. 1929; *s* of George Wilfred Lock and Phyllis Nita (*née* Hollingworth); *m* 1965, Ann Elizabeth Biggs; four *s* one *d. Educ:* Haileybury and ISC; Queens' Coll., Cambridge (MA). British Tabulating Machine Co. Ltd (now ICL), 1954–59; Save & Prosper Group Ltd, 1959–69; American Express, 1969–74; Private Patients Plan Ltd, 1974–85 (Man. Dir, 1975–85). Director: Priplan Investments Ltd, 1979–85; Priplan Services Ltd, 1979–85; PPP Medical Centre Ltd (incorp. Cavendish Medical Centre), 1981–85. Director: Home Concern for the Elderly, 1985–; The Hosp. Management Trust, 1985–; Bd of Management, St Anthony's Hosp., Cheam. Sec., Friends of Children of Great Ormond Street, 1986. Trustee, Eynsham Trust, 1975–83; Gov., PPP Medical Trust Ltd (Dir, 1983–85). Member: Nuffield Nursing Homes Trust, 1979–; Exec. Cttee, Assoc. of Independent Hosps, 1981–. Mem., RSocMed., 1979–. Freeman, Barbers' Co., 1982–. *Recreations:* bridge, music, family activities, entertaining. *Address:* Buckhurst Place, Horsted Keynes, Sussex RH17 7AH. *T:* Danehill 790599.

LOCK, Graham; *see* Lock, T. G.

LOCK, John Arthur, QPM 1975; Deputy Assistant Commissioner, Metropolitan Police, and National Co-ordinator, Regional Crime Squads of England and Wales, 1976–79; *b* 20 Oct. 1922; *s* of Sidney George Lock and Minnie Louise Lock; *m* 1950, Patricia Joyce Lambert; two *d. Educ:* George Palmer Central School, Reading. Royal Air Force, 1941–46; Wireless Operator/Air Gunner; Flying Officer. Joined Metropolitan Police, 1946. *Recreations:* Association football (Vice-Chm., Met. Police FC), tennis, sailing. *Club:* Royal Air Force.

LOCK, Lt-Comdr Sir (John) Duncan, Kt 1978; RN; Chairman, Association of District Councils of England and Wales, 1974–79; *b* 5 Feb. 1918; *s* of Brig. Gen. F. R. E. Lock, DSO, and Mary Elizabeth Lock; *m* 1947, Alice Aileen Smith (*d* 1982); three *d. Educ:* Royal Naval Coll., Dartmouth. Served as regular officer in Royal Navy (retiring at his own request), 1931–58: specialised in navigation and navigated Battleships HMS King George V and Howe, the Cruiser Superb, destroyers and minesweepers. Served War of 1939–45: took part in Battle of Atlantic, Norwegian and N African campaigns, Pacific War and Normandy and Anzio landings. Farmed family estate in Somerset, 1958–61. Admty Compass Observatory as specialist in magnetic compasses, 1962–83. Member of Lloyd's. Eton RDC, 1967–74; Chairman: Bucks Br., RDC Assoc., 1969–74; S Bucks Dist Council, 1985– (Mem., 1973–); Assoc. of Dist Councils of England and Wales Council and Policy Cttee, 1974–79 (Chm. Bucks Br., 1974–); Chm., Rep. Body for England, 1977–; Mem., Adv. Cttee on Local Govt Audit, 1979–82; British Rep., Council of Local and Reg. Authorities of Europe, 1979–; Chm., Local Authorities Management Services and Computer Cttee, 1981–. Chm., Beaconsfield Constituency Conservative Assoc., 1972–75. *Recreations:* gardening, shooting, bee-keeping. *Address:* Fen Court, Oval Way, Gerrards Cross, Bucks SL9 8QD. *T:* Gerrards Cross 882467.

LOCK, Max; *see* Lock, C. M.

LOCK, Stephen Penford, FRCP; MA; Editor, British Medical Journal, since 1975; Governor, Brendoncare Foundation, since 1984; *b* 8 April 1929; *er s* of Wallace Henry Lock, Romford, Essex; *m* 1955, Shirley Gillian Walker, *d* of E. W. Walker, Bridlington, Yorks; one *s* one *d. Educ:* City of London Sch.; Queens' Coll., Cambridge; St Bartholomew's Hosp., London. MA 1953; MB 1954; MRCP 1963; FRCP 1974. Ho. Phys., Bart's, Brompton, and Central Middlesex Hosps, and Med. Officer, RAF Bomber Comd, 1954–57; Jun. Registrar, London Hosp., London, 1958; Jun. Asst Editor, The Lancet, 1959; Registrar in Pathology, Hosp. for Sick Children, Gt Ormond St., London, 1959–61, and at Bart's, 1961–62; Sen. Registrar in Pathology, Lewisham Hosp., London, 1962–64; Asst Editor, British Med. Jl, 1964–69, Sen. Asst Editor, 1969–74, Dep. Editor, 1974–75. Med. Corresp., BBC Overseas Service, 1966–74. Chm., Internat. Gp on Medical Jl Style, 1978. Organiser and/or participant in 65 Postgrad. Courses in Med. Writing in Britain, Finland, Iraq, Iran, Eire, Canada, Australia, NZ, USA, Kuwait, Bahrein, India, Singapore, 1971–; organiser BMJ/ELSE conference: Winchester, 1977; Bath, 1978; Salisbury, 1979; Oxford, 1980; York, 1982; Eastbourne, 1983; Stratford on Avon, 1985; Tunbridge Wells, 1986; organiser European Assoc. of Science Editors/Council of Biology Editors conf., Cambridge, 1984. Member: Council, ASH, 1975– (Chm., policy cttee, 1978); Council, Res. Defence Soc., 1976; Med. Adv. Cttee, British Council, 1976–; Publications Cttee, King's Fund, 1977; Council, European Life Scis Editors, 1977– (Vice-Pres., 1979–82); Council, Med. Insurance Agency, 1978; RCP cttee on dietary fibre, 1978, on smoking, 1982, on relations with the pharmaceutical industry, 1984; Med. Inf. Review Panel, 1979–; Managing Cttee, Bureau of Hygiene and Tropical Diseases, 1981–. Vice-Pres., Internat. Union of the Medical Press, 1976; Pres., European Assoc. of Sci. Editors, 1982–. Vis. Prof. in Medicine, McGill Univ., 1978; Visitor, Acad. Dept of Medicine, Monash Univ., 1982; Foundn Vis. Prof. in Medicine, RCSI, 1986; Lectures: Wade, Keele Univ., 1980; Morgan, Royal Cornwall Hosp., 1984; Rock Carling, Nuffield Provincial Hosps Trust, 1985; Maurice Block, Glasgow Univ., 1986. Trustee, British Med. Students Trust, 1979–. Mem., 14 Editorial Bds of BMA jls. Hon. MSc Manchester, 1985. Donders Medal, Ned. Tijdsch. Geneesk, 1981; Internat. Medal, Finnish Med. Soc. Duodecim, 1981. Officer, first cl., White Rose of Finland, 1982. *Publications:* An Introduction to Clinical Pathology, 1965; Health Centres and Group Practices, 1966; The Enemies of Man, 1968; Better Medical Writing, 1970; Family Health Guide, 1972; Medical Risks of Life, 1976; Thorne's Better Medical Writing, 2nd edn 1977; (ed) Adverse Drug Reactions, 1977; (ed) Remembering Henry, 1977; A Difficult Balance: editorial peer review in medicine, 1985; chapter on jls and journalism in Oxford Companion to Medicine, 1983; articles on haematology and medical writing in British, American, Swiss and Finnish jls. *Recreations:* as much opera as possible (before Stockhausen), hill walking, gardening. *Address:* 115 Dulwich Village, SE21 7BJ. *T:* 01–693 6317. *Club:* Athenæum.

LOCK, (Thomas) Graham; Chief Executive, Amalgamated Metal Corporation plc, since 1983; *b* 19 Oct. 1931; *s* of Robert Henry Lock and Morfydd Lock (*née* Thomas); *m* 1954, Janice Olive Baker Lock (*née* Jones); two *d. Educ:* Whitchurch Grammar School; University College of South Wales and Monmouthshire (BSc Metall); College of Advanced Technology, Aston; Harvard Business School. CEng, FIM, CBIM. Instructor Lieut, RN, 1953–56; Lucas Industries and Lucas Electrical, 1956–61; Dir, Girling Bremsen GmbH, 1961–66; Gen. Man. and Overseas Ops Dir, Girling Ltd, 1966–73; Gen. Man. and Dir, Lucas Service Overseas Ltd, 1973–79; Man. Dir, Industrial Div., Amalgamated Metal Corp., 1979–83; non-exec. Director: Marshall's Universal plc, 1983–; Evode Gp plc, 1985–. *Recreations:* sailing, music, skiing. *Address:* The Cottage, Fulmer Way, Gerrards Cross, Bucks SL9 8AJ. *T:* Gerrards Cross 883200. *Clubs:* Royal Naval Sailing Association (Portsmouth), Royal Southern Yacht (Hamble).

LOCKE, Arthur D'Arcy, (Bobby Locke); professional golfer; Playing Professional at Observatory Golf Club, Johannesburg; *b* Germiston, Transvaal, 20 Nov. 1917; *s* of Charles James Locke; *m* 1943; one *d*; *m* 1958, Mary Fenten, USA. *Educ:* Benoni High Sch. Won Open and Amateur South African Championships, 1935; won Irish, Dutch and New Zealand Open Championships, 1938; French Open Championship, 1952–53; British Open Championship, 1949, 1950, 1952, 1957; Canadian Open, 1947; Mexican Open, 1952; Egyptian Open, 1954; German Open, 1954; Swiss Open, 1954; Australian Open, 1955; Member Professional Golfers' Association (London). Served War of 1939–45, Middle East and Italy as Pilot, South African Air Force. *Publication:* Bobby Locke on Golf, 1953.

LOCKE, Bobby; *see* Locke, A. D'A.

LOCKE, John Howard, CB 1984; Director, Health and Safety Executive, 1975–83; *b* 26 Dec. 1923; *s* of Percy Locke and Josephine Locke (*née* Marshfield); *m* 1948, Eirene Sylvia Sykes; two *d. Educ:* Hymers Coll., Hull; Queen's Coll., Oxford. Ministry of Agriculture, Fisheries and Food, 1945–65; Under-Secretary: Cabinet Office, 1965–66; MoT, 1966–68; Dept of Employment and Productivity, 1968–71; Dep. Sec., Dept of Employment, 1971–74. *Address:* 4 Old Palace Terrace, The Green, Richmond-on-Thames, Surrey. *T:* 01–940 1830; Old Box Trees, East Preston, Sussex.

LOCKETT, Reginald; His Honour Judge Lockett; a Circuit Judge, since 1981; *b* 24 June 1933; *s* of George Alfred Lockett and Emma (*née* Singleton); *m* 1959, Edna (*née* Lowe); one *s* one *d. Educ:* Ashton-in-Makerfield Grammar Sch.; Manchester Univ.; London Univ. (LLB 1954). Solicitor, 1955. Asst Coroner for Wigan, 1963; Dist Registrar and County Court Registrar, Manchester, 1970–81; a Recorder of the Crown Court, 1978–81. Pres., Manchester Law Students' Soc., 1975–77. Vice Pres., The Boys' Bde, 1978– (Dist Pres., NW Dist, 1973–). Reader, Anglican Church, 1970–. Editor, Butterworths Family Law Service, 1983–. *Recreations:* music, photography. *Address:* 7 Blandford Rise, Lostock, Bolton BL6 4JH. *T:* Bolton 68591.

LOCKHART; *see* Bruce Lockhart.

LOCKHART, Brian Alexander; Sheriff in Glasgow and Strathkelvin, since 1981 (in North Strathclyde, 1979–81); *b* 1 Oct. 1942; *s* of John Arthur Hay Lockhart and Norah Lockhart; *m* 1967, Christine Ross Clark; two *s* two *d. Educ:* Glasgow Academy; Glasgow Univ. (BL). Qualified as solicitor, 1964; Partner in Robertson Chalmers & Auld, Solicitors, Glasgow, 1966–79. *Recreations:* fishing, golf, family. *Address:* 18 Hamilton Avenue, Glasgow G41 4JF. *T:* 041–427 1921.

LOCKHART, Frank Roper; a Recorder, since 1985; *b* 8 Dec. 1931; *s* of Clement and Betsy Lockhart; *m* 1958, Brenda Harriett Johnson; one *s* one *d. Educ:* King Edward VI Sch., Retford; Doncaster Grammar Sch.; Univ. of Leeds (LLB Hons). Asst Town Clerk, Southend-on-Sea, 1960–65; Partner, Jefferies, Solicitors, 1965–85. Chairman: Industrial Tribunal, 1983–85; Social Security Tribunal, 1970–85. *Recreations:* golf, tennis, squash. *Address:* 33 Lynton Road, Thorpe Bay, Essex SS1 3BE. *T:* Southend-on-Sea 332311. *Clubs:* Thorpe Hall Golf, Hazards Golf.

LOCKHART, Prof. Robert Douglas, MD, ChM; LLD; FSAScot, FRSE; Regius Professor of Anatomy, University of Aberdeen, 1938–65, now Emeritus Professor; concurrently Curator, Anthropological Museum (Hon. Curator, 1939–79, Consultant 1979–80; room in Museum now named The Lockhart Room by the University); *b* 7 Jan. 1894; *s* of William Lockhart and Elizabeth Bogie. *Educ:* Robert Gordon's Coll., Aberdeen; University, Aberdeen (MB, ChB 1918). Ho. Surg. Aberdeen Royal Infirmary; Surgeon-Probationer, RNVR, 1916; Surgeon-Lt, RN 1918; Lecturer in Anatomy, Aberdeen Univ., 1919; Prof. of Anat., Birmingham Univ. 1931; Dean of Faculty of Medicine, Aberdeen, 1959–62. Past Pres., Anatomical Soc. of Great Britain and Ireland. Hon. LLD Aberdeen, 1965. *Publications:* Chapter, Ways of Living, in Man and Nature, 1926; Living Anatomy, Photographic Atlas of Muscles in Action and Surface Contours, 1948, 7th edn 1974; Myology Section in Cunningham's Anatomy, 1964; Anatomy of the Human Body, 1969; contributor to Kodak Med. Film Library, 1933; Structure and Function of Muscle, 1960 (2nd rev. edn, vol. 1, ed Bourne, 1972). *Recreations:* roses and rhododendrons. *Address:* 25 Rubislaw Den North, Aberdeen AB2 4AL. *T:* Aberdeen 37833.

LOCKHART, Sir Simon John Edward Francis S.; *see* Sinclair-Lockhart.

LOCKHART, Stephen Alexander, CMG 1960; OBE 1949; HM Diplomatic Service, retired; *b* 19 March 1905; *o s* of late Captain Murray Lockhart, RN, Milton Lockhart, and of Leonora Rynd; *m* 1944, Angela Watson; two *s* two *d. Educ:* Harrow; Jesus Coll., Cambridge. Served Lisbon, 1940–43; Ministry of Information, 1943; Press Attaché, Lisbon, 1944, Brussels, 1945; First Sec. (Information), Brussels, 1946–51; Foreign Office, 1951; First Sec., Buenos Aires, 1952–55; UK Rep., Trieste, 1955–57; HM Consul-Gen., Leopoldville, and in French Equatorial Africa, 1957–60; HM Consul-Gen., Zürich, 1960–62; HM Ambassador to Dominican Republic, 1962–65; re-employed in FCO, 1965–70; Hon. Consul, Oporto, 1970–75. *Address:* 10 Shelley Court, Tite Street, SW3; 4 Clarence Lodge, Englefield Green, Egham TW20 0NO.

LOCKHART-MUMMERY, Christopher John; QC 1986; *b* 7 Aug. 1947; *s* of Sir Hugh Lockhart-Mummery, *qv*; *m* 1971, Elizabeth Rosamund Elles; one *s* two *d. Educ:* Stowe; Trinity College, Cambridge (BA). Called to the Bar, Inner Temple, 1971, *Publication:* Specialist Editor, Hill and Redman's Law of Landlord and Tenant, 17th edn, 1982. *Recreations:* fishing, listening to music, opera, gardening. *Address:* 52 Argyll Road, W8 7BS. *T:* 01–937 1289.

LOCKHART-MUMMERY, Sir Hugh (Evelyn), KCVO 1981; MD, MChir; FRCS; Serjeant-Surgeon to the Queen, 1975–83 (Surgeon to HM Household, 1969–75, to the Queen, 1974–75); Consultant Surgeon: King Edward VII's Hospital for Officers since 1968; RAF, 1975–84; Consulting Surgeon: St Mark's Hospital; St Thomas' Hospital; *b* 28 April 1918; *s* of John Percy Lockhart-Mummery, FRCS; *m* 1st, 1946, Elizabeth Jean Crerar (*d* 1981), *d* of Sir James Crerar, KCSI, CIE; one *s*; 2nd, 1985, Jean Elizabeth Hoare (*née* Foote). *Educ:* Stowe Sch.; Trinity Coll., Cambridge; Westminster Hosp. Med. Sch. MB, BCh 1942; FRCS 1943; MChir 1950; MD 1956. Served RAF, 1943–46. Examr in

Surgery, Univ. of London, 1965; Pres., Sect. of Proctology, RSM, 1966. Dir, Med. Sickness Annuity & Life Assce Soc., 1973– (Chm., 1982–). Hon. Fellow, (French) Académie de Proctologie, 1961; Hon. Fellow, Amer. Soc. of Colon and Rectal Surgeons, 1974. *Publications:* chapters in surgical textbooks; articles on surgery of the colon and rectum in Brit. jls. *Recreations:* golf, fishing. *Address:* Duns House, Hannington, near Basingstoke, Hants RG26 5TX. *T:* Kingsclere 298162. *Club:* Royal Air Force.

See also C. J. Lockhart-Mummery.

LOCKLEY, Ven. Harold; Archdeacon of Loughborough, 1963–86, Archdeacon Emeritus since 1986; Post-graduate student, Emmanuel College, Cambridge, since 1986; *b* 16 July 1916; *s* of Harry and Sarah Elizabeth Lockley; *m* 1947, Ursula Margaret, JP, *d* of Rev. Dr H. Wedell and Mrs G. Wedell (*née* Bonhoeffer); three *s*. *Educ:* Loughborough Coll. (Hons Dip. Physical Education); London University; Westcott House, Cambridge. BA Hons 1937, BD Hons 1943, MTh 1949, London Univ.; PhD 1955, Nottingham Univ. Chaplain and Tutor, Loughborough Coll., 1946–51; Vicar of Glen Parva and South Wigston, 1951–58. OCF Royal Leics Regt, 1951–58; Chaplain, Leicester Royal Infirmary Maternity Hospital, 1967–74; Proctor in Convocation of Canterbury, 1960–80; Canon Chancellor of Leicester Cathedral, 1958–63, Vicar of All Saints, Leicester, 1963–78. Sen. Examining Chaplain to Bishop of Leicester, 1951–79. Chm., Anglican Young People's Assoc., 1966–86. Part-time Lectr in Divinity, Univ. of Leicester, 1953–86; Mem., Leics Educn Cttee, 1973–85. *Publications:* Editor, Leicester Cathedral Quarterly, 1960–63. *Recreations:* walking and foreign travel. *Address:* Edgehill Cottage, Loxley, Warwickshire; Emmanuel College, Cambridge. *Club:* Leicestershire (Leicester).

See also Prof. E. A. O. G. Wedell.

LOCKLEY, Ronald Mathias; author and naturalist; *b* 8 Nov. 1903. Hon. MSc Wales, 1977. *Publications:* Dream Island, 1930; The Island Dwellers, 1932; Island Days, 1934; The Sea's a Thief, 1936; Birds of the Green Belt, 1936; I Know an Island, 1938; Early Morning Island, 1939; A Pot of Smoke, 1940; The Way to an Island, 1941; Shearwaters, 1942; Dream Island Days, 1943; Inland Farm, 1943; Islands Round Britain, 1945; Birds of the Sea, 1946; The Island Farmers, 1947; Letters from Skokholm, 1947; The Golden Year, 1948; The Cinnamon Bird, 1948; Birds of Pembrokeshire, 1949; The Charm of the Channel Islands, 1950; (with John Buxton) Island of Skomer, 1951; Travels with a Tent in Western Europe, 1953; Puffins, 1953; (with Rosemary Russell) Bird Ringing, 1953; The Seals and the Curragh, 1954; Gilbert White, 1954; (with James Fisher) Sea-Birds, 1954; Pembrokeshire, 1957; The Pan Book of Cage Birds, 1961; Britain in Colour, 1964; The Private Life of the Rabbit, 1964; Wales, 1966; Grey Seal, Common Seal, 1966; Animal Navigation, 1967; The Book of Bird-Watching, 1968; The Channel Islands, 1968, rev. edn, A Traveller's Guide to the Channel Islands, 1971; The Island, 1969; The Naturalist in Wales, 1970; Man Against Nature, 1970; Seal Woman, 1974; Ocean Wanderers, 1974; Orielton, 1977; Myself when Young, 1979; Whales, Dolphins & Porpoises, 1979; (with Noel Cusa) New Zealand Endangered Species, 1980; The House Above the Sea, 1980; (with Richard Adams) Voyage Through the Antarctic, 1982; Flight of the Storm Petrel, 1983; (with Geoff Moon) New Zealand's Birds, 1983; *edited:* Natural History of Selborne, by G. White, 1949, rev. edn 1976; Nature Lover's Anthology, 1951; The Bird-Lover's Bedside Book, 1958; *compiled:* In Praise of Islands, 1957. *Address:* 6 Calder Place, Auckland 6, New Zealand.

LOCKSPEISER, Sir Ben, KCB 1950; Kt 1946; FRS 1949; FEng, FIMechE, FRAeS; *b* 9 March 1891; *s* of late Leon and Rose Lockspeiser, London; *m* 1920, Elsie Shuttleworth (*d* 1964); one *s* two *d*; *m* 1966, Mary Alice Heywood (*d* 1983). *Educ:* Grocers' Sch.; Sidney Sussex Coll., Cambridge (Hon. Fellow); Royal School of Mines. MA; Hon. DSc Oxford; Hon. DEng Witwatersrand; Hon. DTech, Haifa; Aeronautical Research at Royal Aircraft Establishment, Farnborough, 1920–37; Head of Air Defence Dept, RAE, Farnborough, 1937–39; Asst Dir of Scientific Research, Air Ministry, 1939; Dep. Dir of Scientific Res., Armaments, Min. of Aircraft Production, 1941; Dir of Scientific Research, Ministry of Aircraft Production, 1943; Dir-Gen. of Scientific Research, Ministry of Aircraft Production, 1945; Chief Scientist to Ministry of Supply, 1946–49; Sec. to Cttee of Privy Council for Scientific and Industrial Research, 1949–56; retired 1956. President: Engineering Section of British Association, 1952; Johnson Soc., 1953–54; Council European Organization for Nuclear Research, 1955–57. Hon. Mem., Parly and Scientific Cttee, 1960. Medal of Freedom (Silver Palms), 1946. *Recreations:* music, gardening. *Address:* Birchway, 15 Waverley Road, Farnborough, Hants. *T:* Farnborough, Hants, 543021. *Club:* Athenæum.

LOCKWOOD, Baroness *cr* 1978 (Life Peer), of Dewsbury, W Yorks; **Betty Lockwood;** President, Birkbeck College, London, since 1983; *b* 22 Jan. 1924; *d* of Arthur Lockwood and Edith Alice Lockwood; *m* 1978, Lt-Col Cedric Hall. *Educ:* Eastborough Girls' Sch., Dewsbury; Ruskin Coll., Oxford. Chief Woman Officer and Asst Nat. Agent of Labour Party, 1967–75; Chm., Equal Opportunities Commn, 1975–83. Vice-Chm., Internat. Council of Social Democratic Women, 1969–75; Chm., Adv. Cttee to European Commn on Equal Opportunities for Women and Men, 1982–83. Chairman: Mary Macarthur Educnl Trust, 1971–; Mary Macarthur Holiday Homes, 1971–. Member: Dept of Employment Adv. Cttee on Women's Employment, 1969–83; Adv. Council on Energy Conservation, 1977–80; Council, Advertising Standards Authority, 1983–. Member, Council: Bradford Univ., 1983–; Leeds Univ., 1985–. Hon. Fellow, UMIST, 1986. Hon. DLitt Bradford, 1981; Hon. LLD Strathclyde, 1985. Editor, Labour Woman, 1967–71. *Recreations:* walking and country pursuits, music. *Address:* 6 Sycamore Drive, Addingham, Ilkley LS29 0NY. *Clubs:* Soroptomist, University Women's.

LOCKWOOD, Prof. David, FBA 1976; Professor of Sociology, University of Essex, since 1968; *b* 9 April 1929; *s* of Herbert Lockwood and Edith A. (*née* Lockwood); *m* 1954, Leonore Davidoff; three *s*. *Educ:* Honley Grammar Sch.; London Sch. of Economics. BSc(Econ) London, 1st Cl. Hons 1952; PhD London, 1957. Trainee, textile industry, 1944–47; Cpl, Intell. Corps, Austria, 1947–49. Asst Lectr and Lectr, London Sch. of Economics, 1953–60; Rockefeller Fellow, Univ. of California, Berkeley, 1958–59; Univ. Lectr, Faculty of Economics, and Fellow, St John's Coll., Cambridge, 1960–68. Visiting Professor: Dept of Sociology, Columbia Univ., 1966–67; Delhi Univ., 1975. Mem., SSRC (Chm., Sociol. and Soc. Admin Cttee), 1973–76. *Publications:* The Blackcoated Worker, 1958; (jtly) The Affluent Worker in the Class Structure, 3 vols, 1968–69; numerous articles in jls and symposia. *Address:* 82 High Street, Wivenhoe, Essex. *T:* Wivenhoe 3530.

LOCKWOOD, Sir Joseph (Flawith), Kt 1960; Chairman, Royal Ballet, 1971–85; *b* 14 Nov. 1904. Manager of flour mills in Chile, 1924–28; Technical Manager of Etablissements, Henry Simon Ltd, in Paris and Brussels, 1928–33; Director, 1933; Dir Henry Simon Ltd, Buenos Aires, Chm. Henry Simon (Australia) Ltd, Dir Henry Simon (Engineering Works) Ltd, etc, 1945, Chm. and Managing Dir, Henry Simon Ltd, 1950; Dir, NRDC, 1951–67; Chm., IRC, 1969–71 (Mem., 1966–71); Chm., EMI Ltd and subsidiaries, 1954–74 (Dir, 1954–79); Director: Smiths Industries Ltd, 1959–79; Hawker Siddeley Group, 1963–77; British Domestic Appliances Ltd, 1966–71 (Chm., 1966–70); The Beecham Group, 1966–75; Laird Group Ltd, 1970–84. Member: Engineering Advisory Council, Board of Trade, 1959; Export Council for Europe, 1961–63; Export Credits Guarantee Adv. Council, 1963–67; Council Imperial Soc. of Knights Bach. Director: Sandown Park Ltd, 1969–83; Epsom Grandstand Assoc. Ltd, 1969–83; United Racecourses Ltd, 1969–83. Hon. Treasurer British Empire Cancer Campaign, 1962–67; Chairman: Royal Ballet Sch. Endowment Fund and Governors, Royal Ballet Sch., 1960–78; Young Vic Theatre Company, 1974–75; South Bank Theatre Bd, 1977–84 (Mem., 1968–85); Vice-Pres., Central Sch. of Speech and Drama (Chm., Governors, 1965–68); Mem., Arts Council, 1967–70. CompIEE. *Publications:* Provender Milling—the Manufacture of Feeding Stuffs for Livestock, 1939; Flour Milling (trans. into various languages), 1945. *Address:* c/o National Westminster Bank, Southwell, Notts.

LOCKWOOD, Margaret Mary, CBE 1981; Actress; *b* Karachi, India, 15 Sept. 1916; (*née* Margaret Lockwood); *m* Rupert W. Leon (marr. diss.); one *d*. *Educ:* Sydenham Girls' High Sch. Studied for Stage under Italia Conti and at Royal Academy of Dramatic Art. *Films:* Lorna Doone; Case of Gabriel Perry, 1934; Midshipman Easy; Jury's Evidence; Amateur Gentleman, 1935; Irish for Luck; Beloved Vagabond; Street Singer, 1936; Who's Your Lady Friend; Owd Bob; Bank Holiday, 1937; The Lady Vanishes; A Girl Must Live; Stars Look Down; Night Train to Munich, 1939; Quiet Wedding, 1940; Alibi; Man in Grey, 1942; Dear Octopus; Give Us The Moon; Love Story, 1943; Place of One's Own; I'll Be Your Sweetheart, 1944; Wicked Lady; Bedelia, 1945; Hungry Hill; Jassy, 1946; The White Unicorn, 1947; Look Before You Love, 1948; Cardboard Cavalier; Madness of the Heart, 1949; Highly Dangerous, 1950; Laughing Anne, 1952; Trent's Last Case, 1952; Trouble in the Glen, 1954; Cast A Dark Shadow, 1955; The Slipper and the Rose, 1976. Named top money-making Star in Britain by motion Picture Poll; Motion Picture Herald Fame Poll, 1945 and 1946; Winner Daily Mail Film Award, 1945–46, 1946–47 and 1947–48. *Stage:* tour in Private Lives, 1949; Peter Pan, 1949–50, 1950–51 and 1957–58; Pygmalion, 1951; Spider's Web, Savoy, 1954–56; Subway in the Sky, Savoy, 1957; And Suddenly It's Spring, Duke of York's, 1959–60; Signpost to Murder, Cambridge Theatre, 1962–63; Every Other Evening, Phœnix, 1964–65; An Ideal Husband, Strand, 1965 and Garrick, 1966; The Others, Strand, 1967; On a Foggy Day, St Martin's, 1969; Lady Frederick, Vaudeville, 1970; Relative Values (nat. tour), 1972, Westminster, 1973; Double Edge, Vaudeville, 1975–76; Quadrille (nat. tour), 1977; Suite in Two Keys (nat. tour), 1978; Motherdear, Ambassadors, 1980. *Television:* BBC series (with daughter Julia) The Flying Swan, March-Sept. 1965; Yorkshire TV series, Justice, 1971, 1972–73, 1974. *Recreations:* crossword puzzles and swimming. *Address:* c/o Mrs H. de Leon, Flat 22, The Colonnades, Porchester Square, W2.

LOCKWOOD, Robert; General Director, Overseas Planning and Project Development, General Motors Corporation, 1982–85, retired; *b* 14 April 1920; *s* of Joseph A. Lockwood and Sylvia Lockwood; *m* 1947, Phyllis M. Laing; one *s* one *d*. *Educ:* Columbia Univ. (AB); Columbia Law Sch. (LLB). Attorney, Bar of New York, 1941; US Dist of New York and US Supreme Court, 1952. Pilot, USAAF (8th Air Force), 1944–45. Attorney: Ehrich, Royall, Wheeler & Holland, New York, 1941 and 1946–47; Sullivan & Cromwell, New York, 1947–54; Sec. and Counsel, Cluett, Peabody & Co., Inc., New York, 1955–57; Man. Dir, Cluett, Peabody & Co., Ltd, London, 1957–59; General Motors: Overseas Ops, Planning and Develt, 1960–61; Asst to Man. Dir, GM Argentina, Buenos Aires, 1962; Asst to Man. Dir, and Manager, Parts, Power and Appliances, GM Continental, Antwerp, 1964–66; Branch Man., Netherlands Br., GM Continental, Rotterdam, 1967–68; Man., Planning and Develt, GM Overseas Ops, New York, 1969–73; Vice Pres., GM Overseas Corp., and Gen. Man., Japan Br., 1974–76; Exec. Vice Pres., Isuzu Motors Ltd, Tokyo, 1976; Chm., GM European Adv. Council, 1977–82. *Recreations:* tennis, chess, reading. *Address:* 126 Littlefield Road, Monterey, Calif 93940, USA. *Clubs:* Hurlingham; Tokyo Lawn Tennis (Tokyo).

LOCKWOOD, Walter Sydney Douglas, CBE 1962 (OBE 1948); CEng; FRAeS; FInstProdE; *b* 4 Jan. 1895; *s* of Walter Lockwood, Thetford, Norfolk; *m* 1924, Constance Rose, *d* of T. F. Bayliss, Norwich. *Educ:* Thetford Sch.; Bristol Univ. Served European War, 1914–18: Gloucester Regt, France and Belgium (Belgian Croix de Guerre; despatches; wounded). Joined design staff of Sir W. G. Armstrong Whitworth Aircraft Ltd, 1921; became Works Man., 1944. Armstrong Whitworth Aircraft: Works Dir, 1950; Dir and Gen. Man., 1955; Man. Dir, 1960; Man. Dir, Whitworth Gloster Aircraft Ltd (when Armstrong Whitworth Aircraft and Gloster Aircraft Companies merged), 1961–63 (when Co. dissolved); Dir, Hawker Siddeley Aviation Ltd, 1961–64, retired. Mem. Coun., SBAC, 1960. *Address:* Wayside, Abbey Road, Leiston, Suffolk.

LOCKYER, Rear-Adm. (Alfred) Austin, LVO 1973; Chief Staff Officer (Engineering) to Commander-in-Chief Fleet, 1982–84, retired; Director General, Timber Trade Federation, since 1985; *b* 4 March 1929; *s* of Austin Edmund Lockyer and Jane Russell (*née* Goldman); *m* 1965, Jennifer Ann Simmons; one *s*. *Educ:* Frome County School; Taunton School; Royal Naval Engineering College. Entered RN 1947; Comdr 1965; Staff of Commander Far East Fleet, 1965–67; jssc, 1968–69; Ship Dept, 1969–71; HMY Britannia, 1971–73; Captain 1973; sowc, 1973–74; Naval Ship Production Overseer, Scotland and NI, 1974–76; Dep. Dir, Fleet Maintenance, 1976–78; Dir, Naval Officers Appointments (Engrg), 1978–80; HMS Sultan in Comd, 1980–82; ADC to the Queen, 1981; Rear-Adm. 1982. Governor: Forres Sch., Swanage, 1980– (Chm., 1983–); Sherborne Sch., 1981–. *Recreations:* gardening, listening to good music and watching sport. *Address:* 8 Darlington Place, Bath, Avon BA2 6BX. *Club:* Army and Navy.

LODER, family name of **Baron Wakehurst.**

LODER, Sir Giles Rolls, 3rd Bt, *cr* 1887; DL; *b* 10 Nov. 1914; *o s* of late Capt. Robert Egerton Loder, *s* of 2nd Bt, and late Muriel Rolls, *d* of J. Rolls-Hoare; *S* grandfather, 1920; *m* 1939, Marie, *o c* of Bertram Hanmer Bunbury Symons-Jeune; two *s*. *Educ:* Eton; Trinity Coll., Cambridge (MA). High Sheriff of Sussex, 1948–49; DL West Sussex, 1977. Vice-Pres., RHS, 1983–. VMH 1971. *Recreations:* sailing, horticulture. *Heir:* *s* Edmund Jeune Loder [*b* 26 June 1941; *m* 1966, Penelope Jane (marr. diss. 1971), *d* of Ivo Forde; one *d*]. *Address:* Ockenden House, Cuckfield, Haywards Heath, West Sussex. *T:* Haywards Heath 459433; Leonardslee Gardens, Horsham, Sussex. *Club:* Royal Yacht Squadron.

LODGE, Prof. David John, MA, PhD; FRSL 1976; Professor of Modern English Literature, University of Birmingham, since 1976; *b* 28 Jan. 1935; *s* of William Frederick Lodge and Rosalie Marie Lodge (*née* Murphy); *m* 1959, Mary Frances Jacob; two *s* one *d*. *Educ:* St Joseph's Acad., Blackheath; University College, London (Fellow, 1982). BA hons, MA (London); PhD (Birm). National Service, RAC, 1955–57. British Council, London, 1959–60. Univ. of Birmingham: Asst Lectr in English, 1960–62; Lectr, 1963–71; Sen. Lectr, 1971–73; Reader in English, 1973–76. Harkness Commonwealth Fellow, 1964–65; Visiting Associate Prof., Univ. of California, Berkeley, 1969; Henfield Writing Fellow, Univ. of E Anglia, 1977. Yorkshire Post Fiction Prize, 1975; Hawthornden Prize, 1976; Whitbread Book of the Year Award, 1980. *Publications:* *novels:* The Picturegoers, 1960; Ginger, You're Barmy, 1962; The British Museum is Falling Down, 1965; Out of the Shelter, 1970, rev. edn 1985; Changing Places, 1975; How Far Can You Go?, 1980; Small World, 1984; *criticism:* Language of Fiction, 1966; The Novelist at the Crossroads, 1971; The Modes of Modern Writing, 1977; Working with Structuralism, 1981; Write

On, 1986. *Recreations:* badminton, television, cinema. *Address:* Department of English, University of Birmingham, Birmingham B15 2TT. *T:* 021–472 1301.

LODGE, Prof. Geoffrey Arthur, BSc, PhD, FIBiol; FRSE 1986; Professor of Animal Science, Sultan Qaboos University, Muscat, since 1986; *Educ:* Durham University (BSc). PhD Aberdeen. Formerly Reader in Animal Production, Univ. of Nottingham School of Agriculture, and Principal Research Scientist, Animal Research Inst., Ottawa; Strathcona-Fordyce Prof. of Agriculture, Univ. of Aberdeen, and Principal, North of Scotland Coll. of Agriculture, 1978–86. FRSA. *Publications:* (ed jointly) Growth and Development of Mammals, 1968; contribs to journals and books. *Recreations:* food, malt whisky, anything free. *Address:* PO Box 6281, Ruwi, Muscat, Sultanate of Oman. *Club:* Farmers'.

LODGE, Oliver Raymond William Wynlayne; Regional Chairman of Industrial Tribunals, London (South), since 1980; *b* Painswick, Glos, 2 Sept. 1922; *e s* of Oliver William Foster Lodge and Winifred, (Wynlayne), *o d* of Sir William Nicholas Atkinson, ISO, LLD; *m* 1953, Charlotte, *o d* of Col Arthur Davidson Young, CMG; one *s* two *d*. *Educ:* Bryanston Sch.; King's Coll., Cambridge. BA 1943, MA 1947. Officer-cadet, Royal Fusiliers, 1942. Called to the Bar, Inner Temple, 1945; admitted *ad eundem*, Lincoln's Inn, 1949, Bencher, 1973; practised at Chancery Bar, 1945–74; Permanent Chairman of Industrial Tribunals, 1975–. Member: Bar Council, 1952–56, 1967–71; Supreme Court Rules Cttee, 1968–71; Gen. Comr of Income Tax, Lincoln's Inn, 1983–. *Publications:* (ed) Rivington's Epitome of Snell's Equity, 3rd edn, 1948; (ed) Fraudulent and Voidable Conveyances, article in Halsbury's Laws of England, 3rd edn, 1956; contribs to legal periodicals. *Recreations:* walking, bell-ringing, reading history, formerly sailing. *Address:* Southridge House, Hindon, Salisbury, Wilts. *T:* Hindon 238; 33 The Little Boltons, SW10. *T:* 01–370 5265. *Clubs:* Garrick; Bar Yacht.

LODGE, Sir Thomas, Kt 1974; Consultant Radiologist, United Sheffield Hospitals, 1946–74, retired; Clinical Lecturer, Sheffield University, 1960–74; *b* 25 Nov. 1909; *s* of James Lodge and Margaret (*née* Lowery); *m* 1940, Aileen Corduff; one *s* one *d*. *Educ:* Univ. of Sheffield. MB, ChB 1934, FFR 1945, FRCP 1967, FRCS 1967. Asst Radiologist: Sheffield Radium Centre, 1936; Manchester Royal Infirmary, 1937–38; 1st Asst in Radiology, United Sheffield Hosps, 1938–46; Cons. Adviser in Radiology, DHSS, 1965–74. Fellow, BMA, 1968; Hon. FRSocMed; Hon. FFR RCSI; Hon. FRACR 1963; Hon. FACR 1975; Hon. MSR 1975. Twining Medal, 1945, Knox Lectr, 1962, Pres., 1963–66, Faculty of Radiologists. Hon. Editor, Clinical Radiology, 1954–59. Hon. MD Sheffield, 1985. *Publications:* Recent Advances in Radiology, 3rd edn 1955, 4th edn 1964, 5th edn 1975, 6th edn 1979; articles in Brit. Jl Radiology, Clinical Radiology, etc. *Recreation:* gardening. *Address:* 44 Sussex Square, Brighton, East Sussex BN2 1GE. *T:* Brighton 604242.

LODGE, Thomas C. S.; see Skeffington-Lodge.

LODGE, Tom Stewart, CBE 1967; Director of Research and Statistics, Home Office, 1969–73; retired; *b* 15 Dec. 1909; *s* of George Arthur and Emma Eliza Lodge, Batley, Yorks; *m* 1936, Joan McFadyean (*d* 1961); one *d*. *Educ:* Batley Grammar Sch.; Merton Coll., Oxford. BA Hons Maths 1931, MA 1934; FIA 1939. Prudential Assurance Co., 1931–43; Min. of Aircraft Production, 1943–46; Admty as Superintending Actuary, 1946–50; Statistical Adviser, Home Office, 1950; Statistical Adviser and Dir of Research, Home Office, 1957. Chm., Criminological Scientific Council, Council of Europe, 1975–77 (Mem., 1970–77). *Publications:* articles in British and French jls. *Address:* 16A The Avenue, Coulsdon, Surrey CR3 2BN. *T:* 01–660 3390. *Club:* Civil Service.

LOEHNIS, Anthony David; Executive Director, Bank of England, since 1981; *b* 12 March 1936; *s* of Sir Clive Loehnis, *qv*; *m* 1965, Jennifer Forsyth Anderson; three *s*. *Educ:* Eton; New Coll., Oxford (BA); Harvard Sch. of Public Administration. HM Diplomatic Service, 1960–66; J. Henry Schroder Wagg & Co. Ltd, 1967–80 (on secondment to Bank of England, 1977–79); Associate Dir (Overseas), Bank of England, 1980–81. *Address:* c/o Bank of England, Threadneedle Street, EC2R 8AH. *Club:* Garrick.

LOEHNIS, Sir Clive, KCMG 1962 (CMG 1950); Commander RN (retired); *b* 24 Aug. 1902; *s* of H. W. Loehnis, Barrister-at-Law, Inner Temple; *m* 1929, Rosemary Beryl, *d* of late Major Hon. R. N. Dudley Ryder, 8th Hussars; one *s* one *d*. *Educ:* Royal Naval Colls, Osborne, Dartmouth and Greenwich. Midshipman, 1920; Lt, 1924; qualified in signal duties, 1928; Lt-Comdr, 1932; retired, 1935; AMIEE 1935. Re-employed in Signal Div. Admiralty, 1938; Comdr on retd List, 1942; Naval Intelligence Div., 1942; demobilised and entered Foreign Office, 1945; Dep. Dir, Government Communications Headquarters, 1952–60; Dir, Government Communications HQ, 1960–64. Dep. Chm., Civil Service Selection Bd, 1967–70. *Address:* 12 Eaton Place, SW1X 8AD. *T:* 01–235 6803. *Clubs:* White's, MCC.

See also A. D. Loehnis, Baron Remnant.

LOEWE, Frederick; composer; concert pianist; *b* Vienna, 10 June 1901; *s* of Edmund Loewe, actor. Began career as concert pianist playing with leading European orchestras; went to US, 1924; first musical, Salute to Spring, produced in St Louis, 1937; first Broadway production, Great Lady, 1938; began collaboration with Alan Jay Lerner, *qv*, in 1942, since when has written music for: Day Before Spring, 1945; Brigadoon, 1947 (1st musical to win Drama Critics' Award); Paint Your Wagon, 1951 (best score of year); My Fair Lady, 1956 (many awards); Gigi (film), 1958 (Oscar), (stage) 1974; Camelot, 1960; The Little Prince, 1975 (film). DMus *hc* Univ. of Redlands, Calif; Dr of Fine Arts *hc* Univ. of NYC. Kennedy Center Honors Award for Lifetime Achievement in the Arts, 1986. *Address:* c/o ASCAP, One Lincoln Plaza, New York, NY 10023, USA. *Clubs:* Players', Lambs (New York); Palm Springs Racquet.

LOFTHOUSE, Geoffrey; JP; MP (Lab) Pontefract and Castleford, since Oct. 1978; *b* 18 Dec. 1925; *s* of Ernest and Emma Lofthouse; *m* 1952, Sarah Lofthouse (*d* 1985); one *d*. *Educ:* Featherstone Primary and Secondary Schs. MIPM 1984. Haulage hand in mining industry at age of 14. Personnel Manager, NCB Fryston, 1970–78. Member: Pontefract Borough Council, 1962–74 (Mayor, 1967–68); Wakefield Metropolitan District Council, 1974– (Chm., Housing Cttee). Mem., NUM, 1939–64, APEX, 1970–. JP Pontefract, 1970. *Publication:* A Very Miner MP (autobiog.), 1986. *Recreations:* Rugby League, cricket. *Address:* 67 Carleton Crest, Pontefract, West Yorkshire.

LOFTHOUSE, John Alfred, (Jack), OBE 1967; Director, Britoil, since 1983; Member, British National Oil Corporation, 1980–82; *b* 30 Dec. 1917; *s* of John Duncan Lofthouse and Clara Margaret Smith; *m* 1950, Patricia Ninette Mann (*d* 1956); one *d*. *Educ:* Rutlish Sch., Merton; St Catharine's Coll., Cambridge (BA Hons, MA). Joined ICI Ltd as engr, 1939; Engrg Manager, Petrochemicals Div., 1958; Technical Dir, Nobel Div., 1961; Chm., Petrochems Div., 1967; Dir, Main Bd of ICI Ltd, 1970–80: responsibilities included Personnel Dir, Petrochems, Oil, and Explosives businesses, and Chm., ICI Americas Ltd. *Publications:* contrib. Geographical Jl and engrg jls. *Recreations:* gardening, hill-walking, music. *Address:* Little Paddocks, Streatley, Berks RG8 9RD.

LOFTHOUSE, Reginald George Alfred, FRICS; Convener, Standing Conference on Countryside Sports, since 1978; *b* Workington, 30 Dec. 1916; *m* 1939, Ann Bernardine Bannan; three *d*. *Educ:* Workington Secondary Sch.; with private land agent, Cockermouth. Chartered Surveyor and Land Agent (Talbot-Ponsonby Prizeman). Asst District Officer, Penrith, 1941–42; District Officer, Carlisle, for Cumberland War Agric. Exec. Cttee, 1942–43; Asst Land Comr, West Riding, 1943–46; Land Commissioner: N and E Ridings, 1946–48; Derbs, Leics, Rutland, Northants, 1948–50; Somerset and Dorset, 1950–52; Regional Land Comr, Hdqtrs, 1952–59, and SE Region, 1959–71; Regional Officer, SE Region, Agric., Develt and Adv. Service, 1971–73; Chief Surveyor, MAFF, 1973–76. Chairman: UK Jt Shelter Res. Cttee, 1958–71; Statutory Cttee on Agricl Valuations, 1973–76. Mem., Farming and Wildlife Adv. Gp, 1966–81. Adviser to: Lord Porchester's Exmoor Study, 1977; Nature Conservancy Council, 1978–82; Council for Environmental Conservation, 1980–81. Vis. Lectr in Rural Estate Management and Forestry, Regent Street Polytechnic, 1954–62. Member: Bd of Governors, Coll. of Estate Management, 1963–85 (Chm., 1972–77; Research Fellow, 1982–85, Hon. Fellow 1985; Chm., Centre for Advanced Land Use Studies, 1972–81); Court and Council, Reading Univ., 1973–; Adv. Cttee, Centre for Agricl Strategy, Reading Univ., 1980– (Chm., 1982–); Delegacy for Nat. Inst. for Res. in Dairying, Shinfield, 1974–80; Gen. Council, RICS, 1974–76; RICS Land Agency and Agric. Div. Council, 1974–77. Hon. Life Mem., Cambridge Univ. Land Soc.; Chm. Farm Bldgs Cttee 1973–80, Mem. Engrg and Bldgs Res. Bd 1973–80, Jt Consultative Organisation. Liveryman, Loriners' Co., 1976; Freeman, City of London, 1976. *Publications:* The Berwyn Mountains Area of Wales, 1979; contrib. professional, techn. and countryside jls. *Address:* c/o College of Estate Management, Whiteknights, Reading RG6 2AW. *Clubs:* Athenæum, MCC.

LOFTUS, Viscount; Charles John Tottenham; Head of French Department, Strathcona-Tweedsmuir School, Calgary; *b* 2 Feb. 1943; *e s* and heir of 8th Marquess of Ely, *qv*; *m* 1969, Judith Marvelle, *d* of Dr J. J. Porter, FRS, Calgary, Alberta; one *s* one *d*. *Educ:* Trinity Coll. Sch., Port Hope, Ont; Ecole Internationale de Genève; Univ. of Toronto (MA). Heir: *s* Hon. Andrew John Tottenham, *b* 26 Feb. 1973. *Address:* 1424 Springfield Place SW, Calgary, Alberta T2W 0Y1, Canada.

LOFTUS, Col Ernest Achey, CBE 1975 (OBE (mil.) 1928); TD 1929; DL; MA, MLitt (TCD), BSc Econ. (London), LCP, FRGS, FRSA, MRST; Member RSL; a pedagogue for 74 years and retired 1975 as the oldest civil servant in the world (see Guinness Book of Records); in service of Zambian Government 1963–75; *b* 11 Jan. 1884; *s* of Capt. William Loftus, Master Mariner, Kingston-upon-Hull; *m* 1916, Elsie (*d* 1979), *er d* of Allen Charles Cole, West Tilbury, Essex; two *s*. *Educ:* Archbishop Holgate's Gram. Sch., York; Trinity Coll., Dublin. Senior Geography Master, Palmer's Sch., Grays, Essex, 1906–19; Head of Junior Sch., Southend on Sea High Sch. for Boys, 1919–20; Asst Dir of Educn, Southend-on-Sea, 1920–22; Headmaster, Barking Abbey Sch., 1922–49; a select speaker, Conf. of World Educn Assocs, Oxford, 1935; coined term 'Health Science' and drew up first syllabus of work (London Univ.) in that subject, 1937; an Educn Officer in Kenya, 1953–60, in Nyasaland, 1960–63, in Zambia, 1963–75. Formed two Cadet Corps and raised four Territl Units in Co. Essex; served with The Essex Regt 1910–29; European War in Gallipoli 1915, Egypt 1916, France 1918; Staff Officer for Educn 67th Div., Independent Force and Kent Force, 1917; Comdr, first draft of troops (1500 miners) to be demobilised, Dec. 1918; commanded (as Major) 300 troops, Purfleet Garrison, to prevent sabotage on ships in the river or Tilbury Docks and the oil tanks at Purfleet, during miners' strike, 1921; a pioneer officer in what became RAEC; Lt-Col Commanding 6th Essex Regt, 1925–29; Mem. Essex Territorial Army Association 1925–29; Brevet Col, 1929; served in War of 1939—Pioneer Corps, 1939–42, commanding No 13 (Italian) Group in France and No 31 Group in London, etc.; Founder Hon. Sec. Essex County Playing Fields Association, 1925–29; Hon. Organiser or Sec. various Appeals, in Essex. Mem. Standing Cttee Convocation, London Univ., 1944–53, and Bedell of Convocation, 1946–53. A Chm. Nat. Assistance Board, 1949–53; Mem. Exec. Cttee Essex Playing Fields Assoc., 1925–53; Mem. Thurrock UDC 1946–53, Vice-Chm. 1951–52; Controller, Civil Defence, Thurrock area, 1951–53. Freeman, City of Kingston-upon-Hull, 1968. For some years a Governor, The Strand Sch. (Brixton), Palmer's Sch. (Grays), etc. A Selborne Lectr. DL Essex 1929–75, now inactive. Mason, 1915–; Rotarian (Pres., Barking, 1935), 1930–. *Publications:* Education and the Citizen; History of a Branch of the Cole Family; Growls and Grumbles; A History of Barking Abbey (with H. F. Chettle); A Visual History of Africa, 1953, 16 reprints, 2nd edn 1974; A Visual History of East Africa; and brochures for the East African Literature Bureau. Contributor of feature articles in London Daily and Weekly Press, etc. on Education; author of 8 scenes of Barking Pageant, 1931, and of Elizabethan scene in Ilford Pageant of Essex, 1932. *Recreations:* historical and genealogical research. *Address:* c/o Kingscote, Furze Hill, Kingswood, Surrey KT20 6EP. *Club:* Royal Commonwealth Society.

LOGAN, David Brian Carleton; HM Diplomatic Service; Head of Personnel Operations Department, Foreign and Commonwealth Office, since 1986; *b* 11 Aug. 1943; *s* of Captain Brian Ewen Weldon Logan, RN (Retd) and Mary Logan (*née* Fass); *m* 1967, Judith Margaret Walton Cole; two *s* one *d*. *Educ:* Charterhouse; University College, Oxford. BA. Foreign Office, 1965; served Istanbul, Ankara and FCO, 1965–70; Private Sec. to Parly Under Sec. of State for Foreign and Commonwealth Affairs, 1970–73; First Sec., 1972; UK Mission to UN, 1973–77; FCO, 1977–82; Counsellor, Hd of Chancery and Consul-Gen., Oslo, 1982–86. *Recreations:* music, reading, sailing. *Address:* c/o Foreign and Commonwealth Office, King Charles Street, SW1A 2AH. *Club:* Royal Ocean Racing.

LOGAN, Sir Donald (Arthur), KCMG 1977 (CMG 1965); HM Diplomatic Service, retired; Director, Great Britain/East Europe Centre, since 1980; Chairman, Jerusalem and Middle East Trust Ltd, since 1981; Chairman, St Clare's College, Oxford, since 1984; *b* 25 Aug. 1917; *s* of late Arthur Alfred Logan and Louise Anne Bradley; *m* 1957, Irène Jocelyne Angèle, *d* of Robert Everts (Belgian Ambassador at Madrid, 1932–39) and Alexandra Comnène; one *s* two *d*. *Educ:* Solihull. Fellow, Chartered Insurance Institute, 1939. War of 1939–45: Major, RA; British Army Staff, Washington, 1942–43; Germany, 1945. Joined HM Foreign (subseq. Diplomatic) Service, Dec. 1945; Foreign Office, 1945–47; HM Embassy, Tehran, 1947–51; Foreign Office, 1951–53; Asst Political Agent, Kuwait, 1953–55; Asst Private Sec. to Sec. of State for Foreign Affairs, 1956–58; HM Embassy, Washington, 1958–60; HM Ambassador to Guinea, 1960–62; Foreign Office, 1962–64; Information Counsellor, British Embassy, Paris, 1964–70; Ambassador to Bulgaria, 1970–73; Dep. Permanent UK Rep. to NATO, 1973–75; Ambassador and Permanent Leader, UK Delegn to UN Conf. on Law of the Sea, 1976–77. Leader, UK delegn to Conf. on Marine Living Resources of Antarctica, Buenos Aires and Canberra, 1978–80. Vice-Pres., Internat. Exhibitions Bureau, Paris, 1963–67. *Address:* 6 Thurloe Street, SW7 2ST; (office) 31 Knightsbridge, SW1X 7NH. *T:* 01–245 9771. *Clubs:* Brooks's, Royal Automobile.

LOGAN, Sir Douglas; see Logan, Sir R. D.

LOGAN, Sir Douglas (William), Kt 1959; DPhil, MA, BCL; Principal of the University of London, 1948–75; President, British Universities Sports Board and Federation, 1953–75; Chairman: British Student Sports Federation, 1971–77; Universities Superannuation Scheme Ltd, 1974–77 (Deputy Chairman, 1977–80; Consultant, 1980–86); *b* Liverpool, 27 March 1910; *yr s* of Robert Logan and Euphemia Taylor

Stevenson, Edinburgh; *m* 1st, 1940, Vaire Olive Wollaston (from whom he obtained a divorce); two *s*; 2nd, 1947, Christine Peggy Walker; one *s* one *d*. *Educ:* Liverpool Collegiate Sch.; University Coll., Oxford (Open Classical Scholar). First Classes: Hon. Mods 1930, Lit. Hum. 1932, Jurisprudence, 1933; Oxford Univ. Senior Studentship, 1933; Harmsworth Scholar, Middle Temple, 1933 (Hon. Bencher, 1965); Henry Fellowship Harvard Law Sch., 1935–36; Asst Lecturer, LSE, 1936–37; Barstow Scholarship, 1937; called to Bar, Middle Temple, 1937; Fellow of Trinity Coll., Cambridge, 1937–43; Principal, Ministry of Supply, 1940–44; Clerk of the Court, University of London, 1944–47. Rede Lecturer, 1963. Fellow: Wye Coll., 1970; Imperial Coll., 1974; School of Pharmacy, 1975. Vice-Chm., Association of Commonwealth Univs, 1961–67 (Chm. 1962–63; Hon. Treasurer, 1967–74; Dep. Hon. Treasurer, 1974–84); Vice-Chm., Athlone Fellowship Cttee, 1959–71; Member: Commonwealth Scholarships Commn, 1960–86 (Dep. Chm., 1970–86); Marshall Scholarships Commn, 1961–67; Nat. Theatre Bd, 1962–68; a Governor, Old Vic, 1957–80 (Vice-Chm., 1972–80), and Bristol Old Vic; a Trustee, City Parochial Foundation, 1953–67; Member: Anderson Cttee on Grants to Students, 1958–60; Hale Cttee on Superannuation of Univ. Teachers, 1958–60; Northumberland Cttee on Recruitment to the Veterinary Profession, 1962–64; Maddex Working Party on the Superannuation of Univ. Teachers, 1965–68. Mem. British Delegation to 1st, 2nd, 3rd, and 4th Commonwealth Educn Confs, Oxford, 1959, Delhi, 1962, Ottawa, 1964, and Lagos, 1968; Commonwealth Medical Conf. Edinburgh, 1965. Hon. Mem., Pharmaceutical Soc. Hon. Fellow: LSE, 1962; University Coll., Oxford, 1973; University Coll. London, 1975. Hon. DCL Western Ontario; Hon. DLitt Rhodesia; Hon. LLD: Melbourne, Madras, British Columbia, Hong Kong, Liverpool, McGill, CNAA, London; Hon. FDSRCS; Hon. FRIBA. Chevalier de l'Ordre de la Légion d'Honneur. *Publications:* The Birth of a Pension Scheme—a history of the universities superannuation scheme, 1985; annual reports of the Principal of the University of London, 1948–73. *Address:* Restalrig, Mountain Street, Chilham, Canterbury, Kent CT4 8DQ. *T:* Canterbury 730640. *Club:* Athenæum.

LOGAN, James, CChem; Vice-Chairman, Scottish Arts Council, since 1984; *b* 28 Oct. 1927; *s* of John and Jean Logan; *m* 1959, Anne Brand, singer; one *s* one *d*. *Educ:* Robert Gordon's Inst., Aberdeen. MRIC. Member, Sen. Scientific Staff, Macaulay Inst. for Soil Research, 1949–81. Director, Scotland The What? Revue Co., 1970–; Member: Arts Council of Great Britain, 1984–; Scottish Arts Council, 1983–; Founder/Chm., Friends of Aberdeen Art Gallery and Museums, 1975–77. Queen's Jubilee Medal, 1978. *Recreations:* theatre; hoping The Guardian will be published. *Address:* 53 Fountainhall Road, Aberdeen. *T:* Aberdeen 646914.

LOGAN, Lt-Col John, TD 1945; Vice-Lieutenant, Stirlingshire, 1965–79; *b* 25 May 1907; *s* of Crawford William Logan and Ada Kathleen Logan (*née* Kidston); *m* 1937, Rosaleen Muriel O'Hara (*d* 1967); one *s* one *d*. *Educ:* Eton Coll., Windsor. British American Tobacco Co. Ltd (China), 1928–32; Imperial Tobacco Co. (of Great Britain and Ireland) Ltd, 1932–39. POW in Germany, 1940–45 (Captain, 7th Argyll and Sutherland Hldrs; C O, 1949–50). Imperial Tobacco Co. (of Great Britain and Ireland) Ltd, 1946–67. DL Stirlingshire, 1956. Hon. MA Stirling, 1983. *Publication:* China Old and New, 1981. *Recreation:* fishing. *Address:* Wester Craigend, Stirling FK7 9PX. *T:* Stirling 75025.

LOGAN, Sir (Raymond) Douglas, Kt 1983; grazier (sheep and cattle), since 1944; *b* 31 March 1920; *s* of Raymond Hough Logan and Agnes Eleanor Logan; *m* 1944, Florence Pearl McGill (MBE 1975); one *s* one *d* (and one *s* decd). *Educ:* Thornburgh College, Charters Towers. Served RAAF, 1941–44 (Flying Officer, pilot; trained EATS, Australia, 1941–42; served with 66 Sqdn RAF, 1942–44). Member: Qld Govt Beef Cttee of Enquiry, 1975–77; Qld Meat Industry Orgn and Marketing Authority (now Livestock and Meat Authority of Qld), 1978–; United Graziers Assoc. of Qld; Cattlemen's Union, Qld. *Recreations:* tennis, horse riding, sailing, flying. *Address:* Richmond Downs, Richmond, Qld 4822, Australia.

LOGAN, Robert Faid Bell; Group Chief Executive and Deputy Chairman, Samuel Montagu & Co. (Holdings), since 1985; Chairman, Samuel Montagu & Co. Ltd, since 1986; *b* 30 Nov. 1932; *s* of John Logan and Mary Logan (*née* Bell); *m* 1958, Susan Elizabeth Vokes; three *d*. *Educ:* Berwickshire High School, Duns. British Linen Bank, 1949–50 and 1952–55; RAF, 1950–52; Bank of London & South America, 1955–60; Citibank NA, 1960–81 (Exec. Vice-Pres. Merchant Banking Group); Chief Financial Officer, Continental Grain Co., 1981–83; Group Chief Exec., Grindlays Bank, 1983–85. *Recreations:* shooting, tennis, diving. *Address:* 9 Wilton Street, SW1X 7AF. *Clubs:* Marks, Hurlingham, Queen's; Piping Rock (New York).

LOGAN, Rt. Rev. Vincent; *see* Dunkeld, Bishop of, (RC).

LOGAN, William Philip Dowie, MD, PhD, BSc, DPH, FRCP; epidemiological consultant to various national and international organisations, since 1974; Director, Division of Health Statistics, WHO, 1961–74; *b* 2 Nov. 1914; *s* of late Frederick William Alexander Logan and late Elizabeth Jane Dowie; *m* 1st, Pearl (*née* Piper) (marr. diss.); four *s* two *d* (and one *s* decd); 2nd, Barbara (*née* Huneke). *Educ:* Queen's Park Sch., Glasgow; Universities of Glasgow and London. RAF Med. Branch, 1940–46 (Squadron Leader). Hospital appointments in Glasgow, 1939–40 and 1946. Gen. practice in Barking, Essex, 1947–48; General Register Office, 1948–60 (Chief Medical Statistician, Adviser on Statistics to Ministry of Health, Head of WHO Centre for Classification of Diseases, and Member, WHO panel of experts on Health Statistics). *Publications:* contribs on epidemiology, vital and health statistics in official reports and medical jls. *Address:* 164 Elmer Road, Bognor Regis, West Sussex PO22 6JA; 10 chemin de la Tourelle, 1209 Geneva, Switzerland.

LOGUE, Christopher; *b* 23 Nov. 1926; *s* of John Logue and Molly Logue (*née* Chapman); *m* 1985, Rosemary Hill. *Educ:* Prior Park Coll., Bath; Portsmouth Grammar Sch. Mem., Equity. *Publications: verse:* Wand & Quadrant, 1953; Devil, Maggot & Son, 1956; Songs, 1959; Patrocleia, 1962; ABC, 1966; Pax, 1967; New Numbers, 1969; Twelve Cards, 1972; The Crocodile (illus. Binette Schroeder), 1976; Abecedary (illus. Bert Kitchen), 1977; War Music, 1981; Ode to the Dodo, 1981; *anthologies:* The Children's Book of Comic Verse, 1979; London in Verse, 1982; Sweet & Sour, 1983; The Oxford Book of Pseuds, 1983; The Children's Book of Children's Rhymes, 1986; *plays:* The Trial of Cob & Leach, 1959; (with Harry Cookson) The Lilywhite Boys, 1959; trans. Hugo Claus, Friday, 1971; trans. Brecht and Weill, The Seven Deadly Sins, 1984; The Arrival of the Poet in the City: a melodrama for narrator and seven musicians (music by George Nicholson), 1985; trans. Brecht, Baal, 1985; *prose:* Ratsmagic (illus, Wayne Anderson), 1976; The Magic Circus (illus. Wayne Anderson), 1979; The Bumper Book of True Stories (illus. Bert Kitchen), 1980; contrib. Private Eye, The Times, The Sunday Times, etc; *as Count Palmiro Vicarion:* Lust, a pornographic novel, 1957; (ed) Count Palmiro Vicarion's Book of Limericks, 1957; (ed) Count Palmiro Vicarion's Book of Bawdy Ballads, 1957. *Screen plays:* Savage Messiah (dir Ken Russell), 1972. *Play:* The Story of Mary Frazer, 1962. *Recordings:* Red Bird (with Tony Kinsey and Bill Le Sage), 1960; Songs from The Establishment (singer Annie Ross), 1962; The Death of Patroclus (with Vanessa Redgrave, Alan Dobie and others), 1963. *Film roles:* Swinburne, in Ken Russell's Dante's Inferno, 1966; John Ball, in John Irvin's The Peasants' Revolt, 1969; Cardinal Richelieu, in Ken Russell's The Devils, 1970; TV and stage roles. *Address:* 18 Denbigh Close, W11.

LOISELLE, Gilles; Agent General for Quebec in Rome; *b* 20 May 1929; *s* of Arthur Loiselle and Antoinette Lethiecq; *m* 1962, Lorraine Benoît; one *s* one *d*. *Educ:* Sacred-Heart Coll., Sudbury, Ont. BA Laval. Tafari Makonnen Sch., Addis Ababa, 1951–53; Journalist, Le Droit, Ottawa, 1953–56; Haile Selassie First Day Sch., Addis Ababa, 1956–62; Dir, Behrane Zarie Néo Inst., Addis Ababa, 1958–62; Canadian Broadcasting Corporation: Editor, TV French Network, 1962–63; Quebec and Paris correspondent, French Radio and TV Network, 1963–67; Counsellor, Quebec House, Paris, 1967–72; Dir Gen. of Quebec Govt Communications, 1972–76; Pres., Intergovtl Deptl Cttee for Olympic Year, 1976; Dir, Interparly Relations, Quebec Nat. Assembly, 1977; Agent General for Quebec in London, with responsibility for Scandinavian countries, Iceland, and Ireland, 1977–83; Dep. Minister for Cultural Affairs, Quebec, 1983–85. Founder Mem., Assoc. France-Québec, 1969–72; Member: Council, Office franco-québécois pour la Jeunesse, 1973–76; Inst. of Public Admin; RIIA. *Recreations:* reading, gardening. *Address:* Délégation du Québec, Corso Trieste 16, 00198 Roma, Italy. *Clubs:* Royal Automobile, Royal Commonwealth Society, East India, Devonshire, Sports and Public Schools.

LOKOLOKO, Sir Tore, GCMG 1977; GCVO 1982; OBE; Chairman, Indosuez Niugini Bank, since 1983; *b* 21 Sept. 1930; *s* of Loko Loko Tore and Kevau Sarufa; *m* 1950, Lalahaia Meakoro; four *s* six *d*. *Educ:* Sogeri High Sch., PNG. Dip. in Cooperative, India. Chm., PNG Cooperative Fedn, 1965–68; MP, 1968–77 (two terms); Minister for Health, and Dep. Chm. of National Exec. Council, 1968–72. Rep. PNG: Co-op. Conf., Australia, 1951; S Pacific Conf., Lae, 1964; attended UN Gen. Assembly, 1969, and Trusteeship Council, 1971. Governor-General of Papua New Guinea, 1977–82. KStJ 1979. *Address:* Indosuez Niugini Bank, Burns House, Port Moresby, Papua New Guinea.

LOMAS, Alfred; Member (Lab) London North East, European Parliament, since 1979; Leader, British Labour Group, European Parliament, since 1985; *b* 30 April 1928; *s* of Alfred and Florence Lomas; one *s* one *d*. *Educ:* St Paul's Elem. Sch., Stockport; various further educnl estabs. Solicitor's clerk, 1942–46; Radio Telephony Operator, RAF, 1946–49; various jobs, 1949–51; railway signalman, 1951–59; Labour Party Sec./Agent, 1959–65; Polit. Sec., London Co-op., 1965–79. *Publication:* The Common Market—why we should keep out, 1970. *Recreations:* chess, jogging, arts, sport. *Address:* 23 Hatcliffe Close, SE3 9UE. *T:* 01–852 5433. *Club:* Hackney Labour.

LOMAX, (Janis) Rachel; Under Secretary, HM Treasury, since 1986; *b* 15 July 1945; *d* of William and Dilys Salmon; *m* 1967, Michael Acworth Lomax; two *s*. *Educ:* Cheltenham Ladies' Coll.; Girton Coll., Cambridge (MA); LSE (MSc). HM Treasury: Econ. Assistant, 1968; Econ. Advr, 1972; Sen. Econ. Advr, 1978; Principal Pvte Sec. to Chancellor of the Exchequer, 1985–86. *Address:* HM Treasury, Parliament Street, SW1. *T:* 01–233 4266.

LOMAX, Sir John Garnett, KBE 1953 (MBE 1928); CMG 1944; MC 1917; HM Diplomatic Service, retired; *b* Liverpool, 27 Aug. 1896; *s* of Rev. Canon Edward Lomax and Bessie Garnett; *m* 1922, Feridah Yvette Krajewski; two *s*. *Educ:* Liverpool Coll.; Liverpool Univ. Served European War, France, Belgium, India, and Egypt; Driver, RFA (West Lancs), 1915, Lt 1916. HM Vice-Consul, New Orleans, 1920, Chicago, 1921; Vice-Consul and 2nd Sec. HM Legation, Bogota, 1926–30; 2nd Commercial Sec. HM Embassy, Rio de Janeiro, 1930; transferred to HM Embassy, Rome, 1935; HM Commercial Agent, Jerusalem, 1938; Commercial Counsellor, HM Embassy, Madrid, 1940; HM Legation, Berne, 1941; Commercial Counsellor at Angora, 1943; Minister (commercial), British Embassy, Buenos Aires, 1946–49; Ambassador to Bolivia, 1949–56. *Publication:* The Diplomatic Smuggler, 1965. *Address:* Tanterfyn, Llaneilian, Anglesey, Gwynedd; 803 Nelson House, Dolphin Square, SW1. *Clubs:* Reform, Royal Automobile.

LOMAX, Rachel; *see* Lomax, J. R.

LOMBARD KNIGHT, Eric John Percy Crawford; Director: Kellock Factors Ltd; Sterling Credit Ltd; Kellock Holdings Ltd; *yr s* of late Herbert John Charles and Mary Henrietta Knight; *m* 1933, Peggy Julia (*née* Carter); one *s* one *d*. *Educ:* Ashford Grammar Sch. Served War of 1939–45, RAF. British Mercedes Benz; Bowmaker Ltd; established Lombard Banking, 1947. *Address:* The White House, 18 Limpsfield Road, Sanderstead Village, Surrey. *T:* 01–657 2021.

LOMBE, Edward Christopher E.; *see* Evans-Lombe.

LOMER, Dennis Roy, CBE 1984; Director, Davidson Group Ltd, since 1983; Adviser: Balfour Beatty; Fairey Engineering; *b* 5 Oct. 1923; *s* of Bertie Cecil Lomer and Agnes Ellen Coward; *m* 1949, Audrey May Bick; one *s* one *d*. With Consulting Engineers, 1948–50; joined Electricity Supply Industry, 1952; Project Engr, Transmission Div., 1961; Asst Chief Transmission Engr, 1965; Generation Construction Div. (secondment at Dir level), 1972; Dep. Dir-Gen. (Projects), 1973; Dir-Gen., Transmission Div., 1975; Mem., CEGB, 1977–83. Pres., Welding Inst., 1985–87. FIEE; CBIM. *Recreations:* golf, sailing. *Address:* Henley House, Heathfield Close, Woking, Surrey GU22 7JQ. *T:* Woking 64656. *Club:* West Hill Golf (Surrey).

LOMER, Geoffrey John, CBE 1985; FEng 1984; FIEE; Technical Director, Racal Electronics plc, since 1977; *b* 5 Jan. 1932; *s* of Frederick John Lomer and Dorothy Lomer; *m* 1st, 1955, Pauline Helena May (*d* 1974); one *s* one *d*; 2nd, 1977, Antoinette Ryall; one step *s* one step *d*. *Educ:* St Austell Grammar School; Queens' College, Cambridge (MA). Research Engineer, EMI Research Laboratories, 1953–57; Head of RF Div., Broadcast Equipment Dept, EMI Electronics, 1957–63; Head of Transmitter Lab., Racal Communications, 1963–68; Technical Dir, Racal Mobilcal, 1968–70; Dir in Charge, Racal Communications Equipment, 1970–76; Dep. Man. Dir, Racal Tacticom, 1976–77. *Recreations:* music, theatre. *Address:* Racal Electronics plc, Bracknell, Berks RG12 1RG. *T:* Bracknell 481222.

See also W. M. Lomer.

LOMER, William Michael, PhD; Director, Culham Laboratory, United Kingdom Atomic Energy Authority, since 1981; *b* 2 March 1926; *s* of Frederick John Lomer and Dorothy Lomer; *m* 1952, Pamela Anne Wakelin; one *s* two *d*. *Educ:* St Austell County School; University College of the South West, Exeter (MSc London); Queens' College, Cambridge (MA, PhD). Research Scientist, UKAEA, 1952; AERE Harwell: Divison Head, Theory Div., 1958–62; Division Head, Solid State Physics, 1962–68; Research Director, 1968–81. Hon. Treasurer, Inst. of Physics, 1980–82. FInstP. *Publications:* papers in physics and metallurgical jls. *Recreations:* gardening, walking, painting. *Address:* 7 Hids Copse Road, Cumnor Hill, Oxford. *T:* Oxford 862173.

LONDESBOROUGH, 9th Baron, *cr* 1850; **Richard John Denison;** *b* 2 July 1959; *s* of John Albert Lister, 8th Baron Londesborough, TD, AMICE, and of Elizabeth Ann, *d* of late Edward Little Sale, ICS; *S* father, 1968. *Educ:* Wellington College; Exeter Univ.

LONDON, Bishop of, since 1981; **Rt. Rev. and Rt. Hon. Graham Douglas Leonard;** PC 1981; Dean of the Chapels Royal, since 1981; Prelate of the Order of the British Empire, since 1981; *b* 8 May 1921; *s* of late Rev. Douglas Leonard, MA; *m* 1943, Vivien Priscilla, *d* of late M. B. R. Swann, MD, Fellow of Gonville and Caius Coll., Cambridge; two *s. Educ*: Monkton Combe Sch.; Balliol Coll., Oxford (Hon. Fellow, 1986). Hon. Sch. Nat. Science, shortened course. BA 1943, MA 1947. Served War, 1941–45; Captain, Oxford and Bucks Light Infantry; Army Operational Research Group (Ministry of Supply), 1944–45. Westcott House, Cambridge, 1946–47. Deacon 1947, Priest 1948; Vicar of Ardleigh, Essex, 1952–55; Director of Religious Education, Diocese of St Albans, 1955–58; Hon. Canon of St Albans, 1955–57; Canon Residentiary, 1957–58; Canon Emeritus, 1958; General Secretary, Nat. Society, and Secretary, C of E Schools Council, 1958–62; Archdeacon of Hampstead, Exam. Chaplain to Bishop of London, and Rector of St Andrew Undershaft with St Mary Axe, City of London, 1962–64; Bishop Suffragan of Willesden, 1964–73; Bishop of Truro, 1973–81. Chairman: C of E Cttee for Social Work and the Social Services, 1967–76; C of E Board for Social Responsibility, 1976–83; Churches Main Cttee, 1981–; C of E Board of Education, 1983–; BBC and IBA Central Religious Adv. Cttee, 1984–. Member: Churches Unity Commn, 1977–78, Consultant 1978; Churches Council for Covenanting, 1978–82. An Anglican Mem., Commn for Anglican Orthodox Jt Doctrinal Discussions, 1974–81; one of Archbp of Canterbury's Counsellors on Foreign Relations, 1974. Elected delegate, 5th Assembly WCC, Nairobi, 1975. Entered House of Lords, 1977. Select Preacher to University of Oxford, 1968, 1984. Freeman, City of London, 1970. President: Middlesex Assoc., 1970–73; Corporation of SS Mary and Nicholas (Woodard Schools), 1973–78, Hon. Fellow, 1978. Member Court and Council, City Univ., 1981–86. Hon. DD Episcopal Seminary, Kentucky, 1974; Hon. DCnL Nashotah, USA, 1983. STD Siena Coll., USA, 1984. Episcopal Canon of Jerusalem, 1982; Hon. Bencher, Middle Temple, 1982. *Publications*: Growing into Union (Jt author), 1970; The Gospel is for Everyone, 1971; God Alive: Priorities in Pastoral Theology, 1981; Firmly I Believe and Truly, 1985; Life in Christ, 1986; contrib. to: The Christian Religion Explained, 1960; Retreats Today, 1962; Communicating the Faith, 1969; A Critique of Eucharistic Agreement, 1975; Is Christianity Credible?, 1981; The Cross and the Bomb, 1983; Unholy Warfare, 1983; Synod of Westminster, 1986. *Recreations*: reading, especially biographies; music. *Address*: London House, 8 Barton Street, Westminster, SW1P 3NE. *T*: 01–222 8661. *Clubs*: Athenæum, Garrick.
See also Baron Swann.

LONDON, Archdeacon of; *see* Harvey, Ven. F. W.

LONDON, EAST, Bishop in, (RC); *see* Guazzelli, Rt Rev. Victor.

LONDON, NORTH, Bishop in, (RC); *see* Harvey, Rt Rev. Philip.

LONDON, WEST, Bishop in, (RC); *see* Mahon, Rt Rev. Gerald Thomas.

LONDONDERRY, 9th Marquess of, *cr* 1816; **Alexander Charles Robert Vane-Tempest-Stewart;** Baron Londonderry, 1789; Viscount Castlereagh, 1795; Earl of Londonderry, 1796; Baron Stewart, 1814; Earl Vane, Viscount Seaham, 1823; *b* 7 Sept. 1937; *s* of 8th Marquess of Londonderry and Romaine (*d* 1951), *er d* of Major Boyce Combe, Great Holt, Dockenfield, Surrey; *S* father 1955; *m* 1st, 1958, Nicolette (marr. diss. 1971), *d* of Michael Harrison, Netherhampton, near Salisbury, Wilts; two *d*; 2nd, 1972, Doreen Patricia Wells, *qv*; two *s. Educ*: Eton. *Heir*: *s* Viscount Castlereagh, *qv*. *Address*: Wynyard Park, Billingham, Cleveland TS22 5NF. *T*: Wolviston 317.

LONDONDERRY, Marchioness of; *see* Wells, Doreen P.

LONG, family name of **Viscount Long.**

LONG, 4th Viscount, *cr* 1921, of Wraxall; **Richard Gerard Long;** a Lord in Waiting (Government Whip), since 1979; *b* 30 Jan. 1929; *s* of 3rd Viscount and Gwendolyn (*d* 1959), *d* of Thomas Reginald Hague Cook; *S* father, 1967; *m* 1957, Margaret Frances (marr. diss. 1984), *d* of late Ninian B. Frazer; one *s* one *d* (and one *d* decd); *m* 1984, Catherine Patricia Elizabeth Mier-Woolf, *d* of C.T. Mills-Ede, S Africa. *Educ*: Harrow. Wilts Regt, 1947–49. Opposition Whip, 1974–79. Vice-Pres. and formerly Vice-Chm., Wilts Royal British Legion; Pres., Bath Gliding Club. *Heir*: *s* Hon. James Richard Long, *b* 31 Dec. 1960. *Address*: Vallance Lodge, Kington Magna, Gillingham, Dorset. *Club*: Pratt's.

LONG, (Adrian) Douglas; Managing Director, Newspaper Publishing PLC (The Independent), since 1986; *b* London, 9 Feb. 1925; *s* of late Harold Edgar Long and Kate Long; *m* 1949, Vera Barbara Wellstead; one *s. Educ*: Wandsworth Sch. MBIM. Served Indian Army, 1943–47: Royal Deccan Horse, 43rd Cavalry, Probyns Horse (Captain). Reporter/Feature Writer: Daily Graphic, 1947; Daily Record, Glasgow, 1948–54; Scottish Editor, Daily Herald, 1955–57; Chief News Editor/Features Editor, Daily Herald and Sun newspapers, 1958–68; Gen. Man., Odhams, 1969–71; Mirror Group Newspapers Ltd: Dep. Man. Dir/Dep. Chief Exec., 1972–79; Chief Exec., 1980–84; Group Chief Exec., 1984. Chairman: Syndication Internat., 1975–84; Mirrorair Ltd, 1981–84; Director: Odhams Newspapers Ltd, 1976–84; Mirror M&G Management Ltd, 1976–84; Scottish Daily Record & Sunday Mail, 1977–84; Reed Publishing Pension Trustees Ltd, 1980–84; Reed Publishing Holdings Ltd, 1981–85; Mirror Gp Pension Trustees Ltd, 1981–84. Consultant, Surrey Business Enterprise Ltd, 1985–. Mem., Press Council, 1986–. Member: President's Assoc.; Amer. Management Assoc.; Inst. of Dirs. *Recreations*: theatre, cinema, tennis, swimming. *Address*: 3 Garbrand Walk, Ewell Village, Surrey KT17 1UQ. *Clubs*: Royal Automobile, Sandown Park.

LONG, Athelstan Charles Ethelwulf, CMG 1968; CBE 1964 (MBE 1959); Chairman and President, United Bank International, Cayman Islands, since 1975; Chairman, President and Director of some ten companies; Chairman: Public Service Commission; Planning Appeals Tribunal; *b* 2 Jan. 1919; *s* of Arthur Leonard Long and Gabrielle Margaret Campbell (historical writer and novelist, Marjorie Bowen); *m* 1948, Edit Mäjken Zadie Harriet Krantz, *d* of late Erik Krantz, Stockholm; two *s. Educ*: Westminster Sch.; Brasenose Coll., Oxford. Served War of 1939–45: commnd into RA, 1940; seconded 7th (Bengal) Battery, 22nd Mountain Regt, IA, 1940; served Malaya; POW as Capt., 1942–45. Cadet, Burma Civil Service, 1946–48; Colonial Admin. Service (N Nigeria), 1948; Sen. District Officer, 1958; Resident, Zaria Province, 1959; Perm. Sec., Min. of Animal Health and Forestry, 1959; started new Min. of Information as Perm. Sec., 1960; Swaziland: appointed Govt Sec., 1961; Chief Sec., 1964; Leader of Govt business in Legislative Council and MEC, 1964–67; HM Dep. Comr, 1967–68; Administrator, later Governor, of the Cayman Is, 1968–71; Comr of Anguilla, March–July 1972; Admin. Sec., Inter-University Council, 1972–73. Man. Dir, Anegada Corp. Ltd, 1973–74; Dir and Chm., Cayman Airways, 1977–81. Chm. Governing Council, Waterford Sch., Swaziland, 1963–68. FRAS; FRGS. *Recreations*: travel, tropical farming, reading. *Address*: Box 131, Savannah, Grand Cayman, Cayman Islands, West Indies.

LONG, Christopher William, CMG 1986; HM Diplomatic Service; Assistant Under-Secretary of State (Deputy Chief Clerk and Chief Inspector), Foreign and Commonwealth Office, since 1985; *b* 9 April 1938; *s* of Eric and late May Long; *m* 1972, Patricia, *d* of Dennis and late May Stanbridge; two *s* one *d. Educ*: King Edward's Sch., Birmingham; Balliol Coll., Oxford (Deakin Scholar); Univ. of Münster, W Germany. Served RN, 1956–58. HM Diplomatic Service, 1963–: FO, 1963–64; Jedda, 1965–67; Caracas, 1967–69; FCO, 1969–74; Budapest, 1974–77; Belgrade (CSCE), 1977; Counsellor, Damascus, 1978–80; Counsellor and Dep. Perm. Rep., UKMIS, Geneva, 1980–83; Head, Near East and N Africa Dept, FCO, 1983–85. *Address*: c/o Foreign and Commonwealth Office, King Charles Street, SW1A 2AH.

LONG, Douglas; *see* Long, A. D.

LONG, Gerald; *b* 22 Aug. 1923; *o s* of Fred Harold Long and Sabina Long (*née* Walsh); *m* 1951, Anne Hamilton Walker; two *s* three *d. Educ*: St Peter's Sch., York; Emmanuel Coll., Cambridge. Army Service, 1943–47. Joined Reuters, 1948: served as Reuter correspondent in Germany, France and Turkey, 1950–60; Asst General Manager, 1960; Chief Exec., 1963–81 (Gen. Manager, 1963–73; Man. Dir, 1973–81); Man. Dir, Times Newspapers Ltd, 1981–82; Dep. Chm., News International plc, 1982–84. Chairman: Visnews Ltd, 1968–79; Exec. Cttee, Internat. Inst. of Communications Ltd, 1973–78. Mem., Design Council, 1974–77. CBIM (FBIM 1978). Commander, Royal Order of the Phoenix, Greece, 1964; Grand Officer, Order of Merit, Italy, 1973; Commander, Order of the Lion of Finland, 1979; Chevalier de la Légion d'Honneur, France, 1979; Commander's Cross, Order of Merit, Federal Republic of Germany, 1983. *Recreation*: cooking. *Address*: 15 rue d'Aumale, 75009 Paris, France. *T*: 48 74 67 26; 51 route de Caen, St Martin des Entrees, 14400 Bayeux, France. *T*: 31 92 47 12.

LONG, Hubert Arthur, CBE 1970; Deputy Secretary, Exchequer and Audit Department, 1963–73; *b* 21 Jan. 1912; *s* of Arthur Albert Long; *m* 1937, Mary Louise Parker; three *s. Educ*: Taunton's Sch., Southampton. Entered Exchequer and Audit Department, 1930. *Address*: 2A Hawthorndene Road, Hayes, Kent. *T*: 01–462 4373.

LONG, Ven. John Sanderson, MA; Archdeacon of Ely, Hon. Canon of Ely and Rector of St Botolph's, Cambridge, 1970–81; Archdeacon Emeritus, 1981; *b* 21 July 1913; *s* of late Rev. Guy Stephenson Long and Ivy Marion Long; *m* 1948, Rosamond Mary, *d* of Arthur Temple Forman; one *s* three *d. Educ*: St Edmund's Sch., Canterbury; Queens' Coll., Cambridge; Cuddesdon Theological Coll. Deacon, 1936; Priest, 1937; Curate, St Mary and St Eanswythe, Folkestone, 1936–41. Chaplain, RNVR, 1941–46. Curate, St Peter-in-Thanet, 1946; Domestic Chaplain to the Archbishop of Canterbury, 1946–53; Vicar of: Bearsted, 1953–59; Petersfield with Sheet, 1959–70; Rural Dean of Petersfield, 1962–70. *Recreations*: walking, gardening. *Address*: 23 Thornton Road, Girton, Cambridge CB3 0NP. *T*: Cambridge 276421.

LONG, Olivier; Ambassador; President, Graduate Institute of Public Administration, Lausanne, since 1981; *b* 1915; *s* of Dr Edouard Long and Dr Marie Landry; *m* 1946, Francine Roels; one *s* two *d. Educ*: Univ. de Paris, Faculté de Droit et Ecole des Sciences Politiques; Univ. de Genève. PhD Law, 1938; Rockefeller Foundn Fellow, 1938–39; PhD Pol. Sc., 1943. Swiss Armed Forces, 1939–43; International Red Cross, 1943–46; Swiss Foreign Affairs Dept, Berne, 1946–49; Washington Embassy, 1949–54; Govt Delegate for Trade Agreements, 1955–66; Head of Swiss Delegn to EFTA, 1960–66; Ambassador to UK and Malta, 1967–68; Dir-Gen., GATT, 1968–80. Prof., Graduate Inst. of Internat. Studies, Geneva, 1962–85. Mem., Internat. Red Cross Cttee, 1980–. Trustee, Foundn for Internat. Conciliation, Geneva, 1984–. *Publications*: several on political sciences and trade policies. *Address*: 6 rue Constantin, 1206 Geneva, Switzerland.

LONG, Pamela Marjorie, (Mrs John Nichols); Metropolitan Stipendiary Magistrate, since 1978; *b* 12 Sept. 1930; *d* of late John Holywell Long, AMICE, and Emily McNaughton; *m* 1966, Kenneth John Heastey Nichols, *qv. Educ*: Carlisle and County High School for Girls. Admitted Solicitor of Supreme Court, 1959; private practice, 1959–63; Solicitor's Dept, New Scotland Yard, 1963–77. Mem., Cttee of Magistrates for Inner London, 1984–. *Recreations*: music, riding, watching cricket. *Address*: Greenwich Magistrates' Court, Blackheath Road, SE10 8PG.

LONG, Sir Ronald, Kt 1964; Solicitor; *b* 5 Sept. 1902; *s* of Sydney Richard and Kate Long; *m* 1931, Muriel Annie Harper; one *s* two *d. Educ*: Earls Colne Grammar Sch.; The School, Stamford, Lincs. President, The Law Society, 1963–64. Chm., Stansted Airport Consultative Cttee, 1969–79. *Recreations*: fishing, gardening. *Address*: Ayletts Farm, Halstead, Essex CO9 1QA. *T*: Halstead 472072.

LONG, Captain Rt. Hon. William Joseph, OBE 1985; PC (N Ireland) 1966; JP; Minister of Education, Northern Ireland, 1969–72; MP (Unionist) Ards, Parliament of Northern Ireland, 1962–72; *b* 23 April 1922; *s* of James William Long and Frederica (Walker); *m* 1942, Dr Elizabeth Doreen Mercer; one *s. Educ*: Friends' Sch., Great Ayton, Yorks; Edinburgh Univ.; RMC, Sandhurst. Served Royal Inniskilling Fusiliers, 1940–48. Secretary: NI Marriage Guidance Council, 1948–51; NI Chest and Heart Assoc., 1951–62. Parliamentary Secretary, Min. of Agriculture, NI, 1964–66; Sen. Parliamentary Secretary, Min. of Development, NI, Jan.–Oct. 1966; Minister of Educn, 1966–68; Minister of Home Affairs, Dec. 1968–March 1969; Minister of Develt, March 1969–May 1969. *Recreations*: cricket, horticulture, angling, sailing, model engineering, aviation. *Address*: Lisvarna, Warren Road, Donaghadee, Co. Down. *T*: Donaghadee 2538.

LONGAIR, Prof. Malcolm Sim, PhD; FRSE 1981; Astronomer Royal for Scotland, Regius Professor of Astronomy, University of Edinburgh, and Director of Royal Observatory, Edinburgh, since 1980; *b* 18 May 1941; *s* of James Sim Longair and Lily Malcolm; *m* 1975, Dr Deborah Janet Howard; one *s* one *d. Educ*: Morgan Acad., Dundee; Queen's Coll., Dundee, Univ. of St Andrews (BSc Electronic Physics, 1963); Cavendish Lab., Univ. of Cambridge (MA, PhD 1967). Res. Fellow, Royal Commn for Exhibn of 1851, 1966–68; Royal Soc. Exchange Fellow to USSR, 1968–69; Res. Fellow, 1967–71, and Official Fellow, 1971–80, Clare Hall, Cambridge; Univ. of Cambridge: Univ. Demonstrator in Phys., 1970–75; Univ. Lectr in Phys., 1975–80. Vis. Professor: of Radio Astronomy, Calif Inst. of Technol., 1972; of Astronomy, Inst. for Advanced Study, Princeton, 1978. Editor, Monthly Notices of RAS, 1974–78. Hon. LLD Dundee, 1982. Britannica Award, 1986. *Publications*: (ed) Confrontation of Cosmological Theories with Observational Data, 1974; (ed with J. Einasto) The Large-Scale Structure of the Universe, 1978; (with J. E. Gunn and M. J. Rees) Observational Cosmology, 1978; (ed with J. Warner) The Scientific Uses of the Space Telescope, 1980; High Energy Astrophysics: an informal introduction, 1980; (ed with H. A. Brück and G. Coyne) Astrophysical Cosmology, 1982; Theoretical Concepts in Physics, 1984; over 100 papers, mostly in Monthly Notices of RAS. *Recreations*: music, esp. opera, 19th and 20th Century music and all piano music; art, architecture. *Address*: c/o Royal Observatory, Blackford Hill, Edinburgh EH9 3HJ. *T*: 031–667 3321.

LONGBOTHAM, Samuel; Lord-Lieutenant of the Western Isles, 1975–83; *b* Elgin, Morayshire, 19 March 1908; *s* of George Longbotham and Elizabeth Longbotham (*née* Monks); *m* 1941, Elizabeth Rae, *d* of Donald Davidson, Glasgow; two *s* one *d. Educ*: Elgin. Served War, 1940–46: with RA and Intelligence Corps: commissioned, 1944. Major, Lovat Scouts TA (RA), 1952–60; Major, North Highland ACF, 1968–75. DL Ross and

Cromarty, 1964. *Recreations:* angling, walking, reading, family life. *Address:* 25 Lewis Street, Stornoway, Isle of Lewis, Scotland. *T:* Stornoway 2519.

LONGBOTTOM, Charles Brooke; *b* 22 July 1930; *s* of late William Ewart Longbottom, Forest Hill, Worksop; *m* 1962, Anita, *d* of G. Trapani and Mrs Basil Mavroleon; two *d*. *Educ:* Uppingham. Contested (C) Stockton-on-Tees, 1955; MP (C) York, 1959–66; Parly Private Secretary to Mr Iain Macleod, Leader of the House, 1961–63. Barrister, Inner Temple, 1958; Chairman: Austin & Pickersgill, Shipbuilders, Sunderland, 1966–72; A&P Appledore International Ltd, 1970–79; Seascope Holdings Ltd, 1970–82; Seascope Sale & Purchase, 1970–; Seascope Offshore Ltd, 1978–; Seascope Shipping Ltd, 1982–; Seascope Insurance Holdings Ltd, 1984–86; Seascope Insurance Services Ltd, 1984–; Director: Henry Ansbacher Hldgs Ltd, 1982–; Henry Ansbacher & Co., 1982–; Ansbacher (Guernsey) Ltd, 1982–. Chairman, Ariel Foundation, 1960–. Member: General Advisory Council, BBC, 1965–75; Community Relations Commn, 1968–70. Member of Lloyd's. *Recreations:* shooting, golf and racing. *Address:* 66 Kingston House North, Princes Gate, SW7. *Clubs:* White's, Carlton.

LONGCROFT, James George Stoddart, FCA; FInstPet; Chairman: Tricentrol plc, since 1980; Combined Technologies Corporation plc, since 1981; Mnemos Ltd, since 1982; Senior Partner, Longcrofts, Chartered Accountants, since 1969; *b* 25 Oct. 1929; *s* of Reginald Stoddart Longcroft and Annie Mary Longcroft (*née* Thompson); *m* 1963, Valerie Sylvia Longcroft (*née* Ward); three *s* one *d*. *Educ:* Wellington Coll., Crowthorne, Berks. FBIM. Partner, Longcrofts, Chartered Accountants, 1955; Director 1964, Managing Director 1969, Tricentrol plc. Master, Worshipful Company of Founders, 1978; Mem., Honourable Artillery Co., 1957–. FRSA 1985. *Recreations:* skiing, tennis. *Address:* Chalet Souleiadou, 3780 Gstaad, Switzerland. *Club:* City of London.

LONGDEN, Sir Gilbert (James Morley), Kt 1972; MBE 1944; MA (Cantab), LLB; *b* 16 April 1902; *e s* of late Lieut-Colonel James Morley Longden, Castle Eden, Co. Durham, and of late Kathleen, *d* of George Blacker Morgan, JP; unmarried. *Educ:* Haileybury; Emmanuel Coll., Cambridge. Secretary ICI (India) Ltd, 1930–36; travelled throughout Asia (Middle and Far East) and in North and South America. Student at University of Paris, 1937. Called up from AOER into DLI, 1940; served with 2nd and 36th Divisions in Burma campaigns (MBE (mil.)). Adopted Parliamentary Candidate for Morpeth, 1938; contested (C) Morpeth, 1945; MP (C) SW Herts, 1950–Feb. 1974. UK Representative to Council of Europe, 1953–54; United Kingdom Delegate to 12th and 13th Sessions of United Nations; Past Chairman: British Atlantic Cttee; Conservative Gp for Europe; Great Britain-East Europe Centre. Vice-Chm., British Council. *Publications:* A Conservative Philosophy, 1947; and (jointly): One Nation, 1950; Change is our Ally, 1954; A Responsible Society, 1959; One Europe, 1969. *Recreations:* reading, writing, gardening. *Address:* 89 Cornwall Gardens, SW7 4AX. *T:* 01–584 5666. *Clubs:* Brooks's, Hurlingham.

LONGDEN, Henry Alfred, FEng, FICE, FIMinE; FGS; Director, Trafalgar House Investments Ltd, 1970–76; *b* 8 Sept. 1909; *s* of late Geoffrey Appleby Longden and late Marjorie Mullins; *m* 1935, Ruth, *d* of Arthur Gilliat, Leeds; one *s* four *d*. *Educ:* Oundle; Birmingham Univ. (BSc Hons). Served in Glass Houghton and Pontefract Collieries, 1930; Asst Gen. Manager, Stanton Ironworks Co., 1935; Gen. Manager, Briggs Colliers Ltd, 1940; Director: Blackwell Colliery Co., 1940; Briggs Collieries Co., 1941; New Hucknell Colliery Co., 1941; Area Gen. Manager, 1947, and Production Dir, 1948, NE Div., NCB; Dir-Gen., Production, NCB, 1955; Chm., W Midlands Div., NCB, 1960; Chm. and Chief Exec., Cementation Co. Ltd, 1963–70 (Dep. Chm. and Chief Exec, 1961–63). President: Instn of Mining Engineers, 1958; Engineering Industries Assoc., 1965–71; Member: Engineering Industry Trg Bd, 1967–70; Confedn of British Industry, 1968. Fellow, Fellowship of Engineering, 1977. *Publication:* Cadman Memorial Lecture, 1958. *Recreations:* Rugby football, cricket, tennis, shooting, fishing, sailing. *Address:* Raeburn, Northdown Road, Woldingham, Surrey. *T:* Woldingham 2245.

LONGDEN, Wilson, JP; Vice-Principal, Barnfield College, Luton, since 1973; Commissioner, Manpower Services Commission, since 1983; *b* 26 May 1936; *s* of Harold and Doris Longden; *m* 1966 (marr. diss. 1982); two *s*. *Educ:* Chesterfield Grammar Sch.; Univ. of Hull (BA Hons, Dip Ed); Univ. of Bradford (MSc). National service, RAF, 1955–57; Teacher, Northmount High Sch., Canada, 1961–62; Lectr, Matthew Boulton Tech. Coll., Birmingham, 1962–66, Bingley Coll. of Educn, 1966–67, Margaret McMillan Coll. of Educn, 1967–68, Hatfield Polytechnic, 1968–69, Coventry (Lanchester) Polytechnic, 1969–73. Pres., Assoc. of Vice-Principals of Colleges, 1982–84. JP Luton, 1980. *Publications:* The School Manager's, and the School Governor's Handbook, 1977; Meetings, 1977. *Recreations:* bringing up two sons (and associated housework); playing the piano. *Address:* 311 Turnpike Drive, Luton LU3 3RE. *T:* Luton 573905.

LONGE, Desmond Evelyn, MC 1944; DL; President, later Chairman, Norwich Union Insurance Group, 1964–81; (Vice-President, 1963); Chairman: Norwich Union Life Insurance Society, 1964–81; Norwich Union Fire Insurance Society Ltd, 1964–81; Maritime Insurance Co. Ltd, 1964–81; Scottish Union and National Insurance Co., 1964–81; East Coast Grain Ltd, 1962–82; Napak Ltd, 1962–82; President, D. E. Longe & Co. 1982 (Chairman, 1962–82); *b* 8 Aug. 1914; *y s* of late Rev. John Charles Longe, MA, Spixworth Park, Norfolk; *m* 1944, Isla (*née* Bell); one *s* one *d*. *Educ:* Woodbridge Sch., Suffolk. Director: Eastern Counties Group Ltd, to 1982; Eastern Counties Newspapers Ltd, 1977–82; Norwich Winterthur Holdings Ltd, 1977–81; Anglia TV Ltd, 1970–82. Member: BR Eastern Region Bd, 1969–70; BR London Midland Region Bd, 1971–74; (and Dep. Chm.) BR London and SE Region Bd, 1975–77; BR Property Bd, 1978–82. Mem., E Anglia Econ. Planning Council, 1965–68. A Church Commissioner, 1970–76. Chm., Royal Norfolk Agric. Assoc. (Pres., 1980). DL Norfolk, 1971; High Sheriff, Norfolk, 1975. Croix de Guerre avec Palme (French), 1944. *Recreations:* travel, hunting, fishing. *Address:* Woodton Grange, Bungay, Suffolk. *T:* Woodton 260. *Clubs:* Special Forces, MCC; Norfolk County (Norwich).

LONGFIELD, Dr Michael David; Director, Teesside Polytechnic, since 1980; *b* 28 April 1928; *s* of Edric Douglas Longfield and Dorothy Longfield (*née* Hennessey); *m* 1st, 1952, Ann McDonnell; two *s* two *d*; 2nd, 1970, June Shirley, *d* of late Levi and of Esther Beman; two *s*. *Educ:* Prince Henry's Grammar Sch., Otley; Leeds Univ. BSc, PhD; CEng, MIMechE. Lectr in Mech. Engrg, Univ. of Leeds, 1960–68; Manager, Leeds Univ. Industrial Unit of Tribology, 1968–70; Head of Dept of Mech., Marine and Production Engrg, Liverpool Polytechnic, 1970–72; Asst Dir, Teesside Polytechnic, 1972–80. *Publications:* contribs to engineering and medical engineering journals. *Address:* Plum Tree House, Thirlby, Thirsk, N Yorks YO7 2DJ.

LONGFORD, 7th Earl of, *cr* 1785, **Francis Aungier Pakenham,** KG 1971; PC 1948; Baron Longford, 1759; Baron Silchester (UK), 1821; Baron Pakenham (UK), 1945; *b* 5 Dec. 1905; 2nd *s* of 5th Earl of Longford, KP, MVO; *S* brother (6th Earl) 1961; *m* 1931, Elizabeth (*see* Countess of Longford); four *s* three *d* (and one *d* decd). *Educ:* Eton; New Coll., Oxford, MA. 1st Class in Modern Greats, 1927. Tutor, University Tutorial Courses, Stoke-on-Trent, 1929–31; Cons. Party Economic Res. Dept, 1930–32. Christ Church, Oxford: Lecturer in Politics, 1932; Student in Politics, 1934–46, and 1952–64. Prospective

Parliamentary Labour Candidate for Oxford City, 1938. Enlisted Oxford and Bucks LI (TA), May 1939; resigned commission on account of ill-health, 1940. Personal assistant to Sir William Beveridge, 1941–44; a Lord-in-Waiting to the King, 1945–46; Parliamentary Under-Secretary of State, War Office, 1946–47; Chancellor of the Duchy of Lancaster, 1947–48; Minister of Civil Aviation, 1948–51; First Lord of the Admiralty, May-Oct. 1951; Lord Privy Seal, 1964–65; Secretary of State for the Colonies, 1965–66; Leader of the House of Lords, 1964–68; Lord Privy Seal, 1966–68; Chm., The National Bank Ltd, 1955–63; Dir, Sidgwick and Jackson, 1980–85 (Chm., 1970–80). Chm., Nat. Youth Employment Council, 1968–71; Joint Founder: New Horizon Youth Centre, 1964; New Bridge for Ex-Prisoners, 1956; (also Dir) The Help Charitable Trust, 1986. *Publications:* Peace by Ordeal (The Anglo-Irish Treaty of 1921), 1935 (repr. 1972); (autobiog.) Born to Believe, 1953; (with Roger Opie), Causes of Crime, 1958; The Idea of Punishment, 1961; (autobiog.) Five Lives, 1964; Humility, 1969; (with Thomas P. O'Neill) Eamon De Valera, 1970; (autobiog.) The Grain of Wheat, 1974; Abraham Lincoln, 1974; Jesus Christ, 1974; Kennedy, 1976; St Francis of Assisi, 1978; Nixon, 1980; (with Anne McHardy) Ulster, 1981; Pope John Paul II, 1982; Diary of a Year, 1982; Eleven at No. 10: a personal view of Prime Ministers, 1984; One Man's Faith, 1984; The Search for Peace, 1985; The Bishops, 1986. *Heir:* s Thomas (Frank Dermot) Pakenham, *qv. Address:* Bernhurst, Hurst Green, East Sussex. *T:* Hurst Green 248; 18 Chesil Court, Chelsea Manor Street, SW3. *T:* 01–352 7794; The Help Charitable Trust, 39/41 New Oxford Street, WC1A 1BH. *Club:* Garrick.

See also Lady Rachel Billington, Lady Antonia Fraser, Hon. M. A. Pakenham, A. D. Powell.

LONGFORD, Countess of; Elizabeth Pakenham, CBE 1974; *b* 30 Aug. 1906; *d* of late N. B. Harman, FRCS, 108 Harley Street, W1, and of Katherine (*née* Chamberlain); *m* 1931, Hon. F. A. Pakenham (*see* 7th Earl of Longford); four *s* three *d* (and one *d* decd). *Educ:* Headington Sch., Oxford; Lady Margaret Hall, Oxford (MA). Lectr for WEA and Univ. Extension Lectr, 1929–35. Contested (Lab) Cheltenham, 1935, Oxford, 1950; candidate for King's Norton, Birmingham, 1935–43. Mem., Rent Tribunal, Paddington and St Pancras, 1947–54; Trustee, National Portrait Gall., 1968–78; Member: Adv. Council, V&A Museum, 1969–75; Adv. Bd, British Library, 1976–80; Hon. Life Pres., Women Writers and Journalists, 1979. Hon. DLitt Sussex 1970. *Publications:* (as Elizabeth Pakenham): Points for Parents, 1956; Catholic Approaches (ed), 1959; Jameson's Raid, 1960, new edn 1982; (as Elizabeth Longford) Victoria RI, 1964 (James Tait Black Memorial Prize for Non-Fiction, 1964); Wellington: Years of the Sword, 1969 (Yorkshire Post Prize); Wellington: Pillar of State, 1972; The Royal House of Windsor, 1974; Churchill, 1974; Byron's Greece, 1975; Life of Byron, 1976; A Pilgrimage of Passion: the life of Wilfrid Scawen Blunt, 1979; (ed) Louisa: Lady in Waiting, 1979; Images of Chelsea, 1980; The Queen Mother, a biography, 1981; Eminent Victorian Women, 1981; Elizabeth R, 1983; The Pebbled Shore (autobiog.), 1986. *Recreations:* gardening, reading. *Address:* Bernhurst, Hurst Green, East Sussex. *T:* Hurst Green 248; 18 Chesil Court, Chelsea Manor Street, SW3. *T:* 01–352 7794.

See also Lady Rachel Billington, Lady Antonia Fraser, Hon. M. A. Pakenham, T. F. D. Pakenham.

LONGFORD, Elizabeth; *see* Longford, Countess of.

LONGLAND, Cedric James, LVO 1949; Surgeon, Glasgow Royal Infirmary, 1954–77; *b* 30 Sept. 1914; *s* of Frank Longland; *m* 1945, Helen Mary Cripps; three *d*. *Educ:* Monkton Combe Sch. MB, BS (Hons in Medicine) London, 1937; House Surgeon and Demonstrator of Pathology, St Bartholomew's Hosp.; FRCS, 1939; MS London, 1949. 1 Airborne Division; Lieut RAMC 1942, Temp. Major, RAMC, 1943; SMO Bermuda Command, 1945; First Assistant, Surgical Professorial Unit, St Bartholomew's Hospital, 1947; Assistant Surgical Professorial Unit, University College Hospital, 1951. Bronze Cross (Holland), 1945. *Publications:* articles in Lancet and British Journal of Surgery. *Address:* Malmesbury Lodge, Grittleton, near Chippenham, Wiltshire SN14 6AW. *T:* Castle Combe 782624.

LONGLAND, Sir David (Walter), Kt 1977; CMG 1973; Parliamentary Commissioner for Administrative Investigations, Queensland, 1974–79; *b* 1 June 1909; 2nd *s* of David Longland and Mary McGriskin; *m* 1935, Ada Elizabeth Bowness (*d* 1977); one *s* one *d*. *Educ:* Queensland Govt Primary and Secondary Schs. Queensland Educn Dept, High Sch. teaching, 1926. Appointed: to State Treasury Dept, 1938; Premier's Dept, 1939; (re-apptd) Treasury Dept, 1940; (re-apptd) Premier's Dept, 1942; Officer in Charge of Migration for Qld, 1946; Under-Sec., Dept of Works and Housing, 1957; Chm., Public Service Bd, Qld, 1969. Member: Australian Cerebral Palsy Assoc. (Nat. Pres., 1967–68); Queensland Spastic Welfare League, 1958– (Pres., 1962–); Exec. Dir, Queensland Art Gallery Foundn. FASA, FAIM, FRIPA. *Recreations:* tennis, surfing, reading, gardening. *Address:* Elimbari, Unit 1, 39 Wambool Street, Bulimba Heights, Qld 4171, Australia. *T:* 399–8998. *Club:* Rotary (Brisbane).

LONGLAND, Sir Jack, (Sir John Laurence Longland), Kt 1970; Director of Education, Derbyshire, 1949–70; *b* 26 June 1905; *e s* of late Rev. E. H. Longland and late Emily, *e d* of Sir James Crockett; *m* 1934, Margaret Lowrey, *y d* of late Arthur Harrison, Elvet Garth, Durham; two *s* two *d*. *Educ:* King's Sch., Worcester; Jesus Coll., Cambridge (Rustat Exhibitioner and Scholar). 2nd Class, 1st Part Classical Tripos, 1925; 1st Class, 1st Division, Historical Tripos, Part II, 1926; 1st Class with special distinction, English Tripos, 1927; Charles Kingsley Bye-Fellow at Magdalene Coll., Cambridge, 1927–29; Austausch-student, Königsberg Univ., 1929–30; Lectr in English at Durham Univ., 1930–36; Dir Community Service Council for Durham County, 1937–40; Regional Officer of Nat. Council of Social Service, 1939–40; Dep. Educn Officer, Herts, 1940–42; County Educn Officer, Dorset CC, 1942–49. Athletic Blue; Pres., Cambridge Univ. Mountaineering Club, 1926–27; Member: Mount Everest Expedn, 1933; British East Greenland Expedn, 1935; Pres., Climbers' Club, 1945–48 and Hon. Mem., 1964; Pres., Alpine Club, 1973–76 (Vice-Pres., 1960–61); Member: Colonial Office Social Welfare Adv. Cttee, 1942–48; Develt Commn, 1948–78; Adv. Cttee for Educn in RAF, 1950–57; Adv. Cttee for Educn in Germany, 1950–57; Central Adv. Council for Educn in England and Wales, 1948–51; Nat. Adv. Council on the Training and Supply of Teachers, 1951–; Children's Adv. Cttee of the ITA, 1956–60; Wolfenden Cttee on Sport, 1958–60; Outward Bound Trust Council, 1962–73; Central Council of Physical Recreation Council and Exec., 1961–72; Electricity Supply Industry Training Bd, 1965–66; Royal Commn on Local Govt, 1966–69; The Sports Council, 1966–74 (Vice-Chm. 1971–74); Countryside Commn, 1969–74; Commn on Mining and the Environment, 1971–72; Water Space Amenity Commn, 1973–76; President: Assoc. of Educn Officers, 1960–61; British Mountaineering Council, 1962–65 (Hon. Mem., 1983); Chairman: Mountain Leadership Training Bd, 1964–80; Council for Environmental Educn, 1968–75. *Publications:* literary and mountaineering articles in various books and journals. *Recreations:* walking, books. *Address:* Bridgeway, Bakewell, Derbyshire. *T:* Bakewell 2252. *Clubs:* Savile, Alpine, Achilles.

LONGLAND, Sir John Laurence; *see* Longland, Sir Jack.

LONGLEY, Mrs Ann Rosamund; Head Mistress, Roedean School, since 1984; *b* 5 March 1942; *d* of late Jack Gilroy Dearlove and of Rhoda E.M. Dearlove (*née* Billing); *m*

1964, Stephen Roger Longley (d 1979); one s two d. Educ: Walthamstow Hall School, Sevenoaks; Edinburgh University (MA 1964); PGCE Bristol University, 1984. Wife and mother, 1964–; Teacher, Toorak Coll., Victoria, Australia, 1964–65; Asst Housemistress, Peninsula C of E Sch., Victoria, 1966–67; Residential Teacher, Choate School, Conn, USA, 1968–73; Teacher, Webb School, Calif, 1975–78; Headmistress, Vivian Webb School, Calif, 1981–84. Recreations: tennis, swimming, fishing, walking. Address: Roedean House, Roedean School, Brighton, Sussex BN2 5RQ. T: Brighton 680791. Clubs: New Cavendish; University (Los Angeles).

LONGLEY, Sir Norman, Kt 1966; CBE; DL; retired as Chairman, James Longley (Holdings) Ltd, Building and Civil Engineering Contractors, Crawley, Sussex; b 14 Oct. 1900; s of Charles John Longley and Anna Gibson Marchant; m 1925, Dorothy Lilian Baker; two s one d. Educ: Clifton. West Sussex County Council, 1945–61, Alderman 1957–61. President: National Federation of Building Trades Employers, 1950; International Federation of Building and Public Works Contractors, 1955–57. Hon. Fellow, Institute of Builders. DL West Sussex, 1975. Hon. DSc: Heriot-Watt, 1968; Sussex, 1986. Coronation Medal, 1953. Recreation: horticulture. Address: The Beeches, Crawley, Sussex. T: Crawley 20253.

LONGMAN, Peter Martin; Secretary, Museums and Galleries Commission, since 1984; b 2 March 1946; s of Denis Martin Longman and Mary Joy Longman (née Simmonds); m 1976, Sylvia June Prentice; two d. Educ: Huish's School, Taunton; University College, Cardiff; Univ. of Manchester. Finance Dept and Housing the Arts Officer, Arts Council, 1968–78; Dep. Dir, Crafts Council, 1978–83; Dep. Sec., Museums and Galleries Commn, 1983–84. Dir, Caryl Jenner Productions Ltd, 1983–. Mem., Exec. Council, Textile Conservation Centre Ltd, 1983–85. Publications: Working Party Reports: Training Arts Administrators, Arts Council, 1971; Area Museum Councils and Services, HMSO, 1984; Museums in Scotland, HMSO, 1986; articles on theatre, the arts, museums. Recreations: discovering Britain, listening to music. Address: Museums and Galleries Commission, 7 St James's Square, SW1Y 4JU. T: 01-839 9341.

LONGMORE, Andrew Centlivres; QC 1983; b 25 Aug. 1944; s of John Bell Longmore and Virginia Longmore (née Centlivres); m 1979, Margaret Murray McNair; one s. Educ: Winchester College; Lincoln College, Oxford. MA. Called to the Bar, Middle Temple, 1966. Publications: (co-editor) MacGillivray and Parkington, Law of Insurance, 6th edn 1975, 7th edn 1981. Recreation: fell-walking. Address: 7 King's Bench Walk, Temple, EC4Y 7DS. T: 01-583 0404.

LONGMORE, William James Maitland, CBE 1972; Director: Lloyds Bank International Ltd, 1971–75; Bank of London & South America Ltd, 1960–75; b 6 May 1919; 2nd s of late Air Chief Marshal Sir Arthur Murray Longmore, GCB, DSO; m 1941, Jean, d of 2nd Baron Forres of Glenogil; three d. Educ: Eton Coll. Royal Air Force, 1938–46 (Wing Comdr). Balfour, Williamson & Co. Ltd, 1946–75 (Chm., 1967–75). Vice-Chm., 1966–70, Chm., 1970–71, BNEC for Latin America. Recreations: shooting, sailing. Address: Strete End House, Bishop's Waltham, Hants SO3 1FS. T: Bishop's Waltham 2794. Club: Royal Yacht Squadron.

LONGRIGG, John Stephen, CMG 1973; OBE 1964; HM Diplomatic Service, retired; Administrator, The Common Law Institute of Intellectual Property, since 1983; b 1 Oct. 1923; s of late Brig. Stephen Hemsley Longrigg, OBE; m 1st, 1953, Lydia Meynell (marr. diss. 1965); one s one d; 2nd, 1966, Ann O'Reilly; one s. Educ: Rugby Sch.; Magdalen Coll., Oxford (BA). War Service, Rifle Bde, 1942–45 (despatches). FO, 1948; Paris, 1948; Baghdad, 1951; FO, 1953; Berlin, 1955; Cabinet Office, 1957; FO, 1958; Dakar, 1960; Johannesburg, 1962; Pretoria, 1962; Washington, 1964; FO, 1965–67; Bahrain, 1967–69; FCO, 1969–73; seconded to HQ British Forces, Hong Kong, 1974–76; FCO, 1976–82. Recreation: golf. Address: 2 The Cedars, 3 Westcombe Park Road, Blackheath, SE3 7RE. T: 01-858 1604. Clubs: Reform; Royal Blackheath Golf.
    See also R. E. Longrigg.

LONGRIGG, Roger Erskine; author; b 1 May 1929; s of Brig. S. H. Longrigg, OBE; m 1957, Jane Chichester; three d. Educ: Bryanston Sch.; Magdalen Coll., Oxford (BA Hons Mod. Hist.). Publications: A High Pitched Buzz, 1956; Switchboard, 1957; Wrong Number, 1959; Daughters of Mulberry, 1961; The Paper Boats, 1963; The Artless Gambler, 1964; Love among the Bottles, 1967; The Sun on the Water, 1969; The Desperate Criminals, 1971; The History of Horse Racing, 1972; The Jevington System, 1973; Their Pleasing Sport, 1975; The Turf, 1975; The History of Foxhunting, 1975; The Babe in the Wood, 1976; The English Squire and his Sport, 1977; Bad Bet, 1982. Recreations: trout fishing, racing. Address: Orchard House, Crookham, Hants. T: Aldershot 850333. Clubs: Brooks's, Pratt's.
    See also J. S. Longrigg.

LONGSTRETH THOMPSON, Francis Michael; see Thompson, F. M. L.

LONGUET-HIGGINS, Prof. Hugh Christopher, FRS 1958; DPhil (Oxon); Royal Society Research Professor, University of Sussex, since 1974; b 11 April 1923; e s of late Rev. H. H. L. Longuet-Higgins. Educ: Winchester (schol.); Balliol Coll., Oxford (schol., MA). Research Fellow of Balliol Coll., 1946–48; Lecturer and Reader in Theoretical Chemistry, University of Manchester, 1949–52; Prof. of Theoretical Physics, King's Coll., University of London, 1952–54; FRSE; John Humphrey Plummer Professor of Theoretical Chemistry, University of Cambridge, 1954–67; Royal Soc. Res. Prof., Univ. of Edinburgh, 1968–74; Fellow of Corpus Christi Coll., 1954–67, Life Fellow 1968; Hon. Fellow: Balliol Coll., Oxford, 1969; Wolfson Coll., Cambridge, 1977. A Governor, BBC, 1979–84. Warden, Leckhampton House, 1961–67. Editor of Molecular Physics, 1958–61. For. Mem., Amer. Acad. of Arts and Scis, 1961; Foreign Associate, US National Academy of Sciences, 1968. DUniv York, 1973; DU Essex, 1981; Hon. DSc Bristol, 1983. Harrison Meml Prize, Chemical Soc., 1950. Publications: co-author, The Nature of Mind (Gifford Lectures), 1972; papers on theoretical physics, chemistry and biology in scientific journals. Recreations: music and arguing. Address: Centre for Research on Perception and Cognition, Laboratory of Experimental Psychology, University of Sussex, Falmer, Brighton BN1 9QY.

LONGUET-HIGGINS, Michael Selwyn, FRS 1963; Royal Society Research Professor, University of Cambridge, since 1969; b 8 Dec. 1925; s of late Henry Hugh Longuet and Albinia Cecil Longuet-Higgins; m 1958, Joan Redmayne Tattersall; two s two d. Educ: Winchester Coll. (Schol.); Trinity Coll., Cambridge (Schol.). (BA). Admiralty Research Lab., Teddington, 1945–48; Res. Student, Cambridge, 1948–51; PhD Cambridge, 1951; Rayleigh Prize, 1951; Commonwealth Fund Fellowship, 1951–52; Res. Fellow, Trinity Coll., Cambridge, 1951–55. Nat. Inst. of Oceanography, 1954–69. Visiting Professor: MIT, 1958; Institute of Geophysics, University of California, 1961–62; Univ. of Adelaide, 1964. Prof. of Oceanography, Oregon State Univ., 1967–69. Foreign Associate, US Nat. Acad. of Sci., 1979. Hon. DTech Tech. Univ. of Denmark, 1979; Hon. LLD Glasgow, 1979. Sverdrup Gold Medal, Amer. Meteorolog. Soc., 1983; Internat. Coastal Engrg Award, Amer. Soc. of Civil Engineers, 1984. Publications: papers in applied mathematics,

esp. physical oceanography, dynamics of sea waves and currents. Recreations: music, mathematical toys. Address: Gage Farm, Comberton, Cambridge CB3 7DH.

LONGWORTH, Ian Heaps, PhD; FSA; Keeper of Prehistoric and Romano-British Antiquities, British Museum, since 1973; b 29 Sept. 1935; yr s of late Joseph Longworth and Alice (née Heaps); m 1967, Clare Marian Titford; one s one d. Educ: King Edward VII, Lytham; Peterhouse, Cambridge. Open and Sen. Scholar, Matthew Wren Student, 1957, MA, PhD, Cantab. Temp. Asst Keeper, Nat. Museum of Antiquities of Scotland, 1962–63; Asst Keeper, Dept of British and Medieval Antiquities, Brit. Mus., 1963–69; Asst Keeper, Dept of Prehistoric and Romano-British Antiquities, Brit. Mus., 1969–73. Mem., Ancient Monuments Bd for England, 1977–84. Chm., Area Archaeol. Adv. Cttee for NW England, 1978–79. Hon. Sec., Prehistoric Soc., 1966–74, Vice-Pres., 1976–80; Sec., Soc. of Antiquaries of London, 1974–79, Vice-Pres., 1985–. Publications: Yorkshire (Regional Archaeologies Series), 1965; (with G. J. Wainwright) Durrington Walls—excavations 1966–68, 1971; Collared Urns of the Bronze Age in Great Britain and Ireland, 1984; Prehistoric Britain, 1985; (with I. A. Kinnes) Catalogue of the Excavated Prehistoric and Romano-British Material in the Greenwell Collection, 1985; (ed with J. Cherry) Archaeology in Britain since 1945, 1986; articles in various learned jls on topics of prehistory. Address: 2 Hurst View Road, South Croydon, Surrey CR2 7AG. T: 01-688 4960. Club: MCC.

LONGWORTH, Wilfred Roy, PhD; FRSC, FRACI, FACE; Principal Director (formerly Director), Swinburne Institute of Technology and College of Technical and Further Education, 1970–86; b 13 Dec. 1923; s of Wilfred Arnold Longworth and Jessie Longworth; m 1951, Constance Elizabeth Dean; two d. Educ: Bolton Sch.; Manchester Univ. (BSc, MSc, PhD). FRIC 1963; FRACI 1970; FACE 1976. Works Manager and Chief Chemist, Blackburn & Oliver, 1948–56; postgrad. res., Univ. of Keele, 1956–59; Lectr in Physical Chemistry, Huddersfield Coll. of Technol., 1959–60; Sen. Lectr in Phys. Chem., Sunderland Technical Coll., 1960–64; Head, Dept of Chem. and Biol., Manchester Polytechnic, 1964–70. Pres., World Council on Co-op. Educn, 1983–85. Publications: articles on cationic polymerisation in learned jls. Recreations: lawn bowls, gardening. Address: 35 Fairmont Avenue, Camberwell, Vic 3124, Australia. T: 299 1145. Clubs: Kelvin (Melbourne, Aust.); Hawthorn (Hawthorn, Aust.).

LONSDALE, 7th Earl of (UK), cr 1807; **James Hugh William Lowther,** Viscount and Baron Lowther, 1797; Bt 1764; b 3 Nov. 1922; er s of Anthony Edward, Viscount Lowther (d 1949), and Muriel Frances, Viscountess Lowther (d 1968), 2nd d of late Sir George Farrar, Bt, DSO, and Lady Farrar; S grandfather, 1953; m 1975, Caroline, y d of Sir Gerald Ley, 3rd Bt, TD; one s one d (and three s three d of previous marriages). Educ: Eton. Armed Forces, 1941–46; RAC and East Riding Yeo. (despatches, Captain). Structural engineering, 1947–50. Farmer, forester, and director of associated and local companies in Cumbria; Chairman: Lakeland Investments Ltd and of nine subsid. or associated cos; Chm., Border TV, 1985– (Vice-Chm., 1984–85; Dir, 1960–). Chm., Northern Adv. Council for Sport and Recreation, 1966–71; Member: Northern Region Economic Planning Council, 1964–72; Sports Council, 1971–74; English Tourist Bd, 1971–75; TGO (Pres., 1971–73); Forestry Cttee for GB (Chm., 1974–76); President: NW Area British Legion, 1961–73; NW Div. YMCA, 1962–72; Cumberland and Westmorland NPFA; British Deer Soc., 1963–70; Lake District Naturalists' Trust, 1963–73. Master, Farmers' Co., 1973–74. CBIM; FRSA 1984. Heir: s Viscount Lowther, qv. Address: Askham Hall, Penrith, Cumbria CA10 2PF. T: Hackthorpe 208. Clubs: Brooks's, Turf.

LONSDALE, Maj.-Gen. Errol Henry Gerrard, CB 1969; MBE 1942; Transport Officer-in-Chief (Army) 1966–69; b 26 Feb. 1913; 2nd s of Rev. W. H. M. Lonsdale, Arlaw Banks, Barnard Castle; m 1944, Muriel Allison, d of E. R. Payne, Mugswell, Chipstead; one s one d. Educ: Westminster Sch.; St Catharine's Coll., Cambridge (MA). 2nd Lt, RASC, 1934; Bt Lt-Col 1952; Col 1957; Brig. 1961; Maj.-Gen. 1966. Sudan Defence Force, 1938–43 (despatches); Chief Instr, RASC Officers Trng Centre, 1944–45; AQMG FARELF, 1945–47; CRASC 16 Airborne Div., 1947–48; GSOI, 1948–51; AA & QMG, War Office, 1951–53; Korea, 1953–54; Malaya, 1954–56 (despatches); ACOS, G4 Northern Army Group, 1957–60; DDST, 1st Corps, 1960–62; Comdt RASC Trng Centre, 1962–64; Inspector, RASC, 1964–65; ADC to the Queen, 1964–66; Inspector, RCT, 1965–66; psc; jssc. Col Comdt, RCT, 1969–74. Hon. Colonel: 160 Regt RCT(V), 1967–74; 562 Para Sqdn RCT(V), 1969–78. FCIT (MInstT) 1966. Vice-President: Transport Trust, 1969; Internat. Union for Modern Pentathlon and Biathlon, 1976–80; Pres., Modern Pentathlon Assoc. of Great Britain, 1977– (Chm., 1967); Chm., Inst. of Advanced Motorists, 1971–79, Vice-Pres., 1979. Recreations: modern pentathlon, photography, driving. Address: Stoke House, Stogursey, near Bridgwater, Somerset TA5 1TA. T: Nether Stowey 732763.

LOOKER, Sir Cecil (Thomas), Kt 1969; Chairman, Australian United Corporation Ltd; Principal Partner, Ian Potter & Co., Sharebrokers, 1967–76 (Partner, 1953); Director of various other companies; b 11 April 1913; s of Edward William and Martha Looker; m 1941, Jean Leslyn Withington; one s two d. Educ: Fort Street Boys' High Sch., Sydney; Sydney Univ. (BA). Apptd to Commonwealth Public Service, 1937; Private Sec. to Prime Minister (Rt Hon. later Sir Robert Menzies), 1939–41. War of 1939–45: RANVR, 1942–45. Resigned Commonwealth Public Service, 1946, and joined Ian Potter & Co. Chm., Stock Exchange of Melbourne, 1966–72 (Mem. 1962–78); Pres., Australian Associated Stock Exchanges, 1968–71. Apptd by Dept of Territories as Dir of Papua and New Guinea Development Bank, 1966. Chairman: Exec. Cttee, Duke of Edinburgh's Third Commonwealth Study Conf., Aust., 1966–68; Aust. Adv. Cttee, Duke of Edinburgh's Fifth Study Conf., Canada, 1980. Recreation: farming. Address: 26 Tormey Street, North Balwyn, Victoria 3104, Australia. T: 857–9316. Clubs: Australian, Royal Automobile Club of Victoria (Melbourne) (President).

LOOSLEY, Stanley George Henry, MC 1944; MA Cantab; JP Glos; Headmaster of Wycliffe College, 1947–67; b 18 July 1910; s of Harold D. and Edith M. Loosley; m 1938, Margaret Luker; two s one d. Educ: Wycliffe Coll.; St John's Coll., Cambridge. Asst Master, Wycliffe Coll., 1934–39; War of 1939–45, RA, Sept. 1939–Oct. 1945; Major OC 220 Field Battery, 1941 (despatches, MC); NW Europe Campaign, 1944; sc; Bde Major RA 43 Div., 1945; Senior Asst Master, Wycliffe Coll., 1945–47. A Vice-Pres., Gloucestershire Magistrates Assoc., 1981–. Publication: Wycliffe College—The First Hundred Years, 1982. Recreations: travel, unskilled gardening, walking, looking, listening. Address: Brillings, Chalford Hill, Stroud, Glos. T: Brimscombe 883505. Club: Royal Over-Seas League.

LOPES, family name of **Baron Roborough.**

LORAINE, Dr John Alexander, FRCPEd; FRSE 1978; Senior Lecturer, Department of Community Medicine, University of Edinburgh, since 1979; b 14 May 1924; s of Lachlan Dempster Loraine and Ruth (née Jack); m 1974, Alison Blair. Educ: George Watson's Boys' Coll., Edinburgh; Univ. of Edinburgh. MB ChB (Hons) 1946, PhD 1949, DSc 1959; FRCPEd 1960. House Phys., Royal Infirmary, Edinburgh, under Prof. Sir Stanley Davidson, 1947; Mem., Scientific Staff, MRC Clinical Endocrinology Unit, Edinburgh, 1947–61; Dir of the Unit, 1961–72. Visiting Prof. of Endocrinology, Donner Laboratory and Donner Pavilion, Univ. of Calif., Berkeley, USA, 1964. Hon. Senior Lectr, Dept of Pharmacology, Univ. of Edinburgh, 1965–72; MRC Ext. Sci. Staff, 1972–79; Dir, Centre for Human Ecology, 1978–84. Founder Chm., Doctors and Overpopulation Gp, 1972–; Vice-Chm., Conservation Soc., 1974–. Member: Internat. Union for Scientific Study of Population, 1977–83; Internat. Epidemiological Assoc., 1985–. FRSA. *Publications:* (co-author) Hormone Assays and their Clinical Application, 1958, (co-editor) 4th edn 1976; (co-author) Recent Research on Gonadotrophic Hormones, 1967; (co-author) Fertility and Contraception in the Human Female, 1968; Sex and the Population Crisis, 1970; The Death of Tomorrow, 1972; (ed) Reproductive Endocrinology and World Population, 1973; (ed) Environmental Medicine, 1973; (ed) Understanding Homosexuality: its biological and psychological bases, 1974; Syndromes of the 'Seventies, 1977; (ed) Here Today: world outlooks from the Centre for Human Ecology, 1979; Global Signposts to the 21st Century, 1979; (ed) Environmental Medicine, 2nd edn, 1980; Energy Policies Around the World, 1982; author and co-author of numerous scientific and general pubns dealing with sex hormones, fertility, contraception, population and related issues, incl. women's rights, mineral resources, nuclear proliferation and environmental medicine. *Recreations:* reading modern history and political biography, music, bridge. *Address:* 20 Buckingham Terrace, Edinburgh EH4 3AD. *T:* 031-332 3698. *Club:* University of Edinburgh Staff.

LORAM, Vice-Adm. Sir David (Anning), KCB 1979; LVO 1957; Deputy Supreme Allied Commander Atlantic, 1977–80, retired; Gentleman Usher to The Queen, since 1982; *b* 24 July 1924; *o* surv. *s* of late Mr and Mrs John A. Loram; *m* 1st, 1958, Fiona Beloe (marr. diss. 1981); three *s*; 2nd, 1983, Diana Keigwin. *Educ:* Royal Naval Coll., Dartmouth (1938–41). Awarded King's Dirk. Served War: HMS Sheffield, Foresight, Anson, Zealous, 1941–45. ADC to Governor-Gen. of New Zealand, 1946–48; specialised in Signal Communications, 1949; served in HMS Chequers, 1951; Equerry to the Queen, 1954–57; qualified helicopter pilot, 1955; commanded HMS Loch Fada, 1957; Directing Staff, JSSC, 1959–60; served in HMS Belfast, 1961; Naval Attaché, Paris, 1964–67; commanded HMS Arethusa, 1967; Dir, Naval Ops and Trade, 1970–71; commanded HMS Antrim, 1971; ADC to The Queen, 1972–73; Comdr British Forces, FO Malta, and NATO Comdr SE Mediterranean, 1973–75; Comdt, Nat. Defence Coll., 1975–77. Mem., RN Cresta Team, 1954–59. *Recreations:* country pursuits. *Address:* Broadacre, Cosmore, near Dorchester, Dorset. *T:* Buckland Newton 294. *Club:* Chesapeake.

LORANT, Stefan; *b* 22 Feb. 1901; *m* 1963, Laurie Robertson (marr. diss. 1978); two *s*. *Educ:* Evangelical Gymnasium, Budapest; Academy of Economics, Budapest; Harvard Univ. (MA 1961). Editor: Das Magazin, Leipzig, 1925; Bilder Courier, Berlin, 1926; Muenchner Illustrierte Presse, 1927–33; Weekly Illustrated, 1934; Picture Post, 1938–40; Founder of Lilliput, Editor, 1937–40. Hon. LLD, Knox Coll., Galesburg, Ill., 1958; Dr of Human Letters *hc* Syracuse Univ., NY, 1985. *Publications:* I Was Hitler's Prisoner, 1935; Lincoln, His Life in Photographs, 1941; The New World, 1946, rev. edn 1965; F.D.R., a pictorial biography, 1950; The Presidency, a pictorial history of presidential elections from Washington to Truman, 1951; Lincoln: a picture story of his life, 1952, rev. and enl. edns 1957, 1969; The Life of Abraham Lincoln, 1954; The Life and Times of Theodore Roosevelt, 1959; Pittsburgh, the story of an American city, 1964, rev. and enl. edns 1975, 1980; The Glorious Burden: the American Presidency, 1968, rev. and enl. edn, 1976; Sieg Heil: an illustrated history of Germany from Bismarck to Hitler, 1974; Pete: the story of Peter F. Flaherty, 1978; Ich war Hitler's Gefangener, 1985; Wir vom Film, 1986; My Years in England, fragments to an autobiography, 1986. *Address:* Farview, Lenox, Mass 01240, USA. *T:* Lenox 637–0666.

LORD, Alan, CB 1972; Deputy Chairman and Chief Executive, Lloyd's of London, since 1986; *b* 12 April 1929; *er s* of Frederick Lord and Anne Lord (*née* Whitworth), Rochdale; *m* 1953, Joan Ogden; two *d*. *Educ:* Rochdale; St John's Coll., Cambridge. Entered Inland Revenue, 1950; Private Sec. to Dep. Chm. and to Chm. of the Board, 1952–54; HM Treasury, 1959–62; Principal Private Sec. to First Secretary of State (then Rt Hon. R. A Butler), 1962–63; Comr of Inland Revenue, 1969–73, Dep. Chm. Bd, 1971–73; Principal Finance Officer to DTI, subseq. to Depts of Industry, Trade, and Prices and Consumer Protection, 1973–75; Second Permanent Sec. (Domestic Econ.), HM Treasury, 1975–77. Man. Dir, 1980, Chief Exec., 1982–84, Dunlop Hldgs plc; formerly: Exec. Dir, Dunlop Hldgs; Man. Dir, Dunlop Internat. Ltd, 1978. Director: Allied-Lyons plc, 1979–86; Bank of England, 1983–86; Johnson Matthey Bankers, 1985–86. Chm., CBI Taxation Cttee, 1979–81. Mem. Council of Management, Henley Centre for Forecasting, 1977–82. Governor, NIESR; Trustee, Southern African Studies Trust; Pres., Johnian Soc., 1985–86. *Publications:* A Strategy for Industry (Sir Ellis Hunter Meml Lecture, Univ. of York), 1976; Earning an Industrial Living (1985 Johnian Society Lecture). *Recreations:* reading, gardening, rough-shooting. *Address:* Mardens, Hildenborough, Tonbridge, Kent. *T:* Hildenborough 832268. *Club:* Reform.

LORD, Geoffrey; Secretary and Treasurer, Carnegie United Kingdom Trust, since 1977; *b* 24 Feb. 1928; *s* of Frank Lord and Edith Lord; *m* 1955, Jean; one *s* one *d*. *Educ:* Rochdale Grammar Sch.; Univ. of Bradford (MA Applied Social Studies). AIB. Midland Bank Ltd, 1946–58; Probation and After-Care Service, 1958–76: Dep. Chief Probation Officer, Greater Manchester, 1974–76. FRSA 1985. *Publication:* The Arts and Disabilities, 1981. *Recreations:* philately, walking, gardening, appreciation of the arts. *Address:* 9 Craigleith View, Ravelston, Edinburgh EH4 3JZ. *T:* 031-337 7623. *Club:* New (Edinburgh).

LORD, John Herent; His Honour Judge Lord; a Circuit Judge, since 1978; *b* 5 Nov. 1928; *s* of late Sir Frank Lord, KBE, JP, DL, and of Lady Lord (*née* Rosalie Jeanette Herent), Brussels; *m* 1959, June Ann, *d* of late George Caladine and of Ada Caladine, Rochdale; three *s*. *Educ:* Manchester Grammar Sch.; Merton Coll., Oxford (BA (Jurisprudence), MA). Half Blue, Oxford Univ. lacrosse XII, 1948 and 1949; represented Middlesex, 1950. Called to Bar, Inner Temple, 1951; The Junior of Northern Circuit, 1952; Asst Recorder of Burnley, 1971; a Recorder of the Crown Court, 1972–78. Governor, Bramcote Sch.; Trustee: Friends of Shrewsbury Sch.; Frank Lord Postgraduate Med. Centre. *Recreations:* photography, shooting. *Address:* Three Lanes, Greenfield, Oldham, Lancs. *T:* Saddleworth 2198. *Clubs:* St James's (Manchester); Leander.

LORD, Michael Nicholson; MP (C) Suffolk Central, since 1983; *b* 17 Oct. 1938; *s* of John Lord and Jessie Lord (*née* Nicholson); *m* 1965, Jennifer Margaret (*née* Childs); one *s* one *d*. *Educ:* Christ's College, Cambridge. MA. MBIM; FArborA. Arboricultural consultant. PPS: to Minister of State, MAFF, 1984–85; to Chief Secretary to the Treasury, 1985–. *Recreations:* golf, sailing, gardening, trees. *Address:* House of Commons, SW1A 0AA. *Club:* Farmers'.

LORD, Peter Herent, FRCS; Consultant Surgeon, Wycombe General Hospital, High Wycombe, since 1964; *b* 23 Nov. 1925; *s* of Sir Frank Lord, KBE, JP, DL and Rosalie Jeanette Herent; *m* 1952, Florence Shirley Hirst; two *s* two *d*. *Educ:* Manchester Grammar Sch.; St John's Coll., Cambridge (MA, MChir). St George's Hosp., Salford Royal Hosp., Christie Hosp., Manchester, St Margaret's, Epping, St George's Hosp., 1949–63 (Captain, RAMC, 1952–53). Royal College of Surgeons: H. N. Smith Research Fellow, 1964; Penrose May Teacher, 1970; Mem. Council, 1978–; Vice-Pres., 1986–. *Publications:* Cardiac Pacemakers, 1964; Pilonidal Sinus, 1964; Wound Healing, 1966; Haemorrhoids, 1969; Hydrocoele, 1972, Surgery in Old Age, 1980. *Recreation:* sailing. *Address:* Mayfield, 38 Burkes Road, Beaconsfield, Bucks HP9 1PN. *T:* Beaconsfield 4488.

See also J. H. Lord.

LORD, William Burton Housley, CB 1979; scientific and technological consultant; *b* 22 March 1919; *s* of Arthur James Lord and Elsie Lord (*née* Housley); *m* 1942, Helena Headon Jaques; two *d*. *Educ:* King George V Sch., Southport; Manchester Univ.; London Univ. (External MSc); Trinity Coll., Cambridge (MA). Enlisted Royal Fusiliers, commn S Lancs Regt (served Middle East and N Africa), 1941–46. Cambridge Univ., 1946. Entered Civil Service, 1949; joined Atomic Weapons Res. Estab., 1952; Head of Metallurgy Div., AWRE, 1958; moved to MoD, 1964; Asst Chief Scientific Adviser (Research), 1965; Dep. Chief Scientist (Army), 1968–71; Dir Gen., Establishments, Resources and Programmes (B), MoD, 1971–76; Dir, RARDE, 1976–79. Award for wartime invention of radio proximity fuse, 1952. *Recreations:* amateur radio, walking, orienteering, water sports. *Address:* c/o Barclays Bank, 2 Victoria Street, SW1H 0ND.

LOREN, Sophia; film actress; *b* 20 Sept. 1934; *d* of Ricardo Scicolone and Romilda Villani; *m* 1957, Carlo Ponti, film producer (marriage annulled in Juarez, Mexico, Sept. 1962; marriage in Paris, France, April 1966); two *s*. *Educ:* parochial sch. and Teachers' Institute, Naples. First leading role in, Africa sotto i Mari, 1952; acted in many Italian films, 1952–55; subsequent films include: The Pride and the Passion; Boy on a Dolphin; Legend of the Lost; The Key; Desire under the Elms; Houseboat; The Black Orchid (Venice Film Festival Award, 1958); That Kind of Woman; It Started in Naples; Heller in Pink Tights; The Millionairess; Two Women (Cannes Film Festival Award, 1961); A Breath of Scandal; Madame sans Gêne; La Ciociara; El Cid; Boccaccio 70; Five Miles to Midnight; Yesterday, Today and Tomorrow; The Fall of the Roman Empire; Marriage, Italian Style; Operation Crossbow; Lady L; Judith; A Countess from Hong Kong; Arabesque; Sunflower; The Priest's Wife; The Man of La Mancha; The Verdict; The Voyage; Una Gionnata Particolare; Firepower; Blood Feud. *Publications:* Eat with Me, 1972; Sophia Loren on Woman and Beauty, 1984; *relevant publication:* Sophia: living and loving, by A. E. Hotcher, 1979. *Address:* Chalet Daniel Burgenstock, Luzern, Switzerland.

LORENZ, Dr Konrad, MD, DPhil; Director, Research Station for Ethology, Konrad-Lorenz-Institute, Austrian Academy of Sciences, since 1982; *b* 7 Nov. 1903; *s* of Prof. Dr Adolf Lorenz and Emma Lorenz (*née* Lecher); *m* 1927, Dr Margarethe Lorenz (*née* Gebhardt); one *s* two *d*. *Educ:* High Sch., Vienna; Columbia Univ., New York; Univ. of Vienna. Univ. Asst at Anatomical Inst. of University of Vienna (Prof. Hochstetter), 1928–35; Lectr in Comparative Anat. and Animal Psychol., University of Vienna, 1937–40; University Lectr, Vienna, 1940; Prof. of Psychol. and Head of Dept, University of Königsberg, 1940; Head of Research Station for Physiology of Behaviour of the Max-Planck-Inst. for Marine Biol., 1951; Co-Director, Max-Planck-Inst. for Physiology of Behaviour, 1956–73; Dir, Dept for Animal Sociology, Inst. for Comparative Ethology, Austrian Acad. of Scis, 1973–82. Hon. Prof., University of Münster, 1953 and München, 1957. Nobel Prize for Physiology or Medicine (jtly), 1973. Mem., Pour le Mérite for Arts and Science; Hon. Member: Assoc. for Study of Animal Behaviour, 1950; Amer. Ornithol. Union, 1951, etc; For. Mem., Royal Society, 1964. For. Assoc. Nat. Acad. of Sciences, USA, 1966. Hon. degrees: Leeds, 1962; Basel, 1966; Yale, 1967; Oxford, 1968; Chicago, 1970; Durham, 1972; Birmingham, 1974; Vienna, 1980. Gold Medal, Zoological Soc., New York, 1955; City Prize, Vienna, 1959; Gold Boelsche Medal, 1962; Austrian Distinction for Science and Art, 1964; Prix Mondial, Cino del Duca, 1969. Grosses Verdienstkreuz, 1974; Bayerischer Verdienstorden, 1974. *Publications:* King Solomon's Ring, 1952; Man Meets Dog, 1954; Evolution and Modification of Behaviour, 1965; On Aggression, 1966; Studies in Animal and Human Behaviour, 1970; (jtly) Man and Animal, 1972; Civilized Man's Eight Deadly Sins, 1974; Behind the Mirror, 1977; The World of the Greylag Goose, 1979; The Foundations of Ethology, 1983; articles in Tierpsychologie, Behaviour, etc. *Address:* Adolf-Lorenzgasse 2, A-3422 Altenberg, Austria.

LORIMER, Dr George Huntly, FRS 1986; Research Leader, Central Research Department, E. I. Du Pont de Nemours & Co., since 1978; *b* 14 Oct. 1942; *s* of Gordon and Ellen Lorimer; *m* 1970, Freia (*née* Schulz-Baldes); one *s* one *d*. *Educ:* George Watson's College, Edinburgh; Univ. of St Andrews (BSc); Univ. of Illinois (MS); Michigan State Univ. (PhD). Scientist, Max-Planck Society, Berlin, 1972–74; Research Fellow, Inst. for Advanced Studies, ANU, Canberra, 1974–77; Scientist, Society for Radiation and Environmental Research, Munich, 1977. Mem., Amer. Soc. of Biological Chemists. *Publications:* contribs to Biochemistry, Jl of Biological Chemistry. *Recreations:* music, philately. *Address:* 2025 Harwyn Road, Wilmington, Delaware 19810, USA. *T:* (home) (302) 475–6748; (office) (302) 772–4833.

LORIMER, Hew Martin, OBE 1986; RSA; Sculptor; Representative in Fife of National Trust for Scotland; *b* 22 May 1907; 2nd *s* of late Sir Robert Stodart Lorimer, KBE, Hon. LLD, ARA, RSA, architect, and of Violet Alicia (*née* Wyld); *m* 1936, Mary McLeod Wylie (*d* 1970), 2nd *d* of H. M. Wylie, Edinburgh; two *s* one *d*. *Educ:*Loretto; Edinburgh Coll. of Art, Andrew Grant Scholarship, 1933 and Fellowship, 1934–35. National Library of Scotland, Edinburgh, sculptor of the 7 allegorical figures, 1952–55; Our Lady of the Isles, South Uist, 1955–57; St Francis, Dundee, 1957–59. Hon. LLD Dundee, 1983. *Recreations:* music, travel, home. *Address:* Kellie Castle, Pittenweem, Anstruther, Fife KY10 2RF. *T:* Arncroach 306.

LORIMER, Sir (Thomas) Desmond, Kt 1976; Chairman, Northern Bank Ltd, since 1986 (Director, since 1983; Deputy Chairman, 1985); *b* 20 Oct. 1925; *s* of Thomas Berry Lorimer and Sarah Ann Lorimer; *m* 1957, Patricia Doris Samways; two *d*. *Educ:* Belfast Technical High Sch. Chartered Accountant, 1948; Fellow, Inst. of Chartered Accountants in Ireland, 1957. Practised as chartered accountant, 1952–74; Sen. Partner, Harmood, Banner, Smylie & Co., Belfast, Chartered Accountants, 1960; Chm., Lamont Holdings PLC, 1973–; Dir, Ruberoid PLC, 1972–. Chm., Industrial Develt Bd for NI, 1982–85; Pres., Inst. of Chartered Accountants in Ireland, 1968–69; Chairman: Ulster Soc. of Chartered Accountants, 1960; NI Housing Exec., 1971–75; Mem., Rev. Body on Local Govt in NI, 1970. *Recreations:* gardening and golf. *Address:* Windwhistle Cottage, 6A Circular Road West, Cultra, Holywood, Co. Down BT18 0AT. *T:* Holywood 3323. *Clubs:* Carlton; Royal Belfast Golf, Royal Co. Down Golf (Co. Down).

LÖRINCZ-NAGY, János, Golden Grade of Order of Merit for Labour; Head of Department, Ministry of Foreign Affairs, Hungary, since 1981; *b* 19 Dec. 1931; *m* Ida Lörincz-Nagy; one *d*. *Educ:* Foreign Affairs Acad., Budapest; Coll. of Polit. Sciences, Budapest. Entered Diplomatic Service, 1953; Press Attaché, Peking, 1953–55; 2nd Sec., Djakarta, 1957–61; Dep. Head of Personnel Dept, 1964–68; Ambassador to Ghana, 1968–72; Head of Press Dept, 1972–74; Ambassador, Head of Hungarian Delegn to Internat. Commn of Control and Supervision in Saigon, 1974; Ambassador: to Sweden, 1975–76; to the Court of St James's, 1976–81. *Recreations:* reading and walking. *Address:* Ministry of Foreign Affairs, II Bem József rakpart 47, H-1394 Budapest, Hungary.

LORING, James Adrian, CBE 1979; *b* 22 Nov. 1918; *s* of Francis and Ellen Elizabeth Loring; *m* 1971, Anita Susan (*née* Hunt), JP; one *s* (and one *s* two *d* by previous marr.).

Educ: Central Foundation Sch., London; London Univ. DipEcon; ACIS. Served War, Royal Air Force, 1940–46; CO No 200 Staging Post, Shanghai, 1946. Secretary, Culpeper House Gp of Companies, 1947–49; John Lewis Partnership, 1949–60: Central Merchandise Advisor Advisor (Food), 1949–55; Gen. Manager, Waitrose Gp, 1955–57; Mem., Central Management (specialising in financial matters), 1958–60. Asst Director, Services to Spastics, Spastics Soc., 1960–67; Director, 1967–80; Dir, Camphill Village Trust, 1981. Immediate Past Pres., Internat. Cerebral Palsy Soc., 1984– (Pres., 1978–84). Vice-Chm., Centre on Environment for the Handicapped, 1976–86 (Hon. Life Mem.); Member: Mental Health Film Council, 1964–86; British Cttee of Rehabilitation Internat., 1980–86. *Publications:* ed, Learning Problems of the Cerebral Palsied, 1964; ed, Teaching the Cerebral Palsied Child, 1965; ed, The Spastic School Child and the Outside World, 1966; ed, The Subnormal Child, 1968; ed, Assessment of the Cerebral Palsied Child for Education, 1968. *Recreation:* country life. *Address:* 19 St Mary's Grove, Chiswick, W4 3LL. *T:* 01–995 5721.

LORNE, Marquess of; Torquhil Ian Campbell; *b* 29 May 1968; *s* and *heir* of 12th Duke of Argyll, *qv. Educ:* Craigflower; Cargilfield; Glenalmond Coll. A Page of Honour to the Queen, 1981–83. *Address:* Inveraray Castle, Inveraray, Argyll.

LOSINSKA, Kathleen Mary, (Kate), OBE 1986; President, Civil and Public Services Association, 1979–82 and 1983–86 (a Vice-President, 1982–83); *b* Croydon, Surrey, 5 Oct. 1924; *d* of late James Henry Conway, Border Regt and Dorothea Marguerite Hill; *m* 1942, Stanislaw Losinski (formerly serving Officer, Polish Air Force, subseq. 301 Bomber Sqdn, RAF, retd with rank of Sqdn Leader; awarded Polish Virtuti Militari Cross, Croix de Guerre, Cross of Lorraine, Yugoslav Cross of Valour, etc); one *s. Educ:* Selhurst Grammar Sch., Croydon (matriculation); university of life generally. Entered Civil Service, 1939; with Office of Population Censuses and Surveys. Delegate Mem., Council of Civil Service Unions, 1970– (Chm. 1980–81); Chairman: White Eagle Trust; Solidarnosc Found. Has held all honorary positions, CFSA. Founder Mem., Resistance Internat., 1983–. Governor, Ruskin Coll., 1976, 1979–. Silver Jubilee Medal, 1977. *Recreations:* journalism, reading, music, history, travel; work for the Christian Trade Union and Moderate Trade Union Movements. *Address:* 45 Rectory Park, Sanderstead, South Croydon, Surrey. *T:* 01–657 4834. *Club:* Civil Service.

LOSS, Joshua Alexander, (Joe Loss), LVO 1984; OBE 1978; band-leader; *b* 22 June 1909; *s* of Israel and Ada Loss; *m* 1938, Mildred Blanch Rose; one *s* one *d. Educ:* Jewish Free Sch., Spitalfields; Trinity Coll. of Music; London Coll. of Music. Played as silent film accompanist, Coliseum, Ilford and at Tower Ballroom, Blackpool, 1926; formed own orchestra at Astoria Ballroom, Charing Cross Road, 1930; first broadcast, 1934, then broadcast every week; was one of first West End bands to play in provinces in ballrooms and to top bill in variety theatres; toured through war inc. overseas; joined Mecca, 1959; became resident at Hammersmith Palais. Joined Regal Zonophone record co.; hit record, 1936, with Begin the Beguine (gold disc for sales of a million over 25 years); is now joint longest serving artiste on EMI label, has 50–year contract. First record with EMI I Only Have Eyes For You; hit singles inc. Wheels Cha Cha, The Maigret Theme, The Steptoe Theme; gold discs for long-playing albums inc. Joe Loss Plays Glenn Miller and All Time Party Hits. *Television:* Come Dancing, Bid for Fame, Home Town Saturday Night, and Holiday Parade; was featured in This Is Your Life, 1963 and 1980; panel member, New Faces. Awards: 15 Carl Alan Awards; Musical Express Top Big Band Award, 1963, 1964; Weekend Magazine Top Musical Personality Award, 1964; and Music Publishers' Assoc. Award as outstanding personality of 1976. First dance orch. in western world to appear in China, at Dairen, 1979. Has played for dancing on all QE2 world cruises, at Buckingham Palace and Windsor Castle for over 20 years, and at pre-wedding balls for Princess Margaret, Princess Alexandra and Princess Anne, for Queen's 50th birthday celebrations and for Queen Mother's 80th birthday; Royal Variety Performance, 1980. Queen's Silver Jubilee Medal, 1978. Freeman, City of London, 1979; Liveryman, Musicians' Co., 1983. *Recreations:* motoring, watching television, collecting watches, playing with grandchildren. *Address:* Morley House, Regent Street, W1. *T:* 01–580 1212. *Clubs:* St James's, Middlesex County Cricket (Life Member).

LOSTY, Howard Harold Walter, FEng, FIEE; Secretary, Institution of Electrical Engineers, since 1980; *b* 1 Aug. 1926; *s* of Patrick J. Losty and Edith E. Wilson; *m* 1950, Rosemary L. Everritt; two *d. Educ:* Harvey Grammar Sch, Folkestone; Sir John Cass Coll., London. BSc. GEC Research Laboratories, 1942–53; GEC Nuclear Power Programme, 1953–66; Head of Engineering Div., GEC Research Centre, 1966 71; Dir, GEC Hirst Research Centre, 1971–77; Man. Dir, GEC Electronic Devices Ltd, 1977–80. *Publications:* (co-author) Nuclear Graphite, 1962; some forty technical papers. *Recreations:* walking, listening to music (opera), reading history. *Address:* Shandon, 14 Wyatts Road, Chorleywood, Herts WD3 5TE. *T:* Chorleywood 3568.

LOTEN, Alexander William, CB 1984; CEng, FIMechE; FCIBS; Under Secretary, Department of the Environment, and Director, Mechanical and Electrical Engineering Services, Property Services Agency, 1981–85, retired; *b* 11 Dec. 1925; *s* of late Alec Oliver Loten and of Alice Maud Loten; *m* 1954, Mary Diana Flint; one *s* one *d. Educ:* Churcher's Coll., Petersfield; Corpus Christi Coll., Cambridge Univ. (BA). CEng, FIMechE 1980; FCIBSE 1970. Served War, RNVR, 1943–46 (Air Engr Officer). Engineer: Rolls-Royce Ltd, Derby, 1950–54; Benham & Sons, London, 1954–58; Air Min. Work Directorate, 1958–64; Sen. Engr, 1964–70; Superintending Engr (Mechanical Design), 1970–75, MPBW; Dir of Works, Civil Accommodation, PSA, 1975–81. Pres., CIBS, 1976–77. Lt-Col, Engr and Railway Staff Corps RE, T&AVR, 1979–. *Recreations:* walking, gardening. *Address:* Mansers Farm, Nizels Lane, Hildenborough, Tonbridge, Kent TN11 8NX.

LOTH, David; Editor and Author; *b* St Louis, Missouri, 7 Dec. 1899; *s* of Albert Loth and Fanny Sunshine. *Educ:* University of Missouri. Staff of New York World, 1920–30; Editor and Publisher The Majorca Sun, 1931–34; NY Times, 1934–41; US Govt Information Services, 1941–45; Information Dir, Planned Parenthood Federation of America, 1946–51; Acting Nat. Dir, 1951; Information Dir, Columbia Univ. Bicentennial, 1953–54; Assoc. Nieman Fellow, Harvard Univ., 1957–58; Lecturer, Finch Coll., 1961–65. Senior Editor-Writer, High Sch. Geog. Project of Assoc. of Amer. Geographers, 1967–68. Consultant, Psychological Corp., 1969–76. Contributor to various English, American, and Australian publications. *Publications:* The Brownings; Lorenzo the Magnificent; Charles II; Philip II; Public Plunder; Alexander Hamilton; Lafayette; Woodrow Wilson; Chief Justice; A Long Way Forward; Swope of GE; The Erotic in Literature; Pencoyd and the Roberts Family; Crime Lab.: How High is Up; The City Within a City; Crime in Suburbia; The Marriage Counselor; Gold Brick Cassie; Economic Miracle in Israel; The Tertelines: earth movers; Built to Last; (co-author) American Sexual Behaviour and the Kinsey Report; Report on the American Communist; For Better or Worse; Peter Freuchen's Book of the Seven Seas; The Frigid Wife; The Emotional Sex; Ivan Sanderson's Book of Great Jungles; The Taming of Technology; The Colorado Model for Conservation Education. *Address:* 2227 Canyon Boulevard, 412, Boulder, Colo 80302, USA.

LOTHIAN, 12th Marquess of *cr* 1701; **Peter Francis Walter Kerr,** KCVO 1983; DL; Lord Newbattle, 1591; Earl of Lothian, 1606; Baron Jedburgh, 1622; Earl of Ancram, Baron Kerr of Nisbet, Baron Long-Newton and Dolphingston, 1633; Viscount of Brien, Baron Kerr of Newbattle, 1701; Baron Ker (UK), 1821; Lord Warden of the Stannaries and Keeper of the Privy Seal of the Duke of Cornwall, 1977–83; *b* 8 Sept. 1922; *s* of late Captain Andrew William Kerr, RN, and Marie Constance Annabel, *d* of Capt. William Walter Raleigh Kerr; *S* cousin, 1940; *m* 1943, Antonella, *d* of late Maj.-Gen. Sir Foster Newland, KCMG, CB, and Mrs William Carr, Ditchingham Hall, Norfolk; two *s* four *d. Educ:* Ampleforth; Christ Church, Oxford. Lieut, Scots Guards, 1943. Mem. Brit Delegation: UN Gen. Assembly, 1956–57; European Parliament, 1973; UK Delegate, Council of Europe and WEU, 1959. PPS to Foreign Sec., 1960–63; a Lord in Waiting (Govt Whip, House of Lords), 1962–63, 1972–73; Joint Parliamentary Sec., Min. of Health, April-Oct. 1964; Parly Under-Sec. of State, FCO, 1970–72. Chm., Scottish Council, British Red Cross Soc., 1976–86. Mem., Queen's Body Guard for Scotland (Royal Company of Archers). Mem., Prince of Wales Council, 1976–83. DL, Roxburgh, 1962. Kt, SMO Malta. *Heir: s* Earl of Ancram, *qv. Address:* Melbourne Hall, Derby. *T:* Melbourne 2163; Monteviot, Jedburgh, Roxburghshire. *T:* Ancrum 288; 54 Upper Cheyne Row, SW3. *Clubs:* Boodle's, Beefsteak; New (Edinburgh).

See also Col Sir D. H. Cameron of Lochiel, Earl of Dalkeith, Earl of Euston.

LOTHIAN, Andrew; Sheriff of Glasgow and Strathkelvin, since 1979; *b* 6 Feb. 1942; *s* of Andrew Lothian and Catriona Elizabeth (*née* Gillies); *m* 1st, 1969, Deirdre Edith Shannon; two *s*; 2nd, 1976, Susan Adiel Ogilvie Raeburn; 3rd, 1983, Harriet Jane M'Ewan; two *s. Educ:* Trinity Coll., Glenalmond; Univ. of St Andrews (MA); Univ. of Edinburgh (LLB). Kate's Bard, St Andrews Univ., 1964; Editor, Gambit, 1965–66. Admitted Advocate, 1968. Standing Junior Counsel to Highlands and Islands Development Bd, 1976–79. Hon. Lectr, Univ. of Glasgow, 1984–. Member, Scottish Arts Council Publication Awards Cttee, 1970–73; President, Speculative Soc., 1971. *Publications:* So Many Kinds of Yes (with Alan Davidson), 1962; (contrib.) Glasgow: a celebration, 1984; contrib. Times Educnl Supplement, Blackwood's Magazine, Jl of Law Soc. of Scotland. *Recreations:* ornithology, theatre.

LOTON, Brian Thorley, FTS; Managing Director, Broken Hill Proprietory Co. Ltd, since 1982; *b* Perth, WA, 17 May 1929; *s* of Sir (Ernest) Thorley Loton and Grace (*née* Smith); *m* 1956, Joan Kemelfield; two *s* two *d. Educ:* Hale Sch., Perth; Trinity Coll., Melbourne Univ. (BMetEng 1953). Joined BHP as Cadet 1954; Technical Asst, 1959; Asst Chief Engr, 1961; Gen. Manager Planning and Develt, 1969, Gen. Manager Newcastle Steel Works, 1970; Exec. Gen. Manager Steel Div., 1973; Dir, 1976; Chief Gen. Manager, 1977; Director of numerous subsidiaries. Pres., Australian Mining Industry Council, 1983–84; Mem. Council (Pres., 1982), Aust. Inst. of Mining and Metallurgy, Vice-Chm., Defence Industry Cttee; Member: Aust. Sci. and Tehnol. Council, 1977–80; Aust. Manufg Council, 1977–81; Vict. Govt Long Range Policy Planning Cttee, 1980–82; Aust. Council on Population and Ethnic Affairs, 1980–82. Internat. Counsellor, The Conf. Bd, 1984–. Mem. Faculty Engrg, Melbourne Univ., 1980–83. FIE (Aust); FAIM; FIDA. *Address:* c/o GPO Box 86A, Melbourne, Vic 3001, Australia. *Clubs:* Melbourne, Australian (Melbourne).

LOTT, Dr Bernard Maurice, OBE 1966; Course Tutor, Open University, since 1979; *b* 13 Aug. 1922; *s* of late William Lott and of Margaret Lott (*née* Smith); *m* 1949, Helena, *d* of late Clarence Winkup; one *s* one *d* (and one *s* decd). *Educ:* Bancroft's Sch.; Keble Coll., Oxford (MA); Univ. of London (MA Distinction, PhD); Univ. of Edinburgh (Dip. in Applied Linguistics, Dist.). RN, 1942–46. Brit. Council Lectr in English, Ankara Univ. and Gazi Inst. of Educn, Turkey, 1949–55; Brit. Council Asst Rep., Finland, 1955–57; Prof. of Eng. and Head of Dept, Univ. of Indonesia, 1958–61; Dir of Studies, Indian Central Inst. of Eng., 1961–66; Dep. Controller, Educn Div., Brit. Council, 1966–72; Controller, Eng. Teaching Div., Brit. Council, 1972–75; Brit. Council Representative, Poland, 1975–77; English Language Teaching Develt Adviser, British Council, 1977–79. Hon. Res. Fellow, University Coll. London, 1980–. *Publications:* A Course in English Language and Literature, 1986; Gen. Editor, New Swan Shakespeare series, and edited: Macbeth, 1958, Twelfth Night, 1959, Merchant of Venice, 1962, Hamlet, 1968 (also Open Univ. edn 1970), King Lear, 1974; Much Ado About Nothing, 1977; contribs on teaching of English as foreign lang. to Times Educnl Supp. and Eng. Lang. Teaching Jl. *Recreations:* local studies, music. *Address:* 8 Meadway, NW11 7JT. *T:* 01–455 0918.

LOTT, Air Vice-Marshal Charles George, CB 1955; CBE 1944; DSO 1940; DFC 1940; Royal Air Force, retired; *b* 28 Oct. 1906; *s* of late Charles Lott, Sandown; *m* 1936, Evelyn Muriel Little; two *s* one *d. Educ:* Portsmouth Junior Technical Sch. Joined Royal Air Force as Aircraft Apprentice, 1922; learned to fly at Duxford in No 19 Squadron, 1927–28; Sergeant, 1928; Commissioned 1933 and posted to No 41 Squadron; Iraq, 1935–38; HQ No 11 Gp, 1938–39; Commanded No 43 Squadron, 1939–40 (DFC, wounded, DSO); Temp. Wing Comdr, 1941; HQ 13 Group, 1940–42; Sector Comdr, Fighter Command, 1952; Acting Group Capt. 1942; Temp. Group Captain 1944; RAF Delegation (USA), 1944–45; Group Captain 1947; Air Commodore, 1954; Air Vice-Marshal, 1956; Dir Air Defence, SHAPE, 1955–57; Commandant, Sch. of Land/Air Warfare, Old Sarum, Wilts, 1957–59. Retd 1959. *Address:* Glen Waverley, Hooke Hill, Freshwater, Isle of Wight PO40 9BG. *Club:* Royal Air Force.

LOTT, Felicity Ann; soprano; *b* 8 May 1947; *d* of John Albert Lott and Whyla (*née* Williams); *m* 1st, 1973, Robin Mavesyn Golding (marr. diss. 1982); 2nd, 1984, Gabriel Woolf; one *d. Educ:* Pate's Grammar Sch. for Girls, Cheltenham; Royal Holloway Coll., Univ. of London (BA Hons French); Royal Acad. of Music (LRAM; ARAM 1976; FRAM 1986). Principal rôles with English National Opera, Glyndebourne, Welsh National Opera, Covent Garden, Scottish Opera; operatic rôles in France, Belgium, Germany; recitals, concerts and oratorio performances in UK, Belgium, Canada, France, Holland, Hong Kong, USA; several recordings. Founder Mem., The Songmakers' Almanac. *Recreations:* reading, sleeping. *Address:* c/o Lies Askonas, 186 Drury Lane, WC2B 5QD. *T:* 01–405 1808.

LOTZ, Dr Kurt; German business executive; *b* 18 Sept. 1912; *m* Elizabeth Lony; two *s* one *d. Educ:* August-Vilmar-Schule, Homberg. Joined Police Service, 1932; Lieut 1934. Served Luftwaffe (Gen. Staff; Major), 1942–45. Employed by Brown Boveri & Cie, Dortmund, 1946; Head of Business Div., Mannheim, 1954; Dir 1957; Chm. 1958–67; Mem. Board of Directors in parent company, Baden, Switzerland, 1961; Managing Director, 1963–67. Dep. Chm., 1967–68, Chm., 1968–71, Volkswagenwerk AG. Member: Deutscher Rat für Landespflege. Chm., World Wildlife Fund, Germany, 1980. Mem., Rotary Internat. Hon. Senator, Heidelberg Univ., 1963; Hon. Prof., Technische Universität Carolo Wilhelmina, Brunswick, 1970. Dr rer. pol. *hc* Mannheim, 1963. *Publication:* Lebenserfahrungen: Worüber man in Wirtschaft und Politik auch sprechen sollte, 1978. *Recreations:* hiking, hunting, golf. *Address:* D-6900 Heidelberg, Ludolf-Krehl-Strasse 35, Germany.

LOUDON, John Duncan Ott, FRCSE, FRCOG; Consultant Obstetrician and Gynaecologist, Eastern General Hospital, Edinburgh, since 1960; Senior Lecturer,

University of Edinburgh, since 1962; *b* 22 Aug. 1924; *s* of late James Alexander Law Loudon and Ursula (*née* Ott) *m* 1953, Nancy Beaton (*née* Mann); two *s*. *Educ:* John Watson's Sch., Edinburgh; Wyggeston Sch., Leicester; Univ. of Edinburgh (MB, ChB 1947). FRCSE 1954; FRCOG 1973 (MRCOG 1956). National Service, RAF, 1948–50. House appts, Edinburgh and Cambridge, 1948–52; Registrar, Sen. Registrar and Consultant Obstetrician and Gynaecologist, Simpson Maternity Pavilion and Royal Infirm., Edinburgh, 1954–66. Examiner in Obstetrics and Gynaecology: Univs of Cardiff, Manchester, RCSE and RCOG; formerly Univs of Leeds, Dundee, Glasgow, Aberdeen, Newcastle upon Tyne, RCSI and RACOG. Adviser in Family Welfare to Govt of Malta, 1976–81. Vice Pres., RCOG, 1981–84 (Mem. Council, 1966–72 and 1976–81). *Publications:* papers to obstetric and gynaecol jls. *Recreations:* gardening, golf, travel, food and wine. *Address:* Thorncroft, 94 Inverleith Place, Edinburgh EH3 5PA. *T:* 031–552 1327. *Clubs:* Royal Air Force; Bruntsfield Links Golfing Society (Edinburgh).

LOUDON, John Hugo; Jonkheer (Netherlands title); Knight in the Order of the Netherlands Lion, 1953; Grand Officer, Order of Orange-Nassau, 1965; KBE (Hon.) (Gt Brit.), 1960; Officer, Légion d'Honneur, 1963; holds other decorations; Chairman, Institut Européen d'Administration des Affairs, since 1971; Director, Russell Reynolds Associates Inc., since 1977; *b* 27 June 1905; *s* of Jonkheer Hugo Loudon and Anna Petronella Alida Loudon (*née* van Marken); *m* 1931, Baroness Marie Cornelie van Tuyll van Serooskerken; three *s* (and one *s* decd). *Educ:* Netherlands Lyceum, The Hague; Utrecht Univ., Holland. Doctor of Law, 1929. Joined Royal Dutch/Shell Group of Cos, 1930; served in USA, 1932–38; Venezuela, 1938–47 (Gen. Man., 1944–47); Man. Dir, 1947–52, Pres., 1952–65, Chm., 1965–76, Royal Dutch Petroleum Co.; former Chm., Shell Oil Co. (New York); Vice-Chm. Bd, Royal Netherlands Blast-furnaces & Steelworks, NV, 1971–76; Director: Orion Bank Ltd, 1971–81; Chase Manhattan Corp., 1971–76; Estel NV Hoesch-Hoogovens, 1972–76. Chairman: Internat. Adv. Cttee, Chase Manhattan Bank, 1965–77; Bd, Atlantic Inst., 1969–84; European Adv. Cttee, Ford Motor Co., 1976–83. Mem. Bd Trustees, Ford Foundation, 1966–75; Internat. Pres., World Wildlife Fund, 1977–81. *Recreations:* golf, yachting. *Address:* 48 Lange Voorhout, 2514 EG The Hague, Holland. *T:* 453755; Koekoeksduin, 5 Vogelenzangseweg 2111 HP, Aerdenhout, Holland. *T:* Haarlem 245924. *Clubs:* White's; Royal Yacht Squadron.

LOUDOUN, Countess of (13th in line) *cr* 1633; **Barbara Huddleston Abney-Hastings;** Lady Campbell Baroness of Loudoun, 1601; Lady Tarrinzean and Mauchline, 1638; the 3 English baronies of Botreaux 1368, Stanley 1456, and Hastings 1461, which were held by the late Countess, are abeyant, the Countess and her sisters being *co-heiresses*; *b* 3 July 1919; assumed by deed poll, 1955, the surname of Abney-Hastings in lieu of that of Griffiths; *S* mother, 1960; *m* 1st, 1939 (marr. diss., 1945), Capt. Walter Strickland Lord; one *s*; 2nd, 1945, Capt. Gilbert Frederick Greenwood (*d* 1951); one *s* one *d*; 3rd, 1954, Peter Griffiths (who assumed by deed poll the surname of Abney-Hastings in lieu of his patronymic, 1958); three *d*. *Heir: s* Lord Mauchline, *qv*. *Address:* Mount Walk, Ashby-de-la-Zouch, Leics. *T:* Ashby-de-la-Zouch 415844.

LOUDOUN, Maj.-Gen. Robert Beverley, CB 1973; OBE 1965; Director, Mental Health Foundation, since 1977; *b* 8 July 1922; *s* of Robert and Margaret Loudoun; *m* 1950, Audrey Stevens; two *s*. *Educ:* University College Sch., Hampstead. Served War of 1939–45 (despatches): enlisted Royal Marines, 1940; commissioned, 1941; 43 Commando, Central Mediterranean, 1943–45; 45 Commando, Hong Kong, Malta and Palestine, 1945–48. Instructor, RNC Greenwich, 1950–52; Staff of C-in-C America and West Indies, 1953–55; RN Staff Coll., 1956; Adjt, 40 Commando, Malta and Cyprus, 1958–59; USMC Sch., Quantico, Virginia, 1959–60; MoD, 1960–62; Second-in-Command, 42 Commando, Singapore and Borneo, 1963–64; CO, 40 Commando, Far East, 1967–69; Brig., UK Commandos, Plymouth, 1969–71; Maj.-Gen. RM Training Gp, Portsmouth, 1971–75, retired 1975. Representative Col Comdt, RM, 1983–84. Chm., Jt Shooting Cttee for GB, 1977–82. Freeman, City of London, 1979; Mem., Guild of Freemen, 1982–. *Address:* 2 Warwick Drive, Putney, SW15 6LB. *Club:* Army and Navy.

LOUGH, Prof. John, FBA 1975; Professor of French, University of Durham (late Durham Colleges), 1952–78; *b* 19 Feb. 1913; *s* of Wilfrid Gordon and Mary Turnbull Lough, Newcastle upon Tyne; *m* 1939, Muriel Barker; one *d*. *Educ:* Newcastle upon Tyne Royal Grammar Sch.; St John's Coll., Cambridge; Sorbonne. Major Schol., St John's Coll., 1931; BA, First Cl. Hons Parts I and II Mod. and Medieval Langs Tripos, 1934; Esmond Schol. at British Inst. in Paris, 1935; Jebb Studentship, Cambridge, 1936; PhD 1937, MA 1938, Cambridge. Asst (later Lectr), Univ. of Aberdeen, 1937; Lectr in French, Cambridge, 1946. Leverhulme Res. Fellow, 1973. Hon. Dr, Univ. of Clermont, 1967; Hon. DLitt Newcastle, 1972. Officier de l'Ordre National du Mérite, 1973. *Publications:* Locke's Travels in France, 1953; (ed) selected Philosophical Writings of Diderot, 1953; (ed) The Encyclopédie of Diderot and d'Alembert: selected articles, 1954; An Introduction to Seventeenth Century France, 1954; Paris Theatre Audiences in the 17th and 18th centuries, 1957; An Introduction to Eighteenth Century France, 1960; Essays on the Encyclopédie of Diderot and D'Alembert, 1968; The Encyclopédie in 18th Century England and other studies, 1970; The Encyclopédie, 1971; The Contributors to the Encyclopédie, 1973; (ed with J. Proust) Diderot: Œuvres complètes, vols V-VIII, 1977; (with M. Lough) An Introduction to Nineteenth Century France, 1978; Writer and Public in France, 1978; Seventeenth Century French Drama: the background, 1979; The Philosophes and Post-Revolutionary France, 1982; France Observed in the Seventeenth Century by British Travellers, 1985; articles on French literature and ideas in 17th and 18th centuries in French and English learned jls. *Address:* 1 St Hild's Lane, Durham DH1 1QL. *T:* Durham 3848034.

LOUGHBOROUGH, Lord; Jamie William St Clair-Erskine; *b* 28 May 1986; *s* and *heir* of Earl of Rosslyn, *qv*.

LOUGHBOROUGH, Archdeacon of; *see* Jones, Ven. T. H.

LOUGHEED, Hon. (Edgar) Peter, PC (Can.) 1982; QC (Can.) 1972; Senior Partner, Bennett Jones, barristers and solicitors, Calgary and Edmonton; *b* Calgary, 26 July 1928; *s* of late Edgar Donald Lougheed and Edna Bauld; *m* 1952, Jeanne Estelle Rogers, Edmonton; two *s* two *d*. *Educ:* public and secondary schs, Calgary; Univ. of Alberta (BA, LLB); Harvard Grad. Sch. of Business (MBA). Read law with Calgary firm of lawyers; called to Bar of Alberta, 1955, and practised law with same firm, 1955–56. Joined Mannix Co. Ltd, as Sec., 1956 (Gen. Counsel, 1958, Vice-Pres., 1959, Dir, 1960). Entered private legal practice, 1962. Director: ATCO Ltd; Genstar Corp.; Luscar Ltd; Canadian Pacific; Royal Bank of Canada; Princeton Developments; Maclean Hunter; Northern Telecom; Brascan Ltd; Mem., Internat. Adv. Council, Morgan Grenfell. Advr, Govt of Newfoundland. Lecturer: Alberta Univ.; Calgary Univ. Elected: Provincial Leader of Progressive Conservative Party of Alberta, also Member for Calgary West, 1965; Leader of the Official Opposition, 1967; Premier of Alberta, 1971–85 (re-elected 1975, 1979 and 1982). Hon. Chm., Organizing Cttee, XV Olympic Winter Games. Hon. LLD: St Francis Xavier, 1983; Alberta, 1986. *Recreations:* all team sports (formerly football with Edmonton Eskimos). *Address:* (office) 3200 Shell Centre, 400–4th Avenue SW, Calgary, Alberta T2P OX9, Canada.

LOUGHLIN, Charles William; trade union official; retired 1974; *b* 16 Feb. 1914; *s* of late Charles Loughlin, Grimsby; *m* 1945, May, *d* of David Arthur Dunderdale, Leeds; one *s* (one *d* decd). *Educ:* St Mary's Sch., Grimsby; National Council of Labour Colls. Area Organiser, Union of Shop, Distributive and Allied Workers, 1945–74. MP (Lab) Gloucestershire West, 1959–Sept. 1974; Parly Sec., Min. of Health, 1965–67; Jt Parly Sec., Min. of Social Security, then Dept of Health and Social Security, 1967–68; Parly Sec., Min. of Public Building and Works, 1968–70. *Address:* 22 Templenewsam View, Leeds LS15 0LW. *T:* Leeds 647354.

LOUGHRAN, James; Principal Conductor and Musical Adviser, Hallé Orchestra, 1971–83, Conductor Laureate, since 1983; a Chief Guest Conductor, BBC Welsh Symphony Orchestra, since 1987; *b* 30 June 1931; *s* of James and Agnes Loughran; *m* 1961, Nancy (*née* Coggon); two *s*. *Educ:* St Aloysius' Coll., Glasgow; Bonn, Amsterdam and Milan. FRNCM 1976; FRSAMD 1983. 1st Prize, Philharmonia Conducting Competition, 1961. Asst Conductor, Bournemouth Symphony Orchestra, 1962; Associate Conductor, Bournemouth Symphony Orchestra, 1964; Principal Conductor, BBC Scottish Symphony Orchestra, 1965–71; Chief Conductor, Bamberg Symphony Orchestra, 1979–83. Hon. DMus Sheffield, 1983. *Address:* c/o Harold Holt Ltd, 31 Sinclair Road, W14 0NS.

LOUIS, John Jeffry, Jr; Chairman, Butler Aviation International, Inc., since 1986; Director: Butler International, Inc.; Air Wisconsin, Inc., since 1984; Baxter Travenol Laboratories, since 1984; Gannett Company, Inc., since 1984; Johnson's Wax, since 1961; Walgreen Co., since 1985; *b* 10 June 1925; *s* of John Jeffry Louis and Henrietta Louis (*née* Johnson); *m* 1953, Josephine Peters; one *s* two *d*. *Educ:* Deerfield Academy, Mass; Northwestern Univ., 1943 and 1946; Williams Coll., Mass (BA 1947); Dartmouth Coll., New Hampshire (MBA 1949). Served with AUS, 1943–45. Account Executive, Needham, Louis & Brorby, Inc., Chicago, 1952–58; Director, International Marketing, Johnson's Wax, Wis, 1958–61; Chairman Board: KTAR Broadcasting Co., Ariz., 1961–68; Combined Communications Corp., Chicago, 1968–80. US Ambassador to UK, 1981–83. Trustee: Northwestern Univ., 1967–81, 1984–; Deerfield Acad., 1963–81; Foxcroft Sch., 1975–79; Williams Coll., 1979–81. Trustee, Evanston Hosp., 1959–81, 1984– (Chm., 1962–68). Hon. Master of The Bench, Middle Temple, 1981. *Recreations:* golf, tennis, skiing, shooting. *Address:* Suite 510, One Northfield Plaza, Northfield, Illinois 60093, USA. *Clubs:* Old Elm (Illinois); Pine Valley Golf (New Jersey); Augusta National Golf (Georgia); Gulfstream Golf (Florida).

LOUISY, Rt. Hon. Allan (Fitzgerald Laurent), CBE 1983; PC 1981; Leader of St Lucia Labour Party. Prime Minister of St Lucia, and Minister of Finance, Home Affairs, Information and Tourism, 1979–81; Minister without Portfolio, 1981–82; Minister of Legal Affairs, Jan.-May 1982. *Address:* Laborie, St Lucia, West Indies.

LOUSADA, Sir Anthony (Baruh), Kt 1975; Solicitor; Partner in Stephenson Harwood, 1935–73; Consultant, 1973–81; *b* 4 Nov. 1907; *s* of Julian George Lousada and Maude Reignier Conder; *m* 1st, 1937, Jocelyn (marr. diss. 1960), *d* of late Sir Alan Herbert, CH; one *s* three *d*; 2nd, 1961, Patricia, *d* of late C. J. McBride, USA; one *s* one *d*. *Educ:* Westminster; New Coll., Oxford. Admitted Solicitor, 1933. Min. of Economic Warfare, 1939–44; Min. of Production and War Cabinet Office, 1944–45. Member: Council, Royal College of Art, 1952–79 (Hon. Fellow, 1957; Sen. Fellow, 1967; Vice-Chm., 1960–72; Treasurer, 1967–72; Chm., 1972–79; Hon. Dr 1977); Cttee, Contemp. Art Soc., 1955–71 (Vice-Chm., 1961–71); Fine Arts Cttee, British Council (visited Japan on behalf of Council, 1970, to set up exhibn of sculpture by Barbara Hepworth); GPO Adv. Cttee on Stamp Design, 1968–80; Chairman: Adv. Cttee, Govt Art Collection, 1976–83; British Art Market Standing Cttee, 1984–. Council, Friends of Tate Gallery, 1958– (Hon. Treasurer, 1960–65, Chm., 1971–77); Trustee, Tate Gallery, 1962–69 (Vice-Chm., 1965–67; Chm., 1967–69). One-man exhibns of drawings, Covt Gdn Gall., 1977, 1981. Officer, Order of Belgian Crown, 1945. *Recreations:* painting, sailing. *Address:* The Tides, Chiswick Mall, W4. *T:* 01–994 2257. *Clubs:* Garrick; London Corinthian Sailing.

LOUSTAU-LALANNE, Bernard Michel; International Representative, Performing Right Society Ltd, since 1980; *b* 20 June 1938; *s* of Joseph Antoine Michel Loustau-Lalanne, OBE, and Marie Therese Madeleine (*née* Boullé); *m* 1974, Debbie Elizabeth Temple-Brown (marr. diss. 1983); one *d* and one step-*s*. *Educ:* Seychelles Coll.; St Mary's Coll., Southampton; Imperial Coll., London. Called to the Bar, Middle Temple, London, 1969. Assistant Inspector, Northern Rhodesia Police, 1962–64; Crown Counsel, Seychelles, 1970–72; Sen. State Counsel and Official Notary, 1972–76; Attorney-General, Seychelles, 1976–78; High Comr for Seychelles, in London, 1978–80; concurrently Seychelles Ambassador to USA, and Seychelles Perm. Rep. to UN. *Recreations:* windsurfing, tennis, swimming, scuba diving, reading. *Address:* 2 Albert Mansions, Luxborough Street, W1. *T:* 01–935 4092. *Club:* Seychelles Yacht.

LOUTH, 16th Baron, *cr* 1541, **Otway Michael James Oliver Plunkett;** *b* 19 Aug. 1929; *o s* of Otway Randal Percy Oliver Plunkett, 15th Baron, and Ethel Molly, *d* of Walter John Gallichen, Jersey, Channel Islands; *S* father, 1950; *m* 1951, Angela Patricia Cullinane, Jersey; three *s* two *d*. *Heir: s* Hon. Jonathan Oliver Plunkett, BSc, AMIEE [*b* 4 Nov. 1952; *m* 1981, Jennifer, *d* of Norman Oliver Hodgetts, Coventry; one *s* one *d*]. *Address:* Les Sercles, La Grande Pièce, St Peter, Jersey, Channel Islands.

LOUTIT, John Freeman, CBE 1957; FRS 1963; MA, DM, FRCP; External Scientific Staff Medical Research Council, 1969–75, Visitor at Radiobiology Unit since 1975; *b* 19 Feb. 1910; *s* of John Freeman Loutit, Perth, WA; *m* 1941, Thelma Salusbury; one *s* two *d*. *Educ:* C of E Grammar Sch., Guildford, W Australia; Univs of W Australia, Melbourne, Oxford, London. Rhodes Scholar (W Australia), 1930; BA Oxon 1933, BM, BCh Oxon 1935. Various appointments, London Hosp., 1935–39; MA (Oxon) 1938; Director, South London Blood Supply Depot, 1940–47; DM Oxon, 1946; Dir, Radiobiological Research Unit, AERE Harwell, 1947–69. FRCP 1955. VMD (*hc*) Stockholm, 1965. Officer, Order of Orange-Nassau (Netherlands) 1951. *Publications:* Irradiation of Mice and Men, 1962; Tissue Grafting and Radiation (jointly), 1966; articles in scientific journals. *Recreations:* cooking, gardening. *Address:* 22 Milton Lane, Steventon, Oxon. *T:* Abingdon 831279.

LOVAT, 17th Baron (S) *cr* before 1440 (*de facto* 15th Baron, 17th but for the Attainder); **Simon Christopher Joseph Fraser,** DSO 1942; MC; TD; JP; DL; Baron (UK) 1837; 24th Chief of Clan Fraser of Lovat; *b* 9 July 1911; *s* of 16th Baron and Hon. Laura Lister (*d* 1965), 2nd *d* of 4th Baron Ribblesdale; *S* father, 1933; *m* 1938, Rosamond, *o d* of Sir Delves Broughton, 11th Bt; four *s* two *d*. *Educ:* Ampleforth; Magdalen Coll., Oxford, BA. Lt, Scots Guards, 1932–37, retd. Served War of 1939–45: Capt. Lovat Scouts, 1939; Lt-Col 1942; Brig. Commandos, 1943 (wounded, MC, DSO, Order of Suvarov, Légion d'Honneur, Croix de Guerre avec palme; Norway Liberation Cross). Under-Sec. of State for Foreign Affairs, 1945. DL 1942, JP 1944, Inverness. Awarded LLD (Hon.) by Canadian universities. Order of St John of Jerusalem; Knight of Malta; Papal Order of St Gregory with Collar. *Publication:* March Past, 1978. *Heir: s* Master of Lovat, *qv*. *Address:* Balblair, Beauly, Inverness-shire. *Club:* Cavalry and Guards.

See also Earl of Eldon, Sir Fitzroy Maclean of Dunconnel, Bt, Lord Reay.

LOVAT, Master of; Hon. Simon Augustine Fraser; *b* 28 Aug. 1939; *s* of 17th Baron Lovat, *qv*; *m* 1972, Virginia, *d* of David Grose; two *s* one *d*. *Educ:* Ampleforth Coll. Lieut Scots Guards, 1960. *Address:* Beaufort Castle, Beauly, Inverness-shire.

LOVAT, Sheriff Leonard Scott; Sheriff of South Strathclyde, Dumfries and Galloway at Hamilton, since 1978; *b* 28 July 1926; *s* of late Charles Lovat and Alice (*née* Hunter); *m* 1960, Elinor Frances, *d* of late J. A. McAlister and Mary McAlister; one *s* one *d*. *Educ:* St Aloysius Coll., Glasgow; Glasgow Univ. (BL 1947). Solicitor, 1948; Partner, Jno. Shaughnessy and McColl, Solicitors, Glasgow, 1955–59. Asst to Prof. of Roman Law, Glasgow Univ., 1954–63; Cropwood Fellow, Inst. of Criminology, Univ. of Cambridge, 1971. Procurator Fiscal Depute, Glasgow, 1960; Sen. Asst Procurator Fiscal, Glasgow and Strathkelvin, 1976. *Publications:* Climbers' Guide to Glencoe and Ardgour, 2 vols, 1959, 1965; articles and reviews in legal jls. *Recreations:* music, mountaineering, bird-watching. *Address:* 38 Kelvin Court, Glasgow G12 0AE. *T:* 041-357 0031. *Club:* Alpine.

LOVE, Prof. Andrew Henry Garmany, MD; FRCP, FRCPI; Professor of Medicine since 1983, and Dean of Faculty of Medicine since 1981, Queen's University of Belfast; *b* 28 Sept. 1934; *s* of Andrew and Martha Love; *m* 1963, Margaret Jean Lennox; one *s*. *Educ:* Bangor Endowed Sch., NI; Queen's Univ. of Belfast (BSc Hons 1955; MD 1963). FRCP 1973; FRCPI 1972. Lectr in Physiology, 1960–63 and Lectr in Medicine, 1963–64, QUB; MRC Travelling Fellow, and Hon. Consultant, US Naval Med. Res. Unit-2, Taipei, Taiwan, 1964–65; Sen. Lectr in Medicine, 1966–73 and Prof. of Gastroenterology, 1973–83, QUB (on leave of absence, Res. Fellow, Boston City Hosp., Mass, 1966). Hon. Consultant, SEATO Cholera Labs, Pakistan, 1967–70. Mem., GMC, 1983–. *Publications:* articles in learned jls on gen. medicine, intestinal function, trace element metabolism and nutrition. *Recreations:* golf, sailing. *Address:* The Lodge, New Road, Donaghadee, Co. Down, Northern Ireland BT21 0DU. *T:* Donaghadee 883507. *Clubs:* East India, Devonshire, Sports and Public Schools; Royal Ulster Yacht (Bangor, Co. Down); Royal County Down Golf (Newcastle).

LOVE, Prof. Philip Noel, CBE 1983; Professor of Conveyancing and Professional Practice of Law, since 1974, and Vice-Principal, since 1986, University of Aberdeen (Dean of Faculty of Law, 1979–82); Member, Scottish Law Commission, since 1986; *b* 25 Dec. 1939; *o s* of Thomas Isaac and Ethel Violet Love; *m* 1963, Isabel Leah, *yr d* of Innes Taylor and Leah Wallace Mearns; three *s*. *Educ:* Aberdeen Grammar Sch.; Aberdeen Univ. (MA 1961, LLB 1963). Admitted Solicitor in Scotland, 1963; Advocate in Aberdeen, 1963–; Partner, Campbell Connon & Co., Solicitors, Aberdeen, 1963–74, Consultant, 1974–; Chm., Aurora Instruments Ltd, 1983–. Law Society of Scotland: Mem. Council, 1975–; Examr, 1975–83 (Chm. Examrs, 1977–80); Vice-Pres., 1980–81; Pres., 1981–82. Local Chm., Rent Assessment Panel for Scotland, 1972–; Chm., Sec. of State for Scotland's Expert Cttee on house purchase and sale, 1982–84; Vice-Pres., Scottish Law Agents Soc., 1970; Member: Jt Standing Cttee on Legal Educn in Scotland, 1976–85 (Chm., 1976–80); Rules Council, Court of Session, 1968–; Council, Internat. Bar Assoc., 1983– (Vice-Chm., Legal Educn Div., 1983–); Jt Ethical Cttee, Grampian Health Bd, 1984– (Vice-Chm., 1985; Chm., 1986). Chm., Aberdeen Home for Widowers' Children, 1971–. Hon. Sheriff of Grampian, Highland and Islands, 1978–. *Recreations:* Rugby, keep-fit. *Address:* 3A Rubislaw Den North, Aberdeen AB2 4AL. *T:* Aberdeen 313339. *Clubs:* New (Edinburgh); Royal Aberdeen Golf, Rotary of Aberdeen, Aberdeen Grammar School Former Pupils' Club Centre (Aberdeen).

LOVEDAY, Alan (Raymond); Solo Violinist; *b* 29 Feb. 1928; *s* of Leslie and Margaret Loveday; *m* 1952, Ruth Stanfield; one *s* one *d*. *Educ:* privately; Royal College of Music (prizewinner). Made debut at age of 4; debut in England, 1946; has given many concerts, broadcasts, and made TV appearances, in this country and abroad, playing with all leading conductors and orchestras; repertoire ranges from Bach (which he likes to play on an unmodernised violin), to contemporary music. Prof., RCM, 1955–72. Full-time Mem. and Soloist, Acad. of St Martin-in-the-Fields. *Recreations:* chess, bridge.

LOVEGROVE, Geoffrey David, QC 1969; **His Honour Judge Lovegrove;** a Circuit Judge (formerly County Court Judge), since 1971; *b* 22 Dec. 1919; *s* of late Gilbert Henry Lovegrove; *m* 1959, Janet, *d* of John Bourne; one *s* two *d*. *Educ:* Haileybury; New College, Oxford (MA). Army, 1940–46. Called to the Bar, Inner Temple, 1947; Dep. Chairman, W Sussex Quarter Sessions, 1965–71. Master, Innholders' Company, 1980–81. *Address:* 1 King's Bench Walk, Temple, EC4.

LOVELACE, 5th Earl of, *cr* 1838; **Peter Axel William Locke King;** Baron King and Ockham, 1725; Viscount Ockham, 1838; *b* 26 Nov. 1951; *s* of 4th Earl of Lovelace and of Manon Lis, *d* of Axel Sigurd Transo, Copenhagen, Denmark; *S* father, 1964; *m* 1980, Kirsteen Oihrig, *d* of Calum Kennedy, Leethland House, Leethland, Renfrewshire, and late Anne Gillies Kennedy. *Address:* Torridon House, Torridon, Ross-shire.

LOVELL, Sir (Alfred Charles) Bernard, Kt 1961; OBE 1946; FRS 1955; Director of Jodrell Bank Experimental Station, Cheshire, now Nuffield Radio Astronomy Laboratories, 1951–81; Professor of Radio Astronomy, University of Manchester, 1951–80, now Emeritus Professor; *b* 31 Aug. 1913; *s* of G. Lovell, Oldland Common, Gloucestershire; *m* 1937, Mary Joyce Chesterman; two *s* three *d*. *Educ:* Kingswood Grammar Sch., Bristol; University of Bristol. Asst Lectr in Physics, Univ. of Manchester, 1936–39; Telecommunication Res. Establishment, 1939–45; Physical Laboratories, Univ. of Manchester and Jodrell Bank Experimental Station, Cheshire; Lectr, 1945, Sen. Lectr, 1947, Reader, 1949, in Physics. Reith Lectr, 1958; Lectures: Condon, 1962; Guthrie, 1962; Halley, 1964; Queen's, Berlin, 1970; Brockington, Kingston, Ont, 1970; Bickley, Oxford, 1977; Crookshank, RCR, 1977; Angel Meml, Newfoundland, 1977. Vis. Montague Burton Prof. of Internat. Relations, Univ. of Edinburgh, 1973. Member: ARC, 1955–58; SRC, 1965–70; Amer. Philosophical Soc., 1974–. Pres., RAS, 1969–71; Vice-Pres., Internat. Astronomical Union, 1970–76; Pres., British Assoc., 1975–76. Pres., Guild of Church Musicians, 1976–; Jun. Warden, 1984–85, Sen. Warden, 1985–86, Musicians' Co. Hon. Freeman, City of Manchester, 1977. Hon. Fellow, Society of Engineers, 1964; Hon. Foreign Member American Academy of Arts and Sciences, 1955; Hon. Life Member, New York Academy, 1960; Hon. Member: Royal Swedish Academy, 1962; RNCM, 1981. Hon. LLD: Edinburgh, 1961; Calgary, 1966; Hon. DSc: Leicester, 1961; Leeds, 1966; London, 1967; Bath, 1967; Bristol, 1970; DUniv Stirling, 1974; DUniv Surrey, 1975; Hon. FIEE, 1967; Hon. FInstP, 1976. Duddell Medal, 1954; Royal Medal, 1960; Daniel and Florence Guggenheim International Astronautics Award, 1961; Ordre du Mérite pour la Recherche et l'Invention, 1962; Churchill Gold Medal, 1964; Maitland Lecturer and Silver Medallist, Institution of Structural Engineers, 1964; Second RSA American Exchange Lectr, Philadelphia, 1980; Benjamin Franklin Medal, RSA, 1980; Gold Medal, Royal Astronomical Soc., 1981; Rutherford Meml Lectr, Royal Soc., 1984. Commander's Order of Merit, Polish People's Republic, 1975. *Publications:* Science and Civilisation, 1939; World Power Resources and Social Development, 1945; Radio Astronomy, 1951; Meteor Astronomy, 1954; The Exploration of Space by Radio, 1957; The Individual and The Universe, (BBC Reith Lectures, 1958); The Exploration of Outer Space (Gregynog Lectures, 1961); Discovering the Universe, 1963; Our Present Knowledge of the Universe, 1967; (ed with T. Margerison) The Explosion of Science: The Physical Universe, 1967; The Story of Jodrell Bank, 1968; The Origins and International Economics of Space Exploration, 1973; Out of the Zenith, 1973; Man's Relation to the Universe, 1975; P. M. S. Blackett: a biographical memoir, 1976; In the Centre of Immensities, 1978; Emerging Cosmology, 1981; The Jodrell Bank Telescopes, 1985; many publications in Physical and Astronomical journals. *Recreations:* cricket, gardening, music. *Address:* The Quinta, Swettenham, Cheshire. *T:* Lower Withington 71254. *Clubs:* Athenæum, MCC; Lancashire County Cricket (Vice-Pres., 1981–).

LOVELL, Arnold Henry; Under-Secretary, HM Treasury, 1975–86; *b* 5 Aug. 1926; *s* of Alexander and Anita Lovell; *m* 1950, Joyce Harmer; one *s* one *d*. *Educ:* Hemsworth Grammar Sch., Yorks; London School of Economics (BScEcon, 1st Cl. Hons). HM Treasury: Asst Principal, 1952; Principal, 1956; Asst Financial Adviser to UK High Commn, New Delhi, India, 1962–65; re-joined HM Treasury, Monetary Policy Div., 1965–70; Asst Sec., 1967; Balance of Payments Div., 1970–75; Under-Sec., Fiscal Policy Div., 1975–80, Industry and Agric. Gp, 1980–86. *Recreations:* walking, Stafford bull terriers. *Address:* 12 Bromley Lane, Chislehurst, Kent BR7 5DY. *T:* 01-467 1116.

LOVELL, Kenneth Ernest Walter; Treasurer to the Greater London Council, 1977–80, retired; *b* 25 Oct. 1919; *s* of Ernest John and Alice Lovell; *m* 1946, Vera Mary Pithouse; one *s* two *d*. *Educ:* Ashford County Grammar School. Mem. Chartered Inst. of Public Finance and Accountancy. Middlesex County Council (Finance Dept): Computer Manager, 1961; Asst County Treasurer, 1963. Greater London Council: Asst Treasurer, 1965; Finance Officer, ILEA, 1972. *Recreations:* gardening, cricket, hockey, photography; study of social and economic development of British Isles; study of landscape of British Isles. *Address:* 15 Meadway Close, Staines, Mddx TW18 2PR. *T:* Staines 52806.

LOVELL-DAVIS, family name of **Baron Lovell-Davis.**

LOVELL-DAVIS, Baron *cr* 1974 (Life Peer), of Highgate; **Peter Lovell Lovell-Davis;** Member: Commonwealth Development Corporation, 1978–84; London Consortium, since 1978; *b* 8 July 1924; *s* of late William Lovell Davis and late Winifred Mary Davis; *m* 1950, Jean Graham; one *s* one *d*. *Educ:* Christ's Coll., Finchley; King Edward VI Sch., Stratford-on-Avon; Jesus Coll., Oxford. BA Hons English, MA. Served War, RAF (Pilot), to Flt-Lt, 1943–47. Oxford, 1947–50. Managing Dir, Central Press Features Ltd, 1952–70; Dir, various newspaper and printing cos. Chm., Colour Features Ltd; Chairman: Davis & Harrison Ltd, 1970–73; Features Syndicate, 1971–74; Lee Cooper Licensing Services, 1983–. Mem., Islington DHA, 1982–85. A Lord in Waiting (Govt Whip), 1974–75; Parly Under-Sec. of State, Dept of Energy, 1975–76. Adviser to various Govt Cttees, Health Educn Council, Labour Party and Govt, on media. Vice-Pres., YHA, 1978–; Trustee, Whittington Hosp. Academic Centre, 1980–. *Recreations:* industrial archaeology, inland waterways, bird-watching, walking, sketching and flying kites. *Address:* 80 North Road, Highgate, N6 4AA. *T:* 01-348 3919.

LOVELOCK, Sir Douglas (Arthur), KCB 1979 (CB 1974); First Church Estates Commissioner, since 1983; Chairman, Central Board of Finance of the Church of England, since 1983; *b* 7 Sept. 1923; *s* of late Walter and Irene Lovelock; *m* 1961, Valerie Margaret (*née* Lane); one *s* one *d*. *Educ:* Bec Sch., London. Entered Treasury, 1949; Min. of Supply, 1952; Private Sec. to Permanent Sec., 1953–54; Principal, 1954; Private Sec. to successive Ministers of Aviation (Rt Hon. Peter Thorneycroft and Rt Hon. Julian Amery), 1961–63; Asst Sec., 1963; Under-Sec. (Contracts), Min. of Technology, subseq. Min. of Aviation Supply, 1968–71; Asst Under-Sec. of State (Personnel), MoD, 1971–72; Dep. Sec., DTI, 1972–74, Depts of Trade, Industry, Prices and Consumer Protection, 1974–77; Chm., Bd of Customs and Excise, 1977–83. Chm., Civil Service Benevolent Fund, 1980–83. Chm., Review of Citizens' Advice Bureaux Service, 1983–84. *Recreations:* walking, gardening, outdoor activities generally. *Address:* The Old House, 91 Coulsdon Road, Old Coulsdon, Surrey. *T:* Downland 55211.

LOVELOCK, Prof. James Ephraim, FRS 1974; independent scientist, since 1964; Visiting Professor, University of Reading, since 1967; *b* 26 July 1919; *s* of Tom Arthur Lovelock and Nellie Ann Elizabeth (*née* March); *m* 1942, Helen Mary Hyslop; two *s* two *d*. *Educ:* Strand Sch., London; Manchester and London Univs. BSc, PhD, DSc, ARIC. Staff Scientist, Nat. Inst. for Med. Research, 1941–61; Rockefeller Fellow, Harvard Univ., 1954–55; Yale Univ., 1958–59; Prof. of Chemistry, Baylor Univ. Coll. of Medicine, Texas, 1961–64. Pres., Marine Biol Assoc., 1986–. Mem. Sigma Xi, Yale Chapter, 1959. Hon. ScD East Anglia, 1982. *Publications:* Gaia, 1979; (with Michael Allaby) The Great Extinction, 1983; numerous papers and patents. *Recreations:* walking, painting, computer programming, reading. *Address:* Coombe Mill, St Giles on the Heath, Launceston, Cornwall PL15 9RY.

LOVERIDGE, Joan Mary, OBE 1968; Matron and Superintendent of Nursing, St Bartholomew's Hospital, 1949–67; *b* 14 Aug. 1912; *d* of William Ernest Loveridge. *Educ:* Maidenhead, Berkshire. Commenced training, 1930, Royal National Orthopædic Hospital, W1; St Bartholomew's Hospital, 1933–37; Radcliffe Infirmary, Oxford, Midwifery Training, 1937–38; Night Sister, Ward Sister, Matron's Office Sister, Assistant Matron, St Bartholomew's Hospital. *Address:* 24 Powys, All Saints Road, Sidmouth, Devon.

LOVERIDGE, Sir John (Henry), Kt 1975; CBE 1964 (MBE 1945); Bailiff of Guernsey, 1973–82; Barrister-at-Law; Judge of Appeal for Jersey, 1974–82; *b* 2 Aug. 1912; *e s* of late Henry Thomas and Vera Lilian Loveridge; *m* 1946, Madeleine Melanie, *o d* of late Eugene Joseph C. M. Tanguy; one *s* one *d*. *Educ:* Elizabeth Coll., Guernsey; Univ. of Caen. Called to Bar, Middle Temple, 1950. Advocate of Royal Court of Guernsey, 1951; HM Solicitor-General, Guernsey, 1954–60; HM Attorney-General, Guernsey, 1960–69; Deputy Bailiff of Guernsey, 1969–73. RAFVR, 1954–59. KStJ 1980. *Recreations:* reading, swimming, sport. *Address:* Kinmount, Sausmarez Road, St Martin's, Guernsey. *T:* Guernsey 38038. *Club:* Royal Guernsey Golf.

LOVERIDGE, John Warren, JP; Principal of St Godric's College since 1954; farmer; *b* 9 Sept. 1925; *s* of C. W. Loveridge and Emily (Mickie), *d* of John Malone; *m* 1954, Jean Marguerite, *d* of E. J. Chivers; three *s* two *d*. *Educ:* St John's Coll., Cambridge (MA). Mem., Hampstead BC, 1953–59. Contested (C) Aberavon, 1951, Brixton (LCC), 1952. MP (C) Hornchurch, 1970–74, Upminster, 1974–83 (Member: Parly Select Cttee on Expenditure (Mem. General Purposes Sub-Cttee); Procedure Cttee; Chm., Cons. Smaller Business Cttee, 1979–83). Treasurer/Trustee, Hampstead Conservative Assoc., 1959–74; Pres., Hampstead and Highgate Conservative Assoc., 1986. Vice-Pres., Nat. Council for Civil Defence, 1980–. Pres., Axe Cliff Golf Club. JP West Central Division, 1963. FRAS; FRAgS; MRIIA. Liveryman, Girdlers' Co. *Publications:* God Save the Queen: Sonnets of Elizabeth I, 1981; Hunter of the Moon, 1983; Hunter of the Sun, 1984; (jtly) Moving Forward: small businesses and the economy, 1983. *Recreations:* painting, poetry, historic houses, shooting. *Address:* 2 Arkwright Road, NW3 6AD. *Clubs:* Buck's, Carlton, Hurlingham.

LOVICK, Albert Ernest Fred; Chairman, 1964–68, Director, 1950–68 and 1969–78, Co-operative Insurance Society Ltd; Chairman, Cumbrian Co-operative Society Ltd, Carlisle, since 1972; Director: CWS Ltd, 1949–78; Shoefayre Ltd, 1975–78; *b* 19 Feb. 1912; *s* of late Arthur Alfred Lovick and late Mary Lovick (*née* Sharland); *m* 1934,

Florence Ena Jewell; no *c.* *Educ:* Elementary Sch., Eastleigh, Hants; Peter Symonds, Winchester. Hearne & Partner, rating surveyors, 1928; Eastleigh Co-operative Society, 1929–33; Harwich, Dovercourt and Parkeston CS, 1933–35; Managing Secretary, Basingstoke CS, 1935–49. During War of 1939–45, government cttees. Member, Basingstoke Borough Council, 1946–49. Former Chm., Centratours Ltd. Member: Export Credits Guarantees Advisory Council, 1968–73; Bristol Rent Assessment Cttee, 1973–; Bristol Rent Tribunal, 1973–. Fellow, Co-operative Secretaries Assoc.; FCIS; FCIArb. *Recreations:* golf, gardening. *Address:* 48 Botchergate, Carlisle CA1 1RG; Coedway, Bristol Road, Stonehouse, Glos GL10 2BQ. *T:* Stonehouse 3167. *Club:* Royal Commonwealth Society.

LOVILL, John Roger, CBE 1983; DL; Chairman, Sloane Square Investments, since 1980 (Director since 1960); *b* 26 Sept. 1929; *s* of Walter Thomas Lovill and Elsie Lovill (*née* Page); *m* 1958, Jacqueline (*née* Parker); two *s* one *d.* *Educ:* Brighton Hove and Sussex Grammar School. S. G. Warburg, 1951–55; Dep. Gen. Manager, Securicor Ltd, 1955–60; Director: Municipal Gen. Insce Co., 1984–; Municipal Life Insce Co., 1984–. Contested (C) Ebbw Vale, 1966; Mem., East Sussex CC, 1967–, Leader, 1973–77; Chairman: Local Authority Conditions of Service Adv. Bd, 1978–83; ACC, 1983–86; Leader, Conservative Assoc. of County Councils, 1981–83. DL E Sussex 1983. *Recreations:* opera, politics, marine paintings. *Address:* Little Dene, Beddingham, near Lewes, Sussex. *T:* Glynde 212.

LOW, family name of **Baron Aldington.**

LOW, Sir Alan (Roberts), Kt 1977; Governor, Reserve Bank of New Zealand, 1967–77; Chairman, Dairy Products Prices Authority, since 1977; *b* 11 Jan. 1916; 4th *s* of Benjamin H. Low and Sarah Low; *m* 1940, Kathleen Mary Harrow; one *s* two *d.* *Educ:* Timaru Main Sch.; Timaru Boys' High Sch.; Canterbury University College. MA 1937. Joined Reserve Bank of New Zealand, 1938; Economic Adviser, 1951; Asst Governor, 1960; Deputy Governor, 1962; Governor, 1967. Army Service, 1942–44; on loan to Economic Stabilisation Commission, 1944–46. Hon. Fellow, Bankers' Inst. of NZ, 1977. Hon. LLD Canterbury, 1977. *Publications:* No Free Lunch, 1983; Where DO We Go For Lunch, 1984; contributions to many economic and financial jls. *Recreations:* gardening, music, reading. *Address:* 83 Penrose Street, Lower Hutt, New Zealand. *T:* 699–526. *Club:* Wellington (NZ).

LOW, Prof. Donald Anthony, DPhil; PhD; FAHA, FASSA; Smuts Professor of the History of British Commonwealth and Fellow of Churchill College, University of Cambridge, since 1983; Director, Centre of International Studies, Cambridge, since 1985; *b* 22 June 1927; *o s* of late Canon Donald Low and Winifred (*née* Edmunds); *m* 1952, Isobel Smails; one *s* two *d.* *Educ:* Haileybury and ISC; Univ. of Oxford (MA, DPhil); PhD Cantab 1983. Open Scholar in Modern History, 1944 and Amelia Jackson Sen. Student, 1948, Exeter Coll., Oxford; Lectr, subseq. Sen. Lectr, Makerere Coll., University Coll. of E Africa, 1951–58; Uganda corresp., The Times, 1952–58; Fellow, subseq. Sen. Fellow in History, Res. Sch. of Social Sciences, ANU, 1959–64; Founding Dean of Sch. of African and Asian Studies, and Prof. of Hist., Univ. of Sussex, 1964–72 (Dir, Graduates in Arts and Social Studies, 1970–71); Australian National University: Prof. of History, 1973–83; Dir, Res. Sch. of Pacific Studies, 1973–75; Vice Chancellor, 1975–82. Chm., Educn Adv. Cttee, Aust. Develt Assistance Bureau, 1979–82; Mem. Exec., 1976–82, Dep. Chm., 1980, Aust. Vice-Chancellors' Cttee (Chm., Internat. Relations Cttee, 1979–82); Member: Council, Univ. of Papua New Guinea, 1974–82; Standing Cttee, Aust. Univs Internat. Develt Program, 1975–82; Council, ACU, 1980–82; Cttee, Australian Studies Centre, London Univ., 1983–; Council of Senate, Univ. of Cambridge, 1985–; Governing Body: SOAS, 1983–; Inst. of Develt Studies, Sussex Univ., 1984–; Haileybury, 1985–; Chm., Cttee of Management, Inst. of Commonwealth Studies, London Univ., 1984–. Sen. Visitor Nuffield Coll., Oxford, 1956–57; Vis. Prof., Univ. of Calif, Berkeley, and Chicago Univ., 1967; Smuts Fellow and Vis. Fellow, Clare Hall, Cambridge, 1971–72. Hon. Fellow: Inst. of Develt Studies, UK, 1972; University House, ANU 1983; Kingsley Martin Meml Lectr, Cambridge, 1980. President: African Studies Assoc. of Aust. and Pacific, 1979–82; Asian Studies Assoc. of Aust., 1980–82; British Australian Studies Assoc., 1984–86. Commander of the Order of Civil Merit (Spain), 1984. *Publications:* Buganda and British Overrule, 1900–1955 (with R. C. Pratt), 1960; (ed) Soundings in Modern South Asian History, 1968; (with J. C. Iltis and M. D. Wainwright) Government Archives in South Asia, 1969; Buganda in Modern History, 1971; The Mind of Buganda, 1971; Lion Rampant, 1973; Congress and the Raj 1917–1947, 1977; Oxford History of East Africa: (contrib.) Vol. I, 1963 and Vol. II, 1965; (contrib. and ed jtly) Vol. III, 1976; articles on internat. history in jls. *Address:* Churchill College, Cambridge.

LOW, Dr (George) Graeme (Erick); Director, Atomic Energy Research Establishment, Harwell, since 1986; Member, United Kingdom Atomic Energy Authority, since 1986; *b* Palmerston North, NZ, 29 Nov. 1928; *s* of George Eric Low and Evelyn Edith Low (*née* Gillman); *m* 1st, 1952, Marion Townsend (marr. diss. 1977); two *d*; 2nd, 1985, Joan Kathleen Swinburne. *Educ:* New Plymouth Boys' High Sch., NZ; Canterbury Coll., Univ. of NZ (BSc, MSc); Univ. of Reading (PhD, DSc). FInstP. Special Branch, RNZN, 1952–58; Research Scientist, 1958–68, Head of Materials Physics Div., 1968–70, AERE Harwell; Special Asst to Dir, UKAEA Research Gp, 1970–73; Programme Dir (Applied Nuclear), 1973–76, Research Dir (Industry), 1976–81, Dir of Environmental Research, 1981–83, AERE Harwell; Dir, AEE, Winfrith, 1983–86. *Publications:* papers on semiconductors, neutron beam studies of the solid state, magnetism and management. *Recreations:* reading, walking, family and friends. *Address:* AERE Harwell, Didcot, Oxon OX11 0RA. *T:* Abingdon 24141.

LOW, Sir James (Richard) Morrison-, 3rd Bt, *cr* 1908; DL; DFH, CEng, MIEE; Director, Osborne & Hunter Ltd, Glasgow, since 1956 (Electrical Engineer with firm, since 1952); *b* 3 Aug. 1925; *s* of Sir Walter John Morrison-Low, 2nd Bt and Dorothy Ruth de Quincey Quincey (*d* 1946); *S* father 1955; *m* 1953, Ann Rawson Gordon; one *s* three *d.* *Educ:* Ardvreck; Harrow; Merchiston. Served Royal Corps of Signals, 1943–47; demobilised with rank of Captain. Faraday House Engineering Coll., 1948–52. Chm., Scottish Cttee, Nat. Inspection Council for Electrical Installation Contracting, 1982–; Pres., Electrical Contractors Assoc. of Scotland, 1982–84. Chm., Fife Area Scout Council, 1966–84. Hon. Pipe-Major, Royal Scottish Pipers Soc., 1981–83. DL Fife, 1978. *Recreations:* shooting, piping. *Heir:* *s* Richard Walter Morrison-Low, *b* 4 Aug. 1959. *Address:* Kilmaron Castle, Cupar, Fife. *T:* Cupar 52248. *Clubs:* New, Royal Scottish Pipers Society (Edinburgh).

LOWE, David Alexander; QC 1984; *b* Kilbirnie, Ayrshire, 1 Nov. 1942; *o s* of late David Alexander Lowe and of Rea Sadie Aitchison Lowe (*née* Bridges); *m* 1972, Vivian Anne Langley; three *s* two *d.* *Educ:* Pocklington Sch., York; St John's Coll., Cambridge (schol.; MA; MacMahon Law Student). Called to Bar, Middle Temple, 1965 (Harmsworth Schol.); *ad eundem,* Lincoln's Inn, 1975. In practice at the Chancery Bar, 1966–. *Address:* 3 New Square, Lincoln's Inn, WC2A 3RS. *T:* 01–405 5296.

LOWE, David Bruce Douglas; His Honour Judge Lowe; a Circuit Judge, since 1983; *b* 3 April 1935; *o s* of late Douglas Gordon Arthur Lowe, QC, and of Karen, *e d* of Surgeon Einar Thamsen; *m* 1978, Dagmar, *o d* of Horst and Anneliese Bosse; one *s* three *d* (and one *s* one *d* by a previous marriage). *Educ:* Winchester College; Pembroke Coll., Cambridge (MA). National service, RN, 1953–55. Profumo Scholar, Inner Temple. Called to the Bar, Inner Temple, 1960; Midland and Oxford Circuit (formerly Midland); Prosecuting Counsel to Dept of Trade, 1975–83; a Recorder of the Crown Court, 1980–83. *Recreations:* music, tennis, gardening (formerly rackets and real tennis). *Address:* 7 Lansdowne Crescent, W11. *T:* 01–221 4178. *Club:* Hawks (Cambridge).

LOWE, David Nicoll, OBE 1946; MA, BSc; FRSE; Secretary, Carnegie United Kingdom Trust, 1954–70; *b* 9 Sept. 1909; *s* of George Black Lowe and Jane Nicoll, Arbroath, Angus; *m* 1939, Muriel Enid Bryer, CSP; one *s* three *d.* *Educ:* Arbroath High Sch.; St Andrews Univ. (Kitchener Scholar). MA 1931; BSc (1st Class Hons Botany) 1934; President Union, 1933–34; President Students' Representative Council, 1934–35; Founder President, University Mountaineering Club; Asst Secretary British Assoc. for the Advancement of Science, 1935–40, Secretary 1946–54. War Cabinet Secretariat, 1940–42 and 1945–46; Ministry of Production, 1942–45. Joint Hon. Secretary, Society of Visiting Scientists, 1952–54; Member Executive Cttee: Scottish Council of Social Service, 1953–71; Nat. Trust for Scotland, 1971–81; Member, Countryside Commn for Scotland, 1968–78. Chairman: Scottish Congregational Coll., 1961–68; Pollock Meml Missionary Trust, 1973–84; Governor, Scottish Nat. Meml to David Livingstone, 1974–80. Contributor to Annual Register, 1947–59. Queen's Silver Jubilee Medal, 1977. *Recreations:* those of his family and gardening. *Address:* Caddam, Perth Road, Crieff, Perthshire.

LOWE, Hon. Douglas Ackley; MLC (Ind.) for Buckingham, Tasmania, since 1986; *b* 15 May 1942; *s* of Ackley Reginald Lowe and Dulcie Mary Lowe (*née* Kean); *m* 1962, Pamela June (*née* Grant); two *s* two *d.* *Educ:* St Virgil College, Hobart. Mem. Tasmanian House of Assembly, for Franklin, 1969–86: ALP, 1969–82; Ind., 1982–86. Minister for Housing, 1972; Chief Secretary, 1974; Deputy Premier, 1975–77; Chief Sec. and Minister for Planning and Reorganisation, 1975; Premier, 1977–81; Treasurer, 1980–81; Minister for: Industrial Relations, Planning and the Environment, 1976; Industrial Relations and Health, Aug. 1976; Industrial Relations and Manpower Planning, 1977–79; Economic Planning and Development, 1979–80; Energy, 1979–81. Australian Labor Party: State Sec. 1965–69, State Pres. 1974–75, Tasmanian Section. Tasmanian Deleg. to Aust. Constitutional Convention. Queen's Silver Jubilee Medal, 1977. *Publication:* The Price of Power, 1984. *Address:* (home) 15 Tooma Avenue, Chigwell, Hobart, Tasmania; (office) Parliament House, Hobart, Tasmania. *T:* (002) 302548.

LOWE, Air Chief Marshal Sir Douglas (Charles), GCB 1977 (KCB 1974; CB 1971); DFC 1943; AFC 1946; Chairman, Band III Holdings Ltd, since 1986; Director: Rolls-Royce, since 1984; Royal Ordnance plc, since 1984; *b* 14 March 1922; *s* of John William Lowe; *m* 1944, Doreen Elizabeth (*née* Nichols); one *s* one *d.* *Educ:* Reading School. Joined RAF, 1940; No 75 (NZ) Sqdn, 1943; Bomber Comd Instructors' Sch., 1945; RAF Coll., Cranwell, 1947; Exam. Wing CFS, 1950; Air Min. Operational Requirements, 1955; OC No 148 Sqdn, 1959; Exchange Officer, HQ SAC, USAF, 1961; Stn Comdr Cranwell, 1963; idc 1966; DOR 2 (RAF), MoD (Air), 1967; SASO, NEAF, 1969–71; ACAS (Operational Requirements), 1971–73; AOC No 18 Group, RAF, 1973–75; Controller, Aircraft, MoD Procurement Executive, 1975–82; Chief of Defence Procurement, MoD, Sept. 1982–June 1983. Air ADC to the Queen, 1978–83. Chm., Mercury Communications Ltd, 1984–85. Mem. Council, St John's Sch., Leatherhead, 1984–. CRAeS 1982; CBIM 1984. *Recreations:* gardening, domestic odd-jobbing, photography, theatre, music. *Address:* c/o Lloyds Bank, Byfleet, Surrey. *Club:* Royal Air Force.
See also Baron Glanusk.

LOWE, Air Vice-Marshal Sir Edgar (Noel), KBE 1962 (CBE 1945); CB 1947; Director General of Supply Co-ordination, Ministry of Defence, 1966–70, retired (Inspector General of Codification and Standardisation, 1964); *b* 1905; *s* of late Albert Henry Lowe, Church Stretton, Shropshire; *m* 1948, Mary McIlwraith, *o d* of George M. Lockhart, Stair House, Stair, Ayrshire; one *s* one *d.* Served India, 1934–38; psa 1939; served in France 1939–40 (despatches); Air Commodore, Director of Organisation (Forecasting and Planning), Air Ministry, 1945–47; idc 1949; ADC to the King, 1949–52, to the Queen, 1952–57; Directing Staff, RAF Staff Coll., Bracknell, 1950–51; Director of Organisation, Air Ministry, 1951–53; Deputy Asst Chief of Staff (Logistics), SHAPE, 1953–56; Senior Air Staff Officer, HQ No 41 Group, RAF, 1956–58; AOC No 40 Group, RAF, 1958–61; Director-General of Equipment, Air Ministry, 1961–64. *Address:* Wyndford, 97 Harestone Hill, Caterham, Surrey CR3 6DL. *T:* Caterham 45757. *Club:* Royal Air Force.

LOWE, Frank Budge; Founder, 1981, and Chairman of Lowe Howard-Spink & Bell PLC; Chairman of Lowe Marschalk Worldwide, since 1985; *b* 23 Aug. 1941; *s* of Stephen and Marion Lowe; *m* 1981, Michelle Lowe; one *s* one *d.* *Educ:* Westminster School. Managing Director, Collett Dickenson Pearce, 1972–79. *Recreations:* tennis, ski-ing, shooting. *Address:* 50 Glebe Place, SW3.

LOWE, Geoffrey Colin; aviation consultant since 1980; *b* 7 Sept. 1920; *s* of late Colin Roderick and late Elsie Lowe; *m* 1948, Joan Stephen (*d* 1985); one *d.* *Educ:* Reigate Grammar Sch. GPO, 1937; Exchequer and Audit Dept, 1939. Served War, RAFVR, 1941–46 (Flt-Lt). Asst Principal, Min. of Civil Aviation, 1947; Private Sec. to Permanent Sec., MCA, 1950; Principal, 1950; Colonial Office, 1954–57; Min. of Transport and Civil Aviation, 1957–61; Civil Air Attaché, SE Asia, 1961–64; Asst Sec., Overseas Policy Div., Min. of Aviation, 1964–68; Investment Grants Div., Bd of Trade, 1968–71; Counsellor (Civil Aviation), British Embassy, Washington, 1971–73, Counsellor (Civil Aviation and Shipping), Washington, 1973–74; Under Sec. (Management Services and Manpower), Depts of Industry and Trade, 1974–80. *Recreations:* theatre, crossword puzzles. *Address:* Starlings, 36a Monkhams Avenue, Woodford Green, Essex IG8 0EY. *T:* 01–504 7035.

LOWE, Dr Gordon, FRS 1984; CChem, FRSC; Lecturer in Organic Chemistry, University of Oxford, since 1965; Official Fellow and Tutor in Organic Chemistry, since 1962, and Sub-Rector since 1986, Lincoln College, Oxford; *b* 31 May 1933; *s* of Harry Lowe and Ethel (*née* Ibbetson); *m* 1956, Gwynneth Hunter; two *s.* *Educ:* Imperial Coll. of Science and Technol., Univ. of London (Governors Prize and Edmund White Prize, 1954; Edmund White Prize, 1957; BSc 1954; ARCS 1954; PhD 1957; DIC 1957). DSc Oxon 1985 (MA 1960). CChem, FRSC 1981. University of Oxford: Pressed Steel Res. Fellow, 1957–59; Deptl Demonstrator, 1959–65; Weir Jun. Res. Fellow, University Coll., 1959–61. Irvine Lectr, Univ. of St Andrews, 1984. Member: Biochemistry and Biophysics Cttee, SERC, 1979–82; Molecular Enzymology Cttee, Biochemical Soc., 1978–84; Editorial Adv. Panel, Biochemical Jl, 1981–; Editorial Bd, Bio-organic Chemistry, 1983–. FRSA 1986. Charmian Medal, RSC, 1983. *Publications:* reports on the cysteine proteinases, β-Lactam antibiotics, and chiral phosphate esters; articles in primary chemical and biochemical jls. *Address:* 17 Norman Avenue, Abingdon, Oxon OX14 2HQ. *T:* Abingdon 23029.

LOWE, Dr John; Head, Country Educational Policy Reviews, Education and Training Division, OECD, since 1973; *b* 3 Aug. 1922; *s* of John Lowe and Ellen (*née* Webb); *m* 1949, Margaret James (*d* 1982); two *s* one *d.* *Educ:* Univ. of Liverpool (BA Hons 1950); Univ. of London (CertEd 1951, PhD 1960). Lectr, subseq. Sen. Lectr, Univ. of Liverpool,

1955–63; Dir, Extra-Mural Studies, Univ. of Singapore, 1963–64; Dir, Dept of Adult Educn and Extra-Mural Studies, subsequently Head, Dept of Educnl Studies, Univ. of Edinburgh, 1964–72; OECD: Consultant in field, 1964–; Principal Administrator, 1973–. Sec./Treas., Internat. Congress of Univ. Adult Educn, 1972–76. *Publications:* Adult Education in England and Wales, 1970; (ed) Adult Education and Nation-Building, 1970; (ed) Education and Nation-Building in the Third World, 1971; The Education of Adults: a world perspective, 1975, rev. edn, 1982; (ed) The Clanricarde Letter Book, 1983; articles in educnl and hist. jls. *Recreations:* reading, music, theatre, swimming. *Address:* 3 Rue Ribera, 75016 Paris, France. *T:* 520.2515.

LOWE, John Eric Charles, LVO 1965; MBE 1937; *b* 11 Aug. 1907; 6th *s* of late John Frederick Lowe; *m* 1935, Trudy (*née* Maybury); one *s* two *d. Educ:* Burghley Road Sch., Highgate. Vice-Consul, Jibuti, 1930–37, Harar, 1940; Political Officer, Aden Protectorate, 1940; served in HM Forces, Somaliland and Ethiopia, 1941–46; Senior Asst, Foreign Office, 1947–49; Acting Consul, Suez, 1949; Vice-Consul, Beira, 1950; Vice-Consul, Hamburg, 1951 and Frankfurt, 1953; 2nd Secretary, Helsinki, 1953; Political Agent's Representative, Mina-Al-Ahmadi (Kuwait), 1956; Vice-Consul, Leopoldville, 1959; Consul, Khartoum, 1962; Consul-General, Basra, 1965–67; retired, Sept. 1967. Order of the Two Niles (Sudan), 1965. *Recreations:* gardening, golf, sailing. *Address:* Woodbine, Ewhurst Lane, Northiam, E Sussex. *T:* Northiam 2456.

LOWE, John Evelyn, MA, FSA, FRSA; cultural consultant and author, since 1978, foreign travel specialist, journalist and photographer; Literary Editor, Kansai Time Out, since 1983; *b* 23 April 1928; *s* of late Arthur Holden Lowe; *m* 1956, Susan Helen Sanderson (marr. diss. 1981); two *s* one *d. Educ:* Wellington Coll., Berks; New Coll., Oxford. Served in RAEC, 1947–49 (Sgt Instructor). Victoria and Albert Museum, Dept of Woodwork, 1953–56; Deputy Story Editor, Pinewood Studios, 1956–57; Victoria and Albert Museum: Dept of Ceramics, 1957–61; Assistant to the Director, 1961–64; Dir, City Museum and Art Gall., Birmingham, 1964–69; Dir, Weald and Downland Open Air Museum, 1969–74; Principal, West Dean College, Chichester, West Sussex, 1972–78. Pres., Midlands Fedn of Museums, 1967–69. Member: Exec. Cttee, Midland Arts Centre for Young People, 1964–69; Council of the British School at Rome, 1968–70; Crafts Adv. Cttee, 1973–78. Vis. Prof. in British Cultural Studies, Doshisha Univ., Japan, 1979–81. Trustee: Sanderson Art in Industry Fund, 1968–; Edward James Foundn, 1972–73. *Publications:* Thomas Chippendale, 1955; Japanese Crafts, 1983; Into Japan, 1985; Into China, 1986; major contribs to Encylopædia Britannica and OUP Junior Encyclopedia; articles on applied arts, foreign travel, social history and Japan. *Recreations:* Japan, music, reading, book-collecting, travel. *Address:* 50 Saikata-cho, Ichijo-ji, Sakyo-ku, Kyoto 606, Japan. *T:* 075.722.4546; La Paillole Basse, Cours, 47360 Prayssas, France.

LOWE, Prof. Kenneth Gordon, CVO 1982; MD, FRCP, FRCPE, FRCPGlas; Physician to the Queen in Scotland, 1971–82; Formerly Consultant Physician, Royal Infirmary and Ninewells Hospital, Dundee; Hon. Professor of Medicine, Dundee University, since 1969; *b* 29 May 1917; *s* of Thomas J. Lowe, MA, BSc, Arbroath, and Flora MacDonald Gordon, Arbroath; *m* 1942, Nancy Young, MB, ChB, twin *d* of Stephen Young, Logie, Fife; two *s* one *d. Educ:* Arbroath High Sch.; St Andrews Univ. (MD Hons). Served with RAMC, 1942–46; Registrar, Hammersmith Hosp., Royal Postgrad. Med. Sch., 1947–52; Sen. Lectr in Medicine, St Andrews Univ., 1952–61. *Publications:* (jtly) Regional Anatomy Illustrated, 1983; contribs to med. and scientific jls, mainly on renal, metabolic and cardiac disorders. *Recreations:* reading, fishing. *Address:* 36 Dundee Road, West Ferry, Dundee. *T:* Dundee 78787. *Club:* Flyfishers'.

LOWE, Dr Robert David; Medical Research Consultant, National Heart Foundation of Australia; *b* 23 Feb. 1930; *s* of John Lowe and Hilda Althea Mead; *m* 1952, Betty Irene Wheeler; one *s* three *d. Educ:* Leighton Park Sch.; Emmanuel Coll., Cambridge; UCH Medical School. BCh, MB, MA, MD, PhD Cantab; FRCP, LMSSA. Medical Specialist, RAMC, 1955–59; Research Asst, UCH Med. Sch., 1959–61; St George's Hosp. Med. Sch.: MRC Res. Fellow, 1961–62; Wellcome Sen. Res. Fellow in Clinical Science, 1963–64; Sen. Lectr in Medicine, St Thomas' Hosp. Med. Sch., 1964–70; Hon. Consultant to St Thomas' Hosp., 1966–70; Dean, St George's Hosp. Med. Sch., 1971–82. AUCAS: Exec. Mem., 1967–; Chm., 1972–78. *Publications:* (with B. F. Robinson) A Physiological Approach to Clinical Methods, 1970; papers on peripheral circulation, hypertension, adrenergic mechanisms, central action of angiotensin, control of cardiovascular system. *Recreations:* bridge, squash, hill-walking, sailing. *Address:* c/o National Heart Foundation, Box 2, Woden, ACT 2606, Australia; Brookfield, Tredington, near Shipston-on-Stour, Warwickshire. *T:* Shipston-on-Stour 62426.

LOWE, Robson; philatelist, publisher, editor, author, auctioneer; *b* 7 Jan. 1905; *s* of John Lowe and Gertrude Lee; *m* 1928, Winifred Marie Denne (*d* 1973); two *d. Educ:* Fulham Central Sch. Started own business, 1920; worked on PO Records, 1926; purchased control of Woods of Perth (Printers), 1964; formed Australian co., 1967; joined bd of Christie, Manson & Woods, 1968; formed Italian co., 1969 (founded Il Piccolo for Italian collectors). Chm., Expert Cttee of British Philatelic Assoc., 1941–61; Past Pres., British Philatelic Fedn, 1979–81; Co-founder, Postal History Soc., 1935; Founder: Soc. of Postal Historians, 1950; annual British Philatelic Exhibn, 1965. Mem. jury at internat. philatelic exhibns: first, Durban, 1928; Chm., Cape Town, 1979. Over 1000 lectures. Took over Philatelic Jl of GB, 1958 (still the publisher); Editor, The Philatelist, 1934–74 (centenary, 1966). *Publications:* Philatelic Encyclopaedia (ed), 1935; Handstruck Stamps of the Empire, 1937, 4th edn 1941; Sperati and his Craft, 1953; British Postage Stamps, 1968; (jtly) St Vincent, 1971; Encyclopaedia of Empire Stamps: Europe, 1947, 2nd edn 1951; Africa, 1949; Asia, 1951; Australia, 1962; North America, 1973; monographs (latest, De La Rue Key-plates, 1979); articles in philatelic pubns. *Recreations:* history, philately, study of forgers and forgery. *Address:* Robson Lowe, 47 Duke Street, St James's, SW1Y 6QX. *Clubs:* East India, Devonshire, Sports and Public Schools; Collectors (New York).

LOWE, Sir Thomas (William Gordon), 4th Bt *cr* 1918, of Edgbaston, City of Birmingham; *b* 14 Aug. 1963; *s* of Sir Francis Reginald Gordon Lowe, 3rd Bt and of Franziska Cornelia, *d* of Siegfried Steinkopf; *S* father, 1986. *Educ:* Stowe School; London School of Economics (LLB 1984); Jesus Coll., Cambridge (LLM 1986). Called to the Bar, Inner Temple, 1985. *Heir: b* Christopher Colin Francis Lowe, *b* 25 Dec. 1964. *Address:* 8 Seymour Walk, SW10 9NF.

LOWENSTEIN, Prof. Otto Egon, FRS 1955; FRSE; DSc (Glasgow); PhD (Birmingham); DrPhil (Munich); Honorary Senior Research Fellow, Pharmacology Department (formerly at Neurocommunications Research Unit), Birmingham University Medical School, since 1976 (Leverhulme Emeritus Research Fellow, 1974–76); *b* 24 Oct. 1906; *s* of Julius Lowenstein and Mathilde Heusinger; *m* 1st, Elsa Barbara, *d* of R. Ritter; two *s*; 2nd, Gunilla Marika (*d* 1981), *d* of Prof. Gösta Dohlman; one step *s*; 3rd, Maureen Josephine (*née* McKernan). *Educ:* Neues Realgymnasium, Munich; Munich Univ. Asst, Munich Univ., 1931–33; Research Scholar, Birmingham Univ., 1933–37; Asst Lecturer, University College, Exeter, 1937–38; Senior Lecturer, Glasgow Univ., 1938–52; Mason Prof. of Zoology and Comparative Physiology, Birmingham Univ., 1952–74. President: Assoc. for the Study of Animal Behaviour, 1961–64; Section D, British Assoc., 1962;

Institute of Biology, 1965–67; Member Council, Royal Society, 1968–69. *Publications:* Revision of 6th edn of A Textbook of Zoology (Parker and Haswell), Vol. I; The Senses, 1966; papers in various learned journals on Electrophysiology and Ultrastructure of Sense Organs, esp. inner ear of vertebrates. *Recreations:* music, golf, painting. *Address:* 22 Estria Road, Birmingham B15 2LQ. *T:* 021–440 2526.

LOWNIE, Ralph Hamilton; His Honour Judge Lownie; a Circuit Judge, since 1986; *b* 27 Sept. 1924; *yr s* of James H. W. Lownie and Jesse H. Aitken; *m* 1960, Claudine Therese, *o d* of Pierre Lecrocq, Reims; one *s* one *d. Educ:* George Watson's Coll.; Edinburgh Univ. (MA, LLB, Dip. Admin. Law and Practice). Royal Engineers, 1943–47, NW Europe. WS 1952; enrolled as solicitor, 1953; Mem. Faculty of Advocates 1959; called to Bar, Inner Temple, 1962. Dep. Registrar, Supreme Court of Kenya, 1954–56; Resident Magistrate, 1956–61, Sen. Resident Magistrate, 1961–63, Dep. Registrar-Gen., Kenya, 1963–65; Sen. Magistrate, Bermuda, 1965–72; a Metropolitan Stipendiary Magistrate, 1974–85; a Deputy Circuit Judge, 1976–82; a Recorder, 1983–85. Chm. of Juvenile Courts, 1976–85. Lectr, Kenya Sch. of Law, 1963–65. *Recreations:* hill-walking, military heraldry. *Address:* 57 Greenhill Road, Otford, Kent TN14 5RR.

LOWREY, Air Comdt Dame Alice, DBE 1960; RRC 1954; Matron-in-Chief, Princess Mary's Royal Air Force Nursing Service, 1959–63 (retired); *b* 8 April 1905; *d* of William John Lowrey and Agnes Lowrey (formerly Walters). *Educ:* Yorkshire; Training Sch., Sheffield Royal Hospital. Joined PMRAFNS, 1932; served in Iraq and Aden. Principal Matron: HQ, MEAF and FEAF, 1956–58; HQ, Home Command and Technical Training Command, 1958–59. Air Commandant, 1959. Officer Sister Order of St John, 1959. *Address:* c/o Midland Bank, Attleborough, Norfolk.

LOWRY, family name of **Baron Lowry.**

LOWRY, Baron *cr* 1979 (Life Peer), of Crossgar in the County of Down; **Robert Lynd Erskine Lowry;** PC 1974; PC (NI) 1971; Kt 1971; Lord Chief Justice of Northern Ireland, since 1971; *b* 30 Jan. 1919; *o s* of late William Lowry (Rt Hon. Mr Justice Lowry) and Catherine Hughes Lowry, 3rd *d* of Rev. R. J. Lynd, DD; *m* 1945, Mary Audrey, *o d* of John Martin, 43 Myrtlefield Park, Belfast; three *d. Educ:* Royal Belfast Academical Institution (Porter exhibnr, 1937); Jesus Coll., Cambridge (Hon. Fellow 1977). Entrance Exhibn. (Classics). Scholar, 1939; 1st Class Classical Tripos, Part I, 1939, Part II 1940; MA 1944. Served HM Forces, 1940–46; enlisted Royal Inniskilling Fusilers, 1940; Tunisia, 1942–43 with 38 Irish Inf. Bde; commissioned Royal Irish Fusiliers, 1941; Major, 1945; Hon. Colonel: 7th Bn Royal Irish Fusiliers, 1969–71 (5th Bn, 1967–68); 5th Bn Royal Irish Rangers, 1971–76. Called to the Bar of N Ireland, 1947; Bencher of the Inn of Court, 1955–; Hon. Bencher, Middle Temple, 1973; Hon. Bencher, King's Inns, Dublin, 1973; QC (N Ireland), 1956. Counsel to HM Attorney-General, 1948–56; Judge of the High Court of Justice (NI), 1964–71. Member Departmental Cttees on Charities, Legal Aid and Registration of Title; Dep. Chm., Boundaries Commn (NI) 1964–71; Chairman: Interim Boundary Commn (NI Constituencies), 1967; Permanent Boundary Commn, 1969–71; Dep. Chm., Lord Chancellor's Cttee on NI Supreme Court; Member, Jt Law Enforcement Commn, 1974; Chairman: N Ireland Constitutional Convention, 1975; Council of Legal Educn (NI), 1976–79. Governor, Royal Belfast Academical Instn, 1956–71, Chm., Richmond Lodge Sch., 1956–77; Chm. Governing Bodies Assoc. (NI), 1965. Hon. LLD QUB, 1980; Hon. DLitt NUU, 1981. *Recreations:* golf (Pres., Royal Portrush GC, 1974–); showjumping (Chm., SJAI Exec., 1969–72; Mem. Nat. Equestrian Fedn, 1969–78; Internat. Showjumping Judge, 1973–). *Address:* White Hill, Crossgar, Co. Down. *T:* Crossgar 830397. *Clubs:* Army and Navy, MCC; Royal and Ancient (St Andrews).

LOWRY, Sir (John) Patrick, (Sir Pat), Kt 1985; CBE 1978; Chairman, Advisory, Conciliation and Arbitration Service, since 1981; *b* 31 March 1920; *s* of John McArdle and Edith Mary Lowry; *m* 1952, Sheilagh Mary Davies; one *s* one *d. Educ:* Wyggeston Grammar Sch., Leicester; London Sch. of Economics (evening student). BCom London; CIPM, CBIM. Statistical Clerk, Engineering Employers' Fedn, 1938; served Army, 1939–46; various posts in EEF, 1946–70, Dir 1965–70; Dir of Industrial Relations, British Leyland Motor Corp., 1970, Board Dir 1972; Dir of Personnel, 1975–77, of Personnel and Admin, British Leyland Ltd, 1977–78, of Personnel and External Affairs, 1978–81. Hon. Prof., Sch. of Industrial and Business Studies, Warwick Univ., 1983. Member: UK Employers' Delegn, ILO, 1962, 1963, 1967; Court of Inquiry, Barbican and Horseferry Road Building Disputes, 1967; Court of Inquiry, Grunwick Dispute, 1977. Pres., Inst. of Supervisory Management, 1972–74. FRSA 1984. Hon. LLD Leicester, 1984. *Recreations:* theatre, gardening, fishing. *Address:* Ashfield, Snowdenham Links Road, Bramley, Guildford, Surrey. *T:* Guildford 893289.

LOWRY, Mrs Noreen Margaret, (Nina); Her Honour Judge Lowry; a Circuit Judge, since 1976; *b* 6 Sept. 1925; *er d* of late John Collins, MC, and Hilda Collins; *m* 1st, 1950, Edward Lucas Gardner, QC (marr. diss., 1962); one *s* one *d*; 2nd, 1963, Richard John Lowry, *qv*; one *d. Educ:* Bedford High Sch.; Birmingham Univ. LLB Birmingham, 1947. Called to the Bar, Gray's Inn, 1948. Criminal practice on S Eastern Circuit, Central Criminal Court, Inner London Sessions, etc., practising as Miss Nina Collins; Metropolitan Stipendiary Magistrate, 1967–76. Mem. Criminal Law Revision Cttee, 1975–. *Recreations:* theatre, travel. *Address:* Central Criminal Court, EC4M 7EH.

LOWRY, Sir Pat; *see* Lowry, Sir J. P.

LOWRY, Richard John; QC 1968; **His Honour Judge Richard Lowry;** a Circuit Judge, since 1977; *b* 23 June 1924; *s* of late Geoffrey Charles Lowry, OBE, TD, and late Margaret Spencer Lowry; *m* 1963, Noreen Margaret Lowry, *qv*; one *d. Educ:* St Edward's Sch.; University College, Oxford. RAF, 1943; qualified as pilot and commnd, 1944; No 228 Group Staff Officer, India, 1945; Flt-Lieut, 1946. University College, Oxford, 1942–43 and 1946–48; BA, 1948, MA 1949. Called to Bar, Inner Temple, 1949; Bencher 1977; Member, General Council of Bar, 1965–69. Dep. Chm., Herts QS, 1968; a Recorder, 1972–77. Mem., Home Office Adv. Council on Penal System, 1972–78. *Recreations:* theatre, swimming, fossicking; formerly rowing (Oxford Univ. wartime VIII, 1943). *Address:* Central Criminal Court, EC4M 7EH. *Clubs:* Garrick; Leander (Henley-on-Thames).

LOWRY-CORRY, family name of **Earl of Belmore.**

LOWSON, Sir Ian (Patrick), 2nd Bt *cr* 1951; *b* 4 Sept. 1944; *s* of Sir Denys Colquhoun Flowerdew Lowson, 1st Bt and of Patricia, OStJ, *yr d* of 1st Baron Strathcarron, PC, KC; *S* father, 1975; *m* 1979, Mrs Tanya Du Boulay, *d* of R. F. A. Judge; one *s* one *d. Educ:* Eton; Duke Univ., USA. OStJ. *Heir: s* Henry William Lowson, *b* 10 Nov. 1980. *Address:* 23 Flood Street, SW3 5ST. *Clubs:* Boodle's, Pilgrims; Brook (NY).

LOWTHER, family name of **Earl of Lonsdale** and **Viscount Ullswater.**

LOWTHER, Viscount; Hugh Clayton Lowther; *b* 27 May 1949; *s* and *heir* of 7th Earl of Lonsdale, *qv*, and Tuppina Cecily, *d* of late Captain G. H. Bennet; *m* 1971, Pamela

Middleton; *m* 1986, Angela M., *d* of Captain Peter J. Wyatt, RN and Mrs Christine Wyatt.

LOWTHER, Lt-Col Sir Charles (Douglas), 6th Bt *cr* 1824; Commanding Officer, Queen's Royal Irish Hussars, since 1986; *b* 22 Jan. 1946; *s* of Lt-Col Sir William Guy Lowther, 5th Bt, OBE, and of Grania Suzanne, *d* of late Major A. J. H. Douglas Campbell, OBE; *S* father, 1982; *m* 1975, Florence Rose, *y d* of Colonel Alexander James Henry Cramsie, O'Harabrook, Ballymoney, Co. Antrim; one *s* one *d*. *Educ*: Winchester College. Commissioned, Queen's Royal Irish Hussars, 1966; Regimental Duty UK and BAOR, including ADC to Chief of Defence Staff, 1974–76; Army Staff College, Camberley, 1978–79; Staff appointment, 1981. *Recreations*: polo, shooting, travel. *Heir*: *s* Patrick William Lowther, *b* 15 July 1977. *Address*: National Westminster Bank, 31 Lord Street, Wrexham, Clwyd LL11 1LS. *Club*: Cavalry and Guards.

LOWTHER, John Luke, CBE 1983; JP; Lord Lieutenant for Northamptonshire, since 1984; *b* 17 Nov. 1923; *s* of Col J.G. Lowther, CBE, DSO, MC, TD and the Hon. Mrs Lowther; *m* 1952, Jennifer Jane Bevan; one *s* two *d*. *Educ*: Eton; Trinity College, Oxford. MA 1949. Served King's Royal Rifle Corps, 1942–47; worked for Singer Sewing Co., USA, 1949–51; Managing Dir, own manufacturing Co., 1951–60; farmer, 1960–. CC Northants, 1970–84 (Leader of Council, 1977–81); High Sheriff 1971, DL 1977, JP 1984, Northants. Hon. Col, Royal Anglian Regt (Northamptonshire), TA, 1986–. *Recreations*: shooting, countryman. *Address*: Guilsborough Court, Northampton NN6 8QW. *T*: Northampton 740289. *Club*: Boodle's.

LOXAM, John Gordon; Director of Veterinary Field Services, Ministry of Agriculture, Fisheries and Food, 1983–86; *b* 26 April 1927; *s* of John Loxam and Mary Elizabeth Loxam (*née* Rigby); *m* 1950, Margaret Lorraine Smith; one *d* (and one *s* decd). *Educ*: Lancaster Royal Grammar Sch.; Royal (Dick) Veterinary Coll., Edinburgh. MRCVS. General veterinary practice: Marlborough, 1949–51; Carlisle, 1951–53; Vet. Officer, MAFF, Lincoln, 1953–63; Divisional Veterinary Officer: Tolworth, Surrey, 1963–66; Bury St Edmunds, 1966–71; Dep. Regl Vet. Officer, Leeds, 1971–76; Regl Vet. Officer, Tolworth, 1976–78; Asst Chief Vet. Officer, Tolworth, 1979–83. *Recreations*: gardening, golf; spectator sports, particularly Rugby football; officiating at carriage driving events. *Address*: Boyton, Claremont Avenue, Esher, Surrey KT10 9JD. *T*: Esher 66433. *Clubs*: Farmers', Civil Service; Tyrell's Wood Golf (Leatherhead).

LOY, Francis David Lindley; Stipendiary Magistrate at Leeds since 1974; a Recorder of the Crown Court, since 1983; *b* 7 Oct. 1927; *s* of late Archibald Loy and late Sarah Eleanor Loy; *m* 1954, Brenda Elizabeth Walker; three *d*. *Educ*: Repton Sch.; Corpus Christi Coll., Cambridge. BA Hons (Law) 1950. Royal Navy, 1946–48. Called to the Bar, Middle Temple, 1952; practised North-Eastern Circuit, 1952–72; Recorder (Northern Circuit), 1972; Stipendiary Magistrate of Leeds, 1972–74. Hon. Sec., Soc. of Provincial Stipendiary Magistrates. *Recreations*: reading, English history, walking, wine making. *Address*: 4 Wedgewood Drive, Roundhay, Leeds LS8 1EF; 14 The Avenue, Sheringham, Norfolk. *T*: Sheringham 822697. *Club*: Leeds (Leeds).

LOYD, Christopher Lewis, MC 1943; *b* 1 June 1923; 3rd and *o* surv. *s* of late Arthur Thomas Loyd, OBE, JP, Lockinge, Wantage, Berks, and Dorothy, *d* of late Paul Ferdinand Willert, Headington, Oxford; *m* 1957, Joanna, *d* of Captain Arthur Turberville Smith-Bingham, Milburn Manor, Malmesbury, Wilts; two *s* one *d*. *Educ*: Eton; King's Coll., Cambridge (MA). Served 1942–46, with Coldstream Guards, Captain. ARICS 1952, FRICS 1955. Mem., Jockey Club. Trustee, Wallace Collection, 1973–. JP 1950, DL 1954, Oxfordshire (formerly Berks); High Sheriff of Berkshire, 1961. *Address*: Lockinge, Wantage, Oxfordshire OX12 8QL. *T*: Abingdon 833265. *Club*: Boodle's.

LOYD, Sir Francis Alfred, KCMG 1965 (CMG 1961); OBE 1954 (MBE 1951); *b* 5 Sept. 1916; *s* of Major A. W. K. Loyd, Royal Sussex Regt; *m* 1st, 1946, Katharine Layzell (*d* 1981), *d* of Lt Col S. C. Layzell, MC, Mwatati, Kenya; two *d*; 2nd, 1984, Helen Monica, *widow* of Lt Col C. R. Murray Brown, DSO, Worlington, Suffolk. *Educ*: Eton; Trinity Coll., Oxford (MA). District Officer, Kenya, 1939; Mil. Service, E Africa, 1940–42; Private Secretary to Governor of Kenya, 1942–45; HM Consul, Mega, Ethiopia, 1945; District Comdr, Kenya, 1947–55; Commonwealth Fund Fellowship to USA, 1953–54; Provincial Commissioner, 1956; Permanent Secretary, Governor's Office, 1962–63; HM Commissioner for Swaziland, 1964–68. Dir, London House for Overseas Graduates, 1969–79; Chm., Oxfam Africa Cttee, 1979–85. *Recreations*: golf, gardening. *Address*: 53 Park Road, Aldeburgh, Suffolk. *T*: Aldeburgh 2478. *Clubs*: Army and Navy; Vincent's (Oxford).

LOYD, John Anthony Thomas; QC 1981; a Recorder, since 1985; *b* 18 July 1933; *e s* of Leslie William Loyd and Joan Louisa Loyd; *m* 1963, Rosaleen Iona Ward; one *d* (and one *d* decd). *Educ*: Wycliffe Coll.; Gonville and Caius Coll., Cambridge (BA 1956, MA 1959). RAF Regt, 1951–53. Called to the Bar, Gray's Inn, 1958. *Recreations*: viticulture, sailing. *Address*: 603 Seddon House, Barbican, EC2; Segos, Le Boulvé, Lot, France.

LOYD, Julian St John, CVO 1979; DL; FRICS; Land Agent to HM The Queen, Sandringham Estate, since 1964; *b* 25 May 1926; *s* of General Sir Charles Loyd, GCVO, KCB, DSO, MC and Lady Moyra Loyd; *m* 1960, Mary Emma, *d* of Sir Christopher Steel, GCMG, MVO and Lady Steel; one *s* two *d*. *Educ*: Eton Coll.; Magdalene Coll., Cambridge (MA). FRICS 1955. Partner in Savills, Norwich, 1955–64. DL Norfolk, 1983. *Recreation*: fishing. *Address*: Laycocks, Sandringham, King's Lynn PE35 6EB. *Club*: Army and Navy.

LOYDEN, Edward; MP (Lab) Liverpool, Garston, Feb. 1974–1979 and since 1983; *b* 3 May 1923; *s* of Patrick and Mary Loyden; *m* 1944, Rose Ann; one *s* two *d* (and one *d* decd). *Educ*: Friary RC Elem. School. Shop boy, margarine factory, 1937; Able-Seaman, MN, 1938–46; Seaman Port Worker, Mersey Docks & Harbour Co., 1946–74. Member: Liverpool City Council, 1960 (Dep. Leader, 1983–); Liverpool District Council, 1973; Merseyside Met. CC, 1973; Liverpool Met. Dist Council (St Mary's Ward), 1980–83. Shop Steward, TGWU, 1954, Branch Chm. 1959; Mem. District Cttee, Docks and Waterways, 1967; Mem. Nat. Cttee, TGWU, 1968; Pres., Liverpool Trades Council, 1967; Pres., Merseyside Trades Council, 1974. *Recreations*: full-time political. *Address*: 456 Queens Drive, Walton, Liverpool L4 8UA. *T*: 051–226 4478. *Clubs*: Gillmoss Labour, Woolton Labour.

LOYN, Prof. Henry Royston, DLitt; FSA, FRHistS; FBA 1979; Professor of History, Westfield College, University of London, since 1977 (Vice-Principal, 1980–86); *b* 16 June 1922; *s* of late Henry George Loyn and Violet Monica Loyn; *m* 1950, Patricia Beatrice, *d* of late R. S. Haskew; three *s*. *Educ*: Cardiff High Sch.; University Coll., Cardiff (MA 1949, DLitt 1968). FRHistS 1958; FSA 1968. Dept of History, University Coll., Cardiff: Asst Lectr, 1946; Lectr, 1949; Sen. Lectr, 1961; Reader, 1966; Prof. of Medieval Hist., 1969–77; Dean of Students, 1968–70 and 1975–76; Fellow, 1981. President: Historical Assoc., 1976–79; Glam Hist. Soc., 1975–77; Cardiff Naturalists Soc., 1975–76; Soc. for Medieval Archaeol., 1983– (Vice-Pres., 1971–74); Vice-President: Soc. of Antiquaries, 1983–; RHistS, 1983–. Mem., Ancient Monuments Bd for England, 1982–84. W. N. Medlicott Medal for service to history, Historical Assoc., 1986. *Publications*: Anglo-Saxon England and the Norman Conquest, 1962; Norman Conquest, 1965; Norman Britain,

1966; Alfred The Great, 1967; A Wulfstan MS, Cotton, Nero Ai, 1971; (ed with H. Hearder) British Government and Administration, 1974; (with J. Percival) The Reign of Charlemagne, 1975; The Vikings in Britain, 1977; (with Alan and Richard Sorrell) Medieval Britain, 1977; The Governance of England, vol. 1, 1984; contribs to Eng. Hist. Rev., History, Antiquaries Jl, and Med. Archaeol. *Recreations*: natural history, gardening. *Address*: Westfield College, Kidderpore Avenue, NW3 7ST. *Club*: Athenæum.

LU, Dr Gwei-Djen; Associate Director, East Asian History of Science Library, Cambridge, since 1976; Fellow of Robinson College, Cambridge, 1979–80, Emeritus Fellow, since 1980; *b* 1 Sept. 1904; *d* of Mou-T'ing Lu and Hsiu-Ying Lu. *Educ*: Ming-Tê Sch., Nanking; Ginling Coll., Nanking (BA). PhD Cambridge. Trained as clin. pathologist, Peking Union Med. Coll.; Lectr in Physiology and Biochemistry, St John's Univ., Shanghai; Res. Fellow, Lester Inst. of Med. Research, Shanghai (nutritional biochemistry); research, Cambridge Biochemical Lab., 1937–39, followed by research at Univ. of Calif. Berkeley, Birmingham City Hosp., Alabama, and at Coll. of Physicians and Surgeons, Columbia Univ., NY; staff mem., Sino-British Science Co-operation Office, HM Embassy, Chungking, later Nanking; Prof. of Nutritional Science, Ginling Coll., Nanking, 1947; staff mem., Secretariat, UNESCO, Paris (i/c Nat. Sci. Div., Field Science Co-operation Offices); working with Dr Joseph Needham on Science and Civilisation in China proj., Cambridge, 1957–. Medal for Literature, Ministry of Educn, China. *Publications*: Epicure in China, 1942; (with Dr J. Needham and others) Clerks and Craftsmen in China and the West, 1970; (with Dr J. Needham and others) Science and Civilisation in China, 1971–: Vol. 4, pt 3; Vol. 5, pts 2, 3, 4, 5 and 7; Vol. 6, pts 1, 3 and 4; (with Dr J. Needham) Celestial Lancets: a history and rationale of Acupuncture and Moxa, 1980; Trans-Pacific Echoes and Resonances; Listening Once Again, 1985; The Hall of Heavenly Records: Korean astronomical instruments and clocks 1380–1780, 1986; papers in biochem. and historical jls. *Recreation*: reading, esp. history, economics, politics and sociology. *Address*: 28 Owlstone Road, Cambridge CB3 9JH. *T*: (home) Cambridge 356642, (office) 311545.

LUARD, (David) Evan (Trant); Fellow of St Antony's College, Oxford, since 1957; *b* 31 Oct. 1926; *s* of late Colonel T. B. Luard, DSO, RM. *Educ*: Felsted; King's Coll., Cambridge (Maj. Schol.). Factory worker, 1949–50; HM Foreign Service, 1950–56; served in Hong Kong, Peking, London; resigned, 1956. Oxford City Councillor, 1958–61. Delegate, UN General Assembly, 1967–68. MP (Lab) Oxford, 1966–70 and Oct. 1974–1979; Parly Under-Sec. of State, FCO, 1969–70, 1976–79; contested (SDP) Oxford W and Abingdon, 1983. Apptd by UN Sec.-Gen. to Cttee on Restructuring of UN Economic and Social Activities, 1975; worked for Oxfam, 1980–83. Writer on international affairs. *Publications*: (part author) The Economic Development of Communist China, 1959 (2nd edn 1961); Britain and China, 1962; Nationality and Wealth, 1964; Conflict and Peace in the Modern International System, 1968; The Control of the Sea-bed, 1974; Types of International Society, 1976; International Agencies, the Emerging Framework of Interdependence, 1977; The United Nations, 1978; Socialism without the State, 1979; A History of the United Nations, vol I, 1982; The Management of the World Economy, 1983; Economic Relationships Among States, 1984; War in International Society, 1986; articles in Foreign Affairs, Foreign Policy, International Affairs, World Politics, World Today, The Annals. *Recreations*: music, gardening. *Address*: 35 Observatory Street, Oxford. *T*: Oxford 513302.

LUBBOCK, family name of **Baron Avebury.**

LUBBOCK, Sir Alan, Kt 1963; MA, FSA; *b* 13 Jan. 1897; 6th *s* of Frederic Lubbock, Ide Hill, Kent; *m* 1918, Helen Mary, *d* of late John Bonham-Carter, Adhurst St Mary, Petersfield; two *s*. *Educ*: Eton; King's Coll., Cambridge. Served in Royal Artillery, 1915–19 and 1939–45. Fellow of King's, 1922–28. Hants County Council, 1932–74 (Alderman 1939, Vice-Chairman 1948, Chairman 1955–67); JP (Hants) 1935; DL; High Sheriff of Hants, 1949–; Member: National Parks Commission, 1954–61; Royal Commission on Common Land, 1955; War Works Commission, 1959–64. Chairman: Council, Southampton Univ., 1957–69 (Pro-Chancellor, 1967–83); County Councils Assoc., 1965–69 (Vice-Chairman 1963); Nat. Foundn for Educnl Research, 1967–73. Hon. LLD Southampton, 1969. *Publication*: The Character of John Dryden, 1925. *Address*: Adhurst St Mary, Petersfield, Hants. *T*: Petersfield 63043. *Clubs*: United Oxford & Cambridge University; Leander.

LUBBOCK, Christopher William Stuart; a Master of the Supreme Court (Queen's Bench Division), since 1970; *b* 4 Jan. 1920; 2nd *s* of late Captain Rupert Egerton Lubbock, Royal Navy; *m* 1947, Hazel Gordon, *d* of late Gordon Chapman; one *s* one *d*. *Educ*: Charterhouse; Brasenose Coll., Oxford. Served 1939–46, RNVR. Called to Bar, Inner Temple, 1947. *Recreation*: chatting to music publishers. *Address*: Great Horkesley, Essex. *Club*: Pratt's.

LUCAN, 7th Earl of, *cr* 1795; **Richard John Bingham;** Bt 1632; Baron Lucan, 1776; Baron Bingham (UK), 1934; *b* 18 Dec. 1934; *e s* of 6th Earl of Lucan, MC; *S* father, 1964; *m* 1963, Veronica, *d* of late Major C. M. Duncan, MC, and of Mrs J. D. Margrie; one *s* two *d*. *Educ*: Eton. Lieut (Res. of Officers) Coldstream Guards. *Heir*: *s* Lord Bingham, *qv*.

LUCAS, family name of **Baron Lucas of Chilworth.**

LUCAS; *see* Keith-Lucas.

LUCAS OF CHILWORTH, 2nd Baron *cr* 1946, of Chilworth; **Michael William George Lucas;** Parliamentary Under-Secretary of State, Department of Trade and Industry, since 1984; *b* 26 April 1926; *er s* of 1st Baron and Sonia (*d* 1979), *d* of Marcus Finkelstein, Libau, Latvia; *S* father, 1967; *m* 1955, Ann-Marie, *o d* of Ronald Buck, Southampton; two *s* one *d*. *Educ*: Peter Symond's Sch., Winchester; Luton Technical Coll. Served with Royal Tank Regt. A Lord in Waiting (Govt Whip), 1983–84. Member: House of Lords Select Cttee on Science and Technol., 1980–83; N Atlantic Assembly, 1981–83. TEng(CEI); FIMI (Mem. Council, 1972–76); FInstTA; President: League of Safe Drivers, 1976–80; Inst. of Transport Administration, 1980–83; Vice-Pres., RoSPA, 1980; Mem., Public Policy Cttee, RAC, 1981–83. Governor, Churcher's Coll., Petersfield, 1985–. *Heir*: *s* Hon. Simon William Lucas, late Capt. RE [*b* 6 Feb. 1957. *Educ*: Churcher's Coll., Petersfield; Leicester Univ. (BSc). Geophysicist, USA]. *Address*: House of Lords, SW1A 0PW.

See also Hon. I. T. M. Lucas.

LUCAS OF CRUDWELL, Baroness (10th in line) *cr* 1663 **AND DINGWALL, Lady** (13th in line) *cr* 1609; **Anne Rosemary Palmer;** *b* 28 April 1919; *er d* of Group Captain Howard Lister Cooper, AFC, and Baroness Lucas and Dingwall; *S* mother, 1958; is a *co-heir* to Barony of Butler; *m* 1950, Major the Hon. Robert Jocelyn Palmer, MC, JP, late Coldstream Guards, 3rd *s* of 3rd Earl of Selborne, PC, CH; two *s* one *d*. *Heir*: *er s* Hon. Ralph Matthew Palmer [*b* 7 June 1951; *m* 1978, Clarissa Marie, *d* of George Vivian Lockett, TD; one *d*]. *Address*: The Old House, Wonston, Winchester, Hampshire.

LUCAS, (Charles) Vivian; Chief Executive, Devon County Council, 1974–79; solicitor; *b* 31 May 1914; *s* of Frank and Mary Renshaw Lucas, Malvern, Worcs; *m* 1941, Oonah

Holderness; two *s* two *d*. *Educ:* Malvern Coll.; abroad; London Univ. (LLB). Clerk, Devon County Council, 1972–74; Clerk to the Lieutenancy of Devon, 1972–79. *Recreations:* sport, bridge. *Address:* Highfield Lodge, 7 Salterton Road, Exmouth EX8 2BR. *Club:* Golf and Country (Exeter).

LUCAS, Christopher Charles; Under Secretary, Community and International Policy Division, Department of Energy, 1977–80, retired; *b* 5 June 1920; *s* of Charles Edwin Lucas and Mabel Beatrice Read; *m* 1945, Beryl June Vincent; two *d*. *Educ:* Devonport High Sch.; Balliol Coll., Oxford (Newman Exhibnr). Min. of Fuel, 1946; Central Econ. Planning Staff, 1948; HM Treasury, 1950–70; Cabinet Office, 1970–72; Sec., NEDC, 1973–76, Under-Sec., Dept of Energy, 1976–. *Recreation:* riding. *Address:* Orchard Croft, Withycombe, near Minehead, Somerset. *T:* Dunster 821551.

LUCAS, Sir Cyril (Edward), Kt 1976; CMG 1956; FRS 1966; Director of Fisheries Research, Scotland (Department of Agriculture and Fisheries for Scotland) and Director Marine Laboratory Aberdeen, 1948–70; *b* Hull, Yorks, 30 July 1909; *o s* of late Archibald and Edith Lucas, Hull; *m* 1934, Sarah Agnes (*d* 1974), *o d* of late Henry Alfred and Amy Rose; two *s* one *d*. *Educ:* Grammar Sch., Hull; University Coll., Hull. BSc (London) 1931, DSc (London) 1942. FRSE 1939; Vice-Pres., 1962–64; Neill Prize, 1960. Research Biologist, University Coll., Hull, 1931; Head of Dept of Oceanography, University Coll., Hull, 1942. UK Expert or Delegate to various internat. confs on Marine Fisheries and Conservation, 1948–, and Chm. of research cttees in connexion with these; Chm., Consultative and Liaison Cttees, Internat. Council for Exploration of Sea, 1962–67; Member: Adv. Cttee on Marine Resources Research, FAO, 1964–71 (Chm. 1966–71); Council for Scientific Policy, 1968–70; Nat. Environmental Res. Council, 1970–78. Hon. DSc Hull, 1975; Hon. LLD Aberdeen, 1977. *Publications:* various scientific, particularly on marine plankton and fisheries research in Bulletins of Marine Ecology (Joint Editor), Jl of Marine Biological Assoc., etc and various international jls. *Address:* 16 Albert Terrace, Aberdeen AB1 1XY. *T:* Aberdeen 645568.

LUCAS, Ian Albert McKenzie, CBE 1977; Principal of Wye College, University of London, since 1977; *b* 10 July 1926; *s* of Percy John Lucas and Janie Inglis (*née* Hamilton); *m* 1950, Helen Louise Langerman; one *s* two *d*. *Educ:* Clayesmore Sch.; Reading Univ.; McGill Univ. BSc, MSc; FIBiol; FRAgS. Lectr, Harper Adams Agricl Coll., 1949–50; pig nutrition res., Rowett Res. Inst., Aberdeen, 1950–57 and 1958–61; Res. Fellow, Ruakura Res. Station, New Zealand, 1957–58; Prof. of Agriculture, UCNW, Bangor, 1961–77. Chm., Agricl and Vet. Cttee, British Council, 1978–. Member: MAFF Adv. Council for Agric. and Hortic., 1969–79; Agric. and Vet. Sub-Cttee, UGC, 1972–77; British-Greek Mixed Commn, 1979–. Pres., Sect. M, BAAS, 1983. Member Governing Body: Grassland Res. Inst., 1970–79; RVC, 1978–; E Malling Res. Station, 1978–; Hadlow Agric. Coll., 1978–. *Publications:* scientific papers in Jl Agricl Science, Animal Production, Brit. Jl Nutrition and others. *Recreations:* sailing. *Address:* Court Lodge, Brook, Ashford, Kent TN25 5PF. *T:* Wye 812341. *Club:* Farmers'.

LUCAS, Hon. Ivor Thomas Mark, CMG 1980; HM Diplomatic Service, retired; Assistant Secretary-General, Arab–British Chamber of Commerce, since 1985; *b* 25 July 1927; 2nd *s* of George William Lucas, 1st Baron Lucas of Chilworth, and Sonia Lucas; *m* 1954, Christine Mallorie Coleman; three *s*. *Educ:* St Edward's Sch., Oxford; Trinity Coll., Oxford (MA). Served in Royal Artillery, 1945–48 (Captain). BA Oxon 1951. Entered Diplomatic Service, 1951; Middle East Centre for Arab Studies, Lebanon, 1952; 3rd, later 2nd Sec., Bahrain, Sharjah and Dubai, 1952–56; FO, 1956–59; 1st Sec., Karachi, 1959–62; 1st Sec. and Head of Chancery, Tripoli, 1962–66; FO, 1966–68; Counsellor, Aden, 1968–69 (Chargé d'Affaires, Aug. 1968–Feb. 1969); Dep. High Comr, Kaduna, Nigeria, 1969–71; Counsellor, Copenhagen, 1972–75; Head of Middle East Dept, FCO, 1975–79; Ambassador to Oman, 1979–81, to Syria, 1982–84. *Recreations:* music, cricket, tennis. *Address:* Arab–British Chamber of Commerce, 6 Belgrave Square, SW1. *Clubs:* Royal Commonwealth Society, Royal Over-Seas League.

LUCAS, Ven. John Michael; Archdeacon of Totnes, 1976–81, now Archdeacon Emeritus; *b* 13 June 1921; *s* of Rev. Stainforth John Chadwick Lucas and Dorothy Wybray Mary Lucas; *m* 1952, Catharina Madeleine Bartlett; three *s* (one *d* decd). *Educ:* Kelly Coll., Tavistock; Lichfield Theological Coll. Deacon 1944, priest 1945, dio. Exeter; Asst Curate: Parish of Wolborough, 1944; Parish of Ashburton, 1950; Rector of Weare Giffard with Landcross and Vicar of Monkleigh, 1952; Vicar of Northam, 1962; Vicar of Chudleigh Knighton, 1976–83. *Recreations:* family recreations, garden. *Address:* Wybray House, Shobrooke, Crediton, Devon.

LUCAS, Keith Stephen; Head of Radio, Film and Televison Studies, Christ Church College, Canterbury, since 1984; *b* 28 Aug. 1924; *m* 1969, Rona Stephanie Lucas (*née* Levy); two *s* one *d* (and two step *s*). *Educ:* Royal Coll. of Art (ARCA). London Press Exchange, 1956–64; Prof. of Film and Television, Royal Coll. of Art, 1964–72 (first holder of Chair); Dir, British Film Institute, 1972–78; Television Consultant, BFI, 1979–84. Artistic Dir, Commonwealth Film and TV Fest. and supporting arts prog., Cyprus, 1980. Chairman: Canterbury New Theatre Ltd, 1979–83; Canterbury Theatre and Festival Trust, 1983–86 (Pres., 1986); Vice-Pres., Centre Internat. de Liaison des Ecoles de Cinéma et de Télévision, 1970–72. Governor: North East London Poly., 1971–72; Canterbury Coll. of Art (formerly Canterbury Sch. of Art), 1971–74, 1981–; Maidstone Coll. of Art, 1982–. Hon. Fellow, Royal Coll. of Art, 1972. *Recreations:* writing, painting. *Address:* Cordwainers, Market Place, Charing, Ashford, Kent. *T:* Charing 2420. *Club:* Athenæum.

LUCAS, Percy Belgrave, CBE 1981; DSO 1943 and Bar 1945; DFC 1942; Chairman: GRA Property Trust Ltd, 1965–75 (Managing Director, 1957–65); John Jacobs Golf Consultants Ltd, since 1978; John Jacobs Golf Associates Ltd, since 1985; *b* Sandwich Bay, Kent, 2 Sept. 1915; *y s* of late Percy Montagu Lucas, Prince's, Sandwich, form. of Filby House, Filby, Norfolk; *m* 1946, Jill Doreen, *d* of Lt-Col A. M. Addison, Ascot; two *s* (and one *s* decd). *Educ:* Stowe; Pembroke Coll., Cambridge. Editorial Staff, Express Newspapers, 1937–40. Joined RAFVR, 1939; Commanded: 249 (Fighter) Sqdn, Battle of Malta, 1942; 616 (Fighter) Sqdn, 1943; Coltishall Wing, Fighter Command, 1943; 613 (Mosquito) Sqdn, 2 Gp, 2nd TAF, North-West Europe, 1944–45; Fighter Command, HQ Staff, 1942; Air Defence of Great Britain HQ Staff, 1944; demobilised with rank of Wing Comdr, 1946. Contested (C) West Fulham, 1945; MP (C) Brentford and Chiswick, 1950–59. Capt. Cambridge Univ. Golf team, 1937; Pres. Hawks Club, Cambridge, 1937; English International Golf team, 1936, 1948, 1949 (Capt. 1949); British Walker Cup team, 1936, 1947, 1949 (Capt. 1949). Vice-President: Golf Foundation Ltd, 1983– (Mem. Council, 1966–83; Pres., 1963–66); Nat. Golf Clubs Advisory Assoc., 1969– (Pres., 1963–69); Assoc. of Golf Club Secretaries, 1974– (Pres., 1968–74). Member: General Advisory Council, BBC, 1962–67; Council, National Greyhound Racing Soc. of Great Britain, 1957–72; Policy Cttee, Nat. Greyhound Racing Club Ltd, 1972–77; AAA Cttee of Inquiry, 1967; Exec. Cttee, General Purposes and Finance Cttee; Central Council of Physical Recreation; Management Cttee, Crystal Palace Nat. Sports Centre, 1961–73; Sports Council, 1971–83 (Chm., Finance Cttee, 1978–82; Chm., Sports Trade Adv. Panel, 1972–83); Governor, Stowe Sch., 1964–79. Pres., Old Stoic Soc., 1979–81. Croix de Guerre avec Palmes, 1945. *Publications:* Five-Up (autobiography), 1978; The Sport of Prince's (reflections of a golfer), 1980; Flying Colours: the epic story of Douglas Bader, 1981; Wings of War: airmen of all nations tell their stories 1939–1945, 1983; Out of the Blue: the role of luck in air warfare 1917–66, 1985. *Recreations:* golf, photography. *Address:* 11 Onslow Square, SW7 3NJ. *T:* 01-584 8373. *Clubs:* Naval and Military, Royal Air Force; Sandy Lodge Golf; Walton Heath Golf; Prince's Golf; Royal West Norfolk Golf.

LUCAS, Prof. Raleigh Barclay; Professor of Oral Pathology, University of London, 1954–79, now Emeritus; Consultant Pathologist, Royal Dental Hospital of London, 1950–79; *b* 3 June 1914; *s* of H. Lucas; *m* 1942, Violet Sorrell; one *d* (one *s* decd). *Educ:* George Watson's Coll.; Univ. of Edinburgh. MB, ChB (Edinburgh) 1937; DPH 1939; MD 1945; MRCP 1946; FRCPath 1963; FRCP 1974; FDS RCS 1974. Asst Bacteriologist, Edinburgh Royal Infirmary, 1939–40; Pathologist, Stoke Mandeville Hosp. and Royal Buckinghamshire Hospital, 1947–49; Reader in Pathology, University of London, 1950–54; Dean, Sch. of Dental Surgery, Royal Dental Hospital of London, 1958–73. Examiner in Pathology and Bacteriology for dental degrees, Univs of London, Glasgow, Birmingham, Sheffield, Liverpool and Wales. Served War of 1939–45, Major RAMC; FRSocMed; Fellow and Past Pres., Royal Medical Society; Mem. Pathological Soc. of Great Britain and Ireland; Mem. BMA. *Publications:* Bacteriology for Students of Dental Surgery (jointly), 1954; Pathology of Tumours of the Oral Tissues, 1964; (jtly) Atlas of Oral Pathology, 1985; various articles in medical and scientific journals.

LUCAS, Sir Thomas (Edward), 5th Bt *cr* 1887; MA; FBIM; international industrial strategy consultant; Chairman, TLA Communications Group; *b* 16 Sept. 1930; *s* of late Ralph John Scott Lucas (killed in action, 1941), and Dorothy (*d* 1985), *d* of late H. T. Timson, Tatchbury Mount, Hants; *S* cousin, 1980; *m* 1958, Charmian (*d* 1970), *d* of Col J. S. Powell; one *s*; *m* 1980, Ann Graham Moore. *Educ:* Wellington College; Trinity Hall, Cambridge. *Publications:* Handbook of Vacuum Physics, Vol. 1, part 2, 1964; Patterns of World Social and Economic Change—the next 15 years, 1984; articles in scientific and technical jls. *Heir:* *s* Stephen Ralph James Lucas, *b* 11 Dec. 1963. *Club:* Athenæum.

LUCAS, Vivian; *see* Lucas, C. V.

LUCAS-TOOTH, Sir (Hugh) John, 2nd Bt *cr* 1920, of Bught; *b* 20 Aug. 1932; *s* of Sir Hugh Vere Huntly Duff Munro-Lucas-Tooth of Teananich, 1st Bt and Laetitia Florence, OBE (*d* 1978), *er d* of Sir John Ritchie Findlay, 1st Bt, KBE; *S* father, 1985; *m* 1955, Hon. Caroline, *e d* of Baron Poole, *qv*; three *d*. *Educ:* Eton College; Balliol Coll., Oxford. *Heir:* *cousin* James Lingen Warrand [*b* 6 Oct. 1936; *m* 1960, Juliet Rose, *yr d* of late T. A. Pearn; two *s* one *d*]. *Address:* Parsonage Farm, East Hagbourne, Didcot, Oxon OX11 9LN. *Clubs:* Brooks's, Beefsteak.

LUCE, Hon. Clare Boothe; playwright and author since 1933; *d* of William F. and Ann Snyder Boothe; *m* 1st, 1923, George Tuttle Brokaw; 2nd, 1935, Henry Robinson Luce (*d* 1967). *Educ:* St Mary's Sch., Garden City, Long Island; The Castle, Tarrytown, New York. Associate Editor Vogue, 1930; Associate Editor Vanity Fair, 1931–32; Managing Editor Vanity Fair, 1933–34. Mem. of Congress from 4th District of Connecticut, 1943–47. United States Ambassador to Italy, 1953–57. Mem., President's Foreign Intelligence Adv. Bd, 1973–77, 1982–. Presidential Medal of Freedom, 1983. Holds hon. doctorates. Dame of Magistral Grace, SMO Malta; Kt Gr. Cross, Order of Merit, Italy. *Publications:* Stuffed Shirts, 1933; Europe in the Spring (in England, European Spring), 1940; (ed) Saints For Now, 1952; *plays:* Abide with Me, 1935; The Women, 1936; Kiss the Boys Goodbye, 1938; Margin for Error, 1939; Child of the Morning, 1951; Slam the Door Softly, 1970; *screenplay:* Come to the Stable, 1947; articles to magazines. *Address:* 700 New Hampshire Avenue NW, Washington, DC 20037, USA.

LUCE, Rt. Hon. Richard Napier, PC 1986; MP (C) Shoreham, since 1974 (Arundel and Shoreham, Apr. 1971–1974); Minister of State, Privy Council Office (Minister for the Arts), since 1985; *b* 14 Oct. 1936; *s* of late Sir William Luce, GBE, KCMG, and of Margaret, *d* of late Adm. Sir Trevylyan Napier, KCB; *m* 1961, Rose, *d* of Sir Godfrey Nicholson, Bt, *qv*; two *s*. *Educ:* Wellington Coll.; Christ's Coll., Cambridge. 2nd cl. History. Nat. Service officer, 1955–57, served in Cyprus. Overseas Civil Service, served as District Officer, Kenya, 1960–62; Brand Manager, Gallaher Ltd, 1963–65; Marketing Manager, Spirella Co. of GB; Dir, National Innovations Centre, 1968–71; Chairman: IFA Consultants Ltd, 1972–79; Selanex Ltd, 1973–79; Courtenay Stewart International Ltd, 1975–79; Mem. European Adv. Bd, Corning Glass International, 1975–79. Contested (C) Hitchin, 1970. PPS to Minister for Trade and Consumer Affairs, 1972–74; an Opposition Whip, 1974–75; an Opposition spokesman on foreign and commonwealth affairs, 1977–79; Parly Under Sec. of State, 1979–81, Minister of State, 1981–82 and 1983–85, FCO. *Recreations:* tennis, walking, reading, etc. *Address:* House of Commons, Westminster, SW1.

LUCET, Charles (Ernest); French Ambassador, retired; *b* Paris, 16 April 1910; *s* of Louis Lucet and Madeleine Lucet (*née* Zoegger); *m* 1931, Jacqueline Bardoux; one *s* one *d*. *Educ:* University of Paris. Degree in law, also degree of Ecole Libre des Sciences Politiques. French Embassy, Washington, 1935–Nov. 1942; then joined Free French movement and was apptd to its mission in Washington; attached to Foreign affairs Commissariat in Algiers, 1943; First Sec., Ankara, 1943–45; Asst Dir for Middle Eastern Affairs, Foreign Affairs Min., Paris, 1945–46; First Counsellor: Beirut, 1946; Cairo, 1949; Dept Head of Cultural Relations Div. of Foreign Affairs Min., Paris, 1950–53; rank of Minister Plenipotentiary, 1952; Mem. French Delegn to UN, serving as Dep. Permanent Rep. to UN and to Security Council, 1953–55; Minister Counsellor, French Embassy, Washington, 1955–59; Dir of Political Affairs, Foreign Affairs Min., Paris, 1959–65; Ambassador to USA, 1965–72; Ambassador to Italy, 1972–75. Commandeur de la Légion d'Honneur; Commandeur de l'Ordre National du Mérite; holds foreign decorations. *Address:* 9 rue de Thann, 75017 Paris, France. *T:* 622–5676.

LUCEY, Rear-Adm. Martin Noel, CB 1973; DSC 1944; RN retired; *b* 21 Jan. 1920; *s* of A. N. Lucey; *m* 1947, Barbara Mary Key; two *s* one *d*. *Educ:* Gresham's Sch., Holt. Entered RN, 1938. Served War of 1939–45: qualif. in navigation, 1944; "N" 10th Destroyer Sqdn, 1944. Comdr, 1953; Mem. NATO Defence Coll., 1954; Captain, 1961; Captain "F7" HMS Puma, 1964; Cdre, Sen. Naval Officer, West Indies, 1968; Rear-Adm., 1970; Adm. President, RNC Greenwich, 1970–72; Flag Officer, Scotland and NI, 1972–74. Dir Gen., Nat. Assoc. of British and Irish Millers, 1975–84. Hon. Nat. Sec., Burma Star Assoc., 1984. *Recreation:* painting. *Address:* Oldways, Houghton, Arundel, West Sussex.

LUCIE-SMITH, (John) Edward (McKenzie); poet and art critic; *b* Kingston, Jamaica, 27 Feb. 1933; *s* of John Dudley Lucie-Smith and Mary (*née* Lushington); unmarried. *Educ:* King's Sch., Canterbury; Merton Coll., Oxford (MA). Settled in England, 1946. Education Officer, RAF, 1954–56; subseq. worked in advertising and as free-lance journalist and broadcaster. FRSL. *Publications:* A Tropical Childhood and other poems, 1961 (jt winner, John Llewellyn Rhys Mem. Prize; winner, Arts Coun. Triennial Award); (ed, with Philip Hobsbaum) A Group Anthology, 1963; Confessions and Histories, 1964;

(with Jack Clemo, George MacBeth) Penguin Modern Poets 6, 1964; (ed) Penguin Book of Elizabethan Verse, 1965; What is a Painting?, 1966; (ed) The Liverpool Scene, 1967; (ed) A Choice of Browning's Verse, 1967; (ed) Penguin Book of Satirical Verse, 1967; Thinking about Art, 1968; Towards Silence, 1968; Movements in Art since 1945, 1969; (ed) British Poetry Since 1945, 1970; (with Patricia White) Art in Britain 69–70, 1970; (ed) A Primer of Experimental Verse, 1971; (ed with S. W. Taylor) French Poetry: the last fifteen years, 1971; A Concise History of French Painting, 1971; Symbolist Art, 1972; Eroticism in Western Art, 1972; The First London Catalogue, 1974; The Well Wishers, 1974; The Burnt Child (autobiog.), 1975; The Invented Eye (early photography), 1975; World of the Makers, 1975; (with Celestine Dars) How the Rich Lived, 1976; Joan of Arc, 1976; (with Celestine Dars) Work and Struggle, 1977; Fantin-Latour, 1977; The Dark Pageant (novel), 1977; Art Today, 1977; A Concise History of Furniture, 1979; Super Realism, 1979; Cultural Calendar of the Twentieth Century, 1979; Art in the Seventies, 1980; The Story of Craft, 1981; The Body, 1981; A History of Industrial Design, 1983; Art Terms: an illustrated dictionary, 1984; Art in the Thirties, 1985; American Art Now, 1985; Lives of the Modern Artists, 1986; contribs to Times, Sunday Times, Listener, Spectator, New Statesman, Evening Standard, Encounter, London Magazine, Illustrated London News, etc. *Recreations:* walking the dog, malice. *Address:* c/o Deborah Rogers Ltd, 49 Blenheim Crescent, W11 2EF.

LUCKHOO, Hon. Sir Edward Victor, Kt 1970; QC (Guyana); Order of Roraima, 1979; attached to Luckhoo and Luckhoo, Guyana, 1949–66 and since 1984; *b* Guyana (when Br. Guiana), 24 May 1912; *s* of late E. A. Luckhoo, OBE; *m* 1981, Maureen Moxlow, Batley, Yorks. *Educ:* New Amsterdam Scots Sch.; Queen's Coll., Guyana; St Catherine's Coll., Oxford (BA). Called to Bar, Middle Temple, 1936; QC Guyana 1965. Began career in magistracy as acting Magistrate, Essequibo District, 1943; Magistrate, 1944–47; Judge of Appeal, 1966; Chancellor and President of Court of Appeal, Guyana, 1968–76; Actg Governor-General, 1969–70; Actg Pres. of Guyana, Feb.–March, 1970; High Comr in India and Sri Lanka, 1976–83. Chairman: Customs Tariff Tribunal, 1954–56; Judicial Service Commn, 1966–75; Honours Adv. Council, 1970–76. Mem. Exec. Bd, UNESCO, 1983–. *Address:* 17 Lamaha Street, Georgetown, Guyana.

See also Sir L. A. Luckhoo.

LUCKHOO, Hon. Sir Joseph (Alexander), Kt 1963; President: Bahamas Court of Appeal, since 1982 (Reserve Judge, 1978–81, Judge, 1981–82); Turks and Caicos Court of Appeal, since 1982; *b* 8 June 1917; *e s* of late Joseph Alexander Luckhoo, KC and Irene Luckhoo; *g s* of Moses Luckhoo, official interpreter to the Courts; *m* 1964, Leila Patricia Singh; three *s* one *d*. *Educ:* Queen's Coll., British Guiana; University Coll., London; Middle Temple. BSc London, 1939. Barrister, Middle Temple, 1944; practised at Bar, British Guiana. Crown Counsel, British Guiana, 1949; Legal Draftsman, 1953; acted as Solicitor Gen., British Guiana, 1952, 1954 and 1955; Puisne Judge, British Guiana, 1956; Acting Chief Justice, 1959; Chief Justice, 1960–66; Chief Justice Guyana, 1966; Judge, Court of Appeal, Jamaica, 1967–76; Acting Pres., Court of Appeal, Jamaica, 1972, 1973, and 1974–76; Judge of Ct of Appeal, Turks and Caicos, 1979. Chairman: Judicial Service Commission, 1961–66; Law Reform Cttee, Jamaica, 1973–76. *Publications:* Editor: Law Reports of British Guiana, 1956–58; British Guiana section of West Indian Reports, 1958–61, Jamaica section, 1970–72; Dominion Report Service (Canada), 1977–. *Recreations:* watching cricket and tennis; table tennis. *Address:* 31 Aldenham Crescent, Don Mills, North York, Ontario, Canada.

See also Hon. Sir E. V. Luckhoo, Sir L. A. Luckhoo.

LUCKHOO, Sir Lionel (Alfred), KCMG 1969; Kt 1966; CBE 1962; QC (Guyana) 1954; Judge of Supreme Court, Guyana, 1980, retired; *b* 2 March 1914; 2nd *s* of late Edward Alfred Luckhoo, OBE, Solicitor, and Evelyn Luckhoo; *g s* of Moses Luckhoo, official interpreter to the Courts; *m* Sheila Chamberlin; two *s* three *d*. *Educ:* Queen's Coll., Georgetown, Brit. Guiana; Middle Temple, London. MLC, 1949–51; Mem. State Coun., 1952–53; Minister without Portfolio, 1954–57; Mem. Georgetown Town Council, 1950–64; Mayor, City of Georgetown, 1954, 1955, 1960, 1961 (Dep. Mayor three times); High Comr in UK, for Guyana, May 1966–70; for Barbados, Nov. 1966–70; Ambassador of Guyana and Barbados, to Paris, Bonn and The Hague, 1967–70. Pres., MPCA Trade Union, Brit. Guiana, 1949–52; Pres. of several Unions; has served on Commns of Enquiry, Public Cttees, Statutory Bodies, Legal Cttees, Drafting Cttees, Disciplinary Cttees, etc. Head of Luckhoo & Luckhoo, Legal Practitioners. Chm., Red Cross Soc., 1978. Pres., Guyana Olympic Assoc., 1974–79. Mem. of the Magic Circle. Listed in the Guinness Book of Records as the world's most successful advocate with 245 successful defences in murder cases. Has travelled more than one million miles around the world speaking of Jesus. *Publications:* (jtly) The Fitzluck Theory of Breeding Racehorses, 1960; I Believe, 1968; God is Love, 1975; Life After Death, 1975; The Xmas Story, 1975; Sense of Values, 1975; Dear Atheist, 1977; Dear Boys and Girls, 1978; Dear Adults, 1979; God and Science, 1980; Dear Muslims, 1980; The Question Answered, 1984; The Verdict is Yours, 1985. *Recreation:* cricket. *Address:* Lot 1, Croal Street, Georgetown, Guyana. *Club:* Royal Commonwealth Society (West Indian).

See also Hon. Sir E. V. Luckhoo, Hon. Sir Joseph A. Luckhoo.

LUCY, Sir Edmund J. W. H. C. R. F.; *see* Fairfax-Lucy.

LUDDINGTON, Sir Donald (Collin Cumyn), KBE 1976; CMG 1973; CVO 1974; retired; *b* 18 Aug. 1920; *s* of late F. Norman John Luddington, Ceylon Civil Service, and late M. Myrtle Amethyst Payne; *m* 1945, Garry Brodie Johnston; one *s* one *d*. *Educ:* Dover Coll.; St Andrews Univ. (MA). Served War, Army, 1940–46, KOYLI and RAC, Captain. Hong Kong Govt, 1949–73; Sec. for Home Affairs, 1971–73; Governor, Solomon Islands, 1973–76. Chm., Public Services Commn, Hong Kong, 1977–78; Comr, Indep. Commn against Corruption, Hong Kong, 1978 80. *Recreations:* walking, cycling. *Address:* The Firs, Little Lane, Easingwold, York. *Clubs:* Royal Commonwealth Society; Hong Kong (Hong Kong).

LUDER, (Harold) Owen, CBE 1986; PPRIBA; Chairman and Managing Director, Owen Luder Partnership, since 1978; *b* London, 7 Aug. 1928; *s* of late Edward Charles and Ellen Clara Luder; *m* 1951, Rose Dorothy (Doris) Broadstock; four *d* (one *s* decd). *Educ:* Deptford Park Primary Sch.; Peckham Sch. for Girls; Brixton Sch. of Building; Regent St Polytechnic Sch. of Architecture. ARIBA 1954, FRIBA 1967, PRIBA 1981–83. Private practice in architecture, 1957–; Founder and Sen. Partner, Owen Luder Partnership, 1958–78, when it was one of the first architectural partnerships to convert to an unlimited co. Principal works in commercial and industrial architecture and environmental planning in UK and abroad; consultant to NCB for Vale of Belvoir coal mining project, 1975–. Royal Institute of British Architects: Mem. Council, 1967–80; Hon. Treasurer, 1975–78; Hon. Sec./Treasurer, Commonwealth Assoc. of Architects, 1985–; Chm. Organising Cttee, IUA Congress 1987, 1985–. Pres., Norwood Soc., 1981–. Columnist, Building magazine, 1983–. Occasional radio and TV broadcaster, UK and USA. British Kart Racer, 1961–63; survivor, Lakonia cruise-liner disaster, 1963. FRSA 1984. RIBA Architecture Bronze Medal, 1963; various Civic Trust architectural and housing awards and commendations; Business Columnist of the Year, Publisher magazine, 1985. Arkansas Traveller, USA, 1971. *Publications:* contribs on architectural, planning and building matters to various jls. *Recreations:* writing, swimming, photography, theatre, playing golf badly, supporting Arsenal FC avidly. *Address:* 96 St George's Square, SW1V 3RA. *Club:* Savage.

LUDLOW, Bishop Suffragan of, since 1981; **Rt. Rev. (Stanley) Mark Wood;** *b* 21 May 1919; *s* of Arthur Mark and Jane Wood; *m* 1947, Winifred Ruth, *d* of Edward James Toase; three *s* two *d*. *Educ:* Pontypridd County School; University College, Cardiff; College of the Resurrection, Mirfield. BA (2nd cl. Greek and Latin), Wales. Curate at St Mary's, Cardiff Docks, 1942–45; Curate, Sophiatown Mission, Johannesburg, 1945–47; Rector of Bloemhof, Transvaal, 1947–50; Priest in charge of St Cyprian's Mission, Johannesburg, 1950–55; Rector of Marandellas, Rhodesia, 1955–65; Dean of Salisbury, Rhodesia, 1965–70; Bishop of Matabeleland, 1971–77; Asst Bishop of Hereford, 1977–81; Archdeacon of Ludlow, 1982–83. *Address:* Wistanstow Rectory, Craven Arms, Shropshire SY7 8DG. *T:* Craven Arms 3244.

LUDLOW, Archdeacon of; *see* Griggs, Ven. I. M.

LUDLOW, (Ernest John) Robin, TD 1979; Managing Director, Robin Ludlow & Associates Ltd (Executive Search), since 1981; *b* 2 May 1931; *s* of late Donald Ernest Ludlow, Blandford, Dorset, and Buxted, Sussex; *m* 1970, Sonia Louise Hatfeild; one *s* one *d*. *Educ:* Framlingham Coll., Suffolk. RMA Sandhurst, 1949–52; commissioned RASC, 1952; Staff, RMA Sandhurst, 1954–57; retd 1957. J. Lyons & Co. Ltd, 1957–59; The Economist, 1959–72; Press Sec. to the Queen, 1972–73; Dep. Dir, Aims of Industry, 1973–77; Head of Publicity, Strutt and Parker, 1977; Man. Dir, Kiernan and Co. Ltd (Exec. Search), 1977–79; Partner, Boyden Internat. (Exec. Search), 1979–81. Governor, Clergy Orphan Corp., 1973–83; Chairman: The Yeomanry Benevolent Fund, 1981–; Sharpshooters Yeomanry Assoc., 1973–83. Kent and Co. of London Yeomanry, TA, 1959–69; The Queen's Regt, TA, 1971–78 (Maj.). Member: Gen. Purposes and Finance Cttee, SE, TA&VRA 1973–86; Kent Cttee, TA&VRA, 1973–86. *Recreations:* shooting, gardening, Territorial Army. *Address:* Wingmore Grove Farm, Elham, near Canterbury, Kent. *T:* Elham 553. *Club:* Cavalry and Guards.

LUDWIG, Christa; singer; *b* Berlin, 16 March; *d* of Anton Ludwig, singer, stage director and opera general manager and Eugenie (*née* Besalla), singer; *m* 1st, 1957, Walter Berry (marr. diss. 1970), baritone; one *s*; 2nd, 1972, Paul-Emile Deiber, actor and stage-director. *Educ:* Matura. Staedtische Buehnen, Frankfurt; Landestheater Darmstadt; Landestheater, Hannover; Vienna State Opera; guest appearances in New York, Chicago, London, Berlin, Munich, Tokyo, Milan, Rome, Lucerne, Salzburg, Epidauros, Zürich, Holland, Los Angeles, Cleveland, Saratoga, Bayreuth, Copenhagen, Gent, Montreal, Prague, Budapest and others. Kammersängerin, Austria, 1962; Grand Prix du Disque, 1966; Mozart Medal, Mozartgemeinde, Vienna, 1969; First Class Art and Science, Austria, 1969; Deutscher Schallplattenpreis, 1970; Orphée d'Or, 1970; Prix des Affaires Culturelles, 1972; Vienna Philharmonic Silver Rose, 1980; Hugo Wolf Medal, 1980; Gustav Mahler Medal, 1980; Ehrenring, Staatsoper Vienna, 1980, Hon. Mem., 1981. *Recreations:* listening to music, theatre, concerts, reading. *Address:* c/o Heidrun Artmüller, Goethegasse 1, A-1010 Wien, Austria; Rigistrasse 14, CH-6045 Meggen, Switzerland.

LUFF, Rev. Alan Harold Frank; Precentor and Sacrist of Westminster Abbey, since 1979; *b* 6 Nov. 1928; *s* of Frank Luff and late Elsie Lilian Luff (*née* Down), Bristol; *m* 1956, Enid Meirion, *d* of late Robert Meirion Roberts and Daisy Harker Roberts; three *s* one *d*. *Educ:* Bristol Grammar School; University Coll., Oxford (BA 1951, Dip. Theol. 1952, MA 1954); Westcott House, Cambridge. ARCM 1977. Deacon, 1956; priest, 1957; Assistant Curate: St Mathew, Stretford, Manchester, 1956–59; St Peter, Swinton, Manchester (with charge of All Saints, Wardley), 1959–61; Precentor of Manchester Cathedral, 1961–68; Vicar of Dwygyfylchi (otherwise Penmaenmawr), Gwynedd, dio. Bangor, 1968–79. Chm. designate, Hymn Soc. of Great Britain and Ireland, 1986–87 (Hon. Sec., 1973–86). *Publications:* Hymns and Psalms (composer and author), 1981; contribs to New Christian, Musical Times, Organist's Review, etc. *Recreations:* singing, conducting, cooking. *Address:* 7 Little Cloister, Westminster Abbey, SW1P 3PL. *T:* 01–222 1386.

LUFF, Geoffrey Shadrack, IPFA, FCCA; County Treasurer, Nottinghamshire County Council, since 1984; *b* 12 July 1933; *s* of Shadrack Thomas Luff and Rosie Winifred Luff (*née* Lister); *m* 1956, Gloria Daphne Taylor; one *s* one *d*. *Educ:* Mundella Grammar Sch., Nottingham. Various posts in City Treasury, Nottingham CC, 1949–67; Sen. Technical Asst and Asst Bor. Treasurer, Derby CBC, 1967–73; Asst County Treasurer, Derbyshire CC, 1973–78; Dep. County Treasurer, Nottinghamshire CC, 1978–84. *Recreations:* gardening, birdwatching, photography. *Address:* 1 Thornton Close, Russell Drive, Wollaton, Nottingham NG8 2BG. *T:* Nottingham 283433.

LUFF, Richard William Peter, FRICS; FRSA; Director of Property, British Telecom, since 1984; *b* 11 June 1927; *s* of Victor and Clare Luff; *m* 1950, Betty Chamberlain; no *c*. *Educ:* Hurstpierpoint Coll., Sussex; Coll. of Estate Management. Service in RA, India and UK, 1945–48. Estates and Valuation Dept, MCC, 1949–65; Asst Valuer, GLC, 1968–75; City Surveyor, Corp. of London, 1975–84. Royal Institution of Chartered Surveyors: Mem., Gen. Practice Divl Council, 1973–83; Chm., Valuation and Rating Cttee, 1974–79; Mem., Gen. Council, 1975–; Dep. Chm., Public Affairs Cttee, 1975–79; Pres., 1982–83; Pres., Assoc. of Local Authority Valuers and Estate Surveyors, 1978–79; Hon. Vice-Pres., Cambridge Univ. Land Soc., 1983–. Mem., Furniture History Soc. Master, Chartered Surveyors' Co., 1985. Hon. FISM 1983. *Publications:* Furniture in England—the age of the joiner (with S. W. Wolsey), 1968; articles and papers on compensation and allied property matters; nearly 50 articles on furniture history in Antique Collector, Country Life, and Connoisseur, 1961–73. *Recreations:* collecting antiquarian objects, writing and lecturing on English furniture. *Address:* Blossoms, Broomfield Park, Sunningdale, Ascot, Berks SL5 0JT. *T:* Ascot 23806. *Clubs:* MCC; Surrey County Cricket.

LUFFINGHAM, Prof. John Kingley, FDS RCSE; Professor of Orthodontics, University of Glasgow, since 1976; *b* 14 Aug. 1928; *s* of Alfred Hulbert Carr Luffingham and Frances Tugby; *m* 1968, Elizabeth Margaret Anderson; two *s* one *d*. *Educ:* Haileybury; London Hosp. Med. Coll. (BDS, PhD London); Dip. Orth RCSE. House Surgeon, London Hosp. Med. Coll., 1957–58; Registrar, KCH, 1959–61; Clinical Research Fellow, MRC, 1961–64; Sen. Registrar, Guy's Hosp., 1965–67; Sen. Lectr, Glasgow Univ., 1968–76; Consultant Orthodontist, Greater Glasgow Health Board, 1968–76. *Publications:* articles in dental jls, incl. British Jl of Orthodontics, European Jl of Orthodontics, Archives of Oral Biology. *Recreations:* sailing, skiing. *Address:* Orthodontic Department, University of Glasgow, Glasgow G12 8QQ.

LUFT, Arthur Christian; His Honour Deemster Luft; HM's First Deemster, Clerk of the Rolls and Deputy Governor of the Isle of Man, since 1980; *b* 21 July 1915; *e s* of late Ernest Christian Luft and late Phoebe Luft; *m* 1950, Dorothy, *yr d* of late Francis Manley; two *s*. *Educ:* Bradbury Sch., Cheshire. Served Army, 1940–46. Admitted to Manx Bar, 1940; Attorney-Gen., IOM, 1972–74; Second Deemster, 1974–80. Chairman: IOM Criminal Injuries Compensation Tribunal, 1974–; Prevention of Fraud (Unit Trust) Tribunal, 1974–80; IOM Licensing Appeal Court, 1974–80; Wireless Telegraphy Appeal

Bd for IOM, 1974–80; IOM Income Tax Appeal Comrs, 1980–. Pres., Manx Deaf Soc., 1975–. Pres., IOM Cricket Club, 1980. *Recreations:* theatre, watching cricket, gardening. *Address:* Leyton, Victoria Road, Douglas, Isle of Man. *T:* Douglas 21048. *Clubs:* Ellan Vannin, Manx Automobile (Douglas).

LUKE, 2nd Baron *cr* 1929, of Pavenham; **Ian St John Lawson Johnston,** KCVO 1976; TD; DL; JP; *b* 7 June 1905; *e s* of 1st Baron and Hon. Edith Laura (*d* 1941), *d* of 16th Baron St John of Bletsoe; *S* father, 1943; *m* 1932, Barbara, *d* of Sir FitzRoy Hamilton Anstruther-Gough-Calthorpe, 1st Bt; four *s* one *d*. *Educ:* Eton; Trinity Coll., Cambridge, MA. Life President, Electrolux Ltd, 1978– (Chm., 1963–78); Chm., Gateway Building Society, 1978–; Dir, Ashanti Goldfields Corporation Ltd and other companies; Chm., Bovril Ltd, 1943–70. One of HM Lieutenants, City of London, 1953–. Hon. Col 5th Bn Beds Regt, 1947–62; OC 9th Bn Beds and Herts Regt, 1940–43; Chairman: Area Cttee for National Fitness in Herts and Beds, 1937–39; London Hospitals Street Collections Cen. Cttee, 1943–45; Beds TAA, 1943–46; Duke of Gloucester's Red Cross and St John Fund, 1943–46; Nat. Vice-Pres., Royal British Legion; Chm., National Playing Fields Assoc., 1950–76 (a Vice-Pres., 1977–); an Hon. Sec., Assoc. of British Chambers of Commerce, 1944–52; Mem. of Church Assembly (House of Laity), 1935; Lay Reader, St Alban's dio., 1933–; Mem., International Olympic Cttee, 1952–; President: Incorporated Sales Managers Assoc., 1953–56; Advertising Assoc., 1955–58; Outdoor Advertising Council, 1957; Operation Britain Organisation, 1957–62; London Chamber of Commerce, 1952–55; Inst. of Export, 1973–83; Chm. Governors, Queen Mary Coll., Univ. of London, 1963–82, Fellow, 1980. MFH Oakley Hunt, 1947–49. CC, DL, JP, Bedfordshire. *Heir: s* Hon. Arthur Charles St John Lawson Johnston [*b* 13 Jan. 1933; *m* 1st, 1959, Silvia Maria (marr. diss. 1971), *yr d* of Don Honorio Roigt and Doña Dorothy Goodall de Roigt; one *s* two *d*; 2nd, 1971, Sarah, *d* of Richard Hearne; one *s*]. *Address:* Odell Castle, Odell, Beds MK43 7BB. *T:* Bedford 720240. *Club:* Carlton.

See also Hon. H. de B. Lawson Johnston, Sir I. J. Pitman.

LUKE, Hon. Sir Emile Fashole, KBE 1969 (CBE 1959); Speaker of the House of Representatives, Sierra Leone, 1968–73; *b* 19 Oct. 1895; *s* of late Josiah Thomas Steven Luke and late Dorcas Evangeline Luke; *m* 1929, Sarah Christina Jones-Luke (decd); two *s* one *d*. *Educ:* Wesleyan Methodist High Sch.; Fourah Bay Coll.; Lincoln's Inn. Civil Servant, 1913–19; practised Law, 1926–44; City Councillor, Freetown, 1940–44; Asst Police Magistrate, 1944–45; Police Magistrate, 1945–51; Senior Police Magistrate, 1951; Actg Judge, Bathurst, Gambia, 1953; Actg Puisne Judge, 1951–54; Puisne Judge, Sierra Leone, 1954–59, retired; Acting Chief Justice, in Sierra Leone and Gambia, on various occasions between 1956 and 1968, and Appeal Court Justice on several occasions, 1960–68. Chief Scout, Scouts Assoc., Sierra Leone, 1969 (awarded the Silver Wolf); Bronze Wolf, World Bureau, 1971. DCL (hc) Univ. of Sierra Leone, 1976. Grand Cordon, Order of Cedar of Lebanon, 1971; Grand Cordon, Order of Menelik II, Ethiopia, 1972. *Recreations:* tennis and walking. *Address:* 85 Motor Road, Wilberforce, PO Box 228, Freetown, Sierra Leone. *T:* Freetown 30602. *Clubs:* Royal Commonwealth Society; Freetown Dinner (Freetown).

LUKE, Eric Howard Manley, CMG 1950; FRCSE 1922; FRACS 1932; retired; *b* 18 Aug. 1894; *s* of Sir Charles Luke; *m* 1923, Gladys Anne, *d* of Col J. J. Esson, CMG; one *s* two *d*. *Educ:* Wellington Coll.; Otago Univ.; Edinburgh Univ. MB, ChB, Otago Univ., NZ, 1920; senior surgeon, Wellington Hospital, NZ, 1925–50; Thoracic Surgeon, East Coast Hospitals, 1942–54; Chm. of Council, British Medical Association, NZ Branch, 1944–49; President BMA, NZ Branch, 1950. Has a citrus orchard. OStJ 1940. *Recreations:* formerly Rugby; now bowls and gardening. *Address:* Keri Keri, Bay of Islands, NZ. *Club:* Wellington (Wellington, NZ).

LUKE, Peter (Ambrose Cyprian), MC 1944; writer and dramatist, freelance since 1967; *b* 12 Aug. 1919, *e s* of late Sir Harry Luke, KCMG, DLitt Oxon and Joyce Fremlin; *m* 1st, Carola Peyton-Jones (decd); 2nd, Lettice Crawshaw (marr. diss.); one *d* (one *s* decd); 3rd, June Tobin; two *s* three *d*. *Educ:* Eton; Byam Shaw Sch. of Art; Atelier André Lhote, Paris. Served War, 1939–46 with Rifle Bde in ME, Italy and NW Europe. Sub-Editor, Reuters News Desk, 1946–47; wine trade, 1947–57; Story Editor, ABC TV, 1958–62; Editor, The Bookman (ABC TV), 1962–63; Editor, Tempo (ABC TV Arts Programme), 1963–64; Drama Producer, BBC TV, 1963–67. Dir, Edwards-Mac Liammoir Dublin Gate Theatre Co., 1977–80; Directed, Abbey Theatre, Dublin: Hadrian VII, 1970; directed, Gaiety Theatre, Dublin: Rings for a Spanish Lady, 1978. Author TV plays: Small Fish are Sweet, 1958; Pigs Ear with Flowers, 1960; Roll on Bloomin' Death, 1961; (with William Sansom) A Man on Her Back, 1965; Devil a Monk Wou'd Be, 1966; Honour, Profit and Pleasure, 1985. Produced, Silent Song, BBC TV (Prix Italia, 1967). Wrote and directed films: Anach Cuan (about Sean O Riada), BBC TV, 1967; Black Sound Deep Song (about Federico Garcia Lorca), BBC TV, 1968; wrote stage plays: Hadrian the Seventh, prod. Birmingham Rep. 1967, Mermaid 1968, Theatre Royal, Haymarket and Broadway, 1969 (Antoinette Perry Award nomination, 1968–69); Bloomsbury, Phoenix, 1974; Proxopera (adaptation), Dublin Gate Theatre, 1979; Married Love, The Apotheosis of Marie Stopes, Thorndyke, Leatherhead, 1985. OStJ 1940. *Publications:* The Play of Hadrian VII, 1968; Sisyphus and Reilly, an autobiography, 1972; (ed) Enter Certain Players, Edwards-Mac Liammoir 1928–1978, 1978; Paquito and the Wolf (children), 1981; Telling Tales: selected short stories, 1981; The Other Side of the Hill, a novel of the Peninsular War, 1984; The Mad Pomegranate & the Praying Mantis, Adventure in Andalusia, 1985; translations from the Spanish: Yerma, by Federico Garcia Lorca, 1972; Rings for a Spanish Lady (Anillos para Una Dama) by Antonio Gala, 1974; short stories in: Envoy, Cornhill, Pick of Today's Short Stories, Winter's Tales, Era, New Irish Writing, etc. *Recreations:* conviviality, tauromachy. *Address:* c/o Harvey Unna & Stephen Durbridge Ltd, 24 Pottery Lane, Holland Park, W11 4LZ. *Club:* Kildare Street and University (Dublin).

LUKE, Sir Stephen (Elliot Vyvyan), KCMG 1953 (CMG 1946); *b* 26 Sept. 1905; *o c* of late Brigadier-General Thomas Mawe Luke, CBE, DSO; *m* 1st, 1929, Helen Margaret Reinold; two *s*; 2nd, 1948, Margaret Stych; one *d*. *Educ:* St George's Sch., Harpenden; Wadham Coll., Oxford. Asst Clerk, House of Commons, 1930; Asst Principal, Colonial Office, 1930; Asst Private Sec. to successive Secs of State, 1933–35; seconded to Palestine Administration, 1936–37; Sec., Palestine Partition Commission, 1938; Under-Sec., Cabinet Office, 1947–50; Asst Under-Sec. of State, Colonial Office, 1950–53; Comptroller for Development and Welfare in the West Indies, and British Co-Chm. of Caribbean Commn, 1953–58; Comr for preparation of WI Federal Organisation, 1956–58; Senior Crown Agent for Oversea Governments and Administrations, 1959–68; Interim Comr for the West Indies, May 1962–68; Mem. Exec. Cttee, W India Cttee, 1969–72. Chm., Board of Governors, St George's Sch., Harpenden, 1963–68. Dir, Pirelli Ltd and other companies, 1968–76. *Address:* Merryfields, Breamore, Fordingbridge, Hants. *T:* Downton 22389. *Club:* United Oxford & Cambridge University.

LUKE, William Edgell; Chairman, 1959–79 (Managing Director, 1949–73), Lindustries Ltd (formerly the Linen Thread Co. Ltd) and associated companies at home and abroad; Director: Powell Duffryn Ltd, 1966–79; Bankers Trust (Holdings) Ltd, 1975–78; *b* 9 June 1909; *s* of George Bingley Luke and Violet Edgell; *m* 1st, Muriel Aske Haley (marr. diss.); one *s* one *d*; 2nd, Constance Anne Reid; two *d*. *Educ:* Old Hall, Wellington; Kelvinside Academy, Glasgow. Served War of 1939–45: Major, Intelligence Corps, S Africa and Central America. Mem. Grand Coun., FBI, 1947–73 (Chm. Scottish Council, 1957) (FBI is now CBI); Mem. Council, Aims of Industry, 1958–80; Chm. Industrial Advisers to the Blind Ltd, 1963–67; Pres., UK-S Africa Trade Assoc., 1977–79 (Chm., 1963–77); Mem., Brit. Nat. Export Council, and Chm., BNEC Southern Africa Cttee for Exports to Southern Africa, 1965–68; Mem., BOTB Adv. Council, 1975–78; Trustee, South Africa Foundation. FBIM. Master, Worshipful Company of Makers of Playing Cards, 1958. Mem. Lloyd's. Royal Order, Crown of Yugoslavia, 1944. *Recreations:* golf, music and travel. *Address:* Pickhurst Cottage, High Street Green, Chiddingfold, Surrey GU8 4YB. *Clubs:* Royal Thames Yacht, Travellers'.

LUMBY, Sir Henry, Kt 1973; CBE 1957; DL, JP; Chairman of Lancashire County Council, 1967–73; Chairman, Liverpool Diocesan Board of Finance, 1977–80; *b* 9 Jan. 1909; *m* 1936, Dorothy Pearl Watts; two *s*. *Educ:* Merchant Taylors' Sch., Crosby. Served War of 1939–45 (POW, 1942–45). Mem., Lancs CC, 1946; Alderman, 1956–74; Leader of Conservative Gp, Lancs CC, 1965–74; DL 1965, JP 1951, High Sheriff 1973, Lancashire. *Recreation:* gardening. *Address:* The Dawn, Dark Lane, Ormskirk, Lancs. *T:* Ormskirk 72030.

LUMET, Sidney; film director; *b* Philadelphia, 25 June 1924; *o s* of Baruch and Eugenia Lumet; *m* Rita Gam (marr. diss.); *m* 1956, Gloria Vanderbilt (marr. diss. 1963); *m* 1963, Gail Jones (marr. diss. 1978); two *d*; *m* 1980, Mary Gimbel. *Educ:* Professional Children's Sch., NY; Columbia Univ. Served US Army, SE Asia, 1942–46. Appeared as child actor: Dead End; The Eternal Road; Sunup to Sunday; Schoolhouse on the Lot; My Heart's in the Highlands; Dir, Summer Stock, 1947–49; taught acting, High Sch. of Professional Arts; Associate Dir, CBS, 1950, Dir, 1951–57. *TV shows include:* Danger; Your Are There; Alcoa: The Sacco and Vanzetti Story; Goodyear Playhouse; Best of Broadway; Omnibus. *Films directed include:* Twelve Angry Men, 1957; Stage Struck, 1958; That Kind of Woman, 1959; The Fugitive Kind, 1960; A View from the Bridge, Long Day's Journey into Night, 1962; Fail Safe, 1964; The Pawnbroker, The Hill, 1965; The Group, 1966; The Deadly Affair, 1967; Bye Bye Braverman, Last of the Mobile Hot Shots, Child's Play, The Seagull, 1969; The Anderson Tapes, 1971; The Offence, 1973; Serpico, Murder on the Orient Express, 1974; Dog Day Afternoon, 1975; Network, 1977; Equus, 1977; The Wiz, 1979; Just Tell Me What You Want, 1979; Prince of the City, 1980; Deathtrap, 1981; The Verdict, 1982; Daniel, 1983; Garbo Talks, 1984; Power, 1985; *play:* Caligula, 1960. *Address:* c/o 110 West 57 Street, New York, NY 10019, USA.

LUMLEY, family name of **Earl of Scarbrough.**

LUMLEY, Viscount; Richard Osbert Lumley; *b* 18 May 1973; *s* and *heir* of 12th Earl of Scarbrough, *qv*.

LUMLEY-SAVILE, family name of **Baron Savile.**

LUMSDEN, Sir David (James), Kt 1985; Principal, Royal Academy of Music, since 1982; *b* Newcastle upon Tyne, 19 March 1928; *m* 1951, Sheila Daniels; two *s* two *d*. *Educ:* Dame Allan's Sch., Newcastle upon Tyne; Selwyn Coll., Cambridge. Organ scholar, Selwyn Coll., Cambridge, 1948–51; BA Class I, 1950; MusB (Barclay Squire Prize) 1951; MA 1955; DPhil 1957. Asst Organist, St John's Coll., Cambridge, 1951–53; Res. Student, 1951–54; Organist and Choirmaster, St Mary's, Nottingham, 1954–56; Founder and Conductor, Nottingham Bach Soc., 1954–59; Rector Chori, Southwell Minster, 1956–59; Dir of Music, Keele, 1958–59; Prof. of Harmony, Royal Academy of Music, 1959–61; Fellow and Organist, New Coll., Oxford, and Lectr in the Faculty of Music, Oxford Univ., 1959–76; Principal, RSAMD, Glasgow, 1976–82. Conductor: Oxford Harmonic Soc., 1961–63; Oxford Sinfonia, 1967–70; BBC Scottish Singers, 1977–80; Organist, Sheldonian Theatre, 1964–76; Choragus, Oxford Univ., 1968–72. Harpsichordist to London Virtuosi, 1972–75. Member of Board: Scottish Opera, 1977–83; ENO, 1983–. President: Inc. Assoc. of Organists, 1966–68; ISM, 1984–85; RCO, 1986–; Chairman: NYO, 1985–; Early Music Soc., 1985–. Hugh Porter Lectr, Union Theological Seminary, NY, 1967; Vis. Prof., Yale Univ., 1974–75. Hon. Editor, Church Music Soc., 1970–73. Hon. FRCO 1976; Hon. RAM 1978; FRCM 1980; FRNCM 1981; FRSAMD 1982; Hon. GSM 1984; FLCM 1985; FRSA 1985. *Publications:* An Anthology of English Lute Music, 1954; Thomas Robinson's Schoole of Musicke, 1603, 1971; Articles in: The Listener; The Score; Music and Letters: Galpin Soc. Jl; La Luth et sa Musique; La Musique de la Renaissance, etc. *Recreations:* reading, theatre, photography, travel, hill-walking, etc. *Address:* 47 York Terrace East, NW1; Royal Academy of Music, Marylebone Road, NW1 5HT.

LUMSDEN, George Innes, FRSE; Director, British Geological Survey, since 1985; *b* 27 June 1926; *s* of George Lumsden and Margaret Ann Frances Lumsden (*née* Cockburn); *m* 1958, Sheila Thomson; two *s* one *d*. *Educ:* Banchory Academy; Aberdeen University (BSc). MIGeol. Geological Survey of GB, 1949; District Geologist S Scotland, 1970, Asst Dir and Sen. Officer Scotland, 1980, Inst. of Geol Scis; Dep. Dir, British Geol. Survey, 1982–85. Member: Council of Management, Macaulay Inst. for Soil Research, 1980–; Engineering and Sci. Adv. Cttee, Derby Coll. of Higher Educn, 1983–; Geol. Museum Adv. Panel, 1985–; Chm., Dirs of Western European Geol Surveys' Standing Gp on Envtl Geology, 1984–. *Publications:* papers on geol topics in official Geol Survey. *Recreations:* music, theatre, sport, gardening. *Address:* British Geological Survey, Keyworth, Nottingham NG12 5GG. *T:* Plumtree 6111; 1 Mevell Court, Clumber Road East, The Park, Nottingham NG7 1BD. *T:* Nottingham 414979.

LUMSDEN, James Alexander, MBE 1945; TD 1962; DL; Partner, Maclay, Murray & Spens, Solicitors, Glasgow, 1947–82; *b* 24 Jan. 1915; *s* of late Sir James Robert Lumsden and Lady (Henrietta) Lumsden (*née* Macfarlane Reid); *m* 1947, Sheila, *d* of late Malcolm Cross and Evelyn Cross (*née* Newlands); three *s*. *Educ:* Rugby Sch.; Corpus Christi Coll., Cambridge. BA Cantab, LLB. Director: Bank of Scotland, 1958–85; Weir Group PLC, 1957–84; William Baird PLC, 1959–84; Murray Growth Trust PLC and other companies in Murray Johnstone Group, 1967–85 (Chm., 1971–84); Scottish Provident Instn, 1968–85 (Chm., 1977–83); Burmah Oil Co. Ltd, 1957–76 (Chm., 1971–75). Mem. Jenkins Cttee on Company Law. DL Dunbartonshire, 1966. *Recreations:* shooting and other country pursuits. *Address:* Bannachra, Helensburgh, Dunbartonshire. *T:* Arden 653. *Clubs:* Caledonian; New (Edinburgh); Western (Glasgow).

LUNCH, John, CBE 1975; VRD 1965; FCA, FCIT; Director-General of the Port of London Authority, and Board Member, 1971–76; Chairman: Comprehensive Shipping Group, 1973–75; Transcontinental Air Ltd, 1973–75; *b* 11 Nov. 1919; *s* of late Percy Valentine Lunch and late Amy Lunch (*née* Somerville); *m* 1943, Joyce Barbara Clerke; two *s*. *Educ:* Roborough Sch., Eastbourne. Served War, Lt RNVR, Medit. and Home Fleets, 1939–46 (N Atlantic convoys, Crete, N Africa, Malta convoys, Sicily D-Day landings; Torpedo specialist, 1944), subseq. Permanent RNVR, later RNR; Lt-Comdr RNR, retd list, 1969; Lt-Col RE (TA), Engr and Transport Staff Corps (formerly Engr and Railway Staff Corps), 1971, Col, 1976. In business in City, 1946–48: Asst Man. Dir, Tokenhouse Securities Corp. Ltd, 1947, and dir several cos; British Transport Commn,

1948–61: road and rail transport and ancillary businesses; PLA, 1961; Dir of Finance, also Dir of Commerce, 1966; Asst Dir-Gen., responsible docks and harbour, 1969; Chairman: (and founder) PLA Port Users Consultative Cttee, 1966–71; Internat. Port Develt Cttee, Internat. Assoc. of Ports and Harbors, 1972–76; Pres., Inst. of Freight Forwarders, 1972–73. Chm., London Industrial Chartered Accountants, 1971–72; Member Council: Inst. of Chartered Accountants, 1970–77; Chartered Inst. of Transport, 1973–76. Founder Chm., RNLI Manhood Br., 1976–78; Mem. Cttee of Management, RNLI, 1977–; Pres., RNLI, Hayling Island Lifeboat Station, 1978–; Hon. Art Adviser, RNLI, 1981–. Hon. Life Mem. Internat. Assoc. of Airport and Seaport Police, 1974. CBIM (FBIM 1971); FInstM 1973; FRSA (Council nominee) 1976; HH 1979; Hon. FInstFF 1986. Freeman: City of London, 1970; Watermen & Lightermen's Co. of River Thames, 1970 (Court Mem., 1976–80, Hon. Court Mem., 1980–). ADC to Governor of Louisiana, with rank Adm., 1971–. *Publications:* The Chartered Accountant in Top Management, 1965; A Plan for Britain's Ports, 1975. *Recreations:* sailing, art. *Address:* Twittens, Itchenor, Chichester, West Sussex PO20 7AN. *T:* Birdham 512105; 97A York Mansions, Prince of Wales Drive, SW11 4BN. *T:* 01–622 8100. *Clubs:* Army and Navy; West Sussex County (Chichester); Itchenor Sailing (West Sussex).

LUND, John Walter Guerrier, CBE 1975; FRS 1963; DSc, PhD; Botanist, at Windermere Laboratory of Freshwater Biological Association, 1945–78; Deputy Chief Scientific Officer; *b* 27 Nov. 1912; *s* of George E. Lund and Kate Lund (*née* Hardwick); *m* 1949, Hilda M. Canter; one *s* one *d*. *Educ:* Sedbergh Sch.; Univs of Manchester and London. Demonstrator in Botany, Univ. of Manchester, also Queen Mary Coll. and Chelsea Polytechnic, Univ. of London, 1935–38; Temp. Lectr in Botany, Univ. of Sheffield, 1936; PhD (London) 1939; Staff Biologist, W Midland Forensic Science Laboratory, Birmingham, 1938–45; DSc (London) 1951. *Publications:* papers and articles in scientific jls, symposium vols, etc. *Recreation:* gardening. *Address:* Ellerbeck, Ellerigg Road, Ambleside, Cumbria LA22 9EU. *T:* Ambleside 32369.

LUND, Rodney Cookson; Chairman, National Bus Co., since 1986; *b* 16 June 1936; *s* of late Arthur and Doris Lund; *m* 1964, Lynda Brooks (marr. diss. 1973); one *s*. *Educ:* Wallasey Grammar School; Liverpool University (BCom Hons). Served RAPC, 1957–59 (commissioned). Evans Medical, 1959; Carreras Rothmans, 1960–64; Partner, Urwick Orr & Partners, 1964–66 and 1969–73; Man. Dir, The Mace Voluntary Gp, 1966–69; Vice-Chm., Produce Importers Alliance, 1966–69; Exec. Director: Rank Radio International, 1973–75; British Sugar Corp., 1976–82; Woolworth Holdings, 1982–86. *Recreations:* travel, opera, cooking. *Address:* 18 Billing Road, Chelsea, SW10 9UL. *T:* 01–352 2641; Newbottle Lodge, Kings Sutton, Banbury, Oxon OX17 3DB. *T:* Banbury 811276.

LUNKOV, Nikolai Mitrofanovich; Soviet Ambassador to Italy, since 1980; *b* Pavlovka, Ryazan Region, 7 Jan. 1919; *Educ:* Lomonosov Technical Inst., Moscow. Diplomatic Service, 1943–; Asst Minister of Foreign Affairs, 1951–52; Dep. Political Counsellor, Soviet Control Commn in Germany, 1952–54; Counsellor, Stockholm, 1954–57; Dep. Head, Dept of Internat. Organizations, Ministry of Foreign Affairs, 1957; 3rd European Dept, 1957–59; Head of Scandinavian Dept, Min. of Foreign Affairs, 1959–62; Ambassador to Norway, 1962–68; Head of Dept of Cultural Relations with Foreign Countries, 1968–71; Head of 2nd European Dept, 1971–73; Ambassador to the Court of St James's, 1973–80. Mem. of Collegium of Min. of Foreign Affairs, 1968–73. Awarded orders and medals. *Address:* Embassy of the USSR, Via Gaeta 5, Rome, Italy.

LUNN, Rt. Rev. David Ramsay; *see* Sheffield, Bishop of.

LUNN, Peter Northcote, CMG 1957; OBE 1951; HM Diplomatic Service, retired 1972; *b* 15 Nov. 1914; *e s* of late Sir Arnold Lunn; *m* 1939, Hon. (Eileen) Antoinette (*d* 1976), *d* of 15th Viscount Gormanston; three *s* three *d*. *Educ:* Eton. Joined RA, 1940; served 1940–46 (Malta, Italy and BAOR); entered FO, 1947; Vienna, 1948–50; Berne, 1950–53; Germany, 1953–56; London, 1956–57; Bonn, 1957–62; Beirut, 1962–67; FCO, 1967–72. Mem., Brit. International Ski team, 1931–37, Capt. 1934–37; Capt. British Olympic Ski team, 1936. *Publications:* High-Speed Skiing, 1935; Evil in High Places, 1947; A Skiing Primer, 1948, rev. edn 1951; The Guinness Book of Ski-ing, 1983. *Club:* Ski Club of Great Britain.

LUNNY, William Francis; Sheriff of South Strathclyde, Dumfries and Galloway, since 1984; *b* 10 Dec. 1938; *s* of James F. Lunny and Sarah Ann Crawford or Lunny; *m* 1967, Elizabeth McDermott; two *s* one *d*. *Educ:* Our Lady's High School, Motherwell; Glasgow Univ. (MA, LLB). Solicitor, 1961–67; Depute Procurator Fiscal, 1967–74; Crown Counsel/Legal Draftsman, Antigua, 1974–76; Advocate, 1977. *Recreations:* walking, travelling. *Address:* Sheriff's Chambers, Sheriff Court, Hamilton, Lanarkshire. *T:* Hamilton 282957.

LUNS, Dr Joseph Marie Antoine Hubert; Officer, Order of Orange-Nassau, 1947; Knight Grand Cross, Order of the Netherlands Lion, 1971; Hon. GCMG; Hon. CH 1971; Secretary-General of NATO, 1971–84; *b* 28 Aug. 1911; *m* Baroness E. C. van Heemstra; one *s* one *d*. *Educ:* sec. schs, Amsterdam and Brussels; universities of Leyden, Amsterdam, London and Berlin. Attaché of Legation, 1938; 2nd Sec., 1942; 1st Sec., 1945; Counsellor, 1949. Served in: Min. for For. Affairs, 1938–40; Berne, 1940–41; Lisbon, 1941–43; London, at Netherlands Min. for For. Affairs, 1943–44, and at Netherlands Embassy, 1944–49; Netherlands Delegn to UN, NY, 1942–52; Minister of Foreign Affairs, The Netherlands, 1952–71. MP (Second Chamber, Netherlands), July-Oct. 1956 and March-June 1959. Hon. Fellow, London Sch. of Economics, 1969. Prix Charlemagne, Aachen, 1967; Gustav Stresemann Medal, 1968. Hon. DCL: Harvard, 1970; Oxon, 1972; Exeter, 1974; Dr Humanities, Hope Coll., USA, 1974. Holds numerous foreign orders. *Publications:* The Epic of The Royal Netherlands Navy; articles on Royal Netherlands Navy in Dutch and foreign jls, and articles on international affairs in International Affairs, La Revue Politique, and others. *Recreation:* swimming. *Address:* 117 Avenue Franklin Roosevelt, 1050 Brussels, Belgium. *Clubs:* Athenæum, Reform (Hon. Mem.); Haagsche, De Witte (Netherlands).

LUNT, Maj.-Gen. James Doiran, CBE 1964 (OBE 1958); MA (Oxon); FRGS; FRHistS; Domestic Bursar, and Fellow, Wadham College, Oxford, 1973–83, now Emeritus Fellow; *b* 13 Nov. 1917; *s* of late Brig. W. T. Lunt, MBE, Camberley, Surrey; *m* 1940, Muriel, *d* of late A. H. Byrt, CBE, Bournemouth; one *s* one *d*. *Educ:* King William's Coll., IOM; RMC, Sandhurst. 2nd Lieut, Duke of Wellington's Regt, 1937; served with 4th Bn Burma Rifles, 1939–41; Burma Campaign, 1942; transf. to 16/5th Queen's Royal Lancers, 1949; served with Arab Legion, 1952–55; comd 16/5th Queen's Royal Lancers, 1957–59; comd Fed. Regular Army, Aden, 1961–64; Dir of Admin. Planning (Army), MoD, 1964–66; Defence Adviser to British High Commissioner, India, 1966–68; Chief of Staff, Contingencies Planning, SHAPE, 1969–70; Vice-Adjt-Gen., MoD, 1970–72; Col, 16th/5th The Queen's Royal Lancers, 1975–80. Order of Independence (Jordan), 1956; Commander, Order of South Arabia, 1964. *Publications:* Charge to Glory, 1961; Scarlet Lancer, 1964; The Barren Rocks of Aden, 1966; Bokhara Burnes, 1969; From Sepoy to Subedar, 1970; The Duke of Wellington's Regiment, 1971; 16th/5th The Queen's Royal Lancers, 1973; John Burgoyne of Saratoga, 1975; Imperial Sunset, 1981; Glubb Pasha, 1984; A Hell of a Licking: the retreat from Burma 1941–42, 1986. *Recreations:* fly fishing, writing. *Address:* Hilltop House, Little Milton, Oxon. *T:* Great Milton 242. *Club:* Army and Navy.

LUNT, Rev. Canon Ronald Geoffrey, MC 1943; MA, BD; Rector of Martley, 1974–78; Chief Master, King Edward's School, Birmingham, 1952–74; *b* 25 June 1913; *s* of late Rt Rev. G. C. L. Lunt, DD, Bishop of Salisbury; *m* 1945, Veslemoy Sopp Foss, Oslo, Norway; one *s* two *d*. *Educ:* Eton (King's Scholar); The Queen's Coll., Oxford (Scholar, 1st class Lit. Hum.); Westcott House, Cambridge. Assistant Master, St George's Sch., Harpenden, 1935; Haberdashers' Sch., Hampstead, 1936–37; Deacon, 1938; Priest, 1939; Master in Orders at Radley Coll., Abingdon, 1938–40; CF 1940–45; Middle East, 1941–44 (MC); CF 3rd class, SCF 1 Airborne Division, 1945; Headmaster, Liverpool Coll., 1945–52. Won Cromer Greek Prize, 1937; Page Scholar to USA, 1959; Select Preacher: University of Cambridge, 1948, 1960, Oxford, 1951–53, 1983. Chm., Birmingham Council of Churches, 1957–60; Hon. Canon, Birmingham Cathedral, 1969. Mem., Birmingham Educn Cttee, 1952–74. Life Governor, Queen's Coll., Birmingham, 1957; Trustee, 1954, Chm., 1971–74, E. W. Vincent Trust; Governor, 1952, Sen. Vice-Pres., 1971–72, Pres., 1973, Birmingham and Midland Inst. Pres., Incorporated Assoc. of Head Masters, 1962. Mem., Press Council, 1964–69. BD (Oxon), 1967. *Publications:* Edition of Marlowe's Dr Faustus, 1937, Edward II, 1938; contrib. to Arts v. Science, 1967; articles in Theology, Expository Times, and other journals. *Address:* The Station House, Ledbury, Herefordshire. *T:* Ledbury 3174.

LUPTON, Prof. Thomas; Professor of Organisational Behaviour, University of Manchester, 1966–86; *b* 4 Nov. 1918; *s* of Thomas Lupton, blacksmith, and Jane Lupton (*née* Vowell); *m* 1st, 1942, Thelma Chesney; one *d*; 2nd, 1963, Dr Constance Shirley Wilson; one *s* one *d*. *Educ:* Elem. and Central Sch.; Technical Coll.; Ruskin Coll.; Oriel Coll., Oxford; Univ. of Manchester. DipEconPolSci (Oxon), MA (Oxon), PhD (Manch.). Served War, HM Forces, 1939–41 and 1944–46; Marine Engr, 1932–39, 1941–44. Research Posts: Liverpool Univ., 1951–54; Manchester Univ., 1954–57; Lectr in Sociology, Manchester Univ., 1957–59; Head of Dept of Industrial Admin, Coll. of Advanced Techn., Birmingham, 1959–64; Montague Burton Prof. of Ind. Rel., Univ. of Leeds, 1964–66; Dir, Manchester Business Sch., 1977–83. Gen. Editor, Jl of Management Studies, 1966–76; Dir, Pirelli General Cables Ltd, 1970–77; Member: Civil Service Arbitration Tribunal, 1967–70; Arbitration Panel, Dept of Employment, 1969–; various official commns and tribunals, 1960–. *Publications:* On the Shop Floor, 1963; Industrial Behaviour and Personnel Management, 1964; Management and the Social Sciences, 1966, 3rd edn, 1983; Selecting a Wage Payment System (with D. Gowler), 1969; Job and Pay Comparisons (with A. M. Bowey), 1973; Wages and Salaries (with A. M. Bowey), 1974, rev. edn 1983; articles in Jl of Management Studies, Manchester Sch., Production Engineer, etc. *Recreations:* golf, Association Football. *Address:* 667 Burnage Lane, Manchester M19 1RT. *T:* 061–431 6880.

LUPU, Radu; pianist; *b* 30 Nov. 1945; *s* of Mayer Lupu, lawyer, and Ana Gabor, teacher of languages; *Educ:* Moscow Conservatoire. Debut at age of twelve with complete programme of own music; studied with Florica Muzicescu, Cella Delavrancea, Heinrich Neuhaus and Stanislav Neuhaus. 1st prize: Van Cliburn Competition, 1966; Enescu Internat. Competition, 1967; Leeds Internat. Pianoforte Competition, 1969. Numerous recordings include complete Mozart violin and piano sonatas, complete Beethoven Piano Concertos, 1979. *Recreations:* history, art, sport. *Address:* c/o Harrison/Parrott Ltd, 12 Penzance Place, W11 4PA. *T:* 01–229 9166.

LURGAN, 5th Baron *cr* 1839; **John Desmond Cavendish Brownlow,** OBE 1950; Lieut-Colonel, Grenadier Guards, retired; *b* 29 June 1911; *s* of Captain Hon. Francis Cecil Brownlow (*d* 1932) (3rd *s* of 2nd Baron) and Angela (*d* 1973), *d* of Samuel Radcliffe Platt; *S* cousin, 1984. *Educ:* Eton. *Address:* Pennington House, Lymington, Hants.

LURIA, Prof. Salvador Edward; Sedgwick Professor of Biology, Massachusetts Institute of Technology, 1964–70, Institute Professor since 1970; *b* 13 Aug. 1912; *s* of David Luria and Ester Sacerdote; *m* 1945, Zella Hurwitz; one *s*. *Educ:* Turin Univ. (MD 1935). Res. Fellow, Inst. of Radium, Paris, 1938–40; Res. Asst, Columbia Univ. Medical School, NY, 1940–42; Guggenheim Fellow, Vanderbilt and Princeton Univs, 1942–43; Instructor in Bacteriology, Indiana Univ., 1943–45, Asst Prof., 1944–47, Associate Prof. 1947–50; Prof. of Bacteriology, Illinois Univ., 1950–59; Prof. and Chm. of Dept of Microbiology, MIT, 1959–64. Fellow of Salk Inst. for Biol Studies, 1965–. Associate Editor, Jl Bacteriology, 1950–55; Editor: Virology, 1955–; Biological Abstracts, 1958–62; Member: Editorial Bd, Exptl Cell Res. Jl, 1948–; Advisory Bd, Jl Molecular Biology, 1958–64; Hon. Editorial Advisory Bd, Jl Photochemistry and Photobiology, 1961–. Lecturer: Univ. of Colorado, 1950; Jesup, Notre Dame, 1950; Nieuwand, Notre Dame 1959; Dyer, Nat. Insts of Health, 1963. Member: Amer. Phil Soc.; Amer. Soc. for Microbiology (Pres. 1967–68); Nat. Acad. of Scis; Amer. Acad. of Arts and Scis; AAAS; Soc. Genetic Microbiology; Genetics Soc. of America; Amer Assoc. Univ. Profs; Sigma Xi. Prizes: Lepetit, 1935; Lenghi, 1965; Louisa Gross Horowitz of Columbia University; Nobel Prize for Physiology or Medicine (jtly), 1969. Hon. ScD: Chicago, 1967; Rutgers, 1970; Indiana, 1970. *Recreation:* sculpting. *Address:* Department of Biology, Massachusetts Institute of Technology, Cambridge, Mass 02139, USA.

LURIE, Prof. Alison; writer; Professor of English, Cornell University, since 1976; *b* 3 Sept. 1926; *d* of Harry Lurie and Bernice Stewart; *m* 1948, Jonathan Bishop (marr. diss. 1985); three *s*. *Educ:* Radcliffe Coll., Cambridge, Mass (AB). *Publications:* Love and Friendship, 1962; The Nowhere City, 1965; Imaginary Friends, 1967; Real People, 1969; The War Between the Tates, 1974; Only Children, 1979; Foreign Affairs, 1984 (Pulitzer Prize, 1985); *non-fiction:* The Language of Clothes, 1981; *children's books:* Clever Gretchen, 1980; The Heavenly Zoo, 1980; Fabulous Beasts, 1981. *Address:* c/o English Department, Cornell University, Ithaca, NY 14853, USA.

LUSCOMBE, Prof. David Edward, FSA; FRHistS; FBA 1986; Professor of Medieval History, University of Sheffield, since 1972; *b* 22 July 1938; *s* of Edward Dominic and Nora Luscombe; *m* 1960, MeganPhillips; three *s* one *d*. *Educ:* St Michael's Sch., North Finchley; Finchley Catholic Grammar Sch.; King's Coll., Cambridge (BA, MA, PhD). Fellow, King's Coll., Cambridge, 1962–64; Fellow and Dir of Studies in History, Churchill Coll., Cambridge, 1964–72; Sheffield University: Head of Dept of History, 1973–76, 1979–84; Dean, Faculty of Arts, 1985–87. Leverhulme European Fellow, 1973. *Publications:* The School of Peter Abelard, 1969; Peter Abelard's Ethics, 1971 (trans. Italian, 1976); (ed jtly) Church and Government in the Middle Ages, 1976; (ed jtly) Petrus Abaelardus 1079–1142: Person, Werk und Wirkung, 1980; articles in learned jls. *Recreations:* playing cricket, walking a spaniel. *Address:* 4 Caxton Road, Broomhill, Sheffield S10 3DE. *T:* Sheffield 686355.

LUSCOMBE, Most Rev. Lawrence Edward; *see* Brechin, Bishop of.

LUSH, Christopher Duncan, CMG 1983; HM Diplomatic Service, retired; *b* 4 June 1928; *s* of late Eric Duncan Thomas Lush and of Iris Leonora (*née* Greenfield); *m* 1967, Marguerite Lilian, *d* of Frederick Albert Bolden; one *s*. *Educ:* Sedbergh; Magdalen Coll.,

Oxford. Called to Bar, Gray's Inn, 1953. Asst Legal Adviser, FO, 1959–62; Legal Adviser, Berlin, 1962–65, Dep. Political Adviser, Berlin, 1965–66; FO (later FCO), 1966–69; Head of Chancery, Amman, 1969–71; Head of Aviation and Telecommunications Dept, FCO, 1971–73; Canadian Nat. Defence Coll., 1973–74; Counsellor, Paris, 1974–78; Counsellor, Vienna, 1978–82; Ambassador and UK Perm. Rep. to Council of Europe, Strasbourg, 1983–86. Médaille de Vermeil, Société d'Encouragement au Progrès, 1978. *Publications:* articles in Internat. and Compar. Law Qly, Connoisseur. *Address:* Greywings, Fairlight, Sussex. *Club:* Travellers'.

LUSH, Hon. Sir George (Hermann), Kt 1979, Justice, Supreme Court of Victoria, 1966–83; *b* 5 Oct. 1912; *s* of John Fullarton Lush and Dora Louise Emma Lush; *m* 1943, Winifred Betty Wragge; three *d*. *Educ:* Carey Grammar Sch.; Ormond Coll., Melbourne Univ. (LLM). Admitted, Victorian Bar, 1935; served War, Australian Imperial Forces, 1940–45; Lecturer, Mercantile Law, Melbourne Univ., 1947–55; QC: Victoria 1957, Tasmania 1958. Chairman, Victorian Bar Council, 1964–66; President: Medico-Legal Soc., Victoria, 1962–63; Australian Bar Assoc., 1964–66; Commissioner, Overseas Telecommunications Commn, 1961–66. Chancellor, Monash Univ., 1983– (Mem. Council, 1969–74); Chm. Council, Ormond Coll., 1981–. *Recreations:* tennis, walking. *Address:* 37 Rochester Road, Canterbury, Victoria 3126, Australia. *Clubs:* Melbourne, Melbourne Cricket (Melbourne); Lorne Country (Lorne, Vic.).

LUSH, Maurice Stanley, CB 1944; CBE 1942; MC 1916; *b* 23 Nov. 1896; *s* of late Hubert Stanley Lush; *m* 1930, Diana Ruth, *d* of late Charles Alexander Hill; one *s* two *d*. *Educ:* Tonbridge Sch.; RMA, Woolwich. European War, RA, 1915–19 (MC and Bar); Egyptian Army, 1919–22; Sudan Political Service from 1919; Secretary HM Legation, Addis Ababa, 1919–22; District Commissioner, Sudan, 1922–26; Assistant Civil Secretary Sudan Government, 1926–29; Private Secretary to Governor-General of Sudan, 1929–30; Dep. Governor, Sudan, 1930–35; Sudan Agent, Cairo, 1935–38; Governor, Northern Province, Sudan, 1938–41. War of 1939–45 recalled from RARO as Brig. (despatches thrice); Chief Political Officer, Ethiopia, 1941–42; Military Administrator, Madagascar, 1942; Chief Civil Affairs Officer British Military Administration, Tripolitania, 1942–43; Executive Commissioner and Vice-President, Allied Commission, Italy, 1943–46; Resident representative for Germany and Austria of Intergovernmental Cttee on Refugees, 1946–47; Chief of Mission in Middle East, IRO, 1947–49; Special Representative for Middle East of IRO, 1949–51; Rep. Anglo-Saxon Petroleum Co. (Shell), Libya, 1952–56; Man. Dir, Pakistan Shell Oil Co. Ltd, 1956–59. Vice-Pres., British and Foreign Bible Soc. FRSA. FRGS. Order of the Nile, 3rd Class; Officer, Legion of Merit US, 1945; Comdr Order of Knights of Malta, 1945. *Address:* 3 Carlton Mansions, Holland Park Gardens, W14 8DW. *T:* 01–603 4425. *Club:* Athenæum.

See also Countess of Limerick.

LUSHINGTON, Sir Henry Edmund Castleman, 7th Bt *cr* 1791; *b* 2 May 1909; *s* of Sir Herbert Castleman Lushington, 6th Bt and Barbara Henrietta (*d* 1927), *d* of late Rev. William Greville Hazlerigg; *S* father, 1968; *m* 1937, Pamela Elizabeth Daphne, *er d* of Major Archer R. Hunter, Wokingham, Berks; one *s* two *d*. *Educ:* Dauntsey's Sch. Served War of 1939–45, Flt-Lieut, RAFVR. Metropolitan Police, 1935–58; retired as Superintendent. *Recreations:* gardening, golf. *Heir: s* John Richard Castleman Lushington [*b* 28 Aug. 1938; *m* 1966, Bridget Gillian Margaret, *d* of Colonel John Foster Longfield, Saunton, Devon; three *s*]. *Address:* Carfax, Crowthorne, Berkshire. *T:* Crowthorne 772819. *Club:* East Berks Golf.

LUSTIGER, His Eminence Cardinal Jean-Marie; Archbishop of Paris, since 1981; *b* Paris, 1926. *Educ:* Carmelite Seminary; Institut Catholique de Paris; Sorbonne (Lèsl, LenThéol). Ordained priest, 1954. Chaplain to students, Sorbonne, Paris; Dir, Centre d'étudiants Richelieu, Paris; Parish Priest, Sainte Jeanne de Chantal, Paris, 1969–79; Bishop of Orléans, 1979–81. Cardinal, 1983. *Publications:* Sermons d'un curé de Paris, 1978; Pain de vie, Peuple de Dieu, 1981; Osez croire—Osez vivre, 1985; Freude der Weihnacht, 1985; Premiers pas dans la prière, 1986. *Address:* Maison diocésaine, 8 rue de la Ville-l'Evêque, 75008 Paris, France.

LUSTY, Sir Robert (Frith), Kt 1969; *b* 7 June 1909; *o s* of late Frith Lusty; *m* 1st, 1939, Joan Christie (*d* 1962), *y d* of late Archibald Brownlie, Glasgow; 2nd, 1963, Eileen, *widow* of Dr Denis Carroll. *Educ:* Society of Friends' Co-educational Sch., Sidcot. Joined editorial staff The Kent Messenger, 1927; abandoned journalism for publishing and entered production and editorial departments Messrs Hutchinson and Company, 1928; appointed manager associated company, Messrs Selwyn & Blount, 1933; left in 1935 to join Michael Joseph Ltd, on its formation, resigned as Deputy Chairman, 1956, to become Man. Dir, Hutchinson Publishing Gp, until retirement in 1973; a Governor of the BBC, 1960–68 (Vice-Chairman, 1966–68); Member Council of Publishers' Assoc., 1955–61; Chairman: National Book League, 1949–51 and of its 1951 Festival Cttee; Soc. of Bookmen, 1962–65; Publication Panel, King Edward's Hosp. Fund for London, 1975–83. Liveryman Stationers' Co., 1945; Freeman of City of London. A Governor and Councillor, Bedford Coll., 1965–71. FRSA 1969. *Publication:* Bound to be Read (autobiog.), 1975. *Address:* Broad Close, Blockley, Moreton-in-Marsh, Glos GL5 6DY. *T:* Blockley 700335. *Club:* Garrick.

LUSZTIG, Prof. George, PhD; FRS 1983; Professor of Mathematics, Massachusetts Institute of Technology, Cambridge, USA, since 1978; *b* 20 May 1946; *s* of Akos and Erzsébet Lusztig; *m* 1972, Michal-Nina Abraham; two *d*. *Educ:* Univ. of Bucharest, Rumania; Princeton Univ. (MA, PhD). Asst, Univ. of Timisoara, Rumania, 1969; Mem., Inst. for Advanced Study Princeton, 1969–71; Univ. of Warwick: Res. Fellow, 1971–72; Lectr in Maths, 1972–74; Prof. of Maths, 1974–78. *Publications:* The Discrete Series of GL_n over a Finite Field, 1974; and Characters of Reductive Groups over a Finite Field, 1984. *Address:* 106 Grant Avenue, Newton, Mass 02159, USA. *T:* (617) 964–8579.

LUTHER, Rt. Rev. Arthur William; retired; *b* 21 March 1919; *s* of William and Monica Luther; *m* 1946, Dr Kamal Luther; one *s* two *d*. *Educ:* Nagpur University; India (MA, BT); General Theological Seminary, New York (STD 1957). Deacon, 1943; Priest, 1944; in USA and Scotland for study and parish work, 1952–54; Chaplain to Bishop of Nagpur, 1954; Head Master, Bishop Cotton School, Nagpur, 1954–57; Bishop of Nasik, 1957–70; Bishop of Bombay, 1970–73; held charge of Kolhapur Diocese concurrently with Bombay Diocese, Dec. 1970–Feb. 1972; Bishop, Church of North India, and Reg. Sec. of the Leprosy Mission, 1973–80; Promotional Sec., 1980–84. *Address:* Leprosy Mission Hospital, Poladpur, Dist. Raigad, Maharashtra, India 402303. *T:* Poladpur 24.

LUTOSŁAWSKI, Witold; composer and conductor; *b* Warsaw, 25 Jan. 1913; *m* 1946, Maria Danuta Dygat. *Educ:* Warsaw Conservatoire. Dep. Chief of Music Dept, Polish Radio, 1945–46; teacher of composition: Berkshire Music Center, USA, 1962; Dartington, 1963, 1964; Aarhus, 1968; composer-in-residence: Hopkins Center, USA, 1966; Aldeburgh Fest., 1983. Vice-Pres., Polish Composers' Union, 1973–79. Hon. RAM, 1976; Hon. GSM, 1978. Member: Swedish Royal Acad. of Music; Free Acad. of Arts, Hamburg; Acad. of Arts, Berlin; German Acad. of Arts, E Berlin; Bavarian Acad. of Fine Arts; Amer. Acad. of Arts and Letters; Nat. Inst. of Arts and Letters, NY; Acad. of Fine Arts, France. Hon. Member: Polish Composers' Union; Polish Soc. of Contemp. Music; ISCM; Konzerthausges., Vienna. Hon. Dr: Cleveland Inst. of Music; Northwestern; Evanston, Chicago; Warsaw; Lancaster; Glasgow; Torún; Durham; Cracow. Many prizes include: City of Warsaw Music Prize, 1948; state prizes; Sonning Music Prize, Copenhagen, 1967; Ravel Prize, 1971; Sibelius Prize, 1972; Ernst von Siemens Music Prize, 1983; Solidarnošć (Solidarity) Prize, 1984 (Poland); Univ. of Louisville Grawemeyer Award for music composition, 1985; (jtly) Gold Medal, Royal Philharmonic Soc., 1985. Order of Builder of People's Poland, 1977; Comdr des Arts et des Lettres (France). *Compositions* include: *orchestral:* Symphonic Variations, 1938; 1st Symphony, 1947; Concerto for Orchestra, 1954; Musique Funèbre, 1958; Jeux vénitiens, 1961; 2nd Symphony, 1967; Livre pour orchestre, 1968; Cello concerto, 1970; Mi-parti, 1976; Novelette, 1979; 3rd Symphony, 1983; *chamber:* Overture, 1949; Three Poems of Henri Michaux for choir and orch., 1963; String Quartet, 1964; Paroles tissées for tenor and chamber orch., 1965; Preludes and Fugues for 13 solo strings, 1972; Les espaces du sommeil for baritone and orch., 1975; Double Concerto, 1980; Chain 1, 1983; vocal and choral works, compositions for piano, and children's music; scores and incidental music for theatre, films and radio. Has made many recordings, conducting own compositions. *Address:* Ul. Smiała 39, 01–523 Warsaw, Poland.

LUTTRELL, Lt-Col Geoffrey Walter Fownes, MC 1945; JP; Lord-Lieutenant of Somerset, since 1978; *b* 2 Oct. 1919; *s* of late Geoffrey Fownes Luttrell of Dunster Castle, Somerset; *m* 1942, Hermione Hamilton, *er d* of late Capt. Cecil Gunston, MC, and Lady Doris Gunston. *Educ:* Eton; Exeter Coll., Oxford. Served War of 1939–45, with 15th/19th King's Royal Hussars, 1940–46; North Somerset Yeomanry, 1952–57; Lt-Col 1955; Hon. Col, 6th Bn LI, TAVR, 1977–. Liaison Officer, Ministry of Agriculture, 1965–71. Regional Dir, Lloyds Bank, 1972–83. Member: National Parks Commn, 1962–66; Wessex Regional Cttee, Nat. Trust, 1970–85; SW Electricity Bd, 1969–78; UGC, 1973–76. Pres., Royal Bath and West and Southern Counties Soc., 1983. DL Somerset, 1958–68, Vice Lord-Lieutenant, 1968–78; High Sheriff of Somerset, 1960; JP 1961. Hon. Col Somerset ACF, 1982–. KStJ. *Address:* Court House, East Quantoxhead, Bridgwater, Somerset TA5 1EJ. *T:* Holford 242. *Club:* Cavalry and Guards.

LUTYENS, Mary, (Mrs J. G. Links), FRSL; writer since 1929; *b* 31 July 1908; *y d* of late Sir Edwin Lutyens, OM, KCIE, PRA, and late Lady Emily Lutyens; *m* 1st, 1930, Anthony Sewell (marr. diss. 1945; decd); one *d*; 2nd, 1945, J. G. Links, OBE. *Educ:* Queen's Coll., London; Sydney, Australia. FRSL 1976. *Publications: fiction:* Forthcoming Marriages, 1933; Perchance to Dream, 1935; Rose and Thorn, 1936; Spider's Silk, 1939; Family Colouring, 1940; A Path of Gold, 1941; Together and Alone, 1942; So Near to Heaven, 1943; And Now There is You, 1953; Week-End at Hurtmore, 1954; The Lucian Legend, 1955; Meeting in Venice, 1956; Cleo, 1973; *for children:* Julie and the Narrow Valley, 1944; *autobiography:* To Be Young, 1959; *edited:* Lady Lytton's Court Diary, 1961; (for Krishnamurti) Freedom from the Known, 1969; The Only Revolution, 1970; The Penguin Krishnamurti Reader, 1970; The Urgency of Change, 1971; (with Malcolm Warner) Rainy Days at Brig O'Turk, 1983; *biography:* Effie in Venice, 1965; Millais and the Ruskins, 1967; The Ruskins and the Grays, 1972; Krishnamurti: the years of awakening, 1975; The Lyttons in India, 1979; Edwin Lutyens, 1980; Krishnamurti: the years of fulfilment, 1982; also numerous serials, afterwards published, under pseudonym of Esther Wyndham; contribs to TLS, Apollo, The Cornhill, The Walpole Soc. Jl. *Recreations:* reading, cinema-going. *Address:* 8 Elizabeth Close, Randolph Avenue, W9 1BN. *T:* 01–286 6674.

LUTZ, Marianne Christine, (Mrs C. A. Whittington-Smith); Headmistress, Sheffield High School for Girls (Girls' Public Day School Trust), 1959–83; *b* 9 Dec. 1922; *d* of Dr H. Lutz; *m* 1981, Charles Alexander Whittington-Smith, LLM, FCA. *Educ:* Wimbledon High Sch., GPDST; Girton Coll., Cambridge (Schol.); University of London (DipEd, DipTh). Asst Mistress (History) at: Clergy Daughters' Sch., Bristol, 1946–47; South Hampstead High Sch., GPDST, 1947–59. Former Member: History Textbooks Panel for W Germany (under auspices of FO and Unesco); Professional Cttee, Univ. of Sheffield; Historical Assoc.; Secondary Heads' Assoc.; Schnauzer Club of Great Britain. *Publications:* several in connection with Unesco work and Historical Assoc. *Recreations:* travel, crosswords, books, opera, art and theatre. *Address:* Grendon, Hydro Close, Baslow, Bakewell, Derbyshire DE4 1SH. *T:* Baslow 2152.

LUXMOORE, Rt. Rev. Christopher Charles; *see* Bermuda, Bishop of.

LUXON, Benjamin, CBE 1986; FGSM; baritone; *b* Camborne, Cornwall, 1937; *m* 1969, Sheila Amit; two *s* one *d*. *Educ:* Truro Sch.; Westminster Trng Coll.; Guildhall Sch. of Music. Teacher of Physical Education until becoming professional singer, 1963. Repertoire includes lieder, folk music, Victorian songs and duets, oratorio (Russian, French and English song), and operatic rôles at major opera houses at home and abroad. Major rôles include: Eugene Onegin, Don Giovanni, Wozzeck, Papageno, Julius Caesar, Posa. Numerous recordings. Appointed Bard of the Cornish Gorsedd, 1974. Third prize, Munich Internat. Festival, 1961; Gold Medal GSM, 1963. FGSM 1970; Hon. RAM, 1980; Hon. DMus Exeter, 1980. *Recreations:* collecting English water-colours and drawings; tennis, swimming. *Address:* Bylands House, Dunstable Road, Redbourn, Herts.

LUXTON, William John, CBE 1962; Director, London Chamber of Commerce and Industry, 1964–74 (Secretary, 1958–74); *b* 18 March 1909; *s* of late John Luxton; *m* 1942, Megan, *d* of late John M. Harries; one *s* one *d*. *Educ:* Shebbear Coll., N Devon; London Univ. Wallace Brothers & Co. Ltd (merchant bankers), 1926–38. Called to the Bar, Lincoln's Inn, 1938; Chancery Bar, 1938–40. Served with Royal Armoured Corps, 1940–45. Legal Parliamentary Secretary, Association of British Chambers of Commerce, 1947–53 (Vice-Pres., 1974); Secretary Birmingham Chamber of Commerce, 1953–58; Dir, Fedn of Commonwealth Chambers of Commerce, 1958–74. *Address:* Menchine, Nepcote Lane, Findon Village, Worthing, West Sussex. *T:* Findon 3164.

LUYT, Sir Richard (Edmonds), GCMG 1966 (KCMG 1964; CMG 1960); KCVO 1966; DCM 1942; Vice-Chancellor and Principal, University of Cape Town, 1968–80; *b* 8 Nov. 1915; *m* 1st, 1948, Jean Mary Wilder (*d* 1951); one *d*; 2nd, 1956, Eileen Betty Reid; two *s*. *Educ:* Diocesan Coll., Rondebosch, Cape, SA; Univ. of Cape Town (BA); Trinity Coll., Oxford (MA). Rhodes Scholar from S Africa, 1937. Entered Colonial Service and posted to N Rhodesia, 1940; War Service, 1940–45: with Mission 101, in Ethiopia, 1941, remained in Ethiopia with British Military Mission, for remainder of War. Returned to N Rhodesia, Colonial Service, 1945; transferred to Kenya, 1953; Labour Commissioner, Kenya, 1954–57; Permanent Secretary to various Ministries of the Kenya Government, 1957–60; Secretary to the Cabinet, 1960–61; Chief Secretary, Northern Rhodesia, 1962–64; Governor and C-in-C, British Guiana, 1964–66, until Guyana Independence; Governor-General of Guyana, May-Oct. 1966. Vice-Pres., South African Inst. of Race Relations, 1983–; Nat. Pres., Friends of the Nat. Union of South African Students, 1980–; Governor, Africa Inst. of South Africa, 1968–; Patron, Civil Rights League, 1968–. Hon. LLD: Natal, 1972; Witwatersrand, 1980; Hon. DAdmin Univ. of South Africa, 1980; Hon. DLitt Cape Town, 1982. *Recreations:* gardening, sport, particularly Rugby (Oxford Blue, 1938) and cricket (Oxford Captain 1940) (also played for Kenya at cricket). *Address:* Allandale, 64 Alma Road, Rosebank, Cape, 7700, South

Africa. *T:* 666765. *Clubs:* Royal Commonwealth Society; Nairobi (Kenya); City and Civil Service (Cape Town).

LWOFF, Prof. André Michel; Grand-Croix de la Légion d'Honneur, 1982 (Grand Officier; Commandeur, 1966; Officier, 1960; Chevalier, 1947); Médaille de la Résistance, 1946; Directeur de l'Institut de Recherches Scientifiques sur le Cancer, 1968–72; Professor of Microbiology, Faculté des Sciences, Paris, 1959–68, and Head of Department of Microbial Physiology, Pasteur Institute, 1938–68; *b* Ainay-le-Château, Allier, France, 8 May 1902; *m* 1925, Marguerite Bourdaleix. *Educ:* (Fac. des Sciences et de Méd.) Univ. of Paris. MD (Paris) 1927; DSc (Paris) 1932. With the Pasteur Institute, 1921–. Fellow: Rockefeller Foundn, 1933 and 1935; Salk Inst., 1967; Vis. Professor: MIT, 1960; Harvard Univ., Albert Einstein Med. Sch., New York, 1964. Lectures: Dunham, Harvard, 1947; Marjory Stephenson, Soc. for Gen. Microbiol.; Harvey, 1954; Leuwenhoek, Royal Soc., 1966; Dyer, 1969; Penn, University of Pennsylvania, 1969; MacCormick, Univ. of Chicago, 1969. Hon. Member: Soc. for Gen. Microbiol.; Amer. Soc. of Microbiol.; Amer. Botanical Soc.; Amer. Soc. of Biochem.; Corresp. Mem., Acad. of Med. Sciences of USSR; Foreign Member: Royal Soc., 1958; Hungarian Acad. of Science; Indian Acad. of Science; For. Associate, Nat. Acad. of Scis, USA; For. Associate Mem., Amer. Acad. of Arts and Scis. President: Internat. Assoc. of Societies of Microbiology, 1962; Mouvement Français pour le Planning Familial, 1970–. Exhibitions of paintings: Galerie Alex Maguy, 1960; Galerie Aleph, 1978, 1985. Holds hon. doctorates in science and law at British and other foreign univs. Awarded several prizes and medals from 1928 onwards, both French and foreign, for his work; Nobel Prize for Medicine (jointly), 1965; Leuwenhoek Medal, Royal Netherlands Acad. of Science; Keilin Medal, Biochemical Soc. *Publications:* (with L. Justin-Besançon) Vitamine antipellagreuse et avitaminoses nocotiniques, 1942; L'Evolution physiologique, Collection de microbiologie, Hermann éd., 1944; Problems of Morphogenesis in Ciliates, The Kinetosomes in Development, Reproduction and Evolution, 1950; Biological Order, 1960; Jeux et combats, 1981. *Recreation:* painting. *Address:* 69 avenue de Suffren, 75007 Paris, France. *T:* 47.83.27.82.

LYALL, Andrew Gardiner, CMG 1976; Under Secretary, Department of Transport, 1981–86, retired; *b* 21 Dec. 1929; *s* of late William and Helen Lyall (*née* Gardiner); *m* 1953, Olive Leslie Gennoe White; one *s* one *d*. *Educ:* Kirkcaldy High Sch. Joined MoT, 1951; Asst Shipping Attaché, British Embassy, Washington, DC, 1961–64; Principal, Nationalised Industry Finance and Urban Transport Planning, 1965–70; Asst Sec., Railways Div., 1970–72; seconded to FCO as Counsellor, UK Representation to European Communities, 1972–75; Assistant Secretary: Land Use Planning, DoE, 1975–76; Central Unit on Environmental Pollution, 1976–77; Under Sec., PSA, 1978–81. *Recreations:* photography, travel, historical research. *Address:* 5 Barrowfield, Cuckfield, Haywards Heath, West Sussex. *T:* Haywards Heath 454606. *Club:* Reform.

LYALL, Gavin Tudor; author; *b* 9 May 1932; *s* of J. T. and A. A. Lyall; *m* 1958, Katharine E. Whitehorn, *qv*; two *s*. *Educ:* King Edward VI Sch., Birmingham; Pembroke Coll., Cambridge (MA). RAF, 1951–53 (Pilot Officer, 1952). Journalist with: Picture Post, 1956–57; BBC, 1958–59; Sunday Times, 1959–63. Hon. Consultant, Air Transport Users' Cttee, CAA, 1985– (Mem., 1979–85); Mem., Air Travel Trust Cttee, 1986–. *Publications:* The Wrong Side of the Sky, 1961; The Most Dangerous Game, 1964; Midnight Plus One, 1965; Shooting Script, 1966; Venus with Pistol, 1969; Blame the Dead, 1972; Judas Country, 1975; Operation Warboard, 1976; The Secret Servant, 1980 (televised, 1984); The Conduct of Major Maxim, 1982; The Crocus List, 1985. (As Editor) Freedom's Battle: The RAF in World War II, 1968. *Recreations:* real beer, cooking, military history, model making. *Address:* 14 Provost Road, NW3 4ST. *T:* 01–722 2308. *Clubs:* Royal Air Force, Detection, Groucho.

LYALL, Katharine Elizabeth; *see* Whitehorn, K.

LYALL, William Chalmers, MBE 1952; HM Diplomatic Service, retired; *b* 6 Aug. 1921; *s* of John Brown Lyall and Margaret Angus Leighton Stevenson Lyall; *m* 1948, Janet Lawson McKechnie; two *s* one *d*. *Educ:* Kelty Public and Beath Secondary schools. Min. of Labour, 1940–48; HM Forces, 1941–47; FO, 1948; Hankow, 1948–51; São Paulo, 1952–53; Manila, 1953–55; FO, 1955–57; Caracas, 1957–60; Bahrain, 1960–64; FO, 1964–65; DSAO, 1965–68; FCO, 1968–69; Consul-General, Genoa, 1969–73; FCO, 1973; Counsellor (Administration), Bonn, 1974–78. *Recreations:* music, photography. *Address:* 30 Charles Way, Limekilns, Dunfermline, Fife KY11 3JN. *T:* Limekilns 872044.

LYALL GRANT, Maj.-Gen. Ian Hallam, MC 1944; Director General, Supply Coordination, Ministry of Defence, 1970–75; retired; *b* 4 June 1915; *s* of Col H. F. Lyall Grant, DSO; *m* 1951, Mary Jennifer Moore; one *s* two *d*. *Educ:* Cheltenham Coll.; RMA, Woolwich; Cambridge Univ. (MA). Regular Commission, RE, 1935; service in: India, Burma and Japan, 1938–46 (MC; twice mentioned in despatches); Cyprus and Egypt, 1951–52; Imperial Defence Coll., 1961; Aden, 1962–63; Comdt, Royal School of Mil. Engineering, 1965–67; Maj.-Gen. 1966; Dep. QMG, 1967–70, retired 1970. Col Comdt, RE, 1972–77. *Recreations:* sailing, fishing, paintings, gemmology. *Address:* Kingswear House, Kingswear, S Devon. *T:* Kingswear 359. *Club:* Naval and Military.

LYDDON, (William) Derek (Collier), CB 1984; Chief Planning Officer, Scottish Development Department, 1967–85; *b* 17 Nov. 1925; *s* of late A. J. Lyddon, CBE, and E. E. Lyddon; *m* 1949, Marian Louise Kaye Charlesworth, *d* of late Prof. J. K. Charlesworth, CBE; two *d*. *Educ:* Wrekin Coll.; University Coll., London. BA (Arch.) 1952; ARIBA 1953; DipTP 1954; AMTPI 1963; FRTPI 1973. Depute Chief Architect and Planning Officer, Cumbernauld Development Corp., 1962; Chief Architect and Planning Officer, Skelmersdale Development Corp., 1963–67. Pres., Internat. Soc. of City and Regional Planners, 1981–84. Hon. Prof., Heriot-Watt Univ., 1986; Vis. Prof., Strathclyde Univ., Hon. Fellow: Univ. of Edinburgh; Duncan Jordanstone Coll. of Art, Dundee. Hon. DLitt Heriot-Watt, 1981. *Recreations:* walking, reading. *Address:* 38 Dick Place, Edinburgh EH9 2JB. *T:* 031–667 2266.

LYELL, family name of **Baron Lyell.**

LYELL, 3rd Baron *cr* 1914, of Kinnordy; **Charles Lyell;** Bt, 1894; Parliamentary Under-Secretary of State, Northern Ireland Office, since 1984; *b* 27 March 1939; *s* of 2nd Baron, VC (killed in action, 1943), and Sophie, *d* of Major S. W. and Lady Betty Trafford; *S* father, 1943. *Educ:* Eton; Christ Church, Oxford. 2nd Lieut Scots Guards, 1957–59. CA Scotland. An Opposition Whip, 1974–79; a Lord in Waiting (Govt Whip), 1979–84. Mem., Queen's Body Guard for Scotland (Royal Company of Archers). *Heir:* none. *Address:* Kinnordy House, Kirriemuir, Angus. *T:* Kirriemuir 2848; 20 Petersham Mews, SW7. *T:* 01–584 9419. *Clubs:* Turf, White's.

LYELL, Nicholas Walter; QC 1980; MP (C) Mid Bedfordshire, since 1983 (Hemel Hempstead, 1979–83); Parliamentary Under Secretary of State (Social Security), Department of Health and Social Security, since 1986; a Recorder, since 1985; barrister-at-law; *b* 6 Dec. 1938; *s* of late Sir Maurice Legat Lyell and Veronica Mary Lyell; *m* 1967, Susanna Mary Fletcher; two *s* two *d*. *Educ:* Stowe Sch.; Christ Church, Oxford (MA Hons Mod. Hist.). National Service, commnd Royal Artillery, 1957–59; Walter Runciman & Co., 1962–64; called to the Bar, Inner Temple, 1965, Bencher, 1986; private practice, London (Commercial and Industrial Law), 1965–. Jt Sec., Constitutional Cttee, 1979; PPS to the Attorney General, 1979–. Chm., Soc. of Cons. Lawyers, 1985–86 (Vice-Chm., 1982–85). Vice-Chm., BFSS, 1983–86. *Recreations:* gardening, shooting, drawing. *Address:* Hill Farm, Markyate, St Albans, Herts. *T:* Luton 840783. *Club:* Brooks's.

LYGO, Adm. Sir Raymond (Derek), KCB 1977; FRAeS; CBIM; Chief Executive, British Aerospace PLC, since 1983 (Managing Director, 1983–86); Board Member, British Aerospace PLC, since 1980; Chairman, British Aerospace Inc., since 1983; *b* 15 March 1924; *s* of late Edwin T. Lygo and of Ada E. Lygo; *m* 1950, Pepper Van Osten, USA; two *s* one *d*. *Educ:* Valentine's Sch., Ilford; Ilford County High Sch.; Clark's Coll., Bromley. The Times, 1940; Naval Airman, RN, 1942; CO, HMS Ark Royal, 1969–71; Vice Chief of Naval Staff, 1975–78. British Aerospace: Man. Dir, Hatfield/Lostock Div., 1978–79, Group Dep. Chm., 1980; Chm. and Chief Exec., Dynamics Gp, 1980–82. Dir, CBI Educn Foundn, 1985–. Freeman, City of London, 1985. FRSA. Appeal Pres., Sense, 1983. *Recreations:* building, gardening, joinery. *Address:* British Aerospace PLC, 11 Strand, WC2N 5JT. *Club:* Royal Naval and Royal Albert Yacht (Portsmouth).

LYLE, Lt-Col (Archibald) Michael; JP; Vice Lord-Lieutenant, Perth and Kinross, since 1984; farmer and landowner; *b* 1 May 1919; 3rd *s* of Col Sir Archibald Lyle, 2nd Bt, MC, TD and Lady Lyle; *m* 1942, Hon. Elizabeth Sinclair, *yr d* of 1st Viscount Thurso, KT, CMG, PC; three *d* (and one *d* decd). *Educ:* Eton College; Trinity College, Oxford (BA; MA). Hon. Attaché, Rome, 1938–39; served 1939–45 with The Black Watch, RHR (wounded Normandy, 1944 and discharged, 1945); Lt-Col, The Scottish Horse RAC (TA), 1953–56. Chm., T&AFA, 1959–64. Mem., Royal Company of Archers, Queen's Body Guard for Scotland. Member: Perth and Kinross CC, 1946–74; Tayside Regional Council, 1974–79. Chm., Perth Coll. of Further Educn, 1978–. JP Perth 1950; DL Perthshire 1961. *Recreations:* fishing, shooting, music. *Address:* Riemore Lodge, Dunkeld, Perthshire. *T:* Butterstone 205. *Clubs:* MCC; Puffin's (Edinburgh); Royal Perth Golfing Society.

LYLE, Sir Gavin Archibald, 3rd Bt *cr* 1929; estate manager, farmer; company director; *b* 14 Oct. 1941; *s* of late Ian Archibald de Hoghton Lyle and of Hon. Lydia Yarde-Buller (who *m* 1947, as his 2nd wife, 13th Duke of Bedford; marr. diss. 1960; now Lydia Duchess of Bedford), *d* of 3rd Baron Churston; *S* grandfather, 1946; *m* 1967, Suzy Cooper; five *s* one *d*. *Heir:* *s* Ian Abram Lyle, *b* 25 Sept. 1968. *Address:* Glendelvine, Caputh, Perthshire PH1 4JN. *T:* Caputh 225.

LYLE, Lt-Col Michael; *see* Lyle, Lt-Col A.M.

LYLE, Thomas Keith, CBE 1949; MA, MD, MChir (Cantab); FRCP, FRCS; Consulting Ophthalmic Surgeon: King's College Hospital (Ophthalmic Surgeon, 1938–69); Moorfields Eye Hospital (Ophthalmic Surgeon, 1936–69); National Hospital, Queen Square (Ophthalmic Surgeon, 1936–69); Director, Orthoptic Department, Moorfields Eye Hospital, 1947–69; Dean of Institute of Ophthalmology, British Post-graduate Medical Federation of University of London, 1959–67; Teacher of Ophthalmology, University of London; *b* 26 Dec. 1903; *s* of late Herbert Willoughby Lyle, MD, FRCS, Fircliff, Portishead, Somerset; *m* 1949, Jane Bouverie, *e d* of late Major Nigel Maxwell, RA, and Mrs Maxwell, Great Davids, Kingwood, Henley-on-Thames; one *s* three *d*. *Educ:* Dulwich Coll.; Sidney Sussex Coll., Cambridge (Exhib.); King's College Hospital (Burney Yeo Schol.). Todd medal for Clinical Medicine; House Physician, House Surg., Sen. Surg. Registrar; First Asst Neurol. Dept, King's Coll. Hosp., 1929–33; House Surgeon, Royal Westminster Ophth. Hosp., 1934. Civilian Consultant in Ophth., RAF, 1948–; Mem., Flying Personnel Res. Cttee, RAF, Chm., Vision sub-cttee, 1975; Consultant in Ophth. Dept of Civil Aviation, Board of Trade; Hon. Consultant in Ophth., BALPA. Examiner in Ophthalmology: Bristol Univ., 1947–50; RCS, 1949–55; FRCS (Ophthalmology), 1958–66; FRCSE (Ophthalmology), 1960–70; Mem. Council, Faculty of Ophthalmologists, 1946–69, Pres., 1965–68, and Rep. on Council of RCS, 1958–63; Chm., Specialist Adv. Cttee in Ophthalmology, RCS; Past Mem., International Council of Ophthalmology; Mem. Court of Assts, Soc. of Apothecaries, Master, 1962–63. Order of St John: Deputy Hospitaller, 1960–69; Hospitaller, 1969–81; Chm., Hosp. Cttee; Member Council: Med. Protection Soc.; British Council for the Prevention of Blindness; Vice-Chm., Royal London Soc. for the Blind; Pres., St John Ambulance, Henley-on-Thames Div. Past Pres., Internat. Strabismological Assoc.; Member: Cttee of Management, Inst of Opthalmology; Ophth. Soc. UK, Pres. 1968–70; Orthoptists Bd, Council for Professions Supplementary to Medicine; Soc. Franc. d'Opthalmologie; FRSocMed (Vice-Pres. Ophth. Section, Pres. United Services Section, 1964–66); Hon. Mem. Ophth. Socs of Australia, New Zealand and Greece. Chas H. May Memorial Lectr, New York, 1952; Doyne Memorial Lectr, Oxford, 1953; Alexander Welch Lectr, Edinburgh, 1965; Vis. Lectr, Blindness Res. Foundn, Univ. of the Witwatersrand, SA, 1974. Nettleship Medal, 1959; Richardson Cross Medal, 1972. Served RAFVR, 1939–46, Temp. Air Cdre Cons. in Ophth. RAF overseas (despatches). GCStJ 1980 (KStJ 1960; CStJ 1956); Kt, Order of Holy Sepulchre, 1970. *Publications:* (co-ed with Sylvia Jackson) Practical Orthoptics in the Treatment of Squint, 1937, 5th edn (co-ed with K. C. Wybar) 1967; (co-ed with Hon. G. J. O. Bridgeman) Worth's Squint by F. B. Chavasse, 9th edn 1959; (co-ed with A. G. Cross) May and Worth's Diseases of the Eye, 13th edn 1968; (co-ed with late H. Willoughby Lyle) Applied Physiology of the Eye, 1958; articles in British Jl Ophth., Lancet, BMJ, Med. Press and Circular, etc, chapters in Sorsby's Modern Trends in Ophthalmology, 1948, in Stallard's Modern Practice in Ophthalmology, 1949 and in Rob and Rodney Smith's Operative Surgery, 1958. *Recreations:* gardening, riding, ski-ing. *Address:* Kingsley, Crowsley Road, Shiplake, near Henley-on-Thames, Oxon. *T:* Wargrave 2832. *Clubs:* Royal Air Force, Royal Automobile, Sloane, Ski Club of GB.

LYMBERY, Robert Davison; QC 1967; **His Honour Judge Lymbery;** a Circuit Judge (formerly Judge of County Courts), since 1971; *b* 14 Nov. 1920; *s* of late Robert Smith Lymbery and late Louise Lymbery; *m* 1952, Pauline Anne, *d* of John Reginald and Kathleen Tuckett; three *d*. *Educ:* Gresham's Sch.; Pembroke Coll., Cambridge. Served Army, 1940–46; commissioned 17/21 Lancers, 1941; Middle East, Italy, Greece (Royal Tank Regt), 1942–46, Major. Pembroke Coll., 1939–40, 1946–48 (MA, LLB 1st class hons). Foundation Exhibn. 1948; called to Bar, Middle Temple, 1949; Harmsworth Law Scholar, 1949; practice on Midland Circuit, 1949–71. Recorder of Grantham, 1965–71, now Honorary Recorder; Chairman: Rutland QS, 1966–71 (Dep. Chm., 1962–66); Bedfordshire QS, 1969–71 (Dep. Chm., 1961–69); Commissioner of Assize, 1971. Freeman, City of London, 1983. *Recreations:* various. *Address:* Park Lodge, Knebworth, Herts. *T:* Stevenage 813308; 2 Crown Office Row, Temple, EC4. *T:* 01–353 1365. *Club:* Hawks (Cambridge).

LYMINGTON, Viscount; Oliver Henry Rufus Wallop; *b* 22 Dec. 1981; *s* and *heir* of Earl of Portsmouth, *qv*.

LYMPANY, Miss Moura, CBE 1979; FRAM 1948; concert pianist; *b* Saltash, Cornwall, 18 Aug. 1916; British; *d* of John and Beatrice Johnstone; *m* 1944, Lt-Col Colin Defries (marr. diss. 1950); *m* 1951, Bennet H. Korn, American Television Executive (marr. diss. 1961); one *s* decd. *Educ:* Belgium, Austria, England. First public performance at age of 12, 1929, at Harrogate, playing Mendelssohn G Minor Concerto. Won second prize out of

79 competitors at Ysaye International Pianoforte Competition at Brussels, 1938. Has played in USA, Canada, South America, Australia, New Zealand, India, and all principal European countries. Records for HMV and Decca. Commander of the Order of the Crown, Belgium, 1980. *Recreations:* gardening, tapestry, reading. *Address:* c/o Ibbs & Tillett, 450/452 Edgware Road, W2.

LYNAM, Desmond Michael; sports broadcaster, BBC, since 1969; *b* 17 Sept. 1942; *s* of Edward Lynam and Gertrude Veronica Lynam (*née* Malone); *m* 1965, Susan Eleanor Skinner (marr. diss. 1974); one *s*. *Educ:* Varndean Grammar Sch., Brighton; Brighton Business Coll. ACII. Business career in insurance, until 1967; also freelance journalist; reporter for local radio, 1967–69; sports reporter and presenter, BBC Radio, 1969–78: Sport on 2; Sports Report; commentator on boxing and tennis; also Presenter: Today; various quiz shows; Queen's Jubilee Special; presenter and commentator, BBC TV Sport, 1978–: Grandstand and Sunday Grandstand; main presenter, Commonwealth and Olympic Games, and World Cup; commentator on boxing and football. Dir, CPR Ltd, 1978–. TV Sports Presenter of the Year, TV and Radio Industries Club, 1985. *Publication:* Guide to Commonwealth Games, 1986. *Recreations:* golf, tennis, sailing, Brighton and Hove Albion, reading, theatre. *Address:* c/o BBC, Richmond Way, Shepherds Bush, W14.

LYNCH, Rev. Prebendary Donald MacLeod, CBE 1972; MA; *b* 2 July 1911; *s* of Herbert and Margaret Lynch; *m* 1st, 1941, Ailsa Leslie Leask; three *s* one *d*; 2nd, 1963, Jean Wileman. *Educ:* City of London Sch.; Pembroke Coll., Cambridge; Wycliffe Hall, Oxford. Curate, Christ Church, Chelsea, 1935; Tutor, Oak Hill Theological Coll., 1938; Curate, St Michael's, Stonebridge Park, 1940; Minister, All Saints, Queensbury, 1942; Vicar, St Luke's, Tunbridge Wells, 1950; Principal, Church Army Training Coll., 1953; Chief Sec., Church Army, 1960–76; Preb. of Twiford, St Paul's Cathedral, 1964–76, now Emeritus; Priest-in-Charge of Seal, St Lawrence, dio. Rochester, 1974–85, also of Underriver, 1980–85; RD, Sevenoaks, 1979–84. Chaplain to the Queen, 1969–81. *Publications:* Action Stations, 1981; Chariots of the Gospel, 1982. *Recreations:* reading, walking. *Address:* Flat 2, 20 Grassington Road, Eastbourne, Sussex BN20 7BJ. *T:* Eastbourne 20849.

LYNCH, John; *b* 15 Aug. 1917; *y s* of Daniel Lynch and Norah O'Donoghue; *m* 1946, Mairin O'Connor. *Educ:* Christian Brothers' Schools, N Monastery, Cork; University College, Cork; King's Inns, Dublin. Entered Civil Service (Dept of Justice), 1936; called to Bar, 1945; resigned from Civil Service, became Mem. Munster Bar and commenced practice in Cork Circuit, 1945. Teachta Dala (TD) for Cork, Parlt of Ireland, 1948–81; Parly Sec. to Govt and to Minister for Lands, 1951–54; Minister for: Education, 1957–59; Industry and Commerce, 1959–65; Finance, 1965–66; Leader of Fianna Fail, 1966–79; Taoiseach (Head of Government of Ireland), 1966–73 and 1977–79. Alderman, Co. Borough of Cork, 1950–57; Mem. Cork Sanatoria Board and Cttee of Management, N Infirmary, Cork, 1950–51 and 1955–57; Mem. Cork Harbour Comrs, 1956–57; Vice-Pres., Consultative Assembly of Council of Europe, 1958; Pres., Internat. Labour Conf., 1962. Hon. LLD: Dublin, 1967; Nat. Univ. of Ireland, 1969; Rhode Island Coll., USA, 1980; Hon. DCL N Carolina, 1971. Grand Cross, Order of the Crown (Belgium), 1968. Robert Schumann Gold Medal, 1973. *Address:* 21 Garville Avenue, Rathgar, Dublin 6, Ireland.

LYNCH, Prof. John; Director of Institute of Latin American Studies since 1974 and Professor of Latin American History since 1970, University of London; *b* 11 Jan. 1927; *s* of late John P. Lynch and of Teresa M. Lynch, Boldon Colliery, Co. Durham; *m* 1960, Wendy Kathleen, *d* of late Frederick and of Kathleen Norman; two *s* three *d*. *Educ:* Corby Sch. Sunderland; Univ. of Edinburgh; University College, London. MA Edinburgh 1952; PhD London 1955. Army, 1945–48. Asst Lectr and Lectr in Modern History, Univ. of Liverpool, 1954–61; Lectr in Hispanic and Latin American History, University Coll., London, Reader 1964. Corresp. Member: Academia Nacional de la Historia, Argentina, 1963, Venezuela, 1980; Academia Panameña de la Historia, 1981; Academia Chilena de la Historia, 1985. Order of Andrés Bello, Venezuela, 1979. *Publications:* Spanish Colonial Administration 1782–1810, 1958; Spain under the Habsburgs, vol. 1 1964, vol. 2 1969; (with R. A. Humphreys) The Origins of the Latin American Revolutions, 1808–1826, 1965; The Spanish American Revolutions 1808–1826, 1973; Argentine Dictator: Juan Manuel de Rosas, 1829–52, 1981; (ed) Andrés Bello: the London years, 1982; (contrib.) Cambridge History of Latin America, vol. III 1985, vol. IV 1986. *Address:* 8 Templars Crescent, N3 3QS. *T:* 01–346 1089.

LYNCH, Martin Patrick James; Under Secretary, Overseas Development Administration, Foreign and Commonwealth Office, 1975–83, retired; Assistant Secretary (Administration), British College of Ophthalmic Opticians, since 1984; *b* 4 June 1924; 2nd *s* of late Frederick Lynch, DSM, and late Elizabeth Yeatman; *m* 1959, Anne, *d* of late Major Gerald McGorty, MC, RAMC; two *s* one *d* (and one *s* decd). *Educ:* London Oratory School. BA Hons London. RAF, 1942–49; Exec. Officer, HM Treasury, 1950; Asst Private Sec. to Financial Sec., 1953–54; Private Sec. to Minister Without Portfolio, 1954–55; Principal, 1958; Asst Sec., Min. of Overseas Devel, 1966 and 1971–75; Counsellor, UK Treasury and Supply Delegn, Washington, and UK Alternate Dir, World Bank, 1967–71. FRSA 1973; Chm., Assoc. for Latin Liturgy, 1976– (Mem. Council, 1973–76). *Address:* 29 Boileau Road, W5 3AP. *T:* 01–997 4004. *Club:* Reform.

LYNCH, Patrick, MA; MRIA; Professor of Political Economy (Applied Economics), University College, Dublin, 1975–80, now Emeritus; *b* 5 May 1917; *s* of Daniel and Brigid Lynch, Co. Tipperary and Dublin; *m* Mary Crotty (*née* Campbell), MA. *Educ:* Univ. Coll., Dublin. Fellow Commoner, Peterhouse, Cambridge, 1956. Entered Irish Civil Service, 1941; Asst Sec. to Govt, 1950; Univ. Lectr in Econs, UC Dublin, 1952, Associate Prof., 1966–75. Chm., Aer Lingus, 1954–75; Jt Dep. Chm., Allied Irish Banks, 1976–84. Has acted as economic consultant to OECD, Council of Europe, Dept of Finance, Dublin, Gulbenkian Inst., Lisbon. Directed surveys sponsored by Irish Govt with OECD into long-term Irish educnl needs, 1965, and into requirements of Irish economy in respect of scientific res., develt and technology, 1966; estab. Science Policy Res. Centre in Dept of Applied Econs, UC Dublin, 1969. Mem., various Irish Govt Commns and Cttees, 1952–; Member: Club of Rome, 1973; EEC Economic and Monetary Union 1980 Group, 1974; Nat. Science Council, 1968–78; Higher Educn Authority, 1968–72; Nat. Economic and Social Council, 1973–76; European Science Foundn, 1974–77; Chairman: Medico-Social Research Board, 1966–72; Public Service Adv. Council, 1973–77; Exec. Cttee, Econ. and Social Res. Inst., 1983; Editl Bd, Economic and Social Review; Mem. Editorial Bd, University Review. Chm., Nat. Library of Ireland Soc., 1969–72; Chm., Irish Anti-Apartheid Movement, 1972; Member: Irish Assoc. for Civil Liberty; Movement for Peace in Ireland. Chm., Inst. of Public Administration, 1973–77. Member: Governing Body UC Dublin, 1963–75; Senate NUI, 1972–77; Treasurer, RIA, 1972–80. Hon. DUniv Brunel, 1976; Hon. LLD: Dublin, 1979; NUI, 1985. *Publications:* Planning for Economic Development in Ireland, 1959; (with J. Vaizey) Guinness's Brewery in the Irish Economy, 1960; (jtly) Economics of Educational Costing, 1969; (with Brian Hillery) Ireland in the International Labour Organisation, 1969; (with B. Chubb) Economic Development Planning, 1969; Whither Science Policy, 1980; essays in various symposia, etc; articles in Administration, The Bell, Encycl. Britannica, Econ. History Review, Irish Hist. Studies, Irish Jl of Educn, Statist, Studies, University Review, etc. *Address:* 68 Marlborough Road, Dublin 4, Ireland.

LYNCH-BLOSSE, Sir Richard Hely, 17th Bt *cr* 1622; RAMC, 1975–85, retired; general medical practioner, since 1985; *b* 26 Aug. 1953; *s* of Sir David Edward Lynch-Blosse, 16th Bt, and of Elizabeth, *er d* of Thomas Harold Payne, Welwyn Garden City; *S* father, 1971; *m* 1976, Cara, *o d* of George Sutherland, St Ives, Cambs; two *d*. *Educ:* Royal Free Hosp. Sch. of Medicine. Commnd RAMC, July 1975; LRCP MRCS 1978; MB BS 1979; DRCOG 1983; MRCGP 1984. *Heir: cousin* (Eric) Hugh Lynch-Blosse, OBE [*b* 30 July 1917; *m* 1946, Jean Evelyn, *d* of Commander Andrew Robertson Hair, RD, RNR; one *s* one *d* (and one *d* decd)]. *Address:* The Surgery, Watery Lane, Clifton Hampden, Oxon.

LYNCH-ROBINSON, Sir Niall (Bryan), 3rd Bt *cr* 1920; DSC 1941; late Lieut RNVR; one time Chairman, Leo Burnett Ltd, 1969–78; *b* 24 Feb. 1918; *s* of Sir Christopher Henry Lynch-Robinson, 2nd Bt and Dorothy (*d* 1970), *d* of Henry Warren, Carrickmines, Co. Dublin; *S* father 1958; *m* 1940, Rosemary Seaton, *e d* of Mrs M. Seaton Eller; one *s* one (adopted) *d*. *Educ:* Stowe. Sub-Lieut 1939, Lieut 1940, RNVR; served War of 1939–45 (DSC, Croix de Guerre). Mem. Exec. Cttee, Nat. Marriage Guidance Council. Chm. of Governors, Cranbourne Chase School, 1970–82. *Recreations:* fishing, gardening. *Heir: s* Dominick Christopher Lynch-Robinson, *b* 30 July 1948. *Address:* The Old Vicarage, Ampfield, Romsey, Hants SO51 9BQ.

LYNDEN-BELL, Prof. Donald, FRS 1978; Professor of Astrophysics, University of Cambridge, since 1972; Director, Institute of Astronomy, Cambridge, 1972–77 and since 1982; *b* 5 April 1935; *s* of late Lt-Col L. A. Lynden-Bell, MC and of M. R. Lynden-Bell (*née* Thring); *m* 1961, Ruth Marion Truscott, MA, PhD; one *s* one *d*. *Educ:* Marlborough; Clare Coll., Cambridge (MA, PhD). Harkness Fellow of the Commonwealth Fund, NY, at the California Inst. of Technology and Hale Observatories, 1960–62; Research Fellow and then Fellow and Dir of studies in mathematics, Clare Coll., Cambridge, 1960–65; Asst Lectr in applied mathematics, Univ. of Cambridge, 1962–65; Principal Scientific officer and later SPSO, Royal Greenwich Observatory, Herstmonceux, 1965–72. Visiting Associate, Calif. Inst. of Technology and Hale Observatories, 1969–70. Pres., RAS, 1985–. Eddington Medal, RAS, 1984. FHMAAAS 1985. *Publications:* contrib. to Monthly Notices of Royal Astronomical Soc. *Recreations:* hill walking, golf, squash racquets. *Address:* Institute of Astronomy, The Observatories, Madingley Road, Cambridge CB3 0HA. *T:* Cambridge 337525.

LYNE, Air Vice-Marshal Michael Dillon, CB 1968; AFC (two Bars); DL; *b* 23 March 1919; *s* of late Robert John Lyne, Winchester; *m* 1943, Avril Joy Buckley, *d* of late Lieut-Colonel Albert Buckley, CBE, DSO; two *s* two *d*. *Educ:* Imperial Service Coll.; RAF Coll., Cranwell. Fighter Comd and Middle East, 1939–46; Comdg No 54 Fighter Squadron, 1946–48; Comdg RAF Wildenrath, 1958–60; Air Attaché, Moscow, 1961–63; Commandant, Royal Air Force Coll., Cranwell, 1963–64; Air Officer Commanding No 23 Group, RAF Flying Training Command, 1965–67; Senior RAF Instructor, Imperial Defence Coll., 1968–69; Dir-Gen. Training, RAF, 1970–71; retired. Sec., Diocese of Lincoln, 1971–76. Vice-Chm. (Air), TAVR Assoc. for East Midlands, 1977–84. Vice Chm., Governing Body, Bishop Grosseteste Coll., 1976–. Vice-President: RAF Gliding and Soaring Assoc.; RAF Motor Sport Assoc.; Old Cranwellian Assoc., 1982–. Founder and first Chm., Lincs Microprocessor Soc., 1979–83; Mem. Council, British Computer Soc., 1980–83. President: Lincoln Branch, SCF, 1977–; Grantham Constituency Liberal Assoc., 1979–; No 54 Squadron Assoc., 1981–. DL Lincs, 1973. *Recreations:* sailing, gardening. *Address:* Far End, Far Lane, Coleby, Lincoln LN5 0AH. *T:* Lincoln 810468. *Clubs:* Royal Air Force; Royal Mersey Yacht.

LYNN, Bishop Suffragan of, since 1986; **Rt. Rev. David Edward Bentley;** *b* 7 Aug. 1935; *s* of William Bentley and Florence (*née* Dalgleish); *m* 1962, Clarice Lahmers; two *s* two *d*. *Educ:* Gt Yarmouth Grammar School; Univ. of Leeds (BA English); Westcott House, Cambridge. Deacon 1960, priest 1961; Curate: St Ambrose, Bristol, 1960–62; Holy Trinity with St Mary, Guildford, 1962–66; Rector: Headley, Bordon, 1966–73; Esher, 1973–86. Hon. Canon of Guildford Cathedral, 1980; RD of Emly, 1977–82. Chairman: Guildford dio. Council of Social Responsibility, 1980–86; Guildford dio. House of Clergy, 1977–86. *Recreations:* music; sport, especially clergy cricket; theatre. *Address:* The Old Vicarage, Castle Acre, King's Lynn, Norfolk PE32 2AA. *T:* Castle Acre 553. *Club:* MCC.

LYNN, Archdeacon of; *see* Grobecker, Ven. G. F.

LYNN, Jonathan Adam; director, writer and actor; Company Director of the National Theatre, since 1986; *b* 3 April 1943; *s* of Robin and Ruth Lynn; *m* 1967, Rita Merkelis; one *s*. *Educ:* Kingswood Sch., Bath; Pembroke Coll., Cambridge (MA). Acted in Cambridge Circus, New York, 1964; TV debut, Ed Sullivan Show, 1964; actor in repertory, Leicester, Edinburgh and Bristol Old Vic, and in London; performances include: Green Julia, 1965; Fiddler on the Roof, 1967–68; Blue Comedy, 1968; The Comedy of the Changing Years, 1969; When We Are Married, 1970; Dreyfus, 1982; actor in TV comedy programmes and plays, including: Barmitzvah Boy, 1975; The Knowledge, 1979; Outside Edge, 1982; Diana, 1984; (also scriptwriter) Suspicion, 1986; Artistic Dir, Cambridge Theatre Co., 1977–81 (dir. 19 prodns); *director: London:* The Plotters of Cabbage Patch Corner, 1970; The Glass Menagerie, 1977; The Gingerbread Man, 1977 and 1978; The Unvarnished Truth, 1978; The Matchmaker, 1978; Songbook, 1979 (SWET Award, Best Musical, 1979); Tonight at 8.30, 1981; Arms and the Man, 1981; Pass the Butler, 1982; Loot, 1984; *National Theatre:* A Little Hotel on the Side, 1984; Jacobowski and the Colonel, 1986; *RSC:* Anna Christie, Stratford 1979, London 1980; *Broadway:* The Moony Shapiro Songbook, 1981; *short film:* Mick's People, 1982. *TV scriptwriter:* situation comedies, including: My Brother's Keeper, 2 series, 1974 and 1975 (also co-starred); Yes Minister (also radio scripts), 3 series, 1980, 1981 and 1982; Yes Prime Minister, 1986; *film scriptwriter:* The Internecine Project, 1974; (also dir), Clue, 1986. *Publications:* A Proper Man (novel), 1976; (with Antony Jay) Yes Minister, The Diaries of a Cabinet Minister: Vol. I, 1981; Vol. II, 1982; Vol. III, 1983; (with Antony Jay) The Complete Yes Minister, 1984; (with Antony Jay) Yes Prime Minister, Vol. I, 1986. *Recreation:* working. *Address:* c/o A. D. Peters & Co. Ltd, 10 Buckingham Street, WC2N 6BU.

LYNN, Prof. Richard; Professor of Psychology, University of Ulster, since 1972; *b* 20 Feb. 1930; *s* of Richard and Ann Lynn; *m* 1956, Susan Maher (marr. diss. 1978); one *s* two *d*. *Educ:* Bristol Grammar Sch.; King's Coll., Cambridge. Lectr in Psychology, Univ. of Exeter, 1956–67; Prof. of Psychology, Dublin Economic and Social Res. Inst., 1967–71. US Mensa Award for Excellence, for work on intelligence, 1985. *Publications:* Attention, Arousal and the Orientation Reaction, 1966; The Irish Braindrain, 1969; The Universities and the Business Community, 1969; Personality and National Character, 1971; An Introduction to the Study of Personality, 1972; (ed) The Entrepreneur, 1974; (ed) Dimensions of Personality, 1981; articles on personality, intelligence and social psychology. *Recreation:* do-it-yourself house renovation. *Address:* Dunderg House, Coleraine, Co. Londonderry. *Club:* Arts (Dublin).

LYNN, Dame Vera, (Dame Vera Margaret Lewis), DBE 1975 (OBE 1969); singer; *b* 20 March 1917; *d* of Bertram Samuel Welch and Annie Welch; *m* 1941, Harry Lewis; one *d*. *Educ:* Brampton Rd Sch., East Ham. First public appearance as singer, 1924; joined juvenile troupe, 1928; ran own dancing school, 1932; broadcast with Joe Loss and joined Charlie Kunz, 1935; singer with Ambrose Orch., 1937–40, then went solo; voted most popular singer, Daily Express comp., 1939, and named Forces Sweetheart; own radio show, Sincerely Yours, 1941–47; starred in Applesauce, London Palladium, 1941; sang to troops in Burma, etc, 1944 (Burma Star, 1985); subseq. Big Show (radio), USA; London Laughs, Adelphi; appeared at Flamingo Hotel, Las Vegas, and many TV shows, USA and Britain, including own TV series on Rediffusion, 1955; BBC TV, 1956; BBC 2, 1970; also appearances in Holland, Denmark, Sweden, Norway, Germany, Canada, NZ and Australia; in seven Command Performances, also films and own shows on radio. 14 Gold Records; records include Auf Wiederseh'n (over 12 million copies sold), became first British artiste to top American Hit Parade. Pres., Printers' Charitable Corp., 1980. Hon. Citizen: Winnipeg, 1974; Nashville, Tennessee, 1977. Hon. LLD Memorial Univ. of Newfoundland, 1977 (founded Lynn Music Scholarship, first award, 1982). Freedom: City of London, 1978; City of Corner Brook, Newfoundland, 1981. FInstD. Music Publishers' Award, 1975; Show Business Personality of the Year, Grand Order of Water Rats, 1975; Ivor Novello Award, 1975; Humanitarian Award, Variety Club Internat., 1985. Comdr, Order of Orange-Nassau, Holland. *Publication:* Vocal Refrain (autobiog.), 1975. *Recreations:* gardening, painting, sewing, swimming.

LYNN, Wilfred; Director, National Westminster Bank Ltd (Outer London Board), 1969–73; *b* 19 May 1905; *s* of late Wilfred Crosland Lynn and Alice Lynn; *m* 1936, Valerie, *e d* of late B. M. A. Critchley; one *s* one *d* (twins). *Educ:* Hull Grammar School. Entered National Provincial Bank Ltd, 1921; Asst General Manager, 1952; Joint General Manager, 1953; Chief General Manager, 1961; Director, 1965–69; Dir, North Central Finance Ltd, 1962–70. FIB. *Recreation:* golf. *Address:* c/o National Westminster Bank, 15 Bishopsgate, EC2.

LYNNE, Gillian, (Mrs Peter Land); director, choreographer, dancer, actress; *d* of late Leslie Pyrke and Barbara (*née* Hart); *m* 1980, Peter Land, actor. *Educ:* Baston Sch., Bromley, Kent; Arts Educnl Sch. Leading soloist, Sadler's Wells Ballet, 1944–51; star dancer, London Palladium, 1951–53; role in film, Master of Ballantrae, 1952; lead in Can-Can, Coliseum, 1954–55; Becky Sharp in Vanity Fair, Windsor, 1956; guest principal dancer: Samson and Delilah, Sadler's Wells, 1957; Aida, and Tannhauser, Covent Garden, 1957; Puck in A Midsummer Night's Dream, TV, 1958; star dancer in Chelsea at Nine (featured dance segments), TV, 1958; lead in New Cranks, Lyric, Hammersmith, 1959; roles in Wanda, Rose Marie, Cinderella, Out of My Mind, and lead in revue, 1960–61; leading lady, 5 Past Eight Show, Edinburgh, 1962; conceived, dir., chor. and starred in Collages (mod. dance revue), Edinburgh Fest., 1963, transf. Savoy; *choreographed:* The Owl and the Pussycat (1st ballet), Western Theatre Ballet, 1962; Queen of the Cats, London Palladium, 1962–63; Wonderful Life (1st film), 1963–64; Every Day's a Holiday, and Three Hats for Lisa (musical films), 1964; The Roar of the Greasepaint, and Pickwick, Broadway, 1965; The Flying Dutchman, Covent Garden, 1966; Half a Sixpence (film), 1966–67 (also staged musical nos); How Now Dow Jones, Broadway, 1967; Midsummer Marriage, Covent Garden, 1968; The Trojans, Covent Garden, 1969, 1977; Breakaway (ballet), Scottish Theatre Ballet, 1969; Phil the Fluter, Palace, 1969; Ambassador, Her Majesty's, 1971; Man of La Mancha (film), 1972; The Card, Queen's, 1973; Hans Andersen, London Palladium, 1975; The Way of the World, Aldwych, 1978; My Fair Lady, national tour and Adelphi, 1979; Parsifal, Covent Garden, 1979; (also Associate Dir) Cats, New London, 1981 (Olivier Award, 1981), Broadway 1982, nat. tour, 1983, Los Angeles, Sydney, 1985; Café Soir (ballet), Houston Ballet Co., 1985; *directed and choreographed* The Match Girls, Globe, 1966; Bluebeard, Sadler's Wells Opera, 1966, new prodn, Sadler's Wells Opera, Coliseum, 1969; Love on the Dole (musical), Nottingham Playhouse, 1970; Liberty Ranch, Greenwich, 1972; Once Upon a Time, Duke of York's, 1972; Jasperina, Amsterdam, 1978; Cats, Vienna, 1983 (1st proscenium arch prodn; Silver Order of Merit, Austria, 1984); *directed:* Round Leicester Square (revue), Prince Charles, 1963; Tonight at Eight, Hampstead, 1970 and Fortune, 1971; Lillywhite Lies, Nottingham, 1971; A Midsummer Night's Dream (co-dir.), Stratford, 1977; Tomfoolery, Criterion, 1980; Jeeves Takes Charge, Fortune, 1980, off-Broadway, 1983, Los Angeles, 1985; To Those Born Later, New End, 1981; (Additional Dir) La Ronde, RSC, Aldwych, 1982; (also appeared in) Alone Plus One, Newcastle, 1982; The Rehearsal, Yvonne Arnaud, Guildford and tour, 1983; Cabaret, Strand, 1986; *staged:* England Our England (revue), Princes, 1961; 200 Motels (pop-opera film), 1971; musical nos in Quilp (film), 1974; A Comedy of Errors, Stratford, 1976 (TV musical, 1977); musical As You Like It, Stratford, 1977; Songbook, Globe, 1979; Once in a Lifetime, Aldwych, 1979; new stage act for Tommy Steele, 1979; wedding sequence in Yentl (film), 1982; *choreographed for television:* Peter and the Wolf (narrated and mimed all 9 parts), 1958; At the Hawk's Well (ballet), 1975; There was a Girl, 1975; The Fool on the Hill (1st Colour Special for ABC), with Australian Ballet and Sydney Symph. Orch., staged Sydney Opera House, 1975; Muppet Show series, 1976–80; (also musical staging) Alice in Wonderland, 1985; shows and specials for Val Doonican, Perry Como, Petula Clark, Nana Mouskouri, John Curry, Harry Secombe, Ray Charles, and Mike Burstein; also produced and devised Noel Coward and Cleo Laine specials; *directed for television:* Mrs F's Friends, 1981; Easy Money, 1982; Le Morte d'Arthur (also devised), 1983. *Publications:* (contrib.) Cats, The Book of the Musical; articles in Dancing Times. *Address:* 25 The Avenue, Bedford Park, Chiswick, W4. *Club:* Pickwick.

LYNTON, Norbert Casper; Professor of the History of Art, since 1975, and Dean of the School of European Studies, since 1985, University of Sussex; *b* 22 Sept. 1927; *s* of Paul and Amalie Christiane Lynton; *m* 1st, 1949, Janet Irving; two *s*; 2nd, 1969, Sylvia Anne Towning; two *s*. *Educ:* Douai Sch.; Birkbeck Coll., Univ. of London (BA Gen.); Courtauld Inst., Univ. of London (BA Hons). Lectr in History of Art and Architecture, Leeds Coll. of Art, 1950–61; Sen. Lectr, then Head of Dept of Art History and Gen. Studies, Chelsea Sch. of Art, 1961–70. London Corresp. of Art International, 1961–66; Art Critic, The Guardian, 1965–70; Dir of Exhibitions, Arts Council of GB, 1970–75; Vis. Prof. of History of Art, Open Univ., 1975. Trustee, National Portrait Gallery, 1985–. *Publications:* (jtly) Simpson's History of Architectural Development, vol. 4 (Renaissance), 1962; Kenneth Armitage, 1962; Paul Klee, 1964; The Modern World, 1968; The Story of Modern Art, 1980; Looking at Art, 1981; (jtly) Looking into Paintings, 1985; articles in Burlington Mag., TLS, Studio International, Architectural Design, Art in America, Smithsonian, Leonardo, etc. *Recreations:* art, people, music, travel. *Address:* 28 Florence Road, Brighton BN1 6DJ. *T:* Brighton 509478.

LYON; *see* Bowes Lyon.

LYON, Alexander Ward; Chairman, UK Immigrants Advisory Service, since 1978; *b* 15 Oct. 1931. Contested (Lab) York, 1964, 1983. MP (Lab) York, 1966–83; addtl PPS to the Treasury Ministers, 1969; PPS to Paymaster General, 1969; Opposition Spokesman: on African Affairs, 1970; on Home Affairs, 1971; Min. of State, Home Office, 1974–76. Member: Younger Cttee on Intrusions into Privacy; Select Cttee on Home Affairs, 1979; Chm., PLP Home Affairs Gp, 1979. *Address:* 23 Larkhall Rise, SW4. *T:* 01–720 1525.

LYON, Clare; *see* Short, C.

LYON, (Colin) Stewart (Sinclair), FIA; FSA, FRNS; General Manager (Finance), Group Actuary and Director, Legal & General Group Plc, since 1980; *b* 22 Nov. 1926; *s* of late Col Colin Sinclair Lyon, OBE, TD and Mrs Dorothy Winstanley Lyon (*née* Thomason); *m* 1958, Elizabeth Mary Fargus Richards; four *s* one *d*. *Educ:* Liverpool Coll.; Trinity Coll., Cambridge (MA). FIA 1954; FSA 1972; FRNS 1955. Chief Exec., Victory Insurance Co. Ltd, 1974–76; Chief Actuary, Legal & General Assurance Soc. Ltd, 1976–85. Member: Occupational Pensions Bd, 1979–82; Inquiry into Provision for Retirement, 1983–85; Treasure Trove Reviewing Cttee, 1986–. President: Inst. of Actuaries, 1982–84; British Numismatic Soc., 1966–70 (Sanford Saltus Gold Medal, 1974); Vice-Pres., Guildford Philharmonic Soc., 1974–. Trustee, Disablement Income Gp Charitable Trust, 1967–84; Dir, Disablement Income Gp, 1984–. *Publications:* papers on Anglo-Saxon coinage, particularly in British Numismatic Jl; contrib. Jl of Inst. of Actuaries and Trans Internat. Congress of Actuaries. *Recreations:* numismatics, music, short-wave radio. *Address:* Cuerdale, White Lane, Guildford, Surrey GU4 8PR. *T:* Guildford 573761. *Club:* Actuaries'.

LYON, Mary Frances, ScD; FRS 1973; Head of Genetics Division, Medical Research Council Radiobiology Unit, Harwell, since 1962; *b* 15 May 1925; *e d* of Clifford James Lyon and Louise Frances Lyon (*née* Kirby). *Educ:* King Edward's Sch., Birmingham; Woking Grammar Sch.; Girton Coll., Cambridge (ScD 1968; Hon. Fellow 1985). FIBiol. MRC Scientific Staff, Inst. of Animal Genetics, Edinburgh, 1950–55; MRC Radiobiology Unit, Harwell, 1955–. Clothworkers Visiting Research Fellow, Girton Coll., Cambridge, 1970–71. Foreign Hon. Mem., Amer. Acad. Arts and Scis, 1980 (Amory Prize, 1977). Foreign Associate, US Nat. Acad. of Scis, 1979. Royal Medal, Royal Soc., 1984; Prize for Genetics, Sanremo, Italy, 1985; Gairdner Foundn Award, 1985. *Publications:* papers on genetics in scientific jls. *Address:* MRC Radiobiology Unit, Chilton, Oxon OX11 0RD. *T:* Abingdon 834393.

LYON, Maj.-Gen. Robert, CB 1976; OBE 1964 (MBE 1960); Bursar, Loretto School, Musselburgh, since 1979; *b* Ayr, 24 Oct. 1923; *s* of David Murray Lyon and Bridget Lyon (*née* Smith); *m* 1951, Constance Margaret Gordon (*d* 1982); one *s* one *d*. *Educ:* Ayr Academy. Commissioned, Aug. 1943, Argyll and Sutherland Highlanders. Served Italy, Germany, Palestine, Greece; transf. to Regular Commn in RA, 1947; Regtl Service, 3 RHA in Libya and 19 Field in BAOR, 1948–56; Instr, Mons Officer Cadet Sch., 1953–55; Staff Coll., 1957; DAQMG, 3 Div., 1958–60; jssc, 1960; BC F (Sphinx) Bty 7 PARA, RHA, 1961–62 (Bt Lt-Col); GSO1, ASD2, MoD, 1962–65 (Lt-Col); CO 4 Lt Regt, RA, 1965–67, Borneo (despatches), UK and BAOR (Lt-Col); as Brig.: CRA 1 Div., 1967–69, BAOR; IDC, 1970; Dir Operational Requirements, MoD, 1971–73; DRA (Maj.-Gen.), 1973–75; GOC SW District, 1975–78; retired 1979. Pres., Army Hockey Assoc., 1974–76; Chm., Army Golf Assoc., 1977–78. Chm., RA Council of Scotland, 1984–. Col Comdt RA. Dir, Braemar Civic Amenities Trust, 1986–. HM Comr, Queen Victoria Sch., Dunblane, 1984–. FBIM (MBIM 1978). *Recreations:* golf, fishing, ski-ing. *Address:* Woodside, Braemar, Aberdeenshire, Scotland. *T:* Braemar 667; Loretto School, Musselburgh, East Lothian EH21 7RE. *T:* 031–665 2380. *Club:* New (Edinburgh).

LYON, Stanley Douglas; Deputy Chairman, Imperial Chemical Industries Ltd, 1972–77 (Director, 1968–77); *b* 22 June 1917; *s* of Ernest Hutcheon Lyon and late Helen Wilson Lyon; *m* 1941, May Alexandra Jack; three *s*. *Educ:* George Heriot's Sch., Edinburgh; Edinburgh Univ. (BSc Hons Engrg). AMICE, FBIM. Major, Royal Engrs, 1939–46. ICI Ltd: Engr, Dyestuffs Div., 1946; Engrg Dir, Wilton Works, 1957; Prodn Dir, Agricl Div., 1962; Dep. Chm. 1964, Chm. 1966, Agric. Div. *Recreations:* golf, tennis, gardening, sculpture. *Address:* Bramble Carr, Danby, Whitby, N Yorks.

LYON, Hon. Sterling, PC 1982; QC (Canada) 1960; Counsel, Pitblado & Hoskin, law firm; Premier of Manitoba, 1977–81; *b* 30 Jan. 1927; *s* of David Rufus Lyon and Ella May (*née* Cuthbert); *m* 1953, Barbara Jean Mayers; two *s* three *d*. *Educ:* Portage Collegiate (Governor-General's Medal); United College (BA 1948); Univ. of Manitoba Law Sch. (LLB 1953). Crown Attorney, Manitoba, 1953–57; Member, Manitoba Legislative Assembly, and Executive Council, 1958–69; Attorney-General, 1958–63 and 1966–69; Minister of: Municipal Affairs, 1960–61; Public Utilities, 1961–63; Mines and Natural Resources, 1963–66; Tourism and Recreation, Commissioner of Northern Affairs, 1966–68; Govt House Leader, 1966–69; Leader, Progressive Cons. Party of Manitoba, 1975–83; MLA for Souris-Killarney, 1976–77, for Charleswood, 1977–86; Leader of the Opposition, Manitoba, 1976–77 and 1981–83; Minister of Dominion-Provincial Affairs, 1977–81. Director and General Counsel of national corporation, 1969–74. *Recreations:* hunting, fishing. *Address:* 1900–360 Main Street, Winnipeg, Manitoba R3C 3Z3, Canada. *T:* (204) 9420391. *Club:* Albany (Toronto).

LYON, Stewart; *see* Lyon, C. S. S.

LYON-DALBERG-ACTON, family name of **Baron Acton.**

LYONS, Bernard, CBE 1964; JP; DL; Chairman: UDS Group PLC, 1972–82 (Director, 1954–83; Joint Managing Director, 1966; Managing Director, 1972–79); Colmore Trust Ltd, since 1984; *b* 30 March 1913; *m* 1938, Lucy Hurst; three *s* one *d*. *Educ:* Leeds Grammar Sch. Chairman: Yorkshire and City Properties Ltd, 1956–73; Glanfield Securities, 1958–74. Chm., Yorkshire and NE Conciliation Cttee, Race Relations Bd, 1968–70; Member: Leeds City Council, 1951–65; Community Relations Commn, 1970–72; Govt Adv. Cttee on Retail Distribution, 1970–76. Mem. Court and Council, Univ. of Leeds, 1953–58; Chm., Swarthmore Adult Educn Centre Appeal for Building Extensions, 1957–60. Chm., Leeds Judean Youth Club, 1955–70; Jt Chm., Leeds Br., CCJ, 1955–60; Life Pres., Leeds Jewish Representative Council, 1960–. JP Leeds, 1960; DL West Riding, Yorks, 1971. Hon. LLD Leeds, 1973. *Publications:* The Thread is Strong, 1981; The Narrow Edge, 1985. *Recreations:* farming, forestry, travel, writing. *Address:* Upton Wood, Fulmer, Bucks. *T:* Fulmer 2404.

See also S. R. Lyons.

LYONS, Charles Albert; General Secretary, Transport Salaried Staffs' Association, since 1982; *b* Liverpool, 13 Aug. 1929; *s* of Maurice Lyons and Catherine Jones; *m* 1958, Judith Mary Robinson; three *s*. *Educ:* St Mary's RC Secondary Modern Sch., Fleetwood. Wages Clerk, fishing industry, 1943–47; National Service, RAPC, 1947–49; Clerical Officer, British Rail, 1950–59; Transport Salaried Staffs' Association: Clerical Asst, 1959–64; Scottish Sec., 1965–68; London Midland Div. Officer, 1968–73; Asst Gen. Sec., 1973–77; Senior Asst Gen. Sec., 1977–82; Member: TUC Gen. Council, 1983– (Mem. Committees: Equal Rights; Transport; Public Enterprise; Social Insurance and Indust. Welfare; Employment, Policy and Orgn); Hotels and Catering Industrial Training Bd, 1982–84; Railway Industry Adv. Cttee, 1982–; Jt Council for Railways, EEC; Vice-Chm., ITF Travel Bureau Section, 1979–; individual Mem., Labour Party, 1950–. *Address:* Transport Salaried Staffs' Association, Walkden House, 10 Melton Street, Euston, NW1 2EJ. *T:* 01–387 2101.

LYONS, Dennis John, CB 1972; CEng, FRAeS; Director General of Research, Department of the Environment, 1971–76; *b* 26 Aug. 1916; *s* of late John Sylvester Lyons and of

Adela Maud Lyons; *m* 1939, Elisabeth, *d* of Arnold and Maria Friederika Müller Haefliger, Weggis, Switzerland; five *s* two *d*. *Educ*: Grocers' Company School; Queen Mary Coll., London Univ. (Fellow, 1969). Aerodynamics Dept, Royal Aircraft Estabt, 1937; RAFVR, 1935–41; Aerodynamics Flight Aero Dept, RAE, 1941–51; Head of Experimental Projects Div., Guided Missiles Dept, RAE, 1951; Head of Ballistic Missile Group, GW Dept, 1956; Head of Weapons Dept, RAE, 1962; Dir., Road Research Laboratory, 1965–72. Member: Adv. Board for Res. Councils, 1973–76; SRC, 1973–76; Engineering Bd, SRC, 1970–76; Natural Environment Res. Council, 1973–76. Pres. OECD Road Research Unit, 1968–72. Hon. Mem., Instn Highway Engineers. *Publications*: papers in scientific jls. *Recreations*: ski-ing, pottery-making, philately. *Address*: Summerhaven, Gough Road, Fleet, Hants. *T*: 4773.

LYONS, Edward; QC 1974; LLB; a Recorder of the Crown Court, since 1972; *b* 17 May 1926; *s* of late A. Lyons and of Mrs S. Taylor; *m* 1955, Barbara, *d* of Alfred Katz; one *s* one *d*. *Educ*: Roundhay High Sch.; Leeds Univ. LLB (Hons) 1951. Served Royal Artillery, 1944–48; Combined Services Russian Course, Cambridge Univ., 1946; Interpreter in Russian, Brit. CCG, 1946–48. Called to Bar, Lincoln's Inn, 1952, Bencher, 1983. MP (Lab 1966–81, SDP 1981–83) Bradford E, 1966–74, Bradford W, 1974–83; PPS at Treasury, 1969–70; SDP Parly spokesman: on home affairs, 1981–82; on legal affairs, 1982–83. Member: H of C Select Cttee on European Legislation, 1975–83; SDP Nat. Cttee, 1984–; Chairman: PLP Legal and Judicial Gp, 1974–77; PLP Home Office Gp, 1974–79 (Dep. Chm., 1970–74). Contested: (Lab) Harrogate, 1964; (SDP) Bradford W, 1983; (SDP) Yorkshire West, European Parly Elecn, 1984. Member: Exec. of Justice, 1974–; Amnesty. *Recreations*: history, opera. *Address*: 15 Old Square, Lincoln's Inn, WC2. *T*: 01–831 0801; 59 Westminster Gardens, Marsham Street, SW1. *T*: 01–834 1960; 4 Primley Park Lane, Leeds LS17 7JR. *T*: Leeds 685351; 6 Park Square, Leeds LS1 2NG.

LYONS, Sir Edward Houghton, Kt 1977; FAIM; Chairman, Totalisator Administration Board, Queensland, 1981–85. Formerly Chairman, Katies Ltd, and Gen. Manager, Industrial Acceptance Corp. Ltd; Dir, Bruck (Australia) Ltd. Trustee, National Party. *Address*: 47 Kneale Street, Holland Park Heights, Queensland 4121, Australia. *T*: 49 6461.

LYONS, Hamilton; Temporary Sheriff (Scotland), since 1984; *b* 3 Aug. 1918; *s* of Richard Lyons and Annie Cathro Thomson; *m* 1943, Jean Cathro Blair; two *s*. *Educ*: Gourock High Sch.; Greenock High Sch.; Glasgow Univ. (BL 1940). Practised as Solicitor, Greenock, until 1966; Sheriff Substitute of Inverness, Moray, Nairn and Ross and Cromarty at Stornoway and Lochmaddy, 1966–68; Sheriff of N Strathclyde (formerly Renfrew and Argyll, and Ayr and Bute), 1968–84, retd. Member: Coun. of Law Soc. of Scotland, 1950–66 (Vice-Pres., 1962–63); Law Reform Cttee for Scotland, 1954–64; Cttee of Inquiry on Children and Young Persons, 1961–64; Cttee of Inquiry on Sheriff Courts, 1963–67; Sheriff Court Rules Coun., 1952–66; Scottish Probation Adv. and Trng Coun., 1959–69. *Address*: 14 Cloch Road, Gourock, Inverclyde PA19 1AB. *T*: Gourock 32566.

LYONS, Sir (Isidore) Jack, Kt 1973; CBE 1967; Chairman: J. Lyons, Chamberlayne & Co. Ltd; John David Ltd; H. Allen Smith; UK Advisor, Bain & Co., Boston, Mass; Member, Advisory Board, Bain Capital Fund, Boston, Mass; Financial Advisor, Cranbury Group; Director of other companies; *b* 1 Feb. 1916; *s* of Samuel H. Lyons and Sophia Niman; *m* 1943, Roslyn Marion Rosenbaum; two *s* two *d*. *Educ*: Leeds Grammar Sch. Chm., Leeds Musical Festival, 1955–72, Vice-Pres., 1973; Chm., London Symphony Orchestra Trust, 1970– (Jt Chm., 1963–70), Trustee, 1970– (Hon. Mem., LSO, 1973); Jt Chm., Southwark Rehearsal Hall Trust, 1974–; Chm., Shakespeare Exhibn (quatercentenary celebrations Stratford-upon-Avon), 1964; Mem. Exec. Cttee, Royal Acad. of Dancing, 1964; Life Trustee, Shakespeare Birthplace Trust, 1967; Mem., Culture Adv. Cttee, UNESCO, 1973–, Dep. Chm., Fanfare for Europe, 1972–73; Chm., FCO US Bicentennial Cttee for the Arts, 1973–; Member: Adv. Cttee of Honour, Britain's Salute to NY 1983 Bicentennial; Adv. Council, Britain Salutes NY, 1983. Chairman: Sir Jack Lyons Charitable Trust; Musical Therapy Charity, 1984–85; Dir, Wolf Trap Foundn, USA. Vice-Pres., Anglo-Italian Chamber of Commerce, 1977–. Vice-Pres., Jt Israel Appeal, 1972 (Dep. Chm. 1957); Chm., Fedn of Jewish Relief Organisations, 1958. Member: Canadian Veterans' Assoc., 1964; Pilgrims, 1965. Mem. Council, Internat. Triangle Res. Inst., 1983–. Patron, St Gemma's Hospice. Dep. Chm., Governors of Carmel Coll., 1961–69; Mem. Ct, York Univ., 1965. Hon. FRAM, 1973. DUniv York, 1975. *Recreations*: music, the arts and swimming. *Address*: Blundell House, 2 Campden Hill, W8. *T*: 01–727 2750. *Club*: Carlton.

LYONS, Sir James (Reginald), Kt 1969; JP; Chairman and Company Director, Park Lodge Property Company; Airport Manager, Cardiff Airport, 1955–75; *b* 15 March 1910; *s* of James Lyons; *m* 1937, Doreen Mary Fogg; one *s*. *Educ*: Howard Gardens High Sch.; Cardiff Technical Coll. Served War of 1939–45: Royal Tank Regt, 1940–46 (1939–45 Star, Africa Star, Italy Star, Defence Medal, War Medal of 1939–45). Civil Service, 1929–65: Post Office, Min. of Supply, Min. of Aviation. Mem., Wales Tourist Bd. Glamorgan CC, 1965–74; Cardiff City Council: Councillor, 1949–58; Alderman, 1958–74; Lord Mayor of Cardiff, 1968–69. Mem., BBC Broadcasting Council. Assessor under Race Relations Act, 1976. Pres., Welsh Games Council, 1985–; Chm., Cardiff Horticultural Soc., 1962–. Trustee, Wales and Border Counties TSB. Chairman of Governors: UC Cardiff, 1955–70; St Illtyd's Coll.; Gov., De La Salle Prep. Sch. JP Cardiff, 1966–. OStJ; KCSG. *Recreations*: Rugby football, swimming, tennis. *Address*: 101 Minehead Avenue, Sully, S Glam. *T*: Sully 530403.

LYONS, Dr John, FBA 1973; Master of Trinity Hall, Cambridge, since 1984; *b* 23 May 1932; *s* of Michael A. Lyons and Mary B. Lyons (*née* Sullivan); *m* 1959, Danielle J. Simonet; two *d*. *Educ*: St Bede's Coll., Manchester; Christ's Coll., Cambridge. MA; PhD 1961. Lecturer: in Comparative Linguistics, SOAS, 1957–61; in General Linguistics, Univ. of Cambridge, 1961–64; Prof. of General Linguistics, Edinburgh Univ., 1964–76; Prof. of Linguistics, 1976–84, Pro-Vice-Chancellor, 1981–84, Sussex Univ. DèsL (*hc*) Univ. Catholique de Louvain, 1980; Hon. DLitt Reading, 1986. *Publications*: Structural Semantics, 1964; Introduction to Theoretical Linguistics, 1968; New Horizons in Linguistics, 1970; Chomsky, 1970, 2nd edn 1977; Semantics, vols 1 and 2, 1977; Language and Linguistics, 1981; Language, Meaning and Context, 1981; articles and reviews in learned journals. *Address*: The Master's Lodge, Trinity Hall, Cambridge CB2 1TJ.

LYONS, John, CBE 1986; General Secretary, Engineers' and Managers' Association, since 1977, and Electrical Power Engineers' Association, since 1973; *b* 19 May 1926; *s* of Joseph and Hetty Lyons; *m* 1954, Molly McCall; two *s* two *d*. *Educ*: St Paul's Sch.; Polytechnic, Regent Street; Cambridge Univ. (BA Econ). RN 1944–46. Asst. to Manager of Market Research Dept, Vacuum Oil Co., 1950; Research Officer: Bureau of Current Affairs, 1951; Post Office Engineering Union, 1952–57; Asst. Sec., Instn of Professional Civil Servants 1957–66, Dep. Gen. Sec. 1966–73. Member: TUC Gen. Council, 1983–; Nat. Enterprise Bd, 1975–79; Exec. Cttee PEP, 1975–78; Council, PSI, 1978–80; Adv. Council for Applied R&D, 1978–81; Engrg Council, 1982–86; PO Bd, 1980–81, British Telecommunications Bd, 1981–83; Sec., Electricity Supply Unions' Council (formerly Employees' Nat. Cttee for Electricity Supply Industry), 1976–; Chm., NEDO Working Party on Industrial Trucks, 1977–80. A Vice-Pres., Industrial Participation Assoc. (Mem., Exec. Cttee, 1976). Governor, Kingsbury High School, 1974–86; Member: Court of Governors, LSE, 1978–84; Bd of Governors, London Business Sch., 1986–. FRSA. *Publications*: various papers and articles. *Recreation*: family. *Address*: Engineers' and Managers' Association, Station House, Fox Lane North, Chertsey, Surrey KT16 9HW. *T*: Chertsey 64131.

LYONS, Prof. Malcolm Cameron; Sir Thomas Adams's Professor of Arabic, University of Cambridge, since 1985; Fellow of Pembroke College, Cambridge, since 1957; *b* Indore, India, 11 Feb. 1929; *s* of Harold William Lyons and Florence Katharine (*née* Cameron); *m* 1961, Ursula Schedler. *Educ*: New Park Sch., St Andrews; Fettes Coll.; Pembroke Coll., Cambridge (Major Open Classical Schol., 1946; John Stewart of Rannoch Classical Schol. in Latin and Greek, 1948; Browne Medallist, 1948, 1949; 1st cl. hons Pts I and II, Classical Tripos, 1948, 1949; 1st cl. hons Pts I and II, Oriental Studies, Arabic and Persian, 1953; E. G. Browne Prize, 1953; MA 1954; PhD 1957). RAF, 1949–51, commissioned 1950. University of Cambridge: Asst Lectr in Arabic, 1954–59; Lectr, 1959–84; Reader in Medieval Islamic Studies, 1984–85. Seconded to FO as Principal Instructor, MECAS, Lebanon, 1961–62. Founder Editor: Arabic Technical and Scientific Texts, 1966–78; Jl of Arabic Literature, 1970–. *Publications*: Galen on Anatomical Procedures (with W. Duckworth and B. Towers), 1962; In Hippocratis de Officina Medici, 1963, and De Partibus Artis Medicativae, De Causis Contentivis, De Diaeta in Morbis Acutis (in Corpus Medicorum Graecorum), 1967; An Arabic Translation of Themistius' Commentary on Aristotle's De Anima, 1973; Aristotle's Ars Rhetorica, Arabic version, 1982; (with E. Maalouf) The Poetic Vocabulary of Michel Trad, 1968; (with J. Riley-Smith and U. Lyons) Ayyubids, Mamlukes and Crusaders, 1971; (with D. Jackson) Saladin, The Politics of the Holy War, 1982; articles and reviews in learned jls. *Recreations*: golf, ski-ing, walking. *Address*: Pembroke College, Cambridge CB1 2RF. *T*: Cambridge 352241. *Club*: Royal and Ancient Golf (St Andrews).

LYONS, His Honour Sir Rudolph, Kt 1976; QC 1953; a Circuit Judge, 1972–82; Honorary Recorder of Manchester, 1977–82; *b* 5 Jan. 1912; *er s* of late G. Lyons, Leeds; *m* 1936, Jeannette, *yr d* of late Philip Dante; one *s* two *d*. *Educ*: Leeds Grammar Sch.; Leeds Univ. (LLB). Called to Bar, Gray's Inn, 1934; Mem., Gen. Council of the Bar, 1958–70; Master of the Bench, Gray's Inn, 1961–. Recorder of: Sunderland, 1955–56; Newcastle upon Tyne, 1956–61; Sheffield, 1961–65; Leeds, 1965–70; Recorder and Judge of the Crown Ct of Liverpool, 1970–71; Hon. Recorder of Liverpool, 1972–77. Comr, Central Criminal Court, 1962–70; Comr of Assize, 1969; Leader of N Eastern Circuit, 1961–70; Solicitor-Gen., 1961–65, Attorney-Gen., 1965–70, County Palatine of Durham. Jt Pres., Council, HM Circuit Judges, 1974. Hon. Member: Northern Circuit, 1979; N Eastern Circuit, 1983. Mem. Court, Univ. of Manchester, 1980–. Hon. LLD Leeds, 1982. *Recreations*: gardening, paintings, classical music. *Address*: 8 Brookside, Alwoodley, Leeds LS17 8TD. *T*: Leeds 683274. *Clubs*: Racquet (Liverpool); St James's (Manchester).

LYONS, Stuart Randolph; Managing Director, Royal Doulton Ltd, since 1985; *b* 24 Oct. 1943; 3rd *s* of Bernard Lyons, *qv*; *m* 1969, Ellen Harriet Zion; two *s* one *d*. *Educ*: Rugby (Scholar); King's Coll., Cambridge (Major Scholar; 1st Cl. Hons Pt I Classical Tripos, Cl. II(I) Pt II Classical Tripos; BA 1965, MA 1969). Man. Dir, John Collier Tailoring Ltd, 1969–74 (Chm., 1975–83); Dir, UDS Group plc, 1974–83 (Man. Dir, 1979–83); Chairman: Wm Timpson, 1976–83; Richard Shops, 1982–83. Member: Leeds CC, 1970–74; Yorkshire and Humberside Econ. Planning Council, 1972–75; Clothing EDC, 1976–79; Ordnance Survey Review Cttee, 1978–79; Monopolies and Mergers Commn, 1981–85. Contested (C) Halifax, Feb. and Oct. 1974. *Address*: Minton House, London Road, Stoke-on-Trent ST4 7QD. *T*: Stoke-on-Trent 49171. *Clubs*: Carlton, Hurlingham.

LYONS, Terence Patrick; a consultant, since 1983; Associate Director, Pauline Hyde & Associates Ltd; Director, Industrial Training Services Ltd, since 1980; Senior Visiting Fellow, City University Business School, since 1983; *b* 2 Sept. 1919; *s* of Maurice Peter Lyons and Maude Mary Elizabeth Lyons (*née* O'Farrell); *m* 1945, Winifred Mary Normile; two *d*. *Educ*: Wimbledon Coll.; King's College, London; London Sch. of Economics. CompIPM, FIB. Indian Armd Corps, 1940–46. Unilever Ltd, 1948–54; Philips Electrical Industries Ltd, 1954–60; Ilford Ltd, 1960–66; Dir of Personnel, Staveley Industries Ltd, 1966–69; Exec. Dir (Personnel), 1969–81, Dir, 1981–82, Williams & Glyn's Bank Ltd. Pres., Inst. of Personnel Management, 1971–73; Mem. Council, Inst. Bankers, 1975–81; Chairman: Manpower Services Adv. Panel, CBI, 1975–82; Educn and Trng Cttee, CBI, 1976–77 (Vice-Chm., 1977–82); Council, Fedn of London Clearing Bank Employers, 1976–78 (Mem., 1971–81). Member: Monopolies and Mergers Commn, 1975–81; MSC, 1981–82; EEC Vocational Trng Cttee, 1981–84. Member Council: Open Univ., 1980–; CBI Educn Found, 1976–. *Publications*: The Personnel Function in a Changing Environment, 1971, 2nd edn 1985; contrib. newspapers and personnel management and banking jls. *Recreations*: sailing, golf, music. *Address*: Winter Ride, 2 Rosefield, Kippington Road, Sevenoaks, Kent. *Clubs*: Army and Navy; Wildernesse Golf; Chipstead Sailing.

LYSAGHT, family name of **Baron Lisle.**

LYTHALL, Basil Wilfrid, CB 1966; MA; occasional research consultant; *b* 15 May 1919; *s* of Frank Herbert Lythall and Winifred Mary (*née* Carver); *m* 1942, Mary Olwen Dando; one *s*. *Educ*: King Edward's Sch., Stourbridge; Christ Church, Oxford. Joined Royal Naval Scientific Service, 1940; Admiralty Signal and Radar Establishment, 1940–53; Admiralty Research Laboratory, 1954–57; Asst Dir of Physical Research, Admty, 1957–58; a Dep. Chief Scientist, Admty Signal and Radar Estabt (later Admty Surface Weapons Estabt), 1958–60; first Chief Scientist of Admty Underwater Weapons Estabt, Portland, 1960–64; Member of Admiralty Bd of Defence Council and Chief Scientist (RN), 1964–78; Dep. Controller, R&D Estab., Procurement Exec., 1971–78; Dir, SACLANT Anti-Submarine Warfare Res. Centre, La Spezia, Italy, 1978–81. Chm., Policy Bd, Centre for Operational Res. and Defence Analysis, CAP Scientific Ltd, 1986–. Trustee, National Maritime Museum, 1974–80. UK Mem., Editorial Bd, Naval Forces, 1986–. *Publications*: occasional articles in learned jls. *Recreations*: gardening, sculpture, music. *Address*: 48 Grove Way, Esher, Surrey KT10 8HL. *T*: 01–398 2958.

LYTHGO, Wilbur Reginald, OBE 1964; HM Diplomatic Service, retired; *b* 7 June 1920; *yr s* of late Alfred and Marion Lythgo, Monkton, Ayrshire; *m* 1943, Patricia Frances Sylvia Smith; two *s*. *Educ*: Palmer's Sch., Grays, Essex. Joined Home Office, 1937. Served in RASC, 1939–41 and Indian Army, 1941–46. Rejoined Home Office, 1946; British Information Services, New Delhi, 1948–54; UK High Commn, New Delhi, 1956–59; British High Commn, Ottawa, 1962–66; Head of Office Services and Supply Dept, DSAO, 1966–68; Counsellor, British Embassy, and Consul-Gen., Washington DC, 1968–71; Consul-Gen., Cleveland, Ohio, 1971–73. Hon. Kentucky Col, 1971. *Recreations*: reading, gardening. *Address*: 200 Dovercourt Avenue, Ottawa, Ontario K1Z 7H2, Canada. *T*: (613) 722 3242.

LYTHGOE, Prof. Basil, FRS 1958; Professor of Organic Chemistry, Leeds University, 1953–78, now Emeritus; *b* 18 Aug. 1913; 2nd *s* of Peter Whitaker and Agnes Lythgoe; *m* 1946, Kathleen Cameron, *er d* of H. J. Hallum, St Andrews; two *s*. *Educ*: Leigh Grammar

Sch.; Manchester Univ. Asst Lectr, Manchester Univ., 1938; Univ. Lectr, Cambridge Univ., 1946. Fellow of King's Coll., Cambridge, 1950. *Publications:* papers on chemistry of natural products, in Jl of Chem. Soc. *Recreation:* mountaineering. *Address:* 113 Cookridge Lane, Leeds LS16 7NB. *T:* Leeds 678837.

LYTHGOE, Ian Gordon, CB 1975; company director; *b* 30 Dec. 1914; *s* of John and Susan Lythgoe; *m* 1st, 1939, Marjory Elsie Fleming; three *s*; 2nd, 1971, Mary Margaret Pickard, CBE 1980. *Educ:* Southland Boys' High Sch., Invercargill; Victoria UC, Wellington. MComm (Hons); FCA(NZ). Private Sec., Ministers of Finance, 1944–53; Asst Sec., Treasury, 1962; State Services Commission: Mem., 1964–66; Dep. Chm., 1967–70; Chm., 1971–74. NZ Soc. of Accountants: Mem. Council, 1966–76; Vice-Pres., 1973–74; Pres., 1974–75; Chm., Disciplinary Cttee, 1982– (Mem., 1979–). Mem. Council, Central Inst. of Technology, 1977–86 (Vice Chm., 1978–80, Chm., 1980–86). Member: Commn of Enquiry into Rescue and Fire Safety at Internat. Airports (NZ); Information Authority, 1982–; Commn of Enquiry concerning Ian David Donaldson, 1983. Director: Fletcher Challenge Corp. Ltd (formerly Challenge Corp. Ltd), 1975–84; Philips Electrical Industries Ltd, 1975–. *Recreations:* gardening, reading. *Address:* Winara Avenue, Waikanae, New Zealand. *T:* 35113. *Club:* Wellington (Wellington, NZ).

LYTTELTON, family name of **Viscount Chandos** and of **Viscount Cobham.**

LYTTELTON, Humphrey Richard Adeane; musician; band-leader (specializing in Jazz); journalist; *b* Eton, Bucks, 23 May 1921; *s* of late Hon. George William Lyttelton; *m* 1st, 1948, Patricia Mary Braithwaite (marr. diss. 1952); one *d*; 2nd, 1952, Elizabeth Jill, *d* of Albert E. Richardson; two *s* one *d. Educ:* Sunningdale Sch.; Eton Coll.; Camberwell Sch. of Art; self-taught as regards musical educn. Served War of 1939–45: Grenadier Guards, 1941–46. Cartoonist, Daily Mail, 1949–53. Formed his own band, 1948; leader of Humphrey Lyttelton's Band, and free-lance journalist, 1953–; founded: own record label, Calligraph, 1984; own music publishers, Humph Music. Has composed over 120 original works for his band; numerous recordings and television appearances; jazz festival appearances, Nice, Bracknell, Zürich, Camden, Montreux, Newcastle, Warsaw. Compère, BBC radio jazz programmes: Jazz Scene, Jazz Club, The Best of Jazz, etc. Vice-Pres., Soc. for Italic Handwriting. *Publications:* I Play as I Please, 1954; Second Chorus, 1958; Take It from the Top (autobiog.), 1975; The Best of Jazz: Basin Street to Harlem, 1978; Humphrey Lyttelton's Jazz and Big Band Quiz, 1979; The Best of Jazz 2—Enter the Giants, 1981; Why No Beethoven? the diary of a vagrant musician, 1984; contributor: Melody Maker, 1954–; Reynolds News, 1955–62; Sunday Citizen, 1962–67; Harper's & Queen's, Punch, The Field, High Life. *Recreations:* birdwatching, calligraphy. *Address:* BBC Light Music Department, Broadcasting House, Portland Place, W1A 4WW. *T:* 01–580 4468; (home) Alyn Close, Barnet Road, Arkley, Herts.

LYTTLE, James Brian Chambers; Under Secretary, Department of Finance and Personnel, Northern Ireland, since 1984; *b* 22 Aug. 1932; *s* of late James Chambers Lyttle and of Margaret Kirkwood Billingsley; *m* 1957, Mary Alma Davidson; four *d. Educ:* Bangor Grammar Sch.; Trinity Coll., Dublin (BA 1st Cl. Hons Classics). Entered NI Civil Service as Asst Principal, 1954; Private Sec. to Minister of Commerce, 1960–62; Chief Exec., Enterprise Ulster, 1972–75; Dir, Employment Service, Dept of Manpower Services,

1975–77; Under Secretary, Dept of Commerce, later Dept of Economic Develt, 1978–84; Dir, Industrial Develt Orgn, Dept of Commerce, 1977–81. *Recreations:* reading, walking, music.

LYTTLETON, Prof. Raymond Arthur, MA, PhD; FRS 1955; Emeritus Professor of Theoretical Astronomy, University of Cambridge; Fellow of St John's College, Cambridge; Member, Institute of Astronomy (formerly Institute of Theoretical Astronomy), University of Cambridge, since 1967; *o s* of William John Lyttleton and Agnes (*d* of Patrick Joseph Kelly), Warley Woods, near Birmingham, formerly of Ireland; *m* Meave Marguerite, *o d* of F. Hobden, Parkstone, formerly of Shanghai; no *c. Educ:* King Edward's Grammar Sch., Five Ways; King Edward's Sch., Birmingham; Clare Coll., Cambridge. Wrangler; Tyson Medal for Astronomy. Procter Visiting Fellowship, Princeton Univ., USA; Exptl Officer, Min. of Supply, 1940–42; Technical Asst to Scientific Adviser to the Army Council, War Office, 1943–45. Lectr in Mathematics, 1937–59, Stokes Lectr, 1954–59, Reader in Theoretical Astronomy, 1959–69 (resigned), Univ. of Cambridge. Jacob Siskind Vis. Prof., Brandeis Univ., USA, 1965–66; Vis. Prof., Brown Univ., USA, 1967–68; Halley Lectr, Oxford Univ., 1970; Milne Lectr, Oxford, 1978. Mem. of Council, Royal Society, 1959–61; Geophysical Sec. of Royal Astronomical Soc., 1949–60 and Mem. of Council, 1950–61, 1969–72; Fellow, 1934–; Pres., Milne Soc., 1977–. Hon. Mem., Mark Twain Soc., 1977. Hopkins Prize (for 1951) of Cambridge Philosophical Soc.; Gold Medallist of Royal Astronomical Soc., 1959; Royal Medallist of Royal Society, 1965. *Publications:* The Comets and their Origin, 1953; The Stability of Rotating Liquid Masses, 1953; The Modern Universe, 1956; Rival Theories of Cosmology, 1960; Man's View of the Universe, 1961; Mysteries of the Solar System, 1968; (Play) A Matter of Gravity (produced by BBC, 1968); Cambridge Encyclopædia of Astronomy (co-ed and contrib.), 1977; The Earth and Its Mountains, 1982; papers on astrophysics, cosmogony, cosmology, physics, dynamics, and geophysics in Proc. Royal Soc., Monthly Notices of Royal Astron. Soc., Proc. Camb. Phil Soc., etc. *Recreations:* golf, motoring, music; wondering about it all. *Address:* 165 Huntingdon Road, Cambridge. *T:* 354910; St John's College, Cambridge. *T:* 61621; Institute of Astronomy, Madingley Road, Cambridge. *T:* Cambridge 337548, ext. 7506.

LYTTON, family name of **Earl of Lytton.**

LYTTON, 5th Earl of, *cr* 1880; **John Peter Michael Scawen Lytton;** Baron Wentworth, 1529; Bt 1838; Baron Lytton, 1866; Viscount Knebworth, 1880; *b* 7 June 1950; *s* of 4th Earl of Lytton, OBE, and of Clarissa Mary, *d* of Brig.-Gen. C. E. Palmer, CB, CMG, DSO, RA; *S* father, 1985; *m* 1980, Ursula Alexandra (*née* Komoly); one *d Educ:* Downside; Reading Univ. (BSc, Estate Management), ARICS 1976. *Heir: b* Hon. Thomas Roland Cyril Lawrence Lytton, *b* 10 Aug. 1954.

LYVEDEN, 6th Baron *cr* 1859; **Ronald Cecil Vernon;** retired; *b* 10 April 1915; *s* of 5th Baron Lyveden and Ruby (*née* Shanley) (*d* 1932); *S* father 1973; *m* 1938, Queenie Constance, *d* of Howard Ardern; three *s. Educ:* Te Aroha College. *Heir: e s* Hon. Jack Leslie Vernon [*b* 10 Nov. 1938; *m* 1961, Lynette June, *d* of William Herbert Lilley; one *s* two *d*]. *Address:* 20 Farmer Street, Te Aroha, New Zealand. *T:* 410. *Club:* RSA (Te Aroha).

M

MA LIN, Hon. CBE 1983; PhD; JP; Vice-Chancellor, The Chinese University of Hong Kong, since 1978; *b* 8 Feb. 1925; *s* of late Prof. Ma Kiam and Sing-yu Cheng; *m* 1958, Dr Meng-Hua Chen; three *d*. *Educ:* West China Union Univ., China (BSc); Univ. of Leeds (PhD). Post-doctorate Fellow, University College Hosp. Med. Sch., London, and St James's Hosp., Leeds, 1955–56. Assistant Lectr, 1957–59, and Lectr, 1959–64, in Clinical Chemistry, Dept of Pathology, Univ. of Hong Kong; Chinese University of Hong Kong: part-time Lectr in Chemistry, 1964; Sen. Lectr, 1965–72, Reader, 1972–73, Prof., 1973–78, in Biochemistry; Dean of Faculty of Science, 1973–75. Visiting Biochemist, Hormone Research Laboratory, Univ. of California, San Francisco, 1969. FRSA 1982. Unofficial JP, 1978. Hon. DSc Sussex, 1984. *Publications:* various research papers in academic jls. *Recreations:* swimming, table-tennis. *Address:* The Vice-Chancellor's Residence, The Chinese University of Hong Kong, Shatin, New Territories, Hong Kong. *T:* 0–612581.

MAAN, Bashir Ahmed, JP; DL; Councillor, City of Glasgow District, 1974–84; Bailie, City of Glasgow, 1980–84; Judge, City of Glasgow District Courts; *b* Maan, Gujranwala, Pakistan, 22 Oct. 1926; *s* of Choudhry Sardar Khan Maan and late Mrs Hayat Begum Maan; *m*; one *s* three *d*. *Educ:* D. B. High Sch., Qila Didar Singh; Panjab Univ. Involved in struggle for creation of Pakistan, 1943–47; organised rehabilitation of refugees from India in Maan and surrounding areas, 1947–48; emigrated to UK and settled in Glasgow, 1953; Glasgow Founder Sec., Pakistan Social and Cultural Soc., 1955–65, Pres., 1966–69; Vice-Chm., Glasgow Community Relations Council, 1970–75; Pres., Standing Conf. of Pakistani Orgns in UK, 1974–77; a Dep. Chm., Commn for Racial Equality, 1977–80; Founder Chm., Scottish Pakistani Assoc., 1984–. Councillor, Glasgow Corp., 1970–75; Magistrate, City of Glasgow, 1971–74; Vice-Chm. 1971–74, Chm. 1974–75, Police Cttee, Glasgow Corp.; Police Judge, City of Glasgow, 1974–75; Mem. Exec. Cttee, Glasgow City Labour Party, 1969–70. Contested (Lab) East Fife, Feb. 1974. Mem., BBC Immigrants Programme Adv. Cttee, 1972–80; Convener, Pakistan Bill Action Cttee, 1973; Member: Nat. Road Safety Cttee, 1971–75; Scottish Accident Prevention Cttee, 1971–75; Scottish Gas Consumers' Council, 1978–81; Greater Glasgow Health Bd, 1981–. JP, DL, 1982, Glasgow. *Publications:* articles, contrib. to press. *Recreations:* golf, reading. *Address:* 20 Sherbrooke Avenue, Glasgow G41 4PE. *T:* 041–427 4057. *Club:* Douglas Park Golf.

MAAZEL, Lorin; symphony conductor; *b* 6 March 1930; *s* of Lincoln Maazel and Marie Varencove; *m* 1st, 1952, Miriam Sandbank; two *d*; 2nd, 1969, Israela Margalit; one *s* one *d*; 3rd, 1986, Dietlinde Turban. *Educ:* Pittsburgh University. FRCM 1981. Début as a conductor at age of 9, as violinist a few years later; by 1941 had conducted foremost US Orchestras, including Toscanini's NBC; since 1952, over 500 concerts in Europe and performances at major festivals, including Edinburgh, Bayreuth, Salzburg and Lucerne; in USA: conducted Boston Symphony, New York Philharmonic, Philadelphia Orchestra, and at Metropolitan, 1960 and 1962; Covent Garden début, 1978. Several world tours, including Latin America, Australia, USSR and Japan. Artistic Director of Deutsche Oper Berlin, 1965–71; Music Director, Radio Symphony Orchestra, 1965–75; Associate Principal Conductor, Philharmonia (formerly New Philharmonia) Orchestra, 1970–72, Principal Guest Conductor, 1976–80; Music Director, Cleveland Orchestra, 1972–82, Conductor Emeritus, 1982; Principal Guest Conductor, Orchestre National, 1977–; Director, Vienna State Opera, 1982–84. Has made numerous recordings. Hon. Dr of Music Pittsburgh Univ., 1968; Hon. Dr of Humanities Beaver Coll., 1973; Hon. Dr of Fine Arts, Carnegie-Mellon Univ., Pennsylvania. Commander's Cross of Order of Merit, Federal Republic of Germany, 1977; Officier, Légion d'Honneur, France, 1981. *Address:* c/o Cleveland Orchestra, Severance Hall, 11001 Euclid Avenue, Cleveland, Ohio 44106, USA.

MABBOTT, John David, CMG 1946; President of St John's College, Oxford, 1963–69; *b* 18 Nov. 1898; *s* of late Walter John and Elizabeth Mabbott; *m* 1934, Doreen Roach (*d* 1975). *Educ:* Berwickshire High Sch.; Edinburgh Univ.; St John's Coll., Oxford. Asst Lectr in Classics, Reading Univ., 1922; Asst Lectr in Philosophy, Univ. Coll. of North Wales, 1923; John Locke Scholar, Univ. of Oxford, 1923; Fellow of St John's Coll., Oxford, 1924–63, Tutor, 1930–63, and Hon. Fellow, 1969. *Publications:* The State and the Citizen, 1948; An Introduction to Ethics, 1966; John Locke, 1973; contribs to Philosophy, Proc. Aristotelian Soc., Classical Quarterly, Mind. *Address:* Wing Cottage, Mill Lane, Islip, Oxon. *T:* Kidlington 2360.

MABBS, Alfred Walter, CB 1982; Keeper of Public Records, 1978–82; *b* 12 April 1921; *e s* of James and Amelia Mabbs; *m* 1942, Dorothy Lowley; one *s*. *Educ:* Hackney Downs Sch. Served War, RAF, 1941–46. Asst Keeper, Public Record Office, 1950–66; Principal Asst Keeper, 1967–69; Records Admin. Officer, 1970–73; Dep. Keeper of Public Records, 1973–78. Pres., Internat. Council on Archives, 1980–82. FRHistS 1954. FSA 1979. *Publications:* Guild Stewards Book of the Borough of Calne (vol. vii, Wilts Arch. and Record Soc.), 1953; The Records of the Cabinet Office to 1922, 1966; Guide to the Contents of the Public Record Office, vol. iii (main contributor), 1968; Exchequer of the Jews, vol. iv (jt contrib.), 1972; The Organisation of Intermediate Records Storage (with Guy Duboscq), 1974; articles and reviews in various jls. *Recreations:* golf, reading. *Address:* 14 Acorn Lane, Cuffley, Herts EN6 4JQ. *T:* Cuffley 873660.

MABEY, Richard Thomas; writer and broadcaster; *b* 20 Feb. 1941; *s* of late Thomas Gustavus Mabey and of Edna Nellie (*née* Moore). *Educ:* Berkhamsted Sch.; St Catherine's Coll., Oxford (BA Hons 1964, MA 1971). Lectr in Social Studies, Dacorum Coll. of Further Educn, 1963–65; Sen. Editor, Penguin Books, 1966–73; freelance writer, 1973–. Pres., London Wildlife Trust, 1982–; Member: Nature Conservancy Council, 1982–; Council, Botanical Soc. of the British Isles, 1981–83. Leverhulme Trust Res. Award, 1983–84. *Publications:* (ed) Class, 1967; The Pop Process, 1969; Food for Free, 1972; Children in Primary School, 1972; The Unofficial Countryside, 1973; The Pollution Handbook, 1973; The Roadside Wildlife Book, 1974; Street Flowers, 1976; Plants with a Purpose, 1977; The Common Ground, 1980; The Flowering of Britain, 1980; (ed) Landscape with Figures, 1983; Oak and Company, 1983; In a Green Shade, 1983; Back to the Roots, 1983; (ed) Second Nature, 1984; The Frampton Flora, 1985; Gilbert White: a biography, 1986. *Recreations:* food, woods, walking, gardening. *Address:* 10 Cedar Road, Berkhamsted, Herts. *Club:* Groucho.

MABON, Rt. Hon. (Jesse) Dickson, PC 1977; Chairman: British Indigenous Technology Group, since 1984; A. H. McIntosh Ltd; Hall Russell Offshore plc; *b* 1 Nov. 1925; *s* of Jesse Dickson Mabon and Isabel Simpson Montgomery; *m* 1970, Elizabeth, *o d* of William Zinn, *qv*; one *s*. *Educ:* Possilpark, Cumbrae, North Kelvinside Schools. Worked in coalmining industry before Army service, 1944–48. MB, ChB (Glasgow); DHMSA; MFHom; Visiting Physician, Manor House Hospital, London, 1958–64. Political columnist, Scottish Daily Record, 1955–64; studied under Dr Kissinger, Harvard, 1963. President: Glasgow University Union, 1951–52; Scottish Union of Students, 1954–55; Chairman: Glasgow Univ. Labour Club, 1948–50; National Assoc. of Labour Students, 1949–50. Contested: (Lab) Bute and N Ayrshire, 1951; (Lab and Co-op) W Renfrewshire, 1955; (SDP) Renfrew W and Inverclyde, 1983; (SDP) Lothians, European Parly Election, 1984. MP (Lab and Co-op 1955–81, SDP 1981–83) Greenock, Dec. 1955–1974, Greenock and Port Glasgow, 1974–83; Joint Parly Under-Sec. of State for Scotland, 1964–67; Minister of State, Scottish Office, 1967–70; Dep. Opposition Spokesman on Scotland, 1970–72 (resigned over Labour's attitude to Common Mkt); Minister of State, Dept of Energy, 1976–79. Chairman: UK Labour Cttee for Europe, 1974–76; Scottish Parly Labour Party, 1972–73, 1975–76; Member: Council of Europe, 1970–72 and 1974–76; Assembly, WEU, 1970–72 and 1974–76; North Atlantic Assembly, 1980–82; Chm., European Movement, 1975–76, Dep. Chm., 1979–83. Founder Chm., Manifesto Gp, Parly Lab. Party, 1974–76. Founder Mem., SDP, 1981–; Mem., SDP Nat. Cttee, 1984–. Chm., RGC (Offshore) plc, 1979–82 (Dep. Chm., 1982–83). Chm., Young Volunteer Force Foundn, 1974–76. Fellow: Inst. of Petroleum; Inst. of Directors; Faculty of History of Medicine; Soc. of Apothecaries; FRSA. Freeman of City of London. *Recreations:* golf, theatre. *Address:* 2 Sandringham, Largs KA30 8BT.

MABY, (Alfred) Cedric, CBE 1962; HM Diplomatic Service, retired; *b* 6 April 1915; 4th *s* of late Joseph Maby, Penrose, Monmouthshire; *m* 1944, Anne-Charlotte, *d* of Envoyén Einar Modig, Stockholm; one *s* two *d*. *Educ:* Cheltenham; Keble Coll., Oxford. Joined HM Consular Service, 1939. Served at Peking, 1939, Chungking, 1940, Tsingtao, 1941, Istanbul, 1943, Angora, 1944, Buenos Aires, 1946, Caracas, 1949, Singapore, 1954; Counsellor and Consul-General, Peking, 1957–59 (Chargé d'Affaires, 1957 and 1958); Deputy Consul-General, New York, 1959–62; Counsellor (Commercial) at Vienna, 1962–64; Asst Sec., Min. of Overseas Development, 1964–67; Consul-General, Zürich and Liechtenstein, 1968–71; Dir, Trade Promotion for Switzerland, 1970–71. Member: Governing Body, Church in Wales, 1975–78; Church in Wales Adv. Commn on Church and Society, 1977–. Fellow, Huguenot Soc., London. High Sheriff of Gwynedd, 1976. *Publications:* Dail Melyn o Tseina, 1983; Y Cocatŵ Coch, 1986; contribs to Planet, Y Faner and other Welsh periodicals. *Address:* Cae Canol, Minffordd, Penrhyn-Deudraeth, Gwynedd LL48 6EN.

McADAM, Sir Ian (William James), Kt 1966; OBE 1957; FRCS, FRCSE; *b* 15 Feb. 1917; *s* of W. J. McAdam and Alice Culverwell; *m* 1st, 1939, Hrothgarde Gibson (marr. diss. 1961); one *s* two *d*; 2nd, 1967, Lady (Pamela) Hunt (*née* Medawar). *Educ:* Plumtree Sch., S Rhodesia; Edinburgh Univ. MB, ChB. Cambridge Anatomy Sch., 1940; Dept of Surgery, Edinburgh, 1942; Wilkie Surgical Research Fellow, 1942; Clinical Tutor, Royal Infirmary, Edinburgh, 1942; Surgical Specialist, Uganda, 1946; Senior Consultant, Uganda, 1957; Prof. of Surgery, Makerere Univ., Univ. of E Africa, 1957–72, also Consultant Surgeon Uganda Govt and Kenyatta Hosp., Kenya; Consultant to Nat. Insts of Health, Bethesda, Md, 1973–74. *Publications:* various papers in medical jls. *Recreations:* golf, gardening. *Address:* Box 166, Plettenberg Bay, Cape Province, South Africa.

See also Sir Peter Medawar.

MACADAM, Sir Peter, Kt 1981; Chairman: BAT Industries plc, 1976–82; Libra Bank, since 1984; *b* 9 Sept. 1921; *s* of late Francis Macadam and Marjorie Mary Macadam (*née* Browne); *m* 1949, Ann Musson; three *d*. *Educ:* Buenos Aires, Argentina; Stonyhurst Coll., Lancs. Served as Officer in Queen's Bays, 1941–46. Joined BAT Gp tobacco co., Argentina, 1946; Chm. and Gen. Man., gp co., Argentina, 1955–58; PA in London to Dir resp. for Africa, 1959–60 (travelled widely in Africa); Chm., BAT Hong Kong, 1960–62; BAT Main Bd, 1963 (resp. at times for interest in S and Central Africa, S and Central America and Caribbean); Mem., Chm.'s Policy Cttee with overall resp. for tobacco interests and special interest, USA, Canada and Mexico, 1970; Chm., Tobacco Div. Bd and Dir, Gp HQ Bd, 1973; Vice-Chm., 1975. Dir, National Westminster Bank, 1978–84. Chm., British Nat. Cttee, ICC, 1978–85; Mem. Exec. Cttee, ICC, Paris, 1982–85. Pres., Hispanic and Luso Brazilian Council, 1982–. Hon. FBIM; FRSA 1975. *Recreations:* golf, shooting. *Address:* Layham Hall, Layham, near Hadleigh, Suffolk IP7 5LE. *T:* Hadleigh 822137. *Club:* Canning.

McADAM CLARK, James; *see* Clark, James McAdam.

McADOO, Most Rev. Henry Robert, PhD, STD, DD; *b* 1916; *s* of James Arthur and Susan McAdoo; *m* 1940, Lesley Dalriel Weir; one *s* two *d*. *Educ:* Cork Grammar School; Mountjoy School, Dublin; Deacon, 1939; Priest, 1940; Curate of Holy Trinity Cathedral,

Waterford, 1939–43; Incumbent of Castleventry with Ardfield, 1943–48 (with Kilmeen, 1947–48); Rector of Kilmocomogue, Diocese of Cork, 1948–52; Rural Dean of Glansalney West and Bere, 1948–52; Canon of Kilbrittain in Cork Cathedral, and Canon of Donoughmore in Cloyne Cathedral, 1949–52; Dean of Cork, 1952–62; Canon of St Patrick's Cathedral, Dublin, 1960–62; Bishop of Ossory, Ferns and Leighlin, 1962–77; Archbishop of Dublin and Primate of Ireland, 1977–85. Member, Anglican-Roman Catholic Preparatory Commission, 1967–68; Jt Chm., Anglican-Roman Catholic International Commission, 1969–81 (Canterbury Cross). *Publications:* The Structure of Caroline Moral Theology, 1949; John Bramhall and Anglicanism, 1964; The Spirit of Anglicanism, 1965; Modern Eucharist Agreement, 1973; Modern Ecumenical Documents on Ministry, 1975; Being an Anglican, 1977; Rome and the Anglicans, 1982; The Unity of Anglicanism: Catholic and Reformed, 1983. *Address:* 2 The Paddocks, Dalkey, Co. Dublin. *Club:* Kildare Street and University (Dublin).

McALISKEY, (Josephine) Bernadette, (Mrs Micheal McAliskey); Chairman, Independent Socialist Party, Ireland; *b* 23 April 1947; *d* of late John James Devlin and Elizabeth Devlin; *m* 1973, Micheal McAliskey; three *c. Educ:* St Patrick's Girls' Acad., Dungannon; psychology student at Queen's Univ., Belfast, 1966–69. Youngest MP in House of Commons when elected at age of 21; MP (Ind. Unity) Mid Ulster, Apr. 1969–Feb. 1974. Founder Member and Mem. Exec., Irish Republican Socialist Party, 1975–76. Contested: (Ind) N Ireland, European Parlt, 1979; (People's Democracy), Dublin N Central, Dáil Eireann, Feb. and Nov. 1982. *Publication:* The Price of my Soul (autobiog.), 1969. *Recreations:* walking, folk music, doing nothing, swimming.

McALISTER, Michael Ian, FCA; a Director, Cluff Oil, since 1984; *b* Leeds, Yorkshire, 23 Aug. 1930; *s* of S. McAlister, CBE, and J. A. McAlister (*née* Smith); *m* 1953, Patricia (*née* Evans); four *s* three *d. Educ:* Brazil; France; St John's Coll., Oxford (MA). Articled Clerk, Price Waterhouse, London, 1954–58; Private Sec. to the Duke of Windsor, 1959–61; Investment Manager, Ionian Bank Ltd, London, 1961–67; Managing Dir, Ionian Bank Trustee Co, London, 1967–68; Slater Walker Securities (Australia): Dep. Chm., 1969–70, Chm., 1970–72; Pres., Aust. Associated Stock Exchanges, 1972–74. *Recreations:* game fishing, archery, swimming. *Address:* Cluff Oil PLC, 58 St James's Street, SW1A 1LD.

McALISTER, Maj.-Gen. Ronald William Lorne, CB 1977; OBE 1968 (MBE 1959); Bursar, Wellesley House School, Broadstairs, since 1977; *b* 26 May 1923; 2nd *s* of late Col R. J. F. McAlister, OBE and Mrs T. M. Collins, Bath; *m* 1964, Sally Ewart Marshall; two *d. Educ:* Dreghorn Castle Sch., Edinburgh; Sedbergh School. Commnd 3rd QAO Gurkha Rifles, 1942; Adjt 1/3 GR Burma, 1945 (despatches); Adjt 2/10 GR Malaya, 1950–52 (despatches); Instructor, Sch. of Infantry, 1953–55; psc 1956; Bde Major 99 Gurkha Bde, Malaya, 1957–59 (MBE); jssc 1961–62; Asst Sec., Chiefs of Staff Cttee, 1962–64; 2nd in comd and CO 10th PMO Gurkha Rifles, Borneo, 1964–66 (despatches); Internal Security Duties, Hong Kong, 1967–68 (OBE); Instructor, Jt Services Staff Coll., 1968; comd Berlin Inf. Bde, 1968–71; ndc, Canada, 1971–72; Exercise Controller UK Cs-in-C Cttee, 1972–75; Dep. Commander Land Forces Hong Kong and Maj.-Gen. Brigade of Gurkhas, 1975–77; retired 1977. Col, 10th Princess Mary's Own Gurkha Rifles, 1977–85; Chm., Gurkha Brigade Assoc., 1980–. *Recreations:* golf, gardening. *Address:* The Chalet, 41 Callis Court Road, Broadstairs, Kent. *T:* Thanet 62351. *Clubs:* Army and Navy; Royal St George's Golf, Senior Golfers' Society.

McALISTER, William Harle Nelson; Director, Institute of Contemporary Arts, since 1977; *b* 30 Aug. 1940; *s* of Flying Officer William Nelson (*d* 1940) and Marjorie Isobel (*née* McIntyre); adopted by William Edwyn McAlister (whom she *m* 2nd); *m* 1968, Sarah Stone (marr. diss. 1985); two *s* two *d. Educ:* Sorbonne, Paris; Univ. of Copenhagen (BA Hons Psychology, 1967); University Coll. London. Dir, Almost Free Theatre, 1968–72; Dep. Dir, Inter-Action Trust, 1968–72; Founder Dir, Islington Bus Co., 1972–77; Dir, Battersea Arts Centre, 1976–77. Dir, Sense of Ireland Fest., 1980–; Bd Dir, London International Theatre Fest., 1983; Chm. for the Arts, IT 82 Cttee, 1982. Chm., Recreational Trust, 1972–; Co-Founder, Fair Play for Children, 1974–75; Advr, Task Force Trust, 1972–74; Trustee: Circle 33 Housing Trust, 1972–75; Moving Picture Mime Trust, 1978–80; Shape (Arts for the Disadvantaged), 1979–81. Governor, Holloway Adult Educn Inst., 1974–76. Mem. Court, RCA, 1980–. British Deleg. to Ministerial Conf. on cultural policy, Bulgaria, 1980; British Cultural Deleg., China, 1982. *Publications:* Community Psychology, 1975; EEC and the Arts, 1978; articles on Arts Policy. *Recreations:* angling, tennis, travel. *Address:* 151c Grosvenor Avenue, N5. *T:* 01–226 0205; Institute of Contemporary Arts, Nash House, The Mall, SW1. *T:* 01–930 0493.

McALLISTER, John Brian; Chief Executive, Industrial Development Board for Northern Ireland, since 1985 (Deputy Chief Executive, 1984–85); *b* 11 June 1941; *s* of late Thomas McAllister and of Jane (*née* McCloughan); *m* 1966, Margaret Lindsay Walker; two *d. Educ:* Royal Belfast Academical Instn; Queen's Univ., Belfast (BA Hons). Joined NI Civil Service as Asst Principal, Dept of Educn, 1964; Dep. Principal, Higher Educn Div., 1968; Principal: Secondary Schs Br., 1969; Re-Organisation of Local Govt Br., 1970; Principal, Dept of Finance, 1971, Dept's Central Secretariat, 1972; Asst Sec. 1973, Sen. Asst Sec. 1976, Dep. Sec., 1978–80, Dept of Educn; Dep. Sec., later Under Sec., Dept of Finance, 1980–83; Under Sec., DoE, NI, 1983–84. *Recreations:* watching sport of all kinds, reading, jogging. *Address:* IDB House, Chichester Street, Belfast BT1 4JX.

McALPINE, family name of **Barons McAlpine of Moffat** and **McAlpine of West Green.**

McALPINE OF MOFFAT, Baron *cr* 1980 (Life Peer), of Medmenham in the County of Buckinghamshire; **Robert Edwin McAlpine;** Bt 1918; Kt 1963; Partner, Sir Robert McAlpine & Sons, since 1928; Deputy Chairman, British Nuclear Associates, since 1973; Chairman, Greycoat London Estates Ltd, since 1978; *b* 23 April 1907; *s* of William Hepburn McAlpine and Margaret Donnison; *S* to baronetcy of brother, Sir Thomas George Bishop McAlpine, 4th Bt, 1983; *m* 1930, Ella Mary Gardner Garnett; three *s* one *d. Educ:* Oundle. Joined Sir Robert McAlpine & Sons, 1925. Chm. Trustees, Apprentice Sch. Charitable Trust, 1980–. *Recreations:* breeding race horses, farming, travel, golf, theatre. *Heir* (to baronetcy only): *s* Hon. William Hepburn McAlpine [*b* 12 Jan. 1936; *m* 1959, Jill Benton, *o d* of Lt-Col Sir Peter Fawcett Benton Jones, 3rd Bt, OBE, ACA; one *s* one *d*]. *Address:* Benhams, Fawley Green, Henley-on-Thames, Oxon. *T:* Henley-on-Thames 571246. *Clubs:* Garrick, Buck's, Caledonian, Jockey.

See also Baron McAlpine of West Green.

McALPINE OF WEST GREEN, Baron *cr* 1984 (Life Peer), of West Green in the County of Hampshire; **Robert Alistair McAlpine;** Hon. Treasurer, Conservative and Unionist Party, since 1975, jointly since 1981 (Deputy Chairman, 1979–83); Director, Sir Robert McAlpine & Sons Ltd, since 1963; *b* 14 May 1942; *s* of Lord McAlpine of Moffat, *qv*; *m* 1964, Sarah Alexandra Baron (marr. diss. 1979); two *d*; *m* 1980, Romilly, *o d* of A. T. Hobbs, Cranleigh, Surrey; one *d. Educ:* Stowe. Joined Sir Robert McAlpine & Sons Ltd, 1958. Hon. Treasurer: Europ. Democratic Union, 1978–; Europ. League for Econ. Co-operation, 1974–75, Vice Pres., 1975–. Director: George Weidenfeld Holdings Ltd, 1975–83; ICA, 1972–73. Mem., Arts Council of GB, 1981–82; Vice-President: Friends of Ashmolean Museum, 1969–; Greater London Arts Assoc., 1971–77; Vice-Chm., Contemporary Arts Soc., 1973–80. Pres., British Waterfowl Assoc., 1978–81, Patron 1981–. Member: Friends of V&A Museum, 1976–; Council, English Stage Co., 1973–75. Trustee, Royal Opera House Trust, 1974–80; Dir, Theatre Investment Fund, 1981– (Chm., 1985–). Governor: Polytechnic of the South Bank, 1981–82; Stowe Sch., 1981–84. *Recreations:* the arts, horticulture, aviculture, agriculture. *Address:* West Green House, Hartley Wintney, near Basingstoke, Hants. *Clubs:* Garrick, Carlton, Buck's, Beefsteak.

McALPINE, Christopher; *see* McAlpine, R. D. C.

McALPINE, Robert Douglas Christopher, CMG 1967; HM Diplomatic Service, retired; Director: Baring Brothers, 1969–79; H. Clarkson (Holdings) plc, since 1980; *b* 14 June 1919; *s* of late Dr Douglas McAlpine, FRCP and late Elizabeth Meg Sidebottom; *m* 1943, Helen Margery Frances Cannan; two *s* one *d* (and one *d* decd). *Educ:* Winchester; New Coll., Oxford. RNVR, 1939–46. Entered Foreign Service, 1946. FO, 1946–47; Asst Private Sec. to Sec. of State, 1947–49; 2nd Sec. and later 1st Sec., UK High Commn at Bonn, 1949–52; FO, 1952–54; Lima, 1954–56; Moscow, 1956–59; FO, 1959–62; Dep. Consul-Gen. and Counsellor, New York, 1962–65; Counsellor, Mexico City, 1965–69. *Recreations:* sailing, tennis, fishing, photography. *Address:* Longtree House, Cutwell, Tetbury, Glos GL8 8EB. *Club:* United Oxford & Cambridge University.

McALPINE, Sir Robin, Kt 1969; CBE 1957; Director, Newarthill plc, 1972 (Chairman, 1972–77); Chairman, Sir Robert McAlpine & Sons Ltd, 1967–77; *b* 18 March 1906; *s* of late Sir (Thomas) Malcolm McAlpine, KBE, and late Lady (Maud) McAlpine; *m* 1st, 1939, Nora Constance (*d* 1966), *d* of F. H. Perse; 2nd, 1970, Mrs Philippa Nicolson, *d* of Sir Gervais Tennyson D'Eyncourt, 2nd Bt. *Educ:* Charterhouse. Pres., Federation of Civil Engineering Contractors, 1966–71. *Recreation:* owner and breeder of racehorses. *Address:* Aylesfield, Alton, Hants. *Club:* Jockey.

MacANDREW, family name of **Baron MacAndrew.**

MacANDREW, 2nd Baron *cr* 1959; **Colin Nevil Glen MacAndrew;** *b* 1 Aug. 1919; *s* of 1st Baron MacAndrew, PC, TD, and of Lilian Cathleen, *d* of James Prendergast Curran, St Andrews; *S* father, 1979; *m* 1943, Ursula Beatrice (*d* 1986), *d* of Captain Joseph Steel; two *s* one *d. Educ:* Eton College; Trinity College, Cambridge. Served War, 1939–45. *Recreations:* hunting, racing, golf. *Heir: s* Hon. Christopher Anthony Colin MacAndrew [*b* 16 Feb. 1945; *m* 1975, Sarah, *o d* of Lt-Col P. H. Brazier; one *s* two *d*]. *Address:* Dilston House, Aldborough St John, Richmond, Yorks. *T:* Piercebridge 272.

MACARA, Sir (Charles) Douglas, 3rd Bt *cr* 1911; *b* 19 April 1904; *s* of 2nd Bt and Lillian Mary (*d* 1971), *d* of John Chapman, Boyton Court, East Sutton, Kent; *S* father, 1931; *m* 1926, Quenilda (marr. diss. 1945), *d* of late Herbert Whitworth, St Anne's-on-Sea; two *d* (one *s* decd). *Heir: b* Hugh Kenneth Macara, *b* 17 Jan. 1913.

McARDLE, Michael John Francis, MB, BS (Hons, London), FRCP; Consulting Physician Emeritus for Nervous Diseases, Guy's Hospital; Consulting Physician Emeritus, The National Hospital, Queen Square, WC1; Hon. Consulting Neurologist, Kingston Hospital and St Teresa's Maternity Hospital, Wimbledon, SW19; *b* 1909; *s* of Andrew McArdle; *m* 1955, Maureen MacClancy (*d* 1978). *Educ:* Wimbledon Coll.; Guy's Hospital; Paris. Entrance Scholarship, Arts, Guy's Hospital. Medical Registrar, Guy's Hospital; Asst Medical Officer, Maudsley Hospital. Rockefeller Travelling Fellow in Neurology, 1938. War of 1939–45, Temp. Lt-Col, RAMC and Adviser in Neurology, 21st Army Group. *Publications:* papers on neurological subjects in medical journals. *Recreation:* golf. *Address:* 3 Kingsdown, 115A The Ridgway, SW19 4RL. *T:* 01–946 4149.

McARDLE, Rear-Adm. Stanley Lawrence, CB 1975; LVO 1952; GM 1953; JP; Flag Officer, Portsmouth, and Port Admiral, Portsmouth, 1973–75; retired; *b* 1922; *s* of Theodore McArdle, Lochmaben, Dumfiresshire; *m* 1st, 1945, (Helen) Joyce, *d* of Owen Cummins, Wickham, Hants; one *d*; 2nd, 1962, Jennifer, *d* of Walter Talbot Goddard, Salisbury, Wilts; one *d. Educ:* Royal Hospital Sch., Holbrook, Suffolk. Joined RN, 1938; served War, 1939–45. Lieut 1945; Comdr 1956; Captain 1963. Directorate of Naval Operations and Trade, 1969; Comd HMS Glamorgan, 1970; Dir Naval Trng, Director General, Personal Services and Trng (Naval), 1971–73; Rear Admiral 1972. Dir, Endless Holdings Ltd. JP Wilts, 1977. *Address:* Barn Ridge Cottage, Farley, Salisbury, Wilts.

MACARTHUR, Rev. Arthur Leitch, OBE 1981; MA, MLitt; inducted, Christ Church, Marlow-on-Thames, 1980, retired 1986; *b* 9 Dec. 1913; *s* of Edwin Macarthur and Mary Macarthur (*née* Leitch); *m* 1950, Doreen Esmé Muir; three *s* one *d. Educ:* Rutherford Coll.; Armstrong Coll., Durham Univ. (MA, MLitt Dunelm); Westminster Coll., Cambridge. Ordained, 1937; inducted, Clayport, Alnwick, 1937; served with YMCA in France, 1940. Inducted: St Augustine's, New Barnet, 1944; St Columba's, North Shields, 1950. Gen. Sec., Presbyterian Church of England, 1960–72; Moderator, Presbyterian Church of England, 1971–72; Jt Gen.-Sec., URC, 1972–74; Moderator, URC, 1974–75; Gen. Sec., URC, 1975–80; Moderator, Free Church Federal Council, 1980–81. Vice-Pres., BCC, 1974–77 (Chm., Admin. Cttee, 1969–74). Director: Tavistock Court Ltd; URC Insurance Co., etc. *Recreations:* gardening, golf, walking. *Address:* Haywards Corner, Randalls Green, Chalford Hill, near Stroud, Glos GL6 8HL. *T:* Brimscombe 883700.

MacARTHUR, Brian; Editor-in-Chief, Today, since 1986; *b* 5 Feb. 1940; *o s* of late S. H. MacArthur and of Mrs M. MacArthur; *m* 1975, Bridget Trahair; two *d. Educ:* Brentwood Sch.; Helsby Grammar Sch.; Leeds Univ. (BA). Yorkshire Post, 1962–64; Daily Mail, 1964–66; The Guardian, 1966–67; The Times: Education Correspondent, 1967–70; Dep. Features Editor, 1970–71; Founder Editor, The Times Higher Educn Supplement, 1971–76; Home News Editor, 1976–78; Dep. Editor, Evening Standard, 1978–79; Chief Asst to the Editor, The Sunday Times, 1979–81, Exec. Editor (News), The Times, 1981–82; Jt Dep. Editor, The Sunday Times, 1982–84; Editor, Western Morning News, 1984–85. Hon. MA, Open Univ., 1976. *Publications:* several contribs to educnl and political symposia, incl. (jtly) The Struggle for Education (Nat. Union of Teachers' Centenary), 1970; (jtly) An Interim History of The Open University, in The Open University Opens, 1974. *Recreations:* reading, gardening. *Address:* (office) 70 Vauxhall Bridge Road, SW1V 2RP. *T:* 01–630 1300; (home) 50 Lanchester Road, N6. *T:* 01–883 1855. *Club:* Reform.

MacARTHUR, Mrs Charles; *see* Hayes, Helen.

MACARTHUR, Charles Ramsay, QC (Scot.) 1970; Sheriff of Tayside, Central and Fife, since 1981; *s* of late Alastair and late Joan Macarthur; *m* 1973, Rosemary Valda Morgan (marr. diss. 1982), Edinburgh. *Educ:* Glasgow Univ. (MA, LLB). Served War of 1939–45: joined Royal Navy, 1942; demobilised as Lieut, RNVR, 1946. Solicitor, 1952–59; admitted Scottish Bar, 1960; Standing Junior Counsel, Highlands and Islands Development Board, 1968–70; Sheriff of the Lothians and Borders, 1974–76. *Recreations:* travel, talking. *Address:* Sheriff's Chambers, Sheriff Court, Kirkcaldy, Fife. *Club:* New (Edinburgh).

MacARTHUR, Ian; Director, British Textile Confederation, since 1977; *b* 17 May 1925; *yr s* of late Lt-Gen. Sir William MacArthur, KCB, DSO, MD, DSc, FRCP, KHP; *m* 1957,

Judith Mary, (RGN 1976), *d* of late Francis Gavin Douglas Miller; four *s* three *d*. *Educ:* Cheltenham Coll.; The Queen's Coll., Oxford (Scholar, MA). Contested (U), Greenock Gen. Election, May 1955, also by-election, Dec. 1955; MP (C) Perth and E Perthshire, 1959–Sept. 1974; Chm., Scottish Cons. Mems' Cttee, 1972–73. Introduced, as Private Member's Bills: Law Reform (Damages and Solatium) (Scotland) Act, 1962; Interest on Damages (Scotland) Act, 1971; Social Work (Scotland) Act, 1972; Domicile and Matrimonial Proceedings Act, 1973. An Asst Government Whip (unpaid), 1962–63; a Lord Comr of the Treasury and Govt Scottish Whip, 1963–64; Opposition Scottish Whip, 1964–65; an Opposition Spokesman on Scottish Affairs, 1965–70. Personal Asst to the Prime Minister, Rt Hon. Sir Alec Douglas-Home, Kinross and W Perthshire By Election, Nov. 1963. Hon. Pres., Scottish Young Unionists, 1962–65; Vice-Chm., Cons. Party in Scotland, 1972–75. Formerly Dir of Administration, J. Walter Thompson Co. Ltd. Served War of 1939–45, with RN and RNVR, 1943–46 (King's Badge; Flag Lieut to C-in-C Portsmouth, 1946). FRSA 1984. Gold Cross of Merit, Polish Govt in Exile, 1971. *Address:* 15 Old Palace Lane, Richmond, Surrey. *Clubs:* Naval; Puffin's (Edinburgh).
See also R. A. G. Douglas Miller.

McARTHUR, Dr Thomas Burns, (Tom); English teacher, since 1959; feature writer, since 1962; lecturer and writer on yoga and Indian philosophy, since 1962; author and language consultant, since 1970; Editor, English Today, since 1984; *b* 23 Aug. 1938; *s* of Archibald McArthur and Margaret Burns; *m* 1963, Fereshteh Mottahedin; one *s* two *d*. *Educ:* Glasgow Univ. (MA 1958); Edinburgh Univ. (MLitt 1970; PhD 1978). Officer-Instr, RAEC, 1959–61; Asst Master, Riland Bedford Sch., Warwicks, 1961–63; Head of English, Cathedral and John Connon Sch., Bombay, India, 1965–67; Vis. Prof. in the English of the Media, Rajendra Prasad College of Mass Communication (Bharatiya Vidya Bhavan), Univ. of Bombay, 1965–67; Dir of Extra-Mural English Language Courses, Univ. of Edinburgh, 1972–79; Associate Prof. of English, Université du Québec à Trois-Rivières, Canada, 1979–83. Consultant: Min. of Educn, Quebec, 1980–81; Société pour la promotion de l'enseignement de l'anglais (langue seconde) au Québec, 1980–83; Henson International Television, 1985–86; also on dictionaries and ELT books published by Chambers, Collins, CUP and Longman. *Publications:* Patterns of English series, 1972–74; English for Students of Economics, 1973; (with Beryl Atkins) Collins Dictionary of English Phrasal Verbs, 1974; (ed with A. J. Aitken) Languages of Scotland, 1979; Longman Lexicon of Contemporary English, 1981; A Foundation Course for Language Teachers, 1983; The Written Word, Books 1 and 2, 1984; Worlds of Reference, 1986; Yoga and the Bhagavad-Gita, 1986; Understanding Yoga, 1986. *Recreations:* reading, television, walking, cycling, travel. *Address:* 22–23 Ventress Farm Court, Cherry Hinton Road, Cambridge CB1 4HD. *T:* Cambridge 245934.

MACARTNEY, Sir John Barrington, 6th Bt *cr* 1799, of Lish, Co. Armagh; dairy farmer, retired; *b* 21 Jan. 1917; *s* of John Barrington Macartney (3rd *s* of Sir John Macartney, 3rd Bt; he *d* 1951) and Selina Koch, Hampden, Mackay, Qld, Australia; *S* uncle, Sir Alexander Miller Macartney, 5th Bt, 1960; *m* 1944, Amy Isobel Reinke (*d* 1978); one *s*. *Heir: s* John Ralph Macartney [*b* 24 July 1945; *m* 1966, Suzanne Marie Fowler; four *d*]. *Address:* 37 Meadow Street, North Mackay, Qld 4740, Australia.

MACAULAY, Janet Stewart Alison, MA; Headmistress of St Leonards and St Katharines Schools, St Andrews, 1956–70; *b* 20 Dec. 1909; 3rd *d* of late Rev. Prof. A. B. Macaulay, DD, of Trinity Coll., Glasgow. *Educ:* Laurel Bank Sch., Glasgow; Glasgow Univ.; Somerville Coll., Oxford. BA Oxon 1932; BLitt Oxon 1934; MA Oxon 1936. Asst Mistress, Wycombe Abbey Sch., Bucks, 1933–36; Sutton High Sch. (GPDST), Sutton, Surrey, 1937–45; Headmistress, Blackheath High Sch. (GPDST), 1945–Dec. 1955. Hon. LLD St Andrews, 1977. *Address:* 3 Drummond Place, Edinburgh EH3 6PH.

McAULAY, (John) Roy (Vincent); QC 1978; a Recorder of the Crown Court, since 1975; Barrister-at-law, practising mainly in London and on Midland and Oxford Circuit; a legal assessor to General Medical Council and General Dental Council, since 1981; *b* 9 Sept. 1933; *er s* of Dr John McAulay and Mrs Marty McAulay (*née* Hüni), West Wickham, Kent; *m* 1970, Ruth Hamilton Smith, Sundridge, Kent; one *s* one *d*. *Educ:* Whitgift Sch. (Victoria Scholar); Queens' Coll., Cambridge (MA Hons). National Service, Intelligence Corps, 1951–53. Called to Bar, Gray's Inn, 1957 (Lord Justice Holker Scholar); Recorder, Midland Circuit, 1965–67; Mem., Gen. Council of Bar, 1967–71. Mem. Council, Medico-Legal Soc, 1984–. *Publications:* contrib. Halsbury's Laws of England, 3rd and 4th edns, and other legal pubns. *Recreations:* walking, swimming, animals, sport. *Address:* 1 Harcourt Buildings, Temple, EC4. *T:* 01–353 0375; 5 Montpelier Row, Blackheath, SE3 0RL. *Clubs:* Caledonian; United Services (Nottingham).

McAVOY, Sir (Francis) Joseph, Kt 1976; CBE 1969; Chairman: Queensland and Australian Canegrowers Councils, 1963–82 (Member, 1952–82); Australian Canegrowers Council, 1952–82; retired; *b* 26 Feb. 1910; *s* of William Henry McAvoy and Hanorah Catherine McAvoy; *m* 1936, Mary Irene Doolan; four *s* (one *d* decd). *Educ:* Nudgee Coll., Brisbane; Sacred Heart Convent, Innisfail, Qld. Member: Goondi Mill Suppliers Cttee, 1947–82; Innisfail Canegrowers Exec., 1949–82; Metric Conversion Bd (Aust.), 1970–78; Aust. Immigration Adv. Council, 1964–72; Exec. Council of Agriculture, 1963–82; Exec., Aust. Farmers Fedn, 1969–77, Nat. Farmers Fedn, 1977–82. Vice-Pres., Internat. Fedn of Agricultural Producers, 1968–74. *Recreation:* lawn bowls. *Address:* PO Box 95, Innisfail, Qld 4860, Australia. *T:* 633724. *Clubs:* Rotary, IDB (Innisfail, Qld).

McBAIN, (David) Malcolm, LVO 1972; HM Diplomatic Service; Ambassador to Madagascar, since 1984; *b* 19 Jan. 1928; *s* of David Walker McBain and Lilian J. McBain; *m* 1951, Audrey Yvonne Evison; one *s* three *d*. *Educ:* Sutton County School; London School of Economics (evening student). Min. of Civil Aviation appts in Tripoli, Libya, 1949–51, New Delhi, 1953–54; Diplomatic Service: New Delhi, 1958–61; Kenya, 1963–67; Thailand, 1968–75; Brunei, 1978–81; Texas, 1981–84. Order of Crown of Thailand, 1972. *Recreations:* golf, fishing. *Address:* c/o Foreign and Commonwealth Office, SW1.

McBAIN, Ed; *see* Hunter, Evan.

McBAIN, Malcolm; *see* McBain, D. M.

McBEAN, Angus Rowland; photographer; *b* 8 June 1904; *s* of Clement Phillip James McBean and Irene Sarah Thomas; *m* 1925, Helena Wood (decd). *Educ:* Monmouth Grammar School. Bank Clerk, 1921–24; Assistant in Liberty's Antique Dept, 1924–31; left to become an odd-job man for the theatre, making masks and building scenery; gradually became a full-time photographer of the theatre, 1936–69; also known for his individual approach to portraiture and the use of surrealism for its fun value. *Exhibitions:* 60th birthday, Kodak Gall., 1964; *retrospectives:* Impressions Gall., York, 1976; Nat. Theatre, 1977; Michael Parkin Gall., 1985; Parco Gall., Tokyo, 1986. *Publications:* Stratford Shakespeare Theatre annuals, 1947–53; (with Adrian Woodhouse) Angus McBean, 1982; (with Adrian Woodhouse) Masters of Photography: Angus McBean, 1985. *Recreations:* photography, interior decorating. *Address:* High Street, Debenham, Suffolk. *T:* Debenham 860422.

MACBEATH, Prof. Alexander Murray, PhD (Princeton, NJ); MA (Cantab); Professor of Mathematics and Statistics, University of Pittsburgh, since 1979; *b* 30 June 1923; *s* of late Prof. Alexander Macbeath, CBE; *m* 1951, Julie Ormrod, Lytham St Anne's; two *s*. *Educ:* Royal Belfast Academical Inst.; Queen's Univ., Belfast; Clare Coll., Cambridge. Entrance Schol., Dixon Prize in Maths, Purser Studentship, 1st class hons in Maths, BA, QUB. Temp. post with Foreign Office, 1943–45. Cambridge, 1945–48; Maj. Entrance Schol., Wrangler Math. Tripos, Part II, dist. Part III, BA, Owst Prize. Commonwealth Fund Fellowship, Princeton, NJ, 1948–50; Smith's Prize, 1949; PhD Princeton, 1950. Research Fellow, Clare Coll., Cambridge, 1950–51; MA Cambridge, 1951. Lectr in Maths, Univ. Coll. of North Staffordshire, 1951–53; Prof. of Maths, Queen's Coll., Dundee, 1953–62; Mason Prof. of Pure Maths, Univ. of Birmingham, 1962–79. Visiting Professor: California Inst. of Technology, 1966–67; Univ. of Pittsburgh, 1974–75. *Publications:* Elementary Vector Algebra, 1964; papers in: Jl London Mathematical Soc.; Proc. London Math. Soc.; Proc. Cambridge Philosophical Soc.; Quarterly Jl of Mathematics; Annals of Mathematics; Canadian Jl of Mathematics. *Recreation:* Scottish country dancing. *Address:* 16 Highmeadow Road, Pittsburgh, Pa 15215, USA.

MacBETH, George Mann; writer; *b* Scotland, 1932; *s* of George MacBeth and Amelia Morton Mary Mann; *m* 1955, Elizabeth Browell Robson, *qv* (marr. diss. 1975); *m* 1982, Lisa St Aubin de Téran; one *s*. *Educ:* New Coll., Oxford (read Classics and Philosophy). BBC, 1955–76: Producer, Overseas Talks Dept, 1957; Producer, Talks Dept, 1958; Editor: Poet's Voice, 1958–65; New Comment, 1959–64; Poetry Now, 1965–76. Sir Geoffrey Faber Memorial Award (jtly), 1964; Cholmondeley Award (jtly), 1977. *Publications: poems:* A Form of Words, 1954; The Broken Places, 1963; A Doomsday Book, 1965; The Colour of Blood, 1967; The Night of Stones, 1968; A War Quartet, 1969; The Burning Cone, 1970; Collected Poems 1958–1970, 1971; The Orlando Poems, 1971; Shrapnel, 1973; A Poet's Year, 1973; In The Hours Waiting For The Blood To Come, 1975; Buying a Heart, 1978; Poems of Love and Death, 1980; Poems from Oby, 1982; The Long Darkness, 1983; The Cleaver Garden, 1986; *prose poems:* My Scotland, 1973; *prose:* The Transformation, 1975; The Samurai, 1975; The Survivor, 1977; The Seven Witches, 1978; The Born Losers, 1981; A Kind of Treason, 1982; Anna's Book, 1983; The Lion of Pescara, 1984; Dizzy's Woman, 1986; *anthologies:* The Penguin Book of Sick Verse, 1963; (with J. Clemo and E. Lucie-Smith) Penguin Modern Poets VI, 1964; The Penguin Book of Animal Verse, 1965; (with notes) Poetry, 1900–1965, 1967; The Penguin Book of Victorian Verse, 1968; The Falling Splendour, 1970; The Book of Cats, 1976; Poetry, 1900–1975, 1980; Poetry for Today, 1984; *children's books:* Jonah and the Lord, 1969; The Rectory Mice, 1982; The Story of Daniel, 1986. *Recreation:* Japanese swords. *Address:* St Mary's Hall, Wiggenhall St Mary, King's Lynn, Norfolk.

McBRATNEY, George, CEng, FIMechE; Principal, College of Technology, Belfast, since 1984; *b* 5 May 1927; *s* of George McBratney and Sarah Jane McBratney; *m* 1949, Patricia, (Trissie), McBratney; one *s*. *Educ:* Coll. of Technology, Belfast (BSc(Eng) 1948); Northampton Coll. of Advanced Technol.; QUB (Dip Ed 1976). CEng, FIMechE 1971. Apprentice fitter/draughtsman, Harland and Wolff, Belfast, 1943–47; Teacher, Comber Trades Prep. Sch., 1947–54; College of Technology, Belfast: successively Asst Lectr, Lectr and Sen. Lectr, 1954–67; Asst to Principal, 1967–69; Vice-Principal, 1969–84. *Publications:* Mechanical Engineering Experiments, vols 1 and 2 (with W. R. Mitchell), 1962, vol. 3 (with T. G. J. Moag), 1964; (with T. G. J. Moag) Science for Mechanical Engineering Technicians, vol. 1, 1966. *Recreation:* gardening. *Address:* 16 Glencregagh Drive, Belfast BT6 0NL. *T:* Belfast 796123.

McBREARTY, Tony; Chairman, Central Technical Unit; Councillor (Lab), London Borough of Haringey, since 1975; *b* 26 April 1946; *s* of Patrick and Mary McBrearty; *m* 1969, Heather McGowan; one *s*. Chm. of Personnel Cttee, 1976–79, Chm. of Housing Cttee, 1979–82, Haringey Borough Council; Mem. (Lab) Enfield N, 1981–86, Chm., Housing Cttee, 1982–86, GLC. Prospective Parly Cand. (Lab) W Herts, 1985–. *Recreations:* politics, history. *Address:* 112 Inderwick Road, Hornsey, N8 9JY. *T:* 01–348 8159.

McBRIDE, Commandant (Sara) Vonla (Adair), CB 1979; Director, Central London Region, Lloyds Bank Ltd, since 1980; a Chairman, Civil Service Commissioners' Interview Panel, since 1985; *b* 20 Jan. 1921; *d* of late Andrew Stewart McBride and Agnes McBride. *Educ:* Ballymena Acad., NI; TCD (Moderatorship in Mod. Lit; BA Hons). CBIM. Teacher of English and French, Ballymena Acad., 1942–45; Housemistress, Gardenhurst Sch., Burnham-on-Sea, Somerset, 1945–49. Dir, WRNS, 1976–79 (joined 1949); Hon. ADC to the Queen, 1976–79. Freeman, City of London, 1978. Liveryman, Shipwrights' Co., 1983–. *Publication:* Never at Sea (autobiog.), 1966. *Recreations:* golf, theatre entertaining, continental travel. *Address:* Flat 11, 8 The Paragon, Blackheath, SE3. *T:* 01–852 8673. *Club:* Naval.

MacBRIDE, Seán; Senior Counsel, Irish Bar; Assistant Secretary-General, United Nations, and United Nations Commissioner for Namibia, 1973–77; *b* 26 Jan. 1904; *s* of late Major John MacBride and late Maud Gonne; *m* 1926, Catalina Bulfin; one *s* one *d*. *Educ:* St Louis de Gonzaque, Paris; Mount St Benedict, Gorey, Co. Wexford, Ireland. Was active in movement for Irish independence and suffered imprisonment in 1918, 1922 and 1930; was Sec. to Mr de Valera; decorated by Irish Govt for Military services in Ireland, 1938. Was a journalist for a number of years before being called to Irish Bar, 1937; Irish correspondent for Havas and some American and South African papers before War of 1939–45. Called to Bar, 1937; called to Inner Bar, 1943; holds record of having become a Senior Counsel in a shorter period of time than any other living member of the Bar; defended many sensational capital cases and had an extensive practice in High Court and Supreme Court. Founder, 1946, and Leader of political party, Clann na Poblachta (Republican Party). Member of Dail Eireann, 1947–58; Minister for External Affairs, Eire, 1948–51. Pres., Council of Foreign Ministers of Council of Europe, 1950; Vice-Pres., OEEC, 1948–51; declined ministerial portfolio, June 1954, on ground of inadequate parliamentary representation; delegate to Council of Europe from Ireland, 1954. Trustee, Internat. Prisoners of Conscience Fund; Mem. Exec., Pan-European Union; Consultant to late President K. N'Krumah in relation to forming OAU; Mem., European Round Table; Mem., Ghana Bar; International Congress of Jurists, New Delhi, 1958 and Rio de Janeiro, 1962; Chm., Irish Assoc. of Jurists; one of the founders of Amnesty International and Chm. Internat. Exec., 1961–75; President: Internat. Commn of Jurists (Sec.-Gen. of the Commn, 1963–70, Mem., 1971–); Internat. Peace Bureau, Geneva, 1972–85 (Pres. Emeritus, 1985–); Internat. Commn for Study of Communication Problems, 1977. Mem., Tunisian Acad. of Scis, 1983. LLD (hc): Coll. of St Thomas, Minnesota, 1975; Guelph Univ., Canada, 1977; TCD, 1978; Univ. of Cape Coast, 1978; DLitt (*hc*) Bradford Univ., 1977. Elected to Internat. Gaelic Hall of Fame, 1974; Man of the Year, Irish United Socs, 1975. Nobel Peace Prize (jtly), 1974; Lenin Internat. Prize for Peace, 1977; Amer. Medal of Justice, 1978; Internat. Inst. of Human Rights Medal, 1978; ALECSO Gold Medal, 1985. Commander, Order of Arts and Letters (France), 1984. *Publications:* Civil Liberty, 1948 (pamphlet); Our People—Our Money, 1951; A Message to the Irish People, 1985. *Recreation:* sailing. *Address:* Roebuck House, Clonskea, Dublin 14. *T:* Dublin 694225; International Peace Bureau, 41 rue de Zurich, CH 1201 Geneva, Switzerland.

McBRIDE, Vonla; *see* McBride, S. V. A.

McBRIDE, William Griffith, AO 1977; CBE 1969; MD, FRCOG; FRACOG; Consultant Obstetrician and Gynaecologist: The Women's Hospital, Sydney, 1966–83; Royal Hospital for Women, since 1983; St George Hospital, Sydney, since 1957; *b* 25 May 1927; *s* of late John McBride, Sydney; *m* 1957, Patricia Mary, *d* of late Robert Louis Glover; two *s* two *d*. *Educ:* Canterbury High Sch., Sydney; Univ. of Sydney; Univ. of London. MB, BS Sydney 1950; MRCOG 1954; MD Sydney 1962; FRCOG 1968; FAGO 1972; FRACOG 1979. Resident: St George Hosp., Sydney, 1950; Launceston Hosp., 1951; Med. Supt, Women's Hosp., Sydney, 1955–57; Cons. Gynaecologist, Bankstown Hosp., Sydney, 1957–66. Lectr in Obstetrics and Gynaecology, Univ. of Sydney, 1957–; Examr in Obstetrics and Gynaecology, Univ. of Sydney, 1960–; Medical Dir, Foundation 41 for the study of congenital abnormalities and mental retardation, 1972–. Vis. Prof. of Gynaecology, Univ. of Bangkok, 1968. Mem., WHO Sub-Cttee on safety of oral contraceptives, 1971–. Pres. Sect. of Obstetrics and Gynæcology, AMA, 1966–73. Fellow, Senate of Univ. of Sydney. Member: Faculty of Medicine, Univ. of NSW; Amer. Coll. of Toxicology; Soc. of Reproductive Biology; Endocrine Soc.; Teratology Soc.; Soc. for Risk Analysis. BP Prize of Institut de la Vie, 1971 (for discovery of the teratogenic effects of the drug Thalidomide; first person to alert the world to the dangers of this drug and possibly other drugs). Member: Bd of Dirs, Australian Opera, 1979–82; Australian Opera Council, 1982–. *Publications:* Drugs, 1960–70; contrib. (on Teratogenic Effect of the Drug Thalidomide), Lancet 1961 (London); numerous papers in internat. med. jls and scientific jls. *Recreations:* tennis, swimming, riding, music, cattle breeding. *Address:* Foundation 41, 365 Crown Street, Sydney, NSW 2010, Australia. *T:* 221–3898. *Clubs:* Union, Australian Jockey, Palm Beach Surf, Royal Sydney Golf (all in Sydney).

McBURNEY, Air Vice-Marshal Ralph Edward, CBE 1945; CD; RCAF, retired; *b* Montreal, Quebec, 17 Aug. 1906; *s* of Irville Albert and Lilian McBurney, Saskatoon, Sask.; *m* 1931, Gertrude Elizabeth Bate, Saskatoon; two *s* one *d*. *Educ:* Univs of Saskatchewan and Manitoba. BSc (EE); Commenced flying training as a cadet in RCAF, 1924; Pilot Officer, 1926; employed on Forest Fire Patrols and photographic mapping; Course in RAF School of Army Co-operation and tour as Instructor in RCAF School of Army Co-operation, 1931; Course at RAF Wireless School, Cranwell, and tour as Signals Adviser at Air Force HQ, Ottawa, 1935–36; RAF Staff Coll., Andover, 1939; Dir of Signals, AFHQ, Ottawa, 1939–42; CO, RCAF Station, Trenton, Ont., 1943; CO, RCAF Station, Dishforth, Yorks, 1943; Air Cdre 1944; Base Comdr of 61 Training Base, and later, 64 Operational Base in No 6 (RCAF) Bomber Group of Bomber Comd; SASO of the Group, Dec. 1944; AOC RCAF Maintenance Comd, 1945–46; Senior Canadian Air Force Liaison Officer, London, 1946–48; AOC Air Materiel Comd, RCAF, Ottawa, 1948–52. Business Consultant, 1952–60; Chief, Technical Information Service, Nat. Research Council, Ottawa, 1960–72. Pres., Internat. Fedn for Documentation, 1968–72. *Address:* 2022 Sharon Avenue, Ottawa, Ontario K2A 1L8, Canada.

McBURNIE, Tony; Director General, Institute of Marketing, since 1984; Managing Director: College of Marketing Ltd, since 1985; Marketing Training Ltd, since 1984; Marketing House Publishers Ltd, since 1985; *b* 4 Aug. 1929; *s* of William McBurnie and Bessie McKenzie Harvey McBurnie; *m* 1954, René Keating; one *s* one *d*. *Educ:* Lanark Grammar Sch.; Glasgow Univ. (MA). FInstM 1984. National Service, RAF (FO), 1951–53. Divisional Manager Mullard Ltd, 1958–65; Group Marketing Dir, United Glass Ltd, 1965–69; Chairman and Managing Director: Ravenhead Co. Ltd, 1970–79; United Glass Containers Ltd, 1979–82; Man. Dir, United Glass PT&D Gp, 1982–84; Dir, United Glass Holdings PLC, 1966–84. Pres., Assoc. of Glass Container Manufacturers, 1981–83; Chm., NJIC for Glass Industry, 1982–83; Dir, European Glass Fedn, 1979–83. *Recreations:* golf, swimming, theatre, the arts. *Address:* Moor Hall, Cookham, Berkshire SL6 9QH. *T:* Bourne End (Bucks) 24922. *Club:* Wentworth.

MacCABE, Brian Farmer, MC and Bar, 1942; Honorary President, Foote, Cone & Belding Ltd (London) (Chairman, 1948–78, President, 1978–80); Director and Senior Vice-President, Foote, Cone & Belding Communications Inc. (New York), 1953–80; *b* 9 Jan. 1914; *s* of late James MacCabe and Katherine MacCabe (*née* Harwood); *m* 1940, Eileen Elizabeth Noel Hunter (*d* 1984); one *s*. *Educ:* Christ's Coll., Finchley. Executive, C. R. Casson Ltd, 1934–40. Major RTR (wounded 3 times, Sqdn Comd, Alamein), 1940–45. World-wide Advertising Manager, BOAC, 1945–47; Chm., FCB International Inc. (NY), 1967–74. Mem. Council: Inst. of Practitioners in Advertising, 1951–80 (Pres., 1963–65); Advertising Assoc., 1952–69; Internat. Marketing Programme, 1965–80. Mem., Reith Commn on Advertising, 1962–66; Dir, American Chamber of Commerce, 1971–80; Member: Promotion Cttee, BNEC, 1965–68; Marketing Cttee, Ashridge Management Coll., 1965–78; Advertising Standards Authority, 1969–72; Appeals Cttee, Olympic and Commonwealth Games, 1952–80; Management Cttee, British Sports Assoc. for the Disabled, 1962–65; Nat. Council, Brit. Polio Fellowship, 1959–65. Royal Humane Soc. Medal for saving life at sea, 1934; awards for services to advertising, 1957–. *Recreations:* finalist: (800 metres) Olympic Games, Berlin, 1936; (880 yards) British Commonwealth Games, Sydney, 1938; golf, fishing. *Address:* Somerford, Penn Road, Beaconsfield, Bucks. *T:* Beaconsfield 3365. *Clubs:* Boodle's; Wasps RFC; LAC (Vice-Pres.), Bucks AA (Vice-Pres.), Beaconsfield Golf, Denham Golf.

MacCABE, Prof. Colin Myles Joseph; Head of Production, British Film Institute, since 1985; *b* 9 Feb. 1949; *s* of Myles Joseph MacCabe and Ruth Ward MacCabe; one *s* one *d*. *Educ:* Trinity College, Cambridge (BA English and Moral Scis 1971, MA 1974, PhD 1976); Ecole Normale Supérieure, 1972–73 (pensionnaire anglais). University of Cambridge: Research Fellow, Emmanuel College, 1974–76; Fellow, King's College, 1976–81; Asst Lectr, Faculty of English, 1976–81; Prof. of English Studies, 1981–85, Vis. Prof., 1985–, Strathclyde Univ. Vis. Fellow, School of Humanities, Griffith Univ., 1981, 1984; Chm., John Logie Baird Centre for Research in Television and Film, 1985– (Dir, 1983–85); Mellon Vis. Prof., Univ. of Pittsburgh, 1985. Mem., Edtl Bd, Screen, 1973–81. *Publications:* James Joyce and the Revolution of the Word, 1979; Godard: Images, Sounds, Politics, 1980; (ed) The Talking Cure: essays in psychoanalysis and language, 1981; (ed) James Joyce: new perspectives, 1982; Theoretical Essays: film, linguistics, literature, 1985. *Recreations:* eating, drinking, talking. *Address:* British Film Institute Production Division, 29 Rathbone Street, W1. *T:* 01–636 5587.

McCABE, Eamonn Patrick; Picture Editor, Sportsweek magazine, since 1986; *b* 28 July 1948; *s* of James and Celia McCabe; *m* 1972, Ruth Calvert; one *s* one *d*. *Educ:* Challoner School, Finchley; San Francisco State Coll. Freelance photographer on local papers and with The Guardian for one year; staff photographer, The Observer, 1977–86. Sports photographer of the year, RPS and Sports Council, 1978, 1979, 1981, 1984; News photographer of the year, British Press Awards, 1985. *Publication:* Sports Photographer, 1981. *Recreations:* playing soccer, occasional jogging. *Address:* 58 The Mall, Southgate, N14. *T:* 01–886 5742. *Club:* Nine Elms Dynamos Soccer Team.

McCABE, John, CBE 1985; professional musician; composer and pianist; Director, London College of Music, since 1983; *b* 21 April 1939; *s* of Frank and Elisabeth McCabe; *m* 1974, Monica Christine Smith. *Educ:* Liverpool Institute High Sch. for Boys; Manchester Univ. (MusBac); Royal Manchester Coll. of Music (ARMCM); Hochschule für Musik, Munich. Pianist-in-residence, University Coll., Cardiff, 1965–68; freelance musical criticism, 1966–71. Career as composer and pianist: many broadcasts and recordings as well as concert appearances in various countries. Prizewinner in Gaudeamus Competition for Interpreters of Contemporary Music, Holland, 1969. Recordings incl. 16–record set of complete piano music by Haydn; complete piano music of Nielsen (2 records). Awarded Special Citation by Koussevitsky Internat. Recording Foundn of USA, for recording of Symph. No 2 and Notturni ed Alba, 1974; Special Award by Composers' Guild of Gt Brit. (services to Brit. music), 1975; Ivor Novello Award (TV theme tune, Sam), 1977. Pres., ISM, 1983–84; Chm., Assoc. of Professional Composers, 1984–85. Hon. FRMCM; Hon. FLCM 1983; Hon. FRCM 1984; Hon. RAM 1985. *Publications:* many compositions, incl. three symphonies, two operas, ballets, concerti, orchestral works incl. The Chagall Windows and Hartmann Variations, Notturni ed Alba, for soprano and orch., chamber music, keyboard works, and vocal compositions. Rachmaninov (short biog.), 1974; Bartok's Orchestral Music (BBC Music Guide), 1974; Haydn Piano Sonatas (Ariel Music Guide), 1986. *Recreations:* cricket, snooker, books, films. *Address:* London College of Music, 47 Great Marlborough Street, W1V 2AS; 49 Burns Avenue, Southall, Mddx.

McCAFFREY, Sir Thos Daniel, (Sir Tom McCaffrey), Kt 1979; public affairs consultant; *b* 20 Feb. 1922; *s* of William P. and B. McCaffrey; *m* 1949, Agnes Campbell Douglas; two *s* four *d*. *Educ:* Hyndland Secondary Sch. and St Aloysius Coll., Glasgow. Served War, RAF, 1940–46. Scottish Office, 1948–61; Chief Information Officer, Home Office, 1966–71; Press Secretary, 10 Downing Street, 1971–72; Dir of Information Services, Home Office, 1972–74; Head of News Dept, FCO, 1974–76; Chief Press Sec. to Prime Minister, 1976–79; Chief of Staff to Rt Hon. James Callaghan, MP, 1979–80; Chief Asst to Rt Hon. Michael Foot, MP, 1980–83; Hd, Chief Executive's Office, BPCC, 1983–84; Dir, Public Affairs, and Special Advr to the Publisher, Mirror Gp Newspapers, 1984–85. *Address:* Balmaha, The Park, Great Bookham, Surrey. *T:* Bookham 54171.

MacCAIG, Norman (Alexander), OBE 1979; MA; FRSL; FRSE; ARSA; *b* 14 Nov. 1910; *s* of Robert McCaig and Joan MacLeod; *m* 1940, Isabel Munro; one *s* one *d*. *Educ:* Edinburgh University. MA Hons Classics. FRSL 1965; ARSA 1981; FRSE 1983. Schoolteacher, 1932–67 and 1969–70; Fellow in Creative Writing, Univ. of Edinburgh, 1967–69; Lectr in English Studies, Univ. of Stirling, 1970–72, Reader in Poetry, 1972–77. Travelling Scholarship, Soc. of Authors, 1964; RSL Award (Heinemann Bequest), 1967; Cholmondeley Award, 1975; Scottish Arts Council Awards, 1954, 1966–67, 1970, 1971, 1978, 1980, 1986; Saltire Award, 1985; Queen's Gold Medal for Poetry, 1986. DUniv Stirling, 1981; Hon. DLitt Edinburgh, 1983; Hon. LLD Dundee, 1986. *Publications: poetry:* Far Cry, 1943; The Inward Eye, 1946; Riding Lights, 1955; The Sinai Sort, 1957; A Common Grace, 1960; A Round of Applause, 1962; Measures, 1965; Surroundings, 1966; Rings on a Tree, 1968; A Man in My Position, 1969; The White Bird, 1973; The World's Room, 1974; Tree of Strings, 1977; The Equal Skies, 1980; A World of Difference, 1983; Collected Poems, 1985; (ed anthology) Honour'd Shade, 1959; (with Alexander Scott, ed anthology) Contemporary Scottish Verse, 1970. *Recreations:* fishing, music. *Address:* 7 Leamington Terrace, Edinburgh EH10 4JW. *T:* 031–229 1809. *Club:* Scottish Arts (Edinburgh).

McCALL, Charles James, DA (Edinburgh); ROI 1949, NEAC 1957; artist-painter; *b* 24 Feb. 1907; *s* of late William McCall, Edinburgh; *m* 1945, Eloise Jerwood, *d* of late F. Ward, Bickley, Kent. *Educ:* Edinburgh Univ.; Edinburgh College of Art. RSA Travelling Schol., 1933; Edinburgh College of Art: Travelling Schol., 1936 (Fellow, 1938). Studied in many art galleries in Europe; also in studios in Paris. Returned to London in 1938, exhibiting RA, NEAC, London Group, etc. Commissioned, RE 1940; at end of war taught drawing and painting at Formation College. Has exhibited regularly in London; one-man shows held at: Leicester Galleries, 1950 and 1953; Victor Waddington Galleries, Dublin, 1951; Duveen Graham Galleries, New York, 1955 and 1957; Crane Galleries, Manchester, 1955; Klinkhoff Gallery, Montreal, 1958 and 1960; Whibley Gallery, London, 1963; Federation of British Artists, 1965; Ash Barn Gallery, Stroud, 1965, 1969, 1973; Eaton's Gallery, Winnipeg, Canada, 1966; Nevill Gallery, Canterbury, 1972; Belgrave Gallery, 1975, 1977; Bath Contemporary Festival, 1982–83; Gerber Gallery, Glasgow, 1984; paintings in: Sotheby's Centenary NEAC, 1985; Christie's NEAC Centenary exhibn, 1986. BBC TV Programme on his life and work, 1975; profile in Artist magazine, 1981. Painter of portraits, landscapes, interiors with figures, and of contemporary life. Lord Mayor's Art Award, 1963, 1973, 1977. *Relevant publication:* Interior with Figure, the life and painting of Charles McCall, 1987, by Mitzi McCall. *Recreations:* music, literature, travel. *Address:* 1a Caroline Terrace, SW1W 8JS. *T:* 01–730 8737.

McCALL, Sir (Charles) Patrick (Home), Kt 1971; MBE 1944; TD 1946; solicitor; Clerk of the County Council, 1960–72, Clerk of the Peace, 1960–71, and Clerk of the Lieutenancy, Lancashire, 1960–74; *b* 22 Nov. 1910; *s* of late Charles and Dorothy McCall; *m* 1934, Anne, *d* of late Samuel Brown, Sedlescombe, Sussex; two *s* one *d*. *Educ:* St Edward's Sch., Oxford. Served 1939–45; Substantive Major TA. Hon. Lt-Col. Mem., Economic and Social Cttee, EEC, 1973–78. *Recreations:* travel, walking, swimming, gardening. *Address:* Auchenhay Lodge, Corsock, by Castle Douglas, Kirkcudbrightshire DG7 3HZ. *T:* Corsock 651.

See also R. H. McCall.

McCALL, Christopher Hugh; Junior Counsel to the Attorney General in charity matters, since 1981; *b* 3 March 1944; *yr s* of Robin Home McCall, *qv*; *m* 1981, Henrietta Francesca Sharpe. *Educ:* Winchester (Scholar); Magdalen Coll., Oxford (Demy; BA Maths, 1964; Eldon Law Scholar, 1966). Called to the Bar, Lincoln's Inn, 1966. Second Jun. Counsel to the Inland Revenue in chancery matters, 1977–. Mem, Bar Council, 1973–76; Jt Hon. Treas., Barristers Benevolent Assoc., 1981–86. *Recreations:* music, travel, glass. *Address:* 7 New Square, Lincoln's Inn, WC2A 3QS. *T:* 01–405 1266. *Clubs:* Royal Automobile; Leander (Henley-on-Thames); Climbers.

McCALL, David Slesser; Director since 1970 and Chief Executive since 1976, Anglia Television Ltd; Chief Executive, Anglia Television Group PLC, since 1986; *b* 3 Dec. 1934; *s* of Patrick McCall and Florence Kate Mary Walker; *m* 1968, Lois Patricia Elder. *Educ:* Robert Gordon's Coll., Aberdeen. Mem., Inst. of Chartered Accountants of Scotland, 1958. National Service, 1959–61. Accountant, Grampian Television Ltd, 1961–68; Company Sec., Anglia Television Ltd, 1968–76. Director: Anglia Television Group plc, 1970–; ITN, 1978–86; Ind. Television Publications Ltd, 1971–; Ind. Television Cos Assoc. Ltd, 1976–; Channel Four Television Co., 1981–85; Sodastream Holdings Ltd, 1976–85; Norwich City Football Club, 1979–85; Radio Broadland, 1984–. *Recreations:* sport, travel. *Address:* 168 St Clements Hill, Norwich NR3 4DG. *T:* Norwich 45911. *Club:* Norfolk (Norwich).

McCALL, John Armstrong Grice, CMG 1964; *b* 7 Jan. 1913; 2nd *s* of Rev. Canon J. G. McCall; *m* 1951, Kathleen Mary Clarke; no *c*. *Educ:* Glasgow Academy; Trinity Coll., Glenalmond; St Andrews Univ.; St John's Coll., Cambridge. MA 1st class hons Hist. St Andrews, 1935. Colonial Administrative Service (HMOCS), Nigeria, 1935–67; Cadet, 1936; Class I, 1956; Staff Grade, 1958. Chm., Mid-Western Nigeria Development Corp.,

Benin City, 1966–67, retired 1967. Asst Chief Admin. Officer, East Kilbride Develt Corp., 1967–76. Scottish Rep., Executive Cttee, Nigeria-British Chamber of Commerce, 1977–. Mem. 1969, Vice-Chm. 1971, S Lanarkshire Local Employment Cttee; Mem. Panel, Industrial Tribunals (Scotland), 1972–74; Gen. Sec., Scotland, Royal Over-Seas League, 1978–80. Sec., West Linton Community Council, 1980–83. *Recreations:* golf, walking. *Address:* Burnside, West Linton, Peeblesshire. *T:* West Linton 60488. *Clubs:* Caledonian; Old Glenalmond (Chm., 1978–81); Royal and Ancient (St Andrews).

McCALL, John Donald; Director, Consolidated Gold Fields Ltd, 1959–81 (Chairman, 1969–76); *b* 1 Feb. 1911; *s* of late Gilbert Kerr McCall; *m* 1942, Vere Stewart Gardner; one *s* one *d.* *Educ:* Clifton Coll.; Edinburgh Univ. Gold Mining industry, S Africa, 1930–39. Served War of 1939–45: commissioned, Gordon Highlanders. Joined Consolidated Gold Fields Ltd, London, 1946 (Dir, 1959; Jt Dep. Chm., 1968). Dir, Ultramar plc, 1965–. *Recreations:* gardening, golf. *Address:* 64 Pont Street, SW1. *Club:* Caledonian.

McCALL, Kenneth Murray, DL; Lord Lieutenant of Dumfriesshire, 1970–72; *b* 21 Dec. 1912; *s* of late Major William McCall, DL; *m* 1938, Christina Eve Laurie; two *s* two *d.* *Educ:* Merchiston Castle School. DL Dumfriesshire, 1973. *Recreations:* shooting, golf. *Address:* Caitloch, Moniaive, Thornhill, Dumfriesshire. *T:* Moniaive 211.

McCALL, Sir Patrick; *see* McCall, Sir C. P. H.

McCALL, Robin Home, CBE 1976 (OBE 1969); retired 1976; *b* 21 March 1912; *s* of late Charles and Dorothy McCall; *m* 1937, Joan Elizabeth Kingdon; two *s* one *d.* *Educ:* St Edward's Sch., Oxford. Solicitors Final (Hons), 1935. Served War, RAFVR Night Fighter Controller (Sqdn Ldr); D Day landing Normandy, in command of 15083 GCI, 1944. Asst Solicitor: Bexhill Corp., 1935–39; Hastings Corp., 1939–46; Bristol Corp., 1946–47; Dep. Town Clerk, Hastings, 1947–48; Town Clerk and Clerk of the Peace, Winchester, 1948–72; Sec., Assoc. of Municipal Corporations, later Assoc. of Metropolitan Authorities, 1973–76. Hon. Sec., Non-County Boroughs Cttee for England and Wales, 1958–69; Member: Reading Cttee (Highway Law Consolidation); Morris Cttee (Jury Service); Kennett Preservation Gp (Historic Towns Conservation); Exec. Cttee, European Architectural Heritage Year, 1972–; UK delegn to ECLA (Council of Europe); North Hampshire Hosp. Cttee, 1969–72. Governor, St Swithin's Sch., Winchester, 1978–; Mem., Winchester Excavations Cttee, 1962–. Hon. Freeman, City of Winchester, 1973. *Publications:* contrib. Local Government, Halsbury's Laws, 4th edn, 1980; various articles and reviews on local govt. *Recreations:* gardening, mountains. *Address:* The Hospice, St Giles Hill, Winchester. *T:* Winchester 54101. *Club:* Alpine.

See also C. H. McCall, Sir C. P. H. McCall.

McCALL, William; General Secretary, Institution of Professional Civil Servants, since 1963; *b* 6 July 1929; *s* of Alexander McCall and Jean Corbet Cunningham; *m* 1955, Olga Helen Brunton; one *s* one *d.* *Educ:* Dumfries Academy; Ruskin College, Oxford. Civil Service, 1946–52; Social Insurance Dept, TUC, 1954–58; Asst Sec., Instn of Professional Civil Servants, 1958–63; Mem., Civil Service Nat. Whitley Council (Staff Side), 1963–, Chm. 1969–71, Vice-Chm. 1983. Hon. Treasurer, Parly and Scientific Cttee, 1976–80; Part-time Mem., Eastern Electricity Board, 1977–86; Member: Cttee of Inquiry into Engrg Profession, 1977–79; PO Arbitration Tribunal, 1980–; TUC Gen. Council, 1984–. Mem. Ct, Univ. of London, 1984–. *Address:* Foothills, Gravel Path, Berkhamsted, Herts. *T:* Berkhamsted 4974.

McCALLUM, Archibald Duncan Dugald, TD 1950; MA; Headmaster, Strathallan School, 1970–75; *b* 26 Nov. 1914; *s* of late Dr A. D. McCallum and Mrs A. D. McCallum; *m* 1950, Rosemary Constance, *widow* of Sqdn Ldr John Rhind, RAF, and *d* of William C. Thorne, OBE, Edinburgh; two *s* (one step *s*). *Educ:* Fettes Coll., Edinburgh; St John's Coll., Cambridge (Classical Sizar). Asst Master and Housemaster, Fettes Coll., 1937–39, 1945–51. Served War of 1939–45 (despatches): Home Forces, India, and Burma. Second Master, Strathallan Sch., 1951–56; Headmaster: Christ Coll., Brecon, 1956–62; Epsom Coll., 1962–70. FRSA 1969–75. *Recreations:* golf, reading. *Address:* 1 Church Row Cottages, Burnham Market, King's Lynn, Norfolk. *T:* Fakenham 738518.

McCALLUM, Donald Murdo, CBE 1976; FEng 1982; FRSE; DL; General Manager, Scottish Group, Ferranti plc, 1968–85; Chairman: Ferranti Defence Systems Ltd, since 1984; Ferranti Industrial Electronics Ltd, since 1984; *b* 6 Aug. 1922; *s* of Roderick McCallum and Lillian (*née* McPhee); *m* 1st, 1949, Barbara Black (*d* 1971); one *d*; 2nd, 1974, Mrs Margaret Illingworth (*née* Broadbent). *Educ:* George Watson's Boys' Coll.; Edinburgh Univ. (BSc). FIEE; FRAeS; CBIM. Admiralty Signal Establishment, 1942–46; Standard Telecommunications Laboratories, 1946; Ferranti Ltd, 1947–; Director: Ferranti plc, 1970–; Short Bros Ltd, 1981–. Chairman, Scottish Tertiary Education Adv. Council, 1984–. Mem. Court, Heriot-Watt Univ., 1979–85. Liveryman, Company of Engineers, 1984; Freeman, City of London. DL City of Edinburgh, 1984. DUniv Stirling, 1985; Hon. DSc: Heriot-Watt, 1986; Napier Coll. of Commerce and Technology, Edinburgh, 1986. *Recreations:* photography, fishing. *Address:* 46 Heriot Row, Edinburgh EH3 6EX. *T:* 031–225 9331. *Clubs:* Caledonian; New (Edinburgh).

McCALLUM, Googie; *see* Withers, Googie.

McCALLUM, Ian; *see* McCallum, John.

McCALLUM, Ian Stewart; Vice-Chairman, Sports Council, 1980–86; Sales Manager, Save & Prosper Sales Ltd, since 1985; *b* 24 Sept. 1936; *s* of John Blair McCallum and Margaret Stewart McCallum; *m* 1st, 1957, Pamela Mary (*née* Shave) (marr. diss. 1984); 2nd, 1984, Jean (*née* Lynch); two step *d.* *Educ:* Kingston Grammar Sch. Eagle Star Insurance Co. Ltd, 1953–54; National Service, Highland Light Infantry, 1954–56; Eagle Star Insce Co. Ltd, 1956–58; F. E. Wright and Co., Insurance Brokers, 1958–63; H. Clarkson (Home) Ltd, Insurance Brokers, 1963–68; Save & Prosper Group Ltd, 1968–. Leader, Woking Borough Council, 1972–76 and 1978–81, Dep. Leader, 1981–82; Chm., Assoc. of Dist Councils, 1979–84; Vice-Chairman: Standing Cttee on Local Authorities and Theatre, 1977–81; UK Steering Cttee on Local Authority Superannuation, 1974–84; Member: Local Authorities Conditions of Service Adv. Bd, 1973–84; Consultative Council on Local Govt Finance, 1975–84; Council for Business in the Community, 1981–84; Audit Commn, 1983–86; Health Promotion Res. Trust, 1983–. *Recreations:* swimming, jogging, walking, reading, badminton. *Address:* 5 Minters Orchard, Maidstone Road, St Marys Platt, near Sevenoaks, Kent TN15 8QJ. *T:* Borough Green 883653. *Club:* St Stephen's Constitutional.

McCALLUM, John, BSc, FEng, FRINA, FICE; consultant naval architect; Chief Ship Surveyor, Lloyd's Register of Shipping, 1970–81; *b* 13 Oct. 1920; *s* of Hugh McCallum and Agnes Falconer McCallum (*née* Walker); *m* 1948, Christine Peggy Sowden; two *s.* *Educ:* Allan Glen's Sch., Glasgow; Glasgow Univ. (BSc (First Cl. Hons Naval Architecture) 1943). Apprenticed John Brown & Co., Clydebank, 1938–43; Jun. Lectr, Naval Architecture, Glasgow Univ., 1943–44; Ship Surveyor, Lloyd's Register of Shipping, Newcastle upon Tyne, 1944, Glasgow, 1949, London, 1953; Naval Architect, John Brown & Co., 1961 (Chief Ship Designer, QE2); Technical Dir, John Brown Shipbuilders, 1967, Upper Clyde Shipbuilders, 1969. FRINA (Mem. Council, 1970–; Chm., 1971–73; Vice-Pres., 1975–); FEng 1977; FICE 1978. Mem., IES, 1962– (past Mem. Council); Member: SNAME, 1970–81, Fellow, 1981–; Smeatonian Soc. of Civil Engrs, 1979–; CEI Cttee on Internat. Affairs, 1980–83; Lloyd's Register Technical Cttee, 1981–. Liveryman and Mem. Educn Cttee, Worshipful Co. of Shipwrights, 1975. *Publications:* various technical papers to Royal Soc., RINA, NE Coast IES, Assoc. Tech. Maritime et Aéronautique (1978 Medal), and other Europ. learned socs. *Recreations:* golf, piano, pastel art. *Address:* Dala, Garvock Drive, Kippington, Sevenoaks, Kent TN13 2LT. *T:* Sevenoaks 455462. *Club:* Wildernesse (Sevenoaks).

McCALLUM, John Neil, CBE 1971; Chairman and Executive Producer, Fauna Films, Australia, since 1967, and John McCallum Productions, since 1976; actor and producer; *b* 14 March 1918; *s* of John Neil McCallum and Lilian Elsie (*née* Dyson); *m* 1948, Georgette Lizette Withers (*see* Googie Withers); one *s* two *d.* *Educ:* Oatlands Prep. Sch., Harrogate; Knox Grammar Sch., Sydney; C of E Grammar Sch., Brisbane; RADA. Served War, 2/5 Field Regt, AIF, 1941–45. Actor, English rep. theatres, 1937–39; Stratford-on-Avon Festival Theatre, 1939; Old Vic Theatre, 1940; British films and theatre, 1946–58; films include: It Always Rains On Sunday; Valley of Eagles; Miranda; London stage plays include: Roar Like a Dove; Janus; Waiting for Gillian; J. C. Williamson Theatres Ltd, Australia: Asst Man. Dir, 1958; Jt. Man. Dir, 1959–65; Man. Dir, 1966. Appeared in: (with Ingrid Bergman) The Constant Wife, London, 1973–74; (with Googie Withers) The Circle, London, 1976–77, Australia, 1982–83; (with Googie Withers) The Kingfisher, Australia, 1978–79; The Skin Game, The Cherry Orchard, and Dandy Dick, theatrical tour, England, 1981; The School for Scandal, British Council European tour, 1984; (with Googie Withers, and dir.) Stardust, tours England, 1984, Australia, 1984–85; The Chalk Garden, Chichester Fest., 1986. Author of play, As It's Played Today, produced Melbourne, 1974. Produced television series, 1967–: Boney; Barrier Reef; Skippy; Bailey's Bird. Prod., Attack Force Z (feature film), 1980; Exec. Prod., The Highest Honor (feature film), 1982. Pres., Aust. Film Council, 1971–72. *Publication:* Life with Googie, 1979. *Recreation:* golf. *Address:* 1740 Pittwater Road, Bayview, NSW 2104, Australia. *T:* Sydney 9976879. *Clubs:* Garrick, MCC; Melbourne (Melbourne); Australian, Elanora Country (Sydney).

MAC CANA, Prof. Proinsias; Senior Professor, School of Celtic Studies, Dublin Institute for Advanced Studies, since 1985; *b* 6 July 1926; *s* of George Mc Cann and Mary Catherine Mallon; *m* 1952, Réiltín (*née* Supple); one *s* one *d.* *Educ:* St Malachy's Coll., Belfast; The Queen's Univ., Belfast (BA, MA, PhD); Ecole des Hautes Etudes, Paris. Asst Lectr, Celtic Dept, QUB, 1951–54; University College Wales, Aberystwyth: Asst Lectr in Early Irish, 1955–57; Lectr, 1957–61; Prof., Sch. of Celtic Studies, Dublin Inst. for Advanced Studies, 1961–63; Prof. of Welsh, 1963–71, Prof. of Early (incl. Medieval) Irish, 1971–85, UC Dublin. Co-editor, Ériu (RIA Jl of Irish Studies), 1973–; General editor, Medieval and Modern Welsh Series, Dublin Inst. for Advanced Studies, 1962–. Chm., Governing Bd, Sch. of Celtic Studies, Dublin Inst. for Advanced Studies, 1975–85. PRIA, 1979–82. Hon. LittD Dublin, 1985. *Publications:* Scéalaíocht na Ríthe (collection of early Irish tales trans. into Modern Irish), 1956; Branwen Daughter of Llŷr: the second branch of the Mabinogi, 1958; Celtic Mythology, 1970; The Mabinogi, 1977; Regnum and Sacerdotium: notes on Irish Tradition (Rhŷs Meml Lecture, British Academy), 1979; The Learned Tales of Medieval Ireland, 1980. *Address:* 9 Silchester Road, Glenageary, Co. Dublin. *T:* Dublin 805062. *Club:* Kildare Street and University (Dublin).

McCANCE, Robert Alexander, CBE 1953; FRS 1948; Professor of Experimental Medicine, Medical Research Council and University of Cambridge, 1945–66, now Emeritus; Director, MRC Infantile Malnutrition Research Unit, Mulago Hospital, Kampala, 1966–68; Fellow of Sidney Sussex College; *b* near Belfast, Northern Ireland, 9 Dec. 1898; *s* of Mary L. Bristow and J. S. F. McCance, linen merchant, Belfast; *m* 1922, Mary L. MacGregor (*d* 1965); one *s* one *d.* *Educ:* St Bees Sch., Cumberland; Sidney Sussex Coll., Cambridge. RN Air Service and RAF, 1917–18; BA (Cambridge), 1922; Biochemical Research, Cambridge, 1922–25; qualified in medicine King's Coll. Hosp., London, 1927; MD (Cambridge), 1929; Asst Physician i/c biochemical research, King's Coll. Hosp., London; FRCP 1935; Goulstonian Lectr, RCP, 1936; Humphrey Rolleston Lectr, RCP, 1953; Groningen Univ. Lectr, 1958; Leonard Parsons Lectr, Birmingham Univ., 1959; Lumleian Lectr, RCP, 1962. Reader in Medicine, Cambridge Univ., 1938; War of 1939–45, worked on medical problems of national importance; visited Spain and Portugal on behalf of British Council, 1943, South Africa, 1965; i/c Medical Research Council Unit, Germany, 1946–49. Hon. FRCOG; Hon. Member: Assoc. of American Physicians; American Pediatric Soc.; Swiss Nutrition Soc.; Brit. Pædiatric Assoc.; Nutrition Soc. Gold Medal, West London Medico-Chirurgical Soc., 1949. Conway Evans Prize, RCP and Royal Society, 1960; James Spence Medal, Brit. Pæd. Assoc., 1961. Hon. DSc Belfast, 1964. *Publications:* Medical Problems in Mineral Metabolism (Goulstonian Lectures), 1936; (jointly) The Chemical Composition of Foods; An Experimental Study of Rationing; (jointly) Breads White and Brown; numerous papers on the physiology of the newborn animal. *Recreations:* mountaineering, cycling, gardening. *Address:* 32 Havenfield, Arbury Road, Cambridge CB4 2JY.

McCANN, Hugh James; Chairman, Cultural Relations Committee, Irish Department of Foreign Affairs, since 1981; President, Ireland-France Economic Association, since 1981; *b* 8 Feb. 1916; *e s* of late District Justice Hugh Joseph McCann, BL, and late Sophie McCann, Dublin; *m* 1950, Mary Virginia Larkin, Washington, DC, USA; four *s* one *d.* *Educ:* Belvedere Coll., Dublin; London Sch. of Economics, Univ. of London. Served in Dept of Lands, Dublin, and in Dept of Industry and Commerce, Dublin; Commercial Sec., London, 1944–46; First Sec., Dept of External Affairs, Dublin, 1946–48; Counsellor, Irish Embassy, Washington, DC, 1948–54; Irish Minister to Switzerland and Austria, 1954–56; Asst Sec., Dept of External Affairs, Dublin, 1956–58; Irish Ambassador at the Court of St James's, 1958–62; Sec., Dept of Foreign Affairs, Dublin, 1963–74; Irish Ambassador to France, Perm. Rep. to OECD and to UNESCO, 1974–81, and concurrently Ambassador to Morocco, 1975–81. Dir, Independent Newspapers Ltd, 1982–. Chm., Nat. Cttee for Study of Internat. Affairs, RIA, 1984–. Grand Cross, Order of Leopold II, Belgium, 1968; Grand Officer, National Order of Merit, France, 1981. *Recreations:* golf, reading, swimming, and photography. *Address:* Shenandoah, Mart Lane, Foxrock, Co. Dublin. *Clubs:* Royal Dublin Society, Stephen's Green (Dublin), Woodbrook Golf.

McCANN, His Eminence Cardinal Owen, DD, PhD, BCom; Archbishop Emeritus of Cape Town; Assistant at Pontifical Throne, 1960; Cardinal since 1965 (Titular Church, St Praxedes); *b* 26 June 1907. *Educ:* St Joseph's Coll., Rondebosch, CP; Univ. of Cape Town; Collegium Urbanianum de Propaganda Fide, Rome. Priest, 1935. Editor, The Southern Cross, 1940–48; Administrator, St Mary's Cathedral, Cape Town, 1948–50; Archbishop of Cape Town, 1950–84. Hon. DLitt Univ. of Cape Town, 1968; Hon. Dr Hum. Lett. Coll. of St Joseph, Portland, Maine, USA, 1984. Freeman of City of Cape Town, 1984. *Address:* Oak Lodge, Fair Seat Lane, Wynberg, CP, South Africa; Chancery Office, Cathedral Place, 12 Bouquet Street, Cape Town. *Club:* City and Civil Service (Cape Town).

McCANN, Peter Toland McAree, CBE 1977; JP; DL; Lord Provost of the City of Glasgow and Lord-Lieutenant of the City of Glasgow, 1975–77; *b* 2 Aug. 1924; *s* of Peter

McCann and Agnes (*née* Waddell); *m* 1958, Maura Eleanor (*née* Ferris); one *s. Educ:* St Mungo's Academy; Glasgow Univ. (BL). Solicitor and Notary Public. Pres., Glasgow Univ. Law Soc., 1946; Pres., St Thomas More Soc., 1959. Mem. Glasgow Corp., 1961. Chm., McCann Cttee (Secondary Educn for Physically Handicapped Children), 1971. DL Glasgow, 1978. OStJ 1977. *Recreations:* music, history, model aeroplane making. *Address:* 31 Queen Mary Avenue, Glasgow G42 8DS.

McCARRAHER, David, VRD 1964; **His Honour Judge McCarraher;** a Circuit Judge, since 1984; *b* 6 Nov. 1922; *s* of Colin McCarraher and Vera Mabel McCarraher (*née* Hickley) *m* 1950, Betty Johnson (*née* Haywood); one *s* three *d Educ:* King Edward VI Sch., Southampton; Magdalene Coll., Cambridge (MA Law). RN, 1941–45. Called to the Bar, Lincoln's Inn, 1948; practised Western Circuit until 1952, disbarred at own request to be articled; admitted solicitor, 1955; Sen. Partner in private practice, 1960–84; a Recorder, 1979–84. Mem. Panel, Dep. Circuit Judges, 1973–79. Founder Mem. and Past Pres., Southampton Junior Chamber of Commerce. Governor, King Edward VI Sch., Southampton, 1961–84 (Chm., 1983–84). Sub-Lieut, RNVR, 1943–45, RNVSR, 1946–52; served to Captain RNR, 1969; CO Solent Div., RNR, 1969–72; ADC to the Queen, 1972–73; retired 1975. Hon. Sec., RNR Benevolent Fund, 1973–84. *Recreations:* family, golf, sailing. *Clubs:* Naval; Thames Rowing, Law Society's Yacht; Stoneham Golf (Southampton); Royal Naval Sailing Association (Portsmouth); Southampton Police (Hon. Mem.) (Southampton).

McCARTHY, family name of **Baron McCarthy.**

McCARTHY, Baron *cr* 1975 (Life Peer), of Headington; **William Edward John McCarthy,** DPhil; Fellow of Nuffield College and Oxford Management Centre; University Lecturer in Industrial Relations; engaged in Industrial Arbitration and Chairman of Committees of Inquiry and Investigation, since 1968; *b* 30 July 1925; *s* of E. and H. McCarthy; *m* Margaret McCarthy. *Educ:* Holloway County; Ruskin Coll.; Merton Coll.; Nuffield Coll. MA (Oxon), DPhil (Oxon). Trade Union Scholarship to Ruskin Coll., 1953; Research Fellow of Nuffield Coll., 1959; Research Dir, Royal Commn on Trade Unions and Employers' Assocs, 1965–68; Sen. Economic Adviser, Dept of Employment, 1968–71. Chm., Railway Staff Tribunal, 1973–86; Special Advisor on Industrial Relations to Sec. of State for Social Services, 1975–77; Member: Houghton Cttee on Aid to Political Parties, 1975–76; TUC Independent Review Cttee, 1976; Pres., British Univ. Industrial Relations Assoc., 1975–78; Special Comr, Equal Opportunities Commn, 1977–80; Dep. Chm., Teachers' Nat. Conciliation Cttee, 1979–. Chm., TUC Newspaper Feasibility Adv. Study Gp, 1981–83. Mem., H of L Select Cttee on Unemployment, 1980–82; Opposition front bench spokesman on employment, 1980–. Dir, Harland & Wolff Ltd, 1976–. *Publications:* The Closed Shop in Britain, 1964; The Role of Shop Stewards in British Industrial Relations, 1966; (with V. L. Munns) Employers' Associations, 1967; (with A. I. Marsh) Disputes Procedures in Britain, 1968; The Reform of Collective Bargaining at Plant and Company Level, 1971; (ed) Trade Unions, 1972, 2nd edn, 1985; (with A. I. Collier) Coming to Terms with Trade Unions, 1973; (with N. D. Ellis) Management by Agreement, 1973; (with J. F. O'Brien and V. E. Dowd) Wage Inflation and Wage Leadership, 1975; Making Whitley Work, 1977; (jtly) Change in Trade Unions, 1981; (jtly) Strikes in Post-War Britain, 1983; articles in: Brit. Jl of Industrial Relns; Industrial Relns Jl. *Recreations:* gardening, theatre, ballet. *Address:* 4 William Orchard Close, Old Headington, Oxford. *T:* Oxford 62016. *Club:* Reform.

McCARTHY, Adolf Charles; HM Diplomatic Service, retired; Hon. British Consul at Freiburg, since 1985; *b* 19 July 1922; *s* of Herbert Charles McCarthy and Anna Schnorf; *m* 1949, Ursula Vera Grimm; one *s* two *d. Educ:* London Univ. (BScEcon). Served War, RN, 1942–46. Min. of Agriculture, Fisheries and Food, 1939–64; Min. of Overseas Develt, 1964–66; HM Diplomatic Service, 1966; First Secretary: (Economic), Pretoria, 1968–70; (Commercial), Wellington, 1971–74; Asst Head of Western European Dept, FCO, 1974–77; Consul-Gen., Stuttgart, 1977–82. *Recreations:* music, modern political history. *Address:* Buchenstrasse 4, 7803 Gundelfingen, Federal Republic of Germany. *Club:* Rotary (Waldshut-Säckingen).

McCARTHY, Donal John, CMG 1969; HM Diplomatic Service, retired; *b* 31 March 1922; *s* of Daniel and Kathleen McCarthy. *Educ:* Holloway Sch.; London Univ. Served Royal Navy, 1942–46. Foreign Office, 1946; Middle East Centre for Arab Studies, 1947–48; 3rd and 2nd Sec., Brit. Embassy, Jedda, 1948–51; 2nd Sec., Political Div., Brit. Middle East Office, 1951–55; 1st Sec., FO, 1955–58; Asst Polit. Agent, Kuwait, 1958–60; Brit. High Commn, Ottawa, 1960–63; FO, 1963–64; Counsellor, Brit. High Commn, Aden, and Polit. Adviser to C-in-C Middle East, 1964–67; Head of Aden Dept, FO, 1967–68, of Arabian Dept, FCO, 1968–70; IDC, 1970–71; Minister (Economic and Social Affairs), UK Mission to UN, 1971–73; Ambassador to United Arab Emirates, 1973–77; FCO, 1978–79. *Recreations:* music, sailing, skiing. *Address:* Church Farmhouse, Sudbourne, Suffolk IP12 2BP. *T:* Orford 443. *Clubs:* Travellers', Royal Automobile, Ski Club of Great Britain.

McCARTHY, Eugene Joseph; Writer, since 1971; *b* 29 March 1916; *s* of Michael J. and Anna Baden McCarthy; *m* 1945, Abigail Quigley McCarthy; one *s* three *d. Educ:* St John's Univ., Collegeville (BA); Univ. of Minnesota (MA). Teacher in public schools, 1935–40; Coll. Prof. of Econs and Sociology, and civilian techn Asst in Mil. Intell. for War Dept, 1940–48; US Representative in Congress of 4th District, Minnesota, 1949–58; US Senator from Minnesota, 1959–70. Independent. Holds hon. degrees. *Publications:* Frontiers in American Democracy, 1960; Dictionary of American Politics, 1962; A Liberal Answer to the Conservative Challenge, 1964; The Limits of Power, 1967; The Year of the People, 1969; Other Things and the Aardvark (poetry), 1970; The Hard Years, 1975; (with James Kilpatrick) A Political Bestiary, 1977; Ground Fog and Night (poetry), 1978; The Ultimate Tyranny: the majority over the majority, 1979; Gene McCarthy's Minnesota, 1982; The View from Rappahannock 1984; contribs to Saturday Review, Commonweal, Harper's, New Republic, USA Today. *Address:* Box 22, Woodville, Va, USA.

McCARTHY, Mary, (Mrs James West); writer; *b* 21 June 1912; *m* 1933, Harold Johnsrud; *m* 1938, Edmund Wilson; one *s*; *m* 1946, Bowden Broadwater; *m* 1961, James Raymond West. *Educ:* Annie Wright Seminary; Vassar Coll. Theatre critic, Partisan Review, 1937–57, Editor, Covici Friede, 1937–38; Instructor, Bard Coll., 1945–46; Instructor, Sarah Lawrence Coll., 1948. Lectures and broadcasts, 1952–65. President's Distinguished Visitor, Vassar, 1982; Stevenson Chair of Lit., Bard Coll., 1986–. Horizon award, 1948; Guggenheim Fellow, 1949–50, 1959–60; National Academy of Arts and Letters award, 1957; Nat. Medal for Literature, 1984; Edward MacDowell Medal, 1984; First Rochester Literary Award, 1985. Hon. Dr Letters: Syracuse Univ., 1973; Bard, 1976; Hon. DLitt Hull, 1974; Hon. LLD Aberdeen, 1979; Hon. Dr Litt: Bowdoin, 1981; Maine, 1982. *Publications:* The Company She Keeps, 1942; The Oasis, 1949; Cast a Cold Eye, 1950; The Groves of Academe, 1952; A Charmed Life, 1955; Venice Observed, 1956; Sights and Spectacles, 1956; Memories of a Catholic Girlhood, 1957; The Stones of Florence, 1959; On the Contrary, 1962; The Group, 1963 (filmed 1966); Vietnam, 1967; Hanoi, 1968; The Writing on the Wall and Other Literary Essays, 1970; Birds of

America, 1971; Medina, 1972; The Seventeenth Degree, 1974; The Mask of State: a gallery of Watergate portraits, 1974; Cannibals and Missionaries, 1979; Ideas and the Novel, 1980; Occasional Prose, 1985; essays, journalism, short stories and reviews in the New Yorker, Partisan Review, Horizon, The New York Review of Books, The Observer, etc. *Address:* 141 Rue de Rennes, Paris, France.

McCARTHY, Nicholas Melvyn, OBE 1983; HM Diplomatic Service; Consul-General, Osaka, since 1985; *b* 4 April 1938; *s* of Daniel Alfred McCarthy and Florence Alice McCarthy; *m* 1961, Gillian Eileen Hill; three *s* one *d. Educ:* Queen Elizabeth's Sch., Faversham; London Univ. (BA Hons). Attaché, Saigon, 1961–64; Language Student, then Second Sec., Tokyo, 1964–69; FCO, 1969–73; First Sec., Brussels, 1973–78; FCO, 1978–80; Head of Chancery, Dakar, 1980–84; FCO, 1984–85. *Recreations:* bridge, squash, windsurfing, tennis. *Address:* c/o Foreign and Comonwealth Office, King Charles Street, SW1. *Club:* Sundridge Park Lawn Tennis.

McCARTHY, Patrick Peter; Regional Chairman, Liverpool, Industrial Tribunals, since 1977; *b* 10 July 1919; *er s* of late William McCarthy and Mary McCarthy; *m* 1945, Isabel Mary, *y d* of late Dr Joseph Unsworth, St Helens; two *s* three *d. Educ:* St Francis Xavier's Coll., Liverpool; Liverpool Univ. LLB 1940, LLM 1942. Admitted Solicitor, 1942; in private practice until 1974. Part-time Chm., 1972–74, full-time Chm., 1975–, Industrial Tribunals; part-time Chm., Rent Assessment Cttee, 1972–74. JP Liverpool, 1968–74. *Address:* 19a Gloucester Road, Birkdale, Southport, Merseyside PR8 2AU. *T:* Southport 68061.

McCARTHY, Rt. Hon. Sir Thaddeus (Pearcey), PC 1968; KBE 1974; Kt 1964; Judge of the Court of Appeal of New Zealand, 1963–76, President, 1973–76; Chairman, New Zealand Press Council, since 1978; *b* 24 Aug. 1907; *s* of Walter McCarthy, Napier, merchant; *m* 1938, Joan Margaret Miller; one *s* two *d* (and one *d* decd). *Educ:* St Bede's Coll., Christchurch, New Zealand; Victoria Univ. Coll., Wellington. Master of Laws (1st Class Hons) 1931. Served War of 1939–45 in MEF with 22 Bn 2 NZEF, later as DJAG, 2 NZEF. Practised as Barrister and Solicitor until 1957 when appointed to Supreme Court. Chairman: Royal Commn on State Services, 1961–62; Winston Churchill Memorial Trust, 1966–76; Royal Commissions: on Salary and Wage Fixing Procedures in the State Services, 1968; on Social Security, 1969; on Horse Racing, Trotting and Dog Racing, 1969; on Salaries and Wages in the State Services, 1972; on Nuclear Power Generation, 1976–78; on Maori Land Courts, 1979–; Chm., Security Review Authority and Comr of Security Appeals, 1977–. Chm. Adv. Cttee, NZ Computer Centre, 1977–. Vice-Pres., NZ Sect., Internat. Commn of Jurists. Chm., Queen Elizabeth II Nat. Trust, 1978–84. Fellow, NZ Inst. of Public Admin, 1984. Hon. Bencher, Middle Temple, 1974. Hon. LLD Victoria Univ. of Wellington, 1978. *Recreations:* golf (Captain, Wellington Golf Club, 1952, Pres., 1973–77), sailing. *Address:* 383 Fergusson Drive, Heretaunga, New Zealand. *T:* 286322. *Club:* Wellington (Wellington, NZ) (Pres., 1976–78).

McCARTIE, Rt. Rev. Patrick Leo; Auxiliary Bishop of Birmingham, (RC), and Titular Bishop of Elmham, since 1977; *b* 5 Sept. 1925; *s* of Patrick Leo and Hannah McCartie. *Educ:* Cotton College; Oscott College. Priest, 1949; on staff of Cotton College, 1950–55; parish work, 1955–63; Director of Religious Education, 1963–68; Administrator of St Chad's Cathedral, Birmingham, 1968–77. Pres., Catholic Commn for Racial Justice, 1978–83; Chm., Dept for Christian Citizenship, 1984–. *Recreations:* music, walking. *Address:* 84 St Bernard's Road, Olton, Solihull, W Midlands. *T:* 021–706 9721.

McCARTNEY, Gordon Arthur; Secretary, Association of District Councils, since 1981; *b* 29 April 1937; *s* of Arthur and Hannah McCartney; *m* 1960, Ceris Ysobel Davies; two *d. Educ:* Grove Park Grammar Sch., Wrexham. Articled to Philip J. Walters, MBE (Town Clerk, Wrexham), 1954–59; admitted solicitor, 1959. Asst Solicitor, Birkenhead County Bor. Council, 1959–61; Asst Solicitor, 1961–63, Sen. Asst Solicitor, 1963–65, Bootle County Bor. Council; Dep. Clerk, Wrexham RDC, 1965–73; Clerk, Holywell RDC, 1973–74; Chief Exec., Delyn Bor. Council, 1974–81. Dir, Nat. Transport Tokens Ltd, 1984–. Secretary-General, British Section: IULA, 1984–; CEMR, 1984. *Recreations:* squash, football, cricket, music. *Address:* 1 Kent Drive, Wrexham, Clwyd LL11 2UR. *T:* Wrexham 264355; 203 Frobisher House, Dolphin Square, SW1. *T:* 01–630 8207. *Clubs:* Wellington; Middlesex CCC.

McCARTNEY, Hugh; MP (Lab) Clydebank and Milngavie, since 1983 (Dunbartonshire Central, 1974–83; Dunbartonshire East, 1970–74); *b* 3 Jan. 1920; *s* of John McCartney and Mary Wilson; *m* 1949, Margaret; one *s* two *d. Educ:* Royal Technical Coll., Glasgow; John Street Senior Secondary School. Apprentice in textile industry, 1934–39; entered aircraft engrg industry, Coventry, 1939; joined Rolls Royce, Glasgow, 1941; joined RAF as aero-engine fitter, 1942 and resumed employment with Rolls Royce, 1947; representative with company (now one of GKN group) specialising in manufacture of safety footware, 1951. Joined Ind. Labour Party, 1934; joined Labour Party, 1936. Town Councillor, 1955–70 and Magistrate, 1965–70, Kirkintilloch; Mem., Dunbarton CC, 1965–70. Scottish Regional Whip, 1979–83; Mem., Speaker's Panel of Chairmen, 1984–. *Recreation:* spectating at football matches and athletic meetings (political activities permitting). *Address:* 23 Merkland Drive, Kirkintilloch G66 3PG.

McCARTNEY, (James) Paul, MBE 1965; musician, composer; *b* Allerton, Liverpool, 18 June 1942; *s* of James McCartney and late Mrs McCartney; *m* 1969, Linda Eastman; one *s* two *d*, and one step *d. Educ:* Liverpool Inst. Mem., sch. skiffle group, The Quarrymen, 1958; played with John Lennon and George Harrison as trio, The Moondogs, 1959; toured Scotland with them and Stu Sutcliffe as the Silver Beatles; made 1st official appearance as the Beatles at Litherland Town Hall, nr Liverpool, Dec. 1960; appeared as mem. of Beatles: Sweden, 1963; Royal Variety perf., London, 1963; Paris, Denmark, Hong Kong, Australia, NZ, 1964; TV appearances, USA, and later, coast-to-coast tour, 1964; France, Italy, Spain, USA, 1965; formed MPL group of cos, 1970, and own pop group, Wings, 1971; toured: GB, Europe, 1972–73; UK, Australia, 1975; Europe, USA, 1976. *Songs* (with John Lennon) include: Love Me Do; Please, Please Me; She Loves You; Can't Buy Me Love; I Want to Hold Your Hand; I Saw Her Standing There; Eight Days a Week; Yes It Is; This Boy; All My Loving; Help!; Ticket to Ride; I Feel Fine; I'm A Loser; A Hard Day's Night; No Reply; I'll Follow The Sun; Yesterday; Eleanor Rigby; Yellow Submarine; Penny Lane; All You Need Is Love; Lady Madonna; Hey Jude. *Albums* with The Beatles: Please, Please Me, 1963; With The Beatles, 1963; A Hard Day's Night, 1964; Beatles for Sale, 1965; Help!, 1965; Rubber Soul, 1966; Revolver, 1966; Sgt Pepper's Lonely Hearts Club Band, 1967; Magical Mystery Tour, 1967; The Beatles (White Album), 1968; Yellow Submarine, 1969; Abbey Road, 1969; Let it Be, 1970; subseq. *albums* include: McCartney, 1970; Ram, 1971; Wildlife, 1971; Red Rose Speedway, 1973; Band on the Run, 1973 (2 Grammy Awards); Venus and Mars, 1975; Wings at the Speed of Sound, 1976; Wings over America, 1976; London Town, 1978; Wings Greatest, 1978; Back to the Egg, 1979; McCartney II, 1980; Tug of War, 1982; Pipes of Peace, 1983; Give My Regards to Broad Street, 1984; *Films* (with Beatles): A Hard Day's Night, 1964; Help!, 1965; Yellow Submarine, 1968; Let It Be, 1970; (with Wings) Rockshow, 1981; (wrote, composed score, and acted in) Give My Regards To Broad Street, 1984. *Film scores:* The Family Way, 1967; James Paul McCartney, 1973;

Live and Let Die, 1973; *TV score:* The Zoo Gang (series), 1973. Grammy Awards for best perf. by vocal group and best new artist of 1964 (with other Beatles), Nat. Acad. of Recording Arts and Scis, USA, 1965; Ivor Novello Special Award for Internat. Achievement, 1980; Music Achievement Award, Nat. Acad. of Popular Music, 1981; Ivor Novello Award for Ebony and Ivory, Internat. Hit of the Year, 1982; awards for arrangements and albums. Freeman, City of Liverpool, 1984. *Address:* c/o MPL Communications Ltd, 1 Soho Square, W1V 6BQ. *T:* 01–439 6621.

McCAUGHEY, John Davis; Governor of Victoria, Australia, since 1986; *b* 12 July 1914; *s* of John and Lizzie McCaughey; *m* 1940, Jean Middlemas Henderson; three *s* two *d. Educ:* Pembroke Coll., Cambridge (MA); New Coll., Edinburgh; Presbyterian Coll., Belfast. Ordained in Presbyt. Ch. in Ireland, 1942; Study Sec., SCM, 1946–52; Prof. of NT Studies, Ormond Coll., Univ. of Melbourne, 1953–64, Master of the Coll. 1959–79; Dep. Chancellor, Univ. of Melbourne, 1978–79, 1982–85. Hon. DD Edinburgh, 1966; Hon. LLD Melbourne, 1982. *Publications:* Christian Obedience in the University, 1958; Diversity and Unity in the New Testament Picture of Christ, 1969; articles in Colloquium, Aust. Biblical Rev., etc. *Recreations:* reading, listening, golf. *Address:* Government House, Melbourne, Vic 3004, Australia. *T:* (03) 639971. *Clubs:* Melbourne, Royal Melbourne Golf.

McCAULEY, Air Marshal Sir John Patrick Joseph, KBE 1955 (CBE 1943); CB 1951; *b* 18 March 1899; *s* of late John and Sophia McCauley; *m* 1925, Murielle Mary, *d* of late John Burke, and of Maude Burke; one *s* two *d. Educ:* St Joseph's Coll., Sydney; RMC, Duntroon; Melbourne Univ. (BCom 1936). Grad. RMC 1919; Aust. Staff Corps, 1919–23; RAAF, 1924–; passed RAF Staff Coll., 1933; Flying Instructor's Course, Central Flying Sch., RAF, 1934; Dir Trg, RAAF HQ Melbourne, 1937–38; CO 1 Flying Trg Sch. 1939; CO 1 Eng. Sch., 1940; CO RAAF Stn Sembawang, Malaya, 1941–42; CO RAAF Stn, Palembang 11, Sumatra, 1942; SASO RAAF Darwin, 1942; DCAS, 1942–43; Air Cdre Ops, 2nd TAF France and Germany, 1944–45; DCAS, 1946–47; Chief of Staff, BCOF, Japan, 1947–49; AOC E Area, 1949–53; CAS, RAAF, 1954–57, retd. *Address:* 10 Onslow Gardens, Greenknowe Avenue, Elizabeth Bay, Sydney, NSW 2011, Australia.

McCAVE, Prof. Ian Nicholas, FGS; Woodwardian Professor of Geology, University of Cambridge, since 1985; *b* 3 Feb. 1941; *s* of Thomas Theasby McCave and Gwendoline Marguerite McCave (*née* Langlois); *m* 1972, Susan Caroline Adams (*née* Bambridge); three *s* one *d. Educ:* Elizabeth Coll., Guernsey; Hertford Coll., Oxford (MA, DSc); Brown Univ., USA (PhD). FGS 1963. NATO Research Fellow, Netherlands Inst. for Sea Research, 1967–69; Lectr 1969–76, Reader 1976–84, UEA. Vis. Prof., Oregon State Univ., 1974; Vis. Investigator, Woods Hole Oceanographic Instn, 1978–. *Publications:* (ed) The Benthic Boundary Layer, 1976; over 70 papers in jls. *Recreations:* pottering about in the garden, choral singing. *Address:* Marlborough House, 23 Victoria Street, Cambridge CB1 1JP. *Club:* Royal Channel Islands Yacht (Guernsey).

McCAW, Hon. Sir Kenneth (Malcolm), Kt 1975; QC (Australia) 1972; Attorney-General of New South Wales, 1965–75, retired; *b* 8 Oct. 1907; *s* of Mark Malcolm and Jessie Alice McCaw; *m* 1968, Valma Marjorie Cherlin (*née* Stackpool); *s* one *d. Educ:* matriculated evening college. Left school, 1919; farm and saw-mill hand; clerk, commercial offices and law office, 1922–28; articled law clerk, 1928–33; admitted Solicitor and founded city law firm, 1933; Attorney, Solicitor and Proctor, NSW Supreme Court, until 1965; admitted to NSW Bar, 1965. Councillor, NSW Law Soc., 1945–48. MLA (Lib.) for Lane Cove, NSW, 1947–75, retired. *Publication:* People Versus Power, 1978. *Recreations:* swimming, walking, Braille reading, music, elocution. *Address:* Woodrow House, Charlish Lane, Lane Cove, NSW 2066, Australia. *T:* 427–1900. *Clubs:* Sydney, Lane Cove Businessmen's, (Charter Mem.) Lane Cove Lions (all Sydney/Metropolitan).

McCLEAN, Prof. (John) David; Professor of Law, since 1973, Dean of Faculty of Law, 1978–81, University of Sheffield; *b* 4 July 1939; *s* of Major Harold McClean and Mrs Mabel McClean; *m* 1966, Pamela Ann Loader; one *s* one *d. Educ:* Queen Elizabeth's Grammar Sch., Blackburn; Magdalen Coll., Oxford (DCL, 1984). Called to the Bar, Gray's Inn, 1963. Asst Lectr 1961, Lectr 1963, Sen. Lectr 1968, Univ. of Sheffield. Vis. Lectr in Law, Monash Univ., Melbourne, 1968, Vis Prof., 1978. Vice-Chm., C of E Bd for Social Responsibility, 1978–80. Member: Gen. Synod of C of E, 1970– (Vice-Chm., House of Laity, 1979–85, Chm. 1985–); Crown Appts Commn, 1977–. *Publications:* Criminal Justice and the Treatment of Offenders (jtly), 1969; (contrib.) Halsbury's Laws of England, 4th edn 1974; The Legal Context of Social Work, 1975, 2nd edn 1980; (jtly) Defendants in the Criminal Process, 1976; (ed jtly) Shawcross and Beaumont, Air Law, 4th edn 1977, reissue (new edn of one vol.) 1983; (jtly) Recognition and Enforcement of Judgments, etc, within the Commonwealth, 1977; (ed jtly) Dicey and Morris, Conflict of Laws, 10th edn 1980, 11th edn 1987; Recognition of Family Judgments in the Commonwealth, 1983. *Recreation:* detective fiction. *Address:* 6 Burnt Stones Close, Sheffield S10 5TS. *T:* Sheffield 305794. *Club:* Royal Commonwealth Society.

McCLEAN, Kathleen; *see* Hale, Kathleen.

McCLELLAN, Col Sir (Herbert) Gerard (Thomas), Kt 1986; CBE 1979 (OBE 1960); TD 1955; JP; DL; company director; *b* 24 Sept. 1913; *s* of late George McClellan and Lilian (*née* Fitzgerald); *m* 1939, Rebecca Ann (Nancy) Desforges (*d* 1982); one *s* three *d.* Served War of 1939–45, Loyal (N Lancs) Regt, RA, London Irish Rifles, in ME, N Africa and Italy (wounded; despatches). Commanded 626 HAA (Liverpool Irish) Regt and 470 LAA (3rd West Lancs) Regt, RA TA, 1955–60; County Comdt, W Lancs ACF, 1961–66; Member: W Lancs T&AVRA, 1955–66 (Vice-Chm., 1966–68); NW England and IoM T&AVRA, 1968–70 (Vice-Chm., 1970–75; Chm., 1975–79). Former Mem. (C) for Childwall, Liverpool City Council; Member: Liverpool Cons. Assoc., 1960– (Vice-Chm., 1966–75; Chm., 1975–85); NW Area Cons. Assoc., 1971–; Chm., Wavertree Cons. Assoc., 1962–67 (Pres., 1967–76); President: Garston Cons. Assoc., 1979–; Crosby Cons. Assoc., 1986–. FIAM. DL Lancs later Merseyside, 1967; JP Liverpool, 1968; High Sheriff of Merseyside, 1980–81. *Address:* Westwood, Windermere Road, Hightown, Liverpool L38 3RJ. *T:* 051-929 2269. *Clubs:* Army and Navy; Athenæum (Liverpool).

McCLELLAN, John Forrest; Under Secretary, Industry Department for Scotland (formerly Scottish Economic Planning Department), 1980–85, retired; *b* 15 Aug. 1932; *s* of John McClellan and Hester (*née* Niven); *m* 1956, Eva Maria Pressel; three *s* one *d. Educ:* Ferryhill Primary Sch., Aberdeen; Aberdeen Grammar Sch.; Aberdeen Univ. (MA). Served Army, 2nd Lieut, Gordon Highlanders and Nigeria Regt, RWAFF, 1954–56. Entered Civil Service, 1956; Asst Principal, Scottish Educn Dept, 1956–59; Private Sec. to Perm. Under Sec. of State, Scottish Office, 1959–60; Principal, Scottish Educn Dept, 1960–68; Civil Service Fellow, Glasgow Univ., 1968–69; Asst Sec., Scottish Educn Dept, 1969–77; Asst Under Sec. of State, Scottish Office, 1977–80. Dir, Scottish Internat. Educn Trust, 1986–; Mem., Management Cttee, Hanover (Scotland) Housing Assoc., 1986–. *Recreations:* gardening, walking. *Address:* Grangeneuk, West Linton, Peeblesshire EH46 7HG. *T:* West Linton 60502. *Club:* Royal Scots (Edinburgh).

McCLELLAND, Senator the Hon. Douglas; President of the Australian Senate, since 1983; *b* 5 Aug. 1926; *s* of Alfred McClelland and Gertrude Amy Cooksley; *m* 1950, Lorna Belva McNeill; one *s* two *d. Educ:* Parramatta Boys High School; Metropolitan Business College. Reporter, 1949–61; Mem. NSW ALP Executive, 1956–62; Hon. Dir, St George Hosp., Sydney, 1957–68. Member, Australian Senate for NSW, 1961–; Senate appointments: Minister for the Media, 1972–75; Manager, Govt Business, 1974–75; Special Minister of State, June–Nov. 1975; Opposition spokesman on Admin. Services, 1976–77; Manager, Opposition Business, 1976–77; Dep. Leader of Opposition, May–Dec. 1977; Dep. Pres. and Chm of Cttees, 1981–82. *Recreations:* No 1 supporter, St George Rugby League FC; reading, making friends. *Address:* Parliament House, Canberra, ACT 2600, Australia. *T:* 72 6350. *Clubs:* City Tattersalls (Life Mem.); St George Rugby League Football.

McCLELLAND, George Ewart, CB 1986; Solicitor, Department of Employment, since 1982; *b* 27 March 1927; *s* of George Ewart McClelland and Winifred (*née* Robinson); *m* 1956, Anne Penelope, *yr d* of late Judge Arthur Henry Armstrong; one *s* two *d. Educ:* Stonyhurst Coll.; Merton Coll., Oxford (Classical Scholar; MA). Called to the Bar, Middle Temple, 1952. Entered Solicitor's Dept, Min. of Labour, 1953; Asst Solicitor, 1969; Principal Asst Solicitor, 1978.

McCLELLAND, Prof. (William) Grigor, MA; MBA; Visiting Professor, Durham University Business School, since 1977; Chairman, Washington Development Corporation, since 1977; *b* 2 Jan. 1922; *o c* of Arthur and Jean McClelland, Gosforth, Newcastle upon Tyne; *m* 1946, Diana Avery Close; two *s* two *d. Educ:* Leighton Park; Balliol Coll., Oxford. First Class PPE, 1948. Friends' Ambulance Unit, 1941–46. Man. Dir, Laws Stores Ltd, 1949–65, 1978–85 (Chm., 1966–85); Sen. Res. Fellow in Management Studies, Balliol Coll., 1962–65; Dir, Manchester Business Sch., 1965–77, and Prof. of Business Administration, 1967–77, Univ. of Manchester; Dep. Chm., Nat. Computing Centre, 1966–68. Chm., EDC for the Distributive Trades, 1980–84 (Mem., 1965–70); Member: The Consumer Council, 1963–66; Economic Planning Council, Northern Region, 1965–66; IRC, 1966–71; NEDC, 1969–71; SSRC, 1971–74; North Eastern Industrial Develt Bd, 1977–; Trustee: Anglo-German Foundn for the Study of Industrial Soc., 1973–79; Employment Inst. and Campaign for Jobs, 1985–; Governor: Nat. Inst. of Econ. and Social Research; Leighton Park Sch., 1952–60 and 1962–66; Trustee, 1956–, and Chm., 1965–78, Joseph Rowntree Charitable Trust. CBIM. Hon. DCL Dunelm, 1985. *Publications:* Studies in Retailing, 1963; Costs and Competition in Retailing, 1966; And a New Earth, 1976; (ed) Quakers Visit China, 1957; Editor, Jl of Management Studies, 1963–65. *Recreations:* tennis, ski-ing, fell-walking. *Address:* 66 Elmfield Road, Gosforth, Newcastle upon Tyne NE3 4BD.

MACCLESFIELD, 8th Earl of *cr* 1721; **George Roger Alexander Thomas Parker;** Baron Parker, 1716; Viscount Parker, 1721; DL; *b* 6 May 1914; *e s* of 7th Earl of Macclesfield and Lilian Joanna Vere (*d* 1974), *d* of Major Charles Boyle; *S* father, 1975; *m* 1938, Hon. Valerie Mansfield, *o d* of 4th Baron Sandhurst, OBE; two *s.* DL Oxfordshire, 1965. *Heir: s* Viscount Parker, *qv. Address:* Shirburn, Watlington, Oxon.

MACCLESFIELD, Archdeacon of; *see* Gaisford, Ven. J. S.

McCLEVERTY, Prof. Jon Armistice; Professor of Inorganic Chemistry, since 1980, and Head of Department of Chemistry, since 1984, University of Birmingham; *b* 11 Nov. 1937; *s* of John and Nessie McCleverty; *m* 1963, Dianne Barrack; two *d. Educ:* Univ. of Aberdeen (BSc 1960); Imperial College, London (DIC, PhD 1963); Massachusetts Inst. of Technology. Asst Lectr, part-time, Acton Coll. of Technology, 1962–63; Asst Lectr, then Lectr, Sen. Lectr, and Reader, Univ. of Sheffield, 1964–80. Tilden Lectr, RSC, 1981. RSC Medal, Chem. and Electrochem. of Transition Metals, 1985. *Publications:* numerous articles, principally in Jl of Chem. Soc. *Recreations:* gardening, DIY, travel, traditional jazz. *Address:* Department of Chemistry, University of Birmingham, PO Box 363, Birmingham B15 2TT. *T:* 021–472 1301.

McCLINTOCK, Surg. Rear-Adm. Cyril Lawson Tait, CB 1974; OBE 1964; Medical Officer in Charge, Royal Naval Hospital, Haslar and Command Medical Adviser on staff of Commander-in-Chief Naval Home Command, 1972–75; retired 1975; *b* 2 Aug. 1916; 2nd surv. *s* of late Lawson Tait McClintock, MB, ChB, Loddon, Norfolk; *m* 1966, Freda Margaret, *o d* of late Robert Jones, Caergwle, Denbighshire; two step *s. Educ:* St Michael's, Uckfield; Epsom; Guy's Hospital. MRCS, LRCP 1940; DLO 1955. Joined RN Medical Service, 1940; served War of 1939–45 in Western Approaches, N Africa, Eritrea, India and Singapore; Korea, 1950–51; ENT Specialist, RN Hosps, Port Edgar, Chatham, Hong Kong, Portland, Haslar, Malta and Russell Eve Building, Hamilton, Bermuda; MO i/c RN Hosp. Bighi, Malta, 1969; David Bruce RN Hosp. Mtarfa, Malta, 1970–71; Comd Med. Adviser to C-in-C Naval Forces Southern Europe, 1969–71. QHS 1971–75. FRSocMed 1948; MFCM 1974. CStJ 1973. *Recreations:* cricket, tennis, Rugby refereeing, history. *Address:* 14 Ambleside Court, Alverstoke, Hants PO12 2DJ. *Clubs:* Army and Navy, MCC.

McCLINTOCK, David, TD; writer, naturalist and horticulturist; *b* 4 July 1913; *o s* of Rev. E. L. L. McClintock, Glendaragh, Crumlin, Co. Antrim, and Margaret McClintock, *d* of John Henry Buxton, Easneye, Ware, Herts; *m* Elizabeth Anne, *d* of Maj. V. J. Dawson, Miserden, Glos; two *s* two *d. Educ:* West Downs Sch., Winchester; Harrow Sch.; Trinity Coll., Cambridge. BA 1934, MA 1940. FCA 1938; FLS 1953. 2nd Lieut, Herts Yeomanry RA TA, 1938; HQ 54 Div., Captain, 1941; Intelligence Trng Centre, 1941–43; Major, 1942; Civil Affairs Trng Centre, 1943–44; Lt-Col, 1944; BAOR, 1944–45. K-H Newsletter, 1938–46; Commercial Manager, Air Contractors Ltd, 1946–47; Chief Accountant and Admin. Officer, Coal Utilisation Council, 1951–73. Member: Wild Flower Soc., 1934– (Chm., 1981–, Treasurer, 1978–82); Council, Botanical Soc. of British Isles, 1954–64 (Pres., 1971–73); Council, Kent Trust for Nature Conservation, 1958–62 (Vice-Pres., 1963–); Council, Ray Soc., 1968–72, 1976–80 (Vice-Pres., 1972–76; Pres., 1980–83; Hon. Vice-Pres., 1983–); Council, Linnean Soc., 1970–78 (Vice-Pres., 1971–74; Editl Sec., 1974–78); Plant Variety Rights Adv. Panel for heathers, 1973–; Royal Horticultural Society: Scientific Cttee, 1979– (Vice-Chm., 1983–), Publications Cttee, 1982–; Council, Internat. Dendrology Soc., 1979– (Editor, 1979–83); Council, Nat. Trust, 1980–84. Pres., Kent Field Club, 1978–80. Membre d'Honneur, Soc. Guernesiaise, 1968–. Veitch Meml Medal in gold, 1981. *Publications:* Pocket Guide to Wild Flowers (with R.S.R. Fitter), 1956; Supplement to the Pocket Guide to Wild Flowers, 1957; (jtly) Natural History of the Garden of Buckingham Palace, 1964; Companion to Flowers, 1966; Guide to the Naming of Plants, 1969, 2nd edn 1980; Wild Flowers of Guernsey, 1975; (with J. Bichard) Wild Flowers of the Channel Islands, 1975; Joshua Gosselin of Guernsey, 1976; (with F. Perring and R. E. Randall) Picking Wild Flowers, 1977; (ed) H. J. van de Laar, The Heather Garden, 1978; Guernsey's Earliest Flora, 1982; contribs to several other books and numerous periodicals. *Recreations:* anything to do with wild life and gardening, music, formerly shooting, fishing, tennis etc. *Address:* Bracken Hill, Platt, Sevenoaks, Kent TN15 8JH. *T:* Borough Green 884102. *Clubs:* Horticultural, Linnean Dining.

See also Baron Hazlerigg, C. H. G. Kinahan.

McCLINTOCK, Sir Eric (Paul), Kt 1981; Chairman, Woolworths Ltd, since 1978; *b* 13 Sept. 1918; *s* of Robert and Ada McClintock; *m* 1942, Eva Lawrence; two *s* one *d. Educ:* De La Salle Coll., Armidale; Sydney Univ. (DPA). Supply Dept, Dept of the Navy, Australia, 1935–47; served successively in Depts of Commerce, Agriculture, and Trade, in Washington, New York, Melbourne and Canberra, 1947–61 (1st Asst Sec. on resignation); investment banking, 1962–. Chairman: AFT Ltd; Upper Hunter Newspapers Pty Ltd; Williams Bros Engineering Pty Ltd; G. S. Yuill & Co. Pty Ltd; Yuill Australia Ltd; McClintock Associates Ltd; Aust. Overseas Projects Corp., 1978–84; Dep. Chm., Development Finance Corp. Ltd; Director: Philips Industries Holdings Ltd, 1978–85; Wormalds Internat. Holdings Ltd, 1986–. Chm., Trade Develt Council, 1970–74. President: Royal Life Saving Soc. (NSW); Inst. Public Affairs (NSW). *Recreations:* tennis, golf. *Address:* 16 O'Connell Street, Sydney, NSW, Australia. *T:* 233 5733. *Clubs:* Australian (Sydney); Commonwealth (Canberra).

McCLINTOCK, Nicholas Cole, CBE 1979; Secretary-General of the Order of St John, 1968–81 (Deputy Secretary-General, 1963–68); *b* 10 Sept. 1916; *s* of late Col Robert Singleton McClintock, DSO (3rd *s* of Adm. Sir Leopold McClintock), and Mary Howard, *d* of Sir Howard Elphinstone, VC; *m* 1953, Pamela Sylvia, *d* of late Major Rhys Mansel, Smedmore, Dorset; two *s* two *d. Educ:* Stowe Sch.; Trinity Coll., Cambridge (MA; Capt., Univ. Fencing Team). Entered Colonial Admin. Service, N Nigeria, 1939 but went immediately on War Service with 18th and 28th Field Regts RA, Dunkirk 1940, India and Burma, 1942–45; commanded 1st Field Battery RA in final Burma campaign. Asst Principal, Appointments Dept, CO, Feb.–Oct. 1946; Asst Dist Officer, N Nigeria, 1946–49; Private Sec. to Governor (Sir John Macpherson), 1949–50; Clerk to Exec. Council and Clerk, Legislature, N Nigeria, 1951–53; Sen. Dist Officer and Actg Resident, Kano Province, 1955–59; Admin. Officer Grade 1 and Resident, Bornu Province, 1960–62; retd 1962 to allow for Africanisation of Service. KStJ 1968. *Address:* Lower Westport, Wareham, Dorset BH20 4PR. *T:* Wareham 2943. *Club:* Army and Navy.

McCLINTOCK-BUNBURY, family name of **Baron Rathdonnell.**

McCLOSKEY, Bernard Mary; Deputy Director of Public Prosecutions for Northern Ireland, 1972–84; *b* 7 Aug. 1924; *s* of Felix and Josephine McCloskey; *m* 1952, Rosalie Donaghy; three *s* two *d. Educ:* St Malachy's Coll., Belfast; Queen's Univ., Belfast (LLB (Hons)). Admitted solicitor (Northern Ireland), 1947; private practice, 1947–72. Joint Solicitor to Scarman Tribunal of Enquiry, 1969–71. *Recreations:* swimming, golf. *Address:* c/o Royal Courts of Justice, Chichester Street, Belfast, Northern Ireland BT1 3NX. *T:* Belfast 35111. *Club:* Fortwilliam Golf (Hon. Mem.).

McCLOY, John Jay, DSM, MF (US); Partner, Milbank Tweed, Hadley & McCloy, since 1963; Director and Chairman Executive Committee, Squibb Corporation; Hon. Chairman, Board of the Council on Foreign Relations, Inc.; *b* 31 March 1895; *s* of John Jay McCloy and Anna May Snader; *m* 1930, Ellen Zinsser; one *s* one *d. Educ:* Amherst Coll. (AB); Harvard Univ. (LLB). Admitted to New York Bar, 1921; mem. of law firm of Cravath, de Gersdorff Swaine & Wood, New York City, 1929–40; expert cons. to Sec. of War, 1940; The Asst Sec. of War, 1941–45; Chm. of The Combined Civil Affairs Cttee of Combined Chiefs of Staff; Mem. of law firm of Milbank, Tweed, Hope, Hadley & McCloy, NY City, 1945–47; Pres. International Bank for Reconstruction and Development, Washington, DC, 1947–49; US Military Governor and US High Comr for Germany, Frankfurt, Germany, 1949–52; Mem. State Dept Cttee on Atomic Energy, 1946–47; Counsel, Milbank, Tweed, Hope & Hadley, 1961; Adviser to President Kennedy on Disarmament, 1961; Chairman: Co-ordinating Cttee of the US on Cuban Crisis, 1962–63; Past Chm., Gen. Adv. Cttee on Arms Control and Disarmament; Mem. Exec. Cttee, The Salk Inst., La Jolla, Calif; Hon. Chairman: Atlantic Institute, 1966–68; Chm., Amer. Council on Germany Inc. Mem., President's Commn on the Assassination of President Kennedy; Mem., American and NY Bar Assocs; Mem., Bar Assoc. of City of New York. Director: Dreyfus Corp., NYC; Mercedes-Benz of N America, Inc. Past Chm. and Trustee, Ford Foundation. Chm. Public Oversight Bd, Sec. Practice Section, AICPA, 1978–. Retired Director: The Chase Manhattan Bank (Chm. 1953–60); Metropolitan Life Insurance Co.; Westinghouse Electric Corp.; American Telephone & Telegraph Co; Allied Chemical Corp. Trustee, John M. Olin Foundn. Hon. Trustee: Bd of Trustees, Amherst Coll., Mass (Chm.); Lenox Hill Hosp.; Johns Hopkins Univ.; Trustee, Amer. Sch. of Classical Studies, Athens; Mem., Bd of Overseers to visit Center for Internat. Studies, Harvard Univ. Capt. FA, AEF. Holds numerous hon. degrees both in US and abroad, also Civic Hons. US Presidential Medal of Freedom and Distinguished Service Medal; Grand Officer of Legion of Honour (France); Grand Officer of Order of Merit of the Republic (Italy); Grand Cross of Order of Merit (Federal Republic of Germany). *Publication:* The Challenge to American Foreign Policy, 1953. *Recreations:* tennis and fishing. *Address:* 1 Chase Manhattan Plaza, New York, NY 10005, USA. *Clubs:* Brook, Links, University, Century, Anglers, Recess, Ausable, Clove Valley Rod and Gun (NY); Metropolitan (Washington).

McCLUNE, Rear-Adm. (William) James, CB 1978; *b* Londonderry, 20 Nov. 1921; *s* of James McClune, MBE, Carrickmacross, Co. Monaghan, and Matilda (*née* Burns); *m* 1953, Elizabeth, *yr d* of A. E. D. Prideaux, LDS, Weymouth; one *s* one *d. Educ:* Model Sch. and Foyle Coll., Derry; QUB (BSc 1st Cl. Hons Elec. Eng. 1941); RN Staff Coll., Greenwich (1961); Univ. of Birmingham (Ratcliff Prizeman, MSc 1970); RN War Coll. (1971). Bronze Medal, CGLI, 1940; Belfast Assoc. of Engrs' Prize, 1940, 1941. CEng, MIEE; CBIM. Radar Officer, RNVR, 1941–47: HMS Howe and HMS Cleopatra; Staff of Vice-Adm. (Destroyers), Home Fleet; HMS Vanguard; Eng Dept, GPO, 1947–49; RN, 1949–78; HMS Euryalus and HMS Mermaid; Weapon Elec. Sch.; HMS Collingwood, HMS Barfleur, HMS Albion; ASRE; HMS Eastbourne; Exec. Officer, RNEC, Manadon; Weapons Dept; HMS London; Ship Dept; Defence Fellowship; Admiralty Interview Bd; Captain, HMS Collingwood; Dir, Naval Manning and Trng (Eng); CSO (Engrg) to C-in-C Fleet, 1976–78; Chm. Trustees, Royal Sailors Rests; Admty Governor, RN Benevolent Trust; Mem., RNLI Management Cttee. Chm., South Western Electricity Consultative Council; Chm., Christian Alliance Trust Corp. Chm., Bd of Governors, Monkton Combe Sch. *Recreation:* sailing. *Address:* Harlam Lodge, Lansdown, Bath; 7 Theed Street, SE1. *Clubs:* Royal Commonwealth Society; Royal Naval and Royal Albert Yacht (Portsmouth).

McCLUNEY, Ian; HM Diplomatic Service; Foreign and Commonwealth Office, since 1986; *b* 27 Feb. 1937; *e s* of John McCluney and Annie (*née* Currie); *m* 1962, Elizabeth Mary Walsh; two *s* one *d. Educ:* Orange Hill Grammar Sch.; Edinburgh Univ. (BSc). Served HM Forces, Lieut RASC, 1958–62. Joined FO, 1964; Commerical Attaché, Addis Ababa, 1964–67; Asst Private Sec. to Foreign and Commonwealth Sec., 1969–70; Head, British Interests Section, Baghdad, 1972–74; FCO, 1975–78; Head of Chancery, Kuwait, 1979–82; Consul-Gen., Alexandria, 1982–86. *Recreation:* sailing. *Address:* c/o Foreign and Commonwealth Office, King Charles Street, SW1; 8 Pewley Way, Guildford GU1 3PY. *T:* Guildford 63304. *Club:* Littleton Sailing.

McCLURE, David, RSA 1971 (ARSA 1963); RSW 1965; SSA 1951; painter and printmaker; *b* 20 Feb. 1926; *s* of Robert McClure, MM, and Margaret Helena McClure (*née* Evans); *m* 1950, Joyce Dixon Flanigan; two *s* one *d. Educ:* Queen's Park Sch., Glasgow; Glasgow Univ., 1943–44; (coal-miner, 1944–47); Edinburgh Univ., 1947–49; Edinburgh Coll. of Art, 1947–52 (DA). Travelled in Spain and Italy, 1952–53; on staff of Edinburgh Coll. of Art, 1953–55; one year painting in Italy and Sicily, 1956–57; Duncan of Jordanstone Coll. of Art, Dundee: Lectr, 1957–71, Sen. Lectr, 1971–83; Head of Drawing and Painting, 1983–85. *One man exhibitions:* Palermo, 1957; Edinburgh, 1957, 1961, 1962, 1966, 1969; 14 Scottish Painters, London, 1964; Univ. of Birmingham, 1965; Thackeray Gall., London, 1978; retrospective exhibn, Dundee Art Galls, 1984. *Work in public and private collections:* UK, USA, Canada, Italy. *Publication:* John Maxwell (monograph), 1976. *Recreations:* collecting Victorian china, gardening, the pianoforte, cooking. *Address:* 16 Strawberry Bank, Dundee, Scotland. *T:* Dundee 66959.

McCLURE, Joseph Robert; JP; Councillor, Tyne and Wear County Council, 1974–81 (Chairman, 1977–78); *b* 23 Oct. 1923; *s* of Thomas Render McClure and Catherine Bridget McClure; *m* 1943, Evelyn Joice; one *d. Educ:* Prior Street Sch.; Oakwellgate Sch., Gateshead. Served War, Royal Marines, 1941–46. Elected Councillor, County Borough of Gateshead, 1964, Dep. Mayor, 1973–74. President, Gateshead Royal British Legion, 1976–. JP Gateshead and Blaydon 1979. *Recreation:* bowls. *Address:* 170 Rectory Road, Gateshead, Tyne and Wear. *T:* Gateshead 770709.

McCLUSKEY, family name of **Baron McCluskey.**

McCLUSKEY, Baron *cr* 1976 (Life Peer), of Churchhill in the District of the City of Edinburgh; **John Herbert McCluskey,** a Senator of the College of Justice in Scotland, since 1984; *b* 12 June 1929; *s* of Francis John McCluskey, Solicitor, and Margaret McCluskey (*née* Doonan); *m* 1956, Ruth Friedland; two *s* one *d. Educ:* St Bede's Grammar Sch., Manchester; Holy Cross Acad., Edinburgh; Edinburgh Univ. Harry Dalgety Bursary, 1948; Vans Dunlop Schol., 1949; Muirhead Prize, 1949; MA 1950; LLB 1952. Sword of Honour, RAF Spitalgate, 1953. Admitted Faculty of Advocates, 1955; Standing Jun. Counsel to Min. of Power (Scotland), 1963; Advocate-Depute, 1964–71; QC (Scot.) 1967; Chm., Medical Appeal Tribunals for Scotland, 1972–74; Sheriff Principal of Dumfries and Galloway, 1973–74; Solicitor General for Scotland, 1974–79. Reith Lectr, BBC, 1986. *Recreations:* tennis, pianoforte. *Address:* Court of Session, Parliament House, Edinburgh EH1 1RF. *T:* 031–225 2595. *Club:* Royal Air Force.

McCLUSKIE, Samuel Joseph; Assistant General Secretary, National Union of Seamen, since 1976; *b* 11 Aug. 1932; *s* of James and Agnes McCluskie; *m* 1961, Alice (*née* Potter); one *s* one *d. Educ:* St Mary Primary School, Leith; Holy Cross Academy, Edinburgh. Merchant Navy, 1955; Union Delegate, 1963; Mem., Labour Party Nat. Exec. Cttee, 1974–, Treasurer, 1984–; Chairman, Labour Party, 1983. *Recreations:* coursing, greyhounds, watching Glasgow Celtic. *Address:* 23/7 Ferryfield, Edinburgh. *T:* 031–552 9791; (office) 01–622 5588.

McCOLL, Colin Hugh Verel, CMG 1983; Counsellor, Foreign and Commonwealth Office, since 1977; *b* 6 Sept. 1932; *s* of Dr Robert McColl and Julie McColl; *m* 1st, 1959, Shirley Curtis (*d* 1983); two *s* two *d*; 2nd, 1985, Sally Wyld. *Educ:* Shrewsbury School; The Queen's College, Oxford (BA). Foreign Office, 1956; Third Secretary, Bangkok, 1958, Vientiane, 1960; Second Secretary, FO, 1962; First Secretary, Warsaw, 1966; Consul and First Secretary (Disarmament), Geneva, 1973. *Recreations:* music, walks, cycling, tennis, classics. *Address:* c/o Foreign and Commonwealth Office, SW1. *Club:* Royal Commonwealth Society.

McCOLL, Ian, CBE 1983; Chairman, Scottish Express Newspapers Ltd, 1975–82; *b* 22 Feb. 1915; *e s* of late John and Morag McColl, Glasgow and Bunessan, Isle of Mull; *m* 1968, Brenda, *e d* of late Thomas and Mary McKean, Glasgow; one *d. Educ:* Hillhead High Sch., Glasgow. Served in RAF, 1940–46 (despatches, 1945): Air Crew, Coastal Comd 202 Sqdn. Joined Scottish Daily Express as cub reporter, 1933; held various editorial executive posts; Editor, Scottish Daily Express, 1961–71; Editor, Daily Express, 1971–74; Dir, Express Newspapers Ltd, 1971–82. Contested (L): Dumfriesshire, 1945; Greenock, 1950. Mem., Presbytery of Glasgow and Synod of Clydesdale, 1953–71; Mem., General Assembly Publications Cttee, until 1971; Session Clerk, Sandyford-Henderson Memorial Church of Scotland, Glasgow, 1953–71. Mem., Press Council, 1975–78; a Vice-Pres., Newspaper Press Fund, 1981–. Mem., Inst. of Journalists; Sec., Glasgow branch Nat. Union of Journalists, 1947–48; Mem., Gen. Assembly Bd of Communication, 1983–86. Chm. Media Div., XIII Commonwealth Games, Scotland 1986, 1983–86. Mem., Saints and Sinners Club of Scotland, Chm., 1981–82. *Address:* 12 Newlands Road, Newlands, Glasgow G43 2JB.

McCOLL, Prof. Ian, MS, FRCS, FACS, FRCSE; Professor of Surgery, University of London at the United Medical Schools of Guy's and St Thomas' Hospitals, since 1971; Director of Surgery, since 1985, and Consultant Surgeon, since 1971, Guy's Hospital; Hon. Consultant Surgeon, King's College Hospital, since 1971; Consultant Surgeon to: Edenbridge District Memorial Hospital, since 1978; Lewisham Hospital, since 1983; *b* 6 Jan. 1933; *s* of late Frederick George McColl and Winifred E. McColl, Dulwich; *m* 1960, Dr Jean Lennox, 2nd *d* of Arthur James McNair, FRCS, FRCOG; one *s* two *d. Educ:* Hutchesons' Grammar Sch., Glasgow; St Paul's Sch., London; Guy's Hosp., London. MB, BS 1957; FRCS 1962; FRCSE 1962; MS 1966; FACS 1975. Junior staff appts at St Bartholomew's, Putney, St Mark's, St Peter's, Great Ormond Street, Barnet, St Olave's and Guy's Hosps, 1957–67; Research Fellow, Harvard Med. Sch., and Moynihan Fellowship, Assoc. of Surgeons, 1967; Reader in Surgery, St Bartholomew's Hosp. Med. Coll., 1967 (Sub dean, 1969); Dir of Surgical Unit, Guy's Hosp., 1971–85. Visiting Professor: Univ. of South Carolina, 1974; Johns Hopkins Hosp., 1976. Hon. Consultant in Surgery to the Army, 1982–. External examiner in Surgery to Univs of Newcastle upon Tyne and Cardiff, QUB, TCD and NUI. Royal College of Surgeons: Examr in Pathology, 1970–76; Regl Advr, SE Reg., 1975–80; Mem. Council, 1986; Arris and Gale Lectr, 1964, 1965; Erasmus Wilson Lectr, 1972. Royal Advr, RCSE, 1982–; Medical Advisor, BBC Television, 1976–. Member: Central Health Services Council, 1972–74; Standing Medical Adv. Cttee, 1972–82; Management Cttee, King Edward VII Hospital Fund (Chm., R&D Cttee), 1975–80; Council, Metrop. Hosp. Sunday Fund, 1986–; Chairman: King's Fund Centre Cttee, 1976–; Govt Wkg Pty on Artificial Limb and Appliance Centres in England, 1984–86. Vice-Pres., Coll. of Health, 1981–; Hon. Sec., British Soc. of Gastroenterology, 1970–74. Governor-at-Large for England, Bd of Governors, Amer. Coll. of Surgeons, 1982–. Pres., Mildmay Mission Hosp., 1985–; Governor, Dulwich Coll. Prep. Sch., 1978–. *Publications:* (ed jtly) Intestinal Absorption in Man, 1975; Talking to Patients, 1982; NHS Data Book, 1984; med. articles, mainly on gastroenterology. *Recreation:* forestry. *Address:* 12 Gilkes Crescent, Dulwich Village, SE21 7BS. *T:* 01–693 3084. *Club:* Athenæum.

McCOLOUGH, (Charles) Peter; Chairman, Executive Committee, Xerox Corporation, since 1985; *b* 1 Aug. 1922; *s* of Reginald W. McColough and Barbara Martin McColough; *m* 1953, Mary Virginia White. *Educ:* Dalhousie Univ. (LLB); Harvard Grad. Sch. of Business Administration (MBA). Lehigh Coal & Navigation Co., Philadelphia, 1951–54; Xerox Corp.: Gen. Man., Reproduction Service Centers, 1954–56; Man. Marketing, 1957–59; Gen. Sales Man., 1959–60; Vice-Pres. Sales, 1960–63; Exec. Vice-Pres., Ops,

1963–66; Pres., 1966–68; Pres. and Chief Exec. Officer, 1968–71; Chm., 1971–85. Director: Knight Ridder Inc.; Citibank, NA; Citicorp; Fuji Xerox Co., Ltd; Internat. Executive Service Corps; Union Carbide Corp.; Council on Foreign Relations; Trustee: Eisenhower Exchange Fellowship; Univ. of Rochester; Member: Corp. of Greenwich Hospital Assoc. Inc.; The Business Council; Adv. Council of Industrial Estates Ltd, Nova Scotia. *Address:* Xerox Corporation, Stamford, Conn 06904, USA. *Clubs:* Harvard, River (New York); Belle Haven, Greenwich Country (Connecticut).

McCONE, John A.; US business executive, retired; Chairman, Hendy International Co., 1969–75; *b* 4 Jan. 1902; *s* of Alexander J. McCone and Margaret McCone (*née* Enright); *m* 1938, Rosemary Cooper (*d* 1961); no *c*; *m* 1962, Mrs Theiline McGee Pigott (widow). *Educ:* Univ. of California, Coll. of Engineering. Began as construction engineer, Llewellyn Iron Works; supt Consolidated Steel Corp., 1929; Exec. Vice-Pres. and Dir, 1933–37; Pres. of Bechtel-McCone Corp., Los Angeles, 1937–45; Pres. and Dir, California Shipbuilding Corp., 1941–46; Joshua Hendy Corp., Joshua Hendy Iron Works, 1945–69; Mem. President's Air Policy Commn, 1947–48; Dep. to Sec. of Defense, March-Nov. 1948; Under Sec. of US Air Force, 1950–51. Chm., US Atomic Energy Commn, 1958–61; Dir, Central Intelligence Agency, 1961–65. Chm., Joshua Hendy Corp., 1961–69; holds hon. degrees from Univs and colls in the US. *Recreation:* golf. *Address:* (home) 1543 Riata Road, PO Box 1499, Pebble Beach, Calif 93953, USA. *T:* (408) 625 3266; Norcliffe, The Highlands, Seattle, Washington; PO Box 19, Rock Sound, Eleuthera, Bahamas. *Clubs:* California (Los Angeles); Los Angeles Country (Los Angeles); Pacific Union, Bohemian (San Francisco); Metropolitan, F Street (Washington, DC); The Links (NYC); Cypress Point (Pebble Beach, Calif); Seattle Golf, Ranier (Seattle).

McCONNELL, Albert Joseph, MA, ScD, Hon. DSc: Belfast; Ulster; Hon. ScD Columbia; Hon. LLD NUI; Hon. Fellow of Oriel College, Oxford; Provost of Trinity College, Dublin, 1952–74; Member of Council of State, Ireland, since 1973; *b* 19 Nov. 1903; *s* of Joseph McConnell; *m* 1st, 1934, Hilda (*d* 1966), *d* of late Francis McGuire; 2nd, 1983, Jean (*d* 1985), *d* of late Robert Shekleton. *Educ:* Ballymena Acad.; Trinity Coll., Dublin (Scholar, First Math. Moderator and Univ. Student); Univ. of Rome. Dr of Univ. of Rome, 1928; Mem. of Royal Irish Academy, 1929; ScD (Dublin), 1929; Fellow of Trinity Coll., Dublin, 1930–52; Chm., Governing Board of Sch. of Theoretical Physics, and Mem. Council of Dublin Inst. for Advanced Studies; Lectr in Maths, Trinity Coll., Dublin, 1927–30; Prof. of Natural Philosophy, Univ. of Dublin, 1930–57; Special Univ. Lectr, Univ. of London, 1949; Vis. Professor: Univ. of Alexandria, 1946–47; Univ. of Kuwait, 1970. *Publications:* Applications of the Absolute Differential Calculus, 1931; (ed) The Mathematical Papers of Sir William Rowan Hamilton, vol. II, 1940; Applications of Tensor Analysis, 1957; papers on relativity, geometry and dynamics in various mathematical jls. *Address:* Seafield Lodge, Seafield Road, Killiney, Dublin. *Clubs:* Athenæum; Dublin University (Dublin).

McCONNELL, Comdr Sir Robert Melville Terence, 3rd Bt, *cr* 1900; VRD; RNVR (retired); *b* 7 Feb. 1902; *s* of Sir Joseph McConnell, 2nd Bt, and Lisa (*d* 1956), *d* of late Jackson McGown; *S* father, 1942; *m* 1st, 1928, Rosamond Mary Elizabeth (marr. diss., 1954), *d* of James Stewart Reade, Clonmore, Lisburn, Co. Antrim; three *s* one *d*; 2nd, 1967, Mrs Alice A. M. Hills. *Educ:* Glenalmond; St John's Coll., Cambridge; College of Estate Management, London. Consultant with R. J. McConnell and Co., estate agents, Belfast. *Heir:* *s* Robert Shean McConnell, *b* 23 Nov. 1930. *Address:* Pigeon Hill, Island Road, Killyleagh, Co. Down, N Ireland.

McCONNELL, Rt. Hon. Robert William Brian, PC (N Ireland) 1964; Social Security (formerly National Insurance) Commissioner, Northern Ireland, since 1968; *b* 25 Nov. 1922; *s* of late Alfred E. McConnell, Belfast; *m* 1951, Sylvia Elizabeth Joyce Agnew; two *s* one *d*. *Educ:* Sedbergh Sch.; Queen's Univ., Belfast (BA, LLB). Called to Bar of Northern Ireland, 1948. MP (U) for South Antrim, NI Parlt, 1951–68; Dep. Chm. of Ways and Means, NI Parlt, 1962; Parly Sec. to Min. of Health and Local Govt for N Ireland, 1963; Minister of Home Affairs for Northern Ireland, 1964–66; Minister of State, Min. of Develt, 1966–67; Leader of the House of Commons, NI, 1967–68. Pres., Industrial Court of NI, 1968–81. *Recreation:* cattle breeding. *Address:* 50 Glenavy Road, Knocknadona, Lisburn, Co. Antrim, Northern Ireland. *T:* Lisburn 3432.

MacCONOCHIE, John Angus, MBE 1943; FCIT; Chairman: Furness Withy & Co. Ltd, 1968–72 (Director, 1964–73); Shaw Savill & Albion Co. Ltd, 1968–73 (Director, 1957–73); *b* 12 April 1908; *m* 1938, Peggy, *d* of late Robert Gunson Martindale, MA, Worthing, Sussex; one *s* one *d*. *Educ:* Royal Caledonian Schools, Bushey, Herts. Joined Shaw Savill Line, 1927. Seconded to Min. of War Transport, 1942; served on Staff of Resident Minister for W Africa, Accra; Min. of War Transport Rep. in Gold Coast (MBE); London, 1944; Min. HQ with 21 Army Group; subseq. Paris, Marseilles, Naples. Returned to Shaw Savill Line, 1945: New Zealand, 1949; subseq. Manager for Australia; Gen. Manager for New Zealand, 1953; returned to Britain, 1958; Dir, 1957. Chm., Royal Mail Lines, 1968–73; Director: Economic Insurance, 1967 (Chm. 1969–73); British Maritime Trust, 1966–73; Pacific Steam Navigation Co. Ltd, 1967–73; Pacific Maritime Services, 1967–73; Houlder Bros & Co. Ltd, 1967–73; Whitehall Insurance Co. Ltd, 1967–73; Manchester Liners Ltd, 1968–73; National Bank of New Zealand, 1970 (NZ Bd, 1973–78). Member: Council, Chamber of Shipping; Council of Management, Ocean Travel Development (past Chm.); Cttee, NZ Society (PP); Council Fedn of Commonwealth Chambers of Commerce (a NZ Rep.); British Ship Adoption Soc. (past Chm.); Pres., UK Chamber of Shipping, 1972–73 (Pres.-designate 1971). Patron, Auckland Maritime Soc. *Address:* 36 Barlow Place, Chatswood, Auckland 10, New Zealand. *Club:* Northern (Auckland).

McCONVILLE, Michael Anthony, MBE 1958; writer; *b* 3 Jan. 1925; *s* of late Lt-Col James McConville, MC and late Winifred (*née* Hanley); *m* 1952, Beryl Anne (*née* Jerrett); two *s* four *d*. *Educ:* Mayfield Coll.; Trinity Coll., Dublin. Royal Marines, 1943–46. Malayan Civil Service, 1950–61: served in Perak, Johore, Trengganu, Negri Sembilam, Pahang and Kedah; retd as Chm., Border War Exec. Cttee. CRO (later HM Diplomatic Service), 1961–77: Colombo, 1963–64; Kingston, Jamaica, 1966–67; Ottawa, 1967–71; Consul-Gen., Zagreb, 1974–77. Kesatria Mankgu Negara (Malaya), 1962. *Publications:* (as Anthony McCandless): Leap in the Dark, 1980; The Burke Foundation, 1985; Ascendancy to Oblivion: the story of the Anglo-Irish, 1986; (as Miles Noonan): Tales from the Mess, 1983; (as Patrick Plum): articles and short stories in Blackwoods, etc. *Recreations:* walking, gardening, watching Rugby. *Club:* Kildare Street and University (Dublin).

McCORD, Brig. Mervyn Noel Samuel, CBE 1978 (OBE 1974); MC 1951; retired; *b* 25 Dec. 1929; *s* of Major G. McCord, MBE and Muriel King; *m* 1953, Annette Mary, *d* of C. R. W. Thomson; three *s*. *Educ:* Coleraine, NI; RMA Sandhurst. Commissioned Royal Ulster Rifles, 1949; Korea, 1950–51; School of Infantry, 1958–60; Staff Coll., Camberley, 1961–62; DAQMG, Eastern Command, Canada, 1963–65; BM, HQ 6 Infantry Brigade, 1967–69; JSSC, 1969; GSO1, HQNI, 1970–71; CO, 1st Bn The Royal Irish Rangers, 1971–74; Brig. 1975; Commander, Ulster Defence Regt, 1976–78; Dep. Comdr, Eastern Dist, 1978–81; Brig. King's Div., 1981–84. ADC, 1981–84. Col, The Royal Irish Rangers, 1985– (Dep. Col, 1976–81). Chairman: SHAA, 1986–; SHAA Retirement Homes plc, 1986–. FBIM (MBIM 1978). *Recreations:* cricket, athletics, country sports, gardening. *Address:* c/o Royal Bank of Scotland, Whitehall, SW1. *Club:* Army and Navy.

McCORKELL, Col Michael William, OBE 1964; TD 1954; Lord-Lieutenant, County Londonderry, since 1975; *b* 3 May 1925; *s* of late Captain B. F. McCorkell, Templeard, Culmore, Co. Londonderry and of Mrs E. M. McCorkell; *m* 1950, Aileen Allen, OBE 1975, 2nd *d* of late Lt-Col E. B. Booth, DSO, Darver Castle, Dundalk, Co. Louth, Eire; three *s* one *d*. *Educ:* Aldenham. Served with 16/5 Lancers, 1943–47; Major (TA) North Irish Horse, 1951; Lt-Col 1961; comd North Irish Horse (TA); retd, 1964. T&AVR Col, NI, 1971–74; Brevet Col, 1974; Pres., T&AVR, NI, 1977–; ADC to the Queen, 1972. Co. Londonderry: High Sheriff 1961, DL 1962. *Recreations:* fishing, shooting. *Address:* Ballyarnett, Londonderry, Northern Ireland. *T:* 51239. *Club:* Cavalry and Guards.

MacCORMAC, Richard Cornelius, RIBA; Partner, MacCormac, Jamieson & Prichard, Architects, since 1972; *b* 3 Sept. 1938; *s* of Henry MacCormac, CBE, MD, FRCP and Marion Maud, *d* of B. C. Broomhall, FRCS; *m* 1964, Susan Karin Landen; one *s* (and one *s* decd). *Educ:* Trinity Coll., Cambridge (BA 1962); University College London (MA 1965). RIBA 1967. Served RN, 1957–59. Proj. Archt, London Bor. of Merton, 1967–69; estabd private practice, 1969; taught in Dept of Arch., Cambridge Univ., 1969–75 and 1979–81, Univ. Lectr, 1976–79; Vis. Prof., Univ. of Edinburgh (Dept of Architecture), 1982–85. Dir, Spitalfields Workspace, 1981–. Chm., Good Design in Housing Awards, RIBA London Region, 1977; Mem., Royal Fine Art Commn, 1983–. FRSA 1982. *Publications:* articles in Architectural Review and Archts Jl. *Recreations:* sailing, music, reading. *Address:* 9 Heneage Street, E1 5LJ. *T:* 01–377 9262.

McCORMACK, Arthur Gerard; Director, Population and Development Office, Rome, since 1973; Consultant to United Nations Fund for Population Activities, since 1975; *b* 16 Aug. 1911; *s* of Francis McCormack and Elizabeth Ranard. *Educ:* St Francis Xavier Coll., Liverpool; Durham Univ. (MA Hons History and Econs). Ordained, 1936. Mill Hill Missionary, Africa, 1940–48 (invalided home, 1948); after lengthy illness and convalescence, hosp. chaplain and subseq. teacher-chaplain in secondary modern sch., Widnes; Adviser to Superior Gen., Mill Hill Missionaries, 1963; attended II Vatican Council as expert on population and develt of developing countries, 1963–65; part Founder, Vatican Commn, Justice and Peace (mem. staff for 7 yrs). Special Adviser to Sec. Gen., World Population Conf., Bucharest, 1974. *Publications:* People, Space, Food, 1960; (ed) Christian Responsibility and World Poverty, 1963; World Poverty and the Christian, 1963; Poverty and Population, 1964; The Population Problem, 1970; The Population Explosion and Christian Concern, 1973; Multinational Investment: Boon or Burden for the Developing Countries, 1980; contrib. The Tablet, Population & Develt Rev., Populi, etc. *Recreations:* reading, driving scooter. *Address:* St Joseph's College, Lawrence Street, Mill Hill, NW7 4JX. *T:* 01–959 8493.

McCORMACK, Most Rev. John; *see* Meath, Bishop of, (RC).

McCORMACK, John P(atrick); Vice President, in charge of Latin American and South African Operations, General Motors Corporation, since 1983; *b* New York, 23 Nov. 1923; *s* of John McCormack and Margaret (*née* Bannon); *m* 1952, Mari Martha Luhrs; two *s*. *Educ:* St John's Univ., Jamaica, NY (Bachelor of Business Admin); NY Univ., NYC (LLB). Joined General Motors, 1949; Gen. Clerk, Accounting Dept, NY, 1949, Sen. Clerk 1950, Sen. Accountant 1952; Asst to Treas., Djakarta Br., 1953; Asst Treas., Karachi Br., 1956; Asst Treas., Gen. Motors South African (Pty) Ltd, Port Elizabeth, 1958, Treas. 1961; Asst Finance Man., Overseas Div., NY, 1966; Treas., subseq. Man. Dir, Gen. Motors Continental, Antwerp, 1968; Finance Man., Adam Opel, 1970, Man. Dir and Chm. Bd, 1974; Gen. Dir, European Ops, Gen. Motors Overseas Corp., 1976; Vice Pres. i/c joint ventures and African ops, 1980. *Recreations:* golf, photography. *Address:* c/o General Motors Corporation, General Motors Building, Detroit, Michigan 48202, USA.

McCORMACK, Mark Hume; Chairman and Chief Executive Officer, International Management Group; *b* 6 Nov. 1930; *s* of Ned Hume McCormack and Grace Wolfe McCormack; *m* 1954, Nancy Breckenridge McCormack; two *s* one *d*. *Educ:* Princeton Univ.; William and Mary Coll. (BA); Yale Univ. (LLB). Admitted to Ohio Bar, 1957; Associate in Arter, Hadden, Wykoff & Van Duzer, 1957–63; Partner, 1964–; started Internat. Management Gp, 1962. Commentator for televised golf, BBC. *Publications:* The World of Professional Golf, 1967, 17th edn 1983; Arnie: the evolution of a legend, 1967; The Wonderful World of Professional Golf, 1973; What they don't teach you at Harvard Business School, 1984. *Recreation:* golf. *Address:* No 1300, One Erieview Plaza, Cleveland, Ohio 44114, USA. *T:* 216/522–1200. *Clubs:* Royal & Ancient Golf (St Andrews); Wentworth (Virginia Water); Sunningdale Golf (Berkshire, England); Old Prestwick (Prestwick); Royal Dornoch (Dornoch); Country Club of Cleveland (Ohio).

MacCORMICK, Prof. Donald Neil, FBA 1986; Regius Professor of Public Law, University of Edinburgh, since 1972, Dean of Faculty of Law, 1973–76 and since 1985; *b* 27 May 1941; *yr s* of J. M. MacCormick, MA, LLD (Glasgow) and Margaret I. Miller, MA, BSc (Glasgow); *m* 1965, Caroline Rona Barr, MA (Glasgow); three *d*. *Educ:* High School, Glasgow; Univ. of Glasgow (MA, 1st cl. Philos. and Eng. Lit.); Balliol Coll., Oxford (BA, 1st cl. Jurisprudence; MA); LLD Edinburgh, 1982. Pres., Oxford Union Soc., 1965. Called to the Bar, Inner Temple, 1971. Lecturer, St Andrew's Univ. (Queen's Coll., Dundee), 1965–67; Fellow and Tutor in Jurisprudence, Balliol Coll., Oxford, 1967–72, and CUF Lectr in Law, Oxford Univ., 1968–72; Pro-Proctor, Oxford Univ., 1971–72. Corry Lectr, Queen's Univ., Kingston, Ont, 1981; Vis. Prof., Univ. of Sydney, 1981; Dewey Lectr, NY Univ., 1982. Contested (SNP): Edinburgh North, 1979; Edinburgh, Pentlands, 1983. President: Assoc. for Legal and Social Philosophy, 1974–76; Soc. of Public Teachers of Law, 1983–84. Member: Houghton Cttee on Financial Aid to Political Parties, 1975–76; Broadcasting Council for Scotland, 1985–. FRSE 1986. Hon. LLD Uppsala, 1986. *Publications:* (ed) The Scottish Debate: Essays on Scottish Nationalism, 1970; (ed) Lawyers in their Social Setting, 1976; Legal Reasoning and Legal Theory, 1978; H. L. A. Hart, 1981; Legal Right and Social Democracy: essays in legal and political philosophy, 1982; (with O. Weinberger) Grundlagen des Institutionalistischen Rechtspositivismus, 1985; An Institutional Theory of Law, 1986; contribs to various symposia, jls on law, philosophy and politics. *Recreations:* hill walking, bagpiping, sailing. *Address:* The Old College, Edinburgh EH8 9YL.

See also I. S. MacD. MacCormick.

MacCORMICK, Iain Somerled MacDonald; Director Liaison Manager, British Telecommunications plc, since 1984 (Major Account Manager, 1982); *b* 28 Sept. 1939; *er s* of John MacDonald MacCormick, MA, LLB, LLD and Margaret Isobel MacCormick, MA, BSc; *m* 1964, Micky Trefusis Elsom; two *s* three *d*. *Educ:* Glasgow High Sch.; Glasgow Univ. (MA). Queen's Own Lowland Yeomanry, 1957–67 (Captain). Contested (SNP) Argyll, 1970; MP (SNP) Argyll, Feb. 1974–1979; introduced, as private member's bill, Divorce (Scotland) Act, 1976. Founder Mem., SDP, 1981. Mem., Argyll and Bute District Council, 1979–80. *Recreations:* Rugby football, sailing, local history. *Address:* 102 Mayfield Avenue, W13 9UX. *T:* 01–579 0788. *Club:* Brooks's.

See also Prof. D. N. MacCormick.

McCORMICK, Prof. James Stevenson, FRCPI, FRCGP; FFCM; Professor of Community Health, Trinity College Dublin, since 1973 (Dean of School of Physic, 1974–79); *b* 9 May 1926; *s* of Victor Ormsby McCormick and Margaretta Tate (*née* Stevenson); *m* 1954, Elizabeth Ann Dimond; three *s* one *d. Educ:* The Leys Sch., Cambridge; Clare Coll., Cambridge (BA, MB); St Mary's Hospital, W2. Served RAMC, 1960–62; St Mary's Hosp., 1963; general practice, 1964–73. Chairman: Eastern Health Board, 1970–72; Nat. Health Council, 1984–86. Pres., Irish Coll. of General Practitioners, 1986. Hon. MCFP 1982. *Publications:* The Doctor—Father Figure or Plumber, 1979; papers, espec. on General Practice and Ischaemic Heart Disease. *Recreations:* open air, patients. *Address:* The Barn, Windgates, Bray, Co. Wicklow, Ireland. *T:* Dublin 874113.

McCORMICK, John Ormsby, CMG 1965; MC 1943; HM Diplomatic Service, retired; *b* Dublin, 7 Feb. 1916; *s* of Albert Victor McCormick and Sarah Beatty de Courcy; *m* 1955, Francine Guieu (*née* Pâris); one *d,* one step *s. Educ:* The Leys Sch., Cambridge; New Coll., Oxford. BA Hon. Mods and Greats (Oxford), 1938. Passed Competitive Exam. for Consular Service, 1939, and appointed Asst Officer, Dept of Overseas Trade. Served War of 1939–45, in Royal Corps of Signals, Africa, Sicily, Germany, 1940–45. 2nd Sec. (Commercial), British Embassy, Athens, 1945–47; FO, London, 1948–50; 1st Sec., UK High Commn, Karachi, 1950–52; Consul, New York, 1952–54; transferred to Washington, 1954–55; NATO Defence Coll., 1955; Asst Head, SE Asia Dept, FO, 1956–59; Foreign Service Officer, Grade 6, 1959; Counsellor (Commercial), British Embassy, Djakarta, 1959–62; Corps of Inspectors, FO, 1962–64; Counsellor (Commercial), British Embassy, Ankara, 1965–67; Consul-General, Lyons, 1967–72. *Recreations:* golf, sailing, philosophy. *Address:* Oldfort, Newcastle, Co. Wicklow, Ireland.

McCORQUODALE, Mrs Barbara; *see* Cartland, Barbara H.

McCOWAN, Hon. Sir Anthony (James Denys), Kt 1981; **Hon. Mr Justice McCowan;** a Judge of the High Court, Queen's Bench Division, since 1981; Presiding Judge, South Eastern Circuit, since 1986; *b* 12 Jan. 1928; *yr s* of John Haines Smith McCowan, MBE, and Marguerite McCowan, Georgetown, British Guiana; *m* 1961, Sue Hazel Anne, *d* of late Reginald Harvey and of Mrs Harvey, Braiseworth Hall, Tannington, Suffolk; two *s* one *d. Educ:* Epsom Coll.; (Open Hist. schol.) Brasenose Coll., Oxford (MA, BCL). Called to Bar, Gray's Inn, 1951, Atkin Scholar; Bencher, 1980. Dep. Chm., E Sussex QS, 1969–71; a Recorder of the Crown Court, 1972–81; QC 1972; Leader, SE Circuit, 1978–81. Mem., Parole Bd, 1982–84. *Recreations:* sport, history, travel. *Address:* c/o Royal Courts of Justice, Strand, WC2A 2LL.
See also J. M. Archer.

McCOWAN, Sir Hew Cargill, 3rd Bt, *cr* 1934; *b* 26 July 1930; *s* of Sir David James Cargill McCowan, 2nd Bt and Muriel Emma Annie, *d* of W. C. Willmott; *S* father, 1965. *Heir: b* David William Cargill McCowan, *b* 28 Feb. 1934. *Address:* Vivenda Marbelo, Estrada da Lagoa Azul, Malveira da Serra, Cascais, Portugal.

McCOWEN, Alec, (Alexander Duncan McCowen), CBE 1986 (OBE 1972); actor; *b* 26 May 1925; *s* of Duncan McCowen and Hon. Mrs McCowen. *Educ:* Skinners' Sch., Tunbridge Wells; RADA, 1941. Repertory: York, Birmingham, etc, 1943–50; Escapade, St James's, 1952; The Matchmaker, Haymarket, 1954; The Count of Clérambard, Garrick, 1955; The Caine Mutiny Court Martial, Hippodrome, 1956; Look Back in Anger, Royal Court, 1956; The Elder Statesman, Cambridge, 1958; Old Vic Seasons, 1959–61: Touchstone, Ford, Richard II, Mercutio, Oberon, Malvolio; Dauphin in St Joan; Algy in The Importance of Being Earnest; Royal Shakespeare Company, 1962–63: Antipholus of Syracuse in The Comedy of Errors; Fool, in King Lear; Father Fontana in The Representative, Aldwych, 1963; Thark, Garrick, 1965; The Cavern, Strand, 1965; After the Rain, Duchess, 1967, Golden Theatre, NY, 1967; Hadrian VII, Birmingham, 1967, Mermaid, 1968, New York, 1969; Hamlet, Birmingham, 1970; The Philanthropist, Royal Court, 1970, NY, 1971; Butley, Criterion, 1972; The Misanthrope, National Theatre, 1973, 1975, NY 1975; Equus, National Theatre, 1973; Pygmalion, Albery, 1974; The Family Dance, Criterion, 1976; Antony and Cleopatra, Prospect Co., 1977; solo performance of St Mark's Gospel, Riverside Studios, Mermaid and Comedy, 1978, Globe, 1981, UK tour, 1985; Tishoo, Wyndham's, 1979; The Browning Version, and A Harlequinade, National Theatre, 1980; The Portage to San Cristobal of A. H., Mermaid, 1982; Kipling (solo performance), Mermaid, 1984; The Cocktail Party, Phoenix, 1986. Films include: Frenzy, 1971; Travels with My Aunt, 1972; Stevie, 1978; Never Say Never Again, 1983. TV series, Mr Palfrey of Westminster, 1984. Evening Standard (later Standard) Drama Award, 1968, 1973, 1982; Stage Actor of the Year, Variety Club, 1970. *Publications:* Young Gemini (autobiog.), 1979; Double Bill (autobiog.), 1980; Personal Mark, 1984. *Recreations:* music, gardening.

McCRAE, Alister Geddes, CBE 1973; Chairman: Clyde Port Authority, 1966–77; British Ports Association, 1972–74; *b* 7 Aug. 1909; *s* of Alexander McCrae; *m* 1st, 1938, Margaret Montgomery Reid (*d* 1977); one *s*; 2nd, 1978, Norah Crawford Orr. *Educ:* Kelvinside Academy; High School of Glasgow. Joined: P. Henderson & Co., Shipowners, Glasgow, 1927; Irrawaddy Flotilla Co. Ltd (in Burma), 1933; Served War: Middle East and Burma, 1941–45; Lt-Col, Royal Indian Engrs (despatches). Irrawaddy Flotilla Co. Ltd, 1946–48 (Dep. Gen. Manager, in Burma); re-joined P. Henderson & Co., as Partner, 1948; Sen. Partner and Man. Dir, British & Burmese Steam Navigation Co. Ltd, 1963; retd 1972. Member: Nat. Dock Labour Bd, 1953–57; UK Chamber of Shipping Council, 1954–65; Clyde Navigation Trust, 1962–65; British Transport Docks Bd, 1963–65; Nat. Ports Council, 1967–71; Scottish Economic Council, 1969–74; Aldington/Jones Commn on Docks, 1972; Chm., Clyde Estuary Develt Gp, 1968–71; Dir, Hunterston Develt Co. Ltd, 1970–74. Chm., Glasgow Old People's Welfare Commn (Age Concern), 1969–79, Hon. Pres., 1979–. Freeman, City of London, 1959; Liveryman, Worshipful Co. of Shipwrights, 1959. FRSA. *Publications:* Irrawaddy Flotilla, 1978; (jtly) Tales of Burma, 1981. *Recreations:* country walking, the garden, fishing, the fine arts. *Address:* Belwood, Killearn, Stirlingshire G63 9LG. *Club:* Oriental.

McCRAITH, Col Patrick James Danvers, MC 1943; TD; DL; Solicitor and Notary Public; *b* 21 June 1916; *s* of late Sir Douglas McCraith; *m* 1946, Hon. Philippa Mary Ellis, *yr d* of 1st and last Baron Robins, KBE, DSO, of Rhodesia and Chelsea; one *s* one *d. Educ:* Harrow. 2nd Lieut, Sherwood Rangers Yeomanry, 1935; served War, 1939–45, N Africa and NW Europe (three times wounded); raised and commanded Yeomanry Patrol of Long Range Desert Group, 1940–41; commanded Sherwood Rangers Yeomanry, 1953–57; Bt Colonel, 1958. Hon. Col, B (Sherwood Rangers Yeomanry) Squadron, The Royal Yeomanry, 1968–79. High Sheriff of Nottinghamshire, 1963; DL Notts, 1965. *Address:* Cranfield House, Southwell, Notts. *T:* Southwell 812129. *Clubs:* Special Forces; Nottingham and Notts United Services (Nottingham).

McCREA, Rev. Robert Thomas William; MP (DUP) Mid Ulster, since 1983 (resigned seat Dec. 1985 in protest against Anglo-Irish Agreement; re-elected Jan. 1986); Minister, Free Presbyterian Church of Ulster, since 1967; *b* 6 Aug. 1948; *s* of Robert T. and Sarah J. McCrea; *m* 1971, Anne Shirley McKnight; two *s* three *d. Educ:* Cookstown Grammar Sch.; Theol Coll., Free Presbyterian Church of Ulster. Civil servant, 1966; Free Presbyterian Minister of the Gospel, 1967–. Dist Councillor, Magherafelt, 1973–; Mem. (DUP) Mid Ulster, NI Assembly, 1982–86. Gospel singer and recording artist; Silver, Gold and Platinum Discs for record sales. *Publication:* In His Pathway—the story of the Reverend William McCrea, 1980. *Recreation:* singing. *Address:* 10 Highfield Road, Magherafelt, Co. Londonderry BT45 5JD. *T:* Magherafelt 32664.

McCREA, Sir William (Hunter), Kt 1985; FRS 1952; MA; PhD, ScD (Cambridge); BSc (London); FRSE, FRAS, MRIA; Research Professor of Theoretical Astronomy, University of Sussex, 1966–72, now Emeritus; *b* Dublin, 13 Dec. 1904; *er s* of late Robert Hunter McCrea; *m* 1933, Marian Nicol Core, 2nd *d* of late Thomas Webster, JP, Burdiehouse, Edinburgh; one *s* two *d. Educ:* Chesterfield Grammar Sch.; Trinity Coll., Cambridge (Scholar; University of Göttingen. Wrangler, Rayleigh Prizeman, Sheepshanks Exhibitioner, and Isaac Newton Student, of Cambridge Univ.; Rouse Ball Travelling Student, and Rouse Ball Senior Student, of Trinity Coll.; Comyns Berkeley Bye-Fellow, Gonville and Caius Coll., Cambridge, 1952–53. Lecturer in Mathematics, Univ. of Edinburgh, 1930–32; Reader in Mathematics, Univ. of London, and Assistant Prof., Imperial Coll. of Science, 1932–36; Prof. of Mathematics: Queen's Univ., Belfast, 1936–44; Royal Holloway Coll., Univ. of London, 1944–66 (Hon. Fellow, 1984). Visiting Prof. of Astronomy: Univ. of California, 1956; Case Inst. of Technology, 1964; Univ. of BC, Vancouver, 1975–76; Consulting Astronomer, Kitt Peak National Observatory, Arizona, 1965, 1975; Royal Society Exchange Visitor: to USSR, 1960, 1968; to Mexico, 1971; to Argentina, 1971, 1983; to India, 1976; to Egypt, 1981; For. Visiting Prof. of American Astronomical Soc. and Vis. Prof., Berkeley Astronomy Dept, 1967; first occupant, Chaire Georges Lemaître, Louvain Univ., 1969; Royal Soc. Leverhulme Vis. Prof. of Astronomy, Cairo Univ., 1973; Vis. Prof., Istanbul Univ., 1977, 1978; William Evans Vis. Prof., Otago Univ., 1979. Visiting Lecturer: Univ. of Liège, 1960; Technische Hochschule, Aachen, 1962; various universities in Greece and Turkey (British Council), 1971; York Univ., 1965; Lectures: Harland, Univ. of Exeter, 1970; Larmor, QUB, 1970; Halley, Oxford, 1975; Milne, Oxford, 1985. Temp. Princ. Experimental Officer, Admty, 1943–45; Commnd RAFVR (Training Branch), 1941–45. Mem., Governing Board of School of Theoretical Physics, Dublin Institute for Advanced Studies, 1940–50; Governor: Royal Holloway Coll., 1946–49; Ottershaw Sch., 1947–52; Barclay Sch. for Partially Sighted Girls, 1949–66; Mem. Adv. Council, Chelsea Coll. of Aeronautical and Automobile Engineering, 1958–. Secretary of Section A of British Assoc., 1935–39, Pres. 1966; Pres., Mathematical Assoc., 1973–74 (Hon. Mem., 1985). Joint Editor of The Observatory, 1935–37. Pres., Royal Astronomical Soc., 1961–63 (Sec., 1946–49; Foreign Correspondent, 1968–71; Treasurer, 1976–79). Fellow, Imperial Coll., 1967–; Leverhulme Emeritus Fellow, 1973–75. Mem., Akademie Leopoldina, 1972–. Keith Prize, RSE, 1939–41; Gold Medal, RAS, 1976. Hon. DSc: National Univ., Ireland, 1954; QUB, 1970; Sussex, 1978; Dr *hc* National Univ., Cordoba, Argentina, 1971; Hon. ScD Dublin, 1972. *Publications:* Relativity Physics, 1935; Analytical Geometry of Three Dimensions, 1942; Physics of the Sun and Stars, 1950; trans. A. Unsöld's The New Cosmos, 1969; Royal Greenwich Observatory, 1975; various papers and reviews in mathematical and astronomical journals. *Address:* 87 Houndean Rise, Lewes, East Sussex. *Club:* Athenæum.

McCREERY, Henry Edwin Lewis, QC 1965; **His Honour Judge McCreery;** a Circuit Judge (formerly Judge of County Courts), since 1971; *b* 26 July 1920; *s* of late Rev. William John McCreery, BD, and late Anne Cullen McCreery; *m* 1945, Margaret Elizabeth Booth; two *d. Educ:* St Andrew's Coll., Dublin; Trinity Coll., Dublin. RAF, 1942–47. Called: Irish Bar King's Inns, 1943; English Bar, Middle Temple, 1946 (Bencher, 1971). Dep. Chm., Quarter Sessions: Cornwall, 1966–71; Devon, 1967–71; Recorder of Salisbury, 1969–71. *Recreation:* gardening. *Club:* Royal Air Force.

MacCRINDLE, Robert Alexander, QC 1963; commercial lawyer and partner, Shearman and Sterling; *b* 27 Jan. 1928; *s* of F. R. MacCrindle; *m* 1959, Pauline Dilys, *d* of Mark S. Morgan; one *s* one *d. Educ:* Girvan High Sch.; King's Coll., London; Gonville and Caius Coll., Cambridge. LLB London, 1948. Served RAF, 1948–50, Flt-Lt. LLM Cantab, Chancellor's Medal, 1951. Called to Bar, Gray's Inn, 1952 (Bencher, 1969); Junior Counsel to Board of Trade (Export Credits), 1961–63; Mem., Hong Kong Bar, 1967. Mem., Royal Commn on Civil Liability and Compensation for Personal Injury, 1973–78. Honorary Fellow: American Coll. of Trial Lawyers, 1974; Conseil Juridique (France). *Publication:* McNair's Law of the Air, 1953. *Recreation:* golf. *Address:* 4 Essex Court, Temple, EC4. *T:* 01–583 9191; 88 avenue de Breteuil, 75015 Paris, France. *T:* 567–1193. *Club:* University (New York).

McCRINDLE, Robert Arthur; MP (C) Brentwood and Ongar, since 1974 (Billericay, 1970–74); Consultant: Hogg Robinson Travel Ltd, since 1980; British Caledonian Airways, since 1984; *b* 19 Sept. 1929; *o s* of Thomas Arthur and Isabella McCrindle; *m* 1953, Myra Anderson; two *s. Educ:* Allen Glen's Coll., Glasgow. Vice-Chm., Sausmarez, Carey & Harris, Financial Consultants, 1972–75; Director: Langham Life Assurance Co. Ltd, 1972–76; Worldmark Travel Ltd, 1978–82; Chairman: Cometco Ltd, Commodity Brokers, 1972–78; Citybond Storage. Contested: Dundee (East), 1959; Thurrock, 1964. PPS to Min. of State, Home Office, 1974; Mem., UK Delegn to N Atlantic Assembly, 1977– (Chm., Economic Cttee, 1980–); Parliamentary Consultant: British Transport Police Fedn; British Insurance Brokers' Assoc.; Guild of Business Travel Agents, 1975–78. Nat. Vice-Pres., Corp. of Mortgage Brokers, 1970–76. Fellow, Corp. of Insurance Brokers; AC11. *Address:* 26 Ashburnham Gardens, Upminster, Essex. *T:* Upminster 27152.

McCRIRRICK, Thomas Bryce, FEng, FIEE, FIERE; Director of Engineering, BBC, since 1978; *b* 19 July 1927; *s* of late Alexander McCrirrick and Janet McCrirrick (*née* Tweedie); *m* 1953, Margaret Phyllis Yates; three *s. Educ:* Galashiels Academy; Heriot Watt Coll., Edinburgh; Regent Street Polytechnic, London. BBC Radio, Studio Centres in Edinburgh, Glasgow and London, 1943–46; served RAF, 1946–49; BBC Television, 1949; Engineer-in-Charge Television Studios, 1963; Head of Engineering Television Recording, and of Studio Planning and Installation Dept, 1969; Chief Engineer, Radio Broadcasting, 1970; Asst Dir of Engrg, 1971; Dep. Dir of Engrg, 1976. Pres., Soc. of Electronic and Radio Technicians, 1981–85 (Vice-Pres., 1979–80); Vice-Pres., IERE, 1985–; Dep. Pres., IEE, 1986– (Vice-Pres., 1982–86). FRTS 1980; FBKSTS 1982. *Recreations:* skiing, theatre. *Address:* Oakwood, Knightsbridge Road, Camberley, Surrey GU15 3TS. *T:* Camberley 65309.

McCRONE, Robert Gavin Loudon, CB 1983; FRSE 1983; Secretary of the Industry Department for Scotland (formerly Scottish Economic Planning Department), since 1980, and Chief Economic Adviser at the Scottish Office, since 1972; *b* 2 Feb. 1933; *s* of Robert Osborne Orr McCrone and Laura Margaret McCrone; *m* 1959, Alexandra Bruce Waddell; two *s* one *d. Educ:* Stowe Sch.; St Catharine's Coll., Cambridge (Economics Tripos; MA); University Coll. of Wales, Aberystwyth (Milk Marketing Bd Research Schol. in agricl economics; MSc 1959); Univ. of Glasgow (PhD 1964). Fisons Ltd, 1959–60; Lectr in Applied Economics, Glasgow Univ., 1960–65; Economic Consultant to UNESCO and Mem. Educnl Planning Mission to Libya, 1964; Fellow of Brasenose

Coll., Oxford, 1965–72; Chm., Oxford Univ. Economics Subfaculty, 1968–70; Mem. NEDC Working Party on Agricl Policy, 1967–68; Economic Adviser to House of Commons Select Cttee on Scottish Affairs, 1969–70; Special Economic Adviser to Sec. of State for Local Govt and Regional Planning, 1970; Sen. Economic Adviser and Head of Economics and Statistics Unit, 1970–72, Under-Sec. for Regional Develt, 1972–80, Scottish Office. Vis. Prof. of Economics, Univ. of Strathclyde, 1983–. Member Council: Royal Economic Soc., 1977–82; Scottish Economic Soc., 1982–. Hon. LLD Glasgow 1986. *Publications:* The Economics of Subsidising Agriculture, 1962; Scotland's Economic Progress 1951–60, 1963; Agricultural Integration in Western Europe, 1963; Regional Policy in Britain, 1969; Scotland's Future, 1969; contribs to various economic jls. *Recreation:* walking. *Address:* New St Andrews House, Edinburgh. *T:* 031–556 8400. *Club:* United Oxford & Cambridge University.

McCRORIE, Esther Linda, (Mrs Peter McCrorie); *see* Gray, E. L.

McCRUM, Michael William, MA; Master of Corpus Christi College, Cambridge, since 1980; *b* 23 May 1924; 3rd *s* of Captain C. R. McCrum, RN (retired) and of Ivy Hilda Constance (*née* Nicholson); *m* 1952, Christine Mary Kathleen, *d* of Sir Arthur fforde, GBE; three *s* one *d*. *Educ:* Horris Hill, Newbury; Sherborne Sch.; Corpus Christi Coll., Cambridge. Entrance Scholar to CCC, Dec. 1942. Served RN, 1943–45 (Sub-Lt RNVR, Dec. 1943). CCC, Cambridge, 1946–48; Part I, Class. Tripos, First Class, 1947; Part II, First Class, with distinction, 1948. Asst Master, Rugby School, Sept. 1948–July 1950 (Lower Bench Master, 1949–50); Fellow CCC, Cambridge, 1949; Second Tutor, 1950–51; Tutor, 1951–62; Headmaster, Tonbridge Sch. 1962–70; Head Master of Eton, 1970–80. Lectures: Lansdowne, Univ. of Victoria, BC, 1985; Clayesmore, Blandford Forum, 1986; Member: Council of the Senate, University of Cambridge, 1955–58, 1981–; General Board of Faculties, 1957–62; Financial Bd, 1985–; Chairman: Faculty Bd of Educn, 1981–86; Bd of Extra-Mural Studies, 1982–86, Cambridge. Chairman: HMC, 1974; Joint Educnl Trust, 1984–. Dep. Chm., GBA, 1982–; Mem., Governing Body, Schools Council, 1969–76 (also mem., various cttees); Governor: Bradfield Coll., 1956–62; Eastbourne Coll., 1960–62; King's Sch., Canterbury, 1980–; Sherborne Sch., 1980–; Oakham Sch., 1981–85; United World Coll. of the Atlantic, 1981–; Rugby Sch., 1982–. Trustee, Nat. Heritage Meml Fund, 1984–. Hon. Freeman, Skinners' Co., 1980. *Publication:* (with A. G. Woodhead) Select Documents of the Principates of the Flavian Emperors AD 68–96, 1961. *Address:* The Master's Lodge, Corpus Christi College, Cambridge CB2 1RH. *T:* Cambridge 338029. *Clubs:* Athenæum, United Oxford & Cambridge University, East India, Devonshire, Sports and Public Schools; Hawks (Cambridge).

MacCULLOCH, Dr Malcolm John, MD; DPM; FRCPsych; Medical Director, Park Lane Hospital, Liverpool, and Director of Special Hospitals Research Unit, since 1979; *b* 10 July 1936; *s* of William MacCulloch and Constance Martha MacCulloch; *m* 1962, Mary Louise Beton (marr. diss. 1975); one *s* one *d*; *m* 1975, Carolyn Mary Reid; two *d*. *Educ:* King Edward VII Sch., Macclesfield, Cheshire; Manchester Univ. (MB, ChB, DPM, MD). Consultant Child Psychiatrist, Cheshire Child Guidance Service, 1966–67; Director Univ. Dept, Child Psychiatry and Subnormality, Birmingham Univ., 1967–70; Sen. Lectr, Adult Psychiatry, Univ. of Liverpool, 1970–75; PMO, DHSS, 1975–78; SPMO, Mental Health Div., DHSS, 1979–80. *Publications:* Homosexual Behaviour: therapy and assessment, 1971; Human Sexual Behaviour, 1980; numerous med. papers on aspects of psychiatry. *Recreations:* inventing, playing music. *Address:* Park Lane Hospital, Park Lane, Maghull, Liverpool L31 1HW. *T:* 051–520 2244.

McCULLOCH, Rt. Rev. Nigel Simeon; *see* Taunton, Bishop Suffragan of.

McCULLOUGH, Sir Charles; *see* McCullough, Sir I. C. R.

McCULLOUGH, Hon. Sir (Iain) Charles (Robert), Kt 1981; **Hon. Mr Justice McCullough**; a Judge of the High Court of Justice, Queen's Bench Division, since 1981; *b* 31 July 1931; *o s* of Thomas W. McCullough, *qv*; *m* 1965, Margaret Joyce, JP 1973, *o d* of late David H. Patey, MS, FRCS, of The Middlesex Hospital, W1; one *s* one *d*. *Educ:* Taunton Sch.; Trinity Hall, Cambridge. BA 1955; MA 1960. National Service, 1950–52, commnd Royal Artillery; RA (TA), 1952–54. Called to Bar, Middle Temple, 1956 (Harmsworth Law Schol.); Bencher, 1980. Midland Circuit, 1957–71, Midland and Oxford Circuit, 1972–81; Dep. Chm., Notts QS, 1969–71; QC 1971; a Recorder of the Crown Court, 1972–81. Member: Criminal Law Revision Cttee, 1973–; Gen. Council of the Bar, 1966–70; Parole Bd, 1984–86. Trustee, Uppingham Sch., 1984–. *Address:* Royal Courts of Justice, Strand, WC2. *Club:* Garrick.

McCULLOUGH, Thomas Warburton, CB 1962; OBE 1954; HM Chief Inspector of Factories, Ministry of Labour, 1958–63; *b* 13 March 1901; *o s* of late Robert McCullough and Emma Warburton, *d* of Thomas Rigby; *m* 1928, Lisette Hunter (*d* 1979), *d* of late Henry George Gannaway; one *s*. *Educ:* Ballymena Academy; Glasgow Univ.; Middle Temple. BSc 1925. Engineering training, Glasgow, 1917–25; Valuation Dept, Ministry of Finance, Belfast, 1925; joined Factory Dept, Home Office, 1926. Member Joint Advisory Cttee on Conditions in Iron Foundries, 1947; Hon. Adviser Scottish Industrial Groups Advisory Council, 1951–53; Chairman of numerous Joint Standing Cttees, 1950–56. Member: Home Office Inter-Departmental Cttee on Accidents in the Home, 1954–57; National Industrial Safety Cttee, 1954–57, Executive Cttee, 1958–63, Royal Society for Prevention of Accidents; Industrial Grants Cttee, Dept of Scientific and Industrial Research, 1958–63; Nuclear Safety Advisory Cttee, 1960–63; Technical Adviser (Safety), The United Steel Companies Ltd, 1963–67. Hon. Life Member, Royal Society for Prevention of Accidents, 1963; Hon. Fellow, Institution of Industrial Safety Officers, 1964; Hon. Adviser (Safety) British Steel Corp. (formerly British Iron and Steel Fedn), 1964–74; Pres., London Construction Safety Group, 1963–74. Silver Medal, L'Institut National de Sécurité, Paris, 1961; Industrial Safety Award, RoSPA, 1970. *Publications:* sundry contribs to literature of accident prevention in industry. *Address:* c/o Hon. Mr Justice McCullough, Royal Courts of Justice, Strand, WC2.
See also Sir I. C. R. McCullough.

McCUNN, Peter Alexander, CBE 1980; Deputy Chairman, Cable and Wireless plc, 1978–82 (and Group Managing Director, 1978–81); *b* 11 Nov. 1922; *m* 1943, Margaret Prescott; two *s* (and one *s* decd). *Educ:* Mexborough Grammar Sch.; Edinburgh University. Commnd W Yorks Regt, 1942; served in Normandy, Malta, Italy; left Army, Nov. 1946 (Captain). Joined Cable & Wireless, 1947; Director: Cable & Wireless/Western Union International Inc. of Puerto Rico, 1968–70; Cable & Wireless, 1969– (Exec. Dep. Chm., 1977); Nigerian External Telecommunications Ltd, 1969–72; Sierra Leone External Telecommunications Ltd, 1969–72; Trinidad and Tobago External Telecommunications Ltd, 1972–77; Jamaica International Telecommunications Ltd, 1972–77; Cable and Wireless (Hong Kong) Ltd, 1981–84; Mercury Communications Ltd, 1981–84. FBIM. *Recreations:* music, gardening, swimming, cricket, Association football (now non-active). *Address:* Wychelms, 14 Lime Walk, Pinkneys Green, Maidenhead, Berks. *T:* Maidenhead 24308. *Club:* Exiles (Twickenham).

McCURLEY, Anna Anderson; MP (C) Renfrew West and Inverclyde, since 1983; *b* 18 Jan. 1943; *d* of George Gemmell and Mary (*née* Anderson); *m* 1966, Dr John McCurley; one *d*. *Educ:* Glasgow High Sch. for Girls; Glasgow Univ. (MA); Jordanhill Coll. of Educn (Dip. in Secondary Educn); Strathclyde Univ. Secondary history teacher, 1966–72; College Methods Tutor, Jordanhill Coll. of Educn, 1972–74. Strathclyde Regional Councillor, Camphill/Pollokshaws Div., 1978–82. Mem., Scottish Select Cttee, 1984–. *Recreations:* music, cookery, painting in oils. *Address:* 263A Nithsdale Road, Glasgow G41 5AW. *T:* 041–427 3330.

McCUSKER, Sir James (Alexander), Kt 1983; Founder, Town and Country Permanent Building Society, 1964, Foundation Chairman 1964–83; *b* Perth, WA, 2 Dec. 1913; *m* Mary Martindale McCusker; three *c*. *Educ:* Perth Modern Sch. Served War of 1939–45, 2½ years with 1st Armoured Div. (Sgt). 30 years with Commonwealth Bank of Aust.; resigned 1959, as Sen. Branch Manager in Perth. Chm., State Cttee of Inquiry into Rates and Taxes, 1980. Councillor: WA Permanent Building Socs Assoc., 1964–83 (former Pres.); Aust. Assoc. of Permanent Building Socs; Fellow, Aust. Inst. of Valuers; Member: Council of Rural and Allied Industries; WA Indicative Planning Cttee (Housing). Patron, Paraplegic Assoc. of WA. *Address:* 195 Brookdale Street, Floreat Park, Perth, WA 6014, Australia.

McCUSKER, (James) Harold; MP (UU) Upper Bann, since 1983 (Armagh, 1974–83) (resigned seat Dec. 1985 in protest against Anglo-Irish Agreement; re-elected Jan. 1986); *b* 7 Feb. 1940; *s* of James Harold McCusker and Lily McCusker; *m* 1965, Jennifer Leslie Mills; three *s*. *Educ:* Lurgan Coll.; Stranmillis Coll., Belfast. Teacher, 1961–68; Trng Officer, 1968–73; Production Man., 1973–74. Sec. and Whip, Ulster Unionist Party, Westminster, 1975–76. Member (UU) Armagh and Dep. Leader, Official Unionist Party, NI Assembly, 1982–86. Chm., NI Gas Employers' Bd, 1977–81. *Address:* 33 Seagoe Road, Portadown, Craigavon BT63 5HW. *T:* Portadown 33876; 25 Vincent Square, SW1. *T:* 01–821 7036.

McCUTCHEON, Dr William Alan, FRGS, FSA, MRIA; author, lecturer, teacher and consultant; *b* 2 March 1934; *s* of late William John and of Margaret Elizabeth McCutcheon; *m* 1956, Margaret Craig; three *s*. *Educ:* Royal Belfast Academical Instn; The Queen's University of Belfast (Hugh Wisnom Scholar, 1960; BA (Hons Geog.) 1955, MA 1958, PhD 1962). FRGS 1958; FSA 1970; MRIA 1983. School Teacher (Geography Specialist), Royal Belfast Academical Instn, 1956–62; Director, N Ireland Survey of Industrial Archaeology, 1962–68; Keeper of Technology and Local History, Ulster Museum, Belfast, 1968–77; Dir, Ulster Museum, 1977–82. Vis. Teacher, Glenalmond Coll., 1984, 1986. Chairman: Historic Monuments Council (NI), 1980–85; Jt Cttee on Industrial Archaeology (NI), 1981–85; Member: Malcolm Cttee on Regional Museums in Northern Ireland, 1977–78; Industrial Archaeol. Cttee, Council for British Archaeol., 1981–85. Mem., Internat. Molinological Soc., 1973–. *Publications:* The Canals of the North of Ireland, 1965; Railway History in Pictures, Ireland: vol. 1 1970, vol. 2 1971; (contrib.) Travel and Transport in Ireland, 1973; (contrib.) Folk & Farm, 1976; Wheel and Spindle—Aspects of Irish Industrial History, 1977; The Industrial Archaeology of Northern Ireland, 1980 (Library Assoc. high commendation as an outstanding reference book); (contrib.) Some People and Places in Irish Science and Technology, 1985; (contrib.) An Economic and Social History of Ulster 1820–1939, 1985; numerous papers. *Recreations:* reading, classical music, photography, travel, hill walking, swimming. *Address:* 22 Moira Drive, Bangor, Co. Down, Northern Ireland BT20 4RN. *T:* Bangor 465005.

McDERMID, Ven. Norman George Lloyd Roberts; Archdeacon of Richmond since 1983; *b* 5 March 1927; *s* of Lloyd Roberts McDermid and Annie McDermid; *m* 1953, Vera Wood; one *s* three *d*. *Educ:* St Peter's School, York; St Edmund Hall, Oxford (MA); Wells Theological Coll. Deacon 1951, priest 1952; Curate of Leeds, 1951–56, in charge of St Mary, Quarry Hill, Leeds, 1953–56; Vicar of Bramley, Leeds, 1956–64; Rector of Kirkby Overblow, 1964–80; Stewardship Adviser, Ripon Diocese, 1964–76, Bradford and Wakefield, 1973–76; Vicar of Knaresborough, 1980–83. Hon. Canon of Ripon Cathedral, 1972–; RD of Harrogate, 1977–83. Member: General Synod, 1970–; Church of England Pensions Bd, 1972–78; Redundant Churches Fund, 1977–; Central Bd of Finance of C of E, 1985–. Church Commissioner, 1978–83. *Recreations:* investment, historic churches, pedigree cattle, gardening. *Address:* 62 Palace Road, Ripon, N Yorks HG4 1HA. *T:* Ripon 4342. *Club:* National Liberal.

MacDERMOT, Brian (Charles), CBE 1966; LVO 1961; HM Diplomatic Service, retired; *b* 29 Jan. 1914; *m* 1949, Mary Arden Hunter; seven *s* two *d*. Probationer Vice-Consul, Peking, China, 1936; served at: Hankow, China, 1939–40; Kobe, Japan, 1940–41; Kunming, South China, 1942; Vice-Consul, Shiraz, Persia, 1943; Paris, 1944, promoted Consul, 1945; Foreign Office, 1946; Consul, Beirut, 1948; First Secretary, Belgrade, 1950; First Secretary, Berne, 1951, acted as Charge d'Affaires, 1951, 1952, 1953; transferred to Foreign Office, 1954; transferred to Holy See, 1955, acted as Chargé d'Affaires, 1958, 1959, 1960 and 1961; HM Consul-General, Oporto, 1962–68; Ambassador and Consul-Gen., Paraquay, 1968–72. *Address:* Little Orchard, Wetherden, Stowmarket, Suffolk IP14 3LY.

MacDERMOT, The, (Sir Dermot MacDermot), KCMG 1962 (CMG 1954); CBE 1947; styled Prince of Coolavin; *b* 14 June 1906; 2nd surv. *s* of late Charles Edward, The MacDermot, Prince of Coolavin; *S* brother, 1979; *m* 1934, Betty Steel; three *s*. *Educ:* Stonyhurst Coll.; Trinity Coll., Dublin, LLD *jure dignitatis*, 1964. Joined HM Consular Service in 1929 and served in Tokyo, Yokohama, Kobe and Osaka in Japan, Manila (Philippines), Tamsui (Formosa), New Orleans, and in the Foreign Office. Appointed a Counsellor in the Foreign Office, 1947; Inspector, HM Foreign Service, 1951; HM Minister to Roumania, 1954–56; HM Ambassador to Indonesia, 1956–59; Assistant Under-Secretary, Foreign Office, 1959–61; HM Ambassador to Thailand, 1961–65. *Recreation:* golf. *Heir:* *s* Niall Anthony MacDermot, *b* 25 April 1935. *Address:* Dunlavin, Co. Wicklow, Eire. *Club:* Kildare Street and University (Dublin).

MACDERMOT, Niall, OBE (mil.) 1944; QC 1963; barrister-at-law; Secretary-General, International Commission of Jurists, since Dec. 1970; *b* 10 Sept. 1916; *s* of late Henry MacDermot, KC, Dublin; *m* 1940, Violet Denise Maxwell (marr. diss.); one *s*; *m* 1966, Ludmila Benvenuto. *Educ:* Rugby Sch.; Corpus Christi Coll., Cambridge; Balliol Coll., Oxford. Served in Intelligence Corps, 1939–46; GSO1 HQ 21 Army Group, 1944–45. MP (Lab) Lewisham North, Feb. 1957–59, Derby North, April 1962–1970; Mem. Exec., London Labour Party, 1958–62. Dep. Chm., Beds QS, 1961–64, 1969–72; Recorder of Newark-on-Trent, 1963–64; a Recorder of the Crown Court, 1972–74. Master of the Bench, Inner Temple, 1970–. Financial Sec., Treasury, 1964–67; Minister of State, Min. of Housing and Local Govt, 1967–68. Hon. Treasurer, Justice, 1968–70. Member: Council, Internat. Inst. of Human Rights, Strasbourg, 1972–; Adv. Council, Interights, 1984–; Bd, Internat. Alert, 1985–; Pres., Special NGO Cttee on Human Rights, Geneva, 1973–86, Vice-Pres., 1986–. Founding Mem., Groupe de Bellerive, 1977–. Trustee of Tate Gall., 1969–76. *Address:* PO Box 120, 109 route de Chêne, 1224 Geneva, Switzerland. *T:* Geneva 49.35.45.

MacDERMOTT, Edmond Geoffrey; Metropolitan Stipendiary Magistrate, 1972–84. Called to Bar, Gray's Inn, 1935; Dept of Dir of Public Prosecutions, 1946–72; Asst Dir of Public Prosecutions, 1968–72.

McDERMOTT, Sir Emmet; *see* McDermott, Sir L. E.

MacDERMOTT, Hon. John Clarke; Hon. Mr Justice MacDermott; Judge of the High Court of Northern Ireland, since 1973; *b* 1927; *s* of Baron MacDermott, PC, PC (NI), MC, and of Louise Palmer, *o d* of Rev. J. C. Johnston, DD; *m* 1953, Margaret Helen, *d* of late Hugh Dales, Belfast; four *d. Educ:* Campbell Coll., Belfast; Trinity Hall, Cambridge (BA); QUB. Called to Bar, Inner Temple and Northern Ireland, 1949; QC (NI) 1964. *Address:* Royal Courts of Justice, Belfast, Northern Ireland; 6 Tarawood, Holywood, Co. Down.

McDERMOTT, Sir (Lawrence) Emmet, KBE 1972; Lord Mayor of Sydney, 1969–72; Alderman, Sydney, 1962–77; Dental Surgeon; *b* 6 Sept. 1911; *s* of O. J. McDermott; *m* 1939, Arline Beatrice Olga; one *s* one *d. Educ:* St Ignatius Coll., Sydney; Univ. of Sydney; Northwestern Univ., Chicago. MDS Sydney; DDS Northwestern; FICD, FRACDS, FACD; FAIM 1983. Hon. Consultant Dental Surgeon: Royal Prince Alfred Hosp., 1942–; Eastern Suburbs Hosp., 1945–; Pres., Bd of Control, United Dental Hosp., Sydney, 1967–79; Mem., NSW Dental Bd, 1967–79; Pres., Australian Dental Assoc. (NSW Br.), 1960–61; Councillor, Australian Dental Assoc., 1962–66. Mem., Liberal Party State Council, 1969; Councillor, Sydney County Council, 1973–80, Dep. Chm., 1975–77, Chm., 1977–78. Dir, City Mutual Life Assce Soc. Ltd, 1970–83, Dep. Chm., 1976–83; Member: Sydney Cove Redevelopment Authority, 1971–76; Convocation, Macquarie Univ., 1966–; Australia-Britain Soc. (NSW Br.), Vice-Pres., 1972–77. *Recreations:* golf, swimming (Sydney Univ. Blue), bowls. *Address:* T&G Tower, Hyde Park Square, Park & Elizabeth Streets, Sydney, NSW 2000, Australia. *T:* 264–3660; 20 Carnarvon Road, Roseville, NSW 2069. *T:* 46–2086. *Clubs:* Australian Jockey, Royal Sydney Golf, Elanora Country, Tattersall's, American National, Chatswood Bowling, City Bowling, Warrawee Bowling (all Sydney).

McDERMOTT, Patrick Anthony, MVO 1972; HM Diplomatic Service; Consul-General, and Economic and Financial Adviser to British Military Government, West Berlin, since 1984; *b* 8 Sept. 1941; *e s* of Patrick McDermott and Eileen (*née* Lyons); *m* 1976, Christa, *d* of Emil and Anne-Marie Herminghaus, Krefeld, W Germany; four *s. Educ:* Clapham College, London. FO 1960; Attaché, Mexico City, 1963; Attaché, UK Delegn to UN, NY, 1966; Vice-Consul, Belgrade, 1971; FCO, 1973; Second Sec., Bonn, 1973; First Sec., Paris, 1976; FCO, 1979. *Address:* c/o Foreign and Commonwealth Office, SW1; Longfield, Sidney Road, Walton-on-Thames, Surrey. *T:* Walton-on-Thames 221589.

MACDONALD, family name of **Barons Macdonald** and **Macdonald of Gwaenysgor.**

MACDONALD, 8th Baron *cr* 1776; **Godfrey James Macdonald of Macdonald;** Chief of the Name and Arms of Macdonald; *b* 28 Nov. 1947; *s* of 7th Baron Macdonald, MBE, TD, and of Anne, *o d* of late Alfred Whitaker; *S* father, 1970; *m* 1969, Claire, *e d* of Captain T. N. Catlow, CBE, RN, Gabriel Cottage, Tunstall, Lancs; one *s* three *d. Heir: s* Hon. Godfrey Evan Hugo Thomas Macdonald of Macdonald, yr, *b* 24 Feb. 1982. *Address:* Kinloch Lodge, Isle of Skye. *T:* Isle Ornsay 333. *Club:* New (Edinburgh).

McDONALD, Hon. Lord; Robert Howat McDonald, MC 1944; a Senator of the College of Justice in Scotland, since 1973; *b* 15 May 1916; *s* of Robert Glassford McDonald, and Roberta May Howat, Paisley, Renfrewshire; *m* 1949, Barbara Mackenzie, *d* of John Mackenzie, Badcaul, Ross-shire; no *c. Educ:* John Neilson Institution, Paisley. MA (Glasgow) 1935; LLB (Glasgow) 1937; admitted Faculty of Advocates, 1946; QC (Scot.) 1957. Served with KOSB, 1939–46 (despatches, 1945). Sheriff Principal of Ayr and Bute, 1966–71. Mem., Criminal Injuries Compensation Board, 1964–71; Pres., Industrial Tribunals for Scotland, 1972–73; Chm., Gen. Nursing Council for Scotland, 1970–73; Chm., Mental Welfare Commn for Scotland, 1965–83; Mem., Employment Appeal Tribunal, 1976–86. Chm., Queen's Nursing Inst., Scotland, 1981–. *Address:* Parliament House, Edinburgh. *Club:* New (Edinburgh).

MACDONALD OF GWAENYSGOR, 2nd Baron *cr* 1949, of Gwaenysgor, Flint; **Gordon Ramsay Macdonald;** business consultant; *b* 16 Oct. 1915; *er s* of 1st Baron Macdonald of Gwaenysgor, PC, KCMG; *S* father, 1966; *m* 1941, Leslie Margaret Taylor; three *d. Educ:* Manchester Univ. MA, Economics and Commerce. Served War, 1940–46; Army, Major, Artillery; GSO2 Operations and Intelligence (despatches, Burma). Board of Trade, 1946–53: Principal, 1946–47; UK Trade Comr, Canberra, ACT, 1947–53. With Tube Investments Ltd, and Man. Dir TI (Export) Ltd, 1953–64; Chief Exec., Telecommunications Group, Plessey Co., 1964–67; Chm., Hayek Engrg (UK) Ltd, 1967–76; Chm. and Chief Exec., Ferro Metal and Chemical Comp., and Satra Consultants (UK) Ltd, 1977. *Recreations:* golf, chess. *Heir: b* Hon. Kenneth Lewis Macdonald [*b* 3 Feb. 1921; m 1952, Maureen Margaret Watson-Allan; two *d*]. *Address:* Littleworth House, Littleworth Common, near Burnham, Bucks SL1 8PP.

MACDONALD of Sleat (Btcy); *see under* Bosville Macdonald.

MACDONALD, Alastair John Peter; Deputy Secretary, Department of Trade and Industry, since 1985; *b* 11 Aug. 1940; *s* of Ewen Macdonald and late Hettie Macdonald; *m* 1969, Jane, *d* of late T. R. Morris; one *s* two *d. Educ:* Wimbledon Coll.; Trinity Coll., Oxford. Editorial staff of Spectator, 1962; Financial Times, 1963–68: Washington DC, 1965–66; Features Editor, 1966–68; joined Home Civil Service as Asst Principal, DEA, 1968; Principal, DTI, 1971; Sec., Lord Devlin's Commn into Industrial and Commercial Representation, 1971–72; Asst Sec., DoI, 1975; RCDS, 1980; Under Sec., DTI, 1981. Non-exec. Dir, Rank Leisure Ltd (subsid. of Rank Organisation), 1981–85. *Address:* c/o Department of Trade and Industry, 1 Victoria Street, SW1.

McDONALD, Alex Gordon; Chief Scientific Officer, Department of Health and Social Security, 1975–82; *b* 29 Jan. 1921; *m* 1st, 1942, P. Thomas; 2nd, 1950, J. James; two *d. Educ:* Tiffin Sch., Kingston upon Thames; Royal Coll. of Science (BSc, ARCS). Served RNVR, Lieut (A), Fleet Air Arm, 1939–46. Home Office, 1949; Chief of Staffs, MoD, 1956; Police Research and Develt Br., 1963; DHSS, 1970. Sometime Lectr at: Inst. of Criminology, Inst. of Advanced Legal Study, London Hosp. Sch. of Forensic Pathology, London Sch. of Hygiene and Trop. Med., and Univ. of Warwick Sch. of Business Studies. Member, Bd of Studies in Community Med., London. Hon. Prof. in Industrial and Business Studies, and Dir, Res. Centre on Mathematical Modelling of Clinical Trials, Univ. of Warwick. *Publications:* contrib. learned jls on OR and Systems Analysis. *Recreations:* Basset Hounds, Blood Hounds, needlework, reading. *Address:* 40 Wolsey Road, East Molesey, Surrey KT8 9EN. *Club:* Kennel.

McDONALD, Alexander Gordon; *see* McDonald, Alex G.

McDONALD, Prof. Alexander John, MA (Cantab), LLB, WS; Professor of Conveyancing, University of Dundee (formerly Queen's College), 1955–82, now Emeritus (Dean of the Faculty of Law, 1958–62, 1965); Senior Partner, Thornton Oliver (formerly Thornton, Dickie & Brand), WS, Dundee, 1978–84, now Consultant; *b* 15 March 1919; *o s* of late John McDonald, and Agnes Mary Stewart McDonald; *m* 1951, Doreen Mary, *o d* of late Frank Cook, OBE; two *s* two *d. Educ:* Cargilfield Sch.; Fettes Coll. (open scholar); Christ's Coll., Cambridge (Classical Exhibn, BA 1942); Edinburgh Univ. (Thow Schol. and John Robertson Prize in Conveyancing; LLB with dist., 1949). Admitted as Solicitor and Writer to the Signet, 1950; Lectr in Conveyancing, Edinburgh Univ., 1952–55. *Address:* Hillside, 4 Forthill Road, Broughty Ferry, Dundee. *T:* Dundee 77301.

MACDONALD, Alistair; *b* 23 July 1912; 2nd *s* of late Reginald James Macdonald and Dorothy Bolden; *m* 1941, Myra Jones; one *s* six *d. Educ:* King's Sch., Bruton. Called to the Bar, Inner Temple, 1935. Worked with mentally handicapped children, Sunfield Childrens' Homes, Clent, 1936–40; served in RAF, 1940–45; Air Staff (Intelligence), 1943–45 (despatches). Practice at the Bar and journalism, 1946–48; Legal Assistant, Law Officers Dept, 1948; Legal Sec. to Law Officers of the Crown, 1950–58; Secretary, The Council on Tribunals, 1958–70; Mem., Lord Chancellor's Dept: Consultant to: Royal Inst. of Public Admin, 1970–72; Emerson Coll., Forest Row, Sussex, 1973–. *Publication:* (with R. E. Wraith and P. G. Hutchesson) Administrative Tribunals, 1973. *Address:* South Harbour, Priory Road, Forest Row, E Sussex.

McDONALD, Alistair; Economic Development Officer, Wandsworth Borough Council; *b* 13 March 1925; *e s* of late John Bell McDonald and Mary McDonald; *m* 1954, Isabel Margaret Milne; two *d. Educ:* Fraserburgh Academy; Aberdeen Univ. (BSc 1st Cl. Hons Natural Philosophy). Served RAF and Fleet Air Arm, 1943–46. Malayan Meteorological Service, 1950–56; ICI, 1956–66; Min. of Technology, 1966–70; Dept of Trade and Industry, 1970–74; Dept of Industry, 1974–77; Director, British Shipbuilders (on secondment), 1977–79; Regional Dir, NW Region, Dept of Industry, 1979–83. *Recreation:* golf. *Club:* Caledonian.

MacDONALD, Alistair Archibald, MA, LLB; DL; Sheriff of Grampian, Highland and Islands; at Lerwick and Kirkwall, since 1975; *b* 8 May 1927; *s* of James and Margaret MacDonald; *m* 1950, Jill Russell; one *s* one *d. Educ:* Broughton Sch.; Edinburgh Univ. Served in Army, 1945–48. Called to Scottish Bar, 1954. Formerly Sheriff Substitute, Caithness, Sutherland, Orkney and Zetland at Lerwick, 1961 and at Kirkwall, 1968. DL Shetland Islands, 1986. *Address:* West Hall, Shetland Islands; Hall Cottage, Burray, Orkney. *Club:* Royal Northern (Aberdeen).

MACDONALD, Alistair H.; credit analyst; Deputy Company Secretary: Finance Houses Association; Equipment Leasing Association; *b* 18 May 1925. *Educ:* Dulwich Coll.; Enfield Technical Coll.; Corpus Christi Coll., Cambridge. MP (Lab) Chislehurst, 1966–70. Councillor, Chislehurst and Sidcup UDC, 1958–62; Alderman, 1964–68, Councillor, 1971–, London Borough of Bromley. *Address:* 79 Oakdene Avenue, Chislehurst, Kent BR7 6DZ. *T:* 01–857 8219.

McDONALD, Alistair Ian, CBE 1978; Chairman, Cirkit Holdings PLC, since 1983; Director: Trans Oceanic Trust plc, since 1981; TR Industrial and General Trust PLC, since 1982; TR Trustees Corporation PLC, since 1982; *b* 12 Sept. 1921; *s* of late Angus McDonald and Blanche Elizabeth McDonald; *m* 1947, Olwen (*née* Evans); one *d. Educ:* Greenwich Sch. Served War, RAF, 1940–46. Church Comrs, 1947–81: Dep. Investments Sec., 1966–68; Investments Sec., 1968–81. Director: Datastream Ltd, 1981–82; Trust Union Ltd, 1981–82. Royal Coll. of Nursing: Investment Adviser, 1967–; Vice Pres., 1975–. Chm., Lampada Housing Assoc., 1975–. *Recreations:* golf, gardening, reading. *Address:* Newby, Tower Hill, Horsham, West Sussex. *T:* Horsham 52437. *Clubs:* Caledonian; West Sussex Golf.

McDONALD, Allan Stuart; Headmaster, George Heriot's School, Edinburgh, 1970–83; *b* 20 Aug. 1922; *s* of Allan McDonald and Clementina Peebles (*née* Stuart), both of Edinburgh; *m* 1948, Margaret Wilson, *d* of late James Adams, Paisley and Stranraer, and of Margaret Wilson (*née* Ferguson); one *s* two *d. Educ:* Royal High Sch., Edinburgh; Giffnock and Eastwood Schs, Renfrewshire; Glasgow Univ.; Sorbonne. MA Hons 1944; DipEd 1948. Commnd, Royal Corps of Signals (21st Army Group Signals), 1943–45. Asst Master: Johnstone High Sch., 1948–50; Eastwood Sch., 1950–54; Principal Teacher: Modern Languages, Fortrose Acad., 1954–59; German, George Heriot's Sch., 1959–70; Depute Headmaster, George Heriot's Sch., 1967–70. *Recreations:* formerly Rugby, cricket; now gardening, photography. *Address:* Millbrook House, 36 Mill Street, Dalbeattie DG5 4HE. *T:* Dalbeattie 611231.

MACDONALD, Angus Cameron; His Honour Judge Angus Macdonald; a Circuit Judge, since 1979; *b* 26 Aug. 1931; *o s* of late Hugh Macdonald, OBE, and of Margaret Cameron Macdonald (*née* Westley); *m* 1956, Deborah Anne, *d* of late John Denny Inglis, DSO, MC, JP, and of Deborah Margery Meiklem Inglis (*née* Thomson); three *d. Educ:* Bedford Sch.; Trinity Hall, Cambridge (BA 1954, MA 1960). Nat. service, 1950–51, commissioned, TA, 1951–57. Called to Bar, Gray's Inn, 1955; Resident Magistrate, then Crown Counsel, Nyasaland Govt, 1957–65; Sen. State Counsel, Malawi Govt, 1965–67; practised, NE Circuit, 1967–79; a Recorder of the Crown Court, 1974–79. *Recreations:* singing, fishing. *Address:* 21 Lindisfarne Road, Newcastle upon Tyne NE2 2HE. *T:* Tyneside 2811695; Blaren, Kilninver, by Oban, Argyll. *T:* Kilmelford 246. *Club:* Northern Counties (Newcastle upon Tyne).

MACDONALD, Angus John, (Gus); Director of Programmes, Scottish Television, since 1986; Visiting Professor, Media and Film Studies, Stirling University, since 1985; *b* 20 Aug. 1940; *s* of Colin Macdonald and Jean (*née* Livingstone); *m* 1963, Alice Theresa McQuaid; two *d. Educ:* Scotland Street Sch., Glasgow; Allan Glen's Sch., Glasgow. Marine fitter, 1955–63; Circulation Manager, Tribune, 1963–65; feature writer, The Scotsman, 1965–66; Editor, Financial Scotsman, 1966–67; Granada Television: Editor/Exec. Producer, World in Action, 1969–75; Head of Current Affairs, 1975–82; presenter, variously, Camera, Devil's Advocate, Granada 500, Party conferences, What the Papers Say, World in Action, Union World; ombudsman, Right to Reply (viewers' complaints about independent television), Channel Four, 1982–. Chm. (Founder), Edinburgh Internat. Television Festival, 1976 and 1977; Dep. Chm., Edinburgh Internat. Film Festival, 1975–84. *Publications:* The Documentary Idea and Television Today, 1977; Camera: Victorian eyewitness, 1979. *Recreations:* pictures, moving and still; exploring Scotland past and present. *Address:* Scottish Television, Cowcaddens, Glasgow G2 3PR. *T:* 041–332 9999. *Clubs:* Reform, Royal Automobile, Art (Glasgow).

MACDONALD, Angus Stewart, CBE 1985; DL; FRAgS; farmer; Chairman, Scottish Agricultural Development Council, 1980–86; *b* 7 April 1935; *s* of Angus Macdonald and Mary Macdonald (*née* Anderson); *m* 1959, Janet Ann Somerville; three *s. Educ:* Conon Bridge School; Gordonstoun School. FRAgS 1982. Director: British Wool Marketing Board and Associated Cos; Scottish English Welsh Wool Growers; Grampian Television; Reith & Anderson (Tain & Dingwall) Ltd. Chm., RHAS, 1978–79; Member: Highlands & Islands Develt Bd; Hill Farming Res. Orgn; Panel of Agricl Arbiters. Governor: Gordonstoun School; Aberlour School. DL Ross and Cromarty, 1984. *Recreations:* field sports. *Address:* Torgorm, Conon Bridge, Dingwall, Ross-shire IV7 8DN. *T:* Dingwall 61365.

MacDONALD, Gen. Sir Arthur (Leslie), KBE 1978 (OBE 1953); CB 1969; Director: Carricks Ltd, since 1980; Gas Corporation of Queensland Ltd, since 1983; *b* 30 Jan. 1919; *s* of late Arthur Leslie MacDonald, Yaamba, Queensland; *m* 1940, Joan Bevington, *d* of late Sidney Brady, Brisbane, Queensland; one *d. Educ:* The Southport School, Southport, Queensland; Royal Military College, Duntroon, ACT. Regtl and Staff appts, Aust., ME and New Guinea, 1940–44; Instructor, Staff Coll., Camberley, 1944–45; CO 3rd Bn, The Royal Australian Regt, Korea, 1953–54; Dir of Mil. Ops, AHQ, 1955–56; Senior Aust. Planner, SEATO, Bangkok, 1957–58; Commandant, Jungle Training Centre, Canungra, 1959–60; Dir of Staff Duties, AHQ, 1960–61; Imperial Defence Coll., 1962; Dep. Commander, 1st Div., 1963–64; Commander, Papua New Guinea Comd, 1965–66; Dep. Chief of the General Staff, 1966–67; Commander Australian Force, Viet Nam, 1968–69; Adjutant-Gen., 1969–70; GOC Northern Comd, 1970–73; Chief of Operations, 1973; Vice Chief of Gen. Staff, 1973–75; CGS, 1975–77; Chief of Defence Force Staff, 1977–79, retired. Col Comdt, Royal Aust. Regt, 1981–85. *Address:* 14 Meiers Road, Indooroopilly, Qld 4068, Australia. *Club:* Queensland (Brisbane).

McDONALD, Air Marshal Sir Arthur (William Baynes), KCB 1958 (CB 1949); AFC 1938; CEng, FRAeS 1959; DL; retired; *b* 14 June 1903; *s* of late Dr Will McDonald, OBE, Antigua, BWI; *m* 1928, Mary Julia Gray, Hindhead, Surrey; two *s* two *d. Educ:* Epsom Coll.; Peterhouse, Cambridge (MA). Joined RAF, 1924; served in Singapore, 1933–35; in Air Ministry, 1939–40; Fighter Command, 1941. Appointed Air Defence Commander, Ceylon, 1942; Air Officer Training, Air HQ, India, 1943–44; Air Officer Commanding No. 106 Group, 1945–46; Comdt RAF Staff Coll., Bulstrode and later Andover, 1947–48; Student Imperial Defence Coll., 1949; OC Aeroplane and Armament Experimental Establishment, under the Ministry of Supply, 1950–52; Director-General of Manning, Air Ministry, 1952–55; Commander-in-Chief, Royal Pakistan Air Force, 1955–57; AOC-in-C, RAF Technical Training Comd, 1958–59; Air Mem. for Personnel, Air Council, 1959–61, retired 1962. DL Hampshire, 1965. *Recreation:* sailing (rep. Great Britain in Olympic Games, 1948). *Address:* Five Oaks, Woodside, Lymington, Hants. *Clubs:* Royal Air Force; Royal Lymington Yacht; RAF Sailing Association (Adm.).

McDONALD, David Arthur; Director of Information, Department of the Environment, since 1982; *b* 16 Jan. 1940; *s* of late Campbell McDonald and Ethel McDonald; *m* 1st, 1963, Barbara MacCallum (marr. diss.); one *d*; 2nd, 1971, Mavis Lowe; one *s. Educ:* Campbell College, Belfast; Trinity College, Dublin. BA (Moderatorship) Classics. Asst Master, Classics, Methodist College, Belfast, 1963–66; Press Sec. to Minister of Education, N Ireland, 1967–68; joined Min. of Housing and Local Govt, 1970; Asst Private Sec. to Sec. of State for the Envt, 1974–76; Asst Sec., Local Govt Finance Divs, DoE, 1977–82. Pres., Civil Service Men's Hockey Club, London. *Recreations:* golf, cricket. *Clubs:* Reform; Wimbledon Park Golf.

MACDONALD, David Cameron; Senior UK Adviser to Credit Suisse First Boston, since 1983; Chairman, Pittard Group, since 1985 (Director, 1984); Director: Coutts and Co., since 1980; Sears, since 1981; Merivale Moore, since 1985; *b* 5 July 1936; *s* of James Fraser Macdonald, OBE, FRCS and Anne Sylvia Macdonald (*née* Hutcheson); *m* 1st, 1968, Melody Jane Coles (marr. diss. 1980); two *d*; 2nd, 1983, Mrs Sally Robertson; one *s. Educ:* St George's Sch., Harpenden; Newport Grammar Sch. Admitted a solicitor with Slaughter and May, 1962; joined Philip Hill Higginson Erlangers (now Hill Samuel & Co. Ltd), 1964: Dir, 1968; Dep. Chm., 1979–80; Dir, Hill Samuel Gp Ltd, 1979–80; Chief Exec., Antony Gibbs Holdings Ltd and Chm., Antony Gibbs & Sons, 1980–83; Chm., Bath and Portland Gp, 1982–85. Dir Gen., Panel on Takeovers and Mergers, 1977–79. Adviser to Govt on Upper Clyde Shipbuilders crisis, 1971. Chm., Issuing Houses Assoc., 1975–77. Mem., BTA, 1971–82. Trustee, London City Ballet, 1983–. *Recreations:* music, fishing. *Address:* 13A Bolton Gardens, SW5. *T:* 01–373 1296; Sweetapples Farmhouse, Martin, near Fordingbridge, Hants. *T:* Martin Cross 368.

McDONALD, David Wylie, CMG 1978; DA, RIBA, ARIAS, FHKIA; Secretary for Lands and Works, Hong Kong, 1981–83; MLC Hong Kong, 1974–83; *b* 9 Oct. 1927; *s* of William McDonald and Rebecca (*née* Wylie); *m* 1951, Eliza Roberts Steele; two *d. Educ:* Harris Acad., Dundee; School of Architecture, Dundee Coll. of Art (Lorimer Meml Prize, RIAS, 1950; City Coronation Design Prize, Corporation of Dundee, 1953; DA 1953). Architect with Gauldie, Hardie, Wright and Needham, Chartered Architects, Dundee, 1953–55; Public Works Department, Hong Kong: Architect, 1955; Sen. Architect, 1964; Chief Architect, 1967; Govt Architect, 1970; Principal Govt Architect, 1972; Dir of Building Devel, 1973; Dir of Public Works, 1974. Member: Finance Cttee, Legislative Council, 1974–83; Commonwealth Parly Assoc., 1974–. Director: Mass Transit Railway Corp., Hong Kong, 1975–83; Ocean Park Ltd, Hong Kong, 1976–83; Hong Kong Industrial Estate Corp., 1981–83; Mem., Hong Kong Housing Auth., 1982–83. Mem. Exec. Cttee: Girl Guides Assoc. (Hong Kong Br.), 1977–83; Hong Kong Red Cross, 1981–83. Mem. Cttee of Management, Margaret Blackwood Hsg Assoc., 1984–; Trustee, Scottish Trust for Physically Disabled, 1984–. JP Hong Kong, 1972–83. Silver Jubilee Medal, 1977. *Recreations:* swimming (Coach and Manager, Hong Kong Swimming Team at Commonwealth Games, Christchurch, NZ, 1974), drawing, painting and calligraphy. *Address:* Northbank, Backmuir of Liff, by Dundee DD2 5QT. *T:* Dundee 580483. *Clubs:* Hong Kong (Hong Kong) (Chairman, 1977); Royal Hong Kong Jockey (Hong Kong).

MACDONALD, Prof. Donald Farquhar; Professor of Modern Social and Economic History, University of Dundee, 1967–76 (University of St Andrews, 1955–67); *b* 3 June 1906; 3rd *s* of Donald Macdonald and Annabella Mackenzie; *m* Jeannette Eileen Bickle; one *s. Educ:* Dingwall Academy; Aberdeen Univ. (MA 1st cl. Hons Hist.); Balliol Coll., Oxford (DPhil). University Lecturer, Aberdeeen Univ. and University Coll., Exeter, 1934–41; Ministry of Supply and Ministry of Labour and National Service, 1941–43; Secretary (later General Manager), National Assoc. of Port Employers, 1943–55. *Publications:* Scotland's Shifting Population, 1770–1850, 1937; The State and the Trade Unions, 1960, revised edn 1976; The Age of Transition, 1967, etc. *Address:* 11 Arnhall Drive, Dundee.

MACDONALD, Rev. Donald Farquhar Macleod, CBE 1979; DLit; Principal Clerk of General Assembly of the Church of Scotland, 1972–85; *b* 1 May 1915; *s* of John Murchison Macdonald and Margaret Macleod; *m* 1948, Anne Jane Vance Sinclair; one *s* two *d. Educ:* North Kelvinside Secondary Sch.; Glasgow Univ. (MA, LLB). Ordained to Glasford Parish, 1948; Clerk to Presbytery of Hamilton, 1952–72; Dep. Clerk of General Assembly, 1955–71. *Publications:* (ed) Practice and Procedure in the Church of Scotland, 6th edn, 1977; (ed and comp.) Fasti Ecclesiae Scoticanae, vol. X, 1981. *Recreations:* chess, swimming, gardening. *Address:* 29 Auchingramont Road, Hamilton, Lanarkshire. *T:* Hamilton 423667; 3 Chapmans Place, Elie, Fife. *Club:* Caledonian (Edinburgh).

MACDONALD, Donald Hardman, CMG 1974; *b* 16 May 1908; *s* of Archibald J. H. and Elizabeth Macdonald; *m* 1930, Simone Dumortier; one *s* one *d. Educ:* City of London Sch. Partner, Charles Fulton & Co., London, 1935–39; Bank of England, 1939–49; Chief, Allied Bank Commn, Frankfort, 1949–52; Adviser, Bank of England, 1953–54; Bank for International Settlements, Basle, 1954–73 (Head of Banking Dept, 1972–73). *Recreations:* reading, travel, gardening. *Address:* 5 rue Robert de Traz, 1206 Geneva, Switzerland. *T:* (022) 46.95.46.

MACDONALD, Air Vice-Marshal Donald Malcolm Thomas, CB 1952; RAF retired; *b* 15 Aug. 1909; *s* of late D. P. Macdonald, Tormore, Isle of Skye; *m* 1938, Kathleen Mary de Vere, *d* of late J. T. Hunt, Oxford; one *s* four *d. Educ:* Westminster School. Joined Royal Air Force, 1930. Dir-Gen. of Personal Services, Air Min., 1957–58; Dir-Gen. of Manning, Air Min., 1958–61, retd 1961. Mem. Crofters Commn, 1962–65. Chm., Royal British Legion, Scotland, 1977–81. *Address:* Torbeag, Clachan Seil, by Oban, Argyll. *T:* Balvicar 311.

MACDONALD, Hon. Donald (Stovel), PC (Canada) 1968; lawyer; Partner, McCarthy & McCarthy, since 1978; Director: Boise Cascade Corporation, since 1978; McDonnell Douglas Corporation, since 1978; Du Pont Canada Inc., since 1978; Bank of Nova Scotia, since 1980; Alberta Energy Co. Ltd, since 1981; *b* 1 March 1932; *s* of Donald Angus Macdonald and Marjorie Stovel Macdonald; *m* 1961, Ruth Hutchison, Ottawa; four *d. Educ:* Univ. of Toronto (BA 1951); Osgoode Hall Law Sch. (1955); Harvard Law Sch. (LLM 1956); Cambridge Univ. (Dip. in Internat. Law, 1957). Called to Ont Bar, 1955; Prize in Insurance Law, Law Soc. of Upper Canada, 1955; Rowell Fellow, Canadian Inst. of Internat. Affairs, 1956; McCarthy & McCarthy, law firm, Toronto, 1957–62. Special Lectr, Univ. of Toronto Law Sch., 1978–83. MP Rosedale, 1962–78; Parly Sec. to Ministers of Justice, Finance, Ext. Affairs, Industry, 1963–68; Minister without Portfolio, 1968; Pres., Queen's Privy Council, and Govt House Leader, 1968–70; Minister of National Defence, 1970–72; Minister of Energy, Mines and Resources, 1972–75; Minister of Finance, 1975–77. Chm., Internat. Develt Res. Centre, Canada, 1981–84. Chm., Royal Commn on Econ. Union and Develt Prospects for Canada, 1982–85. LLD (*hc*) St Lawrence Univ., 1974; Hon. DEng Colorado Sch. of Mines, 1976. *Recreations:* fishing, cross-country skiing, tennis. *Address:* 29 Dunvegan Road, Toronto, Ont M4V 2P5, Canada. *T:* 960—1223; (office) PO Box 48, Toronto Dominion Tower, Toronto Dominion Center, Toronto, Ont M5K 1E6, Canada. *T:* 362–1812.

MacDONALD, Douglas George; Managing Director: John Menzies (Holdings) plc, 1971–84; Receptor International Ltd, since 1985; *b* 5 Aug. 1930; *s* of Colin Douglas MacDonald and Jane Grant Stewart; *m* Alexandra von Tschirschky und Boegendorf; one *s. Educ:* Morgan Acad., Dundee; Univ. of St Andrews (BSc). Queen's Own Cameron Highlanders, 1951–57. Potash Ltd, 1957–66; Man. Dir, Wyman Marshall Ltd, 1966–68. Member: National Freight Corp., 1973–80; Scottish Telecommunications Bd, 1973–76; Chm., East Lothian Conservative and Unionist Assoc., 1970–73; Director: Scottish Investment Trust plc, 1977–83; William Muir (Bond 9) Ltd, 1981–; Robert Moss plc, 1981–83; Scottish Life Assce Co. Ltd, 1982–83; Royal Bank of Scotland plc, 1982–85; Chairman: Advent Technol. plc, 1981–; Clan Donald Lands Trust, 1982–. Chm., Scottish Council, Res. Inst. Ltd, 1975–85. Scottish Nat. Orch. Soc., 1984. *Address:* c/o Royal Bank of Scotland, 36 St Andrew Square, Edinburgh EH2 2YB. *Clubs:* Royal Automobile; New (Edinburgh).

McDONALD, Sir Duncan, Kt 1983; CBE 1976; BSc, FH-WC, FRSE, FEng, CBIM, SMIEEE; Chairman, Northern Engineering Industries plc, 1980–86 (Group Managing Director, 1977–80; Chief Executive, 1980–83); *b* 20 Sept. 1921; *s* of Robert McDonald and Helen Orrick; *m* 1955, Jane Anne Guckian; three *s* one *d. Educ:* Inverkeithing Public Sch.; Dunfermline High Sch.; Edinburgh Univ. (BSc). Grad. App., BTH, Rugby, 1942–45; Transformer Design, Research and Develt, BTH, 1945–54. Bruce Peebles Industries Ltd: Chief Transformer Designer, 1954–59; Chief Engr, 1959; Dir and Chief Engr, 1960; Managing Dir, 1962; Chm. and Chief Exec. (and of A. Reyrolle & Co. Ltd), 1974; Reyrolle Parsons Ltd: Dir, 1973–77; Chief Exec., 1976–77. Director: Barclays Bank (Newcastle), 1980; Nat. Nuclear Corp., 1982; General Accident, 1983–. Member: Scottish Council Develt and Industry, 1967– (Vice-Pres., 1984–); Scottish Economic Council, 1975–. FH-WC 1962. Hon. FIEE 1984. Hon. DSc Heriot-Watt, 1982; Hon. DEng Newcastle, 1984. *Publications:* various papers to learned socs, nat. and internat. *Recreation:* fishing. *Address:* Duncliffe, Kinellan Road, Edinburgh EH12 6ES. *T:* 031–337 4814. *Club:* New (Edinburgh).

McDONALD, (Edward) Lawson, MA, MD Cantab; FRCP; FACC; Consultant Cardiologist, National Heart Hospital, since 1961; Cardiologist, to King Edward VII's Hospital for Officers, London, since 1968, to King Edward VII Hospital, Midhurst, since 1970; Senior Lecturer (formerly Lecturer) to the Institute of Cardiology, since 1961; Hon. Consultant Cardiologist, Canadian Red Cross Memorial Hospital, Taplow, since 1960; *b* 1918; *s* of Charles Seaver McDonald, Belfast, NI; *m* 1953, Ellen Greig Rattray (marr. diss. 1972); one *s. Educ:* Felsted Sch.; Clare Coll., Cambridge; Middlesex Hospital; Harvard Univ. House appointments Middlesex Hospital, 1942–43. Temp. Surgeon-Lt, RNVR, 1943–46; served War of 1939–45, in N Atlantic and Normandy Campaigns. RMO, Nat. Heart Hosp., 1946–47; Asst Registrar, Inst. of Cardiology, 1947–48; Med. Registrar, Middlesex Hosp., 1948–49; studied in Stockholm, 1949; Asst to Prof. of Medicine, Middlesex Hosp., 1949–52; Rockefeller Travelling Fellow in Medicine, 1952–53; Asst in Medicine, Med. Dept, Peter Bent Brigham Hosp., Boston, Mass. and Research Fellow in Medicine, Harvard Univ., 1952–53; Clinical and Research Asst, Dept of Cardiology, Middlesex Hosp., 1953–55; Asst Dir, Inst. of Cardiology and Hon. Asst Physician, Nat. Heart Hosp., 1955–61; Physician, and Physician to Cardiac Dept, London Hosp., 1960–78. Member: Bd of Governors, National Heart and Chest Hosps, 1975–82; Council, British Heart Foundn, 1975–83. Visiting Lecturer: American Coll. of Cardiology; Univ. of Toronto, Queen's Univ., Kingston, Ont; Univ. of Bombay; University of Barcelona, Eliseo Migoya Inst. of Cardiology, Bilbao, Spain; Istanbul Univ., Turkey; Univs of Chicago, Cincinnati and Kansas; Harvard Univ.; Mayo Foundation, USA; Univs of Belgrade, Ljubljana and Zagreb, Yugoslavia; Nat. Univ. of Cordoba, Argentine; Univ. of Chile, and Catholic Univ., Santiago; Nat. Univ. of Colombia; Nat. Inst. of Cardiology, Mexico; Nat. Univ. of Mexico; University of San Marcos and University of Cayetano Heredia, Peru; Nat. Univ. of Venezuela. From 1961, has addressed numerous heart societies in Europe, Canada, USA, People's Republic of China, USSR, and South America; St Cyres Lecturer, 1966; First Charles A. Berns Meml Lectr, Albert Einstein Coll. of Medicine, NY, 1973; Vth World Congress of Cardiology Souvenir Orator and Lectr's Gold Medallist, 1977. Advisor to the Malaysian Govt on Cardiac Services. Member: British Cardiac Soc.; Assoc. of Physicians of Great Britain and Ireland, and other societies; FACC; Corresp. Mem. or Hon. Mem. of various socs of Cardiology or Angiology in S America. Hon. Fellow, Turkish Med. Soc.; Internat. Fellow, Council on Clinical Cardiol., Amer. Heart Assoc.; Mem., Italian Soc. of Cardiology; Hon. Member: Pakistan Cardiac Soc.; Scientific Council, Revista Portuguesa de Cardiologia. Member, Most Honourable Order of the Crown of Johore, 1980. Editorial Bd, New Istanbul Contribution to Clinical Science. *Publications:* (ed) Pathogenesis and Treatment of Occlusive Arterial Disease, 1960; Medical and Surgical Cardiology, 1969; (ed) Very Early Recognition of Coronary Heart Disease, 1978; numerous contribs to learned jls; also papers and addresses. *Recreations:* art, ski-ing, mountain walking, sailing. *Address:* 9 Upper Wimpole Street, W1M 7TD. *T:* 01–935 7101; 9 Bentinck Mansions, Bentinck Street, W1M 5RJ. *T:* 01–935 0868.

MacDONALD, Hon. Flora Isabel; MP (Progressive C) Kingston, Ontario, since 1972; Minister for Communications, Canada, since 1986; *b* 3 June 1926. *Educ:* schools in North Sydney, Nova Scotia; Empire Business Coll., Canadian Nat. Defence Coll. With Nat. HQ, Progressive Cons. Party, 1957–66 (Exec. Dir, 1961–66); Nat. Sec., Progressive Cons. Assoc. of Canada, 1966–69; Administrative Officer and Tutor, Dept of Political Studies, Queen's Univ., Kingston, 1966–72. Minister for External Affairs, Canada, 1979–80; Minister of Employment and Immigration, 1984–86. Member: Canadian Inst. of Internat. Affairs; Canadian Civil Liberties Assoc.; Elizabeth Fry Soc., Kingston (former Pres.); Cttee for an Indep. Canada (former exec. dir); Canadian Political Science Assoc. (former dir). *Publications:* papers on political subjects. *Address:* House of Commons, Ottawa, Ont K1A 0A6, Canada.

McDONALD, (Francis) James; President and Chief Operating Officer, General Motors, 1981–87; *b* Saginaw, Mich, 3 Aug. 1922; *s* of Francis and Mary McDonald; *m* 1944, Betty Ann Dettenthaler; two *s* one *d*. *Educ:* General Motors Inst. Served USN, 1944–46 (Lieut). Joined Saginaw Malleable Iron Plant, 1946; Transmission Div., Detroit, 1956–65; Pontiac Motor Div., 1965–68; Dir, Manufacturing Operations, Chevrolet Motor Div., 1968–69; Vice-Pres., and Mem. Admin Cttee, Gen. Motors, 1969; General Manager: Pontiac Motor Div., 1969–72; Chevrolet Motor Div., 1972–74; Exec. Vice-Pres. and a Dir, 1974; Mem. Finance Cttee, 1979; Chm., Exec. and Admin Cttees, 1981. Chm., Res. Inst., William Beaumont Hosp., Mich, 1973–76. *Address:* (office) 3044 West Grand Boulevard, Detroit, Mich 48202, USA.

MACDONALD, George Grant; His Honour Judge Macdonald; a Circuit Judge, since 1972; *b* 5 March 1921; *s* of late Patrick Macdonald, MA, Aberdeen, MB, ChB, Edinburgh, and Charlotte Primrose (*née* Rintoul); *m* 1967, Mary Dolores (*née* Gerrish), *widow* of G. G. Taylor; no *c*. *Educ:* Kelly Coll., Tavistock; Bristol Univ. (LLB (Hons)). Served War of 1939–45: in Royal Navy, Aug. 1941–July 1946, in Western Approaches, and Mine Sweeping, RNVR. Called to Bar, Gray's Inn, 1947; practised on Western Circuit, from Albion Chambers, Bristol; Dep.-Chm., Dorset QS, apptd 1969; Temp. Recorder of Barnstaple, Dec. 1971. *Recreations:* sailing, bridge, chess. *Address:* Hartfield, Wood Green, Fordingbridge, Hants. *T:* Downton 22248. *Club:* Clifton (Bristol).

McDONALD, Graeme Patrick Daniel; Controller of BBC 2, since 1983; *b* 30 July 1930; *s* of Daniel McDonald and Eileen (*née* McLean); unmarried. *Educ:* St Paul's Sch.; Jesus Coll., Cambridge. Entered TV, 1960; Dir, Granada TV, 1960–65; BBC Television: Producer, 1966–76: prodns include Thirty Minute Theatre, 1966–67, Wednesday Play, 1967–70 and Play for Today, 1970–76; Head of Drama Series and Serials, 1977–81; Head of Drama Gp, 1981–83. *Address:* c/o BBC TV, Wood Lane, W12 7RJ.

MACDONALD, Gus; *see* Macdonald, A. J.

MACDONALD, Sir Herbert (George deLorme), KBE 1967 (OBE 1948); JP (Jamaica); retired government officer (Jamaica); company director; sportsman; President Organising Committee, IX Central American and Caribbean Games, 1962, and 8th British Empire and Commonwealth Games, 1966 (compiled and edited history); Chairman, National Sports Ltd (a Government body owning and operating National Stadium and Sports Centre), 1960–67, now President (specially created post); Director: Prospect Beach Ltd; Macdonald Ltd; *b* Kingston, 23 May 1902; *s* of late Ronald Macdonald, JP, planter, and late Louise (*née* Alexander). *Educ:* Wolmer's Boys' Sch., Jamaica; Northeast High Sch., Philadelphia, USA. Clerical and planting activities, 1919–43. Published Sportsman Magazine (with late Sir Arthur Thelwell). Accompanied Jamaica's team to World Olympics, London, 1948, and (as Manager) to Helsinki, 1952, Melbourne, 1956; Chef de Mission, WI Olympic Team to Rome, 1960; Deleg., Tokyo, 1964. Chief Liaison Officer, BWI Central Lab. Org. (USA), 1943–55; Pres., Jamaica Olympic Assoc., 1940–44 and 1956–58; Pres., WI Olympic Assoc. (from inception), 1958–61 (when Polit. Fedn was broken up). Past Pres. etc, various Jamaican sporting assocs and boards; Mem. Exec. Cttee Pan American Sports Organisation which controls Pan American Games; Exec. Sec., Jamaica Tercentenary Celebrations Cttee, 1955. Mem. Bd of Trustees, Wolmer's Sch. Diploma of Merit, 1966 Internat. Olympic Cttee, 1968. Is an Anglican. *Recreations:* all sports; stamp collecting (athletic stamps); represented Jamaica in football and tennis *v* foreign teams, 1925–32. *Address:* 1 Liguanea Row, Kingston 6, Jamaica. *T:* 927–8213. *Clubs:* (Life Mem., past Hon. Sec.) Kingston Cricket (Kingston, Jamaica); Constant Spring Golf.

MACDONALD, Prof. Hugh Ian, OC 1977; Canada Centennial Medal, 1967; Silver Jubilee Medal, 1977; Professor, Department of Economics and Faculty of Administrative Studies, York University, Toronto, since 1974; President Emeritus and Director, York International, since 1984; *b* Toronto, 27 June 1929; *s* of Hugh and Winnifred Macdonald; *m* 1960, Dorothy Marion Vernon; two *s* three *d*. *Educ:* public schs, Toronto; Univ. of Toronto; Oxford Univ. BCom (Toronto), MA (Oxon), BPhil (Oxon). Univ. of Toronto: Lectr in Economics, 1955; Dean of Men, 1956; Asst Prof., Economics, 1962. Govt of Ontario: Chief Economist, 1965; Dep. Provincial Treas., 1967; Dep. Treas. and Dep. Minister of Economics, 1968; Dep. Treas. and Dep. Minister of Economics and Intergovernmental Affairs, 1972. Pres., York Univ., 1974–84. Director: Canadian Gen. Electric Co.; Rockwell Internat. of Canada Ltd; the AGF Cos; CIBA-GEIGY Canada Ltd; Excelsior Life Insurance Co.; Aetna Casualty Co. of Canada; McGraw-Hill Ryerson Ltd; Member, Board of Dirctors: Hockey Canada; London House Assoc. of Canada; CJRT-FM Inc; Computer Museum of Canada; North-South Inst.; Canadian Rhodes Scholars' Foundn; Member, Bd of Governors: York-Finch Hosp.; Member: Bd of Advisors, Internat. Assoc. for Students of Economics and Commerce; Adv. Council, Niagara Inst.; Admin. Bd, Internat. Assoc. of Univs; Council and Exec. Cttee, Interamerican Org. for Higher Educn; Chairman: Bd, Corp. to Promote Innovation Develt for Employment Advancement (Govt of Ontario); Commn on Financing of Elementary and Secondary Educn in Ontario. Chm., Inst. for Political Involvement; Member: Canadian Economics Assoc.; Amer. Economics Assoc.; Royal Economic Soc. (London); Canadian Assoc. for Club of Rome; Inst. of Public Admin of Canada; Lambda Alpha Fraternity (Land Economics); Amer. Soc. for Public Admin; Past President: Empire Club of Canada; Ticker Club; Couchiching Inst. Public Affairs; Past Chm., Toronto Men's Br. of CIIA; Past Mem., Attorney General's Cttee on Securities Legislation. KLJ 1978; Citation of Merit, Court of Canadian Citizenship, 1980. Hon. LLD Toronto, 1974. *Recreations:* hockey, tennis; public service in various organizations. *Address:* 7 Whitney Avenue, Toronto, Ont. M4W 2A7, Canada. *T:* 921–2908; York University, 4700 Keele Street, Downsview, Ont. M3J 1P3, Canada. *T:* 736–5177.

MACDONALD, Prof. Hugh John; Gardiner Professor of Music, University of Glasgow, since 1980; *b* 31 Jan. 1940; *s* of Stuart and Margaret Macdonald; *m* 1st, 1963, Naomi Butterworth; one *s* three *d*; 2nd, 1979, Elizabeth Babb; one *s*. *Educ:* Winchester College; Pembroke College, Cambridge (MA; PhD). Cambridge University: Asst Lectr, 1966–69; Lectr, 1969–71; Fellow, Pembroke Coll., 1963–71; Lectr, Oxford Univ., 1971–80, and Fellow, St John's Coll., 1979. Vis. Prof., Indiana Univ., 1979. Gen. Editor, New Berlioz Edition, 1966–. Szymanowski Medal, Poland, 1983. *Publications:* Berlioz Orchestral Music, 1969; Skryabin, 1978; Berlioz, 1981; articles in New Grove Dict. of Music and Musicians, Musical Times, Music and Letters, Revue de Musicologie. *Recreations:* bridges, typewriters. *Address:* Department of Music, University of Glasgow, Glasgow G12 8QH. *T:* 041–339 8855.

MACDONALD, Iain Smith, MD; FRCPE, FFCM; Chief Medical Officer, Scottish Home and Health Department, since 1985; *b* 14 July 1927; *s* of Angus Macdonald, MA and Jabina Urie Smith; *m* 1958, Sheila Foster; one *s* one *d*. *Educ:* Univ. of Glasgow (MD, DPH). Lectr, Univ. of Glasgow, 1955; Deputy Medical Officer of Health: Bury, 1957; Bolton, 1959; joined Scottish Home and Health Dept, 1964, Dep. Chief Med. Officer, 1974–85. QHP 1984–87. *Address:* 36 Dumyat Drive, Falkirk FK1 5PA. *T:* Falkirk 25100.

MacDONALD, Ian; *see* Mayfield, Hon. Lord.

MACDONALD, Prof. Ian Grant, FRS 1979; Professor of Pure Mathematics, Queen Mary College, University of London, since 1976; *b* 11 Oct. 1928; *s* of Douglas Grant Macdonald and Irene Alice Macdonald; *m* 1954, Margaretha Maria Lodewijk Van Goethem; two *s* three *d*. *Educ:* Winchester Coll.; Trinity Coll., Cambridge (MA). Asst Principal and Principal, Min. of Supply, 1952–57; Asst Lectr, Univ. of Manchester, 1957–60; Lectr, Univ. of Exeter, 1960–63; Fellow, Magdalen Coll., Oxford, 1963–72; Fielden Prof. of Pure Maths, Univ. of Manchester, 1972–76. *Publications:* Introduction to Commutative Algebra (with M. F. Atiyah), 1969; Algebraic Geometry, 1969; articles in math. jls. *Address:* 8 Blandford Avenue, Oxford. *T:* Oxford 515373.

MACDONALD, Ian Wilson, MA; DLitt; CA; *b* Old Cumnock, Ayrshire, 28 May 1907; *s* of late Rev. Alexander B. Macdonald, BD, PhD, Dron, Perthshire, and late Dr Mary B. W. Macdonald; *m* 1933, Helen Nicolson, MA; one *s* two *d*. *Educ:* Perth Academy; Edinburgh Academy. Prof. of Accountancy, Univ. of Glasgow, 1938–50. Partner in Kerr Macleod and Macfarlan, CA, Glasgow, 1933–53. Member: Cttee of Investigation into Port Transport Industry, 1945; Court of Inquiry into Omnibus Industry, 1946, Shipbuilding Industry, 1947, Railwaymen's Wages and Hours of Work, 1947; Arbitrator, Nigerian Railways Labour dispute, 1948; Mem. Gen. Claims Tribunal, 1943–58. Member: Cttee of Inquiry: Fishing Industry, 1957–60; Ports and Harbours, 1961–62; Member: S Scotland Electricity Board, 1956–61; National Ports Council, 1963–67; NRDC, 1959–73; CAA, 1972–75. Chairman: Lloyds and Scottish Ltd, 1959–78; Royal Bank of Scotland Ltd, 1969–72; Dir, Lloyds Bank Ltd, 1961–78; Dep. Chm., National and Commercial Banking Group Ltd, 1969–78. Chm., Scottish Hosps Endowments Res. Trust, 1971–83. *Recreations:* shooting, fishing. *Address:* Seton Court, Gullane, East Lothian EH31 2BD. *Club:* Caledonian.

MacDONALD, Isabel Lillias, (Mrs J. G. MacDonald); *see* Sinclair, I. L.

McDONALD, Iverach; Associate Editor, The Times, 1967–73; Director, The Times Ltd, 1968–73; *b* 23 Oct. 1908; *s* of Benjamin McDonald, Strathcool, Caithness, and Janet Seel; *m* 1935, Gwendoline, *o d* of late Captain Thomas R. Brown; one *s* one *d*. *Educ:* Leeds Gram. Sch. Asst Editor, Yorkshire Post, 1933; sub-editor, The Times, 1935; correspondent in Berlin, 1937; diplomatic correspondent 1938; Asst Editor, 1948; Foreign Editor, 1952; Managing Editor, 1965. War of 1939–45: Capt., Gen. Staff, 1939–40; travelled extensively in Soviet Union, Far East and America; reported all allied conferences after the war, including San Francisco, 1945, Paris, 1946 and 1947, Moscow, 1947, Colombo, 1950, and Bermuda, 1953. Sen. Associate Mem., St Antony's Coll., Oxford, 1976–. *Publications:* A Man of the Times, 1976; The History of The Times, vol. V, 1939–1966, 1984; chapters in: Walter Lippmann and His Times, 1959; The Times History of our Times, 1971. *Address:* Whistlers, Beckley Common, Oxford. *T:* Stanton St John 226.

McDONALD, James; *see* McDonald, F. J.

McDONALD, Sir James, KBE 1967 (CBE 1956; OBE 1948); British Consul (Hon.), Portland, Oregon USA, since 1938; Managing Partner: Macdon & Co.; Kermac Investment Co.; Renfrew Associates; *b* 23 July 1899; *s* of late James McDonald, Renfrew, Scotland; *m* 1933, Anne, *d* of late Peter Kerr, Portland, Ore, USA; one *s* two *d*. *Educ:* Allen Glen's Sch., Glasgow. Lt, RFC (later RAF), 1917–19. Partner McDonald Gattie & Co., 1927–67; President: Norpac Shipping Co., 1940–67; McDonald Dock Co., 1955–72. Trustee: Oregon Historical Soc.; Oregon Parks Foundn. *Recreations:* walking, farming. *Address:* 11626 SW Military Lane, Portland, Ore, USA. *T:* 636–4775; Inchinnan Farm, Wilsonville, Ore, USA. *T:* 625–6914. *Clubs:* Boodle's, Royal Air Force; Arlington, University (Portland, Ore.).

MACDONALD, Prof. James Alexander, BSc (Agric.), PhD (Edinburgh), DSc (St Andrews); Professor of Botany, University of St Andrews, 1961–77, now Emeritus; *b* 17 June 1908; *s* of late James Alexander Macdonald and Jessie Mary Simpson; *m* 1935, Constance Mary Simmie; one *d*. *Educ:* Inverness Royal Academy; Edinburgh Univ.; Steven Scholarship in Agriculture, 1930; DSc with Sykes Gold Medal, 1947. Asst Lecturer in Botany, East of Scot. Coll. of Agriculture, 1932–35; St Andrews University: Lecturer in Botany, 1935–52; Senior Lecturer, 1952–60; Dean, Faculty of Science, 1967–69. Pres., Botanical Soc. of Edinburgh, 1955–57; FRSE 1940 (Council Mem., 1956–59); Vice-Pres. RSE, 1961–64. Fellow, Inst. Biology. Silver Jubilee Medal, 1977. *Publications:* Introduction to Mycology, 1951; scientific papers in Trans Brit. Mycol. Soc., Annals Applied Biol., Mycologia, Proc. and Trans Bot. Soc. Edinburgh, Proc. and Trans Royal Soc. Edinburgh. *Recreations:* golf, fishing, philately. *Address:* 17 Hepburn Gardens, St Andrews, Fife. *Club:* Royal and Ancient (St Andrews).

MACDONALD, John B(arfoot), DDS, MS, PhD; Chairman, Addiction Research Foundation, since 1981 (President and Chief Executive Officer, 1976–81); Executive Director, Council of Ontario Universities, 1968–76; Professor of Higher Education, University of Toronto, 1968–76; *b* 23 Feb. 1918; *s* of Arthur A. Macdonald and Gladys L. Barfoot; *m*; two *s* one *d*; *m* 1967, Liba Kucera; two *d*. *Educ:* Univ. of Toronto, University of Illinois, Columbia Univ. DDS (with hons) Toronto, 1942; MS (Bact) Ill, 1948; PhD (Bact) Columbia, 1953. Lectr, Prev. Dentistry, University of Toronto, and private practice, 1942–44. Canadian Dental Corps, 1944–46 (Capt.) Instr, Bacteriol, University of Toronto, and private practice, 1946–47; Res. Asst, Univ. of Illinois, 1947–48; Kellogg Fellow and Canadian Dental Assoc. Res. Student, Columbia Univ., 1948–49; University of Toronto: Asst Prof. of Bacteriol., 1949–53; Assoc. Prof. of Bacteriol., 1953–56; Chm., Div. of Dental Res., 1953–56; Prof. of Bacteriol., 1956; Cons. in Dental Educn, University of BC, 1955–56; Dir, Forsyth Dental Infirmary, 1956–62 (Cons. in Bacteriol., 1962); Prof. of Microbiol., Harvard Sch., of Dental Med., 1956–62 (Dir of Postdoctoral Studies, 1960–62); President, Univ. of British Columbia, 1962–67. Consultant: Dental Med. Section of Corporate Research Div. of Colgate-Palmolive Co., 1958–62; Donwood Foundn, Toronto, 1967 (Chm. of Bd, 1972–75); Science Council of Canada, 1967–69; Addiction Research Foundn of Ontario, 1968–74 (Mem., 1974–76); Nat. Inst. of Health, 1968– (Mem., Dental Study Sect., 1961–65). Chm., Commn on Pharmaceutical Services of the Canadian Pharmaceutical Assoc., 1967; Mem. and Vice-Chm., Ontario Council of Health, 1981–84; Councillor-at-Large, Internat. Assoc. for Dental Research, 1963, Pres. 1968–69. Fellow, Mem. or Chm. of numerous assocs. etc, both Canadian and international. FACD 1955; Hon. FICD 1965. Hon. AM, Harvard Univ., 1956; Hon. LLD: Univ. of Manitoba, 1962; Simon Fraser Univ., 1965; Hon DSc

Univ. of British Columbia, 1967; Hon. LLD: Wilfred Laurier Univ., 1976; Brock Univ., 1976; Univ. of W Ontario, 1977; Hon. DSc Univ. of Windsor, 1977. *Publications:* Higher Education in British Columbia and a Plan for the Future, 1962, etc.; numerous contribs to learned jls. *Recreations:* golf, fishing. *Address:* Addiction Research Foundation, 33 Russell Street, Toronto, Ontario M5S 2S1, Canada. *T:* 595–6050. *Clubs:* University of BC Faculty, Vancouver (Vancouver); Canadian, Faculty, University of Toronto (Toronto).

MACDONALD, Air Commodore John Charles, CB 1964; CBE 1957; DFC 1940 (Bar 1942); AFC 1941; Chairman, Abbeyfield (Weymouth) Society, since 1979; *b* 25 Dec. 1910; *s* of late Robert Macdonald; *m* 1952, Gladys Joan, *d* of John Hine, Beaminster, Dorset; two *s*. *Educ:* Berkhamsted Sch.; RAF Cadet Coll., Cranwell. Commissioned RAF, 1930. Served War of 1939–45 in Bomber Command; POW Stalag Luft III, 1942–45, escaped April 1945. Commanded RAF Akrotiri during Suez campaign; UK National Military Representative, SHAPE, 1959–61; Comdr RAF East Africa, 1961–64; Min. of Defence, 1964; retd, 1964. Chevalier, Légion d'Honneur, 1958; Croix de Guerre, 1958. *Recreations:* golf, sailing, shooting. *Address:* Woodbine Cottage, Osmington, Dorset. *T:* Preston 833259.

McDONALD, Prof. John Corbett, MD; FRCP, FFCM, FFOM; Professor, School of Occupational Health, McGill University, since 1981 (Head of School, 1981–83); *b* 20 April 1918; *s* of John Forbes McDonald and Sarah Mary McDonald; *m* 1942, Alison Dunstan Wells; one *s* three *d*. *Educ:* London Univ. (MD); Harvard Univ. (MS). DPH, DIH; FRCP (Canada) 1970; FRCP 1976; FFCM 1976; FFOM 1978. Served War, MO, RAMC, 1942–46. Epidemiologist, Public Health Lab. Service, 1951–64 (Dir, Epidemiol Res. Lab., 1960–64); Prof. and Head, Dept of Epidemiology and Health, McGill Univ., Montreal, 1964–76; Prof. of Occupational Health, LSHTM, Univ. of London, 1976–81; Dir, TUC Centenary Inst. of Occupational Health, 1976–81. *Publications:* (ed) Recent Advances in Occupational Health, 1981; papers on epidemiol subjects. *Recreations:* skiing, cycling. *Address:* 536 Pine Avenue West, Montreal, Quebec H2W 1S6, Canada. *Club:* Athenæum.

MacDONALD, John Grant, MBE 1962; HM Diplomatic Service; Ambassador to Paraguay, since 1986; *b* 26 Jan. 1932; *er s* of late John Nicol MacDonald and Margaret MacDonald (*née* Vasey); *m* 1955, Jean, *o c* of late J. K. K. Harrison; one *s* two *d*. *Educ:* George Heriot's School. Entered HM Foreign (later Diplomatic) Service, 1949; FO, 1949; served HM Forces, 1950–52; FO, 1952; Berne, 1954–59; Third sec. and Vice Consul, Havana, 1960–62; FO, 1962; DSAO, 1965; Second, later First Sec. (Comm.), Lima, 1966–71; ndc, Latimer, 1971–72; Parly Clerk of FCO, 1972–75; First Sec. (Comm.), Hd of Trade Promotion Sect., Washington, 1975–79; Hd of Chancery, Dhaka, 1980–81; Hd of Chancery and HM Consul, Bogotá, 1981–84; Counsellor, FCO, 1985–86. *Recreations:* travelling, photography, swimming. *Address:* c/o Foreign and Commonwealth Office, SW1A 2AH. *Clubs:* Naval and Military, Royal Over-Seas League.

MACDONALD, John Reginald, QC 1976; barrister-at-law; *b* 26 Sept. 1931; *s* of Ranald Macdonald and Marion Olive (*née* Kirkby); *m* 1958; one *s* one *d*. *Educ:* St Edward's Sch., Oxford; Queens' Coll., Cambridge. Called to Bar, Lincoln's Inn, 1955, Bencher, 1985. Contested (L): Wimbledon, 1966 and 1970; Folkestone and Hythe, 1983. Chm., Assoc. of Liberal Lawyers, 1973–78. *Recreation:* the theatre. *Address:* 12 New Square, Lincoln's Inn, WC2. *T:* 01–405 3808.

MACDONALD, Kenneth Carmichael, CB 1983; Deputy Under-Secretary of State (Resources and Programmes), Ministry of Defence, since 1985; *b* 25 July 1930; *s* of William Thomas and Janet Millar Macdonald; *m* 1960, Ann Elisabeth (*née* Pauer); one *s* two *d*. *Educ:* Hutchesons' Grammar Sch.; Glasgow Univ. MA (Hons Classics). RAF, 1952–54. Asst Principal, Air Ministry, 1954; Asst Private Sec. to Sec. of State, 1956–57; Private Sec. to Permanent Sec., 1958–61; HM Treasury, 1962–65; MoD, 1965; Asst Sec., 1968; Counsellor (Defence), UK Delegn to NATO, 1973–75; Asst Under-Sec. of State, MoD, 1975, Dep. Under-Sec. of State, 1980. *Recreation:* golf. *Address:* 61 Park Avenue, Bromley, Kent BR1 4EG. *T:* 01–460 6262.

McDONALD, Lawson; *see* McDonald, E. L.

MACDONALD, Dame Margaret; *see* Kidd, Dame Margaret Henderson.

MacDONALD, Margo, (Mrs James Sillars); television and radio presenter and reporter; *b* 19 April 1944; *d* of Robert and Jean Aitken; *m* 1st, 1965, Peter MacDonald (marr. diss. 1980); two *d*; 2nd, 1981, James Sillars, *qv*. *Educ:* Hamilton Academy; Dunfermline Coll. (Diploma of Physical Educn). Contested (SNP) Paisley, Gen. Elec., 1970; MP (SNP) Glasgow (Govan), Nov. 1973–Feb. 1974; contested (SNP): Glasgow (Govan), Gen. Elec., Feb. 1974 and Oct. 1974; Hamilton, by-election, May 1978. Vice-Chm., Scottish National Party, 1972–79 (Senior Vice-Chm., 1974–78); Mem., SNP Nat. Exec., 1980–81; Chm., SNP '79 Group, 1978–81. Director of Shelter (Scotland), 1978–81. *Recreations:* more work, music, swimming. *Address:* 15 Woodburn Terrace, Edinburgh 10.

McDONALD, Dr Oonagh; MP (Lab) Thurrock, since July 1976; *b* Stockton-on-Tees, Co. Durham; *d* of Dr H. D. McDonald. *Educ:* Roan Sch. for Girls, Greenwich; East Barnet Grammar Sch.; Univ. of London (BD Hons 1959; MTh 1962, PhD 1974, King's Coll.). Teacher, St Barnabas Sch., S Woodford, 1959–62; Lectr for Dip. in Sociology, Toynbee Hall, 1964–65; Teacher, Hornsey Grammar Sch. and Boreham Wood Sch., 1964–65; Lectr in Philosophy, Bristol Univ., 1965–76. Contested (Lab.), S Glos, Feb. and Oct. 1974. PPS to Chief Sec. to Treasury, 1977–79; Opposition front bench spokesman on defence, 1981–83, on Treasury and economic affairs, 1983–. Member: Public Accounts Cttee, 1977–78; Select Cttee on Employment, 1981; Jobs and Industry Policy Cttee, 1985–. Member: ASTMS, 1972–; Industrial Policy sub-cttee, Labour Party NEC, 1976–83 (Finance and Economic Affairs sub-cttee, 1978–83). Devised TV documentary, A Woman's Life. *Publications:* (jtly) The Economics of Prosperity, 1980; articles on taxation, child benefit, industrial strategy, etc. *Address:* House of Commons, Westminster, SW1A 0AA. *T:* 01–219 3415, 01–940 5563.

MACDONALD, Patrick Donald, CMG 1953; CVO 1963; *b* 21 July 1909; *s* of late Major E. W. Macdonald and Amy Beatrice Cavalier; *m* 1937, Delia Edith (marr. diss.), 5th *d* of Capt. R. W. Travers, RN (retired); twin *d* (and one *s* decd). *Educ:* Marlborough Coll.; St John's Coll., Cambridge. BA 1931. Cadet officer, Gilbert and Ellice Islands Colony, 1932; Administrative Officer, 1936; Sec. to Government, 1935–36 and 1938–39; Asst Sec., Western Pacific High Commission, 1940–42; Asst Colonial Sec., Trinidad and Tobago, 1942–45. Fiji: Administrative Officer, Grade II, 1946, Grade I, 1947; Asst Colonial Sec., 1946–49; Colonial Secretary, Governor's Deputy and Acting Governor: Leeward Islands, 1950–57; Colonial Sec. and Acting Governor, Fiji, 1957–66; Chm., Public and Police Service Commns, 1966–71. Actg Archivist, Western Pacific Archives, 1974, 1976 and 1978. *Recreations:* swimming and deep-sea fishing. *Address:* Flat 34, St Margarets, London Road, Guildford, Surrey GU1 1TJ. *T:* Guildford 575396.

MACDONALD OF CLANRANALD, Ranald Alexander; 24th Chief and Captain of Clanranald; Chairman and Managing Director, Tektura Ltd; *b* 27 March 1934; *s* of late Captain Kenneth Macdonald of Inchkenneth, DSO, and late Marjory Broad Smith, Basingstoke; *S* kinsman as Chief of Clanranald, 1944; *m* 1961, Jane Campbell-Davys, *d* of late I. E. Campbell-Davys, Llandovery, Carms; two *s* one *d*. *Educ:* Christ's Hospital. Founded: Fairfix Contracts Ltd, 1963; Tektura Wallcoverings, 1970. Chm., British Contract Furnishing Assoc., 1975–76. Lieut (TA) Cameron Highlanders, 1958–68. Mem., Standing Council of Scottish Chiefs, 1957–; Director, Highland Soc. of London, 1959–80; Vice Pres., Caledonian Catholic Assoc. of London. Chief Exec., Clan Donald Lands Trust, 1978–80; Chm., Museum of the Isles, 1981–. Kt of Honour and Devotion SMO Malta, 1982; Kt of Justice Constantinian Order of St George, 1982. *Recreations:* sailing, fishing. *Heir:* *s* Ranald Og Angus Macdonald, younger of Clanranald, *b* 17 Sept. 1963. *Address:* Wester Lix, by Killin, Perthshire FK21 8RD. *T.* (office) 01–226 3034. *Clubs.* Turf, Beefsteak; New, Puffin's (Edinburgh).

McDONALD, Robert Howat; *see* McDonald, Hon. Lord.

MACDONALD, Vice-Adm. Sir Roderick (Douglas), KBE 1978 (CBE 1966); retired; artist, since 1979; *b* Java, 25 Feb. 1921; *s* of Douglas and Marjorie Macdonald; *m* 1st, 1943, Joan Willis (marr. diss. 1980); two *s* (and one *s* decd); 2nd, 1980, Mrs Pamela Bartosik. *Educ:* Fettes. Entered Royal Navy, 1939. Served War: Fleet and Convoy ops throughout 1939–45 (Atlantic, Norway, Mediterranean, Eastern Fleet, East Coast and Normandy). Commanded: HMS Leeds Castle, 1953, also HMS Essington; Sen. Officer, 104th Mine-Sweeping Sqdn and HMS Walkerton, 1957 (despatches, Cyprus); HMS Falmouth, 1961; Comdr, Naval Forces, Borneo, 1965 (CBE); HMS Galatea; Captain (D): Londonderry Sqdn, 1968; First Frigate Sqdn, Far East, 1969; Captain of the Fleet, 1970; HMS Bristol, 1972; COS to C-in-C, Naval Home Command, 1973–76; ADC to the Queen, 1975; COS to Comdr, Allied Naval Forces Southern Europe, 1976–79. One-man exhibitions: Naples, 1978; Edinburgh, 1980; London, 1981, 1983, 1985. Younger Brother of Trinity House; Vice-Pres. 1976–85, and Fellow, Nautical Inst. Pres., Isle of Skye Highland Games. *Address:* Ollach, Braes, Isle of Skye. *Clubs:* Caledonian; Royal Scottish Pipers Society (Edinburgh); Royal Naval Sailing Assoc.

MACDONALD, Maj.-Gen. Ronald Clarence, CB 1965; DSO 1944 and Bar, 1945; OBE 1953; Director, Griffin Farms Ltd, Wilts; *b* 1 Aug. 1911; 2nd *s* of late Col C. R. Macdonald, CMG; *m* 1939, Jessie Ross Anderson (*d* 1986); one *s* one *d*. *Educ:* Rugby; RMC, Sandhurst. Royal Warwicks Regt: Commissioned, 1931; Comdr 2nd Bn, 1945–46; Comdr 1st Bn, 1953–55; Bn Comdr, France, Germany Campaign, 1944–45; Mil. Asst to CIGS, 1946–49; GSO1, HQ, West Africa Comd, 1950–53; Col Gen. Staff, SHAPE, 1955–56; Comdr 10th Inf. Bde Gp, 1956–59; DDI, War Office, 1959–60; Chief of Staff, HQ Middle East Comd, 1960–62; Dep. Chief of Staff, Headquarters, Allied Land Forces, Central Europe, 1962–65; retired, 1965. Col Royal Warwicks Fusiliers, 1963–68; Dep. Col (Warwicks), The Royal Regt of Fusiliers, 1968–74. *Recreation:* golf. *Address:* Grassmead, Beanacre, near Melksham, Wilts.

MACDONALD, Ronald John, CEng, MIMechE; Director-General, Royal Ordnance Factories/Production, 1974–79, retired; *b* 2 Nov. 1919; *s* of Ronald Macdonald and Sarah Jane Macdonald; *m* 1944, Joan Margaret Crew; two *s*. *Educ:* Enfield Grammar Sch.; Enfield Technical Coll. Engrg apprenticeship at Royal Small Arms Factory, Enfield, 1936–40. Army service, REME, in India, China and Hong Kong, 1943–47 (Major). Established Civil Servant, Royal Small Arms Factory, 1948; Royal Ordnance Factory, Radway Green, 1949; ROF Headquarters, Mottingham, 1953; ROF, Blackburn, 1960; Director: ROF, Birtley, Co. Durham, 1964; Ordnance Factories/Ammunition, 1972. *Address:* 72 Lincoln Park, Amersham, Bucks HP7 0DQ. *T:* Amersham 7402. *Club:* Army and Navy.

MacDONALD, Prof. Simon Gavin George, FRSE; Professor of Physics, University of Dundee, since 1973; *b* 5 Sept. 1923; *s* of Simon MacDonald and Jean H. Thomson; *m* 1948, Eva Leonie Austerlitz; one *s* one *d*. *Educ:* George Heriot's Sch., Edinburgh; Edinburgh Univ. (MA (1st Cl. Hons) Maths and Nat. Phil); PhD (St Andrews). FIP 1958, FRSE 1972. Jun. Scientific Officer, RAE, Farnborough, 1943–46; Lectr, Univ. of St Andrews, 1948–57; Senior Lecturer: University Coll. of the West Indies, 1957–62; Univ. of St Andrews, 1962–67; Visiting Prof., Ohio Univ., 1963; University of Dundee: Sen. Lectr, then Prof., 1967–; Dean of Science, 1970–73; Vice-Principal, 1974–79. Convener, Scottish Univs Council on Entrance, 1977–83 (Dep. Convener, 1973–77); Dep. Chm., UCCA, 1983– (Mem. Exec. Cttee, 1977–; Chm., Technical Subcttee, 1979–83). Chm., Bd of Dirs, Dundee Rep. Th., 1975–; Chm., Fedn of Scottish Theatres, 1978–80. *Publications:* Problems and Solutions in General Physics, 1967; Physics for Biology and Premedical Students, 1970, 2nd edn 1975; Physics for the Life and Health Sciences, 1975; articles in physics jls. *Recreations:* bridge, golf, fiction writing. *Address:* 10 Westerton Avenue, Dundee DD5 3NJ. *T:* Dundee 78692. *Club:* Royal Commonwealth Society.

MACDONALD, Rt. Rev. Thomas Brian, OBE 1970; Coadjutor Bishop of Perth, Western Australia, 1964–79, retired; *b* 25 Jan. 1911; *s* of Thomas Joseph Macdonald, MD, and Alice Daisy Macdonald; *m* 1936, Audrey May Collins; three *d*. *Educ:* Mercers' Sch., Holborn, EC. Licentiate of Theology 1932, Aust. Coll. of Theol. Deacon 1934, priest 1935, Diocese of Ballarat, Vic.; Deacon in charge of All Saints, Ballarat, 1934; Priest in charge of Landsborough, 1935; Rector of Williams, Dio. of Bunbury, 1935–39; Rector of Manjimup, WA, 1939–40. Chaplain, Australian Imperial Forces, 1940–44 (despatches). Rector of Christ Church, Claremont, Dio. of Perth, 1944–50; Chaplain of Collegiate Sch. of St Peter, Adelaide, S Australia, 1950–58; Dean of Perth, Western Australia, 1959–61; Archdeacon of Perth, 1961–63. Administrator, Diocese of Perth during 1963 and 1969. *Address:* 33 Thomas Street, Nedlands, WA 6009, Australia. *Club:* Weld (Perth).

MACDONALD, Air Vice-Marshal Thomas Conchar, CB 1962; AFC 1942; MD (retired); *b* 6 Aug. 1909; *s* of John Macdonald, MA, BSc, and Mary Jane Conchar; *m* 1937, Katharine Cairns Frew. *Educ:* Hermitage Sch.; Glasgow High Sch.; University of Glasgow; MB, ChB 1932; MD 1940; DPH (London) 1949. Joined RAF Medical Br., 1933; served in Iraq, Egypt and England, before 1939. War service included RAF Inst. of Aviation Med., Farnborough, as Asst to Consultant in Applied Physiology, 1939–41; USA and Canada, 1941–42; DPMO (Flying) Fighter Command, 1942–45; Far East, 1945–46 (despatches, AFC). Post-war appts include: PMO 2nd TAF (Germany), 1951–53; Dir of Hygiene and Research, Air Min., 1953–56 (Chm. Aero-Medical Panel of Advisory Gp for Research and Develt (AGARD) of NATO); PMO, Bomber Command, 1956–58; PMO Middle East Air Force, 1958–61; PMO Technical Training Command, RAF, 1961–66. Air Vice-Marshal, 1961. QHP 1961–66; CStJ 1961. *Publications:* contributions to various med. jls. *Recreations:* sailing, fishing. *Address:* Wakeners Wood, Midhurst Road, Haslemere, Surrey. *T:* Haslemere 3685. *Club:* Royal Air Force.

McDONALD, William, CA; JP; Chamberlain since 1962, and Secretary since 1971, Company of Merchants of City of Edinburgh; *b* 9 Nov. 1929; *yr s* of late Joseph McDonald and Margaret Pringle (*née* Gibb); *m* 1956, Anne Kidd Laird Donald; one *s* one *d*. *Educ:* Perth Acad. Sec., South Mills and Grampian Investment, Dundee, 1957–62. Clerk and Treasurer, Incorp. of Guildry in Edinburgh, 1975–; Jt Sec., Scottish Council of Independent Schs, 1978–; Dep. Chief Comr for Scotland, Scout Assoc., 1977–79; Mem., High Constables of Edinburgh (Colinton Ward), 1983–. *Recreations:* Scout Association, bridge, golf. *Address:* 4/5 West Grange Gardens, Edinburgh EH9 2RA. *T:* 031–668 1845. *Club:* New (Edinburgh).

McDONALD, Hon. Sir William (John Farquhar), Kt 1958; *b* 3 Oct. 1911; *s* of John Nicholson McDonald and Sarah McDonald (*née* McInnes); *m* 1935, Evelyn Margaret Koch; two *d. Educ:* Scotch Coll., Adelaide, South Australia. Served AIF, 1939–45, Capt. Councillor, Shire of Kowree, 1946–61. MLA, electorate of Dundas, Victoria, 1947–52, 1955–70; Speaker, Legislative Assembly, Victoria, 1955–67; Minister of Lands, Soldier Settlement, and for Conservation, 1967–70. Mem., Exec. Council, Victoria. Trustee, Shrine of Remembrance, 1955–70. Victoria State Pres., Poll Shorthorn Soc. of Aust., 1962–72; Trustee, Royal Agricultural Soc. of Victoria, 1968–. Trustee, Victoria Amateur Turf Club, 1969. *Address:* Brippick, 102 St Georges Road, Toorak, Vic. 3142, Australia. *T:* 241 5839. *Clubs:* Hamilton (Hamilton, Victoria); Australian, Naval and Military (Melbourne).

MACDONALD, Prof. William Weir, PhD, DSc; FIBiol; Selwyn Lloyd Professor of Medical Entomology, since 1980 and Dean since 1983, Liverpool School of Tropical Medicine; *b* 5 Dec. 1927; *s* of William Sutherland Macdonald and Ina Weir; *m* 1950, Margaret Lawrie; two *d. Educ:* Univ. of Glasgow (BSc 1948). MSc 1964, PhD 1965, Univ. of Liverpool; DSc 1973, Univ. of Glasgow; FIBiol 1966. Strang-Steel Scholar, Glasgow Univ., 1948; Colonial Office Res. Scholar, 1949–50; Entomologist, E African Fisheries Res. Org., Uganda, 1950–52; Res. Fellow, Inst. for Med. Res., Kuala Lumpur, 1953–60; Lectr, Sen. Lectr, and Reader, Liverpool Sch. of Trop. Medicine, 1960–76; Prof. of Med. Entomology, London Sch. of Hygiene and Trop. Medicine, 1977–80. Consultant: WHO; various overseas govts; Hon. Consultant on Entomology to the Army. Chalmers Medal, Royal Soc. of Trop. Medicine and Hygiene, 1972. *Publications:* papers on med. entomology in scientific jls. *Recreations:* golf, gardening. *Address:* 10 Headland Close, West Kirby, Merseyside L48 3JP. *T:* 051–625 7857. *Club:* Savage.

MacDONALD SCOTT, Mary, (Mrs Michael MacDonald Scott); *see* Lavin, Mary.

MACDONALD-SMITH, Maj.-Gen. Hugh, CB 1977; Director, Telecommunication Engineering and Manufacturing Association, 1981–87 (Secretary to Council, 1979–80); *b* 8 Jan. 1923; *s* of Alexander and Ada Macdonald-Smith; *m* 1947, Désirée Violet (*née* Williamson); one *s* one *d* (and one *d* decd). *Educ:* Llanelli Grammar Sch.; Llandovery Coll.; Birmingham Univ. BSc. CEng, FIMechE, FIEE. Commissioned REME, 1944; served: India, 1945–47; Singapore, 1956–58; BAOR, 1961–63; Technical Staff Course, 1949–51; Staff Coll., Camberley, 1953; Lt-Col, 1963; Asst Dir, Electrical and Mechanical Engineering, HQ Western Comd, 1963–65; Asst Mil. Sec., MoD, 1965–66; Comd REME, 1 (BR) Corps Troops, 1966–67; Technical Gp, REME, 1967–72; Col, 1967; Brig. 1970; Dep. Dir, Electrical and Mechanical Engineering (Eng. Pol.), (Army), 1972–75; Dir, later Dir Gen., Electrical and Mech. Engrg (Army), 1975–78; retired 1978. Col Comdt, REME, 1978–83; Rep. Col Comdt, REME, 1979–80. Mem., Cttee of Inquiry into Engrg Profession, 1977–79. Mem. Council, IMechE, 1975–76. *Recreations:* golf, gardening, photography. *Address:* c/o Lloyds Bank, Llanelli.

MACDONALD-SMITH, Sydney, CMG 1956; retired; *b* 9 July 1908; *s* of late John Alfred Macdonald-Smith, MB, ChB, FRCSE; *m* 1st, 1935, Joyce (*d* 1966), *d* of Austen Whetham, Bridport, Dorset; one *s* one *d*; 2nd, 1968, Winifred Mary Atkinson, JP, *widow* of Captain T. K. W. Atkinson, RN. *Educ:* Nottingham High Sch.; New Coll., Oxford. Entered Colonial Administrative Service, Nigeria, 1931; Controller of Imports, 1945; Director of Supplies, 1947; Under-Sec., Gold Coast, 1949; Permanent Sec. Ministry of Communications and Works, 1950; Chief Regional Officer, Northern Territories, 1954–57; retired Nov. 1957. *Recreation:* gardening. *Address:* Woodman's, Westbourne, Emsworth, Hants. *T:* Emsworth 372943.

McDONAUGH, James, CBE 1970 (OBE 1965); retired 1973; reappointed 1973–75, Director North Europe Department, British Council; *b* 26 July 1912; *s* of late Edward McDonaugh and late Christina, *d* of William Bissell; *m* 1944, Mary-Eithné Mitchell, *d* of James Vyvyan Mitchell; three *s* two *d. Educ:* Royal Grammar Sch., Worcester; St Edmund Hall, Oxford (Exhibitioner, MA). Asst Master, Ampleforth Coll., 1935–40; War Service, 1940–45; Lecturer, Graz and Innsbruck Univs, 1947–50; Asst Rep., British Council, Austria, 1950–54; Representative, Malta, 1954–58; Dep. Counsellor (Cultural), Bonn, 1958–59; Dep. Rep., Germany, 1958–61; Dir Specialist Tours Dept, 1961–65; Asst Controller, Education Div., 1965; Rep., Germany, 1966–73. *Address:* Old Rectory Cottage, Whitestaunton, Chard, Somerset.

MacDONELL OF GLENGARRY, Air Cdre Aeneas Ranald Donald, CB 1964; DFC 1940; Hereditary 22nd Chief of Glengarry; *b* 15 Nov. 1913; *e s* of late Ranald MacDonell of Glengarry, CBE; *m* 1st, Diana Dorothy (*d* 1980), *yr d* of late Henry Keane, CBE; two *s* one *d*; 2nd, Lois Eirene Frances, *d* of Rev. Gerald Champion Streatfeild; one *s* one *d. Educ:* Hurstpierpoint Coll.; Royal Air Force Coll., Cranwell. No 54 Fighter Sqdn, 1934; Fleet Air Arm, 1935–37; Flying Instructor, 1938–39; Air Ministry, 1939–40; No 64 Fighter Sqdn, 1940–41; POW, 1941–45; Ministry of Defence, 1946–47; HQ Flying Training Command, 1947–49; Chief Flying Instructor, RAF Coll., Cranwell, 1949–51; Ministry of Defence, 1952–54; Senior RAF Instructor, Joint Services Staff Coll., 1954–56; Air Attaché, Moscow, 1956–58; Dir of Management and Work Study, Ministry of Defence, Air Force Dept, 1960–64, retd. *Recreations:* ciné photography, art, travel. *Address:* Elonbank, 23 Castle Street, Fortrose, Ross-shire IV10 8TH. *T:* Fortrose 20121. *Club:* Royal Air Force.

McDONNELL, family name of **Earl of Antrim.**

McDONNELL, Christopher Thomas; Under-Secretary of State, Ministry of Defence, since 1985; *b* 3 Sept. 1931; *s* of Christopher Patrick McDonnell and Jane McDonnell; *m* 1955, Patricia Anne (*née* Harvey) (*d* 1967); three *s* one *d. Educ:* St Francis Xavier's Coll., Liverpool; Corpus Christi Coll., Oxford (MA). WO, 1954; HM Treasury, 1966–68; RCDS, 1973; Asst Under-Sec. of State, MoD, 1976–84.

McDONNELL, His Honour Denis Lane, OBE 1945; a Circuit Judge (formerly a County Court Judge), 1967–86; *b* 2 March 1914; *o c* of late David McDonnell, LLD and Mary Nora (*née* Lane), Riversdale, Sundays Well, Cork and Fairy Hill, Monkstown, Co. Cork and *g s* of Denny Lane, poet and Young Irelander; *m* 1940, Florence Nina (Micky), *d* of late Lt-Col Hugh T. Ryan, DSO and Clare Emily (*née* Conry), Castle View, Ballincollig, Co. Cork; three *d* (and one *s* one *d* decd). *Educ:* Christian Brothers' Coll., Cork; Ampleforth Coll.; Sidney Sussex Coll., Cambridge (MA). Served in RAFVR, Equipment and Admin. and Special Duties Branches, 1940–45 in UK and with No. 84 Gp in NW Europe (Wing Comdr). Called to Bar, Middle Temple, 1936; Bencher, 1965. Practised at Bar, 1938–40 and 1946–67. Hon. Sec., Council of HM Circuit Judges, 1979–83. *Publications:* Kerr on Fraud and Mistake (7th edn, with J. G. Monroe), 1952; titles on carriage in Encyclopædias of Forms and Precedents and Court Forms and Precedents, and in Halsbury's Laws of England; articles in British Tax Review. *Recreations:* family life, listening to music, golf, gardening. *Clubs:* Piltdown Golf, Rye Golf, Woking Golf, Royal Cinque Ports Golf.

McDONNELL, John; Principal Policy Adviser, Camden Borough Council, since 1985; *b* 8 Sept. 1951; *s* of Robert and Elsie McDonnell; *m* 1971, Marilyn Jean Cooper; two *d. Educ:* Great Yarmouth Grammar Sch.; Burnley Technical Coll.; Brunel Univ. (BSc); Birkbeck Coll., Univ. of London (MSc Politics and Sociology). Prodn worker, 1968–72; Research Assistant: NUM, 1976–78; TUC, 1978–82; full-time GLC Councillor, Hillingdon, Hayes and Harlington, 1982–86; Dep. Leader, GLC, 1984–85; Chm., GLC F and GP Cttee, 1982–85. Contested (Lab) Hampstead and Highgate, 1983. Housefather (pt-time) of family unit, children's home, 1972–. *Recreations:* gardening, reading, cycling; generally fermenting the overthrow of capitalism. *Address:* 15 Mulberry Parade, West Drayton, Mddx UB7 9AE. *T:* West Drayton 445706.

McDONNELL, John Beresford William; QC 1984; *b* 26 Dec. 1940; *s* of Beresford Conrad McDonnell and Charlotte Mary McDonnell (*née* Caldwell); *m* 1968, Susan Virginia, *d* of late Wing Comdr H. M. Styles, DSO and of Audrey (*née* Jorgensen, who *m* 2nd, 1947, Gen. Sir Charles Richardson, *qv*); two *s* one *d. Educ:* City of London School (Carpenter Scholar); Balliol College, Oxford (Domus Scholar; Hon. Mention, Craven Scholarship, 1958; 1st Cl. Hon. Mods 1960; 2nd LitHum 1962, 2nd Jurisp 1964; MA); Harvard Law Sch. (LLM 1965). Called to the Bar, Inner Temple, 1968. Pres., Oxford Union Soc. and Amer. Debating Tour, 1962; Harkness Fellowship, 1964–66; Amer. Political Science Assoc. Congressional Fellowship, 1965–66 (attached Rep. Frank Thompson Jr, NJ and Senator George McGovern, SDak); Cons. Research Dept, 1966–69; HM Diplomatic Service, 1969–71, First Sec., Asst Private Sec. to Sec. of State for Foreign and Commonwealth Affairs, 1970–71; practising at Chancery Bar, 1972–. Cllr, Lambeth Borough Council, 1968–69. Chm., Research Cttee, Soc. of Cons. Lawyers, 1986–. London Rowing Club Grand VIII, Henley, 1958. *Address:* 20 Brompton Square, SW3 2AD. *T:* 01–584 1498; 1 New Square, Lincoln's Inn, WC2A 3SA. *T:* 01–405 0884.

MacDOUGALL OF MacDOUGALL, Madam; (Coline Helen Elizabeth); 30th Chief of Clan MacDougall, 1953; *b* 17 Aug. 1904; *e d* of Col Alexander J. MacDougall of MacDougall, 29th Chief, and Mrs Colina Edith MacDougall of MacDougall; *m* 1949, Leslie Grahame-Thomson (who assumed the surname of MacDougall, 1953), RSA, FRIBA, PPRIAS, FSAScot (*d* 1974); resumed surname of MacDougall of MacDougall on succession to Chiefship, 1953. *Educ:* St James's, West Malvern. Served WRNS (Second Officer), 1941–46. *Address:* Dunollie Castle, Oban, Argyll. *T:* Oban 2012.

MacDOUGALL, Brig. David Mercer, CMG 1946; MA; *b* 1904; *m* 1st, 1929, Catherine Crowther; one *d*; 2nd, 1951, Inez Weir, *o d* of late James Hislop Thompson; two *d. Educ:* St Andrews Univ. Cadet Hong Kong Administrative Service, 1928; seconded to Colonial Office as asst principal, Feb. 1937–March 1939; seconded Hong Kong Dept of Information and Sec. Far Eastern Bureau of British Ministry of Information, Oct. 1939; Colonial Office, 1942; British Embassy, Washington, DC, 1943; Dir British Political Warfare Mission, San Francisco, Dec. 1943; Colonial Office, 1944; Brig. Chief Civil Affairs Officer, Hong Kong, 1945; Colonial Sec., Hong Kong, 1946–49; retired, 1949; Order of the Brilliant Star (China), 1946. *Address:* Mercers, Finchingfield, Essex; Blackhill, by Aberfeldy, Perthshire.

MacDOUGALL, Sir (George) Donald (Alastair), Kt 1953; CBE 1945 (OBE 1942); FBA 1966; economist; *b* 26 Oct. 1912; *s* of late Daniel Douglas MacDougall, Glasgow, and late Beatrice Amy Miller; *m* 1st, 1937, Bridget Christabel Bartrum (marr. diss. 1977); one *s* one *d*; 2nd, 1977, Margaret Hall (*see* L. M. MacDougall). *Educ:* Kelvinside Acad., Glasgow; Shrewsbury Sch.; Balliol Coll., Oxford. George Webb Medley Junior (1934) and Senior (1935) Scholarships in Political Economy; Asst Lecturer (later Lecturer) in Economics, University of Leeds, 1936–39; First Lord of the Admiralty's Statistical Branch, 1939–40; Prime Minister's Statistical Branch, 1940–45 (Chief Asst, 1942–45). Work on Reparations and German Industry, Moscow and Berlin, 1945; Mem. of Heavy Clothing Industry Working Party, 1946; Official Fellow of Wadham Coll., Oxford, 1945–50, Domestic Bursar, 1946–48, Hon. Fellow, 1964–; Econ. Dir, OEEC, Paris, 1948–49; Faculty Fellow, Nuffield Coll., 1947–50, Professorial Fellow, 1950–52, Official Fellow, 1952–64, First Bursar, 1958–64, Hon. Fellow, 1967–; Nuffield Reader in Internat. Economics, Oxford Univ., 1950–52; Chief Adviser, Prime Minister's Statistical Branch, 1951–53; Visiting Prof., Australian Nat. Univ., 1959; MIT Center for Internat. Studies, New Delhi, 1961; Dir, Investing in Success Equities, Ltd, 1959–62; Economic Dir, NEDO, 1962–64; Mem. Turnover Tax Cttee, 1963–64; Dir-Gen., Dept of Economic Affairs, 1964–68; Head of Govt Economic Service, and Chief Economic Adviser to the Treasury, 1969–73; Chief Economic Advr, CBI, 1973–84. Mem. Council, Royal Econ. Soc., 1950– (Hon. Sec., 1958–70; Vice-Pres., 1970–72, 1974–; Pres., 1972–74); Pres., Soc. for Strategic and Long Range Planning, 1977–85, Vice-Pres., 1968–77; Vice-Pres., Soc. of Business Economists, 1978–; Chm., Exec. Cttee NIESR, 1974–; Mem., EEC Study Gp on Economic and Monetary Union, 1974–75; Chm., EEC Study Gp on Role of Public Finance in European Economic Integration, 1975–77. Hon. LLD Strathclyde, 1968; Hon. LittD Leeds, 1971; Hon. DSc Aston in Birmingham, 1979. *Publications:* (part author) Measures for International Economic Stability, UN, 1951; The World Dollar Problem, 1957; (part author) The Fiscal System of Venezuela, 1959; The Dollar Problem: A Reappraisal, 1960; Studies in Political Economy (2 vols), 1975; contrib. to Britain in Recovery, 1938, Lessons of the British War Economy, 1951, and to various economic and statistical jls. *Address:* 86A Denbigh Street, Westminster, SW1V 2EX. *T:* 01–821 1998. *Club:* Reform.

MacDOUGALL, Air Cdre Ian Neil, CBE 1964; DFC 1942; Galt Composites Ltd, since 1977; *b* 11 June 1920; *s* of late Archibald MacDougall, Colonial Service, and Helen Grace (*née* Simpson); *m* 1944, Dorothy Eleanor, *d* of late John Frankland; one *s* one *d. Educ:* Morrison's Academy, Crieff; RAF Coll., Cranwell. Commnd Sept. 1939; served in Fighter Sqdns in Battle of Britain, Syrian and Western Desert Campaigns, Malta and in invasions of Sicily and Normandy; War Studies Lectr at RAF Coll., 1948–50 and USAF Academy, Colorado, 1956–58; Asst Air Attaché, Paris, 1950–53; Chief Flying Instructor, RAF Coll., 1953–56; Supt of Flying, Boscombe Down, 1959–62; comd RAF Fighter Stn, Binbrook, 1962–64; SASO 38 Gp, 1964–67; comd Zambian Expedn and Zambian Oil Lift, 1965–66; Air Attaché, Paris, 1967–69; jssc, psc, pfc, cfs; retd Dec. 1969. Mil. Liaison, Rolls Royce and Bristol Composite Materials Ltd, 1970–77. *Recreation:* fishing. *Address:* Swifts Cottage, East Grafton, Marlborough, Wilts SN8 3DB. *T:* Marlborough 810482. *Club:* Royal Air Force.

MacDOUGALL, Laura Margaret, (Lady MacDougall); Hon. Fellow of Somerville College, Oxford, since 1975; Consultant to National Economic Development Office; Economic Consultant to Distillers Co. plc, 1978–84; *d* of George E. Linfoot and Laura Edith Clayton; *m* 1932, Robert L. Hall (now Lord Roberthall) (marr. diss. 1968); two *d*; *m* 1977, Sir Donald MacDougall, *qv. Educ:* Sheffield Girls' High Sch. and High Storrs Grammar Sch.; Somerville Coll., Oxford. Hon. Scholar, 1st Cl. Hons Philosophy, Politics and Economics; Jun. George Webb Medley Scholar. US Govt Office of Price Admin, 1941–44; UNNRA Planning Div., Washington, DC, Sydney and London, 1944–45; Lectr, Lincoln Coll., Oxford, 1946–47; Lectr, 1947–49, and Fellow and Tutor, 1949–75, Somerville Coll., Oxford; University Lectr in Economics, 1949–75. Member: Treasury Purchase Tax Cttee, 1954; Interdeptal Cttee on Economic and Social Research, 1957–58;

Gaitskell Indep. Co-operative Commn, 1958; Min. of Ag. Cttee on the Remuneration of Milk Distributors in the UK, 1962; Reith Indep. Commn on Advertising, 1964; Covent Garden Market Authority Adv. Cttee, 1972; Distributive Trades Industrial Trng Bd's Research Cttee, 1972; EDC for Distributive Trades, 1963–75; Monopolies and Mergers Commn, 1973–76; Past Member: Retail Furnishing and Allied Trades Wages Council; Retail Newsagency, Confectioner and Tobacconist Wages Council. Visiting Prof. MIT, USA, 1961–62. Hon. LLD Nottingham, 1979. *Publications:* US Senate Cttee Print, Effect of War on British Retail Trade, 1943; Distributive Trading: an economic analysis, 1954; Distribution in Great Britain and North America (with Knapp and Winsten), 1961; contribs to: The British Economy, 1945–50, 1962; The British Economy in the 1950s, 1962; (Bolton Cttee, Research Report No 8) The Small Unit in Retail Trade, 1972; numerous contribs to various economic and statistical jls. *Address:* 86A Denbigh Street, Westminster, SW1V 2EX. *T:* 01–821 1998.

MACDOUGALL, Neil; Hon. Mr Justice Macdougall; a Judge of the High Court of Hong Kong, since 1980; *b* 13 March 1932; *s* of Norman Macdougall and Gladys Clare Kennerly. *Educ:* Aquinas Coll., Perth, WA; Univ. of Western Australia (LLB 1954). Admitted Barrister and Solicitor of Supreme Court, WA, 1957, and of High Court of Australia, 1958; Solicitor of Supreme Court of England, 1976, and of Supreme Court of Hong Kong, 1977. Crown Counsel, Hong Kong, 1965; Director of Public Prosecutions, Hong Kong, 1978. *Recreations:* classical music, study of natural history, long distance running, photography. *Address:* 8B Severn Road, The Peak, Hong Kong. *T:* 5–8497077. *Clubs:* Hong Kong, Jockey (all in Hong Kong).

MACDOUGALL, Patrick Lorn, FCA; Chief Executive, Standard Chartered Merchant Bank Ltd, since 1985; *b* 21 June 1939; *s* of late James Archibald Macdougall, WS, and of Valerie Jean Macdougall; *m* 1st, 1967, Alison Noel Offer (marr. diss. 1982); two *s*; 2nd, 1983, Bridget Margaret Young; one *d*. *Educ:* schools in Kenya; Millfield; University Coll., Oxford (MA Jurisprudence). FCA 1976. Called to the Bar, Inner Temple, 1962. Manager, N. M. Rothschild & Sons Ltd, 1967–70; Exec. Dir, Amex Bank (formerly Rothschild Intercontinental Bank Ltd), 1970–77, Chief Exec., 1977–78; Exec. Dir, Jardine Matheson Holdings Ltd, 1978–85. Mem., Internat. Adv. Bd, Creditanstalt–Bankverein, Vienna, 1982–85. *Recreations:* ski-ing, golf, sailboarding, opera, bridge. *Address:* 4 Stanford Road, W8 5QJ. *T:* 01–937 1985. *Clubs:* Royal Automobile; Hongkong, Shek O (Hong Kong).

MacDOWALL, Dr David William, MA, DPhil; FSA, FRAS; Chairman, Society for South Asian Studies (formerly Society for Afghan Studies), since 1982 (Hon. Secretary, 1972–82); *b* 2 April 1930; *o s* of late William MacDowall and late Lilian May MacDowall (*née* Clarkson); *m* 1962, Mione Beryl, *yr d* of late Ernest Harold Lashmar and Dora Lashmar; two *d*. *Educ:* Liverpool Inst.; Corpus Christi Coll., Oxford; British Sch. at Rome. Hugh Oldham Scholar 1947, Pelham Student in Roman History 1951; Barclay Head Prize for Ancient Numismatics, 1953 and 1956. 2nd Lieut Royal Signals, 1952. Asst Principal, Min. of Works, 1955; Asst Keeper, Dept of Coins and Medals, British Museum, 1956; Principal, Min. of Educn, 1960; Principal, Univ. Grants Cttee, 1965; Asst Sec. 1970; Master of Univ. Coll., Durham, 1973; Hon. Lectr in Classics and in Oriental Studies, Univ. of Durham, 1975; Dir, Polytechnic of London, 1980–85. Hon. Treas., Royal Numismatic Soc., 1966–73. *Publications:* Coin Collections, their preservation, classification and presentation, 1978; The Western Coinages of Nero, 1979; (contrib.) Mithraic Studies, 1975; (contrib.) The Archaeology of Afghanistan, 1978; articles in Numismatic Chron., Jl Numismatic Soc. India, Schweizer Münzblätter, Acta Numismatica, S Asian Archaeology, Afghan Studies, S Asian Studies; etc. *Recreations:* travel, antiquities, photography, natural history, gardening, genealogy. *Address:* Admont, Dancers End, Tring, Herts HP23 6JY. *Club:* Athenæum.

McDOWALL, Keith Desmond; Confederation of British Industry: Director of Information, since 1981; Deputy Director General, since 1986; *b* 3 Oct. 1929; *s* of William Charteris McDowall and Edna Florence McDowall; *m* 1957, Shirley Margaret Russell Astbury (marr. diss. 1985); two *d*. *Educ:* Heath Clark Sch., Croydon, Surrey. Served RAF, National Service, 1947–49. South London Press, 1947–55; Daily Mail, 1955–67: Indust. Corresp., 1958; Indust. Editor, 1961–67; Man. Dir, Inca Construction (UK) Co. Ltd, 1967–69; Govt Information Service: successively Chief Inf. Officer, DEA, BoT, Min. of Housing and Local Govt, DoE, and Home Office, 1969–72; Dir of Inf., NI Office, 1972–74; Dir of Inf., Dept of Employment, 1974–78; Man. Dir Public Affairs, British Shipbuilders, 1978–80. Dir, Govan Shipbuilders Ltd, 1978–80. *Publications:* articles in newspapers and various pubns. *Recreations:* sailing, tennis, mingling. *Address:* Confederation of British Industry, Centre Point, 103 New Oxford Street, WC1A 1DU. *Clubs:* Reform; Medway Yacht (Rochester).

McDOWALL, Robert John Stewart, DSc, MD, MRCP; FRCPE; Professor Emeritus in the University of London since 1959; Professor of Physiology, 1923–59, and Dean of Faculty of Medicine and Fellow of King's College, London; Vice-Chairman Medical Advisory Committee and Founder Member, Asthma Research Council; Formerly Examiner for Universities of London, Leeds, Durham, Manchester, Aberdeen, St Andrews, Edinburgh, Sheffield, Bristol, West Indies, Nigeria, RCP, RCS, in India, Egypt, Australasia, and Eire; *b* 1892; *s* of Robert McDowall, Auchengaillie, Wigtonshire, and Fanny Grace Stewart; *m* 1st, 1921, Jessie (*d* 1963), *yr d* of Alexander Macbeth, JP, Pitlochry, Perthshire; two *d*; 2nd, 1964, Dr Jean Rotherham, *d* of Col Ewan Rotherham, TD, DL (Warwickshire). *Educ:* Watson's Coll., Edinburgh; University of Edinburgh (Gold Medal for MD thesis). Assistant and Lecturer in Physiology, University of Edinburgh, 1919–21; Lectr, Experimental Physiology and Experimental Pharmacology, Univ. of Leeds, 1921–23; Lectr in Applied Physiology, London Sch. of Hygiene, 1927–29. Ellis prizeman, 1920; Parkin prizeman, RCP, Edinburgh, 1930; Gunning Victoria Jubilee Cullen Prize, RCP, Edinburgh, 1938; Arris and Gale Lectr, RCS, 1933; Oliver Sharpey Lectr, RCP, 1941; medal of honour, Univ. of Ghent, 1951; has given 3 lecture tours of America. Hon. Fellow: Amer. Acad. of Allergy, 1953; Soc. Française d'Allergie, 1957; European Acad. of Allergy; Finnish Acad. of Allergy. Pres., 4th European Congress of Allergy, 1959; Hon. Mem., British Soc. of Allergy; Extraordinary Mem., British Cardiac Soc. Has been Resident House Physician, Edinburgh Royal Infirmary, and Clinical Tutor in Medicine, Univ. of Edinburgh; served with RAMC, European War, 1914–18, also 1940–41; became DADMS for British Forces in Palestine, Syria, and Cilicia; President, Physiology Sect. British Assoc., 1936; Chairman Board of Intermediate Medical Studies and of Physiology, University of London. *Publications:* Clinical Physiology; The Science of Signs and Symptoms in relation to Modern Diagnosis and Treatment, 4 editions; Handbook of Physiology, 13 editions; The Control of the Circulation of the Blood, 1938, 1957; The Whiskies of Scotland, 1967, 3rd edn 1975 (Swedish, German, Spanish, Japanese and American edns); Editor, The Mind, by various authors; Sane Psychology, 6 reprints; Anatomy and Physiology for students of Physiotherapy (with Smout) and numerous scientific papers. *Recreations:* chess, curling (1st President, Hampstead Curling Club; 1st President, London Watsonian Curling Club; former Pres. and Hon. Mem., Province of London; skipped England against Scotland, 1966 and 1969); golf (Ex-Captain, Life Mem. and Director, Hampstead Golf Club). *Address:* 34 Park Drive, NW11. *T:* 01–455 2858.

See also J. K. Rotherham.

McDOWALL, Robert William, CBE 1977 (OBE 1966); FSA (Lond.); Secretary, Royal Commission on Historical Monuments (England), 1973–79; *b* 13 May 1914; *yr s* of Rev. C. R. L. McDowall; *m* 1939, Avril Betty Everard Hannaford; three *s* one *d*. *Educ:* Eton; Magdalene Coll., Cambridge (MA). Investigator, Royal Commission on Historical Monuments (England), 1936. Served War, with Royal Engineers, 1939–45. Vis. Lectr, UCL, 1979. Mem., Ancient Monuments Bd for England, 1973–79; Pres., Surrey Archaeological Soc., 1975–80; Vice-Pres., Royal Archaeol Inst., 1980 (Hon. Vice-Pres., 1986). Trustee and Mem., Exec. Bd, Weald and Downland Open-Air Mus., 1985. *Publications:* contributor to: Monuments Threatened or Destroyed, 1963; Peterborough New Town, 1969; Shielings and Bastles, 1970, Recording Old Houses, 1980; County Inventories of RCHM; Archaeologia, Antiquaries Jl (and local archaeological jls). *Address:* Chandlers, Ballsdown, Chiddingfold, Surrey. *T:* Wormley 2995.

McDOWALL, Stuart, CBE 1984; Senior Lecturer in Economics, University of St Andrews, since 1967; *b* 19 April 1926; *s* of Robert McDowall and Gertrude Mary Collister; *m* 1951, Margaret Burnside Woods Gyle; three *s*. *Educ:* Liverpool Institute; St Andrews University (MA hons 1950). Personnel Manager, Michael Nairn & Co., 1955–61; Lectr in Econs, St Andrews Univ., 1961–67; Master, United Coll. of St Salvator and St Leonard, 1976–80. Dep. Chm., Central Arbitration Cttee, 1976–; Local Govt Boundary Comr for Scotland, 1983–; Mem., Monopolies and Mergers Commn, 1985–. Sec., Scottish Economic Soc., 1970–76. *Publications:* (with P. R. Draper) Trade Adjustment and the British Jute Industry, 1978; (with H. M. Begg) Industrial Performance and Prospects in Areas Affected by Oil Developments, 1981; articles on industrial economics and regional economics. *Recreations:* golf, hill walking. *Address:* 10 Woodburn Terrace, St Andrews, Fife KY16 8BA. *T:* St Andrews 73247. *Clubs:* Royal Commonwealth Society; Royal and Ancient Golf (St Andrews).

McDOWELL, Prof. Coulter; *see* McDowell, Prof. M. R. C.

McDOWELL, Eric Wallace, CBE 1982; FCA; Chairman, Industrial Development Board for Northern Ireland, since 1986; *b* 7 June 1925; *s* of Martin Wallace McDowell and Edith Florence (*née* Hillock); *m* 1954, Helen Lilian (*née* Montgomery); one *s* two *d*. *Educ:* Royal Belfast Academical Instn. FCA 1957. Served War, 1943–46. Student Chartered Accountant, 1942, qualified 1948; Partner, Wilson Hennessey & Crawford, and (after merger in 1973) Deloitte, Haskins & Sells, 1952–85 (Sen. Partner, Belfast, 1980–85, retd). Dir, Spence Bryson Ltd, 1986–; Trustee and Mem. Bd of Management, TSB of NI, 1986–. Member: Council, Inst. of Chartered Accountants in Ireland, 1968–77 (Pres., 1974–75); NI Econ. Council, 1977–83; Industrial Develt Bd for NI, 1982–; Broadcasting Council for NI, 1983–86. Trustee, Presbyterian Church in Ireland, 1983–. Governor, Royal Belfast Academical Instn, 1959– (Chm. of Governors, 1977–86). *Recreations:* music, drama, foreign travel. *Address:* Beechcroft, 19 Beechlands, Belfast BT9 5HU. *T:* Belfast 668771. *Clubs:* Royal Over-Seas League; Ulster Reform (Belfast).

McDOWELL, George Roy Colquhoun, CEng, FIEE; Chairman and Managing Director, George H. Scholes PLC, since 1972 (Director, since 1969); Chairman, British Standards Institution, since 1985; *b* 1 Sept. 1922; *s* of Robert Henry McDowell and Jean McDowell; *m* 1948, Joan Annie Bryan; two *s*. *Educ:* Coleraine Academical Instn; Queen's Univ., Belfast (BSc Eng). Signals Officer, RAF, 1942–46. Works Manager, Distribn Transformer Div., subseq. Works Manager, Power Transformer Div., Ferranti Ltd, 1950–69; Man. Dir Designate, George H. Scholes, 1969–72. Director: WSK (Electrical), 1980–; Clipsal (UK), 1983–; Thomas Bolton & Johnson, 1984–; L. T. Switchgear, 1984–; Peter Peregrinus, 1985–; LPDL-Wylex Sdn Bhd, Malaysia, 1980–; Clipsal Switchgear Pty, Australia, 1982–. Menvier-Swain Group, 1985–; Chairman: Electrical Installation Equipment Manufacturers' Assoc., 1977–80; British Electrotechnical Cttee, BSI; Electrotechnical Council, BSI; President: British Electrical and Allied Manufacturers' Assoc., 1981–82; IEEIE; Institution of Electrical Engineers: Chm., Power Bd; Chm., Finance Cttee; Mem. Council. Dir, Manchester Chamber of Commerce and Industry, 1980–. Grand Decoration of Honour for Services to the Republic of Austria, 1978. *Recreations:* golf, Rugby, cricket. *Address:* 24 Oak Drive, Bramhall, Stockport, Cheshire SK7 2AD. *T:* 061–439 4552. *Club:* Army and Navy.

McDOWELL, Sir Henry (McLorinan), KBE 1964 (CBE 1959); retired; *b* Johannesburg, S Africa, 10 Dec. 1910; *s* of John McDowell and Margaret Elizabeth Bingham; *m* 1939, Norah, *d* of Walter Slade Douthwaite; one *s* one *d*. *Educ:* Witwatersrand Univ.; Queen's Coll., Oxford; Yale Univ. Served War of 1939–45, 1 Bn Northern Rhodesia Regt, East Africa and South-East Asia, 1940–44. Entered HM Colonial Service (Cadet, Northern Rhodesia), 1938; Clerk, Legislative and Executive Councils, 1945; Assistant Secretary, 1950; Deputy Financial Secretary, 1952. Imperial Defence Coll., 1948; seconded Colonial Office, 1949. Economic and Financial Working Party, in preparation for federation of Rhodesias and Nyasaland, 1953; Federal Treasury, 1954; Secretary, Ministry of Transport, 1955; Secretary, Federal Treasury, 1959–63. Chm., Zimbabwe Board, Barclays Bank Internat. Ltd, 1969–79; Chm. or Dir, other cos in Zimbabwe, 1964–79. Chancellor, Univ. of Rhodesia, 1971–81; Chm. or Mem., governing bodies, educational institutions, Zimbabwe, 1964–79. Hon. LLD Witwatersrand, 1971; Hon. DLitt Rhodesia, 1975. *Recreations:* walking, reading. *Address:* 2 Donne Court, Burbage Road, SE24. *Club:* Harare.

See also J. H. McDowell.

McDOWELL, John Henry, FBA 1983; Fellow and Praelector in Philosophy, University College, Oxford, since 1966; University Lecturer (CUF), Oxford University, since 1967; *b* 7 March 1942; *s* of Sir Henry McDowell, *qv*; *m* 1977, Andrea Lee Lehrke. *Educ:* St John's College, Johannesburg; University College of Rhodesia and Nyasaland; New College, Oxford. BA London; MA Oxon. James C. Loeb Fellow in Classical Philosophy, Harvard Univ., 1969; Visiting Professor: Univ. of Michigan, 1975; Univ. of California, Los Angeles, 1977; Univ. of Minnesota, 1982; Jadavpur Univ., Calcutta, 1983. Sen. Fellow, Council of Humanities, Princeton Univ., 1984. *Publications:* Plato, Theaetetus (trans. with notes), 1973; (ed with Gareth Evans) Truth and Meaning, 1976; (ed) Gareth Evans, The Varieties of Reference, 1982; (ed with Philip Pettit) Subject, Thought, and Context, 1986; articles in jls and anthologies. *Recreations:* reading, music, lawn tennis. *Address:* 131 Cumnor Hill, Oxford OX2 9JA. *T:* Oxford 862454.

McDOWELL, Prof. (Martin Rastall) Coulter, JP; FRAS, FInstP; Professor of Applied Mathematics, since 1969 and Head of Department of Mathematics, since 1982, Royal Holloway and Bedford New College (formerly at Royal Holloway College), University of London; *b* 30 Jan. 1932; *s* of late Richard Whiteside Coulter McDowell and Evelyn Jean McDowell; *m* 1956, Brenda Gordon Blair, *d* of late Robert Cooke Blair and of Mildred Martley Blair; two *s*. *Educ:* Methodist College, Belfast; Queen's University, Belfast (BSc 1953, PhD 1957); Columbia University, NY (MA 1954). Gassiot Research Fellow, QUB, 1956–57; Lectr in Mathematics, Royal Holloway Coll., 1957–64; apptd Teacher, Univ. of London, 1960; Vis. Scholar, Georgia Inst. of Tech., Atlanta, 1959–60; Reader in Appl. Maths, Univ. of Durham, 1964–69; Senior Research Associate, Goddard Space Flight Center, 1967–68; Dean of Science, 1972–75 and 1982–85, RHC, Univ. of London; Member: Council, RHC, 1973–76, 1984–85; Senate, Univ. of London, 1983–85.

JP Surrey, 1981. *Publications:* (with J. P. Coleman) Theory of Ion-Atom Collisions, 1970; (with H. J. W. Kleinpoppen) Electron and Photon Interactions with Matter, 1976; (with A. Ferendici) Atomic Processes in Thermonuclear Plasmas, 1980; (with J. W. Humberston) Positrons in Gases, 1984; papers in learned jls. *Recreations:* Roman archaeology, drinking wine. *Address:* Innisfayle, Heathside Park Road, Woking, Surrey. *T:* Woking 64220.

MACDUFF, Earl of; David Charles Carnegie; *b* 3 March 1961; *s* and *heir* of 3rd Duke of Fife, *qv. Educ:* Eton; Pembroke College, Cambridge (BA Law 1982, MA 1986); Cazenove & Co.; Royal Agricultural College, Cirencester.

MacEACHEN, Hon. Allan Joseph, PC (Canada); Leader of Opposition in the Senate, since 1984; *b* Inverness, Nova Scotia, 6 July 1921; *s* of Angus and Annie MacEachen. *Educ:* St Francis Xavier Univ. (BA 1944); Univ. of Toronto (MA 1946); Univ. of Chicago; MIT. Prof. of Economics, St Francis Xavier Univ., 1946–48; Head of Dept of Economics and Social Sciences; MP (L) Cape Breton Highlands-Canso, Nova Scotia, 1953–84; Special Asst and Consultant on Econ. Affairs to Hon. Lester Pearson, 1958; Minister: of Labour, 1963–65; of Nat. Health and Welfare, 1965–68; of Manpower and Immigration, 1968–70; of External Affairs, 1974–76; of Finance, 1980–82; Sec. of State for External Affairs, 1982–84; Pres., Privy Council and Govt Leader in House of Commons, Canada, 1970–74 and 1976–79; Dep. Prime Minister, 1977–79 and 1980–84; Dep. Leader of the Opposition and Opposition House Leader, 1979–80; called to Senate, 1984, Leader of Govt in Senate, 1984. Hon. Degrees: St Francis Xavier Univ.; Acadia Univ.; Loyola Coll; St Mary's Univ.; Dalhousie Univ.; Wilfrid Laurier Univ. *Address:* The Senate, Ottawa K1A 0A4, Canada.

McEACHRAN, Colin Neil, QC (Scot.) 1982; JD; *b* 14 Jan. 1940; *s* of Eric Robins McEachran and Nora Helen Bushe; *m* 1967, Katherine Charlotte Henderson; two *d. Educ:* Trinity Coll., Glenalmond; Merton Coll., Oxford (BA 1961); Univ. of Glasgow (LLB 1963); Univ. of Chicago (Commonwealth Fellow; JD 1965). Admitted Solicitor, 1966; admitted to Faculty of Advocates, 1968. Solicitor, Glasgow, 1966–67; Advocate Depute, 1975–78. *Recreations:* target rifle shooting (Silver Medal, Commonwealth Games, NZ, 1974), squash. *Address:* 1 Saxe-Coburg Place, Edinburgh EH3 5BR. *T:* 031–332 6820.

MACEDO, Prof. Helder Malta, PhD; Camoens Professor of Portuguese and Head, Department of Portuguese and Brazilian Studies, King's College, London (KQC), since 1982; *b* 30 Nov. 1935; *s* of Adelino José de Macedo and Aida Malta de Macedo; *m* 1960, Suzette Armanda (*née* de Aguiar). *Educ:* Faculty of Law, Univ. of Lisbon; King's Coll., Univ. of London (BA, PhD). Lectr in Portuguese and Brazilian Studies, KCL, 1971–82; Sec. of State for Culture, Portuguese Govt, 1979. Vis. Prof., Harvard Univ., 1981. *Publications:* The Purpose of Praise: 'The Lusiads' of Luís de Camões, 1973; Nós, Uma Leitura de Cesário Verde, 1975, 3rd edn 1986; Do Significado Oculto da 'Menina a Moça', 1977; Poesia 1957–77, 1978; Camões e a Viagem Iniciática, 1980. *Address:* Department of Portuguese and Brazilian Studies, King's College London (KQC), Strand, WC2R 2LS. *T:* 01–836 5454.

McELHERAN, John; Principal Assistant Solicitor (Under Secretary), Ministry of Agriculture, Fisheries and Food, since 1983; *b* 18 Aug. 1929; *s* of late Joseph Samuel McElheran and Hilda McElheran (*née* Veale); *m* 1956, Jean Patricia Durham; one *s* two *d. Educ:* Archbishop Holgate's Grammar Sch., York; St Edmund Hall, Oxford (BA English, DipEd). Solicitor. Short period of teaching; articled clerk, Thomson & Hetherton, York, 1954; Asst Solicitor 1959, Partner 1962, Leathes Prior & Son, Norwich; Senior Legal Asst, Land Commn, Newcastle upon Tyne, 1967; Sen. Legal Asst 1971, Asst Solicitor 1974, Dept of Trade and Industry and successor Depts. *Recreation:* photography. *Address:* 131 Dora Road, SW19 7JT. *T:* 01–946 4037. *Club:* Civil Service.

McELLIGOTT, Neil Martin; Metropolitan Magistrate at Great Marlborough Street Magistrates' Court, 1972–76 (at Old Street Magistrates' Court, 1961–72); *b* 21 March 1915; *s* of Judge E. J. McElligott, KC, Limerick; *m* 1939, Suzanne, *d* of late Air Chief Marshal Sir Arthur Barratt, KCB, CMG, MC, DL; one *d. Educ:* Ampleforth. Served in Royal Air Force, 1935–45. Called to Bar, Inner Temple, 1945, South Eastern Circuit, Recorder of King's Lynn, 1961. *Recreations:* hunting, racing, fishing, gardening. *Address:* Stone Cottage, Abthorpe, near Towcester, Northants.

McELROY, Roy Granville, CMG 1972; LLD, PhD; Pro-Chancellor of the University of Auckland, since 1968; *b* 2 April 1907; *s* of H. T. G. McElroy and Frances C. Hampton; *m* Joan H., *d* of R. O. H. Biss; two *d. Educ:* Auckland Univ.; Clare Coll., Cambridge. LLM NZ 1929; PhD Cantab 1934; LLD NZ 1936. Barrister. Lectr in Law, Auckland Univ., 1936–37. Mem., Auckland City Council, 1938–53; Dep. Mayor of Auckland, 1953, Mayor, 1965–68; Chm., Auckland Metro Planning Cttee, 1953; Mem., Auckland Regional Planning Authority, 1954–66; Chairman: Auckland Old People's Welfare Cttee, 1950–65; NZ Welfare of Aged Persons Distribution Cttee, 1962–75; Sunset Home Inc., 1972–82; Member: Bd of Trustees, NZ Retirement Life Care, 1972–82; Council, Dr Barnardo's in NZ; Auckland Medico-Legal Soc. Consular Agent of France in Auckland, 1948–72; Dean, Auckland Consular Corps, 1965 and 1971. Chm., NZ Section Internat. Commn of Jurists, 1965–72. Chm. Legal Research Foundn, Auckland Univ., 1968–72; Mem., Auckland Univ. Council, 1939–54 and 1960–78; Chm., Auckland Br., NZ Inst. of Internat. Affairs, 1970. FRSA 1971. Hon. DLitt Auckland Univ., 1976. Chevalier de l'Ordre National de la Légion d'Honneur, 1954. *Publications:* Law Reform Act 1936 NZ, 1937; Impossibility of Performance of Contracts, 1942; articles in Modern Law Review, NZ Law Jl, NZ Financial Times. *Recreation:* reading. *Address:* Highpoint, 119 St Stephens Avenue, Parnell, Auckland, New Zealand. *T:* 30–645. *Club:* Northern (Auckland).

McENERY, John Hartnett; author, consultant and conceptual analyst, since 1981; *b* 5 Sept. 1925; *y s* of late Maurice Joseph and Elizabeth Margaret McEnery (*née* Maccabe); *m* 1977, Lilian Wendy, *yr d* of late Reginald Gibbons and Lilian Gibbons (*née* Cox). *Educ:* St Augustine's Sch., Coatbridge; St Aloysius Coll., Glasgow; Glasgow Univ. (MA(Hons)). Served War of 1939–45: RA, 1943–47; Staff Captain, Burma Command, 1946–47. Glasgow Univ., 1947–49. Asst Principal, Scottish Educn Dept, 1949; Principal, 1954; Cabinet Office, 1957; HM Treasury, 1959; Min. of Aviation, 1962; UK Delegn to NATO, 1964; Counsellor (Defence Supply), British Embassy, Bonn, 1966; Asst Sec., Min. of Technology, 1970; Dept of Trade and Industry, 1970–72; Under-Sec. and Regional Dir for Yorks and Humberside, DTI, 1972, Dept of Industry, 1974–76; Under Sec., Concorde and Nationalisation Compensation Div., Dept of Industry, 1977–81. *Publications:* Manufacturing Two Nations—the sociological trap created by the bias of British regional policy against service industry, 1981; Towards a New Concept of Conflict Evaluation, 1985; articles in Jl of Economic Affairs. *Recreations:* various games and sports, chess, travel. *Address:* 56 Lillian Road, SW13 9JF. *Club:* Hurlingham.

McENERY, Peter; actor; Associate Artist, Royal Shakespeare Co.; *b* 21 Feb. 1940; *s* of Charles and Mary McEnery; *m* 1978; one *d. Educ:* various state and private schs. First stage appearance, Brighton, 1956; first London appearance in Flowering Cherry, Haymarket, 1957; *stage:* rôles with RSC include, 1961–: Laertes, Tybalt, Johnny Hobnails in Afore Night Come, Bassanio, Lorenzaccio, Orlando, Sachs in The Jail Diary of Albie Sachs, Pericles, Brutus, Antipholus of Ephesus; other rôles include: Rudge in Next Time I'll Sing to You, Criterion, 1963; Konstantin in The Seagull, Queen's, 1964; Harry Winter in The Collaborators, Duchess, 1973; Trigorin in The Seagull, Lyric, 1975; Made in Bangkok, Aldwych, 1986; directed: Richard III, Nottingham, 1971; The Wound, Young Vic, 1972. *Films* include: Tunes of Glory, 1961; Victim, 1961; The Moonspinners, 1963; Entertaining Mr Sloane, 1970; *television:* Clayhanger, 1976; The Aphrodite Inheritance, 1979; The Jail Diary of Albie Sachs, 1980; Japanese Style, 1982; Pictures, 1983; The Collectors, 1986. *Recreations:* steam railway preservation, ski-ing. *Address:* c/o Norman Boyack, 9 Cork Street, W1X 1PD.

McENTEE, Peter Donovan, CMG 1978; OBE 1963; HM Diplomatic Service, retired; Governor and Commander-in-Chief of Belize, 1976–80; *b* 27 June 1920; *s* of Ewen Brooke McEntee and Caroline Laura Clare (*née* Bayley); *m* 1945, Mary Elisabeth Sherwood; two *d. Educ:* Haileybury Coll., Herts. Served War, HM Forces, 1939–45, KAR (Major). HM Overseas Civil Service, 1946–63: Dist Commissioner; retired as Principal of Kenya Inst. of Administration; First Secretary: Commonwealth Relations Office, 1963; Lagos, 1964–67; Commonwealth Office (later Foreign and Commonwealth Office), 1967–72; Consul-Gen., Karachi, 1972–75. Member Council and Exec. Cttee: Royal Over-Seas League; Royal Commonwealth Soc. for the Blind. *Recreations:* music, natural history, golf. *Address:* Woodlands, Church Lane, Danehill, Sussex RH17 7EU. *Club:* Royal Over-Seas League.

MACER, Dr Richard Charles Franklin, MA, PhD; consultant, since 1985; *b* 21 Oct. 1928; *s* of Lionel William Macer and Adie Elizabeth Macer; *m* 1952, Vera Gwendoline Jeapes; three *d. Educ:* Worthing High Sch.; St John's Coll., Cambridge. Research, St John's Coll., Cambridge, 1949–55, Hutchinson Res. Student, 1952–53; Hd of Plant Pathology Section, Plant Breeding Inst., Cambridge, 1955–66; Dir and Dir of Res., Rothwell Plant Breeders Ltd, Lincs, 1966–72; Prof. of Crop Production, Univ. of Edinburgh, 1972–76; Dir, Scottish Plant Breeding Station, 1976–81; Gen. Manager, Plant Royalty Bureau Ltd, 1981–85. *Publications:* papers on fungal diseases of cereals. *Recreations:* hill walking, archaeology, reading. *Address:* Cherry Trees, 61 Fleetwood, Ely, Cambs CB6 1BH. *T:* Ely 61395. *Club:* Farmers'.

McEVOY, David Dand; QC 1983; barrister-at-law; a Recorder of the Crown Court, since 1979; *b* 25 June 1938; *s* of David Dand McEvoy and Ann Elizabeth McEvoy (*née* Breslin); *m* 1974, Belinda Anne Robertson; three *d. Educ:* Mount St Mary's Coll.; Lincoln Coll., Oxford. BA (PPE). 2nd Lieut The Black Watch, RHR, 1958–59. Called to the Bar, Inner Temple, 1964. *Recreations:* golf, fishing. *Address:* Chambers Court, Longdon, Tewkesbury, Glos GL20 6AS. *T:* Birtsmorton 626. *Club:* Caledonian.

McEVOY, Air Chief Marshal Sir Theodore Newman, KCB 1956 (CB 1951); CBE 1945 (OBE 1941); *b* 21 Nov. 1904; *s* of late Rev. C. McEvoy, MA, Watford; *m* 1935, Marian, *d* of late W. A. E. Coxon, Cairo; one *s* one *d. Educ:* Haberdashers' School; RAF Coll., Cranwell. Served with Fighter Squadrons and in Iraq, 1925–36; psa 1937; Air Ministry, 1938–41; commanded Northolt, 1941; Group Captain Operations, HQ Fighter Command, 1942–43; SASO No 11 Group, 1943; SASO No 84 Group, 1944 (despatches); Air Ministry (DST), 1945–47; idc 1948; AOC No 61 Group, 1949–50; Assistant Chief of Air Staff (Training), 1950–53; RAF Instructor, Imperial Defence Coll., 1954–56; Chief of Staff, Allied Air Forces, Central Europe, 1956–59; Air Secretary, Air Ministry, 1959–62; Air ADC to the Queen, 1959–62; retired, 1962. Vice-President, British Gliding Assoc. Commander Order of Polonia Restituta (Poland), 1942. *Recreations:* gardening, glass engraving. *Address:* 75A Boundstone Road, Rowledge, Farnham, Surrey GU10 4AT. *Club:* Royal Air Force.

McEWAN, Geraldine, (Mrs Hugh Cruttwell); actress; *b* 9 May 1932; *d* of Donald and Norah McKeown; *m* 1953, Hugh Cruttwell, *qv*; one *s* one *d. Educ:* Windsor County Girls' School. Acted with Theatre Royal, Windsor, 1949–51; Who Goes There, 1951; Sweet Madness, 1952; For Better For Worse, 1953; Summertime, 1955; Love's Labour's Lost, Stratford-on-Avon, 1956; The Member of the Wedding, Royal Court Theatre, 1957; The Entertainer, Palace, 1957–58; Stratford-on-Avon, 1958: Pericles; Twelfth Night; Much Ado About Nothing; 1961: Much Ado About Nothing; Hamlet; Everything in the Garden, Arts and Duke of York's, 1962; School for Scandal, Haymarket, and USA, 1962; The Private Ear, and The Public Eye, USA, 1963; Loot, 1965; National Theatre, 1965–71: Armstrong's Last Goodnight; Love For Love; A Flea in Her Ear; The Dance of Death; Edward II; Home and Beauty; Rites; The Way of the World; The White Devil; Amphitryon 38; Dear Love, Comedy, 1973; Chez Nous, Globe, 1974; The Little Hut, Duke of York's, 1974; Oh Coward!, Criterion, 1975; On Approval, Haymarket, 1975; Look After Lulu, Chichester, and Haymarket, 1978; National Theatre: The Browning Version and Harlequinade, 1980; The Provok'd Wife, 1980; The Rivals, 1983; Two Inches of Ivory, 1983; You Can't Take It With You, 1983. *Television series:* The Prime of Miss Jean Brodie, 1978; The Barchester Chronicles, 1982; Mapp and Lucia, 1985, 1986. *Address:* c/o Marmont Management Ltd, Langham House, 302–308 Regent Street, W1.

McEWAN, Ian Russell, FRSL 1982; author; *b* 21 June 1948; *s* of Major (retd) David McEwan and Rose Lilian Violet Moore; *m* 1982, Penny Allen; two *s* two *d. Educ:* Woolverstone Hall Sch.; Univ. of Sussex (BA Hons Eng. Lit.); Univ. of East Anglia (MA Eng. Lit.). Began writing, 1970. *Films:* The Ploughman's Lunch, 1983; Last Day of Summer, 1984. *Publications:* First Love, Last Rites, 1975; In Between the Sheets, 1978; The Cement Garden, 1978; The Imitation Game, 1981; The Comfort of Strangers, 1981; Or Shall we Die? (oratorio), 1982; The Ploughman's Lunch (film script), 1985. *Address:* c/o Jonathan Cape, 32 Bedford Square, WC1B 3EL.

McEWAN, Robin Gilmour, QC (Scot.) 1981; PhD; Sheriff of South Strathclyde, Dumfries and Galloway at Lanark, since 1982; *b* 12 Dec. 1943; *s* of late Ian G. McEwan and of Mary McEwan, Paisley, Renfrewshire; *m* 1973, Sheena, *d* of late Stewart F. McIntyre and of Lilian McIntyre, Aberdour; two *d. Educ:* Paisley Grammar Sch.; Glasgow Univ. (1st Cl. Hons LLB; PhD). Faulds Fellow in Law, Glasgow Univ., 1965–68; admitted to Faculty of Advocates, 1967. Standing Jun. Counsel to Dept of Energy, 1974–76; Advocate Depute, 1976–79. Chm., Industrial Tribunals, 1981–. *Publications:* Pleading in Court, 1980; (with Ann Paton) A Casebook on Damages, 1983. *Recreation:* golf. *Address:* Sheriff Court House, Lanark ML11 7NQ. *Clubs:* New (Edinburgh); Honourable Company of Edinburgh Golfers.

MacEWEN, Ann Maitland, RIBA (DisTP), MRTPI; Planning Consultant; *b* 15 Aug. 1918; *d* of Dr Maitland Radford, MD, DPH, MOH St Pancras, and Dr Muriel Radford; *m* 1st, 1940, John Wheeler, ARIBA, AADip (Hons), Flt-Lt, RAF (killed on active service, 1945); two *d*; 2nd, 1947, Malcolm MacEwen, *qv*; one *d. Educ:* Howell's Sch., Denbigh, N Wales; Architectural Assoc. Sch. of Architecture (AA Dip., RIBA); Assoc. for Planning and Regional Reconstruction Sch. of Planning (SP Dip., MRTPI). Architectural Asst, 1945–46; Planning Asst, Hemel Hempstead New Town Master Plan, 1946–47; Architect-Planner with LCC, 1949–61; Mem., Colin Buchanan's Gp, Min. of Transport, which produced official report, Traffic in Towns, 1961–63; res. work, Transport Section, Civil Engineering Dept, Imperial Coll., 1963–64; Partner, Colin Buchanan and Partners, 1964–73. Senior Lectr, Bristol Univ. Sch. of Advanced Urban Studies, 1974–77; Hon.

Res. Fellow, UCL, 1977–84. Mem., Noise Adv. Council, 1971–73. RIBA Distinction in Town Planning, 1967. *Publications:* National Parks—Cosmetics or Conservation? (with M. MacEwen), 1982; (with Joan Davidson) The Livable City, 1983. *Address:* Manor House, Wootton Courtenay, Minehead, Somerset. *T:* Timberscombe 325.

M'EWEN, Ewen, CBE 1975; MScEng; FRSE; CEng, FIMechE; FASME; Consulting Engineer, since 1980; *b* 13 Jan. 1916; *e s* of Clement M'Ewen and Doris Margaret Pierce-Hope; *m* 1938, Barbara Dorrien, *d* of W. F. Medhurst; two *s* one *d*. *Educ:* Merchiston; University Coll., London. BSc (Eng) 1st class Hons, 1935; MSc (Eng) 1948; Head Memorial Medallist and Prizeman, 1935; Graduate Apprentice David Brown & Sons (Huddersfield) Ltd, 1935–37, Research Engineer, 1937–40, Asst Works Manager, 1940–42; served War of 1939–45, 1942–46: Lt-Col 1943; Lt-Col (Hon. Col) REME (TA retd); Asst Dir, Dept of Tank Design, 1943–46; Asst Chief Engineer, Fighting Vehicles Design Dept, 1946–47; Prof. of Agricultural Engineering, King's Coll., Univ. of Durham, Newcastle upon Tyne, 1947–54, and Reader in Applied Mechanics, 1952–54; Dir Armament R and D Establishment, Fort Halstead, 1955–58; Dir of Engineering, Massey Ferguson Ltd, 1958–63; Dep. Man. Dir, 1963, Man. Dir, 1965–67, Hobourn Group Ltd; Vice-Chm. (Engrg), Joseph Lucas Ltd, 1967–80. Commanded REME 50 (N) Infantry Div. (TA), 1949–52. Hon. Col Durham Univ. OTC, 1955–60. Member: Council, Instn of Mech. Engs, 1961–81 (Vice-Pres., 1970–76; Pres., 1976–77); Design Council, 1971–77; Armed Forces Pay Review Body, 1971–83; Chm., Metrology and Standards Requirements Bd, 1973–77. Chm., Lanchester Polytechnic, Coventry, 1970–73. Fellow, UCL, 1965; Visiting Professor: Imperial Coll., London, 1971–78; UCL, 1978–. Hon. DSc: Heriot-Watt, 1976; Newcastle, 1977. Liveryman, Glaziers Company; Hammerman, Glasgow. *Publications:* papers and articles in Technical Press. *Recreation:* sailing. *Address:* 45 Pearce Avenue, Poole, Dorset BH14 8EG. *T:* Parkstone 742067. *Clubs:* Army and Navy; Royal Thames Yacht; Parkstone Yacht.

McEWEN, Rev. Prof. James Stevenson, DD; Professor of Church History, University of Aberdeen, 1958–77; Master of Christ's College, Aberdeen, 1971–77; *b* 18 Feb. 1910; *s* of Rev. Thomas McEwen and Marjorie Bissett; *m* 1945, Martha M. Hunter, Auchendrane, Alexandria; two *s*. *Educ:* George Watson's Coll., Edinburgh Univ. Ordained Church of Scotland, 1940; held parishes at Rathen, Hawick and Invergowrie; Lecturer in Church History at University of Edinburgh, 1953. *Publication:* The Faith of John Knox, 1961. *Address:* 8 Westfield Terrace, Aberdeen AB2 4RU. *T:* Aberdeen 645413.

McEWEN, Sir John (Roderick Hugh), 5th Bt *cr* 1953; *b* 4 Nov. 1965; *s* of Sir Robert Lindley McEwen, 3rd Bt, of Marchmont and Bardrochat, and of Brigid Cecilia, *d* of late James Laver, CBE, and Veronica Turleigh; *S* brother, 1983. *Heir: cousin* Adam Hugo McEwen, *b* 9 Feb. 1965. *Address:* Whiteside, Greenlaw, Berwickshire.

MacEWEN, Malcolm; journalist; *b* 24 Dec. 1911; *s* of late Sir Alexander MacEwen and of Lady (Mary Beatrice) MacEwen; *m* 1st, 1937, Barbara Mary Stebbing, BSc (*d* 1944); one *d*; 2nd, 1947, Mrs Ann Maitland Wheeler (*see* Ann Maitland MacEwen); one *d* (and two step *d*). *Educ:* Edinburgh Univ. (MA, LLB). Member (Lab) Ross and Cromarty CC, 1938–40; wrote for Daily Worker, mainly as Parliamentary Correspondent, 1944–56; Asst Editor, Architects' Jl, 1956–60; Editor, RIBA Jl, 1964–71; RIBA: Head of Information Services, 1960–66; Publishing Services, 1966–70; Dir, Public Affairs, 1971–72. Leverhulme Res. Fellow, 1972–73; Research Fellow: UCL, 1977–84; Birkbeck Coll., 1985–. Mem., Exmoor Nat. Park Cttee, 1973–81. Hon. Fellow, RIBA, 1974. *Publications:* Crisis in Architecture, 1974; (ed) Future Landscapes, 1976; (with Mrs A. M. MacEwen) National Parks—Cosmetics or Conservation?, 1982; (with G. Sinclair) New Life for the Hills, 1983; (jtly) Countryside Conflicts—The Politics of Farming, 1986. *Address:* Manor House, Wootton Courtenay, Somerset. *T:* Timberscombe 325.

McEWIN, Hon. Sir (Alexander) Lyell, KBE 1954; *b* 29 May 1897; *s* of late A. L. McEwin; *m* 1921, Dora Winifred, *d* of late Mark Williams, Blyth; four *s* one *d*. *Educ:* State Sch.; Prince Alfred Coll., Adelaide. Engaged in farming at Hart, near Blyth, since 1912; Sec., Blyth Agric. Bureau, 1920–26, Pres., 1927–36; Life Mem. State Advisory Bd of Agric., 1930, Chm., 1935–37; Mem. Agric. Settlement Cttee, 1931; Mem. Debt Adjustment Cttee, 1933; Producers' representative for SA on Federal Advisory Cttee for Export Mutton and Beef, prior to appt of Australian Meat Bd, 1934. Entered Legislative Council of South Australian Parliament as Member for Northern District, 1934; Chief Secretary, Minister of Health, and Minister of Mines, 1939–65; Leader of Opposition in Legislative Council, 1965–67; Pres., Legislative Council, S Australia, 1967–75, retired. Councillor, Hart Ward of Hutt and Hill Rivers' District Council, 1932–35; transferred to Blyth Dist Council, 1935–53; retired. Life Mem., South Australian Rifle Assoc. (Chairman, 1948–83); Mem., Commonwealth Council, State Rifle Assocs, 1952–62 (Chm., 1959–62). Chief, Royal Caledonian Society (SA), 1959–68. *Recreation:* bowls. *Address:* 93 First Avenue, St Peters, SA 5069. *T:* 423698.

MACEY, Rear-Adm. David Edward, CB 1984; Gentleman Usher of the Scarlet Rod, Order of the Bath, since 1985; Receiver-General, Canterbury Cathedral, since 1984; *b* 15 June 1929; *s* of Frederick William Charles Macey and Florence May Macey; *m* 1st, 1958, Lorna Therese Verner (decd), *o d* of His Honour Judge Oliver William Verner; one *s* one *d*, and one step *s* two step *d*; 2nd, 1982, Fiona, *o d* of Vice-Adm. Sir William Beloe, KBE, CB, DSC; three step *s*. *Educ:* Sir Joseph Williamson's Mathematical Sch., Rochester; Royal Naval Coll., Dartmouth. Midshipman, 1948; Cruisers, Carriers, Destroyers, 1950–63; Comdr, 1963; Amer. Staff Coll., 1964; Comdr, RNC Dartmouth, 1970; Captain, 1972; Directorate Naval Plans, 1972–74; RCDS, 1975; Dir, RN Staff Coll., 1976–78; Dir, Naval Manpower, 1979–81; Rear-Adm., 1981; Dep. Asst Chief of Staff (Ops), SACEUR, 1981–84. ADC to HM the Queen, 1981. *Recreations:* walking, cricket, cooking. *Address:* Petham Oast, Garlinge Green, Canterbury, Kent CT4 5RT. *Club:* MCC.

MACEY, Air Vice-Marshal Eric Harold, OBE, 1975; Air Officer Commanding and Commandant, Royal Air Force College, Cranwell, since 1985; *b* 9 April 1936; *s* of Harold Fred and Katrina Emma Mary Macey; *m* 1957, Brenda Ann Bracher; one *s* one *d*. *Educ:* Shaftesbury Grammar School; Southampton Tech. Coll. Asst Sci. Officer, Min. of Supply, 1953–54; RAF, 1954; commissioned, 1955; Pilot's Wings, 1956; RAF Staff Coll., 1966; RCDS 1983. *Recreations:* music, walking, DIY. *Address:* Royal Air Force College, Cranwell, Lincs NG34 8HB. *Club:* Royal Air Force.

MACEY, John Percival, CBE 1969; FRICS, FIHM; Chairman, Samuel Lewis Housing Trust, since 1974; Treasurer, Peabody Trust, 1974–81; *b* 3 Dec. 1906; *s* of Edward Macey; *m* 1931, Jill, *d* of Joseph Gyngell; one *s* one *d*. *Educ:* Varndean Grammar Sch., Brighton. Entered LCC service, 1926; Principal Asst, Housing Dept, 1948–51; Dep. Housing Manager, City of Birmingham, 1951–54; Housing Manager, City of Birmingham, 1954–63; Director of Housing to LCC, later GLC, 1964–71. President: Inst. of Housing, 1957 and 1963; Inst. of Housing Managers, 1969; Vice-Pres., Surrey and Sussex Rent Assessment Panel, 1971–79. Served with Royal Engineers, 1939–45 (despatches); retired with rank of Major. *Publications:* Macey on the Housing Finance Act, 1972; The Housing Act, 1974; The Housing Rents and Subsidies Act, 1975; (joint author) Housing Management, 1965, 4th edn (sole author) 1983; papers to professional bodies on housing and allied subjects. *Recreations:* motoring, walking, gardening. *Address:* 7 Bath Court, Kings Esplanade, Hove, East Sussex BN3 2WP. *T:* Brighton 728104.

McFADDEN, Jean Alexandra, JP, MA; Vice Lord Lieutenant of City of Glasgow, since 1980; Principal Teacher of Classics, St Patrick's High School, Coatbridge, since 1972; *b* 26 Nov. 1941; *d* of John and Elma Hogg; *m* 1966, John McFadden. *Educ:* Univ. of Glasgow (MA 1st Cl. Hons Classics). Teacher of Classics, Notre Dame High Sch. for Girls, 1964–70. Entered Local Govt as Mem. of Glasgow Corp. for Cowcaddens Ward, 1971; Mem. for Scotstoun Ward, 1984– (due to boundary changes); Chm., Manpower Cttee, 1974–77; Leader of Labour Group, 1977–; Leader, Glasgow DC, 1980–86. JP Glasgow, 1972; DL 1980. *Recreations:* cycling, theatre, walking, gliding, canoeing. *Address:* 16 Lansdowne Crescent, Glasgow G20 6NQ. *T:* 041–334 3522. *Club:* Tron Theatre (Glasgow).

McFADYEAN, Colin William; Director General, National Playing Fields Association, since 1985; *b* 11 March 1943; *s* of Captain Angus John McFadyean, MC, 1st Bn London Scottish Regt (killed in action, 1944) and Joan Mary McFadyean (*née* Irish); *m* 1970, Jeanette Carol Payne; one *s*. *Educ:* Plymouth Coll.; Bristol Grammar Sch.; Loughborough Coll. of Education; Keele Univ. (DLC hons, Adv. DipEd). Phys. Educn teacher, Birmingham, 1965–67; Phys. Educn Lectr, 1967–72, Sen. Lectr, 1972–74, Cheshire; Dep. Dir, Nat. Sports Centre, Lilleshall, 1974–78; Chief Coach, Jubilee Sports Centre, Hong Kong, 1979–82; Sports Master and House Master, Dulwich Coll., 1983–85. Internat. Rugby career includes: 11 England caps, 1966–68; 4 Tests British Lions *v* NZ, 1966; (captain) *v* Ireland, 1968; (captain) *v* Wales, 1968; scored 5 tries, 1 dropped goal (in 15 Tests); other sport: coach to Hong Kong disabled team to Olympics, Arnhem, 1980; Adviser, Hong Kong table tennis team to World Championships, Yugoslavia, 1981. Broadcaster with Hong Kong TV and commercial radio. *Recreations:* tennis, golf, music. *Address:* 55 Woodland Way, West Wickham, Kent BR4 9LT. *T:* 01–777 6750. *Clubs:* British Sportsman's; England Rugby International's; Moseley Football (Vice-Pres.); Corkscrew Hill Lawn Tennis.

MACFADYEN, Donald James Dobbie, QC (Scot.) 1983; *b* 8 Sept. 1945; *er s* of late Donald James Thomson Macfadyen, Solicitor, Hamilton, and of Christina Dick Macfadyen; *m* 1971, Christine Balfour Gourlay Hunter; one *s* one *d*. *Educ:* Wishaw Public Primary Sch.; Hutchesons' Boys' Grammar Sch., Glasgow; Glasgow Univ. (LLB 1967). Admitted to Faculty of Advocates, 1969; Advocate Depute, 1979–82. *Address:* 42 Northumberland Street, Edinburgh EH3 6JE. *T:* 031–556 6043. *Club:* New (Edinburgh).

McFADZEAN, family name of **Barons McFadzean** and **McFadzean of Kelvinside.**

McFADZEAN, Baron, *cr* 1966 (Life Peer); **William Hunter McFadzean,** KT 1976; Kt 1960; Director, Midland Bank, 1959–81 (Deputy Chairman, 1968–77); Hon. President, BICC plc, 1973 (Managing Director, 1954–61; Chairman, 1954–73); *b* Stranraer, 17 Dec. 1903; *s* of late Henry and of Agnes McFadzean, Stranraer; *m* 1933, Eileen, *e d* of Arthur Gordon, Blundellsands, Lancs.; one *s* one *d*, one adopted *d*. *Educ:* Stranraer Academy and High Sch.; Glasgow Univ. Served articles with McLay, McAllister & McGibbon, Chartered Accountants, Glasgow, 1922–27; qualified as Chartered Accountant, 1927; with Chalmers Wade & Co., 1927–32; joined British Insulated Cables Ltd, as Accountant, 1932 (Financial Secretary, 1937; Exec. Manager, 1942); on amalgamation of British Insulated Cables Ltd and Callender's Cable & Construction Co. Ltd, in 1945, appointed to Board of British Insulated Callender's Cables Ltd as Exec. Director (Dep. Chairman, 1947; Chief Exec. Director, 1950), retd 1973; Chairman: Standard Broadcasting Corp. (UK) Ltd, 1972–79 (Hon. Pres., 1979); Home Oil (UK) Ltd, 1972–78; Scurry-Rainbow (UK) Ltd, 1974–78; Deputy Chairman: RTZ/BICC Aluminium Holdings Ltd, 1967–73; National Nuclear Corp., 1973–80; Canada Life Unit Trust Managers Ltd (Chm., 1971–82); Director: Anglesey Aluminium Ltd, 1968–73; Midland Bank Executor and Trustee Co., 1959–67; English Electric Co., 1966–68; Steel Co. of Wales Ltd, 1966–67; Canadian Imperial Bank of Commerce, 1967–74; Canada Life Assurance Co., 1969–79; Canada Life Assurance Co. of GB, 1971–84 (Dep. Chm., 1971–84); Home Oil Co. Ltd, 1972–77; Standard Broadcasting Corp. Ltd, 1976–79. Pres. FBI, 1959–61. Chairman: Council of Industrial Fedns of EFTA, 1960–63; (Founder) Export Council for Europe, 1960–64 (Hon. Pres. 1964–71); Commonwealth Export Council, 1964–66; British Nat. Export Council, 1964–66 (Pres. 1966–68); President: Brit. Electrical Power Convention, 1961–62; Brit. Nuclear Forum, 1964–66; Coal Trade Benevolent Assoc., 1967–68; Electrical and Electronics Industries Benevolent Assoc., 1968–69. Vice-President: Middle East Assoc., 1965; City of London Soc., 1965–72; British/Swedish Chamber of Commerce, 1963–74. Member: Inst. of Directors, 1954–76 (Council, 1954–74); Min. of Labour Adv. Bd on Resettlement of Ex-Regulars, 1957–60; Bd of Trade Adv. Council on ME Trade, 1958–60; MoT Shipping Adv. Panel, 1962–64; Ct of British Shippers' Council, 1964–74 (Pres., 1968–71); Council, Foreign Bondholders, 1968–74; Anglo-Danish Soc., 1965–75 (Chm., 1969–75; Hon. Pres., 1975); Adv. Cttee, Queen's Award for Industry, 1965–67 (Chm., Review Cttee, 1970). CompIEE 1956. JDipMA 1965. Commander Order of Dannebrog (Denmark), 1964, Grand Commander, 1974; Grande Oficial da Ordem do Infante Dom Henrique, Portugal, 1972. *Address:* 114 Whitehall Court, SW1A 2EL. *T:* 01–930 3160; 16 Lansdown Crescent, Bath, Avon BA1 5EX. *T:* Bath 335487. *Clubs:* Carlton, MCC.

McFADZEAN OF KELVINSIDE, Baron *cr* 1980 (Life Peer), of Kelvinside in the District of the City of Glasgow; **Francis Scott McFadzean;** Kt 1975; Former Director, Shell Transport and Trading Company Ltd; Director: Shell Petroleum Company Ltd, 1964–86; Beecham Group Ltd, 1974–86; Coats Patons Ltd, 1979–86; *b* 26 Nov. 1915; *m* 1938, Isabel McKenzie Beattie; one *d*. *Educ:* Glasgow Univ.; London Sch. of Economics (Hon. Fellow, 1974). MA. BoT, 1938; Treasury, 1939; War Service, 1940–45; Malayan Govt, 1945; Colonial Develt Corp., 1949; Shell Petroleum Co. Ltd, 1952; Man. Dir, Royal Dutch/Shell Group of Companies, 1964–76; Dir, 1964–, Man. Dir 1971, Chm., 1972–76, "Shell" Transport and Trading Co. Ltd; Chairman: Shell International Marine Ltd, 1966–76; Shell Canada Ltd, 1970–76; Shell Petroleum Co. Ltd, 1972–76; British Airways, 1976–79 (Dir, 1975); Rolls Royce Ltd, 1980–83; Dir, Shell Oil Co., 1972–76. Chairman: Trade Policy Research Centre, 1971–82; Steering Bd, Strathclyde Div., Scottish Business Sch., 1970–76; Vis. Prof. of Economics, Strathclyde Univ., 1967–76. Hon. LLD Strathclyde, 1970. Comdr, Order of Oranje Nassau. *Publications:* Galbraith and the Planners, 1968; Energy in the Seventies, 1971; The Operation of a Multi-National Enterprise, 1971; (jtly) Towards an Open World Economy, 1972; The Economics of John Kenneth Galbraith: a study in fantasy, 1977; (jtly) Global Strategy for Growth: a report on North-South issues, 1981. *Address:* House of Lords, SW1A 0PW.
See also Baron Marsh.

McFALL, David (Bernard), RA 1963 (ARA 1955); Sculptor; Master of Sculpture, City and Guilds of London Art School, Lambeth, 1956–75; *b* 21 Dec. 1919; *s* of David McFall and Elizabeth McEvoy; *m* 1972, Alexandra Dane, actress; one *s* one *d*. *Educ:* Art Schools, Birmingham, Lambeth and Royal College of Art. Official Commissions: Unicorns (pair, 12 ft, gilt-bronze) mounted on roof of Bristol New Council House, known as The Bristol Unicorns, 1950; Finials (pair, carved, Portland stone, 10 ft), Zodiac Clock (8 ft, carved stone and cast aluminium), Bronze Portrait Bust (Alderman Frank Sheppard), 1955, same building; Festival of Britain, Boy and Foal (carved stone 5 ft), 1951, now at Missenden Abbey, Bucks. Pocahontas (bronze), 1956; Bust (bronze, Lord Methuen), 1956; Head of Ralph Vaughan Williams, OM (bronze) in Royal Festival Hall, 1957; 8 ft Statues of St Bride and St Paul in St Bride's Church, Fleet Street; Bronze Head of Sir Winston Churchill, in Grocers Hall, 1958; 8 ft 6 ins Bronze Figure of Sir Winston Churchill, 1959 (Woodford Green); Lord Balfour, House of Commons, 1962; Bust (bronze) Lord Brabazon of Tara (Royal Institution); Memorial to Sir Albert Richardson, PPRA, for Crypt of St Paul's Cathedral; Crucifixion (Portland stone), Church of Our Lady of Lourdes, Thames-Ditton; bust (bronze, Lord Ridley) for Univ., Newcastle upon Tyne; The Golden Gazelle, Abu Dhabi, Trucial States; bronze figure of Sir Winston Churchill, trophy for Dame Felicity Peake Essay Prize; The Black Horse for LTB Victoria Line, 1968; stone frieze on Wm Whitfield's extension to Inst. of Chartered Accountants, London, 1969; bust of Sir Thomas Holmes Sellors, Pres., RCS, 1971; Meml to Sir Gerald Kelly, St Paul's Cathedral Crypt, 1973; busts of: Sir George Godber, for RCP; Prof. George Grenfell Baines, for Building Design Partnership, Preston; late Hugh Stenhouse, Glasgow, 1973–74; Oedipus and Jocasta (stone group), W Norwood Library, 1974; posthumous bust of Josiah Wedgwood, Barlaston, Stoke-on-Trent, 1974–75; portrait head of HRH Prince Charles, Duke of Cornwall, 1974–75; Meml to Lord Fraser of Lonsdale, Westminster Abbey, 1976; Official purchase: The Bullcalf (Chantrey Bequest), 1943. Has exhibited at Royal Academy yearly since 1943. *Recreations:* photography, cycling. *Address:* 10 Fulham Park Gardens, SW6 4JX. *T:* 01–736 6532; Natura, Fairlight Cove, Sussex TN35 4DJ.

McFALL, Richard Graham; Chairman, 1980–86, Director, 1976–86, Fleming Enterprise Investment Trust plc (formerly Crossfriars Trust plc); *b* 31 Jan. 1920; 3rd *s* of Henry Joseph Marshall and Sarah Gertrude McFall; *m* 1945, Clara Louise Debonnaire Mitford; one *s* one *d. Educ:* Holmwood Prep. Sch., Lancs; Clifton Coll., Bristol. Joined Pacol Ltd, 1938; Mil. Service, HAC, 1939–40; Colonial Office, 1941–45 (Asst Sec., then Sec., W African Produce Control Bd); Motor & Air Products Ltd, 1946–48; re-joined Pacol Ltd, 1949, Dir 1951; Chm., London Cocoa Terminal Market Assoc., 1954–55; Chm., Cocoa Assoc. of London, 1958–59; Dir 1962–82, Man. Dir 1965–74, Chm., 1970–76, Vice-Chm., 1976–78, Gill & Duffus Group PLC. *Recreations:* golf, bridge. *Address:* Springfold Cottage, Greendene, East Horsley, Surrey. *T:* East Horsley 3282. *Clubs:* Farmers'; Effingham Golf.

McFARLAND, Sir John (Talbot), 3rd Bt *cr* 1914, of Aberfoyle, Co. Londonderry; TD 1967; Chairman: Lanes (Business Equipment), since 1977; R. C. Malseed & Co. Ltd, since 1977; J. T. McFarland Holdings, since 1984; McFarland Farms Ltd, since 1980; Director: Londonderry Gaslight Co., since 1958; G. Kinnaird & Son Ltd, since 1984; *b* 3 Oct. 1927; *s* of Sir Basil Alexander Talbot McFarland, 2nd Bt, CBE, ERD, and Anne Kathleen (*d* 1952), *d* of late Andrew Henderson; *S* father, 1986; *m* 1957, Mary Scott, *d* of late Dr W. Scott Watson, Londonderry; two *s* two *d. Educ:* Marlborough College; Trinity Coll., Oxford. Captain RA (TA), retired 1967. Chairman 1977–84, Director 1984–87: Lanes (Derry) Ltd; Lanes (Fuel) Oils Ltd; Lanes Patent Fuels Ltd; Holmes Coal Ltd; Alexander Thompson & Co. Ltd; Nicholl Ballintyne Ltd; J. W. Corbett Ltd; Wattersons Ltd. Chm., Londonderry Lough Swilly Railway Co., 1978–81; Dir, Donegal Holdings Ltd, 1963–85. Member: Londonderry County Borough Council, 1955–69; NW HMC, 1960–73; Londonderry Port and Harbour Commrs, 1965–73. Jt Chm., Londonderry and Foyle Coll., 1971–76. High Sheriff, Co. Londonderry 1958, City of County of Londonderry 1965–67; DL Londonderry 1962, resigned 1982. *Recreations:* golf, shooting. *Heir: er s* Anthony Basil Scott McFarland, *b* 29 Nov. 1959. *Address:* Dunmore House, Carrigans, Lifford, Co. Donegal. *T:* Letterkenny 40120. *Clubs:* Kildare Street and University (Dublin); Northern Counties (Londonderry).

McFARLANE OF LLANDAFF, Baroness *cr* 1979 (Life Peer), of Llandaff in the County of South Glamorgan; **Jean Kennedy McFarlane;** Professor and Head of Department of Nursing, University of Manchester, since 1974; *b* 1 April 1926; *d* of James and Elvina Alice McFarlane. *Educ:* Howell's Sch., Llandaff; Bedford and Birkbeck Colls, Univ. of London. MA, BSc(Soc); SRN, SCM, HV Tutor's Cert.; FRCN 1976; FCNA 1984. Staff Nurse, St Bartholomew's Hosp., 1950–51; Health Visitor, Cardiff CC, 1953–59; Royal Coll. of Nursing: Organising Tutor, Integrated Course, Educn Div., London, 1960–62; Educn Officer, Birmingham, 1962–66; Res. Project Ldr (DHSS sponsored), London, 1967–69; Dir of Educn, Inst. of Advanced Nursing Educn, London, 1969–71; Univ. of Manchester: Sen. Lectr in Nursing, Dept of Social and Preventive Medicine, 1971–73; Sen. Lectr and Head of Dept of Nursing, 1973–74. Member: Royal Commn on NHS, 1976–79; Commonwealth War Graves Commn, 1983–. Chm., English Bd for Nursing, Midwifery and Health Visiting, 1980–83. Hon. MSc Manchester, 1979; Hon. DSc Ulster, 1981; Hon. DEd CNAA 1983. *Publications:* The Problems of Developing Criteria of Quality for Nursing Care (thesis), 1969; The Proper Study of the Nurse, 1970; (with G. Castledine) The Practice of Nursing using the Nursing Process, 1982. *Recreations:* music, walking, travelling, photography. *Address:* Department of Nursing, University of Manchester, Stopford Building, Oxford Road, Manchester M13 9PT. *T:* 061–273 8241, ext. 182.

MACFARLANE, Dr Alan Donald James, FRAI; FRHistS; FBA 1986; Reader in Historical Anthropology, University of Cambridge, since 1981; *b* 20 Dec. 1941; *s* of Donald Kennedy Macfarlane and Iris Stirling Macfarlane; *m* 1st, 1966, Gillian Ions; one *d*; 2nd, 1981, Sarah Harrison. *Educ:* Sedbergh School; Worcester College, Oxford (MA, DPhil); LSE (MPhil); SOAS (PhD). Senior Research Fellow in History, King's College, Cambridge, 1971–74; Univ. Lectr in Social Anthropology, Cambridge, 1975–81. Lectures: Frazer Meml, 1974; Malinowski Meml, 1978. Rivers Meml Medal, 1984. *Publications:* Witchcraft in Tudor and Stuart England, 1970; The Family Life of Ralph Josselin, 1970; Resources and Population, 1976; (ed) The Diary of Ralph Josselin, 1976; Reconstructing Historical Communities, 1977; Origins of English Individualism, 1978; The Justice and the Mare's Ale, 1981; A Guide to English Historical Records, 1983; Marriage and Love in England, 1986. *Recreations:* walking, gardening, second-hand book hunting. *Address:* 25 Lode Road, Lode, near Cambridge CB5 9ER. *T:* Cambridge 811976.

MacFARLANE, Prof. Alistair George James, FRS 1984; FEng 1981; Professor of Engineering, University of Cambridge, since 1974; Fellow since 1974, Vice-Master since 1980, Selwyn College, Cambridge; *b* 9 May 1931; *s* of George R. MacFarlane; *m* 1954, Nora Williams; one *s. Educ:* Hamilton Academy; Univ. of Glasgow. BSc 1953, DSc 1969, Glasgow; PhD London 1964; MSc Manchester 1973; MA 1974, ScD 1979, Cantab. Metropolitan-Vickers, Manchester, 1953–58; Lectr, Queen Mary Coll., Univ. of London, 1959–65, Reader 1965–66; Reader in Control Engrg, Univ. of Manchester Inst. of Sci. and Technology, 1966–69, Prof. 1969–74. Chm., Cambridge Control Ltd, 1985–. Member: Council, SERC, 1981–85; Computer Board, 1983–. *Publications:* Engineering Systems Analysis, 1964; Dynamical System Models, 1970; A Complex Variable Approach to the Analysis of Linear Multivariable Feedback Systems, 1979; Frequency-Response Methods in Control Systems, 1979; Complex Variable Methods for Linear Multivariable Feedback Systems, 1980; Multivariable Feedback: a quasi-classical approach, 1982. *Address:* 9 Dane Drive, Newnham, Cambridge CB3 9LP.

MACFARLANE, Rev. Alwyn James Cecil; Associate Minister, Scots' Church, Melbourne, since 1986; Parish Minister of Newlands (South), Church of Scotland, 1968–85; Chaplain to the Queen in Scotland, 1977; *b* 14 June 1922; *s* of James Waddell Macfarlane and Ada Cecilia Rankin; *m* 1953, Joan Cowell Harris; one *s* one *d. Educ:* Cargilfield Sch.; Rugby Sch.; Oxford Univ. (MA); Edinburgh Univ. Served War: N Africa, Italy, Greece; Liaison Officer in Black Watch with 12th Bde, 1942–46. Ordained, 1951; served in parishes in Ross-shire, Edinburgh and Glasgow. *Recreations:* photography, walking. *Address:* c/o Scots' Church, 99 Russell Street, Melbourne, Vic 3000, Australia.

MACFARLANE, Anne Bridget; Master of the Court of Protection, since 1982; *b* 26 Jan. 1930; *d* of late Dr David Griffith and Dr Grace Griffith; *m* 1957, James Douglas Macfarlane; two *d. Educ:* nine schools; Bristol Univ. (LLB). Admitted Solicitor, 1954. HM Land Registry, 1966–75; Registrar, Bromley County Court, 1975–82. *Publication:* (contrib.) Atkin's Court Forms, 2nd edn 1983. *Recreation:* collecting Victorian tiles. *Address:* 25 Store Street, WC1E 7BP. *T:* 01–636 6877. *Club:* Law Society.

MACFARLANE, (David) Neil; MP (C) Sutton and Cheam, since Feb. 1974; *b* 7 May 1936; *yr s* of Robert and Dulcie Macfarlane; *m* 1961, June Osmond King, Somerset; two *s* one *d. Educ:* St Aubyn's Prep. Sch.; Bancroft's, Woodford Green. Short Service Commission, Essex Regt, 1955–58; served TA, 265 LAA, RA, 1961–66. Joined Shell Mex and BP, 1959; contested (C): East Ham (North), 1970; Sutton and Cheam, by-election, 1972. Parly Under-Sec. of State, DoE, 1981–85 (with spec. responsibility for Sport, 1981–85, for Children's Play, 1983–85). Mem., All Party Select Cttee on Science and Technology; Parly Under Sec. of State, DES, 1979–81. Mem., National Trust. *Recreations:* golf, swimming, cricket, cricket-watching. *Address:* House of Commons, SW1. *T:* 01–219 3404; 48 Benhill Avenue, Sutton, Surrey. *Clubs:* MCC; Essex County Cricket; Royal & Ancient Golf; Huntercombe Golf.

MacFARLANE, Donald, CBE 1963; HM Diplomatic Service, retired; *b* 26 Oct. 1910; *s* of late Donald MacFarlane, CIE; *m* 1933, Jean Carmen, *d* of late Charles Young, Pitt Manor, Winchester; one *s* decd. *Educ:* Stowe; Queens' Coll., Cambridge. Lamson Paragon Supply Co. Ltd, 1932–39. Served in RA and Intelligence Corps, 1939–46 (despatches); North Africa, Sicily, Italy and France; Colonel, head of Anglo-Greek Information Services, Athens, 1945–46. First Secretary, Foreign Service, 1946; British Embassy, China, 1946–49; Foreign Office, 1949–52; British Embassy: Rio de Janeiro, 1952–55; Counsellor (Commercial), Washington, 1955–58; Lisbon, 1958–60; HM Consul-General, Frankfurt-am-Main, 1960–64, Naples, 1964–67; Head of Nationality and Treaty Dept, FCO, 1967–70. *Recreations:* fishing, ski-ing. *Address:* 27 Lennox Gardens, SW1. *Club:* Flyfishers'.

MACFARLANE, Sir George (Gray), Kt 1971; CB 1965; BSc; Dr Ing (Dresden); FEng; Corporate Director, British Telecommunications plc, since 1984 (Member of the Board, since 1981); *b* 8 Jan. 1916; *s* of late John Macfarlane, Airdrie, Lanarks; *m* 1941, Barbara Grant, *d* of Thomas Thomson, Airdrie, Lanarks; one *s* one *d. Educ:* Airdrie Academy; Glasgow Univ.; Technische Hochschule, Dresden, Germany. On scientific staff, Air Ministry Research Establishment, Dundee and Swanage, 1939–41; Telecommunications Research Establishment (TRE), Malvern, 1941–60; Deputy Chief Scientific Officer (Individual Merit Post), 1954–60; Deputy Director, National Physical Laboratory, 1960–62; Director, Royal Radar Establishment, 1962–67; Controller (Research), Min. of Technology and Min. of Aviation Supply, 1967–71; Controller, Research and Develt Establishments and Research, MoD, 1971–75. Member: PO Review Cttee, 1976–77; PO Bd, 1977–81; NEB, 1980–85 and NRDC, 1981–85 (now British Technology Gp). Mem., Bd of Trustees, Imperial War Museum, 1978–. Deputy-Pres., IEE, 1976–78 (Vice-Pres., 1972–74); Hunter Meml Lecturer, IEE, 1966; Council Mem., Fellowship of Engrg, 1982–86 (Vice-Pres. 1983–86). Hon. LLD Glasgow. Glazebrook Medal and Prize, Inst. of Physics, 1978. *Publications:* papers in IEE, Proc. Phys. Society, Phys. Review. *Recreations:* walking, gardening. *Address:* Red Tiles, Orchard Way, Esher, Surrey. *T:* Esher 63778. *Club:* Athenæum.

McFARLANE, Sir Ian, Kt 1984; Chairman and Managing Director: Southern Pacific Petroleum NL, since 1968; Central Pacific Minerals NL, since 1968; Chairman, Trans Pacific Consolidated Ltd, since 1964; *b* 25 Dec. 1923; *s* of Stuart Gordon McFarlane, CMG, MBE and Mary Grace McFarlane; *m* 1956, Ann, *d* of M. A. Shaw, Salt Lake City, USA; one *s* two *d. Educ:* Melbourne Grammar School; Harrow; Sydney Univ. (BSc, BE); MIT (SM). Served War of 1939–45, RANVR. Morgan Stanley & Co., 1949–59; Mem., Sydney Stock Exchange, 1959–64; Dep. Chm., Magellan Petroleum, 1964–70; Director: International Pacific Corp., 1967–73; Aust. Gen. Insurance Co., 1968–74; Mercantile Mutual Insurance Co., 1969–74; Concrete Construction, 1972–74; International Pacific Aust. Investments, 1972–73; Morgan Stanley Internat., NYC, 1976–80. Mem. Council, Imperial Soc. of Knights Bachelor. Founder, Sir Ian McFarlane Travelling Professorship in Urology. Chm., Royal Brisbane Hosp. Foundn. Life Governor, Royal Prince Alfred Hosp., Sydney; Founding Governor, St Luke's Hosp. Foundn, Sydney. Kentucky Col, 1984. *Address:* 40 Wentworth Road, Vaucluse, NSW 2030, Australia. *Clubs:* Australian (Sydney); Queensland (Brisbane); University (NY); Royal Sydney Golf.

McFARLANE, Prof. Ian Dalrymple, MBE 1946; FBA 1978; Professor of French Literature, University of Oxford, 1971–83, now Emeritus; Professorial Fellow, Wadham College, Oxford, 1971–83, now Emeritus Fellow; *b* 7 Nov. 1915; *s* of James Blair McFarlane and Valérie Edith Liston Dalrymple; *m* 1939, Marjory Nan Hamilton; one *s* one *d. Educ:* Lycée St-Charles, Marseilles; Tormore Sch., Upper Deal, Kent; Westminster Sch.; St Andrews Univ. MA 1st class Hons, 1938; Carnegie Research Scholar, 1938–39. Served 1st Bn Black Watch, RHR, 1940–45. Apptd Lectr in French, Cambridge Univ., 1945; Gonville and Caius Coll.: elected Fellow, 1947; appointed Senior Tutor, 1956; Prof. of French Language and Literature, St Andrews, 1961–70. Zaharoff Lectr, Oxford, 1984; Hon. Faculty Prof., University Coll., Cardiff, 1984. Member, Scottish Cert. of Educn Examination Board, 1964; Member Academic Planning Board, University of Stirling, 1964–67; Mem. Cttee on Research and Develt in Modern Languages, 1966. Pres., MHRA, 1986. Doctor of Univ. of Paris, 1950; Dr *hc*, Univ. of Tours, 1982; Hon. DLitt St Andrews, 1982. Officier des Palmes Académiques, 1971. *Publications:* critical edn of M. Scève's Délie, 1966; Renaissance France 1470–1589, 1974; Buchanan, 1981; The Entry of Henri II into Paris, 1549, 1982; various, in learned periodicals. *Recreations:* cricket, music. *Address:* Wadham College, Oxford.

McFARLANE, James Sinclair, CBE 1986; CEng, FIM, CBIM; Director General, Engineering Employers' Federation, since 1982; *b* 8 Nov. 1925; *s* of John Mills McFarlane and Hannah McFarlane; *m* 1951, Ruth May Harden; three *d. Educ:* Manchester Grammar Sch.; Emmanuel Coll., Cambridge (MA, PhD). CEng, FIM 1961. ICI Ltd, 1949–53; Henry Wiggin & Co. Ltd, 1953–69; Chm. and Man. Dir, Smith-Clayton Forge Ltd (GKN Ltd), 1969–76; Man. Dir, Garringtons Ltd (GKN Ltd), 1976–77; Guest Keen & Nettlefolds Ltd: Gen. Man., Personnel, 1977–79; Exec. Dir, 1979–82. Mem., NEDC, 1982–; a Civil Service Comr (pt-time), 1983–. *Publications:* contrib. scientific and technical jls. *Recreation:* music. *Address:* The Court House, Atch Lench, Evesham, Worcs

WR11 5SP. *T*: Evesham 870225. *Clubs*: Caledonian, United Oxford & Cambridge University.

McFARLANE, Prof. James Walter; Professor of European Literature, University of East Anglia, 1964–82, now Emeritus; *b* 12 Dec. 1920; *s* of James and Florence McFarlane; *m* 1944, Lillie Kathleen Crouch; two *s* one *d*. *Educ*: Bede Grammar Sch., Sunderland; St Catherine's Society, Univ. of Oxford. MA, BLitt 1948. War service, Intell. Corps, 1941–46 (Major); Oxford Soccer blue, 1947; Lectr and Sen. Lectr, Dept of German and Scandinavian Studies, King's Coll., Univ. of Durham, later Univ. of Newcastle upon Tyne, 1947–63; University of East Anglia: Founding Dean of European Studies, 1964–68; Public Orator, 1964–68, 1974–75, 1978–79; Pro-Vice-Chancellor, 1968–71; Professorial Fellow, 1982–86. Vis. Prof., Univ. of Auckland, NZ, 1967; Herbert F. Johnson Vis. Res. Prof., Inst. for Res. in Humanities, Univ. of Wisconsin-Madison, 1983–84. Mem., BBC Gen. Adv. Council, 1970–75; Chm., East Anglia Regional Adv. Council, 1970–75; Chm., Hunworth Crafts Trust, 1973–77; Mem. Exec., Eastern Arts Assoc., 1977–82. Founder Trustee, Norwich Puppet Theatre, 1979; Chm., The Wells Centre, Norfolk, 1981–. Editor, Scandinavica: an International Journal of Scandinavian Studies, 1975–; Man. Editor, Norvik Press. Leverhulme Faculty Fellow in European Studies, 1971–72; Brit. Acad. Wolfson Fellow. Fellow, Det Norske Videnskaps-Akademie, Oslo, 1977; Corresp. Mem., Svenska Litteratursällskapet i Finland, Helsinki, 1977; Foreign Member: Royal Norwegian Soc. of Sciences and Letters, 1982; Royal Danish Acad. of Sciences and Letters, 1983. Hon. Mem., Phi Beta Kappa, 1984. Commander's Cross, Royal Norwegian Order of St Olav, 1975. *Publications*: Ibsen and the Temper of Norwegian Literature, 1960; Discussions of Ibsen, 1962; Henrik Ibsen, 1970; (with Malcolm Bradbury) Modernism: European Literature 1890–1930, 1976; (editor and translator) The Oxford Ibsen, 1960–77: vol. 1, Early Plays, 1970; vol. 2, The Vikings at Helgeland, Love's Comedy, The Pretenders, 1962; vol. 3, Brand, Peer Gynt, 1972; vol. 4, The League of Youth, Emperor and Galilean, 1963; vol. 5, Pillars of Society, A Doll's House, Ghosts, 1961; vol. 6, An Enemy of the People, The Wild Duck, Rosmersholm, 1960; vol. 7, The Lady from the Sea, Hedda Gabler, The Master Builder, 1966; vol. 8, Little Eyolf, John Gabriel Borkman, When We Dead Awaken, 1977; (editor and translator with Janet Garton) Slaves of Love and other Norwegian short stories, 1982; *festschrift*: (ed J. Garton) Facets of European Modernism: essays in honour of James McFarlane, 1985; *translations*: Hamsun's Pan, 1955; Hamsun's Wayfarers, 1980. *Recreation*: domestic odd-jobbery. *Address*: The Croft, Stody, Melton Constable, Norfolk NR24 2EE. *T*: Melton Constable 860505.

MACFARLANE, Sir James (Wright), Kt 1973; PhD; FRSE; CEng, FIEE, FIMechE; JP; DL; Managing Director, Cathcart Investment Co. Ltd, since 1964; *b* 2 Oct. 1908; *s* of late James C. Macfarlane, OBE, MIEE, WhSch; *m* 1937, Claire Ross. *Educ*: Allan Glen's Sch.; Royal Technical Coll. (DRTC); Glasgow Univ. (PhD); London Univ. WhSch and WhSen.Sch. FIFire E. War of 1939–45: Home Guard (Major); Intell.; Lt-Col (TA) Comdg Renfrewshire Bn, Army Cadet Force. Apprentice, Engineer and Director, Macfarlane Engrg Co. Ltd, 1926–; Chm., Macfarlane Engrg Co. Ltd, Cathcart, 1967–69. Past Pres., Assoc. of County Councils in Scotland; Past Mem. various instns; Member: Royal Commn on the Police, 1960–62; Departmental Cttee on the Fire Service, 1968–70. JP 1940; entered local govt, 1944; DL 1962, Renfrewshire; Convener, County of Renfrew, 1967–73. Chm. of Governors, Paisley Coll. of Technology. *Publications*: numerous papers in IEE and IMechE Jls. *Recreations*: motor cycles and cars (vintage), sailing. *Address*: 2 Sandringham Court, Newton Mearns, Glasgow G77 5DT. *T*: 041–639 1842. *Clubs*: RNVR (Scotland); Royal Gourock Yacht (Gourock).

MACFARLANE, Neil; *see* Macfarlane, D. N.

MACFARLANE, Sir Norman (Somerville), Kt 1983; Chairman and Managing Director, Macfarlane Group (Clansman) PLC, since 1973; *b* 5 March 1926; *s* of Daniel Robertson Macfarlane and Jessie Lindsay Somerville; *m* 1953, Marguerite Mary Campbell; one *s* four *d*. *Educ*: High Sch. of Glasgow. Commnd RA, 1945; served Palestine, 1945–47. Founded N. S. Macfarlane & Co. Ltd, 1949; became Macfarlane Group (Clansman) PLC, 1973. Underwriting Mem. of Lloyd's, 1978–; Chairman: The Fine Art Society PLC, 1976–; American Trust PLC, 1984– (Dir, 1980–); Director: Clydesdale Bank PLC, 1980–; General Accident Fire & Life Assce Corp. plc, 1984–; Edinburgh Fund Managers plc, 1980–. Chm., Scottish Industrialists' Council, 1975–; Dir, Glasgow Chamber of Commerce, 1976–79; Member: Council, CBI Scotand, 1975–81; Bd, Scottish Develt Agency, 1979–. Chm., Glasgow Action, 1985–. Vice Chm., Scottish Ballet, 1983– (Dir, 1975–); Dir, Scottish National Orch., 1977–82; Pres., Royal Glasgow Inst. of the Fine Arts, 1976–; Mem., Royal Fine Art Commn for Scotland, 1980–82; Scottish Patron, National Art Collection Fund, 1978–; Governor, Glasgow Sch. of Art, 1976–; Trustee: Nat. Heritage Meml Fund, 1984–; Nat. Galls of Scotland, 1986–. Dir, Third Eye Centre, 1978–81. Chm. Governors, High Sch. of Glasgow, 1979–; Mem. Court, Univ. of Glasgow, 1979–. President: Stationers' Assoc. of GB and Ireland, 1965; Co. of Stationers of Glasgow, 1968–70; Glasgow High Sch. Club, 1970–72. Hon. FRIAS 1984. Hon. LLD Strathclyde, 1986. *Recreations*: golf, cricket, theatre, art. *Address*: Macfarlane Group (Clansman) PLC, Sutcliffe Road, Glasgow G13 1AH; 50 Manse Road, Bearsden, Glasgow. *Clubs*: Art, Royal Scottish Automobile (Glasgow); Glasgow Golf.

MacFARLANE, Maj.-Gen. Robert Goudie, MBE 1952; FRCP; FRCPE; Deputy Secretary, Scottish Council for Postgraduate Medical Education, 1975–84; *b* 1 March 1917; *s* of late Archibald Forsyth MacFarlane and Jessie Robertson Goudie; *m* 1945, Mary Campbell Martin; three *s*. *Educ*: Hillhead High Sch., Glasgow; Glasgow Univ. MB, ChB, 1940; MD 1955; FRCPE 1964; MRCP 1970; FRCP 1979. Served War: commissioned RAMC, 1941; in Madagascar, India, Burma, 1941–45. Specialist in Medicine and Consultant Physician, 1948–; CO, British Mil. Hosp., Iserlohn, 1968–70; Prof. of Mil. Med., Royal Army Medical Coll., 1970–71; Consulting Physician, BAOR, 1971–73. Dir. of Army Medicine and Consulting Physician to the Army, 1973–74. QHP 1973. *Address*: 6 Redholm, Greenheads Road, North Berwick, East Lothian.

MACFARLANE, Robert Gwyn, CBE 1964; MD; FRCP; FRS 1956; retired; *b* 26 June 1907; *o c* of Robert Gray and Eileen Macfarlane; *m* 1936, Hilary, *o c* of H. A. H. and Maude Carson; four *s* one *d*. *Educ*: Highfield Sch., Liphook, Hants; Cheltenham Coll.; St Bartholomew's Hospital, London. MRCS, LRCP, 1933; MB, BS (London), 1933; MD (London), Gold Medal, 1938; MA (Oxford), 1948; FRCP 1960; FRCPS 1986. Sir Halley Stewart Research Fellow, 1935; Asst Clinical Pathologist, Postgrad. Medical School, London, 1936; Asst Bacteriologist, Wellcome Physiological Research Lab., 1939. Major, RAMC, 1944, attached Mobile Bacteriological Research Unit, Normandy and NW Europe. Director, Medical Research Council Blood Coagulation Research Unit, Churchill Hospital, Oxford, 1959–67; Professor of Clinical Pathology, Oxford Univ., 1964–67, now Emeritus (Reader in Haematology, 1957–64); Fellow, All Souls Coll., Oxford, 1963–70, now Quondam Fellow; Clinical Pathologist, Radcliffe Infirmary, Oxford, 1941–67. Pres., Haemophilia Soc., 1982– (Vice-Pres. 1955–82). Cameron Prize, Univ. of Edinburgh, 1968. *Publications*: (with R. Biggs) Human Blood Coagulation and its Disorders (3rd edn, 1962); Howard Florey: the Making of a Great Scientist, 1979; Alexander Fleming: the Man and the Myth, 1984; papers, chapters in books and

encyclopædias on haematological and pathological subjects. *Address*: Mallie's Cottage, Opinan, Laide, Ross-shire.

MACFARLANE, Maj.-Gen. William Thomson, CB 1981; Consultant/Administrator, Sion College, since 1984; *b* Bath, 2 Dec. 1925; *s* of late James and Agnes Macfarlane; *m* 1955, Dr Helen D. Meredith; one *d*. Commissioned Royal Signals, 1947. Served Europe, Near East, ME, and Far East. Commanded 16th Parachute Bde Signal Squadron, 1961–63; Military Asst, Commander FARELF, 1964–66; Comd 1st Div. HQ and Signal Regt, BAOR, 1967–70; Services Mem., Cabinet Office Secretariat, 1970–72; Comd, Corps Royal Signals, 1972–73; Dir of Public Relations (Army), MoD, 1973–75; C of S, UKLF, 1976–78; Chief, Jt Services Liaison Organisation, Bonn, 1978–80. Exec. Dir, Hong Kong Resort Co. Ltd, 1981–84. Col Comdt, Royal Corps of Signals, 1980–86. jssc; psc. FBIM. *Recreations*: golf, music. *Address*: Colts Paddock, Aveley Lane, Farnham, Surrey. *Club*: Naval and Military.

MacFARQUHAR, Sir Alexander, KBE 1952; CIE 1945; Director of Personnel, United Nations, 1962–67; *b* 6 Nov. 1903; *s* of Roderick MacFarquhar; *m* 1929, Berenice Whitburn; one *s*. *Educ*: Aberdeen Univ. (MA 1st class Hons Classics); Emmanuel Coll., Cambridge. Entered ICS 1926; Deputy Commissioner, Ferozepore, 1930; Deputy Commissioner, Amritsar, 1933; Settlement Officer, Amritsar, 1936; Deputy Secretary, Government of India, 1941; Deputy Director-General, Directorate-General of Supply, Government of India, 1943; Dir-Gen. Disposals, India, 1946; Commerce and Education Sec. Govt of Pakistan, 1947–51. Resident Rep. to Pakistan of UN Technical Assistance Board, 1952; Regional Rep. to Far East, of UN Technical Assistance Board, Bangkok, 1955; UN Secretary General's Special Adviser for Civilian Affairs in the Congo, 1960. Chm., Pakistan Soc., 1970–81. Hon. LLD Aberdeen, 1980. HQA, Pakistan, 1981. *Address*: Ottershaw, Beverley Lane, Coombe Hill, Kingston-upon-Thames, Surrey.

See also R. L. MacFarquhar.

MacFARQUHAR, Prof. Roderick Lemonde; Professor of Government, since 1984, Director of Fairbank Center for East Asian Research, since 1986, Harvard University; *b* 2 Dec. 1930; *s* of Sir Alexander MacFarquhar, qv; *m* 1964, Emily Jane Cohen; one *s* one *d*. *Educ*: Fettes Coll.; Oxford Univ. (BA); Harvard Univ. (AM); LSE (PhD). Specialist on China, Daily Telegraph (and later Sunday Telegraph), 1955–61; Founding Editor, China Quarterly, 1959–68; Rockefeller Grantee, 1962; Reporter, BBC TV programme Panorama, 1963–64. Associate Fellow, St Antony's Coll., Oxford, 1965–68. Mem., Editorial Bd, New Statesman, 1965–69; Ford Foundation Grant, 1968; Senior Research Fellow, Columbia Univ., 1969; Senior Research Fellow, RIIA, 1971–74 (Mem. Council, 1978–83); Co-presenter, BBC Gen. Overseas Services 24 Hours prog., 1972–74, 1979–80. Governor, SOAS, 1978–83. Contested: (Lab) Ealing South, 1966; (Lab) Meriden, March 1968; (SDP) Derbys S, 1983. MP (Lab) Belper, Feb. 1974–1979; PPS to Minister of State, FCO, March 1974; resignation accepted, April 1975; reappointed June 1975; PPS to Sec. of State, DHSS, 1976–78. Member: N Atlantic Assembly, 1974–79; Select Cttee for Sci. and Technology, 1976–79; Trilateral Commn, 1976–(Mem. Exec. Cttee, 1976–84); Exec. Cttee, Fabian Soc., 1976–80. Leverhulme Res. Fellow, 1980–83; Fellow, Woodrow Wilson Center, Smithsonian Instn, 1980–81; Vis. Prof. of Govt, Harvard, 1982; Vis. Fellow, St Antony's Coll., Oxford, 1983. *Publications*: The Hundred Flowers, 1960; The Sino-Soviet Dispute, 1961; Chinese Ambitions and British Policy (Fabian Pamphlet), 1966; Sino-American Relations, 1949–71, 1972; The Forbidden City, 1972; The Origins of the Cultural Revolution: Vol. 1, Contradictions among the People 1956–1957, 1974; Vol. 2, The Great Leap Forward 1958–1960, 1983; (ed) China under Mao, 1966; articles in Foreign Affairs, The World Today, Atlantic Monthly, Pacific Affairs, Commentary, etc. *Recreations*: reading, listening to music, travel. *Address*: Fairbank Center, 1737 Cambridge Street, Cambridge, Mass 02138, USA.

MacFEELY, Most Rev. Anthony C.; *b* 4 Feb. 1909. *Educ*: St Columb's Coll., Londonderry; St Patrick's Coll., Maynooth; Irish Coll., Rome. Priest, 1932; Prof., St Columb's Coll., Oct. 1934; Pres., St Columb's Coll., 1950; Parish Priest, Strabane, Co. Tyrone, 1959–65; Bishop of Raphoe, 1965–82. *Recreation*: walking. *Address*: Fernbank, Glebe, Letterkenny, Co. Donegal, Ireland. *T*: Letterkenny 074–21422.

McFEELY, Elizabeth Sarah Anne C.; *see* Craig McFeely.

McFETRICH, Cecil, OBE 1950; Director, Sunderland and Shields Building Society, 1964–86; Partner, C. & K. M. McFetrich, since 1977; *b* 17 Jan. 1911; *y s* of Archibald B. and Hannah B. McFetrich; *m* 1937, Kathleen M. Proom; four *s*. *Educ*: Cowan Terrace Sch., Sunderland; Skerry's Coll., Newcastle upon Tyne. Qual. Chartered Accountant, 1933. After varied industrial and professional experience, joined Bartram & Sons Ltd, South Dock, Sunderland, as Sec., 1936; apptd a Dir, 1939; responsible for sales and marketing, 1945, Man. Dir, 1964–72; Jt Man. Dir, Austin & Pickersgill Ltd, 1968–69, Man. Dir 1969–72, Dep. Chm. and Chm., 1972–75; Founder Dir, A. & P. Appledore Internat. Ltd, 1970–74. Man. Dir, Ward & Davidson Ltd, 1946–75 (Chm. 1975–79); Chm., Sunderland Structural Steel Ltd, 1947–79. Mem., Sunderland Town Council, 1942–51 (Chm. Finance Cttee, 1943–44); Mem., River Wear Commn, 1943–45, 1969–72; served on various Nat. Savings Cttees, 1940–63; Chairman: Sunderland Savings Cttee, 1947–63; N Regional Industrial Savings Cttee, 1956–62. Life Governor, Nat. Children's Home, 1953–81 (Mem., Order of St Christopher, 1982); Pres., Bishopwearmouth Choral Soc., Sunderland, 1962–65. Liveryman, Worshipful Co. of Shipwrights. Freeman by redemption, City of London. Lord Mayor of London's Gold Medal for Export Achievement, 1963. *Recreations*: local history, antiques (especially maps and Sunderland pottery), champagne. *Address*: 8 Belle Vue Drive, Sunderland, Tyne and Wear. *T*: Sunderland 226449. *Clubs*: MCC; Sunderland (Sunderland).

McGAHERN, John, FRSL; author; *b* 12 Nov. 1934; *s* of Francis McGahern and Susan McManus; *m* 1973, Madeline Green. Research Fellow, Univ. of Reading, 1968–71; O'Connor Prof., Colgate Univ., 1969, 1972, 1977, 1979 and 1983. Member: Aosdana Irish Acad of Letters. British Northern Arts Fellow, 1974–76. AE Meml Award, 1962; McCauley Fellowship, 1964; British Arts Council Award, 1967; Soc. of Authors Award, 1975; Amer. Irish Foundn Literary Award, 1985. *Publications*: The Barracks, 1963; The Dark, 1965; Nightlines, 1970; The Leavetaking, 1975; Getting Through, 1978; The Pornographer, 1979; High Ground, 1985. *Address*: c/o Faber & Faber, 3 Queen Square, WC1N 3AU.

McGARRITY, J(ames) Forsyth, CB 1981; MA, MEd, BSc; HM Senior Chief Inspector of Schools (Scotland), 1973–81; *b* 16 April 1921; *s* of late James McGarrity and Margaret Davidson; *m* 1951, Violet S. G. Philp, MA; one *s* one *d*. *Educ*: Bathgate Academy; Glasgow Univ. Schoolmaster, 1949–57; HM Inspector of Schools, 1957–68; HM Chief Inspector of Schools, 1968–73. *Recreations*: golf, gardening. *Address*: 30 Oatlands Park, Linlithgow, Scotland EH49 6AS. *T*: Linlithgow 843258.

McGARVEY, Alan; Chief Executive, Greater London Enterprise Board, 1982–86; *b* 22 June 1942; *s* of William Johnson McGarvey and Rosina McGarvey; *m* 1967, Eileen Cook. *Educ*: Wallsend Grammar Sch.; Coll. of Further Educn; Newcastle Univ. (BSc); Cranfield Sch. of Management (MBA). C. A. Parsons, 1958–64 (apprentice); RTZ, 1968–71; Decca

Gp, 1972–76; MK Electric, 1976–78; Director, Small Company Div., NEB, 1978–82. Labour Party, 1974–; Mem., Wandsworth Borough Council, 1981–86 (Dep. Opposition Leader, 1982–83); Chm., Battersea Constituency Labour Parties, 1978–82. Exec. Mem., Wandsworth CRC, 1973–82; Dir. Battersea Arts Centre Trust, 1982–. Mem., Management Board, Centre for Industrial Development (EEC-ACP Lomé). Governor, Polytech. of South Bank, 1985–. *Recreations:* politics and community affairs, home and garden, science fiction. *Address:* 51 Longbeach Road, SW11 5SS. *T:* 01-228 0230.

McGEE, Prof. James Dwyer, OBE 1952; FRS 1966; MSc Sydney; PhD, ScD, Cantab; CEng; FIEE; FInstP; FRAS; Hon. ARCS; Professor of Applied Physics, 1954–71, now Emeritus, Senior Research Fellow, 1971–80, and Fellow, 1977, Imperial College of Science and Technology, University of London; *b* Canberra, ACT, 17 Dec. 1903; *s* of Francis and Mary McGee; *m* 1944, Hilda Mary, *d* of George Winstone, Takapuna, Auckland, NZ; no *c. Educ:* St Patrick's Coll., Goulburn, NSW; St John's Coll., Sydney Univ. (MSc); Clare Coll., Cambridge (PhD). 1851 Exhibition Scholar from Sydney Univ. to Cambridge. Nuclear physics research, Cavendish Laboratory, Cambridge, 1928–31; Research physicist, Electric and Musical Industries Research Laboratories, Hayes, Middx. Engaged on research on photo-electricity and electronic problems of Television, 1932–39; research on electronic problems in connection with military operations, in particular the use of infra-red light, 1939–45; returned to work on photo-electronic devices for television and other scientific purposes, 1945–54. Rutherford Meml Lecturer, New Zealand, 1982. Awarded Research Fellowship, Carnegie Inst., Washington, 1960; Hon. Research Associate, Carnegie Inst., 1960, 1962, 1966. Hon. Life Mem. IREE(Aust.), 1939. Hon. DSc Salford, 1972; Hon. DTech Brunel, 1978. Awarded prize of Worshipful Company of Instrument Makers, 1968; Callendar Medal, Inst. of Measurement and Control, for contribs to opto-electronics, 1975. *Publications:* chap. on Electronic Generation of Television Signals in Electronics (ed B. Lovell), 1947; ed Vols XII, XVI, XXII, XXVIII, XXXIII, Advances in Electronics: Symposia on Photoelectronic Devices, 1960, 1962, 1966, 1969, 1972; technical papers in Engineering, Physical and Technical Jls. *Recreations:* gardening, music. *Address:* 3E/10 Hilltop Crescent, Fairlight, NSW 2094, Australia. *T:* 949 3723. *Club:* Athenæum.

McGEE, Prof. James O'Donnell; Professor of Morbid Anatomy, University of Oxford, Fellow of Linacre College, Oxford, since Oct. 1975; *b* 27 July 1939; *s* of Michael and Bridget McGee; *m* 1961, Anne Lee; one *s* two *d. Educ:* Univ. of Glasgow. MB, ChB, PhD, MD; MA (Oxon). FRCPath 1986. Various appts in Univ. Dept of Pathology, Royal Infirmary, Glasgow, 1962–69; Roche Inst. of Molecular Biology, Nutley, NJ: MRC Fellow 1969–70; Vis. Scientist 1970–71; Dept of Pathology, Royal Infirmary, Glasgow: Lectr 1971–74; Sen. Lectr, 1974–75. Mem., Scientific Cttee, Cancer Res. Campaign, 1978–. Kettle Meml Lectr, RCPath, 1980; Annual Guest Lecturer: Royal Coll. of Physicians, Ireland, 1986; Royal Acad. of Medicine (Ireland), 1985. Bellahouston Gold Medal, Glasgow Univ., 1973. *Publications:* Biopsy Pathology of Liver, 1980, 2nd edn, 1986; papers in scientific jls on liver disease and non-istopic methods of gene detection. *Recreations:* squash, swimming. *Address:* Nuffield Department of Pathology, Level 1, John Radcliffe Hospital, Headington, Oxford OX3 9DU.

McGEOCH, Vice-Adm. Sir Ian (Lachlan Mackay), KCB 1969 (CB 1966); DSO 1943; DSC 1943; Chairman, Midar (Marine Systems) Ltd; *b* 26 March 1914; 3rd *s* of L. A. McGeoch of Dalmuir; *m* 1937, Eleanor Somers, *d* of Rev. Canon Hugh Farrie; two *s* two *d. Educ:* Pangbourne Coll. Joined RN, 1932. Comd HM Submarine Splendid, 1942–43; Staff Officer (Ops) 4th Cruiser Sqdn, 1944–45; Comd: HMS Fernie, 1946–47; 4th Submarine Squadron, 1949–51; 3rd Submarine Squadron, 1956–57; Dir of Undersurface Warfare, Admiralty, 1959; IDC 1961; Comd HMS Lion 1962–64; Admiral Pres., RNC, Greenwich, 1964–65; Flag Officer Submarines, 1966–67; Flag Officer, Scotland and Northern Ireland, 1968–70. Trustee, Imperial War Museum, 1977–. Pres., RNVR Club (Scotland), 1981–. Mem., The Queen's Body Guard for Scotland, Royal Co. of Archers, 1969–. MPhil Edinburgh, 1975. *Publications:* (jtly) The Third World War: a future history, 1978; The Third World War: the untold story, 1982. *Recreations:* sailing, music. *Address:* Southerns, Castle Hedingham, Essex. *Clubs:* Army and Navy; Royal Yacht Squadron, Royal Naval Sailing Association (Cdre 1968–70), Royal Cruising, Royal Northern and Clyde Yacht.

McGEOUGH, Prof. Joseph Anthony, CEng, FIMechE, FIProdE, MIM; Regius Professor of Engineering and Head of Department of Mechanical Engineering at University of Edinburgh, since 1983; Director, Transfer Technology Ltd, since 1985; *b* 29 May 1940; *s* of late Patrick Joseph McGeough and Gertrude (*née* Darroch); *m* 1972, Brenda Nicholson; two *s* one *d. Educ:* St Michael's Coll., Irvine; Glasgow Univ. (BSc, PhD); Aberdeen Univ. (DSc). Vacation-apprentice, Malcolm & Allan Ltd, at ICI Ardeer, 1957–61; Research Demonstrator, Leicester Univ., 1966; Sen. Res. Fellow, Queensland Univ., 1967; Res. Metallurgist, International Research & Development Co. Ltd, Newcastle upon Tyne, 1968–69; Sen. Res. Fellow, Strathclyde Univ., 1969–72; Lectr 1972–77, Sen. Lectr 1977–80, Reader 1980–83, Dept of Engineering, Aberdeen Univ. Member, IProdE working party on manufacturing information systems, 1984–86. Chm., Dyce Academy College Council, 1980–83; Hon. Vice-Pres., Aberdeen Univ. Athletic Assoc., 1981–87. *Publications:* Principles of Electrochemical Machining, 1974; papers mainly in Journals of: Mech. Engrg Science, Inst. of Mathematics and its Applications, Applied Electrochemistry; various patents. *Recreations:* gardening, golf, athletics. *Address:* 39 Dreghorn Loan, Colinton, Edinburgh EH13 0DF. *T:* 031–441 1302.

McGEOWN, Dr Mary Graham, (Mrs J. M. Freeland), CBE 1985; FRCP, FRCPE, FRCPI; Consultant Nephrologist, since 1962; *b* 19 July 1923; *d* of James Edward McGeown and Sarah Graham Quinn; *m* 1949, Joseph Maxwell Freeland (*d* 1982); three *s. Educ:* Lurgan College; Queen's University of Belfast (MB, BCh, BAO, with hons, 1946; MD, PhD). House Physician and Surgeon, Royal Victoria Hosp., Belfast, 1947–48; Sen. House Physician, Royal Belfast Hosp. for Sick Children, 1948; Asst Lectr in Pathology, 1948–50, in Biochemistry, 1950–53, QUB; res. grant, MRC, 1953–56; Res. Fellow, Royal Victoria Hosp., 1956–58; Belfast City Hospital: Sen. Hosp. MO, 1958–62; Consultant Nephrologist, 1962–; Physician in Admin. Charge, Renal Unit, 1968–. Hon. Reader in Nephrology, QUB, 1972–. Chm., UK Transplant Management Cttee, 1983–; Hon. Treas., Renal Assoc., 1986– (Pres., 1983–86); Pres., Ulster Med. Soc., 1985–86. Chm., Corrigan Club, 1987. Graves Lectr, Royal Acad. of Medicine, Ireland, 1963. Hon. DSc New Univ. of Ulster, 1983. *Publications:* Clinical Management of Electrolyte Disorders, 1983; numerous papers and chapters in books on calcium metabolism, renal stones, phosphate metabolism, parathyroid function and disease, renal transplantation, kidney diseases. *Recreations:* gardening, antique collecting, genealogy. *Address:* 14 Osborne Gardens, Belfast BT9 6LE. *T:* Belfast 669918. *Club:* Royal Commonwealth Society.

McGHEE, George Crews, Legion of Merit; businessman; former diplomat; Director: Mobil Oil Co., since 1969; Procter and Gamble Co., since 1969; American Security & Trust Co., since 1969; Trans World Airlines, since 1976; *b* Waco, Texas, 10 March 1912; *s* of George Summers McGhee and Magnolia (*née* Spruce); *m* 1938, Cecilia Jeanne DeGolyer; two *s* four *d. Educ:* Southern Methodist Univ., Dallas; Univ. of Oklahoma; Oxford Univ. (Rhodes Schol.); Univ. of London. BS (Oklahoma) 1933; DPhil (Oxon) 1937. Served with US Navy, 1943–45 (Asiatic ribbon with three battle stars). Geologist and geophysicist, 1930–40; Oil producer, sole owner, McGhee Production Co., 1940–. Special Asst to Under-Sec of State for Economic Affairs, 1946; Coordinator for Aid to Greece and Turkey, 1947; Asst Sec. of State for Near Eastern, South Asian and African Affairs, 1949; US Ambassador to Turkey, 1951; Consultant, Nat. Security Council, 1958; Mem. President's Cttee to Study Mil. Asst Program, 1958; Counselor of Dept of State and Chm. of State Dept Policy Planning Council, 1961; Under-Sec. of State for Political Affairs, 1961; Bd, Panama Canal Co., 1962; US Ambassador to the Federal Republic of Germany, 1963–68; Ambassador-at-Large, 1968–69. Chairman: English Speaking Union of US, 1969–74; Business Council for Internat. Understanding, 1969–73; Vice-Chm., Inst. for Study of Diplomacy, 1978–; Member Board: Geo. Cttee, Marshall Res. Fund, 1972–; Amer. Council on Germany, 1969–; Resources for Future, 1977–; Asia Foundn, 1974–; Atlantic Council, 1977–; Atlantic Inst. for Internat. Affairs, 1977–; Smithsonian Nat. Associates, 1971– (Chm., 1975–76); Population Crisis Cttee, 1969–; Council of Amer. Ambassadors, 1983–; Amer. Inst. for Contemp. German Studies, 1983–. Member: Inst. of Turkish Studies, 1983–; Sackler Gall. Vis. Cttee, Smithsonian Instn. Trustee: Duke Univ.; Cttee for Economic Develt, 1957–; Aspen Inst. for Humanistic Studies, 1958–; Salzburg Seminar, 1969–; Internat. Civil Service League, 1969–; Folger Library Council, 1983–85. Chm., Saturday Review World, 1974–77. Hon. Fellow, Queen's Coll., Oxford, 1969. Distinguished Service Citation, Univ. of Oklahoma, 1952; Hon. DCL, Southern Methodist Univ., 1953; Hon. LLD: Tulane Univ., 1957; Univ. of Maryland, 1965; Hon. DSc, Univ. of Tampa, 1969. Ouissam Alaouite Cherifien, Govt Morocco, 1950; Hon. Citizen, Ankara, Turkey, 1954; Outstanding Citizen Award, Amer. Friends of Turkey, 1983. *Publications:* Envoy to the Middle World, 1983; contribs to Foreign Affairs, Gewerkschaftliche Rundschau, Werk und Wir, Europa Archiv, Universitas, Ruperto-Carola Weltraumfahrt-Raketentechnik, Europa, Washington Post, New York Times, etc. *Recreations:* hunting, tennis, photography. *Address:* 2808 N Street, NW, Washington, DC 20007, USA; Farmers' Delight, Middleburg, Va, USA. *Clubs:* Bohemian (California); Metropolitan, Cosmos, City Tavern Association (Washington, DC); Brook, Century Association (New York).

McGHIE, James Ironside, CMG 1973; HM Diplomatic Service, retired; *b* 12 Oct. 1915; *s* of William I. McGhie and Annie E. Ratcliffe; *m* 1946, Ellen-Johanne Gran, *d* of Maj. T. Gran, MC, Norway, and Ingeborg Gran (*née* Meinich); two *s* one *d. Educ:* King Henry VIII Sch., Coventry. Journalist, 1933–39. Army, 1940–46, attached Royal Norwegian Army, 1943–46. Entered Foreign Service, 1946; served: Stockholm, Helsinki, FO, Tokyo, FO, Singapore; Dir, British Information Services, Saigon; Head of Chancery, Bucharest; Consul-General, Seattle; Counsellor, Commercial, Stockholm; Minister (Commercial and Econ.), Tokyo; retired, 1975. Special Advr on Japanese market to BOTB, 1975–77; Co-Chm., Japan Task Force, 1976–77. Order of the Rising Sun (Japan) 3rd class, 1975. *Recreations:* Scandinavian studies and translations. *Address:* Poplars, South Street, Faversham, Kent ME13 9NS. *T:* Canterbury 751424.

McGHIE, James Marshall; QC (Scot.) 1983; *b* 15 Oct. 1944; *s* of James Drummond McGhie and Jessie Eadie Bennie; *m* 1968, Ann Manuel Cockburn; one *s* one *d. Educ:* Perth Acad.; Edinburgh Univ. (LLB Hons). Called to the Scottish Bar, 1969; Advocate-depute, 1983–86. *Recreations:* dining and Dunning. *Address:* 3 Lauder Road, Edinburgh EH9 2EW. *T:* 031–667 8325.

MacGIBBON, Dr Barbara Haig, (Mrs John Roberts), FRCPath; Senior Principal Medical Officer, Department of Health and Social Security, since 1983; *b* 7 Feb. 1928; *d* of Ronald Ross MacGibbon and Margaret Fraser; *m* 1954, John Roberts; one *s* one *d. Educ:* Lady Margaret Hall, Oxford; University College Hosp. Registrar, then Res. Assistant, Dept of Haematology, Royal Postgraduate Med. Sch., 1957–64; Sen. Registrar, Sen. Lectr/Hon. Consultant, then Sen. Res. Fellow, Dept of Haematology, St Thomas' Hosp. Med. Sch., 1969–79; SMO, then PMO, Toxicology and Environmental Protection, DHSS, 1979. *Publications:* articles in various med. jls. *Address:* Medical TEP Division, Department of Health and Social Security, Hannibal House, Elephant and Castle, SE1 6TE.

McGILL, Maj.-Gen. Allan, CB 1969; CBE 1964 (OBE 1945; MBE 1943); Director of Electrical and Mechanical Engineering (Army), 1966–69; *b* 28 June 1914; *s* of William McGill; *m* 1945, Kathleen German. *Educ:* George Heriot's, Edinburgh; Heriot-Watt Coll. (now Heriot-Watt Univ.). Served War of 1939–45 (despatches, 1943). Dir, Electrical and Mechanical Engineering, British Army of the Rhine, 1965–66. Brig., 1961; Maj.-Gen., 1966. Col Comdt, REME, 1969–74. CEng, MIMechE. *Recreations:* motor rallying, skiing. *Address:* Tudor House, Vicarage Gardens, Bray, Berks SL6 2AE. *Club:* Army and Navy.

MacGILL, George Roy Buchanan, CBE 1965; General Manager, Cumbernauld Development Corporation, 1956–70; Deputy Chairman, Scottish Special Housing Association, 1971–76; *b* 20 Dec. 1905; *s* of George Buchanan MacGill; *m* 1934, Jean Ferguson Anderson; two *d. Educ:* Glasgow High Sch. Chartered Accountant, 1928. FIMTA 1938. Town Chamberlain, Airdrie, 1932; Burgh Chamberlain, Dunfermline, 1947. *Recreations:* golf, music. *Address:* 28 Roman Court, Bearsden, Glasgow.

McGILL, Maj.-Gen. Nigel Harry Duncan, CB 1966; Chief of Staff to Commandant-General, Royal Marines, 1967–68, retired, 1968; *b* 15 Oct. 1916; *s* of Lt-Col H. R. McGill; *m* 1944, Margaret Constance Killen; two *s* one *d. Educ:* Victoria Coll., Jersey. Commissioned 2nd Lt RM 1934; Maj.-Gen. 1964; Comdr, Portsmouth Group, RM, 1964–67. Representative Col Comdt RM, 1977–78. Exec., Rolls Royce Ltd, 1968–78. *Recreations:* cricket, golf. *Address:* Alderwood, Manor Farm Road, Fordingbridge, Hants.

McGILL, Rt. Rev. Stephen; *see* Paisley, Bishop of, (RC).

McGILLIGAN, Denis Brian; Assistant Solicitor, Ministry of Agriculture, Fisheries and Food, 1973–83; *b* 26 June 1921; *s* of Michael McGilligan, SC, and Mary Georgina McGilligan (*née* Musgrave); *m* 1952, Hazel Patricia Pakenham Keady; one *s* two *d. Educ:* St Gerard's, Bray, Co. Wicklow; Trinity Coll., Dublin (BA). Practised at Irish Bar, 1945–52; Crown Counsel, Sarawak, and Dep. Legal Adviser, Brunei, 1952–58; Senior Magistrate, Sarawak, 1958–59; Acting Puisne Judge, Combined Judiciary, 1959–60; Senior Magistrate, Sarawak, 1960–63; Puisne Judge, Combined Judiciary of Sarawak, North Borneo and Brunei, March, 1963; Judge of the High Court in Borneo, Malaysia, 1963–66. Called to the Bar, Gray's Inn, 1966. *Recreations:* golf, swimming, walking, reading. *Address:* Wychbury, Ringmore Drive, Bigbury on Sea, Devon TQ7 4AU. *T:* Bigbury 810604.

MacGILLIVRAY, Barron Bruce, FRCP; Consultant in Clinical Neurophysiology and Neurology, since 1964, and Dean, School of Medicine, since 1975, Royal Free Hospital; Consultant in Clinical Neurophysiology, National Hospital for Nervous Diseases, since 1971; *b* 21 Aug. 1927; *s* of late John MacGillivray and of Doreene (*née* Eastwood), S Africa; *m* 1955, Ruth Valentine; two *s* one *d. Educ:* King Edward VII Sch., Johannesburg; Univ. of Witwatersrand (BSc Hons 1949); Univ. of Manchester; Univ. of London (MB, BS 1962). FRCP 1973. House Surg., House Phys., Manchester Royal Infirm., 1955–56; RMO, Stockport and Stepping Hill Hosp., 1957–59; Registrar, subseq. Sen. Registrar,

Nat. Hosp. for Nervous Diseases, Queen Sq., London, 1959–64; Res. Fellow, UCLA, 1964–65; Cons., Clin. Neurophysiol., Nat. Hosp. for Nervous Diseases, 1971. Member: NE Thames Regional Health Authority; Senate, Collegiate Council, Univ. of London; Univ. rep., Council, Sch. of Pharmacy and British Postgraduate Med. Fedn; Examr and Teacher, Univ. of London. Pres., Electrophys. Technicians Assoc., 1976–82. FRSocMed. *Publications:* papers in sci. jls on cerebral electrophysiol., epilepsy, computing and cerebral death. *Recreations:* PPL, photography, D-I-Y. *Address:* Rosslyn Tower, 18 St John's Avenue, Putney, SW15 2AA. *T:* 01–788 5213.

MacGILLIVRAY, Prof. Ian, MD, FRCP; FRCOG; Regius Professor of Obstetrics and Gynæcology, University of Aberdeen, 1965–84 (Dean of Medical Faculty, 1976–79), now Emeritus Professor; *b* 25 Oct. 1920; *yr s* of W. and A. MacGillivray; *m* 1950, Edith Mary Margaret Cook; one *s* twin *d*. *Educ:* Vale of Leven Academy, Alexandria; University of Glasgow (MB, ChB 1944; MD 1953); MRCOG 1949, FRCOG 1959; FRCPGlas 1973. Gardiner Research Schol., 1949–51, Lectr in Midwifery, 1951–53, Univ. of Glasgow; Senior Lecturer: in Obstetrics and Gynæcology, Univ. of Bristol, 1953–55; in Midwifery and Gynæcology, Univ. of Aberdeen, 1955–61; Prof. of Obstetrics and Gynæcology, University of London, at St Mary's Hospital Medical Sch., 1961–65. Mem., GMC, 1979–84. Founder Pres., Internat. Soc. for Study of Hypertension in Pregnancy, 1976–80; Pres., Internat. Soc. for Twin Studies, 1980–83; Mem. Council, RCOG, 1974–80. *Publications:* Outline of Human Reproduction, 1963; Combined Textbook of Obstetrics and Gynaecology, 1976; Human Multiple Reproduction, 1976; Pre-eclampsia: the hypertensive disease of pregnancy, 1983; contrib. to: British Medical Journal, Lancet, Journal of Obstetrics and Gynæcology of the British Empire; Clinical Science. *Address:* Errogie, 35A Coombe Lane, Westbury-on-Trym, Bristol BS9 2LD. *T:* Bristol 686218.

McGILVRAY, James William; Director, Fraser of Allander Institute, University of Strathclyde, since 1980; *b* 21 Feb. 1938; *m* 1966, Alison Ann Wingfield; one *s* one *d*. *Educ:* St Columba's Coll., Dublin; Univ. of Edinburgh (MA); Trinity Coll., Dublin (MLitt). Lectr in Econs, TCD, 1962–69; Res. Fellow, Harvard Univ., 1969–70; Sen. Lectr, Univ. of Stirling, 1970–75; Res. Prof., Univ. of Strathclyde, 1975–80. *Publications:* Irish Economic Statistics, 1968, 2nd edn 1983; Use and Interpretation of Medical Statistics (with G. J. Bourke), 1969, 3rd edn 1985; articles in Econometrica, Economic Jl, Rev. of Econs and Statistics, Jl of Reg. Sci., etc. *Recreations:* squash, gardening. *Address:* Gartinstarry Lodge, Buchlyvie, Stirling FK8 3PD. *Club:* Fitzwilliam (Dublin)

MacGINNIS, Francis Robert, CMG 1979; HM Diplomatic Service, retired; Minister and Deputy Commandant, British Military Government, Berlin, 1977–83; *b* 6 March 1924; *s* of late Dr Patrick MacGinnis, Murray House, Chesterfield; *m* 1955, Carolyn, *d* of late Col D. W. McEnery, USA; three *s* two *d*. *Educ:* Stonyhurst; Merton Coll., Oxford (MA). Served with Rifle Bde, 1942–47 (Temp. Captain). Joined HM Foreign (subseq. Diplomatic) Service, 1949; served in London, Washington, Paris and Warsaw; Dir-Gen., British Information Services, New York, 1968–72; Counsellor, Bonn, 1972–76; RCDS, 1976. *Address:* Boîte Postale 47, Fayence 83440, Var, France. *Club:* Travellers'.

McGIRR, Prof. Edward McCombie, CBE 1978; BSc, MD Glasgow; FRCP, FRCPE, FRCPGlas; FACP (Hon.); FFCM; FRSE; Dean, 1974–81, Administrative Dean, 1978–81, and Professor of Administrative Medicine, 1978–81 now Professor Emeritus, Faculty of Medicine, University of Glasgow; Physician, Glasgow Royal Infirmary, 1952–81; Honorary Consultant Physician to the Army in Scotland, 1975–81; *b* 15 June 1916; *yr s* of William and Ann McGirr, Hamilton, Lanarkshire; *m* 1949, Diane Curzon, *y c* of Alexander Woods, MBE, TD, DL, and Edith E. C. Woods, Birmingham and London; one *s* three *d*. *Educ:* Hamilton Academy; Glasgow Univ. BSc 1937; MB, ChB (Hons) Glasgow, 1940; MD (Hons) and Bellahouston Medal, 1960. Served RAMC, 1941–46, in UK, India, Burma, Siam, Indo-China; Medical Specialist; demobilized with hon. rank of Major. Glasgow University: various appointments incl. Lectr and Sen. Lectr in Medicine, at Royal Infirmary, Glasgow, 1947–61; Muirhead Prof. of Medicine, 1961–78. Visitor, Royal Coll. of Physicians and Surgeons of Glasgow, 1968–70, President 1970–72. Member: Medical Appeals Tribunals, 1961–; Nat. Radiological Protection Bd, 1976–83; Scottish Health Service Planning Council, 1977–84 (Chm., 1978–84); Nat. Med. Consultative Cttee, 1977–81; Med. Sub-Cttee, UGC, 1977–81; GNC for Scotland, 1978–83; Greater Glasgow Health Bd, 1979–85; Nat. Bd for Nursing, Midwifery and Health Visiting for Scotland, 1980–83; BBC/IBA Scottish Appeals Adv. Cttee, 1982–; Chairman: Scottish Council for Postgrad. Med. Educn, 1979–85; Scottish Council for Opportunities for Play Experience, 1985–; Professional Adv. Panel, Prince and Princess of Wales Hospice, 1985–. Member: Assoc. of Physicians of Gt Britain and Ireland (mem. of editorial panel, Quarterly Journal of Medicine, 1968–76; Mem. Council, 1972–76); Scottish Soc. of Physicians; Scottish Soc. for Experimental Med. (Treas., 1960–66); Pres., Harveian Soc. of Edin., 1979; Corresp. Member: Amer. Thyroid Assoc.; Medical Research Soc. (mem. of council, 1967–69); Royal Medico-Chirurgical Soc. of Glasgow (Pres., 1965–66). *Publications:* chiefly in relation to thyroid gland dysfunction, nuclear medicine, medical education and policy planning in the NHS. *Recreations:* family life, curling. *Address:* Anchorage House, Bothwell, by Glasgow G71 8NF. *T:* Bothwell 852194. *Club:* Royal Scottish Automobile.

McGLASHAN, John Reid Curtis, CBE 1974; HM Diplomatic Service, retired 1979; *b* 12 Dec. 1921; *s* of late John Adamson McGlashan and Emma Rose May McGlashan; *m* 1947, Dilys Bagnall (*née* Buxton Knight); one *s* two *d*. *Educ:* Fettes; Christ Church, Oxford (Rugger Blue, 1945). RAF (Bomber Command), 1940–45 (POW, 1941–45). Entered Foreign Service, 1953; Baghdad, 1955; Tripoli, 1963; Madrid, 1968; Counsellor, FCO, 1970–79. *Recreations:* gardening, golf, reading, tennis. *Address:* Allendale, Selsey Bill, West Sussex PO20 9DB. *Club:* Vincent's (Oxford).

MacGLASHAN, Maureen Elizabeth; Assistant Director, Research Centre for International Law, Cambridge University, since 1986; *b* 7 Jan. 1938; *d* of Kenneth and Elizabeth MacGlashan. *Educ:* Luton High Sch.; Girton Coll., Cambridge (MA, LLB). Joined FO, 1961; 2nd Sec., Tel Aviv, 1964–67; FCO, 1967–72; Head of Chancery, East Berlin, 1973–75; UK Representation to EEC, 1975–77; seconded to Home Civil Service, 1977–82; Counsellor, Bucharest, 1982–86. *Address:* Research Centre for International Law, 5 Cranmer Road, Cambridge CB3 9BL.

McGLASHAN, Prof. Maxwell Len, FRSC; Professor of Chemistry and Head of the Department of Chemistry, University College London, since 1974; *b* 1 April 1924; *s* of late Leonard Day McGlashan and late Margaret Cordelia McGlashan; *m* 1947, Susan Jane, *d* of late Col H. E. Crosse, MC, OBE, and late Mrs D. Crosse, Patoka Station, Hawkes Bay, NZ. *Educ:* Greymouth, NZ; Canterbury Univ. Coll., Christchurch, NZ; Univ. of Reading. MSc (NZ) 1946, PhD (Reading) 1951, DSc (Reading) 1962. Asst Lectr, 1946–48, Lectr, 1948–53, Sen. Lectr, 1953, in Chemistry, at Canterbury Univ. Coll., Christchurch, NZ. Sims Empire Scholar, 1949–52; Lectr in Chem., Univ. of Reading, 1954–61; Reader in Chem., Univ. of Reading, 1962–64; Prof. of Physical Chem., Univ. of Exeter, 1964–74 (Dean, Faculty of Science, 1973–74). Mem., 1963–65, Vice-Chm., 1965–67, Chm., 1967–71, Commn on Physicochemical Symbols, Terminology, and Units. Chm., Interdivl Cttee on Nomenclature and Symbols, Internat. Union of Pure and Applied Chem., 1971–76; Member: Royal Society Symbols Cttee, 1963–; BSI's Tech. Cttee on physical quantities and units, 1963– (Chm., 1978–); Council, Faraday Soc., 1965–67; Metrication Bd, 1969–80; Comité Consultatif des Unités (Metre Convention), 1969–; Council, Chem. Soc., 1970–73; SRC Chem. Cttee, 1974–76; Data Compilation Cttee, 1974–77; Res. Cttee, British Gas Corp., 1979–; Trustee, Ramsay Meml Fellowships Trust, 1982– (Chm. Adv. Council, 1975–). Editor, Jl of Chemical Thermodynamics, 1969–. *Publications:* Physicochemical Quantities and Units, 1968 (Royal Inst. of Chem.), 2nd edn, 1971; Chemical Thermodynamics, 1979; papers on chemical thermodynamics and statistical mechanics in Proc. Roy. Soc., Trans Faraday Soc., Jl Chem. Thermodynamics, etc. *Recreations:* climbing in the Alps, the theatre. *Address:* 9 Camden Square, NW1 9UY. *T:* 01–267 1583; Department of Chemistry, University College London, 20 Gordon Street, WC1H 0AJ. *T:* 01–387 7050. *Club:* Athenæum.

McGONAGLE, Stephen; Senator, Seanad Éireann, Dublin, since 1983; *b* 17 Nov. 1914; *m*; five *s* one *d*. *Educ:* Christian Brothers', Derry. Chairman, NI Cttee, Irish Congress of Trade Unions, 1959; Vice-Chm., Derry Develt Commn, 1969–71; Pres., Irish Congress of Trade Unions, 1972–73; Mem., NI Economic Council, Indust. Tribunal, Indust. Ct, until 1973; Dist Sec., Irish Transport and General Workers' Union, Dec. 1973; NI Parly Comr For Admin, and Comr for Complaints, 1974–79; Chm., NI Police Complaints Bd, 1977–83. *Recreations:* fishing, boating, reading. *Address:* 10 Kingsfort Park, Derry.

MACGOUGAN, John; Member, Central Arbitration Committee, 1977–83; *b* 21 Aug. 1913; *m* 1941, Lizzie Faulkner; three *s* one *d*. *Educ:* various Northern Ireland Schs; Technical Sch.; Correspondence courses. Accountancy profession, 1930–45. Irish Officer, NUTGW, in charge of all Irish affairs, 1945–69; Gen. Sec., NUTGW, 1969–79. Contested (Irish Labour) N Ireland Parly Elections, Oldpark 1938, Falls Div. 1951; Westminster Parly Election, South Down 1950; Member: Belfast Corporation, 1949–58; Executive, Irish TUC, 1950–69 (Pres. 1957–58 and 1963–64); TUC Gen. Council, 1970–79; MSC, 1977–79; Economic and Social Cttee, EEC, 1978–80. Irish and UK Rep., ILO, 1962–85. *Recreations:* proletarian pastimes. *Address:* 96 Whalley Drive, Bletchley, Milton Keynes, Bucks MK3 6HU. *T:* Milton Keynes 72174.

McGOUGH, Roger; poet; *b* 9 Nov. 1937; *s* of Roger Francis and Mary Agnes McGough; *m* 1970 (marr. diss. 1980); two *s*. *Educ:* St Mary's Coll., Crosby, Liverpool; Hull Univ. (BA, Grad. Cert. Ed.). Fellow of Poetry, Univ. of Loughborough, 1973–75. *Publications:* Watchwords, 1969; After The Merrymaking, 1971; Out of Sequence, 1972; Gig, 1972; Sporting Relations, 1974; In The Glassroom, 1976; Mr Noselighter, 1977; Summer with Monika, 1978; Holiday on Death Row, 1979; Unlucky For Some, 1981; Waving at Trains, 1982; The Great Smile Robbery, 1982; Sky in the Pie, 1983; The Stowaways, 1986; Noah's Ark, 1986; Melting into the Foreground, 1986; contributed to: Penguin Modern Poets, No 10, Mersey Sound, 1967, rev. edn 1983; Oxford Book of 20th Century Verse, 1973; (ed) Strictly Private, 1981; (ed) Kingfisher Book of Comic Verse. *Address:* c/o A. D. Peters, 10 Buckingham Street, WC2N 6BU. *T:* 01–839 2556. *Club:* Chelsea Arts.

McGOVERN, George Stanley; Chairman, Americans for Common Sense; *b* Avon, S Dakota, 19 July 1922; *s* of Rev. Joseph C. McGovern and Francis (*née* McLean); *m* 1943, Eleanor Faye Stegeberg; one *s* four *d*. *Educ:* Dakota Wesleyan Univ. (BA); Northwestern Univ. (MA, PhD). Served World War II, USAAF (DFC). Teacher, Northwestern Univ., 1948–50; Prof. of History and Govt, Dakota Wesleyan Univ., 1950–53. Exec. Sec., S Dakota Democratic Party, 1953–56; Mem., 1st Dist, S Dakota, US House of Reps, 1957–61; Dir, Food for Peace Programme, 1961–62; Senator from South Dakota, 1963–81. Democratic Candidate for US Presidential nomination, 1972. Vis. Prof., University Coll., Dublin, 1982. Mem., Amer. Hist. Assoc. *Publications:* The Colorado Coal Strike, 1913–14, 1953; War Against Want, 1964; Agricultural Thought in the Twentieth Century, 1967; A Time of War, A Time of Peace, 1968; (with Leonard F. Guttridge) The Great Coalfield War, 1972; An American Journey, 1974; Grassroots, an Autobiography, 1978. *Address:* 1825 Connecticut Avenue NW, Suite 213, Washington, DC 20009, USA.

McGOWAN, family name of **Baron McGowan.**

McGOWAN, 3rd Baron, *cr* 1937; **Harry Duncan Cory McGowan;** Partner, Panmure, Gordon & Co., since 1971; *b* 20 July 1938; *e s* of Harry Wilson McGowan, 2nd Baron McGowan, and Carmen, *d* of Sir (James) Herbert Cory, 1st Bt; *S* father, 1966; *m* 1962, Lady Gillian Angela Pepys, *d* of 7th Earl of Cottenham; one *s* two *d*. *Educ:* Eton. *Heir:* *s* Hon. Harry John Charles McGowan, *b* 23 June 1971. *Address:* House of Lords, Westminster, SW1; Highway House, Lower Froyle, Alton, Hants. *T:* Bentley 2104; 12 Stanhope Mews East, SW7. *T:* 01–370 2346. *Club:* Boodle's.

McGOWAN, Alan Patrick, PhD; Head of Department of Ships, National Maritime Museum, since 1971; *b* 16 Nov. 1928; *s* of Hugh McGowan and Alice Chilton; *m* 1958, Betty Eileen, *e d* of Mr and Mrs F. L. MacDougall, Ontario; three *s*. *Educ:* Spring Grove Grammar Sch.; Borough Road Coll.; Univ. of Western Ontario (BA, MA); Univ. of London (PhD). Associate RINA 1980. Served RASC (Air Freight), 1947–49. Asst Master (History), 1953–63; Lectr, Univ. of Western Ont Summer Sch., 1964; Canada Council Fellow, 1964–66; Asst Keeper, Dept of Ships, National Maritime Museum, 1967–71; Associate Prof. of History, Univ. of Western Ont Summer Sch., 1977. Member: Council, Navy Records Soc., 1968–; Adv. Council on Export of Works of Art, 1972–; Victory Adv. Technical Cttee, 1974– (Chm., 1983–); Mary Rose Adv. Cttee, 1974–78; Ships Cttee, Maritime Trust, 1977–; Council, Soc. for Nautical Res., 1981–; Cttee, Falkland Islands Foundn, 1981–83. *Publications:* (ed) Jacobean Commissions of Enquiry, 1608 and 1618, vol. 113 of Navy Records Society, 1971; Royal Yachts, 1975; (with J. Fabb) The Victorian and Edwardian Navy in Photographs, 1976; (ed and prefaced) Steel's Naval Architecture, 1976; Sailor, 1977; (ed and prefaced) Steel's Rigging and Seamanship, 1978; The Century before Steam, 1980; Tiller and Whipstaff, 1981; articles in jls of history and in encyclopaedia. *Recreations:* golf, reading, music. *Address:* c/o National Maritime Museum, Greenwich, SE10 9NF.

McGOWAN, Bruce Henry, MA; FRSA; Headmaster, Haberdashers' Aske's School, Elstree, 1973–Aug. 1987; *b* 27 June 1924; *er s* of late Rt Rev. Henry McGowan, sometime Bishop of Wakefield, and Nora Heath McGowan (*née* Godwin); *m* 1947, Beryl McKenzie (*née* Liggitt); one *s* three *d*. *Educ:* King Edward's Sch., Birmingham; Jesus Coll., Cambridge. War service, Royal Artillery, 1943–46 (India and Burma). Asst Master, King's Sch., Rochester, 1949–53; Senior History Master, Wallasey Gram. Sch., 1953–57; Headmaster: De Aston Sch., Market Rasen, Lincs, 1957–64; Solihull Sch., 1964–73. Page Scholar of the English-Speaking Union, 1961. Member: Church Assembly, 1963–70; Public Schools Commn, 1968–70; Council, Church Schools Co., 1986–; Chairman: Boarding Schools Assoc., 1967–69; Headmasters' Conference, 1985 (Chairman: London Div. 1977; Community Service Cttee, 1976–80; Political and Public Relations Cttee, 1981–84). *Recreations:* foreign travel, walking, music, the theatre. *Address:* (until Aug. 1987) Haberdashers' Aske's School, Elstree, Herts WD6 3AF; 57 Oxford Street, Woodstock, Oxford OX7 1TJ.

McGOWAN, Michael; Member (Lab) Leeds, European Parliament, since 1984; *b* 19 May 1940; *m*; two *s* one *d. Educ:* Leicester University. Formerly: lecturer; BBC journalist; cooperative employment development officer, Kirklees Council, to 1984. *Address:* 3 Grosvenor Terrace, Otley, West Yorks LS21 1HJ.

McGRADY, Edward Kevin; Partner, M. B. McGrady & Co., chartered accountants and insurance brokers; *b* 3 June 1935; *y s* of late Michael McGrady and late Lilian Leatham; *m* 1959, Patricia, *d* of Wm Swail and Margaret Breen; two *s* one *d. Educ:* St Patrick's High Sch., Downpatrick. ACA 1957, FCA 1962. Councillor, Downpatrick UDC, 1961; Chm. of UDC, 1964–73; Vice-Chm., Down District Council, 1973, 1975–76, 1977, Chm. 1974, 1976, 1978, 1981, 1982. 1st Chm. of SDLP, 1971–73; 1st Chm. of SDLP Assembly Party. Mem. (SDLP) S Down: NI Assembly, 1973–75; NI Constitutional Convention, 1975–76; NI Assembly, 1982–86; Head of Office of Executive Planning and Co-ordination (Minister for Co-ordination, Jan.-May 1974); contested (SDLP) Down S, gen. elections, 1979, 1983 and 1986. *Recreations:* golf, badminton, choral work. *Address:* Cois Na Cille, Saul Brae, Downpatrick, Co. Down BT30 6NL. *T:* Downpatrick 2307.

McGRAIL, Prof. Sean Francis, FSA; Visiting Professor of Maritime Archaeology, University of Oxford, since 1986; Chief Archaeologist, National Maritime Museum, since 1976; *b* 1928; *m* 1955, Ursula Anne Yates; one *s* three *d. Educ:* Royal Navy (Master Mariner); Univ. of Bristol (BA); Univ. of London (PhD). FSA 1981. Served RN, 1946–68: Seaman Officer; awarded Wings (pilot), 1952; comd 849 Sqdn, FAA, 1962–63. Undergrad., Univ. of Bristol, 1968–71 (Harry Crook Scholar, 1969–71); Postgrad. Student, Inst. of Archaeology, London, 1972–73; Postgrad. Student (pt-time), UCL, 1973–78; National Maritime Museum, 1972–; Hd of Archaeol Res. Centre, 1976–86. Mem., Dept of Transport Adv. Cttee on Historic Wrecks, 1975–. *Publications:* Building and Trials of a Replica of an Ancient Boat, 1974; Logboats of England and Wales, 1978; Rafts, Boats and Ships, 1981; Ancient Boats, 1983; Ancient Boats of North West Europe, 1986; *edited:* Sources and Techniques in Boat Archaeology, 1977; Medieval Ships and Harbours, 1979; Paul Johnstone, Seacraft of Prehistory, 1980; Brigg 'raft' and her Prehistoric Environment, 1981; Woodworking Techniques before 1500, 1982; Aspects of Maritime Archaeology and Ethnography, 1984; (with J. Coates) Greek Trireme of 5th Century BC, 1984; (with E. Kentley) Sewn Plank Boats, 1985; articles in archaeological and maritime jls. *Recreations:* rearing geese, real ale specialist. *Address:* Institute of Archaeology, 36 Beaumont Street, Oxford OX1 2PG. *T:* Oxford 58850.

McGRATH, Brian Henry; Private Secretary, since 1982, and Treasurer, since 1984, to the Duke of Edinburgh (Assistant Private Secretary, 1982); *b* 27 Oct. 1925; *s* of William Henry and Hermione Gioja McGrath; *m* 1959, Joan Elizabeth Bruce (*née* Gregson-Ellis); two *s*, and one step *d. Educ:* Eton College. Served War of 1939–45, Irish Guards, 1943–46, Lieut. Cannon Brewery Co., 1946–48; Victoria Wine Co.: joined, 1948; Dir, 1949; Chm., 1960–82; Dir, 1960, Chm., 1975–82, Grants of St James's Ltd; Dir, Allied Breweries Ltd (subseq. Allied-Lyons plc), 1970–82; Chm., Broad Street Securities, 1983–. Master of Wine. *Recreations:* golf, tennis, shooting. *Address:* Flat 3, 9 Cheyne Gardens, SW3. *Clubs:* Boodle's, White's.

McGRATH, John Peter; writer; Artistic Director, 7:84 Theatre Companies, since 1971; Director, Freeway Films, since 1983; *b* 1 June 1935; *s* of John Francis McGrath and Margaret McGrath; *m* 1962, Elizabeth Maclennan; two *s* one *d. Educ:* Alun Grammar Sch., Mold; St John's Coll., Oxford. Theatre (playwright), 1958–61; BBC Television, 1960–65; film (screenwriting) and theatre (writing and directing), 1965–70; theatre, with regular forays into television and film, as writer and director, 1970–; founded 7:84 Theatre Co., 1971. Has produced or directed over 75 plays in the theatre; many TV plays performed on BBC and ITV; wrote libretto for Alexander Goehr's opera, Behold the Sun; writes songs and poems. *Publications: plays:* Events While Guarding the Bofors Gun, 1966; Random Happenings in the Hebrides, 1972; Bakke's Night of Fame, 1973; The Cheviot, The Stag and The Black Black Oil, 1974, 2nd edn 1981; The Game's A Bogey, 1974; Fish in the Sea, 1977; Little Red Hen, 1977; Yobbo Nowt, 1978; Joe's Drum, 1979; Blood Red Roses, and Swings and Roundabouts, 1981; *general:* A Good Night Out, 1981. *Address:* c/o 7:84 Theatre Co., 31 Albany Street, Edinburgh.

McGRATH, Dr Patrick Gerard, CB 1981; CBE 1971; Senior Consultant Psychiatrist and Physician Superintendent, Broadmoor Hospital, 1956–81, now Physician Superintendent Emeritus; *b* 10 June 1916; *s* of late Patrick McGrath and Mary (*née* Murray), Glasgow; *m* 1949, Helen Patricia O'Brien; three *s* one *d. Educ:* St Aloysius Coll., Glasgow; Glasgow and Edinburgh Univs. MB, ChB Glasgow 1939; DipPsych Edinburgh 1955; FRCPsych (Vice-Pres., 1978–80), Hon. FRCPsych 1981; FRSocMed. RAMC, 1939–46 (Hon. Lt-Col); various trng posts in psychiatry, Glasgow, London and Colchester, 1946–51; Psychiatrist, Ayrshire, 1951–56. Member: Parole Board, 1982–85; Adv. Council, Inst. of Criminology, Univ. of Cambridge, 1982–86. *Publications:* chapter in Psychopathic Disorder, 1966; Mentally Abnormal Offender, 1968; contrib. Jl of RSH, Cropwood publications, etc. *Recreation:* golf (purely social). *Address:* 18 Heathermount Drive, Crowthorne, Berks. *Club:* East Berks Golf.

McGRATH, Peter William; UK Operations Director, Stone International Plc, since 1982; *b* 19 Nov. 1931; *s* of Major W. P. McGrath and Winifred Clara (née Fill); *m* 1954, Margaret Irene Page; one *s* three *d. Educ:* Boroughmuir Sch.; Royal Liberty Sch.; Univ. of London (Dip. in Econs). Sen. managerial positions in finance and prodn, Ford of Britain and Ford of Germany, 1962–69; Controller of Corporate Finance, BR Bd, 1969–72; Dir of Finance, NFC, 1972–77; Dir of Finance and Systems, Truck and Bus Div., British Leyland, 1977; Man. Dir, British Leyland Internat., 1977–78; Chm. and Man. Dir, BL Components Ltd, 1978–79; Group Man. Dir, Concord Rotaflex, 1980–82. *Recreations:* sailing, military history, opera. *Address:* St Leonard's Forest House, Horsham, West Sussex RH13 6HX. *Club:* Medway Yacht (Rochester).

McGREGOR, family name of **Baron McGregor of Durris.**

McGREGOR OF DURRIS, Baron *cr* 1978 (Life Peer), of Hampstead; **Oliver Ross McGregor;** Chairman, Advertising Standards Authority, since 1980; Professor of Social Institutions in the University of London, 1964–85; Head of Department of Sociology, at Bedford College, 1964–77; Joint Director, Rowntree Legal Research Unit, 1966–84; *b* 25 Aug. 1921; *s* of late William McGregor and late Anne Olivia Ross; *m* 1944, Nellie Weate; three *s. Educ:* Worksop Coll.; University of Aberdeen; London School of Economics (Hon. Fellow 1977). Temp. civil servant, War Office and Ministry of Agriculture, 1940–44. Asst Lecturer and Lecturer in Economic History, University of Hull, 1945–47; Lecturer, Bedford Coll., 1947–60, Reader in University of London, 1960–64; Simon Senior Research Fellow, University of Manchester, 1959–60. Fellow of Wolfson Coll., Oxford, 1972–75; Dir, Centre for Socio-Legal Studies, Univ. of Oxford, 1972–75. Member: Cttee on Enforcement of Judgment Debts, 1965; Cttee on Statutory Maintenance Limits, 1966; Cttee on Land Use (Recreation and Leisure), 1967; National Parks Commission, 1966–68; Independent Television Authority's General Advisory Council, 1967–73; Countryside Commission, 1968–80; Legal Aid Adv. Cttee, 1969–78; Cttee on One-Parent Families, 1969–74; Chairman: Royal Commn on Press, 1975–77 (Mem., 1974); Forest Philharmonic Soc., 1975–. President: Nat. Council for One Parent Families,

1975–; Nat. Assoc. of Citizens' Advice Bureaux, 1981–. Independent Trustee, Reuters, 1984–. Lectures: Fawcett Meml, 1966; James Seth Meml, 1968; Hobhouse Meml, 1971; Maccabaean in Jurisprudence, 1973; Hamlyn, 1979; Eleanor Rathbone Meml, 1979; Ian Gulland, 1980. Hon. LLD Bristol, 1986. *Publications:* Divorce in England, 1957; ed, Lord Ernle, English Farming Past and Present, 6th edn, 1960; (jtly) Separated Spouses, 1970; Social History and Law Reform, 1981; various papers in British Journal of Sociology and other journals. *Address:* The Advertising Standards Authority, Brook House, 2–16 Torrington Place, WC1E 7HN. *T:* 01–580 5555; Far End, Wyldes Close, NW11 7JB. *T:* 01–458 2856. *Club:* Garrick.

McGREGOR, Alistair Gerald Crichton; QC (Scot.) 1982; WS; Assistant Minister, Colinton Parish Church, Edinburgh, since 1986; *b* 15 Oct. 1937; *s* of late James Reid McGregor, CB, CBE, MC, and Dorothy McGregor; *m* 1965, Margaret Lees or McGregor; two *s* one *d. Educ:* Charterhouse; Pembroke Coll., Oxford (BA (Hons) Jurisprudence); Edinburgh Univ. (LLB; BD). Intelligence Corps, 1956–58. Solicitor and WS, 1965–66; Advocate, 1967–82. Clerk to Court of Session Rules Council, 1972–75; Standing Junior Counsel to: SHHD, 1977–79; Scottish Develt Dept, 1979–82. Chm., Family Care (Scotland), 1983–. *Recreations:* squash, tennis. *Address:* 25 Gillespie Road, Edinburgh EH13 0NW. *T:* 031–441 1607. *Clubs:* University Staff, Sports (Edinburgh).

McGREGOR, Dr Angus; Regional Medical Officer, West Midlands Regional Health Authority, since 1979; *b* 26 Dec. 1926; *s* of Dr William Hector Scott McGregor and Dr Olwen May Richards; *m* 1951, May Burke, BA; one *d. Educ:* Solihull Sch.; St John's Coll., Cambridge. MA, MD; FRCP; FFCM; DPH. Junior hospital posts, 1950; Army service, RAMC, 1951–52; general practice, 1953; Asst MOH, Chester, 1954–56; Deputy Medical Officer of Health: Swindon, 1957–58; Hull, 1958–65; MOH and Port MO, Southampton, 1965–74; District Community Physician, East Dorset, 1974–79. Mem. Bd, FCM, RCP, 1982–. FRSA 1986. *Publications:* contrib. papers to medical journals. *Recreation:* piano. *Address:* (home) 68 Gillhurst Road, Birmingham B17 8PB. *T:* 021–427 2450; (office) 146 Hagley Road, Birmingham B16 9PA. *T:* 021–454 4828. *Club:* Royal Over-Seas League.

MacGREGOR, Edward Ian Roy, CMG 1966; HM Diplomatic Service, retired; *b* 4 March 1911; *s* of late John MacGregor and late Georgina Agnes MacGregor (*née* Barbor); *m* 1944, Lilianne, *d* of William Swindlehurst, Washington, DC, USA; one *s* one *d. Educ:* Methodist Coll., Belfast; Queen's Univ., Belfast (MSc). Wing Comdr RAF, 1936–47. Asst Civil Air Attaché, Washington, 1948–52; Ministry of Transport and Civil Aviation, 1952–59; Civil Air Attaché, Washington, 1959–65; Asst Sec., BoT, 1965–67; Counsellor, FO, 1967–68; Consul-Gen., Detroit, 1968–71. *Address:* Spinneys, Brock Way, Virginia Water, Surrey. *T:* Wentworth 3612.

MACGREGOR, Sir Edwin (Robert), 7th Bt *cr* 1828; Assistant Deputy Minister, Ministry of Energy, Mines and Petroleum Resources, Province of British Columbia, Victoria, BC; *b* 4 Dec. 1931; *e s* of Sir Robert McConnell Macgregor, 6th Bt, and of Annie Mary Lane; *S* father, 1963; *m* 1st, 1952, (Margaret Alice) Jean Peake (marr. diss. 1981); one *s* two *d* (and one *s* decd); 2nd, 1982, Helen Linda Herriott; two step *d. Educ:* University of British Columbia. BASc 1955, MASc 1957, Metallurgical Engineering. Member: Assoc. of Professional Engrs, Province of British Columbia; Canadian Inst. of Mining and Metallurgy. *Publications:* contribs to Trans Amer. Inst. of Mining, Metallurgical and Petroleum Engrg, Jl Amer. Chem. Soc. *Recreations:* reading; participation in several outdoor sports such as golf, swimming, fishing, etc.; music. *Heir: s* Ian Grant Macgregor, *b* 22 Feb. 1959. *Address:* 6136 Kirby Road, RR3, Sooke, BC V0S 1N0, Canada.

MacGREGOR, Geddes; *see* MacGregor, J. G.

McGREGOR, Dr Gordon Peter; Principal, College of Ripon and York St John, since 1980; *b* Aldershot, Hants, 13 June 1932; 2nd *s* of William A. K. McGregor and Mary A. McGregor (*née* O'Brien); *m* 1957, Jean Olga Lewis; three *d. Educ:* Bishop Road Jun. Sch., Bristol; St Brendan's Coll., Bristol; Univ. of Bristol (BA Hons); Univ. of East Africa (MEd); Univ. of Sussex (DPhil); Ripon Coll., Wisconsin (DLitt); Dip. Coll. of Teachers of the Blind. Educn Officer, RAF, 1953–56; Asst Master, Worcester Coll. for the Blind, 1956–59; Asst Master, King's Coll., Budo, Uganda, 1959–62; Lecturer in English Language, Makerere Univ. Coll., Uganda 1963–66; Univ. of Zambia: Sen Lecturer in Educn, 1966–68; Reader and Head of Dept of Education, 1968–70; Prof. of Educn, 1970; Principal, Bishop Otter Coll., Chichester, 1970–80. Member: York DHA, 1982–; UK Commn for UNESCO, 1984–; Voluntary Sector Consultative Council, 1985–. FRSA 1976. *Publications:* King's College, Budo, The First Sixty Years, 1967; Educating the Handicapped, 1967; English for Education?, 1968; Teaching English as a Second Language (with J. A. Bright), 1970; English in Africa, (UNESCO), 1971; Bishop Otter College and Policy for Teacher Education 1839–1980, 1981; contrib. Univs Qly, Times Higher Educn Supplement, PNEU Jl. *Recreations:* music, literature, theatre, travel, swimming. *Address:* Principal's House, College of Ripon and York St John, Lord Mayor's Walk, York. *T:* York 56771.

MacGREGOR OF MacGREGOR, Brig. Sir Gregor, 6th Bt, *cr* 1795; ADC 1979; 23rd Chief of Clan Gregor; *b* 22 Dec. 1925; *o s* of Capt. Sir Malcolm MacGregor of MacGregor, 5th Bt, CB, CMG, and Hon. Gylla Lady MacGregor of MacGregor, OBE (*d* 1980); *S* father 1958; *m* 1958, Fanny, *o d* of C. H. A. Butler, Shortgrove, Newport, Essex; two *s. Educ:* Eton. Commissioned Scots Guards, 1944; served War of 1939–45. Served in Palestine, 1947–48; Malaya, 1950–51; Borneo, 1965. Staff Coll. Course, 1960; Brigade Major, 16th Parachute Bde Gp, 1961–63; Joint Services Staff Coll., 1965; commanding 1st Bn Scots Guards, 1966–69; GSO1 (BLO) Fort Benning, USA, 1969–71; Col Recruiting, HQ Scotland, 1971; Lt-Col commanding Scots Guards, 1971–74; Defence and Mil. Attaché, British Embassy, Athens, 1975–78; Comdr, Lowlands, 1978–80. Mem. of the Royal Company of Archers (Queen's Body Guard for Scotland). *Heir: s* Malcolm Gregor Charles MacGregor of MacGregor, Scots Guards, *b* 23 March 1959. *Address:* Bannatyne, Newtyle, Blairgowrie, Perthshire. *T:* Newtyle 314; R-5 Buttonwood Bay, Key Largo, Florida 33037, USA. *T:* 305–852–5740. *Clubs:* Buck's, Pratt's; New (Edinburgh).

McGREGOR, Harvey, QC 1978; DCL; Fellow, since 1972, and Warden, since 1985, New College, Oxford; *b* 25 Feb. 1926; *s* of late William Guthrie Robertson McGregor and Agnes (*née* Reid). *Educ:* Inverurie Acad.; Scarborough Boys' High Sch.; Queen's Coll., Oxford (Hastings Scholar; BA 1951, BCL 1952, MA 1955, DCL 1983). Dr of Juridical Science, Harvard, 1962. Called to the Bar, Inner Temple, 1955, Bencher, 1985. Flying Officer, RAF, 1946–48. Bigelow Teaching Fellow, Univ. of Chicago, 1950–51; Vis. Prof., New York Univ. and Rutgers Univ., 1963–69 (various times). Consultant to Law Commn 1966–73. Pres., Harvard Law Sch. Assoc. of UK, 1981–. Dep. Independent Chm., London Theatre Council, 1971–; Trustee, Oxford Union Soc., 1977–. Mem. Editorial Cttee, Modern Law Review, 1967–. *Publications:* McGregor on Damages, 12th edn 1961–14th edn 1980; (contrib.) International Encyclopedia of Comparative Law, 1972; articles in legal jls. *Recreations:* music, theatre, travel, sailing. *Address:* New College, Oxford OX1 3BN. *T:* Oxford 248451; (chambers) 4 Paper Buildings, Temple, EC4Y 7EX. *T:* 01–353

3366; (residence) Gray's Inn Chambers, Gray's Inn, WC1R 5JA. *T:* 01–242 4942. *Club:* Garrick.

MacGREGOR, Sir Ian, Kt 1986; Non-executive Director, Lazard Brothers & Co., Ltd, since 1986; Limited Partner, Lazard Frères & Co., New York, since 1978; *b* 21 Sept. 1912; *m* Sibyl Spencer; one *s* one *d*. *Educ:* George Watson's Coll., Edinburgh; Hillhead High Sch., Glasgow; Univ. of Glasgow. BSc (1st cl. Hons); Royal Coll. of Science and Technol. (now Univ. of Strathclyde) (Dip. with distinction). Pres. and Chief Exec., 1966, Chm., 1969–77; Amax Inc. (Hon. Chm., 1977–82); Deputy Chairman, BL Ltd, 1977–80; Chm. and Chief Exec., BSC, 1980–83; Chm., NCB, 1983–86. President of the International Chamber of Commerce, Paris, 1978. Hon. degrees from Univs. of Glasgow (LLD), Strathclyde (LLD), Denver (LLD), Montana State (DEng), Rochester (LLD), Colorado Sch. of Mines (DEng), Wyoming (LLD), and Tri-State Coll., Indiana (DSc). Jackling Medal, Amer. Inst. of Mining and Metallurgical Engrs; John Fritz Gold Medal, Amer. Inst. of Mining, Metallurgical and Petroleum Engrs, 1981; Bessemer Gold Medal, Metals Soc., London, 1983. Chevalier, Légion d'Honneur, 1972. *Publication:* The Enemies Within, 1986. *Address:* Lazard Brothers & Co., Ltd, 21 Moorfields, EC2P 2HT.

McGREGOR, Sir Ian (Alexander), Kt 1982; CBE 1968 (OBE 1959); FRS 1981; Professorial Fellow, Department of Tropical Medicine, Liverpool School of Tropical Medicine, since 1981; *b* 26 Aug. 1922; *s* of John McGregor and Isabella (*née* Taylor), Cambuslang, Lanarks; *m* 1954, Nancy Joan, *d* of Frederick Small, Mapledurham, Oxon; one *s* one *d*. *Educ:* Rutherglen Academy; St Mungo Coll., Glasgow. LRCPE, LRCSE, LRFPS(G) 1945; DTM&H 1949; MRCP 1962; FRCP 1967; FFCM 1972; Hon. FRCPGlas 1984. Mil. Service, 1946–48 (despatches). Mem. Scientific Staff, Human Nutrition Research Unit, MRC, 1949–53; Dir, MRC Laboratory, The Gambia, 1954–74, 1978–80; Head of Laboratory of Trop. Community Studies, Nat. Inst. for Med. Research, Mill Hill, 1974–77; Mem., External Staff, MRC, 1981–84. Chm., WHO Expert Cttee on Malaria, 1985–; Member: WHO Adv. Panel on Malaria, 1961–; Malaria Cttee, MRC, 1962–71; Cttee on Nutrition Surveys, Internat. Union of Nutrition Sciences, 1971–75; Tropical Medicine Res. Bd, MRC, 1974–77, 1981–83; Steering Cttee on Immunology of Malaria, WHO, 1978–; Steering Cttee on Applied Field Res. in Malaria, WHO, 1984–; Council, Royal Soc., 1985–86. Lectures: Heath Clark, London Sch. of Hygiene and Tropical Medicine, 1983–84; Fred Soper, Amer. Soc. of Trop. Medicine and Hygiene, 1983. Pres., Royal Soc. of Trop. Medicine and Hygiene, 1983–85 (Vice-Pres., 1981–83). Chalmers Medal, Royal Soc. Trop. Med. and Hygiene, 1963; Stewart Prize, BMA, 1970; Darling Foundn Medal, WHO, 1974; Laveran Medal, Société de Pathologie Exotique de Paris, 1983. Hon. Fellow Liverpool Sch. of Trop. Medicine, 1980; Hon. Mem., Amer. Soc. of Trop. Medicine and Hygiene, 1983. Hon. LLD Univ. of Aberdeen, 1983; Hon. DSc Glasgow, 1984. *Publications:* Scientific papers on infections, nutrition, immunity, child health and community medicine in tropical environments. *Recreations:* ornithology, golf, fishing. *Address:* The Glebe House, Greenlooms, Hargrave, Chester CH3 7RX.

McGREGOR, Ian Alexander, FRCS, FRCSGlas; Director, West of Scotland Regional Plastic and Oral Surgery Unit, since 1980; *b* 6 June 1921; *s* of late Walker McGregor and Mary Duncan (*née* Thompson); *m* 1st, 1950, Christeen Isabel Mackay (decd); three *s*; 2nd, 1970, Frances Mary Vint. *Educ:* North Kelvinside Secondary Sch.; Glasgow Univ. (MB, ChB 1944; ChM 1972). FRCS 1950, FRFPSG 1951, FRCSGlas 1962; Hon. FRACS 1977; Hon. FRCSI 1984; Hon. FRCSE 1985. Served RAMC, 1945–48. Consultant Surgeon, Glasgow Royal Infirmary, 1957–59; Consultant Plastic Surgeon, Greater Glasgow Health Bd, 1959–80. Visitor, 1982–84, Pres., 1984–86, RCPSGlas. Hon. DSc Glasgow, 1986. *Publications:* Fundamental Techniques of Plastic Surgery, 1960, 7th edn 1980; (with W. H. Reid) Plastic Surgery for Nurses, 1966; (with Frances M. McGregor) Cancer of the Face and Mouth, 1986; scientific papers to surgical jls on reconstructive aspects of plastic surgery. *Recreations:* music, literature, golf. *Address:* 7 Ledcameroch Road, Bearsden, Glasgow G61 4AB. *T:* 041–942 3419.

McGREGOR, James Stalker; Chairman, Honeywell Ltd, since 1981; *b* 30 Oct. 1927; *s* of John McGregor and Jean McCabe; *m* 1953, Iris Millar Clark; one *s*. *Educ:* Dumfries Acad.; Royal Tech. Coll., Glasgow (ARTC); Glasgow Univ. BSc (Hons); CEng, MIMechE; CBIM. Production Engr, Rolls Royce Ltd, 1952–56; Sales Engr, Sandvik Swedish Steels, 1956–57; Honeywell Control Systems: Assembly Manager, later Production Control Manager and Admin Manager, 1957–65; Divl Dir, Temperature Controls Gp, 1965–71; Man. Dir, 1971–86. Hon. LLD Strathclyde, 1984. *Recreation:* golf. *Address:* 19 Burgess Wood Road, Beaconsfield, Bucks. *T:* Beaconsfield 2187.

MacGREGOR, Prof. (John) Geddes, DèsL (Sorbonne), DPhil, DD Oxon, BD Edinburgh et Oxon, LLB Edinburgh; FRSL 1948; Distinguished Professor of Philosophy, University of Southern California, 1966–75, now Emeritus; Dean of Graduate School of Religion, 1960–66; first holder of Rufus Jones Chair of Philosophy and Religion, Bryn Mawr, USA, 1949–60; Canon Theologian of St Paul's Cathedral, Los Angeles, 1968–74; *b* 13 Nov. 1909; *o s* of late Thomas and Blanche Geddes MacGregor, Angus; *m* 1941, Elizabeth, *e d* of late Archibald McAllister, Edinburgh; one *s* one *d*. *Educ:* Universities of Edinburgh, Paris, Heidelberg; The Queen's Coll., Oxford. Senior Assistant to Dean of Chapel Royal in Scotland, at St Giles' Cathedral, Edinburgh, 1939–41; served in Civil Defence, War of 1939–45; Minister, Trinity Church, Glasgow, S1, 1941–49; Assistant to Prof. of Logic and Metaphysics, Edinburgh Univ., 1947–49; Examiner: Swarthmore Coll., USA, 1950, 1953, 1955–57; Hebrew Union Coll., USA, 1959, 1961; Occasional Lectr at many US and Canadian Univs (Birks, Montreal, 1976; Warren, Dubuque, 1979; Arnett, Kansas, 1982; Fairchild, Miss, 1982;) Visiting Professor: Univ. of British Columbia, 1963, 1966, 1973; Hebrew Union Coll., 1964–65; Univ. of Santa Clara, 1968; World Campus Afloat (Orient, 1974; Mediterranean, 1975); McGill Univ., Montreal, 1976; Inst. for Shipboard Educn (round-the-world-voyage), 1977; Univ. of Iowa, 1979; Univ. of Saskatchewan, 1979; Vis. Fellow, Dept of Religious Studies, Yale Univ., 1967–68; Vis. Lectr, Rikkyo Univ., Tokyo, 1981; Dir, Amer. Friends of the Univ. of Edinburgh, 1983–86, Adv. Council, 1986–; Hon. Fellow, Emporia State Univ., Kansas, 1982. Diplomate, Internat. Soc. for Philosophical Enquiry, 1986. Special Preacher: St Paul's Cathedral, London, 1969; Westminster Abbey, 1970. Regent, American-Scottish Foundation, Inc., NY; Hon. Chaplain and Historian, St Andrew's Soc. of LA, 1981– (Mem., 1985–86, Vice-Pres., 1986–87, Bd of Trustees). Hon. LHD Hebrew Union, 1978. Hon. Phi Kappa Phi, 1972 (Distinguished Award, 1982). California Literature Award (Gold Medal, non fiction), 1964. *Publications:* Aesthetic Experience in Religion, 1947; Christian Doubt, 1951; Les Frontières de la Morale et de la Religion, 1952; From a Christian Ghetto, 1954; The Vatican Revolution, 1957; The Tichborne Impostor, 1957; The Thundering Scot, 1957; Corpus Christi, 1959; Introduction to Religious Philosophy, 1959; The Bible in the Making, 1959; The Coming Reformation, 1960; The Hemlock and the Cross, 1963; God Beyond Doubt, 1966; A Literary History of the Bible, 1968; The Sense of Absence, 1968; So Help Me God, 1970; Philosophical Issues in Religious Thought, 1973; The Rhythm of God, 1974; He Who Lets Us Be, 1975; Reincarnation in Christianity, 1978; Gnosis, 1979; Scotland Forever Home, 1980; The Nicene Creed, 1981; Reincarnation as a Christian Hope, 1982; The Gospels as a Mandala of Wisdom, 1982; The Christening of Karma, 1984; Apostles Extraordinary, 1986; (ed) Immortality and Human Destiny, 1986. *Recreation:* manual labour. *Address:* 876 Victoria Avenue, Los Angeles, California 90005–3751, USA. *T:* 213–938–4826. *Clubs:* Athenæum, English-Speaking Union, Royal Commonwealth Society; Caledonian (Edinburgh); Union Society (Oxford); Automobile (Los Angeles).

MacGREGOR, Rt. Hon. John (Roddick Russell), OBE 1971; PC 1985; MP (C) South Norfolk, since Feb. 1974; Chief Secretary to HM Treasury, since 1985; *b* 14 Feb. 1937; *s* of late Dr. N. S. R. MacGregor; *m* 1962, Jean Mary Elizabeth Dungey; one *s* two *d*. *Educ:* Merchiston Castle Sch., Edinburgh; St Andrews Univ. (MA, 1st cl. Hons); King's Coll., London (LLB). Univ. Administrator, 1961–62; Editorial Staff, New Society, 1962–63, Special Asst to Prime Minister, Sir Alec Douglas-Home, 1963–64; Conservative Research Dept, 1964–65; Head of Private Office of Rt Hon. Edward Heath, Leader of Opposition, 1965–68; an Opposition Whip, 1977–79; a Lord Comr of HM Treasury, 1979–81; Parly Under-Sec. of State, DoI, 1981–83; Minister of State, MAFF, 1983–85. Hill Samuel & Co. Ltd, 1968–79 (Dir, 1973–79). Chairman: Fedn of University Cons. and Unionist Assocs, 1959; Bow Group, 1963–64; 1st Pres., Conservative and Christian Democratic Youth Community, 1963–65; formerly Treasurer, Federal Trust for Educn and Research; formerly Trustee, European Educnl Research Trust; Governor, Langley Sch., Norfolk, 1976. *Publications:* contrib. The Conservative Opportunity; also pamphlets. *Recreations:* music, reading, travelling, gardening, conjuring. *Address:* House of Commons, SW1A 0AA.

MACGREGOR, John Roy; His Honour Judge Macgregor; a Circuit Judge, since 1974; Honorary Recorder of Margate, 1972–79; *b* Brooklyn, NY, 9 Sept. 1913; 4th *s* of Charles George McGregor, of Jamaica and New York. *Educ:* Bedford School. Called to the Bar, Gray's Inn, 1939; Inner Temple (*ad eundem*), 1968. Served in Royal Artillery, 1939–46; RA (TA) and Special Air Service (TA), 1950–61. Dep. Chm., Cambridgeshire and Isle of Ely QS, 1967–71; a Recorder, 1972–74. Legal Assessor to Gen. Optical Council, 1972–74. *Address:* Nether Gaulrig, Yardley Hastings, Northampton NN7 1HD. *T:* Yardley Hastings 861. *Club:* Special Forces.

MacGREGOR, Neil; *see* MacGregor, R. N.

McGREGOR, Peter, CEng, FIEE; Director, Export Group for the Constructional Industries, since 1984; Chairman, ICTC Ltd, since 1983; *b* 20 May 1926; *s* of Peter McGregor and Margaret Thomson McGregor (*née* McAuslan); *m* 1954, Marion, *d* of H. T. Downer; one *s* one *d*. *Educ:* Cardiff High Sch.; Univ. of Birmingham; London Sch. of Economics (BSc (Econs)); CompIProdE; MInstM; FBIM. National Service, RE, 1946–48. Various appointments, Ferranti Ltd, incl. Works Manager, Distribution Transformer Dept, Sales Manager, Transformer Div., Gen. Manager, Power Div., 1950–74; Dir, Industrie Elettriche di Legnano (Italy), 1970–74; Dir, Oxford Univ. Business Summer Sch., 1972; first Sec. Gen., Anglo-German Foundn for Study of Industrial Soc., 1974–81; Industrial Dir, NEDO, 1981–84. Chm., Textile Machinery EDC, 1982–; Dir, Templeton Technol. Seminar, 1985–86. Member: N American Adv. Gp, BOTB, 1968–74; Europ. Trade Cttee, BOTB, 1981–83; Adv. Bd, Public Policy Centre, 1984–; Cttee on Exchange Rate, Public Policy Centre, 1984–. Industrial Advr to Liberal Party, 1960–73; Chm., Hazel Grove Liberal Assoc., 1971–74; Member: Liberal Party Treasury Panel, 1985–; Liberal Party Industry and Trade Panel, 1985–; contested (L) Ilford South, 1964. Hon. Treasurer, Anglo-German Assoc., 1983–. FRSA. *Publications:* various articles and pamphlets especially on industrial relations, company structure, market economy. *Recreations:* sailing, walking, reading, listening to music, writing, conversation. *Address:* Dacres, Troutstream Way, Loudwater, Rickmansworth, Herts WD3 4LA. *T:* Rickmansworth 776985. *Club:* Caledonian.

MacGREGOR, (Robert) Neil; Director, National Gallery, since 1987; *b* 16 June 1946; *s* of Alexander Rankin MacGregor and Anna Fulton Scobie MacGregor (*née* Neil). *Educ:* Glasgow Acad.; New Coll., Oxford; Ecole Normale Supérieure, Paris; Univ. of Edinburgh; Courtauld Inst. of Art. Mem., Faculty of Advocates, Edinburgh, 1972. Lectr in History of Art and Architecture, Univ. of Reading, 1976; Editor, The Burlington Magazine, 1981–86. *Publications:* contribs to Apollo, The Burlington Magazine, Connoisseur, etc. *Address:* 10 Pembridge Crescent, W11.

MacGREGOR, Susan Katriona, (Sue); Presenter, BBC Radio Four: Woman's Hour, since 1972; Tuesday Call, since 1973; Today, since 1984; It's Your World, since 1985; Conversation Piece (occasional series); *b* 30 Aug. 1941; *d* of Dr James MacGregor and Margaret MacGregor (*née* MacGregor). *Educ:* Herschel School, Cape, South Africa. Announcer/producer, South African Broadcasting Corp., 1962–67; BBC Radio reporter, World at One, World This Weekend, PM, 1967–72. Dir, Municipal Journal Ltd, 1980–. Broadcasting Press Guild Award for Outstanding Contribution to Radio, 1979; Female UK Radio Personality of the Year, Sony Radio Awards, 1983. FRSA. *Recreations:* theatre, cinema, ski-ing, procrastination. *Address:* c/o BBC, Portland Place, W1A 1AA. *T:* 01–580 4468.

McGRIGOR, Captain Sir Charles Edward, 5th Bt, *cr* 1831; Rifle Brigade, retired; Member Royal Company of Archers (HM Body Guard for Scotland); *b* 5 Oct. 1922; *s* of Lieut-Colonel Sir Charles McGrigor, 4th Bt, OBE, and Lady McGrigor, *d* of Edward Lygon Somers Cocks, Bake, St Germans, Cornwall; *S* father, 1946; *m* 1948, Mary Bettine, *e d* of Sir Archibald Charles Edmonstone, 6th Bt; two *s* two *d*. *Educ:* Eton. War of 1939–45 (despatches); joined Army, 1941, from Eton; served with Rifle Bde, N. Africa, Italy, Austria. ADC to Duke of Gloucester, 1945–47, in Australia and England. Exon, Queen's Bodyguard, Yeoman of the Guard, 1970–85. Mem. Cttee of Management and a Vice-Pres., RNLI and Convenor, Scottish Lifeboat Council. *Recreations:* fishing, gardening. *Heir:* *s* James Angus Rhoderick Neil McGrigor, *b* 19 Oct. 1949. *Address:* Upper Sonachan, Dalmally, Argyll. *Club:* Boodle's.

MacGUIGAN, Hon. Mark Rudolph, PC (Can.) 1980; PhD, JSD; **Hon. Mr Justice MacGuigan;** Judge, Federal Court of Appeal, Canada, since 1984; *b* 17 Feb. 1931; *s* of Hon. Mark R. MacGuigan and Agnes V. Trainor; two *s* one *d*. *Educ:* Queen Square Sch.; Prince of Wales (Jun.) Coll.; St Dunstan's Univ., Charlottetown (BA *summa cum laude*); Univ. of Toronto (MA, PhD); Osgoode Hall Law Sch.; Columbia Univ. (LLM, JSD). Admitted to Law Soc. of Upper Canada, 1958. Asst Prof. of Law, 1960–63, and Associate Prof. of Law, 1963–66, Univ. of Toronto; Prof. of Law, Osgoode Hall Law Sch., 1966–67; Dean, Faculty of Law, Univ. of Windsor, 1967–68. MP for Windsor–Walkerville, Ont, 1968–84; Parly Secretary: to Minister of Manpower and Immigration, 1972–74; to Minister of Labour, 1974–75; Opposition Critic of Solicitor Gen., 1979–80; Sec. of State for External Affairs, 1980–82; Minister of Justice, 1982–84. Chairman: House of Commons Special Cttee on Statutory Instruments, 1968–69; Standing Cttee on Justice and Legal Affairs, 1975–79; Sub-Cttee on Penitentiary System in Canada, 1976–77; Co-Chairman, Special Jt Cttee on Constitution of Canada, 1970–72 and 1978. Hon. LLD: Univ. of PEI, 1971; St Thomas Univ., 1981; Law Soc. of Upper Canada, 1983; Univ. of Windsor, Ont, 1983. *Publications:* Cases and Materials on Creditors' Rights, 2nd edn 1967; Jurisprudence: readings and cases, 2nd edn 1966. *Recreations:* running, tennis, skiing, swimming. *Address:* 23 Linden Terrace, Ottawa, Ont K1S 1Z1, Canada. *Clubs:* Rideau, Cercle universitaire (Ottawa).

McGUINNESS, Maj.-Gen. Brendan Peter, CB 1986; General Officer Commanding Western District, 1983–86; *b* 26 June 1931; *s* of Bernard and May McGuinness; *m* 1968, Ethne Patricia (*née* Kelly); one *s* one *d. Educ:* Mount St Mary's College. psc, rcds. Commissioned Royal Artillery, 1950; regimental duty, 1950–60; Staff, 1960–62; sc 1963; Adjutant, 1964–65; Staff, 1965–68 (despatches,Borneo, 1966); Battery Comdr, 1968–70; Staff Coll. Directing Staff, 1970–72; CO 45 Medium Regt, 1972–75; CRA 1st Armd Div., 1975–77; RCDS 1978; MoD Staff, 1979–81; Dep. Comdr, NE District, 1981–83. *Recreations:* tennis, hill walking, beagling. *Address:* Woodside, 53 Baring Road, Beaconsfield, Bucks HP9 2NF. *T:* Beaconsfield 4055. *Club:* Army and Navy.

McGUINNESS, James Henry, CB 1964; Chairman, Scottish Philharmonic Trust, since 1976; *b* 29 Sept. 1912; *s* of James Henry McGuinness, Scotstoun; *m* 1939, Annie Eveline Fordyce, Ayr; one *s* two *d. Educ:* St Aloysius Coll.; Univ. of Glasgow, 1st Cl. Hons Classics 1932, George Clark Fellow; Trinity Coll., Oxford (schol.), 1st cl. Hons Mods, 1934, 1st cl. Lit. Hum. Under-Secretary, Dept of Health for Scotland, 1959–62; Scottish Development Department, 1962–64; Asst Under-Sec. of State, Scottish Office and Chm., Scottish Economic Planning Bd, 1965–72; Sen. Res. Fellow in Politics, Univ. of Glasgow, 1973–74. Mem., Oil Develt Council for Scotland, 1973–75. Chairman: Scottish Baroque Ensemble, 1973–74; Scottish Philharmonic Society Ltd, 1974–78. Hon. MRTPI, 1978. *Address:* 28 Falkland Street, Glasgow G12 9QY; Kendoon, Dalry, Kirkcudbrightshire. *Club:* Scottish Arts.

McGUINNESS, Rt. Rev. James Joseph; *see* Nottingham, Bishop of, (RC).

McGUIRE, Gerald, OBE 1974; Chairman, Countryside Link Group, 1982–86; *b* 12 July 1918; *s* of John Charles McGuire and Adelaide Maud McGuire (*née* Davies); *m* 1942, Eveline Mary Jenkins; one *s* one *d. Educ:* Trinity County Sch., Wood Green. Youth Hostels Association: Reg. Sec., N Yorks, 1944–64; National Countryside and Educn Officer, 1964–74; Dep. Nat. Sec., 1974–82. President: Ramblers Assoc., 1975–78 (Vice Pres., 1978–; Pres., Lake Dist Area, 1983–86); Assoc. of National Park and Countryside Voluntary Wardens, 1978–80. Member: N York Moors Nat. Park Cttee, 1953–72, 1985–; Exec. Cttee, CPRE, 1966–76, 1981–84; Gosling Cttee on Footpaths, 1967–68; Countryside Commn, 1976–79; Commn on Energy and the Environment, 1978–81; Recreation and Conservation Cttee, Yorks Water Authority, 1984–; Yorks Regional Cttee, Nat. Trust, 1985–. Vice President: Open Spaces Soc., 1982– (Vice Chm. 1971–76); Council for National Parks, 1983– (Vice Chm., 1981–83); Vice Chairman: Standing Cttee on Nat. Parks, 1970–76; Council for Environmental Conservation, 1981–82; Trustee, Gatliff Trust, 1983–. Hon. Mem., Cyclists Touring Club, 1978–. Cert. of Merit, Internat. Youth Hostel Fedn, 1983; Richard Schirrmann (Founder's) Medal, German Youth Hostels Assoc., 1983; Nat. Blood Transfusion Service Award for 100 donations, 1983. *Recreations:* reading, music, walking in the countryside. *Address:* 24 Castle Howard Drive, Malton, North Yorks YO17 0BA. *T:* Malton 692521.

McGUIRE, Michael Thomas Francis; MP (Lab) Makerfield, since 1983 (Ince, 1964–83); *b* 3 May 1926; *m* 1954, Marie T. Murphy; three *s* two *d. Educ:* Elementary Schools. Coal miner. Whole-time NUM Branch Secretary, 1957–64. Joined Lab. Party, 1951. PPS to Minister of Sport, 1974–77. Member: Council of Europe, 1977–; WEU, 1977–. *Recreations:* most out-door sports, especially Rugby League football; traditional music, especially Irish traditional music. *Address:* House of Commons, SW1.

McGUIRE, Robert Ely, CMG 1948; OBE 1943; Indian Civil Service (retired); *b* 22 Aug. 1901; *s* of late Major E. C. McGuire, 2nd Bn York and Lancaster Regt; *m* 1930, Barbara, *d* of late Sir Benjamin Heald, ICS, Judge of the High Court of Judicature, Rangoon; one *s* one *d. Educ:* High Sch., Dublin; Trinity Coll., Dublin. MA (Hons). Entered ICS, 1926; Warden, Burma Oilfields, 1932 and 1940–42; Dep. Commissioner, 1932–42. Secretary to Government of Burma (temp. in India), 1942–45. Dep. Director of Civil Affairs, with rank of Brigadier, British Military Administration in Burma, 1945. Divisional Comr, Burma, 1946–47; Secretary to Governor of Burma, 1947 to 4 Jan. 1948 (date of Independence of Burma). Secretary Cement Makers Federation, 1949–64. *Address:* Corofin, Rookery Way, Haywards Heath, West Sussex RH16 4RE. *T:* Haywards Heath 453692. *Club:* East India.

McGURK, Colin Thomas, OBE 1971 (MBE 1963); HM Diplomatic Service, retired; *b* 9 July 1922; *m* 1946, Ella Taylor; one *s. Educ:* St Mary's Coll., Middlesbrough. Served in Army, 1942–45. HM Foreign (subseq. Diplomatic) Service; served in British Embassies, Cairo, Addis Ababa, Ankara; 3rd Sec., HM Legation, Sofia, 1953–55; 2nd Sec. (Commercial), Athens, 1956–58; FO, 1958–62; HM Consul, Stanleyville, 1962; 1st Sec., Yaoundé, Brussels and Kuwait, 1962–70; Commercial Counsellor, Kuwait, 1971–72; Commercial Inspector, FCO, 1972–75; Counsellor (Economic and Commercial), New Delhi, 1975–77 and Canberra, 1977–81. *Recreations:* computer programming, painting, sailing. *Address:* 113 High Street, Burnham-on-Crouch, Essex CM0 8AH. *T:* Maldon 782467. *Club:* Royal Burnham Yacht.

McHALE, Keith Michael; His Honour Judge McHale; a Circuit Judge, since 1980; *b* 26 March 1928; *s* of late Cyril Michael McHale and Gladys McHale; *m* 1966, Rosemary Margaret Arthur; one *s* one *d.* Called to the Bar, Gray's Inn, 1951. *Address:* Oak Lodge, Albemarle Road, Beckenham, Kent.

McHARDY, Prof. William Duff; Regius Professor of Hebrew, Oxford University, and Student of Christ Church, 1960–78; *b* 26 May 1911; *o s* of late W. D. McHardy, Cullen, Banffshire; *m* 1941, Vera (*d* 1984), *y d* of late T. Kemp, York; one *d. Educ:* Fordyce Academy; Universities of Aberdeen, Edinburgh, and Oxford (St John's College). MA, BD (Aberdeen), MA (Edinburgh), DPhil (Oxford). Research Fellow in Syriac, Selly Oak Colleges, Birmingham, 1942; Lecturer in Aramaic and Syriac, University of Oxford, 1945; Samuel Davidson Professor of Old Testament Studies in the University of London, 1948–60. Examiner, Universities of Aberdeen, Cambridge, Durham, Edinburgh, Leeds, London, Oxford and University Colleges of the Gold Coast/Ghana and Ibadan. Hon. Curator of Mingana Collection of Oriental Manuscripts, 1947. Grinfield Lecturer on the Septuagint, Oxford, 1959–61. Dir, New English Bible. Burgess, Royal Burgh of Cullen, 1975. Hon. DD Aberdeen, 1958. Hon. Fellow, Selly Oak Colleges, 1980. *Publications:* articles in journals. *Address:* 2 Ogilvie Park, Cullen, Banffshire. *T:* Cullen 41008.

McHENRY, Donald F.; University Research Professor of Diplomacy and International Affairs, Georgetown University, since 1981; *b* 13 Oct. 1936; *s* of Limas McHenry and Dora Lee Brooks; *m* Mary Williamson (marr. diss.); one *s* two *d. Educ:* Lincoln Senior High Sch., East St Louis, Ill; Illinois State Univ. (BS); Southern Illinois Univ. (MSc); Georgetown Univ. Taught at Howard Univ., Washington, 1959–62; joined Dept of State, 1963; Head of Dependent Areas Section, Office of UN Polit. Affairs, 1965–68; Asst to Sec. of State, US, 1969; Special Asst to Counsellor, Dept of State, 1969–71; Lectr, Sch. of Foreign Service, Georgetown Univ.; Guest Scholar, Brookings Inst., and Internat. Affairs Fellow, Council on Foreign Relations (on leave from State Dept), 1971–73; resigned from State Dept, 1973; Project Dir, Humanitarian Policy Studies, Carnegie Endowment for Internat. Peace, Washington, 1973–76; served in transition team of President Carter, 1976–77; Ambassador and Deputy Rep. of US to UN Security Council,

1977–79, Permanent Rep., 1979; US Ambassador to UN, 1979–81. Director: Internat. Paper Co.; First National Bank of Boston; Bank of Boston Corp.; Smith Kline Beckman Corp.; Coca-Cola; Inst. for Internat. Economics; American Ditchley Foundn; Nat. Inst. for Dispute Resolution. Governor, American Stock Exchange. Trustee: Mount Holyoke Coll.; Ford Foundn; Brookings Instn; Phelps-Stokes Fund. Member, Amer. Polit. Sci. Assoc. Hon. degrees: Dennison, Duke, Eastern Illinois, Georgetown, Harvard, Illinois State, Michigan, Princeton, Southern Illinois, Tufts, and Washington Univs; Amherst, Bates, Boston and Williams Colleges. Superior Honor Award, Dept of State, 1966. Mem. Council on Foreign Relations and Editorial Bd, Foreign Policy Magazine. *Publication:* Micronesia: Trust Betrayed, 1975. *Address:* Georgetown University, 37th and O Streets, NW, Washington, DC 20057, USA.

MACHIN, Arnold, OBE 1965; RA 1956 (ARA 1947); sculptor, FRBS 1955; Master of Sculpture, Royal Academy School, 1958–67; Tutor, Royal College of Art, 1951–58; *b* 1911; *s* of William James Machin, Stoke-on-Trent; *m* 1949, Patricia, *d* of late Lt-Col Henry Newton; one *s. Educ:* Stoke School of Art; Derby School of Art; Royal College of Art. Silver Medal and Travelling Scholarship for Sculpture, 1940; two works in terracotta: St John the Baptist and The Annunciation, purchased by Tate Gallery, 1943; Spring terracotta purchased by President and Council of Royal Academy under terms of Chantrey Bequest, 1947; designed: new coin effigy, 1964, 1967 (decimal coinage); definitive issue of postage stamp, 1967; Silver Wedding commemorative crown, 1972; commemorative Silver Jubilee crown, 1977. *Recreations:* music, garden design. *Address:* 4 Sydney Close, SW3; Garmelow Manor, near Eccleshall, Staffordshire.

MACHIN, David; Managing Director of The Bodley Head Ltd, since 1982 (Joint Managing Director, 1981); *b* 25 April 1934; *s* of late Noel and Joan Machin; *m* 1963, Sarah Mary, *yr d* of late Col W. A. Chester-Master; two *d. Educ:* Eton (Oppidan Scholar); Trinity Coll., Cambridge. National Service, 1952–54 (2nd Lieut Welsh Guards). Editor, William Heinemann Ltd, 1957–66; Literary Agent, Gregson & Wigan Ltd and London International, 1966–68; Partner, A. P. Watt & Son, 1968–70; Director: Jonathan Cape Ltd, 1970–78; Chatto, Bodley Head and Jonathan Cape Ltd, 1977–78, 1981–; Triad Paperbacks Ltd, 1983–; Gen. Sec., The Society of Authors, 1978–81. FRSA. *Publications:* (contrib.) Outlook, 1963; articles in The Author, The Bookseller. *Address:* 53 Westwick Gardens, W14 0BS. *T:* 01–603 4000. *Clubs:* Garrick, Groucho.

MACHIN, Edward Anthony, QC 1973; a Recorder of the Crown Court, since 1976; *b* 28 June 1925; *s* of Edward Arthur Machin and Olive Muriel Smith; *m* 1953, Jean Margaret McKanna; two *s* one *d. Educ:* Christ's Coll., Finchley; New Coll., Oxford. MA 1950; BCL 1950; Vinerian Law Scholar, 1950; Tancred Student, 1950; Cassel Scholar, 1951. Called to Bar, Lincoln's Inn, 1951; Bencher, 1980. *Publications:* Redgrave's Factories Acts, 1962, 1966, 1972; Redgrave's Offices and Shops, 1965 and 1973; Redgrave's Health and Safety in Factories, 1976, 1982; Health and Safety at Work, 1980. *Recreations:* music, sailing, languages. *Address:* Strand End, Strand, Topsham, Exeter. *T:* Topsham 7992; 26 Woodridge Way, Northwood, Mddx. *T:* Northwood 29197. *Club:* Bar Yacht.

MACHIN, George; Secretary, Sheffield Trades and Labour Club, since 1981; *b* 30 Dec. 1922; *s* of Edwin and Ada Machin, Sheffield; *m* 1949, Margaret Ena (*née* Heard); one *s. Educ:* Marlcliffe Sch., Sheffield. Served RAF, 1943–47. Engineering Inspector. Shop Steward, and Mem., Sheffield District Cttee, AUEW. Sec., Sheffield Heeley Constituency Lab. Party, 1966–73. Mem., Sheffield City Council, 1967–74. MP (Lab) Dundee E, March 1973–Feb. 1974; contested (Lab) Dundee E, Oct. 1974. Governor, Granville Coll. of Further Educn, Sheffield, 1968–73. *Recreations:* swimming, walking. *Address:* 104 Norgreave Way, Sheffield S19 5TN.

MACHIN, Kenneth Arthur; QC 1977; **His Honour Judge Machin;** a Circuit Judge, since 1984 (Deputy Circuit Judge, 1976–79); *b* 13 July 1936; *o s* of Thomas Arthur Machin and Edith May Machin; *m* 1983, Amaryllis Francesca (Member of Court of Common Council, Cripplegate Ward, City of London), *o d* of Dr Donald and Lucille Bigley. *Educ:* St Albans School. Called to the Bar, Middle Temple, 1960; South Eastern Circuit and Central Criminal Court; a Recorder of the Crown Court, 1979–84. Freeman, City of London. *Recreations:* painting, martello towers, Scalextric. *Address:* New Court, Temple, EC2. *T:* 01–353 7741; The Penthouse, 502 Ben Jonson House, Barbican, EC2.

McHUGH, James, FEng 1986; Member, British Gas Corporation, since 1979; Managing Director, Production and Supply, since 1982; *b* 4 May 1930; *s* of late Edward McHugh and Martha (*née* Smith); *m* 1953, Sheila (*née* Cape); two *d. Educ:* Carlisle Grammar Sch.; various colls. FIMechE, FIGasE, FInstPet; CBIM. Served Army, National Service. Entered Gas Industry, 1947; technical and managerial appts in Northern and E Midlands Gas Bds; Prodn Engr 1967, Dir of Engrg 1971, W Midlands Gas Bd; Dir of Ops, British Gas Corp., 1975. Mem., Meteorological Cttee, 1981–. *Recreations:* mountaineering, dinghy sailing. *Address:* 16 Miall Park Road, Solihull, W Midlands. *T:* 021–705 0836. *Club:* Royal Automobile.

McHUGH, Dr Mary Patricia; Coroner for Southern District of London, 1965–85; *b* 5 June 1915; *d* of J. C. McHugh, MB, BS, BAO, Royal Univ., Dublin, and Madeleine Jeffroy Leblan, Brittany, France; *m* 1943, E. G. Murphy, FRCS (marr. diss., 1952); one *s* two *d. Educ:* Nymphenburg, Munich, Bavaria; Notre Dame, Clapham; Birmingham Univ. MB, ChB, 1942; PhD Fac. of Laws, London 1976. Birmingham House Physician and Anæsthetist, St Chad's Hospital, Birmingham, 1942–43; General Practice, London, 1944–65. Called to the Bar, Inner Temple, 1959. Past Chm., Whole Time Coroner's Assoc.; Mem., British Academy of Forensic Sciences, 1963; Founder Mem., RCGP; Associate, Inst. of Linguists, 1981; Associate to Res. and Adv. Cttee, Cantab Gp of Toxicology and Biosciences, Cambridge, 1983–. Medico Legal Columnist, Pulse, 1981–. *Publication:* Treasure Trove and the Law (Med. Sci. Law vol. 16 no 2), 1976. *Recreations:* cooking, languages. *Address:* 8 Hitherwood Drive, College Road, Dulwich, SE19. *T:* 01–670 8400.

McILVENNA, Maj.-Gen. John Antony, CB 1980; Director of Army Legal Services, 1978–80, retired; *b* 10 Dec. 1919; *s* of Joseph Henry McIlvenna and Dorothy (*née* Brown); *m* Dr Hildegard Paula Gertrud Overlack; one *s* one *d. Educ:* Royal Grammar School, Newcastle upon Tyne; Hymers Coll., Hull; Durham Univ. LLB 1940. Private, KOYLI; 2nd Lieut, DLI, 1941; despatches 1945; admitted Solicitor, 1947; Captain, Army Legal Services, 1950; served in Hong Kong, Aden, Egypt, Libya and BAOR; Maj.-Gen. and Dir, newly formed Army Legal Corps, 1978. Chm. and Dir, United Services Catholic Assoc., 1979–81, Vice-Pres., 1981–. *Recreations:* swimming, music, history. *Address:* Westfield, Biddenden, Kent TN27 8BB. *Club:* Army and Navy.

McILWAIN, Alexander Edward, CBE 1985; WS; President, Law Society of Scotland, 1983–84; Senior Partner, Leonards, Solicitors, Hamilton, since 1984 (Partner, since 1963); *b* 4 July 1933; *s* of Edward Walker McIlwain and Gladys Edith Horne or McIlwain; *m* 1961, Moira Margaret Kinnaird; three *d. Educ:* Aberdeen Grammar Sch.; Aberdeen Univ. MA 1954; LLB 1956. Pres., Students Representative Council, Univ. of Aberdeen, 1956–57. Commnd RCS, 1957–59, Lieut. Admitted Solicitor in Scotland, 1957; SSC, 1966. Burgh Prosecutor, Hamilton, 1966–75; District Prosecutor, Hamilton, 1975–76;

Dean, Soc. of Solicitors of Hamilton, 1981–83; Vice Pres., Law Soc. of Scotland, 1982–83; Hon. Sheriff, Sheriffdom of South Strathclyde, Dumfries and Galloway at Hamilton, 1982; Temp. Sheriff, 1984. WS 1985. Member: Legal Aid Central Cttee, 1980–83 (Chm., 1985–); Lanarkshire Health Bd, 1981–. Hon. Vice-Pres., Scottish Lawyers for Nuclear Disarmament, 1985. Chm., Lanarkshire Scout Area, 1981–. Hon. Mem., Amer. Bar Assoc., 1983. *Recreations:* work, gardening, listening to music, getting away from the Law Society. *Address:* Craigievar, Bothwell Road, Uddingston, Glasgow G71 7EY. *T:* Uddingston 813368. *Club:* New (Edinburgh).

McILWAIN, Prof. Henry, DSc, PhD; Professor of Biochemistry in the University of London at Institute of Psychiatry, British Postgraduate Medical Federation, 1954–80, now Emeritus; Visiting Professor, Department of Biochemistry, St Thomas's Hospital Medical School, London, since 1980; *b* Newcastle upon Tyne, 20 Dec. 1912; *e s* of John McIlwain, Glasgow, and Louisa (*née* Widdowson), Old Whittington; *m* 1st, 1941, Valerie (*d* 1977), *d* of K. Durston, Bude, Cornwall; two *d*; 2nd, 1979, Marjorie Allan Crennell. *Educ:* King's Coll., Newcastle upon Tyne (University of Durham); The Queen's Coll., Oxford. Leverhulme Research Fellow and later Mem. of Scientific Staff, Medical Research Council, in Council's Dept of Bacterial Chemistry (Middlesex Hosp., London) and Unit for Research in Cell Metabolism (Univ. of Sheffield), 1937–47; Lectr in Biochemistry, Univ. of Sheffield, 1944–47; Senior Lectr (later Reader) in Biochemistry, Inst. of Psychiatry (British Postgraduate Medical Fedn), Univ. of London, 1948–54. Hon. Biochemist, Bethlem Royal Hosp. and Maudsley Hosp., 1948–80. Mem. Editorial Bd, Biochemical Jl, 1947–50; Historian, Internat. Soc. for Neurochemistry, 1984–. Research Associate, Univ. of Chicago, 1951; Visiting Lectr, Univ. of Otago, New Zealand, 1954; Lectr and Medallist, Univ. of Helsinki, 1973; Thudichum Lectr and Medallist, Biochemical Soc., 1975. Dr *hc* Univ. d'Aix-Marseille, 1974. *Publications:* Biochemistry and the Central Nervous System, 1955, 5th edn (with H. S. Bachelard), 1985; Chemotherapy and the Central Nervous System, 1957; (with R. Rodnight) Practical Neurochemistry, 1962; Chemical Exploration of the Brain, 1963; (ed) Practical Neurochemistry, 1975; 250 papers in the Biochemical Journal and other scientific and medical publications. *Address:* 73 Court Lane, SE21 7EF. *T:* 01-693 5334.

McILWRAITH, Arthur Renwick; Sheriff of South Strathclyde, Dumfries and Galloway (formerly Lanark) at Airdrie, 1972–85, now temporary Sheriff; *b* 8 April 1914; *s* of Nicholas Renwick McIlwraith and Adaline Gowans McIlwraith; *m* 1950, Thelma Preston or Sargent; one *s* one *d*. *Educ:* High Sch. of Glasgow; Univ. of Glasgow (MA, LLB). Grad. 1938. Served War: Highland Light Infantry, 1939–45. Solicitor, 1945–72. *Recreation:* fishing. *Address:* Upper Dunbeg, 60A James Street, Helensburgh G84 9LE. *Club:* Nomads (Glasgow).

McINDOE, William Ian, CB 1978; Deputy Chairman, Housing Corporation, since 1986; *b* 11 March 1929; *s* of John McIndoe, Leven, Fife and Agnes Scott; *m* 1st, 1954, Irene Armour Mudie (*d* 1966); one *s* two *d*; 2nd, 1971, Jamesanna Smart (*née* MacGregor). *Educ:* Sedbergh; Corpus Christi Coll., Oxford. 2nd Lieut 2 RHA, 1951–53; CRO, 1953–63, served in Canberra and Salisbury, 1956–62, Private Sec. to Sec. of State, 1962–63; Private Sec. to Sec. of Cabinet, later Asst Sec., Cabinet Office, 1963–66; Scottish Office, 1966–76, Under-Sec., 1971; Dep. Sec., Cabinet Office, 1976–79; Dep. Sec., DoE, 1979–86. *Address:* 35 Fitzgerald Avenue, SW14 8SZ. *T:* 01–878 2626; Innisfree, Station Road, Gifford, E Lothian. *Club:* Royal Commonwealth Society.

McINERNEY, Prof. John Peter; Glanely Professor of Agricultural Policy and Director of Agricultural Economics Unit, University of Exeter, since 1984; *b* 10 Jan. 1939; *s* of Peter McInerney and Eva McInerney; *m* 1961, Audrey M. Perry; one *s* one *d*. *Educ:* Colyton Grammar Sch., Colyford, Devon; Univ. of London (BScAgric Hons); Univ. of Oxford (DipAgricEcons); Iowa State Univ. (DPhil). Lectr in Agricl Econs, Wye Coll., Univ. of London, 1964–66; Lectr and Sen. Lectr in Agricl Econs, Univ. of Manchester, 1967–78; Prof. of Agricl Econs and Management, Univ. of Reading, 1978–84. Research Economist and Cons., World Bank, Washington, DC, 1972–. Phi Kappa Phi 1964, Gamma Sigma Delta 1964. *Publications:* The Food Industry: economics and policy (jtly), 1983; chapters in: Current Issues in Economic Policy, 1975, 2nd edn 1980; Resources Policy, 1982, etc; articles in Jl of Agricl Econs, Amer. Jl of Agricl Econs, Canadian Jl of Agricl Econs, Span. *Recreations:* doing it myself, tentative farming, introspection. *Address:* c/o Agricultural Economics Unit, University of Exeter, Exeter EX4 6TL. *T:* Exeter 263837. *Club:* Templeton Social.

McINERNEY, Hon. Sir Murray (Vincent), Kt 1978; Judge of Supreme Court of Victoria, 1965–83; retired; *b* 11 Feb. 1911; *s* of Patrick McInerney and Kathleen Ierne (*née* Murray); *m* 1st, 1939, Manda Alice Franich (*d* 1973); two *s* five *d*; 2nd, 1975, Frances Mary Branagan (*née* O'Gorman). *Educ:* Christian Brothers' Coll., Pretoria; Xavier Coll., Melbourne; Newman Coll., Univ. of Melb. (MA, LLM). Served War, RANVR, 1942–45 (Lieut). Admitted as barrister and solicitor, 1934; practised at Victorian Bar, 1935–65; QC 1957. Sen. Law Tutor, Newman Coll., 1933–41; Lectr, Law of Evidence and Civil Procedure, Melb. Univ., 1949–62. Pres., Aust. Sect. of Lawasia, 1967–69; Vice-Pres., Law Council of Aust., 1964–65; Dep. Pres., Courts Martial Appeals Tribunal, 1958–65. Mem., Victorian Bar Council, 1952–65 (Chm., 1962, 1963). Chm., Council, State Coll. of Vic., 1973–81. Melb. Univ. Full Blue Athletics, and Aust. Univs Blue Athletics, 1933; Pres., Victorian Amateur Athletics Assoc., 1979–82; Mem., Lawn Tennis Assoc. of Vic. *Publications:* contrib. Aust. Law Jl and Melb. Univ. Law Review. *Recreations:* reading, watching cricket, tennis, athletics. *Address:* 7 Chatfield Avenue, Balwyn, Vic 3103, Australia. *T:* 8175051. *Clubs:* Australian, Celtic, Melbourne Cricket, Royal Automobile of Victoria (Melbourne), West Brighton.

MacINNES, Archibald, CVO 1977; Consultant to HAT Group Ltd, since 1980; Ad Hoc Planning Inspector, Department of the Environment, since 1980; *b* 10 April 1919; *s* of Duncan and Catherine MacInnes; *m* 1950, Nancey Elisabeth Blyth (*d* 1976); one *s* two *d*. *Educ:* Kirkcudbright Academy; Royal Technical Coll., Glasgow. FIMechE. Scott's Shipbuilding and Engineering Co., Greenock, 1937–44; Colonial Service, Nigeria, 1945–59; War Office Works Organisation: Gibraltar, 1959–63; Southern Comd, Salisbury, Wilts, 1963–64; MPBW, Bristol, 1964–68; DoE, Germany, 1968–72; Dir, London Region, PSA, DoE, 1972–79. FBIM. Coronation Medal. *Recreations:* golf, shooting, fishing, gardening. *Address:* Lower Road, Homington, Salisbury, Wilts. *T:* Coombe Bissett 336.

MacINNES, Hamish, OBE 1979; BEM; Founder and Leader, Glencoe Mountain Rescue Team; author and film-maker (mountaineering); Hon. Director, Leishman Memorial Research Centre, Glencoe; *b* 7 July 1930. Dep. Leader, British Everest Expedition, 1975. Has served on Mountain Rescue Cttee for Scotland for 20 years (Past Sec.). Founder and Hon. Pres., Search and Rescue Dog Assoc.; Past Pres., Alpine Climbing Group. Designer of climbing equipment, incl. the first all metal ice axe, terrodactyl ice tools, the MacInnes stretchers, MacInnes Boxes for high altitude mountain camping. Hon. LLD, Glasgow, 1983. *Publications:* Climbing, 1964; Scottish Climbs, 2 vols, 1971, 2nd edn (1 vol.) 1981; International Mountain Rescue Handbook, 1972, 2nd edn 1984 (also USA); Call-Out: mountain rescue, 1973, 3rd edn 1985; Climb to the Lost World, 1974; Death Reel (novel), 1976; West Highland Walks, vols 1 and 2, 1979, Vol. 3, 1983; Look Behind the Ranges, 1979; Scottish Winter Climbs, 1980; High Drama (stories), 1980; Beyond the Ranges, 1984; Sweep Search, 1985; books have been translated into Russian, Japanese and German. *Address:* Achnacone, Glencoe, Argyll PA39 4LA.

McINNES, John Colin; Sheriff of Tayside Central and Fife, since 1974 (at Cupar and Perth); *b* 21 Nov. 1938; *s* of late Mr I. W. McInnes, WS, and of Mrs Lucy McInnes, Cupar, Fife; *m* 1966, Elisabeth Mabel Neilson; one *s* one *d*. *Educ:* Cargilfield Sch., Edinburgh; Merchiston Castle Sch., Edinburgh; Brasenose Coll., Oxford (BA); Edinburgh Univ. (LLB). 2nd Lieut 8th Royal Tank Regt, 1957–58, Lieut Fife and Forfar Yeomanry/Scottish Horse (TA), 1958–64. Advocate, 1963. In practice at Scottish Bar, 1963–73; Tutor, Faculty of Law, Edinburgh Univ., 1965–73; Sheriff of the Lothians and Peebles, 1973–74. Director: R. Mackness & Co. Ltd, 1963–70; Fios Group Ltd, 1970–72 (Chm., 1970–72). Mem. Court, St Andrews Univ., 1983–. Contested (C) Aberdeen North, 1964. *Recreations:* shooting, fishing, ski-ing, gardening, photography. *Address:* Parkneuk, Blebo Craigs, Cupar, Fife KY15 5UG. *T:* Strathkinness 366.

MacINNES, Keith Gordon, CMG 1984; HM Diplomatic Service; Assistant Under-Secretary of State and Principal Finance Officer, Foreign and Commonwealth Office, since 1983; *b* 17 July 1935; *s* of Kenneth MacInnes and Helen MacInnes (*née* Gordon); *m* 1st, 1966, Jennifer Anne Fennell (marr. diss. 1980); one *s* one *d*; 2nd, 1985, Hermione Pattinson. *Educ:* Rugby; Trinity Coll., Cambridge (MA); Pres., Cambridge Union Soc., 1957. HM Forces, 1953–55. FO, 1960; Third, later Second Secretary, Buenos Aires, 1961–64; FO, 1964 (First Sec., 1965); Private Sec. to Permanent Under-Sec., Commonwealth Office, 1965–68; First Sec. (Information), Madrid, 1968–70; FCO, 1970–74; Counsellor and Head of Chancery: Prague, 1974–77; Dep. Perm. Rep., UK Mission, Geneva, 1977–80; Head of Information Dept, FCO, 1980–83. *Recreations:* chess, bridge. *Address:* c/o Foreign and Commonwealth Office, SW1A 2AH.

McINTOSH, family name of **Baron McIntosh of Haringey.**

McINTOSH OF HARINGEY, Baron *cr* 1982 (Life Peer), of Haringey in Greater London; **Andrew Robert McIntosh;** Chairman: IFF Research Ltd, since 1981 (Managing Director, 1965–81); SVP United Kingdom Ltd, since 1983; *b* 30 April 1933; *s* of Prof. A. W. McIntosh and Jenny (*née* Britton); *m* 1962, Naomi Ellen Sargant; two *s*. *Educ:* Haberdashers' Aske's Hampstead Sch.; Royal Grammar Sch., High Wycombe; Jesus Coll., Oxford (MA); Ohio State Univ. (Fellow in Econs, 1956–57). Gallup Poll, 1957–61; Hoover Ltd, 1961–63; Market Res. Manager, Osram (GEC) Ltd, 1963–65. Member: Hornsey Bor. Council, 1963–65; Haringey Bor. Council, 1964–68 (Chm., Develt Control); Greater London Council: Member for Tottenham, 1973–83; Chm., NE Area Bd, 1973–74, W Area Bd, 1974–76, and Central Area Bd, 1976; Opposition Leader on Planning and Communications, 1977–80; Leader of the Opposition, 1980–81. An Opposition spokesman on educn and science, 1985–, on industry matters, 1983–, House of Lords. Chairman: Market Res. Soc., 1972–73; Assoc. for Neighbourhood Councils, 1974–80; Computer Sub-Cttee, H of L Offices Cttee, 1984–; Mem., Metrop. Water Bd, 1967–68. Chm., Fabian Soc., 1985–86 (Mem., NEC, 1981–). Governor, Drayton Sch., Tottenham, 1967–83. Editor, Jl of Market Res. Soc., 1963–67. *Publications:* Industry and Employment in the Inner City, 1979; (ed) Employment Policy in the UK and United States, 1980; Women and Work, 1981; jl articles on theory, practice and findings of survey research. *Recreations:* cooking, reading, music. *Address:* 27 Hurst Avenue, N6 5TX. *T:* 01–340 1496.

See also N. E. S. McIntosh.

McINTOSH, Prof. Angus, FRSE 1978; consultant on English language problems; Director, Middle English Dialect Atlas Project, 1979–86; Forbes Professor of English Language, University of Edinburgh, 1964–79; *b* 10 Jan. 1914; *s* of late Kenneth and Mary McIntosh (*née* Thompson), Cleadon, Sunderland, Co. Durham; *m* 1939, Barbara, *d* of late Dr William Seaman and Mrs Bainbridge (*née* June Wheeler), New York City; two *s* one *d*. *Educ:* Ryhope Grammar Sch., Co. Durham; Oriel Coll., Oxford (BA, 1st Class Hons, English Lang., and Lit., 1934); Merton Coll., Oxford (Harmsworth Scholar); (Dip. of Comparative Philology, University of Oxford, 1936); Harvard Univ. (Commonwealth Fund Fellow, AM, 1937). MA (Oxford) 1938. Lecturer, Dept of English, University College, Swansea, 1938–46. Served War of 1939–45, beginning as trooper in Tank Corps, finishing as Major in Intelligence Corps. University Lecturer in Mediæval English, Oxford, 1946–48; Lecturer in English, Christ Church, Oxford, 1946–47; Student of Christ Church, 1947–48; Prof. of English Language and General Linguistics, Univ. of Edinburgh, 1948–64; Rockefeller Foundation Fellowship, US, June-Sept. 1949; Leverhulme Emeritus Res. Fellow, 1984–86. Pres., Scottish Text Soc., 1977. For. Mem., Finnish Acad. of Science and Letters, 1976. Hon. DPhil Poznan Univ., 1972; Hon. DLitt Durham, 1980. *Publications:* books, articles and reviews on subject of English language and related topics. *Recreations:* tennis, fishing, gardening, painting. *Address:* 32 Blacket Place, Edinburgh EH9 1RL. *T:* 031–667 5791.

MACINTOSH, Dr Farquhar, CBE 1982; Rector (Headmaster), The Royal High School, Edinburgh, since 1972; *b* 27 Oct. 1923; *s* of John Macintosh and Kate Ann Macintosh (*née* MacKinnon); *m* 1959, Margaret Mary Inglis, Peebles; two *s* two *d*. *Educ:* Portree High Sch., Skye; Edinburgh Univ. (MA); Glasgow Univ. (DipEd). Served RN, 1943–46; commnd RNVR, 1944. Headmaster, Portree High Sch., 1962–66; Rector, Oban High Sch., 1967–72. Mem., Highlands and Islands Develt Consultative Council, 1965–82; Chairman: BBC Secondary Programme Cttee, 1972–80; School Broadcasting Council for Scotland, 1981–85; Scottish Examination Bd, 1977–; Scottish Assoc. for Educnl Management and Admin, 1979–82. Chm. of Governors, Jordanhill Coll. of Educn, 1970–72; Mem. Court, Edinburgh Univ., 1975–. FEIS 1970. Hon. DLitt Heriot-Watt, 1980. *Publications:* regular contribs to TES Scotland; contrib. to European Jl of Educn. *Recreations:* hill-walking, occasional fishing, Gaelic. *Address:* 12 Rothesay Place, Edinburgh EH3 7SQ. *T:* (home) 031–225 4404; (office) 031–336 2261. *Clubs:* Scottish Arts, Rotary of Murrayfield and Cramond (Edinburgh).

MacINTOSH, Prof. Frank Campbell; FRS 1954; FRSC 1956; J. M. Drake Professor of Physiology, McGill University, Montreal, Canada, 1949–78, Emeritus Professor since 1980; *b* 24 Dec. 1909; *s* of Rev. C. C. MacIntosh, DD, and Beenie MacIntosh (*née* Matheson); *m* 1938, Mary M. MacKay; two *s* three *d*. *Educ:* Dalhousie Univ., Halifax, NS (MA); McGill Univ. (PhD). Member of research staff, Medical Research Council of Great Britain, 1938. Hon. LLD: Alberta, 1964; Queen's, 1965; Dalhousie, 1976; St Francis Xavier, 1985; Hon. MD Ottawa, 1974; Hon. DSc McGill, 1980. *Publications:* papers in physiological journals. *Address:* Department of Physiology, McGill University, 3655 Drummond Street, Montreal H3G 1Y6, Canada; 145 Wolseley Avenue, Montreal West, H4X 1V8, Canada. *T:* 481–7939.

McINTOSH, Rev. Canon Hugh; Honorary Canon, St Mary's Cathedral, Glasgow, since 1983; *b* 5 June 1914; *s* of Hugh Burns McIntosh and Mary (*née* Winter); *m* 1951, Ruth Georgina, *er d* of late Rev. William Skinner Wilson and Enid (*née* Sanders); two *s* one *d*. *Educ:* Hatfield Coll., Durham (Exhibr); Edinburgh Theological Coll. (Luscombe Schol.). LTh, 1941; BA (dist.), 1942; MA 1945. Deacon and Priest, 1942. Precentor and Senior

Chaplain, St Paul's Cathedral, Dundee, 1942–46; Senior Chaplain, St Mary's Cathedral, Edinburgh, 1946–49; Curate, St Salvador's, Edinburgh, 1949–51; Rector, St Adrian's, Gullane, 1951–54; Rector, St John's, Dumfries, 1954–66; Canon of St Mary's Cathedral, Glasgow, and Synod Clerk of Glasgow and Galloway, 1959; Provost of St Mary's Cathedral, Glasgow, 1966–70; Rector, Christ Church, Lanark, 1970–83. *Recreations:* reading, writing, and (a little) arithmetic. *Address:* 2 Ridgepark Drive, Lanark, Scotland. *T:* Lanark 3458.

McINTOSH, Vice-Admiral Sir Ian (Stewart), KBE 1973 (MBE 1941); CB 1970; DSO 1944; DSC 1942; Management Selection Consultant, 1973–78; *b* 11 Oct. 1919; *s* of late A. J. McIntosh, Melbourne, Australia; *m* 1943, Elizabeth Rosemary Rasmussen; three *s* (one *d* decd). *Educ:* Geelong Grammar Sch. Entered RN, 1938; comd HM Submarine: H44, 1942; Sceptre, 1943–44; Alderney, 1946–48; Aeneas, 1950–51; Exec. Officer, HMS Ark Royal, 1956–58; comd 2nd Submarine Sqn, 1961–63; comd HMS Victorious, 1966–68; Dir-Gen., Weapons (Naval), 1968–70; Dep. Chief of Defence Staff (Op. Req.), 1971–73, retd 1973. Captain, 1959; Rear-Adm., 1968; Vice-Adm., 1971. Chairman: Sea Cadet Assoc., 1973–83; HMS Cavalier Trust, 1974–. *Recreations:* friends, reading, music. *Address:* 19 The Crescent, Alverstoke, Hants. *T:* Gosport 580510. *Club:* Royal Over-Seas League.

MACINTOSH, Joan, (Mrs I. G. Macintosh), CBE 1978; Lay Observer for Scotland (Solicitors (Scotland) Act), since 1982; *b* 23 Nov. 1919; *m* 1952, Ian Gillies Macintosh; one *s* two *d*. *Educ:* Amer. and English schs; Oxford (MA Modern History). BBC, 1941–42; Amer. Div., Min. of Inf., 1942–45; HM Foreign Service, 1945–52; retd on marriage. Voluntary work in India, 1953–69; CAB Organiser, Glasgow, 1972–75; Chm. Council, Insurance Ombudsman Bureau, 1981–85. Member: Royal Commn on Legal Services in Scotland, 1975–80; Chm., Scottish Consumer Council, 1975–80; Vice-Chm., National Consumer Council, 1976–84; Vice-Pres., Nat. Fedn of Consumer Gps, 1982–. Hon. LLD Dundee, 1982. *Recreations:* writing, gardening. *Address:* Wynd End, Auchterarder, Perthshire PH3 1AD. *T:* Auchterarder 2499. *Club:* United Oxford & Cambridge University.

McINTOSH, Prof. Naomi Ellen Sargant, (Lady McIntosh of Haringey); Senior Commissioning Editor, Channel Four Television Company Ltd, since 1981; *b* 10 Dec. 1933; *d* of Tom Sargant, *qv*, and Marie Cerny (*née* Hlouskova); *m* 1st, 1954, Peter Joseph Kelly; one *s*; 2nd, 1962, Andrew Robert McIntosh (now Baron McIntosh of Haringey, *qv*); two *s*. *Educ:* Friends' Sch., Saffron Walden, Essex; Bedford Coll., London (BA Hons Sociology). Social Surveys (Gallup Poll) Ltd, 1955–67; Sen. Lectr in Market Res., Enfield Coll., of Technol., 1967–69; Open University: Sen. Lectr in Res. Methods, 1970–75; Reader in Survey Research, 1975–78; Head, Survey Res. Dept, Inst. of Educnl Technol., 1972–81; Pro Vice-Chancellor (Student Affairs), 1974–78; Prof. of Applied Social Research, 1978–81. Vis. Prof. in Higher Educn (part-time), Univ. of Mass, Amherst, 1974–75. Councillor, and Chm. Children's Cttee, London Bor. of Haringey, 1964–68; Vice-Chm., London Boroughs Trng Cttee (Social Services), 1966–68. Chm., National Gas Consumers' Council, 1977–80. Pres., Nat. Soc. for Clean Air, 1981–83. Member: Council and Exec. Cttee, Social Work Adv. Service, 1966–68; Local Govt Trng Bd, 1967–68; Energy Commn, 1978–79; Commn on Energy and the Environment, 1978–81; Nat. Consumer Council, 1978–81; Adv. Council for Adult and Continuing Educn, 1977–83; Council, Bedford Coll., Univ. of London, 1977–83; Council, Polytechnic of the South Bank, 1982; Gov., Haringey Coll., 1984; Trustee, Nat. Extension Coll., 1975. Mem. RTS, 1982. *Publications:* A Degree of Difference, 1976 (New York 1977); (with A. Woodley) The Door Stood Open, 1980. *Recreation:* gardening. *Address:* 27 Hurst Avenue, N6 5TX. *T:* 01–340 1496.

McINTOSH, Neil Scott Wishart; Director, Voluntary Service Overseas, since 1985; *b* 24 July 1947; *s* of William Henderson McIntosh and Mary Catherine McIntosh; *m* 1971, Genista Mary Tandy; one *s* one *d*. *Educ:* Merchiston Castle Sch., Edinburgh; Univ. of York (BA Politics); London Sch. of Econs (MSc Industrial Relations). Res. Associate, PEP, 1969–73; Res. Dir, Southwark Community Develt Proj., 1973–76; Dir, Shelter, 1976–84. Councillor, London Bor. of Camden, 1971–77; Chm., Housing Cttee, 1974–76. Director: Moonlighter Productions Ltd, 1982–; Stonham Housing Assoc., 1982–. Treasurer, Campaign for Freedom of Information. *Publication:* The Right to Manage?, 1971 (2nd edn 1976). *Recreations:* Rugby, hill walking, theatre. *Address:* 8 Lupton Street, NW5.

MACINTOSH, Sir Robert (Reynolds), Kt 1955; MA, DM, FRCSE, DA; FFARCS; Hon. Fellow: Faculties of Anæsthetists of Australasia, 1950, of Ireland, 1964, of England, 1968; Royal Society of Medicine, 1966; Pembroke College, Oxford, 1965; Nuffield Professor of Anæsthetics, Oxford University, 1937–65; War time Consultant in Anæsthetics, Royal Air Force (Air Cdre); *b* Timaru, New Zealand, 17 Oct. 1897; *s* of C. N. Macintosh. *Educ:* Waitaki, New Zealand; Guy's Hospital. Served European War (despatches), Spanish Civil War (Order of Military Merit); War of 1939–45 (Order of Liberty, Norway). Hon. FRCOG. Dr *hc* Univs of Buenos Aires, Aix-Marseilles and Poznan; Hon. DSc: Univ. of Wales; Med. Coll. of Ohio. *Publications:* Textbooks, Essentials of General Anæsthesia, Physics for the Anæsthetist, Lumbar Puncture and Spinal Analgesia, Local Anæsthesia, Brachial Plexus; articles on anæsthesia in medical and dental journals. *Address:* 326 Woodstock Road, Oxford. *Club:* Royal Air Force.

McINTOSH, Sir Ronald (Robert Duncan), KCB 1975 (CB 1968); Chairman, APV Holdings PLC, since 1982; Director: S. G. Warburg & Co. Ltd; Foseco Minsep, plc; London & Manchester Group plc; *b* 26 Sept. 1919; *s* of late Thomas Steven McIntosh, MD, FRCP, FRCS, and late Christina Jane McIntosh; *m* 1951, Doreen Frances, *o d* of late Commander Andrew MacGinnity, Frinton-on-Sea. *Educ:* Charterhouse (Scholar); Balliol Coll., Oxford. Served in Merchant Navy, 1939–45; Second Mate, 1943–45. Assistant Principal, Board of Trade, 1947; General Manager, Dollar Exports Board, 1949–51; Commercial Counsellor, UK High Commn, New Delhi, 1957–61; Under-Secretary: BoT, 1961–64; DEA, 1964–66; Dep. Under-Sec. of State, Dept of Economic Affairs, 1966–68; Dep. Secretary, Cabinet Office, 1968–70; Dep. Under-Sec. of State, Dept of Employment, 1970–72; Dep. Sec., HM Treasury, 1972–73; Dir-Gen. Nat. Economic Development Office, and Mem. NEDC, 1973–77. Dir, Fisons Ltd, 1978–81. Member: British Overseas Trade Adv. Cttee, 1975–77; Council, CBI, 1980–; Co-Chm., British-Hungarian Round Table, 1980–84. CBIM; FRSA. Hon. DSc Aston, 1977. *Recreations:* sailing, travel. *Address:* 24 Ponsonby Terrace, SW1P 4QA. *Club:* Royal Thames Yacht.

MacINTYRE, Prof. Alasdair Chalmers; W. Alton Jones Professor of Philosophy, Vanderbilt University, since 1982; *b* 12 Jan. 1929; *o s* of Eneas John MacIntyre, MD (Glasgow), and Margaret Emily Chalmers, MB, ChB (Glasgow); *m* 1977, Lynn Sumida Joy; one *s* three *d* by previous marriages. *Educ:* Epsom Coll. and privately; Queen Mary Coll., Univ. of London (Fellow, 1984); Manchester Univ. BA (London); MA (Manchester); MA (Oxon). Lectr in Philosophy of Religion, Manchester Univ., 1951–57; Lectr in Philosophy, Leeds Univ., 1957–61; Research Fellow, Nuffield Coll., Oxford, 1961–62; Sen. Fellow, Council of Humanities, Princeton Univ., 1962–63; Fellow and Preceptor in Philosophy, University Coll., Oxford, 1963–66; Prof. of Sociology, Univ. of Essex, 1966–70; Prof. of History of Ideas, Brandeis Univ., 1970–72; Univ. Prof. in Philos. and Political Sci., Boston Univ., 1972–80; Luce Prof., Wellesley Coll., 1980–82. Pres., Eastern Div., Amer. Phil Assoc., 1984. Fellow, Amer. Acad. of Arts and Scis, 1985. Hon. Mem., Phi Beta Kappa, 1973. Hon. DHL Swarthmore, 1983. *Publications:* Marxism and Christianity, 1954 (revised, 1968); New Essays in Philosophical Theology (ed, with A. G. N. Flew), 1955; Metaphysical Beliefs (ed), 1956; The Unconscious: a conceptual analysis, 1958; A Short History of Ethics, 1965; Secularisation and Moral Change, 1967; Marcuse: an exposition and a polemic, 1970; Sociological Theory and Philosophical Analysis (ed with D. M. Emmet), 1971; Against the Self-Images of the Age, 1971; After Virtue, 1981. *Recreations:* walking, reading trash, cooking, sleeping. *Address:* Department of Philosophy, Vanderbilt University, Nashville, Tennessee 37235, USA.

McINTYRE, Prof. Alasdair Duncan, FRSE 1975; Director of Fisheries Research Services for Scotland, Department of Agriculture and Fisheries for Scotland, since 1983; *b* 17 Nov. 1926; *s* of Alexander Walker McIntyre and Martha Jack McIntyre; *m* 1967, Catherine; one *d*. *Educ:* Hermitage Sch., Helensburgh; Glasgow Univ. BSc (1st class Hons Zoology) 1948; DSc 1973. Scottish Home Department (since 1960, DAFS) Marine Laboratory, Aberdeen: Develt Commn Grant-aided Student, 1948–49; Scientific Officer, 1950; Head, Lab. Environmental Gp, 1973; Dep. Dir, 1977; Dir, 1983. Chairman: UN Gp of Experts on Scientific Aspects of Marine Pollution (GESAMP), 1981–84; Adv. Cttee on Marine Pollution, Internat. Council for the Exploration of the Sea, 1982–84. Hon. Res. Prof., Aberdeen Univ., 1983. *Publications:* some 70 articles in scientific jls on marine ecology and pollution. *Recreations:* cooking, wine, walking. *Address:* 63 Hamilton Place, Aberdeen AB2 4BW. *T:* Aberdeen 645633.

MACINTYRE, Angus Donald, DPhil; Official Fellow and Tutor in Modern History, since 1963, and Acting President, Jan.–July 1987, Magdalen College, Oxford (Senior Tutor, 1966–68; Vice-President, 1981–82); *b* 4 May 1935; *e s* of Major Francis Peter Macintyre, OBE, and Evelyn, *d* of Nicholas Synnott, JP, Furness, Naas, Co. Kildare, Eire; *m* 1958, Joanna Musgrave Harvey, *d* of Sir Richard Musgrave Harvey, 2nd Bt; two *s* one *d*. *Educ:* Wellington; Hertford Coll., Oxford (Baring Scholar); St Antony's Coll., Oxford (MA, DPhil). Coldstream Guards, 1953–55, 1956 (Lieut). Governor, Magdalen Coll. Sch., Brackley, 1965–77; Chm., Thomas Wall Trust, London, 1971–. Gen. Editor, Oxford Historical Monographs, 1971–79; Editor, English Historical Review, 1978–86. FRHistS 1972. *Publications:* The Liberator: Daniel O'Connell and the Irish Parliamentary Party 1830–47, 1965; (ed with Kenneth Garlick) The Diary of Joseph Farington 1793–1821, vols I-II, 1978; vols III-VI, 1979; (contrib.) Thank You Wodehouse by J. H. C. Morris, 1981; (contrib.) Daniel O'Connell: portrait of a Radical, ed Nowlan and O'Connell, 1984; (ed) General Index, English Historical Review, vols LXXI–C, 1956–85, 1986. *Recreations:* cricket, bibliophily. *Address:* Magdalen College, Oxford OX1 4AU. *T:* Oxford 241781. *Club:* MCC.

McINTYRE, Donald Conroy, CBE 1985 (OBE 1977); opera singer, free-lance; *b* 22 Oct. 1934; *s* of George Douglas McIntyre and Mrs Hermyn McIntyre; *m*; three *d*. *Educ:* Mount Albert Grammar Sch.; Auckland Teachers' Trng Coll.; Guildhall Sch. of Music. Debut in Britain, Welsh National Opera, 1959; Sadler's Wells Opera, many roles, 1960–67; Royal Opera, Covent Garden, from 1967; also Vienna, Bayreuth, La Scala, Milan and Metropolitan, NY. Principal roles: Barak, in Die Frau Ohne Schatten, Strauss; Wotan and Wanderer, in The Ring, Wagner; Hollander, Wagner; Heyst, in Victory, Richard Rodney Bennett; Macbeth, Verdi; Scarpia, in Tosca, Puccini; Count, in Figaro, Mozart; Hans Sachs, in Die Meistersinger Von Nurnberg, Wagner; Dr Schön, in Wozzeck, Berg; title role in Cardillac, Hindemith. Bayreuth: Wotan, Wanderer, Hollander; Telramund, in Lohengrin; Klingsor, Amfortas and Gurnemanz in Parsifal; Rocco, in Fidelio. Video and films include: Der Fliegende Holländer, 1975; Electra, 1979; Bayreuth Centenary Ring, 1981; Die Meistersinger, 1984; recordings include Pelléas et Mélisande, Il Trovatore, The Messiah, Oedipus Rex, The Ring, Beethoven's 9th Symphony, Damnation of Faust. *Recreations:* gardening, swimming, tennis. *Address:* 2 Roseneath Close, Orpington, Kent. *T:* Farnborough (Kent) 55368.

MacINTYRE, Rt. Hon. Duncan, PC (NZ) 1980; DSO 1945; OBE 1956; ED; Deputy Prime Minister of New Zealand, 1981–84; *b* 1915; *s* of A. MacIntyre; *m* Diana, *d* of Percy Hunter. Sheep farming, 1933–39 and 1946–. Served War, NZ Army, 1939–46; Territorial Force, 1949–60 (Brig. 1956); Col Comdt RNZAC, 1976. MP (National Party) Hastings, 1960–72, Bay of Plenty, 1975–78, East Cape, 1978–84; Minister: of Lands, of Forests, and i/c of Valuation Dept, 1966–72; of Maori Affairs, 1969–72; for the Environment, 1972; of Agriculture, of Fisheries, and i/c of Rural Banking and Finance Corp., 1975–84; of Island Affairs, 1976–79. *Address:* Taikura, RD4, Waipukurau, New Zealand.

MacINTYRE, Prof. Iain; Professor of Chemical Pathology, University of London, and Director: Department of Chemical Pathology, since 1982, and Endocrine Unit, since 1967, Royal Postgraduate Medical School; Hon. Consultant Pathologist, Hammersmith Hospital, since 1960; *b* 30 Aug. 1924; *s* of John MacIntyre, Tobermory, and Margaret Fraser Shaw, Stratherick, Inverness-shire; *m* 1947, Mabel Wilson Jamieson, MA, *y d* of George Jamieson, Largs, Ayrshire; one *d*. *Educ:* Jordanhill Coll. Sch., Glasgow; Univ. of Glasgow. MB, ChB Glasgow 1947; PhD London 1960; MRCPath 1963 (Founder Mem.), FRCPath 1971; FRCP 1977 (MRCP 1969); DSc London 1970. Asst Clinical Pathologist, United Sheffield Hosps, and Hon. Demonstrator in Biochem., Sheffield Univ., 1948–52; Royal Postgraduate Medical School: Registrar in Chemical Pathology, 1952–54; Sir Jack Drummond Meml Fellow, 1954–56; Asst Lectr in Chem. Path., 1956–59; Reader in Chem. Path., 1963–67. Vis. Scientist, Nat. Insts of Health, Bethesda, 1960–61; Visiting Professor: San Francisco Medical Center, 1964; Melbourne Univ., 1979–80; Vis. Lectr, Insts of Molecular Biol. and Cytol., USSR Acad. of Scis, 1978. Mem., Hammersmith and Queen Charlotte's SHA, 1982–. Chm. Organizing Cttee, Hammersmith Internat. Symposium on Molecular Endocrinology, 1967–79; Member: Orgng Cttee, Hormone and Cell Regulation Symposia, 1976–79; Adv. Council, Workshop on Vitamin D, 1977–79. Pres., Bone and Tooth Soc., 1984–; Member: Cttee, Soc. for Endocrinology, 1978–80; Biochem. Soc.; NIH Alumni Assoc; Amer. Endocrine Soc.; Amer. Soc. for Bone and Mineral Res.; European Calcified Tissue Soc.; Assoc. of Clin. Biochemists. Hon. MD Turin, 1985. Member Editorial Board: Clinical Endocrinology, 1975–79; Molecular and Cellular Endocrinology, 1975–80; Jl of Endocrinological Investigation; Jl of Mineral and Electrolyte Metabolism; Jl of Investigative and Cell Pathol.; Jl of Metabolic Bone Disease and Related Res. Gairdner Internat. Award, Toronto, 1967. *Publications:* articles in endocrinology. *Recreations:* tennis, squash, chess, music. *Address:* Great Broadhurst Farm, Broad Oak, Heathfield, East Sussex TN21 8UX. *T:* Burwash 883515. *Clubs:* Athenæum; Queen's, Hurlingham.

McINTYRE, Ian James; Controller, BBC Radio 3, since 1978; *b* Banchory, Kincardineshire, 9 Dec. 1931; *y s* of late Hector Harold McIntyre, Inverness, and late Annie Mary Michie, Ballater; *m* 1954, Leik Sommerfelt, 2nd *d* of late Benjamin Vogt, Kragerø, Norway; two *s* two *d*. *Educ:* Prescot Grammar Sch.; St John's Coll., Cambridge (Scholar; Med. and Mod. Langs Tripos, Pts I and II; BA 1953; MA); Coll. of Europe, Bruges. Pres., Cambridge Union, 1953. Commnd, Intelligence Corps, 1955–57. Current affairs talks producer, BBC, 1957; Editor, At Home and Abroad, 1959; Man. Trng Organiser, BBC Staff Trng Dept, 1960; Programme Services Officer, ITA, 1961; staff of

Chm., Cons. Party in Scotland, 1962; Dir of Inf. and Res., Scottish Cons. Central Office, 1965; contested (C) Roxburgh, Selkirk and Peebles, 1966; long-term contract, writer and broadcaster, BBC, 1970–76; presenter and interviewer, Analysis, and other programmes on politics, for. affairs and the arts; travelled widely in Europe, N America, Africa, Asia and ME; Controller, BBC Radio 4, 1976–78. *Publications:* The Proud Doers: Israel after twenty years, 1968; (ed and contrib.) Words: reflections on the uses of language, 1975; articles in The Listener. *Recreation:* family life. *Address:* BBC, Broadcasting House, W1A 1AA. *T:* 01–580 4468. *Clubs:* Beefsteak; Union (Cambridge).

McINTYRE, Very Rev. Prof. John, CVO 1985; DD, DLitt; FRSE; Professor of Divinity, University of Edinburgh, 1956–86; Dean of the Order of the Thistle, since 1974; an Extra Chaplain to the Queen in Scotland, 1974–75 and since 1986 (Chaplain to the Queen in Scotland, 1975–86); Moderator of the General Assembly of the Church of Scotland, 1982; *b* 20 May 1916; *s* of late John C. McIntyre, Bathgate, Scotland, and Annie McIntyre; *m* 1945, Jessie B., *d* of late William Buick, Coupar Angus; two *s* one *d*. *Educ:* Bathgate Academy; University of Edinburgh; MA (1938); BD (1941); DLitt (1953). Ordained, 1941; Locum Tenens, Parish of Glenorchy and Inishail, 1941–43; Minister of Parish of Fenwick, Ayrshire, 1943–45; Hunter Baillie Prof. of Theology, St Andrew's Coll., University of Sydney, 1946–56; Principal of St Andrew's Coll., 1950–56; Principal Warden, Pollock Halls of Residence, Univ. of Edinburgh, 1960–71; actg Principal and Vice-Chancellor, Edinburgh Univ., 1973–74, 1979; Principal, New Coll., and Dean of Faculty of Divinity, 1968–74. FRSE 1977 (Vice-Pres., 1983–86). DD *hc* Glasgow, 1961; DHL *hc*, Coll. of Wooster, Ohio, 1983. *Publications:* St Anselm and His Critics, 1954; The Christian Doctrine of History, 1957; On the Love of God, 1962; The Shape of Christology, 1966; articles and reviews in various learned jls of Theology. *Address:* 22/4 Minto Street, Edinburgh EH9 1RQ. *T:* 031–667 1203.

McINTYRE, Air Commodore Kenneth John, CB 1958; CBE 1951; JP; DL; RAF retired; *b* 23 July 1908; *s* of late William Seymour McIntyre and Winifred May McIntyre, Clevedon, Somerset; *m* 1936, Betty Aveley, *o d* of late Lt-Col Percie C. Cooper, Dulwich. *Educ:* Blundell's Sch.; RMC Sandhurst. Commissioned Royal Tank Regt, 1928; served UK and India; seconded to RAF 1934; permanent commission RAF, 1945. Served War of 1939–45 in UK, France and Belgium. Dep. Dir of Organisation, Air Ministry, 1945–47; Joint Services Staff Coll., 1947–48; Group Capt. 1947; Group Capt. Operations, HQ MEAF, 1948–50; idc 1951; SHAPE (Paris), 1952–54; Air Commodore, 1955; Dir of Policy (Air Staff), Air Ministry, 1955–58. Mem., Dorset CC, 1967–, Chm., 1981–; JP Poole, 1967 (Supplementary list, 1978); DL Dorset, 1983. *Address:* The East Penthouse, 57 Branksome Court, Canford Cliffs, Poole, Dorset BH13 7BD. *T:* Canford Cliffs 708250. *Club:* Royal Air Force.

McINTYRE, Robert Douglas, MB, ChB (Edinburgh), DPH (Glasgow); JP; Consultant Chest Physician; *b* Dec. 1913; 3rd *s* of Rev. John E. McIntyre and Catherine, *d* of Rev. William Morison, DD; *m* 1954, Letitia, *d* of Alexander Macleod; one *s*. *Educ:* Hamilton Acad.; Daniel Stewart's Coll.; University of Edinburgh. MP (Scottish Nationalist), Motherwell and Wishaw, April-July 1945. Contested (SNP): Motherwell, 1950; Perth and E Perthshire, 1951, 1955, 1959, 1964; W Stirlingshire, 1966, 1970; Stirling, Falkirk and Grangemouth, by-election 1971, Feb. and Oct. 1974. Chm., 1948–56, Pres., 1958–80, Scottish National Party; Mem., Stirling Town Council (Hon. Treas., 1958–64, Provost, 1967–75); Chancellor's Assessor, Stirling Univ. Court, 1979–; Freeman, Royal Burgh of Stirling, 1975. DUniv Stirling 1976. JP Co. Stirling. *Publications:* numerous articles on Scottish, political and medical subjects, including regular contribs to the Scots Independent. *Recreation:* yachting. *Address:* 8 Gladstone Place, Stirling. *T:* Stirling 3456. *Clubs:* Scottish Arts (Edinburgh); Stirling and County.

McINTYRE, Stuart Charles, MBE; FCIS; *b* 6 Feb. 1912; *s* of James and Eleanor McIntyre; *m* 1938, Edith Irene Walton; two *d*. *Educ:* Dulwich Coll. Served War, RAF, Wing Comdr, 1940–46. Joined Pearl Assurance Co. Ltd, 1930; Dir, 1952, Chm. 1972–77, Pres. 1977–80; Director: Arsenal Football Club Ltd, 1962–; The Charter Trust & Agency Ltd, 1962–82; The Cross Investment Trust Ltd, 1962–82; Property Holding & Investment Trust Ltd, 1965–82; Property Selection & Investment Trust Ltd, 1966–82; Property Selection Finance Ltd, 1966–82. Freeman, City of London; Past Master, Glass Sellers' Company. *Recreation:* Association football. *Address:* Barton, East Close, Middleton-on-Sea, Sussex. *T:* Middleton-on-Sea 3746. *Club:* Royal Air Force.

MACINTYRE, William Ian; Director-General, Energy Efficiency Office, Department of Energy, since 1983; *b* 20 July 1943; *s* of Mr and Mrs R. M. Macintyre; *m* 1967, Jennifer Mary Pitblado; one *s* two *d*. *Educ:* Merchiston Castle School, Edinburgh; St Andrews University. MA (Hons). British Petroleum Co. Ltd, 1965–72; ECGD, 1972–73; DTI, later Dept of Energy, 1973–77; seconded to ICFC, 1977–79; Asst Sec., Dept of Energy, Gas Div., 1979–83; Under-Sec. 1983. Governor: Shene Sch.; East Sheen Primary Sch. *Address:* Department of Energy, Thames House South, Millbank, SW1P 4QJ.

McINTYRE, Prof. William Ian Mackay, PhD; FRCVS; Director, International Trypanotolerance Centre, The Gambia, since 1984; *b* 7 July 1919; *s* of George John and Jane McIntyre; *m* 1948, Ruth Dick Galbraith; three *s*. *Educ:* Altnaharra Primary and Golspie Secondary Sch., Sutherland; Royal (Dick) Veterinary Coll. (MRCVS); University of Edinburgh (PhD). FRCVS 1983. Clinical Asst, Royal (Dick) Veterinary Coll., 1944–48; Lectr, Vet. Med., Royal (Dick) Vet. Coll., 1948–51; Sen. Lectr, Vet. Med., University of Glasgow, 1951–61, Prof. of Vet. Med., 1961–83. Seconded to University of East Africa, University Coll., Nairobi, as Dean, Faculty of Veterinary Science, and Prof., Clinical Studies, 1963–67. *Publications:* various, on canine nephritis, parasitic diseases and vaccines, clinical communications, and African Trypanosomiasis. *Address:* International Trypanotolerance Centre, PO Box 2571, Serrekunda, The Gambia.

McIVOR, Rt. Hon. Basil; *see* McIvor, Rt Hon. W. B.

McIVOR, Donald Kenneth; Chairman of the Board and Chief Executive Officer, Imperial Oil Ltd, since 1982; *b* 12 April 1928; *s* of Kenneth MacIver McIvor and Nellie Beatrice McIvor (*née* Rutherford); *m* 1953, Avonia Isabel Forbes; four *s* one *d*. *Educ:* Univ. of Manitoba (BSc Hons in Geol.). Joined Imperial Oil, 1950; operational and res. assignments, Exploration Dept, 1950–58; gen. planning and res. management positions, 1958–68; Asst Manager and Manager, Corporate Planning, 1968–70; Exploration Manager, 1970–72; Nat. Defence Coll., 1972–73; Sen. Vice-Pres., 1973–75; Exec. Vice-Pres., 1975–77; Vice-Pres., oil and gas exploration and prodn, Exxon Corp., NY, 1977–81; Dep. Chm., Imperial Oil, 1981. *Address:* (office) 111 St Clair Avenue West, Toronto, Ontario M5W 1K3, Canada. *T:* (416) 968–4111. *Club:* York (Toronto).

McIVOR, (Frances) Jill; Northern Ireland Member, Independent Broadcasting Authority, since 1980; *b* 10 Aug. 1930; *d* of Cecil Reginald Johnston Anderson and Frances Ellen (*née* Henderson); *m* 1953, William Basil McIvor, *qv*; two *s* one *d*. *Educ:* Methodist Coll.; Lurgan Coll.; Queen's Univ. of Belfast (LLB Hons). Called to Bar of Northern Ireland, 1980. Asst Librarian (Law), QUB, 1954–55; Tutor in Legal Res., Law Faculty, QUB, 1965–74; editorial staff, NI Legal Qtly, 1966–76; Librarian, Dept of Dir of Public Prosecutions, 1977–79. Chm., Lagan Valley Regional Park Cttee, 1984– (Mem., 1975); Member: Ulster Countryside Cttee, 1984–; Fair Employment Agency, 1984–; Lay Panel, Juvenile Court, 1976–77; GDC, 1979–; Exec., Belfast Voluntary Welfare Soc., 1981–; Court, Univ. of Ulster, 1984–; Adv. Council, Co-operation North, 1985–; Adv. Panel on Community Radio, 1985–. *Publications:* Irish Consultant (and contrib.), Manual of Law Librarianship, 1976; (ed) Elegentia Juris: selected writings of F. H. Newark, 1973; Chart of the English Reports (new edn), 1982. *Recreations:* gardening, bees. *Address:* Larkhill, 98 Spa Road, Ballynahinch, Co. Down. *T:* Ballynahinch 563534. *Club:* Royal Commonwealth Society.

McIVOR, Rt. Hon. (William) Basil, PC (NI) 1971; *b* 17 June 1928; 2nd *s* of Rev. Frederick McIvor, Methodist clergyman and Lilly McIvor; *m* 1953, Frances Jill Anderson (*see* F. J. McIvor); two *s* one *d*. *Educ:* Methodist Coll., Belfast; Queen's Univ., Belfast. LLB 1948. Called to NI Bar, 1950; Jun. Crown Counsel, Co. Down, Sept. 1974; Resident Magistrate, Dec. 1974. MP (UU) Larkfield, NI Parlt, 1969; Minister of Community Relations, NI, 1971–72; Member (UU) for S Belfast, NI Assembly, 1973–75; Minister of Education, NI, 1974. Governor, Campbell Coll., 1975–, Chm., 1983–; Chm., Lagan Coll., Belfast, 1981– (the first integrated RC and Protestant school in NI). *Recreations:* golf, music, gardening. *Address:* Larkhill, 98 Spa Road, Ballynahinch, Co Down. *T:* Ballynahinch 563534. *Club:* Royal Commonwealth Society.

MACK, Alan Frederick, JP; Director, Manchester Chamber of Commerce and Industry, 1971–81; *b* 5 Dec. 1920; *s* of late Stanley Mack and late Sarah Elizabeth Mack; *m* 1953, Ailsa Muriel Wells; two *d*. *Educ:* Manchester Grammar School. War Service, Royal Artillery, Middle East, Italy, 1940–46. Secretary, Textile Finishing Trade Assocs, 1946–68; Commercial Manager, British Textile Employers Assoc., 1968–70. Jt Hon. Sec., NW Industrial Develt Assoc., 1971–81; Hon. Sec., Manchester Post Office Adv. Cttee, 1971–81; Mem., NW Supplementary Benefits Tribunal, 1977–; Hon. Sec., Greater Manchester East County Scout Council, 1974–80; Pres., Manchester Jun. Ch. of Commerce, 1956–57. JP Manchester (Inner), 1974. *Recreations:* reading, gardening, historic buildings. *Address:* 22 Appleby Road, Gatley, Cheadle, Cheshire SK8 4QD. *T:* 061–428 6512.

MACK, Prof. Alan Osborne, MDS; FDS RCS; Professor of Dental Prosthetics, Institute of Dental Surgery, University of London, 1967–80, now Emeritus; Consultant Dental Surgeon, Eastman Dental Hospital; Civilian Consultant in Dental Prosthetics to the Royal Air Force since 1976; *b* 24 July 1918; *s* of Arthur Joseph Mack, Glos, and Florence Emily Mack (*née* Norris); *m* 1943, Marjorie Elizabeth (*née* Westacott); two *s* one *d*. *Educ:* Westbourne Park Sch.; London Univ. LDS RCS 1942; MDS Durham, 1958; FDS RCS 1971. House Surgeon, Royal Dental Hosp., Sch. of Dental Surgery, University of London, 1942–43; served in RAF Dental Branch, 1943–47; Demonstrator, Prosthetics Dept Royal Dental Hosp., 1948; successively Asst Dir, Prosthetics Dept, and Senior Lecturer, London Univ., Royal Dental Hosp., 1949–56; Prof. of Dental Prosthetics, Univ. of Newcastle upon Tyne (formerly King's Coll., Univ. of Durham), 1956–67; Examiner in Dental Prosthetics, Royal Coll. of Surgeons of England, 1956; Examiner, University of Manchester, 1959, Leeds, 1961, Glasgow, 1961, Liverpool, 1965, London, 1965, Edinburgh, 1968, Lagos, 1970, Singapore, Khartoum, 1977; Benghazi, 1978; Examination Visitor, GDC; Advisor, Univ. of Malaya. Mem. Board of Faculty, Royal College of Surgeons, 1959. Pres. British Soc. for Study of Prosthetic Dentistry (BSSPD), 1963. Hon. Consultant, Stoke Mandeville Hosp., 1976; part-time Consultant, John Radcliffe Hosp., 1980–. Vis. Prof., Univ. of Singapore, 1981–. Hon. Mem., Amer. Acad. of Implant Dentures, 1966. *Publications:* Full Dentures, 1971; articles in British Dental Jls. *Recreations:* gardening, pottery. *Address:* Home Farm, London Road, Aston Clinton, Bucks HP22 5HG.

MACK, Keith Robert; Full-time Member and Group Director, Civil Aviation Authority, since 1985; Controller, National Air Traffic Services, since 1985; *b* 2 March 1933; *s* of late David Stanley Mack and of Dorothy Ivy Mack (*née* Bowes); *m* 1960, Eileen Mary Cuttell; two *s* four *d*. *Educ:* Edmonton County School. RAF Pilot, 1951–58; Civilian Air Traffic Control Officer, Scottish and Oceanic Air Traffic Control Centre, 1960–67; RAF Staff College, Bracknell, 1968; NATS HQ, 1969–71; ATC Watch Supervisor, Scottish ATCC, 1972–73; CAA Chief Officer, Cardiff Airport, 1974; NATS HQ, 1975–76; ATC Watch Supervisor, London ATCC, 1977; NATS Dep. Dir of Control (Airspace Policy), 1978–79; Supt, London ATCC, 1980–82; Dep. Controller, NATS, 1983–84. *Recreations:* DIY house refurbishing, cycling, walking, photography. *Address:* National Air Traffic Services, CAA House, 43–59 Kingsway, WC2B 6TE. *T:* 01–379 7311.

MACK SMITH, Denis, FBA 1976; FRSL; Senior Research Fellow, since 1962 and Sub-Warden, 1984–86, All Souls College, Oxford; *b* 3 March 1920; *s* of Wilfrid Mack Smith and Altiora Gauntlett; *m* 1963, Catharine Stevenson; two *d*. *Educ:* St Paul's Cathedral Choir Sch.; Haileybury Coll.; Peterhouse, Cambridge Univ. (organ and history schols). MA Cantab, MA Oxon. Asst Master, Clifton Coll., 1941–42; Cabinet Offices, 1942–46; Fellow of Peterhouse, Cambridge, 1947–62 (Hon. Fellow, 1986); Tutor of Peterhouse, 1948–58; Univ. Lectr, Cambridge, 1952–62. Commendatore dell'Ordine al Merito della Repubblica Italiana. For. Hon. Mem., Amer. Acad. of Arts and Sciences. Oratore Ufficiale della Repubblica di San Marino, 1982. Awards: Thirlwall, 1949; Serena, 1960; Elba, 1972; Villa di Chiesa, 1973; Mondello, 1975; Nove Muse, 1976; Duff Cooper Meml., 1977; Wolfson Literary, 1977; Rhegium Julii, 1983. *Publications:* Cavour and Garibaldi 1860, 1954; Garibaldi, 1957; (jtly) British Interests in the Mediterranean and Middle East, 1958; Italy, a Modern History, 1959 (enlarged edn 1969); Medieval Sicily, 1968; Modern Sicily, 1968; Da Cavour a Mussolini, 1968; (ed) The Making of Italy 1796–1870, 1968; (ed) Garibaldi, 1969; (ed) E. Quinet, Le Rivoluzioni d'Italia, 1970; Victor Emanuel, Cavour and the Risorgimento, 1971; (ed) G. La Farina, Scritti Politici, 1972; Vittorio Emanuele II, 1972; Mussolini's Roman Empire, 1976; Un Monumento al Duce, 1976; Cento Anni di Vita Italiana attraverso il Corriere della Sera, 1978; L'Italia del Ventesimo Secolo, 1978; (ed) G. Bandi, I mille: da Genova a Capua, 1981; Mussolini, 1981; (ed) F. De Sanctis, Un Viaggio Elettorale, 1983; Cavour, 1985; Jt Editor, Nelson History of England, 1962–. *Address:* All Souls College, Oxford. *T:* Oxford 722251; White Lodge, Osler Road, Headington, Oxford. *T:* Oxford 62878.

McKAIG, Adm. Sir (John) Rae, KCB 1973; CBE 1966; *b* 24 April 1922; *s* of late Sir John McKaig, KCB, DSO, and Lady (Annie Wright) McKaig (*née* Lee), *m* 1945, Barbara Dawn, *d* of Dr F. K. Marriott, MC, Yoxford, Suffolk; two *s* one *d*. *Educ:* Loretto Sch. Joined RN as Special Entry Cadet, 1939; served in cruisers and destroyers in Home and Mediterranean Waters, 1940–43; in Amphibious Force S at invasion of Normandy, 1944; in coastal forces until 1945; qual. in Communications, 1945; Commander, 1952; Captain, 1959; served as Dep. to Chief Polaris Exec., 1963–66; comd HM Signal Sch., 1966–68; Rear-Adm., 1968; Asst Chief of Naval Staff (Operational Requirements), 1968–70; Vice-Adm., 1970; Flag Officer, Plymouth, and Port Admiral, Devonport, Comdr Central Sub Area, E Atlantic, and Comdr Plymouth Sub Area, Channel, 1970–73; Adm., 1973; UK Mil. Rep. to NATO, 1973–75. Mem., Royal Patriotic Fund Corp., 1978–. *Recreations:* offshore sailing, shooting, fishing. *Address:* Hill House, Hambledon, Hants. *Clubs:* Army and Navy, Royal Ocean Racing.

McKANE, Prof. William, FRSE 1984; FBA 1980; Professor of Hebrew and Oriental Languages, University of St Andrews, since 1968; Principal of St Mary's College, St Andrews, 1982–86; *b* 18 Feb. 1921; *s* of Thomas McKane and Jemima Smith McKane; *m* 1952, Agnes Mathie Howie; three *s* two *d*. *Educ:* Univ. of St Andrews (MA 1949); Univ. of Glasgow (MA 1952, PhD 1956, DLitt 1980). RAF, 1941–45. University of Glasgow: Asst in Hebrew, 1953–56; Lectr in Hebrew, 1956–65; Sen. Lectr, 1965–68; Dean, Faculty of Divinity, St Andrews, 1973–77. Foreign Sec., Soc. for Old Testament Study, 1981 (Pres., 1978); Chm., Peshitta project (Old Testament in Syriac), Internat. Org. for Study of Old Testament. DD (*hc*) Edinburgh, 1984. Burkitt Medal, British Acad., 1985. *Publications:* Prophets and Wise Men, 1965; Proverbs: a new approach, 1970; Studies in the Patriarchal Narratives, 1979; Jeremiah 1–25 (International Critical Commentary series), 1986; articles and reviews in British and European learned jls. *Recreations:* St Andrews association football blue (1949), walking, including hill walking. *Address:* 51 Irvine Crescent, St Andrews, Fife KY16 8LJ. *T:* St Andrews 73797. *Club:* Royal and Ancient Golf (St Andrews).

MACKANESS, George Bellamy, MB, BS, DPhil; FRS 1976; President, Squibb Institute for Medical Research and Development, since 1976; *b* Sydney, Australia, 20 Aug. 1922; *s* of James V. Mackaness and Eleanor F. Mackaness; *m* 1945, Gwynneth Patterson; one *s*. *Educ:* Sydney Univ. (MB, BS Hons 1945); London Univ. (DCP 1948); Univ. of Oxford (Hon. MA 1949, DPhil 1953). Resident MO, Sydney Hosp., 1945–46; Resident Pathologist, Kanematsu Inst. of Pathology, Sydney Hosp., 1946–47; Dept of Path., Brit. Postgrad. Med. Sch., London Univ., 1947–48 (DCP); ANU Trav. Scholarship, Univ. of Oxford, 1948–51; Demonstrator and Tutor in Path., Sir William Dunn Sch. of Path., Oxford, 1949–53; Dept of Experimental Pathology, Australian National University: Sen. Fellow, 1954–58; Associate Prof. of Exp. Path., 1958–60; Professorial Fellow, 1960–63; Vis. Investigator, Rockefeller Univ., NY, 1959–60; Prof. of Microbiology, Univ. of Adelaide, 1963–65; Dir, Trudeau Inst. for Med. Res., NY, 1965–76; Adjunct Prof. of Path., NY Univ. Med. Center, 1969–. Director: Josiah Macy Jr Foundn, 1982–; Squibb Corp., 1984–. Member: Allergy and Immunol. Study Sect., Nat. Insts of Health, 1967–71; Bd of Sci. Counsellors, Nat. Inst. of Allergy and Infect. Diseases, 1971–75; Armed Forces Epidemicol Bd, 1967–73; Bd of Governors, W. Alton Jones Cell Science Center, 1970–72; Council, Tissue Culture Assoc., 1973–; Bd of Sci. Consultants, Sloan-Kettering Inst. Member: Amer. Assoc. of Immunologists; Amer. Assoc. for Advancement of Science; Reticuloendothelial Soc.; Lung Assoc.; Internat. Union Against Tuberculosis; Amer. Soc. of Microbiologists. Fellow, Amer. Acad. of Arts and Scis, 1978. Paul Ehrlich-Ludwig Darmstaedter Prize, 1975. *Address:* 71 Sutphin Pines, Yardley, Pa 19067, USA. *T:* (215) 295–2362.

MACKAY, family name of **Earl of Inchcape, Lord Reay** and **Barons Mackay of Clashfern** and **Tanlaw.**

MACKAY OF CLASHFERN, Baron *cr* 1979 (Life Peer), of Eddrachillis in the District of Sutherland; **James Peter Hymers Mackay;** PC 1979; FRSE 1984; a Lord of Appeal in Ordinary, since 1985; *b* 2 July 1927; *s* of James Mackay and Janet Hymers; *m* 1958, Elizabeth Gunn Hymers; one *s* two *d*. *Educ:* George Heriot's Sch., Edinburgh. MA Hons Maths and Nat. Philosophy, Edinburgh Univ., 1948; Lectr in Mathematics, Univ. of St Andrews, 1948–50; Major Schol., Trinity Coll., Cambridge, in Mathematics, 1947, taken up 1950; Senior Schol. 1951; BA (Cantab) 1952; LLB Edinburgh (with Distinction) 1955. Admitted to Faculty of Advocates, 1955; QC (Scot.) 1965; Standing Junior Counsel to: Queen's and Lord Treasurer's Remembrancer; Scottish Home and Health Dept; Commissioners of Inland Revenue in Scotland; Sheriff Principal, Renfrew and Argyll, 1972–74; Vice-Dean, Faculty of Advocates, 1973–76; Dean, 1976–79; Lord Advocate of Scotland, 1979–84; a Senator of Coll. of Justice in Scotland, 1984–85. Part-time Mem., Scottish Law Commn, 1976–79. Hon. Master of the Bench, Inner Temple, 1979. Fellow: Internat. Acad. of Trial Lawyers, 1979; Inst. of Taxation, 1981. Dir, Stenhouse Holdings Ltd, 1976–77. Mem., Insurance Brokers' Registration Council, 1977–79. A Comr of Northern Lighthouses, 1975–84. Hon. LLD: Edinburgh, 1983; Dundee, 1983; Strathclyde, 1985. *Publication:* Armour on Valuation for Rating, 5th edn (Consultant Editor), 1985. *Recreation:* walking. *Address:* 19/11 East Parkside, Edinburgh. *T:* 031–667 5995. *Club:* New (Edinburgh).

MACKAY, Alastair, CMG 1966; *b* 27 Sept. 1911; *s* of late Alexander Mackay; *m* 1st, 1939, Janetta Brown Ramsay (*d* 1973); one *s* one *d*; 2nd, 1975, Edith Whicher. *Educ:* George Heriot's Sch.; Edinburgh Univ.; Berlin Univ. Entered HM Treasury, 1940. Member UK Treasury and Supply Delegation, Washington, 1951–54; seconded to Foreign Service Inspectorate, 1957–59; Financial Adviser to the British High Commissioner in India, 1963–66; Under-Sec., HM Treasury, 1967–71; Financial and Development Sec., Gibraltar, 1971–75. *Recreations:* golf, gardening. *Address:* 3 Cloona House, 38 Carlisle Road, Eastbourne, E Sussex BN20 7TD. *T:* Eastbourne 22738.

McKAY, Prof. Alexander Gordon, FRSC 1965; Professor of Classics, McMaster University, since 1957; President, Royal Society of Canada, 1984–87; *b* 24 Dec. 1924; *s* of Alexander Lynn McKay and Marjory Maude Redfern Nicoll McKay; *m* 1964, Helen Jean Zulauf; two step *d*. *Educ:* Trinity Coll., Toronto (Hons BA Classics 1946); Yale Univ. (MA 1947); Princeton Univ. (AM 1948; PhD 1950). Classics faculty: Wells Coll., NY, 1949–50; Univ. of Pennsylvania, 1950–51; Univ. of Manitoba, 1951–52; Mount Allison Univ., 1952–53; Waterloo Coll., Ont., 1953–55; Univ. of Manitoba, 1955–57; McMaster Univ., 1957–: Chm. of Dept, 1962–68, 1976–79; Founding Dean of Humanities, 1968–73; Senator, 1968–73, 1985–. Dist. Vis. Prof., Univ. of Colorado, 1973; Prof. i/c, Intercollegiate Center for Classical Studies in Rome (Stanford Univ.), 1975; Mem. Inst. for Advanced Study, Princeton, 1979, 1981. Dir, Internat. Union of Academics, 1980–83, 1986– (Vice-Pres., 1983–86). Hon. LLD Manitoba, 1986. KStJ 1986. Silver Jubilee Medal, 1977. *Publications:* Naples and Campania: texts and illustrations, 1962; Roman Lyric Poetry: Catullus and Horace, 1962; Vergil's Italy, 1970; Cumae and the Phlegraean Fields, 1972; Naples and Coastal Campania, 1972; Houses, Villas and Palaces in the Roman World, 1975, German edn 1980; Roman Satire, 1976; Vitruvius, Architect and Engineer, 1978; Roma Antiqua: Latium and Etruria, 1986. *Recreations:* surface archaeology, pianoforte, travel. *Address:* 1 Turner Avenue, Hamilton, Ont L8P 3K4, Canada. *T:* 416 526 1331; Royal Society of Canada, 344 Wellington Street, Ottawa, Ont K1A 0N4, Canada. *T:* 613 992 3468. *Clubs:* Princeton (NY); University (Pittsburgh); Tamahaac (Ancaster, Hamilton); Arts and Letters (Toronto); President's (McMaster Univ.); Canadian (Hamilton).

McKAY, Maj.-Gen. Alexander Matthew, CB 1975; FEng 1984; Secretary, Institution of Mechanical Engineers, since 1976; Vice-Chairman, Mechanical Engineering Publications Ltd, since 1976; Chairman, Stocklake Holdings Ltd, since 1976; Director, Northgate Publishing Co. Ltd, since 1978; *b* 14 Feb. 1921; *s* of Colin and Anne McKay; *m* 1949, Betty Margaret Lee; one *s* one *d* (and one *d* decd). *Educ:* Esplanade House Sch.; RN Dockyard Sch.; Portsmouth Polytechnic. FIEE, FIMechE, CBIM, psc, sm; Member: ASME; SAE (USA). Served War of 1939–45 (despatches twice); 2nd Lieut, 1943; Lieut 1944; Captain 1944; Major 1947; Lt-Col 1960; Col 1966; Brigadier 1968; Maj.-Gen. 1972. Served with 6th Airborne Div.; Staff Coll., Quetta, 1954; staff appts include GS02, DAA&QMG, DAQMG, AQMG; Dir, Elect. and Mech. Engrg, Army, 1972–75; Col Comdt, REME, 1974–80. Gen. Sec., IChemE, 1975–76. Mem. Council, IEE, 1973–76. FInstD; FRSE, 1985. Freeman, City of London, 1984; Liveryman, Engineers' Co., 1984–. *Publications:* papers in Proceedings IMechE and REME Institution. *Recreations:* fly fishing, gardening, restoring antique furniture. *Address:* Church Cottage, Martyr Worthy, near Winchester, Hants SO21 1DY. *Clubs:* Caledonian, Institute of Directors.

McKAY, Allen; JP; MP (Lab) Barnsley West and Penistone, since 1983 (Pensistone, July 1978–1983); *b* 5 Feb. 1927; *s* of Fred and Martha Anne McKay; *m* 1949, June Simpson; one *s*. *Educ:* Hoyland Kirk Balk Secondary Modern School; extramural studies, Univ. of Sheffield. Clerical work, Steel Works, 1941–45; general mineworker, 1945–47; Mining Electrical Engineer, 1947–65; NCB Industrial Relations Trainee, 1965–66; Asst Manpower Officer, Barnsley Area, NCB, 1966–78. Opposition Whip, 1981. JP Barnsley, 1971. *Recreation:* reading. *Address:* House of Commons, SW1; 24 Springwood Road, Hoyland, Barnsley, South Yorks S74 0AZ. *T:* Barnsley 743418.

MacKAY, Andrew James; MP (C) Berkshire East, since 1983; Partner, Jones MacKay & Croxford, Estate Agents, since 1974; *b* 27 Aug. 1949; *s* of Robert James MacKay and Olive Margaret MacKay; *m* 1975, Diana Joy (*née* Kinchin) one *s* one *d*. *Educ:* Solihull. Consultant, Birmingham Housing Industries Ltd, 1973–. MP (C) Birmingham, Stechford, Mar. 1977–1979; PPS to Sec. of State for NI, 1986–. Mem., Environment Select Cttee, 1985–86; Sec., Cons. Parly For. Affairs Cttee, 1985–86. Mem., Conservative Party Nat. Exec., 1979–82. *Recreations:* golf, squash, good food. *Address:* House of Commons, SW1A 0AA. *T:* 01–219 4109. *Clubs:* Birmingham (Birmingham); Olton Golf (Solihull); Aberdovey Golf (Wales).

McKAY, Archibald Charles; Sheriff of Glasgow and Strathkelvin, since 1979; *b* 18 Oct. 1929; *s* of Patrick McKay and Catherine (*née* McKinlay); *m* 1956, Ernestine Maria Tobia; one *s* three *d*. *Educ:* Knocknacarry, Co. Antrim; St Aloysius' Coll., Glasgow; Glasgow Univ. (MA, LLB 1954). National Service, 1955–56. Started practice in Glasgow as solicitor, 1957; estabd own firm of solicitors, 1961; apptd to the Bench, 1978. *Recreations:* flying, amateur radio, motor-cycling. *Address:* 18 Dargarvel Avenue, Dumbreck, Glasgow G41 5LU. *T:* 041–427 1525.

MACKAY, A(rthur) Stewart, ROI 1949; Teacher, Hammersmith College of Art, 1960–68, retired; *b* 25 Feb. 1909; British. *Educ:* Wilson's Grammar Sch.; Regent Street Polytechnic School of Art. Art Master, Regent Street Polytechnic School of Art, 1936, Assistant Lecturer, 1936–60. Served War of 1939–45: enlisted Army, Jan. 1942; released with rank of Captain, 1946. Exhibitor: RA (44 pictures exhibited); Paris Salon; ROI; RBA; Leicester Galleries; Imperial War Museum; Royal Scottish Academy; New York. *Publications:* How to Make Lino Cuts, 1935; articles for Artist and Kent Life, 1953, 1963. *Recreations:* reading, writing. *Address:* 4 Dog Kennel Hill, East Dulwich, SE22.

MACKAY, Charles, CB 1986; FIBiol; Chief Agricultural Officer, Department of Agriculture and Fisheries for Scotland, 1975–87; *b* 12 Jan. 1927; *s* of Hugh and Eliza Mackay; *m* 1956, Marie A. K. Mackay (*née* Mitchell); one *s* one *d*. *Educ:* Strathmore Sch., Sutherland; Lairg Higher Grade Sch., Sutherland; Univ. of Aberdeen (BScAgric); Univ. of Kentucky (MSc). Department of Agriculture and Fisheries for Scotland: Temporary Inspector, 1947–48; Asst Inspector, 1948–54; Inspector, 1954–64; Sen. Inspector, 1964–70; Technical Develt Officer, 1970–73; Dep. Chief Agricl Officer, 1973–75. Hon. Order of Kentucky Colonels, 1960. *Recreations:* fishing, golf. *Address:* Dun Dornaig, 35 Boswall Road, Edinburgh EH5 3RP. *T:* 031–552 6063.

MACKAY, Donald George; Under Secretary, Scottish Development Department, since 1985; *b* 25 Nov. 1929; *s* of William Morton Mackay and Annie Tainsh Higgs; *m* 1965, Elizabeth Ailsa Barr; two *s* one *d*. *Educ:* Morgan Academy, Dundee; St Andrews Univ. (MA). National Service, RA. Assistant Principal, Scottish Home Dept, 1953; Asst Private Sec. to Sec. of State for Scotland, 1959; Asst Sec., Royal Commission on the Police, 1960–62; Sec., Royal Commission on Local Govt in Scotland, 1966–69; Asst Sec., Scottish Development Dept, 1969–79; Dept of Agriculture and Fisheries for Scotland: Asst Sec., 1980–83; Under Sec., 1983–85. *Recreations:* hill walking, photography, music. *Address:* 38 Cluny Drive, Edinburgh EH10 6DX. *T:* 031–447 1851.

MacKAY, Prof. Donald Iain; Chairman, PIEDA Ltd, since 1974; Consultant to Secretary of State for Scotland, since 1971; *b* 27 Feb. 1937; *s* of William and Rhona MacKay; *m* 1961, Diana Marjory (*née* Raffan); one *s* two *d*. *Educ:* Dollar Academy; Univ. of Aberdeen (MA). English Electric Co., 1959–62; Lectr in Political Economy, Univ. of Aberdeen, 1962–65; Lectr in Applied Economics, Univ. of Glasgow, 1965–68, Sen. Lectr, 1968–71; Prof. of Political Economy, Univ. of Aberdeen, 1971–76; Prof. of Economics, Heriot-Watt Univ., Edinburgh, 1976–82, Professorial Fellow 1982–. Lister Lectr, British Assoc. for the Advancement of Science, 1974. Director: Edinburgh Financial Trust, 1983–; Adam and Co., 1983–; Chm., Ainslie Investments Ltd, 1983–; City of Edinburgh Life Assurance Co., 1984–. Indep. Mem., Sea Fish Industry Authority, 1982–; Mem., S of Scotland Electricity Bd, 1984–. *Publications:* Geographical Mobility and the Brain Drain, 1969; Local Labour Markets and Wage Structures, 1970; Labour Markets under Different Employment Conditions, 1971; The Political Economy of North Sea Oil, 1975; (ed) Scotland 1980: the economics of self-government, 1977; articles in Econ. Jl, Oxford Econ. Papers, Manch. Sch., Scottish Jl Polit. Econ., Jl Royal Stat. Soc. *Recreations:* tennis, chess, golf. *Address:* Newfield, 14 Gamekeeper's Road, Edinburgh EH4 6LU.

MacKAY, Prof. Donald MacCrimmon, BSc, PhD, FInstP; Professor Emeritus, University of Keele; Joint Editor, Biological Cybernetics; *b* 9 Aug. 1922; *o s* of Dr Henry MacKay; *m* 1955, Valerie Wood; two *s* three *d*. *Educ:* Wick High Sch.; St Andrews Univ. BSc (St Andrews) 1943; PhD (London) 1951. Radar research, Admiralty, 1943–46; Assistant Lecturer in Physics, 1946–48, Lecturer, 1948–59, Reader, 1959–60, King's Coll., London, FKC 1979; Granada Research Prof. of Communication and Neuroscience, Univ. of Keele, 1960–82. Rockefeller Fellow in USA, 1951. Vis. Prof., Univ. of California, 1969; Lectures: Fleming, 1961; Eddington, 1967, Herter, Johns Hopkins Univ., 1971; Foerster, Univ. of California, 1973; Drummond, Univ. of Stirling, 1975; Fremantle, Balliol Coll. Oxford, 1975; Riddell, Univ. of Newcastle, 1977; Pascal, Univ. of Waterloo, 1979; Kelvin, IEE, 1985; Gifford, Univ. of Glasgow, 1986. Foreign Mem., Royal Netherlands Acad. of Arts and Sciences, 1983. Hon. DSc St Andrews, 1986. *Publications:* (with M. E. Fisher) Analogue Computing at Ultra-High Speed, 1962; (ed) Christianity in a Mechanistic Universe, 1965; Freedom of Action in a Mechanistic Universe, 1967; Information, Mechanism and Meaning, 1969; The Clockwork Image, 1974; Science, Chance and Providence, 1978; Human Science and Human Dignity, 1979; Brains, Machines and Persons, 1980; Science and the Quest for Meaning, 1982; Visual Neuroscience, 1986; *chapters in:* Communication Theory, 1953; Information Theory, 1956, 1961; Sensory Communication, 1961; Man and his Future, 1963; Science in its Context, 1964; Information Processing in the Nervous System, 1964; Brain and Conscious Experience, 1966; Structure and Function of Inhibitory Neuronal Mechanisms, 1968; Evoked Brain Potentials, 1969; The Neurosciences, 1971; Non-Verbal Communication, 1972; Handbook of Sensory Physiology, 1973; Cybernetics and Bionics, 1974; Modifying Man: implications and ethics, 1978; Cerebral Correlates of Conscious Experience, 1978;

Motivation, Motor and Sensory Processes of the Brain, 1980; Neural Communication and Control, 1981; Thinking: the expanding frontier, 1983; The Study of Information, 1983; Handbook of Cognitive Neuroscience, 1983; Cognition and Motor Processes, 1984; Models of the Visual Cortex, 1985; scientific papers on electronic computing, information theory, experimental psychology, neurophysiology. *Recreation:* photography. *Address:* The Croft, Keele, Staffs ST5 5AN. *T:* Newcastle (Staffs) 627300.

McKAY, Hon. Sir Donald Norman, KCMG 1978; farmer and politician, New Zealand; Chairman, New Zealand Ports Authority; *b* Waipu, NZ, 28 Nov. 1908; *s* of Angus John McKay; *m* 1934, Miriam Hilda, *d* of A. T. Stehr; two *s* one *d*. *Educ:* Whangarei High Sch.; Auckland Univ. MP, Marsden, NZ, 1954–72; Minister of Health and Social Security, and Minister in Charge of Child Welfare Div., 1962–72. Member: Marsden National Party; Waipu Centenary Celebrations Cttee; Caledonian Soc.; District High Sch. Cttee; Northland Harbour Bd (Chm. 1974–). *Recreations:* bowls, golf; rep. Auckland Univ., Rugby football, 1928–30; N Auckland, cricket, 1932–36. *Address:* Waipu, Northland, New Zealand.

MACKAY, Eric Beattie; Editor of The Scotsman, 1972–85; *b* 31 Dec. 1922; *s* of Lewis Mackay and Agnes Johnstone; *m* 1954, Moya Margaret Myles Connolly (*d* 1981); three *s* one *d*. *Educ:* Aberdeen Grammar Sch.; Aberdeen Univ. (MA). Aberdeen Bon-Accord, 1948; Elgin Courant, 1949; The Scotsman, 1950; Daily Telegraph, 1952; The Scotsman, 1953: London Editor, 1957; Dep. Editor, 1961. *Recreations:* travel, golf, theatre. *Address:* 5 Strathearn Place, Edinburgh EH9 2AL. *T:* 031–447 7737.

MACKAY, Maj.-Gen. Eric MacLachlan, CBE 1971 (MBE 1944); Managing Director, Forum Development Pte Ltd, since 1983; *b* 26 Dec. 1921; *s* of Ian MacLachlan Mackay and Violet Aimée Scott-Smith; *m* 1954, Ruth Thérèse Roth (*d* 1985); one *s*. *Educ:* Fettes Coll., Edinburgh. Served War: enlisted Royal Scots Fusiliers, 1940; commissioned Oct. 1941, Royal Engineers; 2/Lieut-Major, 1st Parachute Sqdn, RE, 1941–45, N Africa, Sicily, Italy, Arnhem, PoW (escaped) Norway. OC, Field Company, 20 Indian Div., French Indo-China, 1945–46; 2 i/c 23 Indian Div. Engrs, Java, 1946; OC, 35 Indian Field Company, Malaya, 1947; Supplementary Engrg Course, SME, 1948; GSO 2 Intell., Jt Intell. Bureau, 1949–50; Staff Coll., 1951; GSO 2, Org. and Equipment, HQ, ALFCE, 1952–53; Sen. Instructor Tactics, SME, 1954–55; OC, 33 Field Sqdn, RE, Cyprus, Suez, 1956–58; GSO 2, Wpns, MoD, 1958–60; JSSC, 1960; 2 i/c 2 Div. Engrs, 1961–62; Chief Engr, Malaysian Army, Borneo/Malaya, 1963–65; GSO 1, Co-ord., Master-Gen. of the Ordnance, 1966–67; Col, GS, RSME, 1968–69; Chief Engr (Brig.): Army Strategic Command, 1970–71; UK Land Forces, 1972; Maj.-Gen. 1973; Chief Engr, BAOR, 1973–76, retired. Managing Director: Cementation Sico Oman Ltd, 1977; Galadari Cementation Pte Ltd, 1978–83; Regional Dir Iraq, Engineering Services Internat., 1981–82. CEng 1976; MICE 1976. DSC (USA), 1944; Pingat Peringatan Malaysia (PPM), 1965. *Recreations:* motoring, skiing, photography.

McKAY, Frederick; *see* McKay, J. F.

MACKAY, Sir (George Patrick) Gordon, Kt 1966; CBE 1962; Director, World Bank, 1975–78; Member, Board of Crown Agents, 1980–82; *b* 12 Nov. 1914; *s* of Rev. Adam Mackay and Katie Forrest (*née* Lawrence); *m* 1954, Margaret Esmé Martin; one *s* two *d*. *Educ:* Gordon Sch., Huntly; Aberdeen Univ. Joined Kenya and Uganda Railways and Harbours (later East African Railways and Harbours), 1938; Chief Asst to Gen. Manager, 1948; Chief Operating Supt, 1954; Dep. General Manager, 1960, General Manager, 1961–64; with World Bank, 1965–78. FCIT (MInstT 1961). OStJ 1964. *Recreation:* golf. *Address:* Well Cottage, Sandhills, Brook, Surrey GU8 5UP. *T:* Wormley 2549. *Club:* Nairobi (Kenya).

MACKAY, Sir Gordon; *see* Mackay, Sir G. P. G.

McKAY, Very Rev. (James) Frederick, CMG 1972; OBE 1964 (MBE 1953); retired; Associate Minister, St Stephen's Uniting (formerly Presbyterian) Church, Sydney, 1974–80; Chairman, Uniting Church Negotiators, NSW, 1976–80; recognised as a foundation minister of Uniting Church in Australia at time of Union, 1977; *b* 15 April 1907; father, Northern Ireland; mother, Australian; *m* 1938, Margaret Mary Robertson; one *s* three *d*. *Educ:* Thornburgh Coll., Charters Towers, Qld; Emmanuel Coll., Brisbane, Qld; University of Queensland. MA; BD. Ordained Minister, Presbyterian Church of Australia, 1935; Patrol Padre, Australian Inland Mission (working with Flynn of the Inland), 1935–41; Chaplain, RAAF, 1941–46; Command Chaplain, Middle East, 1943–45; Minister, Toowong Parish, Qld, 1946–50; Superintendent (succeeding Flynn of the Inland), Aust. Inland Mission, 1951–74, Archivist, 1974–75. Moderator, Presbyterian Church of NSW, 1965; Moderator-Gen., Presbyterian Church of Australia, 1970–73. Editor, Frontier News, 1951–74. Vocational Award, Sydney Rotary, 1972. *Address:* Hawkesbury Village, Chapel Street, Richmond, NSW 2753, Australia. *T:* (045) 78 4561. *Club:* Australian (Sydney).

McKAY, Sir James (Wilson), Kt 1971; JP; DL; former Lord Provost of Edinburgh, and Lord Lieutenant of the County of the City of Edinburgh, 1969–72; *b* 12 March 1912; *s* of John McKay; *m* 1942, Janette Urquhart; three *d*. *Educ:* Dunfermline High Sch.; Portobello Secondary Sch., Edinburgh. Insurance Broker; Man. Dir, John McKay (Insurance) Ltd, Edinburgh; Director: George S. Murdoch & Partners Ltd, Aberdeen; Church of Scotland Insurance Co. Ltd. Served with RN, 1941–46 (Lieut, RNVR). Hon. DLitt Heriot-Watt, 1972. JP Edinburgh, 1972; DL County and City of Edinburgh, 1972. Order of Cross of St Mark (Greek Orthodox Church), 1970; Knight, Order of Orange-Nassau, 1972. *Recreations:* walking, gardening, reading. *Address:* T'Windward, 11 Cammo Gardens, Edinburgh EH4 8EJ. *T:* 031–339 6755. *Clubs:* New (Edinburgh); RNVR (Glasgow); Caledonian (Hon. Mem.) (San Francisco).

MACKAY, John; Headmaster, Bristol Grammar School, 1960–75; *b* 23 June 1914; *s* of William Mackay, Nottingham, and Eliza Mackay; *m* 1952, Margaret Ogilvie; two *s* two *d*. *Educ:* Mundella Grammar Sch., Nottingham; University of Nottingham; Merton Coll., Oxford. BA London (External) 1st Class Hons (English), 1935; Cambridge Teacher's Certificate, 1936. On staff of SCM, 1936–38; English Lecturer, St John's Coll., York, 1938–40. Served War of 1939–45, in Royal Navy, 1940–46. Merton Coll., Oxford, 1946–48; DPhil (Oxon) 1953. English Master, Merchant Taylors' School, Crosby, Liverpool, 1948–54; Second Master, Cheltenham Coll., 1954–60. Chm., HMC, 1970, Treasurer, 1974–75. *Recreations:* literature, gardening, cricket, arguing, senile reminiscence. *Address:* The Old Post Office, Tormarton, Badminton, Avon GL9 1HU. *T:* Badminton 243. *Club:* East India, Devonshire, Sports and Public Schools.

McKAY, Sir John (Andrew), Kt 1972; CBE 1966; QPM 1968; HM Chief Inspector of Constabulary for England and Wales, 1970–72; *b* 28 Nov. 1912; *s* of late Denis McKay, Blantyre, Lanarkshire; *m* 1st, 1947, Gertrude Gillespie Deighan (*d* 1971); two *d*; 2nd, 1976, Mildred Grace Kilday, *d* of Dr Emil Stern and late Grace Mildred Pleasants, San Francisco. *Educ:* Glasgow Univ. MA Glasgow, 1934. Joined Metropolitan Police, 1935; seconded to Army for service with Military Govt in Italy and Austria, 1943–47 (Lt-Col); Asst Chief Constable, then Deputy Chief Constable, Birmingham, 1953–58; Chief Constable of Manchester, 1959–66; HM Inspector of Constabulary, 1966–70. Freeman of City of London, 1972. OStJ 1963. Hon. MA, Manchester, 1966; Hon. Fellow, Manchester Polytechnic, 1971. *Address:* 7357 Oak Leave Drive, Santa Rosa, Calif 95405, USA. *T:* 707–835–8285.

McKAY, Dr John Henderson; Lord Provost, City of Edinburgh District Council, since 1984; *b* 12 May 1929; *s* of Thomas Johnstone McKay and Patricia Madeleine Henderson; *m* 1964, Catherine Watson Taylor; one *s* one *d*. *Educ:* West Calder High School. BA Hons, PhD, Open University. Labourer, clerk, Pumpherston Oil Co. Ltd, 1948–50; National Service, Royal Artillery, 1950–52; Officer and Surveyor, Customs and Excise, 1952–. *Recreations:* gardening, listening to music. *Address:* 2 Buckstone Way, Edinburgh EH10 6PN. *T:* 031–445 2865. *Club:* Civil Service.

MACKAY, John Jackson; MP (C) Argyll and Bute, since 1983 (Argyll, 1979–83); Parliamentary Under Secretary of State, Scottish Office, since 1982; *b* 15 Nov. 1938; *s* of Jackson and Jean Mackay; *m* 1961, Sheena Wagner; two *s* one *d*. *Educ:* Glasgow Univ. (BSc, DipEd). Formerly, Head of Maths Dept, Oban High Sch. *Recreations:* fishing, sailing. *Address:* Innishail, Polvinister Road, Oban, Argyll. *T:* Oban 62678.

MACKAY, Maj.-Gen. Kenneth, CB 1969; MBE 1943; idc, psc; GOC, Field Force Command Australia, Nov. 1973–Feb. 1974, retired; *b* 17 Feb. 1917; *m* 1943, Judith, *d* of F. Littler; two *s* one *d*. *Educ:* University High Sch., Melbourne; RMC Duntroon. Served War of 1939–45: Artillery, and Liaison Officer HQ 9th Australian Division, Middle East, 1940–41; ME Staff Sch., 1942; Bde Maj. 26 Bde, 1942–44; MO 12, War Office, 1944–45; Joint Sec., JCOSA, 1945–48; CO, 67 Inf. Bn, 1948; CO, 3 Bn Royal Aust. Regt, 1949; AHQ, 1949–52; Chief Instructor, Sch. of Tactics and Admin. 1952–55; Asst Aust. Defence Rep. UK, 1955–57; successively Dir of Maintenance, Personnel Admin., Quartering and Military Training, 1957–61; IDC, 1962; Dir Military Operations and Plans, Army HQ, Canberra, 1962–66; Comdr Aust. Force Vietnam, 1966; Commander 1st Division Australian Army, 1967–68; QMG AHQ, 1968–71; GOC Eastern Comd, 1971–73. *Recreations:* fishing, golf. *Address:* 3 Beauchamp Street, Deakin, ACT 2600, Australia. *Clubs:* Australian, Royal Canberra; New South Wales Golf.

McKAY, Mrs Margaret; Public Relations Consultant; *b* Jan. 1911. *Educ:* Elementary. Joined Labour Party 1932. Chief woman officer, TUC, 1951–62; Member of Co-operative Society, 1928–. Held administrative posts with Civil Service Clerical Association and Transport and General Workers' Union. MP (Lab) Clapham, 1964–70. Commander, Order of the Cedar of Lebanon. World Culture Award, Accademia Italia, 1984. *Publications:* Generation in Revolt (pen name Margaret McCarthy), 1953; Women in Trade Union History (TUC), 1954; Arab Voices from the Past; Electronic Arabia, 1974; The Chainless Mind, 1974; Timeless Arabia, 1978; Strangers in Palestine, 1982; Gulf Saga, 1982; Eve's Daring Daughters, 1985. *Address:* PO Box 668, Abu Dhabi, Union of Arab Emirates.

McKAY, Rev. Roy; Hon. Canon, Chichester Cathedral, since 1957; *b* 4 Nov. 1900; *s* of William McKay and Sarah Evelyn (*née* Littlewood); *m* 1927, Mary Oldham Fraser; one *s* one *d*. *Educ:* Marlborough Coll.; Magdalen Coll., Oxford. Curate, S Paul's, Kingston Hill, 1926; Curate-in-charge and Vicar of St Mark's Londonderry, Smethwick, 1928; Vicar of Mountfield, Sussex, 1932; Chaplain of Christ's Chapel of Alleyn's College of God's Gift, Dulwich, 1937; Vicar of Goring-by-Sea, Sussex, 1943; Chaplain of Canford Sch., 1948; Head of Religious Broadcasting, 1955–63; Preacher to Lincoln's Inn, 1958–59; Rector of St James, Garlickhythe, EC4, 1965–70. *Publications:* Tell John (with Bishop G. F. Allen), 1932; The Pillar of Fire, 1933; Take Care of the Sense, 1964; John Leonard Wilson: Confessor for the Faith, 1973. *Address:* 64 Thomas More House, Barbican, EC2.

MACKAY, Sir William (Calder), Kt 1968; OBE 1957; MC 1918; JP; *b* 5 Aug. 1896; *s* of William Scoular Mackay and Anne Armstrong Henderson; *m* 1920, Constance May Harris; one *s*. *Educ:* Hillhead High Sch., Glasgow. Served European War, 1914–18, NZEF (Adjt), France; served War of 1939–45 as Hon. YMCA Comr i/c welfare work in military camps, Air Force stations and naval establishments, Auckland Province. Past Member Board, Auckland Provincial Patriotic Fund; Director, Christchurch YMCA, 1929–33; Director, Auckland YMCA, 1934–45; President, YMCA, 1939–45; Chairman, Campaign Cttee for new Auckland YMCA, 1954; Life Member, YMCA, 1966. Past Member: Council, Auckland Chamber of Commerce; Exec. Cttee, Auckland Provincial Retailers' Assoc.; Auckland City Council, 1948–54; Auckland Harbour Bridge Authority; Council, Auckland, War Memorial Museum (Hon. Life Member, 1962). President, Rotary Club of Auckland, 1944–45; District Gov., Rotary, 1948–49; Member Aims and Objects Cttee, Rotary International, 1949–50. Provincial Comr, Boy Scouts, 1958; Organising Comr for Pan-Pacific Boy Scouts Jamboree, 1959 (Medal of Merit). Patron, Crippled Children Soc. (Mem. Exec., 1935–66, past Vice-Pres., and Pres., 1958–66, Life Mem. 1974, Auckland Branch); Vice-President: NZ Crippled Children Soc., 1964; St John Amb. Assoc. Auckland Centre Trust Bd, 1970; Pres., Nat. Children's Med. Res. Foundn, 1974; Past Area Co-ordinator, Duke of Edinburgh Award for Auckland Province and Mem. NZ Council, 1963. Foundn Mem. Bd, St Andrews Presbyterian Hospital and Hostel for Aged. JP 1940. *Recreations:* fishing, outdoor bowls. *Address:* 416 Remuera Road, Auckland 5, New Zealand. *T:* 502 495. *Club:* Northern (Auckland).

McKAY, William Robert; Clerk of Financial Committees, House of Commons, since 1985; *b* 18 April 1939; *s* of late William Wallace McKay and Margaret H. A. Foster; *m* 1962, Margaret M., *d* of E. M. Fillmore, OBE; twin *d*. *Educ:* Trinity Academy, Leith; Edinburgh Univ. (MA Hons). Clerk in the House of Commons, 1961; Secretary: to the House of Commons Commn, 1981–84; to the Public Accounts Commn, 1985–. *Publications:* (ed) Erskine May's Private Journal 1883–86, 1984; Mr Speaker's Secretaries, 1986; articles in historical periodicals. *Recreation:* dry-stone walling. *Address:* 26 Earl Street, Cambridge CB1 1JR.

MACKAY-TALLACK, Sir Hugh, Kt 1963; Deputy Chairman, The Standard & Chartered Bank PLC, 1972–83; Director, Fleming Japanese Investment Trust PLC (formerly Capital and National Trust Ltd), since 1965 (Chairman, 1970–83); *s* of E. H. Tallack and Deborah Lyle Mackay; unmarried. *Educ:* Kelly Coll., Devon; Heidelberg Univ. Served War of 1939–45, with 17th Dogra Regt, in Middle East and Burma; Private Sec. to C-in-C ALFSEA, and Mil. Sec. (Col) to Admiral Mountbatten, Supreme Allied Comdr, SEAC. Formerly: Chm., Macneill & Barry Ltd (Inchcape Gp) Calcutta; Governor of State Bank of India; Director numerous other cos in India; Chm., Indian Tea Assoc., 1954–55; Vice-Chairman, Tea Board of India, 1954–55; Member Government of India Tea Auction Cttee, 1954–55; Chairman, Ross Inst. of India, 1951–64; Pres., Bengal Chamber of Commerce and Industry and Associated Chambers of Commerce of India, 1962–63. Director: Inchcape & Co. Ltd, 1963–82 (Dep. Chm., 1964–77); Assam Investments Ltd, 1965–81 (Chm., 1965–74); London & Holyrood Trust Ltd, 1973–82; London & Provincial Trust Ltd, 1973–82. Mem., Fedn of Commonwealth Chambers of Commerce. Governor: Nehru Meml Trust; Victoria League. *Recreation:* riding. *Address:* 47 South Street, Mayfair, W1. *T:* 01–493 5670. *Clubs:* White's, Oriental, City of London; Bengal, Tollygunge, Turf (all in Calcutta).

McKEAN, Charles Alexander, FSAScot; FRSA; Secretary and Treasurer, Royal Incorporation of Architects in Scotland, since 1979; *b* 16 July 1946; *s* of John Laurie McKean and Nancy Burns Lendrum; *m* 1975, Margaret Elizabeth Yeo; two *s*. *Educ:* Fettes Coll., Edinburgh; Univ. of Bristol (BA Hons). Regional Secretary, RIBA, 1968–79; Architectural Correspondent, The Times, 1977–83; Trustee, Thirlestane Castle Trust, 1983–; Director, Workshops and Artists Studios Scotland (WASPS), 1980–85; Member: Scottish Arts Council Exhibitions Panel, 1980–83; Adv. Council for the Arts in Scotland, 1984. Bossom Lectr, RSA, 1986. Architectural Journalist of the Year, 1979 and 1983; Building Journalist of the Year, 1983. *Publications:* (with David Atwell) Battle of Styles, 1974; Guide to Modern Buildings in London 1965–75, 1976; Fight Blight, 1977; Architectural Guide to Cambridge and East Anglia 1920–80, 1980; Edinburgh—an illustrated architectural guide, 1982, 3rd edn 1983; (with David Walker) Dundee—an illustrated introduction through its buildings, 1984; Stirling—an illustrated introduction through its buildings, 1984; The Scottish Thirties, 1986. *Recreations:* gardening, topography, books and glass collecting. *Address:* 10 Hill Park Road, Edinburgh EH4 2AW. *T:* 031–336 2753. *Club:* Scottish Arts.

McKEAN, Douglas, CB 1977; Director, Agricultural Mortgage Corporation, since 1978; *b* 2 April 1917; *s* of late Alexander McKean, Enfield, Mddx; *m* 1942, Anne, *d* of late Roger Clayton, Riding Mill, Northumberland; two *s*. *Educ:* Merchant Taylors' Sch.; St John's Coll., Oxford. War Office, 1940; transferred to HM Treasury, 1949; Asst Sec., 1956; Under-Sec., 1962; on loan to Dept of the Environment, 1970–72; retired as Under Sec., HM Treasury, 1977. Dep. Sec., Central Bd of Finance, Church of England, 1978–83. Trustee, Irish Sailors and Soldiers Land Trust, 1980–; Governor, Whitelands Coll., 1984–. *Recreation:* mountain walking. *Address:* The Dower House, Forty Hill, Enfield, Middlesex EN2 9EJ. *T:* 01–363 2365. *Club:* United Oxford & Cambridge University.

McKEARNEY, Philip, CMG 1983; HM Diplomatic Service; Ambassador to Romania, 1983–86; *b* 15 Nov. 1926; *s* of Philip McKearney, OBE; *m* 1950, Jean Pamela Walker; two *s*. *Educ:* City of London Sch.; Hertford Coll., Oxford. 4/7th Dragoon Guards, 1946–53; joined HM Diplomatic Service, 1953; 3rd Sec., British Embassy, Damascus, 1955–56; 1st Sec., British Legation, Bucharest, 1959–62; British Political Agent, Qatar, 1962–65; Counsellor and Consul-Gen., Baghdad, 1968–70; Counsellor, Belgrade, 1970–74; Inspector, FCO, 1975–77; Consul-General: Zagreb, 1977–80; Boston, Mass, 1980–83. *Address:* c/o Foreign and Commonwealth Office, SW1.

McKECHNIE, Sheila Marshall; Director of Shelter, National Campaign for the Homeless, since 1985; *b* Falkirk, 3 May 1948. *Educ:* Falkirk High School; Edinburgh Univ. (MA Politics and History); Warwick Univ. (MA Industrial Relations). Research Asst, Oxford Univ., 1971–72; Asst Gen. Sec., Wall Paper Workers Union Staff Section, 1972–74; WEA Tutor, Manchester, 1974–76; Health and Safety Officer, ASTMS, 1976–85. *Address:* Shelter, 157 Waterloo Road, SE1 8XF. *T:* 01–633 9377.

McKEE, Air Marshal Sir Andrew, KCB 1957 (CB 1951); CBE 1944; DSO 1942; DFC 1941; AFC 1938; *b* 1901; *s* of Samuel Hugh McKee, Eyredale, Oxford, Canterbury, NZ; *m* 1949, Cecelia Tarcille, *er d* of Michael Keating, NZ; two *d*. *Educ:* Christchurch Boys' High Sch., NZ. Joined RAF, 1927. AOC No 205 Group Mediterranean Allied Air Force, 1945–46; Senior Air Staff Officer, MEAF, 1946–47; Comdt OATS, 1947–49; First Comdt, RAF Flying Coll., 1949–51; Air Vice-Marshal, 1952; AOC No 21 Group, 1951–53; Senior Air Staff Officer, Bomber Command, 1953–55; Air Marshal, 1957; Air Officer Commanding-in-Chief, Transport Command, 1955–59, retired. *Address:* 27 Frederick Street, Palmerston North, New Zealand. *Club:* Royal Air Force.

McKEE, Major Sir Cecil; *see* McKee, Major Sir William Cecil.

McKEE, John, RD 1973; QC (NI) 1974; **His Honour Judge McKee;** a County Court Judge, Northern Ireland, since 1981; President: Industrial Tribunals (Northern Ireland), since 1981; Industrial Court (Northern Ireland), since 1982; *b* 18 May 1933; *s* of late Frank McKee and of Mollie A. McKee; *m* 1962, Annette S. Wilson; two *s* one *d*. *Educ:* Strathallan Sch., Scotland; Queen's Univ. of Belfast (BA Hons, LLB Hons). Called to the Bar of NI, 1960; Bar, Middle Temple, 1971; Sen. Bar, NI, 1974; Bar of Republic of Ireland (King's Inns), 1975. Chm., UK Delegn to CCBE, 1979–81. Served RNR; subseq. placed on Retd List with rank of Lt-Comdr RNR, 1952–73; *Publication:* (with Phyllis Bateson) Industrial Tribunals in Northern Ireland, 1981. *Recreation:* golf. *Clubs:* Ulster Reform (Belfast); Royal County Down Golf.

McKEE, Major Sir (William) Cecil, Kt 1959; ERD; JP; Estate Agent; *b* 13 April 1905; *s* of late W. B. McKee and M. G. B. Bulloch; *m* 1932, Florence Ethel Irene Gill; one *d*. *Educ:* Methodist Coll., Belfast; Queen's Univ., Belfast. Alderman, Belfast Corporation, 1934; High Sheriff, Belfast, 1946; Deputy Lord Mayor, 1947, Lord Mayor of Belfast, 1957–59. JP Belfast, 1957. Pres., NI Br., Inst. of Dirs, 1957–59. Served with Royal Artillery in War of 1939–45. KStJ. 1982. Hon. LLD Queen's Univ., Belfast, 1960. *Recreation:* golf. *Address:* 250 Malone Road, Belfast. *T:* Belfast 666979. *Clubs:* Ulster Reform (Belfast); Royal County Down Golf.

McKEE, Dr William James Ernest, MA, MD, FFCM; Regional Medical Advisor, Wessex Regional Health Authority, since 1976; *b* 20 Feb. 1929; *s* of John Sloan McKee, MA, and Mrs Annie Emily McKee (*née* McKinley); *m* Josée Tucker; three *d*. *Educ:* Queen Elizabeth's, Wakefield; Trinity Coll., Cambridge; Queen's Coll., Oxford. MA, MD, BChir (Cantab); LRCP, MRCS, FFCM. Clinical trng and postgrad. clinical posts at Radcliffe Infirmary, Oxford, 1952–57; med. res., financed by Nuffield Provincial Hosps Trust, 1958–61; successive posts in community medicine with Metrop. Regional Hosp. Bds, 1961–69; Sen. Admin. Med. Officer, Liverpool Regional Hosp. Bd, 1970–74; Regional Med. Officer, Mersey RHA, 1974–76. Chm., Regional Med. Officers' Gp; UK Med. Rep., EEC Hosp. Cttee (and Sub-Cttee on Community Co-ordination). *Publications:* papers on tonsillectomy and adenoidectomy in learned jls. *Address:* 22a Bereweeke Avenue, Winchester SO22 6BH. *T:* Winchester 61369.

MacKEIGAN, Hon. Ian Malcolm; Supernumerary Justice of Appeal Division of Supreme Court of Nova Scotia (Chief Justice of Nova Scotia and Chief Justice of Appeal Division of Supreme Court of Nova Scotia, 1973–85); *b* 11 April 1915; *s* of Rev. Dr J. A. MacKeigan and Mabel (*née* McAvity); *m* 1942, Jean Catherine Geddes; two *s* one *d*. *Educ:* Univs of Saskatchewan, Dalhousie and Toronto. BA (Great Distinction) 1934, MA 1935, LLB 1938, Dalhousie; MA Toronto 1939. Member of Nova Scotia and Prince Edward Island Bars; QC (Nova Scotia) 1954. Dep. Enforcement Administrator, Wartime Prices and Trade Bd, Ottawa, 1942–46; Dep. Comr, Combines Investigation Commn, Ottawa, 1946–50; Partner, MacKeigan, Cox, Downie & Mitchell and predecessor firms, Halifax, NS, 1950–73; Chm., Atlantic Develt Bd, 1963–69; Dir, Gulf Oil (Canada) Ltd, 1968–73; Dir, John Labatt Ltd, 1971–73. Hon. LLD Dalhousie, 1975. Centennial Medal, 1967; Jubilee Medal, 1977. *Publications:* articles in Can. Bar Review and Can. Jl Polit. Sci. and Econs. *Recreations:* fishing, golf. *Address:* 833 Marlborough Avenue, Halifax, NS B3H 3G7, Canada. *T:* 429–1043. *Clubs:* Halifax, Saraguay, Ashburn Golf (Halifax).

McKELLEN, Ian (Murray), CBE 1979; actor and director since 1961; *b* 25 May 1939; *s* of Denis Murray McKellen and Margery (*née* Sutcliffe). *Educ:* Wigan Grammar Sch.; Bolton Sch.; St Catharine's Coll., Cambridge (BA; Hon. Fellow, 1982). Pres., Marlowe Soc., 1960–61. Elected to Council of Equity, 1971–72. 1st appearance (stage): Belgrade Theatre, Coventry, in A Man for all Seasons, Sept. 1961. Arts Theatre, Ipswich, 1962–63; Nottingham Playhouse, 1963–64. 1st London appearance: A Scent of Flowers, 1964 (Clarence Derwent Award). National Theatre Co., 1965, Old Vic and Chichester Festival; A Lily in Little India; Man of Destiny/O'Flaherty VC, Mermaid Theatre, EC4; Their Very Own and Golden City, Royal Court, 1966; The Promise, Fortune and Broadway, 1967; White Lies/Black Comedy; Richard II, Prospect Theatre Co., 1968; Recruiting Officer, Chips with Everything, Cambridge Theatre Co., 1968; revived Richard II with Edward II, Edinburgh Festival; British and European Tour; Mermaid and Piccadilly Theatres, 1969–70; Hamlet, British and European Tours and Cambridge Theatre, WC2, 1971. Founder Mem., Actors' Company: Ruling the Roost, 'Tis Pity She's a Whore, Edin. Fest., 1972; Knots, Wood-Demon, Edin. Fest., 1973, and with King Lear, Brooklyn Acad. of Music, Wimbledon Theatre season, 1974; Royal Shakespeare Co.: Dr Faustus, Edin. Fest., 1974; Marquis of Keith, Aldwych, 1974–75; King John, Aldwych, 1975; Ashes, Young Vic, 1975; Too True to Be Good, Aldwych and Globe, 1975; Romeo and Juliet, The Winter's Tale, Macbeth (Plays and Players award, 1976), Stratford, 1976–77; Romeo and Juliet, Macbeth, Pillars of the Community (SWET Award, 1977), Days of the Commune, The Alchemist (SWET Award, 1978), Aldwych and RSC Warehouse, 1977–78; RSC touring company (also artistic dir), 1978: Twelfth Night; Three Sisters; Is There Honey Still for Tea?; solo recitals: Words, Words, Words, Edin. Fest. and Belfast Fest., 1976; repeated with Acting Shakespeare, Edin. and Belfast, 1977; Every Good Boy Deserves Favour, RFH, 1977 and Barbican Centre, 1982; Bent, Royal Court, Criterion, 1979 (SWET Award, 1979); Amadeus, Broadhurst, NY (Drama Desk, NY Drama League, Outer Critics' Circle, and Tony Awards), 1980–81; Acting Shakespeare tour, Israel, Norway, Denmark, Sweden, 1980, Spain, France, Cyprus, Israel, Poland and Romania, 1982, Los Angeles and Ritz, NYC (Drama Desk Award), 1983; Short List, Hampstead, 1983; Cowardice, Ambassadors, 1983; Venice Preserv'd, Wild Honey (Lawrence Olivier Award; Plays and Players Award; NY, 1986–87), Coriolanus (London Standard Award), National, 1984–85; as Associate Dir of NT, produced and acted in: The Duchess of Malfi, The Real Inspector Hound, The Critic, The Cherry Orchard, 1985–86. Directed: Liverpool Playhouse, 1969; Watford and Leicester, 1972; A Private Matter, Vaudeville, 1973; The Clandestine Marriage, Savoy 1975. Films, 1968–: A Touch of Love, The Promise, Alfred the Great, Priest of Love, Scarlet Pimpernel, Plenty, Zina. Has appeared on television, 1966–, incl. Walter, 1982 (RTS Performance Award for 1982), Walter and June, 1983. *Address:* c/o James Sharkey, 15 Golden Square, W1R 3AG. *T:* 01–434 3801/6.

McKELVEY, Air Cdre John Wesley, CB 1969; MBE 1944; CEng, MRAeS; RAF, retired; *b* 25 June 1914; *s* of late Captain John Wesley McKelvey, Enfield, Mddx; *m* 1938, Eileen Amy Carter, *d* of John Charles Carter, Enfield; two *s*. *Educ:* George Spicer Sch., Enfield. RAF Aircraft Apprentice, 1929; commnd 1941 (Eng Branch); served 1939–45, Egypt, Syria, Iraq and Bomber Comd (despatches, 1943); Group Captain 1960; Dep. Dir Intelligence (Tech.), 1962–64; Dir of Aircraft and Asst Attaché, Defence Research and Development, British Embassy, Washington, 1964–66; Air Officer Wales and CO, RAF St Athan, 1966–69; retd Aug. 1969. RAF Benevolent Fund: Sec. (Appeals), 1971–77; Legacies and Trusts Officer, 1977–79. *Recreations:* bowls, gardening, photography. *Address:* Inchmerle, 29 Manorway, Bush Hill Park, Enfield, Mddx EN1 2JD. *T:* 01–360 4054. *Club:* Royal Air Force.

McKELVEY, William; MP (Lab) Kilmarnock and Loudoun, since 1983 (Kilmarnock, 1979–83). *b* Dundee, July 1934; *m*; two *s*. *Educ:* Morgan Acad.; Dundee Coll. of Technology. Joined Labour Party, 1961; formerly Sec. Organiser, Lab. Party, and full-time union official. Mem., Dundee City Council. *Address:* House of Commons, SW1; 41 Main Street, Kilmaurs, Ayrshire.

MACKEN, Frederic Raymond, CMG 1964; *b* 23 Sept. 1903; *s* of Charles Alfred Macken and Ella (*née* Steadman); *m* 1929, Alma Doris (*née* Keesing); one *d*. *Educ:* Whangarei High Sch.; Auckland Univ., New Zealand. LLM (with Hons), 1927. Retired as Commissioner of Inland Revenue for New Zealand, 1964. *Recreations:* bowls, golf. *Address:* 9 Harley Grove, Lower Hutt, Wellington, New Zealand. *T:* 695205. *Club:* Civil Service (Wellington, NZ).

MacKENNA, Sir Bernard Joseph Maxwell, (Sir Brian MacKenna), Kt 1961; Judge of the High Court of Justice (Queen's Bench Division), 1961–77; *b* 12 Sept. 1905; unmarried. Called to the Bar, Inner Temple, Jan. 1932; Western Circuit; QC 1950; Master of the Bench of the Inner Temple, 1958. *Address:* 2 Paper Buildings, Temple, EC4. *T:* 01–353 2123. *Clubs:* Athenæum, Beefsteak.

MacKENNA, Sir Brian; *see* MacKenna, Sir Bernard Joseph Maxwell.

McKENNA, David, CBE 1967 (OBE 1946; MBE 1943); FCIT; Member, British Railways Board, 1968–76 (part-time Member, 1976–78); *b* 16 Feb. 1911; *s* of late Rt Hon. Reginald McKenna and Pamela Margaret McKenna (*née* Jekyll); *m* 1934, Lady Cecilia Elizabeth Keppel, *d* of 9th Earl of Albemarle, MC; three *d*. *Educ:* Eton; Trinity Coll., Cambridge. London Passenger Transport Board, 1934–39, and 1946–55; Asst General Manager, Southern Region of BR, 1955–61; Chief Commercial Officer, HQ, BR, 1962; General Manager, Southern Region of BR, and Chairman Southern Railway Board, 1963–68; Chairman, British Transport Advertising, 1968–81. Mem., Dover Harbour Bd, 1969–80. Dir, Isles of Scilly Steamship Co. War Service with Transportation Service of Royal Engineers, 1939–45; Iraq, Turkey, India and Burma; Lieut-Colonel. Pres., Chartered Inst. of Transport, 1972. Chairman of Governors, Sadler's Wells, 1962–76. Vice-Pres. and Hon. Secretary, Royal College of Music; Chairman of Bach Choir, 1964–76. FRCM. Commandeur de l'Ordre National du Mérite, 1974. *Publications:* various papers on transport subjects. *Recreations:* music, sailing. *Address:* Rosteague, Portscatho, Truro, Cornwall. *Clubs:* Brooks's; Royal Cornwall Yacht (Falmouth).

MacKENNA, Robert Ogilvie, MA, ALA; University Librarian and Keeper of the Hunterian Books and MSS, Glasgow, 1951–78; *b* 21 March 1913; *s* of late Dr John G. MacKenna and Katherine Ogilvie; *m* 1942, Ray, *o d* of late Samuel Mullin, Glasgow. *Educ:* Paisley Grammar Sch.; Glasgow Univ. Assistant Librarian, Glasgow Univ., 1936; Sub-Librarian, Leeds Univ., 1946; Librarian, King's Coll., Newcastle upon Tyne (University of Durham), 1947. Served War as officer, RNVR, 1939–45. Trustee, National Library of Scotland, 1953–79. President, Scottish Library Association, 1966; Chairman, Standing Conference of National and University Libraries, 1967–69. President Scottish Cricket Union, 1968. Editor, The Philosophical Journal, 1976–77. *Publication:* Glasgow University Athletic Club: the story of the first hundred years, 1981. *Recreations:* cricket (played for Scotland, 1935–39 and 1946); hill-walking. *Address:* 2 Turnberry Avenue, Glasgow G11 5AQ. *Club:* College (Glasgow).

McKENNA, Siobhán; actress; *b* Belfast, 24 May 1923; *d* of Prof. Owen McKenna and Margaret O'Reilly; *m* 1946, Denis O'Dea (*d* 1978); one *s*. *Educ:* St Louis Convent, Monaghan; Galway Univ. BA (1st cl. Hons, French, English and Irish Lit.). Holds 5 hon. doctorates in Literature and the Humanities. Apptd to Council of State, Republic of

Ireland, by President Cearbhall Ó Dálaigh, 1975. First stage appearances with Irish trans of plays by Molière, O'Neill, O'Casey, Shaw, Shakespeare, for Irish speaking theatre An Taibhdhearc, Galway, 1940–43; Abbey Theatre, Dublin, 1944–47 (first appearance in Le Bourgeois Gentilhomme). *Plays include:* The White Steed (first London appearance), Embassy and Whitehall, 1947; Fading Mansions (dir, Laurence Olivier), Duchess, 1949; Ghosts, Embassy; Berkeley Square, Queen's; Héloise and Abelard, Duke of York's; Shakespeare season, Stratford-upon-Avon, 1952, with As You Like It, Coriolanus, Macbeth, also Ben Johnson's Volpone; Saint Joan, Arts, 1954, St Martin's, 1955 (first Evening Standard Best Actress Award, 1955), European tour, NY, 1956; The Chalk Garden (first NY appearance), NY, 1955; The Rope-Dancers, NY, 1957; Hamlet (title role), NY, 1957; Shakespeare season, as Viola in Twelfth Night (dir, Tyrone Guthrie), Stratford, Ont., Canada, as Lady Macbeth, Cambridge Shakespeare Fest., USA; Playboy of the Western World, Dublin, Edinburgh and Paris Festivals, then Piccadilly, St Martin's, 1960, European tour (Best Actress, Florence Festival); Captain Brassbound's Conversion, Dublin and Philadelphia, 1961; Saint Joan of the Stockyards, Dublin Festival, 1961, Queen's, 1964; Play with a Tiger, Comedy, 1962; The Cavern, Strand; Laurette, Dublin, 1964; Juno and the Paycock, Gaiety, Dublin, 1966, Toronto, 1973, Abbey, Dublin, 1979; The Loves of Cass Maguire, Abbey, 1967; The Cherry Orchard, Abbey, 1968; On a Foggy Day, St Martin's, 1969; Best of Friends, Strand, 1970; Here are Ladies (one woman show), Criterion, 1970, USA, Canada, Australia, Dublin, 1975; Fallen Angels, Gate, 1975; A Moon for the Misbegotten, Gate, 1976; Plough and the Stars, Abbey, 1977, US tour; Sons of Oedipus, Greenwich, 1977; Sarah Bernhardt in Memoir, Canada and Dublin, 1977, Ambassadors, 1978; Riders to the Sea, Greenwich Fest., 1978; Here are Ladies, Vienna, 1979; The Shadow of a Gunman, Vienna, 1980; Agrippina in Britannicus, Lyric, Hammersmith, 1981; All Joyce, Abbey, 1982. *Plays directed:* St Joan (in Gaelic), Galway, 1943; Daughter from over the Water, Dublin; I must be getting out of this Kip, Dublin, 1968; Tinkers Wedding, Shadow of the Glen, Riders to the Sea, Toronto, 1973; Juno and the Paycock, Mermaid, 1973; Playboy of the Western World, USA, 1967, English tour and Hong Kong, 1977; Rising of the Moon; The Cat and the Moon, Purgatory and A Pot of Broth, Riders to the Sea, Greenwich, 1978; The Shadow of a Gunman, Vienna, 1980; The Midnight Court (in Irish), Peacock, Dublin, 1984. *Films include:* Hungry Hill, Daughter of Darkness, The Lost People (Lejeune Gold Medal), The Adventurers, King of Kings, Doctor Zhivago, Playboy of the Western World, Philadelphia Here I Come, Of Human Bondage, Here are Ladies, Memed. *Television* includes: USA: What Every Woman Knows, The Letter, Cradle Song, The Winslow Boy, Misalliance, Don Juan in Hell, The Rope Dancers, The Last Days of Pompeii; UK: The Aspern Papers, Chez Torpe, The Landlady, Vicious Circle, The Diary of Brigid Hitler, Angels in the Annexe. *Publications:* trans. into Irish: Mary Rose, by J. M. Barrie; Saint Joan, by G. B. Shaw. *Recreations:* reading, walking, theatre-going. *Address:* Highfield Road, Rathgar, Dublin 6, Republic of Ireland.

MACKENZIE; *see* Montagu-Stuart-Wortley-Mackenzie, family name of Earl of Wharncliffe.

MACKENZIE, family name of **Earl of Cromartie.**

MACKENZIE of Gairloch; *see under* Inglis of Glencorse.

McKENZIE, Sir Alexander, KBE 1962; Past Dominion President, New Zealand National Party (1951–62); *b* Invercargill, New Zealand, 1896; *m* 1935, Constance Mary Howard; two *s* two *d*. *Educ:* Isla Bank Primary Sch.; Southland Technical Coll.; Southland Boys' High Sch. Chm., Ponsonby Electorate, NZ Nat. Party, 1938–41; Chm., Auckland Div., NZ Nat. Party, 1941–51. Overseas Rep. for NZ Forest Products Ltd, 1925–29; engaged in Stock and Share Broking, 1929–; Mem. Auckland Stock Exchange; Dir, of companies covering finance, merchandising, manufacturing, etc. Mem. Anglican Church. *Recreations:* trout fishing, surfing, bowling, gardening. *Address:* 54 Wallace Street, Herne Bay, New Zealand. *Club:* Auckland (Auckland, NZ).

MACKENZIE, Sir Alexander Alwyne H. C. B. M.; *see* Muir Mackenzie.

MACKENZIE, Sir (Alexander George Anthony) Allan, 4th Bt, of Glen-Muick, *cr* 1890; CD 1957; retired; *b* 4 Jan. 1913; *s* of late Capt. Allan Keith Mackenzie (3rd *s* of 2nd Bt) and Hon. Louvima, *o d* of 1st Viscount Knollys (she *m* 2nd, 1922, Richard Henry Spencer Checkley); *S* uncle, 1944; *m* 1937, Marjorie McGuire, Vancouver, BC; four *d*. *Educ:* Stowe School. Page of Honour to King George V; Member Royal Canadian Mounted Police, 1932–37; served War of 1939–45, with Seaforth Highlanders of Canada (Captain), in Italy and in NW Europe. Subsequently Black Watch (RHR) of Canada (Regular Army). Canada Centennial Medal, 1967. *Heir: cousin* (James William) Guy Mackenzie [*b* 6 Oct. 1946; *m* 1972, Paulene Patricia Simpson; one *d*].

MACKENZIE, Sir Allan; *see* Mackenzie, Sir (Alexander George Anthony) Allan.

MACKENZIE, Archibald Robert Kerr, CBE 1967; HM Diplomatic Service, retired; *b* 22 Oct. 1915; *s* of James and Alexandrina Mackenzie; *m* 1963, Virginia Ruth Hutchison. *Educ:* Glasgow, Oxford, Chicago and Harvard Universities. Diplomatic Service, with duty at Washington, 1943–45; United Nations, 1946–49; Foreign Office, 1949–51; Bangkok, 1951–54; Cyprus, 1954; Foreign Office, 1955–57; OEEC, Paris, 1957–61; Commercial Counsellor, HM Embassy, Rangoon, 1961–65; Consul-General, Zagreb 1965–69; Ambassador, Tunisia, 1970–73; Minister (Econ. and Social Affairs), UK Mission to UN, 1973–75. Brandt Commission, 1978–80. *Recreation:* golf. *Address:* Strathcashel Cottage, Rowardennan, near Glasgow G63 0AW. *T:* Balmaha 262. *Clubs:* Royal Commonwealth Society; Royal Scottish Automobile (Glasgow).

MACKENZIE, Major Colin Dalzell, MBE 1945; MC 1940; Vice Lord-Lieutenant of Inverness, since 1986; *b* 23 March 1919; *s* of Lt-Col Douglas William Alexander Dalziel Mackenzie, CVO, DSO, DL; *m* 1947, Lady Anne FitzRoy, *d* of 10th Duke of Grafton; one *s* three *d* (and one *s* decd). *Educ:* Eton; RMC Sandhurst. Page of Honour to King George V, 1932–36; joined Seaforth Highlanders, 1939; ADC to Viceroy of India, 1945–46, Dep. Mil. Sec. to Viceroy, 1946–47; retired Seaforth Highlanders, 1949. Mem., Queen's Body Guard for Scotland, Royal Company of Archers, 1959–. Mem., Inverness-shire County Council, 1949–51. *Recreation:* fishing. *Address:* Farr House, Inverness IV1 2XB. *T:* Farr 202. *Clubs:* Turf, Pratt's; New (Edinburgh).

MACKENZIE, Colin Hercules, CMG 1946; *b* 5 Oct. 1898; *o s* of late Maj.-Gen. Sir Colin Mackenzie, KCB, and Ethel, *er d* of Hercules Ross, ICS; *m* 1940, Evelyn Clodagh, 2nd *d* of Charles and Lady Aileen Meade; one *d*. *Educ:* Summerfields; Eton (Schol.); King's Coll., Cambridge (1st Class Hons in Economics. Exhibitioner and Senior Scholar, also Chancellor's Medal for English Verse). Served France with 1st Bn Scots Guards in 1918 (wounded). Served in India and with South-East Asia Command, 1941–45, comd Force 136 (CMG, Officier de la Légion d'Honneur, Dutch Resistance Cross). British Economic Mission to Greece, 1946. Dir, J. and P. Coats Ltd, 1928–65. Chairman: Scottish Council, FBI, 1957–59; Scottish Cttee on Electricity, 1961–62; Scottish Arts Council, 1962–70; Inverness Conservative and Unionist Assoc., 1967–70. Hon. Sheriff Inverness-shire. Hon. LLD St Andrews, 1970. *Address:* Kyle House, Kyleakin, Isle of Skye. *T:* Kyle 4517. *Club:* Special Forces.

MACKENZIE, Colin Scott; Procurator Fiscal, Stornoway, since 1969; Vice Lord-Lieutenant, Western Isles, since 1984; *b* 7 July 1938; *s* of late Major Colin Scott Mackenzie, BL and of Mrs Margaret S. Mackenzie, MA; *m* 1966, Christeen Elizabeth Drysdale McLauchlan. *Educ:* Nicolson Inst., Stornoway; Fettes Coll., Edinburgh; Edinburgh Univ. (BL 1959). Admitted Solicitor and Notary Public, 1960. Partner, C. Scott Mackenzie & Co., 1961–74. Chm., Local Unemployment Tribunal, 1962–74; Procurator Fiscal, Lochmaddy, 1975–82; Burgh Prosecutor, Stornoway, 1971–75; Clerk to the Lieutenancy, 1975; Founding Dean, Western Isles Faculty of Solicitors, 1976–79. Dir, Harris Tweed Assoc. Ltd, 1979–; Trustee, Western Isles Kidney Machine Trust, 1977–; Local Trust Rep., King George V's and Queen Elizabeth II's Silver Jubilee Trusts, 1978–, Co-ordinator, Silver Jubilee Appeal in Western Isles, 1977; County Co-ordinator, Operation Raleigh, 1983–. Pres., Stornoway Rotary Club, 1977; Founding Pres., Stornoway Flying Club, 1972; Chm., Lewis Pipe Band, 1978–. 2nd Lieut T&AVR (List B), 1976; Captain 1st Cadet Bn, Queen's Own Highlanders ACF, 1979. Council Mem for Western Isles, Orkney, Shetland etc, Law Soc. of Scotland, 1985–. JP Fiscal, Lewis, 1971–75; DL Islands Area of Western Isles, 1975. *Recreations:* aviation, boating, fishing, local history, shooting, trying to grow trees. *Address:* Park House, 8 Matheson Road, Stornoway, Western Isles. *T:* Stornoway 2008. *Club:* Royal Scottish Automobile (Glasgow).

McKENZIE, Dan Peter, PhD; FRS 1976; Professor of Earth Sciences, Department of Earth Sciences, Cambridge University, since 1984; Fellow of King's College, Cambridge, 1965–73 and since 1977; *b* 21 Feb. 1942; *s* of William Stewart McKenzie and Nancy Mary McKenzie; *m* 1971, Indira Margaret Misra; one *s*. *Educ:* Westminster Sch.; King's Coll., Cambridge (BA 1963, PhD 1966). Cambridge University: Sen. Asst in Res., 1969–75; Asst Dir of Res., 1975–79; Reader in Tectonics, 1979–84. Hon. MA Cambridge, 1966. (Jtly) Geology and Geophysics Prize, Internat. Balzan Foundn of Italy and Switzerland, 1981. *Publications:* papers in learned jls. *Recreation:* gardening. *Address:* 14 Humberstone Road, Cambridge CB4 1JE. *T:* Cambridge 66794.

MacKENZIE, David Alexander; Civil Servant since 1980; General Secretary, Transport Salaried Staffs' Association, 1973–77; *b* 22 March 1922; *s* of David MacKenzie and Jeannie Ross; *m* 1945, Doreen Joyce Lucas; two *s* one *d*. *Educ:* Merkinch Public Sch.; Inverness High Sch. Entered London Midland Railway Service, 1936. Served in Royal Navy, 1941–45. Transport Salaried Staffs Assoc.: Divisional Sec., 1952–66; Sen. Asst Sec., 1966–68; Asst Gen. Sec., 1968. Former Member: TUC Non-Manual Workers' Cttee; Air Transport and Travel Industry Trng Bd; Hotel and Catering Industry Trng Bd. *Recreations:* golf, reading. *Address:* 19 Grattons Drive, Pound Hill, Three Bridges, West Sussex. *T:* Crawley 513048.

MACKENZIE, David James Masterton, CMG 1957; OBE 1947 (MBE 1944); FRCP; Hon. Research Associate, Department of Medical Microbiology, Medical School, University of Cape Town; Visiting Scientist, Malaria Eradication Program, Communicable Disease Center, Atlanta, Georgia, 1965–69; Director of Medical and Health Services in Hong Kong, 1958–64; Colonial Medical Service, retired; *b* 23 July 1905; *s* of John Henderson Mackenzie and Agnes Masterton; *m* 1934, Patricia Eleanor Margaret Bailey; two *d*. *Educ:* Rutherford College School; Edinburgh Univ. MB, ChB, Edinburgh, 1929; DPH (Edinburgh), 1948; MRCPE 1956, FRCPE 1959. Edinburgh Royal Infirmary, 1930–31. Joined Colonial Medical Service, 1934; DDMS Bechuanaland Protectorate, 1944; DMS Nyasaland, 1949–55; DMS Northern Nigeria, 1955–57. *Recreations:* golf, fishing. *Address:* 8 Avondrust Avenue, Bergvliet, 7945, S Africa. *T:* 72–4541. *Clubs:* Royal Hong Kong Golf; Zomba Gymkhana (Malaŵi).

MACKENZIE, Rear-Adm. David John, CB 1983; FNI; Royal Navy, retired 1983; Director, Atlantic Salmon Trust, since 1985; *b* 3 Oct. 1929; *s* of late David Mackenzie and of Alison Walker Lawrie; *m* 1965, Ursula Sybil Balfour; two *s* one *d*. *Educ:* Cargilfield Sch., Barnton, Edinburgh; Royal Naval Coll., Eaton Hall, Cheshire. Cadet to Comdr, 1943–72: served in East Indies, Germany, Far East, Home and Mediterranean Fleets, and commanded: HMML 6011, HM Ships: Brinkley, Barrington, Hardy, Lincoln, Hermione; Captain 1972; Senior Officers War Course, 1972; commanded HMS Phoenix (NBCD School), 1972–74; Captain F8 in HMS Ajax, 1974–76; Director of Naval Equipment, 1976–78; Captain: HMS Blake, 1979; HMS Hermes, 1980; Rear Admiral 1981; Flag Officer and Port Admiral, Gibraltar, Comdr Gibraltar Mediterranean, 1981–83. Younger Brother of Trinity House, 1971–. Member, Queen's Body Guard for Scotland (Royal Company of Archers), 1976–. Vice Pres., Nautical Inst., 1985–. *Recreations:* shooting and fishing. *Address:* c/o Bank of Scotland, Haymarket Branch, SW1. *Clubs:* New (Edinburgh); Royal Naval Target Rifle (Bisley).

McKENZIE, Dr Donald Francis, FBA 1986; Reader in Textual Criticism, and Professorial Fellow, Pembroke College, University of Oxford, since 1986; *b* 5 June 1931; *s* of Leslie Alwyn Olson McKenzie and Millicent McKenzie; *m* 1951, Dora Mary Haigh; one *s*. *Educ:* Christchurch and Palmerston North Boys' High Schs, NZ; Victoria UC, Wellington, NZ (BA 1954; DipJourn 1955; MA 1957); Corpus Christi Coll., Cambridge (PhD 1961). Public servant, NZ PO, 1949–56; Jun. Lectr, Victoria UC, 1956–57; Victoria University of Wellington: Lectr, 1961; Sen. Lectr, 1961–63; Associate Prof., 1964–69; Prof. of Eng. Lang. and Lit., 1969–87. Fellow, Corpus Christi Coll., Cambridge, 1960–66; Sandars Reader in Bibliography, Cambridge, 1975–76. Panizzi Lectr, British Liby, 1985. Founder-manager, Wai-te-ata Press, 1961–86. Trustee, Nat. Liby of NZ, 1975–85. Pres., Bibliographical Soc., 1982–83; Hon. Mem., Bibliographical Soc. of America, 1986. Corresp. FBA 1980. *Publications:* (ed) Stationers' Company Apprentices 1605–1800, 3 vols, 1961–78; The Cambridge University Press 1696–1712: a bibliographical study, 1966; (ed) A Ledger of Charles Ackers, 1968; (ed) Robert Tailor, The Hogge hath lost his Pearl, 1972; Oral Culture, Literacy and Print in early New Zealand, 1985; Bibliography and the Sociology of Texts, 1986; contribs to bibliographical jls. *Address:* Pembroke College, Oxford OX1 1DW. *T:* Oxford 242271.

MacKENZIE, Rt. Hon. Gregor; *see* MacKenzie, Rt Hon. J. G.

MACKENZIE, Vice-Adm. Sir Hugh (Stirling), KCB 1966 (CB 1963); DSO 1942 and Bar 1943; DSC 1945; *b* 3 July 1913; 3rd *s* of Dr and Mrs T. C. Mackenzie, Inverness; *m* 1946, Helen Maureen, *er d* of Major J. E. M. Bradish-Ellames; one *s* two *d*. *Educ:* Cargilfield Sch.; Royal Naval Coll., Dartmouth. Joined Royal Naval Coll., 1927; qualified in Submarines, 1935. Served throughout War of 1939–45 in Submarines, comdg HMS Thrasher, 1941–43; HMS Tantalus, 1943–45; Comdr 1946; Capt. 1951; Rear-Adm. 1961; Flag Officer, Submarines, 1961–63; Chief Polaris Executive, 1963–68; Vice-Adm. 1964; retired 1968. Chm., Navy League, 1969–74; Dir, Atlantic Salmon Research Trust Ltd, 1969–79 (renamed Atlantic Salmon Trust, 1979), Chm., 1979–83, Vice Pres., 1984–. Hon. Freeman, Borough of Shoreditch, 1942. CBIM. *Recreation:* the country. *Address:* Sylvan Lodge, Puttenham, near Guildford, Surrey. *Club:* Naval and Military.

MACKENZIE, Ian Clayton, CBE 1962; HM Diplomatic Service, retired; Ambassador to Korea, 1967–69; *b* 13 Jan. 1909; *m* 1948, Anne Helena Tylor; one *s* one *d*. *Educ:* Bedford Sch.; King's Coll., Cambridge. China Consular Service, 1932–41; Consul, Brazzaville, 1942–45, Foreign Office, 1945; 1st Sec., Commercial, Shanghai, 1946–49; Santiago, 1949–53; Commercial Counsellor: Oslo, 1953–58; Caracas, 1958–63;

Stockholm, 1963–66. *Address:* Koryo, Armstrong Road, Brockenhurst, Hants SO42 7TA. *T:* Lymington 23453.

MACKENZIE, James, BSc; CEng, FIM, FICeram; Director: Thomas Marshall (Loxley) plc; Geo. Cohen Sons & Co. Ltd; Lloyds Register Quality Assurance Ltd; *b* 2 Nov. 1924; *s* of James Mackenzie and Isobel Mary Chalmers; *m* 1950, Elizabeth Mary Ruttle; one *s* one *d*. *Educ:* Queen's Park Sch., Glasgow; Royal Technical Coll., Glasgow (BSc). The United Steel Companies Ltd, Research and Develt Dept, 1944–67; British Steel Corporation, 1967–85, a Man. Dir, 1976–85. President: Inst. of Ceramics, 1965–67; Metals Soc., 1983–85. *Address:* Westhaven, Beech Waye, Gerrards Cross, Bucks SL9 8BL. *T:* Gerrards Cross 886461. *Club:* Western (Glasgow).

MacKENZIE, James Alexander Mackintosh, FEng 1982; Chief Road Engineer, Scottish Development Department, since 1976; *b* Inverness, 6 May 1928; *m* 1970, Pamela Dorothy Nixon; one *s* one *d*. *Educ:* Inverness Royal Acad. FICE, FIHE. Miscellaneous local govt appts, 1950–63; Chief Resident Engr, Durham County Council, 1963–67; Dep. Dir, 1967–71, Dir, 1971–76, North Eastern Road Construction Unit, MoT, later DoE. *Recreations:* golf, fishing. *Address:* Pendor, 2 Dean Park, Longniddry, East Lothian EH32 0QR. *T:* Longniddry 52643. *Clubs:* Royal Automobile; Royal Scottish Automobile (Glasgow).

MacKENZIE, Rt. Hon. (James) Gregor, PC 1977; MP (Lab) Glasgow, Rutherglen, since 1983 (Rutherglen, May 1964–1983); *b* 15 Nov. 1927; *o s* of late James and Mary MacKenzie; *m* 1958, Joan Swan Provan; one *s* one *d*. *Educ:* Queen's Park Sch.; Royal Technical College; Glasgow Univ. (School of Social Studies). Joined Labour Party, 1944. Contested (Lab): East Aberdeenshire, 1950; Kinross and West Perthshire, 1959. Chm., Scottish Labour League, 1948; Mem. and Magistrate, Glasgow Corporation, 1952–55, 1956–64; PPS to Rt Hon. James Callaghan, MP, 1965–70; Opposition spokesman on Posts and Telecommunications, 1970–74; Parly Under-Sec. of State for Industry, 1974–75; Minister of State for Industry, 1975–76; Minister of State, Scottish Office, 1976–79. JP Glasgow, 1962. *Address:* 6 Restormel House, Chester Way, SE11 4UU. *T:* 01–735 2957. *Club:* Reform.

MacKENZIE, James Sargent Porteous, OBE 1963; *b* 18 June 1916; *s* of late Roderick and Daisy W. MacKenzie; *m* 1944, Flora Paterson; three *s*. *Educ:* Portree High Sch.; Edinburgh Univ. (MA Hons 1939); Glasgow Univ. (Dip. Social Studies 1947). War Service, 1939–45: Captain RA (Combined Ops, Burma and Normandy). Scottish HQ, Min. of Labour, 1947–56; Labour Advr, UK High Commn, New Delhi, 1956–62 (First Sec., 1956, Counsellor, 1959); Ministry of Labour: Asst Controller, Scottish HQ, 1962–65; Dep. Controller, Yorks and Humberside Regional Office, 1965–67; Principal Dep. Controller, Scottish HQ, Dept of Employment, 1967–72; Asst Sec., 1970; Counsellor (Labour) British Embassy, Bonn, 1972–77, retired 1977. Exec. Mem., Church of Scotland Cttee on Church and Nation, 1977–83. *Address:* 11 Baberton Park, Juniper Green, Edinburgh.

McKENZIE, John, CMG 1970; MBE 1947; PhD; HM Diplomatic Service, retired; *b* 30 April 1915; *m* 1943, Sigridur Olafsdóttir; two *s* one *d*. *Educ:* Archbishop Holgate's Grammar Sch., York; Leeds Univ. Lectr, Univ. of Iceland, 1938–40; Second Sec. and Vice-Consul, Reykjavik, 1945; Consul, Helsinki, 1948; First Sec., 1949; Foreign Office, 1950; Sofia, 1953 (Chargé d'Affaires, 1954, 1955, 1956); Baghdad, 1956; Foreign Office, 1958; Counsellor, seconded to Cabinet Office, 1962; Helsinki, 1964 (Chargé d'Affaires, 1965, 1966); Dep. High Comr Calcutta, 1967–70; Ambassador to Iceland, 1970–75. *Address:* 60 Dome Hill, Caterham, Surrey CR3 6EB. *T:* Caterham 42546.

MACKENZIE, Brig. John Alexander, CBE 1955; DSO 1944 and Bar, 1944; MC 1940 and Bar, 1940; retired; *b* 9 March 1915; *s* of late Louis Robert Wilson Mackenzie; *m* 1952, Beryl Cathreen Culver; one *s*. *Educ:* Nautical Coll., Pangbourne; RMC, Sandhurst. 2nd Bn Gloucestershire Regt, 1935–43; Bn Comd, 2nd Bn Lancs Fusiliers, Tunisia, Sicily and Italy Campaigns, 1943–44 (despatches, 1944); Bde Comd: 11 Inf. Bde, Italy, 1944; 10 Inf. Bde, Greece, 1945–46; psc 1947; GSO1 HQ British Troops, Berlin, 1948–49; AAG (Organisation), HQ, BAOR, 1950; jssc 1951; GSO1 HQ Western Comd, 1951–54; Comd: Britcom Sub-area N, S Korea, 1955; Inf. Trng Team, HQ Jordan Arab Army, 1956; Jt Concealment Centre, 1957–58; Small Arms Sch., Hythe, 1958–59; idc 1960; Comd: 1 Bde, Nigeria, 1961–63; 3 Bde, Congo, 1962; Actg GOC, Royal Nigerian Army, 1963; BGS Army Trng, MoD, 1964–67; ADC to the Queen, 1967–70; Comdt and Inspector of Intelligence, 1967–70; retired 1970. *Recreation:* gardening. *Address:* Slaybrook Hall, Sandling Road, Saltwood, Hythe, Kent.

McKENZIE, John Cormack; FEng 1984; FICE; Secretary, Institution of Civil Engineers, since 1982; Managing Director, Thomas Telford Ltd, since 1982; *b* 21 June 1927; *s* of William Joseph McKenzie and Elizabeth Frances Robinson; *m* 1954, Olga Caroline Cleland; three *s* one *d*. *Educ:* St Andrews Coll.; Trinity Coll., Dublin (MA, MAI); Queen's Univ., Belfast (MSc). FIPM, FIEI. McLaughlin & Harvey, and Sir Alexander Gibb & Partners, 1946–48; Asst Lectr, QUB, 1948–50; Edmund Nuttall Ltd, 1950–82, Dir, 1967–82; Chm., Nuttall Geotechnical Services Ltd, 1967–82. Sec. Gen., Commonwealth Engineers' Council, 1983–. *Publications:* papers: Research into some Aspects of Soil Cement, 1952; Engineers: Administrators or Technologists?, 1971; (contrib.) Civil Engineering Procedure, 3rd edn 1979. *Recreations:* philately, collecting ancient pottery, climbing. *Address:* Institution of Civil Engineers, 1 Great George Street, SW1P 3AA. *T:* 01–222 7722. *Club:* Athenæum.

McKENZIE, Prof. John Crawford; Rector, The London Institute, since 1986; *b* 12 Nov. 1937; *s* of Donald Walter McKenzie and Emily Beatrice McKenzie; *m* 1960, Ann McKenzie (née Roberts); two *s*. *Educ:* London School of Economics and Political Science (BScEcon); Bedford Coll., London (MPhil). Lecturer, Queen Elizabeth Coll., Univ. of London, 1961; Dep. Director, Office of Health Econs, 1966; Market Inf. Manager, Allied Breweries Ltd, 1968; various posts, Kimpher Ltd, 1969, finally Chief Exec., Kimpher Marketing Services, 1973; Head of Dept, London Coll. of Printing, 1975; Principal: Ilkley Coll., 1978; Bolton Inst. of Higher Educn, 1982; Rector, Liverpool Poly., 1984–85. Visiting Professor: Queen Elizabeth Coll., 1976–80; Univ. of Newcastle, 1981–. Member: NAB/UGC Continuing Educn Cttee; NAB Good Management Practice Gp. *Publications:* (ed jtly) Changing Food Habits, 1964; (ed jtly) Our Changing Fare, 1966; (ed jtly) The Food Consumer, 1986; many articles in Proc. Nutrition Soc., British Jl Nutrition, Nutrition Bull., etc. *Recreation:* collecting antiquarian books. *Address:* The London Institute, 20 John Prince's Street, W1M 9HE; Flag House, The Green, Chalfont St Giles, Bucks; Roughdown, Heathness Road, Addingham, Ilkley, West Yorks LS29 0PL. *T:* Ilkley 831105. *Clubs:* Athenæum; Athenæum (Liverpool).

McKENZIE, Rear-Adm. John Foster, CB 1977; CBE 1974 (OBE 1962); Member, Planning Tribunal, since 1979; *b* Waiuku, 24 June 1923; *s* of Dr J. C. McKenzie; *m* 1945, Doreen Elizabeth, *d* of Dr E. T. McElligott; one *s* one *d*. *Educ:* Timaru Boys' High Sch.; St Andrews Coll., Christchurch, NZ. Served War of 1939–45: Royal Navy; transferred to Royal New Zealand Navy, 1947; Head, Defence Liaison Staff, London, 1966–68; Imperial Defence Coll., 1969; Asst Chief of Defence Staff (Policy), Defence HQ, NZ, 1970–71;

Deputy Chief of Naval Staff, 1972; Commodore, Auckland, 1973–75; Chief of Naval Staff, and Mem. Defence Council, 1975–77, retired 1977. ADC 1972–75. *Recreations:* gardening, fishing. *Address:* 64 Lohia Street, Khandallah, Wellington 4, New Zealand.

MACKENZIE of Mornish, John Hugh Munro; Chairman: London and Northern Group plc, since 1967; Pauling plc, since 1976; Scottish, English and European Textiles plc, since 1969; Tace plc, since 1967; Goring Kerr PLC, since 1983; *b* 29 Aug. 1925; *s* of Lt-Col John Munro Mackenzie of Mornish, DSO, JP, Mil. Kt of Windsor, Henry VIII Gateway, Windsor Castle, and Mrs E. H. M. Mackenzie (née Taaffe); *m* 1951, Eileen Louise Agate, *d* of Alexander Shanks, OBE, MC, and Mrs Shanks; four *s* one *d* (and one *s* decd). *Educ:* Edinburgh Acad.; Loretto Sch.; Trinity Coll., Oxford (MA (Hons)); Hague Acad. of Internat. Law; Inns of Court Law Schs; McGill Univ., Montreal. Served Army, 1945–49: Captain, The Royal Scots (Royal Regt); war service, Europe; 1st KOSB, A Company, 9th Brigade, 3rd Inf. Div. (despatches, certs of gallantry) and Far East HQ Allied Land Forces SE Asia and HQ Ceylon Army Comd, Staff Captain, Mil. Sec's Branch; HM Guard of Honour, Balmoral, 1946; HQ 3rd Auto Aircraft Div., 1946–47, GSO III. Harmsworth Law Scholar, Middle Temple, 1950; called to the Bar, Middle Temple, 1950. United Dominions Trust Ltd, trainee, ICI Ltd, Legal Asst, Estates Dept, 1951; Hudson's Bay Scholar, 1952–53; ICI Ltd, Buyer Crop and misc. products, 1953–54; Trubenised (GB) Ltd and Associated Cos, Co. Sec. and Legal Advisor, 1955–56; Aspro-Nicholas Ltd, Gp Develt Officer, 1956–57; Knitmaster Holdings, 1957; formed: Grampian Holdings Ltd (Manager and Sec.), 1958, Man. Dir, 1960; London and Northern Gp Ltd (Dep. Chm. and Man. Dir), 1962; Tace plc, 1967 (Chm.); Scottish, English and European Textiles plc, 1969 (Chm.). Seven Queen's Awards for Export won by Group Cos. FRSA, FBIM. *Recreations:* opera, bridge, shooting, fishing, all field sports. *Address:* Mortlake House, Vicarage Road, SW14 8RU; Scaliscro Lodge, Isle of Lewis, Outer Hebrides; Shellwood Manor, Leigh, Surrey RH2 8NX. *Clubs:* Royal Automobile; Royal Scots (Edinburgh).

McKENZIE, Julia Kathleen, (Mrs Jerry Harte); actress and singer; *b* 17 Feb. 1941; *d* of Albion McKenzie and Kathleen Rowe; *m* 1972, Jerry Harte. *Educ:* Guildhall School of Music and Drama. *Stage:* Maggie May, 1965; Mame, 1969; Promises, Promises, 1970; Company, 1972; Cowardy Custard, 1973; Cole, 1974; Side by Side by Sondheim, 1977 (London and Broadway); Norman Conquests, 1978; Ten Times Table, 1979; On the 20th Century, 1981; Guys and Dolls, NT, 1982; Schweyk in 2nd World War, NT, 1982; Woman in Mind, 1986; *films:* Those Glory Glory Days; Hotel Du Lac; *TV series:* Fame is the Spur; Blott on the Landscape; Maggie and Her; Fresh Fields; Sharing Time; Dear Box No; Absent Friends; Julia and Company (TV special), 1986; numerous TV musicals; directed Stepping Out, 1984. *Recreations:* cooking, gardening. *Address:* c/o April Young Ltd, 31 King's Road, SW3. *T:* 01–730 9922.

MACKENZIE, Keith Roderick Turing, OBE 1983; MC; Secretary, Royal and Ancient Golf Club of St Andrews, Fife, Scotland, 1967–83; *b* 19 Jan. 1921; *s* of Henry Roderick Turing Mackenzie and Betty Dalzell Mackenzie; *m* 1949, Barbara Kershaw Miles; two *s* two *d*. *Educ:* Uppingham Sch.; RMC, Sandhurst. Served War: Indian Army, 2/6th Gurkha Rifles, 1940–47 (MC, Italy, 1944). Burmah-Shell Oil Storage and Distributing Co. of India, 1947–65; Shell Company of Rhodesia, 1965–66. *Recreations:* gardening, golf. *Address:* Eden Hill, Kennedy Gardens, St Andrews, Fife KY16 9DJ. *T:* St Andrews 73581. *Clubs:* Royal Cinque Ports Golf (Deal); Royal & Ancient Golf (St Andrews); Royal Porthcawl Golf; Royal St George's Golf; Atlanta Athletic (Georgia); Pine Valley Golf (New Jersey); Royal Calcutta Golf (Calcutta); Royal Harare Golf (Zimbabwe).

MacKENZIE, Kelvin Calder; Editor of The Sun, since 1981; *b* 22 Oct. 1946; *m* 1969, Jacqueline Mary Holland; two *s* one *d*. *Educ:* Alleyn's Sch., Dulwich. Sub-editor, The Sun, 1973, Asst Night Editor, 1976; Managing Editor, New York Post, 1978; Night Editor, The Sun, 1980; Night Editor, Daily Express, 1981. *Recreation:* squash. *Address:* The Sun, 30 Bouverie Street, EC4Y 8DE. *T:* 01–353 3030.

MACKENZIE, Kenneth Edward, CMG 1970; HM Diplomatic Service, retired; *b* 28 April 1910; *s* of late A. E. Mackenzie, Dundee, and late K. M. Mackenzie (née Foley); *m* 1935, Phyllis Edith Fawkes; one *s*. *Educ:* schools in India, Australia and in the UK; University Coll., London. Engineering industry, 1926–29; University Coll., London, 1929–32, BSc (Hons) in civil and mechanical engineering. Inst. of Civil Engineers, 1932–34; Dept of Overseas Trade, 1934–36; HM Embassy, Brussels, 1936–40; interned in Germany, 1940–41; HM Embassy, Tehran, 1942–45. Trade Commissioner: in India, 1945–48; in Malaya, 1949–54; Asst Sec., Bd of Trade, 1954–66; Counsellor (Commercial), HM Embassy, Stockholm, and Chargé d'Affaires *ad interim*, 1966–70; Counsellor (Investment), 1973; Counsellor (Investment), HM Embassy, Copenhagen, 1974–75. *Address:* 11 St James Close, Pangbourne, Berks RG8 7AP. *T:* Pangbourne 2228.

MacKENZIE, Kenneth John; Under Secretary, Scottish Office, since 1985; *b* 1 May 1943; *s* of John Donald MacKenzie and Elizabeth Pennant Johnston Sutherland; *m* 1975, Irene Mary Hogarth; one *s* one *d*. *Educ:* Woodchurch Road Primary School, Birkenhead; Birkenhead School; Pembroke College, Oxford (Exbnr; MA Mod. Hist.); Stanford Univ., Calif (AM Hist.). Scottish Home and Health Dept, 1965; Private Sec. to Jt Parly Under Sec. of State, Scottish Office, 1969–70; Scottish Office Regional Develt Div., 1970–73; Scottish Educn Dept, 1973–76; Civil Service Fellow, Glasgow Univ., 1974–75; Principal Private Sec. to Sec. of State for Scotland, 1977–79; Asst Sec., Scottish Economic Planning Dept, 1979–83; Scottish Office Finance Div., 1983–85; Principal Finance Officer, 1985. *Recreations:* Session Clerk, St Cuthbert's Parish Church, Edinburgh; amateur dramatics. *Address:* 29 Regent Terrace, Edinburgh EH7 5BS. *T:* 031–557 4530. *Club:* National Liberal.

MACKENZIE, Kenneth Roderick, CB 1965; Clerk of Public Bills, House of Commons, 1959–73; *b* 19 April 1908; *s* of late Walter Mackenzie; *m* 1935, Mary Howard, *e d* of late Lt-Col C. H. Coode, RM; three *s* one *d*. *Educ:* Dulwich Coll.; New Coll., Oxford (scholar). 1st class Classical Moderations; 2nd class Literæ Humaniores. Asst clerk, House of Commons, 1930; Clerk of Standing Cttees, 1953. Mem., Cttee on Preparation of Legislation, 1973–74. Officer's Cross, Order of Polonia Restituta, 1964. *Publications:* The English Parliament, 1950; Parliament, 1959; editions of Sir Bryan Fell's Guide to the Palace of Westminster, 1944–72; verse translations of: Słowacki's In Switzerland, 1953; Mickiewicz's Pan Tadeusz, 1964; Virgil's Georgics, 1969; Dante's Divine Comedy, 1979. *Recreation:* gardening. *Address:* Woodnorton, Mayfield, East Sussex TN20 6EJ. *T:* Mayfield 872317.

MacKENZIE, Kenneth William Stewart, CMG 1958; CVO 1975; FRAI; a Director of Studies, Royal Institute of Public Administration (Overseas Unit), since 1976; *b* 30 July 1915; *s* of late W. S. MacKenzie and E. MacKenzie (née Johnson); *m* 1939, Kathleen Joyce Ingram; one *s* one *d*. *Educ:* Whitcliffe Mount Gram. Sch., Cleckheaton; Downing Coll., Cambridge. 1st Cl. Hist. Tripos, Part I, 1935; Class II, Div. I, 1936; 1st Cl. Arch. and Anthrop. Tripos, Section A, 1937, BA 1936, MA 1962. Cadet, Colonial Administrative Service, Basutoland, 1938; Asst Sec., Mauritius, 1944; Administrative Officer, Kenya, 1948; Asst Financial Sec., Kenya, 1950; HM Treasury, 1951–53; Dep. Sec., 1954 and Permanent Sec., 1955, Treasury, Kenya; Minister for Finance and Development and

Financial Sec., Kenya, 1959–62. MLC Kenya, 1955–62; MLA East Africa, 1959–62. Retired, 1963 to facilitate constitutional change. Re-employed as Principal, Colonial Office, 1963; Principal, HM Treasury, 1966–70; Asst Sec., DoE, 1970–75. *Publication:* pamphlet, How Basutoland is Governed, 1944. *Recreations:* reading, gardening. *Address:* Beaumont, 28 Greenhurst Lane, Oxted, Surrey RH8 0LB. *T:* Oxted 3848. *Clubs:* Royal Over-Seas League; Achilles; Nairobi (Nairobi).

MACKENZIE, Maxwell Weir, OC 1972; CMG 1946; Director: Canadian Imperial Bank of Commerce, 1955–77, now Emeritus; Canron Ltd, 1961–77; International Multifoods Corp., 1964–77; Royal Trust, 1960–67; Imperial Life, 1962–75; *b* 30 June 1907; *s* of late Hugh Blair Mackenzie, Gen. Man., Bank of Montreal, Montreal, and Maude Marion Weir; *m* 1931, Jean Roger Fairbairn; two *s* two *d*. *Educ:* Lakefield Preparatory Sch., Lakefield, Ont.; Trinity Coll. School, Port Hope, Ont.; McGill Univ., Montreal (BCom 1928). Joined McDonald, Currie & Co., Chartered Accountants of Montreal, 1928; Mem. Soc. of Chartered Accountants of the Province of Quebec, 1929; Jr Partner, McDonald, Currie & Co., Montreal, 1935; on loan to Foreign Exchange Control Board, Ottawa, 1939–42; to Wartime Prices and Trade Board, Ottawa, 1942–44 (Dep. Chm. 1943–44); Mem., Royal Commission on Taxation of Annuities and Family Corporation, 1944; Dep. Minister of Trade and Commerce, 1945–51; Dep. Minister of Defence Production, Canada, 1951–52; Pres., Canadian Chemical & Cellulose Company, Ltd, 1954–59 (Exec. Vice-Pres., 1952–54). Mem., Economic Council of Canada, 1963–71. Dir, C. D. Howe Res. Inst., 1973–80. Chairman: Royal Commission on Security, 1966; Federal Inquiry into Beef Marketing, 1975. Hon. LLD McGill, 1973. *Recreation:* ski-ing. *Address:* 383 Maple Lane, Rockcliffe Park, Ottawa, Ont K1M 1H7, Canada. *Club:* Rideau (Ottawa).

McKENZIE, Michael; Assistant Registrar, Court of Appeal Criminal Division, since 1986; *b* Hove, Sussex, 25 May 1943; *s* of Robert John McKenzie and Kitty Elizabeth McKenzie; *m* 1964, Peggy Dorothy, *d* of Thomas Edward William Russell and Dorothy Mabel Russell; three *s*. *Educ:* Varndean Grammar Sch., Brighton. Town Clerk's Dept, Brighton, 1961–63; Asst to Clerk of the Peace, Brighton Quarter Sessions, 1963–67; Sen. Clerk of the Court, 1967–70, Dep. Clerk of the Peace, 1970–71, Middlesex Quarter Sessions; Called to the Bar, Middle Temple, 1970; Deputy to Courts Administrator, Middlesex Crown Court, 1972–73; Courts Administrator (Newcastle), NE Circuit, 1974–79; Courts Administrator, Central Criminal Court, and Coordinator for Taxation of Crown Court Costs, S Eastern Circuit, 1979–84; Dep. Circuit Administrator, SE Circuit, 1984–86. Freeman, City of London, 1979. *Recreations:* Northumbrian stick dressing, fell walking. *Address:* Criminal Appeal Office, Royal Courts of Justice, Strand, WC2A 2LL.

MACKENZIE, Sir Robert Evelyn, 12th Bt, *cr* 1673; *b* 15 Feb. 1906; *s* of 11th Bt and Evelyn Mary Montgomery (*d* 1908), *d* of Major-Gen. Sir Edward W. Ward; *S* father, 1935; *m* 1st, 1940, Mrs Jane Adams-Beck (*d* 1953); 2nd, 1963, Mrs Elizabeth Campbell. *Educ:* Eton; Trinity Coll., Cambridge. Mem. of Lloyd's, 1932–71. Intelligence Corps, 1939; British Embassy, Paris, 1944; Foreign Office, 1947; Washington, 1948; Foreign Office, 1951. *Heir: kinsman* Peter Douglas Mackenzie, *b* 1949. *Address:* 44 Chester Square, SW1W 9EA.

MACKENZIE, Sir Roderick McQuhae, 12th Bt *cr* 1703, of Scatwell; FRCP(C); medical practitioner; *b* 17 April 1942; *s* of Captain Sir Roderick Edward François McQuhae Mackenzie, 11th Bt, CBE, DSC, RN and of Marie Evelyn Campbell, *o c* of late William Ernest Parkinson; *S* father, 1986; *m* 1970, Nadezhda, (Nadine), Baroness von Rorbas, *d* of Georges Frederic Schlatter, Baron von Rorbas; one *s* one *d*. *Educ:* Sedbergh; King's College London. MB, BS; MRCP; DCH. *Heir:* *s* Gregory Roderick McQuhae Mackenzie, *b* 8 May 1971. *Address:* 2431 Udell Road NW, Calgary, Alberta T2N 4H9, Canada.

MACKENZIE, Wallace John, OBE 1974; Director, Slough Estates plc, since 1986 (Group Managing Director, 1975–86); *b* 2 July 1921; *s* of Wallace D. Mackenzie and Ethel F. Williamson; *m* 1951, Barbara D. Hopson; two *s* one *d*. *Educ:* Harrow Weald County Grammar Sch. Gen. Manager, Slough Estates Canada Ltd, 1952–72; Dep. Man. Dir, Slough Estates Ltd, 1972–75. Dir, Investors in Industry plc, 1982–; Chm., Trust Parts Ltd, 1985–. Member: Commn for New Towns, 1978–; London Residuary Body, 1985–. *Recreations:* golf, bridge. *Address:* Manitou, Spring Coppice, Lane End, High Wycombe, Bucks. *T:* High Wycombe 881032.

MACKENZIE, Prof. William James Millar, CBE 1963; FBA 1968; Professor of Politics, Glasgow University, 1966–74, now Emeritus; *b* 8 April 1909; *s* of Laurence Millar Mackenzie, WS, Edinburgh; *m* 1943, Pamela Muriel Malyon; one *s* four *d*. *Educ:* Edinburgh Academy; Balliol Coll., Oxford (MA) (Ireland Schol. 1929); Edinburgh Univ. (LLB); Fellow of Magdalen Coll., Oxford, 1933–48; Temp. Civil Servant, Air Ministry, 1939–44; Official War Historian, SOE, 1945–48. Faculty Fellow, Nuffield Coll., 1948; Lecturer in Politics, Oxford Univ., 1948; Prof. of Government, Manchester Univ., 1949–66, Glasgow Univ., 1966–74; Special Comr, for Constitutional Development, Tanganyika, 1952; Co-opted Mem., Manchester City Educn Cttee, 1953–64; apptd Mem., British Wool Marketing Board, 1954–66; Mem. Royal Commn on Local Govt in Greater London, 1957; Constitutional Adviser, Kenya, 1959; Vice-Chm., Bridges Cttee on Training in Public Administration for Overseas Countries, 1962; Member: Maud Cttee on Management in Local Govt, 1964–66; Cttee on Remuneration of Ministers and Members of Parliament, 1963–64; North-West Regional Economic Planning Council, 1965–66; SSRC, 1965–69; Parry Cttee on University Libraries, 1964–67; Chm., Children's Panel Adv. Cttee, Glasgow City, 1973–75. Hon. LLD: Dundee, 1968; Lancaster, 1970; Manchester, 1975; Hon. DLitt Warwick, 1972; Hon. DSc (Econ) Hull, 1981; DUniv Open Univ., 1984. *Publications:* (in part) British Government since 1918, 1950; (jtly) Central Administration in Great Britain, 1957; Free Elections, 1958; (ed with Prof. K. Robinson) Five Elections in Africa, 1959; Politics and Social Science, 1967; (jtly) Social Work in Scotland, 1969; Power, Violence, Decision, 1975; Explorations in Government, 1975; Political Identity, 1977; Biological Ideas in Politics, 1978; Power and Responsibility in Health Care, 1979. *Address:* 12 Kirklee Circus, Glasgow G12 0TW.

MACKENZIE CROOKS, Air Vice-Marshal Lewis, CBE 1963 (OBE 1950); Consultant Adviser in Orthopaedic Surgery, RAF, 1966–70, retired; Locum Consultant in Orthopaedic Surgery, Cornwall, since 1970; *b* 20 Jan. 1909; *s* of David Mackenzie Crooks and Mary (*née* McKechnie); *m* 1936, Mildred, *d* of A. J. Gwyther; two *s* one *d*. *Educ:* Epworth Coll.; Liverpool Univ. MB, ChB 1931; FRCS 1937; ChM (Liverpool) 1945. House Surgeon: Northern Hosp., Liverpool, 1931–32; Shropshire Orthop. Hosp., Oswestry, 1932–33; Sen. House Surgeon: Selly Oak Hosp., Birmingham, 1933–34; All Saints Hosp., London, 1934–35; commnd RAF, 1935; surgical hosp. appts in RAF, 1936–52; overseas service: Palestine, 1937–39; Iraq, 1939–42 (despatches 1941); Egypt, 1950–51. Clinical Tutor, Edinburgh Royal Infirmary, 1947; Cons. in Orthop. Surgery, 1952; Sen. Cons. in Orthop. Surgery, 1955. QHS, 1966–70. *Publication:* article on chondromalaca patellae in Jl of Bone and Joint Surgery. *Recreations:* golf, gardening. *Address:* Trelawney, Harlyn Bay, Padstow, Cornwall PL28 8SF. *T:* Padstow 520631. *Clubs:* Royal Air Force; Trevose Golf, Country (Constantine Bay, Cornwall).

McKENZIE JOHNSTON, Henry Butler, CB 1981; Vice-Chairman, Commission for Local Administration in England, 1982–84 (Commissioner, 1981–84); *b* 10 July 1921; *er s* of late Colin McKenzie Johnston and late Bernardine (*née* Fawcett Butler); *m* 1949, Marian Allardyce Middleton, *e d* of late Brig. A. A. Middleton and Winifred (*née* Salvesen); one *s* two *d*. *Educ:* Rugby. Served with Black Watch (RHR), 1940–46; Adjt 6th Bn, 1944–45; Temp. Major 1945. Staff of HM Embassy, Athens, 1946–47; entered Foreign (subseq. Diplomatic) Service, 1947; Paris, 1948–51; British High Commn, Germany, 1951–54; FO, 1954–56; 1st Sec. (Commercial), Montevideo, 1956–60; FO, 1960–63; Counsellor (Information), Mexico City, 1963–66; Dep. High Comr, Port of Spain, 1966–67; seconded to Min. of Overseas Develt, 1968–70, Consul-Gen., Munich, 1971–73; seconded to Office of Parly Comr, 1973–79, transferred permanently, 1979–81; Dep. Parly Comr for Admin, 1974–81. Mem., Broadcasting Complaints Commn, 1986–. Mem., Social Security Appeal Tribunal, Kensington. Hon. Sec., Southwark Div., SSAFA. *Address:* 6 Pembroke Gardens, W8 6HS. *Clubs:* Athenæum, Hurlingham.

MACKENZIE-KENNEDY, Brig. Archibald Gordon, CBE 1952 (OBE 1949); DSO 1945; Brigadier late Royal Scots; *b* 1904; *s* of late Maj.-Gen. Sir Edward Charles William Mackenzie-Kennedy, KBE, CB; *m* 1937, Jean Katherine (*d* 1981), *d* of H. A. Law, Marble Hill, Ballymore, Co. Donegal. *Educ:* Marlborough; Royal Military College, Sandhurst. 2nd Lt Royal Scots, 1924. Served War of 1939–45: Burma, 1941–45 (DSO; despatches 1943); Lt-Col, 1943; Brig., 1947; Comdr Eritrea District, 1950–52; retd 1955. County Comdt, Ulster Special Constabulary, 1955. *Address:* Tarff Old Manse, Kirkcudbright. *T:* Ringford 219.

MACKENZIE STUART, Hon. Lord; Alexander John Mackenzie Stuart; President of the Court of Justice, European Communities at Luxembourg, since 1984 (Judge of the Court of Justice, 1972–84); a Senator of the College of Justice in Scotland, 1972–73; *b* 18 Nov. 1924; *s* of late Prof. A. Mackenzie Stuart, KC, and Amy Margaret Dean, Aberdeen; *m* 1952, Anne Burtholme Millar, *d* of late J. S. L. Millar, WS, Edinburgh; four *d*. *Educ:* Fettes Coll., Edinburgh (open Schol.); Sidney Sussex Coll., Cambridge (schol. 1949, 1st cl. Pt II Law Tripos, BA 1949, Hon. Fellow, 1977); Edinburgh Univ. (LLB (dist.) 1951). Royal Engineers (Temp. Capt. 1946), 1942–47. Admitted Faculty of Advocates, 1951; QC (Scot.) 1963; Keeper of the Advocates Library, 1970–72. Standing Junior Counsel: to Scottish Home Dept, 1956–57; to Inland Revenue in Scotland, 1957–63. Sheriff-Principal of Aberdeen, Kincardine and Banff, 1971–72. Governor, Fettes College, 1962–72. Hon. Bencher, Middle Temple, 1978; Hon. Mem., Soc. of Public Teachers of Law, 1982. Hon. Prof., Collège d'Europe, Bruges, 1974–77; DUniv. Stirling, 1973; Hon. LLD: Exeter, 1978; Edinburgh, 1978; Glasgow, 1981; Aberdeen, 1983. *Publications:* Hamlyn Lectures: The European Communities and the Rule of Law, 1977; articles in legal publications. *Recreation:* collecting. *Address:* 48 rue de Wormeldange, Rodenbourg, Luxembourg. *T:* 77276; c/o Bank of Scotland, 64 George Street, Edinburgh. *Clubs:* Athenæum; New (Edinburgh); Société de la Pétanque (Les Vans).

McKEOWN, Prof. Patrick Arthur, MSc; FEng 1986; FIProdE; FIQA; FIMechE; Professor of Precision Engineering since 1974, Director of Cranfield Unit for Precision Engineering since 1969, and Head of Department for Design of Machine Systems since 1975, Cranfield Institute of Technology; *b* 16 Aug. 1930; *s* of Robert Matthew McKeown and Augusta (*née* White); *m* 1954, Mary Patricia Heath; three *s*. *Educ:* Cambridge County High Sch. for Boys; Bristol Grammar Sch.; Cranfield Inst. of Technol. (MSc). CEng, MIMechE 1969; FIProdE 1971; FIQA 1973. National Service, RE, 1949–51; Suez Campaign, 1956: Captain RE; port maintenance. Student apprentice, Bristol Aircraft Co. Ltd, Bristol, 1951–54 (HNC National State Scholarship); Cranfield Inst. of Technol., 1954–56; Société Genevoise, Newport Pagnell and Geneva, 1956–68 (Technical and Works Dir, 1965). Vice-Pres., Inst. of Qual. Assurance, 1976. Member: CIRP (Internat. Instn for Prodn Engrg Research); Evaluation Panel, National Bureau of Standards, Washington, USA; Metrology and Standards Requirements Bd, 1983–; Advanced Manufg Technol. Cttee, DTI, 1983–; Vis. Cttee, RCA, 1984–. Fulbright Award (Vis. Prof. of Mechanical Engrg, Univ. of Wisconsin-Madison), 1982; F. W. Taylor Award, Soc. of Manufacturing Engrs, 1983. *Publications:* papers in CIRP Annals. *Recreations:* walking, travel, enjoyment of wine, good food, music, theatre. *Address:* 37 Church End, Biddenham, Bedford MK40 4AR. *T:* Bedford 67678.

McKEOWN, Prof. Thomas, BA British Columbia, PhD McGill, DPhil Oxon, MB, BS London, MD Birmingham, FRCP, FFCM; Professor of Social Medicine, 1945–77, and Pro-Vice-Chancellor, 1974–77, University of Birmingham; *b* 2 Nov. 1912; *s* of William McKeown; *m* 1940, Esmé Joan Bryan Widdowson; one *s* one *d*. *Educ:* Universities: British Columbia; McGill (National Research Council Schol.); Trinity Coll., Oxford (Rhodes Scholar); London (Guy's Hospital: Poulton Research Scholar). Demonstrator in biochemistry, McGill; demonstrator in physiology, Guy's Hosp. Lectures: Cutter, Harvard Sch. of Public Health, 1960; Lowell, Mass, General Hosp., 1963; British Council, Australia, 1963; De Frees, Univ. of Pennsylvania, 1969; Teale, RCP, 1969; BMA Winchester, 1970; Cecil and Ida Green, Univ. of BC, 1975; Osler, McGill, 1979; Alexander D. Langmuir, Center for Disease Control, Atlanta, 1980; James Seth, Univ. of Edinburgh, 1981. Rock Carling Fellow, Nuffield Provincial Hosps Trust, 1976. Jt Editor, Brit. Jl of Preventive and Social Medicine, 1950–58. Hon. FFCM Ireland, 1980; Hon. FACP, 1982; Hon. DSc McGill, 1981. *Publications:* A Balanced Teaching Hospital (jointly), 1965; Medicine in Modern Society, 1965; Introduction to Social Medicine (jt), 1966; Screening in Medical Care (jointly), 1968; Medical History and Medical Care (jt Ed.), 1971; The Modern Rise of Population, 1976; The Role of Medicine, 1976; contributions to scientific journals. *Address:* 23 Hintlesham Avenue, Edgbaston, Birmingham B15 2PH. *T:* 021–454 2810.

MACKEOWN, Thomas Frederick William; Administrator and Secretary, University College Hospital, London, 1946–63; *b* 3 Jan. 1904; *s* of Rev. William Mackeown, Rushbrooke, Co. Cork; *m* 1936, Lorraine, *d* of Major R. Hayes, Sherburn-in-Elmet, Yorks; one *d*. *Educ:* Felsted; Worcester Coll., Oxford (MA). Qualified as Chartered Accountant, 1927. Hospital Administrator: Liverpool Stanley Hospital, 1934–37; Clayton Hospital, Wakefield, 1937–45; Royal Infirmary, Sunderland, 1945–46; Hill Homes, Highgate (actg), 1966; King Edward VII Memorial Hospital, Bermuda, 1967; Vice-Chm., Management Cttee, Harefield and Northwoods Hosps, 1960–74; undertook Hosp. Domestic Staff Survey under aegis of King Edward's Hosp. Fund for London, 1968. Lay FRSocMed, 1974. *Address:* 4 Westhill Court, Millfield Lane, N6. *T:* 01–348 1952.

McKERN, Leo, (Reginald McKern); AO 1983; actor; *b* 16 March 1920; *s* of Norman Walton McKern and Vera (*née* Martin); *m* 1946, Joan Alice Southa (Jane Holland); two *d*. *Educ:* Sydney Techn. High Sch. Engrg apprentice, 1935–37; artist, 1937–40; AIF (Corp., Engrs), 1940–42; actor, 1944; arrived England, 1946; CSEU tour, Germany; Arts Council tours, 1947; Old Vic, 1949–52; Shakespeare Meml Theatre, 1952–54; Old Vic last season, 1962–63; New Nottingham Playhouse, 1963–64; *stage:* Toad of Toad Hall, Princes, 1954; Queen of the Rebels, Haymarket, 1955; Cat on a Hot Tin Roof, Aldwych, 1958; Brouhaha, Aldwych, 1958; Rollo, Strand, 1959; A Man for all Seasons, Globe, 1960; The Thwarting of Baron Bollegrew, RSC, Aldwych, 1965; Volpone, Garrick, 1967; The Wolf, Apollo, 1973; The Housekeeper, Apollo, 1982; Number One, Queen's,

1984; *films:* The Chain, 1985; Murder With Mirrors, 1985; Travelling North, 1986; *television:* Rumpole of the Bailey (series), 1977–; Reilly—Ace of Spies, 1983; Monsignor Quixote, 1985. *Publication:* Just Resting (biographical memoir), 1983. *Recreations:* sailing, swimming, photography, painting, ecology, environment preservation, model making, dolls' house and furniture construction. *Address:* c/o ICM, 388/396 Oxford Street, W1N 9HE.

MACKERRAS, Sir (Alan) Charles (MacLaurin), Kt 1979; CBE 1974; Hon. RAM 1969; Musical Director, Welsh National Opera, since 1987; Principal Guest Conductor, Royal Liverpool Philharmonic Orchestra, since 1986; Guest Conductor: Vienna State Opera; Geneva and Zurich Opera; Royal Opera House Covent Garden; English National Opera; San Francisco Opera; *b* 17 Nov. 1925; *s* of late Alan Patrick and Catherine Mackerras, Sydney, Australia; *m* 1947, Helena Judith (*née* Wilkins); two *d. Educ:* Sydney Grammar Sch. Principal Oboist, Sydney Symphony Orchestra, 1943–46; Staff Conductor, Sadler's Wells Opera, 1949–53; Principal Conductor BBC Concert Orchestra, 1954–56; freelance conductor with most British and many continental orchestras; concert tours in USSR, S Africa, USA, 1957–66; Conductor, Hamburg State Opera, 1966–69; Musical Dir, Sadler's Wells Opera, later ENO, 1970–77; Chief Guest Conductor, BBC SO, 1976–79; Chief Conductor, Sydney Symphony Orch., ABC, 1982–85; frequent radio and TV broadcasts; many commercial recordings, notably Handel series for DGG and Janáček operas for Decca; appearances at many internat. festivals and opera houses. Evening Standard Award for Opera, 1977; Janáček Medal, 1978; Gramophone Record of the Year Award, 1978, 1980 and 1983; Grammy Award for best opera recording, 1981. *Publications:* ballet arrangements of Pineapple Poll and of Lady and the Fool; Arthur Sullivan's lost Cello Concerto, 1986; articles in Opera Magazine, Music and Musicians and other musical jls. *Recreations:* languages, yachting. *Address:* 10 Hamilton Terrace, NW8 9UG. *T:* 01–286 4047. *Club:* Garrick.

MACKESON, Sir Rupert (Henry), 2nd Bt *cr* 1954; *b* 16 Nov. 1941; *s* of Brig. Sir Harry Ripley Mackeson, 1st Bt, and Alethea, Lady Mackeson (*d* 1979), *d* of late Comdr R. Talbot, RN; *S* father, 1964. *Educ:* Harrow; Trinity Coll., Dublin (MA). Captain, Royal Horse Guards, 1967, retd 1968. *Recreations:* art, racing. *Heir:* none.

MACKEY, Most Rev. John, CBE 1983; Bishop of Auckland, NZ, (RC), 1974–82. *Educ:* Auckland Univ. (MA, DipEd); Notre Dame Univ., USA (PhD). Formerly Professor in Theological Faculty, National Seminary of Mosgiel, Dunedin. *Publications:* The Making of a State Education System, 1967; Reflections on Church History, 1975. *Address:* c/o Bishop's House, 36 New Street, Ponsonby, PO Box 47255, Auckland 1, New Zealand. *T:* 764–244.

MACKEY, Prof. William Arthur, TD; St Mungo Professor of Surgery, University of Glasgow, 1953–72, now Emeritus; *b* 1 Oct. 1906; *s* of Arthur Edward Mackey, Schoolmaster, and Elizabeth Annie (*née* Carr); *m* 1939, Joan Margaret Sykes; two *s* two *d. Educ:* Ardrossan Academy; Univ. of Glasgow. MB, ChB (hons). Asst to Prof. of Pathology, Univ. of Glasgow, 1928; Asst to Regius Prof. of Surgery, University of Glasgow, 1931. Hon. FACS. *Recreations:* golf, gardening, repenting plans and pottering around Bohemia. *Address:* Flat 24, Queens Court, East Clyde Street, Helensburgh, Dunbartonshire G84 7AH. *T:* Helensburgh 3659. *Clubs:* Royal Scottish Automobile (Glasgow), Glasgow Golf.

MACKEY, William Gawen; Partner, Ernst & Whinney, since 1952; *b* 22 Sept. 1924; *s* of William Gawen Mackey and Jane Mackey; *m* 1948, Margaret Reeves Vinycomb; two *s. Educ:* Dame Allan's Sch., Newcastle upon Tyne. Qualified Chartered Accountant, 1949. Served RN, 1942–45 (Sub-Lt). Joined Ernst & Whinney, 1952, Newcastle; transf. London, 1973, with responsibility for corporate restructuring and insolvency services in UK. Receiver: Airfix; British Tanners; Laker; Stone-Platt. Chm., Insolvency Services Sub Cttee, CCAB, 1978–82; Dir, Institute Corporate Insolvency Courses, 1974–80. *Publications:* articles and lectures on corporate management, restructuring and insolvency. *Recreations:* opera, France, work. *Address:* 7 Radnor Mews, W2 2SA. *T:* 01–402 0198.

MACKIE; *see* John-Mackie.

MACKIE, family name of **Barons John-Mackie** and **Mackie of Benshie.**

MACKIE OF BENSHIE, Baron *cr* 1974 (Life Peer), of Kirriemuir; **George Yull Mackie,** CBE 1971; DSO 1944; DFC 1944; Chairman: Caithness Glass Ltd, 1966–84; Caithness Pottery Co. Ltd, 1975–84; The Benshie Cattle Co. Ltd; Cotswold Wine Co. (UK) Ltd, since 1983; *b* 10 July 1919; *s* of late Maitland Mackie, OBE, Hon. LLD; *m* 1944, Lindsay Lyall Sharp (*d* 1985), *y d* of late Alexander and Isabella Sharp, OBE, Aberdeen; three *d* (one *s* decd). *Educ:* Aberdeen Grammar Sch.; Aberdeen Univ. Served War of 1939–45, RAF; Bomber Command, (DSO, DFC); Air Staff, 1944. Farming at Ballinshoe, Kirriemuir, from 1945. Contested (L) South Angus, 1959; MP (L) Caithness and Sutherland, 1964–66; contested (L) Scotland NE, European Parliamentary election, 1979. Pres., Scottish Liberal Party, 1983– (Chm., 1965–70); Member: EEC Scrutiny Cttee (D), House of Lords; Liberal Shadow Admin; Exec., Inter-Parly Union; Governing Body, GB/East Europe Centre; Council of Europe, 1986–; WEU, 1986–; Liberal Spokesman, House of Lords: Devolution, Agriculture, Scotland, Industry. Rector, Dundee Univ., 1980–83. Hon. LLD Dundee, 1982. *Publication:* Policy for Scottish Agriculture, 1963. *Address:* Ballinshoe, Kirriemuir, Angus DD8 5QG. *T:* Kirriemuir 73466. *Clubs:* Garrick, Farmers', Royal Air Force.

See also Baron John-Mackie, Sir Maitland Mackie, I. L. Aitken, A. G. Sharp, Sir R. L. Sharp.

MACKIE, Air Cdre (Retd) Alastair Cavendish Lindsay, CBE 1966; DFC 1943 and Bar 1944; Director General, Health Education Council, 1972–82; Director, Ansador Ltd, since 1983; *b* 3 Aug. 1922; *s* of George Mackie, DSO, OBE, MD, Malvern, Worcs and May (*née* Cavendish); *m* 1944, Rachel Goodson; two *s. Educ:* Charterhouse. Royal Air Force, 1940–68; Under Treas., Middle Temple, 1968; Registrar, Architects' Registration Council, 1970; Sec., British Dental Assoc., 1971; Pres., Internat. Union for Health Educn, 1979–82. Vice-Pres., CND, 1986. *Recreation:* allotmenteering. *Address:* 4 Warwick Drive, SW15 6LB. *T:* 01–789 4544. *Club:* Royal Air Force.

MACKIE, Prof. Andrew George; Professor of Applied Mathematics since 1968, Vice-Principal 1980–85, University of Edinburgh; *b* 7 March 1927; *s* of late Andrew Mackie and of Isobel Sigsworth Mackie (*née* Storey); *m* 1959, Elizabeth Maud Mackie (*née* Hebblethwaite); one *s* one *d. Educ:* Tain Royal Acad.; Univ. of Edinburgh (MA); Univ. of Cambridge (BA); Univ. of St Andrews (PhD). Lecturer, Univ. of Dundee, 1948–50; Bateman Res. Fellow and Instructor, CIT, 1953–55; Lecturer: Univ. of Strathclyde, 1955–56; Univ. of St Andrews, 1956–62; Prof. of Applied Maths, Victoria Univ. of Wellington, NZ, 1962–65; Res. Prof., Univ. of Maryland, 1966–68. Visiting Professor: CIT, 1984; Univ. of NSW, 1985. *Publications:* Boundary Value Problems, 1965; numerous contribs to mathematical and scientific jls. *Recreation:* golf. *Address:* Department of Mathematics, The King's Buildings, Mayfield Road, Edinburgh EH9 3JZ. *T:* 031–667 1081, ext. 2700.

MACKIE, Clive David Andrew, FCA, FSS; Secretary-General, Institute of Actuaries, since 1983; *b* 29 April 1929; *s* of David and Lilian Mackie; *m* 1953, Averil Ratcliff; one *s* three *d. Educ:* Tiffin Sch., Kingston-on-Thames. FCA 1956; FSS 1982. Director: cos in Grundy (Teddington) Group, 1959–67; D. Sebel & Co. Ltd, 1967–70; post in admin of higher educn, 1970–73; Dep. Sec., 1973–77 and Sec., 1977–83, Inst. of Actuaries. *Recreations:* music (post 1800), cricket, carpentry, walking. *Address:* Withermere, Burwash, East Sussex TN19 7HN. *T:* Burwash 882427. *Clubs:* Reform, Royal Commonwealth Society, MCC.

MACKIE, Eric Dermott; Chief Executive and Managing Director, Govan Shipbuilders Ltd, since 1979; *b* 4 Dec. 1924; *s* of James Girvan and Ellen Dorothy Mackie; *m* 1950, Mary Victoria Christie; one *s* one *d. Educ:* Coll. of Technology, Belfast. CEng; MIMechE, MIMarE. 1st Class MoT Cert. (Steam and Diesel). Trained with James Mackie & Son (Textile Engrs), 1939–44; Design draughtsman, Harland & Wolff, Belfast, 1944–48; 2nd Engineer (sea-going) in both steam and diesel ships for Union Castle Mail Steamship Co., 1948–53; Harland & Wolff, Belfast, 1953–75: Test Engr; Manager, Shiprepair Dept; Gen. Manager i/c of Southampton branch; Gen. Manager i/c of ship prodn and shiprepair, Belfast; Man. Dir, James Brown Hamer, S Africa, 1975–79; Chief Exec. and Man. Dir of Shiprepair in UK, British Shipbuilders, 1979–81. *Publications:* articles for marine engrg instns on various subjects pertaining to marine engrg and gen. engrg. *Recreations:* golf, swimming, reading. *Address:* Middle Barton, Whittingham, near Alnwick, Northumberland. *T:* Whittingham 648. *Clubs:* Durban, Rand (Johannesburg, SA).

MACKIE, George, DFC 1944; RSW 1968; RDI 1973; freelance graphic artist and painter; Head of Design, Gray's School of Art, Aberdeen, 1958–80 (retd); *b* 17 July 1920; *s* of late David Mackie and late Kathleen Grantham; *m* 1952, Barbara Balmer, ARSA, RSW; two *d.* Served Royal Air Force, 1940–46. Consultant in book design to Edinburgh University Press, 1960–. Paintings in various public and private collections incl. HRH the Duke of Edinburgh's and Scottish Nat. Gall. of Modern Art. *Publication:* Lynton Lamb: Illustrator, 1979. *Address:* 32 Broad Street, Stamford, Lincs. *T:* Stamford 53296; 37 Queensferry Street, Edinburgh. *T:* 031–226 5580. *Club:* Double Crown.

McKIE, Rt. Rev. John David; Assistant Bishop, Diocese of Coventry, 1960–80; Vicar of Great and Little Packington, 1966–80; *b* 14 May 1909; *s* of Rev. W. McKie, Melbourne, Vic; *m* 1952, Mary Lesley, *d* of late Brig. S. T. W. Goodwin, DSO and of Mrs Goodwin, Melbourne, Vic; four *d. Educ:* Melbourne Church of England Grammar Sch.; Trinity Coll., Melbourne Univ.; New Coll., Oxford. BA (Trinity Coll., Melbourne Univ.). 1931; MA (New Coll., Oxford), 1945; Deacon, 1932; Priest, 1934; Asst Chap. Melbourne Church of England Grammar Sch., 1932–33; Chap. and lecturer, Trinity Coll., Melbourne, 1936–39; served War of 1939–45 (despatches): AIF, 1939–44; Asst CG; Vicar Christ Church, South Yarra, 1944–46; Coadjutor, Bishop of Melbourne (with title of Bishop of Geelong) and Archdeacon of Melbourne, 1946–60, Chaplain and Sub-Prelate, Order of St John of Jerusalem, 1949. *Address:* 2 Birdwood Avenue, Mornington, Victoria 3931, Australia.

MACKIE, Lily Edna Minerva, (Mrs John Betts), OBE 1986; Head Mistress, City of London School for Girls, 1972–86; *b* 14 April 1926; *d* of late Robert Wood Mackie and late Lilian Amelia Mackie (*née* Dennis); *m* 1985, John Betts. *Educ:* Plaistow Grammar Sch.; University Coll., London (BA); Lycée de Jeunes Filles, Limoges; Université de Poitiers. Asst Mistress: Ilford County High Sch. for Girls, 1950–59; City of London Sch. for Girls, 1960–64; Head Mistress: Wimbledon County Sch., 1964–69; Ricards Lodge High Sch., Wimbledon, 1969–72. FRSA. *Recreations:* theatre, music, gardening, travel, boating. *Address:* c/o City of London School for Girls, Barbican, EC2Y 8BB. *T:* 01–628 0841.

MACKIE, Sir Maitland, Kt 1982; CBE 1965; JP; Lord-Lieutenant of Aberdeenshire, since 1975; farmer since 1932; *b* 16 Feb. 1912; *s* of late Dr Maitland Mackie, OBE and Mary (*née* Yull); *m* 1st, 1935, Isobel Ross (*d* 1960); two *s* four *d*; 2nd, 1963, Martha Pauline Turner. *Educ:* Aberdeen Grammar Sch.; Aberdeen Univ. (BSCAgric). FEIS 1972; FRAgSS 1974; FInstM. County Councillor, Aberdeenshire, 1951–75 (Convener 1967–75); Chm., NE Develt Authority, 1969–75; Chairman: Jt Adv. Cttee, Scottish Farm Bldgs Investigation Unit, 1963–; Aberdeen Milk Marketing Bd, 1965–82; Peterhead Bay Management Co., 1975–86; Hanover (Scotland) Housing Assoc., 1981–86. Member: Agric. Sub-Cttee, UGC, 1965–75; Bd, Scottish Council for Development and Industry, 1975– (Chm., Oil Policy Cttee, 1975–); Clayson Cttee on Drink Laws in Scotland. Chm., Aberdeen Cable Services, 1983–; Director: Scottish Telecommunications, 1969; Highland Hydrocarbons Ltd, 1978–. Governor: N of Scotland Coll. of Agriculture, 1968–82 (Vice-Chm., 1974–78); Rowett Inst., 1973–82. Burgess of Guild, Aberdeen, 1978. JP 1956. KStJ 1977. Hon. LLD Aberdeen, 1977. *Recreation:* travel. *Address:* Cramond House, 17 Rubislaw Den North, Aberdeen AB2 4AL. *T:* Aberdeen 313587. *Clubs:* Farmers'; Royal Northern (Aberdeen).

See also Barons John-Mackie and Mackie of Benshie.

McKIERNAN, Most Rev. Francis J.; *see* Kilmore, Bishop of, (RC).

MACKILLIGIN, David Patrick Robert; HM Diplomatic Service; Counsellor (Economic, Commercial and Agriculture), Canberra, since 1986; *b* 29 June 1939; *s* of R. S. Mackilligin, CMG, OBE, MC and Patricia (*née* Waldegrave); *m* 1976, Gillian Margar Zuill Walker; two *d. Educ:* St Mary's Coll., Winchester; Pembroke Coll., Oxford (2nd Cl. Hons PPE). Asst Principal, CRO, 1961–62; Third, later Second Sec., Pakistan, 1962–66; Asst Private Sec. to Sec. of State for Commonwealth Relations, 1966–68; Private Sec. to Minister Without Portfolio, 1968–69; Dep. Comr, Anguilla, 1969–71 (Actg Comr, July–Aug. 1970); First Sec., Ghana, 1971–73; First Sec., Head of Chancery and Consul, Cambodia, 1973–75 (Chargé d'Affaires at various times); FCO, 1975–80 (Asst Head of W African Dept, 1978–80); Counsellor (Economic, Commercial and Aid), Indonesia, 1980–85; NATO Defence Coll., Rome, 1985–86. *Recreations:* walking and swimming in remote places, ruins, second-hand bookshops, theatre, literature. *Address:* c/o Foreign and Commonwealth Office, King Charles Street, SW1. *Clubs:* United Oxford & Cambridge University, Royal Commonwealth Society.

McKILLOP, Edgar Ravenswood, CMG 1952; OBE 1942; Company Director; Commissioner of Works and Permanent Head, Ministry of Works, NZ, 1944–55, retired; *b* 26 July 1895; *s* of Alexander McKillop and Jean Cameron; *m* 1930, Marguerita Anne Mary Dennis. *Educ:* Canterbury Univ. Coll., New Zealand. Civil engineer, New Zealand Government engaged on developmental works; railway construction, irrigation and hydro-electric projects. Served 1914–18 with 1st NZEF overseas (twice wounded). Lt-Col NZ Eng. 2nd NZ Exp. Force, in Pacific, 1939–42; Dep. Comr Def. Constr., 1942–44, in NZ and South Pacific. Past mem. Scientific and Industrial Research Council; FICE and past mem. of Council; FNZ Inst. of Engineers and past mem. of Council. *Recreation:* golf. *Address:* PO Box 2071, Raumati Beach, Paraparaumu, New Zealand.

MacKINLAY, Sir Bruce, Kt 1978; CBE 1970; company director; *b* 4 Oct. 1912; *s* of Daniel Robertson MacKinlay and Alice Victoria Rice; *m* 1943, Erica Ruth Fleming; two *s. Educ:* Scotch Coll. Served War, AASC, 1940–45 (Lieut). Director: J. Gadsden Australia

Ltd, 1954–77; Whittakers Ltd, 1975–; Chm. Local Bd, Chamber of Manufactures Insurance Ltd, 1977–. President: WA Chamber of Manufactures, 1958–61; Confedn of WA Industry, 1976–78; WA Employers' Fedn, 1974–75; Fremantle Rotary Club, 1956; Vice-Pres., Associated Chambers of Manufactures of Aust., 1960. Chairman: WA Inst. of Dirs, 1975–77; WA Div., National Packaging Assoc., 1967–69; WA Finance Cttee for the Duke of Edinburgh's Third Commonwealth Study Conf., 1967–68; Mem., Commonwealth Manufg Industries Adv. Council, 1962–70. Leader: Aust. Trade Mission, E Africa, 1968; WA Trade Mission, Italy, 1970; Employers' Rep., Internat. Labour Conf., 1977; Comr, State Electricity Commn, 1961–74. Univ. of Western Australia: Mem. Senate, 1970–; Chm., Master of Business Admin Appeal, 1973. Life Governor, Scotch Coll. Council (Chm., 1969–74); Chm. Nat. Council, Keep Australia Beautiful, 1984– (Mem. 1967–, Chm. 1981–, WA Council); Councillor: Organising Council of Commonwealth and Empire Games, 1962; Aust. Council on Population and Ethnic Affairs, 1981–. Pres., Most Excellent Order of the British Empire, WA Div., 1983–. *Recreations:* swimming, gardening. *Address:* 9B Melville Street, Claremont, WA 6010, Australia. *T:* 3832220. *Clubs:* Weld, WACA, Claremont Football (WA).

McKINLEY, Air Vice-Marshal David Cecil, CB 1966; CBE 1957; DFC 1940; AFC 1944, Bar 1945; RAF; *b* 18 Sept. 1913; *s* of David McKinley, Civil Engineer, and May McKinley (*née* Ward); *m* 1940, Brenda Alice (*née* Ridgway); three *s*. *Educ:* Bishop Foy Sch., Waterford; Trinity Coll., Dublin. Radio Engineering, Ferranti Ltd, 1935. Entered (regular) Royal Air Force, 1935; served continuously since that date; AOC Malta and Dep. C-in-C (Air), Allied Forces, Mediterranean, 1963–65; SASO, Transport Command, 1966, Air Support Command, 1967–68; retired 1968. Freeman, The Guild of Air Pilots and Air Navigators, 1959. FIN 1949. *Recreations:* sailing, fishing, water ski-ing, gardening. *Address:* Sundial Cottage, Fawley, Hants. *T:* Fawley 891031; Midland Bank, Bushey, Herts. *Club:* Royal Air Force.

McKINLEY, John Key; Chairman and Chief Executive Officer, Texaco Inc., since 1980 (President, 1980–83); *b* Tuscaloosa, Ala, 24 March 1920; *s* of Virgil Parks McKinley and Mary Emma (*née* Key); *m* 1946, Helen Grace Heare; two *s* *Educ:* Univ. of Alabama (BS Chem. Engrg, 1940; MS Organic Chemistry, 1941); Harvard Univ. (Graduate, Advanced Management Program, 1962). Served War, AUS, Eur. Theatre of Ops, 1941–45 (Major; Bronze Star). Texaco Inc., 1941–: Asst Dir of Res., Beacon, NY, 1957–59; Asst to the Vice-Pres., 1959–60; Manager of Commercial Develt Processes, 1960; Gen. Man., Worldwide Petrochemicals, NYC, 1960–67, Vice-Pres., Petrochem. Dept, 1967–71 (also Vice-Pres. i/c Supply and Distribution); Sen. Vice-Pres., Worldwide Refining, Petrochems, Supply and Distbn, 1971, Pres. and Dir, 1971–80; Chief Operating Officer and Chm. Exec. Cttee, 1980–. Director: Burlington Industries, Inc.; Merck & Co., Inc.; Manufacturers Hanover Corp.; Hanover Trust Co. Member: Bd of Dirs and Exec. Cttee, Amer. Petroleum Inst.; National Pet. Council. Man. Dir, Met. Opera Assoc., 1980–; National Chm., Met. Opera Centennial Fund, 1980–. Member: Bd of Overseers and Bd of Managers, Meml Sloan-Kettering Cancer Center, 1981–; Bd of Managers, Meml Hosp. for Cancer and Allied Diseases and Sloan-Kettering Inst. for Cancer Res., 1981–. Trustee: Council of the Americas, 1980–; US Council, Internat. Chamber of Commerce, 1981–. Fellow, Amer. Inst. of Chem. Engrs; Sesquicentennial Hon. Prof., Univ. of Alabama; Hon. LLD: Univ. of Alabama, 1972; Troy State Univ., 1974. *Address:* (office) 2000 Westchester Avenue, White Plains, NY 10650, USA; (home) 5 Searles Road, Darien, Conn 06820. *Clubs:* Links, Brook, New York Yacht (NYC); Wee Burn Country (Darien); Augusta (Ga); National Golf, Blind Brook Country (Port Chester, NY); Clove Valley Rod and Gun (LaGrangeville, NY).

McKINNEY, Mrs J. P.; *see* Wright, Judith.

McKINNEY, (Sheila Mary) Deirdre; Her Honour Judge McKinney; a Circuit Judge, since 1981; *b* 20 Oct. 1928; *d* of Patrick Peter McKinney and Mary Edith (*née* Conoley). *Educ:* Convent of the Cross, Boscombe, Bournemouth. Called to the Bar, Lincoln's Inn, 1951; a Recorder of the Crown Court, 1978–81. *Address:* 39 Granville Road, Boscombe, Bournemouth, Dorset. *T:* Bournemouth 423452.

MACKINNON, Angus, DSO 1945; MC 1940; TD; Director, Brown Shipley Holdings Ltd, since 1960; *b* 20 Feb. 1911; *s* of late William and Lucy Vere Mackinnon; *m* 1947, Beatrice Marsinah Neison; two *s*. *Educ:* Eton; Pembroke Coll., Oxford. With Gray Dawes & Co., 1932; Mackinnon Mackenzie & Co, Calcutta, 1933–38. Joined Argyll and Sutherland Highlanders (TA), 1939; served BEF, MEF and BLA (despatches); comd 7th Bn A&SH, 1944–45, 51st Highland Div. Joined Brown Shipley & Co. Ltd, 1946, Chm., 1953–63, retired 1976; Chairman: Agricultural Credit Corp., 1959–75; Accepting Houses Cttee, 1967–70; Australia and New Zealand Banking Gp, 1975–77; Director: Australian Pastoral Co., 1955–71; P&O Steam Navigation Co., 1962–72; Guardian Royal Exchange Assurance, 1968–81; Inchcape & Co. Ltd. Chairman: Royal Nat. Orthopaedic Hosp., 1969–78; Governors, Keil Sch., Dumbarton, 1950–. An Underwriting Member of Lloyd's. *Recreations:* shooting, fishing, golf. *Address:* Hunton Down, Sutton Scotney, Winchester, Hants SO21 3PT. *T:* Sutton Scotney 202. *Clubs:* White's, City.

MacKINNON, Prof. Donald MacKenzie, MA; FRSE 1984; FBA 1978; Norris-Hulse Professor of Divinity, Cambridge University, 1960–78; Fellow of Corpus Christi College, Cambridge, since 1960; *b* Oban, 27 Aug. 1913; *o s* of late D. M. MacKinnon, Procurator Fiscal, and late Grace Isabella Rhind; *m* 1939, Lois, *e d* of late Rev. Oliver Dryer; no *c*. *Educ:* Cargilfield Sch., Edinburgh; Winchester Coll. (scholar); New Coll., Oxford (scholar). Asst in Moral Philosophy (to late Prof. A. E. Taylor) at Edinburgh, 1936–37; Fellow and Tutor in Philosophy at Keble Coll., Oxford, 1937–47; Dir of Course for special courses in Philosophy for RN and RAF cadets at Oxford, 1942–45; Lectr in Philosophy at Balliol Coll., 1945–47; Wilde Lectr in Natural and Comparative Religion at Oxford, 1945–47; Regius Prof. of Moral Philosophy at Aberdeen, 1947–60. Lectures: Scott Holland, 1952; Hobhouse, 1953; Stanton, in the Philosophy of Religion, Cambridge, 1956–59; Gifford, Edinburgh, 1965–66; Prideaux, Exeter, 1966; Coffin, London, 1968; Riddell, Newcastle-upon-Tyne, 1970; D. Owen Evans, Aberystwyth, 1973; Drummond, Stirling, 1977; Martin Wight Meml, LSE, 1979; Boutwood, CCC Cambridge, 1981. President: Aristotelian Soc., 1976–77; Soc. for Study of Theol., 1981–82; Mem., Scottish Episcopal Church. Supporter, CND. Hon. DD Aberdeen, 1961. *Publications:* (ed) Christian Faith and Communist Faith, 1953; The Notion of a Philosophy of History, 1954; A Study in Ethical Theory, 1957; (with Prof. G. W. H. Lampe) The Resurrection, 1966; Borderlands of Theology and other papers, 1968; The Stripping of the Altars, 1969; The Problem of Metaphysics, 1974; Explorations in Theology 5, 1979; Creon and Antigone, 1981; articles, reviews, etc in periodicals and symposia in UK, France, Italy and Germany. *Recreations:* walking, cats, the cinema. *Address:* Dunbar Cottage, 10 Dunbar Street, Old Aberdeen AB2 1UE.

McKINNON, James, CA, FCMA; Director General, Office of Gas Supply, since 1986. *Educ:* Camphill School. CA 1952, FCMA 1956. Company Secretary, Macfarlane Lang & Co. Ltd, Glasgow, 1955–65; Business Consultant, McLintock, Moores & Murray, Glasgow, 1965–67; Finance Director, Imperial Group plc, London, 1967–86. Pres., Inst. of Chartered Accountants of Scotland, 1985–86. *Publications:* papers to learned jls and articles in Accountants' magazine. *Recreation:* ski-ing. *Address:* Office of Gas Supply, Southside, 105 Victoria Street, SW1E 6QT.

McKINNON, Prof. Kenneth Richard, FACE; Vice-Chancellor, University of Wollongong, Australia, since 1981; Chairman, Australian National Commission for UNESCO, since 1984; *b* 23 Feb. 1931; *s* of Charles and Grace McKinnon; *m* 1st, 1956 (marr. diss.); one *s*; 2nd, 1981, Suzanne H., *d* of W. Milligan. *Educ:* Univ. of Adelaide (BA); Univ. of Queensland (BEd); Harvard Univ. (EdD). FACE 1972. Teacher, headmaster and administrator, 1957–65; Dir of Educn, Papua New Guinea, 1966–73; Chairman: Australian Schs Commn, 1973–81; Bd of Educn, Vic, 1982–85. Mem., Australia Council, 1974–77 (Dep. Chm., 1976–77). Consultant in the Arts, Aust. Govt, 1981. *Publications:* Realistic Educational Planning, 1973; articles in jls and papers. *Recreations:* swimming, theatre, music, reading. *Address:* 2 Parrish Avenue, Mt Pleasant, Wollongong, NSW 2519, Australia. *T:* (042) 842–926. *Club:* Commonwealth (Canberra, Australia).

McKINNON, His Honour Neil Nairn, QC 1957; an Additional Judge, Central Criminal Court, 1968–82; *b* 19 Aug. 1909; *s* of late Neil Somerville and Christina McKinnon, Melbourne; *m* 1937, Janet, *d* of late Michael Lilley, Osterley; three *s* four *d*. *Educ:* Geelong Coll.; Trinity Hall, Cambridge (MA). Squadron Leader, RAFVR, Feb. 1940–Dec. 1945. Called to the Bar, Lincoln's Inn, 1937; Bencher, 1964. Recorder of Maidstone, 1961–68. *Recreation:* cricket. *Club:* Hawks (Cambridge).
See also S. N. McKinnon.

MACKINNON, Dame Patricia; *see* Mackinnon, Dame U. P.

MacKINNON, Peter Ralph, DSC 1942; Underwriting Member of Lloyd's, retired 1974; *b* 6 May 1911; *s* of Norman MacKinnon; *m* 1934, Jean Mary, *d* of G. N. Ogilvie; one *s* two *d*. *Educ:* Wellington Coll.; Jesus Coll., Cambridge. Entered Lloyd's, 1931; Underwriting Mem., 1932; Dep. Chm., 1964; Member: Cttee, Lloyd's Underwriters Assoc., 1958–73; Cttee of Lloyd's, 1961–64; Cttee Lloyd's Register of Shipping, 1958. Served War of 1939–45: RNVR, 1940; Combined Ops, Europe, N Africa, India, Malaya, Pacific (DSC, despatches twice); retd as Comdr RNVR, 1945. *Recreations:* golf, tennis. *Clubs:* City University; All England Lawn Tennis; Denham Golf.

McKINNON, Stuart Neil; QC 1980; a Recorder, since 1985; *b* 14 Aug. 1938; *s* of His Honour Neil Nairn McKinnon, *qv*; *m* 1966, Helena Jacoba Sara (*née* van Hoorn); two *d*. *Educ:* King's Coll. Sch., Wimbledon; Council of Legal Educn; Trinity Hall, Cambridge (LLB 1963, MA). Called to the Bar, Lincoln's Inn, 1960. *Recreations:* cricket, golf. *Address:* 1 The Ridgeway, Sanderstead, Surrey CR2 0LG. *T:* 01–657 4379. *Clubs:* Purley Cricket (Purley, Surrey); Croham Hurst Golf (South Croydon).

MACKINNON, Dame (Una) Patricia, DBE 1977 (CBE 1972); *b* Brisbane, 24 July 1911; *d* of Ernest T. and Pauline Bell; *m* 1936, Alistair Scobie Mackinnon; one *s* one *d*. *Educ:* Glennie School and St Margaret's School, Queensland. Member Cttee of Management, Royal Children's Hospital, Melbourne, 1948–79; Vice-President, 1958; President, 1965–79; Chm., Research Bd, 1967–85. *Recreations:* gardening, reading history and biographies. *Address:* 5 Ross Street, Toorak, Vic 3142, Australia. *Club:* Alexandra (Melbourne).

McKINNON, Maj.-Gen. Walter Sneddon, CB 1966; CBE 1961 (OBE 1947); *b* 8 July 1910; *s* of Charles McKinnon and Janet Robertson McKinnon (*née* Sneddon); *m* 1937, Anna Bloomfield Plimmer; four *s* one *d*. *Educ:* Otago Boys High Sch., Dunedin, NZ; Otago Univ. (BSc); commissioned in NZ Army, 1935; various military courses, including Staff Coll., Camberley, England. Served War of 1939–45: Pacific, Italy (Lt-Col; despatches), Japan (occupation) (OBE); Brigadier, 1953; subsequent appointments: Comdr, Southern Mil. Dist (NZ), 1953; Head, NZ Joint Mil. Mission, Washington, DC, 1954–57; Comdr, Northern Military District, 1957–58; Adjutant-General, 1958–62; Quartermaster-General, 1963–65, Maj.-General, 1965; Chief of the General Staff, NZ Army, 1965–67; retired, 1967. Chm., NZ Broadcasting Corp., 1969–74. Member: Taupo Borough Council, 1977–80; Tongariro United Council, 1979–80. Pres., Taupo Regional Museum and Art Centre, 1975–79; Mem., Social Develt Council, New Zealand, 1976–79. *Recreations:* golf, fishing and gardening. *Address:* 43 Birch Street, Taupo, New Zealand. *Clubs:* Wellesley (Wellington); Taupo Golf.

MACKINTOSH, family name of **Viscount Mackintosh of Halifax.**

MACKINTOSH OF HALIFAX, 3rd Viscount *cr* 1957; **John Clive Mackintosh;** Bt 1935; Baron 1948; *b* 9 Sept. 1958; *s* of 2nd Viscount Mackintosh of Halifax, OBE, BEM; *S* father, 1980; *m* 1982, Elizabeth, *o d* of late David G. Lakin; one *s*. *Educ:* The Leys School, Cambridge; Oriel College, Oxford (BA in PPE). President, Oxford Univ. Conservative Assoc., 1979. Chartered accountant. *Recreations:* cricket, bridge, golf. *Heir:* *s* Hon. Thomas Harold George Mackintosh, *b* 8 Feb. 1985. *Address:* House of Lords, SW1. *Clubs:* MCC, Carlton, Coningsby.

MacKINTOSH, Sir Angus (MacKay), KCVO 1972; CMG 1958; HM Diplomatic Service, retired; British High Commissioner in Sri Lanka and Ambassador to the Republic of Maldives, 1969–73; *b* 23 July 1915; *s* of Angus MacKintosh, JP, Inverness; *m* 1947, Robina Marigold, *d* of J. A. Cochrane, MC; one *s* two *d* (and one *d* decd). *Educ:* Fettes Coll., Edinburgh; University College, Oxford (MA, BLitt). Agricultural Economics Research Institute, Oxford, 1938–41; Nuffield Colonial Research, Oxford, 1941–42. Served Army, 1942–46: Adjutant, 2nd Bn Queen's Own Cameron Highlanders; Major; despatches. Entered Colonial Office as Principal, 1946; Principal Private Secretary to Secretary of State, 1950; Assistant Secretary, 1952; seconded to Foreign Service as Dep. Commissioner-General for the UK in SE Asia, 1956–60; seconded to Cabinet Office, 1961–63; HM High Comr for Brunei, 1963–64; Asst Sec., Min. of Defence, 1964–65; Asst Under-Sec. of State, 1965–66; Senior Civilian Instructor, Imperial Defence Coll., 1966–68; Asst Under-Sec. of State, FCO, 1968–69. DK (Brunei), 1963; NSAIV (Maldives), 1972. *Address:* 9 Leven Terrace, Edinburgh EH3 9LW. *T:* 031–229 1091; Fenecreich, Gorthleck, Inverness IV1 2YS. *T:* Gorthleck 652. *Club:* Royal Commonwealth Society.

MACKINTOSH, David Forbes; Headmaster of Loretto, 1945–60; retired; *b* 7 May 1900; *s* of late Very Rev. Professor H. R. Mackintosh, DD; *m* 1930, Caroline Elisabeth, *o d* of Cyril Meade-King, Clifton, Bristol; three *s* one *d*. *Educ:* Merchiston; Oriel Coll., Oxford (MA); Princeton Univ., NJ (AM). Assistant Master at Clifton Coll., 1924–45; Housemaster, 1930–45. Conroy Fellow, St Paul's Sch., USA, 1960. Chm., Scottish Assoc. of Boys' Clubs, 1962–69. *Recreation:* gardening. *Address:* Bowling Green Cottage, Broadwell, by Lechlade, Glos GL7 3QS. *T:* Filkins 336.

MACKINTOSH, Duncan Robert, CBE 1969 (OBE 1948); *b* 4 Oct. 1902; *s* of Duncan H. Mackintosh; *m* 1937, Mary Isa Grant; one *s* three *d*. *Educ:* RN Colleges Osborne and Dartmouth; University Coll., London. Served with Royal Dutch Shell Group of Oil Cos, in China, Middle East and London, 1923–58. Mem. British Council. Chm. Exec. Cttee, Voluntary Service Overseas, (VSO), 1962–70. *Publications:* (with Alan Ayling): A

Collection of Chinese Lyrics, 1965; A Further Collection of Chinese Lyrics, 1969; A Folding Screen, 1974. *Recreations:* bird-watching, gardening. *Address:* Apple Tree Cottage, Oaksey, Malmesbury, Wilts SN16 9TG. *T:* Crudwell 431. *Club:* Athenæum.

MACKINTOSH, (Hugh) Stewart, CBE 1956; Chairman, Scottish Sports Council, 1966–68; Chief Education Officer, Glasgow, 1944–68; *b* 1903; *s* of William Mackintosh, Helmsdale, Sutherland; *m* 1933, Mary, *d* of James Wilson. *Educ:* Helmsdale, Sutherland; Glasgow Univ. (MA, BSc, MEd); Aberdeen Univ. (PhD). Director of Education: Wigtownshire, 1931–37; Aberdeen, 1937–44; Glasgow, 1944. FEIS 1958; Hon. LLD Glasgow, 1969. *Address:* 16 Rowan Crescent, Killearn, Glasgow G63 9RZ; Bayview, Helmsdale, Sutherland.

McKINTOSH, Ian; Partner, Lemon & Co., Swindon, since 1969; a Recorder of the Crown Court, since 1981; *b* 23 April 1938; *s* of Stanley and Gertrude McKintosh; *m* 1967, Alison Rosemary, *e d* of Kenneth Blayney Large and Margaret Wharton Large; two *s* one *d*. *Educ:* Leeds Grammar Sch.; Exeter Coll., Oxford (MA). Admitted Solicitor of the Supreme Court, 1966. Served RAF, 1957–59. Articled to Town Clerk, Chester and to Laces & Co., Liverpool, 1962–66; Dept of Solicitor to Metropolitan Police, New Scotland Yard, 1966–69. *Recreations:* cricket, sailing. *Address:* 33 Long Street, Devizes, Wilts. *Clubs:* MCC, XL.

MACKINTOSH, (John) Malcolm, CMG 1975; Assistant Secretary, Cabinet Office, since 1968; *b* 25 Dec. 1921; *s* of late James M. Mackintosh, MD, and Marjorie Mackintosh; *m* 1946, Elena Grafova; one *s* one *d* (and one *s* decd). *Educ:* Mill Hill; Edinburgh Academy; Glasgow Univ. MA (Hons) 1948. Served War, Middle East, Italy and Balkans, 1942–46; Allied Control Commn, Bulgaria, 1945–46. Glasgow Univ., 1946–48. Programme Organiser, BBC Overseas Service, 1948–60. Foreign Office, engaged on research, 1960–68. *Publications:* Strategy and Tactics of Soviet Foreign Policy, 1962, 2nd edn 1963; Juggernaut: a history of the Soviet armed forces, 1967. *Recreations:* walking, climbing. *Address:* 21 Ravensdale Avenue, N12 9HP. *T:* 01–445 9714. *Club:* Garrick.

MACKINTOSH OF MACKINTOSH, Lt-Comdr Lachlan Ronald Duncan, OBE 1972; JP; 30th Chief of Clan Mackintosh; Lord-Lieutenant of Inverness-shire, since 1985 (Vice-Lieutenant, 1971–85); Chairman, Highland Exhibitions Ltd, 1964–84; *b* 27 June 1928; *o s* of Vice-Adm. Lachlan Donald Mackintosh of Mackintosh, CB, DSO, DSC (*d* 1957); *m* 1962, Mabel Cecilia Helen (Celia), *yr d* of Captain Hon. John Bernard Bruce, RN; one *s* two *d* (and one *d* decd). *Educ:* Elstree; RNC Dartmouth. Flag Lieut to First Sea Lord, 1951; spec. communications, 1954; served in HM Yacht Britannia, 1957; retd 1963. Vice-Pres., Scottish Conservative and Unionist Assoc., 1969–71. DL 1965, CC 1970–75, Inverness-shire; Regional Cllr, Highland Region, 1974–; JP Inverness, 1982. *Heir: s* John Lachlan Mackintosh, younger of Mackintosh, *b* 2 Oct. 1969. *Address:* Moy Hall, Tomatin, Inverness-shire IV13 7YQ. *T:* Tomatin 211. *Club:* Naval and Military.

MACKINTOSH, Malcolm; *see* Mackintosh, J. M.

MACKINTOSH, Prof. Nicholas John, DPhil; Professor of Experimental Psychology, and Professorial Fellow of King's College, University of Cambridge, since 1981; *b* 9 July 1935; *s* of Dr Ian and Daphne Mackintosh; *m* 1st, 1960, Janet Ann Scott; one *s* one *d*; 2nd, 1978, Bundy Wilson; two *s*. *Educ:* Winchester; Magdalen Coll., Oxford. BA 1960, MA, DPhil 1963. Univ. Lectr, Univ. of Oxford, 1964–67; Res. Fellow, Lincoln Coll., Oxford, 1966–67; Res. Prof., Dalhousie Univ., 1967–73; Prof., Univ. of Sussex, 1973–81. Visiting Professor: Univ. of Pennsylvania, 1965–66; Univ. of Hawaii, 1972–73; Bryn Mawr Coll., 1977. Editor, Qly Jl of Experimental Psychology, 1977–84. *Publications:* (ed with W. K. Honig) Fundamental Issues in Associative Learning, 1969; (with N. S. Sutherland) Mechanisms of Animal Discrimination Learning, 1971; The Psychology of Animal Learning, 1974; Conditioning and Associative Learning, 1983; papers in psychological journals. *Address:* King's College, Cambridge CB2 1ST. *T:* Cambridge 351386.

MACKINTOSH, Stewart; *see* Mackintosh, H. S.

McKISSOCK, Sir Wylie, Kt 1971; OBE 1946; MS (London), FRCS; Consulting Neurological Surgeon in London, 1936–71, now retired; Neurological Surgeon, National Hospital for Nervous Diseases, Queen Square and Metropolitan Ear, Nose and Throat Hospital; Neurological Surgeon, Hospital for Sick Children, Great Ormond Street; Neurological Surgeon, St Andrew's Hospital, Northampton; Visiting Neurological Surgeon, Graylingwell Hospital, Chichester, St James's Hospital, Portsmouth, Belmont Hospital, Sutton, and Park Prewett Hospital, Basingstoke; Associate Neurological Surgeon, Royal Marsden Hospital; Director of Institute of Neurology, Queen Square; Surgeon in Charge, Department of Neuro-Surgery, Atkinson Morley Hospital branch of St George's Hospital; Hon. Civil Consultant in Neuro-Surgery to RAF; Hon. Neurological Surgeon, Welsh Regional Hospital Board; Teacher of Surgery, St George's Hospital Medical School (University of London); Member, Panel of Consultants, Royal Navy, British European Airways, British Overseas Airways Corporation; *b* 27 Oct. 1906; *s* of late Alexander Cathie McKissock; *m* 1934, Rachel, *d* of Leonard Marcus Jones, Beckenham, Kent; one *s* two *d*. *Educ:* King's Coll. and St George's Hospital, University of London. Junior University Schol., St George's Hospital, 1928; Laking Memorial Prize, 1932–33 and 1933–34; Rockefeller Schol. in Neuro-Surgery, 1937–38; Casualty Officer, House Surgeon, House Physician, House Surgeon to Ear, Nose, Throat and Eye Depts, Assistant Curator of Museum, Surgical Registrar, Surgical Chief Asst, St George's Hosp.; Surgical Registrar, Maida Vale Hosp. for Nervous Diseases, Hosp. for Sick Children, Great Ormond St, and Victoria Hospital for Children, Tite St. FRSM; Fellow, Society of British Neurological Surgeons (President, 1966); FRCR (Hon.) 1962; Corresponding Member, American Association of Neurological Surgeons, 1968. Hon. DSc, Newcastle upon Tyne, 1966. *Publications:* contributions to medical journals. *Recreations:* wine, food, gardening, ornithology, antagonism to Bureaucracy and the enjoyment of retirement. *Address:* Camus na Harry, Lechnaside, Gairloch, West Ross. *T:* Badachro 224.

MACKLEN, Victor Harry Burton, CB 1975; *b* 13 July 1919; *s* of H. Macklen and A. C. Macklen, Brighton, Sussex; *m* 1950, Ursula Irene Fellows; one *d*. *Educ:* Varndean Sch., Brighton; King's Coll., London. Air Defence Experimental Establishment, 1941; Operational Research Group, 1942; served Army, 1943–49; WO Scientific Staff, 1949–51; Head, Operational Research Section, BAOR, 1951–54; MoD Scientific Staff, 1954–60; Head, Technical Secretariat Reactor Group, UKAEA, 1960–64; Dep. Director, Technical Operations Reactor Group, UKAEA, 1966–67; Asst Chief Scientific Adviser (Studies and Nuclear), MoD, 1967–69; Dep. Chief Scientific Adviser (Projects and Nuclear), MoD, 1969–79. FRSA 1975. *Address:* Stepp House, Hartlip, near Sittingbourne, Kent. *T:* Newington 842591. *Club:* Army and Navy.

MACKLEY, Ian Warren; HM Diplomatic Service; Counsellor, Deputy Head of UK Delegation to Conference on Confidence- and Security-Building Measures and Disarmament in Europe, Stockholm, 1984–86; *b* 31 March 1942; *s* of late Harold William Mackley and of Marjorie Rosa Sprawson (*née* Warren); *m* 1968, Jill Marion (*née* Saunders); three *s*. *Educ:* Ardingly College. FO, 1960; Saigon, 1963; Asst Private Sec. to Ministers of State, FCO, 1967; Wellington, 1969; First Sec., 1972; FCO 1973; Head of Inf. Services, New Delhi, 1976; Asst Head, UN Dept, FCO, 1979; seconded to ICI, 1982. *Recreations:* golf, armchair sport. *Address:* c/o Foreign and Commonwealth Office, SW1A 2AH.

MACKLIN, Sir Bruce (Roy), Kt 1981; OBE 1970; FCA; company director; Chairman: South Australian Gas Company, since 1969; Onkaparinga Textiles Ltd, since 1982; Advertiser Newspapers Ltd, since 1983; *b* 23 April 1917; *s* of Hubert Vivian Macklin and Lillian Mabel Macklin; *m* 1944, Dorothy Potts, Tynemouth, England; two *s* one *d*. *Educ:* St Peter's Coll., Adelaide; St Mark's Coll., Univ. of Adelaide (AUA Commerce). Served RAAF (Aircrew), 1941–45. Practising chartered accountant, 1947–69. Director of seven major Aust. companies; Pres., Aust. Chamber of Commerce, 1967–69. Hon. Consul in S Aust. for Fed. Republic of Germany, 1968–; Leader, Aust. Govt Mission to Papua New Guinea, 1971. Mem. Council of Governors, St Peter's Coll., 1962–69; Mem. Council, Univ. of Adelaide, 1965–71. A Founder, Adelaide Festival of Arts, 1958, Chm. Bd of Governors, 1972–78; Dir, Queen Elizabeth II Silver Jubilee Trust for Young Australians. Silver Jubilee Medal 1977; Commander's Cross, Order of Merit of Fed. Republic of Germany, 1986. *Recreations:* tennis, gardening, music. *Address:* 45 Grenfell Street, Adelaide, SA 5000, Australia. *T:* 212–1533. *Clubs:* Adelaide, Naval, Military and Air Force (South Australia).

MACKLIN, David Drury; Chief Executive, Devon County Council, since 1979; *b* 1 Sept. 1928; *s* of Laurence Hilary Macklin and Alice Dumergue (*née* Tait); *m* 1955, Janet Smallwood; four *s*. *Educ:* Felsted Sch., Essex; St John's Coll., Cambridge. MA. Articled to Baileys Shaw & Gillett, Solicitors, 1951–54; Assistant Solicitor: Coward Chance & Co., 1954–56; Warwickshire CC, 1956–61; Devon CC, 1961–69; Dep. Clerk, Derbyshire CC, 1969–73; Chief Exec., Lincolnshire CC, 1973–79. *Recreations:* rowing, sailing, music, golf, theatre, walking. *Address:* County Hall, Exeter, Devon EX2 4QD. *T:* Exeter 273201.

MACKNIGHT, Dame Ella (Annie Noble), DBE 1969; Consultant Emeritus (Obstetrician and Gynaecologist), Queen Victoria Hospital, Melbourne, since 1964; *b* 7 Aug. 1904; 4th *d* of Dr Conway Macknight. *Educ:* Toorak Coll., Melbourne; Univ. of Melbourne, resident student, Janet Clarke Hall. MB, BS 1928; MD Melbourne 1931; DGO Melbourne 1936; MRCOG 1951; FRCOG 1958; FRACS 1971; FAGO 1973; FRACOG (FAustCOG 1978); Fellow AMA, 1976. Hon. Obstetrician and Gynaecologist, Queen Victoria Hosp., Melbourne, 1935–64; Pres., Queen Victoria Hosp., Melbourne, 1971–77 (Vice-Pres., 1965–71); Hon. Sec., 1963–67, Vice-Pres., 1967–70, Pres., 1970–72, Australian Council, RCOG. Hon. MD Monash, 1972. *Recreation:* golf. *Address:* 692 Toorak Road, Malvern, Victoria 3144, Australia. *Clubs:* Lyceum (Melbourne); Royal Melbourne Golf.

MACKSEY, Kenneth John, MC 1944; freelance author, since 1968, and publisher, since 1982; *b* 1 July 1923; *s* of Henry George Macksey and Alice Lilian (*née* Nightingall); *m* 1946, Catherine Angela Joan Little; one *s* one *d*. *Educ:* Goudhurst Sch.; Sandhurst; Army Staff Coll., Camberley. Served War, RAC: trooper, 1941–44; commnd 141st Regt RAC (The Buffs), 1944; Western Europe, 1944–45; Royal Tank Regt, 1946; served: India, 1947; Korea, 1950; Germany, 1957 and 1960–62; Singapore, 1958–60; retd, 1968. Dep. Editor, Purnell's History of the Second World War, and History of the First World War, 1968–70. Consultant to Canadian Armed Forces, 1981–. Town Councillor, 1972–83. *Publications:* To the Green Fields Beyond, 1965 (2nd edn 1977); The Shadow of Vimy Ridge, 1965; Armoured Crusader: the biography of Major-General Sir Percy Hobart, 1967; Afrika Korps, 1968 (4th edn 1976); Panzer Division, 1968 (4th edn 1976); Crucible of Power, 1969; Tank, 1970 (3rd edn 1975); Tank Force, 1970; Beda Fomm, 1971; Tank Warfare, 1971; Vimy Ridge, 1972; Guinness Book of Tank Facts and Feats, 1972 (3rd edn 1980); The Guinness History of Land Warfare, 1973 (2nd edn 1976); Battle, 1974; The Partisans of Europe, 1975; (jtly) The Guinness History of Sea Warfare, 1975; Guderian, Panzer General, 1975 (2nd edn 1976); (with Joan Macksey) The Guinness Guide to Feminine Achievements, 1975; (jtly) The Guinness History of Air Warfare, 1976; The Guinness Book of 1952, 1977; The Guinness Book of 1953, 1978; The Guinness Book of 1954, 1978; Kesselring: the making of the Luftwaffe, 1978; Rommel: battles and campaigns, 1979; The Tanks, vol. 3, 1979; Invasion, 1980; The Tank Pioneers, 1981; A History of the Royal Armoured Corps, 1914–1975, 1983; Commando Strike, 1985; First Clash, 1985; Technology in War, 1986; contributor to DNB; articles and reviews in RUSI Jl, Army Qly, Brit. Army Rev., and The Tank. *Recreations:* umpiring hockey, listening to music, living in Beaminster. *Address:* Whatley Mill, Beaminster, Dorset DT8 3EN. *T:* Beaminster 862321. *Clubs:* Savage; Social (Beaminster).

McKUEN, Rod; poet, composer, author, performer, columnist, classical composer; *b* Oakland, Calif, 29 April 1933. Has appeared in numerous films, TV, concerts, nightclubs, and with symphony orchestras. Composer: modern classical music; scores for motion pictures and TV. President: Stanyan Records; Discus Records; New Gramophone Soc.; Mr Kelly Prodns; Montcalm Prodns; Stanyan Books; Cheval Books; Biplane Books; Rod McKuen Enterprises; Vice-Pres., Tamarack Books; Dir, Animal Concern; Member, Advisory Board: Fund for Animals; Internat. Educn; Market Theatre, Johannesburg; Member, Board of Directors: National Ballet Theatre; Amer. Dance Ensemble; Amer. Guild of Authors and Composers; Exec. Pres., Amer. Guild of Variety Artists; Member: Amer. Soc. of Composers, Authors and Publishers; Writers' Guild; Amer. Fedn of TV and Radio Artists; Screen Actors' Guild; Equity; Modern Poetry Assoc.; Amer. Guild of Variety Artists; AGAC; Internat. Platform Assoc. Mem., Bd of Governors, National Acad. of Recording Arts and Sciences; Trustee: Univ. of Nebraska; Freedoms Foundn. Nat. spokesperson for Amer. Energy Awareness; Internat. spokesperson for Cttee for Prevention of Child Abuse (also Nat. Bd Mem.). Numerous awards, including: Grand Prix du Disc, Paris, 1966, 1974, 1975 and 1982; Golden Globe Award, 1969; Grammy for best spoken word album, Lonesome Cities, 1969; Entertainer of the Year, 1975; Man of the Year Award, Univ. of Detroit, 1978; awards from San Francisco, LA, Chattanooga, Topeka, Lincoln and Nebraska; Freedoms Foundn Patriot Medal, 1981; Salvation Army Man of the Year, 1982. Over 200 record albums; 41 Gold and Platinum records internationally; nominated Pulitzer Prize in classical music for The City, 1973. *Publications: poetry:* And Autumn Came, 1954; Stanyan Street and Other Sorrows, 1966; Listen to the Warm, 1967; Lonesome Cities, 1968; Twelve Years of Christmas, 1968; In Someone's Shadow, 1969; A Man Alone, 1969; With Love, 1970; Caught in the Quiet, 1970; New Ballads, 1970; Fields of Wonder, 1971; The Carols of Christmas, 1971; And to Each Season, 1972; Pastorale, 1972; Grand Tour, 1972; Come to Me in Silence, 1973; America: an Affirmation, 1974; Seasons in the Sun, 1974; Moment to Moment, 1974; Beyond the Boardwalk, 1975; The Rod McKuen Omnibus, 1975; Alone, 1975; Celebrations of the Heart, 1975; Finding my Father: one man's search for identity (prose), 1976; The Sea Around Me, 1977; Hand in Hand, 1977; Coming Close to the Earth, 1978; We Touch the Sky, 1979; Love's Been Good to Me, 1979; Looking for a Friend, 1980; An Outstretched Hand (prose), 1980; The Power Bright and Shining, 1980; Too Many Midnights, 1981; Rod McKuen's Book of Days, 1981; The Beautiful Strangers, 1981; The Works of Rod McKuen: Vol. 1, Poetry, 1950–82, 1982; Watch for the Wind . . ., 1982; Rod McKuen—1984 Book of Days, 1983; The Sound of Solitude, 1983; Suspension Bridge, 1984; Another Beautiful Day, 1984, vol. 2, 1985; Valentines, 1986; *major classical works:* Symphony No One; Concerto for Guitar and Orchestra; Concerto for Four

Harpsichords; Concerto for Cello and Orch.; Concerto for Bassoon and Orch.; Seascapes; Concerto for Piano and Orchestra; Adagio for Harp and Strings; Piano Variations; The Black Eagle (opera); Birch Trees (Concerto for Orch.); various other classical commns; numerous lyrics; *film and television scores:* Joanna, 1968; Travels with Charley, 1968; The Prime of Miss Jean Brodie (Academy Award Nomination), 1969; Me, Natalie, 1969; The Loner, 1969; A Boy Named Charlie Brown (Academy Award Nomination), 1970; Come to your Senses, 1971; Scandalous John, 1971; Wildflowers, 1971; The Borrowers, 1973; Lisa Bright and Dark, 1973; Hello Again, 1974; Emily, 1975; The Unknown War, 1979; Man to Himself, 1980; Portrait of Rod McKuen, 1982; The Beach, 1984. *Address:* PO Box G, Beverly Hills, Calif 90213, USA.

MACKWORTH, Commander Sir David Arthur Geoffrey, 9th Bt, *cr* 1776; RN retired; *b* 13 July 1912; *o s* of late Vice-Admiral Geoffrey Mackworth, CMG, DSO, and Noel Mabel, *d* of late William I. Langford; *S* uncle, 1952; *m* 1st, 1941, Mary Alice (marr. diss. 1972), *d* of Thomas Henry Grylls; one *s*; 2nd, 1973, Beryl Joan, formerly wife of late Ernest Henry Sparkes, and 3rd *d* of late Pembroke Henry Cockayn Cross and of Jeanie Cross. *Educ:* Farnborough Sch., Hants; RNC Dartmouth. Joined RN 1926; served HMS Eagle, HMS Suffolk, 1939–45; Commander, 1948; Naval Adviser to Director of Guided Weapon Research and Development, Ministry of Supply, 1945–49; retired, 1956. MRIN. *Recreations:* sailing, cruising. *Heir: s* Digby John Mackworth [*b* 2 Nov. 1945; *m* 1971, Antoinette Francesca, *d* of Henry James McKenna, Ilford, Essex; one *d*. *Educ:* Wellington Coll. Served Australian Army Aviation Corps, Malaysia and Vietnam (Lieut). With British Airways Helicopters]. *Address:* 36 Wittering Road, Hayling Island, Hants. *Clubs:* Royal Ocean Racing; Royal Naval and Royal Albert Yacht (Portsmouth); Royal Naval Sailing Association; Royal Yacht Squadron (Cowes).

MACKWORTH-YOUNG, Sir Robert Christopher, (Sir Robin Mackworth-Young), GCVO 1985 (KCVO 1975; CVO 1968; MVO 1961); Librarian, Windsor Castle, and Assistant Keeper of The Queen's Archives, 1958–85, Librarian Emeritus to HM the Queen; *b* 12 Feb. 1920; *s* of late Gerard Mackworth-Young, CIE; *m* 1953, Rosemarie, *d* of W. C. R. Aue, Menton, France; one *s*. *Educ:* Eton (King's Schol.); King's Coll., Cambridge. Pres., Cambridge Union Soc., 1948. Served in RAF, 1939–46. HM Foreign Service, 1948–55; Deputy Librarian, Windsor Castle, 1955–58. Mem. Bd, British Library, 1984–. FSA; Hon. FLA. *Recreations:* music, electronics, ski-ing. *Address:* c/o Baring Brothers & Co. Ltd, 8 Bishopsgate, EC2N 4AE. *Club:* Roxburghe.

McLACHLAN, Angus Henry; journalist; *b* 29 March 1908; *s* of James H. and Mabel McLachlan; unmarried. *Educ:* Scotch Coll., Melbourne; University of Melbourne. Melbourne Herald, 1928–36; joined Sydney Morning Herald, 1936; News Editor, 1937–49; General Manager, John Fairfax & Sons Ltd (publishers of Sydney Morning Herald, Australian Financial Review, Sun), 1949–64, Dir, 1965–80 (Man. Dir, 1965–70). Jt Man. Dir, Australian Associated Press Pty Ltd, 1965–82 (Chairman, 1958–59, 1964–65, 1975–77); Director: Reuters Ltd, London, 1966–71 (Trustee, 1979–84, Chm. 1980–84); Amalgamated Television Services Pty Ltd, 1955–85; Macquarie Broadcasting Holdings Ltd, 1966–80; David Syme & Co. Ltd, Publishers of The Age, 1970–79; Federal Capital Press Ltd, Publishers of Canberra Times, 1970–79; Mem. Council, Library of NSW, 1966–75 (Dep. Pres., 1974–75); Mem., Library Council of NSW, 1975–78; Member, Sydney University Extension Board, 1960–75. *Address:* Box 5303, GPO, Sydney, NSW 2001, Australia. *T:* 233–1550. *Clubs:* Australian, Union (Sydney); Royal Sydney Yacht Squadron.

McLACHLAN, Charles, CBE 1985; QPM 1977; Chief Constable of Nottinghamshire, since 1976; *b* 12 Dec. 1931; *s* of Charles McLachlan and Ruby (*née* Bywater); *m* 1958, Dorothy (*née* Gardner); three *s*. *Educ:* Liverpool Inst. High Sch.; London Univ. (LLB 1962); Keele Univ. (MA 1968). Army Service, 1950–52 (commd RMP, 1951); joined Liverpool City Police, 1953 (promoted through ranks); Chief Inspector, Warwicks, 1966; Chief Supt, Liverpool and Bootle Constab., 1968; Asst Chief Constable (Ops), Lincs, 1970; Dep. Chief Constable, Lincs, 1973. Pres., Assoc. of Chiefs of Police, 1984–85. *Recreations:* caravanning, watching old films. *Address:* Radcliffe-on-Trent, Nottingham. *Club:* Army and Navy.

McLACHLAN, Gordon, CBE 1967; BCom; FCA; Secretary, Nuffield Provincial Hospitals Trust, 1956–86; *b* 12 June 1918; *s* of late Gordon and Mary McLachlan; *m* 1951, Monica Mary Griffin; two *d*. *Educ:* Leith Academy; Edinburgh Univ. Served with RNVR, 1939–46; Gunnery Specialist, 1943–46. Accountant, Edinburgh Corp., 1946–48; Dep. Treas., NW Met. Regional Hosps Bd, 1948–53; Accountant Nuffield Foundn, Nuffield Provincial Hosps Trust, Nat. Corp. for Care of Old People, 1953–56. Asst Dir, Nuffield Foundn, 1955–56. Henry Cohen Lectr, Univ. of Jerusalem, 1969. Consultant, American Hospitals Assoc. and American Hospitals Research and Educational Trust, 1964–65; Member Council, American Hospitals Research and Educational Trust, 1965–74 (citation for meritorious service, AHA, 1976); Mem., Inst. of Medicine, Nat. Acad. of Sciences, Washington DC, 1974–. Parker B. Francis Foundn Distinguished Lectr, Amer. Coll. of Hosp. Admin, 1976. General Editor, Nuffield Provincial Hospitals Trust publications, 1956–86; Consulting Editor, Health Services Research Journal (US), 1966–74. Hon. FRCGP 1978. Hon. LLD Birmingham, 1977. *Publications:* editor of many publications on Nuffield Provincial Hospitals Trust list; contrib. to Lancet, Practitioner, Times, Twentieth Century, etc. *Recreations:* reading, watching ballet, theatre, Rugby football. *Address:* 95 Ravenscourt Road, W6. *T:* 01–748 8211. *Club:* Caledonian.

McLACHLAN, Air Vice-Marshal Ian Dougald, CB 1966; CBE 1954; DFC 1940; Consultant, Northrop Corporation, since 1968; Chairman, Information Electronics, since 1984; *b* Melbourne, 23 July 1911; *s* of Dougald McLachlan, author and teacher, and Bertha Frances (*née* Gilliam); *m* 1946, Margaret Helen Chrystal (marr. diss. 1968); one *d*. *Educ:* Melbourne High Sch.; Royal Military Coll., Duntroon. Imperial Defence Coll., 1954; Dir, Flying Trng, Air Min., London 1955–56; Dep. Chief of Air Staff, Australia, 1959–61; Australian Defence Adviser, Washington, 1962–63; Air Mem. for Supply and Equipment, Australian Air Bd, 1964–68. Chairman: Mainline Corp., 1970–74; Pokolbin Winemakers, 1971–73; Director: Capitol Motors, 1969–75; Reef Oil, 1969–75. *Recreations:* tennis, squash, golf. *Address:* 2 Eastbourne Road, Darling Point, NSW 2027, Australia. *T:* 326–1860. *Clubs:* Australian (Sydney); Naval and Military (Melbourne); Melbourne Cricket, Royal Sydney Golf, Royal Canberra Golf.

McLACHLAN, Peter John, OBE 1983; General Secretary, Belfast Voluntary Welfare Society, since 1980; *b* 21 Aug. 1936; *s* of Herbert John McLachlan and Joan Dorothy McLachlan (*née* Hall); *m* 1965, Gillian Mavis Lowe; two *d*. *Educ:* Magdalen College Sch., Oxford; Queen's Coll., Oxford (schol.; BA Lit. Hum.; MA). Administrative trainee, Min. of Finance, NICS, 1959–62; Administrator, NYO of GB, 1962–65 and 1966–69; Personal Asst to Chm., IPC, 1965–66; Cons. Res. Dept, 1970–72; Exec. Dir, Watney & Powell Ltd, 1972–73; Mem. (Unionist) S Antrim, NI Assembly, 1973–75; Gen. Manager, S. H. Watterson Engineering, 1975–77; Jt Man. Dir, Ulster Metalspinners Ltd, 1976–77; Projects Manager, Peace By Peace Ltd, 1977–79; Sec., Peace People Charitable Trust, 1977–79; Chm., Community of The Peace People, 1978–80. Founder Chairman: NI Fedn of Housing Assocs, 1976–78; Belfast Improved Houses Ltd, 1975–81; Dismas House, 1983–; Chm., NI Peace Forum, 1980–82; Vice-Chm., NI Hospice Ltd, 1981–; Member: Gulbenkian Adv. Cttee on Community Work, 1978–80; The Corrymeela Community; Minister's Adv. Cttee on Community Work, NI, 1982–; Council, Children's Community Holidays, 1982–; Exec. Cttee, NI Children's Holiday Scheme, 1983–; Exec. Cttee, NI Chest, Heart and Stroke Assoc., 1983–; Cttee, Cruse in NI, 1984–; Central Personal Social Services Adv. Cttee, 1984–; Administrative Council: Royal Jubilee Trusts, 1975–81; NI Projects Trust. *Recreations:* piano playing, mountain walking, Corrymeela Singers. *Address:* 79 Antrim Road, Lisburn, Co. Antrim, Northern Ireland. *T:* Lisburn 81339.

MACLAGAN, Michael, FSA; FRHistS, Richmond Herald of Arms, since 1980; *b* 14 April 1914; *s* of Sir Eric Robert Dalrymple Maclagan, KCVO, CBE, and Helen Elizabeth (*née* Lascelles); *m* 1st, 1939, Brenda Alexander (marr. diss. 1946); one *s*; 2nd, 1949, Jean Elizabeth Brooksbank Garnett, *d* of late Lt-Col W. B. Garnett, DSO; two *d* (one *s* decd). *Educ:* Winchester Coll.; Christ Church, Oxford (BA 1st Cl. Hons Modern History, MA). FSA 1948; FRHistS 1961; FSG 1970; FHS 1972. Lectr, Christ Church, Oxford, 1937–39; Fellow of Trinity Coll., 1939–81, Emeritus Fellow 1981, Sen. Proctor, 1954–55. 2/Lieut TA, 1938; served war, 1939–46: 16/5 Lancers; sc; Major, GSOII War Office. Slains Pursuivant, 1948–70; Portcullis Pursuivant, 1970–80. Vis. Professor, Univ. of S Carolina, 1974; Fellow of Winchester Coll., 1975; Sen. Librarian, Oxford Union, 1960–70; Trustee, Oxford Union, 1970. Councillor, Oxford CBC, 1946–74; Sheriff, 1964–65; Lord Mayor of Oxford, 1970–71. Chm., Oxford Dio. Adv. Cttee, 1961–85. OStJ 1952. *Publications:* (ed) Bede: Ecclesiastical History I and II, 1949; Trinity College, 1955, rev. edn 1963; (jtly) The Colour of Heraldry, 1958; (ed) Richard de Bury: Philobiblon, 1960; 'Clemency' Canning, 1962 (Wheatley Gold Medal); City of Constantinople, 1968; (with J. Louda) Lines of Succession, 1981 (trans. French, 1984); articles in DNB, VCH, etc. *Recreations:* real tennis, wine, walking, travel. *Address:* 20 Northmoor Road, Oxford OX2 6UR. *T:* Oxford 58536; Trinity College, Oxford OX1 3BH; College of Arms, Queen Victoria Street, EC4V 4BT. *T:* 01–248 2543. *Clubs:* Cavalry and Guards, Pratt's, City Livery; Oxford Union (Oxford).

MACLAGAN, Noel Francis, DSc, MD, FRCP, FRSC; retired; formerly Professor of Chemical Pathology in University of London at Westminster Medical School, now Emeritus; Chemical Pathologist, Westminster Hospital, 1947–70; *b* 1904; *y s* of late Oscar Frederick and Ada Maclagan, Newcastle and London; *m* 1933, Annemarie, *d* of Curt and Marie Herzog, London; one *s* one *d*. *Educ:* University Coll. Sch.; University Coll., London (First Cl. Hons BSc Chemistry, 1925); Middlesex Hosp. Medical School (MSc London in Biochemistry, 1933). DSc London, 1946; MD London, 1935; MRCP, 1933; FRIC 1946; FRCP 1952. Asst in Courtauld Inst. of Biochemistry, Middlesex Hosp., 1926–33; House Physician Middlesex Hosp., 1932; whole-time worker for Medical Research Council, 1933–34; Biochemist, Westminster Hosp., 1935–46; Pathologist, EMS, 1939–45; Chemical Pathologist at Westminster Hosp. Medical Sch., 1946–47. Chm., Nuffield Project on Clinical Chemistry Labs, 1976–79. Hon. FRSM 1986. Editor, Annals of Clinical Biochemistry, 1974–76. *Publications:* contributions to medical textbooks on various biochemical subjects and articles in scientific journals on thymol turbidity test, thyroid function, lipid metabolism, etc. *Recreations:* music and chess. *Address:* 40 Temple Fortune Lane, NW11. *T:* 01–458 4032.

McLAREN, family name of **Baron Aberconway.**

McLAREN, Dr Anne Laura, FRS 1975; Director, Medical Research Council's Mammalian Development Unit, since 1974; *b* 26 April 1927; *d* of 2nd Baron Aberconway; *m* 1952, Donald Michie (marr. diss.); one *s* two *d*. *Educ:* Univ. of Oxford (MA, DPhil). Post-doctoral research, UCL, 1952–55 and Royal Vet. Coll., London, 1955–59; joined staff of ARC Unit of Animal Genetics at Edinburgh Univ., 1959. Mem., ARC, 1978–83. Mem., Cttee of Managers, Royal Instn, 1976–81. Scientific Medal, Zool Soc. London, 1967. *Publications:* Mammalian Chimaeras, 1976; Germ Cells and Soma, 1980; papers on reproductive biology, embryology, genetics and immunology in sci. jls. *Address:* 9 Steele's Road, NW3 4SG.

McLAREN, Prof. Digby Johns, PhD; FRS 1979; FRSC 1968; Professor, Department of Geology, University of Ottawa, since 1981; *b* 11 Dec. 1919; *s* of James McLaren and Louie Kinsey; *m* 1942, Phyllis Matkin; two *s* one *d*. *Educ:* Sedbergh Sch.; Queens' Coll., Cambridge (BA, MA); Univ. of Michigan (PhD). Served RA (Gunner to Captain), ME and Italy, 1940–46. Field Geologist, Geological Survey of Canada, in Alberta and British Columbia Rocky Mountains, District of Mackenzie, Yukon Territory, Artic Islands, 1948–80; first Dir, Inst. of Sedimentary and Petroleum Geology, Calgary, Alberta, 1967–73; Dir Gen., Geological Survey of Canada, 1973–80; Sen. Science Adviser, Dept of Energy, Mines and Resources, Ottawa, 1981–84. Pres., Commn on Stratigraphy, IUGS, 1972–76; Chm. of Bd, Internat. Geol Correlation Programme, UNESCO-IUGS, 1976–80; IUGS Deleg. to People's Republic of China to advise on participation in international science, 1977. Pres., Geol Soc. of America, 1981; Hon. Mem., Geol Soc. of Germany, 1982; Corresp. Mem., Geol Soc. of France, 1975; Foreign Associate, Nat. Acad. of Scis, USA, 1979. Hon. DSc Ottawa, 1980. Gold Medal (for Pure and Applied Science), Professional Inst. of Public Service of Canada, 1979. *Publications:* 80 memoirs, bulletins, papers, geological maps, and scientific contribs to journals on regional geology, paleontology, geological time, correlation and extinctions. *Recreations:* skiing, swimming, gardening, music. *Address:* 248 Marilyn Avenue, Ottawa, Ont K1V 7E5, Canada. *T:* (613) 737–4360.

MacLAREN, Sir Hamish (Duncan), KBE 1951; CB 1946; DFC; Director of Electrical Engineering, Admiralty, 1945–60; *b* 7 April 1898; *s* of Rev. Peter MacLaren, MA, and Constance Hamilton Simpson; *m* 1927, Lorna Cicely, *d* of late Dr R. P. N. B. Bluett, MC, Harrow; one *s* one *d*. *Educ:* Fordyce Academy, Banffshire; Edinburgh Univ. (BSc 1921). Served European war, 1914–18, in RNVR, RNAS and RAF (DFC and Bar, French Croix de Guerre with Palm). After completing degree at Edinburgh Univ. in 1921 joined British Thomson Houston Co., Rugby, as student apprentice. Awarded Bursary by Commission for Exhibition of 1851 for 1921–23; British Thomson Houston Fellowship to spend one year with the GE Co. of Schenectady, USA, 1923–24; on staff of British Thomson Houston, Rugby, 1924–26; joined Admiralty Service as Asst Electrical Engineer, 1926. In Admiralty Service at HM Dockyards, Chatham, Devonport, at Dir of Dockyards Dept, Admiralty, 1933–37, and in Ceylon, 1931–33; Superintending Electrical Engineer, HM Naval Base, Singapore, 1937–40; Asst Dir, Electrical Engineering Dept, Admiralty, 1940–45. Pres. Instn of Electrical Engineers, 1960–61. Hon. LLD St Andrews, 1954; Hon. DSc Bath, 1970. *Address:* 104 Heath Road, Petersfield, Hants. *T:* Petersfield 4562.

McLAREN, Robin John Taylor, CMG 1982; HM Diplomatic Service; Ambassador to the Philippines, since 1985; *b* 14 Aug. 1934; *s* of late Robert Taylor McLaren and of Marie Rose McLaren (*née* Simond); *m* 1964, Susan Ellen Hatherly; one *s* two *d*. *Educ:* Richmond and East Sheen County Grammar Sch. for Boys; Ardingly Coll.; St John's Coll., Cambridge (Schol.; MA). Royal Navy, 1953–55. Entered Foreign Service, 1958; language student, Hong Kong, 1959–60; Third Sec., Peking, 1960–61; FO, 1961–64; Asst Private Sec. to Lord Privy Seal (Mr Edward Heath), 1963–64; Second, later First Sec., Rome, 1964–68; seconded to Hong Kong Govt as Asst Political Adviser, 1968–69;

First Sec., FCO, 1970–73; Dep. Head of Western Organisations Dept, 1974–75; Counsellor and Head of Chancery, Copenhagen, 1975–78; Head of Hong Kong and Gen. Dept, 1978–79, of Far Eastern Dept, 1979–81, FCO; Political Advr, Hong Kong, 1981–85. *Recreations:* music, China, hill-walking. *Address:* c/o Foreign and Commonwealth Office, SW1A 2AH. *Clubs:* United Oxford & Cambridge University; Hong Kong (Hong Kong).

McLAUCHLAN, Madeline Margaret Nicholls; Head Mistress, North London Collegiate School, 1965–85; *b* 4 June 1922; *o c* of late Robert and Gertrude McLauchlan, Birmingham. *Educ:* King Edward VI Grammar Sch. for Girls, Camp Hill, Birmingham; Royal Holloway College, University of London. Asst Mistress: Shrewsbury High Sch., GPDST, 1944; Manchester High Sch., 1952. Senior Walter Hines Page Scholar, E-SU, 1955. Head Mistress, Henrietta Barnett Sch., 1958. Chm., Schoolboy and Schoolgirl Exchange Cttee, E-SU (Mem., Educn Cttee, 1966); Member: Exec. Cttee, Assoc. of Head Mistresses, 1966–76, Chm., 1974–76; Exec. Cttee, UCCA, 1968–85; Direct Grant Cttee, GBGSA, 1972–; Assisted Places Cttee, ISJC, 1980–85; Council, Westfield Coll., Univ. of London, 1975–78; Council, The Church Schools Co., 1985–; Council, The Francis Holland Schools Trust, 1985–; Vice-Chm., Council, Nat. Youth Orchestra, 1981 (Mem., 1975–). Governor: Imperial Coll., 1968–85; Bedford Coll., 1981–85; St Christopher's Sch., NW3, 1985–. *Recreations:* music, mountain walking, housekeeping. *Address:* Moor Park Coach House, Llanbedr, Crickhowell, Powys. *Club:* English-Speaking Union.

McLAUCHLAN, Thomas Joseph, JP; Stipendiary Magistrate, 1966–82; *b* 15 May 1917; *s* of Alexander and Helen McLauchlan; *m* 1945, Rose Catherine Gray, MA. *Educ:* St Aloysius Coll., Glasgow; Univ. of Glasgow (BL). Law apprentice, 1936–39 and 1946–47. War service, Merchant Navy and RAF Y Section, Signals Intell., Wireless Officer, 1940–46. Legal Asst to Manager of large industrial insurance co., 1947–49; Clerk to Glasgow Police Courts, 1949–66. JP Scotland. *Recreations:* golf, bridge, travel. *Address:* 75 Clouston Street, Glasgow G20 8QW. *T:* 041–946 4222. *Clubs:* Centenary, College (Glasgow).

McLAUGHLAN, Rear-Adm. Ian David, CB 1970; DSC 1941 and Bar, 1953; Admiral Commanding Reserves and Director General, Naval Recruiting, 1970–72, retired; *b* 2 May 1919; *s* of Richard John and Margaret McLaughlan; *m* 1942, Charity Pomeroy Simonds; two *d. Educ:* St Paul's Sch. Entered Navy, 1937; served in destroyers, 1940–45 (despatches three times); comd HMS: Flint Castle, 1948–50; Concord, 1950–52; jssc 1952; Armed Forces Staff Coll., Norfolk, Va, 1953; HMS Jupiter, 1953–55; comd HMS: Chieftain, 1955; Chevron, 1955–56 (despatches); Staff of C-in-C, Portsmouth, 1957–59; Asst Dir of Plans, Admty, 1959–61; Capt. (F), 2nd Frigate Sqdn, 1961–62; idc 1963; Dir, Naval Ops and Trade, 1964–66; comd HMS Hampshire, 1966–67; Chief of Staff to Comdr Far East Fleet, 1967–70. Comdr 1951; Capt. 1958; Rear-Adm. 1968. Commendador d'Aviz, 1956. *Recreations:* gardening, house husbandry. *Address:* The Five Gables, Mayfield, East Sussex. *T:* Mayfield 872218.

McLAUGHLIN, Mrs (Florence) Patricia (Alice), OBE 1975; *b* 23 June 1916; *o d* of late Canon F. B. Aldwell; *m* 1937, Henry, *o s* of late Major W. McLaughlin, of McLaughlin & Harvey Ltd, London, Belfast and Dublin; one *s* two *d. Educ:* Ashleigh House, Belfast; Trinity Coll., Dublin. MP (UU) Belfast West, 1955–64; Hon. Sec., Parly Home Safety Cttee, 1956–64; Deleg. to Council of Europe and WEU, 1959–64. Past Chm., Unionist Soc.; Past Vice-Chm., Women's National Advisory Cttee of Cons. Party; Former Nat. Advisor on Women's Affairs to European Movement. Has been active in voluntary and consumer work for many years; Chairman: Steering Gp on Food Freshness, 1973–75; Housewife's Trust; Former Mem., Exec. Cttee, BSI. Vice-Pres., Royal Society for Prevention of Accidents. *Recreations:* talking and travelling. *Address:* 31 Headbourne Worthy House, Winchester, Hants SO23 7JG.

MacLAURIN, Ian Charter; Chairman, Tesco PLC, since 1985 (Managing Director, 1973–85; Director, 1970); Director, Enterprise Oil PLC, since 1984; *b* Blackheath, 30 March 1937; *s* of Arthur George and Evelina Florence MacLaurin; *m* 1961, Ann Margaret (*née* Collar); one *s* two *d. Educ:* Malvern Coll., Worcs. Served in RAF, 1956–58. Joined Tesco, 1959. Chm., Food Policy Gp, Retail Consortium, 1980–84; Mem., Inst. of Grocery Distribution Management Cttee; Governor and Mem. Council, Malvern Coll. Mem. Cttee, MCC, 1986–. FRSA 1986. Liveryman, Carmen's Co., 1982–. *Recreation:* golf. *Address:* Tesco PLC, Tesco House, Delamere Road, Cheshunt, Herts. *Clubs:* Institute of Directors, Royal Automobile; MCC, Lord's Taverners, XL, Band of Brothers.

MACLAY, family name of **Baron Maclay** and **Viscount Muirshiel.**

MACLAY, 3rd Baron *cr* 1922, of Glasgow; **Joseph Paton Maclay,** DL; Bt 1914; Managing Director: Denholm Maclay Co. Ltd, 1970–83; Denholm Maclay (Offshore) Ltd; Triport Ferries (Management) Ltd, 1975–83; Deputy Managing Director, Denholm Ship Management Ltd, 1982–83; *b* 11 April 1942; *s* of 2nd Baron Maclay, KBE, and of Nancy Margaret, *d* of R. C. Greig, Hall of Caldwell, Uplawmoor, Renfrewshire; *S* father, 1969; *m* 1976, Elizabeth Anne, *o d* of G. M. Buchanan, Delamere, Pokataroo, NSW; two *s* one *d. Educ:* Winchester; Sorbonne Univ. Director: Milton Shipping Co. Ltd, 1970–83; Milton Timber Services Ltd, 1984–; Marine Shipping Mutual Insce Co., 1982–83; Pres., Hanover Shipping Inc., 1982–83. Director: British Steamship Short Trades Assoc, 1978–83; N of England Protection and Indemnity Assoc., 1976–83. Chm., Scottish Br., British Sailors Soc., 1979–81; Vice-Chm., Glasgow Shipowners & Shipbrokers Benevolent Assoc., 1982–83. DL Renfrewshire, 1986. *Heir: s* Hon. Joseph Paton Maclay, *b* 6 March 1977. *Address:* Duchal, Kilmacolm, Renfrewshire.

McLAY, Hon. James Kenneth, (Jim); MP (National Party) for Birkenhead, since 1975; Leader of the National Party, and Leader of the Opposition, New Zealand, 1984–86; *s* of late Robert McLay and of Joyce McLay; *m* 1983, Marcy Farden. *Educ:* St Helier's Sch.; King's Sch.; King's Coll.; Auckland Univ. (LLB 1967). Solicitor in practice on own account, 1971; barrister in practice on own account 1974. Attorney-Gen. and Minister of Justice, 1978–84; Government Spokesperson for Women, 1979–84; Dep. Prime Minster, 1984. *Recreation:* trout fishing. *Address:* Parliament Buildings, Wellington, New Zealand. *T:* 749–176.

MACLEAN, family name of **Baron Maclean.**

MACLEAN, Baron *cr* 1971 (Life Peer), of Duart and Morvern in the County of Argyll; **Charles Hector Fitzroy Maclean;** Bt 1631; KT 1969; GCVO 1971; KBE 1967; Royal Victorian Chain, 1984; PC 1971; JP; 27th Chief of Clan Maclean; a Permanent Lord in Waiting, since 1984; Scots Guards, Major, retired; Lord Lieutenant of Argyll since 1954; Lord High Commissioner, General Assembly of the Church of Scotland, 1984 and 1985; Chief Steward of Hampton Court Palace, since 1985; Lieutenant, Royal Company of Archers (Queen's Body Guard for Scotland); President, Argyll T&AFA; *b* 5 May 1916; *e surv. s* of late Hector F. Maclean and Winifred Joan, *y d* of late J. H. Wilding; *S* grandfather, 1936; *m* 1941, Elizabeth, *er d* of late Frank Mann, Upper Farm House, Milton Lilbourne, Wilts; one *s* one *d. Educ:* Canford Sch., Wimborne. Served War of 1939–45 (despatches). Chief Commissioner for Scotland, Boy Scouts Assoc., 1954–59; Chief Scout of the UK and Overseas Branches, 1959–71; Chief Scout of the Commonwealth, 1959–75; Lord Chamberlain of HM Household, 1971–84; Chancellor, Royal Victorian Order, 1971–84. Patron: Coombe Trust Fund; Roland House; Argyll Div., Scottish Br., British Red Cross Soc.; Hon. Patron, Friends of World Scouting; Vice Patron: Argyll & Sutherland Highlanders Regimental Assoc.; President: T&AFA of Argyll; Argyll Br., Forces Help Soc. and Lord Robert's Workshops; Convenor, Standing Council of Scottish Chiefs; Hon. President: Argyll Co. Scout Council; Toc H; Scouts Friendly Soc.; Vice President: Highland Cattle Soc.; Scottish Br., Nat. Playing Fields Assoc.; (ex officio) Nat. Small-Bore Rifle Assoc.; Camping Club of GB; Trefoil Residential Sch. for Physically Handicapped Children; Casualties Union; Member of Council: Earl Haig Officers Meml Fund; Scottish Naval, Military and Air Forces Veteran Residences; Royal Zoological Soc.; Outward Bound Trust; Life Member: Highland and Agricultural Soc. of Scotland; Highland Cattle Soc.; Scottish Nat. Fatstock Club; Royal Agricultural Soc. of England. JP Argyll, 1955. *Publication:* Only (children's book), 1979. *Recreation:* travelling. *Heir:* (to Baronetcy only): *s* Hon. Lachlan Hector Charles Maclean, Major, Scots Guards, retired [*b* 25 Aug. 1942; *m* 1966, Mary Helen, *e d* of W. G. Gordon; two *s* two *d* (and one *d* decd)]. *Address:* Duart Castle, Isle of Mull. *T:* Craignure 309. *Clubs:* Cavalry and Guards, Pratt's, Royal Commonwealth Society (Mem. Council); Royal Highland Yacht (Oban).

See also D. J. Graham-Campbell.

MACLEAN, Alistair; author; *b* Scotland, 1922. *Educ:* Glasgow Univ. *Publications:* HMS Ulysses, 1955; The Guns of Navarone, 1957 (filmed 1959); South by Java Head, 1958 (filmed 1959); The Last Frontier, 1959 (filmed 1960 as The Secret Ways); Night Without End, 1960; Fear is the Key, 1961 (filmed 1972); The Golden Rendezvous, 1962 (filmed 1977); (for children) All About Lawrence of Arabia, 1962; Ice Station Zebra, 1963 (filmed 1968); When Eight Bells Toll, 1966 (filmed 1970); Where Eagles Dare, 1967 (filmed 1968); Force 10 from Navarone, 1968 (filmed 1978); Puppet on a Chain, 1969 (filmed 1970); Bear Island, 1971 (filmed 1979); Captain Cook, 1972; The Way to Dusty Death, 1973; (introd.) Alistair MacLean Introduces Scotland, ed, A. M. Dunnett, 1972; Breakheart Pass, 1974 (filmed 1975); Circus, 1975; The Golden Gate, 1976; Sea Witch, 1977; Goodbye California, 1977; Athabasca, 1980; River of Death, 1981; Partisans, 1982; Floodgate, 1983; San Andreas, 1984; The Lonely Sea (short stories), 1985; *as Ian Stuart:* The Dark Crusader, 1961; The Satan Bug, 1962 (filmed 1965). *Screen plays:* Where Eagles Dare, Caravan to Vaccares, Puppet on a Chain, Breakheart Pass. *Film for TV:* Hostage Tower, 1980. *Address:* c/o Wm Collins Sons & Co. Ltd, 8 Grafton Street, W1.

McLEAN, Colin, CMG 1977; MBE 1964; HM Diplomatic Service; UK Permanent Representative to the Council of Europe (with the personal rank of Ambassador), since 1986; *b* 10 Aug. 1930; *s* of late Dr L. G. McLean and of H. I. McLean; *m* 1953, Huguette Marie Suzette Leclerc; one *s* one *d. Educ:* Fettes; St Catharine's Coll., Cambridge (MA). 2RHA, 1953–54. District Officer, Kenya, 1955–63; Vice-Principal, Kenya Inst. of Administration, 1963–64; HM Diplomatic Service, 1964; served Wellington, Bogotá and FCO, 1964–77; Counsellor, Oslo, 1977–81; Head of Trade Relations and Export Dept, FCO, 1981–83; High Comr in Uganda, 1983–86. *Recreation:* sailing. *Address:* c/o Foreign and Commonwealth Office, SW1.

MACLEAN, David John; MP (C) Penrith and the Border, since July 1983; *b* 16 May 1953; *s* of John and Catherine Jane Maclean; *m* 1977, Jayalaluna Dawn Gallacher. *Address:* House of Commons, SW1A 0AA.

McLEAN, Denis Bazeley Gordon; Secretary of Defence, New Zealand, since 1979; *b* Napier, NZ, 18 Aug. 1930; *s* of John Gordon McLean and Renée Maitland Smith; *m* 1958, Anne Davidson, Venado Tuerto, Argentina; two *s* one *d. Educ:* Nelson Coll., NZ; Victoria Univ. Coll., NZ (MSc); Rhodes Schol. 1954; University Coll., Oxford (MA). Jun. Lectr in Geology, Victoria UC, 1953–54; joined Dept of External Affairs of NZ Govt, London, 1957; served in: Wellington, 1958–60; Washington, 1960–63; Paris, 1963–66; Kuala Lumpur, 1966–68; Asst Sec. (Policy), MoD, Wellington, 1969–72; RCDS, 1972; Dep. High Comr, London, 1973–77; Dep. Sec. of Defence, NZ, 1977. *Recreations:* walking, modest mountaineering, geology. *Address:* 11 Dekka Street, Wellington, New Zealand. *Clubs:* Travellers'; Wellington (NZ).

MacLEAN, Captain Donald Murdo, DSC 1944; RD 1940; RNR; Retired from Cunard Line, 1962; Commodore Captain Cunard Fleet and commanding RMS Queen Elizabeth, 1960–62; *b* 9 June, 1899; *s* of William MacLean and Isobel (*née* Graham); *m* 1929, Bernice Isobel Wellington; one *s* one *d. Educ:* The Nicholson Sch., Lewis Island. Apprenticed to Cunard Line, 1917–21; served, as Officer, 1921–39. Served War of 1939–45 (despatches): RNR, 1939–46; Trg Comdr RNC, Greenwich, 1941–43; Sen. Officer, 7th Escort Gp, Murmansk and Atlantic and Mediterranean Convoys; Staff Officer C-in-C Mediterranean, 1944–45. Returned to Cunard Line, 1946. ADC to Lord High Comr for Scotland, 1946. *Publications:* Queens' Company, 1965; Cachalots and Messmates, 1973. *Recreations:* sailing, fishing, travel. *Address:* Landfall, 51A Newtown Road, Warsash, Southampton. *T:* Locks Heath 3951. *Club:* Master Mariners (Southampton).

MACLEAN, Sir Donald (Og Grant), Kt 1985; optician, practising in Ayr, since 1965; Deputy Chairman, Scottish Conservative Party, since 1985; *b* 13 Aug. 1930; *s* of Donald Og Maclean and Margaret Maclean (*née* Smith); *m* 1958, Muriel Giles (*d* 1984); one *s* one *d. Educ:* Morrison's Academy, Crieff; Heriot Watt Univ. FBOA; Fellow, British Coll. of Opticians. RAMC, 1952–54. Optical practice: Newcastle upon Tyne, 1954–57; Perth, 1957–65. Chm., Ayr Constituency Cons. Assoc., 1971–75; Scottish Conservative and Unionist Association: Vice-Pres., 1979–83; Pres., 1983–85; Chm., W of Scotland Area, 1977–79; Exec. Mem., Nat. Union, 1979–. Chm., Ayrshire and Arran Local Optical Cttee. *Recreations:* coastal shipping, reading, photography, philately. *Address:* Dun Beag II, 22 Woodend Road, Alloway, Ayr. *Club:* Royal Scottish Automobile (Glasgow).

MACLEAN, Rear-Adm. Euan, CB 1986; FRINA, FIMechE; Director General Fleet Support Policy and Services, 1983–86; *b* 7 July 1929; *s* of John Fraser Maclean and Dorothy Mary Maclean; *m* 1954, Renée Shaw; two *d. Educ:* Coalbrookdale High Sch.; BRNC Dartmouth; RNEC Keyham/Manadon. FRINA 1980; FIMechE 1980. Joined Exec. Br., RN, 1943; transf. to Engr Br., 1947; sea service in HMS Gambia, Ocean, Indefatigable, Defender, Hermes, Eagle and Ark Royal, 1950–72; on loan to Royal Malaysian Navy, 1965–68; Prodn Dept, Portsmouth Dockyard, 1968–71; HMS Ark Royal, 1971–72; Exec. Officer, HMS Sultan, 1973; Dep. Prodn Man., Devonport Dockyard, 1974–77; Fleet Marine Engr Officer, 1977–79; student, RCDS, 1980; Prodn Man., Portsmouth Dockyard, 1981–83. ADC to the Queen, 1982. Comdr 1965, Captain 1974, Rear-Adm. 1983. *Recreation:* rough country. *Address:* c/o National Westminster Bank, The Hard, Portsmouth, Hants PO1 3DU.

MACLEAN of Dunconnel, Sir Fitzroy Hew, 1st Bt, *cr* 1957; CBE (mil.) 1944; 15th Hereditary Keeper and Captain of Dunconnel; *b* 11 March 1911; *s* of Major Charles Maclean, DSO; *m* 1946, Hon. Mrs Alan Phipps, 2nd *d* of 16th Baron Lovat, KT; two *s. Educ:* Eton; Cambridge. 3rd Sec., Foreign Office, 1933; transferred to Paris, 1934, and to Moscow, 1937; 2nd Sec., 1938; transferred to Foreign Office, 1939; resigned from Diplomatic Service, and enlisted as private in Cameron Highlanders; 2nd Lt Aug. 1941; joined 1st Special Air Service Regt Jan. 1942; Capt. Sept. 1942; Lt-Col 1943; Brig.

Comdg British Military Mission to Jugoslav partisans, 1943–45. Lees Knowles Lecturer, Cambridge, 1953. MP (C) Lancaster, 1941–59, Bute and N Ayrshire, 1959–Feb. 1974; Parly Under-Sec. of State for War and Financial Sec. War Office, Oct. 1954–Jan. 1957. Member: UK Delegn to North Atlantic Assembly, 1962–74 (Chm., Mil. Cttee, 1964–74); Council of Europe and WEU, 1972–74. Hon. LLD: Glasgow 1969; Dalhousie 1971; Dundee, 1984; Hon. DLitt Acadia, 1970. French Croix de Guerre, 1943; Order of Kutusov, 1944; Partisan Star (First Class), 1945; Order of Merit, Yugoslavia, 1969; Order of the Yusoslav Star with Ribbon, 1981. *Publications:* Eastern Approaches, 1949; Disputed Barricade, 1957; A Person from England, 1958; Back to Bokhara, 1959; Jugoslavia, 1969; A Concise History of Scotland, 1970; The Battle of Neretva, 1970; To the Back of Beyond, 1974; To Caucasus, 1976; Take Nine Spies, 1978; Holy Russia, 1979; Tito, 1980; The Isles of the Sea, 1985. *Heir: s* Charles Maclean, yr of Dunconnel, *b* 31 Oct. 1946. *Address:* Strachur House, Argyll. *T:* Strachur 242. *Clubs:* White's, Pratt's; Puffin's, New (Edinburgh).

McLEAN, Sir Francis (Charles), Kt 1967; CBE 1953 (MBE 1945); *b* 6 Nov. 1904; *s* of Michael McLean; *m* 1930, Dorothy Mabel Blackstaffe; one *s* one *d*. *Educ:* University of Birmingham (BSc). Chief Engineer, Psychological Warfare Division, SHAEF, 1943–45. Dep. Chief Engineer, BBC, 1952–60; Dep. Dir of Engineering, BBC, 1960–63; Director, Engineering, BBC, 1963–68. Dir, Oxley Developments Ltd, 1961–. Chairman: BSI Telecommunications Industry Standards Cttee, 1960–77; Royal Commn on FM Broadcasting in Australia, 1974. Pres., Newbury Dist Field Club. FIEE. *Publications:* contrib. Journal of IEE. *Address:* Greenwood Copse, Tile Barn, Woolton Hill, Newbury, Berks. *T:* Newbury 253583.

McLEAN, Geoffrey Daniel, QPM 1981; Assistant Commissioner (Territorial Operations), Metropolitan Police, since 1984; *b* 4 March 1931; *s* of late William James McLean and Matilda Gladys (*née* Davies); two *s* two *d*. Following service in RA, joined Metropolitan Police, 1951; Chief Supt, 1969; Staff Officer to HMCIC, Home Office, 1970–72; Comdr, 1975; Graduate, RCDS, 1978; Dep. Asst Comr, 1979; Dep. Comdt, Police Staff Coll., 1981–83. *Recreations:* Chm., Met. Police Race-Walking Club, 1978–; riding. *Address:* New Scotland Yard, Broadway, SW1H 0BG. *T:* 01–230 1212.

MACLEAN, Vice-Adm. Sir Hector Charles Donald, KBE 1962; CB 1960; DSC 1941; JP; DL; *b* 7 Aug. 1908; *s* of late Captain D. C. H. Maclean, DSO, The Royal Scots; *m* 1933, Opre, *d* of late Captain Geoffrey Vyvyan, Royal Welch Fusiliers; one *s* two *d*. *Educ:* Wellington. Special Entry into Navy, 1926; Captain 1948; idc 1951; Comd HMS Saintes and 3rd Destroyer Sqdn, 1952–53; Dir of Plans, Admiralty, 1953–56; Comd HMS Eagle, 1956–57; Chief of Staff, Home Fleet, 1958–59; Chief of Allied Staff, Mediterranean, 1959–62; Vice-Adm. 1960; retired 1962. JP Norfolk, 1963; DL Norfolk, 1977. *Address:* Deepdale Old Rectory, Brancaster Staithe, King's Lynn, Norfolk. *T:* Brancaster 210281. *Club:* Norfolk (Norwich).

MACLEAN, Hector Ronald; Sheriff of North Strathclyde (formerly Renfrew and Argyll) since 1968; *b* 6 Dec. 1931; *s* of Donald Beaton Maclean and Lucy McAlister; *m* 1967, Hilary Elizabeth Jenkins; three *d*. *Educ:* High Sch. of Glasgow; Glasgow Univ. Admitted to Faculty of Advocates, 1959. *Recreation:* golf. *Address:* Barrfield, Houston, Renfrewshire. *T:* Bridge of Weir 612449.

MACLEAN of Pennycross, Rear-Admiral Iain Gilleasbuig, CB 1954; OBE 1944; retired; *b* 25 Nov. 1902; *s* of late Norman H. Maclean; *m* 1st, 1931, Evelyn Marjorie, *d* of late R. A. and Mrs Winton Reid; one step *d*; 2nd, 1973, Nancy Margaret, *widow* of E. A. Barnard. *Educ:* Cargilfield; RN Colleges, Osborne and Dartmouth. Joined RN, 1916; Captain, 1945; Rear-Admiral, 1952; Served War of 1939–45: in Combined Operations, HMS Renown and Admiralty. Imperial Defence Coll., 1951; Dep. Engineer in Chief of the Fleet, 1952–55; retired, Nov. 1955. Director, Marine Development, Brush Group, 1956–60. Research Survey for National Ports Council, 1963–64. *Recreations:* fishing, gardening. *Address:* Pear Tree Cottage, Moorlands Drive, Pinkney's Green, Maidenhead, Berks. *T:* Maidenhead 30287.

McLEAN, Ian Graeme; His Honour Judge McLean; a Circuit Judge since 1980; *b* Edinburgh, 7 Sept. 1928; *s* of Lt-Gen. Sir Kenneth McLean, *qv*; *m* 1957, Eleonore Maria Gmeiner, Bregenz, Austria; two *d*. *Educ:* Aldenham Sch.; Christ's Coll., Cambridge. BA Hons Law 1950; MA 1955. Intell. Corps, 1946–48. Called to English Bar, Middle Temple, Nov. 1951; admitted Faculty of Advocates, Edinburgh, 1985; practised London and on Western Circuit, 1951–55; Crown Counsel, Northern Nigeria, 1955–59; Sen. Lectr and Head of Legal Dept of Inst. of Administration, Northern Nigeria, 1959–62; Native Courts Adviser, 1959–62; returned to English Bar, 1962; practised London and South Eastern Circuit, 1962–70; occasional Dep. Chm., Inner, NE, SW and Mddx Areas, London QS, 1968–70; occasional Dep. Recorder, Oxford, 1969–70; Adjudicator under Immigration Acts, 1969–70; Metropolitan Stipendiary Magistrate, 1970–80. *Publications:* Cumulative Index West African Court of Appeal Reports, 1958; (with Abubakar Sadiq) The Maliki Law of Homicide, 1959; (with Sir Lionel Brett) Criminal Law Procedure and Evidence of Lagos, Eastern and Western Nigeria, 1963; (with Cyprian Okonkwo) Cases on the Criminal Law, Procedure and Evidence of Nigeria, 1966; (with Peter Morrish) A Practical Guide to Appeals in Criminal Courts, 1970; (with Peter Morrish) The Crown Court, an index of common penalties, etc, 1972; (ed, with Peter Morrish) Harris's Criminal Law, 22nd edn, 1972; (with Peter Morrish) The Magistrates' Court, an index of common penalties, 1973; (with Peter Morrish) The Trial of Breathalyser Offences, 1975; A Practical Guide to Criminal Appeals, 1980; A Pattern of Sentencing, 1981; (with John Mulhern) The Industrial Tribunal: a practical guide to employment law and tribunal procedure, 1982; contrib. Archbold's Criminal Pleadings, 38th edn, and Halsbury's Laws of England, 4th edn, title Criminal Law. *Recreations:* family, gardening, writing, languages.

MacLEAN, Dr John Alexander, CBE 1968; Chairman, Northern Regional Hospital Board (Scotland), 1971–74; *b* 12 Oct. 1903; *s* of Donald MacLean, Achiltibuie, Ross-shire; *m* 1935, Hilda M. L. Munro, BSc, Aberdeen; one *s* one *d*. *Educ:* Dingwall Academy; Aberdeen Univ. MA, LLB, PhD; FEIS. Aberdeen Educn Authority: Teacher, 1926–39; Asst Dir of Educn, 1939–43; Dir of Educn, Inverness-shire Educn Authority, 1943–68, retd. Member: Exec. Cttee, National Trust for Scotland, 1967–82; Scottish Council, Royal Over-Seas League, 1969–81; Scottish Arts Council, 1964–68; Sec. of State's Council for Care of Children; Council on School Broadcasting. *Publication:* Sources for History of the Highlands in the Seventeenth Century, 1939. *Recreation:* sport. *Address:* 12 Eriskay Road, Inverness IV2 3LX. *T:* Inverness 231566. *Club:* Royal Over-Seas House (Edinburgh).
See also R. N. M. MacLean.

McLEAN, John Alexander Lowry, QC 1974; Principal Secretary to Lord Chief Justice (formerly Permanent Secretary, Supreme Court of Northern Ireland) and Clerk of the Crown for Northern Ireland, since 1966; *b* 21 Feb. 1921; *o s* of John McLean and Phoebe Jane (*née* Bowditch); *m* 1950, Diana Elisabeth Campbell (*d* 1986), *e d* of S. B. Boyd Campbell, MC, MD, FRCP, and Mary Isabella Ayre, St John's, Newfoundland; one *s* two *d*. *Educ:* Methodist Coll., Belfast; Queen's University Belfast. Served Intell. Corps, 1943–47. Called to Bar of Northern Ireland, 1949. Asst Sec., NI Supreme Court, and Private Sec. to Lord Chief Justice of NI 1956; Under Treas., Hon. Soc. of Inn of Court of NI, 1966; Clerk of Restrictive Practices Court in NI, 1957. Member: Jt Working Party on Enforcement of Judgments of NI Courts, 1963; Lord Chancellor's Cttee on NI Supreme Court, 1966; Lord Chancellor's Foreign Judgments Working Party, 1974. *Publications:* contrib. legal periodicals. *Recreations:* not golf. *Address:* 24 Marlborough Park South, Belfast BT9 6HR. *T:* Belfast 667330; Lifeboat Cottage, Cloughey, Co. Down BT22 1HS. *T:* Portavogie 71313. *Club:* Royal Commonwealth Society.

MacLEAN, Hon. (John) Angus, PC 1957; DFC, CD; Premier of Prince Edward Island, 1979–81; *b* 15 May 1914; *s* of late George A. MacLean; *m* 1952, Gwendolyn Esther M. Burwash; two *s* two *d*. *Educ:* Mount Allison Academy; Summerside High Sch.; Univ. of British Columbia; Mount Allison Univ. BSc. Served War of 1939–45, RCAF: commanded Test and Development Estabt, 1943–45; Missing and Enquiry Unit, Europe, 1945–47, Wing Comdr (despatches). First elected to House of Commons by by-election, June 1951, re-elected 1953, 1957, 1958, 1962, 1963, 1965, 1968, 1972, 1974; Minister of Fisheries in the Diefenbaker Cabinet, 1957–63; elected Leader of PC Party of PEI, 1976; first elected to PEI Legislature at by-election, 1976, re-elected 1978 and 1979. PEI's Comr to EXPO '86. Mem. Royal Air Forces Escaping Soc. (Canadian Br.). Hon. LLD: Mount Allison Univ., 1958; Univ. of PEI, 1985. *Recreations:* genealogical research, bird watching. *Address:* Lewes, RR3, Belle River, Prince Edward Island COA 1B0, Canada. *T:* Murray River, PEI (902) 962–2235. *Clubs:* United Services, Charlottetown, RCAF Association, Masonic Lodge, AF and AM, Royal Canadian Legion, Charlottetown Chamber of Commerce, Canadian (PEI).

McLEAN, (John David) Ruari (McDowall Hardie), CBE 1973; DSC 1943; freelance typographer and author; *b* 10 June 1917; *s* of late John Thomson McLean and late Isabel Mary McLean (*née* Ireland); *m* 1945, Antonia Maxwell Carlisle; two *s* one *d*. *Educ:* Dragon Sch., Oxford; Eastbourne Coll. First studied printing under B. H. Newdigate at Shakespeare Head Press, Oxford, 1936. Industrial printing experience in Germany and England, 1936–38; with The Studio, 1938; Percy Lund Humphries, Bradford, 1939. Served Royal Navy, 1940–45. Penguin Books, 1945–46; Book Designer (freelance), 1946–53; Tutor in Typography, Royal College of Art, 1948–51; Typographic Adviser to Hulton Press, 1953; Founder Partner, Rainbird, McLean Ltd, 1951–58; Founder Editor, and Designer, Motif, 1958–67. Typographic Consultant to The Observer, 1960–64; Hon. Typographic Adviser to HM Stationery Office, 1966–80. Sandars Reader in Bibliography, Univ. of Cambridge, 1982–83; Alexander Stone Lectr in Bibliophily, Univ. of Glasgow, 1984. Member: Nat. Council for Diplomas in Art and Design, 1971; Vis. Cttee of RCA, 1977–83. Crown Trustee, Nat. Library of Scotland, 1981–. Croix de Guerre (French), 1942. *Publications:* George Cruikshank, 1948; Modern Book Design, 1958; Wood Engravings of Joan Hassall, 1960; Victorian Book Design, 1963, rev. edn 1972; Tschichold's Typographische Gestaltung (Trans.), 1967; (ed) The Reminiscences of Edmund Evans, 1967; Magazine Design, 1969; Victorian Publishers' Book-bindings in Cloth and Leather, 1973; Jan Tschichold, Typographer, 1975; Joseph Cundall, 1976; (ed) Edward Bawden: A Book of Cuts, 1979; Thames and Hudson Manual of Typography, 1980; Victorian Publishers' Book-Bindings in Paper, 1983. *Recreations:* sailing, reading, acquiring books. *Address:* Pier Cottage, Carsaig, Pennyghael, Isle of Mull. *Clubs:* Double Crown; New (Edinburgh).

McLEAN, Lieut-General Sir Kenneth Graeme, KCB 1954 (CB 1944); KBE 1951; US Legion of Merit, 1945; Officer, Legion of Honour (France); Croix de Guerre (France); *b* 11 Dec. 1896; *s* of late Arthur H. McLean, WS; *m* 1926, Daphne Winifred Ashburner Steele (*d* 1979); two *s*. *Educ:* Edinburgh Academy; RMA Woolwich. Commissioned RE 1918; served, in Ireland, 1919–20, and with KGO Bengal Sappers and Miners in India, 1923–29; Staff Coll., Quetta, 1930–31; on General Staff, AHQ, India, 1932–36; Assistant Secretary Cttee of Imperial Defence, 1938; Student at Imperial Defence Coll., 1939. Served France and Germany, 1944–45; Deputy Adjutant-General, GHQ, Far East, 1945–46; Dep. Adjutant-General, GHQ, Middle East, 1946; Vice-Adjutant-General, War Office, 1947–49; Chief of Staff, CCG, and Deputy Military Governor, British Zone in Germany, 1949; Military Secretary to the Secretary of State for War, 1949–51; Chief Staff Officer, Ministry of Defence, 1951–52; Special Duty, War Office, 1952–54. Retired, 1954. Colonel Comdt RE, 1956–61. *Address:* Greenways, Melrose, Roxburghshire.
See also I. G. McLean.

MacLEAN, Kenneth Smedley, MD, FRCP; Consultant Physician to Guy's Hospital, 1950–79, now Emeritus; *b* 22 Nov. 1914; *s* of Hugh MacLean and Ida Smedley; *m* 1939, Joan Hardaker; one *s* one *d* (and one *s* decd). *Educ:* Westminster; Clare Coll., Cambridge. MRCS, LRCP, 1939; House appts at Guy's, 1939; MB, BChir 1939. RNVR, 1939–46, Surg.-Lt and Surg.-Lt-Comdr. MRCP 1946; House Officer and Medical Registrar, Guy's Hosp., 1946–48; MD Cantab 1948; FRCP 1954; elected to Assoc. of Physicians of Great Britain and Ireland, 1956. Assistant Director, Dept of Medicine, Guy's Hospital Medical Sch., 1949, Director, 1961–63. Chm., University Hosps Assoc., 1975–78. Pres., Assurance Medical Soc., 1985–87. *Publication:* Medical Treatment, 1957. *Recreation:* golf. *Address:* 7 Icehouse Wood, Oxted, Surrey. *T:* Oxted 6652.

MacLEAN, Murdo; Private Secretary to the Government Chief Whip, since 1979; *b* 21 Oct. 1943; *s* of Murdo MacLean and Johanna (*née* Martin). *Educ:* Glasgow. Temp. Clerk, Min. of Labour Employment Exchange, Govan, Glasgow, 1963–64; BoT, 1964–67; Prime Minister's Office, 1967–72; Dept of Industry, 1972–78. *Address:* c/o 12 Downing Street, SW1. *T:* 01–219 3595/4400.

McLEAN, Lt-Col Neil Loudon Desmond, DSO 1943; *b* 28 Nov. 1918; *s* of Neil McLean; *m* 1949, Daška Kennedy (*née* Ivanović-Banac), Dubrovnik, Jugoslavia. *Educ:* Eton; RMC, Sandhurst. Gazetted Royal Scots Greys, 1938; Palestine Campaign, 1939; served War of 1939–45, Middle East and Far East: Ethiopia under 101 Mission, 1941; Head of First Military Mission to Albania, 1942 and 1943; Lieut-Colonel, 1943; Far East, 1944–45. Contested (C) Preston South, 1950 and 1951; MP (C) Inverness, Dec. 1954–Sept. 1964. Member Highland and Islands Advisory Panel, 1955. Member of Queen's Body Guard for Scotland, Royal Company of Archers. Distinguished Military Medal of Haile Selassie I, 1941. *Publications:* contributions to Chatham House, Royal Central Asian Society Reviews. *Recreations:* travel, riding, shooting, under-water fishing. *Address:* 5 Sheridan Court, Barkston Gardens, SW5. *Clubs:* White's, Buck's, Cavalry and Guards, Pratt's; Highland (Inverness).

McLEAN, Peter Standley, CMG 1985; OBE 1965; Head of East Asia Department, Overseas Development Administration, 1985–87; *b* 18 Jan. 1927; *s* of late William and Alice McLean; *m* 1954, Margaret Ann Minns; two *s* two *d*. *Educ:* King Edward's Sch., Birmingham; Wadham Coll., Oxford (MA). Served Army, 1944–48; Lieut, 15/19th King's Royal Hussars. Colonial Service, Uganda, 1951–65, retired from HMOCS as Permanent Sec., Min. of Planning and Economic Develt; Ministry of Overseas Development: Principal, 1965; Private Sec. to Minister for Overseas Develt, 1973; Head of Eastern and Southern Africa Dept, 1975; Head of Bilateral Aid and Rural Develt Dept, 1979; Minister and UK Perm. Rep to FAO, 1980. *Recreations:* watching sport, DIY, painting. *Address:* 17 Woodfield Lane, Ashtead, Surrey KT21 2BQ. *T:* Ashtead 78146.

McLEAN, Philip Alexander; HM Diplomatic Service; Head of South America Department, Foreign and Commonwealth Office, since 1985; *b* 24 Oct. 1938; *s* of late Wm Alexander McLean and of Doris McLean (*née* Campbell), *m* 1960, Dorothy Helen Kirkby; two *s* one *d. Educ*: King George V Sch., Southport; Keble Coll., Oxford (MA Hons). National Service, RAF, 1956–58. Industry, 1961–68; entered HM Diplomatic Service by Open Supplementary Competition, 1968; Second, later (1969) First, Secretary, FCO; La Paz, 1970–74: Head of Chancery, 1973; FCO, 1974–76; Dep. Director of British Trade Development Office and Head of Industrial Marketing, New York, 1976–80; Counsellor and Consul-Gen., Algiers, 1981–83; Diplomatic Service Inspector, 1983–85. *Recreation:* free time. *Address:* c/o Foreign and Commonwealth Office, SW1; Hill Cottage, Reading Road, Goring-on-Thames, near Reading RG8 0LH. *Club:* United Oxford & Cambridge University.

MacLEAN, Ranald Norman Munro, QC (Scot) 1977; *b* 18 Dec. 1938; *s* of John Alexander Maclean, *qv*; *m* 1963, Pamela Ross; two *s* one *d* (and one *s* decd). *Educ*: Inverness Royal Acad.; Fettes Coll.; Clare Coll., Cambridge Univ. (BA); Edinburgh Univ. (LLB); Yale Univ., USA (LLM). Called to the Scottish Bar, 1964. Advocate Depute, 1972–75, 1979–82, Home Advocate Depute, 1979–82; Standing Jun. Counsel, Health and Safety Exec. (Scotland), 1975–77; Mem., Council on Tribunals, 1985– (Chm., Scottish Cttee, 1985–). Mem., Stewart Cttee on Alternatives to Prosecution, 1977–82. Trustee, Nat. Library of Scotland. Governor, Fettes Coll., 1977–. *Publication:* (ed jtly) Gloag and Henderson, Introduction to the Law of Scotland, 7th edn 1968, 8th edn 1980. *Recreations:* hill walking, Munro collecting, birdwatching. *Address:* 12 Chalmers Crescent, Edinburgh EH9 1TS. *T:* 031–667 6217. *Club:* Scottish Arts (Edinburgh).

MACLEAN, Sir Robert (Alexander), KBE 1973; Kt 1955; DL; Honorary President, Stoddard Holdings Ltd; *b* 11 April 1908; *s* of Andrew Johnston Maclean, JP, Cambuslang, Lanarkshire, and Mary Jane Cameron; *m* 1938, Vivienne Neville Bourke, *d* of Captain Bertram Walter Bourke, JP, Heathfield, Co. Mayo; two *s* two *d. Educ*: High Sch. of Glasgow. JDipMA. President: Glasgow Chamber of Commerce, 1956–58; Association British Chambers of Commerce, 1966–68; Chairman: Council of Scottish Chambers of Commerce, 1960–62; Scottish Cttee, Council of Industrial Design, 1949–58 (Mem., CoID, 1948–58); Council of Management, Scottish Industries Exhibns, 1949, 1954 and 1959; Scottish Exports Cttee, 1966–70; Scottish Industrial Estates Corp., 1955–72 (Mem., 1946–72); Pres., British Industrial Exhibn, Moscow, 1966; Vice-Chm., Scottish Bd for Industry, 1952–60; Member: Pigs and Bacon Marketing Commn, 1955–56; BNEC, 1966–70; Scottish Aerodromes Bd, 1950–61; Export Council for Europe, 1960–64; BoT Trade Exhbns Adv. Cttee, 1961–65; Nat. Freight Corp., 1969–72; Regional Controller (Scotland): Board of Trade, 1944–46; Factory and Storage Premises, 1941–44. Director: Scottish Union & Nat. Insce Co., 1965–68; Scottish Adv. Bd, Norwich Union Insce Gp., 1965–81. Former Vice-Pres., Scottish Council (Develt and Industry), 1955–82. Trustee, Clyde Navigational Trust, 1956–58; Pres., Scottish Youth Clubs, 1959–68. DL Renfrewshire, 1970. CStJ 1975. FRSA; CBIM. Hon. LLD Glasgow, 1970. *Recreations:* golf, fishing. *Address:* South Branchal Farm, Bridge of Weir, Renfrewshire PA11 3SJ. *Clubs:* Carlton; Western (Glasgow).

McLEAN, Ruari; see McLean, J. D. R. McD. H.

McLEAN, Dr Thomas Pearson, FRSE, FInstP, CEng, FIEE; Director, Royal Armament Research and Development Establishment, Ministry of Defence, since 1984; *b* Paisley, 21 Aug. 1930; *s* of Norman Stewart McLean and Margaret Pearson McLean (*née* Ferguson); *m* 1957, Grace Campbell Nokes; two *d. Educ:* John Neilson Instn, Paisley; Glasgow Univ. (BSc, PhD); Birmingham Univ. Royal Radar Estabt (becoming Royal Signals and Radar Estabt, 1976), 1955–80: Head of Physics Gp, 1973–77; Dep. Dir, 1977–80; Under Sec., Dir Gen. Air Weapons and Electronic Systems, MoD, 1980–83. Member: Physics Cttee, SRC, 1968–73; Optoelectronics Cttee, Rank Prize Funds, 1972–81; Council, Inst. of Physics, 1980–84. Hon. Prof. of Physics, Birmingham Univ., 1977–80. Dep. Editor, Jl of Physics C, 1976–77. *Publications:* papers in Physical Rev., Jl of Physics, etc. *Recreations:* music, Scottish country dancing. *Address:* 42 Strickland Way, Orpington, Kent. *T:* Orpington 25816.

MacLEARY, Donald Whyte; principal male dancer with the Royal Ballet since 1959; Repetiteur to the Principal Artists, Royal Ballet, since 1981; *b* Glasgow, 22 Aug. 1937; *s* of Donald Herbert MacLeary, MPS, and Jean Spiers (*née* Leslie). *Educ:* Inverness Royal Academy; The Royal Ballet School. Ballet Master, Royal Ballet, 1975–81. *Classical Ballets:* (full length) Swan Lake, Giselle, 1958; Sleeping Beauty, Cinderella, Sylvia, 1959; Ondine, La Fille Mal Gardée, 1960; (centre male rôle) in Ashton's Symphonic Variations, 1962; Sonnet Pas de Trois, 1964; Romeo and Juliet, 1965; Eugene Onegin, Stuttgart, 1966; Apollo, 1966; Nutcracker, 1968; Swan Lake with N. Makarova, 1972. *Creations:* (1954–74): Solitaire, The Burrow, Danse Concertante, Antigone, Diversions, Le Baiser de la Fée, Jabez and the Devil, Raymonda Pas de Deux (for Frederick Ashton), two episodes in Images of Love; Song of the Earth; Lilac Garden (revival); Jazz Calendar; Raymonda (for Nureyeff); The Man in Kenneth MacMillan's Checkpoint; leading role in Concerto no 2 (Balanchine's Ballet Imperial, renamed); Elite Syncopations, 1974; Kenneth MacMillan's Four Seasons Symphony; the Prince in Cinderella. Toured Brazil with Royal Ballet, Spring 1973. Guest dancer, Scottish Ballet, 1979. *Recreations:* reading, theatre, records (all types); riding, fox hunting, swimming. *Address:* Bunyans Cottage, Wainwood, Preston, Herts; Casa Svetlana, Quinta do Lazo, Algarve, Portugal. *Club:* Queen's.

MACLEHOSE, family name of **Baron MacLehose of Beoch.**

MACLEHOSE OF BEOCH, Baron *cr* 1982 (Life Peer), of Maybole in the District of Kyle and Carrick, and of Victoria in Hong Kong; **Crawford Murray MacLehose,** KT 1983; GBE 1976 (MBE 1946); KCMG 1971 (CMG 1964); KCVO 1975; DL; HM Diplomatic Service, retired; Director, National Westminster Bank, since 1982; Chairman, Victoria League of Commonwealth Friendship, since 1983; *b* 16 Oct. 1917; *s* of Hamish A. MacLehose and Margaret Bruce Black; *m* 1947, Margaret Noël Dunlop; two *d. Educ:* Rugby; Balliol Coll., Oxford. Served War of 1939–45, Lieut, RNVR. Joined Foreign Service, 1947; Acting Consul, 1947, Acting Consul-General, 1948, Hankow; promoted First Secretary, 1949; transferred to Foreign Office, 1950; First Secretary (Commercial), and Consul, Prague, 1951; seconded to Commonwealth Relations Office, for service at Wellington, 1954; returned to Foreign Office and transferred to Paris, 1956; promoted Counsellor, 1959; seconded to Colonial Office and transferred to Hong Kong as Political Adviser; Counsellor, Foreign Office, 1963; Principal Private Secretary to Secretary of State, 1965–67; Ambassador: to Vietnam, 1967–69; to Denmark, 1969–71; Governor and C-in-C, Hong Kong, 1971–82. Chairman: Scottish Trust for the Physically Disabled, 1982–; Margaret Blackwood Housing Assoc., 1982–. Chm. Govs, SOAS, Univ. of London, 1985–. DL Ayr and Arran, 1983. KStJ 1972. *Recreations:* sailing, fishing. *Address:* Beoch, Maybole, Ayrshire. *Clubs:* Athenæum; New (Edinburgh).

MacLELLAN, Maj.-Gen. (Andrew) Patrick (Withy), CB 1981; MBE 1964; Resident Governor and Keeper of the Jewel House, HM Tower of London, since 1984; *b* 29 Nov. 1925; *y s* of late Kenneth MacLellan and Rachel Madeline MacLellan (*née* Withy); *m* 1954, Kathleen Mary Bagnell; one *s* twin *d. Educ:* Uppingham. Commnd Coldstream

Guards, 1944; served Palestine 1945–48, N Africa 1950–51, Egypt 1952–53, Germany 1955–56; psc 1957; DAA&QMG 4th Guards Brigade Group, 1958–59; Mil. Asst to Chief of Defence Staff, 1961–64; Instructor, Staff Coll., Camberley, 1964–66; GSO1 (Plans) Far East Comd, 1966–67; CO 1st Bn Coldstream Guards, 1968–70; Col GS Near East Land Forces, 1970–71; Comdr 8th Inf. Brigade, 1971–72; RCDS 1973; Dep. Comdr and COS, London District, 1974–77; Pres., Regular Commns Bd, 1978–80. Chevalier de la Légion d'Honneur, 1960. *Address:* Queen's House, HM Tower of London, EC3N 4AB. *Clubs:* White's, Pratt's.

McLELLAN, Prof. David; DPhil; Professor of Political Theory, University of Kent, since 1975; *b* 10 Feb. 1940; *s* of Robert Douglas McLellan and Olive May Bush; *m* 1967, Annie Brassart; two *d. Educ:* Merchant Taylors' Sch.; St John's Coll., Oxford (MA, DPhil). Lectr in Politics, Univ. of Kent, 1966–71; Vis. Prof., State Univ. of New York, 1969; Guest Fellow in Politics, Indian Inst. of Advanced Studies, Simla, 1970; Sen. Lectr in Politics, Univ. of Kent, 1972, Reader in Political Theory, 1973. *Publications:* The Young Hegelians and Karl Marx, 1969 (French, German, Italian, Spanish and Japanese edns); Marx before Marxism, 1970, 2nd edn 1972; Karl Marx: The Early Texts, 1971; Marx's Grundrisse, 1971, 2nd edn 1973; The Thought of Karl Marx, 1971 (Portuguese and Italian edns); Karl Marx: His Life and Thought, 1973, 22nd edn 1976 (German, Italian, Spanish, Japanese, Swedish and Dutch edns); Marx (Fontana Modern Masters), 1975; Engels, 1977; Marxism after Marx, 1979; (ed) Marx: the first hundred years, 1983; Karl Marx: the legacy, 1983; Ideology, 1986. *Recreations:* chess, Raymond Chandler, hill walking. *Address:* Eliot College, University of Kent, Canterbury, Kent CT2 7NS. *T:* Canterbury 66822.

McLELLAN, His Honour Eric Burns; a Circuit Judge (formerly County Court Judge), 1970–86; *b* 9 April 1918; *s* of late Stanley Morgan McLellan, Christchurch, Newport, Mon; *m* 1949, Elsa Sarah, *d* of late Gustave Mustaki, Alexandria; one *s* one *d. Educ:* Newport High Sch.; New Coll., Oxford. BA 1939; MA 1967. Served RAF, 1940–46, N Africa, Italy, Egypt, 205 Group; Flt-Lt. Called to Bar, Inner Temple, 1947. Dep. Chm., IoW QS, 1967–72. Official Principal, Archdeaconry of Hackney, 1967–72; Dep. Chm., Workmen's Compensation Supplementation Bd and Pneumoconiosis, Byssinosis and Miscellaneous Diseases Benefit Bd, 1969–70; Mem., Dept of Health and Social Security Adv. Group on Use of Fetuses and Fetal Material for Research, 1970. Governor, Portsmouth Grammar Sch., 1980–. *Publications:* contribs to medico-legal jls. *Recreations:* heraldry and genealogy. *Address:* Lone Barn, Catherington, Hants PO8 0SF. *T:* Hambledon 436. *Clubs:* United Oxford & Cambridge University, Royal Air Force; Leander (Henley-on-Thames).

MacLELLAN, Prof. George Douglas Stephen, MA, PhD (Cantab); CEng; FIMechE, FIEE; Professor and Head of Department of Engineering, University of Leicester, since 1965; *b* Glasgow, 1 Nov. 1922; *e s* of late Alexander Stephen MacLellan. *Educ:* Rugby Sch.; Pembroke Coll., Cambridge. Mech. Sci. Tripos, 1942. Dept of Colloid Science, Cambridge, and Callenders Cable and Construction Co. Ltd, 1942–44; Fellow, Pembroke Coll., 1944–59; Vickers-Armstrong Ltd, Newcastle upon Tyne, 1944–46; University Demonstrator and Lecturer in Engineering, Cambridge, 1947–59; Rankine Professor of Mechanical Engineering (Mechanics and Mechanism), University of Glasgow, 1959–65. Commonwealth Fund Fellow, MIT, 1948–49; Visiting Professor: Michigan State University, 1958; MIT, 1962; NTI, Singapore, 1986. Pres. of the Soc. of Instrument Technology, 1964–65. Member: CNAA, 1970–80; Engrg Bd, SRC, 1971–74; Vis. Cttee, RCA, 1973–82; Council, IMechE, 1974–76; Nominations Cttee, Engrg Council, 1984–; Council, Loughborough Univ. of Technology, 1979–; Chm., Engrg Professors' Conference, 1983–85. *Publications:* contribs to mech. and elec. jls. *Address:* Department of Engineering, The University, Leicester LE1 7RH. *T:* Leicester 554455. *Clubs:* Athenæum, Leander.

MacLELLAN, Sir (George) Robin (Perronet), Kt 1980; CBE 1969; JP; Chairman: Scottish Industrial and Trade Exhibitions Ltd, since 1981 (Director, 1975–79); Bield Housing Trust, Edinburgh, since 1982; Scottish Tourist Board, 1974–80; *b* 14 Nov. 1915; *e s* of George Aikman MacLellan, Glasgow, and Irene Dorothy Perronet Miller, Liverpool; *m* 1941, Margaret, *er d* of Dr Berkeley Robertson, Glasgow; one *s. Educ:* Ardvreck Sch., Crieff; Clifton Coll.; Ecole de Commerce, Lausanne. Chm., George MacLellan Hldgs Ltd, 1965–76; Dep. Chm., British Airports Authority, 1965–75; Pres., Glasgow Chamber of Commerce, 1970–71; Mem., Scottish Industrial Develt Bd, 1972–74. Director: Scottish National Trust plc, 1970–85; Govan Shipbuilders Ltd, 1972–74; Nationwide Building Society, 1971–84; British Tourist Authority, 1974–80; Melville Retirement Homes Ltd, Edinburgh, 1983–. Chm., Crossroads (Scotland) Care Attendant Scheme, 1984–. Dir and Chm. of Governors, Ardvreck Sch. Ltd, 1970–83; Governor, Clifton Coll.; Mem. Council, Scottish Business Sch., 1972–75; Mem. Court, Strathclyde Univ., 1972–76. Member: West Central Scotland Plan Steering Cttee, 1970–75; Scottish Econ. Council, 1968–75; BNEC's Cttee for Exports to Canada, 1964–69; Council, Nat. Trust for Scotland, 1974– (Dep. Chm., 1980–85; Counsellor Emeritus, 1986–); Gen. Adv. Council, IBA, 1976–79; BR Adv. Bd (Scottish), 1977–81. Pres., Soc. of Friends of Glasgow Cathedral, 1978–. A Vice-Pres., Assoc. British Chambers of Commerce, 1975–80; Pres., Inst. of Marketing (Strathclyde Branch), 1980–85; Senior Industrialist, Design Advisory Service, Design Council (funded consultancy scheme), 1983–. Pres., Old Cliftonian Soc., 1983–85. Trustee, Mental Health Foundn, 1982–86. Hon. FRCPS Glas, 1979. JP Dunbartonshire, 1973. OStJ 1972. *Publications:* articles on travel and tourism. *Recreations:* swimming, angling, travelling, keeping friendships in good repair, happy retirement. *Address:* 11 Beechwood Court, Bearsden, Glasgow G61 2RY. *T:* 041–942 3876. *Clubs:* Western (Glasgow); RNVR (Scotland).

MacLELLAN, Maj.-Gen. Patrick; see MacLellan, A. P. W.

MacLELLAN, Sir Robin; see MacLellan, Sir G. R. P.

McLELLAND, Charles James; Deputy Managing Director, BBC Radio, 1980–86; *b* 19 Nov. 1930; *s* of Charles John McLelland and Jessie Steele Barbour; *m* 1961, Philippa Mary Murphy; one *s* three *d. Educ:* Kilmarnock Acad.; Glasgow Acad.; Glasgow Univ. (MA). Commissioned Royal Artillery, 1952–54. Sub-Editor, Leader Writer, Glasgow Herald, 1954–58; Scriptwriter, European Productions, BBC, 1958–61; Head of Programmes, Radio Sarawak, 1962–64; Indian Programme Organiser, BBC, 1964–67; Asst Head, Arabic Service, BBC, 1967–71; Head of Arabic Service, 1971–75; Controller, BBC Radio 2, 1976–80 (also Radio 1, 1976–78). Chm., EBU Radio Prog. Cttee, 1985–86; Pres., Overseas Broadcasters' Club, 1985–. *Recreations:* gardening, reading, flying. *Address:* 79 Gayville Road, SW11 6JW. *Club:* Travellers'.

MacLENNAN, Maj.-Gen. Alastair, OBE 1945; Curator, Royal Army Medical Corps Historical Museum, Mytchett, Hants, 1969–Feb. 1977; *b* 16 Feb. 1912; *s* of Col. Farquhar MacLennan, DSO; *m* 1940, Constance Anne Cook; two *s* one *d. Educ:* Aberdeen Grammar Sch.; University of Aberdeen (MB, ChB). Commissioned Lieut, RAMC, 1934; Captain, 1935; Major, 1942; Lieut-Colonel, 1942; Colonel, 1952; Brigadier, 1964; Maj.-General, 1967; retired 1969. Appointments held include regimental, staff and Ministry of Defence in UK, Malta, NW Europe, India, Malaya, Korea, Egypt and Germany; ADGMS (Army),

Min. of Defence, 1957–61; DDMS, HQ, BAOR, 1961–64; Inspector Army Medical Services, 1964–66; DDMS: 1 (Br) Corps, 1966–67; HQ Eastern Command, 1967–68; Dep. Dir-Gen., Army Med. Services, MoD, 1968–69; Col Comdt, RAMC, 1971–76. US Bronze Star Medal, 1952. OStJ, 1966. QHP, 1968–69. *Publications:* papers on history of military firearms and on Highland Regts in North America 1756–1783. *Recreations:* bird-watching, military history, collecting antique military firearms and swords, vintage motor-cars. *Address:* Gable House, Chequers Lane, North Crawley, Bucks MK16 9LJ. *T:* North Crawley 700.

McLENNAN, Gordon; General Secretary, Communist Party of Great Britain, since 1975; *b* Glasgow, 12 May 1924; *s* of a shipyard worker; *m*; four *c.* *Educ:* Hamilton Crescent Sch., Partick, Glasgow. Engineering apprentice, Albion Motors Ltd, Scotstoun, 1939, later engineering draughtsman. Elected Glasgow Organiser, Communist Party, 1949; Sec., Communist Party in Scotland, 1957; Nat. Organiser, Communist Party of GB, 1966. *Recreations:* golf and other sports; cultural interests. *Address:* 16 St John Street, EC1M 4AL.

MacLENNAN, Hugh; CC (Canada) 1967; Professor, English Literature, McGill University, 1967–79 (Associate Professor, 1951–67), now Professor Emeritus; *b* 20 March 1907; *s* of Dr Samuel John MacLennan and Katherine MacQuarrie; *m* 1st, 1936, Dorothy Duncan (*d* 1957); 2nd, 1959, Frances Aline, *d* of late Frank Earle Walker and Isabella Scott Benson. *Educ:* Dalhousie Univ.; Oriel Coll., Oxford; Graduate Coll., Princeton. Rhodes Schol. (Canada at large), 1928; PhD (Princeton) 1935. Classics Master, Lower Canada Coll., Montreal, 1935–45; writing, 1945–51. FRS Canada, 1953 (Gold Medal, 1951); FRSL, 1959. Governor-General's Award for Fiction, 1945, 1948, 1959; Governor-General's Award for non-fiction, 1949, 1954. Hon. DLitt: Waterloo Lutheran, 1961; Carleton Univ., 1967; Western Ontario, 1953, Manitoba, 1955; Hon. LLD: Dalhousie, 1956, Saskatchewan, 1959; McMaster, 1965; Toronto, 1966; Laurentian, 1966; Sherbrooke, 1967; British Columbia, 1968; St Mary's, 1968; Hon. DCL Bishop's, 1965. *Publications:* Oxyrhynchus: An Economic and Social Study, 1935; Barometer Rising, 1941; Two Solitudes, 1945; The Precipice, 1948; Cross Country (essays), 1949; Each Man's Son, 1951; Thirty and Three (essays), 1954; The Watch That Ends The Night, 1959; Scotchman's Return (essays), 1960; Return of the Sphinx, 1967; Rivers of Canada, 1974; Voices in Time, 1980. *Recreations:* walking, gardening. *Address:* 1535 Summerhill Avenue, Montreal, PQ, Canada. *T:* 932–0475. *Clubs:* Montreal Amateur Athletic Association, McGill Faculty (Montreal).

MACLENNAN, Sir Ian (Morrison Ross), KCMG 1957 (CMG 1951); HM Diplomatic Service, retired; *b* 30 Oct. 1909; *s* of late W. Maclennan, Glasgow; *m* 1936, Margherita Lucas, *d* of late F. Lucas Jarratt, Bedford; one *s* one *d.* *Educ:* Hymers Coll., Hull; Worcester Coll., Oxford. Appointed Colonial Office, 1933; Dominions Office, 1937; UK High Commissioner's Office, Ottawa, 1938; Pretoria, 1945; UK High Commissioner S Rhodesia, 1951–53; Federation of Rhodesia and Nyasaland, 1953–55; Assistant Under-Secretary of State, CRO, 1955–57; UK High Commissioner in Ghana, 1957–59; Ambassador to the Republic of Ireland, 1960–63; High Commissioner in New Zealand, 1964–69. Mem., Gen. Adv. Council, IBA, 1974–82 (Chm., 1979–82). *Address:* 26 Ham Street, Richmond, Surrey. *Club:* Travellers'.

McLENNAN, Sir Ian (Munro), KCMG 1979; KBE 1963 (CBE 1956); President, Australian Academy of Technological Sciences, 1976–83, The Foundation President, since 1983; *b* 30 Nov. 1909; *s* of R. B. and C. O. McLennan; *m* 1937, Dora H., *d* of J. H. Robertson; two *s* two *d.* *Educ:* Scotch Coll., Melbourne; Melbourne Univ. Broken Hill Pty Co. Ltd: Cadet engineer, 1933; Asst Manager, Newcastle Steelworks of BHP Co. Ltd, 1943; Asst Gen. Man., BHP Co. Ltd, 1947; Gen. Man., 1950; Sen. Gen. Man., 1956; Chief Gen. Man., 1959; Man. Dir, 1967–71; Chm., 1971–77; Chairman: BHP-GKN Hldgs Ltd, 1970–78; Tubemakers of Australia Ltd, 1973–79; Australia and New Zealand Banking Group Ltd, and Australia and New Zealand Group Hldgs Ltd, 1977–82; Interscan Australia Pty Ltd, 1978–84; Bank of Adelaide, 1979–80; Henry Jones IXL Ltd, 1981; Elders IXL Ltd, 1981–85; Dir, ICI Australia Ltd, 1976–79. Chairman: Defence (Industrial) Cttee, 1956–75; Ian Clunies Ross Meml Foundn; Australian Mineral Development Laboratories, 1959–67, Mem. Council, 1959–77; Dep. Chm., Immigration Planning Council, 1949–67. Former Dir, International Iron and Steel Inst.; Pres., Australia-Japan Business Co-operation Cttee, 1977–85; Member: Internat. Council, Morgan Guaranty Trust Co. of NY, 1973–79; Australian Mining Industry Council, 1967–77; Australasian Inst. of Mining and Metallurgy (Pres., 1951, 1957 and 1972); Australian Mineral Industries Research Assoc. Ltd, 1958–77; General Motors Australian Adv. Council, 1978–82; Adv. Council, CSIRO, 1979–82. Chm., Queen Elizabeth II Jubilee Trust for Young Australians, 1978–81. For. Associate, Nat. Acad. of Engrg (USA), 1978. FIAM 1978; FAA 1980. *Recreations:* golf, gardening. *Address:* Apt 3, 112–120 Walsh Street, South Yarra, Victoria 3141, Australia. *Clubs:* Melbourne, Athenæum, Australian (all Melbourne); Union (Sydney); Newcastle (Newcastle); Commonwealth (Canberra); Royal Melbourne Golf; Melbourne Cricket.

MACLENNAN, Robert Adam Ross; MP Caithness and Sutherland since 1966 (Lab, 1966–81, SDP, since 1981); Barrister-at-Law; *b* 26 June 1936; *e s* of late Sir Hector MacLennan and Isabel Margaret Adam; *m* 1968, Mrs Helen Noyes, *d* of Judge Ammi Cutter, Cambridge, Mass, and *widow* of Paul H. Noyes; one *s* one *d*, and one step *s.* *Educ:* Glasgow Academy; Balliol Coll., Oxford; Trinity Coll., Cambridge; Columbia Univ., New York City. Called to the Bar, Gray's Inn, 1962. Parliamentary Private Secretary: to Secretary of State for Commonwealth Affairs, 1967–69; to Minister without Portfolio, 1969–70; an Opposition Spokesman: on Scottish Affairs, 1970–71; on Defence, 1971–72; Parly Under-Sec. of State, Dept of Prices and Consumer Protection, 1974–79; opposition spokesman on foreign affairs, 1980–81; SDP spokesman: on agriculture, fisheries and food; on home and legal affairs; Member: House of Commons Estimates Cttee, 1967–69; House of Commons Select Cttee on Scottish Affairs, 1969–70; Public Accounts Cttee, 1979–; Latey Cttee on Age of Majority, 1968; National and Policy Cttees of SDP, 1981–. *Recreations:* theatre, music, the 2,800 square miles of my constituency. *Address:* 74 Abingdon Villas, W8; Hollandmake, Barrock, Caithness.

MacLENNAN OF MacLENNAN, Ronald George; 34th Chief of Clan MacLennan; Chairman, Kintail Museum Company, since 1983; teacher of and lecturer in physical education, 1949–82, retired; *b* 7 Feb. 1925; *s* of George Mitchell MacLennan and Helen Ames Thomson; recognised as Chief of Clan MacLennan, 1978; *m* 1970, Margaret, 2nd *d* of Donald and Jemima MacLennan; one *s* two *d.* *Educ:* Boroughmuir Secondary Sch., Edinburgh; Univ. of Copenhagen (Dip. in Physical Educn). Served War, 1939–45. Editor, Clan MacLennan Newsletter, 1971–. Mem., Standing Council of Scottish Chiefs, 1978–. FSAScot 1969; FRHistS 1970; FRSA 1982. Hon. Col, Oregon National Guard, 1981–; Hon. Ambassador of Scotland to Poland, London, 1981–; Hon. Brig.-Gen., Polish Armed Forces (in exile), 1982–. Hon. DLitt London, 1984. Kt, Order of St Lazarus of Jerusalem, 1976; Kt Comdr's Cross, Order of Polonia Restituta, 1981; Order of Virtuti Militari (1st cl., 1939–45), Poland, 1982; several international knighthoods (including Kt Niadh Nask, 1983 and Kt Grand Cross and Collar, Imperial Constantinian Military Order of St George, 1986), and many other honours, govt and civic receptions, etc, in USA, Canada and Australia. *Publication:* History of the MacLennans, 1978. *Recreations:* history, gardening, kayaking. *Heir:* *s* Ruairidh Donald George MacLennan, yr of MacLennan, *b* 22 April 1977. *Address:* The Old Mill, Dores, Inverness. *T:* Dores 228.

MacLEOD, family name of **Baron MacLeod of Fuinary.**

MACLEOD, family name of **Baroness Macleod of Borve.**

MACLEOD OF BORVE, Baroness *cr* 1971 (Life Peer), of Borve, Isle of Lewis; **Evelyn Hester Macleod,** JP; DL; *b* 19 Feb. 1915; *d* of Rev. Gervase Vanneck Blois (*d* 1961), and Hon. Hester Murray Pakington (*d* 1973), *y d* of 3rd Baron Hampton; *m* 1st, 1937, Mervyn Charles Mason (killed by enemy action, 1940); 2nd, 1941, Rt Hon. Iain Norman Macleod, MP (Minister of Health, 1952–55; Minister of Labour and Nat. Service, 1955–59; Secretary of State for the Colonies, 1959–61; Chancellor of the Duchy of Lancaster and Leader of the House of Commons, 1961–63; Chancellor of the Exchequer, June 1970) (*d* 1970), *e s* of late Norman A. Macleod, MD, Scaliscro, Isle of Lewis; one *s* one *d.* Chairman, Nat. Association of the Leagues of Hospital Friends; first Chm., Nat. Gas Consumers' Council, 1972–77; Member: IBA (formerly ITA), 1972–75; Energy Commn, 1977–78; Metrication Bd, 1978–80. Founder, Crisis at Christmas, 1967; Pres., Nat. Assoc. of Widows, 1976–. Governor, Queenswood Sch., 1978–85. JP Middlesex, 1955; DL Greater London, 1977. *Recreation:* my family. *Address:* House of Lords, SW1; Luckings Farm, Coleshill, Amersham, Bucks.

MacLEOD OF FUINARY, Baron, *cr* 1967 (Life Peer), of Fuinary in Morven; **Very Rev. George Fielden MacLeod,** Bt, 1924; MC; BA Oxford; DD (Glasgow); Moderator of the General Assembly of the Church of Scotland, May 1957–May 1958 (designation, Very Rev.); Founder of the Iona Community (Leader, 1938–67); one of Her Majesty's Chaplains in Scotland; *b* 17 June 1895; 2nd *s* of Sir John MacLeod, 1st Bt; *S* nephew, 1944; *m* 1948, Lorna Helen Janet (*d* 1984), *er d* of late Rev. Donald Macleod, Balvonie of Inshes, Inverness; two *s* one *d.* *Educ:* Winchester; Oriel Coll., Oxford (Hon. Fellow 1969); Edinburgh Univ. Post Graduate Fellow, Union Theological Coll., New York, 1921; Missioner, British Columbia Lumber Camps, 1922; Collegiate Minister, St Cuthbert's Parish Church, Edinburgh, 1926–30; Minister of Govan Parish Church, Glasgow, 1930–38; served European War, 1914–18; Captain Argyll and Sutherland Highlanders (MC and Croix de Guerre); Warrack Lecturer on Preaching at Edinburgh and St Andrews Universities, 1936; Select Preacher, Cambridge Univ., 1943 and 1963; Cunningham Lecturer on Evangelism, 1954; first holder of Fosdick Professorship (Rockefeller Foundation), Union Theological Seminary, New York, 1954–55; Danforth Lecturer, USA Universities, 1960 and 1964. Rector of Glasgow Univ., 1968–71. Pres. and Chm. of Council of International Fellowship of Reconciliation, 1963. DLitt Muskingum Univ., USA; Dr of Laws, Iona Coll., New Rochelle, USA. *Publications:* Govan Calling: a book of Broadcast Sermons and Addresses, 1934; contributor to Way to God Series for the BBC; Speaking the Truth in Love: a book on Preaching, 1936; We Shall Rebuild (the principles of the Iona Community), 1944; Only One Way Left, 1956. *Heir* (to Baronetcy only): *s* Hon. John Maxwell Norman MacLeod, *b* 23 Feb. 1952. *Address:* 23 Learmonth Terrace, Edinburgh EH4 1PG. *T:* 031–332 3262.

MacLEOD, Angus, CBE 1967; Hon. Sheriff of Lothians and Peebles, since 1972; Procurator Fiscal of Edinburgh and Midlothian, 1955–71; *b* 2 April 1906; *s* of late Alexander MacLeod, Glendale, Skye; *m* 1936, Jane Winifred (*d* 1977), *d* of late Sir Robert Bryce Walker, CBE, LLD; three *s.* *Educ:* Hutchesons Grammar Sch.; Glasgow Univ. (MA, LLB). Solicitor, 1929; general practice, 1929–34; Depute Procurator Fiscal, Glasgow and Edinburgh, 1934–42; Procurator Fiscal of Dumfriesshire, 1942–52, of Aberdeenshire, 1952–55; Temp. Sheriff, Scotland, 1973–77. Part-time Chm., VAT Appeal Tribunals, 1973–77. *Recreations:* reading, walking, interested in sport. *Address:* 7 Oxford Terrace, Edinburgh EH4 1PX. *T:* 031–332 5466.

MacLEOD, Aubrey Seymour H.; *see* Halford-MacLeod.

McLEOD, Sir Charles Henry, 3rd Bt, *cr* 1925; *b* 7 Nov. 1924; *o surv. s* of Sir Murdoch Campbell McLeod, 2nd Bt, and Annette Susan Mary (*d* 1964), *d* of Henry Whitehead, JP, 26 Pelham Crescent, SW7; *S* father 1950; *m* 1957, Gillian (*d* 1978), *d* of Henry Bowlby, London; one *s* two *d.* *Educ:* Winchester. *Heir:* *s* James Roderick Charles McLeod, *b* 26 Sept. 1960.

MacLEOD, Donald Alexander; HM Diplomatic Service; Deputy High Commissioner, Bridgetown, since 1984; *b* 23 Jan. 1938; *er s* of late Col Colin S. MacLeod of Glendale, OBE, TD, and of Margaret Drysdale Robertson MacLeod; *m* 1963, Rosemary Lilian Abel (*née* Randle); two *s* two *d.* *Educ:* Edinburgh Academy; Pembroke Coll., Cambridge, 1958–61 (BA). National Service, Queen's Own Cameron Highlanders, 1956–58. HM Foreign Service, 1961; School of Oriental and African Studies, London, 1961–62; British Embassy, Rangoon, 1962–66; Private Sec. to Minister of State, Commonwealth Office, 1966–69; First Secretary, Ottawa, 1969–73; FCO, 1973–78; First Sec./Head of Chancery, Bucharest, 1978–80; Counsellor (Econ. and Commercial), Singapore, 1981–84. *Address:* c/o Foreign and Commonwealth Office, SW1. *Club:* United Oxford & Cambridge University.

MacLEOD, Air Vice-Marshal Donald Francis Graham, CB 1977; Director of Royal Air Force Dental Services, 1973–77, retired; *b* Stornoway, Isle of Lewis, Scotland, 26 Aug. 1917; *s* of Alexander MacLeod; both parents from Isle of Lewis; *m* 1941, Marjorie Eileen (*née* Gracie); one *s* one *d.* *Educ:* Nicolson Inst., Stornoway, Isle of Lewis; St Andrews Univ.; Royal Coll. of Surgeons, Edinburgh. LDS St And. 1940; FDS RCSEd 1955. Qualif. in Dental Surgery, 1940; two years in private practice. Joined Royal Air Force Dental Branch, 1942; served in various parts of the world, mainly in hospitals doing oral surgery. QHDS, 1972. Royal Humane Society Resuscitation Certificate for life saving from the sea in the Western Isles, 1937. *Recreations:* golf, gardening; Captain of Soccer, St Andrews Univ., 1938 (full blue), Captain of Badminton, 1939 (half blue). *Address:* 20 Witchford Road, Ely, Cambs CB6 3DP. *T:* Ely 3164. *Club:* Royal Worlington Golf.

MacLEOD, Hugh Roderick; Chairman, Lloyd's Register of Shipping, since 1983; *b* 20 Sept. 1929; *s* of Neil MacLeod and Ruth MacLeod (*née* Hill); *m* 1958, Josephine Seager Berry (marr. diss. 1985); two *s* one *d.* *Educ:* Bryanston Sch.; St John's Coll., Cambridge. Served 2nd Regt, RHA, 1948–50. Joined The Ben Line Steamers Limited, 1953, Jt Man. Dir, 1964–82; Partner, Wm Thomson & Co., 1959, Director, 1964; Chairman, Associated Container Transportation Ltd, 1975–78. Member: Leith Docks Commn, 1960–65; Forth Ports Authority, 1967–70; National Ports Council, 1977–80; (pt-time) BRB, 1980–86. Chm., Scottish Bd, BR, 1980–82. *Recreations:* outdoor pursuits, music. *Address:* 14 Dawson Place, W2.

McLEOD, Sir Ian (George), Kt 1984; JP; Managing Director, EDP Services Computer Bureau, since 1964; *b* 17 Oct. 1926; *s* of George Gunn McLeod; *m* 1950, Audrey Davis; two *d.* *Educ:* Kearsney College, Natal; Natal University; ACIS. Played for Rosslyn Park Rugby Team, 1951. Chm., London Transport Passengers Cttee, 1979–83; Board Mem., SE Electricity Board, 1983–. Chairman: Croydon Central Cons. Assoc., 1973–76; Greater London Area Conservatives, 1981–84; Cons. Policy Gp for London, 1984–; Vice-Chm.,

Nat. Union of Cons. and Unionist Assocs, 1985–; Mem., Nat. Union Exec. Cttee, Cons. Party, 1974–; Mem., Croydon Borough Council, 1974–78; Dep. Mayor, 1976–77. Governor, Old Palace Girls' Sch., Croydon. JP SE London, 1977. *Recreations:* politics, reading history. *Address:* Pine Ridge, Pine Coombe, Shirley Hills, Croydon, Surrey. *T:* 01–654 4869. *Clubs:* Carlton, MCC.

McLEOD, Rev. John; Church of Scotland Minister, Livingston Ecumenical Team Ministry, since 1974; Chaplain to the Queen in Scotland, since 1978; *b* 8 April 1926; *s* of Angus McLeod and Catherine McDougall; *m* 1958, Sheila McLeod; three *s* two *d. Educ:* Inverness Royal Academy; Edinburgh Univ. (MA); New Coll., Edinburgh. Farming until 1952; at university, 1952–58; ordained, Inverness, 1958. Missionary in India: Jalna, 1959–68; Poona, 1969–74; involved in rural development with special emphasis on development and conservation of water resource; also responsible for pastoral work in Church of N India, St Mary's, Poona, 1970–74; Warden of Nether Dechmont Farm Community Centre, 1977–81. *Recreations:* hill walking, gardening, swimming, music. *Address:* 53 Harburn Avenue, Deans, Livingston, West Lothian EH54 8NH. *T:* Livingston 412392.

MacLEOD OF MacLEOD, John; 29th Chief of MacLeod; *b* 10 Aug. 1935; second *s* of late Captain Robert Wolrige-Gordon, MC, and Joan, *d* of Hubert Walter and Dame Flora MacLeod of MacLeod, DBE; officially recognised in name of MacLeod of MacLeod by decree of Lyon Court, 1951; *S* grandmother, 1976; *m* 1973, Melita Kolin; one *s* one *d. Educ:* Eton. *Heir: s* Hugh Magnus MacLeod, younger of MacLeod. *Address:* Dunvegan Castle, Isle of Skye. *T:* Dunvegan 206.
See also P. Wolrige-Gordon.

McLEOD, Keith Morrison, CBE 1975; Financial Controller, British Airports Authority, 1971–75; *b* 26 May 1920; *yr s* of John and Mary McLeod; *m* 1943, Patricia Carter; two *s* one *d. Educ:* Bancroft's School. FCIT. Asst Auditor, Exchequer and Audit Dept, 1939; served RAF, 1941–46; Asst Principal, Min. of Supply, 1948; Principal, 1950; BJSM, Washington, 1955–57; Asst Sec., Min. of Supply, 1957; Cabinet Office, 1962; Finance Dir, British Airports Authority, 1966. *Address:* 161 Banstead Road, Banstead, Surrey. *T:* 01–393 9005.

McLEOD, Malcolm Donald; Keeper of Ethnography, British Museum, since 1974; *b* 19 May 1941; *s* of Donald McLeod and Ellen (*née* Fairclough); *m* 1st, 1965, Jacqueline Wynborne (marr. diss. 1980); two *s* one *d;* 2nd, 1980, Iris Barry. *Educ:* Birkenhead Sch.; Hertford and Exeter Colls, Oxford. MA, BLitt. Lectr, Dept of Sociology, Univ. of Ghana, 1967–69; Asst Curator, Museum of Archaeology and Ethnology, Cambridge, 1969–74; Lectr, Girton Coll., Cambridge, 1969–74; Fellow, Magdalene Coll., Cambridge, 1972–74. Member: Hist. and Current Affairs Selection Cttee, Nat. Film Archive, 1978–84; Council, Museums Assoc., 1983–; UK Unesco Cultural Adv. Cttee, 1980–85. Hon. Lectr, Anthropology Dept, UCL, 1976–81. Lectures: Marett, Exeter Coll., Oxford, 1982; Sydney Jones, Liverpool Univ., 1984. *Publications:* The Asante, 1980; Treasures of African Art, 1980; (with J. Mack) Ethnic Art, 1984; articles and reviews in learned jls. *Address:* 6 Burlington Gardens, W1X 2EX. *Club:* Athenæum.

MACLEOD, Nigel Ronald Buchanan, QC 1979; a Recorder of the Crown Court, since 1981; *b* 7 Feb. 1936; *s* of Donald Macleod, MB, ChB, and Katherine Ann Macleod; *m* 1966, Susan Margaret (*née* Buckley); one *s* one *d. Educ:* Wigan Grammar Sch.; Christ Church, Oxford (MA, BCL). Served RAF, 1954–56. Called to the Bar, Gray's Inn, 1961, Inner Temple *ad eundem* 1984. Asst Comr, Boundary Commn for England, 1981–85. *Publications:* contribs to legal jls. *Recreations:* sailing, walking. *Address:* The Start, Start Lane, Whaley Bridge, Derbyshire. *T:* Whaley Bridge 2732; 87 Rennie Court, Kings Reach, Upper Ground, SE1. *T:* 01–633 9807.

MACLEOD, Norman Donald, MA, LLB; Advocate; Sheriff Principal of Glasgow and Strathkelvin, since 1986; *b* 6 March 1932; *s* of Rev. John MacLeod, Edinburgh, and late Catherine MacRitchie; *m* 1957, Ursula Jane, *y d* of George H. Bromley, Inveresk; two *s* two *d. Educ:* Mill Hill Sch.; George Watson's Boys' Coll., Edinburgh; Edinburgh Univ.; Hertford Coll., Oxford. Passed Advocate, 1956. Colonial Administrative Service, Tanganyika: Dist. Officer, 1957–59; Crown Counsel, 1959–64; practised at Scots Bar, 1964–67; Sheriff of Glasgow and Strathkelvin (formerly Lanarkshire at Glasgow), 1967–86. *Recreations:* sailing, gardening. *Address:* Sheriffs' Library, Sheriff Court, PO Box 23, 1 Carlton Place, Glasgow. *T:* 041–429 8888.

MACLEOD-SMITH, Alastair Macleod, CMG 1956; retired; *b* 30 June 1916; *s* of late R. A. Smith, MIEE, and Mrs I. Macleod-Smith (*née* Kellner); *m* 1945, Ann (*née* Circuitt); one *s* one *d. Educ:* The Wells House, Malvern Wells, Worcs; Ellesmere Coll., Salop; The Queen's Coll., Oxford. BA Oxon 1938. Entered HM Oversea Service as administrative cadet, Nigeria, 1939; Asst Dist Officer, 1942, Dist Officer, Nigeria, 1949; seconded to Windward Islands as Financial and Economic Adviser, 1949–52; Financial Sec., Western Pacific High Commission, 1952–57; Financial Sec., Sierra Leone, 1957–61. Dir, Selection Trust Ltd, 1967–80; Consultant, National Westminster Bank, 1981–83. *Recreations:* golf, sailing. *Address:* Roughetts Lodge, Coldharbour Lane, Hildenborough, Kent. *Clubs:* United Oxford & Cambridge University; Knole Park Golf.

McLINTOCK, (Charles) Alan, CA; Senior Partner, KMG Thomson McLintock (formerly Thomson McLintock & Co.), chartered accountants, London, since 1982; Partner, Klynveld Main Goerdeler (KMG), since 1979; Chairman: Woolwich Equitable Building Society, since 1984 (Deputy Chairman, 1980–84; Director, since 1970); Govett Oriental Investment Trust (formerly Lake View Investment Trust), since 1975 (Director, since 1971); Govett Atlantic Investment Trust (formerly Stockholders Investment Trust), since 1978; Govett Strategic Investment Trust (formerly Border and Southern Stockholders Investment Trust), since 1975; Ecclesiastical Insurance Office, since 1981 (Director, since 1972); Director: National Westminster Bank Ltd, since 1979; M&G Group, since 1982; *b* 28 May 1925; *s* of late Charles Henry McLintock, OBE, and Alison McLintock; *m* 1955, Sylvia Mary Foster Taylor; one *s* three *d. Educ:* Rugby School. Served Royal Artillery, 1943–47; commnd 1945; Captain RHA 1946. With Thomson McLintock & Co., Chartered Accountants, 1948–; qualified, 1952; Partner, 1954. Chm., Grange Trust, 1973–81 (Dir, 1958–81); Dir, Trust Houses Ltd, 1967–71. Vice-Pres., Metropolitan Assoc. of Building Socs, 1985–. Governor: Rugby Sch., 1973–; Westonbirt Sch., 1977–; Vice-Pres., Clergy Orphan Corp. Cttee, 1984– (Mem., Cttee of Management, 1963–84); Mem., Royal Alexandra and Albert Sch. Bd of Management, 1965–. *Recreations:* music, walking. *Address:* Manor House, Westhall Hill, Burford, Oxon OX8 4BJ. *T:* Burford 2276.

McLINTOCK, Sir William Traven, 3rd Bt, *cr* 1934; *b* 4 Jan. 1931; *s* of Sir Thomas McLintock, 2nd Bt and Jean, *d* of R. T. D. Aitken, New Brunswick; *S* father 1953; *m* 1952, André (marr. diss.), *d* of Richard Lonsdale-Hands; three *s; m* Heather, *d* of Philip Homfray-Davies; one step *s* one step *d. Educ:* Harrow. *Heir: s* Michael William McLintock, *b* 13 Aug. 1958.

McLOUGHLIN, Patrick Alan; MP (C) W Derbyshire, since May 1986; *b* 30 Nov. 1957; *s* of Patrick and Gladys Victoria McLoughlin; *m* 1984, Lynne; one *s. Educ:* Cardinal

Griffin Roman Catholic Sch., Cannock. Mineworker, Littleton Colliery, 1979–85; Marketing Official, NCB, 1985–86. *Address:* House of Commons, SW1.

MACLURE, Sir John (Robert Spencer), 4th Bt *cr* 1898; Headmaster, Croftinloan School, Pitlochry, Perthshire, since 1978; *b* 25 March 1934; *s* of Sir John William Spencer Maclure, 3rd Bt, OBE, and of Elspeth, *er d* of late Alexander King Clark; *S* father, 1980; *m* 1964, Jane Monica, *d* of late Rt Rev. T. J. Savage, Bishop of Zululand and Swaziland; four *s. Educ:* Winchester College. IAPS Diploma. 2nd Lt, 2nd Bn KRRC, 1953–55, BAOR; Lt, Royal Hampshire Airborne Regt, TA. Assistant Master: Horris Hill, 1955–66 and 1974–78; St George's, Wanganui, NZ, 1967–68; Sacred Heart Coll., Auckland, NZ, 1969–70; St Edmund's, Hindhead, Surrey, 1971–74. *Heir: s* John Mark Maclure, *b* 27 Aug. 1965. *Address:* Croftinloan School, Pitlochry, Perthshire PH16 5JR. *T:* Pitlochry 2837.

MACLURE, (John) Stuart, CBE 1982; Editor, Times Educational Supplement, since 1969; *b* 8 Aug. 1926; *s* of Hugh and Bertha Maclure, Highgate, N6; *m* 1951, Constance Mary Butler; one *s* two *d. Educ:* Highgate Sch.; Christ's Coll., Cambridge. MA. Joined The Times, 1950; The Times Educational Supplement, 1951; Editor, Education, 1954–69. Hon. Prof. of Educn, Keele Univ., 1981–84. President: Br. Sect., Comparative Educn Soc. in Europe, 1979; Educnl Sect., BAAS, 1983; Member: Educnl Adv. Council, IBA, 1979–84; Consultative Cttee, Assessment of Performance Unit, 1974–82. Regents' Lecturer, Univ. of California, Berkeley, 1980. Hon. Fellow, City of Sheffield Polytechnic, 1976; Hon. FCP 1985. *Publications:* Joint Editor (with T. E. Utley) Documents on Modern Political Thought, 1956; Editor, Educational Documents, 1816–1963, 1965; A Hundred Years of London Education, 1970; (with Tony Becher) The Politics of Curriculum Change, 1978; (ed with Tony Becher) Accountability in Education, 1979; Education and Youth Employment in Great Britain, 1979; Educational Development and School Building, 1945–1973, 1984. *Address:* 109 College Road, Dulwich, SE21. *Club:* MCC.

McLUSKEY, Very Rev. J(ames) Fraser, MC; MA, BD, DD; Minister at St Columba's Church of Scotland, Pont Street, London, 1960–86; Moderator of the General Assembly of the Church of Scotland, 1983–84; *b* 1914; *s* of James Fraser McLuskey and Margaret Keltie; *m* 1st, 1939, Irene (*d* 1959), *d* of Pastor Calaminus, Wuppertal; two *s;* 2nd, 1966, Ruth Quartermaine (*née* Hunter), *widow* of Lt-Col Keith Briant. *Educ:* Aberdeen Grammar Sch.; Edinburgh Univ. Ordained Minister of Church of Scotland, 1938; Chaplain to Univ. of Glasgow, 1939–47. Service as Army Chaplain, 1943–46 (1st Special Air Service Regt, 1944–46); Sub Warden Royal Army Chaplains' Training Centre, 1947–50; Minister at Broughty Ferry East, 1950–55; Minister at New Kilpatrick, Bearsden, 1955–60. *Publication:* Parachute Padre, 1951. *Recreations:* walking, music, reading. *Address:* 11 Milford Court, Milford-on-Sea, Lymington, Hants SO4 0WF. *T:* Lymington 42162. *Clubs:* Caledonian, Special Forces.

McMAHON, Andrew, (Andy); *b* 18 March 1920; *s* of Andrew and Margaret McMahon; *m* 1944; one *s* one *d. Educ:* District School, Govan. Boilermaker, Govan shipyards, 1936; unemployed, 1971–79. MP (Lab) Glasgow, Govan, 1979–83; first and only Boilermaker to enter House of Commons. Member, Glasgow Dist. Council, 1973–79. Chairman, Scottish Arab Friendship Assoc. *Recreations:* youth work, care and comfort for elderly. *Address:* 21 Morefield Road, Govan, Glasgow G51 4NG.

McMAHON, Sir Brian (Patrick), 8th Bt *cr* 1817; engineer; *b* 9 June 1942; *s* of Sir (William) Patrick McMahon, 7th Bt, and Ruth Stella (*d* 1982), *yr d* of late Percy Robert Kenyon-Slaney; *S* father, 1977; *m* 1981, Kathleen Joan, *d* of late William Hopwood. *Educ:* Wellington. BSc, AIM. Assoc. Mem., Inst of Welding. *Heir: brother* Shaun Desmond McMahon [*b* 29 Oct. 1945; *m* 1971, Antonia Noel Adie]. *Address:* 157B Wokingham Road, Reading, Berks RG6 1LP.

McMAHON, Sir Christopher William, (Sir Kit), Kt 1986; Chairman, Midland Bank, from April 1987 (Chief Executive and Deputy Chairman, 1986–April 1987; Director, since 1986); Deputy Chairman, Samuel Montagu and Co. (Holdings), since 1986; *b* Melbourne, 10 July 1927; *s* of late Dr John Joseph McMahon and late Margaret Kate (*née* Brown); *m* 1st, 1956, Marion Kelso; two *s;* 2nd, 1982, Alison Barbara Braimbridge, *d* of late Dr J. G. Cormie and late Mrs B. E. Cormie. *Educ:* Melbourne Grammar Sch.; Univ. of Melbourne (BA Hons Hist. and English, 1949); Magdalen Coll., Oxford. 1st cl. hons PPE, 1953. Tutor in English Lit., Univ. of Melbourne, 1950; Econ. Asst, HM Treasury, 1953–57; Econ. Adviser, British Embassy, Washington, 1957–60; Fellow and Tutor in Econs, Magdalen Coll., Oxford, 1960–64 (Sen. Tutor, 1961–63); Tutor in Econs, Treasury Centre for Admin. Studies, 1963–64; Mem., Plowden Cttee on Aircraft Industry, 1964–65; entered Bank of England as Adviser, 1964; Adviser to the Governors, 1966–70; Exec. Dir, 1970–80; Dep. Governor, 1980–85. Mem., Steering Cttee, Gp of Thirty, 1978–84; Chm., Working Party 3, OECD, 1980–. Mem. Court, Univ. of London, 1984–; Trustee: Whitechapel Art Gall., 1984–; Royal Opera House Trust, 1984–. *Publications:* Sterling in the Sixties, 1964; (ed) Techniques of Economic Forecasting, 1965. *Recreations:* gardening, walking. *Address:* c/o Midland Bank, 27–32 Poultry, EC2P 2BX. *Club:* Garrick.

MacMAHON, Gerald John, CB 1962; CMG 1955; *b* 26 Sept. 1909; 2nd *s* of late Jeremiah MacMahon and Kathleen MacMahon (*née* Dodd); unmarried. *Educ:* Clongowes Wood Coll., Co. Kildare, Ireland; Emmanuel Coll., Cambridge (BA). Entered Board of Trade, 1933; Asst Sec., 1942. Imperial Defence Coll., 1949. Senior UK Trade Commissioner in India, 1952–58; Under-Sec., Board of Trade 1958–62 and 1964–70; Admiralty, Nov. 1962–64. *Recreation:* golf. *Address:* 19 Lower Park, Putney Hill, SW15. *Club:* Reform.

McMAHON, Hugh Robertson; Member (Lab) Strathclyde West, European Parliament, since 1984; *b* 17 June 1938; *s* of Hugh McMahon and Margaret Fulton Robertson. *Educ:* Glasgow University (MA Hons); Jordanhill College. Assistant Teacher: Largs High School, 1962–63; Stevenston High School, 1963–64; Asst Teacher of History, Irvine Royal Academy, 1964–68; Mainholm Academy, Ayr, 1968–71; Principal Teacher of History, 1971–72, Asst Head Teacher, 1972–84, Ravenspark Academy, Irvine. *Recreations:* golf, reading, walking, languages. *Address:* 6 Whitlees Court, Ardrossan, Ayrshire. *T:* Ardrossan 66692. *Clubs:* Saltcoats Labour; Ravenspark Golf; Irvine Bogside Golf.

McMAHON, Sir Kit; *see* McMahon, Sir C. W.

McMAHON, Rt. Rev. Thomas; *see* Brentwood, Bishop of, (RC).

McMAHON, Rt. Hon. Sir William, GCMG 1977; CH 1972; PC 1966; MP for Lowe, NSW, 1949–82; Prime Minister of Australia, 1971–72; *b* 23 Feb. 1908; *s* of William Daniel McMahon; *m* 1965, Sonia R. Hopkins; one *s* two *d. Educ:* Sydney Grammar Sch.; St Paul's Coll., Univ. of Sydney (LLB, BEc with distinction; Frank Albert Prize for proficiency; John D'Arcy Meml Prize for Public Admin). Practised as solicitor until 1939. Australian Army, 1940–45, Major. Elected to House of Representatives for Lowe, NSW, in gen. elections, 1949, 1951, 1954, 1955, 1958, 1961, 1963, 1966, 1969, 1972, 1974, 1975, 1977, 1980; Minister: for Navy, and for Air, 1951–54 (visited Korea and Japan in that capacity, 1952); for Social Services, 1954–56; for Primary Industry, 1956–58; for

Labour and National Service, 1958–66; Treasurer, Commonwealth of Australia, 1966–69; Minister for External Affairs, later Foreign Affairs, 1969–71. Vice-Pres., Executive Council, 1964–66; Dep. Leader of Liberal Party, 1966–71, Leader, 1971–72; Acting Minister for Trade, Acting Minister for Labour and Nat. Service, Acting Minister in Charge, CSIRO, Acting Minister for National Development, Acting Minister for Territories, and Acting Attorney-Gen., for short periods, 1956–69; Leader of Aust. Delegation to Commonwealth Parliamentary Conf., New Delhi, Nov. 1957–Jan. 1958; Visiting Minister to ILO Conf., Geneva, June 1960 and June 1964; Pres., ILO Asian Regional Conf., Melbourne, Nov.-Dec., 1962; Mem., Bd of Governors, IMF and World Bank, 1966–69. Chm., Bd of Governors, Asian Development Bank, 1968–69. Led Australian delegns to Bangkok, Djakarta, Wellington, Tokyo, Manila and Saigon, 1970. As Prime Minister officially visited: USA, GB, 1971; Indonesia, Malaysia, Singapore, 1972. *Recreations:* squash, swimming. *Address:* 18 Drumalbyn Road, Bellevue Hill, NSW 2023, Australia; Ashleigh Park, Orange, NSW 2800, Australia; 1 Rapallo Avenue, Surfers Paradise, Qld 4127, Australia. *Clubs:* Union, Australian, Australian Jockey (Sydney); Melbourne (Melbourne).

McMANNERS, Rev. Prof. John, DLitt; FBA 1978; Fellow and Chaplain, All Souls College, Oxford, since 1984; *b* 25 Dec. 1916; *s* of Rev. Canon Joseph McManners and Mrs Ann McManners; *m* 1951, Sarah Carruthers Errington; two *s* two *d.* *Educ:* St Edmund Hall, Oxford (Hon. Fellow, 1983); Durham Univ. BA 1st cl. hons Mod. History Oxon, 1939; DipTheol Dunelm, 1947; DLitt Oxon 1980. Military Service, 1939–45 in Royal Northumberland Fusiliers (Major). Priest, 1948; St Edmund Hall, Oxford: Chaplain, 1948; Fellow, 1949; Dean, 1951; Prof., Univ. of Tasmania, 1956–59; Prof., Sydney Univ., 1959–66; Vis. Fellow, All Souls Coll., Oxford, 1965–66; Prof. of History, Univ. of Leicester, 1967–72; Canon of Christ Church and Regius Prof. of Ecclesiastical History, Oxford Univ., 1972–84. Birkbeck Lectr, Cambridge, 1976; John Coffin Meml Lectr, London Univ., 1982; Sir Owen Evans Lectr, Univ. of Wales, 1984; F. D. Maurice Lectr, King's Coll. London, 1985; Zaharoff Lectr, 1985, Hensley Henson Lectr, 1986, Oxford. Dir d'études associé, Ecole Pratique des Hautes Etudes, sect. IV, Paris, 1980–81. Mem., Doctrinal Commn of C of E, 1978–. Trustee, Nat. Portrait Gallery, 1970–78; Mem. Council, RHistS, 1971; Pres., Ecclesiastical Hist. Soc., 1977–78. FAHA 1970. Hon. DLitt Durham, 1984. Officer, Order of King George I of the Hellenes, 1945. *Publications:* French Ecclesiastical Society under the Ancien Régime: a study of Angers in the 18th Century, 1960; (ed) France, Government and Society, 1965, 2nd edn 1971; Lectures on European History 1789–1914: Men, Machines and Freedom, 1966; The French Revolution and the Church, 1969; Church and State in France 1870–1914, 1972; Death and the Enlightenment, 1981 (Wolfson Literary Award, 1982); contrib.: New Cambridge Modern History vols VI and VIII; Studies in Church History, vols XII, XV and XXII. *Recreation:* tennis. *Address:* All Souls College, Oxford. *T:* Oxford 722251.

McMANUS, Francis Joseph; solicitor; *b* 16 Aug. 1942; *s* of Patrick and Celia McManus; *m* 1971, Carmel V. Doherty, Lisnaskea, Co. Fermanagh; two *s* one *d.* *Educ:* St Michael's, Enniskillen; Queen's University, Belfast. BA 1965; Diploma in Education, 1966. Subsequently a Teacher. MP (Unity) Fermanagh and S Tyrone, 1970–Feb. 1974. Founder Mem. and Co-Chm., Irish Independence Party, 1977–. *Address:* Lissadell, Drumlin Heights, Enniskillen, Co. Fermanagh, N Ireland. *T:* Enniskillen 23401.

MacMANUS, John Leslie Edward, TD 1945; QC 1970; **His Honour Judge MacManus;** a Circuit Judge (formerly a Judge of County Courts), since 1971; *b* 7 April 1920; *o s* of E. H. MacManus and H. S. MacManus (*née* Colton); *m* 1942, Gertrude (Trudy) Mary Frances Koppenhagen; two *d.* *Educ:* Eastbourne College. Served 1939–45 with RA: Middle East, Italy, Crete, Yugoslavia; Captain 1942; Major 1945. Called to Bar, Middle Temple, 1947. Dep. Chm., East Sussex QS, 1964–71. *Recreations:* gardening, odd-jobbing, travel. *Address:* The Old Rectory, Twineham, Haywards Heath, West Sussex. *T:* Bolney 221; 1 Crown Office Row, Temple, EC4. *T:* 01–353 1801. *Club:* Sussex Martlets.

McMASTER, Brian John; Managing Director (formerly General Administrator), Welsh National Opera, since 1976; Artistic Director, Vancouver Opera, since 1984; *b* 9 May 1943; *s* of Brian John McMaster and Mary Leila Hawkins. *Educ:* Wellington Coll.; Bristol Univ. LLB. International Artists' Dept, EMI Ltd, 1968–73; Controller of Opera Planning, ENO, 1973–76. *Address:* 1 Cowper Court, Wordsworth Avenue, Cardiff. *T:* Cardiff 497694; 71 Breton House, Barbican, EC2. *T:* 01–638 4365.

McMASTER, Hughan James Michael, RIBA; Chief Architect and Director of Works, Home Office, since 1980; *b* 27 July 1927; *s* of William James Michael and Emly McMaster; *m* 1950; one *s* two *d.* *Educ:* Christ's Coll., Finchley; Regent Street Polytechnic (DipArch). ARIBA 1951. Served RAF, India and Far East, 1946–48. T. P. Bennett and Son, 1951; Gollins Melvin Ward & Partners, 1955; joined Civil Service, 1961; Navy Works, 1961–69; Whitehall Development Gp, Directorate of Home Estate Management and Directorate of Civil Accommodation, 1969–76; Defence Works (PE and Overseas), 1976–80. *Publications:* various articles in architectural jls. *Recreations:* ski-ing, mountaineering, swimming, music. *Address:* c/o Home Office, Abell House, John Islip Street, SW1P 4LH.

McMASTER, Peter, FRICS; Director General, Ordnance Survey, since 1985; *b* 22 Nov. 1931; *s* of Peter McMaster and Ada Nellie (*née* Williams); *m* 1955, Catherine Ann Rosborough; one *s* one *d.* *Educ:* Kelvinside Academy, Glasgow; RMA Sandhurst; RMCS Shrivenham. BScEng London. Called to the Bar, Middle Temple, 1969. Commissioned into Royal Engineers, 1952; served Middle and Far East; retired (major), 1970; joined Civil Service, 1970; W Midland Region, Ordnance Survey, 1970–72; Caribbean Region, Directorate of Overseas Survey, 1972–74; Headquarters, Ordnance Survey, 1974–. *Recreations:* travel, walking, chess. *Address:* Hillhead, Stratton Road, Winchester, Hampshire SO23 8JQ. *T:* Winchester 62684.

McMASTER, Stanley Raymond; *b* 23 Sept. 1926; *o s* of F. R. McMaster, Marlborough Park, Belfast, N Ireland; *m* 1959, Verda Ruth Tynan, SRN, Comber, Co Down, Northern Ireland; two *s* two *d* (and one *d* decd). *Educ:* Campbell Coll., Belfast; Trinity Coll., Dublin (MA, BComm). Called to the Bar, Lincoln's Inn, 1953. Lectr in Company Law, Polytechnic, Regent Street, 1954–59. Parliamentary and Legal Sec., to Finance and Taxation Cttee, Association of British Chambers of Commerce, 1958–59. MP (UU) Belfast E, March 1959–Feb. 1974; contested (UU) Belfast S, Oct. 1974. *Publications:* various articles in legal and commercial journals. *Recreations:* golf, rowing and shooting. *Address:* 31 Embercourt Road, Thames Ditton, Surrey. *Clubs:* Knock Golf, etc.

McMICHAEL, Prof. Andrew James, PhD; Medical Research Council Clinical Research Professor of Immunology, University of Oxford, since 1982; Fellow of Trinity College, Oxford, since 1983; *b* 8 Nov. 1943; *s* of Sir John McMichael, *qv* and Sybil McMichael; *m* 1968, Kathryn Elizabeth Cross; two *s* one *d.* *Educ:* St Paul's Sch., London; Gonville and Caius Coll., Cambridge (MA; BChir 1968; MB 1969); St Mary's Hosp. Med. Sch., London. PhD 1974; MRCP 1971; FRCP 1985. House Physician, St Mary's Hosp., Royal Northern Hosp., Hammersmith Hosp. and Brompton Hosp., 1968–71; MRC Jun. Res. Fellow, National Inst. for Med. Res., 1971–74; MRC Travelling Fellow, Stanford Univ. Med. Sch., 1974–76; Oxford University: Wellcome Sen. Clin. Fellow, Nuffield Depts of Medicine and Surgery, 1977–79; University Lectr in Medicine and Hon. Consultant Physician, 1979–82. *Publications:* (ed with J. W. Fabre) Monoclonal Antibodies in Clinical Medicine, 1982; articles on genetic control of human immune response and transplantation antigens. *Recreations:* reading, walking, sailing. *Address:* 5 The Green, Horton-cum-Studley, Oxford OX9 1AE. *T:* Oxford 817586.

McMICHAEL, Sir John, Kt 1965; MD, FRCP, FRCPE; FRS 1957; Director, British Post-graduate Medical Federation, 1966–71; Emeritus Professor of Medicine, University of London; *b* 25 July 1904; *s* of James McMichael and Margaret Sproat; *m* 1942, Sybil E. Blake (*d* 1965); four *s*; *m* 1965, Sheila M. Howarth. *Educ:* Kirkcudbright Acad.; Edinburgh Univ. Ettles Scholar, 1927; Beit Memorial Fellow, 1930–34. MD (Gold Medal) Edinburgh 1933; MD Melbourne 1965; FRCPE 1940 (Hon. FRCPE 1981); FRCP 1946. Johnston and Lawrence Fellow, Royal Society, 1937–39; Univ. teaching appointments in Aberdeen, Edinburgh and London. Dir, Dept of Medicine, Post-grad. Med. Sch. of London, 1946–66; Mem. Medical Research Council, 1949–53. A Vice-Pres., Royal Soc., 1968–70. Pres., World Congress of Cardiology, 1970. Hon. Member: American Medical Association, 1947; Medical Soc., Copenhagen, 1953; Norwegian Medical Soc., 1954; Assoc. Amer. Physicians, 1959. For. Mem. Finnish Acad. of Science and Letters, 1963; Hon. For. Mem., Acad. Roy. de Med. Belgique, 1971; For. Associate, Nat. Acad. Sci., Washington, 1974. Thayer Lectr, Johns Hopkins Hosp., 1948; Oliver Sharpey Lectr, 1952; Croonian Lectr, 1961, RCP; Watson Smith Lectr RCPEd, 1958. Cullen Prize, RCPEd, 1953. Jacobs Award, Dallas, 1958; Morgan Prof., Nashville, Tenn, 1964. Fellow, Royal Postgrad. Med. Sch., 1972. Moxon Medal, RCP, 1960; Gairdner Award, Toronto, 1960; Wihuri Internat. Prize, Finland, 1968. Harveian Orator, RCP, 1975. Krug Award of Excellence, 1980. Trustee, Wellcome Trust, 1960–77. Hon. FRCPE; Hon. FACP; Hon. LLD Edin.; Hon. DSc: Newcastle; Sheffield; Birmingham; Ohio; McGill; Wales; Hon. ScD Dublin. *Publications:* Pharmacology of the Failing Human Heart, 1951. Numerous papers on: Splenic Anaemia, 1931–35; Cardiac Output in Health and Disease, 1938–47; Lung Capacity in Man, 1938–39; Liver Circulation and Liver Disease, 1932–43. *Recreation:* gardening. *Address:* 2 North Square, NW11 7AA. *T:* 01–455 8731.

See also A. J. McMichael.

MACMILLAN, family name of **Earl of Stockton.**

MACMILLAN OF OVENDEN, Viscount; Alexander Daniel Alan Macmillan; Chairman: Macmillan Ltd, since 1985 (Deputy Chairman, 1984–85); Macmillan Publishers Ltd, since 1980; St Martin's Press, Inc., New York, since 1983; *b* Oswestry, Shropshire, 10 Oct. 1943; *s* of Viscount Macmillan of Ovenden, PC, MP (*d* 1984) and of Katharine Viscountess Macmillan of Ovenden, DBE; *g s* and *heir* of 1st Earl of Stockton, *qv;* *m* 1970, Hélène Birgitte, *o d* of late Alan D. C. Hamilton, Mitford, Northumberland; one *s* two *d.* *Educ:* Eton; Université de Paris; Strathclyde Univ. MBIM 1981. Sub-editor, Glasgow Herald, 1963–65; Reporter, Daily Telegraph, 1965–67, Foreign Correspondent, 1967–68; Chief European Correspondent, Sunday Telegraph, 1968–70; Dir, Macmillan and Co. Ltd, 1970–76; Dep. Chm., Macmillan Ltd, 1976–80. Director: Birch Grove Estates Ltd, 1969–; Book Trade Benevolent Soc., 1976–; National Fedn of Industrial Assocs, 1981–82. Chm., Bookrest Appeal Cttee, 1978–; Pres., Westminster Chamber of Commerce, 1986–; Mem., Lindemann Fellowship Cttee, 1979–, Chm., 1983–; Member: Publishers' Assoc. Council, 1985–; Council, RSNC, 1985–. Hon. Sec., 1975–84, Vice-Chm., 1984–, Carlton Club Political Cttee. Governor: Archbishop Tenison's Grammar Sch. and Foundn, 1979–; Merchant Taylors' Sch., 1980–82; E-SU, 1980–84. Liveryman: Worshipful Co. of Merchant Taylors, 1972; Worshipful Co. of Stationers and Newspaper Maker, 1973. *Recreations:* shooting, fishing, motor racing, conversation. *Heir:* *s* Hon. Daniel Maurice Alan Macmillan, *b* 9 Oct. 1974. *Address:* Flat 4, 46 Tite Street, SW3 4JA. *T:* 01–352 7596; Pooks, Chelwood Gate, near Haywards Heath, West Sussex RH17 7DG. *T:* Chelwood Gate 554. *Clubs:* Carlton, Beefsteak, Buck's, Pratt's, Royal Automobile, White's.

McMILLAN, Alan Austen, CB 1986; Solicitor to the Secretary of State for Scotland, since 1984; *b* 19 Jan. 1926; *s* of Allan McMillan and Mabel (*née* Austin); *m* 1949, Margaret Moncur; two *s* two *d.* *Educ:* Ayr Acad.; Glasgow Univ. Served in Army, 1944–47. Qualified Solicitor in Scotland, 1949; Legal Assistant, Ayr Town Council, 1949–55; Scottish Office: Legal Assistant, 1955–62; Sen. Legal Assistant, 1962–68; Asst Solicitor, 1968–82, seconded to Cabinet Office Constitution Unit, 1977–78; Dep. Solicitor, 1982–84. *Recreations:* reading, music, theatre. *Address:* 28A Polwarth Terrace, Edinburgh. *T:* 031–337 1451. *Club:* Civil Service.

MACMILLAN, Sir (Alexander McGregor) Graham, Kt 1983; Director, Scottish Conservative Party, 1975–84; Chairman, M & P Financial Services Ltd, since 1986 (Director, since 1984); *b* 14 Sept. 1920; *s* of James Orr Macmillan and Sarah Dunsmore (*née* Graham); *m* 1947, Christina Brash Beveridge; two *s* two *d.* *Educ:* Hillhead High Sch., Glasgow. Served War, RA, 1939–46. Conservative Agent: W Lothian, 1947–50; Haltemprice, 1950–53; Bury St Edmunds, 1953–60; Dep. Central Office Agent, NW Area, 1960–61; Central Office Agent, Yorks Area, 1961–75. Chm., Bury St Edmunds Round Table, 1959–60; Hon. Sec., Suffolk Assoc. of Boys' Clubs, 1986–. Governor, Leeds Grammar Sch., 1968–75. *Recreations:* fishing, watching cricket and rugby. *Address:* 46 Crown Street, Bury St Edmunds, Suffolk. *T:* Bury St Edmunds 704443. *Club:* St Stephen's Constitutional.

MACMILLAN, Alexander Ross, FIBScot, CBIM; Director, Clydesdale Bank PLC, since 1974 (Chief General Manager, 1971–82); *b* 25 March 1922; *s* of Donald and Johanna Macmillan; *m* 1961, Ursula Miriam Grayson; two *s* one *d.* *Educ:* Tain Royal Acad. FIBScot 1969; CBIM 1980. Served War, RAF, 1942–46 (despatches, King's Birthday Honours, 1945). Entered service of N of Scotland Bank Ltd, Tain, 1938; after War, returned to Tain, 1946; transf. to Supt's Dept, Aberdeen, and thereafter to Chief Accountant's Dept, Clydesdale Bank, Glasgow, 1950, on amalgamation with N of Scotland Bank; Chief London Office, 1952; Gen. Manager's Confidential Clerk, 1955; Manager, Piccadilly Circus Br., 1958; Supt of Branches, 1965; Gen. Manager's Asst, 1967; Asst Gen. Man., 1968. Director: Caledonian Applied Technology Ltd, 1982–; Highland-North Sea Ltd, 1982– (Chm., 1982–); John Laing plc, 1982–86; Martin-Black PLC, 1982–85; Radio Clyde plc, 1982–; Scottish Develt Finance Ltd, 1982–; Kelvin Technology Develts Ltd, 1982–; The High Sch. of Glasgow Ltd, 1979–; Compugraphics Internat. Ltd, 1983–; TEG Products Ltd, 1986–; Chm., First Northern Corporate Finance Ltd, 1983–. Chm., Nat. House Bldg Council (Scotland), 1982–. Mem. Court, Univ. of Glasgow, 1981–. Freeman, Royal Burgh of Tain, 1975. *Recreation:* golf. *Address:* St Winnins, 16 Ledcameroch Road, Bearsden G61 4AB. *T:* 041–942 6455. *Club:* Golf (Killermont).

McMILLAN, Col Donald, CB 1959; OBE 1945; Chairman, Cable & Wireless Ltd, and associated companies, 1967–72; *b* 22 Dec. 1906; *s* of Neil Munro McMillan and Isabella Jamieson; *m* 1946, Kathleen Ivy Bingham; one *s.* *Educ:* Sloane Sch., Chelsea; Battersea Polytechnic. Post Office Engineering Dept, 1925–54; Director External Telecommunications, Post Office External Telecommunications Executive, 1954–67. BSc

Eng (London); FIEE. *Publications:* contribs to Institution Engineers Journal, Post Office Institution Engineers Journal. *Recreations:* golf and gardening. *Address:* 46 Gatehill Road, Northwood, Mddx. *T:* Northwood 22682. *Club:* Grim's Dyke Golf.

McMILLAN, Rt. Rev. Monsignor Donald Neil; Parish Priest, St Teresa's Church, Filton, Bristol, since 1985; *b* 21 May 1925; *s* of Daniel McMillan and Mary Cameron McMillan (*née* Farrell). *Educ:* St Brendan's Coll., Bristol; Prior Park Coll., Bath; Oscott Coll., Sutton Coldfield. Ordained Priest, Dio. Clifton, 1948; Curate: Bath, 1948–49; Gloucester, 1949–51; Taunton, 1951. Commissioned Army Chaplain, 1951; Served: BAOR, 1961–63, 1966–68, 1975–77; Middle East, 1956–59, 1968–70; Far East, 1952–55; Principal RC Chaplain and Vicar Gen. (Army), 1977–81; Parish Priest, St Augustine's Church, Matson Lane, Gloucester, 1981–85. Apptd Prelate of Honour by Pope Paul VI, 1977. *Recreations:* reading, walking. *Address:* St Teresa's, 71 Gloucester Road North, Filton, Bristol BS12 7PL. *T:* Bristol 692593. *Clubs:* Army and Navy, Challoner.

McMILLAN, Prof. Duncan; John Orr Professor of French Language and Romance Linguistics, University of Edinburgh, 1955–80, now Emeritus; *b* London, 1914; *o s* of late Duncan McMillan and Martha (*née* Hastings); *m* 1945, Geneviève, *er d* of late M and Mme Robert Busse, Paris; one *s*. *Educ:* Holbeach Rd LCC; St Dunstan's Coll.; University Coll., London (Troughton Schol., Rothschild Prizeman, Univ. Postgrad. Student); Sorbonne, Paris (Clothworkers Schol., British Inst. in Paris). BA, PhD (London); Diplôme de l'Ecole des Hautes Etudes, Paris. Army, 1940–46. Lecteur d'anglais, Univ. of Paris, 1938–40; Lectr in French and Romance Philology, Univ. of Aberdeen, 1946–50, Univ. of Edinburgh, 1950–55. Founder Mem., Société Rencesvals, 1955, Pres., British Sect., 1956–59; Member Council: Société des anciens textes français, 1963; Société de Linguistique romane, 1977–83. Chevalier de la Légion d'Honneur, 1958; Médaille d'Honneur, Univ. of Liège, 1962. *Publications:* La Chanson de Guillaume (Société des anciens textes français), 2 vols, 1949–50; (in collaboration with Madame G. McMillan) An Anthology of the Contemporary French Novel, 1950; Le Charroi de Nîmes, 1972, 2nd edn 1978. *Address:* 11 rue des Prés Hauts, 92290 Châtenay Malabry, France. *T:* (1) 4660 3713. *Club:* Scottish Arts (Edinburgh).

McMILLAN, Prof. Edwin Mattison; Professor of Physics, University of California, 1946–73, now Professor Emeritus; *b* Redondo Beach, Calif, 18 Sept. 1907; *s* of Edwin Harbaugh McMillan and Anna Marie (*née* Mattison); *m* 1941, Elsie Walford Blumer; two *s* one *d*. *Educ:* Calif Institute of Technology (MS); Princeton Univ. (PhD). Univ. of California: National Research Fellow, 1932–34; Research Assoc., 1934–35; Instructor, 1935–36; Asst Prof., 1936–41; Assoc. Prof., 1941–46. Leave of absence for war research, 1940–45. Mem. of staff of Radiation Laboratory, Univ. of Calif., 1934–; Assoc. Dir, 1954–58; Dir, 1958–71; Dir, Lawrence Berkeley Laboratory, 1971–73; Mem. General Advisory Cttee to Atomic Energy Commission, 1954–58. Member: Commission on High Energy Physics of International Union for Pure and Applied Physics (IUPAP), 1960–66; Scientific Policy Cttee of Stanford Linear Accelerator Center (SLAC), 1962–66; Physics Adv. Cttee, Nat. Accelerator Lab. (NAL), 1967–69; Trustee, Univs Research Assoc., 1969–84; Chm., Cl. I, Nat. Acad. of Sciences, 1968–71. Fellow Amer. Physical Soc. Member: Nat. Acad. of Sciences (USA); American Philosophical Soc.; Fellow, Amer. Acad. of Arts and Sciences. Research Corp. 1950 Scientific Award, 1951; (jtly) Nobel Prize in Chemistry, 1951; (jtly) Atoms for Peace Award, 1963; Alumni Dist. Service Award, Calif. Inst. of Tech., 1966; Centennial Citation, Univ. of California, Berkeley, 1968. Hon. DSc, Rensselaer Polytechnic Institute; Hon. DSc, Gustavus Adolphus Coll. *Address:* 1401 Vista Road, El Cerrito, Calif 94530, USA.

MACMILLAN, Rev. Gilleasbuig Iain; Minister of St Giles', The High Kirk of Edinburgh, since 1973; Chaplain to the Queen in Scotland, since 1979; *b* 21 Dec. 1942; *s* of Rev. Kenneth M. Macmillan and Mrs Mary Macmillan; *m* 1965, Maureen Stewart Thomson; one *d*. *Educ:* Oban High School; Univ. of Edinburgh. MA, BD. Asst Minister, St Michael's Parish, Linlithgow, 1967–69; Minister of Portree Parish, Isle of Skye, 1969–73. Extra Chaplain to the Queen in Scotland, 1978–79. Hon. Chaplain: Royal Scottish Academy; Royal Coll. of Surgeons of Edinburgh; Soc. of High Constables of City of Edinburgh. *Recreations:* reading, friends, the country, America. *Address:* St Giles' Cathedral, Edinburgh EH1 1RE. *T:* 031-225 4363. *Club:* New (Edinburgh).

MACMILLAN, Sir Graham; *see* Macmillan, Sir A. M. G.

MACMILLAN, Iain Alexander, CBE 1978; LLD; Sheriff of South Strathclyde, Dumfries and Galloway at Hamilton, since 1981; *b* 14 Nov. 1923; *s* of John and Eva Macmillan; *m* 1954, Edith Janet (*née* MacAulay); two *s* one *d*. *Educ:* Oban High Sch.; Glasgow Univ. (BL). Served war, RAF, France, Germany, India, 1944–47. Glasgow Univ., 1947–50. Subseq. law practice; Sen. Partner, J. & J. Sturrock & Co., Kilmarnock, 1952–81. Law Society of Scotland: Mem. Council, 1964–79; Pres., 1976–77. Chm. Lanarkshire Br., Scottish Assoc. for Study of Delinquency, 1986–. Pres., Rotary Club, Kilmarnock, 1979–80. Hon. LLD Aberdeen, 1975. *Publications:* contribs Jl Law Soc. of Scotland. *Recreation:* golf. *Address:* 2 Castle Drive, Kilmarnock. *T:* Kilmarnock 25864.

MacMILLAN, Jake; *see* MacMillan, John.

MACMILLAN, Sir (James) Wilson, KBE 1976 (CBE 1962, OBE 1951); Governing Director, Macmillan Brothers Ltd; President, British Red Cross and Scout Association; *b* 1906; *m* Beatrice Woods. Served in Legislature for many years; formerly Minister of Education, Health and Housing. British Red Cross Badge of Honour, Class I, 1964. *Address:* 3 St Edward Street, Belize City, Belize.

McMILLAN, John, CBE 1969; *b* 29 Jan. 1915; *s* of late William McArthur McMillan, Sydney, NSW; *m* 1958, Lucy Mary, *d* of late Edward Moore, DSO; three *s* two *d*. *Educ:* Scots Coll., Sydney. Manager, Internat. Broadcasting Co. Ltd, London, 1936–38; Manager, EMI Ltd, developing the long-playing record, 1938–39. Served War: joined horsed cavalry as trooper, 1939; commissioned, S Wales Borderers, 1940; OC No 1 Field Broadcasting Unit, British Forces Network, and Telecommns Dir in interim NW German PO, 1945–46 (despatches). Asst, and later Chief Asst, to Controller, BBC Light Programme, 1946–53; USA television, 1954; Manager, Associated Broadcasting Develt Co., London, 1954–55; Controller of Programmes, later Gen. Man. and Dir Rediffusion Television Ltd, 1955–68; Director: Independent Television News Ltd, 1955–68; Global Television Services Ltd, 1960–68; Dir of Special Events and Sport, ITV, 1965–71; Sen. rep. of ITV cos at EBU (Geneva and Brussels), 1968–71. Member: ITA Programme Policy Cttee, 1960–68; Independent Television Standing Consultative Cttee, 1964–68; Independent Television Cos Assoc. (Chm., Finance and General Purposes Cttee), 1964–68; UK Consortium of Communications Satellite Cttee (INTELSAT), Washington DC, 1964–68. Dir, Theatre Royal Windsor Co., 1963–79; Man. Dir, Brompton Production Co. Ltd, 1971–77; Chm. and Man. Dir, Sportsdata Ltd, 1978–80; Chm., Vernons Viewdata Services Ltd, 1978–80. Co-author with Ronald A. Perry, Backstage, for television, 1986. *Recreations:* swimming, gardening, study of 1919–39 European history. *Address:* c/o Lloyds Bank, 6 Pall Mall, SW1.

MacMILLAN, Prof. John, (Jake), PhD Glasgow; DSc Bristol; FRS 1978; CChem, ARIC; Alfred Capper Pass Professor of Organic Chemistry, since 1985, Head of Department of Organic Chemistry, since 1983, University of Bristol; *b* 13 Sept. 1924; *s* of John MacMillan and Barbara Lindsay; *m* 1952, Anne Levy; one *s* two *d*. *Educ:* Lanark Grammar Sch.; Glasgow Univ. Res. Chemist, Akers Res. Labs, ICI Ltd, 1949; Associate Res. Manager, Pharmaceuticals Div., ICI Ltd, 1962; Lectr in Org. Chemistry, Bristol Univ., 1963, Reader 1968, Prof. 1978. Pres., Internat. Plant Growth Substance Assoc., 1973–76. *Publications:* research papers in learned jls on natural organic products, esp. plant growth hormones. *Recreations:* golf, gardening, theatre, music. *Address:* 1 Rylestone Grove, Bristol BS9 3UT. *T:* Bristol 620535.

MacMILLAN, Sir Kenneth, Kt 1983; Principal Choreographer to the Royal Ballet, Covent Garden, since 1977; Artistic Associate, American Ballet Theatre, since 1984; *b* 11 Dec. 1929; *m* 1974, Deborah Williams. *Educ:* Great Yarmouth Gram. Sch. Started as Dancer, Royal Ballet; became Choreographer, 1953; Dir of Ballet, Deutsche Oper, Berlin, 1966–69; Resident Choreographer, and Dir, Royal Ballet, 1970–77. First professional ballet, Danses Concertantes (Stravinsky-Georgiades). Principal ballets: The Burrow; Solitaire; Agon; The Invitation; Romeo and Juliet; Diversions; La Création du Monde; Images of Love; The Song of the Earth; Concerto; Anastasia; Cain and Abel; Olympiad; Triad; Ballade; The Poltroon; Manon; Pavanne; Elite Syncopations; The Four Seasons; Rituals; Requiem; Mayerling; My Brother, My Sisters; La Fin du Jour; Gloria; Isadora; Valley of Shadows; Different Drummer; The Wild Boy; Requiem (Andrew Lloyd Webber). Has devised ballets for: Ballet Rambert, American Ballet, Royal Ballet Sch., theatre, television, cinema, musical shows. Directed: Ionesco's plays, The Chairs and The Lesson, New Inn, Ealing, 1982; The Dance of Death, Royal Exchange, Manchester, 1983; The Kingdom of Earth, Hampstead Theatre Club, 1984. Dr *hc* Edinburgh, 1976. Evening Standard Ballet Award, 1979; Ballet Award, SWET Managers, 1980 and 1983. *Recreation:* cinema. *Address:* c/o Royal Opera House, Covent Garden, WC2.

MACMILLAN, Matthew, CBE 1983 (OBE 1977); Vice-Principal, since 1985, and Professor of English (formerly English Language), since 1983, University College, University of East Asia, Macau; *b* 14 July 1926; *s* of David Craig Macmillan and late Barbara Cruikshank Macmillan (*née* Gow); *m* 1949, Winifred (*née* Sagar); one *s* two *d*. *Educ:* Robert Gordon's Coll., Aberdeen; Aberdeen Univ. (MA Hons); Manchester Univ. (Teacher's Dip.) Served Royal Air Force, 1944–47. Schoolmaster, Chatham House Grammar Sch., Ramsgate, 1951–57; Sen. Lectr, Univ. of Science and Technology, Kumasi, Ghana, 1958–62; Associate Prof., University Coll. of Cape Coast, Ghana, 1962–64; Prof. of English, Univ. of Khartoum, The Sudan, 1965–70; British Council, London: Director, English-Teaching Information Centre, 1970–72; Dep. Controller, English Teaching Div., 1972–74; Asst Educn Adviser (English Studies), British Council, India, 1974–78; Controller, English Lang. and Lit. Div., British Council, 1978–83. *Publications:* articles on the teaching of English as a second/foreign language. *Recreations:* gardening, walking. *Address:* Manor House Cottage, Old Road, Elham, Canterbury, Kent CT4 6UL. *T:* Elham 427; University College, University of East Asia, PO Box 3001, Macau. *Clubs:* Athenæum, Royal Commonwealth Society.

MACMILLAN, Prof. Robert Hugh; Professor of Vehicle Design and Head of School of Automotive Studies, 1977–82, Dean of Engineering, 1980–82, Cranfield Institute of Technology; *b* 27 June 1921; *s* of H. R. M. Macmillan and E. G. Macmillan (*née* Webb); *m* 1950, Anna Christina Roding, Amsterdam; one *s* two *d*. *Educ:* Felsted Sch.; Emmanuel Coll., Cambridge. Technical Branch, RAFVR, 1941; Dept of Engrg, Cambridge Univ., 1947; Prof. of Mech. Engrg, Swansea, 1956; Dir, Motor Industry Res. Assoc., 1964–77. Associate Prof., Warwick Univ., 1965–77. Mem. Council, Loughborough Univ., 1966–81; Chm. Council, Automobile Div., IMechE, 1976–77; Mem., Noise Adv. Council, 1970–77. Approved Lectr for NADFAS, 1985–; official guide, Winslow Hall, 1985–. Editor, The Netherlands Philatelist, 1984–. FRSA; MIEE; FIMechE; FRPSL. *Publications:* Theory of Control, 1951; Automation, 1956; Geometric Symmetry, 1978; Dynamics of Vehicle Collisions, 1983. *Recreations:* music, philately, national heritage. *Address:* 43 Church Road, Woburn Sands, Bucks MK17 8TG. *T:* Milton Keynes 584011. *Clubs:* Royal Air Force, Royal Automobile.

MACMILLAN, Wallace, CMG 1956; retired; *b* 16 Oct. 1913; *s* of late David Hutchen Macmillan and late Jean Wallace, Newburgh, Fife; *m* 1947, Betty Bryce, *d* of late G. R. Watson and Margaret Bryce; three *s*. *Educ:* Bell-Baxter Sch.; University of St Andrews; Kiel Univ.; Corpus Christi Coll., Oxford. Administrative Officer, Tanganyika, 1937; District Officer, 1947; Administrator of Grenada, BWI, 1951–57. Acted as Governor, Windward Is, periods 1955. Federal Establishment Sec. (subsequently Permanent Sec., Min. of Estabts and Service Matters), Federation of Nigeria, 1957–61. Dir, Management Selection Ltd, 1961–78. *Recreations:* bridge, chess, golf. *Address:* Whiteside House, Kilrenny, Anstruther, Fife. *T:* Anstruther 310570.

MACMILLAN, Sir Wilson; *see* Macmillan, Sir J. W.

McMILLAN-SCOTT, Edward; Member (C) York, European Parliament, since 1984; *b* 15 Aug. 1949; *s* of Walter Theodore Robin McMillan-Scott, ARIBA and Elizabeth Maud Derrington Hudson; *m* 1972, Henrietta Elizabeth Rumney Hudson, solicitor; two *d*. *Educ:* Blackfriars School, Llanarth; Blackfriars School, Laxton; Exeter Technical College. Tour director in Europe, Scandinavia, Africa and USSR, 1968–75; PR exec., then parly consultant, 1976–84; political adviser to Falkland Islands Govt, London office 1983–84. European Parliament: Member: Youth Cttee, 1984–; Budget Cttee, 1985–; Sec., 1979 Cttee (Cons. back-bench cttee), 1984–. *Publication:* Mulberry; the artificial harbours, 1979 (with Sir Bruce White). *Recreations:* music, reading. *Address:* European Parliament, 2 Queen Anne's Gate, SW1. *Club:* St Stephen's Constitutional.

McMINN, Prof. Robert Matthew Hay; Part-time Senior Lecturer in Anatomy, Royal Free Hospital School of Medicine, since 1984; *b* 20 Sept. 1923; *o s* of late Robert Martin McMinn, MB, ChB, Auchinleck and Brighton, and Elsie Selene Kent; *m* 1948, Margaret Grieve Kirkwood, MB, ChB, DA; one *s* one *d*. *Educ:* Brighton Coll. (Schol.); Univ. of Glasgow. MB, ChB 1947, MD (commendation) 1958, Glasgow; PhD Sheffield 1956; FRCS 1978. Hosp. posts and RAF Med. Service, 1947–50; Demonstrator in Anatomy, Glasgow Univ., 1950–52; Lectr in Anatomy, Sheffield Univ., 1952–60; Reader 1960–66, Prof. of Anatomy 1966–70, King's Coll., London Univ.; Sir William Collins Prof. of Human and Comparative Anatomy, RCS, Conservator, Hunterian Museum, RCS, and Prof. of Anatomy, Inst. of Basic Med. Scis, London Univ., 1970–82, prematurely retd. Examnr, RCP&S Glasgow; late Examnr to RCS and Univs of London, Cambridge, Edinburgh, Belfast, Singapore, Malaya and Makerere. Arris and Gale Lectr, RCS, 1960; Arnott Demonstrator, RCS, 1970. Former Treas., Anatomical Soc. of Gt Britain and Ireland; Foundn Sec., British Assoc. of Clinical Anatomists; FRSocMed; Member: Amer. Assoc. of Anatomists; Amer. Assoc. of Clinical Anatomists; British Soc. of Gastroenterology; BMA; Trustee, Skin Res. Foundn. *Publications:* Tissue Repair, 1969; The Digestive System, 1974; The Human Gut, 1974; Colour Atlas of Human Anatomy, 1977; Colour Atlas of Head and Neck Anatomy, 1981; Colour Atlas of Foot and Ankle Anatomy, 1982; Colour Atlas of Applied Anatomy, 1984; Picture Tests in Human Anatomy, 1986; The Human Skeleton, 1986; articles in various med. and sci. jls.

Recreations: motoring, photography, archaeology, short-wave radio. *Address:* 74 Dorling Drive, Ewell, Epsom, Surrey. *T:* 01–393 6839.

McMINNIES, John Gordon, OBE 1965; HM Diplomatic Service, retired 1977; *b* 1 Oct. 1919; *s* of late William Gordon McMinnies and Joyce Millicent McMinnies; *m* 1947, Mary (*née* Jackson) (*d* 1978), novelist. *Educ:* Bilton Grange; Rugby Sch.; Austria (language trng). Reporter: Western Mail, 1938; Reuters, 1939. Served War, Army, 1940–46: comd R Troop, RHA; retd, Major. HM Diplomatic Service (Athens, Warsaw, Bologna, Malaysia, Cyprus, Nairobi, Lusaka, New Delhi), 1946–77; retd, Counsellor. *Recreations:* crazy paving, crosswords, cricketology, the sea. *Address:* Villa Woodland, Avenue de Verdun, Ajaccio, Corsica. *T:* (95) 23–13–42.

McMULLAN, Rt. Rev. Gordon; *see* Down and Dromore, Bishop of.

McMULLAN, Henry Wallace, OBE 1967; Member of Independent Broadcasting Authority (formerly Independent Television Authority), 1971–74; *b* 20 Feb. 1909; *s* of William Muir McMullan and Euphemia McMullan; *m* 1934, Roberta Tener Gardiner; three *s. Educ:* King William's Coll., IOM. Worked on Belfast Telegraph and Belfast Newsletter; Producer and Commentator, BBC NI, 1930; Lt-Comdr RNVR, Map Room, Admty, 1939; Head of Programmes, BBC NI, 1945–69. *Recreations:* gardening, watching and listening to people, television and radio. *Address:* 119 Garner Crescent, Nanaimo, British Columbia, Canada. *Club:* Naval.

McMULLAN, Michael Brian; His Honour Judge McMullan; a Circuit Judge, since 1980; *b* 15 Nov. 1926; *s* of Joseph Patrick McMullan and Frances McMullan (*née* Burton); *m* 1960, Rosemary Jane Margaret, *d* of Stanley Halse deL. de Ville; one *s* two *d. Educ:* Manor Farm Road Sch.; Tauntons Sch., Southampton; The Queen's College, Oxford (MA). Called to the Bar, Gray's Inn, 1960. National Service, Army, 1946–48. Colonial Administrative Service: Gold Coast and Ghana, Political Administration Ashanti, Min. of Finance, Accra, Agricl Development Corp., 1949–60. In practice as Barrister, SE Circuit, 1961–80; a Recorder of the Crown Court, 1979. *Club:* United Oxford & Cambridge University.

McMULLEN, Rear-Admiral Morrice Alexander, CB 1964; OBE 1944; Flag Officer, Admiralty Interview Board, HMS Sultan, Gosport, 1961–64, retired; Director, Civil Defence for London, 1965–68; *b* Hertford, 16 Feb. 1909; *m* 1st, 1946, Pamela (*née* May) (marr. diss. 1967), *widow* of Lt-Comdr J. Buckley, DSC, RN; two step *s*; 2nd, 1972, Peggy, *widow* of Comdr Richard Dakeyne, RN; two step *s* one step *d. Educ:* Oakley Hall, Cirencester; Cheltenham Coll. Entered Royal Navy, as Paymaster Cadet, HMS Erebus, 1927. Appts prewar included: S Africa Station, 1929–32; China Station, 1933–36; Asst Sec. to Lord Chatfield, First Sea Lord, 1936–38; Served War of 1939–45 (despatches, OBE); Atlantic, North Sea, Norwegian waters; served in HMS Prince of Wales (battle with Bismarck, and Atlantic Charter Meeting); HQ, Western Approaches, 1941–43; Member Allied Anti-Submarine Survey Board, 1943; served Mediterranean, 1944–45 (Anzio Landing, re-entry into Greece, invasion of S. France). Post-war appointments at home included Dep. Dir Manning (Suez operation), 1956–58, and Captain of Fleet to C-in-C Far East Station, Singapore, 1959–61. Chairman Royal Naval Ski Club, 1955–58. *Recreations:* fishing, sailing, gardening. *Address:* 3 The Crescent, Alverstoke, Hants. *T:* Gosport 582974. *Clubs:* Naval and Military, Royal Cruising, Royal Naval Sailing Association.

McMULLIN, Rt. Hon. Duncan Wallace, PC 1980; **Rt. Hon. Mr Justice McMullin;** Judge of Court of Appeal, New Zealand, since 1979; *b* 1 May 1927; *s* of Charles James McMullin and Kathleen Annie Shout; *m* 1955, Isobel Margaret, *d* of Robert Ronald Atkinson; two *s* two *d. Educ:* Auckland Grammar Sch.; Univ. of Auckland (LLB). Judge of Supreme Court, 1970. Chm., Royal Commn on Contraception, Sterilisation and Abortion in NZ, 1975–77. *Recreations:* boating, farming. *Address:* Jerningham Apartments, Oriental Terrace, Wellington, New Zealand. *T:* Wellington 849–009. *Club:* Wellington (Wellington, NZ).

McMURRAY, David Bruce, MA; Headmaster, Oundle School, since 1984; *b* 15 Dec. 1937; *s* of late James McMurray, CBE, and of Kathleen McMurray (*née* Goodwin); *m* 1962, Antonia Murray; three *d. Educ:* Loretto Sch.; Pembroke Coll., Cambridge (BA, MA). National service, Royal Scots, 1956–58, 2nd Lieut. Pembroke Coll., Cambridge, 1958–61; Asst Master, Stowe Sch., 1961–64; Fettes College: Asst Master, 1964–72; Housemaster, 1972–76; Headmaster, Loretto Sch., 1976–84. HM Comr, Queen Victoria Sch., Dunblane, 1977–; Mem., Edinburgh Fest. Council, 1980–84. CCF Medal, 1976. *Recreations:* cricket, golf, sub-aqua diving, poetry. *Address:* Cobthorne, West Street, Oundle, Peterborough. *T:* Peterborough 73536. *Clubs:* East India, Devonshire, Sports and Public Schools, MCC, Free Foresters.

MacMURRAY, Mary Bell McMillan, (Mrs Ian Mills); QC 1979; Barrister-at-Law; a Recorder of the Crown Court, since 1978; *d* of Samuel Bell MacMurray and Constance Mary MacMurray (*née* Goodman); *m* 1971, Ian Donald Mills. *Educ:* Queen Margaret's School, Escrick, York. Called to the Bar, Lincoln's Inn, 1954, Bencher, 1986. Coronation Medal, 1953. *Recreation:* golf. *Address:* 46 Grainger Street, Newcastle upon Tyne. *T:* Tyneside 2321980; 1 Moor Court, Whitburn, Sunderland, Tyne and Wear. *T:* Whitburn 292152. *Clubs:* Durham County; Whitburn Golf; Boldon Golf.

McMURTRIE, Group Captain Richard Angus, DSO 1940; DFC 1940; Royal Air Force, retired; *b* 14 Feb. 1909; *s* of Radburn Angus and Ethel Maud McMurtrie; *m* 1st, 1931, Gwenyth Mary (*d* 1958), 3rd *d* of Rev. (Lt-Col) H. J. Philpott; no *c*; 2nd, 1963, Laura, 4th *d* of Wm H. Gerhardi. *Educ:* Royal Grammar Sch., Newcastle on Tyne. First commissioned in Territorial Army (72nd Brigade, RA), 1927; transferred to Royal Air Force, 1929, as Pilot Officer; served in No 2 (AC) Squadron, 1931–32, and Fleet Air Arm (442 Flight, and 822 Squadron in HMS Furious), 1932–33; Cranwell, 1934–35; Flt Lieut, 1935; Calshot and No. 201 (Flying Boat) Squadron, 1935–38; Squadron Leader, 1938, and commanded Recruits Sub-Depot, RAF, Linton-on-Ouse; served War of 1939–45 (despatches thrice, DFC, DSO); No 269 GR Squadron, 1939–41; Wing Commander, 1940; HQ No 18 Group RAF, 1941; Group Captain, commanding RAF Station, Sumburgh (Shetlands), 1942–43; HQ Coastal Command, 1943; RAF Staff Coll., Air Ministry, Whitehall, and HQ Transport Command, 1944; commanded RAF Station, Stoney Cross, Hants, 1945; and formed and commanded No. 61 Group (Reserve Command), 1946; Joint Services Mission, Washington, DC, 1946–49; commanded RAF Station, Cardington, 1949–52; HQ No 1 Group, RAF, 1952–54; Royal Naval College, Greenwich, 1954; HQ, Supreme Allied Commander, Atlantic (NATO), Norfolk, Virginia, USA, 1954–56; HQ, Coastal Command, RAF, Northwood, Mddx, 1957–59, now farming. *Recreations:* sailing, photography. *Address:* Rose in Vale Farm, Constantine, Falmouth, Cornwall TR11 5PU. *T:* Falmouth 40338. *Clubs:* RAF Yacht (Hon. Life Mem.), Royal Cornwall Yacht.

McMURTRY, Roland Roy; QC 1970; High Commissioner for Canada in the United Kingdom, since 1985; *b* 31 May 1932; *s* of Roland Roy McMurtry and Doris Elizabeth Belcher; *m* 1957, Ria Jean Macrae; three *s* three *d. Educ:* St Andrew's Coll., Aurora, Ont; Trinity Coll., Univ. of Toronto (BA Hons); Osgoode Hall Law Sch., Toronto (LLB).

Called to the Bar of Ontario, 1958. Partner, Benson, McMurtry, Percival & Brown, Toronto, 1958–75. Elected to Ontario Legislature, 1976; re-elected, 1977 and 1981; Attorney General for Ontario, 1975–85; Solicitor General for Ontario, 1978–82. Hon. LLD: Univ. of Ottawa, 1983; Law Soc. of Upper Canada, 1984. *Recreations:* painting, skiing, tennis. *Address:* Canadian High Commission, 1 Grosvenor Square, W1X 0AB. *T:* 01–629 9492. *Clubs:* Albany, Badminton and Racket (Toronto).

MACNAB, Brigadier Sir Geoffrey (Alex Colin), KCMG 1962 (CMG 1955); CB 1951; retired; *b* 23 Dec. 1899; *s* of Brig.-General Colin Macnab, CMG; *m* 1930, Norah (*d* 1981), *d* of Captain H. A. Cramer Roberts, Folkestone. *Educ:* Wellington Coll.; RMC Sandhurst. 1st Commission, 1919, Royal Sussex Regt; Instr, Small Arms Sch., Hythe, 1925–28; Captain, Argyll and Sutherland Highlanders, 1931; Staff Coll., Camberley, 1930–31; GSO 3, WO, 1933–35; BM 10 Infantry Bde, 1935–38; Military Attaché, Prague and Bucharest, 1938–40; served War of 1939–45, campaigns Western Desert, Greece, Crete; Brigadier, 1944; Military Mission, Hungary, 1945; DMI, Middle East, 1945–47; Military Attaché, Rome, 1947–49; Military Attaché, Paris, 1949–54; retired 1954. Service in Ireland, Germany, Far East, India, Middle East. Secretary, Government Hospitality Fund, 1957–68. *Address:* Stanford House, Stanford, Ashford, Kent. *T:* Sellindge 2118. *Clubs:* Army and Navy, MCC.

MACNAB OF MACNAB, James Charles; The Macnab; 23rd Chief of Clan Macnab; Executive, Hill Samuel Investment Services Ltd, since 1982; *b* 14 April 1926; *e s* of Lt-Col James Alexander Macnabb, OBE, TD (*de jure* 21st of Macnab), London, SW3, and late Mrs G. H. Walford, Wokingham, Berks; *S gt uncle,* Archibald Corrie Macnab, (*de facto*) 22nd Chief, 1970; *m* 1959, Hon. Diana Mary, *er d* of Baron Kilmany, PC, MC, and of Monica Helen, (Lady Kilmany), OBE, JP, *o c* of late Geoffrey Lambton, 2nd *s* of 4th Earl of Durham; two *s* two *d. Educ:* Cothill House; Radley Coll.; Ashbury Coll., Ottawa. Served in RAF and Scots Guards, 1944–45; Lieut, Seaforth Highldrs, 1945–48. Asst Supt, Fedn of Malaya Police Force, 1948; retd, 1957. CC, Perth and Kinross Jt County Council, 1964–75; Dist Councillor, 1961–64; Mem., Central Regional Council, 1978–82. Member, Royal Company of Archers, Queen's Body Guard in Scotland. JP 1968. *Recreations:* shooting, travel. *Heir: s* James William Archibald Macnab, younger of Macnab, *b* 22 March 1963. *Address:* West Kilmany House, Kilmany, Cupar, Fife KY15 4QW. *T:* Gauldry 247. *Club:* New (Edinburgh).

McNAB JONES, Robin Francis, FRCS; Surgeon: ENT Department, St Bartholomew's Hospital, since 1961; Royal National Throat, Nose and Ear Hospital, 1962–83; *b* 22 Oct. 1922; *s* of E. C. H. Jones, CBE, and M. E. Jones, MBE; *m* 1950, Mary Garrett; one *s* three *d. Educ:* Manchester Grammar Sch.; Dulwich Coll.; Med. Coll., St Bartholomew's Hosp. (MB BS 1945); FRCS 1952. Ho. Surg., St Bart's, 1946–47; MO, RAF, 1947–50; Demonstrator of Anatomy, St Bart's, 1950–52; Registrar, Royal Nat. Throat, Nose and Ear Hosp., 1952–54; Sen. Registrar, ENT Dept, St Bart's, 1954–59; Lectr, Dept of Otolaryngology, Univ. of Manchester, 1959–61; Dean, Inst. of Laryngology and Otology, Univ. of London, 1971–76; Vice-Pres., St Bart's Hosp. Med. Coll., 1984–. Mem., Court of Examiners, 1972–78, and Mem. Council (for Otolaryngology), 1982–, RCS; External Examiner, RCSI, 1980–83. Hon. Sec., Sect. of Otology, 1965–68, Pres., Sect. of Laryngology, 1981–82, RSocMed. *Publications:* various chapters in standard med. textbooks; contribs to med. jls. *Recreations:* tennis, ski-ing, golf, fishing, gardening. *Address:* 108 Harley Street, W1N 1AF. *T:* 01–935 7811; 52 Oakwood Avenue, Beckenham, Kent BR3 2PJ. *T:* 01–650 0217.

MACNAGHTEN, Sir Patrick (Alexander), 11th Bt *cr* 1836; farmer; *b* 24 Jan. 1927; *s* of Sir Antony Macnaghten, 10th Bt, and of Magdalene, *e d* of late Edmund Fisher; *S* father, 1972; *m* 1955, Marianne, *yr d* of Dr Erich Schaefer and Alice Schaefer, Cambridge; three *s. Educ:* Eton; Trinity Coll., Cambridge (BA Mechanical Sciences). Army (RE), 1945–48. Project Engineer, Cadbury Bros (later Cadbury Schweppes), 1950–69; in General Management, Cadbury-Schweppes Ltd, 1969–84. *Recreations:* fishing, shooting. *Heir: s* Malcolm Francis Macnaghten, *b* 21 Sept. 1956. *Address:* Dundarave, Bushmills, Co. Antrim, Northern Ireland. *T:* Bushmills 31215.

MACNAGHTEN, Robin Donnelly, MA; Headmaster of Sherborne, since 1974; *b* 3 Aug. 1927; 2nd *s* of late Sir Henry P. W. Macnaghten and of Lady Macnaghten; *m* 1961, Petronella, *er d* of late Lt-Col A. T. Card and Mrs Card; two *s* one *d. Educ:* Eton (Schol.); King's Coll., Cambridge (Schol.). 1st cl. Class. Tripos Pt I, 1947; 1st cl. with dist. Pt II, 1948; Browne Medallist; MA 1954. Travelled in Italy and Turkey, 1949. Asst, Mackinnon Mackenzie & Co., Bombay, 1949–54. Asst Master, Eton Coll., 1954, and Housemaster, 1965. Hon. Sec. and Treas., OEA, 1970–79; Pres., Old Shirburnian Soc., 1984–85. *Publication:* trans. Vita Romana (by U. E. Paoli), 1963. *Recreations:* numismatics (FRNS), walking, gardening. *Address:* Abbey Grange, Sherborne, Dorset DT9 3AP. *T:* Sherborne 812025. *Club:* Western India Turf (Bombay).

McNAIR, family name of **Baron McNair.**

McNAIR, 2nd Baron *cr* 1955, of Gleniffer; **Clement John McNair;** *b* 11 Jan. 1915; *s* of 1st Baron McNair, CBE, QC, and Marjorie (*d* 1971), *yr d* of late Sir Clement Meacher Bailhache; *S* father, 1975; *m* 1941, Vera, *d* of Theodore James Faithfull; two *s* one *d. Educ:* Shrewsbury; Balliol Coll., Oxford. Served War of 1939–45, Major, RA. Substitute Mem., Council of Europe and WEU, 1979–84. Dep. Liberal Whip, H of L, 1985–. *Publications:* Wagonload, 1971; A Place Called Marathon, 1976. *Heir: s* Hon. Duncan James McNair, *b* 26 June 1947. *Address:* House of Lords, SW1.

McNAIR, Archie, (Archibald Alister Jourdan); Chairman: Thomas Jourdan Group, since 1971; Mary Quant Group of Companies, since 1955; *b* 16 Dec. 1919; *s* of late Donald McNair and Janie (*née* Jourdan); *m* 1954, Catherine Alice Jane, *d* of late John and of Margaret Fleming; one *s* one *d. Educ:* Blundell's. Articled to Ford Simey & Ford, Solicitors, Exeter, 1938. Served War, 1939–45: River Thames Formation. Photographer, 1950–57; Co-founder, Mary Quant Gp of Cos, 1955; Founder, Thomas Jourdan Gp, 1971. *Recreations:* fruit farming, carving wood, tennis, chess. *Address:* c/o Thomas Jourdan plc, 6 Park Street, Windsor, Berks SL4 1LU. *T:* Windsor 857951. *Club:* Turf.

McNAIR, Air Vice-Marshal James Jamieson; Principal Medical Officer, Headquarters Support Command, Royal Air Force, 1974–77, retired; *b* 15 June 1917; *s* of Gordon McNair and Barbara MacNaughton; *m* 1945, Zobell Pyper (*d* 1977). *Educ:* Kirkcudbright Academy; Huntly Gordon Sch.; Aberdeen Univ.; London Sch. of Hygiene and Tropical Medicine; Liverpool Sch. of Tropical Medicine. MB, ChB; FFCM; DPH; DTM&H. Sqdn Med. Officer, UK, N Africa, Sicily, Italy, 1942–45; OC, RAF Sch. of Hygiene at Home and Egypt, 1946–51; SMO, 66, 21 and 25 Gp HQ at Home, 1951–57; SMO Air HQ and OC RAF Hosp. Ceylon, 1957–59; OC RAF Inst. of Hygiene, 1959–62; DGMS Staff, Air Min., 1962–65; OC RAF Hosp. Changi, Singapore, 1965–67; PMO HQ's Fighter Comd, 1967–68; OC Jt Service Med. Rehabilitation Unit, 1968–71; Dir of Health and Research, MoD (Air), 1971–74; Dep. Dir GMS RAF, 1974; QHP 1974–77. CStJ. *Recreations:* golf, gardening, travel. *Address:* Wakenills Cottage, Hedgehog Lane, Haslemere, Surrey GU27 2PJ. *T:* Haslemere 51389. *Clubs:* Royal Air Force; Hankley Common Golf.

MACNAIR, Maurice John Peter; His Honour Judge Macnair; a Circuit Judge since 1972; *b* 27 Feb. 1919; *s* of late Brig. J. L. P. Macnair and Hon. Mrs J. L. P. Macnair; *m* 1952, Vickie Reynolds, *d* of Hugh Reynolds; one *s* two *d. Educ:* Bembridge Sch.; St Paul's Sch.; St Edmund Hall, Oxford. BA 1947. Served War of 1939–45, Western Desert, Sicily, Italy; wounded 1944; Captain, RA. Called to Bar, Gray's Inn, 1948. Dep. Chm., W Sussex QS, 1968–72. *Address:* Lambeth County Court, Cleaver Street, SE11.

McNAIR, Thomas Jaffrey, MD, PRCSEd, FRCS; Surgeon to the Queen in Scotland, since 1977; Consultant Surgeon, Royal Infirmary of Edinburgh, since 1961; *b* 1 March 1927; *s* of David McMillan McNair and Helen (*née* Rae); *m* 1951, Dr Sybil Monteith Dick Wood; one *s* one *d. Educ:* George Watson's Coll.; Univ. of Edinburgh (MB, ChB, MD). Ho. Surg., Registrar, Clinical Tutor, Royal Infirmary of Edin., 1949–60; MO, Marlu, Gold Coast, 1950. Served as Flt Lt, RAF, 1951–53. Lectr in Clin. Surgery, Univ. of Edin., 1960; Instr in Surgery, Univ. of Illinois, USA, 1960; Consultant Surgeon: Eastern Gen. Hosp., 1961–64; Chalmers Hosp., 1964–81. Hon. Sen. Lectr in Clin. Surg., Univ. of Edin., 1976–. RCSEd: Pres., 1985–; Examr, 1964–. *Publications:* Emergency Surgery, 8th and 9th edns, 1967 and 1972; various, on surgical subjects. *Recreations:* golf, sailing. *Address:* 8 Learmonth Terrace, Edinburgh EH4 1PQ. *T:* 031–332 1576; Easter Carrick, Chapel Green, Earlsferry, Fife. *Clubs:* New (Edinburgh); Golf House (Elie).

McNAIR-WILSON, Michael; *see* McNair-Wilson, R. M. C.

McNAIR-WILSON, Patrick Michael Ernest David; MP (C) New Forest, since 1968 (Lewisham West, 1964–66); Consultant; *b* 28 May 1929; *s* of Dr Robert McNair-Wilson; *m* 1953, Diana Evelyn Kitty Campbell Methuen-Campbell, *d* of Hon. Laurence Methuen-Campbell; one *s* four *d. Educ:* Eton. Exec. in French Shipping Co., 1951–53; various appointments at Conservative Central Office, 1954–58; Staff of Conservative Political Centre, 1958–61; Director, London Municipal Society, 1961–63; Executive with The British Iron and Steel Federation, 1963–64. Opposition Front Bench Spokesman on fuel and power, 1965–66; Vice-Chm., Conservative Parly Power Cttee, 1969–70; PPS to Minister for Transport Industries, DoE, 1970–74; Opposition Front Bench Spokesman on Energy, 1974–76. Editor of The Londoner, 1961–63. *Recreations:* sailing, pottery. *Address:* House of Commons, SW1A 0AA.

See also R. M. C. McNair-Wilson.

McNAIR-WILSON, (Robert) Michael (Conal); MP (C) Newbury, since 1974 (Walthamstow East, 1969–74); *b* 12 Oct. 1930; *y s* of late Dr Robert McNair-Wilson and of Mrs Doris McNair-Wilson; *m* 1974, Mrs Deidre Granville; one *d. Educ:* Eton College. During national service, 1948–50, was commissioned in Royal Irish Fusiliers. Farmed in Hampshire, 1950–53. Journalist on various provincial newspapers, and did freelance work for BBC in Northern Ireland, 1953–55. Joined Sidney-Barton Ltd, internat. public relations consultants, Dir, 1961–79; consultant to Extel Advertising and Public Relations Ltd (when it acquired Sidney-Barton), 1979–. Contested (C) Lincoln, Gen. Elec., 1964; PPS to Minister of Agriculture, 1979–83. Mem. Council, Bow Group, 1965–66; Jt Secretary: UN Parly Gp, 1969–70; Cons. Greater London Members Gp, 1970–72; Cons. Constitution Cttee, 1986; Sec., 1969–70, Vice-Chm., 1970–72, Chm., 1972–74, Cons. Aviation Cttee; Member Select Cttee on: Nationalised Industries, 1973–79; Members Interests, 1986–; Dep. Chm., Air Safety Gp, 1979–. Mem. Council, Air League, 1972–76. Mem. Ct, Reading Univ., 1979–. First MP on kidney dialysis. *Publications:* Blackshirt, a biography of Mussolini (jointly), 1959; No Tame or Minor Role, (Bow Group pamphlet on the Common Market) (jointly), 1963. *Recreations:* golf, sailing, skiing, riding. *Address:* House of Commons, SW1.

See also P. M. E. D. McNair-Wilson.

McNALLY, Tom; Director-General, Retail Consortium, since 1985; Director, British Retailers Association, since 1985; *b* 20 Feb. 1943; *s* of John P. McNally and Elizabeth May (*née* McCarthy); *m* 1970, Eileen Powell. *Educ:* College of St Joseph, Blackpool; University Coll., London (BScEcon). President of Students' Union, UCL, 1965–66; Vice-Pres., Nat. Union of Students, 1966–67; Asst Gen. Sec. of Fabian Society, 1966–67; Labour Party researcher, 1967–68; Internat. Sec. of Labour Party, 1969–74; Political Adviser to: Foreign and Commonwealth Sec., 1974–76; Prime Minister, 1976–79. MP (Lab 1979–81, SDP 1981–83) Stockport S; SDP Parly spokesman on educn and sport, 1981–83. Mem., Select Cttee on Industry and Trade, 1979–83. Contested (SDP) Stockport, 1983. Public Affairs Adviser, GEC, 1983–84. *Recreations:* playing and watching sport, reading political biographies. *Address:* The Retail Consortium, Commonwealth House, 1 New Oxford Street, WC1.

McNAMARA, (Joseph) Kevin; MP (Lab) Hull North, since 1983 (Kingston-upon-Hull North, Jan. 1966–1974; Kingston-upon-Hull Central, 1974–83); *b* 5 Sept. 1934; *s* of late Patrick and Agnes McNamara; *m* 1960, Nora (*née* Jones), Warrington; four *s* one *d. Educ:* various primary schools; St Mary's Coll., Crosby; Hull Univ. (LLB). Head of Dept of History, St Mary's Grammar Sch., Hull, 1958–64; Lecturer in Law, Hull Coll. of Commerce, 1964–66. Opposition spokesman on defence, 1982–83, on defence and disarmament, 1983–85, dep. opposition spokesman on defence, 1985–. Member: Select Cttee on For. Affairs (former Chm., Overseas Develt Sub-Cttee); Parly Assembly, NATO; Vice-Chm., Economic Cttee, NATO; former Chairman: Select Cttee on Overseas Develt; PLP NI Gp; Sec., Parly Gp, TGWU. Former Mem., UK Delegn to Council of Europe. Commendatore, Order Al Merito della Repubblica Italiana, 1977. *Recreations:* family and outdoor activities. *Address:* House of Commons, SW1; 128/130 Cranbrook Avenue, Hull HU6 7ST.

McNAMARA, Most Rev. Kevin; *see* Dublin, Archbishop of, and Primate of Ireland, (RC).

McNAMARA, Air Chief Marshal Sir Neville (Patrick), KBE 1981 (CBE 1972); AO 1976; AFC 1961; Royal Australian Air Force, retired 1984; *b* Toogoolawah, Qld, 17 April 1923; *s* of late P. F. McNamara; *m* 1950, Dorothy Joan Miller; two *d. Educ:* Christian Brothers Coll., Nudgee, Qld. Enlisted RAAF, 1941; commnd 1944; Fighter Pilot WWII with No 75 Sqdn, Halmaheras and Borneo; served with No 77 Sqdn in Japan on cessation of hostilities; Air Traffic Control duties, HQ NE Area, 1948; Flying Instructor, Central Flying Sch., 1951–53; operational tour with No 77 Sqdn in Korean War; Pilot Trng Officer, HQ Trng Comd, 1954–55; Staff Officer, Fighter Operations Dept Air, 1955–57; CO No 25 Sqdn W Australia, 1957–59; CO No 2 Operational Conversion Unit, 1959–61; CO and Sen. Air Staff Officer, RAAF Staff, London, 1961–63; Director of Personnel (Officers), Dept Air, 1964–66; OC RAAF Contingent, Thailand, 1966–67; Air Staff Officer, RAAF Richmond, 1967–69; Dir-Gen., Organisation Dept Air, 1969–71; Comdr RAAF Forces Vietnam, 1971–72; Aust. Air Attaché, Washington, 1972–75; Dep. Chief of Air Staff, 1975–79; Chief of Air Staff, 1979–82; Chief of Defence Force Staff, 1982–84. RAAF psc, pfc, jssc. *Recreations:* golf, fishing. *Address:* 19 Jukes Street, Hackett, Canberra, ACT 2602, Australia. *T:* 498196. *Clubs:* Commonwealth, Royal Canberra Golf (Canberra).

McNAMARA, Robert Strange; Medal of Freedom with Distinction; Director: Corning Glass Works, since 1981; TWA, since 1981; Royal Dutch Petroleum, since 1981; The Washington Post, since 1981; Bank of America, since 1981; *b* San Francisco, 9 June 1916; *s* of Robert James McNamara and Clara Nell (*née* Strange); *m* 1940, Margaret McKinstry Craig (decd); one *s* two *d. Educ:* University of California (AB); Harvard Univ. (Master of Business Administration); Asst Professor of Business Administration, Harvard, 1940–43. Served in USAAF, England, India, China, Pacific, 1943–46 (Legion of Merit); released as Lieut-Colonel. Joined Ford Motor Co., 1946; Executive, 1946–61; Controller, 1949–53; Asst General Manager, Ford Div., 1953–55; Vice-President, and General Manager, Ford Div., 1955–57; Director, and Group Vice-President of Car Divisions, 1957–61, President, 1960–61; Secretary of Defense, United States of America, 1961–68; Pres., The World Bank, 1968–81. Trustee: Ford Foundn; Brookings Instn. Hon. degrees from: Harvard, Calif, Mich, Columbia, Ohio, Princeton, NY, Notre Dame, George Washington, Aberdeen, St Andrews and Fordham Univs; Williams, Chatham and Amherst Colls. Phi Beta Kappa. Albert Pick Jr Award, Univ. of Chicago (first recipient), 1979; Albert Einstein Peace Prize, 1983; Franklin D. Roosevelt Freedom from Want Medal, 1983; Amer. Assembly Service to Democracy Award; Dag Hammarskjöld Hon. Medal; Extrepreneurial Excellence Medal, Yale Sch. of Organization and Management. *Publications:* The Essence of Security, 1968; One Hundred Countries, Two Billion People: the dimensions of development, 1975; The McNamara Years at the World Bank, 1981. *Address:* 2412 Tracy Place, NW, Washington, DC 20008, USA.

McNAUGHT, John Graeme; a Recorder of the Crown Court, since 1981; *b* 21 Feb. 1941; *s* of Charles William McNaught and Isabella Mary McNaught; *m* 1966, Barbara Mary Smith; two *s* one *d. Educ:* King Edward VII Sch., Sheffield; The Queen's Coll., Oxford (BA Jurisprudence, 1962). Bacon Scholar, Gray's Inn, 1962; called to the Bar, Gray's Inn, 1963. *Address:* Ryton House, Lechlade, Glos GL7 3AR. *T:* Faringdon 52286.

McNAUGHTON, Lt-Col Ian Kenneth Arnold; Chief Inspecting Officer of Railways, Department of Transport, 1974–82; *b* 30 June 1920; *er s* of late Brig. F. L. McNaughton, CBE, DSO and Betty, *d* of late Rev. Arnold Pinchard, OBE; *m* 1946, Arthea, *d* of late Carel Begeer, Voorschoten, Holland; two *d. Educ:* Loretto Sch.; RMA Woolwich; RMCS Shrivenham. BScEng, CEng, FIMechE, FCIT, FIRSE. 2nd Lieut RE, 1939; served War of 1939–45, NW Europe (Captain) (despatches); GHQ MELF, 1949 (Major); Cyprus, 1955; OC 8 Rly Sqdn, 1958; Port Comdt Southampton, 1959 (Lt-Col); SOI Transportation HQ BAOR, 1960; retd 1963. Inspecting Officer of Rlys, Min. of Transport, 1963. Chm., Rlys Industry Adv. Cttee, Health and Safety Commn, 1978–82. *Recreations:* gardening, foreign travel. *Address:* Chawton Glebe, Alton, Hants. *T:* Alton 83395.

MACNAUGHTON, Prof. Sir Malcolm (Campbell), Kt 1986; MD; FRCPG; FRCOG; FRSE; Muirhead Professor of Obstetrics and Gynaecology, University of Glasgow, since 1970; *b* 4 April 1925; *s* of James Hay and Mary Robieson Macnaughton; *m* 1955, Margaret-Ann Galt; two *s* three *d. Educ:* Glasgow Academy; Glasgow Univ. (MD). Lectr, Univ. of Aberdeen, 1957–61; Sen. Lectr, Univ. of St Andrews, 1961–66; Hon. Sen. Lectr, Univ. of Dundee, 1966–70. Pres., RCOG, 1984–. *Publications:* Combined Textbook of Obstetrics and Gynaecology (ed jtly), 9th edn 1976; (ed and contrib.) Handbook of Medical Gynaecology, 1985; numerous papers in obstetric, gynaecological, endocrine and general medical jls. *Recreations:* fishing, walking, curling. *Address:* Beechwood, 15 Boclair Road, Bearsden, Glasgow G61 2AF. *T:* 041–942 1909. *Clubs:* Royal Scottish Automobile, Glasgow Academical (Glasgow).

McNEE, Sir David (Blackstock), Kt 1978; QPM 1975; Commissioner, Metropolitan Police, 1977–82; non-executive director and adviser to a number of public limited companies; *b* 23 March 1925; *s* of John McNee, Glasgow, Lanarkshire; *m* 1952, Isabella Clayton Hopkins; one *d. Educ:* Woodside Senior Secondary Sch., Glasgow. Joined City of Glasgow Police, 1946. Apptd Dep. Chief Constable, Dunbartonshire Constabulary, 1968; Chief Constable: City of Glasgow Police, 1971–75; Strathclyde Police, 1975–77. Lectures: Basil Henriques, Bristol Univ., 1978; London, in Contemporary Christianity, 1979; Dallas, Glasgow, 1980; Peter le Neve Foster Meml, RSA, 1981. President: Royal Life Saving Soc., 1982–; National Bible Soc. of Scotland 1983–; Glasgow Battalion, Boys' Brigade, 1984–; Hon. Vice-Pres., Boys' Bde, 1980–; Vice-Pres., London Fedn of Boys Clubs, 1982–. Member: Lord's Taverners, 1981–; Saints and Sinners Club of Scotland, 1982–. Patron, Scottish Motor Neurone Assoc., 1982–. Freeman of the City of London, 1977. FBIM 1977; FRSA 1981. CStJ 1978. *Publication:* McNee's Law, 1983. *Recreations:* fishing, golf, music. *Clubs:* Caledonian, Naval (Hon. Mem.).

McNEICE, Sir (Thomas) Percy (Fergus), Kt 1956; CMG 1953; OBE 1947; *b* 16 Aug. 1901; *s* of late Canon W. G. McNeice, MA, and Mary Masterson; *m* 1947, Yuen Peng Loke, *d* of late Dr Loke Yew, CMG, LLD; one *s* one *d. Educ:* Bradford Grammar Sch.; Keble Coll., Oxford (MA). Malayan Civil Service, 1925; Captain, Straits Settlements Volunteer Force (Prisoner of War, 1942–45); MLC, Singapore, 1949; MEC 1949; President of the City Council, Singapore, 1949–56, retired. FZS. *Recreations:* bird watching, walking and swimming. *Address:* Cathay Apartments, 22 Handy Road No 12–02, Singapore 0922. *Club:* Royal Commonwealth Society.

MACNEIL OF BARRA, Prof. Ian Roderick; The Macneil of Barra; 46th Chief of Clan Macneil and of that Ilk; Baron of Barra; Wigmore Professor of Law, Northwestern University, since 1980; *b* 20 June 1929; *s* of Robert Lister Macneil of Barra and Kathleen, *d* of Orlando Paul Metcalf, NYC, USA; *m* 1952, Nancy, *e d* of James Tilton Wilson, Ottawa, Canada; two *s* one *d* (and one *s* decd). *Educ:* Univ. of Vermont (BA 1950); Harvard Univ. (LLB 1955). Lieut, Infty, Army of US, 1951–53 (US Army Reserve, 1950–69, discharged honorably, rank of Major). Clerk, US Court of Appeals, 1955–56; law practice, Concord, NH, USA, 1956–59. Cornell Univ., USA: Asst Prof. of Law, 1959–62; Associate Prof., 1962–63; Prof. of Law, 1962–72 and 1974–76; Ingersoll Prof. of Law, 1976–80; Prof. of Law, Univ. of Virginia, 1972–74. Vis. Prof. of Law, Univ. of East Africa, Dar es Salaam, Tanzania, 1965–67; Guggenheim Fellow, 1978–79; Vis. Fellow, Wolfson Coll., Oxford, 1979. Hon. Vis. Fellow, Faculty of Law, Edinburgh Univ., 1979. Member: American Law Inst.; Standing Council of Scottish Chiefs. FSAScot. *Publications:* Bankruptcy Law in East Africa, 1966; (with R. B. Schlesinger, *et al*) Formation of Contracts: A Study of the Common Core of Legal Systems, 1968; Contracts: Instruments of Social Co-operation-East Africa, 1968; (with R. S. Morison) Students and Decision Making, 1970; Contracts: Exchange Transactions and Relations, 1971, 2nd edn 1978; The New Social Contract, 1980. *Heir:* *s* Roderick Wilson Macneil, Younger of Barra, *b* 22 Oct. 1954. *Address:* 3500 Lake Shore Drive, Chicago, Ill 60657, USA; Kisimul Castle, Isle of Barra, Scotland. *T:* Castlebay 300. *Club:* New (Edinburgh).

McNEIL, John Struthers, CBE 1967; Chief Road Engineer, Scottish Development Department, 1963–69; *b* 4 March 1907; *s* of R. H. McNeil, Troon; *m* 1931, Dorothea Yuille; two *s. Educ:* Ayr Academy; Glasgow Univ. BSc Hons, Civil Engineering, 1929; FICE 1955. Contracting and local government experience, 1929–35; joined Ministry of Transport as Asst Engineer, 1935; Divisional Road Engineer, NW Div. of England, 1952–55; Asst Chief Engineer, 1955–57; Dep. Chief Engineer, 1957–63. Telford Gold Medal, ICE. *Publications:* contribs. to technical journals. *Recreations:* fishing, gardening. *Address:* 306–250 Douglas Street, Victoria, BC V8V 2P4, Canada.

MacNEIL, Most Rev. Joseph Neil; *see* Edmonton (Alberta), Archbishop of, (RC).

McNEILL, Hon. Sir David (Bruce), Kt 1979; **Hon. Mr Justice McNeill;** a Judge of the High Court of Justice, Queen's Bench Division, since 1979; Member, Restrictive Practices Court, since 1981; *b* 6 June 1922; *s* of late Ferguson and Elizabeth Bruce McNeill; *m* 1949, Margaret Lewis; one *s* three *d*. *Educ:* Rydal Sch.; Merton Coll., Oxford. BCL, MA Oxon, 1947. Called to Bar, Lincoln's Inn, 1947 (Cassel Schol.); Bencher, 1974; Northern Circuit, Leader, 1974–78, Presiding Judge, 1980–84. Lecturer in Law, Liverpool Univ., 1948–58. QC 1966; Recorder of Blackburn, 1969–71; Recorder of the Crown Court, 1972–78. Mem., Parole Bd, 1986–. Member: Bar Council, 1968–72; Senate of the Inns of Court and the Bar, 1975–81 (Vice-Chm., 1976–77; Chm., 1977–78). Hon. Member: American Bar Assoc.; Canadian Bar Assoc. Hon. LLD Liverpool, 1982. Commissioned into Reconnaissance Corps, 1943; served in N Africa, Sicily, Italy, Germany. *Address:* Royal Courts of Justice, Strand, WC2A 2LL.

McNEILL, Sir James (Charles), Kt 1978; AC 1986; CBE 1972; FASA; FAIM; Chairman, The Broken Hill Proprietary Co. Ltd, 1977–84; *b* 29 July 1916; *s* of Charles Arthur Henry McNeill and Una Beatrice Gould; *m* 1942, Audrey Evelyn Mathieson; one *s*. *Educ:* Newcastle Boys' High Sch., NSW. Chm., Tubemakers of Aust. Ltd, 1978–86; Dir, ANZ Bank, 1982–86. Member: Internat. Adv. Council, Morgan Guaranty Trust Co. of NY; AT & T (International). Member: Aust. Govt Consultative Cttee on Relations with Japan; Chm., Aust.–Japan Business Forum, 1985–86; Vice-Pres., Aust.–Japan Business Consultative Council, 1977–86. Member: Council, Monash Univ. (Chm., Finance Cttee); Finance Adv. Cttee, Walter & Eliza Hall Inst. for Med. Res. Hon. DSc Newcastle, NSW, 1981; Hon. Dr jur, Monash Univ., 1986. *Recreations:* music, farming, gardening. *Address:* 104 Mont Albert Road, Canterbury, Victoria 3126, Australia. *T:* 836.4924. *Clubs:* Australian (Pres.), Athenæum, Melbourne (all Melbourne); Frankston Golf.

McNEILL, Maj.-Gen. John Malcolm, CB 1963; CBE 1959 (MBE 1942); *b* 22 Feb. 1909; *s* of Brig.-General Angus McNeill, CB, CBE, DSO, TD, Seaforth Highlanders, and Lilian, *d* of Maj.-General Sir Harry Barron, KCVO; *m* 1939, Barbara, *d* of Colonel C. H. Marsh, DSO, Spilsby, Lincs; two *d*. *Educ:* Imperial Service Coll., Windsor; RMA, Woolwich. 2nd Lieut, RA, 1929. Served Western Desert, Sicily, Italy, N.W. Europe and Burma, 1939–45; Commanded 1st Regt RHA, 1948–51; Student Imperial Defence Coll., 1952; Dep. Secretary, Chiefs of Staff Cttee, Ministry of Defence, 1953–55; Comdr RA 2nd Div. 1955–58; Comdt School of Artillery, 1959 60; Commander, British Army Staff, and Military Attaché, Washington, DC, 1960–63; Col Comdt RA, 1964–74. Principal Staff Officer to Sec. of State for Commonwealth Relations, 1964–69. ADC to the Queen, 1958–60. *Address:* Hole's Barn, Pilton, Shepton Mallet, Som. *T:* Pilton 212. *Clubs:* Army and Navy, English-Speaking Union.

McNEILL, Peter Grant Brass, PhD; Sheriff of Lothian and Borders at Edinburgh, since 1982; *b* 3 March 1929; *s* of late William Arnot McNeill and late Lillias Philips Scrimgeour; *m* 1959, Matilda Farquhar Rose, *d* of Mrs Christina Rose; one *s* three *d*. *Educ:* Hillhead High Sch., Glasgow; Morrison's Academy, Crieff; Glasgow Univ. MA (Hons Hist.) 1951; LLB 1954; Law apprentice, Biggart Lumsden & Co., Glasgow, 1952–55; Carnegie Fellowship, 1955; Faulds Fellowship, 1956–59; Scottish Bar, 1956; PhD, 1961. Hon. Sheriff Substitute of Lanarkshire, and of Stirling, Clackmannan and Dumbarton, 1962; Standing Junior Counsel to Scottish Development Dept (Highways), 1964; Advocate Depute, 1964; Sheriff of Lanarks, subseq. of Glasgow and Strathkelvin, at Glasgow, 1965–82. Pres., Sheriffs' Assoc., 1982–85. *Publications* (ed) Balfour's Practicks (Stair Society), 1962–63; (ed jtly) An Historical Atlas of Scotland *c* 400–*c* 1600, 1975; Adoption of Children in Scotland, 1982; legal and historical articles in Encyclopaedia Britannica, Juridical Review, Scots Law Times, Glasgow Herald, etc. *Recreations:* legal history, gardening, bookbinding. *Address:* Sheriffs' Chambers, Sheriff Court House, Lawnmarket, Edinburgh EH1 2NS. *T:* 031–226 7181.

McNEISH, Prof. Alexander Stewart, FRCP; Professor of Paediatrics and Child Health, and Director of the Institute of Child Health, University of Birmingham, since 1980; *b* 13 April 1938; *s* of Angus Stewart McNeish and Minnie Howieson (*née* Dickson); *m* 1963, Joan Ralston (*née* Hamilton); two *s* one *d*. *Educ:* Glasgow Acad.; Univ. of Glasgow (MB); Univ. of Birmingham (MSc). FRCP 1977; FRCPGlas 1985. Sen. Lectr in Paediatrics and Child Health, Univ. of Birmingham, 1970–76; Foundn Prof. of Child Health, Univ. of Leicester, 1976–80. Mem., GMC, 1984–. *Publications:* papers on paediatric gastroenterology in Lancet, BMJ and in Archives of Disease in Childhood. *Recreations:* golf, music. *Address:* 128 Westfield Road, Edgbaston, Birmingham B15 3JQ. *T:* 021–454 6081. *Clubs:* Athenæum; Blackwell Golf.

McNICOL, David Williamson, CBE 1966; Australian Diplomatic Service, retired; *b* 20 June 1913; *s* of late Donald McNicol, Adelaide; *m* 1947, Elsa Margaret, *d* of N. J. Hargrave, Adelaide; one *s*. *Educ:* Carey Grammar Sch., Melbourne; Kings Coll., Adelaide; Adelaide Univ. (BA). RAAF, 1940–45, Pilot, 201 and 230 Sqdns RAF, Atlantic, Madagascar, Italy and Dodecanese. Australian Minister to Cambodia, Laos and Vietnam, 1955–56; idc 1957; Australian Comr to Singapore, 1958–60; Asst Sec., Dept of External Affairs, Australia, 1960–62; Australian High Comr to Pakistan, 1962–65 and to New Zealand, 1965–68; Australian Ambassador to Thailand, 1968–69; Australian High Comr to Canada, 1969–73; Dep. High Comr for Australia in London, 1973–75; Ambassador to S Africa, and High Comr to Botswana, Lesotho and Swaziland, 1975–77. *Recreations:* golf, gardening. *Address:* 18 Fishburn Street, Red Hill, ACT 2603, Australia. *Clubs:* Naval and Military (Melbourne); Royal Canberra Golf.

McNICOL, Prof. George Paul, FRSE 1984; Principal and Vice-Chancellor, University of Aberdeen, since 1981; Member, Aberdeen Local Board, Bank of Scotland, since 1983; *b* 24 Sept. 1929; *s* of Martin and Elizabeth McNicol; *m* 1959, Susan Ritchie; one *s* two *d*. *Educ:* Hillhead High Sch., Glasgow; Univ. of Glasgow. MD, PhD, FRCP, FRCPG, FRCPE, FRCPath. House Surg., Western Infirmary, Glasgow, 1952; House Phys., Stobhill Gen. Hosp., Glasgow, 1953; Regimental MO, RAMC, 1953–55; Asst, Dept Materia Medica and Therapeutics, Registrar, Univ. Med. Unit, Stobhill Gen. Hosp., 1955–57; Univ. Dept of Medicine, Royal Infirmary, Glasgow: Registrar, 1957–59; Hon. Sen. Registrar, 1961–65; Lectr in Medicine, 1963–65; Hon. Cons. Phys., 1966–71; Sen. Lectr in Medicine, 1966–70; Reader in Medicine, 1970–71; Prof. of Medicine and Hon. Cons. Phys., Leeds Gen. Infirmary, 1971–81; Chm., Bd of Faculty of Medicine, Leeds Univ., 1978–81. Harkness Fellow, Commonwealth Fund, Dept of Internal Medicine, Washington Univ., 1959–61; Hon. Clinical Lectr and Hon. Cons. Phys., Makerere UC Med. Sch. Extension, Kenyatta Nat. Hosp., Nairobi (on secondment from Glasgow Univ.), 1965–66. Chm. Med. Adv. Cttee, Cttee of Vice-Chancellors and Principals, 1985–; Mem., British Council Cttee on Internat. Co-op. in Higher Educn, 1985–; Former Mem., Adv. Council on Misuse of Drugs. Chm., Part I Examining Bd, Royal Colls of Physicians (UK). Chm., Bd of Governors, Rowett Res. Inst., 1981–; Mem., Bd of Governors, N of Scotland Coll. of Agriculture, 1981–. FRSA 1985. Hon. FACP. Foreign Corresp. Mem., Belgian Royal Acad. of Medicine, 1985. *Publications:* papers in sci. and med. jls on thrombosis and bleeding disorders. *Recreations:* sailing, skiing. *Address:* University Office, Regent Walk, Aberdeen AB9 1FX. *T:* Aberdeen 40241; Chanonry Lodge, 13 The Chanonry, Old Aberdeen AB2 1RP. *Clubs:* Athenæum, Caledonian; Royal Northern & University (Aberdeen).

See also A. H. Smallwood.

McNICOLL, Vice-Adm. Sir Alan (Wedel Ramsay), KBE 1966 (CBE 1954); CB 1965; GM 1941; Australian Ambassador to Turkey, 1968–73; *b* 3 April 1908; 2nd *s* of late Brig.-Gen. Sir Walter McNicoll and Lady McNicoll; *m* 1st, 1937, Ruth, *d* of late W. N. Timmins; two *s* one *d*; 2nd, 1957, Frances, *d* of late J. Chadwick. *Educ:* Scotch Coll., Melbourne; Royal Australian Naval Coll. Joined Navy, 1922; Lieut, 1930; Captain, 1949; Rear-Admiral, 1958; Dep. Chief of Naval Staff, 1951–52; Commanded 10th Destroyer Flotilla, 1950; HMAS Australia, 1953–54; IDC, 1955; 2nd Naval Member, Commonwealth Naval Board, 1960–61; Commanded Australian Fleet, 1962–64; Vice-Admiral, 1965; Chief of Naval Staff, Australia, 1965–68. Comdr of Order of Orange Nassau, 1955. *Publications:* Sea Voices (verse), 1931; trans., Odes of Horace, 1979. *Recreations:* music, fly-fishing. *Address:* 6 Hutt Street, Yarralumla, ACT 2600, Australia.

See also Very Rev. Prof. H. Chadwick, Sir J. E. Chadwick, W. O. Chadwick.

McNISH, Althea Marjorie, (Althea McNish Weiss), CMT 1976; freelance textile designer, since 1957; *b* Trinidad; *d* of late J. Claude McNish, educnl reformer, and late Margaret (*née* Bourne); *m* 1969, John Weiss. *Educ:* Port-of-Spain, by her father and others; London Coll. of Printing; Central School of Art and Crafts; Royal Coll. of Art. NDD, DesRCA; FSIAD (FSIA 1968, MSIA 1960). Painted throughout childhood; after design educn in London, freelance practice, with commns from Ascher and Liberty's, 1957; new techniques for laminate murals, for SS Oriana and hosp. and coll. in Trinidad; Govt of Trinidad and Tobago travelling schol., 1962; interior design (for Govt of Trinidad and Tobago) in NY, Washington and London, 1962. Cotton Bd trav. schol. to report on export potential for British printed cotton goods in Europe, 1963; textile designs in exhibn, Inprint, Manch. and London, 1964–71; collection of dress fabric designs for ICI and Tootal Thomson for promotion of Terylene Toile, 1966; special features for Daily Mail Ideal Home Exhibn, 1966–78; interior design for Sec.-Gen. of Commonwealth, 1975; bedlinen collection for Courtaulds, 1978; (with John Weiss) textile design devolt for BRB, 1978–; textile hangings for BRB Euston offices, 1979–; banners for Design Centre, 1981; (with John Weiss) improvements to London office of High Comr for Trinidad and Tobago, 1981; advr on exhibn design for Govt of Trinidad and Tobago, Commonwealth Inst., 1982–. Member: Design Council selection panels for Design Awards and Design Index, 1968–; Design Council, 1974–81; Design Council's Jubilee Souvenir Selection Panel, 1976, Royal Wedding Souvenir Selection Panel, 1981; textile designs in exhibns of Design Council and BoT: USA, 1969; Sweden, 1969; London, 1970; London and USA, 1972. Paintings and hangings in exhibitions include: London, 1954–, one-man exhibn of hangings, Peoples Gall., 1982; Jamaica, 1975; Magazine Workspace, Leicester, 1983. (With John Weiss) exhibited textile designs, Amsterdam, 1972–74, Design Council, London, 1975–, Lille, 1981–; etched silver dishes, London, 1973–; hangings, Kilkenny, 1981; printed textiles, Commonwealth Fest. Art Exhibn, Brisbane, 1982. Research tours: Czechoslovakia, 1968; Yugoslavia, 1972; Tunisia, 1974; Caribbean and N America, 1976. Vis. Lectr, Central Sch. of Art and Crafts and other colls and polytechnics, 1960–; Advisory Tutor in Furnishing and Surface Design, London Coll. of Furniture, 1972–. External assessor for educnl and professional bodies, incl. SIAD and NCDAD/CNAA, 1966–; Mem. jury for Leverhulme schols, 1968; Judge: Portuguese textile design comp., Lisbon, 1973; 'Living' Design Awards, 1974. Mem., London Local Adv. Cttee, IBA, 1981–. Vice-Pres., SIAD, 1977–78; Mem., Fashion and Textiles Design Bd, CNAA, 1975–78; Mem. Gov. Body, Portsmouth Coll. of Art, 1972–81. *BBC-TV:* studio setting for Caribbean edn of Full House, 1973. Has appeared, with work, in films for COI and Gas Council. Chaconia Medal (Gold) (Trinidad and Tobago), 1976, for service to art and design. *Publications:* textile designs prod. in many countries, and published in Designers in Britain and design jls. *Recreations:* ski-ing, travelling, music, gardening. *Address:* 142 West Green Road, N15 5AD. *T:* 01–800 1686. *Club:* Soroptimist.

MACONCHY, Elizabeth, (Mrs W. R. Le Fanu), CBE 1977; FRCM; Hon. RAM; composer of serious music; *b* 19 March 1907; of Irish parentage; *d* of Gerald E. C. Maconchy, Lawyer, and Violet M. Poë; *m* 1930, William Richard Le Fanu (author of Bibliography of Edward Jenner, 1951, Betsy Sheridan's Journal, 1960, etc); two *d*. *Educ:* privately; Royal College of Music, London. Held Blumenthal Scholarship and won Sullivan Prize, Foli and other exhibitions, at RCM; pupil of Vaughan-Williams; travelled with Octavia Scholarship, 1929–30. First public performance: Piano Concerto with Prague Philharmonic Orchestra, 1930. Sir Henry Wood introduced "The Land", Promenade Concerts, 1930. Has had works performed at 3 Festivals of International Society for Contemporary Music (Prague, 1935; Paris, 1937; Copenhagen, 1947). Largest output has been in Chamber Music; String Quartets played as a series in BBC Third Programme, 1955, 1975. Chairman: Composers Guild of Great Britain, 1960; Soc. for Promotion of New Music, 1972–75 (Pres., 1977–). Hon. Fellow, St Hilda's Coll., Oxford, 1978. *Compositions:* Suite for Orchestra, The Land; Nocturne; Overture, Proud Thames (LCC Coronation Prize, 1953); Dialogue for piano and orchestra; Serenata Concertante for violin and orchestra, 1963; Symphony for double string orchestra; Concertino for: bassoon and string orchestra; Piano and chamber orchestra; Concerto for oboe, bassoon and string orchestra; Variazioni Concertanti for oboe, clarinet, bassoon, horn and strings, 1965; Variations for String Orchestra; twelve String Quartets (No 5, Edwin Evans Prize; No 9, Radcliffe Award, 1969); Oboe Quintet (Daily Telegraph Prize); Violin Sonata; Cello Divertimento; Duo for 2 Violins; Duo for Violin and Cello; Variations for solo cello; Reflections, for oboe, clarinet, viola and harp (Gedok International Prize, 1961); Clarinet Quintet; Carol Cantata, A Christmas Morning; Samson and the Gates of Gaza for chorus and orchestra, 1964; 3 settings of Gerard Manley Hopkins for soprano and chamber orchestra; Sonatina for harpsichord and Notebook for harpsichord, 1965; Three Donne settings, 1965; Nocturnal for unaccompanied chorus, 1965; Music for brass and woodwind, 1966; An Essex Overture, 1966; 6 Miniatures for solo violin, 1966; Duo for piano duet, 1967; Extravaganza, The Birds, after Aristophanes, 1968; And Death shall have no Dominion for chorus and brass, 3 Choirs Festival, 1969; The Jesse Tree, masque for Dorchester Abbey, 1970; Music for double-bass and piano, 1971; Ariadne (C. Day Lewis), for soprano and orch., King's Lynn Festival, 1971; Faustus, scena for tenor and piano, 1971; Prayer Before Birth, for women's voices, 1971; 3 Bagatelles for oboe and harpsichord, 1972; oboe quartet, 1972; songs for voice and harp, 1974; The King of the Golden River, opera for children, 1975; Epyllion, for solo cello and strings, Cheltenham Festival, 1975; Sinfonietta, for Essex Youth Orch., 1976; Pied Beauty, and Heaven Haven (G. M. Hopkins), for choir and brass, Southern Cathedrals Fest., 1976; Morning, Noon and Night, for harp, Aldeburgh Fest., 1977; Sun, Moon and Stars (Traherne), song cycle for soprano and piano, 1977; Heloise and Abelard, for 3 soloists, chorus and orch., 1977–78; The Leaden Echo & the Golden Echo (Hopkins), for choir and 3 instruments, 1978; Contemplation, for cello and piano, 1978; Colloquy, for flute and piano, 1979; Romanza, for solo viola and 11 instruments, 1979; Creatures, for mixed voices, 1979; Fantasia, for clarinet and piano, 1980; Little Symphony, for Norfolk Youth Orch., 1980; 4 Miniatures for chorus, 1981; Trittico for 2 oboes, bassoon and harpsichord, 1981; Piccola Musica for string trio, 1981; My Dark Heart, for soprano and 6 instruments, for RCM cent., 1982; Wind Quintet, 1982; L'Horloge (Baudelaire), for soprano, clarinet and piano, 1982; Music for Strings, for large body of strings, 1983; Proms, 1983; 5 Sketches for Solo Viola, 1983; O Time Turn Back, chorus with cello, 1983; Narration for solo cello, 1984; Still Falls the Rain for double choir, 1984; Excursion for solo bassoon, 1985; Life Story for string orchestra, 1985; Butterflies for soprano and piano, 1986; songs, piano pieces, etc; Three One-Act Operas (The Sofa, The Three Strangers, The Departure). *Address:* Shottesbrook, Boreham, Chelmsford, Essex. *T:* Chelmsford 467 286.

MACOUN, Michael John, CMG 1964; OBE 1961; QPM 1954; Overseas Police Adviser, and Inspector-General of Police, Dependent Territories, Foreign and Commonwealth Office, 1967–79, retired; Police Training Adviser, Ministry of Overseas Development, 1967–79; *b* 27 Nov. 1914; *o s* of late John Horatio Macoun, Comr of Chinese Maritime Customs; *m* 1940, Geraldine Mabel, *o d* of late Brig.-Gen. G. C. Sladen, CB, CMG, DSO, MC; two *s*. *Educ:* Stowe Sch., Buckingham; Univ. of Oxford (MA). At Metropolitan Police Coll., 1938; Tanganyika Police, 1939–42, 1945–58; Inspector-Gen. of Police, Uganda, 1959–64; Directing Staff, Police Coll., Bramshill, 1965; Commonwealth Office, 1966. Lecture tour: of USA, under auspices of British Information Services, 1964; of Eastern Canada, for Assoc. of Canadian Clubs, 1966. War Service, 1943–44. Colonial Police Medal, 1951; OStJ 1959. *Recreations:* travel, walking. *Address:* Furzedown, Rowledge, near Farnham, Surrey. *T:* Frensham 3196. *Club:* Royal Commonwealth Society.

McPARTLIN, Noel; Advocate, since 1976; Sheriff of Grampian, Highland and Islands at Elgin, since 1985; *b* 25 Dec. 1939; *s* of Michael Joseph McPartlin and Ann Dunn or McPartlin; *m* 1965, June Anderson Whitehead; three *s* three *d*. *Educ:* Galashiels Acad.; Edinburgh Univ. (MA, LLB). Solicitor in Glasgow, Linlithgow and Stirling, 1964–76. Sheriff of Grampian, Highland and Islands at Peterhead and Banff, 1983–85. *Recreation:* country life. *Address:* Rowan Lodge, Mayne Road, Elgin. *Club:* Peterhead ACC.

McPETRIE, Sir James (Carnegie), KCMG 1966 (CMG 1961); OBE 1953; Honorary Fellow, Department of Public Law, Dundee University, since 1976; *b* 29 June 1911; *er s* of late James Duncan McPetrie and late Elizabeth Mary Carnegie; *m* 1941, Elizabeth, *e d* of late John Howie; one *d*. *Educ:* Madras Coll., St Andrews; Univ. of St Andrews; Jesus Coll., Oxford (Scholar), MA (St Andrews) 1933; BA Oxon 1937, MA 1972; Harmsworth Schol., Middle Temple, 1937; Barrister, Middle Temple, 1938. Served War of 1939–45, Royal Artillery and staff of JAG (India); commissioned, 1940; Major, 1944. Legal Asst, Commonwealth Relations Office and Colonial Office, 1946, Sen. Legal Asst, 1947, Asst Legal Adviser, 1952; Legal Adviser, Colonial Office, 1960, Commonwealth Office, 1966, FCO, 1968–71; retired from HM Diplomatic Service, 1971; temporary mem. Legal Staff, DoE, 1972–75. Chm., UNESCO Appeals Bd, 1973–79. Mem. Court, Univ. of St Andrews, 1982–86. *Address:* 52 Main Street, Strathkinness, St Andrews, Fife KY16 9SA. *T:* Strathkinness 235.

McPETRIE, James Stuart, CB 1960; *b* 13 June 1902; *s* of John McPetrie and Mary (*née* Simpson); *m* 1st, 1931, Helen Noreen McGregor (*d* 1974); one *s*; 2nd, 1975, Myra, *widow* of John F. Pullen. *Educ:* Robert Gordon's Coll., Aberdeen; Aberdeen Univ. National Physical Laboratory, 1925–43; Radio Physicist, British Supply Mission, Washington, DC, 1943–44; Research Superintendent, Signals Research and Development Establishment, Ministry of Supply, 1944–50; Head of Radio Dept, Royal Aircraft Establishment, 1950–58; Dir-Gen. of Electronics Research and Development at Ministry of Aviation, 1958–62; Consulting Electronic Engineer, 1962–; Dir, Racal Electronics, 1965–69. *Publications:* series of papers on various aspects of radio research to learned societies. *Address:* 3 Edenhurst Court, Parkhill Road, Torquay, Devon TQ1 2DD.

MacPHAIL, Bruce Dugald, FCA; Managing Director, Peninsular and Oriental Steam Navigation Co., since 1985; *b* 1 May 1939; *s* of Dugald Ronald MacPhail and Winifred Marjorie MacPhail; *m* 1st, 1963, Susan Mary Gregory (*d* 1975); three *s*; 2nd, 1983, Caroline Ruth Grimston Curtis-Bennett (*née* Hubbard). *Educ:* Haileybury Coll.; Balliol Coll., Oxford (MA); Harvard Business Sch., Mass, USA (MBA). FCA 1976. Articled, Price Waterhouse, 1961–65; Harvard Business Sch., 1965–67; Hill Samuel & Co. Ltd, 1967–69; Finance Director: Sterling Guarantee Trust Ltd, 1969–74; Town & City Properties Ltd, 1974–76; Man. Dir, Sterling Guarantee Trust, 1976–85. Gov., Royal Ballet Sch., 1982–. *Recreations:* reading, wine, scuba diving. *Address:* Thorpe Lubenham Hall, Lubenham, Market Harborough, Leics LE16 9TR. *T:* Market Harborough 33960.

MACPHAIL, Sheriff Iain Duncan; Sheriff of Lothian and Borders, since 1982; *b* 24 Jan. 1938; *o s* of Malcolm John Macphail and late Mary Corbett Duncan; *m* 1970, Rosslyn Graham Lillias, *o d* of E. J. C. Hewitt, MD, TD, Edinburgh; one *s* one *d*. *Educ:* George Watson's Coll.; Edinburgh and Glasgow Univs. MA Hons History Edinburgh 1959, LLB Glasgow 1962. Admitted to Faculty of Advocates, 1963; in practice at Scottish Bar, 1963–73; Faulds Fellow in Law, Glasgow Univ., 1963–65; Lectr in Evidence and Procedure, Strathclyde Univ., 1968–69 and Edinburgh Univ., 1969–72; Standing Jun. Counsel to Scottish Home and Health Dept and to Dept of Health and Social Security, 1971–73; Extra Advocate-Depute, 1973; Sheriff of Lanarks, later Glasgow and Strathkelvin, 1973–81; Sheriff of Tayside, Central and Fife, 1981–82. Examiner in legal subjects, Glasgow and Edinburgh Univs, 1979–. Chm., Scottish Assoc. for Study of Delinquency, 1978–81. *Publications:* Law of Evidence in Scotland (Scottish Law Commn), 1979; articles and reviews in legal jls. *Recreations:* music, theatre, reading and writing. *Address:* Sheriff Court House, Court Square, Linlithgow EH49 7EQ. *T:* Linlithgow 842922. *Club:* New (Edinburgh).

MACPHERSON, family name of **Barons Drumalbyn, Macpherson of Drumochter** and **Strathcarron.**

MACPHERSON OF DRUMOCHTER, 2nd Baron, *cr* 1951; **(James) Gordon Macpherson;** Chairman and Managing Director of Macpherson, Train & Co. Ltd, and Subsidiary and Associated Companies, since 1964; Chairman, A. J. Macpherson & Co. Ltd (Bankers), since 1973; founder Chairman, Castle Dairies (Caerphilly) Ltd; *b* 22 Jan. 1924; *s* of 1st Baron (*d* 1965) and Lucy Lady Macpherson of Drumochter; (*d* 1984); *S* father, 1965; *m* 1st, 1947, Dorothy Ruth Coulter (*d* 1974); two *d* (one *s* decd); 2nd, 1975, Catherine, *d* of Dr C. D. MacCarthy; one *s* two *d*. *Educ:* Loretto; Wells House, Malvern. Served War of 1939–45, with RAF; 1939–45 Campaign medal, Burma Star, Pacific Star, Defence Medal, Victory Medal. Founder Chm. and Patron, British Importers Confedn, 1972–. Member: Council, London Chamber of Commerce, 1958–73; (Gen. Purposes Cttee, 1959–72); East European Trade Council, 1969–71; PLA, 1973–76; Exec. Cttee, W India Cttee, 1959–83 (Dep. Chm. and Treasurer, 1971, Chm. 1973–75). Freeman of City of London, 1969; Mem., Butchers' Co., 1969–. Governor, Brentwood Sch. JP Essex, 1961–76; Dep. Chm., Brentwood Bench, 1972–76; Mem. Essex Magistrates Court Cttee, 1974–76. Hon. Game Warden for Sudan, 1974; Chief of Scottish Clans Assoc. of London, 1972–74. FRSA 1971; FRES 1940; FZS 1965. *Recreations:* shooting, fishing, golf. *Heir: s* Hon. James Anthony Macpherson, *b* 27 Feb. 1979. *Address:* Kyllachy, Tomatin, Inverness-shire. *T:* Tomatin 212. *Clubs:* Boodle's, East India, Devonshire, Sports and Public Schools, Shikar; Thorndon Park, House of Lords Yacht; Royal and Ancient (St Andrews); Nairn Golf.

MACPHERSON, Sheriff Alexander Calderwood; a Sheriff of South Strathclyde, Dumfries and Galloway, at Hamilton, since 1978; *b* 14 June 1939; *s* of Alexander and Jean Macpherson; *m* 1st, 1963, Christine Isobel Hutchison; two *s*; 2nd, 1984, Eileen Mary Joyce or Gray. *Educ:* Glasgow Academy; Glasgow Univ. (MA 1959, LLB 1962). Qualified as solicitor, 1962; private practice, 1962–78; part-time Assistantship in Private Law at Glasgow Univ., 1962–69; Partner in West, Anderson & Co., Solicitors, Glasgow, 1968–78; Lectr in Evidence and Procedure at Strathclyde Univ., 1969–78. Chairman, Glasgow North and East Br., Multiple Sclerosis Soc., 1973–. *Recreations:* piping (especially Piobaireachd), fishing, fly tying, reading. *Address:* Sheriff Court, Hamilton, Lanarks ML3 6AA. *Clubs:* Glasgow Highland, Glasgow Art, Royal Scottish Automobile, Bohemian (all Glasgow); Royal Scottish Pipers' Society (Edinburgh).

MACPHERSON, Rt. Rev. Colin; *see* Argyll and the Isles, Bishop of, (RC).

MACPHERSON, Colin, MA; CA; Senior Partner, Smith & Williamson, Chartered Accountants, since 1973 (Partner, since 1959); *b* 17 Feb. 1927; *s* of Ian Macpherson and Anna Elizabeth McLean; *m* 1st, 1951, Christian Elizabeth Randolph; two *s* one *d*; 2nd, 1981, Judith Margaret Jackson, *widow* of Brig. Tom Jackson. *Educ:* Eton; Trinity Coll., Cambridge (MA). Director: Sun Life Assce, 1968–; Keystone Investment, 1975–. Dep. Chm., 1976–78, Chm., 1978–82, Commn for New Towns. Mem., Pilcher Cttee on Commercial Property Develt, 1975; Vice-Chairman: Guide Dogs for the Blind, 1976–; Regents Coll., 1985–. *Recreations:* skiing, shooting. *Address:* The Mill, Droxford, Hants SO3 1QS. *Clubs:* Oriental, City of London.

MacPHERSON, Donald, CIE 1946; *b* 22 March 1894; *s* of D. MacPherson, Edinburgh; *m* 1931, Marie Elizabeth (decd), *d* of John Nicholson, Sydney, NSW; two *d*. *Educ:* Royal High Sch. and Univ., Edinburgh. Indian Civil Service; District Magistrate, Bengal, 1928; Commissioner of Excise, 1935; Commissioner of Division, 1944. Retired, 1947. *Address:* 51 Marlborough Mansions, Cannon Hill, NW6 1JS. *T:* 01–435 4358.

MACPHERSON, Sir Keith (Duncan), Kt 1981; company director; Chief Executive since 1975, and Chairman since 1977, The Herald and Weekly Times Ltd, Melbourne; *b* 12 June 1920; *m* 1946, Ena Forester McNair; three *s* two *d*. *Educ:* Scotch Coll., Melbourne. Joined The Herald and Weekly Times Ltd, 1938; Sec., 1959–64; Asst Gen. Man., 1965–67; Gen. Man., 1968–70; Dir, 1974. Chairman: Australian Newsprint Mills Holdings Ltd, 1978– (Vice-Chm., 1976–78); West Australian Newspapers Ltd, 1981– (Dir, 1970; Man. Dir, 1970–75); South Pacific Post Pty Ltd (New Guinea Newspapers), 1965–70; Queensland Press Ltd, 1983– (Dep. Chm., 1981–83, Dir, 1978). Director: Tasman Pulp & Paper Co. Ltd, 1977–78; Davies Bros Ltd, 1975–; New Nation Publishing Ltd, Singapore, 1974–81. Pres., Australian Newspapers Council, 1968–70; Chairman: Newspaper Proprietors' Assoc. of Melbourne, 1968–70; Media Council of Aust., 1969–70. *Recreations:* swimming, gardening. *Address:* Gleneagles, 24 Balwyn Road, Canterbury, Vic 3126, Australia. *T:* 836–8571. *Clubs:* Melbourne, Athenæum, Melbourne Cricket, Royal Automobile of Victoria, Victoria Racing, Victoria Amateur Turf, Moonee Valley Racing (Melbourne); American National (Sydney).

M'PHERSON, Prof. Philip Keith, CEng, FIMechE, FIEE, FBIM; Professor of Systems Engineering and Management (formerly Systems Science), and Pro-Vice-Chancellor, since 1982, The City University; *b* 10 March 1927; *s* of Ven. Kenneth M'Pherson and Dulce M'Pherson; *m* 1975, Rosalie Margaret, *d* of Richard and Mary Fowler. *Educ:* Marlborough Coll.; Royal Naval Engineering Coll.; Royal Naval Coll., Greenwich; Massachusetts Inst. of Technology (SM); MA Oxon. Engineer Officer, Royal Navy, 1948–59; research in Admiralty Gunnery Estabt, 1955–59, retired as Lt-Comdr, 1959. Head, Dynamics Gp, Atomic Energy Estabt, UKAEA, 1959–65, SPSO, 1963; Fellow of St John's Coll., Oxford, 1965–67. Member: Executive Cttee, UK Automation Council, 1964–68; SRC Control Engrg Cttee, 1970–75; Chairman: IMechE Automatic Control Gp, 1967–69; IEE Systems Engrg Gp Cttee, 1966–69; IEE Control and Automation Div., 1967–69; IMechE Management of Innovation Cttee, 1984–; IEE Systems Engrg Cttee, 1984–; Soc. for General Systems Research (UK), 1973–76. Vis. Scholar, Internat. Inst. of Applied Systems Analysis, Austria, 1976–77; Adjunct Prof., Xian Jiaotong Univ., China, 1980–84. Freeman, City of London, 1985; Liveryman, Engineers' Co., 1986. *Publications:* many papers in the scientific literature. *Recreations:* life at home, walking in lonely places, history of naval technology, making things. *Address:* The City University, Northampton Square, EC1V 0HB. *T:* 01–253 4399.

MACPHERSON, Roderick Ewen; Fellow, King's College, Cambridge, since 1942; Registrary, University of Cambridge, 1969–83; *b* 17 July 1916; *s* of Ewen Macpherson, Chief Charity Commissioner, and Dorothy Mildred Hensley; *m* 1941, Sheila Joan Hooper, *d* of H. P. Hooper; two *s* two *d*. *Educ:* Eton College; King's College, Cambridge. Math. Tripos, Part II, Wrangler; Math. Tripos, Part III, Distinction; Smith's Prizeman, 1940. Served RAFVR, 1940–46, Navigator (Radio). Fellow, King's Coll., Cambridge, 1942–; Third Bursar, King's College, 1947–50, Second Bursar, 1950–51, First Bursar, 1951–62; University Treasurer, Univ. of Cambridge, 1962–69; Member: Council of the Senate, 1957–62; Financial Board, 1955–62. *Recreations:* gardening, hill-walking. *Address:* Orion, Coton Road, Grantchester, Cambridge CB3 9NX. *T:* Cambridge 840266.

MACPHERSON, Ronald Thomas Stewart, (Tommy), CBE (mil.) 1968; MC 1943, Bars 1944 and 1945; TD 1960; DL; Chairman: Allstate Insurance Co., since 1983 (Director, since 1980); Birmid Qualcast, since 1984 (Director, since 1982); Cosmopolitan Textile Co. Ltd, since 1984 (Director, since 1983); Employment Conditions Abroad Ltd, since 1984; Webb-Bowen International Ltd, since 1984; *b* 4 Oct. 1920; 5th *s* of late Sir Thomas Stewart Macpherson, CIE, LLD, and Lady (Helen) Macpherson, (*née* Cameron); *m* 1953, Jean Henrietta, *d* of late David Butler Wilson; two *s* one *d*. *Educ:* Edinburgh Acad.; Cargilfield; Fettes Coll. (scholar); Trinity Coll., Oxford (1st open classical scholar; MA 1st Cl. Hons PPE). Athletics Blue and Scottish International; British Team World Student Games, Paris, 1947; represented Oxford in Rugby football and hockey, 1946–47. Reader Middle Temple. 2nd Lieut. Queen's Own Cameron Highlanders TA, 1939; Scottish Commando, 1940; POW, 1941–43, escaped 1943; Major 1943; served Special Forces with French and Italian Resistance, 1944–45. Consultant, Italo-Yugoslav Border Commn, 1946. Comd 1st Bn London Scottish TA, 1961–64; Col TA London Dist, 1964–67. Mem., Queen's Body Guard for Scotland (Royal Co. of Archers). Chm., 1961–79, Pres., 1979–, Achilles Club; Vice-Pres., Newtonmore Camanachd Club. Chm., Mallinson-Denny Gp, 1981–82 (Man. Dir, 1967–81); Exec. Dir, Brooke Bond Gp plc, 1981–82; Director: Transglobe Expedition Ltd, 1978–83; C. H. Industrials PLC, 1983–; Scottish Mutual Assurance Soc., 1982–; NCB, 1983–86; TSB Scotland, 1986–, and other cos; UK Consultant, Sears Roebuck & Co., Chicago. Dep. Chm., ABCC, 1986–; Vice-Pres., London Chamber of Commerce, 1985– (Chm., Council, 1980–82). Member: Council, CBI (Chm., London and SE Reg., CBI, 1975–77); Scottish Council, London; Prices and Incomes Bd, 1968–69; Council, GBA, 1979–83; Council, Strathclyde Univ. Business Sch. Governor, Fettes Coll. Prime Warden, Co. of Dyers, 1985–86. FRSA, FBIM. DL 1977, High Sheriff, 1983–84, Greater London. Chevalier, Légion d'Honneur, and Croix de Guerre with 2 palms, France; Medaglia d'Argento and Resistance Medal, Italy; Kt of St Mary of Bethlehem. *Recreations:* shooting, outdoor sport, languages. *Address:* 4

Somers Crescent, W2 2PN. *T:* 01–262 8487; Balavil, Kingussie, Inverness-shire PH21 1LU. *T:* Kingussie 470. *Clubs:* Hurlingham, MCC.
See also Baron Drumalbyn.

MacPHERSON, Stewart Myles; Radio Commentator; Journalist; Variety Artist; Special Events Coordinator, Assiniboia Downs Racetrack, Winnipeg; *b* Winnipeg, Canada, 29 Oct. 1908; *m* 1937, Emily Comfort; one *s* one *d*. *Educ:* Canada. Started broadcasting, 1937, on ice hockey; War Correspondent. Commentator on national events and world championships. Question Master, Twenty Questions and Ignorance is Bliss. Compère, Royal Command Variety Performance, 1948; Dir of Programs, C-Jay Television, Winnipeg, 1960. *Publication:* The Mike and I, 1948; *relevant publication:* Highlights with Stewart MacPherson, by John Robertson, 1980. *Recreations:* golf, bridge, poker. *Address:* 709–3200 Portage Avenue, Winnipeg, Manitoba, Canada. *T:* (204) 889–0210.

MACPHERSON, Tommy; *see* Macpherson, R. T. S.

MACPHERSON OF CLUNY (and Blairgowrie), Hon. Sir William (Alan), Kt 1983; TD 1966; **Hon. Mr Justice Macpherson of Cluny;** Judge of the High Court of Justice, Queen's Bench Division, since 1983; Presiding Judge, Northern Circuit, since 1985; Cluny Macpherson; 27th Chief of Clan Macpherson; *b* 1 April 1926; *s* of Brig. Alan David Macpherson, DSO, MC, RA (*d* 1969) and late Catherine Richardson Macpherson; *m* 1962, Sheila McDonald Brodie; two *s* one *d*. *Educ:* Wellington Coll., Berkshire; Trinity Coll., Oxford (MA). Called to Bar, Inner Temple, 1952; Bencher, 1978; QC 1971; a Recorder of the Crown Court, 1972–83. Mem., Bar Council and Senate, 1981–83. Served, 1944–47, in Scots Guards (Capt.). Commanded (Lt-Col) 21st Special Air Service Regt (TA), 1962–65, Hon. Col, 1983–; Mem., Queen's Body Guard for Scotland, Royal Co. of Archers, 1977–. Gov., Royal Scottish Corporation, 1972–. *Recreations:* golf, fishing; Past Pres., London Scottish FC. *Heir: s* Alan Thomas Macpherson yr of Cluny and Blairgowrie. *Address:* Newton Castle, Blairgowrie, Perthshire; Royal Courts of Justice, Strand, WC2A 2LL. *Clubs:* Caledonian, Highland Society of London; Blairgowrie Golf.

McQUAIL, Paul Christopher; Under Secretary, Department of the Environment, since 1977; *b* 22 April 1934; *s* of Christopher McQuail and Anne (*née* Mullan); *m* 1964, Susan Adler; one *s* one *d*. *Educ:* St Anselm's, Birkenhead; Sidney Sussex Coll., Cambridge. Min. of Housing and Local Govt, 1957; Principal, 1962; Asst Sec., 1969; DoE, 1970; Special Asst to Permanent Sec. and Sec. of State, 1972–73; Sec., Royal Commn on the Press, 1974–77; Chief Exec., Hounslow Bor. Council, 1983–85 (on secondment). Mem., Environment and Planning Cttee, ESRC, 1983–. *Recreations:* harmless pleasures. *Address:* 158 Peckham Rye, SE22. *T:* 01–693 2865.

MACQUAKER, Donald Francis; solicitor; Partner, T. C. Young & Son, Glasgow, since 1957; Chairman, Greater Glasgow Health Board, since 1983 (Member since 1973); *b* 21 Sept. 1932; *s* of Thomas Mason Macquaker, MC, MA, BL and Caroline Bertha Floris Macquaker; *m* 1964, Susan Elizabeth, *d* of Mr and Mrs W. A. K. Finlayson, High Coodham, Symington, Ayrshire; one *s* one *d*. *Educ:* Winchester Coll.; Trinity Coll., Oxford (MA); Univ. of Glasgow (LLB). Admitted Solicitor, 1957. Mem. Bd of Management, Glasgow Royal Maternity Hosp. and associated hosps, 1965–74 (Vice-Chm., 1972–74); Convener, Finance and Gen. Purposes Cttee, Greater Glasgow Health Bd, 1974–83. *Recreations:* shooting, fishing, travelling, gardening. *Address:* Blackbyres, by Ayr KA7 4TS. *T:* Alloway 41088. *Clubs:* The Western (Glasgow); Leander (Henley-on-Thames).

McQUARRIE, Albert; MP (C) Banff and Buchan, since 1983 (Aberdeenshire East, 1979–83); *b* 1 Jan. 1918; *s* of Algernon Stewart McQuarrie and Alice Maud Sharman; *m* 1945, Roseleen McCaffery (*d* 1986); one *s*. *Educ:* Highlanders Acad., Greenock; Greenock High Sch.; Royal Coll. of Science and Technology. MSE, PEng. Served in HM Forces, 1939–45 (Officer in RE). Chm., A. McQuarrie & Son (Great Britain) Ltd, 1946–; Consultant, Bredero Homes Ltd, 1976–; Dir, Energy Explorations Ltd. Former Dean of Guild, Gourock Town Council; former Chm., Fyvie/Rothienorman/Monquhitter Community Council. Chm., British/Gibraltar All Party Gp; Vice Chm., Conservative Fisheries Sub Cttee; Mem., Select Cttee on Agriculture. Member: Council, Soc. of Engineers, 1978–; Turriff Branch, British Legion. Hon Patron, North Eastern Junior Football Assoc.; Hon. Mem., Fraserburgh Junior Football Club. *Recreations:* golf, bridge, music, soccer. *Address:* Teuchar Lodge, Cuminestown, Aberdeenshire AB5 8HR. *T:* Mintlaw 2531; 21 Sancroft Street, Kennington, SE11 5UG. *T:* 01–582 4345. *Clubs:* Challoner (Chm.); Royal Scottish Automobile (Mem. Council, 1978–); Turriff Golf.

MACQUARRIE, Rev. Prof. John, TD 1962; FBA 1984; Lady Margaret Professor of Divinity, University of Oxford, and Canon of Christ Church, 1970–86; *b* 27 June 1919; *s* of John Macquarrie and Robina Macquarrie (*née* McInnes); *m* 1949, Jenny Fallow (*née* Welsh); two *s* one *d*. *Educ:* Paisley Grammar Sch.; Univ. of Glasgow. MA 1940; BD 1943; PhD 1954; DLitt 1964; DD Oxon 1981. Royal Army Chaplains Dept, 1945–48; St Ninian's Church, Brechin, 1948–53; Lecturer, Univ. of Glasgow, 1953–62; Prof. of Systematic Theology, Union Theological Seminary, NY, 1962–70. Consultant, Lambeth Conf., 1968 and 1978. Governor: St Stephen's Hse, Oxford, 1970–; Pusey House, Oxford, 1975–. Hon. degrees: STD: Univ. of the South, USA, 1967; General Theological Seminary, New York, 1968; DD: Univ. of Glasgow, 1969; Episcopal Seminary of SW, Austin, Texas, 1981; Virginia Theol Seminary, 1981. *Publications:* An Existentialist Theology, 1955; The Scope of Demythologising, 1960; Twentieth Century Religious Thought, 1963; Studies in Christian Existentialism, 1965; Principles of Christian Theology, 1966; God-Talk, 1967; God and Secularity, 1967; Martin Heidegger, 1968; Three Issues in Ethics, 1970; Existentialism, 1972; Paths in Spirituality, 1972; The Faith of the People of God, 1972; The Concept of Peace, 1973; Thinking about God, 1975; Christian Unity and Christian Diversity, 1975; The Humility of God, 1978; Christian Hope, 1978; In Search of Humanity, 1982; In Search of Deity (Gifford Lectures), 1984; Theology, Church and Ministry, 1986. *Address:* 206 Headley Way, Headington, Oxford OX3 7TA. *T:* Oxford 61889.

MACQUEEN, Angus, CMG 1977; Director, The British Bank of the Middle East, 1970–79 (Chairman, 1975–78); Member, London Advisory Committee, The Hongkong and Shanghai Banking Corporation, 1975–78; Chairman, Incotes Ltd, 1975–85; *b* 7 April 1910; *s* of Donald Macqueen and Catherine Thomson; *m* 1st, 1940, Erica A. L. Sutherland (marr. diss.); one *d*; 2nd, 1950, Elizabeth Mary Barber; one *s* one *d*. *Educ:* Campbeltown Grammar Sch. Joined Union Bank of Scotland, 1927; Imperial Bank of Persia (now The British Bank of the Middle East), 1930; overseas service in Iraq, Iran, Kuwait, Aden, Lebanon, Morocco; Gen. Manager, 1965–70. Director: The British Bank of the Middle East (Morocco), 1961–70; The Bank of Iran and the Middle East, 1965–74; Bank of North Africa, 1965–70. Member: London Chamber of Commerce (Middle East Section), 1962–66; Council, Anglo-Arab Assoc., 1968–75; Corona (Overseas Students) Housing Assoc., 1969–81. AIB (Scot.). National Cedar Medal, Lebanon, 1960. *Recreations:* walking, foreign travel. *Address:* 18 Montagu Square, W1H 1RD. *T:* 01–935 9015. *Club:* Oriental.

MacQUEEN, Prof. John; Professor of Scottish Literature and Oral Tradition, since 1972, and Director, School of Scottish Studies, since 1969, University of Edinburgh; *b* 13 Feb. 1929; *s* of William L. and Grace P. MacQueen; *m* 1953, Winifred W. McWalter; three *s*. *Educ:* Hutchesons' Boys' Grammar Sch.; Glasgow Univ.; Cambridge Univ. MA English Lang. and Lit., Greek, Glasgow; BA, MA Archaeology and Anthropology, Section B, Cambridge. RAF, 1954–56 (Flying Officer). Asst Prof. of English, Washington Univ., Missouri, 1956–59; Lectr in Medieval English and Scottish Literature, 1959–63, Masson Prof. of Medieval and Renaissance Literature, 1963–72, Univ. of Edinburgh. Barclay Acheson Vis. Prof. of Internat. Relations, Macalester Coll., Minnesota, 1967; Vis. Prof. in Medieval Studies, Australian Nat. Univ., 1971; Winegard Vis. Prof., Univ. of Guelph, Ont, 1981. Chairman: British Branch, Internat. Assoc. of Sound Archives, 1978–80; Exec. Cttee, Scottish Nat. Dictionary Assoc., 1978–; Mem., Scottish Film Council, 1981– (Chm., Archive Cttee, 1980–). Hon. DLitt NUI, 1985. *Publications:* St Nynia, 1961; (with T. Scott) The Oxford Book of Scottish Verse, 1966; Robert Henryson, 1967; Ballattis of Luve, 1970; Allegory, 1970; (ed with Winifred MacQueen) A Choice of Scottish Verse, 1470–1570, 1972; Progress and Poetry, 1982; Numerology, 1985; articles and reviews in learned jls. *Recreations:* music, walking, archaeology. *Address:* 12 Orchard Toll, Edinburgh EH4 3JF. *T:* 031–332 1488; Slewdonan, Damnaglaur, Drummore, Stranraer DG9 9QN. *Clubs:* University Staff, Scottish Arts (Edinburgh).

McQUIGGAN, John, MBE 1955; independent consultant; Executive Director, United Kingdom-South Africa Trade Association Ltd, 1978–86; retired at own request from HM Diplomatic Service, 1977; *b* 24 Nov. 1922; *s* of John and Sarah Elizabeth McQuiggan; *m* 1950, Doris Elsie Hadler; three *s* one *d*. *Educ:* St Edwards Coll., Liverpool. Served War, in RAF, 1942–47 (W Africa, Europe and Malta). Joined Dominions Office, 1940; Administration Officer, British High Commission, Canberra, Australia, 1950–54; Second Sec., Pakistan, Lahore and Dacca, 1954–57; First Sec. (Inf.), Lahore, 1957–58; Dep. Dir, UK Inf. Services, Australia (Canberra and Sydney), 1958–61; Dir, Brit. Inf. Services, Eastern Nigeria (Enugu), 1961–64; Dir, Brit. Inf. Services in Uganda, and concurrently First Sec., HM Embassy, Kigali, Rwanda, 1964–69; W African Dept, FCO, 1969–73; HM Consul, Chad, 1970–73 (London based); Dep. High Comr and Counsellor (Econ. and Commercial), Lusaka, Zambia, 1973–76. Dir-Gen., Brit. Industry Cttee on South Africa, 1986. Mem., Royal African Soc.; MIPR 1964; Mem., Internat. Public Relations Assoc., 1975. Fellow, Inst. of Dirs. *Publications:* pamphlets and contribs to trade and economic jls. *Recreations:* tennis, carpentry, craftwork. *Address:* 7 Meadowcroft, Bickley, Kent BR1 2JD. *T:* 01–467 0075. *Clubs:* Royal Commonwealth Society, Royal Over-Seas League, Institute of Directors, Belfry.

McQUILLAN, William Rodger; HM Diplomatic Service, retired; *b* 18 March 1930; *s* of late Albert McQuillan and Isabella Glen McQuillan; *m* 1970, Sheriell May Fawcett; one *s* two *d*. *Educ:* Royal High Sch., Edinburgh; Edinburgh Univ.; Yale Univ. Served RAF, 1954–57. Asst Sec., Manchester Univ. Appointments Board, 1957–65; HM Diplomatic Service, 1965–83: First Sec., CRO, 1965; Lusaka, 1968, Head of Chancery, 1969; First Sec. (Commercial), Santiago, Chile, 1970; Counsellor and HM Consul, Guatemala City, 1974; Head of Inf. Policy Dept, FCO, 1978–81; Ambassador to Iceland, 1981–83. *Recreations:* hill walking, scribbling.

MacQUITTY, James Lloyd, OBE 1983; QC (NI) 1960; Chairman, Ulster Television Ltd, 1977–83; *b* 2 Nov. 1912; *s* of James MacQuitty and Henrietta Jane (*née* Little); *m* 1941, Irene Frances McDowell. *Educ:* Campbell Coll. and Methodist Coll., Belfast; St Catherine's Coll., Oxford (MA); Trinity Hall, Cambridge (MA, LLM). Vice-Pres., Cambridge Univ. Conservative Assoc., 1936. HG Instructor, 1940–43; HAA, 1943–44. Called to English Bar, 1938, to NI Bar, 1941. Chairman: Compensation Appeals Tribunal; Compensation Tribunal for Loss of Employment through Civil Unrest; Wages Councils in NI; Arbitrator under the Industrial Courts Act 1919, 1958–78; Mem., Industrial Injuries Adv. Council, 1960–86. Before reorganisation in 1973 of Local Govt in NI, was Chm. of former Jt Adv. Bds for Local Authorities' Services, Municipal Clerks, Rural Dist Clerks and County Chief Educn Officers and County Surveyors. Vice-Chm., Management Cttee, Glenlola Collegiate Sch., 1964–75; Chm., Trustees of Ulster Folk and Transport Museum, 1976–85 (Vice-Chm., 1969–76). Freeman, City of London, 1967. Chevalier de l'Ordre de St Lazare, 1962. *Recreations:* swimming, sailing. *Address:* 10 Braemar Park, Bangor, Co. Down, Northern Ireland. *T:* Bangor 454420. *Clubs:* Carlton; Royal Ulster Yacht.

MacRAE, (Alastair) Christopher (Donald Summerhayes); HM Diplomatic Service; Political Counsellor and Head of Chancery, Paris, since 1983; *b* 3 May 1937; *s* of Dr Alexander Murray MacRae and Dr Grace Maria Lynton Summerhayes MacRae; *m* 1963, Mette Willert; two *d*. *Educ:* Rugby; Lincoln Coll., Oxford (BA Hons English); Harvard (Henry Fellow in Internat. Relations). RN, 1956–58. CRO, 1962; 3rd, later 2nd Sec., Dar es Salaam, 1963–65; ME Centre for Arab Studies, Lebanon, 1965–67; 2nd Sec., Beirut, 1967–68; FCO, 1968–70; 1st Sec. and Head of Chancery: Baghdad, 1970–71; Brussels, 1972–76; attached European Commn, Brussels, on special unpaid leave from FCO, 1976–78; Ambassador to Gabon, 1978–80, and to Sao Tomé and Principé (non-resident), 1979–80; Head of W Africa Dept, FCO, 1980–83, and Ambassador (non-resident) to Chad, 1982–83. *Recreation:* trying to keep fit. *Address:* c/o Foreign and Commonwealth Office, King Charles Street, SW1A 2AH. *Club:* Royal Commonwealth Society.

MACRAE, Christopher, CBE 1956; MA, DPhil; Vice-President, Ashridge Management College, since 1969 (Principal, 1962–69); *b* 6 Jan. 1910; *s* of John Tait Macrae and Mary (*née* Mackenzie), Kintail, Ross-shire; *m* 1939, Mary Margaret Campbell Greig, *er d* of Robert Elliott, Glasgow; two *s* one *d* (*er d* decd in infancy). *Educ:* Dingwall Acad.; Glasgow Univ. (MA); New Coll., Oxford (DPhil). Civil Servant, 1937–46; Chief Exec. Scottish Counc. (Devel. and Industry), 1946–56; Prof. of Industrial Admin., The Royal Coll. of Science and Technology, Glasgow, and Head of Chesters Residential Management Educn Centre, 1956–62. *Publications:* various articles and papers. *Recreations:* reading, music, walking, climbing, sailing. *Address:* Cluain, Tomnacroich, by Aberfeldy, Perthshire PH15 2LJ. *T:* Kenmore 298.

MacRAE, Prof. Donald Gunn; Martin White Professor of Sociology, University of London, since 1978 (Professor of Sociology, University of London, since 1961); *b* 20 April 1921; *o s* of Donald MacRae and Elizabeth Maud Gunn; *m* 1948, Helen Grace McHardy; two *d*. *Educ:* various schools in Scotland; Glasgow High Sch.; Glasgow Univ.; Balliol Coll., Oxford. MA Glasgow 1942; BA 1945, MA 1949, Oxon. Asst Lectr, LSE, 1945; Univ. Lectr in Sociology, Oxford, 1949; Reader in Sociology, London Univ., 1954; Prof. of Sociology: UC Gold Coast, 1956; Univ. of California, Berkeley, 1959; Fellow, Center for Advanced Studies in Behavioral Sciences, Stanford, 1967. Vis. Prof., Univ. of the Witwatersrand, 1975. Member: Council, CNAA (Chm. Cttee for Arts and Social Studies, to 1978); Archbp of Canterbury's Gp on Divorce Law, 1964–66; Gaitskell Commn of Inquiry into Advertising, 1962–66; Internat. Council on the Future of the University, 1973–82. Editor, British Jl of Sociology, from formation to 1965. *Publications:* Ideology and Society, 1960; (ed) The World of J. B. Priestley, 1967; (ed with intro.) The Man Versus the State, by Herbert Spencer, 1969; Ages and Stages, 1973; Max Weber,

1974. *Recreations:* talking, music, walking. *Address:* Flat 1, 1 Church Road, Highgate, N6. *T:* 01–348 9506; 33 Liverpool Road, Walmer, Kent. *Club:* Athenæum.

McRAE, Frances Anne, (Mrs Hamish McRae); *see* Cairncross, F. A.

McRAE, Hamish Malcolm Donald; Financial Editor, The Guardian, since 1975; *b* 20 Oct. 1943; *s* of Donald and Barbara McRae (*née* Budd); *m* 1971, Frances Anne Cairncross, *qv*; two *d. Educ:* Fettes College; Trinity College, Dublin (BA Hons Economics and Political Science). Liverpool Post, 1966–67; The Banker, 1967–72 (Asst Editor, 1969, Dep. Editor, 1971); Editor, Euromoney, 1972–74; Wincott Foundn financial journalist of the year, 1979. *Publications:* (with Frances Cairncross) Capital City: London as a financial centre, 1973, 4th edn 1985; (with Frances Cairncross) The Second Great Crash, 1975; Japan's role in the emerging global securities market, 1985. *Recreations:* walking, ski-ing, cooking. *Address:* 6 Canonbury Lane, N1 2AP.

MACRAE, John Esmond Campbell, CMG 1986; DPhil; HM Diplomatic Service; Ambassador to Senegal, since 1985; concurrently Ambassador (non-resident) to Guinea, Guinea-Bissau, Mali, Mauritania and Cap Verde, since 1985; *b* 8 Dec. 1932; *s* of Col Archibald Campbell Macrae, IMS, and Euretta Margaret Skelton; *m* 1962, Anne Catherine Sarah Strain; four *s. Educ:* Sheikh Bagh Sch., Kashmir; Fettes Coll., Edinburgh; Christ Church Oxford (Open Scholar); Princeton, USA. DPhil, MA; FRGS. Atomic Energy and Disarmament Dept, Foreign Office, 1959–60; 2nd Sec., British Embassy, Tel Aviv, 1961–64; 1st Secretary: Djakarta, 1964; Vientiane, 1964–66; FO, NE African Dept, 1966; Central Dept, 1967–69; Southern African Dept, 1970–72; UK Mission to the UN, New York (dealing with social affairs, population and outer space), 1972–75; Counsellor, Science and Technology, Paris, 1975–80; Head of Cultural Relns Dept, FCO, 1980–85; RCDS, 1985. *Recreations:* swimming, travel, music. *Address:* c/o Foreign and Commonwealth Office, Whitehall, SW1A 2AH. *Club:* Royal Geographic.

MACRAE, Col Robert Andrew Alexander Scarth, MBE 1953; JP; Lord-Lieutenant of Orkney, since 1972 (Vice-Lieutenant, 1967–72); Farmer; *b* 14 April 1915; *s* of late Robert Scarth Farquhar Macrae, Grindelay House, Orphir, Orkney; *m* 1945, Violet Maud, *d* of late Walter Scott MacLellan; two *s. Educ:* Lancing; RMC Sandhurst. 2nd Lt Seaforth Highlanders, 1935; Col 1963; retd 1968. Active Service: NW Europe, 1940–45 (despatches, 1945); Korea, 1952–53; E Africa, 1953–54. Member: Orkney CC, 1970–74; Orkney Islands Council, 1974–78; Vice Chairman: Orkney Hospital Bd, 1971–74; Orkney Health Bd, 1974–79. Hon. Sheriff, Orkney, 1974. DL, Co. of Orkney, 1946; JP Orkney, 1975. *Recreations:* sailing, fishing. *Address:* Grindelay House, Orkney. *T:* Orphir 228. *Clubs:* Army and Navy; New, Puffin's (Edinburgh).

MACREADY, Sir Nevil (John Wilfrid), 3rd Bt *cr* 1923; CBE 1983; Managing Director, Mobil Oil Co. Ltd, 1975–85; Chairman: Crafts Council, since 1984; Horseracing Advisory Council, since 1986; *b* 7 Sept. 1921; *s* of Lt-Gen. Sir Gordon (Nevil) Macready, 2nd Bt, KBE, CB, CMG, DSO, MC, and Elisabeth (*d* 1969), *d* of Duc de Noailles; *S* father 1956; *m* 1949, Mary, *d* of late Sir Donald Fergusson, GCB; one *s* three *d. Educ:* Cheltenham; St John's Coll., Oxford. Served in RA (Field), 1942–47 (despatches); Staff Captain, 1945. BBC European Service, 1947–50. Vice-Pres. and Gen. Manager, Mobil Oil Française, 1972–75. Pres., Inst. of Petroleum, 1980–82. Pres., Royal Warrant Holders' Assoc., 1979–80. *Recreations:* racing, fishing, theatre, music. *Heir:* *s* Charles Nevil Macready [*b* 19 May 1955; *m* 1981, Lorraine, *d* of Brian McAdam; one *s* one *d*]. *Address:* The White House, Odiham, Hants. *T:* Odiham 2976. *Clubs:* Boodle's, Naval and Military; Jockey (Paris).

MacRITCHIE, Prof. Farquhar, CBE 1968; MA, LLB (Aberdeen); Professor of Conveyancing at Aberdeen University, 1946–74; Consultant, Burnett & Reid, Advocates, Aberdeen, since 1979; *b* 1 Nov. 1902; *s* of Donald MacRitchie, Isle of Lewis; *m* 1941, Isobel, *d* of William Ross, Aberdeen; one *s* decd. *Educ:* Aberdeen Univ. Asst Lecturer in Law, Aberdeen Univ., 1940–45; Lecturer in Mercantile Law, Aberdeen Univ., 1945–46. Hon. Sheriff in Aberdeen. Convener, Legal Education Cttee, Law Soc. of Scotland, 1955–70; Vice-Pres., Law Soc. of Scotland, 1963. Mem. of firm of Morice & Wilson, Advocates, Aberdeen, 1939–79. Hon. LLD Edinburgh, 1965. *Recreation:* golf. *Address:* 60 Rubislaw Den North, Aberdeen AB2 4AN. *T:* 35458. *Club:* University (Aberdeen).

McROBERT, Rosemary Dawn Teresa, OBE 1985; Deputy Director, Consumers' Association, since 1980; *b* Maymyo, Burma, 29 Aug. 1927; *e d* of late Lt-Col Ronald McRobert, IMS, and Julie Rees. *Educ:* privately and at Gloucestershire College of Educn. Journalist and broadcaster on consumer subjects, 1957–63; Founder editor, Home Economics, 1954–63; Chief Information Officer, Consumer Council, 1965–70; Consumer Representation Officer, Consumers' Assoc., 1971–73; Adviser on consumer affairs in DTI and Dept of Prices and Consumer Protection, 1973–74; Dir, Retail Trading Standards Assoc., 1974–80. Member Council: Inst. of Consumer Ergonomics, 1974–81; Consumers' Assoc., 1974–79; Advertising Standards Authority, 1974–80; Member: Adv. Council on Energy Conservation, 1974–82; Design Council, 1975–84; Post Office Review Cttee, 1976; Policyholders' Protection Bd, 1976–; Nuffield Enquiry into Pharmacy Services, 1984–86. Chm., Management Cttee, Camden Consumer Aid Centres, 1977–80. Liveryman, Glovers' Co., 1979. *Address:* 57 Lawford Road, NW5 2LG. *Club:* Reform.

MACRORY, Sir Patrick (Arthur), Kt 1972; Director, Rothman Carreras Ltd, 1971–82; Barrister-at-Law; *b* 21 March 1911; *s* of late Lt-Col F. S. N. Macrory, DSO, DL, and Rosie, *d* of Gen. Brabazon Pottinger; *m* 1939, Elizabeth, *d* of late Rev. J. F. O. Lewis and of Mrs Lewis; three *s* (one *d* decd). *Educ:* Cheltenham Coll.; Trinity Coll., Oxford (MA). Called to the Bar, Middle Temple, 1937. Served War, 1939–45, Army. Unilever Ltd: joined 1947; Secretary, 1956; Director, 1968–71; retd. Dir, Bank of Ireland Gp, 1971–79; Chm., Merchant Ivory Productions, 1976–. Mem., Northern Ireland Development Council, 1956–64; Gen. Treasurer, British Assoc. for Advancement of Science, 1960–65; Chm., Review Body on Local Govt in N Ireland, 1970; Pres., Confedn of Ulster Socs, 1980–84 (Chm., 1974–79); Member: Commn of Inquiry into Industrial Representation, 1971–72; Cttee on the Preparation of Legislation, 1973. Mem. Council, Cheltenham Coll. (Dep. Pres., 1980–83). *Publications:* Borderline, 1937; Signal Catastrophe—the retreat from Kabul 1842, 1966, repr. as Kabul Catastrophe: the retreat of 1842, 1986; Lady Sale's Journal, 1969; The Siege of Derry, 1980; Days that are Gone, 1983. *Recreations:* golf, military history. *Address:* Amberdene, Walton-on-the-Hill, Tadworth, Surrey. *T:* Tadworth 3086. *Clubs:* Athenæum, Army and Navy; Walton Heath Golf; Castlerock Golf (Co Londonderry).

McSHARRY, Deirdre; Editor-in-Chief, Country Living, since 1986; *b* 4 April 1932; *d* of late Dr John McSharry and of Mrs Mary McSharry. *Educ:* Dominican Convent, Wicklow; Trinity Coll., Dublin. Woman's Editor, Daily Express, 1962–66; Fashion Editor, The Sun, 1966–72; Editor, Cosmopolitan, 1973–85. Magazine Editor of the Year, 1981. *Recreations:* architecture, gardening. *Address:* 37 Addison Avenue, W11.

McSHINE, Hon. Sir Arthur Hugh, TC; Kt 1969; Chief Justice of Trinidad and Tobago, 1968–71; Acting Governor-General, Trinidad and Tobago, 1972; *b* 11 May 1906; *m* Dorothy Mary Vanier; one *s* one *d. Educ:* Queen's Royal Coll., Trinidad. Called to Bar, Middle Temple, 1931. Practised at Trinidad Bar for eleven years; Magistrate, 1942;

Senior Magistrate, 1950; Puisne Judge, 1953; Justice of Appeal, 1962. Acting Governor-Gen., Trinidad and Tobago, 1970. *Recreations:* music and chess (Pres., Caribbean Chess Fedn and Trinidad Chess Assoc.); flying (holder of private pilot's licence). *Address:* 6 River Road, Maraval, Port-of-Spain, Trinidad. *Clubs:* Trinidad and Tobago Turf, Trinidad and Tobago Yacht.

MACTAGGART, Fiona; Councillor (Lab), London Borough of Wandsworth, since 1986; *b* 12 Sept. 1953; *d* of Ian Auld Mactaggart and Rosemary Belhaven. *Educ:* Cheltenham Ladies' Coll.; King's Coll., London (BA Hons). Gen. Sec., London Students' Organisation, 1977–78; Vice-Pres., 1978–80, Nat. Sec., 1980–81, NUS; Gen. Sec., Jt Council for Welfare of Immigrants, 1982–86. *Address:* 61 Taybridge Road, SW11 5PX. *T:* 01–228 4468.

MACTAGGART, Sir Ian (Auld), 3rd Bt *cr* 1938; Managing Director The Western Heritable Investment Company and Director of several Property and other Companies; *b* Glasgow, 19 April 1923; *e s* of Sir John (Jack) Mactaggart, 2nd Bt, Nassau, Bahamas; *S* father 1960; *m* 1946, Rosemary (marr. diss. 1969), *d* of Sir Herbert Williams, 1st Bt, MP; two *s* two *d. Educ:* Oundle; Clare Coll., Cambridge. Served with Royal Engineers in India, 1942–45. Contested (U) Gorbals div. of Glasgow, 1945; contested (C) Fulham, 1970. Mem. (C) London County Council, for Fulham, 1949–51. Chm., Soc. for Individual Freedom. *Heir:* *s* John Auld Mactaggart [*b* 21 Jan. 1951; *m* 1977, Patricia, *y d* of late Major Harry Alastair Gordon]. *Address:* 2A Westmoreland Terrace, SW1. *T:* 01–834 8062. *Club:* English-Speaking Union.

McTAGGART, Robert; MP (Lab) Glasgow Central, since June 1980; *b* 2 Nov. 1945; *s* of Robert and Mary McTaggart; *m* 1966, Elizabeth Jardine; one *s* two *d. Educ:* St Constantine's, St Bartholomew's and Holyrood. Apprentice Marine Plumber, 1962–67; Trigonometrical Calculator, 1968–72; Pipework Planner, 1972–80. EETPU Shop Steward, 1971–77. Joined Labour Party, 1969; Glasgow Corporation Councillor, 1974–75, District Councillor 1977–80; Parliamentary Election Agent, 1978–80. *Recreations:* watching football, athletics, playing draughts, snooker, reading. *Address:* 61 St Mungo Avenue, Townhead, Glasgow G4 0PL. *T:* 041–552 7346.

MACTAGGART, William Alexander, CBE 1964; JP; Chairman, 1960–70, and Managing Director, 1945–68, Pringle of Scotland Ltd, Knitwear Manufacturers, Hawick; *b* 17 Aug. 1906; *o s* of late William Alexander and Margaret Mactaggart, Woodgate, Hawick; *m* 1932, Marjorie Laing Innes; two *s* one *d. Educ:* Sedbergh Sch., Yorks. Joined Robert Pringle & Son Ltd (later Pringle of Scotland Ltd), 1925; Dir, 1932; Joint Managing Dir, 1933. Served War of 1939–45: Captain, RASC, Holland, Belgium, France, 1942–45. Elder of Lilliesleaf Parish Church. *Address:* Bewlie House, Lilliesleaf, Melrose, Roxburghshire TD6 9ER. *T:* Lilliesleaf 267.

MacTAGGART, Air Vice-Marshal William Keith, CBE 1976 (MBE 1956); CEng, FIMechE; FRAeS; FBIM; Managing Director, MPE Ltd, since 1984; *b* 15 Jan. 1929; *s* of Duncan MacTaggart and Marion (*née* Keith); *m* 1st, 1949 Christina Carnegie Geddes (marr. diss. 1977); one *s* two *d*; 2nd, 1977, Barbara Smith Brown, *d* of Adm. Stirling P. Smith, late USN, and Mrs Smith; one step *d. Educ:* Aberdeen Grammar Sch.; Aberdeen Univ. (BScEng 1948). FIMechE 1973; FRAeS 1974; FBIM 1978. Commnd RAF, 1949; 1949–67: Engr Officer; Pilot; AWRE, Aldermaston (Montebello and Maralinga atomic trials); attended RAF Staff Coll., and Jt Services Staff Coll.; Def. Intell.; Systems Analyst, DOAE, West Byfleet, and MoD (Air); Head of Systems MDC, RAF Swanton Morley, 1968; OC RAF Newton, 1971 (Gp Captain); Dep. Comd Mech. Engr, HQ Strike Comd, 1973; Dir of Air Armament, MoD (PE), 1973 (Air Cdre); RCDS, 1977; Vice-Pres. (Air), Ordnance Bd, 1978 (Air Vice-Marshal), Pres., 1978–80. Dep. Chm., Tomash Holdings Ltd, 1980–84. *Recreations:* music, travel. *Address:* 11 Rectory Meadow, Southfleet, Gravesend, Kent DA13 9NY. *T:* Southfleet 3962; MPE Ltd, Brunswick Road, Cobbs Wood, Ashford, Kent TN23 1EB. *T:* Ashford 23404. *Club:* Royal Air Force.

MacTHOMAS OF FINEGAND, Andrew Patrick Clayhills; 19th Chief of Clan MacThomas (Mac Thomaidh Mhor); *b* 28 Aug. 1942; *o s* of late Captain Patrick Watt MacThomas of Finegand and of Elizabeth, *d* of late Becket Clayhills-Henderson, Invergowrie, Angus; *S* father 1970; *m* 1985, Anneke Cornelia Susanna, *o d* of A. and S. Kruyning-Van Hout, Netherlands. *Educ:* St Edward's, Oxford. Public relations, Barclays Bank, London. FSA (Scot.) 1973. Pres., Clan MacThomas Soc., 1970–; Hon. Vice-Pres., Clan Chattan Assoc., 1970–. *Recreations:* steeplechasing, travelling, promoting Scotland. *Heir:* sister Elizabeth Gillian MacThomas, *b* 15 Feb. 1949. *Address:* c/o Clan MacThomas Society, 29 Bennan Gardens, Broughty Ferry, Dundee, Angus.

McTIERNAN, Rt. Hon. Sir Edward (Aloysius), PC 1963; KBE 1951; Justice of the High Court of Australia, 1930–76; *b* 16 Feb. 1892; *s* of Patrick and Isabella McTiernan; *m* 1948, Kathleen, *d* of Sidney and Ann Lloyd, Melbourne. *Educ:* Marist Brothers' High Sch., Sydney; Sydney Univ. (BA, LLB, 1st cl. Hons). Admitted to Bar, NSW, 1917; Lecturer in Law, Sydney Univ.; NSW Parliament, 1920–27; Attorney-Gen., 1920–22 and 1925–27; NSW Govt Representative in London, 1926; MHR for Parkes, Commonwealth Parl., 1928; Papal Chamberlain, 1927. *Address:* 36 Chilton Parade, Warrawee, Sydney, NSW 2074, Australia. *Club:* Australian (Sydney).

MacVICAR, Rev. Kenneth, MBE (mil.) 1968; DFC 1944; Chaplain in ordinary to the Queen in Scotland, since 1974; Minister of Kenmore and Lawers, Perthshire, since 1950; *b* 25 Aug. 1921; *s* of Rev. Angus John MacVicar, Southend, Kintyre; *m* 1946, Isobel Guild McKay; three *s* one *d. Educ:* Campbeltown Grammar Sch.; Edinburgh Univ.; St Andrews Univ. (MA); St Mary's Coll., St Andrews. Mem., Edinburgh Univ. Air Squadron, 1941; joined RAF, 1941: Pilot, 28 Sqdn, RAF, 1942–45, Flt Comdr, 1944–45 (despatches, 1945). Chaplain, Scottish Horse and Fife and Forfar Yeomanry/Scottish Horse, TA, 1953–65. Convener, Church of Scotland Cttee on Chaplains to HM Forces, 1968–73. Clerk to Presbytery of Dunkeld, 1955–. District Councillor, 1951–74. *Recreation:* golf. *Address:* Manse of Kenmore, Aberfeldy, Perthshire PH15 2HE. *T:* Kenmore 218.

MACVICAR, Neil, QC (Scotland) 1960; MA, LLB; Sheriff of Lothian and Borders (formerly the Lothians and Peebles), at Edinburgh, 1968–85; *b* 16 May 1920; *s* of late Neil Macvicar, WS; *m* 1949, Maria, *d* of Count Spiridon Bulgari, Corfu; one *s* two *d. Educ:* Loretto Sch.; Oriel Coll., Oxford; Edinburgh Univ. Served RA, 1940–45. Called to Scottish Bar, 1948. Chancellor, Dio. of Edinburgh, 1961–74. Chm. of Govs, Dean Orphanage and Cauvin's Trust, 1967–85. *Address:* 149 Warrender Park Road, Edinburgh EH9 1DT. *T:* 031–228 1618; Kapoutsi, Gastouri, Corfu, Greece. *Club:* New (Edinburgh).

McVITTIE, Maj.-Gen. Charles Harold, CB 1962; CBE 1953; *b* 6 Aug. 1908; *s* of Col R. H. McVittie, CB, CMG, CBE; *m* 1939, Margaret Wark (*d* 1984), *d* of Dr T. Divine, Huddersfield; two *s. Educ:* Haileybury; Brighton Coll.; Sandhurst. 2nd Lt Queen's Own Royal West Kent Regt, 1928; transferred to RAOC, 1935; Served War of 1939–45, ADOS Singapore Fortress, 1941–42; POW, 1942–45; comd Vehicle Organization, 1948–50; DOS, GHQ Farelf, 1951–53; comd Technical Stores Organization, 1953–56; comd RAOC Trg Centre, 1956–60; Comdr Stores Organization, RAOC, 1960–63. Hon. Col AER Units RAOC, 1961–64. Col Commandant, RAOC, 1965–69. *Recreation:*

fencing (Blue, Sandhurst, 1928). *Address:* Clovers, Garelochhead, Dunbartonshire. *T:* Garelochhead 810266.

McVITTIE, George Cunliffe, OBE 1946; MA Edinburgh, PhD Cantab; Professor of Astronomy, University of Illinois, 1952–72, Emeritus Professor, 1972; Hon. Professor of Theoretical Astronomy, University of Kent at Canterbury, 1972–85; *b* 5 June 1904; *e s* of Frank S. McVittie; *m* 1934, Mildred Bond (*d* 1985), *d* of Prof. John Strong, CBE; no *c*. *Educ:* Edinburgh Univ.; Christ's Coll., Cambridge. Asst Lecturer, Leeds Univ., 1930–34; Lecturer in Applied Mathematics, Liverpool Univ., 1934–36; Reader in Mathematics, King's Coll., London, 1936–48; Prof. of Mathematics, Queen Mary Coll., London, 1948–52. War service with Meteorological Office, Air Ministry, and a Dept of the Foreign Office, 1939–45. FRS (Edinburgh), 1943. Mem. Sub-Cttee of Meteorological Research Cttee, 1948–52. Jt Editor of The Observatory, 1938–48. Jt Exec. Editor of Quarterly Journal of Mechanics and Applied Mathematics, 1947–51; Pres., Commn on Galaxies, Internat. Astronomical Union, 1967–70; Sec., American Astronomical Soc., 1961–69. Minor Planet 2417 named "McVittie" by IAU, 1984. Hon. DSc Kent, 1985. *Publications:* Cosmological Theory, 1937; General Relativity and Cosmology, 1956, 2nd edn, 1965; Fact and Theory in Cosmology, 1961; (ed) Problems of Extra-galactic Research, 1962; papers on Relativity and its astronomical applications, classical mechanics, etc., Proc. Royal Soc. and other journals. *Address:* 74 Old Dover Road, Canterbury, Kent CT1 3AY. *Club:* Athenæum.

McWATTERS, George Edward; Chairman: HTV Ltd, since 1986; HTV West, since 1969; *b* India, 17 March 1922; *s* of Lt-Col George Alfred McWatters and Ellen Mary Christina McWatters (*née* Harvey); *m* 1st, 1946, Margery Robertson (*d* 1959); 2nd, 1960, Joy Anne Matthews; one *s*. *Educ:* Clifton Coll., Bristol. Vintners' Scholar, 1947. Served War of 1939–45: enlisted ranks Royal Scots, 1940; commissioned 14th Punjab Regt, Indian Army, 1941–46. John Harvey & Sons (family wine co.): joined, 1947; Dir, 1951; Chm., 1956–66; estab. a holding co. (Harveys of Bristol Ltd), 1962, but Showerings took over, 1966, and he remained Chm. until resignation, Aug. 1966; Chm., John White Footwear Holdings Ltd, later Ward White Gp Ltd, 1967–82; Actg Chm., HTV Group plc, 1985. Dir, Martins Bank, 1960–70; Local Adv. Dir (Peterborough), Barclays Bank, 1970–82; Local Dir (Northampton), Commercial Union Assce Co., 1969–82. Mem., CBI Grand Council, 1970–82. Mem. Cttee, Automobile Assoc., 1962–. Chairman: Appeal Cttee, Avon Wildlife Trust, 1982; St John Council, Avon, 1983. Governor: Clifton Coll., 1958–; Kimbolton Sch., 1970–82. City Councillor, Bristol, 1950–53. JP, Bristol, 1960–67; JP, Marylebone, 1969–71; High Sheriff, Cambridgeshire, 1979. *Recreations:* tennis, swimming, walking. *Address:* Burrington House, Burrington, Bristol BS18 7AD. *T:* Blagdon 62291. *Clubs:* Buck's, MCC.

McWATTERS, Stephen John; Headmaster, The Pilgrims' School, 1976–83, retired; *b* 24 April 1921; *er s* of late Sir Arthur Cecil McWatters, CIE; *m* 1957, Mary Gillian, *o d* of late D. C. Wilkinson and Mrs G. A. Wilkinson; one *s* two *d*. *Educ:* Eton (Scholar); Trinity Coll., Oxford (Scholar, MA). 1st Cl. Class. Mods, 1941. Served in The King's Royal Rifle Corps, 1941–45. Distinction in Philosophy section of Litterae Humaniores, Oxford, 1946. Asst Master, Eton Coll., 1947–63 (Master in Coll., 1949–57, Housemaster, 1961–63); Headmaster, Clifton Coll., 1963–75. *Recreations:* music, bird-watching. *Address:* 26 Edgar Road, Winchester. *T:* Winchester 67523.

McWEENY, Prof. Roy; Professor of Theoretical Chemistry, University of Pisa, since 1982; *b* 19 May 1924; *o s* of late Maurice and Vera McWeeny; *m* 1947, Patricia M. Healey (marr. diss. 1979); one *s* one *d*. *Educ:* Univ. of Leeds; University Coll., Oxford. BSc (Physics) Leeds 1945; DPhil Oxon 1949. Lectr in Physical Chemistry, King's Coll., Univ. of Durham, 1948–57; Vis. Scientist, Physics Dept, MIT, USA, 1953–54; Lectr in Theoretical Chemistry, Univ. Coll. of N Staffs, 1957–62; Associate Dir, Quantum Chemistry Gp, Uppsala Univ., Sweden, 1960–61; Reader in Quantum Theory, 1962–64, Prof. of Theoretical Chemistry, 1964–66, Univ. of Keele; Prof. of Theoretical Chem., 1966–82, and Hd of Chemistry Dept, 1976–79, Sheffield Univ. Vis. Prof., America, Japan, Europe. *Publications:* Symmetry, an Introduction to Group Theory and its Applications, 1963; (with B. T. Sutcliffe) Methods of Molecular Quantum Mechanics, 1969; Spins in Chemistry, 1970; Quantum Mechanics: principles and formalism, 1972; Quantum Mechanics: methods and basic applications, 1973; Coulson's Valence, 3rd rev. edn 1979; contrib. sections in other books and encyclopædias; many research papers on quantum theory of atomic and molecular structure in Proc. Royal Soc., Proc. Phys. Soc., Phys. Rev., Revs. Mod. Phys., Jl Chem. Phys., etc. *Recreations:* drawing, sculpture, travel. *Address:* Via Pietro Giordani 16, Gello, Pisa, Italy.

McWHINNIE, Donald; Freelance Director, Stage and Television, since 1960; *b* 16 Oct. 1920; *s* of Herbert McWhinnie and Margaret Elizabeth (*née* Holland). *Educ:* Rotherham Gram. Sch.; Gonville and Caius Coll., Cambridge. MA Cantab 1941. Served War of 1939–45: RAF, 1941–46. Joined BBC, 1947; Asst Head of Drama (Sound), 1953–60, resigned. Theatrical productions include: Krapp's Last Tape, Royal Court, 1958; The Caretaker, Arts and Duchess, 1960, Lyceum, NY, 1961; The Duchess of Malfi, Aldwych, 1960; Three, Arts and Criterion, 1961; The Tenth Man, Comedy, 1961; A Passage to India, Ambassador, NY, 1962; Everything in the Garden, Arts and Duke of York's, 1962; Macbeth, Royal Shakespeare, 1962; Rattle of a Simple Man, Garrick, 1962, Booth, NY, 1963; Doctors of Philosophy, Arts, 1962; The Doctor's Dilemma, Haymarket, 1963; Alfie, Mermaid and Duchess, 1963; Out of the Crocodile, Phœnix, 1963; The Fourth of June, St Martin's, 1964; End Game, Aldwych, 1964; The Creeper, St Martin's, 1965; All in Good Time, Royale, NY, 1965; The Cavern, Strand, 1965; This Winter's Hobby, US Tour, 1966; The Astrakhan Coat, Helen Hayes, NY, 1967; Happy Family, St Martin's, 1967; Tinker's Curse, Nottingham Playhouse, 1968; Vacant Possession, Nottingham Playhouse, 1968; Hamlet, Covent Garden, 1969; No Quarter, Hampstead, 1969; There'll be Some Changes Made, Fortune, 1969; The Apple Cart, Mermaid, 1970; A Hearts and Minds Job, Hampstead, 1971; Meeting at Night, Duke of York's, 1971; Endgame, and Play and Other Plays, Royal Court, 1976; Translations, Hampstead and Nat. Theatre, 1981; Hedda Gabler, Cambridge, 1982; Lovers Dancing, Albery, 1983; also numerous television productions for BBC and ITV. *Publication:* The Art of Radio, 1959. *Address:* 16 Chepstow Place, W2. *T:* 01–229 2120.

McWHIRTER, Norris Dewar, CBE 1980; author, publisher, broadcaster; Director, Guinness Superlatives Ltd, since 1954 (Managing Director, 1954–76); *b* 12 Aug. 1925; *er (twin) s* of William Allan McWhirter, Managing Director of Associated Newspapers and Northcliffe Newspapers Group, and Margaret Williamson; *m* 1957, Carole, *d* of George H. Eckert; one *s* one *d*. *Educ:* Marlborough; Trinity Coll., Oxford. BA (Internat. Rel. and Econs), MA (Contract Law). Served RN, 1943–46: Sub-Lt RNVR, 2nd Escort Gp, Atlantic; minesweeping Pacific. Dir, McWhirter Twins Ltd, 1950; Chm., Wm McWhirter & Sons, 1955–86; co-founder, Redwood Press (Chm., 1966–72); Dir, Gieves Group, Ltd, 1972–. Founder Editor (with late Ross McWhirter till 1975) and compiler, Guinness Book of Records, 1955–86 (1st edn 1955), Adv. Editor, 1986–; by 1986, 245 edns in 25 languages; over 53 million sales. Athletics Correspondent: Observer, 1951–67; Star, 1951–60; BBC TV Commentator, Olympic Games, 1960–72; What's In the Picture, 1957; The Record Breakers, 1972–84. Mem., Sports Council, 1970–73. Chm., Freedom Assoc., 1983– (Dep. Chm., 1975–83). Pres., Marlburian Club, 1983–84. Contested (C) Orpington, 1964, 1966. *Publications:* Get To Your Marks, 1951; (ed) Athletics World, 1952–56; Dunlop Book of Facts, 5 edns, 1964–73; Guinness Book of Answers, 1976, 5th edn 1985; Ross: story of a shared life, 1976; Guinness Book of Essential Facts (US), 1979. *Recreations:* family tennis, ski-ing, watching athletics (Oxford 100 yds, Scotland 1950–52, GB in Norway 1951) and Rugby football (Mddx XV, 1950). *Address:* c/o 33 London Road, Enfield EN2 6DJ. *T:* 01-367 4567. *Clubs:* Caledonian; Vincent's (Oxford); Achilles.

McWHIRTER, Prof. Robert, CBE 1963, FRCSEd, FRCPEd, FRCR; FRSE; Professor of Medical Radiology, Edinburgh University, 1946–70; Director of Radiotherapy, Royal Infirmary, Edinburgh, 1935–70; President, Medical and Dental Defence Union of Scotland, since 1959; *b* 8 Nov. 1904; *s* of Robert McWhirter and Janet Ramsay Gairdner; *m* 1937, Dr Susan Muir MacMurray; one *s*. *Educ:* Girvan Academy; Glasgow and Cambridge Universities. MB, ChB (High Commendn), Glasgow, 1927; FRCS Edinburgh 1932; DMRE Cambridge, 1933; FFR 1939. Formerly: Student, Mayo Clinic; British Empire Cancer Campaign Research Student, Holt Radium Institute, Manchester; Chief Assistant, X-Ray Dept, St Bartholomew's Hospital, London. Member, British Institute of Radiology; Pres., Sect. of Radiology, RSM, 1956; Fellow Royal College of Radiologists (Twining Memorial Medal, 1943; Skinner Memorial Lecturer, 1956; Warden, 1961–66; Knox Memorial Lecturer, 1963, Pres. 1966–69); Past Pres., Internat. Radio Therapists Visiting Club; Hon. Member, American Radium Society; Membre Corresp. Etranger, Société Française d'Electro-Radiologie Médicale, 1967; Membro d'onore, Società Italiana della Radiologia Medica e Medicine Nucleare, 1968; Hon. Member: Sociedade Brasileira de Patologia Mamária, 1969; Nippon Societas Radiologica, 1970; Groupe Européen des Radiotherapeutes, 1971. Caldwell Memorial Lecturer, American Roentgen Ray Society, 1963; Hon. Fellow: Australasian College of Radiologists, 1954; American College of Radiology, 1965; Faculty of Radiologists, RCSI, 1967. Gold Medal, Nat. Soc. for Cancer Relief, 1985. *Publications:* contribs to medical journals. *Recreation:* golf. *Address:* 2 Orchard Brae, Edinburgh EH4 1NY. *T:* 031–332 5800. *Club:* University (Edinburgh).

McWIGGAN, Thomas Johnstone, CBE 1976; Secretary General, European Organisation for Civil Aviation Electronics, since 1979; *b* 26 May 1918; *s* of late Thomas and Esther McWiggan; *m* 1947, Eileen Joyce Moughton; two *d*. *Educ:* UC Nottingham. Pharmaceutical Chemist. FIEE, FRAeS, SMIEEE. Signals Officer (Radar), RAFVR, 1941–46. Civil Air Attaché (Telecommunications) Washington, 1962–65; Dir of Telecommunications (Plans), Min. of Aviation, 1965; Dir of Telecommunications (Air Traffic Services), BoT, 1967; Dir Gen. Telecommunications, Nat. Air Traffic Services, 1969–79 (CAA, 1972–79). *Publications:* various technical papers. *Recreations:* photography, cabinet-making, gardening. *Address:* The Squirrels, Liberty Rise, Addlestone, Weybridge, Surrey. *T:* Weybridge 43068. *Club:* St George's Hill Tennis.

MacWILLIAM, Very Rev. Alexander Gordon; Dean of St Davids, since 1984; *b* 22 Aug. 1923; *s* of Andrew George and Margaret MacWilliam; *m* 1951, Catherine Teresa (*née* Bogue); one *s*. *Educ:* Univ. of Wales (BA Hons Classics, 1943); Univ. of London (BD 2nd Cl. Hons, 1946, PhD 1952, DipEd 1962). Deacon 1946, priest 1947; Curate of Penygroes, Gwynedd, 1946–49; Minor Canon, Bangor Cathedral, 1949–55; Rector of Llanfaethlu, Gwynedd, 1955–58; Head of Dept of Theology, Trinity Coll., Carmarthen, Dyfed, 1958–74; Head of School of Society Studies, Trinity Coll. (Inst. of Higher Education, Univ. of Wales), 1974–84; Canon of St Davids Cathedral and Prebendary of Trefloden, 1978. Examining Chaplain to Bishop of St Davids, 1969. Vis. Prof. of Philosophy and Theology, Central Univ. of Iowa, USA, 1983. *Publications:* contribs to Learning for Living (Brit. Jl of Religious Education), UCW Jl of Educn. *Recreations:* travel to archaeological sites and art centres, classical music, food and wine. *Address:* The Deanery, St Davids, Dyfed. *T:* St Davids 720202.

McWILLIAM, (Frederick) Edward, CBE 1966; Sculptor; *b* 30 April 1909; *yr s* of Dr William Nicholson McWilliam, Banbridge, County Down, Ireland; *m* 1932, Elizabeth Marion Crowther; two *d*. *Educ:* Campbell Coll., Belfast; Slade School of Fine Art; Paris. Served War of 1939–45, RAF, UK and Far East. Member of Staff, Slade Sch. of Fine Art, London Univ., 1947–66. Mem. Art Panel, Arts Council, 1960–68. First one-man exhib., sculpture, London Gall., 1939; subsequently Hanover Gallery, 1949, 1952, 1956; Waddington Galleries, 1961, 1963, 1966, 1968, 1971, 1973, 1976, 1979, 1984; Dawson Gallery, Dublin; Felix Landau Gallery, Los Angeles; retrospective exhibitions: Belfast, Dublin, Londonderry, 1981; Warwick Arts Trust, 1982. Has exhibited in International Open-Air Exhibitions, London, Antwerp, Arnheim, Paris. Work included in British Council touring exhibitions USA, Canada, Germany, South America. Fellow, UCL, 1972. Hon. DLit Belfast, 1964. *Relevant Publication:* McWilliam, Sculptor, by Roland Penrose, 1964. *Address:* 8A Holland Villas Road, W14 8BP.

McWILLIAM, John David; MP (Lab) Blaydon, since 1979; *b* 16 May 1941; *s* of Alexander and Josephine McWilliam; *m* 1965, Lesley Mary Catling; two *d*. *Educ:* Leith Academy; Heriot Watt Coll.; Napier College of Science and Technology. Post Office Engineer, 1957–79. Councillor, Edinburgh CC, 1970–75 (last Treasurer of City of Edinburgh and only Labour one, 1974–75); Commissioner for Local Authority Accounts in Scotland, 1974–78. Member: Scottish Council for Technical Educn, 1973–85; Select Cttee on Educn, Science and the Arts, 1980–83; Select Cttee on Procedure, 1984–; Services Cttee (Chm., Computer sub-cttee, 1983–). Dep. to the Shadow Leader of the House of Commons, 1983; Opposition Whip, 1984–. Mem., Gen. Adv. Council, BBC, 1984–. *Recreations:* reading, listening to music, angling. *Address:* 16 Farndale Close, Winlaton, Blaydon on Tyne. *T:* Blaydon 4424 88. *Clubs:* Bleach Green Labour (Blaydon); Chopwell Social; Chopwell RAOB (Chopwell); Dunston Social, Dunston Mechanics Institute (Dunston); Ryton Social (Ryton); Blackhall Mill Social (Blackhall Mill); Greenside and District Social.

McWILLIAM, Michael Douglas; Group Managing Director, Standard Chartered Bank, since 1983; *b* 21 June 1933; *s* of Douglas and Margaret McWilliam; *m* 1960, Ruth Arnstein; two *s*. *Educ:* Cheltenham Coll.; Oriel Coll., Oxford (MA); Nuffield Coll., Oxford (BLitt). Kenya Treasury, 1958; Samuel Montagu & Co., 1962; joined Standard Bank, subseq. Standard Chartered Bank, 1966; Gen. Manager, 1973. *Address:* c/o Standard Chartered Bank, 38 Bishopsgate, EC3. *Club:* Royal Commonwealth Society.

McWILLIAM, William Nicholson, CB 1960; *b* 26 Nov. 1897; *er s* of W. N. McWilliam, MD, Banbridge, Co. Down; *m* 1927, V. Maureen, *er d* of H. H. Mussen, Asst Chief Crown Solicitor; one *s* two *d*. *Educ:* Excelsior Academy, Banbridge; Campbell Coll., Belfast; Trinity Coll., Dublin. Served European War, 1916–18, Lieut, RGA, 1916–18. BA, BAI, 1921. Entered NI Civil Service, 1922; Asst Sec. to Cabinet, NI, 1945–57; Dep. Clerk of the Privy Council, NI, 1945–57; Permanent Sec., Min. of Labour and National Insurance, NI, 1957–62 (retired). Member Boundary Commn for NI, 1963–69. *Address:* Garryard, 34 Massey Avenue, Belfast BT4 2JT. *T:* Belfast 63179.

MADANG, Archbishop of, (RC), since 1976; **Most Rev. Leo Arkfeld,** CBE (Hon.) 1976; *b* 4 Feb. 1912; *s* of George Arkfeld and Mary Siemer. *Educ:* St Mary's Seminary,

Techny, Ill., USA (BA). Bishop of Wewak, Papua New Guinea, 1948–76; Administrator Apostolic of Wewak, 1976. *Address:* Box 750, Madang, Papua New Guinea. *T:* 82–2707.

MADDEN, (Albert) Frederick (McCulloch), DPhil; Reader in Commonwealth Government, Oxford, 1957–84; Professorial Fellow of Nuffield College, 1958–84, Emeritus Fellow since 1984; *b* 27 Feb. 1917; *e s* of A. E. and G. McC. Madden; *m* 1941, Margaret, *d* of Dr R. D. Gifford; one *s* one *d*. *Educ:* privately, by mother; Bishop Vesey's Grammar Sch.; Christ Church, Oxford. Boulter and Gladstone exhibns; BA 1938, BLitt 1939, DPhil 1950. Dep. Sup., Rhodes House Library, 1946–48; Beit Lectr, 1947–57; Sen. Tutor to Overseas Service Courses, 1950–; Dir, Inst. of Commonwealth Studies, 1961–68; Vice-Chm., History Bd, 1968–73. Canadian Vis. Fellow, 1970; Vis. Prof., Cape Town, 1973; Vis. Fellow, Res. Sch., ANU, 1974. Dir, Hong Kong admin. course, 1975–86. Dir, Prospect Theatre, 1963–66. FRHistS 1952. *Publications:* (with V. Harlow) British Colonial Developments, 1774–1834, 1953; (with K. Robinson) Essays in Imperial Government, 1963; chapter in Cambridge History of British Empire III, 1959; Imperial Constitutional Documents, 1765–1965, 1966; (with W. Morris-Jones) Australia and Britain, 1980; (with D. K. Fieldhouse) Oxford and the Idea of Commonwealth, 1982; Perspectives on Imperialism and Decolonisation (Festschrift), 1984; Select Documents on the Constitutional History of the British Empire: Vol. I, The Empire of the Bretaignes 1165–1688, 1985; Vol. II, The Classical Period of the Firtst British Empire 1689–1783, 1986; reviews in English Historical Review, etc. *Recreations:* acting; photographing islands and highlands, hill towns, country houses, churches; Renaissance art; writing music and listening. *Address:* Oak Apples, Shotover Hill, Oxford. *T:* Oxford 62972.

MADDEN, Admiral Sir Charles (Edward), 2nd Bt, *cr* 1919; GCB 1965 (KCB 1961; CB 1955); Vice Lord-Lieutenant of Greater London, 1969–81; *b* 15 June 1906; *s* of Admiral of the Fleet Sir Charles E. Madden, 1st Bart, GCB, OM, and Constance Winifred (*d* 1964), 3rd *d* of Sir Charles Cayzer, 1st Bart; *S* father, 1935; *m* 1942, Olive, *d* of late G. W. Robins, Caldy, Cheshire; one *d*. *Educ:* Royal Naval Coll., Osborne. ADC to the Queen, 1955. Served War: Exec. Officer, HMS Warspite, 1940–42 (despatches); Captain, HMS Emperor, 1945 (despatches); Naval Asst to 1st Sea Lord, 1946–47. Captain, 1946; Rear-Admiral, 1955; Vice-Admiral, 1958; Admiral, 1961. Chief of Naval Staff, NZ, 1953–55; Dep. Chief of Naval Personnel, 1955–57; Flag Officer, Malta, 1957–59; Flag Officer, Flotillas, Home Fleet, 1959–60; C-in-C Plymouth, 1960–62; C-in-C Home Fleet and NATO C-in-C Eastern Atlantic Command, 1963–65; retired, 1965. Chairman, Royal National Mission to Deep Sea Fishermen, 1971–81 (Dep. Chm., 1966–71); Vice-Chairman, Sail Training Assoc., 1968–70. Trustee: National Maritime Museum, 1968– (Chm., 1972–77); Portsmouth Royal Naval Museum, 1973–77. Chm., Standing Council of the Baronetage, 1975–77. Dep. Warden, Christ Church, Victoria Rd, 1970–86. Grand Cross of Prince Henry the Navigator, Portugal, 1960. *Recreation:* painting. *Heir:* *b* Lieut-Colonel John Wilmot Madden, MC, 1944, RA [*b* 1916; *m* 1941, Beatrice Catherine Sievewright; two *s* one *d*]. *Address:* 21 Eldon Road, W8. *Club:* Arts.

MADDEN, Rear-Admiral Colin Duncan, CB 1966; CBE 1964; LVO 1954; DSC 1940 and Bar, 1944; Registrar and Secretary, Order of the Bath, 1979–85; *b* 19 Aug. 1915; *s* of late Archibald Maclean Madden, CMG, and Cecilia Catherine Moor; *m* 1943, Agnes Margaret, *d* of late H. K. Newcombe, OBE, Canada and London, and Eleanor Clare; two *d*. *Educ:* RN Coll., Dartmouth. During War of 1939–45, took part in blocking Ijmuiden harbour and Dutch evacuation; Navigating Officer of 7th Mine Sweeping Flotilla; HMS Arethusa; Assault Group J1 for invasion of Europe, and HMS Norfolk. Thence HMS Triumph. Commander, 1950; Comd HMS Crossbow, 1952; staff of Flag Officer Royal Yachts, SS Gothic and Comdr (N) HM Yacht Britannia, for Royal Commonwealth Tour, 1953–54; Captain, Naval Attaché, Rome; Captain D 7 in HMS Trafalgar; IDC. Comd HMS Albion, 1962; Rear-Admiral, 1965; Senior Naval Member Directing Staff, Imperial Defence Coll., 1965–67; retired, 1967. Dir, Nat. Trade Devel Assoc., 1967–69. Gentleman Usher of the Scarlet Rod to the Order of the Bath, 1968–79. Dir Gen., Brewers' Soc., 1969–80. *Recreations:* sailing, gardening, fishing, tapestry. *Clubs:* Army and Navy, Royal Cruising.

MADDEN, Frederick; *see* Madden, A. F. McC.

MADDEN, Max; MP (Lab) Bradford West, since 1983; *b* 29 Oct. 1941; *s* of late George Francis Leonard Madden and Rene Frances Madden; *m* 1972, Sheelagh Teresa Catherine Howard. *Educ:* Lascelles Secondary Modern Sch.; Pinner Grammar Sch. Journalist: East Essex Gazette; Tribune (political weekly); Sun, London; Scotsman, London; subseq. Press and Information Officer, British Gas Corp., London; Dir of Publicity, Labour Party, 1979–82. MP (Lab) Sowerby, Feb. 1974–1979. *Address:* House of Commons, SW1A 0AA.

MADDEN, Michael; Under Secretary, Ministry of Agriculture, Fisheries and Food, since 1985; *b* 12 Feb. 1936; *s* of late Harold Madden and Alice Elizabeth (*née* Grenville); *m* 1960 (marr. diss. 1977); two *s* one *d*. *Educ:* King Edward VII Sch., Sheffield. Exec. Officer, Min. of Transport and Civil Aviation, 1955; Ministry of Agriculture, Fisheries and Food: Asst Principal, 1963–67; Asst Private Sec. to Minister, 1966–67; Principal, 1967; Asst Sec. (as Head, Tropical Foods Div.), 1973; Head, Management Services Gp, 1985. *Recreations:* walking, eating and drinking with friends, music, planning expeditions. *Address:* 3 Stratford Lodge, Stratford Road, Watford WD1 3QQ. *T:* Watford 32897.

MADDISON, Vincent Albert, CMG 1961; TD 1953; *b* 10 Aug. 1915; *s* of late Vincent Maddison; *m* 1954, Jennifer Christian Bernard; two *s* one *d*. *Educ:* Wellingborough Sch.; Downing Coll., Cambridge (MA). Colonial Administrative Service, 1939. Served War of 1939–45: Ethiopian and Burma Campaigns. District Officer, Kenya, 1947; seconded to Secretariat, 1948; Director, Trade and Supplies, 1953; Secretary, 1954, Perm. Secretary, 1957–63, Min. of Commerce and Industry; retired from Kenya Government, 1963; Chairman: East African Power and Lighting Co. Ltd, 1965–70; Tana River Development Co. Ltd, 1965–70; The Kenya Power Co. Ltd 1965–70; Director: Nyali Ltd, 1966–70; Kisauni Ltd, 1966–70; East African Trust and Investment Co. Ltd, 1966–70; East African Engineering Consultants, 1966–70. *Recreations:* ski-ing, gardening, sailing. *Address:* Edifici la Neu, Arinsal, La Massana, Andorra. *Club:* Muthaiga Country (Kenya).

MADDOCK, Sir Ieuan, Kt 1975; CB 1968; OBE 1953; FRS 1967; FEng 1975; Chairman: Fulmer Research Institute, since 1978; Sira Institute, since 1978; Corporate Consulting Group, since 1979; Enterprise Capital Ltd, since 1983; Amazon Computers, since 1983; Deputy Chairman, International General Electric Co. of New York Ltd, since 1983; Director, Cogent Ltd, since 1982; *b* 29 March 1917; British; *m* 1943, Eurfron May Davies; one *s*. *Educ:* Gowerton Grammar Sch., Glamorgan; University of Wales, Swansea (Hon. Fellow, 1985). Entered Government service, Explosives Res. and Develt, 1940; Principal Scientific Officer, Armament Res. Dept, Fort Halstead, 1949; Head of Field Experiments Div., Atomic Weapons Research Establishment, 1960; directed UK Research programme for Nuclear Test Ban Treaty, 1957–66; Dep. Controller B, 1965–67, Controller (Industrial Technology) 1967–71, Min. of Technology; Chief Scientist: DTI, 1971–74; DoI, 1974–77; Dir, Nat. Physical Laboratory, 1976–77. Principal of St Edmund Hall, Oxford, 1979–82 (Hon. Fellow, 1982). Director: Prutec, 1980–82; Chubb & Sons Ltd, 1978–84. Sec., BAAS, 1977–81. Vis. Prof., Imperial Coll., London, 1977–79. Member: SRC, 1973–77; NERC, 1973–77; Science Cons. Cttee to BBC, 1969–80 (Chm., 1977–80); ABRC, 1973–77; Adv. Council for Applied R&D, 1977–80; Gen. Adv. Council, BBC, 1977–80; Ct, Brunel Univ., 1979–82; Ct, Cranfield Coll. of Technology, 1969–77; Ct, Surrey Univ., 1974–79; Ct, University Coll. of Swansea, 1981–. President: IERE, 1973–75; IMGTechE, 1976; Dep. Chm., Nat. Electronics Council, 1977–80; Vice-Pres., ASLIB, 1977–. For. Mem., Royal Swedish Acad. of Engrg Science, 1975. Hon. FIQA. Hon. Fellow: Manchester Polytechnic, 1977; Polytechnic of Wales, 1982; IERE, 1983; Hon. Mem., CGLI, 1986. Hon. DSc: Wales, 1970; Bath, 1978; Reading, 1980; Salford, 1980; Hon. DTech CNAA, 1980; DUniv Surrey, 1983. *Publications:* in various scientific and technical jls. *Address:* 13 Darell Road, Caversham, Reading, Berks. *T:* Reading 474096.

MADDOCKS, Arthur Frederick, CMG 1974; HM Diplomatic Service, retired; Ambassador and UK Permanent Representative to OECD, Paris, 1977–82; *b* 20 May 1922; *s* of late Frederick William Maddocks and Celia Elizabeth Maddocks (*née* Beardwell); *m* 1945, Margaret Jean Crawford Holt; two *s* one *d*. *Educ:* Manchester Grammar Sch.; Corpus Christi Coll., Oxford. Army, 1942–46; Foreign (later Diplomatic) Service, 1946–: Washington, 1946–48; FO, 1949–51; Bonn, 1951–55; Bangkok, 1955–58; UK Delegn to OEEC, 1958–60; FO, 1960–64; UK Delegn to European Communities, Brussels, 1964–68; Political Adviser, Hong Kong, 1968–72; Dep. High Comr and Minister (Commercial), Ottawa, 1972–76. Mem., OECD Appeals Tribunal, 1984–. *Address:* Lynton House, 83 High Street, Wheatley, Oxford OX9 1XP. *Club:* Hong Kong (Hong Kong).

MADDOCKS, Bertram Catterall; a Recorder of the Crown Court, since 1983; *b* 7 July 1932; *s* of His Honour George Maddocks and of Mary Maddocks (*née* Day); *m* 1964, Angela Vergette Forster; two *s* one *d*. *Educ:* Malsis Hall, near Keighley; Rugby; Trinity Hall, Cambridge (schol.; MA; Law Tripos Part 2 1st Cl. 1955). Nat. Service, 2nd Lieut, RA, 1951; Duke of Lancaster's Own Yeomanry (TA), 1958–67. Called to the Bar, Middle Temple, 1956; Harmsworth Schol.; Mem., Lincoln's Inn. Pt-time Chm., VAT Tribunals, 1977–. *Recreations:* real tennis, lawn tennis, ski-ing, bridge. *Address:* Moor Hall Farm, Prescot Road, Aughton, Lancashire L39 6RT. *T:* Aughton Green 421601. *Club:* Manchester Tennis and Racquet.

MADDOCKS, Sir Kenneth (Phipson), KCMG 1958 (CMG 1956); KCVO 1963; *b* 8 Feb. 1907; *s* of Arthur P. Maddocks, Haywards Heath, Sussex; *m* 1st, 1951, Elnor Radcliffe, CStJ (*d* 1976), *d* of late Sir E. John Russell, OBE, FRS; no *c*; 2nd, 1980, Patricia Josephine, *d* of Algernon and Irma Hare Duke and *widow* of Sir George Mooring, KCMG. *Educ:* Bromsgrove Sch.; Wadham Coll., Oxford. Colonial Administrative Service, Nigeria, 1929; Civil Secretary, Northern Region, Nigeria, 1955–57; Dep. Governor, 1957–58. Acting Governor, Northern Region, Nigeria, 1956 and 1957. Governor and Commander-in-Chief of Fiji, 1958–63; Dir and Secretary, E Africa and Mauritius Assoc., 1964–69. KStJ. *Recreations:* fishing, gardening. *Address:* 11 Lee Road, Aldeburgh, Suffolk. *T:* Aldeburgh 3443.

MADDOCKS, Rt. Rev. Morris Henry St John; Hon. Assistant Bishop, Diocese of Bath and Wells, since 1983; Adviser on the Ministry of Health and Healing to Archbishops of Canterbury and York, since 1983; *b* 28 April 1928; *s* of late Rev. Canon Morris Arthur Maddocks and Gladys Mabel Sharpe; *m* 1955, Anne Sheail; no *c*. *Educ:* St John's Sch., Leatherhead; Trinity Coll., Cambridge; Chichester Theological Coll. BA 1952, MA 1956, Cambridge. Ordained in St Paul's Cathedral, London, 1954. Curate: St Peter's, Ealing, 1954–55; St Andrews, Uxbridge, 1955–58; Vicar of: Weaverthorpe, Helperthorpe and Luttons Ambo, 1958–61; S Martin's on the Hill, Scarborough, 1961–71; Bishop Suffragan of Selby, 1972–83. Chm., Churches' Council for Health and Healing, 1982–85 (Co-Chm., 1975–82). *Publications:* The Christian Healing Ministry, 1981; The Christian Adventure, 1983; Journey to Wholeness, 1986. *Recreations:* golf, music, painting. *Address:* 39 St Ann Street, Salisbury, Wilts SP1 2DP. *T:* Salisbury 331096. *Clubs:* Army and Navy, Royal Society of Medicine.

MADDOCKS, William Henry, MBE 1975; General Secretary, National Union of Dyers, Bleachers and Textile Workers, 1979–82; *b* 18 Feb. 1921; *m* 1944, Mary Holdsworth; one *d*. *Educ:* Eastwood Elem. Sch.; Holycroft Council Sch., Keighley. W of England full-time Organiser for National Union of Dyers, Bleachers and Textile Workers, 1963. JP Gloucestershire, 1968. *Clubs:* Trades (Shipley, W Yorks); Yeadon Trades Hall (Yeadon, W Yorks).

MADDOX, Sir (John) Kempson, Kt 1964; VRD 1948; Hon. Consulting Physician: Royal Prince Alfred Hospital, Sydney; Royal Hospital for Women, Sydney; *b* Dunedin, NZ, 20 Sept. 1901; *s* of Sidney Harold Maddox and Mabel Kempson; *m* 1940, Madeleine Scott; one *s* one *d*. *Educ:* N Sydney Boys' High Sch.; Univ. of Sydney. MD, ChM (Sydney) 1924; MRCP 1928; FRACP 1935; FRCP 1958; Hon. FACP 1980. Served War of 1939–45, Surgeon Comdr, RANR. President: BMA (NSW), 1950; Cardiac Soc. of Australia and NZ, 1958; Asian-Pacific Soc. of Cardiology, 1960–64; Internat. Soc. of Cardiology, 1966–70; Vice-Pres., Nat. Heart Foundation of Australia, 1960–64 (Pres. NSW Div.); FACC 1965; FACP 1968; Hon. Pres., Internat. Soc. of Cardiology, 1970–. Hon. AM (Singapore) 1963. Chevalier de l'Ordre de la Santé Publique, France, 1961; Comendador, Orden Hispolito Unanue (Peru), 1968. *Recreations:* golf, fishing. *Address:* 8 Annandale Street, Darling Point, Sydney, NSW 2027, Australia. *T:* 32–1707. *Clubs:* Australian (Sydney); Royal Sydney Golf.

MADDOX, John (Royden); writer and broadcaster; Editor, Nature, 1966–73 and since 1980; *b* 27 Nov. 1925; *s* of A. J. and M. E. Maddox, Swansea; *m* 1st, 1949, Nancy Fanning (*d* 1960); one *s* one *d*; 2nd, 1960, Brenda Power Murphy; one *s* one *d*. *Educ:* Gowerton Boys' County Sch.; Christ Church, Oxford; King's Coll., London. Asst Lecturer, then Lecturer, Theoretical Physics, Manchester Univ., 1949–55; Science Correspondent, Guardian, 1955–64; Affiliate, Rockefeller Institute, New York, 1962–63; Asst Director, Nuffield Foundation, and Co-ordinator, Nuffield Foundation Science Teaching Project, 1964–66; Man. Dir, Macmillan Journals Ltd, 1970–72; Dir, Macmillan & Co. Ltd, 1968–73; Chm., Maddox Editorial Ltd, 1972–74; Dir, Nuffield Foundn, 1975–80. Member: Royal Commn on Environmental Pollution, 1976–81; Genetic Manipulation Adv. Gp, 1976–80; British Library Adv. Council, 1976–81; Council on Internat. Develt, 1977–79; Chm. Council, Queen Elizabeth Coll., 1980–85; Mem. Council, King's Coll. London (KQC), 1985–. *Publications:* (with Leonard Beaton) The Spread of Nuclear Weapons, 1962; Revolution in Biology, 1964; The Doomsday Syndrome, 1972; Beyond the Energy Crisis, 1975. *Address:* Macmillan Journals Ltd, 4 Little Essex Street, WC2; 9 Pitt Street, W8. *T:* 01–937 9750. *Club:* Athenæum.

MADDRELL, Dr Simon Hugh Piper, FRS 1981; Fellow of Gonville and Caius College, Cambridge, since 1964; Senior Principal Scientific Officer, Agricultural and Food Research Council Unit of Insect Neurophysiology and Pharmacology (formerly Unit of Invertebrate Chemistry and Physiology), Cambridge University, since 1968; *b* 11 Dec. 1937; *s* of Hugh Edmund Fisher Maddrell and Barbara Agnes Mary Maddrell; *m* 1961, Anna Myers; three *s* one *d*. *Educ:* Peter Symonds' Sch., Winchester; St Catharine's Coll., Cambridge. BA, MA, PhD 1964, ScD 1978. Res. Fellow, Dalhousie Univ., Canada,

1962–64; College Fellow and Lectr, Gonville and Caius Coll., Cambridge, 1968–. Financial Sec., Co. of Biologists Ltd, 1965–. Scientific Medal, Zool Soc. of London, 1976. *Publication*: Neurosecretion, 1979. *Recreations*: cycling, golf, gardening, wine-tasting, cinema. *Address*: Gonville and Caius College, Cambridge; Ballamaddrell, Ballabeg, Arbory, Isle of Man. *T*: Castletown (IOM) 822787.

MADEL, William David; MP (C) Bedfordshire South West, since 1983 (South Bedfordshire, 1970–83); *b* 6 Aug. 1938; *s* of late William R. Madel and of Eileen Madel (*née* Nicholls); *m* 1971, Susan Catherine, *d* of late Lt-Comdr Hon. Peter Carew; one *s* one *d*. *Educ*: Uppingham Sch.; Keble Coll., Oxford. MA Oxon 1965. Graduate Management Trainee, 1963–64; Advertising Exec., Thomson Organisation, 1964–70. PPS to Parly Under-Sec. of State for Defence, 1973–74, to Minister of State for Defence, 1974. Vice-Chairman: Cons. Backbench Employment Cttee, 1974–81; Cons. Backbench Educn Cttee, 1981–. *Recreations*: cricket, tennis, reading. *Address*: 120 Pickford Road, Markyate, Herts. *Clubs*: Carlton, Coningsby; Mid-Cheshire Pitt (Chester).

MADELUNG, Prof. Wilferd Willy Ferdinand; Laudian Professor of Arabic, University of Oxford, since 1978; *b* 26 Dec. 1930; *s* of Georg Madelung and Elisabeth (*née* Messerschmitt); *m* 1963, A. Margaret (*née* Arent); one *s*. *Educ*: Eberhard Ludwig Gymnasium, Stuttgart; Univs of Georgetown, Cairo, Hamburg. PhD (Hamburg). Cultural Attaché, W German Embassy, Baghdad, 1958–60. Vis. Professor, Univ. of Texas, Austin, 1963; Privatdozent, Univ. of Hamburg, 1963–64; University of Chicago: Asst Prof., 1964; Associate Prof., 1966; Prof. of Islamic History, 1969. Guggenheim Fellowship, 1972–73. Decoration of Republic of Sudan (4th cl.), 1962. *Publications*: Der Imam al-Qāsim ibn Ibrāhīm und die Glaubenslehre der Zaiditen, 1965; Religious Schools and Sects in Medieval Islam, 1985; articles in learned jls and Encyc. of Islam. *Recreation*: travel. *Address*: The Oriental Institute, Pusey Lane, Oxford OX1 2LE. *T*: Oxford 59272.

MADEN, Margaret; Director, Islington Sixth Form Centre, since 1983; *b* 16 April 1940; *d* of Clifford and Frances Maden. *Educ*: Arnold High Sch. for Girls, Blackpool; Leeds Univ. (BA Hons); Univ. of London Inst of Educn (PGCE). Asst Teacher of Geography, Stockwell Manor Comprehensive Sch., SW9, 1962–66; Lectr, Sidney Webb Coll. of Educn, 1966–71; Dep. Head, Bicester Comprehensive Sch., Oxon, 1971–75; Headmistress, Islington Green Comprehensive Sch., 1975–82. *Publications*: contributions to: Dear Lord James, 1971; Teachers for Tomorrow (ed Calthrop and Owens), 1971; Education 2000 (ed Wilby and Pluckrose), 1979; The School and the University, an International Perspective (ed Burton R. Clark), 1984. *Recreations*: American painting, writing and films; politics, gardening.

MADGE, Charles Henry; *b* 10 Oct. 1912; *s* of Lieut-Colonel C. A. Madge and Barbara (*née* Hylton Foster); *m* 1st, Kathleen Raine (marr. diss.); one *s* one *d*; 2nd, Inez Pearn (*d* 1976); one *s* one *d*; 3rd, Evelyn Brown (*d* 1984). *Educ*: Winchester Coll. (Scholar); Magdalene Coll., Cambridge (Scholar). Reporter on Daily Mirror, 1935–36; founded Mass-Observation, 1937; directed survey of working-class saving and spending for National Institute of Economic and Social Research, 1940–42; Research staff of PEP, 1943; Director, Pilot Press, 1944; Social Development Officer, New Town of Stevenage, 1947; Prof. of Sociology, Univ. of Birmingham, 1950–70. Mission to Thailand on UN Technical Assistance, 1953–54. UNESCO Missions to India, 1957–58, to South-East Asia, 1959 and 1960 and Leader of Mission to Ghana for UN Economic Commission for Africa, 1963. *Publications*: The Disappearing Castle (poems), 1937; The Father Found (poems), 1941; part-author of Britain by Mass-Observation, 1938, and other books connected with this organisation; War-time Pattern of Saving and Spending, 1943; (ed) Pilot Papers: Social Essays and Documents, 1945–47; Society in the Mind, 1964; (with Barbara Weinberger) Art Students Observed, 1973; (with Peter Willmott) Inner City Poverty in Paris and London, 1981; (ed with Mary-Lou Jennings) Pandaemonium, by Humphrey Jennings, 1985; contributions to Economic Journal, Town Planning Review, Human Relations, etc. *Address*: 28 Lynmouth Road, N2.

MADGE, James Richard, CB 1976; Deputy Secretary, Department of the Environment, on secondment as Chief Executive, Housing Corporation, 1973–84; *b* 18 June 1924; *s* of James Henry Madge and Elisabeth May Madge; *m* 1955, Alice June Annette (*d* 1975), *d* of late Major Horace Reid, Jamaica; two *d*. *Educ*: Bexhill Co. Sch.; New Coll., Oxford. Pilot in RAFVR, 1942–46. Joined Min. of Civil Aviation, 1947; Principal Private Secretary: to Paymaster-General, 1950–51; to Minister of Transport, 1960–61; Asst Secretary, Min. of Transport, 1961–66; Under-Sec., Road Safety Gp, 1966–69; Head of Policy Planning, 1969–70; Under-Sec., Housing Directorate, DoE, 1971–73. *Recreations*: lawn tennis, swimming, furniture-making. *Address*: 56 Gordon Place, Kensington, W8. *T*: 01–937 1927.

MADIGAN, Sir Russel (Tullie), Kt 1981; OBE 1970; Deputy Chairman, CRA Ltd, since 1978; *b* 22 Nov. 1920; *s* of Dr Cecil T. Madigan and Wynnis K. Wollaston; *m* 1st, 1942, Margaret Symons (decd); four *s* one *d*; 2nd, 1981, Satsuko Tamura. *Educ*: Univ. of Adelaide (BScEng 1941, BE 1946, ME 1954, LLB 1960). FSASM 1941; FTS. Director: APV Hldgs PLC; National Commercial Union Ltd; Chm., APV Asia Pacific Ltd; Australian Mineral Foundn; Pres., Australian Inst. of Internat. Affairs; Councillor: Pacific Basin Economic Council; Australasian Inst. of Mining and Metallurgy; Australian Acad. of Technological Scis. *Recreations*: flying, farming, music. *Address*: 60 Broadway, East Camberwell, Victoria 3126, Australia. *T*: 82 6152. *Clubs*: Athenæum, Melbourne, Royal Melbourne Golf.

MAEGRAITH, Brian Gilmore, CMG 1968; TD (2 bars) 1975; MA, MB, MSc, DPhil; FRCP, FRCPE, FRACP; Alfred Jones and Warrington Yorke Professor of Tropical Medicine, School of Tropical Medicine, Liverpool University, 1944–72, now Professor Emeritus; Hon. Senior Research Fellow, Department of Tropical Paediatrics, since 1978, and Dean, 1946–75, Vice-President, since 1975, Liverpool School of Tropical Medicine; *b* 26 Aug. 1907; *s* of late A. E. R. Maegraith, Adelaide, S Australia; *m* 1934, Lorna Langley, St Peters, Adelaide; one *s*. *Educ*: St Peter's and St Mark's Colleges, Adelaide University (MB 1930); Magdalen and Exeter Colleges, Oxford (Rhodes Scholar, Rolleston Memorial Prize). Beit Memorial Fellow, 1932–34; Medical Fellow, Exeter Coll., Oxford, 1934–40; University Lecturer and Demonstrator in Pathology, Dean of Faculty of Medicine, Oxford Univ., 1938–44; War of 1939–45, OC Army Malaria Research Unit. Med. Advisory Cttee ODM, 1963–72. Tropical Med. Research Board, MRC, 1960–65, 1966–69, Cttees on Malaria and Abnormal Haemoglobins, 1960–69; Hon. Consulting Physician, Liverpool Royal Infirmary; Hon. Consultant in Trop. Med., RAF (Consultant 1964–76); Hon. Malariologist, Army, 1967–73; Adviser: Council for Health in Socio-economic Developments, Thailand, 1964–; Faculty Tropical Medicine, Bangkok, 1959–; Reg. Trop. Medicine and Public Health Project, SE Asian Ministers of Educn Orgn. Sec.-Gen., Council of Institutes of Tropical Medicine, Europe and USSR, 1969–72 (Hon. Life Pres., 1972–); Pres., Royal Society Tropical Medicine, 1969–71 (Vice-Pres., 1949–51 and 1957–59; Chalmers Gold Medal, 1951); Vis. Prof., Univ. of Alexandria, 1956; Lectures: Litchfield, Oxford, 1955; Maurice Bloch, Glasgow, 1969; Heath Clark, London, 1970; Craig, US Soc. Trop. Med., 1976; Justus Ström, Stockholm, 1980. Membre d'Honneur: de Soc. Belg. de Méd. Tropicale; Soc. de Pathologie Exotique, Paris; Hon. Member American, Canadian and German Socs of Tropical Medicine and Hygiene. Hon. Fellow: St Mark's Coll., 1956–; London Sch. of Hygiene and Tropical Med., 1980–. Hon. DSc Bangkok, 1966; MD (Emeritus) Athens, 1972. Le Prince Award and Medal, Soc. of Tropical Medicine, USA, 1954; Bernhard Nocht Medal (Hamburg), 1957; Mary Kingsley Medal, Liverpool Sch. of Trop. Med., 1973; Jubilee Medal, Swedish Med. Acad., 1980; Anniv. Plaque, Faculty of Trop. Medicine, Bangkok, 1980. Tritabhorn, Order of the White Elephant, Thailand, 1982. KLJ 1977. *Publications*: Pathological Processes in Malaria and Blackwater Fever, 1948; Clinical Tropical Diseases, 5th edn, 1970, to 8th edn 1984; Tropical Medicine for Nurses (with A. R. D. Adams), 1956, 5th edn (with H. M. Gilles), 1980; (with C. S. Leithead) Clinical Methods in Tropical Medicine, 1962; Exotic Diseases in Practice, 1965; (with H. M. Gilles) Management and Treatment of Diseases in the Tropics, 1970; One World, 1973; papers and articles in technical and scientific journals on various subjects. *Address*: 23 Eaton Road, Cressington Park, Liverpool L19 0PN. *T*: 051–427 1133; Department of Tropical Paediatrics, Liverpool School of Tropical Medicine, Liverpool L3 5QA. *T*: 051–708 9393. *Clubs*: Athenæum; Athenæum (Liverpool).

MAEHLER, Prof. Herwig Gustav Theodor, FBA 1986; Professor of Papyrology, University College London, since 1981; *b* 29 April 1935; *s* of Ludwig and Lisa Maehler; *m* 1963, Margaret Anderson; two *d*. *Educ*: Katharineum Lübeck (Grammar Sch.); Univs of Hamburg (PhD Classics and Classical Archaeol.), Tübingen and Basel. British Council Schol., Oxford, 1961–62; Res. Assistant, Hamburg Univ., 1962–63, Hamburg Univ. Liby, 1963–64; Keeper of Greek Papyri, Egyptian Mus., W Berlin, 1964–79; Habilitation for Classics, 1975, Lectr in Classics, 1975–79, Free Univ. of W Berlin; Reader in Papyrology, UCL, 1979–81. Corresp. Mem., German Archeol Inst., 1979. *Publications*: Die Auffassung des Dichterberufs im frühen Griechentum bis zur Zeit Pindars, 1963; Die Handschriften des S Jacobi-Kirche Hamburg, 1967; Urkunden römischer Zeit, (BGU XI), 1968; Papyri aus Hermupolis (BGU XII), 1974; Die Lieder des Bakchylides, 2 vols, 1982; editions for Bacchylides and Pindar, 1970, 1984; articles in learned jls. *Address*: Department of Greek, University College London, Gower Street, WC1E 6BT. *T*: 01-387 7050.

MAFFEY, family name of **Baron Rugby.**

MAGAREY, Sir (James) Rupert, Kt 1980; FRCS, FRACS: Senior Visiting Consultant Surgeon, The Queen Elizabeth Hospital, Adelaide, 1979–84; *b* 21 Feb. 1914; *s* of Dr Rupert Eric Magarey and Elsie Emily (*née* Cowell); *m* 1940, (Catherine) Mary Gilbert; one *s* two *d* (and one *d* decd). *Educ*: St Peter's Coll., Adelaide; St Mark's Coll., Univ. of Adelaide (MB, BS 1938; MS 1951). FRCS 1949; FRACS 1950. Served War, RAAMC, 1939–46: despatches, Syria, 1941; Captain, subseq. Major; retd with rank of Lt-Col. Hon. Asst Surgeon, Royal Adelaide Hosp., 1950–58; Hon. Surgeon, 1958–70, and Sen. Vis. Surgeon, 1970–79, Queen Elizabeth Hosp., Adelaide. Pres., AMA, 1976–79 (Pres. SA Br., 1969–70); Mem. Ct of Examrs, RACS, 1960–; Hon. Fellow, Royal Aust. Coll. of Gen. Practitioners, 1978; Hon. Life Governor, Aust. Post-Grad. Fedn in Medicine, 1980. Silver Jubilee Medal, 1977. *Publications*: scientific articles in British Jl of Surgery and in Med. Jl of Australia. *Recreations*: music, the theatre, tennis, golf, rowing, beef cattle breeding. *Address*: 175 North Terrace, Adelaide, SA 5000, Australia. *T*: 51 5528. *Clubs*: Adelaide (Adelaide); Royal Adelaide Golf (Seaton, Adelaide).

MAGEE, Bryan; writer; Hon. Senior Research Fellow in History of Ideas, King's College London (KQC), since 1984; *b* 12 April 1930; *s* of Frederick Magee and Sheila (*née* Lynch); *m* 1954, Ingrid Söderlund (marr. diss.); one *d*. *Educ*: Christ's Hospital; Lycée Hôche, Versailles; Keble Coll., Oxford (Open Scholar). Pres., Oxford Union, 1953; MA 1956. Henry Fellow in Philosophy, Yale, 1955–56. Theatre Critic, The Listener, 1966–67; regular columnist, The Times, 1974–76. Current Affairs Reporter on TV; Critic of the Arts on BBC Radio 3; own broadcast series include: Conversations with Philosophers, BBC Radio 3, 1970–71; Men of Ideas, BBC TV 2, 1978. Silver Medal, RTS, 1978. Contested (Lab): Mid-Bedfordshire, Gen. Elec., 1959; By-Elec., 1960; MP (Lab 1974–82, SDP 1982–83) Leyton, Feb. 1974–1983; contested (SDP) Leyton, 1983. Elected to Critics' Circle, 1970, Pres., 1983–84. Judge for Evening Standard annual Opera Award, 1973–84. Lectr in Philosophy, Balliol Coll., Oxford, 1970–71; Visiting Fellow of All Souls Coll., Oxford, 1973–74; Vis. Schol. in Philos., Harvard, 1979, Sydney Univ., 1982. Governor, 1979–, Mem. Council, 1982–, Ditchley Foundn. *Publications*: Crucifixion and Other Poems, 1951; Go West Young Man, 1958; To Live in Danger, 1960; The New Radicalism, 1962; The Democratic Revolution, 1964; Towards 2000, 1965; One in Twenty, 1966; The Television Interviewer, 1966; Aspects of Wagner, 1968; Modern British Philosophy, 1971; Popper, 1973; Facing Death, 1977; Men of Ideas, 1978; The Philosophy of Schopenhauer, 1983. *Recreations*: music, theatre, travel. *Address*: 12 Falkland House, Marloes Road, W8 5LF. *T*: 01–937 1210. *Clubs*: Beefsteak, Brooks's, Garrick.

MAGEE, Reginald Arthur Edward, FRCSI, FRCOG; Consultant Gynaecologist, Belfast; President, Royal College of Surgeons in Ireland, since 1986 (Vice-President, 1984–86); *b* 18 Aug. 1914; *s* of James and Ellen Magee; *m* 1945, Gwladys Susannah (*née* Chapman); two *d*. *Educ*: Campbell Coll., Belfast (Sen. Science Prizeman); Queen's Univ., Belfast (MB, BCh, BAO, 1937). FRCSI 1947; FRCOG 1963 (MRCOG 1947). Mem. Students' Rep. Council, QUB; Mem., Univ. Athletic Team; Prizeman, Diseases of Children, Royal Belfast Hosp. for Sick Children. Demonstr in Physiol., QUB; House Surgeon, later Resident Surg. Officer, Royal Victoria Hosp., Belfast; House Surg. and Asst in Plastic Surgery, N Staffs Royal Infirm.; House Surg., Royal Maternity Hosp., Belfast; Jun., later Sen. Tutor in Obs, QUB; Temp. Consultant Gen. Surgery, Belfast City Hosp.; Obstet. and Gynaecologist, Massereene Hosp., and Antrim and Newtownards Dist Hosp.; post-grad. studies, Radium Inst., Stockholm; Clin. Teacher in Obs and Gynae., Clin. Lectr and Examr, QUB; Sen. Obstet., Royal Maternity Hosp., Belfast, and Sen. Gynaecologist, Royal Victoria Hosp., Belfast, and Ulster Hosp., Belfast, 1948–79; Administrative Med. Officer, Royal Gp of Hospitals, Belfast, 1979–84. Vis. Professor: Univ. of Basrah; Univ. of Baghdad; Vis. Lectr, Univ. of Cairo. Mem., NI Council for Post-grad. Med. Educn. Formerly: Chairman: Gp Med. Adv. Cttee, Royal Hosps, Belfast; Computer Cttee, Royal Victoria Hosp.; Member: Council, Jt Nurses and Midwives Council (also Lectr); Management Cttee, Ulster Hosp., Belfast; Royal Maternity Hosp. Cttee; Standing Cttee of Convocation, QUB. NI Hospitals Authority: formerly Chairman: Policy and Planning Cttee; Nurses and Midwives Cttee; Grading Cttee; Grading Appeals Cttee; formerly Mem., Exec. Cttee. Councillor: RCSI, 1974–; RCOG, 1972–78; Mem., Inst. of Obs and Gynae., Royal Coll. of Physicians of Ireland; Fellow, Ulster Med. Soc. (formerly Mem. Council); Mem., Ulster Obstet. and Gynaecol Soc. (formerly Pres.). Chm., Unionist Party of NI; Official Unionist Mem. for S Belfast, NI Assembly, 1973: Mem., Cttee of Privileges, Cttee on Finance, and Cttee on Health and Social Services; Leader of Pro-Assembly Unionist Back Bench Cttee; Mem., Public Accounts Cttee, NI; Advisor, Sunningdale Conf., 1973. Mem. Senate, QUB, 1979–82. Pres., Old Campbellian Soc., 1979. *Publications*: A Modern Record System of Obstetrics, 1963; A Computerised System of Obstetric Records, 1970; Royal Maternity Hospital Clinical Reports, and Ulster Hospital Clinical Reports, 1963–77; monographs on obstetric and gynaecological subjects; various hospital service reports. *Recreations*: riding, horse breeding, travel, photography.

Address: Montpelier, 96 Malone Road, Belfast BT9 5HP. *T:* Belfast 666765. *Clubs:* Athenæum, Royal Over-Seas League, English-Speaking Union; Kildare Street and University (Dublin).

MAGGS, Air Vice-Marshal William Jack, CB 1967; OBE 1943; MA; Fellow and Domestic Bursar, Keble College, Oxford, 1969–77, Emeritus Fellow since 1981; *b* 2 Feb. 1914; *s* of late Frederick Wilfrid Maggs, Bristol; *m* 1940, Margaret Grace, *d* of late Thomas Liddell Hetherington, West Hartlepool; one *s* one *d*. *Educ:* Bristol Grammar Sch.; St John's Coll., Oxford (MA). Management Trainee, 1936–38. Joined RAF, 1939; Unit and Training duties, 1939–42; Student, Staff Coll., 1942; Planning Staffs, and participated in, Algerian, Sicilian and Italian landings, 1942–44; SESO Desert Air Force, 1944; Jt Admin. Plans Staff, Cabinet Offices, Whitehall, 1945–48; Instructor, RAF Coll., Cranwell, 1948–50; comd No 9 Maintenance Unit, 1950–52; exchange officer at HQ, USAF Washington, 1952–54; Student Jt Services Staff Coll., 1954–55; No 3 Maintenance Unit, 1955–57; Dep. Director of Equipment, Air Ministry, 1958–59; SESO, HQ, NEAF, Cyprus, 1959–61; Student, Imperial Defence Coll., 1962; Director of Mech. Transport and Marine Craft, Air Ministry, 1963–64; Director of Equipment, Ministry of Defence (Air), 1964–67; SASO, RAF Maintenance Comd, 1967–69. Group Captain, 1958; Air Commodore, 1963; Air Vice-Marshal, 1967. Governor, Bristol Grammar Sch., 1980–. *Recreations:* golf, gardening. *Address:* Hillside, Noke, near Oxford OX3 9TT. *T:* Kidlington 3139. *Club:* Royal Air Force.

MAGILL, Air Vice-Marshal Graham Reese, CB 1966; CBE 1962 (OBE 1945); DFC 1941 and Bar, 1943; retired Jan. 1970; *b* 23 Jan. 1915; *s* of late Robert Wilson Magill and late Frances Elizabeth Magill, Te Aroha, NZ; *m* 1942, Blanche Marie Colson; two *s*. *Educ:* Te Aroha High Sch.; Hamilton Technical Coll., NZ. Joined Royal Air Force, 1936. Served War of 1939–45, Sudan and Eritrea (despatches 1941), Egypt, UK, NW Europe; subsequently, UK, Egypt, France. Director of Operations (Bomber and Reconnaissance), Air Ministry, 1959–62; Commandant, RAF College of Air Warfare, Manby, Lincs, 1963–64; Director-General of Organisation (RAF), Ministry of Defence, 1964–67; AOC, 25 Group, RAF, 1967–68; AOC 22 Group, RAF, 1968–69. *Recreations:* generally interested in sport and gentle sailing. *Address:* Calle Guillermo Cifre de Colonia, 30, Pollensa, Majorca. *Club:* Royal Air Force.

MAGILL, Sir Ivan Whiteside, KCVO 1960 (CVO 1946); FRCS 1951; FFARCS; MB, BCh, Belfast, 1913; DA 1935; formerly Hon. Consulting Anæsthetist, Westminster, Brompton and St Andrew's, Dollis Hill, Hospitals; *b* Larne, 1888; *s* of Samuel Magill; *m* 1916, Edith (*d* 1973), *d* of Thomas Robinson Banbridge. *Educ:* Larne Grammar Sch.; Queen's Univ., Belfast. Formerly: Consultant Army, Navy, EMS; Senior Anæsthetist, Queen's Hospital, Sidcup; Anæsthetist, Seamens Hospital, Greenwich; Res. MO, Stanley Hospital, Liverpool; Examiner, DA; Robert Campbell Memorial Orator, Belfast, 1939; Bengué Memorial Lecturer, Royal Institute of Public Health, 1950; Hon. Member: Liverpool Medical Institution; American Society of Anæsthesiologists; New York State Society of Anæsthesiologists; British Assoc. of Plastic Surgeons; Canadian Society of Anæsthetists; Hon. Fellow: Royal Society of Medicine, 1956; Faculty of Anæsthetists, Royal College of Surgeons, 1958; Assoc. of Anæsthetists of Great Britain and Ireland, 1958; Hon. FFARCSI, 1961. Henry Hill Hickman Medal, 1938; John Snow Medal, 1958; Canadian Anæsthetists Society Medal, 1963; Medal, American Assoc. of Plastic Surgeons, 1965; Gillies Mem. Lecturer, British Assoc. of Plastic Surgeons, 1965; Ralph M. Waters Prize, Chicago, 1966. Hon. DSc, Belfast, 1945. Frederic Hewitt Lecturer for 1965. *Publications:* contributions and chapters in various medical journals. *Recreation:* trout fishing. *Address:* c/o Royal Bank of Scotland, Holts Branch, Kirkland House, Whitehall, SW1.

MAGINNIS, John Edward, JP; *b* 7 March 1919; *s* of late Edward Maginnis, Mandeville Hall, Mullahead, Tanderagee; *m* 1944, Dorothy, *d* of late R. J. Rusk, JP, of Cavanaleck, Fivemiletown, Co. Tyrone; one *s* four *d*. *Educ:* Moyallon Sch., Co. Down; Portadown Technical Coll. Served War of 1939–45, Royal Ulster Constabulary. MP (UU) Armagh, Oct. 1959–Feb. 1974. JP, Co. Armagh, 1956. Group Secretary, North Armagh Group, Ulster Farmers' Union, 1956–59; Member, Co. Armagh Agricultural Society. *Recreations:* football, hunting, shooting. *Address:* Mandeville Hall, 68 Mullahead Road, Tandragee, Craigavon, Co. Armagh, N Ireland BT62 2LB. *T:* Tandragee 840260.

MAGINNIS, Ken; MP (UU) Fermanagh and South Tyrone, since 1983 (resigned seat Dec. 1985 in protest against Anglo-Irish Agreement; re-elected Jan. 1986); *b* 21 Jan. 1938; *m* 1961, Joy Stewart; two *s* two *d*. *Educ:* Royal Sch., Dungannon; Stranmillis Coll., Belfast. Served UDR, 1970–81, commissioned 1972, Major. Party spokesman on internal security and defence. Mem., Dungannon District Council, 1982–; Mem. (UU) Fermanagh and S Tyrone, NI Assembly, 1982–86. Contested (UU) Fermanagh and S Tyrone, Aug. 1981. Mem., H of C Select Cttee on Defence. *Address:* House of Commons, SW1A 0AA; 10 Springfield Lane, Mullaghmore, Dungannon, Co. Tyrone.

MAGNIAC, Rear-Admiral Vernon St Clair Lane, CB 1961; *b* 21 Dec. 1908; *s* of late Major Francis Arthur Magniac and of Mrs Beatrice Caroline Magniac (*née* Davison); *m* 1947, Eileen Eleanor (*née* Witney); one *s* one *d* (and one *d* decd). *Educ:* Clifton Coll. Cadet, RN, 1926; Served in HM Ships Courageous, Effingham, Resolution and Diamond, 1931–37; RN Engineering Coll., 1937–39; HMS Renown, 1940–43; Combined Ops, India, 1943–45; HM Ships Fisgard, Gambia, and Nigeria, 1945–50; HM Dockyards Chatham, Malta and Devonport, 1950–62. *Recreations:* golf, fishing. *Address:* Marlborough, Down Park, Yelverton, Devon.

MAGNUS, Hilary Barrow, TD; QC 1957; Social Security (formerly National Insurance) Commissioner, 1964–82; *b* 3 March 1909; *yr s* of late Laurie Magnus, 34 Cambridge Square, W2; *b* and *heir-pres.* to Sir Philip Magnus-Allcroft, *qv*; *m* 1950, Rosemary, *d* of G. H. Masefield and *widow* of Quentin Hurst; one *s* one *d* and one step *s*. *Educ:* Westminster; Christ Church, Oxford. Barrister, Lincoln's Inn, 1933 (Bencher, 1963; Treasurer, 1982). Served War of 1939–45, Rifle Brigade TA (Lieut-Colonel). JP (Kent) 1948. *Recreations:* reading, gardening. *Address:* Cragmore House, Church Street, Wye, Ashford, Kent TN25 5BJ. *T:* Wye 812036; 3 Temple Gardens, EC4. *T:* 01–353 7884. *Clubs:* Garrick, Beefsteak.

MAGNUS, Philip; *see* Magnus-Allcroft, Sir Philip.

MAGNUS, Prof. Philip Douglas, FRS 1985; Professor of Chemistry, Indiana University, since 1981; *b* 15 April 1943; *s* of Arthur Edwin and Lillian Edith Magnus; *m* 1963, Andrea Claire (*née* Parkinson); two *s*. *Educ:* Imperial College, Univ. of London (BSc, ARCS, PhD, DSc). Asst Lectr, 1967–70, Lectr, 1970–75, Imperial College; Associate Prof., Ohio State Univ., 1975–81. Corday Morgan Medal, RSC, 1978. *Publications:* papers in leading chemistry jls. *Recreations:* golf, chess, teasing the cat. *Address:* 2224 Sussex Drive, Bloomington, Indiana 47401, USA. *T:* (812) 335–7174.

MAGNUS, Samuel Woolf; Justice of Appeal, Court of Appeal for Zambia, 1971; Commissioner, Foreign Compensation Commission, 1977–83; *b* 30 Sept. 1910; *s* of late Samuel Woolf Magnus; *m* 1938, Anna Gertrude, *o d* of Adolph Shane, Cardiff; one *d*. *Educ:* University Coll., London. BA Hons, 1931. Called to Bar, Gray's Inn, 1937. Served War of 1939–45, Army. Practised in London, 1937–59. Treas., Assoc. of Liberal Lawyers, Mem. Council, London Liberal Party and Pres., N Hendon Liberal Assoc., until 1959. Contested (L) Central Hackney, 1945. Partner in legal firm, Northern Rhodesia, 1959–63; subseq. legal consultant. QC 1964, MLC 1962, MP Jan.-Oct. 1964, Northern Rhodesia; MP, Zambia, 1964–68. Puisne Judge, High Court for Zambia, 1968. Chm., Law, Parly and Gen. Purposes Cttee, Bd of Deputies of British Jews, 1979–83. *Publications:* (with M. Estrin) Companies Act 1947, 1947; (with M. Estrin) Companies: Law and Practice, 1948, 5th edn 1978, and Supplement, 1981; (with A. M. Lyons) Advertisement Control, 1949; Magnus on Leasehold Property (Temporary Provisions) Act 1951, 1951; Magnus on Landlord and Tenant Act 1954, 1954; Magnus on Housing Repairs and Rents Act 1954, 1954; Magnus on the Rent Act 1957, 1957; (with F. E. Price) Knight's Annotated Housing Acts, 1958; (with Tovell) Magnus on Housing Finance, 1960; (with M. Estrin) Companies Act 1967, 1967; Magnus on the Rent Act 1968, 1969; Magnus on Business Tenancies, 1970; Magnus on the Rent Act 1977, 1978; contributor: Law Jl; Halsbury's Laws of England; Encycl. of Forms and Precedents; Atkin's Court Forms and Precedents. *Recreations:* writing, photography, enthusiastic spectator at all games, preferably on TV. *Address:* 33 Apsley House, Finchley Road, St John's Wood, NW8. *T:* 01–586 1679. *Clubs:* MCC, Middlesex CC.

MAGNUS-ALLCROFT, Sir Philip, 2nd Bt, *cr* 1917; CBE 1971; MA; FRSL; FRHistS; author; *b* 8 Feb. 1906; *er s* of late Laurie Magnus and Dora, *e d* of late Sir I. Spielman, CMG; *S* grandfather, 1933; *m* 1943, Jewell Allcroft, Stokesay Court, Onibury, Shropshire, *d* of late Herbert Allcroft and of Mrs John Rotton. Formally assumed surname of Allcroft (in addition to that of Magnus), 1951. *Educ:* Westminster Sch.; Wadham Coll., Oxford. Civil Service, 1928–32 and 1946–50. Served War of 1939–45 in Royal Artillery and Intelligence Corps (Iceland and Italy); Major. CC 1952, CA 1968–74, Salop (Chairman, Planning Cttee, 1962–74; formerly: Chm., Records Cttee; Vice-Chm., Educn Cttee); Chairman of Governors, Attingham Coll.; JP Salop, 1953–71 (Chm., Juvenile Ct). Trustee, National Portrait Gall., 1970–77. Mem., Mercia Regional Cttee, Nat. Trust, 1973–81. Governor, Ludlow Grammar Sch., 1952–77. *Publications:* (as Philip Magnus): Life of Edmund Burke, 1939; Selected Prose of Edmund Burke (with Introduction), 1948; Sir Walter Raleigh, 1951 (revised edns, 1956, 1968); Gladstone—A Biography, 1954; Kitchener—Portrait of an Imperialist, 1958 (revised edn, 1968); King Edward the Seventh, 1964. *Recreations:* travel, gardening. *Heir:* *b* Hilary Barrow Magnus, *qv*. *Address:* Stokesay Court, Onibury, Craven Arms, Shropshire SY7 9BD. *T:* Bromfield 372 and 394. *Clubs:* Brooks's, Beefsteak, Pratt's.

MAGNUSSON, Magnus, MA (Oxon); FRSE 1980; FRSA 1983; writer and broadcaster; *b* 12 Oct. 1929; *s* of late Sigursteinn Magnusson, Icelandic Consul-Gen. for Scotland, and Ingibjorg Sigurdardottir; *m* 1954, Mamie Baird; one *s* three *d* (and one *s* decd). *Educ:* Edinburgh Academy; Jesus Coll., Oxford (MA). Subseq. Asst Editor, Scottish Daily Express and Asst Editor, The Scotsman. Presenter, various television and radio programmes including: Chronicle; Mastermind; Pebble Mill at One; BC, The Archaeology of the Bible Lands; Tonight; Cause for Concern; All Things Considered; Living Legends; Vikings!; Scottish Television Personality of the Year, 1974. Editor: The Bodley Head Archaeologies; Popular Archaeology, 1979–80. Chairman: Ancient Monuments Bd for Scotland, 1981–; Stewards, York Archaeol Trust; Scottish Churches Architectural Heritage Trust, 1978–85; Scottish Youth Theatre, 1976–78; Mem., Bd of Trustees, Nat. Museums of Scotland, 1985–; Pres., RSPB, 1985–; Hon. Vice-President: Age Concern Scotland; RSSPCC. Rector, Edinburgh Univ., 1975–78. FSAScot 1974. D *hc* Edinburgh, 1978; DUniv York, 1981. Knight of the Order of the Falcon (Iceland), 1975, Knight Commander, 1986; Silver Jubilee Medal, 1977; Iceland Media Award, 1985. *Publications:* Introducing Archaeology, 1972; Viking Expansion Westwards, 1973; The Clacken and the Slate (Edinburgh Academy, 1824–1974), 1974; Hammer of the North (Norse mythology), 1976, 2nd edn, Viking Hammer of the North, 1980; BC, The Archaeology of the Bible Lands, 1977; Landlord or Tenant? a view of Irish history, 1978; Iceland, 1979; Vikings!, 1980; Magnus on the Move, 1980; Treasures of Scotland, 1981; Lindisfarne: The Cradle Island, 1984; Iceland Saga, 1987; translations (all with Hermann Pálsson): Njal's Saga, 1960; The Vinland Sagas, 1965; King Harald's Saga, 1966; Laxdaela Saga, 1969; (all by Halldor Laxness): The Atom Station, 1961; Paradise Reclaimed, 1962; The Fish Can Sing, 1966; World Light, 1969; Christianity Under Glacier, 1973; (by Samivel) Golden Iceland, 1967; contributor: The Glorious Privilege, 1967; The Future of the Highlands, 1968; Strange Stories, Amazing Facts, 1975; Pass the Port, 1976; Book of Bricks, 1978; Chronicle, 1978; Discovery of Lost Worlds, 1979; Living Legends, 1980; The Hammer and the Cross, 1980; Pass the Port Again, 1981; Second Book of Bricks, 1981; introduced: Ancient China, 1974; The National Trust for Scotland Guide, 1976; Karluk, 1976; More Lives Than One?, 1976; Atlas of World Geography, 1977; Face to Face with the Turin Shroud, 1978; Modern Bible Atlas, 1979; Household Ghosts, 1981; Great Books for Today, 1981; The Voyage of Odin's Raven, 1982; Robert Burns: Bawdy Verse & Folksongs, 1982; Mastermind 4, 1982; Northern Voices, 1984; The Village, 1985; Secrets of the Bible Seas, 1985; edited: Echoes in Stone, 1983; Readers Digest Book of Facts, 1985. *Recreations:* digging and delving. *Address:* Blairskaith House, Balmore-Torrance, Glasgow G64 4AX. *T:* Balmore 20226. *Clubs:* Athenæum; New (Edinburgh).

MAGOR, Major (Edward) Walter (Moyle), CMG 1960; OBE 1956 (MBE 1947); DL; *b* 1 June 1911; *e s* of late Edward John Penberthy Magor, JP, Lamellen, St Tudy, Cornwall, and Gilian Sarah Magor, JP; *m* 1939, Daphne Davis (*d* 1972), *d* of late Hector Robert Lushington Graham, Summerhill, Thomastown, Co. Kilkenny; two *d*. *Educ:* Marlborough; Magdalen, Oxford; Magdalene, Cambridge. MA. Indian Army, 1934–47; RARO, 10th Hussars, 1949–61; Indian Political Service, 1937–39 and 1943–47; Colonial Administrative Service, 1947–61; Kenya: Asst Chief Secretary, 1953; Permanent Secretary, Ministry of Defence, 1954; Acting Minister for Defence, 1956; Secretary to the Cabinet, 1958. Home Civil Service, DTI, formerly BoT, 1961–71; Asst Secretary, 1964; retired 1971. Chm., St John Council for Cornwall, 1973–78. Editor, RHS Rhododendron and Camellia Yearbook, 1974–82; Chm., RHS Rhododendron and Camellia Gp, 1976–80. President: Cornwall Garden Soc., 1981–84; Royal Cornwall Agricl Assoc., 1983. DL Cornwall, 1974; High Sheriff of Cornwall, 1981. CStJ 1978 (OStJ 1975). Médaille de la Belgique Reconnaissante, 1961; Veitch Meml Medal, RHS, 1986. Lord of the Manor of Kellygreen. *Recreation:* gardening (Mem., Garden Soc.). *Address:* Lamellen, St Tudy, Cornwall PL30 3NR. *T:* Bodmin 850207. *Club:* Army and Navy.

MAGUIRE, (Albert) Michael, MC 1945, MM 1943; QC 1967; *b* 30 Dec. 1922; *s* of late Richard Maguire and Ruth Maguire. *Educ:* Hutton Grammar Sch.; Trinity Hall, Cambridge (BA 1948). Served War of 1939–45, North Irish Horse (Captain), in Africa (MM) and Italy (MC). Inns of Court Regt, 1946. War Crimes Investigation Unit, 1946. Called to the Bar, Middle Temple, 1949 (Harmsworth Scholar); Bencher, 1973; Leader, Northern Circuit, 1980–84. Last Recorder of Carlisle (1970–71). *Address:* Goldsmith Building, Temple, EC4Y 7BL; Chestnuts, Lower Bank Road, Fulwood, Preston, Lancs. *T:* Preston 719291. *Club:* United Oxford & Cambridge University.

MAGUIRE, (Benjamin) Waldo, OBE 1973; *b* 31 May 1920; *s* of Benjamin Maguire and Elizabeth Ann Eldon; *m* 1944, Lilian Joan Martin; four *s*. *Educ:* Portadown Coll.;

Trinity Coll., Dublin. BA 1st cl. hons Philosophy. Intell. Service, WO and FO, 1942–45; BBC Latin American Service, 1945; BBC Radio News, 1946–55; BBC TV News, 1955; Editor, BBC TV News, 1962–64; Controller, News and Public Affairs, NZ Broadcasting Corp., 1965–66; BBC Controller, NI, 1966–72; Head of Information Programmes, NZ TV2, 1975–76. *Recreations:* conversation, angling. *Address:* 116 Park Avenue, Ruislip, Mddx. *T:* Ruislip 35981.

MAGUIRE, Air Marshal Sir Harold John, KCB 1966 (CB 1958); DSO 1946; OBE 1949; Director, Commercial Union Assurance Co., 1975–82 (Political and Economic Adviser, 1972–79); *b* 12 April 1912; *s* of Michael Maguire, Maynooth, Ireland, and Harriett (*née* Warren), Kilkishen, Co. Clare, Ireland; *m* 1940, Mary Elisabeth Wild, Dublin; one *s* one *d*. *Educ:* Wesley Coll., Dublin; Dublin Univ. Royal Air Force Commn, 1933; service in flying boats, 230 Sqdn, Egypt and Far East, 1935–38; commanded night fighter sqdn, UK, 1939–40 and day fighter sqdn, 1940; OC 266 (Fighter) Wing, Dutch E Indies, 1942; POW, Java, 1942; Staff Coll., 1947; Fighter Command Staff Duties, 1948–50; OC, RAF, Odiham, 1950–52; Senior Air Staff Officer, Malta, 1952–55; staff of CAS, Air Ministry, 1955–58; Senior Air Staff Officer, HQ No 11 Group, RAF, 1958–59; AOC No 13 Group, RAF, 1959–61; AOC No 11 Group, Fighter Command, 1961–62; SASO Far East Air Force, 1962–64; ACAS (Intelligence), 1964–65; Dep. Chief of Defence Staff (Intelligence), 1965–68; retired, 1968; Dir-Gen. of Intelligence, MoD, 1968–72. *Address:* c/o Lloyds Bank, 6 Pall Mall, SW1. *Club:* Royal Air Force.

MAGUIRE, Hugh, FRAM; violinist and conductor; Leader: Melos Ensemble, since 1972; Royal Opera House, Covent Garden, since 1983; Professor of Violin, Royal Academy of Music, since 1957; Director of Strings, Britten-Pears School for Advanced Music Studies, since 1978; *b* 2 Aug. 1926; *m* 1953, Suzanne Lewis, of International Ballet; two *s* three *d*. *Educ:* Belvedere Coll., SJ, Dublin; Royal Academy of Music, London (David Martin); Paris (Georges Enesco). Leader: Bournemouth Symphony Orchestra, 1952–56; London Symphony Orchestra, 1956–62; BBC Symphony Orchestra, 1962–67; Cremona String Quartet, 1966–68; Leader, Allegri String Quartet, 1968–76. Artistic Dir, Irish Youth Orch. String coach, European Commn Youth Orch. Mem., Irish Arts Council. Hon. MMus Hull, 1975; Hon. DLitt Univ. of Ulster, 1986. Harriet Cohen Internat. Award; Councils Gold Medal (Ireland), 1963; Cobbett Medal, Musicians' Co., 1982. *Address:* Manor Farm, Benhall, Suffolk IP17 1HN. *T:* Saxmundham 3245.

MAGUIRE, Mairead C.; *see* Corrigan-Maguire.

MAGUIRE, Michael; *see* Maguire, A. M.

MAGUIRE, Rt. Rev. Robert Kenneth, MA, DD; Assistant to the Primate, Anglican Church of Canada, since 1980; *b* 31 March 1923; *s* of late Robert Maguire and late Anne Crozier; unmarried. *Educ:* Trinity Coll., Dublin. BA 1945; Divinity Testimonium, 1947. Deacon, 1947; Priest, 1948. Curate of: St Mark, Armagh, 1947–49; St James the Apostle, Montreal, 1949–52; Dean of Residence, Trinity Coll., Dublin, 1952–60; Curate-in-charge of St Andrew's, Dublin, 1954–57; Minor Canon of St Patrick's Cathedral, Dublin, 1955–58; Dean and Rector of Christ Church Cathedral, Montreal, 1961–62; Bishop of Montreal, 1963–75. Co-ordinator: Canadian Conf., Theology '76, 1975–76; North American Consultation on the Future of Ministry, 1979–80. DD (*jure dig.*): Dublin Univ., 1963; Montreal Diocesan Theolog. Coll., 1963; DCL (*hc*), Bishop's Univ., Lennoxville, Qué., 1963. *Address:* 4875 Dundas Street West, Apt 304, Islington, Ontario M9A 1B3, Canada.

MAGUIRE, Waldo; *see* Maguire, B. W.

MAHATHIR bin MOHAMAD, Datok Seri Dr; MHR for Kubang Pasu, since 1974; Prime Minister of Malaysia, since 1981, and Minister of Home Affairs, since 1986; *b* 20 Dec. 1925. *Educ:* Sultan Abdul Hamid Coll.; College of Medicine, Singapore. Medical Officer, Kedah and Perlis, 1953–57; in private practice, 1957–64. MHR for Kota Star Selatan, 1964–69; Mem., Senate, 1972–74; Minister of: Education, 1974–77; Trade and Industry, 1977–81; Dep. Prime Minister, 1976–81; Minister of Defence, 1981–86. President, United Malays Nat. Organisation, 1981– (Mem., Supreme Council, 1972–). Chm., Food Industries of Malaysia Co., 1973. *Publication:* The Malay Dilemma, 1969. *Address:* Office of the Prime Minister, Kuala Lumpur, Malaysia.

MAHER, Terence; Metropolitan Stipendiary Magistrate, since 1983; an Assistant Recorder, since 1985; *b* 20 Dec. 1941; *s* of late John Maher and of Bessie Maher; *m* 1965 (marr. diss. 1983); two *d*. *Educ:* Burnley Grammar Sch.; Univ. of Manchester. LLB (hons). Admitted Solicitor, 1966; articled to Town Clerk, Burnley; Asst Sol., City of Bradford, 1966–68; Prosecuting Sol., Birmingham Corp., 1968–70; Dep. Pros. Sol., Thames Valley Police, 1970–73; Asst Sol. and partner, Cole & Cole, Oxford, 1973–83. Gen. Sec., Univ. of Manchester Students' Union, 1962–63; Chm., Chipping Norton Round Table, 1975–76; Treasurer/Vice-Chm. and Chm., Oxford and District Solicitors' Assoc., 1980–83; Mem., Law Society Standing Cttee on Criminal Law, 1980–85; a Chm., Inner London Juvenile Courts. Mem. Editl Bd, Jl of Criminal Law. *Recreations:* walking, reading, anything to do with France and the French. *Address:* c/o Magistrates' Court, Old Street, EC1. *Club:* Frewen (Oxford).

MAHER, Very Rev. William Francis, SJ; Provincial Superior of the English Province of the Society of Jesus, 1976–81; *b* 20 June 1916. *Educ:* St Ignatius' College, Stamford Hill; Heythrop College, Oxon. STL. Entered the Society of Jesus, 1935; ordained priest, 1948; Principal, Heythrop College, 1974–76. *Address:* 20 Colston Street, Bristol BS1 5AE.

MAHLER, Dr Halfdan; Director-General, World Health Organization, since 1973; *b* 21 April 1923; *m* 1957, Dr Ebba Fischer-Simonsen; two *s*. *Educ:* Univ. of Copenhagen (MD, EOPH). Planning Officer, Internat. Tuberculosis Campaign, Ecuador, 1950–51; Sen. WHO Med. Officer, Nat. TB Programme, India, 1951–61; Chief MO, Tuberculosis Unit, WHO/HQ, Geneva, 1961–69; Dir, Project Systems Analysis, WHO/HQ, Geneva, 1969–70; Asst Dir-Gen., WHO, 1970–73. Hon. FRSM 1976; Hon. Fellow: Indian Soc. for Malaria and other Communicable Diseases, Delhi; Faculty of Community Med., RCP, 1975; Hon. Professor: Univ. Nacional Mayor de San Marcos, Lima, Peru, 1980; Fac. of Medicine, Univ. of Chile, 1982; Beijing Med. Coll., China, 1983; Hon. Fellow: LSHTM, 1979; Coll. of Physicians and Surgeons, Dacca, Bangladesh, 1980; Hon. Member: Soc. médicale de Genève; Union internat. contre la Tuberculose; Société Française d'Hygiène, de Médecine Sociale et Génie Sanitaire, 1977; Hon. Life Mem., Uganda Medical Assoc., 1976; Assoc. Mem., Belgian Soc. of Trop. Med. FRCP 1981. Hon. LLD Nottingham, 1975; Hon. MD: Karolinska Inst., 1977; Charles Univ., Prague, and Mahidol Univ., Bangkok, 1982; Hon. Dr de l'Univ. Toulouse (Sciences Sociales), 1977; Hon. Dr Public Health, Seoul Nat. Univ., 1979; Hon DSc Univ. of Lagos, 1979; Hon. Dr Med. Warsaw Med. Acad., 1980; Hon. Dr Faculty of Medicine, Univ. of Ghent, Belgium, and Universidad Nacional Autonoma de Nicaragua, Managua, 1983. Grand Officier: l'Ordre Nat. du Bénin, 1975; l'Ordre Nat. Voltaïque, 1978; l'Ordre du Mérite, République du Sénégal, 1982; White Rose Order of Finland, 1983; Commandeur, l'Ordre National du Mali, 1982. Jane Evangelisty Purkyne Medal, Prague, 1974; Comenius Univ. Gold Medal, Bratislava, 1974; Carlo Forlanini Gold Medal, 1975; Ernst Carlsens Foundn Prize, Copenhagen, 1980; Georg Barfred-Pedersen Prize, Copenhagen, 1982; List of Honour, Internat. Dental Fedn, 1984. *Publications:* papers etc on the epidemiology and control of tuberculosis, the political, social, economic and technological priority setting in the health sector, and the application of systems analysis to health care problems. *Recreations:* sailing, skiing. *Address:* (home) 12 chemin du Pont-Ceard, 1290 Versoix, Switzerland; (office) World Health Organization, Avenue Appia, 1211 Geneva 27, Switzerland.

MAHLER, Kurt, FAA 1965; FRS 1948; PhD, DSc; Professor Emeritus, Australian National University, since 1975; *b* 1903. *Educ:* Univs of Frankfurt and Göttingen. Research work at Univs of Göttingen, Groningen, and Manchester. Asst Lecturer at Manchester Univ., 1937–39, 1941–44; Lecturer, 1944–47; Senior Lecturer, 1948–49; Reader, 1949–52; Prof. of Mathematical Analysis, 1952–63; Prof. of Mathematics, Institute of Advanced Studies, ANU, 1963–68; Prof. of Mathematics, Ohio State Univ., USA, 1968–72. De Morgan Medal, 1971; Thomas Ranken Lyle Medal, 1977. *Publications:* Lectures on Diophantine Approximations, 1961; Introduction to p-adic Numbers and their Functions, 1973, 2nd edn 1980; Lectures on Transcendental Numbers, 1976; papers on different subjects in pure mathematics (Theory and Geometry of Numbers) in various journals, from 1928. *Recreations:* Chinese, photography. *Address:* Mathematics Department, Institute of Advanced Studies, Australian National University, Canberra, PO Box 4, ACT 2601, Australia.

MAHLER, Prof. Robert Frederick, FRCP, FRCPE; Consultant Physician, Clinical Research Centre, Northwick Park Hospital, Harrow, since 1979; *b* 31 Oct. 1924; *s* of Felix Mahler and Olga Lowy; *m* 1951, Maureen Calvert; two *s*. *Educ:* Edinburgh Academy; Edinburgh Univ. BSc; MB, ChB. Research fellowships and univ. posts in medicine, biochemistry and clinical pharmacology at various med. schs and univs: in Gt Britain: Royal Postgrad. Med. Sch., Guy's Hosp., Manchester, Dundee, Cardiff; in USA: Harvard Univ., Univ. of Indiana; in Sweden: Karolinska Inst., Stockholm; Prof. of Med., Univ. of Wales, 1970–79. Member: MRC, 1977–81; Commonwealth Scholarship Commn, 1980–; Council, Imperial Cancer Res. Fund, 1984–; Res. Cttee, British Diabetic Assoc., 1984–; Scientific Co-ord. Cttee, Arthritis and Rheumatism Council, 1986–. *Publications:* contribs to British and Amer. med. and scientific jls. *Recreations:* opera, music, theatre. *Address:* 14 Manley Street, NW1. *T:* 01–586 1198. *Club:* Royal Society of Medicine.

MAHMUD HUSAIN, Syed Abul Basher; Chief Justice of Bangladesh, 1975–78; *b* 1 Feb. 1916; *s* of late Syed Abdul Mutakabbir Abul Hasan, eminent scholar; *m* 1936, Sufia Begum; three *s* five *d*. *Educ:* Shaistagonj High Sch.; M. C. Coll., Sylhet; Dacca Univ. (BA, BL). Pleader, Judge's Court, Dacca, 1940–42; Hon. Supt, Darul-Ulum Govt-aided Sen., Madrassa, Dacca, 1937–42; Additional Govt Pleader, Habiganj, 1943–48; Advocate, Dacca High Ct Bar, 1948–51; Attorney, Fed. Ct of Pakistan, 1951, Advocate, 1953, Sen. Advocate, Supreme Ct of Pakistan, 1958; Asst Govt Pleader, High Ct of E Pakistan, 1952–56; Sen. Govt Pleader, 1956–65; Actg Advocate-Gen., E Pakistan for some time; Judge: High Ct of E Pakistan, 1965; High Ct of Bangladesh, 1972; Appellate Div. of High Ct of Bangladesh, Aug. 1972; Appellate Div. of Supreme Ct of Bangladesh, Dec. 1972. Mem. Bar Council, High Ct, Dacca, 1958–66; Chm., Enrolment Cttee, E Pakistan Bar Council, 1966–69; played important role in Muslim League and Pakistan Movement. Member: Coll. Rover Crew, 1933–34; Dacca Univ. OTC, 1935–39; Local Bd, Habiganj, 1944–50; Councillor: Assam Provincial Muslim League, 1944–47; All India Muslim League, 1945–47; All Pakistan Muslim League, 1947–55; Member: Constituent Assembly of Pakistan, 1949–54; Commonwealth Parly Assoc., 1950–54; Inter-Parly Union, 1950–54; Pakistan Tea Bd, 1951–54; Exec. Council, Univ. of Dacca, 1952–54; Local Adv. Cttee, East Bengal Rlwy, 1952–54; Dir, Pakistan Refugees Rehabilitation Finance Corp., 1953–54. Leader of Hajj Delegn of Bangladesh, 1975; attended Internat. Islamic Conf., London, 1976 (Chm., Third Session). *Address:* 56/1, Shah Saheb Lane, Narinda, Dhaka, Bangladesh. *T:* 238986.

MAHON, Sir Denis; *see* Mahon, Sir J. D.

MAHON, Sir George Edward John, 6th Bt, *cr* 1819; *b* 22 June 1911; *s* of 5th Bt and late Hon. Edith Dillon, 2nd *d* of 4th Lord Clonbrock; *S* father, 1926; *m* 1st, 1938, Audrey Evelyn (*d* 1957), *o c* of late Dr Walter Jagger and late Mrs Maxwell Coote; two *s* one *d*; 2nd, 1958, Suzanne, *d* of late Thomas Donnellan, Pirbright, Surrey, and late Mrs Donnellan; one *d*. *Heir:* *s* Col William Walter Mahon, Irish Guards [*b* 4 Dec. 1940; *m* 1968, Rosemary Jane, *yr d* of Lt-Col M. E. Melvill, West Linton, Peebles-shire; one *s* two *d*]. *Address:* 7 Waltham Terrace, Blackrock, Co. Dublin. *T:* Dublin 880473.

MAHON, Rt. Rev. Gerald Thomas; Auxiliary Bishop of Westminster (Bishop in West London) (RC) and Titular Bishop of Eanach Duin since 1970; *b* 4 May 1922; *s* of George Elborne Mahon and Mary Elizabeth (*née* Dooley). *Educ:* Cardinal Vaughan Sch., Kensington; Christ's Coll., Cambridge. Priest, 1946. Teaching, St Peter's Coll., Freshfield, 1950–55; missionary work in Dio. of Kisumu, Kenya, 1955–63; Superior General of St Joseph's Missionary Society of Mill Hill, 1963–70. *Address:* 34 Whitehall Gardens, Acton, W3 9RD.

MAHON, Sir (John) Denis, Kt 1986; CBE 1967; MA Oxon; FBA 1964; Art Historian; Trustee of the National Gallery, 1957–64 and 1966–73; Member, Advisory Panel, National Art Collections Fund; *b* 8 Nov. 1910; *s* of late John FitzGerald Mahon (4th *s* of Sir W. Mahon, 4th Bt) and Lady Alice Evelyn Browne (*d* 1970), *d* of 5th Marquess of Sligo. *Educ:* Eton; Christ Church, Oxford. Has specialised in the study of 17th-Century painting in Italy and has formed a collection of pictures of the period; is a member of the Cttee of the Biennial Exhibitions at Bologna, Italy; was awarded, 1957, Medal for Benemeriti della Cultura by Pres. of Italy for services to criticism and history of Italian art; Archiginnasio d'Oro, City of Bologna, 1968; Serena Medal for Italian Studies, British Acad., 1972. Elected Accademico d'Onore, Clementine Acad., Bologna, 1964; Corresp. Fellow: Accad. Raffaello, Urbino, 1968; Deputazione di Storia Patria per le provincie di Romagna, 1969. Hon. Citizen, Cento, 1982. Hon. DLitt, Newcastle, 1969. *Publications:* Studies in Seicento Art and Theory, 1947; Mostra dei Carracci, Catalogo critico dei Disegni, 1956 (1963); Poussiniana, 1962; Catalogues of the Mostra del Guercino (Dipinti, 1968; Disegni, 1969); contributed to: Actes of Colloque Poussin, 1960; Friedlaender Festschrift, 1965; Problemi Guardeschi, 1967; articles, including a number on Caravaggio and Poussin, in art-historical periodicals, *eg*, The Burlington Magazine, Apollo, The Art Bulletin, Journal of the Warburg and Courtauld Institutes, Bulletin of the Metropolitan Museum of New York, Gazette des Beaux-Arts, Art de France, Paragone, Commentari, Zeitschrift für Kunstwissenschaft; has collaborated in the compilation of catalogues raisonnés of exhibitions, *eg*, Artists in 17th Century Rome (London, 1955), Italian Art and Britain (Royal Academy, 1960), L'Ideale Classico del Seicento in Italia (Bologna, 1962), Omaggio al Guercino (Cento, 1967). *Address:* 33 Cadogan Square, SW1. *T:* 01–235 7311, 01–235 2530.

MAHON, Peter, JP; *b* 4 May 1909; *s* of late Alderman Simon Mahon, OBE, JP, Bootle, Liverpool; *m* 1935, Margaret Mahon (*née* Hannon). *Educ:* St James Elementary Sch.; St Edward's Coll. (Irish Christian Brothers). One of the longest serving Local Govt representatives in GB (42 years); Bootle Borough Council, 1933–70 (Mayor, 1954–55); Liverpool City Council, 1970–75; Liverpool DC, 1973–80 (Mem. (L) Old Swan Ward);

Chm. or Dep. Chm. numerous cttees; Mem. Nat. Cttee of TGWU. Prospective Parly Candidate (Lab) Blackburn, 1952–54, contested (Lab) Preston, 1962–64; MP (Lab) Preston South, 1964–70; contested Liverpool Scotland, April 1971, as first Against Abortion candidate in UK; expelled from Labour Party. Talked out first Abortion Bill, House of Commons, 1966. *Recreations:* football and swimming enthusiast; fond of music. *Address:* Seahaven, Burbo Bank Road, Blundellsands, Liverpool L23 8TA.

MAHONY, Francis Joseph, CB 1980; OBE 1972; President, Repatriation Review Tribunal, Australia, 1979–84; *b* 15 March 1915; *s* of Cornelius J. Mahony and Angela M. Heagney; *m* 1939, Mary K. Sexton; seven *s* one *d*. *Educ:* De La Salle Coll., Armidale; Sydney Univ. (LLB 1940). Served War, CMF and AIF, 1942–44. Called to the Bar, Supreme Court of NSW, 1940; Commonwealth Crown Solicitor's Office, 1941; admitted Practitioner, High Ct of Australia, 1950; admitted Solicitor, Supreme Ct of NSW, 1952; Dep. Commonwealth Crown Solicitor, NSW, 1963–70; Dep. Sec., Attorney-Gen.'s Dept, Canberra, 1970–79. Leader, Aust. Delegn to Diplomatic Conf. on Humanitarian Law Applicable in Armed Conflicts, 1974–77. Chairman: Criminology Res. Council, 1972–79; Bd of Management, Aust. Inst. of Criminology, 1973–79; Mem. UN Cttee, Crime Prevention and Control, 1980–83. *Recreations:* tennis, golf. *Address:* 92 Cliff Avenue, Northbridge, NSW 2063, Australia. *T:* (02) 95 1853. *Clubs:* Sydney Cricket Ground; Northbridge Golf.

MAHONY, Lt-Col John Keefer, VC 1944; *b* 30 June 1911; *s* of Joseph Jackson and Louise Mary Mahony; *m* 1950, Bonnie Johnston, Ottawa; two *d*. *Educ:* Duke of Connaught Sch., New Westminster, BC, Canada. On editorial staff of Vancouver Daily Province (newspaper) until outbreak of war of 1939–45; mem. Canadian Militia (equivalent of British Territorials) from 1936 until going on active service in Sept. 1939. Served War of 1939–45 (VC): (Canada, UK, Africa, Italy) Westminster Regt, Canadian Army; Major, 1943. Liaison Officer, US Dept of the Army, Washington, DC, 1954; retd as AA and QMG, Alberta Area, 1963. Exec. Dir, Junior Achievement of London, Inc. *Recreations:* swimming, lacrosse, baseball. *Address:* 657 Santa Monica Road, London, Ontario, Canada.

MAHY, Brian Wilfred John, PhD, ScD; Director, Animal Virus Research Institute, since 1984; *b* 7 May 1937; *s* of Wilfred Mahy and Norah Dillingham; *m* 1959, Valerie Pouteaux; two *s* one *d*. *Educ:* Elizabeth Coll., Guernsey; Univ. of Southampton (BSc, PhD); Univ. of Cambridge (MA, ScD). Res. Biologist, Dept of Cancer Res., London Hosp. Med. Coll., Univ. of London, 1962–65; Asst Dir, Res. Virology, Dept of Pathology, Cambridge Univ., 1965–79; Fellow and Tutor, University (Wolfson) Coll., 1967–75; Librarian, Wolfson Coll., 1975–80; Huddersfield Lectr in Special Path. (Virology), 1979–84; Head, Div. of Virology, Cambridge, 1979–84. Vis. Prof., Univ. of Minnesota, 1968; Eleanor Roosevelt Internat. Cancer Fellow, Dept of Microbiol., Univ. of California, San Francisco, 1973–74; Vis. Prof., Inst. für Virologie, Univ. of Würzburg, 1980–81. Convener, Virus Group, 1980–84, Mem. Council, 1983–, Soc. for General Microbiology. FRSocMed 1985. *Publications:* (jtly) The Biology of Large RNA Viruses, 1970; Negative Strand Viruses, 1975; Negative Strand Virus and the Host Cell, 1978; Lactic Dehydrogenase Virus, 1975. A Dictionary of Virology, 1981; Virus Persistence, 1982; The Microbe 1984: pt 1, Viruses, 1984; Virology: a practical approach, 1985; numerous articles on animal virology in learned jls. *Recreation:* playing the violin in chamber and orchestral groups. *Address:* Animal Virus Research Institute, Pirbright, Woking, Surrey GU24 0NF. *T:* Worplesdon 232442.

MAIDEN, Colin James, ME, DPhil; Vice-Chancellor, University of Auckland, New Zealand, since 1971; *b* 5 May 1933; *s* of Henry A. Maiden; *m* 1957, Jenefor Mary Rowe; one *s* three *d*. *Educ:* Auckland Grammar Sch.; Univ. of Auckland, NZ; Oxford Univ. ME(NZ), DPhil (Oxon). Post-doctorate research, Oxford Univ., Oxford, Eng. (supported by AERE, Harwell), 1957–58; Head of Hypersonic Physics Section, Canadian Armament Research and Develt Estabt, Quebec City, Canada, 1958–60; Sen. Lectr in Mechanical Engrg, Univ. of Auckland, 1960–61; Head of Material Sciences Laboratory, Gen. Motors Corp., Defense Research Laboratories, Santa Barbara, Calif, USA, 1961–66; Manager of Process Engineering, Gen. Motors Corp., Technl Centre, Warren, Michigan, USA, 1966–70. Director: Farmers Trading Co. Ltd, 1973–; Winstone Ltd, 1978–; Fisher & Paykel Ltd, 1978–. Chairman: NZ Energy R&D Cttee, 1974–81; Liquid Fuels Trust Bd, 1978–; NZ Synthetic Fuels Corp. Ltd, 1980–. NZ Agent for Joint NZ/US Sci. and Technol Agreement, 1974–81. Thomson Medal, Royal Soc. NZ, 1986; Medal, Univ. of Bonn, 1983. *Publications:* numerous scientific and technical papers. *Recreations:* tennis, golf. *Address:* 1 Fern Avenue, Auckland, New Zealand. *T:* 685600. *Clubs:* Vincent's (Oxford); Northern, Rotary (Auckland); Remuera Racquets, Eden Epsom Tennis, International Lawn Tennis of NZ, Auckland Golf.

MAIDMENT, Kenneth John, MA; Emeritus Fellow, Merton College, Oxford; *b* 29 Oct. 1910; *s* of Francis George Maidment and Jessie Louisa Taylor; *m* 1937, Isobel Felicity, *d* of Archibald Leitch; one *s* three *d*. *Educ:* Bristol Gram. Sch.; Merton Coll., Oxford. Hertford Scholar, 1929; First Class Classical Hon. Mods, 1930; Craven Scholar, 1930; First Class Litt. Hum., 1932; Junior Research Fellow, Merton Coll., 1932–34; Fellow and Classical Tutor, Jesus Coll. (Oxford), 1934–38; Fellow and Classical Tutor, Merton Coll., 1938–49; Oxford and Bucks Lt Infantry, 1940; seconded War Office, 1941; liaison duties in US, 1942–45, Lt-Col; University Lecturer in Greek Literature, 1947–49; Principal, Auckland Univ. Coll., 1950–57; Vice-Chancellor, Univ. of Auckland, 1957–71. Governor, Bristol Grammar Sch., 1972–79. Hon. LLD Auckland. *Publications:* critical edition and translation of Antiphon and Andocides (Loeb Library), 1940; contribs to classical journals. *Address:* 9 Highfield Avenue, Headington, Oxford.

MAIDSTONE, Viscount; Daniel James Hatfield Finch Hatton; *b* 7 Oct. 1967; *s* and *heir* of 16th Earl of Winchilsea, *qv*.

MAIDSTONE, Bishop Suffragan of; *no appointment at time of going to press.*

MAIDSTONE, Archdeacon of; *see* Smith, Ven. A. M. P.

MAILER, Norman; *b* 31 Jan. 1923; *s* of Isaac Barnett Mailer and Fanny Schneider; *m* 1st, 1944, Beatrice Silverman (marr. diss., 1951); one *d*; 2nd, 1954, Adèle Morales (marr. diss., 1962); two *d*; 3rd, 1962, Lady Jeanne Campbell (marr. diss., 1963); one *d*; 4th, 1963, Beverly Bentley; two *s*; 5th, Carol Stevens; one *d*; 6th, Norris Church; one *s*. *Educ:* Harvard. Infantryman, US Army, 1944–46. Co-founder of Village Voice, 1955; an Editor of Dissent, 1953–63. Democratic Candidate, Mayoral Primaries, New York City, 1969. Directed films: Wild 90, 1967; Beyond the Law, 1967; Maidstone, 1968. Pulitzer Prize for Fiction, 1980. *Publications:* The Naked and the Dead, 1948; Barbary Shore, 1951; The Deer Park, 1955 (dramatized, 1967); Advertisements for Myself, 1959; Deaths For The Ladies, 1962; The Presidential Papers, 1963; An American Dream, 1964; Cannibals and Christians, 1966; Why Are We In Vietnam?, 1967 (a novel); The Armies of the Night, 1968 (Pulitzer Prize, 1969); Miami and the Siege of Chicago, 1968 (National Book Award, 1969); Of a Fire on the Moon, 1970; The Prisoner of Sex, 1971; Existential Errands, 1972; St George and the Godfather, 1972; Marilyn, 1973; The Faith of Graffiti, 1974; The Fight, 1975; Some Honorable Men, 1975; Genius and Lust, 1976; A Transit to Narcissus, 1978; The Executioner's Song, 1979; Of a Small and Modest Malignancy, Wicked and Bristling with Dots, 1980; Of Women and Their Elegance, 1980; The Essential Mailer, 1982; Ancient Evenings, 1983; Tough Guys Don't Dance, 1984. *Address:* c/o Rembar, 19 W 44th Street, New York, NY 10036, USA.

MAILLART, Ella (Kini); Explorer; *b* 20 Feb. 1903; Swiss father and Danish mother; unmarried. *Educ:* Geneva; and also while teaching French at two schools in England. Took to the seas at 20, cruising with 3 ton Perlette, 10 ton Bonita, 45 ton Atalante-all these manned by girls; then 120 ton Volunteer, 125 ton Insoumise; in Mediterranean, Biscay, Channel; sailed for Switzerland Olympic Games, Paris, 1924 single-handed competition; Hockey for Switzerland as captain in 1931; Ski-ed for Switzerland in the FIS races in 1931–34; went to Russia for 6 months, 1930; travelled in Russian Turkestan for 6 months 1932; went to Manchoukuo for Petit Parisien, 1934; returned overland accompanied by Peter Fleming, via Koko Nor; travelled overland to Iran and Afghanistan in 1937 and 1939, in South India, 1940–45, Nepal, 1951, Everest Base Camp, 1965. Fellow RGS, London; Member: Royal Soc. for Asian Affairs; Club des Explorateurs, Paris. Sir Percy Sykes Medal. *Publications:* Parmi la Jeunesse Russe, 1932; Des Monts Célestes aux Sables Rouges, 1934 (in English as Turkestan Solo, 1934, repr. 1985); Oasis Interdites, 1937 (in English as Forbidden Journey, 1937, repr. 1983); Gipsy Afloat, 1942; Cruises and Caravans, 1942; The Cruel Way, 1947, repr. 1986; Ti-Puss, 1952; The Land of the Sherpas, 1955. *Recreations:* ski-ing, gardening. *Address:* c/o David Higham Associates Ltd, 5–8 Lower John Street, W1; 10 Avenue G. Vallette, 1206 Geneva, Switzerland. *T:* Geneva 46.46.57; Atchala, Chandolin sur Sierre, Switzerland. *Clubs:* Kandahar; (hon.) Ski Club de Dames Suisse; (hon.) Ski Club of Great Britain; (hon.) Alpine.

MAIN, Frank Fiddes, CB 1965; FRCPEd; Chief Medical Officer, Ministry of Health and Social Services, Northern Ireland, 1954–68, retired; *b* 9 June 1905; *s* of Frank and Mary Main, Edinburgh; *m* 1931, Minnie Roberta Paton; two *s* two *d*. *Educ:* Daniel Stewart's Coll., Edinburgh; Edinburgh Univ. MB, ChB 1927; DPH 1931; MRCPEd 1954; FRCPEd 1956. Medical Officer of Health, Perth, 1937–48; Senior Administrative Medical Officer, Eastern Regional Hosp. Bd (Scotland), 1948–54. Crown Mem., Gen. Med. Council, 1956–69. QHP 1956–59. *Recreation:* golf. *Address:* Bruce's Cottage, Kilconquhar, Elie, Fife KY9 1LG. *T:* Colinsburgh 312.

MAIN, John Roy, QC 1974; **His Honour Judge Main;** a Circuit Judge, since 1976; *b* 21 June 1930; *yr s* of late A. C. Main, MIMechE; *m* 1955, Angela de la Condamine Davies, *er d* of late R. W. H. Davies, ICS; two *s* one *d*. *Educ:* Portsmouth Grammar Sch.; Hotchkiss Sch., USA; Brasenose Coll., Oxford (MA). Called to Bar, Inner Temple, 1954; a Recorder of Crown Court, 1972–76. Mem. Special Panel, Transport Tribunal, 1970–76; Dep. Chm., IoW QS, 1971. *Recreations:* walking, gardening, music. *Address:* 4 Queen Anne Drive, Claygate, Surrey KT10 0PP. *T:* Esher 66380.

MAIN, Sir Peter (Tester), Kt 1985; ERD 1964; Director: W. A. Baxter and Sons Ltd, since 1985; John Fleming and Co. Ltd, since 1985; Chairman: The Boots Company Ltd, 1982–85 (Director, 1973–85); Inveresk Research International; *b* 21 March 1925; *s* of late Peter Tester Main and Esther Paterson (*née* Lawson); *m* 1952, Dr Margaret Fimister, MB, ChB (*née* Tweddle) (*d* 1984); two *s* one *d*. *Educ:* Robert Gordon's Coll., Aberdeen; Univ. of Aberdeen (MB, ChB 1948, MD 1963; Hon. LLD 1986). MRCPE 1981, FRCPE 1982. Captain, RAMC, 1949–51; MO with Field Ambulance attached to Commando Bde, Suez, 1956; Lt-Col RAMC (AER), retd 1964. House Surg., Aberdeen Royal Infirmary, 1948; House Physician, Woodend Hosp., Aberdeen, 1949; Demonstrator, Univ. of Durham, 1952; gen. practice, 1953–57; joined Res. Dept, Boots, 1957; Dir of Res., 1968; Man. Dir, Industrial Div., 1979–80; Vice-Chm., The Boots Co. Ltd, 1980–81. Chm., Cttee of Inquiry into Teachers' Pay and Conditions, Scotland, 1986; Member: NEDC, 1984–85; Scottish Health Service Policy Board, 1985–; Scottish Develt Agency. Governor, Henley Management Coll., 1983–. CBIM (FBIM 1978). *Recreations:* fly fishing, Scottish music. *Address:* Lairig Ghru, Dulnain Bridge, Grantown-on-Spey, Moray PH26 3NT. *Clubs:* Naval and Military, Flyfishers'.

MAINGARD de la VILLE ès OFFRANS, Sir (Louis Pierre) René, (Sir René Maingard), Kt 1982; CBE 1961; company chairman and director, Mauritius; Chairman, Colonial Steamships Co. Ltd, since 1948; *b* 9 July 1917; *s* of Joseph René Maingard de la Ville ès Offrans and Véronique Hugnin; *m* 1946, Marie Hélène Françoise Raffray; three *d*. *Educ:* St Joseph's Coll.; Royal Coll. of Mauritius; Business Training Corp., London. Clerk, Rogers & Co. Ltd, 1936, Man. Dir, 1948. Chairman: Rogers & Co. Ltd, 1956–82; Mauritius Steam Navigation Co. Ltd, 1964–; Mauritius Portland Cement Co. Ltd, 1960–; De Chazal du Mée Associates Ltd, 1982–. Director: Mauritius Commercial Bank Ltd, 1956–; New Mauritius Dock Co. Ltd, 1948–. Formerly, Consul for Finland in Mauritius. Chevalier 1st Cl., Order of the White Rose, Finland, 1973. *Recreations:* golf, fishing, boating. *Address:* Pereybere, Grand'Baie, Mauritius. *T:* 03 85 49; Rogers & Co. Ltd, PO Box 60, Port Louis. *T:* 08 68 01. *Clubs:* Royal Air Force; Dodo, Mauritius Naval & Military Gymkhana (Mauritius).

MAINI, Sir Amar (Nath), Kt 1957; CBE 1953 (OBE 1948); *b* Nairobi, 31 July 1911; *e s* of late Nauhria Ram Maini, Nairobi, Kenya, and Ludhiana, Punjab, India; *m* 1935, Ram Saheli Mehra (*d* 1982), Ludhiana; two *s*. *Educ:* Govt Indian Sch., Nairobi; London Sch. of Economics (BCom, Hons 1932). Barrister-at-law, Middle Temple, London, 1933. Advocate of High Court of Kenya, and of High Court of Uganda. Sometime an actg MLC, Kenya, and Mem. Nairobi Municipal Council. From 1939 onwards, in Uganda; associated with family cotton business of Nauhria Ram & Sons (Uganda) Ltd. Formerly: Mem. Kampala Township Authority, Chm., Kampala Municipal Council, 1st Mayor of Kampala (1950–55); Dep. Chm., Uganda Electricity Board; Member: Uganda Development Corporation; Lint Marketing Board; Civil Defence Bd; Asian Manpower Cttee; Transport Bd; Supplies Bd; Immigration Advisory Bd; Advisory Bd of Health; Railway Advisory Council; Advisory Bd of Commerce; Rent Restriction Bd; Makerere Coll. Assembly, etc. Past Pres. Central Council of Indian Assocs in Uganda; Indian Assoc., Kampala; served on Cttees of Cotton Association. Formerly: Mem. Uganda Legislative and Exec. Councils; Development Council, Uganda; EA Legislative Assembly; EA Postal Advisory Bd; EA Transport Adv. Council; EA Air Adv Council, etc. Minister for Corporations and Regional Communications in the Government of Uganda, 1955–58; Minister of Commerce and Industry in Uganda, 1958–61; Speaker, E African Central Legislative Assembly, 1961–67; Mem., E African Common Market Tribunal, 1967–69. Dep. Chm. Kenya Broadcasting Corp., 1962–63. *Recreations:* walking, listening. *Address:* 55 Vicarage Road, East Sheen, SW14 8RY. *T:* 01–878 1497. *Clubs:* Reform; Nairobi.

MAINLAND, Prof. William Faulkner, MA; Professor of German, University of Sheffield, 1953–70; *b* 31 May 1905; *s* of late George Mainland and of Ada (*née* Froggatt); *m* 1930, Clarice Vowles, *d* of late A. E. Brewer; no *c*. *Educ:* George Heriot's Sch.; Univ. of Edinburgh. 1st Class Hons. Vans Dunlop Schol. in German; Postgrad. studies in London under late Prof. J. G. Robertson, and in Germany. Asst for French and German at London Sch. of Economics, 1929–30; thereafter attached to German Depts of Univs of: Manitoba, 1930; Manchester, 1935; London (UC, 1937, King's Coll., 1938, Birkbeck Coll., 1938); Sheffield, 1946; Leeds, 1947. Voluntary evening tutor in German, HM Prison, Wormwood

Scrubs, 1938; Public Orator, Univ. of Sheffield, 1968–70. *Publications:* German for Students of Medicine, 1938; German Lyrics of the Seventeenth Century (with Prof. August Closs), 1941; E. T. A. Hoffmann, Der goldene Topf (Editor), 1942, 2nd edn, 1945; Schiller, Uber naive und sentimentalische Dichtung (Editor), 1951; Schiller and the Changing Past, 1957; Wilhelm Tell in metrical translation with commentary, 1972; chapters on Th. Storm, H. Sudermann, Fr. v. Unruh, H. Kasack, in German Men of Letters, 1961–66; Schiller, Jungfrau v. Orleans (Editor with Prof. E. J. Engel), 1963; Schiller, Wilhelm Tell (Editor), 1968. Reviews and articles on German and Dutch literature. *Recreations:* drawing, painting; Lithuanian language studies. *Address:* Apt 3, 46 Sale Hill, Sheffield S10 5BX. *T:* Sheffield 665759. *Club:* University Staff (Sheffield).

MAINWARING, Captain Maurice K. C.; *see* Cavenagh-Mainwaring.

MAIR, Prof. Alexander; FRSE 1980; Professor of Community and Occupational Medicine (formerly of Public Health and Social Medicine), University of Dundee, 1954–82, now Emeritus; *m* 1945, Nancy Waddington; two *s* one *d. Educ:* Aberdeen Univ. MB, ChB, 1942, DPH, 1948, MD (Hons), 1952 (Aberdeen); DIH (London) 1955; FRCPE 1966; FFCM 1976; FFOM 1979. RAMC 1942–46. Lecturer, Univ. of Aberdeen, 1948–52; Senior Lecturer, Univ. of St Andrews, at Dundee, 1952–54. Formerly Founder and Dir, Scottish Occupational Health Laboratory Service, Ltd; Member: Steering Cttee, East of Scotland Occupational Health Service; Nat. Adv. Cttee for Employment of Disabled; Asbestos Adv. Cttee, 1976–; Adv. Cttee, Health and Safety Exec., 1976–82; Industrial Injuries Adv. Council, 1977–82; formerly Chm., Scottish Cttee for Welfare of Disabled and Sub-Cttee on Rehabilitation; Consultant, Occupational Health, to RN in Scotland. First Chm., British Soc. for Agriculture Labour Science. Occasional consultant to WHO, Geneva. *Publications:* Student Health Services in Great Britain and Northern Ireland, 1966; (jointly) Custom and Practice in Medical Care, 1968; Hospital and Community II, 1969; Sir James Mackenzie, MD, 1973 (Abercrombie Award); contrib.: Cerebral Palsy in Childhood and Adolescence, 1961; Further Studies in Hospital and Community, 1962; numerous publications on Researches into Occupational Diseases, especially Silicosis, Byssinosis, etc. *Address:* Tree Tops, Castle Roy, Broughty Ferry, Angus. *T:* 78727. *Club:* Caledonian.

MAIR, Alexander, MBE 1967; Chief Executive and Director, Grampian Television Ltd, since 1970; *b* 5 Nov. 1922; *s* of Charles Mair and Helen Dickie; *m* 1953, Margaret Isobel Gowans Rennie. *Educ:* Skene, Aberdeenshire; Webster's Business Coll., Aberdeen; Sch. of Accountancy, Glasgow. Associate, ICMA, 1953. Chief Accountant, Bydand Holdings Ltd, 1957–60; Company Sec., Grampian Television, 1961–70; apptd Dir, 1967; Director: ITN, 1980–; Cablevision (Scotland) Ltd, 1983–; TV Publication Ltd, 1970–. Chairman: British Regional Television Assoc., 1973–75; ITCA Management Cttee, 1980–. Pres., Aberdeen Junior Chamber of Commerce, 1960–61. Mem. Council, Aberdeen Chamber of Commerce, 1973. FRSA 1973. *Recreations:* golf, ski-ing, gardening. *Address:* Ravenswood, 66 Rubislaw Den South, Aberdeen AB2 6AX. *T:* Aberdeen 317619. *Club:* Royal Northern (Aberdeen).

MAIR, John Magnus; Director of Social Work, Edinburgh, 1969–75; Lecturer in Social Medicine, University of Edinburgh, 1959–75; *b* 29 Dec. 1912; *s* of Joseph Alexander Mair and Jane Anderson; *m* 1940, Isobelle Margaret Williamson (*d* 1969); three *s. Educ:* Anderson Inst., Lerwick; Univs of Aberdeen (MB, ChB) and Edinburgh (DPH). MFCM. Asst GP, Highlands and Islands Medical Service, 1937–40; RAMC, 1940–45; Edinburgh Public Health Dept (latterly Sen. Depute Medical Officer of Health), 1945–69. *Recreation:* golf. *Address:* 30 Honiton Gardens, Corby, Northants NN18 8BW. *Clubs:* Edinburgh University Staff; Grampian (Corby).

MAIR, Prof. William Austyn, CBE 1969; MA; FEng 1984; Francis Mond Professor of Aeronautical Engineering, University of Cambridge, 1952–83; Head of Engineering Department, 1973–83; Fellow of Downing College, Cambridge, 1953–83, Hon. Fellow, 1983; *b* 24 Feb. 1917; *s* of William Mair, MD; *m* 1944, Mary Woodhouse Crofts; two *s. Educ:* Highgate Sch.; Clare Coll., Cambridge. Aerodynamics Dept, Royal Aircraft Establishment, Farnborough, 1940–46; Dir, Fluid Motion Laboratory, Univ. of Manchester, 1946–52. Mem. various cttees, Aeronautical Research Council, 1946–80. Dir, Hovercraft Development Ltd, 1962–81. John Orr Meml Lectr, S Africa, 1983. Chm., Editorial Bd, Aeronautical Qly, 1975–81. FRAeS (Silver Medal 1975). *Publications:* papers on aerodynamics. *Address:* 74 Barton Road, Cambridge. *T:* Cambridge 350137. *Club:* United Oxford & Cambridge University.

MAIS, family name of **Baron Mais.**

MAIS, Baron, *cr* 1967 (Life Peer); **Alan Raymond Mais,** GBE 1973 (OBE (mil.) 1944); TD 1944; ERD 1958; FEng 1977; DL; JP; Colonel; Director, Royal Bank of Scotland, 1969–81; Chairman, Peachey Property Corporation, 1977–81; *b* July 1911; *s* of late Capt. E. Mais, Mornington Court, Kensington; *m* 1936, Lorna Aline, *d* of late Stanley Aspinall Boardman, Addiscombe, Surrey; two *s* one *d. Educ:* Banister Court, Hants; Coll. of Estate Management, London Univ. Commissioned RARO, Royal West Kent Regt, 1929; transf. RE 1931; Major 1939, Lt-Col 1941, Col 1944; served War of 1939–45; France, BEF 1939–40 (despatches); Special Forces, MEF, Iraq and Persia, 1941–43 (despatches); Normandy and NW Europe, 1944–46 (OBE, despatches), wounded; CRE 56 Armd Div., TA, 1947–50; CO 101 Field Engr Regt, 1947–50, Hon. Col, 1950–63; Comd Eng Gp, AER, 1951–54; DDES, AER, 1954–58. Worked for Richard Costain and other cos on Civil Engrg Works at home and abroad, 1931–38; Private Practice, A. R. Mais & Partners, Structural Engineers & Surveyors, 1938–39 and 1946–48. Dir Trollope & Colls Ltd, Bldg and Civil Engrg contractors and subsid. cos, 1948–68, Chm. and Man. Dir 1963–68; Chairman: City of London Insurance Co. Ltd, 1970–77; Hay-MSL Consultants, 1969–81; Director: Nat. Commercial Bank of Scotland, 1966–69; Slag Reduction Co. Ltd, 1962–85. Member: EDC Cttee for Constructional Industry, 1964–68; Marshall Aid Commemoration Commn, 1964–74. Treasurer: Royal Masonic Hosp., 1973–; Fellowship of Engrg, 1977–81. City University: Mem., Court and Council, 1965–; Chancellor, 1972–73; Pro-Chancellor, 1979–84. Governor, The Hon. Irish Soc., 1978–80. Lieut, City of London, 1963–81; Alderman, Ward of Walbrook, 1963–81; Sheriff, 1969–70; Lord Mayor of London, 1972–73. JP London (City Bench), 1963–83; DL: Co. London (later Greater London), 1951–76; Kent, 1976–. Master: Cutlers' Co., 1968–69; Paviors' Co., 1975–76; Marketors' Co., 1983–84. FICE 1953 (Hon. FICE 1975); FIStructE, MSocCE (France), FIArb, FRICS, KStJ 1973. Hon. BSc; Hon. DSc: City, 1972; Ulster, 1981. Order of Patriotic War (1st class), USSR, 1942; Order of Aztec Eagle, Mexico, 1973; Order of Merit, Mexico, 1973. *Publications:* Yerbury Foundation Lecture, RIBA, 1960; Bossom Foundation Lecture, 1971. *Recreations:* family, Territorial Army. *Address:* Griffins, Sundridge Avenue, Bromley, Kent; Le Fontagnes, Roi Soleil, Antibes. *Clubs:* City Livery, Army and Navy, London Welsh.

MAIS, Francis Thomas; Secretary, Royal Northern College of Music, since 1982; *b* 27 June 1927; *s* of Charles Edward Mais and Emma (*née* McLoughlin); *m* Margaret Edythe Evans; one *d. Educ:* Barnsley Grammar Sch.; Christ's Coll., Cambridge. Joined Ministry, later Dept, of Commerce, NI, 1951; Dep. Sec., 1973–79; Permanent Sec., 1979–81;

Permanent Sec., Dept of Manpower Services, 1981–82. *Address:* 3 Kingston Avenue, Didsbury, Manchester. *T:* 061–445 7532.

MAIS, Hon. Sir (Robert) Hugh, Kt 1971; Judge of the High Court of Justice, Queen's Bench Division, 1971–82; *b* 14 Sept. 1907; *s* of late Robert Stanley Oliver Mais, Chobham, Surrey; *m* 1938, Catherine, *d* of J. P. Pattinson; one *s. Educ:* Shrewsbury Sch.; Wadham Coll., Oxford (MA, 1948, Hon. Fellow, 1971). Called to the Bar, 1930, Bencher, Inner Temple, 1971; Mem. of Northern Circuit. Chancellor of the Diocese of: Manchester, 1948–71; Carlisle, 1950–71; Sheffield, 1950–71. Judge of County Courts: Circuit No 37 (West London), 1958–60; Circuit No 42 (Marylebone), 1960–71. Dep. Chm., Berkshire QS, 1964–71; Commissioner of Assize: SE Circuit, 1964, 1967; Oxford Circuit, 1968, 1969; NE Circuit, 1971. Mem., Winn Cttee on Personal Injuries Litigation. Served as Wing Comdr, RAF, 1940–44. *Recreations:* fishing, golf. *Address:* Ripton, Streatley-on-Thames, Berks. *T:* Goring 872397.

MAISEY, Prof. Michael Norman, FRCP; FRCR; Philip Harris Professor of Radiological Sciences, United Medical and Dental Schools of Guy's and St Thomas's Hospitals, since 1984; Consultant Physician in Endocrinology and Nuclear Medicine, Guy's Hospital, since 1973; *b* 10 June 1939; *s* of Harold Lionel Maisey and Kathleen Christine Maisey; *m* 1965, Irene Charlotte (*née* Askay); two *s. Educ:* Caterham Sch.; Guy's Hosp. Med. Sch. (BSc, MD). ABNM 1972; FRCP 1980. House appts, 1964–66; Registrar, Guy's Hosp., 1966–69; Fellow, Johns Hopkins Med. Instns, 1970–72; Sen. Registrar, Guy's Hosp., 1972–73. Hon. Consultant to the Army in Endocrinology and Nuclear Medicine, 1978–. *Publications:* Nuclear Medicine, 1980; Clinical Nuclear Medicine, 1982; papers on thyroid disease and nuclear medicine. *Recreations:* sailing, jazz appreciation. *Address:* Guy's Hospital, St Thomas Street, SE1 9RT. *T:* 01–407 7600.

MAISNER, Air Vice-Marshal Aleksander, CB 1977; CBE 1969; AFC 1955; Director, Industry and Parliament Trust, since 1984; *b* 26 July 1921; *s* of Henryk Maisner and Helene Anne (*née* Brosin); *m* 1946, Mary (*née* Coverley); one *s* one *d. Educ:* High Sch. and Lyceum, Czestochowa, Poland; Warsaw Univ. Labour Camps, USSR, 1940–41; Polish Artillery, 1941–42; Polish Air Force, 1943–46; joined RAF, 1946; Flying Trng Comd, 1946–49; No 70 Sqdn Suez Canal Zone, 1950–52; No 50 Sqdn RAF Binbrook, 1953–55; No 230 (Vulcan) OCU, RAF Waddington, 1955–59; psa 1960; OC Flying Wing, RNZAF Ohakea, 1961–62; Dirg Staff, RAF Staff Coll., Andover, 1963–65; DD Air Plans, MoD, 1965–68; CO, RAF Seletar, Singapore, 1969–71; Asst Comdt, RAF Coll., Cranwell, 1971–73; Dir, Personnel (Policy and Plans), MoD, 1973–75; Asst Air Sec., 1975; Dir-Gen. of Personnel Management, RAF, 1976. Personnel Exec., Reed Internat. Ltd, 1977–82. Governor, Shiplake Coll., 1978–. Pres., Polish Air Force Assoc., 1982–. *Recreations:* walking, gardening, reading. *Address:* 14 Orchard Close, Shiplake, Henley-on-Thames, Oxon RG9 4BU. *T:* Wargrave 2671. *Club:* Royal Air Force.

MAISONROUGE, Jacques Gaston; Director-General of Industry, France, since 1986; *b* Cachan, Seine, 20 Sept. 1924; *s* of Paul Maisonrouge and Suzanne (*née* Cazas); *m* 1948, Françoise Andrée Féron; one *s* four *d. Educ:* Lycée Voltaire and Saint Louis, Paris. Studied engineering; gained dip. of Ecole Centrale des Arts et Manufactures. Engineer, 1948; various subseq. appts in IBM Corp., France; Chm. and Chief Exec. Officer, IBM World Trade Europe/ME/Africa Corp., 1974–81; Pres., IBM Europe, 1974–81; Sen. Vice-Pres., 1972–84, and Mem. Bd of Dirs, 1983–84, IBM Corp.; Chm., IBM World Trade Corp., 1976–84. Director: Philip Morris Inc.; L'Air Liquide, 1964–86; Councillor, French Chamber of Commerce, USA, 1964. Chm., Bd of Trustees, Ecole Centrale des Arts et Manufactures, 1976–. Officier Ordre de la Légion d'Honneur; Commander: Ordre National du Mérite; des Palmes Académiques; Order of Merit of the Italian Republic; Order of Saint Sylvester; Order of Star of North (Sweden); Grand Officer, Order of Malta. *Recreations:* interested in sport (tennis, riding). *Club:* Automobile of France.

MAITLAND, family name of **Earl of Lauderdale.**

MAITLAND, Viscount; Master of Lauderdale; **Ian Maitland;** Assistant Regional Manager, Middle East Banking Division, National Westminster Bank, since 1975; *b* 4 Nov. 1937; *s* and *heir* of Earl of Lauderdale, *qv; m* 1963, Ann Paule, *d* of Geoffrey Clark; one *s* one *d. Educ:* Radley Coll., Abingdon; Brasenose Coll., Oxford (MA Modern History). Various appointments since 1960; with Hedderwick Borthwick & Co., 1970–75. Royal Naval Reserve (Lieutenant), 1963–73. *Recreations:* photography, sailing. *Heir:* s Master of Maitland, *qv. Address:* 150 Tachbrook Street, SW1. *Club:* Royal Ocean Racing.

MAITLAND, Master of; Hon. John Douglas Maitland; *b* 29 May 1965; *s* and *heir* of Viscount Maitland, *qv. Educ:* Emanuel School; Radley College; Van Mildert College, Durham. *Recreations:* cycling, camping, sailing. *Address:* 150 Tachbrook Street, SW1.

MAITLAND, Alastair George, CBE 1966; Consul-General, Boston, 1971–75, retired; *b* 30 Jan. 1916; *s* of late Thomas Douglas Maitland, MBE, and Wilhelmina Sarah Dundas; *m* 1943, Betty Hamilton (*d* 1981); two *s* one *d. Educ:* George Watson's Coll., Edinburgh; Universities of Edinburgh (MA First Class Hons), Grenoble and Paris, Ecole des Sciences Politiques. Vice-Consul: New York, 1938; Chicago, 1939; New York, 1939; Los Angeles, 1940; apptd to staff of UK High Commissioner at Ottawa, 1942; apptd to Foreign Office, 1945; Brit. Middle East Office, Cairo, 1948; Foreign Office, 1952; UK Delegation to OEEC, Paris, 1954; Consul-General: at New Orleans, 1958–62; at Jerusalem, 1962–64; at Cleveland, 1964–68; Dir-Gen., British Trade Develt Office, NY, 1968–71. Hon. LLD Lake Erie Coll., Ohio, 1971. CStJ. *Recreations:* music, golf, gardening, reading. *Address:* Heath, Mass 01346, USA.

MAITLAND, Sir Donald (James Dundas), GCMG 1977 (CMG 1967); Kt 1973; OBE 1960; Director: Slough Estates, since 1983; Northern Engineering Industries, since 1986; *b* 16 Aug. 1922; *s* of Thomas Douglas Maitland and Wilhelmina Sarah Dundas; *m* 1950, Jean Marie Young, *d* of Gordon Young; one *s* one *d. Educ:* George Watson's Coll.; Edinburgh Univ. Served India, Middle East, and Burma, 1941–47 (Royal Scots; Rajputana Rifles). Joined Foreign Service, 1947; Consul, Amara, 1950; British Embassy, Baghdad, 1950–53; Private Sec. to Minister of State, Foreign Office, 1954–56; Director, Middle East Centre for Arab Studies, Lebanon, 1956–60; Foreign Office, 1960–63; Counsellor, British Embassy, Cairo, 1963–65; Head of News Dept, Foreign Office, 1965–67; Principal Private Sec. to Foreign and Commonwealth Secretary, 1967–69; Ambassador to Libya, 1969–70; Chief Press Sec., 10 Downing St, 1970–73; UK Permanent Rep. to UN, 1973–74; Dep. Under-Sec. of State, FCO, 1974–75; UK Mem., Commonwealth Group on Trade, Aid and Develt, 1975; Ambassador and UK Perm. Rep. to EEC, 1975–79; Dep. to Perm. Under-Sec. of State, FCO, Dec. 1979–June 1980; Perm. Under-Sec. of State, Dept of Energy, 1980–82. Chm., Independent Commn for World-Wide Telecommunications Develt, 1983–85. Advr to British Telecom, 1985–. Govt Dir, Britoil, 1983–85. Chairman: UK National Cttee for World Communications Year, 1983; Christians for Europe, 1984–. Member: Commonwealth War Graves Commn, 1983–; British Co-ordinator, Indo-British Colloquium, 1984–. *Recreations:* hill-walking, music. *Address:* Murhill Farm House, Limpley Stoke, Bath BA3 6HH. *T:* Limpley Stoke 3157.

MAITLAND, Sir Richard John, 9th Bt, *cr* 1818; farmer; *b* 24 Nov. 1952; *s* of Sir Alexander Keith Maitland, 8th Bt, and of Lavender Mary Jex, *y d* of late Francis William Jex Jackson, Kirkbuddo, Forfar; *S* father, 1963; *m* 1981, Carine, *er d* of J. St G. Coldwell, Somerton, Oxford; one *s* one *d*. *Educ:* Rugby; Exeter Univ. (BA Hons 1975); Edinburgh Sch. of Agriculture. *Heir: s* Charles Alexander Maitland, *b* 3 June 1986. *Address:* Burnside, Forfar, Angus.

MAITLAND DAVIES, Keith Laurence; Metropolitan Stipendiary Magistrate, since 1984; *b* 3 Feb. 1938; *s* of Wyndham Matabele Davies, QC and Enid Maud Davies; *m* 1964, Angela Mary (*née* Fraser-Jenkins); two *d* one *s*. *Educ:* Winchester; Christ Church, Oxford (MA). Called to the Bar, Inner Temple, 1962; private practice, 1962–84. *Address:* c/o 1 Paper Buildings, Temple, EC4.

MAITLAND-MAKGILL-CRICHTON; *see* Crichton.

MAITLAND SMITH, Geoffrey; Chief Executive, since 1978, and Chairman, since 1985, Sears plc (formerly Sears Holdings plc); chartered accountant; *b* 27 Feb. 1933; *s* of Philip John Maitland Smith and Kathleen (*née* Goff). *Educ:* University Coll. Sch., London. Partner, Thornton Baker & Co., Chartered Accountants, 1960–70; Sears Holdings plc: Dir, 1971–; Dep. Chm., 1978–85; Jt Chm., 1984; Chairman: British Shoe Corp. Ltd, 1984–; Butler Shoe Corp. (USA), 1984–; Lewis's Investment Trust Ltd, 1985– (Dep. Chm., 1978–85); Selfridges Ltd, 1985– (Dep. Chm., 1978–85); Garrard & Co. Ltd, 1985– (Dep. Chm., 1978–85); Mappin & Webb Ltd, 1985– (Dep. Chm., 1978–85); Mallett plc, 1986–; Director: Asprey & Co. plc, 1980–; Central Independent Television plc, 1983–85; Courtaulds plc, 1983–; Imperial Group plc, 1984–86; Midland Bank plc, 1986–. Mem. Council, University Coll. Sch. Liveryman, Worshipful Co. of Gardeners. *Recreations:* opera, music. *Address:* (office) 40 Duke Street, W1A 2HP. *T:* 01–408 1180. *Club:* Cripplegate Ward.

MAITLAND-TITTERTON, Major David Maitland, TD 1947; Marchmont Herald of Arms to Court of Lord Lyon, since 1982; *b* 8 Aug. 1904; *s* of Rev. Charles Henry Titterton and Anna Louise, *d* of Rear-Adm. Lewis Maitland; *m* 1929, Mary Etheldritha, *y d* of Senator Rt Hon. James Graham Leslie, sometime HM Lieutenant, Co. Antrim; two *s*. *Educ:* Queens' Coll., Cambridge (MA). Commissioned, 1924; Ayrshire Yeo., 1926; Asst Dist Officer, Political Service, Nigeria, 1927–32; Instructor, 124 OCTU, Llandrindod Wells, 1939; served War of 1939–45; Major 1942; comd School of Artillery, Nigeria, 1943; Liaison Officer with Polish Army, 1944; Staff Officer with 51 Highland Div., 1954–63. Falkland Pursuivant Extraordinary, 1969–71; Ormond Pursuivant, 1971–84. OStJ. Knight Grand Cross, Order of St Lazarus. *Recreations:* racing, books, print collecting. *Address:* Moberty, Craigton of Airlie, by Kirriemuir, Angus DD8 5NW. *T:* Craigton 249. *Clubs:* Cavalry and Guards (Life Mem.); County (Ayr); Caledonian, Puffin's (Edinburgh).

MAITLIS, Prof. Peter Michael, FRS 1984; Professor of Chemistry, Sheffield University, since 1972; *b* 15 Jan. 1933; *s* of Jacob Maitlis and Judith Maitlis; *m* 1959, Marion (*née* Basco); three *d*. *Educ:* Univ. of Birmingham (BSc 1953); Univ. of London (PhD 1956, DSc 1971). Asst Lectr, London Univ., 1956–60; Fulbright Fellow and Res. Associate, Cornell Univ., 1960–61, Harvard Univ., 1961–62; Asst Prof, 1962–64, Associate Prof., 1964–67, Prof., 1967–72, McMaster Univ., Hamilton, Ont, Canada; Prof. of Inorganic Chemistry, Univ. of Sheffield, 1972–. Chm., Chemistry Cttee, SERC, 1985–. Fellow, Alfred P. Sloan Foundn, USA, 1968–70; Tilden Lectr, RSC, London, 1979–80; Sir Edward Frankland Prize Lectr, RSC, 1985. Member: Royal Soc. of Chemistry (formerly Mem., Chem. Soc.), 1952– (Pres., Dalton Div., 1985–); Amer. Chemical Soc., 1963–. E. W. R. Steacie Prize (Canada), 1971; Medallist, RSC (Noble Metals and their Compounds), 1981. *Publications:* The Organic Chemistry of Palladium, vols 1 and 2, 1971; many research papers in learned jls. *Recreations:* travel, music, reading (especially thrillers), swimming. *Address:* Department of Chemistry, The University, Sheffield S3 7HF. *T:* Sheffield 768555, ext. 4480.

MAJITHIA, Dr Sir Surendra Singh, Kt 1946; Industrialist; *b* 4 March 1895; *s* of late Hon. Sardar Bahadur Dr Sir Sundar Singh Majithia, CIE, DOL; *m* 1921, Lady Balbir Kaur (*d* 1977), *d* of late General Hazura Singh, Patiala. *Educ:* Khalsa Collegiate High Sch.; Khalsa Coll., Amritsar. Chairman, Saraya Sugar Mills Ltd, Sardarnagar; Senior Managing Partner, Saraya Surkhi Mill, Sardarnagar; Dir, Punjab & Sind Bank Ltd, Amritsar. Member: Khalsa College Council, Amritsar; Akal College Council, Gursagar; UP Fruit Development Board, Lucknow. President, Chairman, etc., of many educational foundations and social activities. Past member, various Advisory and Consultative Cttees. Chairman, Lady Parsan Kaur Charitable Trust (Educnl Soc.), Sardarnagar; Patron: Wrestling Federation of India; UP Badminton Assoc.; Life Mem., Internal Soc. of Krishna Consciousness; Hon. Mem., Mark Twain Soc., USA; Member, Garden Advisory Cttee, Gorakhpur. Hon. DLitt Gorakhpur, 1970. *Address:* PO Sardarnagar, Dist Gorakhpur, Uttar Pradesh, India. *Clubs:* Gorakhpur, Nepal (Gorakhpur).

MAJOR; *see* Henniker-Major, family name of Baron Henniker.

MAJOR, John; MP (C) Huntingdon, since 1983 (Huntingdonshire, 1979–83); Minister of State for Social Security, Department of Health and Social Security, since 1986; *b* 29 March 1943; *s* of Thomas Major and Gwendolyn Minny Coates; *m* 1970, Norma Christina Elizabeth (*née* Johnson); one *s* one *d*. *Educ:* Rutlish. AIB. Banker, Standard Chartered Bank: various executive posts in UK and overseas, 1965–79. Contested (C) St Pancras North (Camden), Feb. 1974 and Oct. 1974; PPS to Ministers of State at the Home Office, 1981–83; an Asst Govt Whip, 1983–84; a Lord Comr of HM Treasury (a Govt Whip), 1984–85; Parly Under-Sec. of State for Social Security, DHSS, 1985–86. Member, Lambeth Borough Council, 1968–71 (Chm. Housing Cttee, 1970–71). Jt Sec., Cons. Parly Party Environment Cttee, 1979–81; Parly Consultant, Guild of Glass Engravers, 1979–83. Mem. Bd, Warden Housing Assoc., 1975–83. Pres., Eastern Area Young Conservatives, 1983–85. *Recreations:* opera, cricket. *Address:* Finings, Great Stukeley, Huntingdon, Cambs.

MAJOR, Kathleen, FBA 1977; Professor (part-time) of History, University of Nottingham, 1966–71; Principal of St Hilda's College, Oxford, 1955–65; Hon. Fellow, St Hilda's College, 1965; *b* 10 April 1906; *er d* of late George Major and Gertrude Blow. *Educ:* various private schools; St Hilda's College, Oxford. Honour School of Modern History, 1928; BLitt 1931. Librarian, St Hilda's College, 1931. Archivist to the Bishop of Lincoln, 1936; Lecturer, 1945, subsequently Reader in Diplomatic in the University of Oxford, until July 1955. Hon. Secretary, Lincoln Record Society, 1935–56 and 1965–74, Hon. Gen. Editor, 1935–75. Member Academic Planning Board for the University of Lancaster, 1962, and of Academic Advisory Cttee, 1964–70. Trustee of the Oxford Preservation Trust, 1961–65; a Vice-Pres., RHistS, 1967–71, Hon. Vice-Pres., 1981–; Pres., Lincoln Civic Trust, 1980–84. Hon. DLitt Nottingham, 1961. *Publications:* (joint editor with late Canon Foster) Registrum Antiquissimum of the Cathedral Church of Lincoln, vol. IV, 1938, (sole editor) vols V-X, 1940–73; *Acta Stephani Langton*, 1950; The D'Oyrys of South Lincolnshire, Norfolk and Holderness, 1984; (with S. R. Jones and J. Varley) A Survey of Ancient Homes in Lincoln, Fascicule I, Minster Yard I, 1984; articles in English Hist. Review, Journal of Ecclesiastical Hist., etc. *Recreation:* reading. *Address:* 21 Queensway, Lincoln. *Club:* English-Speaking Union.

MAJURY, Maj.-Gen. James Herbert Samuel, CB 1974; MBE 1961; Senior Steward, National Greyhound Racing Club, since 1976; *b* 26 June 1921; *s* of Rev. Dr M. Majury, BA, DD, and Florence (*née* Stuart), Antrim, N Ireland; *m* 1948, Jeanetta Ann (*née* Le Fleming); two *s*. *Educ:* Royal Academical Institution, Belfast; Trinity College, Dublin. Royal Ulster Rifles, 1940; attached 15 Punjab Regt, 1942; seconded South Waziristan Scouts, 1943–47; Korean War, 1949 (Royal Ulster Rifles); Prisoner of War, Korea, 1950–53 (despatches 1954); Parachute Regiment, 1957–61; Comd Royal Irish Fusiliers, 1961–62; Comd 2nd Infantry Bde, 1965–67; GOC West Midland District, 1970–73. idc 1968. Col. Comdt, The King's Division, 1971–75, Col The Royal Irish Rangers, 1972–77; Hon. Col, 2nd Bn Mercian Volunteers, 1975–79. *Recreations:* golf, racing. *Address:* Hollybrook, Colemans Hatch, Hartfield, E Sussex TN7 4HH. *T:* Forest Row 2489. *Clubs:* Naval and Military, XL; Royal Ashdown Forest Golf, Bluemantles Cricket.

MAKAROVA, Natalia; dancer; *b* Leningrad, 21 Nov. 1940; *m* 1976, Edward Karkar; one *s*. *Educ:* Vaganova Ballet Sch.; Leningrad Choreographic Sch. Mem., Kirov Ballet, 1959–70; London début, as Giselle, Covent Garden, 1961; joined American Ballet Theatre, 1970; formed dance co., Makarova & Co., 1980; Guest Artist: Royal Ballet, Covent Garden, 1972; London Festival Ballet, 1984. Has danced many classical and contemporary rôles in UK, Europe and USA, 1970–; appearances include: La Bayadère (which she also staged, and choreographed in part), NY Met, 1980, Manchester, 1985; On Your Toes, London and NY, 1984–86. Honoured Artist of RSFSR, 1970. *Publications:* A Dance Autobiography, 1979; On Your Toes, 1984. *Address:* c/o Herbert Breslin Inc., 119 W 57th Street, New York, NY 10019, USA.

MAKEPEACE, John, FSIAD, FBIM, FRSA; furniture designer and maker, since 1961; established workshops at Farnborough Barn, Banbury, 1964, moved to Parnham in 1976; Founder and Director, The Parnham Trust and The School for Craftsmen in Wood, since 1977; *b* 6 July 1939; *m* 1964, Ann Sutton (marr. diss. 1979). *Educ:* Denstone Coll., Staffs. Trained in cabinet-making with Keith Cooper, 1957–59; study tours of Scandinavia 1957, N America 1961, Italy 1968, W Africa 1972, N America 1974. Most work in private collections; exceptions incl. Oxford Centre for Management Studies; Attlee Room, Toynbee Hall; Keble College, Oxford; Reed Internat.; Jones Lang Wootton; RSA. *Public Collections:* Cardiff Museum; Fitzwilliam Museum, Cambridge; Leeds; Museum für Kunsthandwerk, Frankfurt; V&A Museum. *Exhibitions:* Herbert Art Gall., Coventry, 1963; New Art Centre, London, 1971; Science Centre, Toronto, 1974; Mitsukoshi, Tokyo, 1975; Wohndesign, Dusseldorf, 1975; Fine Art Soc., London, 1977; Interieur, Kortrijk, Belgium, 1978; Parnham in London, 1979; Parnham at Nat. Theatre, 1980; Inscape, Barbican Centre, 1981; Parnham at Royal Show, with students graduating from Parnham, 1981; Crafts Council Open, 1984; *Consultancies/Lectures:* Mem., Crafts Council, 1972–77; develt of wood products in India, 1975 (EEC); furniture design for Jammu and Kashmir Govt Industries, 1977 (Commonwealth Secretariat); Design Education, Belgrade Univ., 1978 (British Council); Artist in Context, Study Day at V&A Mus., 1979; Chm., Wood Programme, World Crafts Conf., Kyoto, Japan, 1979; co-ordinated Internat. Wood Turning Seminar, 1980; Internat. Wood Carving Seminar, 1982; Lecture tour of Australia, 1980 (Aust. Crafts Bd and Headmasters' Conf.); Selector for The Maker's Eye, 1982; Loughborough Design Lecture, 1982. *Television Films:* Made by Makepeace (dir, Sir Peter Hall), 1975; History of English Furniture, 1978; Heritage in Danger, 1979; First Edition (dir, Tony Palmer), 1980; Touch Wood (dir, John Read), 1982. Winner, Observer Kitchen Comp., 1971; Six Guild Marks, Worshipful Co. of Furniture Makers, 1977. *Address:* Parnham House, Beaminster, Dorset DT8 3NA. *T:* Beaminster 862204.

MAKGILL, family name of **Viscount of Oxfuird.**

MAKGILL CRICHTON MAITLAND, Major John David; Lord-Lieutenant of Renfrewshire, since 1980; *b* 10 Sept. 1925; *e s* of late Col Mark Edward Makgill Crichton Maitland, CVO, DSO, DL, JP, The Island House, Wilton, Salisbury, Wilts, and late Patience Irene Fleetwood Makgill Crichton Maitland (*née* Fuller); *m* 1954, Jean Patricia (*d* 1985), *d* of late Maj.-Gen. Sir Michael Creagh, KBE, MC, Pigeon Hill, Homington, Salisbury; one *s* one *d*. *Educ:* Eton. Served War, 1944–45, Grenadier Guards. Continued serving until 1957 (temp. Major, 1952; retd 1957), rank Captain (Hon. Major). Governor, West of Scotland Agricl Coll.; Renfrew CC, 1961–75. DL Renfrewshire 1962, Vice-Lieutenant 1972–80. *Address:* Houston House, Houston, by Johnstone, Renfrewshire. *T:* Bridge of Weir 612545.

MAKHULU, Most Rev. Walter Paul Khotso; *see* Central Africa, Archbishop of.

MAKINS, family name of **Baron Sherfield.**

MAKINS, Sir Paul (Vivian), 4th Bt *cr* 1903; Company Director, 1962–73; *b* 12 Nov. 1913; *yr s* of Sir Paul Makins, 2nd Bt, and Gladys Marie (*d* 1919), *d* of William Vivian, Queen's Gate, London; *S* brother, 1969; *m* 1945, Maisie (*d* 1986), *d* of Major Oswald Pedley and *widow* of Major C. L. J. Bowen, Irish Guards; no *c*. *Educ:* Eton Coll.; Trinity Coll. Cambridge (MA). Commissioned in Welsh Guards, 1935. Served War of 1939–45: France, 1940; Italy, 1944–45. Dir and Sec. Vitalba Co. Ltd (Gibraltar), 1962–73; Dir, Compañia Rentistica SA (Tangier), 1967–73. Kt of Magistral Grace, SMO Malta, 1955; JP Gibraltar, 1964–70. *Heir:* none. *Address:* Casas Cortijo 135, Sotogrande, Provincia de Cadiz, Spain. *Clubs:* Cavalry and Guards, Pratt's.

See also Archbishop of Southwark.

MAKINSON, William, CBE 1977; Director, the Grundy Group, since 1980; *b* 11 May 1915; *s* of Joshua Makinson and Martha (*née* Cunliffe); *m* 1952, Helen Elizabeth Parker; one *s* three *d*. *Educ:* Ashton-in-Makerfield Grammar Sch.; Manchester Univ. Asst Lecturer, Electronics, Manchester Univ., 1935–36; Education Officer, RAF Cranwell, 1936–39; RAE Farnborough, 1939–52; Hon. Squadron-Ldr, RAF, 1943–45; Superintendent, Blind Landing Experimental Unit, 1952–55; Defence Research Policy Staff, 1955–56; Managing Director, General Precision Systems Ltd, 1956–64; Group Jt Managing Director, Pullin, 1964–65; Mem., NRDC, 1967–80 (Man. Dir, 1974–80, Chief Exec., Engrg Dept, 1965–74). *Publications:* papers to Royal Aeronautical Society. *Recreation:* golf. *Address:* Ridings, Snows Paddock, Snows Ride, Windlesham, Surrey. *T:* Ascot 22431. *Clubs:* Athenæum, Directors.

MAKKAWI, Dr Khalil; Chevalier, Order of Cedars, Lebanon; Director of Political Affairs, Ministry of Foreign Affairs, Beirut, since 1983; *b* 15 Jan. 1930; *s* of Abdel Basset Makkawi and Rosa Makkawi; *m* 1958, Zahira Sibaei; one *s* one *d*. *Educ:* Amer. Univ. of Beirut (BA Polit. Science); Cairo Univ. (MA Polit. Science); Colombia Univ., NY, USA (PhD Internat. Relations). Joined Lebanese Min. of Foreign Affairs, 1957; UN Section at Min., 1957–59; Attaché to Perm. Mission of Lebanon to UN, New York, 1959, Dep. Perm. Rep., 1961–64; First Sec., Washington, 1964–66; Chief of Internat. Relations Dept, Min. of For. Affairs, Beirut, 1967–70; Counsellor, London, 1970–71; Minister Plenipotentiary, London, 1971–73; Ambassador to: German Democratic Republic, 1973–78; Court of St James's 1978–83; Republic of Ireland, 1979–83. Mem., Lebanese

Delegn to UN Gen. Assembly Meetings, 14th-32nd Session. *Recreations:* sports, music. *Address:* Ministry of Foreign Affairs, Beirut, Lebanon.

MALAND, David; barrister; *b* 6 Oct. 1929; *s* of Rev. Gordon Albert Maland and Florence Maud Maland (*née* Bosence); *m* 1953, Edna Foulsham; two *s. Educ:* Kingswood Sch.; Wadham Coll., Oxford. BA 2nd class Mod. Hist., 1951; MA 1957; Robert Herbert Meml Prize Essay, 1959. Nat. service commn RAF, 1951–53. Asst Master, Brighton Grammar Sch., 1953–56; Senior History Master, Stamford Sch., 1957–66; Headmaster: Cardiff High Sch., 1966–68; Denstone Coll., 1969–78; High Master, Manchester Grammar Sch., 1978–85. Chm., Assisted Places Sub-Cttee of Headmasters' Conf., 1982–83. Called to the Bar, Gray's Inn, 1986. Governor: Stonyhurst Coll., 1973–80; Abingdon Sch., 1979–; GPDST, 1984–. *Publications:* Europe in the Seventeenth Century, 1966; Culture and Society in Seventeenth Century France, 1970; Europe in the Sixteenth Century, 1973; Europe at War, 1600–1650, 1980; (trans.) La Guerre de Trente Ans, by Pagès, 1971; articles and reviews in History. *Address:* Windrush, Underhill Lane, Westmeston, Hassocks, East Sussex BN6 8XG.

MALCOLM, Lt-Col Arthur William Alexander, CVO 1954 (MVO 1949); *b* 31 May 1903; *s* of Major Charles Edward Malcolm, London; *m* 1928, Hester Mary, *d* of S. F. Mann, Lawrenny-Caramut, Victoria, Australia; two *s. Educ:* Repton. 2nd Lieut, Welsh Guards, 1924; psc 1938; served War of 1939–45 (POW); Lieut-Colonel, 1945; comd 3rd, 2nd and 1st Bn, Welsh Guards, 1945–49. ADC to Governor of Victoria, Australia, 1926–28. Asst Military Attaché, British Embassy, Paris, 1950–52; retired from Army, 1952. Private Secretary to Governor of South Australia, 1953–55; Queen's Foreign Service Messenger, 1955–68. *Recreation:* golf. *Address:* Faraway, Sandwich Bay, Kent. *T:* Sandwich 612054. *Clubs:* Army and Navy; Royal St George's Golf, Prince's Golf (Sandwich).

MALCOLM, Sir David (Peter Michael), 11th Bt *cr* 1665; *b* 7 July 1919; *s* of Sir Michael Albert James Malcolm, 10th Bt, and Hon. Geraldine Margot (*d* 1965), *d* of 10th Baron Digby; *S* father, 1976; *m* 1959, Hermione, *d* of Sir David Home, Bt, *qv;* one *d. Educ:* Eton; Magdalene Coll., Cambridge (BA). Served with Scots Guards, 1939–46 (Major). Mem., Inst. of Chartered Accountants of Scotland, 1949. Member: Stock Exchange, 1956–80; Stock Exchange Council, 1971–80. *Recreations:* shooting, golf. *Heir: cousin* Lt-Col Arthur William Alexander Malcolm, *qv. Address:* Whiteholm, Gullane, East Lothian EH31 2BD. *Club:* New (Edinburgh).

MALCOLM, Derek Elliston Michael; film critic, The Guardian, since 1971; Director, London International Film Festival, since 1984; *b* 12 May 1932; *s* of J. Douglas Malcolm and Dorothy Taylor; *m* 1962, Barbara Ibbott (marr. diss. 1966); one *d. Educ:* Eton; Merton College, Oxford (BA Hons Hist.). Actor, amateur rider (National Hunt), 1953–56; Drama Critic, Gloucestershire Echo, 1956–62; Sub-Editor, The Guardian, 1962–69; Racing correspondent, The Guardian, 1969–71. Pres., Critics' Circle of UK, 1980 (Chm., Film Section, 1978–81); Chm., UK Section, Internat. Critics Group, 1982–. Internat. Publishing Co.'s Critic of the Year, 1972. *Publication:* Robert Mitchum, 1984. *Recreations:* cricket, tennis, squash, music. *Address:* 28 Avenue Road, Highgate, N6. *T:* 01–348 2013.

MALCOLM, Dugald, CMG 1966; CVO 1964; TD 1945; HM Diplomatic Service, retired; Minister to the Holy See, 1975–77; *b* 22 Dec. 1917; 2nd *s* of late Maj.-Gen. Sir Neill Malcolm, KCB, DSO, and Lady (Angela) Malcolm; *m* 1957, Patricia Anne Gilbert-Lodge (*d* 1976), *widow* of Captain Peter Atkinson-Clark; one *d* one *step d. Educ:* Eton; New Coll., Oxford. Served Argyll and Sutherland Highlanders, 1939–45; discharged wounded. Appointed Foreign Office, Oct. 1945; Served Lima, Bonn, Seoul; HM Vice-Marshal of the Diplomatic Corps, 1957–65; Ambassador: to Luxembourg, 1966–70; to Panama, 1970–74. Member Queen's Body Guard for Scotland (Royal Company of Archers). *Address:* Flat 11, 33 Cranley Gardens, SW7 3BD. *T:* 01–244 7079. *Clubs:* Travellers', Boodle's.

MALCOLM, Ellen, RSA 1976 (ARSA 1968); *b* 28 Sept. 1923; *d* of John and Ellen Malcolm; *m* 1962, Gordon Stewart Cameron, *qv. Educ:* Aberdeen Acad.; Gray's Sch. of Art, Aberdeen. DA (Aberdeen) 1944. Teacher of Art, Aberdeen Grammar Sch. and Aberdeen Acad., 1945–62. Paintings in public galleries in Southend, Aberdeen, Perth, Milngavie, Edinburgh, and in private collections in Scotland, England, Wales, America, Switzerland, Sweden and Australia. Chalmers-Jervise Prize, 1946; Guthrie Award, Royal Scottish Acad., 1952; David Cargill Award, Royal Glasgow Inst., 1973. *Recreation:* reading. *Address:* 7 Auburn Terrace, Invergowrie, Dundee DD2 5AB. *T:* Invergowrie 318.

MALCOLM, George (John), CBE 1965; musician; *b* London, 28 Feb. 1917; *o s* of George Hope Malcolm, Edinburgh, and Johanna Malcolm. *Educ:* Wimbledon Coll.; Balliol Coll., Oxford (Scholar); Royal College of Music (Scholar). MA, BMus (Oxon). Served in RAFVR, 1940–46. Master of the Cathedral Music, Westminster Cathedral, 1947–59, training unique boys' choir for which Benjamin Britten wrote Missa Brevis, Op. 63. Now mainly known as harpsichordist, pianist and conductor (making frequent concert tours). Cobbett Medal, Worshipful Company of Musicians, 1960; Hon. RAM, 1961; Hon. Fellow, Balliol Coll., Oxford, 1966; FRCM 1974; Hon. DMus, Sheffield, 1978. Papal Knight of the Order of St Gregory the Great, 1970. *Address:* 99 Wimbledon Hill Road, SW19 7QT.

MALCOLM, Gerald; see Malcolm, W. G.

MALCOLM, Prof. John Laurence; Regius Professor of Physiology, University of Aberdeen, 1959–75, retired; *b* 28 Aug. 1913; *s* of late Professor J. Malcolm, Dunedin, New Zealand; *m* 1st, 1940, Sylvia Bramston (*d* 1958), *d* of late Basil B. Hooper, Auckland, New Zealand; one *s* one *d;* 2nd, 1961, Margaret Irvine Simpson (*d* 1967), *d* of late Colonel J. C. Simpson, Skene, Aberdeenshire. *Publications:* contributions to the Proceedings of Royal Society, Journal of Physiology, Journal of Neuro-physiology. *Address:* Heath Cottage, Crathie, Aberdeenshire AB3 5UP.

MALCOLM, (William) Gerald, CB 1976; MBE 1943; Member, Planning Appeals Commission (NI), 1978–83; Permanent Secretary, Department of the Environment for Northern Ireland, 1974–76; *b* Stirling, 19 Dec. 1916; *s* of late John and Jane M. Malcolm; *m* 1949, Margaret Cashel. *Educ:* High Sch. of Stirling; Glasgow Univ. (MA) (Hons French and German, 1945); London Univ. (BA 1945). Served War, Army, 1939–46: RASC and Intelligence Corps; Major, 1944; Africa and Italy Stars, 1939–45. Min. of Home Affairs for NI, Asst Principal, 1948; Min. of Agriculture for NI: Principal, 1956; Asst Sec., 1962; Sen. Asst Sec., 1966; Dep. Sec., 1970. *Recreations:* angling, swimming, ornithology, nature.

MALCOLMSON, Kenneth Forbes, MA, BMus (Oxon), FRCO; Precentor and Director of Music, Eton College, 1956–71; *b* 29 April 1911; *m* 1972, Mrs B. Dunhill. Organ Scholar, Exeter Coll., Oxford, 1931–35; Commissioner, Royal School of Church Music, 1935–36; Temporary Organist, St Alban's Cathedral, 1936–37; Organist, Halifax Parish Church, 1937–38; Organist and Master of the Music, Newcastle Cathedral, 1938–55.

Recreations: gardening, swimming, walking. *Address:* Dixton House, Dixton Road, Monmouth, Gwent NP5 3PR. *T:* Monmouth 4509.

MALDEN; see Scott-Malden.

MALDEN, Viscount; Frederick Paul de Vere Capell; In charge of Pastoral Care, Curriculum Development and Music, Skerton County Primary School, Lancaster, since 1981; *b* 29 May 1944; *s* and *heir* of 10th Earl of Essex, *qv. Educ:* Skerton Boys' School; Lancaster Royal Grammar School; Didsbury College of Education, Manchester; Northern School of Music. ACP, LLCM(TD). Assistant teacher, Marsh County Junior School, 1966–72; Deputy Head, 1972–75; Acting Head, 1975–77; Deputy Head Teacher, Marsh County Primary School, 1977–78; Head Teacher, Cockerham Parochial CE School, Cockerham, Lancaster, 1979–80. A Patron, Internat. Centre for Child Studies, 1983–. FRSA. *Recreations:* music, hi-fi. *Address:* 35 Pinewood Avenue, Brookhouse, Lancaster LA2 9NU.

MALE, Peter John Ellison, CMG 1967; MC 1945; HM Diplomatic Service, retired; Ambassador to Czechoslovakia, 1977–80; *b* 22 Aug. 1920; *s* of late H. J. G. Male and late Mrs E. A. Male; *m* 1947, Patricia Janet Payne; five *s* two *d. Educ:* Merchant Taylors' Sch.; Emmanuel Coll., Cambridge. HM Forces, 1940–45. HM Foreign Service (now HM Diplomatic Service), 1946; served in: Damascus, 1947–49; Wahnerheide, 1949–53; London, 1953–55; Guatemala City, 1955–57; Washington, 1957–60; London, 1960–62; Oslo, 1962–66; Bonn, 1966–70; New Delhi, 1970–74; Asst Under-Sec. of State, FCO, 1974–77. *Recreations:* gadgets, gardening. *Address:* Swinley Edge, Coronation Road, Ascot, Berks. *Club:* United Oxford & Cambridge University.

MALEK, Redha; Algerian Ambassador to the Court of St James's, 1982–84; *b* 21 Dec. 1931; *m* 1963, Rafida Cheriet; two *s* one *d. Educ:* Algiers; Paris. BA. Mem. Governing Bd, Gen. Union of Moslem Algerian Students, 1956; Dir and Editor in Chief, El Moudjahid, party newspaper of Front de la Libération Nationale, 1957–62; Ambassador to: Yugoslavia, 1963–65; France, 1965–70; USSR, 1970–77; Minister of Information and Culture, Algeria, 1977–79; Ambassador to USA, 1979–82 (negotiated release of the 52 American hostages in Iran, 1980–81). Mem. and spokesman, Algerian delegn to negotiations of Evian, 1961–62; Member, Drafting Committee: Programme of Tripoli, setting out FLN political programme, 1962; Nat. Charter, 1976. Mem., Central Cttee, FLN, 1979–. *Address:* c/o Ministry of Foreign Affairs, Algiers, Algeria.

MALENKOV, Georgi Maximilianovich; Manager of Ust-Kamenogorsk Hydro-Electric Station, 1957–63, retired; *b* Orenburg, 1901; *m* 1st (marr. diss.); 2nd, Elena Khrushcheva. *Educ:* Moscow Higher Technical Coll. Member of the Communist Party, 1920–; Member of Organisation Bureau of Central Cttee of the Communist Party, 1934; Member Cttee for State Defence, 1941; Member Cttee for Economic Rehabilitation of Liberated Districts, 1943; Dep.-Chairman, Council of Ministers, 1946; Dep.-Chairman, Council of Ministers of the Soviet Union, 1955–57 (Dep.-Chairman, 1946, Chairman, 1953–55); Minister of Electric Power Stations, 1955–57. Holds title Hero of Socialist Labour, Hammer and Sickle Gold Medal, Order of Lenin (twice).

MALET, Colonel Sir Edward William St Lo, 8th Bt, *cr* 1791; OBE 1953; 8th King's Royal Irish Hussars; retired; *b* 27 Nov. 1908; *o s* of Sir Harry Charles Malet, DSO, OBE, 7th Bt and Mildred Laura (*d* 1951), *d* of Captain H. S. Swiney, Gensing House, St Leonards; *S* father, 1931; *m* 1935, Baroness Benedicta Maasburg (*d* 1979), *e d* of Baron William von Maasburg; one *s* two *d. Educ:* Dover Coll.; Christ Church, Oxford. BA. Dep.-Chief Civil Affairs Officer, HQ, British Troops, Egypt, 1953–55. President Bridgwater Division, Conservative Assoc., 1959. High Sheriff of Somerset, 1966. *Heir: s* Harry Douglas St Lo Malet, late Lieut, The Queen's Royal Irish Hussars, now Special Reserve [*b* 26 Oct. 1936; *m* 1967, Julia Harper, Perth, WA; one *s. Educ:* Downside; Trinity Coll., Oxford]. *Address:* Chargot, Washford, Somerset. *Club:* Cavalry and Guards. *See also* Maj.-Gen. E. H. A. Beckett.

MALIK, Bidhubhusan; *b* 11 Jan. 1895; *s* of Raibahadur Chandrasekhar Malik, Chief Judge, Benares State; *m* 1916, Leelabati, *d* of Saratkumar Mitra, Calcutta; two *s. Educ:* Central Hindu Coll., Benares (graduated, 1917); Ewing Christian Coll. (MA in Economics, 1919); Allahabad Univ. (LLB 1919); LLD (*hc*), Saugur Univ. Vakil, Allahabad High Court, 1919; started practice in the civil courts in Benares; left for England in Sept. 1922; called to Bar, Lincoln's Inn, 1923; joined Allahabad High Court Bar, 1924; Member of Judicial Cttee of Benares State, 1941; Special Counsel for Income Tax Dept, 1943; Judge, Allahabad High Court, 1944; Chief Justice, High Court, Allahabad, Dec. 1947; thereafter Chief Justice, UP, from 26 July 1948–55, excepting 3 March-1 May 1949, when acted as Governor, Uttar Pradesh. Commissioner for Linguistic Minorities in India, 1957–62. Member: Constitutional Commission for the Federation of Malaya, 1956–57; Air Transport Council of India, 1955–62; National Integration Commn, India. Constitutional Adviser to Mr Jomo Kenyatta and the Kenya African National Union, Lancaster House Conference, London, 1961–62; Constitutional Expert for Republic of Congo appointed by UNO, Aug.-Oct. 1962; Constitutional Adviser to Kenya Government, Kenya Independence Conference, Lancaster House, Sept.-Oct. 1963; Adviser, Mauritius Constitutional Conference, London, Sept.-Nov. 1965. Vice-Chancellor, Calcutta Univ., 1962–68 (Life-Mem. Senate); President: Jagat Taran Educn Soc., 1924–; Jagat Taran Degree Coll., 1924–; Jagat Taran Inter Coll., 1924–; Jagat Taran Golden Jubilee Eng. Med. Sch. and Hindi Med. Primary Sch., 1924–; Harijan Ashram Degree Coll., Allahabad, 1968–. Former Mem. Council, Ewing Christian Coll., Pres., Old Boys' Assoc., 1976–. Founder Mem., Lions Club, Allahabad, 1959–60; Rotary Club: Pres., Allahabad; Mem., Allahabad and Calcutta. Founder President: Golf Club, Allahabad, 1949–55; Allahabad Badminton Assoc., 1949–55. *Address:* 23 Muir Road, Allahabad, India.

MALIM, Rear-Adm. Nigel Hugh, CB 1971; LVO 1960; FIMechE; FIMarE; *b* 5 April 1919; *s* of late John Malim, Pebmarsh, and Brenda Malim; *m* 1944, Moonyeen, *d* of late William and Winefride Maynard; two *s* one *d. Educ:* Weymouth Coll.; RNEC Keyham. Cadet, RN, 1936; HMS Manchester, 1940–41; HMS Norfolk, 1942; RNC Greenwich, 1943–45; HMS Jamaica, 1945–47; Staff of RNEC, 1948–50; Admty, 1951–54; HMS Triumph, 1954–56; Admty, 1956–58; HM Yacht Britannia, 1958–60; District Overseer, Scotland, 1960–62; Asst. and later Dep., Dir Marine Engrg, 1962–65; idc 1966; Captain, RNEC Manadon, 1967–69; Chief Staff Officer Technical to C-in-C, W Fleet, 1969–71, retd. Man. Dir, Humber Graving Dock & Engrg Co. Ltd, 1972–82. Chm., Fabric Council, Lincoln Cathedral, 1985–. *Recreations:* offshore racing and cruising. *Address:* The Old Vicarage, Caistor, Lincoln LN7 6UG. *Clubs:* Royal Ocean Racing, Royal Naval Sailing Association.

MALIN, Peter; see Conner, Rearden.

MALIN, Prof. Stuart Robert Charles; Head of Astronomy and Navigation, National Maritime Museum, since 1982; Visiting Professor, Department of Physics and Astronomy, University College London, since 1983; *b* 28 Sept. 1936; *s* of Cecil Henry Malin and Eleanor Mary Malin (*née* Howe); *m* 1963, Irene Saunders; two *d. Educ:* Royal Grammar Sch., High Wycombe; King's College, London. BSc 1958, PhD 1972, DSc 1981; FInstP 1971; CPhys 1985; FRAS 1961 (Mem. Council, 1975–78). Royal Greenwich Observatory,

Herstmonceux: Asst Exptl Officer, 1958; Scientific Officer, 1961; Sen. Scientific Officer, 1965; Institute of Geological Science, Herstmonceux and Edinburgh: PSO, 1970; SPSO (individual merit), 1976, and Hd of Geomagnetism Unit, 1981. Cape Observer, Radcliffe Observatory, Pretoria, 1963–65; Vis. Scientist, Nat. Center for Atmospheric Res., Boulder, Colorado, 1969; Green Schol., Scripps Instn of Oceanography, La Jolla, 1981. *Publications:* (with Carole Stott) The Greenwich Meridian, 1984; Spaceworks, 1985; contribs to scientific jls. *Recreation:* croquet. *Address:* 30 Wemyss Road, Blackheath, SE3 0TG. *T:* 01–318 3712.

MALINS, Humfrey Jonathan; MP (C) North West Croydon, since 1983; *b* 31 July 1945; *s* of Rev. Peter Malins and Lilian Joan Malins; *m* 1979, Lynda Ann; one *s* one *d*. *Educ:* St John's Sch., Leatherhead; Brasenose Coll., Oxford (MA Hons Law). College of Law, Guildford, 1967; joined Tuck and Mann, Solicitors, Dorking, 1967, qual. as solicitor, 1971; Partner, Tuck and Mann, 1973. Councillor, Mole Valley DC, Surrey, 1973–83 (Chm., Housing Cttee, 1980–81). Contested: Toxteth Division of Liverpool, Feb. and Oct. 1974; E Lewisham, 1979. *Recreations:* Rugby football, golf, gardening. *Address:* Highbury, Westcott Street, Westcott, Dorking, Surrey RH4 3NU. *T:* Dorking 885554. *Clubs:* Coningsby; Vincent's (Oxford); Richmond Rugby Football; West Sussex Golf.

MALJERS, Floris Anton; Chairman, Unilever NV, and Vice Chairman, Unilever PLC, since 1984; *b* 12 Aug. 1933; *s* of A. C. J. Maljers and L. M. Maljers-Kole; *m* 1958, J. H. Maljers-de Jongh; two *s* (one *d* decd). *Educ:* Univ. of Amsterdam. Joined Unilever, 1959; various jobs in the Netherlands until 1965; Man. Dir, Unilever-Colombia, 1965–67; Man. Dir, Unilever-Turkey, 1967–70; Chairman, Van den Bergh & Jurgens, Netherlands, 1970–74; Co-ordinator of Man. Group, edible fats and dairy, and Dir of Unilever NV and Unilever PLC, 1974–. Member, Unilever's Special Committee, 1982–. *Address:* 34 Cadogan Place, SW1. *T:* 01–235 2879.

MALLABAR, Sir John (Frederick), Kt 1969; FCA; Senior Partner, J. F. Mallabar & Co., Chartered Accountants, 1929–80; *b* 19 July 1900; *e s* of Herbert John Mallabar and Gertrude Mallabar, *d* of Hugh Jones, Barrow; *m* 1st, 1931, Henrietta, *d* of George Goodwin-Norris; 2nd, 1949, Annie Emily (Pat), *d* of Charles Mealing, Princes Risborough, and *widow* of Richard Howard Ford, Bodweni, Merionethshire; no *c*. An External Underwriting Member of Lloyd's. Chairman: Ruston & Hornby, 1964–66; Harland and Wolff Ltd, 1966–70; former Chairman: Franco-British Electrical Co.; Villiers Engrg Co.; Agricl Central Trading; NFU Seeds; Combined Telephone Hldgs; Kelvin Bergins; former Director: local Bd, Martins Bank; Plessey Co.; Chubb & Son; S. G. Warburg Finance & Develt; David Brown Corp. etc. Chm., Cttee on Govt Industrial Establishments, 1968–70. *Recreations:* stalking, salmon fishing. *Address:* 39 Arlington House, St James's, SW1. *Club:* Carlton.

MALLABY, Christopher Leslie George, CMG 1982; HM Diplomatic Service; Deputy Secretary, Cabinet Office, since 1985; *b* 7 July 1936; *s* of late Brig. A. W. S. Mallaby, CIE, OBE, and Margaret Catherine Mallaby (*née* Jones); *m* 1961, Pascale Françoise Thierry-Mieg; one *s* three *d*. *Educ:* Eton; King's Coll., Cambridge. British Delegn to UN Gen. Assembly, 1960; 3rd Sec., British Embassy, Moscow, 1961–63; 2nd Sec., FO, 1963–66; 1st Sec., Berlin, 1966–69; 1st Sec., FCO, 1969–71; Harvard Business Sch., 1971; Dep. Dir, British Trade Develt Office, NY, 1971–74; Counsellor and Head of Chancery, Moscow, 1975–77; Head of Arms Control and Disarmament Dept, FCO, 1977–79, Head of East European and Soviet Dept, 1979–80, Head of Planning Staff, 1980–82, FCO; Minister, Bonn, 1982–85. *Recreations:* fishing, reading, travel. *Address:* c/o Foreign and Commonwealth Office, SW1A 2AH. *Club:* Beefsteak.

MALLALIEU, Ann; a Recorder, since 1985; *b* 27 Nov. 1945; *d* of Sir (Joseph Percival) William Mallalieu and of Lady Mallalieu; *m* 1979, Timothy Felix Harold Cassel, *qv*; two *d*. *Educ:* Holton Park Girls' Grammar Sch., Wheatley, Oxon; Newnham Coll., Cambridge (MA, LLM). (First woman) Pres., Cambridge Union Soc., 1967. Called to the Bar, Inner Temple, 1970; Mem., Gen. Council of the Bar, 1973–75. *Recreations:* sheep, hunting, poetry, horseracing. *Address:* 6 King's Bench Walk, Temple, EC4Y 7DR. *T:* 01–583 0410.

MALLE, Louis; Film Director; *b* 30 Oct. 1932; *s* of Pierre Malle and Françoise Béghin; one *s*; *m* 1980, Candice Bergen. *Educ:* Paris Univ.; Institut d'Etudes Politiques. Television, 1953; Asst to Comdt Cousteau on the Calypso, 1953–55. Films: Co-prod. Le Monde du Silence, 1955 (Palme d'Or, Cannes); Collab. techn of Robert Bresson for Un Condamné a mort s'est echappé, 1956; Author and Producer of: Ascenseur pour l'échafaud, 1957 (Prix Louis-Delluc, 1958); Les Amants, 1958 (Prix spécial du Jury du Festival de Venise, 1958); Zazie dans le métro, 1960; Vie privée, 1962; Le Feu Follet (again, Prix spécial, Venise, 1963); Viva Maria, 1965 (Grand Prix du Cinéma français); Le Voleur, 1966; Histoires extraordinaires (sketch), 1968; Inde 68, 1968; Calcutta, 1969 (prix de la Fraternité); Phantom India, 1969; Le Souffle au Coeur, 1971 (nominated Best Screenplay, US Acad. Awards, 1972); Humain, trop humain, 1972; Place de la République, 1973; Lacombe Lucien, 1974; Black Moon, 1975; Pretty Baby, 1977; (dir) Atlantic City, 1979 (Jt winner, Golden Lion, Venice Film Fest., 1980; Best Director, BAFTA awards, 1982; nominated Best Film and Best Director, US Acad. Awards, 1982); My Dinner With André, 1981; (dir) Crackers, 1984; (dir) Alamo Bay, 1985; (dir, cameraman) God's Country (for Public TV), 1985. *Address:* c/o NEF, 15 rue du Louvre, 75001 Paris, France.

MALLET, Sir Ivo; *see* Mallet, Sir W. I.

MALLET, John Valentine Granville, FSA; FRSA; Keeper, Department of Ceramics, Victoria and Albert Museum, since 1976; *b* 15 Sept. 1930; *s* of late Sir Victor Mallet, GCMG, CVO, and Lady Mallet (*née* Andreae); *m* 1958, Felicity Ann Basset; one *s*. *Educ:* Winchester Coll.; Balliol Coll., Oxford (BA Modern History). Mil. service in Army: commnd; held temp. rank of full Lieut in Intell. Corps, 1949–50. Messrs Sotheby & Co., London, 1955–62; Victoria and Albert Museum: Asst Keeper, Dept of Ceramics, 1962; Sec. to Adv. Council, 1967–73. Indep. Mem., Design Selection Cttee, Design Council, 1981–. Mem., Court of Assistants, Fishmongers' Co., 1970–, Prime Warden, 1983–84. *Publications:* articles on ceramics in Burlington Magazine, Apollo, Trans English Ceramic Circle, and Faenza. *Recreation:* tennis. *Address:* Victoria and Albert Museum, South Kensington, SW7 2RL.

See also P. L. V. Mallet.

MALLET, Philip Louis Victor, CMG 1980; HM Diplomatic Service, retired; *b* 3 Feb. 1926; *e s* of late Sir Victor Mallet, GCMG, CVO and Christiana Jean, *d* of Herman A. Andreae; *m* 1953, Mary Moyle Grenfell Borlase; three *s*. *Educ:* Winchester; Balliol Coll., Oxford. Army Service, 1944–47. Entered HM Foreign (subseq. Diplomatic) Service, 1949; served in: FO, 1949; Baghdad, 1950–53; FO, 1953–56; Cyprus, 1956–58; Aden, 1958; Bonn, 1958–62; FO, 1962–64; Tunis, 1964–66; FCO, 1967–69; Khartoum, 1969–73; Stockholm, 1973–76; Head of Republic of Ireland Dept, FCO, 1977–78; High Comr in Guyana and non-resident Ambassador to Suriname, 1978–82. *Address:* Wittersham House, Wittersham, Kent TN30 7ED. *Club:* Brooks's.

See also J. V. G. Mallet.

MALLET, Roger; Chairman, North Western Electricity Board, 1972–76, retired; *b* 7 June 1912; British; *m* 1942, Kathleen Els Walker; two *s* two *d*. *Educ:* Eastbourne Coll.; Trinity Hall, Cambridge. BA Mech. Sci. Tripos; CEng, FIEE. West Cambrian Power Co., S Wales, 1937–40; Buckrose Light & Power Co., Yorks, 1940–45; Shropshire, Worcestershire and Staffordshire Electric Power Co., 1945–47; Midlands Electricity Board, 1948–72. *Recreation:* golf. *Address:* 75 Carrwood, Hale Barns, Cheshire WA15 0ER. *T:* 061–980 3214.

MALLET, Sir (William) Ivo, GBE 1960; KCMG 1951 (CMG 1945); retired as Ambassador to Spain (1954–60); *b* 7 April 1900; *yr s* of late Sir Charles Mallet; *m* 1929, Marie-Angèle (*d* 1985), *d* of Joseph Wierusz-Kowalski; two *s* one *d*. *Educ:* Harrow; Balliol Coll., Oxford. Entered Diplomatic Service, 1925. Served in Constantinople, Angora, London, Berlin, Rome; Asst Private Secretary to Secretary of State for Foreign Affairs, 1938–41; Acting Counsellor in FO, 1941; Counsellor, 1943; Consul-General, Tangier, 1946; Asst Under-Secretary, Foreign Office, 1949; HM Ambassador, Belgrade, 1951. *Address:* Chalet La Combe, Rossinière, Vaud, Switzerland.

See also R. A. Farquharson.

MALLETT, Edmund Stansfield; Director of Applications Programmes, European Space Agency, Paris, 1981–85, retired; *b* 21 April 1923; *s* of Cecil Finer Mallett and Elsie Stansfield; *m* 1953, Nancy Campbell (*d* 1983); three *s*; *m* 1985, Jocelyn Maynard Ghent. *Educ:* Bradford Grammar Sch.; Leeds Univ. (BSc). CEng, MIEE; FBIS. Gramophone Co., 1944; Fairey Aviation Co., 1948; Royal Aircraft Establishment: joined 1950; Head, Data Transmission and Processing Div., 1961; Supt, Central Unit for Scientific Photography, 1966; Head, Instrumentation Div., 1968; Head of Instruments Br., Min. of Technol., 1969; Head of Instrumentation and Ranges Dept, RAE, 1971; Director Space, DoI, 1976; Under Sec., and Head of Res. and Technol. Requirements and Space Div., DoI, 1978; Dir, Nat. Maritime Inst., 1979. *Publications:* papers and articles on instrumentation and measurement. *Recreations:* music, art, genealogy, solving problems. *Address:* 580 Prospect Avenue, Rockcliffe Park, Ottawa, Ontario K1M 0X7, Canada. *T:* 748 7219.

MALLETT, Francis Anthony, CBE 1984; Chief Executive, South Yorkshire County Council, 1973–84; Clerk of the Lieutenancy, South Yorkshire, 1974–84; solicitor; *b* 13 March 1924; *s* of Francis Sidney and Marion Mallett; *m* 1956, Alison Shirley Melville, MA; two *s* one *d*. *Educ:* Mill Hill; London Univ. (LLB). Army, 1943–47: commissioned, Royal Hampshire Regt, 1944; served in Middle East, Italy and Germany. Staff Captain, 160 (South Wales) Infty Bde, 4th (Infty) Bde and 4th (Guards) Bde, successively, 1946 and 1947. Second Dep. Clerk, Hertfordshire CC, 1966–69; Dep. Clerk, West Riding CC, 1969–74. Chairman: Assoc. of Local Authority Chief Execs, 1979–84; Crown Prosecution Service Staff Commn, 1985–; Mem, W Yorks Residuary Body, 1985–. *Recreations:* gardening, fishing, tennis. *Address:* Aketon Springs, Follifoot, Harrogate, N Yorks. *T:* Spofforth 395. *Club:* Lansdowne.

MALLETT, Ven. Peter, CB 1978; AKC; Chaplain-General to the Forces, 1974–80; Managing Director, Inter-Church Travel, since 1982; *b* 1925; *s* of Edwin and Beatrice Mallett; *m* 1958, Joan Margaret Bremer; one *s* two *d*. *Educ:* King's Coll., London; St Boniface Coll., Warminster, Wilts. Deacon, 1951, priest, 1952. Curate, St Oswald's, Norbury, S London, 1951–54. Joined Royal Army Chaplains' Dept (CF), 1954, and has served overseas in Far East, Aden, Germany (despatches, Malaya, 1957). Has been Senior Chaplain of Aden Brigade, and at RMA, Sandhurst; Dep. Asst Chaplain-General, Berlin, 1968, in N Ireland, 1972; Asst Chaplain-General, BAOR, 1973. QHC 1973. Canon, dio. of Europe, 1982. OStJ 1976. Hon. DLitt Geneva Theol Coll., 1976. *Address:* Everleigh Cottage, The Hollow, Shrewton, near Salisbury, Wilts. *T:* Shrewton 620847. *Clubs:* Army and Navy, Naval and Military (Hon.).

MALLIN, Very Rev. Stewart Adam Thomson, CSG; Dean of Moray, Ross and Caithness, since 1983; Rector of St James, Dingwall and St Anne's, Strathpeffer, since 1977; *b* 12 Aug. 1924; *s* of George Garner Mallin and Elizabeth Thomson. *Educ:* Lasswade Secondary School; Coates Hall Theological Coll., Edinburgh. Deacon 1961, priest 1962; Curate, St Andrew's Cathedral, Inverness, 1961–64; Itinerant Priest, Diocese of Moray, Ross and Caithness, 1964–68; Priest-in-Charge of St Peter and the Holy Rood, Thurso, and St John's, Wick, 1968–77; Member of CSG, 1968–; Canon of St Andrew's Cathedral, Inverness, 1974. Hon. Chaplain, British Legion. Associate, Order of the Holy Cross (USA). *Recreations:* amateur drama, amateur opera. *Address:* The Parsonage, 4 Castle Street, Dingwall, Ross-shire. *T:* Dingwall 62204. *Club:* Rotary (Thurso, then Dingwall).

MALLINSON, Anthony William; Senior Partner, Slaughter and May, 1984–86; *b* 1 Dec. 1923; *s* of Stanley Tucker Mallinson and Dora Selina Mallinson (*née* Burridge); *m* 1955, Heather Mary Gardiner. *Educ:* Cheam School; Marlborough College; Gonville and Caius College, Cambridge (Exbnr 1948, Tapp Post-Graduate Scholar, 1949, BA, LLM). Served RA, 1943–47, Major. Admitted solicitor, England and Wales, 1952, Hong Kong, 1978; Partner, Slaughter and May, 1957–86; Solicitor to Fishmongers' Co., 1964–86. Mem. London Bd, Bank of Scotland, 1985–; Dir, Outwich Investment Trust, 1986–. Mem., BoT Cttee examining British Patent System (Banks Cttee), 1967–70; Chm., Cinematograph Films Council, 1973–76. Hon. Legal Adviser to Accounting Standards Cttee, 1982–86; Member: Council, Section on Business Law, Internat. Bar Assoc., 1984–; Exec. Cttee, Essex County Cricket Club, 1986–. *Recreations:* sport watching, particularly cricket, reading. *Address:* 15 Douro Place, W8 5PH. *T:* 01–937 2739. *Clubs:* Royal Commonwealth Society, MCC.

MALLINSON, Dennis Hainsworth; Director, National Engineering Laboratory, East Kilbride, Department of Industry, 1974–80; *b* 22 Aug. 1921; *s* of David and Anne Mallinson; *m* 1945, Rowena Mary Brooke; one *s* two *d*. *Educ:* Leeds Univ. (BSc). RAE, 1942, early jet engines; Power Jets (R&D) Ltd, later Nat. Gas Turbine Estabt, 1944–63; Min. of Aviation and successors: Asst Dir, 1963; Dir, 1964; Dir-Gen., Engines, Procurement Exec., MoD, 1972–74. Vis. Prof., Strathclyde Univ., 1976–82. Member Council: Instn Engrs and Shipbuilders in Scotland, 1977–80; Scottish Assoc. of Metals, 1976–78. *Address:* 19 Rossett Holt Close, Harrogate HG2 9AD.

MALLINSON, John Russell; Under Secretary (Legal), Department of Trade and Industry, since 1985; *b* 29 June 1943; *s* of Wilfred and Joyce Helen Mallinson; *m* 1968, Susan Rebecca Jane Godfree; one *s* one *d*. *Educ:* Giggleswick Sch.; Balliol Coll., Oxford (Keasbey Schol. 1963; BA). Solicitor (Hons.), 1972. Asst Solicitor, Coward Chance, 1972–74; Sen. Legal Assistant, DTI, 1974–79; Assistant Solicitor: Law Officers' Dept, AG's Chambers, 1979–81; DTI, 1982–84. *Recreations:* conversation, music, food and wine. *Address:* 4 Nunappleton Way, Hurst Green, Surrey RH8 9AW. *T:* Oxted 4775.

MALLINSON, Sir Paul; *see* Mallinson, Sir W. P.

MALLINSON, William Arthur, CBE 1978; FEng 1985; CBIM; consultant engineer; Vice Chairman, Smiths Industries PLC, 1978–85; *b* 12 June 1922; *s* of Arthur Mallinson and Nellie Jane Mallinson; *m* 1948, Muriel Ella Parker; two *d*. *Educ:* William Hulme's Grammar Sch., Manchester; Faculty of Technol., Manchester Univ. (BScTech 1st Cl. Hons). MIEE, MIMechE, MRAeS; FBIM 1976. Electrical Officer, Tech. Br., RAFVR, 1943–47; Elec. Designer, Electro-Hydraulics Ltd, 1947–51; Ferranti Ltd: Proj. Engr, GW

Dept, 1951–55; Chief Engr, Aircraft Equipment Dept, 1955–68; Smiths Industries Ltd, 1968–85: Technical Dir, then Gen. Man., Aviation Div.; Divl Man. Dir; Main Bd Dir; Corporate Man. Dir. Member: Airworthiness Requirements Bd, CAA, 1981–85; Electronics and Avionics Requirements Bd, DTI, 1983–85 (Chm., Aviation Cttee, 1984–85). *Recreations:* music, horticulture. *Address:* Chestnut Cottage, Dukes Covert, Bagshot, Surrey GU19 5HU. *T:* Bagshot 72479.

MALLINSON, Sir (William) Paul, 3rd Bt, *cr* 1935; MA, BM, BCh, FRCP; FRCPsych; Hon. Consulting Psychiatrist to St George's Hospital, SW1; Civilian Consultant Emeritus in Psychiatry to Royal Navy; Chairman, Wm Mallinson & Denny Mott Ltd, 1962–73; *b* 6 July 1909; *s* of Sir William Mallinson, 2nd Bt, and Mabel (*d* 1948), *d* of J. W. Rush, Tunbridge Wells; *S* father, 1944; *m* 1st, 1940, Eila Mary (marr. diss. 1968; she *d* 1985), *d* of Roland Graeme Guy, Hastings, NZ; one *s* two *d*; 2nd, 1968, Margaret Cooper, BA, MB, BS (served in FO during war, 1939–45), *d* of S. A. Bowden, Barnstaple, Devon. *Educ:* Westminster; Christ Church, Oxford; St Thomas's Hospital. Served RNVR, 1940–46, Surgeon Lieut-Commander. First class Order of the Family, Brunei, 1973. *Heir: s* William John Mallinson [*b* 8 Oct. 1942; *m* 1968, Rosalind Angela (marr. diss.), *o d* of Rollo Hoare, Dogmersfield, Hampshire; one *s* one *d*]. *Address:* 25 Wimpole Street, W1. *T:* 01–580 7919; Meadow Lea, Northclose Road, Bembridge, Isle of Wight. *T:* Isle of Wight 872239. *Clubs:* Athenæum, MCC; Royal Thames Yacht.

MALLON, Seamus; MP (SDLP) Newry and Armagh, since Jan. 1986; *b* 17 Aug. 1936; *s* of Francis P. Mallon and Jane O'Flaherty; *m* 1966, Gertrude Cush; one *d*. *Educ:* St Joseph's Coll. of Educn. Member: NI Assembly, 1973–74 and 1982; NI Convention, 1975–76; Irish Senate, 1981–82; Armagh Dist Council, 1973–. Author of play, Adam's Children, prod. radio, 1968, and stage, 1969. *Recreations:* angling, gardening. *Address:* 5 Castleview, Markethill, Armagh BT60 1QP. *T:* Markethill 551351.

MALLORIE, Air Vice-Marshal Paul Richard, CB 1979; AFC 1947; retired RAF, 1980; Military Command and Control Systems Consultant; *b* 8 March 1923; *s* of late Rev. W. T. Mallorie and Margaret Mallorie; *m* 1951, Ursula Joyce Greig; three *s* one *d*. *Educ:* King's Sch., Canterbury. Flying Instructor, 1945; India and Middle East, 1946–49; Air Ministry, 1951–53; Staff Coll., 1954; No 139 Sqdn, 1955–57; JSSC, 1960; UK Mil. Advisers' Rep., SEATO, Bangkok, 1963–66; OC RAF Wittering, 1967–68; IDC, 1969; Min. of Defence, 1974–76; Asst Chief of Staff (Info. Systems), SHAPE, 1976–79. Res. Fellow, NATO, 1981–82. *Recreations:* gardening, computers. *Address:* c/o Barclays Bank, Framlingham, Woodbridge, Suffolk. *Club:* Royal Air Force.

MALLOWS, Surg. Rear-Adm. Harry Russell; Senior Medical Officer, Shell Centre, 1977–85; *b* 1 July 1920; *s* of Harry Mallows and Amy Mallows (*née* Law); *m* 1942, Rhona Frances Wyndham-Smith; one *s* two *d*. *Educ:* Wrekin Coll.; Christ's Coll., Cambridge (MA, MD); UCH, London. FFCM, FFOM, DPH, DIH. SMO, HM Dockyards at Hong Kong, Sheerness, Gibraltar and Singapore, 1951–67; Naval MO of Health, Scotland and NI Comd, and Far East Stn, 1964–68; Dir of Environmental Medicine, Inst. of Naval Medicine, 1970–73; Comd MO, Naval Home Comd, 1973–75; QHP, 1974–77; Surgeon Rear-Adm. (Ships and Estabts), 1975–77; retd 1977. CStJ 1976. *Publications:* articles in BMJ, Royal Naval Med. Service Jl, Proc. RSM. *Recreations:* music, travel. *Address:* 1 Shear Hill, Petersfield, Hants GU31 4BB. *T:* Petersfield 63116. *Club:* Naval.

MALMESBURY, 6th Earl of *cr* 1800; **William James Harris;** TD 1944 (2 Clasps); JP; DL; Baron Malmesbury, 1788; Viscount FitzHarris, 1800; Official Verderer of the New Forest, 1966–74; Lord-Lieutenant and Custos Rotulorum of Hampshire, 1973–82; served Royal Hampshire Regiment, TA; *b* 18 Nov. 1907; *o s* of 5th Earl and Hon. Dorothy Gough-Calthorpe (*d* 1973), CBE (Lady of Grace, Order of St John of Jerusalem, Order of Mercy, with bar), *y d* of 6th Lord Calthorpe; *S* father 1950; *m* 1932, Hon. Diana Carleton, *e d* of 6th Baron Dorchester, OBE; one *s* two *d*. *Educ:* Eton; Trinity Coll., Cambridge (MA). Vice-Pres. of the Cambridge Univ. Conservative Association, 1930; Professional Associate of Surveyors Institution, 1937. Personal Liaison Officer to Min. of Agric., SE Region, 1958–64; Mem., Agric. and Forestry Cttee, RICS, 1953–69; Chm., Hants Agric. Exec. Cttee, 1959–67; Cttee which produced White Paper on the Growing Demand for Water, 1961. Dir, Mid-Southern Water Co., 1961–78. Chairman: Hants Br., Country Landowners Assoc., 1954–56; T&AFA, Hants and IoW, 1960–68; first Chm., Eastern Wessex TA&VRA, 1968–70 (Vice-Pres., 1973–78; Pres., 1978–80); Hon. Col, 65th (M) Signal Regt, R Sigs (TA), 1959–66; Hon. Col, 2nd Bn The Wessex Regt (V), 1970–73. Mem. Basingstoke RDC, 1946–52; County Councillor, Hants CC, 1952; Vice-Lt, Co. Southampton, 1960–73; DL Hants, 1955 and 1983. Master, Worshipful Co. of Skinners, 1952–53. KStJ 1973. Coronation Medal, 1937, 1953; Silver Jubilee Medal, 1977. *Heir: s* Viscount FitzHarris, *qv*. *Address:* Greywell Hill, Basingstoke, Hants RG25 1DB. *T:* Odiham 2033. *Club:* Royal Yacht Squadron (Vice-Cdre, 1971–77).

See also J. N. Maltby.

MALMESBURY, Bishop Suffragan of, since 1983; **Rt. Rev. Peter James Firth;** *b* 12 July 1929; *s* of Atkinson Vernon Firth and Edith Pepper; *m* 1955, Felicity Mary Wilding; two *s* two *d* (and one long-term foster *d*). *Educ:* Stockport Grammar School; Emmanuel Coll., Cambridge (Open Exhibnr, MA, DipEd); St Stephen's House Theol Coll., Oxford. Ordained, 1955; Assistant Curate, St Stephen's, Barbourne in Worcester, 1955–58; Priest-in-charge, Church of the Ascension, Parish of St Matthias, Malvern Link, Worcs, 1958–62; Rector of St George's, Abbey Hey, Gorton in Manchester, 1962–66; Religious Broadcasting Assistant, North Region, BBC, 1966–67; Religious Broadcasting Organiser and Senior Producer, Religious Programmes, BBC South and West, Bristol, 1967–83. Internat. Radio Festival winner, Seville, 1975. *Publication:* Lord of the Seasons, 1978. *Recreations:* theatre, photography, music, travel, Manchester United. *Address:* 7 Ivywell Road, Bristol BS9 1NX. *T:* Bristol 685931.

MALONE, Hon. Sir Denis (Eustace Gilbert), Kt 1977; **Hon. Mr Justice Malone;** Puisne Judge of the Commonwealth of the Bahamas, since 1979; *b* 24 Nov. 1922; *s* of Sir Clement Malone, OBE, QC, and Lady Malone; *m* 1963, Diana Malone (*née* Traynor). *Educ:* St Kitts-Nevis Grammar Sch.; Wycliffe Coll., Stonehouse, Glos; Lincoln Coll., Oxford (BA). Called to Bar, Middle Temple, 1950. Royal Air Force, Bomber Comd, 1942–46. Attorney General's Chambers, Barbados, WI, 1953–61, Solicitor-Gen., 1958–61; Puisne Judge: Belize, 1961–65; Trinidad and Tobago, 1966–74; Chief Justice of Belize, 1974–79. *Recreations:* tennis, swimming, walking, bridge, reading. *Address:* c/o The Supreme Court, PO Box N8167, Nassau, Bahamas.

MALONE, (Peter) Gerald; MP (C) Aberdeen South, since 1983; an Assistant Government Whip, since 1986; *b* 21 July 1950; *s* of P. A. and J. Malone; *m* 1981, Dr Anne S. Blyth. *Educ:* St Aloysius Coll., Glasgow; Glasgow Univ. (MA, LLB). Admitted solicitor, 1972. PPS to Parly Under Secs of State, Dept of Energy, 1985–. *Recreations:* opera, motoring. *Address:* 32 Albyn Lane, Aberdeen AB1 6XF. *T:* Aberdeen 571779. *Clubs:* Art (Glasgow); Royal Northern University, Aberdeen Conservative (Aberdeen).

MALONE-LEE, Michael Charles; Director of Establishments and Personnel (HQ), Department of Health and Social Security, since 1984; *b* 4 March 1941; *s* of Dr Gerard Brendan and Theresa Malone-Lee; *m* 1971, Claire Frances Cockin; two *s*. *Educ:* Stonyhurst College; Campion Hall, Oxford (MA). Ministry of Health, 1968; Principal Private Sec. to Sec. of State for Social Services, 1976–79; Asst Sec., 1977; Area Administrator, City and East London AHA, 1979–81; District Administrator, Bloomsbury Health Authy, 1982–84; Under Secretary, 1984. *Recreation:* natural history. *Address:* 31 Underhill, Moulsford, Oxon OX10 9JH.

MALONEY, Michael John, JP; MA; Headmaster, Kamuzu Academy, Malaŵi, since 1986; *b* 26 July 1932; *s* of John William Maloney and Olive Lois Maloney; *m* 1960, Jancis Ann (*née* Ewing); one *s* one *d*. *Educ:* St Alban's Sch.; Trinity Coll., Oxford (MA). Nat. Service, 2nd Lieut RA, served with RWAFF, 1955–57. May & Baker Ltd, 1957–58; Asst Master, Shrewsbury Sch., 1958–66; Sen. Science Master, Housemaster, Dep. Headmaster, Eastbourne Coll., 1966–72; Headmaster, Welbeck Coll., 1972–85. JP Worksop, 1975. *Publication:* (with D. E. P. Hughes) Advanced Theoretical Chemistry, 1964. *Recreations:* Rugby football, ornithology, cryptography. *Address:* Kamuzu Academy, PO Box 1, Mtunthama, Malaŵi. *Club:* East India, Devonshire, Sports and Public Schools.

MALOTT, Deane Waldo; President Cornell University, Ithaca, NY, 1951–63, President Emeritus, 1963; Consultant, Association of American Colleges, 1963–70; *b* 10 July 1898; *s* of Michael Harvey Malott and Edith Gray Johnson; *m* 1925, Eleanor Sisson Thrum; one *s* two *d*. *Educ:* Univ. of Kansas (AB); Harvard Univ. (MBA). Asst Dean, Harvard Business Sch., 1923–29; Assoc. Prof. of Business, 1933–39; Vice-Pres., Hawaiian Pineapple Co., Honolulu, 1929–33; Chancellor, Univ. of Kansas, 1939–51. Educational Advisor, Ops Analysis Div., US Army Air Corps, 1943–45; Mem., Business Council, Washington, DC, 1944–; Trustee: Corning Museum of Glass, 1952–73; Teagle Foundation, 1952–85; William Allen White Foundation, 1952–; Kansas Univ. Endowment Assoc., 1962–; Pacific Tropical Botanical Garden, 1964–; Mem. Bd, Univ. of Kansas Alumni Assoc., 1974–; Director: General Mills, Inc., 1948–70; Citizens Bank, Abilene, Kans, 1944–73; Pitney-Bowes, Inc., 1951–71; First Nat. Bank, Ithaca, NY, 1951–83; Owens-Corning Fiberglas Corp., 1951–72; Lane Bryant, Inc., 1963–77; Servomation Corp., 1963–74. Mem., Adv. Bd, Security Northstar Bank, 1983–. Hon. LLD: Washburn Univ., 1941; Bryant Coll., 1951; Hamilton Coll., 1951; Univ. of California 1954; Univ. of Liberia, 1962; Univ. of New Hampshire, 1963; Emory Univ., 1963; Juniata Coll., 1965; DCS, Univ. of Pittsburgh, 1957; Hon. DHL, Long Island Univ., 1967. Holds foreign Orders. *Publications:* Problems in Agricultural Marketing, 1938; (with Philip Cabot) Problems in Public Utility Management, 1927; (with J. C. Baker) Introduction to Corporate Finance, 1936; (with J. C. Baker and W. D. Kennedy) On Going into Business, 1936; (with B. F. Martin) The Agricultural Industries, 1939; Agriculture—the Great Dilemma (an essay in Business and Modern Society), 1951. *Address:* 322 Wait Avenue, Cornell University, Ithaca, NY 14850, USA. *Clubs:* University, Cornell (New York); Bohemian (San Francisco).

MALPAS, Prof. James Spencer, DPhil; FRCP; FRCR; Consultant Physician, St Bartholomew's Hospital, since 1973; Professor of Medical Oncology, since 1979, and Director, Imperial Cancer Research Fund Medical Oncology Unit, since 1976, St Bartholomew's Hospital; *b* 15 Sept. 1931; *s* of Tom Spencer Malpas, BSc, MICE and Hilda Chalstrey; *m* 1957, Joyce May Cathcart; two *s*. *Educ:* Sutton County Grammar Sch.; St Bartholomew's Hosp., London Univ. Schol. in Sci., 1951; BSc Hons, 1952; MB BS, 1955; DPhil, 1965; FRCP 1971; FRCR 1983. Junior appts in medicine, St Bartholomew's Hosp. and Royal Post-Grad. Med. Sch.; Nat. Service in RAF, 1957–60; Aylwen Bursar, St Bartholomew's Hosp., 1961; Lectr in Medicine, Oxford Univ., 1962–65; St Bartholomew's Hospital: Sen. Registrar in Medicine, 1966–68; Sen. Lectr in Medicine, 1968–72; Dean of Medical Coll., 1969–72. Cooper Res. Schol. in Med., 1966, 1967, 1968. Examiner in Medicine: Univ. of Oxford, 1974; Univ. of London, 1985, 1986. Asst Registrar, RCP, 1975–80; Lockyer Lectr, RCP, 1978; Skinner Lectr, RCR, 1986. *Publications:* contrib. many medical textbooks; papers in BMJ, Brit. Jl Haematology, Jl Clinical Pathology, etc. *Recreations:* travel, history, painting, ski-ing, sailing. *Address:* 36 Cleaver Square, SE11 4DP. *T:* 01–735 7566.

MALPAS, Robert, CBE 1975; FEng 1978; FIMechE, FIChemE, FIMH; a Managing Director, British Petroleum, since 1983; *b* 9 Aug. 1927; *s* of late Cheshyre Malpas and of Louise Marie Marcelle Malpas; *m* 1956, Josephine Dickenson. *Educ:* Taunton Sch.; St George's Coll., Buenos Aires; Durham Univ. BScMechEng (1st Cl. Hons). Joined ICI Ltd, 1948; moved to Alcudia SA (48.5 per cent ICI), Spain, 1963; ICI Europa Ltd, Brussels, 1965; Chm., ICI Europa Ltd, 1973; ICI Main Board Dir, 1975–78; Pres., Halcon International Inc., 1978–82. Member: Engineering Council, 1983– (Vice-Chm., 1984); ACARD, 1983–86. Hon. DTech Loughborough, 1983; DUniv Surrey, 1984. Order of Civil Merit, Spain, 1967. *Recreations:* sport, music. *Address:* Britannic House, Moor Lane, EC2. *Clubs:* Royal Automobile; River (NY); Real Automóvil Club de España (Madrid).

MALTA, Archbishop of, (RC), since 1977; **Most Rev. Joseph Mercieca,** STD, JUD; *b* Victoria, Gozo, 11 Nov. 1928. *Educ:* Gozo Seminary; Univ. of London (BA); Gregorian Univ., Rome (STD); Lateran Univ., Rome (JUD). Priest, 1952; Rector of Gozo Seminary in late 1960s; Permanent Judge at Sacred Roman Rota and Commissioner to Congregation for the Sacraments and Congregation for the Doctrine of the Faith, 1969; Auxiliary Bishop of Malta, and Vicar-General, 1974–77. *Address:* Archbishop's Palace, Valletta, Malta.

MALTBY, Antony John, JP; DL; MA; Headmaster of Trent College since 1968; *b* 15 May 1928; *s* of late G. C. Maltby and Mrs Maltby (*née* Kingsnorth); *m* 1959, Jillian Winifred (*née* Burt); four *d*. *Educ:* Clayesmore Sch., Dorset; St John's Coll., Cambridge. BA Hons (History) 1950; MA. Schoolmaster: Dover Coll., 1951–58; Pocklington Sch., 1958–68. JP Ilkeston, 1980; DL Derbyshire, 1984. *Recreations:* squash, travel. *Address:* Westhorpe Drive, Long Eaton, Nottingham NG10 4BU. *T:* Nottingham 732737; (home) Nottingham 734550. *Clubs:* East India, Devonshire, Sports and Public Schools; Hawks (Cambridge).

MALTBY, John Newcombe; Executive Chairman, The Burmah Oil plc, since 1983; *b* 10 July 1928; *s* of Air Vice-Marshal Sir Paul Maltby, KCVO, KBE, CB, DSO, AFC, DL and Winifred Russell Paterson; *m* 1956, Lady Sylvia Veronica Anthea Harris, *d* of Earl of Malmesbury, *qv*; one *s* two *d*. *Educ:* Wellington Coll.; Clare Coll., Cambridge (MA Mech. Scis). Shell Internat. Petrolem, 1951–69; Founder and Man. Dir, Panocean Shipping & Terminals, 1969–75; Man. Dir, Panocean-Anco Ltd, 1975–79; Dir, The Burmah Oil plc, 1980–82, Dep. Chm., 1982–83. Dir, J. Bibby and Sons plc, 1984–. *Recreations:* history, gardening, sailing. *Address:* Broadford House, Stratfield Turgis, Basingstoke, Hants RG27 0AS. *Club:* Naval and Military.

MALVERN, 3rd Viscount *cr* 1955, of Rhodesia and of Bexley, Kent; **Ashley Kevin Godfrey Huggins;** *b* 26 Oct. 1949; *s* of 2nd Viscount Malvern, and of Patricia Marjorie, *d* of Frank Renwick-Bower, Durban, S Africa; *S* father, 1978. *Heir: uncle* Hon. (Martin) James Huggins, *b* 13 Jan. 1928.

MAMALONI, Solomon; MP (People's Alliance Party), 1977; Prime Minister of Solomon Islands, 1981–85; *b* 1943. *Educ:* King George VI School; Te-Aute College, NZ. Exec. Officer, Civil Service, later Clerk to Legislative Council; MP Makira, 1970–76, West

Makira, 1976–77; Chief Minister, British Solomon Islands, 1974–76; founder and leader, People's Progress Party (merged with Rural Alliance Party to form People's Alliance Party, 1979); Man. Dir, Patosha Co., 1977. *Address:* c/o Office of the Prime Minister, Honiara, Guadalcanal, Solomon Islands.

MAMBA, George Mbikwakhe; High Commissioner for the Kingdom of Swaziland to UK, since 1978; concurrently High Commissioner to Malta, Ambassador to Denmark, Sweden and Norway, and Permanent Delegate to UNESCO; *b* 5 July 1932; *s* of Ndabazebelungu Mamba and Getrude Mthwalose Mamba, and *g s* of late Chief Bokweni Mamba; *m* 1960, Sophie Sidzandza Sibande; three *s* two *d. Educ:* Franson Christian High Sch.; Swazi National High Sch.; Morija Teacher Trng Coll.; Cambridge Inst. of Educn; Nairobi Univ. Head Teacher, Makhonza Mission Sch., 1956–60; Teacher, Kwaluseni Central Sch., 1961–65; Head Teacher, Enkamheni Central Sch., 1966–67; Inspector of Schs, Manzini Dist, 1969–70; Welfare/Aftercare Officer, Prison Dept, 1971–72; Counsellor, Swaziland High Commn, Nairobi, 1972–77. Vice-Pres., Swaziland NUT, 1966–67. Field Comr, Swaziland Boy Scouts Assoc., 1967–68, Chief Comr, 1971–72. *Publication:* Children's Play, 1966. *Recreations:* scouting, reading. *Address:* Kingdom of Swaziland High Commission, 58 Pont Street, SW1. *T:* 01–581 4976.

MAMO, Sir Anthony (Joseph) Kt 1960; OBE 1955; *b* 9 Jan. 1909; *s* of late Joseph Mamo and late Carola (née Brincat); *m* 1939, Margaret Agius; one *s* two *d. Educ:* Royal Univ. of Malta. BA 1931; LLD 1934. Mem. Statute Law Revision Commn, 1936–42; Crown Counsel, 1942–51; Prof., Criminal Law, Malta Univ., 1943–57; Dep. Attorney-Gen., 1952–54, Attorney-Gen., 1955, Malta; Chief Justice and President, Court of Appeal, Malta, 1957–71; President, Constitutional Court, Malta, 1964–71; Governor-General, Malta, 1971–74; President, Republic of Malta, 1974–76. QC (Malta) 1957. Hon. DLitt Malta, 1969; Hon. LLD Libya, 1971. KStJ 1969. *Publications:* Lectures on Criminal Law and Criminal Procedure delivered at the University of Malta. *Address:* 49 Stella Maris Street, Sliema, Malta. *T:* 30708. *Club:* Casino (1852).

MAMOULIAN, Rouben; stage and screen director; producer; author; *b* 8 Oct. 1897; *s* of Zachary Mamoulian and Virginia Kalantarian; *m* Azadia Newman, Washington, DC. *Educ:* Lycée Montaigne, Paris; Gymnasium, Tiflis; Univ., Moscow. First English production, Beating on the Door, at St James's Theatre, London, Nov. 1922; arrived in Rochester, New York, Aug. 1923; from that date to summer of 1926 was Director of Production at the Eastman Theatre, producing Grand Operas, Operettas, Dramas, and stage presentations, among which were the following: Carmen, Faust, Boris Godounoff, Shanewis, Gilbert and Sullivan Operettas, Sister Beatrice, etc; also organised and was Director of the Eastman Theatre Sch.; came to New York at the end of 1926; started there as a Director of the Theatre Guild Sch.; first production of a play on Broadway, 10 Oct. 1927, Porgy, for the Theatre Guild; Porgy was followed by direction of the following plays on Broadway: Marco Millions, Congai, Wings over Europe, These Modern Women, RUR, The Game of Love and Death, A Month in the Country, A Farewell to Arms, and Solid South; also an opera at the Metropolitan Opera House, Hand of Fate, with L. Stokowski and the Philadelphia Orchestra; Opera Porgy and Bess (music by George Gershwin) for Theatre Guild, New York, 1935; in Los Angeles and San Francisco, 1938. Directed following motion pictures: Applause 1928; City Streets and Dr Jekyll and Mr Hyde, 1932; Love Me Tonight, and Song of Songs, 1933; Queen Christina, 1933 and We Live Again, 1934; Becky Sharp (Technicolor), 1935; The Gay Desperado, 1936; High, Wide and Handsome, 1937; Golden Boy, 1939; The Mark of Zorro, 1940; Blood and Sand (Technicolor), 1941; Rings on Her Fingers, 1942; Summer Holiday (technicolor musical, based on Eugene O'Neill's Ah Wilderness), 1947; Silk Stockings (musical film, cinemascope, color) 1957. *Stage productions:* Oklahoma!, 1943; Sadie Thompson, 1944, and Carousel, 1945, St Louis Woman, 1946, musical dramas in New York; Lost In The Stars (musical tragedy), 1949; Arms And The Girl (musical play), 1950, New York; Oklahoma! (for Berlin Arts Festival), 1951; Adolph Zukor's Golden Jubilee Celebration, Hollywood, 1953; Carousel (New Prod.), Los Angeles and San Francisco, 1953; Oklahoma!, new production for Paris, Rome, Milan, Naples and Venice, 1955. Co-Author (with Maxwell Anderson) of musical play The Devil's Hornpipe (made musical film Never Steal Anything Small), 1959. World Première Perf. of Shakespeare's Hamlet, A New Version, Lexington, Ky, 1966. Tributes and retrospective showings: NY, 1967, 1970, 1971; London, 1968; Montreal, Beverly Hills and Washington, 1970; Amer. Inst. for Advanced Studies, San Francisco, Toronto and Univs of Calif. at LA, S Florida and Yale, 1971; Hollywood, 1972; UCLA, Hollywood, Paris, San Sebastian, 1973; Washington DC, 1974; Univ. of California, Univ. of S California, 1975; Calif State Coll., 1976; Amer. Film Inst., 1976, 1977; Hollywood, N Carolina State Univ., 1977. Guest of Honour: Republics of Armenia and Georgia, 1971; Internat. Film Festivals, Moscow 1971, Iran 1974, Australia 1974, San Sebastian 1974, Boston 1976. Lectures, and appears on TV. Award of Excellence, Armenian Amer. Bicentennial Commemoration Cttee Inc., 1976. *Publications:* Abigayil, 1964; Hamlet Revised and Interpreted, 1965; contrib. Scoundrels and Scalawags, 1968; Ararat, 1969; Foreword to Chevalier, 1973. *Recreations:* swimming, horseback riding, and reading detective stories. *Address:* 1112 Schuyler Road, Beverly Hills, Calif 90210, USA.

MAN, Archdeacon of; *see* Willoughby, Ven. D. A.

MAN, Maj.-Gen. Christopher Mark Morrice, CB 1968; OBE 1958; MC 1945; retired; *b* 20 April 1914; *s* of late Rev. M. L. Man, MA, and late Evelyn Dora Man, Tenterden, Kent; *m* 1940, Georgina, *d* of late James Marr, Edinburgh; no *c. Educ:* Eastbourne Coll.; Emmanuel Coll., Cambridge. (MA). Lieut, Middlesex Regt, 1936; 1st Bn, The Middlesex Regt, 1937–45. Commanded Army Air Transport Training and Development Centre, 1953–55; GSO 1, WO, 1955–57; comdg Infantry Junior Leaders Battalion, 1957–59; comdg 125 Infantry Bde (TA), 1959–62; Head of Commonwealth Liaison Mission, UN Command, Korea and British Military Attaché, Seoul, 1962–64; GOC 49th Infantry Div. TA and N Midland District, 1964–67; Colonel, The Middlesex Regt, 1965–66; Pres., Regular Army Commn, 1967–69; Dep. Colonel The Queen's Regt, 1967–69, Hon. Colonel, 1970–71. Private, Atholl Highlanders, 1969. *Address:* The Clock Tower Flat, Blair Castle, Blair Atholl, Pitlochry, Perthshire PH18 5TL. *T:* Blair Atholl 452.

MANASSEH, Leonard Sulla, OBE 1982; RA 1979 (ARA 1976); FRIBA; Partner, Leonard Manasseh Partnership (formerly Leonard Manasseh & Partners), since 1950; *b* 21 May 1916; *s* of late Alan Manasseh and Esther (née Elias); *m* 1st, 1947 (marr diss. 1956); two *s*; 2nd, 1957, Sarah Delaforce; two *s* one *d. Educ:* Cheltenham College; The Architectural Assoc. Sch. of Architecture (AA Dip.). ARIBA 1941, FRIBA 1964; FSIA 1965; RWA 1972. Asst Architect, CRE N London and Guy Morgan & Partners; teaching staff, AA and Kingston Sch. of Art, 1941–43; Fleet Air Arm, 1943–46; Asst Architect, Herts CC, 1946–48; Senior Architect, Stevenage New Town Develt Corp., 1948–50; won Festival of Britain restaurant competition, 1950; started private practice, 1950; teaching staff, AA Sch. of Architecture, 1951–59; opened office in Singapore and Malaysia with James Cubitt & Partners (Cubitt Manasseh & Partners), 1953–54. Member: Council, Architectural Assoc., 1959–66 (Pres., 1964–65); Council of Industrial Design, 1965–68; Council, RIBA 1968–70, 1976–82 (Hon. Sec., 1979–81); Council, National Trust, 1977–; Ancient Monuments Bd, 1978–84; Bd, Chatham Historic Dockyard Trust, 1984–. Pres.,

Franco-British Union of Architects, 1978–79. FRSA 1967. *Work includes:* houses, housing and schools; industrial work; conservation plan for Beaulieu Estate; Nat. Motor Museum, Beaulieu; Wellington Country Park, Stratfield Saye; Pumping Station, Weymouth; British Museum refurbishment. *Publications:* Office Buildings (with 3rd Baron Cunliffe), 1962, Japanese edn 1964; Snowdon Summit Report (Countryside Commission), 1974; Eastbourne Harbour Study (Trustees, Chatsworth Settlement), 1976; (jtly) planning reports and studies. *Recreations:* photography, travel, sketching, watching aeroplanes, being optimistic. *Address:* 6 Bacon's Lane, Highgate, N6 6BL. *T:* 01–340 5528. *Club:* Athenæum.

MANBY, Mervyn Colet, CMG 1964; QPM 1961; retired; *b* 20 Feb. 1915; *s* of late Harold B. and Mary Manby (née Mills), late of Petistree, Suffolk; *m* 1949, Peggy Aronson, Eastern Cape, South Africa; one *s* one *d. Educ:* Bedford Sch., Bedford; Pembroke Coll., Oxford (MA). Colonial Police Service, 1937; Malaya, 1938–47; Basutoland, 1947–54; Kenya, 1954–64. Dep. Inspector General, Kenya Police, 1961–64; retired, 1964. United Nations Technical Assistance Adviser to Government of Iran, 1965–70; UN Div. of Narcotic Drugs, 1971–75; special consultant, UN Fund for Drug Abuse Control, 1975. Mem. Council, Inst. for Study of Drug Dependence, 1975–78. *Address:* Old Well Cottage, Barham, Canterbury, Kent CT4 6PB. *T:* Canterbury 381369.

MANCE, Jonathan Hugh, QC 1982; barrister; *b* 6 June 1943; *e s* of late Sir Henry Stenhouse Mance and of Lady (Joan Erica Robertson) Mance; *m* 1973, Mary Howarth Arden; one *s* two *d. Educ:* Charterhouse; University Coll., Oxford (MA). Called to the Bar, Middle Temple, 1965. Worked in Germany, 1965. *Publications:* (asst editor) Chalmer's Sale of Goods, 1981; (ed jtly) Sale of Goods, Halsbury's Laws of England, 4th edn 1983. *Recreations:* tennis, languages, music. *Address:* 11 Frognal Lane, NW3 7DG. *T:* 01–794 8011. *Club:* Cumberland Lawn Tennis.

MANCHAM, Sir James Richard Marie, KBE 1976; international trade consultant, since 1981; President, Republic of the Seychelles, 1976–77 (Prime Minister of Seychelles, 1975–76; Chief Minister, 1970–75); *b* 11 Aug. 1939; adopted British nationality, 1984; *e s* of late Richard Mancham and Evelyne Mancham, MBE (née Tirant); *m* 1963, Heather Jean Evans (marr. diss. 1974); one *s* one *d; m* 1985, Catherine Olsen; one *s. Educ:* Seychelles Coll.; Wilson Coll., London. Called to Bar, Middle Temple, 1961. Auditeur Libre à la Faculté de Droit ès Sciences Economiques, Univ. of Paris, 1962; Internat. Inst. of Labour Studies Study Course, Geneva, Spring 1968. Legal practice, Supreme Court of Seychelles. Seychelles Democratic Party (SDP), Pres. 1964; Mem. Seychelles Governing Council, 1967; Leader of Majority Party (SDP), 1967; Mem., Seychelles Legislative Assembly, 1970–76; led SDP to Seychelles Constitutional Conf., London, 1970 and 1976. Founder, Seychelles Weekly, 1962. Lecturer, 1981, on struggle for power in Indian Ocean, to US and Eur. univs and civic gps. Hon. Citizen: Dade County, Florida, 1963; New Orleans, 1965. FRSA 1968. Cert. of Merit for Distinguished Contribn to Poetry, Internat. Who's Who in Poetry, 1974. Officier de la Légion d'Honneur, 1976; Grande Médaille de la Francophonie, 1976; Grande médaille vermeille, Paris, 1976; Quaid-i-Azam Medallion (Pakistan), 1976; Gold Medal for Tourism, Mexico, 1977; Gold Medal of Chamber of Commerce and Industries of France, 1977; Gold Medal des Excellences Européennes, 1977. *Publications:* Reflections and Echoes from Seychelles, 1972 (poetry); L'Air des Seychelles, 1974; Island Splendour, 1980; Paradise Raped, 1983; Galloo - The undiscovered paradise, 1984; New York's Robin Island, 1985. *Recreations:* travel, water sports, tennis, writing. *Address:* c/o Lloyds Bank, 81 Edgware Road, W2 2HY. *Clubs:* Royal Automobile, Annabel's, Les Ambassadeurs, Wig and Pen; El Morocco, Intrepids (NY); Régine (Paris); Griffin (Geneva).

MANCHESTER, 12th Duke of, *cr* 1719; **Angus Charles Drogo Montagu;** Baron Montagu, Viscount Mandeville, 1620; Earl of Manchester, 1626; *b* 9 Oct. 1938; *yr s* of 10th Duke of Manchester, OBE, and Nell Vere (*d* 1966), *d* of Sydney Vere Stead, Melbourne; *S* brother, 1985; *m* 1st, 1961, Mary Eveleen (marr. diss. 1970), *d* of Walter Gillespie McClure; two *s* one *d*; 2nd, 1971, Diane Pauline (marr. diss. 1985), *d* of Arthur Plimsaul. *Educ:* Gordonstoun. *Heir: s* Viscount Mandeville, *qv*.

MANCHESTER, Bishop of, since 1979; **Rt. Rev. Stanley Eric Francis Booth-Clibborn;** *b* 20 Oct. 1924; *s* of Eric and Lucille Booth-Clibborn; *m* 1958, Anne Roxburgh Forrester, *d* of late Rev. William Roxburgh Forrester, MC; two *s* two *d. Educ:* Highgate School; Oriel Coll., Oxford (MA); Westcott House, Cambridge. Served RA, 1942–45; Royal Indian Artillery, 1945–47, Temp. Captain. Curate, Heeley Parish Church, Sheffield, 1952–54, The Attercliffe Parishes, Sheffield, 1954–56; Training Sec., Christian Council of Kenya, 1956–63; Editor-in-Chief, East African Venture Newspapers, Nairobi, 1963–67; Leader, Lincoln City Centre Team Ministry, 1967–70; Vicar, St Mary the Great, University Church, Cambridge, 1970–79. Hon. Canon, Ely Cathedral, 1976–79. Member: Div. of Internat. Affairs, BCC, 1968–80; BCC delegn to Namibia, 1981. Moderator, Movement for Ordination of Women, 1979–82. Introduced to House of Lords, 1985. *Recreations:* photography, tennis, listening to music. *Address:* Bishopscourt, Bury New Road, Manchester M7 0LE. *T:* 061–792 2096/1779. *Club:* Royal Commonwealth Society.

MANCHESTER, Dean of; *see* Waddington, Very Rev. R. M.

MANCHESTER, Archdeacon of; *see* Harris, Ven. R. B.

MANCHESTER, William; author; Purple Heart (US) 1945; Fellow, East College, since 1968, writer in residence since 1974, Adjunct Professor of History since 1979, Wesleyan University; *b* 1 April 1922; *s* of William Raymond Manchester and Sallie E. R. (née Thompson); *m* 1948, Julia Brown Marshall; one *s* two *d. Educ:* Springfield Classical High School; Univ. of Massachusetts; Dartmouth Coll., NH; Univ. of Missouri. Served US Marine Corps, 1942–45. Reporter, Daily Oklahoman, 1945–46; Reporter, foreign corresp., war corresp., Baltimore Sun, 1947–55; Man. editor, Wesleyan Univ. Publications, 1955–65; Fellow, Center for Advanced Studies, 1959–60, Lectr in English, 1968–69, Wesleyan Univ. Trustee, Friends of Univ. of Massachusetts Library, 1970–76, Pres., 1970–72; Mem., Soc. of Amer. Historians. Guggenheim Fellow, 1959; Dr of Humane Letters: Univ. of Mass, 1965; Univ. of New Haven, 1979; Dag Hammarskjold Internat. Prize in Literature, 1967; Overseas Press Club (New York) Award for Best Book of the Year on Foreign Affairs, 1968; Univ. of Missouri Medal, 1969; Connecticut Book Award, 1974; President's Cabinet Award, Detroit Univ., 1981; Frederick S. Troy Medal, 1981; McConaughy Award, 1981; Distinguished Public Service Award, Conn Bar Assoc., 1985. *Publications:* Disturber of the Peace, 1951 (publ. UK as The Sage of Baltimore, 1952); The City of Anger, 1953; Shadow of the Monsoon, 1956; Beard the Lion, 1958; A Rockefeller Family Portrait, 1959; The Long Gainer, 1961; Portrait of a President, 1962; The Death of a President, 1967; The Arms of Krupp, 1968; The Glory and the Dream, 1974; Controversy and other Essays in Journalism, 1976; American Caesar, 1978; Goodbye, Darkness, 1980; The Last Lion, vol. 1, Visions of Glory, 1983; One Brief Shining Moment, 1983; contrib. to Encyclopedia Britannica and to periodicals. *Recreation:* photography. *Address:* Wesleyan University, Middletown, Conn 06457, USA. *T:* 203–347–9422, ext. 2388. *Clubs:* Century, Williams (New York), University (Hartford).

MANCROFT, family name of **Baron Mancroft.**

MANCROFT, 2nd Baron, *cr* 1937, of Mancroft in the City of Norwich; Bt, *cr* 1932; **Stormont Mancroft Samuel Mancroft;** KBE 1959 (MBE 1945); TD 1950; MA; Chairman, British Greyhound Racing Board, 1977–85; *b* 27 July 1914; *s* of 1st Baron and Phœbe (*d* 1969), 2nd *d* of Alfred Chune Fletcher, MRCS; *S* father, 1942; *m* 1951, Mrs Diana Elizabeth Quarry, *o d* of Lieut-Colonel Horace Lloyd; one *s* two *d*. *Educ:* Winchester; Christ Church, Oxford. Called to Bar, Inner Temple, 1938; Member of Bar Council, 1947–51; Member St Marylebone Borough Council, 1947–53; a Lord in Waiting to the Queen, 1952–54; Parliamentary Under-Secretary for Home Dept, Oct. 1954–Jan. 1957; Parliamentary Secretary, Min. of Defence, Jan.-June 1957; Minister without Portfolio, June 1957–Oct. 1958, resigned. Dir, GUS, 1958–66; Dep. Chm., Cunard Line Ltd, 1966–71; Chm., Horserace Totalisator Bd, 1972–76; Mem., Council on Tribunals, 1972–80; President: The Institute of Marketing, 1959–63; St Marylebone Conservative Assoc., 1961–67; London Tourist Board, 1963–73. Served RA (TA), 1939–46; Lieut-Colonel (despatches twice, MBE); commissioned TA, 1938; rejoined TA 1947–55. Hon. Col Comdt, RA, 1970–80. Croix de Guerre. *Publications:* Booking the Cooks (essays from Punch), 1969; A Chinaman in My Bath, 1974; Bees in some Bonnets, 1979. *Heir: s* Hon. Benjamin Lloyd Stormont Mancroft, *b* 16 May 1957. *Address:* 29 Margaretta Terrace, SW3 5NU. *T:* 01–352 7674. *Clubs:* Pratt's; West Ham Boys.

MANDELSON, Peter Benjamin; Director of Campaigns and Communications, Labour Party, since 1985; *b* 21 Oct. 1953; *s* of George Mandelson and Mary (*née* Morrison). *Educ:* Hendon County Grammar Sch.; St Catherine's Coll., Oxford (Hons degree, PPE). Econ. Dept, TUC, 1977–78; Chm., British Youth Council, 1978–80; producer, LWT, 1982–85. Mem. Council, London Bor. of Lambeth, 1979–82. *Publications:* Youth Unemployment: causes and cures, 1977; Broadcasting and Youth, 1980. *Recreations:* swimming, country walking. *Address:* 1 Brick End, Foy, Ross-on-Wye, Herefordshire HR9 6QZ. *T:* Ross-on-Wye 62981.

MANDELSTAM, Prof. Joel; FRS 1971; Iveagh Professor of Microbiology, and Fellow of Linacre College, University of Oxford, 1966–Sept. 1987, Emeritus Fellow from Sept. 1987; *b* S Africa, 13 Nov. 1919; *s* of Leo and Fanny Mandelstam; *m* 1954, Dorothy Hillier; one *s* one *d*; *m* 1975, Mary Maureen Dale. *Educ:* Jeppe High Sch., Johannesburg; University of Witwatersrand; Queen Elizabeth Coll., London. Lecturer, Medical Sch., Johannesburg, 1947; Scientific Staff, Nat. Institute for Med. Research, London, 1952–66. Fulbright Fellow, US, 1958–59; Vis. Prof., Univ. of Adelaide, 1971. Mem., ARC, 1973–83. Leewenhoek Lectr, Royal Soc., 1975. Editorial Board, Biochemical Journal, 1960–66. *Publications:* Biochemistry of Bacterial Growth (with K. McQuillen), 1968; articles in journals and books on microbial biochemistry. *Address:* Microbiology Unit, Department of Biochemistry, South Parks Road, Oxford. *T:* Oxford 56733; (from Sept. 1987) 13 Cherwell Lodge, Water Eaton Road, Oxford OX2 7QN.

MANDELSTAM, Prof. Stanley, FRS 1962; Professor of Physics, University of California. *Educ:* University of the Witwatersrand, Johannesburg, Transvaal, South Africa (BSc); Trinity Coll., Cambridge (BA). PhD, Birmingham. Formerly Professor of Math. Physics, University of Birmingham; Prof. Associé, Univ. de Paris Sud, 1979–80 and 1984–85. *Publications:* (with W. Yourgrau) Variational Principles in Dynamics and Quantum Theory, 1955 (revised edn, 1956); papers in learned journals. *Address:* Department of Physics, University of California, Berkeley, California 94720, USA.

MANDER, Sir Charles (Marcus), 3rd Bt, *cr* 1911; Underwriting Member of Lloyd's; Director: Manders (Holdings) Ltd, 1951–58; Mander Brothers Ltd, 1948–58; Headstaple Ltd, since 1977; Chairman, London & Cambridge Investments Ltd, since 1984; *b* 22 Sept. 1921; *o s* of Sir Charles Arthur Mander, 2nd Bart, and late Monica Claire Cotterill, *d* of G. H. Neame; *S* father, 1951; *m* 1945, Maria Dolores Beatrice, *d* of late Alfred Brodermann, Hamburg; two *s* one *d*. *Educ:* Eton Coll., Windsor; Trinity Coll., Cambridge. Commissioned Coldstream Guards, 1942; served War of 1939–45, Canal Zone, 1943; Italy, 1943, Germany, 1944; War Office (ADC to Lieut-General R. G. Stone, CB), 1945. Chm., Arlington Securities Ltd, 1977–83. High Sheriff of Staffordshire, 1962–63. *Recreations:* shooting, music. *Heir: s* Charles Nicholas Mander [*b* 23 March 1950; *m* 1972, Karin Margareta, *d* of Arne Norin; three *s* one *d*]. *Address:* Little Barrow, Moreton-in-Marsh, Glos. *T:* Cotswold 30265; Greville House, Kinnerton Street, SW1. *T:* 01–235 1669. *Clubs:* Boodle's; Royal Thames Yacht.

MANDER, Michael Harold; His Honour Judge Mander; a Circuit Judge, since 1985; *b* 27 Oct. 1936; *e s* of late Harold and Ann Mander; *m* 1960, Janis Mary Dodd, *er d* of late Revd Charles and Edna Dodd. *Educ:* Workington Grammar School; Queen's College, Oxford (BA, 2nd cl. hons Jurisp.; Rigg Exbnr). Nat. Service, RA (2nd Lieut) to 1957. Articled clerk; solicitor, 2nd cl. hons, 1963; called to the Bar, Inner Temple, 1972. Asst Recorder, 1982–85. Dep. Chm., Agricultural Lands Tribunal, 1983–85. *Recreation:* life under the Wrekin. *Address:* Garmston, Eaton Constantine, Shrewsbury SY5 6RL. *T:* Cressage 288. *Clubs:* East India; Wrekin Rotary (Hon. Mem.).

MANDER, Noel Percy, MBE 1979; FSA; Managing Director, N. P. Mander Ltd, since 1946; *b* 19 May 1912; *s* of late Percy Mander and Emily Pike, Hoxne, Suffolk; *m* 1948, Enid Watson; three *s* two *d*. *Educ:* Haberdashers Aske's Sch., Hatcham. Organ building from 1930, interrupted by war service with RA (Hampshire Bde) in N Africa, Italy and Syria, 1940–46. FSA 1974. Mem., Nat. Council of Christians and Jews (former Chm., N London Council). Governor, Sir John Cass Foundn. Liveryman, Musicians' Co.; Past Master, Parish Clerks' Co. of City of London; Mem., Art Workers' Guild. Churchill Life Fellow, Westminster Coll., Fulton, 1982; Hon. Dr Arts Westminster Coll., 1984. Builder of Winston Churchill Meml Organ, Fulton, Missouri, and organs in many parts of world; organ builder to St Paul's Cathedral London and Canterbury Cathedral, and to HM Sultan of Oman. *Publications:* St Lawrence Jewry, A History of the Organs from the Earliest Times to the Present Day, 1956; St Vedast, Foster Lane, A History of the Organs from Earliest Times to the Present Day, 1961; St Vedast Foster Lane, in the City of London: a history of the 13 United Parishes, 1973; (with C. M. Houghton) St Botolph Aldgate: a history of the organs from the Restoration to the Twentieth Century, 1973. *Recreations:* archaeology, horology, reading. *Address:* The Street, Earl Soham, Woodbridge, Suffolk. *T:* Earl Soham 312; The Lodge, St Peter's Organ Works, St Peter's Close, E2 7AF. *T:* 01–739 4746. *Club:* Savage.

MANDER, Lady (Rosalie), (R. Glynn Grylls), MA Oxon; Biographer; Lecturer; Cornish ancestry; *m* 1930, Sir Geoffrey Mander (*d* 1962), sometime MP for East Wolverhampton; one *d* (and one *s* decd). *Educ:* Queen's Coll., Harley Street, London; Lady Margaret Hall, Oxford. Lectures frequently in USA. *Publications:* Mary Shelley, 1936; Trelawny, 1950; Portrait of Rossetti, 1965; Mrs Browning, 1980. *Address:* Wightwick Manor, Wolverhampton, Staffs; 35 Buckingham Gate, SW1.

MANDEVILLE, Viscount; Alexander Charles David Drogo Montagu; *b* 11 Dec. 1962; *s* and *heir* of 12th Duke of Manchester, *qv*.

MANDI, Lt-Col Raja (Sir) Joginder Sen Bahadur of; KCSI 1931; *b* 20 Aug. 1904; *s* of late Mian Kishan Singh; *m* 1930, *d* of late Kanwar Prithiraj Sinhji, Rajpipla; two *s* two *d*. *Educ:* Queen Mary's Coll. and Aitchison Coll., Lahore. Ascended Gadi, 1913; full ruler, 1925. Visited various countries. Ambassador of Republic of India to Brazil, 1952–56; Member of Lok Sabha, 1957–62. Hon. Lt-Col 3rd/17th Dogra Regt and Bengal Sappers and Miners. *Address:* Bhawani Palace, Mandi, Mandi District (HP) 175001, India.

MANDUELL, John, CBE 1982; FRAM, FRCM, FRNCM, FRSAMD; composer; Principal, Royal Northern College of Music, since 1971; *b* 2 March 1928; *s* of Matthewman Donald Manduell, MC, MA, and Theodora (*née* Tharp); *m* 1955, Renna Kellaway; three *s* one *d*. *Educ:* Haileybury Coll.; Jesus Coll., Cambridge; Royal Acad. of Music. FRAM 1964; FRNCM 1974; FRCM 1980; FRSAMD 1982; Hon. FTCL 1973. BBC: music producer, 1956–61; Head of Music, Midlands and E Anglia, 1961–64; Chief Planner, The Music Programme, 1964–68; Univ. of Lancaster: Dir of Music, 1968–71; Mem. Court and Council, 1972–77, 1979–. Prog. Dir, Cheltenham Festival, 1969–. Arts Council: Mem. Council, 1976–78, 1980–84; Mem. Music Panel, 1971–76, Dep. Chm., 1976–78, Chm., 1980–84; Mem. Touring Cttee, 1975–80, Chm., 1976–78; Mem. Trng Cttee, 1973–77. Mem. Music Adv. Cttee, British Council, 1963–72, Chm., 1973–80; Chm. Music Panel, North West Arts, 1973–79; Chm., British Arts Fests Assoc., 1981– (Vice-Chm., 1977–81); European Music Year (1985): Dep. Chm. UK Cttee, 1982–85; Member: Eur. Organising Cttee, 1982–86; Eur. Exec. Bureau, 1982–86; Internat. Prog. Cttee, 1982–84; Mem. Exec. Cttee, Composers' Guild of GB, 1984–; Gulbenkian Foundn Enquiry into Trng Musicians; Governor: Chetham's Sch., 1971–; National Youth Orch., 1964–73, 1978–; President: Lakeland Sinfonia, 1972–; Jubilate Choir, 1979–; Director: London Opera Centre, 1971–79; Associated Bd of Royal Schools of Music, 1971–; Northern Ballet Theatre, 1973–; Manchester Palace Theatre Trust, 1978–; London Orchestral Concert Bd, 1980–; Lake Dist Summer Music, 1984–. Hon. Member: Roy. Soc. of Musicians, 1972; Chopin Soc. of Warsaw, 1973. Engagements and tours as composer, conductor and lectr in Canada, Europe, Hong Kong, S Africa and USA. Chairman: BBC TV Young Musicians of the Year, 1978, 1980; Munich Internat. Music Comp., 1982, 1984, 1985; Chm. or mem., national and internat. music competition juries. FRSA 1981; Fellow, Manchester Polytechnic, 1983. First Leslie Boosey Award, Royal Phil. Soc. and PRS, 1980. *Publications:* (contrib.) The Symphony, ed Simpson, 1966; *compositions:* Overture, Sunderland Point, 1969; Diversions for Orchestra, 1970; String Quartet, 1976; Prayers from the Ark, 1981; Double Concerto, 1985. *Recreations:* cricket; travel; French life, language and literature. *Address:* Royal Northern College of Music, Oxford Road, Manchester M13 9RD. *T:* 061–273 6283.

MANGHAM, Maj.-Gen. William Desmond, CB 1978; Director, The Brewers' Society, since 1980; *b* 29 Aug. 1924; *s* of late Lt-Col William Patrick Mangham and Margaret Mary Mangham (*née* Donnachie); *m* 1960, Susan, *d* of late Col Henry Brabazon Humfrey; two *s* two *d*. *Educ:* Ampleforth College. 2nd Lieut RA, 1943; served India, Malaya, 1945–48; BMRA 1st Div. Egypt, 1955; Staff, HQ Middle East, Cyprus, 1956–58; Instructor, Staff Coll., Camberley and Canada, 1962–65; OC 3rd Regt Royal Horse Artillery, 1966–68; Comdr RA 2nd Div., 1969–70; Royal Coll. of Defence Studies, 1971; Chief of Staff, 1st British Corps, 1972–74; GOC 2nd Div., 1974–75; VQMG, MoD, 1976–79. Colonel Commandant: RA, 1979–; RHA, 1983–. *Recreations:* shooting, golf, tennis. *Address:* 42 Portman Square, W1H 0BB. *Club:* Army and Navy.

MANGO, Prof. Cyril Alexander, FBA 1976; Bywater and Sotheby Professor of Byzantine and Modern Greek, Oxford University, since 1973; *b* 14 April 1928; *s* of Alexander A. Mango and Adelaide Damonov; *m* 1st, 1953, Mabel Grover; one *d*; 2nd, 1964, Susan A. Gerstel; one *d*; 3rd, 1976, Maria C. Mundell. *Educ:* Univ. of St Andrews (MA); Univ. of Paris (Dr Univ Paris). From Jun. Fellow to Lectr in Byzantine Archaeology, Dumbarton Oaks Byzantine Center, Harvard Univ., 1951–63; Lectr in Fine Arts, Harvard Univ., 1957–58; Visiting Associate Prof. of Byzantine History, Univ. of California, Berkeley, 1960–61; Koraës Prof. of Modern Greek and of Byzantine History, Language and Literature, King's Coll., Univ. of London, 1963–68; Prof. of Byzantine Archaeology, Dumbarton Oaks Byzantine Center, 1968–73. FSA. *Publications:* The Homilies of Photius, 1958; The Brazen House, 1959; The Mosaics of St Sophia at Istanbul, 1962; The Art of the Byzantine Empire, Sources and Documents, 1972; Architettura bizantina, 1974; Byzantium, 1980; Byzantium and its Image, 1984; Le Développement Urbain de Constantinople, 1985. *Address:* Exeter College, Oxford.

MANGOLD, Thomas Cornelius; Reporter, BBC TV Panorama, since 1976; *b* 20 Aug. 1934; *s* of Fritz Mangold and Dorothea Mangold; *m* 1972, Valerie Ann Hare (*née* Dean); three *d*. *Educ:* Dorking Grammar Sch. Reporter, Croydon Advertiser, 1952. Served RA, 1952–54. Reporter: Croydon Advertiser, 1955–59; Sunday Pictorial, 1959–62; Daily Express, 1962–64; BBC TV News, 1964–70; BBC TV 24 Hours, later Midweek, 1970–76. *Publications:* (jtly) The File on the Tsar, 1976; (jtly) The Tunnels of Cu Chi, 1985. *Recreations:* writing, playing Blues harp. *Address:* c/o BBC TV, Lime Grove, W12. *T:* 01–743 8000. *Club:* Stocks.

MANGWAZU, Timon Sam, MA Oxon; Group Managing Director, Press (Holdings) Ltd, 1980 (Deputy Managing Director, 1978–80); Chairman, National Bank of Malaŵi, since 1980; *b* 12 Oct. 1933; *s* of Sam Isaac Mangwazu, Farmer; *m* 1958, Nelly Kathewera; three *s* three *d*. *Educ:* Ruskin Coll., Oxford; Brasenose Coll., Oxford (BA; MA 1976). Teacher at Methodist Sch., Hartley, S Rhodesia, 1955; Clerical Officer, Government Print, Agricultural Dept and Accountant General's Dept, 1956–62; Asst Registrar of Trade Unions, Ministry of Labour, 1962–63; Malaŵi Ambassador, West Germany, Norway, Sweden, Denmark, Netherlands, Belgium, Switzerland and Austria, 1964–67; High Comr in London for Republic of Malaŵi, and Ambassador to Belgium, Portugal, Netherlands and Holy See, 1967–69; Brasenose Coll., Oxford, 1969–72; Malaŵi Ambassador to EEC, Belgium and the Netherlands, 1973–78. Mem. Council, Univ. of Malaŵi; Chm., Bd of Governors, Malaŵi Polytechnic. *Recreation:* fishing. *Address:* Press (Holdings) Ltd, PO Box 30238, Capital City, Lilongwe 3, Malaŵi.

MANHOOD, Harold Alfred; Writer; *b* 6 May 1904; *m* 1937. *Educ:* Elementary Schooling. *Publications:* Nightseed, 1928; Gay Agony (novel), 1930; Apples by Night, 1932; Crack of Whips, 1934; Fierce and Gentle, 1935; Sunday Bugles, 1939; Lunatic Broth, 1944 (collections of short stories); Selected Stories, 1947; A Long View of Nothing (short stories), 1953. *Address:* Holmbush, near Henfield, W Sussex.

MANKIEWICZ, Joseph Leo; American writer and film director; *b* 11 Feb. 1909; *s* of Frank Mankiewicz and Johanna (*née* Blumenau); *m* 1939, Rosa Stradner (*d* 1958); two *s* (and one *s* by previous marriage); *m* 1962, Rosemary Matthews; one *d*. *Educ:* Columbia Univ. (AB 1928). Has written, directed and produced for the screen, 1929–. President, Screen Directors' Guild of America, 1950. Films include: Manhattan Melodrama, Fury, Three Comrades, Philadelphia Story, Woman of the Year, Keys of the Kingdom, A Letter to Three Wives (Academy Awards for Best Screenplay and Best Direction), No Way Out, All About Eve (Academy Awards for Best Screenplay and Best Direction), People Will Talk, Five Fingers, Julius Caesar, The Barefoot Contessa, Guys and Dolls; The Quiet American; Suddenly Last Summer; The Honey Pot; There Was a Crooked Man; Sleuth. Directed La Bohème for Metropolitan Opera, 1952. Formed own company, Figaro Inc., 1953, dissolved 1961. Fellow, Yale Univ., 1979–. Work in progress on The Performing

Woman (when and how women came to perform the roles of women on the stages of the Western theatre). Received Screen Directors' Guild Award, 1949 and 1950; Screen Writers' Guild Award for best American comedy, 1949 and 1950; Laurel Award, Writers Guild of America, 1963; D. W. Griffith Award, Directors Guild of America, for Lifetime Achievement, 1986. Erasmus Award, City of Rotterdam, 1984. Order of Merit (Italy), 1965; Hon. Citizen of Avignon (France), 1980. *Address:* Guard Hill Road, Bedford, NY 10506, USA.

MANKOWITZ, Wolf; author; Honorary Consul to the Republic of Panama in Dublin, 1971; *b* 7 Nov. 1924; *s* of Solomon and Rebecca Mankowitz; *m* 1944, Ann Margaret Seligmann; four *s*. *Educ:* East Ham Grammar Sch.; Downing Coll., Cambridge (MA, English Tripos). Adjunct Prof. of English, Univ. of New Mexico, 1982–86. *Publications: novels:* Make Me An Offer, 1952; A Kid for Two Farthings, 1953; Laugh Till You Cry, 1955 (USA); My Old Man's a Dustman, 1956; Cockatrice, 1963; The Biggest Pig in Barbados, 1965; Penguin Wolf Mankowitz, 1967; Raspberry Reich, 1979; ¡ Abracadabra !, 1980; The Devil in Texas, 1984; *short stories:* The Mendelman Fire, 1957; The Blue Arabian Nights, 1973; The Day of the Women and The Night of the Men (fables), 1977; *histories:* Wedgwood, 1953, 3rd repr. 1980; The Portland Vase, 1953; An Encyclopaedia of English Pottery and Porcelain, 1957; *biography:* Dickens of London, 1976; The Extraordinary Mr Poe, 1978; Mazeppa, 1982; *poetry:* 12 Poems, 1971; *plays:* The Bespoke Overcoat and Other Plays, 1955; Expresso Bongo (musical), 1958–59; Make Me An Offer (musical), 1959; Belle, 1961 (musical); Pickwick, 1963 (musical); Passion Flower Hotel (musical), 1965; The Samson Riddle, 1972; Stand and Deliver! (musical), 1972; The Irish Hebrew Lesson, 1978; Samson and Delilah, 1978; Casanova's Last Stand, 1980; Iron Butterflies, 1986; *films:* Make Me An Offer, 1954; A Kid for Two Farthings, 1954; The Bespoke Overcoat, 1955; Expresso Bongo, 1960; The Millionairess, 1960; The Long and The Short and The Tall, 1961; The Day the Earth Caught Fire, 1961; The Waltz of the Toreadors, 1962; Where The Spies Are, 1965; Casino Royale, 1967; The Assassination Bureau, 1969; Bloomfield, 1970; Black Beauty, 1971; Treasure Island, 1972; The Hebrew Lesson (wrote and dir.), 1972; The Hireling, 1973; Almonds and Raisins (a treatment of Yiddish films, 1929–39), 1984; *television:* Dickens of London, 1976. *Recreation:* sleeping. *Address:* The Bridge House, Ahakista, Co. Cork. *T:* Kilcrohane 11. *Club:* Savile.

MANKTELOW, Rt. Rev. Michael Richard John; *see* Basingstoke, Bishop Suffragan of.

MANLEY, Ivor Thomas, CB 1984; Deputy Secretary, Department of Energy, since 1981; *b* 4 March 1931; *s* of Frederick Stone and Louisa Manley; *m* 1952, Joan Waite; one *s* one *d*. *Educ:* Sutton High Sch., Plymouth. Entered Civil Service, 1951; Principal: Min. of Aviation, 1964–66; Min. of Technology, 1966–68; Private Secretary: to Rt Hon. Anthony Wedgwood Benn, 1968–70; to Rt Hon. Geoffrey Rippon, 1970; Principal Private Sec. to Rt Hon. John Davies, 1970–71; Asst Sec., DTI, 1971–74; Department of Energy: Under-Sec., Principal Estabt Officer, 1974–78, Under Sec., Atomic Energy Div., 1978–81. UK Governor, IAEA, 1978–81; Mem., UKAEA, 1981–86. *Recreations:* walking, reading. *Address:* 28 Highfield Avenue, Aldershot, Hants GU11 3BZ. *T:* Aldershot 22707.

MANLEY, Hon. Michael Norman; Leader of the Opposition, Jamaican Parliament, 1969–72, and since 1980; President, People's National Party, Jamaica, since 1969 (Member, Executive, since 1952); MP for Central Kingston, Jamaica, since 1967; President, National Workers Union, since 1984; *b* St Andrew, Jamaica, 10 Dec. 1924; *s* of late Rt Excellent Norman W. Manley, QC, and of Edna Manley (*née* Swithenbank); *m* 1972, Beverly Anderson; one *s* one *d*; one *s* two *d* by previous marriages. *Educ:* Jamaica Coll.; London Sch. of Economics (BSc Econ Hons). Began as freelance journalist, working with BBC, 1950–51; returned to Jamaica, Dec. 1951, as Associate Editor of Public Opinion, 1952–53; Sugar Supervisor, Nat. Workers' Union, 1953–54; Island Supervisor and First Vice-Pres., 1955–72; Mem. Senate, 1962–67; Prime Minister of Jamaica, 1972–80. Has held various posts in Labour cttees and in Trade Union affairs; organised strike in sugar industry, 1959, which led to Goldenberg Commn of Inquiry. Vice-Pres., Socialist Internat., 1978. Hon. Doctor of Laws Morehouse Coll., Atlanta, 1973. UN Special Award for contrib. to struggle against apartheid, 1978; Joliot Curie Medal, World Peace Council, 1979. Order of the Liberator, Venezuela, 1973; Order of Mexican Eagle, 1975; Order of Jose Marti, Cuba, 1975. *Publications:* The Politics of Change, 1974; A Voice at the Workplace, 1976; The Search for Solutions, 1977; Jamaica: Struggle in the Periphery, 1982. *Recreations:* sports, music, gardening, reading. *Address:* 89 Old Hope Road, Kingston 6, Jamaica.

MANN, Bruce Leslie Home D.; *see* Douglas-Mann.

MANN, Eric John; Controller, Capital Taxes Office, 1978–81; *b* 18 Dec. 1921; *s* of Percival John Mann and Marguerite Mann; *m* 1960, Gwendolen Margaret Salter; one *s* one *d*. *Educ:* University Coll. Sch., Hampstead; Univ. of London (LLB). Entered Inland Revenue, 1946; Dep. Controller, Capital Taxes Office, 1974. *Publications:* (ed jtly) Green's Death Duties, 5th-7th edns, 1962–71. *Address:* Lawn Gate Cottage, Moccas, Herefordshire HR2 9LF.

MANN, Dr Felix Bernard; medical practitioner; *b* 10 April 1931; *s* of Leo and Caroline Mann. *Educ:* Shrewsbury House; Malvern Coll.; Christ's Coll., Cambridge; Westminster Hosp. MB, BChir, LMCC. Practised medicine or studied acupuncture in England, Canada, Switzerland, France, Germany, Austria and China. Founder, Medical Acupuncture Soc. *Publications:* Acupuncture; the ancient Chinese art of healing, 1962, 2nd edn 1971; The Treatment of Disease by Acupuncture, 1963; The Meridians of Acupuncture, 1964; Atlas of Acupuncture, 1966; Acupuncture: cure of many diseases, 1971; Scientific Aspects of Acupuncture, 1977; also edns in Italian, Spanish, Dutch, Finnish, Portuguese, German, Japanese and Swedish; contrib. various jls on acupuncture. *Recreations:* walking in the country and mountains. *Address:* 15 Devonshire Place, W1N 1PB. *T:* 01–935 7575. *Club:* Royal Society of Medicine.

MANN, (Francis) George, CBE 1983; DSO 1942; MC 1941; Director, 1977–87, and non-executive Deputy Chairman, 1980–86, Extel Group; *b* 6 Sept. 1917; *s* of Frank Mann and Enid Mann (*née* Tilney); *m* 1949, Margaret Hildegarde (*née* Marshall Clark); three *s* one *d*. *Educ:* Eton; Cambridge Univ. BA. Served War of 1939–45, Scots Guards (DSO, MC). Director: Mann Crossman and Paulin, Watney Mann, Watney Mann and Truman Brewers, 1946–77. Middlesex County Cricket Club: first played, 1937; Captain, 1948–49; Pres., 1983–87; captained England in SA, 1948–49 and against NZ, 1949. Chairman: TCCB, 1978–83; Cricket Council, 1983. *Address:* The Old Rectory, West Woodhay, Newbury, Berks. *T:* Inkpen 243. *Club:* MCC (Pres., 1984–85).

MANN, Frederick (Francis) Alexander, CBE 1980; FBA 1974; LLD, DrJur; Solicitor of the Supreme Court, since 1946; Partner, Herbert Smith & Co., 1957–83, now Consultant; Hon. Professor of Law in the University of Bonn, since 1960; *b* 11 Aug. 1907; *s* of Richard Mann and Ida (*née* Oppenheim); *m* 1933, Eleonore (*née* Ehrlich) (*d* 1980); one *s* two *d*. *Educ:* Univ of Geneva, Munich, Berlin (DrJur) and London (LLD). Asst, Faculty of Law, Univ. of Berlin, 1929–33; German lawyer, 1933; Internat. Law Consultant, London, 1933–46; Solicitor, 1946; Mem., Legal Div., Allied Control Council (British Element), Berlin, 1946. Member: Lord Chancellor's Standing Cttee for Reform of Private Internat. Law, 1952–64; numerous Working Parties of Law Commn. Member: Council, British Inst. of Internat. and Comparative Law; Rapporteur, 1952–73, Monetary Law Cttee, Internat. Law Assoc. Special Consultant, Cttee on Foreign Money Liabilities, Council of Europe, 1964–67; Chm., Cttee on Place of Payment, Council of Europe, 1968–71. Counsel for Belgium in Barcelona Traction Case, The Hague, 1969–70; Counsel for Federal Republic of Germany in Young Loan Case, Koblenz and Bonn, 1979–80. Mem., Editorial Cttee, British Year Book of International Law. Mem., Institut de Droit International. Lectures at Acad. of Internat. Law at The Hague, 1959, 1964, 1971 and 1984, and at numerous Univs in England, Austria, Belgium, Germany, Switzerland and USA; Blackstone Lectr, Oxford, 1978; Hon. Prof. of Legal Ethics, Univ. of Birmingham, 1985–86. Hon. Mem., Amer. Soc. of Internat. Law, 1980. Hon. DrJur: Kiel, 1978; Zürich, 1983. Alexander von Humboldt Prize, Alexander von Humboldt Foundn, Bonn, 1984. Grand Cross of Merit, Federal Republic of Germany, 1977, with Star, 1982. *Publications:* The Legal Aspect of Money, 1938, 4th edn 1982 (trans. German, 1960, Spanish, 1986); Studies in International Law, 1973; Foreign Affairs in English Courts, 1986; numerous articles on international law, the conflict of laws, and monetary law in English and foreign legal pubns and periodicals. *Recreations:* music, walking. *Address:* Flat 4, 56 Manchester Street, W1. *T:* 01–487 4735. *Club:* Athenæum.

See also A. C. Thomas, P. Vogelpoel.

MANN, George; *see* Mann, F. G.

MANN, John Frederick; Director of Education, London Borough of Harrow, since 1984; *b* 4 June 1930; *e s* of Frederick Mann and Hilda G. (*née* Johnson); *m* 1966, Margaret (*née* Moore); one *s* one *d*. *Educ:* Poole and Tavistock Grammar Schs; Trinity Coll., Oxford (MA). Asst Master, Colchester Royal Grammar Sch., 1954–61; Admin. Asst, Leeds County Bor., 1962–65; Asst Educn Officer, Essex CC, 1965–67; Dep. Educn Officer, Sheffield County Bor., 1967–78; Sec., Schools Council for the Curriculum and Exams, 1978–83. Member: Iron and Steel Industry Trng Bd, 1975–78; Exec., Soc. of Educn Officers, 1976–78; Sch. Broadcasting Council, 1979–83; Council, British Educn Management and Admin Soc., 1979–84. Governor, Welbeck Coll., 1975–84. Hon. Fellow: Sheffield Polytechnic, 1980; Coll. of Preceptors, 1986. FBIM; FRSA. JP Sheffield, 1976–79. *Publications:* Education, 1979; contrib. to Victoria County History of Essex, Local Govt Studies, and Educn. *Recreations:* travel, books, theatre, gardening. *Address:* 109 Chatsworth Road, NW2 4BH. *T:* 01–459 5419. *Club:* Royal Commonwealth Society.

MANN, Martin Edward, QC 1983; *b* 12 Sept. 1943; *s* of S. E. Mann and M. L. F. Mann; *m* 1966, Jacqueline Harriette (*née* Le Maître); two *d*. *Educ:* Cranleigh Sch. Called to the Bar, Gray's Inn, 1968 (Lord Justice Holker Sen. Exhibn), Lincoln's Inn, 1973 (*Ad eund*). Mem., Senate of the Inns of Court and the Bar, 1979–82. *Publication:* (jtly) What Kind of Common Agricultural Policy for Europe, 1975. *Recreations:* ski-ing/mountaineering, running, walking, riding, swimming, cricket, reading, theatre, opera, ballet, music, gardening, target shooting. *Address:* 7 Stone Buildings, Lincoln's Inn, WC2A 3UJ. *T:* 01–404 0946; Kingston St Mary, Somerset. *Clubs:* Royal Automobile; Exeter Centre Fire Pistol.

MANN, Hon. Sir Michael, Kt 1982; **Hon. Mr Justice Mann;** a Judge of the High Court of Justice, Queen's Bench Division, since 1982; *b* 9 Dec. 1930; *s* of late Adrian Bernard Mann, CBE and of Mary Louise (*née* Keen); *m* 1957, Jean Marjorie (*née* Bennett), MRCVS; two *s*. *Educ:* Whitgift; King's Coll., London (LLB, PhD; FKC 1984). Called to Bar, Gray's Inn, 1953, Bencher 1980; practised, 1955–82; Junior Counsel to the Land Commn (Common Law), 1967–71; QC 1972; a Recorder of the Crown Court, 1979–82. Asst Lectr 1954–57, Lectr 1957–64, in Law, LSE; part-time Legal Asst, FO, 1954–56. Inspector, Vale of Belvoir Coal Inquiry, 1979–80. *Publications:* (ed jtly) Dicey, Conflict of Laws, 7th edn, 1957; Dicey and Morris, Conflict of Laws, 8th edn 1967 to 10th edn, 1980. *Address:* The Royal Courts of Justice, WC2A 2LL. *Club:* Athenæum.

MANN, Rt. Rev. Michael Ashley; Dean of Windsor, since 1976; Chairman, St George's House; Register, Order of the Garter, since 1976; Domestic Chaplain to the Queen, since 1976; *b* 25 May 1924; *s* of late H. G. Mann and F. M. Mann, Harrow; *m* 1949, Jill Joan Jacques; one *d* (and one *s* decd). *Educ:* Harrow Sch.; RMC Sandhurst; Wells Theological Coll.; Graduate School of Business Admin., Harvard Univ. Served War of 1939–45: RMC, Sandhurst, 1942–43; 1st King's Dragoon Guards, 1943–46 (Middle East, Italy, Palestine). Colonial Admin. Service, Nigeria, 1946–55. Wells Theological Coll., 1955–57; Asst Curate, Wolborough, Newton Abbot, 1957–59; Vicar: Sparkwell, Plymouth, 1959–62; Christ Church, Port Harcourt, Nigeria, 1962–67; Dean, Port Harcourt Social and Industrial Mission; Home Secretary, The Missions to Seamen, 1967–69; Residentiary Canon, 1969–74, Vice-Dean, 1972–74, Norwich Cathedral; Adviser to Bp of Norwich on Industry, 1969–74; Bishop Suffragan of Dudley, 1974–76. Church Comr, 1977–85; Comr, Royal Hospital Chelsea, 1985–. Trustee: Imperial War Museum, 1980–; Army Museums Ogilby Trust, 1984–. Governor, Harrow Sch. (Chm., 1980–). CBIM; FRSA. *Publications:* A Windsor Correspondence, 1984; And They Rode On, 1984. *Recreations:* military history, philately, ornithology. *Address:* The Deanery, Windsor Castle, Berks SL4 1NJ. *T:* Windsor 865561. *Club:* Cavalry and Guards.

MANN, Murray G.; *see* Gell-Mann.

MANN, Patricia Kathleen Randall, (Mrs Pierre Walker); Head of External Affairs, J. Walter Thompson Group, and Vice-President, JWT International, since 1981; Editor, Consumer Affairs, since 1978; Member, Monopolies and Mergers Commission, since 1984; *b* 26 Sept. 1937; *d* of late Charles Alfred Mann and of Marjorie Lilian Mann (*née* Heath); *m* 1962, Pierre George Armand Walker; one *d*. *Educ:* Clifton High School, Bristol. FCAM, FIPA; CBIM. Joined J. Walter Thompson Co., 1959, Copywriter, 1959–77, Head of Public Affairs, 1978. Director: Valor plc, 1985–; Woolwich Equitable Building Soc., 1983–. Member: Council, Inst. of Practitioners in Advertising, 1965– (Hon. Sec., 1979–83); Advertising Creative Circle, 1965–; Council, Nat. Advertising Benevolent Soc., 1973–77; Council, Advertising Standards Authy, 1973–; Board, European Assoc. of Advertising Agencies, 1984–; Nat. Gas Consumers Council, 1981–; Board, UK Centre for Economic and Envtl Develt, 1984–. Governor: CAM Educn Foundn, 1971–77; Admin. Staff Coll., Henley, 1976–; Mem. Ct and Council, Brunel Univ., 1976–. Mem., Awards Nomination Panel, RTS, 1974–78. Mackintosh Medal, Advertising Assoc., 1977. *Publications:* 150 Careers in Advertising, 1971; Advertising, 1979; (ed) Advertising and Marketing to Children, 1980. *Recreations:* word games, watching showjumping. *Address:* c/o J. Walter Thompson, 40 Berkeley Square, W1X 6AD. *T:* 01–629 9496. *Clubs:* Reform, Women's Advertising, London Cornish Association.

MANN, Rt. Rev. Peter Woodley; *see* Dunedin, Bishop of.

MANN, Ronald; Deputy Chairman, Grindlays Bank Ltd, 1964–77; Director, Grindlays Holdings Ltd, 1969–78; *b* 22 April 1908; *s* of Harry Ainsley Mann and Millicent (*née*

Copplestone); *m* 1935, Beatrice Elinor Crüwell Wright; one *s* three *d*. *Educ:* Cranleigh Sch., Surrey. The Eastern Produce and Estates Co. Ltd: Asst, Ceylon, 1930–35; Man., Ceylon, 1935–46; Man. Dir, London, 1947–71; Chm., Eastern Produce Holdings Ltd, 1957–71. *Recreations:* golf, gardening. *Address:* Fernhurst Place, Fernhurst, near Haslemere, Surrey. *T:* Haslemere 52220. *Club:* Oriental.

MANN, Sir Rupert (Edward), 3rd Bt *cr* 1905; *b* 11 Nov. 1946; *s* of Major Edward Charles Mann, DSO, MC (*g s* of 1st Bt) (*d* 1959), and of Pamela Margaret, *o d* of late Major Frank Haultain Hornsby; *S* great uncle, 1971; *m* 1974, Mary Rose, *d* of Geoffrey Butler, Stetchworth, Newmarket; two *s*. *Educ:* Malvern. *Heir: s* Alexander Rupert Mann, *b* 6 April 1978. *Address:* Billingford Hall, Diss, Norfolk. *Clubs:* MCC; Norfolk.

MANN, Thaddeus Robert Rudolph, CBE 1962; FRS 1951; Biochemist; Professor of the Physiology of Reproduction, University of Cambridge, 1967–76, now Emeritus (Reader in Physiology of Animal Reproduction, 1953–67); Fellow of Trinity Hall, Cambridge, since 1961; Member of the Staff of Agricultural Research Council, 1944–76; *b* 1908; *s* of late William Mann and Emilia (*née* Quest); *m* 1934, Dr Cecilia Lutwak-Mann. *Educ:* Trin. Hall, Cambridge; MD Lwòw 1935, PhD Cantab 1937, ScD Cantab 1950; Rockefeller Research Fellow, 1935–37; Beit Mem. Research Fellow, 1937–44. Dir, ARC Unit of Reproductive Physiology and Biochemistry, Cambridge, 1954–76. Awarded Amory Prize of Amer. Academy of Arts and Sciences, 1955; Senior Lalor Fellow at Woods Hole, 1960; Vis. Prof. in Biology at Florida State Univ., 1962; Vis. Prof. in Biological Structure and Zoology, Univ. of Washington, 1968; Vis. Scientist, Reproduction Res. Br., Nat. Insts of Health, USA, 1978–82. Gregory Pincus Meml Lectr, 1969; Albert Tyler Meml Lectr, 1970. For. Member: Royal Belgian Acad. of Medicine, 1970; Polish Acad. of Science, 1980. Hon. doctorate: of Veterinary Medicine, Ghent, 1970, Hanover, 1977; of Natural Scis, Cracow, 1973. Cavaliere Ufficiale, Order of Merit (Italy), 1966. *Publications:* The Biochemistry of Semen, 1954; The Biochemistry of Semen and of the Male Reproductive Tract, 1964; (with C. Lutwak-Mann) Male Reproductive Function and Semen—Themes and Trends in Physiology, Biochemistry and Investigative Andrology, 1981; Spermatophores—Development, Structure, Biochemical Attributes and Role in the Transfer of Spermatozoa, 1984; papers on Carbohydrate Metabolism of Muscle, Yeast and Moulds, on Metaloprotein Enzymes, and on Biochemistry of Reproduction. *Address:* 1 Courtney Way, Cambridge CB4 2EE.

MANN, William Neville, MD, FRCP; Consultant Physician Emeritus, Guy's Hospital, 1976; *b* 4 April 1911; *s* of William Frank Mann and Clara, *d* of John Chadwick; *m* Pamela, *yr d* of late H. E. Chasteney; two *s* four *d*. *Educ:* Alleyn's Sch.; Guy's Hospital. MB, BS (London), 1935; MRCP 1937; MD (London), 1937; FRCP, 1947. House Physician, Demonstrator of Pathology and Medical Registrar, Guy's Hospital, 1935–39. Served, 1940–45, in RAMC in Middle East and Indian Ocean (Temp. Lt-Col). Physician, Guy's Hosp., 1946–76. Hon. Visiting Physician to Johns Hopkins Hosp., Baltimore, USA. Physician: to HM Household, 1954–64; to HM the Queen, 1964–70; King Edward VII's Hosp. for Officers, 1965–76. Sen. Censor and Sen. Vice-Pres., RCP, 1969–70. Hon. DHL Johns Hopkins, 1986. *Publications:* Clinical Examination of Patients (jointly), 1950; The Medical Works of Hippocrates (jointly), 1950. Editor, Conybeare's Text-book of Medicine, 16th edn, 1975. *Address:* 90 Alleyn Road, SE21 8AH. T: 01–670 2451. *Club:* Garrick.

MANN, William Somervell; Radio Broadcaster on music since 1949; Associate Editor, Opera, since 1954; *b* 14 Feb. 1924; *s* of late Gerald and Joyce Mann; *m* 1948, Erika Charlotte Emilie Sohler; four *d*. *Educ:* Winchester Coll.; Magdalene Coll., Cambridge (BA, MusB). Music Critic, Cambridge Review, 1946–48; Asst Music Critic, The Times, 1948–60, Chief Music Critic 1960–82. Artistic Dir, Bath Fest., 1985. Member: ISM; CAMRA; Royal Musical Assoc.; The Critics' Circle (Pres., 1963–64). *Publications:* Introduction to the Music of J. S. Bach, 1950; (contrib. to symposium) Benjamin Britten, 1952; (contrib. to): The Concerto, 1952; The Record Guide, 1955; Chamber Music, 1957; The Analytical Concert Guide (English Editor), 1957; (contrib.) Music and Western Man, 1958; Let's Fake an Opera (with F. Reizenstein), 1958; Richard Strauss's Operas, 1964; Wagner's The Ring, Introduction and Translation, 1964; (contrib. to symposium) Michael Tippett, 1965; Wagner's Tristan, Introduction and Translation, 1968; The Operas of Mozart, 1977; (contrib.) Opera on Record, vol. 1 1979, vol. 2 1983, vol. 3 1984; Music in Time, 1982; (contrib.) The Book of the Violin, 1984; trans. Schwinger, Penderecki, 1986; contributor: opera guides to Aida, 1982, Arabella, 1985 and La Bohème, 1983; Musical Times, Opera, Opernwelt, The Gramophone, Internat. Concert and Opera Guide. *Recreations:* camping, winemaking, destructive gardening, phillumenism, interior decoration, food and drink, foreign languages, crosswords, shove-halfpenny, Mah-Jong, making music. *Address:* The Old Vicarage, Coleford, Bath BA3 5NG. *T:* Mells 812245.

MANNERS, family name of **Baron Manners,** and **Duke of Rutland.**

MANNERS, 5th Baron *cr* 1807; **John Robert Cecil Manners;** Partner, Osborne, Clarke & Co., Solicitors, Bristol, retired; *b* 13 Feb. 1923; *s* of 4th Baron Manners, MC, and of Mary Edith, *d* of late Rt Rev. Lord William Cecil; *S* father, 1972; *m* 1949, Jennifer Selena, *d* of Ian Fairbairn; one *s* two *d*. *Educ:* Eton; Trinity College, Oxford. Served as Flt-Lieut, RAFVR, 1941–46. Solicitor to the Supreme Court, 1949. Official Verderer of the New Forest, 1983–. *Recreations:* hunting and shooting. *Heir: s* Hon. John Hugh Robert Manners [*b* 5 May 1956; *m* 1983, Lanya Mary Jackson, *d* of late Dr H. E. Heitz and of Mrs Ian Jackson]. *Address:* Sabines, Avon, Christchurch, Dorset. *Clubs:* Brooks's; Constitutional (Bristol).

MANNERS, Elizabeth Maude, TD 1962; MA; Headmistress of Felixstowe College, Suffolk, 1967–79; Member, East Anglia Regional Health Authority, 1982–85; *b* 20 July 1917; *d* of William George Manners and Anne Mary Manners (*née* Sced). *Educ:* Stockton-on-Tees Sec. Sch.; St Hild's Coll., Durham Univ. BA (Dunelm) 1938; MA 1941. Teacher of French at: Marton Grove Sch., Middlesbrough, 1939–40; Ramsey Gram. Sch., IOM, 1940–42; Consett Sec. Sch., Durham, 1942–44; Yarm Gram. Sch., Yorks, 1944–54; Deputy Head, Mexborough Gram. Sch., Yorks, 1954–59; Head Mistress, Central Gram. Sch. for Girls, Manchester, 1959–67. Vice-President: Girl Guides Assoc., Co. Manchester, 1959–67; Suffolk Agric. Assoc., 1967–82. Member: Educn Cttee, Brit. Fedn of Univ. Women, 1966–68; Council, Bible Reading Fellowship, 1973–81; Cttee, E Br., RSA, 1974–; Cttee, ISIS East, 1974–79. Mem., Suffolk CC, 1977–85 (Member: Educn Cttee, 1977–85; Staff Joint and Personnel Cttees, 1981–85; Vice-Chm., Secondary Educn Cttee, 1981–85); Mem., Suffolk War Pensions Cttee, 1980–. Sponsor, the Responsible Society, 1982–. Chm. Governors, Felixstowe Deben High Sch., 1985–. Enlisted ATS (TA), 1947; commissioned, 1949. FRSA 1972. Coronation Medal, 1953. *Publications:* The Vulnerable Generation, 1971; The Story of Felixstowe College, 1980. *Recreations:* foreign travel, theatre, motoring, good food and wine. *Address:* 6 Graham Court, Hamilton Gardens, Felixstowe, Suffolk.

MANNERS, Prof. Gerald; Professor of Geography, University College London, since 1980; Chairman, Sadler's Wells Foundation and Trust, since 1986 (Governor, since 1978, Vice-Chairman, 1982–86); *b* 7 Aug. 1932; *s* of George William Manners and Louisa Hannah Manners; *m* 1st, 1959, Anne (*née* Sawyer) (marr. diss. 1982); one *s* two *d*; 2nd, 1982, Joy Edith Roberta (*née* Turner); one *s*. *Educ:* Wallington County Grammar School; St Catharine's College, Cambridge (MA). Lectr in Geography, University Coll. Swansea, 1957–67; Reader in Geography, UCL, 1967–80. Vis. Schol., Resources for the Future, Inc., Washington DC, 1964–65; Vis. Associate, Jt Center for Urban Studies, Harvard and MIT, 1972–73. Dir, Economic Associates Ltd, 1964–74. Member: Council, Inst. of British Geographers, 1967–70; LOB 1970–80; SE Economic Planning Council, 1971–79; Council, TCPA, 1980–; Subscriber, Centre for Environmental Studies Ltd, 1981–. Specialist Advr to H of C Select Cttee on Energy, 1980–; Advr to Assoc. for Conservation of Energy, 1981–; Chairman: Regl Studies Assoc., 1981–84; RSA Panel of Inquiry into regl problem in UK, 1982–83. Mem., Central Governing Body, City Parochial Foundn, 1977–. Trustee, Chelsea Physic Garden, 1980–83. Mem. Court, City Univ., 1985–. *Publications:* Geography of Energy, 1964, 2nd edn 1971; South Wales in the Sixties, 1964; Changing World Market for Iron Ore 1950–1980, 1971 (ed) Spatial Policy Problems of the British Economy, 1971; Minerals and Man, 1974, Regional Development in Britain, 1974, 2nd edn 1980; Coal in Britain, 1981; Office Policy in Britain, 1986; contribs to edited volumes and learned jls. *Recreations:* music, dance, theatre, walking, undergardening. *Address:* 105 Barnsbury Street, N1 1EP. *T:* 01–607 7920.

MANNING, Frederick Allan, CVO 1954; ISO 1971; JP; retired, 1970; Commissioner for Transport, Queensland, 1967–70, (Deputy Commissioner, 1960–67); *b* Gladstone, Qld, Australia, 27 Aug. 1904; British parentage; *m* 1934, Phyllis Maud Fullerton; no *c*. *Educ:* Central Boys' State Sch. and Boys' Gram. Sch., Rockhampton, Qld. Entered Qld State Public Service as Clerk in Petty Sessions Office, Rockhampton, 1920; Clerk of Petty Sessions and Mining Registrar, 1923; Stipendiary Magistrate and Mining Warden, 1934; Petty Sessions Office, Brisbane, 1926; Relieving Clerk of Petty Sessions and Mining Registrar, 1931 (all parts of State); seconded to Commonwealth Govt for service in Qld Directorate of Rationing Commission, 1942; Asst Dep. Dir of Rationing, 1943. Dep. Dir, 1944, for Qld; returned to Qld Public Service, 1947; Sec., Dept of Transport, 1947–60; JP, Qld, 1925–. Coronation Medal, 1953; State Dir, Royal Visit to Queensland, 1954 (CVO). Exec. Vice-Chm, Qld Road Safety Coun., and Qld Rep. Aust. Road Safety Coun., 1962. Mem., Greyhound Racing Control Bd of Queensland, 1971–77. *Recreation:* bowls. *Address:* 126 Indooroopilly Road, Taringa, Brisbane, Qld 4068, Australia. *T:* 370–1936. *Club:* Tattersalls (Brisbane).

MANNING, Frederick Edwin Alfred, CBE 1954; MC 1919; TD 1937; BSc (Eng.); Hon. MA London; Hon. DEng NSTC; Hon. LLD RMC of Canada; Hon. DSc City; CEng; FIMechE; FIEE; FINucE; DPA (London); retired; *b* 6 April 1897; *s* of late Francis Alfred Manning and late Ellen Lavinia Manning; *m* 1927, Alice Beatrice Wistow, BSc; one *s* one *d* (and one *s* decd.). *Educ:* Christ's Hospital; St Olave's; Univ. of London. Academic Diploma of Mil. Studies, Univ. of London; Certificate in Statistics, Univ. of Vienna. War Service, 1915–20 (Order of St Stanislas, 2nd Class; Order of St Vladimir, 4th Class); RE (TA) 1920–38; Royal Signals (TA), 1938–52. Hon. Col, Univ. of London OTC, 1958–68, retired 1968, retaining rank of Col. Entered GPO 1925; idc 1937; Home Office and Min. of Home Security, 1938–41; GPO, 1941; SHAEF, 1943–45; Asst Sec., Foreign Office (Allied Commission for Austria), 1945–47; GPO, 1947; Dir of the Post Office in Wales and Border Counties, 1950–59; Adviser on Athlone Fellowship Scheme, 1961–72; Chm. Boards for the CS Commn, 1961–68; Hon. Sen. Treas., Univ. of London Union, 1928–52, Chm. of Union Court, 1952–69, Chm., Sports Finance Cttee, 1969–74; Mem. of Senate, Univ. of London, 1952–74 (Chm. Military Educ. Cttee, 1952–55); First Chm. of Convocation, The City Univ., 1967–70; Vice-Pres., Univs in London Catholic Chaplaincy Assoc., 1970–. Metrop. Special Constabulary (Comdt, GPO Div.), 1931–41. KSG 1972. *Recreations:* gardening, Rotary (Pres. Shepperton, 1964–65). *Address:* 1 Range Way, Shepperton, TW17 9NW. *T:* Walton-on-Thames 223400. *Club:* Royal Commonwealth Society.

MANNING, Air Cdre Frederick John, CB 1954; CBE 1948; retired, 1967; *b* 5 May 1912; *s* of late Frederick Manning; *m* 1937, Elizabeth Anwyl, *er d* of late Rev. Æ. C. Ruthven-Murray, BA, Bishop Burton, Beverley; four *d* (and one *s* decd). Cadet, P&OSN Co., 1928; Midshipman, RNR, 1929; Actg Sub-Lt, RNR, 1933; Pilot Officer, RAF, 1934; Flt Lt, 269 Squadron, 1938; Actg Group Capt., 1942; Dir of Organisation (Establishments), Air Ministry, 1944–45 (actg Air Commodore); commanding RAF Station Shaibah, Abu Sueir Shallufa, 1945–47 (acting Group Capt.); Group Capt., Organisation, HQ, RAF, Mediterranean and Middle East, 1947–48; Senior Air Adviser, and Dep. Head of Mission, British Services Mission, Burma, 1949–52; Senior Officer i/c Administration HQ Transport Command, 1952; Dep. Dir of Work Study, Air Ministry, 1956–59; Dir of Manning (2) Air Ministry, 1960–63; Air Officer Administration: HQ Near East Air Force, 1963–65; HQ Fighter Comd, 1965–67. *Address:* Myrtle Cottage, Eynsham, Oxford. *Club:* Royal Air Force.

MANNING, Dr Geoffrey, CBE 1986; FInstP; Director, Rutherford Appleton Laboratory, Science and Engineering Research Council, since 1981; *b* 31 Aug. 1929; *s* of Jack Manning and Ruby Frances Lambe; *m* 1951, Anita Jacqueline Davis; two *s* one *d*. *Educ:* Tottenham Grammar Sch.; Imperial Coll., London Univ. BSc, PhD; ARCS. Asst Lectr in Physics, Imperial Coll., 1953–55; Research worker: English Electric Co., 1955–56; Canadian Atomic Energy Co., 1956–58; Calif Inst. of Technol., 1958–59; AERE, 1960–65; Rutherford Laboratory, Science Research Council: Gp Leader, 1965–69; Dep. Dir, 1969–79; Head of High Energy Physics Div., 1969–75; Head of Atlas Div., 1975–79; Dir, Rutherford (Rutherford & Appleton Labs), 1979–81. Glazebrook Medal and Prize, Inst. of Physics, 1986. *Recreations:* golf, squash, ski-ing. *Address:* 38 Sunningwell Village, Abingdon, Oxon OX13 6RB. *T:* Oxford 736123.

MANNING, Jane Marian; freelance concert and opera singer (soprano), since 1965; *b* 20 Sept. 1938; *d* of Gerald Manville Manning and Lily Manning (*née* Thompson); *m* 1966, Anthony Edward Payne, composer. *Educ:* Norwich High Sch.; Royal Academy of Music (LRAM 1958); Scuola di Canto, Cureglia, Switzerland. GRSM 1960, ARCM 1962. London début (Park Lane Group), 1964; first BBC broadcast, 1965; regular appearances in leading concert halls and festivals in UK and Europe, with leading orchestras and conductors. Specialist in contemporary music (over 200 world premières given); Warsaw Autumn Fest., 1975–78; début Henry Wood Promenade Concerts, 1972; Wexford Opera Fest., 1976; Scottish Opera, 1978; Brussels Opera, 1980. Canadian début, 1977; tours of Australia and New Zealand, 1978, 1980, 1982, 1984, 1986; tours of USA, 1981, 1983, 1985, 1986; Milhaud Vis. Prof., Mills Coll. Oakland, 1983 and 1986; many broadcasts and gramophone recordings, lectures and master classes. Lucie Stern Vis. Prof., Mills Coll., Oakland, 1981. Vice Pres., SPNM, 1984–. Member: Internat. Jury, Gaudeamus Young Interpreters Competition, Holland, 1976, 1979, 1987; Jury, Eur. Youth Competition for Composers, Eur. Cultural Foundn, 1985. Hon. ARAM 1972, Hon. FRAM 1984. Special award, Composers Guild of Gt Britain, 1973. *Publications:* (chapter in) How Music Works, 1981; New Vocal Repertory in the English Language: an introduction, 1986; articles in Composer, and Music and Musicians. *Recreations:* cooking, cinema, ornithology. *Address:* 2 Wilton Square, N1 3DL. *T:* 01–359 1593.

MANNING, Thomas Henry, OC 1974; zoologist; *b* 22 Dec. 1911; *s* of Thomas E. and Dorothy (*née* Randall) Manning, Shrublands, Dallington, Northampton; *m* 1938, Ella

Wallace Jackson. *Educ:* Harrow; Cambridge. Winter journey across Lapland, 1932–33; Survey and Zoological work on Southampton Island, 1933–35; Leader, Brit. Canadian-Arctic Exped., 1936–41; Royal Canadian Navy, 1941–45; Geodetic Service of Canada, 1945–47; Leader Geographical Bureau Expedition to Prince Charles I. (Foxe Basin), 1949; Zoological and Geographical work in James Bay, 1950; Leader Defence Research Board Expeditions: Beaufort Sea, 1951; Banks Island, 1952, 1953; Nat. Mus. Canadian Expedition; King William Island, Adelaide Peninsula, 1957, Prince of Wales Island, 1958. FRGS (Patron's Gold Medal, 1948). Hon. LLD McMaster, 1979. Bruce Memorial Prize (Royal Society of Edinburgh, RPS, RSGS), 1944; Massey Medal, Royal Canadian Geographical Soc., 1977. Guggenheim Fellow, 1959. *Publications:* The Birds of North Western Ungava, 1949; Birds of the West James Bay and Southern Hudson Bay Coasts, 1952; Birds of Banks Island, 1956; Mammals of Banks Island, 1958; A Biological Investigation of Prince of Wales Island, 1961; articles in The Auk, Journal Mamm. and Geog. Journal, Canadian Geog. Jl, Canadian Field-Naturalist, Arctic, Nat. Mus. Can. Bull., Canadian Jl of Zool., Syllogeus. *Recreations:* shooting, book-binding, cabinet-making, farming. *Address:* RR4, Merrickville, Ont., Canada. *T:* 269–4940.

MANNINGHAM-BULLER, family name of **Viscount Dilhorne.**

MANS, Maj.-Gen. Rowland Spencer Noel, CBE 1971 (OBE 1966, MBE 1956); Director, Military Assistance Office, 1973–76, retired; *b* 16 Jan. 1921; *s* of Thomas Frederick Mans and May Seigenberg; *m* 1945, Veeo Ellen Sutton; three *s*. *Educ:* Surbiton Grammar Sch.; RMC, Sandhurst; jssc, psc. Served War, Queen's Royal Regt and King's African Rifles, 1940–45. Regtl and Staff Duty, 1945–59; Instr, Staff Colleges, Camberley and Canada, 1959–63; Comd, 1st Tanganyika Rifles, 1963–64; Staff Duty, Far East and UK, 1964–68; Comd, Aldershot, 1969–72; DDPS (Army), 1967–73. Col, Queen's Regt, 1978–83 (Dep. Col (Surrey), 1973–77). Defence consultant and writer on defence and political affairs. Mem., Hampshire CC, 1984–. *Publications:* Kenyatta's Middle Road in a Changing Africa, 1977; Canada's Constitutional Crisis, 1978. *Recreations:* writing, reading, gardening. *Address:* Kirke House, Sway Road, Brockenhurst, Hants. *T:* Lymington 22291. *Clubs:* Army and Navy; Royal Lymington Yacht.

MANSAGER, Felix Norman, KBE (Hon.) 1976 (Hon. CBE 1973); Honorary Director, Hoover Co. USA (President-Chairman, Hoover Co. and Hoover World-wide Corporation, 1966–75); Director, Hoover Ltd UK (Chairman, 1966–75); *b* 30 Jan. 1911; *s* of Hoff Mansager and Alice (*née* Qualseth); *m* Geraldine (*née* Larson); one *s* two *d*. *Educ:* South Dakota High Sch., Colton. Joined Hoover Co. as Salesman, 1929; Vice-Pres., Sales, 1959; Exec. Vice-Pres. and Dir, 1961. Dir, Belden and Blake Energy Co. Member: Council on Foreign Relations; Newcomen Soc. in N America; Trustee, Graduate Theological Union (Calif); The Pilgrims of the US; Assoc. of Ohio Commodores; Masonic Shrine (32nd degree Mason); Mem. and Governor, Ditchley Foundn; Member Board of Trustees: Ohio Foundn of Indep. Colls; Indep. Coll. Funds of America. Hon. Mem., World League of Norsemen. Marketing Award, British Inst. of Marketing, 1971. Executive Prof. of Business (Goodyear Chair), Univ. of Akron (Mem. Delta Sigma Pi; Hon. Mem., Beta Sigma Gamma). Hon. Fellow, UC Cardiff, 1973. Hon. Dr of Laws Capital Univ., 1967; Hon. LLD Strathclyde, 1970; Hon. DHL Malone Coll., Canton, Ohio, 1972; Hon. PhD Walsh Coll., Canton, 1974; Hon. Dr Humanities Wartburg Coll., Waverly, Iowa, 1976; Medal of Honor, Vassa Univ., Finland, 1973; Person of Year, Capital Univ. Chapter of Tau Pi Phi, 1981. Grand Officer, Dukes of Burgundy, 1968; Chevalier: Order of Leopold, 1969; Order of St Olav, Norway, 1971; Legion of Honour, France, 1973; Grande Officiale, Order Al Merito della Republica Italiana, 1975. *Recreation:* golf. *Address:* 3421 Lindel Court NW, Canton, Ohio 44718, USA. *Clubs:* Metropolitan (NYC); Congress Lake Country (Hartville, Ohio); Torske (Hon.) (Minneapolis).

MANSEL, Rev. Canon James Seymour Denis, KCVO 1979 (LVO 1972); Extra Chaplain to the Queen, since 1979; Assistant Priest, St Margaret's, Westminster, since 1980; Priest Vicar, Westminster Abbey, since 1983; *b* 18 June 1907; *e s* of Edward Mansel, FRIBA, Leamington, and Muriel Louisa (*née* Denis Browne); *m* 1942, Ann Monica (*d* 1974), *e d* of Amyas Waterhouse, MD, Boars Hill, Oxford, and Ruth (*née* Gamlen); one *d*. *Educ:* Brighton Coll.; Exeter Coll., Oxford (MA); Westcott House. Asst Master, Dulwich Coll., 1934–39; Asst Master, Chaplain and House Master, Winchester Coll., 1939–65; Sub-Dean of HM Chapels Royal, Deputy Clerk of the Closet, Sub-Almoner and Domestic Chaplain to the Queen, 1965–79; Canon and Prebendary of Chichester Cathedral, 1971–81, Canon Emeritus, 1981. Mem., Winchester City Coun., 1950–56. JP: City of Winchester, 1964; Inner London Commn, 1972. FSA. ChStJ. *Address:* 15 Sandringham Court, Maida Vale, W9 1UA. *Club:* Athenæum.
See also R. E. Jack.

MANSEL, Sir Philip, 15th Bt, *cr* 1621; FInstSM; Managing Director of Eden-Vale Engineering Co. Ltd; *b* 3 March 1943; *s* of Sir John Mansel, 14th Bt and Hannah, *d* of Ben Rees; *S* father, 1947; *m* 1968, Margaret, *o d* of Arthur Docker; one *s* one *d*. *Heir: s* John Philip Mansel, *b* 19 April 1982. *Address:* 4 Redhill Drive, Fellside Park, Whickham, Newcastle upon Tyne NE16 5TY.

MANSEL-JONES, David; Chairman, Huntingdon Research Centre plc, 1978–86 (Vice-Chairman, 1974–78); *b* 8 Sept. 1926; *o s* of Rees Thomas Jones and Ceinwen Jones; *m* 1952, Mair Aeronwen Davies; one *s*. *Educ:* St Michael's Sch., Bryn; London Hospital. MB, BS 1950; MRCP 1973. Jun. Surgical Specialist, RAMC; Dep. Med. Dir, Wm R. Warner & Co. Ltd, 1957–59; Med. Dir, Richardson-Merrell Ltd, 1959–65; formerly PMO, SMO and MO, Cttee on Safety of Drugs; formerly Med. Assessor, Cttee on Safety of Medicines; Consultant to WHO, 1970–; Senior PMO, Medicines Div., DHSS, 1971–74. Vis. Prof., Gulbenkian Science Inst., Portugal, 1981; Examiner, Dip. Pharm. Med., Royal Colls of Physicians, UK, 1980–. *Publications:* papers related to safety of medicines. *Recreations:* music, painting. *Address:* 9 Aldeburgh Lodge Gardens, Aldeburgh, Suffolk. *T:* Aldeburgh 3136.

MANSEL LEWIS, David Courtenay; Lord-Lieutenant of Dyfed, since 1979 (Lieutenant, 1974–79; HM Lieutenant for Carmarthenshire, 1973–74); JP; *b* 25 Oct. 1927; *s* of late Charlie Ronald Mansel Lewis and Lillian Georgina Warner, *d* of Col Sir Courtenay Warner, 1st Bt, CB; *m* 1953, Lady Mary Rosemary Marie-Gabrielle Montagu-Stuart-Wortley, OBE, JP, 4th *d* of 3rd Earl of Wharncliffe; one *s* two *d*. *Educ:* Eton; Keble Coll., Oxford (BA). Served in Welsh Guards, 1946–49; Lieut 1946, RARO. High Sheriff, Carmarthenshire, 1965; JP 1969; DL 1971. FRSA; KStJ. *Recreations:* music, sailing. *Address:* Stradey Castle, Llanelli, Dyfed. *T:* Llanelli 774626. *Clubs:* Lansdowne; Cruising Association.

MANSELL, Gerard Evelyn Herbert, CBE 1977; Managing Director, External Broadcasting, BBC, 1972–81; Deputy Director-General, BBC, 1977–81; retired; *b* 16 Feb. 1921; 2nd *s* of late Herbert and of Anne Mansell, Paris; *m* 1956, Diana Marion Sherar; two *s*. *Educ:* Lycée Hoche, Versailles; Lycée Buffon, Paris; Ecole des Sciences Politiques, Paris; Chelsea Sch. of Art. Joined HM Forces, 1940; served in Western Desert, Sicily and NW Europe, 1942–45 (despatches). Joined BBC European Service, 1951; Head, Overseas Talks and Features Dept, 1961; Controller, BBC Radio 4 (formerly Home Service), and Music Programme, 1965–69; Dir of Programmes, BBC, Radio, 1970. Chairman: British Cttee, Journalists in Europe, 1978–; Jt Adv. Cttee on Radio Journalism Trng, 1981–; Sony Radio Awards Organising Cttee, 1983–; Mem., Communication and Cultural Studies Bd, CNAA, 1982–. Chm., New Hampstead Garden Suburb Trust, 1984–. FRSA 1979. French Croix de Guerre, 1945. *Publications:* Tragedy in Algeria, 1961; Let Truth be Told, 1982. *Address:* 46 Southway, NW11.

MANSER, Michael John; architect in private practice, Manser Associates (formerly Michael Manser Associates), since 1961; President, Royal Institute of British Architects, 1983–85; *b* 23 March 1929; *s* of Edmund George Manser and Augusta Madge Manser; *m* 1953, Dolores Josephine Bernini; one *s* one *d*. *Educ:* Sch. of Architecture, Polytechnic of Central London (DipArch). RIBA 1954. Intermittent architectural journalism, including: News Editor, Architectural Design, 1961–64; Architectural Correspondent, The Observer, 1963–65. Councillor, RIBA, 1977–80 and 1982. Hon. Fellow, Royal Architectural Inst. of Canada, 1985. Civic Trust Awards, 1967 and 1973; Award for Good Design in Housing, DoE, 1975; Heritage Year Award, 1975; Structural Steel Award, BSC, 1976; Commendation and Arch. Award, RIBA, 1977. *Publication:* (with José Manser) Planning Your Kitchen, 1976. *Recreations:* going home, architecture, music, books, boats, sketching, gardening (under supervision). *Address:* Morton House, Chiswick Mall, W4 2PS.

MANSERGH, Vice-Adm. Sir (Cecil) Aubrey (Lawson), KBE 1953; CB 1950; DSC 1915; retired; *b* 7 Oct. 1898; *s* of Ernest Lawson Mansergh and Emma Cecilia Fisher Hogg; *m* 1st, 1928, Helen Raynor Scott (*d* 1967); one *s* (and one *s* decd); 2nd, 1969, Dora, *widow* of Comdr L. H. L. Clarke, RN. *Educ:* RN Colleges Osborne and Dartmouth. Served European War, 1914–18; Comdr, 1932; Captain, 1938; Commanded HMNZS Achilles, 1942 and HMNZS Leander, 1943, in Pacific; Commodore 1st Cl., Admiralty, 1944–46; Commanded HMS Implacable, 1946–47; Rear-Adm. 1948; Vice-Controller of Navy and Dir of Naval Equipment, 1948–50; Commanded 2nd Cruiser Squadron, 1950–52; Vice-Adm., 1951. Pres., Royal Naval Coll., Greenwich, 1952–54, retired Dec. 1954. *Address:* 102 High Street, Rottingdean, Sussex BN2 7HF. *T:* Brighton 32213.

MANSERGH, Prof. (Philip) Nicholas (Seton), OBE 1945; DPhil 1936; DLitt Oxon 1960; LittD Cantab 1970; FBA 1973; Master of St John's College, Cambridge, 1969–79, Fellow 1955–69 and since 1979; Editor-in-chief, India Office Records on the Transfer of Power, 1967–82 (12 volumes); Hon. Fellow: Pembroke College, Oxford, 1954; Trinity College, Dublin, 1971; *b* 27 June 1910; *yr s* of late Philip St George Mansergh and late Mrs E. M. Mansergh, Grenane House, Tipperary; *m* 1939, Diana Mary, *d* of late G. H. Keeton, Headmaster's Lodge, Reading; three *s* two *d*. *Educ:* Abbey Sch., Tipperary; College of St Columba, Dublin; Pembroke Coll., Oxford. Sec. OU Politics Research Cttee and Tutor in Politics, 1937–40; Empire Div., Ministry of Information, 1941–46; Dir, 1944–46; Asst Sec., Dominions Office, 1946–47; Abe Bailey Research Prof. of British Commonwealth Relations, RIIA, 1947–53; Smuts Prof. of History of British Commonwealth, Univ. of Cambridge, 1953–April 1970, now Emeritus Professor. Visiting Professor: Nat. Univ. of Australia, 1951; Univ. of Toronto, 1953; Duke Univ., NC, 1957 and 1965 (W. K. Boyd Prof. of History); Indian Sch. of International Studies, New Delhi, 1958 and 1966; Jawaharlal Nehru Univ., 1980; Reid Lecturer, Acadia Univ., 1960; Smuts Meml Lectr, Cambridge Univ., 1976. Member: Editorial Board, Annual Register, 1947–73; Gen. Advisory Council, BBC, 1956–62; Adv. Council on Public Records, 1966–76; Councillor, RIIA, 1953–57; Chm. Faculty Board of History, 1960–62, Bd of Graduate Studies, 1970–73, Cambridge Univ. *Publications:* The Irish Free State: Its Government and Politics, 1934; The Government of Northern Ireland, 1936; Ireland in the Age of Reform and Revolution, 1940; Advisory Bodies (Jt Editor), 1941; Britain and Ireland, 1942, 2nd edn 1946; The Commonwealth and the Nations, 1948; The Coming of the First World War, 1949; Survey of British Commonwealth Affairs (2 vols), 1931–39, 1952 and 1939–52, 1958; Documents and Speeches on Commonwealth Affairs, 1931–62 (3 vols), 1953–63; The Multi-Racial Commonwealth, 1955; (jointly) Commonwealth Perspectives, 1958; South Africa, 1906–1961, 1962; The Irish Question, 1840–1921, 1965, 3rd edn 1975; The Commonwealth Experience, 1969, 2nd edn 1982; Prelude to Partition, 1978. *Recreation:* lawn mowing. *Address:* The Lodge, Little Shelford, Cambridge CB2 5EW. *Clubs:* Royal Commonwealth Society; Kildare Street and University (Dublin).

MANSFIELD, family name of **Baron Sandhurst.**

MANSFIELD AND MANSFIELD, 8th Earl of, *cr* 1776 and 1792 (GB); **William David Mungo James Murray;** JP, DL; Baron Scone, 1605; Viscount Stormont, 1621; Baron Balvaird, 1641; (Earl of Dunbar, Viscount Drumcairn, and Baron Halldykes in the Jacobite Peerage); Hereditary Keeper of Bruce's Castle of Lochmaben; First Crown Estate Commissioner, since 1985; *b* 7 July 1930; *o s* of 7th Earl of Mansfield and Mansfield, and of Dorothea Helena (*d* 1985), *y d* of late Rt Hon. Sir Lancelot Carnegie, GCVO, KCMG; *S* father, 1971; *m* 1955, Pamela Joan, *o d* of W. N. Foster, CBE; two *s* one *d*. *Educ:* Eton; Christ Church, Oxford. Served with Scots Guards, Malayan campaign, 1949–50. Called to Bar, Inner Temple, 1958; Barrister, 1958–71. Mem., British Delegn to European Parlt, 1973–75; an opposition spokesman in the House of Lords, 1975–79; Minister of State: Scottish Office, 1979–83; NI Office, 1983–84. Mem., Tay Salmon Fisheries Bd, 1971–79. Director: General Accident, Fire and Life Assurance Corp. Ltd, 1972–79, 1985–; American Trust, 1985–; Punneys of Scotland, 1985–. Ordinary Dir, Royal Highland and Agricl Soc., 1976–79. President: Fédn des Assocs de Chasse de l'Europe, 1977–79; Scottish Assoc. for Care and Resettlement of Offenders, 1974–79; Scottish Assoc. of Boys Clubs, 1976–79; Royal Scottish Country Dance Soc., 1977–; Chm., Scottish Branch, Historic Houses Assoc., 1976–79. Mem., Perth CC, 1971–75; Hon. Sheriff for Perthshire, 1974; JP 1975, DL 1980, Perth and Kinross. *Heir: s* Viscount Stormont, *qv*. *Address:* Scone Palace, Perthshire PH2 6BE; 16 Thorburn House, Kinnerton Street, SW1. *Clubs:* White's, Pratt's, Turf, Beefsteak.

MANSFIELD, Rear-Adm. David Parks, CB 1964; *b* 26 July 1912; *s* of Comdr D. Mansfield, RD, RNR; *m* 1939, Jean Craig Alexander (*d* 1984); one *s* one *d*. *Educ:* RN Coll., Dartmouth; RN Engineering Coll., Keyham. Lt (E) 1934; HMS Nelson, 1934–36; Staff of C-in-C Med., 1936–39; HMS Mauritius, 1939–42; Lt-Comdr (E) 1942; HMS Kelvin, 1942–43; Chatham Dockyard, 1943–46; Comdr (E) 1945; Admty (Aircraft Maintenance Dept), 1946–49; Staff of FO Air (Home), 1949–51; HMS Kenya, 1951–53; RN Engrg Coll., 1953–55; Captain 1954; RNAS Anthorn (in command), 1955–57; RN Aircraft Yard, Fleetlands (Supt.), 1957–60; Admty Dir of Fleet Maintenance, 1960–62; Rear-Adm. 1963; Rear-Adm. Aircraft, on Staff of Flag Officer Naval Air Command, 1963–65. *Recreation:* family affairs. *Address:* The Outlook, Salisbury Road, St Margaret's Bay, Dover, Kent. *T:* Dover 852237. *Club:* Army and Navy.

MANSFIELD, Vice-Adm. Sir (Edward) Gerard (Napier), KBE 1974; CVO 1981; retired 1975; *b* 13 July 1921; *s* of late Vice-Adm. Sir John Mansfield, KCB, DSO, DSC, and Alice Talbot Mansfield; *m* 1943, Joan Worship Byron, *d* of late Comdr John Byron, DSC and Bar, and late Frances Byron; two *d*. *Educ:* RNC, Dartmouth. Entered Royal Navy, 1935. Served War of 1939–45 in destroyers and Combined Ops (despatches), taking part in landings in N Africa and Sicily. Comdr, 1953; comd HMS Mounts Bay, 1956–58; Captain 1959; SHAPE, 1960–62; Captain (F) 20th Frigate Sqdn, 1963–64; Dir of Defence Plans (Navy), 1965–67; Cdre Amphibious Forces, 1967–68; Senior Naval Member, Directing Staff, IDC, 1969–70; Flag Officer Sea Training, 1971–72; Dep. Supreme Allied Comdr, Atlantic, 1973–75. Chairman: Assoc. of RN Officers, 1975–86; Council, Operation Raleigh, 1984–. Chm., Crondall Parish Council, 1977–81. Mem. Admin. Council, Royal Jubilee Trusts, 1978–81. *Recreations:* golf, gardening. *Address:* White Gate House, Heath Lane, Ewshot, Farnham, Surrey GU10 5AH. *T:* Aldershot 850325. *Club:* Army and Navy.

MANSFIELD, Prof. Eric Harold, FRS 1971; FEng 1976; Visiting Professor, Department of Mechanical Engineering, University of Surrey, since 1984; formerly Chief Scientific Officer (individual merit), Royal Aircraft Establishment, 1980–83; *b* 24 May 1923; *s* of Harold Goldsmith Mansfield and Grace Phundt; *m* 1st, 1947, Mary Ola Purves Douglas (marr. diss. 1973); two *s* one *d*; 2nd, 1974, Eunice Lily Kathleen Shuttleworth-Parker. *Educ:* St Lawrence Coll., Ramsgate; Trinity Hall, Cambridge. MA, ScD; FRAeS, FIMA. Research in Structures Department, Royal Aircraft Establishment, Farnborough, Hants, 1943–83. Member: British Nat. Cttee for Theoretical and Applied Mechanics, 1973–79; Gen. Assembly of IUTAM, 1976–80; Council, Royal Soc., 1977–78. UK winner (with I. T. Minhinnick), World Par Bridge Olympiad, 1951. Editorial Advisory Boards: Internat. Jl of Non-linear Mechanics, 1965–; Internat Jl of Mechanical Scis, 1977–84. *Publications:* The Bending and Stretching of Plates, 1964; Bridge: the ultimate limits, 1986; contribs to: Proc. Roy. Soc., Phil. Trans., Quarterly Jl Mech. Applied Math., Aero Quarterly, Aero Research Coun. reports and memos, and to technical press. *Recreations:* duplicate bridge, palaeontology, snorkling. *Address:* Manatoba, Dene Close, Lower Bourne, Farnham, Surrey GU10 3PP. *T:* Farnham 713558.

MANSFIELD, Sir Gerard; *see* Mansfield, Sir E. G. N.

MANSFIELD, Sir Philip (Robert Aked), KCMG 1984 (CMG 1973); HM Diplomatic Service, retired; Ambassador to the Netherlands, 1981–84; *b* 9 May 1926; *s* of Philip Theodore Mansfield, CSI, CIE; *m* 1953, Elinor Russell MacHatton; two *s*. *Educ:* Winchester; Pembroke Coll., Cambridge. Grenadier Guards, 1944–47. Sudan Political Service, 1950–54. Entered HM Diplomatic Service, 1955; served in: Addis Ababa, Singapore, Paris, Buenos Aires; Counsellor and Head of Rhodesia Dept, FCO, 1969–72; RCDS, 1973; Counsellor and Head of Chancery, 1974–75, Dep. High Comr, 1976, Nairobi; Asst Under Sec. of State, FCO, and Comr for British Indian Ocean Territory, 1976–79; Ambassador and Dep. Perm. Representative to UN, 1979–81. *Recreations:* sailing, bird watching, gardening. *Address:* Gill Mill, Stanton Harcourt, Oxford. *T:* Witney 2554. *Clubs:* Royal Commonwealth Society; Aberdare Country (Kenya).

MANSFIELD COOPER, Prof. Sir William, Kt 1963; LLM; Professor of Industrial Law, University of Manchester, 1949–70, now Professor Emeritus; Vice-Chancellor of the University, 1956–70; *b* Newton Heath, Manchester, 20 Feb. 1903; *s* of William and Georgina C. Cooper; *m* 1936, Edna Mabel, *o c* of Herbert and Elizabeth Baker; one *s*. *Educ:* Elementary Sch.; Ruskin Coll., 1931–33; Manchester Univ., 1933–36 (LLB, Dauntesey Jun. Law Schol., Dauntesey Special Prizeman in International Law). Grad. Res. Schol., 1936–37; Lecturer WEA (LLM 1938). University of Manchester: Asst Lecturer, 1938; Lecturer, 1942; Asst to Vice-Chancellor, 1944; Registrar and Senior Lecturer in Law, 1945; Professor of Industrial and Commercial Law, 1949, continuing as Joint Registrar until 1952; Acting Vice-Chancellor, Nov. 1953–May 1954 and July 1954–Oct. 1954. Called to the Bar (Gray's Inn), 1940. Chairman John Rylands Library, 1956–70; Chairman Cttee of Vice-Chancellors and Principals, 1961–64; President, Council of Europe Cttee on Higher Education and Research, 1966–67; Vice-President, Standing Conference of European Rectors and Vice-Chancellors, 1964–69. Dep. Chm., Cttee of Inquiry into London Univ., 1970–72. Hon. Mem., Manchester Royal Coll. Music, 1971. Hon. LLD: Manitoba, 1964; Liverpool, 1970; Manchester, 1970; Hon. DLitt Keele, 1967; Hon. DSc Kharkov, 1970; Hon. DHL Rochester, 1970. Hon. Fellow, Manchester Inst. Science and Technology, 1972. *Publications:* Outlines of Industrial Law, 1947, 6th edn by John C. Wood, 1972; papers and reviews in learned journals. *Recreations:* gardening, bird-watching. *Address:* Fieldgate Cottage, Meldreth, Royston, Herts. *Club:* Athenæum.

MANT, Prof. (Arthur) Keith, MD; FRCP; FRCPath; Emeritus Professor of Forensic Medicine, University of London, since 1984; *b* 11 Sept. 1919; *s* of George Arthur Mant and Elsie Muriel (*née* Slark); *m* 1947, Heather Smith, BA; two *s* one *d*. *Educ:* Denstone Coll., Staffs; St Mary's Hosp., Paddington. MB BS 1949, MD 1950; MRCS, LRCP 1943; FRCPath 1967; MRCP 1977; FRCP 1982. Dept Obst. and Gynæc., St Mary's Hosp., 1943; RAMC, i/c Path. Section, War Crimes Gp, 1945–48 (Major); Registrar (ex-service), Med. Unit, St Mary's Hosp., 1948–49; Dept of Forensic Medicine, Guy's Hospital, Univ. of London: Research Fellow, 1949–55; Lectr, 1955–66; Reader in Forensic Med., 1966–74; Prof. of Forensic Med., 1974–84; Head of Dept, 1972–84. Sen. Lectr in Forensic Med., 1965, Hon. Consultant in Forensic Med., 1967–84, KCH. WHO Consultant, Sri Lanka, 1982 and 1984. Visiting Lectr in Med. Jurisprudence and Toxicology, St Mary's Hosp., 1955–84; British Council Lectr, India, 1979; Visiting Professor: Univ. of Jordan, 1985; Nihon Univ., Japan, 1985. Lectures: Niels Dungal Meml, Reykjavic, 1979; J. B. Firth Meml, London, 1981; W. D. L. Fernando Meml, Sri Lanka, 1982; Douglas Kerr Meml, London, 1985. Examiner in Forensic Medicine: NUI, 1960; St Andrews Univ., 1967; Dundee Univ., 1968; RCPath, 1971; Soc. of Apothecaries, 1971; Univ. of Riyadh, Saudi Arabia, 1976; Univ. of Garyounis-Libya, 1976; Univ. of Tripoli, 1979. A. D. Williams Distinguished Scholar Fellowship, Univ. Med. Coll. of Virginia, 1963 and 1968. President: Internat. Assoc. in Accident and Traffic Med., 1972–83 (now Pres. Emeritus); British Acad. of Forensic Sci., 1975–76; Past Pres., Forensic Sci. Soc., British Assoc. in Forensic Med.; Vice-Pres., Medico-Legal Soc. Nat. correspondent for GB, Internat. Acad. of Legal and Social Med.; Corresp. Mem., Amer. Acad. of Forensic Sci.; Corresp. For. Mem., Soc. de Méd. Légale; Hon. Member: Brazilian Assoc. for Traffic Med.; Soc. de Méd. Légale, Belgium; Mem., Editorial Bd, Internat. Reference Org. in Forensic Med. (INFORM); English Editor, Zeitschrift für Rechtsmedizin; Internat. Editorial Bd, Excerpta Medica (Forensic Sci. abstracts). Fellow: Indian Acad. of Forensic Sci.; Indian Assoc. in Forensic Medicine; Swedish Soc. of Med. Scis. Hon. DMJ(Path) Soc. of Apothecaries, 1979. *Publications:* Forensic Medicine: observation and interpretation, 1960; Modern Trends in Forensic Medicine, Series 3, 1973; (ed) Taylor's Principles and Practice of Medical Jurisprudence, 13th edn, 1984; contribs to med. and sci. literature. *Recreations:* fishing, orchid culture. *Address:* 29 Ashley Drive, Walton-on-Thames, Surrey KT12 1JT. *T:* Walton-on-Thames 225005. *Club:* Athenæum.

MANT, Sir Cecil (George), Kt 1964; CBE 1955; consultant and company director; Consultant to Corporation of London, 1972–83; Project Co-ordinator for Barbican Arts Centre, 1972–81; *b* 24 May 1906; *o s* of late George Frederick Mant and Beatrice May Mant; *m* 1940, Hilda Florence (*née* Knowles); three *d*. *Educ:* Trinity County Sch.; Hornsey School of Art; Northern Polytechnic School of Architecture. ARIBA 1929, FRIBA 1944, resigned 1970. Entered HM Office of Works, 1928. Visiting Lecturer in Architecture and Building to Northern Polytechnic, 1930–39; Departmental Liaison Officer to Works and Buildings Priority Cttee, 1939–40. Ministry of Public Building and Works: Deputy Director-General of Works, 1950–60; Director-General of Works, 1960–63; Controller-Gen. of Works, 1963–67. Served as member and chairman of various cttees, to British Standards Institution and Codes of Practice; Departmental Working Parties and Investigating Boards, Civil Service Commission Selection Boards, Joint Min. of Works and P.O. Study Group on P.O. Buildings Costs and Procedure, etc. Assessor to Advisory Cttee on Building Research, 1958–67; Member, Architecture Consultative Cttee, Hammersmith College of Art and Building, 1966–75. Mem., Ct of Assts, Guild of Freemen of City of London, 1972–. *Address:* 44 Hamilton Court, Maida Vale, W9 1QR. *T:* 01-286 8719. *Clubs:* City Livery, Arts.

MANT, Keith; *see* Mant, A. K.

MANTELL, Charles Barrie Knight; QC 1979; **His Honour Judge Mantell;** a Circuit Judge, since 1985; *b* 30 Jan. 1937; *s* of Francis Christopher Knight Mantell and Elsie Mantell; *m* 1960, Anne Shirley Mantell; two *d*. *Educ:* Manchester Grammar Sch.; Manchester Univ. (LLM). Called to the Bar, Gray's Inn, 1960. Flying Officer, RAF, 1958–61. In practice at Bar, London and Manchester, 1961–82; a Recorder of the Crown Court, 1978–82; Judge of Supreme Court, Hong Kong, 1982–85. *Recreations:* golf, reading, watching cricket. *Address:* Hartstone House, Shaugh Prior, Plymouth, Devon PL7 5EP. *Clubs:* Lansdowne; Big Four (Manchester); Hong Kong (Hong Kong).

MANTHORP, Rev. Brian Robert, MA; FCollP; Headmaster, Worcester College for the Blind, since 1980; *b* 28 July 1934; *s* of Alan Roy Manthorp and Stella Manthorp; *m* 1955, Jennifer Mary Caradine; three *s* one *d*. *Educ:* Framlingham Coll.; Pembroke Coll., Oxford (MA Hons English); Westcott House, Cambridge. Instructor Lieut, RN, 1955–58. Ordained priest, Guildford, 1961. Assistant Master, Charterhouse, 1958–65; Head of English: Lawrence Coll., Pakistan, 1965–67; Aitchison Coll., Pakistan, 1968–70; Oakbank Sch., Keighley, 1970–73; Headmaster, Holy Trinity Senior Sch., Halifax, 1973–80. *Publication:* Fifty Poems for Pakistan, 1971. *Recreations:* sport, sketching. *Address:* The Headmaster's House, Worcester College for the Blind, Whittington Road, Worcester WR5 2JU. *T:* Worcester 356599; The Brew House, High Street, Chipping Campden, Glos.

MANTLE, Philip Jaques, CMG 1952; *b* 7 Aug. 1901; 2nd *s* of late Paul Mantle; *m* 1930, Gwendolen, *d* of late John Webb, CMG, CBE, MC; one *s* one *d*. *Educ:* Bancroft's Sch., Woodford; St John's Coll., Oxford (Scholar, Goldsmiths' exhibitioner, 1st class Mod. Hist. Finals). Entered Inland Revenue Dept, 1923 (Taxes); Secretaries' office, 1928; Asst Secretary Min. of Supply, 1940, Board of Trade, 1942; Deputy Head, Administration of Enemy Property Dept, 1949; Controller-General, 1955–57; Companies Dept, 1957–61; with Charity Commission, 1962; retired 1966. *Address:* 10 Lonsdale Road, Cannington, near Bridgwater, Som TA5 2JR. *T:* Combwich 652477.

MANTON, 3rd Baron, *cr* 1922, of Compton Verney; **Joseph Rupert Eric Robert Watson;** DL; Landowner and Farmer; *b* 22 Jan. 1924; *s* of 2nd Baron Manton and Alethea (*d* 1979), 2nd *d* of late Colonel Philip Langdale, OBE; *S* father, 1968; *m* 1951, Mary Elizabeth, twin *d* of Major T. D. Hallinan, Ashbourne, Glounthaune, Co. Cork; two *s* three *d*. *Educ:* Eton. Joined Army, 1942; commissioned Life Guards, 1943; Captain, 1946; retired, 1947; rejoined 7th (QO) Hussars, 1951–56. DL Humberside, 1980. *Recreations:* hunting, shooting, racing. *Heir:* *s* Capt. the Hon. Miles Ronald Marcus Watson, Life Guards [*b* 7 May 1958; *m* 1984, Elizabeth, *e d* of J. R. Story; one *s*]. *Address:* Houghton Hall, Sancton, York. *T:* Market Weighton 73234. *Clubs:* White's, Jockey.

See also Baron Hesketh.

MANTON, Prof. Irene, BA, ScD, PhD; FRS 1961; Emeritus Professor of Botany, University of Leeds; retired 1969. *Educ:* Girton Coll., Cambridge (Hon. Fellow 1985). BA 1926, PhD 1930, ScD 1940, Cambridge. Has made studies with the light and electron microscope on the ultramicroscopic structure of plants, and studies on the cytology and evolution of ferns. Hon. Member: Danish Acad. of Sciences and Letters, 1953; Deutsche Akad. Leopoldina, 1967; Amer. Acad. of Arts and Sciences, 1969. Hon. DSc: McGill Univ., Canada, 1958; Durham Univ., 1966; Lancaster Univ., 1979; Leeds Univ., 1985; Hon. Doctorate, Oslo Univ., 1961. *Publications:* Problems of Cytology and Evolution in the Pteridophyta, 1950; papers in scientific journals. *Address:* 15 Harrowby Crescent, West Park, Leeds LS16 5HP.

MANUEL, Joseph Thomas, CBE 1970; QPM 1967; one of HM's Inspectors of Constabulary, 1963–74; *b* 10 June 1909; *s* of George and Lucy Manuel; *m* 1933, Millicent Eveline Baker; one *s*. *Educ:* Dorchester Boys' Sch., Dorchester, Dorset. Joined Metropolitan Police, 1929. Served in Allied Military Government, Italy (rank of Captain and Major), 1943–46. Returned Metropolitan Police and promoted: Superintendent, 1954; Chief Superintendent, 1957; Dep. Commander, 1958; Commander 1959. *Recreations:* walking, motoring. *Address:* Cranbrook, Pyrford Road, West Byfleet, Weybridge, Surrey KT14 6RE. *T:* Byfleet 46360.

MANVELL, (Arnold) Roger, PhD (London), DLitt (Sussex); film historian, biographer; scriptwriter and lecturer; Professor of Film, since 1975, and University Professor, since 1982, Boston University; Director: Rationalist Press Association Ltd; Pemberton Publishing Co. Ltd, etc; *b* 10 Oct. 1909; *s* of Canon A. E. W. Manvell; *m* 1981, Françoise, *d* of René Nautré, Antibes, France. *Educ:* Wyggeston Sch., Leicester; King's Sch., Peterborough; University College, Leicester; Univ. of London. Schoolmaster and Lecturer in adult education, 1931–37; Lecturer in Literature and Drama, Dept Extramural Studies, University of Bristol, 1937–40; Ministry of Information, specialising in film work, 1940–45; Research Officer, BFI, 1945–47; Dir, British Film Acad., 1947–59; Consultant to BAFTA and Editor of its Jl, 1959–76. Associate Editor, New Humanist (formerly Humanist), 1967–75. Has lectured on film subjects for BFI, British Council and other authorities in Great Britain, US, Canada, Far East, India, Caribbean, W Africa and most European countries; regular broadcaster, 1946–, including BBC's long-established programme The Critics. Visiting Fellow, Sussex Univ.; Bingham Prof. of Humanities, Louisville Univ., 1973. Governor, London Film School, 1966–74; Vice-Chm., Nat. Panel for Film Festivals, 1974–76; Member Cttee of Management, Society of Authors, 1954–57, 1965–68; Chairman: Society of Lecturers, 1959–61; Radiowriters' Assoc., 1962–64; Authors' Club, 1972–75. Hon. DFA New England Coll., USA, 1972; Hon. DLitt: Leicester, 1974; Louisville, 1979. Scholar-Teacher of the Year Award for 1984–85, Boston Univ. Commander of the Order of Merit of the Italian Republic, 1970; Order of Merit (First Class) of German Federal Republic, 1971. *Publications:* Film, 1944, revised 1946 and 1950; A Seat at the Cinema, 1951; On the Air (a study of broadcasting in sound and vision), 1953; The Animated Film, 1954; The Film and the Public, 1955; The Dreamers (novel), 1958; The Passion (novel), 1960; The Living Screen (a study of film and TV), 1961; What is a Film?, 1965; This Age of Communication, 1967; New Cinema in Europe, 1966; The July Plot (television play), 1966; New Cinema in the USA, 1968; Ellen Terry, 1968; New Cinema in Britain, 1969; SS and Gestapo, 1969; Sarah Siddons, 1970; Shakespeare and the Film, 1971; The Conspirators: 20 July 1944, 1971; Goering, 1972; Films and the Second World War, 1974; Charles Chaplin, 1974; Love Goddesses of the Movies, 1975; The Trial of Annie Besant, 1976; Theater and Film, 1979; Ingmar Bergman, 1980; Art and Animation, 1980; (ed and contributed) Experiment in the Film, 1949; (contributed) Twenty Years of British Film, 1947; collaborated: with Rachel Low in The History of the British Film 1896–1906, 1948; with Paul Rotha in revised edn of Movie Parade, 1950; with John Huntley in The Technique of Film Music, 1957; with John Halas in The Technique of Film Animation, 1959, Design in Motion, 1962, and Art in Movement, 1970; with Michael Fleming in Images of Madness: the portrayal of insanity in the feature film, 1985; with Heinrich Fraenkel in: Dr Goebbels, 1959, Hermann Goering, 1962, The July Plot, 1964, Heinrich Himmler, 1965, The Incomparable Crime, 1967, The Canaris Conspiracy, 1969, History of the German Cinema, 1971, Hess, 1971, Inside Adolf Hitler, 1973 (revd as Adolf Hitler, the Man and the Myth, 1977; enlarged UK edn, 1978), The Hundred Days to Hitler, 1974; Editor: Three British Screenplays, 1950; Penguin Film Review, 1946–49; The Cinema, 1950–52; The Year's Work in the Film (for British Council), 1949 and 1950; International Encyclopedia of Film, 1972; for over thirty years contrib. on Cinema to the Annual Register; contributed to Encyclopædia Britannica, journals at home and overseas concerned with history and art of the film and history of the Nazi régime. *Recreation:* travel abroad. *Address:* 15 Above Town, Dartmouth, Devon TQ6 9RG.

MANWARING, Randle (Gilbert), MA; FSS, FPMI; poet and author; retired company director; *b* 3 May 1912; *s* of late George Ernest and Lilian Manwaring; *m* 1941, Betty Violet, *d* of H. P. Rout, Norwich; three *s* one *d*. *Educ:* private schools. MA Keele, 1982. Joined Clerical, Medical and Gen. Life Assce Soc., 1929. War service, RAF, 1940–46, W/Cdr; comd RAF Regt in Burma, 1945. Clerical, Medical & Gen. Pensions Rep., 1950; joined C. E. Heath & Co. Ltd, 1956: Asst Dir, 1960, Dir, 1964, Man. Dir. 1969; Founder Dir (Man.), C. E. Heath Urquhart (Life and Pensions), 1966–71, and a Founder Dir, Excess Life Assce Co., 1967–75; Dir, Excess Insurance Group, 1975–78; Insurance Adviser, Midland Bank, 1971; first Man. Dir, Midland Bank Ins. Services, 1972–74, Vice-Chm., 1974–77, Dir, 1977–78. Chm., Life Soc., Corp. of Insce Brokers, 1965–66; Dep. Chm., Corp. of Insce Brokers, 1970–71; Pres., Soc. of Pensions Consultants, 1968–70. Chairman of Governors: Luckley-Oakfield Sch., 1972–83; Northease Manor Sch., 1972–84. Diocesan Reader (Chichester), 1968–; Mem., Diocesan Synod, 1985–. Chm., Vine Books Ltd; Dir, Crusaders Union Ltd, 1960– (Vice-Pres., 1983–). Chm. of Trustees, Careforce, 1980–. *Publications:* The Heart of this People, 1954; A Christian Guide to Daily Work, 1963; Thornhill Guide to Insurance, 1976; The Run of the Downs, 1984; From Controversy to Co-existence, 1985; *poems:* Posies Once Mine, 1951; Satires and Salvation, 1960; Under the Magnolia Tree, 1965; Slave to No Sect, 1966; Crossroads of the Year, 1975; From the Four Winds, 1976; In a Time of Unbelief, 1977; Poem Prayers for Growing People, 1980; The Swifts of Maggiore, 1981; In a Time of Change, 1983; Collected Poems, 1986; contrib. poems and articles to learned jls in GB and Canada. *Recreations:* music, reading, following cricket. *Address:* Marbles Barn, Newick, Lewes, East Sussex BN8 4LG. *T:* Newick 3845. *Clubs:* Royal Air Force, MCC.

MANZIE, (Andrew) Gordon, CB 1983; Second Permanent Secretary and Chief Executive, Property Services Agency, Department of the Enviroment, since 1984; *b* 3 April 1930; *s* of late John Mair and Catherine Manzie; *m* 1955, Rosalind Clay; one *s* one *d*. *Educ:* Royal High Sch. of Edinburgh; London Sch. of Economics and Political Science (BScEcon). Joined Civil Service as Clerical Officer, Scottish Home Dept, 1947. National Service, RAF, 1949. Min. of Supply: Exec. Officer (Higher Exec. Officer, 1957). Private Sec. to Perm. Sec., Min. of Aviation, 1962; Sen. Exec. Officer, 1963; Principal, 1964; Sec. to Cttee of Inquiry into Civil Air Transport (Edwards Cttee), 1967; Asst Sec., Dept of Trade and Industry, on loan to Min. of Posts and Telecommunications, 1971; Dept of Industry, 1974; Under-Sec., Dir, Office for Scotland, Depts of Trade and Industry, 1975; Under Sec., Scottish Economic Planning Dept, 1975–79; Dir, Industrial Develt Unit, 1980–81, Dep. Sec., 1980–84, Dept of Industry (Dept of Trade and Industry, 1983–84). *Recreations:* golf, reading. *Address:* 28 Manor Links, Bishop's Stortford, Herts CM23 5RA. *Club:* Caledonian.

MANZINI, Raimondo; Gran Croce, Ordine Merito Repubblica, 1968; GCVO (Hon.) 1969; former Secretary-General at Italian Ministry of Foreign Affairs, retired; *b* Bologna, 25 Nov. 1913. *Educ:* Univ. of California (Berkeley); Clark Univ., Mass. (MA); Dr of Law, Bologna Univ. Entered Diplomatic Service, 1940; Sec. to Italian Legation, Lisbon, 1941–43; Ministry of Foreign Affairs in Brindisi (1943) and Salerno (1944); Sec. to Italian Embassy, London, 1944–47; Consul General for Congo, Nigeria and Gold Coast, 1947–50; Consul General, Baden Baden, 1951–52; Head of Information Service, CED, Paris, 1952–53; Ministry of Foreign Affairs, 1953–55; Adviser to the Minister of Foreign Trade, 1955–58; Chef de Cabinet of Minister for Foreign Affairs, 1958; Diplomatic Adviser to the Prime Minister, 1958–59; Advr to Minister of Industry, 1960–64; Perm. Rep. to OECD, Paris, 1965–68; Ambassador to the Court of St James's, 1968–75. Commandeur, Légion d'Honneur (France), 1976. *Address:* Villa Bellochio, 83 Boulevard de Garavan, Menton, France.

MANZÙ, Giacomo; sculptor and painter; stage designer; *b* 22 Dec. 1908; *s* of Angelo and Maria Manzoni; marr. diss.; three *s* decd. *Educ:* Milan. Professor of Sculpture, Brera Accad., Milan, 1941–54; International Summer Acad., Salzburg, 1954–60. Grazioli Prize, Milan, 1934; Prize of Esposizione Universale, Paris, 1937; Sculpture Prize, Venice Biennale, 1948; Society of Portrait Sculptors' International Award (Jean Masson Davidson Medal), 1965; Internat. Feltrinelli Prize, Nat. Acad. of Arts, Rome, 1984. Works include: Cathedral main door, Salzburg, 1958, and re-designing of bronze doors of St Peter's, Rome, 1963 (commission won in open international competition); façade of Palace of Italy, NY, 1965; The Door of Peace and War, St Laurenz Church, Rotterdam, 1968. Exhibitions of Sculptures, Paintings and Drawings: La Cometa, Rome, 1937; Buenos Aires, 1949; Hanover Gall., London, 1953, 1965; NY, 1957; Haus der Kunst, Munich, 1959; Tate Gall., 1960; NY, Tokyo, Moscow, Leningrad, and Kiev, 1966; Bordeaux, 1969; Prague and Tokyo, 1973; Salzburg and Budapest, 1974; Rome, 1975; Moscow and Münster, 1976; (retrospective exhibn) Hamilton, Ont., 1980, and in 8 other Canadian cities, 1981; Tokyo, 1982, 1983; travelling exhibn to 8 Japanese Museums, 1983; Oslo and tour of Norway, 1986; Florence, 1986. Established permanent collection of his most important works at Ardea, near Rome, 1969, donated to the Republic of Italy, 1981; Sala Manzù established at Accademia Carrara, Bergamo, 1982; Bronze figure set up, Chamber of Commerce, Augsburg, 1983; Sala Manzù, Hermitage Mus., Leningrad, 1986. Hon. RA; Hon. RSA; Hon. Member: American Academy of Arts and Letters; National Academies of Argentina, Belgium and Rome; Accademia di Belle Arti Sovietica; Acad. Européenne des Sciences, des Arts et des Lettres, Paris; Akad. der Kunst, Berlin; Acad. des Beaux Arts, Paris; For. Hon. Mem., Amer. Acad. of Arts and Sci., 1978. Hon. Dr RCA 1971. Premio Internazionale Lenin per la pace, 1966. Medaglia d'Oro Benemeriti, Scuola, Cultura, Arte (Italy), 1981. *Publication:* La Porta di S Pietro, 1965; *relevant publications include:* J. Rewald, Giacomo Manzù, 1966; B. Heynold von Graefe, The Doors of Rotterdam, 1969. *Address:* 00040 Ardea, Rome, Italy.

MAPLES, Ven. Jeffrey Stanley; Archdeacon of Swindon and Hon. Canon Diocesan, Bristol Cathedral, 1974–82, Archdeacon Emeritus, 1982; *b* 8 Aug. 1916; *o s* of Arthur Stanley and Henrietta Georgina Maples; *m* 1945, Isobel Eileen Mabel Wren; four *s* (and one *s* decd). *Educ:* Downing Coll., Cambridge; Chichester Theological Coll. Asst Curate St James, Milton, Portsmouth, 1940–46; Asst Curate, Watlington, Diocese of Oxford, 1946–48. Vicar of Swinderby, Dio. Lincoln, and Diocesan Youth Chaplain, 1948–50; Vicar of St Michael-on-the-Mount, Lincoln, and Director of Religious Education: for Lincoln Dio., 1950–56; for Salisbury Dio., 1956–63; Canon of Lincoln, 1954–56; Chancellor of Salisbury Cathedral, 1960–67; Director of the Bible Reading Fellowship, 1963–67; Proctor in Convocation for Salisbury Diocese, 1957–70; Canon Emeritus of Salisbury Cathedral, 1967–; Vicar of St James, Milton, Portsmouth, 1967–74; Rural Dean of Portsmouth, 1968–73; Hon. Canon, Portsmouth Cathedral, 1972–74. *Address:* 88 Exeter Street, Salisbury, Wilts SP1 2SE. *T:* Salisbury 23848.

MAPLES, John Cradock; MP (C) West Lewisham, since 1983; *b* 22 April 1943; *s* of Thomas Cradock Maples and Hazel Mary Maples. *Educ:* Marlborough Coll., Wiltshire; Downing Coll., Cambridge; Harvard Business Sch., USA. Self employed lawyer and businessman. *Recreations:* sailing, skiing, cooking and wine. *Address:* House of Commons, SW1.

MAPLES EARLE, Ven. E. E.; *see* Earle.

MAR, Countess of (*suo jure*, 31st in line from Ruadri, 1st Earl of Mar, 1115); Premier Earldom of Scotland by descent; Lady Garioch, *c* 1320; **Margaret of Mar;** *b* 19 Sept. 1940; *er d* of 30th Earl of Mar, and Millicent Mary Salton; *S* father, 1975; recognised in surname "of Mar" by warrant of Court of Lord Lyon, 1967, when she abandoned her second forename; *m* 1st, 1959, Edwin Noel Artiss (marr. diss. 1976); one *d*; 2nd, 1976, (cousin) John Salton (marr. diss. 1981); 3rd, 1982, J. H. Jenkin, MA (Cantab), FRCO, LRAM, ARCM. Lay Mem., Immigration Appeal Tribunal, 1985–. Patron, Dispensing Doctors' Assoc., 1985–. Governor, King's Sch., Gloucester, 1984–. *Heir: d* Mistress of Mar, *qv*. *Address:* St Michael's Farm, Great Witley, Worcester WR6 6JB. *T:* Great Witley 608.

MAR, Mistress of; Lady Susan Helen of Mar; *b* 31 May 1963; *d* and *heiress* of Countess of Mar, *qv*. *Educ:* King Charles I School, Kidderminster; Christie College, Cheltenham. *Address:* 7 Allestree Road, SW6 6AD. *T:* 01–385 8480.

MAR, 13th Earl of, *cr* 1565, **and KELLIE,** 15th Earl of, *cr* 1619; **John Francis Hervey Erskine;** Baron Erskine, 1429; Viscount Fentoun, 1606; Baron Dirleton, 1603; Premier Viscount of Scotland; Hereditary Keeper of Stirling Castle; Representative Peer for Scotland, 1959–63; Major Scots Guards; retired 1954; Major, Argyll and Sutherland Highlanders (TA) retired 1959; Lord Lieutenant of Clackmannan, since 1966; *b* 15 Feb. 1921; *e s* of late Lord Erskine (John Francis Ashley Erskine), GCSI, GCIE; *S* grandfather, 1955; *m* 1948, Pansy Constance (OBE, 1984; Pres., UK Cttee for UNICEF, 1979–84; Chm., Youth at Risk Adv. Gp; Hon. Pres., Girls Bde, Scotland; Chm. and Vice-Chm., Scottish Standing Conf., Voluntary Youth Orgns, 1967–81. Elder of Church of Scotland. JP 1971; CStJ 1983), *y d* of late General Sir Andrew Thorne, KCB; three *s* one *d*. *Educ:* Eton; Trinity Coll., Cambridge. 2nd Lieut, Scots Guards, 1941; served in Egypt, N. Africa, Italy and Germany with 2nd Bn Scots Guards and HQ 201 Guards' Brigade, 1942–45 (wounded, despatches). Staff Coll., Camberley, 1950; DAAG, HQ, 3rd Infantry Div., 1951–52. DL Clackmannanshire, 1954, Vice-Lieutenant, 1957, JP 1962; County Councillor for Clackmannanshire, 1955–75 (Vice-Convener, 1961–64); Chairman: Forth Conservancy Board, 1957–68; Clackmannanshire T&AFA, 1961–68. An Elder of the Church of Scotland. Member of the Queen's Body Guard for Scotland (Royal Company of Archers). KStJ 1966. *Heir: s* Lord Erskine, *qv*. *Address:* Claremont House, Alloa, Clackmannanshire FK10 2JF. *T:* Alloa 212020. *Club:* New (Edinburgh).

MARA, Rt. Hon. Ratu Sir Kamisese Kapaiwai Tuimacilai, GCMG 1983; KBE 1969 (OBE 1961); PC 1973; Tui Nayau; Tui Lau; Prime Minister of Fiji, since 1970, and Minister for Foreign Affairs and Civil Aviation; Hereditary High Chief of the Lau Islands; *b* 13 May 1920; *s* of late Ratu Tevita Uluilakeba, Tui Nayau; *m* 1951, Adi Lady Lala Mara (Roko Tui Dreketi); three *s* five *d*. *Educ:* Fiji; Sacred Heart Coll., NZ; Otago Univ., NZ; Wadham Coll., Oxford (MA), Hon. Fellow, 1971; London Sch. of Economics (Dip. Econ. & Social Admin.), Hon. Fellow, 1985. Administrative Officer, Colonial Service, Fiji, Oct. 1950; Fijian MLC, 1953–, and MEC, 1959–61 (elected MLC and MEC, 1959). Member for Natural Resources and Leader of Govt Business; Alliance Party, 1964–66 (Founder of Party); Chief Minister and Mem., Council of Ministers, Fiji, 1967. Hon. Dr of Laws: Univ. of Guam, 1969; Univ. of Papua New Guinea, 1982; Hon. LLD: Univ. of Otago, 1973; New Delhi, 1975; Hon. DPolSc Korea, 1978; Hon. Dr Tokai Univ., 1980; DU Univ. of South Pacific, 1980. Man of the Pacific Award, 1984. Grand Cross, Order of Lion, Senegal, 1975; Order of Diplomatic Service Merit, Korea, 1978. *Recreations:* athletics, cricket, Rugby football, golf, fishing. *Address:* 11 Battery Road, Suva, Fiji. *T:* 311629. *Clubs:* United Oxford & Cambridge University, Achilles (London); Defence (Suva, Fiji).

MARAJ, Dr James Ajodhya; Permanent Secretary, Ministry of Foreign Affairs, Fiji, since 1986; High Commissioner for Fiji to India, since 1986; Vice-Chancellor, University of the South Pacific, 1975–82 (Hon. Professor of Education, since 1978); *b* 28 Sept. 1930; *s* of Ramgoolam Maraj and Popo Maraj; *m* 1951, Etress (*née* Ouditt); two *s* two *d*. *Educ:* St Mary's Coll. and Govt Teachers' Coll., Trinidad; Univ. of Birmingham (BA, PhD). FRICS 1981. Teacher, Lectr, 1947–60; Sen. Lectr, Univ. of West Indies, 1965–70; Head, Inst. of Educn, UWI, 1968–70; Dir, Educn Div., Commonwealth Secretariat, 1970–72; Commonwealth Asst Sec.-Gen., 1973–75; Sen. Evaluation Officer, The World Bank, 1982–84; High Comr for Fiji in Australia, Malaysia and Singapore, 1985–86. External Examr, Educn Adviser and Consultant to WHO and to several countries; Chm. or Sec. nat. or internat. commns. Hon. DLitt Loughborough, 1980; DU Univ. of South Pacific, 1983. Gold Medal of Merit, Trinidad and Tobago, 1974; Pacific Person of the Year, Fiji Times, 1978; Dist. Scholar's Award, British Council, 1979. Chevalier de la Légion d'Honneur, France, 1982. *Publications:* miscellaneous research papers. *Recreations:* sport: cricket, squash, horse-racing; poetry, music. *Address:* Ministry of Foreign Affairs, Government Buildings, Suva, Fiji. *Clubs:* Athenæum, Royal Commonwealth Society, Royal Over-Seas League.

'MARC'; *see* Boxer, C. M. E.

MARCEAU, Marcel; Chevalier de la Légion d'Honneur; Officier de l'Ordre National du Mérite; Commandeur des Arts et Lettres de la République Française; mime; Founder and Director, Compagnie de Mime Marcel Marceau, since 1949; Director, International School of Mime of Paris Marcel Marceau; *b* Strasbourg, 22 March 1923; *s* of Charles and Anne Mangel; two *s* two *d*. *Educ:* Ecole des Beaux Arts; Arts Décoratifs, Limoges; Ecole Etienne Decroux; Ecole Charles Dullin. First stage appearance, in Paris, 1946; with Barrault/Renaud Co., 1946–49; founded his company, 1949; since then has toured constantly, playing in 65 countries. Created about 100 pantomimes (most famous are The Creation of the World, The Cage, The Maskmaker, The Tree, Bip Liontamer, Bip hunts Butterfly, Bip plays David and Goliath, Bip at a Society Party, Bip in the Modern and Future Life, Bip Soldier, etc), and 26 mimodrames, and in particular the character 'Bip' (1947); *Mimodrames:* Bip et la fille des rues, 1947; Bip et L'Oiseau, 1948; Death Before Dawn, 1948; The Fair, 1949; The Flute Player, 1949; The Overcoat, 1951; Moriana and Galvan, Pierrot of Montmartre, 1952; Les Trois Perruques, 1953; Un Soir aux Funambules, 1953; La Parade en bleu et noir, 1956; le 14 juillet, 1956; Le Mont de Piété,

1956; Le Loup de Tsu Ku Mi, 1956; Le Petit Cirque, 1958; Les Matadors, 1959; Paris qui rit, Paris qui pleure, 1959; Don Juan, 1964; Candide, 1970, with Ballet de l'Opéra de Hambourg; *films:* The Overcoat, 1951; Barbarella, 1967; Scrooge (BBC London), 1973; Shanks, US, 1973; Silent Movie, 1976. Has made frequent TV appearances and many short films for TV, incl. Pantomimes, 1954, A Public Garden, 1955, Le mime Marcel Marceau, 1965, The World of Marcel Marceau, 1966, 12 short films with Enc. Brit., NY, 1974. Member: Acad. of Arts and Letters (DDR); Akad. der schönen Künste, Munich. Emmy Awards (US), 1955, 1968. Hon. Dr, Univ. of Oregon; Dr *hc* Univ. of Princeton, 1981. Gold Medal of Czechoslovak Republic (for contribution to cultural relations). *Publications:* Les 7 Péchés Capitaux (lithographs); Les Rêveries de Bip (lithographs), La Ballade de Paris et du Monde (text, lithographs, water-colours, drawings in ink and pencil); Alphabet Book; Counting Book; L'Histoire de Bip (text and lithographs); The Third Eye (lithoprint). *Recreations:* painting, poetry, fencing. *Address:* Compagnie de Mime Marcel Marceau, 21 rue Jean-Mermoz, 75008 Paris, France. *T:* 225 06 05 and 256 32 76.

MARCH AND KINRARA, Earl of; Charles Henry Gordon-Lennox; DL; *b* 19 Sept. 1929; *s* and *heir* of 9th Duke of Richmond and Gordon, *qv*; *m* 1951, Susan Monica, *o d* of late Colonel C. E. Grenville-Grey, CBE, Hall Barn, Blewbury, Berks; one *s* four *d*. *Educ:* Eton; William Temple Coll. 2nd Lieut, 60th Rifles, 1949–50. Chartered Accountant, 1956. Dir of Industrial Studies, William Temple Coll., 1964–68; Chancellor, Univ. of Sussex, 1985– (Treasurer, 1979–82). Church Commissioner, 1963–76; Mem. Gen. Synod of Church of England, formerly Church Assembly, 1960–80 (Chm., Bd for Mission and Unity, 1967–77); Mem., Central and Exec. Cttees, World Council of Churches, 1968–75; Chairman: Christian Orgn Res. and Adv. Trust, 1965–; House of Laity, Chichester Diocesan Synod, 1976–79; Vice-Chm., Archbishop's Commn on Church and State, 1966–70; Pres., Voluntary and Christian Service, 1982–. Mem., W Midlands Regional Economic Planning Council, 1965–68; Chm., Goodwood Group of Cos, 1969–; Dir, Radio Victory Ltd, 1982–. Historic Houses Association: Hon. Treas., 1975–82; Chm., SE Region, 1975–78; Dep. Pres., 1982–; President: Sussex Rural Community Council, 1973–; British Horse Soc., 1976–78; South of England Agricultural Soc., 1981–82; Vice-Pres., SE England Tourist Bd, 1974–; Chairman: Rugby Council of Social Service, 1961–68; Dunford Coll. (YMCA), 1969–82; Dir, Country Gentlemen's Assoc. Ltd, 1975–. Chairman: of Trustees, Sussex Heritage Trust, 1978–; Chichester Cathedral Develt Trust, 1985–. DL W Sussex, 1975. CBIM 1982. Medal of Honour, British Equestrian Fedn, 1983. *Heir: s* Lord Settrington, *qv*. *Address:* Goodwood House, Chichester, W Sussex. *T:* (office) Chichester 774107; (home) Chichester 774760.

See also Lord N. C. Gordon Lennox.

MARCH, Derek Maxwell, CBE 1982 (OBE 1973); HM Diplomatic Service; High Commissioner in Kampala, since 1986; *b* 9 Dec. 1930; *s* of Frank March and Vera (*née* Ward); *m* 1955, Sally Annetta Riggs; one *s* two *d*. *Educ:* Devonport High Sch.; Birkbeck Coll., London. National Service, RAF, 1949–51. Joined HM Diplomatic Service, 1949; FO, 1951; Bonn, 1955; Vice Consul, Hanover, 1957; Asst Trade Comr, Salisbury, 1959; Consul, Dakar, 1962; First Secretary: FO, 1964; Rawalpindi, 1968; Peking, 1971; FCO, 1974; Counsellor, seconded to Dept of Trade, 1975; Senior British Trade Comr, Hong Kong, 1977–82; Counsellor, seconded to DTI, 1982–86. *Recreations:* golf, cricket, Rugby Union. *Address:* c/o Foreign and Commonwealth Office, SW1; Soke House, The Soke, Alresford, Hants. *T:* Alresford 2588. *Clubs:* MCC, East India, Devonshire, Sports and Public Schools; Hong Kong (Hong Kong); Alresford Golf.

MARCH, Henry Arthur, MA (Oxon); *b* 14 March 1905; *s* of late Edward Gerald March, MD, Reading; *m* 1943, Mary (*d* 1968), *d* of late Rev. P. P. W. Gendall, Launceston; two *s* one *d*. *Educ:* Leighton Park Sch.; St John's Coll., Oxford. Asst Master, Merchant Taylors' Sch., 1929–39; Head of Modern Language side, 1940–54, and Housemaster, 1945–54, Charterhouse; Headmaster, Cranleigh Sch., 1954–59; Temp. Asst Master, Marlborough Coll., 1959–61; Asst Master, 1961–65. Acting Headmaster, Charterhouse, 1964. *Address:* Horsna Parc, St Tudy, Bodmin, Cornwall.

MARCH, Lionel John, ScD; FRSA; Professor and Head of Architecture/Urban Design Program, Graduate School of Architecture and Urban Planning, University of California, Los Angeles, since 1984; *b* 26 Jan. 1934; *o s* of Leonard James March and Rose (*née* Edwards); *m* 1st, 1960, Lindsey Miller (marr. diss. 1984); one *s* two *d*; 2nd, 1984, Maureen Vidler; one step *s* two step *d*. *Educ:* Hove Grammar Sch. for Boys; Magdalene Coll., Cambridge (MA, ScD). FIMA, FRSA. Nat. Service: Sub-Lt, RNVR, 1953–55. Harkness Fellow, Commonwealth Fund, Harvard Univ. and MIT, 1962–64; Asst to Sir Leslie Martin, 1964–66; Lectr in Architecture, Univ. of Cambridge, 1966–69; Dir, Centre for Land Use and Built Form Studies, Univ. of Cambridge, 1969–73; Prof., Dept of Systems Design, Univ. of Waterloo, Ontario, 1974–76; Prof. of Design, Faculty of Technology, Open Univ., 1976–81; Rector and Vice-Provost, RCA, 1981–84. Chm., Applied Res. of Cambridge Ltd, 1969–73. Mem., Governing Body, Imperial Coll. of Science and Technology, 1981–84. General Editor (with Leslie Martin), Cambridge Urban and Architectural Studies, 1970–; Editor, Environment and Planning B, Planning and Design, 1974–. *Publications:* (with Philip Steadman) The Geometry of Environment, 1971; (ed with Leslie Martin) Urban Space and Structures, 1972; (ed) The Architecture of Form, 1976. *Address:* The How House, 2422 Silver Ridge Avenue, Silver Lake, Los Angeles, Calif 90039, USA. *T:* (213) 661–7907.

MARCH, Prof. Norman Henry; Coulson Professor of Theoretical Chemistry, University of Oxford, since 1977; Fellow of University College, Oxford, since 1977; *b* 9 July 1927; *s* of William and Elsie March; *m* 1949, Margaret Joan Hoyle; two *s*. *Educ:* King's Coll., London Univ. University of Sheffield: Lecturer in Physics, 1953–57; Reader in Theoretical Physics, 1957–61; Prof. of Physics, 1961–72; Prof. of Theoretical Solid State Physics, Imperial Coll., Univ. of London, 1973–77. Hon. DTech Chalmers, Gothenburg, 1980. *Publications:* The Many-Body Problem in Quantum Mechanics (with W. H. Young and S. Sampanthar), 1967; Liquid Metals, 1968; (with W. Jones) Theoretical Solid State Physics, 1973; Self-Consistent Fields in Atoms, 1974; Orbital Theories of Molecules and Solids, 1974; (with M. P. Tosi) Atomic Dynamics in Liquids, 1976; (with M. Parrinello) Collective Effects in Solids and Liquids, 1983; (with S. Lundqvist) The Theory of the Inhomogeneous Electron Gas, 1983; (with M. P. Tosi) Coulomb Liquids, 1984; (with M. P. Tosi) Polymers, Liquid Crystals and Low-Dimensional Solids, 1984; (with R. A. Street and M. P. Tosi) Amorphous Solids and the Liquid State, 1985; Chemical Bonds outside Metal Surfaces, 1986; (with P. N. Butcher and M. P. Tosi) Crystalline Semiconducting Materials and Devices, 1986; many scientific papers on quantum mechanics and statistical mechanics in Proceedings Royal Society, Phil. Magazine, etc. *Recreations:* music, chess, cricket. *Address:* Elmstead, 6 Northcroft Road, Englefield Green, Egham, Surrey. *T:* Egham 3078.

MARCH, Valerie, (Mrs Andrew March); *see* Masterson, V.

MARCHAMLEY, 3rd Baron, *cr* 1908, of Hawkstone; **John William Tattersall Whiteley;** late Lieutenant, Royal Armoured Corps; *b* 24 April 1922; *s* of 2nd Baron and Margaret Clara (*d* 1974), *d* of Thomas Scott Johnstone of Glenmark, Waipara, New Zealand; *S* father, 1949; *m* 1967, Sonia Kathleen Pedrick; one *s*. Served War of 1939–45, Captain, 19th King George V Own Lancers. *Heir: s* Hon. William Francis Whiteley, *b* 27 July 1968. *Address:* Whetcombe, North Huish, South Brent, Devon.

MARCHANT, Catherine; *see* Cookson, C.

MARCHANT, Edgar Vernon; Director, Paddington Building Society, since 1977; *b* 7 Dec. 1915; *s* of E. C. Marchant; *m* 1945, Joyce Allen Storey; one *s* two *d*. *Educ:* Marlborough Coll.; Lincoln Coll., Oxford. Engr, Bahrain Petroleum Co., 1938; various technical and scientific posts in Min. of Aircraft Production, Min. of Supply and RAF, 1940–51; Principal, Min. of Supply, 1951; Principal, BoT, 1955; Asst Sec., BoT, 1959; Asst Registrar of Restrictive Trading Agreements, 1964; Asst Sec., Dept of Economic Affairs, 1966; Nat. Board for Prices and Incomes: Asst Sec., 1967–68; Under-Sec., 1968–71; Under-Sec., DTI, later Dept of Industry, 1971–75. *Recreations:* gardening, messing about in boats. *Address:* 87 New Forest Drive, Brockenhurst, Hants SO4 7QT. *Clubs:* Royal Southampton Yacht, Royal Lymington Yacht.

MARCHANT, Ven. George John Charles; Archdeacon Emeritus and Canon Emeritus of Durham, since 1983; *b* 3 Jan. 1916; *s* of late T. Marchant, Little Stanmore, Mddx; *m* 1944, Eileen Lillian Kathleen, *d* of late F. J. Smith, FCIS; one *s* three *d*. *Educ:* St John's Coll., Durham (MA, BD); Tyndale Hall, Bristol. Deacon 1939, priest 1940, London; Curate of St Andrew's, Whitehall Park, N19, 1939–41; Licence to officiate, London dio., 1941–44 (in charge of Young Churchmen's Movement); Curate of St Andrew-the-Less, Cambridge (in charge of St Stephen's), 1944–48; Vicar of Holy Trinity, Skirbeck, Boston, 1948–54; Vicar of St Nicholas, Durham, 1954–74; Rural Dean of Durham, 1964–74; Hon. Canon of Durham Cathedral, 1972–74; Archdeacon of Auckland and Canon Residentiary, Durham Cathedral, 1974–83. Member of General Synod, 1970–80 (Proctor in Convocation for Dio. Durham). Chm. Editorial Bd, Anvil, 1983–. *Publications:* book reviews. *Recreations:* record-music, bird watching, gardening. *Address:* 28 Greenways, Eaton, Norwich NR4 6PE. *T:* Norwich 58295.

MARCHANT, Sir Herbert (Stanley), KCMG 1963 (CMG 1957); OBE 1946; MA Cantab; *b* 18 May 1906; *s* of E. J. Marchant; *m* 1937, Diana Selway, *d* of C. J. Selway, CVO, CBE; one *s*. *Educ:* Perse Sch.; St John's Coll., Cambridge (MA 1929). Asst Master, Harrow Sch., 1928–39; Foreign Office, 1940–46; Consul, Denver, Colorado, USA, 1946–48; First Secretary, British Legation, Bucharest, 1948–49; Counsellor, British Embassy, Paris, 1950–52; Consul-General, Zagreb, 1952–54; Land Commissioner and Consul-General for North Rhine/Westphalia, 1954–55; Consul-General, Düsseldorf, 1955–57; Consul-General, San Francisco, 1957–60; Ambassador to Cuba, 1960–63; Ambassador to Tunisia, 1963–66. Asst Dir, Inst. of Race Relations, 1966–68; UK Representative, UN Cttee for Elimination of Racial Discrimination, 1969–73. Chm., British-Tunisian Soc., 1970–74. *Publications:* Scratch a Russian, 1936; His Excellency Regrets, 1980. *Recreations:* mountains, spear fishing, theatre. *Club:* Travellers'.

MARCHWOOD, 3rd Viscount *cr* 1945, of Penang and of Marchwood, Southampton; **David George Staveley Penny;** Bt 1933; Baron 1937; Director, Moët & Chandon (London) Ltd; *b* 22 May 1936; *s* of 2nd Viscount Marchwood, MBE and Pamela (*d* 1979), *o d* of John Staveley Colton-Fox; *S* father, 1979; *m* 1964, Tessa Jane, *d* of W. F. Norris; three *s*. *Educ:* Winchester College. 2nd Lt, Royal Horse Guards (The Blues), 1955–57. Joined Schweppes Ltd, 1958, and held various positions in the Cadbury Schweppes group before joining his present company. *Recreations:* cricket, shooting, racing. *Heir: s* Hon. Peter George Worsley Penny, *b* 8 Oct. 1965. *Address:* Filberts, Aston Tirrold, near Didcot, Oxon. *T:* Blewbury 850386. *Clubs:* White's, MCC.

MARCUS, Frank Ulrich; playwright; Television Critic for Plays International Magazine, since 1984; *b* Breslau, Germany, 30 June 1928; *s* of late Frederick and Gertie Marcus; *m* 1951, Jacqueline (*née* Sylvester); one *s* two *d*. *Educ:* Bunce Court Sch., Kent (evac. to Shropshire during war); St Martin's Sch. of Art, London. Actor, Dir, Scenic Designer, Unity Theatre, Kensington (later Internat. Theatre Gp). Theatre Critic, Sunday Telegraph, 1968–78. *Stage plays:* Minuet for Stuffed Birds, 1950; The Man Who Bought a Battlefield, 1963; The Formation Dancers, 1964; The Killing of Sister George, 1965 (3 'Best Play of the Year' Awards: Evening Standard, Plays and Players, Variety); Cleo, 1965; Studies of the Nude, 1967; Mrs Mouse, Are You Within?, 1968; The Window, 1969; Notes on a Love Affair, 1972; Blank Pages, 1972; Carol's Christmas, 1973; Beauty and the Beast, 1975; Portrait of the Artist (mime scenario), 1977; Blind Date, 1977; The Ballad of Wilfred the Second, 1978; The Merman of Orford (mime scenario), 1978; *television plays:* A Temporary Typist, 1966; The Glove Puppet, 1968; *radio plays:* The Hospital Visitor, 1980; The Beverley Brooch, 1981; The Row over La Ronde, 1982; *translations:* Schnitzler's Reigen, 1952 (as La Ronde, TV, 1982); Liebelei (TV), 1954; Anatol, 1976; Molnar's The Guardsman, 1978 (first perf., 1969); Kaiser's From Morning Till Midnight, 1979; Hauptmann's The Weavers, 1980. *Publications:* The Formation Dancers, 1964; The Killing of Sister George, 1965; The Window, 1968; Mrs Mouse, Are You Within?, 1969; Notes on a Love Affair, 1972; Blank Pages, 1973; Beauty and the Beast, 1977; Blind Date, 1977; contribs to: Behind the Scenes, 1972; Those Germans, 1973; On Theater, 1974 (US), etc, also to London Magazine, Plays and Players, Dramatists' Quarterly (US), New York Times, etc. *Recreation:* observing. *Address:* 8 Kirlegate, Meare, Glastonbury, Somerset BA6 9TA. *T:* Meare Heath 398; c/o Margaret Ramsay Ltd, 14a Goodwin's Court, St Martin's Lane, WC2.

MARDELL, Peggy Joyce, CBE 1982; Regional Nursing Officer, North West Thames Regional Health Authority, 1974–82; *b* 8 July 1927; *d* of Alfred Edward and Edith Mary Mardell. *Educ:* George Spicer Sch., Enfield; Highlands Hosp., London (RFN); E Suffolk Hosp., Ipswich (Medallist, SRN); Queen Charlotte's Hosp. Battersea Coll. of Further Educn (Hons Dip., RNT). Queens Inst. of District Nursing, Guildford, 1951–52 (SCM); Ward Sister, Night Sister, Bethnal Green Hosp., 1953–55; Sister Tutor, Royal Surrey County Hosp., 1957–64; Asst Regional Nursing Officer, NE Metrop. Regional Hosp. Bd, 1964–70; Chief Regional Nursing Officer, NW Metrop. Regional Hosp. Bd, 1970–74. Lectr, British Red Cross, 1958–60; Examr, Gen. Nursing Council, 1962–70; Nurse Mem., Surrey AHA, 1977–82; Member: Royal Coll. of Nursing; Regional Nurse Trng Cttee, 1970–82; Assessor for Nat. Nursing Staff Cttee, 1970–82. *Recreations:* renovating old furniture, gardening, reading. *Address:* 19 East Meads, Guildford, Surrey. *T:* Guildford 575906.

MARDEN, John Louis, CBE 1976; JP; Former Chairman, Wheelock, Marden and Co. Ltd; *b* Woodford, Essex, 12 Feb. 1919; *s* of late George Ernest Marden; *m* 1947, Anne Harris; one *s* three *d*. *Educ:* Gresham Sch., Norfolk; Trinity Hall, Cambridge (MA). Served War, as Captain 49th Regt RHA, in N Africa, France and Germany, 1940–46. Joined Wheelock, Marden & Co. Ltd, as trainee (secretarial and shipping, then insurance side of business), 1946; Dir of company, 1952, Chm., 1959. Chm., Hong Kong Shipowners' Assoc., 1978–. JP Hong Kong, 1964. *Recreations:* golf, water ski-ing, ski-ing. *Address:* PO Box 85, Hong Kong.

MARDER, Bernard Arthur; QC 1977; **His Honour Judge Marder;** a Circuit Judge, since 1983; *b* 25 Sept. 1928; *er s* of late Samuel Marder and Marie Marder; *m* 1953, Sylvia

Levy; one *s* one *d. Educ:* Bury Grammar Sch.; Manchester Univ. (LLB 1951). Called to the Bar, Gray's Inn, 1952. A Recorder of the Crown Court, 1979–83. Formerly Asst Comr, Local Govt and Parly Boundary Commns; Chm., Panel of Inquiry into W Yorks Structure Plan, 1979. *Recreations:* music, theatre, wine, rambling. *Address:* 4/5 Gray's Inn Square, Gray's Inn, WC1R 5AY.

MARDON, Lt-Col (John) Kenric La Touche, DSO 1945; TD 1943; DL; MA; JP; Vice Lord-Lieutenant, Avon, 1974–80; Chairman, Mardon, Son & Hall, Ltd, Bristol, 1962–69; Director, Bristol & West Building Society, 1969–82; *b* 29 June 1905; *e s* of late Evelyn John Mardon, Halsway Manor, Crowcombe and late Maud Mary (*née* Rothwell); *m* 1933, Dulcie Joan, 3rd *d* of late Maj.-Gen. K. M. Body, CB, CMG, OBE; two *s* one *d. Educ:* Clifton; Christ's Coll., Cambridge. Commissioned in Royal Devon Yeomanry, 1925; Major, 1938; Lieut-Colonel, RA, 1942; served War of 1939–45, in N.W. Europe, 1944–45 (despatches). JP Somerset, 1948; High Sheriff of Somerset, 1956–57; DL 1962. Master, Society of Merchant Venturers, Bristol, 1959–60; Governor, Clifton Coll., 1957. Pres., Bristol YMCA, 1969–79. *Recreations:* shooting, lawn tennis, squash rackets (rep. Cambridge v. Oxford, 1925). *Address:* 4 Rivers Street, Bath BA1 2PZ. *T:* Bath 337725. *Club:* Bath and County (Bath).

MAREK, John, PhD; MP (Lab) Wrexham, since 1983; *b* 24 Dec. 1940; *m* 1964, Anne. *Educ:* Univ. of London (BSc (Hons), PhD). Lecturer in Applied Mathematics, University College of Wales, Aberystwyth, 1966–83. Junior opposition frontbench spokesman on health, 1985–. *Publications:* various research papers. *Recreation:* basketball. *Address:* 44 Percy Road, Wrexham, Clwyd LL13 7EF. *T:* Wrexham 264152.

MARENGO, Kimon Evan; *see* Kem.

MARGADALE, 1st Baron, *cr* 1964, of Islay, Co. Argyll; **John Granville Morrison,** TD; JP; DL; Lord-Lieutenant of Wiltshire, 1969–81; Member Royal Company of Archers (Queen's Body Guard for Scotland); *b* 16 Dec. 1906; *s* of late Hugh Morrison; *m* 1928, Hon. Margaret Esther Lucie Smith (*d* 1980), 2nd *d* of 2nd Viscount Hambleden; three *s* one *d. Educ:* Eton; Magdalene Coll., Cambridge. Served 1939–45 with Royal Wilts Yeomanry; in MEF, 1939–42. MP (C) Salisbury Division of Wilts, 1942–64; Chairman, Conservative Members' (1922) Cttee, 1955–64. Yeomanry Comdt and Chm., Yeomanry Assoc., 1965–71; Hon. Col, The Royal Wiltshire Yeomanry Sqdn, 1965–71; Hon. Col, The Royal Yeomanry, 1965–71; Dep. Hon. Col, The Wessex Yeomanry, 1971–. JP 1936, High Sheriff, 1938, DL 1950, Wilts. MFH S and W Wilts Foxhounds, 1932–66. KStJ 1972. *Heir: s* Major Hon. James Ian Morrison, *qv. Address:* Fonthill House, Tisbury, Wilts. *T:* Tisbury 870202; Eallubus, Bridgend, Argyll. *Clubs:* Turf, Jockey, White's.

See also Hon. C. A. Morrison, Hon. M. A. Morrison, Hon. P. H. Morrison.

MARGÁIN, Hugo B.; GCVO; Ambassador of Mexico to the United States, 1965–70 and 1977–82; *b* 13 Feb. 1913; *s* of Cesar R. Margáin and Maria Teresa Gleason de Margáin; *m* 1941, Margarita Charles de Margáin; two *s* three *d* (and one *s* decd). *Educ:* National Univ. of Mexico (UNAM); National Sch. of Jurisprudence (LLB). Prof. of Constitutional Law, 1947, of Constitutional Writs, 1951–56, and of Fiscal Law, 1952–56, Univ. of Mexico. Govt posts include: Dir-Gen., Mercantile Transactions Tax, 1951–52, and Dir-Gen., Income Tax, 1952–59, Min. for Finance. Official Mayor, Min. for Industry and Commerce, 1959–61; Dep. Minister of Finance, Sept. 1961–Dec. 1964; Sec. of Finance, Aug. 1970–May 1973; Ambassador to the UK, 1973–77. Chm., Nat. Commn on Corporate Profit-Sharing (ie labour participation), 1963–64; Govt Rep. on Bd of Nat. Inst. for Scientific Res., 1962–63 (Chm. of Bd, 1963–64). Holds hon. degrees from univs in USA. Hon. GCVO 1975. *Publications:* Avoidance of Double Taxation Based on the Theory of the Source of Taxable Income, 1956; Preliminary Study on Tax Codification, 1957; (with H. L. Gumpel) Taxation in Mexico, 1957; Civil Rights and the Writ of Amparo in Administrative Law, 1958; The Role of Fiscal Law in Economic Development, 1960; Profit Sharing Plan, 1964; Housing Projects for Workers (Infonavit), 1971. *Recreations:* riding, swimming. *Address:* Ministerio de Relaciones Exteriores, Avenue Nonoalco, Matelolco, México 3, DF, México.

MARGASON, Geoffrey, CEng, FICE, FIHE; FBIM; Director, Transport and Road Research Laboratory, Crowthorne, since 1984 (Deputy Director, 1980–84); *b* 19 Sept. 1933; *s* of Henry and Edna Margason; *m* 1958, Bernice Thompson; one *s* two *d. Educ:* Humberston Foundation Sch., Cleethorpes; Loughborough College of Advanced Technology (DLCEng). With British Transport Commission and Mouchel Associates, Consulting Engineers, until 1960; Transport and Road Research Laboratory: Researcher in Geotechnics, 1960–69; Research Manager in Construction Planning, Scottish Br. and Transport Planning, 1969–75; Sen. Research Manager in Transport Operations, 1975–78; Head of Research and Science Policy Unit, Depts of Environment and Transport, 1978–80. *Publications:* papers in jls of various professional instns and to nat. and internat. confs on range of topics in highway transportation; reports of TRRL. *Recreations:* sailing, caravanning. *Address:* Transport and Road Research Laboratory, Old Wokingham Road, Crowthorne, Berks RG11 6UA. *T:* Crowthorne 773131. *Club:* Frensham Pond (Farnham).

MARGERISON, Thomas Alan; author, journalist and broadcaster on scientific subjects; *b* 13 Nov. 1923; *s* of late Ernest Alan Margerison and Isabel McKenzie; *m* 1950, Pamela Alice Tilbrook; two *s. Educ:* Huntingdon Grammar Sch.; Hymers Coll., Hull; King's Sch., Macclesfield; Sheffield University. Research Physicist, 1949; film script writer, Film Producers Guild, 1950; Scientific Editor, Butterworths sci. pubns, Ed. Research, 1951–56; Man. Editor, Heywood Pubns and National Trade Press, 1956. First Scientific Editor, The New Scientist, 1956–61; Science Corresp., Sunday Times, 1961; Dep. Editor, Sunday Times Magazine, 1962; Man. Dir, Thomson Technical Developments Ltd, 1964; Dep. Man. Dir, 1967–69, Chief Exec., 1969–71, London Weekend Television; Dir, 1966, Chm., 1971–75, Computer Technology Ltd. Chm., Communications Cttee, UK Nat. Commn for UNESCO. Worked for many years with Tonight team on BBC. Responsible for applying computers to evening newspapers in Reading and Hemel Hempstead. *Publications:* articles and television scripts, indifferent scientific papers; (ed) popular science books. *Recreation:* sailing. *Club:* Savile.

MARGESSON, family name of **Viscount Margesson.**

MARGESSON, 2nd Viscount *cr* 1942, of Rugby; **Francis Vere Hampden Margesson;** *b* 17 April 1922; *o s* of 1st Viscount Margesson, PC, MC, and Frances H. Leggett (*d* 1977), New York; *S* father, 1965; *m* 1958, Helena, *d* of late Heikki Backstrom, Finland; one *s* three *d. Educ:* Eton; Trinity Coll., Oxford. Served War of 1939–45, as Sub-Lt, RNVR. A Director of Thames & Hudson Publications, Inc., New York, 1949–53. ADC to Governor of the Bahamas, 1956; Information Officer, British Consulate-General, NY, 1964–70. *Heir: s* Lt the Hon. Richard Francis David Margesson, Coldstream Guards, *b* 25 Dec. 1960. *Address:* Ridgely Manor, Box 245, Stone Ridge, New York, NY 12484, USA.

MARGETSON, Sir John William Denys, KCMG 1986 (CMG 1979); HM Diplomatic Service; Ambassador to the Netherlands, since 1984; *b* 9 Oct. 1927; *yr s* of Very Rev. W. J. Margetson and Marion Jenoure; *m* 1963, Miranda, *d* of Sir William Menzies Coldstream, *qv* and Mrs Nancy Spender; one *s* one *d. Educ:* Blundell's; St John's Coll., Cambridge. Lieut, Life Guards, 1947–49. Colonial Service, District Officer, Tanganyika, 1951–60 (Private Sec. to Governor, Sir Edward Twining, subseq. Lord Twining, 1956–57); entered Foreign (subseq. Diplomatic) Service, 1960; The Hague, 1962–64; speech writer to Foreign Sec., Rt Hon. George Brown, MP, subseq. Lord George-Brown, 1966–68; Head of Chancery, Saigon, 1968–70; Counsellor 1971, seconded to Cabinet Secretariat, 1971–74; Head of Chancery, UK Delegn to NATO, 1974–78; Ambassador to Vietnam, 1978–80; seconded to MoD as Senior Civilian Instructor, RCDS, 1981–82; Ambassador and Dep. Perm. Rep. to UN, NY, 1983–84. Pres., Trusteeship Council, 1983–84. FRSA. *Recreation:* music. *Address:* c/o Foreign and Commonwealth Office, SW1. *Clubs:* Brooks's; Haagsche (The Hague).

MARGETTS, Frederick Chilton, CBE 1966 (MBE 1943); Consultant, Containerisation; *b* 2 Nov. 1905; *m* 1929, Dorothy Walls; one *d. Educ:* Driffield Grammar Sch.; St Martin's Grammar Sch., Scarborough. Asst Operating Supt, LNER Scotland, 1946; BR Scotland, 1949; Chief Operating Supt, BR Scotland, 1955; Chief Traffic Manager, 1958, Asst General Manager, 1959, General Manager, 1961, BR York; Member BR Cttee, 1962; Operating Mem., BR Board, 1962–67. *Publication:* Records of the York Cordwainers Company from circa 1395, 1983. *Recreations:* œnology, history of ancient gilds. *Address:* 9 Riseborough House, York YO3 6NQ. *T:* York 26207.

MARGRIE, Victor Robert, CBE 1984; FSIAD; studio potter; *b* 29 Dec. 1929; *s* of Robert and Emily Miriam Margrie; *m* 1955, Janet Smithers; three *d. Educ:* Southgate County Grammar Sch.; Hornsey Sch. of Art (now Mddx Polytechnic) (NDD, ATD 1952). FSIAD 1975. Part-time teaching at various London art colls, 1952–56; own workshop, making stoneware and latterly porcelain, 1954–71; Head of Ceramics Dept, Harrow Sch. of Art, 1963–71 (founded Studio Pottery Course); Sec., Crafts Adv. Cttee, 1971–77; Dir, Crafts Council, 1977–84; own studio, Bristol, 1985. One-man exhibns, British Craft Centre (formerly Crafts Centre of GB), 1964, 1966 and 1968; represented in V&A Museum and other collections. Vice-Chm., Crafts Centre of GB, 1965; Member: Cttee for Art and Design, DATEC, 1979–84; Cttee for Art and Design, CNAA, 1981–84; Design Bursaries Bd, RSA, 1980–84; Working Party, Gulbenkian Craft Initiative, 1985–; Fine Art Adv. Cttee, British Council, 1983–; UK National Commn for UNESCO, 1984–85 (also Mem., Culture Adv. Cttee); Adv. Council, V&A Mus., 1979–84; Craftsmen Potters Assoc., 1960–; Internat. Acad. of Ceramics, 1972–. Ext. Examiner, Royal Coll. of Art: Dept of Ceramics and Glass, 1977; Dept of Silversmithing and Jewellery, 1978–80. Governor: Herts Coll. of Art and Design, 1977–79; Camberwell Sch. of Art and Crafts, 1975–84; W Surrey Coll. of Art and Design, 1978–; Loughborough Coll. of Art and Design, 1984–. *Publications:* contributed to: Oxford Dictionary of Decorative Arts, 1975; Europaischt Keramik Seit 1950, 1979; Lucie Rie, 1981; contrib. specialist pubns and museum catalogues. *Address:* 3 The Polygon, Clifton, Bristol BS8 4PW. *T:* Bristol 277527.

MARJORIBANKS, (Edyth) Leslia, JP; MA; Headmistress, The Henrietta Barnett School, London, since 1973; *b* 17 Feb. 1927; *d* of late Stewart Dudley Marjoribanks and late Nancye (*née* Lee) *Educ:* Cheltenham Ladies' Coll.; Girton Coll., Cambridge (BA Hons Hist. 1951, MA 1955); Hughes Hall, Cambridge (Certif. Educn 1952). Talbot Heath, Bournemouth: Asst History Mistress, 1952–57; Head of History Dept, 1957–68; Headmistress, Holly Lodge High Sch., Liverpool, 1969–73. Mem. Governing Council, Examinations Cttee and Curriculum Sub-Cttee of North-West Sec. Schs Exam. Board, 1969–73. JP City of Liverpool, 1971–73, Inner London, 1976. *Recreations:* gardening, cookery. *Address:* 29 Park Farm Close, N2 0PU. *T:* 01–883 6609.

MARJORIBANKS, Sir James Alexander Milne, KCMG 1965 (CMG 1954); Chairman, Scotland in Europe, since 1979; *b* 29 May 1911; *y s* of Rev. Thomas Marjoribanks, DD, and Mary Ord, *d* of William Logan, Madras CS; *m* 1936, Sonya Patricia (*d* 1981), *d* of David Stanley-Alder, Alderford Grange, Sible Hedingham, Essex, and Sylvia Marie Stanley; one *d. Educ:* Merchiston; Edinburgh Academy; Edinburgh Univ. (MA, 1st class hons). Entered Foreign Service, Nov. 1934; HM Embassy, Peking, 1935–38; Consulate-General, Hankow, 1938; Marseilles, 1939–40; Consul, Jacksonville, 1940–42; Vice-Consul, New York, 1942–44; Asst to UK Political Rep., Bucharest, 1944–45; Foreign Office, 1945–49; Dep. to Secretary of State for Foreign Affairs in Austrian Treaty negotiations, 1947–49; Official Secretary, UK High Commn, Canberra, 1950–52; Dep. Head of UK Delegation to High Authority of European Coal and Steel Community, 1952–55; Cabinet Office, 1955–57; HM Minister (Economic), Bonn, 1957–62; Asst Under-Secretary of State, Foreign Office, 1962–65; Ambassador and Head of UK Delegn to European Economic Community, European Atomic Energy Community and ECSC, 1965–71. Director: Scottish Council (Develt and Industry), 1971–81 (Vice-Pres., 1981–83); The Distillers Co. Ltd, 1971–76; Governing Mem., Inveresk Research International, 1978–. Gen. Council Assessor, Edinburgh Univ. Ct, 1975–79. *Recreations:* hill walking, croquet. *Address:* 13 Regent Terrace, Edinburgh EH7 5BN; Lintonrig, Kirk Yetholm, Roxburghshire TD5 8PH. *Club:* New (Edinburgh).

MARJORIBANKS, Leslia; *see* Marjoribanks, E. L.

MARK, James, MBE 1943; Under-Secretary, Ministry of Overseas Development, 1965–74, retired; *b* 12 June 1914; *s* of late John Mark and Louisa Mary (*née* Hobson); *m* 1941, Mary Trewent Rowland; three *s* two *d. Educ:* William Hulme's Grammar Sch., Manchester; Trinity Coll., Cambridge; Universities of Munich and Münster. MA 1939. PhD 1939, Cambridge. Intelligence Corps, 1940–46. Principal, Control Office for Germany and Austria, 1946–48; HM Treasury, 1948–64; Asst Secretary, 1950; Economic Counsellor, Washington, 1951–53. Jt Editor, Theology, 1976–83. *Publications:* The Question of Christian Stewardship, 1964; articles and reviews on theological and related subjects. *Recreations:* reading, music, theatre. *Address:* 6 Manorbrook, SE3. *T:* 01–852 9289.

See also Sir Robert Mark.

MARK, Sir Robert, GBE 1977; Kt 1973; QPM 1965; Commissioner, Metropolitan Police, 1972–77 (Deputy Commissioner, 1968–72); Chairman, Forest Mere Ltd, since 1978; Director, Control Risks Ltd, since 1982; *b* Manchester, 13 March 1917; *y s* of late John Mark and Louisa Mark (*née* Hobson); *m* 1941, Kathleen Mary Leahy; one *s* one *d. Educ:* William Hulme's Grammar Sch., Manchester. Constable to Chief Superintendent, Manchester City Police, 1937–42, 1947–56; Chief Constable of Leicester, 1957–67; Assistant Commissioner, Metropolitan Police, 1967–68. Vis. Fellow, Nuffield Coll., Oxford, 1970–78 (MA Oxon 1971). Member: Standing Advisory Council of Penal System, 1966; Adv. Cttee on Police in Northern Ireland, 1969; Assessor to Lord Mountbatten during his Inquiry into Prison Security, 1966. Royal Armoured Corps, 1942–47: Lieut, Phantom (GHQ Liaison Regt), North-West Europe, 1944–45; Major, Control Commission for Germany, 1945–47. Lecture tour of N America for World Affairs Council and FCO, Oct. 1971; Edwin Stevens Lecture to the Laity, RCM, 1972; Dimbleby Meml Lecture (BBC TV), 1973. Dir, Phoenix Assurance Co. Ltd, 1977–85. Mem. Council, AA, 1977–; Governor and Mem. Admin. Bd, Corps of Commissionaires, 1977–; Hon. Freeman, City of Westminster, 1977. Hon. LLM Leicester Univ., 1967; Hon. DLitt Loughborough, 1976; Hon. LLD: Manchester, 1978; Liverpool, 1978. KStJ

1977. *Publications*: Policing a Perplexed Society, 1977; In the Office of Constable, 1978. *Address*: Esher, Surrey KT10 8LU.
See also James Mark.

MARKALL, Most Rev. Francis, SJ; *b* 24 Sept. 1905; *e s* of late Walter James Markall and Alice Mary Gray, London. *Educ*: St Ignatius' College, London. Entered Society of Jesus, 1924; continued classical and philosophical studies, 1926–31; Assistant Master, Stonyhurst College, 1931–34; theological studies, 1934–38; Missionary in Rhodesia, 1939–56; Titular Archbishop of Cotieo and Coadjutor with right of succession to Archbishop of Salisbury, April 1956; Archbishop of Salisbury and Metropolitan of Province of Rhodesia, Nov. 1956; retired, 1976. *Address*: House of Adoration, PO Box EH79, Emerald Hill, Harare, Zimbabwe. *Club*: Harare (Harare).

MARKHAM, Sir Charles (John), 3rd Bt, *cr* 1911; *b* 2 July 1924; *s* of Sir Charles Markham, 2nd Bt, and Gwladys, *e d* of late Hon. Rupert Beckett; *S* father 1952; *m* 1949, Valerie, *o d* of Lt-Col E. Barry-Johnston, Makuyu, Kenya; two *s* one *d*. *Educ*: Eton. Served War of 1939–45, Lieut in 11th Hussars (despatches). Vice-Chm., Nairobi Co. Council, 1953–55; MLC Kenya, 1955–60. Pres., Royal Agricultural Soc., Kenya, 1958. KStJ 1973. *Heir*: *s* Arthur David Markham [*b* 6 Dec. 1950; *m* 1977, Carolyn, *yr d* of Captain Mungo Park; two *d*]. *Address*: PO Box 42263, Nairobi, Kenya, East Africa. *Club*: Cavalry and Guards.

MARKING, Sir Henry (Ernest), KCVO 1978; CBE 1969; MC 1944; CompRAeS 1953; FCIT; Chairman, Rothmans UK Ltd, 1979–86; Director: Rothmans International Ltd, 1979–86; Barclays International Ltd, 1977–86; *b* 11 March 1920; *s* of late Isaac and Hilda Jane Marking. *Educ*: Saffron Walden Gram. Sch.; University Coll., London. Served War of 1939–45: 2nd Bn The Sherwood Foresters, 1941–45; North Africa, Italy and Middle East; Adjutant, 1944–45. Middle East Centre of Arab Studies, Jerusalem, 1945–46. Admitted solicitor, 1948. Asst Solicitor, Cripps, Harries, Hall & Co., Tunbridge Wells, 1948–49; Asst Solicitor, 1949, Sec., 1950, Chief Exec., 1964–72, Chm., 1971–72, BEA; Mem. Bd, BOAC, 1971–72; Mem., British Airways Board, 1971–80 (Man. Dir, 1972–76; Dep. Chm., 1972–77). Mem., 1969–77, Chm., 1977–84, British Tourist Authority. Trustee and Vice-Chm., Leonard Cheshire Foundn, 1962–. FBIM 1971. *Club*: Reform.

MARKOVA, Dame Alicia, DBE 1963 (CBE 1958); **(Dame Lilian Alicia Marks);** Prima Ballerina Assoluta; Professor of Ballet and Performing Arts, College-Conservatory of Music, University of Cincinnati, since 1970; President, London Festival Ballet, since 1986; *b* London 1910; *d* of Arthur Tristman Marks and Eileen Barry. With Diaghilev's Russian Ballet Co., 1925–29; Rambert Ballet Club, 1931–33; Vic-Wells Ballet Co., 1933–35; Markova-Dolin Ballet Co., 1935–37; Ballet Russe de Monte Carlo, 1938–41; Ballet Theatre, USA, 1941–46. Appeared with Anton Dolin, guest and concert performances, 1948–50. Co-Founder and Prima Ballerina, Festival Ballet, 1950–51; Guest Prima Ballerina: Buenos Aires, 1952; Royal Ballet, 1953 and 1957; Royal Danish Ballet, 1955; Scala, Milan, 1956; Teatro Municipal, Rio de Janeiro, 1956; Festival Ballet, 1958 and 1959; Guest appearances at Metropolitan Opera House, New York, 1952, 1953–54, 1955, 1957, 1958; Dir, Metropolitan Opera Ballet, 1963–69; produced Les Sylphides for Festival Ballet and Aust. Ballet, 1976, for Royal Ballet School and Northern Ballet Theatre, 1978, for Royal Winnipeg Ballet, Canada, 1979. Guest Professor: Royal Ballet Sch., 1973–; Paris Opera Ballet, 1975; Australian Ballet Sch., 1976; Yorkshire Ballet Seminars, 1975–; Pres., All England Dance Competition, 1983–. Vice-Pres., Royal Acad. of Dancing, 1958–; Governor, Royal Ballet, 1973–; President: London Ballet Circle, 1981–; Trust of the Arts Educational Schs, 1984–. Concert, television and guest appearances (general), 1952–61. BBC series, Markova's Ballet Call, 1960; Masterclass, BBC2, 1980. Queen Elizabeth II Coronation Award, Royal Acad. of Dancing, 1963. Hon. DMus: Leicester, 1966; East Anglia, 1982. *Publications*: Giselle and I, 1960; Markova Remembers, 1986. *Address*: c/o Barclays Bank, 451 Oxford Street, W1.

MARKS, family name of **Baron Marks of Broughton.**

MARKS OF BROUGHTON, 2nd Baron, *cr* 1961; **Michael Marks;** *b* 27 Aug. 1920; *o s* of 1st Baron and Miriam (*d* 1971), *d* of Ephraim Sieff; *S* father 1964; *m*; one *s* two *d*. *Heir*: son.

MARKS, Bernard Montague, OBE 1984; Life President, Alfred Marks Bureau Group of Companies, 1985 (Managing Director, 1946–81 and Chairman, 1946–84); *b* 11 Oct. 1923; *s* of Alfred and Elizabeth Marks; *m* 1956, Norma Renton; two *s*. *Educ*: Highgate Public Sch.; Royal Coll. of Science. Served Somerset LI, seconded to RWAFF (Staff Capt.), 1944–46. Chm. or Vice-Chm., Fedn of Personnel Services of GB, 1965–79, 1983–84. Mem., Equal Opportunities Commn, 1984–86. *Publication*: Once Upon A Typewriter, 1974. *Recreations*: bridge, golf, ski-ing. *Address*: Cossyns, Albury Road, Burwood Park, Walton-on-Thames, Surrey. *Club*: St George's Hill Golf.

MARKS, John Emile, CBE 1970; Chairman: Peckerbond Ltd; Exclusive Environments Ltd; *m* 1975, Averil May Hannah (*née* Davies); two *s* two *d* by former marriage. *Educ*: Eton College. Served War of 1939–45 (despatches 1944). *Recreations*: tennis, golf. *Address*: Shaldon, Devon.

MARKS, John Henry, MD; FRCGP; General Practitioner, Boreham Wood, since 1954; Chairman of Council, British Medical Association, since 1984; *b* 30 May 1925; *s* of Lewis and Rose Marks; *m* 1954, Shirley Evelyn, *d* of Alic Nathan, OBE; one *s* two *d*. *Educ*: Tottenham County Sch.; Edinburgh Univ. MD; FRCGP; D(Obst)RCOG. Served RAMC, 1949–51. Chairman: Herts LMC, 1966–71; Herts Exec. Council, 1971–74; Member: NHS Management Study Steering Cttee, 1971–72; Standing Med. Adv. Cttee, 1984–; Council for Postgrad. Med. Educn, 1984–. British Medical Association: Fellow, 1976; Member: Gen. Med. Services Cttee, 1968– (Dep. Chm., 1974–79); Council, 1973–; GMC, 1979–84; Chm., Representative Body, 1981–84. *Publications*: The Conference of Local Medical Committees and its Executive: an historical view, 1979; papers on the NHS and general medical practice. *Recreations*: philately, walking, gardening. *Address*: Brown Gables, Barnet Lane, Elstree, Herts WD6 3RQ. *T*: 01–953 7687.

MARKS, Kenneth; *b* 15 June 1920; *s* of Robert P. Marks, Electrician and Edith Collins, Cotton Weaver; *m* 1944, Kathleen Lynch; one *s* one *d*. *Educ*: Peacock Street Sch., Gorton; Central High Sch., Manchester; Didsbury Coll. of Education. Worked in offices of LNER, 1936–40. Joined ranks, Grenadier Guards, 1940–42; commnd into Cheshire Regt, 1942–46 (Capt.); served in Middle East, Malta, Italy, NW Europe and Germany as Infantry Platoon and Company Comdr. Taught in Manchester schs, 1946–67; Headmaster, Clough Top Sec. Sch. for Boys, 1964–67. MP (Lab) Gorton, Nov. 1967–1983; Parliamentary Private Secretary: to Rt Hon. Anthony Crosland, 1969–70; to Roy Hattersley, 1974–75; to Rt Hon. Harold Wilson, 1975; Opposition Whip, 1971–72; Parly Under-Sec. of State, DoE, 1975–79. Member: House of Commons Select Cttee for Educn and Science, 1968–70; Select Cttee on Expenditure, 1974–75; Exec. Cttee, CPA, 1972–75; Exec. Cttee, UK Br., IPU, 1981–83. Chm., Parly Labour Party Educn Gp, 1972–75, NW Reg. Gp, 1974–83; Mem., N Atlantic Assembly, 1974–75, 1979–83. Vice-Pres., YHA, 1980–. Voluntary worker, CAB, 1983–. *Address*: 50 Boothfield, Knutsford, Cheshire WA16 8JU.

MARKS, Prof. Shula Eta; Director, since 1983, and Professor of Commonwealth History, since 1984, Institute of Commonwealth Studies, University of London; *b* Cape Town, S Africa, 14 Oct. 1936; *d* of Chaim and Frieda Winokur; *m* 1957, Isaac M. Marks; one *s* one *d*. *Educ*: Univ. of Cape Town (Argus Scholar, 1958–59; BA 1959). PhD London, 1967. Came to London, 1960; Lectr in the History of Southern Africa, SOAS and Inst. of Commonwealth Studies, 1963–76, Reader, 1976–83; Vice-Chancellor's Visitor to NZ, 1978. Dir, Ford Foundn Grant to Univ. of London on S African History, 1975–78; Pres., African Studies Assoc. of UK, 1978. Editor, Jl of African History, 1971–77; Mem. Council, Jl of Southern African Studies, 1974– (Founding Mem., 1974). *Publications*: Reluctant Rebellion: an assessment of the 1906–8 disturbances in Natal, 1970; (ed with A. Atmore) Economy and Society in Pre-industrial South Africa, 1980; (ed with R. Rathbone) Industrialization and Social Change in South Africa, 1870–1930, 1982; (ed with P. Richardson) International Labour Migration: historical perspectives, 1983; chapters in Cambridge Hist. of Africa, vols 3, 4 and 6; contrib. Jl of African Hist. and Jl of Southern African Studies. *Address*: Institute of Commonwealth Studies, 27–28 Russell Square, WC1B 5DS. *T*: 01–580 5876.

MARKUS, Rika, (Rixi), MBE 1975 (for services to Bridge); Bridge journalist and author; *b* 27 June 1910; *d* of Michael and Louise Scharfstein; *m* 1929, Salomon Markus (marr. diss. 1947); one *d* decd. *Educ*: Vienna and Dresden. Turned to bridge after a severe illness; arrived in London, March 1938 (3 days after Hitler occupied Austria; parents lived already in London). Bridge correspondent of: The Guardian and Weekly Guardian, 1955– (organizer of Eastern Bridge Guardian Tournament); Harpers & Queen (organizer of Championship for Women); formerly of the Evening Standard; writes for Express Syndication Gp; commentator and contributor to Daily Bulletin on major European and world championships. Organises annual bridge match between House of Lords and House of Commons (Challenge Cup donated by The Guardian); matches held with parliamentarians and players in other countries, *eg* France, Holland, Dubai, USA, Sweden and Morocco; player in Master Bridge, Channel Four TV series, 1983. Acclaimed as best woman player in the world; European Bridge Champion, 1935 and 1936; World Champion, 1937; 1st Woman Grand Master, 1973; Charles Goren Award for the player of the year, 1976; 4 Olympic titles; 5 World titles; 10 Eur. Championships; many national and internat. titles. *Publications*: Bid Boldly, Play Safe, 1965; Common-Sense Bridge, 1972; Aces and Places, 1972; Bridge around the World, 1977; Improve Your Bridge, 1977; Play Better Bridge with Rixi Markus, 1978; Table Tales by Rixi Markus, 1979; Bridge with Rixi, 1983; More Deadly than the Male, 1984; Best Bridge Hands, 1985; The Rixi Markus Book of Bridge, 1985. *Recreations*: music, cooking, watching all sports, theatre. *Address*: 22 Lowndes Lodge, Cadogan Place, SW1X 9RZ. *T*: 01–235 7377. *Club*: St James Bridge.

MARKUS, Prof. Robert Austin, FBA 1985; Professor of Medieval History, Nottingham University, 1974–82, now Emeritus; *b* 8 Oct. 1924; *s* of Victor Markus and Lily Markus (*née* Elek); *m* 1955, Margaret Catherine Bullen; two *s* one *d*. *Educ*: Univ. of Manchester (BSc 1944; MA 1948; PhD 1950). Mem., Dominican Order, 1950–54; Asst Librarian, Univ. of Birmingham, 1954–55; Liverpool University: Sub-Librarian, 1955–59; Lectr, Sen. Lectr, Reader in Medieval Hist., 1959–74. Pres., Ecclesiastical Hist. Soc., 1978–79. *Publications*: Christian Faith and Greek Philosophy (with A. H. Armstrong), 1964; Saeculum: history and society in the theology of St Augustine, 1970; Christianity in the Roman world, 1974; From Augustine to Gregory the Great, 1983; contribs to Jl of Ecclesiastical Hist., Jl of Theol Studies, Byzantion, Studies in Church Hist., etc. *Recreation*: music. *Address*: 100 Park Road, Chilwell, Beeston, Nottingham NG9 4DE. *T*: Nottingham 255965.

MARLAND, Michael, CBE 1977; Headmaster, North Westminster Community School, since 1980; *b* 28 Dec. 1934; *m* 1st, 1955, Eileen (*d* 1968); four *s* one *d*; 2nd, 1971, Rose. *Educ*: Christ's Hospital Sch.; Sidney Sussex Coll., Cambridge (MA). Head of English, Abbey Wood Sch., 1961–64; Head of English and subseq. Dir of Studies, Crown Woods Sch., 1964–71; Headmaster, Woodberry Down Sch., 1971–79. Hon. Prof., Dept of Educn, Univ. of Warwick, 1980–. Member: many educn cttees, incl. Bullock Cttee, 1972–75; Educn and Human Develt Cttee, ESRC (formerly SSRC), 1983–; Nat. Book League Council, 1984; Finniston Cttee on Technol. in Educn, 1985–; Chairman: Schools Council English Cttee, 1978–81; Books in Curriculum Res. Project, 1982–; Royal Ballet Educn Adv. Council, 1983–; Nat. Assoc. for Pastoral Care in Educn, 1982–86; Royal Opera House Educnl Adv. Council, 1984–; Nat. Textbook Ref. Library Steering Cttee, 1984–. Mem., Paddington and N Kensington DHA, 1982–84. *Publications*: Towards The New Fifth, 1969; The Practice of English Teaching, 1970; Peter Grimes, 1971; Head of Department, 1971; Pastoral Care, 1974; The Craft of the Classroom, 1975; Language Across the Curriculum, 1977; Education for the Inner City, 1980; Departmental Management, 1981; Sex Differentiation and Schooling, 1983; Short Stories for Today, 1984; Meetings and Partings, 1984; School Management Skills, 1985; General Editor of: Blackie's Student Drama Series; Longman Imprint Books; The Times Authors; Heinemann Organisation in Schools Series; contrib. Times Educnl Supplement. *Recreations*: music, literature. *Address*: 22 Compton Terrace, N1 2UN. *T*: 01–226 0648; The Green Farmhouse, Cranmer Green, Walsham-le-Willows, Bury St Edmunds, Suffolk. *T*: 483.

MARLAND, Paul; MP (C) Gloucestershire West, since 1979; *b* 19 March 1940; *s* of Alexander G. Marland and Elsa May Lindsey Marland; *m* 1965, Penelope Anne Barlow (marr. diss. 1982); one *s* two *d*; *m* 1984, Caroline Ann Rushton. *Educ*: Gordonstoun Sch., Elgin; Trinity Coll., Dublin (BA, BComm). Hopes Metal Windows, 1964; London Press Exchange, 1965–66; farmer, 1967–. Jt PPS to Financial Sec. to the Treasury and Economic Sec., 1981–83, to Minister of Agriculture, Fisheries and Food, 1983–. *Recreations*: skiing, shooting, riding, ballet. *Address*: Ford Hill Farm, Temple Guiting, Cheltenham, Glos. *T*: Guiting Power 232. *Club*: Boodle's.

MARLBOROUGH, 11th Duke of, *cr* 1702; **John George Vanderbilt Henry Spencer-Churchill;** DL; Baron Spencer, 1603; Earl of Sunderland, 1643; Baron Churchill, 1685; Earl of Marlborough, 1689; Marquis of Blandford, 1702; Prince of the Holy Roman Empire; Prince of Mindelheim in Suabia; late Captain Life Guards; *b* 13 April 1926; *s* of 10th Duke of Marlborough and Hon. Alexandra Mary Hilda Cadogan, CBE (*d* 1961), *d* of late Henry Arthur, Viscount Chelsea; *S* father, 1972; *m* 1st, 1951, Susan Mary (marr. diss., 1960; she *m* 1962, Alan Cyril Heber-Percy), *d* of Michael Hornby, *qv*; one *s* one *d* (and one *s* decd); 2nd, 1961, Mrs Athina Livanos (marr. diss. 1971; she *d* 1974), *d* of late Stavros G. Livanos, Paris; 3rd, 1972, Rosita Douglas; one *s* one *d* (and one *s* decd). *Educ*: Eton. Lieut Life Guards, 1946; Captain, 1953; resigned commission, 1953. Chairman: Martini & Rossi, 1979–; London Paperweights Ltd, 1974–. President: Thames and Chilterns Tourist Board, 1974–; Oxfordshire Branch, CLA, 1978–; Oxfordshire Assoc. of Boys' Clubs, 1972–; Oxford Br., SSAFA, 1977–; Sports Aid Foundn (Southern), 1981–; Oxford United Football Club, 1964–. CC 1961–64, Oxfordshire; JP 1962; DL 1974. *Heir*: *s* Marquis of Blandford, *qv*. *Address*: Blenheim Palace, Woodstock, Oxon. *Clubs*: Portland, White's.

MARLER, Dennis Ralph Greville, FRICS; Chairman, Capital & Counties plc, since 1985; *b* 15 June 1927; *s* of late Greville Sidney Marler, JP, FRICS and Ivy Victoria (*née*

Boyle); *m* 1952, Angela (*née* Boundy); one *s* one *d*. *Educ:* Marlborough. Served Royal Lincolnshire Regt, Palestine, 1945–48; articled pupil, Knight, Frank & Rutley, 1948–50; Partner, Marler & Marler, 1950–83; Capital & Counties: Asst Man. Dir, 1962–66; Jt Man. Dir, 1966–76; Man. Dir, 1976–85; Chm., Knightsbridge Green Hotel Ltd, 1966–. Member: NEDO Working Party for Wood Report (Public Client and Construction Industry), 1974–75; Adv. Bd, Dept of Construction Management, Univ. of Reading, 1981–; Cttee of Management, Pension Fund and other Property Unit Trusts, 1985–; DHSS Nat. Property Adv. Gp, 1984–; FCO *ad hoc* Adv. Panel on Diplomatic Estate, 1985–. A Vice-Pres., TCPA, 1983–; Pres., British Property Fedn, 1983–84. Mem. Ct of Assistants, Merchant Taylors' Co., 1984–. CBIM, FRSA. *Recreations:* reading, golf, travel. *Address:* 13 Whaddon House, William Mews, SW1X 9HG. *T:* 01–245 6139; 13 Slipway Cottages, Rock, Cornwall. *T:* Trebetherick 2141. *Clubs:* Royal Thames Yacht, St Stephen's Constitutional, Roehampton; St Enodoc Golf.

MARLEY, 2nd Baron *cr* 1930, of Marley in the County of Sussex; **Godfrey Pelham Leigh Aman;** *b* 6 Sept. 1913; *s* of 1st Baron Marley and Octable Turquet, Lady Marley (*d* 1969); *S* father 1952; *m* 1956, Catherine Doone Beal. *Educ:* Bedales Sch; Univ. of Grenoble. Royal Marines, 1939–45. *Heir:* none. *Address:* 104 Ebury Mews, SW1. *T:* 01–730 4844; House of Lords, SW1.

MARLING, Sir Charles (William Somerset), 5th Bt *cr* 1882; *b* 2 June 1951; *s* of Sir John Stanley Vincent Marling, 4th Bt, OBE, and Georgina Brenda (Betty) (*d* 1961), *o d* of late Henry Edward FitzRoy Somerset; *S* father, 1977; *m* 1979, Judi P. Futrille; two *d*. *Address:* The Barn, The Street, Eversley, Hants.

MARLOW, Antony Rivers; MP (C) Northampton North, since 1979; *b* 17 June 1940; *s* of late Major Thomas Keith Rivers Marlow, MBE, RE retd, and Beatrice Nora (*née* Hall); *m* 1962, Catherine Louise Howel (*née* Jones); three *s* two *d*. *Educ:* Wellington Coll.; RMA Sandhurst; St Catharine's Coll., Cambridge (2nd Cl. Hons (1) Mech. Sciences, MA). Served Army, 1958–69; retd, Captain RE; management consultant and industrial/commercial manager, 1969–79. *Recreations:* livestock farming, Rugby spectator, opera, ballet. *Address:* House of Commons, SW1A 0AA.

MARLOW, Roy George; HM Diplomatic Service; Consul General, Karachi, since 1985; *b* 24 April 1931; *s* of George Henry Marlow and May Marlow (*née* Wright); *m* 1st, 1959, Hilary Ann Charlesworth (marr. diss. 1975); one *s* two *d*; 2nd, 1976, Vali Ceballos; one step *s* one step *d*. *Educ:* Nottingham High Sch.; Jesus Coll., Cambridge (BA). United Africa Group (Unilever): Manchester, 1953–56, 1958–59, 1961–65; Nigeria, 1956–58, 1959–61. Joined Foreign and Commonwealth Office, 1966; First Secretary (Commercial): Calcutta, 1967–70; Bogotá, 1971–73; FCO, 1973–76; Head of Chancery, Quito, 1976–79; Counsellor (Commercial), Manila, 1980–83; Ambassador to Dominican Republic, 1983–85. *Recreations:* music, tennis. *Address:* c/o Foreign and Commonwealth Office, SW1; Flat 4, 40 Redcliffe Square, SW10. *T:* 01–370 6005.

MARLOWE, Hugh; *see* Patterson, Harry.

MARMION, Prof. Barrie P.; Visiting Professor, Department of Pathology, University of Adelaide (Adelaide Medical School), since 1985; *b* 19 May 1920; *s* of J. P. and M. H. Marmion, Alverstoke, Hants; *m* 1953, Diana Ray Newling, *d* of Dr P. Ray Newling, Adelaide, SA; one *d*. *Educ:* University Coll. and University Coll. Hosp., London. MD London 1947, DSc London 1963, FRCPath 1962, FRCPA 1964, FRCPE 1970, FRACP 1984. House Surg., UCH, 1942; Bacteriologist, Public Health Laboratory Service, 1943–62; Rockefeller Trav. Fellow, at Walter and Eliza Hall Inst., Melbourne, 1951–52; Foundation Prof., Microbiology, Monash Univ., Melbourne, Australia, 1962–68; Prof. of Bacteriology, Univ. of Edinburgh, 1968–78; Dir, Div. of Virology, Inst. of Med. and Vet. Science, Adelaide, 1978–85, retd. *Publications:* (ed) Mackie and McCartney's Medical Microbiology, 13th edn 1978; numerous papers on bacteriology and virology. *Recreations:* swimming, music. *Address:* Department of Pathology, University of Adelaide, North Terrace, Adelaide, SA 5000, Australia.

MARNAN, His Honour John Fitzgerald, MBE 1944; QC 1954; a Circuit Judge, lately sitting at Central Criminal Court, 1972–80, retired; *b* 23 Jan. 1908; *s* of late T. G. Marnan, Irish Bar; *m* 1st, 1934, Morwenna (marr. diss., 1958), *d* of late Sir Keith Price; one *s* (and one *s* decd); 2nd, 1958, Mrs Diana Back (marr. diss., 1963), *o d* of late Comdr Charles Crawshay, RN (retd), and late Mrs M. L. Greville; 3rd, 1966, Joanna, *o d* of late Maj.-Gen. W. N. Herbert, CB, CMG, DSO. *Educ:* Ampleforth; Trinity Coll., Oxford. Commnd TA (Oxford Univ. OTC), 1929. Called to Bar, 1931; joined Chester and N Wales Circuit; joined Supplementary Reserve, Irish Guards, 1936; served War of 1939–45 (MBE, despatches); Western Europe with Irish Guards, and on staff of 15th (Scottish) Div.; Major (GSO2), 1944. A Metropolitan Magistrate, 1956–58, resigned. Crown Counsel in the Ministry of Legal Affairs, Kenya Government, 1958–59; Federal Justice of the Federal Supreme Court, the West Indies, 1959–62; subseq. Justice of Appeal of the British Caribbean Court of Appeal. Sat as Commissioner at Crown Courts, at Manchester, 1962–63, at Liverpool, 1963, and at Central Criminal Court, 1964–66; a Dep. Chm., Greater London Sessions, 1966–68; Chm., NE London QS, 1968–71. *Recreation:* field sports. *Address:* Cottrells, Dinton, near Salisbury, Wilts. *T:* Teffont 315. *Club:* Cavalry and Guards.

MARNHAM, Harold, MBE 1945; QC 1965; Barrister-at-Law; Leader of Parliamentary Bar, 1967–74; *b* 14 July 1911; *y s* of late Arthur Henry Marnham and late Janet Elizabeth Marnham; *m* 1947, Hilary, *y d* of late Ernest Jukes; two *s*. *Educ:* Stellenbosch Boys' High Sch.; Stellenbosch Univ.; Jesus Coll., Cambridge. Called to Bar, Gray's Inn, 1935; Bencher, 1969. Served War 1939–45; BEF, 1939–40; BLA, 1944–45 (despatches); 2nd Lt RA (TA); Capt. 1940; Major 1942; Lt-Col 1945. Dep. Chm., Oxfordshire QS, 1966–71. Chm., Industrial Tribunals, 1975–79. *Address:* Brook House, 7 Quay Street, Halesworth, Suffolk. *T:* Halesworth 2805. *Clubs:* Hawks (Cambridge); Leander (Henley-on-Thames).

MAROWITZ, Charles; Associate Director, Los Angeles Theater Center, since 1984; *b* 26 Jan. 1934; Austrian mother, Russian father; *m* 1982, Jane Elizabeth Allsop. *Educ:* Seward Park High Sch.; University Coll. London. Dir, In-Stage Experimental Theatre, 1958; Asst Dir, Royal Shakespeare Co., 1963–65; Artistic Director: Traverse Theatre, 1963–64; Open Space Theatre London, 1968–81; Open Space Theatre of Los Angeles, 1982. Drama Critic: Encore Magazine, 1956–63; Plays and Players, 1958–74; The Village Voice, 1955–; The NY Times, 1966–. West End Director: Loot, Criterion, 1967; The Bellow Plays, Fortune, 1966; Fortune and Men's Eyes, Comedy, 1969; productions abroad: Woyzeck, 1965, The Shrew, 1979, Nat. Theatre, Bergen; Hedda, 1978, Enemy of the People, 1979, Nat. Theatre, Oslo; Measure for Measure, Oslo New Theatre, 1981; The Father, Trondheim, 1981; A Midsummer Night's Dream, Odense, Denmark; Tartuffe, Molde, Norway; productions: in Los Angeles: Artaud at Rodez, 1982; Sherlock's Last Case, 1984; in Seattle: Ah Sweet Mystery of Life, 1981. Order of the Purple Sash, 1969. *Publications:* The Method as Means, 1960; The Marowitz Hamlet, 1967; A Macbeth, 1970; Confessions of a Counterfeit Critic, 1973; Open Space Plays, 1974; Measure for Measure, 1975; The Shrew, 1975; Artaud at Rodez, 1976; Variations on The Merchant of Venice; The Act of Being, 1977; The Marowitz Shakespeare, 1978; New Theatre Voices of the 50s and 60s, 1981; Sex Wars, 1982; Prospero's Staff, 1986; Potboilers (collection of plays), 1986. *Recreation:* balling. *Address:* 3058 Sequit Drive, Malibu, Calif 90265, USA.

MARPLES, Brian John; Emeritus Professor of Zoology, University of Otago, NZ; *b* 31 March 1907; 2nd *s* of George and Anne Marples; *m* 1931, Mary Joyce Ransford; two *s*. *Educ:* St Bees Sch.; Exeter Coll., Oxford. Lecturer in Zoology, Univ. of Manchester, 1929–35; Lecturer in Zoology, Univ. of Bristol, 1935–37; Prof. of Zoology, Univ. of Otago, NZ, 1937–67. *Publications:* Freshwater Life in New Zealand, 1962; various technical zoological and archaeological papers. *Address:* 1 Vanbrugh Close, Old Woodstock, Oxon.

MARQUAND, Prof. David (Ian); Professor of Contemporary History and Politics, Salford University, since 1978; *b* 20 Sept. 1934; *s* of Rt Hon. Hilary Marquand, PC; *m* 1959, Judith Mary (*née* Reed); one *s* one *d*. *Educ:* Emanuel Sch.; Magdalen Coll., Oxford; St Antony's Coll., Oxford (Sen. Schol.). 1st cl. hons Mod. Hist., 1957. Teaching Asst, Univ. of Calif., 1958–59; Leader Writer, The Guardian, 1959–62; Research Fellow, St Antony's Coll., Oxford, 1962–64; Lectr in Politics, Univ. of Sussex, 1964–66. Contested (Lab) Barry, 1964; (SDP) High Peak, 1983; MP (Lab) Ashfield, 1966–77; PPS to Minister of Overseas Develt, 1967–69; Jun. Opposition Front-Bench Spokesman on econ. affairs, 1971–72; Member: Select Cttee on Estimates, 1966–68; Select Cttee on Procedure, 1968–73; Select Cttee on Corp. Tax, 1971; British Deleg. to Council of Europe, 1970–73. Chief Advr, Secretariat-Gen., European Commission, 1977–78. Vis. Scholar, Hoover Instn, Stanford, USA, 1985–86. Mem., Nat. Steering Cttee, SDP, 1981–. Member Board: Aspen Inst., Berlin, 1982–; Public Policy Centre (formerly Social Scis Res. Trust), 1983–. Thomas Jefferson Meml Lectr, Univ. of Calif at Berkeley, 1981. George Orwell Meml Prize (jtly), 1980. *Publications:* Ramsay MacDonald, 1977; Parliament for Europe, 1979; The Politics of Nostalgia, 1980; Taming Leviathan, 1980; (with David Butler) European Elections and British Politics, 1981; (ed) John Mackintosh on Politics, 1982; contrib. to: The Age of Austerity, 1964; A Radical Future, 1967; Coalitions in British Politics, 1978; Britain in Europe, 1980; The Political Economy of Tolerable Survival, 1980; The Rebirth of Britain, 1982; European Monetary Union Progress and Prospects, 1982; Social Theory and Political Practice, 1982; The Changing Constitution, 1985; articles and reviews in The Guardian, The Times, The Sunday Times, New Statesman, Encounter, Commentary, etc. *Recreation:* walking. *Address:* c/o University of Salford, Salford M5 4WT.

MÁRQUEZ, Gabriel García; Colombian novelist; *b* 1928; *m* Mercedes García Márquez; two *s*. *Educ:* Univ. of Bogotá; Univ. of Cartagena. Corresp., El Espectador, Rome and Paris; formed Cuban Press Agency, Bogotá; worked for Prensa Latina, Cuba, later as Dep. Head, NY office, 1961; lived in Venezuela, Cuba, USA, Spain, Mexico; returned to Colombia, 1982. Rómulo Gallegos Prize, 1972; Nobel Prize for Literature, 1982. *Publications:* La hojarasca, 1955 (Leaf Storm, 1973); El colonel no tiene quien la escriba, 1961 (No One Writes to the Colonel, 1971); La mala hora, 1962 (In Evil Hour, 1980); Los funerales de la Mamá Grande, 1962; Cien años de soledad, 1967 (One Hundred Years of Solitude, 1970); La increíble y triste historia de la cándida Eréndira, 1972 (Innocent Erendira and other stories, 1979); El otoño del patriarca, 1975 (The Autumn of the Patriarch, 1977); Crónica de una muerte anunciada, 1981 (Chronicle of a Death Foretold, 1982); (with P. Mendoza) El olor de la Guayaba, 1982 (Fragrance of Guava, ed T. Nairn, 1983). *Address:* c/o Jonathan Cape Ltd, 32 Bedford Square, WC1B 3EL.

MARQUIS, family name of **Earl of Woolton.**

MARQUIS, James Douglas, DFC 1945; Managing Director, Irvine Development Corporation, 1972–81; *b* 16 Oct. 1921; *s* of James Charles Marquis and Jessica Amy (*née* Huggett); *m* 1945, Brenda Eleanor, *d* of Robert Reyner Davey; two *s*. *Educ:* Shooters Hill Sch., Woolwich. Local Govt, 1938–41. Served War: RAF: 1941–46 (RAF 1st cl. Air Navigation Warrant, 1945), Navigation Officer, 177 Sqdn, 224 Gp, and AHQ Malaya (Sqdn Ldr 1945). Local Govt, 1946–56; Harlow Develt Corp., 1957–68; Irvine Develt Corp.; Chief Finance Officer, 1968–72; Dir of Finance and Admin., 1972. Pres., Ayrshire Chamber of Industries, 1979–80. FRMetS 1945; IPFA 1950; FCIS 1953. *Publication:* An Ayrshire Sketchbook, 1979. *Recreations:* sketching and painting (five one-man exhibns, incl. one in Sweden; works in collections: Rhodesia, Japan, Sweden, Norway, Denmark, Australia, USA, Canada); angling, gardening, ornithology, golf. *Address:* 3 Knoll Park, Ayr KA7 4RH. *T:* Alloway 42212. *Club:* Royal Air Force.

MARR, Allan James, CBE 1965; Director and Chairman, EGS Co. Ltd; *b* 6 May 1907; *s* of late William Bell Marr and Hilda May Marr; *cousin* and *heir pres.* to Sir Leslie Lynn Marr, 2nd Bt, *qv*; *m* 1935, Joan de Wolf Ranken; one *s* two *d*. *Educ:* Oundle; Durham Univ. Apprenticeship, Joseph L. Thompson & Sons Ltd, 1926–31; joined Sir James Laing & Sons Ltd, 1932. Dir, Doxford and Sunderland Shipbuilding and Eng. Co. Ltd; retd from all shipbldg activities, 1973. Pres. Shipbuilding Conf., 1963–65; Fellow of North-East Coast Inst. of Engineers and Shipbuilders (Pres., 1966–68); Mem., RINA. Chm., Research Council of British Ship Research Assoc., 1965–73. *Recreation:* photography. *Address:* Dalesford, Thropton, Morpeth, Northumberland NE65 7JE.

MARR, (Sir) Leslie Lynn, (2nd Bt, *cr* 1919, but does not use the title); MA Cambridge; painter and draughtsman; late Flight Lieutenant RAF; *b* 14 Aug. 1922; *o s* of late Col John Lynn Marr, OBE, TD, (and *g s* of 1st Bt,) and Amelia Rachel, *d* of late Robert Thompson, Overdinsdale Hall, Darlington; *S* grandfather 1932; *m* 1st, 1948, Dinora Delores Mendelson (marr. diss. 1956); one *d*; 2nd, 1962, Lynn Heneage; two *d*. *Educ:* Shrewsbury; Pembroke Coll., Cambridge. Has exhibited at Ben Uri, Drian, Woodstock, Wildenstein, Whitechapel, Campbell and Franks Galls, London; also in Norwich, Belfast, Birmingham, Newcastle upon Tyne, Bristol and Paris. *Publication:* From My Point of View, 1979. *Heir: cousin* Allan James Marr, *qv*. *Address:* c/o Lloyds Bank, Holt, Norfolk.

MARRACK, Rear-Adm. Philip Reginald, CB 1979; CEng, FIMechE, FIMarE; *b* 16 Nov. 1922; *s* of Captain Philip Marrack, RN and Annie Kathleen Marrack (*née* Proud); *m* 1954, Pauline Mary (*née* Haag); two *d*. *Educ:* Eltham Coll.; Plymouth Coll.; RNC Dartmouth; RN Engineering Coll., Manadon. War service at sea, HM Ships Orion and Argus, 1944–45; Advanced Engineering Course, RNC Greenwich, 1945–47; HM Submarines Templar and Token, 1947–50; served in Frigate Torquay, Aircraft Carriers Glory and Hermes, and MoD; Captain 1965; Commanded Admiralty Reactor Test Estab., Dounreay, 1967–70; CSO (Mat.) on Staff of Flag Officer Submarines, and Asst Dir (Nuclear), Dockyard Dept, 1970–74; Rear-Adm. 1974; Dir, Naval Ship Production, 1974–77; Dir, Dockyard Production and Support, 1977–81, retd. *Recreations:* fly fishing, gardening, viticulture, wine making. *Address:* c/o Barclays Bank, Princess Street, Plymouth PL1 2HA.

MARRE, Sir Alan (Samuel), KCB 1970 (CB 1955); Parliamentary Commissioner for Administration, 1971–76; ex officio Member, Council on Tribunals, 1971–76; *b* 25 Feb. 1914; *s* of late Joseph and late Rebecca Marre; *m* 1943, Romola Mary (*see* Lady Marre); one *s* one *d*. *Educ:* St Olave's and St Saviour's Grammar Sch., Southwark; Trinity Hall, Cambridge (Major open Schol.) John Stewart of Rannoch Schol. and 1st cl. hons Class. Trip. Parts I and II. Ministry of Health: Asst Principal, 1936; Principal, 1941; Asst Sec.,

1946; Under-Sec., 1952–63; Under-Sec., Ministry of Labour, 1963–64; Dep. Sec.: Ministry of Health, 1964–66; Min. of Labour (later Dept of Employment and Productivity), 1966–68; Second Perm. Under-Sec. of State, Dept of Health and Social Security, 1968–71. Health Service Comr for England, Wales and Scotland, 1973–76; ex officio Mem. Commns for Local Admin, 1974–76. Chairman: Age Concern England, 1977–80; Crown Housing Assoc., 1978–; Rural Dispensing Cttee, 1983–. Mem., British Nutrition Foundn, 1981– (Chm., 1983–85). Vice-Chm., Adv. Cttee on Distinction Awards for Consultants, 1979–85. Trustee, Whitechapel Art Gall., 1977–83. *Recreations:* reading, walking, travel. *Address:* 44 The Vale, NW11 8SG. *T:* 01–458 1787. *Clubs:* Athenæum, MCC.

MARRE, Romola Mary, (Lady Marre), CBE 1979; Chairman, BBC and IBA Central Appeals Advisory Committee, since 1984 (Member since 1980); *b* 25 April 1920; *d* of late Aubrey John Gilling and Romola Marjorie Angier; *m* 1943, Sir Alan Samuel Marre, *qv*; one *s* one *d*. *Educ:* Chelmsford County High Sch. for Girls; Bedford Coll., Univ. of London. BA Hons Philosophy. Asst Principal (Temp.), Min. of Health, 1941–42; Sgt, subseq. Jun. Comdr, ATS Officer Selection Bd, 1942–45. Organiser, West Hampstead Citizen's Advice Bureau, 1962–65; Dep. Gen. Sec., Camden Council of Social Service, 1965–73; Adviser on Community Health Councils to DHSS, 1974–75; Chm., London Voluntary Service Council (formerly London Council of Social Service), 1974–84. Member: Lord Chancellor's Adv. Cttee on Legal Aid, 1975–80; Milk Marketing Bd, 1973–82; Dep. Chm., Royal Jubilee Trusts, 1981–; Chairman: Volunteer Centre, 1973–78; Adv. Gp on Hospital Services for children with cancer in North Western Region, Jan.-June 1979; Prince of Wales' Adv. Gp on Disability, 1982–84; Cttee on Future of Legal Profession, 1986–. Founder Pres., Barnet Voluntary Service Council, 1979–; Chm., COPE UK, 1981–. Trustee, City Parochial Foundn, 1975–. *Recreations:* cooking, gardening, walking, talking. *Address:* 44 The Vale, NW11 8SG. *T:* 01–458 1787.

MARRINER, Sir Neville, Kt 1985; CBE 1979; conductor; Founder and Director, Academy of St Martin in the Fields, since 1956; Music Director, Stuttgart Radio Symphony Orchestra, since 1984; *b* 15 April 1924; *s* of Herbert Henry Marriner and Ethel May Roberts; *m* 1955, Elizabeth Mary Sims; one *s* one *d*. *Educ:* Lincoln Sch.; Royal College of Music (ARCM). Taught music at Eton Coll., 1948; Prof., Royal Coll. of Music, 1950. Martin String Quartet, 1949; Jacobean Ensemble, 1951; London Symphony Orchestra, 1954; Music Director: Los Angeles Chamber Orchestra, 1968–77; Minnesota Orchestra, 1979–86. Artistic Director: South Bank Summer Music, 1975–77; Meadow Brook Festival, Detroit Symphony Orchestra, 1979–83. Hon. ARAM; Hon. FRCM 1983. *Club:* Garrick.

MARRIOTT, Bryant Hayes; Controller Radio Two, BBC, since 1983; *b* 9 Sept. 1936; *s* of Rev. Horace Marriott and Barbara Marriott; *m* 1963, Alison Mary Eyles; one *s* two *d*. *Educ:* Tormore Sch., Upper Deal, Kent; Marlborough Coll., Wilts; New Coll., Oxford (MA). Joined BBC, 1961–: Studio Manager, 1961; Producer, 1963; Staff Training Attachments Officer, 1973; Chief Asst to Controller Radio 1 and 2, 1976; Head of Recording Services, 1979. *Recreations:* gardening, sailing, drumming. *Address:* c/o BBC, Broadcasting House, W1A 1AA. *T:* 01–580 4468. *Club:* Brancaster Staithe Sailing.

MARRIOTT, John Miles; Principal, Grant Thornton, Chartered Accountants, Manchester, since 1986; *b* 11 Oct. 1935; *s* of Arthur James Marriott and May Lavinia (*née* Goodband); *m* 1967, Josephine Anne (*née* Shepherd). *Educ:* High Pavement Grammar Sch., Nottingham. CIPFA 1962; MBCS 1970. E Midlands Electricity Bd, Nottingham (incl. 2 yrs National Service in RAF), 1952–60; Morley Bor. Council, 1960–62; Wolverhampton County Bor. Council, 1962–67; Asst Bor. Treasurer, Torbay Co. Bor. Council, 1967–70; Dep. Bor. Treas., 1970–72, and Bor. Treas., 1972–73, Ipswich Co. Bor. Council; Dir of Finance, Bolton Metrop. Bor. Council, 1973–78; County Treasurer, Greater Manchester Council, 1978–86. Non-exec. Dir, Phillips & Drew Fund Management Ltd. *Publications:* papers in prof. jls. *Recreations:* golf, reading, bird watching, motoring. *Address:* 12 Martinsclough, Lostock, Bolton BL6 4PF. *T:* Bolton 47444.

MARRIOTT, Sir Ralph G. C. S.; *see* Smith-Marriott.

MARRIS, Prof. Robin Lapthorn; Professor of Economics, 1981–86, and Head of Department of Economics, 1983–86, Birkbeck College, University of London, now Professor Emeritus; *b* 31 March 1924; *s* of Eric Denyer Marris, CB, and late Phyllis, *d* of T. H. F. Lapthorn, JP; *m* 1st, 1949, Marion Ellinger; 2nd, 1954, Jane Evelina Burney Ayres; one *s* two *d*; 3rd, 1972, Anne Fairclough Mansfield; one *d*. *Educ:* Bedales Sch.; King's Coll., Cambridge. BA 1946, ScD 1968, Cantab. Asst Principal, HM Treasury, 1947–50; UN, Geneva, 1950–52; Fellow of King's Coll., Cambridge, 1951–76; Lectr, 1951–72, Reader, 1972–76, in Econs, Univ. of Cambridge; Prof. 1976–81 and Chm., 1976–79, Dept of Economics, Univ. of Maryland. Vis. Prof., Univ. California, Berkeley, 1961, and Harvard, 1967; Dir, World Economy Div., Min. of Overseas Develt, 1964–66. Mem., Vis. Cttee, Open Univ., 1982–. *Publications:* Economic Arithmetic, 1958; The Economic Theory of Managerial Capitalism, 1964; The Economics of Capital Utilisation, 1964; (with Adrian Wood) The Corporate Economy, 1971; The Corporate Society, 1974; The Theory and Future of the Corporate Economy and Society, 1979; contrib. Econ. Jl, Rev. Econ. Studies, Economica, Jl Manchester Stat. Soc., Jl Royal Stat. Soc., Amer. Econ. Rev., Qly Jl of Econs, Economie Appliquée, etc. *Recreations:* cooking, ski-ing, sailing. *Address:* Lingard House, Chiswick Mall, W4 2PJ.

See also S. N. Marris.

MARRIS, Stephen Nicholson; Senior Fellow, Institute for International Economics, Washington, since 1983; *b* 7 Jan. 1930; *s* of Eric Denyer Marris, CB, and Phyllis May Marris (*née* Lapthorn); *m* 1955, Margaret Swindells; two *s* one *d*. *Educ:* Bryanston School; King's College, Cambridge. MA, PhD. Parker of Waddington Research Student, Cambridge Univ., 1952–53; Nat. Inst. of Economic and Social Research, 1953–54; economist and international civil servant; with Org. for European Economic Co-operation, later Org. for Economic Co-operation and Development (OECD), 1956–83; Dir, Economics Branch, 1970; Economic Advr to Sec.-Gen., 1975. Vis. Res. Prof. of Internat. Economics, Brookings Instn, Washington DC, 1969–70. Hon. Dr Stockholm Univ., 1978. *Publication:* Deficits and the Dollar: the world economy at risk, 1985. *Recreation:* sailing. *Address:* Institute for International Economics, 11 Dupont Circle NW, Washington, DC 20036, USA. *T:* (202) 328–0583.

See also R. L. Marris.

MARRISON, Dr Geoffrey Edward; Tutor, Carlisle Diocesan Training Institute, since 1984; Director and Keeper, Department of Oriental Manuscripts and Printed Books, British Library, London, 1974–83; *b* 11 Jan. 1923; *s* of John and Rose Marrison; *m* 1958, Margaret Marian Millburn; one *s* three *d*. *Educ:* SOAS, Univ. of London; Bishops' Coll. Cheshunt; Kirchliche Hochschule, Berlin. BA Malay 1948, PhD Linguistics 1967, London. Indian Army, 1942–46. SOAS, 1941–42 and 1946–49; ordained Priest, Singapore, 1952; in Malaya with USPG, 1952–56; Vicar of St Timothy, Crookes, Sheffield, 1958–61; Linguistics Adviser British and Foreign Bible Soc., 1962–67, incl. service in Assam, 1962–64. Asst Keeper, British Museum, 1967–71, Dep. Keeper 1971–74. Mem., Koninklijk Instituut voor Taal-, Land- en Volkenkunde, The Netherlands, 1983–. Hon. Canon of All Saints Pro-Cathedral, Shillong, 1963. FRAS. *Publications:* The Christian Approach to the Muslim, 1958; articles in Jl Malayan Branch Royal Asiatic Soc., Bible Translator. *Recreation:* ethno-linguistics of South and South East Asia. *Address:* 1 Ainsworth Street, Ulverston, Cumbria LA12 7EU. *T:* Ulverston 56874.

MARS-JONES, Hon. Sir William (Lloyd), Kt 1969; MBE 1945; **Hon. Mr Justice Mars-Jones;** a Judge of the High Court of Justice, Queen's Bench Division, since 1969; *b* 4 Sept. 1915; *s* of Henry and Jane Mars Jones, Llansannan, Denbighshire; *m* 1947, Sheila Mary Felicity Cobon; three *s*. *Educ:* Denbigh County Sch.; UCW, Aberystwyth (LLB Hons); St John's Coll., Cambridge (BA). Entrance Schol., Gray's Inn, 1936; Pres. Students' Rep. Counc. and Central Students' Rep. Counc., UCW, 1936–37; MacMahon Studentship, 1939; Barrister-at-Law, 1941, QC 1957. War of 1939–45, RNVR (MBE); Lt-Comdr RNVR 1945. Contested W Denbigh Parly Div., 1945. Joined Wales and Chester Circuit, 1947, Presiding Judge, 1971–75. Recorder of: Birkenhead, 1959–65; Swansea, 1965–68; Cardiff, 1968–69; Dep. Chm., Denbighshire Quarter Sessions, 1962–68. Bencher, Gray's Inn, 1964, Treasurer, 1982. Comr of Assize, Denbigh and Mold Summer Assize, 1965. Member: Bar Council, 1962; Home Office Inquiry into allegations against Metropolitan Police Officers, 1964; Home Secretary's Adv. Council on Penal System, 1966–68. President: N Wales Arts Assoc., 1976–; UCNW, Bangor, 1983–. Hon. LLD UCW, Aberystwyth, 1973. *Recreations:* singing, acting, guitar. *Address:* Royal Courts of Justice, Strand, WC2. *T:* 01–936 6056. *Club:* Garrick.

MARSACK, Hon. Sir Charles (Croft), KBE 1981 (CBE 1962); **Hon. Mr Justice Marsack;** Judge, Fiji Court of Appeal, since 1957; *b* 7 May 1892; *s* of Richard Marsack and Mary Ann Marsack; *m* 1918, Ninette Padiou; two *s*. *Educ:* Auckland Univ., New Zealand (BA, LLB). Legal practice, New Zealand, 1914–39, except for overseas service with NZ Rifle Brigade, 1915–18; service with 2 NZEF, Middle East and Italy, 1939–45. New Zealand Stipendiary Magistrate, 1945–47; Chief Justice, Western Samoa, 1947–62; Independent Chairman, Fiji Sugar Industry, 1962–70. *Publications:* Samoan Medley, 1961, 2nd edn 1964; Teach Yourself Samoan, 1962, 3rd edn 1973. *Recreation:* gardening. *Address:* PO Box 3751, Samabula, Suva, Fiji. *T:* Suva 383150. *Club:* Returned Servicemen's (Suva).

MARSDEN, Allen Gatenby, CBE 1945; FCIT; Hon. President of International Transport-Users Commission, Paris; *b* 13 Sept. 1893; *s* of late William Allen Marsden, OBE, and Marianne Turvey; *m* 1st, 1918, Mabel Kathleen Buckley (*decd*); one *s* two *d*; 2nd, 1933, Janet Helen Williamson (*d* 1982); one *s*. *Educ:* Wadham House, Hale; Bedford Grammar Sch. Joined staff of London & North-Western Railway as a probationer, 1909; served European War with commission in 8th Bn Manchester Regt, TF, 1914–16, in Egypt, Cyprus and Gallipoli, invalided home with rank of Capt.; under Dir-Gen. of Transportation, France, 1917; Transport and Storage Div., Min. of Food, 1917–18; Traffic Asst, Ministry of Transport, 1920; transport manager of Cadbury Bros Ltd, Bournville, 1921; subsequently transport Supervisor, Cadbury-Fry Joint Transport until 1940; Dir of Transport, Ministry of Food, Aug. 1940–May 1946; Transport Adviser to Bd of Unilever Ltd, 1946–58. On retirement apptd Independent Mem., Scottish Agricultural Wages Bd, 1959–65. Chairman: Transport Cttee, CBI, 1946–58; British Gen. Transport Cttee, ICC; Vice-Pres., Internat. Container Bureau, Paris, 1948–58; Pres., Internat. Transport Users Commn, Paris, 1948–58. Commerce and industry rep., Central Transport Consultative Cttee for GB, 1946–58; former Mem. Council, CIT (British Transport Commn Award for paper on Traders and the Transport Act, 1949). *Recreations:* golf, fishing. *Address:* 64 Heathfield Road, Audlem, near Crewe, Cheshire. *T:* Audlem 811555.

MARSDEN, Arthur Whitcombe, MSc, DIC, ARCS; formerly Education Officer/Technical Editor, Animal Production and Health Division, FAO, Rome, 1964–73; *b* Buxton, Derbyshire, 14 June 1911; *o s* of late Hubert Marsden and Margaret Augusta Bidwell; *m* 1940, Ailsa Anderson, *yr d* of late William Anderson McKellar, physician, and Jessie Reid Macfarlane, of Glasgow and Chester-le-Street, Co. Durham; one *s* two *d*. *Educ:* St Paul's; Imperial Coll. (Royal College of Science), London. BSc Special and ARCS, 1933; research in agricultural (royal chemistry at Imperial Coll., 1933–36; research asst, 1936; demonstrator, 1937; asst lecturer, 1939; MSc and DIC, 1940. Temp. Instr Lieut RN, 1942; HMS Diomede, 1943; HMS King Alfred, 1944; RN Coll., Greenwich, and HMS Superb, 1945. Lecturer, Imperial Coll., London, 1946; Dept Head, Seale-Hayne Agricultural Coll., Newton Abbot, 1946–48; dir of research to grain companies in Aberdeen, 1948–49. Dir of Commonwealth Bureau of Dairy Science and Technology, Shinfield, Reading, 1950–57; Organising Secretary: 15th International Dairy Congress, London, 1957–60; 2nd World Congress of Man-made Fibres, 1960–63. Hon. Sec., Agriculture Group, Soc. of Chem. Industry, 1947–52, Chm., 1954–56; Organising Cttee of 2nd International Congress of Crop Protection, London, 1949; delegate on OEEC Technical Assistance Mission in USA and Canada, 1951; toured research centres in Pakistan, India, Australia, NZ and USA, Oct. 1954–Feb. 1955. *Publications:* papers in scientific journals. *Recreations:* gardening, music, meeting and talking to people, especially from developing countries. *Address:* 109 Willingdon Road, Eastbourne, East Sussex BN21 1TX. *T:* Eastbourne 33602.

MARSDEN, Prof. Charles David, DSc; FRCP; FRS 1983; Professor of Neurology, Institute of Psychiatry and King's College Hospital, London, 1972–Oct 1987, Professor of Clinical Neurology, Institute of Neurology and National Hospitals for Nervous Diseases, Queen Square, from Oct. 1987; *b* 15 April 1938; *s* of Charles Moustaka Marsden, CBE and Una Maud Marsden; *m* 1961, Jill Slaney Bullock; two *s* three *d*; *m* 1979, Jennifer Sandom. *Educ:* Cheltenham Coll.; St Thomas's Hosp. Med. Sch. (MSc 1960; MB, BS 1963). FRCP 1975 (MRCP 1965); MRCPsych 1978. Sen. House Physician, National Hosp. for Nervous Diseases, 1968–70; Sen. Lectr in Neurol., Inst. of Psych. and King's Coll. Hosp., 1970–72. *Publications:* papers on human movement disorders, motor physiology, and basal ganglia pharmacology. *Recreation:* the human brain. *Address:* Department of Neurology, Institute of Psychiatry, De Crespigny Park, SE5 8AF. *T:* 01–703 5411, ext. 136; (from Oct. 1987) Institute of Neurology and National Hospitals for Nervous Diseases, Queen Square, WC1. *Club:* Athenæum.

MARSDEN, Frank; JP; *b* Everton, Liverpool, 15 Oct. 1923; *s* of Sidney Marsden and Harriet Marsden (*née* Needham); *m* 1943, Muriel Lightfoot; three *s*. *Educ:* Abbotsford Road Sec. Mod. Sch., Liverpool. Served War, with RAF Bomber Command, 115 Sqdn (Warrant Officer), 1941–46. Joined Lab. Party and Co-op. Movement, 1948. MP (Lab) Liverpool, Scotland, Apr. 1971–Feb. 1974. Local Councillor: Liverpool St Domingo Ward, May 1964–67; Liverpool Vauxhall Ward, 1969–71; Knowsley DC, 1976–. Chm. Liverpool Markets, 1965–67; Past Mem. Exec. Cttee: Liverpool Trades Council; Liverpool Lab. Party. JP (City of Liverpool), 1969. *Recreations:* jazz music, gardening. *Address:* 2 Thunderbolt Cottage, 6 Alder Lane, Knowsley, Prescot, Merseyside. *T:* 051–546 1959.

MARSDEN, Leslie Alfred, CMG 1966; *b* 25 Sept. 1921; *s* of late William Marsden, Stanmore, Middx, and of Kitty Marsden; *m* 1947, Doris Winifred, *d* of late Walter Richard Grant and of Winifred Grant; two *d*. *Educ:* Kingsbury County Sch. Served War: The Queen's Own Royal West Kent Regt, 1940–42; 14th Punjab Regt, Indian Army,

1942–46; serving in India, Burma and Thailand; retd as Hon. Major. Joined Nigeria Police Force, 1946; Commissioner of Police, 1964; Asst Inspector-General, 1966–68. Associate Director, Sierra Leone Selection Trust, 1969; Security Adviser, Standard Telephones and Cables Ltd, 1970–82; retired 1982. Nigeria Police Medal, 1964; Queen's Police Medal, 1964; Colonial Police Medal, 1958. *Recreations:* walking, reading, public affairs. *Address:* Ashbank, 14 Orchard Rise, Groombridge, Sussex. *T:* Groombridge 486.

MARSDEN, Sir Nigel (John Denton), 3rd Bt *cr* 1924, of Grimsby; gardener since 1983; *b* 26 May 1940; *s* of Sir John Denton Marsden, 2nd Bt and of Hope, *yr d* of late G. E. Llewelyn; *S* father, 1985; *m* 1961, Diana Jean, *d* of Air Marshal Sir Patrick Hunter Dunn, *qv*; three *d. Educ:* Ampleforth College, York. Vice-Chairman and Managing Director of family business, Consolidated Fisheries Ltd, of Grimsby, 1973 until 1982, when Company ceased trading and was sold. *Recreations:* walking, shooting, family. *Heir: b* Simon Neville Llewelyn Marsden [*b* 1 Dec. 1948; *m* 1970, Catherine Thérèse, *d* of late Brig. James Charles Windsor-Lewis, DSO, MC; *m* 1984, Caroline, *y d* of John Stanton, Houghton St Giles, Norfolk]. *Address:* The Homestead, 1 Grimsby Road, Waltham, Grimsby, South Humberside DN37 0PS. *T:* Grimsby 822166.

MARSDEN, Rear-Adm. Peter Nicholas; Senior Naval Member, Directing Staff, Royal College of Defence Studies, since 1985; *b* 29 June 1932; *s* of Dr James Pickford Marsden and Evelyn (*née* Holman); *m* 1956, Jean Elizabeth Mather; two *s* one *d. Educ:* Felsted Sch., Essex. Joined RN, 1950; Commander, 1968; Captain, 1976; Commodore, Admiralty Interview Bd, 1983–84. *Recreations:* golf, beagling, gardening. *Address:* c/o National Westminster Bank, Standishgate, Wigan, Lancs.

MARSDEN, Susan; Assistant Director, National Association of Citizens' Advice Bureaux, since 1985; *b* 6 Dec. 1931; *d* of late John Marsden-Smedley and Agatha (*née* Bethell). *Educ:* Downe House Sch.; Girton Coll., Cambridge (MA). Called to the Bar, Middle Temple, 1957. Worked in consumer organisations in Britain and US, 1957–65; Senior Research Officer, Consumer Council, 1966–70; Legal Officer, Nuffield Foundation Legal Advice Research Unit, 1970–72; Exec. Dir, 1972–78, and Course Dir, 1978–81, Legal Action Gp (Editor, LAG Bulletin, 1972–78); Sec., Public Sector Liaison, RIBA, 1981–84. Chm., Greater London CAB Service, 1979–85; Member: Council, National Assoc. of CAB, 1980–84; Royal Commn on Legal Services, 1976–79. *Publication:* Justice Out of Reach, a case for Small Claims Courts, 1969. *Recreations:* tree planting and preservation, gardening, looking at modern buildings. *Address:* Flat 5, 28 Newlay Lane, Horsforth, Leeds LS18 4LE. *T:* Leeds 580936.

MARSDEN, William; HM Diplomatic Service; Head, East Africa Department, Foreign and Commonwealth Office, and Commissioner, British Indian Ocean Territory, since 1985; *b* 15 Sept. 1940; *s* of Christopher Marsden and Ruth (*née* Kershaw); *m* 1964, Kaja Collingham; one *s* one *d. Educ:* Winchester Coll.; Lawrenceville Sch., USA; Trinity Coll., Cambridge (MA); London Univ. (BSc Econs). FO, 1962–64; UK Delegn to NATO, 1964–66; Rome, 1966–69; seconded as Asst to Gen. Manager, Joseph Lucas Ltd, 1970; First Sec., FCO, 1971–76; First Sec. and Cultural Attaché, Moscow, 1976–79; Asst Head, European Community Dept, FCO, 1979–81; Counsellor, UK Representation to EEC, 1981–85. Chm., Twickenham Town Cttee, 1981–. MBIM. *Address:* c/o Foreign and Commonwealth Office, SW1A 2AH.

MARSDEN-SMEDLEY, Susan; *see* Marsden.

MARSH, family name of **Baron Marsh.**

MARSH, Baron *cr* 1981 (Life Peer), of Mannington in the County of Wiltshire; **Richard William Marsh;** PC 1966; Kt 1976; FCIT; Chairman: Newspaper Publishers' Association, since 1976; TV-am, since 1983 (Deputy Chairman, 1980–83); Lee Cooper Group, since 1982; *b* 14 March 1928; *s* of William Marsh, Belvedere, Kent; *m* 1st, 1950, Evelyn Mary (marr. diss. 1973), *d* of Frederick Andrews, Southampton; two *s*; 2nd, 1973, Caroline Dutton (*d* 1975); 3rd, 1979, Felicity, *d* of Baron McFadzean of Kelvinside, *qv. Educ:* Jennings Sch., Swindon; Woolwich Polytechnic; Ruskin Coll., Oxford. Health Services Officer, National Union of Public Employees, 1951–59; Mem., Clerical and Administrative Whitley Council for Health Service, 1953–59; MP (Lab) Greenwich, Oct. 1959–April 1971; promoted Offices Act 1961; Member: Select Cttee Estimates, 1961; Chm. Interdepartmental Cttee to Co-ordinate Govt Policy on Industrial Training, 1964; Parly Sec., Min. of Labour, 1964–65; Joint Parly Sec., Min. of Technology, 1965–66; Minister of Power, 1966–68; Minister of Transport, 1968–69. Chairman: British Railways Bd, 1971–76; British Iron and Steel Consumers' Council, 1977–82; Allied Investments Ltd, 1977–81; Member: NEDC, 1971–; Freight Integration Council, 1971–. Chairman: Michael Saunders Management Services, 1970–71; Allied Medical Group, 1977–81; Deputy Chairman: United Medical Enterprises Ltd, 1978–81; Lopex PLC, 1986–; Director: National Carbonising Co. Ltd (Chm., NCC Plant and Transport), 1970–71; Concord Rotoflex International Ltd, 1970–71; European Bd, 1979–, Main Bd, 1984–, Imperial Life of Canada; Imperial Life of Canada UK, 1983–; Advisor: Nissan Motor Co., 1981–; Fujitec, 1982–. Pres., Council ECSC, 1968. Governor: British Transport Staff Coll. (Chm.); London Business Sch. *Publication:* Off the Rails (autobiog.), 1978. *Address:* c/o 6 Bouverie Street, EC4Y 8AY. *Clubs:* Reform, Buck's.

MARSH, Ven. Bazil Roland, BA; Archdeacon of Northampton, Non-Residentiary Canon of Peterborough, and Rector of St Peter's, Northampton, since 1964; *b* Three Hills, Alta, Canada, 11 Aug. 1921; *s* of late Ven. Wilfred Carter Marsh and late Mary Jean (*née* Stott), Devil's Lake, North Dakota, USA; *m* 1946, Audrey Joan, *d* of late Owen George Oyler, farmer, of Brookmans Park, Hatfield, and Alma Lillian Oyler; three *s* one *d. Educ:* State schs in USA and Swindon, Wilts; Leeds Univ.; Coll. of the Resurrection, Mirfield, Yorks. Curate of: St Mary the Virgin, Cheshunt, Herts, 1944–46; St John Baptist, Coventry, 1946–47; St Giles-in-Reading, Berks, 1947–51; Rector of St Peter's, Townsville, Qld, Australia, 1951–56; Vicar of St Mary the Virgin, Far Cotton, Northampton, 1956–64. *Address:* 11 The Drive, Northampton NN1 4RZ. *T:* Northampton 714015. *Club:* Royal Commonwealth Society.

MARSH, Gordon Victor, MA; FHA; Deputy Health Service Commissioner, since 1982; *b* 14 May 1929; *s* of late Ven. Wilfred Carter Marsh, Devil's Lake, North Dakota, USA and Rosalie (*née* Holliday); *m* Millicent, *e d* of late Christopher Thomas and Edith Rowsell; one *s* one *d. Educ:* Grammar Schs, Swindon; Keble Coll., Oxford (MA); Inst. of Health Service Administrators (FHA 1964); Sloan Business Sch., Cornell Univ., USA. NHS admin. posts, England and Wales, 1952–72; Administrator and Sec., Bd of Governors, UCH, 1972–74; Area Administrator, Lambeth, Southwark and Lewisham AHA(T), 1974–82. Vice-Chm., Assoc. of Chief Administrators of Health Authorities, 1980–82; Member: Council, National Assoc. of Health Authorities, 1979–82; Adv. Bd, Coll. of Occupational Therapists, 1974–. Chm., Trelawn Cttee of Richmond Fellowship, 1970–83; Hon. Sec. to Congregational Meeting and Wandsman, St Paul's Cathedral, 1980–. *Publications:* articles in professional jls. *Recreations:* music, gardening. *Address:* Springwater, St Lucian's Lane, Wallingford, Oxon OX10 9ER. *T:* Wallingford 36660. *Club:* United Oxford & Cambridge University.

MARSH, Rt. Rev. Henry Hooper, MA, DD; *b* 6 Oct. 1898; *s* of Rev. Canon Charles H. Marsh, DD; *m* Margaret D. Heakes; one *s* one *d. Educ:* University College, Toronto, BA 1921; Wycliffe College, Toronto, 1924, MA 1925; DD 1962. Deacon, 1924; Priest, 1925; Curate of St Anne, Toronto, 1924–25; Curate of St Paul, Toronto, 1925–30; Priest-in-charge of St Timothy's Mission, City and Diocese of Toronto, 1930–36; Rector, Church of St Timothy, 1936–62; Canon of Toronto, 1956–62; Bishop of Yukon, 1962–67. Canadian Centennial Medal, 1967. *Recreation:* bird watching. *Address:* Hedgerows, RR6, Cobourg, Ont K9A 4J9, Canada.

MARSH, (Henry) John, CBE 1967; international management consultant, writer and lecturer; director of companies; Chairman, New Product Management Group Ltd, since 1983; *b* 1913; *s* of late Jasper W. P. Marsh and Gladys M. Carruthers; *m* 1950, Mary Costerton; two *s* two *d. Educ:* Chefoo Sch., China; Queen Elizabeth's Grammar Sch., Wimborne. Commerce, China, 1930–32; Shanghai Volunteer Force, 1930–32; engineering apprenticeship and apprentice supervisor, Austin Motor Co., 1932–39. Served War of 1939–45, Royal Army Service Corps TA, 48th and 56th Divisions; Singapore Fortress; BEF France, 1940; Malaya, 1941–42 (despatches twice); Prisoner of War, 1942–45; released with rank of Major, 1946. Personnel Officer, BOAC, 1946–47; Dir of Personnel Advisory Services, Institute of Personnel Management, 1947–49; Dir, Industrial (Welfare) Soc., 1950–61; British Institute of Management: Dir, later Dir-Gen., 1961–73; Asst Chm. and Counsellor, 1973–75. Mem., Nat. Coal Board, 1968–74. Hon. Administrator, Duke of Edinburgh's Study Conference, 1954–56; Chairman:. Brit. Nat. Conference on Social Work, 1957–60; VSO, 1957–60; Member: Youth Service Cttee, 1958–59; BBC General Advisory Council, 1959–64; Advisory Cttee on Employment of Prisoners, 1960–63; Council for Technical Educn and Training for Overseas Countries, 1961–74; UK Advisory Council on Education for Management, 1962–66; Russell Cttee on Adult Educn, 1969–72; Court, Univ. of Cranfield, 1962–69; Court, Univ. of Surrey, 1969–79; Food Manufacturing EDC, 1967–69; Adv. Council, Civil Service College, 1970–77; UK Mem., Commonwealth Team of Industrial Specialists, 1976–78. Governor, King's Coll. Hosp., 1971–74. British Information Service Lecture Tours: India and Pakistan, 1959 and 1963; Nigeria, 1964; Malaysia, 1965; Australia, 1967; Latin America, 1971, 1973; Malaysia, NZ, 1974. FIAM 1969; Hon. Fellow, Canadian Inst. of Management, 1973; CBIM (FBIM 1967); FIMC 1980. Hon. CIPM 1985. Hon. DSc Bradford, 1968. Verulam Medal, 1976. *Publications:* Introduction to Human Relations at Work, 1952; People at Work, 1957; Partners in Work Relations, 1960; Work and Leisure Digest, 1961; Pursuit of God, 1968; Ethics in Business, 1970; Organisations of the Future, 1980; Late Glimpses (verse), 1984; lectures: Ardeshir Dalal Memorial Lecture, India, 1953; The Clarke Hall Lecture, 1957; E. W. Hancock Lecture, 1960; MacLaren Memorial Lecture, 1962; Tullis Russell Lecture, 1967; Allerdale-Wyld Lecture, 1972; RSA Lecture, 1973; Geden Foster Lecture, 1977; Chester Lecture, 1978; Stantonbury Lecture, 1981. *Recreations:* music, counselling, idling. *Address:* 13 Frank Dixon Way, Dulwich, SE21 7ET.

MARSH, Jean Lyndsey Torren; actress; Artistic Director, Adelphi University Theatre, Long Island, New York, 1981–83; *b* 1 July 1934; *d* of Henry Charles and Emmeline Susannah Marsh; *m* 1955, Jon Devon Roland Pertwee (marr. diss. 1960). Began as child actress and dancer; *films:* danced in Tales of Hoffmann, Where's Charley?, etc; Return to Oz; acted in repertory companies: Huddersfield, Nottingham, etc; Broadway debut in Much Ado About Nothing, 1959; West End debut, Bird of Time, 1961; *stage:* Habeas Corpus, The Importance of Being Earnest, Too True to be Good, Twelfth Night, Blithe Spirit, Whose Life is it Anyway?, Uncle Vanya, On the Rocks, Pygmalion, Hamlet; *television:* co-created and co-starred (Rose) in series Upstairs Downstairs; series, Nine to Five. Hon. DH Maryland Coll., NY, 1980. *Publications:* The Illuminated Language of Flowers, 1978; articles for Sunday Times and Washington Post. *Recreations:* cross-country skiing, reading, cooking, eating. *Address:* Hamstead Farm Cottage, Drift Lane, Chidham, W Sussex.

MARSH, Prof. the Rev. John, CBE 1964; MA (Edinburgh et Oxon), DPhil (Oxon); DD (Hon.) Edinburgh; Moderator, Free Church Federal Council, 1970–71; Principal, Mansfield College, Oxford, 1953–70; *b* 5 Nov. 1904; *s* of George Maurice and Florence Elizabeth Ann Marsh, East Grinstead, Sussex; *m* 1934, Gladys Walker, *y d* of George Benson and Mary Walker, Cockermouth, Cumberland; two *s* one *d. Educ:* The Skinners Company Sch., Tunbridge Wells; Yorkshire United Coll., Bradford; Edinburgh Univ.; Mansfield Coll. and St Catherine's Soc., Oxford; Marburg Univ. Lecturer, Westhill Training Coll., 1932; Minister, Congregational Church, Otley, Yorks, 1934; Tutor and Chaplain, Mansfield Coll., Oxford, 1938; Prof. of Christian Theology, The University, Nottingham, 1949–53. Gray Lectr, Duke Univ., NC; Reinecke Lectr, Prot. Episc. Semin., Alexandria, Va, 1958. Delegate: First Assembly, World Council of Churches, Amsterdam, 1948; Second Assembly, Evanston, Ill., 1954; Third Assembly, New Delhi, 1961; Fourth Assembly, Uppsala, 1968. Sec. World Conference on Faith and Order's Commn on "Intercommunion"; Chm., Section 2 of British Council of Churches Commn on Broadcasting, 1949; Mem., Working Cttee, Faith and Order Dept, World Council of Churches, 1953; Sec., European Commission on Christ and the Church, World Council of Churches, 1955; Mem. Central Religious Advisory Cttee to BBC, 1955–60; Mem. Sub-Cttee of CRAC acting as Religious Advisory Panel to ITA, 1955–65; Chm. British Council of Churches Commn of Faith and Order, 1960–62. Mem. Central Cttee, World Council of Churches, 1961–68; Chm. Division of Studies, World Council of Churches, 1961–68; Select Preacher, University of Oxford, 1962; Chm. Congregational Union of England and Wales, 1962–63; Chairman: Inter-Church Relationships Cttee, Congregational Church in England and Wales, 1964–67; Board of Faculty of Theology, Oxford Univ., 1966–68; Exec. Cttee, Congregational Church in England and Wales, 1966–72; Joint Chm. Joint Cttee for Conversations between Congregationalists and Presbyterians, 1965–72; Lay Vice-Chm., Derwent Deanery Synod, 1979–82. Chm., Buttermere Parish Council, 1973–80. Governor, Westminster Coll., Oxford, 1967–70. *Publications:* The Living God, 1942; Congregationalism Today, 1943; (jtly) A Book of Congregational Worship, 1948; (Jt Ed.) Intercommunion, 1952; contrib. Biblical Authority Today, 1951; and Ways of Worship, 1951; The Fulness of Time, 1952; The Significance of Evanston, 1954; trans. Stauffer, Theology of the New Testament, 1955; A Year with the Bible, 1957; contributed to Essays in Christology for Karl Barth, 1957; Amos and Micah, 1959; trans. Bultmann, The History of the Synoptic Tradition, 1963; Pelican Commentary on St John's Gospel, 1968; Jesus in his Lifetime, 1981. *Recreations:* water colour painting, wood turning. *Address:* Dale House, High Lorton, Cockermouth, Cumbria CA13 9UQ. *T:* Lorton 650.

MARSH, John; *see* Marsh, H. J.

MARSH, Leonard George, MEd; Principal, Bishop Grosseteste College, since 1974; *b* 23 Oct. 1930; third *c* of late Ernest Arthur Marsh and Anne Eliza (*née* Bean); *m* 1953, Ann Margaret Gilbert; one *s* one *d. Educ:* Ashford (Kent) Grammar Sch.; Borough Road Coll., London Inst. of Educn; Leicester Univ. Teachers' Certif., Academic Dip. Lectr in Educn and Mathematics, St Paul's Coll., Cheltenham, 1959–61; Lectr, 1961–63, Sen. Lectr, 1963–65, Principal Lectr and Head of Postgraduate Primary Educn Dept, 1965–74,

Goldsmiths' Coll., London. Visiting Lectr, Bank Street Coll., New York, and Virginia Commonwealth Univ.; former Consultant, OECD, Portugal; Educnl Consultant, Teacher Trng Proj., Botswana, 1981; Specialist tour to India for British Council. Member: Gen. Adv. Council, IBA, 1977–82; N Lincolnshire AHA, 1984–; Chm., Nat. Assoc. for Primary Educn, 1981–83. *Publications:* Let's Explore Mathematics, Books 1–4, 1964–67; Children Explore Mathematics, 1967, 3rd edn 1969; Exploring Shapes and Numbers, 1968, 2nd edn 1970; Exploring the Metric System, 1969, 2nd edn 1969; Exploring the Metric World, 1970; Approach to Mathematics, 1970; Alongside the Child in the Primary School, 1970; Let's Discover Mathematics, Books 1–5, 1971–72; Being A Teacher, 1973; Helping your Child with Maths—a parents' guide, 1980; The Guinness Mathematics Book, 1980; The Guinness Book for Young Scientists, 1982. *Recreations:* photography, theatre going, films. *Address:* The Principal's House, Bishop Grosseteste College, Lincoln LN1 3DY. *T:* Lincoln 28241; Broomfields, The Meadow, Chislehurst, Kent BR7 6AA. *T:* 01–467 6311.

MARSH, Nevill Francis, CBE 1969; Director-General, St John Ambulance, 1972–76; *b* 13 Aug. 1907; *m* 1935, Betty (*née* Hide); one *s* one *d. Educ:* Oundle Sch., Northants; Clare Coll., Cambridge (MA). Traction Motor Design Staff, Metropolitan-Vickers Electrical Co. Ltd, 1930–32; Mid-Lincolnshire Electric Supply Co. Ltd: Dist Engineer, 1932–38; Engineer and Manager, 1938–48; Chief Commercial Officer, E Midlands Electricity Board, 1948–55; Dep.-Chm., N Eastern Electricity Board, 1955–57; Dep.-Chm., E Midlands Electricity Board, 1957–59; Chm., East Midlands Electricity Board, 1959–61; a Dep. Chm., Electricity Council, 1962–71; Chm., British Electrotechnical Cttee, 1970–72. Dir for Gtr London, St John Ambulance Assoc., 1971–72. Also formerly: Dir, Altrincham Electric Supply Ltd, and Public Utilities (Elec.) Ltd, and Supervising Engineer, Campbeltown & Mid-Argyll Elec. Supply Co. Ltd, and Thurso & District Elec. Supply Co. Ltd. FIEE; Pres. of Assoc. of Supervising Electrical Engineers, 1966–68. KStJ 1973. *Publications:* jt contrib. Jl Inst. Electrical Engineers, 1955. *Address:* Stocksfield, First Avenue, Frinton-on-Sea, Essex CO13 9EZ. *T:* Frinton 2995. *Club:* Royal Air Force.

MARSH, Norman Stayner, CBE 1977; QC 1967; Law Commissioner, 1965–78; Member, Royal Commission on Civil Liability and Compensation for Personal Injury, 1973–78; *b* 26 July 1913; 2nd *s* of Horace Henry and Lucy Ann Marsh, Bath, Som; *m* 1939, Christiane Christinnecke, 2nd *d* of Professor Johannes and Käthe Christinnecke, Magdeburg, Germany; two *s* two *d. Educ:* Monkton Combe Sch.; Pembroke Coll., Oxford (2nd Class Hons, Final Honour Sch. of Jurisprudence, 1935; 1st Cl. Hons BCL; Hon. Fellow, 1978). Vinerian Scholar of Oxford Univ., Harmsworth Scholar of Middle Temple, called to Bar, 1937; practice in London and on Western Circuit, 1937–39; Lieut-Col Intelligence Corps and Control Commission for Germany, 1939–46. Stowell Civil Law Fellow, University Coll., Oxford, 1946–60; University Lecturer in Law, 1947–60; Estates Bursar, University Coll., 1948–56; Secretary-General, International Commission of Jurists, The Hague, Netherlands, 1956–58. Member: Bureau of Conference of Non-Governmental Organisations with Consultative Status with the United Nations, 1957–58; Internat. Cttee of Legal Science (Unesco), 1960–63. Dir of British Institute of International and Comparative Law, 1960–65. Mem., Younger Cttee on Privacy, 1970–72. Hon. Vis. Prof. in Law, KCL, 1972–77. Vice-Chm., Age Concern, England, 1979–86. General editor, International and Comparative Law Quarterly, 1961–65; Mem., Editorial Board, 1965–. *Publications:* The Rule of Law as a supra-national concept, in Oxford Essays in Jurisprudence, 1960; The Rule of Law in a Free Society, 1960; Interpretation in a National and International Context, 1974; (editor and part-author) Public Access to Government-held Information, 1986; articles on common law and comparative law in English, American, French and German law jls. *Address:* Wren House, 13 North Side, Clapham Common, SW4. *T:* 01–622 2865.

MARSHALL, family name of **Barons Marshall of Goring** and **Marshall of Leeds.**

MARSHALL OF GORING, Baron *cr* 1985 (Life Peer), of South Stoke in the County of Oxfordshire; **Walter Charles Marshall;** Kt 1982; CBE 1973; FRS 1971; Chairman, Central Electricity Generating Board, since 1982; *b* 5 March 1932; *s* of late Frank Marshall and Amy (*née* Pearson); *m* 1955, Ann Vivienne Sheppard; one *s* one *d. Educ:* Birmingham Univ. Scientific Officer, AERE, Harwell, 1954–57; Research Physicist: University of California, 1957–58; Harvard Univ., 1958–59; AERE, Harwell: Group Leader, Solid State Theory, 1959–60; Head of Theoretical Physics Div., 1960–66; Dep. Dir, 1966–68; Dir, 1966–75; Chief Scientist, Dept of Energy, 1974–77; United Kingdom Atomic Energy Authority: Dir, Research Gp, 1969–75; Mem., 1972–82; Dep. Chm., 1975–81; Chm., 1981–82. Member: NRDC, 1969–75; NEDC, 1984–; Chairman: Adv. Council on R&D for Fuel and Power, 1974–77; Offshore Energy Technology Bd, 1975–77. Fellow, Royal Swedish Acad. of Engrg Scis, 1977; For. Associate, Nat. Acad. of Engineering, USA. Hon. Fellow, St Hugh's Coll., Oxford, 1983; Hon. DSc Salford, 1977. Editor, Oxford Internat. Series of Monographs on Physics, 1966–. Maxwell Medal, 1964; Glazebrook Medal, 1975. FBIM. Freeman, City of London, 1984. *Publications:* Thermal Neutron Scattering, 1971; research papers on magnetism, neutron scattering and solid state theory. *Recreations:* gardening, origami. *Address:* c/o Central Electricity Generating Board, Sudbury House, 15 Newgate Street, EC1. *T:* 01–634 6101.

MARSHALL OF LEEDS, Baron *cr* 1980 (Life Peer), of Shadwell in the City of Leeds; **Frank Shaw Marshall,** Kt 1971; solicitor; Chairman, Municipal Mutual Insurance Co., since 1978 (Managing Trustee, since 1970); Director, since 1962, and Vice-President, since 1985, Leeds & Holbeck Building Society (President, 1967–69 and 1977–79); Deputy Chairman, Dartford International Ferry Terminal Ltd, since 1985; Director, Barr & Wallace Arnold Trust PLC, since 1953; director of other companies; *b* Wakefield, 26 Sept. 1915; 4th *s* of Charles William Marshall and Edith Marshall; *g g s* of Charles Marshall (*b* Wakefield, 1827), of New York, Philadelphia and Columbia, Missouri, who fought in American Civil War; *m* 1941, Mary, *e c* of Robert and Edith Barr, Shadwell House, Leeds; two *d. Educ:* Queen Elizabeth's Sch., Wakefield; Downing Coll., Cambridge (scholar; MA, LLM; Associate Fellow, 1986). Served War, 1940–46: Captain RTR; SO JAG's Dept, WO. Leeds City Council: Leader, and Chm. Finance Cttee, 1967–72; Alderman, 1967–73. Chairman: NE Leeds Cons. Assoc., 1962–65; City of Leeds Cons. Assoc., 1967–69; Yorks Provincial Area, Nat. Union of Cons. and Unionist Assocs, 1976–78; Conservative and Unionist Party: Mem., Nat. Exec., 1968–; Mem., Gen. Purposes Cttee, 1969 and 1976–; Mem., Adv. Cttee on Policy, 1977–; a Vice-Chm., Nat. Union, 1978–79; a Vice-Chm. of the Cons. Party, 1979–85; Mem., Sub-Cttee 'A', House of Lords Select Cttee on Eur. Communities, 1985. Special Advr to Govt on Third London Airport Proj., 1972. Chairman: Maplin Develt Authority, 1973–74; Leeds and Bradford Airport, 1968–69; Leeds Grand Theatre and Opera House Ltd, 1969–72; Local Govt Inf. Office of England and Wales, 1968–73; Assoc. of Municipal Corps of England, Wales and NI, 1968–73; Local Authorities Conditions of Service Adv. Bd, 1971–73; Steering Cttee on Local Authority Management Structures, 1972–73; Marshall Inquiry on Govt of Greater London, 1977–78; Yorks Reg. Cttee, RSA, 1972–84; President: Leeds Law Soc., 1975–76; Leeds Philosophical and Literary Soc., 1981–83; Inst. of Transport Admin, 1983–; Vice-Pres., Building Socs Assoc., 1979–. Member: Yorks and Humberside Econ. Planning Council, 1971–74; Adv. Cttee on Local Govt Audit, 1979–82; Uganda

Resettlement Bd, 1972–73; BBC North Regional Council, 1969–72; Leeds Radio Council, BBC, 1969–73; Exec. Cttee, AA, 1974– (a Vice-Chm., 1983–85). Member Court: Leeds Univ., 1965–84 (Mem. Council, 1965–72 and 1975–); Bradford Univ., 1967–71; Univ. of York, 1981–; Mem., Council of Management, Univ. of Buckingham (formerly University Coll. at Buckingham), 1975–85; Vice-Chm., Bd of Governors, Centre for Environmental Studies, 1971–80. Hon. Freedom, City of Leeds, 1976. FRSA. *Publications:* The Marshall Report on Greater London, 1978; contrib. Local Government and other jls; press articles. *Recreations:* theatre, reading. *Address:* House of Lords, SW1A 0PW.

MARSHALL, Mrs Alan R.; *see* Marshall, V. M.

MARSHALL, Alan Ralph; HM Chief Inspector of Schools, Department of Education and Science, since 1985; *s* of Ralph Marshall and Mabel Mills; *m* 1958, Caterina Gattico; one *s* one *d. Educ:* Shoreditch College (Teacher's Cert. 1953); London Univ. (Dip Ed 1959; MPhil 1965); Eastern Washington State Univ. (MEd 1964); Stanford Univ. (MA 1969). Teacher, schools in UK and USA, 1954–62; Lectr, Shoreditch Coll., 1962–68; Vis. Prof., Eastern Washington State Univ., 1964–65; Field Dir, Project Technology, Schools Council, 1970–72; Nat. Centre for School Technology, 1972–73; Course Team Chm., Open Univ., 1973–76; HM Inspector, DES, 1976–. *Publications:* (ed) School Technology in Action, 1974; (with G. T. Page and J. B. Thomas) International Dictionary of Education, 1977; articles in jls. *Recreations:* travel, reading, various crafts. *Address:* Department of Education and Science, Elizabeth House, SE1. *T:* 01-934 9806.

MARSHALL, Alexander Badenoch, (Sandy Marshall); Chairman, Commercial Union Assurance Co. plc, since 1983 (Director, since 1970); Vice-Chairman: The Maersk Co. Ltd, since 1983 (Director, since 1980); The Boots Co. PLC, since 1985 (Director since 1981); Director, Royal Bank of Canada, since 1985; *b* 31 Dec. 1924; *m* 1961, Mona Kurina Douglas Kirk, South Africa; two *s* one *d. Educ:* Trinity Coll., Glenalmond; Worcester Coll., Oxford (MA). Served War, Sub-Lieut RNVR, 1943–46. P&O Group of Companies: Mackinnon Mackenzie & Co., Calcutta, 1947–59; Gen. Manager, British India Steam Navigation Co., 1959–62; Man. Dir, Trident Tankers Ltd, 1962–68; Dir, 1968–72, Man. Dir, 1972–79, Peninsular and Oriental Steam Navigation Co.; Chm., Bestobell Plc, 1979–85. Co-Chm., British-N American Cttee, 1984–. *Recreations:* family, gardening. *Address:* Crest House, Woldingham, Surrey CR3 7DU. *T:* Woldingham 2299. *Clubs:* Oriental; Tollygunge (Calcutta).

MARSHALL, Arthur; *see* Marshall, Charles A. B.

MARSHALL, Arthur C.; *see* Calder-Marshall.

MARSHALL, Sir Arthur Gregory George, Kt 1974; OBE 1948; DL; Chairman and Joint Managing Director, Marshall of Cambridge (Engineering) Ltd, since 1942; *b* 4 Dec. 1903; *s* of David Gregory Marshall, MBE, and Maude Edmunds Wing; *m* 1931, Rosemary Wynford Dimsdale, *d* of Marcus Southwell Dimsdale; two *s* one *d. Educ:* Tonbridge Sch.; Jesus Coll., Cambridge. Engrg, MA. Joined Garage Company of Marshall (Cambridge) Ltd, 1926, which resulted in estabt of Aircraft Company, now Marshall of Cambridge (Engineering) Ltd, 1929. Chm., Aerodrome Owners Assoc., 1964–65; Member: Air Cadet Council, 1951–59 and 1965–76; Adv. Council on Technology, 1967–70. Hon. Old Cranwellian, 1979; CRAeS 1980. DL 1968, High Sheriff of Cambridgeshire and Isle of Ely, 1969–70. *Recreations:* Cambridge Athletics Blue, Olympic Team Reserve, 1924; flying (pilot's licence) since 1928. *Address:* Horseheath Lodge, Linton, Cambridge CB1 6PT. *T:* Cambridge 891318. *Clubs:* Royal Air Force; Hawks (Cambridge).

MARSHALL, Arthur Hedley, CBE 1956; MA; BSc (Econ); PhD; City Treasurer, Coventry, 1944–64, retired; Senior Research Fellow in Public Administration, Birmingham University, 1964–74; Visiting Lecturer, City University, 1977–83; *b* 6 July 1904; *s* of Rev. Arthur Marshall; *m* 1933, Margaret L. Longhurst; one *s. Educ:* Wolverhampton Grammar Sch.; London Sch. of Economics. Incorporated Accountant (Hons), 1934; Fellow Institute Municipal Treasurers and Accountants and Collins gold medal, 1930 (Pres. 1953–54); DPA (London) 1932. Chm. Royal Institute of Public Administration, 1952–53; Adviser in Local Govt to Sudan Govt, 1948–49; and to Govt of British Guiana, 1955. Chm., Cttee on Highway Maintenance, 1967–70; Member: Colonial Office Local Government Advisory Panel, 1950–; Central Housing Adv. Cttee, 1957–65; Cttee for Training Public Administration in Overseas Countries, 1961–62; Arts Council Drama Panel, 1965–76; Arts Council, 1973–76; Uganda Commission, 1961; Kenya Commission, 1962; Royal Commission on Local Government in England, 1966–69. Hon. LLD Nottingham, 1972. *Publications:* Local Authorities: Internal Financial Control, 1936; Consolidated Loans Funds of Local Authorities (with J. M. Drummond), 1936; Report on Local Government in the Sudan, 1949, and on British Guiana, 1955; Financial Administration in Local Government, 1960; Financial Management in Local Government, 1974; Local Authorities and the Arts, 1974; various contribs to learned jls on Local Government, Accountancy, and administration of the arts. *Recreation:* music. *Address:* 39 Armorial Road, Coventry CV3 6GH. *T:* Coventry 414652. *Club:* Reform.
   See also N. H. Marshall.

MARSHALL, Arthur Stirling-Maxwell, CBE 1986 (OBE 1979); HM Diplomatic Service; Ambassador to People's Democratic Republic of Yemen, since 1986; *b* 29 Jan. 1929; *s* of Victor Stirling-Maxwell Marshall and Jeannie Theodora Hunter; *m* 1st, 1955, Eleni Kapralou, Athens (*d* 1969); one *s* two *d*; 2nd, 1985, Cheryl Mary Hookens, Madras. *Educ:* Daniel Stewart's Coll., Edinburgh. Served Royal Navy, 1947–59. Foreign Office, 1959; Middle East Centre for Arab Studies, Lebanon, 1959–61; Political Officer, British Political Agency, Bahrain, 1961–64; Attaché, Athens, 1964–67; Information Officer, Rabat, Morocco, 1967–69; Commercial Secretary: Nicosia, Cyprus, 1970–75; Kuwait, 1975–79; Deputy High Commissioner, Madras, 1980–83; Counsellor, Kuwait, 1983–85. *Recreations:* music, nature. *Address:* c/o Foreign and Commonwealth Office, SW1. *Clubs:* Oriental, Royal Commonwealth Society; Madras (Madras).

MARSHALL, Bruce; novelist; *b* 24 June 1899; *s* of Claude Niven Marshall, Edinburgh; *m* 1928, Phyllis, *d* of late William Glen Clark, Edinburgh; one *d. Educ:* Edinburgh Acad.; Trinity Coll., Glenalmond; St Andrews and Edinburgh Univs. Served in Royal Irish Fusiliers, 1914–18 War and in Royal Army Pay Corps and Intelligence in War of 1939–45; MA Edinburgh, 1924; B Com. Edinburgh, 1925; admitted a mem. of the Soc of Accountants in Edinburgh, 1926. *Publications:* Father Malachy's Miracle, 1931; Prayer for the Living, 1934; The Uncertain Glory, 1935; Yellow Tapers for Paris, 1943; All Glorious Within, 1944; George Brown's Schooldays, 1946; The Red Danube, 1947; Every Man a Penny, 1950; The White Rabbit, 1952; The Fair Bride, 1953; Only Fade Away; Thoughts of my Cats, 1954; Girl in May, 1956; The Bank Audit, 1958; A Thread of Scarlet, 1959; The Divided Lady, 1960; A Girl from Lübeck, 1962; The Month of the Falling Leaves, 1963; Father Hilary's Holiday, 1965; The Bishop, 1970; The Black Oxen, 1972; Urban the Ninth, 1973; Operation Iscariot, 1974; Marx the First, 1975; Peter the Second, 1976; The Yellow Streak, 1977; Prayer for a Concubine, 1978; Flutter in the Dovecot, 1986. *Address:* c/o Lloyds Bank, 6 Pall Mall, SW1.

MARSHALL, (Charles) Arthur (Bertram), MBE 1944; journalist and author; *b* 10 May 1910; *s* of Charles Frederick Bertram Marshall and Dorothy (*née* Lee). *Educ:* Edinburgh House, Lee-on-Solent, Hampshire; Oundle Sch.; Christ's Coll., Cambridge (MA). Schoolmaster and Housemaster, Oundle Sch., 1931–54; Private Sec. to Lord Rothschild, 1954–58; TV Script Editor for H. M. Tennent Ltd, 1958–64. Has written for New Statesman, 1935–81; regular columnist, 1976–81; broadcaster, in variety and more serious programmes, 1934–. American Bronze Star, 1945. *Publications:* Nineteen to the Dozen, 1953; (ed) New Statesman Competitions, 1955; Salome Dear, NOT in the Fridge, 1968; Girls Will Be Girls, 1974; I SAY!, 1977; I'll Let You Know, 1981; Whimpering in the Rhododendrons, 1982; Smile Please, 1982; Life's Rich Pageant, 1984; Giggling in the Shrubbery, 1985. *Recreations:* reading, sitting in the sun. *Address:* Pound Cottage, Christow, Exeter, Devon EX6 7LX. *T:* Christow 52236. *Club:* Reform.

MARSHALL, Colin Marsh; Chief Executive, British Airways, since 1983; *b* 16 Nov. 1933; *s* of Marsh Edward Leslie and Florence Mary Marshall; *m* 1958, Janet Winifred (*née* Cracknell); one *d. Educ:* University College Sch., Hampstead. Progressively, cadet purser to Dep. Purser, OSNC, 1951–58; Hertz Corp., 1958–64: management trainee, Chicago and Toronto, 1958–59; Gen. Man., Mexico, Mexico City, 1959–60; Asst to Pres., New York, 1960; Gen. Manager: UK London, 1961–62; UK Netherlands and Belgium, London, 1962–64; Avis Inc., 1964–79: Reg. Man./Vice-Pres., Europe, London, 1964–66; Vice-Pres. and Gen. Man., Europe and ME, London, 1966–69; Vice-Pres. and Gen. Man., International, London, 1969–71; Exec. Vice-Pres. and Chief Operating Officer, New York, 1971–75; Pres. and Chief Operating Officer, New York, 1975–76; Pres. and Chief Exec. Officer, New York, 1976–79; Norton Simon Inc., New York, 1979–81: Exec. Vice-Pres. and Sector Exec.; Mem., Office of the Chm.; co-Chm. of Avis Inc.; Sears Holdings plc, 1981–83: Dir and Dep. Chief Exec. Member: South Bank Bd, 1985–; British Tourist Authority Bd, 1986–. *Recreations:* tennis, skiing. *Address:* c/o British Airways Head Office, PO Box 10, Heathrow Airport London, Hounslow, Mddx TW6 2JA. *T:* 01-562 5474. *Club:* Queen's.

MARSHALL, David; MP (Lab) Glasgow, Shettleston, since 1979 (sponsored by TGWU); former transport worker; *b* May 1941; *m*; two *s* one *d. Educ:* Larbert, Denny and Falkirk High Schs; Woodside Sen. Secondary Sch., Glasgow. Joined Labour Party, 1962; former Lab. Party Organiser for Glasgow; Member: TGWU; Select Cttee, Scottish Affairs; Hon. Sec., Scottish Gp of Labour MPs; Private Member's Bill, The Solvent Abuse (Scotland) Act, May 1983. Member: Glasgow Corp., 1972–75; Strathclyde Reg. Council, 1974–79 (Chm., Manpower Cttee); Chm., Manpower Cttee, Convention of Scottish Local Authorities; Mem., Local Authorities Conditions of Service Adv. Bd. *Address:* House of Commons, SW1; 32 Enterkin Street, Glasgow G32 7BA.

MARSHALL, Sir Denis (Alfred), Kt 1982; solicitor; with Barlow Lyde & Gilbert, 1947–83, now a consultant; *b* 1 June 1916; *s* of Frederick Herbert Marshall and Winifred Mary Marshall; *m* 1st, 1949, Joan Edith Straker (*d* 1974); one *s*; 2nd, 1975, Jane Lygo. *Educ:* Dulwich Coll. Served War: HAC, 1939; XX Lancs Fusiliers (Temp. Major), 1940–46. Articled to Barlow Lyde & Gilbert, Solicitors, 1932–37; admitted Solicitor, 1937. Mem. Council, Law Soc., 1966–, Vice-Pres., 1980–81, Pres., 1981–82. Member: Insurance Brokers Registration Council, 1979–; Criminal Injuries Compensation Bd, 1982–. *Recreations:* sailing, gardening. *Address:* Redways, Warfleet Road, Dartmouth, S Devon. *Clubs:* Naval and Military; Royal Dart Yacht, Lloyds Yacht.

MARSHALL, Dr Edmund Ian; Lecturer in Management Science, University of Bradford, since 1984; *b* 31 May 1940; *s* of Harry and Koorali Marshall; *m* 1969, Margaret Pamela, *d* of John and Maud Antill, New Southgate, N11; one *d. Educ:* Magdalen Coll., Oxford (Mackinnon Schol.). Double 1st cl. hons Maths, and Junior Mathematical Prize, Oxon, 1961; PhD Liverpool, 1965. Various univ. appts in Pure Maths, 1962–66; mathematician in industry, 1967–71. Mem., Wallasey County Borough Council, 1963–65. Contested (L) Louth Div. of Lincs, 1964 and 1966; joined Labour Party, 1967. MP (Lab) Goole, May 1971–1983; PPS to Sec. of State for NI, 1974–76, to Home Sec., 1976–79; Chm., Trade and Industry sub-cttee of House of Commons Expenditure Cttee, 1976–79; Mem., Chairmen's Panel in House of Commons, 1981–82; Opposition Whip, 1982–83; joined SDP, 1985; prospective parly cand. (SDP/Alliance) Bridlington, 1986–. Member: British Methodist Conf., 1969–72, 1980 and 1985–87; World Methodist Conf., 1971; British Council of Churches, 1972–78. *Publications:* (jtly) Europe: What Next? (Fabian pamphlet), 1969; Parliament and the Public, 1982; various papers in mathematical and other jls. *Recreations:* genealogy, music. *Address:* 14 Belgravia Road, Wakefield, West Yorks WF1 3JP. *Club:* Yorks County Cricket.

MARSHALL, Dr Frank Graham, FIEE; Managing Director, Plessey Research Roke Manor (formerly Plessey Electronic Systems Research), since 1983; *b* 28 March 1942; *s* of Frank and Vera Marshall; *m* 1965, Patricia Anne (*née* Bestwick); two *s* one *d. Educ:* Birmingham Univ. (BSc Physics); Nottingham Univ. (PhD Physics). FIEE 1984. Joined Royal Signals and Radar Estabt (MoD) (Physics and Electronic Device Res.), 1966; Sen. Principal Scientific Officer, 1975–80; seconded to HM Diplomatic Service as Science and Technology Counsellor, Tokyo, 1980–82. (Jtly) IEEE Best Paper award, 1973; (jtly) Wolfe Award, 1973. *Publications:* numerous papers on electronic signal processing devices in various jls. *Recreations:* country life, electronics. *Address:* Plessey Research Roke Manor, Romsey, Hants.

MARSHALL, Fredda, (Mrs Herbert Marshall); *see* Brilliant, F.

MARSHALL, Geoffrey, MA, PhD; FBA 1971; Fellow and Tutor in Politics, The Queen's College, Oxford, since 1957; *b* 22 April 1929; *s* of Leonard William and Kate Marshall; *m* 1957, Patricia Ann Christine Woodcock; two *s. Educ:* Arnold Sch., Blackpool, Lancs; Manchester Univ. MA Manchester, MA Oxon, PhD Glasgow. Research Fellow, Nuffield Coll., 1955–57. Andrew Dixon White Vis. Prof., Cornell Univ., Ithaca, NY, 1985–. Mem. Oxford City Council, 1965–74; Sheriff of Oxford, 1970–71. *Publications:* Parliamentary Sovereignty and the Commonwealth, 1957; Some Problems of the Constitution (with G. C. Moodie), 1959; Police and Government, 1965; Constitutional Theory, 1971; Constitutional Conventions, 1984. *Recreation:* middle-aged squash. *Address:* The Queen's College, Oxford. *T:* Oxford 248411.

MARSHALL, George Wicks, CMG 1974; MBE 1955; BEM 1946; *b* 6 March 1916; *e s* of G. L. Marshall, Highbury, London, N5; *m* 1946, Mary Cook Kirkland. General Post Office, 1930–48. Served War, Royal Artillery (HAA), 1940–46. Board of Trade, 1948–56; Trade Commn Service, 1956–65; Asst Trade Comr, Nairobi, 1956; Trade Comr: Accra, 1958, Colombo, 1961; Principal Trade Comr, Hong Kong, 1963; Dep. Controller, BoT office for Scotland, 1965; Dep. Dir, Export Services Br., 1967; seconded to HM Diplomatic Service as Counsellor (Commercial) HM Embassy, Copenhagen, 1969–76. Asst Gen. Sec., 1976–78, Gen. Sec., 1978–81, Assoc. of First Div. Civil Servants. Mem. Cttee of Management, 1977–, Vice Chm., 1983–, Civil Service Retirement Fellowship. *Recreations:* theatre, television, working. *Address:* 30 Withdean Avenue, Goring by Sea, West Sussex BN12 4XD. *T:* Worthing 45158. *Clubs:* Royal Commonwealth Society; Hong Kong (Hong Kong).

MARSHALL, Prof. Herbert Percival James; film, theatre and TV producer, director, scriptwriter, author and translator; *b* London, 20 Jan. 1906; *s* of Percival Charles Marshall and Anne Marshall (*née* Organ); *m* 1935, Fredda Brilliant, *qv. Educ:* Elementary Sch., Ilford; evening classes, LCC; Higher Inst. of Cinematography, Moscow, USSR. Began as Asst Film Editor, Empire Marketing Bd Film Unit, 1929–30; Asst Dir various Moscow theatres; Drama Dir, Moscow Radio (English), 1933–35; Founder, Dir, Unity Theatre; prod. documentary films, Spanish Civil War; Principal, Unity Theatre Trng Sch.; Lectr, LCC Evening Insts, 1935–39; Founder and Artistic Dir, Neighbourhood Theatre, S Kensington; Script-writer (with Fredda Brilliant) and Associate Producer (Ealing Studios), 1939–40; apptd Dir, Old Vic (theatre bombed); toured England; Dir for Sadler's Wells Opera Co.; Lectr, RADA, 1940–41; i/c of production, Russian, Czech, Polish and Yugoslav films for Europe (8 langs); broadcasts, BBC, in Russian, 1942–45; Lectr on film art, Amer. Univ., Biarritz, 1945–46; Indep. Film Producer: prod. for J. Arthur Rank, Min. of Educn, NCB, etc; prod., scripted and dir. (with Fredda Brilliant), Tinker (Edinburgh Festival Award), 1946–50; dir. Man and Superman, Arena Theatre (Fest. of Brit.), 1951; prod. official Mahatma Gandhi Biog. Documentary, etc, India, 1951–55; Exec. Producer, TV closed circuit and films for Advision Ltd, London, 1955–56; Film Producer for Govt of India; Principal, Natya Acad. of Dramatic Art, Bombay; Producer, Natya Nat. Theatre Company, 1957–60; Dir, Centre for Soviet and E European Studies, Southern Illinois Univ., apptd Prof., Academic Affairs, 1970, Prof. Emeritus 1979. Theatre Architecture Consultant to various projects: Indian Nat. Theatres, 1955–59; Centre 42, London, 1962; Morrison Civic Arts Centre, Lambeth, 1965; Samuel Beckett Theatre, Oxford Univ., 1968–. Lecturer: RCA and NY Univ., 1965; Univ. of Illinois, and Oxford Univ., 1968; Himachal Pradesh Univ., Hong Kong Univ., La Trobe Univ., Monash Univ., Univ. of Melbourne, 1972. Many well-known actors and actresses have been produced or directed by him. FRSA 1967. Mather Schol. of the Year, Case Western Reserve, Ohio, 1972. *Publications:* (ed) International Library of Cinema and Theatre (20 vols), 1946–56; Mayakovsky and His Poetry, 1964 (London); Hamlet Through the Ages (jointly), 1953 (London); Ira Aldridge, The Negro Tragedian (with Mildred Stock), 1953 (London, New York); Poetry of Voznesensky (London and New York) and Yevtushenko (London and New York), 1965; Stanislavsky Method of Direction (London and New York), 1969; Anthology of Soviet Poetry, 1970; (ed) Pictorial History of the Russian Theatre, 1978; (ed and introd) Battleship Potemkin, 1979; Masters of the Soviet Cinema: crippled creative biographies, 1983; (trans.) Memoirs of Sergei Eisenstein, vol. 1, Immoral Memories, 1983; *scores:* English Text and Lyrics, Ivan the Terrible (Oratorio by S. Prokoviev and S. M. Eisenstein), 1962 (Moscow); English Texts: 13th and 14th Symphonies, and Execution of Stepan Razin, by D. Shostakovich; Mayakovsky Oratorio Pathetique, by G. Sviridov, 1974, etc. *Recreations:* reading and TV. *Address:* 1204 Chautauqua Street, Carbondale, Ill 62901, USA; Southern Illinois University, Carbondale, Ill 62901, USA.

MARSHALL, Howard Wright; retired; Under Secretary, Department of Transport, 1978–82; *b* 11 June 1923; *s* of Philip Marshall, MBE, and Mary Marshall; *m* 1st (marr. diss.); two *s*; 2nd, 1963, Carol Yvonne (*née* Oddy); one *d. Educ:* Prudhoe West Elementary, Northumberland; Queen Elizabeth Grammar Sch., Hexham. Served War, RAF, 1941–46; POW, 1943–45. Min. of Health, Newcastle upon Tyne, 1940; Regional Offices, Ministries of Health, Local Govt and Planning, Housing and Local Govt, 1948–55; HQ, Min. of Housing and Local Govt, 1955–59; National Parks Commn, 1959–62; Min. of Housing and Local Govt, later DoE, 1962; Asst Sec., 1968; Under Sec., 1976; Regional Dir, Eastern Region, Depts of Environment and Transport, 1976–78; Chm., East Anglia Regional Economic Planning Bd, 1976–78. *Recreations:* gardening, sport. *Address:* Brackenwood, Farthing Green Lane, Stoke Poges, Bucks. *T:* Fulmer 2974. *Clubs:* Caterpillar; Wexham Park Golf and Leisure.

MARSHALL, James; *b* 13 March 1941; *m* 1962, Shirley, *d* of W. Ellis, Sheffield; one *s* one *d. Educ:* City Grammar Sch., Sheffield; Leeds Univ. BSc, PhD. Joined Lab Party, 1960. Mem., Leeds City Council, 1965–68; Leicester City Council: Mem., 1971–76; Chm., Finance Cttee, 1972–74; Leader, 1974. Contested (Lab): Harborough, 1970; Leicester South, Feb. 1974, 1983. MP (Lab) Leicester S, Oct. 1974–1983; an Asst Govt Whip, 1977–79. *Address:* Flat 15, The Woodlands, 31 Knighton Road, Leicester. *T:* Leicester 708237.

MARSHALL, John, MA; JP; Headmaster, Robert Gordon's College, Aberdeen, 1960–77; *b* 1 July 1915; *s* of Alexander Marshall and Margaret Nimmo Carmichael; *m* 1940, May Robinson Williamson; two *d. Educ:* Airdrie Acad.; Glasgow Univ. MA (1st cl. hons Classics), 1935; Medley Memorial Prizeman, History 1934; John Clark Schol., Classics, 1935. Asst Master: Bluevale Sch., 1937–39; Coatbridge Sec. Sch., 1939–41; Principal Teacher of Classics, North Berwick High Sch., 1941–50; Rector, North Berwick High Sch., 1950–60. Mem., Adv. Coun. on Educn for Scotland, 1955–57; Trustee, Scottish Sec. Schools Travel Trust, 1960–78 (Chm., 1971–78; Sec., 1978–80); Pres., Headmasters' Assoc. of Scotland, 1962–64; Member: Gen. Teaching Coun. for Scotland, 1966–70; Exec. Cttee, UCCA, 1970–78; Coordinator, Scottish Scheme of Oxford Colls' Admissions, 1978–84. JP City of Aberdeen, 1967. *Publications:* numerous articles on educational subjects. *Recreations:* fishing, photography, writing, language studies. *Address:* 11 Hazledene Road, Aberdeen AB1 8LB. *T:* Aberdeen 38003. *Club:* Royal Northern and University (Aberdeen).

MARSHALL, Prof. John, FRCP, FRCPE; Professor of Clinical Neurology in the University of London, since 1971; Dean of Institute of Neurology, since 1982; *b* 16 April 1922; *s* of James Herbert and Bertha Marshall; *m* 1946, Margaret Eileen Hughes; two *s* three *d. Educ:* Univ. of Manchester (MB ChB 1946, MD 1951, DSc 1981). FRCPE 1957, FRCP 1966; DPM 1952. Sen. Registrar, Manchester Royal Infirmary, 1947–49; Lt-Col RAMC, 1949–51; MRC research worker, 1951–53; Sen. Lectr in Neurology, Univ. of Edinburgh, 1954–56; Reader in Clinical Neurology, Univ. of London, 1956–71. Chm., Attendance Allowance Bd, 1982–. Knight of the Order of St Sylvester (Holy See), 1962, KCSG 1986 (KSG 1964). Auenbrugger Medal, Univ. of Graz, 1983. *Publications:* The Management of Cerebrovascular Disease, 1965, 3rd edn 1976; The Infertile Period, Principles and Practice, 1963, 2nd rev. edn 1969. *Recreations:* gardening, walking. *Address:* 203 Robin Hood Way, SW20 0AA. *T:* 01-942 5509.

MARSHALL, John Alexander, CB 1982; General Secretary, Distressed Gentlefolk's Aid Association, since 1982; *b* 2 Sept. 1922; *s* of James Alexander Marshall and Mena Dorothy Marshall; *m* 1947, Pauline Mary (*née* Taylor); six *s. Educ:* LCC elem. sch.; Hackney Downs School. Paymaster General's Office, 1939; FO, 1943; HM Treasury, 1947: Principal, 1953; Asst Sec., 1963; Under-Sec., 1972; Cabinet Office, 1974–77; Northern Ireland Office, 1977–82, Dep. Sec., 1979–82. *Recreations:* literature, music. *Address:* 48 Long Lane, Ickenham, Mddx. *T:* Ruislip 72020.

MARSHALL, John Leslie; Member (C) London North, European Parliament, since 1979; Director, Kitcat & Aitken & Co., since 1986; *b* 19 Aug. 1940; *s* of late Prof. William Marshall and Margaret Marshall; *m* 1978, Susan Elizabeth, *d* of David Mount, Petham, Kent; two *s. Educ:* Glasgow Academy; St Andrews Univ. (MA). ACIS. Asst Lecturer in Economics, Glasgow Univ., 1962–66; Lectr in Economics, Aberdeen Univ.,

1966–70; Mem., London Stock Exchange; Carr Sebag & Co., 1979–82; Partner, Kitcat & Aitken, 1983–86. Contested (C): Dundee East, 1964 and 1966; Lewisham East, Feb. 1974; prospective parly cand. (C), Hendon S, 1985–. Member: Aberdeen Town Council, 1968–70; Ealing Borough Council, 1971–86 (Chm., Finance Bd, 1978–82; Chm., Local Services Cttee, 1982–84). *Publications:* articles on economics in several professional jls; pamphlets on economic questions for Aims. *Recreations:* watching cricket and Rugby; gardening, bridge, theatre. *Address:* 2 Birkdale Road, W5 1JZ. *T:* 01–991 0162. *Clubs:* Carlton; Middlesex County Cricket.

MARSHALL, John Robert Neil, CMG 1977; MBE 1968; *b* 15 July 1922; *s* of William Gilchrist Marshall and Mabel Marshall. *Educ:* Wisbech Grammar Sch.; Balliol Coll., Oxford (MA). Nigerian Administrative Service, 1950–79 (Adviser, Local Govt Reforms, 1976–79); Ahmadu Bello University (Institute of Administration), Zaria, 1979–81, retired 1981. *Address:* 2 Saxon Lane, Seaford, East Sussex. *T:* Seaford 895447. *Club:* Royal Commonwealth Society.

MARSHALL, Rt. Hon. Sir John (Ross), PC 1966; GBE 1974; CH 1973; BA, LLM; Prime Minister of New Zealand, Feb.-Nov. 1972; Leader of the Opposition, 1972–74; Chairman of Directors, National Bank of New Zealand, 1975–83; *b* Wellington, 5 March 1912; *s* of Allan Marshall; *m* 1944, Margaret Livingston; two *s* two *d*. *Educ:* Whangarei High Sch.; Otago Boys' High Sch.; Victoria Univ. Coll. Barrister and Solicitor, 1936; served War, with 2nd NZEF, Pacific Is and Italy, 1941–46 (Inf. Major); MP (Nat.) for Mount Victoria, 1946–54, for Karori, 1954–75; Lectr in Law, Victoria Univ. Coll., 1948–51, Vis. Fellow, 1975–82; Minister, Asst to Prime Minister, in charge of State Advances Corp., Public Trust Office and Census and Statistics Dept, 1949–54; Minister of Health, 1951–54, and Information and Publicity, 1951–57; Attorney-Gen. and Minister of Justice, 1954–57; Dep. Prime Minister, 1957; Dep. Leader of the Opposition, 1957–60; Minister of Customs, 1960–61; Minister of Industries and Commerce, 1960–69; Attorney-General, 1969–71; Dep. Prime Minister, and Minister of Overseas Trade, 1960–72; Minister of Labour and Immigration, 1969–72. NZ Rep. at Colombo Plan Conf., New Delhi, 1953; visited US on Foreign Leader Grant, April 1958; NZ Representative: GATT, 1961, 1963, 1966, and ECAFE, 1962, 1964, 1966, 1968, 1970; Commonwealth Prime Ministers' Conf., 1962; Commonwealth Trade Ministers' Conf., 1963, 1966; Commonwealth Parly Conf., 1965; UN 25th Annual Session, NY, 1970; ILO Conf., Geneva, 1971; EEC Negotiations, 1961–71. Mem., Adv. Council, World Peace through Law. Chairman: NZ Commn for Expo 70; Nat. Develt Council, 1969–72; Cttee of Registration of Teachers, 1976–77. Chairman: Philips Electrical Industries, 1974–84; Contractors Bonding Corp., 1975–; Norwich Winterthur Insurance (NZ) Ltd, 1977–82; DRG (NZ) Ltd, 1975–; Williams Property Hldgs Ltd, 1983–; Director: Norwich Union Insurance Soc.; Hallenstein Bros Ltd, 1974–82. Consultant Partner, Buddle Findlay, 1974–86. Pres., Bible Soc. in NZ, 1978–80; World Vice Pres., United Bible Socs, 1982–; Patron, World Vision in NZ; Chm., NZ Internat. Festival of the Arts. Hon. Bencher, Gray's Inn. Hon. LLD Wellington, 1975. *Publications:* The Law of Watercourses, 1957; Memoirs, 1983; *for children:* The Adventures of Dr Duffer, 1978; More Adventures of Dr Duffer, 1979; Dr Duffer and the Treasure Hunt, 1980; Dr Duffer and his Australian Adventures, 1981. *Recreations:* fishing, golf, breeding Connemara ponies. *Address:* 22 Fitzroy Street, Wellington, NZ. *T:* 736.631.

MARSHALL, Margaret Anne; concert and opera singer; soprano; *b* 4 Jan. 1949; *d* of Robert and Margaret Marshall; *m* 1970, Dr Graeme Griffiths King Davidson; two *d*. *Educ:* High School, Stirling; Royal Scottish Academy of Music and Drama (DRSAMD). Performances in Festival Hall, Barbican, Covent Garden; concerts and opera in major European events; numerous recordings. First Prize, Munich International Competition, 1974. *Recreations:* squash, golf. *Address:* 46 Borestone Place, Stirling FK7 0PL. *T:* Stirling 74921. *Club:* Gleneagles Country.

MARSHALL, Mark Anthony; HM Diplomatic Service; Head of Finance Department, Foreign and Commonwealth Office, since 1984; *b* 8 Oct. 1937; *s* of late Thomas Humphrey Marshall, CMG and of Nadine, *d* of late Mark Hambourg; *m* 1970, Penelope Lesley Seymour; two *d*. *Educ:* Westminster Sch.; Trinity Coll., Cambridge (BA). MECAS, 1958; Third Sec., Amman, 1960; FO, 1962; Commercial Officer, Dubai, 1964; FO, 1965; Aden, 1967; First Sec., 1968; Asst Dir of Treasury Centre for Admin. Studies, 1968; UK Delegn to Brussels Conf., 1970; First Sec./Head of Chancery, Rabat, 1972; First Sec., FCO, 1976; Counsellor: Tripoli, 1979–80; Damascus, 1980–83. *Recreations:* swimming, golf, fell walking. *Address:* c/o Foreign and Commonwealth Office, King Charles Street, SW1.

MARSHALL, Martin John, CMG 1967; HM Diplomatic Service, retired; *b* 21 March 1914; *s* of late Harry Edmund Marshall and late Kate Ann (*née* Bishop); *m* 1938, Olive Emily Alice, *d* of Thomas and Olive King; two *d*. *Educ:* Westminster City Sch.; London Sch. of Economics, University of London. Customs and Excise Officer, 1935–39; Technical Officer, Min. of Aircraft Prod., 1940–46; Principal, Min. of Supply, 1947–50. Called to Bar, Gray's Inn, 1947. Trade Commissioner: Montreal, 1950–52; Atlantic Provinces, 1953; Alberta, 1954–57; Principal Trade Commissioner: Montreal, 1957–60; Calcutta (for Eastern India), 1961–63; Dep. High Comr, Sydney, 1963–67; Consul-General, Cleveland, Ohio, 1968–71; Dep. High Comr, Bombay, 1971–74. Dir, Finance/Administration, Royal Assoc. for Disability and Rehabilitation, 1977–79. *Recreation:* golf. *Address:* 8 Sunnyside Place, SW19 4SJ. *T:* 01–946 5570. *Club:* Royal Wimbledon Golf.

MARSHALL, Michael; *see* Marshall, R. M.

MARSHALL, Rt. Rev. Michael Eric, MA; Founding Episcopal Director, Anglican Institute, St Louis, Missouri, since 1984; an Assistant Bishop, Diocese of London, since 1984; *b* Lincoln, 14 April 1936. *Educ:* Lincoln Sch.; Christ's Coll., Cambridge (Tancred Scholar, Upper II: Hist. Pt 1 and Theol Pt 1a, MA); Cuddesdon Theological Coll. Deacon, 1960; Curate, St Peter's, Spring Hill, Birmingham, 1960–62; Tutor, Ely Theological Coll. and Minor Canon of Ely Cath., 1962–64; Chaplain in London Univ., 1964–69; Vicar of All Saints', Margaret Street, W1, 1969–75; Bishop Suffragan of Woolwich, 1975–84. Founder and Director: Inst. of Christian Studies, 1970; Internat. Inst. for Anglican Studies, 1982; Member: Gen. Synod, 1970, also Diocesan and Deanery Synods; Liturgical Commn; Anglican/Methodist Liaison Commn until 1974; SPCK Governing Body; USPG Governing Body; Exam. Chap. to Bp of London, 1974. Has frequently broadcast on BBC and commercial radio; also lectured, preached and broadcast in Canada and USA. *Publications:* A Pattern of Faith, 1966 (co-author); Glory under Your Feet, 1978; Pilgrimage and Promise, 1981; Renewal in Worship, 1982; The Anglican Church, Today and Tomorrow, 1984; Christian Orthodoxy Revisited, USA 1985; The Gospel Conspiracy in the Episcopal Church, 1986; Founder and co-editor, Christian Quarterly. *Recreations:* music, cooking. *Address:* The Anglican Institute, 6330 Ellenwood Avenue, PO Box 11887, St Louis, Missouri 63105, USA; 18 Andrewes House, The Barbican, EC2. *Club:* University (St Louis, Mo, USA).

MARSHALL, Noël Hedley, CMG 1986; HM Diplomatic Service; Minister, Moscow, since 1986; *b* 26 Nov. 1934; *s* of Arthur Hedley Marshall, *qv*. *Educ:* Leighton Park Sch.; Lawrenceville Sch., NJ (E-SU Exchange Scholar, 1953–54); St John's Coll., Cambridge (BA 1957; Sir Joseph Larmor Award, 1957). Pres., Cambridge Union Soc., 1957. Entered Foreign (later Diplomatic) Service; FO, 1957–59; Third Sec., Prague, 1959–61; FO, 1961–63; Second (later First) Sec., Moscow, 1963–65; CRO, 1965–66; First Sec. (Economic): Karachi, 1966–67; Rawalpindi, 1967–70; Chargé d'affaires *ai*, Ulan Bator, 1967; FCO, 1970–74; First Sec. (later Counsellor) Press, Office of UK Permanent Rep. to European Communities, Brussels, 1974–77; NATO Defence Coll., Rome, 1977–78; Counsellor, UK Delegn to Cttee on Disarmament, Geneva, 1978–81; Head of N America Dept, FCO, 1982–85; Overseas Inspector, 1985–86. *Recreations:* sailing, the theatre. *Address:* c/o Foreign and Commonwealth Office, SW1. *Clubs:* Royal Ocean Racing; Europe House.

MARSHALL, Norman Bertram, MA, ScD; FRS 1970; Professor and Head of Department of Zoology and Comparative Physiology, Queen Mary College, University of London, 1972–77, now Professor Emeritus; *b* 5 Feb. 1915; *s* of Arthur Harold and Ruby Eva Marshall; *m* 1944, Olga Stonehouse; one *s* three *d*. *Educ:* Cambridgeshire High Sch.; Downing Coll., Cambridge. Plankton Biologist, Dept of Oceanography, UC Hull, 1937–41; Army (mostly involved in operational research), 1941–44; seconded from Army for Service in Operation Tabarin to Antarctic, 1944–46; British Museum (Natural History): Marine fishes, 1947–72; Sen. Principal Scientific Officer, 1962–72. In charge of Manihine Expedns to Red Sea, 1948–50; Senior Biologist, Te Vega Expedn, 1966–67. Polar Medal (Silver), 1948; Rosenstiel Gold Medal for distinguished services to marine science; Senior Queen's Fellow in Marine Science, Aust., 1982. *Publications:* Aspects of Deep Sea Biology, 1954; The Life of Fishes, 1965; Explorations in the Life of Fishes, 1970; Ocean Life, 1971; Developments in Deep Sea Biology, 1979; various papers in learned jls. *Recreations:* music, fishing, golf. *Address:* 6 Park Lane, Saffron Walden, Essex. *T:* Saffron Walden 22528.

MARSHALL, Prof. Sir (Oshley) Roy, Kt 1974; CBE 1968; Vice-Chancellor, Hull University, 1979–85, Emeritus Professor since 1985; *b* 21 Oct. 1920; *s* of Fitz Roy and Corene Carmelita Marshall; *m* 1945, Eirwen Lloyd; one *s* three *d*. *Educ:* Harrison Coll., Barbados, WI; Pembroke Coll., Cambridge; University Coll., London (Fellow, 1985). Barbados Scholar, 1938; BA 1945, MA 1948 Cantab; PhD London 1948. Barrister-at-Law, Inner Temple, 1947. University Coll., London: Asst Lecturer, 1946–48; Lecturer, 1948–56; Sub-Dean, Faculty of Law, 1949–56; Prof. of Law and Head of Dept of Law, Univ. of Sheffield, 1956–69, Vis. Prof. in Faculty of Law, 1969–80; on secondment to University of Ife, Ibadan, Nigeria, as Prof. of Law and Dean of the Faculty of Law, 1963–65; Vice-Chancellor, Univ. of West Indies, 1969–74; Sec.-Gen., Cttee of Vice-Chancellors and Principals, 1974–79. Chairman: Commonwealth Educn Liaison Cttee, 1974–81; Cttee on Commonwealth Legal Co-operation, 1975; Commonwealth Standing Cttee on Student Mobility, 1982–; Council for Educn in the Commonwealth, 1985–; Review Cttee on Cave Hill Campus, Univ. of WI, 1986; Member: Police Complaints Bd, 1977–81; Council, RPMS, 1976–83; Council, ACU, 1979–85; Management Cttee, Universities Superannuation Scheme Ltd, 1980–85; Chm., Bd of Governors, Hymers Coll., Hull, 1985–; Vice-Chm., Governing Body of Commonwealth Inst., 1980–81; Trustee, Commonwealth Foundn, 1981. Hon. LLD: Sheffield, 1972; West Indies, 1976; Hull, 1986. *Publications:* The Assignment of Choses in Action, 1950; A Casebook on Trusts (with J. A. Nathan), 1967; Theobald on Wills, 12th edn, 1963. *Recreations:* racing and cricket. *Address:* 4 Thorpe Leys, Lockington, near Driffield YO25 9SP. *Club:* Royal Commonwealth Society.

MARSHALL, Percy Edwin Alan J.; *see* Johnson-Marshall.

MARSHALL, Peter, QPM 1979; Commissioner of Police for the City of London, 1978–85; *b* 21 June 1930; *s* of late Christopher George Marshall and Sylvia Marshall; *m* 1954, Bridget Frances Humphreys; three *s* one *d*. *Educ:* St Clement Danes Holborn Estate Grammar Sch. Trooper, 8th Royal Tank Regt, 1948–50. Police Officer, Metropolitan Police, 1950–78. *Recreations:* riding, reading, relaxing. *Address:* The Cottage, Cock Lane, Elham, Canterbury, Kent CT4 6TL.

MARSHALL, Sir Peter (Harold Reginald), KCMG 1983 (CMG 1974); Commonwealth Deputy Secretary General (Economic), since 1983; *b* 30 July 1924; 3rd *s* of late R. H. Marshall; *m* 1957, Patricia Rendell Stoddart (*d* 1981); one *s* one *d*. *Educ:* Tonbridge; Corpus Christi Coll., Cambridge. RAFVR, 1943–46. HM Foreign (later Diplomatic) Service, 1949–83: FO, 1949–52; 2nd Sec. and Private Sec. to Ambassador, Washington, 1952–56; FO, 1956–60; on staff of Civil Service Selection Board, 1960; 1st Sec. and Head of Chancery, Baghdad, 1961, and Bangkok, 1962–64; Asst Dir of Treasury Centre for Administrative Studies, 1965–66; Counsellor, UK Mission, Geneva, 1966–69, Counsellor and Head of Chancery, Paris, 1969–71; Head of Financial Policy and Aid Dept, FCO, 1971–73; Asst Under-Sec. of State, FCO, 1973–75; UK Rep. on Econ. and Social Council of UN, 1975–79; Ambassador and UK Perm. Rep. to Office of UN and Other Internat. Organisations at Geneva, 1979–83. *Recreations:* music, golf. *Address:* Commonwealth Secretariat, Marlborough House, Pall Mall, SW1Y 5HX. *T:* 01–839 3411. *Club:* Travellers'.

MARSHALL, Prof. Peter James, DPhil; Rhodes Professor of Imperial History, King's College, London, since 1980; *b* 28 Oct. 1933; *s* of Edward Hannaford Marshall and Madeleine (*née* Shuttleworth). *Educ:* Wellington College; Wadham Coll., Oxford (BA 1957, MA, DPhil 1962). Military service, King's African Rifles, Kenya, 1953–54. Assistant Lecturer, Lecturer, Reader, Professor, History Dept, King's Coll., London, 1959–80. Editor, Journal of Imperial and Commonwealth History, 1975–81; Associate Editor, Writings and Speeches of Edmund Burke, 1976–. *Publications:* Impeachment of Warren Hastings, 1965; Problems of Empire: Britain and India 1757–1813, 1968; (ed, with J. A. Woods) Correspondence of Edmund Burke, vol. VII, 1968; The British Discovery of Hinduism, 1972; East India Fortunes, 1976; (ed) Writings and Speeches of Edmund Burke, vol. V, 1981; (with Glyndwr Williams) The Great Map of Mankind, 1982; articles in Economic History Rev., History, Modern Asian Studies, etc. *Address:* 7 Malting Lane, Braughing, Ware, Herts SG11 2QZ. *T:* Ware 822 232.

MARSHALL, Air Cdre Philippa Frances, CB 1971; OBE 1956; Director of the Women's Royal Air Force, 1969–73; *b* 4 Nov. 1920; *d* of late Horace Plant Marshall, Stoke-on-Trent. *Educ:* St Dominic's High Sch., Stoke-on-Trent. Joined WAAF, 1941; Comd WRAF Admin. Officer, Strike Comd, 1968–69, Air Cdre 1969; ADC, 1969–73. *Recreations:* music, cookery. *Club:* Royal Air Force.

MARSHALL, Sir Robert (Braithwaite), KCB 1971 (CB 1968); MBE 1945; Chairman, National Water Council, 1978–82; *b* 10 Jan. 1920; *s* of Alexander Halford Marshall and Edith Mary Marshall (*née* Lockyer); *m* 1945, Diana Elizabeth Westlake; one *s* three *d*. *Educ:* Sherborne Sch.; Corpus Christi Coll., Cambridge. Mod. Langs, Pt I, 1938–39; Economics Pts I and II, 1945–47. BA Cambridge. Foreign Office temp. appointment, 1939–45. Entered Home Civil Service, 1947; Ministry of Works, 1947–50; Private Sec. to Sec., Cabinet Office, 1950–53; Min. of Works, 1953–62; Min. of Aviation, 1962–66; Min. of Power, 1966–69; Min. of Technology, 1969–70; Under-Sec., 1964; Dep. Sec. 1966; Second Perm. Sec., 1970; Secretary (Industry), DTI, 1970–73; Second Permanent Sec., DoE, 1973–78. Chm., Cair Ltd, 1985–. Trustee, Wateraid and other trusts. Mem.

Council, Surrey Univ., 1975–; Chm. Governors, W Surrey Coll. of Art, 1985–. Coronation Medal, 1953. *Recreations:* travel, gardening, music and arts. *Address:* Brooklands, Lower Bourne, Farnham, Surrey. *T:* Frensham 2879.

MARSHALL, Robert Leckie, OBE 1945; Principal, Co-operative College, and Chief Education Officer, Co-operative Union Ltd, 1946–77; *b* 27 Aug. 1913; *s* of Robert Marshall and Mary Marshall; *m* 1944, Beryl Broad; one *s*. *Educ:* Univ. of St Andrews (MA Mediaeval and Modern History; MA 1st Cl. Hons English Lit.); Commonwealth Fellow, Yale Univ. (MA Polit. Theory and Govt). Scottish Office, 1937–39. Served War, 1939–46: RASC and AEC; finally Comdt, Army Sch. of Educn. Pres., Co-op. Congress, 1976. Missions on Co-op. develt to Tanganyika, Nigeria, India, Kenya, S Yemen and Thailand. Member: Gen. Adv. Council and Complaints Rev. Bd, IBA, 1973–77; Monopolies and Mergers Commn, 1976–82; Distributive Studies Bd, Business Educn Council, 1976–79; Chm., Quest House, Loughborough, 1980–; Vice-Chm., Charnwood Community Council, 1980–. Hon. MA Open Univ., 1977; Hon. DLitt Loughborough Univ. of Technol., 1977. Editor, Jl of Soc. for Co-operative Studies, 1967–. *Publications:* Lippen on Angus—a celebration of North Angus Co-operative Society, 1983; contribs to educnl and co-op jls. *Recreations:* walking, reading, swimming, golf. *Address:* Holly Cottage, 15 Beacon Road, Woodhouse Eaves, Loughborough, Leics LE12 8RN. *T:* Woodhouse Eaves 890612.

MARSHALL, (Robert) Michael; MP (C) Arundel since Feb. 1974; *b* 21 June 1930; *s* of Robert Ernest and late Margaret Mary Marshall, Brookside Cottages, Hathersage; *m* 1972, Caroline Victoria Oliphant, *d* of late Alexander Hutchison of Strathairly; two step *d*. *Educ:* Bradfield Coll.; Harvard and Stanford Univs. MBA Harvard 1960. Joined United Steel Cos Ltd, 1951; Branch Man., Calcutta, 1954–58; Man. Dir, Bombay, 1960–64; Commercial Dir, Workington, 1964–66; Man. Dir, Head Wrightson Export Co. Ltd, 1967–69; Management Consultant, Urwick Orr & Partners Ltd, 1969–74. Parly Under-Sec. of State, DoI, 1979–81. Vice-Chairman: Cons. Party Parly Industry Cttee, 1976–79; All Party Parly Cttee on Management, 1974–79; Parly Information Technology Cttee, 1982–; Mem., Select Cttee on Defence, 1982–; Parly Adviser: British Aerospace, 1982–; Cable and Wireless, 1982–; SWET, 1984–. Member: Equity; BAFTA. Hon. DL New England Coll., 1982. FRSA. *Publications:* Top Hat and Tails: the story of Jack Buchanan, 1978; (ed) The Stanley Holloway Monologues, 1979; More Monologues and Songs, 1980; The Book of Comic and Dramatic Monologues, 1981; The Timetable of Technology, 1982; No End of Jobs, 1984. *Recreations:* writing books and for radio and TV, cricket commentating, golf. *Address:* Old Inn House, Slindon, Arundel, W Sussex. *Clubs:* Garrick, MCC, Lord's Taverners; Sussex; Royal & Ancient Golf (St Andrews), Goodwood Golf.

MARSHALL, Maj.-Gen. Roger Sydenham, CB 1974; TD 1948; Director of Army Legal Services, Ministry of Defence, 1971–73, retired; *b* 15 July 1913; 2nd *s* of Robert Sydenham Cole Marshall and Enid Edith Langton Cole; *m* 1940, Beryl Marie, *d* of William Vaughan Rayner; one *d*. Solicitor, Supreme Court, 1938. Commnd N Staffs Regt, TA, 1933; mobilised TA, 1939; comd 365 Batt. 65th Searchlight Regt, RA, 1942–44; Trans. Army Legal Services, 1948; DADALS: HQ MELF, 1948–49; HQ E Africa, 1949–52; GHQ MELF, 1952–53; WO, 1953–55; ADALS: WO, 1955–56; HQ BAOR, 1956–58; WO, 1960–61; HQ E Africa Comd, 1961–62; DDALS, GHQ FARELF, 1962–63; Col Legal Staff, WO, 1964–69; Brig. Legal Staff, 1969–71; Maj.-Gen. 1971. *Recreations:* golf, reading history. *Address:* Higher Campscott Farm, Lee, N Devon. *T:* Ilfracombe 62885.

MARSHALL, Sir Roy; *see* Marshall, Sir O. R.

MARSHALL, Maj.-Gen. Roy Stuart, CB 1970; OBE 1960; MC 1945; MM 1940; *b* 28 Oct. 1917; *s* of Andrew Adamson Marshall and Bessie Marshall, Whitley Bay, Northumberland; *m* 1946, Phyllis Mary Rawlings; two *s*. *Educ:* Whitley Bay and Monkseaton High Sch. Joined TA 88 (West Lancs) Field Regt, 1939; commd into RA, 1942; War Service in Europe and Middle East, 1939–45; Staff Coll., Camberley, 1947; GSO 2, 2 Inf. Div., 1948–50; DAA & QMG, 6 Inf. Bde, 1950–51; jssc 1952–53; AA & QMG, 1 (BR) Corps, 1958–60; CO 12th Regt RA, 1960–62; Comdr 7th Artillery Bde, 1962–64; Indian Nat. Def. Coll., 1965; Maj.-Gen. RA, BAOR, 1966–69; Dep. Master-General of the Ordnance, 1969–70, retired; Col Comdt, RA, 1972–77. Dynamics Group, British Aerospace, 1970–82. *Recreations:* fishing, golf, bridge. *Address:* Sherford Place East, Taunton.

MARSHALL, Thomas Daniel; Member, Newcastle City Council, since 1986; *b* 6 Nov. 1929; *s* of James William and Leonora Mary Marshall; *m* 1953, Eileen James; one *s*. *Educ:* St George's RC Elementary Sch., Bell's Close, Newcastle upon Tyne; Ruskin Coll.; Open Univ. Post Office, then Nat. Assistance Board, 1960; DHSS, 1966. Councillor, Newburn UDC, 1967; Mem., Tyne and Wear CC, 1974–86 (Chm., 1978–79). Chairman: Microprocessor Application Research Inst. Ltd; Tyne and Wear Enterprise Trust; Director: Tyne and Wear Innovation Centre and Development Co.; Bowes Railway Co.; Trustee: MEA Trust; Industrial Monuments Trust; Building Preservation Trust Ltd. *Recreation:* reading. *Address:* 7 Hallow Drive, Throckley, Newcastle upon Tyne NE15 9AQ. *T:* Newcastle upon Tyne 670956. *Clubs:* Grange Welfare; Newburn Memorial (Newcastle).

MARSHALL, Thurgood; Associate Justice of US Supreme Court, since 1967; *b* 2 July 1908; *s* of William C. and Norma A. Marshall; *m* 1st, 1929, Vivian Burey (*d* 1955); 2nd, 1955, Cecilia A. Suyat; two *s*. *Educ:* Lincoln Univ. (AB 1930); Howard Univ. Law Sch. Admitted Maryland Bar, 1933. Special Counsel, NAACP, 1938–50 (Asst, 1936–38); Dir, NAACP Legal Defense and Educ. Fund, 1940–61. Judge, 2nd Circuit Court of Appeals, 1961–65; Solicitor-Gen. of USA, 1965–67. Holds hon. doctorates at many US Univs. Spingarn Medal, 1946.

MARSHALL, Valerie Margaret, (Mrs A. R. Marshall); Investment Executive, Scottish Development Agency, since 1980; *b* 30 March 1945; *d* of Ernest Knagg and Marion Knagg; *m* 1972, Alan Roger Marshall; two *s* one *d*. *Educ:* Brighton and Hove High Sch.; Girton Coll., Cambridge (MA); London Graduate Sch. of Business Studies (MSc). LRAM. Financial Controller, ICFC, 1969–80. Member: Scottish Cttee, Design Council, 1975–77; Monopolies and Mergers Commn, 1976–81. *Recreations:* music, ballet, collecting antiquarian books, walking, entertaining. *Address:* Kilmore, 16 Dalkeith Avenue, Dumbreck, Glasgow G41 5BJ. *T:* 041–427 0096.

MARSHALL, William; Assistant Under-Secretary of State, Ministry of Defence (Navy), 1968–72, retired; *b* 30 Sept. 1912; *e s* of late Allan and Julia Marshall, Whitecraigs, Renfrewshire; *m* 1st, 1940, Jessie Gardner Miller (*d* 1962); one *s*; 2nd, 1963, Doreen Margaret Read. *Educ:* Allan Glen's Sch., Glasgow; Glasgow Univ. MA Glasgow 1932, LLB (*cum laude*) Glasgow 1935. War of 1939–45: Temp. Asst Principal, Air Ministry, 1940; Service with Royal Navy (Ord. Seaman), and Admin. Staff, Admty, 1941. Private Sec. to Permanent Sec. of Admty (Sir J. G. Lang), 1947–48; Principal Private Sec. to successive First Lords of Admty (Lord Hall, Lord Packenham and Rt Hon. J. P. L. Thomas, later Lord Cilcennin), 1951–54; Asst Sec. in Admty, 1954; on loan to HM Treasury, 1958–61; returned to Admiralty, 1961. Chm., cttee to review submarine escape trng, 1974. *Recreations:* golf, travel, gardening. *Address:* 37 West Drive, Cheam, Surrey. *T:* 01–642 3399. *Club:* Banstead Downs Golf.

MARSHALL-ANDREWS, Robert Graham; a Recorder of the Crown Court, since 1982; *b* 10 April 1944; *s* of Robin and Eileen Nora Marshall; *m* 1968, Gillian Diana Elliott; one *s* one *d*. *Educ:* Mill Hill Sch.; Univ. of Bristol (LLB). Called to the Bar, Gray's Inn, 1967; Recorder, Oxford and Midland Circuit, 1982–. *Recreations:* theatre, reading, Rugby (watching). *Address:* 4 Paper Buildings, Temple, EC4. *T:* 01–353 3366.

MARSHALL EVANS, David; *see* Evans.

MARSHAM, family name of **Earl of Romney.**

MARSHAM, Thomas Nelson, CBE 1976 (OBE 1964); BSc, PhD; FRS 1986; FEng 1986; MIEE, MInstP, FInstF; Managing Director, Northern Division, since 1977, Member, since 1979, United Kingdom Atomic Energy Authority; part-time Director, British Nuclear Fuels Ltd, since 1979; *b* 10 Nov. 1923; *s* of late Captain Thomas Brabban Marsham, OBE, and Jane Wise Marsham (*née* Nelson); *m* 1958, Dr Sheila Margaret Griffin; two *s*. *Educ:* Merchant Taylors' Sch., Crosby; Univ. of Liverpool (BSc, PhD). Ocean Steam Ship Co., 1941–46; Oliver Lodge Fellow, Univ. of Liverpool, 1951–53; joined UKAEA, 1953; Reactor Manager, Calder Hall Nuclear Power Station, 1955–57; Dep. Gen. Man., Windscale and Calder Works, 1958–64; Dir, Technical Policy, Reactor Gp, 1964–77. Mem., Adv. Council on R&D for Fuel and Power, 1974–. Mem. Council, Univ. of Liverpool, 1980–84. *Publications:* papers in scientific jls on nuclear physics. *Recreations:* sailing, Rugby football. *Address:* Whitecroft, Broseley Avenue, Culcheth, Warrington WA3 4HL. *T:* Culcheth 2948. *Clubs:* Naval, East India, Devonshire, Sports and Public Schools.

MARSLAND, Prof. Edward Abson; Vice-Chancellor and Principal, University of Birmingham, 1981– Oct. 1986; *b* Coventry, 18 May 1923; *s* of T. Marsland; *m* 1957, Jose, *d* of J. H. Evans; one *s* two *d*. *Educ:* King Edward's Sch. and Univ. of Birmingham. BDS (1st cl. hons), PhD, FDSRCS, FRCPath. House Surgeon, Gen. and Dental Hosps, Birmingham, 1946; Birmingham University: Research Fellow, 1948–50; Lectr in Dental Pathology, 1950–58; Sen. Lectr, 1958–64; Prof. of Oral Pathology, 1964–81; Pro-Vice-Chancellor, 1977–79; Vice-Principal, 1979–81; Dir, Birmingham Dental Sch., 1969–74. Chm., Co-ord. Cttee for Welfare of Handicapped, Birmingham, 1972–81; Pres., West Midlands Council for Disabled People, 1985– (Chm., 1977–83); Vice-Pres., Midlands Council for Preparatory Trng of Disabled, 1983– (Vice-Chm., 1976–83); Mem., W Midlands RHA, 1984–. Pres., Blue Coat Sch., Birmingham, 1984–; Mem., Council, Edgbaston C of E Coll. for Girls, Birmingham, 1984–. *Publications:* An Atlas of Dental Histology, 1957; A Colour Atlas of Oral Histopathology, 1975; scientific papers in various jls. *Recreations:* gardening, music, motoring. *Address:* 43 Edgbaston Park Road, Edgbaston, Birmingham B15 2RS. *T:* 021–454 6565.

MARSON, Air Vice-Marshal John, CB 1953; CBE 1950; CEng; RAF (retired); *b* 24 Aug. 1906; *s* of late Wing Comdr T. B. Marson, MBE, and late Mrs E. G. Marson, (*née* Atkins); *m* 1935, Louise Joy Stephen Paterson; two *s*. *Educ:* Oakham Sch. RAF Coll., Cranwell, 1924–26. STSO, HQ, Coastal Command, 1949–50; AOC 42 Group, 1951–54; Pres., Ordnance Board, 1956–57 (Vice-Pres., 1954–56); Dir-Gen. of Technical Services, 1957–58; AOC 24 Group, 1959–61. *Recreations:* sailing, golf. *Address:* Marygold, Aldeburgh, Suffolk IP15 5HF. *Clubs:* Royal Air Force; Royal Cruising; Cruising Association; Aldeburgh Golf.

MARTELL, Edward Drewett; Chairman of The Freedom Group, since 1953; *b* 2 March 1909; *e s* of E. E. Martell and Ethel Horwood; *m* 1932, Ethel Maud Beverley; one *s*. *Educ:* St George's Sch., Harpenden. In Coal trade, 1926–28, then entered journalism. Past: News Editor, World's Press News; Gen. Manager, The Saturday Review; Managing Editor, Burke's Peerage and Burke Publishing Co.; Sports staff of The Star. Served War of 1939–45, with RAC (Capt.). On demobilisation established own bookselling and publishing company. Mem. LCC, 1946–49; contested (L) Rotherhithe, 1946, and N. Hendon, 1950; East Ham (Ind.), 1957; SE Bristol (Nat. Fellowship C), 1963; Dep. Chm., Liberal Central Assoc., 1950–51; Trustee, Winston Churchill Birthday Trust, 1954. Founded: Free Press Soc., 1955; People's League for the Defence of Freedom, 1956 (first Chm.); Anti-Socialist Front, 1958; National Fellowship (co-founder), 1962; New Daily (also Editor), 1960. *Publications:* (with R. G. Burnett) The Devil's Camera, 1932; (with R. G. Burnett) The Smith Slayer, 1940; The Menace of Nationalisation, 1952; The Menace of the Trade Unions, 1957; Need the Bell Toll?, 1958; (with Ewan Butler) Murder of the News-Chronicle and the Star, 1960; Wit and Wisdom-Old and New, 1961; A Book of Solutions, 1962. *Recreations:* lawn tennis; Sherlock Holmes and Father Brown. *Address:* BM Box 2044, WC1.

MARTELL, Vice-Adm. Sir Hugh (Colenso), KBE 1966 (CBE 1957); CB 1963; *b* 6 May 1912; *s* of late Engineer Capt. A. A. G. Martell, DSO, RN (Retd) and late Mrs S. Martell. *Educ:* Edinburgh Academy; RNC Dartmouth. Royal Navy, 1926–67, retired; served War, 1940–45 (despatches): Gunnery Officer in HMS Berwick and HMS Illustrious. Naval Adviser to Dir Air Armament Research and Development, Min. of Supply, 1952–54; Capt. (F) 7 and in Comd HMS Bigbury Bay, 1954–55; Overall Operational Comdr, Nuclear Tests, in Monte Bello Is as Cdre, 1956; IDC, 1957; Capt., HMS Excellent, 1958; Dir of Tactical and Weapons Policy, Admiralty and Naval Mem. Defence Research Policy Staff, Min. of Defence, 1959–62; Admiral Commanding Reserves and Dir-Gen. of Naval Recruiting, 1962–65; Chief of Allied Staff, Mediterranean, Aegean and Black Sea, 1965–67. *Recreation:* sailing. *Club:* Naval.

MARTEN, Francis William, CMG 1967; MC 1943; formerly Counsellor, Foreign and Commonwealth Office; *b* 8 Nov. 1916; *er s* of late Vice-Adm. Sir Francis Arthur Marten and late Lady Marten (*née* Phyllis Raby Morgan); *m* 1940, Hon. Avice Irene Vernon (*d* 1964); one *s* one *d*; 2nd, 1967, Miss Anne Tan; one *s*. *Educ:* Winchester Coll.; Christ Church, Oxford. Served HM Forces, 1939–46. Entered HM Foreign Service, 1946; served FO, 1946–48; Washington, 1948–52; FO, 1952–54; Teheran, 1954–57; NATO Defence Coll., Paris, 1957–58; Bonn, 1958–62; Leopoldville, 1962–64; Imperial Defence Coll., 1964–65; Dep. High Comr, Eastern Malaysia, 1965–67; ODM, 1967–69. *Recreations:* ski-ing, gardening. *Address:* 113 Pepys Road, SE14. *T:* 01–639 1060.

MARTIN; *see* Holland-Martin.

MARTIN, Archer John Porter, CBE 1960; FRS 1950; MA, PhD; *b* 1 March 1910; *s* of Dr W. A. P. and Mrs L. K. Martin; *m* 1943, Judith Bagenal; two *s* three *d*. *Educ:* Bedford Sch.; Peterhouse, Cambridge, Hon. Fellow, 1974. Nutritional Lab., Cambridge, 1933–38; Chemist, Wool Industries Research Assoc., Leeds, 1938–46; Research Dept, Boots Pure Drug Co., Nottingham, 1946–48; staff, Medical Research Council, 1948–52; Head of Phys. Chem. Div., National Inst. of Medical Research, 1952–56; Chemical Consultant, 1956–59; Director, Abbotsbury Laboratories Ltd, 1959–70; Consultant to Wellcome Research Laboratories, 1970–73. Extraordinary Prof., Technological Univ. of Eindhoven, 1965–73; Professorial Fellow, Univ. of Sussex, 1973–78; Invited Prof. of Chemistry,

Ecole Polytechnique Fédérale de Lausanne, 1980–84. Berzelius Gold Medal, Swedish Medical Soc., 1951; (jointly with R. L. M. Synge) Nobel Prize for Chemistry, 1952; John Scott Award, 1958; John Price Wetherill Medal, 1959; Franklin Institute Medal, 1959; Leverhulme Medal, Royal Society, 1963; Koltoff Medal, Acad. of Pharmaceutical Science, 1969; Callendar Medal, Inst. of Measurement and Control, 1971. Hon. DSc Leeds, 1968; Hon. LLD Glasgow, 1973. *Address:* 47 Roseford Road, Cambridge CB4 2HA. *Club:* Chemists' (New York).

MARTIN, Bruce; *see* Martin, R. B.

MARTIN, Charles Edmund, MA; Headmaster, Bristol Grammar School, since 1986; *b* 19 Sept. 1939; *s* of late Flight Lieut Charles Stuart Martin and of Sheila Martin; *m* 1966, Emily Mary Bozman; one *s* one *d*. *Educ:* Lancing College; Selwyn College, Cambridge (Hons English; MA); Bristol University (PGCE). VSO, Sarawak, 1958–59; Asst Master, Leighton Park School, Reading, 1964–68; Day Housemaster and Sixth Form Master, Sevenoaks School, 1968–71; Head of English Dept and Dep. Headmaster, Pocklington School, 1971–80; Headmaster, King Edward VI Camp Hill Boys' School, Birmingham, 1980–86. *Recreations:* travel, hill walking, theatre, ornithology, bee keeping. *Address:* 47 Hampton Park, Redland, Bristol, Avon BS6 6LQ.

MARTIN, Christopher George; Director of Personnel, British Broadcasting Corporation, since 1981; *b* 29 May 1938; *s* of George and Lizbette Martin; *m* 1st, 1960, Moira Hughes (marr. diss. 1975); one *s* one *d*; 2nd, 1981, Elizabeth Buchanan Keith; one *s* decd. *Educ:* Beckenham Sch., Kent. Royal Marines, 1956–62. Group Personnel Manager: Viyella Internat., 1964–70; Great Universal Stores, 1970–74; Personnel Dir, Reed Paper & Board, 1974–76; UK Personnel Dir, Air Products Ltd, 1976–78; Gp Personnel Controller, Rank Organisation Ltd, 1978–81. CBIM 1984; FIPM 1984. *Publication:* contrib. Jl of Textile Inst. *Recreations:* music, sailing. *Address:* c/o BBC, Broadcasting House, W1A 1AA. *T:* 01–580 4468. *Clubs:* Brook's.

MARTIN, Prof. David Alfred, PhD; Professor of Sociology, London School of Economics and Political Science, London University, since 1971; Professor of Human Values, Southern Methodist University, Dallas, Texas, since 1986; *b* 30 June 1929; *s* of late Frederick Martin and late Rhoda Miriam Martin; *m* 1st, 1953, Daphne Sylvia Treherne (*d* 1975); one *s*; 2nd, 1962, Bernice Thompson; two *s* one *d*. *Educ:* Richmond and East Sheen Grammar Sch.; Westminster Coll. (DipEd 1952); Westcott House, Cambridge. BSc (Ext.) 1st Cl. Hons, London Univ., 1959; PhD 1964. School teaching, 1952–59; postgrad. scholar, LSE, 1959–61; Asst Lectr, Sheffield Univ., 1961–62; Lectr, LSE, 1962–67, Reader, 1967–71; JSPS Scholar, Japan, 1978–79. Lectures: Cadbury, Birmingham Univ., 1973; Ferguson, Manchester Univ., 1977; Gore, Westminster Abbey, 1977; Firth, Nottingham Univ., 1980; Forwood, Liverpool Univ., 1982; Prideaux, Exeter Univ., 1984; Select Preacher, Cambridge Univ., 1979. Pres., Internat. Conf. of Sociology of Religion, 1975–83. Ordained Deacon, 1983, Priest 1984. *Publications:* Pacifism, 1965; A Sociology of English Religion, 1967; The Religious and the Secular, 1969; Tracts against the Times, 1973; A General Theory of Secularisation, 1978; Dilemmas of Contemporary Religion, 1978; (ed) Crisis for Cranmer and King James, 1979; The Breaking of the Image, 1980; (ed jtly) Theology and Sociology, 1980; (ed jtly) No Alternative, 1981; (ed jtly) Unholy Warfare, 1983; contrib. Encounter, TLS, THES, Daedalus, TES. *Recreation:* piano accompaniment. *Address:* London School of Economics and Political Science, Houghton Street, Aldwych, WC2A 2AE. *T:* 01–405 7686; Cripplegate Cottage, 174 St John's Road, Woking, Surrey GU22 9NP. *T:* Woking 62134.

MARTIN, David Weir; Member (Lab) Lothians, European Parliament, since 1984; *b* 26 Aug. 1954; *s* of William Martin and Marion Weir; *m* 1979, Margaret Mary Cook; one *d*. *Educ:* Liberton High School; Heriot Watt University (BA Econs). Stockbroker's clerk, 1970–74; animal rights campaigner, 1975–79. Lothian Regional Councillor, 1982–84. Vice-Pres., National Playbus Assoc., 1985–; Mem. Cttee, Scottish Soc. for Prevention of Vivisection, 1985–. Dir, St Andrew Animal Fund, 1986. *Recreations:* soccer, reading. *Address:* (office) Ruskin House, 15 Windsor Street, Edinburgh EH7 5LA. *T:* 031–557 0936; (home) 7 Mortonhall Park Gardens, Edinburgh EH17 8SL. *T:* 031–664 9178.

MARTIN, Prof. Derek H.; Professor of Physics, Queen Mary College, University of London, since 1967; *b* 18 May 1929; *s* of Alec Gooch Martin and Winifred Martin; *m* 1951, Joyce Sheila Leaper; one *s* one *d*. *Educ:* Hitchin Boys' Grammar Sch.; Eastbourne Grammar Sch.; Univ. of Nottingham. BSc; PhD. Queen Mary College, London: Lectr, 1954–58, 1962–63; Reader in Experimental Physics, 1963–67; Dean, Faculty of Science, 1968–70; Head of Dept of Physics, 1970–75. DSIR Res. Fellow, 1959–62; Vis. Prof., Univ. of Calif, Berkeley, 1965–66. Member: Astronomy, Space and Radio Bd, SRC, 1975–78; Bd, Athlone Press, 1973–79; Royal Greenwich Observatory Cttee, 1977–80; Senate, Univ. of London, 1981–. Fellow, Inst. of Physics (Hon. Sec., 1984–); Member: Optical Soc. of America; Inst. of Electrical and Electronic Engrs; Internat. Astronomical Union. NPL Metrology Award, 1983. Editor, Advances in Physics, 1974–84. *Publications:* Magnetism in Solids, 1967; Spectroscopic Techniques, 1967; numerous articles and papers in Proc. Royal Soc., Jl of Physics, etc. *Address:* Hermanus, Hillwood Grove, Brentwood, Essex. *T:* Brentwood 210546. *Club:* Athenæum.

MARTIN, Douglas Whitwell; Chairman, Gill & Duffus Ltd, 1964–70; President, Gill & Duffus Group PLC, 1973–85; *b* 17 Feb. 1906; *s* of Rev. T. H. Martin, MA, and Lily Janet Vaughan Martin; *m* 1st, 1931, Jessie Milroy Lawrie (*d* 1965); three *s*; 2nd, 1967, Margaret Helen Simms, FCIS. *Educ:* Rossall Sch.; Lausanne University. Member of staff, Export Dept of Lever Brothers Ltd, 1923–27; joined Gill & Duffus Ltd, 1929. Underwriting Member of Lloyd's, 1950–69. *Recreations:* reading, theatre. *Address:* 74 Fort George, St Peter Port, Guernsey, CI. *T:* Guernsey 25381.

MARTIN, (Francis) Troy K.; *see* Kennedy Martin.

MARTIN, Frank Vernon, RE 1961 (ARE 1955); MA; MSIA; Wood Engraver; Etcher; Book Illustrator; Head of Department of Graphic Arts, Camberwell School of Art, 1976–80, Senior Lecturer since 1965 and Teacher of Etching and Engraving since 1953; *b* 14 Jan. 1921; *er s* of late Thomas Martin; *m* 1942, Mary Irene Goodwin; three *d*. *Educ:* Uppingham Sch.; Hertford Coll., Oxford; St Martin's Sch. of Art. History Schol., Hertford Coll., Oxford. Served War of 1939–45, Army, 1941–46. Book illustrations for Folio Society, Hutchinson, Geoffrey Bles, Burns Oates, Vine Press and other publishers. One-man exhibitions of prints and drawings, London, 1956, 1961 and 1968; works represented in: Victoria and Albert Museum; Manchester City Art Gallery; Whitworth Art Gallery, Manchester; Fitzwilliam, Cambridge; other public collections at home and abroad. Sec., Royal Society of Painter-Etchers and Engravers, 1956–57. Hon. Academician, Accademia delle Arti del Disegno, Florence, 1962. *Publications:* articles, book reviews, etc, on Engraving and the Graphic Arts. *Recreation:* photography. *Address:* Studio L, 416 Fulham Road, SW6. *T:* 01–385 1089; 55 St Mary's Grove, W4. *T:* 01–736 8896.

MARTIN, Frederick Royal, BSc, CEng, FICE, FIStructE; Under-Secretary, Department of the Environment and Director, Defence Services II, Property Services Agency, 1975–79, retired; *b* 10 Oct. 1919; *e s* of late Frederick Martin and Lois Martin (*née* Royal); *m* 1946, Elsie Winifred Parkes (*d* 1984); one *s* three *d*. *Educ:* Dudley Grammar Sch.; Univ. of Birmingham (BSc (Hons)). Asst Engr, Birmingham, Tame and Rea Dist Drainage Bd, 1940; entered Air Min. Directorate-Gen. of Works, as Engrg Asst, 1941; Asst Civil Engr: Heathrow, Cardington, London, 1944–48; Civil Engr: Cambridge, Iraq, Jordan, Persian Gulf, London, 1948–54; Sqdn Leader, RAF, 1949–52; Sen. CE, London, 1954–58; Suptg CE, London, also Chief Engr, Aden, Aden Protectorate, Persian Gulf and E Africa, 1958–62; Suptg CE, Exeter, 1962–64; Min. of Public Bdg and Works, Area Officer, Bournemouth, 1964–66; Suptg CE, Directorate of Civil Engrg Develt, 1966–70; Asst Dir, 1970–72; Dir of Directorate of Social and Research Services, Property Services Agency, 1972; Chief Engineer, Maplin Develt Authority, 1973–74. Crampton Prize, ICE, 1946. *Publications:* various papers and articles to Instn Civil Engrs, etc, on airfield pavements. *Recreations:* looking at medieval building, reading, gardening. *Address:* 25 East Avenue, Bournemouth, Dorset BH3 7BS. *T:* Bournemouth 25858.

MARTIN, Geoffrey; *see* Martin, T. G.

MARTIN, Geoffrey Haward, CBE 1986; DPhil; FSA, FRHistS; Keeper of Public Records, since 1982; *b* 27 Sept. 1928; *s* of late Ernest Leslie Martin and of Mary H. Martin (*née* Haward); *m* 1953, Janet, *d* of late Douglas Hamer, MC and of Enid Hamer; three *s* one *d*. *Educ:* Colchester Royal Grammar Sch.; Merton Coll., Oxford (MA, DPhil); Univ. of Manchester. FSA 1975; FRHistS 1958. Univ. of Leicester (formerly University Coll. of Leicester): Lectr in Econ. History, 1952–65; Reader in History, 1966–73; Prof. of History, 1973–82; Public Orator, 1971–74; Dean, Faculty of Arts, 1972–75; Pro-Vice-Chancellor, 1979–82. Vis. Prof. of Medieval History, Carleton Univ., Ottawa, 1958–59 and 1967–68; Vis. Res. Fellow, Merton Coll., Oxford, 1971. Chairman: Board of Leicester University Press, 1975–82; British Records Assoc., 1982–; Commonwealth Archivists' Assoc., 1984–; Arts and Humanities Res. Degrees, CNAA, 1986–. Selection Cttee, Miners' Welfare National Educn Fund, 1978–84. Vice-Pres., RHistS, 1984–. Hon. Gen. Editor, Suffolk Record Soc., 1956–. Besterman Medal, Library Assoc., 1972. *Publications:* The Town: a visual history, 1961; Royal Charters of Grantham, 1963; (with Sylvia McIntyre) Bibliography of British and Irish Municipal History, vol. 1, 1972; Ipswich Recognizance Rolls: a calendar, 1973; contribs to various learned jls. *Recreations:* fell-walking, adjusting phrases, gardening. *Address:* 27 Woodside House, Woodside, Wimbledon, SW19 7QN. *T:* 01–946 2570. *Clubs:* Royal Commonwealth Society, United Oxford & Cambridge University.

MARTIN, Air Marshal Sir Harold Brownlow Morgan, KCB 1971 (CB 1968); DSO 1943 (Bar 1944); DFC 1942 (Bar 1943, 1944); AFC 1948; *b* Edgecliffe, 27 Feb. 1918; *s* of the late J. H. O. M. Martin, MD, and of Colina Elizabeth Dixon; *m* 1944, Wendy Lawrence, *d* of late Grenville Outhwaite, Melbourne; two *d*. *Educ:* Bloomfields; Sydney; Randwick. Served war, 1939–45, Bomber Comd; took part in raid on Möhne dam, 1943. psa 1945; won Britannia Flying Trophy, 1947; Air Attaché, British Embassy, Israel, 1952–55; jssc, 1958; idc, 1965. SASO, Near East Air Force and Jt Services Chief of Staff, 1966–67; Air Vice-Marshal 1967; AOC No 38 Gp, Air Support Command, 1967–70; Air Marshal 1970; C-in-C, RAF Germany, and Commander, NATO 2nd Tactical Air Force, 1970–73; Air Member for Personnel, MoD, 1973–74, retired. ADC to HM the Queen, 1963. Hawker Siddeley International Ltd: Advr, 1974–75, Principal, Beirut, 1975–78, Middle East Future Markets; Market Advr, Hawker Siddeley PE Ltd, 1979. Oswald Watt Memorial Medal. *Recreations:* flying, horse racing, tennis, travel. *Clubs:* Royal Air Force, Arts, Hurlingham.

MARTIN, Lt-Gen. Henry James, CBE 1943; DFC; Chief of Defence Staff, South African Defence Force, retired; *b* 10 June 1910; *s* of Stanley Charles Martin and Susan C. Fourie; *m* 1940, Renée Viljoen; one *s* two *d*. *Educ:* Grey Coll. Sch., Bloemfontein; Grey Univ. Coll., Bloemfontein. Joined S African Air Force, 1936, and played important rôle in British Empire Training Scheme in South Africa; commanded No 12 Sqdn in Western Desert (DFC, Croix Militaire de première classe Belgique); commanded No 3 Wing (a unit of Desert Air Force) and campaigned from El Alamein to Tunis; returned to Union, 1943. *Recreations:* rugger (represented Orange Free State, 1931–34, Transvaal, 1935–37, South Africa, 1937), bowls. *Address:* 34 Crescent Road, Waterkloof Ridge, Pretoria, 0181, S Africa. *Club:* Harlequins Bowling.

MARTIN, Ian; Secretary General, Amnesty International, since 1986 (Head of Asia Research Department, 1985–86); *b* 10 Aug. 1946; *s* of Collin and Betty Martin; *m* 1977, Vivien Stern. *Educ:* Brentwood Sch.; Emmanuel Coll., Cambridge; Harvard Univ. Ford Foundn Representative's Staff, India, 1969–70, Pakistan, 1970–71, Bangladesh, 1972; Community Relations Officer, Redbridge Community Relations Council, 1973–75; Gen. Sec., Jt Council for the Welfare of Immigrants, 1977–82 (Dep. Gen. Sec., 1976–77; Exec. Cttee Mem., 1982–); Gen. Sec., The Fabian Soc., 1982–85. Member: Exec. Cttee, NCCL, 1983–85; Redbridge and Waltham Forest AHA, 1977–82; Redbridge HA, 1982–83. Councillor, London Borough of Redbridge, 1978–82. *Publications:* Immigration Law and Practice (with Larry Grant), 1982; chapters on: Racial Equality, in Labour and Equality, Fabian Essays, 1980; Racism in Immigration Law and Practice, in Civil Liberties, Cobden Trust Essays, 1984. *Address:* 22 Sidney Square, E1 2EY. *T:* 01–790 0281.

MARTIN, James Arthur, CMG 1970; FASA; company director; *b* 25 July 1903; *s* of late Arthur Higgins Martin and Gertrude, *d* of George Tippins. *Educ:* Stawell and Essendon High Schools, Victoria; Melbourne Univ. FASA 1924. Joined The Myer Emporium Ltd, Melbourne, 1918; The Myer Emporium (SA) Ltd, Adelaide, 1928, Man. Dir 1936, Chm. and Man. Dir, 1956–68, retd; Dir, Myer (Melbourne) Ltd, department store, 1936–68, retd. *Recreations:* gardening, walking, motoring. *Address:* 17 Hawkers Road, Medindie, SA 5081, Australia. *T:* Adelaide 442535. *Clubs:* South Australian Cricket, South Australian Jockey (Adelaide).

MARTIN, Maj.-Gen. James Mansergh Wentworth, CB 1953; CBE 1944; late 8th King George V's Own Light Cavalry; *b* 5 Aug. 1902; *er s* of late James Wentworth Martin, Castle Jane, Glanmire, Co. Cork, Ireland, and late Mrs J. Wentworth Martin, Great Meadow, Hambledon, Surrey; *m* 1944, Mrs Jean Lindsay Barnes (*d* 1978), *d* of late Sir Henry Cowan, MP. *Educ:* Charterhouse; Royal Military Academy, Woolwich. Joined RFA 1922; with Royal West African Frontier Force, 1925–27; Private Sec. to Governor of Assam, 1928–29; transferred to Indian Army, 1930. During War of 1939–45, Persia and Iraq, Syria, Tunisia, Sicily, Italy and Burma; Brig., Gen. Staff, 1943–44. Comd 1st Indian Armoured Bde, 1945–47, transferred to Royal Scots Greys, Jan. 1948; Chief of Staff, British Forces in Trieste, 1948–49; Comd 9th Armoured Brigade, 1949–51; Dep. Chief of Staff Allied Land Forces Central Europe, Fontainebleau, 1951–53; GOC Salisbury Plain District, 1953–56; retired Sept. 1956. Liveryman of the Merchant Taylors' Company. *Address:* Great Meadow, Hambledon, Godalming, Surrey. *T:* Wormley 2665.

MARTIN, Janet, (Mrs K. P. Martin); Social Services Officer, Test Valley, since 1978; Member, Press Council, 1973–78; *b* Dorchester, Dorset, 8 Sept. 1927; *d* of James Wilkinson and Florence Steer; *m* 1951, Peter Martin (Payroll Services Manager, Southampton Health Dist); one *s* one *d*. *Educ:* Dorchester Grammar Sch., Dorset; Weymouth Tech. Coll.; occupational training courses. PA to Group Sec., Herrison HMC, 1949; admin./clerical work, NHS and other, 1956; social research fieldwork, mainly

NHS (Wessex mental health care evaluation team), and Social Services (Hants CC and Nat. Inst. for Social Work), 1967–76; residential social worker (children with special needs), Southampton, 1976–78. Interviewer, MRC 'National' Survey, 1970–85; Psychosexual Counsellor, Aldermoor Clinic, 1981–84. *Recreations:* local history, local pub. *Address:* 35 West Tytherley, near Salisbury, Wilts. *T:* Lockerley 40892.

MARTIN, John Christopher; Deputy Chief Scientific Officer (Special Merit), United Kingdom Atomic Energy Authority, since 1974; *b* 21 Sept. 1926; *s* of late Percy Martin and Marjorie Etta Caselton. *Educ:* Edward Alleyn's Sch.; King's Coll., London (BSc (Hons Physics) 1946). MoS, Fort Halstead, Sept. 1947; Woolwich Arsenal, 1950; UKAEA/MoD, AWRE, Aldermaston, Nov. 1952–. USA Defense Nuclear Agency Exceptional Public Service Gold Medal, 1977. *Publications:* contribs to learned jls. *Recreations:* friends, food, snorkling, science fiction and fact (not always distinguishable). *Address:* Boundary Hall, Tadley, Basingstoke, Hants.

MARTIN, Brig. John Douglas K.; *see* King-Martin.

MARTIN, Vice-Adm. Sir John (Edward Ludgate), KCB 1972 (CB 1968); DSC 1943; FNI; retired; Lieutenant-Governor and Commander-in-Chief of Guernsey, 1974–80; *b* 10 May 1918; *s* of late Surgeon Rear-Admiral W. L. Martin, OBE, FRCS and Elsie Mary Martin (*née* Catford); *m* 1942, Rosemary Ann Deck; two *s* two *d*. *Educ:* RNC, Dartmouth. Sub Lt and Lt, HMS Pelican, 1938–41; 1st Lt, HMS Antelope, 1942; navigation course, 1942; Navigation Officer, 13th Minesweeping Flotilla, Mediterranean, 1943–44, including invasions N Africa, Sicily, Pantelleria, Salerno; RNAS Yeovilton, 1944; Navigation Officer: HMS Manxman and HMS Bermuda, 1944–46; HMS Nelson, 1947; HMS Victorious, 1948; Staff Coll., 1949; Navigation Officer, HMS Devonshire, 1950–51; Dirg Staff, Staff Coll., 1952–54; Jt Services Planning Staff, Far East, 1954–55; Exec. Off., HMS Superb, 1956–57; Jt Services Staff Coll., 1958; Dep. Dir Manpower Planning and Complementing Div., Admty, 1959–61; Sen. Naval Off., W Indies, 1961–62; Comdr Brit. Forces Caribbean Area, 1962–63; Capt. Britannia Royal Naval Coll., Dartmouth, 1963–66; Flag Officer, Middle East, 1966–67; Comdr, British Forces Gulf, 1967–68 (despatches); Dir-Gen., Naval Personal Services and Training, 1968–70; Dep. Supreme Allied Comdr, Atlantic, 1970–72. Comdr 1951; Captain 1957; Rear-Adm. 1966. Pres., Nautical Inst., 1975–78. *Recreations:* fishing, shooting, beagling (Jt Master Britannia Beagles, 1963–66), sailing. *Clubs:* Army and Navy; Royal Naval Sailing Association; Royal Yacht Squadron.

MARTIN, John Francis Ryde; HM Diplomatic Service; Counsellor and Head of Chancery, Lagos, since 1984; *b* 8 Feb. 1943; *s* of Frank George Martin and Phyllis Mary Wixcey; *m* 1st, 1966, Hélène Raymonde Henriette Pyronnet (marr. diss. 1984); two *s*; 2nd, 1985, Kathleen Marie White. *Educ:* Bedford School; Brasenose College, Oxford (MA); Bologna Center, Johns Hopkins Univ. FCO, 1966; Buenos Aires, 1968–70; Athens, 1970–74; Private Sec. to Minister of State, FCO, 1976–78; Nicosia, 1978–81; Asst Sec., Internat. Telecommunications, DTI, 1983–84. *Recreations:* travel, collecting, bibliomania. *Address:* c/o Foreign and Commonwealth Office, SW1. *Club:* Travellers'.

MARTIN, Sir (John) Leslie, Kt 1957; RA 1986; MA, PhD Manchester; MA Cantab; MA Oxon; Hon. LLD Leicester, Hull, Manchester; DUniv Essex; FRIBA; Professor of Architecture, University of Cambridge, 1956–72; Emeritus Professor, 1973; Fellow, Jesus College, Cambridge, 1956–73, Hon. Fellow 1973, Emeritus Fellow, 1976; *b* 17 Aug. 1908; *s* of late Robert Martin, FRIBA; *m*, Sadie Speight, MA, ARIBA; one *s* one *d*. *Educ:* Manchester Univ. Sch. of Architecture. Asst Lectr, Manchester Univ. Sch. of Architecture, 1930–34; Head of Sch. of Architecture, Hull, 1934–39; Principal Asst Architect, LMS Railway, 1939–48; Dep. Architect, LCC, 1948–53; Architect to the LCC, 1953–56. Slade Prof. of Fine Art, Oxford, 1965–66; Ferens Prof. of Fine Art, Hull, 1967–68; William Henry Bishop Vis. Prof. of Architecture, Univ. of Yale, 1973–74; Lethaby Prof., RCA, 1981. Lectures: Gropius, Harvard, 1966; Cordingley, Manchester, 1968; Kenneth Kassler, Princeton, 1974; annual, Soc. Arch. Historians, 1976; Townsend, UCL, 1976; Convocation, Leicester, 1978. Consultant to Gulbenkian Foundn, Lisbon, 1959–69. Buildings include: work in Cambridge and for Univs of Cambridge, Oxford, Leicester and Hull; RSAMD, Glasgow; Gall. of Modern Art, Gulbenkian Foundn, Lisbon. Mem. Council, RIBA, 1952–58 (Vice-Pres., 1955–57); Mem. Royal Fine Art Commn, 1958–72. RIBA Recognised Schs Silver Medallist, 1929; Soane Medallist, 1930; London Architecture Bronze Medallist, 1954; RIBA Distinction in Town Planning, 1956; Civic Trust Award, Oxford, 1967; Commend. Cambridge, 1972; Concrete Soc. Award, Oxford, 1972; Royal Gold Medal for Architecture, RIBA, 1973. Hon. Mem. Assoc. of Finnish Architects, Accademico corrispondente National Acad. of S Luca, Rome. Comdr, Order of Santiago da Espada, Portugal. *Publications:* Jt Editor, Circle, 1937, repr. 1971; The Flat Book, 1939 (in collab. with wife); Whitehall: a Plan for a National and Government Centre, 1965; The Framework of Planning (Inaugural Lecture) Hull, 1967; Jt Editor, Cambridge Urban and Architectural Studies, Vol. I: Urban Space and Structure, 1972; Building and Ideas (1933–83) from the Studio of Leslie Martin, 1983; contrib. various jls; papers include: An Architect's Approach to Architecture; Education Without Walls; Education Around Architecture; Notes on a Developing Architecture. *Address:* The Barns, Church Street, Great Shelford, Cambridge. *T:* Cambridge 842399. *Club:* Athenæum.

MARTIN, Sir John (Miller), KCMG 1952; CB 1945; CVO 1943; British High Commissioner in Malta, 1965–67; *b* 15 Oct. 1904; *s* of late Rev. John Martin; *m* 1943, Rosalind Julia, 3rd *d* of late Sir David Ross, KBE; one *s*. *Educ:* The Edinburgh Acad.; Corpus Christi Coll., Oxford (Scholar, MA; Hon. Fellow, 1980). Entered Civil Service (Dominions Office), 1927; seconded to Malayan Civil Service, 1931–34; Sec. of Palestine Royal Commission, 1936; Private Sec. to the Prime Minister (Rt Hon. Winston Churchill), 1940–45 (Principal Private Sec. from 1941); Asst Under-Sec. of State, 1945–56, Dep. Under-Sec. of State, 1956–65, Colonial Office. KStJ 1966. *Publication:* contrib. to Action This Day-Working with Churchill, 1968. *Address:* The Barn House, Watlington, Oxford. *T:* Watlington 2487.

MARTIN, Prof. John Powell; Professor of Sociology and Social Administration, University of Southampton, since 1967; *b* 22 Dec. 1925; *s* of Bernard and Grace Martin; *m* 1st, 1951, Sheila Feather (marr. diss. 1981); three *s*; 2nd, 1983, Joan Higgins. *Educ:* Leighton Park Sch., Reading; Univ. of Reading (BA); London Sch. of Economics and Political Science (Certif. in Social Admin., PhD); Univ. of Cambridge (MA). Lectr, London Sch. of Economics, 1953–59; Asst Dir of Research, Inst. of Criminology, Univ. of Cambridge, 1960–66; Fellow, King's Coll., Cambridge, 1964–67. Hill Foundn Vis. Prof., Univ. of Minnesota, 1973; Vis. Fellow, Yale Law Sch., 1974. Mem., Jellicoe Cttee on Boards of Visitors of Penal Instns, 1974–75. *Publications:* Social Aspects of Prescribing, 1957; Offenders as Employees, 1962; The Police: a study in manpower (with Gail Wilson), 1969; The Social Consequences of Conviction (with Douglas Webster), 1971; (ed) Violence and the Family, 1978; (jtly) The Future of the Prison System, 1980; Hospitals in Trouble, 1984; (with J. B. Coker) Licensed to Live, 1985; articles in: Lancet, British Jl of Criminology, British Jl of Sociology, International Review of Criminal Policy, etc. *Recreations:* sailing, photography, do-it-yourself. *Address:* Department of Sociology and Social Administration, The University, Southampton SO9 5NH. *T:* Southampton 559122. *Club:* Lymington Town Sailing.

MARTIN, John Sinclair, CBE 1977; farmer; *b* 18 Sept. 1931; *s* of Joseph Martin and Claire Martin, Littleport, Ely; *m* 1960, Katharine Elisabeth Barclay, MB, BS; three *s* one *d*. *Educ:* The Leys Sch., Cambridge; St John's Coll., Cambridge (MA, Dip. in Agriculture). Chairman: Littleport and Downham IDB, 1971–; JCO Arable Crops and Forage Bd, 1973–76; Eastern Regional Panel, MAFF, 1981–86 (Mem., 1972–78); Great Ouse Local Land Drainage Cttee, AWA, 1983– (Vice-Chm., 1974–83). Member: Eastern Counties Farmers' Management Cttee, 1960–72; ARC, 1968–78; Great Ouse River Authority, 1970–74; Lawes Agricl Trust Cttee, 1982–84; MAFF Priorities Bd, 1984–. Chairman: Ely Br., NFU, 1963; Cambs NFU, 1979. High Sheriff, Cambs, 1985–86. *Address:* Denny Abbey, Waterbeach, Cambridge CB5 9PQ. *T:* Cambridge 860282. *Club:* Farmers'.

MARTIN, John William Prior; HM Diplomatic Service; Counsellor, Foreign and Commonwealth Office, since 1985; *b* 23 July 1934; *er s* of Stanley Gordon Martin and Frances Heather (*née* Moore); *m* 1960, Jean Fleming; three *s* one *d*. *Educ:* CIM Sch., Chefoo and Kuling; Bristol Grammar Sch.; St John's Coll., Oxford (MA). National Service, 1953–55 (2nd Lieut Royal Signals). Joined FO, 1959; Beirut, 1960; Saigon, 1963; Language Student, Hong Kong, 1965–67; Dar es Salaam, 1968; FCO, 1971; Singapore, 1974; FCO, 1978; Kuala Lumpur, 1982. *Address:* c/o Foreign and Commonwealth Office, SW1A 2AH.

MARTIN, Jonathan Arthur; Head of Sport, BBC Television, since 1981; *b* 18 June 1942; *s* of Arthur Martin and Mabel Gladys Martin (*née* Bishop); *m* 1967, Joy Elizabeth Fulker; two *s*. *Educ:* Gravesend Grammar School; St Edmund Hall, Oxford (BA 1964, English). Joined BBC as general trainee, 1964; producer, Sportsnight 1969; producer, Match of the Day, 1970; editor, Sportsnight and Match of the Day, 1974; exec. producer, BBC TV Wimbledon tennis coverage, 1979–81; producer, Ski Sunday and Grand Prix, 1978–80; managing editor, Sport, 1980. *Recreations:* skiing, watching sport, watching television. *Address:* Arkle, Valentine Way, Chalfont St Giles, Bucks HP8 4JB; BBC, Kensington House, W14. *T:* 01–743 1272.

MARTIN, Mrs Kenneth Peter; *see* Martin, Janet.

MARTIN, Prof. Laurence Woodward; DL; Vice-Chancellor, University of Newcastle upon Tyne, since 1978; *b* 30 July 1928; *s* of Leonard and Florence Mary Martin; *m* 1951, Betty Parnall; one *s* one *d*. *Educ:* St Austell Grammar Sch.; Christ's Coll., Cambridge (MA); Yale Univ. (MA, PhD). Flying Officer, RAF, 1948–50; Instr, Yale Univ., 1955–56; Asst Prof., MIT, 1956–61; Rockefeller Fellow for Advanced Study, 1958–59; Associate Prof., Sch. of Advanced Internat. Studies, The Johns Hopkins Univ., 1961–64; Wilson Prof. of Internat. Politics, Univ. of Wales, 1964–68; Prof. of War Studies, King's Coll., Univ. of London, 1968–77, Fellow 1983–; Research Associate, Washington Center of Foreign Policy Research, 1964–76, 1979–; Vis. Prof., Univ. of Wales, 1985–. Lees-Knowles Lectr, Cambridge, 1981; BBC Reith Lectr, 1981. Director: Tyne Tees Television; European-American Inst. for Security Res., 1977–. Member: SSRC, 1969–76 (Chm. Res. Grants Bd); Res. Council, Georgetown Center of Strategic Studies, 1969–77, 1979–; Council, IISS, 1975–83. Consultant, Univ. of California, Los Alamos Scientific Laboratory. DL Tyne and Wear, 1986. *Publications:* The Anglo-American Tradition in Foreign Affairs (with Arnold Wolfers), 1956; Peace without Victory, 1958; Neutralism and Non-Alignment, 1962; The Sea in Modern Strategy, 1967; (jtly) America in World Affairs, 1970; Arms and Strategy, 1973; (jtly) Retreat from Empire?, 1973; (jtly) Strategic Thought in the Nuclear Age, 1979; The Two-Edged Sword, 1982; Before the Day After, 1985. *Address:* University of Newcastle upon Tyne, Newcastle upon Tyne NE1 7RU.

MARTIN, Leonard Charles James; Under-Secretary, Overseas Development Administration, FCO (formerly Ministry of Overseas Development), 1968–80, retired; *b* 26 June 1920; *s* of Leonard Howard Martin and Esther Martin (*née* Avis); *m* 1945, Althea Lilian Charles; three *d*. *Educ:* Brighton, Hove and Sussex Grammar Sch.; London Sch. of Economics. Served RAFVR, 1941–45. Min. of Educn, and Dept of Educn and Science, 1946–64; ODM, 1965–80. UK Permanent Delegate to UNESCO, 1965–68; Mem. Exec. Bd, UNESCO, 1974–78 (Chm., 1976–78). *Address:* 87 Downside, Shoreham-by-Sea, West Sussex BN4 6HF.

MARTIN, Sir Leslie; *see* Martin, Sir J. L.

MARTIN, Leslie Vaughan; Hon. Research Fellow, Exeter University; *b* 20 March 1919; *s* of late Hubert Charles Martin and late Rose Martin (*née* Skelton) *m* 1949, Winifred Dorothy Hopkins; one *s* one *d*. *Educ:* Price's Sch., Fareham. FIA 1947. Served with RAMC and REME, 1940–46. Deptl Clerical Officer, Customs and Excise, 1936–38; joined Govt Actuary's Dept, 1938; Asst Actuary, 1949; Actuary, 1954; Principal Actuary, 1962; Directing Actuary (Superann. and Research), 1974–79. Mem. Council, Inst. of Actuaries, 1971–76; Vice-Chm., CS Medical Aid Assoc., 1976–79. Churchwarden, St Barnabas, Dulwich, 1965–70, 1977–79, Vice-Chm. of Parish Council, 1970–79; Treasurer: Morchard Bishop Parochial Church Council, 1980–83; Cadbury Deanery Synod, 1981–. *Recreations:* crosswords, chess, scrabble. *Address:* Pickwick House, Down St Mary, Crediton, Devon EX17 6EQ. *T:* Copplestone 581.

MARTIN, Michael John; MP (Lab) Springburn Division of Glasgow, since 1979; *b* 3 July 1945; *s* of Michael and Mary Martin; *m* 1965, Mary McLay; one *s* one *d*. *Educ:* St Patrick's Boys' Sch., Glasgow. Sheet metal worker; AUEW Shop Steward, Rolls Royce, Hillington, 1970–74; Trade Union Organiser, 1976–79; Mem., and sponsored by, Nat. Union of Sheet Metal Workers, Coppersmiths and Heating and Domestic Engineers; PPS to Rt Hon. Denis Healey, MP, 1981–83; Mem., Select Cttee for Trade and Industry, 1983–. Councillor: for Fairfield Ward, Glasgow Corp., 1973–74; for Balornock Ward, Glasgow DC, 1974–79. *Recreations:* hill walking, local history. *Address:* 144 Broomfield Road, Balornock, Glasgow G21 3UE.

MARTIN, Oliver Samuel, QC 1970; **His Honour Judge Martin;** a Circuit Judge, since 1975; *b* 26 Nov. 1919; *s* of Sidney Edward Martin and Nita Martin; *m* 1st, 1954, Marion Eve (marr. diss. 1982); two *s*; 2nd, 1982, Gloria Audrey. *Educ:* King's College Sch., Wimbledon; London University. Served RNVR, 1939–46. Called to Bar, Gray's Inn, 1951. Dep. Chm. E Sussex QS, 1970–71; a Recorder of the Crown Court, 1972–75. *Recreations:* golf, music, reading, writing, holidays. *Address:* c/o Bloomsbury County Court, Marylebone Road, NW1.

MARTIN, Patrick William, TD; JP; MA; Headmaster of Warwick School, 1962–77; *b* 20 June 1916; *e s* of Alan Pattinson Martin, Bowness-on-Windermere, Westmorland; *m* 1939, Gwendoline Elsie Helme, MA, St Hilda's Coll., Oxford; two *d*. *Educ:* Windermere Grammar Sch.; Balliol Coll., Oxford. 2nd cl. hons in Modern History, Balliol Coll., 1937. Asst Master, Abingdon Sch., Berks, 1938–40. Commissioned in TA, 1938; served War of 1939–45, on active service with Royal Artillery; Staff College, Quetta; GSO 2, and 1 HQRA 14th Army in Burma (despatches); British Mil. Mission to Belgium, 1946. Schoolmaster, 1946–49; Asst Dir of Educn, Brighton, 1950–52; Headmaster: Chipping Norton Grammar Sch., 1952–57; Lincoln Sch., 1958–62. Chm., Midland Div.,

Headmasters' Conf., 1972–; Pres., Headmasters' Assoc., 1976; Treasurer, Warwick Univ., 1983–. CC Warwickshire, 1977–85 (Leader, 1981–83). JP Warwicks 1966, Dep. Chm., Warwick Petty Sessions. *Publications:* History of Heart of England Building Society, 1981; articles in educational and other periodicals. *Recreations:* books, music, foreign countries and people; being alone in the countryside. *Address:* 80 High Street, Kenilworth, Warwicks. *T:* Kenilworth 54140.

MARTIN, Hon. Paul Joseph James, PC (Canada) 1945; CC (Canada) 1976; QC (Canada); High Commissioner for Canada in the United Kingdom, 1974–79; *b* Ottawa, 23 June 1903; *s* of Philip Ernest Martin and Lumina Marie Chouinard; *m* 1937, Alice Eleanor Adams; one *s* one *d. Educ:* Pembroke Separate Schs; St Alexandre Coll.; St Michael's Coll.; University of Toronto (MA); Osgoode Hall Law Sch., Toronto; Harvard Univ. (LLM); Trinity Coll., Cambridge; Geneva Sch. of Internat. Studies. Wilder Fellow, 1928; Alfred Zimmern Schol., 1930; Barrister-at-Law; Partner, Martin, Laird & Cowan, Windsor, Ont, 1934–63; QC 1937. Lectr, Assumption Coll., 1931–34. Can. Govt Deleg., 19th Ass. League of Nations, Geneva, 1938; Parl. Asst to Minister of Labour, 1943; Deleg. to ILO Confs, Phila, 1944, London, 1945. Apptd Sec. of State, 1945. Deleg. to 1st, 4th, 7th, 9th, 10th General Assembly, UN (Chm. Can. Del., 9th, 18th, 19th, 20th, 21st). Deleg. 1st, 3rd, 5th sessions, Economic and Social Council, 1946–47. Minister of National Health and Welfare, Dec. 1946–June 1957; Sec. of State for External Affairs, 1963–68; Pres., N Atlantic Council, 1965–66; Govt Leader in Senate, Canada, 1968–74. First elected to Canadian House of Commons, Gen. Elec., 1935; Rep. Essex East until 1968; apptd to Senate, 1968. Chancellor, Wilfrid Laurier Univ., 1972–. Holds several hon. doctorates. Hon. Life Mem., Canadian Legion. Christian Culture Award, 1956. Freedom, City of London, 1977. Hon. LLD Cambridge, 1980. *Address:* 2021 Ontario Street, Windsor, Ontario N8Y 1N3, Canada. *Clubs:* Rideau (Ottawa); Beach Grove Golf and Country (Windsor, Ont).

MARTIN, Peter; *see* Martin, R. P.

MARTIN, Maj.-Gen. Peter Lawrence de Carteret, CBE 1968 (OBE 1964); Vice-President, Lady Grover's Hospital Fund for Officers' Families, since 1985 (Chairman, 1975–85); Member: National Executive Committee, Forces Help Society, since 1975; Ex-Services Mental Welfare Society, since 1977; *b* 15 Feb. 1920; *s* of late Col Charles de Carteret Martin, MD, ChD, IMS and of Helen Margaret Hardinge Grover; *m* 1st, 1949, Elizabeth Felicia (marr. diss. 1967), *d* of late Col C. M. Keble; one *s* one *d*; 2nd, 1973, Mrs Valerie Singer. *Educ:* Wellington Coll.; RMC Sandhurst. FBIM 1979 (MBIM 1970). Commnd Cheshire Regt, 1939; BEF (Dunkirk), 1940; Middle East, 1941; N Africa 8th Army, 1942–43 (despatches); invasion of Sicily, 1943; Normandy landings and NW Europe, 1944 (despatches); Palestine, 1945–47; GSO2 (Int.), HQ British Troops Egypt, 1947; Instructor, RMA Sandhurst, 1948–50; psc 1951; Bde Major 126 Inf. Bde (TA), 1952–53; Chief Instructor MMG Div. Support Weapons Wing, Sch. of Infantry, 1954–56; Malayan Ops, 1957–58 (despatches); DAAG GHQ FARELF, 1958–60; CO 1 Cheshire, N Ireland and BAOR, 1961–63; AA&QMG Cyprus District, 1963–65; comd 48 Gurkha Inf. Bde, Hong Kong, 1966–68; Brig. AQ HQ Army Strategic Comd, 1968–71; Dir, Personal Services (Army), 1971–74. Col The 22nd (Cheshire) Regt, 1971–78; Col Comdt, Mil. Provost Staff Corps, 1972–74. Services Advr, Variety Club of GB, 1976–86. *Recreations:* golf, tennis, reading and watching 1 Cheshire winning Athletics championships. *Club:* Army and Navy.

MARTIN, Peter Lewis, CBE 1980; building services engineer, retired; *b* 22 Sept. 1918; *s* of George Lewis and Madeleine Mary Martin; *m* 1949, Elizabeth Grace, *d* of John David Melling; two *d. Educ:* Wyggeston Boys Sch., Leicester; Kibworth Beauchamp Grammar Sch.; Leicester Coll. of Art and Technology; Borough Polytechnic. CEng; MConsE. Apprenticed to engrg contractor, 1934–39. Served War, 1940–46, RAF Engrg Branch. Joined consulting engrg practice of Dr Oscar Faber, 1947; Partner, 1961–83; Consultant, 1983–85. Pres., IHVE, 1971–72; Chairman: Heating and Ventilating Res. Assoc., 1967–69; Assoc. of Consulting Engrs, 1983–84; Member: Cttee for Application of Computers to the Construction Industry, 1970–72; Technical Data on Fuel Cttee, World Energy Conf., 1971–77; Construction and Housing Res. Adv. Council, 1975–77; Building Services Bd, CNAA, 1975–80; Engrg Council, 1982–86. Vis. Prof., Univ. of Strathclyde, 1974–85; Hon. DSc Strathclyde, 1985. Governor, Herts Coll. of Building, 1970–74. Master, Plumbers' Co., 1979–80; Liveryman: Fanmakers' Co., 1971–; Engineers' Co., 1983–. Silver Medal, 1956, Bronze Medal, 1968, Gold Medal, 1976, IHVE. *Publications:* (jtly) Heating and Air Conditioning of Buildings, by Faber and Kell, 5th edn 1971, 6th edn 1979; contribs to engrg jls and confs. *Recreation:* avoiding gardening. *Address:* Quietways, Lower Bodham, Holt, Norfolk NR25 6PS. *T:* Holt 712591. *Clubs:* City Livery, Lansdowne.

MARTIN, Most Rev. Pierre, Officer, Legion of Honour, 1967; President, Episcopal Conference of The Pacific, since 1971; Former Archbishop of Noumea (1966–71); *b* 22 Feb. 1910. *Educ:* Univ. de Lyon; Lyon Séminaire and in Belgium. Priest, 1939. POW, Buchenwald and Dachau Camps, until 1945. Séminaire de Missions d'Océanie, Lyon: Professor, 1945–47; Supérieure, 1947–53; Provincial, Sté de Marie, Paris, 1953–56; Bishop of New Caledonia, 1956. Apostolic Administrator of the Diocese of Port-Vila, 1976–77. *Address:* CEPAC, PO Box 1200, Suva, Fiji.

MARTIN, Prof. Raymond Leslie, MSc, PhD, ScD, DSc; FRACI, FRSC, FAA; Professor of Chemistry, Monash University, Melbourne, since 1987 (Vice-Chancellor, 1977–87); *b* 3 Feb. 1926; *s* of Sir Leslie Harold Martin, CBE, FRS, FAA and of Gladys Maude Elaine, *d* of H. J. Bull; *m* 1954, Rena Lillian Laman; three *s* one *d. Educ:* Scotch Coll., Melbourne; Univ. of Melb. (BSc, MSc); Sidney Sussex Coll., Cambridge (PhD, ScD). FRACI 1956; FRSC (FRIC 1974); FAA 1971. Resident Tutor in Chemistry, Queen's Coll., Melb., 1947–49 (Fellow, 1979); Sidney Sussex Coll., Cambridge: 1851 Exhibn Overseas Scholar, 1949–51; Sen. Scholar, 1952–54; Res. Fellow, 1951–54; Sen. Lectr, Univ. of NSW, 1954–59; Section Leader, 1959–60, and Associate Res. Manager, 1960–62, ICIANZ; Prof. of Inorganic Chem., 1962–72, and Dean of Faculty of Science, 1971, Univ. of Melb.; Australian National University, Canberra: Prof. of Inorganic Chem., Inst. of Advanced Studies, 1972–77, Prof. Emeritus 1977; Dean, Res. Sch. of Chem., 1976–77; DSc. Vis. Scientist: Technische Hochschule, Stuttgart, 1953–54; Bell Telephone Labs, NJ, 1967; Vis. Prof., Columbia Univ., NY, 1972. Royal Aust. Chemical Institute: Smith Medal, 1968; Olle Prize, 1974; Inorganic Medal, 1978; Fed. Pres., 1968–69. Chm., Internat. Commn on Atomic Weights and Isotopic Abundances, 1983–. Dir, Winston Churchill Meml Trust (and Chm., Vic Regional Cttee), 1983–. *Publications:* papers and revs on physical and inorganic chem. mainly in jls of London, Amer. and Aust. Chem. Socs. *Recreations:* golf; lawn tennis (Cambridge Univ. team *v* Oxford, Full Blue; Cambs County Colours). *Address:* Department of Chemistry, Monash University, Clayton, Vic 3168, Australia. *Clubs:* Melbourne (Melbourne); Hawks (Cambridge).

MARTIN, Col Robert Andrew St George, OBE 1959 (MBE 1949); JP; Lord-Lieutenant and Custos Rotulorum of Leicestershire since 1965; *b* 23 April 1914; *o s* of late Major W. F. Martin, Leics Yeo., and late Violet Anne Philippa (*née* Wynter); *m* 1950, Margaret Grace (JP Leics 1967), *e d* of late J. V. Buchanan, MB, ChB and late Waiata Buchanan (*née* Godsal); one *s. Educ:* Eton Coll.; RMC Sandhurst. Commissioned Oxf. and Bucks Lt Inf., 1934; ADC to Gov.-Gen. of S Africa, 1938–40; war service 4 Oxf. and Bucks, 1940–42; 2/7 R Warwick Regt, 1942–44; 5 DCLI, 1944–45 in NW Europe (despatches); DAMS, HQ ALFSEA, 1946; Mil. Asst to C of S, GHQ, SEALF, 1946–49 (MBE); Chief Instr, School of Mil. Admin., 1949–50; 1 Som. LI, 1950–52; AMS, HQ BAOR, 1952–54; 1 Oxf. and Bucks, 1954–55; Military Sec. to Gov.-Gen. of Australia, 1955–57; Comd 1 Oxf. and Bucks Lt Inf. and 1 Green Jackets, 1957–59; Bde Col Green Jackets Bde, 1959–62; Comd Recruiting and Liaison Staff, HQ Western Command, 1962–65. Pres., E Midlands TA&VRA, 1968–86. Hon. LLD Leicester, 1984. JP Leics, 1965. KStJ 1966. Order of Orange Nassau, 1950. *Recreations:* hunting, shooting, gardening. *Address:* The Brand, Woodhouse Eaves, Loughborough, Leics LE12 8SS. *T:* Woodhouse Eaves 890269. *Clubs:* Army and Navy, MCC.

MARTIN, (Robert) Bruce, QC 1977; a Recorder of the Crown Court, since 1978; *b* 2 Nov. 1938; *s* of Robert Martin and Fay Martin; *m* 1967, Elizabeth Georgina (*née* Kiddie); one *s* one *d. Educ:* Shrewsbury Sch.; Liverpool Univ. (LLB Hons 1959). Called to the Bar, Middle Temple, 1960. Chm., The Bob Martin Co. and associated cos, 1980–. Mem., Mersey RHA, 1983–. *Recreations:* music, golf, fishing. *Address:* 5 Essex Court, Temple, EC4 9AH. *T:* 01-353 4365; 4 Montpelier Terrace, SW7. *T:* 01-584 0649. *Club:* Royal Birkdale Golf.

MARTIN, Robin Geoffrey; Chairman, Hewetson Holdings Ltd, since 1980; *b* 9 March 1921; *s* of Cecil Martin and Isabel Katherine Martin (*née* Hickman); *m* 1946, Margery Chester Yates; two *s* one *d. Educ:* Cheltenham Coll.; Jesus Coll., Cambridge (MA). FIQ. Tarmac Ltd: Dir 1955; Gp Man. Dir 1963; Dep. Chm. 1967; Chm. and Chief Exec., 1971–79; Dir, Serck Ltd, 1971, Dep. Chm., 1974, Chm., 1976–81; Director: Burmah Oil Co,. 1975–85; Ductile Steels Ltd, 1977–82. Mem., Midlands Adv. Bd, Legal and General Assurance Soc. Ltd, 1977–84. Chm., Ironbridge Gorge Develt Trust, 1976–78. Life Governor, Birmingham Univ., 1970–85. *Recreations:* golf, sailing, ski-ing. *Club:* East India, Devonshire, Sports and Public Schools.

MARTIN, Roger John Adam; HM Diplomatic Service; Counsellor and Deputy High Commissioner, Harare, since 1983; *b* 21 Jan. 1941; *s* of late Geoffrey (Richard Rex) Martin and of Hazel (*née* Matthews); *m* 1972, Ann Cornwell (*née* Sharp); one *s. Educ:* Westminster School; Brasenose College, Oxford (BA). VSO, Northern Rhodesia, 1959–60; Commonwealth Office, 1964–66; Second Sec., Djakarta, 1967, Saigon, 1968–70; First Sec., FCO, 1971–74, Geneva, 1975–79; seconded to Dept of Trade, as Head of Middle East/North Africa Br., 1981–83. *Recreations:* walking, ski-ing, archaeology, music. *Address:* Coxley House, Coxley, near Wells, Somerset. *T:* Wells 72180.

MARTIN, Ronald, MBE 1945; *b* 7 Nov. 1919; *o s* of late Albert and Clara Martin; *m* 1943, Bettina, *o d* of late H. E. M. Billing; one *d. Educ:* St Olave's Grammar Sch. Asst Traffic Superintendent, GPO, 1939. Served War of 1939–45, Royal Signals, NW Europe. GPO: Asst Princ., 1948; Princ., 1950; Treasury, 1954; Princ. Private Sec. to PMG, 1955; Staff Controller, GPO, London, 1956; Asst Sec., 1957; Dir Establishments and Organisation, GPO, 1966; Dir Telecommunications Personnel, 1967; Dir of Marketing, Telecommunications HQ, 1968–75; Sen. Dir, Customer Services, 1975–79. *Recreations:* music, motoring, horology. *Address:* 23 Birch Close, Send, Woking, Surrey GU23 7BZ.

MARTIN, (Roy) Peter, MBE 1970; author; *b* 5 Jan. 1931; *s* of Walter Martin and Annie Mabel Martin; *m* 1st, 1951, Marjorie Peacock (marr. diss. 1960); 2nd, Joan Drumwright (marr. diss. 1977); two *s*; 3rd, 1978, Catherine Sydee. *Educ:* Highbury Grammar Sch.; Univ. of London (BA 1953, MA 1956); Univ. of Tübingen. Nat. Service (RAF Educn Branch), 1949–51. Worked as local govt officer, schoolteacher and tutor in adult educn; then as British Council officer, 1960–83; service in Indonesia, Hungary (Cultural Attaché) and Japan (Cultural Counsellor). *Publications:* (with Joan Martin) Japanese Cooking, 1970; (as James Melville): The Wages of Zen, 1979; The Chrysanthemum Chain, 1980; A Sort of Samurai, 1981; The Ninth Netsuke, 1982; Sayonara, Sweet Amaryllis, 1983; Death of a Daimyo, 1984; The Death Ceremony, 1985; Go Gently Gaijin, 1986. *Recreations:* music, things Japanese. *Address:* c/o Curtis Brown, 162–168 Regent Street, W1R 5TB. *Club:* Travellers'.

MARTIN, Rupert Claude, MA; JP; *b* 2 July 1905; *s* of late Col C. B. Martin, CMG; *m* 1931, Ellen (*d* 1966), *d* of Henry Wood, Guernsey, CI; one *s* two *d. Educ:* Shrewsbury Sch.; Queen's Coll., Oxford (Classical Scholar), 2nd Class in Greats, 1927; Asst Master at St Paul's Sch., 1927–37; House Master, 1930–37; Headmaster of King's Sch., Bruton, Som., 1937–46, Governor, 1949–; representative of British Council in Switzerland, 1946–48; Headmaster, St Dunstan's, Burnham-on-Sea, 1948–66. Vice-Chm., Incorporated Assoc. of Preparatory Schs, 1957. *Publications:* (Lands and Peoples Series) Switzerland; Italy; Spain; Morocco; Looking at Italy; Looking at Spain. *Recreations:* mountaineering, travel. *Address:* Quantocks, Burnham on Sea, Som. *Clubs:* MCC, I Zingari, Free Foresters, Alpine; Vincent's, Authentics (Oxford).

MARTIN, Samuel Frederick Radcliffe, CB 1979; First Legislative Draftsman, 1973–79; *b* 2 May 1918; 2nd *s* of late William and Margaret Martin; *m* 1947, Sarah, *y d* of late Rev. Joseph and Margaret McKane; three *s. Educ:* Royal Belfast Academical Instn; Queen's Univ., Belfast (LLB). Called to Bar, Gray's Inn, 1950. Examr, Estate Duty Office, NI, 1939; Professional Asst, Office of Parly Draftsmen, 1956. Legal Adviser to Examiner of Statutory Rules, NI, 1979–81; Asst Comr, Local Govt Boundaries' Commn, 1983–84. Northern Ireland Editor, Current Law. *Publications:* articles in NI Legal Qly and Gazette of Incorp. Law Soc. *Recreation:* golf. *Address:* Brynburn, 196 Upper Road, Greenisland, Co. Antrim. *T:* Whiteabbey 62417.

MARTIN, Sir Sidney (Launcelot), Kt 1979; FRSC; Pro Vice-Chancellor, University of the West Indies, and Principal, Cave Hill Campus, 1964–83, retired; *b* 27 Sept. 1918; *s* of Sidney A. Martin and Miriam A. Martin (*née* McIntosh); *m* 1944, Olga Brett (*née* Dolphin); three *s. Educ:* Wolmers Boys' Sch., Jamaica (Jamaica schol. 1937); Royal College of Science, Imperial Coll. London, 1938–42 (BScChem, ARCS, DIC; Fellow, 1981); MSc London. FRIC 1949 (ARIC 1940). Materials Research Laboratory, Phillips Electrical Ltd, Surrey, 1942; Head. Phys. Chem. Div., 1946–49; University College of the West Indies, later University of the West Indies: Lectr, 1949–52, Sen. Lectr, 1952–63, in Phys. Chem.; Warden, Taylor Hall, 1954–64; Acting Registrar, on secondment, 1961–63; Registrar, 1963–66; Principal, Cave Hill, and Pro Vice-Chancellor on secondment, 1964–66, substantively, 1966–83; Hon. LLD Univ. of West Indies, 1984. Chairman: Sci. Res. Council of Jamaica, 1961–64; Barbados Nat. Council for Sci. and Technology, 1977–84; Member: Bd of Management, Coll. of Arts, Sci. and Technology, Jamaica, 1958–64; Educnl Adv. Cttee, Jamaica, 1960–64; Public Services Commn of Barbados, 1964–69; Bd of Management, Codrington Coll., Barbados, 1969–84. Member: Faraday Soc., London, 1943–68; Chemical Soc., London, 1942–; RSA, 1972–. Queen's Silver Jubilee Medal, 1977. *Publications:* articles in various chemical and physical jls. *Recreations:* bridge, reading. *Address:* c/o University of the West Indies, Cave Hill Campus, PO Box 64, Barbados. *T:* 51310.

MARTIN, Thomas Ballantyne; b 1901; s of late Angus Martin, FRCSE, Newcastle upon Tyne, and Robina, d of Thomas Pringle, Middleton Hall, Wooler, Northumberland; m 1953, Jean Elisabeth, e d of Lt-Col O. D. Bennett and Audrey, d of Sir Hamilton Grant, 12th Bt of Dalvey; two d. Educ: Cambridge Univ. (MA). MP (C) Blaydon Div. of Co. Durham, 1931–35. Political Correspondent of Daily Telegraph, 1937–40. RAFVR; Squadron Leader, Middle East Intelligence Centre, 1940–43; Adviser on Public Relations to UK High Comr in Australia, 1943–45; Sec. of United Europe Movement, 1947–48; Sec. to British all-party delegn to Congress of Europe at The Hague. Mem., London Stock Exchange, 1949–74, retired. Address: Noad's House, Tilshead, Salisbury, Wilts SP3 4RY. T: Shrewton 620258. Clubs: Army and Navy, Pratt's.

MARTIN, (Thomas) Geoffrey; Head of European Community's Press and Information Services, South East Asia, since 1985; b 26 July 1940; s of Thomas Martin and Saidee Adelaide (née Day); m 1968, Gay (Madeleine Annesley) Brownrigg; one s two d. Educ: Queen's Univ., Belfast (BSc Hons). President, National Union of Students of England, Wales and Northern Ireland, 1966–68; City of London: Banking, Shipping, 1968–73; Director, Shelter, 1973–74; Diplomatic Staff, Commonwealth Secretariat, 1974–79; Head of EC Office, NI, 1979–85. Address: Commission of the European Communities, Delegation in South East Asia, Thai Military Bank Building, 34 Phya Thai Road, Bangkok, Thailand. Club: Travellers'.

MARTIN, Victor Cecil, OBE; HM Diplomatic Service, retired; b 12 Oct. 1915; s of late Cecil Martin and Isabel Katherine Martin (née Hickman). Educ: Cheltenham Coll.; Jesus Coll., Cambridge (Scholar; Classical Tripos Parts 1 and 2; MA). Asst Principal, Board of Education, 1939. Served Intelligence Corps, 1940–45; Major 1944, Persia and Iraq Force. Principal, Min. of Education, 1946; transferred to CRO, 1948; British High Commn, New Delhi, 1951–54, 1956–60; Asst Sec., CRO, 1962; Head of West Africa Dept, 1961–64; Head of S Asia Dept, 1964–66; Head of Cultural Relations Dept, 1966–68; Dep. High Comr, Madras, 1968–71; Special Adviser to High Comr, British High Commn, New Delhi, 1972–75. Recreations: ornithology, travel. Address: 76 Swan Court, Flood Street, SW3. Clubs: United Oxford & Cambridge University, Royal Commonwealth Society.

MARTIN, William McChesney, Jun.; Counselor, Riggs National Bank, Washington, DC, since 1970; b St Louis, Mo, 17 Dec. 1906; s of William McChesney Martin and Rebecca (née Woods); m 1942, Cynthia Davis; one s two d. Educ: Yale Univ. (BA 1928); Benton Coll. of Law, St Louis, 1931. Graduate student (part time), Columbia Univ., 1931–37. Served in bank examination dept of Federal Reserve Bank of St Louis, 1928–29; Head of statistics dept, A. G. Edwards & Sons, St Louis, 1929–31; partner, May 1931–July 1938. Mem., New York Stock Exch., June 1931–July 1938; Gov., 1935–38; Chm. Cttee on Constitution, 1937–38; Sec. Conway Cttee to reorganize the Exchange, 1937–38; Chm. Bd and Pres. pro. tem. May-June 1938; Pres. July 1938–April 1941. Asst Exec. President's Soviet Protocol Cttee and Munitions Assignments Board, Wash., DC, 1942; appointed Mem. Export-Import Bank, Nov. 1945; Chm. and Pres., 1946–49 (as Chm. of Federal Reserve Board, serves on National Advisory Council on Internat. Monetary and Financial Problems). Asst Sec. of the Treasury, Feb. 1949–April 1951; Chm., Bd of Governors, Fed. Reserve System, 1951–70; US Exec. Dir, IBRD, 1949–52. Dir of several corporations. Trustee: Berry Schs, Atlanta, Ga; Johns Hopkins Univ., Baltimore; Nat. Geographic Soc. Holds numerous Hon. Degrees from Univs in USA and Canada. Drafted, Selective Service Act, private, US Army, 1941, Sergeant, GHQ Army War Coll., 1941; Commnd 1st Lt, Inf., Feb. 1942; Captain Aug. 1942; Major, 1943; Lt-Col 1944; Col 1945. Legion of Merit, 1945. Recreations: tennis, squash. Address: 2861 Woodland Drive, NW, Washington, DC 20008, USA; (office) 888 17th Street, NW, Washington, DC 20006, USA. Clubs: West Side Tennis, Yale; Metropolitan, Jefferson Island, Alibi (Washington); Chevy Chase (Md).

MARTIN-BATES, James Patrick, MA; JP; FCIS; CBIM; Director: Atkins Holdings Ltd; Avery's Ltd, 1970–77; Charringtons Industrial Holdings Ltd, 1972–77; Hutchinson Ltd, 1958–78; b 17 April 1912; er s of late R. Martin-Bates, JP, Perth, Scotland; m 1939, Clare, d of late Prof. James Miller, MD, DSc; one s two d. Educ: Perth Academy; Glenalmond; Worcester Coll., Oxford. BA 1933; MA 1944. Lamson Industries, 1933–36; Dorman Long & Co. Ltd, 1936–38; PE Group, 1938–61: Man. Dir, Production Engineering Ltd, 1953–59; Vice-Chm., PE Holdings, 1959–61. Principal, Administrative Staff Coll., Henley-on-Thames, 1961–72. Chm., Management Consultants Association, 1960; Member: Council, British Institute of Management, 1961–66; UK Advisory Council on Education for Management, 1961–66; Council, Glenalmond, 1963–82; Bd of Visitors, HM Borstal, Huntercombe, 1964–67; The Council for Technical Education and Training for Overseas Countries, 1962–73; Council, University Coll., Nairobi, 1965–68; Council, Chartered Institute of Secretaries, 1965–74; EDC for Rubber Industry, 1965–69; Council, Univ. of Buckingham (formerly University Coll. at Buckingham), 1977–. Governor, Aylesbury Grammar Sch., 1983–. UN Consultant in Iran, 1972–78. High Sheriff of Buckinghamshire, 1974; Chm., Marlow Bench, 1978–82. FCIS 1961; FBIM 1960; Fellow Internat. Acad. of Management, 1964. DUniv Buckingham, 1986. Burnham Medal, BIM, 1974. Publications: various articles in Management Journals. Recreations: golf, fishing. Address: Ivy Cottage, Fingest, near Henley-on-Thames, Oxon RG9 6QD. T: Turville Heath 202. Clubs: Caledonian; Leander; Royal and Ancient (St Andrews).

MARTIN-BIRD, Col Sir Richard Dawnay, Kt 1975; CBE 1971 (OBE (mil.) 1953); TD 1950; DL; Chairman and Joint Managing Director, Yates Brothers Wine Lodges Ltd, Manchester; b 19 July 1910; s of late Richard Martin Bird and Mildred, 2nd d of late Peter Peel Yates; m 1935, Katharine Blanche, d of Sir Arthur Selborne Jelf, CMG; one s three d (and one s decd). Educ: Charterhouse. Served with 8th (Ardwick) Bn, The Manchester Regt (TA), 1936–53; war service 1939–45; Lt-Col comdg, 1947–53; Hon. Col, 1953–67; Hon. Col, The Manchester Regt (Ardwick and Ashton) Territorials, 1967–71; Dep. Comdr, 127 Inf. Bde (TA), 1953–57 and 1959–63; Regtl Councillor, The King's Regt, 1967–; ADC (TA) to the Queen, 1961–65; Chairman: E Lancs T&AFA, 1963–68; TA&VRA for Lancs, Cheshire and IoM, later TA&VRA for NW England and IoM, 1968–75; Vice-Chm., Council, TA&AVR Assocs, 1973–75; Mem., TAVR Adv. Cttee, 1973–75. Pres., Wine and Spirit Assoc. of GB, 1978–79. DL Lancs 1964–74, Cheshire 1974; High Sheriff Greater Manchester, 1976–82. Address: Stockinwood, Chelford, Cheshire SK11 9BE. T: Chelford 523. Clubs: Army and Navy; St James's (Manchester); Winckley (Preston).

MARTIN-JENKINS, Christopher Dennis Alexander; Editor, The Cricketer International, since 1981; cricket correspondent, BBC; b 20 Jan. 1945; s of Dennis Frederick Martin-Jenkins, qv; m 1971, Judith Oswald Hayman; two s one d. Educ: Marlborough; Fitzwilliam Coll., Cambridge (BA (Modern Hist.); MA). Dep. Editor, The Cricketer, 1967–70; Sports Broadcaster, 1970–73; Cricket Correspondent, 1973–80, 1984–, BBC. Publications: Testing Time, 1974; Assault on the Ashes, 1975; MCC in India, 1977; The Jubilee Tests and the Packer Revolution, 1977; In Defence of the Ashes, 1979; Cricket Contest, 1980; The Complete Who's Who of Test Cricketers, 1980; The Wisden Book of County Cricket, 1981; Bedside Cricket, 1981; Twenty Years On: cricket's years of change, 1984; Cricket: a way of life, 1984; (ed) Cricketer Book of Cricket Eccentrics, 1985; (ed) Seasons Past, 1986. Recreations: cricket, Rugby fives, tennis, golf, gardening, walking. Address: The Cricketer, 29 Cavendish Road, Redhill, Surrey RH1 4AH. T: Redhill 72217. Clubs: Eccentric, MCC; I Zingari, Free Foresters, Arabs, Marlborough Blues, Cranleigh Cricket, Albury Cricket, Rudgwick Cricket, Horsham Cricket, Surrey Cricket.

MARTIN-JENKINS, Dennis Frederick, TD 1945; Chairman, Ellerman Lines Ltd, 1967–81 (Managing Director, 1967–76); chairman or director of many other companies; b 7 Jan. 1911; 2nd s of late Frederick Martin-Jenkins, CA and late Martha Magdalene Martin-Jenkins (née Almeida); m 1937, Rosemary Clare Walker, MRCS, LRCP; three s. Educ: St Bede's Sch., Eastbourne; Marlborough College. FCIT. Served RA, 1939–45 (Lt-Col). Insce, 1930–35; joined Montgomerie & Workman Ltd, 1935; transf. City Line Ltd, 1938; transf. Hall Line Ltd, 1947 (Dir 1949); Dir, Ellerman Lines Ltd and associated cos, 1950. Chamber of Shipping of UK: Mem. 1956 (Hon. Mem., 1975); Vice-Pres. 1964; Pres. 1965; Chm., Deep Sea Liner Section, 1969–76; Chairman: Gen. Council of British Shipping for UK, 1963; Internat. Chamber of Shipping, 1971–77; Past Chm., London Gen. Shipowners' Soc.; formerly Member: Mersey Docks and Harbour Bd; Bd of PLA; Nat. Dock Labour Bd; Exec. Cttee, Nat. Assoc. of Port Employers; Mem., British Transport Docks Bd, 1968–81. Recreations: golf, gardening. Address: Wragmoor, Bantham, Kingsbridge, S Devon TQ7 3AJ. T: Kingsbridge 560427. Clubs: United Oxford & Cambridge University; Woking Golf, Royal Cinque Ports Golf, Thurlestone Golf.
See also C. D. A. Martin-Jenkins.

MARTINDALE, Air Vice-Marshal Alan Rawes, CB 1984; FBIM, FIPDM; Royal Air Force, retired; District General Manager, Hastings Health Authority, since 1985; b 20 Jan. 1930; s of late Norman Martindale and Edith (née Rawes); m 1952, Eileen Alma Wrenn; three d. Educ: Kendal Grammar Sch.; University Coll., Leicester (BA History, London Univ., 1950). Commissioned RAF, 1951; served, 1951–71: RAF Driffield, Oakington, Eindhoven, Stafford, Wickenby, Faldingworth and Marham; Instructor, RAF Coll., Cranwell; Staff AHQ Malta; RAF Staff Coll., Bracknell, MoD, Jt Services Staff Coll. (student and Directing Staff), and HQ Maintenance Comd; Dep. Dir of Supply Management, MoD, Harrogate, 1971–72; Comd Supply Officer, RAF Germany, 1972–74; Dir of Supply Management, MoD, Harrogate, 1974–75; RCDS, 1976; Air Cdre Supply and Movements, RAF Support Comd, 1977; Dep. Gen. Man., NAMMA, 1978–81; Dir of Supply Policy (RAF), MoD, 1981–82; Dir Gen. of Supply (RAF), 1982–84; retd 1985. Recreations: shooting, gardening, mountain walking, squash. Address: Taylors Cottage, Mountfield, Robertsbridge, East Sussex TN32 5JZ. Club: Royal Air Force.

MARTINEAU, Charles Herman; Chairman, Electricity Consultative Council for South of Scotland, 1972–76; b 3 Sept. 1908; s of Prof. Charles E. Martineau, Birmingham; m 1939, Margaret Shirley Dolphin; two s one d. Educ: King Edward's Sch., Birmingham. Jas Williamson & Son Ltd, Lancaster and Nairn-Williamson Ltd, Kirkcaldy: Man. Dir, 1952–66. Part-time Mem., S of Scotland Electricity Bd, 1971–76. Mem., Fife CC, 1967 (Vice-Convener, 1970–73); Mem., Fife Regional Council, 1978–82. Recreations: chess, golf. Address: Gladsmuir, Hepburn Gardens, St Andrews, Fife. T: St Andrews 73069. Club: Royal and Ancient (St Andrews).
See also Rt Rev. R. A. S. Martineau.

MARTINEAU, Rt. Rev. Robert Arnold Schürhoff, MA; b 22 Aug. 1913; s of late Prof. C. E. Martineau, MA, MCom, FCA, and Mrs Martineau, Birmingham; m 1941, Elinor Gertrude Ap-Thomas; one s two d. Educ: King Edward's Sch., Birmingham; Trinity Hall, Cambridge; Westcott House, Cambridge. Tyson Medal for Astronomy, 1935. Deacon 1938, priest 1939; Curate, Melksham, 1938–41. Chaplain: RAFVR, 1941–46; RAuxAF, 1947–52. Vicar: Ovenden, Halifax, 1946–52; Allerton, Liverpool, 1952–66; St Christopher, San Lorenzo, Calif, 1961–62. Hon. Canon of Liverpool, 1961–66; Rural Dean of Childwall, 1964–66. Proctor in Convocation, 1964–66. Bishop Suffragan of Huntingdon, 1966–72; Residentiary Canon of Ely, 1966–72; Bishop of Blackburn, 1972–81. First Jt Chm., C of E Bd of Educn and Nat. Soc. for Promoting Religious Educn, 1973–79. Chm., Central Readers Bd, C of E, 1971–76. Publications: The Church in Germany in Prayer (ed jtly), 1937; Rhodesian Wild Flowers, 1953; The Office and Work of a Reader, 1970; The Office and Work of a Priest, 1972; Moments that Matter, 1976; Preaching through the Christian Year; Truths that Endure, 1977; Travelling with Christ, 1981. Recreations: gardening, swimming. Address: Gwenallt, Park Street, Denbigh, Clwyd LL16 3DB.
See also C. H. Martineau.

MARTINEZ ZUVIRIA, Gen. Gustavo; historian; Argentine Ambassador to the Court of St James's, 1970–74; b 28 Dec. 1915; s of Dr Gustavo Martinez Zuviria and Matilde de Iriondo de Martinez Zuviria; m 1940, Maria Eugenia Ferrer Deheza; five s four d (and one s decd). Educ: Col. El Salvador, Buenos Aires; Mount St Mary's Coll. (Nr Sheffield); San Martin Mil. Academy. Promoted to 2nd Lt, 1938; Capt. 1951. He participated in attempt to overthrow the Peron regime; imprisoned, but when Peron was overthrown, he continued career in Army; among other posts he served in: Cavalry Regt No 12, 1940; Granaderos a Caballo, 1944; Cavalry Regt No 7, 1945; Military Sch.: Instr of cadets, 1944; Asst Dir and Dir of Sch., 1958. Mil. Attaché to Peru, 1955; Chief of 3rd Regt of Cavalry, 1957; Chief of Staff, Argentine Cav. Corps, 1961; Dir, in Superior War Staff Coll., 1962; Dir, Sch. of Cav. and Cav. Inspector, 1963; Comdr, 2nd Cav. Div., 1964; 2nd Comdr, 3rd Army Corps, 1965; Comdr, 1st Army Corps, 1966; Comdr, Southern Joint Forces, 1969; retd from Army and was designated Sec. of State in Intelligence (Secretario de Informaciones de Estado), in 1970. Presidente dela Comisión de Caballería, 1974–76. Member: Genealogical Studies Centre, 1962; Nat. Sanmartinian Historical Academy, 1966; Nat. Acad. of History, 1978. Lectured in Paris and Brussels, Feb. 1978, on bicentenary of birth of Gen. San Martín. Holds several foreign orders. Publications: numerous (related to professional and historical subjects); notably Los tiempos de Mariano Necochea, 1961 (2nd edn, 1969) (1st award mil. lit. and award Fundación Eguiguren); Retreta del Desierto, 1956 (14 edns); José Pidsudski; San Martin y O'Brien, 1963; Historia de Angel Pacheco, 1969. Recreations: riding, shooting. Address: Avenida del Libertador 15249, 1640 Acassuso, Buenos Aires, Argentina. Clubs: Naval and Military, Travellers', Hurlingham, Turf (all in London); Cowdray Park Polo (Sussex); Circulo Militar, Jockey (Buenos Aires); Club Social de Paraná (Entre Rios).

MARTINS, (Virgilio) Armando; Ambassador; Professor, Institute of Oriental Studies, University of Lisbon, since 1980; b 1 Sept. 1914; s of José Júlio Martins and Elvira Janeiro; m 1959, Ingrid Bloser; one s one d. Educ: Coimbra and Lisbon Univs. Degree in Law. Entered Foreign Service, 1939; Attaché, Foreign Min., Lisbon, 1941; Consul: Leopoldville, 1943; Liverpool, 1947; Sydney, 1949; special mission, NZ, 1951; First Sec., Tokyo, 1952; Brussels, 1955; Substitute of Permanent Rep. to NATO, 1956; Minister, 2nd Cl., Foreign Min., Lisbon, 1959; NATO, 1961; Ambassador to: Tokyo, 1964; Rome, 1971; the Court of St James's, 1977–79. Publications: books on internat. law, social questions, literary criticism, history, poetry, and the theatre. Recreations: oriental studies reading, writing. Address: 40 Avenida de Portugal, 2765 Estoril, Portugal.

MARTONMERE, 1st Baron, *cr* 1964; **John Roland Robinson,** PC 1962; GBE 1973; KCMG 1966; Kt 1954; MA, LLB; Governor and C-in-C of Bermuda, 1964–72; *b* 22 Feb. 1907; *e s* of Roland Walkden Robinson, Solicitor, Blackpool; *m* 1930, Maysie, *d* of late Clarence Warren Gasque; one *d* (one *s* decd). *Educ:* Trinity Hall, Cambridge. Barrister-at-law, 1929 (Certificate of Honour and Buchanan Prize Lincoln's Inn, 1928); MP (U) Widnes Division of Lancs, 1931–35, Blackpool, 1935–45, S Blackpool, 1945–64. W/Cdr RAFVR, 1940–45. Pres. Royal Lancs Agricultural Society, 1936; Past Pres. Assoc. of Health and Pleasure Resorts; Past Pres. Residential Hotels Assoc. of Great Britain. Past Chm. Conservative Party Commonwealth Affairs Cttee; Chm. Gen. Council, Commonwealth Parliamentary Assoc., 1961–62. Past Dep. Chm. United Kingdom Branch, Commonwealth Parliamentary Association. Hon. Freeman, Town of St George and City of Hamilton (Bermuda). Officer, Legion of Merit (USA). *Heir: g s* John Stephen Robinson, *b* 10 July 1963. *Address:* Romay House, Tuckers Town, Bermuda; El Mirador, Lyford Cay, PO Box 7776, Nassau, Bahamas. *Clubs:* Carlton; Royal Lytham and St Annes Golf (St Annes); Royal Yacht Squadron (Cowes); Lyford Cay (Bahamas); Hon. Life Member: Royal Bermuda Yacht, Mid-Ocean (Bermuda).

MARTY, Cardinal François, Chevalier de la Légion d'honneur; *b* Pachins, Aveyron, 18 May 1904; *s* of François Marty, cultivateur, and Zoé (*née* Gineste). *Educ:* Collège de Graves et Villefranche-de-Rouergue; Séminaire de Rodez; Institut Catholique de Toulouse (Dr en Th.). Priest, 1930. Vicaire: Villefranche-de-Rouergue, 1932; Rodez, 1933; Parish Priest: Bournazel, 1940; Rieupeyroux, 1943; Archpriest, Millau, 1949; Vicar-General, Rodez, 1951; Bishop of Saint Flour, 1952; Coadjutor Archbishop, 1959, and Archbishop of Reims, 1960; Archbishop of Paris, 1968–81. Cardinal, 1969. Pres., Comité Episcopal of Mission de France, 1965; Mem. Bureau, then Vice-Pres., Perm. Council of French Episcopate, 1966, and Pres., French Episcopal Conf., 1969–75, responsable des Catholiques orientaux. Member: Rome Commission for Revision of Canon Law; Congregations: Divine Worship; Clergy; Eastern Church. *Address:* Monteils, 12200 Villefranche de Rouergue, France.

MARTYN, Charles Roger Nicholas; Master of the Supreme Court, since 1973; *b* 10 Dec. 1925; *s* of Rev. Charles Martyn; *m* 1960, Helen, *d* of Frank Everson; two *s* one *d*. *Educ:* Charterhouse, 1939–44; Merton Coll., Oxford, 1947–49. MA (Hons) Mod. Hist. Joined Regular Army, 1944; commissioned 60th Rifles (KRRC), 1945; CMF, 1946–47; special release, 1947. Articles, 1950–52, and admitted as solicitor, 1952. Sherwood & Co., Parly Agents (Partner), 1952–59; Lee, Bolton & Lee, Westminster (Partner), 1961–73; Notary Public, 1969. Mem. and Dep. Chm., No 14 Legal Aid Area Cttee, 1967–73; Hon. Legal Adviser to The Samaritans (Inc), 1955–73. Chm., Family Welfare Assoc., 1973–78; Member: Gtr London Citizens' Advice Bureaux Management Cttee, 1974–79; Council, St Gabriel's Coll. (Further Education), Camberwell, 1973–77 (Vice-Chm); Goldsmiths' Coll. Delegacy, 1977–. *Recreations:* walking, sailing (Vice-Cdre, Thames Barge Sailing Club, 1962–65), observing people, do-it-yourself, nigrology. *Address:* 29 St Albans Road, NW5 1RG. *T:* 01-267 1076.

MARTYN, Joan, OBE 1962; Governor Class II, HM Prison Commission; Governor, Bullwood Hall, 1962–64, retired; *b* 9 Aug. 1899; 3rd *d* of George Harold and Eve Martyn. *Educ:* Municipal Coll., Grimsby; Queenwood, Eastbourne; Bedford Physical Training Coll. (diploma). Staff of St Mary's Coll., Lancaster Gate, London, W2, 1919–36; staff of HM Borstal Institution, Aylesbury, 1937 (Governor 1946–59); Governor, HM Borstal, Cardiff, 1959–62. *Address:* 57 Bargate, Grimsby, S Humberside.

MARTYN-HEMPHILL, family name of **Baron Hemphill.**

MARWICK, Prof. Arthur John Brereton, FRHistS; Professor of History, The Open University, since 1969; *b* 29 Feb. 1936; *s* of William Hutton Marwick and Maeve Cluna Brereton; unmarried; one *d*. *Educ:* George Heriot's School, Edinburgh; Edinburgh Univ. (MA, DLitt); Balliol Coll., Oxford (BLitt). Asst Lectr in History, Univ. of Aberdeen, 1959–60; Lectr in History, Univ. of Edinburgh, 1960–69; Dean and Dir of Studies in Arts, Open Univ., 1978–84. Vis. Prof. in History, State Univ. of NY at Buffalo, 1966–67; Vis. Scholar, Hoover Instn and Vis. Prof., Stanford Univ., 1984–85; Directeur d'études invité, l'Ecole des Hautes Etudes en Sciences Sociales, Paris, 1985. *Publications:* The Explosion of British Society, 1963; Clifford Allen, 1964; The Deluge, 1965; Britain in the Century of Total War, 1968; The Nature of History, 1970; War and Social Change in the Twentieth Century, 1974; The Home Front, 1976; Women at War 1914–1918, 1977; Class: image and reality in Britain, France and USA since 1930, 1980; (ed) Illustrated Dictionary of British History, 1980; British Society since 1945, 1982; Britain in Our Century, 1984; (ed) Class in the Twentieth Century, 1986; contribs to English Hist. Review, Amer. Hist. Review, Jl of Contemporary Hist. *Recreations:* wine, women, football. *Address:* 67 Fitzjohns Avenue, Hampstead, NW3 6PE. *T:* 01–794 4534. *Clubs:* Open University Football, Open University Tennis.

MARWICK, Sir Brian (Allan), KBE 1963 (CBE 1954; OBE 1946); CMG 1958; *b* 18 June 1908; *s* of James Walter Marwick and Elizabeth Jane Flett; *m* 1934, Riva Lee, *d* of Major H. C. Cooper; two *d*. *Educ:* University of Cape Town; CCC, Cambridge. Administrative Officer: Swaziland, 1925–36; Nigeria, 1937–40; Swaziland, 1941–46; First Asst Sec.: Swaziland, 1947–48; Basutoland, 1949–52; Dep. Resident Comr and Govt Sec., Basutoland, 1952–55; Administrative Sec. to High Comr for Basutoland, the Bechuanaland Protectorate and Swaziland, 1956; Resident Comr, Swaziland, 1957–63; HM Comr, Swaziland, 1963–64; Permanent Secretary: Min. of Works and Town Planning Dept, Nassau, Bahamas, 1965–68; Min. of Educn, Bahamas, 1968–71. *Publication:* The Swazi, 1940. *Recreation:* golf. *Address:* Sea Bank, Shore Road, Castletown, Isle of Man. *T:* Castletown 823782.

MARX, Enid Crystal Dorothy, RDI 1944; Painter and Designer; *b* London, 20 Oct. 1902; *y d* of Robert J. Marx. *Educ:* Roedean Sch.; Central Sch. of Arts and Crafts; Royal College of Art Painting Sch. Designing and printing handblock printed textiles, 1925–39. Exhibited in USA and Europe; various works purchased by Victoria and Albert Museum, Musée des Arts Décoratifs, Boston Museum, Scottish Arts Council, Sheffield Art Gall., etc. Mem. Society of Wood Engravers. Wood engraving and autolithography pattern papers, book jackets, book illustration and decorations, trademarks, etc; designed moquettes and posters for LPTB. Industrial designing for printed and woven furnishing fabrics, wallpapers, ceramics, plastics. Fellow, RCA, 1982, FRSA, FSIAD; original mem. National Register of Industrial Designers of Central Institute of Art and Design. Mem. of Bd of Trade design panel on utility furniture. Designed postage stamps: ½d-2d for first issue Elizabeth II; Christmas 1976 issue. Lectures on textiles and folk art. *Publications:* (jointly) English Popular and Traditional Art, 1947; (with Margaret Lambert), English Popular Art, 1951; articles and broadcasts on aspects of industrial design in various countries; author and illustrator of twelve books for children. *Recreations:* study of popular art in different countries; gardening. *Address:* The Studio, 39 Thornhill Road, Barnsbury Square, N1. *T:* 01–607 2286.

MARY LEO, Sister; *see* Leo, Dame Sister Mary.

MARYCHURCH, Sir Peter (Harvey), KCMG 1985; Director, Government Communications Headquarters, since 1983; *b* 13 June 1927; *s* of Eric William Alfred and Dorothy Margaret Marychurch; *m* 1965, June Daphne Ottaway (*née* Pareezer). *Educ:* Lower School of John Lyon, Harrow. Served RAF, 1945–48. Joined GCHQ, 1948; Asst Sec. 1975; Under Sec. 1979; Dep. Sec. 1983. *Recreations:* theatre, music (especially opera), gardening. *Address:* Government Communications Headquarters, Priors Road, Cheltenham, Glos. *Club:* Naval and Military.

MARYON DAVIS, Dr Alan Roger, FFCM; Chief Medical Officer, Health Education Council, since 1984; Hon. Senior Lecturer in Community Medicine, St Mary's Hospital Medical School, since 1985; Hon. Consultant, Paddington and North Kensington Health Authority, since 1985; *b* 21 Jan. 1943; *s* of Cyril Edward Maryon Davis and Hilda May Maryon Davis; one *s*; *m* 1981, Glynis Anne Davies; two *d*. *Educ:* St Paul's Sch.; St John's Coll., Cambridge (MA 1968; MB BChir 1970); St Thomas's Hosp. Med. Sch.; London Sch. of Hygiene and Tropical Medicine. MSc (Social Med.) London 1978; MRCP 1972, FFCM 1986. Early med. career in gen. medicine and rheumatology, later in community medicine; MO, Health Educn Council, 1977–84. Regular broadcaster on health matters, 1975–; BBC radio series: Action Makes the Heart Grow Stronger (Med. Journalist's Assoc. Radio Award), 1983; Back in 25 Minutes, 1985; Not Another Diet Programme, 1986; *television series:* Your Mind in Their Hands, 1982; Consider Yourself, 1983; Body Matters, 1985, 1986; Save a Life, 1986. *Publications:* Family Health and Fitness, 1981; Body Facts, 1984; (with J. Thomas) Diet 2000, 1984. *Recreations:* eating well, drinking well, singing (not so well) with the humorous group Instant Sunshine. *Address:* 33 Lillieshall Road, Old Town, Clapham, SW4 0LN. *T:* 01-720 5659.

MASCALL, Rev. Canon Eric Lionel, DD Oxon, DD Cantab, BSc London; FBA 1974; an Hon. Canon of Truro Cathedral, with duties of Canon Theologian, 1973–84, now Canon Emeritus; Professor of Historical Theology, London University, at King's College, 1962–73, now Professor Emeritus; Dean, Faculty of Theology, London University, 1968–72; *b* 12 Dec. 1905; *s* of John R. S. Mascall and S. Lilian Mascall, *née* Grundy; unmarried. *Educ:* Latymer Upper Sch., Hammersmith; Pembroke Coll., Cambridge (Scholar); Theological Coll., Ely. BSc (London) 1926; BA (Wrangler) 1927, MA 1931, BD 1943, DD 1958 Cantab; DD Oxon, 1948. Sen. Maths Master, Bablake Sch., Coventry, 1928–31; ordained, 1932; Mem., Oratory of the Good Shepherd, 1938–; Asst Curate, St Andrew's, Stockwell Green, 1932–35; St Matthew's, Westminster, 1935–37; Sub-warden, Scholae Cancellarii, Lincoln, 1937–45; Lecturer in Theology, Christ Ch., Oxford, 1945–46; Student and Tutor of Christ Ch., Oxford, 1946–62, Emeritus Student, 1962–; University Lectr in Philosophy of Religion, 1947–62; Chaplain at Oxford to Bishop of Derby, 1947–48; Commissary to Archbishop of Cape Town, 1964–73; Examining Chaplain to: Bishop of Willesden, 1970–73; Bishop of Truro, 1973–81; Bishop of London, 1981–. Visiting Professor: Gregorian Univ., Rome, 1976; Pontifical Coll. Josephinum, Columbus, Ohio, 1977; Lectures: Bampton, Oxford, 1956; Bampton, Columbia, 1958; Boyle, 1965–66; Charles A. Hart Memorial, Cath. Univ. of America, Washington, DC, 1968; Gifford, Univ. of Edinburgh, 1970–71. FKC, 1968–. Hon. DD St Andrews, 1967. *Publications:* Death or Dogma, 1937; A Guide to Mount Carmel, 1939; Man, his Origin and Destiny, 1940; The God-Man, 1940; He Who Is, 1943, rev. edn 1966; Christ, the Christian and the Church, 1946; Existence and Analogy, 1949; Corpus Christi, 1953, rev. edn 1965; Christian Theology and Natural Science, 1956; Via Media, 1956; Words and Images, 1957; The Recovery of Unity, 1958; The Importance of Being Human, 1958; Pi in the High, 1959; Grace and Glory, 1961; Theology and History (Inaugural Lecture), 1962; Theology and Images, 1963; Up and Down in Adria, 1963; The Secularisation of Christianity, 1965; The Christian Universe, 1966; Theology and The Future, 1968; (jt author) Growing into Union, 1970; The Openness of Being, 1971; Nature and Supernature, 1976; Theology and the Gospel of Christ, 1977, rev. edn 1984; Whatever Happened to the Human Mind, 1980; Jesus: who he is and how we know him, 1985; Compliments of the Season, 1985; The Triune God, 1986; Editor: The Church of God, 1934; The Mother of God, 1949; The Angels of Light and the Powers of Darkness, 1954; The Blessed Virgin Mary, 1963; contribs to: Man, Woman and Priesthood, 1978; When Will Ye Be Wise?, 1983. *Address:* 30 Bourne Street, SW1W 8JJ. *T:* 01–730 2423. *Club:* Athenæum.

MASCHLER, Thomas Michael; Chairman of Jonathan Cape Ltd, since 1970; *b* 16 Aug. 1933; *s* of Kurt Leo Maschler and of Rita Masseron (*née* Lechner); *m* 1970, Fay Coventry; one *s* two *d*. *Educ:* Leighton Park School. Production Asst, Andre Deutsch, 1955; Editor, MacGibbon & Kee, 1956–58; Fiction Editor, Penguin Books, 1958–60; Jonathan Cape: Editorial Dir, 1960; Man. Dir, 1966. Associate Producer, The French Lieutenant's Woman (film), 1981. *Publications:* (ed) Declarations, 1957; (ed) New English Dramatists Series, 1959–63. *Address:* 32 Bedford Square, WC1B 3EL.

MASEFIELD, John Thorold, CMG 1986; HM Diplomatic Service; Head of Far Eastern Department, Foreign and Commonwealth Office, since 1985; *b* 1 Oct. 1939; *e s* of Dr Geoffrey Bussell Masefield, DSc and Mildred Joy Thorold Masefield (*née* Rogers); *m* 1962, Jennifer Mary, *d* of Rev. Dr H. C. Trowell, OBE and late K. M. Trowell, MBE; two *s* one *d* (and one *d* decd). *Educ:* Dragon Sch., Oxford; Repton Sch.; St John's Coll., Cambridge (Scholar) (MA). Joined CRO, 1962; Private Sec. to Permanent Under Sec., 1963–64; Second Secretary: Kuala Lumpur, 1964–65; Warsaw, 1966–67; FCO, 1967–69; First Sec., UK Delegn to Disarmament Conf., 1970–74; Dep. Head, Planning Staff, FCO, 1974–77; Far Eastern Dept, FCO, 1977–79; Counsellor, Head of Chancery and Consul Gen., Islamabad, 1979–82; Head of Personnel Services Dept, FCO, 1982–85. *Recreations:* fruit and vegetables. *Address:* c/o Foreign and Commonwealth Office, SW1A 2AH. *Club:* Royal Commonwealth Society.

MASEFIELD, Sir Peter (Gordon), Kt 1972; MA Cantab; CEng; Hon. FRAeS; FCIT; Chairman, Project Management Ltd, since 1972; Deputy Chairman, British Caledonian Aviation Group Plc, since 1978; Director: Worldwide Estates Ltd, since 1972; Nationwide Building Society, since 1973; *b* Trentham, Staffs, 19 March 1914; *e s* of late Dr W. Gordon Masefield, CBE, MRCS, and Marian A. Masefield (*née* Lloyd-Owen); *m* 1936, Patricia Doreen, 3rd *d* of late Percy H. Rooney, Wallington, Surrey; three *s* one *d*. *Educ:* Westminster Sch.; Chillon Coll., Switzerland; Jesus Coll., Cambridge (BA (Eng) 1935). On Design Staff, The Fairey Aviation Co. Ltd, 1935–37; Pilot's licence, 1937–70; joined The Aeroplane newspaper, 1937, Technical Editor, 1939–43; Air Correspondent Sunday Times, 1940–43; War Corresp. with RAF and US Army Eighth Air Force on active service, 1939–43; Editor, The Aeroplane Spotter, 1941–43; Chm. Editorial Cttee, The Inter-Services Journal on Aircraft Recognition, MAP, 1942–45; Personal Adviser to the Lord Privy Seal (Lord Beaverbrook) and Sec. of War Cabinet Cttee on Post War Civil Air Transport, 1943–45; first British Civil Air Attaché, British Embassy, Washington, DC, 1945–46 (Signator to Anglo-American Bermuda Air Agreement, 1946); Dir-Gen. of Long Term Planning and Projects, Ministry of Civil Aviation, 1946–48; Chief Executive and Mem. of Board of BEA, 1949–55; Managing Dir, Bristol Aircraft Ltd, 1956–60; Man. Dir, Beagle Aircraft Ltd, 1960–67, Chm., 1968–70; Dir, Beagle Aviation Finance Ltd, 1962–71. Chm., British Airports Authority, 1965–71. Chm., Nat. Jt Council for Civil Air Transport, 1950–51; Member: Cairns

Cttee on Aircraft Accident Investigation, 1960; Min. of Aviation Advisory Cttees on Civil Aircraft Control and on Private and Club Flying and Gliding; Aeronautical Research Council, 1958–61; Board, LTE, 1973–82 (Chm., London Transport, 1980–82). Mem., Cambridge Univ. Appointments Bd, 1956–69. Director, Pressed Steel Co. Ltd, 1960–68. RAeS: Chm., Graduates and Students Sect., 1937–39; Mem. Council, 1945–65; Pres., 1959–60; British Commonwealth and Empire Lectr, 1948; RAeS/AFITA Bleriot Meml Lectr, 1966; Pres., Inst. Transport, 1955–56 (Brancker Meml Lectr, 1951, 1967); President: Inst. of Travel Managers, 1967–70; Assoc. of British Aviation Consultants; Chairman: Bd of Trustees, Imperial War Museum, 1977–78; Industry Year, 1986; Littlewood Meml Lectr, Soc. of Automotive Engrs (USA), 1971. Mem. Council, Royal Aero Club (Chm., Aviation Cttee, 1960–65; Chm., 1968–70). Mem., HMS Belfast Trust; Chm., Bd of Governors, Reigate Grammar Sch., 1979–; Governor, Ashridge Management Coll., 1981–. Pres., IRTE, 1979–81. FRSA (Chm. Council, 1977–79; Vice-Pres., 1979–); CBIM. Hon. FAIAA; Hon. FCASI; Hon. DSc Cranfield, 1977; Hon. DTech Loughborough, 1977. Liveryman, Guild of Air Pilots and Air Navigators; Freeman, City of London. *Publications:* To Ride the Storm, 1982; articles on aviation, transport, management, and First World War. *Recreations:* reading, writing, gardening. *Address:* Rosehill, Doods Way, Reigate, Surrey RH2 0JT. *T:* Reigate 42396. *Clubs:* Athenæum, Royal Aero; National Aviation (Washington).

MASERI, Attilio, MD; FRCP; FACC; Sir John McMichael Professor of Cardiovascular Medicine, Royal Postgraduate Medical School, University of London, since 1979; *b* 12 Nov. 1935; *s* of Adriano and Antonietta Albini, Italian nobles; *m* 1960, Countess Francesca Maseri Florio di Santo Stefano; one *s*. *Educ:* Classic Lycée Cividale, Italy; Padua Univ. Med. Sch. Special bds in Cardiology, 1963, in Nuclear Medicine, 1965, Italy. Research fellow: Univ. of Pisa, 1960–65; Columbia Univ., NY, 1965–66; Johns Hopkins Univ., Baltimore, 1966–67; University of Pisa: Asst Prof., 1967–70; Prof. of Internal Medicine, 1970; Prof. of Cardiovascular Pathophisiology, 1972–79; Prof. of Medicine (Locum), 1977–79. Chevalier d'honneur et devotion, SMO Malta. *Publications:* Myocardial Blood Flow in Man, 1972; Primary and Secondary Angina, 1977; Perspectives on Coronary Care, 1979; articles in major internat. cardiological and med. jls. *Recreations:* skiing, tennis, sailing. *Address:* 51 Lennox Gardens, SW1X 0DF. *T:* 01–584 9223. *Club:* Queen's.

MASHAM OF ILTON, Baroness *cr* 1970 (Life Peer); **Susan Lilian Primrose Cunliffe-Lister, (Countess of Swinton);** *b* 14 April 1935; *d* of Sir Ronald Sinclair, 8th Bt and Reba Blair (who *m* 2nd, 1957, Lt-Col H. R. Hildreth, MBE; she *d* 1985), *d* of Anthony Inglis, MD; *m* 1959, Lord Masham (now Earl of Swinton, *qv*); one *s* one *d* (both adopted). *Educ:* Heathfield School, Ascot; London Polytechnic. Has made career in voluntary social work. Mem., Peterlee and Newton Aycliffe New Town Corp., 1974–85. Vice-Chm., All-Party Parly Drug Misuse Cttee, 1984–; Member: Parly All-Party Disabled Cttee; Parly All-Party Penal Affairs Cttee. President: N Yorks Red Cross, 1963–; Yorks Assoc. of the Disabled, 1963–; Chm., Spinal Injuries Assoc., 1974–; Member: Yorks RHA, 1980–; Bd of Visitors, Wetherby Youth Custody Centre, 1963–; Selection Cttee, Winston Churchill Meml Trust, 1980–; Mem. and Governor, Ditchley Foundn, 1980–. Hon. FRCGP, 1981. Hon. MA Open Univ., 1981; Hon. degree, York Univ., 1985. *Recreations:* breeding highland ponies, swimming, table tennis, fishing, flower decoration, gardening. *Address:* Dykes Hill House, Masham, near Ripon, N Yorks. *T:* Ripon 89241; 46 Westminster Gardens, Marsham Street, SW1. *T:* 01–834 0700

See also Sir J. R. N. B. Sinclair, Bt.

MASHONALAND; *see* Harare.

MASIRE, Quett Ketumile Joni, LLD; JP; President of Botswana, since 1980; *b* 23 July 1925; *m* 1957, Gladys Olebile; three *s* three *d*. *Educ:* Kanye; Tiger Kloof. Founded Seepapitso Secondary School, 1950; reporter, later Dir, African Echo, 1958; Mem., Bangwaketse Tribal Council, Legislative Council (former Mem., Exec. Council); founder Mem., Botswana Democratic Party; Mem., Legislative Assembly (later National Assembly), 1965; Dep. Prime Minister, 1965–66; Vice-Pres. and Minister of Finance, 1966–80 and of Development Planning, 1967–80. *Address:* State House, Private Bag 001, Gaborone, Botswana. *T:* 55444; PO Box 70, Gaborone, Botswana. *T:* 53391.

MASLIN, David Michael E.; *see* Eckersley-Maslin.

MASON, family name of **Baron Blackford.**

MASON, Alan Kenneth, ISO 1983; HM Diplomatic Service, retired 1979; *b* 18 May 1920; *s* of Richard Mason and Mary Mason (*née* Williams); *m* 1948 (marr. diss.); two *s*; *m* 1979, Marion Basden. *Educ:* Westcliff High School. Served with British and Indian Army, India, Burma, 1940–46. Customs and Excise, 1946–48; Min. of Works, 1949–65 (Sec., Ancient Monuments Bds, 1958–63); Diplomatic Service, 1965: Head of Chancery, Jakarta, 1967–70; Dep. Defence Sec., Hong Kong, 1972–75; Consul-General, Hanover, 1975–78; Dep. Sec. for Security, Hong Kong, 1979–84. *Recreations:* archæology, bird watching, Chinese porcelain, walking, bridge. *Address:* Tregunter, Charlcombe Lane, Lansdown, Bath. *Clubs:* Royal Commonwealth Society; Hong Kong (Hong Kong).

MASON, Hon. Sir Anthony (Frank), KBE 1972 (CBE 1969); **Hon. Mr Justice Mason;** Justice, High Court of Australia, since 1972; *b* Sydney, 21 April 1925; *s* of F. M. Mason; *m* 1950, Patricia Mary, *d* of Dr E. N. McQueen; two *s*. *Educ:* Sydney Grammar Sch.; Univ. of Sydney. BA, LLB. RAAF Flying Officer, 1944–45. Admitted to NSW Bar, 1951; QC 1964. Commonwealth Solicitor-General, 1964–69; Judge, Court of Appeal, Supreme Court of NSW, 1969–75. Vice-Chm., UN Commn on Internat. Trade Law, 1968. Mem. Council, ANU, 1969–72; Pro-Chancellor, ANU, 1972–75; Hon. LLD ANU, 1980. *Recreations:* gardening, tennis, swimming. *Address:* Judges' Chambers, High Court of Australia, PO Box E435, Canberra, ACT 2600, Australia.

MASON, Arthur Malcolm; Director, Reckitt & Colman Ltd, 1958–79 (Chairman, 1970–77); *b* 19 Dec. 1915; British parents; *m* 1938, Mary Hall (*d* 1981); one *s* (one *d* decd). *Educ:* Linton House, London; Blundells School. Trainee, Unilever Ltd, 1934–38; Chiswick Products Ltd: Asst Sales Man., 1938; Sales and Advertising Man., 1939; Dir, 1943; Chm., 1957; Reckitt & Colman Holdings Ltd: Assoc. Dir, 1957; Dir, 1958; Vice-Chm., 1965–70. FInstD. OStJ 1975. *Recreations:* sailing, sea fishing, gardening. *Address:* Cambisgate, Pier Road, Seaview, Isle of Wight. *T:* Seaview 3389. *Clubs:* Seaview Yacht, Brading Haven Yacht.

MASON, Sir (Basil) John, Kt 1979; CB 1973; FRS 1965; DSc (London); Director-General of the Meteorological Office, 1965–83; President, University of Manchester Institute of Science and Technology, since 1986; *b* 18 Aug. 1923; *s* of late John Robert and Olive Mason, Docking, Norfolk; *m* 1948, Doreen Sheila Jones; two *s*. *Educ:* Fakenham Grammar Sch.; University Coll., Nottingham. Commissioned, Radar Branch RAF, 1944–46. BSc 1st Cl. Hons Physics (London), 1947, MSc 1948; DSc (London) 1956. Shirley Res. Fellow, Univ. of Nottingham, 1947; Asst Lectr in Meteorology, 1948, Lectr, 1949, Imperial Coll.; Warren Res. Fellow, Royal Society, 1957; Vis. Prof. of Meteorology, Univ. of Calif, 1959–60; Prof. of Cloud Physics, Imperial Coll. of Science and Technology (Univ. of London), 1961–65. Dir, Royal Soc. prog. on Acidification of Surface Waters, 1983–; Chm., WMO/ICSU Scientific Cttee, World Climate Res. Prog., 1984–. Hon. Gen. Sec. British Assoc., 1965–70; President: Physics Section, British Assoc., 1965; Inst. of Physics, 1976–78; BAAS, 1982–83; Pres., 1968–70, Hon. Mem., 1985, Royal Meteorol. Soc.; a Vice-Pres., 1976–, and Treasurer, 1976–86, Royal Soc. UK Perm. Rep., World Meteorological Orgn, 1965–83 (Mem. Exec. Cttee, 1966–75 and 1977–83). Member: ABRC, 1983–; Astronomy, Space Radio Bd, SERC, 1981–85. Chm. Council, 1970–75, Pro-Chancellor, 1979–85, Surrey Univ. Lectures: James Forrest, ICE, 1967; Kelvin, IEE, 1968; Dalton, RIC, 1968; Bakerian, Royal Soc., 1971; Hugh MacMillan, IES, 1975; Symons, Royal Meteorol. Soc., 1976; Halley, Oxford, 1977. Hon. Fellow: Imperial Coll. of Science and Technology, 1974; UMIST, 1979. Hon. DSc: Nottingham, 1966; Durham, 1970; Strathclyde, 1975; City, 1980; Sussex, 1983. Hugh Robert Mill Medal, Royal Meteorol. Soc., 1959; Charles Chree Medal and Prize, Inst. Physics and Phys. Soc., 1965; Rumford Medal, Royal Soc., 1972; Glazebrook Medal, Inst. Physics, 1974; Symons Meml Gold Medal, Royal Meteorol. Soc., 1975. *Publications:* The Physics of Clouds, 1957, 2nd edn 1971; Clouds, Rain and Rain-Making, 1962, 2nd edn 1975; papers in physics and meteorological journals. *Recreations:* foreign travel, music. *Address:* 64 Christchurch Road, East Sheen, SW14 7AW. *T:* 01–876 2557.

MASON, Brewster; actor; Associate Artist, Royal Shakespeare Company, since 1965; *b* Kidsgrove, Staffs, 30 Aug. 1922; *s* of Jesse Mason and Constance May Kemp; *m* 1st, 1948, Lorna Whittaker (marr. diss.); one *d*; 2nd, 1966, Kate Meredith. *Educ:* privately; Royal Naval Colls; RADA (Bancroft Gold Medal); Guildhall Sch. of Music and Drama (Hons. Grad.). First appeared as a professional actor at Lyric, Hammersmith, as Flt/Sgt John Nabb in An English Summer, Sept. 1948, followed by London appearances to 1960; took over part of Gen. Allenby in Ross, Haymarket, 1960. First appearance in New York, at Henry Miller Theatre, Sept. 1962, as Sir Lewis Eliot in The Affair. Joined RSC, Aldwych, London, Feb. 1963, to play Kent in King Lear, subseq. appearing at Royal Shakespeare, Stratford, July 1963, as Earl of Warwick in trilogy The Wars of the Roses; since 1963 has appeared in repertory at Stratford and Aldwych, in productions including The Birthday Party, 1964; Hamlet, 1965; Macbeth, All's Well that Ends Well, 1967; Julius Caesar, Merry Wives of Windsor, 1968; Major Barbara, King Henry VIII, 1970; Othello in Othello, 1972; Falstaff in Henry IV and Merry Wives of Windsor, 1975; at National Theatre: The Trojan War Will Not Take Place, and You Can't Take It With You, 1983; Venice Preserv'd, Wild Honey, 1984. Director, Shakespeare Festivals in New England; lectures on Drama and Acting at Univ. of California (Irvine). *Films include:* The Dam Busters, Private Potter, etc. *TV:* first appeared on television, 1953, subseq. playing leading parts, including: Abel Wharton in The Pallisers, 1974; Mr Voysey in The Voysey Inheritance, 1979. FGSM 1976. *Recreations:* golf, painting. *Address:* c/o ICM, 388–396 Oxford Street, W1. *Clubs:* Garrick, Naval; Stage Golfing; Players (New York).

MASON, Prof. David Kean, BDS, MD; FRCSGlas, FDSRCPS Glas, FDSRCSE, FRCPath; Professor of Oral Medicine and Head of the Department of Oral Medicine and Pathology, University of Glasgow Dental School, since 1967; Dean of Dental Education, University of Glasgow, since 1980; *b* 5 Nov. 1928; *s* of George Hunter Mason and Margaret Kean; *m* 1967, Judith Anne Armstrong; two *s* one *d*. *Educ:* Paisley Grammar Sch.; Glasgow Acad.; St Andrews Univ. (LDS 1951, BDS 1952); Glasgow Univ. (MB, ChB 1962, MD (Commendation) 1967). FDSRCSE 1957; FDSRCPS Glas 1967; FRCSGlas 1973; FRCPath 1976 (MRCPath 1967). Served RAF, Dental Br., 1952–54. Registrar in Oral Surgery, Dundee, 1954–56; gen. dental practice, 1956–62; Vis. Dental Surgeon, Glasgow Dental Hosp., 1956–62, Sen. Registrar 1962–64; Sen. Lectr in Dental Surgery and Pathology, Univ. of Glasgow, 1964–67; Hon. Consultant Dental Surgeon, Glasgow, 1964–67. Chm., National Dental Consultative Cttee, 1976–80 and 1983–; Member: Medicines Commn, 1976–80; Dental Cttee, MRC, 1973–; Physiol Systems Bd, MRC, 1976–80; GDC, 1976– (Mem., Disciplinary Cttee, 1980–); Dental Cttee, UGC, 1977– (Chm., 1983–); Jt Cttee for Higher Trng in Dentistry, 1977–; Dental Strategy Rev. Gp, 1980–81; Scientific Prog. Cttee, FDI, 1980–; Consultant to Commn on Dental Res., FDI, 1973–80. President: W of Scotland Br., BDA, 1983–84; British Soc. for Dental Res., 1984–; Convener, Dental Council, RCPGlas, 1977–80. Lectures: Charles Tomes, RCS, 1975; Holme, UCH, London, 1977; Caldwell Meml, Univ. of Glasgow, 1983; Evelyn Sprawson, London Hosp. Med. Coll., 1984. John Tomes Prize, RCS, 1979. *Publications:* (jtly) Salivary Glands in Health and Disease, 1975; (jtly) Introduction to Oral Medicine, 1978; (jtly) Self Assessment: Manual I, Oral Surgery, 1978; Manual II, Oral Medicine, 1978; (ed jtly) Oral Manifestations of Systemic Disease, 1980. *Recreations:* golf, tennis, gardening, enjoying the pleasures of the countryside. *Address:* Greystones, Houston Road, Kilmacolm, Renfrewshire PA13 4NY. *Clubs:* Royal Scottish Automobile (Glasgow); Royal & Ancient Golf, Elie Golf House, Kilmacolm Golf.

MASON, Vice-Adm. Dennis Howard, CB 1967; CVO 1978; *b* 7 Feb. 1916; *s* of Wilfred Howard Mason, Broadwater, Ipswich, and Gladys (Mouse) Mason (*née* Teague), Trevenson, Cornwall; *m* 1940, Patricia D. M. (*née* Hood); three *d*. *Educ:* Royal Naval Coll., Dartmouth. Served War of 1939–45, Coastal Forces, Frigates and Destroyers; Comdr 1951; Captain 1956; Senior Naval Officer, Northern Ireland, 1961–63; Dir RN Tactical Sch., 1964–65; Rear-Adm. 1965; Chief of Staff to Commander, Far East Fleet, 1965–67; Vice-Adm. 1968; Comdt, Jt Services Staff Coll., 1968–70, retired 1970. ADC 1964. With Paper and Paper Products Industry Training Bd, 1971–72; Warden, St George's House, Windsor Castle, 1972–77. Mem., East Hants DC, 1979–. *Recreations:* fishing, gardening. *Address:* Church Cottage, East Meon, Hants. *T:* East Meon 466.

MASON, Vice-Adm. Sir Frank (Trowbridge), KCB 1955 (CB 1953); FEng; Hon. FIMechE; FIMarE; retired; Member of Council for Scientific and Industrial Research, 1958–63 (Vice-Chairman, 1962); *b* 25 April 1900; *s* of late F. J. Mason, MBE, JP; *m* 1924, Dora Margaret Brand; one *s* two *d*. *Educ:* Ipswich Sch. RNC, Keyham, 1918; HMS Collingwood, 1918; HMS Queen Elizabeth, 1919–21; HMS Tiger, 1921; RN Coll., Greenwich, 1921–22; RN Engineering Coll., Keyham, 1922–23; HMS Malaya, 1923–25; HMS Rodney, 1929 and 1933–34; HMS Galatea, 1937–39; Fleet Gunnery Engineer Officer, Home Fleet, 1943–44; Chief Gunnery Engineer Officer and Dep. Dir of Naval Ordnance, 1947–48; idc 1949; Deputy Engineer-in-Chief of The Fleet, 1950–52; Staff of C-in-C The Nore, 1952–53; Engineer-in-Chief of the Fleet, 1953–57, retired. Commander, 1934; Captain, 1943; Rear-Adm., 1950; Vice-Adm., 1953. Parsons Memorial Lectr, 1956. Chm. Steering Cttee, Nat. Engineering Laboratory, 1958–69, Chm. Adv. Board, 1969, Chm. Adv. Cttee, 1973–75; Mem. Steering Cttee, Nat. Physical Laboratory, 1966–68; Chm., Froude Cttee, 1966. Mem. Council, Institution of Mechanical Engineers, 1953–57, and 1961 (Vice-Pres., 1962, Pres., 1964); Institute of Marine Engineers: Chm., Panel of Jt Nuclear Marine Propulsion, 1957; Mem. Council, 1958–60; Vice-Chm., 1961; Chm., 1962; Pres., 1967. Dep. Chm., Schools Science and Technology Cttee, 1968; Mem. Governing Body: National Council for Technological Awards, 1960–64; Royal Naval Sch., Haslemere, 1953–83; Ipswich Sch., 1961–72; Further Education Staff Coll., 1964–74; Navy League, 1967–75; Hurstpierpoint Coll., 1966–80; Brighton Polytechnic, 1969–73; Mem. Council and Exec. Cttee, City and Guilds of London Inst., 1968–77, Vice Chm., 1970–77, Hon. FCGI 1977. Chm., Standing Conf. on Schools Science and Technology, 1971–75, Vice-Pres., 1975. Founder Fellow, Fellowship of Engineering, 1976. Asst to Court, Worshipful Co. of Shipwrights. Mem. Smeatonian Soc. of Civil Engineers (Pres., 1977); Hon. MIPlantE. High Steward of Ipswich, 1967 (life appointment). *Address:*

Townfield House, 114 High Street, Hurstpierpoint, W Sussex BN6 9PX. *T*: Hurstpierpoint 833375. *Clubs*: Naval, MCC.
See also Ven. R. J. Mason.

MASON, Sir Frederick (Cecil), KCVO 1968; CMG 1960; HM Diplomatic Service, retired; *b* 15 May 1913; *s* of late Ernest Mason and Sophia Charlotte Mason (*née* Dodson); *m* 1941, Karen Rørholm; two *s* one *d* (and two *d* decd). *Educ*: City of London Sch.; St Catharine's Coll., Cambridge. Vice-Consul: Antwerp, 1935–36; Paris, 1936–37; Leopoldville, 1937–39; Elisabethville, 1939–40; Consul at Thorshavn during British occupation of Faroes, 1940–42; Consul, Colon, Panama, 1943–45; First Sec., British Embassy, Santiago, Chile, 1946–48; First Sec. (Information), Oslo, 1948–50; Asst Labour Adviser, FO, 1950–53; First Sec. (Commercial), UK Control Commission, Bonn, 1954–55; Counsellor (Commercial), HM Embassy, Athens, 1955–56; Counsellor (Economic), HM Embassy, Tehran, 1957–60; Head of Economic Relations Dept, Foreign Office, 1960–64; Under-Sec., Ministry of Overseas Development, 1965, and CRO, 1966; Ambassador to Chile, 1966–70; Under-Sec. of State, FCO, Oct. 1970–Apr. 1971; Ambassador and Perm. UK Rep. to UN and other Internat. Orgns, Geneva, 1971–73. Dir, New Court Natural Resources, 1973–83. British Mem., Internat. Narcotics Control Bd, Geneva, 1974–77. Chm., Anglo-Chilean Soc., 1978–82. Grand Cross, Chilean Order of Merit, 1968. *Recreations*: ball games, walking, painting. *Address*: The Forge, Ropley, Hants. *T*: Ropley 2285. *Club*: Canning.

MASON, (George Frederick) Peter, QC 1963; **His Honour Judge Mason;** a Circuit Judge, since 1970; *b* 11 Dec. 1921; *s* of George Samuel and Florence May Mason, Keighley, Yorks; *m* 1st, 1950 (marr. diss. 1977); two *s* two *d* (and one *d* decd); 2nd, 1981, Sara, *er d* of Sir Robert Ricketts, Bt, *qv*. *Educ*: Lancaster Royal Grammar Sch.; St Catharine's Coll., Cambridge. Open Exhibnr St Catharine's Coll., 1940. Served with 78th Medium Regt RA (Duke of Lancaster's Own Yeo.) in Middle East and Italy, 1941–45, latterly as Staff Capt. RA, HQ 13 Corps. History Tripos Pt 1, 1st cl. hons with distinction, 1946; called to Bar, Lincoln's Inn, 1947. MA 1948; Cholmeley Schol., 1949. Asst Recorder of Huddersfield, 1961; Dep. Chairman: Agricultural Land Tribunal, W Yorks and Lancs, 1962; West Riding of Yorks Quarter Sessions, 1965–67; Recorder of York, 1965–67; Dep. Chm., Inner London QS, 1970; Dep. Chm., NE London QS, 1970–71; Senior Judge: Snaresbrook Crown Ct, 1974–81; Inner London Crown Court, 1983–. Freeman, City of London, 1977. Liveryman, Wax Chandlers' Co., 1980–. *Recreations*: music, golf, sailing, carpentry. *Address*: Inner London Sessions House, Newington Causeway, SE1. *T*: 01–407 7111. *Clubs*: Athenæum; Hawks.

MASON, James Stephen; Parliamentary Counsel, since 1980; *b* 6 Feb. 1935; *s* of Albert Wesley Mason and Mabel (*née* Topham); *m* 1961, Tania Jane Moeran; one *s* two *d*. *Educ*: Windsor County Grammar Sch.; Univ. of Oxford (MA, BCL). Called to the Bar, Middle Temple, 1958; in practice, 1961–67; Office of Parly Counsel, 1967–. *Recreations*: reading, walking and playing the piano. *Club*: United Oxford & Cambridge University.

MASON, Sir John; *see* Mason, Sir B. J.

MASON, Sir John (Charles Moir), KCMG 1980 (CMG 1976); Chairman: Thorn-EMI (Australia) Ltd, since 1985; Lloyd's Bank (NZA), Sydney, since 1985; Vickers Shipbuilders (Australia) Ltd, since 1985; Australian Natural Foods Holdings Ltd, since 1985; Board of Advice, Spencer Stuart and Associates, Sydney, since 1985; *b* 13 May 1927; *o s* of late Charles Moir Mason, CBE and late Madeline Mason; *m* 1954, Margaret Newton; one *s* one *d*. *Educ*: Manchester Grammar Sch.; Peterhouse, Cambridge. Lieut, XX Lancs Fusiliers, 1946–48; BA 1950, MA 1955, Cantab; Captain, Royal Ulster Rifles, 1950–51 (Korea); HM Foreign Service, 1952; 3rd Sec., FO, 1952–54; 2nd Sec. and Private Sec. to Ambassador, British Embassy, Rome, 1954–56; 2nd Sec., Warsaw, 1956–59; 1st Sec., FO, 1959–61; 1st Sec. (Commercial), Damascus, 1961–65; 1st Sec. and Asst Head of Dept, FO, 1965–68; Dir of Trade Develt and Dep. Consul-Gen., NY, 1968–71; Head of European Integration Dept, FCO, 1971–72; seconded as Under-Sec., ECGD, 1972–75; Asst Under-Sec. of State (Economic), FCO, 1975–76; Ambassador to Israel, 1976–80; High Commissioner to Australia, 1980–84. Director: Wellcome (Australia) Ltd, 1985–; Fluor (Australia) Ltd, 1985–; Prudential (Australia) Ltd, 1985–; Pirelli Ericsson, Australia. Chm., North Shore Heart Foundn, Sydney, 1986–; Director: Churchill Meml Trust, Aust., 1985–; Australian Opera Foundn, 1985–. *Address*: 147 Dover Road, Dover Heights, NSW 2030, Australia; c/o Lloyds Bank, 6 Pall Mall, SW1. *Clubs*: Athenæum; Melbourne (Melbourne); Union (Sydney).

MASON, Prof. John Kenyon French, CBE 1973; Regius Professor of Forensic Medicine, University of Edinburgh, 1973–85, now Emeritus; *b* 19 Dec. 1919; *s* of late Air Cdre J. M. Mason, CBE, DSC, DFC and late Alma French; *m* 1943, Elizabeth Latham (decd); two *s. Educ*: Downside Sch.; Cambridge Univ.; St Bartholomew's Hosp. MD, FRCPath, DCP, DMJ, DTM&H. Joined RAF, 1943; Dir of RAF Dept of Aviation and Forensic Pathology, 1956; retd as Group Captain, Consultant in Pathology, 1973. Pres., British Assoc. in Forensic Medicine, 1981–83. L. G. Groves Prize for Aircraft Safety, 1957; R. F. Linton Meml Prize, 1958; James Martin Award for Flight Safety, 1972; Douglas Weightman Safety Award, 1973; Swiney Prize for Jurisprudence, 1978; Lederer Award for Aircraft Safety, 1985. *Publications*: Aviation Accident Pathology, 1962; (ed) Aerospace Pathology, 1973; Forensic Medicine for Lawyers, 1978, 2nd edn 1983; (ed) The Pathology of Violent Injury, 1978; Law and Medical Ethics, 1983; papers in medical jls. *Address*: 66 Craiglea Drive, Edinburgh EH10 5PF. *Club*: Royal Air Force.

MASON, Rt. Rev. Kenneth Bruce, AM 1984; Chairman, Australian Board of Missions, General Synod of the Anglican Church of Australia, since 1983; *b* 4 Sept. 1928; *s* of Eric Leslie Mason and Gertrude Irene (*née* Pearce); unmarried. *Educ*: Bathurst High Sch.; Sydney Teachers' Coll.; St John's Theological Coll., Morpeth; Univ. of Queensland. Deacon, 1953; Priest, 1954. Primary Teacher, 1948–51; St John's Theological Coll., Morpeth, 1952–53 (ThL); Member, Brotherhood of the Good Shepherd, 1954; Parish of: Gilgandra, NSW, 1954–58; Darwin, NT, 1959–61; Alice Springs, NT, 1962; University of Queensland, 1963–64 (BA, Dip Div); resigned from Brotherhood, 1965; Trinity Coll., Melbourne Univ.: Asst Chaplain, 1965; Dean, 1966–67; Bishop of the Northern Territory, 1968–83. Member, Oratory of the Good Shepherd, 1962, Superior, 1981–. *Recreations*: listening to music, railways. *Address*: ABM House, 91 Bathurst Street, Sydney, NSW 2000, Australia. *T*: 02–264–1021.

MASON, Ven. Lancelot, MBE 1984; MA; Archdeacon of Chichester, 1946–73; Canon Residentiary of Chichester Cathedral, 1949–73, now Canon Emeritus; *b* 22 July 1905; *s* of late Canon A. J. Mason, DD; unmarried. *Educ*: RN Colls Osborne and Dartmouth; Trinity Coll., Cambridge. Deacon, 1928; Priest, 1929; Rector of Plumpton, 1938; Chaplain RNVR, 1939–46 (despatches). Chm., Friends of Rampton Hosp., 1976–. *Address*: The Stables, Morton Hall, Retford, Notts. *T*: Retford 705477.

MASON, Monica; Senior Principal Dancer, Royal Ballet; Principal Répétiteur, Royal Ballet, since 1984; *b* 6 Sept. 1941; *d* of Richard Mason and Mrs E. Fabian; *m* 1968, Austin Bennett. *Educ*: Johannesburg, SA; Royal Ballet Sch., London. Joined Royal Ballet in Corps de Ballet, 1958; created role of Chosen Maiden in Rite of Spring, 1962; also created roles in: Diversions, Elite Syncopations, Electra, Manon, Romeo and Juliet, Rituals, Adieu, Isadora, The Four Seasons, The Ropes of Time. Assistant to the Principal Choreographer, Royal Ballet, 1980–84. *Address*: Royal Opera House, Covent Garden, WC2.

MASON, Dr Pamela Georgina Walsh, FRCPsych; Senior Principal Medical Officer (Under Secretary), Department of Health and Social Security, since 1979; *d* of late Captain George Mason and Marie Louise Walsh; god-daughter and ward of late Captain William Gregory, Hon. Co. of Master Mariners; *m* 1st, 1949, David Paltenghi (*d* 1961); two *s*; 2nd, 1965, Jan Darnley-Smith. *Educ*: Christ's Hosp. Sch.; Univ. of London, Royal Free Hosp. Sch. of Medicine (MRCS, LRCP, 1949; MB, BS 1950). DPM 1957; MRCPsych 1971. Various appointments at: Royal Free Hosp., 1951–53; Maudsley Hosp. and Bethlem Royal Hosp., 1954–58; Guy's Hosp., 1958–60; Home Office, 1961–71; DHSS, 1971–. Vis. Psychiatrist, Holloway Prison, 1962–67; Adviser: C of E Children's Soc., 1962–; Royal Philanthropic Soc., 1962–; WRAF Health Educn Scheme, 1962–67. Chairman: WHO Working Gp on Youth Advisory Services, 1976; WHO Meeting of Nat. Mental Health Advrs, 1979. Member: Council of Europe Select Cttee of Experts on Alcoholism, 1976–77; Cttee of Experts on Legal Problems in the Medical Field, 1979–80. FRSocMed. QHP 1984–. *Publications*: contribs to various professional jls and Govt pubns. *Recreations*: antiquities, humanities, ballet, films, tennis, seafaring and expeditions. *Address*: Blindwell House, Nether Stowey, Bridgwater, Som. *T*: Nether Stowey 732707.

MASON, Peter; *see* Mason, G. F. P.

MASON, Peter Geoffrey, MBE 1946; High Master, Manchester Grammar School, 1962–78; *b* 22 Feb. 1914; *o s* of Harry Mason, Handsworth, Birmingham; *m* 1st, 1939, Mary Evelyn Davison (marr. diss.); three *d*; 2nd, 1978, Elizabeth June Bissell (*d* 1983); 3rd, 1985, Marjorie Payne. *Educ*: King Edward's Sch., Birmingham; Christ's Coll., Cambridge (Scholar). Goldsmith Exhibitioner, 1935; Porson Scholar, 1936; 1st Class, Classical Tripos, Pts 1 and 2, 1935, 1936. Sixth Form Classical Master, Cheltenham Coll., 1936–40, Rugby Sch., 1946–49; Headmaster, Aldenham Sch., 1949–61. War Service, 1940–46: commissioned into Intelligence Corps, 1940; various staff appointments including HQ 21 Army Group; later attached to a dept of the Foreign Office. Member: Advisory Cttee on Education in the Colonies, 1956; ITA Educnl Adv. Council, 1964–69; Council, University of Salford; Council, British Volunteer Programme (Chm., 1966–74); Chairman: Council of Educn for World Citizenship, 1966–83; Reg. Conf. on IVS, 1972–82. *Publications*: Private Education in the EEC, 1983; Private Education in the USA and Canada, 1985; Private Education in Australia and New Zealand, 1986; articles and reviews in classical and educational journals. *Recreations*: travel, fly-fishing, walking. *Address*: Leeward, Longborough, Moreton-in-Marsh, Glos GL56 0QR. *T*: Cotswold 30147. *Club*: Athenæum.

MASON, Philip, CIE 1946; OBE 1942; writer; *b* 19 March 1906; *s* of Dr H. A. Mason, Duffield, Derbs; *m* 1935, Eileen Mary, *d* of Courtenay Hayes, Charmouth, Dorset; two *s* two *d*. *Educ*: Sedbergh; Balliol. 1st Cl. Hons Philosophy, Politics and Economics, Oxford, 1927; MA 1952; DLitt 1972. ICS: Asst Magistrate United Provinces, 1928–33; Under-Sec., Government of India, War Dept, 1933–36; Dep. Commissioner Garhwal, 1936–39; Dep. Sec. Govt of India, Defence Co-ordination and War Depts, 1939–42; Sec. Chiefs of Staff Cttee, India, and Head of Conf. Secretariat, SE Asia Command, 1942–44; represented War Dept in Central Assembly, 1946; Joint Sec. to Government of India, War Dept, 1944–47; Tutor and Governor to the Princes, Hyderabad, 1947; retd from ICS, 1947. Mem. Commn of Enquiry to examine problems of Minorities in Nigeria, 1957. Dir of Studies in Race Relations, Chatham House, 1952–58; Dir, Inst. of Race Relations, 1958–69. Chairman: National Cttee for Commonwealth Immigrants, 1964–65; Exec. Cttee, UK Council for Overseas Student Affairs, 1969–75; Trustees, S African Church Develt Trust, 1976–83 (Pres., 1983–). Hon. Fellow, Sch. of Oriental and African Studies, 1970; Hon. DSc Bristol, 1971. *Publications*: (as Philip Woodruff): Call the Next Witness, 1945; The Wild Sweet Witch, 1947; Whatever Dies, 1948; The Sword of Northumbria, 1948; The Island of Chamba, 1950; Hernshaw Castle, 1950; Colonel of Dragoons, 1951; The Founders, 1953; The Guardians, 1954; (as Philip Mason): Racial Tension, 1954; Christianity and Race, 1956; The Birth of a Dilemma, 1958; Year of Decision, 1960; (ed) Man, Race and Darwin, 1960; Common Sense about Race, 1961; Prospero's Magic, 1962; (ed) India and Ceylon: Unity and Diversity, 1967; Patterns of Dominance, 1970; Race Relations, 1970; How People Differ, 1971; A Matter of Honour, 1974; Kipling: The Glass The Shadow and The Fire, 1975; The Dove in Harness, 1976; A Shaft of Sunlight, 1978; Skinner of Skinner's Horse, 1979; The English Gentleman, 1982; A Thread of Silk, 1984; The Men who Ruled India (abridged from The Founders, and The Guardians), 1985. *Recreation*: living in the country. *Address*: Hither Daggons, Cripplestyle, Alderholt, near Fordingbridge, Hants. *T*: Cranborne 318. *Club*: Travellers'.

MASON, Richard; author; *b* 16 May 1919. *Educ*: Bryanston School. *Publications*: novels: The Wind Cannot Read, 1947; The Shadow and the Peak, 1949; The World of Suzie Wong, 1957; The Fever Tree, 1962. *Address*: c/o A. M. Heath & Co. Ltd, 40–42 William IV Street, WC2N 4DD.

MASON, Air Vice-Marshal Richard Anthony, CBE 1981; Air Secretary, since 1985; *b* 22 Oct. 1932; *s* of William and Maud Mason; *m* 1956, Margaret Stewart; one *d*. *Educ*: Bradford Grammar Sch.; St Andrews Univ. (MA); London Univ. (MA). Commissioned RAF, 1956; Director of Defence Studies, 1977; Director of Personnel (Ground), 1982; Deputy Air Secretary, 1984. *Publications*: Air Power in the Next Generation (ed), 1978; Readings in Air Power, 1979; (with M. J. Armitage) Air Power in the Nuclear Age, 1981; The RAF Today and Tomorrow, 1982; British Air Power in the 1980s, 1984; The Soviet Air Forces, 1986; War in the Third Dimension, 1986; Air Power and Technology, 1986; articles in internat. jls on defence policy and strategy. *Recreations*: Rugby, writing, gardening. *Address*: c/o Lloyds Bank, Cox & King's Branch, Pall Mall, SW1. *Club*: Royal Air Force.

MASON, Ven. Richard John; Archdeacon of Tonbridge, since 1977; Minister of St Luke's, Sevenoaks, since 1983; *b* 26 April 1929; *s* of Vice-Adm. Sir Frank Mason, *qv*. *Educ*: Shrewsbury School. Newspaper journalist, 1949–55; Lincoln Theological College, 1955–58; Asst Curate, Bishop's Hatfield, Herts, 1958–64; Domestic Chaplain to Bishop of London, 1964–69; Vicar of Riverhead with Dunton Green, Kent, 1969–73; Vicar of Edenbridge, 1973–83, also Priest in Charge of Crockham Hill, 1981–83. *Address*: St Luke's House, 30 Eardley Road, Sevenoaks, Kent TN13 1XT. *T*: Sevenoaks 452462.

MASON, Prof. Sir Ronald, KCB 1980; FRS 1975; Professor of Chemistry, University of Sussex, since 1971, Pro-Vice-Chancellor, 1977; Chairman, Hunting Engineering Ltd, since 1987 (Deputy Chairman, 1985–87); *b* 22 July 1930; *o s* of David John Mason and Olwen Mason (*née* James); *m* 1952, E. Pauline Pattinson; three *d*; *m* 1979, Elizabeth Rosemary Grey-Edwards. *Educ*: Univs of Wales and London (Fellow, University College Cardiff, 1981). Research Assoc., British Empire Cancer Campaign, 1953–61; Lectr, Imperial Coll., 1961–63; Prof. of Inorganic Chemistry, Univ. of Sheffield, 1963–71; Chief Scientific Advr, MoD, 1977–83. Vis. Prof., Univs in Australia, Canada, France, Israel, NZ and US, inc. A. D. Little Prof., MIT, 1970; Univ. of California, Berkeley, 1975; Ohio State Univ., 1976; North Western Univ., 1977; Prof. associé, Univ. de

Strasbourg, 1976; Erskine Vis. Prof., Christchurch, NZ, 1977; Prof., Texas, 1982; Vis. Prof. of Internat. Relns, UCW, 1985–. SRC: Mem., 1971–75; Chm. Chemistry Cttee, 1969–72; Chm. Science Bd, 1972–75; Data Cttee, 1975; Member: Chief Scientist's Requirement Bd, DTI later Dept of Industry, 1973; BBC Adv. Group, 1975–79. Adv. Bd, Res. Councils, 1977–83. Schmidt Meml Lectr, Israel, 1977. Hon. DSc Wales, 1986. Corday-Morgan Medallist, 1965, and Tilden Lectr, 1970, Chemical Society; Medal and Prize for Structural Chem., Chem. Soc., 1973. *Publications:* (ed) Advances in Radiation Biology, 1964 (3rd edn 1969); (ed) Advances in Structure Analysis by Diffraction Methods, 1968 (6th edn 1978); (ed) Physical Processes in Radiation Biology, 1964; many papers in Jl Chem. Soc., Proc. Royal Soc., etc, and on defence issues. *Address:* Chestnuts Farm, Weedon, Bucks HP22 4NH. *Club:* Athenæum.

MASON, Rt. Hon. Roy, PC 1968; MP (Lab) Barnsley Central, since 1983 (Barnsley, March 1953–1983); *b* 18 April 1924; *s* of Joseph and Mary Mason; *m* 1945, Marjorie, *d* of Ernest Sowden; two *d*. *Educ:* Carlton Junior Sch.; Royston Senior Sch.; London Sch. of Economics (TUC Scholarship). Went underground at 14 years of age, 1938–53; NUM branch official, 1947–53; mem. Yorks Miners' Council, 1949. Labour party spokesman on Defence and Post Office affairs, 1960–64; Minister of State (Shipping), Bd of Trade, 1964–67; Minister of Defence (Equipment), 1967–April 1968; Postmaster-Gen., April-June 1968; Minister of Power, 1968–69; President, Bd of Trade, 1969–70; Labour party spokesman on Civil Aviation, Shipping, Tourism, Films and Trade matters, 1970–74; Secretary of State for: Defence, 1974–76; Northern Ireland, 1976–79; opposition spokesman on agriculture, fisheries and food, 1979–81. Mem., Council of Europe and WEU, 1973. Chm., Yorkshire Gp of Labour MPs, 1972–74; Chm., Miners Gp of MPs, 1974, Vice-Chm., 1980. Consultant: Amalgamated Distilled Products, 1971–74; H. P. Bulmer, 1971–74; Imperial Tobacco, 1984–. *Recreation:* work, provided one stays on top of it. *Address:* 12 Victoria Avenue, Barnsley, S Yorks.

MASON, Prof. Stephen Finney, FRS 1982; FRSC; Professor of Chemistry, King's College, University of London, since 1970; *b* 6 July 1923; *s* of Leonard Stephen Mason and Christine Harriet Mason; *m* 1955, Joan Banus; three *s*. *Educ:* Wyggeston Sch., Leicester; Wadham Coll., Oxford. MA, DPhil, DSc. Demonstrator, Mus. of Hist. of Sci., Oxford Univ., 1947–53; Research Fellow in Med. Chemistry, ANU, 1953–56; Reader in Chemical Spectroscopy, Univ. of Exeter, 1956–64; Prof. of Chemistry, Univ. of East Anglia, 1964–70. *Publications:* A History of the Sciences: main currents of scientific thought, 1953; Molecular Optical Activity and the Chiral Discriminations, 1982; articles in Jl Chem. Soc., 1945–. *Recreations:* history and philosophy of science. *Address:* Department of Chemistry, King's College, Strand, WC2R 2LS. *T:* 01-836 5454.

MASON, Sydney, FSVA; Chairman and Managing Director, The Hammerson Property Investment and Development Corporation plc, since 1958 (Director since 1949); *b* 30 Sept. 1920; *s* of Jacob Mason and Annie (*née* Foreman); *m* 1945, Rosalind Victor. FSVA 1962. Manager, Land Securities plc, 1943–49. Mem., Gen. Council, British Property Fedn, 1974–. Chm. Exec., Lewis W. Hammerson Meml Home for the Elderly, 1959–80; Mem. Exec., Norwood Orphanage, 1958–76 (Chm., 1968–76). Liveryman, Worshipful Co. of Masons, 1971. *Recreation:* painting in oils and acrylics. *Address:* Bolney Court, Lower Shiplake, Henley-on-Thames, Oxon RG9 3NR. *T:* Wargrave 2095. *Clubs:* Naval, City Livery, Royal Thames Yacht.

MASON, Timothy Ian Godson; Director, Scottish Arts Council, since 1980; *b* 11 March 1945; *s* of Ian Godson Mason and Muriel (*née* Vaile); *m* 1975, Marilyn Ailsa Williams; one *d* one *s*. *Educ:* St Alban's Sch., Washington, DC; Bradfield Coll., Berkshire; Christ Church, Oxford (MA). Assistant Manager, Oxford Playhouse, 1966–67; Assistant to Peter Daubeny, World Theatre Season, London, 1967–69; Administrator: Ballet Rambert, 1970–75; Royal Exchange Theatre, Manchester, 1975–77; Director, Western Australian Arts Council, 1977–80. *Recreations:* the arts, family. *Address:* 37 Park Road, Trinity, Edinburgh EH6 4LA.

MASON, Walter W.; *see* Wynne Mason.

MASON, William Ernest, CB 1983; Deputy Secretary (Fisheries and Food), Ministry of Agriculture, Fisheries and Food, since 1982; *b* 12 Jan. 1929; *s* of Ernest George and Agnes Margaret Mason; *m* 1959, Jean (*née* Bossley); one *s* one *d*. *Educ:* Brockley Grammar Sch.; London Sch. of Economics (BScEcon). RAF, 1947–49; Min. of Food, 1949–54; MAFF, 1954; Principal 1963; Asst Sec. 1970; Under Sec., 1975; Fisheries Sec., 1980. Member: Econ. Develt Cttee for Distrib. Trades, 1975–80; Econ. Develt Cttee for Food and Drink Manufg Inds, 1976–80. *Recreations:* music, reading, gardening. *Address:* The Haven, Fairlie Gardens, SE23 3TE. *T:* 01-699 5821. *Club:* Reform.

MASRI, Taher Nashat; Order of Al-Kawkab, Jordan, 1974; Hon. GBE; Foreign Minister of Jordan, since 1984; *b* 5 March 1942; *s* of Nashat Masri and Hadiyah Solh; *m* 1968, Samar Bitar; one *s* one *d*. *Educ:* North Texas State Univ. (BBA 1965). Central Bank of Jordan, 1965–73; MP Nablus Dist, 1973–75; Minister of State for Occupied Territories Affairs, 1973–74; Ambassador to: Spain, 1975–78; France, 1978–83; Belgium (non-resident), 1978–80; Britain, 1983–84; Perm. Delegate to UNESCO, 1978–83. Grand Cross, Order of Civil Merit, Spain, 1977; Order of Isabel the Catholic, Spain, 1978; Commander, Legion of Honour, France, 1981. *Address:* Ministry of Foreign Affairs, PO Box 35217, Amman, Jordan. *T:* 44361.

MASSEREENE, 13th Viscount, *cr* 1660, **AND FERRARD,** 6th Viscount, *cr* 1797; **John Clotworthy Talbot Foster Whyte-Melville Skeffington;** Baron of Loughneagh, 1660; Baron Oriel, 1790; Baron Oriel (UK), 1821; DL; *b* 23 Oct. 1914; *s* of 12th Viscount (*d* 1956) and Jean Barbara (*d* 1937), *e d* of Sir John Stirling Ainsworth, MP, JP, 1st Bt, of Ardanaiseig, Argyllshire; *S* father 1956; *m* 1939, Annabelle Kathleen, *er d* of late Mr and Mrs Henry D. Lewis, Combwell Priory, Hawkhurst, Kent; one *s* one *d*. *Educ:* Eton. Lt, Black Watch SR, 1933–36, re-employed, 1939–40 (invalided); retired; served in Small Vessels Pool, Royal Navy, 1944. Mem. IPU Delegation to Spain, 1960; Whip, Conservative Peers Cttee (IUP), House of Lords, 1958–65, Jt Dep. Chm., 1965–70; introduced in House of Lords: Deer Act, 1963; Riding Establishments Act, 1964; Export of Animals for Research Bill, 1968; Riding Establishments Act, 1970; Valerie Mary Hill and Alan Monk (Marriage Enabling) Bill, 1984; moved debates on Overseas Information Services and other matters. Pres., Monday Club, 1981–; Member: CPA delegn to Malaŵi, 1976; Select Cttee on Anglian Water Authority Bill, 1976. Posts in Cons. Constituency organisations incl. Pres., Brighton, Kemp Town Div., Vice-Pres. and former Treasurer, Ashford Div. Chm. and Dir of companies. Driver of leading British car, Le Mans Grand Prix, 1937. One of original pioneers in commercial develt of Cape Canaveral, Florida; promoted first scheduled air service Glasgow-Oban-Isle of Mull, 1968; presented operetta Countess Maritza at Palace Theatre, London. Comr, Hunterston Ore Terminal Hearing, Glasgow, 1973. Pres., of Charitable and other organisations incl.: Ponies of Britain; Kent Hotels and Restaurants Assoc. Pres., Canterbury Br., RNLI. Former Mem., Senechal Council, Canterbury Cathedral. Chief, Scottish Clans Assoc. of London, 1974–76. Chm. Kent Branch Victoria League. Treas., Kent Assoc. of Boys' Clubs. Master, Ashford Valley Foxhounds, 1953–54; Vice-Pres., Animal Welfare Year, 1976–77. Commodore, House of Lords Yacht Club, 1972–85. Freeman, City of London, and Mem. Worshipful Company of Shipwrights. Gold Staff Officer, Coronation, 1953. FZS. DL Co. Antrim, 1957–. Cross of Comdr, Order of Merit, SMO Malta, 1978. *Publications:* The Lords, 1973; contributes articles to newspapers, chiefly sporting and natural history. *Recreations:* all field sports; farming; forestry; racing. *Heir: s* Hon. John David Clotworthy Whyte-Melville Foster Skeffington [*b* 3 June 1940; *m* 1970, Ann Denise, *er d* of late Norman Rowlandson; two *s* one *d*]. *Address:* Knock, Isle of Mull, Argyll. *T:* Aros 356; (Seat) Chilham Castle, Kent. *T:* Canterbury 730319. *Clubs:* Carlton, Turf, Pratt's, Royal Yacht Squadron.

MASSEVITCH, Prof. Alla; Vice-President of the Astronomical Council of the USSR Academy of Sciences since 1952; Professor of Astrophysics, Moscow University, since 1946; Vice-President, USSR Peace Committee, 1977; *b* Tbilisi, Georgia, USSR, 9 Oct. 1918; *m* 1942; one *d*. *Educ:* Moscow Univ. Lectured at the Royal Festival Hall, London, and at the Free Trade Hall, Manchester, etc., on The Conquest of Space, 1960; she is in charge of network of stations for tracking Sputniks, in Russia. Pres. Working Group 1 (Tracking and Telemetring) of COSPAR (Internat. Cttee for Space Research) 1961–66. Pres., Commission 35 (Internal Structure of Stars) of the Internat. Astronom. Union, 1967–70; Dep. Sec. Gen., UNISPACE 82 (UN Conf. on Exploration and Peaceful Uses of Outer Space), Vienna, 1981–83. Chm., Space Science Studies Cttee, Internat. Acad. of Astronautics, 1983–. Foreign Member: Royal Astronomical Soc., 1963; Indian Nat. Acad. of Sciences, 1979; Austrian Acad. Scis, 1985; Internat. Acad. Astronautics, 1964. Vice-Pres., Inst. for Soviet-American Relations, 1967; Mem. Board, Soviet Peace Cttee, and Internat. Peace Cttee, 1965. Internat. Award for Astronautics (Prix Galabert), 1963; Govtl decorations, USSR, Sign of Honour, 1963, Red Banner, 1975; USSR State Prize, 1975. Hon. Scientist Emeritus, 1978. *Publications:* Use of Satellite Tracking Data for Geodesy (monograph), 1980; 131 scientific papers on the internal structure of the stars, stellar evolution, and optical tracking of artificial satellites, in Russian and foreign astronomical and geophysical journals. *Address:* 48 Pjatnitskaja Street, Moscow, USSR. *T:* 2315461; 1 Vostania Square 403, Moscow. *Club:* Club for Scientists (Moscow).

MASSEY, Anna (Raymond); actress; *b* 11 Aug. 1937; *d* of late Raymond Massey and of Adrianne Allen; *m* 1958, Jeremy Huggins (marr. diss., 1963); one *s*. *Educ:* London; New York; Switzerland; Paris; Rome. *Plays:* The Reluctant Debutante, 1955; Dear Delinquent, 1957; The Elder Statesman, 1958; Double Yolk, 1959; The Last Joke, 1960; The Miracle Worker, 1961; The School for Scandal, 1962; The Doctor's Dilemma, 1963; The Right Honourable Gentleman, 1964; The Glass Menagerie, 1965; The Prime of Miss Jean Brodie, 1966; The Flip Side, 1967; First Day of a New Season, 1967; This Space is Mine, 1969; Hamlet, 1970; Spoiled, 1971; Slag, 1971; Jingo, 1975; Play, Royal Court, 1976; The Seagull, Royal Court, 1981; *at National Theatre:* Heartbreak House, 1975; Close of Play, 1979; Summer; The Importance of Being Earnest; A Kind of Alaska, and Family Voices, in Harold Pinter trio Other Places, 1982; King Lear, 1986. *Films:* Gideon's Day, 1957; Peeping Tom, 1960; Bunny Lake is Missing, 1965; The Looking Glass War, 1969; David Copperfield, 1969; De Sade, 1971; Frenzy, 1972; A Doll's House, 1973; Sweet William, 1979; The Corn is Green, 1979; Five Days One Summer, 1982; Another Country, 1984; The Chain, 1985. *Films for television:* Journey into the Shadows, Sakharov, 1984; Sacred Hearts, 1985; Hotel du lac, 1986; numerous appearances in TV plays. *Address:* c/o Jeremy Conway Ltd, Eagle House, 109 Jermyn Street, SW1.
See also D. R. Massey.

MASSEY, Daniel (Raymond); actor; *b* London, 10 Oct. 1933; *s* of late Raymond Massey and of Adrianne Allen; *m* 1st, Adrienne Corri (marr. diss.); 2nd, Penelope Alice Wilton; one *d*. *Educ:* Eton; King's Coll., Cambridge. Connaught Theatre, Worthing, 1956–57. *Plays:* The Happiest Millionaire, Cambridge, 1957; Living for Pleasure, Garrick, 1958; Make Me an Offer (musical), New, 1959; The School for Scandal, Haymarket, 1962; The Three Musketeers, and A Subject of Scandal and Concern, Nottingham, 1962; She Loves Me (musical), NY, 1963; Julius Caesar, Royal Court, 1964; A Month in the Country, and Samson Agonistes, Guildford, 1965; Barefoot in the Park, Piccadilly, 1965; The Rivals, Haymarket, 1966; The Importance of Being Earnest, Haymarket, 1967; Spoiled, Glasgow, 1970; Abelard and Heloise, Wyndham's, 1970; Three Sisters, and Trelawny of The Wells, 1971; Becket, Guildford, 1972; Popkiss, Globe, 1972; Gigi, NY, 1973; Bloomsbury, Phoenix, 1974; The Gay Lord Quex, Albery, 1975; Othello, Nottingham, 1976; Rosmersholm, Haymarket, 1977; Don Juan comes back from the War, Betrayal, Nat. Theatre, 1978; The Philanderer, Nat. Theatre, 1979; Appearances, May Fair, 1980; Man and Superman, The Mayor of Zalamea, The Hypochondriac, Nat. Theatre, 1981; The Time of Your Life, Twelfth Night, Measure for Measure, RSC, 1983; Breaking the Silence, Waste, RSC, 1984. *Films:* include: Girls at Sea, 1957; Upstairs and Downstairs; The Entertainer; The Queen's Guard, 1960; Go to Blazes, 1962; Moll Flanders, 1966; Star, 1968; The Incredible Sarah, 1977; The Cat and the Canary, 1978; Escape to Victory, 1981. *TV: serials:* Roads to Freedom, 1970; The Golden Bowl, 1972; Good Behaviour, 1982; Intimate Contact, 1987; numerous plays. Best Supporting Actor, Hollywood Golden Globe Award, 1968; Actor of the Year, SWET Award, 1981. *Recreations:* golf, classical music, gardening. *Address:* c/o Michael Whitehall, 125 Gloucester Road, SW7.

MASSEY, Roy Cyril; Organist and Master of the Choristers, Hereford Cathedral, since 1974; *b* 9 May 1934; *s* of late Cyril Charles Massey and of Beatrice May Massey; *m* 1975, Ruth Carol Craddock Grove. *Educ:* Univ. of Birmingham (BMus); privately with David Willcocks. FRCO (CHM); ADCM; ARCM; FRSCM (for distinguished services to church music) 1972. Organist: St Alban's, Conybere Street, Birmingham, 1953–60; St Augustine's, Edgbaston, 1960–65; Croydon Parish Church, 1965–68; Warden, RSCM, 1965–68; Conductor, Croydon Bach Soc., 1966–68; Special Comr of RSCM, 1964–; Organist to City of Birmingham Choir, 1954–; Organist and Master of Choristers, Birmingham Cath., 1968–74; Dir of Music, King Edward's Sch., Birmingham, 1968–74. Conductor, Hereford Choral Soc., 1974–; Conductor-in-Chief, alternate years Associate Conductor, Three Choirs Festival, 1975–; Advisor on organs to dioceses of Birmingham and Hereford, 1974–. Mem. Council and Examiner, RCO, 1970–; Mem., Adv. Council, 1976–78, Council, 1984–, RSCM. President: Birmingham Organists' Assoc., 1970–75; Cathedral Organists' Assoc., 1982–84. Fellow, St Michael's Coll., Tenbury, 1976 85. *Recreations:* motoring, old buildings, Dutch organs. *Address:* 14 College Cloisters, Hereford HR1 2NG. *T:* Hereford 272011. *Club:* Conservative (Hereford).

MASSEY, Prof. Vincent, PhD; FRS 1977; Professor of Biological Chemistry, University of Michigan, since 1963; *b* 28 Nov. 1926; *s* of Walter Massey and Mary Ann Massey; *m* 1950, Margot Eva Ruth Grünewald; one *s* two *d*. *Educ:* Univ. of Sydney (BSc Hons 1947); Univ. of Cambridge (PhD 1953). Scientific Officer, CSIRO, Australia, 1947–50; Ian McMaster Scholar, Cambridge, 1950–53, ICI Fellow, 1953–55; Researcher, Henry Ford Hosp., Detroit, 1955–57; Lectr, then Sen. Lectr, Univ. of Sheffield, 1957–63. Vis. Prof., Univ. of Ill, 1960; Vis. Prof., Univ. of Konstanz, Germany, 1973–74, Permanent Guest Prof., 1975–. *Publications:* Flavins and Flavoproteins (ed jtly), 1982; over 200 articles in scholarly jls and books. *Recreations:* walking, sailing, gardening. *Address:* Department of Biological Chemistry, University of Michigan, Ann Arbor, Mich 48109, USA. *T:* (313) 7647196.

MASSEY, William Edmund Devereux, CBE 1961; retired from HM Diplomatic Service; *b* 1901; *m* 1942, Ingrid Glad-Block, Oslo; one *d*. Entered Foreign Office, 1922;

served in diplomatic and consular posts in Poland, France, Japan, Brazil, Roumania, Sweden, Luxembourg, Germany (Chargé d'Affaires); Ambassador and Consul-General to Nicaragua, 1959–61. Hon. Consul for Nicaragua in London, 1969–79. Freeman of City of London. Chm., UK Permanent Cttee on Geographical Names for Official Use, 1965–81; UK Deleg., 2nd UN Conf. on Geographical Names, 1972. FRGS. OStJ 1945. Grand Ducal Commemorative Medal, Luxembourg, 1953.

MASSIGLI, René, (Hon.) GCVO 1950; (Hon.) KBE 1938; (Hon.) CH 1954; Grand Cross, Legion of Honour, 1954; *b* 22 March 1888; *s* of late Charles Massigli and late Marguerite Michel; *m* 1932, Odette Boissier; one *d*. *Educ:* Ecole normale supérieure. Mem. of the Ecole Française de Rome, 1910–13; Chargé de cours at the University of Lille, 1913–14; Gen. Sec. at the Conference of Ambassadors, 1920; Maître des Requêtes at the Conseil d'Etat, 1924–28; Ministre plénipotentiaire, Head of the League of Nations' Section at the Ministry of Foreign Affairs, 1928–33; Asst Dir of Political Section at the Ministry of Foreign Affairs, 1933–37, Dir, 1937–38; Ambassador to Turkey, 1939–40; escaped from France, 1943; Commissioner for Foreign Affairs, French Cttee of National Liberation, 1943–44; French Ambassador to Great Britain, Sept. 1944–Jan. 1955; Sec.-Gen. at the Quai d'Orsay, Jan. 1955–June 1956; retired 1956. French Pres., Channel Tunnel Study Gp, 1958–69. *Publications:* Quelques Maladies de l'Etat, 1958; La Turquie devant la guerre, 1964; Une Comédie des Erreurs, 1978. *Address:* 3 avenue Robert Schuman, 75007 Paris, France.

MASSINGHAM, John Dudley, CMG 1986; HM Diplomatic Service; High Commissioner to Guyana and non-resident Ambassador to Suriname, since 1985; *b* 1 Feb. 1930; *yr s* of Percy Massingham and Amy (*née* Sanders); *m* 1952, Jean Elizabeth Beech; two *s* two *d*. *Educ:* Dulwich Coll.; Magdalene Coll., Cambridge (MA); Magdalen Coll., Oxford. HM Overseas Civil Service, N Nigeria, 1954–59; BBC, 1959–64; HM Diplomatic Service, 1964–: First Secretary, CRO, 1964–66; Dep. High Comr and Head of Chancery, Freetown, 1966–70; FCO, 1970–71; seconded to Pearce Commn, Jan.-May 1972; First Sec. (Information), later Aid (Kuala Lumpur), 1972–75; First Sec. and Head of Chancery, Kinshasa, 1976–77; Chief Sec., Falkland Islands Govt, 1977–79; Consul-General, Durban, June-Dec. 1979; Counsellor (Economic and Commercial), Nairobi, 1980–81; Governor and C-in-C, St Helena, 1981–84. *Recreations:* bird watching, avoiding physical exercise. *Address:* c/o Foreign and Commonwealth Office, SW1; 24 Cherry Orchard, Pershore, Worcs. *Club:* Royal Commonwealth Society.

MASSY, family name of **Baron Massy.**

MASSY, 9th Baron *cr* 1776 (Ire.); **Hugh Hamon John Somerset Massy;** *b* 11 June 1921; *o s* of 8th Baron, and Margaret, 2nd *d* of late Richard Leonard, Meadsbrook, Ashbourne, Co. Limerick, and *widow* of Dr Moran, Tara, Co. Meath; *S* father 1958; *m* 1943, Margaret, *d* of late John Flower, Barry, Co. Meath; four *s* one *d*. *Educ:* Clongowes Wood Coll.; Clayesmore Sch. Served War, 1940–45, Private, RAOC. *Heir: s* Hon. David Hamon Somerset Massy, *b* 4 March 1947.

MASSY-GREENE, Sir (John) Brian, Kt 1972; Chairman: Pacific Dunlop (formerly Dunlop Olympic) Ltd, since 1979 (Director since 1968; Vice-Chairman, 1977–79); Hazelton Air Services Holdings Ltd, since 1984; Santos Ltd, since 1984 (Director, since 1984); *b* Tenterfield, NSW, 20 April 1916; *s* of late Sir Walter Massy-Greene, KCMG, and Lula May Lomax; *m* 1942, Margaret Elizabeth Ritchie Sharp, *d* of late Dr Walter Alexander Ramsay Sharp, OBE; two *s* two *d*. *Educ:* Sydney C of E Grammar Sch.; Geelong Grammar Sch.; Clare Coll., Cambridge (MA). Served War 1939–45: New Guinea, AIF, as Lieut, 1942–45. Joined Metal Manufacturers Ltd, as Staff Cadet, 1939; later transferred to their wholly-owned subsid. Austral Bronze Co. Pty Ltd; Gen. Manager, 1953–62. Managing Dir, 1962–76, and Chm., 1966–77, Consolidated Gold Fields Australia Ltd; Chairman: The Bellambi Coal Co. Ltd, 1964–72; Goldsworthy Mining Ltd, 1965–76; The Mount Lyell Mining & Railway Co. Ltd, 1964–76; Lawrenson Alumasc Holdings Ltd, 1964–73 (Dir, 1962–73); Commonwealth Banking Corp., 1985– (Dir, 1968–; Dep. Chm., 1975–85); Director: Associated Minerals Consolidated Ltd, 1962–76; Commonwealth Mining Investments (Australia) Ltd, 1962–72 and 1978–; Consolidated Gold Fields Ltd, London, 1963–76; Dalgety Australia Ltd, 1967–78 (Dep. Chm., 1975–78); Zip Holdings Ltd, 1964–73; Australian European Finance Corp., 1975–; Nat. Mutual Life Assoc. Ltd, 1977–85. Member: Exec. Cttee, Australian Mining Industry Council, 1967–78 (Pres. 1971); Manuf. Industries Adv. Council, 1968–77; NSW Adv. Cttee, CSIRO, 1968–75. Mem., Aust. Inst. Mining and Metallurgy. FAIM; FIEAust. *Recreations:* farming, fishing, flying. *Address:* 1/7 Quambi Place, Edgecliff, NSW 2027, Australia. *T:* 326–1429. *Club:* Australian.

MASTEL, Royston John, CVO 1977; CBE 1969; Assistant Commissioner (Administration and Operations), Metropolitan Police, 1972–76; *b* 30 May 1917; *s* of late John Mastel and late Rose Mastel (*née* Gorton); *m* 1940, Anne Kathleen Johnson; two *s*. *Educ:* Tottenham Grammar School. Joined Metropolitan Police as Constable, 1937; Pilot, RAF, 1941–45; Metro. Police: Sergeant 1946; Inspector 1951; Supt 1955; Comdr, No 2 District, 1966; subseq. Dep. Asst Comr, Head of Management Services Dept and D Dept (Personnel); Asst Comr (Personnel and Training), 1972. OStJ 1976. *Recreations:* Rugby football, golf. *Address:* The Retreat, Nottage, Porthcawl.

MASTERS, Rt. Rev. Brian John; *see* Edmonton, Area Bishop of.

MASTERSON, Valerie, (Mrs Andrew March); opera and concert singer; *d* of Edward Masterson and Rita McGrath; *m* 1965, Andrew March; one *s* one *d*. *Educ:* Holt Hill Convent; studied in London and Milan on scholarship, and with Edwardo Asquez. Début, Landestheater Salzburg; appearances with: D'Oyly Carte Opera, Glyndebourne Festival Opera, ENO, Royal Opera, Covent Garden, etc; appears in principal opera houses in Paris, Aix-en-Provence, Toulouse, Munich, Geneva, Barcelona, Milan, San Francisco, Chile, etc; leading roles in: La Traviata, Le Nozze di Figaro, Manon, Faust, Alcina, Die Entführung aus dem Serail, Così fan tutte, La Bohème, Semele (SWET award, 1983), Die Zauberflöte, Julius Caesar, Rigoletto, Romeo and Juliet, Carmen, Count Ory, Mireille, Louise, Idomeneo, Les Dialogues des Carmélites; The Merry Widow; Xerxes; Orlando. Recordings include: La Traviata; Elisabetta, Regina d'Inghilterra; Der Ring des Nibelungen; The Merry Widow; Julius Caesar; Scipione; several Gilbert and Sullivan operas. Broadcasts regularly on radio and TV. *Recreations:* tennis, swimming, ice skating. *Address:* c/o Music International, 13 Ardilaun Road, Highbury, N5 2QR.

MATABELELAND, Bishop of, since 1977; **Rt. Rev. Robert William Stanley Mercer;** *b* 10 Jan. 1935; *s* of Harold Windrum Mercer and Kathleen Frampton. *Educ:* Grey School, Port Elizabeth, S Africa; St Paul's Theological Coll., Grahamstown, SA (LTh). Deacon 1959, priest 1960, Matabeleland; Asst Curate, Hillside, Bulawayo, 1959–63; Novice, CR, 1963; professed, 1965; at Mirfield, 1963–66; at St Teilo's Priory, Cardiff, 1966–68; Prior and Rector of Stellenbosch, S Africa, 1968–70; deported from SA, 1970; Chaplain, St Augustine's School, Penhalonga, Rhodesia, 1971–72; Rector of Borrowdale, Salisbury, Rhodesia, 1972–77. Sub-Prelate, Order of St John of Jerusalem, 1981. *Address:* Box 2422, Bulawayo, Zimbabwe. *T:* 61370.

MATACA, Most Rev. Petero; *see* Suva, Archbishop of, (RC).

MATANE, Sir Paulias (Nguna), Kt 1986; CMG 1980; OBE 1975; Secretary, Foreign Affairs, Papua New Guinea, 1980–85; *b* 5 July 1932; *s* of Ilias Maila Matane and Elsa Toto; *m* 1957, Kaludia Peril Matane; two *s* two *d*. *Educ:* Teacher's College (Dip. Teaching and Education). Asst Teacher, Tauran Sch., PNG, 1957, Headmaster, 1958–61; School Inspector, 1962–66; Dist Sch. Inspector and Dist Educn Officer, 1967–68; Supt, Teacher Educn, 1969; Foundn Mem., Public Schs Bd, 1969–70; Sec., Dept of Business Develt, 1971–74; Ambassador to USA, Mexico and UN, and High Comr to Canada, 1975–80. Hon. DTech Univ. of Technol., Lae, 1985; Hon. PhD Univ. of PNG, 1986. UN 40th Anniv. Medal, 1985. *Publications:* Kum Tumun of Minj, 1966; A New Guinean Travels through Africa, 1971; My Childhood in New Guinea, 1972; What Good is Business?, 1972; Two New Guineans Travel through SE Asia, 1974; Aimbe the Challenger, 1974; Aimbe the School Dropout, 1974; Aimbe the Magician, 1976; Aimbe the Pastor, 1979. *Recreations:* reading, gardening, squash, fishing, writing. *Address:* PO Box 680, Rabaul, Papua New Guinea. *Clubs:* Tamukavar, Tauran Ex Student and Citizens', Cathay.

MATCHAN, Leonard Joseph; Hon. Life President, Cope Allman International Ltd; Chairman, Guarantee Trust of Jersey Ltd, to 1979; *b* 26 March 1911; *s* of late George Matchan and Elsie Harriet Greenleaf; *m* 1933, Kathleen Artis; one *s* one *d*. *Educ:* Trinity, Croydon. FACCA; JDipMA; Certified Accountant. Vice President and European General Manager, Max Factor, Hollywood, 1936–49. Practice as accountant, 1950–55. President, Toilet Preparations Assoc., 1940–48. *Recreation:* work. *Address:* Island of Brecqhou, Channel Islands. *T:* Guernsey 25000 and Sark 2222.

MATE, Rt. Rev. Martin; *see* Newfoundland, Eastern, and Labrador, Bishop of.

MATES, Lt-Col Michael John; MP (C) East Hampshire, since 1983 (Petersfield, Oct. 1974–1983); *b* 9 June 1934; *s* of Claude John Mates; *m* 1959, Mary Rosamund Paton (marr. diss. 1980); two *s* two *d*; *m* 1982, Rosellen, *d* of Mr and Mrs W. T. Bett; one *d*. *Educ:* Salisbury Cathedral Sch.; Blundell's Sch.; King's Coll., Cambridge (choral schol.). Joined Army, 1954; 2nd Lieut, RUR, 1955; Queen's Dragoon Guards, RAC, 1961; Major, 1967; Lt-Col, 1973; resigned commn 1974. Vice-Chairman: Cons. NI Cttee, 1979–81 (Sec., 1974–79); Cons. Home Affairs Cttee, 1979–; Chm., All-Party Anglo-Irish Gp, 1979–; Mem., Select Cttee on Defence, 1979–; introduced: Farriers Registration Act, 1975; Rent Amendment Act, 1985. Farriers' Co.: Liveryman, 1975–; Asst, 1981; Master, 1986. *Address:* House of Commons, SW1A 0AA.

MATHER, Carol; *see* Mather, David Carol MacDonell.

MATHER, (David) Carol (Macdonell), MC 1944; MP (C) Esher since 1970; *b* 3 Jan. 1919; *s* of late Loris Emerson Mather, CBE; *m* 1951, Hon. Philippa Selina Bewicke-Copley, *o d* of 5th Baron Cromwell, DSO; one *s* three *d*. *Educ:* Harrow; Trinity Coll., Cambridge. War of 1939–45: commissioned Welsh Guards, 1940; served in Western Desert Campaigns, 1941–42; PoW, 1942; escaped, 1943; NW Europe, 1944–45; wounded, 1945; Palestine Campaign, 1946–48. Asst Mil. Attaché, British Embassy, Athens, 1953–56; GSO 1, MI Directorate, War Office, 1957–61; Mil. Sec. to GOC-in-C, Eastern Command, 1961–62; retd as Lt-Col., 1962. Conservative Research Dept, 1962–70; contested (C) Leicester (NW), 1966; an Opposition Whip, 1975–79; a Lord Comr of HM Treasury, 1979–81; Vice-Chamberlain of HM Household, 1981–83; Comptroller of HM Household, 1983–86. FRGS. *Address:* House of Commons, SW1A 0AA. *Club:* Brooks's.

See also Sir W. L. Mather.

MATHER, John Douglas, FCIT; CBIM; Chief Executive, National Freight Consortium plc, since 1984; *b* 27 Jan. 1936; *s* of John Dollandson and Emma May Mather; *m* 1958, Hilda Patricia (*née* Kirkwood); one *s* (one *d* decd). *Educ:* Manchester Univ. (BACom, MAEcon). MIPM. Personnel Management: Philips Electrical, 1959–66; Convoys Ltd, 1966–67; Personnel Management, Transport Management, National Freight Company, 1967–. Mem., Worshipful Co. of Carmen. *Recreations:* golf, gardening, travel. *Address:* St Giles House, Love Lane, Kings Langley, Hertfordshire WD4 9HW. *T:* Kings Langley 63063. *Clubs:* Royal Automobile; Woburn Golf and Country.

MATHER, Sir Kenneth, Kt 1979; CBE 1956; FRS 1949; DSc (London), 1940; Professor Emeritus and Hon. Senior Fellow in Genetics, University of Birmingham, since 1984 (Hon. Professor of Genetics, 1971–84); *b* 22 June 1911; *e c* and *o s* of R. W. Mather; *m* 1937, Mona Rhodes; one *s*. *Educ:* Nantwich and Acton Grammar Sch.; University of Manchester (BSc 1931). Ministry of Agriculture and Fisheries Research Scholar, 1931–34; Lecturer in Galton Laboratory, University Coll., London, 1934–37; Rockefeller Research Fellow, at California Institute of Technology and Harvard University, 1937–38; Head of Genetics Dept, John Innes Horticultural Institution, 1938–48; Professor of Genetics, University of Birmingham, 1948–65; Vice-Chancellor, Univ. of Southampton, 1965–71, now Emeritus Prof. Member: Agricultural Research Council, 1949–54, 1955–60, and 1969–79; Science Research Council, 1965–69; Academic Adv. Cttee of Bath Univ. of Technology, 1967–71; DHSS Cttee on the Irradiation of Food, 1967–74; Cttee on Medical Aspects of Chemicals in Food and the Environment, 1972–74; Genetic Manipulation Adv. Gp, 1976–78; Wessex Regional Hosp. Bd, 1968–71. Hon. LLD Southampton, 1972; Hon. DSc: Bath, 1975; Manchester, 1980; Wales, 1980. *Publications:* The Measurement of Linkage in Heredity, 1938; Statistical Analysis in Biology, 1943; Biometrical Genetics, 1949, 3rd edn 1982; Human Diversity, 1964; The Elements of Biometry, 1967; Genetical Structure of Populations, 1973; (jointly): The Elements of Genetics, 1949; Genes, Plants and People, 1950; Introduction to Biometrical Genetics, 1977; many papers on Genetics, Cytology, and Statistics. *Address:* Department of Genetics, University of Birmingham, B15 2TT. *T:* 021–472 1301; The White House, 296 Bristol Road, Edgbaston, Birmingham B5 7SN. *T:* 021–472 2093. *Club:* Athenæum.

MATHER, Leonard Charles, CBE 1978; Chairman, United Dominions Trust, 1974–81; Director, Midland Bank, 1968–84; a life Vice-President, Institute of Bankers, since 1970; *b* 10 Oct. 1909; *s* of Richard and Elizabeth Mather; *m* 1937, Muriel Armor Morris. *Educ:* Oldershaw Sch., Wallasey. BCom. (London). Entered Midland Bank, Dale Street, Liverpool, 1926; transf. to London, 1937; served in Gen. Managers' Dept at Head Office, 1937–45; Man., Bolton, 1945–48; Princ., Legal Dept, 1948–50; Asst Gen. Man., 1950–56; Gen. Man., Midland Bank Executor & Trustee Co. Ltd, 1956–58; Jt Gen. Man., Midland Bank Ltd, 1958–63; Asst Chief Gen. Man., 1964–66; Dep. Chief Gen. Man., 1966–68; Chief Gen. Man., 1968–72; Vice-Chm., 1972–74; Director: Midland Bank Trust Co. Ltd, 1968–74; Midland & International Banks Ltd, 1969–74; Montagu Trust, 1969–74; Chm., European Banks' International Co. SA, 1972–74 (Dir, 1970); Dep. Chm., Euro-Pacific Finance Corp. Ltd, 1970–74. FCIS; FIB (Dep. Chm., 1967–69; Pres., 1969–70); Hon. FIB 1974. Hon. DLitt Loughborough, 1978. *Publications:* The Lending Banker, 1955; Banker and Customer Relationship and the Accounts of Personal Customers, 1956; The Accounts of Limited Company Customers, 1958; Securities Acceptable to the Lending Banker, 1960. *Recreations:* golf, bridge. *Address:* Rochester House, Parkfield, Seal, Sevenoaks, Kent. *T:* Sevenoaks 61007.

MATHER, Sir William (Loris), Kt 1968; CVO 1986; OBE 1957; MC 1945; TD and 2 clasps 1949; MA, CEng; Vice-Lieutenant of Cheshire, since 1975; Chairman: Neolith

Chemicals Ltd, since 1983; Advanced Manufacturing Technology Group, since 1985; *b* 17 Aug. 1913; *s* of Loris Emerson Mather, CBE; *m* 1937, Eleanor, *d* of Prof. R. H. George, Providence, RI, USA; two *s* two *d*. *Educ:* Oundle; Trinity Coll., Cambridge (MA Engrg and Law, 1939). Commissioned Cheshire Yeomanry, 1935; served War of 1939–45: Palestine, Syria, Iraq, Iran, Western Desert, Italy, Belgium, Holland, Germany (wounded twice, MC); Instructor, Staff Coll., Camberley, and GSO1, 1944–45. Chm., Mather & Platt Ltd, 1960–78; Divisional Dir, BSC, 1968–73; Chm., CompAir Ltd, 1978–83 (Dir, 1973–83). Director: District Bank, 1960–84; National Westminster Bank, 1970–84 (Chm., Northern Bd, 1972–84); Manchester Ship Canal Co. Ltd, 1970–84; Imperial Continental Gas Assoc. Ltd, 1980–84. Chairman: NW Regional Economic Planning Council, 1968–75; Inst. of Directors, 1979–82 (Manchester Inst. of Dirs, 1967–72); British Pump Manufrs Assoc., 1970–73; President: Manchester Chamber of Commerce, 1964–66 (Emeritus Dir, 1978); Manchester Guardian Soc. for Protection of Trade, 1971–85; British Mech. Engrg Confedn, 1975–78; Civic Trust for the NW, 1979– (Chm., 1961–78); Vice Pres., Assoc. of British Chambers of Commerce, 1979–85; Pres., Mech. Engrg Council, 1978–80; Member: Council of Industrial Design, 1960–71; Engineering Industries Council, 1976–80; Council, Duchy of Lancaster, 1977–85. Member Court: Manchester Univ., 1956–; Salford Univ., 1968–; Royal College of Art, 1967–85; Mem. Council, Manchester Business Sch., 1964–85; Governor: Manchester University Inst. of Science and Technology (Pres., 1976–85; Hon. Fellow, 1986); Manchester Grammar Sch., 1965–80; Feoffee, Chetham's Hosp. Sch., 1961–; Pres., Manchester YMCA, 1982– (Chm., 1953–82). Hon. Fellow, Manchester Coll. of Art and Design, 1967; Hon. DEng Liverpool, 1980; Hon. LLD Manchester, 1983. Comdr, Cheshire Yeomanry, 1954–57; Col and Dep. Comdr, 23 Armoured Bde, TA, 1957–60; ADC to the Queen, 1961–66. CBIM; FRSA. DL City and County of Chester, 1963; High Sheriff of Cheshire, 1969–70. *Recreations:* field sports, winter sports, golf, swimming. *Address:* Whirley Hall, Macclesfield, Cheshire SK10 4RN. *T:* Macclesfield 22077. *Clubs:* Naval and Military, Leander.
See also D. C. M. Mather.

MATHERS, Sir Robert (William), Kt 1981; Chairman and Managing Director, Mathers Enterprises Ltd (footwear retailing chain), Australia, since 1973; *b* 2 Aug. 1928; *s* of William Mathers and Olive Ida (*née* Wohlsen); *m* 1957, Betty Estelle Greasley; three *d*. *Educ:* Church of England Grammar Sch., E Brisbane. FAIM; FRMIA 1982. General Manager/Director, Mathers Enterprises Ltd, 1963; Dep. Chm., Bligh Coal Ltd, 1980–. Mem. Council: Retailers Assoc. of Qld, 1960–; Inst. of Public Affairs, 1978–; Griffith Univ., 1978–; Australian Bicentennial Authority, 1980–; Cllr, Enterprise Australia, 1983–; Member: Finance Adv. Cttee for XII Commonwealth Games, 1979; Australiana Fund, 1980–; Finance Adv. Cttee, Australian Stockman's Hall of Fame and Outback Heritage Centre, 1984–; Council, Duke of Edinburgh's Sixth Commonwealth Study Conf., 1984–86; Dep. Chm., Organising Cttee, Brisbane Olympics, 1985–; Past Pres., Footwear Retailers Assoc. Trustee: WWF, Australia, 1981–; Queensland Art Gall. Foundn, 1983– (Founding Cttee Mem., 1979–). Fellow: Inst. of Dirs in Australia, 1973; Company Directors' Assoc. of Australia, 1981; FAMI 1984. Cavaliere, Order of Merit (Italy), 1983. *Recreations:* golf, tennis, swimming. *Address:* 1 Wybelenna Street, Kenmore, Queensland 4069, Australia. *T:* (07) 378 5503. *Clubs:* Rotary, Royal Queensland Yacht Squadron, Tattersalls, Milton Tennis, Rugby Union, Indooroopilly Golf (Brisbane).

MATHESON, Duncan, MA, LLM; a Recorder of the Crown Court, since 1985. *Address:* 1 Crown Office Row, Temple, EC4Y 7HH.

MATHESON, Sir (James Adam) Louis, KBE 1976 (MBE 1944); CMG 1972; FTS; FEng; Vice-Chancellor, Monash University, Melbourne, 1959–76; Chancellor, Papua New Guinea University of Technology, 1973–75; Chairman, Australian Science and Technology Council, 1975–76; *b* 11 Feb. 1912; *s* of William and Lily Edith Matheson; *m* 1937, Audrey Elizabeth Wood; three *s*. *Educ:* Bootham Sch., York; Manchester Univ. (MSc 1933). Lectr, Birmingham Univ., 1938–46 (PhD 1946); Prof. of Civil Engineering, Univ. of Melbourne, Australia, 1946–50; Beyer Prof. of Engineering, Univ. of Manchester, 1951–59. Hon. FICE (Mem. Council, 1965); FIStructE (Vice-Pres., 1967–68); Hon. FIEAust (Mem. Council, 1961–81, Vice-Pres., 1970–74, Pres., 1975–76); Fellow, Aust. Acad. of Technological Scis, 1976; Fellow, Fellowship of Engrg, 1980. Member: Mission on Technical Educn in W Indies, 1957; Royal Commn into failure of King's Bridge, 1963; Ramsay Cttee on Tertiary Educn in Victoria, 1961–63; CSIRO Adv. Council, 1962–67; Exec., Aust. Council for Educational Research, 1964–69; Interim Council, Univ. of Papua New Guinea, 1965–68; Enquiry into Post-Secondary Educn in Victoria, 1976–78; Chairman: Council, Papua New Guinea Inst. of Technology, 1966–73; Aust. Vice-Chancellors' Cttee, 1967–68; Assoc. of Commonwealth Univs, 1967–69; Newport Power Stn Review Panel, 1977; Schools Commn Buildings Cttee, 1977–81; Victorian Planning and Finance Cttee, Commonwealth Schools Commn, 1979–83; Sorrento Harbour Inquiry, 1984. Trustee, Inst. of Applied Science (now Science Mus. of Victoria), 1963–83 (Pres., 1969–73). Dir, Nauru Phosphate Corp., 1977–79. Hon. DSc Hong Kong, 1969; Hon. LLD: Manchester, 1972; Monash, 1975; Melbourne, 1975. Kernot Meml Medal, 1972; Peter Nicol Russell Medal, 1976. *Publications:* Hyperstatic Structures: Vol. 1, 1959; Vol. 2, 1960; Still Learning, 1980; various articles on engineering and education. *Recreations:* music, woodcraft. *Address:* 26/166 West Toorak Road, South Yarra, Victoria 3141, Australia. *Club:* Melbourne.

MATHESON, Very Rev. James Gunn; Moderator of General Assembly of Church of Scotland, May 1975–76; *b* 1 March 1912; *s* of Norman Matheson and Henrietta Gunn; *m* 1937, Janet Elizabeth Clarkson; three *s* one *d* (and one *d* decd). *Educ:* Inverness Royal Academy; Edinburgh Univ. (MA, BD). Free Church of Olrig, Caithness, 1936–39; Chaplain to HM Forces, 1939–45 (POW Italy, 1941–43); St Columba's Church, Blackhall, Edinburgh, 1946–51; Knox Church, Dunedin, NZ, 1951–61; Sec. of Stewardship and Budget Cttee of Church of Scotland, 1961–73; Parish Minister, Portree, Isle of Skye, 1973–79; retired 1979. Hon. DD Edinburgh, 1975. *Publications:* Do You Believe This?, 1960; Saints and Sinners, 1975; contrib. theol jls. *Recreations:* gardening, fishing. *Address:* Husabost, Totaig, Dunvegan, Isle of Skye. *Club:* New (Edinburgh).

MATHESON, Maj.-Gen. John Mackenzie, OBE 1950; TD 1969; Postgraduate Dean, Faculty of Medicine, University of Edinburgh, 1971–80; *b* Gibraltar, 6 Aug. 1912; *s* of late John Matheson and late Nina Short, Cape Town; *m* 1942, Agnes, *d* of Henderson Purves, Dunfermline; one *d*. *Educ:* George Watson's Coll., Edinburgh; Edinburgh Univ. (Vans Dunlop Schol.). MB, ChB 1936; MRCP 1939; MD 1945; FRCSEd 1946; FRCS 1962; FRCP 1972. Royal Victoria Hosp. Tuberculosis Trust Research Fellow, 1936–37; Lieut, RAMC (TA), 1936. Served War of 1939–45: Middle East, N Africa and Italy; Regular RAMC Commn, 1944 (despatches). Clinical Tutor, Surgical Professorial Unit, Edinburgh Univ., 1947–48; Med. Liaison Officer to Surgeon-Gen. US Army, Washington, DC, 1948–50; Asst Chief, Section Gen. Surgery, Walter Reed Army Hosp., Washington, DC, 1950–51; Cons. Surgeon: MELF, 1963–64; BAOR, 1967; Far East, 1967–69; Jt Prof. Mil. Surg., RAM Coll. and RCS of Eng., 1964–67; Brig. 1967; Comdt and Dir of Studies, Royal Army Med. Coll., 1969–71. QHS 1969–71. Hon. Col, 205 (Scottish) Gen. Hosp., T&AVR, 1978–80. Alexander Medal, 1961; Simpson-Smith Memorial Lectr,

1967; Gordon-Watson Lectr, RCS of Eng., 1967. Senior Fellow, Assoc. of Surgeons of GB and Ireland; British Medical Association: Mem., Armed Forces Cttee, 1983–86; Mem., Bd of Educn and Science, 1985–86; Pres., Lothian Div., 1978–80. President: Scottish Br., Royal Soc. of Tropical Medicine and Hygiene, 1978–80; Military Surgical Soc., 1984–86; Vice-Pres., Edinburgh Univ. Graduates Assoc., 1985–86; Chm. Council, Edinburgh Royal Infirmary Samaritan Soc., 1983–. FRSocMed. *Publications:* (contrib.) Military Medicine, in Dictionary of Medical Ethics, 1977; papers (on gun-shot wounds, gas-gangrene and sterilisation) to medical jls. *Recreation:* travel. *Address:* 2 Orchard Brae, Edinburgh EH4 1NY.

MATHESON, Sir Louis; *see* Matheson, Sir J. A. L.

MATHESON, Stephen Charles Taylor; Director of Information Technology, Inland Revenue, since 1984; *b* 27 June 1939; *s* of Robert Matheson and Olive Lovick; *m* 1960, Marna Rutherford Burnett; two *s*. *Educ:* Aberdeen Grammar Sch.; Aberdeen Univ. (MA hons English Lang. and Lit., 1961). HM Inspector of Taxes, 1961–70; Principal, Bd of Inland Revenue, 1970–75; Private Sec. to Paymaster General, 1975–76, to Chancellor of the Exchequer, 1976–77; Bd of Inland Revenue, 1977; Project Manager, Computerisation of Pay As You Earn Project; Under Sec., 1984. *Publication:* Maurice Walsh, Storyteller, 1985. *Recreations:* Scottish and Irish literature, book collecting, cooking, music. *Address:* 7 Lamberts Road, Surbiton, Surrey. *T:* 01–390 0685.

MATHESON OF MATHESON, Sir Torquhil (Alexander), 6th Bt *cr* 1882, of Lochalsh; Chief of Clan Matheson; one of HM Body Guard of the Honourable Corps of Gentlemen at Arms, since 1977; *b* 15 Aug. 1925; *s* of General Sir Torquhil George Matheson, 5th Bt, KCB, CMG; *S* father, 1963, *S* kinsman as Chief of Clan Matheson, 1975; *m* 1954, Serena Mary Francesca, *o d* of late Lt-Col Sir Michael Peto, 2nd Bt; two *d*. *Educ:* Eton. Served War of 1939–45; joined Coldstream Guards, July 1943; commnd, March 1944; 5th Bn Coldstream Guards, NW Europe, Dec. 1944–May 1945 (wounded). Served with 3rd Bn Coldstream Guards: Palestine, 1945–48 (despatches); Tripoli and Egypt, 1950–53; seconded King's African Rifles, 1961–64. Captain, 1952; Major, 1959; retd 1964. 4th Bn, Wilts Regt, TA, 1965–67; Royal Wilts Territorials (T&AVR III), 1967–69. *Heir* (to Baronetcy and Chiefship): *b* Major Fergus John Matheson, late Coldstream Guards [*b* 22 Feb. 1927; *m* 1952, Hon. Jean Elizabeth Mary Willoughby, *yr d* of 11th Baron Middleton, KG, MC, TD; one *s* two *d*. One of HM Body Guard of the Honourable Corps of Gentlemen at Arms, since 1979]. *Address:* Standerwick Court, Frome, Som. *Clubs:* Army and Navy; Leander (Henley-on-Thames).

MATHEW, John Charles, QC 1977; *b* 3 May 1927; *s* of late Sir Theobald Mathew, KBE, MC, and Lady Mathew; *m* 1952, Jennifer Jane Mathew (*née* Lagden); two *d*. *Educ:* Beaumont Coll. Served, Royal Navy, 1945–47. Called to Bar, Lincoln's Inn, 1949; apptd Junior Prosecuting Counsel to the Crown, 1959; First Sen. Prosecuting Counsel to the Crown, 1974–77. Elected a Bencher of Lincoln's Inn, 1970. *Recreations:* golf, backgammon, cinema. *Address:* 47 Abingdon Villas, W8. *T:* 01–937 7535. *Club:* Garrick.

MATHEW, Theobald David; Windsor Herald of Arms, since 1978; *b* 7 April 1942; *s* of Robert Mathew, Porchester Terrace, London, and West Mersea Hall, Essex, solicitor, and Joan Alison, *d* of Sir George Young, Bt, MVO, of Formosa. *Educ:* Downside; Balliol Coll., Oxford (MA). Green Staff Officer at Investiture of HRH the Prince of Wales, 1969; Rouge Dragon Pursuivant of Arms, 1970; Dep. Treasurer, Coll. of Arms, 1978–. OStJ 1986. *Recreations:* cricket and sailing. *Address:* 76 Clifton Hill, NW8. *T:* 01–624 8448; College of Arms, EC4V 4BT. *T:* 01–248 0893. *Clubs:* Athenæum, MCC; Middlesex CCC, Royal Harwich Yacht.

MATHEWS, Rev. Arthur Kenneth, OBE 1942; DSC 1944; Vicar of Thursley, 1968–76; Rural Dean of Godalming, 1969–74; *b* 11 May 1906; *s* of late Reverend Canon A. A. and Mrs Mathews; *m* 1936, Elisabeth, *d* of late E. M. Butler and Mrs Butler; no *c*. *Educ:* Monkton Combe Sch.; Balliol Coll., Oxford (Exhibitioner); Cuddesdon Theol. Coll. Deacon 1932, priest 1933, at Wakefield; Asst Curate of Penistone; Padre of the Tanker Fleet of the Anglo-Saxon Petroleum Co. Ltd; licensed to officiate, Diocese of Wakefield, 1935–38; Vicar of Forest Row, 1938–44; Temp. Chaplain, RNVR, 1939–44 (Chaplain HMS Norfolk, 1940–44); on staff of Christian Frontier Council, 1944–46; Vicar of Rogate and Sequestrator of Terwick, 1946–54; Rural Dean of Midhurst, 1950–54; Hon. Chaplain to Bishop of Portsmouth, 1950–55; Commissary to: Bishop of Singapore, 1949–64; Bishop of Wellington, 1962–72; Student of Central Coll. of Anglican Communion at St Augustine's Coll., Canterbury, 1954–55; Dean and Rector of St Albans, 1955–63; Rector of St Peter's, Peebles, 1963–68. Hon. Chaplain to Bishop of Norwich, 1969–71. Member: Council, Marlborough Coll., 1953–74; Governing Body, Monkton Combe Sch., 1959–77. *Recreations:* walking and gardening. *Address:* The Tallat, Westwell, near Burford, Oxon OX8 4JT.
See also Baroness Brooke of Ystradfellte.

MATHEWSON, George Ross, CBE 1985; BSc, PhD, MBA; CEng, MIEE; Chief Executive and Member, Scottish Development Agency, since 1981; *b* 14 May 1940; *s* of George Mathewson and Charlotte Gordon (*née* Ross); *m* 1966, Sheila Alexandra Graham (*née* Bennett); two *s*. *Educ:* Perth Academy; St Andrews Univ. (BSc, PhD); Canisius Coll., Buffalo, NY (MBA). Assistant Lecturer, St Andrews Univ., 1964–67; various posts in Research & Development, Avionics Engineering, Bell Aerospace, Buffalo, NY, 1967–72; joined Industrial & Commercial Finance Corp., Edinburgh, 1972; Area Manager, Aberdeen, 1974, and Asst General Manager and Director, 1979. Dir, Scottish Investment Trust Ltd, 1981–; Chairman: Scottish Development Finance Ltd, 1981–; Glasgow Garden Festival 1988 Ltd. Vis. Prof., Strathclyde Business Sch., 1984–. CBIM 1986. Hon. LLD Dundee, 1983. *Publications:* various articles on engineering/finance. *Recreations:* geriatric Rugby, golf, business. *Address:* Larach-Beg, Corsee Road, Banchory, Kincardineshire, Scotland. *T:* Banchory 3482. *Club:* Aberdeen Petroleum.

MATHIAS, Surg. Rear-Adm. (D) Frank Russell Bentley; retired 1985; Director, Naval Dental Services, 1983–85, and Deputy Director of Defence Dental Services (Organisation), Ministry of Defence, 1985; *b* 27 Dec. 1927; *s* of Thomas Bentley Mathias and Phebe Ann Mathias; *m* 1954, Margaret Joyce (*née* Daniels); one *s* one *d*. *Educ:* Narberth Grammar Sch.; Guy's Hosp., London. LDSRCS Eng. 1952. House Surgeon, Sussex County Hosp., Brighton, 1952–53; joined RN, 1953; principal appointments: Staff Dental Surgeon, Flag Officer Malta, 1972; Flotilla Dental Surgeon, Flag Officer Submarines, 1972–74; Comd Dental Surgeon, Flag Officer Naval Air Comd, 1974–76; Dep. Dir, Naval Dental Services, 1976–80; Comd Dental Surgeon to C-in-C Naval Home Comd, 1980–83. QHDS 1982–85. OStJ 1981.

MATHIAS, Lionel Armine, CMG 1953; *b* 23 Jan. 1907; *s* of Hugh Henry Mathias and Amy Duncan Mathias (*née* Mathias); *m* 1935, Rebecca Gordon Rogers (*d* 1984); two *d* (and one *d* decd). *Educ:* Christs Coll., New Zealand; St Paul's Sch.; Keble Coll., Oxford. Appointed Asst District Commissioner, Uganda, 1929; Labour Commissioner, 1949–53; Member: Uganda Exec. Council, 1948, Legislative Council, 1949–53; Kampala Municipal Council, 1952–53; Uganda Students Adviser, 1953–62; Chm., Uganda Britain Soc., 1964–65. *Address:* Little Copt Farm, Shoreham, Sevenoaks, Kent. *T:* Otford 2040.

MATHIAS, Pauline Mary; Headmistress, More House School, since 1974; *b* 4 Oct. 1928; *d* of Francis and Hilda Donovan; *m* 1954, Prof. Anthony Peter Mathias; two *s*. *Educ:* La Retraite High School; Bedford College, London (BA Hons; DipEd). Head of English Dept, London Oratory Sch., 1954–64; Sen. Lectr in English and Admissions Tutor, Coloma Coll. of Education, 1964–74. Pres., Girls' Schs Assoc., 1982–83; Vice-Pres., Women's Careers Foundn, 1985–. Chm., ISIS, 1984–86. Governor: E-SU, 1986–; St Felix Sch., Southwold; New Hall Sch., Chelmsford; Westminster Cathedral Choir Sch.; Orwell Park Prep. Sch. *Recreations:* embroidery, golf, birdwatching, bicycling in France. *Address:* 22 Pont Street, SW1; 18 Lee Road, Aldeburgh, Suffolk. *Club:* University Women's.

MATHIAS, Prof. Peter, CBE 1984; MA, LittD; FBA 1977; Chichele Professor of Economic History, University of Oxford, and Fellow of All Souls College, Oxford, since 1969; *b* 10 Jan. 1928; *o c* of John Samuel and Marion Helen Mathias; *m* 1958, Elizabeth Ann, *d* of Robert Blackmore, JP, Bath; two *s* one *d*. *Educ:* Colston's Sch., Bristol; Jesus Coll., Cambridge (Schol.). 1st cl. (dist) Hist. Tripos, 1950, 1951; LittD Oxon, 1985. Research Fellow, Jesus Coll., Cambridge, 1952–55; Asst Lectr and Lectr, Faculty of History, Cambridge, 1955–68; Dir of Studies in History and Fellow, Queens' Coll., Cambridge, 1955–68; Tutor, 1957–68; Senior Proctor, Cambridge Univ., 1965–66. Vis. Professor: Univ. of Toronto, 1961; School of Economics, Delhi, 1967; Univ. of California, Berkeley, 1967; Univ. of Pa, 1972; Virginia Gildersleeve, Barnard Coll., Columbia Univ., 1972; Johns Hopkins Univ., 1979; ANU, Canberra, 1981; Geneva, 1986. Chairman: Business Archives Council, 1968–72 (Vice-Pres., 1980–84; Pres., 1984–); Econ. and Social History Cttee, SSRC, 1975–77 (Mem., 1970–77); Acad. Adv. Council, University Coll., Buckingham, 1979–84 (Mem., 1984–); Wellcome Trust Adv. Panel for History of Medicine, 1981–; Mem., ABRC, 1983–; Treasurer, Econ. Hist. Soc., 1968–; Hon. Treasurer, British Acad., 1980–; International Economic History Association: Sec., 1959–62; Pres., 1974–78; Hon. Pres., 1978–; Member: Exec. Cttee, Internat. Inst. of Economic History Francesco Datini, Prato, 1972–; Jerusalem Cttee, 1978–. Foreign Mem., Royal Danish Acad., 1982. Curator, Bodleian Library, 1972–. FRHistS 1972 (Vice-Pres., 1976–80). Hon. DLitt Buckingham, 1985. Asst Editor, Econ. Hist. Rev., 1955–57. *Publications:* The Brewing Industry in England 1700–1830, 1959; English Trade Tokens, 1962; Retailing Revolution, 1967; The First Industrial Nation, 1969, rev. edn 1983; (ed) Science and Society 1600–1900, 1972; The Transformation of England, 1979; General Editor, Cambridge Economic History of Europe, 1968–. *Recreation:* travel. *Address:* All Souls College, Oxford. *T:* Oxford 722251.

MATHIAS, Sir Richard Hughes, 2nd Bt, *cr* 1917; Member London Stock Exchange, 1948–84; *b* 6 April 1905; *s* of Sir Richard Mathias, 1st Bt, and Annie, *y d* of Evan Hughes, Cardiff; *S* father 1942; *m* 1st, 1937, Gladys Cecilia Turton (marr. diss., 1960), *o d* of late Edwin Hart, New Hextalls, Bletchingley, Surrey; two *d*; 2nd, 1960, Mrs Elizabeth Baird Murray (*d* 1972), *er d* of late Dr and Mrs Miles of Hendrescythan, Creigiau, Glamorgan; 3rd, 1973, Mrs Hilary Vines (*d* 1975), Malaga, Spain. *Educ:* Eton; Balliol Coll., Oxford. RAF 1940–46 (Staff appt Air Ministry, 1942–46). Mem. Council Royal Nat. Mission to Deep Sea Fishermen, 1953–54. Fellow Corp. of S Mary and S Nicolas (Woodard Schs), 1965–80; Mem. Council, Hurstpierpoint Coll., 1965–80 (Chm., 1967–74). *Address:* 8 Oakwood Court, Abbotsbury Road, W14 8JU. *T:* 01–602 2635. *Club:* Reform (Chm., 1964–65).

MATHIAS, Prof. William (James), CBE 1985; DMus, FRAM; composer, conductor, pianist; Professor and Head of the Department of Music, University College of North Wales, Bangor, since 1970; *b* 1 Nov. 1934; *s* of James Hughes Mathias and Marian (*née* Evans); *m* 1959, Margaret Yvonne Collins; one *d*. *Educ:* University Coll. of Wales, Aberystwyth (Robert Bryan Schol.); Royal Academy of Music (Lyell-Taylor Schol.). DMus Wales, 1966; FRAM 1965 (LRAM 1958). Lectr in Music, UC of N Wales, Bangor, 1959–68; Sen. Lectr in Music, Univ. of Edinburgh, 1968–69. Member: Welsh Arts Council, 1974–81 (Chm., Music Cttee, 1982–); Music Adv. Cttee, British Council, 1974–83; ISCM (British Section), 1976–80; BBC Central Music Adv. Cttee, 1979–; Welsh Adv. Cttee, British Council, 1979–; Council, Composers' Guild of GB, 1982–; Bd of Governors, Nat. Museum of Wales, 1973–78; Artistic Dir, N Wales Music Festival, 1972–; Vice-Chm., British Arts Fests Assoc., 1983–; Vice-Pres., RCO, 1985. Governor, NYO of GB, 1985–. Arnold Bax Society Prize, 1968; John Edwards Meml Award, 1982. *Publications include:* Piano Concerto No 2, 1964; Piano Concerto No 3, 1970; Harpsichord Concerto, 1971; Harp Concerto, 1973; Clarinet Concerto, 1976; Horn Concerto, 1984; Organ Concerto, 1984; *orchestral compositions:* Divertimento for string orch., 1961; Serenade for small orch., 1963; Prelude, Aria and Finale, 1966; Symphony No 1, 1969; Festival Overture, 1973; Celtic Dances, 1974; Vistas, 1977; Laudi, 1978; Vivat Regina (for brass band), 1978; Helios, 1978; Requiescat, 1979; Dance Variations, 1979; Investiture Anniversary Fanfare, 1979; Reflections on a theme by Tomkins, 1981; Symphony No 2: Summer Music (commnd by Royal Liverpool Philharmonic Soc.), 1983; Ceremonial Fanfare (for 2 trumpets), 1983; Anniversary Dances (for centenary of Univ. Coll. Bangor), 1985; *chamber compositions:* Sonata for violin and piano, 1963; Piano Sonata, 1965; Divertimento for flute, oboe and piano, 1966; String Quartet, 1970; Capriccio for flute and piano, 1971; Wind Quintet, 1976; Concertino, 1977; Zodiac Trio, 1977; Clarinet Sonatina, 1978; String Quartet No 2, 1981; Piano Sonata No 2, 1984; Violin Sonata No 2, 1984; Piano Trio, 1986; Flute Sonatina, 1986; String Quartet No 3, 1986; *choral and vocal compositions:* Wassail Carol, 1965; Three Medieval Lyrics, 1966; St Teilo, 1970; Ave Rex, 1970; Sir Christemas, 1970; Culhwch and Olwen, 1971; A Babe is born, 1971; A Vision of Time and Eternity (for contralto and piano), 1974; Ceremony after a fire raid, 1975; This Worlde's Joie, 1975; Carmen Paschale, 1976; Elegy for a Prince (for baritone and orch.), 1976; The Fields of Praise (for tenor and piano), 1977; A Royal Garland, 1978; Nativity Carol, 1978; A May Magnificat, 1980; Shakespeare Songs, 1980; Songs of William Blake (for mezzo-soprano and orch.), 1980; Rex Gloriae (four Latin motets), 1981; Te Deum, for soli, chorus and orchestra (commnd for centenary of the Chapel at Haddo House), 1981; Lux Aeterna, for soli, chorus and orchestra (commnd for Three Choirs Fest.), 1982; Salvator Mundi: a carol sequence, 1983; Angelus, 1984; Four Welsh Folk Songs, 1984; The Echoing Green, 1985; O Aula Nobilis (for opening of Orangery at Westonbirt Sch. by TRH Prince and Princess of Wales), 1985; Veni Sancte Spiritus (Hereford Three Choirs Fest.), 1985; Gogoneddawg Arglwydd (for Nat. Youth Choir of Wales), 1985; *organ compositions:* Variations on a Hymn Tune, 1963; Partita, 1963; Postlude, 1964; Processional, 1965; Chorale, 1967; Toccata giocosa, 1968; Jubilate, 1975; Fantasy, 1978; Canzonetta, 1978; Antiphonies, 1982; Organ Concerto, 1984; Berceuse, 1985; Recessional, 1986; A Mathias Organ Album, 1986; *anthems and church music:* O Sing unto the Lord, 1965; Make a joyful noise, 1965; Festival Te Deum, 1965; Communion Service in C, 1968; Psalm 150, 1969; Lift up your heads, 1970; O Salutaris Hostia, 1972; Gloria, 1972; Magnificat and Nunc Dimittis, 1973; Alleluya Psallat, 1974; Missa Brevis, 1974; Communion Service (Series III), 1976; Arise, shine, 1978; Let the people praise thee, O God (anthem composed for the wedding of the Prince and Princess of Wales), 1981; Praise ye the Lord, 1982; All Wisdom is from the Lord, 1982; Except the Lord build the House, 1983; A Grace, 1983; Jubilate Deo, 1983; O how amiable, 1983; Tantum ergo, 1984; Let us now praise famous men, 1984; Alleluia! Christ is risen, 1984; Missa Aedis Christi—in memoriam William Walton, 1984; Salve Regina, 1986; O clap your hands (for BoT 200th anniv.), 1986; Let all the world in every corner sing (for RSCM 50th anniv.), 1987; *opera:* The Servants (libretto by Iris Murdoch), 1980. *Address:* Y Graigwen, Cadnant Road, Menai Bridge, Anglesey, Gwynedd LL59 5NG. *T:* Menai Bridge 712392. *Clubs:* Athenæum; Cardiff and County (Cardiff).

MATHIAS, Winifred Rachel, CBE 1974; Lord Mayor of City of Cardiff, May 1972–May 1973; Member, Local Government Boundary Commission for Wales, 1974–79; *b* 11 Feb. 1902; *d* of Charles and Selina Vodden; *m* 1923, William John Mathias (*d* 1949). *Educ:* Howard Gardens High Sch. Sec., ship-owning co., 1919–23. Member, Cardiff City Council, 1954–74; Alderman, 1967–74; formerly Mem., Estates, Public Works, Civic Buildings and Children's Cttees; Deputy Chairman: Health Cttee, 1961–64, 1967–74; Welfare Cttee, 1961–64 (Mem., 1954–70; Chm., 1967–70); Mem., Educn Cttee, 1956–74; Chairman: Social Services, 1970–74; all Primary Schs, 1965–70; Primary Schs Gp 3, 1970–74. Governor, Coll. of Food Technology and Commerce, 1957– (Dep. Chm., 1960–63, Chm., 1963–74). Life Mem., Blind Council (rep. of City Council); Mem., Management Cttee, "The Rest", Porthcawl, 1954–; Past Mem., Whitchurch Hosp. Gp; Founder Mem., Danybryn Cheshire Home, 1961– (Pres., 1986–); Mem., Cardiff Council for the Elderly (Cartref Cttee). *Recreations:* reading, music, needlework, travel. *Address:* 19 Timbers Square, Cardiff CF2 3SH. *T:* Cardiff 483853. *Club:* Roath Conservative (Life Vice-Pres.) (Cardiff).

MATHIESON, Janet Hilary; *see* Smith, J. H.

MATHIESON, William Allan Cunningham, CB 1970; CMG 1955; MBE 1945; consultant to international organisations; *b* 22 Feb. 1916; *e s* of Rev. William Miller Mathieson, BD, and Elizabeth Cunningham Mathieson (*née* Reid); *m* 1946, Elizabeth Frances, *y d* of late Henry Marvell Carr, RA; two *s*. *Educ:* High Sch. of Dundee; Edinburgh and Cambridge Univs. Joined Colonial Office, 1939; served War, 1940–45; Royal Artillery in UK, France and Germany (Major, despatches). Rejoined Colonial Office, 1945; Middle East Dept, 1945–48; Private Sec. to Minister of State, 1948–49; Asst Sec., Colonial Office, 1949; Counsellor (Colonial Affairs) UK Delegn to UN, New York, 1951–54; Head of East African Department, CO, 1955–58; Minister of Education, Labour and Lands, Kenya, 1958–60; Under-Sec., Dept of Technical Co-operation, 1963–64; Under-Sec., 1964–68, Dep. Sec., 1968–75, Min. of Overseas Development; Consultant, UN Develt Prog., 1976–81. Chm., Executive Council, Commonwealth Agricultural Bureaux, 1963; Member: Exec. Bd, Unesco, 1968–74; Bd of Trustees, Internat. Centre for Maize and Wheat Improvement (Mexico), 1976–86; Council, ODI, 1977–; Council, Commonwealth Soc. for the Deaf, 1979–; Bd of Management, LSHTM, 1981–84; Bd of Governors, Internat. Centre for Insect Physiol. and Ecol., Nairobi, 1985–; Chm., Bd of Trustees, Internat. Service for Nat. Agr. Res., 1980–84. Hon. Fellow, Queen Elizabeth House, Oxford, 1973. FRSA. *Recreations:* photography, travel. *Address:* 13 Sydney House, Woodstock Road, W4.

MATILAL, Prof. Bimal Krishna, PhD; Spalding Professor of Eastern Religions and Ethics, University of Oxford, since 1976; Fellow, All Souls College, since 1976; *b* 1 June 1935; *s* of Hare Krishna Matilal and Parimal Matilal; *m* 1958, Karabi Chatterjee; one *s* one *d*. *Educ:* Univ. of Calcutta (BA Hons 1954, MA 1956); Harvard Univ. (AM 1963, PhD 1965). Lectr, Sanskrit Coll., Calcutta Univ., 1957–65; Asst Prof., Univ. of Toronto, 1965–67, Associate Prof., 1967–71; Associate Prof., Univ. of Pennsylvania, 1969–70; Vis. Sen. Fellow, SOAS, Univ. of London, 1971–72; Prof., Univ. of Toronto, 1971–77. Visiting Professor: Univ. of California, Berkeley, 1979; Victoria Univ. of Wellington, NZ, 1980; Chicago Univ., 1983; Vis. Fellow, Harvard Univ., 1982; Fellow, Japan Soc. for Promotion of Scis, 1984; Sacklar Vis. Fellow, Tel-Aviv Univ., 1985. Mem., Wolfson Coll., Oxford, 1984–. Founder-Editor, Jl of Indian Philosophy, 1971–. *Publications:* The Navya-nyāya Doctrine of Negation, 1968; Epistemology, Logic and Grammar in Indian Philosophical Analysis, 1971; The Logical Illumination of Indian Mysticism, 1977; The Central Philosophy of Jainism, 1981; Logical and Ethical Issues in Indian Religions, 1982; (ed) Analytical Philosophy in Comparative Perspective, 1985; Logic, Language and Reality, 1985; Perception, 1986; contrib. Nyāya-Vaiśesika Literature. *Recreation:* gardening. *Address:* Oriental Institute, University of Oxford, Oxford.

MATLHABAPHIRI, Gaotlhaetse Utlwang Sankoloba; High Commissioner for Botswana in the United Kingdom, since 1986; concurrently Ambassador (non-resident) to Romania and Yugoslavia; *b* 6 Nov. 1949; *s* of late Sankoloba and Khumo Matlhabaphiri; one *d*. *Educ:* Diamond Corporation Training Sch.; London; Friederick Ebert Foundn, Gaborone (Labour Economics). Clerk, Standard Chartered Bank, 1971–72; teacher, also part-time Dep. Head Master, Capital Continuation Classes, Gaborone, 1971–72; diamond sorter valuator, 1973–79; Gen. Sec., Botswana Democratic Party Youth Wing, 1977–85; MP Botswana, 1979–80; Asst Minister of Agriculture, 1979–85; Mem., Central Cttee, Botswana Democratic Party, 1982–85; Ambassador of Botswana to Nordic countries, 1985–86. Asst Gen. Sec., Bank Employees Union, 1972; Gen. Sec., Botswana Diamond Sorters Valuators Union, 1976–79; Chm., Botswana Fedn of Trade Unions, 1979. Governor, IFAD, 1980–84. *Recreations:* footballer, athlete; choral music. *Address:* Botswana High Commission, 6 Stratford Place, W1N 9AE. *T:* 01–499 0031. *Clubs:* Royal Over-Seas League, Royal Commonwealth Society; Gaborone Township Rollers, Tsholetsa (Gaborone).

MATOKA, Hon. Peter Wilfred; High Commissioner for Zambia in Zimbabwe, since 1984; Senior Regional Advisor, Economic Commission for Africa, United Nations, Addis Ababa, 1979–83; *b* 8 April 1930; member of Lunda Royal Family; *m* 1957, Grace Joyce; two *s* one *d*. *Educ:* Mwinilunga Sch.; Munali Secondary Sch.; University Coll. of Fort Hare (BA Rhodes); American Univ., Washington (Dipl. Internat. Relations). Minister: of Information and Postal Services, 1964–65; of Health, 1965–66; of Works, 1967; of Power, Transport and Works, 1968; of Luapula Province, 1969; High Comr for Zambia in UK and Ambassador to the Holy See, 1970–71; Minister of Health, 1971–72; Minister of Local Govt and Housing, 1972–77; Minister of Economic and Technical Co-operation, 1977–79; MP for Mwinilunga in Parlt of Zambia. Mem. Central Cttee, United National Independence Party, 1971–. Pres., AA of Zambia, 1969–70 (Vice-Pres. 1970–71). Kt of St Gregory the Great, 1964; Kt, UAR, 1964; Kt, Ethiopia, 1965. *Recreations:* fishing, shooting, discussion, photography. *Address:* Zambian High Commission, Harare, Zimbabwe; 19 Chisiza Crescent, Lusaka, Zambia. *Club:* Royal Automobile.

MATOLENGWE, Rt. Rev. Patrick Monwabisi; a Bishop Suffragan of Cape Town, since 1976; *b* 12 May 1937; *s* of David and Emma Matolengwe; *m* 1967, Crecentia Nompumelelo (*née* Nxele); three *s* two *d*. *Educ:* Healdtown Institution, Fort Beaufort (matric.); Lovedale Teacher Training Coll., Alice; Bishop Gray Coll., Cape Town; Federal Theol Sem., Alice (Cert. Theol.). Teaching, 1959–60; Court Interpreter, 1960–61; theological studies, 1962–65; Curacy at Herschel, Dio. Grahamstown, 1965–68; Rector of Nyanga, Dio. Cape Town, 1968–76. *Recreations:* scouting, singing, music, reading, tennis. *Address:* Bishop's House, 79 Kildare Road, Newlands, Cape Town, 7700, S Africa. *T:* Cape Town 64–2444.

MATTHEW, Chessor Lillie, FRIBA, FRIAS, MRTPI; JP; Principal, Duncan of Jordanstone College of Art, Dundee, 1964–78, retired; *b* 22 Jan. 1913; *s* of William Matthew and Helen Chessor Matthew (*née* Milne); *m* 1939, Margarita Ellis; one *s*. *Educ:*

Gray's School of Art; Robert Gordon's Coll., Aberdeen. Diploma in Architecture. Lectr, Welsh Sch. of Architecture, Cardiff, 1936–40. Served RAF, 1940–46, Flt-Lt. Sen. Lectr, Welsh Sch. of Architecture, Cardiff, 1946–57; Head of Sch. of Architecture, Duncan of Jordanstone Coll. of Art, Dundee, 1958–64. *Recreations:* hill walking, foreign travel. *Address:* Craigmhor, 36 Albany Road, West Ferry, Dundee DD5 1NW. *T:* Dundee 78364.

MATTHEW, (Henry) Colin Gray, DPhil; Fellow and Tutor in Modern History, St Hugh's College, Oxford, since 1978; Lecturer in Gladstone Studies, Christ Church, Oxford, since 1970; *b* 15 Jan. 1941; *s* of Henry Johnston Scott and Joyce Mary Matthew; *m* 1966, Sue Ann (*née* Curry); two *s* one *d. Educ:* Sedbergh Sch.; Christ Church, Oxford (MA, DPhil); Makerere Coll., Univ. of E Africa (DipEd). Education Officer, Grade IIA, Tanzanian Civil Service, 1963–66; Student of Christ Church, Oxford, 1976–78. Literary Dir, RHistS, 1985–. Editor, The Gladstone Diaries, 1972–. *Publications:* The Liberal Imperialists, 1973; (ed) The Gladstone Diaries: vols 3 and 4 (with M. R. D. Foot), 1974; vols 5 and 6, 1978; vols 7 and 8, 1982; vol. 9, 1986; Gladstone 1809–1874, 1986; contributor to: Studies in Church History, vol. xv, Oxford Illustrated History of Britain, 1984, and learned jls. *Recreations:* fishing, bag-pipe playing, second-hand book buying. *Address:* 107 Southmoor Road, Oxford. *T:* Oxford 57341 or 57959.

MATTHEWMAN, Keith; QC 1979; **His Honour Judge Matthewman;** a Circuit Judge, since 1983; *b* 8 Jan. 1936; *e s* of late Lieut Frank Matthewman and Elizabeth Matthewman; *m* 1962, Jane (*née* Maxwell); one *s. Educ:* Long Eaton Grammar Sch.; University College London (LLB). Called to the Bar, Middle Temple, 1960. Commercial Assistant, Internat. Div., Rolls-Royce Ltd, 1961–62; practice at the Bar, 1962–83, Midland Circuit, later Midland and Oxford Circuit; a Recorder of the Crown Court, 1979–83. Mem. Cttee, Council of HM's Circuit Judges, 1984–. Mem., Heanor UDC, 1960–63. *Recreations:* gardening, cine photography. *Address:* c/o Crown Court, Nottingham NG1 7EJ. *Club:* United Services (Nottingham).

MATTHEWS, family name of Baron Matthews.

MATTHEWS, Baron *cr* 1980 (Life Peer), of Southgate in the London Borough of Enfield; **Victor Collin Matthews,** FRSA, CBIM; Trafalgar House plc: Deputy Chairman, 1973–85; Group Managing Director, 1968–77; Group Chief Executive, 1977–83; Chairman (non-exec.), Ellerman Holdings, since 1983; *b* 5 Dec. 1919; *s* of A. and J. Matthews; *m* 1942, Joyce Geraldine (*née* Pilbeam); one *s. Educ:* Highbury. Served RNVR, 1939–45. Chairman: Trafalgar House Develt Hldgs, 1970–83; Cunard Steam-Ship Co., 1971–83; Ritz Hotel (London), 1976–83; Trafalgar House Construction Hldgs, 1977–83; Express Newspapers plc, 1977–85 (Chief Exec., 1977–82); Cunard Cruise Ships, 1978–83; Cunard Line, 1978–83; Evening Standard Co. Ltd, 1980–85; Fleet Publishing Internat. Hldgs Ltd, 1978–82; Fleet Hldgs, 1982–85; Director: Associated Container Transportation (Australia) Ltd, 1972–83; Cunard Crusader World Travel Ltd, 1974–; Racecourse Holdings Trust Ltd, 1977–; Associated Communications Corp. plc, 1977–82; Goldquill Ltd, 1979–83; Darchart Ltd, 1980–83; Garmaine Ltd, 1980–83. *Recreations:* racehorse owner, cricket, golf. *Address:* Waverley Farm, Mont Arthur, St Brelades, Jersey, Channel Islands. *Clubs:* MCC, Royal Automobile; Royal & Ancient Golf.

MATTHEWS, David Napier, CBE 1976 (OBE 1945); MA, MD, MCh (Cambridge); FRCS; Hon. FDSRCS; retired; Consulting Plastic Surgeon, University College Hospital and Hospital for Sick Children; Civilian Consultant in Plastic Surgery to the Royal Navy since 1954; *b* 7 July 1911; *m* 1940, Betty Eileen Bailey Davies; two *s* one *d. Educ:* Leys Sch., Cambridge; Queens' Coll., Cambridge; Charing Cross Hosp. Qualified as doctor, 1935. Surgical Registrar, Westminster Hospital, until 1940; Surgeon Plastic Unit, East Grinstead, 1939–41; Surgical Specialist, RAFVR, 1941–46; Plastic Surgeon: UCH and Hosp. for Sick Children, 1946–76; Royal Nat. Orthopædic Hosp., 1947–54; King Edward's Hosp. for Officers, 1972–80. Adviser in Plastic Surgery, DHSS, 1962–77. Consulting Practice as Surgeon 1946–80; Hunterian Professor, RCS, 1941, 1944, 1976; President: British Assoc. of Plastic Surgeons, 1954 and 1971; Plastic Section, RSM, 1970–71; Sec., Harveian Soc. of London, 1951, Vice-Pres., 1954, Pres., 1962; Gen. Sec. Internat. Confederation for Plastic Surgery, 1959; Pres., Chelsea Clinical Soc., 1962. *Publications:* Surgery of Repair, 1943, 2nd edn, 1946; (Ed.) Recent Advances in the Surgery of Trauma, 1963; chapters in surgical books; contrib. to Lancet, BMJ and Post Graduate Jl etc. *Recreation:* fishing. *Address:* River Walk, Shooters Hill, Pangbourne, Reading RG8 7DU. *T:* Pangbourne 4476.

MATTHEWS, Prof. Denis (James), CBE 1975; Concert Pianist; (first) Professor of Music, University of Newcastle upon Tyne, 1971–84; *b* Coventry, 27 Feb. 1919; *o s* of Arthur and Elsie Randall Matthews; *m* 1941, Mira Howe (marr. diss., 1960); one *s* three *d*; *m* 1963, Brenda McDermott (marr. diss. 1985); one *s* one *d. Educ:* Warwick. Thalberg Scholar, 1935, Blumenthal Composition Scholar, 1937, at RAM; studied with Harold Craxton and William Alwyn; Worshipful Co. of Musicians' Medal, 1938; first public appearances in London at Queen's Hall and National Gallery, 1939; has broadcast frequently, made records, given talks on musical subjects; soloist at Royal Philharmonic Society's concerts, May and Nov. 1945; toured USA and visited Potsdam with Royal Air Force Orchestra, 1944–45; Vienna Bach Festival, 1950; Canada, 1951, 1957, 1963; South Africa, 1953, 1954, 1962; Poland, 1956, 1960; Egypt and Far East, 1963; World Tour, 1964; N Africa, 1966; W and E Africa, 1968; Latin America, 1968, 1970; Australia, 1977, 1979. Mem., Arts Council of GB, 1972–73. Favourite composers: Bach, Mozart, Beethoven, Wagner. Hon. DMus: St Andrews, 1973; Hull, 1978; Hon. DLitt Warwick, 1982. Cobbett Medal, Musicians' Co., 1973. *Publications:* piano pieces, works for violin, 'cello; In Pursuit of Music (autobiog.), 1966; Beethoven Piano Sonatas, 1968; Keyboard Music, 1972; Brahms's Three Phases, 1972; Brahms Piano Music, 1978; Toscanini, 1982; Beethoven, 1985. *Recreations:* astronomy, filing-systems, reading aloud. *Address:* 6 Reddings Road, Moseley, Birmingham B13 8LN.

MATTHEWS, Douglas, BA; FLA; Librarian, The London Library, since 1980; *b* 23 Aug. 1927; *s* of Benjamin Matthews and Mary (*née* Pearson); *m* 1968, Sarah Maria Williams; two *d. Educ:* Acklam Hall Sch., Middlesbrough; Durham Univ. Assistant: India Office Library, 1952–62; Kungl. Biblioteket, Stockholm, 1956–57; Librarian, Home Office, 1962–64; Dep. Librarian, London Library, 1965–80. *Address:* 1 Priory Terrace, Mountfield Road, Lewes, Sussex BN7 2UT. *T:* Lewes 475635. *Club:* Garrick.

MATTHEWS, Dr Drummond Hoyle, VRD 1967; FRS 1974; Senior Research Associate, Scientific Director, British Institutions Reflection Profiling Syndicate, at the University of Cambridge, since 1982; Fellow, Wolfson College, Cambridge, since 1980; *b* 5 Feb. 1931; *s* of late Captain C. B. and late Mrs E. M. Matthews; *m* 1963, Elizabeth Rachel McMullen (marr. diss. 1980); one *s* one *d. Educ:* Bryanston Sch.; King's Coll., Cambridge. BA 1954, MA 1959, PhD 1962. RNVR, 1949–51, retd 1967. Geologist, Falkland Islands Dependencies Survey, 1955–57; returned to Cambridge (BP student), 1958; Research Fellow, King's Coll., 1960; Sen. Asst in Research, Dept of Geophysics, 1960; Asst Dir of Research, 1966; Reader in Marine Geology, 1971. Balzan Prize (jtly), 1982. *Publications:* papers on marine geophysics in jls and books. *Recreations:* walking, sailing. *Address:* British Institutions Reflection Profiling Syndicate, Bullard Laboratories, Madingley Road, Cambridge. *Clubs:* Antarctic, Cruising Association.

MATTHEWS, Edwin James Thomas, TD 1946; Chief Taxing Master of the Supreme Court, 1979–83 (Master, 1965–78); *b* 2 May 1915; *s* of Edwin Martin Matthews (killed in action, 1917); *m* 1939, Katherine Mary Hirst, BA (Oxon.), Dip. Soc. Sc. (Leeds); two *d. Educ:* Sedbergh Sch., Yorks. Admitted as Solicitor of Supreme Court, 1938; practice on own account in Middlesbrough, 1938–39. Served in Royal Artillery, 1939–46, UK, France and Belgium (Dunkirk 1940); released with rank of Major. Partner, Chadwick Son & Nicholson, Solicitors, Dewsbury, Yorks, 1946–50; Area Sec., No. 6 (W Midland) Legal Aid Area Cttee of Law Soc., 1950–56; Sec. of Law Soc. for Contentious Business (including responsibility for administration of Legal Aid and Advice Schemes), 1956–65. Toured Legal Aid Offices in USA for Ford Foundation and visited Toronto to advise Govt of Ontario, 1963. Mem., Council, British Academy of Forensic Sciences, 1965–68. Special Consultant to NBPI on Solicitors' Costs, 1967–68; General Consultant, Law Soc., 1983–84. Member: Lord Chancellor's Adv. Cttee on Legal Aid, 1972–77; Working Party on Legal Aid Legislation, 1974–76; Working Party on the Criminal Trial, 1980–83; Supreme Ct Procedure Cttee, 1982–83. Lectr, mainly on costs and remuneration for solicitors and counsel, for Coll. of Law, Legal Studies and Services Ltd and to various provincial Law Socs. *Publications:* contrib. Halsbury's Laws of England, 1961 and Atkins Encyclopaedia of Forms and Precedents, 1962; (with Master Graham-Green) Costs in Criminal Cases and Legal Aid, 1965; (jointly) Legal Aid and Advice Under the Legal Aid and Advice Acts, 1949 to 1964, 1971; (ed jtly) Supreme Court Practice; contribs to legal journals. *Recreations:* trout fishing, theatre, gardening, French wines. *Address:* The Old Garden, Dunorlan Park, Tunbridge Wells, Kent. *T:* Tunbridge Wells 24027.

MATTHEWS, Prof. Ernest, DDS, PhD, MSc, ARCS, DIC, FDSRCS; Director of Prosthetics, University of Manchester, 1935–70, now Professor Emeritus; *b* 14 Dec. 1904; *s* of James Alfred Matthews, Portsmouth; *m* 1928, Doris Pipe (decd); one *d* (two *s* decd). *Educ:* Imperial Coll., London; Cambridge; Guy's Hospital, London. Demonstrator and Lecturer, Guy's Hospital Medical and Dental Schs, 1926–34; Prosthetic Dental Surgeon, Manchester Royal Infirmary, 1937; Dean and Dir, Turner Dental Sch., 1966–69; Cons. Dental Surgeon, Christie Hosp., 1945; Hon. Adviser in Dental Surgery to Manchester Regional Hospital Board, 1951. Silver Jubilee Medal, 1977. *Recreation:* gardening. *Address:* 16 The Spain, Petersfield, Hants GU32 3LA.

MATTHEWS, Prof. Geoffrey, MA, PhD; FIMA; Shell Professor of Mathematics Education, Centre for Science and Mathematics Education, Chelsea College, University of London, 1968–77, now Emeritus; *b* 1 Feb. 1917; *s* of Humphrey and Gladys Matthews; *m* 1st, 1941, Patricia Mary Jackson; one *s* one *d*; 2nd, 1972, Julia Comber. *Educ:* Marlborough; Jesus Coll., Cambridge (MA); PhD (London). Wiltshire Regt, Intelligence Officer 43rd (Wessex) Div., 1939–45, Captain (dispatches, 1945; US Bronze Star, 1945). Teacher: Haberdashers' Aske's Sch., 1945–50; St Dunstan's Coll., 1950–64, Dep. Head and head of mathematics dept; Organiser, Nuffield Mathematics Teaching Project, 1964–72; Co-director (with Julia Matthews), Schools Council Early Mathematical Experiences project, 1974–79; Co-dir (with Prof. K. W. Keohane) SSRC funded prog. Concepts in Secondary Sch. Maths and Sci., 1974–79. Presenter of BBC TV programmes in series Tuesday Term, Middle School Mathematics, and Children and Mathematics; consultant to BBC series Maths in a Box and You and Me, and to ATV series Towards Mathematics. Consultant to maths teaching projects in Italy, Greece, Portugal, Sri Lanka and Thailand; has lectured extensively abroad. Pres., Mathematical Assoc., 1977–78; Founder Mem., Commonwealth Assoc. of Sci. and Maths Educators, 1964; Member: Internat. Cttee, 3rd Congress, ICME, 1976; Council, Inst. of Maths and its Applications, 1978–81; Cttee, Soc. of Free Painters and Sculptors, 1978–. *Publications:* Calculus, 1964; Matrices I & II, 1964; Mathematics through School, 1972; papers in Proc. Kon. Akad. Wetensch. (Amsterdam); numerous articles in Math. Gaz., etc. *Recreations:* sculpture, travel. *Address:* 50 Sydney Road, Bexleyheath, Kent DA6 8HG. *T:* 01–303 4301.

MATTHEWS, George Lloyd; Archivist, Communist Party of Great Britain; *b* 24 Jan. 1917; *s* of James and Ethel Matthews, Sandy, Beds; *m* 1940, Elisabeth Lynette Summers; no *c. Educ:* Bedford Modern Sch.; Reading Univ. Pres., Reading Univ. Students Union, 1938–39; Vice-Pres., Nat. Union of Students, 1939–40; Vice-Pres., University Labour Fedn, 1938–39. County Chm., Nat. Union of Agricultural Workers, 1945–49; Mem. Exec. Cttee, Communist Party, 1943–79; Asst Gen. Sec., Communist Party, 1949–57; Asst Editor, 1957–59, Editor, 1959–74, Daily Worker, later Morning Star; Head of Press and Publicity Dept, Communist Party of GB, 1974–79. *Recreation:* music. *Address:* c/o Communist Party, 16 St John Street, EC1M 4AY. *T:* 01–251 4406.

MATTHEWS, Gordon (Richards), CBE 1974; FCA; *m* 1st, 1934, Ruth Hillyard Brooks (*d* 1980); one *s* one *d* (and one *d* decd); 2nd, 1982, Freda E. Evans (*née* Ledger). *Educ:* Repton Sch. Chartered Accountant, 1932. Contested (U) General Election, Deritend, Birmingham, 1945, and Yardley, Birmingham, 1950; MP (C) Meriden Division of Warwicks, 1959–64; PPS to the Postmaster-General, 1960–64. Hon. Treas., Deritend Unionist Assoc., 1937–45; Hon. Sec., Birmingham Unionist Association, 1948–53. Pres. City of Birmingham Friendly Soc., 1957–64; Mem. Board of Management, Linen and Woollen Drapers Institution and Cottage Homes, 1950–65 (Pres. of Appeal, 1954–55); Chm. of Exec. Cttee, Birmingham Area of YMCA, 1951–59; Mem., Nat. Council and Nat. Exec. Cttee, YMCA, 1968–71; Chm., Finance Cttee, YWCA, Birmingham Area, 1965–72. Chm., Oxfordshire Br., CPRE, 1978–81; voluntary warden, Cotswold area of outstanding natural beauty, 1985–. Pres., West Midlands Cons. Council, 1983–85 (Dep. Chm., 1967–70; Chm., 1970–73). *Recreations:* fly-fishing and foreign travel. *Address:* 12 Cherry Orchard Close, Chipping Campden, Glos GL55 6DH. *T:* Evesham 840626.

MATTHEWS, Henry Melvin; Managing Director, Texaco Ltd, since 1982; *b* 26 Feb. 1926; *s* of Phillip Lawrence and Agnes K. Matthews; *m* 1947, Margaret Goodridge; one *s* two *d. Educ:* Columbia University; Tufts Univ. (BSNS, BSME). General Manager, Texaco Europe, USA, 1976; Vice Pres. Manufacture and Marketing, Texaco Europe, USA, 1980. *Recreations:* tennis, golf, swimming, gardening, music (choir), YMCA, Congregational Church. *Address:* 24 Parkside, Knightsbridge, SW1X 7JR. *Clubs:* Queen's; Field (New Canaan, USA).

MATTHEWS, Horatio Keith, CMG 1963; MBE 1946; JP; HM Diplomatic Service, 1948–74; *b* 4 April 1917; *s* of late Horatio Matthews, MD and of Ruth Matthews (*née* McCurry); *m* 1940, Jean Andrée Batten; two *d. Educ:* Epsom Coll.; Gonville and Caius Coll., Cambridge. Entered Indian Civil Service, 1940, and served in Madras Presidency until 1947; appointed to Foreign Service, 1948; First Sec., 1949; Lisbon, 1949; Bucharest, 1951; Foreign Office, 1953; Imperial Defence Coll., 1955; Political Office with Middle East Forces, Cyprus, 1956; Counsellor, 1958; Counsellor, UK High Commission, Canberra, 1959; Political Adviser to GOC Berlin, 1961; Corps of Inspectors, Diplomatic Service, 1964; Minister, Moscow, 1966–67; High Commissioner in Ghana, 1968–70; UN Under-Sec.-Gen. for Admin and Management, 1971–72; Asst Under-Sec. of State, MoD (on secondment), 1973–74. Mem., Bd of Visitors, HM Prison, Albany, 1976–82. JP

IoW 1975. *Address:* Elm House, Bembridge, IoW. *T:* Isle of Wight 872327. *Club:* Royal Commonwealth Society.

MATTHEWS, Jeffery Edward, FSIAD; freelance graphic designer and consultant, since 1952; *b* 3 April 1928; *s* of Henry Edward Matthews and Sybil Frances (*née* Cooke); *m* 1953, (Sylvia Lilian) Christine (*née* Hoar); one *s* one *d*. *Educ:* Alleyn's; Brixton Sch. of Building (Interior Design; NDD). AIBD 1951; FSIAD 1978. Graphic designer with J. Edward Sander, 1949–52; part-time tutor, 1952–55. Lettering and calligraphy assessor for SIAD, 1970–. Designs for Post Office: decimal to pay labels, 1971; fount of numerals for definitive stamps, 1981; stamps: United Nations, 1965; British bridges, 1968; definitives for Scotland, Wales, NI and IOM, 1971; Royal Silver Wedding, 1972; 25th Anniversary of the Coronation, 1978; London, 1980; 80th birthday of the Queen Mother, 1980; Christmas, 1980; Wedding of Prince Charles and Lady Diana Spencer, 1981; Quincentenary of College of Arms, 1984; 60th birthday of the Queen, 1986; Wedding of Prince Andrew and Sarah Ferguson, 1986; also first-day covers, postmarks, presentation packs, souvenir books and posters; one of three stamp designers featured in PO film, Picture to Post, 1969. Other design work includes: title banner lettering and coat of arms, Sunday Times, 1968; cover design and lettering for official prog., Royal Wedding, 1981; official heraldry and symbols, HMSO; hand-drawn lettering, COI; stamp designs, first-day covers, calligraphy, packaging, promotion and bookbinding designs, logotypes, brand images and hand-drawn lettering, for various firms including Unicover Corp., USA, Harrison & Sons Ltd, Metal Box Co., DRG, Reader's Digest Assoc. Ltd, Encyc. Britannica Internat. Ltd, ICI and H. R. Higgins (Coffee-man) Ltd. Work exhibited in A History of Bookplates in Britain, V&A Mus., 1979. Citizen and Goldsmith of London (Freedom by Patrimony), 1949. *Publications:* (contrib.) Designers in Britain, 1964, 1971; (contrib.) 45 Wood-engravers, 1982. *Recreations:* furniture restoration, playing the guitar, gardening, DIY. *Address:* 46 Kings Hall Road, Beckenham, Kent BR3 1LS. *T:* 01–778 2689.

MATTHEWS, John; Director, of Engineering Research, Agricultural and Food Research Council, since 1986; *b* 4 July 1930; *s* of John Frederick Matthews and Catherine Edith Matthews (*née* Terry); *m* 1982, Edna Agnes Luckhurst; two *d*. *Educ:* Royal Latin School, Buckingham. BSc (Physics) London. CPhys, FInstP; CEng. Scientist, GEC Res. Labs, 1951–59; National Institute of Agricultural Engineering: joined 1959; Head of Tractor Performance Dept, 1967–73; Head of Tractor and Cultivation Div., 1973–83; Asst Dir, 1983–84; Dir, 1984–86. Formerly Chm., Technical Cttees, Internat. Standards Orgn and OECD; Pres., Inst. of Agricl Engineers, 1986–. Fellow, Ergonomics Soc. Research Medal, RAgS, 1983. *Publications:* (contrib.) Fream's Elements of Agriculture, 1984; contribs to other books and jls on agricultural engineering and ergonomics. *Recreations:* farming, gardening, Lions International club, travel. *Address:* Church Cottage, Tilsworth, Leighton Buzzard, Beds. *T:* (home) Leighton Buzzard 210204; (office) Silsoe (0525) 60000.

MATTHEWS, Dr John Duncan, FRCPE; Consultant Physician, Royal Infirmary, Edinburgh, 1955–86; Hon. Senior Lecturer, University of Edinburgh, 1976–86; *b* 19 Sept. 1921; *s* of Joseph Keith Matthews and Ethel Chambers; *m* 1945, Constance Margaret Moffat; two *s*. *Educ:* Shrewsbury; Univ. of Cambridge (BA); Univ. of Edinburgh (MB, ChB). FRCPE 1958. Surgeon, High Constables and Guard of Honour, Holyrood House, 1961–. Hon. Consultant in Medicine to the Army in Scotland, 1974–86; Examr in Medicine, Edinburgh and Cambridge Univs. Vice-Pres., RCPE, 1982–85; Mem./Chm., various local and national NHS and coll. cttees. Sec., Edinburgh Medical Angling Club, 1963–. *Publications:* occasional articles in med. jls on diabetes and heart disease. *Recreations:* cricket (Free Foresters, Grange, and Scotland), fishing. *Address:* 14 Moray Place, Edinburgh EH3 6DT. *T:* 031–225 4863.

MATTHEWS, L(eonard) Harrison, FRS 1954, MA, ScD; Scientific Director, Zoological Society of London, 1951–66; *b* 12 June 1901; *s* of Harold Evan Matthews and Ruby Sarah Matthews (*née* Harrison); *m* 1924, Dorothy Hélène Harris; one *s* one *d*. *Educ:* Bristol Grammar Sch.; King's Coll., Cambridge. BA Hons 1st Class Nat. Sci. Trip., 1922; Vintner Exhibitioner King's Coll., University Frank Smart Prize. Has carried out biological researches in Africa, S America, Arctic and Antarctic, etc. Mem. of scientific staff "Discovery" Expedition, 1924; special lectr in Zoology, Univ. of Bristol, 1935; Radio Officer, Anti-Aircraft Command, 1941; Sen. Scientific Officer, Telecommunications Research Establishment, 1942; Radar liaison duties with RAF, 1943–45; Research Fellow, Univ. of Bristol, 1945. Pres. Section D, British Assoc. for the Advancement of Science, 1959; President: British Academy of Forensic Science, 1962; Ray Soc., 1965; Chm., Seals Sub-Cttee, NERC, 1967–71; Tsetse Fly and Trypanosomiasis Cttee, CO, 1955–63. Member Council: Marine Biological Assoc. of UK, 1944–51; Zoological Soc. of London, 1943–45, 1946–49, 1950–51 (Vice-Pres., 1944–45, 1947–49, 1950–51; Silver Medal, 1986); Inst. of Biology, 1954–57; Linnean Soc., of London, 1953–57; Sec., 1947–48, Pres., 1960, Assoc. of British Zoologists; Chm., World List of Scientific Periodicals, 1959–66; Acad. Mem., Assoc. of British Sci. Writers, 1956. Has made numerous sound and TV broadcasts. *Publications:* South Georgia, the Empire's Subantarctic Outpost, 1931; Wandering Albatross, 1951; British Mammals (New Naturalist), 1952; Amphibia and Reptiles, 1952; Sea Elephant, 1952; Beasts of the Field, 1954; Animals in Colour, 1959; The Senses of Animals (with Maxwell Knight), 1963; (ed) The Whale, 1968; The Life of Mammals, Vol. I, 1969, Vol. II, 1971; Introd., Darwin's Origin of Species, 1972; Introd. and explanatory notes, Waterton's Wanderings in South America, 1973; Man and Wildlife, 1975; Penguin, 1977 (with Foreword by HRH The Duke of Edinburgh); The Life of the Whale, 1978; The Seals and the Scientists, 1979; Mammals in the British Isles, 1982; numerous scientific papers on zoological subjects in jls of learned socs, Discovery Reports, Philosophical Transactions, Encyclopædia Britannica, etc. *Address:* The Old Rectory, Stansfield, via Sudbury, Suffolk CO10 8LT. *Club:* Explorers' (New York).

MATTHEWS, Maj.-Gen. Michael, CB 1984; Engineer in Chief (Army), 1983–85; Secretary, Council of TAVR Associations, since 1986; *b* 22 April 1930; *s* of late W. Matthews and of M. H. Matthews; *m* 1955, Elspeth Rosemary, *d* of late Lt-Col Sir John Maclure, 3rd Bt, OBE, and of Lady Maclure; two *s* two *d*. *Educ:* King's Coll., Taunton, Somerset. CompICE, 1984; FBIM. rcds, psc. Commissioned, Royal Engineers, 1951; served overseas, Egypt, Cyprus, Jordan, Kenya, Aden and BAOR; DAA and QMG HQ 24 Inf. Bde, Kenya, 1962–65; OC, Indep. Para Sqn RE, UK and Aden, 1965–67; GSO1 (DS) Staff College, Camberley, 1968–70; CO 35 Engr Regt, BAOR, 1970–72; Col GS Ops, Exercise Planning Staff and Trg, HQ BAOR, 1972–74; CCRE, HQ1 (BR) Corps, BAOR, 1974–76; RCDS 1977; DQMG HQ BAOR, 1978–80; Dir of Personal Services (Army), 1980–83. Col Comdt, RE, 1985–; Hon. Colonel: Southampton Univ. OTC, 1985–; 131 Indep. Commando Sqn RE (V), 1985–. *Recreations:* Rugby, cricket, hockey, hang gliding. *Address:* c/o Lloyds Bank, Chagford, Newton Abbot, Devon. *Clubs:* Army and Navy, MCC.

MATTHEWS, Michael Gough; Director, Royal College of Music, since 1985; *b* 12 July 1931; *s* of late Cecil Gough Matthews and of Amelia Eleanor Mary Matthews. *Educ:* Chigwell School; Royal College of Music (Open Scholarship, 1947; Hopkinson Gold Medal, 1953; ARCM, FRCM 1972); ARCO; Diploma del Corso di Perfezionamento St Cecilia, Rome. Diploma of Honour and Prize, Chopin Internat. Piano Competition, 1955; Italian Govt Scholarship, 1956; Chopin Fellowship, Warsaw, 1959. Pianist; recitals, broadcasts, concerts, UK, Europe and Far East. Supervisor Junior Studies, RSAMD, 1964–71; Royal College of Music: Dir, Junior Dept, and Prof. of Piano, 1972–75; Registrar, 1975; Vice-Dir, 1978–84. Hon. FLCM 1976; Hon. RAM 1979; FRSAMD 1986; FRSA. *Publications:* various musical entertainments; arranger of educational music. *Recreation:* gardening. *Address:* Royal College of Music, Prince Consort Road, SW7 2BS. *T:* 01–589 3643. *Club:* Athenæum.

MATTHEWS, Mrs Pamela Winifred, (Mrs Peter Matthews), BSc (Econ.); Principal, Westfield College (University of London), 1962–65; *b* 4 Dec. 1914; *d* of Lt-Col C. C. Saunders-O'Mahony; *m* 1938, H. P. S. Matthews (*d* 1958); one *s* one *d*. *Educ:* St Paul's Girls' Sch.; London Sch. of Economics. Royal Institute of International Affairs, 1938–39; Foreign Office, 1939–40; The Economist Newspaper, 1940–43; Foreign Office, 1943–45; Reuters, 1945–61; Nat. Inst. for Social Work Trg, 1961–62. Independent Mem., Advertising Standards Authority, 1964–65; Industrial Tribunal rep. for CAB, 1974–84. Governor: Northwood Coll., Middlesex, 1962–86; Cardinal Manning Boys' RC School, 1980–. *Publications:* diplomatic correspondence for Reuters. *Recreations:* travel, theatre. *Address:* 1 Edwardes Place, Kensington High Street, W8 6LR. *T:* 01–603 8458.

MATTHEWS, Paul Taunton, CBE 1975; MA, PhD; FRS 1963; Vice-Chancellor, Bath University, 1976–83; *b* 19 Nov. 1919; *s* of Rev. Gordon Matthews and Janet (*née* Viney); *m* 1947, Margit Zohn; two *s* two *d*. *Educ:* Mill Hill Sch.; Clare Coll., Cambridge. Research Fellow, Inst. for Advanced Study, Princeton, USA, 1950–51; ICI Research Fellow, Cambridge, 1951–52; Lectr, Univ. of Birmingham, 1952–57; Visiting Prof., Univ. of Rochester, USA, 1957; Imperial College, London: Reader in Theoretical Physics, 1957–62; Prof. of Theoretical Physics, 1962–76; Head of Dept of Physics, 1971–76; Dean, RCS, 1972–75. Mem., SRC, 1970–74; Chm., SRC Nuclear Physics Bd, 1972–74; Mem., Scientific Policy Cttee, CERN, Geneva, 1972–78; Chm., Radioactive Waste Management Adv. Cttee, 1983–. Hon. DSc Bath, 1983. Adams Prize, Cambridge, 1958; Rutherford Medal and Prize, IPPS, 1979. *Publications:* Quantum Mechanics, 1963 (USA); Nuclear Apple, 1971; papers on elementary particle physics in Proc. Royal Soc., Phil. Mag., Phys. Review, Nuovo Cimento, Review Mod. Phys., Annals of Physics. *Address:* 64 Highsett, Hills Road, Cambridge.

MATTHEWS, Percy; *b* 24 July 1921; *s* of Samuel and Minnie Matthews; *m* 1946, Audrey Rosenthal; one *s* two *d*. *Educ:* Parmiters Sch., London. Hon. Fellow, St Peter's Coll., Oxford. Mem. Management Cttee, Royal Postgrad. Med. Sch., Hammersmith Hosp.; Freeman, City of London. *Recreations:* painting, golf. *Address:* Hotel del Golf, Apt 204, Las Brisas, Marbella, Málaga, Spain.

MATTHEWS, Mrs Peter; *see* Matthews, Mrs Pamela W.

MATTHEWS, Sir Peter (Alec), Kt 1975; AO 1980; Chairman, Pegler-Hattersley plc, 1979–July 1987 (Director, 1977–87); Director: Lloyds Bank, since 1974 (Chairman, Central London Regional Board, since 1978); British Electric Traction Plc since 1976; Sun Alliance and London Insurance, since 1979; Cookson Group (formerly Lead Industries Group), since 1980; Hamilton Oil Great Britain, since 1981; Lloyds & Scottish, since 1983; *b* 21 Sept. 1922; *s* of Major Alec Bryan Matthews and Elsie Lazarus Barlow; *m* 1946, Sheila Dorothy Bunting; four *s* one *d*. *Educ:* Shawnigan Lake Sch., Vancouver Island; Oundle Sch. Served Royal Engineers (retired as Major), 1940–46. Joined Stewarts and Lloyds Ltd, 1946; Director of Research and Technical Development, 1962; Member for R&D, BSC, 1968–70, Dep. Chm., 1973–76; Vickers PLC: Man. Dir, 1970–79; Chm., 1980–84. Chm., Armed Forces Pay Review Body, 1984–; Mem., Top Salaries Review Body, 1984–. Member: BOTB, 1973–77; Export Guarantees Adv. Council, 1973–78; Status Review Cttee, ECGD, 1983–84; Pres., Sino-British Trade Council, 1983–85. Member: NRDC, 1974–80; Engineering Industries Council, 1976– (Chm., 1980–); Adv. Council for Applied R&D, 1976–80. Pres., Engineering Employers Fedn, 1982–84; Chm., Council, University Coll., London, 1980– (Hon. Fellow, 1982). CBIM, FRSA. *Recreations:* sailing, gardening. *Address:* Ladycross House, Dormansland, Surrey RH7 6NP. *Club:* Royal Yacht Squadron (Cowes).

MATTHEWS, Prof. Peter Bryan Conrad, FRS 1973; MD, DSc; Professor of Sensorimotor Physiology, since 1987 and Student of Christ Church since 1958, University of Oxford; *b* 23 Dec. 1928; *s* of Prof. Sir Bryan Matthews, CBE, FRS; *m* 1956, Margaret Rosemary Blears; one *s* one *d*. *Educ:* Marlborough Coll.; King's Coll., Cambridge; Oxford Univ. Clinical School. Oxford University: Univ. Lectr in Physiology, 1961–77; Reader, 1978–86; Tutor, Christ Church, 1958–86. Sir Lionel Whitby Medal, Cambridge Univ., 1959; Robert Bing Prize, Swiss Acad. of Med. Science, 1971. *Publications:* Mammalian Muscle Receptors and their Central Actions, 1972; papers on neurophysiology in various scientific jls. *Address:* University Laboratory of Physiology, Parks Road, Oxford OX1 3PT. *T:* Oxford 57451.

MATTHEWS, Prof. Peter Hugoe, FBA 1985; Professor and Head of Department of Linguistics, and Fellow of St John's College, University of Cambridge, since 1980; *b* 10 March 1934; *s* of John Hugo and Cecily Eileen Emsley Matthews; *m* 1984, Lucienne Marie Jeanne Schleich; one step *s* one step *d*. *Educ:* Montpellier Sch., Paignton; Clifton Coll.; St John's Coll., Cambridge (MA 1960). Lectr in Linguistics, UCNW, 1961–65 (on leave Indiana Univ., Bloomington, 1963–64); University of Reading: Lectr in Linguistic Science, 1965–69; Reader, 1969–75; Prof., 1975–80 (on leave as Fellow, King's Coll., Cambridge, 1970–71, and as Fellow, Netherlands Inst. of Advanced Study, Wassenaar, 1977–78). An Editor, Jl of Linguistics, 1970–79. *Publications:* Inflectional Morphology, 1972; Morphology, 1974; Generative Grammar and Linguistic Competence, 1979; Syntax, 1981; articles esp. in Jl of Linguistics. *Recreations:* cycling, bird-watching. *Address:* 10 Fendon Close, Cambridge CB1 4RU. *T:* Cambridge 247553; 112 Avenue Victor Hugo, Luxembourg. *T:* (010 352) 24146.

MATTHEWS, Sir Peter (Jack), Kt 1981; CVO 1978; OBE 1974; QPM 1970; DL; Chief Constable of Surrey, 1968–82; *b* 25 Dec. 1917; *s* of Thomas Francis Matthews and Agnes Jack; *m* 1944, Margaret, *er d* of Cecil Levett, London; one *s*. *Educ:* Blackridge Public Sch., West Lothian. Joined Metropolitan Police, 1937; Flt-Lt (pilot) RAF, 1942–46; Metropolitan Police, 1946–65; seconded Cyprus, 1955; Chief Supt P Div. 1963–65; Chief Constable: of East Suffolk, 1965–67; of Suffolk, 1967–68. President: British Section, Internat. Police Assoc., 1964–70 (Internat. Pres. 1966–70); Assoc. of Chief Police Officers of England, Wales and NI, 1976–77 (Chm., Sub-Cttee on Terrorism and Allied Matters, 1976–82; Rep. at Interpol, 1977–80); Chief Constables' Club, 1980–81; Vice-Chm., Home Office Standing Adv. Cttee on Police Dogs, 1982– (Chm., 1978–82; Chm., Training Sub-Cttee, 1972–82); led British Police Study Team to advise Singapore Police, 1982; specialist advr to Parly Select Cttee on Defence, 1984; Mem., MoD Police Review Cttee, 1985. Lecture tour of Canada and USA, 1979; Lectr, Airline Training Associates Ltd, 1984–. CBIM 1978. DL Surrey, 1981. Final Reader, HM The Queen's Police Gold Medal Essay Competition, 1983–. *Club:* Royal Air Force.

MATTHEWS, Richard Bonnar, CBE 1971; QPM 1965; Chief Constable, Warwickshire, 1964–76 (Warwickshire and Coventry, 1969–74); *b* 18 Dec. 1915; *er s* of late Charles Richard Matthews, Worthing; *m* 1943, Joan, *d* of late Basil Worsley, Henstridge, Som;

two d. *Educ:* Stowe School. Served War of 1939–45, Lieut, RNVR. Joined Metropolitan Police, 1936; Asst Chief Constable, E Sussex, 1954–56; Chief Constable of Cornwall and Isles of Scilly, 1956–64. Chm., Traffic Cttee, Assoc. of Chief Police Officers, 1973–76. Mem., Williams Cttee on Obscenity and Film Censorship, 1977–79; Chm., CS selection bds, 1979–85. Founder, Adv. Cttee on Beach Life Saving for Cornwall, 1959. *Recreations:* ski-ing, fishing, gardening. *Address:* Smoke Acre, Great Bedwyn, Marlborough, Wilts SN8 3LP. *T:* Marlborough 870584. *Club:* Naval.

MATTHEWS, Prof. Richard Ellis Ford, ScD, FRS 1974, FRSNZ, FNZIC; Professor of Microbiology, Department of Cell Biology, University of Auckland, New Zealand, since 1962; *b* Hamilton, NZ, 20 Nov. 1921; *s* of Gerald Wilfrid Matthews and Ruby Miriam (*née* Crawford); *m* 1950, Lois Ann Bayley; three *s* one *d*. *Educ:* Mt Albert Grammar Sch.; Auckland University Coll.; Univ. of Cambridge. MSc (NZ), PhD, ScD (Cantab). Postdoctoral Research Fellow, Univ. of Wisconsin, 1949. Plant Diseases Div., DSIR, Auckland, NZ: Mycologist, 1950–53; Sen. Mycologist, 1954–55; (on leave from DSIR as a visiting worker at ARC Virus Research Unit, Molteno Inst., Cambridge, 1952–56); Sen. Principal Scientific Officer, DSIR, 1956–61; Head of Dept of Cell Biology, Univ. of Auckland, 1962–77, 1983–85. Pres., Internat. Cttee for Taxonomy of Viruses, 1975–81. *Publications:* Plant Virus Serology, 1957; Plant Virology, 1970, 2nd edn 1981; over 130 original papers in scientific jls. *Recreations:* gardening, sea fishing, bee keeping. *Address:* 1019 Beach Road, Torbay, Auckland 10, New Zealand. *T:* Auckland 4037709; (summer residence) RD4 Hikurangi.

MATTHEWS, Prof. Robert Charles Oliver, CBE 1975; FBA 1968; Master of Clare College, Cambridge, since 1975; Professor of Political Economy, Cambridge University, since 1980; *b* 16 June 1927; *s* of Oliver Harwood Matthews, WS, and Ida Finlay; *m* 1948, Joyce Hilda Lloyds; one *d*. *Educ:* Edinburgh Academy; Corpus Christi Coll., Oxford (Hon. Fellow, 1976). Student, Nuffield Coll., Oxford, 1947–48; Lectr, Merton Coll., Oxford, 1948–49; University Asst Lectr in Economics, Cambridge, 1949–51, and Univ. Lectr, 1951–65. Fellow of St John's Coll., Cambridge, 1950–65. Visiting Prof., University of California, Berkeley, 1961–62; Drummond Prof. of Political Economy, Oxford, and Fellow of All Souls Coll., 1965–75. Chm., SSRC, 1972–75. Managing Trustee, Nuffield Foundn, 1975–; Trustee, Urwick Orr and Partners Ltd, 1978–86. Pres., Royal Econ. Soc., 1984–86; Mem., OECD Expert Group on Non-inflationary Growth, 1975–77. Chm., Bank of England Panel of Academic Consultants, 1977–. FIDE Internat. Master of chess composition, 1965. For. Hon. Mem., Amer. Acad. of Arts and Scis, 1985. Hon. DLitt Warwick, 1980. *Publications:* A Study in Trade Cycle History, 1954; The Trade Cycle, 1958; (with F. H. Hahn) Théorie de la Croissance Economique, 1972; (ed) Economic Growth: trends and factors, 1981; (with C. H. Feinstein and J. C. Odling-Smee) British Economic Growth 1856–1973, 1982; (ed with G. B. Stafford) The Grants Economy and Collective Consumption, 1982; (ed) Slower Growth in the Western World, 1982; (ed with J. R. Sargent) Contemporary Problems of Economic Policy: essays from the CLARE Group, 1983; articles in learned journals. (With M. Lipton and J. M. Rice) Chess Problems: Introduction to an Art, 1963. *Address:* The Master's Lodge, Clare College, Cambridge. *Club:* Reform.

MATTHEWS, Ronald Sydney, CB 1978; Deputy Secretary, Department of Health and Social Security, 1976–81; *b* 26 July 1922; *s* of George and Louisa Matthews; *m* 1945, Eleanor Bronwen Shaw; one *s* one *d*. *Educ:* Kingsbury County School. RAF, 1940–46. Clerical Officer, Min. of Health, 1939; Principal 1959; Private Sec. to Minister of Health, 1967–68; Private Sec. to Sec. of State for Social Services, 1968–69; Asst Sec. 1968; Under-Sec., DHSS, 1973–76. *Recreations:* walking, gardening, reading. *Address:* 4 Saxon Rise, Winterborne Stickland, Blandford Forum, Dorset DT11 0PQ.

MATTHEWS, Sir Russell, Kt 1982; OBE 1971; company director; retired civil engineer; *b* 26 July 1896; *s* of Robert and Grace Matthews; *m* 1932, Elizabeth Mary Brodie; two *s* two *d*. *Educ:* New Plymouth Boys' High Sch.; London Sch. of Engineering. Formed Matthews & Kirkby and ran business as Man. Dir, 1936–42, then sole Proprietor, Matthews & Co., at that time the country's leading road sealing contractor; Founder Chm., and Dir, Ivon Watkins Dow, 1944–62; Founder Director: Kaikariki Sand & Gravel Co., 1944–68; R. J. Burkitt, 1956–; Pacific Constructors, 1958–71; Russell Matthews Industries, 1959–80; Taranaki Hldgs, 1959–; Fitzroy Engineering, 1960–80; Maxwell Machines, 1962–71; Technic Industries, 1965–80; Aid Industries, 1967–71; Technic Group, 1969–80; Asphaltic Construction, 1971–80. *Recreation:* gardening. *Address:* Tupare, 487 Mangorei Road, New Plymouth, New Zealand. *T:* 86480.

MATTHEWS, Sir Stanley, Kt 1965; CBE 1957; professional footballer; *b* Hanley, Stoke-on-Trent, 1 Feb. 1915; *s* of late Jack Matthews, Seymour Street, Hanley; *m* 1st, 1935, Elizabeth Hall Vallance (marr. diss. 1975); one *s* one *d*; 2nd, 1975, Gertrud (Mila) Winterova. *Educ:* Wellington Sch., Hanley. Played in first Football League match, 1931; first played for England, 1934, and fifty-five times subsequently; Blackpool FC, 1947–61 (FA Cup, 1953); Stoke City FC, 1961–65. Freedom of Stoke-on-Trent, 1963. *Publication:* The Stanley Matthews Story, 1960. *Recreations:* golf, tennis. *Address:* 5250 Lakeshore Road, Burlington, Ont L7L 5L2, Canada. *Club:* National Sporting.

MATTHEWS, Thomas Stanley; journalist; *b* 16 Jan. 1901; *s* of late Rt Rev. Paul Matthews, sometime Bishop of New Jersey, and late Elsie Procter; *m* 1st, 1925, Juliana Stevens Cuyler (*d* 1949); four *s*; 2nd, 1954, Martha Gellhorn; 3rd, 1964, Pamela, *widow* of Lt-Col V. Peniakoff. *Educ:* Park Hill, Lyndhurst, Hants; Shattuck Sch. (Minn.); St Paul's Sch. (Concord, NH); Princeton Univ.; New Coll., Oxford (MA; Hon. Fellow, 1986). Doctor of Humane Letters, Kenyon Coll., Ohio; Doctor of Letters, Rollins Coll., Florida. Editorial staff: The New Republic, 1925–29; Time, 1929; Exec. Editor, Time, 1942; Managing Editor Time, 1943–50, Editor, 1950–53. *Publications:* To the Gallows I Must Go, 1931; The Moon's No Fool, 1934; The Sugar Pill, 1957; Name and Address, 1960; O My America!, 1962; The Worst Unsaid (verse), 1962; Why So Gloomy? (verse), 1966; Great Tom: notes towards the Definition of T. S. Eliot, 1974; Jacks or Better, 1977 (Under the Influence, UK, 1979); Journal to the End of the Day, 1979; Cut Out the Poetry, 1982; Joking Apart, 1983; Tell Me About It, 1985; Angels Unawares, 1985. *Address:* Cavendish Hall, Cavendish, Suffolk. *T:* Clare 296. *Clubs:* Athenæum, Buck's; Century Association, Coffee House, Princeton (New York); Reading Room (Newport, RI); Nassau (Princeton, NJ).

MATTHEWS, Rt. Rev. Timothy John; BA, DCL; LST, STh; Chaplain, Bishop's College School. *Educ:* Bishop's Univ., Lennoxville. Deacon 1932, priest 1933, Edmonton; Vicar of Viking, 1933–37; Incumbent of Edson, 1937–40; Rector of Coaticook, 1940–44; Lake St John, 1944–52; Rector and Archdeacon of Gaspé, 1952–57; Rector of Lennoxville, 1957–71; Archdeacon of St Francis, 1957–71; Bishop of Quebec, 1971–77. *Address:* 23 High Street, Lennoxville, PQ J1M 1E6, Canada. *Clubs:* St George's (Sherbrooke); Hole-in-One, Lennoxville Golf, Milby Golf; Lennoxville Curling.

MATTHEWS, Prof. Walter Bryan; Professor of Clinical Neurology, University of Oxford, 1970–Sept. 1987; Fellow of St Edmund Hall, Oxford, 1970–Sept. 1987; *b* 7 April 1920; *s* of Very Rev. Dr Walter Robert Matthews; *m* 1943, Margaret Forster; one *s* one *d*. *Educ:* Marlborough Coll.; University Coll., Oxford. MA, DM, FRCP. RAMC,

1943–46. Senior Registrar, Oxford, 1948; Chief Asst, Dept of Neurology, Manchester Royal Infirmary, 1949–52; Senior Registrar, King's College Hosp., 1952–54; Consultant Neurologist, Derbyshire Royal Infirmary, 1954–68; Consultant Neurologist, Manchester Royal Infirmary and Crumpsall Hosp., 1968–70. President: Section of Neurology, RSM, 1981; Assoc. of British Neurologists, 1982. Osler Orator, RCP, 1981. Editor-in-Chief, Jl of Neurological Scis, 1977–83. *Publications:* Practical Neurology, 1963, 3rd edn 1975; (with H. G. Miller) Diseases of the Nervous System, 1972, 3rd edn 1979; (ed) Recent Advances in Clinical Neurology I, 1975, II, 1978, IV, 1984; Multiple Sclerosis: the facts, 1978; (ed) McAlpine's Multiple Sclerosis, 1985; papers in Brain, Quarterly Jl of Medicine, etc. *Recreation:* walking. *Address:* Sandford House, Sandford-on-Thames, Oxford. *Club:* United Oxford & Cambridge University.

MATTHÖFER, Hans; Member of the Bundestag (Social Democrat), since 1961; *b* Bochum, 25 Sept. 1925; *m* Traute Matthöfer (*née* Mecklenburg). *Educ:* primary sch.; studied economics and social sciences in Frankfurt/Main and Madison, Wis, USA, 1948–53 (grad. Economics). Employed as manual and clerical worker, 1940–42; Reich Labour Service, 1942; conscripted into German Army, 1943 (Armoured Inf.), final rank NCO. Joined SPD (Social Democratic Party of Germany), 1950; employed in Economics Dept, Bd of Management, IG Metall (Metalworkers' Union) and specialized in problems arising in connection with automation and mechanization, 1953 (Head of Trng and Educn Dept, 1961). Member, OEEC Mission in Washington and Paris, 1957–61; Vice-Pres., Gp of Parliamentarians on Latin American Affairs (Editor of periodical Esprés Español until end of 1972); Mem., Patronage Cttee of German Section of Amnesty Internat.; Pres., Bd of Trustees, German Foundn for Developing Countries, 1971–73; Parly State Sec. in Federal Min. for Economic Co-operation, 1972; Federal Minister for Research and Technology, 1974, for Finance, 1978–82, for Posts and Telecommunications, 1982. Mem. of Presidency and Treasurer, SPD, 1985–. *Publications:* Der Unterschied zwischen den Tariflöhnen und den Effektivverdiensten in der Metallindustrie der Bundesrepublik, 1956; Technological Change in the Metal Industries (in two parts), 1961–62; Der Beitrag politischer Bildung zur Emanzipation der Arbeitnehmer—Materialien zur Frage des Bildungsurlaubs, 1970; Streiks und streikähnliche Formen des Kampfes der Arbeitnehmer im Kapitalismus, 1971; Für eine menschliche Zukunft—Sozialdemokratische Forschungs—und Technologie-politik, 1976; Humanisierung der Arbeit und Produktivität in der Industriegesellschaft, 1977, 1978, 1980; numerous articles on questions of trade union, development, research and finance policies. *Address:* Schreyerstrasse 38, 6242 Kronberg im Taunus, W Germany.

MATTINGLY, Alan; Director (formerly Secretary), Ramblers' Association, since 1974; *b* 19 May 1949; *s* of Alexander and Patricia Mattingly; *m* 1980, Wendy Mallard. *Educ:* The Latymer Sch., Edmonton; St John's Coll., Cambridge (BA). Chm., Council for Nat. Parks, 1979–83; Vice-Pres., Countrywide Holidays Assoc., 1980–. Mem., (Lab) Newham Borough Council, 1980–86, Dep. Leader, 1983–85. *Publications:* Tackle Rambling, 1981; Walking in the National Parks, 1982. *Recreations:* walking, orienteering. *Address:* 45 Tonbridge Crescent, Kenton, Middlesex.

MATTINGLY, Dr Stephen, TD 1964; FRCP; Consultant Physician, Middlesex Hospital, 1958–81; Consultant Physician, 1956–82 and Medical Director, 1972–82, Garston Manor Rehabilitation Centre; Hon. Consultant in Rheumatology and Rehabilitation to the Army, 1976–81; *b* 1 March 1922; *s* of Harold Mattingly, CBE and Marion Grahame Meikleham; *m* 1945, Brenda Mary Pike; one *s*. *Educ:* Leighton Park Sch.; UCH (MB, BS); Dip. in Physical Med., 1953. FRCP 1970. House-surg., UCH, 1947; Regtl MO, 2/10 Gurkha Rifles, RAMC Far East, 1947–49; House-surg. and Registrar, UCH, 1950–55; Sen. Registrar, Mddx Hosp., 1955–56. Reg. Med. Consultant for London, S-Eastern, Eastern and Southern Regions, Dept of Employment, 1960–74. Mem., Attendance Allowance Bd, 1978–83. Lt-Col RAMC TA, 1952–67. *Publications:* (contrib.) Progress in Clinical Rheumatology, 1965; (contrib.) Textbook of Rheumatic Diseases, ed Copeman, 1969; (contrib.) Fractures and Joint Injuries, ed Watson Jones, 5th edn 1976, 6th edn 1982; (ed) Rehabilitation Today, 1977, 2nd edn 1981. *Recreation:* gardening. *Address:* Highfield House, Little Brington, Northants. *T:* Northampton 770271.

MATTURI, Sahr Thomas, CMG 1967; BSc, PhD; farmer; High Commissioner in London for Sierra Leone, 1978–80; retired from Sierra Leone Foreign Service; *b* 22 Oct. 1925; *s* of Sahr and Konneh Matturi; *m* 1956, Anna Adella Stephens; two *s* one *d*. *Educ:* University Coll., Ibadan; Hull Univ. School Teacher, 1944–47, 1954–55; University Lecturer, 1959–63; Principal, Njala Univ. Coll., 1963–76; Vice-Chancellor, Univ. of Sierra Leone, 1968–70; Acting Vice-Chancellor and Pro Vice-Chancellor, 1972–74, Pro Vice-Chancellor, 1966–68, 1970–72, 1973–75. Ambassador of Sierra Leone to Italy, Austria and Yugoslavia, and Perm. Rep. to UN Specialised Agencies in Rome, Geneva and Vienna, 1977–78. Chm., W African Exams Council, 1971–76. Mem., British Mycol. Soc. LLD *hc* Hull, 1981. FRSA. *Recreations:* cricket, lawn tennis, shooting. *Address:* c/o Jaiama Secondary School, Private Mail Bag, Koidu Town, Sierra Leone.

MATUTES JUAN, Abel; Spanish Member, Commission of the European Communities, since 1986; *b* 31 Oct. 1941; *s* of Antonio Matutes and Carmen Juan; *m* Nieves Prats Prats; one *s* three *d*. *Educ:* University of Barcelona (Law and Economic Sciences). Prof., Barcelona Univ., 1963; Vice-Pres., Employers Organization for Tourism, Ibiza-Formentera, 1964–79; Mayor of Ibiza, 1970–71; Senator, Ibiza and Formentera in Alianza Popular (opposition party), 1977–79; Vice-Pres., Alianza Popular, 1979–85 (Pres., Economy Cttee); Pres., Nat. Electoral Cttee; Spokesman for Economy and Finance, Grupo Popular in Congress (Parlt). *Recreation:* tennis. *Address:* Avenue Val au Bois 7, 1980 Kraainem, Belgium. *Clubs:* Golf Rocalliza (Ibiza); de Campo (Ibiza).

MAUCHLINE, Lord; Michael Edward Abney-Hastings; ranger with New South Wales Pastures Protection Board; *b* 22 July 1942; *s* and *heir* of Countess of Loudoun (13th in line), *qv* and *s* of Captain Walter Strickland Lord (whose marriage to the Countess of Loudoun was dissolved, 1945; his son assumed, by deed poll, 1946, the surname of Abney-Hastings in lieu of his patronymic); *m* 1969, Noelene Margaret McCormick, 2nd *d* of Mr and Mrs W. J. McCormick, Barham, NSW; two *s* three *d* (of whom one *s* one *d* are twins). *Educ:* Ampleforth. *Address:* 74 Coreen Street, Jerilderie, NSW 2716, Australia.

MAUD, Hon. Humphrey John Hamilton, CMG 1982; HM Diplomatic Service; Assistant Under-Secretary of State, Foreign and Commonwealth Office, since 1985; *b* 17 April 1934; *s* of Baron Redcliffe-Maud, GCB, CBE and of Jean, *yr d* of late J. B. Hamilton, Melrose; *m* 1963, Maria Eugenia Gazitua; three *s*. *Educ:* Eton; King's Coll., Cambridge (Scholar; Classics and History); MA. Instructor in Classics, Univ. of Minnesota, 1958–59; entered Foreign Service, 1959; FO, 1960–61; Madrid, 1961–63; Havana, 1963–65; FO, 1966–67; Cabinet Office, 1968–69; Paris, 1970–74; Nuffield Coll., Oxford (Econs), 1974–75; Head of Financial Relations Dept, FCO, 1975–79; Minister, Madrid, 1979–82; Ambassador, Luxembourg, 1982–85. *Recreation:* music ('cellist). *Address:* 31 Queen Anne's Grove, Bedford Park, W4 1HW. *Club:* United Oxford & Cambridge University.

MAUDE, family name of **Viscount Hawarden** and **Baron Maude of Stratford-upon-Avon.**

MAUDE OF STRATFORD-UPON-AVON, Baron *cr* 1983 (Life Peer), of Stratford-upon-Avon in the county of Warwickshire; **Angus Edmund Upton Maude;** Kt 1981; TD; PC 1979; author and journalist; *b* 8 Sept. 1912; *o c* of late Col Alan Hamer Maude, CMG, DSO, TD, and late Dorothy Maude (*née* Upton); *m* 1946, Barbara Elizabeth Earnshaw, *o d* of late John Earnshaw Sutcliffe, Bushey; two *s* two *d. Educ:* Rugby Sch. (Scholar); Oriel Coll., Oxford (MA). Financial journalist, 1933–39: The Times, 1933–34; Daily Mail, 1935–39. Commissioned in RASC (TA), May 1939; served in RASC 1939–45, at home and in North Africa (PoW, Jan. 1942–May 1945); Major 56th (London) Armd Divl Column RASC (TA), 1947–51. Dep. Dir of PEP, 1948–50; Dir, Cons. Political Centre, 1951–55; Editor, Sydney Morning Herald, 1958–61. MP (C) Ealing (South), 1950–57, (Ind. C), 1957–58, (C) Stratford-upon-Avon, Aug. 1963–1983; a Dep. Chm., Cons. Party, 1975–79 (Chm. Res. Dept, 1975–79); Paymaster Gen., 1979–81. Contested S Dorset, by-election, Nov. 1962. *Publications:* (with Roy Lewis) The English Middle Classes, 1949; Professional People, 1952; (with Enoch Powell) Biography of a Nation, 1955; Good Learning, 1964; South Asia, 1966; The Common Problem, 1969. *Address:* Old Farm, South Newington, near Banbury, Oxon. *Club:* Carlton.
See also P. D. G. Hayter, Hon. F. A. A. Maude.

MAUDE, Hon. Francis Anthony Aylmer; MP (C) Warwickshire North, since 1983; an Assistant Government Whip, since 1985; *b* 4 July 1953; *s* of Baron Maude of Stratford-upon-Avon, *qv*; *m* 1984, Christina Jane, *yr d* of late Peter Hadfield, Shrewsbury. *Educ:* Abingdon Sch.; Corpus Christi Coll., Cambridge (BA (Hons) History; Avory Studentship; Halse Prize). Called to Bar, Inner Temple, 1977 (scholar; Forster Boulton Prize); member of chambers of Rt Hon. Sir Michael Havers, QC, MP. Councillor, Westminster CC, 1978–84. PPS to Minister of State for Employment, 1984–85. *Recreations:* skiing, cricket, reading, music. *Address:* House of Commons, SW1. *T:* 01–219 3438.

MAUDE-ROXBY, John Henry; Chairman: Cameron Choat and Partners, since 1977; Maude-Roxby, Sussman Associates, since 1978; *b* 4 March 1919; *m* 1966, Katherine Jewell; one *s. Educ:* Radley Coll.; Hertford Coll., Oxford (BA). ACIS. Regular Army Officer, Royal Artillery, 1939–59. Allied Suppliers Ltd, 1959–73 (Chm. and Man. Dir, 1972–73); Dir, Cavenham Ltd, 1972–73; Dep. Chm. and Man. Dir, Morgan Edwards Ltd, 1973–74; Dir Gen., Inst. of Grocery Distribution, 1974–77. Regional Trading Manager, Mercia Region, Nat. Trust, 1979–84. *Recreations:* shooting, golf, gardening. *Address:* Cedar Cottage, Batch Valley, All Stretton, Shropshire SY6 6JW. *T:* Church Stretton 722481. *Clubs:* Army and Navy; Vincent's (Oxford).

MAUDSLAY, Major Sir (James) Rennie, GCVO 1980 (KCVO 1972; CVO 1967); KCB 1979; MBE 1945; Keeper of the Privy Purse and Treasurer to the Queen, 1971–81 (Assistant Keeper, 1958–71); Extra Equerry to the Queen, since 1973; *b* 13 Aug. 1915; *o s* of late Joseph Maudslay and of Mrs Ruth Maudslay (*née* Partridge), Pinewood Copse, Boundstone, Farnham, Surrey; *m* 1951, (Jane) Ann, *d* of A. V. McCarty, Helena, Arkansas; two *s* one *d. Educ:* Harrow Sch. 2nd Lt, KRRC, 1938; served 1938–45 (despatches five times); Hon. Major, 1945. Chm., Mid-Southern Water Co. Mem. of Lloyd's. Pres., Farnham Conservative Assoc., 1954–57; Pres., Maudslay Soc., 1963–65; Hon. Mem., Jun. Instn of Engineers. Employed Lord Chamberlain's Office, 1952–53. Holds Order of: Verdienst (Germany), 1958; Taj (Iran), 1959; Dakshuna Bahu (Nepal), 1960; Legion of Honour (France), 1960; Crown of Thai (Thailand), 1960; Phœnix (Greece), 1963; Al Kawkab (Jordan), 1966; Ordine al Merito della Repubblica (Italy), 1969; Order of Kroonorde (Netherlands), 1972; Order of Merit (Germany), 1972; Order of Star (Afghanistan), 1972; Order of Dannebrog (Denmark), 1974. *Recreations:* shooting, gardening. *Address:* 12 Bradbourne Street, SW6 4RE. *Clubs:* White's, MCC.

MAUGHAN, Air Vice-Marshal Charles Gilbert, CB 1976; CBE 1970; AFC; an Independent Panel Inspector, Department of the Environment, since 1983; *b* 3 March 1923. *Educ:* Sir George Monoux Grammar Sch.; Harrow County Sch. Served War, Fleet Air Arm (flying Swordfishes and Seafires), 1942–46. Joined RAF, 1949, serving with Meteor, Vampire and Venom sqdns in Britain and Germany; comd No 65 (Hunter) Sqdn, Duxford, Cambridgeshire (won Daily Mail Arch-to-Arc race, 1959). Subseq. comd: No 9 (Vulcan) Sqdn; flying bases of Honington (Suffolk) and Waddington (Lincs); held a staff post at former Bomber Comd, Air Staff (Ops), Strike Command, 1968–70; Air Attaché, Bonn, 1970–73; AOA Strike Command, 1974–75; SASO RAF Strike Command, 1975–77. Gen. Sec., Royal British Legion, 1978–83. *Address:* Whitestones, Tresham, Wotton-under-Edge, Glos GL12 7RW.

MAULEVERER, (Peter) Bruce; QC 1985; a Recorder, since 1985; *b* 22 Nov. 1946; *s* of late Algernon Arthur Mauleverer and Hazel Mary Mauleverer; *m* 1971, Sara (*née* Hudson-Evans); two *s* two *d. Educ:* Sherborne School; University College, Univ. of Durham (BA 1968). Called to the Bar, Inner Temple, 1969. Hon. Sec.-Gen., Internat. Law Assoc., 1986–. *Recreations:* sailing, skiing, travel. *Address:* Eliot Vale House, Eliot Vale, Blackheath, SE3 0UW. *T:* 01–852 2070.

MAUND, Rt. Rev. John Arthur Arrowsmith, CBE 1975; MC 1946; Chaplain to the Beauchamp Community, Malvern, since 1983; *b* 1909; *s* of late Arthur Arrowsmith and Dorothy Jane Maund, Worcester, England; *m* 1948, Catherine Mary Maurice, Bromley, Kent; no *c. Educ:* Worcester Cathedral King's Sch.; Leeds Univ.; Mirfield Theological Coll. BA Leeds 1931; Asst Priest, All Saints and St Laurence, Evesham, Worcs, 1933–36; Asst Priest, All Saints, Blackheath, London, 1936–38; Asst Priest, Pretoria Native Mission, Pretoria, South Africa, 1938–40; CF 1940–46 (despatches, 1942); Asst Priest, Pretoria Native Mission, in charge Lady Selborne, Pretoria, 1946–50; Bishop of Lesotho, 1950–76 (diocese known as Basutoland, 1950–66). Fellow Royal Commonwealth Society. *Recreation:* horse riding. *Address:* Chaplain's House, The Beauchamp Community, Newlands, Malvern, Worcs WR13 5AX. *T:* Malvern 68072.

MAUNDER, Prof. Leonard, OBE 1977; BSc; PhD; ScD; FEng; FIMechE; Professor of Mechanical Engineering, since 1967 (Professor of Applied Mechanics, 1961), Dean of the Faculty of Applied Science, 1973–78, University of Newcastle upon Tyne; *b* 10 May 1927; *s* of Thomas G. and Elizabeth A. Maunder; *m* 1958, Moira Anne Hudson; one *s* one *d. Educ:* Grammar Sch., Swansea; University Coll. of Swansea (BSc); Edinburgh Univ. (PhD); Massachusetts Institute of Technology (ScD). Instructor, 1950–53, and Asst Prof., 1953–54, in Dept of Mech. Engrg, MIT; Aeronautical Research Lab., Wright Air Development Center, US Air Force, 1954–56; Lecturer in Post-Graduate Sch. of Applied Dynamics, Edinburgh Univ., 1956–61. Christmas Lectr, Royal Instn, 1983. Member: NRDC, 1976–; SRC Engrg Bd, 1976–80; Adv. Council on R&D for Fuel and Power, Dept of Energy, 1981–; British Technology Gp, 1981–; Dep. Chm., Newcastle Hospitals Management Cttee, 1971–73. President: Internat. Fedn Theory of Machines and Mechanisms, 1976–79; Engrg, BAAS, 1980. Vice-Pres., IMechE, 1975–80. *Publications:* (with R. N. Arnold) Gyrodynamics and Its Engineering Applications, 1961; Machines in Motion, 1986; numerous papers in the field of applied mechanics. *Address:* Stephenson Building, The University, Newcastle upon Tyne NE1 7RU.

MAUNDRELL, Rev. Canon Wolseley David; Rector of Rye, East Sussex, since 1982; Rural Dean of Rye, 1978–84; Canon and Prebendary of Chichester Cathedral, since 1981; *b* 2 Sept. 1920; *s* of late Rev. William Herbert Maundrell, RN, and Evelyn Helen Maundrell; *m* 1950, Barbara Katharine Simmons (*d* 1985); one *s* one *d. Educ:* Radley Coll.; New Coll., Oxford. Deacon, 1943; Priest, 1944; Curate of Haslemere, 1943; Resident Chaplain to Bishop of Chichester, 1949; Vicar of Sparsholt and Lainston, Winchester, 1950; Rector of Weeke, Winchester, 1956; Residentiary Canon of Winchester Cathedral, 1961–70 (Treasurer, 1961–70; Vice-Dean, 1966–70). Examining Chaplain to Bishop of Winchester, 1962–70; Asst Chaplain of Holy Trinity Church, Brussels, 1970–71; Vicar of Icklesham, E Sussex, 1972–82. *Address:* The Rectory, Gun Garden, Rye, East Sussex. *T:* Rye 222430.

MAURICE, Dr Rita Joy; Director of Statistics, Home Office, since 1977; *b* 10 May 1929; *d* of A. N. Maurice and F. A. Maurice (*née* Dean). *Educ:* East Grinstead County Sch.; University Coll., London. BSc (Econ) 1951; PhD 1958. Asst Lectr, subseq. Lectr in Economic Statistics, University Coll., London, 1951–58; Statistician, Min. of Health, 1959–62; Statistician, subseq. Chief Statistician, Central Statistical Office, 1962–72; Head of Economics and Statistics Div. 6, Depts of Industry, Trade and Prices and Consumer Protection, 1972–77. Mem. Council, Royal Statistical Soc., 1978–82. *Publications:* articles in statistical jls.

MAUROY, Pierre; Mayor of Lille, since 1973; *b* 5 July 1928; *s* of Henri Mauroy and Adrienne Mauroy (*née* Bronne) *m* 1951, Gilberte Deboudt; one *s. Educ:* Lycée de Cambrai; Ecole normale nationale d'apprentissage de Cachan. Joined Young Socialists at age of 16 (Nat. Sec., 1950–58); teacher of technical educn, Colombes, 1952; Sec.-Gen., Syndicat des collèges d'enseignement technique de la Fédération de l'Education nationale, 1955–59; Sec., Fedn of Socialist Parties of Nord, 1961; Mem., Political Bureau, 1963, Dep. Gen. Sec., 1966, Socialist Party; Mem. Exec. Cttee, Fédération de la gauche démocratique et socialiste, 1965–68; First Sec., Fedn of Socialist Parties of Nord and Nat. Co-ordination Sec., Socialist Party, 1971–79. Member, from Le Cateau, and Vice-Pres., Conseil Gen. du Nord, 1967–73; Town Councillor and Deputy Mayor of Lille, 1971, Vice-Pres., Town Corp., 1971–81; Deputy, Nord, 1973–81; Prime Minister of France, 1981–84. Pres., Regional Council, Nord-Pas-de-Calais, 1974–81; Socialist Rep. and Vice-Pres., Political Commn, EEC, 1979–81. Political Dir, Action Socialiste Hebdo, 1979–; Pres., Fédération nationale Léo Lagrange. *Publications:* Héritiers de l'avenir, 1977; C'est ici le chemin, 1982. *Address:* 38 avenue Charles-Saint-Venant, 59000 Lille, France.

MAVOR, Air Marshal Sir Leslie (Deane), KCB 1970 (CB 1964); AFC 1942; DL; FRAeS; *b* 18 Jan. 1916; *s* of William David Mavor, Edinburgh; *m* 1947, June Lilian Blackburn; four *s. Educ:* Aberdeen Grammar Sch. Commissioned RAF 1937. Dir of Air Staff Briefing, Air Ministry, 1961–64; AOC, No 38 Group, 1964–66; Asst CAS (Policy), 1966–69; AOC-in-C, RAF Training Comd, 1969–72; retd Jan. 1973. Principal, Home Office Home Defence Coll., 1973–80; Co-ordinator of Voluntary Effort in Civil Defence, 1981–84. DL N Yorks, 1976. *Recreations:* golf, fishing, shooting, gliding. *Address:* Barlaston House, Alne, Yorks. *Clubs:* Royal Air Force, Yorkshire.

MAVOR, Michael Barclay, CVO 1983; MA; Headmaster, Gordonstoun School, since 1979; *b* 29 Jan. 1947; *s* of William Ferrier Mavor and Sheena Watson Mavor (*née* Barclay); *m* 1970, Jane Elizabeth Sucksmith; one *s* one *d. Educ:* Loretto School; St John's Coll., Cambridge (Exhibn and Trevelyan Schol.). MA (English); CertEd. Woodrow Wilson Teaching Fellow, Northwestern Univ., Evanston, Ill, 1969–72; Asst Master, Tonbridge Sch., 1972–78; Course Tutor (Drama), Open Univ., 1977–78. *Recreations:* theatre, writing, golf, fishing, cricket. *Address:* Gordonstoun School, Elgin, Moray IV30 2RF. *T:* Hopeman 830445. *Club:* Hawks (Cambridge).

MAVOR, Ronald Henry Moray, CBE 1972; author; Professor and Head, Department of Drama, University of Saskatchewan; *b* 13 May 1925; *s* of late Dr O. H. Mavor, CBE (James Bridie) and Rona Bremner; *m* 1959, Sigrid Bruhn; one *s* one *d* (and one *d* decd). *Educ:* Merchiston Castle Sch.; Glasgow Univ. MB, ChB 1948, MRCP(Glas) 1955. In medical practice until 1957, incl. periods in RAMC, at American Hosp., Paris, and Deeside Sanatoria. Drama Critic, The Scotsman, 1957–65; Dir, Scottish Arts Council, 1965–71. Vice-Chm., Edinburgh Festival Council, 1975–81 (Mem., 1965–81); Mem. Gen. Adv. Council, BBC, 1971–76; Mem. Drama Panel, British Council, 1973–79. Vis. Lectr on Drama, Guelph, Ontario, and Minneapolis, 1976; Vis. Prof., Univ. of Saskatchewan, 1977–78, 1979–81. *Plays:* The Keys of Paradise, 1959; Aurelie, 1960; Muir of Huntershill, 1962; The Partridge Dance, 1963; A Private Matter (originally A Life of the General), 1973; The Quartet, 1974; The Doctors, 1974; Gordon, 1978; A House on Temperance, 1980. *Publications:* Art the Hard Way, in, Scotland, 1972; A Private Matter (play), 1974. *Address:* 15 Church Hill, Edinburgh EH10 4BG; 417 Lansdowne Avenue, Saskatoon, Sask. S7N 1C8. *T:* (306) 242 3523.

MAVROGORDATO, John George, CMG 1952; *b* 9 May 1905; 2nd *s* of late George Michel and Irene Mavrogordato. *Educ:* Charterhouse; Christ Church, Oxford (BA 1927). Called to Bar, Gray's Inn, 1932; practised at Chancery Bar, 1932–39. Asst Dir, Ministry of Aircraft Production, 1943. Advocate-Gen., Sudan Government, 1946; Legal Adviser to Governor-Gen. of the Sudan, 1953; Senior Legal Counsel, Ministry of Justice, Sudan, 1958–61; retired, 1961. MBOU. *Publications:* A Hawk for the Bush, 1960; A Falcon in the Field, 1966; Behind the Scenes (autobiog.), 1982. *Recreations:* ornithology, wild life conservation.

MAW, (John) Nicholas; composer; *b* 5 Nov. 1935; *s* of Clarence Frederick Maw and Hilda Ellen (*née* Chambers); *m* 1960, Karen Graham; one *s* one *d. Educ:* Wennington Sch., Wetherby, Yorks; Royal Academy of Music. Studied in Paris with Nadia Boulanger and Max Deutsch, 1958–59. Fellow Commoner in Creative Arts, Trinity Coll., Cambridge, 1966–70; Visiting Professor of Composition: Yale Music Sch., 1984–85; Boston Univ., 1986. Midsummer Prize, Corp. of London, 1980. Compositions include: *operas:* One-Man Show, 1964; The Rising of The Moon, 1970; *for orchestra:* Sinfonia, 1966; Sonata for Strings and Two Horns, 1967; Serenade, for small orchestra, 1973, 1977; Life Studies, for 15 solo strings, 1973; Odyssey, 1974–86; Summer Dances, 1981; Spring Music, 1983; *for instrumental soloist and orchestra:* Sonata Notturna, for cello and string orchestra, 1985; *for voice and orchestra:* Nocturne, 1958; Scenes and Arias, 1962; *chamber music:* String Quartet, 1965; Chamber Music for wind and piano quintet, 1962; Flute Quartet, 1981; String Quartet no 2, 1983; *instrumental music:* Sonatina for flute and piano, 1957; Essay for organ, 1961; Personae for piano, nos I-III, 1973, IV–VI, 1985; *vocal music:* Five Epigrams for chorus, 1960; Round for chorus and piano, 1963; The Voice of Love, for mezzo soprano and piano, 1966; Six Interiors, for high voice and guitar, 1966; Five Irish Songs, for mixed chorus, 1972; Reverdie, five songs for male voices, 1975; Nonsense Rhymes, songs and rounds for children, 1975–76; La Vita Nuova, for soprano and chamber ensemble, 1979; The Ruin, for double choir and solo horn, 1980. *Address:* c/o Faber Music Ltd, 3 Queen Square, WC1N 3AU.

MAWBY, Colin (John Beverley); Choral Director, Radio Telefis Eireann, since 1981; *b* 9 May 1936; *e s* of Bernard Mawby and Enid Mawby (*née* Vaux); unmarried. *Educ:* St Swithun's Primary Sch., Portsmouth; Westminster Cathedral Choir Sch.; Royal Coll. of Music. Organist and Choirmaster of Our Lady's Church, Warwick St, W1, 1953; Choirmaster of Plymouth Cath., 1955; Organist and Choirmaster of St Anne's, Vauxhall, 1957; Asst Master of Music, Westminster Cath., 1959; Master of Music, 1961–75; Dir of

Music, Sacred Heart, Wimbledon, 1978–81. Conductor: Westminster Chamber Choir, 1971–78; Westminster Cathedral String Orchestra, 1971–78; New Westminster Chorus, 1972–80; Horniman Singers, 1979–80; Culwick Choral Soc., 1981–85. Prof. of Harmony, Trinity Coll. of Music, 1975–81. Director (Catholic) Publisher, L. J. Cary & Co., 1963; Vice-Pres., Brit. Fedn of *Pueri Cantores*, 1966; Member: Council, Latin Liturgical Assoc., 1969; Adv. Panel, Royal Sch. of Church Music, 1974; Music Sub-Cttee, Westminster Arts Council, 1974. Broadcaster and recording artist; free lance journalism. *Publications:* Church music including nine Masses, Anthems, Motets and Holy Week music. *Recreations:* gardening, wine drinking. *Address:* Gerrardstown, Garlow Cross, Navan, Co. Meath, Ireland. *T:* Navan 29394.

MAWBY, Raymond Llewellyn; *b* 6 Feb. 1922; *m* 1944; one *d* (one *s* decd). *Educ:* Long Lawford Council Sch., Warwicks. One-time Pres. Rugby branch Electrical Trades Union; one-time mem. of Rugby Borough Council. MP (C) Totnes, 1955–83; Asst Postmaster-Gen., 1963–64. *Address:* 29 Applegarth Avenue, Newton Abbot, S Devon.

MAWER, Air Cdre Allen Henry, DFC 1943; *b* 16 Dec. 1921; *s* of Gordon Mawer and Emily Naomi Mawer (*née* Block); *m* 1st, 1947, Pamela Mitchell (*d* 1982), *d* of David Thomas; one *s* one *d*; 2nd, 1982, Elizabeth Mary Stokes. *Educ:* Bancroft's School. Joined RAF, 1940; bomber and special duties ops, 1941–45; psc 1956; Stn Comdr, RAF Scampton, 1965–68; idc 1968; Comdt RAF Coll. of Air Warfare, 1969–71; Air Cdre Plans, HQ Strike Comd, RAF, 1971–73; Air Comdr, Malta, 1973–75, retd. Gen. Manager, Basildon Develt Corp., 1975–78; Man. Dir, Docklands Develt Organisation, 1979–80. Croix de Guerre, France, 1944. *Recreations:* painting, golf, shooting. *Address:* 68 High Street, Burnham-on-Crouch, Essex CM0 8AA. *Clubs:* Royal Air Force; Royal Burnham Yacht; Burnham Golf.

MAWER, Ronald K.; *see* Knox-Mawer.

MAWHINNEY, Brian Stanley; MP (C) Peterborough, since 1979; Under Secretary of State for Northern Ireland, since 1986; *b* 26 July 1940; *s* of Frederick Stanley Arnot Mawhinney and Coralie Jean Mawhinney; *m* 1965, Betty Louise Oja; two *s* one *d*. *Educ:* Royal Belfast Academical Instn; Queen's Univ., Belfast (BSc); Univ. of Michigan, USA (MSc); Univ. of London (PhD). Asst Prof. of Radiation Research, Univ. of Iowa, USA, 1968–70; Lectr, subsequently Sen. Lectr, Royal Free Hospital School of Medicine, 1970–84. Mem., MRC, 1980–83. Mem., Gen. Synod of C of E, 1985–. PPS to Ministers of State, 1982–83, to Minister of State, June 1983–84, HM Treasury; PPS to Sec. of State for Employment, 1984–85, to Sec. of State for NI, 1985–86. Vice-Pres., Cons. Trade Unionists, 1984–; Mem., AUT. Contested (C) Stockton on Tees, Oct. 1974. *Publication:* (jtly) Conflict and Christianity in Northern Ireland, 1976. *Recreations:* sport, reading. *Address:* House of Commons, SW1A 0AA.

MAWREY, Richard Brooks; QC 1986; *b* 20 Aug. 1942; *s* of Philip Stephen Mawrey and Alice Brooks Mawrey; *m* 1965, Gillian Hargaret Butt; one *d*. *Educ:* Rossall School; Magdalen College, Oxford (BA, 1st class Hons Law, 1963; Eldon Law Scholar, 1964; MA 1967). Albion Richardson Scholar, Gray's Inn, 1964; called to the Bar, Gray's Inn, 1964; Lectr in Law, Magdalen College, Oxford, 1964–65, Trinity College, Oxford, 1965–69. *Publications:* (specialist editor) Consumer Credit Legislation, 1983; Butterworth's County Court Precedents, 1985. *Recreations:* history, opera, cooking. *Address:* 2 Harcourt Buildings, Temple, EC4Y 9DB. *T:* 01–583 9020.

MAWSON, David; JP; DL; RIBA; FSA; Partner, Feilden and Mawson, Architects, Norwich, since 1957; *b* 30 May 1924; *s* of John William Mawson and Evelyn Mary Mawson (*née* Bond); *m* 1951, Margaret Kathlyn Norton; one *s* one *d*. *Educ:* Merchant Taylors' Sch., Sandy Lodge; Wellington Coll., NZ; Auckland Univ., NZ; Kingston-upon-Thames Coll. of Art. Royal Navy, 1945–47. Chartered Architect, 1952–. Architect, Norwich Cathedral, 1977–. Chairman: Norfolk Soc. (CPRE), 1971–76 (Vice Pres. 1976–); 54 Gp, 1982–; Friends of Norwich Museums, 1985–; Founder and Chm., British Assoc. of Friends of Museums, 1973–; Founder Pres., World Fedn of Friends of Museums, 1975–81, Past Pres., 1981–. Mem., Cttee of Nat. Heritage, 1973–; Trustee, Norfolk Historic Bldgs Trust, 1975–. Mem., Norfolk Assoc. of Architects, 1952– (Pres., 1979–81); Hon. Treas., Heritage Coordination Gp, 1981–. Pres., Norfolk Club, 1986–87 (Vice-Pres., 1985–86). JP Norwich, 1972; DL Norfolk, 1986. FRSA 1982; FSA 1983. *Publication:* paper on British Museum Friends Socs in Proc. of First Internat. Congress of Friends of Museums, Barcelona, 1972; contrib. Jl of Royal Soc. of Arts. *Recreations:* tennis, yachting. *Address:* Gonville Hall, Wymondham, Norfolk NR18 9JG. *T:* Wymondham 602166. *Club:* Norfolk (Norwich).

MAWSON, Stuart Radcliffe; Consultant Surgeon, Ear Nose and Throat Department, King's College Hospital, London, 1951–79, Head of Department, 1973–79; *b* 4 March 1918; *s* of late Alec Robert Mawson, Chief Officer, Parks Dept, LCC, and Ena (*née* Grossmith), *d* of George Grossmith Jr, Actor Manager; *m* 1948, June Irene, *d* of George Percival; two *s* two *d*. *Educ:* Canford Sch.; Trinity Coll., Cambridge; St Thomas's Hosp., London. BA Cantab 1940, MA 1976; MRCS, LRCP 1943; MB, BChir Cantab 1946; FRCS 1947; DLO 1948. House Surg., St Thomas's Hosp., 1943; RMO XIth Para. Bn, 1st Airborne Div., Arnhem, POW, 1943–44; Chief Asst, ENT Dept, St Thomas's Hosp., 1950; Consultant ENT Surgeon: King's Coll. Hosp., 1951; Belgrave Hosp. for Children, 1951; Recog. Teacher of Oto-Rhino-Laryngology, Univ. of London, 1958. Chm., KCH Med. Cttee and Dist Management Team, 1977–79. FRSocMed (Pres. Section of Otology, 1974–75); Liveryman, Apothecaries' Soc.; former Mem. Council, Brit. Assoc. of Otolaryngologists. *Publications:* Diseases of the Ear, 1963, 4th edn 1979; (jtly) Essentials of Otolaryngology, 1967; (contrib.) Scott-Brown's Diseases of the Ear, Nose and Throat, 4th edn 1979; (contrib.) Modern Trends in Diseases of the Ear, Nose and Throat, 1972; Arnhem Doctor, 1981; numerous papers in sci. jls. *Address:* Whinbeck, Knodishall, Saxmundham, Suffolk. *Clubs:* Aldeburgh Golf, Aldeburgh Yacht.

MAXEY, Peter Malcolm, CMG 1982; HM Diplomatic Service; Ambassador and Deputy Permanent Representative to UN, New York, 1984–86; *b* 26 Dec. 1930; *m* 1st, 1955, Joyce Diane Marshall; two *s* two *d*; 2nd, Christine Irene Spooner. *Educ:* Bedford Sch.; Corpus Christi Coll., Cambridge. Served HM Forces, 1949–50. Entered Foreign Office, 1953; Third Sec., Moscow, 1955; Second Sec., 1956; First Sec., Helsinki, 1962; Moscow, 1965; First Sec. and Head of Chancery, Colombo, 1968; seconded to Lazard Bros, 1971; Inspector, 1972; Deputy Head UK Delegation to CSCE, Geneva, 1973; Head of UN Dept, FCO, 1974; NATO Defence Coll., Rome, 1977; Dublin, 1977; on secondment as Under Sec., Cabinet Office, 1978–81; Ambassador, GDR, 1981–84. *Address:* c/o Foreign and Commonwealth Office, SW1.

MAXTON, John Alston; MP (Lab) Glasgow, Cathcart, since 1979; *b* Oxford, 5 May 1936; *s* of John Maxton, agr. economist, and Jenny Maxton; *m* Christine Maxton; three *s*. *Educ:* Lord Williams' Grammar Sch., Thame; Oxford Univ. Lectr in Social Studies, Hamilton Coll. Chm., Assoc. of Lectrs in Colls of Educn, Scotland; Member: Educnl Inst. of Scotland; Socialist Educnl Assoc. Joined Lab. Party, 1970. Mem., ASTMS. *Recreations:* family and golf. *Address:* House of Commons, SW1.

MAXWELL, family name of **Barons de Ros** and **Farnham.**

MAXWELL, Hon. Lord; Peter Maxwell; a Senator of the College of Justice in Scotland, since 1973; *b* 21 May 1919; *s* of late Comdr and late Mrs Herries Maxwell, Munches, Dalbeattie, Kirkcudbrightshire; *m* 1941, Alison Susan Readman; one *s* two *d* (and one *s* decd). *Educ:* Wellington Coll.; Balliol Coll., Oxford; Edinburgh Univ. Served Argyll and Sutherland Highlanders, and late RA, 1939–46. Called to Scottish Bar, 1951; QC (Scotland) 1961; Sheriff-Principal of Dumfries and Galloway, 1970–73. Mem., Royal Commn on Legal Services in Scotland, 1976–80; Chm., Scottish Law Commn, 1981–. *Address:* 1c Oswald Road, Edinburgh EH9 2HE. *T:* 031–667 7444.

MAXWELL, Colonel (Arthur) Terence, TD; *b* 19 Jan. 1905; *s* of late Brig.-Gen. Sir Arthur Maxwell, KCB, CMG, DSO, and late Eva Jones; *m* 1935, Beatrice Diane, *d* of late Rt Hon. Sir J. Austen Chamberlain, KG, PC, MP, and late Ivy Muriel Dundas, GBE; two *s* one *d*. *Educ:* Rugby; Trinity Coll., Oxford, MA. Travelled in Africa as James Whitehead travelling student, 1926–27, and in South America; Barrister-at-Law, 1929; served 7th City of London Regt Post Office Rifles, 1923–35; Captain TA Reserve of Officers, 1935. Capt. KRRC 1940; Staff Coll., 1941; Leader Ministry of Economic Warfare Mission to the Middle East with rank of Counsellor, 1941–42; Col General Staff, AFHQ, 1943–44; Deputy Chief, Military Government Section; attached SHAEF etc. British Rep., Investments Cttee, ILO, 1937–77. A Managing Dir, Glyn, Mills & Co., bankers, until 1945; Chm., Powers-Samas Accounting Machines Ltd, 1952–70; Dep. Chm., International Computers and Tabulators Ltd, 1959–67, Chm., 1967–68; Chm., International Computers (Holdings) Ltd, 1968, Dep. Chm. 1969; Chm. Computer Leasings Ltd, 1963–69; Director: Vickers Ltd, 1934–75; Aust. and NZ Banking Group Ltd, and its predecessors, 1935–76; Steel Co. of Wales, 1948–67; English Steel Corp. Ltd, 1954–67. Vice-Chm. Cttee on Rural Bus Services (1959), Ministry of Transport; Vice-Pres. and Treas. City and Guilds of London Institute, 1959–67; Mem. Delegacy of City and Guilds Coll., Imperial Coll., University of London, 1959–64. *Recreation:* forestry. *Address:* Roveries Hall, Bishop's Castle, Shropshire. *T:* Bishop's Castle 638402; Flat 7, 52 Onslow Square, SW7. *T:* 01–589 0321. *Club:* Carlton.

MAXWELL, Sir Aymer, 8th Bt of Monreith, *cr* 1681; Hon. Captain Scots Guards; *b* 7 Dec. 1911; *s* of late Lt-Col Aymer Maxwell, Royal Naval Div., Captain Grenadier Guards and Lovat Scouts, and Lady Mary Percy, 5th *d* of 7th Duke of Northumberland; *S* grandfather 1937. *Educ:* Eton; Magdalene Coll., Cambridge. BA (Hon.). *Heir: nephew* Michael Eustace George Maxwell, *b* 28 Aug. 1943. *Address:* Monreith, Wigtownshire. *T:* Portwilliam 248; 11 Lansdowne House, Lansdowne Road, W11 3LP. *T:* 01–727 6394.

MAXWELL, David Campbell F.; *see* Finlay-Maxwell.

MAXWELL of Ardwell, Col Frederick Gordon, CBE 1967; TD; FCIT; *b* 2 May 1905; *s* of late Lt-Col Alexander Gordon Maxwell, OBE, Hon. Corps of Gentlemen-at-Arms; *m* 1st, 1935, Barbara Margaret (decd), *d* of late Edward Williams Hedley, MBE, MD, Thursley, Surrey; two *s* (one *d* decd); 2nd, 1965, True Hamilton Exley, *d* of Francis George Hamilton, Old Blundells Cottage, Tiverton, Devon. *Educ:* Eton. OC 2nd Bn The London Scottish, 1939–42; GSO1, 52nd (Lowland) Div., 1943–44, served in Holland and Germany (despatches); GSO1, Allied Land Forces SE Asia, 1945; OC 1st Bn The London Scottish, 1947–50. Joined London Transport, 1924; Operating Manager (Railways), London Transport, 1947–70, retired 1971. Mem., Co. of London T&AFA, 1947–68; Lt-Col RE (T&AVR, IV), 1956–70; Regimental Col, The London Scottish, 1969–73. DL, Co. of London, 1962; DL, Greater London, 1966–81. OStJ 1969. *Address:* 41 Cheyne Court, Cheyne Place, SW3 5TS. *T:* 01–352 9801. *Clubs:* Naval and Military, Highland Brigade.

MAXWELL, (Ian) Robert; MC 1945; Chairman, Mirror Group Newspapers Ltd (publisher of Daily Mirror, Daily Record, Sunday Mail, Sunday Mirror, The People, Sporting Life, Sporting Life Weekender, since 1984, of the London Daily News, and Sportsweek, since 1986); Founder and Publisher, Pergamon Press, Oxford, New York and Paris, since 1949; Publisher, China Daily in Europe, since 1986; Chairman: BPCC (formerly BPC) plc, since 1981; British Cable Services Ltd (Rediffusion Cablevision), since 1984; Chairman and Chief Executive, British Newspaper Printing Corporation plc, since 1983; Director: SelecTV, since 1982; Hollis plc, since 1982; Central Television plc, since 1983; The Solicitors' Law Stationery Society plc, since 1985; Mirrorvision, since 1985; Clyde Cablevision Ltd, since 1985; Premiere, since 1986; Philip Hill Investment Trust, since 1986; Reuters Holdings plc, since 1986; *b* 10 June 1923; *s* of Michael and Ann Hoch; *m* 1945, Elisabeth (*née* Meynard); three *s* four *d* (and one *s* one *d* decd). *Educ:* self-educated. Served War of 1939–45 (MC). In German Sect. of Foreign Office (Head of Press Sect., Berlin), 1945–47. Chm., Robert Maxwell & Co. Ltd, 1948–; Dir, Computer Technology Ltd, 1966–77; Chm. and Chief Exec., Internat. Learning Systems Corp. Ltd, 1968–69; Dir, Gauthier-Villars (Publishers), Paris, 1961–70; Co-Chm., Scottish News Enterprises Ltd, 1975; Chm., Commonwealth Games (Scotland 1986) Ltd, 1986; Pres., European Satellite Television Broadcasting Consortium, 1986–. MP (Lab) Buckingham, 1964–70. Chm., Labour Nat. Fund Raising Foundn, 1960–69; Chm., Labour Working Party on Science, Govt and Industry, 1963–64; Mem., Council of Europe (Vice-Chm., Cttee on Science and Technology), 1968. Contested (Lab) Buckingham, Feb. and Oct. 1974. Treasurer, The Round House Trust Ltd (formerly Centre 42), 1965–83; Chairman: Media Cttee, NSPCC Centenary Appeal (1984), 1984; GB-Sasakawa Foundn, 1985–; Dir, Bishopsgate Trust, 1984–. Chm., Oxford Utd FC, 1982–. Kennedy Fellow, Harvard Univ., 1971. Hon. Mem., Acad. of Astronautics, 1974; Member: Club of Rome, 1979– (Exec. Dir, British Gp); Council, Newspaper Publishers' Assoc., 1984–. Co-produced films: Mozart's Don Giovanni, Salzburg Festival, 1954; Bolshoi Ballet, 1957; Swan Lake, 1968; Producer, DODO the Kid from Outer Space (children's TV series), 1968. Hon. DSc Moscow State Univ., 1983; Hon. Dr of Science, Polytech. Univ. of NY, 1985. Royal Swedish Order of Polar Star (Officer 1st class), 1983; Bulgarian People's Republic Order Stara Planina (1st class), 1983; Comdr, Order of Merit with Star, Polish People's Republic, 1986. Gen. Editor, Leaders of the World series, 1980–. *Publications:* The Economics of Nuclear Power, 1965; Public Sector Purchasing, 1968; (jt author) Man Alive, 1968. *Recreations:* chess, football. *Address:* Headington Hill Hall, Oxford OX3 0BB. *T:* Oxford 64881; 01-353 0246.

MAXWELL, Sir Nigel Mellor H.; *see* Heron-Maxwell.

MAXWELL, Patrick; Solicitor; *b* 12 March 1909; *e s* of late Alderman Patrick Maxwell, Solicitor, Londonderry; *m* 1st, 1935 (wife *d* 1962); two *d*; 2nd, 1969. *Educ:* Convent of Mercy, Artillery Street, Londonderry; Christian Brothers Sch., Brow-of-the-Hill, Londonderry; St Columb's Coll., Londonderry. Solicitor, 1932; entered Londonderry Corporation as Councillor, 1934; resigned as protest against re-destribution scheme, 1937; Leader of Anti-Partition Party in Londonderry Corporation from 1938; did not seek re-election, 1946; first Chairman of Irish Union Association, 1936; Chairman of Derry Catholic Registration Association, 1934–52. MP (Nat) Foyle Division of Londonderry City, Northern Ireland Parliament, 1937–53. Resident Magistrate, 1968–80. President: Law Society of Northern Ireland, 1967–68 (Vice-Pres., 1966–67); Londonderry Rotary Club, 1958–59; Chm. Rotary in Ireland, 1963–64; Mem., Council, International Bar Association, 1968. *Address:* 3 Talbot Park, Londonderry. *T:* Londonderry 51425.

MAXWELL, Peter; *see* Maxwell, Hon. Lord.

MAXWELL, Robert; *see* Maxwell, I. R.

MAXWELL, Sir Robert (Hugh), KBE 1961 (OBE 1942); *b* 2 Jan. 1906; *s* of William Robert and Nancy Dockett Maxwell; *m* 1935, Mary Courtney Jewell; two *s*. Comdr of Order of George I of Greece, 1961; Order of Merit of Syria. *Address:* Court Hay, Charlton Adam, Som. *Club:* Athens (Athens).

MAXWELL, Col Terence; *see* Maxwell, Col A. T.

MAXWELL, Rear-Adm. Thomas Heron, CB 1967; DSC 1942; idc, jssc, psc; Director-General of Naval Training, Ministry of Defence, 1965–67; retired, 1967; *b* 10 April 1912; *s* of late H. G. Maxwell; *m* 1947, Maeve McKinley; two *s* two *d*. *Educ:* Campbell Coll., Belfast; Royal Naval Engineering Coll. Cadet, 1930; Commander, 1946; Captain, 1956; Rear-Adm., 1965. *Address:* Tokenbury, Shaft Road, Bath, Avon.

MAXWELL-HYSLOP, Robert John, (Robin); MP (C) Tiverton Division of Devon since Aug. 1960; *b* 6 June 1931; 2nd *s* of late Capt. A. H. Maxwell-Hyslop, GC, RN, and late Mrs Maxwell-Hyslop; *m* 1968, Joanna Margaret, *er d* of Thomas McCosh; two *d*. *Educ:* Stowe; Christ Church, Oxford (MA). Hons Degree in PPE Oxon, 1954. Joined Rolls-Royce Ltd Aero Engine Div., as graduate apprentice, Sept. 1954; served 2 years as such, then joined Export Sales Dept; PA to Sir David Huddie, Dir and GM (Sales and Service), 1958; left Rolls-Royce, 1960. Contested (C) Derby (North), 1959. Chm., Anglo-Brazilian Parly Gp. Member: Trade and Industry Select Cttee, 1971–; Standing Orders Cttee, 1977–; Procedure Select Cttee, 1978–. Governor, Casa do Brazil. *Recreations:* motoring, South American history. *Address:* 4 Tiverton Road, Silverton, Exeter, Devon.

MAXWELL-SCOTT, Dame Jean (Mary Monica), DCVO 1984 (CVO 1969); Lady in Waiting to HRH Princess Alice, Duchess of Gloucester, since 1959; *b* 8 June 1923; *d* of Maj.-Gen. Sir Walter Maxwell-Scott of Abbotsford, Bt, CB, DSO, DL and Mairi MacDougall of Lunga. *Educ:* Couvent des Oiseaux, Westgate-on-Sea. VAD Red Cross Nurse, 1941–46. *Recreations:* gardening, reading, horses. *Address:* Abbotsford, Melrose, Roxburghshire TD6 9BQ. *T:* Galashiels 2043. *Club:* New Cavendish.

MAXWELL SCOTT, Sir Michael Fergus, 13th Bt *cr* 1642; *b* 23 July 1921; *s* of Rear-Adm. Malcolm Raphael Joseph Maxwell Scott, DSO (*d* 1943), and Fearga Victoria Mary (*d* 1969) *e d* of Rt Hon. Sir Nicholas Roderick O'Conor, PC, GCB, GCMG; *S* to baronetcy of kinsman, Sir Ralph (Raphael) Stanley De Marie Haggerston, 1972; *m* 1963, Deirdre Moire, *d* of late Alexander McKechnie; two *s* one *d*. *Educ:* Ampleforth; Trinity College, Cambridge. *Publication:* Stories of Famous Scientists, 1965. *Recreations:* sailing, fishing, gardening. *Heir:* *s* Dominic James Maxwell Scott, *b* 22 July 1968. *Address:* 10 Evelyn Mansions, Carlisle Place, SW1. *T:* 01–828 0333. *Club:* Army and Navy.

MAY, family name of **Baron May.**

MAY, 3rd Baron, *cr* 1935, of Weybridge; **Michael St John May**; 3rd Bt, *cr* 1931; late Lieut, Royal Corps of Signals; *b* 26 Sept. 1931; *o s* of 2nd Baron May and *d* of George Ricardo Thomas; *S* father 1950; *m* 1st, 1958, Dorothea Catherine Ann (marr. diss. 1963), *d* of Charles McCarthy, Boston, USA; 2nd, 1963, Jillian Mary, *d* of Albert Edward Shipton, Beggars Barn, Shutford, Oxon; one *s* one *d*. *Educ:* Wycliffe Coll., Stonehouse, Glos; Magdalene Coll., Cambridge. 2nd Lieut, Royal Signals, 1950. *Recreations:* flying, travel. *Heir:* *s* Hon. Jasper Bertram St John May, *b* 24 Oct. 1965. *Address:* Gautherns Barn, Sibford Gower, Oxon.

MAY, Anthony Tristram Kenneth; QC 1979; a Recorder, since 1985; *b* 9 Sept. 1940; *s* of late Kenneth Sibley May and Joan Marguérite (*née* Oldaker); *m* 1968, Stella Gay Pattisson; one *s* two *d*. *Educ:* Bradfield Coll.; Worcester Coll., Oxford (Trevelyan Scholar 1960, Hon. Scholar 1962; MA). Inner Temple Scholar, 1965; called to the Bar, 1967, Bencher, 1985. Jun. Counsel to DoE for Land Commn Act Matters, 1972. Chm., Guildford Choral Soc. *Recreations:* gardening, music, books. *Address:* 10 Essex Street, Outer Temple, WC2R 3AA. *T:* 01–240 6981.

MAY, Prof. Brian Albert; Head, Silsoe College (formerly National College of Agricultural Engineering), since 1976; Professor of Agricultural Engineering, since 1982, and Dean, Faculty of Agricultural Engineering, Food Production and Rural Land Use, since 1977, Cranfield Institute of Technology; *b* 2 June 1936; *s* of Albert Robert and Eileen May; *m* 1961, Brenda Ann Smith; three *s*. *Educ:* Faversham Grammar Sch.; Aston Univ., Birmingham. FRAgS. Design Engineer, Massey Ferguson, 1958–63; National College of Agricultural Engineering: Lectr, 1963–68; Sen. Lectr, 1968–72; Principal Lectr, 1972–75; Head of Environmental Control and Processing Dept, 1972–75; Prof. of Environmental Control and Processing, Cranfield Inst. of Technol., 1975–82. Dir, British Agricl Export Council, 1985–. Member: Res. Requirements Bd on Plants and Soils, AFRC; Engrg Adv. Cttee, AFRC; Standing Cttee on University Entrance Requirements; Agric. and Vet. Cttee, British Council. Pres., IAgrE, 1984–86; Mem. Council, Royal Agricl Soc. of England. Governor, British Soc. for Res. in Agricl Engrg, 1979–. *Publications:* Power on the Land, 1974; papers in agricl and engrg jls. *Recreations:* cricket, gardening, reading. *Address:* Fairfield Greenway, Campton Shefford, Beds SG17 5BN. *T:* Hitchin 813451. *Club:* Farmers'.

MAY, Charles Alan Maynard, FEng, FIEE, FBCS; lately Senior Director, Development and Technology, British Telecom; retired 1984; *b* 14 April 1924; *s* of late Cyril P. May and Katharine M. May; *m* 1947, Daphne, *o d* of late Bertram Carpenter; one *s* two *d*. *Educ:* The Grammar Sch., Ulverston, Cumbria; Christ's Coll., Cambridge (Mech. Sciences tripos 1944, MA). CEng, FIEE 1967; FBCS 1968. Served REME and Indian Army, 1944–47. Entered Post Office Engrg Dept, 1948; Head of Electronic Switching Gp, 1956; Staff Engr, Computer Engrg Br., 1966; Dep. Dir (Engrg), 1970; Dir of Research, Post Office, later British Telecom, 1975–83. Dir, SIRA Ltd, 1982–. Chm., IEE Electronics Divl Bd, 1977–78; Member: Council, IEE, 1970–72 and 1976–80; BBC Engrg Adv. Cttee, 1978–84; Adv. Cttee on Calibration and Measurement, 1978–83; Adv. Cttee, Dept of Electronic and Electrical Engrg, Sheffield Univ., 1979–82; Communications Systems Adv. Panel, Council of Educnl Technology, 1980–83; Ind. Adv. Bd, Sch. of Eng. and Applied Scis, Sussex Univ., 1981–84; Council, ERA Technology, 1983–. Graham Young Lectr, Glasgow Univ., 1979. Vis. Examr, Imperial Coll., Univ. of London, 1980–82; External Examnr, NE London Polytechnic, 1982–86. Governor, Suffolk Coll. of Higher and Further Educn, 1980–83. FRSA 1985. *Publications:* contribs on telecommunications to learned jls. *Recreations:* gardening, caravanning, playing the piano and organ. *Address:* Sherbourne, Glendene Avenue, East Horsley, Leatherhead, Surrey KT24 5AY. *T:* East Horsley 2521.

MAY, Gordon Leslie, OBE 1982; Consultant, Keene Marsland, solicitors, since 1984; *b* 19 Nov. 1921; *s* of A. Carveth May and Isobella May; *m* 1945, Nina Cheek; one *s* two *d*. *Educ:* Worcester College for the Blind; Manchester Univ. War service, 1939–45. Admitted Solicitor, 1947; South Eastern Gas Board: Solicitor, 1956; Secretary, 1961; Executive Board Member, 1968; British Gas Corporation: Dep. Chairman, SW Region, 1974; Sec., 1977–84; Mem. Executive, 1982–84. Mem. Exec. Council, RNIB, 1975–; Chm. Bd of Governors, Worcester Coll. for the Blind, 1980–. Liveryman, Solicitors' Co., 1963. *Recreation:* sailing. *Address:* Walsall House, High Street, Upnor, Rochester, Kent ME2 4XG. *T:* Medway 716163. *Clubs:* Royal Automobile; Medway Yacht (Upnor); Alderney Sailing.

MAY, Graham; retired from Civil Service, 1981; *b* 15 Dec. 1923; *s* of Augustus May; *m* 1952, Marguerite Lucy Griffin; four *s*. *Educ:* Gravesend County Sch. for Boys; Balliol Coll., Oxford (BA). War Service, Royal Artillery, 1942–46. Asst Principal, Min. of Works, 1948, Principal 1952; seconded to Treasury, 1961–63; Asst Sec., MPBW, 1963; Under Sec., DoE, 1972–81. *Address:* 2 West Cross, Tenterden, Kent TN30 6JL.

MAY, Harry Blight, MD, FRCP, retired; Director of Clinical Laboratories, The London Hospital, 1946–74; Consultant Pathologist to Royal Navy, 1950–74; *b* 12 Nov. 1908; *s* of John and Isobel May, Plymouth, Devon; *m* 1949, Dorothy Quartermaine; no *c*. *Educ:* Devonport; St John's Coll., Cambridge (Scholar). 1st cl. Natural Science Tripos, 1929. Postgraduate study Harvard Medical Sch., 1936. Dean, Faculty of Medicine, Univ. of London, 1960–64; Dean of Med. and Dental Sch., The London Hosp. Med. Coll., 1953–68; Mem. Senate, Univ. of London; Mem. Governing Body, Royal Veterinary Coll.; Examiner, Royal College of Physicians of London and Univ. of Oxford. *Publications:* Clinical Pathology (6th edn), 1951; papers on Antibacterial Agents and other medical subjects. *Address:* 3 Littlemead, Littleworth Road, Esher, Surrey. *T:* Esher 62394.

MAY, John; Councillor, Tyne and Wear County Council, 1974–86 (Vice-Chairman, 1978–79, Chairman, 1979–80); *b* 24 May 1912; *s* of William and Sara May; *m* 1939, Mary Peacock (*d* 1980); two *s*. *Educ:* Holystone Council Sch., Newcastle upon Tyne. Councillor: Seaton Valley UDC, 1949–74 (Chm., 1963–64 and 1972–73); Northumberland CC, 1970–74; Tyne and Wear County Council: Chairman, Transport Cttee, 1980–86 (Vice-Chm., 1977–80). *Address:* 7 Etal Close, Shiremoor, Newcastle upon Tyne, Tyne and Wear. *T:* Tyneside 2533204.

MAY, Rt. Hon. Sir John (Douglas), Kt 1972; PC 1982; **Rt. Hon. Lord Justice May**; a Lord Justice of Appeal, since 1982; *b* 28 June 1923; *s* of late E. A. G. May, Shanghai, and of Mrs May, Whitelands House, SW3; *m* 1958, Mary, *er d* of Sir Owen Morshead, GCVO, KCB, DSO, MC, and Paquita, *d* of J. G. Hagemeyer; two *s* one *d*. *Educ:* Clifton Coll.; Balliol Coll., Oxford. Lieut (SpSc) RNVR, 1944–46. Barrister-at-Law, Inner Temple, 1947, Master of the Bench, 1972; QC 1965; Recorder of Maidstone, 1971; Leader, SE Circuit, 1971; Presiding Judge, Midland and Oxford Circuit, 1973–77; a Judge of the High Ct, Queen's Bench Division, 1972–82; a Judge of the Employment Appeal Tribunal, 1978–82. Mem., Parole Bd, 1977–80, Vice-Chm., 1980; Chm., Inquiry into UK Prison Services, 1978–79. *Address:* c/o Royal Courts of Justice, Strand, WC2. *Club:* Vincent's (Oxford).

MAY, John Otto, CBE 1962 (OBE 1949); HM Diplomatic Service; retired; *b* 21 April 1913; *s* of late Otto May, FRCP, MD; *m* 1939, Maureen McNally; one *d*. *Educ:* Sherborne; St John's Coll., Cambridge. Apptd to Dept of Overseas Trade, 1937. Private Sec. to Comptroller-General, 1939; Asst Commercial Secretary: Copenhagen, 1939; Helsinki, 1940; Ministry of Economic Warfare (Representative in Caracas), 1942–44; First Sec. (Commercial): Rome, 1945, Bucharest, 1948; Foreign Office, 1950–53; First Sec., Helsinki, 1954. Acted as Chargé d'Affaires in 1954, 1955, and 1956; Counsellor (Commercial) and Consul-General, HM Embassy, Athens, 1957–60; Consul-General: Genoa, 1960–65; Rotterdam, 1965–68; Gothenburg, 1968–72. Coronation Medal, 1953. *Recreations:* travel, photography, walking, philately. *Address:* 6 Millhedge Close, Cobham, Surrey KT11 3BE. *T:* Cobham 64645. *Club:* United Oxford & Cambridge University.

MAY, Sir Kenneth Spencer, Kt 1980; CBE 1976; Director, The News Corporation Ltd, since 1980; *b* 10 Dec. 1914; *s* of late N. May; *m* 1943, Betty C. Scott; one *s* one *d*. *Educ:* Woodville High School. Editorial staff, News, 1930; political writer, 1946–59; Asst Manager, News, Adelaide, 1959–64, Manager, 1964–69; Dir, News Ltd, 1969–; Man. Dir, News Ltd, Aust., 1977–80; Chm., Mirror Newspapers Ltd and Nationwide News Pty Ltd, 1969–80; Director: Independent Newspapers Ltd, Wellington, NZ, 1971–84; Santos Ltd, 1980–83. *Address:* 26 Waterfall Terrace, Burnside, SA 5066, Australia.

MAY, Paul, CBE 1970; retired 1970; *b* 12 July 1907; *s* of William Charles May and Katharine Edith May; *m* 1st, 1933, Dorothy Ida Makower (*d* 1961); two *s* one *d*; 2nd, 1969, Frances Maud Douglas (*née* Tarver); two step *s*. *Educ:* Westminster; Christ Church, Oxford (MA). United Africa Co. Ltd, 1930–32; John Lewis Partnership, 1932–40; Min. of Aircraft Production, 1940–45; John Lewis Partnership, 1945–70 (Dep. Chm., 1955–70). Mem. Exec. Cttee, Land Settlement Assoc. Ltd, 1962–71. *Recreations:* walking, reading, etc. *Address:* Chesterford, Whittingham, Northumberland. *T:* Whittingham 642.

MAY, Peter Barker Howard, CBE 1981; Lloyd's Insurance Broker since 1953; Underwriting Member of Lloyd's, 1962; Director, Willis Faber & Dumas (UK) Ltd, since 1976; *b* 31 Dec. 1929; *m* 1959, Virginia, *er d* of A. H. H. Gilligan; four *d*. *Educ:* Charterhouse; Pembroke Coll., Cambridge (MA). Cambridge cricket and football XIs v. Oxford, 1950, 1951 and 1952; Surrey County Cricket Cap, 1950; played cricket for England v S Africa 1951, v India 1952, v Australia 1953, v W Indies 1953, v Pakistan, Australia and New Zealand 1954; captained England 41 times, incl. v S Africa, 1955, v Australia 1956, v S Africa 1956–57, v W Indies, 1957, v New Zealand 1958, v Australia, 1958–59, v India, 1959, v West Indies, 1959–60, v Australia, 1961. Chm., England Cricket Selection Cttee, 1982–. *Publications:* Peter May's Book of Cricket, 1956; A Game Enjoyed, 1985. *Recreations:* golf, eventing. *Address:* Homestead Farm, Selborne, near Alton, Hants. *T:* Selborne 216. *Clubs:* MCC (Pres., 1980–81), Surrey County Cricket.

MAY, Richard George; a Recorder, since 1985; *b* 12 Nov. 1938; *s* of George William May, MB, and Phyllis May; *m* 1974, Radmila Monica, *er d* of late J. D. A. Barnicot, OBE, and Elizabeth Barnicot; one *s* two *d*. *Educ:* Haileybury; Selwyn Coll., Cambridge. National Service, 2nd Lieut, DLI, 1958–60. Called to the Bar, Inner Temple, 1965; Midland and Oxford Circuit. Contested (Lab): Dorset South, 1970; Finchley, 1979. Councillor, Westminster CC, 1971–78 (Leader of the Opposition, 1974–77). *Publications:* (ed jtly) Phipson on Evidence, 12th edn 1976, 13th edn 1982; Criminal Evidence, 1986. *Address:* Devereux Chambers, Devereux Court, WC2R 3JJ. *T:* 01–353 7534.

MAY, Prof. Robert McCredie, FRS 1979; Chairman, University Research Board, since 1977 and Class of 1877 Professor of Zoology, since 1975, Princeton University; *b* 8 Jan. 1936; *s* of Henry W. May and Kathleen M. May; *m* 1962, Judith (*née* Feiner); one *d*. *Educ:* Sydney Boys' High Sch.; Sydney Univ. BSc 1956, PhD (Theoretical Physics) 1959. Gordon Mackay Lectr in Applied Maths, Harvard Univ., 1959–61; Sydney Univ.: Sen. Lectr in Theoretical Physics, 1962–64; Reader, 1964–69; Personal Chair, 1969–73; Prof. of Biology, Princeton Univ., 1973–; Vis. Prof., Imperial Coll., 1975–; visiting appointments at: Harvard, 1966; California Inst. of Technology, 1967; UKAEA Culham Lab., 1971; Magdalen Coll., Oxford, 1971; Inst. for Advanced Study, Princeton, 1972; King's Coll., Cambridge, 1976. *Publications:* Stability and Complexity in Model Ecosystems, 1973, 2nd edn 1974; Theoretical Ecology: Principles and Applications, 1976, 2nd edn 1981; Population Biology of Infectious Diseases, 1982; Exploitation of Marine Communities, 1984; articles in mathematical, biol and physics jls. *Recreations:* tennis, running, bridge. *Address:* Biology Department, Princeton University, Princeton, NJ 08544, USA. *T:* (609) 452–3830. *Club:* Athenæum.

MAY, Valentine Gilbert Delabere, CBE 1969; Director, Yvonne Arnaud Theatre, Guildford, since 1975; *b* 1 July 1927; *s* of Claude Jocelyn Delabere May and Olive Gilbert; *m* 1st, 1955, Penelope Sutton; one *d*; 2nd, 1980, Petra Schroeder; one *d*. *Educ:* Cranleigh Sch.; Peterhouse Coll., Cambridge. Trained at Old Vic Theatre Sch. Director: Ipswich Theatre, 1953–57; Nottingham Playhouse, 1957–61; Bristol Old Vic Company, 1961–75. Plays directed for Bristol Old Vic which subseq. transf. to London incl.: War and Peace, 1962; A Severed Head, 1963; Love's Labour's Lost, 1964 (which also went on a British Council European tour); Portrait of a Queen, 1965; The Killing of Sister George, 1965; The Italian Girl, 1968; Mrs Mouse, Are You Within, 1968; Conduct Unbecoming, 1969; It's a Two-Foot-Six Inches Above the Ground World, 1970; Poor Horace, 1970; Trelawny, 1972; The Card, 1973. Plays directed for Arnaud Theatre transferred to London: Baggage, 1976; Banana Ridge, 1976; The Dark Horse, 1978; House Guest, 1981. Dir, Little Me, Prince of Wales, 1984. Overseas prodns include: Romeo and Juliet, and Hamlet (NY and USA tour); The Taming of the Shrew (Hong Kong Fest. and Latin America tour); Broadway prodns: A Severed Head; Portrait of a Queen; The Killing of Sister George; Conduct Unbecoming; Murder Among Friends. Hon. MA Bristol, 1975. *Recreations:* reading, architecture, music, astronomy. *Address:* Yvonne Arnaud Theatre, Millbrook, Guildford, Surrey GU1 3UX. *T:* Guildford 64571.

MAYALL, Sir (Alexander) Lees, KCVO 1972 (CVO 1965); CMG 1964; HM Diplomatic Service, retired; Ambassador to Venezuela, 1972–75; *b* 14 Sept. 1915; *s* of late Alexander Mayall, Bealings End, Woodbridge, Suffolk, and Isobel, *d* of F. J. R. Hendy; *m* 1st, 1940, Renée Eileen Burn (marr. diss., 1947); one *d*; 2nd, 1947, Hon. Mary Hermione Ormsby Gore, *e d* of 4th Baron Harlech, KG, PC, GCMG; one *s* two *d*. *Educ:* Eton; Trinity Coll., Oxford (MA). Entered HM Diplomatic Service, 1939; served with armed forces, 1940; transferred to HM Legation, Berne, 1940–44; First Secretary: HM Embassy, Cairo, 1947–49, Paris, 1952–54; Counsellor, HM Embassy: Tokyo, 1958–61; Lisbon, 1961–64; Addis Ababa, 1964–65; Vice-Marshal of the Diplomatic Corps, 1965–72. President: West Wilts Conservative Assoc., 1984–; Bath Preservation Trust, 1986–. *Recreations:* travelling, reading. *Address:* Sturford Mead, Warminster, Wilts. *T:* Chapmanslade 219. *Clubs:* Travellers', Beefsteak.

MAYCOCK, Sir William d'Auvergne, Kt 1978; CBE 1970 (MBE 1945); LVO 1961; MD, FRCP, FRCPath; Superintendent, Elstree Laboratories, 1949–73, and Director of Blood Products Laboratory, 1973–78, Lister Institute of Preventive Medicine; retired; *b* 7 Feb. 1911; *s* of William Perren Maycock, MIEE, and Florence Marion, *d* of Alfred Hart; *m* 1940, Muriel Mary, *d* of Duncan Macdonald, Toronto; two *s*. *Educ:* The King's School, Canterbury; McGill Univ., Montreal. MD McGill, 1935; FRCP, MRCS, FRCPath. Demonstrator in Pathology, McGill Univ., 1935; Leverhulme Scholar, RCS of Eng., 1936–39; Dept of Physiology, St Thomas's Hosp. Med. Sch., 1939. Served in RAMC, 1939–45: Temp. Col, AMS, 1945. Mem. Staff of Lister Inst., London, 1946–48: Consultant Adviser in Transfusion, Min. of Health (later Dept of Health and Social Security), 1946–78; Hon. Cons. in Transfusion and Resuscitation to War Office (later Min. of Defence), 1946–78. Oliver Memorial Award for Blood Transfusion, 1955; Karl Landsteiner Gold Medal, Netherlands Red Cross Soc., 1978; Guthrie Medal, RAMC, 1979; Pres., Brit. Soc. for Haematology, 1966–67. *Publications:* scientific and other papers. *Recreations:* various. *Address:* 59 Ivinghoe Road, Bushey, Herts. *Club:* Athenæum.

MAYER BROWN, Prof. Howard; *see* Brown, Prof. H. M.

MAYFIELD, Hon. Lord; Ian MacDonald, MC 1945; a Senator of the College of Justice in Scotland, since 1981; *b* 26 May 1921; *s* of H. J. and J. M. MacDonald; *m* 1946, Elizabeth de Vessey Lawson; one *s* one *d*. *Educ:* Colston's Sch., Bristol; Edinburgh Univ. (MA, LLB). Served 1939–46: Royal Tank Regt (Capt.). TA Lothians and Border Horse, later Queen's Own Lowland Yeomanry, 1948–62. Called to Bar, 1952; QC (Scot.) 1964. Mem., Criminal Injuries Compensation Board, 1972–74. Sheriff Principal of Dumfries and Galloway, Feb.-Dec. 1973; Pres., Industrial Tribunals for Scotland, 1973–81. *Recreation:* sport. *Address:* 16 Mayfield Terrace, Edinburgh EH9 1SA. *T:* 031–667 5542. *Clubs:* Caledonian; Hon. Company of Edinburgh Golfers.

MAYFIELD, Rt. Rev. Christopher John; *see* Wolverhampton, Bishop Suffragan of.

MAYHEW, family name of **Baron Mayhew.**

MAYHEW, Baron *cr* 1981 (Life Peer), of Wimbledon in Greater London; **Christopher Paget Mayhew;** *b* 12 June 1915; *e s* of late Sir Basil Mayhew, KBE; *m* 1949, Cicely Elizabeth Ludlam; two *s* two *d*. *Educ:* Haileybury Coll. (Scholar); Christ Church, Oxford (Open Exhibitioner, MA). Junior George Webb-Medley Scholar (Economics), 1937; Pres., Union Soc., 1937. Gunner Surrey Yeomanry RA; BEF Sept. 1939–May 1940; served with BNAF and CMF; BLA 1944 (despatches); Major, 1944. MP (Lab) S Norfolk, 1945–50; MP (Lab) Woolwich East, later Greenwich, Woolwich East, June 1951–July 1974; PPS to Lord Pres. of the Council, 1945–46; Parly Under-Sec. of State for Foreign Affairs, 1946–50; Minister of Defence (RN), 1964, resigned 1966; left Lab. Party, joined Lib. Party, 1974; MP (L) Greenwich, Woolwich East, July-Sept. 1974; contested (L): Bath, Oct. 1974 and 1979; Surrey, for European Parlt, 1979; London SW, for European Parlt, Sept. 1979; Chief Liberal Party Spokesman on Defence, 1980; Pres., Alliance Action Gp for Electoral Reform. Chairman: Middle East International (Publishers) Ltd; ANAF Foundn; former Chm., MIND (Nat. Assoc. for Mental Health). *Publications:* Planned Investment—The Case for a National Investment Board, 1939; Socialist Economic Policy, 1946; "Those in Favour . . ." (television play), 1951; Dear Viewer . . ., 1953; Men Seeking God, 1955; Commercial Television: What is to be done?, 1959; Coexistence Plus, 1962; Britain's Role Tomorrow, 1967; Party Games, 1969; (jtly) Europe: the case for going in, 1971; (jtly) Publish It Not . . .: the Middle East cover-up, 1975; The Disillusioned Voter's Guide to Electoral Reform, 1976. *Recreations:* music, golf. *Address:* 39 Wool Road, Wimbledon, SW20 0HN. *Club:* National Liberal.

MAYHEW, Rt. Hon. Sir Patrick (Barnabas Burke), Kt 1983; PC 1986; QC 1972; MP (C) Tunbridge Wells, since 1983 (Royal Tunbridge Wells, Feb. 1974–1983); Solicitor General, since 1983; *b* 11 Sept. 1929; *o surv. s* of late A. G. H. Mayhew, MC; *m* 1963, Jean Elizabeth Gurney *d* of John Gurney; four *s*. *Educ:* Tonbridge; Balliol Coll., Oxford (MA). President, Oxford Union Society, 1952. Commnd 4th/7th Royal Dragoon Guards, national service and AER, captain. Called to Bar, Middle Temple, 1955, Bencher 1980. Contested (C) Camberwell and Dulwich, in Gen. Election, 1970. Parly Under Sec. of State, Dept of Employment, 1979–81; Minister of State, Home Office, 1981–83. Mem. Exec., 1922 Cttee, 1976–79; Vice Chm., Cons. Home Affairs Cttee, 1976–79. *Address:* House of Commons, SW1.

MAYHEW-SANDERS, Sir John (Reynolds), Kt 1982; MA; FCA; Chairman, Heidrick and Struggles UK, since 1985; Director, Rover Group (formerly BL plc), since 1980; *b* 25 Oct. 1931; *e s* of Jack Mayhew-Sanders, FCA; *m* 1958, Sylvia Mary, *d* of George S. Colling; three *s* one *d*. *Educ:* Epsom Coll.; RNC, Dartmouth; Jesus Coll., Cambridge (MA Engrg). FCA 1958. RN, 1949–55. Mayhew-Sanders & Co., Chartered Accountants,

1955–58; P-E Consulting Gp Ltd, 1958–72; Chief Exec., 1975–83, and Chm., 1978–83, John Brown PLC (Dir, 1972–83); Dir, Dowty Gp, 1982–85. Member: Management Bd, Engineering Employers' Fedn, 1977–81; BOTB, 1980–83; BBC Consultative Gp on Industrial and Business Affairs, 1981–83; Chm., Overseas Project Bd, 1980–83; Pres., British-Soviet Chamber of Commerce, 1982–; Vice-Pres., Inst. of Marketing, 1982–. Governor, Sadler's Wells Foundn, 1983–. CBIM 1980; FRSA 1983. *Recreations:* fishing, shooting, gardening, music. *Address:* Heidrick and Struggles, 25-28 Old Burlington Street, W1X 2BD; Earlstone House, Burghclere, Hants. *T:* Burghclere 288.

MAYLAND, Rev. Canon Ralph, VRD 1962 and bar 1972; Canon and Treasurer of York Minster, since 1982; *b* 31 March 1927; *s* of James Henry and Lucy Mayland; *m* 1959, Jean Mary Goldstraw; one *d* and one adopted *d*. *Educ:* Cockburn High Sch., Leeds; Leeds City Training Coll.; Westminster Coll., London Univ.; Ripon Hall, Oxford. Schoolteacher, 1945–46; RN, 1946–51; perm. commn, RNR, 1952, Chaplain, 1961–82; 3rd yr student, 1951–52; schoolteacher, 1952–57; theol student, 1957–59. Curate of Lambeth, 1959–62; Priest-in-charge, St Paul's, Manton, Worksop, 1962–67; Vicar, St Margaret's, Brightside, 1968–72; Chaplain, Sheffield Industrial Mission, 1968–75; Vicar, St Mary's, Ecclesfield, 1972–82; Chaplain to Master Cutler, 1979–80. Life Mem., Royal Naval Assoc. *Recreations:* collecting Victorian children's literature, goat-keeping and rearing. *Address:* 3 Minster Court, York YO1 2JJ. *T:* York 25599.

MAYNARD, Brian Alfred, CBE 1982; FCA, CBIM; Partner, Coopers & Lybrand, Chartered Accountants, 1950–81; *b* 27 Sept. 1917; *s* of late Alfred A. Maynard and Clarissa L. (*née* Shawe); *m* 1946, Rosemary Graham, *y d* of late Col E. C. Boutflower; two *s*. *Educ:* Leighton Park Sch.; Cambridge Univ. (MA). RNVR Commission, 1939–46, served Middle East and Europe. Member: Oxford Univ. Appts Cttee, 1959–81; Cttee of Duke of Edinburgh's Award Scheme, 1961–67; Council, Industry for Management Educn, 1968–81; Cttee of Enquiry into the Financial Control of Catering in the Services, 1973; Cttee of Enquiry into Problems facing the Nat. Theatre, 1978; Council for the Securities Industry, 1978; City Panel of Takeovers and Mergers, 1978; Chm., Adv. Cttee on Local Govt Audit, 1979–82. Mem. Council, Inst. of Chartered Accountants in England and Wales, 1968–81 (Pres., 1977–78); Chairman: London Soc. of Chartered Accountants, 1966–67; Management Consultants Assoc., 1970; Pres., Inst. of Management Consultants, 1974; Vice-Pres., European Fedn of Management Consultants Assoc., 1972–75; Pres., OECD Mission to USA, on Computers, 1960. *Recreations:* racing, shooting, CPRE. *Address:* Cowage Farm, Hilmarton, Calne, Wilts SN11 8RZ. *T:* Hilmarton 397; 5 Redanchor Close, Chelsea, SW3 5DW. *T:* 01–352 6777.

MAYNARD, Edwin Francis George; Overseas Business Consultant; Member, Export Council Advisory Panel; HM Diplomatic Service, retired; Deputy High Commissioner, Calcutta, 1976–80; *b* 23 Feb. 1921; *s* of late Edwin Maynard, MD, FRCS, DPH, and late Nancy Frances Tully; *m* 1945, Patricia Baker; one *s* one *d*; *m* 1963, Anna McGettrick; two *s*. *Educ:* Westminster. Served with Indian Army (4/8th Punjab Regt and General Staff) (Major, GSO II), Middle East and Burma, 1939–46. BBC French Service, 1947; Foreign Office, 1949; Consul and Second Sec., Jedda, 1950; Second Later First, Sec., Benghazi, 1952; FO 1954; Bogota, 1956; Khartoum, 1959; FO, 1960; Baghdad, 1962; Founder Dir, Diplomatic Service Language Centre, 1966; Counsellor, Aden, 1967; Counsellor, New Delhi, 1968–72; Minister (Commercial), 1972–76; Chargé d'Affaires, 1974–75, Buenos Aires. *Recreations:* shooting, fishing, languages, gardening. *Address:* Littlebourne Court, Littlebourne, Canterbury, Kent. *Club:* Brooks's.

MAYNARD, Prof. Geoffrey Walter; Director of Economics, Europe and Middle East, Chase Manhattan Bank, 1977–86 (Economic consultant, 1974); Director, Chase Manhattan Ltd, 1977–86; *b* 27 Oct. 1921; *s* of Walter F. Maynard and Maisie Maynard (*née* Bristow); *m* 1949, Marie Lilian Wright; two *d*. *Educ:* London School of Economics. BSc(Econ); PhD. Lectr and Sen. Lectr, UC of S Wales, Cardiff, 1951–62; Economic Consultant, HM Treasury 1962–64; Economic Advr, Harvard Univ. Develt Adv. Gp in Argentina, 1964–65; University of Reading: Reader, 1966–68; Prof. of Economics, 1968–76; Vis. Prof. of Economics, 1976–. Editor, Bankers' Magazine, 1968–72; Under-Sec. (Econs), HM Treasury, 1972–74 (on leave of absence); Dep. Chief Economic Advr, HM Treasury, 1976–77; occasional consultant, IBRD, Overseas Develt Administration of FCO. Mem., Econ. Affairs Cttee, ESRC, 1982–85. Mem. Governing Body, Inst. of Develt Studies, Sussex, 1984–. *Publications:* Economic Development and the Price Level, 1962; (jtly) International Monetary Reform and Latin America, 1966; (jtly) A World of Inflation, 1976; chapters in: Development Policy: theory and practice, ed G. Papanek, 1968; Commonwealth Policy in a Global Context, ed Streeten and Corbet, 1971; Economic Analysis and the Multinational Enterprise, ed J. Dunning, 1974; Special Drawing Rights and Development Aid (paper), 1972; articles in Economic Jl, Oxford Economic Papers, Jl of Development Studies, World Development, etc. *Address:* Flat 219, Queens Quay, 58 Upper Thames Street, EC4. *Club:* Reform.

MAYNARD, Joan; *see* Maynard, V. J.

MAYNARD, Air Chief Marshal Sir Nigel (Martin), KCB 1973 (CB 1971); CBE 1963; DFC 1942; AFC 1946; *b* 28 Aug. 1921; *s* of late Air Vice-Marshal F. H. M. Maynard, CB, AFC, and of Irene (*née* Pim); *m* 1946, Daphne, *d* of late G R. P. Llewellyn, Baglan Hall, Abergavenny; one *s* one *d*. *Educ:* Aldenham; RAF Coll., Cranwell. Coastal Comd, UK, Mediterranean, W Africa, 1940–43; Flt-Lieut 1942; Sqdn-Ldr 1944; Mediterranean and Middle East, 1944; Transport Comd, 1945–49; comd 242 Sqdn on Berlin Air Lift; Air Staff, Air Min., 1949–51; Wing Comdr 1952; psa 1952; Staff Officer to Inspector Gen., 1953–54; Bomber Comd, 1954–57; jssc 1957; Gp Capt. 1957; SASO 25 Gp, 1958–59; CO, RAF Changi, 1960–62; Gp Capt. Ops, Transport Comd, 1963–64; Air Cdre 1965; Dir of Defence Plans (Air), 1965; Dir of Defence Plans and Chm. Defence Planning Staff, 1966; idc 1967; Air Vice-Marshal, 1968; Commandant, RAF Staff College, Bracknell, 1968–70; Commander, Far East Air Force, 1970–71; Air Marshal, 1972; Dep. C-in-C, Strike Command, 1972–73; C-in-C RAF Germany, and Comdr, 2nd Allied Tactical Air Force, 1973–76; Air Chief Marshal 1976; C-in-C, RAF Strike Command, and C-in-C, UK Air Forces, 1976–77. ADC to the Queen, 1961–65. *Recreations:* tennis, squash, shooting. *Address:* Manor House, Piddington, Bicester, Oxon. *T:* Brill 238270. *Clubs:* Naval and Military, Royal Air Force; MCC.

MAYNARD, Roger Paul; Counsellor, Aviation and Shipping, British Embassy, Washington, since 1982; *b* 10 Feb. 1943; *s* of Leonard John Maynard and May Gertrude Blake; *m* 1966, Ruth Elizabeth Wakeling; three *s* (including twin *s*). *Educ:* Purley Grammar Sch., Surrey; Queens' Coll., Cambridge (MA Hons Economics). Asst Principal, Bd of Trade, 1965; Second Secretary, UK Mission to UN and Internat. Organisations, Geneva, 1968; Principal: Dept of Industry, Shipbuilding Division, 1972; Dept of Trade, Airports Policy, 1975; Asst Sec., Dept of Industry, Air Division, 1978. *Recreations:* cricket, other sports, music. *Address:* British Embassy, 3100 Massachusetts Avenue, Washington, DC 20008, USA. *T:* 202 462 1340.

MAYNARD, (Vera) Joan; JP; MP (Lab) Sheffield, Brightside, since Oct. 1974; *b* 1921. Mem. Labour Party Nat. Exec. Cttee, 1972–82, 1983–; Sec., 1956–78, Chm., 1978–, Yorks Area, Agricl and Allied Workers National Trade Group TGWU (formerly Nat.

Union of Agricl and Allied Workers), sponsored as MP by the Union; Mem., Parly Select Cttee on Agriculture; Vice-Chm., Labour Party, 1980–81. Chair, Campaign Gp of Lab. MPs. Vice Pres., Rural District Councils Assoc. JP Thirsk, 1950. *Address:* House of Commons, SW1A 0AA.

MAYNARD SMITH, Prof. John, FRS 1977; Professor of Biology, University of Sussex, 1965–85, now Emeritus; *b* 6 Jan. 1920; *s* of Sidney Maynard Smith and Isobel Mary (*née* Pitman); *m* 1941; two *s* one *d. Educ:* Eton Coll.; Trinity Coll., Cambridge (BA Engrg, 1941); UCL (BSc Zool., 1951; Fellow, 1979). Aircraft stressman, 1942–47; Lectr in Zool., UCL, 1952–65; first Dean of Biol Sciences, Univ of Sussex, 1965 72. For. Associate, US Nat. Acad. of Scis, 1982. Hon. DSc Kent, 1983. *Publications:* The Theory of Evolution, 1958, 3rd edn 1975; Mathematical Ideas in Biology, 1968; On Evolution, 1972; Models in Ecology, 1974; The Evolution of Sex, 1978; Evolution and the Theory of Games, 1982; The Problems of Biology, 1985. *Recreations:* gardening, fishing, talking. *Address:* The White House, Kingston Ridge, Lewes, East Sussex. *T:* Lewes 4659.

MAYNE, Prof. David Quinn, FRS 1985; Professor of Control Theory, since 1971, and Head of Department of Electrical Engineering, since 1984, Imperial College of Science and Technology; *b* 23 April 1930; *s* of Leslie Harper Mayne and Jane Theresa Quin; *m* 1954, Josephine Mary Hess; three *d. Educ:* Univ. of the Witwatersrand, Johannesburg (BSc (Eng), MSc); DIC, PhD, DSc London. FIEE, FIEEE. Lectr, Univ. of Witwatersrand, 1950–54, 1956–59; R&D Engineer, British Thomson Houston Co., Rugby, 1955–56; Imperial College: Lectr, 1959–67, Reader, 1967–71; Sen. Sci. Res. Fellow, 1979–80. Research Consultant, at Univs of California (Berkeley), Lund, Newcastle NSW, 1974–. Vis. Prof., Academia Sinica, Beijing, Shanghai and Guanzhou, 1981. Corresp. Mem., Nacional Acad. de Ingenieria, Mexico, 1983. *Publications:* Differential Dynamic Programming, vol. 24 in Modern Analytic and Computational Methods in Science and Mathematics (with D. H. Jacobson, ed R. Bellman), 1970; Geometric Methods in System Theory, proc. NATO Advanced Study Inst., (ed. with R. W. Brockett), 1973; contribs to learned jls. *Recreation:* walking. *Address:* 123 Elgin Crescent, W11 2JH. *T:* 01–229 1744.

MAYNE, Eric; Under Secretary, Department of Economic Development, Northern Ireland, since 1982; *b* 2 Sept. 1928; *s* of Robert P. Mayne and Margaret Mayne; *m* 1954, Sarah Boyd (*née* Gray); three *s* two *d. Educ:* Bangor Grammar Sch. Univ. of Reading (BSc); Michigan State Univ. (MS). Horticultural Advisor, Min. of Agriculture, NI, 1949–56; Kellogg Foundation Fellow, 1956–57; Horticultural Advisor, HQ Min. of Agriculture, NI, 1957–64; Principal Officer, 1964–67; Gen. Manager, NI Agric. Trust, 1967–74; Sen. Asst Secretary, Dept of Agriculture, NI, 1974–79; Dep. Sec., Dept of Manpower Services, NI, 1979–82. *Recreations:* gardening, winemaking. *Address:* Netherleigh, Massey Avenue, Belfast BT4 2JP.

MAYNE, John Fraser, CB 1986; Principal Establishment and Finance Officer, Department of Health and Social Security, since 1986; *b* 14 Sept. 1932; *s* of late John Leonard Mayne and Martha Laura (*née* Griffiths); *m* 1958, Gillian Mary (*née* Key); one *s* one *d. Educ:* Dulwich Coll.; Worcester Coll., Oxford. National Service, Royal Tank Regt, 1951–53. Air Min., 1956–64; HM Treasury, 1964–67; MoD, 1967–70; Asst Private Sec. to Sec. of State for Defence, 1968–70; Cabinet Office and Central Policy Rev. Staff, 1970–73; MoD, 1973–78; Private Sec. to Sec. of State for Def., 1975–76; Asst Under-Sec. of State (Air Staff), 1976–78; Principal Establishments and Finance Officer, NI Office, 1979–81; Dir Gen. of Management Audit, MoD, 1981–83; Dep. Sec., Cabinet Office (MPO), 1984–86. Mem. Council, RUSI, 1986–. Freeman, City of London, 1983. FBIM 1981; FIPM 1984. *Recreations:* music, fell-walking, cooking, work. *Club:* United Oxford & Cambridge University.

MAYNE, Very Rev. Michael Clement Otway; Dean of Westminster, since 1986; *b* 10 Sept. 1929; *s* of Rev. Michael Ashton Otway Mayne and Sylvia Clementina Lumley Ellis; *m* 1965, Alison Geraldine McKie; one *s* one *d. Educ:* King's Sch., Canterbury; Corpus Christi Coll., Cambridge (MA); Cuddesdon Coll., Oxford. Curate, St John the Baptist, Harpenden, 1957–59; Domestic Chaplain to the Bishop of Southwark, 1959–65; Vicar of Norton, Letchworth, 1965–72; Head of Religious Progs, BBC Radio, 1972–79; Vicar of Great St Mary's, Cambridge (the University Church), 1979–86. *Publications:* Prayers for Pastoral Occasions, 1982; (ed) Encounters, 1985. *Recreations:* theatre, bird-watching, books. *Address:* The Deanery, Westminster, SW1. *T:* 01–222 2953.

MAYNE, Richard (John); writer; broadcaster; *b* 2 April 1926; *s* of John William Mayne and Kate Hilda (*née* Angus); *m* 1st, Margot Ellingworth Lyon; 2nd, Jocelyn Mudie Ferguson; two *d. Educ:* St Paul's Sch., London; Trinity Coll., Cambridge (1st Cl. Hons Pts I and II, Hist. Tripos; MA and PhD). War service, Royal Signals, 1944–47. Styring, Sen., and Res. Scholar, and Earl of Derby Student, Trinity Coll., Cambridge, 1947–53; Leverhulme European Scholar, Rome, and Rome Corresp., New Statesman, 1953–54; Asst Tutor, Cambridge Inst. of Educn, 1954–56; Official: ECSC, Luxembourg, 1956–58; EEC, Brussels, 1958–63; Dir of Documentation Centre, Action Cttee for United States of Europe, and Personal Asst to Jean Monnet, Paris, 1963–66; Paris Corresp., Encounter, 1966–71; Co-Editor, 1985–; Vis. Prof., Univ. of Chicago, 1971; Dir of Federal Trust for Educn and Res., 1971–73; Head of UK Offices, 1973–79, Special Advr, 1979–80, EEC. *Publications:* The Community of Europe, 1962; The Institutions of the European Community, 1968; The Recovery of Europe, 1970 (rev. edn 1973); The Europeans, 1972; (ed) Europe Tomorrow, 1972; (ed) The New Atlantic Challenge, 1975; (trans.) The Memoirs of Jean Monnet, 1978 (Scott-Moncrieff Prize, 1979); Postwar: the dawn of today's Europe, 1983; (ed) Western Europe: a handbook, 1986; Europe: a hundred windows, 1987. *Recreations:* travel, sailing, fell-walking. *Address:* Albany Cottage, 24 Park Village East, Regent's Park, NW1. *T:* 01–387 6654. *Clubs:* Europe House; Les Misérables (Paris).

MAYNE, Mrs Roger; see Jellicoe, P. A.

MAYNE, William; writer; *b* 16 March 1928; *s* of William and Dorothy Mayne. *Educ:* Cathedral Choir Sch., Canterbury, 1937–42 (then irregularly). Has pursued a career as novelist and has had published a large number of stories for children and young people— about 66 altogether, beginning in 1953 and going on into the foreseeable future. Lectr in Creative Writing, Deakin Univ., Geelong, Vic, Aust., academic years, 1976 and 1977; Fellow in Creative Writing, Rolle Coll., Exmouth, 1979–80. Library Assoc.'s Carnegie Medal for best children's book of the year (1956), 1957. *Address:* c/o David Higham Associates, 5–8 Lower John Street, Golden Square, W1R 4HA.

MAYNEORD, Prof. William Valentine, CBE 1957; FRS 1965; Emeritus Professor of Physics as Applied to Medicine, University of London; formerly Director of Physics Department, Institute of Cancer Research, Royal Cancer Hospital; *b* 14 Feb. 1902; *s* of late Walter Mayneord; *m* 1963, Audrey Morrell, Kingston-upon-Thames. *Educ:* Prince Henry's Grammar Sch., Evesham; Birmingham Univ. BSc 1921, MSc 1922, DSc 1933. Chairman: Internat. Commn on Radiological Units, 1950–53; MRC Cttee on Protection against Ionising Radiations, 1951–58; Member: Internat. Commn on Radiological Protection, 1950–58; UK Delegn to UN Scientific Cttee on the Effects of Atomic Radiation, 1956–57; MRC Cttee on Hazards to Man of Nuclear and Allied Radiations,

1955–60; President: British Inst. of Radiology, 1942–43; 1st Internat. Conf. on Medical Physics, 1965; Internat. Orgn for Medical Physics, 1965–69; Consultant: UKAEA, 1945–70; CEGB; WHO; Mem. Council and Scientific Cttee, Imp. Cancer Research Fund, 1965–73. A Trustee, National Gallery, 1966–71 (Mem., 1952–81, Chm., 1966–71, Hon. Adv. Scientific Cttee). Many awards and hon. memberships of British and foreign learned societies incl. RSocMed. Coronation Medal, 1953; Gold Medals: Royal Swedish Acad. of Science, 1965; Faculty of Radiologists (now RCR), 1966; Univ. of Arizona, 1974. Sievert Award, Internat. Radiation Protection Assoc., 1977; Beclère Prize and medal, Internat. Soc. of Radiology, 1985. Hon. LLD Aberdeen, 1969; DUniv Surrey, 1978. *Publications:* Physics of X-Ray Therapy, 1929; Some Applications of Nuclear Physics to Medicine, 1950; Radiation and Health, 1964; Carcinogenesis and Radiation Risk, 1975; articles on chemical carcinogenesis, and on applications of physics to medicine and radiation hazards. *Recreation:* Italian Renaissance art and literature, particularly Dante. *Address:* 7 Downs Way Close, Tadworth, Surrey KT20 5DR. *T:* Tadworth 2297.

MAYO, 10th Earl of, *cr* 1785; **Terence Patrick Bourke;** Baron Naas, 1766; Viscount Mayo, 1781; Lieut RN (retired); Managing Director, Irish Marble Ltd, Merlin Park, Galway; *b* 26 Aug. 1929; *s* of Hon. Bryan Longley Bourke (*d* 1961) and Violet Wilmot Heathcote Bourke (*d* 1950); *S* uncle, 1962; *m* 1952, Margaret Jane Robinson Harrison; three *s. Educ:* St Aubyns, Rottingdean; RNC Dartmouth. Lieut, RN, 1952; Fleet Air Arm, 1952; Suez, 1956; Solo Aerobatic Displays, Farnborough, 1957; invalided, 1959. Mem., Gosport Borough Council, 1961–64; Pres., Gosport Chamber of Trade, 1962; Gov., Gosport Secondary Schs, 1963–64. Mem., Liberal Party, 1963–65; contested (L) Dorset South, 1964. *Recreations:* sailing, riding, shooting, fishing. *Heir: s* Lord Naas, *qv. Address:* Doon House, Maam, Co. Galway, Eire. *Clubs:* Naval; County Galway.

MAYO, Col (Edward) John, OBE 1976; Director General, Help the Aged, since 1983; *b* 24 May 1931; *s* of Rev. Thomas Edward Mayo, JP, and Constance Muriel Mayo; *m* 1961, Jacqueline Margaret Anne Armstrong, MBE 1985, Lieut WRAC, *d* of late Brig. C. D. Armstrong, CBE, DSO, MC; one *s. Educ:* King's Coll., Taunton. Commissioned into Royal Regt of Artillery, 1951; served Malta and N Africa 36 HAA Regt, 1951–55; ADC to Governor of Malta, 1953–54; 2nd Regt RHA, BAOR, 1955–58; ADC to C-in-C BAOR/Comdr Northern Army Gp, 1958–60; 20 Field Regt, RA UK, 1960–61; Adjt 20 Field Regt, RA Malaya, 1961–63; Adjt 254 (City of London) Regt RA(TA), 1963–64; Instr RMA, Sandhurst, 1964–66; GS03 Mil. Operations, MoD, 1966–68; Second in Comd 20 Heavy Regt, RA BAOR, 1968–70; GS02 Instr Staff Coll., 1970–72; commanded 17 Trng Regt and Depot RA, 1972–74, and The Depot Regt RA, 1974–75; GS01 Public Relations MoD, 1976–79; Col GS; Public Information BAOR, 1979–83; retired 1983. Trustee: HelpAge India; HelpAge Kenya; Bd Mem., HelpAge Sri Lanka. Mem., Adv. Council, Centre for Policy on Ageing. *Publications:* miscellaneous articles on military matters. MIPR 1981. *Recreations:* fishing, gardening, sailing, riding, travelling, collecting and restoring antiques. *Address:* Help the Aged, St James's Walk, EC1R 0BE. *T:* 01–253 0253; Sehore House, Tekels Avenue, Camberley, Surrey. *T:* Camberley 29653. *Clubs:* Army and Navy, Special Forces, MCC.

MAYO, Eileen; artist, author, printmaker and painter. *Educ:* Clifton High School; Slade School of Art. Exhibited Royal Academy, London Group, United Society of Artists, Festival of Britain, etc; works acquired by British Council, British Museum, Victoria and Albert Museum, Contemporary Art Society, and public galleries in UK, USA, Australia and NZ. Designer of Australian mammals series of postage stamps, 1959–62, and Barrier Reef series, 1966; four Cook Bicentenary stamps, NZ, 1969, and other NZ stamps, 1970–78, and three for Christmas 1985. *Publications:* The Story of Living Things; Shells and How they Live; Animals on the Farm, etc. *Recreations:* printmaking, gardening.

MAYO, Col John; see Mayo, Col E. J.

MAYO, Rear-Adm. Robert William, CB 1965; CBE 1962; *b* 9 Feb. 1909; *s* of late Frank Mayo, Charminster; *m* 1st, 1942, Sheila (*d* 1974), *d* of late John Colvill, JP, of Campbeltown; one *s*; 2nd, 1980, Mrs Betty Washbrook. *Educ:* Weymouth Coll.; HMS Conway. Royal Naval Reserve and officer with Royal Mail Steam Packet Co., 1926–37; Master's Certificate; transferred to Royal Navy, 1937. Served War, 1939–45; Korea, 1952; Capt., 1953; Rear-Adm., 1964; retired, 1966. Sheriff Substitute of Renfrew and Argyll at Campbeltown. *Recreations:* gardening, fishing, yachting. *Address:* Bellgrove, Campbeltown, Argyll. *T:* Campbeltown 52101. *Club:* Royal Scottish Automobile.

MAYO, Simon Herbert; Hon. Mr Justice Mayo; a Judge of the High Court of Hong Kong, since 1980; *b* 15 Nov. 1937; *s* of late Herbert and Marjorie Mayo; *m* 1966, Catherine Yin Ying Young; one *s* one *d. Educ:* Harrow Sch. Admitted a solicitor, England and Wales, 1961, Hong Kong, 1963; called as barrister and solicitor, W Australia, 1967. Asst Legal Advr, GEC, 1961; Asst Solicitor, Deacons, Solicitors, Hong Kong, 1963; in private practice, WA, 1967; Asst Registrar, 1968, Registrar, 1976, Supreme Court of Hong Kong. *Recreations:* golf, music, literature, walking. *Address:* Supreme Court, Hong Kong. *T:* 5–8214417. *Clubs:* Hong Kong, Hong Kong Cricket, Sheko Country (Hong Kong).

MAYOH, Raymond Blanchflower; Under Secretary, Department of Health and Social Security, 1979–83, retired; *b* 11 Nov. 1925; *s* of Charles and Isabella Mayoh; *m* 1956, Daphne Yvonne Bayliss; one *s* one *d* (and one *s* decd). *Educ:* Colwyn Bay County Sch.; University College of North Wales. Assistant Principal, Ministry of Pensions, 1950; Principal, Ministry of Health, 1955; Assistant Secretary, 1965. *Recreations:* gardening, bird watching. *Address:* 20 Willingale Way, Thorpe Bay, Southend-on-Sea, Essex SS1 3SL. *T:* Southend 586650.

MAYOR, Hugh Robert; QC 1986; barrister; a Recorder of the Crown Court, since 1982; *b* 12 Oct. 1941; *s* of George and Grace Mayor; *m* 1970, Carolyn Ann Stubbs; one *s* one *d. Educ:* Kirkham Grammar Sch.; St John's Coll., Oxford (MA). Lectr, Univ. of Leicester, 1964 (MA). Called to the Bar, Gray's Inn, 1968. *Recreation:* sailing. *Address:* 33 Eastgate, Hallaton, Leics LE16 8UB. *T:* Hallaton 200.

MAYS, Colin Garth; HM Diplomatic Service; High Commissioner to the Bahamas, since 1986; *b* 16 June 1931; *s* of William Albert Mays and Sophia May Mays (*née* Pattinson); *m* 1956, Margaret Patricia, *d* of Philemon Robert Lloyd and Gladys Irene (*née* Myers); one *s. Educ:* Acklam Hall Sch.; St John's Coll., Oxford (Heath Harrison Scholar). Served in Army, 1949–51; entered HM Foreign (subseq. Diplomatic) Service, 1955; FO, 1955–56; Sofia, 1956–58; Baghdad, 1958–60; FO, 1960; UK Delegn to Conf. of 18 Nation Cttee on Disarmament, Geneva, 1960; Bonn, 1960–65; FO, 1965–69; Prague, 1969–72; FCO, 1972–77; Head of Information Administration Dept, 1974–77; Counsellor (Commercial), Bucharest, 1977–80; seconded to PA Management Consultants, 1980–81; Diplomatic Service Overseas Inspector, 1981–83; High Comr, Seychelles, 1983–86. Liveryman, Painter-Stainers' Co., 1981. *Recreations:* sailing, swimming, travel. *Address:* c/o Foreign and Commonwealth Office, King Charles Street, SW1A 2AH. *Club:* Travellers'.

MAZRUI, Prof. Ali A., DPhil; Professor of Political Science, University of Michigan, since 1974; Research Professor, University of Jos, Nigeria; *b* Kenya, 24 Feb. 1933; *s* of

Al'Amin Ali Mazrui, Judge of Islamic Law, and Safia Suleiman Mazrui; marr. diss.; three *s*. *Educ:* Univ. of Manchester (BA with distinction 1960); Columbia Univ. (MA 1961); Oxford Univ. (DPhil 1966). Makerere University, Kampala, Uganda: Lectr, 1963–65; Prof. and Head of Dept of Political Science, 1965–69; Dean, Faculty of Social Sciences, 1967–73. Vis. Prof., Univs of London, Chicago, Manchester, Harvard, Nairobi, Calif (LA), Northwestern, Singapore, Australia, Stanford, Cairo, Sussex, Colgate and Leeds, 1965–78. Pres., African Studies Assoc. of USA, 1978–79; Vice-Pres., Internat. Congress of African Studies, 1978–. BBC Reith Lectr, 1979; Presenter, The Africans (BBC TV series), 1986. *Publications:* Towards a Pax Africana, 1967; Violence and Thought, 1969; The Trial of Christopher Okigbo (novel), 1971; Cultural Engineering and Nation-Building in East Africa, 1972; Soldiers and Kinsmen in Uganda, 1975; A World Federation of Cultures: an African perspective, 1976; Africa's International Relations, 1977; Political Values and the Educated Class in Africa, 1978; Sex in Politics and Modern History, 1979; The African Condition (The Reith Lectures), 1980; (with Michael Tidy) Nationalism and New States of Africa, 1984. *Address:* 1517 Wells, Ann Arbor, Mich 48104, USA. *T:* 313–668–7842.

MBEKEANI, Nyemba W.; Chief Executive, Mkulumadzi Farm Bakeries Ltd, since 1981; *b* 15 June 1929; Malawi parentage; *m* 1950, Lois Mosses (*née* Chikankheni); two *s* three *d*. *Educ:* Henry Henderson Institute, Blantyre; London Sch. of Economics (Economic and Social Administration, 1963). Local Government Officer, 1945–58; political detention in Malawi and Southern Rhodesia, 1959–60; Business Executive, 1960–61; Local Govt Officer, 1963–64; Foreign Service, 1964; High Commissioner for Malawi in London, 1964–67; Ambassador to USA and Permanent Rep. at the UN, 1967–72; Ambassador to Ethiopia, 1972–73; Gen. Manager, Malaŵi Housing Corp., 1973–81. Farmer, company director, tea broker, baker, confectioner. *Recreation:* flower gardening. *Address:* PO Box 2095, Blantyre, Malaŵi. *T:* 640–504; *Telex:* 4847 Lumadzi.

M'BOW, Amadou-Mahtar; Director-General of Unesco, since Nov. 1974; *b* 20 March 1921; *s* of Fara-N'Diaye M'Bow and N'Goné Casset, Senegal; *m* 1951, Raymonde Sylvain; one *s* two *d*. *Educ:* Univ. of Paris. Teacher, Rosso Coll., Mauritania, 1951–53; Dir, Service of Fundamental and Community Educn, Senegal, 1953–57; Min. of Education and Culture, 1957–58; Teacher at Lycée Faidherbe, St-Louis, Senegal, 1958–64; Prof., Ecole Normale Supérieure, Dakar, 1964–66; Minister of Educn, 1966–68; Mem. Nat. Assembly, Senegal, 1968–70; Minister of Culture, Youth and Sports 1968–70; Asst Dir-Gen. for Educn, UNESCO, 1970–74. Member: Acad. des Sciences d'Outre-Mer, 1977; Acad. of Kingdom of Morocco, 1981; Hon. Mem., Royal Acad. Fine Arts, San Temo, Spain, 1977; For. Mem., Acad. of Athens, 1983. Hon. Professor: Ecole normale supérieure, Dakar, 1979; Indep. Univ. of Santo Domingo, 1978; Nat. Indep. Univ. of Mexico, 1979; Hon. Dr: Buenos Aires, 1974; Granada (Lit. and Phil.), Sherbrooke (Educn), West Indies (Laws), 1975; Open, Kliment Okhridski, Sofia, Nairobi (Lit.), 1976; Malaya (Lit.), Philippines (Laws); Venice (Geog.), Uppsala (Soc. Scis), Moscow (Soc. Scis), Paris I, 1977; Andes (Philos.), Peru (Educn Scis), Haiti, Tribhunvan Univ., Nepal (Lit.), State Univ., Mongolia, Khartoum (Law), Sri Lanka, 1978; Charles Univ., Prague (Phil.), Tashkent, Québec, 1979; Nat. Univ. of Zaïre, Madras, Belgrade, Ivory Coast, Sierra Leone, 1980; Univ. Gama Filho, Brazil, 1981; Nat. Univ. of Lesotho, 1981; Univ. of Benin, 1981; Technical Univ. of Middle East, Ankara, 1981; Univ. of Ankara, 1981, Univ. of Gand, Belgium, 1982; Nat. Univ. of Seoul, 1982; State Univ. of Kiev, 1982; Laval Univ., Quebec, 1982; Quaid-i-Azam Univ., Islamabad, 1983; Jawaharlal Nehru Univ., New Delhi, 1983; Aix-Marseilles Univ., 1983; Beijing Univ., China, 1983; Kim Il Sung Univ., PDR of Korea (Pedagogy), 1983; Lucknow Univ., India (Lit.), 1983; Chulalongkorn Univ., Thailand (Pedagogy), 1983; Sokoto Univ., Nigeria (Lit.), 1984; Grand Tribute, Univ. Candido Mendes, Brazil, 1981. Order of Merit, Senegal; Grand Cross: Order of the Liberator, Order of Andres Bello and Order of Francisco de Miranda, Venezuela; Order of Merit and Juan Montalvo National Order of Merit (Educn), Ecuador; Order of Miguel Antonio Caro y Rufino José Cuervo, Colombia; Order of Stara Planina, Bulgaria; Order of the Sun, Peru; Order of Merit of Duarte, Sanchez and Mella, Dominican Republic; National Order of the Lion, Senegal; Order of Alphonso X the Sabio, Spain; Order of the Southern Cross and Order of Merit of Guararapes, Brazil; Order of Distinguished Diplomatic Service Merit, Republic of Korea; Order of Sikatuna, Philippines; Order of Merit, Indonesia; Order of Merit, Syrian Arab Republic; Order of Merit, Jordan; Order of the Arab Republic of Egypt; Order of Felix Varela, Cuba; Grand Officer: National Order of Ivory Coast; National Order of Guinea; Order of Merit, Cameroon; National Order of Merit, Mauritania; Order of Independence, Tunisia; Commander: Order of Academic Palms; National Order of Upper Volta; Order of the Gabonese Merit; Order of Arts and Letters, France; Grand Medal, Order of the Inconfidência, State of Minas Gerais, Brazil; Medal: Order of Merit of Caetés, Olinda, Brazil; Order of Manual José Hurtado, Panama; Order of National Flag, PDR of Korea; Order of Meritorious Action, Libya; Superior Decoration for Education, Jordan. Man and his World Peace Prize, Canada, 1978; Gold Medal of Olympic Order, 1981; Gold Medal of ALECSO (Arab Educnl, Cultural and Scientific Orgn), 1981; Internat. Dimitrov Prize, 1982. *Publications:* Le temps des peuples, ed R. Laffont, 1982; Where the Future Begins, 1982; Hope for the Future, 1984; numerous monographs, articles in educnl jls, textbooks, etc. *Address:* 7 Place de Fontenoy, 75700 Paris, France. *T:* 577.16.10.

MEACHER, Michael Hugh; MP (Lab) Oldham (West) since 1970; *b* 4 Nov. 1939; *s* of George Hubert and Doris May Meacher; *m* 1962, Molly Christine (*née* Reid); two *s* two *d*. *Educ:* Berkhamsted Sch., Herts; New College, Oxford. Greats, Class 1. Sec. to Danilo Dolci Trust, 1964; Research Fellow in Social Gerontology, Univ. of Essex, 1965–66; Lecturer in Social Administration: Univ. of York, 1967–69; London Sch. of Economics, 1970. Parly Under-Secretary of State: DoI, 1974–75; DHSS, 1975–76; Dept of Trade, 1976–79; Mem., Shadow Cabinet, 1983–; chief opposition spokesman on health and social security, 1983–. Mem., Treasury Select Cttee, 1980–83 (a Chm. of its sub-cttee). Chm., Labour Co-ordinating Cttee, 1978–83; Member: Nat. Exec.'s Campaign for Press Freedom; Labour Party NEC, 1983–. Vis. Prof., Univ. of Surrey, Dept of Sociology, 1980–. *Publications:* Taken for a Ride: Special Residential Homes for the Elderly Mentally Infirm, a study of separatism in social policy, 1972; Fabian pamphlets, The Care of the Old, 1969; Wealth: Labour's Achilles Heel, in Labour and Equality, ed P. Townsend and N. Bosanquet, 1972; Socialism with a Human Face, 1981; numerous articles. *Recreations:* music, sport, reading. *Address:* 45 Cholmeley Park, N6.

MEAD, (William Howard) Lloyd; *b* 14 April 1905; *yr s* of late F. J. Mead; *m* 1951, Mary Pattinson, *e d* of late L. Borthwick Greig, Kendrew, S Africa. *Educ:* Marlborough; London Univ. BSc (Econ.) Hons. Industrial and Commercial Law, 1925. Chartered Accountant, 1930; RNVR 1938. Served War of 1939–45: in HMS Orion, 1939–41; Flag Lt to Vice-Adm. at Dover, 1942–45. Lt-Comdr (Sp) RNVR, retired, 1950. Clerk to the Vintners' Co., 1947–69. Dir, Royal Insurance Gp (London Bd), 1967–69. *Address:* 20 Bowen Court, The Drive, Hove, East Sussex BN3 3JF.

MEAD, Prof. William Richard; Professor and Head of Department of Geography, University College, London, 1966–81, now Emeritus Professor; *b* 29 July 1915; *s* of William Mead and Catharine Sarah Stevens; unmarried. *Educ:* Aylesbury Gram. Sch. (Foundation Governor, 1981–); London Sch. of Economics (Hon. Fellow 1979). DSc(Econ) London, 1968. Asst Lectr and Lectr, University of Liverpool, 1947–49; Rockefeller Fellowship, held in Finland, 1949–50; Lectr, 1950, Reader, 1953, University Coll., London. Chm. Council, Sch. of Slavonic and E European Studies, 1978–80. Chm., Anglo-Finnish Soc., 1966–; President: Inst. of British Geographers, 1971; Geog. Assoc., 1981–82; Hon. Sec., Royal Geographical Society, 1967–77 (Vice Pres., 1977–81, Hon. Vice-Pres., 1981–). Hon. Member: Finnish Geog. Soc.; Fenno-Ugrian Soc.; Porthan Soc.; Sydsvenska geografiska sällskapet; Det norske Videnskaps. Akademi, 1976. Gill Memorial Award, 1951, Founder's Medal, 1980, RGS; Wahlberg Gold Medal, Swedish Geographical Soc., 1983. Dr *hc*, University of Uppsala, 1966; DPhil *hc*, Univ. of Helsinki, 1969. Chevalier, Swedish Order of Vasa, 1962; Comdr, Orders of: Lion of Finland, 1963 (Chevalier, 1953); White Rose of Finland, 1976; Polar Star of Sweden, 1977. *Publications:* Farming in Finland, 1953; Economic Geography of Scandinavian States and Finland, 1958; (with Helmer Smeds) Winter in Finland, 1967; Finland (Modern Nations of the World Series), 1968; (with Wendy Hall) Scandinavia, 1972; The Scandinavian Northlands, 1973; (with Stig Jaatinen) The Åland Islands, 1974; An Historical Geography of Scandinavia, 1981; other books on Norway, Canada and USA. *Recreations:* riding, music. *Address:* 6 Lower Icknield Way, Aston Clinton, near Aylesbury, Bucks.

MEADE, family name of **Earl of Clanwilliam.**

MEADE, Eric Cubitt, FCA; Senior Partner, Deloitte Haskins & Sells, Chartered Accountants, 1982–85; Member, Audit Commission, since 1986; *b* 12 April 1923; *s* of William Charles Abbott Meade and Vera Alicia Maria Meade; *m* 1960, Margaret Arnott McCallum; two *s* one *d*. *Educ:* Ratcliffe College. FCA 1947. Served War, Hampshire Regt, 1942–46; N Africa, Italy, prisoner of war, 1944–45; Captain. Chartered Accountant, 1947. Mem. Council, Inst. of Chartered Accountants in England and Wales, 1969–79 (Chm., Parly and Law Cttee, 1974–76; Chm., Investigation Cttee, 1976–77); Chm., Consultative Cttee., Accountancy Bodies Ethics Cttee, 1977–83; Mem. Council, Nat. Assoc. of Security Dealers and Investment Managers, 1986–. *Recreations:* tennis, gardening. *Address:* 56 Hurlingham Court, Ranelagh Gardens, Fulham, SW6 3UP. *T:* 01–736 5382. *Club:* Hurlingham.

MEADE, Sir Geoffrey; *see* Meade, Sir R. G. A.

MEADE, James Edward, CB 1947; FBA 1951; MA Oxon, MA Cantab; Hon. Dr, Universities of Basel, Bath, Essex, Glasgow, Hull and Oxford; Hon. Fellow: London School of Economics; Oriel College, Oxford; Hertford College, Oxford; Christ's College, Cambridge; *b* 23 June 1907; *s* of Charles Hippisley Meade and Kathleen Cotton-Stapleton; *m* 1933, Elizabeth Margaret, *d* of Alexander Cowan Wilson; one *s* three *d*. *Educ:* Malvern Coll.; Oriel Coll., Oxford; Trinity Coll., Cambridge. 1st Class Hon. Mods 1928; 1st Class Philosophy, Politics, and Economics, 1930. Fellow and Lecturer in Economics, 1930–37, and Bursar, 1934–37, Hertford Coll., Oxford; Mem. Economic Section of League of Nations, Geneva, 1938–40. Economic Asst (1940–45), and Dir (1946–47), Economic Section Cabinet Offices. Prof. of Commerce, with special reference to International Trade, London Sch. of Economics, 1947–57; Prof. of Political Economy, Cambridge, 1957–68; Nuffield Res. Fellow, 1969–74, and Fellow, Christ's Coll., Cambridge, 1957–74. Member: Coun. of Royal Economic Society, 1945–62 (Pres., 1964–66, Vice-Pres., 1966–); Council of Eugenics Soc., 1962–68 (Treasurer 1963–67). Visiting Prof., Australian National Univ., 1956. Pres. Section F, British Assoc. for the Advancement of Science, 1957; Chm. Economic Survey Mission, Mauritius, 1960. Trustee of Urwick, Orr and Partners Ltd, 1958–76. Governor: Nat. Inst. of Economic and Social Research, 1947–; LSE, 1960–74; Malvern Coll., 1972–. Chm., Cttee of Inst. for Fiscal Studies, 1975–77 (producing report on The Structure and Reform of Direct Taxation, 1978). Hon. Mem., Amer. Economic Assoc., 1962; For. Hon. Member: Soc. Royale d'Econ. Politique de Belgique, 1958; Amer. Acad. of Arts and Sciences, 1966; For. Associate, Nat. Acad. of Sciences, USA, 1981. (Jtly) Nobel Prize for Economics, 1977. *Publications:* Public Works in their International Aspect, 1933; The Rate of Interest in a Progressive State, 1933; Economic Analysis and Policy, 1936; Consumers' Credits and Unemployment, 1937; League of Nations' World Economic Surveys for 1937–38 and 1938–39; The Economic Basis of a Durable Peace, 1940; (with Richard Stone) National Income and Expenditure, 1944; Planning and the Price Mechanism, 1948; The Theory of International Economic Policy, Vol. I, 1951, Vol. II, 1955; A Geometry of International Trade, 1952; Problems of Economic Union, 1953; The Theory of Customs Unions, 1955; The Control of Inflation, 1958; A Neo-Classical Theory of Economic Growth, 1960; Three Case Studies in European Economic Union, 1962 (Joint Author); Efficiency, Equality, and the Ownership of Property, 1964; Principles of Political Economy, Vol. 1, The Stationary Economy, 1965, Vol. 2, The Growing Economy, 1968, Vol. 3, The Controlled Economy, 1972, Vol. 4, The Just Economy, 1976; The Theory of Indicative Planning, 1970; The Theory of Externalities, 1973; The Intelligent Radical's Guide to Economic Policy, 1975; Stagflation, vol. 1, Wage Fixing, 1982, vol. 2, (jtly) Demand Management, 1983; Alternative Systems of Business Organisation and of Workers' Remuneration, 1986. *Address:* 40 High Street, Little Shelford, Cambridge CB2 5ES. *T:* Cambridge 842491.

See also Prof. P. S. Dasgupta, T. W. Meade, Sir Geoffrey Wilson, Prof. R. C. Wilson, S. S. Wilson.

MEADE, Patrick John, OBE 1944; consultant in meteorology to various international organisations; Director of Services, and Deputy Director-General, Meteorological Office, 1966–73; *b* 23 Feb. 1913; *s* of late John Meade, Caterham, Surrey; *m* 1937, Winifred Jessie, *d* of Bertram Kent, Fawley, Hants; one *s* one *d* (and one *s* decd). *Educ:* Sir Joseph Williamson's Math. Sch., Rochester; Imperial Coll. of Science and Technology (Royal College of Science). ARCSc, BSc; Lubbock Mem. Prize in Maths, London Univ., 1933. Entered Met. Office, 1936; Southampton, 1937; Flt Lt RAFVR, Fr., 1939–40; Sqdn Leader, Sen. Met. Off., GHQ Home Forces, 1940–42; Wing Comdr (Gp Capt. 1944), Chief Met. Off., MAAF, 1943–45; Chief Met. Off., ACSEA, 1945–46; Head of Met. Office Trng Sch., 1948–52; London Airport, 1952–55; Research, 1955–60; idc 1958; Dep. Dir for Outstations Services, 1960–65. Hon. Sec., Royal Meteorological Society, 1956–61, Vice-Pres., 1961–63. *Publications:* papers in jls on aviation meteorology and on meteorological aspects of air pollution, atmospheric radioactivity and hydrology. *Recreations:* music, gardening. *Address:* Luccombe, Coronation Road, South Ascot, Berks. *T:* Ascot 23206.

MEADE, Sir (Richard) Geoffrey (Austin), KBE 1963; CMG 1953; CVO 1961; *b* 8 March 1902; *s* of late Austin Meade, MA; *m* 1929, Elizabeth Ord, MA Oxon, 2nd *d* of late G. J. Scott, JP; three *d*. *Educ:* Ecole Alsacienne, Paris; Balliol Coll., Oxford. BA 1925. Entered Consular Service, 1925; served at Tangier, 1927, Salonica, 1929, Aleppo, 1930, Athens, 1931, Salonica, 1933, Tangier, 1935, Valencia, 1939, Crete, 1940, FO, 1941, Dakar, 1943, Tetuan, 1943, Cassablanca, 1945; Istanbul, 1947; idc, 1950; Marseilles, 1951; Tangier, 1956; Düsseldorf, 1957; Milan, 1958–62. Retired, 1962. *Address:* Baker's Close, 104 Lower Radley, Abingdon, Oxon OX14 3BA. *T:* Abingdon 21327.

MEADE, Thomas Wilson, DM; FRCP, FFCM; Director, Medical Research Council Epidemiology and Medical Care Unit, Northwick Park Hospital, Harrow, since 1970;

Hon. consultant in epidemiology, Northwick Park Hospital; *b* 21 Jan. 1936; *s* of James Edward Meade, *qv*; *m* 1962, Helen Elizabeth Perks; one *s* two *d*. *Educ:* Westminster Sch.; Christ Church, Oxford; St Bartholomew's Hosp. Sen. Lectr, Dept of Public Health, London Sch. of Hygiene and Tropical Medicine (on secondment to Schieffelin Leprosy Research Sanatorium, S India, 1969–70), 1968–70. Hon. Dir, Cardiovascular Epidemiology Res. Gp, British Heart Foundn, 1982–. Member: MRC Physiological Systems and Disorders Bd, 1974–78; MRC Health Services Res. Panel and Cttee, 1981–; Chm., Adv. Panel (to CSM) on Collection of data relating to Adverse Reactions to Pertussis Vaccine, 1977–81. Member: British Cardiac Soc.; Assoc. of Physicians. *Publications:* papers on thrombosis, chronic disability, leprosy. *Recreations:* oboe, growing vegetables. *Address:* 28 Cholmeley Crescent, N6 5HA. *T:* 01–340 6260. *Club:* Leander (Henley-on-Thames).

MEADE-KING, Charles Martin, MA; Headmaster, Plymouth College, 1955–73, retired; *b* 17 Aug. 1913; *s* of late G. C. Meade-King, solicitor, Bristol; *m* 1948, Mary (*née* Frazer); one *s* one *d*. *Educ:* Clifton Coll.; Exeter Coll., Oxford (Stapeldon Scholar). Asst Master, King's Sch., Worcester, 1935–38; Asst Master, Mill Hill Sch., 1938–40. Intelligence Corps, 1940–45. Housemaster, Mill Hill Sch., 1945–55. *Recreations:* history, arts, games. *Address:* Whistledown, Yelverton, near Plymouth. *T:* Yelverton 852237.

MEADEN, Rt. Rev. John Alfred, DD, MA, LTh; *b* 16 Feb. 1892. *Educ:* Queen's Coll., Newfoundland; University Coll., Durham, England. LTh Durham, 1916, BA 1917, MA 1935. Deacon, 1917, Nova Scotia for Newfoundland; Priest, 1918, Newfoundland. Incumbent of White Bay, 1917–21; Rector of Burin, 1921–29; Pouch Cove, 1929–34; Sec.-treasurer of Executive Cttee of Newfoundland Diocesan Synod, 1934–47; Examining Chaplain to the Bishop of Newfoundland, 1943–47; Canon of St John Baptist's Cathedral, St John's, Newfoundland, 1938–57. Principal of Queen's Coll., St John's, 1947–57. Bishop of Newfoundland, 1956–65. Hon. DCL, Bishop's Univ., Lennoxville, 1957; Hon. DD, Trinity Coll., Toronto, 1959; Hon. LLD, Memorial Univ. of Nfld, 1961. *Address:* Saint Luke's Homes, Topsail Road, St John's, Newfoundland, Canada.

MEADOWCROFT, Michael James; MP (L) Leeds West, since 1983; *b* 6 March 1942; *m*; one *s* one *d*. *Educ:* King George V Sch., Southport; Bradford Univ. (MPhil 1978). Chm., Merseyside Regl Young Liberal Orgn, 1961; Liberal Party Local Govt Officer, 1962–67; Sec., Yorks Liberal Fedn, 1967–70; Asst Sec., Joseph Rowntree Social Service Trust, 1970–78; Gen. Sec., Bradford Metropolitan Council for Voluntary Service, 1978–83. Member: Leeds City Council, 1968–83; W Yorks MCC, 1973–76, 1981–83. Dir, Leeds Grand Theatre and Opera House, 1971–83. Chm., Liberal Party Assembly Cttee, 1977–81. Contested (L) Leeds W, Feb. and Oct. 1974. *Publications:* Liberal Party Local Government Handbook (with Pratap Chitnis), 1963; Success in Local Government, 1971; Liberals and a Popular Front, 1974; Local Government Finance, 1975; A Manifesto for Local Government, 1975; The Bluffer's Guide to Politics, 1976; Liberal Values for a New Decade, 1980; Social Democracy—Barrier or Bridge?, 1981; Liberalism and the Left, 1982; Liberalism and the Right, 1983. *Recreations:* music (including jazz), cricket. *Address:* Waterloo Lodge, 72 Waterloo Lane, Bramley, Leeds LS13 2JF. *T:* Leeds 576232. *Clubs:* National Liberal; Armley Liberal, Bramley Liberal, Burley Liberal, Kirkstall Liberal, New Wortley Liberal, Upper and Lower Wortley Liberal (Leeds).

MEADOWS, Bernard William; sculptor; Professor of Sculpture, Royal College of Art, 1960–80; *b* Norwich, 19 Feb. 1915; *s* of W. A. F. and E. M. Meadows; *m* 1939, Marjorie Winifred Payne; two *d*. *Educ:* City of Norwich Sch. Studied at Norwich Sch. of Art, 1934–36; worked as Asst to Henry Moore, 1936–40; studied at Royal College of Art, 1938–40 and 1946–48. Served with RAF, 1941–46. Commissioned by Arts Council to produce a work for Festival of Britain, 1951. Rep. (Brit. Pavilion) in Exhib. of Recent Sculpture, Venice Biennale, 1952; in Exhib., Kassel, Germany, 1959, etc. Exhibited in International Exhibitions of Sculpture (Open Air): Battersea Park, 1951, 1960; Musée Rodin, Paris, 1956; Holland Park, 1957; in 4th International Biennial, São Paulo, Brazil, 1957; also in Exhibns (Open Air) in Belgium and Holland, 1953–. *One man exhibitions:* Gimpel Fils, London, 1957, 1959, 1963, 1965, 1967; Paul Rosenberg, New York, 1959, 1962, 1967; Taranman, London, 1979. *Works in Collections:* Tate Gallery; Victoria and Albert Museum; Arts Council; British Council; Museum of Modern Art, New York; also in public collections in N and S America, Israel, Australia, and in Europe. Mem., Royal Fine Art Commn, 1971–76. Awarded Italian State Scholarship, 1956. *Publication:* 34 etchings and box (for Molloy by Samuel Beckett), 1967. *Address:* 34 Belsize Grove, NW3. *T:* 01–722 0772.

MEADOWS, Robert; company director, motor trade; Lord Mayor of Liverpool, 1972–73; *b* 28 June 1902; *m* 1st, 1926, Ivy L. Jenkinson (*d* 1963); three *s*; 2nd, 1967, Nora E. Bullen. *Educ:* locally and Bootle Technical Coll. Engineering, 1917–21. Liverpool: City Councillor, Fairfield Ward, 1945; City Alderman, Princes Park Ward, 1961–74. Pres., Exec. Cttee, Broadgreen Conservative Assoc. *Recreations:* motor vehicle development, property improvement, landscape gardening. *Address:* 161A Prescot Road, Liverpool L7 0LD. *T:* 051–228 6441.

MEADOWS, Swithin Pinder, MD, BSc, FRCP; Consulting Physician: Westminster Hospital; National Hospital, Queen Square; Moorfields Eye Hospital; *b* 18 April 1902; *er s* of late Thomas and late Sophia Florence Meadows; *m* 1934, Doris Steward Noble; two *s* two *d*. *Educ:* Wigan Grammar Sch.; University of Liverpool; St Thomas' Hosp. Kanthack Medal in Pathology; Owen T. Williams Prize; House Physician and House Surgeon, Liverpool Royal Infirmary; House Physician, Royal Liverpool Children's Hospital; Medical Registrar and Tutor, St Thomas' Hosp.; RMO National Hosp., Queen Square; Medical First Asst, London Hosp.; Examiner in Neurology and Medicine, University of London; Hosp. Visitor, King Edward's Hosp. Fund for London; Mem., Assoc. of British Neurologists; Hon. Mem., Aust. Assoc. of Neurologists; Hunterian Prof., Royal College of Surgeons, 1952; Pres., Section of Neurology, Royal Society of Medicine, 1965–66; Visiting Prof., University of California, San Francisco, 1954; Doyne Meml Lectr, Oxford Ophthalmological Congress, 1969. Neurologist, British European Airways; Vice-Pres., Newspaper Press Fund. *Publications:* contributions to medical literature. *Recreations:* walking, music, country life. *Address:* 45 Lanchester Road, Highgate N6 4SX.

MEAKIN, Wilfred, CB 1982; CEng, FIMechE; Executive Director, Royal Ordnance plc, since 1986; Chairman, Royal Ordnance Inc., since 1986; *b* 1925. *Educ:* engineering apprenticeship in industry. Served War of 1939–45, RN. Technical Asst, ROF, Maltby, 1951; posts in ROF and former Inspectorate of Armaments; Asst Dir, ROF, Blackburn, 1966–72; Dir, ROF, Birtley, 1972–75; Dir, ROF Leeds, during 1975; Dir-Gen., Ordnance Factories (Weapons and Fighting Vehicles), 1975–79; Chief Exec. and Dep. Chm., Bd of ROF, later Royal Ordnance plc, 1979–86. Hon. CGIA. *Address:* Royal Ordnance plc, Griffin House, PO Box 288, The Strand, WC2N 5BB.

MEANEY, Sir Patrick (Michael), Kt 1981; Chairman: The Rank Organisation Plc, since 1983 (Director since 1979); A. Kershaw and Sons PLC, since 1983; Deputy Chairman: Midland Bank, since 1984 (Director, since 1979); Horserace Betting Levy Board, since 1985; *b* 6 May 1925; *m* Mary June Kearney; one *s*. *Educ:* Wimbledon College; Northern Polytechnic. HM Forces, 1941–47. Joined Thomas Tilling Ltd, 1961; Dir 1961, Man. Dir and Chief Exec. 1973–83. Director: Cable and Wireless PLC, 1978–84; ICI PLC, 1981–; Metropolitan and Country Racecourse Mgt Hldgs Ltd, 1985–; Racecourse Technical Services Ltd, 1985–; MEPC PLC, 1986–; Member, Internat. Adv. Board: EMF Foundn, 1979–; Cement Roadstone PLC, 1985–. Member Council: British North American Cttee and Res. Assoc., 1979–; CBI, 1979–; London Chamber of Commerce and Industry, 1977–82; Chm., Govt Review Cttee on Harland & Wolff, 1980; Mem., Conference Bd, 1982–. CBIM 1976; FInstM 1981. Pres., Inst. of Marketing, 1981–. *Recreations:* sport, music, education. *Address:* Stambourne House, Totteridge Village, N20 8JP. *T:* (office) 01–629 7454. *Clubs:* Garrick, Harlequins, British Sportsman's.

MEARS, Rt. Rev. John Cledan; *see* Bangor, Bishop of.

MEATH, 14th Earl of, *cr* 1627; **Anthony Windham Normand Brabazon;** Baron Ardee, Ireland, 1616; Baron Chaworth, of Eaton Hall, Co. Hereford, UK, 1831; late Major Grenadier Guards; *b* 3 Nov. 1910; *o s* of 13th Earl of Meath, CB, CBE and Lady Aileen Wyndham-Quin (*d* 1962), *d* of 4th Earl of Dunraven; *S* father 1949; *m* 1940, Elizabeth Mary, *d* of late Capt. Geoffrey Bowlby, Royal Horse Guards, and of Hon. Mrs Geoffrey Bowlby, *qv*; two *s* two *d*. *Educ:* Eton; RMC Sandhurst. Joined Grenadier Guards, 1930. ADC to Governor of Bengal, 1936; Capt., 1938; served War of 1939–45, Grenadier Guards (wounded); Major, 1941; retired, 1946. *Heir: s* Lord Ardee, *qv*. *Address:* Killruddery, Bray, Co. Wicklow, Ireland.

MEATH, Bishop of, (RC), since 1968; **Most Rev. John McCormack;** *b* 25 March 1921; *s* of Peter McCormack and Bridget Mulvany. *Educ:* St Finian's Coll., Mullingar; Maynooth Coll.; Lateran Univ., Rome. Priest, 1946. Ministered: Multyfarnham, 1950–52; St Loman's Hosp., 1952–58; Mullingar, 1958–68; Diocesan Sec., 1952–68. *Address:* Bishop's House, Dublin Road, Mullingar, Co. Westmeath, Ireland. *T:* Mullingar 48841/42038.

MEATH AND KILDARE, Bishop of, since 1985; **Most Rev. Walton Newcombe Francis Empey;** *b* 26 Oct. 1934; *m* 1960, Louise E. Hall; three *s* one *d*. *Educ:* Portora Royal School and Trinity College, Dublin. Curate Assistant, Glenageary, Dublin, 1958–60; Parish Priest, Grand Falls, NB, Canada, 1960–63; Parish Priest, Edmundston, NB, 1963–66; Incumbent, Stradbally, Co. Laois, Ireland, 1966–71; Dean of St Mary's Cathedral and Rector, Limerick City Parish, 1971–81; Bishop of Limerick and Killaloe, 1981–85. *Recreations:* reading, fishing and walking. *Address:* Ivy House, Leixlip, Co. Kildare, Ireland.

MEDAWAR, Nicholas Antoine; QC 1984; a Recorder of the Crown Court, since 1985; *b* 25 April 1933; *e s* of Antoine Medawar and Innes (*née* Macbeth); *m* 1st, 1962, Joyce Catherine (*née* Crosland-Boyle) (marr. diss.); one *s* (one *d* decd); 2nd, 1977, Caroline Mary, *d* of Harry Samuel Collins, of Nottingham and Buckley. *Educ:* Keswick School; Trinity College, Dublin. BA Mod., LLB. Called to the Bar, Gray's Inn, 1957. Nat. Service, RASC, 1957–59, 2nd Lieut. *Recreations:* skittles, walking, mathematical diversions. *Address:* 2/11 Wedderburn Road, Hampstead, NW3 5QS. *T:* 01–794 0876; 4 Paper Buildings, Temple, EC4Y 7EX. *T:* 01–353 3420.

MEDAWAR, Sir Peter (Brian), OM 1981; CH 1972; Kt 1965; CBE 1958; MA, DSc (Oxford); FRS 1949; Hon. FBA 1981; medical scientist; President, Royal Postgraduate Medical School, since 1981; Member, Scientific Staff, Medical Research Council, 1962–84; *b* 28 Feb. 1915; *s* of Nicholas Medawar and Edith Muriel Dowling; *m* 1937, Jean Shinglewood, *d* of Dr C. H. S. Taylor; two *s* two *d*. *Educ:* Marlborough Coll.; Magdalen Coll., Oxford. Christopher Welch Scholar and Senior Demy of Magdalen Coll., 1935; Fellow of Magdalen Coll., 1938–44, 1946–47; Fellow of St John's Coll., 1944 (Hon. Fellow, 1986); Mason Prof. of Zoology, Birmingham Univ., 1947–51; Jodrell Prof. of Zoology and Comparative Anatomy, University Coll., London, 1951–62; Dir, Nat. Inst. for Medical Research, Mill Hill, 1962–71, Dir Emeritus, 1975. Lectures: Croonian, Royal Society, 1958; Reith, 1959; Dunham, Harvard Med. Sch., 1959; Romanes, 1968; Danz, Washington Univ., 1984. Prof. of Experimental Medicine, Royal Institution, 1977–83. Pres., Brit. Assoc. for the Advancement of Science, 1968–69; Member: Agricultural Research Council, 1952–62; University Grants Cttee, 1955–59; Royal Commn on Med. Educn, 1965–68; Bd of Scientific Consultants, Meml Sloan-Kettering Cancer Centre; Inst. of Cellular Pathology, Brussels. Foreign Member: New York Acad. of Sciences, 1957; Amer. Acad. Arts and Sciences, 1959; Amer. Philosophical Soc., 1961; National Acad. of Sciences, 1965; Indian Acad. of Sciences, 1967. Hon. Fellow: St Catherine's Coll., 1960; Magdalen Coll., 1961; University Coll., London, 1971; London Sch. of Economics, 1975; Wolfson Coll., Oxford, 1981; American Coll. of Physicians, 1964; Royal College Physicians and Surgeons, Canada, 1966; RCS, 1967; RSE, 1965; RCPE, 1966; RCPath, 1971; RCP, 1974; Prof. at Large, Cornell Univ., 1965; Royal Medal of Royal Society, 1959, Copley Medal, 1969. Nobel Prize for Medicine, 1960; Kalinga Prize (India), 1985. Hon. ScD Cambridge; Hon. D de l'Univ.: Liège; Brussels; Hon. DSc: Aston, Birmingham, Hull, Glasgow, Brazil, Alberta, Dundee, Dalhousie, British Columbia, Chicago, Exeter, Florida, Gustavus Adolphus Coll., Harvard, Southampton, London, Queen's Univ. Glasgow. *Publications:* The Uniqueness of the Individual, 1957; The Future of Man, 1960; The Art of the Soluble, 1967; Induction and Intuition, 1969; The Hope of Progress, 1972; (with J. S. Medawar) Life Science, 1977; Advice to a Young Scientist, 1979; Pluto's Republic, 1982; (with J. S. Medawar) Aristotle to Zoos, 1983; The Limits of Science, 1984; Memoir of a Thinking Radish, 1986. *Address:* Clinical Research Centre, Watford Road, Harrow, Mddx HA1 3UJ; 25 Downshire Hill, NW3.
See also Sir Ian McAdam.

MEDD, Patrick William, OBE 1962; QC 1973; **His Honour Judge Medd;** a Circuit Judge, since 1981; *b* 26 May 1919; *s* of E. N. Medd; *m* 1st, 1945, Jeananne Spence Powell (marr. diss.); three *d*; 2nd, 1971, Elizabeth Spinks D'Albuquerque. *Educ:* Uppingham Sch.; Selwyn Coll., Cambridge. Served in Army, 1940–46, S Staffs Regt and E African Artillery, Major. Called to Bar, Middle Temple, 1947, Bencher 1969; Mem. Gen. Council of the Bar, 1965–67. Dep. Chm., Shropshire QS, 1967–71; Jun. Counsel to Comrs of Inland Revenue, 1968–73; Recorder of Abingdon, 1964–71 (Hon. Recorder, 1972–); a Recorder of the Crown Court, 1972–81. Chm., Bd of Referees, and Finance Act 1960 Tribunal, 1978–; UK rep., panel of arbitrators, Internat. Centre for Settlement of Investment Disputes, 1979–; Co-Pres., Nat. Reference Tribunal for Coalmining Ind., 1985–. *Publications:* (jtly) The Rule of Law, 1955; (jtly) Murder, 1956; (jtly) A Giant's Strength, 1958; Romilly, 1968. *Recreation:* gardening. *Address:* c/o The Crown Court, Oxford.

MEDHURST, Brian; Managing Director (Overseas Division), Prudential Assurance Company Ltd, and Director, Prudential Corporation, since 1985; *b* 18 March 1935; *s* of late Eric Gilbert Medhurst and of Bertha May (*née* Kinggett); *m* 1960, Patricia Anne Beer; two *s* one *d*. *Educ:* Godalming Grammar Sch.; Trinity Coll., Cambridge (MA). FIA 1962 (Mem. Council, 1982–). Joined Prudential Assurance Co. Ltd, 1958; Deputy Investment Manager, 1972; Investment Manager, 1975; Jt Chief Investment Manager, 1981; Gen. Manager, 1982. *Recreations:* squash, golf, piano duets, tree felling. *Address:* Longacre, Fitzroy Road, Fleet, Hants GU13 8JJ. *T:* Fleet 4159. *Clubs:* North Hants Golf; Royal Aldershot Officers'.

MEDLEY, (Charles) Robert (Owen), CBE 1982; RA 1986; Painter and Theatrical Designer; Chairman, Faculty of Painting, British School at Rome, 1966–77; *b* 19 Dec. 1905; *s* of late C. D. Medley, and A. G. Owen. *Educ:* Gresham's Sch., Holt. Studied art in London and Paris; Art Dir of the Group Theatre and designed the settings and costumes for plays by T. S. Eliot, W. H. Auden, Christopher Isherwood, Louis Macneice, and Verdi's Othello, Sadler's Wells Theatre, Coppelia, Sadler's Wells Theatre Ballet; exhibited in London and New York World's Fair; pictures bought by: Tate Gallery; V. & A. (collection of drawings); Walker Art Gallery, Liverpool; City Art Gallery, Birmingham, and other provincial galleries; National Gallery of Canada, Ontario; Contemporary Art Society; Arts Council for Festival of Britain, 1951. Official War Artist, 1940. Retrospective Exhibitions: Whitechapel Art Gallery, 1963; Mus. of Modern Art, Oxford, then touring, 1984. Diocletian in Sebastiane (film), 1976. *Publications:* (illustr.) Milton's Samson Agonistes, 1981; Drawn from the Life, a memoir (autobiog.), 1983. *Address:* 10 Gledhow Gardens, SW5 0AY.

MEDLICOTT, Michael Geoffrey; Chief Executive, British Tourist Authority, since 1986; *b* 2 June 1943; *s* of Geoffrey Henry Medlicott and Beryl Ann Medlicott (*née* Burchell); *m* 1973, Diana Grace Fallaw; one *s* three *d. Educ:* Downside School; Lincoln College, Oxford (Scholar; MA). P&O Cruises: Gen. Manager, Fleet, 1975–80; Gen. Manager, Europe, 1980–83; Dir, Europe, 1983–86; Man. Dir, Swan Hellenic, 1983–86; Man. Dir, P&O Air Holidays, 1980–86; Dir, P&O Travel, 1980–84. Mem., Council of Management, Passenger Shipping Assoc., 1983–86. *Recreations:* philately, theatre, gardening, tennis. *Address:* 7 Glebe Avenue, Enfield, Middx EN2 8NZ. *T:* 01-363 3189.

MEDLICOTT, Prof. William Norton, CBE 1983; DLit, MA (London); FRHistS; Stevenson Professor of International History, University of London, 1953–67; Professor Emeritus, 1967; Senior Editor of Documents on British Foreign Policy, 1919–39, since 1965; *b* 11 May 1900; *s* of William Norton Medlicott (Editor, Church Family Newspaper, 1905–11) and Margaret Louisa McMillan; *m* 1936, Dr Dorothy Kathleen Coveney, Univ. Lectr and palaeographer (*d* 1979). *Educ:* Aske's Sch., Hatcham; University College, London; Institute of Historical Research. Gladstone Prizeman, Hester Rothschild Prizeman, UCL; Lindley Student, Univ. of London. Mil. service, Beds Herts Regt, 1918–20. Lecturer, University Coll., Swansea, 1926–45; Visiting Prof., Univ. of Texas, USA, 1931–32; Principal, Board of Trade, 1941–42; official historian, Ministry of Economic Warfare, 1942–58; Prof. of History, University Coll. of the South West, 1946–53; Vice-Principal, 1953. Creighton Lectr, Univ. of London, 1968. Fellow of UCL. Hon. Fellow LSE. Travel and research in US, 1946, 1952, and 1957; Hon. Sec. Historical Association, 1943–46, Pres., 1952–55. Mem. editl bd, Annual Register, 1947–71; Chm. editorial board, International Affairs, 1954–62. Mem. Institute for Advanced Studies, Princeton, 1952, 1957; Chm. British Co-ordinating Cttee for Internat. Studies. Mem. Council, Chatham House, 1955–71. Hon. DLitt: Wales, 1970; Buckingham, 1984; Hon. LittD Leeds, 1977. *Publications:* The Congress of Berlin and After, 1938, new edn 1963; British Foreign Policy since Versailles, 1940, new edn, 1968; The Economic Blockade, vol. i, 1952, vol. ii, 1959; Bismarck, Gladstone, and the Concert of Europe, 1956; The Coming of War in 1939, 1963; Bismarck and Modern Germany, 1965; Contemporary England, 1914–1964, 1967, rev. edn 1976; Britain and Germany: The Search for Agreement, 1930–1937, 1969; (with D. K. Coveney) Bismarck and Europe, 1971; (with D. K. Coveney) The Lion's Tail, 1971; (ed) Documents on British Foreign Policy 1919–1939, 2nd series, vols x-xxi, 1969–84; numerous articles and reviews. *Address:* 172 Watchfield Court, Sutton Court Road, W4 4NE. *T:* 01-995 7287. *Club:* Athenæum.

MEDLYCOTT, Sir Mervyn (Tregonwell), 9th Bt *cr* 1808, of Ven House, Somerset; *b* 20 Feb. 1947; *s* of Thomas Anthony Hutchings Medlycott (*d* 1970) (2nd *s* of 7th Bt) and of Mrs Cecilia Mary Medlycott, Cowleaze, Edmondsham, Dorset, *d* of late Major Cecil Harold Eden; *S* uncle, 1986. Genealogist; Member: AGRA; HHA; Vice-Pres., Somerset and Dorset Family History Soc., 1984– (Founder and Hon. Sec., 1975–77; Chm., 1977–84). Heir: none. *Address:* The Manor House, Sandford Orcas, Sherborne, Dorset DT9 4SB. *T:* Corton Denham 206.

MEDWAY, Lord; John Jason Gathorne-Hardy; *b* 26 Oct. 1968; *s* and heir of 5th Earl of Cranbrook, *qv*.

MEDWIN, Robert Joseph G.; *see* Gardner-Medwin.

MEECHIE, Brig. Helen Guild, CBE 1986; Member, Royal College of Defence Studies, since 1987; ADC to the Queen, since 1986; *b* 19 Jan. 1938; *d* of John Strachan and Robina Guild Meechie. *Educ:* Morgan Academy, Dundee; St Andrew's University (MA). Commissioned 1960; served in UK, Cyprus and Hong Kong, 1961–76, in UK and Germany, 1977–82; Dir, WRAC, 1982–86. Hon. ADC to the Queen, 1982–86. Hon. Col, Tayforth Univs OTC, 1986–. Gov., Royal Soldiers' Daughters' Sch., 1984–. Freeman, City of London, 1983. CBIM 1986. Hon. LLD Dundee, 1986. *Recreations:* golf, gardening, travel. *Address:* c/o Clydesdale Bank, 31 St James's Street, SW1A 1HW.

MEEK, Brian Alexander, OBE 1982; JP; Convener and Leader of the Administration, Lothian Regional Council, since 1982; *b* 8 Feb. 1939; *s* of Walter Harold Meek and Elsbeth Dearden Meek; *m* 1st, 1962, Glenda (*née* Smith) (marr. diss. 1983); one *s* one *d*; 2nd, 1983, Frances (*née* Horsburgh). *Educ:* Royal High Sch. of Edinburgh; Edinburgh Commercial Coll. Sub-editor, The Scotsman and Edinburgh Evening Dispatch, 1958–63; Features and Leader Writer, Scottish Daily Express, 1963–74; Rugby Football Correspondent, Scottish Daily Express and Sunday Express, 1974–. Councillor: Edinburgh Corp., 1969–74; Edinburgh Dist Council, 1974–82 (Chm., Recreation Cttee, 1974–77); Lothian Regional Council, 1974– (Leader, Conservative Opposition, 1974–82). Magistrate, Edinburgh, 1971, JP 1974. *Recreations:* golf, theatre, cinema, travel. *Address:* Lothian Regional Chambers, Parliament Square, Edinburgh EH1 1TT. *T:* 031–229 9292. *Club:* Caledonian (Edinburgh).

MEEK, Charles Innes, CMG 1961; Chief Executive, 1962–81, Chairman, 1973–81, White Fish Authority; *b* 27 June 1920; *er s* of late Dr C. K. Meek; *m* 1947, Nona Corry Hurford; two *s* one *d. Educ:* King's Sch., Canterbury; Magdalen Coll., Oxford (MA). Demyship, Magdalen Coll., Oxford, 1939. Served in Army, 1940–41; District Officer, Tanganyika, 1941; Principal Asst Sec., Tanganyika, 1958; Permanent Sec., Chief Secretary's Office, 1959; Permanent Sec. to Prime Minister, Sec. to Cabinet, 1960; Government Dir, Williamson Diamonds; Head of the Civil Service, Tanganyika, 1961–62, retd. FRSA 1969. *Publications:* occasional articles in Journal of African Administration, etc. *Recreations:* travel, Times crossword. *Address:* 2 Hiham Green, Winchelsea, E Sussex TN36 4HB. *T:* Rye 226640. *Club:* Royal Commonwealth Society.

MEEK, Prof. John Millar, CBE 1975; DEng; FEng 1976; FInstP; FIEE; David Jardine Professor of Electrical Engineering, University of Liverpool, 1946–78; Public Orator, 1973–76, and Pro-Vice-Chancellor, 1974–77, University of Liverpool; *b* Wallasey, 21 Dec. 1912; *s* of Alexander Meek and Edith Montgomery; *m* 1942, Marjorie, *d* of Bernard Ingleby; two *d. Educ:* Monkton Combe Sch.; University of Liverpool. College Apprentice, Metropolitan-Vickers Electrical Co. Ltd, 1934–36; Research Engineer, Metropolitan-Vickers Electrical Co. Ltd, 1936–38, 1940–46. Commonwealth Fund Research Fellow,

Physics Dept, University of California, Berkeley, 1938–40. Mem. of Council, IEE, 1945–48, 1960–63 (Vice-Pres. 1964–68, Pres., 1968–69), Faraday Medal, 1975. Mem., IBA (formerly ITA), 1969–74. Hon. DSc Salford, 1971. *Publications:* The Mechanism of the Electric Spark (with L. B. Loeb), 1941; Electrical Breakdown of Gases (with J. D. Craggs), 1953, new edn 1978; High Voltage Laboratory Technique (with J. D. Craggs), 1954; papers in various scientific journals concerning research on electrical discharges in gases. *Recreations:* golf, gardening, theatre. *Address:* 4 The Kirklands, West Kirby, Merseyside. *T:* 051–625 5850. *Club:* Royal Commonwealth Society.

MEEK, Marshall, CEng; FRINA; FIMarE; Director, British Maritime Technology, since 1986 (Deputy Chairman, 1985–86); *b* 22 April 1925; *s* of Marshall Meek and Grace R. Smith; *m* 1957, Elfrida M. Cox; three *d. Educ:* Bell Baxter School, Cupar; Glasgow University (BSc). Caledon Shipbuilding Co., 1942–49; BSRA, 1949–53; Dir, Ocean Fleets, 1953–79; Head of Technology, British Shipbuilders, 1979–84; Managing Dir, National Maritime Inst., 1984–85. Vice-Pres., RINA, 1979–; Pres., NE Coast Inst. of Engrs and Shipbuilders, 1984–. *Publications:* numerous papers to RINA and other marine jls. *Recreations:* gardening, reading. *Address:* Redstacks, Tranwell Woods, Morpeth, Northumberland NE61 6AG. *Club:* Caledonian.

MEERES, Norman Victor, CB 1963; Under-Secretary, Ministry of Defence, 1971–73, retired; *b* 1 Feb. 1913; *m* 1938, Elizabeth Powys Fowler; two *s* one *d. Educ:* Sloane Sch., Chelsea; Magdalene Coll., Cambridge. Asst Principal, Air Ministry, 1935; Principal, 1940, Asst Sec., 1944, Ministry of Aircraft Prod.; Asst Sec., Min. of Supply, 1946; Under Secretary: Min. of Supply, 1956; Min. of Aviation, 1959–67; seconded to Dipl. Service in Australia, with title Minister (Defence Research and Civil Aviation), 1965–68; Under-Sec., Min. of Technology, 1969–70. ARCM (piano teaching), 1974. *Recreations:* music, lawn tennis. *Address:* 89 Grove Way, Esher, Surrey. *T:* 01–398 1639.

MEESE, Edwin, III; lawyer; Attorney General, United States of America, since 1985; *b* Oakland, Calif, 1931; *s* of Edwin Meese Jr and Leone Meese; *m* 1958, Ursula Herrick; one *s* one *d* (and one *s* decd). *Educ:* Oakland High Sch.; Yale Univ. (BA 1953); Univ. of Calif at Berkeley (JD 1958). Dep. Dist Attorney, Alameda County, 1959–67; Sec. of Legal Affairs to Gov. of Calif, Ronald Reagan, 1967–69; Exec. Assistant and C of S to Gov. of Calif, 1969–75; Vice-Pres., Rohr Industries, 1975–76; Attorney at Law, 1976–80; Dir, Center for Criminal Justice Policy and Management, Univ. of Calif, San Diego, 1977–81; Prof. of Law, Univ. of San Diego Law Sch., 1978–81; Counsellor to Pres. of USA, 1981–85. Hon. LLD: Delaware Law Sch.; Widener Univ.; Univ. of San Diego; Valparaiso Univ.; California Lutheran Coll. *Publications:* contribs to professional jls. *Address:* Department of Justice, Constitution Avenue and 10th Street NW, Washington, DC 20530, USA.

MEGAHY, Thomas; Member (Lab) SW Yorkshire, European Parliament, since 1979; *b* 16 July 1929; *s* of Samuel and Mary Megahy; *m* 1954, Jean (*née* Renshaw); three *s. Educ:* Wishaw High Sch.; Ruskin Coll., Oxford, 1953–55; College of Educn (Technical), Huddersfield, 1955–56 and 1968–69; London Univ. (external student), 1959–63. BScEcon London; DipEcon and PolSci Oxon; DipFE Leeds. Left school at 14 to work on railway; National Service, RN, 1947–49; railway signalman, 1950–53. Lecturer: Rotherham Coll. of Technology, 1956–59; Huddersfield Technical Coll., 1960–65; Park Lane Coll., Leeds, 1965–79. European Parliament: Dep. Leader, British Labour Group of MEPs, 1985–; Member: Social Affairs Cttee, 1984–; Institutional Affairs Cttee, 1981–. Active member of Labour Party, 1950–; Chm., Scottish Labour League of Youth; Executive Mem., Dewsbury CLP, 1962–. Councillor, Mirfield UDC, 1963–74; Leader, Kirklees Metropolitan Borough Council, 1973–76; Opposition Leader, 1976–78. Member, Yorks and Humberside REPC, 1974–77; Vice-President, AMA, 1979–; Yorks and Humberside Develt Assoc., 1981–. *Address:* 6 Lady Heton Grove, Mirfield, West Yorks WF14 9DY. *T:* Mirfield 492680.

MEGARRY, Rt. Hon. Sir Robert (Edgar), Kt 1967; PC 1978; FBA 1970; a Judge of the Chancery Division of the High Court of Justice, 1967–76; the Vice-Chancellor: of that Division, 1976–81; of the Supreme Court, 1982–85; *b* 1 June 1910; *e s* of late Robert Lindsay Megarry, OBE, MA, LLB, Belfast, and of late Irene, *d* of Maj.-Gen. E. G. Clark; *m* 1936, Iris, *e d* of late Elias Davies, Neath, Glam; three *d. Educ:* Lancing Coll.; Trinity Hall, Cambridge (Hon. Fellow, 1973). MA, LLD (Cantab); Music Critic, Varsity, 1930–32; Solicitor, 1935–41; taught for Bar and Solicitors' exams, 1935–39; Mem., Faculty of Law, Cambridge Univ., 1939–40; Certificate of Honour, and called to Bar, Lincoln's Inn, 1944, in practice, 1946–67; QC 1956–67; Bencher, Lincoln's Inn, 1962, Treasurer 1981. Principal, 1940–44, and Asst Sec., 1944–46, Min. of Supply; Book Review Editor and Asst Ed., Law Quarterly Review, 1944–67; Dir of Law Society's Refresher Courses, 1944–47; Sub-Lector, Trinity Coll., Cambridge, 1945–46; Asst Reader, 1946–51, Reader, 1951–67, Hon. Reader, 1967– in Equity in the Inns of Court (Council of Legal Educn); Member: Gen. Council of the Bar, 1948–52; Lord Chancellor's Law Reform Cttee, 1952–73; Senate of Inns of Court and Bar, 1966–70, 1980–82; Adv. Council on Public Records, 1980–85; Consultant to BBC for Law in Action series, 1953–66; Chairman: Notting Hill Housing Trust, 1967–68; Bd of Studies, and Vice-Chm., Council of Legal Educn, 1969–71; Friends of Lancing Chapel, 1969–; Incorporated Council of Law Reporting, 1972–; Comparative Law Sect., British Inst. of Internat. and Comp. Law, 1977–; President: Soc. of Public Teachers of Law, 1965–66; Lancing Club, 1974–; Selden Soc., 1976–79. Visiting Professor: New York Univ. Sch. of Law, 1960–61; Osgoode Hall Law Sch., Toronto, 1964; Lectures: John F. Sonnett, Fordham Univ., 1982; Tyrrell Williams, Washington Univ., St Louis, 1983; Leon Ladner, Univ. of British Columbia, 1984. Visitor: Essex Univ., 1983–; Clare Hall, Cambridge, 1984–. Hon. LLD: Hull, 1963; Nottingham, 1979; Law Soc. of Upper Canada (Osgoode Hall), 1982. Hon. Life Member: Canadian Bar Assoc., 1971; Amer. Law Inst., 1985. *Publications:* The Rent Acts, 1939, 10th edn 1967; A Manual of the Law of Real Property, 1946, 6th edn (ed D. J. Hayton), 1982; Lectures on the Town and Country Planning Act, 1947, 1949; Miscellany-at-Law, 1955; (with Prof. H. W. R. Wade QC) The Law of Real Property, 1957, 5th edn 1984; Lawyer and Litigant in England (Hamlyn Lectures, 1962); Arabinesque-at-Law, 1969; Inns Ancient and Modern, 1972; A Second Miscellany-at-Law, 1973; Editor, Snell's Equity, 23rd edn 1947, 27th edn (with P. V. Baker, QC), 1973; contrib. to legal periodicals. *Recreations:* heterogeneous. *Address:* The Institute of Advanced Legal Studies, 17 Russell Square, WC1B 5DR. *T:* 01–637 1731; 5 Stone Buildings, Lincoln's Inn, WC2A 3XT. *T:* 01–242 8607.

MEGAW, Arthur Hubert Stanley, CBE 1951; MA Cantab; FSA; *b* Dublin, 1910; *s* of late Arthur Stanley Megaw; *m* 1937, Elene Elektra, *d* of late Helias Mangoletsi, Koritsa, Albania; no *c. Educ:* Campbell Coll., Belfast; Peterhouse, Cambridge. Walston Student (University of Cambridge), 1931. Macmillan Student, British School of Archæology at Athens, 1932–33, Asst Dir, 1935–36; Dir of Antiquities, Cyprus, 1936–60; Field Dir, Byzantine Institute, Istanbul, 1961–62; Dir, British Sch. of Archæology, Athens, 1962–68. CStJ, 1967. *Publications:* (with A. J. B. Wace) Hermopolis Magna-Ashmunein, Alexandria, 1959; (with E. J. W. Hawkins) The Church of the Panagia Kanakariá in Cyprus, its Mosaics and Frescoes, 1977; various papers in archæological journals. *Recreation:* travel. *Address:* 27 Perrin's Walk, NW3; 4–6 Anapiron Polemou, Athens 140, Greece.

MEGAW, Rt. Hon. Sir John, PC 1969; Kt 1961; CBE 1956; TD 1951; a Lord Justice of Appeal, 1969–80; *b* 16 Sept. 1909; 2nd *s* of late Hon. Mr Justice Megaw, Belfast; *m* 1938, Eleanor Grace Chapman; one *s* two *d*. *Educ:* Royal Academical Institution, Belfast; St John's Coll., Cambridge Univ. (open schol. in classics; Hon. Fellow, 1967); Harvard Univ. Law Sch. (Choate Fellowship). Served War, 1939–45; Col, RA. Barrister-at-Law, Gray's Inn, 1934 (Certificate of Honour, Bar Final exam.); Bencher, 1958; Treasurer, 1976; QC 1953; QC (N Ire.) 1954; Recorder of Middlesbrough, 1957–61; Judge of the High Court of Justice, Queen's Bench Div., 1961–69; Pres., Restrictive Practices Court, 1962–68. Chm., Cttee of Inquiry into Civil Service Pay, 1981–82. Visitor: New Univ. of Ulster, 1976; Univ. of Ulster, 1984. Hon. LLD Queen's Univ., Belfast, 1968. Legion of Merit (US), 1946 Played Rugby football for Ireland, 1934, 1938. *Address:* 14 Upper Cheyne Row, SW3.

MEGGESON, Michael; Solicitor and Notary Public; Partner, Warner, Goodman & Streat; a Recorder of the Crown Court, since 1981; *b* 6 Aug. 1930; *s* of Richard Ronald Hornsey Meggeson and Marjorie Meggeson; *m* 1975, Alison Margaret (*née* Wood). *Educ:* Sherborne; Gonville and Caius Coll., Cambridge. BA 1953; MA 1963. Nat. Service, RA, 1949–50; 5th Bn Royal Hampshire Regt, TA, 1950–63. Admitted a Solicitor, 1957; Asst Solicitor, 1957–59, Partner, 1959–, Warner & Sons, subseq. Warner Goodman & Co., and Warner, Goodman & Streat; Dep. Circuit Judge, 1978–81. Mem. Cttee, Solicitors Staff Pension Fund, 1980–; Pres., Hampshire Incorp. Law Soc., 1981–82. *Recreations:* sailing, golf, gardening, music. *Address:* Church Farm, Langrish, near Petersfield, Hants GU32 1RQ. *T:* Petersfield 4470. *Clubs:* Royal Ocean Racing; Royal Southern Yacht (Hamble); Hayling Island Golf.

MEHAFFEY, Rt. Rev. James; *see* Derry and Raphoe, Bishop of.

MEHEW, Peter; Assistant Under Secretary of State (Civilian Management) (C), Ministry of Defence, 1984–86; *b* 22 Jan. 1931; *er s* of Oliver Mehew and Elsie (*née* Cox); *m* 1956, Gwyneth Sellors (*d* 1982); one *s* one *d*. *Educ:* Bishop Wordsworth's Sch.; St Catharine's Coll., Cambridge (BA 1954). Asst Principal, Admiralty, 1954, Principal 1959; Assistant Secretary: CSD, 1970–73; MoD, 1973–80; Dep. Head, UK Delegn to Negotiations on Mutual and Balanced Force Reductions, 1975–77; Asst Under Sec. of State (Sales Admin), MoD, 1981–83. Fellow Commoner, CCC Cambridge, 1980. *Address:* 87 Hitchen Hatch Lane, Sevenoaks, Kent. *T:* Sevenoaks 455641. *Club:* Royal Commonwealth Society.

MEHROTRA, Prakash Chandra; High Commissioner for India in London, 1984; *b* 26 Feb. 1925; *s* of F. Gopalji Mehrotra and M. Raj Dulari; *m* 1978, Priti Mehrotra; one *s* four *d*. *Educ:* Allahabad University; arts graduate; Sec., Univ. Union, 1945–46. Business, 1947–76; Mem. Parliament (Rajya Sabha), 1976–81; Sec., Congress (I) Parly Party, 1980–81; Governor, Assam and Meghalaya, 1981–84. *Recreations:* music, sports, gardening. *Address:* 20A/4 Gokhale Marg, Lucknow, India.

MEHROTRA, Prof. Ram Charan, MSc, DPhil, PhD, DSc; Director, Special Assistance Programme, University of Rajasthan, Jaipur, since 1979 (Professor of Chemistry, 1979–83, now Emeritus); *b* 16 Feb. 1922; *s* of late R. B. Mehrotra; *m* 1944, Suman; one *s* two *d*. *Educ:* Allahabad Univ. (MSc 1943, DPhil 1948); London Univ. (PhD 1952, DSc 1964). Research Chemist, Vigyan Kala Bhawan, Meerut, 1943–44; Lectr, Allahabad Univ., 1944–54; Reader, Lucknow Univ., 1954–58; Prof., 1958–62, Dean, Faculty of Science, 1959–62, Gorakhpur Univ.; Prof., 1962–74, Dean, Faculty of Science, 1962–65, Chief Rector, 1965–67, Vice-Chancellor, 1968–69 and 1972–73, Rajasthan Univ., Jaipur; Vice-Chancellor, Univ. of Delhi, 1974–79. Mem., UGC, 1982–. President: Chemistry Section, Indian Sci. Congress, 1967; Indian Chemical Soc., 1976–77; Indian Science Congress, 1978–79; Vice-Pres., Indian Nat. Science Acad., 1977–78; Member: Inorganic Chem. Div., IUPAC, 1977–81; Inorganic Nomenclature Commn, 1981–. Sir S. S. Bhatnagar award, 1965; Fedn of Indian Chambers of Commerce and Industry award, 1975; Prof. T. R. Seshadri's Birthday Commem. Medal, 1976; P. C. Ray Meml Medal, 1981; Golden Jubilee Medal, Inst. of Science, Bombay, 1983. Hon. DSc Meerut, 1976. *Publications:* treatises on: Metal Alkoxides and Metal β-Diketonates and Allied Derivatives, 1978; Metal Carboxylates, 1983; numerous research papers in nat. and internat. jls of chemistry; contribs to chemistry progress reports of Chem. Soc. London. *Recreation:* photography. *Address:* P4, University Campus, Jaipur 302004, India. *T:* (office) 60088; (home) 76275.

MEHTA, Ved Parkash; staff writer, New Yorker, since 1961; *b* Lahore, 21 March 1934; 2nd *s* of late Dr Amolak Ram Mehta, former Dep. Director General of Health Services, Govt of India, and of Shanti Devi Mehta (*née* Mehra); naturalized citizen of USA, 1975; *m* 1983, Linn Fenimore Cooper, *d* of late William L. Cary; one *d*. *Educ:* Arkansas Sch. for the Blind; Pomona Coll.; Balliol Coll., Oxford; Harvard Univ. BA Pomona, 1956; BA Hons Mod. Hist. Oxon, 1959; MA Harvard, 1961. Phi Beta Kappa, 1955. Hazen Fellow, 1956–59; Harvard Prize Fellow, 1959–60; Guggenheim Fellow, 1971–72, 1977–78; Ford Foundn Travel and Study Grantee, 1971–76, Public Policy Grantee, 1979–82; MacArthur Prize Fellow, 1982–87; Vis. Schol., Case Western Reserve, 1974; Beatty Lectr, McGill Univ., 1979; Vis. Prof., Bard Coll., 1985, 1986. Mem. Council on Foreign Relations, 1979. Mem. Usage Panel, Amer. Heritage Dictionary, 1982. Hon. DLitt: Pomona, 1972; Bard, 1982; Williams, 1986. Assoc. of Indians in America Award, 1978; Distinguished Service Award, Asian/Pacific Americans Liby Assoc., 1986. *Publications:* Face to Face, 1957 (Secondary Educn Annual Book Award, 1958; BBC dramatization on Home prog., serial reading on Light prog., 1958; reissued 1967, 1978; Excerpts, 1981); Walking the Indian Streets, 1960 (rev. edn 1971); Fly and the Fly-Bottle, 1963, 2nd edn 1983 introd. Jasper Griffin; The New Theologian, 1966; Delinquent Chacha (fiction), 1967; Portrait of India, 1970; John Is Easy to Please, 1971; Mahatma Gandhi and his Apostles, 1977; The New India, 1978; Photographs of Chachaji, 1980; A Family Affair: India under three Prime Ministers, 1982; Three Stories of the Raj (fiction), 1986; *autobiographical series:* Daddyji, 1972; Mamaji, 1979; Vedi, 1982; The Ledge Between the Streams, 1984; Sound-Shadows of the New World, 1986; numerous translations; articles and stories in Amer., British and Indian newspapers and magazines from 1957, inc. Ved Mehta: a bibliography, in Bulletin of Bibliography, March 1985. Writer and commentator of TV documentary film, Chachaji: My Poor Relation, PBS, 1978, BBC, 1980 (DuPont Columbia Award for Excellence in Broadcast Journalism, 1977–78). *Recreation:* listening to Indian and Western music. *Address:* c/o The New Yorker, 25 West 43rd Street, New York, NY 10036, USA. *T:* 212–840–3800; (home) 139 East 79th Street, New York, NY 10021, USA; (country) Dark Harbor, Me 04848, USA. *Club:* Century Association (NY) (Trustee, 1973–75).

MEHTA, Zubin; Music Director, New York Philharmonic, since 1978; Music Director for life, Israel Philharmonic Orchestra (Musical Adviser, 1962–78); *b* 29 April 1936; *s* of Mehli Mehta; *m* 1st, 1958, Carmen Lasky (marr. diss. 1964); one *s* one *d*; 2nd, 1969, Nancy Kovack. *Educ:* St Xavier's Coll., Bombay; Musikakademie, Vienna. First Concert, Vienna, 1958; first prize internat. comp., Liverpool, 1958; US debut, Philadelphia Orch., 1960; debut with Israel and Vienna Philharmonic Orchs, 1961; apptd Music Director, Montreal Symphony Orch., 1961; European tour with this orch., 1962; guest conducting, major European Orchs, 1962; Music Dir, Los Angeles Philharmonic Orch., 1962–78; Artistic Dir, Maggio Musicale Fiorentino, 1986–. Opera debut, Montreal, Tosca, 1964;

debut Metropolitan Opera, Aida, 1965; operas at Metropolitan incl.: Tosca, Turandot, Otello, Carmen, Mourning becomes Elektra (world première), Trovatore, etc. Tours regularly with New York Philharmonic and Israel Philharmonic Orchs and occasionally with Vienna Phil. Orch.; regular guest conducting with Vienna Phil., Berlin Phil., Orch. de Paris. Hon. Doctorates: Colgate Univ.; Brooklyn Coll.; Westminster Coll.; Occidental Coll.; Sir George Williams Univ., Canada; Weizmann Inst. of Science, Israel; Tel-Aviv Univ. Holds numerous awards; Padma Bhushan (India), 1967; Commendatore of Italy. *Address:* New York Philharmonic, Avery Fisher Hall, Broadway and 65th Street, New York, NY 10023, USA. *T:* (212) 580–8700.

MEIGGS, Russell, MA; FBA 1961; *b* 1902; *s* of William Herrick Meiggs, London; *m* 1941, Pauline Gregg; two *d*. *Educ:* Christ's Hospital; Keble Coll., Oxford. Fellow of Keble Coll., 1930–39; Fellow and Tutor in Ancient History, Balliol Coll., Oxford, 1939–70, Hon. Fellow, 1970; Univ. Lectr in Ancient History, 1939–70; Praefectus of Holywell Manor, 1945–69. Vis. Prof., Swarthmore Coll., 1960, 1970–71, 1974, 1977–78; Kipling Fellow, Marlborough Coll., Vermont, 1967. For. Mem., Amer. Philosophical Soc., 1981. DHL Swarthmore Coll., 1971. *Publications:* Home Timber Production, 1939–1945, 1949; (ed jtly) Sources for Greek History between the Persian and Peloponnesian Wars, new edn, 1951; (ed) Bury's History of Greece, 3rd edn, 1951, 4th edn, 1975; Roman Ostia, 1960, 2nd edn, 1974; (ed with David Lewis) Selection of Greek Historical Inscriptions to the end of the 5th century BC, 1969; The Athenian Empire, 1972; Trees and Timber in the Ancient Mediterranean World, 1983. *Recreations:* gardening, America. *Address:* The Malt House, Garsington, Oxford.

MEINERTZHAGEN, Daniel; Chairman: Royal Insurance plc, 1974–85; Alexanders Discount plc, 1981–84; *b* 2 March 1915; *e s* of Louis Ernest Meinertzhagen, Theberton House, Leiston, Suffolk and Gwynedd, *d* of Sir William Llewellyn, PRA; *m* 1940, Marguerite, *d* of A. E. Leonard; two *s*. *Educ:* Eton; New Coll., Oxford. Served War of 1939–45, RAFVR (Wing Comdr). Joined Lazard Brothers, 1936; Man. Dir 1954; Dep. Chm. 1971; Chm., 1973–80. Former Chm., Mercantile Credit Co. Ltd, Raeburn Investment Trust Ltd, and Whitehall Trust; Former Director: S. Pearson & Son Ltd; Pearson Longman Ltd; W. T. Henley's Telegraph Works Co. Ltd; Rootes Motors Ltd; Trollope & Colls Ltd; Costain Group Ltd; Brixton Estate plc; Tozer Kemsley & Millbourn (Hldgs) plc. *Address:* 82 Old Church Street, Chelsea, SW3 6EP. *T:* 01–352 5150. *Club:* White's.
See also Sir Peter Meinertzhagen.

MEINERTZHAGEN, Sir Peter, Kt 1980; CMG 1966; General Manager, Commonwealth Development Corporation, 1973–85; *b* 24 March 1920; *y s* of late Louis Ernest Meinertzhagen, Theberton House, Leiston, Suffolk and Gwynnedd, *d* of Sir William Llewellyn, PRA; *m* 1949, Dido Pretty; one *s* one *d*. *Educ:* Eton. Served Royal Fusiliers, 1940–46 (Croix de Guerre, France, 1944). Alfred Booth & Co., 1946–57; Commonwealth Development Corporation, 1958–85. Member: Council, London Chamber of Commerce, 1968–69; Council, Overseas Develt Inst., 1979–85. *Address:* 59 Cleaver Square, SE11 4EA. *T:* 01–735 6263. *Club:* Muthaiga Country (Nairobi).
See also D. Meinertzhagen.

MEIRION-JONES, Prof. Gwyn Idris, FSA 1981; Head of Geography, since 1970, and Professor, since 1983, City of London Polytechnic; *b* 24 Dec. 1933; *e s* of Maelgwyn Meirion-Jones and Enid Roberts, Manchester; *m* 1961, Monica, *e d* of George and Marion Havard, Winchester. *Educ:* North Manchester Grammar School; King's College London (BSc, MPhil, PhD). National Service, RAF, 1954–56. Schoolmaster, 1959–68; Lectr in Geography, Kingston Coll. of Technology, 1968; Sen. Lectr i/c Geography, 1969, Principal Lectr i/c, 1970, Sir John Cass Coll., later City of London Polytechnic. Leverhulme Research Fellow, 1985–87. British Assoc. for the Advancement of Science: Sec., 1973–78, Recorder, 1978–83, Section H (Anthropology); Mem. Council, 1977–80; Mem. Gen. Cttee, 1977–83; Ancient Monuments Society: Mem. Council, 1974–79 and 1983–; Hon. Sec., 1976–79; Vice-Pres., 1979–; Editor, Medieval Village Res. Gp, 1978–86; Editor, 1985–. Mem., Royal Commn on Historical Monuments of England, 1985–; Pres., Domestic Buildings Res. Gp (Surrey), 1986–; Mem., Comité Scientifique des Musées du Finistère, 1984–. Hon. Corresp. Mem., Soc. Jersiaise, 1980. Exhibitions: vernacular architecture of Brittany, on tour 1982–85; Architecture vernaculaire en Bretagne (15e–20e siècles), Rennes and tour, 1984–86. *Publications:* La Maison traditionelle (bibliog.), 1978; The Vernacular Architecture of Brittany, 1982; papers in sci., archaeol and ethnol jls. *Recreations:* walking, listening to music. *Address:* City of London Polytechnic, Old Castle Street, E1 7NT. *T:* 01–283 1030; 11 Avondale Road, Fleet, Hants GU13 9BH. *T:* Fleet 614300. *Club:* Athenæum.

MEKIE, David Eric Cameron, OBE 1955; FRCSEd; FRSEd; FRCPEd; Conservator, Royal College of Surgeons of Edinburgh, 1955–74; *b* 8 March 1902; *s* of Dr D. C. T. Mekie and Mary Cameron; *m* 1930, Winifred Knott (*d* 1970); two *s* one *d*. *Educ:* George Watson's Coll., Edinburgh; University of Edinburgh. MB, ChB 1925; FRCSEd 1928; FRSEd 1962; MRCP 1962; FRCPEd, 1966. Tutor, Dept of Clinical Surgery, University of Edinburgh, 1928–33; Ernest Hart Scholar, 1931–33; Professor of Clinical Surgery and Surgery, University of Malaya, 1935–55 (now Prof. Emeritus). Dir, Postgrad. Bd for Medicine, Edinburgh, 1960–71; Postgrad. Dean of Medicine, Edinburgh Univ., 1970–71. Surgeon, Singapore General Hospital and Hon. Surgical Consultant, Far East Command. *Publications:* Handbook of Surgery, 1936; (ed with Sir James Fraser) A Colour Atlas of Demonstrations in Surgical Pathology, 1983; numerous surgical papers. *Recreations:* fishing, gardening. *Address:* 58 Findhorn Place, Edinburgh EH9 2NW. *T:* 031–667 6472.

MELANESIA, Archbishop of, since 1975; **Most Rev. Norman Kitchener Palmer,** CMG 1981; MBE 1975; Bishop of Central Melanesia; *b* 2 Oct. 1928; *s* of Philip Sydney and Annie Palmer; *m* 1960, Elizabeth Lucy Gorringe; three *s* one *d*. *Educ:* Kokeqolo, Pawa, Solomon Is; Te Aute, NZ; Ardmore, NZ (Teachers' Cert.); St John's Theological Coll., NZ (LTh; ordained deacon, 1964). Appts in Solomon Islands: Deacon/Teacher, Pawa Secondary (Anglican), 1966; priest, Pawa, 1966; Priest/Headmaster: Alanguala Primary, 1967–69; St Nicholas Primary, 1970–72; Dean, St Barnabas Cathedral, 1973–75. Member, Public Service Advisory Bd, 1971–75. *Address:* Archbishop's House, PO Box 19, Honiara, Solomon Islands. *T:* 22339.

MELBOURNE, Archbishop of, and Metropolitan of the Province of Victoria, since 1984; **Most Rev. David John Penman;** *b* 8 Aug. 1936; *s* of John James and Irene May Penman; *m* 1962, Jean Frances (*née* Newson); one *s* three *d*. *Educ:* Keith St School, Wanganui, NZ; Intermediate School, Wanganui and Hutt Valley High Sch., NZ; Teachers' Coll., Wellington; Univ. of New Zealand (BA 1962); Christchurch Theol Coll. (LTh 1964); Univ. of Karachi, Pakistan (MA 1970, PhD 1977, Sociology and Islam). Teacher in Hutt Valley and Palmerston North, NZ, 1957–59; Asst Curate, Christ Church Anglican Church, Wanganui, 1961–64; Missionary work with NZ Church Missionary Soc. in W Asia and Middle East, 1965–75; Principal, St Andrew's Hall, CMS Federal Training Coll., Melbourne, Aust., 1976–79; Vicar of All Saints' Anglican Church, Palmerston North, NZ, 1979–82; a Bishop Coadjutor, Dio. Melbourne, 1982–84.

Recreations: sport, music, stamp collecting and reading. *Address:* Bishopscourt, 120 Clarendon Street, East Melbourne, Victoria 3002, Australia.

MELBOURNE, Archbishop of, (RC), since 1974; **Most Rev. Thomas Francis Little,** KBE 1977; DD, STD; *b* 30 Nov. 1925; *s* of Gerald Thompson Little and Kathleen McCormack. *Educ:* St Patrick's Coll., Ballarat; Corpus Christi Coll., Werribee; Pontifical Urban Coll., Rome. STD Rome, 1953. Priest 1950; Asst Priest, Carlton, 1953–55; Secretary, Apostolic Deleg. to Aust., NZ and Oceania, 1955–59; Asst Priest, St Patrick's Cathedral, Melbourne, 1959–65; Dean, 1965–70; Episcopal Vicar for Lay Apostolate, 1969; Pastor, St Ambrose, Brunswick, 1971–73; Auxiliary Bishop, Archdiocese of Melbourne, 1972; Bishop, 1973. *Address:* St Patrick's Cathedral, Melbourne, Vic. 3002, Australia. *T:* 622.2233.

MELBOURNE, Bishops Coadjutor of; *see* Grant, Rt Rev. J. A.; Shand, Rt Rev. D. H. W.

MELCHETT, 4th Baron *cr* 1928; **Peter Robert Henry Mond;** Bt 1910; *b* 24 Feb. 1948; *s* of 3rd Baron Melchett and of Sonia Elizabeth (who *m* 2nd, 1984, A. A. Sinclair, *qv*), *er d* of Lt-Col R. H. Graham; *S* father, 1973. *Educ:* Eton; Pembroke Coll., Cambridge (BA); Keele Univ. (MA). Res. Worker, LSE and Addiction Res. Unit, 1973–74. A Lord in Waiting (Govt Whip), 1974–75; Parly Under-Sec. of State, DoI, 1975–76; Minister of State, NI Office, 1976–79. Chm., working party on pop festivals, 1975–76; Chm., Community Industry, 1979–85. Chairman: Wildlife Link, 1979–; Greenpeace Environmental Trust, 1986–; Pres., Ramblers' Assoc., 1981–84. Mem., Friends of Release. *Address:* House of Lords, SW1.

MELCHIOR-BONNET, Christian; author; Director and founder, since 1946, Historia, Journal de la France; *b* Marseille, 10 April 1904; *s* of Daniel-Joseph Melchior-Bonnet and Geneviève (*née* de Luxer); *m* 1930, Bernardine Paul-Dubois-Taine (*g d* of the historian Taine, herself a historian, author of several historical works, recipient of Grand Prix Gobert of Académie Française); two *s* one *d*. *Educ:* St Jean de Béthune, Versailles; Ecole du Louvre, Faculté de droit de Paris. Secretary to Pierre de Nolhac, de l'Académie française, historian, at Jacquemart-André museum, 1927–36; formerly, Editor-in-Chief, Petit Journal, 1936–45 and Flambeau; Dir, historical and religious series of Editions Flammarion, 1932–46; Literary Dir, Fayard editions, 1946–67; Director of the reviews: Oeuvres Libres, 1946–64; Historia, 1946–; A la Page, 1964–69; Co-dir, Jardin des Arts; Literary Adviser to Nouvelles Littéraires, 1946–70. Privy Chamberlain to every Pope since 1946, incl. Pope John Paul II. Membre du jury: Prix Historia; Prix de la Fondation de France; Prix des Ambassadeurs. Officier de la Légion d'honneur; Commandeur de l'Ordre national du Mérite; Officier des Arts et des Lettres, et décorations étrangères. Prix du Rayonnement, Académie française, 1963. *Publications:* Scènes et portraits historiques de Chateaubriand, 1928; Les Mémoires du Comte Alexandre de Tilly, ancien page de la reine Marie-Antoinette, 1929; Les Mémoires du Cardinal de Retz, 1929; Principes d'action de Salazar, 1956; Le Napoléon de Chateaubriand, 1969; et nombreuses éditions de mémoires historiques. *Address:* 17 Boulevard de Beauséjour, 75016 Paris, France.

MELDRUM, Andrew, CBE 1962 (OBE 1956); KPM; Chief Inspector of Constabulary for Scotland, 1966–69, retired; *b* 22 April 1909; *s* of late Andrew Meldrum, Burntisland, Fife; *m* 1937, Janet H., *d* of late Robert Crooks, Grangemouth; one *s* one *d*. *Educ:* Burntisland, Fife. Joined Stirlingshire Police, 1927; Deputy Chief Constable, Inverness Burgh, 1943, Chief Constable, 1946; Chief Constable, County of Angus, 1949; Chief Constable of Fife, 1955; Inspector of Constabulary for Scotland, 1965–66. King's Police Medal, 1952. *Recreation:* golf. *Club:* Royal Burgess Golfing Society of Edinburgh.

MELDRUM, Keith Cameron; Director of Veterinary Field Service, Ministry of Agriculture, Fisheries and Food, since 1986; *b* 19 April 1937; *s* of Dr Walter James Meldrum and Mrs Eileen Lydia Meldrum; *m* 1982, Vivien Mary (*née* Fisher); two *s* one *d*. *Educ:* Uppingham; Edinburgh Univ. Qualified as veterinary surgeon, 1961; general practice, Scunthorpe, 1961–63; joined MAFF, Oxford, 1963; Divl Vet. Officer, Tolworth, 1972, Leamington Spa, 1975; Dep. Regional Vet. Officer, Nottingham, 1978; Regional Vet. Officer, Tolworth, 1980; Asst Chief Vet. Officer, Tolworth, 1983. *Recreations:* competitive target rifle shooting, outdoor activities. *Address:* The Orchard, Swaynes Lane, Merrow, Guildford, Surrey GU1 2XX. *T:* Guildford 65197. *Clubs:* Farmers'; North London Rifle (Bisley).

MELGUND, Viscount; Gilbert Timothy George Lariston Elliot-Murray-Kynynmound; *b* 1 Dec. 1953; *s* and *heir* of 6th Earl of Minto, *qv*; *m* 1983, Diana, *yr d* of Brian Trafford; one *s*. *Educ:* Eton; North East London Polytechnic (BSc Hons 1983). ARICS. Lieut, Scots Guards, 1972–76. *Heir:* *s* Hon. Gilbert Francis Elliot-Murray-Kynynmound, *b* 15 Aug. 1984. *Club:* White's.

MELHUISH, Michael Ramsay, CMG 1982; HM Diplomatic Service; High Commissioner to Zimbabwe, since 1985; *b* 17 March 1932; *s* of late Henry Whitfield Melhuish and Jeanette Ramsay Pender Melhuish; *m* 1961, Stella Phillips; two *s* two *d*. *Educ:* Royal Masonic Sch., Bushey; St John's Coll., Oxford (BA). FO, 1955; MECAS, 1956; Third Sec., Bahrain, 1957; FO, 1959; Second Sec., Singapore, 1961; First Sec. (Commercial) and Consul, Prague, 1963; First Sec. and Head of Chancery, Bahrain, 1966; DSAO (later FCO), 1968; First Sec., Washington, 1970; Counsellor, Amman, 1973; Head of N America Dept, FCO, 1976; Counsellor (Commercial), Warsaw, 1979–82; Ambassador, Kuwait, 1982–85. *Recreations:* tennis, golf. *Address:* c/o Foreign and Commonwealth Office, SW1A 2AH. *Club:* United Oxford & Cambridge University.

MELIA, Dr Terence Patrick; Chief Inspector, Further and Higher Education, HM Inspectorate of Schools, since 1985; *b* 17 Dec. 1934; *s* of John and Kathleen Melia (*née* Traynor); *m* 1976, Madeline (*née* Carney); one *d*. *Educ:* Sir John Deanes Grammar Sch., Northwich; Leeds Univ. (PhD). CChem, FRSC. Technical Officer, ICI, 1961–64; Lectr, then Sen. Lectr, Salford Univ., 1964–70; Principal, North Lindsey Coll. of Technology, 1970–74; HM Inspector of Schools, 1974–; Regional Staff Inspector, 1982–84. *Publications:* Masers and Lasers, 1967; papers on thermodynamics of polymerisation, thermal properties of polymers, effects of ionizing radiation, chemical thermodynamics, nucleation kinetics, thermal properties of transition metal compounds and gas kinetics. *Recreations:* golf, gardening. *Address:* 24 Beechwood Park, Boxmoor, Hemel Hempstead, Herts HP3 0DY. *Clubs:* Royal Commonwealth Society, Sloane.

MELINSKY, Rev. Canon (Michael Arthur) Hugh; Principal, Northern Ordination Course, since 1978; *b* 25 Jan. 1924; *s* of late M. M. Melinsky and Mrs D. M. Melinsky; *m* 1949, Renate (*née* Ruhemann); three *d*. *Educ:* Whitgift Sch., Croydon; Christ's Coll., Cambridge (BA 1947, MA 1949); London Univ. Inst. of Education (TDip 1949); Ripon Hall, Oxford. Asst Master: Normanton Grammar Sch., 1949–52; Lancaster Royal Grammar Sch., 1952–57. Curate: Wimborne Minster, 1957–59; Wareham, 1959–61; Vicar of St Stephen's, Norwich, 1961–68; Chaplain of Norfolk and Norwich Hosp., 1961–68; Hon. Canon and Canon Missioner of Norwich, 1968–73; Chief Sec., ACCM, 1973–77. Chairman: C of E Commn on Euthanasia, 1972–75; Inst. of Religion and Medicine, 1973–77; Mem., Social Policy Cttee, C of E Bd for Social Responsibilty, 1982–; Mem. Cttee for Theological Educn, ACCM, 1985–. Hon. Res. Fellow, Dept of Theol Studies, Manchester Univ., 1984. *Publications:* The Modern Reader's Guide to Matthew, 1963; the Modern Reader's Guide to Luke, 1963; Healing Miracles, 1967; (ed) Religion and Medicine, 1970; (ed) Religion and Medicine 2, 1973; Patterns of Ministry, 1974; (ed) On Dying Well, 1975; Foreword to Marriage, 1984. *Address:* 75 Framingham Road, Brooklands, Sale, Cheshire M33 3RH. *T:* 061–962 7513.

MELLAART, James, FSA; FBA 1980; Lecturer in Anatolian Archaeology, Institute of Archaeology, University of London, since 1964; *b* 14 Nov. 1925; *s* of J. H. J. Mellaart and A. D. Van Der Beek; *m* 1954, Arlette Meryem Cenani; one *s*. *Educ:* University College, London. BA Hons (Ancient Hist. and Egyptology) 1951. Archaeol field surveys in Anatolia as Scholar and Fellow of British Inst. of Archaeol. at Ankara, 1951–56; excavations at Hacilar, 1957–60; Asst Dir, British Inst. of Archaeol. at Ankara, 1959–61; excavations at Çatal Hüyük, Turkey, 1961–63 and 1965; Foreign Specialist, Lectr at Istanbul Univ., 1961–63. Corresp. Mem., German Archaeol Inst., 1961. *Publications:* Earliest Civilisations of the Near East, 1965; The Chalcolithic and Early Bronze Ages in the Near East and Anatolia, 1966; Çatal Hüyük, a Neolithic Town in Anatolia, 1967; Excavations at Hacilar, 1970; The Neolithic of the Near East, 1975; The Archaeology of Ancient Turkey, 1978; chapters in Cambridge Ancient History; numerous articles in Anatolian Studies, etc. *Recreations:* geology, Turkish ceramics, clan history, Gaelic and classical music, Seljuk art. *Address:* 13 Lichen Court, 79 Queen's Drive, N4 2BH. *T:* 01–802 6984.

MELLANBY, Kenneth, CBE 1954 (OBE 1945); ScD Cantab; ecological consultant and editor; *b* 26 March 1908; *s* of late Emeritus-Professor A. L. Mellanby; *m* 1933, Helen Neilson Dow, MD (marr. diss.); one *d*; *m* 1948, Jean Copeland, MA, JP; one *s*. *Educ:* Barnard Castle Sch.; King's Coll., Cambridge (Exhibitioner). Research Worker, London Sch. of Hygiene and Trop. Med., 1930–36 and 1953–55; Wandsworth Fellow, 1933; Sorby Research Fellow of Royal Society of London, 1936; Hon. Lecturer, University of Sheffield; CO (Sqdn Ldr RAFVR) Sheffield Univ. Air Sqdn. Dir Sorby Research Institute, 1941; first Principal, University Coll., Ibadan, Nigeria, 1947–53; Major, RAMC (Specialist in Biological Research), overseas service in N Africa, SE Asia, etc.; Dep. Dir, Scrub Typhus Research Laboratory, SEAC; Reader in Medical Entomology, University of London, 1945–47; Head of Dept of Entomology, Rothamsted Experimental Station, Harpenden, Herts, 1955–61; first Dir, Monks Wood Experimental Station, Huntingdon, 1961–74. Vice-Pres. and Mem. Council, Royal Entomological Soc. of London, 1953–56; Pres. Assoc. for Study of Animal Behaviour, 1957–60; Member: Inter-university Council for Higher Education Overseas, 1960–75; ARC Research Cttee on Toxic Chemicals; Council, and Chm., Tropical Group, Brit. Ecological Soc.; Nat. Exec., Cambs Br., CPRE (also Pres.); Council for Science and Technology Insts, 1976–77 (Chm.); Council for Environmental Science and Engrg, 1976– (Chm., 1981–); Pres., Sect. D (Zoology), 1972, and Sect. X (General), 1973, British Assoc.; Vice-Pres. of the Institute of Biology, 1967, Pres., 1972–73; Vice-Pres., Parly and Scientific Cttee; first Hon. Life Mem., Assoc. for Protection of Rural Australia. Hon. Professorial Fellow, University Coll. of S Wales; Hon. Prof. of Biology, Univ. of Leicester. Essex Hall Lectr, 1971. Fellow, NERC. Mem. Editorial Bd, New Naturalist series. Hon. Life Prof., Central London Polytechnic, 1980; DUniv Essex, 1980. Hon. DSc: Ibadan, 1963; Bradford, 1970; Leicester, 1972; Sheffield, 1983. First Charter Award, Inst. of Biology, 1981. *Publications:* Scabies, 1943, new edn 1973; Human Guinea Pigs, 1945, new edn 1973; The Birth of Nigeria's University, 1958, new edn 1975; Pesticides and Pollution, 1967; The Mole, 1971; The Biology of Pollution, 1972; Can Britain Feed Itself?, 1975; Talpa, the story of a mole, 1976; Farming and Wildlife, 1981; many scientific papers on insect physiology, ecology, medical and agricultural entomology; ed, Monographs on Biological Subjects; British Editor of Entomologia Experimentalis et Applicata; Editor, Environmental Pollution. *Recreation:* austere living. *Address:* 38 Warkworth Street, Cambridge CB1 1ER. *T:* Cambridge 328733. *Club:* Athenæum.

MELLERS, Prof. Wilfrid Howard, OBE 1982; DMus; Composer; Professor of Music, University of York, 1964–81, now Emeritus; *b* 26 April 1914; *s* of Percy Wilfrid Mellers and Hilda Maria (*née* Lawrence); *m* 1950, Peggy Pauline (*née* Lewis); two *d*. *Educ:* Leamington Coll.; Downing Coll., Cambridge. BA Cantab 1939; MA Cantab 1945; DMus Birmingham 1962. FGSM. Supervisor in English and College Lecturer in Music, Downing Coll., Cambridge, 1945–48; Staff Tutor in Music, Extra Mural Dept, University of Birmingham, 1949–60; Visiting Mellon Prof. of Music, University of Pittsburgh, USA, 1960–62; Vis. Prof., City Univ., 1984–. Hon. DPhil City, 1981. *Publications:* Music and Society, 1946; Studies in Contemporary Music, 1948; François Couperin and the French Classical Tradition, 1950, 2nd edn 1986; Music in the Making, 1951; Man and his Music, 1957; Harmonious Meeting, 1964; Music in a New Found Land, 1964; Caliban Reborn: renewal in 20th-century music, 1967 (US), 1968 (GB); Twilight of the Gods: the Beatles in retrospect, 1973; Bach and the Dance of God, 1981; Beethoven and the Voice of God, 1983; A Darker Shade of Pale: a backdrop to Bob Dylan, 1984; Angels of the Night: women jazz and pop singers in the Twentieth Century, 1986; The Masks of Orpheus, 1986; *compositions* include: Canticum Incarnations, 1960; Alba in 9 Metamorphoses, 1962; Rose of May, 1964; Life-Cycle, 1967; Yeibichai, 1968; Canticum Resurrectionis, 1968; Natalis Invicti Solis, 1969; The Word Unborn, 1970; The Ancient Wound, 1970; De Vegetabilis et Animalibus, 1971; Venery for Six Plus, 1971; Sunflower: the Quaternity of William Blake, 1972–73; The Key of the Kingdom, 1976; Rosae Hermeticae, 1977; Shaman Songs, 1980; The Wellspring of Loves, 1981; Hortus Rosarium, 1986. *Address:* 5 Wilmington House, Highbury Crescent, N5 1RU. *T:* 01–607 8889.

MELLERSH, Air Vice-Marshal Francis Richard Lee, CB 1977; DFC 1943 and Bar 1944; Air Officer Flying and Officer Training, HQ Training Command, 1974–77; *b* 30 July 1922; *s* of Air Vice-Marshal Sir Francis Mellersh, KBE, AFC; *m* 1967, Elisabeth Nathalie Komaroff; two *s* one *d*. *Educ:* Winchester House Sch.; Imperial Service College. Joined RAFVR, 1940; Nos 29, 600 and 96 Sqdns, 1941–45; various staff and flying appts, 1946–57; Dirg Staff, RAF Staff Coll., 1957–59; Staff of Chief of Defence Staff, 1959–61; Dep. Dir Ops (F), 1961–63; OC RAF West Raynham, 1965–67; Chief Current Plans, SHAPE, 1967–68; RCDS 1969; SASO, RAF Germany, 1970–72; ACDS (Ops), 1972–74. *Address:* Rother Lea, Lossenham Lane, Newenden, Kent. *Club:* Royal Air Force.

MELLING, Cecil Thomas, CBE 1955; MScTech, CEng, Hon. FIEE, FIMechE, Sen. FInstE, CBIM; *b* Wigan, 12 Dec. 1899; *s* of William and Emma Melling; *m* 1929, Ursula Thorburn Thorburn; two *s* one *d* (and one *s* and one *d* decd). *Educ:* Manchester Central High Sch.; College of Technology, University of Manchester. 2nd Lieut RE 1918. Metropolitan Vickers Electrical Co. Ltd, 1920–34; Yorkshire Electric Power Co., 1934–35; Edmundson's Electricity Corporation Ltd, 1935–43. Borough Electrical Engineer, Luton, 1943–48. Chm., Eastern Electricity Board, 1948–57; Member: British Electricity Authority, 1952–53 and 1957; Electricity Council, 1957–61 (a Dep. Chm., 1961–65); Clean Air Council, 1961–64; Adv. Cttee on R&D, 1961–64. Chm. Utilization Sect., Institution of Electrical Engineers, 1949–50, Vice-Pres., IEE, 1957–62, Pres., 1962–63; Chm. of Council, British Electrical Development Association, 1951–52; Founder-Chm. 1945, and Pres. 1947, Luton Electrical Soc.; Pres. Ipswich & District

Electrical Assoc., 1948–57; Chm. of Council, British Electrical and Allied Industries Research Assoc., 1953–55; Pres. Assoc. of Supervising Electrical Engineers, 1952–54; Chm., British Nat. Cttee for Electro-Heat, 1958–68; Mem. Council, BIM, 1961–78; Vice-Pres. Internat. Union for Electro-Heat, 1964–68, Pres., 1968–72; Pres., Manchester Technol. Assoc., 1967; Pres., British Electrotechnical Approvals Bd, 1974–84 (Chm., 1964–73); Chm., Electricity Supply Industry Trg Bd, 1965–68; Vice-Pres., Union of Internat. Engineering Organisations, 1969–75. Founder Chm., Soc. of Retired Chartered Engrs in SE Kent, 1982–83. *Publications:* contribs to Proc. Engineering Instns and Confs. *Address:* Durham, The Grand, Folkestone. *Club:* Athenæum.

MELLISH, family name of **Baron Mellish.**

MELLISH, Baron *cr* 1985 (Life Peer), of Bermondsey in Greater London; **Robert Joseph Mellish;** PC 1967; Deputy Chairman, London Docklands Development Corporation, since 1981; *b* 1913; *m*; five *s*. Served War of 1939–45, Captain RE, SEAC. Official, TGWU, 1938–46. MP (Lab 1946–82, Ind. 1982) Bermondsey, Rotherhithe 1946–50, Bermondsey 1950–74, Southwark, Bermondsey 1974–82. PPS to Minister of Pensions, 1951 (to Minister of Supply, 1950–51); Jt Parly Sec., Min. of Housing, 1964–67; Minister of Public Building and Works, 1967–69; Parly Sec. to Treasury and Govt Chief Whip, 1969–70 and 1974–76; Opposition Chief Whip, 1970–74. Chm., London Regional Lab. Party, 1956–77. *Address:* House of Lords, SW1.

MELLON, James, CMG 1979; HM Diplomatic Service; Director-General for Trade and Investment, USA, and Consul-General, New York, since 1986; *b* 25 Jan. 1929; *m* 1st, 1956, Frances Murray (*d* 1976); one *s* three *d*; 2nd, 1979, Mrs Philippa Shuttleworth (*née* Hartley). *Educ:* Glasgow Univ (MA). Dept of Agriculture for Scotland, 1953–60; Agricultural Attaché, Copenhagen and The Hague, 1960–63; FO, 1963–64; Head of Chancery, Dakar, 1964–66; UK Delegn to European Communities, 1967–72; Counsellor, 1970; Hd of Sci. and Technol. Dept, FCO, 1973–75; Commercial Counsellor, East Berlin, 1975–76; Head of Trade Relations and Export Dept, FCO, 1976–78; High Comr in Ghana and Ambassador to Togo, 1978–83; Ambassador to Denmark, 1983–86. *Address:* c/o Foreign and Commonwealth Office, SW1. *Club:* Travellers'.

MELLON, Paul, Hon. KBE 1974; Hon. RA 1978; Trustee, National Gallery of Art, Washington, DC, since 1945 (President, 1963–79; Chairman, 1979–); *b* 11 June 1907; *s* of late Andrew William Mellon and late Nora McMullen Mellon; *m* 1st, 1935, Mary Conover (decd); one *s* one *d*; 2nd, 1948, Rachel Lambert. *Educ:* Choate Sch., Wallingford, Conn; Yale Univ.; Univ. of Cambridge (BA 1931; MA 1938; Hon. LLD 1983). Trustee: Andrew W. Mellon Foundn (successor to merged Old Dominion and Avalon Foundns), 1969–; A. W. Mellon Educational and Charitable Trust, Pittsburgh, 1930–; Trustee, Virginia Mus. of Fine Arts, Richmond, Va, 1938–68, 1969–79. Member: Amer. Philosophical Soc., Philadelphia, 1971; Grolier Soc.; Soc. of Dilettanti; Roxburghe Club. Hon. Citizen, University of Vienna, 1965. Yale Medal, 1953; Horace Marden Albright Scenic Preservation Medal, 1957; Distinguished Service to Arts Award, Nat. Inst. Arts and Letters, 1962; Benjamin Franklin Medal, Royal Society of Arts, 1965, Benjamin Franklin Fellow, 1969; Alumni Seal Prize Award, Choate Sch., 1966; Skowhegan Gertrude Vanderbilt Whitney Award, 1972; Horserace Writers' and Reporters' Assoc. award (owner), 1982. Hon. FRIBA 1978. Hon. DLitt, Oxford Univ., 1961; Hon. LLD, Carnegie Inst. of Tech., 1967; Hon. DHL, Yale, 1967. *Recreations:* fox-hunting, thoroughbred breeding and racing, sailing, swimming. *Address:* (office) 1729 H Street NW, Washington, DC 20006, USA; (home) Oak Spring, Upperville, Va 22176. *Clubs:* Buck's; Travellers (Paris); Jockey, Knickerbocker, Links, Racquet and Tennis, River, Yale (New York); Metropolitan, 1925 F Street (Washington).

MELLOR, David, OBE 1981; DesRCA; RDI 1962; FSIAD; designer, manufacturer and retailer; Chairman, Crafts Council, 1982–84; *b* 5 Oct. 1930; *s* of Colin Mellor; *m* 1966, Fiona MacCarthy; one *s* one *d*. *Educ:* Sheffield College of Art; Royal College of Art (DesRCA and Silver Medal, 1953, Hon. Fellow 1966); British School at Rome. Set up silver-smithing workshop, Sheffield, 1954; designer and maker of silver for Worshipful Co. of Goldsmiths, Cutlers' Co., Southwell Minster, Essex Univ., Darwin Coll., Cambridge, among others, and range of silver tableware for use in British embassies; designer of fountain in bronze for Botanic Gdns, Cambridge, 1970; concurrently opened industrial design office. Consultancies, 1954–, include: Walker & Hall, Abacus Municipal, Glacier Metal, ITT, Post Office, British Rail, James Neill Tools; Cons. to DoE on design of traffic signals, 1965–70, and on design of automatic half-barrier crossing, as result of Gibbens report, 1969; Chm., Design Council Cttee of Inquiry into standards of design in consumer goods in Britain, 1982–84, Mem., Art and Design Working Gp, Nat. Adv. Body for Local Auth. Higher Educn, 1982–84. Trustee, V & A Museum, 1984–. *Work in collections:* Goldsmiths' Co., V&A, Sheffield City Mus., Mus. of Modern Art, NY. *Exhibitions:* Stedjelick Mus., Amsterdam, 1968; Nat. Mus. of Wales, 1972. Designer for retrospective exhibn A Century of British Design 1880–1980, 1979. *Awards:* Design Centre: 1957, 1959, 1962, 1965, 1966; Design Council: 1974, 1977; RSA Presidential Award for Design Management, 1981. Liveryman, Goldsmiths' Co., 1980; Freeman, Cutlers' Co. of Hallamshire, 1981. FSIAD 1964. Hon. Fellow, Sheffield City Polytechnic, 1979; Hon. DLitt Sheffield Univ., 1986. *Address:* Broom Hall, Broomhall Road, Sheffield S10 2DU. *T:* Sheffield 664124.

MELLOR, Prof. David Hugh, FBA 1983; Professor of Philosophy, University of Cambridge, since 1986; Vice-Master, Darwin College, Cambridge, since 1983; *b* 10 July 1938; *s* of Sydney David Mellor and Ethel Naomi Mellor (*née* Hughes). *Educ:* Manchester Grammar School; Pembroke College, Cambridge (BA Nat. Scis and Chem. Eng, 1960; MA; PhD 1968); Univ. of Minnesota (Harkness Fellowship; MSc Chem. Eng, 1962). Technical Officer, ICI Central Instruments Lab., 1962–63; Research Student in Philosophy, Pembroke Coll., 1963–68; Fellow, Pembroke Coll., 1965–70; Fellow, Darwin Coll., Cambridge, 1971–; Univ. Asst Lectr in Philosophy, 1965–70, Univ. Lectr in Philosophy, 1970–83; Univ. Reader in Metaphysics, 1983–85. Vis. Fellow in Philosophy, ANU, 1975; Radcliffe Trust Fellow in Philosophy, 1978–80. Pres., British Soc. for the Philos. of Science, 1985–86. Editor: British Journal for the Philosophy of Science, 1968–70; Cambridge Studies in Philosophy, 1978–82. *Publications:* The Matter of Chance, 1971; Real Time, 1981; articles in Mind, Analysis, Philosophy of Science, Philosophy, Philosophical Review, Ratio, Isis, British Jl for Philosophy of Science. *Recreation:* theatre. *Address:* 25 Orchard Street, Cambridge CB1 1JS. *T:* Cambridge 65979.

MELLOR, David John; MP (C) Putney, since 1979; Minister of State, Home Office, since 1986; *b* 12 March 1949; *s* of Mr and Mrs Douglas H. Mellor; *m* 1974, Judith Mary Hall; two *s*. *Educ:* Swanage Grammar Sch.; Christ's Coll., Cambridge (BA Hons 1970). FZS 1981. Called to the Bar, Inner Temple, 1972; in practice thereafter. Chm., Cambridge Univ. Conservative Assoc., 1970; contested West Bromwich E, Oct. 1974. PPS to Leader of Commons and Chancellor of the Duchy of Lancaster, 1981; Parly Under-Sec. of State, Dept of Energy, 1981–83, Home Office, 1983–86. Sec., Cons. Parly Legal Cttee, 1979–81; Vice-Chm., Greater London Cons. Members Cttee, 1980–81. Special Trustee, Westminster Hosp., 1980–; Mem. Council, NYO, 1981–. *Recreations:* classical music, reading, football. *Address:* House of Commons, SW1. *T:* 01–219 5481.

MELLOR, Derrick, CBE 1984; HM Diplomatic Service; retired; re-employed at Foreign and Commonwealth Office, since 1984; *b* 11 Jan. 1926; *s* of William Mellor and Alice (*née* Hurst); *m* 1954, Kathleen (*née* Hodgson); two *s* one *d*. Served Army, 1945–49. Board of Trade, 1950–57; Trade Commission Service, 1958–64: served Kuala Lumpur and Sydney; HM Diplomatic Service, 1964–: served Copenhagen, Caracas, Asuncion and London. *Recreations:* tennis, golf, skiing. *Address:* 91 Frant Road, Tunbridge Wells, Kent. *T:* Tunbridge Wells 30117. *Clubs:* Royal Commonwealth Society, Travellers'.

MELLOR, Hugh Wright; Secretary and Director, National Corporation for Care of Old People (now Centre for Policy on Ageing), 1973–80; *b* 11 Aug. 1920; *s* of William Algernon and Katherine Mildred Mellor; *m* 1944, Winifred Joyce Yates. *Educ:* Leys Sch., Cambridge; London Univ. (BScEcon). Friends Relief Service, 1940–45; Sec., St Albans Council of Social Service, 1945–48; Community Develt Officer, Hemel Hempstead Develt Corp., 1948–50; Asst Sec., Nat. Corp. for Care of Old People, 1951–73. Chm., Hanover Housing Assoc., 1980–85. *Publication:* The Role of Voluntary Organisations in Social Welfare, 1985. *Recreations:* walking, reading, music. *Address:* Lark Rise, Risborough Road, Great Kimble, Aylesbury, Bucks HP17 0XS. *Club:* Royal Commonwealth Society.

MELLOR, Brig. James Frederick McLean, CBE 1964 (OBE 1945); Norfolk County Commandant, Army Cadet Force, 1969–72; *b* 6 June 1912; *s* of late Col A. J. Mellor, RM, Kingsland, Hereford; *m* 1942, Margaret Ashley, *d* of Major F. A. Phillips, DSO, Holmer, Hereford; one *s* one *d*. *Educ:* Radley Coll.; Faraday House. C. A. Parsons, 1933; Yorkshire Electric Power, 1935. Commnd in Regular Army as Ordnance Mechanical Engr, 1936; France, Belgium, Dunkirk, 1940; Burma, Malaya, HQ, SEAC, 1944–47 (despatches, 1945); Brig. A/Q Northern Comd, 1961–64; Dir of Technical Trng and Inspector of Boys' Trng (Army), MoD, 1966–69; ADC to the Queen, 1963–69. Various appts in engineering and technical educn. Chm., IMechE Eastern Branch, 1971–72. DFH, FIMechE, FIEE. *Address:* Pinewood, Saxlingham Road, Blakeney, Holt, Norfolk NR25 7PB. *T:* Cley 740990. *Clubs:* Naval and Military, Royal Automobile; Norfolk (Norwich).

MELLOR, Sir John Francis, 3rd Bt *cr* 1924, of Culmhead, Somerset; accountant; *b* 9 March 1925; *s* of Sir John Serocold Paget Mellor, 2nd Bt and of Rachel Margaret, *d* of Sir Herbert Frederick Cook, 3rd Bt; *S* father, 1986; *m* 1948, Alix Marie, *d* of late Charles François Villaret. *Educ:* Eton. Served War of 1939–45 with RASC and Intelligence Corps. *Heir:* none.

MELLOR, John Walter; a Recorder of the Crown Court, 1972–74 and 1978–82; *b* 24 Sept. 1927; *s* of William Mellor and Ruth (*née* Tolson); *m* 1957, Freda Mary (*née* Appleyard); one *s* three *d*. *Educ:* Grammar Sch., Batley; Leeds Univ. (LLB). Called to Bar, Gray's Inn, 1953. *Recreations:* golf, sailing, visiting West Cork. *Address:* 171 Scotchman Lane, Morley, Leeds, W Yorks. *T:* Morley 4093. *Clubs:* Morley Rugby Union; Crookhaven Yacht.

MELLOR, Kenneth Wilson, QC 1975; **His Honour Judge Mellor;** a Circuit Judge, since 1984; *m* 1957, Sheila Gale; one *s* three *d*. *Educ:* King's College Cambridge (MA, LLB). RNVR (Sub Lieut). Called to the Bar, Lincoln's Inn, 1950. Dep. Chm., Hereford QS, 1969–71; a Recorder, 1972–84. Chm., Agricultural Land Tribunal (West Midlands). *Address:* 5 Fountain Court, Steelhouse Lane, Birmingham B4 6DR; 1 Paper Buildings, Temple, EC4.

MELLOR, Ronald William, CBE 1984; FEng; FIMechE; Executive Director, Product Development, Ford Motor Co., since 1985; *b* 8 Dec. 1930; *s* of William and Helen Edna Mellor; *m* 1956, Jean Sephton; one *s* one *d*. *Educ:* Highgate School; King's College London (BSc Eng). Ford Motor Co.: Manager Cortina Product Planning, 1964; Manager Truck Product Planning, 1965; Chief Research Engineer, 1969; Chief Engine Engineer, 1970; Chief Body Engineer, Ford Werke AG, W Germany, 1974; Vice Pres. Car Engineering, Ford of Europe Inc., 1975; Dir, Ford Motor Co., 1983. Thomas Hawksley Lectr, IMechE, 1983. *Recreation:* yachting. *Address:* Ford Motor Co. Ltd, R & E Centre, Laindon, Basildon, Essex SS15 6EE. *T:* Basildon 403000. *Club:* Haven Ports Yacht (Levington).

MELLOWS, Prof. Anthony Roger, TD 1969; PhD, LLD; Solicitor of the Supreme Court, and Professor of the Law of Property in the University of London, since 1974; Head of Department of Laws, King's College, London, since 1984; *b* 30 July 1936; *s* of L. B. and M. P. Mellows; *m* 1973, Elizabeth, *d* of Ven. B. G. B. Fox, MC, TD, and of Hon. Margaret Joan Fox, *d* of 1st Viscount Davidson, PC, GCVO, CH, CB. *Educ:* King's Coll., London. LLB 1957; LLM 1959; PhD 1962; BD 1968; LLD 1973; Fellow 1980. Commissioned Intelligence Corps (TA), 1959, Captain 1964; served Intell. Corps (TA) and (T&AVR) and on the Staff, 1959–71; RARO, 1971–. Admitted a solicitor, 1960; private practice, 1960–; Sen. Partner, Messrs Alexanders. Chm., London Law International Ltd, 1973–; Dep. Chm., James Wilkes PLC, 1982–. Asst Lectr in Law, King's Coll., London, 1962, Lectr, 1964, Reader, 1971; Dir of Conveyancing Studies, 1969; Dean, Fac. of Laws, Univ. of London, 1981–84, and of Fac. of Laws, KCL, 1981–85; Mem. Council, KCL, 1972–80; Trustee: Kincardine Foundn, 1972–84; Nineveh Trust, 1985–; London Law Trust, 1968– (Chm. Trustees). AKC, London, 1957; FRSA 1959. CStJ 1985 (OStJ 1981; Mem. Council, 1981–). Freeman of the City of London, 1963. *Publications:* Local Searches and Enquiries, 1964, 2nd edn 1967; Conveyancing Searches, 1964, 2nd edn 1975; Land Charges, 1966; The Preservation and Felling of Trees, 1964; The Trustee's Handbook, 1965, 3rd edn 1975; Taxation for Executors and Trustees, 1967, 6th edn 1984; (jtly) The Modern Law of Trusts, 1966, 5th edn 1983; The Law of Succession, 1970, 4th edn 1983; Taxation of Land Transactions, 1973, 3rd edn 1982. *Address:* 22 Devereux Court, Temple Bar, WC2R 3JJ. *Club:* Athenæum.

MELLY, (Alan) George (Heywood); professional jazz singer; with John Chilton's Feetwarmers, since 1974; *b* 17 Aug. 1926; *s* of Francis Heywood and Edith Maud Melly; *m* 1955, Victoria Vaughan (marr. diss. 1962); one *d*; *m* 1963, Diana Margaret Campion Dawson; one *s* and one step *d*. *Educ:* Stowe School. Able Seaman, RN, 1944–47. Art Gallery Asst, London Gallery, 1948–50; sang with Mick Mulligan's Jazz Band, 1949–61. Wrote Flook strip cartoon balloons (drawn by Trog (Wally Fawkes)), 1956–71. Critic, The Observer: pop music, 1965–67; TV, 1967–71; films, 1971–73. Film scriptwriter: Smashing Time, 1968; Take a Girl Like You, 1970. Pres., British Humanist Assoc., 1972–74. Critic of the Year, IPC Nat. Press Awards, 1970. *Publications:* I Flook, 1962; Owning Up, 1965; Revolt into Style, 1970; Flook by Trog, 1970; Rum Bum and Concertina, 1977; (with Barry Fantoni) The Media Mob, 1980; Tribe of One: Great Naive and Primitive Painters of the British Isles, 1981; (with Walter Dorin) Great Lovers, 1981; Mellymobile, 1982; (ed) Edward James, Swans Reflecting Elephants: my early years, 1982; Scouse Mouse, 1984; It's All Writ Out for You: the life and work of Scottie Wilson, 1986. *Recreations:* trout fishing, singing and listening to blues of 1920s, collecting modern paintings. *Address:* 33 St Lawrence Terrace, W10 5SR. *Clubs:* Colony Room, Chelsea Arts.

MELMOTH, Christopher George Frederick Frampton, CMG 1959; South Asia Department, International Bank for Reconstruction and Development, 1962–75, retired; *b* 25 Sept. 1912; *s* of late George Melmoth and Florence Melmoth; *m* 1946, Maureen Joan (*née* Brennan); three *d*. *Educ:* Sandringham Sch., Forest Gate. Accountant Officer, Co-ordination of Supplies Fund, Malta, 1942–45; Administrative Officer, Hong Kong, 1946–55; Minister of Finance, Uganda, 1956–62. *Recreations:* tennis, golf, walking. *Address:* Hoptons Field, Kemerton, Tewkesbury, Glos.

MELONEY, Mrs W. B.; *see* Franken, Rose.

MELROSE, Prof. Denis Graham; Professor of Surgical Science, Royal Postgraduate Medical School, 1968–83, Emeritus since 1983; *b* 20 June 1921; *s* of late Thomas Robert Gray Melrose, FRCS and Floray Collings; *m* 1945, Ann, *d* of late Kathleen Tatham Warter; two *s*. *Educ:* Sedbergh Sch.; University Coll., Oxford; UCH London. MA, BM, BCh, MRCP, FRCS. Junior appts at Hammersmith Hosp. and Redhill County Hosp., Edgware, 1945; RNVR, 1946–48; subseq. Lectr, later Reader, Royal Postgrad. Med. Sch.; Nuffield Travelling Fellow, USA, 1956; Fulbright Fellow, 1957; Associate in Surgery, Stanford Univ. Med. Sch., 1958. *Publications:* numerous papers in learned jls and chapters in books, particularly on heart surgery, heart lung machine and med. engrg. *Recreations:* sailing, ski-ing. *Address:* 62 Belvedere Court, Upper Richmond Road, SW15. *Club:* Royal Naval Sailing Association.

MELVILL JONES, Prof. Geoffrey, FRS 1979; FRSC 1979; FCASI; FRAeS; Hosmer Research Professor of Physiology, McGill University, Montreal, since 1978 (Associate Professor, 1961–68, Full Professor, since 1968); Director, Aerospace (formerly Aviation) Medical Research Unit, McGill University, since 1961; *b* 14 Jan. 1923; *s* of Sir Bennett Melvill Jones, CBE, AFC, FRS and Dorothy Laxton Jotham; *m* 1953, Jenny Marigold Burnaby; two *s* two *d*. *Educ:* King's Choir Sch.; Dauntsey's Sch.; Cambridge Univ. (BA, MA, MB, BCh). Appointments in UK, 1950–61: House Surgeon, Middlesex Hosp., 1950; Sen. Ho. Surg., Otolaryngology, Addenbrooke's Hosp., Cambridge, 1950–51; MO, RAF, 1951; Scientific MO, RAF Inst. of Aviation Medicine, Farnborough, Hants, 1951–55; Scientific Officer (external staff), Medical Research Council of Gt Britain, 1955–61. Fellow, Aerospace Medical Assoc., 1969; FCASI 1965; FRAeS 1981. *Publications:* Mammalian Vestibular Physiology, 1979 (NY); Adaptive Mechanisms in Gaze Control, 1985; research papers in physiological jls. *Recreations:* outdoor activities, music. *Address:* Aerospace Medical Research Unit, McGill University, Room 1223, McIntyre Building, 3655 Drummond Street, Montreal, Quebec H3G 1Y6, Canada. *T:* (514) 392–4217.

MELVILLE; *see* Leslie Melville, family name of Earl of Leven and Melville.

MELVILLE, 9th Viscount *cr* 1802; **Robert David Ross Dundas**; Baron Duneira 1802; *b* 28 May 1937; *s* of Hon. Robert Maldred St John Melville Dundas (2nd *s* of 7th Viscount) (killed in action, 1940), and of Margaret Connell (who *m* 2nd, 1946, Gerald Bristowe Sanderson), *d* of late Percy Cruden Ross; *S* uncle, 1971; *m* 1982, Fiona Margaret Stilgoe, *d* of late Roger and of Mrs Stilgoe, Stogumber, Som; two *s*. *Educ:* Wellington College. District Councillor, Lasswade, Midlothian; Mem., Midlothian CC, 1964–67. Pres., Lasswade Civic Soc. Lieutenant, Ayrshire Yeomanry; Captain (Reserve), Scots Guards. *Recreations:* fishing, shooting, golf, chess. *Heir:* *s* Hon. Robert Henry Kirkpatrick Dundas, *b* 23 April 1984. *Address:* Solomon's Court, Chalford, near Stroud, Glos. *T:* Brimscombe 882128; 3 Roland Way, Fulham, SW7. *Clubs:* Cavalry and Guards, Turf; House of Lords Motor; Midlothian County; Bonnyrigg and District Ex-Servicemen's.

MELVILLE, Anthony Edwin; Headmaster, The Perse School, Cambridge, 1969–Aug. 1987; *b* 28 April 1929; *yr s* of Sir Leslie Melville, *qv*; *m* 1964, Pauline Marianne Surtees Simpson, *d* of Major A. F. Simpson, Indian Army; two *d*. *Educ:* Sydney Church of England Grammar Sch.; Univ. of Sydney (BA); King's Coll., Cambridge (MA). Sydney Univ. Medal in English, 1950; Pt II History Tripos, 1st cl. with dist., 1952; Lightfoot Schol. in Eccles. History, 1954. Asst Master, Haileybury Coll., 1953. *Recreations:* reading, gardening. *Address:* 80 Glebe Road, Cambridge. *T:* Cambridge 247964. *Club:* East India, Devonshire, Sports and Public Schools.

MELVILLE, Sir Eugene, KCMG 1965 (CMG 1952); HM Diplomatic Service, retired; Director-General, British Property Federation, 1974–80; *b* 15 Dec. 1911; *s* of George E. Melville; *m* 1937, Elizabeth, *d* of Chas M. Strachan, OBE; two *s* one *d*. *Educ:* Queen's Park Sch., Glasgow; St Andrews Univ. (Harkness Residential Scholar; 1st cl. Hons Classics; 1st cl. Hons Economics). Appointed to Colonial Office, 1936; Colonies Supply Mission, Washington, 1941–45; PS to Sec. of State for Colonies, 1945–46; Financial Adviser, Control Commission for Germany, 1949–52; Asst Under-Sec. of State, Colonial Office, 1952; Asst Under-Sec. of State, Foreign Office, 1961; Minister (Economic), Bonn, 1962–65; Permanent UK Delegate to EFTA and GATT, 1965; Ambassador and Permanent UK Representative to UN and other Internat. Organisations at Geneva, 1966–71; Special Advr, Channel Tunnel Studies, 1971–73. Sec-Gen., Malta Round Table Conf., 1955; Hon. Treasurer, British Sailors' Soc.; Chm., Aldeburgh Festival, Snape Maltings Foundn, 1976–81, Pres., 1981–86. *Address:* Longcroft, Aldeburgh, Suffolk. *Club:* Reform.

MELVILLE, Sir Harry (Work), KCB 1958; FRS 1941; FRSC; PhD Edinburgh and Cantab; DSc Edinburgh; MSc Birmingham; Principal, Queen Mary College, University of London, 1967–76; *b* 27 April 1908; *s* of Thomas and Esther Burnett Melville; *m* 1942, Janet Marian, *d* of late Hugh Porteous and Sarah Cameron; two *d*. *Educ:* George Heriot's Sch., Edinburgh; Edinburgh Univ. (Carnegie Res. Scholar); Trinity Coll., Cambridge (1851 Exhibitioner). Fellow of Trinity College, Cambridge, 1933–44. Meldola Medal, Inst. of Chemistry, 1936; Davy Medal, Royal Society, 1955; Colwyn Medal, Instn of the Rubber Industry. Asst Dir, Colloid Science Laboratory, Cambridge, 1938–40; Prof. of Chemistry, Univ. of Aberdeen, 1940–48; Scientific Adviser to Chief Superintendent Chemical Defence, Min. of Supply, 1940–43; Superintendent, Radar Res. Station, 1943–45; Mason Prof. of Chemistry, Univ. of Birmingham, 1948–56. Chief Scientific Adviser for Civil Defence, Midlands Region, 1952–56; Bakerian Lecture, Royal Society, 1956. Member: Min. of Aviation Scientific Adv. Council, 1949–51; Adv. Council, Dept of Scientific and Industrial Res., 1946–51; Res. Council, British Electricity Authority, 1949–56; Royal Commn on Univ. Educn in Dundee, 1951–52; Res. Council, DSIR, 1961–65; Chm., Adv. Council on Research and Develt, DTI, 1970–74; Member: Nuclear Safety Adv. Cttee, DTI, 1972–; Cttee of Managers, Royal Institution, 1976–; Sec. to Cttee of the Privy Council for Scientific and Industrial Research, 1956–65; Chm., SRC, 1965–67. Mem., London Electricity Bd, 1968–75. Mem., Parly and Scientific Cttee, 1971–75; Pres., Plastics Inst., 1970–75. Hon. LLD Aberdeen; Hon. DCL Kent; Hon. DSc: Exeter; Birmingham; Liverpool; Leeds; Heriot-Watt; Essex; Hon. DTech Bradford. *Publications:* papers in Proceedings of Royal Society, etc. *Address:* Norwood, Dodds Lane, Chalfont St Giles, Bucks. *T:* 2222. *Club:* Athenæum.

MELVILLE, James; *see* Martin, R. P.

MELVILLE, Sir Leslie Galfreid, KBE 1957 (CBE 1953); Member of the Board of the Reserve Bank, Australia, 1959–63, and 1965–74; Member, Commonwealth Grants Commission, 1979–82 (Chairman, 1966–74); *b* 26 March 1902; *s* of Richard Ernest Melville and Lilian Evelyn Thatcher; *m* 1925, Mary Maud Scales; two *s*. *Educ:* Sydney Church of England Grammar Sch. Bachelor of Economics, University of Sydney, 1925; Public Actuary of South Australia, 1924–28; Prof. of Economics, University of Adelaide, 1929–31; Economic Adviser to Commonwealth Bank of Australia, 1931–49; Asst Gov. (Central Banking) Commonwealth Bank of Australia, 1949–53; Mem. of Commonwealth Bank Bd, 1951–53; Exec. Dir of International Monetary Fund and International Bank for Reconstruction and Development, 1950–53. Mem. of Cttees on Australian Finances and Unemployment, 1931 and 1932; Financial Adviser to Australian Delegates at Imperial Economic Conference, 1932; Financial Adviser to Australian Delegate at World Economic Conference, 1933; Mem. of Financial and Economic Advisory Cttee, 1939; Chm. of Australian Delegation to United Nations Monetary Conf. at Bretton Woods, 1944; Mem. of Advisory Council of Commonwealth Bank, 1945–51; Chm. UN Sub-Commn on Employment and Economic Stability, 1947–50; Member: Immigration Planning Council, 1956–61; Develt Adv. Service of Internat. Bank, 1963–65; Chm. of Tariff Bd, Australia, 1960–62; Chm., Tariff Adv. Cttee of Papua and New Guinea, 1969–71. Vice-Chancellor Australian National Univ., Canberra, ACT, 1953–60. Hon. LLD: Toronto, 1958; ANU, 1978; Hon. DSc Econ Sydney, 1980. *Address:* 71 Stonehaven Crescent, Canberra, ACT 2600, Australia. *Club:* Commonwealth.

See also A. E. Melville.

MELVILLE, Sir Ronald (Henry), KCB 1964 (CB 1952); *b* 9 March 1912; *e s* of Henry Edward Melville; *m* 1940, Enid Dorcas Margaret, *d* of late Harold G. Kenyon, Ware; two *s* one *d*. *Educ:* Charterhouse; Magdalene Coll., Cambridge. 1st Class Classical Tripos, Pts I and II, Charles Oldham Scholarship. Entered Air Ministry, 1934; Private Sec. to Chief of Air Staff, 1936, to Sec. of State, 1940; Asst Under-Sec., 1946; Dep. Under-Sec., 1958; Dep. Under-Sec., War Office, 1960–63; Second Permanent Under-Sec. of State, Ministry of Defence, 1963–66; Permanent Sec., Ministry of Aviation, 1966; Permanent Sec., attached Civil Service Dept, 1971–72; Director: Electronic Components Industry Fedn, 1972–81; Westland Aircraft, 1974–83. Chairman: Nat. Rifle Assoc., 1972–84 (Captain, GB Rifle Team, touring USA and Canada, 1976, and for Kolapore match in UK, 1977); Jt Shooting Cttee for GB, 1985–; Pres., Herts Rifle Assoc., 1960–; Member Council: Herts TAA, 1960–80; Herts Soc., 1963–; ACFA, 1972–84. *Recreations:* rifle shooting, painting, bird-watching, gardening. *Address:* The Old Rose and Crown, Braughing, Ware, Herts. *Club:* Brooks's.

MELVILLE-ROSS, Timothy David; Director and Chief General Manager, Nationwide Building Society, since 1985; *b* 3 Oct. 1944; *s* of Antony Stuart Melville-Ross and Anne Barclay Fane; *m* 1967, Camilla Mary Harlackenden; two *s* one *d*. *Educ:* Uppingham School; Portsmouth College of Technology (Dip Business Studies, 2nd cl. hons). FCIS; CBIM. British Petroleum, 1963–73; Rowe, Swann & Co., stockbrokers, 1973–74; Nationwide Building Society, 1974–. FRSA. *Recreations:* music, reading, bridge, tennis, the countryside. *Address:* Little Bevills, Bures, Suffolk CO8 5JN. *T:* Bures 227424.

MELVIN, Air Cdre James Douglas, CB 1956; OBE 1947; idc 1956; retired; Property Manager, Coutts & Co.; *b* 20 Feb. 1914; *s* of William Adamson Melvin, The Square, Turriff, Aberdeenshire, and Agnes Fyffe, The Hunghar, Kirriemuir; *m* 1946, Mary Wills; one *d* (one *s* decd). *Educ:* Turriff Secondary Sch. Apprentice, Halton, 1930; Cadet, Cranwell, 1933. Dep. Dir Organization, Air Ministry, 1951–53; Group Capt. Organization, MEAF, 1953–55; Dir of Organization, Air Ministry, 1957–61, retd. *Address:* Kyrenia Cottage, Old Bosham, Sussex. *Club:* Royal Air Force.

MELVIN, John Turcan, TD and star; MA Cantab; *b* 19 March 1916; *m* 1951, Elizabeth Ann Parry-Jones; one *s* three *d*. *Educ:* Stowe Sch.; Trinity Coll., Cambridge; Berlin Univ. (Schol.). Asst Master, Sherborne Sch., 1938. Served with Dorset Regt, 1939–46. Housemaster, Sherborne Sch., 1950; Headmaster, Kelly Coll., 1959–72; Hd of German Dept, Foster's Sch., 1972–75; Sixth Form Tutor, Sherborne Sch., 1975–82. Governor: Hall Sch. Trust, Wincanton; St Francis Sch., Hook. *Recreations:* walking, reading, tennis, dramatics. *Address:* Culverhayes Lodge, Sherborne, Dorset. *Club:* English-Speaking Union.

MELVYN HOWE, Prof. George; *see* Howe, Prof. G. M.

MENAUL, Air Vice-Marshal Stewart William Blacker, CB 1963; CBE 1957; DFC 1941; AFC 1942; Defence Consultant: Institute for Study of Conflict; Institute for Foreign Policy Analysis, Cambridge, Mass; *b* 17 July 1915; 2nd *s* of late Captain W. J. Menaul, MC, and Mrs M. Menaul, Co. Armagh, N Ireland; *m* 1943, Hélène Mary, *d* of late F. R. Taylor; one *s* one *d*. *Educ:* Portadown; RAF Coll., Cranwell. Bomber Command Squadrons, 1936–39; on outbreak of war serving with No 21 Sqdn until 1940; Flying Instructor, 1940–41; No 15 Sqdn, 1941–42; Air Staff No 3 Gp, Bomber Command, 1943; Pathfinder Force, 1943–45; RAF Staff Coll., 1946; Air Ministry, 1947–49; Imperial Defence Coll., 1950–51; Air Ministry, Dep. Dir of Operations, 1951–54; Comd British Atomic Trials Task Forces, Monte Bello and Maralinga (Australia), 1955–56; Commanding Officer, Bombing Sch., Lindholme, 1957–58; Air Officer Administration, Aden, 1959–60; Senior Air Staff Officer, Headquarters Bomber Command, 1961–65; Commandant, Joint Services Staff Coll., 1965–67; Dir-Gen., RUSI, 1968–76. *Publications:* Soviet War Machine, 1980; Countdown: Britain's strategic nuclear forces, 1980. *Recreations:* ornithology, painting. *Address:* The Lodge, Frensham Vale, Lower Bourne, Farnham, Surrey. *Club:* Royal Air Force.

MENDE, Dr Erich; Member of the Bundestag, German Federal Republic, 1949–80; *b* 28 Oct. 1916; *m* 1948, Margot (*née* Hattje); three *s* one *d*. *Educ:* Humane Coll., Gross-Strehlitz; Universities of Cologne and Bonn (Dr jur). Military service in Infantry Regt 84, Gleiwitz. Served War of 1939–45, Comdr of a Regt (wounded twice, prisoner of war); Major, 1944. Co-founder of FDP (Free Democratic Party), 1945; Mem. Exec. Cttee, British Zone, FDP, 1947; Parliamentary Group of FDP: Whip, and Mem. Exec. Cttee, 1950–53; Dep. Chm., 1953; Chm., 1957; Chm. of FDP, 1960–68; joined CDU, 1970. Vice-Chancellor and Minister for All-German Affairs, Federal Republic of Germany, 1963–66. Mem., CDU Hessen, 1970. *Publications:* autobiography: Das verdammte Gewissen 1921–1945, 1982; Die neue Freiheit 1945–1961, 1984; Von Wende zu Wende 1962–1982, 1986. *Address:* Am Stadtwald 62, 53 Bonn 2, Germany.

MENDIS, Vernon Lorraine Benjamin; Chairman, Sri Lanka Telecommunications Board, Colombo, since 1985; *b* 5 Dec. 1925; *m* 1953, Padma Rajapathirana; one *s*. *Educ:* Univ. of Ceylon (BA Hons History, 1948). Post Grad. Master of Philosophy, Sch. of Oriental and African Studies, Univ. of London, 1966; PhD Colombo Univ., 1986. High Commissioner for Sri Lanka: in Canada, 1974–75; in UK, 1975–77; Ambassador for Republic of Sri Lanka in France, 1978–80; UNESCO Rep. in Egypt and Sudan, 1980–85. *Publications:* The Advent of the British to Ceylon 1760–1815, 1971; Currents of Asian History, 1981; Foreign Relations of Sri Lanka, earliest times to 1965, 1982; British Governors and Colonial Policy in Sri Lanka. *Recreations:* hiking, bird watching. *Address:* Office of the Chairman, Sri Lanka Telecommunications Board, c/o Ministry of Posts & Telecommunications, Lotus Road, Colombo 1, Sri Lanka. *Club:* Travellers'.

MENDL, James Henry Embleton; His Honour Judge Mendl; a Circuit Judge since 1974; *b* 23 Oct. 1927; *s* of late R. W. S. Mendl, barrister and author, and of Dorothy Williams Mendl (*née* Burnett), and *g s* of late Sir S. F. Mendl, KBE; *m* 1971, Helena Augusta Maria Schrama, *d* of late J. H. and H. H. Schrama-Jekat, The Netherlands. *Educ:* Harrow; University Coll., Oxford (MA). Called to Bar, Inner Temple, 1953; South Eastern Circuit. Commissioned, Worcestershire Regt, 1947; served: Egypt, with 2nd N

Staffs, 1947–48; with Royal Signals (TA), 1952–54, and Queen's Royal Regt (TA) (Captain, 1955), 1954–56. Councillor, Royal Borough of Kensington and Chelsea, 1964–74 (Vice-Chm., Town Planning Cttee, 1969; Chm. (Vice-Chm. 1970), Libraries Cttee, 1971). Contested (C) Gateshead East, 1966. *Recreations:* music, skiing. *Address:* 1 Wetherby Place, SW7 4NU. *T:* 01–373 1518.

MENDOZA, June Yvonne, RP; ROI; artist; *d* of John Morton and Dot (*née* Mendoza), musicians; *m* Keith Ashley V. Mackrell; one *s* three *d. Educ:* Lauriston Girls' Sch., Melbourne; St Martin's Sch. of Art. Period of variety of illustration, design etc, also worked as actress in all media. Philippines, 1960–65, Australia, 1969–73. Member: RP 1970; ROI 1968. Extensive portrait work in public and private collections, British and internat. Portraits include: Queen Elizabeth II; Duke of Edinburgh; Prince of Wales; Princess of Wales; Princess Anne; Duke of Norfolk; Rt Rev. Lord Coggan; Margaret Thatcher; A. J. P. Taylor; Sir John Gorton; Ratu Sir Kamisese Mara; Alistair Cooke; Tom Stoppard; Dame Marie Rambert; Lord Clark; group portraits; personal series of musicians include: Dame Joan Sutherland, Yehudi Menuhin; Sir Michael Tippett; Antal Dorati; Sir Colin Davis. Occasional lectures. Hon. DLitt Bath, 1986. *Recreations:* music, theatre, travel. *Address:* 34 Inner Park Road, SW19.

MENDOZA, Maurice, CVO 1982; MSM 1946; heritage consultant; Under Secretary, Ancient Monuments and Historic Buildings, Department of the Environment, 1978–81; *b* 1 May 1921; *e s* of Daniel and Rachel Mendoza; *m* 1949, Phyllis Kriger. *Educ:* Sir Henry Raine's Foundation. Dip. Sociology London. Clerical Officer, HM Office of Works, 1938; served Royal Signals and Cheshire Yeo., 1941–46 (Sgt); Mil. Mission to Belgium, 1944–46; Organisation Officer, Treasury, 1956–61; Principal, MPBW, 1963; Asst Sec. 1968; DoE, 1970; Under-Sec., 1973; Dir of Manpower and Management Services, DoE and later, also Dept of Transport, 1974–78. Chairman: Friends of the Ridgeway, 1982–; Common Land Forum, 1984–; Hon. Consultant to Temple Bar Trust, 1982–. Hon. Mem., 10th Battalion Transportation Corps, US Army, 1977. *Recreations:* theatre, walking, photography. *Address:* 45 Grange Grove, Canonbury, N1 2NP. *Clubs:* Athenæum, Civil Service.

MENDOZA, Vivian P.; *see* Pereira-Mendoza.

MENDOZA-ACOSTA, Vice-Adm. Felix; Venezuelan Ambassador to the Court of St James's, 1979–82; *b* 21 Feb. 1929; *s* of José Mendoza and Virginia Mendoza (*née* Acosta); *m* 1954, Patricia Hill; one *s* two *d. Educ:* Naval Academy, Venezuela; Naval Coll., USA. Professor, Naval Academy, Venezuela, 1957–59; held high appointments at High Court of Admiralty, Min. of Defence, 1960–72; Director, Naval Academy, 1973; Chief of Operations, Headquarters, High Court of Admiralty, 1974, Commander in Chief, 1976; Chief of General Staff, 1977; Inspector General of Armed Forces, 1978; in charge, Min. of Defence, on several occasions, 1978–79. Orden: del Libertador Simón Bolívar; Francisco de Miranda; Gen. Urdaneta; Andrés Bello; Diego de Lozada; naval decorations: Spain, Italy, Colombia, Argentina, Bolivia, Peru, Venezuela; Cross, 1st Cl.: Land Forces of Venezuela, Air Force of Venezuela, Naval Merit, National Guard. *Recreations:* walking, reading, music, conversation with family. *Address:* c/o Ministry of Foreign Affairs, Carácas, Venezuela. *Clubs:* Les Ambassadeurs, Hurlingham, Annabel's, Belfry, White Elephant, Casanova; Officers' (Carácas).

MENEMENCIOGLU, Turgut; *b* Istanbul, 8 Oct. 1914; *s* of Muvatfak and Kadriye Menemencioğlu; *m* 1944, Nermin Moran; two *s. Educ:* Robert Coll., Istanbul; Geneva Univ. Joined Turkish Min. of Foreign Affairs, 1939; Permanent Delegate, European Office, UN Geneva, 1950–52; Counsellor, Turkish Embassy, Washington, 1952; Dir-Gen., Econ. Affairs, Min. of Foreign Affairs, 1952–54; Dep. Permanent Rep. to UN, 1954–60; Ambassador to Canada, 1960; Permanent Rep. to UN, 1960–62; Ambassador to USA, 1962–67; High Polit. Adviser, Mem., High Polit. Planning Bd, Min. of Foreign Affairs, 1967–68; Sec.-Gen., CENTO, 1968–72; Adviser, Min. of Foreign Affairs, 1972; Ambassador of Turkey to the Court of St James's, 1972–78; Sen. Polit. Adviser, Min. of Foreign Affairs, 1978–80. Turkish Representative, Turkish-Greek Cultural Relations Cttee, 1982. *Address:* Inünü Cad 31/12, Taksim, Istanbul, Turkey.

MENEVIA, Bishop of, (RC), since 1983; **Rt. Rev. James Hannigan;** *b* Co. Donegal, 15 July 1928. Ordained priest, 1954. Chm., Catholic Educn Council, 1984–. *Address:* Bishop's House, Sontley Road, Wrexham, Clwyd LL13 7EW. *T:* Wrexham 262726.

MENHENNET, Dr David; Librarian of the House of Commons, since 1976; *b* 4 Dec. 1928; *s* of William and Everill Menhennet, Redruth, Cornwall; *m* 1954, Audrey, *o d* of William and Alice Holmes, Accrington, Lancs; two *s. Educ:* Truro Sch., Cornwall; Oriel Coll., Oxford (BA 1st Cl. Hons 1952); Queen's Coll., Oxford. Open Scholarship in Mod. Langs, Oriel Coll., Oxford, 1946; Heath Harrison Trav. Scholarship, 1951; Bishop Fraser Res. Scholar, Oriel Coll., 1952–53; Laming Fellow, Queen's Coll., Oxford, 1953–54; Zaharoff Trav. Scholarship, 1953–54. MA 1956, DPhil 1960, Oxon. Library Clerk, House of Commons Library, 1954; Asst Librarian i/c Res. Div., 1964–67; Dep. Librarian, 1967–76. Mem., Study of Parliament Gp, 1964–; Chm. Adv. Cttee, Bibliographic Services, British Library, 1986– (Mem., 1975–86). Associate, Inst. of Cornish Studies, 1974–. FRSA 1966. Gen. Editor, House of Commons Library Documents series, 1972–. *Publications:* (with J. Palmer) Parliament in Perspective, 1967; The Journal of the House of Commons: a bibliographical and historical guide, 1971; (ed with D. C. L. Holland) Erskine May's Private Journal, 1857–1882, 1972; (contrib.) The House of Commons in the Twentieth Century, ed S. A. Walkland, 1979; (contrib.) The House of Commons: Services and Facilities 1972–1982, ed M. Rush, 1983; articles in Lib. Assoc. Record, Parliamentarian, Parly Affairs, Polit. Qly, New Scientist, Contemp. Rev., Jl of Librarianship, Jl of Documentation. *Recreations:* walking, gardening, visiting old churches, music. *Address:* (office) House of Commons Library, SW1A 0AA. *T:* 01–219 3635. *Club:* Athenæum.

MENNEER, Stephen Snow, CB 1967; retired, 1970, as Assistant Under-Secretary of State, Department of Health and Social Security; *b* 6 March 1910; *s* of Sydney Charles Menneer, LLD, and Minnie Elizabeth Menneer; *m* 1935, Margaret Longstaff Smith (*d* 1976); one *s* one *d. Educ:* Rugby Sch.; Oriel Coll., Oxford. Min. of Information, 1939; Min. of National Insurance, 1948; Under-Sec., Min. of Pensions and Nat. Insurance, then Min. of Social Security, 1961. *Address:* Pennyhop, Burrington, Umberleigh, N Devon.

MENON, Prof. Mambillikalathil Govind Kumar, MSc, PhD; FRS 1970; Member, Planning Commission, Government of India, since 1982; Scientific Adviser to the Prime Minister, since 1986; *b* 28 Aug. 1928; *s* of Kizhekepat Sankara Menon and Mambillikalathil Narayaniamma; *m* 1955, Indumati Patel; one *s* one *d. Educ:* Jaswant Coll., Jodhpur; Royal Inst. of Science, Bombay (MSc); Univ. of Bristol (PhD). Tata Inst. of Fundamental Research: Reader, 1955–58; Associate Prof., 1958–60; Prof. of Physics and Dean of Physics Faculty, 1960–64; Senior Prof. and Dep. Dir (Physics), 1964–66, Dir, 1966–75. Chm., Electronics Commn, and Sec., Dept of Electronics, Govt of India, 1971–78; Scientific Advr to Minister of Defence, Dir-Gen. of Defence Res. and Develt Orgn, and Sec. in the Ministry of Defence for Defence Res., 1974–78; Dir-Gen., Council of Scientific and Industrial Res., 1978–81; Sec. to Govt of India, Dept of Science and Technology, 1978–82; Chm., Commn for Addtnl Sources of Energy, 1981–82; Chm., Science Adv. Cttee to the Cabinet, 1982–85; Pres., India Internat. Centre, 1983–; Mem., UN Sec.-Gen.'s Adv. Cttee on Application of Sci. and Technol. to Develt, 1972–79 (Chm. for 2 yrs); Special Advr, Internat. Fedn of Insts for Advanced Study, Stockholm. Fellow: Indian Acad. of Sciences (Pres., 1974–76); Indian Nat. Science Acad. (Pres., 1981–82); Pres., Indian Sci. Congress Assoc., 1981–82; Hon. Fellow: Nat. Acad. of Sciences, India; Indian Inst. of Sciences, Bangalore: For. Hon. Member: Amer. Acad. of Arts and Scis; USSR Acad. of Scis; Mem., Pontifical Acad. of Scis, Vatican; Hon. Pres., Asia Electronics Union; Hon. Mem., Instn of Electrical & Electronics Engrs Inc., USA. Hon. DSc: Jodhpur Univ., 1970; Delhi Univ., 1973; Sardar Patel Univ., 1973; Allahabad Univ., 1977; Roorkee Univ., 1979; Banaras Hindu Univ., 1981; Jadavpur Univ., 1981; Sri Venkateswara Univ., 1982; Indian Inst. of Tech. Madras, 1982; Andhra Univ., 1984; Utkal Univ., 1984; Aligarh Muslim Univ., 1986; Hon. Dr Engrg Stevens Inst. of Tech., USA, 1984. Royal Commn for Exhibn of 1851 Senior Award, 1953–55; Shanti Swarup Bhatnagar Award for Physical Sciences, Council of Scientific and Industrial Research, 1960; Khaitan Medal, RAS, 1973; Pandit Jawaharlal Nehru Award for Sciences, Madhya Pradesh Govt, 1983; G. P. Chatterjee Award, 1984; Om Prakash Bhasin Award for Science and Technol., 1985; C. V. Raman Medal, INSA, 1985; J. C. Bose Triennial Gold Medal, Bose Inst.; National Awards: Padma Shri, 1961; Padma Bhushan, 1968; Padma Vibhushan, 1985. *Publications:* 110, on cosmic rays and elementary particle physics. *Recreations:* photography, bird-watching. *Address:* Yojana Bhavan, Parliament Street, New Delhi 110001, India. *T:* (office) 382148; (home) 301–8974. *Clubs:* National Liberal; United Services (Bombay); India International Centre (New Delhi).

MENOTTI, Gian Carlo; Composer; Founder and President, Spoleto Festival; *b* Cadegliano, Italy, 7 July 1911. *Educ:* The Curtis Institute of Music, Philadelphia, Pa. Has been resident in the United States since 1928. Teacher of Composition at Curtis Inst. of Music, 1948–55. First performances of works include: Amelia Goes to the Ball (opera), 1936; The Old Maid and the Thief (radio opera), 1939 (later staged); The Island God, 1942; Sebastian (Ballet), 1943; Piano Concerto in F, 1945; The Medium (opera), 1946 (later filmed); The Telephone (opera), 1947; Errand into the Maze (ballet), 1947; The Consul (opera), 1950 (Pulitzer Prize); Apocalypse (orchestral), 1951; Amahl and the Night Visitors (television opera), 1951; Violin Concerto in A Minor, 1952; The Saint of Bleeker Street (opera), 1954 (Pulitzer Prize); The Unicorn, The Gorgon, and the Manticore, 1956; Maria Golovin (television opera), 1958; The Last Savage (opera), 1963; The Death of the Bishop of Brindisi (oratorio), 1963; Martin's Lie (opera), 1964; Canti della Lontananza (song cycle), 1967; Help, Help, the Globolinks (opera), 1968; The Leper (drama), 1970; Triplo Concerto a Tre (symphonic piece), 1970; The Most Important Man (opera), 1971; Fantasia for 'cello and orch., 1971; Tamu-Tamu (opera), 1973; The Egg (opera), 1976; The Trial of the Gypsy (opera), 1976; Landscapes & Remembrances, for chorus and orch., 1976; Symphony no 1, 1976; Chip & his Dog (opera), 1978, Juana la Loca (opera), 1979; Mass, O Pulchritudo, 1979; Song of Hope (cantata), 1980; A Bride from Pluto (opera), 1982; St Teresa (cantata), 1982; The Boy Who Grew Too Fast (opera), 1982; wrote libretto for Vanessa (opera, by Samuel Barber), 1958. *Publications:* his major works have been published, also some minor ones; he is the author of all his libretti, most of which have been written in English. *Address:* c/o Thea Dispeker, 59 East 54th Street, New York, NY 10022, USA; Yester House, Gifford, Haddington, East Lothian EH41 4JF.

MENSFORTH, Sir Eric, Kt 1962; CBE 1945; MA Cantab; FEng; FIMechE; FRAeS; Hon. FIProdE; Vice Lord-Lieutenant, South Yorkshire, 1974–81; President, Westland Aircraft Ltd, 1979–85; (Director, 1968–83; Managing Director 1938–45; Vice-Chairman, 1945–53, 1968–71; Chairman, 1953–68); Director, John Brown & Co. Ltd, 1948–83 (Deputy Chairman, 1959–78); *b* 17 May 1906; 2nd *s* of late Sir Holberry Mensforth, KCB, CBE; *m* 1934, Betty, *d* of late Rev. Picton W. Francis; three *d. Educ:* Altrincham County High Sch.; University Coll. Sch.; King's Coll., Cambridge (Price Exhibn) (1st class mechanical sciences tripos). Engineering work at Woolwich Arsenal, Mather & Platt Ltd, Bolckow Vaughan Ltd, Kloecknerwerke A. G., Dorman Long Ltd, English Electric Ltd, Markham & Co. Ltd, T. Firth & John Brown Ltd, Firth Brown Tools Ltd, Wickman Ltd, Boddy Industries Ltd, Rhodesian Alloys Ltd, Normalair Ltd; Chief Production Adviser to Chief Executive, Ministry of Aircraft Production, 1943–45. Master Cutler, Sheffield, 1965–66. Chairman: EDC for Electronics Industry, 1968–70; Cttee on Quality Assurance, 1968–70; Council of Engineering Instns, 1969–72; Governing Body, Sheffield Polytechnic, 1969–75; Member: British Productivity Council, 1964–69; Royal Ordnance Factories Bd, 1968–72; Council, RGS, 1968–70; Treasurer, British Assoc. for Advancement of Science, 1970–75; a founder Vice-Pres., Fellowship of Engineering, 1977; President: S Yorks Scouts' Assoc., 1969–76; CPRE (Sheffield and Peak District Branch), 1975–. Hon. Fellow, Sheffield City Polytech. Hon. DEng Sheffield, 1967; Hon. DSc Southampton, 1970. DL S (formerly WR) Yorks, 1971–86. *Publications:* Air Frame Production, 1947 (Instn Prize, IMechE); Future of the Aeroplane (Cantor Lectures), 1959; Production of Helicopters and Hovercraft (Lord Sempill Lecture, IProdE), 1964; Future of Rotorcraft and Hovercraft (Cierva Meml Lecture, RAeS), 1967; Extracts from the Records of the Cutlers' Company, 1972; Family Engineers, 1981. *Address:* 42 Oakmead Green, Woodcote Side, Surrey KT18 7JS. *Club:* Alpine.

MENTER, Sir James (Woodham), Kt 1973; MA, PhD, ScD Cantab; FRS 1966; FInstP; Principal, Queen Mary College, London University, 1976–86; *b* 22 Aug. 1921; *s* of late Horace Menter and late Jane Anne Lackenby; *m* 1947, Marjorie Jean, *d* of late Thomas Stodart Whyte-Smith, WS; two *s* one *d. Educ:* Dover Grammar Sch.; Peterhouse, Cambridge. PhD 1949, ScD 1960. Experimental Officer, Admty, 1942–45; Research, Cambridge Univ., 1946–54 (ICI Fellow, 1951–54; Sir George Beilby Mem. Award, 1954); Tube Investments Research Laboratories, Hinxton Hall, 1954–68; Dir of Research and Develt, Tube Investments Ltd, 1965–76. Director: Tube Investments Res. Labs, 1961–68; Tube Investments Ltd, 1965–; Round Oak Steelworks Ltd, 1967–76; British Petroleum Co., 1976–; Steetley Co., 1981–85. Member: SRC, 1967–72; Cttee of Inquiry into Engrg Profession, 1977–79; a Vice-Pres., Royal Society, 1971–76, Treasurer, 1972–76; Royal Institution: a Manager, 1982–84; a Vice-Pres., 1983–85; Chm. Council, 1984–85. Fellow, Churchill Coll., Cambridge, 1966. President: Inst. of Physics, 1970–72; Metals Soc., 1976; Dep. Chm., Adv. Council Applied R&D, 1976–79. Mem. (part-time), BSC, 1976–79. Mem., Ct of Governors, City of London Polytechnic, 1982–85. Hon. DTech Brunel, 1974. Bessemer Medal, Iron and Steel Inst., 1973; Glazebrook Medal and Prize, Inst. of Physics, 1977. *Publications:* scientific papers in Proc. Royal Society, Advances in Physics, Jl Iron and Steel Inst., etc. *Recreation:* fishing. *Address:* Carie, Rannoch Station, Perthshire. *T:* Kinloch Rannoch 341.

MENTETH, Sir James (Wallace) Stuart-, 6th Bt, *cr* 1838; *b* 13 Nov. 1922; *e s* of 5th Bt and Winifred Melville (*d* 1968), *d* of Daniel Francis and *widow* of Capt. Rupert G. Raw, DSO; *S* father, 1952; *m* 1949, Dorothy Patricia, *d* of late Frank Greaves Warburton; two *s. Educ:* Fettes; St Andrews Univ.; Trinity Coll., Oxford (MA). Served War of 1939–45, with Scots Guards, 1942–44; on active service in North Africa and Italy (Anzio) (severely wounded). *Recreations:* motoring, swimming, gardening, ornithology. *Heir: s* Charles Greaves Stuart-Menteth [*b* 25 Nov. 1950; *m* 1976, Nicola St Lawrence; three *d* (one *s* decd)]. *Address:* Nutwood, Auchencairn, Castle-Douglas, Kirkcudbrightshire DG7 1QZ.

MENTZ, Donald; Director General, Commonwealth Agricultural Bureaux International, since 1985; b 20 Oct. 1933; s of Stanley Mentz and Marie Agnes (née Bryant); m 1959, Mary Josephine (née Goldsworthy); one s two d. Educ: Hampton High School, Victoria; Dookie Agricultural College, Victoria (DDA); Melbourne Univ. (BAgSci); Australian Nat. Univ. (BEcon). Dept of External Territories, Australia, 1969–73; Aust. Develt Assistance Bureau, Dept of Foreign Affairs, 1973–77; Dept of Business and Consumer Affairs, 1977–78; Dir of Operations, Asian Develt Bank, Philippines, 1979–81; Dep. Sec., Dept of Business and Consumer Affairs, Aust., 1981–82; Dep. Sec., Dept of Territories and Local Govt., 1983–84. Recreations: ski-ing, gardening. Address: Flat 1, 25 Longridge Road, Earls Court, SW5 9SB. T: 01–835 1208. Club: Commonwealth (Canberra).

MENUHIN, Sir Yehudi, KBE 1965; violinist, conductor; b New York, 22 April 1916; adopted British nationality, 1985; s of Moshe and Marutha Menuhin; m 1938, Nola Ruby, d of George Nicholas, Melbourne, Australia; one s one d; m 1947, Diana Rosamond, d of late G. L. E. Gould and late Lady Harcourt (Evelyn Suart); two s. Educ: private tutors; studied music under Sigmund Anker and Louis Persinger, in San Francisco; Georges Enesco, Rumania and Paris; Adolph Busch, Switzerland. Made début with orchestra, San Francisco, aged 7, Paris, aged 10, New York, 11, Berlin, 13; since then has played with most of world's orchestras and conductors; has introduced among contemp. works Sonata for Violin alone, by Béla Bartók (composed for Mr Menuhin), as well as works by William Walton, Ben-Haim, Georges Enesco, Pizzetti, Ernest Bloch, etc. During War of 1939–45 devoted larger part of his time to concerts for US and Allied armed forces and benefit concerts for Red Cross, etc (500 concerts). Series of concerts in Moscow (by invitation), 1945; seven visits to Israel, 1950–; first tour of Japan, 1951; first tour of India (invitation of Prime Minister), 1952. Largely responsible for cultural exchange programme between US and Russia, 1955, and for bringing Indian music and musicians to West. Initiated his own annual music festival in Gstaad, Switzerland, 1957, and in Bath, 1959–68; Jt Artistic Dir, Windsor Festival, 1969–72. Founder, Live Music Now, 1977. Founded Yehudi Menuhin Sch. of Music, Stoke d'Abernon, Surrey, 1963; Founder/Pres., Internat. Menuhin Music Acad., Gstaad, 1976; Pres., Trinity Coll. of Music, 1971; Associate Conductor and Pres., Royal Philharmonic Orch., 1982–. Hon. Fellow, St Catharine's Coll., Cambridge, 1970; Hon. DMus: Oxford, 1962; Cambridge, 1970; Sorbonne, 1976, Toronto, 1984, and 10 other degrees from Brit. Univs. Freedom of the City of Edinburgh, 1965; City of Bath, 1966. He records for several companies, both as soloist and as Conductor of Menuhin Festival Orch., with which has toured USA, Australia, NZ and Europe; appears regularly on American and British Television. Gold Medal, Royal Philharmonic Soc., 1962; Jawaharlal Nehru Award for International Understanding, 1970; Sonning Music Prize, Denmark, 1972; Handel Medal, NY; City of Jerusalem Medal; Peace Prize, Börsenverein des Deutschen Buchhandels, 1979; Albert Medal, RSA, 1981; Una Vita Nella Musica, Omaggio a Venezia, 1983; Grande Plaque du Bimillenaire de Paris, 1984; Ernst von Siemens Prize, 1984; Moses-Mendelssohn-Preis des Landes Berlin. Decorations include: Grand Officier de la Légion d'Honneur, 1986; Commander: Order of Arts and Letters (France); Order of Leopold (Belgium); Officer, Ordre de la Couronne (Belgium); Kt Comdr Order of Merit (Fed. Rep. of Germany); Royal Order of the Phœnix (Greece); Comdr, Order of Orange-Nassau (Netherlands); Grand Cross, Order of Merit (FRG); Hon. Citizen of Switzerland, 1970. Publications: The Violin: six lessons by Yehudi Menuhin, 1971; Theme and Variations, 1972; Violin and Viola, 1976; Sir Edward Elgar: My Musical Grandfather (essay), 1976; (autobiography) Unfinished Journey, 1977; The Music of Man, 1980; (with Christopher Hope) The King, the Cat and the Fiddle, (children's book), 1983; Life Class, 1986; Relevant Publication: Yehudi Menuhin, The Story of the Man and the Musician, by Robert Magidoff, 1956 (USA); Conversations with Menuhin, by Robin Daniels, 1979. Films: Stage Door Canteen; Magic Bow; The Way of Light (biog.). Television series: The Music of Man. Address: Anglo-Swiss Artists' Management, 16 Muswell Hill Road, Highgate, N6 5UG. Clubs: Athenæum, Garrick.
See also J. C. M. Benthall.

MENZIES, John Maxwell; Chairman, John Menzies Holdings Ltd, since 1952; b 13 Oct. 1926; s of late John Francis Menzies and of Cynthia Mary Graham; m 1953, Patricia Eleanor, d of late Comdr Sir Hugh Dawson, Bt, CBE and Lady Dawson; four d. Educ: Eton. Lieut Grenadier Guards. Berwickshire CC, 1954–57. Director: Scottish American Mortgage Co., 1959–63; Standard Life Assurance Co., 1960–63; Vidal Sassoon Inc., 1969–80; Gordon & Gotch plc, 1970–85; Atlantic Assets Trust, 1973– (Chm., 1983–); Independent Investment Co. plc, 1973– (Chm., 1983–); Nimslo International, 1980–; Rocky Mountains Oil & Gas, 1980–85; Ivory & Sime plc, 1980–83; Personal Assets PLC, 1981–; Bank of Scotland, 1984–; Guardian Royal Exchange, 1985–. Trustee, Newsvendors' Benevolent Instn, 1974– (Pres., 1968–74). Mem., Royal Co. of Archers, HM's Body Guard for Scotland. Recreations: farming, shooting, reading, travel. Address: Kames, Duns, Berwickshire. T: Leitholm 202. Clubs: Turf, Boodle's; New (Edinburgh).

MENZIES, Dame Pattie (Maie), GBE 1954; b 2 March 1899; d of late Senator J. W. Leckie; m 1920, Robert Gordon Menzies (Rt Hon. Sir Robert Menzies, KT, AK, CH, QC, FRS; Prime Minister of the Commonwealth of Australia, 1939–41 and 1949–66) (d 1978); one s one d (and one s decd). Educ: Fintona Girls' Sch., Melbourne; Presbyterian Ladies' Coll., Melbourne. Address: 7 Monaro Close, Kooyong, Vic 3144, Australia. Club: Alexandra (Melbourne).

MENZIES, Sir Peter (Thomson), Kt 1972; Director: National Westminster Bank Ltd, 1968–82; Commercial Union Assurance Co. Ltd, 1962–82; b 15 April 1912; s of late John C. Menzies and late Helen S. Aikman; m 1938, Mary McPherson Alexander, d of late John T. Menzies and late Agnes Anderson; one s one d. Educ: Musselburgh Grammar Sch.; University of Edinburgh. MA, 1st Class Hons Math. and Natural Philosophy, 1934. Inland Revenue Dept, 1933–39; Treasurer's Dept, Imperial Chemical Industries Ltd, 1939–56 (Asst Treas. 1947, Dep. Treas. 1952); Director: Imperial Chemical Industries Ltd, 1956–72 (Dep. Chm., 1967–72); Imperial Metal Industries Ltd, 1962–72 (Chm., 1964–72). Part-time Mem., CEGB, 1960–72; Mem., Review Body on Doctors' and Dentists' Remuneration, 1971–83; Chairman: Electricity Council, 1972–77; London Exec. Cttee, Scottish Council (Develt and Industry), 1977–82. A Vice-Pres., Siol na Meinnrich; Pres., UNIPEDE, 1973–76; Vice-Pres. and Gen. Treas., BAAS, 1982–. FInstP; CompIEE. Address: Kit's Corner, Harmer Green, Welwyn, Herts. T: Welwyn 4386. Club: Caledonian.

MENZIES-WILSON, William Napier, CBE 1985; Chairman, Viking Resources Trust, since 1986; Director: Ocean Transport & Trading plc, Liverpool, since 1973 (Chairman, 1980–86); National Freight Consortium, since 1986; b 4 Dec. 1926; s of James Robert Menzies-Wilson and Jacobine Napier Williamson-Napier; m 1953, Mary Elizabeth Darnell Juckes; two s one d. Educ: Winchester; New Coll., Oxford (MA); North Western Univ., Chicago. Joined Stewarts & Lloyds Ltd, 1950; Managing Director, Stewarts & Lloyds of South Africa Ltd, 1954–61, Chairman, 1961; Director, Stewarts & Lloyds Ltd, 1964; Dir, Supplies & Transport, British Steel Corporation, 1967–73; Chm., Wm Cory & Son Ltd, 1973–77; Dir, Overseas Containers Holdings, 1979–; Dunlop Holdings, 1982–84. Pres., Gen. Council of British Shipping, 1984–85; Mem. Exec. Bd, Lloyd's

Register of Shipping, 1984–. Recreations: shooting, golf, gardening. Address: Last House, Old, Northampton NN6 9RH. T: Northampton 781346.

MERCER, Rt. Rev. Eric Arthur John; b 6 Dec. 1917; s of Ambrose John Mercer, Kent; m 1951, Rosemary Wilma, d of John William Denby, Lincs; one s one d. Educ: Dover Gram. Sch.; Kelham Theol. Coll. Enlisted Sherwood Foresters, 1940; Capt. and Adjt, 14th Foresters, 1943; served Italy (despatches), 1944; Staff Coll., Haifa, 1944; DAA&QMG, 66 Inf. Bde, Palestine, 1945; GSO2 (SD), HQ, MEF, 1945. Returned Kelham Theol. Coll., 1946–47. Ordained, Chester; Curate, Coppenhall, Crewe, 1947–51; Priest in charge, Heald Green, 1951–53; Rector, St Thomas', Stockport, 1953–59; Chester Diocesan Missioner, 1959–65; Rector, Chester St Bridget, 1959–65; Hon. Canon of Chester Cathedral, 1964; Bishop Suffragan of Birkenhead, 1965–73; Bishop of Exeter, 1973–85. Church Commissioners: Dep. Chm., Pastoral Cttee, 1976–85; Mem., Bd of Governors, 1980–85. Nat. Chm., CEMS, 1974–78. Publication: (contrib.) Worship in a Changing Church, 1965. Address: c/o The Vicarage, Hindon, Salisbury SP3 6ER. T: Hindon 362.

MERCER, John Charles Kenneth; a Recorder of the Crown Court, 1975–82; b 17 Sept. 1917; s of late Charles Wilfred Mercer and Cecil Maud Mercer; m 1944, Barbara Joan, d of late Arnold Sydney Whitehead, CB, CBE, and Maud Ethel Whitehead; one s one d. Educ: Ellesmere Coll.; Law Sch., Swansea University Coll. (LLB). Solicitor. War Service, 1940–45, Captain RA. Partner, Douglas-Jones & Mercer, 1946–. Mem., Royal Commn on Criminal Procedure, 1978–81; Mem., SW Wales River Authority, 1960–74. Recreations: fishing, shooting, golf, watching sport. Address: 334 Gower Road, Killay, Swansea, West Glamorgan. T: Swansea 202931. Clubs: City and County, Clyne Golf (Swansea).

MERCER, Dr Robert Giles Graham; Headmaster, Stonyhurst College, since 1985; b 30 May 1949; s of late Leonard and Florence Elizabeth Mercer; m 1974, Caroline Mary Brougham; one s. Educ: Austin Friars School, Carlisle; Churchill College, Cambridge (Scholar; 1st cl. Hist. Tripos, Pts I and II; MA); St John's College, Oxford (Sen. Schol., DPhil). Head of History, Charterhouse, 1974–76; Asst Principal, MoD, 1976–78; Dir of Studies and Head of History, Sherborne School, 1979–85. Publication: The Teaching of Gasparino Barzizza, 1979. Recreations: art, music, travel, swimming. Address: St Philip's, Stonyhurst, Blackburn, Lancs BB6 9PT. T: Stonyhurst 247.

MERCER, Rt. Rev. Robert William Stanley; see Matabeleland, Bishop of.

MERCER NAIRNE PETTY-FITZMAURICE, family name of **Marquess of Lansdowne.**

MERCHANT, Ismail; film producer, since 1960; Partner, Merchant Ivory Productions, since formation, 1961; b 25 Dec. 1936; s of Noormohamed Haji Abdul Rehman and Hazra Memon. Educ: St Xavier's Coll., Bombay (BA); New York Univ. (MBA). Collaborator with Ruth Prawer Jhabvala and James Ivory on most of the following: feature films: The Householder, 1963; Shakespeare Wallah, 1965 (won Best Actress award, Berlin Film Fest., 1965); The Guru, 1969; Bombay Talkie, 1970; Savages, 1972; The Wild Party, 1975; Roseland, 1977; The Europeans, 1979 (official Brit. entry, Cannes Film Fest.); Quartet, 1981; Heat and Dust, 1982 (Brit. entry, Cannes Film Fest.); The Bostonians, 1984 (feature, Cannes Film Fest.); A Room with a View, 1986; shorts: The Creation of Woman, 1960 (Academy award nomination); Helen, Queen of the Nautch Girls, 1973; (directed) Mahatma and the Mad Boy, 1973; Sweet Sounds, 1976; television: Adventures of a Brown Man in Search of Civilization, 1971 (BBC); Autobiography of a Princess, 1975 (TV special, NY); Hullabaloo over Georgie and Bonnie's Pictures, 1978 (feature, LWT); Jane Austen in Manhattan, 1980 (feature, LWT and Polytel); (directed for Channel 4) The Courtesans of Bombay, 1983. Publication: Ismail Merchant's Indian Cuisine, 1986. Recreations: squash, bicycling, cooking. Address: 400 East 52nd Street, New York, NY 10022, USA. T: 212 759 3694; 32 Motlabai Street, Bombay, India. T: 378–376.

MERCHANT, John Richard; Principal Finance and Establishment Officer, Crown Prosecution Service, since 1986; b 4 June 1945; s of William Henry Merchant and Eileen Merchant; m 1966, Eileen McGill, two s. Educ: Gravesend Grammar Sch.; Sheffield Univ. (BSc); Cranfield Inst. of Technol. (MSc). FIS. Lyons Bakery Ltd, 1966–69; Lectr, Cranfield Inst. of Technol., 1969–75; Statistician, MoD, 1975–79; Chief Statistician, CS Coll., 1979–82; Asst Sec., Cabinet Office (MPO), 1982–84; Principal Finance and Estabt Officer, DPP, 1984–86; Under Sec., 1985. Recreations: Nigerian postal history, fishing. Address: 4/12 Queen Anne's Gate, SW1H 9AZ. T: 01-213 3931.

MERCHANT, Piers Rolf Garfield; MP (C) Newcastle upon Tyne Central, since 1983; b 2 Jan. 1951; s of Garfield Frederick Merchant and Audrey Mary Rolfe-Martin; m 1977, Helen Joan Burrluck; one d. Educ: Nottingham High School; Univ. of Durham. BA (Hons) Law and Politics, MA Political Philosophy. Reporter, Municipal Correspondent, Chief Reporter, Dep. News Editor, The Journal, 1973–80; News Editor, The Journal, 1980–82; Editor, Conservative Newsline, 1982–84. Co-Chm., Freeflow of Information Cttee, Internat. Parly Gp. Mem., Senior Common Room, University Coll., Durham. Publications: newspaper articles and features. Recreations: swimming, walking, genealogy, electronics, computers. Address: 5 Carlton Terrace, Low Fell, Gateshead NE9 6DE. T: Tyneside 4876201; 01–630 9294; (office) 01–219 4584.

MERCHANT, Rev. Prof. William Moelwyn, FRSL; writer and sculptor; b 5 June 1913; s of late William Selwyn and Elizabeth Ann Merchant, Port Talbot, Glamorgan; m 1938, Maria Eluned Hughes, Llanelly; one s one d. Educ: Port Talbot Grammar Sch.; (Exhibnr) University Coll., Cardiff. BA, 1st Cl. English hons 1933; 2nd Cl. 1st div. Hist., 1934; MA 1950; DLitt 1960; Hon. Fellow, University Coll., Cardiff, 1981. Hist. Master, Carmarthen Grammar Sch., 1935; English Master, Newport High Sch., 1936; English Lectr, Caerleon Trg Coll., 1937; University Coll. Cardiff: Lectr in Eng. Lang. and Lit., 1939; Sen. Lectr, 1950; Reader, 1961; Prof. of English, Univ. of Exeter, 1961–74; Vicar of Llanddewi Brefi, dio. St Davids, 1974–78; Hon. Lectr, All Saints Church, Leamington Spa, 1979. Fellow, Folger Shakespeare Library, Washington, DC, and Fulbright Fellow, 1957; Woodward Lectr, Yale Univ., 1957; Dupont Lectr, Sewanee Univ., Tenn, 1963; Willett Prof. of English and Theology, Univ. of Chicago, 1971. Founded Rougemont Press, 1970 (with Ted Hughes, Eric Cleave and Paul Merchant). Welsh Cttee of Arts Council of Gt Brit., 1960 and 1975–; Council, Llandaff Festival, 1958–61. Consultant and script-writer on film, The Bible, Rome, 1960–64. Ordained to Anglican Orders, 1940; Examining Chaplain to the Bishop of Salisbury; Canon of Salisbury Cathedral, 1967–73, Canon Emeritus, 1973 (Chancellor, 1967–71); Mem., Archbishops' Commn on Faculty Jurisdiction, 1979–. Founded Llanddewi Brefi Arts Fest., 1975. FRSL 1976; Hon. Fellow, University Coll. of Wales, Aberystwyth, 1975. Hon HLD Wittenberg Univ., Ohio, 1973. Publications: Wordsworth's Guide to the Lakes (illus. John Piper), 1952 (US 1953); Reynard Library Wordsworth, 1955 (US 1955); Shakespeare and the Artist, 1959; Creed and Drama, 1965; (ed) Merchant of Venice, 1967; (ed) Marlowe's Edward the Second, 1967; Comedy, 1972; Tree of Life (libretto, music by Alun Hoddinott), 1972; Breaking the Code (poems), 1975; (ed) Essays and Studies, 1977; No Dark Glass (poems), 1979; R. S. Thomas, a critical evaluation, 1979; Confrontation of Angels (poems), 1986; Jeshua (novel), 1986; articles in Times Literary Supplement, Warburg Jl, Shakespeare Survey, Shakespeare Quarterly, Shakespeare Jahrbuch, Encyc. Britannica, etc. *Recreations:* theatre, typography, sculpting (one-man exhibns at Exeter, Cardiff, Swansea, Plymouth, Southampton, Aberystwyth, Glasgow, Stirling, Birmingham, 1971–). *Address:* 16 St Mary's Road, Leamington Spa, Warwicks. *T:* Leamington 314253.

MERCIECA, Most Rev. Joseph; *see* Malta, Archbishop of, (RC).

MEREDITH, John Michael; barrister-at-law; a Recorder of the Crown Court, since 1976; *b* 23 Oct. 1934; *s* of late John Stanley Meredith and of Lily Meredith; *m*; one *s* three *d*. *Educ:* Crossley and Porter Schs, Halifax, Yorks; Leeds Univ. (LLB Hons 1956). Called to the Bar, Gray's Inn, 1958. *Recreations:* shooting, sailing. *Address:* 78 Broomfield Avenue, Halifax, West Yorks. *T:* Halifax 64321. *Clubs:* Pwllheli Sailing (N Wales); Queen's Sports (Halifax).

MEREDITH, Richard Alban Creed, MA; Head Master of Monkton Combe School, since 1978; *b* 1 Feb. 1935; *s* of late Canon R. Creed Meredith; *m* 1968, Hazel Eveline Mercia Parry; one *s* one *d*. *Educ:* Stowe Sch.; Jesus Coll., Cambridge. Asst Master (Modern Langs), 1957–70, Housemaster, 1962–70, King's Sch., Canterbury; Headmaster, Giggleswick Sch., 1970–78. *Recreations:* walking, foreign travel, music, gardening. *Address:* Head Master's House, Shaft Road, Monkton Combe School, Bath BA2 7HH. *T:* Limpley Stoke 3278.

MEREDITH DAVIES, (James) Brian; *see* Davies.

MERIFIELD, Anthony James; Director of Health Authority Liaison, Department of Health and Social Security, since 1986; *b* 5 March 1934; *s* of late Francis Bertram Merifield and Richardina (*née* Parker); *m* 1980, Pamela Pratt. *Educ:* Chesterfield Sch.; Shrewsbury Sch.; Wadham Coll., Oxford (BA). National Service, 1952–54, Royal Tank Regt. HM Overseas Civil Service, Kenya, 1958–65; Department of Health and Social Security: Principal, 1965–71; Asst Sec., 1971–77; Under Secretary, 1978–82; Under Sec., NI Office, 1982–85. *Address:* 49 Carson Road, SE21 8HT. *T:* 01-670 1546. *Club:* Royal Commonwealth Society.

MERITT, Benjamin Dean; Visiting Scholar, University of Texas, since 1973; *b* Durham, North Carolina, 31 March 1899; *s* of Arthur Herbert Meritt and Cornelia Frances Dean; *m* 1st, 1923, Mary Elizabeth Kirkland; two *s*; 2nd, 1964, Lucy T. Shoe. *Educ:* Hamilton Coll. (AB 1920, AM 1923, LLD 1937); American Sch. of Class. Studies at Athens. AM Princeton 1923, PhD 1924, LittD 1947; DLitt Oxford, 1936; LLD Glasgow, 1948; LHD: University of Pennsylvania, 1967; Brown Univ., 1974; Dr *hc* Sch. of Philosophy, Univ. of Athens, 1970. Instr Greek Univ. of Vermont, 1923–24; Brown Univ., 1924–25; Asst Prof. Greek, Princeton, 1925–26; Asst Dir, Am. Sch. of Class. Studies at Athens, 1926–28; Associate Prof. Greek and Latin, University of Michigan, 1928–29, Prof. 1929–33; Visiting Prof. Am. Sch. Class. Studies at Athens, 1932–33; Dir Athens Coll., 1932–33; Francis White Prof. of Greek, Johns Hopkins, 1933–35; lecturer at Oxford, 1935; Annual Prof. Am Sch. of Class. Studies at Athens, 1936, 1954–55, 1969–70; Eastman Prof., Oxford Univ., 1945–46; Sather Prof., University of California, 1959; Prof. of Greek Epigraphy, Inst. for Advanced Study, Princeton, NJ, 1935–69, Emeritus, 1969–; Vis. Prof., Univ. of Texas, 1972; Member: American Philosophical Soc.; German Archae. Inst.; Fellow American Academy of Arts and Sciences; Corr. fellow British Academy; hon. councillor, Greek Archæ. Soc.; hon. mem. Michigan Acad. of Sciences, Arts and Letters, Society for the Promotion of Hellenic Studies; Assoc. Mem., Royal Flemish Acad.; Foreign Mem., Acad. of Athens; Pres. Amer. Philological Assoc., 1953. Commander: Order of the Phœnix (Greece); Order of George I (Greece). *Publications:* The Athenian Calendar in the Fifth Century, 1928; Supplementum Epigraphicum Graecum, Vol. V (with Allen B. West), 1931; Corinth, Vol. VIII, Part I-Greek Inscriptions, 1931; Athenian Financial Documents, 1932; The Athenian Assessment of 425 BC (with Allen B. West), 1934; Documents on Athenian Tribute, 1937; The Athenian Tribute Lists (with H. T. Wade-Gery and M. F. McGregor), Vol. I, 1939, Vol. II, 1949, Vol. III, 1950, Vol. IV, 1953; Epigraphica Attica, 1940; The Chronology of Hellenistic Athens (with W. K. Pritchett), 1940; The Athenian Year, 1961; The Athenian Agora Vol. XV: The Athenian Councillors (with J. S. Traill), 1974; articles in Hesperia 1933–81, Proceedings of the American Philosophical Soc. and other jls. *Address:* 712 W 16th Street, Austin, Texas 78701, USA.

MERLE, Robert; Croix du Combattant, 1945; Officier de l'Instruction publique, 1953; Professor of English Literature, University of Paris X, Nanterre, since 1965; Titular Professor: University of Rennes, Brittany, since 1944 (on leave, 1950–51); University of Toulouse, since 1957; University of Caen-Rouen, since 1960; University of Algiers, since 1963; *b* 29 Aug. 1908; father an officer; *m* 1st; one *d*; *m* 2nd, 1949; three *s* one *d*; 3rd, 1965; one *s*. *Educ:* Lycée Michelet, Paris; Sorbonne, Paris. Professor, 1934. Mobilised, 1939; Liaison agent with BEF (prisoner, 1940–43). *Publications:* Oscar Wilde, 1948; Week-end à Zuydcoote, 1949 (awarded Prix Goncourt); La Mort est mon métier, 1953; L'Ile, 1962 (awarded Prix de la Fraternité) (translated, as The Island, 1964); Un Animal doué de raison, 1967 (translated, as The Day of the Dolphin, 1969); Derrière la vitre, 1970; Malevil, 1972 (Campbell Award, USA); Les hommes protégés, 1974 (translated, as The Virility Factor, 1977); Madrapour, 1976; Fortune de France, 1978; En nos vertes années, 1979; Paris ma bonne ville, 1980; Le Prince que voilà, 1982; La violente amour, 1983; La Pique du jour, 1985; Le Jour ne se lève pas pour nous, 1986; *plays:* Flamineo (inspired by Webster's White Devil), 1953; Nouveau Sisyphe; *historical essays:* Moncada, 1965; Ben Bella, 1965; translations, articles. *Recreations:* swimming, tennis, yachting. *Address:* La Malmaison, Grosrouvre, 78490 Montfort L'Amaury, France.

MERLO, David, CEng; Director of Research, British Telecommunications plc, since 1983; *b* 16 June 1931; *s* of Carlo G. Merlo and Catherine E. Merlo (*née* Stringer); *m* 1952, Patricia Victoria Jackson; two *s*. *Educ:* Kilburn Grammar Sch., London; London Univ. (BScEng 1st Cl. Hons 1954); W. B. Esson schol. of IEE, 1953, and IEE Electronics Premium, 1966. CEng 1967, FIEE 1973. Post Office Research Br., 1948; Executive Engineer, 1955; Sen. Scientific Officer, 1959; Principal Sci. Officer, 1967; Head of Division, 1974; Dep. Director of Research, 1977. Visiting Lecturer: Northampton Polytechnic, 1955–61; Regent Street Polytechnic, 1960–69; Governor, Suffolk College of Higher and Further Education, 1984–. Served on numerous technical committees in telecommunications field. Patent award, 1970. *Publications:* miscellaneous contribs to learned jls. *Recreations:* reading, photography, wine. *Address:* Heather Lodge, Levington, Ipswich IP10 0NA. *T:* Nacton 508.

MERMAGEN, Air Commodore Herbert Waldemar, CB 1960; CBE 1945 (OBE 1941); AFC 1940; retired, 1960; Director, Sharps, Pixley Ltd (Bullion Brokers), 1962–77; *b* 1 Feb. 1912; *s* of late L. W. R. Mermagen, Southsea; *m* 1937, Rosemary, *d* of late Maj. Mainwaring Williams, DSO and late Mrs Tristram Fox, Cheltenham; two *s*. *Educ:* Brighton Coll., Sussex. Joined RAF, 1930; 43(F) Sqdn, 1931–34; Instructor CFS, 1936–38; Squadron Leader, 1938; served War of 1939–45 in Fighter Command, UK, Middle East, France and Germany (SHAEF); AOC British Air Command, Berlin, 1945–46; Sen. RAF Liaison Officer, UK Services Liaison Staff, Australia, 1948–50; AOC, RAF Ceylon, 1955–57; Air Officer i/c Administration, Headquarters, RAF Transport Command, 1958–60. Air Commodore, 1955. Comdr Legion of Merit (USA), 1946; Medal for Distinguished Services (USSR), 1945; Chevalier, Légion d'Honneur (France) 1951. *Recreations:* rugby (RAF (colours), Sussex, Richmond), golf, gardening. *Address:* Allandale, Vicarage Street, Painswick, Glos. *Club:* Royal Air Force.

MERRELLS, Thomas Ernest; Lord Mayor of Cardiff, 1970–71; *b* 5 Aug. 1891; *s* of Thomas Arthur Merrells, OBE, JP, and Kate Merrells, Swansea; *m* 1922, Vera Pughe Charles; one *s* one *d*. *Educ:* Bishop Gore Grammar Sch., Swansea. Served European War, 1914–18, in France; commissioned in Welsh Regt; seconded to HQ Staff, Royal Engineers, 1917; War of 1939–45: Chm., S Wales Area Nat. Dock Labour Bd; Mem., Exec. Cttee, Regional Port Director of Bristol Channel. Dep. Chm., S Wales Fedn of Port Employers, 1926–47, and Chm., Jt Conciliation Cttee for S Wales Ports. Councillor, City of Cardiff, 1951–74; Alderman, 1966–74. Freeman of City of London, 1971. Chevalier, Order of Mérite Social (France), 1958. *Recreation:* golf. *Address:* 5/11 Conway Road, Cardiff. *T:* Cardiff 398391. *Clubs:* Cardiff Athletic and Rugby; Cardiff Golf.

MERRETT, Charles Edwin, CBE 1979; Area Organiser, Union of Shop, Distributive and Allied Workers, 1948–83, retired; *b* 26 Jan. 1923; *s* of Charles and Eva Merrett; *m* 1950, Mildred Merrett; two *s*. *Educ:* Palfrey Senior Boys' Sch., Walsall. Bristol City Council: Councillor, 1957–, Leader, 1974–78; Lord Mayor of Bristol, 1978–79, Dep. Lord Mayor, 1979–80. Member: Policy Cttee, Assoc. of District Councils, 1974–78; Jt Consultative Cttee on Local Govt Finance, 1975–78; Chm., Adv. Council, BBC Radio Bristol, 1979–83. *Recreations:* watching sport, music, theatre. *Address:* 13 Gainsborough Square, Lockleaze, Bristol BS7 9XA. *T:* Bristol 515195.

MERRICKS, Walter Hugh; Secretary, Professional and Public Relations, The Law Society, since 1985; *b* 4 June 1945; 2nd *s* of Dick and late Phoebe Merricks, Icklesham, Sussex; *m* 1982, Olivia Montuschi; one *s* one *d*, and one step *s*. *Educ:* Bradfield College, Berks; Trinity College, Oxford. MA Hons (Jurisp). Articled Clerk with Batt, Holden, 1968–70; admitted Solicitor, 1970; Hubbard Travelling Scholar, Montreal, 1971; Dir, Camden Community Law Centre, 1972–76; Lectr in Law, Brunel Univ., 1976–81; legal affairs writer, New Law Journal, 1982–85. Member: Royal Commn on Criminal Procedure, 1978–81; Fraud Trials (Roskill) Cttee, 1984–86. *Address:* 32 Cholmeley Crescent, N6 5HA. *T:* 01–341 0406; c/o The Law Society, 113 Chancery Lane, WC2A 1PL. *T:* 01–242 1222.

MERRIFIELD, Prof. Robert Bruce; Professor, since 1966, John D. Rockefeller Jr Professor, since 1984, Rockefeller University; *b* 15 July 1921; *s* of George and Lorene Merrifield; *m* 1949, Elizabeth L. Furlong; one *s* five *d*. *Educ:* Univ. of California, Los Angeles (BA 1943, Chemistry; PhD 1949, Biochemistry). Chemist, Philip R. Park Research Foundn, 1943–44; Research Asst, UCLA Med. Sch., 1948–49; Asst to Associate Prof., Rockefeller Inst. for Med. Research, 1949–66. Nobel Guest Prof., Uppsala, 1968. Member: Amer. Chem. Soc.; Amer. Soc. of Biological Chemists; Amer. Inst. of Chemists; Nat. Acad. of Sciences. Associate Editor, Internat. Jl of Peptide and Protein Research; Mem. Editl Bd of Analytical Biochemistry. Numerous hon. degrees from Amer. univs and colls. Lasker Award for Basic Med. Research, 1969; Gairdner Award, 1970; Intra-Science Award, 1970; Amer. Chem. Soc. Award for Creative Work in Synthetic Organic Chemistry, 1972; Nichols Medal, 1973; Instrument Specialties Co. Award, Univ. of Nebraska, 1977; Alan E. Pierce Award, 1979; Nobel Prize in Chemistry, 1984. Order of San Carlos (Columbia), 1984. *Publications:* numerous papers in sci. jls, esp. on peptide chemistry, solid phase peptide synthesis. *Address:* The Rockefeller University, 1230 York Avenue, New York, NY 10021, USA. *T:* (212) 570–8244.

MERRIMAN, Dr Basil Mandeville; FRAS, FRAI, FRGS; *b* 28 March 1911; *s* of Thomas Henry Merriman and Ida, *d* of Mandeville Blackwood Phillips; *m* 1938, Yvonne Flavelle (*d* 1974); one *s*. *Educ:* Colet Court Prep. Sch.; St Paul's School; St Bartholomew's Hospital Med. Coll.; MRCS, LRCP 1934. House Appointments, St Bartholomew's Hosp., 1934–36; post graduate studies, Berlin, Vienna, Prague, 1936–38; Medical Adviser, British Drug Houses, 1938; Med. Dir, Carter Foundn, 1956; Consultant, Home Office Prison Department, 1963. FRAS 1972; Fellow, Royal Soc. for Asian Affairs, 1973; FRAI 1974; FRGS 1976. *Publications:* contribs to medical and social jls on drug action and drug addiction and their relationship to crime, also various related aspects of social anthropology. *Recreation:* travel of all forms, particularly Asiatic (journeys mainly in Arab Asia, Central Asiatic region, and Japan). *Address:* 85 Holland Park, W11 3RZ. *T:* 01–727 8228.

MERRIMAN, Air Vice-Marshal Henry Alan, CB 1985; CBE 1973; AFC 1957, and Bar 1961; defence and aerospace consultant; Managing Director, Lazard Defence Fund (Management) Ltd; *b* 17 May 1929; *s* of Henry Victor Merriman and Winifred Ellen Merriman; *m* 1965, Mary Brenda Stephenson; three *d*. *Educ:* Hertford Grammar Sch.; RAF Coll., Cranwell. Graduate, Empire Test Pilots Sch. FRAeS 1977. Commnd, 1951; Qual. Flying Instr, 263 F Sqdn, Empire Test Pilots Sch., Fighter Test Sqdn, A&AEE, Central Fighter Establt, and RAF Staff Coll., 1952–63; Personal Air Sec. to Minister of Defence for RAF, 1964–66; Jt Services Staff Coll., 1966; OC Fighter Test Sqdn, A&AEE, 1966–69; HQ 38 Gp, 1969–70; Stn Comdr, RAF Wittering, 1970–72; RCDS, 1973; CO Empire Test Pilots Sch., 1974–75; Comdt, A&AEE, 1975–77; Dir, Operational Requirements (1), 1977–81; Mil. Dep. to Head of Defence Sales, 1981–84. Queen's Commendation for Valuable Services in the Air, 1956. *Recreations:* sailing, gardening. *Address:* c/o Lloyds Bank, Cox's and King's Branch, 6 Pall Mall, SW1. *Clubs:* Royal Air Force; Poole Yacht.

MERRIMAN, James Henry Herbert, CB 1969; OBE 1961; MSc, MInstP, FEng, FIEE, FIEETE; Chairman, National Computing Centre, 1977–83; Member for Technology, Post Office Corporation, 1969–76; *b* 1 Jan. 1915; *s* of Thomas P. Merriman, AMINA and A. Margaretta Jenkins; *m* 1942, Joan B. Frost; twin *s* one *d*. *Educ:* King's Coll. Sch., Wimbledon; King's Coll., University of London. BSc (Hons) 1935; MSc (Thesis) 1936. Entered GPO Engrg Dept (Research), 1936; Officer i/c Castleton Radio Stn, 1940; Asst Staff Engr, Radio Br., 1951; Imp. Def. Coll., 1954; Dep. Dir, Organisation and Methods, HM Treasury, 1956; GPO: Dep. Engr-in-Chief, 1965; Sen. Dir Engrg, 1967. Chairman: NEDO Sector Working Party on Office Machinery, 1979–83; NEDO Information Technology Cttee, 1980–83 (Mem. NEDO Electronics EDC, 1980–83); SERC/DoI/Industry Project Universe Steering Cttee, 1981–83; Home Office Radio Spectrum Review Cttee, 1982–83. Vis. Prof. of Electronic Science and Telecommunications, Strathclyde Univ., 1969–79. Governor, Imperial College, Univ. of London, 1971–83; Chm., Inspec, 1975–79; Dir, Infoline, 1976–80; Member: Nat. Electronics Council, 1969–76; Computer Bd for Univ. and Res. Councils, 1976–81; Exec. Bd, BSI, 1981–85 (Chm. Council for Inf. Systems); Science Museum Adv. Council, 1976–81; Council, Spurgeon's Coll., 1972–. Mem. Council, IEE, 1965–80 (Chm. Electronics Div. Bd, 1968; Vice-Pres., 1969–72, Dep. Pres., 1972; Pres., 1974–75; Hon. FIEE 1981; Faraday Lectr, 1969–70); Royal Instn Discourse, 1971. FKC 1972. Mem., Hon. Soc. of Cymmrodorion, 1979–. Hon. DSc Strathclyde, 1974. *Publications:* contribs to scientific and professional jls on tele-communications and inf. technology subjects.

Recreations: walking, music, cactus growing. *Address*: 5 Melville Avenue, Copse Hill, W Wimbledon, SW20. *T*: 01–946 9870.

MERRISON, Sir Alexander Walter, (Sir Alec Merrison), Kt 1976; DL; FRS 1969; Vice-Chancellor, University of Bristol, 1969–84; *b* 20 March 1924; *s* of late Henry Walter and Violet Henrietta Merrison; *m* 1st, 1948, Beryl Glencora Le Marquand (*d* 1968); two *s*; 2nd, 1970, Maureen Michèle Barry; one *s* one *d*. *Educ*: Enfield Gram. Sch.; King's Coll., London. BSc (London) 1944; PhD (Liverpool) 1957. Res. in Radio Wave Propagation, as Experimental Officer, Signals Research and Development Establishment, Christchurch, 1944–46; Research in Reactor and Nuclear Physics, as Sen. Scientific Officer, AERE, Harwell, 1946–51; Research in Elementary Particle Physics, as Leverhulme Fellow and Lecturer, Liverpool Univ., 1951–57; Physicist, European Organisation for Nuclear Research (CERN) Geneva, 1957–60; Prof. of Experimental Physics, Liverpool Univ., 1960–69, and Dir, Daresbury Nuclear Physics Lab., SRC, 1962–69. Chairman: Cttee of Inquiry into Design and Erection of Steel Box Girder Bridges, 1970–73; Cttee of Inquiry into the Regulation of the Medical Profession, 1972–75; Royal Commn on NHS, 1976–79; Adv. Bd for the Research Councils, 1979–83 (Mem., 1972–73); Cttee of Vice-Chancellors and Principals, 1979–81; ACU, 1982–83; Management Cttee, Univs Superannuation Scheme, 1984–. Chm., Bristol Regional Bd, Lloyds Bank and Dir, Lloyds Bank UK Management Bd, 1983–; Director: Bristol Evening Post, 1979–; Western Provident Assoc., 1983– (Chm., 1985–); Bristol Waterworks Co., 1984–; Lloyds Bank PLC, 1986–. Charles Vernon Boys Prizeman of Inst. of Physics and the Physical Soc., 1961, Mem. Council, 1964–66, 1983–, Pres., 1984–86. Member: Council for Scientific Policy, 1967–72; Nuclear Power Adv. Bd, 1973–76; Adv. Council for Applied R&D, 1979–83; Cttee of Inquiry into Academic Validation of Public Sector Higher Educn, 1984–; Pres. Council, CERN, 1982–85. Governor, Bristol Old Vic Trust, 1969–, Chm., 1971–. Mem. Haberdashers' Co., 1982; Freeman, City of London, 1982. FRSA 1970; FKC 1973. DL Avon, 1974, High Sheriff, 1986–87. Hon. FFCM 1980; Hon. FIStructE 1981; Hon. FRCPsych 1983. Hon. LLD Bristol, 1971; Hon. DSc: Ulster, 1976; Bath, 1977; Southampton, 1980; Leeds, 1981; Liverpool 1982. *Publications*: contrib. to scientific jls on nuclear and elementary particle physics. *Address*: The Manor, Hinton Blewett, Bristol BS18 5AN. *Club*: Athenæum.

MERRITT, Prof. John Edward; educational research in association with Charlotte Mason College and Community Education Development Centre, Coventry, since 1985; Emeritus Fellow, Leverhulme Trust, since 1986; *b* 13 June 1926; *s* of Leonard Merritt and Janet (*née* Hartford); *m* 1948, Denise Edmondson; two *s*. *Educ*: Univ. of Durham (BA); Univ. of London (DipEdPsychol). ABPsS; FRSA. Sandhurst, 1945–46; Trng Officer, Border Regt, 1946–48. Educnl Psychologist, Lancs LEA, 1957–59; Sen. Educnl Psychologist, Hull LEA, 1959–63; Lectr, Inst. of Educn, Univ. of Durham, 1964–71; Prof. of Teacher Educn, Open Univ., 1971–85, retd. Pres., UK Reading Assoc., 1969–70; Chm., 5th World Congress on Reading, Vienna, 1974; Mem., Nat. Cttee of Inquiry into Reading and Use of English (Bullock Cttee), 1973–75. FRSA. *Publications*: Reading and the Curriculum (ed), 1971; A Framework for Curriculum Design, 1972; (ed jtly) Reading Today and Tomorrow, 1972; (ed jtly) The Reading Curriculum, 1972; Perspectives on Reading, 1973; What Shall We Teach, 1974; numerous papers in educnl jls. *Recreations*: fell walking, climbing, theatre. *Address*: Wetherlam, 20 Fisherbeck Park, Ambleside, Cumbria LA22 0AJ. *T*: Ambleside 32259.

MERRIVALE, 3rd Baron, *cr* 1925, of Walkhampton, Co. Devon; **Jack Henry Edmond Duke;** *b* 27 Jan. 1917; *o s* of 2nd Baron Merrivale, OBE, and Odette, *d* of Edmond Roger, Paris; *S* father 1951; *m* 1st, 1939, Colette (marr. diss. 1974), *d* of John Douglas Wise, Bordeaux, France; one *s* one *d*; 2nd, 1975, Betty, *widow* of Paul Baron. *Educ*: Dulwich; Ecole des Sciences Politiques, Paris. Served War of 1939–45, RAF, 1940; Flight-Lieut, 1944 (despatches). Formerly Chm., Scotia Investments Plc; Pres., Inst. of Traffic Administration, 1953–70; Chairman: Anglo-Malagasy Soc., 1961; British Cttee for Furthering of Relations with French-speaking Africa, 1973. Founder Mem., Club de Dakar, 1974. Freeman, City of London, 1979. FRSA 1964. Chevalier, Nat. Order of Malagasy, 1968. *Recreations*: sailing, riding, photography. *Heir*: *s* Hon. Derek John Philip Duke, *b* 16 March 1948. *Address*: 16 Brompton Lodge, SW7 2JA. *T*: 01–581 5678.

MERSEY, 4th Viscount *cr* 1916, of Toxteth; **Richard Maurice Clive Bigham;** Baron 1910; Master of Nairne; film director; *b* 8 July 1934; *e s* of 3rd Viscount Mersey, and of 12th Lady Nairne, *qv*; *S* father, 1979; *m* 1961, Joanna, *d* of John A. R. G. Murray, *qv*; one *s*. *Educ*: Eton and Balliol. Irish Guards, 1952–54 (final rank Lt). Films incl. documentaries for Shell, LEPRA and Government. Various awards in London and Venice. FRGS. *Heir*: *s* Hon. Edward John Hallam Bigham, *b* 23 May 1966. *Address*: 1 Rosmead Road, W11 2JG. *T*: 01–727 5057.

MERTENS DE WILMARS, Baron Josse (Marie Honoré Charles); Grand Croix de l'Ordre de la Couronne; Chevalier de l'Ordre de Léopold; Judge, 1967–84, and President, 1980–84, Court of Justice of the European Communities; Emeritus Professor, Faculty of Law, Catholic University of Leuven, since 1971; Member of the University Curatorium; *b* 12 June 1912; *s* of (Marie Antoine Joseph) Albert Mertens de Wilmars and Jeanne Eugénie Marie Anne Meert; *m* 1939, Elisabeth Simone M. Hubertine van Ormelingen; three *s* five *d*. *Educ*: Abdijschool, Zevenkerke, Bruges; Catholic Univ. of Leuven (Dr in Law, Dr in Pol. and Diplomatic Science). Hon. Assessor, Legislative Dept of Council of State (Conseil d'Etat) (Assessor, 1950–52). Member: Chambre des Représentants de Belgique (Lower House of Parlt), 1951–62; former Mem., Bar Council. Hon. Mem., Bar of Antwerp. CStJ. Groot kruis von de Orde van Orange Nassau (Neth.); Grand Croix de l'Ordre de la Couronne de Chêne (Lux.); Gross Kreus des Verdienstordens der Bundesrepublik Deutschland. *Publications*: several works on Belgian and European Law. *Address*: 192 Jan Van Rijswijcklaan, B-2020 Antwerpen, Belgium. *T*: 03/238–07–68.

MERTHYR, Barony of (*cr* 1911); title disclaimed by 4th Baron; *see under* Lewis, Trevor Oswin.

MERTON, Viscount; Simon John Horatio Nelson; *b* 21 Sept. 1971; *s* and *heir* of 9th Earl Nelson, *qv*.

MERTON, John Ralph, MBE 1942; painter; *b* 7 May 1913; *s* of late Sir Thomas Merton, KBE, FRS; *m* 1939, Viola Penelope von Bernd; two *d* (and one *d* decd). *Educ*: Eton; Balliol Coll., Oxford. Served War of 1939–45 (MBE); Air Photo reconnaissance research, Lieut-Col 1944. Works include: Mrs Daphne Wall, 1948; The Artist's daughter, Sarah, 1949; Altar piece, 1952; The Countess of Dalkeith, at Drumlanrig, 1958; A myth of Delos, 1959; Clarissa, 1960; Lady Georgina Pelham, Mrs Julian Sheffield, 1970; Sir Charles Evans, 1973; Iona Colquhoun Duchess of Argyll, 1982; Triple Portrait of Sir David Piper, 1984 (in Nat. Portrait Gall.). Legion of Merit (USA), 1945. *Recreations*: music, making things, underwater photography. *Address*: Pound House, Oare, near Marlborough, Wilts; Fourth Floor, 50 Cadogan Square, SW1. *Club*: Garrick.

See also R. A. Morritt.

MERTON, Patrick Anthony, MD; FRS 1979; Professor of Human Physiology, Cambridge University, since 1984; Fellow of Trinity College, Cambridge, since 1962; Hon. Consultant to the National Hospital, Queen Square, London, since 1979; *b* 8 Oct. 1920; *s* of late Gerald Merton, MC, PhD, FRAS; *m* 1951, Anna Gabriel Howe; one *s* three *d* *Educ*: The Leys; Beaumont; Trinity Coll., Cambridge (MB 1946; MD 1982); St Thomas's Hosp. On staff of MRC's Neurol. Res. Unit, National Hosp., Queen Sq., 1946–57; Nobel Inst. for Neurophysiology, Stockholm, 1952–54; Lectr in Physiol., 1957–77, Reader, 1977–84, Univ. of Cambridge; Hon. Sen. Res. Fellow, Royal Postgrad. Med. Sch., 1981–82. *Publications*: papers on control of muscular contraction mainly in Jl of Physiol. *Address*: 12 Lansdowne Road, Cambridge CB3 0EU. *T*: Cambridge 359991.

MERVYN DAVIES, David Herbert; *see* Davies, D. H. M.

MESSEL, Prof. Harry, CBE 1979; BA, BSc, PhD (NUI) 1951; Professor and Head of the School of Physics, and Director of Science Foundation for Physics, University of Sydney, Australia, since 1952; *b* 3 March 1922. *Educ*: Rivers Public High Sch., Rivers, Manitoba. Entered RMC of Canada, 1940, grad. with Governor-General's Silver Medal, 1942. Served War of 1939–45: Canadian Armed Forces, Lieut, Canada and overseas, 1942–45. Queen's Univ., Kingston, Ont., 1945–48; BA 1st Cl. Hons in Mathematics, 1948, BSc Hons in Engineering Physics, 1948; St Andrews Univ., Scotland, 1948–49; Institute for Advanced Studies, Dublin, Eire, 1949–51; Sen. Lectr in Mathematical Physics, University of Adelaide, Australia, 1951–52. Mem., Aust. Atomic Energy Commn, 1974–81; Vice-Chm. (Aust.) Species Survival Commn, IUCN, 1978–. *Publications*: Chap. 4, Progress in Cosmic Ray Physics, vol. 2, (North Holland Publishing Company), 1953; co-author and editor of: A Modern Introduction to Physics (Horwitz-Grahame, Vols I, II, III, 1959, 1960, 1962); Selected Lectures in Modern Physics, 1958; Space and the Atom, 1961; A Journey through Space and the Atom, 1962; The Universe of Time and Space, 1963; Light and Life in the Universe, 1964; Science for High School Students, 1964; Time, 1965; Senior Science for High School Students, 1966; (jt) Electron-Photon Shower Distribution Function, 1970; (jt) Multistrand Senior Science for High School Students, 1975; Australian Animals and their Environment, 1977; Time and Man, 1978; Tidal Rivers in Northern Australia and their Crocodile Populations (19 monographs), 1979–86; The Study of Populations, 1985; editor of: From Nucleus to Universe, 1960; Atoms to Andromeda, 1966; Apollo and the Universe, 1967; Man in Inner and Outer Space, 1968; Nuclear Energy Today and Tomorrow, 1969; Pioneering in Outer Space, 1970; Molecules to Man, 1971; Brain Mechanisms and the Control of Behaviour, 1972; Focus on the Stars, 1973; Solar Energy, 1974; Our Earth, 1975; Energy for Survival, 1979; The Biological Manipulation of Life, 1981; Science Update, 1983; numerous papers published in: Proc. Physical Soc., London; Philosophical Magazine, London; Physical Review of America. *Recreations*: water ski-ing, hunting, fishing and photography. *Address*: University of Sydney, Sydney, NSW 2006, Australia. *T*: 692 2537, 692 3383.

MESSERVY, Sir (Roney) Godfrey (Collumbell), Kt 1986; Chairman and Chief Executive, Lucas Industries plc, since 1980 (Managing Director, 1974; Deputy Chairman, 1979); *b* 17 Nov. 1924; *s* of late Roney Forshaw Messervy and Bertha Crosby (*née* Collumbell); *m* 1952, Susan Patricia Gertrude, *d* of late Reginald Arthur Nunn, DSO, DSC, RNVR, and of Adeline Frances Nunn; one *s* two *d*. *Educ*: Oundle; Cambridge Univ. Served War, RE, 1943–47: Parachute Sqdn (Captain). CAV (Mem. of Lucas Group): joined as trainee, 1949; Dir of Equipment Sales, 1963; Dir and Gen. Man., 1966 (also dir of various Lucas subsids at home and abroad). Director: Joseph Lucas Ltd, 1971–; Joseph Lucas (Industries) Ltd, 1972–; Costain Group plc, 1978–. Member: Council, Birmingham Chamber of Industry and Commerce, 1979– (Vice-Pres., 1980–82, Pres., 1982–83); Council, SMMT, 1980– (Mem. Exec. Cttee; Vice-Pres., 1984); Engrg Industries Council, 1980–; Nat. Defence Industries Council, 1980–; Council, CBI, 1982–; BOTB, 1984–; Vice-Pres., EEF, 1982. Freeman, Worshipful Co. of Ironmongers, 1977, Liveryman, 1979. Hon. DSc Aston in Birmingham, 1982. *Recreations*: farming, field sports, flying, photography. *Address*: Lucas Industries plc, Great King Street, Birmingham B19 2XF. *T*: 021–554 5252.

MESSIAEN, Olivier; Grand Officier de la Légion d'Honneur; Grand Croix de l'Ordre national du Mérite; Commandeur des Arts et des Lettres; Member, Institut de France; composer and organist; *b* Avignon, 10 Dec. 1908; *s* of Pierre Messiaen and Cécile Sauvage; *m* 1st, Claire Delbos (*d* 1959); one *s*; 2nd, 1961, Yvonne Loriod (pianist). *Educ*: Lycée de Grenoble; Conservatoire Nat. supérieur de musique, Paris (7 1st prizes). Organist, Trinité, Paris, 1930; co-founder Jeune-France Movement, 1936. Professor: Ecole Normale and Schola Cantorum, 1936–39; of Harmony, Paris Conservatoire, 1941–47; of Analysis, Aesthetics and Rhythm, 1947–; of Composition, 1966–. Mem. Council, Order of Arts and Letters, 1975–. Member: Royal Academy; Acads of Brussels, Madrid, Stockholm. Erasmus Prize, 1971; Sibelius Prize, 1971; Von Siemens Prize, 1975; Léonie Sonning Prize, 1977; Bach-Hamburg Prize, 1979; Liebermann Prize, 1983; Wolf Foundn (Israel) Prize, 1983; Académie Berlin Prize, 1984; Inamori of Tokyo Prize, 1985. *Works for organ include*: Le Banquet Céleste, 1928; Le Diptyque, 1929; L'Ascension, 1933; La Nativité du Seigneur, 1935; Les Corps Glorieux, 1939; Messe de la Pentecôte, 1949; Livre d'Orgue, 1951; Méditations sur le Mystère de la Sainte Trinité, 1969; Livre du Saint Sacrement, 1984–85; *other works include*: Préludes, 1929; Poèmes pour Mi, 1936; Chants de Terre et de Ciel, 1938; Quatuor pour la Fin du Temps, 1941; Visions de l'Amen, 1943; Vingt Regards sur l'Enfant Jésus, 1944; Trois Petites Liturgies de la Présence Divine, 1944; Harawi, 1945; Turangalila–Symphonie, 1946–48; Cinq Rechants, 1949; Etudes de Rythme, 1949; Réveil des Oiseaux, 1953; Oiseaux exotiques, 1955; Catalogue d'Oiseaux, 1956–58; Chronochromie, 1959; Sept Haïkaï, 1963; Couleurs de la Cité Céleste, 1964; Et Exspecto Resurrectionem Mortuorum, 1965; La Transfiguration de Notre Seigneur, Jésus-Christ, 1969; La Fauvette des Jardins (for piano), 1970; Des Canyons aux Etoiles, 1970–74; Saint François d'Assise (opera), 1975–83.

MESSITER, Air Commodore Herbert Lindsell, CB 1954; 2nd *s* of late Col Charles Bayard Messiter, DSO, OBE, Barwick Park, Yeovil, Som, and Alice Lindsell; *m* 1933, Lucy Brenda Short; one *d*. *Educ*: Bedford Sch. Served War of 1939–45 (despatches 4 times): Egypt, N Africa, Belgium, Germany. Command Engineer Officer, Far East Air Force, 1950–52; Senior Technical Staff Officer, Bomber Command, RAF, 1952–56; Senior Technical Staff Officer, Middle East Air Force, 1956–59, retired. *Address*: c/o Lloyds Bank, 6 Pall Mall, SW1; Lion Cottage, Grateley, Hants. *Club*: Royal Air Force.

MESSMER, Pierre Auguste Joseph; Grand Officier de la Légion d'Honneur; Compagnon de la Libération; Croix de Guerre, 1939–45; Médaille de la Résistance; Député (RPR) from Moselle, since 1968; *b* Vincennes (Seine), 20 March 1916; *s* of Joseph Messmer, industrialist, and of Marthe (*née* Farcy); *m* 1947, Gilberte Duprez. *Educ*: Lycées Charlemagne and Louis-le Grand; Faculty of Law, Paris; Ecole Nationale de la France d'Outre-Mer. Pupil Administrator of Colonies, 1938. Served War of 1939–45: Free French Forces, 1940; African Campaigns (Bir-Hakeim), France, Germany; parachuted Tonkin; PoW of Vietminh, 1945. Sec.-Gen., Interministerial Cttee of Indochina, 1946; Dir of Cabinet of E. Bollaert (High Commissioner, Indochina), 1947–48; Administrator-in-Chief of France Overseas, 1950; Governor: of Mauritania, 1952, of Ivory Coast, 1954–56; Dir of Cabinet of G. Defferre (Minister, France Overseas), Jan.-April 1956; High Commissioner: Republic of Cameroon, 1956–58; French Equatorial Africa, 1958; French West Africa, July 1958–Dec. 1959; Minister of Armed Forces: (Cabinets: M.

Debré, 5 Feb. 1958–14 April 1962; G. Pompidou, April-Nov. 1962, 6 Dec. 1962–7 Jan. 1966, 8 Jan. 1966–1 April 1967, 7 April 1967–10 July 1968; M. Couve de Murville, 12 July 1968–20 June 1969); Minister of State in charge of Depts and Territories Overseas, Feb. 1971–72; Prime Minister, 1972–74; Mem. European Parliament, 1979–84. Pres., RPR Federal Cttee, Moselle, 1969–. Mayor of Sarrebourg, 1971–. Officer, American Legion. *Recreations:* tennis, sailing. *Address:* 1 rue du Général Delanne, 92 Neuilly-sur-Seine, France.

MESTEL, Prof. Leon, PhD; FRS 1977; Professor of Astronomy, University of Sussex, since 1973; *b* 5 Aug. 1927; *s* of late Rabbi Solomon Mestel and Rachel (*née* Brodetsky); *m* 1951, Sylvia Louise Cole; two *s* two *d. Educ:* West Ham Secondary Sch., London; Trinity Coll., Cambridge (BA 1948, PhD 1952). ICI Res. Fellow, Dept of Maths, Univ. of Leeds, 1951–54; Commonwealth Fund Fellow, Princeton Univ. Observatory, 1954–55; University of Cambridge: Univ. Asst Lectr in Maths, 1955–58; Univ. Lectr in Maths, 1958–66; Fellow of St John's Coll., 1957–66; Vis. Mem., Inst. for Advanced Study, Princeton, 1961–62; J. F. Kennedy Fellow, Weizmann Inst. of Science, Israel, 1966–67; Prof. of Applied Maths, Manchester Univ., 1967–73. *Publications:* Magnetohydrodynamics (with N. O. Weiss), 1974 (Geneva Observatory); papers, revs and conf. reports on different branches of theoretical astrophysics. *Recreations:* reading, music. *Address:* 13 Prince Edward's Road, Lewes, E Sussex BN7 1BJ. *T:* Lewes 472731.

MESTON, family name of **Baron Meston.**

MESTON, 3rd Baron *cr* 1919, of Agra and Dunottar; **James Meston;** *b* 10 Feb. 1950; *s* of 2nd Baron Meston and of Diana Mary Came, *d* of Capt. O. S. Doll; *S* father, 1984; *m* 1974, Jean Rebecca Anne, *d* of John Carder; one *s* one *d. Educ:* Wellington College; St Catharine's Coll., Cambridge (MA). Barrister, Middle Temple, 1973. *Heir: s* Hon. Thomas James Dougall Meston, *b* 21 Oct. 1977. *Address:* Queen Elizabeth Building, Temple, EC4. *T:* 01–583 7837. *Club:* Hawks (Cambridge).

METCALF, David Michael, DPhil, DLitt; Keeper of Heberden Coin Room, Ashmolean Museum, Oxford, since 1982; Fellow of Wolfson College, Oxford, since 1982; *b* 8 May 1933; *s* of Rev. Thomas Metcalf and Gladys Metcalf; *m* 1958, Dorothy Evelyn (*née* Uren); two *s* one *d. Educ:* St John's College, Cambridge. MA, DPhil, DLitt; FSA. Asst Keeper, Ashmolean Museum, 1963. Sec., Royal Numismatic Soc., and Editor, Numismatic Chronicle, 1974–84. *Publications:* Coinage in South-eastern Europe 820–1396, 1979; Coinage of the Crusades and the Latin East, 1983; (ed with D. H. Hill) Sceattas in England and on the Continent, 1984; articles on numismatics in various jls. *Address:* 40 St Margaret's Road, Oxford.

METCALF, Dr Donald, AO 1976; FRS 1983, FRACP, FRCPA, FAA; Head of Cancer Research Unit, Walter and Eliza Hall Institute of Medical Research, Melbourne, since 1965; *b* 26 Feb. 1929; *s* of Donald Davidson Metcalf and Enid Victoria Metcalf (*née* Thomas); *m* 1954, Josephine Emily Lentaigne; four *d. Educ:* Sydney University. MD, BSc (med). Resident MO, Royal Prince Alfred Hosp., Sydney, 1953–54; Surgeon-Lieut, RANR, 1953–58; Carden Fellow in Cancer Res., 1954–65, Asst Director and Head of Cancer Res. Unit, 1965–, Walter and Eliza Hall Inst. Vis. Fellow, Harvard Med. Sch., 1956–58; Visiting Scientist: Roswell Park Meml Inst., Buffalo, 1966–67; Swiss Inst. for Experimental Cancer Res., Lausanne, 1974–75; Radiobiological Res. Inst., Rijswijk, 1980–81; Royal Soc. Guest Res. Fellow, Cambridge Univ., 1981. *Publications:* The Thymus, 1966; (with M. A. S. Moore) Haemopoietic Cells, 1971; Hemopoietic Colonies, 1977; numerous scientific papers on cancer and leukaemia. *Recreations:* music, tennis. *Address:* 268 Union Road, Balwyn, Victoria 3103, Australia. *T:* (03) 836–1343.

METCALF, Malcolm, MC 1944; DL; Chairman, Surrey County Council, 1978–81; *b* 1 Dec. 1917; *s* of Charles Almond Metcalf and Martha Fatherly Atkins Metcalf; *m* 1945, Charis Thomas; two *s. Educ:* Merchant Taylors' Sch., Crosby. ACIS. Army service, 1939–46. Contested (C) Barrow-in-Furness, 1959; Mem., Surrey CC, 1965– (Leader, 1973–77; Vice-Chm., 1977–78); Member: Metrop. Water Board, 1965–74 (Vice-Chm. 1971–72); Thames Conservancy, 1970–74; Thames Water Authority, 1973–78, 1981–. Mem., Assoc. of County Councils, 1975–. DL Surrey, 1979. *Address:* 1 The Lodge, Watts Road, Thames Ditton KT7 0DE. *T:* 01–398 3057. *Clubs:* MCC, Burhill Golf (Walton-on-Thames).

METCALFE, Prof. David Henry Harold; Professor of General Practice, University of Manchester School of Medicine, since 1978; Director, DHSS Urban Primary care research unit, since 1978; *b* 3 Jan. 1930; *s* of Henry R. Metcalfe and Mary Metcalfe (*née* Evans); *m* 1957, Anne (*née* Page); three *s. Educ:* Leys School, Cambridge; Cambridge Univ. (clinical course at Liverpool) (MA, MB, BChir); MSc Manchester. FRCGP; MFCM. United Liverpool Hosps, 1956–58; Principal in gen. practice, Hessle, E Yorks, 1969–70; Asst Prof. in Family Medicine, Univ. of Rochester, NY, 1970–72; Sen. Lectr (GP), Dept of Community Health, Nottingham Univ. Med. Sch., 1972–78. Vice-Chm., RCGP, 1983–84. *Publications:* papers on medical information handling, doctor-patient communication, patterns of general practice, and medical educn. *Recreations:* photography, sailing, hill walking. *Address:* 8 Netherwood Road, Manchester M22 4BQ. *T:* 061–998 1974.

METCALFE, Hugh, OBE 1969; FEng; FRAeS; Director, since 1982, and Deputy Chief Executive (Operations), since 1986, British Aerospace plc; *b* 26 June 1928; *s* of Clifford and late Florence Ellen Metcalfe; *m* 1952, Pearl Allison Carter; three *s. Educ:* Harrow County Grammar School; Imperial College, Univ. of London. BSc, ARCS. RAF, 1946–48; joined Bristol Aeroplane Co., 1951; technical and management appts; Divisional Dir, 1974; British Aerospace Dynamics Group: Group Dir, Naval Weapons, 1978; Man. Dir, Bristol Div., 1980; Man. Dir, Hatfield Div., 1981; Chief Exec., 1982; Dep. Man. Dir (Dynamics), BAe, 1985. RAeS gold medal, 1984. *Recreation:* choral music. *Address:* c/o British Aerospace plc, 11 Strand, WC2. *T:* 01–930 1020. *Clubs:* Athenæum; Leander; Savage's (Bristol).

METCALFE, Air Commodore Joan, CB 1981; RRC 1976; Director of RAF Nursing Services, and Matron in Chief, Princess Mary's Royal Air Force Nursing Service, 1978–81; *b* 8 Jan. 1923; *d* of late W. and S. H. Metcalfe. *Educ:* West Leeds High Sch. for Girls; Leeds Coll. of Commerce. St James's Hosp., Leeds, 1943–47 (SRN); St James's Hosp. and Redcourt Hostel, Leeds, 1947–48 (SCM), PMRAFNS 1948. Served in RAF Hospitals in Egypt, Iraq, Libya, Cyprus, Germany, Singapore, and UK. Sen. Matron, 1970; Principal Matron, 1973. QHNS 1978 81. OStJ 1977. *Recreations:* classical music, theatre, needlework, gardening, non-fiction literature. *Address:* 10 Amport Close, Harestock, Winchester, Hants SO22 6LP. *T:* Winchester 880260. *Club:* Royal Air Force.

METCALFE, Stanley Gordon; Managing Director, Ranks Hovis McDougall Ltd, since 1981; *b* 20 June 1932; *s* of Stanley Hudson Metcalfe and Jane Metcalfe; *m* 1968, Sarah Harter; two *d. Educ:* Leeds Grammar Sch.; Pembroke Coll., Oxford (MA). Commnd Duke of Wellington's Regt, 1952. Trainee, Ranks, Hovis McDougall, 1956–59; Director, Stokes & Dalton, Leeds, 1963–66; Managing Director, McDougalls, 1966–69; Director, Cerebos Ltd, 1969–70; Managing Director: RHM Overseas Ltd, 1970–73; RHM Cereals Ltd, 1973–79; Director, Ranks Hovis McDougall Ltd, 1979. President, Nat. Assoc. of British and Irish Millers, 1978. *Recreations:* cricket, golf, theatre. *Address:* The Oast House, Lower Froyle, Alton, Hants GU34 4LX. *T:* Bentley 22310. *Clubs:* United Oxford and Cambridge University, MCC, IZ, Arabs.

METFORD, Prof. John Callan James; Professor of Spanish, 1960–81, now Emeritus Professor, Head of Department of Hispanic and Latin American Studies, 1973–81, University of Bristol; *b* 29 Jan. 1916; *s* of Oliver Metford and Florence Stowe Thomas; *m* 1944, Edith Donald; one *d. Educ:* Porth Grammar Sch.; Universities of Liverpool, Yale and California. Commonwealth Fund Fellow, 1939–41; British Council Lecturer in Brazil, 1942–44; Regional Officer, Latin American Department of the British Council, 1944–46; Lectr in Latin American Studies, Univ. of Glasgow, 1946–55; Bristol University: Head of Dept of Spanish and Portuguese, 1955–73; Prof., 1960–81; Dean of Faculty of Arts, 1973–76; Chm., Sch. of Modern Langs, 1976–79. Vis. Prof., Lehigh Univ., USA, 1968–69. Chm., Council of Westonbirt Sch., 1976–83; Mem., Central Cttee of Allied Schs, 1970–83; Governor, Coll. of St Matthias, Bristol, 1960–79; Mem., St Matthias Trust; Professorial Mem., Council of Univ. of Bristol, 1972–74. Mem., Diocesan Adv. Cttee, Bristol, 1984–. *Publications:* British Contributions to Spanish and Spanish American Studies, 1950; San Martín the Liberator, 1950, 2nd edn 1970; Modern Latin America, 1964; The Golden Age of Spanish Drama, 1969; Falklands or Malvinas?, rev. edn of J. Goebel: The Struggle for the Falkland Islands, 1982; Dictionary of Christian Lore and Legend, 1983; The Christian Year, 1986; articles in Bull. of Spanish Studies, Bull. of Hispanic Studies, Liverpool Studies in Spanish, International Affairs, Contemporary Review, etc. *Recreations:* opera, iconography. *Address:* 2 Parry's Close, Bristol BS9 1AW. *T:* Bristol 682284.

METHUEN, family name of **Baron Methuen.**

METHUEN, 6th Baron *cr* 1838; **Anthony John Methuen,** ARICS; *b* 26 Oct. 1925; *s* of 5th Baron Methuen and Grace (*d* 1972), *d* of Sir Richard Holt, 1st Bt; *S* father, 1975. *Educ:* Winchester; Royal Agricultural Coll., Cirencester. Served Scots Guards and Royal Signals, 1943–47. Lands Officer, Air Ministry, 1951–62; QALAS 1954. *Recreation:* shooting. *Heir: b* Hon. Robert Alexander Holt Methuen [*b* 22 July 1931; *m* 1958, Mary Catharine Jane, *d* of Ven. C. G. Hooper, *qv*; two *d.*] *Address:* Corsham Court, Wilts. *Club:* Lansdowne.

METTERS, Dr Jeremy Stanley, FRCOG; Deputy Chief Scientist, Department of Health and Social Security, since 1986; *b* 6 June 1939; *s* of late Thomas Lee Metters and Henrietta Currey; *m* 1962, Margaret Howell; two *s* one *d. Educ:* Eton; Magdalene College, Cambridge; St Thomas' Hosp. (MB BChir 1963, MA 1965). MRCOG 1970, FRCOG 1982. House officer posts, St Thomas' Hosp. and Reading, 1963–66; Lectr in Obst. and Gyn., St Thomas' Hosp., 1968–70; Registrar in Radiotherapy, 1970–72; DHSS 1972; SPMO (Under Sec.), 1984. Mem., Council of Europe Cttee on Ethical and Legal Problems relating to Human Genetics, 1983–85. *Publications:* papers in med. and sci. jls. *Recreations:* touring and travel, DIY, preserved steam railways. *Address:* 8 Lauriston Road, SW19. *T:* 01–947 1322.

METZGER, Rev. Prof. Bruce Manning; George L. Collord Professor of New Testament Language and Literature, Princeton Theological Seminary, 1964–84, now Emeritus; *b* Middletown, Pa, 9 Feb. 1914; *o s* of late Maurice R. Metzger and Anna Manning Metzger; *m* 1944, Isobel Elizabeth, *e d* of late Rev. John Alexander Mackay, DD; two *s. Educ:* Lebanon Valley Coll. (BA 1935); Princeton Theol Seminary (ThB 1938, ThM 1939); Princeton Univ. (MA 1940, PhD 1942, Classics). Ordained, United Presbyterian Church, USA, 1939; Princeton Theological Seminary: Teaching Fellow in NT Greek, 1938–40; Instr. in NT, 1940–44; Asst Prof., 1944–48; Associate Prof., 1948–54; Prof., 1954–64. Vis. Lectr, Sem. Theol. Presbyt. do Sul, Campinas, Brazil, 1952; Schol. in Residence, Tyndale Hse, Cambridge, 1969; Dist. Vis. Prof., Fuller Theol Sem., 1970; Vis. Fellow: Clare Hall, Cambridge, 1974; Wolfson Coll., Oxford, 1979; Vis. Prof., Gordon-Conwell Theol Sem., 1978; Lectr, New Coll. for Advanced Christian Studies, 1978; many lectures to some 100 other academic instns on 5 continents. Chairman, Amer. Cttee on Versions, Internat. Greek NT Project, 1950–; Secretary: Panel of Translators, Rev. Standard Version of Apocrypha, 1952–57; Amer. Textual Criticism Seminar, 1954–56; Member: Kurat. of Vetus Latina Inst., Beuron, 1959–; Adv. Cttee, Inst. of NT Textual Res. Münster, Germany, 1961–; Inst. for Advanced Study, Princeton, 1964 and 1974; Chairman: Cttee on Trans., Amer. Bible Soc., 1964–70; Amer. Exec. Cttee, Internat. Greek NT Project, 1970–; NT Section, Rev. Standard Version Bible Cttee, 1971–. President: Soc. of Biblical Lit., 1971; Stud. Novi Test. Soc., 1971–72; N Amer. Patristic Soc., 1972; Corresp. Fellow Brit. Acad., 1978; Hon. Fellow and Corresp. Mem., Higher Inst. of Coptic Studies, Cairo, 1955; Mem., Amer. Philosophical Soc., 1986–. Hon. DD: Lebanon Valley Coll., 1951 (also Dist. Alumnus award of Alumni Assoc. 1961); St Andrews, 1964; Hon. DTheol Münster, 1971; Hon. LHD Findlay Coll., 1962; Hon. DLitt Potchefstroom, 1985. *Publications:* The Saturday and Sunday Lessons from Luke in the Greek Gospel Lectionary, 1944; Lexical Aids for Students of New Testament Greek, 1946, enlarged edn 1955 (trans. Malagasy, Korean); A Guide to the Preparation of a Thesis, 1950, 2nd edn 1961; Index of Articles on the New Testament and the Early Church Published in Festschriften, 1951, Supplement 1955; Annotated Bibliography of the Textual Criticism of the New Testament, 1955; (jtly) The Text, Canon, and Principal Versions of the Bible, 1956; An Introduction to the Apocrypha, 1957 (trans. Korean); Index to Periodical Literature on the Apostle Paul, 1960, 2nd edn 1970; Lists of Words Occurring Frequently in the Coptic New Testament (Sahidic Dialect), 1961; (jtly) The Oxford Concise Concordance to the Revised Standard Version of the Holy Bible, 1962; (jtly) The Oxford Annotated Bible, 1962; Chapters in the History of New Testament Textual Criticism, 1963; The Text of the New Testament, its Transmission, Corruption, and Restoration, 1964 (trans. German, Japanese, Korean, Chinese); The Oxford Annotated Apocrypha, 1965; The New Testament, its Background, Growth, and Content, 1965 (trans. Chinese, Korean); Index to Periodical Literature on Christ and the Gospels, 1966; Historical and Literary Studies, Pagan, Jewish, and Christian, 1968; A Textual Commentary on the Greek New Testament, 1971; The New Oxford Annotated Bible with the Apocrypha, expanded edn 1977; The Early Versions of the New Testament, their Origin, Transmission, and Limitations, 1977; New Testament Studies, Philological, Versional, and Patristic, 1980; Manuscripts of the Greek Bible, an Introduction to Greek Palaeography, 1981 (trans. Japanese); (general editor) Reader's Digest Condensed Bible, 1982; ed, New Testament Tools and Studies, ten vols, 1960–80; co-ed, The Greek New Testament, 1966, 3rd edn 1975; numerous articles in learned jls and encycs. *Recreations:* reading, woodworking. *Address:* 20 Cleveland Lane, Princeton, New Jersey 08540, USA. *T:* (609) 924–4060. *Club:* Nassau (Princeton, New Jersey).

MEXBOROUGH, 8th Earl of, *cr* 1766; **John Christopher George Savile;** Baron Pollington, 1753; Viscount Pollington, 1766; *b* 16 May 1931; *s* of 7th Earl of Mexborough, and of Josephine Bertha Emily, *d* of late Captain Andrew Mansel Talbot Fletcher; *S* father, 1980; *m* 1st, 1958, Elizabeth Hariot (marr. diss. 1972), *d* of 6th Earl of Verulam; one *s* one *d*; 2nd, 1972, Mrs Catherine Joyce Vivian, *d* of late J. K. Hope, CBE; one *s* one *d. Heir: s* Viscount Pollington, *qv. Address:* Arden Hall, Hawnby, York. *T:* Bilsdale 348. *Clubs:* Turf; All England Lawn Tennis and Croquet.

MEYER, Prof. Alfred, MD; FRCPsych; Professor of Neuropathology in the University of London, Institute of Psychiatry, 1949–56, retired; *b* 3 Feb. 1895; *m* 1949, Nina Cohen. Assoc. Prof. of Neurology at University of Bonn, 1931; Rockefeller Research Fellow in Pathological Laboratory, Maudlsey Hosp., London, 1933; Neuropathologist in the Pathological Laboratory, Maudsley Hospital, 1943. Honorary Member: German Soc. of Neurology and Psychiatry; French Soc. of Neuro-Surgery; Brit. Soc. of Neuropathology. *Publications:* (jt) Prefrontal Leucotomy and Related Operations: anatomical aspects, 1954; (jt) Neuropathology, 1958, 2nd edn 1963; Historical Aspects of Cerebral Anatomy, 1971; articles on neuroanatomical and neuropathological subjects. *Address:* 38 Wood Lane, N6 5UB.

MEYER, Sir Anthony John Charles, 3rd Bt, *cr* 1910; MP (C) Clwyd North West, since 1983 (West Flint, 1970–83); *b* 27 Oct. 1920; *o s* of Sir Frank Meyer, MP, 2nd Bt, Ayot House, Ayot St Lawrence, Herts; *S* father, 1935; *m* 1941, Barbadee Violet, *o c* of late A. Charles Knight, JP, and of Mrs Charles Knight, Herne Place, Sunningdale; one *s* three *d*. *Educ:* Eton (Capt. of Oppidans); New Coll., Oxford. Served Scots Guards, 1941–45 (wounded); HM Treasury, 1945–46; entered HM Foreign Service, 1946; HM Embassy, Paris, 1951; 1st Sec., 1953; transferred to HM Embassy, Moscow, 1956; London, 1958. MP (C) Eton and Slough, 1964–66. Cons. Research Dept, 1968. PPS to Chief Sec., Treasury, 1970–72; PPS to Sec. of State for Employment, 1972–74. Chm., Franco-British Parly Relations Cttee, 1979–; Vice-Chm., Cons. European Affairs Cttee, 1979–; Mem., Panel of Chairmen, House of Commons, 1985–. Trustee of Shakespeare National Memorial Theatre. Founder and Dir of political jl, Solon, 1969. Officier, Légion d'Honneur, France, 1983. *Publication:* A European Technological Community, 1966. *Recreations:* music, travel, skiing, cooking. *Heir: s* Anthony Ashley Frank Meyer [*b* 23 Aug. 1944; *m* 1966, Susan Mathilda (marr. diss. 1980), *d* of John Freestone; one *d*]. *Address:* Cottage Place, Brompton Square, SW3. *T:* 01–589 7416; Rhewl House, Llanasa, Flints. *Club:* Beefsteak.

MEYER, Christopher John Rome; HM Diplomatic Service; Head of News Department, Foreign and Commonwealth Office, since 1984; *b* 22 Feb. 1944; *s* of Flight Lieut R. H. R. Meyer (killed in action 1944) and Mrs E. P. L. Meyer (now Mrs D. F. Macdonald); *m* 1976, Françoise Elizabeth Hedges (*née* Winskill); two *s* one step *s*. *Educ:* Lancing College; Peterhouse, Cambridge (MA History); Johns Hopkins Sch. of Advanced Internat. Studies, Bologna. Third Sec., FO, 1966–67; Army Sch. of Education, 1967–68; Third, later Second, Sec., Moscow, 1968–70; Second Sec., Madrid, 1970–73; First Sec., FCO, 1973–78; First Sec., UK Perm. Rep. to European Communities, 1978–82; Counsellor and Hd of Chancery, Moscow, 1982–84. *Address:* c/o Foreign and Commonwealth Office, King Charles Street, SW1A 2AH.

MEYER, Rt. Rev. Conrad John Eustace; *see* Dorchester, Area Suffragan of.

MEYER, Michael Leverson; free-lance writer since 1950; *b* London, 11 June 1921; 3rd and *y s* of Percy Barrington Meyer and Eleanor Rachel Meyer (*née* Benjamin); unmarried; one *d*. *Educ:* Wellington Coll.; Christ Church, Oxford (MA). Operational Res. Section, Bomber Comd HQ, 1942–45; Lectr in English Lit., Uppsala Univ., 1947–50. Vis. Prof. of Drama, Dartmouth Coll., USA, 1978. Mem. Editorial Adv. Bd, Good Food Guide, 1958–72. FRSL. Gold Medal, Swedish Academy, 1964. Knight Commander, Polar Star (1st class), Sweden, 1977. *Publications:* (ed, with Sidney Keyes, and contrib.) Eight Oxford Poets, 1941; (ed) Collected Poems of Sidney Keyes, 1945; (ed) The Minos of Crete, by Sidney Keyes, 1948; The End of the Corridor (novel), 1951; The Ortolan (play), 1967; Henrik Ibsen: The Making of a Dramatist, 1967; Henrik Ibsen: The Farewell to Poetry, 1971; Henrik Ibsen: The Top of a Cold Mountain, 1971 (Whitbread Biography Prize, 1971); Lunatic and Lover (play), 1981; (ed) Summer Days, 1981; Ibsen on File, 1985; Strindberg: a biography, 1985; File on Strindberg, 1986; *translated:* The Long Ships, by Frans G. Bengtsson, 1954; Ibsen: Brand, The Lady from the Sea, John Gabriel Borkman, When We Dead Awaken, 1960; The Master Builder, Little Eyolf, 1961; Ghosts, The Wild Duck, Hedda Gabler, 1962; Peer Gynt, An Enemy of the People, The Pillars of Society, 1963; The Pretenders, 1964; A Doll's House, 1965; Rosmersholm, 1966; Emperor and Galilean, 1986; Strindberg: The Father, Miss Julie, Creditors, The Stronger, Playing with Fire, Erik the Fourteenth, Storm, The Ghost Sonata, 1964; A Dream Play, 1973; To Damascus, Easter, The Dance of Death, The Virgin Bride, 1975. *Recreations:* real tennis, eating, sleeping. *Address:* 4 Montagu Square, W1H 1RA. *T:* 01–486 2573. *Clubs:* Savile, Garrick, MCC.

MEYER, Rollo John Oliver, (Jack), OBE 1967; Co-founder, Byron College, Athens, 1986; Rector and Director of Remedial Education Centre; *b* 15 March 1905; *s* of Canon Rollo Meyer and Arabella Ward; *m* 1931, Joyce Symons; one *d* (and one *d* decd). *Educ:* Haileybury Coll.; Pembroke Coll., Cambridge. MA 1926. Cottonbroker, Gill & Co., Bombay, 1926–29; Private Tutor, Limbdi and Porbandar, 1929–30; Headmaster, Dhrangadhra Palace Sch., 1930–35; Founder, and first Headmaster of: Millfield School, 1935–71; Edgarley Hall Preparatory Sch., Glastonbury, 1945–71; Headmaster, 1973–77, and Pres., 1977–80, Campion Sch., Athens; Founder, 1979, and first Headmaster, St Lawrence Coll., Athens, resigned 1986. *Recreations:* teaching, dreaming, talking, chess. *Address:* 12 Milton Lane, Wells, Somerset BA5 2QS. *T:* Wells 72080; Byron College, Athens, Greece. *Clubs:* MCC, English-Speaking Union.

MEYJES, Sir Richard (Anthony), Kt 1972; DL; Director: Portals Holdings Ltd; Foseco Minsep Ltd; *b* 30 June 1918; *s* of Anthony Charles Dorian Meyjes and late Norah Isobel Meyjes; *m* 1939, Margaret Doreen Morris; three *s*. *Educ:* University College School, Hampstead. War Service, RASC, Sept. 1939–Jan. 1946 (temp. Captain). Qualified as Solicitor, June 1946; Legal Dept, Anglo-Saxon Petroleum Co., 1946–56; Manager, Thailand and Vietnam Division, Shell International Petroleum Co., 1956–58; Marketing Manager, Shell Co. of Philippines, Ltd, Manila, 1958–61; President, 1961–64; Head of Regional Marketing Div., Shell International Petroleum Co., London, 1964–66; Marketing Coordinator, 1966–70. Seconded to HM Govt (Mr Heath's Admin) as Head of Business Team, 1970–72; Dir and Group Personnel Co-ordinator, Shell International Petroleum Co. Ltd, 1972–76. Chm. Council, Univ. of Surrey, 1980–85. DL, 1983, High Sheriff, 1984, Surrey. Master, Worshipful Co. of Spectacle Makers, 1985–. CBIM; FInstD; FRSA. Officer of Philippine Legion of Honour, 1964. *Recreations:* gardening, walking. *Address:* Longhill House, The Sands, near Farnham, Surrey. *T:* Runfold 2601. *Clubs:* City Livery, Institute of Directors.

MEYNELL, Dame Alix (Hester Marie), (Lady Meynell), DBE 1949; *b* 2 Feb. 1903; *d* of late Surgeon Commander L. Kilroy, RN, and late Hester Kilroy; *m* 1946, Sir Francis Meynell, RDI (*d* 1975); no *c*. *Educ:* Malvern Girls' Coll.; Somerville Coll., Oxford. Joined civil service, Board of Trade, 1925. Seconded to the Monopolies and Restrictive Practices Commission as Sec., 1949–52; Under-Sec., Board of Trade, 1946–55; resigned from the Civil Service, 1955. Called to the Bar, 1956. Man. Dir, Nonesuch Press Ltd, 1976–. Member: SE Gas Board, 1963–69 (Chm. Cons. Council, 1956–63); Harlow New Town Corpn, 1956–65; Performing Right Tribunal, 1956–65; Cttees of Investigation for England, Scotland and Great Britain under Agricultural Marketing Acts, 1956–65; Monopolies Commn, 1965–68; Cosford RDC, 1970–74. *Recreations:* family bridge, entertaining my friends and being entertained. *Address:* The Grey House, Lavenham, Sudbury, Suffolk. *T:* Lavenham 247526.

MEYNELL, Benedict William; Hon. Director-General, Commission of the European Communities, since 1981; *b* 17 Feb. 1930; *s* of late Sir Francis Meynell, RDI, and of Lady (Vera) Meynell, MA; *m* 1st, 1950, Hildamarie (*née* Hendricks); two *d*; 2nd, 1967, Diana (*née* Himbury). *Educ:* Beltane Sch.; Geneva Univ. (Licencié-ès-sciences politiques); Magdalen Coll., Oxford (Doncaster schol.; MA). Asst Principal, Bd of Inland Revenue, 1954–56; Asst Principal, BoT, 1957–59, Principal, 1959–68; Principal British Trade Commissioner, Kenya, 1962–64; Board of Trade: Principal Private Sec. to Pres., 1967–68; Asst Sec., 1968–70; Commercial Counsellor, Brit. Embassy, Washington, DC, 1970–73; a Dir, EEC, responsible for relations with Far East, and for commercial safeguards and textiles negotiations, 1973–77, for relations with N America, Japan and Australasia, 1977–81. *Publications:* (paper) International Regulation of Aircraft Noise, 1971; (contrib.) Japan and Western Europe, ed Tsoukalis and White, 1982; A Survey of External Relations, in Yearbook of European Law 1982. *Address:* 49 rue Père Eudore Devroye, 1040 Bruxelles, Belgium. *T:* 736 4916.

MEYNELL, Laurence Walter, (Robert Eton); Author; *b* Wolverhampton, 1899; *y s* of late Herbert and Agnes Meynell; *m* 1932, Shirley Ruth (*d* 1955), *e d* of late Taylor Darbyshire; one *d*; *m* 1956, Joan Belfrage (*née* Henley) (*d* 1986). *Educ:* St Edmund's Coll., Old Hall, Ware. After serving in the Honourable Artillery Company became successively schoolmaster, estate agent and finally professional writer; Royal Air Force in War of 1939–45 (despatches). Literary Editor, Time and Tide, 1958–60, Past Pres. Johnson Soc. *Publications:* as *Robert Eton:* The Pattern; The Dividing Air; The Bus Leaves for the Village; Not In Our Stars; The Journey; Palace Pier; The Legacy; The Faithful Years; The Corner of Paradise Place; St Lynn's Advertiser; The Dragon at the Gate; as *Laurence Meynell:* Bluefeather; Paid in Full; The Door in the Wall; The House in the Hills; The Dandy; Third Time Unlucky; His Aunt Came Late; The Creaking Chair; The Dark Square; Strange Landing; The Evil Hour; The Bright Face of Danger; The Echo in the Cave; The Lady on Platform One; Party of Eight; The Man No One Knew; Give me the Knife; Saturday Out; Famous Cricket Grounds; Life of Sir P. Warner; Builder and Dreamer; Smoky Joe; Too Clever by Half; Smoky Joe in Trouble; Rolls, Man of Speed; Young Master Carver; Under the Hollies; Bridge Under the Water; Great Men of Staffordshire; Policeman in the Family; James Brindley; Sonia Back Stage; The Young Architect; District Nurse Carter; The Breaking Point; One Step from Murder; The Abandoned Doll; The House in Marsh Road; The Pit in the Garden; Virgin Luck; Sleep of the Unjust; Airmen on the Run; More Deadly Than the Male; Double Fault; Die by the Book; Week-end in the Scampi Belt; Death of a Philanderer; The Curious Crime of Miss Julia Blossom; The End of the Long Hot Summer; Death by Arrangement; A Little Matter of Arson; A View from the Terrace; The Fatal Flaw; The Thirteen Trumpeters; The Woman in Number Five; The Fortunate Miss East; The Fairly Innocent Little Man; The Footpath; Don't Stop For Hooky Hefferman; Hooky and the Crock of Gold; The Lost Half Hour; Hooky Gets the Wooden Spoon; Parasol in the Park; The Secret of the Pit; The Visitor; The Open Door; as *A. Stephen Tring* (for children): The Old Gang; The Cave By the Sea; Penny Dreadful; Barry's Exciting Year; Penny Triumphant; Penny Penitent; Penny Dramatic; Penny in Italy; Penny Goodbye. *Recreations:* walking, trying to write a play. *Address:* 9 Clifton Terrace, Brighton BN1 3HA. *Club:* Authors'.

MEYNER, Robert Baumle; Lawyer since 1934; Governor, State of New Jersey, USA, 1954–62; *b* 3 July 1908; *s* of late Gustave H. Meyner and Sophia Baumle Meyner; *m* 1957, Helen Day Stevenson. *Educ:* Lafayette Coll. (AB); Columbia Univ. Law Sch. (LLB). State Senator from Warren County, 1948–52; Senate Minority (Democrat) Leader, 1950; Director: Phillipsburg (NJ) National Bank and Trust Co.; NJ State Safety Council; Hon. degrees: Dr of Laws: Rutgers (The State Univ.) 1954; Lafayette Coll., 1954; Princeton Univ., 1956; Long Island Univ., 1958; Fairleigh Dickinson Univ., 1959; Syracuse Univ., 1960; Lincoln Univ., 1960; Colorado Coll., 1961. *Address:* (business) Suite 2500, Gateway 1, Newark, New Jersey 07102, USA; 16 Olden Lane, Princeton, NJ 08540, USA; 372 Lincoln Street, Phillipsburg, NJ 08865, USA. *Clubs:* River, Princeton (New York); Essex, 744 (Newark, NJ); Pomfret (Easton, Pa); Prettybrook Tennis (Princeton).

MEYRICK, Sir David (John Charlton), 4th Bt *cr* 1880; *b* 2 Dec. 1926; *s* of Colonel Sir Thomas Frederick Meyrick, 3rd Bt, TD, DL, JP, and Ivy Frances (*d* 1947), *d* of Lt-Col F. C. Pilkington, DSO; *S* father, 1983; *m* 1962, Penelope Anne, *d* of late Comdr John Bertram Aubrey Marsden-Smedley, RN; three *s*. *Educ:* Eton; Trinity Hall, Cambridge (MA). FRICS. *Heir: s* Timothy Thomas Charlton Meyrick, *b* 5 Nov. 1963. *Address:* Bush House, Gumfreston, Tenby, Dyfed SA70 8RA.

MEYRICK, Lt-Col Sir George David Eliott Tapps Gervis, 6th Bt, *cr* 1791; MC 1943; *b* 15 April 1915; *o s* of Major Sir George Llewelyn Tapps Gervis Meyrick, 5th Bt, and Marjorie (*née* Hamlin) (*d* 1972); *S* father 1960; *m* 1940, Ann, *d* of Clive Miller; one *s* one *d*. *Educ:* Eton; Trinity Coll., Cambridge (BA). 2nd Lieut, 9th Queen's Royal Lancers, 1937. Served War of 1939–45 (wounded, MC): BEF, 1940; Middle East, 1941–43; Italy, 1945; Captain, 1940; Lt-Col, 1947; retired, 1952. Dir, Southampton FC, 1953–. High Sheriff, Anglesey, 1962. *Recreations:* shooting, travel. *Heir: s* George Christopher Cadafael Tapps Gervis Meyrick [*b* 10 March 1941; *m* 1968, Jean Louise Montagu Douglas Scott, *d* of late Lt-Col Lord William Scott and of Lady William Scott, Beechwood, Melrose, Scotland; two *s* one *d*]. *Address:* Hinton Admiral, Christchurch, Dorset. *T:* Highcliffe 72887; Bodorgan, Anglesey, Gwynedd. *T:* Bodorgan 840204. *Club:* Cavalry and Guards.

MEYSEY-THOMPSON, Sir (Humphrey) Simon, 4th Bt *cr* 1874; *b* 31 March 1935; *s* of Guy Herbert Meysey-Thompson (*d* 1961), and Miriam Beryl Meysey-Thompson (*d* 1985); *S* kinsman, Sir Algar de Clifford Charles Meysey-Thompson, 1967. *Address:* 10 Church Street, Woodbridge, Suffolk. *T:* Woodbridge 2144.

MIALL, (Rowland) Leonard, OBE 1961; Research Historian; *b* 6 Nov. 1914; *e s* of late Rowland Miall and S. Grace Miall; *m* 1st, 1941, Lorna (*d* 1974), *o d* of late G. John Rackham; three *s* one *d*; 2nd, 1975, Sally Bicknell, *e d* of late Gordon Leith. *Educ:* Bootham Sch., York (Scholar); Freiburg Univ.; St John's Coll., Cambridge (Sizar), MA. Pres. Cambridge Union, 1936; Ed. Cambridge Review, 1936. Lectured in US, 1937; Sec. British-American Associates, 1937–39; joined BBC; inaugurated talks broadcast to Europe, 1939; BBC German Talks and Features Editor, 1940–42. Mem. British Political Warfare Mission to US, 1942–44 (Dir of News, San Francisco, 1943; Head of New York Office, 1944); Personal Asst to Dep. Dir-Gen., Political Warfare Exec., London, 1944; attached to Psychological Warfare Division of SHAEF, Luxembourg, 1945. Rejoined BBC: Special Correspondent, Czechoslovakia, 1945; Actg Diplomatic Corresp., 1945; Chief Corresp. in US, 1945–53; Head of Television Talks, 1954; Asst Controller, Current Affairs and Talks, Television, 1961; Special Asst to Dir of Television, planning start of BBC-2, 1962; Asst Controller, Programme Services, Television, BBC, 1963–66; BBC Rep. in US, 1966–70; Controller, Overseas and Foreign Relations, BBC, 1971–74; Research Historian, BBC, 1975–84. Inaugurated BBC Lunchtime Lectures, 1962; Advisor, Cttee on Broadcasting, New Delhi, 1965; Delegate to Commonwealth Broadcasting Confs, Jamaica, 1970, Kenya, 1972, Malta, 1974. Dir, Visnews Ltd (Dep. Chm., 1984–85);

Overseas Dir, BAFTA, 1974–; Mem. Council, RTS, 1984–. FRTS 1986; FRSA. Cert. of Appreciation, NY City, 1970. *Publication:* Richard Dimbleby, Broadcaster, 1966. *Recreations:* gardening, doing it oneself. *Address:* Maryfield Cottage, Taplow, Maidenhead, Berks SL6 0EX. *T:* Burnham 4195. *Clubs:* Garrick; Metropolitan (Washington); Union (Cambridge).

MICHAEL, David Parry Martin, CBE 1972; MA; Headmaster, Newport High School, Gwent, 1960–76; Secretary (part-time) University College Cardiff Press Board, since 1976; *b* 21 Dec. 1910; *m* 1937, Mary Horner Hayward; one *s*. *Educ:* University Coll., Cardiff (Fellow, 1981). Major, RAOC, combined ops, 1941–46 (despatches). Asst Master, Bassaleg Gram. Sch., Mon., 1935–41 and 1946–50; Headmaster, Cathays High Sch. for Boys, Cardiff, 1950–60. Member, Council, University Coll., Cardiff, 1961–; Governing Body, Church in Wales, 1963–. Governor, Nat. Library of Wales, 1967–; Member: Broadcasting Council for Wales, 1969–73; Exec. Cttee, SE Wales Arts Assoc., 1975–. Pres., Incorporated Assoc. of Headmasters, 1968; Mem., HMC, 1971–76; Pres., Welsh Secondary Schools Assoc., 1973. Editor, Welsh Secondary Schools' Review, 1965–76. *Publications:* The Idea of a Staff College, 1967; Guide to the Sixth Form, 1969; Arthur Machen, 1971; Town Walks, 1977; The Mapping of Monmouthshire, 1985; articles and reviews in educational and other jls. *Recreations:* collecting Victorian Staffordshire portrait figures; setting and solving crosswords (pseudonym, Egma). *Address:* 28 Fields Road, Newport, Gwent. *T:* Newport (Gwent) 62747.

MICHAEL, Dr Duncan, FEng 1984; Director, Ove Arup and Partners, since 1977; *b* 26 May 1937; *s* of Donald Michael and Lydia Cameron MacKenzie; *m* 1960, Joan Clay; two *s* one *d*. *Educ:* Beauly Public School; Inverness Royal Academy. BSc Edinburgh; PhD Leeds. FICE; FIStructE; FHKIE. Lectr, Leeds Univ., 1961; Engineer, Ove Arup Partnership, 1962. Member: Council, IStructE, 1977–80, 1983–; SE Asia Trade Adv. Group, BOTB, 1982–85; Civil Engineering Cttee, SERC, 1980–83. *Publications:* lectures and engineering papers in technical jls. *Recreations:* garden, Scottish archaeology, opera. *Address:* 22 Cromwell Road, Teddington, Middx TW11 9EN. *T:* 01–977 3158. *Club:* Caledonian.

MICHAEL, Prof. Ian David Lewis; King Alfonso XIII Professor of Spanish Studies, University of Oxford, since 1982; Fellow, Exeter College, Oxford, since 1982; *b* 26 May 1936; *o s* of late Cyril George Michael and of Glenys Morwen (*née* Lewis). *Educ:* Neath Grammar Sch.; King's Coll., London (BA First Class Hons Spanish 1957); PhD Manchester 1967. University of Manchester: Asst Lectr in Spanish, 1957–60; Lectr in Spanish, 1960–69; Sen. Lectr in Spanish, 1969–70; University of Southampton: Prof. of Spanish and Hd of Spanish Dept, 1971–82; Dep. Dean, Faculty of Arts, 1975–77, 1980–82; Sen. Curator and Chm., Univ. Library Cttee, 1980–82. Leverhulme Faculty Fellow in European Studies (at Madrid), 1977–78. *Publications:* The Treatment of Classical Material in the Libro de Alexandre, 1970; Spanish Literature and Learning to 1474, in, Spain: a Companion to Spanish studies, 1973, 3rd edn 1977; The Poem of the Cid, 1975, new edn 1984; Poema de Mio Cid, 1976, 2nd edn 1979; Gwyn Thomas, 1977; chapter on Poem of My Cid in New Pelican Guide to English Literature. I ii, 1983; articles in various learned jls and Festschriften. *Recreations:* horticulture; collecting Art Nouveau and Art Déco, particularly ceramics; writing pseudonymous fiction. *Address:* Exeter College, Oxford. *T:* Oxford 53152. *Clubs:* Organon; Neath Cricket (a Vice-Pres.).

MICHAEL, Ian (Lockie), CBE 1972; Deputy Director, Institute of Education, University of London, 1973–78; *b* 30 Nov. 1915; 4th *c* of late Reginald Warburton Michael and Margaret Campbell Kerr; *m* 1942, Mary Harborne Bayley, *e c* of late Rev. William Henry Bayley; one *s* one *d*. *Educ:* St Bees Sch.; private study. BA (London) 1938; PhD (Bristol) 1963. Schoolmaster: St Faith's Sch., Cambridge, 1935–40; Junior Sch., Leighton Park, 1941–45, Headmaster, 1946–49; Lectr in Educn, Bristol Univ., 1950–63; Prof. of Educn, Khartoum Univ., 1963–64; Vice-Chancellor, Univ. of Malaŵi, 1964–73. Leverhulme Emeritus Fellowship, 1978–79, 1979–80; Vis. Prof. of Educn, Univ. of Cape Town, 1981. Hon. DLitt Malaŵi, 1974. *Publication:* English Grammatical Categories and the Tradition to 1800, 1970. *Address:* 10A Downfield Road, Bristol BS8 2TJ.

MICHAEL, Peter Colin, CBE 1983; CBIM; Chairman, UEI plc, since 1986 (Deputy Chairman, 1981–85); *b* 17 June 1938; *s* of Albert and Enid Michael; *m* 1962, Margaret Baldwin; two *s*. *Educ:* Whitgift Sch., Croydon; Queen Mary Coll., Univ. of London (BSc Elec. Engrg; Fellow, 1983); CBIM 1982. Chairman: Micro Consultants Group, 1969–85; Quantel Ltd, 1974–; Databasix Ltd, 1986–. Member: Adv. Council for Applied R&D, 1982–85; NCB, 1983–86; ACARD Sub-Gp on Annual Review of Govt Funded R&D, 1985–86. Lectures: Humphrey Davies, QMC, 1984; IEE Electronics, 1984. Freeman, Goldsmiths' Co., 1984. Freeman, City of London, 1984. FRSA 1984. Hon. FBKSTS 1981. The Guardian Young Businessman of the Year, 1982. *Recreations:* squash, tennis, opera. *Address:* 20 West Mills, Newbury, Berks RG14 5HG. *T:* Newbury 48222.

MICHAELS, Prof. Leslie, MD; FRCPath, FRCP(C); Professor of Pathology, Institute of Laryngology and Otology, since 1973 (Dean, 1976–81); *b* 24 July 1925; *s* of Henry and Minnie Michaels; *m* Edith (*née* Waldstein); two *d*. *Educ:* Parmiter Sch., London; King's Coll., London; Westminster Med. Sch., London (MB, BS; MD). FRCPath 1963, FRCP(C) 1962. Asst Lectr in Pathology, Univ. of Manchester, 1955–57; Lectr in Path., St Mary's Hosp. Med. Sch., London, 1957–59; Asst Prof. of Path., Albert Einstein Coll. of Medicine, New York, 1959–61; Hosp. Pathologist, Northern Ont, Canada, 1961–70; Sen. Lectr, Inst. of Laryn. and Otol., 1970–73. *Publications:* Pathology of the Larynx, 1984; Ear, Nose and Throat Histopathology, 1987; scientific articles in jls of medicine, pathology and otolaryngology. *Recreations:* reading, music, walking. *Address:* Romany Ridge, Hillbrow Road, Bromley, Kent BR1 4JL.

MICHAELS, Michael Israel, CB 1960; *b* 22 Dec. 1908; *m* 1932, Rosina, *e d* of late Joseph Sturges; one *s* one *d*. *Educ:* City of London College; London Sch. of Economics (Social Science Research Scholar, 1931). Asst Sec., New Survey London Life and Labour, 1932–34. Deputy Director, Programmes and Statistics, Ministry of Supply, 1940–45. Asst Sec., Ministry of Health, 1946–54; Under-Sec., Atomic Energy Office, 1955–59; Office of the Minister for Science (Atomic Energy Division), 1959–64; Under-Sec., Min. of Technology, 1964–71, retired. British Mem., Bd of Governors, Internat. Atomic Energy Agency, 1957–71. *Recreations:* music, gardening, history. *Address:* The Mill House, Kelsale, Saxmundham, Suffolk. *T:* Saxmundham 3142.

MICHALOPOULOS, André, CBE 1937 (OBE 1919); FRSA; Professor Emeritus of Classical Literatures and Civilizations, since 1964, Professor 1957–64, Fairleigh-Dickinson University; *b* 1897; *m* 1st, 1924, Aspasia Eliasco; one *s* two *d*; 2nd, 1964, Countess Eleanor von Etzdorf. *Educ:* St Paul's Sch., London; Oriel Coll., Oxford (Scholar). BA 1st Cl. Hons Litt Hum., 1920; MA 1927; Priv. Sec. to Eleutherios Venizelos, Prime Minister of Greece, 1917 and 1921–24; Mem. Greek Delegation, Lausanne Peace Conference, 1922–23; Civil Governor of Lemnos, Imbros, Tenedos, and Samothrace, 1918–19; Governor of Corfu and adjacent islands, 1924–25; left Public Service for business, 1925; Managing Dir of Athens-Piraeus Water Coy; Dir of several Banking, Industrial, and Commercial Corpns in Athens; Pres. of the Anglo-Hellenic League, Athens, 1935–45; broadcast nightly English news commentary from Athens during Greco-Italian War, 1940–41; joined Greek forces in Crete, April 1941; Gen. Sec. of Nat. Cttee of Greeks of Egypt for resistance, May 1941; followed Greek Govt to S Africa, Aug. 1941; Mem. Greek Cabinet (Minister of Information in London, Washington and Cairo), Sept. 1941–May 1943. Lectured and broadcast extensively in S Africa, Great Britain, USA, Canada, 1941–43; Minister Plenipotentiary for Greece i/c information in America, 1945–46; Special Adviser on American Affairs to Royal Greek Embassy in Washington, 1950–67; Mem., Supreme Educnl Council of Greek Orthodox Archdiocese in N and S America, 1962–70. Visiting Professor, Kansas City University, 1949. Participated as Chm. or panel-mem., in Invitation to Learning programme, Columbia Broadcasting System, 1947–65; Master of Ceremonies and political and literary commentator on weekly Hellenic Television Hour, New York, 1955–56. Broadcast to Greece on Voice of America programme, 1950–55. Participated in annual American Foreign Policy Conf., Colgate Univ., 1951–61; has lectured and broadcast in the 48 States of USA and in Canada. Archon, Order of St Andrew; Grand Protonotary of Oecumenical Patriarchate of Constantinople, 1967. Commander Order of George I (Greece) with swords, 1941; Commander Order of the Phœnix (Greece), 1936; Chevalier Legion of Honour (France), 1934; Commander Order of Orange Nassau (Netherlands), 1939. FRSA 1936; Mem. Academy of American Poets, 1956; Mem. Poetry Society of America, 1957. Fellow, Ancient Monuments Soc. (London), 1958. Hon. LittD Westminster Coll., Utah. *Publications:* Homer, an interpretative study of the Iliad and Odyssey, 1965; and Greek Fire: a collection of broadcasts, articles and addresses, 1943; two collections of Verse 1923 and 1928; contribs to Encyclopedia Americana and Funk & Wagnall's Reference Encyclopaedia; chapts and articles in Greek, English, Scottish, American, Canadian, Egyptian, French, and South African books, reviews and newspapers; weekly book reviews for King Features Syndicate (USA), 1959–75. *Address:* The Normandy, 1120 North Shore Drive, Apt 1103, St Petersburg, Florida 33701, USA. *T:* 813–823–6352.

MICHALOWSKI, Jerzy; Polish diplomat; *b* 26 May 1909; *s* of Andrzej and Maria Michalowski; *m* 1947, Mira Krystyna; two *s*. *Educ:* University of Warsaw. Asst In Polish Inst. of Social Affairs, 1933–36; Dir of Polish Workers Housing Organisation, 1936–39; Chief of Housing Dept of Warsaw City Council, 1945; Counsellor of Polish Embassy in London, 1945–46; Deputy Deleg. of Poland to UN, March-Nov. 1946; Ambassador of Republic of Poland to the Court of St James's 1946–53; Head of a department, Ministry of Foreign Affairs, Warsaw, 1953–54; Under Sec. of State for Educ., 1954–55; Deleg. of Poland to the Internat. Commn in Vietnam, 1955–56; Permanent Representative of Poland to UN, 1956–60; Dir-Gen., in Ministry of Foreign Affairs, Warsaw, 1960–67; Ambassador to USA, 1967–71. Pres. of ECOSOC, UN, 1962. *Publications:* Unemployment of Polish Peasants, 1934; Housing Problems in Poland (publ. by League of Nations), 1935; The Big Game for the White House, 1972. *Recreations:* tennis and winter sports. *Address:* Al. I Armii WP 16/20, Warsaw, Poland.

MICHELIN, Reginald Townend, CMG 1957; CVO 1953; OBE 1952; General Manager: Agualta Vale Estates, Jamaica, 1958–64; Jamaica Tourist Board, 1964–73; *b* 31 Dec. 1903; *s* of V. A. Michelin, Planter, Jamaica; *m* 1940, Nina Gladys Faulkner, Iffley, Oxford; one *s* one *d*. *Educ:* Exeter Sch., England. Sub-Inspector, Police, Jamaica, 1924; Inspector, Police, Leeward Islands, 1928; Asst Commissioner of Police, Nigeria, 1930; Comr of Police, Barbados, 1949; Commissioner of Police, Jamaica, 1953–58, retd. *Address:* Western Mews, Winslow, Bucks.

MICHELL, Keith; actor since 1948; *b* Adelaide; *s* of Joseph Michell and Alice Maud (*née* Aslat); *m* 1957, Jeannette Sterke; one *s* one *d*. *Educ:* Port Pirie High Sch.; Adelaide Teachers' Coll.; Sch. of Arts and Crafts; Adelaide Univ.; Old Vic Theatre School. Formerly taught art. *Stage:* First appearance, Playbox, Adelaide, 1947; Young Vic Theatre Co., 1950–51; first London appearance, And So To Bed, 1951; Shakespeare Meml. Theatre Co., 1952–56, inc. Australian tour, 1952–53 (Henry IV Part 1, As You Like It, Midsummer Night's Dream, Troilus and Cressida, Romeo and Juliet, Taming of the Shrew, All's Well That Ends Well, Macbeth, Merry Wives of Windsor); Don Juan, Royal Court, 1956; Old Vic Co., 1956 (Antony and Cleopatra, Much Ado about Nothing, Two Gentlemen of Verona, Titus Andronicus); Irma La Douce, Lyric, 1958, Washington, DC, 1960 and Broadway, 1960–61; The Chances, Chichester Festival, 1962; The Rehearsal, NY, 1963; The First Four Hundred Years, Australia and NZ, 1964; Robert and Elizabeth, Lyric, 1964; The King's Mare, 1966; Man of La Mancha, 1968–69, NY, 1970; Abelard and Heloise, 1970, Los Angeles and NY, 1971; Hamlet, Globe, 1972; Dear Love, Comedy, 1973; The Crucifer of Blood, Haymarket, 1979; On the Twentieth Century (musical), Her Majesty's, 1980; Pete McGynty and the Dreamtime (own adap. of Peer Gynt), Melbourne Theatre Co., 1981; Captain Beaky Christmas Show, Lyric, Shaftesbury Ave., 1981–82; The Tempest, Brisbane, 1982; opened Keith Michell Theatre, Port Pirie, with one-man show, 1982; Amadeus (UK tour), 1983; La Cage Aux Folles, San Francisco and NY, 1984, Sydney and Melbourne, 1985; *Chichester Festival Theatre:* Artistic Director, 1974–77; Tonight We Improvise, Oedipus Tyrannus, 1974; Cyrano de Bergerac, Othello, 1975; (dir and designed) Twelfth Night, 1976; Monsieur Perrichon's Travel, 1976; The Apple Cart, 1977; (dir and designed) In Order of Appearance, 1977; Murder in the Cathedral (Chichester Cathedral), 1977; toured Australia with Chichester Co., 1978 (Othello, The Apple Cart); acted in: On the Rocks, 1982; Jane Eyre, 1986. *Films include:* Dangerous Exile; The Hell Fire Club; Seven Seas to Calais; The Executioner; House of Cards; Prudence and the Pill; Henry VIII and his Six Wives; Moments. *Television includes:* Henry VIII in the Six Wives of Henry VIII (series), 1972; Keith Michell at Chichester, 1974. Many recordings. First exhibn of paintings, 1959; subseq. exhibns at John Whibley Gall., London and Wright Hepburn and Webster Gall., NY, Century Gall., Henley, Wylma Wayne Gall., London. Many awards. *Publications:* ed and illus. (lithographs), Twelve Shakespeare Sonnets, 1981; illus. and recorded Captain Beaky series, 1975–. *Recreations:* painting, photography, swimming, riding. *Address:* c/o London Management and Representation Ltd, 235 Regent Street, W1.

MICHELL, Michael John; Head of Air Division, Department of Trade and Industry, since 1984; *b* 12 Dec. 1942; *s* of John Martin Michell and Pamela Mary Michell; *m* 1st, 1965, Pamela Marianne Tombs (marr. diss. 1978); two *s* (one *d* decd); 2nd, 1978, Alison Mary Macfarlane; two *s*. *Educ:* Marlborough College; Corpus Christi College, Cambridge (BA 1964). Min. of Aviation, 1964; Private Sec. to Sir Ronald Melville, 1968–69; Concorde Div., 1969–73; Sec. to Sandilands Cttee on inflation accounting, 1973–75; Private Sec. to Sec. of State for Industry, 1975–77; HM Treasury, 1977–80; Industrial Policy Div., Dept. of Industry, 1980–82; RCDS 1983. *Recreations:* tapestry, glass collecting, reading, gardening. *Address:* Department of Trade and Industry, 20 Victoria Street, SW1. *T:* 01–215 3006.

MICHELL, Prof. Robert Hall, FRS 1986; Professor of Biochemistry, University of Birmingham, since 1986; *b* 16 April 1941; *s* of Rowland Charles Michell and Elsie Lorna Michell; one *s* one *d*. *Educ:* Crewkerne School, Somerset; Univ. of Birmingham (BSc Med. Biochem. and Pharmacol. 1961; PhD Med. Biochem. 1964; DSc 1978). Research Fellow, Birmingham, 1965–66, 1968–70, Harvard Med. Sch., 1966–68; Birmingham University: Lectr in Biochemistry, 1970–81; Sen. Lectr, 1981–84; Reader, 1984–86. Mem., Physiol. Systems and Disorders Bd, MRC, 1985–. Member, Editorial Boards: Jl

Neurochem., 1975–80; Cell Calcium, 1979–; Biochem. Jl, 1983–. *Publications:* (with J. B. Finean and R. Coleman) Membranes and their Cellular Functions, 1974, 3rd edn 1984; (ed with J. B. Finean) Membrane Structure, vol. 1 of New Comprehensive Biochemistry, 1981; contribs to Nature, Biochem. Jl and sci. jls. *Recreations:* birdwatching, wilderness. *Address:* 59 Weoley Park Road, Birmingham B29 6QZ. *T:* 021–472 1356.

MICHELMORE, Clifford Arthur, CBE 1969; Television Broadcaster and Producer; Managing Director: Michelmore Enterprises Ltd, since 1969; Communications Consultants Ltd, since 1969; *b* 11 Dec. 1919; *s* of late Herbert Michelmore and Ellen Alford; *m* 1950, Jean Metcalfe (Broadcaster); one *s* one *d*. *Educ:* Cowes Senior Sch., Isle of Wight. Entered RAF, 1935; commnd 1940; left RAF 1947. Head, Outside Broadcasts and Variety, BFN, 1948; Dep. Station Dir, BFN, also returned to freelance as Commentator and Producer, 1949. Entered Television, 1950. Man. Dir, RM/EMI Visual Programmes, 1971–81. Has taken part in numerous radio and television programmes in Britain, Europe and the USA. Introduced: "Tonight" series, 1957–65; 24 Hours series, 1965–68; General Election Results programmes, 1964, 1966, 1970; So You Think . . . ., 1966–; Our World, 1967; With Michelmore (interviews); Talkback; Apollo Space Programmes, 1960–70; Holiday, 1969–; Chance to Meet, 1970–73; Wheelbase, 1972; Getaway, 1975; Globetrotter, 1975; Opinions Unlimited, 1977–79; Presenter: Day by Day (Southern TV), 1980; Sudden Change (HTV), 1982; Cliff Michelmore Show (BBC Radio), 1982–83; Home on Sunday (BBC TV), 1983–; Waterlines (BBC Radio Four), 1984–; Helpline (BBC TV), 1986–. Made films: Shaping of a Writer, 1977; Hong Kong: the challenge, 1978. FRSA, 1975. Television Society Silver Medal, 1957; Guild of TV Producers Award, Personality of the Year, 1958; TV Review Critics Award, 1959; Variety Club Award, 1961. *Publications:* (ed) The Businessman's Book of Golf, 1981; Cliff Michelmore's Holidays By Rail, 1986; (with Jean Metcalfe) Two-Way Story (autobiog.), 1986; contribs to Highlife, Financial Weekly; various articles on television, broadcasting and travel. *Recreations:* golf, reading and doing nothing. *Address:* White House, Reigate, Surrey; Brookfield, Bembridge, Isle of Wight. *T:* Reigate 45014. *Clubs:* Garrick, Royal Air Force.

MICHELMORE, Sir Walter Harold Strachan, Kt 1958; MBE 1945; Company Director; *b* Chudleigh, Devon, 4 April 1908; 2nd *s* of late Harold G. Michelmore; *m* 1933, Dorothy Walrond (*d* 1964), *o c* of late E. W. Bryant; one *d*; *m* 1967, Mrs Dulcie Mary Scott, *d* of late Leonard Haughton. *Educ:* Sherborne Sch.; Balliol Coll., Oxford. Joined Bird & Co., Calcutta, 1929. Served Indian Army (Staff), 1940–46 (MBE). Chm., Indian Mining Assoc., 1947–48. Managing Dir, Bird & Co. (Pvt) Ltd and F. W. Heilgers & Co. (Pvt) Ltd, Calcutta, 1948–63; Dep. Chm., 1955, Chm. 1961; retired 1963. Pres. Bengal Chamber of Commerce and Industry and Associated Chambers of Commerce of India, 1957. *Recreations:* golf, fishing, gardening. *Address:* Derriwong, 33 Derriwong Road, Round Corner, via Dural, NSW 2158, Australia. *Clubs:* Oriental, Queen's; Bengal (Calcutta); Australian (Sydney).

MICHENER, James Albert; Author; *b* New York City, 3 Feb. 1907; *s* of Edwin Michener and Mabel (*née* Haddock); *m* 1st, 1935, Patti Koon (marr. diss. 1948); 2nd, 1948, Vange Nord (marr. diss., 1955); 3rd, 1955, Mari Yoriko Sabusawa; no *c*. *Educ:* Swarthmore Coll., Pennsylvania; St Andrews Univ., Scotland; Harvard Coll., Mass. Teacher, George Sch., Pa, 1933–36; Prof., Colorado State Coll. of Educn, 1936–41; Visiting Prof., Harvard, 1940–41; Associate Editor, Macmillan Co., 1941–49. Member: Adv. Cttee on the arts, US State Dept, 1957; Adv. Cttee, US Information Agency, 1970–76; Cttee to reorganise USIS, 1976. Served with USNR on active duty in South Pacific, 1944–45. Sec., Pennsylvania Constitutional Convention, 1968. Hon. DHL, LLD, LittD, DSci and DHum, from numerous univs. US Medal of Freedom, 1977. *Publications:* Unit in the Social Studies, 1940; Tales of the South Pacific (Pulitzer prize for fiction), 1947; The Fires of Spring, 1949; Return to Paradise, 1951; The Voice of Asia, 1951; The Bridges at Toko-ri, 1953; Sayonara, 1954; Floating World, 1955; The Bridge at Andau, 1957; (with A. Grove Day) Rascals in Paradise, 1957; Selected Writings, 1957; The Hokusai Sketchbook, 1958; Japanese Prints, 1959; Hawaii, 1959; Caravans, 1964; The Source, 1965; Iberia, 1968; Presidential Lottery, 1969; The Quality of Life, 1970; Kent State, 1971; The Drifters, 1971; Centennial, 1974; Michener on Sport, 1977; Chesapeake, 1978; The Covenant, 1980; (with A. Grove Day) Rascals in Paradise, 1980; United States of America, 1982; Space, 1982; Poland, 1983; (ed) Future of Social Studies, for NEA, 1940. *Recreations:* photography, philately, tennis. *Address:* Pipersville, Pa 18947, USA.

MICHENER, Rt. Hon. Roland, CC, CMM, CD; Royal Victorian Chain, 1973; PC (Canada) 1962; QC (Canada); Governor-General and Commander-in-Chief of Canada, 1967–Jan. 1974; Barrister associated as Counsel with Lang, Michener, Cranston, Farquharson & Wright, Toronto, since 1974; Chairman of Council, Duke of Edinburgh's Fifth Commonwealth Study Conference, Canada 1980; Hon. Chairman of Board: National Trust Co., Toronto; Teck Corporation Ltd; Director, Pamour Porcupine Mines Ltd; etc; *b* Lacombe, Alta, 19 April 1900; *s* of late Senator Edward Michener and Mary Edith (*née* Roland), Lincoln Co., Ontario; *m* 1927, Norah Evangeline, *d* of Robert Willis, Manitoba; two *d* (and one *d* decd). *Educ:* Universities of Alberta and Oxford. BA (Alta) 1920; Rhodes Scholar for Alta, 1919; BA 1922, BCL 1923, MA 1929, Oxon. Served with RAF, 1918. Called to Bar, Middle Temple, 1923; Barrister, Ontario, 1924; KC 1943. Practising lawyer with Lang, Michener & Cranston, Toronto, 1924–57. Mem. Ontario Legislature for St David, Toronto, 1945–48, and Provincial Sec. for Ontario, 1946–48; elected to Canadian House of Commons, 1953; re-elected 1957 and 1958; elected Speaker, 1957 and May 1958; Canadian High Commissioner to India and Ambassador to Nepal, 1964–67. Chancellor, Queen's Univ., 1974–80. Gen. Sec. for Canada, Rhodes Scholarships, 1936–64. Mem. Bd of Governors, Toronto Stock Exchange, 1974–76. Formerly: Governor, Toronto Western Hosp.; Hon. Counsel, Chm. of Exec. Cttee (Pres., 1974–79), Canadian Inst. of Internat. Affairs; Hon. Counsel, Red Cross Ont Div.; Chm. of Exec., Canadian Assoc. for Adult Educn; Officer and Dir of various Canadian mining and financial companies. Chancellor and Principal Companion, Order of Canada, 1967–74; Chancellor and Comdr, Order of Military Merit, 1972–74. KJStJ (Prior for Canada), 1967. Hon. Fellow: Hertford Coll., Oxford, 1961; Acad. of Medicine, Toronto, 1967; Trinity Coll., Toronto, 1968; Frontier Coll., Toronto, 1972; Royal Canadian Mil. Inst., 1975; Heraldry Soc. of Canada, 1976; Hon. FRCP(C) 1968; Hon. FRAIC, 1968; Hon. FRSC, 1975. Hon. Mem., Canadian Medical Assoc., 1968; Hon. Bencher, Law Soc. of Upper Canada, 1968. Hon. LLD: Ottawa, 1948; Queen's, 1958; Laval, 1960; Alberta, 1967; St Mary's, Halifax, 1968; Toronto, 1968; RMC Canada, 1969; Mount Allison, Sackville, NB, 1969; Brock, 1969; Manitoba, 1970; McGill, 1970; York, Toronto, 1970; British Columbia, 1971; Jewish Theol Seminary of America, 1972; New Brunswick, 1972; Law Soc. of Upper Canada, 1974; Dalhousie, 1974; Hon. DCL: Bishop's, 1968; Windsor, 1969; Oxford Univ., 1970. *Address:* PO Box 10, First Canadian Place, Toronto, Ontario M5X 1A2, Canada; (home) 24 Thornwood Road, Toronto, Ontario M4W 2S1.

MICHIE, David Alan Redpath, RSA 1972 (ARSA 1964); RGI 1984; Head, School of Drawing and Painting, Edinburgh College of Art, since 1982; *b* 30 Nov. 1928; *s* of late James Michie and late Anne Redpath, OBE, ARA, RSA; *m* 1951, Eileen Anderson Michie; two *d*. *Educ:* Edinburgh Coll. of Art (DA). National Service, 1947–49; Edinburgh Coll. of Art, 1949–53 (studied painting); travelling scholarship, Italy, 1953–54; Lectr in Painting, Gray's Sch. of Art, Aberdeen, 1958–62; Lectr in Painting, Edinburgh Coll. of Art, 1962–, Vice-Principal, 1974–77. Vis. Prof. of Painting, Acad. of Fine Art, Belgrade, 1979. Member: Gen. Teaching Council for Scotland, 1976–80; Edinburgh Festival Soc., 1976–. Pres., Soc. of Scottish Artists, 1961–63. One Man Exhibitions: Mercury Gallery, London, 1967, 1969, 1971, 1974, 1980, 1983; Mercury Gall., Edinburgh, 1986; Lothian Region Chambers, 1977; Scottish Gall., Edinburgh, 1980. *Recreation:* fishing. *Address:* 17 Gilmour Road, Edinburgh EH16 5NS. *T:* 031–667 2684.

MICHIE, Prof. Donald, DPhil (Oxon), DSc (Oxon); Chief Scientist, Turing Institute, Glasgow, since 1986 (Director of Research, 1984–86); Visiting Professor, University of Strathclyde, since 1984; Adjunct Professor of Computer Science, University of Illinois, since 1979; Technical Director, Intelligent Terminals Ltd, since 1984; *b* 11 Nov. 1923; *s* of late James Kilgour Michie and Marjorie Crain Michie; *m* 1st, 1949, Zena Margaret Davies (marr. diss.); one *s*; 2nd, 1952, Anne McLaren (marr. diss.); one *s* two *d*; 3rd, 1971, Jean Elizabeth Crouch. *Educ:* Rugby Sch.; Balliol Coll., Oxford (Schol., MA). Sci. Fellow Zool Soc. of London, 1953; Fellow Royal Soc. Edinburgh 1969; Fellow Brit. Computer Soc., 1971. War Service in FO, Bletchley, 1942–45; Res. Associate, Univ. of London, 1952–58; Univ. of Edinburgh: Sen. Lectr, Surg. Science, 1958; Reader in Surg. Science, 1962; Dir of Expermtl Programming Unit, 1965; Chm. of Dept of Machine Intelligence and Perception, 1966; Prof. of Machine Intelligence, 1967–84, Prof. Emeritus, 1984–; Dir, Machine Intelligence Res. Unit, 1974–84. Royal Soc. Lectr in USSR, 1965; Wm Withering Lectr, Univ. of Birmingham, 1972; Vis. Lectr, USSR Acad. Sci., 1973, 1985; Geo. A. Miller Lectr, Univ. of Illinois, 1974, 1984; Herbert Spencer Lectr, Univ. of Oxford, 1976; Samuel Wilks Meml Lectr, Princeton Univ., 1978; Vis. Fellow, St Cross Coll., Oxford, 1970; Visiting Professor: Stanford Univ., 1962, 1978; Syracuse Univ., USA, 1970, 1971; Virginia Polytechnic Inst. and State Univ., 1974; Univ. of California at Santa Cruz, 1975; Dartmouth Coll., USA, 1975; Illinois Univ., 1976; Carnegie Mellon Univ., 1977; Case Western Reserve Univ., 1978; McGill Univ., 1979. Chief Editor, Machine Intelligence series, 1967–. Chm., A. M. Turing Trust, 1975–86. *Publications:* (jtly) An Introduction to Molecular Biology, 1964; On Machine Intelligence, 1974, 2nd edn 1986; Machine Intelligence and Related Topics, 1982; (jtly) The Creative Computer, 1984 (The Knowledge Machine, USA, 1985); papers in tech. and sci. jls. *Recreations:* chess, travel. *Address:* 10 Bellevue Crescent, Edinburgh; 15 Canal Street, Oxford. *Club:* New (Edinburgh).

MICHIE, William; MP (Lab) Sheffield Heeley, since 1983; *b* 24 Nov. 1935; marr. diss.; two *s*. *Educ:* Abbeydale Secondary Sch., Sheffield. Nat. Service, RAF, 1957–59. Formerly: apprentice electrician; maintenance electrician; Lab. Technician, Computer Applications; unemployed, 1981–83. Joined Labour Party, 1965; Co-op. Party, 1966. Mem., AEU (formerly AUEW), 1952– (Br. Trustee; former Standing Orders Cttee Deleg., Lab. Party Yorks Regl Conf.; AEU sponsored MP, 1984–). Member: Sheffield City Council, 1970–84 (Chairman: Planning, 1974–81; Employment, 1981–83; Gp Sec./Chief Whip, 1974–83); South Yorks CC, 1974–86 (Area Planning Chm., 1974–81). *Recreations:* pub darts, tending allotment. *Address:* House of Commons, SW1. *T:* 01–219 6248; 54 Pinstone Street, Sheffield S1 2HN. *T:* Sheffield 701881.

MICKLETHWAIT, Sir Robert (Gore), Kt 1964; QC 1956; Chief National Insurance Commissioner, 1966–75 (Deputy Commissioner, 1959; National Insurance Commissioner and Industrial Injuries Commissioner, 1961); *b* 7 Nov. 1902; 2nd *s* of late St J. G. Micklethwait, KC and Annie Elizabeth Micklethwait (*née* Aldrich-Blake); *m* 1936, Philippa J., 2nd *d* of late Sir Ronald Bosanquet, QC; three *s* one *d*. *Educ:* Clifton Coll.; Trinity Coll., Oxford (2nd Class Lit. Hum., MA). Called to Bar, Middle Temple, 1925, Bencher, 1951; Autumn Reader, 1964; Dep. Treasurer, 1970, Treasurer, 1971. Oxford Circuit; Gen. Coun. of the Bar, 1939–40 and 1952–56; Supreme Court Rule Cttee, 1952–56. Royal Observer Corps, 1938–40; Civil Asst, WO, 1940–45; Recorder of Worcester, 1946–59. Deputy Chm., Court of Quarter Sessions for County of Stafford, 1956–59. Hon. LLD Newcastle upon Tyne, 1975. Hon. Knight, Hon. Soc. of Knights of the Round Table, 1972. *Publication:* The National Insurance Commissioners (Hamlyn Lectures), 1976. *Address:* 71 Harvest Road, Englefield Green, Surrey TW20 0QR. *T:* Egham 32521.

MIDDLEDITCH, Edward, MC 1945; RA 1973 (ARA 1968); ARCA 1951; painter; Head of Fine Art Department, Norwich School of Art, since 1964; Keeper of the Royal Academy Schools, since 1985; *b* 23 March 1923; *s* of Charles Henry Middleditch and Esme Buckley; *m* 1947, Jean Kathleen Whitehouse; one *d*. *Educ:* Mundella School, Nottingham; King Edward VI Grammar Sch., Chelmsford; Royal College of Art. Served Army, 1942–47, France, Germany, India, W Africa; commissioned Middx Regt 1944. Eleven Exhibitions, London, 1954–74; contrib. to mixed exhibitions: Paris; Rome; Venice Biennale, 1956; Six Young Painters, 1957; Pittsburgh Internat., 1958; Whitechapel, 1959; English Landscape Tradition in the 20th Century, 1969; British Painting '74, 1974; 25 Years of British Painting, 1977; The Forgotten Fifties, 1984, etc. Gulbenkian Foundn Scholarship, 1962; Arts Council of GB Bursary, 1964; Arts Council of NI Bursary, 1968. Paintings in private and public collections, including: Tate Gall.; Arts Council; V & A Museum; Contemporary Art Soc.; Manchester City Art Gall.; Ferens Art Gall., Hull; Nat. Gall. of Victoria; Nat. Gall. of S Aust.; Nat. Gall. of Canada; Chrysler Art Museum, Mass; Toledo Museum of Art, Ohio. *Address:* c/o New Arts Centre, 41 Sloane Street, SW1.

MIDDLEMORE, Sir William Hawkslow, 2nd Bt, *cr* 1919; *b* 10 April 1908; *s* of 1st Bt and Mary, *d* of late Rev. Thomas Price, Selly Oak, Birmingham; *S* father, 1924; *m* 1934, Violet Constance (*d* 1976), *d* of Andrew Kennagh, Worcester. *Heir:* none.

MIDDLESBROUGH, Bishop of, (RC), since 1978; **Rt. Rev. Augustine Harris;** *b* 27 Oct. 1917; *s* of Augustine Harris and Louisa Beatrice (*née* Rycroft). *Educ:* St Francis Xavier's Coll., Liverpool; Upholland Coll., Lancs. Ordained, 1942; Curate at: St Oswald's, Liverpool, 1942–43; St Elizabeth's, Litherland, Lancs, 1943–52; Prison Chaplain, HM Prison, Liverpool, 1952–65; Sen. RC Priest, Prison Dept, 1957–66; English Rep. to Internat. Coun. of Sen. Prison Chaplains (RC), 1957–66; Titular Bishop of Socia and Auxiliary Bishop of Liverpool, 1965–78. Mem. Vatican Delegn to UN Quinquennial Congress on Crime, London, 1960 and Stockholm, 1965; Liaison between English and Welsh Hierarchy (RC) and Home Office, 1966–; Episcopal Moderator to Fédération Internationale des Associations Médicales Catholiques, 1967–76; Episcopal Pres., Commn for Social Welfare (England and Wales), 1972–83; Chm., Dept for Social Responsibility, Bishops Conf. of Eng. and Wales, 1984–. Mem. Central Religious Advisory Council to BBC and IBA, 1974–78. *Publications:* articles for criminological works. *Address:* Bishop's House, 16 Cambridge Road, Middlesbrough, Cleveland TS5 5NN.

MIDDLESBROUGH, Auxiliary Bishop of, (RC); *see* O'Brien, Rt Rev. T. K.

MIDDLESEX, Archdeacon of; *see* Raphael, Ven. T. J.

MIDDLETON, 12th Baron *cr* 1711; **Digby Michael Godfrey John Willoughby,** MC 1945; DL; Bt 1677; *b* 1 May 1921; *er s* of 11th Baron Middleton, KG, MC, TD, and Angela Florence Alfreda (*d* 1978), *er d* of Charles Hall, Eddlethorpe Hall, Malton, Yorks; *S* father, 1970; *m* 1947, Janet, *o d* of General Sir James Marshall-Cornwall, KCB, CBE, DSO, MC; three *s*. *Educ:* Eton; Trinity Coll., Cambridge. BA 1950; MA 1958. Served War of 1939–45: Coldstream Guards, 1940–46; NW Europe, 1944–45 (despatches, MC, Croix de Guerre); Hon. Col, 2nd Bn Yorkshire Volunteers, TAVR, 1976–. Chm., Legal and Parly Cttee, CLA, 1973–79; Pres., CLA, 1981–83; Member: Yorks and Humberside Econ. Planning Council, 1968–79; Nature Conservancy Council, 1986. DL 1963, JP 1958, CC 1964–74, ER of Yorks; CC N Yorks, 1974–77. *Heir: s* Hon. Michael Charles James Willoughby [*b* 14 July 1948; *m* 1974, Hon. Lucy Sidney, *y d* of Viscount De L'Isle, *qv*; two *s* three *d*]. *Address:* Birdsall House, Malton, N Yorks. *T:* North Grimston 202. *Club:* Boodle's.

MIDDLETON, Bishop Suffragan of, since 1982; **Rt. Rev. Donald Alexander Tytler;** *b* 2 May 1925; *s* of Alexander and Cicely Tytler; *m* 1948, Jane Evelyn Hodgson; two *d*. *Educ:* Eastbourne College; Christ's College, Cambridge (MA); Ridley Hall, Cambridge. Asst Curate of Yardley, Birmingham, 1949; SCM Chaplain, Univ. of Birmingham, 1952; Precentor, Birmingham Cathedral, 1955; Diocesan Director of Education, Birmingham, 1957; Vicar of St Mark, Londonderry and Rural Dean of Warley, dio. Birmingham, 1963; Canon Residentiary of Birmingham Cathedral, 1972; Archdeacon of Aston, 1977–82. *Publications:* Operation Think, 1963; (contrib.) Stirrings (essays), 1976. *Recreations:* music, gardening. *Address:* The Hollies, Manchester Road, Rochdale, Lancs OL11 3QY. *T:* Rochdale 358550.

MIDDLETON, Donald King, CBE 1981; HM Diplomatic Service, retired; British High Commissioner, Papua New Guinea, 1977–82; Member, Council, Voluntary Service Overseas, since 1983; *b* 24 Feb. 1922; *s* of late Harold Ernest Middleton and Ellen Middleton; *m* 1945, Marion Elizabeth Ryder; one *d*. *Educ:* King Edward's Sch., Birmingham; Saltley College. Min. of Health, 1958–61; joined Commonwealth Relations Office, 1961; First Sec., British High Commn, Lagos, 1961–65; Head of Chancery, British Embassy, Saigon, 1970–72; British Dep. High Commissioner, Ibadan, 1973–75; HM Chargé d'Affaires, Phnom Penh, 1975; seconded to NI Office, Belfast, 1975–77. *Address:* Stone House, Ledgemoor, near Weobley, Herefordshire HR4 8RN. *Club:* Royal Commonwealth Society.

MIDDLETON, Drew, CBE (Hon.); Military Correspondent of The New York Times, since 1970; *b* 14 Oct. 1914; *o s* of E. T. and Jean Drew Middleton, New York; *m* 1943, Estelle Mansel-Edwards, Dinas Powis, Glamorgan; one *d*. *Educ:* Syracuse Univ., Syracuse, New York. Correspondent: for Associated Press in London, 1939; for Associated Press in France, Belgium, London, Iceland, with the British Army and RAF, 1939–42; for The New York Times with US and British Forces in North Africa, Sicily, Britain, Normandy, Belgium and Germany, 1942–45; Chief Correspondent: in USSR, 1946–47; in Germany, 1948–53; in London, 1953–63; in Paris, 1963–65; UN, 1965–69; European Affairs Correspondent, 1969–70. Correspondent at four meetings of Council of Foreign Ministers, also Potsdam and Casablanca Conferences. Medal of Freedom (US). English-Speaking Union Better Understanding Award, 1955. Doctor of Letters (*hc*) Syracuse Univ., 1963. *Publications:* Our Share of Night, 1946; The Struggle for Germany, 1949; The Defence of Western Europe, 1952; The British, 1957; The Sky Suspended, 1960; The Supreme Choice: Britain and the European Community, 1963; Crisis in the West, 1965; Retreat From Victory, 1973; Where Has Last July Gone?, 1974; Can America Win the Next War?, 1975; Submarine, 1976; Duel of the Giants, 1977; Crossroads of Modern War, 1983; (jtly) This War Called Peace, 1984. *Recreations:* tennis, the theatre. *Address:* The New York Times, 229 W 43rd Street, New York, NY 10036, USA. *Clubs:* Beefsteak, Press, Garrick; Travellers' (Paris); The Brook, Century (New York).

MIDDLETON, Edward Bernard; Partner, Pannell Kerr Forster; on secondment to Department of Trade and Industry as Director in Industrial Development Unit, since 1984; *b* 5 July 1948; *s* of Bernard and Bettie Middleton; *m* 1971, Rosemary Spence Brown; three *s*. *Educ:* Aldenham Sch., Elstree; Chartered Accountant, 1970. Joined London office of Pannell Kerr Forster, 1971; Nairobi office, 1973; Audit Manager, London office, 1975; Partner, 1979. Mem. sub-cttee, Consultative Cttee of Accountancy Bodies, 1980–84. *Recreations:* sailing, walking, photography. *Address:* 4 Cecil Close, Manor Links, Bishops Stortford, Herts CM23 5RD. *T:* Bishops Stortford 58684.

MIDDLETON, Francis; Advocate; Sheriff (formerly Sheriff Substitute) of Glasgow and Strathkelvin (formerly of Lanarkshire) at Glasgow, 1956–78; Temporary Sheriff, 1979; *b* 21 Nov. 1913; Scottish; *m* 1942, Edith Muir; two *s* one *d*. *Educ:* Rutherglen Academy; Glasgow Univ. MA, LLB 1937. Practising as Solicitor, 1937–39; volunteered Sept. 1939; Cameronian Scottish Rifles; commissioned to 6th Battn 11th Sikh Regt, Indian Army, 1940; Captain 1940; Major 1942, injured; Interpreter 1st Class in Hindustani, 1943; posted to Judge Advocate's Branch, 1944; released Dec. 1945. Admitted Faculty of Advocates in Scotland, 1946. Sheriff Substitute of Inverness, Moray, Nairn and Ross and Cromarty, 1949–52, Fife and Kinross, 1952–56. Dir, YMCA, Glasgow. Chairman: Scottish Assoc. of Dowsers; Child and Family Trust. Mem., Rotary Club. *Recreations:* reading, gardening. *Address:* 23 Kirklee Road, Glasgow G12 0RQ.

MIDDLETON, Sir George (Humphrey), KCMG 1958 (CMG 1950); HM Diplomatic Service, retired; Chairman, London Funding and Management plc, since 1985; President, Supernova plc, since 1985; *b* 21 Jan. 1910; *e s* of George Close Middleton and Susan Sophie (*née* Harley, subsequently Elphinstone); *m* Marie Elisabeth Camille Françoise Sarthou, Bordeaux; one *s*; one step *s* one step *d*. *Educ:* St Lawrence Coll., Ramsgate; Magdalen Coll., Oxford. Entered Consular Service, 1933, Vice-Consul, Buenos Aires; transferred to Asuncion, 1934, with local rank of 3rd Sec. in Diplomatic Service; in charge of Legation, 1935; transferred to New York, 1936; to Lemberg (Lwow), 1939; local rank of Consul; in charge of Vice-Consulate at Cluj, 1939–40; appointed to Genoa, 1940, to Madeira, 1940, to Foreign Office, 1943; 2nd Sec. at Washington, 1944; 1st Sec. 1945; transferred to FO, 1947; Counsellor, 1949; Counsellor, British Embassy, Tehran, Jan. 1951; acted as Chargé d'Affaires, 1951 and 1952 (when diplomatic relations severed); Dep. High Comr for UK, in Delhi, 1953–56; British Ambassador at Beirut, 1956–58; Political Resident in the Persian Gulf, 1958–61; British Ambassador to: Argentina, 1961–64; United Arab Republic, 1964–66. Mem. *Ad hoc* Cttee for UN Finances, 1966. Consultant, Industrial Reorganisation Corporation, 1967–68; Director: Michael Rice Ltd; C. E. Planning Ltd; East West Group (Europe) Ltd; Liberty Life Assurance Co. Ltd; Britarge Ltd; Decor France Ltd; Johnson and Bloy Holdings; Chm., Exec. Cttee, British Road Fedn, 1972; Chief Executive, British Industry Roads Campaign, 1969–76. Chairman: Bahrain Soc.; Anglo-Peruvian Soc.; British Moroccan Soc. FRSA. Comdr, Order of Merit, Peru. *Recreations:* fishing, tennis, talking. *Address:* 1 Carlyle Square, SW3 6EX. *T:* 01–352 2962. *Clubs:* Travellers', Pratt's, Royal Automobile.

MIDDLETON, Sir George (P.), KCVO 1962 (CVO 1951; MVO 1941); MB, ChB (Aberdeen); Medical Practitioner, retired 1973; Surgeon Apothecary to HM Household at Balmoral Castle, 1932–73; *b* Schoolhouse, Findhorn, Morayshire, 26 Jan. 1905; *s* of late A. Middleton, FEIS, Kincorth, Elgin; *m* 1931, Margaret Wilson (*d* 1964), *er d* of late A. Silver; one *s* one *d*. *Educ:* Findhorn; Forres Academy; Aberdeen Univ. Entered the Faculty of Medicine, 1921; Graduated, 1926, Bachelor of Medicine and Bachelor of Surgery, Ogston Prize and 1st medallist in Senior Systematic Surgery, 1st Medallist in Operative Surgery, House Surgeon Ward X, and House Physician Ward 4, Aberdeen Royal Infirmary, 1926; went to practice in Sheffield, 1927; Asst to Sir Alexander Hendry, 1928; into partnership, 1929; partnership dissolved, 1931; taken into partnership, Dr James G. Moir, 1948. *Recreations:* golf, Association football, bowling. *Address:* Highland Home, Ballater, Aberdeenshire AB3 5RP. *TA:* Highland Home, Ballater. *T:* Ballater 55478.

MIDDLETON, Kenneth William Bruce; formerly Sheriff of Lothian and Borders at Edinburgh and Haddington; *b* Strathpeffer, Ross-shire, 1 Oct. 1905; 2nd *s* of W. R. T. Middleton; *m* 1st, 1938, Ruth Beverly (marr. diss. 1972), *d* of W. H. Mill; one *s* one *d*; 2nd, 1984, Simona Vere, *d* of T. C. Pakenham, *widow* of N. Iliff. *Educ:* Rossall Sch.; Merton Coll., Oxford; Edinburgh Univ. BA Oxford, LLB Edinburgh; called to Scottish Bar, 1931; Vans Dunlop Scholar in International Law and Constitutional Law and History, Edinburgh Univ.; Richard Brown Research Scholar in Law, Edinburgh Univ.; served War of 1939–45 with Royal Scots and Seaforth Highlanders; attached to Military Dept, Judge Advocate-Gen.'s Office, 1941–45. Sheriff-Substitute, subseq. Sheriff: Perth and Angus at Forfar, 1946–50; Lothians and Peebles, later Lothian and Borders, at Edinburgh and Haddington, 1950–86. *Publication:* Britain and Russia, 1947. *Address:* Cobblers Cottage, Ledwell, Middle Barton, Oxon.

MIDDLETON, Lawrence John, CMG 1985; PhD; HM Diplomatic Service; Ambassador to the Republic of Korea, since 1986; *b* 27 March 1930; *s* of John James Middleton and Mary (*née* Horgan); *m* 1963, Sheila Elizabeth Hoey; two *s* one *d*. *Educ:* Finchley Catholic Grammar Sch.; King's Coll., London (BSc 1951, PhD 1954). Scientific Officer, ARC, 1954–60 and 1962–63; Cons. to FAO and to UN Cttee on Effects of Atomic Radiation, 1960–62; CENTO Inst. of Nuclear Science, 1963–65; Principal, Min. of Agriculture, 1966–68; First Sec., FO, 1968; Washington, 1969–71; Kuala Lumpur, 1971–74; Counsellor (Commercial), Belgrade, 1974–78; Dir of Research, FCO, 1978–80; Cabinet Office, 1980–82; Counsellor, UK Delegn to Conf. on Disarmament, Geneva, 1982–84; Sen. DS, RCDS, 1984–86. *Publications:* articles on plant physiology and nuclear science in biology, 1954–63. *Address:* c/o Foreign and Commonwealth Office, SW1; 373A Woodstock Road, Oxford.

MIDDLETON, Rear Adm. Linley Eric, CB 1986; DSO; FRAeS; FBIM; Flag Officer, Naval Air Command, 1984–87. Joined Royal Navy, 1952. Served HMS Centaur, HMS Eagle, HMS Mounts Bay and HMS Victorious, 1954–63; BRNC Dartmouth, 1964–65; CO, 809 Naval Air Squadron in HMS Hermes, 1966–67; CO, HMS Whitby, 1970–71; Staff of Flag Officer, Naval Air Comd, 1971–73; Commanding Officer: HMS Undaunted, 1973–74; HMS Apollo, 1974–75; Chief Staff Officer to Flag Officer Carriers & Amphibious Ships, 1975–77; Dir, Naval Air Warfare, 1978–79; CO, HMS Hermes, 1980–82; Asst Chief of Naval Staff (Ops), 1983–84.

MIDDLETON, Michael Humfrey, CBE 1975; Director, Civic Trust, since 1969; *b* 1 Dec. 1917; *s* of Humfrey Middleton and Lilian Irene (*née* Tillard); *m* 1954, Julie Margaret Harrison; one *s* two *d*. *Educ:* King's Sch., Canterbury. Art Critic, The Spectator, 1946–56; Art Editor and Asst Editor, Picture Post, 1949–53; Exec. Editor, Lilliput, 1953–54; Editor, House and Garden, 1955–57; Sec. and Dep. Dir, Civic Trust, 1957–69; Mem. Council, Soc. of Industrial Artists and Designers, 1953–55, 1968–70; UK Sec.-Gen., European Architectural Heritage Year, 1972–75. Member: Adv. Cttee on Trunk Road Assessment, 1977–80; UK Commn for UNESCO, 1976–80. FSIA; Hon. Fellow, RIBA, 1974. Film scripts include A Future for the Past, 1972. Council of Europe Pro Merito Medal, 1976. *Publications:* Soldiers of Lead, 1948; Group Practice in Design, 1967; contributor to many conferences and jls, at home and abroad, on art, design and environmental matters. *Recreation:* looking. *Address:* 46 Holland Park Avenue, W11. *T:* 01–727 9136.

MIDDLETON, Sir Peter (Edward), KCB 1984; Permanent Secretary, HM Treasury, since 1983; *b* 2 April 1934; *m* 1964, Valerie Ann Lindup; one *s* one *d*. *Educ:* Sheffield City Grammar Sch.; Sheffield Univ. (BA; Hon. DLitt 1984); Bristol Univ. Served RAPC, 1958–60. HM Treasury: Senior Information Officer, 1962; Principal, 1964; Asst Director, Centre for Administrative Studies, 1967–69; Private Sec. to Chancellor of the Exchequer, 1969–72; Treasury Press Secretary, 1972–75; Head of Monetary Policy Div., 1975; Under Secretary, 1976; Dep. Sec., 1980–83. Vis. Fellow, Nuffield Coll., Oxford, 1981. Mem. Council, Manchester Business Sch., 1985–; Governor: London Business Sch., 1984–; Ditchley Foundn, 1985–. *Address:* HM Treasury, Parliament Street, SW1. *Club:* Reform.

MIDDLETON, Ronald George, DSC 1945; solicitor; *b* 31 July 1913; *o s* of late Sir George Middleton; *m* 1959, Sybil Summerscale (*d* 1976); no *c*. *Educ:* Whitgift Middle Sch.; University Coll., London. Solicitor, 1936. RNVR, 1939–47 (Lt-Comdr); Radar Officer HMS Queen Elizabeth, 1944–45; Fleet Radar Officer, Indian Ocean, 1945. Partner, Coward, Chance & Co., 1949, Senior Partner, 1972–80. Part-time Mem., NBPI, 1965–68. *Recreation:* sailing. *Address:* Quin, Wineham, Henfield, W Sussex. *T:* Cowfold 236. *Clubs:* Reform, Garrick, Royal Ocean Racing.

MIDDLETON, Stanley; novelist; *b* Bulwell, Nottingham, 1 Aug. 1919; *y s* of Thomas and Elizabeth Ann Middleton; *m* 1951, Margaret Shirley, *y d* of Herbert and Winifred Vera Welch; two *d*. *Educ:* High Pavement Sch.; University Coll., Nottingham (later Univ. of Nottingham); Hon. MA Nottingham, 1975. Served Army (RA and AEC), 1940–46. Head of English Dept, High Pavement Coll., Nottingham, 1958–81. Judith E. Wilson Vis. Fellow, Emmanuel Coll., Cambridge, 1982–83. *Publications:* novels: A Short Answer, 1958; Harris's Requiem, 1960; A Serious Woman, 1961; The Just Exchange, 1962; Two's Company, 1963; Him They Compelled, 1964; Terms of Reference, 1966; The Golden Evening, 1968; Wages of Virtue, 1969; Apple of the Eye, 1970; Brazen Prison, 1971; Cold Gradations, 1972; A Man Made of Smoke, 1973; Holiday (jtly, Booker Prize 1974), 1974; Distractions, 1975; Still Waters, 1976; Ends and Means, 1977; Two Brothers, 1978; In A Strange Land, 1979; The Other Side, 1980; Blind Understanding, 1982; Entry into Jerusalem, 1983; The Daysman, 1984; Valley of Decision, 1985; An After Dinner's Sleep, 1986. *Recreations:* music, walking, listening, argument. *Address:* 42 Caledon Road, Sherwood, Nottingham NG5 2NG. *T:* Nottingham 623085. *Club:* PEN.

MIDDLETON, Sir Stephen Hugh, 9th Bt, *cr* 1662; *b* 1909; *s* of Lt Hugh Jeffery Middleton, RN, 3rd *s* of Sir Arthur Middleton, 7th Bt; *S* uncle 1942; *m* 1962, Mary (*d* 1972), *d* of late Richard Robinson. *Educ:* Eton; Magdalene Coll., Cambridge. *Heir: b* Lawrence Monck Middleton [*b* 23 Oct. 1912; *m* 1984, Primrose Westcombe]. *Address:* Belsay Castle, Northumberland.

MIDGLEY, Eric Atkinson, CMG 1965; MBE 1945; HM Diplomatic Service, retired; *b* 25 March 1913; *s* of Charles Ewart Midgley, Keighley, Yorks; *m* 1937, Catherine Gaminara; two *d*. *Educ:* Christ's Hosp.; Merton Coll., Oxford. Indian Civil Service, 1937; Trade Commissioner at Delhi, 1947; Board of Trade, 1957; Commercial Counsellor at

The Hague, 1960; Minister (Economic) in India, 1963–67; Minister (Commercial), Washington, 1967–70; Ambassador to Switzerland, 1970–73. *Recreation:* sailing. *Address:* 2 Wellington Place, Captains Row, Lymington, Hants. *Club:* Royal Lymington Yacht.

MIDLETON, 11th Viscount *cr* 1717, of Midleton, Ireland; **Trevor Lowther Brodrick;** Baron Brodrick, Midleton, Ireland, 1715; Baron Brodrick, Peper Harow, 1796; *b* 7 March 1903; *s* of William John Henry Brodrick, OBE (*d* 1964) (*g s* of 7th Viscount), and Blanche Sophia Emily (*d* 1944), *e d* of F. A. Hawker; *S* to viscountcy of cousin, 2nd Earl of Midleton, MC, 1979; *m* 1940, Sheila Campbell MacLeod, *d* of Charles Campbell MacLeod. *Educ:* privately. *Recreations:* photography and gardening. *Heir: nephew* Alan Henry Brodrick [*b* 4 Aug. 1949; *m* 1978, Julia Helen, *d* of Michael Pitt; two *s* one *d*]. *Address:* Frogmore Cottage, 105 North Road, Bourne, Lincolnshire PE10 9BU.

MIDWINTER, Eric Clare, MA, DPhil; Director, Centre for Policy on Ageing, since 1980; *b* 11 Feb. 1932; *m*; two *s* one *d*. *Educ:* St Catharine's Coll., Cambridge (BA Hons History); Univs of Liverpool (MA Educn) and York (DPhil). Educational posts, incl. Dir of Liverpool Educn Priority Area Project, 1955–75; Head, Public Affairs Unit, Nat. Consumer Council, 1975–80. Chairman: Council, Adv. Centre for Educn, 1976–84; London Transport Users Consultative Cttee, 1977–84; London Regional Passengers' Cttee, 1984–. *Publications:* Victorian Social Reform, 1968; Law and Order in Victorian Lancashire, 1968; Social Administration in Lancashire, 1969; Nineteenth Century Education, 1970; Old Liverpool, 1971; Projections: an education priority project at work, 1972; Social Environment and the Urban School, 1972; Priority Education, 1972; Patterns of Community Education, 1973; ed, Teaching in the Urban Community School, 1973; ed, Pre-School Priorities, 1974; Education and the Community, 1975; Education for Sale, 1977; Make 'Em Laugh: famous comedians and their world, 1978; Schools and Society, 1980; W. G. Grace: his life and times, 1981; Age is Opportunity: education and older people, 1982; (ed) Mutual Aid Universities, 1984; The Wage of Retirement: the case for a new pensions policy, 1985; Fair Game: myth and reality in sport, 1986; Caring for Cash: the issue of private domiciliary care, 1986; chapters in: Fit to Teach, 1971; Comparative Development in Social Welfare, 1972; Year Book of Social Policy, 1972; Cities, Communities and the Young, 1973; Equality and City Schools, 1973; Better Social Services, 1973; Education and Social Action, 1975; Action-Research in Community Development, 1975. *Recreations:* sport, comedy. *Address:* Nuffield Lodge Studio, Regent's Park, NW1. *T:* 01-722 8871.

MIDWINTER, Prof. John Edwin, OBE 1984; PhD; FRS 1985; FEng 1984; British Telecom Professor of Optoelectronics, Department of Electronic Engineering, University College London, since 1984; *b* 8 March 1938; *s* of Henry C. and Vera J. Midwinter; *m* 1961, Maureen Anne Holt; two *s* two *d*. *Educ:* St Bartholomew's Grammar Sch., Newbury, Berks; King's Coll., Univ. of London (BSc Physics, 1961; AKC 1961). PhD Physics, London (ext.), 1968. MInstP 1973; FIEE 1980; FIEEE 1983. Joined RRE, Malvern, as Scientific Officer, 1961 (research on lasers and non-linear optics); Sen. Scientific Officer, 1964–68; Perkin Elmer Corp., Norwalk, Conn, USA, 1968–70; Res. Center, Materials Research Center, Allied Chemical Corp., Morristown, NJ, USA, 1970–71; Head of Optical Fibre Develt, PO Res. Centre, Martlesham, 1971–77; Head, Optical Communications Technol., British Telecom Res. Labs, 1977–84. Vis. Professor: Queen Mary Coll., London, 1979–84; Southampton Univ., 1979–84. Chm., Project 208, Cttee of Science and Technology, EEC, 1977–85. Member: Cttee, IEE Electronics Div. Bd, 1979–82; IEEE COMSOC Internat. Activities Council, 1982–; Optoelectronics Adv. Cttee, Rank Prize Fund, 1983–. Lectures: Bruce Preller, RSE, 1983; Clifford Patterson, Royal Soc.,1983; Cantor, RSA, 1984. Electronics Div. Premium, IEE, 1976. Editor, Optical and Quantum Electronics, 1972–; Associate Editor, Jl of Lightwave Technology, IEEE, 1983–. *Publications:* Applied Non-Linear Optics, 1972; Optical Fibers forTransmission, 1979 (Best Book in Technol. Award, Amer. Publishers' Assoc., 1980); over 70 papers on lasers, non-linear optics and optical communications. *Recreations:* country and mountain walking, skiing, bird-watching, cycling, micro-computing. *Address:* Department of Electronic Engineering, University College London, Torrington Place, WC1E 7JE. *T:* 01-388 0427, 01-387 7050.

MIDWINTER, Stanley Walter, CB 1982; RIBA, FRTPI; architect and planning consultant; Chief Planning Inspector (Director of Planning Inspectorate), Departments of the Environment and Transport, 1978–84; *b* 8 Dec. 1922; *s* of late Lewis Midwinter and Beatrice (*née* Webb); *m* 1954, Audrey Mary Pepper; one *d*. *Educ:* Regent Street Polytechnic Sch.; Sch. of Architecture (DipArch, ARIBA 1948); Sch. of Planning and Res. for Regional Develt (AMTPI 1952, FRTPI 1965); Dip. in Sociol., Univ. of London, 1976. Served War, RE, 1942–46: N Africa, Italy, Greece. Planning Officer, LCC, 1949–54; Bor. Architect and Planning Officer, Larne, NI, 1955–60; joined Housing and Planning Inspectorate, 1960; Dep. Chief Inspector, 1976. Assessor at Belvoir Coalfield Inquiry, 1979. Town Planning Institute: Exam. Prize, 1952; Thomas Adams Prize, 1955; President's Prize, 1958. *Publications:* articles in TPI Jl. *Address:* 2 Prospect Place, Beechen Cliff, Bath BA2 4QP.

MIERS, Sir (Henry) David (Alastair Capel), KBE 1985; CMG 1979; HM Diplomatic Service; Under Secretary of State, Foreign and Commonwealth Office, since 1986; *b* 10 Jan. 1937; *s* of Col R. D. M. C. Miers, DSO, QO Cameron Highlanders, and Honor (*née* Bucknill); *m* 1966, Imelda Maria Emilia, *d* of Jean-Baptiste Wouters, Huizingen, Belgium; two *s* one *d*. *Educ:* Winchester; University Coll., Oxford. Tokyo, 1963; Vientiane, 1966; Private Sec. to Minister of State, FO, 1968; Paris, 1972; Counsellor, Tehran, 1977–79; Hd, Middle Eastern Dept, FCO, 1980–83; Ambassador to Lebanon, 1983–85. *Address:* c/o Foreign and Commonwealth Office, SW1.

MIFSUD BONNICI, Dr Carmelo, LLD; MP; Prime Minister of Malta, since 1984; Minister of Education, since 1983; Minister of the Interior, since 1984; Leader of the Labour Party, since 1984; *b* 17 July 1933; *s* of Lorenzo Mifsud Bonnici, MD, and Catherine (*née* Buttigieg). *Educ:* Govt sch. and Lyceum, Malta; Univ. of Malta (BA, LLD); Univ. Coll. London. Lectr in Industrial and Fiscal Law, Univ. of Malta, 1969–. Legal Consultant, General Workers' Union, 1969–83; Dep. Leader, Labour Party, responsible for party affairs, 1980–82; Designate Leader of the Labour Party, 1982; co-opted to Parlt, 1982, Minister of Labour and Social Services, 1982–83; Sen. Dep. Prime Minister, 1983–84. *Recreation:* reading. *Address:* Kastilja, Valletta, Malta.

MIKARDO, Ian; MP (Lab) Bow and Poplar, since 1983 (Poplar, 1964–74; Tower Hamlets, Bethnal Green and Bow, 1974–83); *b* 9 July 1908; *m* 1932, Mary Rosette; two *d*. *Educ:* Portsmouth. MP (Lab) Reading, 1945–50, South Div. of Reading, 1950–55, again Reading, 1955–Sept. 1959. Member: Nat. Exec. Cttee of Labour Party, 1950–59, and 1960–78 (Chm., 1970–71); Internat Cttee of Labour Party (Chm., 1973–78); Chm., Parly Labour Party, March-Nov. 1974; Chm., Select Cttee on Nationalized Industries, 1966–70. Pres., ASTMS, 1968–73; Vice-Pres., Socialist International, 1978–83 (Hon. Pres. 1983–). *Publications:* Centralised Control of Industry, 1944; Frontiers in the Air, 1946; (with others) Keep Left, 1947; The Second Five Years, 1948; The Problems of Nationalisation, 1948; (jtly) Keeping Left, 1950; The Labour Case, 1950; It's a Mug's Game, 1951; Socialism or Slump, 1959. *Address:* House of Commons, SW1A 0AA. *T:* 01-219 5007.

MIKES, George, LLD (Budapest); Author; *b* Siklós, Hungary, 15 Feb. 1912; *s* of Dr Alfred Mikes and Margit Gál; *m* 1st, 1941, Isobel Gerson (marr. diss.; she *d* 1986); one *s*; 2nd, 1948, Lea Hanak (*d* 1986); one *d*. *Educ:* Cistercian Gymnasium, Pécs; Budapest Univ. Theatrical critic on Budapest newspapers, 1931–38; London correspondent of Budapest papers, 1938–41; working for Hungarian Service of BBC, 1941–51. Pres., PEN in Exile, 1972–80. Governor, London Oratory School, 1978–. *Publications:* How to be an Alien, 1946; How to Scrape Skies, 1948; Wisdom for Others, 1950; Milk and Honey, 1950; Down with Everybody!, 1951; Shakespeare and Myself, 1952; Über Alles, 1953; Eight Humorists, 1954; Little Cabbages, 1955; Italy for Beginners, 1956; The Hungarian Revolution, 1957; East is East, 1958; A Study in Infamy, 1959; How to be Inimitable, 1960; Tango, 1961; Switzerland for Beginners, 1962, new edn 1975; Mortal Passion, 1963; Prison (ed), 1963; How to Unite Nations, 1963; Eureka!, 1965; (with the Duke of Bedford) Book of Snobs, 1965; How to be Affluent, 1966; Not by Sun Alone, 1967; Boomerang, 1968; The Prophet Motive, 1969; Humour-In Memoriam, 1970; The Land of the Rising Yen, 1970; (with Duke of Bedford) How to run a Stately Home, 1971; Any Souvenirs?, 1971; The Spy Who Died of Boredom, 1973; Charlie, 1976; How to be Decadent, 1977; Tsi-Tsa, 1978; English Humour for Beginners, 1980; How to be Seventy, 1982; The Virgin and the Bull (play), 1982; How to be Poor, 1983; Arthur Koestler, the Story of a Friendship, 1983; How to be a Guru, 1984; How to be a Brit, 1984; How to be God, 1986. *Recreations:* tennis, cooking, and not listening to funny stories. *Address:* 1B Dorncliffe Road, SW6. *T:* 01–736 2624. *Clubs:* Garrick, Hurlingham, PEN.

MILBANK, Sir Anthony (Frederick), 5th Bt *cr* 1882; farmer and landowner since 1977; *b* 16 Aug. 1939; *s* of Sir Mark Vane Milbank, 4th Bt, KCVO, MC, and of Hon. Verena Aileen, Lady Milbank, *yr d* of 11th Baron Farnham, DSO; *S* father, 1984; *m* 1970, Belinda Beatrice, *yr d* of Brig. Adrian Gore, DSO; two *s* one *d*. *Educ:* Eton College. Brown, Shipley & Co. Ltd, 1961–66; M&G Securities Ltd, 1966–77. *Recreations:* outdoor sports. *Heir: s* Edward Mark Somerset Milbank, *b* 9 April 1973. *Address:* Barningham Park, Richmond, N Yorks DL11 7DW.

MILBORNE-SWINNERTON-PILKINGTON, Sir T. H.; *see* Pilkington.

MILBOURN, Dr Graham Maurice; Director, National Institute of Agricultural Botany, since 1981; *b* 4 Sept. 1930; *s* of late Frank McLaren Milbourn, BSc and Winifred May Milbourn; *m* 1956, Louise Lawson; three *s*. *Educ:* Reading Univ. (BSc, MSc, PhD). Asst Lectr, Reading Univ., 1953–56; Radiobiological Lab., ARC, 1956–61; Sen. Lectr, Crop Production, Wye Coll., London Univ., 1961–77; Prof. of Crop Production, Sch. of Agric., Edinburgh Univ., 1977–81. *Publications:* papers on physiology of cereals and vegetables, uptake of radio-nucleides by crops. *Recreation:* sailing. *Address:* National Institute of Agricultural Botany, Huntingdon Road, Cambridge CB3 0LE. *T:* Cambridge 276381.

MILBURN, Sir Anthony (Rupert), 5th Bt *cr* 1905; landowner; *b* 17 April 1947; *s* of Major Rupert Leonard Eversley Milburn (*yr s* of 3rd Bt) (*d* 1974) and of Anne Mary, *d* of late Major Austin Scott Murray, MC; *S* uncle, 1985; *m* 1977, Olivia Shirley, *y d* of Captain Thomas Noel Catlow, CBE, RN; one *s* one *d*. *Educ:* Hawtreys, Savernake Forest; Eton College; Cirencester Agricultural Coll. ARICS. Company Director. *Recreations:* sporting and rural pursuits. *Heir: s* Patrick Thomas Milburn, *b* 4 Dec. 1980. *Address:* Guyzance Hall, Acklington, Morpeth, Northumberland. *T:* Alnwick 711247. *Club:* New (Edinburgh).

MILBURN, Donald B.; *see* Booker-Milburn.

MILBURN, Very Rev. Robert Leslie Pollington, MA; FSA; *b* 28 July 1907; *er s* of late George Leslie and Elizabeth Esther Milburn; *m* 1944, Margery Kathleen Mary, *d* of Rev. Francis Graham Harvie; one *d* (one *s* decd). *Educ:* Oundle; Sidney Sussex Coll., Cambridge; New Coll., Oxford. Asst Master, Eton Coll., 1930–32; Select Preacher, University of Oxford, 1942–44; Fellow and Chaplain of Worcester Coll., Oxford, 1934–57, Tutor, 1945–57, Estates Bursar, 1946–57 (Junior Bursar, 1936–46), Hon. Fellow, 1978. University Lectr in Church History, 1947–57; Bampton Lectr, 1952. Examining Chaplain to Bishop of St Edmundsbury and Ipswich, 1941–53, to Bishop of Southwark, 1950–57, to Bishop of Oxford, 1952–57; Dean of Worcester, 1957–68, now Emeritus; Master of the Temple, 1968–80. Mem. of Oxford City Council, 1941–47. A Trustee, Wallace Collection, 1970–76. Grand Chaplain, United Grand Lodge of England, 1969. *Publications:* Saints and their Emblems in English Churches, 1949; Early Christian Interpretations of History, 1954; articles in Journal of Theological Studies and Church Quarterly Review. *Address:* 5 St Barnabas, Newland, Malvern, Worcs WR13 5AX.

MILCHSACK, Dame Lilo, Hon. DCMG 1972 (Hon. CMG 1968); Hon. CBE 1958; Initiator, 1949, and Hon. Chairman, since 1982, Deutsch-Englische Gesellschaft eV (Hon. Secretary, 1949–77; Chairman, 1977–82); *b* Frankfurt/Main; *d* of Prof. Dr Paul Duden and Johanna Bertha (*née* Nebe); *m* Hans Milchsack; (*d* 1984); two *d*. *Educ:* Univs of Frankfurt, Geneva and Amsterdam. Awarded Grosses Bundesverdienstkreuz, 1959, with Stern, 1985. *Recreations:* gardening, reading. *Address:* An der Kalvey 11, D-4000 Düsseldorf 31–Wittlaer, Germany. *T:* Düsseldorf 40 13 87.

MILDON, Arthur Leonard, QC 1971; **His Honour Judge Mildon;** a Circuit Judge, since 1986; *b* 3 June 1923; *er s* of late Rev. Dr W. H. Mildon, Barnstaple; *m* 1950, Iva, *er d* of late G. H. C. Wallis, Plymouth; one *s* one *d*. *Educ:* Kingswood Sch., Bath; Wadham Coll., Oxford (MA). Pres., Oxford Univ. Liberal Club, 1948. Army Service, 1942–46: Lieut, 138th (City of London) Field Regt, RA; Captain, 1st Army Group, RA. Called to Bar, Middle Temple, 1950, Bencher, 1979; Member of Western Circuit; Dep. Chm., Isle of Wight QS, 1967–71; a Recorder, 1972–85. Mem., Bar Council, 1973–74. *Recreation:* sailing. *Address:* 2 Crown Office Row, Temple, EC4. *T:* 01–583 8155. *Clubs:* Hampshire (Winchester); Royal Solent Yacht.

MILEDI, Prof. Ricardo, MD; FRS 1970; Distinguished Professor, University of California, Irvine, since 1984; *b* Mexico City, 15 Sept. 1927; *m* 1955, Ana Carmen (Mela) Garces; one *s*. *Educ:* Univ. Nacional Autónoma, Mexico City. BSc 1948; MD 1954. Research at Nat. Inst. of Cardiology, Mexico, 1952–55; Rockefeller Travelling Fellowship at ANU, 1956–58; research at Dept of Biophysics, UCL, 1958–84. *Address:* Laboratory of Cellular and Molecular Neurobiology, Department of Psychobiology, University of California, Irvine, Calif 92717, USA. *T:* (714) 856–5693; 9 Gibbs Court, Irvine, Calif 92717, USA. *T:* (714) 856–2677.

MILES, family name of **Baron Miles.**

MILES, Baron *cr* 1979 (Life Peer), of Blackfriars in the City of London; **Bernard James Miles,** Kt 1969; CBE 1953; Actor; Founder, with his wife, of the Mermaid Theatre, Puddle Dock, EC4, 1959 (first opened in North London, 1950); *b* 27 Sept. 1907; *s* of Edwin James Miles and Barbara Fletcher; *m* 1931, Josephine Wilson; one *s* two *d*. *Educ:* Uxbridge County Sch.; Pembroke Coll., Oxford (Hon. Fellow, 1969). Hon. DLitt, City

Univ., 1974. First stage appearance as Second Messenger in Richard III, New Theatre, 1930; appeared in St Joan, His Majesty's, 1931; spent 5 years in repertory as designer, stage-manager, character-actor, etc; frequent appearances on West End Stage from 1938. Entered films, 1937, and has written for, directed, and acted in them. First went on Music-hall stage, London Palladium, etc., 1950. Mermaid Theatre seasons: Royal Exchange, 1953; Macbeth, Dido and Aeneas, As You Like It, Eastward Ho! Formed Mermaid Theatre Trust which built City of London's first theatre for 300 years, the Mermaid, Puddle Dock, EC4. Opened May 1959, with musical play Lock Up Your Daughters. *Publications:* The British Theatre, 1947; God's Brainwave, 1972; Favourite Tales from Shakespeare, 1976; (ed with J. C. Trewin) Curtain Calls, 1981. *Address:* House of Lords, SW1A 0PW

MILES, Prof. Albert Edward William, LRCP; MRCS; FDS; DSc; Professor of Dental Pathology at The London Hospital Medical College, 1950–76, retired; Hon. Curator, Odontological Collection, Royal College of Surgeons of England, since 1955; *b* 15 July 1912; *m* 1st, 1939, Sylvia Stuart; one *s* decd; 2nd, 1979, Diana Cross. *Educ:* Stationers' Company Sch.; Charing Cross and Royal Dental Hosps. John Tomes Prize, RCS, 1954–56. Part-time Lectr, Anatomy Dept, London Hosp. Med. Coll., 1977–85. Charles Tomes Lecturer, RCS, 1957; Evelyn Sprawson Lectr, London Hosp. Med. Coll., 1977. Hunterian Trustee, 1978–. Howard Mummery Meml Prize, 1976; Colyer Gold Medal, RCS, 1978. Exec. Editor, Archives of Oral Biology, 1969–. *Publications:* contrib. to scientific literature. *Address:* 1 Cleaver Square, Kennington, SE11. *T:* 01–735 5350. *Clubs:* Tetrapods, Zoo.

MILES, Anthony John; Executive Publisher, Globe Communications Corporation, Florida, USA, since 1985; *b* 18 July 1930; *s* of Paul and Mollie Miles; *m* 1975, Anne Hardman. *Educ:* High Wycombe Royal Grammar Sch. On staff of (successively): Middlesex Advertiser; Nottingham Guardian; Brighton Evening Argus. Daily Mirror: Feature writer, 1954–66; Asst Editor, 1967–68; Associate Editor, 1968–71; Editor, 1971–74; Mirror Group Newspapers: Editorial Dir, 1975–84; Dep. Chm., 1977–79 and 1984; Chm., 1980–83. Dir, Reuters Ltd, 1978–84. Member: Press Council, 1975–78; British Exec. Cttee, IPI, 1976–84; Council, CPU, 1983–84; Appeal Chm. 1982–83, Vice-Pres., 1983–, Newspaper Press Fund. *Address:* 5401 Broken Sound Boulevard, NW, Boca Raton, Florida, USA. *Club:* Reform.

MILES, Sir (Arnold) Ashley, Kt 1966; CBE 1953; FRS 1961; MA, MD, FRCP, FRCPath; Professor of Experimental Pathology, University of London, 1952–71, now Emeritus Professor; Director of the Lister Institute of Preventive Medicine, London, 1952–71; Deputy Director, Department of Medical Microbiology, London Hospital Medical College, since 1976 (Fellow, London Hospital Medical College, 1986); Hon. Consultant in Microbiology, London Hospital, 1976; *b* 20 March 1904; *s* of Harry Miles, York; *m* 1930, Ellen Marguerite, *d* of Harald Dahl, Cardiff; no *c*. *Educ:* Bootham Sch., York; King's Coll., Cambridge, Hon. Fellow, 1971; St Bartholomew's Hosp., London. Demonstrator in Bacteriology, London Sch. of Hygiene and Tropical Medicine, 1929; Demonstrator in Pathol., University of Cambridge, 1931; Reader in Bacteriology, British Postgraduate Medical Sch., London, 1935; Prof. Bacteriology, University of London, 1937–45; Acting Dir Graham Medical Research Laboratories, University Coll. Hosp. Medical Sch., 1943–45; London Sector Pathologist, Emergency Medical Services, 1939–44; Dir, Medical Research Council Wound Infection Unit, Birmingham Accident Hosp., 1942–46; Dep. Dir, 1947–52 and Dir of Dept of Biological Standards, 1946–52, National Institute for Medical Research, London. MRC grant holder, Clinical Res. Centre, 1971–76. Mem., MRC, 1957–61 and 1967–68; Biological Sec. and Vice-Pres., Royal Society, 1963–68. President: Soc. Gen. Microbiology, 1957–59 (Hon. Mem., 1972); Internat. Assoc. Microbiological Socs, 1974–78. Trustee, Beit Memorial Fellowships, 1970–81. For. Corresp., Acad. de Médecine de Belgique, 1972. Hon. Member: Amer. Soc. for Microbiol., 1974; Amer. Assoc. of Pathologists, 1977; Deutsche Gesellschaft für Hygiene und Mikrobiologie, 1978; British Acad. of Forensic Scis, 1978; Path. Soc. of GB, 1980; Fellow, World Acad. Art and Science, 1975; Hon. Fellow: Infectious Diseases Soc. of Amer., 1979; RSocMed, 1981; Hon. FInstBiol, 1975; Consejero de Honor, Consejo Superior de Investigaciones Científicas, Madrid, 1966. Hon. DSc, Newcastle, 1969. *Publications:* (with G. S. Wilson and M. T. Parker) Topley and Wilson's Principles of Bacteriology, Virology and Immunity, 1945, 7th edn 1985; various scientific papers. *Recreations:* various. *Address:* Department of Medical Microbiology, London Hospital Medical College, Turner Street, E1 2AD. *T:* 01–377 7644; 7 Holly Place, Hampstead, NW3 6QU. *T:* 01–435 5811.

MILES, Mrs Caroline Mary; Chairman, Oxfordshire Health Authority, since 1984; Market Development Consultant, Harwell Research Laboratory, since 1981; Director of Development, Foundation for the Study of Christianity and Society, since 1983; *b* 30 April 1929; *d* of Brig. A. J. R. M. Leslie, OBE. *Educ:* numerous schools; Somerville Coll., Oxford. HM Treasury, 1953–54; NIESR, 1954–56 and 1964–67; attached to UN Secretariat, NY, 1956–63. Associate Mem., Nuffield Coll., Oxford, 1972–74. Member: Textile Council, 1968–71; Inflation Accounting Cttee (Sandilands Cttee), 1974–75; Monopolies and Mergers Commn, 1975–84; NEB, 1976–79. Trustee, The Tablet, 1982–; Governor, Ditchley Foundn, 1983–. *Publications:* Lancashire Textiles, A Case Study of Industrial Change, 1968; numerous papers and articles. *Recreations:* music, picnics, poohsticks. *Address:* Millbrook, Brookend, Chadlington, Oxford OX7 3NF. *T:* Chadlington 309.

MILES, Prof. Charles William Noel, CBE 1980; Head of Department of Land Management and Development, 1968–81, Dean of Faculty of Urban and Regional Studies, 1972–75, and Professor Emeritus 1981, University of Reading; Chairman, Agricultural Wages Board for England and Wales, 1972–81; *b* 3 Nov. 1915; 2nd *s* of late Lt-Col Sir Charles W. Miles, 5th Bt; *m* 1940, Jacqueline (Dickie) Cross; one *d* (one *s* decd). *Educ:* Stowe Sch.; Jesus Coll., Cambridge (MA). FRICS. Army Service, 1939–46; Univ. Demonstrator and Univ. Lectr, Dept of Estate Management, Cambridge, 1946–54; Chief Agent to Meyrick Estates in Hants and Anglesey, 1954–68; Agent to Bisterne Estate, 1957–68. Pres., Chartered Land Agents Soc., 1965–66; Mem., Cambs AEC, 1953–54; Mem., SE Region Adv. Cttee of Land Commn, 1967–70. Mem., Yates Cttee on Recreation Management Trng, 1977–82. Leverhulme Trust Emeritus Fellowship, 1982–84. *Publications:* Estate Finance and Business Management, 1953, 4th edn 1981; Estate Accounts, 1960; Recreational Land Management, 1977; (co-ed) Walmesley's Rural Estate Management, 6th edn, 1978. *Recreations:* walking, gardening, theatre. *Address:* Wheelers, Vicarage Lane, Mattingley, Basingstoke, Hants RG27 8LF. *T:* Heckfield 357. *Club:* Farmers'.

See also Sir W. N. M. Miles, Bt.

MILES, Dillwyn, FRGS 1946; The Herald Bard, since 1967; Director, Dyfed Rural Council, 1975–81; Chairman, National Association of Local Councils, since 1977; *b* 25 May 1916; *s* of Joshua Miles and Anne Mariah (*née* Lewis), Newport, Pembrokeshire; *m* 1944, Joyce Eileen (*d* 1976), *d* of Lewis Craven Ord, Montreal and London; one *s* one *d*. *Educ:* Fishguard County Sch.; University College of Wales, Aberystwyth. Served War of 1939–45, Middle East, Army Captain. National Organiser Palestine House, London, 1945–48; Extra mural Lectr, Univ. of Wales, 1948–51; Community Centres Officer, Wales, 1951–54; Gen. Sec., Pembrokeshire Community Council, 1954–75. Founder: Jerusalem Welsh Soc., 1940; W Wales Tourist Assoc., 1962; Assoc. of Trusts for Nature Conservation in Wales, 1973; Hon. Sec., W Wales Naturalists Trust, 1958–75 (Vice-Pres., 1975–). Grand Sword Bearer, Gorsedd of Bards of Isle of Britain, 1959–67 (Mem. Bd, 1945–). Member: Pembrokeshire CC, 1947–63; Cemaes RDC, 1947–52; Newport Parish Council, 1946–52; Haverfordwest Bor. Council, 1957–63; Pembrokeshire Coast Nat. Park Cttee, 1952–75; Exec. Cttee, Council for Protection of Rural Wales, 1946–64; Nature Conservancy's Cttee for Wales, 1966–73; Council, Soc. for Promotion of Nature Reserves, 1961–73; Countryside in 1970 Cttee for Wales, 1969–70; Sports Council for Wales, 1965–69; Mental Health Rev. Tribunal for Wales, 1959–71; Rent Trib. for Wales, 1966–; Court of Govs, Nat. Libr. for Wales, 1963–64; Court of Govs, Univ. of Wales, 1957–66; Pembroke TA Assoc., 1956–59; Council for Small Industries in Wales, 1968–72; Age Concern Wales, 1972–77; Exec. Cttee, Nat. Council for Social Service, 1978–81; Exec. Cttee, NPFA, 1977–81; Council, Royal Nat. Eisteddfod of Wales, 1967–; Prince of Wales Cttee, 1971–80 (former Chm., Dyfed Projects Gp); Welsh Environment Foundn, 1971–80; Heraldry Soc., 1974–; Rural Voice, 1980–. Former Chairman: Further Educn and Libraries and Museums Cttees, Pembs CC; Pembs Cttee, Arthritis and Rheumatism Council; Pembs Jun. Ch. of Commerce; Pembs Community Health Council; Policy and Welsh Cttees, Nat. Assoc. of Local Councils. Chairman: Pembs PO and Telecom Adv. Cttee, 1984– (Vice-Chm., 1971–84); Wales Playing Fields Assoc., 1965–81. Editor: The Pembrokeshire Historian, 1955–81; Nature in Wales, 1970–80. Mayor of Newport, Pembs, 1950, 1966, 1967, 1979, and Sen. Alderman. Mayor and Adm. of the Port, Haverfordwest, 1961, Sheriff 1963, Burgess Warden 1974. Broadcaster, TV and radio, 1936–. *Publications:* ed, Pembrokeshire Coast National Park, 1973, 2nd impr. 1978; (jtly) Writers of the West, 1974; The Sheriffs of the County of Pembroke, 1975; The Royal National Eisteddfod of Wales, 1978; A Pembrokeshire Anthology, 1982; The Castles of Pembrokeshire, 1979, rev. edn 1983; Portrait of Pembrokeshire, 1984. *Recreations:* natural history, local history, books, food and wine. *Address:* Castle Hill, Haverfordwest, Dyfed, Wales SA61 2EG. *T:* Haverfordwest 3400. *Clubs:* Savile, Wig and Pen; Pembrokeshire County (Haverfordwest).

MILES, (Frank) Stephen, CMG 1964; HM Diplomatic Service, retired; *b* 7 Jan. 1920; *s* of Harry and Mary Miles; *m* 1953, Margaret Joy (*née* Theaker); three *d*. *Educ:* John Watson's Sch., Edinburgh; Daniel Stewart's Coll., Edinburgh; St Andrews Univ. (MA); Harvard Univ. (Commonwealth Fellowship; MPA). Served with Fleet Air Arm, 1942–46 (Lt (A) RNVR). Scottish Home Dept, 1948; FCO (previously CRO), 1948–80; served in: New Zealand, 1949–52; E and W Pakistan, 1954–57; Ghana, 1959–62; Uganda, 1962–63; British Dep. High Commissioner, Tanzania, 1963–65 (Acting High Commissioner, 1963–64); Acting High Commissioner in Ghana, March-April 1966; Consul-Gen., St Louis, 1967–70; Dep. High Comr, Calcutta, 1970–74; High Comr, Zambia, 1974–78; High Comr, Bangladesh, 1978–79. A Dir of Studies, Overseas Services Unit, RIPA, 1980–83. Councillor: Tandridge DC, Surrey, 1982–; Limpsfield Parish Council, 1983–. *Recreations:* cricket, tennis, golf. *Address:* Maytrees, 71 Park Road, Limpsfield, Oxted, Surrey RH8 0AN. *T:* Oxted 3132. *Clubs:* Royal Commonwealth Society, MCC.

MILES, Geoffrey, OBE 1970; HM Diplomatic Service, retired; Consul-General, Perth, Western Australia, 1980–82; *b* 25 Oct. 1922; *s* of late Donald Frank Miles and Honorine Miles (*née* Lambert); *m* 1946, Mary Rozel Cottle; one *s* one *d*. *Educ:* Eltham College. Joined Home Civil Service (Min. of Shipping), 1939; War service as pilot in RAF, 1941–46 (commnd 1945); Min. of Transport, 1946–50; British Embassy, Washington 1951; Sec., Copper-Zinc-Lead Cttee, Internat. Materials Conf., Washington 1952–53; BoT, 1953–55; Asst Trade Comr, Perth, 1955–59; Second Sec., Ottawa, 1960–63; First Sec., Salisbury, 1963–66, Dublin, 1967–71; Trade Comr (later Consul) and Head of Post, Edmonton, 1971–75, Consul-Gen., 1976–78; Consul-Gen., Philadelphia, 1979–80. *Recreations:* music, golf, amateur radio. *Address:* Farthings, Appledram Lane, Chichester, W Sussex PO20 7PE. *Clubs:* Royal Air Force; British Officers (Philadelphia); Goodwood Golf.

MILES, Adm. Sir Geoffrey John Audley, KCB 1945 (CB 1942); KCSI 1947; *b* 2 May 1890; 3rd *s* of Audley Charles Miles and Eveline Cradock-Hartopp; *m* 1918, Alison Mary Cadell (*d* 1981); two *s*. *Educ:* Bedford; HMS Britannia. Joined the Royal Navy, served with Submarines and Destroyers during European War, 1914–18; later appointments include: Dep. Dir Staff Coll., Dir Tactical Sch.; Capt. HMS Nelson, 1939–41; Rear-Adm., 1941; Vice-Adm., 1944; Adm., 1948. Head of Mil. Mission in Moscow, 1941–43; Flag Officer Comdg Western Mediterranean, 1944–45; C-in-C, Royal Indian Navy, 1946–47. *Address:* Holyport Lodge, The Green, Holyport, Maidenhead, Berks SL6 2JA. *Club:* Naval and Military.

MILES, Prof. Hamish Alexander Drummond; Barber Professor of Fine Arts and Director of the Barber Institute, University of Birmingham, since 1970; *b* 19 Nov. 1925; *s* of J. E. (Hamish) Miles and Sheila Barbara Robertson; *m* 1957, Jean Marie, *d* of T. R. Smits, New York; two *s* two *d*. *Educ:* Douai Sch.; Univ. of Edinburgh (MA); Balliol Coll., Oxford. Served War: Army, 1944–47. Asst Curator, Glasgow Art Gallery, 1953–54; Asst Lectr, then Lectr in the History of Art, Univ. of Glasgow, 1954–66; Vis. Lectr, Smith Coll., Mass, 1960–61; Prof. of the History of Art, Univ. of Leicester, 1966–70. Trustee, National Galleries of Scotland, 1967–; Mem., Museums and Galleries Commn, 1983–. *Publications:* (jtly) The Paintings of James McNeill Whistler, 2 vols, 1980; sundry articles and catalogues. *Recreations:* beekeeping and woodland management. *Address:* 37 Carpenter Road, Birmingham B15 2JJ; Burnside, Kirkmichael, Blairgowrie, Perthshire PH10 7NA.

MILES, Prof. Herbert William, MSc (Bristol), DSc (Manchester). Adviser and Lecturer in Entomology, University of Manchester, 1927–42; Advisory Entomologist, University of Bristol (Long Ashton Research Station), 1942–46; Deputy Provincial Director (West Midland Province), National Agricultural Advisory Service, 1946–47; Prof. of Horticulture, Wye Coll., London Univ., 1947–65, now Emeritus. Hon. Consultant in Horticulture to RASE, 1948–75. President: Lincolnshire Naturalists' Union, 1938; Assoc. of Applied Biology, 1956. Officier, Ordre du Mérite Agricole, 1974. *Publications:* (with Mary Miles, MSc) Insect Pests of Glasshouse Crops, revised edn 1947; original papers on Economic Entomology in leading scientific journals; original studies on the biology of British sawflies. *Address:* 2 Wood Broughton, Grange-over-Sands, Cumbria.

MILES, John Edwin Alfred, CBE 1979 (OBE 1961; MBE 1952); HM Diplomatic Service, retired; *b* 14 Aug. 1919; *s* of late John Miles and late Rose Miles (*née* Newlyn); *m* 1952, Barbara Fergus Ferguson; two *s* one *d*. *Educ:* Hornsey County Sch. Apptd to Dominions Office, 1937. Served War: joined Queen's Royal West Surrey Regt, 1940; commissioned in N Staffordshire Regt, 1941; attached Royal Indian Army Service Corps, 1942 (Maj. 1943); released, Sept. 1946, and returned to Dominions Office. Served in: Wellington, NZ, 1948–51; Calcutta, 1953–56; CRO, 1957–61; Trinidad (on staff of Governor-Gen.), 1961; Jamaica (Adviser to Governor, and later First Sec. in British High Commission), 1961–64; Wellington, NZ, 1964–68; Counsellor, 1968; Accra, Ghana,

1968–71; Dep. High Comr, Madras, India, 1971–75; High Comr to Swaziland, 1975–79. *Address:* Cartref, Ladyegate Road, Dorking, Surrey. *T:* Dorking 884346.

MILES, John Seeley, FSIAD, FSTD; typographer and partner in design group, Banks and Miles; *b* 11 Feb. 1931; *s* of Thomas William Miles and Winifred (*née* Seeley); *m* 1955, Louise Wilson; one *s* two *d*. *Educ:* Beckenham and Penge Grammar Sch.; Beckenham School of Art. FSIAD 1973; FSTD 1974. UN travelling schol. to Netherlands to practise typography and punch cutting under Jan van Krimpen and S. L. Hartz, 1954–55; Assistant to Hans Schmoller at Penguin Books, 1955–58; joined Colin Banks, *qv,* to form design partnership, Banks and Miles, 1958. Consultant to: Zoological Soc., Regent's Park and Whipsnade, 1958–82; Expanded Metal Co., 1960–83; Consumers' Assoc., 1964–; British Council, 1968–83; The Post Office, 1972–83; E Midlands Arts Assoc., 1974–79; Curwen Press, 1970–72; Basilisk Press, 1976–79; Enschedé en Zn, Netherlands, 1980–; British Telecom, 1980–; British Airports Auth., 1983–; typographic advisor, HMSO, 1985–; design advisor: Agricl Inf. Workshop, Udaipur, India, 1973; Monotype Corp., 1985–. Member, PO Design Adv. Cttee, 1972–76; American Heritage Lectr, New York, 1960; held seminar, Graphic Inst., Stockholm, 1977 and 1986. Chairman: Wynkyn de Worde Soc., 1973–74; Arbitration Cttee, Assoc. Typographique Internationale, 1984–. Governor, Central School of Arts and Crafts, 1978–85; External examr, London Coll. of Printing, 1984–. Mem. CGLI, 1986. Exhibitions: London, 1971, 1978; Amsterdam and Brussels, 1977. *Publications:* articles and reviews in professional jls. *Recreations:* gardening, painting, reading aloud. *Address:* 24 Collins Street, Blackheath, SE3 0GU. *T:* 01–318 4739. *Clubs:* Arts, Double Crown.

MILES, Dame Margaret, DBE 1970; BA; Headmistress, Mayfield School, Putney, 1952–73; *b* 11 July 1911; 2nd *d* of Rev. E. G. Miles and Annie Miles (*née* Jones). *Educ:* Ipswich High Sch., GPDST; Bedford Coll., Univ. of London (Fellow, 1982). History teacher: Westcliff High Sch., 1935–39; Badminton Sch., 1939–44; Lectr, Dept of Educn, University of Bristol, 1944–46; Headmistress, Pate's Grammar Sch., Cheltenham, 1946–52. Member: Schools Broadcasting Council, 1958–68; Educ. Adv. Council, ITA, 1962–67; Nat. Adv. Council on Trng and Supply of Teachers, 1962–65; BBC Gen. Adv. Council, 1964–73; Campaign for Comprehensive Educn, 1966– (Chm., 1972; Pres., 1979–); RSA Council, 1972–77; British Assoc., 1974–79; Council, Chelsea Coll., Univ. of London, 1965–82; former Mem., Council, Bedford Coll., Univ. of London (Vice-Chm.); Chairman: Adv. Cttee on Develt Educn, ODM, 1977–79; Central Bureau for Educl Visits and Exchanges, 1978–82; Vice-Chm., Educ. Adv. Cttee, UK Nat. Commn for Unesco, till 1985. Chm., Meirionnydd Br., Council for Protection of Rural Wales, 1982–; Pres., British Assoc. for Counselling, 1980–. Hon. Fellow, Chelsea Coll., London, 1985. Hon. DCL, Univ. of Kent at Canterbury, 1973. *Publications:* And Gladly Teach, 1965; Comprehensive Schooling, Problems and Perspectives, 1968. *Recreations:* opera, films, reading, gardening, golf, walking, travel when possible. *Address:* Tanycraig, Pennal, Machynlleth SY20 9LB. *Clubs:* University Women's; Aberdovey Golf.

MILES, Oliver; see Miles, R. O.

MILES, Peter Charles H.; see Hubbard-Miles.

MILES, Sir Peter (Tremayne), KCVO 1986; Keeper of the Privy Purse and Treasurer to the Queen, since 1981; Receiver-General, Duchy of Lancaster, since 1981; *b* 26 June 1924; *er s* of late Lt-Col E. W. T. Miles, MC; *m* 1956, Philippa Helen Tremlett; two *s* one *d*. *Educ:* Eton Coll.; RMC, Sandhurst. First The Royal Dragoons, 1944–49; J. F. Thomasson & Co., 1949–59; Gerrard & National Discount Co. Ltd, 1959–80 (Managing Director, 1964–80). Director: P. Murray-Jones Ltd, 1966–75; Astley & Pearce Holdings Ltd, 1975–80 (Chm., 1978–80). Mem., Prince of Wales' Council, 1981–. *Address:* 15 St James's Palace, SW1A 1BG. *T:* 01–930 5642; Mill House, Southrop, Lechlade, Gloucestershire. *T:* Southrop 287. *Clubs:* Cavalry and Guards, Pratt's, White's; Swinley Forest Golf.

MILES, (Richard) Oliver, CMG 1984; HM Diplomatic Service; Ambassador to Luxembourg, since 1985; *b* 6 March 1936; *s* of George Miles and Olive (*née* Clapham); *m* 1968, Julia, *d* of late Prof. J. S. Weiner; three *s* one *d*. *Educ:* Ampleforth Coll.; Merton Coll., Oxford (Oriental Studies). Entered Diplomatic Service, 1960; served in Abu Dhabi, Amman, Aden, Mukalla, Nicosia, Jedda; Counsellor, Athens, 1977–80; Head of Near East and N Africa Dept, FCO, 1980–83; Ambassador, Libya, 1984. *Recreations:* bird-watching, singing, playing the flute. *Address:* c/o Foreign and Commonwealth Office, SW1A 2AH. *Club:* Travellers'.

MILES, Roger Steele, PhD, DSc; Head, Department of Public Services, British Museum (Natural History), since 1975; *b* 31 Aug. 1937; *s* of John Edward Miles and Dorothy Mildred (*née* Steele); *m* 1960, Ann Blake; one *s* one *d*. *Educ:* Malet Lambert High Sch., Hull; King's Coll., Univ. of Durham (BSc, PhD, DSc). Sen. Res. Award, DSIR, 1962–64; Sen. Res. Fellow, Royal Scottish Museum, 1964–66; Sen. Scientific Officer, 1966–68; Sen. Sci. Officer, BM (Nat. Hist.), 1968–71, Principal Sci. Officer, 1971–74. Hon. Fellow, Columbia Pacific Univ., 1983. *Publications:* 2nd edn, Palaeozoic Fishes, 1971 (1st edn, J. A. Moy-Thomas, 1939); (ed, with P. H. Greenwood and C. Patterson) Interrelationships of Fishes, 1973; (ed, with S. M. Andrews and A. D. Walker) Problems in Vertebrate Evolution, 1977; (with others) The Design of Educational Exhibits, 1982; papers and monographs on anatomy and palaeontology of fishes, articles on museums, in jls. *Recreations:* music, twentieth century art and architecture. *Address:* 3 Eagle Lane, Snaresbrook, E11 1PF. *T:* 01–989 5684.

MILES, Surgeon Rear-Adm. Stanley, CB 1968; FRCP, FRCS; Vice President, International Trauma Foundation, since 1982 (Chairman, 1978–82); *b* 14 Aug. 1911; *s* of late T. C. Miles, Company Dir, Sheffield; *m* 1939, Frances Mary Rose; one *s* one *d*. *Educ:* King Edward VII Sch.; University of Sheffield. MSc Sheffield, 1934; MB, ChB, 1936; DTM&HEng, 1949; MD, 1955; FRCP 1971, FRCS 1971. Joined RN Medical Service, 1936; served in China, W Africa, Pacific and Mediterranean Fleets. Medical Officer-in-Charge, RN Medical Sch. and Dir of Medical Research, 1961; Consultant in Physiology; Med. Officer-in-Charge, Royal Naval Hosp., Plymouth, 1966–69. Surg. Captain 1960; Surg. Rear-Adm. 1966. Dean, Postgraduate Med. Studies, Univ. of Manchester, 1969–76. Gilbert Blane Medal, RCS, 1957. QHP 1966–69. CStJ 1968. *Publication:* Underwater Medicine, 1962. *Recreations:* tennis, golf. *Address:* 15 Solent Drive, Barton-on-Sea, New Milton, Hants BH25 7AW.

MILES, Stephen; see Miles, F. S.

MILES, William; Chief Executive, West Yorkshire County Council, and Clerk of the Lieutenancy, West Yorkshire, 1984–86; *b* 26 Sept. 1933; *s* of William and Gladys Miles; *m* 1961, Jillian Anne Wilson; three *s*. *Educ:* Wyggeston School, Leicester; Trinity Hall, Cambridge (MA, LLM). Solicitor. Asst Solicitor, Leicester, Doncaster and Exeter County Boroughs, 1960–66; Asst Town Clerk, Leicester Co. Borough, 1966–69; Dep. Town Clerk, Blackpool Co. Borough, 1969–73; City Legal Adviser, Newcastle upon Tyne, 1973–74; Chief Exec., Gateshead Borough Council, 1974–84. *Recreations:* bridge, hill walking, sport. *Address:* 23 Moor Crescent, Gosforth, Newcastle upon Tyne. *T:* Tyneside 2851996.

MILES, Sir William (Napier Maurice), 6th Bt *cr* 1859; retired architect; *b* 19 Oct. 1913; *s* of Sir Charles William Miles, 5th Bt, OBE; *S* father, 1966; *m* 1946, Pamela, *d* of late Capt. Michael Dillon; one *s* two *d*. *Educ:* Stowe; University of Cambridge (BA). Architectural Assoc. Diploma, 1939. *Recreations:* swimming, motor-cycling. *Heir: s* Philip John Miles, *b* 10 Aug. 1953. *Address:* Old Rectory House, Walton-in-Gordano, near Clevedon, Avon. *T:* Clevedon 873365. *Club:* Royal Western Yacht.

See also Prof. C. W. N. Miles.

MILFORD, 2nd Baron *cr* 1939; **Wogan Philipps;** Bt 1919; farmer and painter; *b* 25 Feb. 1902; *e s* of 1st Baron Milford; *S* father, 1962; *m* 1st, 1928, Rosamond Nina Lehmann, *qv;* one *s* (and one *d* decd); 2nd, 1944, Cristina, Countess of Huntingdon (who *d* 1953); 3rd, 1954, Tamara Rust. *Educ:* Eton; Magdalen Coll., Oxford. Member of International Brigade, Spanish Civil War. Former Member of Henley on Thames RDC; Communist Councillor, Cirencester RDC, 1946–49; has taken active part in building up Nat. Union of Agric. Workers in Gloucestershire and served on its county cttee. Prospective Parly cand. (Lab), Henley on Thames, 1938–39; contested (Com) Cirencester and Tewkesbury, 1950. Has held one-man exhibitions of paintings in London, Milan and Cheltenham and shown in many mixed exhibns. *Heir: s* Hon. Hugo John Laurence Philipps [*b* 27 Aug. 1929; *m* 1st, 1951 (marr. diss., 1958); one *d*; 2nd, 1959, Mary (marr. diss. 1984), *e d* of Baron Sherfield, *qv;* three *s* one *d*]. *Address:* Flat 2, 8 Lyndhurst Road, Hampstead, NW3 5PX.

See also Hon. R. H. Philipps.

MILFORD, John Tillman; a Recorder, since 1985; *b* 4 Feb. 1946; *s* of late Dr Roy Douglas Milford and Jessie Milford; *m* 1975, Mary Alice, *d* of Dr E. A. Spriggs of Wylam, Northumberland; three *d*. *Educ:* The Cathedral School, Salisbury; Hurstpierpoint; Exeter Univ. (LLB). Called to the Bar, Inner Temple, 1969; in practice on NE Circuit, 1970–. *Recreations:* fishing, shooting, gardening. *Address:* Hill House, Haydon Bridge, Hexham, Northumberland. *T:* Haydon Bridge 234.

MILFORD, Rev. Canon Theodore Richard; Master of the Temple, 1958–68; *b* 10 June 1895; *e s* of Robert Theodore Milford, MA, and Elspeth Barter; *m* 1st, 1932, Nancy Dickens Bourchier Hawksley; two *d*; 2nd, 1937, Margaret Nowell Smith; two *d*. *Educ:* Denstone; Fonthill, East Grinstead; Clifton; Magdalen Coll., Oxford; Westcott House, Cambridge. Served European War, 1914–18, 19th Royal Fusiliers, 1914; Oxford & Bucks LI, 1915–19 (Mesopotamia, 1916–18); Magdalen Coll., Oxford, 1919–21; BA (1st Cl. Lit. Hum), 1921; Union Christian Coll., Alwaye, Travancore, 1921–23; St John's Coll., Agra, 1923–24, 1926–30, 1931–34; Sec. Student Christian Movement, 1924–26 and 1935–38; Westcott House, 1930–31; Deacon, 1931; Priest, 1934 (Lucknow); Curate All Hallows, Lombard Street, 1935–37; Vicar of St Mary the Virgin, Oxford (University Church), 1938–47; Canon and Chancellor of Lincoln, 1947–58; Canon of Norton Episcopi, Lincoln Cathedral, 1947–68, Canon Emeritus, 1968. Chm., Oxfam, 1942–47 and 1960–65, Emeritus 1965. Greek Red Cross (Bronze), 1947. *Publications:* Foolishness to the Greeks, 1953; The Valley of Decision, 1961; Belated Harvest (verse), 1978. *Recreations:* music, chess. *Address:* 1 Kingsman Lane, Shaftesbury, Dorset SP7 8HD. *T:* Shaftesbury 2843.

MILFORD HAVEN, 4th Marquess of, *cr* 1917; **George Ivar Louis Mountbatten;** Earl of Medina, 1917; Viscount Alderney, 1917; *b* 6 June 1961; *s* of 3rd Marquess of Milford Haven, OBE, DSC, and of Janet Mercedes, *d* of late Major Francis Bryce, OBE; *S* father, 1970. *Heir: b* Lord Ivar Alexander Michael Mountbatten, *b* 9 March 1963. *Address:* Moyns Park, Birdbrook, Essex.

MILINGO, Most Rev. Emanuel; Former Archbishop of Lusaka (Archbishop, 1969–83); Special Delegate to the Pontifical Commission for Tourism and Immigration, since 1983; *b* 13 June 1930; *s* of Yakobe Milingo Chilumbu and Tomaide Lumbiwe Miti. *Educ:* Kachebere Seminary, Malawi; Pastoral Inst., Rome; University Coll., Dublin. Curate: Minga Parish, Chipata Dio., 1958–60; St Mary's Parish, 1960–61; Chipata Cathedral, 1963–64; Parish Priest, Chipata Cathedral, 1964–65; Sec. for Communications at Catholic Secretariat, Lusaka, 1966–69. Founder, The Daughters of the Redeemer, Congregation for young ladies, 1971. *Publications:* Amake-Joni, 1972; To Die to Give Life, 1975; Summer Lectures for the Daughters of the Redeemer, 1976; The Way to Daughterhood; My God is a Living God, 1981; Lord Jesus, My Lord and Saviour, 1982; Demarcations, 1982; The Flower Garden of Jesus the Redeemer; My Prayers Are Not Heard; Precautions in the Ministry of Deliverance. *Recreation:* music. *Address:* Pontificia Commissione per la Pastorale delle Migrazioni e del Turismo, Palazzo San Calisto, Vatican City.

MILKINA, Nina, (Mrs A. R. M. Sedgwick); Hon. RAM; concert pianist; *b* Moscow, 27 Jan. 1919; *d* of Jacques and Sophie Milkine; *m* 1943, Alastair Robert Masson Sedgwick, Dir Nielsen Sedgwick International; one *s* one *d*. *Educ:* privately. Musical studies with the late Leon Conus of the Moscow Conservatoire and at the Paris Conservatoire, also with Profs Harold Craxton and Tobias Matthay, London. First public appearance at age of 11 with Lamoureux Orchestra, Paris; has since been broadcasting, televising, and touring in Great Britain and abroad. Was commissioned by BBC to broadcast series of all Mozart's piano sonatas; invited to give Mozart recital for bicentenary celebration of Mozart's birth, Edinburgh Festival; recorded for Westminster Co. of New York, and Pye Record Co., London. Widely noted for interpretation of Mozart's piano works. *Publications:* works for piano. *Recreations:* swimming, chess, fly fishing. *Address:* 20 Paradise Walk, SW3 4JL.

MILKOMANE, G. A. M.; see Sava, George.

MILL, Rear-Adm. Ernest, CB 1960; OBE 1944; Director General, Aircraft, Admiralty, 1959–62; *b* 12 April 1904; *s* of Charles and Rosina Jane Mill; *m* 1939, Isobel Mary Neilson (*d* 1971). *Educ:* Merchant Venturers Sch. Fleet Engr Officer on staff of C-in-C, Mediterranean, 1957; Rear-Adm., 1958. *Recreations:* sailing, fishing. *Club:* Army and Navy.

MILL, Laura Margaret Dorothea, OBE 1962; MB, ChB, DipPsych; Medical Commissioner, Mental Welfare Commission for Scotland, 1962–63, retired; *b* 28 Nov. 1897; *d* of Rev. William Alexander Mill, MA and Isabel Clunas. *Educ:* The Park Sch., Glasgow; Glasgow Univ. House Surg., Samaritan Hosp. for Women, and Royal Maternity Hospital, Glasgow, House Physician, Royal Hospital for Sick Children, and Senior Medical Officer Out-patient Dispensary, Glasgow; Resident Medical Officer, York General Dispensary; Asst Physician, Riccartsbar Mental Hosp., Paisley, and Murray Royal Mental Hosp., Perth; Clinical Medical Officer, Glasgow Public Health Dept. Dep. Medical Commissioner, Gen. Board of Control for Scotland, 1936; Medical Commissioner, Gen. Board of Control for Scotland (later Mental Welfare Commission), 1947, and Senior Medical Officer, Dept of Health for Scotland. *Address:* 12 Ettrick Road, Edinburgh EH10 5BJ. *T:* 031–229 7982.

MILLAIS, Sir Ralph (Regnault), 5th Bt *cr* 1885; *b* 4 March 1905; *s* of Sir Geoffroy William Millais, 4th Bt, and Madeleine Campbell (*d* 1963), *d* of C. H. Grace; *S* father, 1941; *m* 1st, 1939, Felicity Caroline Mary Ward Robinson (marr. diss.), *d* of late Brig.-Gen. W. W. Warner, CMG; one *s* one *d*; 2nd, 1947, Irene Jessie (marr. diss. 1971; she *d* 1985), *er d* of E. A. Stone, FSI; 3rd, 1975, Babette Sefton-Smith, *yr d* of Maj.-Gen. H. F.

Salt, CB, CMG, DSO. *Educ:* Marlborough; Trinity Coll., Cambridge. Business career. Joined RAFVR at outbreak of war, 1939, Wing Comdr. *Recreations:* fishing, travel and the restoration of famous Vintage and Historic cars. *Heir:* *s* Geoffroy Richard Everett Millais, *b* 27 Dec. 1941. *Address:* Gate Cottage, Winchelsea, East Sussex.

MILLAN, Rt. Hon. Bruce, PC 1975; MP (Lab) Glasgow, Govan, since 1983 (Glasgow, Craigton, 1959–83); *b* 5 Oct. 1927; *s* of David Millan; *m* 1953, Gwendoline May Fairey; one *s* one *d*. *Educ:* Harris Academy, Dundee. Chartered Accountant, 1950–59. Chm. Scottish Labour Youth Council, 1949–50. Contested: West Renfrewshire, 1951, Craigton Div. of Glasgow, 1955. Parly Under-Sec. of State: for Defence, (RAF), 1964–66; for Scotland, 1966–70, Minister of State, Scottish Office, 1974–76; Sec. of State for Scotland, 1976–79; opposition spokesman on Scotland, 1979–83. *Address:* 10 Beech Avenue, Glasgow G41 5BY. *T:* 041–427 6483.

MILLAR, family name of **Baron Inchyra.**

MILLAR, Betty Phyllis Joy; Regional Nursing Officer, South Western Regional Health Authority, 1973–84; *b* 19 March 1929; *o d* of late Sidney Hildersly Millar and May Phyllis Halliday. *Educ:* Ursuline High Sch. for Girls; Dumbarton Academy; Glasgow Royal Infirm.; Glasgow Royal Maternity Hosp.; Royal Coll. of Nursing, London. RGN 1950; SCM 1953; NA (Hosp.) Cert. 1961. Theatre Sister, Glasgow Royal Infirm., 1953–54; Ward and Theatre Sister, Henry Brock Meml Hosp., 1954–55; Nursing Sister, Iraq Petroleum Co., 1955–57; Clinical Instructor, Exper. Scheme of Nurse Trng, Glasgow, 1957–60; Admin. Student, Royal Coll. of Nursing, 1960–61; 2nd Asst Matron, Glasgow Royal Infirm., 1961–62; Asst Nursing Officer, Wessex Regional Hosp. Bd, 1962–67; Matron, Glasgow Royal Infirm., 1967–69; Chief Regional Nursing Officer, SW Regional Hosp. Bd, 1969–73. WHO Fellowship to study nursing services in Scandinavia, 1967. Mem. Jt Bd of Clinical Nursing Studies, 1970–82. *Address:* Pinedrift, 45 Stoneyfields, Easton-in-Gordano, Bristol BS20 0LL. *T:* Pill 2709.

MILLAR, Prof. Fergus Graham Burtholme, DPhil; FSA; FBA 1976; Camden Professor of Ancient History, and Fellow of Brasenose College, Oxford University, since 1984; *b* 5 July 1935; *s* of late J. S. L. Millar and of Jean Burtholme (*née* Taylor); *m* 1959, Susanna Friedmann; two *s* one *d*. *Educ:* Edinburgh Acad.; Loretto Sch.; Trinity Coll., Oxford (1st Cl. Lit. Hum.). Fellow: All Souls Coll., Oxford, 1958–64; Queen's Coll., Oxford, 1964–76; Prof. of Ancient History, UCL, 1976–84. Conington Prize, 1963. Vice-Pres., Soc. for the Promotion of Roman Studies, 1977–. FSA 1978. Corresp. Mem., German Archaeolog. Inst., 1978. Editor, Jl of Roman Studies, 1975–79. *Publications:* A Study of Cassius Dio, 1964; The Roman Empire and its Neighbours, 1967; (ed with G. Vermes) E. Schürer, history of the Jewish people in the age of Jesus Christ (175 BC-AD 135), Vol. I, 1973, Vol. II, 1979, Vol. III, parts 1 and 2 (ed with G. Vermes and M. D. Goodman), 1986; The Emperor in the Roman World (31 BC-AD 337), 1977, (ed with E. Segal) Caesar Augustus: seven aspects, 1984. *Address:* Brasenose College, Oxford OX1 4AJ; 80 Harpes Road, Oxford OX2 7QL. *T:* Oxford 55782.

MILLAR, George, DSO 1944; MC; farmer and writer; *b* 19 Sept. 1910; 2nd *s* of Thomas Andrew Millar, architect, and Mary Reid Morton; *m* 1945, Isabel Beatriz, *d* of Montague Paske-Smith, CMG, CBE; no *c*. *Educ:* Loretto; St John's, Cambridge. Architect, 1930–32; journalist, with Daily Telegraph and Daily Express, 1934–39; Paris correspondent Daily Express, 1939; served War of 1939–45, The Rifle Bde; escaped from German POW camp to England, then served as agent in France; Chevalier de la Légion d'Honneur; Croix de Guerre avec Palmes. Tenant farmer, 400 acres, 1962; increased to 1000 acres, 1966. *Publications:* Maquis, 1945; Horned Pigeon, 1946; My Past was an Evil River, 1946; Isabel and the Sea, 1948; Through the Unicorn Gates, 1950; A White Boat from England, 1951; Siesta, 1952; Orellana, 1954; Oyster River, 1963; Horseman, 1970; The Bruneval Raid, 1974; Road to Resistance, 1979. *Recreation:* sailing. *Address:* Sydling St Nicholas, Dorset. *T:* Cerne Abbas 205. *Clubs:* Royal Cruising; Royal Yacht Squadron (Cowes).

MILLAR, Ian Alastair D.; *see* Duncan Millar.

MILLAR, John Stanley, CBE 1979; County Planning Officer, Greater Manchester Council, 1973–83; *b* 1925; *s* of late Nicholas William Stanley Millar and late Elsie Baxter Millar (*née* Flinn); *m* 1961, Patricia Mary (*née* Land); one *d*. *Educ:* Liverpool Coll.; Univ. of Liverpool. BArch, DipCD, PPRTPI, RIBA. Planning Asst, then Sen. Asst Architect, City of Liverpool, 1948–51; Sectional Planning Officer, then Dep. Asst County Planning Officer, Lancs CC 1951–61; Chief Asst Planning Officer, then Asst City Planning Officer, City of Manchester, 1961–64; City Planning Officer, Manchester, 1964–73. *Publications:* papers in professional and technical jls. *Recreations:* walking, listening to music, travel, the sea. *Address:* 55 Stanneylands Drive, Wilmslow, Cheshire SK9 4EU. *T:* Wilmslow 523616.

MILLAR, Sir Oliver Nicholas, KCVO 1973 (CVO 1963; MVO 1953); FBA 1970; Surveyor of the Queen's Pictures, since 1972; *b* 26 April 1923; *er s* of late Gerald Millar, MC and late Ruth Millar; *m* 1954, Delia Mary, 2nd *d* of late Lt-Col Cuthbert Dawnay, MC; one *s* three *d*. *Educ:* Rugby; Courtauld Institute of Art, University of London (Academic Diploma in History of Art). Unable, for medical reasons, to serve in War of 1939–45. Asst Surveyor of the King's Pictures, 1947–49, Dep. Surveyor 1949–72. Trustee, Nat. Portrait Gallery, 1972–. Member: Reviewing Cttee on Export of Works of Art, 1975–; Exec. Cttee, Nat. Art Collections Fund, 1986–; Management Cttee, Courtauld Inst., 1986–. FSA. *Publications:* Gainsborough, 1949; William Dobson, Tate Gallery Exhibition, 1951; English Art, 1625–1714 (with Dr M. D. Whinney), 1957; Rubens's Whitehall Ceiling, 1958; Abraham van der Doort's Catalogue, 1960; Tudor, Stuart and Early Georgian Pictures in the Collection of HM the Queen, 1963; Zoffany and his Tribuna, 1967; Later Georgian Pictures in the Collection of HM the Queen, 1969; Inventories and Valuations of the King's Goods, 1972; The Age of Charles I (Tate Gallery Exhibn), 1972; The Queen's Pictures, 1977; Sir Peter Lely (Nat. Portrait Gall. Exhibn), 1978; Van Dyck in England (Nat. Portrait Gall. Exhibn), 1982; articles in the Burlington Magazine, etc; numerous catalogues, principally for The Queen's Gallery. *Recreations:* drawing, gardening, cricket, golf. *Address:* Yonder Lodge, Penn, Bucks. *T:* Penn 2124. *Club:* Brooks's.

MILLAR, Peter Carmichael, OBE 1978; Deputy Keeper of HM Signet, since 1983; Partner in law firm, Aitken, Kinnear & Co., WS, since 1963; *b* 19 Feb. 1927; *s* of late Rev. Peter Carmichael Millar, OBE, DD and of Ailsa Ross Brown Campbell or Millar; *m* 1953, Kirsteen Lindsay Carnegie, *d* of late Col David Carnegie, CB, OBE, TD, DL, Dep. Gen. Manager, Clydesdale Bank; two *s* two *d*. *Educ:* Aberdeen Grammar Sch.; Glasgow Univ.; St Andrews Univ.; Edinburgh Univ. MA, LLB; WS. Served RN, 1944–47. Partner in law firm, Messrs W. & T. P. Manuel, WS, 1954–62. Clerk to Soc. of Writers to HM Signet, 1964–83. Chairman: Church of Scotland Gen. Trustees, 1973–85; Mental Welfare Commn for Scotland, 1983–. *Recreations:* golf, hill-walking, music. *Address:* 25 Cramond Road North, Edinburgh EH4 6LY. *T:* 031–336 2069. *Clubs:* New (Edinburgh); Hon. Co. of Edinburgh Golfers, Bruntsfield Links Golfing Society.

MILLAR, Sir Ronald (Graeme), Kt 1980; playwright and screenwriter; Deputy Chairman, Theatre Royal Haymarket, since 1977; *b* 12 Nov. 1919; *s* of late Ronald Hugh Millar and Dorothy Ethel Dacre Millar (*née* Hill). *Educ:* Charterhouse; King's Coll., Cambridge. Served as Sub-Lt, RNVR, 1940–43 (invalided out). Began in the Theatre as an actor. First stage appearance, London, Swinging the Gate, Ambassadors', 1940, subseq. in Mr Bolfry, The Sacred Flame, Murder on the Nile, Jenny Jones, (own play) Zero Hour, 1944. Ealing Studios, 1946–48, worked on Frieda, Train of Events, etc; screenwriter, Hollywood, 1948–54: So Evil My Love, The Miniver Story, Scaramouche, Rose-Marie, The Unknown Man, Never Let Me Go, Betrayed. Plays produced in London: Frieda, 1946; Champagne for Delilah, 1948, Waiting for Gillian, 1954; The Bride and the Bachelor, 1956; The More the Merrier, 1960; The Bride Comes Back, 1960; The Affair (from C. P. Snow novel), 1961, The New Men (from C. P. Snow), 1962; The Masters (from C. P. Snow), 1963; (book and lyrics) Robert and Elizabeth (musical), 1964; Number 10, 1967; Abelard and Heloise, 1970; The Case in Question (from C. P. Snow), 1975; A Coat of Varnish (from C. P. Snow), 1982. *Recreations:* all kinds of music, all kinds of people. *Address:* 7 Sheffield Terrace, W8. *T:* 01–727 8361. *Clubs:* Brooks's, Dramatists'.

MILLAR, Prof. William Malcolm, CBE 1971; MD; Crombie-Ross Professor of Mental Health, University of Aberdeen, 1949–77; *b* 20 April 1913; *s* of Rev. Gavin Millar, BD, Logiealmond, Perthshire, and Margaret Malcolm, Stanley, Perthshire; *m* 1st, 1941, Catherine McAuslin Rankin; two *s* four *d*; 2nd, 1981, Maria Helen Ramsay. *Educ:* George Heriot's Sch., Edinburgh; Edinburgh Univ. MB, ChB (Edinburgh) 1936; MD (Edinburgh) 1939; Dip. Psych. (Edinburgh) 1939; MRCPE 1958; FRCPE 1962. Asst Physician, Royal Edinburgh Hospital for Mental Disorders, 1937–39. Served 1939–46 (Lieut, Captain, Major), Specialist in Psychiatry, RAMC. Senior Lecturer, Dept of Mental Health, Aberdeen Univ., 1946–49. Dean, Faculty of Medicine, 1965–68. Member: MRC, 1960–64; Mental Welfare Commn for Scotland, 1964–78. FBPsS 1946. *Publications:* contributions to various learned journals. *Recreations:* golf, chess, gardening. *Address:* 35 Beechgrove Avenue, Aberdeen AB2 4HE.

MILLAR-CRAIG, Hamish, CMG 1960; OBE 1958; Public Finance Consultant; *b* 25 Sept. 1918; *yr s* of late Captain David Millar-Craig and late Winifred Margaret Cargill; *m* 1953, Rose Ernestine Boohene. *Educ:* Shrewsbury; Keble Coll., Oxford. Served War of 1939–45, 2nd Lt Royal Scots, 1940; Colonial Civil Service, Gold Coast, 1940–57; Ghana Civil Service, 1957–62; Reader in Public Administration (UN Technical Assistance), Ghana Institute of Public Administration, 1962–65; Dir, E African Staff Coll., 1965–69; Adviser, Min. of Finance, Somalia, 1969–71; Bursar, UNITAR, 1972–77; Adviser: St Kitts-Nevis, 1978; Micronesia, 1980; Ghana, 1980–82; Antigua and Barbuda, 1982–84; Belize, 1986. Economic Development Institute, Washington, 1957–58. *Recreation:* philately. *Address:* c/o Lloyds Bank, Taunton, Somerset TA1 1HN.

MILLARD, Sir Guy (Elwin), KCMG 1972 (CMG 1957); CVO 1961; HM Diplomatic Service, retired; *b* 22 Jan. 1917; *s* of Col Baldwin Salter Millard, and Phyllis Mary Tetley; *m* 1st, 1946, Anne, *d* of late Gordon Mackenzie; one *s* one *d*; 2nd, 1964, Mary Judy, *d* of late James Dugdale and of Pamela, Countess of Aylesford; two *s*. *Educ:* Charterhouse; Pembroke Coll., Cambridge. Entered Foreign Office, 1939. Served Royal Navy, 1940–41. Asst Private Sec., to Foreign Sec., 1941–45; British Embassy, Paris, 1945–49, Ankara, 1949–52; Imperial Defence Coll., 1953; Foreign Office, 1954, Counsellor, 1955; Private Sec. to Prime Minister, 1955–56; British Embassy, Tehran, 1959–62; Foreign Office, 1962–64; Minister, UK Delegation to NATO, 1964–67; Ambassador to Hungary, 1967–69; Minister, Washington, 1970–71; Ambassador to Sweden, 1971–74; Ambassador to Italy, 1974–76. Chm., British-Italian Soc., 1977–83. Grand Officer, Order of Merit, Italy, 1981. *Address:* Fyfield Manor, Southrop, Glos. *T:* Southrop 234. *Club:* Boodle's.

MILLARD, Raymond Spencer, CMG 1967; PhD; FICE; FInstHT; consulting engineer; Director of Technical Affairs, British Aggregate Construction Materials Industries, since 1983; *b* 5 June 1920; *s* of Arthur and Ellen Millard, Ashbourne, Derbs; *m* 1st, 1945, Irene Guy (marr. diss.); one *s* one *d*; 2nd, 1977, Sheila Taylor (*née* Akerman). *Educ:* Queen Elizabeth Grammar Sch., Ashbourne; University Coll., London (BSc (Eng)). RE and civil engineering contracting, 1941–44. Road Research Laboratory, 1944–74: Hd of Tropical Section, 1955–65; Dep. Dir, 1965–74; Partner, Peter Fraenkel & Partners, Asia, 1974–76; Highway Engrg Advisor, World Bank, 1976–82. *Publications:* scientific and technical papers on road planning and construction. *Recreations:* bonsai culture, painting, travel. *Address:* Drapers Cottage, 93 High Street, Odiham, Basingstoke, Hants RG25 1LB.

MILLEN, Brig. Anthony Tristram Patrick; Defence Advisor to British High Commissioner, Ottawa, Canada, 1980–83; *b* 15 Dec. 1928; *s* of Charles Reginald Millen and Annie Mary Martin; *m* 1954, Mary Alice Featherston Johnston; two *s* two *d* (and one *s* decd). *Educ:* Mount St Mary's Coll. AMBIM. 5th Royal Inniskilling Dragoon Guards, 1948; served in Germany, Korea, Cyprus, N Ireland, Hong Kong, USA. *Publications:* articles in US military jls. *Recreation:* sailing. *Club:* Rideau (Ottawa).

MILLER, (Alan) Cameron; MA; LLB; FCIT; advocate; Master at Fettes College, since 1974; Temporary Sheriff, 1979–82; *b* 10 Jan. 1913; *o s* of late Arthur Miller, Edinburgh; *m* 1945, Audrey Main; one *s* one *d*. *Educ:* Fettes Coll.; Edinburgh Univ. MA 1934; LLB 1936; Advocate, 1938; served War of 1939–45, RN; Interim Sheriff-Substitute at Dundee, 1946; Sheriff-Substitute of Inverness, Moray, Nairn, Ross and Cromarty, at Fort William, 1946–52; Legal Adviser (Scotland): British Transport Commn, 1952–62; BR Board, 1962–73. Chm., Inst. of Transport (Scotland), 1971–72. *Recreations:* golf and music. *Address:* 42 Great King Street, Edinburgh, Scotland. *Clubs:* Arts (Edinburgh); HCEG.

MILLER, Alan John McCulloch, DSC 1941, VRD 1950; Chairman, Miller Insulation Ltd, since 1975; *b* 21 April 1914; *s* of late Louis M. Miller and Mary McCulloch; *m* 1940, Kirsteen Ross Orr; three *s* one *d*. *Educ:* Kelvinside Academy; Strathclyde Univ. CEng, MRINA, MIESS, FBIM, FRSA. Family engrg business, 1933–39. Commnd RNVR (Clyde Div.), 1938; served RN, 1939–45: Far East, Indian Ocean, S Atlantic, HMS Dorsetshire, then destroyers; in comd, HMS Fitzroy, Wolverine, Holderness, St Nazaire, Dieppe raids, Russian convoys, 1943–44; psc 1944. Rejoined family business, 1945, until sold to Bestobell Ltd, 1951; Dir, Bestobell Ltd, 1951–73, Chm. and Man. Dir, 1965–73; Chm. and Man. Dir, Wm Simons & Co. Ltd, Shipbuilders, 1956–60; Chairman: Dev West Ltd, 1973–76; Low & Bonar, 1977–82; Miller Insulation Ltd, 1975–86. Chm., BNEC Southern Africa Cttee, 1970, until abolished. Member: Sports Council, 1973–80; Central Council of Physical Recreation. *Recreations:* sailing, golf, ski-ing, shooting. *Address:* Windlefield, Windlesham, Surrey GU20 6AA. *T:* Bagshot 72980. *Clubs:* Army and Navy, Royal Thames Yacht, Royal Ocean Racing, Royal Cruising; Royal and Ancient (St Andrews); Sunningdale Golf; Royal Northern Yacht.

MILLER, Alastair Cheape, MBE 1948; TD; Prison Governor, retired 1972; *b* 13 March 1912 (twin-brother); *s* of John Charles Miller, Banker, Glasgow, and Jessie Amelia Miller; *m* 1943, Elizabeth S. Hubbard (marr. diss. 1967); one *s* one *d*. *Educ:* Melville Coll., Edinburgh; Bedford Sch., Bedford. Territorial Army, 1930–46; War Service (Gibraltar and Italy); 5th Bedfs and Herts Regt, 1st Herts Regt and 4th KOYLI, 1948–51. Barclays Bank Ltd; Junior Clerk to Cashier, 1929–45. Housemaster, Approved Sch., April-Nov. 1946. Prison Service: Asst Governor, Wakefield, Dec. 1946–Jan. 1953; Governor: Dover, 1953–59; Winchester, 1959–62; Hindley Borstal, 1962–65; Parkhurst Prison, 1966–70;

Pentonville, 1970–72. Associated with St Mungo Community Trust i/c Old Charing Cross Hosp. project for homeless people, 1974–75. Freeman, City of London, 1980. *Publication:* Inside Outside, 1976. *Recreations:* golf, sailing. *Address:* 3 White Hart Street, SE11 4EP. *Clubs:* Civil Service; Hampstead Golf; Seaford Golf (Seaford); Newport Golf (Pembs); Cowes Corinthian Yacht (Cowes); Royal Solent Yacht (Yarmouth); Newport Boat (Pembroke).

MILLER, Alexander Ronald, CBE 1970; Chairman, Motherwell Bridge Holdings Ltd, since 1958 (Managing Director, 1958–85); *b* 7 Nov. 1915; *s* of Thomas Ronald Miller and Elise Hay. *Educ:* Craigflower; Malvern Coll.; Royal Coll. of Science and Technology. Royal Engineers and Royal Bombay Sappers and Miners, 1940–46. Member: Scottish Council, CBI (formerly FBI), 1955–82 (Chm., 1963–65); Council, CBI, 1982–; Design Council (formerly CoID), 1965–71 (Chm. Scottish Cttee, 1965–67); Scottish Economic Planning Council, 1965–71 (Chm., Industrial Cttee, 1967–71); British Railways (Scottish) Board, 1966–70; British Rail Design Panel, 1966–82; Gen. Convocation, Univ. of Strathclyde, 1967–; Steering Cttee, W Central Scotland Plan, 1970–75; Lanarkshire Area Health Bd, 1973–85 (Chm., 1973–77); Oil Develt Council for Scotland, 1973–78; Instn of Royal Engineers; BIM Adv. Bd for Scotland, 1974–; Coll. Council, Bell Coll. of Technology, Hamilton, 1976–; Lloyd's Register of Shipping Scottish Cttee, 1977–, Gen. Cttee, 1982–; Lloyd's Register Quality Assce Ltd, 1984–; Incorporation of Hammermen, Merchants' House of Glasgow. Chm., Management Cttee, Scottish Health Servs Common Servs Agency, 1977–83. Pres., Lanarkshire (formerly Hamilton and Other Districts) Br., Forces Help Soc. and Lord Roberts Workshops, 1979–. A Burgess of the City of Glasgow. DUniv Stirling, 1986. FRSA; AIMechE; CBIM. *Address:* Lairfad, Auldhouse, by East Kilbride, Lanarks. *T:* East Kilbride 63275. *Clubs:* Directors; Royal Scottish Automobile (Glasgow), Western (Glasgow).

MILLER, Arjay; Dean, and Professor of Management, Graduate School of Business, Stanford University, 1969–79, now Dean Emeritus; Vice-Chairman, Ford Motor Company, 1968–69 (President, 1963–68); *b* 4 March 1916; *s* of Rawley John Miller and Mary Gertrude Schade; *m* 1940, Frances Marion Fearing; one *s* one *d. Educ:* University of California at Los Angeles (BS with highest hons, 1937). Graduate Student and Teaching Asst, University of California at Berkeley, 1938–40; Research Technician, Calif. State Planning Bd, 1941; Economist, Federal Reserve Bank of San Francisco, 1941–43. Captain, US Air Force, 1943–46. Asst Treas, Ford Motor Co., 1947–53; Controller, 1953–57; Vice-Pres. and Controller, 1957–61; Vice-Pres. of Finance, 1961–62; Vice-Pres., Staff Group, 1962–63. Member, Board of Directors: Litton Industries, Inc.; Utah Internat. Inc.; The Washington Post Co.; Santa Fe Southern Pacific Co.; Trustee: Eisenhower Exchange Fellowships; Brookings Instn, Washington; Internat. Exec. Service Corps; Andrew W. Mellon Foundn; Urban Inst. Mem., Nat. Bd of the Smithsonian Associates. Member, Board of Directors: SRI International; William and Flora Hewlett Foundn; UN Assoc. of USA; Councillor, The Conference Board. Hon. LLD: Univ. of California (LA), 1964; Whitman Coll., 1965; Univ. of Nebraska, 1965; Ripon Coll., 1980; Washington Univ., St Louis, 1982. *Address:* 225 Mountain Home Road, Woodside, Calif 94062, USA. *Clubs:* Bohemian, Pacific Union (San Francisco).

MILLER, Arthur; playwright; *b* 17 Oct. 1915; *s* of Isadore Miller and Augusta Barnett; *m* 1940, Mary Grace Slattery (marr. diss.); one *s* one *d*; *m* 1956, Marilyn Monroe (marr. diss. 1961; she *d* 1962); *m* 1962, Ingeborg Morath; one *d. Educ:* University of Michigan, USA (AB). Pres. of PEN Club, 1965–69. *Publications:* Honors at Dawn, 1936; No Villains (They Too Arise), 1937; The Pussycat and the Expert Plumber who was a Man, 1941; William Ireland's Confession, 1941; The Man who had all the Luck, 1944; That They May Win, 1944; Situation Normal (reportage), 1944; Focus (novel), 1945; Grandpa and the Statue, 1945; The Story of Gus, 1947; All My Sons (play) (New York Drama Critics Award, 1948), 1947; Death of A Salesman (play) (New York Drama Critics Award, 1949, Pulitzer Prize, 1949), 1949, filmed, 1985; The Crucible (play), 1953; A View from the Bridge (play), 1955, filmed, 1962; A Memory of Two Mondays (play), 1955; Collected Plays, 1958; The Misfits (motion picture play), 1960; Jane's Blanket, 1963; After the Fall (play), 1963; Incident at Vichy (play), 1964; I Don't Need You Anymore (collected stories), 1967; The Price (play), 1968; (jt author) In Russia, 1969; Fame, and the Reason Why, 1970; The Portable Arthur Miller, 1971; The Creation of the World and Other Business (play), 1972, musical version, Up From Paradise, 1974; (with Inge Morath) In the Country, 1977; (ed Robert Martin) The Theater Essays of Arthur Miller, 1978; (with Inge Morath) Chinese Encounters, 1979; The American Clock (play), 1980; Playing for Time (play) (Peabody Award, CBS-TV, 1981); Salesman in Beijing, 1984; Two Way Mirror, 1985; contrib. stories and essays to Esquire, Colliers, Atlantic Monthly, etc. *Address:* c/o Kay Brown, ICM, 40 W 57th Street, New York, NY 10019, USA.

MILLER, Barry; Director General of Defence Quality Assurance, Ministry of Defence, Procurement Executive, since 1986; *b* 11 May 1942; *s* of Lt-Col Howard Alan Miller and Margaret Yvonne Richardson; *m* 1968, Katrina Elizabeth Chandler; one *s* one *d. Educ:* Lancaster Royal Grammar Sch. Exec. Officer, RAE Farnborough, 1961; Asst Principal, MoD, London, 1965; Principal: Defence Policy Staff, 1967; Naval Personnel Div., 1969; Equipment Secretariat (Army), 1972; Defence Secretariat, 1973; CSD, 1975; Asst Secretary: Civilian Management, 1977; Defence Secretariat, 1980; RCDS 1984; Asst Sec., Management Services (Organisation), 1985. *Address:* Ministry of Defence, Royal Arsenal West, Woolwich, SE18 6ST.

MILLER, Sir Bernard; *see* Miller, Sir O. B.

MILLER, Bruce; *see* Miller, John D. B.

MILLER, Cameron; *see* Miller, A. C.

MILLER, Maj.-Gen. David Edwin, CB 1986; CBE 1980 (OBE 1973); MC 1967; Chief of Staff Live Oak, SHAPE, 1984–86, retired; *b* 17 Aug. 1931; *s* of late Leonard and Beatrice Miller; *m* 1958, Mary Lamley Fisher; two *s. Educ:* Loughton Sch., Essex; Royal Military Academy, Sandhurst. psc, jssc, ndc. Commissioned, Border Regt, 1951; Comd 1st Bn King's Own Royal Border Regt, 1971–73; Instructor, National Defence Coll., 1973–76; Colonel GS MoD, 1976–78; Comd Ulster Defence Regt, 1978–80; Dep. Chief of Staff Headquarters BAOR, 1980–83. Colonel, King's Own Royal Border Regt, 1981–. *Recreations:* wine, clocks, sailing. *Address:* c/o Barclays Bank PLC, 210 Fore Street, N18 2QF. *Club:* Army and Navy.

MILLER, David Quentin; Metropolitan Stipendiary Magistrate, since 1982; a Recorder, since 1986; *b* 22 Oct. 1936; *s* of Alfred Bowen Badger and Mair Angharad Evans. *Educ:* Ellesmere Coll., Shropshire; London Sch. of Econs and Pol. Science, London Univ. (LLB Hons 1956). Called to the Bar, Middle Temple, 1958; admitted Barrister and Solicitor of the Supreme Court of NZ, 1959. In practice, SE Circuit, 1960–82. *Recreations:* history, walking, gardening, art, music. *Address:* 31 Edinburgh Gardens, Windsor, Berks SL4 2AN. *T:* Windsor 866597.

MILLER, Donald C.; *see* Crichton-Miller.

MILLER, Donald John; FEng; Chairman, South of Scotland Electricity Board, since 1982; *b* 1927; *s* of John Miller and Maud (*née* White); *m* 1973, Fay Glendinning Herriot; one *s* two *d. Educ:* Banchory Academy; Univ. of Aberdeen. BSc(Eng); FEng 1981; FIMechE, FIEE. Metropolitan Vickers, 1947–53; British Electricity Authority, 1953–55; Preece, Cardew and Rider (Consulting Engrs), 1955–66; Chief Engr, North of Scotland Hydro-Electric Bd, 1966–74; Dir of Engrg, then Dep. Chm., SSEB, 1974–82. *Publications:* papers to IEE. *Recreations:* gardening, hill walking, sailing. *Address:* Puldohran, Gryffe Road, Kilmacolm. *T:* Kilmacolm 3652.

MILLER, Sir Douglas; *see* Miller, Sir I. D.

MILLER, Sir Douglas (Sinclair), KCVO 1972; CBE 1956 (OBE 1948); HM Overseas Colonial Service, retired; *b* 30 July 1906; British parentage; m 1933, Valerie Madeleine Carter; one *d. Educ:* Westminster Sch.; Merton Coll., Oxford. HM Overseas Colonial Service, 1930–61: Supt of Native Educn, N Rhodesia, 1930–45; Director of Education: Basutoland, 1945–48; Nyasaland, 1948–52; Uganda, 1952–58; Kenya, 1958–59; Dir of Educn and Permanent Sec., Min. of Educn, Kenya, 1959–60; Temp. Minister of Educn, Kenya, 1960–61; Sec., King George's Jubilee Trust, 1961–71; Develt Adviser, Duke of Edinburgh's Award Scheme, 1971–85. *Address:* The Lodge, 70 Grand Avenue, Worthing, Sussex. *T:* Worthing 501195. *Clubs:* Royal Commonwealth Society; Kampala (Uganda).

MILLER, Edward, FBA 1981; Master, Fitzwilliam College, Cambridge, 1971–81, Hon. Fellow, 1981; *b* Acklington, Northumberland, 16 July 1915; *e s* of Edward and Mary Lee Miller; *m* 1941, Fanny Zara Salingar; one *s. Educ:* King Edward VI's Grammar Sch., Morpeth; St John's Coll., Cambridge (Exhibnr, Schol.). BA 1937; MA 1945; Strathcona Res. Student, 1937–39, Fellow, 1939–65, and Hon. Fellow, 1974, St John's Coll., Cambridge. Nat. Service, 1940–45 in Durham Light Inf., RAC and Control Commn for Germany; Major. Dir of Studies in History, 1946–55 and Tutor, 1951–57, St John's Coll., Cambridge; Asst Lectr in History, 1946–50 and Lectr, 1950–65, University of Cambridge; Warden of Madingley Hall, Cambridge, 1961–65; Prof. of Medieval Hist., Sheffield Univ., 1965–71. FRHistS; Chm., Victoria Co. Histories Cttee of Inst. Hist. Research, 1972–79; Dep. Chm., Cttee to review Local Hist., 1978–79; Mem., St Albans Res. Cttee. Chm., Editorial Bd, History of Parliament Trust. Hon. LittD Sheffield, 1972. *Publications:* The Abbey and Bishopric of Ely, 1951; Portrait of a College, 1961; (Jt Ed.) Cambridge Economic History of Europe, vol. iii, 1963; Historical Studies of the English Parliament, 2 vols, 1970; (jtly) Medieval England: rural society and economic change, 1978; articles in Victoria County Histories of Cambridgeshire and York, Agrarian History of England and Wales, vol. ii, English Hist. Rev., Econ. History Rev., Trans Royal Historical Society, Past and Present, etc. *Recreations:* with advancing years watching any form of sport, especially Rugby and cricket. *Address:* 36 Almoners Avenue, Cambridge CB1 4PA. *T:* Cambridge 246794.

MILLER, Edward; Director of Education, Strathclyde, since 1974; *b* 30 March 1930; *s* of Andrew and Elizabeth Miller; *m* 1955; two *s. Educ:* Eastbank Academy; Glasgow Univ. (MA, MEd). Taught at Wishaw High Sch., 1955–57 and Whitehill Secondary Sch., 1957–59; Depute Dir of Educn, West Lothian, 1959–63; Sen. Asst Dir of Educn, Stirlingshire, 1963–66; Depute, later Sen. Depute Dir of Educn, Glasgow, 1966–74. Hon. MLitt Glasgow Coll. of Technology, 1985. *Recreations:* golf, reading, sailing. *Address:* 58 Heather Avenue, Bearsden, Glasgow G61 3JG.

MILLER, Air Chief Marshal Frank Robert, CC (Canada) 1972; CBE 1946; CD; retired from military service, 1966; Director, United Aircraft of Canada Ltd, 1967–76; *b* Kamloops, BC, April 1908; *m* Dorothy Virginia Minor, Galveston, Texas. *Educ:* Alberta Univ. (BSc, Civil Engrg). Joined RCAF, 1931. Served War of 1939–45: commanded Air Navigation Schs at Rivers, Man., and Penfield Ridge, NB, and Gen. Reconnaissance Sch., Summerside, PEI; subseq. Dir of Trng Plans and Requirements and Dir of Trng, Air Force HQ; service overseas with Can. Bomber Gp as Station Comdr, later Base Comdr, 1944; Tiger Force, 1945 (despatches); Chief SO (later AOC), Air Material Comd, 1945; US Nat. War Coll., 1948; Air Mem. Ops and Trng, Air Force HQ, 1949; Vice Chief of Air Staff, 1951; Vice Air Deputy, SHAPE HQ, Paris, 1954; Dep. Minister, Dept of Nat. Defence, 1955; Chm., Chiefs of Staff, 1960; first Pres., NATO Mil. Cttee, 1963–64; Chief of Defence Staff, Canada, 1964–66. Air Chief Marshal, 1961. Hon. LLD Alta, 1965; Hon. DScMil, RMC Canada, 1968. *Recreations:* golf, fishing. *Address:* 1654 Brandywine Drive, Charlottesville, Va 22901, USA.

MILLER of Glenlee, Sir (Frederick William) Macdonald, 7th Bt *cr* 1788; *b* 21 March 1920; *e s* of Sir Alastair George Lionel Joseph Miller of Glenlee, 6th Bt; *S* father, 1964; *m* 1947, Marion Jane Audrey Pettit; one *s* one *d. Educ:* Tonbridge. Conservative Agent for: Whitehaven, 1947–50; Wembley North, 1950–52; North Norfolk, 1952–65; Lowestoft, 1965–82; political consultant, 1982–85. County Councillor, Suffolk, 1977– (Chm. Education Cttee, 1985–; Vice-Chm. of Council, 1986–). Chm., Eastern Sea Fisheries Jt Cttee, 1981–83. Mem., Suffolk FPC. *Recreation:* gardening. *Heir: s* Stephen William Macdonald Miller of Glenlee, FRCS [*b* 20 June 1953; *m* 1978, Mary Owens; one *s* one *d. Educ:* Rugby; St Bartholomew's Hosp.]. *Address:* Ivy Grange Farm, Westhall, Halesworth, Suffolk IP19 8RN. *T:* Ilketshall 265.

MILLER, G(eorge) William; Chairman, G. William Miller & Co., Inc., Merchant Banking, since 1983; *b* Oklahoma, USA, 9 March 1925; *s* of James Dick Miller and Hazle Deane Miller (*née* Orrick); *m* 1946, Ariadna Rogojarsky. *Educ:* Borger High Sch.; Amarillo Junior Coll.; US Coast Guard Acad. (BS); School of Law, Univ. of California, Berkeley (JD). Served as US Coast Guard Officer, Pacific Area, 1945–49, stationed (one year) in China. Admitted to Bar of California, 1952, New York Bar 1953; law practice with Cravath, Swaine & Moore, NYC, 1952–56. Joined Textron Inc., Providence, RI, 1956; Vice-Pres. 1957; Treas. 1958; Pres. 1960; Chief Exec. 1968–78, also Chm., 1974–78; Sec. of the Treasury, USA, 1979–81; private investments and business ventures, 1981–83. Director: Federated Department Stores; Anderson, Clayton & Co.; Repligen Corp.; Private Satellite Network; Georgetown Industries Inc.; Systems Management American Corp. Chm. Bd of Governors of Federal Reserve System of US, 1978–79. Chm., The Conference Board, 1977–78; Chm., National Alliance of Business, 1978; Chm., US Industrial Payroll Savings Cttee, 1977. Mem., State Bar, California. Chm., Supervisory Cttee, The Schroder Venture Trust, 1983–. Phi Delta Phi. *Recreations:* music, golf. *Address:* 1215 19th Street NW, Washington, DC 20036, USA. *Clubs:* Chevy Chase (Maryland); The Brook (NY); Burning Tree (Bethesda, Md); Lyford Cay (Bahamas).

MILLER, Hilary Duppa, (Hal Miller); MP (C) Bromsgrove, since 1983 (Bromsgrove and Redditch, Feb. 1974–1983); Vice-Chairman of the Conservative Party Organisation, and Parliamentary Private Secretary to the Chairman, since 1984; *b* 6 March 1929; *s* of Lt-Comdr John Bryan Peter Duppa-Miller, *qv*; *m* 1st, 1956, Fiona Margaret McDermid; two *s* two *d*; 2nd, 1976, Jacqueline Roe, *d* of T. C. W. Roe and of Lady Londesborough; one *s* one *d. Educ:* Eton; Merton Coll., Oxford; London Univ. MA (Oxon) 1956; BSc (Estate Management) (London), 1962. With Colonial Service, Hong Kong, 1955–68. Company Director. Contested: (C), 1962, Barrow-in-Furness, 1970; Bromsgrove by-elec. May 1971. PPS to Sec. of State for Defence, 1979–81, to Chancellor of the Duchy of Lancaster, 1981, resigned; Mem., UK delegn to Council of Europe, 1974–76. Jt Chm., All Party

Motor Industry Gp, 1978. Fellow, Econ. Develt Inst. of World Bank, Washington. *Recreations:* sailing, fell walking, cricket, Rugby refereeing. *Address:* House of Commons, SW1A 0AA. *Clubs:* St Stephen's; Vincent's (Oxford); Aston Fields Royal British Legion (Bromsgrove); Eton Ramblers, Free Foresters, Blackheath Football.
See also Michael Miller.

MILLER, Sir Holmes; *see* Miller, Sir J. H.

MILLER, Mrs Horrie; *see* Durack, Dame M.

MILLER, Mrs Hugh; *see* Katzin, Olga.

MILLER, Sir (Ian) Douglas, Kt 1961; FRCS; Hon. Consulting Neurosurgeon, since 1960 (Hon. Neurosurgeon, 1948), St Vincent's Hospital, Sydney, and Repatriation General Hospital; Chairman of Board, St Vincent's Hospital, 1966–76; Dean of Clinical School, St Vincent's Hospital, Sydney, 1931–64; *b* Melbourne, 20 July 1900; *m* 1939, Phyllis Laidley Mort; three *s* two *d*. *Educ:* Xavier Coll., Melbourne; University of Sydney. MB, ChM Sydney 1924; FRCS 1928. Hon. Asst Surgeon, St Vincent's Hosp., Sydney, 1929; Lectr in Surgical Anat., Univ. Sydney, 1930; Hon. Surg., Mater. Hosp. Sydney, 1934; Hon. Surg., St Vincent's Hosp., 1939; Major AIF, Surgical Specialist, 1940; Lt-Col (Surgical CO), 102 AGH, 1942; o/c Neurosurgical Centre, AIF. Chairman: Community Systems Foundn of Aust., 1965–72; Foundn of Forensic Scis, Aust. President: RACS, 1957–59 (Mem. Ct of Examrs, 1946; Mem. Council, 1947); Asian Australasian Soc. of Neurological Surgeons, 1964–67. Chairman: Editorial Cttee, ANZ Jl of Surgery, 1958–73; Editorial Bd, Modern Medicine in Australia, 1970–. Hon. FRCSE 1980. Hon. AM 1964, Hon. LittD 1974, Singapore; Hon. MD Sydney, 1979. *Publications:* A Surgeon's Story, 1985; Earlier Days, 1970; contrib. Med. Jl of Aust., 1956, 1960. *Recreation:* agriculture. *Address:* 149 Macquarie Street, Sydney, NSW 2000, Australia. *T:* BU 5077, JJ 2431. *Club:* Australian (Sydney).

MILLER, Dr Jacques Francis Albert Pierre, AO 1981; FRS 1970; FAA 1970; Head of Experimental Pathology Unit, Walter and Eliza Hall Institute of Medical Research, since 1966; *b* 2 April 1931; French parents; *m* 1956, Margaret Denise Houen. *Educ:* St Aloysius' Coll., Sydney. BSc (Med.) 1953, MB, BS 1955, Sydney; PhD 1960, DSc 1965, London. Sen. Scientist, Chester Beatty Res. Inst., London, 1960–66; Reader, Exper. Pathology, Univ. of London, 1965–66. For. Mem., Académie Royale de Médicine de Belgique, 1969; For. Associate, US Nat. Acad. Scis, 1982. Langer-Teplitz Cancer Research Award (USA), 1965; Gairdner Foundn Award (Canada), 1966; Encyclopaedia Britannica (Australia) Award, 1966; Scientific Medal of Zoological Soc. of London, 1966; Burnet Medal, Austr. Acad. of Scis, 1971; Paul Ehrlich Award, Germany, 1974; Rabbi Shai Shacknai Meml Prize, Hadassah Med. Sch., Jerusalem, 1978; Saint-Vincent Internat. Prize for Med. Res., Italy, 1983. *Publications:* over 285 papers in scientific jls and several chapters in books, mainly dealing with thymus and immunity. *Recreations:* music, photography, art, literature. *Address:* Walter and Eliza Hall Institute of Medical Research, Royal Melbourne Hospital PO, Parkville, Victoria 3050, Australia. *T:* 345–2555.

MILLER, James, RSA 1964; RSW 1934; Artist, Painter; *b* 25 Oct. 1893; *s* of William Miller and Margaret Palmer; *m* 1934, Mary MacNeill, MA (*d* 1973); no *c*. *Educ:* Woodside Sch.; Sch. of Art, Glasgow. Teaching, 1917–47. Commissioned by Artists' Adv. Coun. of Min. of Information to make drawings of buildings damaged by enemy action in Scotland, 1939–41; travelled extensively in Spain looking at buildings and making drawings; made drawings for Pilgrim Trust, 1942. Paintings have been bought by Bradford, Newport, Glasgow, Dundee, Hertford, Paisley, Nat. Gall. of S Australia, Melbourne, Aberdeen, Dumbarton, Perth, Arts Council of GB (Scotland) and Muirhead Bequest, Edinburgh. Has held several one-man shows in Glasgow; retrospective exhibn, Glasgow Art Club, 1986. *Recreations:* listening to gramophone records, reading. *Address:* Tigh-na-bruaich, Dunvegan, Isle of Skye. *Club:* Art (Glasgow).

MILLER, James, CBE 1986; Chairman and Managing Director, Miller Group Ltd (formerly James Miller & Partners), since 1970; *b* 1 Sept. 1934; *s* of Sir James Miller, GBE, and of Lady Ella Jane Miller; *m* 1st, 1959, Kathleen Dewar; one *s* two *d*; 2nd, 1969, Iris Lloyd-Webb; one *d*. *Educ:* Edinburgh Acad.; Harrow Sch.; Balliol Coll., Oxford (MA Engrg Sci.). Joined James Miller & Partners, 1958; Board Mem., 1960. *Recreation:* shooting. *Address:* Miller Group Ltd, Miller House, 18 South Groathill Avenue, Edinburgh EH4 2LW. *T:* 031–332 2585. *Club:* City Livery.

MILLER, Lt-Comdr John Bryan Peter Duppa-, GC and King's Commendation 1941; *b* 22 May 1903; *er s* of Brian Stothert Miller, JP, Posbury, Devon, and Mary (*née* Sadler); *m* 1st, 1926, Barbara, *d* of Stanley Owen, 1st Viscount Buckmaster, GCVO; three *s*; 2nd, 1944, Clare, *d* of Francis Egerton Harding, JP, Old Springs, Market Drayton; 3rd, 1977, Greta, *d* of B. K. G. Landby, Royal Vasa Order, Gothenburg, Sweden. *Educ:* Rugby Sch.; Hertford Coll., Oxford. Dep. County Educn Officer, Hants, 1930–35; Asst Sec., Northants Educn Cttee, 1936–39; Torpedo and Mining Dept, Admty, 1940–45; a Dep. Dir-Gen., Trade and Econs Div., Control Commn for Germany, 1945; Inspector-Gen., Min. of Educn, Addis Ababa, 1945–47; Educn Dept, Kenya, 1947–57; Chm. of European Civil Servants' Assoc., and formation Chm. Staff Side, Central Whitley Coun. for Civil Service; Sec. to Kenya Coffee Marketing Bd, 1960–61; Sec. to Tanganyika Coffee Bd, 1961–62; Asst Sec. and Marketing Officer, Min. of Lands and Settlement, Kenya, 1963–65. *Publication:* Saints and Parachutes, 1951. *Recreations:* yachting, economics. *Address:* Box 222, Somerset West, 7130, South Africa. *Club:* Reform.
See also H. D. Miller, Michael Miller.

MILLER, Prof. J(ohn) D(onald) Bruce; Professor of International Relations, Research School of Pacific Studies, Australian National University, since 1962; *b* 30 Aug. 1922; *s* of Donald and Marion Miller, Sydney, Australia; *m* Margaret Martin (*née* MacLachlan); one *s*. *Educ:* Sydney High Sch.; University of Sydney. BEc, 1944; MEc 1951; MA Cantab 1978. Announcer and Talks Officer, Australian Broadcasting Commission, Sydney and Canberra, 1939–46; Staff Tutor, Department of Tutorial Classes, University of Sydney, 1946–52; Asst Lecturer in Political Science and International Relations, London Sch. of Economics, 1953–55; Lecturer in Politics, University Coll., Leicester, 1955–57; Prof. of Politics, University of Leicester, 1957–62; Dean of Social Sciences, 1960–62; Public Orator, 1961–62. Visiting Professor: Indian Sch. of International Studies, 1959; Columbia Univ., New York, 1962, 1966, 1981; Yale, 1977; Princeton, 1984, 1986; Overseas Vis. Fellow, St John's Coll., and Smuts Vis. Fellow, Cambridge Univ., 1977–78; Macrossan Lectr, University of Queensland, 1966. Member: Aust. Population and Immigration Council, 1975–81; Aust. Res. Grants Cttee, 1975–81. Joint Editor, Journal of Commonwealth Political Studies, 1961–62; Editor, Australian Outlook, 1963–69; Chm., Editorial Adv. Bd for Austr. documents on foreign relations, 1971–77; Austr. Nat. Commn for UNESCO, 1982–84. FASSA 1967 (Treas., 1979–83). *Publications:* Australian Government and Politics, 1954, 4th edn with B. Jinks 1970; Richard Jebb and the Problem of Empire, 1956; Politicians (inaugural), 1958; The Commonwealth in the World, 1958; The Nature of Politics, 1962; The Shape of Diplomacy (inaugural), 1963; Australia and Foreign Policy (Boyer Lectures), 1963; The Disintegrating Monolith (ed with T. H. Rigby), 1965; Britain and the Old Dominions, 1966; Australia, 1966; The Politics of the Third World, 1966; (ed) India, Japan, Australia: Partners in Asia?, 1968; Survey of Commonwealth Affairs: problems of expansion and attrition 1953–1969, 1974; (ed) Australia's Economic Relations, 1975; The EEC and Australia, 1976; The World of States, 1981; Ideology and Foreign Policy, 1982; Norman Angell and the Futility of War, 1986; (ed) Australians and British, 1986. *Recreations:* books, garden, dachshund. *Address:* 16 Hutt Street, Yarralumla, ACT 2600, Australia. *T:* Canberra 813138. *Clubs:* National Press, Commonwealth (Canberra).

MILLER, Sir John Francis C.; *see* Compton Miller.

MILLER, John Harmsworth; architect in private practice; *b* 18 Aug. 1930; *s* of Charles Miller and Brenda Borrett; *m* 1st, 1957, Patricia Rhodes (marr. diss. 1975); two *d*; 2nd, 1985, Su Rogers. *Educ:* Charterhouse; Architectural Assoc. Sch. of Architecture (AA Dip. Hons 1957). ARIBA 1959. Private practice, Colquhoun and Miller, 1961–; works include: Forest Gate High Sch., West Ham (Newham), 1965; Chemistry Labs, Royal Holloway Coll., London Univ., 1970; Melrose Activity Centre, Milton Keynes Develt Corp. (Commendation, Steel Awards, 1975); Pillwood House, Feock, Cornwall (RIBA Regional Award, 1975); Housing, Caversham Road/Gaisford Street, Camden, 1978; single person flats, Hornsey Lane, Haringey, 1980; Oldbrook, Milton Keynes (Silver Medal, Architectural Design; Highly Commended, Housing Design and Civic Trust Awards); Whitechapel Art Gall. extension, 1985. Exhibition Designs for Arts Council: Dada and Surrealism Reviewed, 1978; Ten Modern Houses, 1980; Picasso's Picassos, 1981; Adolf Loos, 1985. Assessor: Grand Buildings Competition, Trafalgar Square. Tutor: RCA and AA, 1961–73; Cambridge Sch. of Arch., 1969–70; Prof. of Environmental Design, RCA, 1975–85, Fellow 1976, Hon. Fellow, 1985. FRSA 1985. Vis. Prof., Sch. of Arch., UC Dublin, 1985. Vis. Critic: Cornell Univ. Sch. of Arch., Ithaca, 1966, 1968 and 1971; Princeton Univ. Sch. of Arch., NJ, 1970; Dublin Univ. Sch. of Arch., 1972–73; Univ. of Toronto, 1985. *Publications:* contribs to architect. jls. *Address:* 23 Regent's Park Road, NW1. *T:* 01–267 5800.

MILLER, Sir John Holmes, 11th Bt *cr* 1705, of Chichester, Sussex; *b* 1925; *er s* of 10th Bt and of Netta Mahalah Bennett; *S* father 1960; *m* 1950, Jocelyn Robson Edwards, Wairoa, NZ; two *d*. *Heir:* *b* Harry Holmes Miller [*b* 1927; *m* 1954, Gwynedd Margaret Sheriff; one *s* two *d*].

MILLER, John Ireland; Vice-President, Methodist Conference of Great Britain, 1973–74; *b* 20 June 1912; *s* of John William Miller and Emma Miller (*née* Minkley); *m* 1943, Vida Bertha Bracher; one *s* one *d*. *Educ:* Hardye's School, Dorchester; Taunton School, Taunton. Admitted Solicitor and Member of Law Society, 1933. HM Coroner: Poole Borough, 1972–74 (Deputy Coroner, 1939–72); East Dorset, 1974–85. Dir, Farney Close School Ltd. *Address:* 25 Merriefield Drive, Broadstone, Dorset BH18 8BW. *T:* Broadstone 694057. *Club:* National Liberal.

MILLER, Air Vice-Marshal John Joseph, CB 1981; Director, Institute of Personnel Management, since 1983; *b* 27 April 1928; *s* of Frederick George Miller and Freda Ruth Miller; *m* 1950, Adele Mary Colleypriest; one *s* two *d*. *Educ:* Portsmouth Grammar School. Commissioned RAF, 1947; called to the Bar, Gray's Inn, 1958; CO RAF Support Unit Fontainbleau, 1965; Directing Staff, RAF Staff Coll., 1967; DGPS (RAF) Staff, MoD, 1970; Group Captain Admin., RAF Halton, 1971; Comd Accountant, HQ Strike Comd, 1973; RCDS 1975; Dir, Personnel Management (Policy and Plans) RAF, MoD, 1976; Asst Chief of Defence Staff (Personnel and Logistics), 1978–81; Head of Administrative Branch, RAF, 1979–83; Dir Gen., Personal Services, RAF, 1982–83. *Recreations:* walking, swimming, theatre, music, collecting (especially antiquarian books). *Address:* IPM House, 34 Camp Road, Wimbledon, SW19 4UW. *T:* 01–946 9100. *Club:* Royal Air Force.

MILLER, Lt-Col Sir John (Mansel), KCVO 1974 (CVO 1966); DSO 1944; MC 1944; Crown Equerry, since 1961; *b* 4 Feb. 1919; 3rd *s* of Brig.-Gen. Alfred Douglas Miller, CBE, DSO, DL, JP, Royal Scots Greys, and of Ella Geraldine Fletcher, Saltoun, E Lothian. *Educ:* Eton; RMA, Sandhurst. 2nd Lieut Welsh Guards, 1939; Adjt 1942–44; ADC to F-M Lord Wilson, Washington, DC, 1945–47; Regtl Adjt, 1953–56; Brigade Major 1st Guards Brigade, 1956–58; comd 1st Bn Welsh Guards, 1958–61. President: Coaching Club, 1975–82; Nat. Light Horse Breeding Soc. (HIS), 1982; British Driving Soc., 1982–; Royal Windsor Horse Show Club, 1985–; Horse Rangers Assoc., 1985–; Patron, Side Saddle Assoc., 1984–. *Recreations:* hunting, shooting, polo, driving. *Address:* Shotover House, Wheatley, Oxon. *T:* Wheatley 2450; The Crown Equerry's House, Buckingham Palace, SW1. *T:* 01–930 4832. *Clubs:* Pratt's, White's.

MILLER, Dr Jonathan Wolfe, CBE 1983; Director; Research Fellow in Neuropsychology, University of Sussex; *b* 21 July 1934; *s* of late Emanuel Miller, DPM, FRCP; *m* 1956, Helen Rachel Collet; two *s* one *d*. *Educ:* St Paul's Sch.; St John's Coll., Cambridge (MB, BCh 1959; Hon. Fellow 1982). Res. Fellow in Hist. of Med., UCL, 1970–73. Associate Director, Nat. Theatre, 1973–75. Mem., Arts Council, 1975–76. Vis. Prof. in Drama, Westfield Coll., London, 1977–; Fellow, UCL, 1981–. Co-author and appeared in Beyond the Fringe, 1961–64; stage directing in London and NY, 1965–67; *television:* Editor, BBC Monitor, 1965; directed films for BBC TV (incl. Alice in Wonderland), 1966; The Body in Question, BBC series, 1978; Exec. Producer, BBC Shakespeare series, 1979–81; *stage:* School for Scandal, 1968, The Seagull, 1969, The Malcontent, 1973, Nottingham Playhouse; King Lear, The Merchant of Venice, Old Vic, 1970; The Tempest, Mermaid, 1970; Hamlet, Arts Theatre, Cambridge, 1970; Danton's Death, 1971, School for Scandal, 1972, Measure for Measure, 1974, Marriage of Figaro, 1974, The Freeway, 1974, Nat. Theatre; The Taming of the Shrew, 1972, The Seagull, 1973, Chichester; Family Romances, 1974, The Importance of Being Earnest, 1975, All's Well, 1975, Greenwich; Three Sisters, Cambridge, 1976; She Would If She Could, Greenwich, 1979; Long Day's Journey Into Night, Haymarket, 1986; *film:* Take a Girl Like You, 1970; *operas:* Arden must die, Sadler's Wells Theatre, 1974; The Cunning Little Vixen, Glyndebourne, 1975 and 1977; English National Opera: The Marriage of Figaro, 1978; The Turn of the Screw, 1979; Arabella, 1980; Otello, 1981; Rigoletto, 1982, 1985; Don Giovanni, 1985; The Magic Flute, 1986; Tosca, 1986; The Mikado, 1986; Kent Opera: Cosi Fan Tutte, 1975; Rigoletto, 1975; Orfeo, 1976; Eugene Onegin, 1977; La Traviata, 1979; Falstaff, 1980, 1981; Fidelio, 1982, 1983. Hon. DLitt Leicester, 1981. Silver Medal, Royal TV Soc., 1981. *Publications:* McLuhan, 1971; (ed) Freud: the man, his world, his influence, 1972; The Body in Question, 1978; Subsequent Performances, 1986. *Recreation:* deep sleep. *Address:* 63 Gloucester Crescent, NW1. *T:* 01–485 6973.

MILLER, Maj.-Gen. Joseph Esmond, MC 1943; retired; *b* 22 Sept. 1914; *s* of Col J. F. X. Miller, OBE; *m* 1946, Kathleen Veronica Lochée-Bayne; one *s*. *Educ:* St George's Coll., Weybridge; London Univ. (St Bartholomew's Hosp.). MRCS, LRCP; MRCGP; MFCM; MBIM. Qualified, July 1940. Fellow RoySocMed; Mem., BMA. Served War of 1939–45: commissioned in RAMC, Dec. 1940 (ante-dated Sept. 1940); RAMC Depot, 1940–42; Airborne Forces, 1942–45: N Africa, Sicily, Italy, Holland, Germany. RAMC Depot, 1945–47; Staff Coll., 1948; DADMS, HQ MELF, Egypt, 1949–50; CO, 35 Field Amb., Tripoli and Egypt, 1950–54; SMO, RMA Sandhurst, 1954–57; CO, 4 Field Amb., Germany, 1957–59; CO, 10 Bde Gp Med. Co., Aden, 1959–61; ADMS, Middle East

Command, Aden, 1961; Chief Instr, RAMC Depot, 1961–65; CO, BMH Hong Kong, 1965–68; ADMS, 4 Div., Germany, 1968–69; DDMS: HQ BAOR, 1969–71; HQ Scotland (Army), 1971–72; HQ UKLF, 1972–73; DMS, HQ UKLF, 1973–76. QHS 1973–76. CStJ 1975. *Recreations:* golf, gardening. *Address:* The Beechings, Folly Close, Salisbury, Wilts SP2 8BU. *T:* Salisbury 21423.

MILLER, Sir (Joseph) Holmes, Kt 1979; OBE 1958; Surveyor, New Zealand; Partner, Spencer, Holmes Miller and Jackson, Wellington, NZ; *b* Waimate, NZ, 12 Feb. 1919; *s* of Samuel Miller; *m* 1947, Marjorie, *d* of Harold Tomlinson; one *s* one *d. Educ:* Willowbridge Sch.; Waimate High Sch.; Victoria Univ., Wellington, NZ (BA). DSc 1979. Served War, 2 NZEF, 1940–44; NZ Artillery (wounded, Tunisia, 1943). Surveyor, Lands and Survey Dept, on rehabilitation farms, geodetic survey; consulting surveyor, Masterton, 1952–55; Wellington, 1959–. Fulton Medallion Exploratory Surveys, Fiordland, 1949; Expedition, Antipodes and Bounty Is, 1950; Dep. Leader, NZ Trans-Antarctic Expedn, 1955–58; Leader, NZ Expedn, Oates Land, Antarctica, 1963–64. Member: NZ Antarctic Soc. (Pres. 1960–63); NZ Inst. Surveyors, 1960–68 (Pres. 1969–71); NZ Survey Bd, 1962–71; NZ Geographic Bd, 1966–; Nature Conservation Council, 1972–. NZ Delegate to SCAR, Paris, 1964, Wyoming, 1974. *Publications:* numerous, on Antarctic and surveying literature. *Address:* 95 Amritsar Street, Khandallah, Wellington, New Zealand.

MILLER, Prof. Karl Fergus Connor; Lord Northcliffe Professor of Modern English Literature, University College London, since 1974; Editor, London Review of Books, since 1979; *b* 2 Aug. 1931; *s* of William and Marion Miller; *m* 1956, Jane Elisabeth Collet; two *s* one *d. Educ:* Royal High School, Edinburgh; Downing Coll., Cambridge. Asst Prin., HM Treasury, 1956–57; BBC TV Producer, 1957–58; Literary Editor, Spectator, 1958–61; Literary Editor, New Statesman, 1961–67; Editor, Listener, 1967–73. *Publications:* (ed) Poetry from Cambridge, 1952–54, 1955; (ed, with introd.) Writing in England Today: The Last Fifteen Years, 1968; (ed) Memoirs of a Modern Scotland, 1970; (ed) A Listener Anthology, August 1967–June 1970, 1970; (ed) A Second Listener Anthology, 1973; (ed) Henry Cockburn, Memorials of his Time, 1974; Cockburn's Millennium, 1975; (ed, with introd.) Robert Burns, 1981; Doubles: studies in literary history, 1985. *Recreation:* football. *Address:* 26 Limerston Street, SW10.

MILLER, Dr Kenneth Allan Glen, FEng; FIMechE; CBIM; Director-General, The Engineering Council, since 1982; *b* 27 July 1926; *s* of Dr Allan Frederick Miller and Margaret Hutchison (*née* Glen); *m* 1954, Dorothy Elaine Brown; three *s. Educ:* Upper Canada Coll., Toronto; Trinity Hall, Cambridge (BA 1946; MA 1950); PhD Wales, 1949. Res. Asst to Prof. of Physics, Aberystwyth, 1946; joined ICI, Billingham, 1949; various posts on production and design, 1949–59; seconded to BTC, 1959–60; Asst Tech. Manager, 1960, Engrg Manager, 1963, Engrg Dir, 1965, HOC Div., ICI; Engrg Advr, ICI, 1971; Managing Director: APV Co., 1974; APV Holdings, 1977–82. Member: Cttee for Industrial Technol., 1972–76; UGC, 1981–83; Chm., Steering Cttee for Manufrg Adv. Service, 1977–82. Mem. Council, Fellowship of Engrg, 1982–85. *Recreations:* gardening, photography. *Address:* 4 Montrose Gardens, Oxshott, Surrey KT22 0UU. *T:* Oxshott 2093. *Clubs:* Caledonian; Leander.

MILLER of Glenlee, Sir Macdonald; *see* Miller of Glenlee, Sir F. W. M.

MILLER, Prof. Marcus Hay, PhD; Professor of Economics, since 1978, Director, Parliamentary Policy Unit, since 1985, University of Warwick; *b* 9 Sept. 1941; *s* of J. Irvine Miller and Rose H. (*née* Moir); *m* 1967, Margaret Ellen Hummel (marr. diss.); two *d. Educ:* Price's Sch., Fareham, Hants; University Coll., Oxford (BA 1st Cl. PPE); Yale Univ. (Henry Fellowship, MA, PhD Econ). Lecturer, London School of Economics, 1967–76; Prof. of Economics, Univ. of Manchester, 1976–78. Economist, 1972–73, Houblon-Norman Fellow, 1981–82, Bank of England; Vis. Associate Prof. of Internat. Finance, Univ. of Chicago, 1976; Vis. Prof. of Public and Internat. Affairs, Princeton Univ., 1983. Member, Academic Panel, HM Treasury, 1976– (Chm., 1979–80); Adviser, House of Commons Select Cttee on the Treasury and Civil Service, 1980–81. Mem. Management Cttee, NIESR, 1980–. Mem., Economic Policy Gp, SDP, 1981–. *Publications:* joint editor: Monetary Policy and Economic Activity in West Germany, 1977; Essays on Fiscal and Monetary Policy, 1981; papers on macro and monetary economics, incl. effects of UK entry into EEC, reform of UK monetary system, inflation, exchange rates and liquidity preference, in Amer. Economic Rev., Economica, Nat. Inst. Economic Rev., Oxford Economic Papers, Rev. of Economic Studies. *Recreations:* swimming, orienteering. *Address:* Department of Economics, University of Warwick, Coventry CV4 7AL. *T:* Coventry 24011, ext. 2484.

MILLER, Mrs Mary Elizabeth H.; *see* Hedley-Miller.

MILLER, Maurice Solomon, MB; MP (Lab) East Kilbride, since 1974 (Glasgow Kelvingrove, 1964–74); *b* 16 Aug. 1920; *s* of David Miller; *m* 1944, Renée, *d* of Joseph Modlin, Glasgow; two *s* two *d. Educ:* Shawlands Academy, Glasgow; Glasgow University. MB, ChB 1944. Mem. of Glasgow Corporation since 1950; Bailie of Glasgow, 1954–57; JP Glasgow, 1957. Asst Govt Whip, 1968–69. Visited Russia as mem. of medical delegation, 1955. *Publication:* Window on Russia, 1956. *Address:* House of Commons, SW1; 82 Springkell Avenue, Glasgow G41 4EH.

MILLER, Michael, RD 1966; QC 1974; Barrister since 1958; *b* 28 June 1933; 2nd *s* of John Bryan Peter Duppa-Miller, *qv*; *m* 1958, Mary Elizabeth, *e d* of Donald Spiers Monteagle Barlow, *qv*; two *s* two *d. Educ:* Dragon Sch., Oxford; Westminster Sch. (King's Scholar); Christ Church, Oxford (Westminster Scholar). BA Lit. Hum. 1955; MA 1958. Ord. Seaman, RNVR, 1950; Sub-Lt 1956; qual. submarines, 1956; Navigating Officer, HMS Solent, 1956; Armaments Officer: HMS Sturdy, 1956–57; HMS Tally Ho, 1957; Lt-Comdr RNR. Called to Bar, Lincoln's Inn, 1958, Bencher 1984; practice at Chancery Bar from 1958; Mem. Bar Council, 1972–74; Mem. Senate of Inns of Court and Bar, 1974–76. *Recreations:* sailing, music, chess, football. *Address:* 8 Stone Buildings, Lincoln's Inn, WC2.

See also H. D. Miller.

MILLER, Sir (Oswald) Bernard, Kt 1967; *b* 25 March 1904; *s* of late Arthur Miller and of Margaret Jane Miller; *m* 1931, Jessica Rose Marie ffoulkes (*d* 1985); three *s. Educ:* Sloane Sch.; Jesus Coll., Oxford (Hon. Fellow, 1968); Stanhope Prize, 1925; BA 1927; MA 1930. Joined John Lewis Partnership, 1927; Dir, 1935; Chm., 1955–72. Chm., Retail Distributors Assoc., 1953; Member: Council of Industrial Design, 1957–66; Monopolies Commission, 1961–69; EDC for Distributive Trades, 1964–71. Chm. Southern Region, RSA, 1974–80; Mem. Council, RSA, 1977–82. Treasurer, Southampton Univ., 1974–82, Chm. Council, 1982–, Pro-Chancellor, 1983–. Hon. LLD Southampton, 1981. *Publication:* Biography of Robert Harley, Earl of Oxford, 1927. *Recreations:* fishing, gardening, opera and theatre. *Address:* The Field House, Longstock, Stockbridge, Hants. *T:* Andover 810627.

MILLER, Rev. Canon Paul William; Canon Residentiary of Derby Cathedral, 1966–83, Canon Emeritus since 1983; Chaplain to the Queen, since 1981; *b* 8 Oct. 1918; *s* of F. W. Miller, Barnet. *Educ:* Haileybury; Birmingham Univ. (Dip. Theology). Served in ranks with Sherwood Foresters, 1939–45; POW of Japanese, 1942–45; despatches 1946. Deacon, 1949; Curate: of Staveley, Derbyshire, 1949–52; of Matlock, Derbyshire, 1952–55; Vicar of Codnor, Derbyshire, 1955–61; Novice, Community of the Resurrection, Mirfield, 1961–63; Priest-in-charge, Buxton, 1963–64; Chaplain, Derby Cathedral, 1964–66. *Recreations:* painting, travel. *Address:* 15 Forester Street, Derby DE1 1PP. *T:* Derby 44773.

MILLER, Peter Francis Nigel, RIBA, FSIAD; Senior Partner, Purcell Miller Tritton and Partners, Architects, Surveyors and Design Consultants, Norwich, London, Sevenoaks, Winchester and Colchester, since 1973; *b* 8 May 1924; *s* of Francis Gerald Miller and Dorothy Emily (*née* Leftwich); *m* 1950, Sheila Gillian Branthwayt, ARCA FSIAD, (*née* Stratton); one *s* two *d. Educ:* King's Sch., Canterbury; Sch. of Architecture, Coll. of Art, Canterbury. ARIBA 1952; FRIBA 1968; MSIA 1956; FSIA 1968. Served army, 1942–47, NW Europe, Austria, Italy and India; commnd Duke of Cornwall's LI, 1943. Private practice: Peter Miller and Sheila Stratton, 1954; Miller and Tritton, 1956; Purcell Miller and Tritton, 1965. Surveyor to the Fabric of Ely Cathedral, 1974–; Architect, Cathedral of St John the Baptist, Norwich, 1976–. Vice-Pres., SIAD, 1976. *Recreations:* deer stalking, shooting, wildfowling, fishing. *Address:* Thornage Hall, Holt, Norfolk NR25 7QH. *T:* Melton Constable 860305; 64 Bethel Street, Norwich NR2 1NR. *T:* Norwich 20438. *Club:* Norfolk (Norwich).

MILLER, Peter North; Chairman, Lloyd's, since 1984; *b* 28 Sept. 1930; *s* of Cyril Thomas Gibson Risch Miller, CBE and Dorothy Alice North Miller, JP; *m* 1st, 1955, Katharine Mary; two *s* one *d*; 2nd, 1979, Boon Lian (Leni). *Educ:* Rugby; Lincoln Coll., Oxford (MA Hons). National Service, Intelligence Corps, 1949–50. Joined Lloyd's, 1953; qualified as barrister, 1954; Partner, Thos. R. Miller & Son (Insurance), 1959, Sen. Partner, 1971–; Chm., Thos R. Miller & Son (Insurance) Group, 1971–83; Partner, Thos R. Miller & Son (Underwriting Agents), 1969–83; Dir, Thos R. Miller & Son (Underwriting Agents) Ltd, 1983–. Dep. Chm., Lloyd's Insurance Brokers' Asoc., 1974–75, Chm. 1976–77; Mem., Cttee of LLoyd's, 1977–80 and 1982–; in charge of team responsible for passage of LLoyd's Bill (Fisher), 1980–82. Member: Baltic Exchange, 1966–; Insurance Brokers' Registration Council, 1977–81; Vice-Pres., British Insce Brokers' Assoc., 1978; Chm., British Cttee of Bureau Veritas, 1980–. *Recreations:* all sport (except cricket), including tennis, running, sailing; wine, music, old churches, gardening. *Address:* Sarratt, Coombe End, Kingston-upon-Thames, Surrey KT2 7DQ. *T:* 01–942 6724. *Clubs:* Brooks's, City of London; Vincent's (Oxford); Thames Hare and Hounds.

MILLER, Sir Richard Hope, Kt 1955; Chairman, North West Region, Arthritis and Rheumatism Council, since 1974; President: Tatton Division Conservative Association, since 1983 (Chairman, Knutsford Division, 1975–83); David Lewis Epileptic Centre, since 1977; *b* 26 July 1904; 2nd *s* of late Hubert James Miller, The Old Court House, Knutsford, Cheshire, and of Elsa Mary Colimann; unmarried. *Educ:* Wellington Coll.; Trinity Hall, Cambridge. BA 1925; MA 1930. Served War of 1939–46: commissioned in 7th Bn (TA) The Manchester Regt; Adjutant 1941; Major 1945; served in Staff appointments (Britain, Ceylon, and Singapore), 1942–46. Hon. Sec., Greater Manchester and Area Br., Inst. of Dirs, 1966–81. Pres., Cheshire County Lawn Tennis Assoc., 1981–82. *Recreations:* skiing, tennis. *Address:* 9 Carrwood, Knutsford, Cheshire WA16 8NG. *T:* Knutsford 3422; National Westminster Bank, Knutsford, Cheshire.

MILLER, Robert Alexander Gavin D.; *see* Douglas Miller.

MILLER, Robin Anthony; a Recorder of the Crown Court, since 1978; *b* 15 Sept. 1937; *s* of William Alexander Miller, CBE, BEM, and Winifred Miller; *m* 1962, Irene Joanna Kennedy; two *s* one *d. Educ:* Devonport High Sch., Plymouth; Wadham Coll., Oxford (MA). Called to the Bar, Middle Temple, 1960. *Address:* St Michael's Lodge, 192 Devonport Road, Stoke, Plymouth, Devon PL1 5RD. *T:* Plymouth 564943.

MILLER, Prof. Ronald, MA, PhD, FRSE, FRSGS; Professor of Geography, Glasgow University, 1953–76; Dean of the Faculty of Science, 1964–67; *b* 21 Aug. 1910; *o c* of late John Robert Miller and Georgina Park; *m* 1940, Constance Mary Phillips, SRN, SCM; one *s* one *d. Educ:* North Queensferry; Stromness Acad.; Edinburgh Univ. Silver Medal, Royal Scottish Geographical Soc.; MA 1931; Carnegie Research Fellowship at Marine Laboratory of Scottish Home Dept, Aberdeen, 1931–33; PhD 1933; Asst Lecturer Manchester Univ., 1933–36; Education Officer, Nigeria, 1936–46; Royal West African Frontier Force, 1939–44; Lecturer, Edinburgh Univ., 1947–53. Guest Lecturer: University of Montpellier, 1957; University of Oslo and Handelshłyskole Bergen, 1966; Simon Fraser Univ., 1967; Ife, 1969. Pres., RSGS, 1974–77. *Publications:* (with MacNair) Livingstone's Travels; The Travels of Mungo Park; (with Tivy) ed. The Glasgow Region, 1958; (with Watson) Ogilvie Essays, 1959; Africa, 1967; Orkney, 1976; papers in geographical journals. *Address:* Ruah, 20 South End, Stromness, Orkney. *T:* Stromness 850594.

MILLER, Ronald Kinsman; Solicitor of Inland Revenue, since 1986; *b* 12 Nov. 1929; *s* of William Miller and Elsie May Kinsman; *m* 1952, Doris Alice Dew; one *s* one *d. Educ:* Colchester Royal Grammar Sch. Served RN, 1948–50. Called to the Bar, Gray's Inn, 1953. Joined Inland Revenue, 1950; Asst Solicitor, 1971; Law Officers' Dept, 1977–79; Principal Asst Solicitor, 1981–86. *Recreations:* gardening, reading, music. *Address:* 4 Liskeard Close, Chislehurst, Kent BR7 6RT. *T:* 01–467 8041. *Club:* Athenæum.

MILLER, Comdr Ronald S.; *see* Scott-Miller.

MILLER, Dr Roy Frank; Vice-Principal, Royal Holloway and Bedford New College, University of London, since 1985; *b* 20 Sept. 1935; *s* of Thomas R. Miller and Margaret Ann Tattum; *m* 1961, Ruth Naomi Kenchington; one *s. Educ:* Wembley County Grammar Sch.; University Coll. SW England, Exeter; Royal Holloway Coll. BSc, PhD; CPhys, FInstP. Teacher, Halbutt Secondary Modern Sch., 1957; Royal Holloway College: Demonstrator, 1957, Asst Lectr, 1960, Lectr, 1963, Sen. Lectr, 1973, Physics Dept; Vice-Principal, 1978–81; Acting Principal, 1981–82; Principal, 1982–85. Research Associate and Teaching Fellow, Case Western Reserve Univ., Ohio, USA, 1967–68. Mem. Senate, Univ. of London, 1981–85; Chm., Cttee of Management, Inst. of Classical Studies, Univ. of London, 1983–; Trustee and Governor, Strode's Foundn, Strode's Coll., Egham. MRI; FRSA. *Publications:* articles in Jl Phys C, Phil. Mag., Vacuum. *Recreations:* mountaineering, squash, music. *Address:* Royal Holloway and Bedford New College, University of London, Egham Hill, Egham, Surrey TW20 0EX. *T:* Egham 34455. *Club:* Athenæum.

MILLER, Rudolph Valdemar Thor C.; *see* Castle-Miller.

MILLER, Sir Stephen (James Hamilton), KCVO 1979; MD, FRCS; Consulting Ophthalmic Surgeon, retired 1986; Hospitaller, St John Ophthalmic Hospital, Jerusalem, since 1980; Surgeon-Oculist: to the Queen, 1974–80; to HM Household, 1965–74; Ophthalmic Surgeon: St George's Hospital, 1951–80; National Hospital, Queen Square, 1955–78; King Edward VII Hospital for Officers, 1965–80; Surgeon, Moorfields Eye Hospital, 1954–80; Recognised Teacher in Ophthalmology, St George's Medical School and Institute of Ophthalmology, University of London, retired; *b* 19 July 1915; *e s* of late Stephen Charles Miller and Isobel Hamilton; *m* 1949, Heather P. Motion; three *s. Educ:* Arbroath High Sch.; Aberdeen Univ. House Physician and Surgeon, Royal Infirmary,

Hull, 1937–39. Surgeon Lieut-Comdr RNVR, 1939–46 (Naval Ophthalmic Specialist, RN Aux. Hosp., Kilmacolm and RN Hosp., Malta). Resident Surgical Officer, Glasgow Eye Infirmary, 1946; Registrar and Chief Clinical Asst, Moorfields Eye Hosp., 1947–50; Registrar St George's Hosp., 1949–51; Research Associate, Institute of Ophthalmology, 1949–80. Ophthalmic Surgeon, Royal Scottish Corp.; Advr in Ophthalmol., BUPA; Civilian Consultant in Ophthalmol. to RN and MoD, 1971–80. Member: Med. Commn for Accident Prevention. FRSocMed (Hon. Mem., Sect. of Ophthalmol.); Fellow Faculty of Ophthalmology; Editor, British Journal of Ophthalmology, 1973–83; Mem. Editorial Bd, Ophthalmic Literature; Ophthalmological Soc. of UK; Oxford Ophthalmological Congress (Master, 1969–70); Examiner in Ophthalmology for Royal Colls and Brit. Orthoptic Bd; RCS and RCSE. Mem. Exec. Cttee, London Clinic, 1975–85; Governor, Moorfields Eye Hosp., 1961–67 and 1974–77. Trustee: Frost Foundn Charity; Guide Dogs for the Blind. Hon. Mem., Amer. Acad. of Ophthalmology. Freeman, City of London; Liveryman, Soc. of Apothecaries. Doyne Medal, 1972; Montgomery Medal, 1974. KStJ 1978. *Publications:* Modern Trends in Ophthalmology, 1973; Operative Surgery, 1976; Parsons Diseases of the Eye, 1984; articles in BMJ, Brit. Jl of Ophthalmology, Ophthalmic Literature. *Recreations:* golf, fishing. *Address:* Sherma Cottage, Pond Road, Woking GU22 0JT. *T:* Woking 62287. *Clubs:* Caledonian; Woking and Muirfield Golf.

MILLER, Terence George, TD 1960; MA Cantab; Director, Polytechnic of North London, 1971–80; *b* 16 Jan. 1918; *o s* of late George Frederick Miller, Cambridge, and late Marion Johnston, Port William, Wigtownshire; *m* 1944, Inga Catriona, 3rd *d* of Austin Priestman, MD, Folkestone, Kent; one *s* three *d*. *Educ:* Perse (foundn schol.); Jesus Coll., Cambridge (schol.). Wiltshire Prizeman, 1939. Served War of 1939–45: RA, Special Forces, Glider Pilot Regt; TA, 1947–67 (Lt.-Col. 1964). Harkness Scholar, 1948; Research Fellow, Jesus Coll., 1949–54. University Demonstrator, 1948; Lectr in Geology, Univ. of Keele, 1953; Sen. Lectr, 1963, Prof. of Geography, Univ. of Reading, 1965–67; Principal, University Coll. of Rhodesia, 1967–69; Vis. Prof., Reading Univ., 1969–71. *Publications:* Geology, 1950; Geology and Scenery in Britain, 1953; scientific papers in various jls. *Recreations:* military history, sailing, beachcombing, listening. *Address:* 29 Wodehouse Terrace, Falmouth, Cornwall. *T:* Falmouth 316657.

MILLER, Walter George, IPFA; FCCA; City Treasurer, Bristol, since 1980; *b* 2 March 1932; *s* of Bert and Rosina Miller; *m* 1956, Sheila Mary Daw; one *s* two *d*. *Educ:* Howardian High Sch., Cardiff. Clerk, City Treasurer's Dept, Cardiff, 1948–50. Served RA, Hong Kong and Korea, 1950–52. Audit Asst, City Treasurer's Dept, Cardiff, 1952–55; Accountant, Treasurer's Dept: Nairobi, 1955–58; Cardiff, 1958–60; Caerphilly, 1960–63; Ilford, 1963–65; Redbridge, 1965; Bromley, 1965–68; Asst Borough Treasurer, Bromley, 1968–72; Bristol: Asst City Treasurer, 1972–73; Dep. City Treasurer, 1973–80. Governor, St Joseph's Sch., Portishead. *Publications:* contrib. local government and accountancy press. *Recreations:* writing and lecturing on local government and allied topics; gardening. *Address:* 4 Nore Road, Portishead, Bristol BS20 9HN. *T:* Bristol 848559.

MILLER, William; *see* Miller, George William.

MILLER, Comdr William Ronald, OBE 1984; Royal Navy (retired); *b* 6 Dec. 1918; *y s* of Col Joseph Sidney Miller, DSO and Florence Eva Drabble; *m* 1942, Betty Claelia Otto, Richmond, Natal; one *d*. *Educ:* Cranleigh Sch., Surrey. Entered RN, 1936. Sec. to Flag Officer (Submarines), 1955–57; Exec. Asst to Dep. Supreme Allied Comdr Atlantic (as Actg Capt.), 1958–60; Sec. to C-in-C Home Fleet (as Actg Capt.), 1960–62; Sec. to C-in-C Portsmouth (as Actg Capt.), 1963–65; retd from RN at own request, 1966. Called to Bar, Lincoln's Inn, 1958. Clerk, Worshipful Co. of Haberdashers, 1966–83 (Liveryman, 1969, Assistant *hc*, 1980). *Recreations:* golf, swimming, gardening. *Address:* 1 Great George Street, Godalming, Surrey. *T:* Godalming 22965.

MILLER JONES, Hon. Mrs; *see* Askwith, Hon. B. E.

MILLER PARKER, Agnes; *see* Parker, A. M.

MILLES-LADE, family name of **Earl Sondes.**

MILLETT, Hon. Sir Peter (Julian), Kt 1986; **Hon. Mr Justice Millett;** a Judge of the High Court of Justice, Chancery Division, since 1986; *b* 23 June 1932; *s* of late Denis Millett and Adele Millett; *m* 1959, Ann Mireille, *d* of late David Harris; two *s* (and one *s* decd). *Educ:* Harrow; Trinity Hall, Cambridge (Schol.; MA). Nat. Service, RAF, 1955–57 (Flying Officer). Called to Bar, Middle Temple, 1955, *ad eundem* Lincoln's Inn, 1959 (Bencher, 1980), Singapore, 1976, Hong Kong, 1979; at Chancery Bar, 1958–86; QC 1973. Examnr and Lectr in Practical Conveyancing, Council of Legal Educn, 1962–76. Junior Counsel to Dept of Trade and Industry in Chancery matters, 1967–73. Mem., General Council of the Bar, 1971–75. Outside Mem., Law Commn on working party on co-ownership of matrimonial home, 1972–73; Mem., Dept of Trade Insolvency Law Review Cttee, 1977–82. *Publications:* contrib. to Halsbury's Laws of England, Encycl. of Forms and Precedents; articles in legal jls. *Recreations:* philately, bridge, The Times crossword. *Address:* Royal Courts of Justice, Strand, WC2; 18 Portman Close, W1H 9HJ. *T:* 01–935 1152; St Andrews, Kewhurst Avenue, Cooden, Sussex.

MILLGATE, Prof. Michael Henry, PhD; FRSC; FRSL; Professor of English, Toronto University, since 1967; *b* 19 July 1929; *s* of Stanley Millgate and Marjorie Louisa (*née* Norris); *m* 1960, Jane, *d* of Maurice and Marie Barr. *Educ:* St Catharine's Coll., Cambridge (MA); Michigan Univ.; Leeds Univ. (PhD). FRSC 1982. Tutor-Organizer, WEA, E Lindsey, 1953–56; Lectr in English Lit., Leeds Univ., 1958–64; Prof. of English and Chm. of the Dept, York Univ., Ont, 1964–67. Killam Sen. Res. Schol., 1974–75, Killam Res. Fellow, 1986–87; John Simon Guggenheim Meml Fellow, 1977–78. FRSL 1984. *Publications:* William Faulkner, 1961; (ed) Tennyson: Selected Poems, 1963; American Social Fiction, 1964; (ed jtly) Transatlantic Dialogue, 1966; The Achievement of William Faulkner, 1966; (ed jtly) Lion in the Garden, 1968; Thomas Hardy: his career as a novelist, 1971; (ed with R. L. Purdy) The Collected Letters of Thomas Hardy, vols I-VI, 1978–87; Thomas Hardy: a biography, 1982; (ed) The Life and Work of Thomas Hardy, 1985. *Address:* 75 Highland Avenue, Toronto, Ont M4W 2A4, Canada. *T:* (416) 920 3717.

MILLICHIP, Frederick Albert, (Bert); Chairman, The Football Association, since 1981 (Member of Council, since 1970); *b* 5 Aug. 1914; *s* of late Hugh Bowater Millichip; *m* 1950, Joan Barbara Brown; one *s* one *d*. *Educ:* Solihull Sch., Warwicks. Qualified as Solicitor, 1950; Sen. Partner, Sharpe & Millichip, 1959–. Served War, 1939–45, in England, N Africa, Sicily and Italy; joined S Staffs Regt as private, commnd RA (Captain). Member: UEFA Organising Cttee for European Championship, 1981–; FIFA Organising Cttee for World Cup, 1983–; Chm., FA Disciplinary Cttee, 1978–81. West Bromwich Albion Football Club: Dir, 1964–84; Chm., 1976–83; Pres., 1984–. *Recreation:* golf. *Address:* Fairlight, 52 Twatling Road, Barnt Green, Birmingham B45 8HU. *T:* 021–445 4688. *Club:* Blackwell Golf (Blackwell, Worcs).

MILLIGAN, James George; QC (Scot.) 1972; *b* 10 May 1934; *s* of Rt Hon. Lord Milligan; *m* 1st, 1961, Elizabeth Carnegie Thomson (*d* 1982), *e d* of late Hon. Lord Migdale and Louise (*née* Carnegie; later Mrs Thomson); two *s* three *d*; 2nd, 1985, Elizabeth Cynthia Rae Ashworth, *widow* of Rupert S. H. Ashworth, and *y d* of P. Rae Shepherd. *Educ:* St Mary's Sch., Melrose; Rugby Sch.; Oxford Univ. (BA); Edinburgh Univ. (LLB). Admitted to Faculty of Advocates, 1959; Standing Junior Counsel to the Scottish Home and Health Dept and Dept of Health and Social Security in Scotland; Advocate-Depute, 1971–78; Chm., Med. Appeal Tribunal (Scotland), 1979–. Chm., RSSPCC Edinburgh, 1978–. *Publication:* (contrib. small part of) Armour on Valuation for Rating, 3rd edn, 1961. *Recreation:* golf. *Address:* 1 South Lauder Road, Edinburgh EH9 2LL. *T:* 031–667 4858. *Clubs:* New (Edinburgh); Honourable Company of Edinburgh Golfers (Muirfield).

MILLIGAN, Terence Alan, (Spike Milligan); actor; author; *b* 16 April 1918; *s* of late Captain L. A. Milligan, MSM, RA retd, and of Florence Winifred Milligan; *m* (wife *d* 1978); one *s* three *d*; *m* 1983, Shelagh Sinclair. *Educ:* Convent of Jesus and Mary, Poona; Brothers de La Salle, Rangoon; SE London Polytechnic, Lewisham. Appearances (comedy) as Spike Milligan: *stage:* The Bed-Sitting Room; Son of Oblomov; Ben Gunn, in Treasure Island, Mermaid, 1973, 1974; One man shows, 1979, 1980; writer, Ubu Roi, 1980; Spike Milligan and Friends, Lyric, 1982; *radio:* Goon Show (inc. special performance, 1972, to mark 50th Anniversary of BBC); Best British Radio Features Script, 1972; *TV:* Show called Fred, ITV; World of Beachcomber, BBC; Q5, BBC; Oh in Colour, BBC; A Milligan for All Seasons, BBC, 1972–73; Marty Feldman's Comedy Machine, ITV (writing and appearing; awarded Golden Rose and special comedy award, Montreux, 1972); The Melting Pot, BBC, 1975; Q7, BBC series, 1977; Q8, 1978; Q9, 1979; TV Writer of the Year Award, 1956; *films:* The Magic Christian, 1971; The Devils, 1971; The Cherry Picker, 1972; Digby the Biggest Dog in the World, 1972; Alice's Adventures in Wonderland, 1972; The Three Musketeers, 1973; The Great McGonagall, 1975; The Last Remake of Beau Geste, 1977; The Hound of the Baskervilles, 1978; Monty Python Life of Brian, 1978; History of the World, Part 1, 1980; Yellowbeard, 1983. *Publications:* Dustbin of Milligan, 1961; Silly Verse for Kids, 1963; Puckoon, 1963; The Little Pot Boiler, 1965; A Book of Bits, 1965; Milliganimals, 1968; The Bedside Milligan, 1968; The Bed-Sitting Room (play), 1969; The Bald Twit Lion, 1970; Adolf Hitler, My Part in his Downfall, 1971 (filmed 1973; on record, 1980); Milligan's Ark, 1971; Small Dreams of a Scorpion, 1972; The Goon Show Scripts, 1972; Rommel: Gunner Who?, 1973; (for children) Badjelly the Witch, 1973; (with J. Hobbs) The Great McGonagall Scrapbook, 1975; The Milligan Book of Records, Games, Cartoons and Commercials, 1975; Dip the Puppy, 1975; Transports of Delight, 1975; William McGonagal, the truth at last, 1976; Monty, His Part in my Victory, 1976; Goblins (with Heath Robinson illus), 1978; Mussolini, His Part in my Downfall, 1978; Open Heart University, 1978; Spike Milligan's Q Annual, 1979; Get in the Q Annual, 1980; Unspun Socks from a Chicken's Laundry, 1981; Indefinite Articles and Scunthorpe, 1981; The 101 Best and Only Limericks of Spike Milligan, 1982; (for children) Sir Nobonk and the Terrible, Awful, Dreadful, Naughty, Nasty Dragon (illus. by Carol Barker), 1982; The Goon Cartoons, 1982; More Goon Cartoons, 1983; There's A Lot Of It About, 1983; The Melting Pot, 1983; Spike Milligan's Further Transports of Delight, 1985; Where have all the Bullets Gone? (autobiog.), 1985; Floored Masterpieces with Worse Verse (illus. by Tracey Boyd), 1985. *Recreations:* restoration of antiques, oil painting, water colours, gardening, eating, drinking, talking, wine, jazz. *Address:* 9 Orme Court, W2. *T:* 01–727 1544.

MILLIGAN, Veronica Jean Kathleen; Senior Partner, Civlec Advisory Industrial Development Services, industrial consultants, since 1966; Director, Vantage Engineering & Maintenance Ltd, since 1985; *b* 11 March 1926; *d* of Gilbert John O'Neill and Jennie Kathleen Robertson; *m* 1945, Francis Sutherland Milligan; one *s* (and one *s* decd). *Educ:* Pontypridd Intermediate Grammar Sch.; University Coll., Cardiff (BA Wales, DipEd); (evenings) Polytechnic of Wales (HNC Elect. and Endorsements, Dip. Management Studies). CEng, MIEE; MBIM. Sch. teacher, Glam Educn Authority, 1948–51; Grad. Trainee/Senior Elec. Engr, Electricity Supply Industry, 1952–65. Manpower Adviser/Consultant to Manpower and Productivity Services, Dept of Employment (on secondment), 1969–73; Chm. and Dir, RTR Engineering Ltd, 1982–86. Pres., Women's Engrg Soc., 1977–79; Chm., E Wales Area, IEE, 1976–77 and Mem. Council, 1976–78. Member: Gwent AHA, 1976–; Gwent FPC, 1985–; National Water Council, 1977–80; Industrial Tribunals Panel, 1977–83; Commn on Energy and Environment, 1978–; Management Adv. Panel for Craftsmen, DHSS, 1979–; Nat. Staff Cttee for Works Staff, DHSS, 1981–82; Rent Assessment Panel, 1981–; Monitoring Cttee, Nat. Financial Incentive Scheme for NHS Maintenance Depts, 1982–. *Publications:* short papers in learned jls. *Recreations:* industrial careers advice to schools, industrial history, landscaping, walking. *Address:* Park Cottage, Rhiwderin, Newport, Gwent NP1 9RP. *T:* Newport 893557, Pontypool 2401/2311.

MILLIGAN, Wyndham Macbeth Moir, MBE 1945; TD 1947; Principal of Wolsey Hall, Oxford, 1968–80, retired; *b* 21 Dec. 1907; *s* of Dr W. Anstruther Milligan, MD, London, W1; *m* 1941, Helen Penelope Eirene Cassavetti, London, W1; three *s* two *d*. *Educ:* Sherborne; Caius Coll., Cambridge (Christopher James Student, 1931; 1st Cl. Classical Tripos, Parts 1 and 2). Asst Master, Eton Coll., 1932–, House Master, Eton Coll., 1946; Warden, Radley Coll., 1954–68. Served 1939–45, with Scots Guards, in NW Europe (Major). Former Chm., N Berks Area Youth Cttee. Governor: St Mary's, Wantage (Chm.); Reed's Sch., Cobham; Lay Chm., Vale of White Horse Deanery Synod; Mem., Administrative Council, King George's Jubilee Trust. FRSA 1968. *Recreations:* gardening, sketching. *Address:* Church Hill House, Stalbridge, Sturminster Newton, Dorset DT10 2LR. *T:* Stalbridge 62815.

MILLING; *see* Crowley-Milling.

MILLING, Peter Francis, MB, BChir, FRCS; formerly: Surgeon, Ear, Nose and Throat Department, University College Hospital; Surgeon in charge, Throat and Ear Department, Brompton Hospital; Consultant Ear, Nose and Throat Surgeon: Epsom District Hospital; Oxted and Limpsfield Cottage Hospital; Visiting Laryngologist Benenden Chest Hospital. *Educ:* Cambridge University. BA Hons, 1937; MRCS, LRCP, 1940; MA, MB, BChir, 1941; FRCS, 1946. Formerly Chief Assistant, Ear, Nose and Throat Department, St Thomas' Hospital; Chief Clinical Assistant and Registrar, Ear, Nose and Throat Department, Guy's Hosp.; Surgical Registrar, Ear, Nose and Throat Dept, Royal Cancer Hospital. Member British Association of Otolaryngologists. *Publications:* contributions to medical text-books and journals. *Address:* 3 Homefield Park, Ballasalla, Isle of Man. *T:* Douglas 823072.

MILLINGTON, Anthony Nigel Raymond; HM Diplomatic Service; Head of Chancery, Tokyo, since 1985; *b* 29 Jan. 1945; *s* of Raymond and Nancy Millington; *m* 1969, Susan Carolyn (*née* Steilberg); two *s*. *Educ:* Univ. of Grenoble; Trinity College, Cambridge (BA); Univ. of Chicago. Joined FCO, 1968; Tokyo, 1969–76; FCO, 1976–80; Paris, 1980–84; Japanese National Defence College, 1984–85. *Recreations:* squash, tennis, walking in the countryside. *Address:* c/o Foreign and Commonwealth Office, SW1A 2AH.

MILLINGTON, Air Commodore Edward Geoffrey Lyall, CB 1966; CBE 1946; DFC 1943; Manager, Regional Defence Sales, SE Asia, Orient Lloyd Pte Ltd, since 1985;

b 7 Jan. 1914; *s* of late Edward Turner Millington, Ceylon CS; *m* 1st, 1939, Mary Bonynge (marr. diss. 1956), *d* of W. Heaton Smith, FRCS; 2nd, 1956, Anne Elizabeth, *d* of Robert Brennan. *Educ:* Nautical Coll., Pangbourne. Served Cameron Highlanders, Palestine, 1936 (despatches); War of 1939–45, RAF, in N Africa, Sicily, Italy (actg Gp Capt.; despatches); Air Cdre, 1960; Comdr, RAF Persian Gulf, 1964–66; Air Commander, Zambia Air Force, 1968–70; Air Defence Adviser, Singapore Air Defence Command, 1970–72. psc; idc; Order Mil. Valour (Poland). *Address:* c/o Royal Bank of Scotland, Holt's Branch, 22 Whitehall, SW1. *Club:* Royal Air Force.

MILLINGTON, Wing Comdr Ernest Rogers, DFC 1945; Teacher in charge of Teachers' Centre, London Borough of Newham, 1967–80, retired; Founder, and Editor, Project, 1967–80; *b* 15 Feb. 1916; *s* of Edmund Rogers Millington and Emily Craggs; *m* 1st, 1937 (marr. diss. 1974); four *d*; 2nd, 1975, Ivy Mary Robinson. *Educ:* Chigwell Sch., Essex; College of S Mark and S John, Chelsea; Birkbeck Coll., London Univ. Clerk; Accountant; Company Sec.; served War of 1939–45, soldier, gunner officer, pilot RAF, instructor and heavy bomber, CO of a Lancaster Sqdn. MP (Commonwealth) for Chelmsford, 1945–50. Re-joined Royal Air Force, 1954–57. Head of Social Educn, Shoreditch Comprehensive Sch., London, 1965–67. *Publications:* (edited) A Study of Film, 1972; The Royal Group of Docks, 1977; A Geography of London, 1979; National Parks, 1980. *Recreations:* Francophilia, travel, writing. *Address:* 85 Upminster Road, Hornchurch, Essex. *T:* Hornchurch 43852; Villa Martine, Couze St Front, 24150 Lalinde, France.

MILLNER, Ralph; QC 1965; Visiting Lecturer in Italian, University of Leicester, since 1980; *b* 25 Jan. 1912; *o s* of Ralph Millner, Merchant, Manchester; *m* 1st, 1935, Bruna, *d* of Arturo Rosa, Este, Italy (marr. diss. 1949); one *d* decd; 2nd, 1949, Monica, *d* of Prof. P. W. Robertson, Wellington, NZ; one *s* two *d. Educ:* William Hulme's Grammar Sch., Manchester; Clare Coll., Cambridge (MA); Bedford Coll., London (BA, Italian). Called to English Bar, Inner Temple, 1934; Ghana Bar (Gold Coast), 1950; Sierra Leone Bar, 1957; Nigerian Bar and S Cameroons Bar, 1959; Guyana Bar (formerly British Guiana), 1961; has also appeared in courts of Aden and Kenya. Lectr in Italian, QUB, 1972–77. Member: Soc. for Italian Studies; Haldane Soc. *Address:* 69 Anson Road, N7 0AS.

MILLOTT, Prof. Norman; Emeritus Professor, University of London, since 1976; Director of the University Marine Biological Station, Millport, 1970–76; *b* 24 Oct. 1912; *s* of Reuben Tomlinson Millott and Mary Millott (*née* Thistlethwaite); *m* 1939, Margaret Newns; three *d. Educ:* The Brunts Sch., Mansfield, Notts; Univs of Sheffield (BSc 1935, MSc 1936, DSc 1961), Manchester, Cambridge (PhD 1944). Demonstrator in Zoology, Manchester Univ., 1935–36; Rouse Ball Student, Trinity Coll., Cambridge, 1936–38; Lectr in Zoology, Manchester Univ., 1938–40 and 1945–47. Commissioned RAFVR Technical Branch, 1940–45. Prof. of Zoology, University Coll. of the West Indies, 1948–55; Prof. of Zoology, Bedford Coll., London Univ., 1955–70. Staff Councillor, 1957–60, and Dean of Faculty of Science, Bedford Coll., 1958–60; Chm. of Board of Studies in Zoology, Univ. of London, 1961–65; Chm. Photobiology Group, UK, 1960–62; Chm. Academic Advisory Board, Kingston-upon-Thames Technical Coll., 1960–66; Vice-Pres., International Congress of Photobiology, 1964; Mem. Council, Scottish Marine Biological Assoc., 1971–76. Royal Society Vis. Prof., Univ. of Malta, 1976–77; Hon. Res. Fellow, Univ. Marine Biological Station, Millport. Governor, Bedford Coll., London Univ., 1976–82. *Publications:* scientific papers chiefly on invertebrate morphology, histology, physiology, and biochemistry. *Address:* Dunmore House, Millport, Isle of Cumbrae, Scotland.

MILLS, family name of Viscount Mills.

MILLS, 2nd Viscount, *cr* 1962; **Roger Clinton Mills**; Bt 1953; Baron 1957; management consultant, since 1983; Chairman, Harrogate District Health Authority, since 1984; *b* 14 June 1919; *o s* of 1st Viscount Mills, PC, KBE, and Winifred Mary (*d* 1974), *d* of George Conaty, Birmingham; *S* father, 1968; *m* 1945, Joan Dorothy, *d* of James Shirreff; one *s* two *d. Educ:* Canford Sch.; Jesus Coll., Cambridge. Served War as Major, RA, 1940–46. Administrative Officer, Colonial Service, Kenya, 1946–63. Barrister, Inner Temple, 1956. *Heir: s* Hon. Christopher Philip Roger Mills [*b* 20 May 1956; *m* 1980, Lesley, *er d* of Alan Bailey, Lichfield, Staffs]. *Address:* Whitecroft, Abbey Road, Knaresborough, N Yorks. *T:* Harrogate 866201.

MILLS, Maj.-Gen. Alan Oswald Gawler; Director-General of Artillery, Ministry of Defence (Army), 1967–69, retired; *b* 11 March 1914; *o s* of John Gawler Mills; *m* 1941, Beata Elizabeth de Courcy Morgan Richards; one *s* one *d. Educ:* Marlborough Coll.; RMA, Woolwich. Commissioned RA, 1934; Hong Kong, 1938–45; Br. Jt Services Mission, USA, 1951–53; Techn SO Grade I, Min. of Supply, 1955–57; Mil. Dir of Studies, RMCS, 1957–61; Sen. Mil. Officer, Royal Armament Research and Develt Estabt, 1961–62; BGS, WO, 1962–65; Dir, Guided Weapons Trials, Min. of Aviation, 1966. *Recreations:* sailing, ski-ing. *Address:* 3 Seafield Terrace, Seaview, IoW. *T:* Seaview 3166; 9 Redburn Street, Chelsea, SW3 4DA. *T:* 01–351 4272. *Clubs:* Island Sailing (Cowes); Seaview Yacht.

MILLS, Major Anthony David; *b* 14 Dec. 1918; *y s* of late Maj.-Gen. Sir Arthur Mills, CB, DSO; *m* 1948, Anne (*née* Livingstone); two *d. Educ:* Wellington Coll.; RMC, Sandhurst. Commnd Indian Army, 1939, 9th Gurkha Rifles; served War of 1939–45, NW Frontier and Burma, regimental duty and various staff appts; seconded Indian Para. Regt, 1944; retd from Army 1948. Apptd Asst Sec., All England Lawn Tennis Club and Wimbledon Championships, 1948, Sec. Treasurer, and Sec.-Gen., 1963–79. *Recreations:* golf, dog walking, consulting Who's Who. *Address:* c/o All England Lawn Tennis Club, Church Road, Wimbledon, SW19 5AE. *Clubs:* Naval and Military, Queen's (Hon.); All England Lawn Tennis; Royal Wimbledon Golf.

MILLS, Barbara Jean Lyon; QC 1986; a Recorder of the Crown Court, since 1982; *b* 10 Aug. 1940; *d* of John and Kitty Warnock; *m* 1962, John Angus Donald Mills; four *c. Educ:* St Helen's Sch., Northwood; Lady Margaret Hall, Oxford (Gibbs Scholar, 1961; MA). Called to the Bar, Middle Temple, 1963. Jun. Treasury Counsel, Central Criminal Court, 1981–86. *Recreation:* my family. *Address:* 3 Temple Gardens, Temple, EC4Y 9AU. *T:* 01–353 3533.

MILLS, Prof. Bernard Yarnton, AC 1976; FRS 1963; FAA 1959; DSc Eng; Professor of Physics (Astrophysics), University of Sydney, 1965–85, Emeritus Professor 1986; *b* 8 Aug. 1920; *s* of Ellice Yarnton Mills and Sylphide Mills. *Educ:* King's Sch., New South Wales; University of Sydney. BSc 1940, DSc Eng 1959 (Sydney). Joined the then Council for Scientific and Industrial Research and worked on Develt of mil. radar systems; after working for many years on radioastronomy he joined Sydney Univ. to form a radioastronomy group in Sch. of Physics, 1960; Reader in Physics, 1960–65; responsible for Mills Cross radio-telescope, near Hoskinstown, NSW. Lyle Medal of Australian Academy of Science, 1957. *Publications:* (jtly) A Textbook of Radar, 1946; many contribs to sci. jls in Australia, England and America, mainly on subjects of radioastronomy and astrophysics. *Address:* 52 Victoria Street, Roseville, NSW 2069, Australia.

MILLS, Vice-Adm. Sir Charles (Piercy), KCB 1968 (CB 1964); CBE 1957; DSC 1953; *b* 4 Oct. 1914; *s* of late Capt. Thomas Piercy Mills, Woking, Surrey; *m* 1944, Anne Cumberlege; two *d. Educ:* RN College, Dartmouth. Joined Navy, 1928; Comdr 1947; Capt. 1953; Rear-Adm. 1963; Vice-Adm. 1966. Served War of 1939–45, Home Waters, Mediterranean and Far East; Korea, 1951–52; Flag Officer, Second in Command, Far East Fleet, 1966–67; C-in-C Plymouth, 1967–69; Lieut-Governor and C-in-C Guernsey, 1969–74. US Legion of Merit, 1955. KStJ 1969. *Recreations:* golf, yachting. *Address:* Park Lodge, Aldeburgh, Suffolk. *T:* Aldeburgh 2115.

MILLS, Edward (David), CBE 1959; FRIBA; Architect and Design Consultant in private practice since 1937; Senior Partner, Edward D. Mills & Partners, Architects, London, since 1956; *b* 19 March 1915; *s* of Edward Ernest Mills; *m* 1939, Elsie May Bryant; one *s* one *d. Educ:* Ensham Sch.; Polytechnic Sch. of Architecture. ARIBA 1937, FRIBA 1946. Mem. of RIBA Council, 1954–62 and 1964–69; Chm. RIBA Bd of Architectural Education, 1960–62 (Vice-Chm., 1958–60); Pres., Soc. of Architectural Illustrators, 1975–. RIBA Alfred Bossom Research Fellow, 1953; Churchill Fellow, 1969. FSIA 1975; Mem., Uganda Soc. of Architects. Chm., Faculty Architecture, British School at Rome. Architect for British Industries Pavilion, Brussels Internat. Exhibn, 1958; works include: St Andrews Cathedral, Mbale, Uganda; Nat. Exhibn Centre, Birmingham; churches, schools, industrial buildings, research centres, flats and houses in Great Britain and overseas. *Publications:* The Modern Factory, 1951; The New Architecture in Great Britain, 1953; The Modern Church, 1956; Architects Details, Vols 1–6, 1952–61; Factory Building, 1967; The Changing Workplace, 1971; Planning, 5 vols, 9th edn 1972, 10th edn (combined Golden Jubilee vol.), 1985; The National Exhibition Centre, 1976; Building Maintenance and Preservation, 1980; Design for Holidays and Tourism, 1983; contribs to RIBA journal, Architectural Review, etc. *Recreations:* photography, foreign travel. *Address:* Gate House Farm, Newchapel, Lingfield, Surrey. *T:* Lingfield 832241.

MILLS, Eric Robertson, CBE 1981; Registrar of the Privy Council, 1966–83; *b* 27 July 1918; *s* of late Thomas Piercy Mills, Woking, Surrey; *m* 1950, Shirley Manger; two *d. Educ:* Charterhouse; Trinity Coll., Cambridge (BA). Served Royal Artillery, 1939–46; Major 1944. Called to Bar, Inner Temple, 1947; Mem. of Western Circuit. Dep. Judge Advocate, 1955; Chief Clerk, Judicial Cttee of Privy Council, 1963. *Publications:* contribs to legal text books. *Address:* Lamber Green, St Catherines Drive, Guildford, Surrey GU2 5HE. *T:* Guildford 37218.

MILLS, Prof. Eric William, AM 1986; CChem, FRSC; FRACI; Director, South Australian Institute of Technology, 1978–85, retired; *b* 22 April 1920; *s* of William and Lucy Margaret Mills; *m* 1945, Inge Julia Königsberger; three *d. Educ:* Liverpool Institute; Univ. of Liverpool (BSc, PhD). Chemist, British Insulated Cables, 1941–45; Research Chemist, British Oxygen Co., 1948–49; Sen. Lectr, Birmingham College of Advanced Technology, 1949–52; Head of Dept, Rutherford Coll. of Technology, 1952–57; Principal: Carlisle Technical Coll., 1959–60; Chesterfield Coll. of Technology, 1960–63; Asst Dir, SA Inst. of Technology, 1964–77. *Address:* 3 Pam Street, Beaumont, SA 5066, Australia. *T:* 79–6674.

MILLS, Sir Frank, KCVO 1983; CMG 1971; HM Diplomatic Service, retired; Chairman, Camberwell Health Authority, since 1984; *b* 3 Dec. 1923; *s* of Joseph Francis Mills and Louisa Mills; *m* 1953, Trilby Foster; one *s* two *d. Educ:* King Edward VI Sch., Nuneaton; Emmanuel Coll., Cambridge. RAFVR, 1942–45. CRO, 1948; served in: Pakistan, 1949–51; S Africa, 1955–58; Malaysia, 1962–63; Singapore, 1964–66; India, 1972–75; High Comr, Ghana, 1975–78; Private Sec. to Sec. of State, 1960–62; RCDS, 1971; Dir of Communications, FCO, 1978–81; High Comr, Bangladesh, 1981–83. Chm. Council, Royal Commonwealth Soc. for the Blind, 1985. *Recreations:* golf, sailing. *Address:* 14 Sherborne Road, Chichester, W Sussex PO19 3AA. *Clubs:* Royal Commonwealth Society; Dulwich and Sydenham Golf; Goodwood Golf.

MILLS, Maj.-Gen. Giles Hallam, CB 1977; CVO 1984; OBE 1964; retired; *b* 1 April 1922; 2nd *s* of late Col Sir John Digby Mills, TD, Bisterne Manor, Ringwood, Hampshire, and of Lady Mills; *m* 1947, Emily Snowden Hallam, 2nd *d* of late Captain W. H. Tuck, Perrywood, Maryland, USA, and of Mrs Tuck; two *s* one *d. Educ:* Eton Coll. Served War: 2nd Lieut, KRRC, 1941; 1st Bn, KRRC, N Africa, Italy (Adjt, despatches), 1943–47. Staff Coll., 1951; Armed Forces Staff Coll. (US), 1959; Mil. Asst to CIGS, 1961–63; CO, 2 Green Jackets, KRRC, 1963–65; Admin. Staff Coll., Henley, 1965; Regtl Col, Royal Green Jackets, 1966–67; Comd, 8 Infty Bde, 1968–69; IDC 1970; Comd, British Army Staff and Mil. Attaché, Washington, 1971–73; Divl Brig., The Light Div., 1973–74; Dir of Manning (Army), 1974–77, retd. Major and Resident Governor, HM Tower of London, and Keeper of the Jewel House, 1979–84. *Publications:* Annals of The King's Royal Rifle Corps, vol. VI (with Roger Nixon), 1971, vol. VII, 1979. *Recreations:* gardening, bird-watching, fishing, shooting, history. *Address:* Leeland House, Twyford, Winchester, Hants SO21 1NP. *Club:* Army and Navy.

MILLS, Maj.-Gen. Graham; *see* Mills, Maj.-Gen. W. G. S.

MILLS, Harold Hernshaw; Under Secretary, Scottish Development Department, since 1984; *b* 2 March 1938; *s* of Harold and Margaret Mills; *m* 1973, Marion Elizabeth Beattie, MA. *Educ:* Greenock High Sch.; Univ. of Glasgow (BSc, PhD). Cancer Research Scientist, Roswell Park Memorial Inst., Buffalo, NY, 1962–64; Lectr, Glasgow Univ., 1964–69; Principal, Scottish Home and Health Dept, 1970–76; Asst Secretary: Scottish Office, 1976–81; Privy Council Office, 1981–83; Scottish Development Dept, 1983–84. *Publications:* scientific papers in jls of learned socs on the crystal structure of chemical compounds. *Address:* 21 Hatton Place, Edinburgh EH9 1UB. *T:* 031–667 7910.

MILLS, Herbert Horatio, MC 1944; Rector of the Edinburgh Academy, 1962–77; *b* Jan. 1917; *s* of Edward Charles and Sarah Mills. *Educ:* Marling Sch.; St Catharine's Coll., Cambridge (PhD). Commonwealth Fellow, University of Pennsylvania, USA, 1950. Asst Master, Sedbergh Sch., 1953–62. *Recreations:* mountaineering; Cambridge Rugby XV, 1947, 1948. *Clubs:* Alpine; Scottish Mountaineering; Scottish Arts (Edinburgh).

MILLS, Iain Campbell; MP (C) Meriden, since 1979; *b* 21 April 1940; *s* of John Steel Mills and Margaret Leitch; *m* 1971, Gaynor Lynne Jeffries. *Educ:* Prince Edward Sch., Salisbury, Rhodesia. Dunlop Rhodesia Ltd, 1961–64; Dunlop Ltd, UK, 1964–79 (latterly Marketing Planning Manager). Parly Private Secretary: to Minister of State for Industry, 1981–82; to Sec. of State for Employment, 1982–83; to Sec. of State for Trade and Industry, 1983–85; to Chancellor of Duchy of Lancaster, 1985–. Chm., Community Trade Mark Cttee, 1984–; Vice-Chm., Transport Safety Cttee, 1984–. *Address:* House of Commons, SW1A 0AA.

MILLS, Ivor; Head of Public Affairs and Deputy Director, Corporate Relations, British Telecommunications plc, since 1981; *b* 7 Dec. 1929; *e s* of John Mills and Matilda (*née* Breen); *m* 1956, Muriel, *o d* of Wilson and Muriel Hay; one *s* one *d. Educ:* High sch.; Stranmillis Coll.; Queen's Univ., Belfast. Radio and television journalist, and freelance writer, Ulster TV, 1959, and Southern TV, 1963; freelance writer/editor/producer/ presenter, contrib. to BBC World Service and Home Radio Networks, and ITV Regions, 1964; joined ITN as Reporter, 1965; newscaster with wide experience in preparation and presentation of ITN's News Bulletins, 1967–78; Head of Public Affairs, Post Office, 1978. Media consultant. *Recreations:* art, music, theatre, tennis, food, wine. *Address:* British Telecommunications plc, British Telecom Centre, 81 Newgate Street, EC1A 7AJ.

MILLS, Ivor Henry, FRCP; Professor of Medicine in the University of Cambridge since 1963; Fellow Churchill College, Cambridge; Hon. Consultant to United Cambridge Hospitals; *b* 13 June 1921; 3rd *s* of late J. H. W. Mills and late Priscilla Mills; *m* 1947, Sydney Elizabeth Puleston (*née* Roberts); one *s* one *d*. *Educ:* Selhurst Grammar Sch., Croydon; Queen Mary Coll., London; Trinity Coll., Cambridge. BSc (London) 1942; PhD (London) 1946; BA (Cantab) 1948; MB, BChir Cantab 1951; MRCP 1953; MD Cantab 1956; MA Cantab 1963; FRCP 1964. Pres. Cambridge Univ. Medical Soc., 1947–48; Sen. Schol., Trinity Coll., Cambridge, 1948; MRC (Eli Lilly) Trav. Fellow, 1956; Vis. Scientist, Nat. Inst. of Health, 1957; Lectr in Medicine and Chem. Path., St Thomas's Hosp. Medical Sch., 1954; Reader in Medicine, St Thomas's Hosp. Medical Sch., London, 1962. Vis. Prof. in Physiology and Medicine, N Carolina Med. Sch., USA, 1972. Mem., Hunter Working Party on Medical Administrators, 1970–72. Sec., Soc. for Endocrinology, 1963–71; Mem. Council, RCP, 1971–74. Pro-Censor, RCP, 1974–75, Censor, 1975–76; Chm., Scientific Adv. Cttee, Mason Med. Res. Foundation, 1982–. Hon. FACP. *Publications:* Clinical Aspects of Adrenal Function, 1964; contrib. Lancet, Science Jl of Endocr., Clin. Science, etc. *Recreation:* gardening. *Address:* Addenbrooke's Hospital, Cambridge.

MILLS, John; *see* Mills, Laurence J.

MILLS, John F. F. P.; *see* Platts-Mills.

MILLS, Sir John (Lewis Ernest Watts), Kt 1976; CBE 1960; Actor, Producer, Director; *b* 22 Feb. 1908; *m* 1941, Mary Hayley Bell, playwright; one *s* two *d*. *Educ:* Norwich. 1st appearance, stage, 1929. *Plays:* Cavalcade, London Wall, Words and Music, Five O'clock Girl, Give Me a Ring, Jill Darling, Floodlight, Red Night, We at the Cross Roads, Of Mice and Men, Men in Shadow, Duet for Two Hands, etc.; Old Vic Season, 1938; Top of the Ladder; Figure of Fun, Aldwych; Ross, New York, 1961; Power of Persuasion, Garrick, 1963; Veterans, Royal Court, 1972; At the End of the Day, Savoy, 1973; The Good Companions, Her Majesty's, 1974; Separate Tables, Apollo, 1977; Goodbye, Mr Chips, Chichester Fest., 1982; Little Lies, Wyndham's, 1983; The Petition, NT, 1986; When the Wind Blows (TV play), 1986. *Films:* The Midshipmaid, Britannia of Billingsgate, Brown on Resolution, OHMS, Cottage To Let, The Young Mr Pitt, We Dive at Dawn, In Which We Serve, The Way to the Stars, Great Expectations, So Well Remembered, The October Man, Scott of the Antarctic, The History of Mr Polly, The Rocking Horse Winner, Morning Departure, Mr Denning Drives North, Gentle Gunman, The Long Memory, Hobson's Choice, The Colditz Story, The End of the Affair, Above Us the Waves, Town on Trial, Escapade, Its Great to be Young, The Baby and the Battleship, War and Peace, Around the World in Eighty Days, Dunkirk, Ice Cold in Alex, I Was Monty's Double, Summer of the Seventeenth Doll, Tiger Bay, Swiss Family Robinson, The Singer not the Song, Tunes of Glory, Flame in the Streets, The Valiant, Tiara Tahiti, The Chalk Garden, The Truth about Spring, King Rat, Operation X Bow, Red Waggon, Sky West and Crooked (directed), The Wrong Box, The Family Way, Chuka, Showdown, Oh What a Lovely War, The Return of the Boomerang, Ryan's Daughter (Best Supporting Actor Award, Oscar Award, 1971), Run Wild, Run Free, Emma Hamilton, Dulcima, Lamb, Young Winston, Oklahoma Crude, Trial by Combat, The Devil's Advocate, Great Expectations, The Big Sleep, Zulu Dawn, The 39 Steps, The Human Factor, Gandhi, Masks of Death, Murder with Mirrors, A Woman of Substance. Tribute to Her Majesty (film documentary), 1986. *TV series:* The Zoo Gang, 1974; Quatermass, 1979; Tales of the Unexpected, 1979, 1980, 1981; Young at Heart, 1980, 1981, 1982. Member: SFTA (Vice-Pres.); RADA Council, 1965–; Chm., Stars Organization for Spastics, 1975–79. Patron Life Mem., Variety Club. *Publications:* Up in the Clouds, Gentlemen Please (autobiog.), 1980; Book of Famous Firsts, 1984. *Recreations:* ski-ing, golf, painting. *Address:* c/o ICM, 388 Oxford Street, W1. *Clubs:* Garrick, St James's.

MILLS, John Robert, BSc; CEng, FIEE; CPhys, MInstP; Under Secretary and Deputy Director (Systems) Royal Signals and Radar Establishment, Ministry of Defence, 1976–77, retired; *b* 12 Nov. 1916; *s* of Robert Edward Mills and Constance H. Mills; *m* 1950, Pauline Phelps; two *s*. *Educ:* Kingston Grammar Sch., Kingston-upon-Thames; King's Coll., London (BSc 1939); MInstP; FIEE, 1971. Air Ministry Research Estab., Dundee, 1939; RAE Farnborough, 1940–42; TRE, later RRE, Malvern, 1942–60; Supt (Offensive), Airborne Radar, RRE, 1954–60; Asst Dir, Electronics R and D (Civil Aviation), Min. of Aviation, 1960–61; Head of Radio Dept, RAE Farnborough, 1961–65; Electronics Div., Min. of Technology, 1965–67; Div, Signals R&D Establishment, Christchurch, 1967–76. *Publications:* (jointly) Radar article in Encyclopædia Britannica; various papers in journals. *Address:* Timberstones, 44 Montagu Road, Highcliffe, Christchurch, Dorset.

MILLS, (John) Vivian G., DLitt; *b* 22 Sept. 1887; *s* of late Comdr J. F. Mills, ISO, RN (retd); *m* 1st, 1915, Lilian (*d* 1947), *d* of late A. Brisley; no *c*; 2nd, 1968, Marguerite Mélanie (*d* 1983), *d* of late Jean Hoffman. *Educ:* privately; Merton Coll., Oxford; Classical Mods and Lit Hum; MA 1946; DLitt 1974. Barrister-at-law, Middle Temple, 1919; Cadet, Malayan Civil Service, 1911; qualified in Chinese, 1914; held various administrative, legal and judicial appointments, 1914–28; Solicitor-Gen., Straits Settlements, 1928–32; acting Attorney-Gen., and Mem. of the Executive and Legislative Councils, 1932; Commissioner of Currency, 1932; Puisne Judge, Straits Settlements, 1933; Judge, Johore, 1934; retired, 1940; Attached to office of Federal Attorney-Gen., Sydney, Australia, 1944–45; Additional Lecturer in Chinese Law, School of Oriental and African Studies, London, 1946–47; Pres. of Malayan Branch, Royal Asiatic Society, 1937; Joint Hon. Sec., 1950–53, Hon. Mem. 1983, Hakluyt Soc. *Publications:* Eredia's Malaca, Meridional India and Cathay, 1930; Malaya in the Wu-pei-chi Charts, 1937; (trans. and ed) Ma Huan: Ying-yai sheng-lan, The Overall Survey of the Ocean's Shores, 1970; various official publications. *Recreations:* Oriental research and watching first-class cricket. *Address:* Bellaria 62, 1814 La Tour de Peilz, Switzerland. *Club:* Athenæum.

MILLS, John William, OBE 1945; QC 1962; *b* 24 Oct. 1914; *s* of late John William Mills, OBE and Jessie Mills; *m* 1942, Phyllis Mary, *yr d* of late Arthur Gibson Pears; no *c*. *Educ:* Clifton; Corpus Christi Coll., Cambridge (MA). Called to Bar, Middle Temple, 1938; Bencher, 1968; Treasr, 1985. Lt-Col, Royal Signals, 1944; Comdr, Royal Signals, 46 Div., 1944. Member: Bar Council, 1961–64; Clifton Coll. Council, 1967–80. *Publications:* The Building Societies Act, 1960, 1961, Wurtzburg and Mills, Building Society Law, 1964–. *Recreations:* sailing, golf. *Address:* 38 Adam and Eve Mews, W8. *T:* 01–937 1259; 11 Old Square, Lincoln's Inn, WC2. *T:* 01–430 0341; Greenleas, Highleigh, Chichester, Sussex. *T:* Sidlesham (024 356) 396.

MILLS, (Laurence) John, CBE 1978; FEng 1978; Chairman, Osprey Belt Company Ltd, since 1986; Member, 1974–82, a Deputy Chairman, 1982–84, National Coal Board; *b* 1 Oct. 1920; *s* of late Archibald John and Annie Ellen Mills; *m* 1944, Barbara May (*née* Warner); two *s*. *Educ:* Portsmouth Grammar Sch.; Birmingham Univ. BSc (Hons); Hon. FIMinE, CIMEMME; CBIM. Mining Student, Houghton Main Colliery Co. Ltd, 1939; Corps of Royal Engrs, 1942–46, Major 1946; various mining appts, Nat. Coal Bd, 1947–67; Chief Mining Engr, HQ NCB, 1968; Area Dir, N Yorks Area, 1970; Area Dir, Doncaster Area, 1973. Chm., British Mining Consultants Ltd, 1983–85; Director: Coal Develts (Queensland) Ltd, 1980–84; Capricorn Coal Management Pty Ltd, 1981–84; Coal Develts (German Creek) Pty Ltd, 1980–84; German Creek Pty Ltd, 1981–84; Burnett and Hallamshire Holdings plc, 1986–. Member: Mining Qualifications Bd, 1975–83; Safety in Mines Res. Adv. Bd, 1975–83; Adv. Council on Res. Develt for Fuel and Power, 1981–83. Pres., IMinE, 1975. Silver Medal, Midland Counties Instn of Engrs, 1959 and 1962; Douglas Hay Medal, IMinE, 1977; Clerk Maxwell Medal, Assoc. of Mining, Electrical and Mech. Engrs (now IMEMME), 1979; Robens Coal Science Lecture Gold Medal, 1981; Institution Medal, IMinE, 1982. *Publications:* techn. papers in Trans IMinE. *Recreation:* coastal and inland waterway cruising. *Address:* Units 3/4 Bowers Parade, Harpenden, Herts AL5 2SH.

MILLS, Lawrence William Robert, JP; Official Member, Legislative Council, Hong Kong, since 1983; Regional Secretary, Hong Kong and Kowloon, since 1983; *b* London, 7 May 1934; *s* of William H. Mills and E. May Mills; *m* 1964, Amy Kwai Lan (*née* Poon), Shanghai and Hong Kong; two *d*. *Educ:* Reigate Grammar Sch., Surrey. National Service: RN, 1953; Intell. Corps, 1954. Formerly, Jun. Exec., K. F. Mayer Ltd, London. Hong Kong Govt (Mem. of HMOCS): Exec. Officer, Cl. II, 1958; Asst Trade Officer, 1960; Trade Officer, 1964; Sen. Trade Officer, 1968; Principal Trade Officer, 1969; Asst Dir of Commerce and Industry, 1971; Chief Trade Negotiator, 1974–75, 1977–79, 1981–83; Counsellor (Hong Kong Affairs), Hong Kong Office, UK Mission, Geneva, 1976–77; Director of Trade, Hong Kong, 1977–79, 1981–83; Comr of Industry, 1979–81. *Recreation:* music (classical jazz). *Address:* City and New Territories Administration, World Shipping Centre 12/F, Harbour City, Kowloon, Hong Kong. *Clubs:* Hong Kong, Hong Kong Country (Hong Kong).

MILLS, Leif Anthony; General Secretary, Banking, Insurance and Finance Union (formerly National Union of Bank Employees), since 1972; Member, Monopolies and Mergers Commission, since 1982; *b* 25 March 1936; *s* of English father and Norwegian mother; *m* 1958, Gillian Margaret Smith; two *s* two *d*. *Educ:* Balliol Coll., Oxford. BA Hons PPE. Commnd in Royal Military Police, 1957–59. Trade Union Official, Nat. Union of Bank Employees, 1960–: Research Officer, 1960; Asst Gen. Sec., 1962; Dep. Gen. Sec., 1968. Mem. various arbitration tribunals; Member: TUC Non-Manual Workers Adv. Cttee, 1967–72; TUC Gen. Council, 1983–; Office of Manpower Economics Adv. Cttee on Equal Pay, 1971; Chm., TUC Financial Services Cttee, 1983–. Member: Cttee to Review the Functioning of Financial Institutions, 1977–80; CS Pay Res. Unit Bd, 1978–81; BBC Consultative Gp on Social Effects of Television, 1978–80; Armed Forces Pay Review Body, 1980–. Contested (Lab) Salisbury, 1964, 1965 (by-elecn). *Publications:* biography (unpublished), Cook: A History of the Life and Explorations of Dr Frederick Albert Cook, SPRI ms 883, Cambridge, 1970. *Recreations:* rowing, chess. *Address:* 31 Station Road, West Byfleet, Surrey. *T:* Byfleet 42829. *Clubs:* United Oxford & Cambridge University; Oxford University Boat, Weybridge Rowing.

MILLS, Leonard Sidney, CB 1970; Deputy Director General (2), Highways, Department of the Environment, 1970–74; *b* 20 Aug. 1914; *s* of late Albert Edward Mills; *m* 1940, Kathleen Joyce Cannicott; two *s*. *Educ:* Devonport High Sch.; London Sch. of Economics; Birkbeck Coll., University of London. Entered Exchequer and Audit Dept, 1933; transferred to Min. of Civil Aviation, 1946; Asst Sec., 1950; Min. of Transport: Under-Sec., 1959; Chief of Highway Administration, 1968–70. Commonwealth Fund Fellow, 1953–54. *Recreations:* walking, croquet, photography, gardening. *Address:* Pine Rise, 7A Bedlands Lane, Budleigh Salterton, Devon.

MILLS, Mary Bell McMillan, (Mrs Ian Mills); *see* MacMurray, M. B. McM.

MILLS, Neil McLay; Chairman, Sedgwick Group plc, 1979–84; *b* 29 July 1923; *yr s* of late L. H. Mills and Mrs Mills; *m* 1950, Rosamund Mary Kimpton, *d* of Col and Hon. Mrs A. C. W. Kimpton; two *s* two *d*. *Educ:* Epsom Coll.; University Coll. London. Served War, 1940–46: commnd RN; Lieut RNVR; Coastal Forces (mentioned in despatches, 1944). Joined Bland Welch & Co. Ltd, 1948; Exec. Dir, 1955; Chm., 1965–74; Chm., Bland Payne Holdings Ltd, 1974–79. Underwriting Mem. of Lloyd's, 1955–. Director: Montagu Trust Ltd, 1966–74; Midland Bank Ltd, 1974–79; Wadlow Grosvenor International Ltd, 1984–; Citicorp Insurance Group Inc., 1985–; Polly Peck International PLC, 1985–. Vice-President: Insurance Inst. of London, 1971–84; British Insurance Brokers Assoc., 1978–84 (Mem., Internat. Insurance Brokers Cttee); Mem. Cttee, Lloyd's Insurance Brokers Assoc., 1974–77. Member: Church Army Board, 1957–64 (Vice-Chm., 1959–64); Council, Oak Hill Theol Coll., 1958–62. Trustee and Governor, Lord Mayor Treloar Trust, 1975–81. *Recreations:* farming, mowing. *Address:* 15 Markham Square, SW3. *T:* 01–584 3995; The Dower House, Upton Grey, near Basingstoke, Hants. *T:* Basingstoke 862435. *Clubs:* City of London, Pilgrims.
See also Sir Peter (McLay) Mills.

MILLS, Sir Peter (Frederick Leighton), 3rd Bt, *cr* 1921; *b* 9 July 1924; *s* of Major Sir Frederick Leighton Victor Mills, 2nd Bt, MC, RA, MICE, and Doris (*née* Armitage); *S* father 1955; *m* 1954, Pauline Mary, *d* of L. R. Allen, Calverton, Notts; one *s* (one adopted *d* decd). *Educ:* Eastbourne Coll.; Cedara Coll. of Agriculture, University of Natal (BSc Agric.). Served HM Forces, 1943–47. CS, Fedn Rhodesia and Nyasaland, 1953; with Rhodesia Min. of Agric., 1964–. *Heir:* *s* Michael Victor Leighton Mills, *b* 30 Aug. 1957. *Address:* Henderson Research Station, P Bag 2004, Mazowe, Zimbabwe.

MILLS, Sir Peter (McLay), Kt 1982; MP (C) Torridge and West Devon since 1983 (Torrington, 1964–74, Devon West 1974–83); *b* 22 Sept. 1921; *m* 1948, Joan Weatherley; one *s* one *d*. *Educ:* Epsom; Wye Coll. Parly Sec., MAFF, 1972; Parly Under-Sec. of State, NI Office, 1972–74. Member: European Legislation Cttee, EEC, 1974–79; Select Cttee on Foreign Affairs, 1980–82; Dep. Chm., CPA, 1982–85; Chairman: Cons. Agriculture Cttee, 1979–; Houses of Parlt Christian Fellowship, 1970–. *Recreations:* work and staying at home for a short time. *Address:* House of Commons, SW1. *T:* 01–219 4093.

MILLS, Peter William; QC (Can.) 1985; Vice President and General Counsel since 1980 and Director since 1982, The Woodbridge Company Limited; Director, Hudson's Bay Company, since 1985; *b* 22 July 1942; *s* of Joseph Roger Mills and Jane Eveyln (*née* Roscoe); *m* 1967, Eveline Jane (*née* Black); two *s*. *Educ:* Dalhousie Univ. Law Sch. (LLB); Dalhousie Univ. (BComm). Barrister and solicitor, Ont, Canada; with McInnes, Cooper and Robertson, Halifax, 1967; Solicitor, Canadian Pacific Ltd, Montreal and Toronto, 1967–71; Dir, Cammell Laird Shipbuilders Ltd, 1971–76; Mem. Org. Cttee for British Shipbuilders, 1976–77; Manager, Currie, Coopers & Lybrand Ltd, Toronto, 1977–79; Dir, Corporate Develt, FP Publications Ltd, 1979–80. *Recreations:* golf, sailing, travel, reading. *Address:* The Woodbridge Company Limited, 65 Queen Street West, Toronto, Ont M5H 2M8, Canada; 390 Glencairn Avenue, Toronto, Ont M5N 1V1. *Clubs:* Board of Trade, York Downs Golf and Country (Toronto); Royal Liverpool Golf (Hoylake); Royal Nova Scotia Yacht Squadron.

MILLS, Richard Michael; Chairman, since 1979, and Chief Executive, since 1970, Bernard Delfont Ltd; *b* 26 June 1931; *s* of Richard Henry Mills and Catherine Keeley; *m* 1st, 1960, Lynda Taylor (marr. diss. 1967); one *d*; 2nd, 1983, Sheila White; one *s*. Commenced working in the theatre as an Assistant Stage Manager in 1948, and worked in every capacity, including acting and stage management. Joined Bernard Delfont Ltd, 1962; Dir, 1967; Dep. Chm. and Chief Exec., 1970; Chm. and Chief Exec., 1979; Managing Director: Prince of Wales Theatre, 1970–; Prince Edward Theatre, 1978–. Member: Nat. Theatre Bd, 1976–; Finance and Gen. Purposes Cttee, NT, 1976–; Drama Panel, Arts Council of GB, 1976–77; English Tourist Bd, 1982–85. Shows worked on in the West End, 1948–62, include: I Remember Mama, Tuppence Coloured, Medea, Adventure Story, Anne Veronica, The Devil's General, I Capture the Castle, No Escape, Three Times a Day, The Sun of York, To my Love, Be my Guest, Hunter's Moon, The Iceman Cometh, Brouhaha, Detour after Dark, The Ginger Man, Sound of Murder, Will You Walk a Little Faster, Pool's Paradise, Belle, Come Blow your Horn. With Lord Delfont has presented in the West End: The Good Old Bad Old Days, Mardi Gras, Brief Lives, Queen Daniella, Cinderella, Henry IV, Harvey, Sammy Cahn's Songbook, Streetcar Named Desire, Good Companions, It's All Right if I Do It, Charley's Aunt, An Evening with Tommy Steele, Gomes, The Wolf, Danny La Rue Show, Beyond the Rainbow, Dad's Army, Plumber's Progress, Paul Daniels Magic Show, Underneath the Arches, Little Me, and over 100 pantomimes and summer season shows. *Recreations:* golf, poker. *Address:* Prince of Wales Theatre, Coventry Street, W1. *T:* 01–930 9901. *Clubs:* Royal Automobile; Wentworth Golf, Royal Mid-Surrey Golf.

MILLS, Robert Ferris; Under Secretary, Department of Health and Social Services, Northern Ireland, since 1983; *b* 21 Sept. 1939; *s* of Robert and Rachel Mills; *m* 1st, 1968, Irene Sandra Miskelly (marr. diss. 1978); one *s* one *d*; 2nd, 1984, Frances Elizabeth Gillies; two step *d. Educ:* Sullivan Upper School, Holywood, Co. Down; Queen's Univ., Belfast (BA Hons). Inland Revenue, 1961–64; Min. of Commerce, NI, 1964–68; Dept of Housing and Local Govt, 1968–71; Dept of the Environment, NI, 1971–74; Asst Sec., Dept of Health and Social Services, NI, 1975–83. *Recreations:* golf, tennis. *Address:* Dundonald House, Belfast BT7 3SS.

MILLS, Air Cdre Stanley Edwin Druce, CB 1968; CBE 1959; Royal Air Force, retired; *b* 1913; *s* of Edwin J. Mills; *m* 1938, Joan Mary, *d* of Robert Ralph James; one *s* one *d. Educ:* Collegiate Sch., Bournemouth, RAF Staff Coll. Entered RAF 1939; served RAF Middle East and Italy, 1942–45; Station Comdr, RAF Innsworth, 1957–60; Comd Accountant, RAF Germany, 1960–63; Dir of Personnel (Policy) (Air), MoD, 1963–65; Dir of Personal Services (Air), MoD, 1966–68. Bursar, Roedean Sch., 1968–73. FCA. *Recreation:* travel. *Address:* Maryland, Lullington Close, Seaford, E Sussex. *Club:* Royal Air Force.

MILLS, Stratton; *see* Mills, W. S.

MILLS, Vivian; *see* Mills, J. V. G.

MILLS, Wilbur Daigh; lawyer and politician, USA; tax consultant, Shea & Gould (Mirabelli & Gould), since 1977; *b* Kensett, Ark, 24 May 1909; *s* of Ardra Pickens Mills and Abbie Lois Daigh; *m* 1934, Clarine Billingsley; two *d. Educ:* Hendrix Coll.; Harvard Law Sch. Admitted to State Bar of Arkansas, 1933; in private legal practice, Searcy; County and Probate Judge, White County, 1934–38; Cashier, Bank of Kensett, 1934–35. Mem., US House of Representatives, 1939–76 (Chm., Ways and Means Cttee, 1958–74). Democrat. *Address:* (office) 1627 K Street NW, Washington, DC 20006, USA; Kensett, Arkansas 72082, USA.

MILLS, Maj.-Gen. (William) Graham (Stead), CBE 1963; *b* 23 June 1917; *s* of William Stead Mills and Margaret Kennedy Mills; *m* 8 July 1941, Joyce Evelyn (*née* Ransom) (*d* 1981); three *s. Educ:* Merchiston Castle Sch., Edinburgh. Regtl duty, Royal Berks Regt, in India, 1938–43; Staff Coll., India, 1944; GSO2 and GSO1, Ops HQ 14th Army, Burma, 1944–45; WO and Washington, USA, 1946–50; Regtl duty with Parachute Regt, comdg 17th Bn, The Parachute Regt, 1958–60; GSO1, 2 Div. BAOR, 1956–58; Regtl Col The Parachute Regt, 1960–62; Comdg TA Brigade, Winchester, 1963–64; Brig. GS, HQ Middle East Comd, Aden, 1965–66; Imperial Defence Coll., Student, 1967; GOC West Midland District, 1968–70. *Recreations:* normal. *Address:* Inglenook, Field Dalling, Holt, Norfolk. *T:* Binham 388.

MILLS, (William) Stratton; Partner in Mills, Selig & Bailie, Solicitors, Belfast; Company Director; *b* 1 July 1932; *o s* of late Dr J. V. S. Mills, CBE, Resident Magistrate for City of Belfast, and Margaret Florence (*née* Byford); *m* 1959, Merriel E. R. Whitla, *o d* of late Mr and Mrs R. J. Whitla, Belfast; three *s. Educ:* Campbell Coll., Belfast; Queen's Univ., Belfast (LLB). Vice-Chm., Federation of University Conservative and Unionist Assocs, 1952–53 and 1954–55; admitted a Solicitor, 1958. MP (UU) Belfast N, Oct. 1959–Dec. 1972; MP (Alliance) Belfast N, Apr. 1973–Feb. 1974; PPS to Parly Sec., Ministry of Transport, 1961–64; Member: Estimates Cttee, 1964–70; Exec. Cttee, 1922 Cttee, 1967–70, 1973; Hon. Sec. Conservative Broadcasting Cttee, 1963–70, Chm., 1970–73; Mem., Mr Speaker's Conference on Electoral Law, 1967. Mem., One Nation Gp, 1972–73. Chm., Ulster Orchestra Soc. Ltd, 1980–. *Address:* (office) 20 Callender Street, Belfast 1. *T:* Belfast 243878; (home) 17 Malone Park, Belfast 9. *T:* Belfast 665210. *Clubs:* Carlton; Reform (Belfast).

MILLS-OWENS, Richard Hugh, CBE 1972; Puisne Judge, Hong Kong, 1967–71, retired (also 1961–64); Chief Justice, Fiji, 1964–67; *b* Jan. 1910; *s* of George Edward Owens and Jessie Mary Mills; *m* 1935, Elizabeth Ann Hiles (*d* 1968); two *s. Educ:* Rhyl Grammar Sch. Admitted Solicitor, 1932; Clifford's Inn Prizeman; Barrister-at-law, 1956, Middle Temple. Practised in Wales (including service with Carmarthenshire County Council) until 1949 when joined Colonial Legal Service as a Registrar of Titles; Principal Registrar, Kenya; Crown Counsel and Legal Draftsman, 1952; Magistrate, 1956, District Judge, 1958, Hong Kong. *Address:* Westwood, Hangersley, Ringwood, Hants.

MILLSON, John Albert; Assistant Under-Secretary of State, Ministry of Defence, 1972–78; *b* 4 Oct. 1918; *s* of late George Charles Millson and Annie Millson, London; *m* 1953, Megan Laura Woodiss; one *s* one *d. Educ:* St Olave's. Entered Air Min., 1936; Private Sec. to Parly Under-Sec. of State for Air, 1947–50; Principal, Air Min., 1955; Asst Sec., MoD, 1961; Asst Under-Sec. of State, 1972. Chm. of Governors, Homefield Prep. Sch., Sutton, 1975. *Recreations:* walking, listening to music. *Address:* 9 The Highway, Sutton, Surrey. *T:* 01–642 3967.

MILLWARD, William, CB 1969; CBE 1954; with Government Communications Headquarters, 1946–74, retired (Superintending Director, 1958–69); *b* 27 Jan. 1909; *s* of William John and Alice Millward; *m* 1937, Nora Florella Harper; one *s* one *d. Educ:* Solihull Sch.; St Catherine's Society, Oxford. Asst Master, Dulwich Coll., 1930–41; RAF, 1941–46. *Recreations:* music, reading, walking. *Address:* 37 Pegasus Court, St Stephen's Road, Cheltenham. *T:* Cheltenham 525732.

MILMAN, Sir Dermot (Lionel Kennedy), 8th Bt, *cr* 1800; *b* 24 Oct. 1912; *e s* of Brig.- Gen. Sir Lionel Charles Patrick Milman, 7th Bt, CMG, and Marjorie Aletta (*d* 1980), *d* of Col A. H. Clark-Kennedy, late Indian Civil Service; *S* father, 1962; *m* 1941, Muriel, *o d* of J. E. S. Taylor, King's Lynn; one *d. Educ:* Uppingham; Corpus Christi Coll., Cambridge. BA 1934, MA 1938. Served War of 1939–45, Royal Army Service Corps, in France, Belgium and Burma (despatches), Major. Hon. Major, RCT (formerly RARO, RASC). British Council service overseas and home, 1946–76, retired 1976. Chairman: Assoc. for British-Arab Univ. Visits; Phyllis Konstam Meml Trust; India Arise Fund. *Heir: b* Malcolm Douglas Milman [*b* 18 May 1915; *m* 1940, Sheila Maud (marriage dissolved), *d* of Albert Maurice Dudeney; two *d*]. *Address:* 7 Old Westhall Close, Warlingham, Surrey. *T:* Upper Warlingham 4843.

MILMO, Sir Helenus (Patrick Joseph), Kt 1964; DL; Judge of High Court of Justice, Queen's Bench Division, 1964–82; *b* 24 Aug. 1908; 3rd *s* of late Daniel Milmo, Furbough, Co. Galway, Eire; *m* 1st, 1933, Joan Frances (*d* 1978), *d* of late Francis Morley, London; two *s* three *d* (and one *d* decd); 2nd, 1980, Anne (Nan), *widow* of F. B. Brand. *Educ:* Downside; Trinity Coll., Cambridge. Barrister, Middle Temple, 1931; Bencher, 1955; QC 1961; Dep. Treasurer, 1972; Treasurer 1973. Civil Asst, General Staff, War Office, 1940–45. Dep. Chm., West Sussex QS, 1960–64. DL Sussex, 1962. *Recreations:* hunting, fishing, wine. *Address:* Arborfield, Castlegate, West Chiltington, West Sussex RH20 2NJ. *T:* West Chiltington 2398. *Clubs:* Garrick, MCC.
    See also P. H. Milmo.

MILMO, John Boyle Martin; QC 1984; a Recorder of the Crown Court, since 1982; *b* 19 Jan. 1943; *s* of Dermod Hubert Francis Milmo, MB BCh and Eileen Clare Milmo (*née* White). *Educ:* Downside Sch.; Trinity Coll., Dublin. MA, LLB. Called to the Bar, Lincoln's Inn, 1966. *Recreations:* opera, discography. *Address:* 24 The Ropewalk, Nottingham NG1 5EF. *T:* Nottingham 472581. *Club:* United Services (Nottingham).

MILMO, Patrick Helenus; QC 1985; *b* 11 May 1938; *s* of Sir Helenus Milmo, *qv; m* 1968, Marina, *d* of late Alexis Schiray and of Xenia Schiray, rue Jules Simon, Paris; one *s* one *d. Educ:* Downside; Trinity Coll., Cambridge (BA 1961). Harmsworth Scholar; called to the Bar, Middle Temple, 1962. *Recreations:* wine, horse-racing, cinema. *Address:* 10 South Square, Gray's Inn, WC1; 7 Baalbec Road, N5. *Club:* Lansdowne.

MILNE, family name of **Baron Milne.**

MILNE, 2nd Baron, *cr* 1933, of Salonika and of Rubislaw, Co. Aberdeen; **George Douglass Milne,** TD; *b* 10 Feb. 1909; *s* of 1st Baron Milne, GCB, GCMG, DSO, Field Marshal from 1928, and Claire Marjoribanks, MBE, DGStJ (*d* 1970), *d* of Sir John N. Maitland, 5th Bt; *S* father, 1948; *m* 1940, Cicely, 3rd *d* of late Ronald Leslie; two *s* one *d. Educ:* Winchester; New Coll., Oxford. Mem., Inst. of Chartered Accountants of Scotland. Partner, Arthur Young McClelland Moores Co., 1954–73; Dir, London & Northern Group Ltd, 1973– (Dep. Chm., 1981). Master of the Grocers' Company, 1961–62. Served War of 1939–45, Royal Artillery (TA); prisoner of war, 1941; NWEF and MEF (wounded, despatches). *Recreation:* art: has exhibited RA, ROI, RP. *Heir: s* Hon. George Alexander Milne, *b* 1 April 1941. *Address:* 33 Lonsdale Road, Barnes, SW13. *T:* 01–748 6421; (business) Essex Hall, Essex Street, WC1. *T:* 01–836 9261.

MILNE, Alasdair David Gordon; Director-General of the BBC, since 1982; *b* 8 Oct. 1930; *s* of late Charles Gordon Shaw Milne and of Edith Reid Clark; *m* 1954, Sheila Kirsten Graucob; two *s* one *d. Educ:* Winchester Coll.; New Coll., Oxford (Hon. Fellow, 1985). Commnd into 1st Bn Gordon Highlanders, 1949. Hon. Mods Oxon 1952; BA Oxon Mod. Langs, 1954. Joined BBC, 1954; Dep. Editor, 1957–61, Editor, 1961–62, of Tonight Programme; Head of Tonight Productions, 1963–65; Partner, Jay, Baverstock, Milne & Co., 1965–67; rejoined BBC, Oct. 1967; Controller, BBC Scotland, 1968–72; Dir of Programmes, 1973–77; Man. Dir, 1977–82, BBC TV; Dep. Dir-Gen., BBC, 1980–82. Vice-Pres., RTS, 1986–. DUniv Stirling, 1983. *Recreations:* piping, salmon fishing, golf, tennis. *Address:* c/o BBC, Broadcasting House, W1A 1AA. *T:* 01–580 4468.

MILNE, (Alexander) Berkeley, OBE 1968; HM Diplomatic Service, retired; *b* 12 Feb. 1924; *s* of George and Mary Milne; *m* 1952, Patricia Mary (*née* Holderness); one *s* two *d. Educ:* Keith Grammar and Buckie High Schs, Banffshire, Scotland; Univ. of Aberdeen (MA (Hons Mental Phil.) 1943); University Coll., Oxford (BA (Hons Persian and Arabic) 1949). 3/2nd Punjab Regt, Indian Army: service in India and Java, 1943–46. Scarborough Schol., Tehran Univ., 1950–51; Lectr in Persian, Edinburgh Univ., 1951–52. Foreign Office, 1952–53; BMEO, Cyprus, 1953–54; Third, later Second Sec., Tehran, 1954–57; FO, 1958–61; Second, later First Sec., Brussels, 1961–64; FO (later FCO), 1964–65; First Sec., British Residual Mission, Salisbury, Rhodesia, 1966–67; First Sec., Jedda, Saudi Arabia, 1968–70; FCO, 1971–74; Counsellor, Tehran, 1974–77; GCHQ, 1978–83. Consultant, Oman Govt, 1983–86. *Recreations:* gardening, reading; playing chamber music, preferably second violin in string quartets. *Address:* 3 Paragon Terrace, Cheltenham, Glos. *T:* Cheltenham 34849.

MILNE, Alexander Taylor; Fellow of University College London; Secretary and Librarian, Institute of Historical Research, University of London, 1946–71; *b* 22 Jan. 1906; *s* of late Alexander Milne and Shanny (*née* Taylor); *m* 1960, Joyce Frederica Taylor, Dulwich. *Educ:* Christ's Coll., Finchley; University Coll., London. BA History Hons 1927; Diploma in Education, 1928; MA (London), 1930; FRHistS, 1938; Vice-Pres., Historical Assoc., 1956–70, Pres., 1970–73; Asst Officer and Librarian, Royal Historical Society, 1935–40; Hon. Librarian, 1965–70. Fellow, Huntington Library, Calif, 1975. Served War of 1939–45: Buffs and Maritime Artillery, 1940–42; Army Bureau of Current Affairs, 1942–44; Research Dept, FO, 1944–46. Director, History Today, 1962–79. *Publications:* History of Broadwindsor, Dorset, 1935; Catalogue of the Manuscripts of Jeremy Bentham in the Library of University College, London, 1937, 2nd edn 1961; Writings on British History, 1934–45: a Bibliography (8 vols), 1937–60; Centenary Guide to Pubns of Royal Historical Society, 1968; (part-author) Historical Study in the West, 1968; (ed) Librarianship and Literature, essays in honour of Jack Pafford, 1970; (ed) Correspondence of Jeremy Bentham, vols. IV and V, 1788–1797, 1981; contribs to Cambridge History of the British Empire, Encyclopædia Britannica and learned journals. *Recreation:* golf. *Address:* 9 Frank Dixon Close, Dulwich, SE21 7BD. *T:* 01–693 6942. *Clubs:* Athenæum, Dulwich (1772).

MILNE, Andrew McNicoll, MA; Editor, Conference and Common Room (HMC magazine), since 1983; *b* 9 March 1937; *s* of late John McNicoll Milne and Daviona K. Coutts; *m* 1963, Nicola Charlotte, 2nd *d* of Ian B. Anderson and Sylvia Spencer; two *d. Educ:* Bishop Wordsworth's Sch., Salisbury; Worcester Coll., Oxford (MA 1961). Oundle: apptd, 1961; Head of History Dept, 1966–70; Housemaster, 1968–75; Second Master, 1975–79; Headmaster, The King's Sch., Worcester, 1979–83. *Publications:* Metternich, 1975; contrib. to Practical Approaches to the New History. *Recreations:* music (classical and jazz), reading, writing. *Address:* Chapel Cottage, Thornage, Holt, Norfolk. *T:* Melton Constable 860928.

MILNE, Berkeley; *see* Milne, A. B.

MILNE, Denys Gordon, (Tiny), CBE 1982; Chairman, Occupational and Environmental Health-Spar Ltd, since 1986; *b* 12 Jan. 1926; *s* of late Dr George Gordon Milne and of

Margaret (*née* Campbell); *m* 1951, Pamela Mary Senior; two *s* one *d*. *Educ*: Epsom Coll.; Brasenose Coll., Oxford (MA Hons Mod. History). Pilot Officer, RAF Regt, RAFVR, 1944–47. Colonial Admin. Service, Northern Nigeria, 1951–55; British Petroleum Company, 1955–81, retired as Man. Dir and Chief Exec., BP Oil Ltd; Dir, Business in the Community, 1981–84. Director: Silkolene Lubricants Plc, 1981–; Fluor (GB) Ltd, 1981–; The Weir Group Plc, 1983–. Member: Scottish Economic Council, 1978–81; Adv. Cttee on Energy Conservation, 1980–81. President: UK Petroleum Industry Assoc., 1980–81 (Vice-Pres., 1979–80); Inst. of Petroleum, 1978–80. Trustee, Nat. Motor Mus. Member, Court of Assistants: Tallow Chandlers' Co.; Carmen's Co. *Recreations*: gardening, cruising. *Address*: Westbury, Old Lane, St Johns, Crowborough, East Sussex. *T*: Crowborough 2634. *Clubs*: Caledonian, Royal Air Force; Inanda (Johannesburg).

MILNE, Maj.-Gen. Douglas Graeme; retired; Civilian Medical Officer, Ministry of Defence, 1979–84; Deputy Director General Army Medical Services, 1975–78; *b* 19 May 1919; *s* of George Milne and Mary Panton; *m* 1944, Jean Millicent Gove; one *d*. *Educ*: Robert Gordon's Coll.; Aberdeen Univ. MB, ChB, FFCM, DPH. Commnd into RAMC, 1943; service in W Africa, Malta, Egypt, BAOR, Singapore; Dir of Army Health and Research, 1973–75. QHS 1974–78. Col Comdt, RAMC, 1979–84. OStJ 1976. *Recreations*: gardening, reading. *Address*: 17 Stonehill Road, SW14 8RR. *T*: 01–878 2828.

MILNE, Ian Innes, CMG 1965; OBE 1946; a Senior Clerk, House of Commons, 1969–76; *b* 16 June 1912; *e s* of Kenneth John Milne, CBE, and Maud Innes; *m* 1939, Marie Mange; one *d*. *Educ*: Westminster Sch.; Christ Church, Oxford. Advertising, 1935–40; RE, 1940–46 (Lieut-Col). FO, 1946–68; 2nd Sec., Teheran, 1948–51; 1st Sec., Berne, 1955–56; 1st Sec., Tokyo, 1960–63; retired 1968. US Legion of Merit (Off.), 1946. *Recreations*: cricket, music, gardening. *Address*: c/o Lloyds Bank, 79 Brompton Road, SW3.

MILNE, James L.; *see* Lees-Milne.

MILNE, Sir John (Drummond), Kt 1986; Chairman, Blue Circle Industries PLC, since 1983; Director: The Dickinson Robinson Group PLC, since 1973; Royal Insurance PLC, since 1982; *b* 13 Aug. 1924; *s* of Frederick John and Minnie Elizabeth Milne; *m* 1948, Joan Akroyd; two *s* two *d*. *Educ*: Stowe Sch.; Trinity Coll., Cambridge. Served Coldstream Guards, 1943–47. APCM (now Blue Circle Industries): management trainee, 1948; Asst to Director i/c Overseas Investments, 1953; President, Ocean Cement, Vancouver, 1957; Director, APCM, 1964, Man. Dir and Chief Exec., 1975; Chm. and Managing Director, BCI, 1983. *Recreations*: golf, shooting, ski-ing. *Address*: Chilton House, Chilton Candover, Hants. *Clubs*: Boodle's, MCC; Berkshire Golf.

MILNE, Hon. Kenneth Lancelot, CBE 1971; chartered accountant; *b* 16 Aug. 1915; *s* of F. K. Milne, Adelaide; *m* 1st, 1941, Mary (*d* 1980), *d* of E. B. Hughes; two *s* one *d*; 2nd, 1982, Joan Constance Lee, *d* of Claude W. J. Lee. *Educ*: St Peter's Coll., Adelaide. Entered Public Practice as a Chartered Acct, 1946; Elected to State Council, 1951, Chm. 1958–60, Mem. Gen. Council, 1956–60. Served with RAAF, 1940–45, attaining rank of Flt Lieut. Municipality of Walkerville: Councillor, 1960; Mayor, 1961–63; Municipal Assoc. 1961 (Pres. 1964–65); Pres. SA Br Aust. Inst. of Internat. Affairs, 1958–60; Mem. Faculty of Economics, University of Adelaide, 1963–65; Agent Gen. and Trade Comr for S Aust. in UK, 1966–71. MLC (Australian Democrat) SA, 1979–85 (Parlt Leader, 1983–85). President: SA Branch, Royal Overseas League, 1975–; Royal Life Saving Soc. of SA, 1977–. Chm., State Govt Insce Commn, 1971–79; Mem., Commn on Advanced Educn, 1973–77. Freeman, City of London, 1970. *Publications*: Ostrich Heads, 1937; Forgotten Freedom, 1952; The Accountant in Public Practice, 1959. *Recreations*: rowing, tennis, conchology. *Address*: 50 Birch Road, Stirling, SA 5152. *T*: 339 3674. *Clubs*: Adelaide, Adelaide Rowing (SA).

MILNE, Prof. Malcolm Davenport, MD, FRCP; FRS 1978; Professor of Medicine, University of London, at Westminster Medical School, 1961–80, now Emeritus; *b* 22 May 1915; *s* of Alexander Milne and Clara Lilian Milne (*née* Gee); *m* 1941 Mary Milne (*née* Thorpe); one *s* one *d*. *Educ*: Stockport Sch.; Univ. of Manchester (BSc, MD, ChB). Ho. Phys., Manchester Royal Inf., 1939–40. Served War, RAMC, 1940–46 (despatches 1942). Sen. Registrar in Med., Manchester, 1946–49; Lectr in Med.: Manchester, 1949–52; Postgrad. Med. Sch., London, 1952–61. *Publications*: numerous articles relating to renal and metabolic diseases in appropriate scientific jls. *Recreations*: horticulture, haute cuisine, mathematics. *Address*: 19 Fieldway, Berkhamsted, Herts HP4 2NX. *T*: Berkhamsted 4704. *Club*: Athenæum.

MILNE, Maurice, CB 1976; FEng 1980; Deputy Director General of Highways, Department of the Environment, 1970–76; retired; *b* 22 July 1916; *s* of James Daniel Milne, stone mason, and Isabella Robertson Milne; *m* 1947, Margaret Elizabeth Stewart Monro; one *d* decd. *Educ*: Robert Gordon's Coll., Aberdeen; Aberdeen University. BScEng (1st cl. Hons); FICE, FIStructE, FIHT, FRTPI. Chief Asst, D. A. Donald & Wishart, Cons. Engrs, Glasgow, 1947–48; Sen. Engr and Chief Engr, Crawley Develt Corp., 1948–59; Engr, Weir Wood Water Board, 1953–57; County Engr and Surveyor, W Sussex CC, 1960–68; Dir, S Eastern Road Construction Unit, MoT, 1968–70. Chairman: Downland Housing Soc. Ltd, 1978–83; London and SE Region Anchor Housing Assoc., 1982–; Humane Research Trust, 1983–. Trustee, Rees Jeffreys Road Fund, and Rees Jeffreys Vis. Lectr, Univ. of Southampton, 1976–. Hon. Sec., County Surveyors' Soc., 1963–67; Pres., Instn Highway Engineers, 1974–75; Mem. Council, ICE, 1967–71 and 1972–75; Pres., Perm. Internat. Assoc. of Road Congresses, 1977–84. *Publications*: contributions to Jl Instn of Civil, Municipal and Highway Engrs. *Recreations*: gardening, camping, hill walking, photography. *Address*: Struan, Walton Lane, Bosham, Chichester, West Sussex. *T*: Bosham 573304.

MILNE, Norman; Sheriff of North Strathclyde at Campbeltown and Oban, 1975–81, retired; *b* 31 Dec. 1915; *s* of William Milne and Jessie Ferguson; *m* 1947, Phyllis Christina Philip Rollo; no *c*. *Educ*: Logie Central Sch., Dundee. Solicitor, 1939. Army, 1939–46: active service in Madagascar, Sicily, Italy, and Germany (despatches). Procurator Fiscal Depute: Perth, 1946–51; Edinburgh, 1951–55; Senior Depute Fiscal, Glasgow, 1955–58; Procurator Fiscal: Banff, 1959–64; Kirkcaldy, 1964–65; Paisley, 1965–71; Edinburgh, 1971–75. *Recreation*: sailing. *Address*: The Anchorage, Machrihanish, Argyll.

MILNE, Peter Alexander, PhD, FIMechE, FIMarE, MNECInst; Member of the Board, British Shipbuilders, since 1981, Board Member for Merchant Ship and Enginebuilding, since 1985; *b* 23 April 1935; *s* of late Alexander Ogston Milne and of Lilian Winifred Milne (*née* Murray); *m* 1961, Beatrice Taylor Reid; two *d*. *Educ*: Tynemouth Sch.; Harwell Reactor Sch. BSc Marine Engrg Univ. of Durham 1957; PhD Applied Sci. Univ. of Newcastle 1960. Practical experience with apprenticeship at Wallsend Slipway & Engineering and at sea with Union Castle Mail Steamship; Trainee Manager, Swan Hunter Gp, 1961; Technical Dir, Swan Hunter Shipbuilders, 1970–74, Man. Dir, 1974–77; British Shipbuilders HQ at formation of Corp., 1977; Man. Dir, Shipbuilding Ops, 1978–80, Bd Mem. for Engrg, 1981–83, Man. Dir, Merchant and Composite Div., 1984, British Shipbuilders. Dir, Vosper Thornycroft, 1978–80. Bd Mem., SMTRB, 1971–75; Chm., BSI Ind. Cttee, 1972–76; Dir, Lloyds Register of Shipping, 1984–. Vis. Lectr in Marine Engrg, Newcastle Univ., 1970–75. Liveryman, Shipwrights' Co., 1984–. *Publications*: papers related to science and industry. *Recreations*: squash, cricket. *Address*: 104 Holywell Avenue, Whitley Bay, Tyne and Wear. *T*: Whitley Bay 2522708.

MILNE HOME, Captain Archibald John Fitzwilliam, DL; RN, retired; Member of Queen's Body Guard for Scotland (Royal Company of Archers) since 1963; *b* 4 May 1909; *e s* of late Sir John Milne Home; *m* 1936, Evelyn Elizabeth, *d* of late Comdr A. T. Darley, RN; three *s* one *d*. *Educ*: RNC Dartmouth. Joined RN, 1923: Comdr 1946; Captain 1952; retd 1962; ADC to the Queen, 1961–62. Chm., Whitbread (Scotland), 1968–73. Chm., SE Region, Scottish Woodland Owners Assoc., 1966–78. DL Selkirkshire, 1970. Cross of Merit, SMO Malta, 1963. *Recreations*: shooting, fishing. *Address*: Horsemill House, Bemersyde, Melrose, Roxburghshire TD6 9DP.
See also *J. G. Milne Home.*

MILNE HOME, John Gavin, TD; FRICS; Vice-Lord-Lieutenant of Dumfries and Galloway, since 1983; *b* 20 Oct. 1916; *s* of Sir John Hepburn Milne Home and Lady (Mary Adelaide) Milne Home; *m* 1942, Rosemary Elwes; two *s* one *d*. *Educ*: Wellington College; Trinity College, Cambridge. BA Estate Management. Served with King's Own Scottish Borderers (4th Bn), 1939–45 (TA 1938–49); Factor for Buccleuch Estates Ltd and Duke of Buccleuch on part of Scottish estates, 1949–74; Mem., Dumfries County Council, 1949–75; DL Dumfries 1970. *Recreations*: fishing and shooting. *Address*: Kirkside of Middlebie, Lockerbie, Dumfriesshire. *T*: Ecclefechan 204.
See also *Captain A. J. F. Milne Home.*

MILNE-WATSON, Sir Michael, 3rd Bt *cr* 1937; Kt 1969; CBE 1953; MA; Director, Rose Thomson Young (Underwriting) Ltd, since 1982; *b* 16 Feb. 1910; *yr s* of Sir David Milne-Watson, 1st Bt, and Olga Cecily (*d* 1952), *d* of Rev. George Herbert; *S* brother, 1982; *m* 1940, Mary Lisette, *d* of late H. C. Bagnall, Auckland, New Zealand; one *s*. *Educ*: Eton; Balliol Coll., Oxford. Served War of 1939–45. RNVR, 1943–45. Joined Gas Light & Coke Co., 1933; Managing Dir, 1945; Governor, 1946–49; Chairman: North Thames Gas Board, 1949–64; Richard Thomas & Baldwins Ltd, 1964–67; The William Press Group of Companies, 1969–74; a Dep. Chm., BSC, 1967–69 (Mem. Organizing Cttee, 1966–67); Mem., Iron and Steel Adv. Cttee, 1967–69. Director: Industrial and Commercial Finance Corp. Ltd, 1963–80; Commercial Union Assurance Co. Ltd, 1968–81; Finance for Industry Ltd, 1974–80; Finance Corp. for Industry Ltd, 1974–80. President: Soc. of British Gas Industries Guild, 1970–71; Pipeline Industries Guild, 1971–72. Vice-Pres., BUPA, 1981– (Chm., 1976–81). Liveryman, Grocers' Co., 1947. Governor: Council, Reading Univ., 1971–82 (Pres., 1975–80); Nuffield Nursing Homes Trust. *Heir*: *s* Andrew Michael Milne-Watson [*b* 10 Nov. 1944; *m* 1st, 1970, Beverley Jane Gabrielle (marr. diss. 1981), *e d* of Philip Cotton, Majorca; one *s* one *d*; 2nd, 1983, Gisella Tisdall; one *s*]. *Address*: 39 Cadogan Place, SW1X 9RX; Oakfield, Mortimer, Berks. *T*: Burghfield Common 2373. *Clubs*: Athenæum, MCC; Leander.

MILNER, family name of **Baron Milner of Leeds.**

MILNER OF LEEDS, 2nd Baron, *cr* 1951; **Arthur James Michael Milner,** AE 1952; Partner, Milners, Curry & Gaskell, Solicitors, London; *b* 12 Sept. 1923; *o s* of 1st Baron Milner of Leeds, PC, MC, TD and Lois Tinsdale (*d* 1982), *d* of Thomas Brown, Leeds; *S* father, 1967; *m* 1951, Sheila Margaret, *d* of Gerald Hartley, Leeds; one *s* two *d*. *Educ*: Oundle; Trinity Hall, Cambridge (MA). Served: RAFVR, 1942–46, Flt Lt; 609 (W Riding) Sqn, RAuxAF, 1947–52, Flt Lt. Admitted Solicitor, 1951. Opposition Whip, House of Lords, 1971–74. Member: Clothworkers' Co.; Pilgrims; Hon. Treas, Soc. of Yorkshiremen in London, 1967–70. *Heir*: *s* Hon. Richard James Milner, *b* 16 May 1959. *Address*: 2 The Inner Court, Old Church Street, SW3 5BY. *Club*: Royal Air Force.

MILNER, Prof. Brenda (Atkinson), OC 1984; OQ 1985; FRS 1979, FRSC 1976; Professor of Psychology, Department of Neurology and Neurosurgery, McGill University, and Head of Neuropsychology Research Unit, Montreal Neurological Institute, since 1970; *b* 15 July 1918; *d* of Samuel Langford and Clarice Frances Leslie (*née* Doig). *Educ*: Univ. of Cambridge (BA, MA, ScD); McGill Univ. (PhD). Experimental Officer, Min. of Supply, 1941–44; Professeur Agrégé, Inst. de Psychologie, Univ. de Montréal, 1944–52; Res. Associate, Psychology Dept, McGill Univ., 1952–53; Lectr, 1953–60, Asst Prof., 1960–64, Associate Prof., 1964–70, Dept of Neurology and Neurosurgery, McGill Univ. Hon. LLD Queen's Univ., Kingston, Ont, 1980; Hon. DSc: Manitoba, 1982; Lethbridge, 1986; Mount Holyoke, 1986. Izaak Walton Killam Prize, Canada Council, 1983; Hermann von Helmholtz Prize, Inst. for Cognitive Neuroscience, USA, 1984. Grand Dame of Merit, Order of Malta, 1985. *Publications*: mainly articles in neurological and psychological jls. *Address*: Montreal Neurological Institute, 3801 University Street, Montreal, Quebec H3A 2B4, Canada. *T*: (514) 284–4518.

MILNER, Sir (George Edward) Mordaunt, 9th Bt *cr* 1716; *b* 7 Feb. 1911; *er s* of Brig.-Gen. G. F. Milner, CMG, DSO; *S* cousin (Sir William Frederick Victor Mordaunt Milner, 8th Bt) 1960; *m* 1st, 1935, Barbara Audrey (*d* 1951), *d* of Henry Noel Belsham, Hunstanton, Norfolk; two *s* one *d*; 2nd, 1953, Katherine Moodie Bisset, *d* of D. H. Hoey, Dunfermline. *Educ*: Oundle. Served War of 1939–45, Royal Artillery. Stipendiary Steward, Jockey Club of South Africa, 1954–59; Steward, Cape Turf Club, 1959–75; Steward, Jockey Club of SA, 1977–80. Mem. Council, Thoroughbred Breeders Assoc., 1975–82. *Publications*: (novels) Inspired Information, 1959; Vaulting Ambition, 1962; The Last Furlong, 1965. *Heir*: *s* Timothy William Lycett Milner, *b* 11 Oct. 1936. *Address*: Natte Valleij, Klapmuts, Cape, S Africa. *T*: 02251–5171. *Clubs*: Rand (Johannesburg); Jockey Club of SA.

MILNER, Joseph, CBE 1975; QFSM 1962; Chief Officer of the London Fire Brigade, 1970–76; *b* 5 Oct. 1922; *e s* of Joseph and Ann Milner; *m* 1943, Bella Grice (*d* 1976), *e d* of Frederick George Flinton; one *s* one *d*; *m* 1976, Anne Cunningham, *e d* of J. Cunningham. *Educ*: Ladybarn Sch., Manchester. Served King's Regt (Liverpool), 1940–46: India/Burma, 1943–46 (Wingate's Chindits). Nat. Fire Service, 1946–48; North Riding Fire Bde, 1948–50; Manchester Fire Bde, 1950–51; Hong Kong Fire Bde, 1951–60; Dep. Dir, Hong Kong Fire Services, 1961–65; Dir, Hong Kong Fire Services, and Unit Controller, Auxiliary Fire Service, 1965–70. Mem., Hong Kong Council, Order of St John, 1965–70; JP Hong Kong, 1965–70. Regional Fire Commander (designate), London, 1970–76. Mem. Bd, Fire Service College, 1970–76; Mem., Central Fire Brigades Adv. Council, 1970–76; Adviser, Nat. Jt Council for Local Authority Fire Brigades, 1970–76; Chm., London Fire Liaison Panel, 1970–76; Mem., London Local Adv. Cttee, IBA, 1974–78; Fire Adviser, Assoc. of Metrop. Authorities. Vice-President: Fire Services Nat. Benevolent Fund (Chm., 1975–77); GLC Br., Royal British Legion. Mem., Caston Parish Council, 1980–; Community Controller, Civil Defence, 1981–; Fellow, Instn of Fire Engineers; Associate Mem., Inst. of British Engineers; Associate, LCSP. OStJ 1971. *Recreations*: walking, poetry, hacking, horse management, remedial therapies. *Address*: Lam Low, Caston, Attleborough, Norfolk NR17 1DD. *T*: Caston 697. *Club*: Hong Kong (Hong Kong).

MILNER, Sir Mordaunt; *see* Milner, Sir G. E. M.

MILNER, Ralph; *see* Millner, Ralph.

MILNER, Ven. Ronald James; Archdeacon of Lincoln, since 1983; *b* 16 May 1927; *s* of Maurice and Muriel Milner; *m* 1950, Audrey Cynthia Howard; two *s* two *d* (and one *d* decd). *Educ:* Hull Grammar School; Pembroke Coll., Cambridge (MA); Wycliffe Hall, Oxford. Succentor, Sheffield Cathedral, 1953–58; Vicar: Westwood, Coventry, 1958–64; St James, Fletchamstead, Coventry, 1964–70; Rector of St Mary's, Southampton, 1970–73; Rector of the Southampton Team Ministry, 1973–83. *Recreations:* ornithology, walking, music. *Address:* 2 Ashfield Road, Sleaford, Lincs. *T:* Sleaford 307149.

MILNER-BARRY, Sir (Philip) Stuart, KCVO 1975; CB 1962; OBE 1946; Ceremonial Officer, Civil Service Department (formerly Treasury), 1966–77; *b* 20 Sept. 1906; *s* of late Prof. E. L. Milner-Barry; *m* 1947, Thelma Tennant Wells; one *s* two *d*. *Educ:* Cheltenham Coll.; Trinity Coll., Cambridge (Major Schol.). 1st Class Hons, Classical Tripos (Pt I), Moral Science Tripos (Pt II). With L. Powell Sons & Co., Stockbrokers, 1929–38; Chess Correspondent, The Times, 1938–45; temporary civil servant, a Dept of the Foreign Office, 1940–45; Principal, HM Treasury, 1945; Asst Sec., 1947; Dir of Organisation and Methods, Treasury, 1954–58; Dir of Establishments and Organisation, Min. of Health, 1958–60; Under-Sec., Treasury, 1954–66. *Recreations:* Chess: British Boy Champion, 1923; British Championship Second, 1953; mem. British Internat. teams, 1937–61; Pres. British Chess Fedn, 1970–73; walking. *Address:* 43 Blackheath Park, SE3. *T:* 01–852 5808. *Club:* Brooks's.

MILNES COATES, Sir Anthony (Robert), 4th Bt *cr* 1911; BSc, MB BS, MD, MRCS, MRCP; *b* 8 Dec. 1948; *s* of Sir Robert Edward James Clive Milnes Coates, 3rd Bt, DSO, and of Lady Patricia Ethel, *d* of 4th Earl of Listowel; *S* father, 1982; *m* 1978, Harriet Ann Burton; two *d*. *Educ:* Eton; St Thomas's Hospital, London University. BSc; MRCS 1973; MB BS 1973; MRCP (UK) 1978; MD 1984. *Address:* Hereford Cottage, 135 Gloucester Road, SW7. *T:* 01–373 3451. *Club:* Brooks's.

MILNES WALKER, Robert; *see* Walker, R. M.

MILOSLAVSKY, Dimitry T.; *see* Tolstoy, Dimitry.

MILOSZ, Czeslaw; poet, author; Professor of Slavic Languages and Literatures, University of California, Berkeley, 1961–78, now Emeritus; *b* Lithuania, 30 June 1911; naturalised US citizen, 1970; *s* of Aleksander and Weronika Milosz. *Educ:* High Sch., Wilno; Univ. of Wilno. MJuris 1934. Programmer, Polish Nat. Radio, 1935–39; Mem., Polish diplomatic service, Washington, Paris, 1945–50. Vis. Lectr, Univ. of Calif, Berkeley, 1960–61. Guggenheim Fellow, 1976. Member: Polish Inst. Letters and Scis in America; PEN Club in Exile. Hon. LittD Michigan, 1977; Hon. doctorate, Catholic Univ. of Lublin, 1981. Prix Littéraire Européen, Les Guildes du Livre, Geneva, 1953; Neustadt Internat. Prize for Literature, Univ. of Oklahama, 1978; citation, Univ. of Calif, Berkeley, 1978; Nobel Prize for Literature, 1980. *Publications:* Poemat o czasie zastyglym (Poem on Time Frozen), 1933; Trzy zimy (Three Winters), 1936; Ocalenie (Rescue), 1945; Zniewolony umysl (The Captive Mind), 1953; Zdobycie wladzy, 1953, trans. as The Usurpers (in US as Seizure of Power), 1955; Dolina Issy, 1955, trans. as The Issa Valley, 1981; Swiatlo dzienne (Daylight), 1955; Traktat poetycki (Poetic Treatise), 1957; Rodzinna Europa, 1958, trans. as Native Realm, 1968; Postwar Polish Poetry, 1965; Widzenia nad Zatoka San Francisco (Views from San Francisco Bay), 1969; The History of Polish Literature, 1970; Prywatne obowiazki (Private Obligations), 1972; Selected Poems, 1973, rev. edn 1981; Ziemia Ulro (The Land of Ulro), 1977; Emperor of the Earth, 1977; Bells in Winter, 1978; Hymn o perle, 1982; Visions from San Francisco Bay, 1983; The Witness of Poetry, 1983; Separate Notebooks, 1984; The Land of Ultro, 1985. *Address:* Department of Slavic Languages and Literatures, 5416 Dwinelle Hall, University of California, Berkeley, Calif 94720, USA.

MILROY, Rev. Dominic Liston, OSB; MA; Headmaster, Ampleforth College, since 1980; *b* 18 April 1932; *s* of Adam Liston Milroy and Clarita Burns. *Educ:* Ampleforth Coll.; St Benet's Hall, Oxford (1st Cl. Mod. Langs, MA). Entered Ampleforth Abbey, 1950; teaching staff, Ampleforth Coll., 1957–74; Head of Mod. Langs, 1963–74; Housemaster, 1964–74; Prior of Internat. Benedictine Coll. of S Anselmo, Rome, 1974–79. *Address:* Ampleforth College, York YO6 4ER. *T:* Ampleforth 224.

MILSOM, Stroud Francis Charles; QC 1985; FBA 1967; Professor of Law, Cambridge University, and Fellow of St John's College, Cambridge, since 1976; *b* 2 May 1923; *yr s* of late Harry Lincoln Milsom and Isobel Vida Collins; *m* 1955, Irène, *d* of late Witold Szereszewski, Wola Krysztoporska, Poland. *Educ:* Charterhouse; Trinity Coll., Cambridge. Admiralty, 1944–45. Called to the Bar, Lincoln's Inn, 1947, Hon. Bencher, 1970; Commonwealth Fund Fellow, Univ. of Pennsylvania, 1947–48; Yorke Prize, Univ. of Cambridge, 1948; Prize Fellow, Fellow and Lectr, Trinity Coll., Cambridge, 1948–55; Fellow, Tutor and Dean, New Coll., Oxford, 1956–64; Prof. of Legal History, London Univ., 1964–76. Selden Society: Literary Dir, 1964–80; Pres., 1985–. Mem., Royal Commn on Historical Manuscripts, 1975–. Vis. Lectr, New York Univ. Law Sch., several times, 1958–70; Visiting Professor: Yale Law Sch., several times, 1968–86; Harvard Law Sch. and Dept of History, 1973; Associate Fellow, Trumbull Coll., Yale Univ., 1974–; Charles Inglis Thomson Prof., Colorado Univ. Law Sch., 1977. Maitland Meml Lectr, Cambridge, 1972; Addison Harris Meml Lectr, Indiana Univ. Law Sch., 1974; Vis. Prof. and Wilfred Fullagar Lectr, Monash Univ., 1981. Foreign Mem., Amer. Phil Soc., 1984. Hon. LLD: Glasgow, 1981; Chicago, 1985. Ames Prize, Harvard, 1972; Swiney Prize, RSA/RCP, 1974. *Publications:* Novae Narrationes (introd., trans. and notes), 1963; introd. reissue Pollock and Maitland, History of English Law, 1968; Historical Foundations of the Common Law, 1969, 2nd edn 1981; The Legal Framework of English Feudalism, 1976; Studies in the History of the Common Law (collected papers), 1985. *Address:* St John's College, Cambridge CB2 1TP; 113 Grantchester Meadows, Cambridge CB3 9JN. *T:* Cambridge 354100. *Club:* Athenæum.

MILSTEIN, César, PhD; FRS 1975; Scientific Staff of Medical Research Council, since 1963; Fellow, Darwin College, University of Cambridge, since 1981; Head, Division of Protein and Nucleic Acid Chemistry, MRC Laboratory of Molecular Biology, since 1983; *b* 8 Oct. 1927; *s* of Lázaro and Máxima Milstein; *m* 1953, Celia Prilleltensky. *Educ:* Colegio Nacional de Bahia Blanca; Univ. Nacional de Buenos Aires; Fitzwilliam Coll., Cambridge (Hon. Fellow 1982). Licenciado en Ciencias Quimicas 1952; Doctor en Quimica 1957; PhD Cantab 1960. British Council Fellow, 1958–60; Staff of Instituto Nacional de Microbiologia, Buenos Aires, 1957–63; Head of Div. de Biologia Molecular, 1961–63; Staff of MRC Laboratory of Molecular Biology, 1963–: Mem. Governing Bd, 1975–79; Head of Sub-div. of Protein Chemistry, 1969–83. For. Associate, Nat. Acad. of Scis, USA, 1981. Hon. FRCP, 1983. Biochem. Soc. Ciba Medal, 1978; Rosenstiel Medal, 1979; Avery-Landsteiner Preis, 1979; Rosenberg Prize, 1979; Mattia Award, 1979; Gross Horwitz Prize, 1980; Koch Preis, 1980; Wolf Prize in Med., 1980; Wellcome Foundn Medal, 1980; Gimenez Diaz Medal, 1981; William Bate Hardy Prize, Camb. Philos. Soc., 1981; Sloan Prize, General Motors Cancer Res. Foundn, 1981; Gairdner Award, Gairdner Foundn, 1981; Royal Medal, Royal Soc., 1982; Nobel Prize for Physiology or Medicine (with Prof. N. Jerne and Dr G. Koehler), 1984. Silver Jubilee Medal, 1977. *Publications:* original papers and review articles on structure, evolution and genetics of immunoglobulins and phosphoenzimes. *Recreations:* open air activities, cooking. *Address:* Medical Research Council Laboratory of Molecular Biology, Hills Road, Cambridge CB2 2QH. *Club:* Sefe (Cambridge).

MILSTEIN, Nathan; violinist; *b* Odessa, Russia, 31 Dec. 1904; *s* of Miron and Maria Milstein; *m* 1945, Thérèse Weldon; one *d*. *Educ:* with Prof. Stoliarsky, in Odessa; with Leopold Auer, at Royal Conservatory, St Petersburg; studied with Eugène Isaye, Le Zoot, Belgium. Many tours in Russia, 1920–26; left Russia, 1926; annual tours throughout Europe, also in North, Central and South America, from 1920, except for war years. Hon. Mem., Acad. of St Cecilia, Rome, 1963. Commandeur, Légion d'Honneur, 1983 (Officier, 1967); Ehrenkreuz, Austria, 1963. *Address:* c/o Shaw Concerts Inc., 1995 Broadway, New York, NY 10023, USA; 17 Chester Square, SW1.

MILTON, Derek Francis; HM Diplomatic Service; Minister-Counsellor, Mexico City, since 1984; *b* 11 Nov. 1935; *s* of Francis Henry Milton and Florence Elizabeth Maud Kirby; *m* 1st, 1960, Helge Kahle; two *s*; 2nd, 1977, Catherine Walmsley. *Educ:* Preston Manor County Grammar Sch., Wembley; Manchester Univ. (BA Hons Politics and Modern History, 1959). Served RAF, 1954–56. Colonial Office, 1959–63; Asst Private Sec. to Commonwealth and Colonial Sec., 1962–64; Commonwealth Prime Ministers' Meeting Secretariat, 1964; First Secretary: CRO (later FO), 1964–67; UK Mission to UN, New York, 1967–71; Rome, 1972–75; FCO, 1975–77; Counsellor: Civil Service Res. Fellow, Glasgow Univ., 1977–78; Caracas, 1978–79; Dept of Trade, 1980–82; Overseas Inspectorate, 1982–84. *Recreations:* QPR Football Club, Polish films, The Guardian, travel, languages. *Address:* c/o Foreign and Commonwealth Office, King Charles Street, SW1A 2AH.

MILTON-THOMPSON, Surg. Rear-Adm. Godfrey James, QHP 1982; FRCP; Medical Director General (Naval) and Deputy Surgeon General (Research and Training), Ministry of Defence, since 1985; *b* 25 April 1930; *s* of Rev. James Milton-Thompson and May LeMare (*née* Hoare); *m* 1952, Noreen Helena Frances, *d* of Lt-Col Sir Desmond Fitzmaurice, *qv*; three *d*. *Educ:* Eastbourne Coll.; Queens' Coll., Cambridge (MA); St Thomas' Hosp. (MB BChir); FRCP 1974 (MRCP 1961); DCH 1963. Joined Royal Navy, 1955; after general service and hosp. appts at home and abroad, Cons. Phys., RN Hosp., Plymouth, 1967–70 and 1972–75; Hon. Research Fellow, St Mark's Hosp., London, 1969–71; Prof. of Naval Medicine, 1975–80; RCDS 1981; Dep. Medical Director General (Naval), 1982–84; Surg. Rear-Adm. (Operational Med. Services), 1984–85. Member: Medical Research Soc., 1971–; British Soc. of Gastroenterology, 1972–. Errol-Eldridge Prize, 1974; Gilbert Blane Medal, 1976. CStJ 1986. *Publications:* on clinical pharmacology of the gastro-intestinal tract and therapy of peptic ulcer, etc, in med. jls. *Recreations:* fishing, paintings and painting, literature. *Address:* c/o Barclays Bank PLC, 44 High Street, Gosport, Hants. *Club:* Naval and Military.

MILVERTON, 2nd Baron *cr* 1947, of Lagos and of Clifton; **Rev. Fraser Arthur Richard Richards;** Rector of Christian Malford with Sutton Benger and Tytherton Kellaways, since 1967; *b* 21 July 1930; *s* of 1st Baron Milverton, GCMG, and Noelle Benda, *d* of Charles Basil Whitehead; *S* father, 1978; *m* 1957, Mary Dorothy, BD, *d* of late Leslie Fly, ARCM, Corsham, Wilts; two *d*. *Educ:* De Carteret Prep. Sch., Jamaica; Ridley Coll., Ontario; Clifton Coll.; Egerton Agric. Coll., Kenya; Bishop's Coll., Cheshunt. Royal Signals, 1949–50; Kenya Police, 1952–53. Deacon 1957, priest 1958, dio. Rochester; Curate: Beckenham, 1957–59; St John Baptist, Sevenoaks, 1959–60; Great Bookham, 1960–63; Vicar of Okewood with Forest Green, 1963–67. *Recreations:* family, reading, current affairs and history; enjoys music and walking; interested in tennis, swimming, cricket and Rugby Union. *Heir:* *b* Hon. Michael Hugh Richards [*b* 1 Aug. 1936; *m* 1960, Edna Leonie, *y d* of Col Leo Steveni, OBE, MC; one *s*]. *Address:* House of Lords, Westminster, SW1A 0PW.

MIMPRISS, Trevor Walter, MS; FRCS; Hon. Consultant; retired, 1970, as: Surgeon to St Thomas' Hospital; Surgeon-in-Charge, Urological Division, St Peter's Hospital, Chertsey, Surrey; *b* 12 May 1905; *s* of late S. T. Mimpriss, Bromley, Kent; *m* 1938, Eleanor Joan, *d* of Gordon Innes; two *s* one *d*. *Educ:* Brighton Coll.; St Thomas' Hospital, London Univ. FRCS 1932; MS London 1935. Cheselden Medal for Surgery, St Thomas' Hospital, 1932; Louis Jenner Research Scholarship, 1936–37. Hunterian Professor of Royal College of Surgeons, 1938. *Publications:* various papers in medical journals. *Recreations:* shooting, fishing, golf. *Address:* Muskoka, Kingsley Green, Haslemere, Surrey.

MIMS, Prof. Cedric Arthur, MD, FRCPath; Professor of Microbiology, Guy's Hospital Medical School, London, since 1972; *b* 9 Dec. 1924; *s* of A. H. and Irene Mims; *m* 1952, Valerie Vickery; two *s* two *d*. *Educ:* Mill Hill Sch.; University Coll. London (BSc (Zool)); Middlesex Hosp. Med. Sch. (MB, BS, BSc, MD). Medical Research Officer, East African Virus Research Inst., Entebbe, Uganda, 1953–56; Research Fellow and Professorial Fellow, John Curtin Sch. of Med. Research, Australian Nat. Univ., Canberra, 1957–72; Rockefeller Foundn Fellow, Children's Hosp. Med. Centre, Boston, USA, 1963–64; Visiting Fellow, Wistar Inst., Philadelphia, USA, 1969–70. *Publications:* The Biology of Animal Viruses (jtly), 1974; The Pathogenesis of Infectious Disease, 1976, rev. edn 1982; (with D. O. White) Viral Pathogenesis and Immunology, 1984; numerous papers on the pathogenesis of virus infections. *Address:* Sheriff House, Hammingden Lane, Ardingly, Sussex RH17 6SR. *T:* Ardingly 892243.

MINCHINTON, Prof. Walter Edward; Professor of Economic History, University of Exeter, 1964–86 (Head of Department, 1964–84); *b* 29 April 1921; *s* of late Walter Edward and Annie Border Minchinton; *m* 1945, Marjorie Sargood; two *s* two *d*. *Educ:* Queen Elizabeth's Hosp., Bristol; LSE, Univ. of London. 1st cl. hons BSc (Econ). FRHistS. War Service, RAOC, REME, Royal Signals (Lieut), 1942–45. UC Swansea: Asst Lectr, 1948–50; Lectr, 1950–59; Sen. Lectr, 1959–64. Rockefeller Research Fellow, 1959–60. Visiting Professor: Fourah Bay Coll., Sierra Leone, 1965; La Trobe Univ., Australia, 1981–82. Chairman: Confedn for Advancement of State Educn, 1964–67; Devon History Soc., 1967–; Exeter Industrial Arch. Gp, 1967–; SW Maritime History Soc., 1984–; British Agricultural History Soc., 1968–71 (Mem. Council, 1952–86); Export Research Group, 1971–72; Exeter Educn Cttee, 1972; Devon Historic Buildings Trust, 1980– (Mem. Council. 1967–). Pres., Assoc. for the History of the Northern Seas, 1982–; Vice-Pres., Internat. Commn for Maritime History, 1968–80 (Mem. Council, 1985–; Mem. Council, British Cttee, 1974–); Council Member: Economic History Soc., 1955–66; Soc. for Nautical Research, 1969–72, 1978–81. Alexander Prize, RHistS, 1953. General Editor: Exeter Papers in Economic History, 1964–; British Records Relating to America in Microform, 1962–. *Publications:* The British Tinplate Industry: a history, 1957; (ed) The Trade of Bristol in the Eighteenth Century, 1957; Industrial Archaeology in Devon, 1968; (ed) Politics and the Port of Bristol in the Eighteenth Century, 1963; (ed) Essays in Agrarian History, 1968; (ed) Industrial South Wales 1750–1914, essays in Welsh economic history, 1969; (ed) Mercantilism, System or Expediency?, 1969; The Growth of English Overseas Trade in the Seventeenth and Eighteenth Centuries, 1969; Wage Regulation in Pre-industrial England, 1972; Devon at Work, 1974; Windmills of Devon, 1977; (with Peter Harper) American Papers in the House of Lords Record Office: a guide, 1983; A Limekiln Miscellany: the South-West and South Wales, 1984; A Guide to Industrial Archaeological Sites in Britain, 1984; Exeter's Water Supply, 1986; Devon's Industrial

Past: a guide, 1986; articles in Econ. History Review, Explorations in Entrepreneurial History, Mariner's Mirror, Trans RHistS, etc. *Recreations:* walking, music, industrial archaeology, squash. *Address:* 53 Homefield Road, Exeter EX1 2QX. *T:* Exeter 77602.

MINFORD, Prof. (Anthony) Patrick (Leslie); Edward Gonner Professor of Applied Economics, University of Liverpool, since 1976; *b* 17 May 1943; *s* of Leslie Mackay Minford and Patricia Mary (*née* Sale); *m* 1970, Rosemary Irene Allcorn; two *s* one *d*. *Educ:* Horris Hill; Winchester Coll. (scholar); Balliol Coll., Oxford (schol.; BA); London Sch. of Economics (grad. studies; MScEcon, PhD). Economic Asst, Min. of Overseas Development, London, 1966; Economist, Min. of Finance, Malawi, 1967–69; Economic Adviser: Director's Staff, Courtaulds Ltd, 1970–71; HM Treasury, 1971–73, and HM Treasury Delegn in Washington DC, 1973–74; Visiting Hallsworth Fellow, Manchester Univ., 1974–75; Editor, NIESR Review, 1975–76. *Publications:* Substitution Effects, Speculation and Exchange Rate Stability, 1978; (jtly) Unemployment—Cause and Cure, 1983, 2nd edn 1985; Rational Expectations and the New Macroeconomics, 1983; articles in learned jls on monetary and international economics. *Address:* Department of Economic and Business Studies, University of Liverpool, PO Box 147, Liverpool L69 3BX.

MINGAY, (Frederick) Ray; Under Secretary, Investment and Development Division, Department of Trade and Industry, since 1986; *b* 7 July 1938; *s* of Cecil Stanley and Madge Elizabeth Mingay; *m* 1963, Joan Heather Roberts; three *s* one *d*. *Educ:* Tottenham Grammar Sch.; St Catharine's Coll., Cambridge (BA); London Univ. (Postgrad. Pub. Admin.). FBIM. Nat. Service (2nd Lt RAEC) 1959–61. Administration, St Thomas' Hosp., 1961; Min. of Transport, 1962–64; BoT, 1964; Chrysler (UK) Ltd, 1968–70; Consul (Commercial), Milan, 1970–73; Asst Sec., Dept of Trade, 1973–78; Counsellor (Commercial), Washington, 1978–83; Under Sec., Mechanical and Electrical Engrg Div., DTI, 1983–86. *Address:* Department of Trade and Industry, Ashdown House, 123 Victoria Street, SW1E 6RB.

MINHINNICK, Sir Gordon (Edward George), KBE 1976 (OBE 1950); Cartoonist, New Zealand Herald, 1930–76, retired; *b* 13 June 1902; *s* of Captain P. C. Minhinnick, RN, and Anne Sealy; *m* 1928, Vernor Helmore; one *s* (one *d* decd). *Educ:* Kelly Coll., Tavistock, Devon. Came to NZ, 1921; studied architecture for 4 years; Cartoonist: NZ Free Lance, 1926; Sun, Christchurch, and Sun, Auckland, 1927. *Address:* Apartment 219, Northbridge, Akoranga Drive, Northcote, Auckland, New Zealand.

MINION, Stephen, OBE 1954; JP; DL; *b* 2 June 1908; *s* of Stephen and Elizabeth Minion; *m* 1935, Ada, *d* of George and Jane Evans; no *c*. *Educ:* Liverpool Technical and Commercial Colleges. Formerly Man. Dir, The Lancashire & Cheshire Rubber Co. Ltd, retired 1980. City Councillor 1940, Alderman 1961, Lord Mayor 1969–70, Liverpool. JP Liverpool, 1954; High Sheriff Merseyside, 1976; DL Merseyside, 1976. *Recreations:* outdoor sports, reading, history, theatre and music. *Address:* Glen Cairn, 223 Booker Avenue, Liverpool L18 9TA. *T:* 051–724 2671. *Club:* Athenæum (Liverpool).

MINNITT, Robert John, CMG 1955; *b* 2 April 1913; *s* of Charles Frederick Minnitt and Winifred May Minnitt (*née* Buddle); *m* 1st, 1943, Peggy Christine Sharp (*d* 1973); one *s* two *d*; 2nd, 1975, Hon. Primrose Keighley Muncaster, *widow* of Claude Muncaster. *Educ:* Marlborough Coll.; Trinity Coll., Cambridge. Appointed to Colonial Administrative Service, Hong Kong, 1935; Chief Sec., Western Pacific High Commission, 1952–58, retired. Furniture designer and craftsman, 1960–66; temp. Civil Servant, CO, 1966; FCO, 1968–69. *Address:* Whitelocks, Sutton, Pulborough, W Sussex. *T:* Sutton 216.

MINOGUE, Hon. Sir John (Patrick), Kt 1976; QC; Law Reform Commissioner, Victoria, 1977–82; *b* 15 Sept. 1909; *s* of John Patrick Minogue and Emma Minogue; *m* 1938, Mary Alicia O'Farrell. *Educ:* St Kevin's Coll., Melbourne; Univ. of Melbourne (LLB). Australian Army, 1940–46; GSO1 HQ 1 Aust. Corps and HQ New Guinea Force, 1942–43 (mentioned in despatches); GSO1 Aust. Mil. Mission, Washington, 1945–46. Solicitor, Bendigo, 1937–39; called to the Bar, Melbourne, 1939; QC Victoria 1957, NSW 1958; Papua New Guinea: Judge, Supreme Court, 1962; Chief Justice, 1970–74. Vice-Pres., Aust. Section, Internat. Commn of Jurists, 1965–76. Member: Council and Faculty of Law, Univ. of Papua New Guinea, 1965–74 (Pro-Chancellor, 1972–74); Law Faculty, Melbourne Univ., 1975–79; Law Faculty, Monash Univ., 1977–82. Pres., Graduate Union, Melbourne Univ., 1983–86. Hon. LLD Papua New Guinea, 1974. *Recreations:* reading, conversation, golf. *Address:* 13 Millicent Avenue, Toorak, Vic 3142, Australia. *T:* (03) 240 9034. *Clubs:* Melbourne, Naval and Military, Royal Automobile of Victoria, Melbourne Cricket (Melbourne).

MINOGUE, Maj.-Gen. Patrick John O'Brien; retired; *b* 28 July 1922; *s* of Col M. J. Minogue, DSO, MC, late East Surrey Regt, and Mrs M. V. E. Minogue; *m* 1950, June Elizabeth (*née* Morris); one *s* two *d*. *Educ:* Brighton Coll.; RMCS. CBIM, FBCS, FIWSP, FIMH; jssc, psc, ato. Indian Army, 1942–46; East Surrey Regt, 1947; RAOC, 1951; served UK, BAOR, USA, Cyprus; Col, 1969; Brig., 1971; Insp. RAOC, 1971–73; Comdt, Central Ord. Depot, Bicester, 1973–75; Maj.-Gen. 1975; Comdr, Base Orgn, RAOC, 1975–78. Hon. Col, RAOC (TAVR), 1975–78; Col Comdt, RAOC, 1980–. Group Systems Controller, Lansing Bagnall Ltd, 1978–81; Chm., LT Electronics, 1979–81. *Recreations:* cricket, sailing (Cdre Wayfarer Class, UK, 1975), golf, shooting, gun-dogs, athletics. *Address:* Apartado 4, Listonero, Cortijo Grande, Turre, Almeria, Spain. *Clubs:* Army and Navy, MCC; Army Sailing Association; Milocarian Athletic; Staff College (Camberley); Cortijo Grande Golf, Spanish Golf Fedn.

MINTO, 6th Earl of, *cr* 1813; **Gilbert Edward George Lariston Elliot-Murray-Kynynmound,** OBE 1986 (MBE (mil.) 1955); Bt 1700; Baron Minto, 1797; Viscount Melgund, 1813; JP; DL; late Captain Scots Guards; *b* 19 June 1928; *er s* of 5th Earl of Minto and Marion, OBE (*d* 1974), *d* of G. W. Cook, Montreal; *S* father, 1975; *m* 1st, 1952, Lady Caroline Child-Villiers (from whom he obtained a divorce, 1965), *d* of 9th Earl of Jersey; one *s* one *d*; 2nd, 1965, Mary Elizabeth (*b* 29 Dec. 1936; *d* 24 Jan. 1983), *d* of late Peter Ballantine and of Mrs Ballantine, Gladstone, New Jersey, USA. *Educ:* Eton; RMA, Sandhurst. Served Malaya, 1949–51; ADC to C-in-C FARELF, 1951, to CIGS, 1953–55, to HE Governor and C-in-C Cyprus, 1955; transferred to RARO, 1956. Brigadier, Queen's Body Guard for Scotland (Royal Company of Archers). Director, Noel Penny Turbines Ltd, 1971–. Regional Councillor (Hermitage Div.), Borders Region, 1974–80, 1986 ; Chm., Scottish Council on Alcohol, 1973–; Dep. Traffic Comr for Scotland, 1975–81; Pres., S of Scotland Chamber of Commerce, 1980–82 (Exec. Vice-Pres., 1978–80). JP Roxburghshire, 1961–; DL Borders Region, Roxburgh, Ettrick and Lauderdale, 1983–. *Heir: s* Viscount Melgund, *qv*. *Address:* Minto, Hawick, Scotland. *T:* Denholm 321. *Club:* Puffin's (Edinburgh).

MINTO, Prof. Alfred, FRCPsych; Associate Professor of Psychiatry, University of Calgary, and Clinical Director of Forensic Psychiatry, Calgary General Hospital, Alberta, since 1986; *b* 23 Sept. 1928; *s* of Alfred Minto and Marjorie Mavor Goudie Leask; *m* 1949, Frances Oliver Bradbrook; two *s* two *d*. *Educ:* Aberdeen Central Sch.; Aberdeen Univ. (MB ChB 1951); DPM RCS&P London 1961; MRCPsych 1972, FRCPsych 1974. House Physician, Huddersfield Royal Inf., 1952; Sen. House Officer/Jun. Hosp. Med. Officer, Fairmile Hosp., Wallingford, 1952–56; Sen. Registrar, St Luke's Hosp., Middlesbrough, 1956–59; Sen. Hosp. Med. Officer, 1959–63, Conslt Psychiatrist, 1963, Mapperley Hosp., Nottingham; Conslt Physchiatrist i/c, Alcoholism and Drug Addiction Service, Sheffield RHB, 1963–68; Conslt Psychiatrist, St Ann's and Mapperley Hosps, 1968–81; Med. Dir, Rampton Hosp., 1981–85. Clinical Teacher, Nottingham Univ. Med. Sch., 1971–85; Special Lectr in Forensic Psych., Nottingham Univ., 1982–85. Conslt Psychiatrist, CS Comrs, 1964–85. *Publications:* Key Issues in Mental Health, 1982; papers on alcoholism, community care, toxoplasmosis. *Recreations:* books, people. *Address:* Calgary General Hospital, Department of Psychiatry, #G2–039 841 Centre Avenue East, Calgary, Alberta T2E 0A1, Canada.

MINTOFF, Hon. Dominic, (Dom), BSc, BE&A, MA, A&CE; MP; MLA (Malta Labour Party), since 1947; Prime Minister of Malta, 1971–84; Leader of Labour Party, 1949–84; *b* Cospicua, 6 Aug. 1916; *s* of Lawrence Mintoff and late Concetta (*née* Farrugia); *m* 1947, Moyra de Vere Bentick; two *d*. *Educ:* Govt Elem. Sch., Seminary and Lyceum, Malta; Univ. of Malta (BSc 1937; BE&A, A&CE 1939); Hertford Coll., Oxford (Govt Travelling Scholar; Rhodes Scholar; MA Engrg Science). Practised as civil engineer in Britain, 1941–43, and as architect in Malta, 1943–. Gen. Sec. Malta Labour Party, 1936–37; Mem., Council of Govt and Exec. Council, 1945; Dep. Prime Minister and Minister for Works and Reconstruction, 1947–49 (resigned); Prime Minister and Minister of Finance, 1955–58; resigned office in 1958 to lead the Maltese Liberation Movement; Leader of Opposition, 1962–71; Minister of Foreign Affairs, 1971–81; Minister of the Interior, 1976–81 and 1983–84. Mem., Labour delegns to UK, 1945, 1947, 1948 and 1949. Negotiated removal of British Military base, 1971 and other foreign mil. bases by 1979. Dr *hc* Univ. of Pol. Studies, Ponterios, Greece, 1976. Order of the Republic, Libya, 1971; Grand Cordon: Order of the Republic, Tunisia, 1973; Order of Oissam Alaouite, 1978. *Publications:* scientific, literary and artistic works. *Recreations:* horse-riding, swimming, water skiing, boċċi. *Address:* The Olives, Tarxien, Malta.

MINTON, Yvonne Fay, CBE 1980; mezzo-soprano; *er d* of R. T. Minton, Sydney; *m* 1965, William Barclay; one *s* one *d*. *Educ:* Sydney Conservatorium of Music. Elsa Stralia Scholar, Sydney, 1957–60; won Canberra Operatic Aria Competition, 1960; won Kathleen Ferrier Prize at s'Hertogenbosch Vocal Competition, 1961. Joined Royal Opera House as a Principal Mezzo-Soprano, 1965. Major roles include: Octavian in Der Rosenkavalier; Dorabella in Cosi Fan Tutte; Marina in Boris Godounov; Helen in King Priam; Cherubino in Marriage of Figaro; Orfeo in Gluck's Orfeo; Sextus in La clemenza di Tito; Dido in The Trojans at Carthage; Kundry in Parsifal; Charlotte in Werther; Countess Geschwitz in Lulu. Recordings include Octavian in Der Rosenkavalier, Mozart Requiem, Elgar's The Kingdom, etc. Guest Artist with Cologne Opera Company, Oct. 1969–. Hon. RAM 1975. *Recreations:* reading, gardening. *Address:* c/o Ingpen and Williams, 14 Kensington Court, W8. *T:* 01–937 5158.

MIQUEL, Raymond Clive, CBE 1981; Chairman and Chief Executive, Belhaven Brewery Group plc, since 1986; *b* 28 May 1931; *m* 1958; one *s* two *d*. *Educ:* Allan Glen's Sch., Glasgow; Glasgow Technical Coll. Joined Arthur Bell & Sons Ltd as Works Study Engineer, 1956; Production Controller, 1958; Production Director, 1962; Dep. Managing Director, 1965; Man. Dir, 1968–85; Dep. Chairman, 1972; Chm., 1973–85. Chairman: Towmaster Transport Co. Ltd, 1974–86; Canning Town Glass Ltd, 1974–86; Wellington Importers Ltd, 1984–86; Gleneagles Hotels PLC, 1984–86. Vis. Prof. in Business Develt, Glasgow Univ., 1985–. *Address:* Whitedene, Caledonian Crescent, Gleneagles, Perthshire, Scotland. *T:* Auchterarder 2642.

MIRON, Wilfrid Lyonel, CBE 1969 (OBE 1945; MBE 1944); TD 1950; JP; DL; Regional Chairman (Midlands), National Coal Board, 1967–76 and Regional Chairman (South Wales), 1969–76; National Coal Board Member (with Regional responsibilities), 1971–76; *b* 27 Jan. 1913; *s* of late Solman Miron and late Minnie Pearl Miron; *m* 1958, Doreen (*née* Hill); no *c*. *Educ:* Llanelli Gram. Sch. Admitted Solicitor, 1934; private practice and Legal Adviser to Shipley Collieries and associated companies. TA Commn, Sherwood Foresters, 1939; served War of 1939–45: Home Forces, 1939; France and Dunkirk, 1940; IO 139 Inf. Bde and GSO3 Aldershot Dist, 1941–42; Staff Coll., Quetta, 1942 (SC); DAAG 17 Ind. Div., 1943–44, and AA&QMG 17 Ind. Div., 1944–45, Chin Hills, Imphal, Burma (despatches, 1944). E Midlands Div. NCB: Sec. and Legal Adviser, 1946–51; Dep. Chm., 1951–60; Chm., 1960–67. Pres., Midland Dist Miners' Fatal Accident Relief Soc.; Chairman: E Mids Regional Planning Council, 1976–79 (Mem., 1965–76); (part-time), Industrial Tribunals, 1976–85. Dir, Nottingham Theatre Trust Ltd. Freeman (by redemption) City of London; Master, Pattenmakers' Company, 1979–80. Hon. Lieut-Col. JP Notts, 1964 (Chairman: Nottingham PSD, 1982–83; Notts Magistrates' Cts Cttee, 1981–83); DL Notts, 1970. FRSA 1965. OStJ 1961. *Publications:* Bitter Sweet Seventeen, 1946; articles and papers in mining and other jls. *Recreations:* cricket, music, reading, crosswords. *Address:* Briar Croft, School Lane, Halam, Newark, Notts. *T:* Southwell 812446. *Clubs:* Army and Navy, MCC; XL; Nottingham and Notts United Services (Nottingham).

MIRRLEES, Prof. James Alexander, FBA 1984; Edgeworth Professor of Economics, University of Oxford, and Fellow of Nuffield College, since 1968; *b* 5 July 1936; *s* of late George B. M. Mirrlees; *m* 1961, Gillian Marjorie Hughes; two *d*. *Educ:* Douglas-Ewart High Sch., Newton Stewart; Edinburgh Univ.; Trinity Coll., Cambridge. MA Edinburgh Maths, 1957; BA Cantab Maths, 1959; PhD Cantab Econs, 1963. Adviser, MIT Center for Internat. Studies, New Delhi, 1962–63; Cambridge Univ. Asst Lectr in Econs and Fellow of Trinity Coll., 1963, University Lectr, 1965; Adviser to Govt of Swaziland, 1963; Res. Assoc., Pakistan Inst. of Develt Econs, Karachi, 1966–67. Vis. Prof., MIT, 1968, 1970, 1976. Mem., Treasury Cttee on Policy Optimisation, 1976–78. Econometric Society: Fellow, 1970; Vice-Pres., 1980, Pres., 1982. For. Hon. Mem., Amer. Acad. of Arts and Scis, 1981; Hon. Mem., Amer. Economic Assoc., 1982. Hon. DLitt Warwick, 1982. *Publications:* (joint author) Manual of Industrial Project Analysis in Developing Countries, 1969; (ed jtly) Models of Economic Growth, 1973; (jt author) Project Appraisal and Planning, 1974; articles in economic jls. *Recreations:* reading detective stories and other forms of mathematics, playing the piano, travelling, listening. *Address:* Nuffield College, Oxford; 11 Field House Drive, Oxford OX2 7NT. *T:* Oxford 52436.

MIRRLEES, Robin Ian Evelyn Stuart de la Lanne-; Richmond Herald of Arms, 1962–67; *b* Paris, 13 Jan. 1925; grandson of Ambassador La Lanne; godson of 11th Duke of Argyll; one *s*. *Educ:* Merton Coll., Oxford (MA). Several language diplomas. Served India, 1942–46; Captain RA, 1944; Gen. Staff, New Delhi, 1946; Embassy Attaché, Tokyo, 1947; Rouge Dragon Pursuivant of Arms, 1952–62 (and as such attended Coronation). Co-editor, Annuaire de France, 1966–. ADC to HM the King of Yugoslavia, 1963–70. Has raised substantial funds for humanitarian organisations; undertook restoration of Inchdrewer Castle, Scotland, and others; Laird of Island of Bernera, pop. 350. Freeman of City of London, 1960. Patrician of San Marino, 1964. Succeeded to the title of Comte de Lalanne (France), 1962 and titular Prince of Coronata. Various foreign orders of knighthood. *Recreations:* foxhunting, piloting, travelling, painting, sculpture, mystic philosophy. *Address:* 25 Holland Park Avenue, W11; 115 Rue de la Pompe, Paris 16me; Inchdrewer Castle, Banff, Scotland; Villa Lambins-Lalanne, Le Touquet, France;

Schloss Ratzenegg, Carinthia, Austria. *Clubs:* Buck's; Puffin's (Edinburgh); Travellers' (Paris).

MIRVISH, Edwin, OC; *b* 24 July 1914; *s* of David and Anna Mirvish; *m* 1941, Anne Maklin; one *s*. *Educ:* Toronto. Proprietor: Ed Mirvish Enterprises and other cos; several restaurants; Royal Alexandra Theatre, Toronto; Old Vic Theatre, 1982–. Hon. LLD Trent Univ., 1967; Hon. PhD Univ. of Waterloo, 1969; Fellow, Ryerson Technical Inst., 1981. Award of Merit, City of Toronto. *Recreation:* ballroom dancing. *Address:* 581 Bloor Street West, Toronto, Ontario M6G 1K3, Canada. *T:* 416–537–2111. *Clubs:* Empire, Canadian, Arts and Letters, Variety (Toronto).

MISCAMPBELL, Norman Alexander, QC 1974; MP (C) Blackpool North since 1962; barrister; a Recorder of the Crown Court, since 1977; *b* 20 Feb. 1925; *s* of late Alexander and Eileen Miscampbell; *m* 1961, Margaret Kendall; two *s* two *d*. *Educ:* St Edward's Sch., Oxford; Trinity Coll., Oxford. Called to Bar, Inner Temple, 1952, Bencher 1983; N Circuit. Mem., Hoylake UDC, 1955–61. Contested (C) Newton, 1955, 1959. *Address:* House of Commons, SW1; 7 Abbey Road, West Kirby, Wirral, Merseyside.

MISCHLER, Norman Martin; Chairman: Hoechst UK Ltd, 1975–84; Hoechst Ireland Ltd, 1976–84; Berger Jenson & Nicholson Ltd, 1979–84; *b* 9 Oct. 1920; *s* of late Martin Mischler and Martha Sarah (*née* Lambert); *m* 1949, Helen Dora Sinclair; one *s* one *d*. *Educ:* St Paul's Sch., London; St Catharine's Coll., Cambridge (MA). Cricket Blue, 1946. Indian Army, 1940; served in Burma Campaign; released, rank of Major, 1946. Joined Burt, Boulton & Haywood, 1947, Vice-Chm. 1963; Dep. Man. Dir, Hoechst UK Ltd, 1966; Chairman: Harlow Chemical Co. Ltd, 1972–74; Kalle Infotec Ltd, 1972–74; Director: Berger, Jenson & Nicholson Ltd, 1975–84; Ringsdorff Carbon Co. Ltd, 1968–84; Vice-Chm., German Chamber of Industry and Commerce in London, 1974–84; Mem. Council, Chemical Industries Assoc. Ltd, 1975–84. Liveryman, Paviors Co.; Freeman, City of London. Officer's Cross, German Order of Merit, 1985. *Recreations:* cricket, opera, and theatre. *Address:* Scott House, Earsham Street, Bungay, Suffolk. *Club:* Hawks (Cambridge).

MISHCON, family name of **Baron Mishcon.**

MISHCON, Baron *cr* 1978 (Life Peer), of Lambeth in Greater London; **Victor Mishcon;** DL; Solicitor; Senior Partner, Victor Mishcon & Co.; *b* 14 Aug. 1915; *s* of Rabbi Arnold and Mrs Queenie Mishcon; *m* 1976, Joan Estelle Conrad; two *s* one *d* by previous marr. *Educ:* City of London Sch. Mem. Lambeth Borough Coun., 1945–49 (Chm. Finance Cttee, 1947–49); Mem. London CC for Brixton, 1946–65 (Chairman: Public Control Cttee, 1947–52; Gen. Purposes Cttee, 1952–54; Council, April 1954–55; Supplies Cttee, 1956–57; Fire Brigade Cttee, 1958–65); Mem. GLC for Lambeth, 1964–67 (Chm., Gen. Purposes Cttee, 1964–67). Mem., Inner London Educn Authority, 1964–67. Chm. Governors, Cormont and Loughborough Secondary Schools, 1947–60; Governor: Stockwell Manor Sch., 1960–78 (Chm. of Governors, 1960–67, 1970–78); JFS Comprehensive Sch., 1970–85; Philippa Fawcett Coll. of Educn, 1970–80. Member: Standing Joint Cttee, Co. of London Sessions, 1950–65 (Vice-Chm. 1959–61); Nat. Theatre Board, 1965–67, 1968– (Mem., Finance and General Purposes Cttee); South Bank Theatre Board, 1977–82; London Orchestra Bd, 1966–67; Exec. Cttee, London Tourist Board, 1965–67; Government Cttee of Enquiry into London Transport, 1953–54; Departmental Cttee on Homosexual Offences and Prostitution, 1954–57; Jt Cttee with House of Commons on Consolidation of Bills, 1983–85; Law Sub-Cttee, House of Lords European Communities Cttee, 1978–86; House of Lords Select Cttee on Procedure, 1981–83. Vice-Chm., Council of Christians and Jews, 1976–77; Vice-Pres., Bd of Deputies of British Jews, 1967–73; Chm., Inst. of Jewish Studies, UCL; Hon. President, Brit. Technion Soc.; Mem. Bd of Governors, Technion, Israel; Vice-Pres. (Past Pres.) Assoc. of Jewish Youth; Pres., British Council of the Shaare Zedek Hosp., Jerusalem. Contested (Lab) NW Leeds, 1950, Bath, 1951, Gravesend, 1955, 1959. DL Greater London. Comdr Royal Swedish Order of North Star, 1954; Star of Ethiopia, 1954. *Address:* House of Lords, SW1.

MISKIN, Sir James (William), Kt 1983; QC 1967; **His Honour Judge Sir James Miskin;** Recorder of London, since 1975; *b* 11 March 1925; *s* of late Geoffrey Miskin and Joyce Miskin; *m* 1st, 1951, Mollie Joan Milne; two *s* two *d*; 2nd, 1980, Sheila Joan Collett, widow. *Educ:* Haileybury; Brasenose Coll., Oxford (MA). Sub-Lt, RNVR, 1943–46. Oxford, 1946–49 (Sen. Heath Harrison Exhibnr). Called to Bar, Inner Temple, 1951; Bencher, 1976; Mem. of Bar Council, 1964–67, 1970–73. Dep. Chm., Herts QS, 1968–71; a Recorder of the Crown Court, 1972–75; Leader of SE Circuit, 1974–75. City of London Magistrate, 1976. Chm., Bd of Discipline, LSE, 1972–75. Appeals Steward, British Boxing Bd of Control, 1972–75; Chm., Inner London Probation After Care Cttee, 1979–. One of HM Lieutenants, City of London, 1976–. Liveryman, Worshipful Co. of Curriers; Hon. Liveryman, Worshipful Co. of Cutlers. *Recreations:* golf, gardening. *Clubs:* Vincent's (Oxford); All England Lawn Tennis.

MISKIN, Raymond John, CEng, FIMechE, FIProdE, MRAeS, FIQA; Secretary, Institution of Production Engineers, since 1976; *b* 4 July 1928; *s* of late Sydney George Miskin and Hilda (*née* Holdsworth); *m* 1951 (marr. diss. 1981); one *d* (one *s* decd). *Educ:* Woking Grammar Sch.; Southall Technical Coll. The Fairey Aviation Co. Ltd: apprentice, 1945–49; develt engr, 1949–59; Dep. Chief Inspector, 1959–63; Quality Control Manager and Chief Inspector, Graviner Ltd, 1963–69; Sec., Inst. of Qual. Assurance, 1969–73; Dep. Sec., IProdE, 1973–76. Dir, IPRODE Ltd, 1976–. Mem. Council and Hon. Treasurer, Inst. of Qual. Assurance, 1963–69; Member: Bd, Nat. Council for Qual. and Reliability, 1969–81 (Chm., 1975–77); Amer. Soc. for Qual. Control. Hon. FIIPE 1979. Liveryman, Engineers' Co. Freeman, City of London. Internat. Industrial Management Award, San Fernando Valley Engineers Council, USA, 1978; Internat. Achievement Award, Los Angeles Council of Engrs, 1981; GTE (Hungary) Technical Achievement Medal, 1984. *Publications:* articles in technical pubns. *Recreation:* golf. *Address:* Institution of Production Engineers, 66 Little Ealing Lane, W5 4XX. *Clubs:* Athenæum; Burhill Golf (Surrey).

MISSELBROOK, (Bertram) Desmond, CBE 1972; FRSE 1978; Chairman, Livingston Development Corporation, 1972–78; *b* 28 May 1913; *s* of late C. J. and E. P. Misselbrook; *m* 1949, Anne, *er d* of late F. O. Goodman; two *s*. *Educ:* Chatham House, Ramsgate; Bristol Univ. Admiralty Psychologist, 1942–45. Lectr in Psychology and Dir, Unit of Applied Psychology, Edinburgh Univ., 1945–49; Senr Res. Fellow in Business Studies, 1970–71, Hon. Fellow, 1971. Personnel Adviser, 1949, Dir. 1955, Dep. Chm. 1963–70, British-American Tobacco Co. Ltd; Chm., Evershed and Vignoles Ltd, 1961–65; Chm., Mardon Packaging International Ltd, 1962–70; Dir, 1963, Dep. Chm. 1966–69, Wiggins Teape Ltd; Dir, Charterhouse Gp Ltd, 1969–72; Deputy Chairman: Standard Life Assurance Co., 1977–80 (Dir, 1970–84); Anderson Mavor Ltd, 1971–74; Chairman: Anderson Strathclyde Ltd, 1974–77; Seaforth Maritime Ltd, 1977–78. Mem. Council, British Inst. of Management, 1967–72 (a Vice-Chm., 1969); Chairman: Bd of Governors, Oversea Service, 1963–70; Construction Ind. Trng Bd, 1970–73; Council, Scottish Business Sch., 1972–77; Economic Development Cttees for Building and Civil Engineering Industries, 1969–72; Member: Adv. Council on Social Work (Scotland), 1970–74; Economic Consultant, Scottish Office, 1970–72. Hon. DSc Edinburgh, 1977. *Recreations:* fishing, gardening, walking. *Address:* Kenbank House, Dalry, Castle Douglas, Kirkcudbrightshire DG7 3TX. *T:* Dalry 424.

MITCHAM, Heather, (Mrs Anthony Mitcham); a Metropolitan Stipendiary Magistrate, since 1986; *b* 19 Dec. 1941; *d* of Louis George Pike and Dorothy Evelyn (*née* Milverton); *m* 1964, Anthony John Mitcham; one *s* one *d*. *Educ:* The King's Sch., Ottery St Mary. Called to the Bar, Gray's Inn, 1964. Examiner, Estate Duty Office, 1960–67; Dep. Chief Clerk, Inner London Magistrates' Court Service, 1967–78; Chief Clerk, Inner London Juvenile Courts, 1978–85; Senior Chief Clerk: Thames Magistrates' Court, 1985; S Western Magistrates' Court, 1986. *Recreations:* riding, horses, gardening. *Address:* c/o Magistrates' Court, Bow Street, WC2E 7AS.

MITCHELL, Adrian; writer; *b* 24 Oct. 1932; *s* of James Mitchell and Kathleen Fabian. *Educ:* Greenways Sch.; Dauntsey's Sch.; Christ Church, Oxford. Worked as reporter on Oxford Mail, Evening Standard, 1955–63; subseq. free-lance journalist for Daily Mail, Sun, Sunday Times, New Statesman; Granada Fellow, Univ. of Lancaster, 1968–69; Fellow, Center for Humanities, Wesleyan Univ., 1972; Resident Writer, Sherman Theatre, Cardiff, 1974–75; Vis. writer, Billericay Comp. Sch., 1978–80; Judith E. Wilson Fellow, Cambridge Univ., 1980–81; Resident writer, Unicorn Theatre for Children, 1982–83. *Plays:* Marat/Sade (stage adaptation), RSC, 1964; Tyger, NT, 1971; Man Friday, 7:84 Theatre Co., 1973 (TV 1972, Screenplay 1975); Mind Your Head, Liverpool Everyman, 1973; Daft as a Brush (TV), 1975; A Seventh Man, Hampstead, 1976; White Suit Blues, Nottingham, Edinburgh and Old Vic, 1977; Houdini, Amsterdam, 1977; Glad Day (TV), 1978; Uppendown Mooney, Welfare State Theatre Co., 1978; The White Deer, Unicorn Theatre, 1978; Hoagy, Bix and Wolfgang Beethoven Bunkhaus, King's Head Theatre, 1979; In the Unlikely Event of an Emergency, Bath, 1979; Peer Gynt (adaptation), Oxford Playhouse, 1980; The Mayor of Zalamea (adaptation), NT, 1981; You Must Believe All This (TV), 1981; The Tragedy of King Real, Welfare State Theatre Co., 1982; Mowgli's Jungle, Contact Theatre, Manchester, 1982; A Child's Christmas in Wales (with Jeremy Brooks), Great Lakes Fest., 1983; The Wild Animal Song Contest, Unicorn Theatre, 1983; Life's a Dream (adaptation with John Barton), RSC Stratford, 1983, Barbican, 1984; Animal Farm (lyrics), NT, 1984; C'Mon Everybody, Tricycle Theatre, 1984; The Great Theatre of the World (adaptation), Mediaeval Players, 1984; The Government Inspector, NT, 1985; Satie Day/Night, Lyric Studio, Hammersmith, 1986. *Publications: novels:* If You See Me Comin', 1962; The Bodyguard, 1970; Wartime, 1973; *poetry:* Poems, 1964; Out Loud, 1968; Ride the Nightmare, 1971; The Apeman Cometh, 1975; For Beauty Douglas, (Collected Poems 1953–1979), 1982; On the Beach at Cambridge, 1984; Nothingmas Day, 1984; *for children:* The Baron Rides Out, 1985; The Baron on the Island of Cheese, 1986; also plays. *Address:* c/o Fraser and Dunlop Scripts Ltd, 91 Regent Street, W1R 8RU. *Clubs:* Ronnie Scott's; Royal Free Hospital Recreation.

MITCHELL, Alec Burton, MA; CEng, MIMechE, FRINA; Director, Admiralty Marine Technology Establishment, 1977–84, retired; Scientific Adviser to Director General Ships, Ministry of Defence, 1981–84; *b* 27 Aug. 1924; *er s* of Ronald Johnson Mitchell and Millicent Annie Mitchell; *m* 1952, Barbara, *d* of Arthur Edward and Katie Florence Jane Archer; three *s*. *Educ:* Purley County Sch.; St. John's Coll., Cambridge (MA). Mechanical Sciences Tripos, Cambridge, 1944. Aeronautical Engineer with Rolls Royce Ltd, Hucknall, 1944–46; Grad. apprentice and gas turbine design engr with English Electric Co Ltd, Rugby, 1946–48. Joined RN Scientific Service, 1948; Dep. Head of Hydrodynamic Research Div., Admty Research Lab., 1961; promoted Dep. CSO, 1966; Dep. Dir, Admty Research Laboratory, 1973, Dir, 1974–77. *Publications:* numerous scientific papers on hydrodynamics and under-water propulsion systems. *Recreations:* golf, photography, wood-work. *Address:* 32 Ormond Crescent, Hampton, Mddx TW12 2TH.

MITCHELL, Alexander Graham, CBE 1973; DFM 1945; *b* 2 Nov. 1923; *s* of Alexander Mitchell and Evelyn Mitchell (*née* Green); *m* 1954, Pamela Ann Borman; three *d*. *Educ:* Dulwich College; Downing Coll., Cambridge (Exhibnr; MA). Served RAF, 1942–45. Clerk to Governors, Dame Allan's Schs, Newcastle. Sudan Government Civil Service, 1951–55; HM Overseas Civil Service, 1955; Western Pacific High Commission: various posts in British Solomon Islands Protectorate and British Residency, New Hebrides, 1955–71; Sec., Financial Affairs, British Residency, 1968–71; Administrator, Turks and Caicos Is, 1971–73, Governor 1973–75; sabbatical, 1975–76, retired June 1977. *Recreations:* ancient and military history. *Address:* The Dene, Stocksfield, Northumberland NE43 7PB. *Club:* Royal Over-Seas League.

MITCHELL, Angus; *see* Mitchell, J. A. M.

MITCHELL, Air Cdre Sir (Arthur) Dennis, KBE 1977; CVO 1961; DFC 1944, and Bar, 1945; AFC 1943; an Extra Equerry to the Queen since 1962; *b* 26 May 1918; 2nd *s* of Col A. Mitchell, DSO, Carrickfergus, Belfast, N Ireland; *m* 1949, Comtesse Mireille Caroline Cornet de Ways Ruart; one *s*. *Educ:* Nautical Coll., Pangbourne; RAF Coll., Cranwell; Army Staff Coll., Camberley; RAF Flying Coll., Manby. Joined RAF, 1936. Served 1938–45, India, Burma, UK and NW Europe; RAF Delegn, Belgium, 1948–49; US Air Force, 1951–53; HQ Allied Air Forces Central Europe, NATO, Fontainebleau, 1953–56; o/c RAF Cottesmore Bomber Comd, 1959–62; Dep. Captain and Captain of the Queen's Flight, 1956–59 and 1962–64; ADC to the Queen, 1958–62. Founder: Brussels Airways; Aero Distributors SA; Aero Systems SA; Gen. Agent, Spantax SA. French Croix de Guerre, 1945. *Recreation:* golf. *Address:* 10 chemin des Chasseurs, 1328 Ohain, Belgium. *T:* 653.13.01; (office) (2)653.00.33. *Clubs:* Royal Air Force, Naval and Military.

MITCHELL, Austin Vernon, DPhil; MP (Lab) Great Grimsby, since 1983 (Grimsby, Apr. 1977–1983); *b* 19 Sept. 1934; *s* of Richard Vernon Mitchell and Ethel Mary Mitchell; *m* 1st, Patricia Dorothea Jackson (marr. diss.); two *d*; 2nd, Linda Mary McDougall; one *s* one *d*. *Educ:* Woodbottom Council Sch.; Bingley Grammar Sch.; Manchester Univ. (BA, MA); Nuffield Coll., Oxford (DPhil). Lectr in History, Univ. of Otago, Dunedin, NZ, 1959–63; Sen. Lectr in Politics, Univ. of Canterbury, Christchurch, NZ, 1963–67; Official Fellow, Nuffield Coll., Oxford, 1967–69; Journalist, Yorkshire Television, 1969–71; Presenter, BBC Current Affairs Gp, 1972–73; Journalist, Yorkshire TV, 1973–77. *Publications:* New Zealand Politics In Action, 1962; Government By Party, 1966; The Whigs in Opposition 1815–1830, 1969; Politics and People in New Zealand, 1970; Yorkshire Jokes, 1971; The Half-Gallon Quarter-Acre Pavlova Paradise, 1974; Can Labour Win Again, 1979; Westminster Man, 1982; The Case for Labour, 1983; Four Years in the Death of the Labour Party, 1983. *Recreation:* worriting (*sic*). *Address:* 1 Abbey Park Road, Grimsby, South Humberside; House of Commons, SW1. *T:* 01–219 4559. *Clubs:* Willows Social (Grimsby); AEU (Saltaire, Shipley).

MITCHELL, Prof. Basil George, DD; FBA 1983; Nolloth Professor of the Philosophy of the Christian Religion, Oxford University, 1968–84; Fellow of Oriel College, 1968–84, now Emeritus; *b* 9 April 1917; *s* of George William Mitchell and Mary Mitchell (*née* Loxston); *m* 1950, Margaret Eleanor Collin; one *s* three *d*. *Educ:* King Edward VI Sch., Southampton; Queen's Coll., Oxford (Southampton Exhibitioner. 1st cl. Lit Hum 1939).

Served Royal Navy, 1940–46; Lt RNVR 1942, Instructor Lt RN 1945. Lectr, Christ Church, Oxford, 1946–47; Fellow and Tutor in Philosophy, Keble Coll., Oxford, 1947–67, Emeritus Fellow, 1981; Sen. Proctor, 1956–57; Hebdomadal Council, 1959–65. Vis. Prof., Princeton Univ., 1963; Stanton Lectr in Philosophy of Religion, Cambridge Univ., 1959–62; Edward Cadbury Lectr, University of Birmingham, 1966–67; Gifford Lectr, Glasgow Univ., 1974–76; Nathaniel Taylor Lectr, Yale, 1986. Vis. Prof., Colgate Univ., 1976. Member: C of E Working Parties on Ethical Questions, 1964–78; Doctrine Commn, 1978–84. Chm., Ian Ramsey Centre, 1985–. Hon. DD Glasgow, 1977; Hon. DLitHum Union Coll., Schenectady, 1979. *Publications:* (ed) Faith and Logic, 1957; Law, Morality and Religion in a Secular Society, 1967; Neutrality and Commitment, 1968; (ed) The Philosophy of Religion, 1971; The Justification of Religious Belief, 1973; Morality: Religious and Secular, 1980; articles in philosophical and theological periodicals. *Address:* Bridge House, Wootton, Woodstock, Oxford. *T:* Woodstock 811265.

MITCHELL, Bob; *see* Mitchell, R. C.

MITCHELL, Charles Julian Humphrey; *see* Mitchell, Julian.

MITCHELL, Lt-Col Colin (Campbell); former soldier and politician; *b* 17 Nov. 1925; *o s* of Colin Mitchell, MC, and Janet Bowie Gilmour; *m* 1956, Jean Hamilton Susan Phillips; two *s* one *d.* *Educ:* Whitgift Sch. British Army, 1943; commissioned Argyll and Sutherland Highlanders, 1944, serving in Italy (wounded); Palestine, 1945–48 (wounded); Korea, 1950–51; Cyprus, 1958–59; Borneo, 1964 (brevet Lt-Col); Aden, 1967 (despatches). Staff appts as ADC to GOC-in-C Scottish Command; Directorate of Mil. Ops (MO4), WO; Qualified Camberley Staff Coll., 1955; subsequently: GSO2, 51st Highland Div. (TA); Bde Major, King's African Rifles, and GSO1 Staff of Chief of Defence Staff at MoD. Retired at own request, 1968; subseq. Special Correspondent, Vietnam; specially employed: Rhodesia, 1975–79; Mexico, 1980; Afghanistan, 1983. MP (C) W Aberdeenshire, 1970–Feb. 1974 (not seeking re-election); PPS to Sec. of State for Scotland, 1972–73. Vice-Pres., Royal Scottish Country Dance Soc. Freedom of City of London, 1979. *Publication:* Having Been A Soldier, 1969. *Recreations:* reading, travel. *Address:* Hill House, Swanton Morley, Dereham, Norfolk NR20 4QB. *T:* Swanton Morley 206. *Club:* Garrick.

MITCHELL, David Bower; MP (C) Hampshire North West, since 1983 (Basingstoke, 1964–83); Minister of State for Transport, since 1986; *b* June 1928; *er s* of James Mitchell, Naval Architect; *m* 1954, Pamela Elaine Haward; two *s* one *d.* *Educ:* Aldenham. Farming, 1945–50; businessman, wine merchant, 1951–79. An Opposition Whip, 1965–67; PPS to Sec. of State for Social Services, 1970–74; Parly Under Sec. of State, DoI, 1979–81, NI Office, 1981–83, Dept of Transport, 1983–85. Chm., Cons. Smaller Business Cttee, 1974–79. *Recreations:* gardening, wine-tasting. *Address:* 46 Eaton Terrace, SW1. *T:* 01–730 4470. *Club:* Carlton.

MITCHELL, Sir Dennis; *see* Mitchell, Sir A. D.

MITCHELL, Sir Derek (Jack), KCB 1974 (CB 1967); CVO 1966; Senior Adviser, Shearson Lehman Brothers International, since 1979; Director: Bowater Industries PLC (formerly Bowater Corporation), since 1979; Bowater Inc., since 1984; Standard Chartered PLC, since 1979; Independent Director, The Observer Ltd, since 1981; *b* 5 March 1922; *s* of late Sidney Mitchell, Schoolmaster, and Gladys Mitchell; *m* 1944, Miriam, *d* of late F. E. Jackson; one *s* two *d.* *Educ:* St Paul's Sch.; Christ Church, Oxford. Served War of 1939–45: Royal Armoured Corps and HQ London District, 1942–45. Asst Principal HM Treasury, 1947; Private Sec. to Economic Sec., 1948–49; Private Sec. to Permanent Sec. and Official Head of Civil Service (Sir Edward Bridges), 1954–56; Principal Private Sec. to: Chancellor of Exchequer (Mr Reginald Maudling), 1962–63; The Prime Minister (Mr Harold Wilson, previously Sir Alec Douglas-Home), 1964–66; Under-Sec., 1964; Dep. Under-Sec. of State, Dept of Economic Affairs, 1966–67; Dep. Sec., Min. of Agriculture, Fisheries and Food, 1967–69; Economic Minister and Head of UK Treasury and Supply Delegn, Washington, (also UK Executive Director for IMF and IBRD), 1969–72; Second Permanent Sec. (Overseas Finance), HM Treasury, 1973–77. Dir, Guinness Mahon & Co., 1977–78; Mem., PLA, 1979–82. Member: Council, University Coll., London, 1978–82; Nat. Theatre Bd, 1977–; Treasurer, Nat. Theatre Foundn, 1982–; Governing Trustee, Nuffield Provincial Hospitals Trust, 1978–. *Recreations:* opera, theatre, concerts, travel. *Address:* 9 Holmbush Road, Putney, SW15 3LE. *T:* 01–788 6581. *Club:* Garrick.
See also E. F. Jackson.

MITCHELL, Douglas Svärd; Controller of Personnel and Administrative Services, Greater London Council, 1972–78; *b* 21 Aug. 1918; *er s* of late James Livingstone Mitchell and Hilma Josefine (*née* Svärd); *m* 1943, Winifred Thornton Paterson, *d* of late William and Ellen Paterson; one *s* two *d.* *Educ:* Morgan Academy, Dundee. Royal Ordnance Factories, 1937–51; Principal, Min. of Supply, 1951–55; Dir of Personnel and Admin., in Industrial, Production and Engineering Groups, UKAEA, 1955–63; Authority Personnel Officer for UKAEA, 1963–64; Dir of Establishments, GLC, 1964–72. *Address:* The Manor House, Horncastle, Lincolnshire. *T:* Horncastle 3553.

MITCHELL, Prof. Edgar William John, CBE 1976; FRS 1986; Dr Lee's Professor of Experimental Philosophy, Oxford University and Fellow of Wadham College, Oxford, since 1978; Chairman, Science and Engineering Research Council, since 1985; *b* Kingsbridge, S Devon, 25 Sept. 1925; *s* of late Edgar and Caroline Mitchell; *m* 1985, Prof. Margaret Davies (*née* Brown); one *s* by previous *m.* *Educ:* Univs of Sheffield (BSc, MSc) and Bristol (PhD). FInstP. Metropolitan Vickers Research Dept, 1946–48, 1950–51; Univ. of Bristol, 1948–50; Univ. of Reading, 1951–78; Prof. of Physics, 1961–78; Dean, Faculty of Science, 1966–69; Dep. Vice-Chancellor, 1976–78. Member: SERC (formerly SRC), 1970–74, 1982–85 (Mem., 1965–70, Chm., 1967–70, Physics Cttee; Chm., Neutron Beam Res. Cttee, 1966–74; Mem., Nuclear Physics Bd, 1980–); Management Bd, British National Space Centre, 1986–; devised scheme for extensive University use of nuclear res. reactors for condensed matter res. Acting Jt Dir, 1973, Mem., 1973–, Sci. Council of Inst. Laue-Langevin, Grenoble; Member: Comité de Direction, Solid State Physics Lab., Ecole Normale and Univ. of Paris VI, 1975–79; Exec. Cttee, Univ. Council for Non-Academic Staff, 1979–82; UGC Phys. Sci. Cttee, 1982–85; Council, Inst. of Physics, 1982–; Chairman: SE Reg. Computing Cttee, 1974–76; Science Planning Gp for Spallation Neutron Source, 1980 85. *Publications:* numerous papers on solid state physics. *Recreations:* good food, opera, motoring, physics. *Address:* Clarendon Laboratory, Parks Road, Oxford OX1 3PU; Science and Engineering Research Council, Polaris House, North Star Avenue, Swindon SN2 1ET.

MITCHELL, Mrs Eric; *see* Shacklock, Constance.

MITCHELL, Ewan; *see* Janner, Hon. G. E.

MITCHELL, Rear-Adm. Geoffrey Charles, CB 1973; retired 1975; Director, The Old Granary Art and Craft Centre, Bishop's Waltham, Hants, since 1976; *b* 21 July 1921; *s* of William C. Mitchell; *m* 1955, Jocelyn Rainger, Auckland, NZ; one *s* two *d.* *Educ:* Marlborough College. Joined RN 1940; Captain 1961; Director Officer Recruiting, 1961–63; Captain (F), 2nd Frigate Sqdn, 1963–65; Director Naval Ops and Trade, 1965–67; Comdr, NATO Standing Naval Force Atlantic, 1968–69; Director Strategic Policy, to Supreme Allied Comdr Atlantic, 1969–71; Rear Adm. 1971; Dep. Asst Chief of Staff (Ops), SHAPE, 1971–74; Chm., RNR and Naval Cadet Forces Review Bd, 1974–75. *Recreations:* golf, tennis, painting, music, languages, sailing. *Address:* Willowpool, Lockhams Road, Curdridge, Southampton. *T:* Botley 2403.

MITCHELL, Prof. George Archibald Grant, OBE 1945; TD 1950; Professor of Anatomy and Director of Anatomical Laboratories, Manchester University, 1946–74, now Professor Emeritus; late Dean of Medical School and Pro-Vice-Chancellor; *b* 11 Nov. 1906; *s* of George and Agnes Mitchell; *m* 1933, Mary Cumming; one *s* two *d.* *Educ:* Fordyce Academy; Aberdeen Central Sch.; Aberdeen Univ. MB, ChB (1st Cl. Hons), 1929; ChM 1933; MSc (Manchester); DSc (Aberdeen) 1950; FRCS 1968. Lecturer in Anatomy, 1930–33, in Surgery, 1933–34, Aberdeen Univ.; Surgical Specialist, Co. Caithness, 1934–37; Sen. Lecturer in Anatomy, Aberdeen Univ., 1937–39. Chm., Internat. Anatomical Nomenclature Commn, 1970–75. Pres., 3rd European Anatomical Congress; Pres., S Lancs and E Cheshire BMA Br. Council, 1972–73; Mem. Ct of Examnrs, RCS, 1950–68; Mem. Bd of Governors, United Manchester Hosps, 1955–74; Past President: Anatomical Soc. of GB and Ireland; Manchester Med. Soc. Served War, 1939–45: Surgical Specialist, Officer i/c No. 1 Orthopædic Centre, MEF; Officer i/c Surgical Divs, Adviser in Penicillin and Chemotherapy, 21 Army Gp. Hon. Alumnus, Univ. of Louvain, 1944; Hon. Member: Société Med. Chir. du Centre; Assoc. des Anatomistes; Amer. Assoc. Anat.; British Assoc. Clin. Anat. Chevalier First Class Order of the Dannebrog. *Publications:* The Anatomy of the Autonomic Nervous System, 1952; Basic Anatomy (with E. L. Patterson), 1954; Cardiovascular Innervation, 1956; ed Symposium, Penicillin Therapy and Control in 21 Army Group, 1945. Sections in: Penicillin (by Sir A. Fleming), 1946; Medical Disorders of the Locomotor System (by E. Fletcher), 1947; British Surgical Practice (by Sir Rock Carling and Sir J. Patterson Ross), 1951; Peripheral Vascular Disorders (by Martin, Lynn, Dible and Aird), 1956; Essentials of Neuroanatomy, 1966; Encyclopaedia Britannica, 15th edn; Editor, Nomina Anatomica, 1966. Numerous articles in Jl Anatomy, British Jl Surg., Jl Bone and Joint Surg., Brit. Jl Radiol., BMJ, Lancet, Acta Anat., Nature, Brit. Jl Urol., Edinburgh Medical Jl, Jl Hist. Med., Aberdeen Univ. Rev., Ann. Méd. Chir. du Centre, etc. *Recreations:* music, studying archaeology. *Address:* 16 Fellpark Road, Northern Moor, Manchester M23 0EU. *T:* 061–998 8579.

MITCHELL, George Francis, FRS 1973; MRIA; Pro-Chancellor, University of Dublin, since 1985; *b* 15 Oct. 1912; *s* of late David William Mitchell and late Frances Elizabeth Kirby; *m* 1940, Lucy Margaret Gwynn; two *d.* *Educ:* High Sch., Dublin; Trinity Coll., Dublin (MA, MSc); FTCD 1945. Joined staff of Trinity Coll., Dublin, 1934; Professor of Quaternary Studies, 1965–79. Pres., Internat. Union for Quaternary Research, 1969–73. MRIA 1939, PRIA 1976–79. HRHA 1981; Hon. Life Mem., RDS, 1981; Hon. Member: Prehistoric Soc., 1983; Quaternary Res. Assoc., 1983; Hon. FRSE 1984. DSc (*hc*): Queen's Univ., Belfast, 1976; NUI, 1977; fil.D (*hc*) Uppsala, 1977. *Publications:* The Irish Landscape, 1976; Treasures of Early Irish Art, 1977. *Address:* Townley Hall, Drogheda, Co. Louth, Republic of Ireland. *T:* Drogheda 38218.

MITCHELL, Sir Hamilton, KBE 1969; Barrister and Solicitor, in private practice, New Zealand; *b* 24 Feb. 1910; *s* of Ernest Hamilton Mitchell and Catherine Mitchell; *m* 1st, 1938, Marion Frances Norman; two *s* one *d*; 2nd, 1980, Dorothy Good. *Educ:* Auckland Grammar Sch.; New Zealand Univ. (LLM). Practice on own account, 1941–. Served 2nd NZEF, 1943–46 (Captain, Egypt and Italy). President: Disabled Servicemen's Re-establishment League, 1959–63; NZ Returned Services Assoc., 1962–74; Vice-President: World Veterans' Fedn, 1964–66; British Commonwealth Ex-Services League, 1962–74; Judge, Courts Martial Appeal Court, 1962–82; Dep. Chm., Winston Churchill Trust, 1966–76; Chairman: National Art Gallery Management Council, 1967–73; Canteen Fund Bd, 1967–84; NZ Patriotic Fund, 1970–84; Nat. War Meml Council, 1973–; War Pensions Appeal Bd, 1978–83; Dep. Chm., Rehabilitation League, NZ, 1970–86. Pres., Wellington Show Assoc., 1980–85. *Address:* 78 Orangikaupapa Road, Wellington, New Zealand. *T:* 757224. *Clubs:* Wellesley (Wellington); Royal New Zealand Yacht Squadron.

MITCHELL, Harold Charles, CIE 1947; Indian Police (retired); *b* 7 March 1896; *s* of late Daniel Charles Mitchell and late Helen Mitchell; *m* 1923, Edna Evadne Bion (*d* 1982); one *d.* *Educ:* Fairfield. RNVR, Bristol, 1912–19 (Pay Lt). Joined Indian Police, 1920; served as Dist Supt of Police, Bareilly, Benares, Cawnpore, Meerut and other UP districts; Central Intelligence Officer, UP and Ajmer, Home Dept Govt of India; Special Branch, CID, UP; Dep. Inspector-Gen. of Police, CID, UP; Personal Asst to Inspector-Gen. of Police, UP; Dep. Inspector-Gen. of Police, UP HQ and Railways. Pres., Indian Police (UK) Assoc, 1979–. *Recreations:* formerly golf, fishing. *Address:* 41 Clarefield Court, North End Lane, Sunningdale, Ascot, Berks. *T:* Ascot 23962. *Club:* Naval.

MITCHELL, Harvey Allan; Head of Cultural and International Services, Lothian Regional Council, 1975–83; *b* 23 Sept. 1932; *s* of Robert Mutter Mitchell and Margaret Massey Mitchell; *m* 1970, Karin Katharina Rapp, Tailfingen, Germany; two *s* one *d.* *Educ:* Edinburgh Univ. (MA Hons). Freelance Journalist, 1955–56; Press Officer, Rank Organization, 1956–58; Sen. Staff, Voice & Vision, 1958–60; Sen. Staff, Barnet & Reef (NY), 1961; Public Relations Administrator, Merck & Co., New York and Brussels, 1962–65; Asst to Vice-Pres., Massey-Ferguson (Toronto), 1965–67. Gen. Manager, New Philharmonia Orch., 1968–72; Dir of Develt, Tayside, 1972–75; Dir, Scottish Occupational Health Service, 1972; Chm., Duntrune House Develts Ltd, 1972. *Publications:* articles on philosophy and the arts. *Recreations:* tennis, bridge, travel.

MITCHELL, Helen Josephine; *see* Watts, H. J.

MITCHELL, Ian Edward; Manager, CKS Products Ltd, since 1982; *b* 24 Dec. 1932; *s* of George Thomas Mitchell and Lorna May Mitchell. *Educ:* Queensland, Australia. Town Clerk's Dept, Brisbane City Council, 1953–65; Gen. Sec., British Film Producers Assoc. Ltd, 1966–81; Co. Sec. and Dir, Central Casting Ltd, 1970–81; Administrator, Fedn of Specialised Film Producers Assocs, 1970–80. Manager, Vicars Saunderson and Partners, 1981–82. *Recreations:* amateur theatricals, opera, swimming, tennis.

MITCHELL, James; writer these many years; *b* South Shields, 12 March 1926; *s* of James Mitchell and Wilhelmina Mitchell; *m* 1968, Delia, *d* of Major and Mrs K. J. McCoy; two *s.* *Educ:* South Shields Grammar Sch.; St Edmund Hall, Oxford (BA 1948, MA 1950); King's Coll., Newcastle upon Tyne, Univ. of Durham (DipEd 1950). Worked in rep. theatre, 1948, then in shipyard, travel agency and Civil Service; taught for some fifteen years in almost every kind of instn from secondary modern sch. to coll. of art. Free-lance writer: novels; more than a hundred television scripts; several screenplays and a theatre play. *Publications:* Here's a Villain, 1957; A Way Back, 1959; Steady Boys, Steady, 1960; Among Arabian Sands, 1963; The Man Who Sold Death, 1964; Die Rich, Die Happy, 1965; The Money that Money can't Buy, 1967; The Innocent Bystanders, 1969; Ilion like a Mist, 1969; A Magnum for Schneider, 1969; The Winners, 1970; Russian Roulette, 1973; Death and Bright Water, 1974; Smear Job, 1975; When the Boat Comes In, 1976; The Hungry Years, 1976; Upwards and Onwards, 1977; The Evil Ones, 1982; Sometimes

You Could Die, 1985; Dead Ernest, 1986. *Recreations:* travel, military history, aristology. *Address:* 15 Zetland House, Marloes Road, W8 5LB. *Club:* Lansdowne.

MITCHELL, James; Social Security Commissioner, since 1980; *b* 11 June 1926; *s* of James Hill Mitchell and Marjorie Kate Mitchell (*née* Williams); *m* 1957, Diane Iris Mackintosh; two *d.* *Educ:* Merchiston Castle Sch., Edinburgh; Brasenose Coll., Oxford, 1944–45 and 1948–51 (Open Exhibnr, BCL, MA). Served RAFVR, 1945–48. Assistant Master, Edge Grove Preparatory Sch., Herts, 1952–55; called to the Bar, Middle Temple, 1954; private practice as barrister/solicitor, Gold Coast/Ghana, 1956–58; practice as barrister, London, 1958–80. Most Hon. Order of Crown of Brunei, 3rd Cl. 1959, 2nd Cl. 1972. *Recreations:* sailing, walking, railways, the Jacobites. *Address:* (office) 6 Grosvenor Gardens, SW1W 0DH. *T:* 01–730 9236.

MITCHELL, Rt. Hon. James Fitzallen; PC 1985; MP for the Grenadines, since 1966; Prime Minister of St Vincent and the Grenadines, since 1984; *b* 15 May 1931; *s* of Reginald and Lois Mitchell; *m* 1965, Patricia Parker; three *d.* *Educ:* Imperial College of Tropical Agriculture (DICTA); University of British Columbia (BSA). Agronomist, 1958–65; owner, Hotel Frangipani, Bequia, 1966–; Minister of Trade, Agriculture and Tourism, 1967–72; Premier, 1972–74. Order of the Liberator, Venezuela, 1972. *Publication:* World Fungicide Usage, 1967. *Recreations:* farming, yachting, windsurfing. *Address:* Bequia, St Vincent, West Indies. *T:* 809–458–3263. *Club:* Bequia Sailing.

MITCHELL, (James Lachlan) Martin, RD 1969; Sheriff of Lothian and Borders (formerly Lothians and Peebles), since 1974 (as a floating Sheriff, 1974–78, and at Edinburgh, 1978); *b* 13 June 1929; *o s* of late Dr L. M. V. Mitchell, OBE, MB, ChB and Harriet Doris Riggall. *Educ:* Cargilfield; Sedbergh; Univ. of Edinburgh. MA 1951, LLB 1953. Admitted Mem. Faculty of Advocates, 1957; Standing Junior Counsel in Scotland to Admty Bd, 1963–74. Nat. Service, RN, 1954–55; Sub-Lt (S) RNVR 1954; Perm. Reserve, 1956; Comdr RNR 1966, retd 1974. *Recreations:* fishing, photography, gramophone. *Address:* 3 Great Stuart Street, Edinburgh EH3 6AP. *T:* 031–225 3384. *Club:* New (Edinburgh).

MITCHELL, Jeremy George Swale Hamilton; Under Secretary, and Director, National Consumer Council, 1977–86; *b* 25 May 1929; *s* of late George Oswald Mitchell and late Agnes Josephine Mitchell; *m* 1956, Margaret Mary Ayres (separated); three *s* one *d.* *Educ:* Ampleforth; Brasenose and Nuffield Colls, Oxford (MA). Dep. Research Dir, then Dir of Information, Consumers' Assoc. (Which?), 1958–65; Asst Sec., Nat. Econ. Develt Office, 1965–66; Scientific Sec., then Sec., SSRC, 1966–74; Under Sec., and Dir of Consumer Affairs, Office of Fair Trading, 1974–77. Mem., Economic Devt Cttee for the Distributive Trades, 1981–; Vice-Chm., Nat. Council on Gambling, 1981–. *Publications:* (ed) SSRC Reviews of Research, series, 1968–73; (ed jtly) Social Science Research and Industry, 1971; Betting, 1972; (ed) Marketing and the Consumer Movement, 1978. *Recreation:* Swinburne. *Address:* 214 Evering Road, E5 8AJ.

MITCHELL, Prof. Joan Eileen, (Mrs James Cattermole); Professor of Political Economy, University of Nottingham, 1978–85; *b* 15 March 1920; *d* of late Albert Henry Mitchell, Paper Merchant, and Eva Mitchell; *m* 1956, James Cattermole; one *s* one *d.* *Educ:* Southend-on-Sea High Sch.; St Hilda's Coll., Oxford. Economist, Min. of Fuel and Power, 1942; Tutor, St Anne's Coll., Oxford, 1945; Economist, BoT, 1947; Research Officer, Labour Party, 1950; Lectr in Econs, Nottingham Univ., 1952, Reader in Econs, 1962. Mem., NBPI, 1965–68; personal economic adviser to Sec. of State for Prices and Consumer Protection, 1974–76. Member: Cttee to Review the Functioning of Financial Institutions, 1977–80 (Chm. Res. Panel); Standing Commn on Pay Comparability, 1979–81. *Publications:* Britain in Crisis 1951, 1963; Groundwork to Economic Planning, 1966; The National Board for Prices and Incomes, 1972; Price Determination and Prices Policy, 1978. *Recreations:* gardening, cooking, highbrow music. *Address:* 15 Ranmoor Road, Gedling, Nottingham. *Club:* National Liberal.

MITCHELL, (John) Angus (Macbeth), CB 1979; CVO 1961; MC 1946; Secretary, Scottish Education Department, 1976–84; *b* 25 Aug. 1924; *s* of late John Fowler Mitchell, CIE and of Sheila Macbeth, MBE; *m* 1948, Ann Katharine Williamson; two *s* two *d.* *Educ:* Marlborough Coll.; Brasenose Coll., Oxford (Junior Hulme Scholar); BA Modern Hist., 1948. Served Royal Armoured Corps, 1943–46: Lieut, Inns of Court Regt, NW Europe, 1944–45; Captain East African Military Records, 1946. Entered Scottish Education Dept, 1949; Private Sec. to Sec. of State for Scotland, 1958–59; Asst Sec., Scottish Educn Dept, 1959–65; Dept of Agriculture and Fisheries for Scotland, 1965–68; Scottish Development Dept, 1968; Asst Under-Secretary of State, Scottish Office, 1968–69; Under Sec., Social Work Services Gp, Scottish Educn Dept, 1969–75; Under Sec., SHHD, 1975–76. Chairman: Scottish Marriage Guidance Council, 1965–69; Working Party on Social Work Services in NHS, 1976; Working Party on Relationships between Health Bds and Local Authorities, 1976; Consultative Cttee on the Curriculum, 1976–80; Stirling Univ. Court, 1984–; Scottish Action on Dementia, 1985–; Mem., Commn for Local Authority Accounts in Scotland, 1985–. Hon. Fellow, Edinburgh Univ. Dept of Politics, 1984–. Hon. LLD Dundee, 1983. Kt, Order of Oranje-Nassau (Netherlands), 1946. *Recreations:* old Penguins; genealogy. *Address:* 20 Regent Terrace, Edinburgh EH7 5BS. *T:* 031–556 7671. *Clubs:* Royal Commonwealth Society; New (Edinburgh).

MITCHELL, John Gall, QC (Scot.) 1970; a Social Security (formerly National Insurance) Commissioner, since 1979; *b* 5 May 1931; *s* of late Rev. William G. Mitchell, MA; *m* 1959, Anne Bertram Jardine (*d* 1986); three *s* one *d.* *Educ:* Royal High Sch., Edinburgh; Edinburgh Univ. (MA, LLB). Advocate 1957. Standing Junior Counsel, Customs and Excise, Scotland, 1964–70; Chairman: Industrial Tribunals, Scotland, 1966–80; Legal Aid Supreme Court Cttee, Scotland, 1974–79; Pensions Appeals Tribunal, Scotland, 1974–80. Hon. Sheriff of Lanarkshire, 1970–74. *Address:* Rosemount, Park Road, Eskbank, Dalkeith, Midlothian.

MITCHELL, John Matthew, CBE 1976; PhD; Assistant Director-General, 1981–84, Senior Research Fellow, 1984–85, British Council; retired; *b* 22 March 1925; *s* of Clifford George Arthur Mitchell and Grace Maud Jamson; *m* 1952, Eva Maria von Rupprecht; three *s* one *d.* *Educ:* Ilford County High Sch.; Worcester Coll., Oxford; Queens' Coll., Cambridge (MA). PhD Vienna. Served War, RN, 1944–46. British Council: Lectr, Austria, 1949–52 and Egypt, 1952–56; Scotland, 1957–60; Dep. Rep., Japan, 1960–63; Reg. Dir, Zagreb, 1963–66; Reg. Rep., Dacca, 1966–69; Dep. Controller, Home Div., 1969–72; Rep., Federal Republic of Germany, 1973–77; Controller, Educn, Medicine and Sci. Div., 1977–81. Vis. Fellow, Wolfson Coll., Cambridge, 1972–73; former Lectr, univs of Vienna, Cairo and Tokyo. Mem., Inst. of Linguists. *Publications:* International Cultural Relations, 1986; verse, short stories and trans. from German. *Recreations:* ski-ing, theatre, cinema, opera. *Address:* The Cottage, Pains Hill Corner, Pains Hill, Limpsfield, Surrey. *T:* Limpsfield Chart 3354. *Clubs:* National Liberal; Tandridge Golf.

MITCHELL, Prof. John Richard Anthony, FRCP; Foundation Professor of Medicine, Nottingham Medical School, since 1967; Consultant Physician, Nottingham Hospitals, since 1968; *b* 20 Oct. 1928; *s* of Richard and Elizabeth Mitchell; *m* 1954, Muriel Joyce Gibbon; two *s* two *d.* *Educ:* Manchester Univ. (BSc, MB ChB, MD); St Catherine's Coll., Oxford (MA, DPhil). Junior clinical posts, Manchester, 1953–54; Medical Specialist, RAMC, 1955–57; Registrar and Lectr, Regius Prof., Oxford, 1957–61; MRC Research Fellow, Oxford, 1961–63; First Asst, Oxford, 1963–68; Fellow, Linacre Coll., Oxford, 1964–68; Adviser in general medicine to DHSS, 1968–81. Pres., Assoc. of Physicians of GB and Ireland, 1982–83. Chm., Atherosclerosis Discussion Gp, 1986–. *Publications:* Arterial Disease, 1965; numerous papers on aspects of vascular disease. *Recreations:* music, getting on to water (sea and canal), local history, natural history, arguing. *Address:* Department of Medicine, University Hospital, Nottingham NG7 2UH. *T:* Nottingham 700111.

MITCHELL, John Wesley, FRS 1956; PhD, DSc; Senior Research Fellow and Emeritus Professor, University of Virginia, since 1979; *b* 3 Dec. 1913; *s* of late John Wesley Mitchell and late Lucy Ruth Mitchell; *m* 1976, Virginia Hill; one step *d* of former marriage. *Educ:* Canterbury University Coll., Christchurch, NZ; Univ. of Oxford. BSc 1934. MSc 1935, NZ; PhD 1938, DSc 1960, Oxford. Reader in Experimental Physics in the Univ. of Bristol, 1945–59; Prof. of Physics, Univ. of Virginia, 1959–63; Dir of the National Chemical Laboratory, Oct. 1963–Aug. 1964; William Barton Rogers Prof. of Physics, Univ. of Virginia, 1964–79. *Publications:* various on photographic sensitivity and on plastic deformation of crystals in scientific journals. *Recreations:* mountaineering, colour photography. *Address:* Department of Physics, University of Virginia, Charlottesville, Virginia 22901, USA. *Clubs:* Athenæum; Cosmos (Washington, DC).

MITCHELL, Joseph Rodney; Director General of Defence Accounts, Ministry of Defence, 1973, retired; *b* 11 March 1914; *s* of late Joseph William and Martha Mitchell, Sheffield; *m* 1936, Marian Richardson; two *s* three *d.* *Educ:* Sheffield Central Secondary School. FCCA, ACMA, ACIS. Works Recorder and Junior Costs Clerk, United Steel Cos Ltd, Sheffield, 1930–35; Senior Accounts Clerk, Cargo Fleet Iron Co. Ltd, Middlesbrough, 1936–39; Royal Ordnance Factories, 1940–55: Chief Exec. Officer, 1951–55; Min. of Supply/Aviation/Technology, 1956–71: Dir of Accounts, 1967–71; Dep. Dir Gen. of Defence Accounts, MoD, 1971–72. *Recreation:* hill-walking. *Address:* 4 Orchard Court, Hathersage Road, Grindleford, Sheffield S30 1JH.

MITCHELL, Prof. Joseph Stanley, CBE 1951; FRS 1952; FRCP; Emeritus Regius Professor of Physic, University of Cambridge, since 1975; engaged on work in the Research Laboratories of the Clinical School, Radiotherapeutic Centre, Addenbrooke's Hospital, Cambridge; Fellow, St John's College, Cambridge, 1936–39, and since 1943; *b* 22 July 1909; *s* of late Joseph Brown Mitchell and Ethel Maud Mary Arnold, Birmingham; *m* 1934, Dr Lilian Mary Buxton, MA, MB, ChB (*d* 1983); one *s* one *d.* *Educ:* Marlborough Road Council Sch., Birmingham; King Edward's High Sch., Birmingham; Univ. of Birmingham (Nat. Scis Tripos Pt II, Cl. I Physics, 1931); St John's Coll., Cambridge (MB, BChir 1934; MA 1935; PhD 1937; MD 1957). DMR RCS 1943; FFR 1954; MRCP 1956, FRCP 1958. Formerly House Physician, Gen. Hosp., Birmingham; Beit Meml Med. Res. Fellow, Colloid Science Lab., Cambridge, 1934–37; Resident Radiological Officer, Christie Hosp., Manchester, 1937–38; Radiotherapist, EMS, 1939; Univ. of Cambridge: Asst in Res. in Radiotherapy, Dept of Medicine, 1938; Regius Prof. of Physic, 1957–75; Prof. of Radiotherapeutics, 1946–57 and 1975–76; Dir, Radiotherapeutic Centre, Addenbrooke's Hospital, Cambridge, 1943–76; i/c med. investigations, National Res. Council Lab., Montreal, 1944–45. Chm. 1971–77 and Vice-Chm. 1977–79, Faith Courtauld Unit for Human Studies in Cancer, KCH, London; Leverhulme Emeritus Fellow, Univ. of Cambridge Clinical Sch., Res. Lab, 1976–77; Hon. Consultant, AEA, 1951–. Pres., British Section, Anglo-German Med. Soc., 1959–68; Hon. Mem., German Roentgen Soc., 1967; Foreign Fellow, Indian Natural Science Acad., 1975. Linacre Lectr, St John's Coll., Cambridge, 1970. DSc (*hc*) Birmingham, 1958. Pirogoff Medal, Acad. of Medicine, USSR, 1967. *Publications:* Studies in Radiotherapeutics, 1960; Cancer, if curable why not cured?, 1971; (with M. Cohen) Cobalt 60 Teletherapy: a compendium of international practice, 1984; papers in scientific and med. jls on mechanism of therapeutic action of radiations and on develt of radioactive compounds for treatment of cancer. *Recreations:* walking, modern languages. *Address:* Thorndyke, Huntingdon Road, Girton, Cambridge CB3 0LG. *T:* Cambridge 276102; Research Laboratories, Radiotherapeutic Centre, Addenbrooke's Hospital, Hills Road, Cambridge CB2 2QQ. *T:* Cambridge 243619.

MITCHELL, Julian; writer; *b* 1 May 1935; *s* of late William Moncur Mitchell and of Christine Mary (*née* Browne). *Educ:* Winchester; Wadham Coll. Oxford. Mem., Literature Panel, Arts Council, 1966–69. John Llewellyn Rhys Prize, 1965; Somerset Maugham Award, 1966. *Publications: novels:* Imaginary Toys, 1961; A Disturbing Influence, 1962; As Far As You Can Go, 1963; The White Father, 1964; A Circle of Friends, 1966; The Undiscovered Country, 1968; *biography:* (with Peregrine Churchill) Jennie: Lady Randolph Churchill, 1974; *translation:* Henry IV (Pirandello), 1979 (John Florio Prize, 1980); *plays:* Half-Life, 1977; The Enemy Within, 1980; Another Country, 1981 (SWET play of the year, 1982; filmed, 1984); Francis, 1983; After Aida (or Verdi's Messiah), 1986; (adapted from Ivy Compton-Burnett): A Heritage and Its History, 1965; A Family and a Fortune, 1975. Television plays include: Shadow in the Sun; A Question of Degree; Rust; Abide With Me (Internat. Critics Prize, Monte Carlo, 1977); adaptations of: Persuasion; The Alien Corn; Staying On; The Good Soldier; The Mysterious Stranger; The Weather in the Streets; series, Jennie, Lady Randolph Churchill, 1974. *Recreations:* local history, fishing. *Address:* 2 Castle Rise, Llanvaches, Newport, Gwent NP6 3BS. *T:* Newport 400848.

MITCHELL, Keith Kirkman, OBE; Lecturer in Physical Education, University of Leeds, since 1955; *b* 25 May 1927; *s* of John Stanley Mitchell and Annie Mitchell; *m* 1950, Hannah Forrest; two *s.* *Educ:* Loughborough Coll. (Hons Dip. in Physical Educn). Phys. Educn Master, Wisbech Grammar Sch., 1950–52; Dir of Phys. Recreation, Manchester YMCA, 1952–55. Chm. Exec. Cttee, CCPR, 1981–; Mem., Sports Council, 1976–. Dir, 1953–84, Pres., 1985–, English Basketball Assoc. *Recreations:* basketball, photography, gardening. *Address:* 7 Park Crescent, Guiseley, West Yorks LS20 8EL. *T:* Guiseley 75248.

MITCHELL, Leslie Herbert, CBE 1955 (OBE 1949); *b* 28 May 1914; *s* of J. W. and A. J. Mitchell; *m* 1937, Margaret Winifred Pellow; three *s.* *Educ:* Christ's Hospital. Served War of 1939–45 in HM Forces in NW Europe. 2nd Sec., British Embassy, Copenhagen, 1945–50; 1st Sec., British Embassy, Washington, 1953–56; 1st Sec., Bonn, 1956–57; FO, retd 1968. Order of Dannebrog (Denmark), 1947. *Recreations:* music, railways. *Address:* 2 Lakeside Court, East Approach Drive, Cheltenham, Glos. *Club:* New (Cheltenham).

MITCHELL, Martin; *see* Mitchell, J. L. M.

MITCHELL, Very Rev. Patrick Reynolds; Dean of Wells, since 1973; *b* 17 March 1930; *s* of late Lt-Col Percy Reynolds Mitchell, DSO; *m* 1959, Mary Evelyn (*née* Phillips); three *s* one *d.* *Educ:* Eton Coll.; Merton Coll., Oxford (MA Theol); Wells Theol Coll. Officer in Welsh Guards (National Service), 1948–49. Deacon, 1954; priest, 1955; Curate at St Mark's, Mansfield, 1954–57; Priest-Vicar of Wells Cathedral and Chaplain of Wells Theological Coll., 1957–60; Vicar of St James', Milton, Portsmouth, 1961–67; Vicar of Frome Selwood, Somerset, 1967–73; Director of Ordination Candidates for Bath and Wells, 1971–74. Res. Fellow, Merton Coll., Oxford, 1984. Member: Adv. Bd for

Redundant Churches, 1978–; Cathedrals Adv. Commn for England, 1981–. FSA 1981. *Address:* The Dean's Lodging, 25 The Liberty, Wells, Somerset. *T:* Wells 72192.

MITCHELL, Dr Peter Dennis, FRS 1974; Director of Research, Glynn Research Institute (formerly Laboratories), since 1964; *b* 29 Sept. 1920; *s* of Christopher Gibbs Mitchell, Mitcham, Surrey; *m* 1958, Helen, *d* of Lt-Col Raymond P. T. ffrench, late Indian Army; three *s* one *d. Educ:* Queens Coll., Taunton; Jesus Coll., Cambridge; BA 1943; PhD 1950; Hon. Fellow, 1980. Dept of Biochem., Univ. of Cambridge, 1943–55, Demonstrator 1950–55; Dir of Chem. Biol. Unit, Dept of Zoology, Univ. of Edinburgh, 1955–63, Sen. Lectr 1961–62, Reader 1962–63. Sir Hans Krebs Lect. and Medal, Fed. European Biochem. Socs, 1978; Fritz Lipmann Lectr, Gesellschaft für Biol. Chem., 1978; Humphry Davy Meml Lectr, RIC and Chilterns and Mddx Sect. of Chem. Soc., at Royal Instn of London, 1980; James Rennie Bequest Lectr, Univ. of Edinburgh, 1980. For. Associate, Nat. Acad. of Scis, USA, 1977; Hon. Member: Soc. for Gen. Microbiology, 1984; Japanese Biochem. Soc., 1984. Hon. Dr rer. nat. Tech. Univ., Berlin, 1976; Hon. DSc: Exeter, 1977; Chicago, 1978; Liverpool, 1979; Bristol, 1980; Edinburgh, 1980; Hull, 1980; Hon. ScD: East Anglia, 1981; Cambridge, 1985; DUniv York, 1982. CIBA Medal and Prize, Biochem. Soc., for outstanding research, 1973; (jtly) Warren Trienniel Prize, Trustees of Mass Gen. Hosp., Boston, 1974; Louis and Bert Freedman Foundn Award, NY Acad. of Scis, 1974; Wilhelm Feldberg Foundn Prize, 1976; Lewis S. Rosenstiel Award, Brandeis Univ., 1977; Nobel Prize for Chemistry, 1978; Copley Medal, Royal Society, 1981; Medal of Honour, Athens Municipal Council, 1982. *Publications:* Chemiosmotic Coupling in Oxidative and Photosynthetic Phosphorylation, 1966; Chemiosmotic Coupling and Energy Transduction, 1968; papers in scientific jls. *Recreations:* enjoyment of family life, home-building and creation of wealth and amenity, restoration of buildings of architectural and historical interest, music, thinking, understanding, inventing, making, sailing. *Address:* Glynn House, Bodmin, Cornwall PL30 4AU. *T:* Cardinham 540.

MITCHELL, Richard Charles, (Bob); Lecturer in Business Studies, Eastleigh College of Further Education, since 1984; *b* 22 Aug. 1927; *s* of Charles and Elizabeth Mitchell; *m* 1950, Doreen Lilian Gregory; one *s* one *d. Educ:* Taunton's Sch., Southampton; Godalming County Gram. Sch.; Southampton Univ. BSc(Econ) Hons 1951. Bartley County Sec. Sch.: Senior Master and Head of Maths and Science Dept, 1957–65; Dep. Headmaster, 1965–66. MP (Lab) Southampton Test, 1966–70; MP (Lab 1971–81, SDP 1981–83) Southampton, Itchen, May 1971–1983. Contested (SDP) Southampton, Itchen, 1983; Prosp. Parly Cand. (SDP) Southampton, Itchen, 1986–. Mem., European Parlt, 1975–79. Member: Bureau of European Socialist Gp, 1976–79; Chairman's Panel, House of Commons, 1979–83. *Recreation:* postal chess (rep. Brit. Correspondence Chess Assoc. against other countries). *Address:* 49 Devonshire Road, Polygon, Southampton. *T:* Southampton 221781.

MITCHELL, Robert, OBE 1984; Councillor, Greater London Council, 1964–86; *b* 14 Dec. 1913; *s* of Robert Mitchell and Lizzie Mitchell (*née* Snowdon); *m* 1946, Reinholda Thoretta L. C. Kettlitz; two *s* one step *s. Educ:* West Ham Secondary Sch.; St John's Coll., Cambridge (MA Hons NatSci). Councillor, Wanstead and Woodford Council, 1958–65, Dep. Mayor, 1960–61. Chairman: GLC, 1971–72; Fire Brigade and Ambulance Cttees, 1967–71; Nat. Jt Negotiating Cttee for Local Authority Fire Brigades, 1970–71; Covent Gdn Jt Develt Cttee, 1972–73; Professional and Gen. Services Cttee, 1977–79; Greater London Jt Supply Bd, 1977–79. Member: CBI Cttee on State Intervention in Private Industry, 1976–78; London and SE Reg. Council, 1969–79; Smaller Firms Council, 1977–79; Policy Cttee, AMA, 1978–79. Wanstead and Woodford Conservative Association: Vice-Chm., 1961–65; Chm., 1965–68; Vice-Pres., 1968–; contested (C) West Ham South, 1964 and 1966 gen. elecs. Represented: Cambridge Univ., swimming and water polo, 1932–35 (Captain, 1935); England and Gt Britain, water polo, 1934–48, incl. Olympic Games, 1936 and 1948; Gt Britain, swimming and water polo, World Univ. Games, 1933, 1935; Rest of World *v* Champions, water polo, Univ. Games, 1935; Captain, 1946–49, Pres., 1955–56, Plaistow United Swimming Club; London Rep., Cambridge Univ. Swimming Club, 1953–75. Mem. Cttee, Crystal Palace Nat. Sports Centre, 1965–. Verderer, Epping Forest, 1976–; Mem., Lea Valley Regl Park Auth., 1982–85. Trustee, London Ecology Centre, 1985–. Liveryman, Worshipful Co. of Gardeners, 1975. Governor: Chigwell Sch., 1966– (Vice-Chm., 1968–); Loughton Coll. of Further Educn, 1984–.Grand Officer, Order of Orange Nassau (Holland), 1972; Order of Star (Afghanistan), 1971; Order of Rising Sun (Japan), 1971. *Publications:* newspaper and magazine articles mainly on countryside and political subjects. *Recreation:* planting trees, then sitting watching them grow. *Address:* Hatchwood House, Nursery Road, Loughton, Essex IG10 4EF. *T:* 01–508 9135; Little Brigg, Bessingham, Norfolk NR11 7JR. *Clubs:* Carlton, City Livery; Hawks (Cambridge).

MITCHELL, Maj.-Gen. Robert Imrie, OBE 1958 (MBE 1945); retired; *b* 25 Jan. 1916; *s* of James I. Mitchell; *m* 1947, Marion Lyell. *Educ:* Glasgow Academy; Glasgow Univ. BSc 1936, MB, ChB 1939. FFCM. 2/Lt 1937, Lieut 1938 (TA Gen. List); Lieut, RAMC, 1939; served war 1939–45 (despatches 1945); Captain 1940; Major 1947; Lt-Col 1958; Col 1962; Brig. 1968; DDMS, I (British) Corps, BAOR, 1968–69; Maj.-Gen. 1969; DDMS, Army Strategic Command, 1969–71; DMS, BAOR, 1971–73. QHP 1970–73. Hon. Colonel, Glasgow and Strathclyde Univs. OTC TA, 1977–82. OStJ 1966. *Recreations:* shooting, fishing, golf. *Address:* Hallam, Gargunnock, Stirlingshire FK8 3BQ. *T:* Gargunnock 600. *Clubs:* Naval and Military; Royal Scottish Automobile (Glasgow).

MITCHELL, Hon. Dame Roma (Flinders), DBE 1982 (CBE 1971); Chancellor, University of Adelaide, since 1983 (Senior Deputy Chancellor, 1972–83); Senior Puisne Judge, Supreme Court of South Australia, 1979–83 (Judge of Supreme Court, 1965–83); *b* 2 Oct. 1913; *d* of Harold Flinders Mitchell and Maude Imelda Victoria (*née* Wickham). *Educ:* St Aloysius Coll., Adelaide; Univ. of Adelaide (LLB 1934). Admitted as Practitioner, Supreme Court of SA, 1934; QC 1962 (first woman QC in Australia). Chairman: Parole Bd of SA, 1974–81; Criminal Law Reform Cttee of SA, 1971–81; Human Rights Commn of Australia, 1981–; State Heritage Cttee of SA, 1978–81; National Chm., Winston Churchill Meml Trust, 1984– (Dep. Chm., 1975–84); National Pres., Australian Assoc. of Ryder-Cheshire Foundn, 1979–. Member: Council for Order of Australia, 1980–; Bd of Governors, Adelaide Festival of Arts, 1981–84. Boyer Lectr, ABC, 1975. *Recreations:* theatre, music, art, swimming, walking. *Address:* 256 East Terrace, Adelaide, SA 5000, Australia. *T:* 223 5373. *Clubs:* Queen Adelaide, Lyceum (Adelaide).

MITCHELL, Prof. Ross Galbraith, MD, FRCPE, DCH; Professor of Child Health, University of Dundee and Pædiatrician, Ninewells Hospital, Dundee, 1973–85, now Emeritus; *b* 18 Nov. 1920; *s* of late Richard Galbraith Mitchell, OBE and Ishobel, *d* of late James Ross, Broadford, Skye; *m* 1950, June Phylis Butcher; one *s* three *d. Educ:* Kelvinside Acad.; University of Edinburgh. MB, ChB Edinburgh, 1944. Surg-Lt, RNVR, 1944–47; Jun. hosp. posts, Liverpool, London, Edinburgh, 1947–52; Rockefeller Res. Fellow, Mayo Clinic, USA, 1952–53; Lectr in Child Health, Univ. of St Andrews, 1952–55; Cons. Pædiatrician, Dundee Teaching Hosps, 1955–63; Prof. of Child Health, Univ. of Aberdeen, Pædiatrician, Royal Aberdeen Children's and Aberdeen Maternity Hosps, 1963–72; Univ. of Dundee: Dean, Faculty of Medicine and Dentistry, 1978–81; Mem. Court, 1982–85. Chairman: Scottish Adv. Council on Child Care, 1966–69; Specialist Adv. Cttee on Pædiatrics, 1975–79; Academic Bd, British Pædiatric Assoc., 1975–78; Spastics Internat. Med. Pubns, 1981–85; Mac Keith Press, London, 1986–; Mem., GMC, 1983–86. President: Harveian Soc., Edinburgh, 1982–83; Scottish Paediatric Soc., 1982–84. For. Corresp. Mem., Amer. Acad. of Cerebral Palsy and Developmental Medicine. Jt Editor, Developmental Medicine and Child Neurology, 1968–80. *Publications:* Disease in Infancy and Childhood, (7th edn) 1973; Child Life and Health (5th edn), 1970; Child Health in the Community (2nd edn), 1980; contribs to textbooks of paediatrics, medicine and obstetrics and articles in scientific and medical jls. *Recreations:* Celtic language and literature, fishing. *Address:* Craigard, Abertay Gardens, Barnhill, Dundee DD5 2SQ.

MITCHELL, Sir (Seton) Steuart (Crichton), KBE 1954 (OBE 1941); CB 1951; *b* 9 March 1902; *s* of A. Crichton Mitchell, DSc, FRSE; *m* 1929, Elizabeth (*née* Duke); no *c. Educ:* Edinburgh Acad.; RN Colls, Osborne and Dartmouth. Joined Royal Navy as Cadet, 1916; at sea in HMS Hercules, Grand Fleet, 1918, subsequently served in HM Ships Ramillies, Sportive, Tomahawk, Marlborough; qualified as Gunnery Specialist, 1927–29, subsequently Gunnery Officer of HM Ships Comus and Frobisher; Naval Ordnance Inspection Dept and Asst Supt of Design, 1931–39; War of 1939–45, Inspector of Naval Ordnance, in charge of Admiralty Ordnance contracts in Switzerland, 1939–40, in USA, 1940–44; Chief Engineer and Supt, in charge of Armament Design Establishment, Min. of Supply, 1945; Controller, Guided Weapons and Electronics, Min. of Supply, 1951–56; Controller, Royal Ordnance Factories, 1956–59; Controller, Guided Weapons and Electronics, Ministry of Aviation, 1959–62; Mem., BTC, Feb.-Nov. 1962; Vice-Chm., British Railways Bd, Nov. 1962–64; Chairman: Machine Tool Industry EDC, 1964–; Shipbuilding Industry Trng Bd, 1964–; Mem., Central Trng Council, 1965–; Adviser (part-time) to Min. of Technology, 1965–; Mem. Scottish Economic Planning Council, 1965–67; Mem. Nat. Economic Develt Council, 1967–70. Chm., Carrier Engineering Co., 1968–70; Director: Parkinson Cowan Ltd, 1964–71; Plessey Numerical Controls Ltd, 1970–73. Officer Legion of Merit (USA), 1945. *Recreations:* music, gardening, antiques. *Address:* 137 Swan Court, Chelsea Manor Street, SW3 5RY. *T:* 01–352 5571.

MITCHELL, Stephen George; QC 1986; a Recorder, since 1985; *b* 19 Sept. 1941; *s* of Sydney Mitchell and Joan Mitchell (*née* Dick); *m* 1978, Alison Clare (*née* Roseveare); two *d. Educ:* Bedford Sch.; Hertford Coll., Oxford (MA). Called to the Bar, Middle Temple, 1964; Second Prosecuting Counsel to the Crown, Inner London Crown Court, 1975; Central Criminal Court: a Junior Prosecuting Counsel to the Crown, 1977; a Senior Prosecuting Counsel to the Crown, 1981–86. Editor, Archbold's Criminal Pleading Evidence and Practice, 1972–. *Publication:* (ed) Phipson on Evidence, 11th edn, 1970. *Address:* 6 King's Bench Walk, Temple, EC4Y 7DR. *T:* 01–583 0410.

MITCHELL, Sir Steuart Crichton; *see* Mitchell, Sir S. S. C.

MITCHELL, Terence Croft; Keeper of Western Asiatic Antiquities, British Museum, since 1985; *b* 17 June 1929; *s* of late Arthur Croft Mitchell and Evelyn Violet Mitchell (*née* Ware). *Educ:* Holderness School, New Hampshire, USA; Bradfield Coll., Berks; St Catharine's Coll., Cambridge (MA 1956). REME Craftsman, 1947–49. Asst Master, St Catherine's Sch., Almondsbury, 1954–56; Resident Study, Tyndale House, Cambridge, 1956–58; European Rep., Aust. Inst. of Archaeology, 1958–59; Dept of Western Antiquities, British Museum, 1959, Dep. Keeper, 1974, Acting Keeper, 1983–85. *Publications:* Sumerian Art at Ur and Al-'Ubaid, 1969; (ed) Sir Leonard Woolley, Ur Excavations VIII, The Kassite Period and the Period of the Assyrian Kings, 1965; VII, The Old Babylonian Period, 1976; (ed) Music and Civilization, 1980; chapters on Israel and Judah in Cambridge Ancient History, rev. edn III, 1982; articles and reviews. *Recreations:* music, reading, landscape gardening. *Address:* 32 Mallord Street, Chelsea, SW3 6DU. *T:* 01–352 3962. *Club:* Athenæum.

MITCHELL, Warren; *b* 14 Jan. 1926; *s* of Montague and Annie Misell, later Mitchell; *m* 1952, Constance Wake; three *s. Educ:* Southgate Co. Sch.; University Coll., Oxford; RADA. Demobbed RAF, 1946. First professional appearance, Finsbury Park Open Air Theatre, 1950; Theophile in Can-Can, Coliseum, 1954; Crookfinger Jake in The Threepenny Opera, Royal Court and Aldwych, 1956; Mr Godboy in Dutch Uncle, Aldwych, 1969; Satan in Council of Love, Criterion, 1970; Herbert in Jump, Queen's, 1971; Ion Will in The Great Caper, Royal Court, 1974; The Thoughts of Chairman Alf, Stratford E, 1976; Willie Loman in Death of a Salesman, Nat. Theatre, 1979; Ducking Out, Duke of York's, 1983; *films include:* Diamonds Before Breakfast; Assassination Bureau; Best House in London; Till Death Us Do Part; Moon Zero Two; Whatever Happened to Charlie Farthing; Jabberwocky; Stand Up Virgin Soldiers; Meetings with Remarkable Men; Norman Loves Rose; The Chain; *television:* Alf Garnett in Till Death Us Do Part, BBC, 1966–78, and In Sickness and in Health, BBC, 1985; Shylock in Merchant of Venice, BBC, 1981; Till Death, ITV, 1981; The Caretaker, BBC, 1981. TV Actor of the Year Award, Guild of Film and TV Producers, 1966; Actor of Year Award: Evening Standard, 1979; Soc. of West End Theatres, 1979; Plays and Players, 1979. *Recreations:* sailing, tennis, playing clarinet. *Address:* c/o ICM, 388/396 Oxford Street, W1N 9HE.

MITCHELL, William Eric Marcus, MC; MB; BS London; FRCS; FRCSC; MRCP; DPH; Surgeon, genito-urinary specialist, Consulting Surgeon, Royal Jubilee Hospital, Victoria, BC, retired; *b* 29 April 1897; *e s* of Dr J. F. Mitchell, formerly of Bangor, Co. Down; *m* 1922, Catherine, *d* of W. F. Hamilton, of Ashwick, NZ; one *d*; *m* 1958, Margery, *d* of D. O. Thomas, Victoria, BC. *Educ:* Campbell Coll., Belfast; St Bartholomew's Hosp., University of London. Served as a Lt with the 11th Battalion Royal Irish Rifles in France, 1916 (wounded, MC); various prizes during sch. and Univ. career; House Surg., St Bartholomew's Hosp.; Chief Asst to a Surgical Unit, St Bartholomew's Hosp.; Clinical Asst, St Peter's Hosp., London; Pres., Abernethian Soc., St Bartholomew's Hosp. War of 1939–45, Lt-Col RAMC, Officer in Charge Surgical Div. No 13 Gen. Hosp. MEF. *Publications:* Health, Wealth and Happiness, 1969; numerous papers on surgical subjects published in the Lancet, the Canadian Medical Association Journal, St Bartholomew's Hospital Journal. *Recreations:* fishing, ski-ing, mountaineering. *Address:* 2171 Granite Street, Oak Bay, Victoria, BC V8S 3G8, Canada. *TA:* Victoria, BC. *Club:* Alpine Club of Canada.

MITCHELL, Rt. Rev. Mgr. William Joseph; Rector, Pontifical Beda College, Rome, since 1978; *b* 4 Jan. 1936; *s* of William Ernest and Catherine Mitchell. *Educ:* St Brendan's Coll., Bristol; Corpus Christi Coll., Oxford (MA); Séminaire S Sulpice, Paris; Gregorian Univ., Rome (LCL). Ordained Priest, Pro-Cathedral, Bristol, 1961; Curate, Pro-Cathedral, Bristol, 1963–64; Secretary to Bishop of Clifton, 1964–75; Parish Priest, St Bernadette, Bristol, 1975–78. Prelate of Honour, 1978. *Address:* Pontificio Collegio Beda, Viale di S Paolo 18, 00146 Rome, Italy. *T:* Rome 5561700; Loretto, 4 Stonehill, Hanham, Bristol BS15 3HL. *T:* Bristol 674306.

MITCHELL COTTS, Sir R. C.; *see* Cotts.

MITCHELL-THOMSON, family name of **Baron Selsdon.**

MITCHENSON, Francis Joseph Blackett, (Joe Mitchenson); Joint Founder and Director, The Raymond Mander and Joe Mitchenson Theatre Collection, since 1939 (Theatre Collection Trust, since 1977); *b* 4 Oct.; *s* of Francis William Mitchenson and Sarah Roddam. *Educ:* privately; Fay Compton Studio of Dramatic Art. First appeared on stage professionally in Libel, Playhouse, London, 1934; acted in repertory, on tour and in London, until 1948. With Raymond Mander, founded Theatre Collection, 1939; War Service with Royal Horse Artillery, invalided out, 1943; returned to stage, and collab. with Raymond Mander on many BBC progs. Collection subject of an Aquarius programme, 1971; many theatrical exhbns, incl. 50 Years of British Stage Design, for British Council, USSR, 1979. Archivist to: Sadler's Wells; Old Vic. Mem., Soc. of West End Theatre Awards Panel, 1976–78. *Publications:* with Raymond Mander: Hamlet Through the Ages, 1952 (2nd rev. edn 1955); Theatrical Companion to Shaw, 1954; Theatrical Companion to Maugham, 1955; The Artist and the Theatre, 1955; Theatrical Companion to Coward, 1957; A Picture History of British Theatre, 1957; (with J. C. Trewin) The Gay Twenties, 1958; (with Philip Hope-Wallace) A Picture History of Opera, 1959; (with J. C. Trewin) The Turbulent Thirties, 1960; The Theatres of London, 1961, illus. by Timothy Birdsall (2nd rev. edn, paperback, 1963; 3rd rev. edn 1975); A Picture History of Gilbert and Sullivan, 1962; British Music Hall: A Story in Pictures, 1965 (rev. and enlarged edn 1974); Lost Theatres of London, 1968 (2nd edn, rev. and enlarged, 1976); Musical Comedy: A Story in Pictures, 1969; Revue: A Story in Pictures, 1971; Pantomime: A Story in Pictures, 1973; The Wagner Companion, 1977; Victorian and Edwardian Entertainment from Old Photographs, 1978; Introd. to Plays, by Noël Coward (4 vols), 1979; Guide to the W. Somerset Maugham Theatrical Paintings, 1980; contribs to and revs in Encyc. Britannica, Theatre Notebook, and Books and Bookmen. *Recreations:* collecting anything and everything theatrical, sun bathing. *Address:* 5 Venner Road, Sydenham, SE26 5EQ. *T:* 01–778 6730; The Mansion, Beckenham Place, Kent. *T:* 01–650 9322; (office) 01–658 7725.

MITCHISON, Avrion; *see* Mitchison, N. A.

MITCHISON, Dr Denis Anthony, CMG 1984; Professor of Bacteriology, Royal Postgraduate Medical School, 1971–84; Director, Medical Research Council's Unit for Laboratory Studies of Tuberculosis, 1956–84; retired; *b* 6 Sept. 1919; *e s* of Baron Mitchison, CBE, QC, and of Naomi Margaret Mitchison, *qv*; *m* 1940, Ruth Sylvia, *d* of Hubert Gill; two *s* two *d*. *Educ:* Abbotsholme Sch.; Trinity Coll., Cambridge; University Coll. Hosp., London (MB, ChB). House Physician Addenbrooke's Hosp., Royal Berkshire Hosp.; Asst to Pathologist, Brompton Hosp.; Prof. of Bacteriology (Infectious Diseases), RPGMS, 1968–71. FRCP; FRCPath. *Publications:* numerous papers on bacteriology and chemotherapy of tuberculosis. *Recreation:* computer programming. *Address:* 14 Marlborough Road, Richmond, Surrey. *T:* 01–940 4751.

See also J. M. Mitchison, N. A. Mitchison.

MITCHISON, Prof. John Murdoch, ScD; FRS 1978; FRSE 1966; Professor of Zoology, University of Edinburgh, since 1963; *b* 11 June 1922; *s* of Lord Mitchison, CBE, QC, and of N. Haldane (*see* Naomi M. Mitchison); *m* 1947, Rosalind Mary Wrong; one *s* three *d*. *Educ:* Winchester Coll.; Trinity Coll., Cambridge. Army Operational Research, 1941–46; Sen. and Research Scholar, Trinity Coll., Cambridge, 1946–50; Fellow, Trinity Coll., Cambridge, 1950–54; Edinburgh University: Lectr in Zoology, 1953–59; Reader in Zoology, 1959–62; Dean, Faculty of Science, 1984–85; Mem. of Court, 1971–74, 1985–. J. W. Jenkinson Memorial Lectr, Oxford, 1971–72. Member: Council, Scottish Marine Biol. Assoc., 1961–67; Exec. Cttee, Internat. Soc. for Cell Biology, 1964–72; Biol Cttee, SRC, 1972–75; Royal Commn on Environmental Pollution, 1974–79; Science Bd, SRC, 1976–79; Working Gp on Biol Manpower, DES, 1968–71; Adv. Cttee on Safety of Nuclear Installations, Health and Safety Exec., 1981–84. Pres., British Soc. for Cell Biology, 1974–77. FInstBiol 1963. *Publications:* The Biology of the Cell Cycle, 1971; papers in scientific jls. *Address:* Great Yew, Ormiston, East Lothian EH35 5NJ. *T:* Pencaitland 340530.

See also D. A. Mitchison, N. A. Mitchison.

MITCHISON, Naomi Margaret, CBE 1985; (Lady Mitchison since 1964, but she still wishes to be called Naomi Mitchison); *b* Edinburgh, 1 Nov. 1897; *d* of late John Scott Haldane, CH, FRS, and Kathleen Trotter; *m* 1916, G. R. Mitchison (*d* 1970), CBE, QC, created a Baron (Life Peer), 1964; three *s* two *d*. *Educ:* Dragon Sch., Oxford; home student, Oxford. Officier d'Académie Française, 1924; Argyll CC, 1945–65, on and off; Highland and Island Advisory Panel, 1947–65; Highlands and Islands Develt Consult. Council, 1966–76; Tribal Mother to Bakgatla, Botswana, 1963–. DUniv.: Stirling, 1976; Dundee, 1985; DLitt Strathclyde, 1983. Hon. Fellow: St Anne's Coll., Oxford, 1980; Wolfson Coll., Oxford, 1983. *Publications:* The Conquered, 1923; When the Bough Breaks, 1924; Cloud Cuckoo Land, 1925; The Laburnum Branch, 1926; Black Sparta, 1928; Anna Comnena, 1928; Nix-Nought-Nothing, 1928; Barbarian Stories, 1929; The Hostages, 1930; Comments on Birth Control, 1930; The Corn King and the Spring Queen, 1931; The Price of Freedom (with L. E. Gielgud), 1931; Boys and Girls and Gods, 1931; The Powers of Light, 1932; (ed) An Outline for Boys and Girls, 1932; The Delicate Fire, 1933; Vienna Diary, 1934; The Home, 1934; We Have Been Warned, 1935; Beyond this Limit, 1935; The Fourth Pig, 1936; Socrates (with R. H. S. Crossman), 1937; An End and a Beginning, 1937; The Moral Basis of Politics, 1938; The Kingdom of Heaven, 1939; As It was in the Beginning (with L. E. Gielgud), 1939; The Blood of the Martyrs, 1939; (ed) Re-educating Scotland, 1944; The Bull Calves, 1947; Men and Herring (with D. Macintosh), 1949; The Big House, 1950; Spindrift (*play:* with D. Macintosh), Citizens' Theatre, Glasgow, 1951; Lobsters on the Agenda, 1952; Travel Light, 1952; The Swan's Road, 1954; Graeme and the Dragon, 1954; The Land the Ravens Found, 1955; To the Chapel Perilous, 1955; Little Boxes, 1956; Behold your King, 1957; The Far Harbour, 1957; Five Men and a Swan, 1958; Other People's Worlds, 1958; Judy and Lakshmi, 1959; The Rib of the Green Umbrella, 1960; The Young Alexander, 1960; Karensgaard, 1961; The Young Alfred the Great, 1962; Memoirs of a Space Woman, 1962; (ed) What the Human Race is Up To, 1962; The Fairy who Couldn't Tell a Lie, 1963; When we Become Men, 1965; Ketse and the Chief, 1965; Return to the Fairy Hill, 1966; Friends and Enemies, 1966; The Big Surprise, 1967; African Heroes, 1968; Don't Look Back, 1969; The Family at Ditlabeng, 1969; The Africans: a history, 1970; Sun and Moon, 1970; Cleopatra's People, 1972; A Danish Teapot, 1973; Sunrise Tomorrow, 1973; Small Talk: memoirs of an Edwardian childhood (autobiog.), 1973; A Life for Africa, 1973; Oil for the Highlands?, 1974; All Change Here (autobiog.), 1975; Solution Three, 1975; Snake!, 1976; The Two Magicians, 1979; The Cleansing of the Knife, 1979; You May Well Ask (autobiog.), 1979; Images of Africa, 1980; The Vegetable War, 1980; Mucking Around, 1980; What Do You Think Yourself, Scottish Stories, 1982; Not By Bread Alone, 1983; Among You Taking Notes, 1985. *Recreation:* keeping up with the family. *Address:* Carradale House, Carradale, Campbeltown, Scotland.

See also D. A. Mitchison, J. M. Mitchison, N. A. Mitchison.

MITCHISON, Prof. (Nicholas) Avrion, FRS 1967; Jodrell Professor of Zoology and Comparative Anatomy, University College, London, since 1970; *b* 5 May 1928; 3rd *s* of Baron Mitchison, CBE, QC, and of Naomi Margaret Mitchison, *qv*; *m* 1957, Lorna

Margaret, *d* of Maj.-Gen. J. S. S. Martin, CSI; two *s* three *d*. *Educ:* Leighton Park Sch.; New Coll., Oxford (MA 1949). Fellow of Magdalen College, 1950–52; Commonwealth Fund Fellow, 1952–54; Lecturer, Edinburgh Univ., 1954–61; Reader, Edinburgh Univ., 1961–62; Head of Div. of Experimental Biology, Nat. Inst. for Med. Research, 1962–71. Hon. MD Edinburgh, 1977. *Publications:* articles in scientific journals. *Address:* 14 Belitha Villas, N1.

See also D. A. Mitchison, J. M. Mitchison.

MITFORD, family name of **Baron Redesdale.**

MITFORD, Jessica Lucy, (Mrs Jessica Treuhaft); author; *b* 11 Sept. 1917; *d* of 2nd Baron Redesdale; *m* 1st, Esmond Marcus David Romilly (*d* 1941); one *d*; 2nd, 1943, Robert Edward Treuhaft; one *s*. Distinguished Prof., San José State Univ., Calif, 1973–74. *Publications:* (as Jessica Mitford): Hons and Rebels, 1960; The American Way of Death, 1963; The Trial of Dr Spock, 1969; Kind and Usual Punishment, 1974; The American Prison Business, 1975; A Fine Old Conflict, 1977; The Making of a Muckraker, 1979; Faces of Philip: a memoir of Philip Toynbee, 1984. *Address:* 6411 Regent Street, Oakland, Calif 94618, USA.

MITFORD, Rupert Leo Scott B.; *see* Bruce-Mitford.

MITFORD-SLADE, Patrick Buxton; Partner, Cazenove & Co., since 1972; Managing Director, Cazenove Money Brokers, since 1986; *b* 7 Sept. 1936; *s* of late Col Cecil Townley Mitford-Slade and Phyllis, *d* of E. G. Buxton; *m* 1964, Anne Catharine Stanton, *d* of Major Arthur Holbrow Stanton, MBE; one *s* two *d*. *Educ:* Eton Coll.; RMA Sandhurst. Commissioned 60th Rifles, 1955, Captain; served Libya, NI, Berlin and British Guyana; Adjt, 1st Bn The Royal Green Jackets, 1962–65; Instructor, RMA Sandhurst, 1965–67. Stockbroker, Cazenove & Co., 1968–. Asst Sec., Panel on Takeovers and Mergers, 1970–72; Mem., Stock Exchange, 1972– (Mem. Council, 1976–; Dep. Chm., 1982–85); Chm., City Telecommunications Cttee, 1983–. Chm., Officers' Assoc., 1985–. *Recreations:* shooting, fishing. *Address:* Damales House, Hartley Wintney, Basingstoke, Hants. *Club:* City of London.

MITHEN, Dallas Alfred, CB 1983; Chairman, Forestry Training Council, since 1984; Commissioner for Harvesting and Marketing, Forestry Commission, 1977–83; *b* 5 Nov. 1923; *m* 1st, 1947, Peggy (*née* Clarke) (decd); one *s* one *d*; 2nd, 1969, Avril Teresa Dodd (*née* Stein). *Educ:* Maidstone Grammar Sch.; UC of N Wales, Bangor. BSc (Forestry). Fleet Air Arm, 1942–46. Joined Forestry Commission as District Officer, 1950; Dep. Surveyor, New Forest and Conservator SE (England), 1968–71; Senior Officer (Scotland), 1971–75; Head of Forest Management Div., Edinburgh, 1975–76. Pres., Inst. of Chartered Foresters, 1984–86; Pres., Forestry Section, BAAS, 1985. Trustee, Central Scotland Woodland Trust, 1985–. *Recreations:* gardening, swimming, walking. *Address:* Kings Knot, Bonnington Road, Peebles EH45 9HF. *T:* Peebles 20738.

MITMAN, Frederick S., CBE 1941; *b* 21 April 1900; *s* of late William and Elizabeth Mitman; *m* 1925, Helen McNary; one *s* one *d*. *Educ:* Lehigh Univ., USA (Deg. of Engineer of Mines, 1923). Dir of Light Alloys and Magnesium (Sheet and Strip) Control, Ministry of Aircraft Production, 1939–41; Co-ordinator of Aircraft Supplies for Fighter and Naval Aircraft, Ministry of Aircraft Production, 1940–41; Adviser on Light Metals Fabrication, Ministry of Aircraft Production, 1941–42. *Address:* 10 Campden House Close, Kensington, W8. *T:* 01–937 9071.

MITSAKIS, Prof. Kariofilis; Professor of Modern Greek Literature, University of Athens, since 1978; *b* 12 May 1932; *s* of Christos and Crystalli Mitsakis; *m* 1966, Anthoula Chalkia; two *s*. *Educ:* Univs of Thessaloniki (BA, PhD), Oxford (MA, DPhil) and Munich. Scientific Collaborator, National Research Foundn of Greece, 1959–62; Associate Prof. of Byzantine and Modern Greek Literature, Univ. of Maryland, 1966–68; Chm. of Dept of Comparative Literature, Univ. of Maryland, 1967–68; Sotheby and Bywater Prof. of Byzantine and Modern Greek Language and Literature, Univ. of Oxford, 1968–72; Prof. of Modern Greek Lit., Univ. of Thessaloniki, 1972–75; Dir, Inst. for Balkan Studies, Thessaloniki, 1972–80. *Publications:* Problems Concerning the Text, the Sources and the Dating of the Achilleid, 1962 (in Greek); The Greek Sonnet, 1962 (in Greek); The Language of Romanos the Melodist, 1967 (in English); The Byzantine Alexanderromance Romance from the Cod. Vindob. theol. gr. 244, 1967 (in German); Byzantine Hymnography, 1971 (in Greek); Petrarchism in Greece, 1973 (in Greek); Introduction to Modern Greek Literature, 1973 (in Greek); Homer in Modern Greek Literature, 1976 (in Greek); George Viziynos, 1977 (in Greek); Modern Greek Prose: the generation of the '30s, 1978 (in Greek); Modern Greek Music and Poetry, 1979 (in Greek and English); March Through the Time, 1982; The Living Water, 1983; contribs to Balkan Studies, Byzantinisch-Neugriechische Jahrbücher, Byzantinische Zeitschrift, Comparative Literature Studies, Diptycha, Etudes Byzantines-Byzantine Studies, Glotta, Hellenika, Jahrbuch der Oesterreichischen Byzantinischen Gesellschaft, Nea Hestia, etc. *Recreations:* music, travelling. *Address:* University of Athens, Faculty of Philosophy, 33 Hippocratous Street, Athens 10680, Greece.

MITTERRAND, François Maurice Marie; Grande Croix de l'Ordre National de la Légion d'Honneur; Croix de Guerre (1939–45); President of the French Republic, since 1981; advocate; *b* Jarnac, Charente, 26 Oct. 1916; *s* of Joseph Mitterrand and Yvonne (*née* Lorrain); *m* 1944, Danielle Gouze; two *s*. *Educ:* Coll. Saint-Paul, Angoulême; Facultés de droit et des lettres, Univ. of Paris. Licencié en droit, Lic. ès lettres; Dip. d'études supérieures de droit public. Served War, 1939–40 (prisoner, escaped); Rosette de la Résistance). Missions to London and to Algiers, 1943; Sec.-Gen., Organisation for Prisoners of War, War Victims and Refugees, 1944–46. Deputy from Nièvre, 1946–58 and 1962–81; Minister for Ex-Servicemen, 1947–48; Sec. of State for Information, attached Prime Minister's Office, 1948–49; Minister for Overseas Territories, 1950–51; Chm., UDSR, 1951–52; Minister of State, Jan.-Feb. 1952 and March 1952–July 1953; Deleg. to Council of Europe, July-Sept. 1953; Minister of the Interior, June 1954–Feb. 1955; Minister of State, 1956–57; Senator, 1959–62; Candidate for Presidency of France, 1965, 1974; Pres., Fedn of Democratic and Socialist Left, 1965–68; First Sec., Socialist Party, 1971–81. Vice-Pres., Socialist International, 1972–. Pres., Conseil général de la Nièvre, 1964–. *Publications:* Aux frontières de l'Union française, 1953; Presence française et abandon, 1957; La Chine au défi, 1961; Le Coup d'Etat permanent, 1964; Ma part de vérité, 1969; Un socialisme du possible, 1970; La rose au poing, 1973; La paille et le grain, 1975; Politique 1, 1977; L'Abeille et l'architecte, 1978; Ici et maintenant, 1980; Politique 2, 1981; Reflexions sur la politique exterieure de la France, 1986; numerous contribs to the Press. *Recreation:* golf. *Address:* Palais de l'Elysée, 75008 Paris, France; (private) 22 rue de Bièvre, 75005 Paris, France.

MITTLER, Prof. Peter Joseph, CBE 1981; MA, PhD, MEd; FBPsS; Professor of Special Education, Director, Centre for Educational Guidance and Special Needs, Department of Education, since 1973, and Director, Hester Adrian Research Centre, 1968–82, University of Manchester; *b* 2 April 1930; *s* of Dr Gustav Mittler and Gertrude Mittler; *m* 1955, Helle Katscher; three *s*. *Educ:* Merchant Taylors' Sch., Crosby; Pembroke Coll., Cambridge (MA); PhD London; MEd Manchester. Clinical Psychologist, Warneford and Park Hosps, Oxford, 1954–58; Principal Psychologist, Reading Area Psychiatric Services, 1958–63; Lectr in Psychology, Birkbeck Coll., Univ. of London, 1963–68. Chm., Nat Develt Gp for Mentally Handicapped, 1975–80; Pres., Internat. League of Socs for Persons with Mental Handicap, 1982–86 (Vice-Pres., 1978–82). FRSA 1984. *Publications:* ed, Psychological Assessment of Mental and Physical Handicaps, 1970; The Study of Twins, 1971; ed, Assessment for Learning in the Mentally Handicapped, 1973; ed, Research to Practice in Mental Retardation (3 vols), 1977; People not Patients, 1979; (jtly) Teaching Language and Communication to the Mentally Handicapped, (Schools Council), 1979; (ed jtly) Advances in Mental Handicap Research, 1980; (ed) Frontiers of Knowledge in Mental Retardation (2 vols), 1981; (ed jtly) Approaches to Partnership: professionals and parents of mentally handicapped people, 1983; (ed jtly) Aspects of Competence in Mentally Handicapped People, 1983; (ed jtly) Issues in Staff Training, 1986; papers in medical and educnl jls. *Recreations:* music, travel. *Address:* 3 Dorset Avenue, Bramhall, Stockport SK7 3NU. *T:* 061–485 6491.

MITTON, Rev. Dr Charles Leslie, BA; MTh; PhD; Principal of Handsworth College, Birmingham, 1955–70 (Tutor, 1951–55); *b* 13 Feb. 1907; *s* of Rev. Charles W. Mitton, Bradford, Yorks; *m* 1937, Margaret J. Ramage; one *s* one *d. Educ:* Kingswood Sch., Bath; Manchester Univ.; Didsbury Coll., Manchester. Asst Tutor at Wesley Coll., Headingley, 1930–33; Minister in Methodist Church at: Dunbar, 1933–36; Keighley, 1936–39; Scunthorpe, 1939–45; Nottingham, 1945–51; Tutor in New Testament Studies at Handsworth Coll., Birmingham, 1951–70. Editor of Expository Times, 1965–76. Hon. DD, Aberdeen Univ., 1964. *Publications:* The Epistle to the Ephesians: Authorship, Origin and Purpose, 1951; Pauline Corpus of Letters, 1954; Preachers' Commentary on St Mark's Gospel, 1956; The Good News, 1961; The Epistle of James, 1966; Jesus: the fact behind the faith, 1974; The Epistle to the Ephesians: a commentary, 1976; Your Kingdom Come, 1978. *Recreations:* Rugby football, Association football, cricket, tennis. *Address:* 14 Cranbrook Road, Handsworth, Birmingham B21 8PJ. *T:* 021–554 7892.

MKONA, Callisto Matekenya, DSM (Malaŵi) 1966; Hon. GCVO 1985; High Commissioner for Malaŵi in London, since 1981; also concurrently accredited to Denmark, France, Norway, Portugal, Sweden and Switzerland; *b* 4 June 1930; *s* of late Benedicto Mkona and of Martha Matekenya Mkona; *m* 1971, Helen Victoria (*née* Sazuze); two *s* two *d. Educ:* Zomba, Malaŵi; Urbanian Univ., Rome (DCL, Dip. Soc. Scis). Secondary School teacher, 1962–64; Mission Educn Liaison Officer, 1964–67; Educn Attaché (First Sec.), Washington and London, 1967–71; Ambassador to Ethiopia, 1971–72; Minister, Washington, 1972–73; High Comr in Zambia, 1973–75; Ambassador in Bonn, 1975–78; Dep. Principal Sec., Min. of External Affairs, 1978–79; Principal Sec., Office of the President and Cabinet, 1979–81. *Recreations:* reading, walking, tennis, golf. *Address:* Malaŵi High Commission, 33 Grosvenor Street, W1X 0DE. *T:* 01–491 4172. *Clubs:* Travellers' (Hon. Mem.), Hurlingham (Hon. Mem.).

MLINARIC, David; interior decorator and designer, since 1964; founded David Mlinaric Ltd, 1964; *b* 12 March 1939; *s* of Franjo and Mabel Mlinaric; *m* 1969, Martha Laycock; one *s* two *d. Educ:* Downside Sch.; Bartlett Sch. of Architecture; University Coll. London. Private and commercial interior decorating, often in historic bldgs, 1964–; Chapel, Trinity College, Dublin, 1977; decorating for National Trust, 1978–, includes: Beningbrough Hall, York; Assembly Rooms, Bath; Nostell Priory, Wakefield; decorating for FCO, 1982–, includes Washington, Paris and Brussels embassies. Houses for pop musicians: Mick Jagger, 1968–69; Eric Clapton, 1969–70; Roger Waters, 1980; Bill Wyman, 1983; Interiors: St Antony's Coll., Oxford, 1970; St John's Coll., Oxford, 1976; TCD, 1977; Magdalene Coll., Cambridge, 1979; Le Gavroche Restaurant, London, 1981; Barings Bank, London, 1983; Curzon House, London, 1984. *Recreations:* gardening, sightseeing. *Address:* 38 Bourne Street, SW1W 8JA. *T:* 01–730 9072.

MOATE, Roger Denis; MP (C) Faversham since 1970; Insurance Broker; *b* 12 May 1938; *m;* one *s* one *d. Educ:* Latymer Upper Sch., Hammersmith. Joined Young Conservative Movement, in Brentford and Chiswick, 1954: Vice-Chm., Greater London Area Young Conservatives, 1964; contested (C) Faversham, Gen. Elec., 1966. *Recreation:* skiing. *Address:* House of Commons, SW1; The Old Vicarage, Knatchbull Road, SE5.

MOBBS, Sir (Gerald) Nigel, Kt 1986; DL; Chairman and Chief Executive, Slough Estates plc, since 1976; Director, Barclays Bank PLC, since 1979; *b* 22 Sept. 1937; *s* of Gerald Aubrey Mobbs and Elizabeth (*née* Lanchester); *m* 1961, Hon. Pamela Jane Marguerite Berry, 2nd *d* of 2nd Viscount Kemsley, *qv;* one *s* twin *d. Educ:* Marlborough Coll.; Christ Church, Oxford. Joined Slough Estates plc, 1961; Director, 1963, Man. Dir, 1971. Director: principal subsidiaries; Charterhouse Gp, 1974–84 (Chm., 1977–83); Woolworth Holdings PLC, 1982–; Cookson Gp plc, 1985–; Barclays International Ltd, 1986–; Barclays Bank Trust Co. Ltd, 1973–86 (Chm., 1985–86); Chairman: Slough Occupational Health Service, 1976–; Slough Social Fund, 1975–; Property Services Agency Adv. Bd, 1980–86; Aims of Industry, 1985–. Pres., Slough & Dist Chamber of Commerce, 1969–72; Vice-Pres., Assoc. of British Chambers of Commerce, 1976– (Chm. 1974–76); Pres., British Property Fedn, 1979–81. Pres., Bucks Assoc. of Boys' Clubs, 1984–. Mem. Council, Univ. of Buckingham, 1983–. CBIM. Renter Warden, Spectacle Makers' Co., 1985–. Hon. Fellow, Coll. of Estate Management. High Sheriff, 1982, DL, 1985, Bucks. *Recreations:* riding, hunting, ski-ing, golf, travel. *Address:* Widmer Lodge, Lacey Green, Aylesbury, Bucks HP17 0RJ. *T:* Hampden Row 265.

MOBERLY, Sir John (Campbell), KBE 1984; CMG 1976; HM Diplomatic Service, retired; Chairman, Middle East Consultants Ltd; *b* 27 May 1925; *s* of Sir Walter Moberly, GBE, KCB, DSO; *m* 1959, Patience, *d* of Major Sir Richard George Proby, 1st Bt, MC; two *s* one *d. Educ:* Winchester College; Magdalen College, Oxford. War Service in Royal Navy, 1943–47 (despatches). Entered HM Foreign (now Diplomatic) Service, 1950; Political Officer, Kuwait, 1954–56; Political Agent, Doha, 1959–62; First Secretary, Athens, 1962–66; Counsellor, Washington, 1969–73; Dir, Middle East Centre for Arab Studies, 1973–75; Ambassador, Jordan, 1975–79; Asst Under-Sec. of State, FCO, 1979–82; Ambassador, Iraq, 1982–85. CStJ 1979. *Recreations:* mountain walking and climbing, skiing, swimming. *Address:* 35 Pymers Mead, West Dulwich, SE21 8NH. *T:* 01–670 2680; The Cedars, Temple Sowerby, Penrith, Cumbria. *T:* Kirkby Thore 61437. *Clubs:* Royal Automobile; Leander (Henley-on-Thames).

MOBERLY, Sir Patrick (Hamilton), KCMG 1986 (CMG 1978); HM Diplomatic Service; Ambassador to South Africa, since 1984; *b* 2 Sept. 1928; *yr s* of G. H. Moberly; *m* 1955, Mary Penfold; two *s* one *d. Educ:* Winchester; Trinity Coll., Oxford (MA). HM Diplomatic Service, 1951–; diplomatic posts in: Baghdad, 1953; Prague, 1957; Foreign Office, 1959; Dakar, 1962; Min. of Defence, 1965; Commonwealth Office, 1967; Canada, 1969; Israel, 1970; FCO, 1974; Asst Under-Sec. of State, 1976–81; Ambassador to Israel, 1981–84. *Recreations:* tennis, sailing, opera. *Address:* c/o Foreign and Commonwealth Office, SW1A 2AH. *Club:* United Oxford & Cambridge University.

MOBERLY, Maj.-Gen. Richard James, CB 1957; OBE 1944; retired, 1960, and became Director, Communications Electronic Equipment, War Office, until 1964; *b* 2 July 1906; *o s* of late J. E. Moberly; *m* 1st, 1935, Mary Joyce Shelmerdine (*d* 1964); three *d;* 2nd, 1971, Mrs Vivien Mary Cameron (*d* 1981), *d* of Victor Bayley, CIE, CBE. *Educ:* Haileybury; Royal Military Academy, Woolwich. Commissioned Royal Signals, 1926; India, 1928–35; comd 1st Airborne Div. Signal Regt, 1942–43; CSO 1st Airborne Corps, 1943–45; Comdt Indian Signal Trng Centre, 1946–47; Dep. Comdt, Sch. of Signals, 1949–52; Dep. Dir of Signals, WO, 1952–54; CSO, Northern Army Gp, 1954–57; Signal Officer-in-Chief, WO, 1957–60. Col Comdt, Royal Signals, 1960–66. Comr for Dorset, St John Ambulance, 1968–76. KStJ 1986. *Address:* Steeple Cottage, Westport Road, Wareham, Dorset BH20 4PR. *T:* Wareham 2697.

MOCATTA, Sir Alan Abraham, Kt 1961; OBE 1944; Judge of the High Court of Justice (Queen's Bench Division), 1961–81, Member, 1961–81, President, 1970–81, Restrictive Practices Court; *b* 1907; *s* of Edward L. Mocatta and Flora Gubbay; *m* 1930, Pamela Halford, JP; four *s. Educ:* Clifton Coll.; New Coll., Oxford (exhbnr); 1st cl. History, 1928, 2nd cl. Jurisprudence, 1929; MA. Called to the Bar, Inner Temple, 1930; Bencher, 1960, Treas., 1982; Northern circuit; QC 1951. Served War of 1939–45: 2nd Lieut 12 LAA Regt, RA, TA, 1939; Bde Major, 56 AA Bde, 1940–41; GSO (2) AA HQ BTNI, 1941–42; Lt-Col GS, Army Council Secretariat, War Office, 1942–45. Chm., Council of Jews' Coll., 1945–61; Vice-Pres., Board of Elders, Spanish and Portuguese Jews' Congregation, London, 1961–67, Pres., 1967–82; Chm. Treasury Cttee on Cheque Endorsement, 1955–56. Joint editor, 14th-19th editions of Scrutton on Charter Parties; Editor, 3rd edn Rowlatt on Principal and Surety; Mem., Adv. Panel for 4th edn of Halsbury's Laws of England. *Address:* 18 Hanover House, NW8 7DX. *T:* 01–722 2857; 10 Breakwater Road, Bude, Cornwall. *T:* Bude 2745. *Club:* MCC.

MODIGLIANI, Prof. Franco; Professor of Economics and Finance, Massachusetts Institute of Technology, since 1962; Institute Professor, since 1970; *b* Rome, 1918; *s* of Enrico Modigliani and Olga (*née* Flaschel); *m* 1939, Serena Calibi; two *s. Educ:* Univ. of Rome (DJur 1939); DSocSci New Sch. for Social Research, New York, 1944. Instr in Economics and Statistics, New Jersey Coll. for Women, 1942; Instr, Associate in Economics and Statistics, Bard Coll. of Columbia Univ., 1942–44; Lectr, 1943–44, Asst Prof. of Math. Econ. and Econometrics, 1946–48, New Sch. for Social Research; Res. Associate and Chief Statistician, Inst. of World Affairs, NY, 1945–48; Res. Consultant, Cowles Commn for Res. in Economics, Univ. of Chicago, 1949–54; Associate Prof., 1949, Prof. of Economics, 1950–52, Univ. of Illinois; Prof. of Econ. and Indust. Admin, Carnegie Inst. of Technology, 1952–60; Prof. of Economics, Northwestern Univ., 1960–62. Social Science Research Council: Mem., Bd of Dirs, 1963–68; Mem., Cttee on Econ. Stability and Growth, 1970–; Jt Chm., Adv. Sub-Cttee on MIT-Pennsylvania SSRC Model, 1970–81; Mem., Sub-Cttee on Monetary Res., 1970–77. Academic Consultant, Bd of Governors, Federal Reserve System, 1966–; Sen. Adviser, Brookings Panel on Econ. Activity, 1971–; Consultant, Bank of Italy, Rome; Mem., Consiglio Italiano per le Scienze Sociali, 1974–; Perm. Mem., Conf. on Income and Wealth, Nat. Bureau of Econ. Res. Member: Editl Adv. Bd, Antitrust Law and Economics Review, 1985–; Adv. Bd, Jl of Money, Credit and Banking, 1969–. Mem., Nat. Acad. of Scis, 1973–; Fellow, Econometric Soc., 1949; Fellow, 1960–, Council Mem., 1978–80, Amer. Acad. of Arts and Scis. Numerous hon. degrees. Nobel Prize in Economic Science, 1985. Kt Grand Cross, Italy, 1985. *Publications:* National Incomes and International Trade (with Hans Neisser), 1953; (jtly) Planning Production, Inventories and Work Forces, 1960; (with Kalman J. Cohen) The Role of Anticipations and Plans in Economic Behavior and their Use in Economic Analysis and Forecasting, 1961; (with Ezio Tarantelli) Mercato del Lavoro, Distribuzione del Reddito e Consumi Privati, 1975; (ed with Donald Lessard) New Mortgage Designs for Stable Housing in an Inflationary Environment, 1975; The Collected Papers of Franco Modigliani, 3 vols, 1980; contribs to Corriere Della Sera, periodicals and learned jls. *Address:* Massachusetts Institute of Technology, Sloan School of Management, 50 Memorial Drive, Cambridge, Mass 02139, USA.

MOERAN, Edward Warner; *b* 27 Nov. 1903; *s* of E. J. Moeran. *Educ:* Christ's Coll., Finchley; University of London. Solicitor. MP (Lab) South Beds, 1950–51. Pres., W London Law Soc., 1971–72. Chm., Solicitors' Ecology Gp, 1972–74. *Publications:* Practical Conveyancing, 1949; Invitation to Conveyancing, 1962; Practical Legal Aid, 1970; (jtly) Social Welfare Law, 1977; Legal Aid Summary, 1978; Introduction to Conveyancing, 1979. *Recreation:* gardening. *Address:* 6 Frognal Gardens, Hampstead, NW3 6UX.

MOFFAT, Lt-Gen. Sir (William) Cameron, KBE 1985 (OBE 1975); QHS 1984; FRCS; Surgeon General/Director General Army Medical Services, Ministry of Defence, since 1985; *b* 8 Sept. 1929; *s* of William Weir Moffat and Margaret Garrett; *m* 1953, Audrey Watson; one *s. Educ:* King's Park Sch., Glasgow; Univ. of Glasgow, Western Infirmary (MB ChB). DTM&H. House Surgeon, Western Inf., Glasgow, 1952; Ship's Surg., Anchor Line, 1953; MO Seaforth Highlanders, 1954; SMO Edinburgh, 1956–57; Hammersmith Hosp., 1962; Birmingham Accident Hosp., 1964; Surg., RAAF Hosp. Malaya, 1965–67; Cons. Surg., BMH Rinteln, 1968–70; Prof. Military Surgery, RAM Coll. and RCS, 1970–75; CO BMH Rinteln, 1978–80; Comd MED HQ 1 (Br) Corps, 1980–83; PMO, UKLF, 1983–84. CStJ 1985. *Publications:* contribs to surgical text books and jls on missile wounds and their management. *Recreations:* golf, travel, bird-watching. *Address:* Defence Medical Services Directorate, First Avenue House, High Holborn, WC1V 6HE.

MOFFATT, Prof. Henry Keith, PhD; FRS 1986; Professor of Mathematical Physics, University of Cambridge, since 1980; Fellow, Trinity College, Cambridge, 1961–76, and since 1980; *b* 12 April 1935; *s* of Frederick Henry Moffatt and Emmeline Marchant Fleming; *m* 1960, Katharine, (Linty), Stiven, *d* of Rev. D. S. Stiven, MC, DD; two *s* two *d. Educ:* George Watson's Coll., Edinburgh; Edinburgh Univ. (BSc); Cambridge Univ. (BA, PhD). Lecturer in Mathematics, Cambridge Univ., and Director of Studies in Mathematics, Trinity Coll., 1961–76; Tutor, 1971–75; Sen. Tutor, 1975; Professor of Applied Mathematics, Bristol Univ., 1977–80. Visiting appts, Stanford Univ. and Johns Hopkins Univ., 1965, Univ. of Paris VI, 1975–76. Syndic, Cambridge University Press, 1984–. Co-editor, Journal of Fluid Mechanics, 1966–83. *Publications:* Magnetic Field Generation in Electrically Conducting Fluids, 1978 (Russian edn 1980); papers in fluid mechanics and dynamo theory in Jl Fluid Mech. and other jls. *Recreations:* squash, genealogy. *Address:* 6 Banham's Close, Cambridge. *T:* Cambridge 63338.

MOGG, Gen. Sir John, GCB 1972 (KCB 1966; CB 1964); CBE 1960; DSO 1944; Bar, 1944; Vice Lord-Lieutenant, Oxfordshire, since 1979; Deputy Supreme Allied Commander, Europe, 1973–76; *b* 17 Feb. 1913; *s* of late Capt. H. B. Mogg, MC and late Alice Mary (*née* Ballard); *m* 1939, Cecilia Margaret Molesworth; three *s. Educ:* Malvern Coll.; RMC Sandhurst. Coldstream Guards, 1933–35; RMC Sandhurst (Sword of Honour) 1935–37; commissioned Oxfordshire and Buckinghamshire Light Infantry, 1937. Served War of 1939–45 (despatches); comd 9 DLI (NW Europe), 1944–45; Instructor, Staff Coll., 1948–50; Commander 10th Parachute Bn, 1950–52; Chief Instructor, School of Infantry, Warminster, 1952–54; Instructor (GSO1), Imperial Defence Coll., 1954–56; Comdr, Commonwealth Brigade Gp, Malaya, 1958–60; Meritorious Medal (Perak, Malaya); Dir of Combat Development, War Office, 1961–62; Comdt, Royal Military Academy, Sandhurst, 1963–66; Comdr 1st (British) Corps, 1966–68; GOC-in-C Southern Comd, 1968; GOC-in-C Army Strategic Comd, 1968–70; Adjutant-Gen., MoD (Army), 1970–73. ADC Gen. to the Queen, 1971–74. Col Comdt:

Army Air Corps, 1963–74; The Royal Green Jackets, 1965–73; Hon. Col, 10th Parachute Bn, TA, 1973–78. Kermit Roosevelt Lectr, 1969. President: Army Cricket Assoc.; Army Saddle Club, 1969; Army Boxing Assoc., 1970; Army Parachute Assoc., 1971; BHS, 1972; Ex Services Mental Welfare Soc.; Army Benevolent Fund, 1980– (Chm., 1976); Normandy Veterans Assoc., 1984–; Chairman: Army Free Fall Parachute Assoc., 1970; Army Football Assoc., 1960–63; Royal Soldiers' Daughters Sch., 1976; Operation Drake for Young Explorers, 1978–; Operation Drake Fellowship, 1980–83; Royal Internat. Horse Show, 1979; Vice-Pres., Operation Raleigh. Pres., Council Services Kinema Corp., 1970. Dir, Lloyds Bank S Midland Regional Bd, 1976. Member Council: Wessex TA&VRA, 1976; British Atlantic Cttee, 1977. Comr, Royal Hospital Chelsea, 1976. Governor: Malvern College, 1967; Bradfield College, 1977; Chm. of Governors, Icknield Sch., 1981–. Hon. Liveryman, Fruiterers' Co. DL Oxfordshire, 1979. *Recreations:* cricket, most field sports, helicopter pilot. *Address:* Church Close, Watlington, Oxon. *Clubs:* Army and Navy, Flyfishers', MCC, Cavalry and Guards, Pitt.

MOGG, John Frederick; Under Secretary, European Commercial and Industrial Policy Division, Department of Trade and Industry, since 1986; *b* 5 Oct. 1943; *s* of Thomas W. Mogg and Cora M. Mogg; *m* 1967, Anne Smith; one *d* one *s*. *Educ:* Bishop Vesey's Grammar Sch., Sutton Coldfield; Birmingham Univ. (BA Hons). Rediffusion Ltd, 1965–74; Principal: Office of Fair Trading, 1974–76; Dept of Trade (Insurance Div.), 1976–79; First Sec., UK Perm. Representation, Brussels, 1979–82; Asst Sec., DTI (Minerals and Metals Div.), 1982–85; PPS to Sec. of State for Trade and Industry, 1985–86. *Address:* 19 East Drive, Brighton, Sussex BN2 2BQ.

MOGG, Sir William R.; *see* Rees-Mogg.

MOHAMED ALI, Ibrahim; Ambassador of Sudan to the Court of St James's, since 1985; *b* 13 Sept. 1932; *s* of Mohamed Ali Ibrahim and Batul Ali El Hag; *m* 1962, Alawia Ramzi Hussein; three *s* one *d*. *Educ:* Univ. of Cairo (BA; Dip. Inst. Pol. Sci.). Joined Min. of Foreign Affairs as Third Sec., 1957; served with Sudan Embassies in Athens, Belgrade, Dar es Salaam, Jeddah, Moscow; Diplomatic course at LSE, 1965; Ambassador to: Kuwait, 1972–74; Ivory Coast, 1974–76; Chief of State Protocol, 1976–78; Ambassador to: Canada, 1978–80; Spain, 1980–83; Under Sec., Min. of For. Affairs, 1984–85. Grand Cross, Order of Isobel la Católica (Spain), 1983; Officer of Legion of Honour (France). *Recreations:* fishing, sports (football, table tennis), photography. *Address:* (office) Sudanese Embassy, 3 Cleveland Row, St James's, SW1; (home) 42 Aylestone Avenue, NW6.

MOHYEDDIN, Zia; actor; producer and director, Central TV, since 1980; *b* 20 June 1931; *m* 1974, Nahid Siddiqui; three *s*. *Educ:* Punjab University (BA Hons). Freelance directing for Aust. broadcasting, 1951–52; RADA, 1953–54; Pakistan stage appearances, 1956–59; UK stage, 1959–71; Dir Gen., Pakistan Nat. Performing Ensemble, to 1977; *stage:* appearances include: A Passage to India, 1960; The Alchemist, 1964; The Merchant of Venice, 1966; Volpone, 1967; The Guide, 1968; On The Rocks, 1969; Measure for Measure, 1981; *films:* Lawrence of Arabia, 1961; Sammy Going South, 1963; The Sailor from Gibraltar; Khartoum, 1965; Ashanti, 1982; Assam Garden, 1985; *television series:* The Hidden Truth, 1964; Gangsters, 1979; Jewel in the Crown, 1983; King of the Ghetto, 1986. *Recreations:* reading, bridge, watching cricket. *Address:* c/o Plunkett Greene Ltd, 91 Regent Street, W1. *Club:* Savile.

MOI, Hon. Daniel arap, EGH, EBS; President of Kenya, since 1978; Minister of Defence, since 1979; *b* Rift Valley Province, 1924. *Educ:* African Inland Mission Sch., Kabartonjo; Govt African Sch., Kapsabet. Teacher, 1946–56. MLC, 1957; Mem. for Baringo, House of Representatives, 1963–78; Minister for Educn, 1961; Minister for Local Govt, 1962–64; Minister for Home Affairs, 1964–67; Vice-Pres. of Kenya, 1967–78. Chm., Kenya African Democratic Union (KADU), 1960; Pres., Kenya African Nat. Union (KANU) for Rift Valley Province, 1966; Pres. of KANU, 1978–. Chm., Rift Valley Provincial Council. Former Member: Rift Valley Educn Bd; Kalenjin Language Cttee; Commonwealth Higher Educn Cttee; Kenya Meat Commn; Bd of Governors, African Girls' High Sch., Kikuyu. *Address:* Office of the President, PO Box 30510, Nairobi, Kenya; State House, PO Box 40530, Nairobi, Kenya.

MOIR, Sir Ernest Ian Royds, 3rd Bt, *cr* 1916; *b* 9 June 1925; *o s* of Sir Arrol Moir, 2nd Bt, and Dorothy Blanche, *d* of Admiral Sir Percy Royds, CB, CMG; *S* father, 1957; *m* 1954, Margaret Hanham Carter; three *s*. *Educ:* Rugby; Cambridge Univ. (BA). Served War of 1939–45 in Royal Engineers. *Heir: s* Christopher Ernest Moir, *b* 22 May 1955. *Address:* Three Gates, 174 Coombe Lane West, Kingston, Surrey. *T:* 01–942 7394. *Club:* Royal Automobile.

MOIR, (George) Guthrie, MA; *b* 30 Oct. 1917; *s* of James William and May Flora Moir; *m* 1951, Sheila Maureen Ryan, SRN; one *s* two *d*. *Educ:* Berkhamsted; Peterhouse, Cambridge. Officer, 5th Suffolk Regt, 1940–46, POW Singapore, 1942. Chief Officer (with Countess (Edwina) Mountbatten of Burma), St John Ambulance Bde Cadets, 1947–50; Dir, European Youth Campaign, 1950–52; Chm., later Pres., World Assembly of Youth, 1952–56; Education Adviser, Hollerith Tab. Machine Co., 1957; adopted Bradenham Manor (Disraeli's) as a training centre; Asst Controller and Exec. Producer, Rediffusion TV, 1958–68; Controller of Educn and Religious Programmes, Thames TV, 1968–76. Serious damage under train in Sept. 1974, and in hospitals till recently. Member: Gen. Synod (formerly House of Laity, Church Assembly), 1956–75; Bd of Church Army, 1973–; Mem. Council, Reading Univ. Mem. Cttee Athenæum, 1974–. Contested (L) Aylesbury Div., 1950. CC Bucks, 1949–75; President: Old Berkhamstedians Assoc., 1974; Ivinghoe Beacon Villages, 1973; started Green Park in adjoining delicious Rothschild country (Chm., Youth Centre). Vice Pres., St John, Bucks. Papal Bene Merenti Medal 1970, for services to religious and educational broadcasting. FRSA 1980. OStJ. *Publications:* (ed) Why I Believe, 1964; (ed) Life's Work, 1965; (ed) Teaching and Television: ETV Explained, 1967; The Suffolk Regiment, 1969; Into Television, 1969; (ed) Beyond Hatred, 1969; contribs to Times, Times Ed. Supplement, Church Times, Contemporary Review, Frontier, etc. Many TV series, including This Week; Dialogue with Doubt; Royalist and Roundhead; Best Sellers; Treasures of the British Museum; (with Nat. Trust) A Place in the Country; A Place in History; A Place in Europe. *Recreations:* golf, poetry, churches, mountains. *Address:* The Old Rectory, Aston Clinton, Aylesbury, Bucks. *T:* Aylesbury 630393. *Club:* Nikaean.

MOIR CAREY, D. M.; *see* Carey.

MOISEIWITSCH, Prof. Benjamin Lawrence; Professor of Applied Mathematics since 1968, and Head of Department of Applied Mathematics and Theoretical Physics since 1977, Queen's University of Belfast; *b* London, 6 Dec. 1927; *s* of Jacob Moiseiwitsch and Chana Kotlerman; *m* 1953, Sheelagh M. McKeon; two *s* two *d*. *Educ:* Royal Liberty Sch., Romford; University Coll., London (BSc, 1949, PhD 1952). Sir George Jessel Studentship in Maths, UCL, 1949; Queen's University, Belfast: Lectr and Reader in Applied Maths, 1952–68; Dean, Faculty of Science, 1972–75. MRIA 1969. *Publications:* Variational Principles, 1966; Integral Equations, 1977; articles on theoretical atomic physics in scientific jls. *Address:* 21 Knocktern Gardens, Belfast, Northern Ireland BT4 3LZ. *T:* Belfast 658332.

MOISEIWITSCH, Tanya, (Mrs Felix Krish), CBE 1976; designer for the theatre; *b* 3 Dec. 1914; *d* of late Benno Moiseiwitsch, CBE, and 1st wife, Daisy Kennedy; *m* 1942, Felix Krish (decd). *Educ:* various private schs; Central School of Arts and Crafts, London; Scenic painting student at Old Vic, London. Abbey Theatre, Dublin, 1935–39; Q. Theatre, 1940; 1st West End prod. Golden Cuckoo, Duchess, 1940; Weekly Repertory, Oxford Playhouse, 1941–44. Stage designs include: Bless the Bride, Adelphi, 1947; Peter Grimes, Covent Garden, 1947; Beggar's Opera, English Opera Group, Aldeburgh Festival, 1948; Treasure Hunt, Apollo, 1949; Home at Seven, Wyndham's, 1950; The Holly and the Ivy, Lyric (Hammersmith) and Duchess, 1950; Captain Carvallo, St James's, 1950; Figure of Fun, Aldwych, 1951. Has designed for Old Vic Company since 1944; at Playhouse, Liverpool, 1944–45; at Theatre Royal, Bristol, 1945–46; productions for Old Vic Company include: (at New Theatre): Uncle Vanya, The Critic, Cyrano de Bergerac, 1945–46, The Cherry Orchard, 1948, A Month in the Country, 1949; (at Old Vic): Midsummer Night's Dream, 1951, Timon of Athens, 1952, Henry VIII, 1953; Two Gentlemen of Verona, 1957. Has designed for Royal Shakespeare Theatre, Stratford upon Avon: Henry VIII, 1950; The History Cycle (assisted by Alix Stone), 1951; Othello, 1954; Measure for Measure, 1956; Much Ado about Nothing (scenery), 1958; All's Well that Ends Well, 1959; also for 1st, and subsequent seasons, Shakespearean Festival, Stratford, Ont, incl. Cymbeline, 1970; The Imaginary Invalid, 1974; All's Well that Ends Well, 1977; Mary Stuart (costumes), 1982; Tartuffe, 1983; (with Polly Scranton Bohdanetzky) The Government Inspector, Stratford, Ont, 1985; for The Matchmaker, Edinburgh Festival, 1954, and New York, 1955; for Cherry Orchard, Piccolo Teatro, Milan, 1955; for Merchant of Venice, Habimah Theatre, Israel, 1959; Tyrone Guthrie Theatre, Minneapolis, USA: 1963: Hamlet, The Miser, Three Sisters; 1964: St Joan, Volpone; 1965: The Way of the World; Cherry Orchard; 1966: As You Like It; Skin of our Teeth (with Carolyn Parker); 1967: The House of Atreus; Metropolitan Opera, New York: Peter Grimes, 1967; Rigoletto, 1977; La Traviata, 1981; National Theatre: Volpone, 1968; The Misanthrope, 1973; Phaedra Britannica, 1975; The Double Dealer, 1978; Macook's Corner, Ulster Players, Belfast, 1969; Caucasian Chalk Circle, Sheffield Playhouse, 1969; Swift, Abbey Theatre, Dublin, 1969; Uncle Vanya, Minneapolis, 1969; The Barber of Seville, Brighton Festival, 1971; (with J. Jensen) The Government Inspector (costumes), USA, 1973; Australian Tour for Elizabethan Theatre Trust, 1974; The Misanthrope, St James' Theater, NY, 1975; The Voyage of Edgar Allan Poe (world première), Minnesota Opera Co., USA, 1976; Œdipus the King and Œdipus at Colonus (costumes and masks), Adelaide Fest., 1978; Red Roses for Me, Abbey Theatre, Dublin, 1980; The Clandestine Marriage, Compass Theatre Co. tour and Albery, 1984. Cons. designer, Crucible Theatre, Sheffield, 1971–73. For Granada TV, King Lear (costumes), 1983. Diplôme d'Honneur, Canadian Conference of the Arts; Hon. Fellow, Ontario Coll. of Art, 1979. Hon. DLitt: Birmingham, 1964; Waterloo, Ont, 1977. *Address:* c/o National Westminster Bank, 185 Sloane Street, SW1.

MOKAMA, Hon. Moleleki Didwell, BA, LLM (Harvard), LLM (London); Barrister-at-Law; Advocate of the Supreme Court of Botswana; Attorney-General of Botswana, since 1969; Member of Parliament *ex officio* and Member of the Cabinet *ex officio*; *b* 2 Feb. 1933; *e s* of Mokama Moleleki and Baipoledi Moleleki, Maunatlala, Botswana; *m* 1962, Kgopodiso Vivien Robi; one *s*. *Educ:* Moeng; Fort Hare; London Univ.; Inner Temple. Crown Counsel to Botswana Govt, 1963–66; High Comr for Botswana in London, 1966–69; Botswana Ambassador Extraordinary and Plenipotentiary: to France, 1967–69; to Germany, 1967–69; to Sweden, 1968–69; to Denmark, 1968–69. Hon. Mem., American Soc. of International Law, 1965. *Recreations:* swimming, shooting, hunting, photography. *Address:* Attorney-General's Chambers, Private Bag 009, Gaborone, Botswana.

MOLAPO, Mooki Motsarapane; High Commissioner for Lesotho in the United Kingdom, 1979–82; *b* 28 April 1928; *s* of Motsarapane and Mathebe Molapo; *m* 1958, Emily Mamanasse Thamae; three *s* one *d*. *Educ:* Lesotho (then Basutoland) High School. Government Service, 1950–83, retired. *Recreations:* football fan, walking, movies, theatre. *Address:* PO Box 1574, Maseru 100, Lesotho.

MOLESWORTH, family name of **Viscount Molesworth.**

MOLESWORTH, 11th Viscount, *cr* 1716 (Ireland); **Richard Gosset Molesworth;** Baron Philipstown, 1716; secretarial work since 1959; *b* 31 Oct. 1907; *s* of 10th Viscount and Elizabeth Gladys Langworthy (*d* 1974); *S* father, 1961; *m* 1958, Anne Florence Womersley, MA (*d* 1983); two *s*. *Educ:* Lancing Coll.; private tutors. Farmed for many years. Freeman, City of London, 1978. Served War, in RAF, 1941–44 (Middle East, 1941–43). *Recreations:* foreign travel, music. *Heir: s* Hon. Robert Bysse Kelham Molesworth, *b* 4 June 1959. *Address:* Garden Flat, 2 Bishopswood Road, Highgate, N6. *T:* 01–348 1366.

MOLESWORTH, Allen Henry Neville; Chief Accountant, Property, British Telecom plc, since 1984; *b* 20 Aug. 1931; *s* of late Roger Bevil Molesworth (Colonel RA), and of Iris Alice Molesworth (*née* Kennion); *m* 1970, Gail Cheng Kwai Chan. *Educ:* Wellington Coll., Berks; Trinity Coll., Cambridge (MA). FCA, FCMA, MIMC. 2nd Lt, 4th Queen's Own Hussars, Malaya, 1950. Project Accounts, John Laing & Sons (Canada) Ltd, 1954–58; Singleton Fabian & Co., Chartered Accountants, 1959–63; Consultant: Standard Telephones & Cables Ltd, 1963–67; Coopers & Lybrand Associates Ltd, 1967–76: India, 1970; Kuwait, 1971; France, 1972; New Hebrides, 1972; Laos, 1974; Tonga, 1975; Financial and Admin. Controller, Crown Agents, 1976–84. *Recreations:* shooting, skiing, music, restoring antiques. *Address:* c/o Lloyds Bank, Cox's & King's Branch, 6 Pall Mall, SW1. *Clubs:* 1900, Coningsby.

MOLESWORTH-ST AUBYN, Lt-Col Sir (John) Arscott, 15th Bt *cr* 1689, of Pencarrow; MBE 1963; DL; JP; *b* 15 Dec. 1926; *s* of Sir John Molesworth-St Aubyn, 14th Bt, CBE, and Celia Marjorie (*d* 1965), *d* of Lt-Col Valentine Vivian, CMG, DSO, MVO; *S* father, 1985; *m* 1957, Iona Audrey Armatrude, *d* of late Adm. Sir Francis Loftus Tottenham, KCB, CBE; two *s* one *d*. *Educ:* Eton. 2nd Lieut KRRC 1946; Captain 1954; psc 1959; Major 1961; jssc 1964; served Malaya and Borneo, 1961–63 and 1965; Royal Green Jackets, 1966; Lt-Col 1967; retd 1969. County Comr, Scouts, Cornwall, 1969–79. Mem., Cornwall River Authority, 1969–74; Chm. Devon Exec. Cttee, 1975–77, and Vice-Chm. Cornwall Exec. Cttee, 1985–, Country Landowners Assoc.; Chairman: West Local Land Drainage Cttee, SW Water Authority, 1974–; Wessex Region, Historic Houses Assoc., 1981–83. Pres., Royal Cornwall Agricl Assoc., 1976; Mem. Council, Devon County Agricl Assoc., 1979–82; JP Devon, 1971; DL Cornwall, 1971; High Sheriff Cornwall, 1975. *Recreations:* shooting, ornithology. *Heir: s* William Molesworth-St Aubyn, *b* 23 Nov. 1958. *Address:* Pencarrow, Bodmin, Cornwall. *T:* St Mabyn 449; Tetcott Manor, Holsworthy, Devon. *T:* North Tamerton 220. *Clubs:* Army and Navy; Cornish 1768.

MOLEYNS; *see* Eveleigh-De-Moleyns.

MOLLISON, Prof. Patrick Loudon, CBE 1979; MD; FRCP; FRCPath; FRCOG; FRS 1968; Professor of Hæmatology, St Mary's Hospital Medical School, London University, 1962–79, now Emeritus Professor; Hon. Consultant Immunohaematologist, North

London Blood Transfusion Centre, since 1983; *b* 17 March 1914; *s* of William Mayhew Mollison, Cons. Surgeon (ENT), Guy's Hospital; *m* 1st, 1940, Dr Margaret D. Peirce (marr. diss., 1964); three *s*; 2nd, 1973, Dr Jennifer Jones. *Educ:* Rugby Sch.; Clare Coll., Cambridge; St Thomas' Hosp., London. MD Cantab 1944; FRCP 1959; FRCPath 1963; FRCOG *ad eund*, 1980. House Phys., Medical Unit, St Thomas' Hosp., 1939; Medical Officer, S London Blood Supply Depot, 1939–43; RAMC, 1943–46; Dir, MRC Blood Transfusion Res. Unit, Hammersmith Hosp., 1946–60; part-time Dir, MRC Experimental Hæmatology Unit, 1960–79; Hon. Lectr, then Sen. Lectr, Dept of Medicine, Post-grad. Medical Sch., 1948; Consultant Hæmatologist: Hammersmith Hosp., 1947–60; St Mary's Hosp., 1960–79. Hon. FRSM 1979; Landsteiner Meml Award, USA, 1960; P. Levine Award, USA, 1973; Oehlecker Medal, Germany, 1974. *Publications:* Blood Transfusion in Clinical Medicine, 1951 (7th edn 1983); papers on red cell survival and blood group antibodies. *Recreations:* music, gardening, golf. *Address:* 60 King Henry's Road, NW3 3RR. *T:* 01–722 1947.

MOLLO, Joseph Molelekoa Kaibe; Ambassador of the Kingdom of Lesotho to Denmark (also accredited to Sweden, Norway, Finland, Iceland, German Democratic Republic and Poland), since 1983; *b* 7 May 1944; *s* of Kaibe and Cyrian Mollo; *m* 1972, Makaibe; two *s* two *d*. *Educ:* Univ. of Botswana, Lesotho and Swaziland (BA Admin); Univ. of Saskatchewan (MCEd); Carleton Univ. (working on a Master's degree in Political Science since 1978). Asst Sec., Min. of Finance, 1971; Comr of Co-operatives, 1973; Dep. Perm. Sec., Finance, 1975; High Comr, Canada, 1976; Perm. Sec., Finance, 1980; High Comr in London, 1982–83. Unpublished thesis: Profit versus Co-operation: the struggle of the Western Co-operative College. *Recreations:* jogging, dancing, music, soccer. *Address:* Embassy of the Kingdom of Lesotho, Østerkildevej 14, DK-2820 Gentofte, Copenhagen, Denmark.

MOLLO, Victor; Bridge Correspondent, The Mail on Sunday, since 1982; Bridge Editor, Methuen, since 1985; Bridge Cruise Director: P&O, 1973–74; Norwegian-America Line, 1975; *b* St Petersburg, 17 Sept. 1909; Russian parents; *m* 1952, Jeanne Victoria Forbes. *Educ:* privately in Paris; Cordwalles, Surrey (Prep. Sch.); Brighton Coll.; London School of Economics, London Univ. Freelance journalism, also reading French and Russian texts for publishers, 1927–40; sub editor and editor, European Services (now External) BBC, 1940 till retirement in Oct. 1969. Bridge Correspondent, The Evening Standard, 1970–75; Bridge Editor: Faber & Faber, 1966–79; Pelham Books, 1980–82. *Publications:* Streamlined Bridge, 1947; Card-Play Technique (in collab. with N. Gardener), 1955; Bridge for Beginners (in collab. with N. Gardener) 1956; Bridge Psychology, 1958; Will You Be My Partner?, 1959; Bridge: Modern Bidding, 1961; Success at Bridge, 1964; Bridge in the Menagerie, 1965; Confessions of an Addict, 1966; The Bridge Immortals, 1967; Victor Mollo's Winning Double, 1968; Bridge: Case for the Defence, 1970; (with E. Jannersten) Best of Bridge, 1972; Bridge in the Fourth Dimension, 1974; Instant Bridge, 1975; (with Aksel J. Nielson) Defence at Bridge, 1976; Bridge Unlimited, 1976; Bridge Course Complete, 1977; The Finer Arts of Bridge, 1977; Masters and Monsters, 1978; Streamline Your Bidding, 1979; Streamline Your Card Play, 1981; Bridge à la Carte, 1982; Winning Bridge, 1983; You Need Never Lose at Bridge, 1983; I Challenge You, 1984; The Other Side of Bridge, 1984; Tomorrow's Textbook, 1985; The Compleat Bridge Player, 1986; also Pocket Guides: ACOL: Winning Bidding, 1969 and Winning Defence, Winning Conventions. Contributing Editor to the Official Encyclopaedia of Bridge. Regular contributor to Bridge Magazines in USA, France, Denmark, Norway and Sweden and to Bridge Magazine in Britain. *Recreations:* gastronomy, conversation, bridge. *Address:* 801 Grenville House, Dolphin Square, SW1. *Club:* St James's Bridge.

MOLLOY, family name of **Baron Molloy.**

MOLLOY, Baron *cr* 1981 (Life Peer), of Ealing in Greater London; **William John Molloy,** FRGS; *b* 26 Oct. 1918; *m* Eva Lewis; one *d*; *m* 1980, Doris Paines, *d* of Joseph Foxton. *Educ:* elementary sch., Swansea; University Coll., Swansea (Political Economy, extra-mural). Served Field Coy, RE, 1939–46. Member: TGWU 1936–46; Civil Service Union, 1946–52; Co-op and USDAW, 1952; Parliamentary Adviser: COHSE, 1974–; Civil Service Union, 1974–79. Editor, Civil Service Review, 1947–52; Chm., Staff-Side Whitley Council, Germany and Austria Sections, FO, 1948–52, and Staff-Side Lectr, 1946–52. Leader, Fulham Borough Council, 1959–62. MP (Lab) Ealing N, 1964–79; former Vice-Chm., Parly Labour Party Gp for Common Market and European Affairs; Chm., PLP Social Services Gp, 1974; Parly Adviser, London Trades Council Transport Cttee, 1968–79; Mem., House of Commons Estimates Cttee, 1968–70; PPS to Minister of Posts and Telecom., 1969–70. Member: CPA, 1964; IPU, 1964 (Mem. Exec., 1984–); Assemblies, Council of Europe and WEU, 1969–73; European Parlt, 1976–79. Mem., Parly and Scientific Cttee, 1982–; EC Mem., CAABY; Mem., Parly and Scientific Assoc. Political Consultant: Confedn of Health Service Employess, 1980–; British Library Assoc., 1984–; former Adviser to Arab League. Pres., Metropolitan Area, Royal British Legion, 1984–; Hon. Pres., London Univ. Union, 1983–; Mem. Court, Reading Univ., 1968–; Mem. Exec. Council, RGS, 1976–. Fellow, World Assoc. of Arts and Sciences. *Recreations:* horse-riding, music. *Address:* 2a Uneeda Drive, Greenford, Mddx. *T:* (office) 01–219 6710.

MOLLOY, Michael John; Editor in Chief, Mirror Group, since 1985; Editor, Sunday Mirror, since 1986; *b* 22 Dec. 1940; *s* of John George and Margaret Ellen Molloy; *m* 1964, Sandra June Foley; three *d*. *Educ:* Ealing School of Art. Sunday Pictorial, 1956; Daily Sketch, 1960; Daily Mirror, 1962–85: Editor, Mirror Magazine, 1969; Asst Editor, 1970; Dep. Editor, 1975; Editor, Dec. 1975–1985; Dir, Mirror Group Newspapers, 1976–. *Publications:* The Black Dwarf, 1985; The Kid from Riga, 1986. *Recreations:* reading, writing. *Address:* Mirror Group Newspapers Ltd, 33 Holborn, EC1. *T:* 01–353 0246. *Club:* Reform.

MOLONY, Thomas Desmond, 3rd Bt. Does not use the title, and his name is not on the Official Roll of Baronets.

MOLOTOV, Vyacheslav Mikhailovich, (*pseudonym* of V. M. Skryabin); Soviet diplomat; *b* Kirov district (Vyatka), 9 March 1890; son of a ship assistant; as mem. of students' Marxist circles in Kazan, took part in first Revolution, 1905; joined Bolshevik section of Russian Social Democratic Labour Party and organised students, 1906; arrested and deported to Vologda, organised Vologda railwaymen; graduated, 1909, organised students, Petrograd; contributed to Zvezda; part-founder with Stalin and sec. of Pravda, 1911; exiled from Petrograd for political activity, 1912; continued Party work from suburbs, organising elections and work of Party deputies in Duma, 1913; reorganised Moscow Bolshevik Party; exiled to Irkutsk, Siberia, 1915; escaped, returned to Petrograd and appointed mem. of Russian Bureau of Bolshevik Central Committee, 1916; mem. of executive of Petrograd Soviet and of military revolutionary cttee, 1917; chm. of People's Economy Council, Northern Region, 1918; chm. Nijegorodsky regional executive, 1919; sec. of Donets Regional Party cttee, 1920; elected mem. and sec. of Central Cttee of Communist Party of Soviet Union and candidate mem. of Political Bureau, 1921; mem. of Political Bureau of CPSU; worked against Zinovievists, Leningrad, 1926; elected mem. of Central Executive Cttee of Russian Soviet Socialist Republic, 1927; sec., Moscow cttee of CPSU; worked against Bukharinists in Moscow, 1928; elected mem. of Presidium of Central Executive Cttee of USSR, 1929; chm. of Council, of People's Commissars of USSR, 1930–41; 1st Dep. Chm., Council of People's Commissars, 1941–46; Dep. Chm., State Defence Cttee, 1941–45; took part in Teheran, Crimean, Potsdam and San Francisco Conferences; Leader of Soviet Delegn to Paris Peace Conf., 1946, to UN Gen. Assemblies, 1945–48; People's Commissar for For. Affairs, 1939–46, For. Min., 1946–49, 1953–56; First Dep. Chm. of USSR Council of Ministers, 1953–57; Min. of State Control, 1956–57; Dep. to Supreme Soviet, 1937–57; Soviet Ambassador to Mongolia, 1957–60; Chief Permanent Representative of the Soviet Union (rank Ambassador) to the International Atomic Energy Agency, Vienna, 1960–62. Hon. Mem. USSR Acad. of Sciences, 1946. Hero of Socialist Labour (and Hammer and Sickle Medal), 1943; Order of Lenin (4 awards). *Publications:* In the Struggle for Socialism, 1934; Articles and Speeches, 1935–36, 1937; Problems of Foreign Policy, 1948. *Address:* c/o Ministry of Social Security, 14 Shabolovka, Moscow, USSR.

MOLSON, family name of **Baron Molson.**

MOLSON, Baron, *cr* 1961, of High Peak (Life Peer); **(Arthur) Hugh (Elsdale) Molson,** PC 1956; President, Council for Protection of Rural England, 1971–80 (Chairman, 1968–71); *b* 29 June 1903; *o surv. s* of late Major J. E. Molson, MP, Gainsborough, and Mary, *d* of late A. E. Leeson, MD; *m* 1949, Nancy, *d* of late W. H. Astington, Bramhall, Cheshire. *Educ:* Royal Naval Colleges, Osborne and Dartmouth; Lancing; New Coll., Oxford. Pres. of Oxford Union, 1925; 1st Class Hons Jurisprudence. Served 36 Searchlight Regt, 1939–41. Staff Captain 11 AA, Div., 1941–42. Barrister-at-Law, Inner Temple, 1931; Political Sec., Associated Chambers of Commerce of India, 1926–29; Contested Aberdare Div. of Merthyr Tydfil, 1929; MP (U) Doncaster, 1931–35. MP (U) The High Peak Div. of Derbyshire, 1939–61. Parly Sec., Min. of Works, 1951–53; Joint Parly Sec., Min. of Transport and Civil Aviation, Nov. 1953–Jan. 1957; Minister of Works, 1957–Oct. 1959. Mem., Monckton Commission on Rhodesia and Nyasaland, 1960; Chm., Commn of Privy Counsellors on the dispute between Buganda and Bunyoro, 1962. *Publications:* articles in various reviews on political and other subjects. *Address:* 20 Marsham Court, Marsham Street, SW1P 4JY. *T:* 01–828 2008. *Clubs:* Athenæum, Carlton.

MOLYNEAUX, Rt. Hon. James Henry; PC 1983; JP; MP (UU) Lagan Valley, since 1983 (Antrim South, 1970–83); Leader, Ulster Unionist Party, since 1979; *b* 27 Aug. 1920; *s* of late William Molyneaux, Seacash, Killead, Co. Antrim; unmarried. *Educ:* Aldergrove Sch., Co. Antrim. RAF, 1941–46. Vice-Chm., Eastern Special Care Hosp. Man. Cttee, 1966–73; Chm. Antrim Br., NI Assoc. for Mental Health, 1967–70; Hon. Sec., S Antrim Unionist Assoc., 1964–70; Vice-Pres., Ulster Unionist Council, 1974. Mem. (UU) S Antrim, NI Assembly, 1982–86. Leader, UU Party, House of Commons, 1974–. Dep. Grand Master of Orange Order and Hon. PGM of Canada; Sovereign Grand Master, Commonwealth Royal Black Instn, 1971. JP Antrim, 1957; CC Antrim, 1964–73. *Recreations:* gardening, music. *Address:* Aldergrove, Crumlin, Co. Antrim, N Ireland. *T:* Crumlin 52545.

MOLYNEUX, James Robert M.; *see* More-Molyneux.

MOLYNEUX, Wilfrid, FCA; *b* 26 July 1910; *s* of Charles Molyneux and Mary (*née* Vose); *m* 1937, Kathleen Eleanor Young; one *s* one *d*. *Educ:* Douai Sch. With Cooper Brothers & Co., 1934–67; Finance Mem., BSC, 1967–71. *Address:* 105 Park Road, Brentwood, Essex CM14 4TT.

MOMIGLIANO, Prof. Arnaldo Dante, Hon. KBE 1974; DLitt (Turin); FBA 1954; Professor of Ancient History in the University of London at University College, 1951–75; Alexander White Visiting Professor, University of Chicago, 1959 and since 1975; *b* 5 Sept. 1908; *s* of late Riccardo Momigliano and late Ilda Levi; *m* 1932, Gemma Segre; one *d*. *Educ:* privately, and at Univs of Turin and Rome. Professore Incaricato di Storia Greca, Univ. of Rome, 1932–36; Professore Titolare di Storia Romana, 1936–38, Professore Ordinario di Storia Romana in soprannumero, 1945–64, Univ. of Turin, *Id*, 1964–, Scuola Normale Superiore of Pisa. Lecturer in Ancient History, 1947–49, Reader in Ancient History, 1949–51, University of Bristol; research work in Oxford, 1939–47. Sather Prof. in Classics, Univ. of California, 1961–62; J. H. Gray Lectr, Univ. of Cambridge, 1963; Wingate Lectr, Hebrew Univ. of Jerusalem, 1964; Vis. Prof. and Lauro de Bosis Lectr, Harvard Univ., 1964–65; C. N. Jackson Lectr, Harvard Univ., 1968; Jerome Lectr, Michigan Univ., 1971–72; Vis. Schol., Harvard, 1972; Trevelyan Lectr, Cambridge Univ., 1973; Flexner Lectr, Bryn Mawr, 1974; Grinfield Lectr on the Septuagint, Oxford, 1978–82; Efroymson Lectr, Hebrew Union Coll., Cincinnati, 1978; Chr. Gauss Lectr, Princeton, 1979; Lurcy Prof., Univ. of Chicago, 1982; Vis. Fellow: Peterhouse, Cambridge, 1983–85; Princeton Univ., 1984; Vis. Prof., Ecole Normale Supérieure, Paris, 1984. Socio Nazionale: Accademia dei Lincei, 1961 (corresp. mem., 1947–61); Arcadia, 1967; Accademia delle Scienze di Torino, 1968; Istituto di Studi Romani, 1970 (corresp. mem., 1954–70); Istituto Studi Etruschi, 1973. Foreign Member: Royal Dutch Academy; Amer. Philosophical Soc.; Amer. Acad. of Arts and Scis; Institut de France; Corresp. Mem., German Archæological Institute, 1935; Hon. Mem., Amer. Hist. Assoc., 1964. Pres., Soc. for Promotion of Roman Studies, 1965–68. Hon. MA Oxford; Hon. DLitt: Bristol, 1959; Edinburgh, 1964; Oxford, 1970; Cambridge, 1971; London, 1975; Chicago, 1976; Leiden, 1977; Urbino, 1978; Marburg, 1986; Hon. DHL: Columbia, 1974; Brandeis, 1977; Hebrew Union Coll., 1980; Bard Coll., 1983; Yale, 1985; Hon. DPhil: Hebrew Univ., 1974; Tel-Aviv Univ., 1981. Hon. Fellow: Warburg Inst., 1975; UCL, 1976; Peterhouse, 1985. Premio Cantoni, Univ. of Florence, 1932; Premio Feltrinelli for historical res. (Accademia dei Lincei award), 1960; Kaplun Prize for historical res., Hebrew Univ., 1975; Gold Medal, Italian Min. of Educn, 1977; Kenyon Medal, British Acad., 1981; Premio Sila per la saggistica, Cosenza Univ., 1985. Co-editor of Rivista Storica Italiana, 1948–. *Publications:* La composizione della Storia di Tucidide, 1930; Prime Linee di storia della tradizione maccabaica, 1931 (2nd edn 1968); Claudius, 1934 (2nd edn 1961); Filippo il Macedone, 1934; La storiografia sull' impero romano, 1936; Contributo alla storia degli studi classici, 1955; Secondo Contributo alla storia degli studi classici, 1960; Terzo Contributo alla storia degli studi classici, 1966; Studies in Historiography, 1966; (ed) Paganism and Christianity in the Fourth Century, 1963 (trans. Italian); Quarto contributo alla storia degli studi classici, 1969; The Development of Greek Biography, 1971 (trans. Italian, Japanese); Introduzione Bibliografica alla Storia Greca fino a Socrate, 1975; Quinto Contributo alla Storia degli studi classici, 1975; Alien Wisdom, the limits of Hellenization, 1975, 2nd edn 1978 (trans. Italian, German, French, Spanish); Essays on Historiography, 1977; Sesto Contributo alla Storia degli Studi Classici, 1981; La Storiografia Greca, 1982 (trans. Spanish, 1984); Problèmes d'historiographie ancienne et moderne, 1983; New Paths of Classicism in the Nineteenth Century, 1983; (ed) Aspetti di Hermann Usener filologo della religione, 1983; (ed) Aspetti dell'opera di G. Dumézil, 1983; Sui Fondamenti della Storia Antica, 1984; Settimo Contributo alla Storia degli Studi Classici, 1984; Tra Storiae Storicismo, 1985; Ottavo Contributo alla Storia degli Studi Classici, 1987; contribs to Cambridge Ancient History, Jl of Roman Studies, History and Theory, Jl of Warburg Inst., Daedalus, Enciclopedia Italiana, Encycl.

Britannica, Encycl. Judaica, Encycl. of Religion. *Recreation*: walking. *Address*: Department of Classics, University of Chicago, Chicago, Ill 60637, USA.

MONAGHAN, Rt. Rev. James; Titular Bishop of Cell Ausaille and Bishop Auxiliary to Archbishop of St Andrews and Edinburgh since 1970; Parish Priest of Holy Cross, Edinburgh, since 1959; *b* Bathgate, 11 July 1914; *s* of Edward and Elizabeth Monaghan. *Educ*: St Aloysius' Coll., Glasgow; Blairs Coll., Aberdeen; Scots Coll., Valladolid; St Kieran's Coll., Kilkenny, Ireland. Priest, 1940; Secretary, 1953; Vicar-Gen. for Archdio. St Andrews and Edinburgh, 1958–. *Address*: 252 Ferry Road, Edinburgh EH5 3AN. *T*: 031–552 3957.

MONCEL, Lt-Gen. Robert William, OC 1968; DSO 1944; OBE 1944; CD 1944; retired 1966; *b* 9 April 1917; *s* of René Moncel and Edith Brady; *m* 1939, Nancy Allison, *d* of Ralph P. Bell; one *d*. *Educ*: Selwyn House Sch.; Bishop's Coll. Sch. Royal Canadian Regt, 1939; Staff Coll., 1940; Bde Major 1st Armd Bde, 1941; comd 18th Manitoba Dragoons, 1942; GSO1, HQ 2 Cdn Corps, 1943; comd 4th Armd Bde, 1944; Dir Canadian Armd Corps, 1946; Nat. War Coll., 1949; Canadian Jt Staff, London, 1949–54; Comdr 3 Inf. Bde, 1957; QMG, 1960; GOC Eastern Comd, 1963; Comptroller Gen., 1964; Vice-Chief of the Defence Staff, Canada, 1965–66. Col, 8th Canadian Hussars. Chm., Fishermen's Memorial Hosp., 1980–; Mem. Bd of Regents, Mount Allison Univ., 1983–. Croix de Guerre, France, 1944; Légion d'Honneur, France, 1944. Hon. LLD Mount Allison Univ., 1968. *Recreations*: fishing, sailing, golf. *Address*: High Head, Murder Point, Nova Scotia B0J 2E0. *Clubs*: Royal Ottawa Golf; Royal St Lawrence Yacht; Royal Nova Scotia Yacht.

MONCK, family name of **Viscount Monck.**

MONCK, 7th Viscount *cr* 1801; **Charles Stanley Monck;** Baron Monck, 1797; Baron Monck (UK), 1866; *b* 2 April 1953; *s* of 6th Viscount Monck, OBE, and of Brenda Mildred (who *m* 1985, Brig. G. M. Palmer) *d* of G. W. Adkins, Harpenden; *S* father, 1982. *Educ*: Eton. BTech. *Heir: b* Hon. George Stanley Monck [*b* 12 April 1957; *m* 1986, Camilla E. V., *d* of late John Naylor]. *Address*: Pilgrim's Farm, Overton, Hants RG25 3DS.

MONCK, Nicholas Jeremy; Deputy Secretary (Industry), HM Treasury, since 1984; *b* 9 March 1935; *s* of Bosworth Monck and Stella Mary (*née* Cock); *m* 1960, Elizabeth Mary Kirwan; three *s*. *Educ*: Eton; King's Coll., Cambridge; Univ. of Pennsylvania. Asst Principal, Min. of Power, 1959–62; NEDO, 1962–65; NBPI, 1965–66; Senior Economist, Min. of Agriculture, Tanzania, 1966–69; HM Treasury, 1969–; Asst Sec., 1971; Principal Private Sec. to Chancellor of the Exchequer, 1976–77; Under Sec., 1977–84. Mem., BSC, 1978–80. *Address*: 31 Lady Margaret Road, Kentish Town, NW5 2NG. *T*: 01–485 8474.

MONCKTON, family name of **Viscount Galway** and **Viscount Monckton of Brenchley.**

MONCKTON OF BRENCHLEY, 2nd Viscount *cr* 1957; **Maj.-Gen. Gilbert Walter Riversdale Monckton,** CB 1966; OBE 1956; MC 1940; DL; retired, 1967; Chairman, Defence Systems Ltd; Director, Gulf Guarantee Trust; *b* 3 Nov. 1915; *o s* of 1st Viscount Monckton of Brenchley, PC, GCVO, KCMG, MC, QC, and Mary A.S. (*d* 1964), *d* of Sir Thomas Colyer-Fergusson, 3rd Bt; *S* father, 1965; *m* 1950, Marianna Laetitia (Dame of Honour and Devotion, SMO Malta (also Cross of Merit), OStJ, Pres., St John's Ambulance, Kent, 1975–80, High Sheriff of Kent, 1981–82), 3rd *d* of late Comdr Robert T. Bower; four *s* one *d. Educ*: Harrow; Trinity Coll., Cambridge. BA 1939, MA 1942. 2/Lt 5th Royal Inniskilling Dragoon Guards, SR 1938; Reg. 1939; France and Belgium, 1939–40; Staff Coll., 1941; Bde Major Armd Bde, 1942; Comd and Gen. Staff Sch., USA, 1943; Sqdn Ldr, 3rd King's Own Hussars, 1944, Italy and Syria; Sqdn Ldr, 5th Royal Inniskilling Dragoon Gds, 1945. RAF Staff Coll., 1949; GSO2, 7th Armd Div., 1949; Sqdn Ldr and 2 i/c 5th Royal Inniskilling Dragoon Gds, Korea and Egypt, 1951–52; GSO1, Mil. Ops, WO, 1954–56; Mil. Adv., Brit. Delegn, Geneva Confs on Indo-China and Korea, 1954; transf. 12th Royal Lancers and comd, 1956–58; Comdr Royal Armd Corps, 3rd Div., 1958–60; psc, idc 1961; Dep. Dir, Personnel Admin., WO, 1962; Dir of Public Relations, WO (subseq. MoD), 1963–65; Chief of Staff, HQ BAOR, 1965–67; Col 9th/12th Royal Lancers (Prince of Wales's), 1967–73; Hon. Col, Kent and Sharpshooters Yeomanry Sqdn, 1974–79. President: Kent Assoc. of Boys' Clubs, 1965–78; Inst. of Heraldic and Genealogical Studies, 1965; Kent Archæological Soc., 1968–75; Medway Productivity Assoc., 1968–72; Kent Co. Rifle Assoc., 1970–75; Anglo-Belgian Union, 1973–83; Chm., Thurnham Parish Council, 1968–70. DL Kent, 1970. Liveryman Broderers' Co., Master 1978; KStJ; Chm., Council of Order of St John for Kent, 1969–75; SMO Malta: Bailiff, Grand Cross of Obedience (Chancellor of the British Assoc., 1963–68, Vice-Pres., 1968–74, Pres., 1974–83); Grand Cross of Merit, 1980; Comdr, Order of Crown (Belgium), 1965; Bailiff, Grand Cross of Justice, Constantinian Order of St George, 1975; Grand Officer, Order of Leopold II (Belgium), 1978. *Recreation*: archaeology. *Heir: s* Hon. Christopher Walter Monckton, *qv. Address*: Runhams Farm, Runham Lane, Harrietsham, Maidstone, Kent ME17 1NJ. *T*: Maidstone 850313. *Clubs*: Brooks's, Cavalry and Guards, MCC; Casino Maltese (Valetta).

MONCKTON, Hon. Christopher Walter; Assistant Editor, Today, since 1986; Special Adviser to the Prime Minister's Policy Unit (Home Affairs), since 1982; *b* 14 Feb. 1952; *s* and *heir* of Viscount Monckton of Brenchley, *qv. Educ*: Harrow; Churchill Coll., Cambridge; University Coll., Cardiff. BA 1973, MA 1977 (Cantab); Dip. Journalism Studies (Wales), 1974. Standing Cttee, Cambridge Union Soc., 1973; Treas., Cambridge Univ. Conservative Assoc., 1973. Reporter, Yorkshire Post, 1974–75, Leader-Writer, 1975–77; Press Officer, Conservative Central Office, 1977–78; Editor-designate, The Universe, 1978, Editor, 1979–81; Managing Editor, Telegraph Sunday Magazine, 1981–82; Leader-Writer, The Standard, 1982. Freeman, City of London, and Liveryman, Worshipful Co. of Broderers, 1973–. Member: Internat. MENSA Ltd, 1975–; St John Amb. Brigade (Wetherby Div.), 1976–77; Hon. Soc. of the Middle Temple, 1979–; RC Mass Media Commn, 1979–; Secretary: Economic Acctg Study Gp, 1980–81, Forward Strategy Gp, 1981, Health Study Gp, 1981–, Employment Study Gp, 1982–, Centre For Policy Studies. Vis. Lectr in Business Studies, Columbia Univ., NY, 1980. Editor, Not the Church Times, 1982. Kt SMO, Malta, 1973; OStJ 1973. *Publications*: The Laker Story (with Ivan Fallon), 1982; Anglican Orders: null and void?, 1986. *Recreations*: walking, talking, stalking. *Address*: 71 Albert Road, Richmond, Surrey. *T*: 01–940 6528. *Clubs*: Brooks's, Beefsteak, Pratt's.

MONCKTON-ARUNDELL, family name of **Viscount Galway.**

MONCREIFF, family name of **Baron Moncreiff.**

MONCREIFF, 5th Baron *cr* 1873; **Harry Robert Wellwood Moncreiff;** Bt, Nova Scotia 1626, UK 1871; Lt-Col (Hon.) RASC, retired; *b* 4 Feb. 1915; *s* of 4th Baron; *S* father, 1942; *m* 1952, Enid Marion Watson (*d* 1985), *o d* of Major H. W. Locke, Belmont, Dollar; one *s. Educ*: Fettes Coll., Edinburgh. Served War of 1939–45 (despatches). Retired, 1958. *Recreations*: Rugby football, tennis, shooting. *Heir: s* Hon. Rhoderick Harry Wellwood Moncreiff [*b* 22 March 1954; *m* 1982, Alison Elizabeth Anne, *d* of late James

Duncan Alastair Ross]. *Address*: Tulliebole Castle, Fossoway, Kinross-shire. *T*: Fossoway 236.

MONCRIEFF, William S.; *see* Scott-Moncrieff.

MONCTON, Archbishop of, (RC), since 1972; **Most Rev. Donat Chiasson;** *b* Paquetville, NB, 2 Jan. 1930; *s* of Louis Chiasson and Anna Chiasson (*née* Godin). *Educ*: St Joseph's Univ., NB; Holy Heart Seminary, Halifax, NS; Theological and Catechetical studies, Rome and Lumen Vitae, Belgium. *Address*: PO Box 248, Chartersville, Moncton, NB, Canada. *T*: 389.9531.

MOND, family name of **Baron Melchett.**

MONDALE, Walter Frederick; Vice-President of the United States of America, 1977–81; Counsel with Winston & Strawn, since 1981; *b* Ceylon, Minnesota, 5 Jan. 1928; *s* of Rev. Theodore Sigvaard Mondale and Claribel Hope (*née* Cowan); *m* 1955, Joan Adams; two *s* one *d. Educ*: public schs, Minnesota; Macalester Coll., Univ. of Minnesota (BA *cum laude*); Univ. of Minnesota Law Sch. (LLB). Served with Army, 1951–53. Admitted to Minn. Bar, 1956; private law practice, Minneapolis, 1956–60; Attorney-Gen., Minnesota, 1960–64; Senator from Minnesota, 1964–76. Democratic Candidate for Vice-Pres., USA, 1976, 1980; Mem., Democratic Farm Labor Party. *Publication*: The Accountability of Power. *Address*: 2550 M Street NW, Washington, DC 20037, USA.

MONDAY, Horace Reginald, CBE 1967 (OBE 1958); JP; *b* 26 Nov. 1907; *s* of late James Thomas Monday, Gambia Civil Servant, and late Rachel Ruth Davis; *m* 1932, Wilhelmina Roberta Juanita, *d* of late William Robertson Job Roberts, a Gambian businessman; one *s. Educ*: Methodist Mission Schools, in Banjul, The Gambia; correspondence course with (the then) London Sch. of Accountancy. Clerk, 1925–48; Asst Acct, Treasury, 1948–52; Acct and Storekeeper, Marine Dept, 1953–54; Acct-Gen., The Gambia Govt, 1954–65; Chm., Gambia Public Service Commn, 1965–68; High Comr for The Gambia in the UK and NI, 1968–71. MP Banjul Central, 1977–82. Chairman: Management Cttee, Banjul City Council, 1971–79; Gambia Utilities Corp., 1972–76. Dir, Gambia Currency Bd, 1964–68; Governor, Gambia High Sch., 1964–68; Pres., Gambia Red Cross Soc., 1967–68. JP 1944. Comdr, National Order of Republic of Senegal, 1968. *Address*: Rachelville, 24 Clarkson Street, Banjul, The Gambia. *T*: Banjul 511.

MONE, Rt. Rev. John Aloysius; Titular Bishop of Abercorn; an Auxiliary Bishop of Glasgow, (RC), since 1984; *b* 22 June 1929; *s* of Arthur Mone and Elizabeth Mone (*née* Dunn). *Educ*: Holyrood Secondary School, Glasgow; Séminaire Saint Sulpice, Paris; Institut Catholique, Paris (Faculty of Social Studies). Ordained Priest, Glasgow, 1952. Scottish National Chaplain, Girl Guides, 1971–; Chm., Scottish Catholic Internat. Aid Fund, 1974–75, Pres./Treas., 1985–; Chm., Scottish Catholic Marriage Advisory Council, 1982–84. *Recreations*: watching soccer (attending if possible), playing golf (when time!), playing the piano. *Address*: 89 Muiryfauld Drive, Glasgow G31 5RU. *T*: 041–556 5533.

MONERAWELA, Chandra; High Commissioner in London for Sri Lanka, since 1984; *b* 8 Sept. 1937; *m* 1965, Rupa Devi De Silva; one *s* two *d. Educ*: Trinity College, Kandy; University of Ceylon, Peradeniya. BA Hons Econ. Dept. of Fisheries, 1960; Sri Lanka Overseas Service, 1961; served Peking, and Washington DC; Chargé d'affaires of Sri Lanka in Thailand, and Perm. Rep. to ESCAP, 1974–80; Chief of Protocol, 1971–74, Dir, Economic Affairs, 1980–83, Ministry of Foreign Affairs; High Comr for Sri Lanka in Singapore, 1984; represented Sri Lanka at meetings, conferences and commissions in Asia, Australia, Europe, Pacific and USA. *Recreations*: athletics, cricket, rugby football, golf. *Address*: High Commission of the Democratic Socialist Republic of Sri Lanka, 13 Hyde Park Gardens, W2. *T*: 01–262 1845.

MONEY, Ernle (David Drummond); Barrister-at-Law; *b* 17 Feb. 1931; *s* of late Lt-Col E. F. D. Money, DSO, late 4th Gurkha Rifles, and of Sidney, *o d* of D. E. Anderson, Forfar; *m* 1960, Susan Barbara, *d* of Lt-Col D. S. Lister, MC, The Buffs; two *s* two *d. Educ*: Marlborough Coll.; Oriel Coll., Oxford (open scholar). Served in Suffolk Regt, 1949–51, and 4th Bn, Suffolks Regt (TA), 1951–56; MA Hons degree (2nd cl.) in mod. hist., 1954. Tutor and lecturer, Swinton Conservative Coll., 1956. Called to Bar, Lincoln's Inn (Cholmeley Scholar), 1958. Mem., Bar Council, 1962–66. MP (C) Ipswich, 1970–Sept. 1974; Opposition Front Bench Spokesman on the Arts, 1974; Sec., Parly Cons. Arts and Amenities Cttee, 1970–73, Vice-Chm., 1974; Vice-Pres., Ipswich Cons. Assoc., 1979–. Regular columnist, East Anglian Daily Times. Governor, Woolverstone Hall Sch., 1967–70; co-opted Mem., GLC Arts Cttee, 1972–73; Mem., GLC Arts Bd, 1974–76; Mem., Cttee of Gainsborough's Birthplace, Sudbury. Fine Arts Correspondent, Contemporary Review, 1968–. Pres., Ipswich Town Football Club Supporters, 1974–; Vice-Pres., E Suffolk and Ipswich Branch, RSPCA, 1974–. *Publications*: (with Peter Johnson) The Nasmyth Family of Painters, 1970; Margaret Thatcher, First Lady of the House, 1975; regular contrib. various periodicals and newspapers on antiques and the arts. *Recreations*: music, pictures and antiques, watching Association football. *Address*: 1 Gray's Inn Square, WC1R 5AA. *T*: 01–405 8946; High House Farm, Rendlesham, near Woodbridge, Suffolk. *T*: Eyke 335. *Clubs*: Carlton; Ipswich and Suffolk (Ipswich).

MONEY, George Gilbert; Director, Barclays Bank International Ltd, 1955–81 (Vice-Chairman, 1965–73); *b* 17 Nov. 1914; 2nd *s* of late Maj.-Gen. Sir A. W. Money, KCB, KBE, CSI and late Lady Money (*née* Drummond). *Educ*: Charterhouse Sch. Clerk, L. Behrens & Soehne, Bankers, Hamburg, 1931–32; Clerk, Barclays Bank Ltd, 1932–35, Dir 1972–73; joined Barclays Bank DCO (now Barclays Bank PLC), London, 1935; served in Egypt, Palestine, Cyprus, Ethiopia, Cyrenaica, E Africa, 1936–52; Local Dir, W Indies, 1952; Director: Barclays Bank of California, 1965–75; Bermuda Provident Bank Ltd, 1969; Barclays Bank of the Netherlands, Antilles NV, 1970; Republic Finance Corp. Ltd, 1972; Republic Bank Ltd, 1972; Barclays Bank of Jamaica Ltd, 1972–77; Barclays Australia Ltd, 1972–75; New Zealand United Corp., 1972–75; Chairman: Bahamas Internat. Trust Co. Ltd, 1970–72; Cayman Internat. Trust Co. Ltd, 1970–72; Mem., Caribbean Bd, Barclays Bank PLC. *Recreations*: water ski-ing, fishing, bridge. *Address*: 54 Lombard Street, EC3.

MONEY-COUTTS, family name of **Baron Latymer.**

MONEY-COUTTS, David Burdett; Chairman, Coutts & Co., since 1976 (Managing Director, 1970–86); *b* 19 July 1931; *s* of Hon. Alexander B. Money-Coutts (2nd *s* of 6th Baron Latymer, TD), and Mary E., *er d* of Sir Reginald Hobhouse, 5th Bt; *m* 1958, Penelope Utten Todd; one *s* two *d. Educ*: Eton; New Coll., Oxford (MA). National Service, 1st Royal Dragoons, 1950–51; Royal Glos Hussars, TA, 1951–67. Joined Coutts & Co., 1954; Dir, 1958. Director: National Discount Co., 1964–69; Gerrard & National, 1969– (Dep. Chm. 1969–); United States & General Trust Corp., 1964–73; Charities Investment Managers (Charifund), 1964– (Chm., 1984–); (Regional), SE Reg., National Westminster Bank, 1969– (Chm., 1986–); National Westminster Bank, 1976–; Dun & Bradstreet, 1973–; Phoenix Assurance, 1978–85 (Dep. Chm., 1984–85); Sun Alliance & London Insurance, 1984–. Member: Kensington and Chelsea and Westminster AHA,

1974–82 (Vice-Chm., 1978–82); Bloomsbury HA, 1982– (Vice-Chm., 1982–); Health Educn Council, 1973–77. Middlesex Hospital: Governor, 1962–74 (Dep. Chm. Governors, 1973–74); Chm., Finance Cttee, 1965–74; Mem., Med. Sch. Council, 1963– (Chm., 1974–). Trustee, Multiple Sclerosis Soc., 1967–. Hon. Treas., Nat. Assoc. of Almshouses, 1960–; Hon. Sec., Old Etonian Trust, 1969–76, Chm. Council, 1976–. *Recreations:* odd jobs, living in the country. *Address:* Magpie House, Peppard Common, Henley-on-Thames, Oxon RG9 5JG. *T:* Rotherfield Greys 497. *Club:* Leander (Henley-on-Thames).

MONGER, George William; Under-Secretary, Cabinet Office, since 1986; *b* 1 April 1937; *s* of George Thomas Monger and Agnes Mary (*née* Dates). *Educ:* Holloway Sch., Jesus Coll., Cambridge (PhD 1962). Entered Home Civil Service (Admin. Class), 1961: Min. of Power, Min. of Technol., DTI, and Dept of Energy; Principal, 1965; Asst Sec., 1972; Under-Sec., Electricity Div., 1976, Coal Div., 1979, Dept of Energy; Social Services Gp, 1981, Fiscal Policy Gp, 1983, HM Treasury. Alexander Prize, RHistS, 1962. *Publication:* The End of Isolation: British Foreign Policy, 1900–1907, 1963. *Address:* Lochalsh, Christ Church Lane, Hadley Green, Barnet, Herts. *T:* 01–449 7887. *Club:* United Oxford & Cambridge University.

MONIBA, Harry Fumba, PhD; Vice-President, Interim National Assembly, Liberia, since 1984; *b* 22 Oct. 1937; *s* of Mr Moniba and Mrs Janga Sando Moniba; *m* 1969, Minita Kollie; three *s* two *d. Educ:* Cuttington Univ. Coll., Liberia (all-round student award; BSEd, *cum laude*); State University of New York, New Paltz (MSc); New York Univ., NY (post grad. studies); Michigan State Univ., USA (PhD African Hist. and Internat. Relations). Teacher and Registrar, also Vice Principal, Holy Cross Bolahun Mission Schs, 1968–70; Special Asst and Dir of Research, Min. of Educn, 1975–76; First Secretary and Consul, Liberian Embassy: Washington DC, 1976–80; Ottawa, Canada, 1978–80; Asst Minister of Foreign Affairs for European Affairs, Min. of Foreign Affairs, 1980–81; Ambassador to London, 1981–84, and (non-resident) to the Holy See, 1983–84. *Recreations:* reading, soccer, fishing, hunting, dancing. *Address:* c/o Capitol Building, Capitol Hill, Monrovia, Liberia, West Africa.

MONIER-WILLIAMS, Evelyn Faithfull; His Honour Judge Monier-Williams; a Circuit Judge since 1972; *b* 29 April 1920; *o s* of late R. T. Monier-Williams, OBE, Barrister-at-Law, and Mrs G. M. Monier-Williams; *m* 1948, Maria-Angela Oswald (*d* 1983); one *s* one *d. Educ:* Charterhouse; University Coll., Oxford (MA). Admitted to Inner Temple, 1940; served Royal Artillery, 1940–46 in UK, Egypt, Libya, Tunisia, Sicily (8th Army), France, Low Countries and Germany; called to Bar, Inner Temple, 1948; South Eastern Circuit; Master of the Bench, Inner Temple, 1967; Mem. Senate of Four Inns of Court, 1969–73; Mem. Council, Selden Soc., 1970; Mem., Council of Legal Educn, 1971, Vice Chm., 1974; Mem., Adv. Cttee on Legal Educn, 1979. Livery, Glaziers Company, 1974. *Recreation:* collecting old books. *Address:* Inner Temple, EC4.

MONIZ DE ARAGÃO, José Joaquim de Lima e Silva; *b* Rio de Janeiro, Brazil, 12 May 1887; *m* 1926, Isabel Rodrigues Alves; two *s. Educ:* Faculty of Law, Rio de Janeiro. Attached to Ministry of Foreign Affairs, Rio de Janeiro, 1908; 2nd Sec., Washington, 1911; 1st Sec., Monte-Video, Madrid, Rome, 1913; Counsellor, Berlin, 1915–18; Counsellor, Brazilian Delegn Peace Conf., Versailles, 1919; Counsellor, Berlin, 1920–25; Minister, League of Nations, Geneva, 1926; Minister Delegate, Internat. Labour Office, Geneva, 1928–29; Minister, Copenhagen, Caracas, 1929–33; Under-Sec. of State for Foreign Affairs, Rio de Janeiro, 1934; Ambassador to Berlin, 1935–38; Brazilian Ambassador to Court of St James's, 1940–52. Brazilian Delegate to UNO Assembly in London, 1945; Chief Brazilian Delegate to: UNESCO Assembly, London, 1945, Paris, 1946; UNRRA Assembly, London, 1946; Internat. Cttee for Refugees in London, 1944, 1945, Paris, 1946. Mem. Royal Philatelic Society. Knight Grand Cross of the Royal Victorian Order, Gt Brit. (Hon. GCVO); Comdr Order of the British Empire (Hon. CBE). *Address:* Avenida Atlântica no 2242, 10 andar, Rio de Janeiro, Brazil. *Clubs:* Rotary, Jockey, Automovel (Rio de Janeiro).

MONK, Alec; *see* Monk, D. A. G.

MONK, Rear-Adm. Anthony John, CBE 1973; Appeals Organizer, The Royal Marsden Hospital Cancer Fund, since 1984; *b* 14 Nov. 1923; *s* of Frank Leonard and Barbara Monk; *m* 1951, Elizabeth Ann Samson; four *s* one *d. Educ:* Whitgift Sch.; RNC Dartmouth; RNEC Keyham. MSc, BScEng, FIMarE, FRAeS, FIMechE. Engr Cadet, 1941; served War of 1939–45, Pacific Fleet; flying trng, Long Air Engrg Course, Cranfield, 1946; RN Air Stn Ford; RNEC Manadon, 1950; Prodn Controller and Man., RN Aircraft Yard, Belfast, 1953–56; Mem. Dockyard Work Measurement Team, subseq. Engr Officer HMS Apollo, Techn. Asst to Dir-Gen. Aircraft, Sqdn Engr Officer to Flag Officer Aircraft Carriers, 1963–65; Asst Dir of Marine Engrg, 1965–68; Dir of Aircraft Engrg, 1968; Comd Engrg Officer to Flag Officer Naval Air Comd; Naval Liaison Officer for NI and Supt RN Aircraft Yard, Belfast, 1970; Port Admiral, Rosyth, 1974–76; Rear-Adm. Engineering to Flag Officer Naval Air Comd, 1976–78. Comdr 1956; Captain 1964; Rear-Adm. 1974. Dir Gen., Brick Develt Assoc., 1979–84. *Recreation:* swimming (ASA teacher). *Address:* 7 London Road, Widley, Portsmouth PO7 5AT.

MONK, Arthur James; Director, Components, Valves and Devices, Ministry of Defence, 1981–84, retired; *b* 15 Jan. 1924; *s* of late Rev. Arthur S. Monk, AKC, and late Lydia E. Monk; *m* 1953, Murial V. Peacock; one *s* two *d. Educ:* Latymer Upper School, Hammersmith; London Univ. BSc Hons Physics 1953; FIEE 1964. Served RAF, 1943–48. Services Electronic Research Labs, 1949–63; Asst Director (Co-ord. Valve Development), MoD, 1963–68; Student, Imperial Defence Coll., 1969; idc 1970; Admiralty Underwater Weapons Establishment, 1970–73; Dep. Director, Underwater Weapons Projects (S/M), MoD, 1973–76; Counsellor, Def. Equipment Staff, Washington, 1977–81. *Publications:* papers on electronics in jls of learned societies. *Recreations:* caravan touring, photography, do-it-yourself. *Address:* 63 Wyke Road, Weymouth, Dorset DT4 9QN. *T:* Weymouth 782338.

MONK, (David) Alec (George); Chairman and Chief Executive, The Dee Corporation PLC, since 1981; *b* 13 Dec. 1942; *s* of Philip Aylmer and Elizabeth Jane Monk; *m* 1965, Jean Ann Searle; two *s* two *d. Educ:* Jesus College, Oxford. MA (PPE). Research Staff, Corporate Finance and Taxation, Sheffield Univ., 1966 and London Business Sch., 1967; Senior Financial Asst, Treasurer's Dept, Esso Petroleum Co., 1968; various positions with The Rio Tinto-Zinc Corp., 1968–77, Dir, 1974–77; Vice-Pres. and Dir, AEA Investors Inc., 1977–81. Vis. Indust. Fellow, Manchester Business Sch., 1984. Hon. Fellow, St Hugh's Coll., Oxford, 1985. *Publication:* (with A. J. Merrett) Inflation, Taxation and Executive Remuneration, 1967. *Recreations:* sports, reading. *Address:* The Dee Corporation, Silbury Court, 418 Silbury Boulevard, Milton Keynes MK9 2NB.

MONK BRETTON, 3rd Baron *cr* 1884; **John Charles Dodson,** DL; *b* 17 July 1924; *o s* of 2nd Baron and Ruth (*d* 1967), 2nd *d* of late Hon. Charles Brand; *S* father, 1933; *m* 1958, Zoë Diana Scott; two *s. Educ:* Westminster Sch.; New Coll., Oxford (MA). DL E Sussex, 1983. *Recreations:* hunting, farming. *Heir: s* Hon. Christopher Mark Dodson, *b* 2 Aug. 1958. *Address:* Shelley's Folly, Cooksbridge, near Lewes, East Sussex. *T:* Barcombe 231. *Club:* Brooks's.

MONKS, Constance Mary, OBE 1962; *b* 20 May 1911; *d* of Ellis Green and Bessie A. Green (*née* Burwell); *m* 1937, Jack Monks (decd); one *s* (decd). *Educ:* Wheelton County Sch.; Chorley Grammar Sch.; City of Leeds Training Coll. Apptd Asst Teacher, 1931. Started retail business as partner with husband, 1945. Councillor (C), Chorley (N Ward), 1947–67, Alderman, 1967–74; Mayor of Chorley, 1959–60; Mem. Lancs CC, 1961–64. MP (C) Chorley, Lancs, 1970–Feb. 1974. JP Chorley, 1954. *Recreations:* reading, needlework. *Address:* Withnell Fold Hall, Withnell Fold, near Chorley, Lancs.

MONKS, John Stephen; Head of Organisation and Industrial Relations Department, Trades Union Congress, since 1977; *b* 5 Aug. 1945; *s* of Charles Edward Monks and Bessie Evelyn Monks; *m* 1970, Francine Jacqueline Schenk; two *s* one *d. Educ:* Ducie Technical High Sch., Manchester; Nottingham Univ. (BA Econ). Joined TUC, 1969. Mem. Council, ACAS, 1979–. *Recreations:* squash, gardening. *Address:* 3 Queenswood Road, Forest Hill, SE23 2QR. *T:* 01–699 4292.

MONKSWELL, 5th Baron *cr* 1885; **Gerard Collier;** Service Administration Manager since 1984; *b* 28 Jan. 1947; *s* of William Adrian Larry Collier and Helen (*née* Dunbar); *S* to disclaimed barony of father, 1984; *m* 1974, Ann Valerie Collins; two *s* one *d. Educ:* Portsmouth Polytechnic (BSc Mech. Eng, 1971); Slough Polytechnic (Cert. in Works Management 1972). Labourer, van driver, lathe setter/operator, fruit juice factory operative, until 1967. Massey Ferguson Manfg Co. Ltd: Product Quality Engineer, 1972; Service Administration Manager, 1984. *Recreations:* politics, swimming, movies. *Heir: s* Hon. James Adrian Collier, *b* 29 March 1977. *Address:* 513 Barlow Moor Road, Chorlton, Manchester M21 2AQ. *T:* (home) 061–881 3887; (office) 061–865 4400.

MONMOUTH, Bishop of, since 1986; **Rt. Rev. Royston Clifford Wright;** *b* 4 July 1922; *s* of James and Ellen Wright; *m* 1945, Barbara Joyce Nowell; one *s* one *d. Educ:* Univ. of Wales, Cardiff (BA 1942); St Stephen's House, Oxford. Deacon 1945, priest 1946; Curate: Bedwas, 1945–47; St John Baptist, Newport, 1947–49; Walton-on-the-Hill, Liverpool, 1949–51; Chaplain RNVR, 1950; Chaplain RN, 1951–68; Vicar of Blaenavon, Gwent, 1968–74; RD of Pontypool, 1973–74; Canon of Monmouth, 1974–77; Rector of Ebbw Vale, Gwent, 1974–77; Archdeacon of Monmouth, 1977; Archdeacon of Newport, 1977–86. *Recreations:* four grandchildren; listening to Baroque music. *Address:* Bishopstow, Newport, Gwent NP9 4EA. *T:* Newport (Gwent) 63510.

MONMOUTH, Dean of; *see* Jenkins, Very Rev. F. G.

MONOD, Prof. Théodore, DèsSc; Officier de la Légion d'Honneur, 1958; Professor Emeritus at National Museum of Natural History, Paris (Assistant 1922, Professor, 1942–73); *b* 9 April 1902; *s* of Rev. Wilfred Monod and Dorina Monod; *m* 1930, Olga Pickova; two *s* one *d. Educ:* Sorbonne (Paris). Docteur èssciences, 1926. Sec.-Gen. (later Dir) of l'Institut Français d'Afrique Noire, 1938; Prof., Univ. of Dakar, 1957–59; Doyen, Science Faculty, Dakar, 1957–58. Mem., Academy of Sciences; Member: Acad. des Sciences d'Outre-Mer; Académie de Marine; Corresp. Mem., Académie des Sciences de Lisbonne and Académie Royale des Sciences d'Outre-Mer. Dr *hc* Köln, 1965, Neuchâtel, 1968. Gold Medallist, Royal Geographical Soc., 1960; Gold Medallist, Amer. Geographical Soc., 1961; Haile Sellassie Award for African Research, 1967. Comdr, Ordre du Christ, 1953; Commandeur, Mérite Saharien, 1962; Officier de l'Ordre des Palmes Académiques, 1966, etc. *Publications:* Méharées, Explorations au vrai Sahara, 1937; L'Hippopotame et le philosophe, 1942; Bathyfolages, 1954; (ed) Pastoralism in Tropical Africa, 1976; L'Emeraude des Garamantes, Souvenirs d'un Saharien, 1984; many scientific papers in learned jls. *Address:* 14 quai d'Orléans, 75004 Paris, France. *T:* 43 26 79 50; Muséum national d'Histoire naturelle, 57 rue Cuvier, 75005 Paris, France. *T:* 43 31 40 10.

MONRO, Sir Hector (Seymour Peter), Kt 1981; AE; JP; DL; MP (C) Dumfries since 1964; *b* 4 Oct. 1922; *s* of late Capt. Alastair Monro, Cameron Highlanders, and Mrs Monro, Craigcleuch, Langholm, Scotland; *m* 1949, Elizabeth Anne Welch, Longstone Hall, Derbs; two *s. Educ:* Canford Sch.; King's Coll., Cambridge. RAF, 1941–46, Flight Lt; RAuxAF, 1946–53 (AE 1953). Mem. of Queen's Body Guard for Scotland, Royal Company of Archers. Dumfries CC, 1952–67 (Chm. Planning Cttee, and Police Cttee). Chm. Dumfriesshire Unionist Assoc., 1958–63; Scottish Cons. Whip, 1967–70; a Lord Comr of HM Treasury, 1970–71; Parly Under-Sec. of State, Scottish Office, 1971–74; Opposition Spokesman on: Scottish Affairs, 1974–75; Sport, 1974–79; Parly Under-Sec. of State (with special responsibility for sport), DoE, 1979–81; Chairman: Scottish Cons. Members Cttee, 1983–; Cons. Parly Cttee on Sport, 1984–85. Vice Chm., Cons. Members Agricl Cttee, 1983–. Mem. Dumfries T&AFA, 1959 67; Hon. Air Cdre, No 2622 RAuxAF Regt Sqdn, 1982–. Member: Area Executive Cttee, Nat. Farmers' Union of Scotland; Nature Conservancy Council, 1982–; Council, Nat. Trust for Scotland 1983–. Pres., Auto-cycle Union, 1983–. JP 1963, DL 1973, Dumfries. *Recreations:* Rugby football (Mem. Scottish Rugby Union, 1958–77, Vice-Pres., 1975, Pres., 1976–77); golf, flying, country sports, vintage sports cars. *Address:* Williamwood, Kirtlebridge, Dumfriesshire. *T:* Kirtlebridge 213. *Clubs:* Royal Air Force, MCC; Royal Scottish Automobile (Glasgow).

MONRO DAVIES, William Llewellyn, QC 1974; **His Honour Judge Monro Davies;** a Circuit Judge, since 1976; *b* 12 Feb. 1927; *s* of Thomas Llewellyn Davies and Emily Constance Davies; *m* 1956, Jean, *d* of late E. G. Innes; one *s* one *d. Educ:* Christ Coll., Brecon; Trinity Coll., Oxford (MA, LitHum). Served in RNVR, 1945–48 (Sub-Lt). Called to the Bar, Inner Temple, 1954. Mem., Gen. Council of the Bar, 1971–75. A Recorder of the Crown Court, 1972–76. *Recreations:* the theatre and cinema; watching Rugby football. *Address:* Farrar's Buildings, Temple, EC4Y 7BD. *T:* 01–583 9241. *Clubs:* Garrick; Bristol Channel Yacht (Mumbles).

MONROE, John George; Social Security (formerly National Insurance) Commissioner since 1973; *b* 27 July 1913; *s* of late Canon Horace G. Monroe, Vicar of Wimbledon and Sub-dean of Southwark and of Frances Alice Monroe (*née* Stokes); *m* 1943, Jane Reynolds; one *s* two *d. Educ:* Marlborough Coll.; Oriel Coll., Oxford. Called to Bar, Middle Temple, 1937; Master of the Bench, 1967. *Publications:* (ed, with Judge McDonnell *qv*) Kerr on Fraud and Mistake, 7th edn; The Law of Stamp Duties, 1954 (5th edn, with R. S. Nock, 1976). *Address:* Highmead, Birchwood Grove Road, Burgess Hill, West Sussex. *T:* Burgess Hill 3350.

MONSELL, 2nd Viscount *cr* 1935, of Evesham; **Henry Bolton Graham Eyres Monsell;** *b* 21 Nov. 1905; *s* of 1st Viscount Monsell, PC, GBE, and Caroline Mary Sybil, CBE (*d* 1959), *d* of late H. W. Eyres, Dumbleton Hall, Evesham; *S* father, 1969. *Educ:* Eton. Served N Africa and Italy, 1942–45 (despatches); Lt-Col Intelligence Corps. US Medal of Freedom with bronze palm, 1946. *Recreation:* music. *Address:* The Mill House, Dumbleton, Evesham, Worcs. *Club:* Travellers'.
See also P. M. Leigh Fermor.

MONSON, family name of **Baron Monson.**

MONSON, 11th Baron *cr* 1728; **John Monson;** Bt *cr* 1611; *b* 3 May 1932; *e s* of 10th Baron and of Bettie Northrup (who *m* 1962, Capt. James Arnold Phillips), *d* of late E. Alexander Powell; *S* father, 1958; *m* 1955, Emma, *o d* of late Anthony Devas, ARA, RP;

three s. *Educ:* Eton; Trinity Coll., Cambridge (BA). Pres., Soc. for Individual Freedom. *Heir: s* Hon. Nicholas John Monson [*b* 19 Oct. 1955; *m* 1981, Hilary, *o d* of Kenneth Martin, Nairobi and Diani Beach; one *s* one *d*]. *Address:* Manor House, South Carlton, Lincoln. *T:* 730263.

MONSON, Sir (William Bonnar) Leslie, KCMG 1965 (CMG 1950); CB 1964; HM Diplomatic Service, retired; *b* 28 May 1912; *o s* of late J. W. Monson and Selina L. Monson; *m* 1948, Helen Isobel Browne. *Educ:* Edinburgh Acad.; Hertford Coll., Oxford. Entered Civil Service (Dominions Office) 1935; transferred to Colonial Office, 1939; Asst Sec., 1944; seconded as Chief Sec. to West African Council, 1947–51; Asst Under-Sec. of State, Colonial Office, 1951–64; British High Commissioner in the Republic of Zambia, 1964–66; Dep. Under-Sec. of State, Commonwealth Office, later FCO, 1967–72. Dir, Overseas Relations Branch, St John Ambulance, 1975–81. KStJ 1975. *Address:* Golf House, Goffers Road, Blackheath, SE3. *Club:* United Oxford & Cambridge University.

MONTAGU; *see* Douglas-Scott-Montagu.

MONTAGU, family name of **Duke of Manchester, Earldom of Sandwich,** and **Baron Swaythling.**

MONTAGU OF BEAULIEU, 3rd Baron *cr* 1885; **Edward John Barrington Douglas-Scott-Montagu;** Chairman, Historic Buildings and Monuments Commission, since 1983; *b* 20 Oct. 1926; *o s* of 2nd Baron and Pearl (who *m* 2nd, 1936, Captain Hon. Edward Pleydell-Bouverie, RN, MVO, *s* of 6th Earl of Radnor), *d* of late Major E. B. Crake, Rifle Brigade, and Mrs Barrington Crake; *S* father, 1929; *m* 1st, 1959, Elizabeth Belinda (marr. diss. 1974), *o d* of late Capt. the Hon. John de Bathe Crossley, and late Hon. Mrs Crossley; one *s* one *d*; 2nd, 1974, Fiona Herbert; one *s. Educ:* St Peter's Court, Broadstairs; Ridley Coll., St Catharines, Ont; Eton Coll.; New Coll., Oxford. Late Lt Grenadier Guards; released Army, 1948. Founded Montagu Motor Car Museum, 1952 and World's first Motor Cycle Museum, 1956; created Nat. Motor Museum Trust, 1970, to administer new Nat. Motor Museum at Beaulieu, opened 1972. Mem., Develt Commn, 1980–84. President: Museums Assoc., 1982–84; Historic Houses Assoc., 1973–78; Union of European Historic Houses, 1978–81; Fédération Internationale des Voitures Anciennes, 1980–83; Southern Tourist Bd; Assoc. of Brit. Transport Museums; English Vineyards Assoc.; Vice-Pres., Inst. of Motor Industry; Chancellor, Wine Guild of UK; Patron, Assoc. of Independent Museums. FRSA. Commodore: Royal Southampton Yacht Club; Beaulieu River Sailing Club; Vice Cdre, H of L Yacht Club. Founder and Editor, Veteran and Vintage Magazine, 1956–79. *Publications:* The Motoring Montagus, 1959; Lost Causes of Motoring, 1960; Jaguar, A Biography, 1961; The Gordon Bennett Races, 1963; Rolls of Rolls-Royce, 1966; The Gilt and the Gingerbread, 1967; Lost Causes of Motoring: Europe, vol. i, 1969, vol. ii, 1971; More Equal than Others, 1970; History of the Steam Car, 1971; The Horseless Carriage, 1975; Early Days on the Road, 1976; Behind the Wheel, 1977; Royalty on the Road, 1980; Home James, 1982. *Heir: s* Hon. Ralph Douglas-Scott-Montagu, *b* 13 March 1961. *Address:* Palace House, Beaulieu, Hants SO42 7ZN. *T:* Beaulieu 612345; Flat 11, 24 Bryanston Square, W1. *T:* 01–262 2603. *Clubs:* Historical Commercial Vehicle (Pres.), Disabled Drivers Motor (Pres.), Show Biz Car (Pres.), Steam Boat Assoc. of Gt Britain (Vice-Pres.), and mem. of many historic vehicle clubs.

See also Sir E. John Chichester, Bt.

MONTAGU, (Alexander) Victor (Edward Paulet); *b* 22 May 1906; *S* father, 1962, as 10th Earl of Sandwich, but disclaimed his peerages for life, 24 July 1964; *m* 1st, 1934, Rosemary, *d* of late Major Ralph Harding Peto; two *s* four *d*; 2nd, 1962, Anne, MBE (*d* 1981), *y d* of Victor, 9th Duke of Devonshire, KG, PC. *Educ:* Eton; Trinity Coll., Cambridge. MA (Nat. Sciences). Lt 5th (Hunts) Bn The Northamptonshire Regt, TA, 1926; served France, 1940, and afterwards on Gen. Staff, Home Forces. Private Sec. to Rt Hon. Stanley Baldwin, MP, 1932–34; Treasurer, Junior Imperial League, 1934–35; Chm., Tory Reform Cttee, 1943–44. MP (C) South Dorset Div. (C 1941, Ind. C 1957, C 1958–62); contested (C) Accrington Div. Lancs, Gen. Elec., 1964. *Publications:* Essays in Tory Reform, 1944; The Conservative Dilemma, 1970; articles in Quarterly Review, 1946–47. *Heir:* (to disclaimed peerages): *s* John Edward Hollister Montagu, *qv. Address:* Mapperton, Beaminster, Dorset. *Clubs:* Carlton, Royal Automobile.

MONTAGU, Prof. Ashley; *b* 28 June 1905; *o c* of Charles and Mary Ehrenberg; *m* 1931, Helen Marjorie Peakes; one *s* two *d. Educ:* Central Foundation Sch., London; Univ. of London; Univ. of Florence; Columbia Univ. (PhD 1937). Research Worker, Brit. Mus. (Natural Hist.), 1926; Curator, Physical Anthropology, Wellcome Hist. Mus., London, 1929; Asst-Prof. of Anatomy, NY Univ., 1931–38; Dir, Div. of Child Growth and Develt, NY Univ., 1931–34; Assoc.-Prof. of Anat., Hahnemann Med. Coll. and Hosp., Phila, 1938–49; Prof. and Head of Dept of Anthropology, Rutgers Univ., 1949–55; Dir of Research, NJ Cttee on Growth and Develt, 1951–55. Chm., Anisfield-Wolf Award Cttee on Race Relations, 1950–. Vis. Lectr, Harvard Univ., 1945; Regent's Prof., Univ. of Calif, Santa Barbara, 1961; Lectr, Princeton Univ., 1978–83, and Dir, Inst. Natural Philosophy, 1979–85. DSc, Grinnell Coll., Iowa, 1967; DLitt Ursinus Coll., Pa, 1972. Distinguished Service Award, Amer. Anthropological Assoc., 1984; Phi Delta Kappa Distinguished Service Award, 1985. *Publications:* Coming Into Being Among the Australian Aborigines, 1937, 2nd edn 1974; Man's Most Dangerous Myth: The Fallacy of Race, 1942, 5th edn 1974; Edward Tyson, MD, FRS (1650–1708): And the Rise of Human and Comparative Anatomy in England, 1943; Introduction to Physical Anthropology, 1945, 3rd edn 1960; Adolescent Sterility, 1946; On Being Human, 1950, 2nd edn 1970; Statement on Race, 1951, 3rd edn 1972; On Being Intelligent, 1951, 3rd edn 1972; Darwin, Competition, and Cooperation, 1952; The Natural Superiority of Women, 1953, 3rd edn 1974; Immortality, 1955; The Direction of Human Development, 1955, 2nd edn 1970; The Biosocial Nature of Man, 1956; Education and Human Relations, 1958; Anthropology and Human Nature, 1957; Man: His First Million Years, 1957, 2nd edn 1969; The Reproductive Development of the Female, 1957, 3rd edn 1979; The Cultured Man, 1958; Human Heredity, 1959, 2nd edn 1963; Anatomy and Physiology (with E. B. Steen), 2 vols, 1959, 2nd edn 1984; A Handbook of Anthropometry, 1960; Man in Process, 1961; The Humanization of Man, 1962; Prenatal Influences, 1962; Race, Science and Humanity, 1963; The Dolphin in History (with John Lilly), 1963; The Science of Man, 1964; Life Before Birth, 1964, 2nd edn 1978; The Human Revolution, 1965; The Idea of Race, 1965; Man's Evolution (with C. Loring Brace), 1965; Up the Ivy, 1966; The American Way of Life, 1967; The Anatomy of Swearing, 1967; The Prevalence of Nonsense (with E. Darling), 1967; The Human Dialogue (with Floyd Matson), 1967; Man Observed, 1968; Man: His First Two Million Years, 1969; Sex, Man and Society, 1969; The Ignorance of Certainty (with E. Darling), 1970; Textbook of Human Genetics (with M. Levitan), 1971, 2nd edn 1977; Immortality, Religion and Morals, 1971; Touching: the human significance of the skin, 1971, 3rd edn 1986; The Elephant Man, 1971, 2nd edn 1979; Man and the Computer (with S. S. Snyder), 1972; (ed) The Endangered Environment, 1973; (ed) Frontiers of Anthropology, 1974; (ed) Culture and Human Development, 1974; (ed) The Practice of Love, 1974; (ed) Race and IQ, 1975; The Nature of Human Aggression, 1976; Human Evolution (with C. L. Brace), 1977; The Human Connection (with F. Matson), 1979; Growing Young, 1981; The

Dehumanization of Man (with F. Matson), 1983; Humanity Speaking to Mankind, 1986; Editor: Studies and Essays in the History of Science and Learning; The Meaning of Love, 1953; Toynbee and History, 1956; Genetic Mechanisms in Human Disease, 1961; Atlas of Human Anatomy, 1961; Culture and the Evolution of Man, 1962; International Pictorial Treasury of Knowledge, 6 vols, 1962–63; The Concept of Race, 1964; The Concept of the Primitive, 1967; Culture: Man's Adaptive Dimension, 1968; Man and Aggression, 1968; The Origin and Evolution of Man, 1973; Learning Non-Aggression, 1978; Sociobiology Examined, 1980; Science and Creationism, 1983. *Recreations:* book collecting, gardening. *Address:* 321 Cherry Hill Road, Princeton, NJ 08540, USA. *T:* 609 924–3756.

MONTAGU, Hon. David Charles Samuel; Deputy Chairman, J. Rothschild Holdings plc, since 1984; *b* 6 Aug. 1928; *e s* and *heir* of 3rd Baron Swaythling, *qv*, and Mary Violet, *e d* of Major Levy, DSO; *m* 1951, Christiane Françoise (Ninette), *d* of Edgar Dreyfus, Paris; one *s* one *d* (and one *d* decd). *Educ:* Eton; Trinity Coll., Cambridge. Exec. Dir, 1954, Chm., 1970–73, Samuel Montagu & Co. Ltd; Chm. and Chief Exec., Orion Bank, 1974–79; Chairman: Ailsa Investment Trust plc, 1981; Derby Trust plc; Fleming Overseas Investment Trust PLC; Director: Ashdown Investment Trust PLC; Drayton Japan Trust plc; Philip Hill Investment Trust PLC; Precious Metals Trust PLC; London Weekend Television; The Daily Telegraph; Rothmans International plc; STC plc; Trades Union Unit Trust Managers Ltd; London Cttee, Ottoman Bank; Pacific Investment Trust PLC. *Recreations:* shooting, racing, theatre. *Address:* 14 Craven Hill Mews, W2 3DY. *T:* 01–724 7860; (office) 15 St James's Place, SW1A 1NN. *T:* 01–493 8111. *Clubs:* White's, Portland, Pratt's.

MONTAGU, Jennifer Iris Rachel, PhD; FBA 1986; Curator of the Photograph Collection, Warburg Institute, since 1971; *b* 20 March 1931; *d* of late Hon. Ewen Edward Samuel Montagu, CBE, QC. *Educ:* Brearley Sch., New York; Benenden Sch., Kent; Lady Margaret Hall, Oxford (BA; Hon. Fellow 1985); Warburg Inst., London (PhD). Assistant Regional Director, Arts Council of Gt Britain, North West Region, 1953–54; Lecturer in the History of Art, Reading Univ., 1958–64; Asst Curator of the Photograph Collection, Warburg Inst., 1964–71. Slade Prof., Cambridge, and Fellow Jesus Coll., Cambridge, 1980–81. Member: Academic Awards Cttee, British Fedn of University Women, 1963–; Executive Cttee, National Art-Collections Fund, 1973–; Consultative Cttee, Burlington Magazine, 1975–; Cttee, The Jewish Museum, 1983–. *Publications:* Bronzes, 1963; (with Jacques Thuillier) Catalogue of exhibn Charles Le Brun, 1963; Alessandro Algardi, 1985 (special Mitchell Prize); articles in learned periodicals. *Address:* 10 Roland Way, SW7 3RE. *T:* 01–373 6691; Warburg Institute, Woburn Square, WC1H 0AB.

MONTAGU, John Edward Hollister; (Viscount Hinchingbrooke, but does not use the title); journalist; Information Officer, Christian Aid, since 1974; *b* 11 April 1943; *er s* of Victor Montagu, *qv*, and *heir* to disclaimed Earldom of Sandwich; *m* 1968, Caroline, *o d* of Canon P. E. C. Hayman, Cocking, W Sussex; two *s* one *d. Educ:* Eton; Trinity College, Cambridge. *Address:* 69 Albert Bridge Road, SW11 4QE.

MONTAGU, Montague Francis Ashley; *see* Montagu, A.

MONTAGU, Victor; *see* Montagu, A. V. E. P.

MONTAGU DOUGLAS SCOTT, family name of **Duke of Buccleuch.**

MONTAGU-POLLOCK, Sir Giles Hampden; *see* Pollock.

MONTAGU-POLLOCK, Sir William H., KCMG 1957 (CMG 1946); *b* 12 July 1903; *s* of Sir M. F. Montagu-Pollock, 3rd Bt; *m* 1st, 1933, Frances Elizabeth Prudence (marr. diss. 1945), *d* of late Sir John Fischer Williams, CBE, KC; one *s* one *d*; 2nd, 1948, Barbara, *d* of late P. H. Jowett, CBE, FRCA, RWS; one *s. Educ:* Marlborough Coll.; Trinity Coll., Cambridge. Served in Diplomatic Service at Rome, Belgrade, Prague, Vienna, Stockholm, Brussels, and at Foreign Office; British Ambassador, Damascus, 1952–53 (Minister, 1950–52); British Ambassador: to Peru, 1953–58; to Switzerland, 1958–60; to Denmark, 1960–62. Retired from HM Foreign Service, 1962. Governor, European Cultural Foundation; Vice-President: European Acad. GB; Soc. for Promotion of New Music. *Recreation:* washing up. *Address:* Flat 181, Coleherne Court, SW5. *T:* 01–373 3685; Playa Blanca, Yaiza, Lanzarote, Canary Islands.

MONTAGU-STUART-WORTLEY-MACKENZIE, family name of **Earl of Wharncliffe.**

MONTAGUE, family name of **Baron Amwell.**

MONTAGUE, Francis Arnold, CMG 1956; retired; *b* 14 June 1904; *s* of late Charles Edward Montague, OBE, author and journalist, and of Madeleine Montague (*née* Scott), Manchester; *m* 1939, Fanny Susanne, *d* of late E. S. Scorer and Mrs C. D. Scorer; one *d. Educ:* Cargilfield Sch., Edinburgh; Rugby Sch.; Balliol Coll., Oxford. Tanganyika: served in Game Preservation Dept, 1925–28; Cadet, Colonial Administrative Service, 1928; Dist Officer, 1938; Private Sec. to Governor, 1938–40; Asst Chief Sec., 1948; Administrative Sec., Sierra Leone, 1950–58; retired from Colonial Service, Jan. 1958. Deputy-Chairman: Public Service Commn, Uganda, 1958–63; Public Service Commn, Aden, 1963. Mem., Oxon CC, 1964–73, Witney (Oxon) RDC, 1966–74; W Oxon Dist. Council, 1973–76. *Recreation:* gardening. *Address:* Dolphin House, Westhall Hill, Fulbrook OX8 4BJ. *T:* Burford 2147. *Club:* Lansdowne.

MONTAGUE, Michael Jacob, CBE 1970; Chairman: Valor PLC, since 1965 (Managing Director, 1963); National Consumer Council, since 1984; Member, Ordnance Survey Advisory Board, since 1983; *b* 10 March 1932; *s* of David Elias Montague and Eleanor Stagg. *Educ:* High Wycombe Royal Grammar Sch.; Magdalen Coll. Sch., Oxford. Founded Gatehill Beco Ltd, 1958 (sold to Valor Co., 1962). Chm., English Tourist Bd, 1979–84; Mem., BTA, 1979–84. President: BAIE, 1983–85; Young European Management Assoc.; Gov., Nat. Inst. of Hardware; Chairman: Asia Cttee, BNEC, 1968–71; Immigration Cttee, Kent Social Service. Non-exec. Dir, President Entertainments PLC, 1985–; Mem. Council, Royal Albert Hall, 1985–. *Address:* 17 Stratford Road, W8.

MONTAGUE BROWNE, Anthony Arthur Duncan, CBE 1965 (OBE 1955); DFC 1945; Director: Security Pacific Trust (Bahamas) Ltd; UK public and private companies; a Managing Director, Gerrard and National PLC, 1974–83 (Director, 1967–74); *b* 8 May 1923; *s* of late Lt-Col A. D. Montague Browne, DSO, OBE, Bivia House, Goodrich, Ross-on-Wye, and Violet Evelyn (*née* Downes); *m* 1st, 1950, Noel Evelyn Arnold-Wallinger (marr. diss. 1970); one *d*; 2nd, 1970, Shelagh Macklin (*née* Mulligan). *Educ:* Stowe; Magdalen Coll., Oxford: abroad. Pilot RAF, 1941–45. Entered Foreign (now Diplomatic) Service, 1946; Foreign Office, 1946–49; Second Sec., British Embassy, Paris, 1949–52; seconded as Private Sec. to Prime Minister, 1952–55; seconded as Private Sec. to Rt Hon. Sir Winston Churchill, 1955–65; Counsellor, Diplomatic Service, 1964; seconded to HM Household, 1965–67; Trustee and Chm. of Council, Winston Churchill Memorial Trust; Mem. Council, Univs Fedn for Animal Welfare, 1985; Chm., Internat. Certificate of

Deposit Market Assoc., 1980–82. *Address:* c/o R3 Section, Lloyds Bank, Cox's & King's Branch, 6 Pall Mall, SW1. *Clubs:* Boodle's, Pratt's.

MONTAGUE-JONES, Brigadier (retd) Ronald, CBE 1944 (MBE 1941); jssc; psc; *b* 10 Dec. 1909; *yr s* of late Edgar Montague Jones, until 1931 Headmaster of St Albans Sch., Herts, and of late Emmeline Mary Yates; *m* 1937, Denise Marguerite (marr. diss.), *y d* of late General Sir Hubert Gough, GCB, GCMG, KCVO; one *s*; *m* 1955, Pamela, *d* of late Lieut-Col Hastings Roy Harington, 8th Gurkha Rifles, and late Hon. Mrs Harington; one *s*. *Educ:* St Albans; RMA, Woolwich; St John's Coll., Cambridge (BA 1933, MA 1937). 2nd Lieut RE 1930; Temp. Brig. 1943; Bt Lt-Col 1952; Brig. 1958. Egypt, 1935; Palestine, 1936–39 (despatches twice); War of 1939–45 (MBE, CBE, US Bronze Star, Africa Star, 1939–45 Star, Italy Star, Burma Star, General Service Medal with Clasps Palestine, SE Asia and Malaya). CC Dorset, for Swanage (East), 1964–74, Swanage, 1974–85. *Address:* 10 Battlemead, Swanage, Dorset BH19 1PH. *T:* Swanage 423186.

MONTEAGLE OF BRANDON, 6th Baron *cr* 1839; **Gerald Spring Rice;** late Captain, Irish Guards; one of HM Body Guard, Hon. Corps of Gentlemen-at-Arms, since 1978; *b* 5 July 1926; *s* of 5th Baron and Emilie de Kosenko (*d* 1981), *d* of Mrs Edward Brooks, Philadelphia, USA; *S* father 1946; *m* 1949, Anne, *d* of late Col G. J. Brownlow, Ballywhite, Portaferry, Co. Down; one *s* three *d* (of whom two are twins). *Educ:* Harrow. Member: London Stock Exchange, 1958–76; Lloyd's, 1978–. *Heir: s* Hon. Charles James Spring Rice, *b* 24 Feb. 1953. *Address:* 242A Fulham Road, SW10. *Clubs:* Cavalry and Guards, Pratt's; Kildare Street and University (Dublin).

MONTEATH, Robert Campbell, CBE 1964; County Clerk, Treasurer and Local Taxation Officer, Kirkcudbright, 1946–72, and Clerk to the Lieutenancy, since 1966; *b* 15 June 1907; *s* of Gordon Drysdale Monteath, Dumbarton; *m* 1936, Sarah McGregor, *d* of John Fenwick, Dumbarton; two *s* one *d*. *Educ:* Dumbarton Academy; Glasgow Univ. Dep. County Clerk, Dunbartonshire, 1937–46; Dep. Civil Defence Controller, 1939–46; Hon. Sheriff, Kirkcudbright, 1966–. Past District Governor, Rotary Internat., District 102. *Address:* Gortonbrae, Townhead, Kirkcudbright. *T:* Townhead 251. *Clubs:* Royal Over-Seas League; Royal Scottish Automobile (Glasgow).

MONTEFIORE, Harold Henry S.; *see* Sebag-Montefiore.

MONTEFIORE, Rt. Rev. Hugh William; *see* Birmingham, Bishop of.

MONTEITH, Charles Montgomery; Fellow of All Souls College, Oxford, since 1948; *b* 9 Feb. 1921; *s* of late James Monteith and Marian Monteith (*née* Montgomery). *Educ:* Royal Belfast Academical Instn; Magdalen Coll., Oxford (Demy 1939, Sen. Demy 1948, MA 1948, BCL 1949). Sub-Warden, All Souls Coll., Oxford, 1967–69. Served War, Royal Inniskilling Fusiliers, India and Burma (Major), 1940–45. Called to the Bar, Gray's Inn, 1949; joined Faber & Faber, 1953, Dir, 1954, Vice-Chm., 1974–76, Chm., 1977–80. Dir, Poetry Book Soc., 1966–81; Member: Literature Panel, Arts Council of GB, 1974–78; Library Adv. Council for England, 1979–81. Hon. DLitt: Ulster, 1980; Kent, 1982. *Address:* c/o Faber & Faber Ltd, 3 Queen Square, WC1. *T:* 01–278 6881. *Clubs:* Beefsteak, Garrick.

MONTEITH, Rt. Rev. George Rae, BA; *b* 14 Feb. 1904; *s* of John Hodge Monteith and Ellen (*née* Hall); *m* 1st, 1931, Kathleen Methven Mules; two *s* one *d*; 2nd, 1982, Hilary Llewellyn Etherington. *Educ:* St John's Coll., Auckland; Univ. of New Zealand. BA 1927. Deacon, 1928; priest, 1929; Curate: St Matthew's, Auckland, 1928–30; Stoke-on-Trent, 1931–33; Vicar of: Dargaville, NZ, 1934–37; Mt Eden, Auckland, NZ, 1937–49; St Mary's Cathedral Parish, Auckland, 1949–69; Dean of Auckland, 1949–69; Vicar-General, 1963–76; Asst Bishop of Auckland, NZ, 1965–76. *Address:* 7 Cathedral Place, Auckland 1, NZ. *T:* 734.449.

MONTEITH, Prof. John Lennox, FRS 1971; FRSE 1972; Director of Resource Management Programme, International Crops Research Institute for the Semi-Arid Tropics, since 1987 (Visiting Scientist, 1984); *b* 3 Sept. 1929; *s* of Rev. John and Margaret Monteith; *m* 1955, Elsa Marion Wotherspoon; four *s* one *d*. *Educ:* George Heriot's Sch.; Univ. of Edinburgh; Imperial Coll., London. BSc, DIC, PhD, FInstP, FIBiol. Mem. Physics Dept Staff, Rothamsted Experimental Station, 1954–67; Prof. of Environmental Physics, 1967–86, Dean of Faculty of Agricl Sci., 1985–86, Nottingham Univ. Governor, Grassland Res. Inst., 1976–83. Vice Pres., British Ecological Soc., 1977–79; Pres., Royal Meteorol Soc., 1978–80. Member: NERC, 1980–84; British Nat. Cttee for the World Climate Programme, 1980–86; Lawes Agricl Trust Cttee, 1983–86. Nat. Res. Council Senior Res. Associate, Goddard Space Flight Center, Md, USA, 1985; Clive Behrens Lectr, Leeds Univ., 1986. Buchan Prize, RMetS, 1962; Solco Tromp Award, Internat. Soc. of Biometeorology, 1983. *Publications:* Instruments for Micrometeorology (ed), 1972; Principles of Environmental Physics, 1973; (ed with L. E. Mount) Heat Loss from Animals and Man, 1974; (ed) Vegetation and the Atmosphere, 1975; (ed with C. Webb) Soil Water and Nitrogen, 1981; papers on Micrometeorology and Crop Science in: Quarterly Jl of RMetSoc.; Jl Applied Ecology, etc. *Recreations:* music, photography. *Address:* ICRISAT, Patancheru PO, AP 502324, India. *T:* Hyderabad 224016; School of Agriculture, Sutton Bonington, Loughborough, Leics LE12 5RD. *T:* Nottingham 506101.

MONTEITH, Lt-Col Robert Charles Michael, OBE 1981; MC 1943; TD 1945; JP; Vice Lord-Lieutenant of Lanarkshire since 1964; Land-owner and Farmer since 1950; *b* 25 May 1914; *s* of late Major J. B. L. Monteith, CBE, and late Dorothy, *d* of Sir Charles Nicholson, 1st Bt; *m* 1950, Mira Elizabeth, *e d* of late John Fanshawe, Sidmount, Moffat; one *s*. *Educ:* Ampleforth Coll., York. CA (Edinburgh), 1939. Served with Lanarkshire Yeomanry, 1939–45: Paiforce, 1942–43; MEF, 1943–44; BLA, 1944–45. Contested (U) Hamilton Division of Lanarkshire, 1950 and 1951. Member: Mental Welfare Commn for Scotland, 1962–84; E Kilbride Develt Corp., 1972–76. DL 1955, JP 1955, CC 1949–64, 1967–74, Lanarkshire; Chm., Lanark DC, later Clydesdale DC, 1974–. Mem. Queen's Body Guard for Scotland, Royal Company of Archers. Mem. SMO of Knights of Malta; OStJ 1973. *Recreations:* shooting, curling. *Address:* Cranley, Cleghorn, Lanark. *T:* Carstairs 330. *Clubs:* New, Puffins (Edinburgh).

MONTGOMERIE, family name of **Earl of Eglinton.**

MONTGOMERIE, Lord; Hugh Archibald William Montgomerie; *b* 24 July 1966; *s* and *heir* of 18th Earl of Eglinton and Winton, *qv*.

MONTGOMERY, family name of **Viscount Montgomery of Alamein.**

MONTGOMERY OF ALAMEIN, 2nd Viscount *cr* 1946, of Hindhead; **David Bernard Montgomery,** CBE 1975; Managing Director, Terimar Services (Overseas Trade Consultancy), since 1974; Director: Northern Engineering Industries, since 1981; Korn/Ferry International, since 1977; *b* 18 Aug. 1928; *s* of 1st Viscount Montgomery of Alamein, KG, GCB, DSO, and Elizabeth (*d* 1937), *d* of late Robert Thompson Hobart, ICS; *S* father, 1976; *m* 1st, 1953, Mary Connell (marr. diss. 1967); one *s* one *d*; 2nd, 1970, Tessa, *d* of late Gen. Sir Frederick Browning, GCVO, KBE, CB, DSO, and of Lady Browning, DBE (*see* Dame Daphne du Maurier). *Educ:* Winchester; Trinity Coll., Cambridge (MA). Shell International, 1951–62; Yardley International (Director), 1963–74; Chm., Antofagasta (Chile) and Bolivia Railway Co., 1980–82. Editorial Adviser, Vision Interamericana, 1974–. Chm., Economic Affairs Cttee, Canning House, 1973–75; Pres., British Industrial Exhibition, Sao Paulo, 1974. Councillor, Royal Borough of Kensington and Chelsea, 1974–78. Hon. Consul, Republic of El Salvador, 1973–77. Pres., Anglo-Argentine Soc., 1977–; Chairman: Hispanic and Luso Brazilian Council, 1978–80; Brazilian Chamber of Commerce in GB, 1980–82. Patron, D-Day and Normandy Fellowship, 1980–. President: Redgrave Theatre, Farnham, 1977–; Restaurateurs Assoc. of GB, 1982–; Centre for International Briefing, Farnham Castle, 1985–. Governor, Amesbury Sch., 1976–. *Heir: s* Hon. Henry David Montgomery [*b* 2 April 1954, *m* 1980, Caroline, *e d* of Richard Odey, Hotham Hall, York; one *d*]. *Address:* Isington Mill, Alton, Hants GU34 4PW. *T:* Bentley (0420) 23126. *Clubs:* Garrick; Royal Fowey Yacht.

MONTGOMERY, Alan Everard, PhD; HM Diplomatic Service; Counsellor, GATT/UNCTAD, UKMIS Geneva, since 1983; *b* 11 March 1938; *s* of Philip Napier Montgomery and Honor Violet Coleman (*née* Price); *m* 1960, Janet Barton; one *s* one *d*. *Educ:* Royal Grammar Sch., Guildford; County of Stafford Training Coll. (Cert. of Educn); Birkbeck Coll., London (BA Hons, PhD). Served Mddx Regt, 1957–59. Teacher, Staffs and ILEA, 1961–65; Lectr, Univ. of Birmingham, 1969–72; entered FCO, 1972; 1st Secretary: FCO, 1972–75; Dhaka, 1975–77; Ottawa, 1977–80; FCO, 1980–83. *Publications:* (contrib.) Lloyd George: 12 essays, ed A. J. P. Taylor, 1971; contrib. Cambridge Hist. Jl. *Recreations:* historic buildings, jazz, swimming, camping, theatre. *Address:* c/o Foreign and Commonwealth Office, King Charles Street, SW1A 2AH.

MONTGOMERY, Sir (Basil Henry) David, 9th Bt, *cr* 1801, of Stanhope; JP; DL; landowner; Chairman, Forestry Commission, since 1979; *b* 20 March 1931; *s* of late Lt-Col H. K. Purvis-Montgomery, OBE, and of Mrs C. L. W. Purvis-Russell-Montgomery (*née* Maconochie Welwood); *S* uncle, 1964; *m* 1956, Delia, *o d* of Adm. Sir (John) Peter (Lorne) Reid, GCB, CVO; one *s* four *d* (and one *s* decd). *Educ:* Eton. National Service, Black Watch, 1949–51. Member: Nature Conservancy Council, 1973–79; Tayside Regional Authority, 1974–79. Hon. LLD Dundee, 1977. DL Kinross-shire, 1960, Vice-Lieutenant 1966–74; JP 1966; DL Perth and Kinross, 1975. *Heir: s* James David Keith Montgomery [*b* 13 June 1957; *m* 1983, Elizabeth, *e d* of E. Lyndon Evans, Pentyrch, Mid-Glamorgan; one *s*. Served The Black Watch, RHR, 1976–86]. *Address:* Kinross House, Kinross. *T:* Kinross 63416.

MONTGOMERY, (Charles) John, CBE 1977; Director: Lloyds Bank Plc, 1972–84 (a Vice-Chairman, 1978–84); Lloyds Bank International, 1978–84; Yorkshire Bank, 1980–84; *b* 18 Feb. 1917; *s* of late Rev. Charles James Montgomery; *m* 1950, Gwenneth Mary McKendrick; two *d*. *Educ:* Colwyn Bay Grammar School. Served with RN, 1940–46. Entered Lloyds Bank, 1935; Jt Gen. Man. 1968; Asst Chief Gen. Man. 1970; Dep. Chief Gen. Man. 1973; Chief Gen. Man., 1973–78. Pres., Inst. of Bankers, 1976–77, Vice Pres., 1977–. Chm., Chief Exec. Officers' Cttee, Cttee of London Clearing Bankers, 1976–78. *Recreations:* walking, photography. *Address:* High Cedar, 6 Cedar Copse, Bickley, Kent. *T:* 01–467 2410. *Clubs:* Naval, Overseas Bankers.

MONTGOMERY, Sir David; *see* Montgomery, Sir B. H. D.

MONTGOMERY, David, CMG 1984; OBE 1972; HM Diplomatic Service, retired; *b* 29 July 1927; *s* of late David Montgomery and of Mary (*née* Walker Cunningham); *m* 1955, Margaret Newman; one *s* one *d*. GPO, Glasgow, 1941–45; Royal Navy, 1945–48; GPO, Glasgow, 1948–49; Foreign Office, 1949–52; Bucharest, 1952–53; FO, 1953–55; Bonn, 1955–58; Düsseldorf, 1958–61; Rangoon, 1961–63; Ottawa, 1963–64; Regina, Saskatchewan, 1964–65; FCO, 1966–68; Bangkok, 1968–72; Zagreb, 1973–76; FCO, 1976–79; Dep. High Comr to Barbados, 1980–84, also (non-resident) to Antigua and Barbuda, Dominica, Grenada, St Kitts and Nevis, St Lucia, St Vincent and the Grenadines, 1980–84; FCO, 1984–85. *Recreations:* golf, music (light and opera). *Address:* 8 Ross Court, Putney Hill, SW15 3NY. *Club:* Royal Over-Seas League.

MONTGOMERY, David John; Editor, News of the World, since 1985; *b* 6 Nov. 1948; *s* of William John and Margaret Jean Montgomery; *m* 1971, Susan Frances Buchanan Russell. *Educ:* Queen's University, Belfast (BA Politics/History). Sub-Editor, Daily Mirror, London/Manchester, 1973–78; Assistant Chief Sub-Editor, Daily Mirror, 1978–80; Chief Sub-Editor, The Sun, 1980; Asst Editor, Sunday People, 1982; Asst Editor, News of the World, 1984. *Address:* The News of the World, Virginia Street, Wapping, E1 9BH. *T:* 01–481 4100.

MONTGOMERY, Prof. Desmond Alan Dill, CBE 1981 (MBE 1943); MD; FRCP, FRCPI; Chairman, Northern Ireland Council for Postgraduate Medical Education, since 1979; *b* 6 June 1916; 3rd *s* of late Dr and Mrs J. Howard Montgomery, China and Belfast; *m* 1941, Dr Susan Holland, 2nd *d* of late Mr and Mrs F. J. Holland, Belfast; one *s* one *d*. *Educ:* Inchmarlo Prep. Sch.; Campbell Coll.; Queen's Univ., Belfast (3rd, 4th and final yr scholarships; MB, BCh, BAO 1st Cl. Hons 1940; MD (Gold Medal) 1946). Sinclair Medal in Surgery, Butterworth Prize in Medicine, Prize in Mental Disease, QUB. MRCP 1948, FRCP 1964; FRCPI 1975; FRCOG (*ae*) 1981. Served War, RAMC, 1941–46: Temp. Major India Comd; DADMS GHQ India, 1943–45. House Physician and Surgeon, Royal Victoria Hosp., Belfast, 1940–41, Registrar, 1946; Registrar, Royal Postgrad. Med. Sch. and Hammersmith Hosp., and National Heart Hosp., London, 1946–48; Royal Victoria Hosp., Belfast: Sen. Registrar, 1948–51; Consultant Physician, 1951–79, Hon. Consultant 1980–; Physician i/c Sir George E. Clark Metabolic Unit, 1958–79; Endocrinologist, Royal Maternity Hosp., Belfast, 1958–79; Hon. Reader in Endocrinol., Dept of Medicine, QUB, 1969–75, Hon. Prof., 1975–. Hon. Secretary: Royal Victoria Med. Staff Cttee, 1964–66 (Chm., 1975–77); Ulster Med. Soc., 1954–58 (Pres., 1975–76). Member: NI Council for Health and Personal Social Services, 1974–83 (Chm., Central Med. Adv. Cttee, 1974–83, Mem. 1983–); NI Med. Manpower Adv. Cttee, 1974–83; Distinction and Meritorious Awards Cttee, 1975– (Chm., 1982–); Faculty of Medicine, QUB, 1969– (Chm., Ethical Cttee, 1975–81); Senate, QUB, 1979–; GMC, 1979–84. Member: BMA; Assoc. of Physicians of GB and NI; Eur. Thyroid Assoc.; Corrigan Club (Chm., 1969); Irish Endocrine Soc. (1st Chm., Founder Mem.); Internat. Soc. for Internal Medicine; formerly Mem., Eur. Soc. for Study of Diabetes; Hon. Mem., British Dietetic Assoc. Lectured in USA, India, Greece, Australia and Nigeria; visited Russia on behalf of British Council, 1975. Pres., Belfast City Mission, 1973, Mem., Bd of Trustees, Presbyterian Church in Ireland. DSc (*hc*) NUI, 1980. Jt Editor, Ulster Med. Jl, 1974–84. *Publications:* (contrib.) Whitla's Dictionary of Treatment, 1957; (contrib.) Good Health and Diabetes, 1961, 3rd edn 1976; (contrib.) R. Smith, Progress in Clinical Surgery, 1961; (with R. B. Welbourn) Clinical Endocrinology for Surgeons, 1963; (contrib.) Progress in Neurosurgery, 1964; (with R. B. Welbourn) Medical and Surgical Endocrinology, 1975; (contrib.) M. D. Vickers, Medicine for Anaesthetists, 1977; articles in med. jls on endocrinology, diabetes mellitus and related subjects. *Recreations:* travel, photography, music, gardening, philately. *Address:* 59 Church Road, Newtownbreda, Belfast BT8 4AN. *T:* Belfast 648326; 15 Carrickmore Road, Ballycastle BT54 6QS. *T:* Ballycastle 62361.

MONTGOMERY, Sir Fergus; *see* Montgomery, Sir (William) Fergus.

MONTGOMERY, Prof. George Lightbody, CBE 1960; TD 1942; MD, PhD, FRCPE, FRCPGlas, FRCPath, FRCSE; FRSE; Professor of Pathology, University of Edinburgh, 1954–71, now Emeritus; *b* 3 Nov. 1905; *o s* of late John Montgomery and Jeanie Lightbody; *m* 1933, Margaret Sutherland, 3rd *d* of late A. Henry Forbes, Oban; one *s* one *d*. *Educ:* Hillhead High Sch., Glasgow; Glasgow Univ. MB, ChB, 1928; Commendation and RAMC Memorial Prize; PhD (St Andrews), 1937; MD Hons and Bellahouston Gold Medal (Glasgow), 1946. House Physician, House Surgeon, Glasgow Royal Infirmary, 1928–29; Lecturer in Clinical Pathology, Univ. of St Andrews, 1931–37; Lecturer in Pathology of Disease in Infancy and Childhood, Univ. of Glasgow, 1937–48; Asst Pathologist, Glasgow Royal Infirmary, 1929–31; Asst Pathologist, Dundee Royal Infirmary, 1931–37; Pathologist, Royal Hospital for Sick Children, Glasgow, 1937–48; Professor of Pathology (St Mungo-Notman Chair), Univ. of Glasgow, 1948–54. Chm. Scottish Health Services Council, 1954–59. Hon. Member: Pathological Soc. Gt Britain and Ireland; BMA. Col (Hon.) Army Medical Service. *Publications:* numerous contribs to medical and scientific journals. *Recreation:* music. *Address:* 2 Cumin Place, Edinburgh EH9 2JX. *T:* 031–667 6792. *Club:* New (Edinburgh).

MONTGOMERY, Group Captain George Rodgers, CBE 1946; DL; RAF (Retired); Secretary, Norfolk Naturalists' Trust, 1963–75; Hon. Appeal Secretary, and Member of the Court, University of East Anglia, since Nov. 1966; *b* 31 May 1910; *s* of late John Montgomery, Belfast; *m* 1st, 1932, Margaret McHarry Heslip (*d* 1981), *d* of late William J. Heslip, Belfast; two *s*; 2nd, 1982, Margaret Stephanie, *widow* of Colin Vanner Hedworth Foulkes. *Educ:* Royal Academy, Belfast. Commnd in RAF, 1928; retd 1958. Served in UK and ME, 1928–38. War of 1939–45: Bomber Comd, NI, Air Min. and ME. Served UK, Japan and W Europe, 1946–58: Comdr RAF Wilmslow, 1946–47; Air Adviser to UK Polit. Rep. in Japan, and Civil Air Attaché, Tokyo, 1948–49; Chief Instr RAF Officers' Advanced Trg Sch., 1950; Comdt RAF Sch. of Admin, Bircham Newton, 1951–52; Comdr RAF Hednesford, 1953–54; DDO (Estabts) Air Min. and Chm. RAF Western European Estabts Cttee, Germany, 1955–57. On retirement, Organising Sec. Friends of Norwich Cathedral, 1959–62; Appeal Sec., Univ. of East Anglia, 1961–66; Hon. Vice-President: Norfolk Naturalists' Trust, 1979–; Broads Soc., 1983–; Mem., Great Bustard Trust Council, 1972–. DL Norfolk, 1979. *Recreations:* river cruising, gardening. *Address:* 24 Cathedral Close, Norwich, Norfolk. *T:* Norwich 628024. *Club:* Royal Air Force.

MONTGOMERY, Hugh Bryan Greville; Managing Director, Andry Montgomery group of companies (organisers, managers and consultants in exhibitions), since 1952; *b* 26 March 1929; *s* of Hugh Roger Greville Montgomery, MC, and Molly Audrey Montgomery (*née* Neele). *Educ:* Repton; Lincoln Coll., Oxford (MA PPE). Founder member, Oxford Univ. Wine and Food Soc. Consultant and adviser on trade fairs and developing countries for UN; Consultant, Internat. Garden Festival, Liverpool, 1984. Chairman: Brit. Assoc. of Exhibn Organisers, 1970; Union des Foires Internat. Bldg Specialised Cttee, 1975–; Internat. Cttee, Amer. Nat. Assoc. of Exposition Managers, 1980–82; British Exhibn Promotion Council, 1982–83; Chm. of Trustees of ECHO (Supply of Equipment to Charity Hosps Overseas), 1978–; Vice-Chm., Bldg Conservation Trust, 1979– (Chm. Interbuild Fund, 1972–); Trustee, The Cubitt Trust, 1982–; Hon. Treas., Contemporary Art Soc., 1980–82; Mem. Council, Design and Industries Assoc., 1983–85; Member Executive Committee: CGLI, 1974–; Nat. Fund for Research into Crippling Diseases, 1970–; Mem. Adv. Bd, Hotel Inst. for Management, Montreux. Master, Worshipful Co. of Tylers and Bricklayers, 1980–81 (Trustee, Charitable and Pension Trusts). Silver Jubilee Medal, 1977. *Publications:* Industrial Fairs and Developing Countries (UNIDO), 1975; Going into Trade Fairs (UNCTAD/GATT), 1982; contrib. to Internat. Trade Forum (ITC, Geneva). *Recreations:* collecting contemparary art, theatre, wine tasting. *Address:* 11 Manchester Square, W1M 5AB. *T:* 01–486 1951; Snells Farm, Amersham Common, Bucks HP7 9QN. *Clubs:* United Oxford & Cambridge University, City Livery.

MONTGOMERY, John; *see* Montgomery, C. J.

MONTGOMERY, John Matthew; Clerk of the Salters' Company, since 1975; *b* 22 May 1930; *s* of Prof. George Allison Montgomery, QC, and Isobel A. (*née* Morison); *m* 1956, Gertrude Gillian Richards; two *s* one *d*. *Educ:* Rugby Sch.; Trinity Hall, Cambridge (MA). Various commercial appointments with Mobil Oil Corporation and First National City Bank, 1953–74. Member, Executive Committee: Nat. Assoc. of Almshouses, 1980–; Age Concern, Gtr London, 1985–. Member: Council, Surrey Trust for Nature Conservation Ltd, 1965– (Chm., 1973–83; Vice-Pres., 1983–); Council, Royal Soc. for Nature Conservation, 1980–; Conservation Cttee, Botanical Soc. of British Isles, 1982–. Founder Mem., London Wildlife Trust, 1981–; Hon. Sec., Conservation Assoc. of Botanical Socs, 1985–. *Recreations:* various natural history interests. *Address:* Dunedin, Red Lane, Claygate, Esher, Surrey KT10 0ES. *T:* Esher 64780.

MONTGOMERY, Col John Rupert Patrick, OBE 1979; MC 1943; *b* 25 July 1913; *s* of George Howard and Mabella Montgomery; *m* 1st, 1940, Alice Vyvyan Patricia Mitchell (*d* 1976); one *s* two *d*; 2nd, 1981, Marguerite Beatrice Chambers (*née* Montgomery). *Educ:* Wellington Coll.; RMC, Sandhurst. Commissioned, Oxfordshire and Buckinghamshire LI, 1933; Regimental Service in India, 1935–40 and 1946–47. Served War, in Middle East, N Africa and Italy, 1942–45. Commanded 17 Bn Parachute Regt (9 DLI), 1953–56; SHAPE Mission to Portugal, 1956–59; retired, 1962. Sec., Anti-Slavery Soc., 1963–80. Silver Medal, RSA, 1973. *Address:* The Oast House, Buxted, Sussex. *Club:* Army and Navy.

MONTGOMERY of Blessingbourne, Captain Peter Stephen; Vice-Lieutenant of County Tyrone, Northern Ireland, 1971–79; *b* 13 Aug. 1909; 2nd *s* of late Maj.-Gen. Hugh Maude de Fellenberg Montgomery, CB, CMG, DL, RA, and late Mary, 2nd *d* of Edmund Langton and Mrs Massingberd, Gunby Hall, Lincs. *Educ:* Wellington Coll.; Trinity Coll., Cambridge (MA). Founder, 1927, and Conductor until 1969, of Fivemiletown Choral Soc.; employed with BBC in N Ireland and London, 1931–47; Asst Music Dir and Conductor, BBC Northern Ireland Symphony Orchestra, 1933–38. Served War of 1939–45: Captain, Royal Intelligence Corps, ADC to Viceroy of India (FM Earl Wavell), 1945–46. Mem. BBC Northern Ireland Advisory Council, 1952–71, and BBC Gen. Adv. Council, 1963–71. Hon. ADC to Governor of Northern Ireland (Lord Wakehurst), 1954–64; Member: National Trust Cttee for NI, 1955–75; Bd of Visitors, HM Prison, Belfast (Chm. 1971); Friends of National Collections of Ireland; Bd of Arts Council of NI (Pres., 1964–74). JP 1959, DL 1956, Co. Tyrone; High Sheriff of Co. Tyrone, 1964. Hon. LLD Queen's Univ. Belfast, 1976. Silver Jubilee Medal, 1977. *Address:* Blessingbourne, Fivemiletown, Co. Tyrone, Northern Ireland. *Clubs:* Oriental; Ulster (Belfast); Tyrone County (Omagh).

MONTGOMERY, Sir (William) Fergus, Kt 1985; MP (C) Altrincham and Sale, since Oct. 1974; *b* 25 Nov. 1927; *s* of William Montgomery and late Winifred Montgomery; *m* Joyce, *d* of George Riddle. *Educ:* Jarrow Grammar Sch.; Bede Coll., Durham. Served in Royal Navy, 1946–48; Schoolmaster, 1950–59. Nat. Vice-Chm. Young Conservative Organisation, 1954–57, National Chm., 1957–58; contested (C) Consett Division, 1955; MP (C): Newcastle upon Tyne East, 1959–64; Brierley Hill, Apr. 1967–Feb. 1974; contested Dudley W, Feb. 1974; PPS to Sec. of State for Educn and Science, 1973–74, to Leader of the Opposition, 1975–76. Mem. Executive, CPA, 1983–. Councillor, Hebburn UDC, 1950–58. Has lectured extensively in the USA. *Recreations:* bridge, reading, going to theatre. *Address:* 181 Ashley Gardens, Emery Hill Street, SW1. *T:* 01–834 7905; 6 Groby Place, Altrincham, Cheshire. *T:* 061–928 1983.

MONTGOMERY CUNINGHAME, Sir John Christopher Foggo, 12th Bt *cr* 1672, of Corsehill, Ayrshire and Kirktonholm, Lanarkshire; Chairman: Ronald A. Lee PLC; Euromax Electronics Ltd; Director: Artemis Energy Co.; Inertia Dynamics Corp.; C. H. Rugg Ltd and other companies; *b* 24 July 1935; 2nd *s* of Col Sir Thomas Montgomery-Cuninghame, 10th Bt, DSO (*d* 1945), and of Nancy Macaulay (his 2nd wife), *d* of late W. Stewart Foggo, Aberdeen (she *m* 2nd, 1946, Johan Frederik Christian Killander); *b* of Sir Andrew Mongtomery-Cuninghame, 11th Bt; *S* brother, 1959; *m* 1964, Laura Violet, *d* of Sir Godfrey Nicholson, Bt, *qv*; three *d*. *Educ:* Fettes; Worcester Coll., Oxford (MA). 2nd Lieut, Rifle Brigade (NS), 1955–56; Lieut, London Rifle Brigade, TA, 1956–59. *Recreation:* fishing. *Heir:* none. *Address:* The Old Rectory, Brightwalton, Newbury, Berks.

MONTGOMERY WATT, Prof. William; *see* Watt.

MONTLAKE, Henry Joseph; solicitor; Senior Partner, H. Montlake & Co., since 1954; a Recorder of the Crown Court, since 1983; *b* 22 Aug. 1930; *s* of Alfred and Hetty Montlake; *m* 1952, Ruth Rochelle Allen; four *s*. *Educ:* Ludlow Grammar Sch., Ludlow; London Univ. (LLB 1951). Law Soc.'s final exam., 1951; admitted Solicitor, 1952. National Service, commnd RASC, 1953. Dep. Registrar of County Courts, 1970–78; Dep. Circuit Judge and Asst Recorder, 1978–83. Chm., Ilford Round Table, 1962–63; Pres., Assoc. of Jewish Golf Clubs and Socs, 1984– (Sec., 1977–84). *Recreations:* golf, The Times crossword, people, travel. *Address:* Chelston, 5 St Mary's Avenue, Wanstead, E11 2NR. *T:* 01–989 7228. *Clubs:* Wig and Pen; Dyrham Park Golf; Abridge Golf (Chm. 1964, Captain 1965).

MONTMORENCY, Sir Arnold Geoffroy de; *see* de Montmorency.

MONTREAL, Archbishop of, (RC), since 1968; **Most Rev. Paul Grégoire,** OC 1979; *b* Verdun, 24 Oct. 1911. *Educ:* Ecole Supérieure Richard; Séminaire de Ste-Thérèse; Univ. of Montreal. Priest, 1937; became Professor, but continued his studies: PhD, STL, LèsL, MA (Hist.), dip. in pedagogy. Subseq. became Director, Séminaire de Ste-Thérèse; Prof. of Philosophy of Educn at l'Ecole Normale Secondaire and at l'Institut Pédagogique; Chaplain of the Students, Univ. of Montreal, 1950–61; consecrated Bishop, 1961, and became auxiliary to Archbishop of Montreal; Vicar-General and Dir of Office for the Clergy; Apostolic Administrator, Archdiocese of Montreal, Dec. 1967–Apr. 1968. Pres., Episcopal Commn on Ecumenism (French sector), 1965. Has presided over several Diocesan Commns (notably Commn for study of the material situation of the Clergy), 1965–68. Member: Canadian delegn to Bishop's Synod, Rome, 1971; Sacred Congregation for the Clergy, 1979. Dr *hc*: Univ. of Montreal, 1969; St Michael's Coll., Winooski, Vt, 1970. *Address:* Archbishop's House, 1071 Cathedral Street, Montreal, Quebec H3B 2V4, Canada.

MONTREAL, Bishop of, since 1975; **Rt. Rev. Reginald Hollis;** *b* 18 July 1932; *s* of Jesse Farndon Hollis and Edith Ellen Lee; *m* 1957, Marcia Henderson Crombie; two *s* one *d*. *Educ:* Selwyn Coll., Cambridge; McGill Univ., Montreal. Chaplain and Lectr, Montreal Dio. Theol Coll., 1956–60; Chaplain to Anglican Students, McGill Univ.; Asst Rector, St Matthias' Church, Westmount, PQ, 1960–63; Rector, St Barnabas' Church, Pierrefonds, PQ, 1963–70; Rector, Christ Church, Beaconsfield, PQ, 1971–74; Dir of Parish and Dio. Services, Dio. Montreal, 1974–75. Hon. DD 1975. *Address:* 3630 Mountain Street, Montreal, PQ H3G 2A8, Canada.

MONTROSE, 7th Duke of, *cr* 1707; **James Angus Graham;** *cr* Baron Graham before 1451; Earl of Montrose, 1505; Bt of Nova Scotia, 1625; Marquis of Montrose, 1645; Duke of Montrose, Marquis of Graham and Buchanan, Earl of Kincardine, Viscount Dundaff, Baron Aberuthven, Mugdock, and Fintrie, 1707; Earl and Baron Graham (Peerage of England), 1722; Hereditary Sheriff of Dunbartonshire; *b* 2 May 1907; *e s* of 6th Duke of Montrose, KT, CB, CVO, VD, and Lady Mary Douglas-Hamilton, OBE (*d* 1957), *d* of 12th Duke of Hamilton; *S* father, 1954; *m* 1st, 1930, Isobel Veronica (marr. diss. 1950), *yr d* of late Lt-Col T. B. Sellar, CMG, DSO; one *s* one *d*; 2nd, 1952, Susan Mary Jocelyn, *widow* of Michael Raleigh Gibbs and *d* of late Dr J. M. Semple; two *s* two *d*. *Educ:* Eton; Christ Church, Oxford. Lt-Comdr RNVR. MP for Hartley-Gatooma in Federal Assembly of Federation of Rhodesia and Nyasaland, 1958–62; Minister of Agriculture, Lands, and Natural Resources, S Rhodesia, 1962–63; Minister of Agric., Rhodesia, 1964–65; (apptd in Rhodesia) Minister of External Affairs and Defence, 1966–68. *Heir:* *s* Marquis of Graham, *qv*. *Address:* Dalgoram, PO Box 1, Baynesfield, Natal, 3770, South Africa; (Seat) Auchmar, Drymen, Glasgow.

MOODY, Helen Wills; *see* Roark, H. W.

MOODY, John Percivale, OBE 1961; Counsellor to the Board, Welsh National Opera Co.; *b* 6 April 1906; *s* of Percivale Sadleir Moody; *m* 1937, Helen Pomfret Burra; one *s* decd. *Educ:* Bromsgrove; Royal Academy Schools. In publishing in the City, 1924–26; Painting; Academy Schs, 1927–28, various London Exhibitions; taught at Wimbledon Art Sch., 1928–29. Studied opera Webber Douglas Sch. Derby Day under Sir Nigel Playfair, Lyric, Hammersmith, 1931. West End plays include: The Brontës, Royalty, 1932; Hervey House, His Majesty's, 1935; After October, Criterion, 1936; played in Old Vic seasons 1934, 1937; Ascent of F6, Dog Beneath the Skin, Group Theatre, 1935; Dir Old Vic Sch., 1940–42. AFS Clerkenwell, 1940 (wounded and discharged). Producer Old Vic Co., Liverpool, 1942–44; Birmingham Repertory Theatre, 1944–45; Carl Rosa Opera Co., 1945; Sadler's Wells Opera Co., 1945–49; Drama Dir, Arts Council of Great Britain, 1949–54; Dir, Bristol Old Vic Co., 1954–59; Dir of Productions, 1960, and Jt Artistic Dir, 1970, Welsh Nat. Opera. First productions in England of Verdi's Simone Boccanegra, 1948, Nabucco, 1952, and The Battle of Legnano, 1960; Rimsky's May Night, 1960; also for Welsh Nat. Opera: Rossini's William Tell, 1961; Macbeth, 1963; Moses, 1965; Carmen, 1967; Boris Godunov, 1968; Simone Boccanegra, 1970; Rigoletto, 1972; The Pearl Fishers, 1973; What the Old Man Does is Always Right, Fishguard Festival, 1977. With wife, new translations of Carmen, Simone Boccanegra, Macbeth, La Traviata, The Pearl Fishers, Prince Igor, May Night, Battle of Legnano, William Tell, Moses and Fidelio. *Publications:* (with Helen Moody) translations of: The Pearl Fishers, 1979; Carmen, 1982; Moses, 1986. *Recreations:* swimming, gardening, painting. *Address:* 2 Richmond Park Road, Bristol BS8 3AT. *T:* Bristol 734436.

MOODY, Leslie Howard; General Secretary, Civil Service Union, 1977–82; *b* 18 Aug. 1922; *s* of George Henry and Edith Jessie Moody; *m* 1944, Betty Doreen Walton; two *s*. *Educ:* Eltham College. Telephone Engineer, General Post Office, 1940–53. Served Royal Signals, Far East, 1944–47. Asst Sec., Civil Service Union, 1953, Dep. Gen. Sec., 1963. *Recreations:* walking, music, theatre, educating management. *Address:* 68 Shearman Road, Blackheath, SE3 9HX. *T:* 01–318 1040. *Club:* Civil Service.

MOODY, Peter Edward, CBE 1981; Deputy Chairman, Prudential Corporation, since 1984 (a Director, since 1981); Director: Equity Capital Trustee Ltd, since 1985; The Laird Group, since 1981; Investors in Industry Group plc, since 1981; Triton Petroleum Ltd, since 1971; *b* 26 Aug. 1918; *s* of late Edward Thomas Moody and Gladys (*née* Flint); *m* 1945, Peggy Elizabeth *d* of Edward Henry Causer and Elizabeth Theodora (*née* Finke); one *s* one *d*. *Educ:* Christ's Coll., Finchley. FIA. Prudential Assurance Co. Ltd: Dep. Investment Manager, 1960; Jt Sec. and Chief Investment Manager, 1973–80; Jt Sec. and Group Chief Investment Manager, Prudential Corp., 1979–80; Director: United Dominions Trust, 1972–81; British American and General Trust, 1981–85; Inmos International, 1981–84. Institute of Actuaries: Hon. Sec., 1968–70; Vice-Pres., 1972–75; Pres., 1978–80. *Publications:* contrib. Jl of Inst. of Actuaries. *Recreation:* golf. *Address:* 46 Brookmans Avenue, Brookmans Park, Herts AL9 7QJ.

MOOKERJEE, Sir Birendra Nath, Kt 1942; MA Cantab, MIE (India); Partner of Martin & Co. and Burn & Co., Managing Director, Martin Burn Ltd, Engineers, Contractors, Merchants, Shipbuilders, etc; Chairman Steel Corporation of Bengal Ltd; President Calcutta Local Board of Imperial Bank of India; Director Darjeeling Himalayan Railway Co. Ltd and many other companies; *b* 14 Feb. 1899; *s* of late Sir Rajendra Nath Mookerjee, KCIE, KCVO, MIE (India), FASB, DSc (Eng); *m* 1925, Ranu Priti Adhikari, *d* of Phani Bhusan Adhikari, late Professor Benares Hindu Univ.; one *s* two *d*. *Educ:* Bishop's Collegiate Sch., Hastings House, Calcutta; Bengal Engineering Coll.; Trinity Coll., Cambridge. Mem., Viceroy's Nat. Defence Council; Adviser, Roger Mission; Mem., Munitions Production Adv. Cttee. Fellow Calcutta Univ.; Sheriff of Calcutta 1941. *Address:* Martin Burn Ltd, Martin Burn House, 12 Mission Row, Calcutta 1, India; 7 Harington Street, Calcutta 16. *Clubs:* National Liberal; Calcutta, Calcutta Polo, Royal Calcutta Turf, Calcutta South, Cricket Club of India (Calcutta), etc.

MOOLLAN, Sir (Abdool) Hamid (Adam), Kt 1986; QC (Mauritius) 1976; *b* 10 April 1933; *s* of Adam Sulliman Moollan and Khatija Moollan; *m* 1966, Sara Sidiot; three *s*. *Educ:* Soonee Surtee Musalman Society Aided School; Royal College School; King's College London (LLB); Faculté de Droit, Univ. de Paris. Called to the Bar, Middle Temple, 1956; joined Mauritian Bar, 1960. *Recreations:* tennis, horse racing, hunting, fishing. *Address:* (home) Railway Road, Phoenix, Mauritius. *T:* 864983; (chambers) 43 Sir William Newton Street, Port-Louis, Mauritius. *T:* 20794. *Clubs:* Royal Over-Seas League; Mauritius Gymkhana, Mauritius Turf.

MOOLLAN, Hon. Sir Cassam (Ismael), Kt 1982; Chief Justice, Supreme Court of Mauritius, since 1982; Acting Governor-General, several occasions in 1984, 1985, 1986; Commander-in-Chief of Mauritius, 1984; *b* 26 Feb. 1927; *s* of Ismael Mahomed Moollan and Fatimah Nazroo; *m* 1954, Rassoulbibie Adam Moollan; one *s* two *d*. *Educ:* Royal Coll., Port Louis and Curepipe; London Sch. of Econs and Pol. Science (LLB 1950). Called to the Bar, Lincoln's Inn, 1951. Private practice, 1951–55; Dist Magistrate, 1955–58; Crown Counsel, 1958–64; Sen. Crown Counsel, 1964–66; Solicitor Gen., 1966–70; QC (Mauritius) 1969; Puisne Judge, Supreme Court, 1970; Sen. Puisne Judge, 1978. Editor, Mauritius Law Reports, 1982–. Chevalier, Légion d'Honneur (France), 1986. *Recreations:* table tennis, tennis, bridge, Indian classical and semi-classical music. *Address:* Supreme Court, Port Louis, Mauritius. *T:* 21905; 22 Hitchcock Avenue, Quatre Bornes, Mauritius. *T:* 546949. *Club:* Gymkhana (Port Louis).

MOON, Sir Edward, 5th Bt *cr* 1887; MC 1944; retired; *b* 23 Feb. 1911; *s* of Jasper Moon (*d* 1975) (*g s* of 1st Bt) and Isabel Moon (*née* Logan) (*d* 1961); *S* cousin, Sir John Arthur Moon, 4th Bt, 1979; *m* 1947, Mary, *d* of late Captain B. D. Conolly, RAMC. *Educ:* Sedbergh. Farming, Kenya, 1934–62. Served 1939–45, King's African Rifles (Major). *Recreations:* gardening, cooking, fishing and all games. *Heir:* *b* Roger Moon [*b* 17 Nov. 1914; *m* 1950, Meg, *d* of late Arthur Mainwaring Maxwell, DSO, MC; three *d*]. *Address:* c/o Midland Bank, Oswestry, Salop.

MOON, Sir (Edward) Penderel, Kt 1962; OBE 1941; *b* 13 Nov. 1905; *s* of Dr R. O. Moon, FRCP; *m* 1966, Pauline Marion (marr. diss.), *d* of Rev. W. E. C. Barns. *Educ:* Winchester; New Coll., Oxford (MA). Fellow of All Souls College, Oxford, 1927–35 and 1965–72. Entered ICS, 1929, resigned, 1944; Sec., Development Board and Planning Advisory Board, Govt of India; Min. of Revenue and Public Works, Bahawalpur State; Chief Comr, Himachal Pradesh; Chief Comr, Manipur; Adviser, Planning Commission. Editor, India Office Records on Transfer of Power, 1972–82. *Publications:* Strangers in India; The Future of India; Warren Hastings and British India; Divide and Quit; Gandhi and Modern India; Disbelief in God; (ed) Wavell: the Viceroy's Journal. *Recreations:* hunting, shooting and singing. *Address:* Manor Farm, Wotton Underwood, Aylesbury, Bucks.

MOON, Sir Penderel; *see* Moon, Sir E. P.

MOON, Sir Peter (James Scott), KCVO 1979; CMG 1979; HM Diplomatic Service; Ambassador to Kuwait, since 1985; *b* 1 April 1928; *m* 1955, Lucile Worms; three *d*. Home Office, 1952–54; CRO, 1954–56; Second Sec., Cape Town/Pretoria, 1956–58; Principal, CRO, 1958–60; First Sec., Colombo, 1960–63; Private Sec. to Sec. of State for Commonwealth Relations, 1963–65; First Sec., UK Mission to UN, New York, 1965–69; Counsellor, FCO, 1969–70; Private Sec. to Prime Minister, 1970–72; NATO Defence Coll., 1972; seconded to NATO Internat. Staff, Brussels, 1972–75; Counsellor, Cairo, 1975–78; Ambassador to Madagascar (non-resident), 1978–79; High Comr in Tanzania, 1978–82; High Comr in Singapore, 1982–85. *Address:* c/o Foreign and Commonwealth Office, SW1.

MOON, Sir Peter Wilfred Giles Graham-, 5th Bt, *cr* 1855; *b* 24 Oct. 1942; *s* of Sir (Arthur) Wilfred Graham-Moon, 4th Bt, and 2nd wife, Doris Patricia, *yr d* of Thomas Baron Jobson, Dublin; *S* father, 1954; *m* 1967, Sarah Gillian Chater (formerly *m* Major Antony Chater; marr. diss. 1966), *e d* of late Lt-Col Michael Lyndon Smith, MC, MB, BS, and Mrs Michael Smith; two *s*. *Recreations:* shooting, golf. *Heir:* *s* Rupert Francis Wilfred Graham-Moon, *b* 29 April 1968. *Address:* Old Whistley Farm, Potterne, Devizes, Wilts SN10 5TD. *T:* Devizes 4388. *Clubs:* Cricketers; Royal Cork Yacht.

MOON, Philip Burton, FRS 1947; Poynting Professor of Physics in the University of Birmingham, 1950–74, now Emeritus; Dean of the Faculty of Science and Engineering, 1969–72; *b* 17 May 1907; *o s* of late F. D. Moon; *m* 1st, 1937, Winifred F. Barber (*d* 1971); one *s* one *d*; 2nd, 1974, Lorna M. Aldridge. *Educ:* Leyton County High Sch.; Sidney Sussex Coll., Cambridge. *Publications:* Artificial Radioactivity, 1949; various papers on physics. *Address:* 8 Oaks Road, Church Stretton, Shropshire SY6 7AX. *T:* Church Stretton 722497.

MOONEY, Bel; writer and broadcaster; *b* 8 Oct. 1946; *d* of Edward and Gladys Mooney; *m* 1968, Jonathan Dimbleby, *qv*; one *s* one *d*. *Educ:* Trowbridge Girls' High School; University College London. Freelance journalist, 1970–79; columnist: Daily Mirror, 1979–80; Sunday Times, 1982–83; The Listener, 1984–86; contributor to The Times, 1970–; *television:* interview series: Mothers By Daughters, 1983; The Light of Experience Revisited, 1984; Fathers By Sons, 1985; film biographies. *Publications:* The Year of the Child, 1979; Liza's Yellow Boat, 1980; The Windsurf Boy, 1983; Differences of Opinion (collected journalism), 1984; I Don't Want To!, 1985; The Anderson Question, 1985; (with Gerald Scarfe) Father Kissmass and Mother Claws, 1985; The Stove Haunting, 1986. *Recreations:* reading, music, art, friends. *Address:* c/o David Higham Associates, 5 Lower John Street, W1. *T:* 01–437 7888. *Club:* Groucho.

MOONMAN, Eric; Director, Centre for Contemporary Studies, since 1979; *b* 29 April 1929; *s* of Borach and Leah Moonman; *m* 1962, Jane; two *s* one *d*. *Educ:* Rathbone Sch., Liverpool; Christ Church, Southport; Univs of Liverpool and Manchester. Dipl. in Social Science, Liverpool, 1955. Human Relations Adviser, British Inst. of Management, 1956–62; Sen. Lectr in Industrial Relations, SW Essex Technical Coll., 1962–64; Sen. Research Fellow in Management Sciences, Univ. of Manchester, 1964–66. MSc Manchester Univ., 1967. MP (Lab) Billericay, 1966–70, Basildon, Feb. 1974–1979; PPS to Minister without Portfolio and Sec. of State for Educn, 1967–68. Chairman: All-Party Parly Mental Health Cttee, 1967–70 and 1974–79; New Towns and Urban Affairs Cttee, Parly Labour Party, 1974–79. Chm., Zionist Fedn, 1975–80; Sen. Vice-Pres., Bd of Deputies, 1985–. Member: Stepney Council, 1961–65 (Leader, 1964–65); Tower Hamlets Council, 1964–67. Chm., Islington HA, 1981–. Mem., Council, Toynbee Hall Univ. Settlement (Chm., Finance Cttee); Governor, BFI, 1974–80. FRSA. *Publications:* The Manager and the Organization, 1961; Employee Security, 1962; European Science and Technology, 1968; Communication in an Expanding Organization, 1970; Reluctant Partnership, 1970; Alternative Government, 1984. *Recreations:* football, theatre, cinema. *Address:* 1 Beacon Hill, N7.

MOORBATH, Dr Stephen Erwin, FRS 1977; Reader in Geology, Oxford University, since 1978; Fellow of Linacre College, since 1970; *b* 9 May 1929; *s* of Heinz Moosbach and Else Moosbach; *m* 1962, Pauline Tessier-Varlêt; one *s* one *d*. *Educ:* Lincoln Coll., Oxford Univ. (MA 1957, DPhil 1959). DSc Oxon 1969. Asst Experimental Officer, AERE, Harwell, 1948–51; Undergrad., Oxford Univ., 1951–54; Scientific Officer, AERE, Harwell, 1954–56; Research Fellow: Oxford Univ., 1956–61; MIT, 1961–62; Sen. Res. Officer, Oxford Univ., 1962–78. Wollaston Fund, Geol Soc. of London, 1968; Liverpool Geol Soc. Medal, 1968; Murchison Medal, Geol Soc. of London, 1978; Steno Medal, Geol Soc. of Denmark, 1979. *Publications:* contribs to scientific jls and books. *Recreations:* music, philately, travel, linguistics. *Address:* 53 Bagley Wood Road, Kennington, Oxford OX1 5LY. *T:* Oxford 739507.

MOORCRAFT, Dennis Harry; Under-Secretary, Inland Revenue, 1975–81; *b* 14 Aug. 1921; *s* of late Harry Moorcraft and Dorothy Moorcraft (*née* Simmons); *m* 1945, Ingeborg Utne, Bergen, Norway; one *s* one *d*. *Educ:* Gillingham County Grammar Sch. Tax Officer, Inland Revenue, 1938. RNVR, 1940–46. Inspector of Taxes, 1948; Sen. Inspector of Taxes, 1956; Principal Inspector of Taxes, 1963. *Recreations:* gardening, garden construction, croquet.

MOORE, family name of **Earl of Drogheda** and **Baron Moore of Wolvercote.**

MOORE, Viscount; Henry Dermot Ponsonby Moore; photographer; *b* 14 Jan. 1937; *o s* and *heir* of 11th Earl of Drogheda, *qv*; *m* 1st, 1968, Eliza Lloyd (marr. diss. 1972), *d* of Stacy Barcroft Lloyd, Jr, and Mrs Paul Mellon; 2nd, 1978, Alexandra, *d* of Sir Nicholas Henderson, *qv*; two *s*. *Educ:* Eton; Trinity College, Cambridge. *Publications:* (as Derry Moore): (with Brendan Gill) The Dream Come True, Great Houses of Los Angeles, 1980; (with George Plumptre) Royal Gardens, 1981; (with Sybilla Jane Flower) Stately Homes of Britain, 1982; (with Henry Mitchell) Washington, Houses of the Capital, 1982; (with Michael Pick) The English Room, 1984; (with Alvilde Lees-Milne) The Englishwoman's House, 1984. *Heir:* *s* Hon. Benjamin Garrett Henderson Moore, *b* 21 March 1983. *Address:* 40 Ledbury Road, W11 2AB. *Clubs:* Garrick, Travellers'.

MOORE OF WOLVERCOTE, Baron *cr* 1986 (Life Peer), of Wolvercote in the City of Oxford; **Philip Brian Cecil Moore,** GCB 1985 (KCB 1980; CB 1973); GCVO 1983 (KCVO 1976); CMG 1966; QSO 1986; PC 1977; Private Secretary to the Queen and Keeper of the Queen's Archives, 1977–86; *b* 6 April 1921; *s* of late Cecil Moore, Indian Civil Service; *m* 1945, Joan Ursula Greenop; two *d*. *Educ:* Dragon Sch.; Cheltenham Coll. (Scholar); Oxford Univ. Classical Exhibitioner, Brasenose Coll., Oxford, 1940. RAF Bomber Command, 1940–42 (prisoner of war, 1942–45). Brasenose Coll., Oxford, 1945–46 (Hon. Fellow 1981). Asst Private Sec. to First Lord of Admiralty, 1950–51; Principal Private Sec. to First Lord of Admiralty, 1957–58; Dep. UK Commissioner, Singapore, 1961–63; British Dep. High Comr in Singapore, 1963–65; Chief of Public Relations, MoD, 1965–66; Asst Private Secretary to the Queen, 1966–72, Dep. Private Secretary, 1972–77. Vice-Pres., SPCK. *Recreations:* golf, Rugby football (Oxford Blue, 1945–46; International, England, 1951), hockey (Oxford Blue, 1946), cricket (Oxfordshire). *Address:* Hampton Court Palace, East Molesey, Surrey. *Clubs:* Athenæum, MCC.

MOORE, Alexander Wyndham Hume S.; *see* Stewart-Moore.

MOORE, Antony Ross, CMG 1965; *b* 30 May 1918; *o s* of late Arthur Moore and late Eileen Maillet; *m* 1st, 1941, Philippa Weigall (marr. diss.); two *d*; 2nd, 1963, Georgina Mary Galbraith (*see* G. M. Moore); one *s*. *Educ:* Rugby; King's Coll., Cambridge. Served in Friends Ambulance Unit, 1939–40; HM Forces, 1940–46. Apptd Mem. Foreign (subseq. Diplomatic) Service, Nov. 1946; transf. to Rome, 1947; FO, Nov. 1949; 1st Sec., 1950; transf. to Tel Aviv, 1952; acted as Chargé d'Affaires, 1953, 1954; apptd Consul, Sept. 1953; FO, 1955; UK Perm. Delegn to UN, NY, 1957; Counsellor and transf. to IDC, 1961; FO, 1962–64; Internat. Fellow, Center for Internat. Affairs, Harvard Univ., 1964–65; Regional Information Officer, Middle East, British Embassy, Beirut, 1965–67; Head of Eastern Dept, FO, 1967; retd from HM Diplomatic Service, Dec. 1968. Dir, Iranian Selection Trust, 1969–72. *Address:* Touchbridge, Boarstall, Aylesbury, Bucks. *T:* Brill 238247.

MOORE, Bobby; *see* Moore, Robert.

MOORE, Brian; novelist; *b* 25 Aug. 1921; *s* of James Bernard Moore, FRCS, Northern Ireland, and Eileen McFadden; *m* Jean Denney. Guggenheim Fellowship (USA), 1959; Canada Council Senior Fellowship (Canada), 1960; Scottish Arts Council Internat. Fellowship, 1983. National Institute of Arts and Letters (USA) Fiction Award 1960; Governor-Gen. of Canada's Award for Fiction, 1960; W. H. Smith Award (UK), 1973; James Tait Black Meml Award, 1975, etc. *Publications:* *novels:* The Lonely Passion of Judith Hearne, 1955; The Feast of Lupercal, 1956; The Luck of Ginger Coffey, 1960; An Answer from Limbo, 1962; The Emperor of Ice-Cream, 1965; I am Mary Dunne, 1968; Fergus, 1970; The Revolution Script, 1972; Catholics, 1972 (W. H. Smith Literary Award, 1973); The Great Victorian Collection, 1975 (James Tait Black Meml Award, 1976; Governor Gen. of Canada's Award for Fiction, 1976); The Doctor's Wife, 1976; The Mangan Inheritance, 1979; The Temptation of Eileen Hughes, 1981; Cold Heaven, 1983; Black Robe, 1985 (Heinemann Award, RSL, 1986); *non-fiction:* Canada (with Editors of Life), 1964. *Address:* c/o Curtis Brown Ltd, 10 Astor Place, New York, NY 10003, USA.

MOORE, Brian Baden; Football Commentator/Presenter: London Weekend Television, since 1968; Mid-Week Sports Special, Thames Television, since 1978; *b* 28 Feb. 1932; *m* 1955, Betty (*née* Cole); two *s. Educ:* Cranbrook Sch., Kent. Sports Sub-Editor, World Sports, 1954–56; journalist: Exchange Telegraph, 1956–58; The Times, 1958–61; Football Commentator/Presenter, BBC Radio, 1961–68. Presenter, Brian Moore Meets (TV documentary series), 1979–. *Publication:* The Big Matches 1970–1980, 1980. *Recreations:* being at home, animal care. *Address:* c/o London Weekend Television, South Bank Television Centre, Kent House, Upper Ground, SE1 9LT. *T:* 01–261 3434.

MOORE, Charles Hilary; Editor, The Spectator, since 1984; *b* 31 Oct. 1956; *s* of Richard and Ann Moore; *m* 1981, Caroline Mary Baxter. *Educ:* Eton Coll.; Trinity Coll., Cambridge (BA Hons History). Joined editorial staff of Daily Telegraph, 1979, leader writer, 1981–83; Assistant Editor and political columnist, The Spectator, 1983–84. *Publications:* (ed with C. Hawtree) 1936, 1986; (with A. N. Wilson and G. Stamp) The Church in Crisis, 1986. *Address:* 60 Ripplevale Grove, N1. *T:* 01–607 8872. *Club:* Beefsteak.

MOORE, Air Vice-Marshal Charles Stuart, CB 1962; OBE 1945; *b* London, 27 Feb. 1910; *s* of late E. A. Moore and E. B. Moore (*née* Druce); *m* 1st, 1937, Anne (*d* 1957), *d* of Alfred Rogers; 2nd, 1961, Jean Mary, *d* of John Cameron Wilson; one *d. Educ:* Sutton Valence Sch.; RAF Coll., Cranwell. Commissioned in General Duties Branch, Dec. 1930; served in Egypt, 1932–34 and 1936–41; Sqdn Ldr 1938; Sudan, 1941–42; Wing Comdr 1940; 11 Group, 1943–44; Gp Capt. 1943; OC, OTU, 1944–45; Gp Capt. Org., HQFC, 1945–46; Staff Coll., Bracknell, 1946–47; Dep. Dir Plans, Air Ministry, London, 1947–49; Student, US National War Coll., Washington, 1949–50; Staff of USAF Air War Coll., Alabama, 1950–53; Air Commodore, 1953; AOC 66 Group, 1953–55; Dir of Intelligence, Air Ministry, London, 1955–58; AOA, NEAF, 1958–62; Actg Air Vice-Marshal, 1960; retired, 1962. Joined HM Foreign Service, Oct. 1962; posted to British Embassy, Tehran, Iran; left HM Diplomatic Service, March 1969. *Recreations:* music, photography and travelling. *Address:* Ferndene, The Avenue, Crowthorne, Berks. *T:* Crowthorne 772300. *Club:* Royal Air Force.

MOORE, Cicely Frances (Mrs H. D. Moore); *see* Berry, C. F.

MOORE, David James Ladd; Under Secretary, HM Treasury, since 1985; *b* 6 June 1937; *s* of James and Eilonwy Moore; *m* 1968, Kay Harrison; two *s. Educ:* King Edward VI Sch., Nuneaton; Brasenose Coll., Oxford (BA). PO, 1961–67 (Asst Principal 1961, Principal 1966); Cabinet Office, 1967–69; HM Treasury, 1969–80 (Asst Sec. 1973); Under Secretary: Cabinet Office, 1980–82; HM Treasury, 1982–83; Inland Revenue (Principal Finance Officer), 1983–85. *Recreations:* reading, theatre, tennis, family. *Address:* 183 Hampstead Way, NW11 7YB.*T:* 01–455 5945.

MOORE, Maj.-Gen. Denis Grattan, CB 1960; DL; retired; *b* 15 March 1909; *s* of Col F. G. Moore, CBE and Marian, *d* of Very Rev. W. H. Stone, Dean of Kilmore; *m* 1st, 1932, Alexandra, *d* of W. H. Wann; two *d*; 2nd, 1946, Beatrice Glynn, *d* of W. S. Williamson; one adopted *d. Educ:* Wellington Coll.; Royal Military College, Sandhurst (cadet schol., 1928). Commissioned 1929, Royal Inniskilling Fusiliers; RMCS, 1935–37 (pac, sac); Sec., Ordnance Bd, 1938; Staff Coll., Quetta, 1939–40 (psc); GHQ India, 1940; GSO1, HQ Tenth Army, 1941; special duties, N Persia, 1941–42; Asst Dir of Artillery (Weapons), HQ Eighth Army, 1943–44; GSO1, War Office, 1946 (Technical and Scientific Intell.); Parachute Regt, 1948–50; Mil. Security Bd, Berlin, 1950; comd 1 Inniskillings, 1951–52; GSO1 (Col) War Office, 1952–54 (Technical Intell.); comd 47 Infantry Bde, TA, 1954–57; Dep. Comd, RMCS, 1957–58; Dir of Weapons and Development, War Office, 1958–60; Dir of Equipment Policy, War Office, 1960–61; Chief, Jt Services Liaison Staff, BAOR, 1961–63. Col, The Royal Inniskilling Fusiliers, 1960–66. Chm., Ulster Timber Growers Organisation, 1965–81. High Sheriff, Co. Tyrone, 1969; DL Co. Tyrone, 1974. *Publications:* pamphlets and articles on the oceanic forest. *Recreation:* palæontological research (forest and fish). *Address:* 26 Headbourne Worthy House, Winchester SO23 7JG. *T:* Winchester 881631. *Club:* Naval and Military.

MOORE, Mrs D(oris) Langley, OBE 1971; FRSL; Founder (1955) and former Adviser, Museum of Costume, Assembly Rooms, Bath; author. Has done varied literary work in connection with films, television, and ballet, and has specialized in promoting the study of costume by means of exhibns and lectures in England and abroad. Designer of clothes for period films. *Publications: fiction:* A Winter's Passion, 1932; The Unknown Eros, 1935; They Knew Her When . . ., 1938 (subseq. re-published as A Game of Snakes and Ladders); Not at Home, 1948; All Done by Kindness, 1951; My Caravaggio Style, 1959; *non-fiction:* Anacreon: 29 Odes, 1926; The Technique of the Love Affair, 1928; Pandora's Letter Box, A Discourse on Fashionable Life, 1929; E. Nesbit, A Biography, 1933 (rev. 1966); The Vulgar Heart, An Enquiry into the Sentimental Tendencies of Public Opinion, 1945; The Woman in Fashion, 1949; The Child in Fashion, 1953; Pleasure, A Discursive Guide Book, 1953; The Late Lord Byron, 1961; Marie and the Duke of H, The Daydream Love Affair of Marie Bashkirtseff, 1966; Fashion through Fashion Plates, 1771–1970, 1971; Lord Byron: Accounts Rendered, 1974 (Rose Mary Crawshay Prize, awarded by British Academy, 1975); Ada, Countess of Lovelace, 1977; Doris Langley Moore's Book of Scraps, 1984; (with June Langley Moore): Our Loving Duty, 1932; The Pleasure of Your Company, 1933. *Recreation:* Byron research. *Address:* 5 Prince Albert Road, NW1.

MOORE, Dudley Stuart John; actor (stage, films, TV and radio); composer (film music and incidental music for plays, etc); *b* 19 April 1935; *s* of Ada Francis and John Moore; *m* Suzy Kendall (marr. diss.); *m* Tuesday Weld (marr. diss.); one *s. Educ:* County High Sch., Dagenham, Essex; Magdalen Coll., Oxford (BA, BMus). *Stage:* Beyond the Fringe, 1960–62 (London), 1962–64 (Broadway, New York); Vic Lewis, John Dankworth Jazz Bands, 1959–60; composed incidental music, Royal Court Theatre (various plays), 1958–60. *BBC TV:* own series with Peter Cook: Not only . . . but also, 1964, 1966, 1970; in the sixties, *ITV:* Goodbye again; Royal Command Performance. Play it again Sam, Woody Allen, Globe Theatre, 1970. *BBC TV Series:* It's Lulu, not to mention Dudley Moore, 1972. Behind the Fridge, Cambridge Theatre, 1972–73; Good Evening, Broadway, New York, 1973–74; Tour of USA, 1975. Various TV and radio guest spots with Jazz piano trio. *Films* 1966–: The Wrong Box, 30 is a Dangerous Age Cynthia, Bedazzled, Monte Carlo or Bust, The Bed-sitting room, Alice in Wonderland, The Hound of the Baskervilles, Foul Play, "10", Wholly Moses, Arthur, Six Weeks, Unfaithfully Yours, Lovesick, Romantic Comedy, Best Defense, Mickey & Maude, Santa Claus—The Movie. *Film music* composed for: Bedazzled, 30 is a dangerous age Cynthia, The Staircase, Inadmissable Evidence, Six Weeks, and various TV films. *Publication:* Dud and Pete: The Dagenham Dialogues, 1971. *Recreations:* films, theatre, music. *Address:* c/o Louis Pitt, ICM, 8899 Beverly Boulevard, Los Angeles, Calif 90048, USA. *Club:* White Elephant.

MOORE, Rt. Rev. Edward Francis Butler, DD; *b* 1906; *s* of Rev. W. R. R. Moore; *m* 1932, Frances Olivia Scott; two *s* two *d. Educ:* Trinity Coll., Dublin (MA, PhD, DD). Deacon, 1930; Priest, 1931; Curate, Bray, 1930–32; Hon. Clerical Vicar, Christ Church Cathedral, Dublin, 1931–35; Curate, Clontarf, 1932–34; Incumbent, Castledermot with Kinneagh, 1934–40; Greystones, Diocese of Glendalough, 1940–49; Chaplain to Duke of Leinster, 1934–40; Rural Dean, Delgany 1950–59; Canon of Christ Church, Dublin,

1951–57; Archdeacon of Glendalough, 1957–59; Bishop of Kilmore and Elphin and Ardagh, 1959–81. *Recreations:* tennis, golf, fishing. *Address:* Drumlona, Sea Road, Kilcoole, Co. Wicklow, Ireland. *Club:* Royal Dublin Society (Dublin).

MOORE, Sir Edward Stanton, 2nd Bt *cr* 1923; OBE 1970; *b* 1910; *s* of Major E. C. H. Moore (killed, Vimy Ridge, 1917) and Kathleen Margaret (*d* 1970), *d* of H. S. Oliver, Sudbury, Suffolk; *S* grandfather, 1923; *m* 1946, Margaret, *er d* of T. J. Scott-Cotterell. *Educ:* Mill Hill Sch.; Cambridge. RAF 1940–46; Wing Cdr Special Duties; Managing Director, Spain and Western Mediterranean, BEA, 1965–72. Pres., British Chamber of Commerce in Spain, 1969–71; Dir, European British Chambers of Commerce, 1970–72. FCIT 1960. *Heir:* none. *Address:* Church House, Sidlesham, Sussex. *T:* Sidlesham 369. *Clubs:* Cruising Association, Royal Yachting Association, Chichester Yacht.

MOORE, the Worshipful Chancellor the Rev. E(velyn) Garth; barrister-at-law; Chancellor, Vicar-General and Official Principal of Diocese of Durham since 1954, of Diocese of Southwark since 1948 and of Diocese of Gloucester since 1957 (and Official Principal of Archdeaconries of Lewisham, Southwark, Kingston-on-Thames and Ely); Vicar, Guild Church of St Mary Abchurch, London, 1972, Priest-in-Charge since 1980; Fellow of Corpus Christi College, Cambridge, since 1947, and formerly Lecturer in Law (Director of Studies in Law, 1947–72); High Bailiff of Ely Cathedral since 1961; President, Churches' Fellowship for Psychical and Spiritual Studies, 1963–83; *b* 6 Feb. 1906; *y s* of His Honour the late Judge (Robert Ernest) Moore and late Hilda Mary, *d* of Rev. John Davis Letts; unmarried. *Educ:* The Hall, Belsize Sch.; Durham Sch.; Trinity Coll., Cambridge (MA); Cuddesdon Theol Coll., 1962. Deacon, 1962; Priest, 1962. Called to Bar, Gray's Inn, 1928; SE Circuit. Formerly: Tutor of Gray's Inn; Lector of Trinity Coll., Cambridge; Mem. Gen. Council of Bar and of Professional Conduct Cttee. Commnd 2nd Lt RA, 1940; Major on staff of JAG; served at WO and throughout Great Britain, N Ireland, Paiforce, Middle East (for a time local Lt-Col), Greece, etc. Mem. of Church Assembly (for Dio. Ely), 1955–62; a Church Comr, 1964–77; Mem., Legal Adv. Commn (formerly Legal Bd of C of E), 1956–86 (Chm., 1972–86). JP and Dep. Chm. of QS, Hunts, 1948–63 and Cambs, 1959–63; Lectr in Criminal Procedure, Council of Legal Educn, 1957–68, Lectr in Evidence, 1952–68. Council, St David's Coll., Lampeter, 1949–65 and Westcott House, 1961–65; Mem. Governing Body, St Chad's Coll., Durham, 1955–78. Legal Assessor to Disciplinary Cttee, RCVS, 1963–68. Pres., Sion Coll., 1977–78. Vis. Prof., Khartoum Univ., 1961. Mere's Preacher, Cambridge Univ., 1965. DCL Lambeth, 1986. *Publications:* An Introduction to English Canon Law, 1966; 8th Edn (with Suppl.) of Kenny's Cases on Criminal Law; (jt) Ecclesiastical Law, in Halsbury's Laws of England (3rd edn); Believe it or Not: Christianity and psychical research, 1977; The Church's Ministry of Healing, 1977; (ed jtly) Macmorran Elphinstone and Moore's A Handbook for Churchwardens and Parochial Church Councillors, 1980; (with Timothy Briden) Moore's English Canon Law, 1985; various contribs mainly to legal and theological jls. *Recreations:* travel, architecture, furniture, etc, psychical research. *Address:* Corpus Christi College, Cambridge. *T:* 359418; 1 Raymond Buildings, Gray's Inn, WC1. *T:* 01–242 3734; St Mary Abchurch, EC4. *T:* 01–626 0306. *Clubs:* Gresham; Pitt (Cambridge).

MOORE, Maj.-Gen. (retired) Frederick David, CB 1955; CBE 1954; *b* 27 Nov. 1902; *s* of Sir Frederick W. Moore; *m* 1932, Anna Morrell Hamilton (*d* 1974), *d* of Col T. H. M. Clarke, CMG, DSO; one *s. Educ:* Wellington Coll.; RMA Woolwich. Commnd in RFA, 1923. Served War of 1939–45: BEF 1940, 5th Regt RHA; BLA, 1944–45, CO 5th Regt RHA and CRA 53rd (W) Div.; GOC 5th AA Group, 1953–55; retd, 1956. DL Beds, 1958, Vice-Lieutenant, 1964–70. Officer Order of Crown (Belgian); Croix de Guerre (Belgian), 1940, with palm, 1945. *Recreations:* country pursuits. *Address:* Riverview, Bunclody, Co. Wexford, Ireland. *T:* Enniscorthy 77184. *Club:* Army and Navy.

MOORE, Geoffrey Ernest, CBE 1977; FCIS, FIMI; Director, Vauxhall Motors Ltd (Chairman, 1979–81); *b* 31 Dec. 1916; *s* of late Charles Frederick Moore and Alice Isobel (*née* Large); *m* 1950, Olive Christine Moore; one *s* one *d. Educ:* Dunstable Grammar Sch. FCIS 1975; FIMI 1973. Served War, Armed Forces, 1939–45. Joined Vauxhall Motors, 1933; returned to Vauxhall Motors, Sales Dept, 1946; Asst Sales Manager, 1953; Domestic Sales Manager, 1955; Sales Dir, 1967; Dir of Govt and Public Relations, 1971; Dir of Personnel and Govt and Public Relations, 1974; Chm., Stampings Alliance Ltd (Vauxhall Subsid.), 1974–; Asst to Man. Dir, 1975. Vice-Pres., Inst. of Motor Industry, 1972–83; Pres., Luton Indust. Coll., 1984– (Vice-Pres., 1973–84); Pres., SMMT, 1981–82; Member: Eastern Reg. Council, CBI, 1975–79; Council, CBI, 1981–84; Exec. Council, Soc. of the Irish Motor Industry, 1981–. Trustee, National Motor Mus., Beaulieu; Hon. Pres., Luton Coll. of Higher Educn. Silver Jubilee Medal, 1977. *Recreations:* golf, gardening. *Address:* Glebe Cottage, Little Gaddesden, Berkhamsted, Herts HP4 1PB. *T:* Little Gaddesden 2431.

MOORE, Geoffrey Herbert; Professor of American Literature and Head of the Department of American Studies, University of Hull, 1962–82, now Professor Emeritus; *b* 10 June 1920; *e s* of late Herbert Jonathan Moore, Norwich; *m* 1947, Pamela Marguerite (marr. diss. 1962), *d* of Bertram Munn, Twickenham; one *s* one *d. Educ:* Mitcham Grammar Sch.; Emmanuel Coll., Cambridge; Univ. of Paris. 1st Cl. English Tripos, Cambridge, 1946; MA 1951. War Service (Air Ministry and RAF), 1939–43. Instr in English, Univ. of Wisconsin, 1947–49; Vis. Prof. of English, Univs of Kansas City and New Mexico, 1948, 1949; Asst Prof. of English, Tulane Univ., 1949–51; Vis. Prof. of English, Univ. of Southern California and Claremont Coll., 1950; Extra Mural Lectr, London and Cambridge Univs, 1951–52; Editor and Producer, BBC Television Talks, 1952–54; Rose Morgan Prof., Univ. of Kansas, 1954–55; Lectr in Amer. Lit., Manchester Univ., 1955–59; Vis. Lectr, Univs of Mainz, Göttingen and Frankfurt, 1959; Rockefeller Fellow, Harvard Univ., 1959–60; Sen. Lectr in Amer. Lit., Manchester Univ., 1960–62; Dean, Faculty of Arts, Univ. of Hull, 1967–69. Visiting Lecturer: Univs of Montpellier, Aix-en-Provence and Nice, 1967, 1971; Univs of Frankfurt, Heidelberg, Mainz, Saarbrücken, Tübingen, 1967, 1968; Univs of Perpignan, Turin, Florence, Pisa, Rome, New Delhi, Hyderabad, Madras, Bombay, Calcutta, 1971; Fellow, Sch. of Letters, Indiana Univ., Summer 1970; Visiting Professor: York Univ., Toronto, 1969–70; Univ. of Tunis, Spring 1970, 1971; Harvard, 1971; Univs of Düsseldorf, Heidelberg, Freiburg, Mainz, 1972; Univs of Teheran, Shiraz, Isfahan, Mashad, 1978; Univs of Berlin, Bremen, Osnabrück, 1981; Univs of Münster, Duisburg, Bonn, Düsseldorf, Aachen, 1982; Univ. of Göttingen, 1983; Univs of Madrid, Bilbao, Barcelona, 1985; Research Fellow; Univ. of California at San Diego, 1974; Rockefeller Centre, Bellagio, 1979. Mem. Cttee, British Assoc. for Amer. Studies, 1957–60. Sen. Scholar Award, Amer. Coun. of Learned Socs, 1965. Editor and Founder, The Bridge (Cambridge lit. mag.), 1946; reviewer, Financial Times, 1976–; Gen. Editor of Henry James for Penguin Books, 1981–. *Publications:* Voyage to Chivalry (under pseud.), 1947; Poetry from Cambridge in Wartime, 1947; The Penguin Book of Modern American Verse, 1954, 2nd rev. edn 1983; (ed) 58 Short Stories by O. Henry, 1956; Poetry Today, 1958; American Literature and the American Imagination, 1964; American Literature, 1964; The Penguin Book of American Verse, 1977, 2nd edn 1983; articles in TLS, Amer. Mercury, BBC Quarterly, Kenyon Review,

Review of English Lit., The Year's Work in English Studies, Jl of American Studies, Studi Americani and other scholarly and literary jls. *Recreations:* swimming, driving. *Club:* Savile.

MOORE, George; Chairman, Grayne Marketing Co. Ltd, since 1978; *b* 7 Oct. 1923; *s* of George Moore and Agnes Bryce Moore; *m* 1946, Marjorie Pamela Davies; three *s. Educ:* University Coll. and Royal Technical Coll., Cardiff (Jt Engineering Diploma); Hull Univ. (Post Graduate Diploma in Economics). Graduate Engineer, Electricity Authority, 1948–50; Development Engineer, Anglo-Iranian Oil Co., Abadan, 1950–52; Chief Electrical Engineer, Distillers' Solvents Div., 1952–58; Management Consultant, Urwick, Orr & Partners, 1958–64; Executive Dir, Burton Group, 1964–66; Group Managing Dir, Spear & Jackson International Ltd and Chm., USA Subsidiary, 1966–75; Dir of cos in Sweden, France, India, Australia, Canada, S Africa, 1966–75; Under Sec. and Regional Industrial Dir, NW Regional Office, DoI, 1976–78; Dir, Cordel Corporate Develt Ltd, 1978–. *Recreations:* golf, sailing. *Address:* Leasgill House, Leasgill, near Milnthorpe, Cumbria. *Club:* Reform.

MOORE, George; Member, South Yorkshire County Council, 1974–86 (Chairman, 1978–79); *b* 29 Jan. 1913; *s* of Charles Edward Moore and Edith Alice Moore; *m* 1943, Hannah Kenworthy; two *d. Educ:* Woodhouse, Sheffield. Started work in pit at 14 yrs of age, 1927; worked in hotel business, 1930; publican in own right for several yrs, after which went into fruit and vegetable business, first as retailer and eventually as wholesaler and partner in small co. Served in RAF for short period during war. Elected to Barnsley Bor. Council, 1961: served as Vice Chm., Health and Housing Cttee, and Vice Chm., Fire and Licensing Dept; Chairman: Barnsley and Dist Refuse Disposal Cttee, 1959–64; Sanitary Cttee, Barnsley, 1963–73; first Chm., Fire Service Cttee, S Yorks CC, 1974–78. Chm., Barnsley Community Health Council, 1974–. *Recreation:* aviculture. *Address:* 34 Derwent Road, Athersley South, Barnsley, S Yorks S71 3QT. *T:* Barnsley 6644.

MOORE, His Honour George Edgar; HM First Deemster and Clerk of the Rolls, Isle of Man, 1969–74; *b* 13 July 1907; *er s* of Ramsey Bignall Moore, OBE, formerly HM Attorney-General for Isle of Man, and Agnes Cannell Moore; *m* 1937, Joan Mary Kissack; one *s* one *d. Educ:* Rydal School. Served in RAF, 1940–45 (Sqdn Ldr). Admitted to Manx Bar, 1930; Attorney-General for Isle of Man, 1957–63; HM Second Deemster, 1963–69; MLC; Chairman: IoM Criminal Injuries Compensation Tribunal, 1967–69; IoM Income Tax Appeal Comrs, 1969–74; Tynwald Common Market Select Cttee, 1970–74; Mem., Exec. Council Manx Museum and Nat. Trust, 1970–74; Chm. of Directors: Commercial Bank of Wales (IoM) Ltd, 1975–84; Securicor (IoM) Ltd, 1975–83; Trustee, Manx Blind Welfare Soc.; Pres., Isle of Man Badminton Assoc., 1953–72; Chm., Manx War Work Trust; Hon. County Representative of Royal Air Force Benevolent Assoc., 1948–72. *Address:* Brookdale, 8 Cronkbourne Road, Douglas, Isle of Man. *Club:* Ellan Vannin (IoM).

MOORE, George Herbert, MSc; FPS; FRSC; *b* 1 June 1903; *s* of late R. Herbert Moore and Mabel Moore, Bath; *m* 1931, Dora, *d* of Frederick and Emily Blackmore, Bath; one *d. Educ:* King Edward's Sch., Bath; Bath Coll. of Chemistry and Pharmacy. FPS 1928, FRIC 1943; MSc Bristol 1953. Merchant Venturers' Technical Coll., Bristol; Lectr in Pharmaceutical Chemistry, 1929–38; Head of Science Dept, 1938–50; Vice-Principal, Bristol Coll. of Technology, 1950–54; Principal, Bristol Coll. of Science and Technology, 1954–66; Vice-Chancellor, Bath Univ., 1966–69. Vice-Pres. Royal Inst. of Chemistry, 1955–57. Hon. LLD Bath, 1968. *Publication:* University of Bath: the formative years 1949–69, 1982. *Recreations:* music, photography. *Address:* Hilcot, Horsecombe Vale, Combe Down, Bath BA2 5QR. *T:* Bath 837417.

MOORE, Mrs (Georgina) Mary, MA; Principal, St Hilda's College, Oxford, since 1980; *b* 8 April 1930; *yr d* of late Prof. V. H. Galbraith, FBA, and late Georgina Rosalie Galbraith (*née* Cole-Baker); *m* 1963, Antony Ross Moore, *qv*; one *s. Educ:* The Mount Sch., York; Lady Margaret Hall, Oxford (1st Cl. Hons Modern History 1951; MA; Hon. Fellow, 1981). Joined HM Foreign (later Diplomatic) Service, 1951; posted to Budapest, 1954; UK Permanent Delegn to United Nations, New York, 1956; FO, 1959; First Secretary, 1961; resigned on marriage. A Trustee: British Museum, 1982–; Rhodes Trust, 1984–. JP Bucks 1977–82. Under pseudonym Helena Osborne has written plays for television and radio, including: The Trial of Madame Fahmy, Granada TV, 1980; An Early Lunch, BBC Radio, 1980; An Arranged Marriage, BBC Radio, 1982. *Publications:* (also as Helena Osborne): *novels:* The Arcadian Affair, 1969; Pay-Day, 1972; White Poppy, 1977; The Joker, 1979. *Address:* St Hilda's College, Oxford. *T:* Oxford 241821; Touchbridge, Boarstall, Aylesbury, Bucks. *T:* Brill 238247. *Club:* University Women's.

See also J. H. Galbraith.

MOORE, Gerald, CBE 1954; FRCM; pianoforte accompanist; *b* Watford, Herts, 30 July 1899; *e s* of David Frank Moore, Tiverton, Devon; *m* Enid Kathleen, *d* of Montague Richard, Beckenham, Kent. *Educ:* Watford Grammar Sch.; Toronto Univ. Studied piano in Toronto; toured Canada as a boy pianist; returning to England, devoted himself to accompanying and chamber music. Associated with world's leading singers and instrumentalists. Festivals of Edinburgh, Salzburg, Holland, etc. Retired from concert platform, 1967. Ensemble Classes in USA, Tokyo, Stockholm, Helsinki, Dartington Hall, Salzburg Mozarteum, London S Bank Fest. Awarded Cobbett Gold Medal, 1951, for services to Chamber Music; Pres. Incorporated Soc. of Musicians, 1962. FRCM 1980. Hon. RAM 1962. Grand Prix du Disque: Amsterdam, 1968, 1970; Paris, 1970; Granados Medal, Barcelona, 1971; Hugo Wolf Medal, Vienna, 1973. Hon. DLitt Sussex, 1968; Hon. MusD Cambridge, 1973. *Publications:* The Unashamed Accompanist, 1943, rev. edn 1957, enlarged edn 1984; Careers in Music, 1950; Singer and Accompanist, 1953, repr. 1982; Am I Too Loud?, 1962; The Schubert Song Cycles, 1975; Farewell Recital, 1978; Poet's Love and other Schumann Songs, 1981; Furthermoore: interludes in an accompanist's life, 1983; Collected Memoirs, 1986; arrangements of songs and folk songs. *Recreations:* walking, reading, bridge. *Address:* Pond House, Penn, Bucks. *T:* Penn 3038.

MOORE, Gordon Charles; Chief Executive, City of Bradford Metropolitan Council, since 1974; *b* 23 July 1928; *s* of John Edward and Jessie Hamilton Moore; *m* 1956, Ursula Rawle; one *s* two *d. Educ:* Uppingham; St Catharine's Coll., Cambridge (MA, LLM). Solicitor. CBIM. Legal Asst, Cambs CC, 1955–56; Asst Solicitor: Worcester CB, 1956–58; Bath CB, 1958–60; Sen. Asst Solicitor: Bath CB, 1960–63; Croydon CB, 1963–65; Asst Town Clerk, Croydon LB, 1965; Dep. Town Clerk, Bradford CB, 1965–68, Town Clerk, 1968–73. FRSA. Silver Jubilee Medal, 1977. *Recreations:* music, railways, supporting Yorkshire County Cricket. *Address:* City Hall, Bradford, West Yorks BD1 1HY. *T:* Bradford 752001.

MOORE, Sir Harry, (Henry Roderick); Kt 1978; CBE 1971; *b* 19 Aug. 1915; *er s* of late Roderick Edward Moore; *m* 1944, Beatrice Margaret, *d* of late Major J. W. Seigne; one *s* one *d. Educ:* Malvern Coll.; Pembroke Coll., Cambridge. Qualified as mem. of Institute of Chartered Accountants, 1939. Served War of 1939–45: North Africa, Italy, Europe; 2nd Lt Royal Fusiliers, 1939; Lt-Col, 1944. Director: Hill Samuel Group Ltd, 1949–80; Estates House Investment Trust Ltd, 1975–76; Chairman: Associated Engineering Ltd, 1955–75; Staveley Industries, 1970–79; Molins plc, 1978–86; Vice-

Chm., Philip Hill Investment Trust plc, 1949–86. Chm., Bd of Governors, The London Hospital, 1960–74; Mem. Council, British Heart Foundn; Dep. Chm., Adv. Panel on Institutional Finance in New Towns, 1970–81; Chm., North East Thames RHA, 1974–84. High Sheriff of Bucks, 1966. *Address:* Huntingate Farm, Thornborough, near Buckingham MK18 2DE. *T:* Buckingham 812241; 70 Chesterfield House, Chesterfield Gardens, W1Y 5TD. *T:* 01–491 0666. *Clubs:* White's, Pratt's; Leander; Rand (Johannesburg).

MOORE, Sir Henry Roderick; *see* Moore, Sir Harry.

MOORE, Rt. Rev. Henry Wylie; General Secretary, Church Missionary Society, since 1986; *b* 2 Nov. 1923; *m* 1951, Betty Rose Basnett; two *s* three *d. Educ:* Univ. of Liverpool (BCom 1950); Wycliffe Hall, Oxford. MA (Organization Studies) Leeds, 1972. LMS Railway Clerk, 1940–42. Served War with King's Regt (Liverpool), 1942–43; Rajputana Rifles, 1943–46. Curate: Farnworth, Widnes, 1952–54; Middleton, 1954–56; CMS, Khuzistan, 1956–59; Rector: St Margaret, Burnage, 1960–63; Middleton, 1963–74; Home Sec. and later Executive Sec., CMS, 1974–83; Bishop in Cyprus and the Gulf, 1983–86. *Recreation:* family life. *Address:* Church Missionary Society, 157 Waterloo Road, SE1 8UU.

MOORE, Maj.-Gen. Sir Jeremy; *see* Moore, Maj.-Gen. Sir John J.

MOORE, Hon. Sir John (Cochrane), AC 1986; Kt 1976; President, Australian Conciliation and Arbitration Commission, 1973–85; *b* 5 Nov. 1915; *s* of E. W. Moore and L. G. Moore; *m* 1946, Julia Fay, *d* of Brig. G. Drake-Brockman; two *s* two *d. Educ:* N Sydney Boys' High Sch.; Univ. of Sydney (BA, LLB). Private, AIF, 1940; R of O Hon. Captain 1945. Admitted NSW Bar, 1940; Dept of External Affairs, 1945; 2nd Sec., Aust. Mission to UN, 1946; practice, NSW Bar, 1947–59; Dep. Pres., Commonwealth Conciliation and Arbitration Commn, 1959–72, Actg Pres. 1972–73. Chm. (Pres.), Aust. Council of Nat. Trusts, 1969–82; President: Nat. Trust of Aust. (NSW), 1966–69; Ind. Relations Soc. of NSW, 1972–73; Ind. Relations Soc. of Aust., 1973–74. Pres., NSW Br., Scout Assoc. of Aust., 1978–82. *Recreations:* swimming, reading. *Address:* 10 The Grange, McAuley Place, Waitara, NSW 2077, Australia. *T:* 2308506. *Club:* Athenæum (Melbourne).

MOORE, Rt. Hon. John (Edward Michael), PC 1986; MP (C) Croydon Central since Feb. 1974; Secretary of State for Transport, since 1986; *b* 26 Nov. 1937; *s* of Edward O. Moore; *m* 1962, Sheila Sarah Tillotson; two *s* one *d. Educ:* London Sch. of Economics (BSc Econ). Nat. Service, Royal Sussex Regt, Korea, 1955–57 (commnd). Chm. Conservative Soc., LSE, 1958–59; Pres. Students' Union, LSE, 1959–60. Took part in expedn from N Greece to India overland tracing Alexander's route, 1960. In Banking and Stockbroking instns, Chicago, 1962–65; Democratic Precinct Captain, Evanston, Ill, USA, 1962; Democratic Ward Chm. Evanston, Illinois, 1964; Dir, 1968–79, Chm., 1975–79, Dean Witter Internat. Ltd. An Underwriting Mem. of Lloyds, 1978–. Conservative Councillor, London Borough of Merton, 1971–74; Chm., Stepney Green Conservative Assoc., 1968; a Vice-Chm., Conservative Party, 1975–79. Parly Under-Sec. of State, Dept. of Energy, 1979–83; HM Treasury: Economic Sec., June–Oct. 1983; Financial Sec., 1983–86. Mem. Ct of Governors, LSE, 1977–. *Address:* House of Commons, SW1A 0AA.

MOORE, Captain John Evelyn, RN; Editor: Jane's Fighting Ships, since 1972; Jane's Naval Review, since 1982; *b* Sant Ilario, Italy, 1 Nov. 1921; *s* of William John Moore and Evelyn Elizabeth (*née* Hooper); *m* 1st, 1945, Joan Pardoe; one *s* two *d*; 2nd, Barbara (*née* Kerry). *Educ:* Sherborne Sch., Dorset. Served War: entered Royal Navy, 1939; specialised in hydrographic surveying, then submarines, in 1943. Commanded HM Submarines: Totem, Alaric, Tradewind, Tactician, Telemachus. RN Staff course, 1950–51; Comdr, 1957; attached to Turkish Naval Staff, 1958–60; subseq. Plans Div., Admty; 1st Submarine Sqdn, then 7th Submarine Sqdn in comd; Captain, 1967; served as: Chief of Staff, C-in-C Naval Home Command, Defence Intell. Staff; retired list at own request, 1972. FRGS 1942. Editor, Forces Naval Review, 1981–83. *Publications:* Jane's Major Warships, 1973; The Soviet Navy Today, 1975; Submarine Development, 1976; (jtly) Soviet War Machine, 1976; (jtly) Encyclopaedia of World's Warships, 1978; (jtly) World War 3, 1978; Seapower and Politics, 1979; Warships of the Royal Navy, 1979; Warships of the Soviet Navy, 1981; (jtly) Submarine Warfare: today and tomorrow, 1986. *Recreations:* gardening, swimming, archaeology. *Address:* Elmhurst, Rickney, Hailsham, Sussex BN27 1SF. *T:* Eastbourne 763294. *Clubs:* Naval, Anchorites.

MOORE, Maj.-Gen. Sir (John) Jeremy, KCB 1982 (CB 1982); OBE (mil.) 1973; MC 1952, Bar 1962; consultant; Director-General: Food Manufacturers' Federation, 1984–85; Food and Drink Federation, 1984–85; *b* 5 July 1928; *s* of Lt-Col Charles Percival Moore, MC, and Alice Hylda Mary (*née* Bibby); *m* 1966, Veryan Julia Margaret Acworth; one *s* two *d. Educ:* Brambletye Sch.; Cheltenham Coll. Joined RM as Probationary 2/Lt, 1947; training until 1950 (HMS Sirius, 1948); Troop subaltern, 40 Commando RM, 1950–53 (MC Malayan Emergency 1952); Housemaster, RM School of Music, 1954; ADC to MGRM Plymouth Gp, 1954–55; Instructor, NCO's Sch., RM, 1955–57; Adjt, 45 Cdo RM, 1957–59; Instr, RMA Sandhurst, 1959–62; Adjt and Company Comdr, 42 Cdo RM, 1962–63 (Bar to MC Brunei Revolt 1962); Australian Staff Coll., 1963–64; GSO2 Operations, HQ 17 Gurkha Div., 1965; Asst Sec., Chiefs of Staff Secretariat, MoD, 1966–68; HMS Bulwark, 1968–69; Officer Comdg, Officers Wing Commando Trng Centre RM, 1969–71; CO 42 Cdo RM, 1972–73 (OBE operational, NI 1973); Comdt RM School of Music (Purveyor of Music to the Royal Navy), 1973–75; RCDS 1976; Comdr 3rd Cdo Bde RM, 1977–79; Maj. Gen. Commando Forces, RM, 1979–82; Comdr, Land Forces, Falkland Islands, May–July 1982; MOD, 1982–83, retired. Pres., British Biathlon Team, 1984–. Mem. Council, Cheltenham Coll.; Governor, Knighton House Sch., Blandford. *Recreations:* music (no performing ability except on a gramophone), painting, sailing, hill walking. *Address:* c/o Lloyds Bank, Cox's and King's Branch, 6 Pall Mall, SW1. *Club:* Edward Bear (RMA Sandhurst).

MOORE, Sir John (Michael), KCVO 1983; CB 1974; DSC 1944; Second Crown Estate Commissioner, 1978–83; *b* 2 April 1921; *m* 1986, Jacqueline Cingel, MBE. *Educ:* Whitgift Middle Sch.; Selwyn Coll., Cambridge. Royal Navy, 1940–46. Royal Humane Society Bronze Medal, 1942. Ministry of Transport, 1946; Joint Principal Private Sec. to Minister (Rt Hon. Harold (later Lord) Watkinson), 1956–59; Asst Sec., 1959; Under-Sec. (Principal Estabt Officer), 1966; Under-Sec., DoE, 1970–72; Dep. Sec., CSD, 1972–78. *Recreations:* sailing, walking hills and mountains. *Address:* 38 Daniells Walk, Lymington, Hants SO41 9PN. *T:* Lymington 79963.

MOORE, Dr John Michael; Headmaster, The King's School, Worcester, since 1983; *b* 12 Dec. 1935; *s* of Roy Moore, *qv*; *m* 1960, Jill Mary Maycock; one *s. Educ:* Rugby Sch.; Clare Coll., Cambridge (John Stewart of Rannoch Scholar, 1956; George Charles Winter Warr Scholar, 1957; 1st Cl. Hons Classical Tripos; MA; PhD 1960). Asst Master: Winchester Coll., 1960–64; Radley Coll., 1964–83; Jun. Fellow, Center for Hellenic Studies, Washington, DC, 1970–71. Silver Jubilee Medal, 1977. *Publications:* The Manuscript Tradition of Polybius, 1965; (ed with P. A. Brunt) Res Gestae Divi Augusti, 1967, repr. with corrections 1973; (with J. J. Evans) Variorum, 1969; Timecharts, 1969;

Aristotle and Xenophon on Democracy and Oligarchy, 1975, 2nd edn 1983; articles and reviews in Gnomon, Jl Soc. for Promotion of Hellenic Studies, Classical Qly, Greek, Roman and Byzantine Studies. *Recreations:* painting, gardening, travel. *Address:* 9 College Green, Worcester WR1 2LH.

MOORE, John Royston, CBE 1983; BSc, CChem, FRSC; Chairman, Bradford Health Authority, since 1982; *b* 2 May 1921; *s* of late Henry Roland and Jane Elizabeth Moore; *m* 1947, Dorothy Mackay Hick, *d* of late Charles and Edith Mackay Hick; two *s*. *Educ:* Manchester Central Grammar Sch.; Univ. of Manchester (BSc Hons). War service, research and manufacture of explosives. Lecturer in schools and college, Manchester; Principal, Bradford Technical Coll., 1959–75; Sen. Vice Principal and Dir of Planning and Resources, Bradford Coll., 1975–80, retired. Chm., Wool, Jute and Flax ITB, 1981–83. Leader, Baildon Urban DC, 1965–68; Councillor, West Riding CC, until 1973; West Yorkshire MCC: Member, 1973–86; Leader, 1978–81; Leader of the Opposition, 1981–86. President, Baildon Conservative Assoc., 1975–; past Chm., Conservative Nat. Adv. Cttee on Educn. Hon. Mem., and Councillor, City and Guilds of London Inst., 1977–. Hon. MA Bradford, 1986. *Recreations:* music, history, bridge. *Address:* Bicknor, 33 Station Road, Baildon, Shipley, West Yorkshire BD17 6HS. *T:* Bradford 581777.

MOORE, Prof. Leslie Rowsell, BSc, PhD, DSc, CEng, FIMinE, FGS; Consultant Geologist; Professor of Geology, University of Sheffield, 1949–77, now Emeritus Professor; *b* 23 June 1912; *m* 1946, Margaret Wilson MacRae (*d* 1985); one *s*. *Educ:* Midsomer Norton Grammar Sch.; Bristol Univ. Univ. of Bristol, 1930–37; Lecturer and Senior Lecturer, Cardiff, 1939–46; Research Dir, Univ. of Glasgow, 1946–48; Reader in Geology, Univ. of Bristol, 1948–49. *Publications:* contributions to: Quarterly Journal Geol. Soc., London; Geological Magazine; S Wales Inst. Engineers. *Recreations:* soccer, cricket, golf. *Address:* Moorside, The Bent, Curbar, near Sheffield S30 1YD.

MOORE, Mary; *see* Moore, G. M.

MOORE, Michael; *see* Stuart, M. M.

MOORE, Noel Ernest Ackroyd; Under-Secretary, Management and Personnel Office (formerly Civil Service Department), 1975–86, and Principal of Civil Service College, 1981–86, retired; *b* 25 Nov. 1928; *s* of late Rowland H. Moore and Hilda Moore (*née* Ackroyd); *m* 1954, Mary Elizabeth Thorpe; two *s*. *Educ:* Penistone Grammar Sch., Yorks; Gonville and Caius Coll., Cambridge (MA; Half-Blue for chess). Asst Principal, Post Office, 1952; Asst Private Sec. to Postmaster General, 1955–56; Private Sec. to Asst PMG, 1956–57; Principal, 1957; Sec., Cttee of Inquiry on Decimal Currency, 1961–63; Treasury, 1966; Asst Sec., 1967; Sec., Decimal Currency Bd, 1966–72; Civil Service Dept, 1972. *Publication:* The Decimalisation of Britain's Currency (HMSO), 1973. *Address:* 30 Spurgate, Hutton, Brentwood, Essex CM13 2LA. *T:* Brentwood 216988.

MOORE, (Sir) Norman Winfrid (3rd Bt *cr* 1919; has established his claim but does not use the title); Senior Principal Scientific Officer, Nature Conservancy Council, 1965–83 (Principal Scientific Officer, 1958–65); Visiting Professor of Environmental Studies, Wye College, University of London, 1979–83; *b* 24 Feb. 1923; *s* of Sir Alan Hilary Moore, 2nd Bt; *S* father 1959; *m* 1950, Janet, *o d* of late Mrs Phyllis Singer; one *s* two *d*. *Educ:* Eton; Trinity Coll., Cambridge. Served War, 1942–45, Germany and Holland (wounded, POW). *Heir:* *s* Peter Alan Cutlack Moore [*b* 21 Sept. 1951. *Educ:* Eton; Trinity Coll., Cambridge (MA); DPhil Oxon]. *Address:* The Farm House, Swavesey, Cambridge.

MOORE, Patrick Caldwell-, OBE 1968; free-lance author since 1968; *b* 4 March 1923; *s* of late Capt. Charles Caldwell-Moore, MC, and of Mrs Gertrude Lilian Moore. *Educ:* privately (due to illness). Served with RAF, 1940–45: Navigator, Bomber Command. Concerned in running of a school, 1945–52; free-lance author, 1952–65; Dir of Armagh Planetarium, 1965–68. TV Series, BBC, The Sky at Night, 1957–; radio broadcaster. Composed and performed in Perseus and Andromeda (opera), 1975, and Theseus, 1982. Pres., British Astronomical Assoc., 1982–84. Honorary Member: Astronomic-Geodetic Soc. of USSR, 1971; Royal Astronomical Soc. of New Zealand, 1983. Editor, Year Book of Astronomy, 1962–. Lorimer Gold Medal, 1962; Goodacre Gold Medal, 1968; Arturo Gold Medal (Italian Astronomical Socs), 1969; Jackson-Gwilt Medal, RAS, 1977; Roberts-Klumpke Medal, Astronom. Soc. of Pacific, 1979. Hon. DSc Lancaster, 1974. *Publications:* More than 60 books, mainly astronomical, including The Amateur Astronomer, 1970; Atlas of the Universe, 1970, rev. edn 1981; Guide to the Planets, 1976; Guide to the Moon, 1976; Can You Speak Venusian?, 1977; Guide to the Stars, 1977; Guide to Mars, 1977; (jtly) Out of the Darkness: the Planet Pluto, 1980; The Unfolding Universe, 1982; Travellers in Space and Time, 1983; (jtly) The Return of Halley's Comet, 1984; Stargazing, 1985; Exploring the Night Sky with Binoculars, 1986; The A–Z of Astronomy, 1986. *Recreations:* cricket, chess, tennis, music, xylophone playing (composer of music in records The Ever Ready Band Plays Music by Patrick Moore, 1979 and The Music of Patrick Moore, 1986). *Address:* Farthings, 39 West Street, Selsey, West Sussex. *Clubs:* Lord's Taverners; Sussex County Cricket.

MOORE, Very Rev. Peter Clement; Dean of St Albans, since 1973; *b* 4 June 1924; *s* of Rev. G. G. Moore and Vera (*née* Mylrea); *m* 1965, Mary Claire, *o d* of P. A. M. Malcolm and Celia (*née* Oldham); one *s* one *d*. *Educ:* Cheltenham Coll.; Christ Church, Oxford (MA, DPhil); Cuddesdon Coll., Oxford. Minor Canon of Canterbury Cathedral and Asst Master, Cathedral Choir School, 1947–49; Curate of Bladon with Woodstock, 1949–51; Chaplain, New Coll., Oxford, 1949–51; Vicar of Alfrick with Lulsley, 1952–59; Hurd Librarian to Bishop of Worcester, 1953–62; Vicar of Pershore with Pinvin and Wick, 1959–67; Rural Dean of Pershore, 1965–67; Canon Residentiary of Ely Cathedral, 1967–73; Vice-Dean, 1971–73. Select Preacher, Oxford Univ., 1986–87. Member: Archbishops' Liturgical Commission, 1968–76; General Synod, 1978–85; Governing Body, SPCK. Liveryman, Worshipful Co. of Glaziers and Painters of Glass. Trustee, Historic Churches Preservation Trust. *Publications:* Tomorrow is Too Late, 1970; Man, Woman and Priesthood, 1978; Footholds in the Faith, 1980; Crown in Glory, 1982; Bishops: but what kind?, 1982; In Vitro Veritas, 1985; The Synod of Westminster, 1985. *Recreations:* gardening, music, fishing, barrel organs. *Address:* The Deanery, St Albans, Herts AL1 1BY. *T:* St Albans 52120; Thruxton House, Thruxton, Hereford. *T:* Wormbridge 376. *Club:* United Oxford & Cambridge University.

MOORE, Prof. Peter Gerald, TD 1963; PhD; FIA; Professor of Statistics and Operational Research, London Business School, since 1965, Principal, since 1984 (Deputy Principal, 1972–84); *b* Richmond, Surrey, 5 April 1928; *s* of Leonard Moore and late Ruby Moore; *m* 1958, Margaret Gertrude Sonja Enevoldson Thomas, Dulwich; two *s* one *d*. *Educ:* King's College Sch., Wimbledon; University Coll. London (BSc (1st Cl. Hons Statistics), PhD; Rosa Morison Meml Medal 1949). Served with 3rd Regt RHA, 1949–51, TA, 1951–65, Major 1963. Lectr, UCL, 1951–57; Commonwealth Fund Fellow, Princeton, NJ, 1953–54; Asst to Economic Adviser, NCB, 1957–59; Head of Statistical Services, Reed Paper Gp, 1959–65. Director: Shell UK, 1969–72; Copeman Paterson Ltd, 1978–; Martin Paterson Associates, 1984–; Partner, Duncan C. Fraser, 1974–77. Member: Review Body on Doctors' and Dentists' Pay, 1971–; Cttee on 1971 Census Security, 1971–73; UGC, 1979–84 (Vice-Chm., 1980–83); Cons. to Wilson Cttee on Financial Instns, 1977–80. Mem. Council, Royal Statistical Soc., 1966–78 (Hon. Sec., 1968–74, Guy Medal, 1970); Pres., Inst. of Actuaries, 1984–86 (Mem. Council, 1966–; Vice-Pres., 1973–76); Member: Internat. Stat. Inst., 1972– (Council, 1985–); Council, Internat. Actuarial Assoc, 1984–; Industry and Employment Cttee, ESRC, 1983–; Chm., Conf. of Univ. Management Schs, 1974–76; a Governor: London Business Sch., 1968–; NIESR, 1985–; Sevenoaks Sch., 1984–. CBIM 1986. Hon. DSc Heriot-Watt, 1985. J. D. Scaife Medal, Instn of Prodn Engrs, 1964. *Publications include:* Principles of Statistical Techniques, 1958, 2nd edn 1969; (with D. E. Edwards) Standard Statistical Calculations, 1965; Statistics and the Manager, 1966; Basic Operational Research, 1968, 3rd edn 1986; Risk and Business Decisions, 1972; (jtly) Case Studies in Decision Analysis, 1975; (with H. Thomas) Anatomy of Decisions, 1976; Reason by Numbers, 1980; The Business of Risk, 1983; articles in professional jls. *Recreations:* golf, walking, travel (particularly by train). *Address:* London Business School, Sussex Place, Regent's Park, NW1 4SA. *T:* 01–262 5050. *Clubs:* Athenæum; Knole Park Golf.

MOORE, Philip John, BMus; FRCO; Organist and Master of the Music, York Minster, since 1983; *b* 30 Sept. 1943; *s* of Cecil and Marjorie Moore; one *s* two *d*. *Educ:* Royal Coll. of Music (ARCM, GRSM). BMus Dunelm; FRCO 1965. Asst Music Master, Eton Coll., 1965–68; Asst Organist, Canterbury Cathedral, 1968–74; Organist and Master of the Choristers, Guildford Cathedral, 1974–83. *Publications:* anthems, services, organ music, song cycles, chamber music. *Recreation:* day-dreaming. *Address:* 1 Minster Court, York YO1 2JJ.

MOORE, Richard Valentine, GC 1940; CBE 1963; BSc (Eng); FIMechE; FIEE; retired; Managing Director (Reactor Group), UK Atomic Energy Authority, 1961–76; Member, 1971–76; *b* 14 Feb. 1916; *s* of Randall and Ellen Moore; *m* 1944, Ruby Edith Fair; three *s*. *Educ:* Strand Sch., London; London Univ. County of London Electric Supply Co., 1936–39. RNVR, 1939–46; HMS Effingham, 1939–40; HMS President, 1940–41; HMS Dido, 1942–44; British Admiralty Delegn, Washington, DC, 1944–46; Lieut-Comdr 1944. AERE Harwell, 1946–53; Dept of Atomic Energy, Risley, 1953; Design and Construction of Calder Hall, 1953–57; Chief Design Engineer, 1955; UKAEA, 1955; Dir of Reactor Design, 1958–61. Faraday Lectr, 1966. Hon. DTech Bradford, 1970. *Publications:* various papers to technical institutions. *Recreations:* golf, gardening. *Address:* Culleen House, Cann Lane, Appleton, Ches. *T:* Warrington 61023. *Club:* Naval.

MOORE, Robert, (Bobby Moore), OBE 1967; professional footballer; Football Manager/Director, Southend United Football Club, (3rd Division), 1983–86; *b* 12 April 1941; *m* 1962, Christina Elizabeth Dean (marr. diss. 1986); one *s* one *d*. Captained: England Youth, at 17 years old (18 caps); England Under 23 (8 caps); made 108 appearances for England (the record number for England, and a world record until 1978), 90 as Captain (equalling Billy Wright's record). League debut for West Ham against Manchester United, Sept. 1958; England debut against Peru, 1962; played in World Cup, in Chile, 1962; Captained England for first time, against Czechoslovakia, 1963. Footballer of the Year, 1963–64; Holder of: FA Cup Winners' medal, 1964; European Cup Winners' medal, 1965; named Player of Players in World Cup (England the Winner), 1966; transferred to Fulham Football Club, 1974–77; played 1,000 matches at senior level. Manager, Oxford City Football Club, 1979–81; Coach: Eastern Ath. FC, Hong Kong, 1982–83; Carolina Lightnin, N Carolina, 1983. *Publication:* Bobby Moore (autobiog.), 1976. *Address:* 164 Mountdale Gardens, Leigh on Sea, Essex.

MOORE, Robert, CBE 1973; Commissioner for Local Administration in Scotland, 1975–78; *b* 2 Nov. 1915; *m* 1940, Jean Laird Dick; two *s*. *Educ:* Dalziel High Sch., Motherwell; Glasgow Univ. (BL). Admitted solicitor, 1939. Town Clerk, Port Glasgow, 1943–48; Secretary, Eastern Regional Hosp. Bd, 1948–60; Principal Officer: Scottish Hosp. Administrative Staffs Cttee, 1960–74; Manpower Div., Scottish Health Service, 1974–75. Lectr in Administrative Law, St Andrews Univ., 1960–65; External Examr in Administrative Law, Glasgow Univ., 1967–71. Mem., Scottish Cttee, Council on Tribunals, 1964–82. *Address:* (home) 93 Greenbank Crescent, Edinburgh EH10 5TB. *T:* 031–447 5493.

MOORE, Roger; actor; *b* London, 14 Oct. 1927; *m* 1st, Doorn van Steyn (marr. diss. 1953); 2nd, 1953, Dorothy Squires (marr. diss. 1969); 3rd, Luisa Mattioli; two *s* one *d*. *Educ:* RADA. Golden Globe World Film Favourite Award, 1980. Stage début, Androcles and the Lion. *TV series include:* Ivanhoe, 1958; The Alaskans, 1960–61; Maverick, 1961; The Saint, 1962–69 (dir some episodes); The Persuaders, 1972–73; *films include:* The Last Time I Saw Paris, 1954; The Interrupted Melody, 1955; The King's Thief, 1955; Diane, 1956; The Miracle, 1959; Rachel Cade, 1961; Gold of the Seven Saints, 1961; The Rape of the Sabine Women, 1961; No Man's Land, 1961; Crossplot, 1969; The Man Who Haunted Himself, 1970; Live and Let Die, 1973; The Man With The Golden Gun, 1974; Gold, 1974; That Lucky Touch, 1975; Street People, 1975; Shout at the Devil, 1975; Sherlock Holmes in New York, 1976; The Spy Who Loved Me, 1976; The Wild Geese, 1977; Escape to Athena, 1978; Moonraker, 1978; North Sea Hijack, 1979; The Sea Wolves, 1980; Sunday Lovers, 1980; For Your Eyes Only, 1980; The Cannonball Run, 1981; Octopussy, 1983; The Naked Face, 1983; A View to a Kill, 1985. *Publication:* James Bond Diary, 1973. *Address:* c/o London Management Ltd, 235 Regent Street, W1.

MOORE, Roy, CBE 1962; *b* 10 Jan. 1908; *s* of Harry Moore and Ellen Harriet Post; *m* 1st, 1934, Muriel Edith (*d* 1959), *d* of late C. E. E. Shill; two *s*; 2nd, 1963, Lydia Elizabeth Newell Park, *widow* of David Park, Berkeley, Calif. *Educ:* Judd Sch., Tonbridge; King's Coll., London. 2nd Cl. Hons English, 1928; AKC 1928; MA 1931; Carter Prize for English Verse. Chief English Master, Mercers' Sch., London, 1931–40. Served War of 1939–45, Squadron Leader RAF Bomber Command, 1941–45. Head Master: Lawrence Sheriff Sch., Rugby, 1945–51; Mill Hill Sch., 1951–67. Fellow King's Coll., London, 1956. *Address:* 138 Santo Tomas Lane, Santa Barbara, Calif 93108, USA. *Club:* Athenæum.
See also J. M. Moore.

MOORE, Thomas William, JP; Chairman (since inception) of Trojan Metals Ltd, Carseview Holdings Ltd, Dundee Timber Market Ltd, Inverlaw Property Co. Ltd; *b* 9 Aug. 1925; Scottish; *m* 1945, Mary Kathleen Thompson; four *s* two *d*. *Educ:* Stobswell Secondary Sch.; Leicester Coll. of Art and Technology. MBIM. Contested (Lab), Perth and East Perthshire, 1959. Lord Provost of Dundee, and Lord Lieutenant of County of City of Dundee, 1973–75; Chairman: Tay Road Bridge Jt Cttee, 1973; Tayside Steering Cttee. FInstD. *Recreations:* golf, reading. *Address:* 85 Blackness Avenue, Dundee. *Club:* Royal Automobile.

MOORE, Sir William (Roger Clotworthy), 3rd Bt *cr* 1932; TD 1962; *b* 17 May 1927; *s* of Sir William Samson Moore, 2nd Bt, and Ethel Cockburn Gordon (*d* 1973); *S* father, 1978; *m* 1954, Gillian, *d* of John Brown, Co. Antrim; one *s* one *d*. *Educ:* Marlborough; RMC, Sandhurst. Lieut Royal Inniskilling Fusiliers, 1945; Major North Irish Horse, 1956. High Sheriff, Co. Antrim, 1964. *Heir:* *s* Richard William Moore [*b* 8 May 1955. *Educ:* Portora; RMA. Lieut Royal Scots, 1974]. *Address:* c/o Grindlay's Bank, 13 St James's Square, SW1. *Clubs:* Boodle's, Army and Navy.

MOORE-BICK, Martin James; QC 1986; *b* 6 Dec. 1946; *s* of John Ninian Moore-Bick and Kathleen Margaret Moore-Bick (*née* Beall); *m* 1974, Tessa Penelope Gee; two *s* two *d*. *Educ:* The Skinners' Sch., Tunbridge Wells; Christ's Coll., Cambridge (MA). Called to the Bar, Inner Temple, 1969. *Recreations:* early music, gardening, reading. *Address:* (chambers) 3 Essex Court, Temple, EC4Y 9AL. *T:* 01–583 9294; Little Bines, Witherenden Hill, Burwash, E Sussex TN19 7JE. *T:* Burwash 883284.

MOORE-BRABAZON, family name of **Baron Brabazon of Tara.**

MOORER, Admiral Thomas Hinman; Defense Distinguished Service Medal, 1973; Navy DSM 1965, 1967, 1968, 1970; Army DSM 1974; Air Force DSM 1974; Silver Star 1942; Legion of Merit, 1945; DFC 1942; Purple Heart, 1942; Presidential Unit Citation, 1942; Vice Chairman of Board, Blount Inc.; Board Member, Fairchild Industries; *b* Mount Willing, Alabama, 9 Feb. 1912; *s* of Dr R. R. Moorer and Hulda Hill Hinson, Eufaula, Ala; *m* 1935, Carrie Ellen Foy Moorer; three *s* one *d*. *Educ:* Cloverdale High Sch., Montgomery, Ala; USN Acad.; Naval Aviation Trg Sch.; Naval War Coll. First ship, 1933; serving at Pearl Harbour in Fleet Air Wing, Dec. 1941; Pacific and East Indies areas, 1942; Mining Observer, C-in-C, US Fleet in UK, 1943; Strategic Bombing Survey in Japan, 1945; Naval Aide to Asst Sec. of Navy (Air), 1956; CO, USS Salisbury Sound, 1957; Special Asst to CNO, 1959; Comdr, Carrier Div. Six, 1960; Dir, Long Range Objectives Group, CNO, 1962; Comdr Seventh Fleet, 1964; C-in-C: US Pacific Fleet, 1965; Atlantic and Atlantic Fleet, and Supreme Allied Commander, Atlantic, 1965–67; Chief of Naval Operations, 1967–70; Chm., Jt Chiefs of Staff, USA, 1970–74, retired US Navy 1974. Captain 1952; Rear-Adm. 1958; Vice-Adm. 1962; Adm. 1964. Holds seventeen foreign decorations. Hon. LLD Auburn, 1968; Hon. DH Samford, 1970; Hon. Dr Mil. Science, The Citadel, 1983. *Recreations:* golfing, fishing, hunting. *Address:* 6901 Lupine Lane, McLean, Va 22101, USA. *Clubs:* Brook (New York); International (Washington, DC); US Naval Inst. (Annapolis, Md); Army-Navy Country (Arlington, Va); Chevy Chase (Chevy Chase, Md).

MOORES, Hon. Frank Duff; Chairman, Government Consultants International; Chairman and Chief Executive Officer: Torngat Investments Inc.; SSF (Holdings) Inc.; Director: Atlantic Container Express Ltd; Mercedes-Benz Canada Inc.; Premier of the Province of Newfoundland, 1972–78; *b* 18 Feb. 1933; *s* of Silas Wilmot Moores and Dorothy Duff Moores; *m* 1982, Beth Champion; two *s* six *d* by former marriages. *Educ:* United Church Academy, Carbonear; St Andrew's Coll., Aurora, Ont. MP, Canada, for Bonavista-Trinity-Conception, 1968–71; MHA for Humber W, Newfoundland, 1971; Pres., Progressive Conservative Party in Canada, 1969; Leader, Progressive Conservative Party, Newfoundland, 1970–79. Mem., Royal Commn on Economic Prospects of Newfoundland. Dir, Council for Canadian Unity; Gov., Olympia Trust. Is a Freemason. Hon. LLD, Meml Univ. of Newfoundland, 1975. *Recreations:* tennis, reading, fishing, hunting, golf. *Address:* St John's, Newfoundland, Canada. *Clubs:* Rideau (Ottawa); Mid Ocean (Bermuda).

MOORES, Sir John, Kt 1980; CBE 1972; Founder of the Littlewoods Organisation, 1924, Chairman, 1924–77 and 1980–82, Life President, 1982; *b* Eccles, Lancs, 25 Jan. 1896; *s* of John William Moores and Louisa (*née* Fethney); *m* 1923 Ruby Knowles; two *s* two *d*. *Educ:* Higher Elementary Sch. Founded: Littlewoods Pools, 1924; Littlewoods Mail Order Stores, 1932; Littlewoods Stores, 1936. Hon. Freeman, City of Liverpool, 1970; Hon. LLB Liverpool, 1973; first winner of Liverpool Gold Medal for Achievement, 1978. *Recreations:* painting, languages, sport, travel. *Address:* c/o The Littlewoods Organisation PLC, JM Centre, Old Hall Street, Liverpool L70 1AB. *T:* 051–235 2222.
See also Baron Grantchester, Peter Moores.

MOORES, Peter; Director: The Littlewoods Organization, since 1965 (Chairman, 1977–80); Singer & Friedlander, since 1978; *b* 9 April 1932; *s* of Sir John Moores, *qv*; *m* 1960, Luciana Pinto (marr. diss. 1984); one *s* one *d*. *Educ:* Eton; Christ Church, Oxford; Wiener Akademie der Musik und darstellenden Kunst. Worked in opera prodn at Glyndebourne and Vienna State Opera; sponsor of complete recordings in English of: Wagner's Der Ring des Nibelungen, La Traviata, Otello, Rigoletto, Mary Stuart and Julius Caesar by the English National Opera. Trustee, Tate Gall., 1978–85; Governor of the BBC, 1981–83. Hon. MA Christ Church, 1975. Gold Medal of the Italian Republic, 1974. *Recreations:* water-skiing, wind-surfing, shooting, fishing. *Address:* Parbold Hall, Parbold, near Wigan, Lancs. *Club:* Boodle's.

MOOREY, (Peter) Roger (Stuart), DPhil; FBA 1977; FSA; Keeper, Department of Antiquities, Ashmolean Museum, Oxford, since 1983; Fellow of Wolfson College, since 1976; *b* 30 May 1937; *s* of late Stuart Moorey and Freda (*née* Harris). *Educ:* Mill Hill Sch.; Corpus Christi Coll., Oxford (MA, DPhil). FSA 1967. Nat. Service, 1956–58, Intelligence Corps. Asst Keeper, 1961–73, Sen. Asst Keeper, 1973–82, Ashmolean Museum, Oxford. Editor of Levant, 1968–86. *Publications:* Catalogue of the Ancient Persian Bronzes in the Ashmolean Museum, 1971; Ancient Persian Bronzes in the Adam Collection, 1974; Biblical Lands, 1975; Kish Excavations 1923–1933, 1978; Cemeteries of the First Millennium BC at Deve Hüyük, 1980; Excavation in Palestine, 1981; (ed) C. L. Woolley, Ur of the Chaldees, revd edn of Excavations at Ur, 1982; (with B. Buchanan) Catalogue of Ancient Near Eastern Seals in the Ashmolean Museum, II, 1984; Materials and Manufacture in Ancient Mesopotamia: the evidence of archaeology and art, 1985; museum booklets and articles in learned jls. *Recreations:* travel, walking. *Address:* Ashmolean Museum, Oxford. *T:* Oxford 512651.

MOORHOUSE, (Cecil) James (Olaf); Member (C) London South and Surrey East, European Parliament, since 1984 (London South, 1979–84); spokesman on external economic relations for European Democratic Group, since 1984; *b* 1 Jan. 1924; *s* of late Captain Sidney James Humphrey Moorhouse and Anna Sophie Hedvig de Lövenskiold; *m* 1958, Elizabeth Clive Huxtable, Sydney, Aust.; one *s* one *d*. *Educ:* St Paul's School; King's Coll. and Imperial Coll., Univ. of London. BSc (Eng); DIC (Advanced Aeronautics); CEng. Designer with de Havilland Aircraft Co., 1946–48; Project Engr, BOAC, 1948–53; Technical Advr 1953–68, and Environmental Conservation Advr 1968–72, Shell International Petroleum; Environmental Advr, Shell Group of Companies in UK, 1972–73; Group Environmental Affairs Advr, Rio-Tinto Zinc Corp., 1973–80, Consultant, 1980–84. Contested (C) St Pancras North, 1966 and 1970. European Parliament: spokesman on transport for European Democratic Gp, 1979–84; Chm., delegn to N Europe and Nordic Council, 1979–84; First Vice-Chm, delegn to EFTA, 1984–. *Publications:* numerous articles and papers. *Recreations:* badminton, cycling, reading, travelling. *Address:* 14 Buckingham Palace Road, SW1W 0QP. *Clubs:* Institute of Directors, Royal Automobile; Croydon Conservative.

MOORHOUSE, Geoffrey; writer; *b* Bolton, Lancs, 29 Nov. 1931; *s* of William Heald and Gladys Heald (*née* Hoyle, subseq. Moorhouse) and step *s* of Richard Moorhouse; *m* 1st, 1956, Janet Marion Murray; two *s* one *d* (and one *d* decd); 2nd, 1974, Barbara Jane Woodward (marr. diss. 1978); 3rd, 1983, Marilyn Isobel Edwards. *Educ:* Bury Grammar School. Royal Navy, 1950–52; editorial staff: Bolton Evening News, 1952–54; Grey River Argus (NZ), Auckland Star (NZ), Christchurch Star-Sun (NZ), 1954–56; News Chronicle, 1957; (Manchester) Guardian, 1958–70 (Chief Features Writer, 1963–70).

FRGS 1972; FRSL 1982. *Publications:* The Other England, 1964; The Press, 1964; Against All Reason, 1969; Calcutta, 1971; The Missionaries, 1973; The Fearful Void, 1974; The Diplomats, 1977; The Boat and The Town, 1979; The Best-Loved Game, 1979 (Cricket Soc. Award); India Britannica, 1983; Lord's, 1983; To the Frontier, 1984 (Thomas Cook Award, 1984). *Recreations:* music, hill-walking, looking at buildings, watching cricket and Rugby League football. *Address:* Park House, Gayle, near Hawes, North Yorkshire DL8 3RT. *T:* Hawes 456. *Club:* Lancashire County Cricket.

MOORHOUSE, James; *see* Moorhouse, C. J. O.

MOORHOUSE, (Kathleen) Tessa; Registrar, Family Division of the High Court of Justice, since 1982; *b* 14 Sept. 1938; *d* of late Charles Elijah Hall, MRCVS and of Helen Barbara Hall; *m* 1959, Rodney Moorhouse. *Educ:* Presentation Convent, Derbyshire; Leeds Univ.; King's Coll., London. Called to the Bar, Inner Temple, 1971. Asst, Jardine's Bookshop, Manchester, 1953–56; student, Leeds Univ., 1956–59; teacher of educationally subnormal, 1959–61; student, King's Coll., London, 1961–62; Classifier, Remand Home, 1962–64; Lectr in Law, 1964–71; barrister in practice, 1971–82. *Address:* Somerset House, Strand, WC2R 1LP. *T:* 01–405 7641; 4 Brick Court, Temple, EC4Y 9AD. *T:* 01–353 7506.

MOORMAN, Rt. Rev. John Richard Humpidge, MA, DD, Cambridge; LittD: Leeds; St Bonaventure, USA; FSA; Hon. Fellow of Emmanuel College; *b* Leeds, 4 June 1905; 2nd *s* of late Professor F. W. Moorman; *m* 1930, Mary Caroline Trevelyan (*see* M. C. Moorman). *Educ:* Gresham's School, Holt; Emmanuel College, Cambridge. Curate of Holbeck, Leeds, 1929–33; of Leighton Buzzard, 1933–35; Rector of Fallowfield, Manchester, 1935–42; Hon. and Examining Chaplain to Bishop of Manchester, 1940–44; Vicar of Lanercost, 1945–46, and Examining Chaplain to Bishop of Carlisle, 1945–59; Principal of Chichester Theological Coll. and Chancellor of Chichester Cathedral, 1946–56; Prebendary of Heathfield in Chichester Cathedral, 1956–59; Bishop of Ripon, 1959–75. Delegate-observer to 2nd Vatican Council, 1962–65. Hale Memorial Lectr, Evanston, USA, 1966. Chairman: Anglican members, Anglican-Roman Catholic Preparatory Commn, 1967–69; Advisory Council for Religious Communities, 1971–80. Member, Jt Internat. Commn of the Roman Catholic Church and the Anglican Communion, 1969–83. Pres., Henry Bradshaw Soc., 1977–. *Publications:* Sources for the Life of S Francis of Assisi, 1940; Church Life in England in the Thirteenth Century, 1945; A New Fioretti, 1946; B. K. Cunningham, a Memoir, 1947; S Francis of Assisi, 1950, 2nd edn 1976; The Grey Friars in Cambridge (Birkbeck Lectures), 1952; A History of the Church in England, 1953; The Curate of Souls, 1958; The Path to Glory, 1960; Vatican Observed, 1967; A History of the Franciscan Order, 1968; The Franciscans in England, 1974; Richest of Poor Men, 1977; The Anglican Spiritual Tradition, 1983; Medieval Franciscan Houses, 1983. *Recreations:* country life, music. *Address:* 22 Springwell Road, Durham. *T:* Durham 3863503.

MOORMAN, Mrs Mary Caroline; *b* 19 Feb. 1905; *d* of George Macaulay Trevelyan, OM, CBE, FRS, FBA, and Janet Penrose Ward, CH; *m* 1930, Rt Rev. J. R. H. Moorman, *qv*. *Educ:* Berkhamsted Sch. for Girls; Somerville Coll., Oxford. BA 1926; MA 1950. Chm., Trustees of Dove Cottage, 1974–77. Hon. Lectr, Sch. of English, Leeds Univ., 1970–, and Dept of English, Durham Univ., 1980–. Hon. LittD: Leeds, 1967; Durham, 1968. *Publications:* William III and the Defence of Holland, 1672–73, 1930; William Wordsworth, A Biography: vol. 1, The Early Years, 1957, vol. 2, The Later Years, 1965 (James Tait Black Meml Prize, 1965); (ed) Letters of William and Dorothy Wordsworth, vol. II, The Middle Years: Part 1, 1806–1811, 2nd edn (rev. and ed), 1969; vol. III, The Middle Years: Part 2, 1812–1820, 2nd edn (rev. and ed with A. G. Hill), 1970; (ed) The Journals of Dorothy Wordsworth, 1971, new edn 1976; George Macaulay Trevelyan, a Memoir, 1980. *Recreations:* country walking, bird-watching. *Address:* 22 Springwell Road, Durham DH1 4LR. *T:* Durham 3863503.

MOORTHY, Arambamoorthy Thedchana; Sri Lanka Foreign Service, retired; private academic research and writing, since 1984; *b* 10 Aug. 1928; *s* of late Mr Arambamoorthy and Mrs Nesamma Arambamoorthy; *m* 1959, Suseela T. Moorthy, *d* of Justice P. Sri Skanda Rajah; one *s* two *d*. *Educ:* BAEcon Hons (Sri Lanka). Called to Bar, Gray's Inn, 1965. Entered Foreign Service of Sri Lanka, 1953; Second Secretary: Indonesia, 1955–57; China, 1957–59; First Secretary: London, 1961–63; Federal Republic of Germany, 1964–66; Chargé d'Affaires, ai, Thailand, and Permanent Representative of Sri Lanka to Economic Commn for Asia and Far East, 1969; Chargé d'Affaires, ai, Iraq, 1970; Ambassador in Pakistan, 1978–Dec. 1980, and concurrently, Jan-Dec. 1980, Ambassador to Iran with residence in Islamabad; High Comr in London, 1981–84; Ministry of Foreign Affairs, Colombo, 1984. *Address:* 10 Montreal Road, Lammack, Blackburn BB2 7BY.

MOOSONEE, Bishop of, since 1980; **Rt. Rev. Caleb James Lawrence;** *b* 26 May 1941; *s* of James Otis Lawrence and Mildred Viola Burton; *m* 1966, Maureen Patricia Cuddy; one *s* two *d*. *Educ:* Univ. of King's College. BA (Dalhousie Univ.) 1962; BST 1964. Deacon 1963, priest 1965; Missionary at Anglican Mission, Great Whale River, Quebec, 1965–75; Rector of St Edmund's Parish, Great Whale River, 1975–79; Canon of St Jude's Cathedral, Frobisher Bay, Diocese of The Arctic, 1974; Archdeacon of Arctic Quebec, 1975–79; Bishop Coadjutor, Diocese of Moosonee, Jan.-Nov. 1980. Hon. DD, Univ. of King's Coll., Halifax, NS, 1980. *Recreations:* reading, photography. *Address:* The Diocese of Moosonee, Synod Office, Box 841, Schumacher, Ontario PON 1G0, Canada. *T:* 705–264–9759.

MOOTHAM, Sir Orby Howell, Kt 1962; *b* 17 Feb. 1901; *s* of Delmé George Mootham, ARIBA; *m* 1st, 1931, Maria Augusta Elisabeth Niemöller (*d* 1973); one *s* one *d*; 2nd, 1977, Mrs Beatrix Douglas Ward, *widow* of Basil Ward, FRIBA. *Educ:* Leinster House Sch., Putney; London Univ. MSc (Econ). Called to Bar, Inner Temple, 1926 (Yarborough-Anderson Schol., 1924; Hon. Bencher, 1958). An Advocate of Rangoon High Court, 1927–40; DJAG, Army in Burma, 1940–41, thereafter service in Dept of JAG in India and as Chief Judicial Officer, Brit. Mil. Admin., Burma (despatches). Actg Judge, Rangoon High Court, 1945–46; Judge, Allahabad High Court, 1946–55; Chief Justice, 1955–61. Chm., Allahabad Univ. Enquiry Cttee, 1953–54; Legal Adviser's Dept, CRO, 1961–63. Deputy-Chairman of QS: Essex, 1964–71; Kent, 1965–71; Surrey, 1970–71; a Recorder of the Crown Court, 1972. Chm., Med. Appeals Tribunal, 1963–73; Mem. Governing Body, Froebel Educational Inst., 1965–79. *Publications:* Burmese Buddhist Law, 1939; The East India Company's Sadar Courts 1801–34, 1983; articles in Brit. Year Book of Internat. Law and other legal jls. *Address:* 3 Paper Buildings, Temple, EC4Y 7EU. *T:* 01–353 1310. *Club:* Athenæum.

MORAES, Dom; Indian poet and author; *b* 1938; *s* of Frank Moraes (Editor of the Indian Express and biographer of Nehru); *m* 1970, Leela Naidu. *Educ:* Jesus Coll., Oxford. Read English, 1956–59. Took up residence in England at age of 16, after world-wide travel and a 2-yr stay in Ceylon. On loan to Govt of India from UNFPA, for a period. *Publications:* A Beginning (poems), 1957 (Hawthornden Prize, 1958); Gone Away (Travel), 1960; Poems, 1960; John Nobody (poems), 1965; The Brass Serpent (trans. from Hebrew poetry), 1964; Poems 1955–65 (collected poems), 1966; My Son's Father (autobiography),

1968; The People Time Forgot, 1972; The Tempest Within, 1972; A Matter of People, 1974; (ed) Voices for Life (essays), 1975; Mrs Gandhi, 1980; Bombay, 1980. *Recreation*: thinking. *Address*: c/o Praeger Publishers Inc., 521 Fifth Avenue, 12th floor, New York, NY 10017, USA.

MORAHAN, Christopher Thomas; television, film and theatre director; National Theatre Associate, since 1977; *b* 9 July 1929; *s* of Thomas Hugo Morahan and Nancy Charlotte Morahan (*née* Barker); *m* 1st, 1954, Joan (*née* Murray) (decd); two *s* one *d*; 2nd, 1973, Anna (*née* Wilkinson, acting name Anna Carteret); two *d*. *Educ*: Highgate; Old Vic Theatre School. Directing for ATV, 1957–61; freelance director in TV for BBC and ITV, 1961–71; Head of Plays, BBC TV, 1972–76; National Theatre, 1977– (Dep. to Director, 1979–80). *Stage*: Little Murders, RSC, 1967; This Story of Yours, 1968; Flint, 1970; The Caretaker, 1972; for National Theatre: State of Revolution, Brand, Strife, The Philanderer, Richard III, The Wild Duck, Sisterly Feelings, Man and Superman, Wild Honey (London Standard, Olivier, British Theatre Assoc. and Plays and Players Awards for Best Dir of the Year, 1984); *film*: Clockwise, 1986; *televison series*: Emergency Ward 10; The Orwell Trilogy; Talking to a Stranger; Fathers and Families; Jewel in the Crown (Internat. Emmy Award, BAFTA Best Series Dir Award, BAFTA Desmond Davis Award, 1984; Peabody Award, 1985; Golden Globe Award, Primetime Emmy Award, 1985). Best Play direction award, SFTA, 1969. *Recreations*: photography, bird watching. *Address*: c/o Michael Whitehall Ltd, 125 Gloucester Road, SW7 4TE. *T*: 01–244 8466.

MORAN, 2nd Baron *cr* 1943; **Richard John McMoran Wilson**, KCMG 1981 (CMG 1970); *b* 22 Sept. 1924; *er s* of 1st Baron Moran, MC, MD, FRCP, and Dorothy (*d* 1983), MBE, *d* of late Samuel Felix Dufton, DSc; *S* father, 1977; *m* 1948, Shirley Rowntree Harris; two *s* one *d*. *Educ*: Eton; King's Coll., Cambridge. Served War of 1939–45; Ord. Seaman in HMS Belfast, 1943; Sub-Lt RNVR in Motor Torpedo Boats and HM Destroyer Oribi, 1944–45. Foreign Office, 1945; Third Sec., Ankara, 1948; Tel-Aviv, 1950; Second Sec., Rio de Janeiro, 1953; First Sec., FO, 1956; Washington, 1959; FO 1961; Counsellor, British Embassy in S Africa, 1965; Head of W African Dept, FCO, 1968–73, Ambassador to Chad (non-resident), 1970–73; Ambassador to Hungary, 1973–76, to Portugal, 1976–81; High Comr in Canada, 1981–84. Grand Cross, Order of the Infante (Portugal), 1978. *Publications*: (as John Wilson): C. B.: a life of Sir Henry Campbell-Bannerman, 1973 (Whitbread Award, 1973); Fairfax, 1985. *Recreations*: fishing, fly-tying, bird-watching. *Heir*: *s* Hon. James McMoran Wilson [*b* 6 Aug. 1952; *m* 1980, Hon. Jane Hepburne-Scott, *y d* of Lord Polwarth, *qv*]. *Address*: House of Lords, SW1A 0PW. *Clubs*: Beefsteak, Flyfishers'.
See also Baron Mountevans, Hon. G. H. Wilson.

MORAN, Rt. Rev. Monsignor John, CBE 1985; Principal RC Chaplain and Vicar General (Army), 1981–85; *b* 3 Dec. 1929; *s* of Thomas Moran and Gertrude May (*née* Sheer). *Educ*: De La Salle Coll., Sheffield; Ushaw Coll., Durham. Ordained Priest, Leeds Diocese, 1956; Curate, Dewsbury, 1956–60; Prison Chaplain, Armley, 1960–61; commissioned Army Chaplain, 1961; service in BAOR, Singapore, Malaya, Hong Kong, UK; Chaplain, RMA Sandhurst, 1968–70; Staff Chaplain, 1970–71; Senior Chaplain, HQ BAOR, 1977–79, and HQ UKLF, 1979–80. *Recreations*: music, rivers, clocks. *Address*: St Aidan's, Baildon Road, Baildon, West Yorks. *T*: Bradford 583032.

MORAN, Prof. Patrick Alfred Pierce, FRS 1975; FAA; Visiting Fellow, Social Psychiatry Research Unit, Australian National University, since 1983; Professor of Statistics, Australian National University, 1952–82, now Emeritus; *b* 14 July 1917; *s* of late Herbert Michael Moran and of Eva Moran; *m* 1946, Jean Mavis Frame; two *s* one *d*. *Educ*: St Stanislaus Coll., Bathurst, NSW; Univs of Sydney (DSc) and Cambridge (ScD). Exper. Officer, Min. of Supply, 1940–42; Australian Sci. Liaison Officer, London, 1942–45; Baylis Student, Cambridge, 1945–46; Sen. Res. Officer, Oxford Inst. of Statistics, 1946–51; Lectr in Maths, Trinity Coll., Oxford, 1949–51; Univ. Lectr in Maths, Oxford, 1951. Mem. Council, Australian Acad. of Scis, 1971–74; Vice-Pres., Internat. Statistical Inst., 1971–73, 1975–77. Hon. FSS. Lyle Medal, Australian Acad. of Scis, 1963; Pitman Medal, Statistical Soc. of Aust., 1982. *Publications*: The Theory of Storage, 1960; The Random Processes of Evolutionary Theory, 1962; (with M. G. Kendall) Geometrical Probability, 1963; Introduction to the Theory of Probability, 1968. *Address*: 17 Tennyson Crescent, Forrest, Canberra, ACT 2603, Australia. *T*: Canberra 731140.

MORAN, Thomas, CBE 1946; ScD; DSc; Scientific Adviser, Home Grown Cereals Authority, 1966–69; Director of Research, Research Association of British Flour Millers, 1939–66, retired; *b* 1899; *s* of late Thomas Moran; *m* 1st, 1924, Elizabeth Ann Flynn (*d* 1952); one *s* one *d* (and one *d* decd); 2nd, 1959, June Patricia Martin. *Educ*: St Francis Xavier's Coll., Liverpool; Liverpool Univ.; Gonville and Caius Coll., Cambridge. Sir John Willox Schol., 1920, Univ. Scholar, 1920, Liverpool Univ.; served European War, 1914–18, with Liverpool Scottish (KLR), 1917–19; with DSIR at Low Temperature Station, Cambridge, 1922–39. Mem. Advisory Scientific Cttee, Food Defence Plans Dept, 1938–39; Dir of Research and Dep. Scientific Adviser, Min. of Food, 1940–46; UK delegate, Quadripartite Food Conf., Berlin, Jan. 1946. Mem. Council, British Nutrition Foundation, 1967–70. *Publications*: Bread (with Lord Horder and Sir Charles Dodds), 1954; papers on different aspects of Food Science in scientific and medical journals, 1922– ; reports on applied food research published by HM Stationery Office. *Address*: 5 Amhurst Court, Grange Road, Cambridge CB3 9BH. *T*: Cambridge 354548.

MORAVIA, Alberto; Italian author; Member of European Parliament, since 1984; *b* 28 Nov. 1907; *s* of Carlo and Teresa de Marsanich; *m* 1941, Elsa Morante (*d* 1985); *m* 1986, Carmen Llera; one step *s*. Chevalier de la Légion d'Honneur (France), 1952. *Publications*: *novels*: Gli indifferenti, 1929 (Eng. trans.: The Time of Indifference, 1953); Le ambizioni sbagliate, 1935; La mascherata, 1941 (Eng. trans.: The Fancy Dress Party, 1948); Agostino, 1944 (Eng. trans.: Agostino, 1947); La Romana, 1947 (Eng. trans.: The Woman of Rome, 1949); La disubbidienza, 1948 (Eng. trans: Disobedience, 1950); L'amore Coniugale, 1949 (Eng. trans.: Conjugal Love, 1951); Il Conformista, 1951 (Eng. Trans.: The Conformist, 1952); La Ciociara, 1957 (Eng. trans.: Two Women, 1958); La Noia, 1961 (Viareggio Prize) (Eng. trans.: The Empty Canvas, 1961); The Fetish, 1965; L'attenzione, 1965 (Eng. trans.: The Lie, 1966); La vita interiore, 1978 (Eng. trans: Time of Desecration, 1980); 1934, 1983; *short stories*: (and selections in Eng.); La bella vita, 1935; L'imbroglio, 1937; I sogni del pigro, 1940; L'amante infelice, 1943; L'epidemia, 1945; Racconti, 1952 (Eng. trans.: Bitter Honeymoon, and the Wayward Wife, 1959); Racconti romani, 1954 (Eng. trans.: Roman Tales, 1956); Nuovi racconti romani, 1959; L'automa, 1964; Una cosa è una cosa, 1966; Il Paradiso, 1970 (Eng. trans.: Paradise, 1971); Io e lui, 1971 (Eng. trans.: The Two of Us, 1971); Un'altra vita, 1973 (Eng. trans.: Lady Godiva and Other Stories, 1975); The Voice of the Sea, 1978; Erotic Tales, 1985; *essays*: L'uomo come fine e altri saggi, 1964 (Eng. trans.: Man as an End, 1966); Impegno Controvoglia, 1980; *plays*: Beatrice Cenci, 1955; Il mondo è quello che è, 1966; Il dio Kurt, 1967; La Vita è Gioco, 1970; *travel*: La rivoluzione culturale in Cina, 1967 (Eng. trans: The Red Book and The Great Wall, 1968); Which Tribe Do You Belong To?, 1974. *Address*: Lungotevere della Vittoria 1, 00195 Rome, Italy. *T*: 3603698.

MORAY, 20th Earl of, *cr* 1562; **Douglas John Moray Stuart**; Lord Abernethy and Strathearn, 1562; Lord Doune, 1581; Baron of St Colme, 1611; Baron Stuart (GB), 1796;

b 13 Feb. 1928; *e s* of 19th Earl of Moray and Mabel Helen Maud Wilson (*d* 1968); *S* father, 1974; *m* 1964, Lady Malvina Murray, *er d* of 7th Earl of Mansfield and Mansfield; one *s* one *d*. *Educ*: Trinity Coll., Cambridge (BA), FLAS 1958. *Heir*: *s* Lord Doune, *qv*. *Address*: Doune Park, Doune, Perthshire. *T*: Doune 333; Darnaway Castle, Forres, Moray, Scotland. *Club*: New (Edinburgh).

MORAY, ROSS AND CAITHNESS, Bishop of, since 1970; **Rt. Rev. George Minshull Sessford**; *b* Aintree, Lancs, 7 Nov. 1928; *o s* of Charles Walter Sessford and Eliza Annie (*née* Minshull); *m* 1952, Norah (*d* 1985), *y d* of David Henry Hughes and Ellen (*née* Whitely); three *d*. *Educ*: Warbreck Primary Sch.; Oulton High and Liverpool Collegiate Schs; St Andrews Univ. (MA). Curate, St Mary's Cathedral, Glasgow, 1953; Chaplain, Glasgow Univ., 1955; Priest-in-Charge, Cumbernauld New Town, 1958; Rector, Forres, Moray, 1966. *Recreations*: Lanchester motor cars, donkey breeding, sailing. *Address*: Spynie House, 96 Fairfield Road, Inverness, Scotland IV3 5LL. *T*: Inverness 231059.

MORAY, ROSS AND CAITHNESS, Dean of; see Mallin, Very Rev. S. A. T.

MORAY, Edward Bruce D.; see Dawson-Moray.

MORCOM, Rev. Canon Anthony John; *b* 24 July 1916; *s* of late Dr Alfred Farr Morcom and Sylvia Millicent Morcom (*née* Birchenough); *m* 1st, 1955, Pamela Cappel Bain (*d* 1963); 2nd, 1965, Richenda, *widow* of Frederick Williams. *Educ*: Repton; Clare Coll., Cambridge; Cuddesdon Coll. Curate: St Mary Magdalene, Paddington, 1939–42; St Mary the Virgin, Pimlico, 1942–47; Domestic Chaplain to the Bishop of London, 1947–55; Archdeacon of Middx, 1953–66; Vicar of St Cyprian's, Clarence Gate, 1955–66; Vicar of St Mary the Less, Cambridge, 1966–73; Rural Dean of Cambridge, 1971–73; Residentiary Canon, Ely Cathedral, 1974–84; Vice-Dean, 1981–84. *Recreation*: travel. *Address*: 33 Porson Road, Cambridge CB2 2ET. *T*: Cambridge 62352. *Clubs*: United Oxford & Cambridge University, MCC.

MORCOM, John Brian; a Social Security Commissioner, since 1981; *b* 31 May 1925; *s* of Albert John Morcom and Alice Maud Morcom (*née* Jones), Carmarthen; *m* 1st, 1958, Valerie Lostie de Kerhor Rivington (*d* 1960); one *s*; 2nd, 1965, Sheila Myfanwy Adams-Lewis (*d* 1986); one *d*. *Educ*: Queen Elizabeth Grammar Sch., Carmarthen; Balliol Coll., Oxford (State schol., 1943; MA). Bevin Ballottee, Oakdale Colliery, 1944; Medical Orderly, RAMC, Talgarth Mil. Mental Hosp. and BMH Suez, 1944–47. Called to the Bar, Inner Temple, 1952, Lincoln's Inn, 1955; Wales and Chester Circuit, 1954–81. *Publications*: Estate Duty Saving, 1959, 5th edn 1972; (jtly) Capital Transfer Tax, 1976, 2nd edn 1978. *Recreations*: Welsh genealogy, forestry. *Address*: Social Security Commission, 6 Grosvenor Gardens, SW1W 0DH. *Clubs*: Royal Commonwealth Society, London Welsh Association.

MORCOS-ASAAD, Prof. Fikry Naguib; Professor of Architecture, Department of Architecture and Building Science, University of Strathclyde, 1970–85; *b* 27 Sept. 1930; *s* of Naguib and Marie A. Morcos-Asaad; *m* 1958, Sarah Ann (*née* Gribben); three *s*. *Educ*: Cairo Univ. (BArch); Georgia Inst. of Techn. (MArch); MIT (SM); IIT (PhD). FRIAS. Lectr in Architecture, Fac. of Engrg, Cairo Univ., 1952–54 and 1958–63; Dir of Structural Studies, Sch. of Arch., Univ. of Liverpool, 1963–70; Design Critic and Vis. Prof. in Arch. Engrg, Calif State Polytechnic Univ., 1969, 1970 and 1973; Visiting Professor of Architecture: Assuit Univ., Egypt, 1980; Univ. of Jordan, Amman, 1985. Research into: culture and arch.; housing design in hot, dry climates; prefabricated multi-storey housing in developing countries. Comr, Royal Fine Art Commn for Scotland; formerly Mem. Educn Cttee, Architects Registration Council of UK; former Member Council: Glasgow Inst. of Architects; Royal Incorp. of Architects in Scotland; Mem. Council, Glasgow Coll. of Building and Printing. Mem., Rotary International. *Publications*: Circular Forms in Architecture, 1955; High Density Concretes for Radiation Shielding, 1956; Structural Parameters in Multi-Storey Buildings under Dynamic Loading, 1956; The Egyptian Village, 1956; Architectural Construction, vol. 1 1960, vol. 2 1961; Plastic Design in Steel, 1975; Large-span Structures, 1976; Brickwork: some pertinent points, 1978; Design and Building for a Tropical Environment, 1978; various papers on structural form in architecture. *Recreations*: renovation of antique clocks, gardening, reading, travelling. *Address*: Staneacre House, Townhead Street, Hamilton ML3 7BP. *T*: Hamilton 420644. *Clubs*: Burns, Hamilton Civic Society (Hamilton).

MORDA EVANS, Raymond John; see Evans.

MORDAUNT, Sir Richard (Nigel Charles), 14th Bt *cr* 1611; (does not use the title at present); *b* 12 May 1940; *s* of Lt-Col Sir Nigel John Mordaunt, 13th Bt, MBE, and Anne (*d* 1980), *d* of late Arthur F. Tritton; *S* father, 1979; *m* 1964, Myriam Atchia; one *s* one *d*. *Educ*: Wellington. *Heir*: *s* Kim John Mordaunt, *b* 11 June 1966.

MORDECAI, Sir John Stanley, Kt 1962; CMG 1956; formerly Secretary, Development Planning, University of the West Indies; *b* 21 Oct. 1903; *s* of Segismund T. and Marie A. Mordecai; *m* 1st, 1929, Pearl K. Redmond (*d* 1947); two *s* four *d*; 2nd, 1951, Phyllis M. Walcott; two *s*. *Educ*: Wolmer's Boys' High Sch., Jamaica; Syracuse Univ., New York, USA. MSc (Pub. Adm.). Entered public service as clerical asst in Treasury, Jamaica, 1920; Finance officer, 1942; asst treasurer, 1944; asst sec. in charge of local government secretariat, 1946; trade administrator and sec. trade control board, 1949; principal, seconded to Colonial Office, 1950; Executive Sec. Regional Economic Cttee of the West Indies, British Guiana and British Honduras, with headquarters in Barbados, 1952–56; Federal Sec., West Indies Federation, 1956–60 (Special work on preparatory arrangements for Federation, 1955–58); Dep. Gov.-Gen., WI Fedn, 1960–62; Gen. Manager, Jamaica Industrial Develt Corp., 1962–63. Fellow, Princeton Univ., NJ, 1964–66. Chairman: Jamaica Public Services Commn, 1962; Cttee of Inquiry into Sugar Ind., 1969. *Publication*: The West Indies, 1968. *Recreations*: horse racing, music. *Address*: 34 Mona Road, Kingston 6, Jamaica.

MORE, Sir Jasper, Kt 1979; JP, DL; *b* 31 July 1907; *s* of Thomas Jasper Mytton More and Lady Norah, *d* of 5th Marquess of Sligo; *m* 1944, Clare Mary Hope-Edwardes, Netley, Shropshire, *d* of Capt. Vincent Coldwell, 4th Indian Cavalry; no *c*. *Educ*: Eton (Schol.); King's Coll., Cambridge. Barrister, Lincoln's Inn, 1930, and Middle Temple, 1931; Harmsworth Law Schol., 1932; in practice, 1930–39. Served War of 1939–45; in Min. of Economic Warfare, MAP and Light Metals Control, 1939–42; commissioned as legal officer in Military Govt, 1943; with Allied Commission (Italy), 8th Army and 5th Army, 1943–45; Legal Adviser, Military Govt, Dodecanese, 1946. MP (C) Ludlow, 1960–79; An Asst Government Whip, Feb.-Oct. 1964; Asst Opposition Whip, 1964–70; Vice-Chamberlain, HM Household, 1970–71. JP Salop, 1950; DL Salop, 1955; CC Salop, 1958–70, 1973–85. *Publications*: The Land of Italy, 1949; The Mediterranean, 1956; A Tale of Two Houses, 1978; The Land of Egypt, 1980; (contrib.) Shell Guide to English Villages, 1980. *Recreations*: travel, landscape gardening. *Address*: Linley Hall, Bishop's Castle, Shropshire. *Clubs*: Travellers', Brooks's, Naval and Military.

MORE, Norman, FRICS; Consultant, Grimley and Son, Chartered Surveyors, Birmingham, London and Manchester, and others, since 1985; Member, West Midlands

Regional Board, Trustee Savings Bank Group, since 1984; *b* 20 Dec. 1921; *s* of Herbert and Anna More; *m* 1952, Kathleen Mary Chrystal; two *s* one *d*. *Educ:* Royal High Sch., Edinburgh; Edinburgh Univ. FRICS 1970 (ARICS 1951). Served in Royal Engineers, Middle East, N Africa, Italy, Greece and Germany, Major, 1941–48. Surveyor, Directorate of Lands and Accommodation, Min. of Works, 1948–58; Sen. Valuer, City Assessor's Office, Glasgow Corporation, 1958–63; Valuation and Estates Officer, East Kilbride Development Corp., 1963–65; Redditch Development Corporation: Chief Estates Officer, 1965–79; Man. Dir, 1979–85. Chairman, West Midlands Br., Royal Instn of Chartered Surveyors, 1974–75. *Publications:* press articles and contribs to jls. *Recreations:* music, sport. *Address:* Mead Cottage, 192 Loxley Road, Stratford-upon-Avon, Warwickshire CV37 7DU. *T:* Stratford-upon-Avon 293763. *Club:* East India, Devonshire, Sports and Public Schools.

MORE-MOLYNEUX, James Robert, OBE 1983; Vice Lord Lieutenant of Surrey, since 1983; Chairman, Loseley Co-Partnership & Loseley Park Farms; *b* 17 June 1920; *s* of Brig. Gen. Francis Cecil More-Molyneux-Longbourne, CMG, DSO and Gwendoline Carew More-Molyneux; *m* 1948, Susan Bellinger; one *s*. *Educ:* Eton; Trinity Hall, Cambridge. War service in 4/7th Royal Dragoon Guards and 14th PWO The Scinde Horse, 1941–46; Founder Chm., Guildway Ltd, 1947–85 (introduced first manufactured timber frame houses with brick cladding to UK, 1960); founded Loseley Co-Partnership, 1950; opened Loseley House to public, 1950–; founded Loseley Dairy Products, 1967; part-time Dir, Seeboard, 1975–84. Founder: Loseley & Guildway Charitable Trust, 1973; Loseley Christian Trust, 1983. Mem. Exec. Cttee, Industrial Participation Assoc., 1952–77; President: Surrey Assoc. of Youth Clubs; Friends of Brookwood Hosp.; Friends of Milford Hosp. High Sheriff of Surrey, 1974; DL Surrey 1976. Bledisloe Gold Medal for Landowners, RASE, 1984. *Recreations:* countryside, riding, Christian Healing Ministry. *Address:* Loseley Park, Guildford, Surrey GU3 1HS. *T:* Guildford 66090. *Club:* Farmers'.

MOREAU, Jeanne; Chevalier, Ordre National du Mérite, 1970; Chevalier de la Légion d'Honneur, 1975; actress; *b* 23 Jan. 1928; *d* of Anatole-Désiré Moreau and Kathleen Moreau (*née* Buckley); *m* 1949, Jean-Louis Richard (marr. diss.); one *s*; *m* 1977, William Friedkin (marr. diss.). *Educ:* Collège Edgar-Quinet; Conservatoire national d'art dramatique. Comédie Française, 1948–52; Théâtre National Populaire, 1953. Over 60 films including: Les amants, 1958; Les liaisons dangereuses, 1959; Le dialogue des Carmelites, 1959; Moderato cantabile, 1960; Jules et Jim, 1961; La Baie des Anges, 1962; Journal d'une femme de chambre, 1963; Viva Maria, 1965; Mademoiselle, 1965; The Sailor from Gibraltar, 1965; The Immortal Story, 1966; Great Catherine, 1967; The Bride wore Black, 1967; Monte Walsh, 1969; Chère Louise, 1971; Nathalie Granger, 1972; La Race des Seigneurs, 1974; Mr Klein, 1976; Lumière (also Dir), 1976; Le Petit Théâtre de Jean Renoir, 1976; Madame Rosa, 1978; L'Intoxe, 1980; Querelle, La Truite, 1982. Officier des Arts et des Lettres (Chevalier, 1966). *Recreation:* reading. *Address:* c/o Artmédia, 10 avenue George V, 75008 Paris, France.

MORELAND, Robert John; company director; *b* 21 Aug. 1941; *s* of Samuel John Moreland and late Norah Mary, (Molly) (*née* Haines). *Educ:* Glasgow Acad.; Dean Close Sch., Cheltenham; Univ. of Nottingham (BA Econs); Inst. of World Affairs, Conn, and Warwick Univ. (postgrad. work). Civil Servant, Govt of NS, Canada, 1966–67, Govt of NB, 1967–72; Sen. Economist, W Central Scotland Planning Study, 1972–74; Management Consultant, Touche Ross and Co., London, 1974–; Director: Drucestyle Ltd, 1985–; Five Valleys Radio, 1982–; Consultant: Warmington Gp, 1984–; Westminster and City Conferences Ltd, 1985–. Contested (C) Pontypool, Oct. 1974; Mem. (C) Staffs, European Parlt, 1979–84, contested same seat, 1984; Chm., Eur. Cttee, Bow Gp, 1977–78; Vice-Chm., Conservative Gp for Europe. *Publications:* contrib. to Crossbow. *Recreations:* tennis, skiing, watching cricket, wine and beer drinking. *Address:* 7 Vauxhall Walk, SE11 5JT. *T:* 01–582 2613. *Clubs:* Carlton, Royal Automobile; Conservative (Burslem); Conservative (Cannock); Conservative (Burntwood).

MORELL, Joan, (Mrs André Morell); *see* Greenwood, Joan.

MORETON, family name of **Earl of Ducie.**

MORETON, Lord; David Leslie Moreton; *b* 20 Sept. 1951; *s* and *heir* of 6th Earl of Ducie, *qv*; *m* 1975, Helen, *er d* of M. L. Duchesne; one *s* one *d*. *Educ:* Cheltenham College; Wye Coll., London Univ. (BSc 1973). *Heir:* *s* Hon. James Berkeley Moreton, *b* 6 May 1981. *Address:* Talbots End Farm, Cromhall, Glos.

MORETON, Sir John (Oscar), KCMG 1978 (CMG 1966); KCVO 1976; MC 1944; HM Diplomatic Service, retired; Director, Wates Foundation, since 1978; Gentleman Usher of the Blue Rod, Order of St Michael and St George, since 1979; *b* 28 Dec. 1917; *s* of Rev. C. O. Moreton; *m* 1945, Margaret Katherine, *d* of late Sir John Fryer, KBE, FRS; three *d*. *Educ:* St Edward's Sch., Oxford; Trinity Coll., Oxford (MA). War Service with 99th (Royal Bucks Yeomanry) Field Regt RA, 1939–46: France, Belgium, 1940; India, Burma, 1942–45. Colonial Office, 1946; Private Sec. to Perm. Under-Sec. of State, 1949–50; seconded to Govt of Kenya, 1953–55; Private Sec. to Sec. of State for Colonies (Rt Hon. Alan Lennox-Boyd), 1955–59; transf. to CRO, 1960; Counsellor, British High Commn, Lagos, 1961–64; IDC 1965; Asst Under-Sec. of State, CRO, 1965–66, CO 1966–68, FCO 1968–69; Ambassador to Vietnam, 1969–71; High Comr, Malta, 1972–74; Dep. Perm. Representative, with personal rank of Ambassador, UK Mission to UN, NY, 1974–75; HM Minister, British Embassy, Washington, 1975–77. Governor, St Edward's Sch., Oxford, 1980–. Hon. DL Hanover Coll., Indiana, 1976. *Recreations:* tennis; formerly athletics (Oxford Blue and International, 880 yds, 1939). *Address:* Woodside House, Woodside Road, Cobham, Surrey. *Club:* Army and Navy.

MOREY, Rev. Dom Adrian, MA, DPhil, LittD; FRHistS; Superior, Downside House of Studies, Cambridge; *b* 10 April 1904; *s* of late John Morey and Charlotte Helen Morey (*née* Nelson). *Educ:* Latymer Upper Sch.; Christ's Coll., Cambridge (Schol.); Univ. of Munich. 1st cl. hons Hist. Tripos Pts I and II, Cambridge. Housemaster, Downside Sch., 1934; Bursar, Downside Abbey and Sch., 1946–50; Headmaster, Oratory Sch., Reading, 1953–67; Rector, St Wulstan's, Little Malvern, Worcs, 1967–69. *Publications:* Bartholomew of Exeter, 1937; (with Prof. C. N. Brooke) Gilbert Foliot and His Letters, 1965; The Letters and Charters of Gilbert Foliot, 1967; The Catholic Subjects of Elizabeth I, 1977; David Knowles: a memoir, 1979; articles in English Hist. Review, Jl Eccles. History, Cambridge Hist. Jl. *Address:* Benet House, Mount Pleasant, Cambridge. *T:* Cambridge 354637.

MORFEE, Air Vice-Marshal Arthur Laurence, CD; CB 1946; CBE 1943; retired; *b* 27 May 1897; *s* of George Thomas Morfee; *m* Estelle Lillian, *d* of William Edward Hurd of South Carolina, USA; one *s* one *d*. *Educ:* Finchley County Sch. Canadian Army from 1915; served France and Belgium, 19th Can. Inf. (wounded); joined RAF 1918; Air Board (Civil Service), 1921–24; appointed RCAF 1924; psa Andover, Eng., 1933; Air Vice-Marshal, 1945; retd 1949. Dir of Air Cadet League; Vice-Chm., Nova Scotia Div., Corps of Commissionaires. US Legion of Merit (Comdr), 1949. *Address:* 380 St George Street, Annapolis Royal, NS, Canada.

MORGAN; *see* Elystan-Morgan.

MORGAN; *see* Vaughan-Morgan.

MORGAN, Ven. Alan Wyndham; Archdeacon of Coventry since 1983; *b* 22 June 1940; *s* of A. W. Morgan; *m* 1965, Margaret Patricia, *d* of W. O. Williams; one *s* one *d*. *Educ:* Boys' Grammar School, Gowerton; St David's Coll., Lampeter (BA 1962); St Michael's Coll., Llandaff. Deacon 1964, priest 1965; Assistant Curate: Llangyfelach with Morriston, 1964–69; Cockett, 1969–72; St Mark with St Barnabas, Coventry, 1972–73; Team Vicar, St Barnabas, Coventry East, 1973–77; Bishop's Officer for Social Responsibility, Diocese of Coventry, 1978–83. Mem., Gen. Synod, 1980–; Chm. House of Clergy, Coventry Diocesan Synod. Vice Chairman: Nat. Council for Voluntary Organisations; Coventry Health Authority, 1983–; Chairman: Coventry Drugs Adv. Cttee, 1983–; Myton Hamlet Hospice Trustees, 1985–. *Address:* c/o Church House, Palmerston Road, Earlsdon, Coventry CV5 6FJ; Corley Rectory, Corley, Coventry, W Midlands CV7 8AA.

MORGAN, Anthony Hugh; HM Diplomatic Service; Counsellor, Vienna, since 1982; *b* 27 March 1931; *s* of late Cyril Egbert Morgan and Muriel Dorothea (*née* Nash); *m* 1957, Cicely Alice Voysey; two *s* one *d*. *Educ:* King's Norton Grammar Sch.; Birmingham Univ. (BA 1952). Served HM Forces (RAF Educn Br.), 1952–55. Joined HM Foreign (later Diplomatic) Service, 1956; Cairo, then Cyprus, 1956; Khartoum, 1957; FO, 1959; Saigon, 1962; Second Sec., 1963; UK Delegn to NATO, 1965; First Sec., 1968; FCO, 1969; First Sec. and Head of Chancery, Calcutta, 1973; FCO, 1976; Dep. Head of Inf. Policy Dept, 1977; Counsellor (Information), Brussels, 1977–79; Counsellor (Commercial), Copenhagen, 1979–82. Comdr, Order of Dannebrog, Denmark, 1979. *Recreations:* listening to music, looking at pictures. *Address:* c/o Foreign and Commonwealth Office, SW1. *Club:* Royal Air Force.

MORGAN, Arthur William Crawford, (Tony Morgan); Executive Chairman, Wistech PLC, since 1984; *b* 24 Aug. 1931; *s* of Arthur James and Violet Morgan; *m* 1955, Valerie Anne Williams; three *s*. *Educ:* Hereford High Sch.; Westcliff High Sch. Governor, BBC, 1972–77. Sailed Olympic Games, Tokyo; Silver Medal, Flying Dutchman, 1964; Jt Yachtsman of the Year, 1965; Member: British Olympic Yachting Appeal, 1970; Royal Yachting Assoc. Council, 1968–72. FRSA. *Publications:* various technical papers. *Recreations:* squash, skiing, sailing. *Address:* Bovingdon, Marlow Common, Bucks SL7 2QR. *T:* Marlow 75983.

MORGAN, Rear-Adm. Brinley John, CB 1972; *b* 3 April 1916; *s* of Thomas Edward Morgan and Mary Morgan (*née* Parkhouse); *m* 1945, Margaret Mary Whittles; three *s*. *Educ:* Abersychan Grammar Sch.; University Coll., Cardiff (BSc 1937). Entered Royal Navy as Instr Lt, 1939. Served War of 1939–45: Cruisers Emerald and Newcastle, 1939–41; Aircraft Carrier Formidable, 1941–43; Naval Weather Service (Admty Forecast Section), 1943–45. Staff of C-in-C Medit., 1945–48; HQ, Naval Weather Service, 1948–50; Staff of Flag Officer Trg Sqdn in HM Ships Vanguard, Indefatigable and Implacable, 1950–52; Instr Comdr, 1951; Lectr, RN Coll., Greenwich, 1952–54; Headmaster, RN Schools, Malta, 1954–59; Instr Captain, 1960; Staff of Dir, Naval Educn Service, 1959–61 and 1963–64; Sen. Officers' War Course, 1961; HMS Ganges, 1961–63; Dean, RN Engineering Coll., Manadon, 1964–69; Instr Rear-Adm., 1970; Dir, Naval Educn Service, 1970–75, retired. Dir, Admin, SSRC, 1975–80. *Address:* 11 Selwyn House, Manor Fields, Putney Hill, SW15. *T:* 01–789 3269.

MORGAN, Rev. Chandos Clifford Hastings Mansel, CB 1973; MA; Rector, St Margaret Lothbury, City of London, since 1983; *b* 12 Aug. 1920; *s* of Llewelyn Morgan, Anglesey; *m* 1946, Dorothy Mary (*née* Oliver); one *s*. *Educ:* Stowe; Jesus Coll., Cambridge (MA); Ridley Hall, Cambridge. Curate of Holy Trinity, Tunbridge Wells, 1944–51; staff of Children's Special Service Mission, 1947–51; Chaplain, RN, 1951; served in HM Ships: Pembroke, 1951; Vengeance and Ceylon, 1952; Drake, 1954; Theseus, 1956; Ocean, 1957; Caledonia, 1958; Adamant, 1960; Jufair, 1961; Heron, 1963; Ark Royal, 1965; Collingwood, 1967; Royal Arthur, 1969; Chaplain of the Fleet and Archdeacon of the Royal Navy, 1972–75; QHC 1972–75. Chaplain, Dean Close Sch., Cheltenham, 1976–83. *Recreations:* riding, shooting, sailing, gardening, etc. *Address:* Westwood Farmhouse, West Lydford, Somerton, Somerset. *T:* Wheathill 301; 603 Gilbert House, Barbican, EC2Y 8BD. *T:* 01–588 3343.

MORGAN, Clifford Isaac, CVO 1986; OBE 1977; Head of Outside Broadcasts Group, BBC Television, since 1975; *b* 7 April 1930; *m* 1955, Nuala Martin; one *s* one *d*. *Educ:* Tonyrefail Grammar School, South Wales. Played International Rugby Union for Wales, British Lions and Barbarians. Joined BBC, 1958, as Sports Organiser, Wales; Editor, Sportsview and Grandstand, 1961–64; Producer, This Week, 1964–66; freelance writer and broadcaster, 1966–72; Editor, Sport Radio, 1972–74; Head of Outside Broadcasts, Radio, 1974–75. Pres., London Glamorgan Soc., 1974–. Chm., Saints and Sinners Club, 1984–85. *Recreation:* music. *Address:* BBC Television, W14.

MORGAN, Cyril Dion, OBE 1970; TD 1945; FCIS; Secretary, Institution of Structural Engineers, 1961–82; *b* 30 Aug. 1917; *y s* of late Robert Dymant Morgan and of Nell (*née* Barrett); *m* 1948, Anthea Grace Brown; two *d*. *Educ:* Sloane Sch., Chelsea; City of London Coll. Served War, North Africa, Italy, 1939–46. Secretary: Inst. of Road Transport Engineers, 1948–53; British Road Fedn, 1953–61. Hon. Fellow, IStructE, 1983. FRSA. *Publications:* articles/reports in Proc. Instn of Structural Engrs. *Recreation:* gardening. *Address:* 8 Wyatts Close, Chorleywood, Herts WD3 5TF. *T:* Chorleywood 5202.

MORGAN, (David) Dudley; retired from Theodore Goddard & Co., Solicitors, 1983; *b* 23 Oct. 1914; *y s* of Thomas Dudley Morgan; *m* 1948, Margaret Helene, *o d* of late David MacNaughton Duncan, Loanhead, Midlothian; two *d*. *Educ:* Swansea Grammar Sch.; Jesus Coll., Cambridge (MA, LLB). War Service with RAF in Intell. Br., UK, 1940–42 and Legal Br., India, 1942–46; Wing Comdr 1945. Admitted Solicitor, 1939, with Theodore Goddard & Co.; Partner 1948; Senior Partner, 1974–80; Consultant, 1980–83. Director: Crown House PLC; Pritchard Services Group PLC, and other companies. An Underwriting Member of Lloyd's. *Recreation:* gardening. *Address:* St Leonard's House, St Leonard's Road, Nazeing, Waltham Abbey, Essex EN9 2HG. *T:* Nazeing 2124. *Club:* Carlton.

MORGAN, David Gethin; County Treasurer, Avon County Council, since 1973; *b* 30 June 1929; *s* of Edgar and Ethel Morgan; *m* 1955, Marion Brook. *Educ:* Jesus Coll., Oxford (MA Hons English). IPFA, FInstAM(Dip). Graduate Accountancy Asst, Staffordshire CC, 1952–58; Computer Systems Officer, Sen. O&M Officer, Cheshire CC, 1958–62; County Management Services Officer, Durham CC, 1962–65; Leicestershire CC: Asst County Treasurer, 1965–68; Dep. County Treasurer, 1968–73. *Publication:* Vol. XV Financial Information Service (IPFA). *Recreations:* local history, church architecture, tai chi. *Address:* 6 Wyecliffe Road, Henleaze, Bristol, Avon BS9 4NH. *T:* Bristol 629640.

MORGAN, David Glyn; His Honour Judge Glyn Morgan; a Circuit Judge, since 1984; *b* 31 March 1933; *s* of late Dr Richard Glyn Morgan, MC, and Nancy Morgan; *m* 1959, Ailsa Murray Strang; three *d*. *Educ:* Mill Hill Sch.; Merton Coll., Oxford (MA). Called to Bar, Middle Temple, 1958; practised Oxford Circuit, 1958–70; Wales and Chester Circuit, 1970–84. A Recorder of the Crown Court, 1974–84. 2nd Lieut, The

Queen's Bays, 1955; Dep. Col. 1st The Queen's Dragoon Guards, 1976. *Recreations:* riding, fishing, Rugby football, gardening. *Address:* 2 Harcourt Buildings, Temple, EC4Y 9DB. *T:* 01–353 8549; 30 Park Place, Cardiff. *T:* Cardiff 41121. *Clubs:* Cavalry and Guards; Cardiff and County (Cardiff); Newport (Mon) Constitutional.

MORGAN, Sir David John H.; *see* Hughes-Morgan.

MORGAN, Dennis, OBE 1972; FEng 1983; Chief Executive, Dowty Group PLC, 1983–86; *b* 25 Oct. 1928; *s* of Thomas Wells and Ellen Morgan; *m* 1953, Hazel Wood; two *s* one *d. Educ:* Durham Univ. (BSc Hons). FIMinE. Asst Undermanager, Linton Colliery, NCB, 1953–54; Undermanager 1954–56, Manager 1956–58, Montague Colliery, NCB; Manager, Weetslade Colliery, NCB, 1958–60; Dowty Mining: Regional Mining Engr, 1960–64; Sen. Mining Engr, 1964–65; Sales Manager, 1965–67; Export Dir, 1967–70; Dep. Man. Dir, 1970–72; Dowty Meco: Man. Dir Designate, 1972–73; Man. Dir, 1973–76; Dowty Group: Div. Man. Dir, Mining Div., 1976–83; Board Mem., 1977; Dep. Chief Exec. (Chief Exec. Designate), 1981. *Recreation:* sailing.

MORGAN, Rev. Dewi, (David Lewis); Rector, St Bride's Church, Fleet Street, EC4, 1962–84; a Prebendary of St Paul's Cathedral, 1976–84, now Prebendary Emeritus; *b* 5 Feb. 1916; *s* of David and Anne Morgan; *m* 1942, Doris, *d* of Samuel and Ann Povey; two *d. Educ:* Lewis Sch., Pengam; University Coll. Cardiff (BA); St Michael's Coll., Llandaff. Curate: St Andrew's, Cardiff, 1939–43; Aberdare, 1943–46; Aberavon, 1946–50. Soc. for the Propagation of the Gospel: Press Officer, 1950–52, Editorial and Press Sec., 1952–62; Editor, St Martin's Review, 1953–55; Associate Editor: Church Illustrated, 1955–67; Anglican World, 1960–67; Priest-in-charge, St Dunstan-in-the-West, 1978–80. Hon. FIPR 1984. Publicity Club of London Cup for services to advertising, 1984. Freeman of City of London, 1963. *Publications:* Expanding Frontiers, 1957; The Bishops Come to Lambeth, 1957; Lambeth Speaks, 1958; The Undying Fire, 1959; 1662 And All That, 1961; But God Comes First, 1962; Agenda for Anglicans, 1963; Seeds of Peace, 1965; Arising From the Psalms, 1965; God and Sons, 1967. Edited: They Became Anglicans, 1959; They Became Christians, 1966; The Church in Transition, 1970; The Phoenix of Fleet Street, 1973. *Recreation:* sleeping. *Address:* 217 Rosendale Road, West Dulwich, SE21 8LW. *T:* 01–670 1308. *Club:* Athenæum.

MORGAN, Douglas; IPFA; County Treasurer, Lancashire County Council, since 1985; *b* 5 June 1936; *s* of late Douglas Morgan and of Margaret Gardner Morgan; *m* 1960, Julia (*née* Bywater); two *s. Educ:* High Pavement Grammar Sch., Nottingham. IPFA 1963 (4th place in final exam. and G. A. Johnston (Dundee) Prize). Nat. Service, RAF, 1954–56. Nottingham CBC, 1952–61; Herefordshire CC, 1961–64; Berkshire CC, 1964–67; Asst Co. Treas., W Suffolk CC, 1967–70; Asst, later Dep., Co. Treas., Lindsey CC, 1970–73; Dep. Co. Treas., Lancashire CC, 1973–85. Chm., NW & N Wales Region, CIPFA, 1985–86. Treas., Lancs Cttee, Royal Jubilee & Prince's Trust, 1985–; Hon. Treas., Lancs Playing Fields Assoc., 1985–. *Publications:* articles for Public Finance & Accountancy and other local govt jls. *Recreations:* golf, jazz, playing "gypsy" in a motor caravan. *Address:* 8 Croyde Road, St Annes-on-Sea, Lancs FY8 1EX. *T:* (home) St Annes 725808; (office) Preston 264701. *Club:* Fairhaven Golf.

MORGAN, Dudley; *see* Morgan, David D.

MORGAN, Prof. Edwin (George), OBE 1982; Titular Professor of English, University of Glasgow, 1975–80, now Emeritus; *b* 27 April 1920; *s* of Stanley Lawrence Morgan and Margaret McKillop Arnott. *Educ:* Rutherglen Academy; High Sch. of Glasgow; Univ. of Glasgow. MA 1st Cl. Hons, Eng. Lang. and Lit., 1947. Served War, RAMC, 1940–46. University of Glasgow: Asst, 1947, Lectr, 1950, Sen. Lectr, 1965, Reader, 1971, in English. Cholmondeley Award for Poets, 1968; Hungarian PEN Meml Medal, 1972; Scottish Arts Council Book Awards, 1968, 1973, 1975, 1977, 1978, 1983 and 1985; Soros Translation Award, NY, 1985. Visual/concrete poems in many internat. exhibns, 1965–. Opera librettos (unpublished): The Charcoal-Burner, 1969; Valentine, 1976; Columba, 1976; Spell, 1979. Hon. DLitt. Loughborough, 1981. *Publications: poetry:* The Vision of Cathkin Braes, 1952; Beowulf, 1952; The Cape of Good Hope, 1955; Poems from Eugenio Montale, 1959; Sovpoems, 1961; (ed) Collins Albatross Book of Longer Poems, 1963; Starryveldt, 1965; Emergent Poems, 1967; Gnomes, 1968; The Second Life, 1968; Proverbfolder, 1969; Penguin Modern Poets 15, 1969; Twelve Songs, 1970; The Horseman's Word, 1970; (co-ed) Scottish Poetry 1–6, 1966–72; Glasgow Sonnets, 1972; Wi the Haill Voice, 1972; Instamatic Poems, 1972; The Whittrick, 1973; From Glasgow to Saturn, 1973; Fifty Renascence Love-Poems, 1975; Rites of Passage, 1976; The New Divan, 1977; Colour Poems, 1978; Platen: selected poems, 1978; Star Gate, 1979; (ed) Scottish Satirical Verse, 1980; Poems of Thirty Years, 1982; Grafts/Takes, 1983; Master Peter Pathelin, 1983; Sonnets From Scotland, 1984; Selected Poems, 1985; From the Video Box, 1986; *prose:* Essays, 1974; East European Poets, 1976; Hugh MacDiarmid, 1976. *Recreations:* photography, scrapbooks, walking in cities. *Address:* 19 Whittingehame Court, Glasgow G12 0BG. *T:* 041–339 6260.

MORGAN, Edwin John; Director, Civil Service Selection Board, 1981–87; *b* 10 Jan. 1927; *s* of Thomas Grosvenor Morgan and Florence (*née* Binmore); *m* 1954, Joyce Beryl, *o d* of Reginald and Gladys Ashurst, Bebington, Wirral; two *s* one *d. Educ:* Dauntsey's Sch.; St Edmund Hall, Oxford (Sen. Scholar, BA 1st Cl. Hons 1951). Served Army, Intell. Corps, Palestine and Cyprus, 1944–48. Lecteur d'anglais, Ecole normale supérieure, Paris, 1952; Asst, Dept of French Studies, Glasgow Univ., 1953; Asst Principal, Air Min., 1957, Principal, 1960; MoD, 1965; Registrar, RMCS, 1968; Asst Sec., 1970; CSD, 1971; CS Commn, 1975; Under Sec., 1980; CS Comr, 1980–85. FIPM 1985. *Recreations:* reading, walking, music, swimming, domesticity. *Address:* c/o Civil Service Commission, Kirkland House, 24 Whitehall, SW1A 2ED. *T:* 01–210 6695. *Club:* Civil Service.

MORGAN, Ellis, CMG 1961; HM Diplomatic Service, retired; *b* 26 Dec. 1916; *s* of late Ben Morgan and of Mary Morgan, The Grove, Three Crosses, Gower, S Wales; *m* 1st, 1948, Molly Darby (marr. diss.); three *d*; 2nd, 1975, Mary, *d* of late Slade Baker Stallard-Penoyre; one *s* twin *d* (one decd). *Educ:* Swansea Grammar Sch. (Bishop Gore Sch.). Dep. Librarian, County Borough of Swansea, 1937–39. Commissioned Royal Artillery, 1941; served War of 1939–45, in India, Burma, Malaya, 1943–47. Entered Foreign (subseq. Diplomatic) Service, 1948; 3rd Sec., 1948–50, 2nd Sec., 1951–53, subseq. 1st Sec., British Embassy, Rangoon; 1st Sec., British Embassy, Bangkok, 1954–55; 1st Sec., Office of Commissioner-Gen., Singapore, 1957–60; Student at Imperial Defence Coll., 1961; Counsellor: UK High Commission, New Delhi, 1964; FO, later FCO, 1966–73; Political and Economic Adviser, Commercial Union Assurance, 1973–79. *Club:* Farmers'.

MORGAN, Sir Ernest (Dunstan), ORSL; KBE 1971 (OBE 1951; MBE 1940); DCL; JP; *b* 17 Nov. 1896; *s* of Thomas William Morgan and Susan Barnett; *m* 1st, 1918, Elizabeth Mary Agnes Collier; one *d*; 2nd, 1972, Monica Fredericka Davies; one *s* three *d. Educ:* Zion Day School, Freetown; Methodist Boys' High School, Freetown. Government Dispenser, 1914–20; Druggist, 1917–. MHR Sierra Leone, 1956–61; Member: Freetown City Council, 1938–44; Fourah Bay Coll. Council, 1950–54; Chairman: Blind Welfare Soc., 1946–52; Public Service Commn, 1948–52. JP Sierra Leone, 1952. *Recreation:*

tennis. *Address:* 15 Syke Street, Freetown, Sierra Leone. *T:* Freetown 23155 and 22366. *Club:* Freetown Dinner.

MORGAN, (Frank) Leslie, MBE 1973; Chairman, Morgan Bros (Mid Wales) Ltd, since 1959; Chairman, Development Board for Rural Wales (Mid Wales Development), since 1981; *b* 7 Nov. 1926; *s* of Edward Arthur Morgan and Beatrice Morgan; *m* 1962, Victoria Stoker (*née* Jeffery); one *s* two *d. Educ:* Llanfair Primary Sch.; Llanfair Grammar Sch.; University College of Wales (BA Econ Hons). Post graduate trainee and parts executive in motor industry, 1950–56. Chairman and President, Montgomery Conservative Assoc., 1964–81; Member, Welsh Council, 1970–79; Dep. Chm., Mid Wales New Town Development Corp., 1973–77; Director: Develt Corp. for Wales, 1981–83; Wales Adv. Bd, Abbey National Bldg Soc., 1982–; Member: Development Bd for Rural Wales, 1977–81; Welsh Development Agency, 1981–; Wales Tourist Bd, 1982–; Infrastructure Cttee, BTA, 1982–; Design Council Welsh Cttee, 1981–85. Pres., Montgomeryshire Agricl Soc., 1986. *Recreations:* reading, travel, jogging, swimming, cycling. *Address:* Wentworth House, Llangyniew, Welshpool, Powys SY21 9EL. *T:* Llanfair-Caereinion 810462.

MORGAN, Col Frank Stanley, CBE 1940; ERD 1954; DL; JP; *b* 10 Jan. 1893; *s* of F. A. Morgan, Commissioner Imperial Chinese Customs; *m* 1918, Gladys Joan (*d* 1953), *d* of Lt-Col H. M. Warde, CBE, DL Kent; no *c*; *m* 1956, Minnie Helen Pine, MBE, TD, DL, Lt-Col WRAC, The Manor House, Great Barrow, Cheshire. *Educ:* Marlborough; Christ Church, Oxford. Served European War, 1914–18; public work in Wales; Territorial and Reserve Service, 1919–39; Air Formation Signals, France, North Africa, Italy, Middle East, 1939–45; DL, Glamorgan, 1946; JP 1951; Hon. Col 50 and 81 AF Signal Regts, 1952–60. *Address:* Herbert's Lodge, Bishopston, Swansea. *T:* Bishopston 4222.

MORGAN, Geoffrey Thomas; Under Secretary, Cabinet Office (Management and Personnel Office), Director of Public Appointments Unit, since 1985; *b* 12 April 1931; *s* of late Thomas Evan Morgan and Nora (*née* Flynn); *m* 1960, Heather, *d* of late William Henry Trick and of Margery Murrell Wells; two *d. Educ:* Roundhay Sch. National Service, Royal Signals, 1950–52; joined Civil Service, 1952; served in Mins of Supply and Aviation, 1952–65; HM Treasury, 1965–68 and 1981–83; CSD, 1968–81; seconded to Arthur Guinness Son & Co., 1970–72; Adviser to World Bank in Washington, 1977–78; Cabinet Office (MPO), 1983–. *Recreation:* planting mulberry trees for posterity and the silkworm. *Address:* 29 The Green, Twickenham, Mddx TW2 5TU. *T:* 01–894 3858.

MORGAN, George Lewis Bush; Chief Registrar, Bank of England, 1978–83; *b* 1 Sept. 1925; *s* of late William James Charles Morgan and Eva Averill Morgan (*née* Bush); *m* 1949, Mary Rose (*née* Vine); three *s. Educ:* Cranbr Sch., Kent. Captain, Royal Sussex Regt, 1943–47. Entered Bank of England, 1947; Asst Chief Accountant, 1966; Asst Sec., 1969; Dep. Sec., 1973. *Recreations:* tennis, golf, gardening. *Address:* Hill Top House, Five Ashes, Mayfield, East Sussex TN20 6HT.

MORGAN, Geraint; *see* Morgan, W. G. O.

MORGAN, Graham, CMG 1954; FICE; Chartered Civil Engineer; *b* 12 July 1903; *m* 1931, Alice Jane Morgan; three *d. Educ:* King Henry VIII Grammar Sch., Abergavenny; University Coll., Cardiff. BSc Civil Engineering, Wales, 1923; Asst Engineer: Newport, Mon., 1924; Devon CC, 1924; Federated Malay States, 1926; Sen. Exec. Engineer, Malayan Public Works Service, 1941; State Engineer, Johore, 1948; Dir of Public Works, Tanganyika, 1950–Sept. 1954, retired. FICE (Mem. of Council, 1953–55). *Address:* 2 Cooper Place, Headington Quarry, Oxford.

MORGAN, Guy, FRIBA; AIStructE; FRSA; BA; Senior Partner, in architectural practice; *b* 14 June 1902; *s* of late Francis Morgan and Miriam Hanley; *m* 1937, Violet Guy (*d* 1986); one *d* (one *s* decd). *Educ:* Mill Hill; Cambridge; University Coll., London. Andrew Taylor Prizeman, 1923. Lecturer and Year Master, Architectural Assoc., 1931–36. In practice, 1927–; principal works include: large blocks of flats and offices in London and Provinces; aircraft factories and air bases; town planning schemes and housing in England and abroad; agricultural buildings and country houses; ecclesiastical and hospital works; film studios; racing and sports stadia. Past Joint Master, Cowdray Foxhounds. Past Master of Worshipful Company of Woolmen. *Recreations:* foxhunting, sailing, travel; music. *Address:* Lower House Farm, Fernhurst, Haslemere, Surrey. *T:* Haslemere 53022; 12A Eaton Square, SW1. *T:* 01–235 5101. *Club:* Royal Thames Yacht.

MORGAN, Gwenda, RE 1961; Wood Engraver; *b* 1 Feb. 1908; *d* of late William David Morgan, JP, and late Mary Morgan. *Educ:* Brighton and Hove High Sch. Studied Art at Goldsmiths' Coll. Sch. of Art, and at Grosvenor Sch. of Modern Art under Iain Macnab. Women's Land Army, 1939–46. Exhibited in London, provincial and foreign exhibitions. Work represented in Victoria and Albert Museum, Brighton Art Gallery, Herefordshire Museum and Ashmolean Museum, Oxford. *Publication:* The Wood Engravings of Gwenda Morgan, 1985. *Address:* Ridge House, Petworth, West Sussex.

MORGAN, Gwyn; *see* Morgan, J. G.

MORGAN, Prof. Henry Gemmell; Professor of Pathological Biochemistry, University of Glasgow, since 1965; *b* 25 Dec. 1922; *s* of John McIntosh Morgan, MC, MD, FRCPE, and Florence Ballantyne; *m* 1949, Margaret Duncan, BSc, MB, ChB; one *d. Educ:* Dundee High Sch.; Merchiston Castle Sch., Edinburgh; Univ. of St Andrews at University Coll., Dundee. BSc 1943; MB, ChB (distinction), 1946; FRCPE 1962; FRCPGlas 1968; FRCPath 1970; FRSE 1971. Hon. Consultant, Royal Infirmary, Glasgow, 1966–. Pres., Assoc. of Clinical Biochemists (UK), 1985– (Chm., 1982–85). Ext. Examnr, Clinical Biochemistry, Univ. of Dublin; Examnr in primary FRCS, RCPGlas. Chm., Scottish Br., Nutrition Soc., 1967–68. Adviser to Greater Glasgow Health Ed, SHHD. *Publications:* chapters; papers in medical jls. *Recreations:* golf, foreign travel, history. *Address:* Royal Infirmary, Glasgow G4 0SF; Firwood House, 8 Eaglesham Road, Newton Mearns, Glasgow. *T:* 041–639 4404. *Club:* Athenæum.

MORGAN, Hugh Travers, CMG 1966; HM Diplomatic Service, retired; Ambassador to Austria, 1976–79; *b* 3 Aug. 1919; *s* of Dr Montagu Travers Morgan, CMG, MC; *m* 1959, Alexandra Belinoff; two *s* one *d. Educ:* Winchester Coll.; Magdalene Coll., Cambridge. RAF, 1939–45, prisoner-of-war in Germany, 1941–45. Entered HM Diplomatic Service, 1945, and served: New York, 1946–48; Moscow, 1948–50; Foreign Office, 1950–53; Canadian National Defence Coll., 1953–54; Mexico City, 1954–57; Foreign Office, 1957–58; UK Delegation to Conference on Nuclear Tests, Geneva, 1958–61; Peking (Counsellor), 1961–63; Political Adviser to the British Commandant, Berlin, 1964–67; FCO, 1967–70; Ambassador, Peru, 1970–74; Asst Under-Sec. of State, FCO, 1974–75. Grand Cross, Peruvian Order of Merit, 1985. *Address:* 42 Waldemar Avenue, SW6.

MORGAN, Janet; writer and consultant; Adviser to the Board, Granada Group PLC, since 1986; *b* 5 Dec. 1945; *e d* of Frank Morgan and Shiela Sadler. *Educ:* Newbury Co. Girls Grammar Sch.; St Hugh's Coll., Oxford. MA, DPhil Oxon, MA Sussex. Kennedy Meml Scholar, Harvard Univ., 1968–69; Student, Nuffield Coll., Oxford, 1969–71; Res.

Fellow, Wolfson Coll., Oxford and Res. Officer, Univ. of Essex, 1971–72; Res. Fellow, Nuffield Coll., Oxford, 1972–74; Lectr in Politics, Exeter Coll., Oxford, 1974–76; Dir of Studies, St Hugh's Coll., Oxford, 1975–76 and Lectr in Politics, 1976–78; Mem., Central Policy Rev. Staff, Cabinet Office, 1978–81. Vis. Fellow, All Souls Coll., Oxford, 1983. Dir, Satellite Television PLC, 1981–83; Special Advr to Dir-Gen., BBC, 1983–86. Vice-Pres., Videotext Industries Assoc., 1985–. Trustee, Amer. Sch. in London, 1985–. Member: Lord Chancellor's Adv. Council on Public Records; Editorial Bd, Political Quarterly. *Publications:* The House of Lords and the Labour Government 1964–70, 1975; Reinforcing Parliament, 1976; (ed) The Diaries of a Cabinet Minister 1964–70 by Richard Crossman, 3 vols 1975, 1976, 1977; (ed) Backbench Diaries 1951–63 by Richard Crossman, 1980; (ed with Richard Hoggart) The Future of Broadcasting, 1982; Agatha Christie: a biography, 1984. *Recreations:* music, sea-bathing, gardens, housekeeping, making ice cream. *Address:* c/o David Higham Associates Ltd, 5–8 Lower John Street, Golden Square, W1R 4HA. *T:* 01–437 7888.

MORGAN, John Albert Leigh, CMG 1982; HM Diplomatic Service; Ambassador to Mexico, since 1986; *b* 21 June 1929; *s* of late John Edward Rowland Morgan, Bridge, Kent; *m* 1st, 1961, Hon. Fionn Frances Bride O'Neill (marr. diss. 1975), *d* of 3rd Baron O'Neill, Shane's Castle, Antrim; one *s* two *d*; 2nd, 1976, Angela Mary Eleanor, *e d* of Patrick Warre Rathbone, Woolton, Liverpool; one *s* one *d. Educ:* London School of Economics (Hon. Fellow, 1984). Served in Army, 1947–49; entered Foreign Service, 1951; FO, 1951–53; 3rd Sec. and Private Sec. to HM Ambassador, Moscow, 1953–56; 2nd Sec., Peking, 1956–58; FO, 1958–63; 1st Sec., 1960; Head of Chancery, Rio de Janeiro, 1963–64; FO, 1964–65; Chargé d'Affaires, Ulan Bator, 1965; Moscow, 1965–67; FO, 1968; Head of Far Eastern Dept, FCO, 1970–72; Head of Cultural Relations Dept, FCO, 1972–80; Ambassador and Consul Gen. to Republic of Korea, 1980–83; Ambassador to Poland, 1983–86. Served on Earl Marshal's Staff for State Funeral of Sir Winston Churchill, 1965, and for Investiture of Prince of Wales, 1969. Governor, LSE, 1971–. Fellow, Royal Asiatic Soc.; Hon. Life Member: Royal Philharmonic Orch.; GB-China Centre. Hon. DSc (Politics) Korea Univ., 1983. *Address:* c/o Foreign and Commonwealth Office, SW1. *Club:* Travellers'.

MORGAN, John Alfred; Chief Executive, Investment Management Regulatory Organisation Ltd, since 1986; *b* 16 Sept. 1931; *s* of late Alfred Morgan and of Lydia Amelia Morgan; *m* 1959, Janet Mary Sclater-Jones; one *d. Educ:* Rugeley Grammar Sch.; Peterhouse, Cambridge (BA). Investment Research, Cambridge, 1953–59; Investment Manager, S. G. Warburg & Co. Ltd, 1959–67; Director: Glyn, Mills & Co., 1967–70; Finance and Investment, Williams & Glyn's Bank Ltd, 1970–76; Rothschild Asset Management, 1976–78; Central Trustee Savings Bank Ltd, 1982–; Zurich Life Assce Co. Ltd, 1970–; Sealink UK Ltd, 1983–85. Gen. Manager, British Railways Pension Funds, 1978–86. Chm., Post Office Users' Nat. Council, 1978–82. *Recreations:* music, contemporary art, fell walking. *Address:* 5 Grange Road, Highgate, N6 4AR. *Club:* Reform.

MORGAN, (John) Gwyn(fryn); Representative of the Commission of the European Community in Turkey, since 1983; *b* 16 Feb. 1934; *s* of Arthur G. Morgan, coal miner, and Mary Walters; *m* 1960, Joan Margaret Taylor (marr. diss. 1974); one *d*; *m* Colette Anne Rumball; two *s* one *d. Educ:* Aberdare Boys' Grammar Sch.; UCW Aberystwyth. MA Classics 1957; Dip. Educn 1958. Senior Classics Master, The Regis Sch., Tettenhall, Staffs, 1958–60; Pres., National Union of Students, 1960–62; Sec.-Gen., Internat. Student Conf. (ISC), 1962–65; Head of Overseas Dept, British Labour Party, 1965–69; Asst Gen. Secretary, British Labour Party, 1969–72; Chef de Cabinet to Mr George Thomson, 1973–75; Head of Welsh Inf. Office, EEC, 1975–79; a Dir, Development Corp. for Wales, 1976–81, Hon. Consultant in Canada 1981–83; Head of EEC Press and Inf. Office for Canada, 1979–83. Mem., Hansard Commn on Electoral Reform, 1975–76. Adjunct Prof., Univ. of Guelph, 1980–. *Publications:* contribs to numerous British and foreign political jls. *Recreations:* cricket, Rugby football, crosswords, wine-tasting. *Address:* Kuleli Sokak 15, Ghaziosmanpaşa, Ankara, Turkey. *Clubs:* Royal Commonwealth Society, Reform; Cardiff and County; Cercle Universitaire, (Ottawa); Mount Stephens (Montreal).

MORGAN, John Lewis, OBE 1981; Member (C), Test Valley Borough Council, since 1974; Chairman, Association of District Councils, since 1984; *b* 12 May 1919; *s* of Charles Lewis Morgan and Elsie Winifred (*née* Smith); *m* 1943, Grace Barnes; one *s* three *d. Educ:* St Paul's Sch. Member: Wherwell Parish Council, 1947– (Chm., 1962–); Andover RDC, 1950–74 (Vice-Chm., 1960–72; Chm., 1972–74; Chm. of Finance, 1956–74); Hampshire CC, 1956–66; Mayor of Test Valley, 1977–78 and 1978–79. Mem., Assoc. of Dist Councils, 1974– (Vice-Chm., 1983–84; Chm. of Housing and Environmental Health, 1979–83); Pres., IULA/CEMR (British Sections), 1984– (Chm., 1980–84); Chairman: Eur. Affairs Cttee, IULA, The Hague, 1981–; Town Planning and Environmental Health, CLRAE, Strasbourg, 1983–; Vice-Chm., CEMR, Paris, 1981–. Church lay reader. *Recreations:* keen supporter of Southampton Football Club; avid gardener. *Address:* Dancing Ledge, Wherwell, Andover, Hants SP11 7JS. *T:* Andover 74296.

MORGAN, John William Harold, FEng 1978; Chairman, AMEC plc, since 1984 (Director, since 1983); Director: Hill Samuel & Co., since 1983; Simon Engineering plc, since 1983; *b* 13 Dec. 1927; *s* of John Henry and Florence Morgan; *m* 1952, Barbara (*née* Harrison); two *d. Educ:* Wednesbury Boys' High Sch.; Univ. of Birmingham (BScEng, 1st Cl. Hons). FIMechE, MIEE; CBIM. National Service commn with RAF, 1949–51. Joined English Electric Co., Stafford, as design engr, subseq. Chief Development Engr (Machines), 1953; Chief Develt Engr (Mechanical), 1957; Chief Engr (DC Machines), 1960; Product Div. Manager, 1962; Gen. Man., Electrical Machines Gp, 1965; Managing Director, English Electric-AEI Machines Gp (following merger with GEC/AEI), 1968; Asst Man. Dir and main board director, GEC plc, 1973–83. Dep. Chm., Petbow Holdings, 1983–86. Royal Society's S. G. Brown award for an outstanding contrib. to promotion and development of mechanical inventions, 1968. *Recreations:* craft activities, particularly woodworking. *Address:* Mullion, Whitmore Heath, near Newcastle, Staffs ST5 5HY. *T:* Newcastle (Staffs) 680462.

MORGAN, Kenneth, OBE 1978; Director, Press Council, since 1980; *b* 3 Nov. 1928; *s* of Albert E. and Lily M. Morgan; *m* 1950, Margaret Cynthia, *d* of Roland E. Wilson; three *d. Educ:* Stockport Grammar School. Reporter, Stockport Express, 1944; Army, 1946, commissioned, 1947 (served Palestine, Egypt, GHQ MELF); journalism, 1949; Central London Sec., NUJ, 1962; Nat. Organiser, NUJ, 1966; Gen. Sec., NUJ, 1970–77; Mem. of Honour, 1978. Press Council: Consultative Mem., 1970–77; Jt Sec., 1977–78; Dep. Dir and Conciliator, 1978–79. Director: Journalists in Europe Ltd, 1982–; Reuters Founder's Share Co., 1984–. Mem. Exec. Cttee: Printing and Kindred Trades Fedn, 1970–73; Nat. Fedn of Professional Workers, 1970–77; Fedn of Broadcasting Unions, 1970–77; Confedn of Entertainment Unions, 1970–77; Bureau, Internat. Fedn of Journalists, 1970–78. Member: NEDC for Printing and Publishing Industry, 1970; Printing Industries Cttee, TUC, 1974–77; Printing and Publishing Industries Trng Bd, 1975–77; Jt Standing Cttee, Nat. Newspaper Industry, 1976–77; British Cttee, Journalists in Europe, 1977–; C of E General Synod Cttee for Communications Press Panel, 1981–84; CRE Media Gp, 1981–85; Internat. Ombudsman Inst., 1983–; Trustee, Reuters, 1984–.

Associate Mem. IPI, 1980; FRSA 1980. *Publication:* Press Conduct in the Sutcliffe Case, 1983. *Recreations:* theatre, military history, inland waterways. *Address:* 1 Salisbury Square, EC4Y 8AE. *T:* 01–353 1248; 151 Overhill Road, Dulwich, SE22 0PT. *T:* 01–693 6585. *Club:* Press.

MORGAN, Dr Kenneth Owen, FBA 1983, FRHistS 1964; Fellow and Praelector, Modern History and Politics, The Queen's College, Oxford, since 1966; *b* 16 May 1934; *s* of David James Morgan and Margaret Morgan (*née* Owen); *m* 1973, Jane Keeler; one *s* one *d. Educ:* University College School, London; Oriel College, Oxford. MA, DPhil 1958, DLitt 1985. University College, Swansea: Lectr in History Dept, 1958–66 (Sen. Lectr, 1965–66); Hon. Fellow, 1985. Amer. Council of Learned Socs Fellow, Columbia Univ., 1962–63; Vis. Prof., Columbia Univ., 1965. Member: Council, RHistS, 1983–86; Bd of Celtic Studies, 1972–; Council, University Coll. of Wales, Aberystwyth, 1972–84. Editor, Welsh History Review, 1961–. *Publications:* Wales in British Politics, 1963, 3rd edn 1980; David Lloyd George, 1963, 2nd edn 1982; Freedom or Sacrilege?, 1966; Keir Hardie, 1967; The Age of Lloyd George, 1971, 3rd edn 1978; (ed) Lloyd George: Family Letters, 1973; Lloyd George, 1974; Keir Hardie: radical and socialist, 1975, 2nd edn 1984 (Arts Council prize, 1976); Consensus and Disunity, 1979, 2nd edn 1986; (with Jane Morgan) Portrait of a Progressive, 1980; Rebirth of a Nation: Wales 1880–1980, 1981, 2nd edn 1982 (Arts Council prize, 1982); David Lloyd George, 1981; Labour in Power 1945–1951, 1984, 2nd edn 1985; (ed jtly) Welsh Society and Nationhood, 1984; (ed) The Oxford Illustrated History of Britain, 1984; (ed) The Sphere Illustrated History of Britain, 1985; many articles, reviews etc. *Recreations:* music, sport, travel. *Address:* The Croft, 63 Millwood End, Long Hanborough, Oxon OX7 2BP. *T:* Freeland 881341.

MORGAN, Kenneth Smith; Editor of the Official Report (Hansard), House of Commons, since 1979; *b* 6 Aug. 1925; *er s* of Edward and Florence Morgan; *m* 1952, Patricia Hunt; one *s* one *d. Educ:* Battersea and Dartford Grammar Schools. Commissioned Royal West Kent Regt, 1944; Burma, 1944–46. Weekly newspapers, 1947–51; Derby Evening Telegraph, 1951–52; Reuters Parliamentary Staff, 1952–54; joined Official Report, 1954; Dep. Asst Editor, 1972, Dep. Editor, 1978. Founded Commonwealth Hansard Editors Assoc., 1984. *Publication:* The Falklands Campaign: a digest of parliamentary debates on the Falklands, 1982. *Recreations:* Napoleonic warfare history, model soldiers, cricket, bridge. *Address:* Official Report (Hansard), House of Commons, SW1A 0AA.

MORGAN, Leslie; see Morgan, F. L.

MORGAN, Leslie James Joseph; a Recorder of the Crown Court, since 1975; *b* Ballina, NSW, 2 June 1922; *er s* of late Bertram Norman Morgan and Margaret Mary Morgan, MA (*née* Meere); *m* 1949, Sheila Doreen Elton Williamson; one *s* one *d. Educ:* Bournemouth Sch.; University Coll., Southampton. LLB (London) 1943. Served, Home Guard, 1940, Radio Security Service, 1941–43. Solicitor (Distinction) 1944; general practice in Bournemouth, 1944–. Chairman: Southern Area Legal Aid Cttee, 1973–74; Bournemouth Exec. Council (NHS), 1962–74; Dorset Family Practitioner Cttee, 1974–77; Law Society's Standing Cttee on Criminal Law, 1979–82 and Contentious Business Cttee, 1982–85; Member: Council, Law Society, 1973–85; Matrimonial Causes Rule Cttee, 1978–82; Crown Court Rule Cttee, 1982–; Mental Health Review Tribunal, 1982–; President: Bournemouth and Dist Law Soc., 1972–73; Soc. of Family Practitioner Cttees, 1975–76. *Publications:* articles on aspects of short wave radio. *Recreations:* music, reading, amateur radio (G2HNO). *Address:* 4 Tree Tops, Martello Park, Canford Cliffs, Poole, Dorset BH13 7BA. *T:* Canford Cliffs 708405. *Club:* Reform.

MORGAN, Michael Hugh, CMG 1978; HM Diplomatic Service, retired; Ambassador to the Philippines, 1981–85; *b* 18 April 1925; *s* of late H. P. Morgan; *m* 1957, Julian Bamfield; two *s. Educ:* Shrewsbury Sch.; Downing College, Cambridge; School of Oriental and African Studies, London Univ. Army Service 1943–46. HMOCS Malaya, 1946–56. Foreign Office, 1956–57; First Secretary, Peking, 1957–60; Belgrade 1960–64; attached to Industry, 1964; First Secretary, FCO, 1964–68; Counsellor and Head of Chancery, Cape Town/Pretoria, 1968–72; Counsellor, Peking, 1972–75; Inspector, FCO, 1975–77; High Comr, Sierra Leone, 1977–81. *Address:* Strefford House, Strefford, Craven Arms, Shropshire SY7 8DE.

MORGAN, Rear-Adm. Sir Patrick (John), KCVO 1970; CB 1967; DSC 1942; Flag Officer, Royal Yachts, 1965–70, retired; *b* 26 Jan. 1917; *s* of late Vice-Adm. Sir Charles Morgan, KCB, DSO; *m* 1944, Mary Hermione Fraser-Tytler, *d* of late Col Neil Fraser-Tytler, DSO, Aldourie Castle, Inverness, and of Mrs C. H. Fraser-Tytler, *qv*; three *s* one *d. Educ:* RN College, Dartmouth. Served War of 1939–45 (despatches, DSC). Naval Attaché, Ankara, 1957–59; Imperial Defence Coll. 1960; Asst Chief of Staff, Northwood, 1961–62; Commanding Officer, Commando Ship, HMS Bulwark, 1963–64. *Recreations:* sports. *Address:* Swallow Barn, Well Road, Crondall, Farnham, Surrey GU10 5PW. *T:* Aldershot 850107.

MORGAN, Peter Trevor Hopkin, QC 1972; **His Honour Judge Hopkin Morgan;** a Circuit Judge, since 1972; Liaison Judge to Gwent Magistrates, and Justice of the Peace, since 1973; a Judge of the Provincial Court of the Church in Wales, since 1980; *b* 5 Feb. 1919; *o s* of Cyril Richard Morgan and Muriel Arceta (*née* Hole); *m* 1942, Josephine Mouncey, *d* of Ben Travers, CBE, AFC; one *s* three *d. Educ:* Mill Hill Sch.; Magdalen Coll., Oxford (BA). Called to Bar, Middle Temple, 1949; Wales and Chester Circuit; Lectr in Law, Univ. of Wales (Cardiff and Swansea), 1950–55. Liveryman, Fishmongers' Company. *Recreation:* inland waterways. *Address:* Itton Court, Chepstow NP6 6BW. *T:* Chepstow 3935. *Club:* Garrick.

MORGAN, Rev. Philip; General Secretary, British Council of Churches, since 1980; *b* 22 June 1930; *s* of David Lewis and Pamela Morgan; *m* 1954, Greta Mary Hanson; one *s* one *d. Educ:* Overdale Coll.; Selly Oaks Colls; Univ. of Birmingham (BA Hons Theology). Ordained 1952; Ministries: Aberfan, Godreaman, Griffithstown, Merthyr Tydfil and Treharris, 1952–58; Eltham, London, 1958–62; Leicester and South Wigston, 1962–67; General Secretary, Churches of Christ in GB and Ireland, 1967–80. Moderator, URC, 1984–85. Hon. DD Christian Theological Seminary, USA, 1980. *Recreations:* hill walking, Celtic history, steam railways. *Address:* 8 Cliveden Place, SW1. *T:* 01–730 3033.

MORGAN, Richard Martin, MA; Headmaster, Cheltenham College, since 1978; *b* 25 June 1940; *s* of His Honour Trevor Morgan, MC, QC, and late Leslie Morgan; *m* 1968, Margaret Kathryn, *d* of late Anthony Agutter and of Mrs Launcelot Fleming; three *d. Educ:* Sherborne Sch.; Caius Coll., Cambridge (MA, DipEd); York Univ. Assistant Master, Radley Coll., 1963; Housemaster, 1969. Member, Adv. Council, Understanding British Industry, 1977–79. *Recreations:* reading, music, games. *Address:* College House, Cheltenham, Glos GL53 7LD. *T:* Cheltenham 24841. *Clubs:* Free Foresters', Jesters'.

MORGAN, Robin Milne; Principal: Daniel Stewart's and Melville College, Edinburgh, since 1977; The Mary Erskine School, since 1979; *b* 2 Oct. 1930; *o s* of Robert Milne Morgan and Aida Forsyth Morgan; *m* 1955, Fiona Bruce MacLeod Douglas; three *s* one *d. Educ:* Mackie Academy, Stonehaven; Aberdeen Univ. (MA); London Univ. (BA, External). Nat. Service, 2nd Lieut The Gordon Highlanders, 1952–54; Asst Master: Arden House Prep. Sch., 1955–60; George Watson's Coll., 1960–71; Headmaster,

Campbell Coll., Belfast, 1971–76. *Recreations:* music, archaeology, fishing, climbing, deer-stalking. *Address:* Daniel Stewart's and Melville College, Queensferry Road, Edinburgh EH4 3EZ.

MORGAN, Roger Hugh Vaughan Charles; Librarian, House of Lords, since 1977; *b* 8 July 1926; *s* of late Charles Langbridge Morgan, FRSL, and Hilda Vaughan, FRSL; *m* 1st, 1951, Harriet Waterfield (marr. diss. 1965), *d* of Gordon Waterfield; one *s* one *d* (and one *s* decd); 2nd, 1965, Susan Vogel Marrian, *d* of Hugo Vogel, Milwaukee, USA; one *s*. *Educ:* Downs Sch., Colwall; Phillips Acad., Andover, USA; Eton Coll.; Brasenose Coll., Oxford. MA. Grenadier Guards, 1944–47 (Captain, 1946). House of Commons Library, 1951–63; House of Lords Library, 1963–. *Address:* 30 St Peter's Square, W6 9UH. *T:* 01–741 0267; Cliff Cottage, Laugharne, Dyfed. *Clubs:* Garrick, Beefsteak.
See also Marchioness of Anglesey.

MORGAN, Prof. Roger Pearce; Visiting Fellow, Centre for International Studies, London School of Economics, since 1987; *b* 3 March 1932; *s* of Donald Emlyn Morgan and Esther Mary Morgan (*née* Pearce); *m* 1957, Annie-Françoise, (Annette) Combes; three *s* one *d*. *Educ:* Wolverton Grammar Sch.; Leighton Park Sch.; Downing Coll., Cambridge (MA 1957; PhD 1959); Univs of Paris and Hamburg. Staff Tutor, Dept of Extra-Mural Studies, London Univ., 1957–59; Asst Lectr and Lectr in Internat. Politics, UCW, Aberystwyth, 1959–63; Lectr in Hist. and Internat. Relations, Sussex Univ., 1963–67; Asst, then Dep. Dir of Studies, RIIA, 1968–74; Prof. of European Politics, 1974–78, and Dean, Sch. of Human and Environmental Studies, 1976–78, Loughborough Univ.; Head of European Centre for Political Studies, PSI, 1978–86. Visiting Professor: Columbia Univ., 1965; Johns Hopkins Univ., 1969–70; Cornell Univ., 1972; Surrey Univ., 1980–84; Res. Associate, Center for Internat. Affairs, Harvard, 1965–66; Visiting Lecturer: Cambridge Univ., 1967; LSE, 1974, 1980–; Associate Mem., Nuffield Coll., Oxford, 1980–83; Hon. Professorial Fellow, UCW, Aberystwyth, 1980–84, Hon. Prof., 1985–. Frequent broadcaster; Lectr at RCDS, CS Coll., RNC, etc. Member: Council: RIIA, 1976–85, 1986–; Centre for European Policy Studies, Brussels, 1982–; Adv. Council, Austrian Inst. for Internat. Affairs, 1979–; Academic Council: European Forum, Alpbach, 1980–; Wilton Park, 1982–83. Trustee, Gilbert Murray Trust, 1973–. *Publications:* The German Social Democrats and the First International 1864–72, 1965; Modern Germany, 1966; (ed jtly) Britain and West Germany: changing societies and the future of foreign policy, 1971 (German edn, 1970); West European Politics since 1945, 1972; (ed) The Study of International Affairs, 1972; High Politics, Low Politics: toward a foreign policy for Western Europe, 1973; The United States and West Germany 1945–1973: a study in alliance politics, 1974 (German edn 1975); West Germany's Foreign Policy Agenda, 1978; (ed jtly) Moderates and Conservatives in Western Europe, 1982 (Italian edn 1983); (ed jtly) Partners and Rivals in Western Europe: Britain, France and Germany, 1986; (ed) Regionalism in European Politics, 1986; contribs to symposia and jls. *Recreations:* music, travel, watching cricket. *Address:* 32 Cruden Street, N1 8NH. *T:* 01–359 0526. *Clubs:* Europe House, PEN; Middlesex County Cricket, Surrey County Cricket.

MORGAN, Tom, CBE 1982; DL; JP; Lord Provost of the City of Edinburgh and Lord Lieutenant of the City and County of Edinburgh, 1980–84; *b* 24 Feb. 1914; *s* of Thomas Morgan; *m* 1940, Mary Montgomery, *d* of Stephen McLauchlan; two *s*. *Educ:* Longside Public Sch., Aberdeenshire; Aberdeen Univ.; W of Scotland Coll. of Agriculture. Unigate Ltd for 36 yrs (Regional Dir for Scotland). Member, Edinburgh Corp., 1954–71 and Edinburgh DC, 1977–84. Chairman: Edinburgh Festival Soc., 1980–84; Edinburgh Mil. Tattoo Policy Cttee, 1980–84. Formerly: Magistrate; City Treasurer; Curator of Patronage, Univ. of Edinburgh; Governor, George Heriot's Trust; Governor, Edinburgh and E of Scotland Coll. of Agric.; Dir, Edinburgh Chamber of Commerce and Manufactures; Pres., Edinburgh City Business Club; Gen. Comr of Income Tax; Chm., Edinburgh Abbeyfield Soc. DL Edinburgh, 1984. OStJ. *Recreations:* golf, gardening. *Address:* 400 Lanark Road, Edinburgh EH13 0LX.

MORGAN, Tony; *see* Morgan, A. W. C.

MORGAN, Rt. Rev. Mgr. Vaughan Frederick John, CBE 1982; Principal Roman Catholic Chaplain (Naval), and Vicar General for the Royal Navy, 1979–84; Chaplain, The Oratory School, since 1984; *b* Upper Hutt, New Zealand, 21 March 1931; *o s* of late Godfrey Frederick Vaughan Morgan and Violet (Doreen) Vaughan Morgan. *Educ:* The Oratory Sch., S Oxon; Innsbruck Univ. Ordained, 1957; Archdiocese of St Andrews and Edinburgh, 1959–62; entered Royal Navy as Chaplain, 1962. Prelate of Honour to HH Pope John Paul II, 1979. *Publications:* contribs to journals. *Recreations:* music, swimming, painting, heraldry. *Address:* The Oratory School, Woodcote, Reading RG8 0PJ. *T:* Checkendon 680207. *Club:* Army and Navy.

MORGAN, Walter Thomas James, CBE 1959; FRS 1949; Director, Lister Institute of Preventive Medicine, London, 1972–75 (Deputy Director, 1952–68); *b* London, 5 Oct. 1900; *s* of Walter and Annie E. Morgan; *m* 1930, Dorothy Irene Price; one *s* two *d*. *Educ:* Univ. of London. Grocers' Company Scholar, 1925–27; Beit Memorial Med. Res. Fellow, 1927–28; First Asst and Biochemist, Lister Institute Serum Dept (Elstree), 1928–37; Rockefeller Research Fellow (Eidgenössiche Tech. Hochschule, Zürich), 1937. Reader, 1938–51, Lister Inst.; Prof. of Biochemistry, Univ. of London, 1951–68, now Prof. Emeritus. PhD 1927, DSc 1937, London Univ.; DrSc (Tech.) Zürich, 1938; FRIC 1929. Hon. Secretary: Biochemical Soc., 1940–45; Biological Council, 1944–47. Chm. Bd of Studies, Biochem., Univ. of London, 1954–57; Member: Scientific Advisory Council, 1956–60; MRC, 1966–70. Mem., Lawes Agricl Trust Cttee, 1964–76. Guest Lecturer, 100th meeting of Gesellschaft Deutscher Naturforscher und Ärzte, Germany, 1959; Royal Society: Croonian Lectr, 1959; Vice-Pres., 1961–64; Royal Medal, 1968. Vis. Prof., Japan Soc. for Promotion of Science, 1979. Hon. Member: Biochem. Soc., 1969; Internat. Soc. Blood Transfusion, 1980; Hon. FRCP 1982. MD *hc* Basel, 1964; DSc *hc* Michigan, 1969. Conway Evans Prize (Royal College of Physicians, London), 1964. (Jointly) Landsteiner Memorial Award (USA), 1967. (Jointly) Paul Ehrlich and Ludwig Darmstädter Prizes (Germany), 1968. *Publications:* papers on biochemistry, immunology and pathology. *Address:* Division of Immunochemical Genetics, Medical Research Council, Clinical Research Centre, Watford Road, Harrow, Mddx HA1 3UJ. *T:* 01–844 5311; 57 Woodbury Drive, Sutton, Surrey. *T:* 01–642 2319. *Club:* Athenæum.

MORGAN, Prof. William Basil; Professor of Geography since 1971, and Head of Geography Department since 1982, King's College London; *b* 22 Jan. 1927; *s* of William George Morgan and Eunice Mary (*née* Heys); *m* 1954, Joy Gardner; one *s* one *d*. *Educ:* King Edward's Sch., Birmingham; Jesus Coll., Oxford (MA); PhD Glasgow. Assistant, Glasgow Univ., 1948; Lecturer: University Coll., Ibadan, Nigeria, 1953; Univ. of Birmingham, 1959; Reader in Geography, KCL, 1967. *Publications:* West Africa (with J. C. Pugh), 1969; (with R. J. C. Munton) Agricultural Geography, 1971; Agriculture in the Third World: a spatial analysis, 1978; (with R. P. Moss) Fuelwood and rural energy production and supply in the humid tropics, 1981; contribs to geographical and other learned jls and to various conf. collections. *Address:* 57 St Augustine's Avenue, South Croydon, Surrey CR2 6JQ. *T:* 01–688 5687.

MORGAN, (William) Geraint (Oliver), QC 1971; a Recorder of the Crown Court, since 1972; *b* Nov. 1920; *m* 1957, J. S. M. Maxwell; two *s* two *d*. *Educ:* University Coll. of Wales, Aberystwyth; Trinity Hall, Cambridge. Served War of 1939–45 with Royal Marines; demobilised with Rank of Major, 1946. Called to the Bar, Gray's Inn, 1947; Squire Law Scholar; Holt Scholar; Northern Circuit. ACIArb. MP (C) Denbigh, Oct. 1959–1983. *Address:* 2nd Floor, Fruit Exchange Building, Victoria Street, Liverpool.

MORGAN, Air Vice-Marshal William Gwyn, CB 1968; CBE 1960 (OBE 1945); RAF, retired 1969; *b* 13 Aug. 1914; *s* of T. S. Morgan; *m* 1962, Joan Russell. *Educ:* Pagefield Coll., Swansea. Joined Royal Air Force, 1939; Group Capt., 1958; Command Acct, HQ, FEAF, 1962; Air Commodore, 1965; DPS (2), RAF, 1965–66; AOA Technical Training Comd, 1966–68, Training Comd, 1968–69. Air Vice-Marshal, 1967; jssc; psc; FCCA; ACMA. *Recreation:* fell walking. *Address:* c/o Lloyds Bank, 6 Pall Mall, SW1. *Club:* Royal Air Force.

MORGAN, Rt. Hon. William James, PC (Northern Ireland) 1961; JP; Member (UUUC), for North Belfast, Northern Ireland Constitutional Convention, 1975–76; *b* 1914; *m* 1942; two *s* one *d*. Retired company director. MP, Oldpark Div. of Belfast, 1949–58, Clifton Div. of Belfast, 1959–69, NI Parlt; Minister: of Health and Local Government, Northern Ireland, 1961–64; of Labour and National Insurance, 1964; of Health and Social Services, 1965–69; Mem. (U), N Belfast, NI Assembly, 1973–75. *Address:* Thornleigh, 45 Tullynagardy Road, Newtownards, Co. Down, N Ireland. *T:* Newtownards 817906.

MORGAN-GILES, Rear-Adm. Sir Morgan (Charles), Kt 1985; DSO 1944; OBE 1943 (MBE 1942); GM 1941; DL; *b* 19 June 1914; *e s* of late F. C. Morgan-Giles, OBE, MINA, Teignmouth, Devon; *m* 1946, Pamela (*d* 1966), *d* of late Philip Bushell, Sydney, New South Wales; two *s* four *d*; *m* 1968, Marigold, *d* of late Percy Lowe. *Educ:* Clifton Coll. Entered Royal Navy, 1932; served on China Station, and in destroyers. War Service: Atlantic convoys and Mediterranean; Tobruk garrison and Western Desert, 1941; with RAF, 1942; Sen. Naval Officer, Vis. (Dalmatia) and liaison with Commandos and Marshal Tito's Partisan Forces, 1943–44. Captain 1953; Chief of Naval Intelligence, Far East, 1955–56; Captain (D) Dartmouth Training Sqdn, 1957–58; HMS Belfast, in command, 1961–62; Rear-Adm. 1962; Adm. Pres., Royal Naval Coll., Greenwich, 1962–64; retd 1964. MP (C) Winchester, May 1964–79. Vice-Chm., Conservative Defence Cttee, 1965–75. Chm., HMS Belfast Trust, 1971–78; a Vice-Pres., RNLI, 1985–. Renter Warden, Ct of Assts, Shipwrights' Company, 1986–87. DL Hants, 1983. *Recreations:* sailing, country pursuits. *Address:* Frenchmoor Farm, West Tytherley, Salisbury SP5 1NU. *T:* Lockerley 41045. *Clubs:* Carlton; Royal Yacht Squadron; Australian (Sydney).
See also Baron Killearn.

MORGAN HUGHES, David; *see* Hughes, David M.

MORGAN JONES, John; *see* Jones, J. M.

MORGAN-OWEN, John Gethin, CB 1984; MBE 1945; QC 1981; Judge Advocate General, 1979–84; Joint Chairman, Disciplinary Appeal Committee, Institute of Chartered Accountants, since 1985; *b* 22 Aug. 1914; *o s* of late Maj.-Gen. L. I. G. Morgan-Owen, CB, CMG, CBE, DSO, West Dene, Beech, Alton; *m* 1950, Mary, *d* of late F. J. Rimington, MBE, Master Mariner; two *s* one *d*. *Educ:* Shrewsbury; Trinity Coll., Oxford (BA). Called to Bar, Inner Temple, 1938; Wales and Chester Circuit, 1939; practised at Cardiff, 1939–52. 2nd Lieut Suppl. Reserve, S Wales Borderers, 1939; served 2nd Bn SWB, 1939–44: N Norway, 1940; NW Europe, 1944–45; DAA&QMG, 146 Inf. Bde, 1944–45; Hon. Major. Dep. Judge Advocate, 1952: Germany, 1953–56; Hong Kong, 1958–60; Cyprus, 1963–66; AJAG, 1966; DJAG, Germany, 1970–72; Vice JAG, 1972–79. *Recreations:* bad tennis, inland waterways, beagling. *Address:* St Nicholas House, Kingsley, Bordon, Hants GU35 9NW. *T:* Bordon 2040. *Club:* Army and Navy.

MORI, Haruki; Adviser to Japanese Foreign Office, since 1975; *b* 1911; *m* 1940, Tsutako Masaki; four *s*. *Educ:* Univ. of Tokyo. Ministry of Foreign Affairs, served USA and Philippines, 1935–41; Head of Economic Section, Dept of Political Affairs, 1950–53; Counsellor, Italy, 1953–55, Asian Affairs Bureau, 1955–56; Private Sec. to Prime Minister, 1956–57; Dep. Dir-Gen., Economic Affairs Bureau, 1957; Dir-Gen., American Affairs Bureau, 1957–60; Minister Plenipotentiary to UK, 1960–63, to France, 1963–64; Ambassador to OECD, 1964–67; Dep. Vice-Minister for Foreign Affairs, 1967–70; Vice-Minister for Foreign Affairs, 1970–72; Japanese Ambassador to the Court of St James's, 1972–75. *Recreation:* golf. *Address:* c/o Ministry of Foreign Affairs, Tokyo, Japan.

MORIARTY, Gerald Evelyn, QC 1974; a Recorder of the Crown Court, since 1976; *b* 23 Aug. 1928; *er s* of late Lt-Col G. R. O'N. Moriarty and Eileen Moriarty (*née* Moloney); *m* 1961, Judith Mary, *er d* of Hon. William Robert Atkin; four *s*. *Educ:* Downside Sch.; St John's Coll., Oxford (MA). Called to the Bar, Lincoln's Inn, 1951, Bencher, 1983. *Address:* 15 Campden Street, W8 7EP. *T:* 01–727 4593. *Club:* Reform.

MORIARTY, Brig. Joan Olivia Elsie, CB 1979; RRC 1977; Matron-in-Chief and Director of Army Nursing Services, 1976–80; *b* 11 May 1923; *d* of late Lt-Col Oliver Nash Moriarty, DSO, RA, and Mrs Georgina Elsie Moriarty (*née* Moore). *Educ:* Royal Sch., Bath; St Thomas' Hosp. (nursing); Queen Charlotte's Hosp. (midwifery). SRN. VAD, Somerset, 1941–42; joined QAIMNS (R), 1947; Reg. QAIMNS (later QARANC), 1948, retired Jan. 1981; appts incl.: Staff Captain, WO; Instr, Corps Trng Centre; Liaison Officer, MoD; served in UK, Gibraltar, BAOR, Singapore, Malaya, Cyprus; Matron, Mil. Hosp., Catterick, 1973–76; Comdt, QARANC Trng Centre, Aldershot, 1976. Major 1960; Lt-Col 1971; Col 1973; Brig. 1977. QHNS, 1977–80. Governor, Royal Sch., Bath, 1979–. OStJ 1977. *Recreation:* country pursuits. *Address:* 95 Church Street, Atworth, Melksham, Wilts SN12 8JA. *Club:* Naval and Military.

MORIARTY, Michael John; Deputy Under-Secretary of State and Principal Establishment Officer, Home Office, since 1984; *b* 3 July 1930; *er s* of Edward William Patrick Moriarty, OBE, and May Lilian Moriarty; *m* 1960, Rachel Milward, *d* of J. S. Thompson and late Isobel F. Thompson; one *s* two *d*. *Educ:* Reading Sch., Reading; St John's Coll., Oxford (Sir Thomas White schol.; MA Lit. Hum.). Entered Home Office as Asst Principal, 1954; Private Sec. to Parliamentary Under-Secretaries of State, 1957–59; Principal, 1959; Civil Service Selection Bd, 1962–63; Cabinet Office, 1965–67; Asst Sec., 1967; Private Sec. to Home Sec., 1968; Head of Crime Policy Planning Unit, 1974–75; Asst Under-Sec. of State, 1975–84; seconded to NI Office, 1979–81; Broadcasting Dept, 1981–84. UK Representative, 1976–79, and Chm., 1978–79, Council of Europe Cttee on Crime Problems. *Publications:* contributions to: Proceedings of Conference on Criminal Policy, 1975; Penal Policy-Making in England, 1977. *Recreations:* music, walking, family pursuits. *Address:* 36 Willifield Way, Hampstead Garden Suburb, NW11 7XT. *T:* 01–455 8439.

MORICE, Prof. Peter Beaumont, DSc, PhD; FICE, FIStructE; Professor of Civil Engineering, University of Southampton, since 1958; *b* 15 May 1926; *o s* of Charles and Stephanie Morice; *m* 1952, Margaret Ransom; one *s* two *d*. *Educ:* Barfield Sch.; Farnham Grammar Sch.; University of Bristol; University of London. Surrey County Council,

1947–48; Research Div., Cement and Concrete Assoc., 1948–57. *Publications:* Linear Structural Analysis, 1958; Prestressed Concrete, 1958; papers on structural theory in various learned journals. *Recreations:* sailing, reading, listening to music. *Address:* 65 Shaftesbury Avenue, Highfield, Southampton. *T:* 556624.

MORINI, Erica; concert violinist; *b* Vienna, 5 Jan. 1910; *m* 1938, Felice Siracusano; no *c.* *Educ:* at age of 4 years under father, Prof. Oscar Morini, and then under Prof. Ottocar Sevcik, masterclass of Viennese Conservatory, at age of 8. Debut under Arthur Nikisch, at age of 9, in Leipzig Gewandhaus (Beethoven Festival); from there on Concert-tours to: Australia, Asia, Africa, Europe; to USA, 1920. Hon. Mem., Sigma Alpha Beta. Hon. MusD: Smith Coll., Mass, 1955; New England Conservatory of Music, Mass, 1963. *Recreations:* mountain climbing and chamber music. *Address:* 1200 Fifth Avenue, New York, NY 10029, USA.

MORISHIMA, Prof. Michio, FBA 1981; Sir John Hicks Professor of Economics, since 1984, London School of Economics and Political Science (Professor of Economics, 1970–84); *b* 18 July 1923; *s* of Kameji and Tatsuo Morishima; *m* 1953, Yoko; two *s* one *d.* Assistant Professor: Kyoto Univ., 1950–51; Osaka Univ., 1951–63; Prof., Osaka Univ., 1963–69. *Publications:* Equilibrium, Stability and Growth, 1964; Theory of Economic Growth, 1969; The Working of Econometric Models, 1972; Marx's Economics, 1973; Theory of Demand: real and monetary, 1973; The Economic Theory of Modern Society, 1976; Walras' Economics, 1977; Value, Exploitation and Growth, 1978; Why Has Japan 'Succeeded'?, 1982; The Economics of Industrial Society, 1985. *Address:* Ker, Greenway, Hutton Mount, Brentwood, Essex CM13 2NP. *T:* Brentwood 219595.

MORISON, Hon. Lord; Alastair Malcolm Morison; a Senator of the College of Justice, Scotland, since 1985; *b* 12 Feb. 1931; 2nd *s* of Sir Ronald Peter Morison, QC (Scotland); *m* 1st, 1957, Lindsay Balfour Oatts (marr. diss. 1977); one *s* one *d*; 2nd, 1980, Birgitte Hendil. *Educ:* Cargilfield; Winchester Coll.; Edinburgh Univ. Admitted to Faculty of Advocates, 1956; QC (Scotland) 1968. *Recreations:* golf, fishing. *Address:* 6 Carlton Terrace, Edinburgh EH7 5DD. *T:* 031–556 6766. *Club:* New (Edinburgh).

MORISON, Hugh; Under Secretary, Scottish Home and Health Department, since 1984; *b* 22 Nov. 1943; *s* of Archibald Ian Morison and Enid Rose Morison (*née* Mawer); *m* 1971, Marion Smithers; two *d.* *Educ:* Chichester High School for Boys; St Catherine's Coll., Oxford (MA English Language and Literature; DipEd). Asst Principal, SHHD, 1966–69; Private Sec. to Minister of State, Scottish Office, 1969–70; Principal: Scottish Educn Dept, 1971–73; Scottish Economic Planning Dept, 1973–74; Offshore Supplies Office, Dept of Energy, 1974–75; Scottish Economic Planning Dept, 1975–82, Asst Sec., 1979; Gwilym Gibbon Res, Fellow, Nuffield Coll., Oxford, 1982–83; Scottish Development Dept, 1983–84. *Publication:* The Regeneration of Local Economies, 1987. *Recreations:* hill walking, cycling, sailing, music, looking at ruins. *Address:* 26 Hartington Place, Edinburgh EH10 4LE. *T:* 031–229 5206. *Club:* Royal Commonwealth Society.

MORISON, Air Vice-Marshal Richard Trevor, CBE 1969 (MBE 1944); RAF retired; President, Ordnance Board, 1971–72; *s* of late Oscar Colin Morison and Margaret Valerie (*née* Cleaver); *m* 1964, Rosemary June Brett; one *s* one *d.* *Educ:* Perse Sch., Cambridge; De Havilland Sch. of Aeronautical Engineering. Commnd in RAF, 1940; RAF Staff Coll., 1952; Sen. Techn. Officer, RAF Gaydon, 1955–57; HQ Bomber Comd, 1958–60; STSO HQ 224 Group, Singapore, 1960–61; Dir of Techn. Services, Royal NZ Air Force, 1961–63; Comd Engrg Officer, HQ Bomber Comd, 1963–65; Air Officer i/c Engrg, HQ Flying Training Comd, 1966–68; Air Officer i/c Engrg, HQ Training Comd RAF, 1968–69; Vice-Pres. (Air) Ordnance Bd, 1969–70. *Recreation:* cabinet making. *Address:* Meadow House, Chedgrave, Loddon, Norfolk. *Club:* Royal Air Force.

MORISON, Thomas Richard Atkin, QC 1979; barrister-at-law, since 1960; *b* 15 Jan. 1939; *s* of Harold Thomas Brash Morison and Hon. Nancy Morison; *m* 1963, Judith Rachel Walton Morris; one *s* one *d.* *Educ:* Winchester Coll.; Worcester Coll., Oxford, 1959–62 (MA). Passed final Bar examinations, 1959; called to the Bar, Gray's Inn, 1960; pupil in Chambers, 1962–63; started practice, 1963. Mem. Court of Assistants, Grocers' Co., 1982–. *Recreations:* reading, walking, cooking. *Address:* Fountain Court, Temple, EC4. *T:* 01–353 7356. *Club:* Oriental.

MORITA, Akio; Chairman and Chief Executive Officer, Sony Corporation, since 1976; *b* Nagoya, Japan, 26 Jan. 1921; *m* 1950, Yoshiko Kamei; two *s* one *d.* *Educ:* Osaka Imperial Univ. (BSc Physics). Sony Corporation, Tokyo: co-founder, 1946; Man. Dir, 1947–55; Sen. Man. Dir, 1955–56; Exec. Vice-Pres., 1959–71; Pres., 1971–76; Sony Corporation of America: Pres., 1960–66, Chm., 1966–72; Chm. Finance Cttee, 1972–74; Chm. Exec. Cttee, 1974–77; Chm. Finance Cttee, 1977–81; Chm., Exec. Cttee, 1981–. Dir, IBM World Trade Americas/Far East Corp., 1972–77; Mem., Internat. Council, Morgan Guaranty Trust Co. Chm., Cttee on Internat. Industrial Co-operation. Exchange, Keidanren (Fedn of Economic Organization), 1981–; Vice-Chm., Keidanren, 1986–. Albert Medal, RSA, 1982. Officier de la Légion d'Honneur, France, 1984. *Publications:* Gakureki Muyooron (Never Mind Education Records), 1966; Shin Jitsuryoku Shugi (A New Merit System), 1969. *Recreations:* music, golf, tennis. *Address:* Sony Corporation, 6–7–35 Kitashinagawa, Shinagawa-ku, Tokyo 141, Japan. *T:* 03–448–2600.

MORLAND, Martin Robert, CMG 1985; HM Diplomatic Service; Ambassador to Burma, since 1986; *b* 23 Sept. 1933; *e s* of Sir Oscar Morland, GBE, KCMG and of Alice, *d* of Rt Hon. Sir F. O. Lindley, PC, GCMG; *m* 1964, Jennifer Avril Mary Hanbury-Tracy; two *s* one *d.* *Educ:* Ampleforth; King's Coll., Cambridge (BA). Nat. Service, Grenadier Guards, 1954–56; British Embassy, Rangoon, 1957–60; News Dept, FO, 1961; UK Delegn to Common Market negotiations, Brussels, 1962–63; FO, 1963–65; UK Disarmament Delegn, Geneva, 1965–67; Private Sec. to Lord Chalfont, 1967–68; European Integration Dept, FCO, 1968–73; Counsellor, 1973–77, Rome (seconded temporarily to Cabinet Office to head EEC Referendum Information Unit, 1975); Hd of Maritime Aviation and Environment Dept, FCO, 1977–79; Counsellor and Head of Chancery, Washington, 1979–82; seconded to Hardcastle & Co. Ltd, 1982–84; Under-Sec., Cabinet Office, 1984–86. *Address:* c/o Foreign and Commonwealth Office, SW1. *Club:* Garrick.

MORLAND, Michael, QC 1972; a Recorder of the Crown Court, since 1972; *b* 16 July 1929; *e s* of Edward Morland, Liverpool, and Jane Morland (*née* Beckett); *m* 1961, Lillian Jensen, Copenhagen; one *s* one *d.* *Educ:* Stowe; Christ Church, Oxford (MA). 2nd Lieut, Grenadier Guards, 1948–49; served in Malaya. Called to Bar, Inner Temple, 1953, Bencher 1979; practises on Northern Circuit. Mem., Criminal Injuries Compensation Bd, 1980–. *Address:* 12 King's Bench Walk, Temple, EC4Y 7EL. *T:* 01–353 5892.

MORLEY; *see* Hope-Morley, family name of Baron Hollenden.

MORLEY, 6th Earl of, *cr* 1815; **John St Aubyn Parker**, JP; Lt-Col, Royal Fusiliers; Lord-Lieutenant of Devon, since 1982; Chairman: Farm Industries Ltd, Truro, since 1970; Plymouth Sound Ltd, since 1974; Henry Norrington & Son Ltd, since 1980; *b* 29 May 1923; *e s* of Hon. John Holford Parker (*y s* of 3rd Earl), Pound House, Yelverton, Devon; *S* uncle, 1962; *m* 1955, Johanna Katherine, *d* of Sir John Molesworth-St Aubyn, 14th Bt, CBE; one *s* one *d.* *Educ:* Eton. 2nd Lt, KRRC, 1942; served NW Europe, 1944–45; Palestine and Egypt, 1945–48; transferred to Royal Fusiliers, 1947; served Korea, 1952–53; Middle East, 1953–55 and 1956; Staff Coll., Camberley, 1957; Comd, 1st Bn Royal Fusiliers, 1965–67. Director: Lloyds Bank Ltd, 1974–78; Lloyds Bank UK Management Ltd, 1979–86. Mem., Devon and Co. Cttee, Nat. Trust, 1969–84; President: Plymouth Incorporated Chamber of Trade and Commerce, 1970–; Cornwall Fedn of Chambers of Commerce and Trader Assocs, 1972–79; West Country Tourist Bd, 1971–. Governor: Seale-Hayne Agric. Coll., 1973; Plymouth Polytechnic, 1975–82 (Chm., 1977–82). Pres., Council of Order of St John for Devon, 1979. DL 1973, Vice Lord-Lieutenant, 1978–82, Devon. JP Plymouth, 1972. *Heir:* *s* Viscount Boringdon, *qv.* *Address:* Pound House, Yelverton, Devon. *T:* Yelverton 853162.

MORLEY, Cecil Denis, CBE 1967; Secretary General, The Stock Exchange, London, 1965–71; retired; *b* 20 May 1911; *s* of Cornelius Cecil Morley and Mildred Irene Hutchinson; *m* 1936, Lily Florence Younge; one *s.* *Educ:* Clifton; Trinity Coll., Cambridge. Solicitor. Asst Sec., Share & Loan Dept, Stock Exchange, 1936; Sec. to Coun. of Stock Exchange, 1949. Served War of 1939–45, Major RA (TA). *Recreations:* travel, gardening. *Address:* Bearsward, Coastal Road, Kingston Gorse, West Sussex BN16 1SJ. *T:* Rustington 782837.

MORLEY, Eric Douglas; Chairman of Miss World Group plc, which he brought to the USM in 1983; orphaned age 11; *m* Julia Evelyn; four *s* one *d.* *Educ:* grammar schools and Army; 4 yrs training ship, Exmouth; joined Royal Fusiliers as band boy, 1934; left Army, 1945 (Captain, RASC motorboats). Joined Mecca, 1946 as Publicity Sales Manager; left 1978 as Chm. and Chief Exec.; Dir, Grand Metropolitan Group, 1970–78. Creator of Come Dancing, 1949 (longest running TV series in history; originator of Miss World contest, 1951, which has raised over $20 million for charity worldwide. Pres., Variety Clubs Internat., world's greatest children's charity, 1977–79; Chief Barker, Variety Club of GB, 1973; Pres., Outward Bound Trust. Trustee, KCH; Mem., Camberwell DHA. Freeman, City of London. Introduced commercial bingo to UK, 1961; formed and was first chm. of most trade assocs in entertainment and gaming. Contested (C) Southwark, Dulwich, 1974 and 1979 (reduced maj. of then Attorney Gen. from 7,500 to 122). *Publication:* Miss World Story, 1967. *Recreations:* French horn, all forms of sport; completed his first-ever marathon for charity, 1982. *Address:* St Giles House, 49/50 Poland Street, W1. *Club:* MCC.

MORLEY, Sir Godfrey (William Rowland), Kt 1971; OBE 1944; TD 1946; *b* 15 June 1909; *o s* of late Arthur Morley, OBE, KC, and late Dorothy Innes Murray Forrest; *m* 1st, 1934, Phyllis Dyce (*d* 1963), *d* of late Sir Edward Duckworth, 2nd Bt; two *s* two *d*; 2nd, 1967, Sonia Gisèle, *d* of late Thomas Ritchie; two *s.* *Educ:* Westminster; Christ Church, Oxford (MA). Solicitor, 1934; Partner in Allen & Overy, 1936, Senior Partner, 1960–75. Joined Territorial Army, 1937; served War of 1939–45, Rifle Bde and on Staff in Middle East and Italy (despatches); Lt-Col 1944. Law Society: Mem. Council, 1952–73; Vice-Pres., 1969–70; Pres., 1970–71. Member: Lord Chancellor's Law Reform Cttee, 1957–73; Cttee on Legal Educn of Students from Africa, 1960; Cttee of Management, Inst. of Advanced Legal Studies, 1961–77; CBI Company Affairs Cttee, 1972; Law Adv. Panel, British Council, 1974–82; Council, Selden Soc., 1975– (Pres., 1979–82). Dir, Bowater Corp. Ltd, 1968–79. Trustee, Thalidomide Children's Trust, 1980–84. Hon. Mem., Canadian Bar Assoc., 1970. Bronze Star Medal (US), 1945. *Address:* Hunter's Lodge, Warren Drive, Kingswood, Tadworth, Surrey KT20 6PT. *T:* Mogador 832485. *Clubs:* Athenæum, Boodle's.

See also Sir William Lindsay.

MORLEY, Herbert, CBE 1974; Director: Ellison-Morlock, since 1985; Bridon Ltd, 1973–85; *b* 19 March 1919; *s* of George Edward and Beatrice Morley; *m* 1942, Gladys Hardy; one *s* one *d.* *Educ:* Almondbury Grammar Sch., Huddersfield; Sheffield Univ. (Assoc. Metallurgy); Univ. of Cincinnati (Post-Grad. Studies in Business Admin). Dir and Gen. Works Man., Samuel Fox & Co. Ltd, 1959–65; Dir and Gen. Man., Steel Peech Tozer, 1965–68; Dir, United Steel Cos, 1966–70; British Steel Corporation: Dir, Northern Tubes Gp, 1968–70; Man. Dir, Gen. Steel Div., 1970–73; Man. Dir, Planning and Capital Develt, 1973–76. Chm., Templeborough Rolling Mills Ltd., 1977–82. *Recreations:* music, cricket lover, weekend golfer. *Address:* Honeysuckle Cottage, Firbeck, near Worksop, Notts S81 8JY. *T:* Rotherham 815710.

MORLEY, John; actor and playwright; Pantomime Writer for Triumph Apollo Ltd, since 1973; *b* 24 Dec. 1924; *s* of Austin Morley and Patricia (*née* Bray). *Educ:* Uppingham; St John's Coll., Cambridge; RADA. Served War: commnd Coldstream Guards, 1943. Wrote Coldstream Guards pantomime, Dick Whittington and his kit, 1944; performed in and wrote two revues and pantomime, St John's Coll., Cambridge, 1947–48; perf. in and co-author of Cambridge Footlights Revue, 1948; performed in: Private View, Fortune, 1948; Birmingham Rep., 1949; Bob's Your Uncle, Theatre Royal, Stratford, and Music at Midnight, Her Majesty's, 1950; Victorian Music Hall, Players, 1951; Fancy Free, Prince of Wales, 1951–53; Northampton Rep., 1953; Call Me Madam tour, 1953–54; After the Ball, Globe, 1954; Jubilee Girl, Victoria Palace, 1956; The Crystal Heart, Saville, and Love à la Carte, Richmond, 1958; Marigold, Savoy, 1959; Follow that Girl, Vaudeville, 1960; performer and writer, Café de Paris, 1955–60; pantomime writer for Howerd and Wyndham, 1964–73; author of: songs for The Art of Living, Criterion, 1960–61; (jtly) Puss in Boots, London Palladium, 1963; (jtly) Houdini, Man of Magic, Piccadilly, 1966; (jtly) The Littlest Clown, Round House, 1972; Aladdin, BBC Radio, 1980; Big Night Out (Thames Television variety series), 1963–66 (incl. The Beatles Night Out, Blackpool Night Out, Boxing Night Out); BBC Television pantomimes: Babes in the Wood, 1972; The Basil Brush Pantomime, 1980; Aladdin and the Forty Thieves, 1983; BBC Children's Television series: Crazy Bus, 1972; Captain Bonny the pirate, 1973–74; Children's Television Revue, 1975; Basil Brush, 1979–81; has written 148 pantomimes. *Publications:* (jtly) The Magic of Houdini, 1978; (jtly) The Performing Arts, 1980; Pinocchio (children's musical), 1983; The Wind in the Willows (children's musical), 1984; pantomimes: Aladdin; Jack and the Beanstalk; Sinbad the Sailor; Goldilocks and the Three Bears; Robinson Crusoe; Dick Whittington. *Recreations:* architecture, furniture, travel, New York, Wagnerian opera, history of pantomime, British folklore, the Industrial Revolution. *Address:* 4 Stafford Terrace, W8 4SN. *T:* 01–937 5575.

MORLEY, John Harwood, FMA; Keeper of Furniture and Interior Design, Victoria and Albert Museum, since 1985; *b* 5 Dec. 1933; *s* of George Frederick Morley and Doris Simpson Morley; *m* 1960, Jacqueline Morgan; three *d.* *Educ:* Henry Mellish Grammar Sch.; Exeter Coll., Oxford (MA). FMA 1965. Archivist, Ipswich Corp., 1958–59; Art Asst, Herbert Art Gall., Coventry, 1959–61; Keeper of Art, Leicester Museums, 1961–65; Director: Bradford City Museums, 1965–68; Royal Pavilion, Art Gall. and Museums, Brighton, 1968–85. Mem. Council, Nat. Trust, 1985–; Chairman (and Founder Member): Decorative Arts Soc. 1890–1940, 1975–; The Brighton Soc., 1973–75; Sec. (and Founder Mem.), Friends of the Royal Pavilion, 1972–85; Trustee, Edward James Foundn, 1976–82; Patron, Thirties Soc.; Mem. Council, Attingham Summer Sch. Trust, 1983–. *Publications:* Death, Heaven and the Victorians, 1971; Designs and Drawings: The Making of the

Royal Pavilion, 1984; articles and reviews in Apollo, The Connoisseur, and Decorative Arts Soc. Bull. *Recreations:* music, gardening, reading, museums and houses. *Address:* 11 Vine Place, Brighton, East Sussex BN1 3HE.

MORLEY, Malcolm A.; artist; *b* 1931. *Educ:* Camberwell Sch. of Arts and Crafts; Royal Coll. of Art (ARCA 1957). *One Man Exhibitions:* Kornblee Gall., NY, 1957, 1964, 1967, 1969; Galerie Gerald Piltzer, Paris, 1973; Stefanotty Gall., NY, 1973, 1974; Clocktower Gall., Inst. for Art & Urban Resources, 1976; Galerie Jurka, Amsterdam, 1977; Galerie Jollenbeck, Cologne, 1977; Nancy Hoffman Gall., NY, 1979; Suzanne Hilberry Gall., Birmingham, Miss., 1979; Xavier Fourcade, NY, 1981, 1982, 1984; Galerie Nicholine Pon, Zurich, 1984; Ponova Gall., Toronto, 1984; Fabian Carlsson Gall., London, 1985; *major exhibitions:* Wadsworth Atheneum, Hartford, Conn, 1980; Akron Art Mus., 1982; retrospective, Whitechapel Art Gall., also shown in Europe and USA, 1983–84; *work in collections:* Met. Mus. of Art, NY; Fordham Univ., NY; Detroit Inst. of Art; Hirshhorn Mus. and Sculpture Gdn, Washington; Lousiana Mus., Humlebaek, Denmark; Neue Galerie der Stadt Aachen; Utrecht Mus.; Mus. of Contemp. Art, Chicago; Munson-Williams-Proctor Inst., Utica, NY. First Turner Prize, Tate Gall., 1984. *Address:* c/o Xavier Fourcade Inc., 36 East 75th Street, New York, NY 10021, USA.

MORLEY, Robert, CBE 1957; Actor-Dramatist; *b* Semley, Wilts, 26 May 1908; *s* of Major Robert Morley and Gertrude Emily Fass; *m* 1940, Joan North Buckmaster, *d* of Dame Gladys Cooper, DBE; two *s* one *d. Educ:* Wellington Coll. Originally intended for diplomatic career; studied for stage at RADA. First appearance in Treasure Island, Strand Theatre, 1929; appeared in provinces; established repertory (with Peter Bull) at Perranporth, Cornwall; parts include: Oscar Wilde in play of that name, Gate, 1936, and Fulton (first New York appearance), 1938; Alexandre Dumas in The Great Romancer, Strand, 1937; Higgins in Pygmalion, Old Vic, 1937; Sheridan Whiteside in The Man Who Came to Dinner, Savoy, 1941; Prince Regent in The First Gentleman, New, 1945, and Savoy; Arnold Holt in Edward My Son, His Majesty's and Lyric, 1947, Martin Beck Theatre, New York, 1948; toured Australia, 1949–50; The Little Hut, Lyric, 1950; Hippo Dancing, Lyric, 1954; A Likely Tale, Globe, 1956; Fanny, Drury Lane, 1957; Hook, Line and Sinker, Piccadilly, 1958; A Majority of One, Phœnix, 1960; A Time to Laugh, Piccadilly, 1962; Halfway Up The Tree, Queen's, 1968; How the Other Half Loves, Lyric, 1970; A Ghost on Tiptoe, Savoy, 1974; Banana Ridge, Savoy, 1976. Directed: The Tunnel of Love, Her Majesty's Theatre, 1957; Once More, with Feeling, New Theatre, 1959. Entered films, 1937; *films:* Marie Antoinette; Major Barbara; Young Mr Pitt; Outcast of the Islands; The African Queen; Curtain Up; Mr Gilbert and Mr Sullivan; The Final Test; Beat the Devil; The Rainbow Jacket; Beau Brummell; The Good Die Young; Quentin Durward; Loser Takes All; Law and Disorder; The Journey; The Doctor's Dilemma; Libel; The Battle of the Sexes; Oscar Wilde; Go to Blazes; The Young Ones; The Boys; The Road to Hong Kong; Nine Hours to Rama; The Old Dark House; Murder at the Gallop; Take her, She's Mine; Hot Enough for June; Sold in Egypt; Topkapi; Of Human Bondage; Those Magnificent Men in Their Flying Machines; Ghengis Khan; ABC Murders; The Loved One; Life at the Top; A Study in Terror; Way Way Out; Finders Keepers; Hotel Paradiso; Le Tendre Voyou; Hot Millions; Sinful Davey; Song of Norway; Oliver Cromwell; When Eight Bells Toll; Doctor in Trouble; Theatre of Blood; Too Many Cooks; The Human Factor. Hon. DLitt Reading, 1980. *Publications:* Short Story, 1935; Goodness How Sad, 1937; Staff Dance, 1944; (with Noel Langley) Edward My Son, 1948; (with Ronald Gow) The Full Treatment, 1953; Hippo Dancing, 1953; (with Dundas Hamilton) Six Months Grace, 1957; (with Sewell Stokes) Responsible Gentleman (autobiography), 1966; A Musing Morley, 1974; Morley Marvels, 1976; (ed) Robert Morley's Book of Bricks, 1978; (ed) Robert Morley's Book of Worries, 1979; Morley Matters, 1980; The Best of Morley, 1981; The Second Book of Bricks, 1981. *Recreations:* conversation, horse racing. *Address:* Fairmans, Wargrave, Berks.

See also S. R. Morley.

MORLEY, Sheridan Robert; Drama Critic and Arts Editor, Punch, since 1975; London Drama Critic, International Herald Tribune, since 1979; *b* Ascot, Berks, 5 Dec. 1941; *s* of Robert Morley, *qv* and Joan Buckmaster; *m* 1965, Margaret Gudejko; one *s* two *d. Educ:* Sizewell Hall, Suffolk; Merton Coll., Oxford (MA Hons) 1964). Newscaster, reporter and scriptwriter, ITN, 1964–67; interviewer, Late Night Line Up, BBC2, 1967–71; Presenter, Film Night, BBC2, 1972; Dep. Features Editor, The Times, 1973–75. Regular presenter: Kaleidoscope, BBC Radio 4; Meridian, BBC World Service; frequent radio and TV broadcasts on the performing arts, incl. Broadway Babes, and Song By Song by Sondheim (Radio 2) and Sheridan Morley Meets (BBC1). Mem., Drama Panel, British Council, 1982–. Narrator: Side by Side by Sondheim, Guildford and Norwich, 1981–82; (also devised), Noël and Gertie (Coward anthology), King's Head, London, 1983, Sonning, 1985. *Publications:* A Talent to Amuse: the life of Noël Coward, 1969; Review Copies, 1975; Oscar Wilde, 1976; Sybil Thorndike, 1977; Marlene Dietrich, 1977; Gladys Cooper, 1979; (with Cole Lesley and Graham Payn) Noël Coward and his Friends, 1979; The Stephen Sondheim Songbook, 1979; Gertrude Lawrence, 1981; (ed, with Graham Payn) The Noël Coward Diaries, 1982; Tales from the Hollywood Raj, 1983; Shooting Stars, 1983; The Theatregoers' Quiz Book, 1983; Katharine Hepburn, 1984; The Other Side of the Moon, 1985; (ed) Bull's Eyes, 1985; Ingrid Bergman, 1985; The Great Stage Stars, 1986; Spread a Little Happiness, 1986; ed, series of theatre annuals and film and theatre studies, incl. Punch at the Theatre, 1980; contribs to The Times, Evening Standard, Radio Times, Mail on Sunday, Playbill (NY), High Life and The Australian. *Recreations:* talking, swimming, eating, narrating Side by Side by Sondheim and Noël and Gertie. *Address:* c/o Punch, 23 Tudor Street, EC4. *T:* 01–583 9199.

MORLEY, Very Rev. William Fenton, CBE 1980; Dean Emeritus of Salisbury, since 1977; *b* 5 May 1912; *s* of Arthur Fenton and Margaret Morley; *m* 1937, Marjorie Rosa, *d* of Joseph Temple Robinson, Frinton; one *s* one *d. Educ:* St David's, Lampeter; Oriel Coll., Oxford; Wycliffe Hall, Oxford; University of London. Ordained, 1935; Curate of: Ely, Cardiff, 1935–38; Porthcawl, S Wales, 1938–43; Officiating Chaplain to the Forces, 1941–43; Vicar of Penrhiwceiber, 1943–46; Rector of Haseley, Oxon, 1946–50; Director of Music and Lecturer in Hebrew at Cuddesdon Coll., Oxon, 1946–50; Examiner in Hebrew and New Testament Greek, 1947–59 and External Lecturer in Biblical and Religious Studies, 1950–61, Univ. of London; Chaplain and Lecturer of St Gabriel's Training Coll., 1956–61; Education Sec. to Overseas Council of Church Assembly, 1950–56; Warburton Lectr, Lincoln's Inn, 1963–65; Chairman: Church of England Deployment and Payment Commission, 1965–68; Church of England Pensions Bd, 1974–80; Bath and Wells Diocesan Education Council, 1978–82. Public Preacher to Diocese of Rochester, 1950–56; Canon Residentiary and Precentor of Southwark Cathedral, 1956–61; Vicar of Leeds, Rural Dean of Leeds and Hon. Canon of Ripon, 1961–71; Dean of Salisbury, 1971–77. Editor, East and West Review, 1953–64. Chaplain to HM's Household, 1965–71; Church Comr, 1968–77. *Publications:* One Church, One Faith, One Lord, 1953; The Church to Which You Belong, 1955; The Call of God, 1959; Preaching through the Christian Year: Year 4, 1974, Year 6, 1977. *Recreations:* music, writing. *Address:* 7 Cavendish Place, Bath, Avon BA1 2UB. *Club:* Royal Commonwealth Society.

MORLEY-JOHN, Michael, CBE 1979; RD 1970; Judge of the Supreme Court of Hong Kong, 1973–78; *b* 22 May 1923; *s* of late Clifford Morley-John and Norah (*née* Thompson); *m* 1951,'Sheila Christine Majendie; one *s* one *d. Educ:* Wycliffe Coll.; Univ. of Bristol (LLB). Called to the Bar, Gray's Inn, 1950. Hong Kong: Crown Counsel, 1951; Dir of Public Prosecutions, 1961; Acting Solicitor Gen., 1966–67; Dist Judge, 1967; Judicial Comr, State of Brunei, 1974. Acting Comdr, RNR, 1973. *Recreations:* tennis, stamp collecting, sailing. *Address:* The Coach House, Woodland Way, Milford-on-Sea, Hants SO41 0NB. *T:* Lymington 44824. *Clubs:* Milford and South Hants (Milford-on-Sea); Royal Ocean Racing; Bar Yacht; Hong Kong, Hong Kong Kennel (former Pres.) (Hong Kong).

MORLING, Col Leonard Francis, DSO 1940; OBE 1946; TD 1942; Architect; *b* 2 Nov. 1904, British; 2nd *s* of late Ernest Charles Morling and Frances Ruth Baldwin; unmarried. *Educ:* Brighton Hove and Sussex Grammar Sch. Architect, 1927–36; Mem. of firm, C. Morling Ltd, Builders and Contractors, Seaford, 1936–39; social work, in London, 1948–50, Malaya, 1950–55; Personnel and Welfare Work, London, 1956–59, Australia, 1960–63, London, 1964. Comnd. Territorial Army, 1924; Capt. 1930; Major, 1934; Lt-Col 1943; Col 1946; served France and Flanders (despatches, DSO); Persia, Iraq and India. *Publication:* Sussex Sappers, 1972. *Address:* c/o Lloyds Bank, Seaford, East Sussex.

MORLING, Norton Arthur; Member, Civil Aviation Authority, 1972–75; *b* 13 Feb. 1909; *o s* of Norton and Edith Morling, Hunsdon, Herts; *m* 1942, Rachel Paterson, *d* of James and Elizabeth Chapman, Johannesburg, SA; one *s* one *d. Educ:* Hertford Grammar Sch.; Cambridge Univ. (MA); Birmingham Univ. (MCom). Joined Turner & Newall Ltd as Management Trainee, 1931. War Service, N Africa and Italy, 1942–45 (despatches); Lt-Col 1944; ADS&T, AFHQ, 1944–45. Dir, and in some cases Chm., of various subsid. and associated companies, UK and overseas, 1946–64, including Turner Brothers Asbestos Co. Ltd and Ferodo Ltd: Gp Dir, 1957–67; Financial Dir, 1964–67; seconded as Industrial Advr to Nat. Economic Develt Office, 1967–70; Mem., Air Transport Licensing Bd, 1971–72. *Recreation:* gardening. *Address:* Little Brook House, Over Wallop, Stockbridge, Hants SO20 8HT. *T:* Andover 781296.

MORNINGTON, Earl of; Arthur Gerald Wellesley; *b* 31 Jan. 1978; *s* and *heir* of Marquess of Douro, *qv.*

MORO, Peter, CBE 1977; FRIBA, FSIAD; Architect; *b* 27 May 1911; *s* of Prof. Ernst Moro and Grete Hönigswald; *m* 1940, Anne Vanneck (marr. diss. 1984); three *d. Educ:* Stuttgart, Berlin and Zürich. Swiss Dip. Architecture, 1936; FRIBA 1948; FSIA 1957. Practice with Tecton, 1937–39; Mem. Exec. Cttee, Mars Gp, 1938; Lectr, Sch. of Arch., Regent Street Polytechnic, 1941–47; LCC Associated Architect, Royal Festival Hall, 1948–51; Tutor, Architectural Assoc., 1954–55. External Examiner: Strathclyde Univ., 1973, 1975; Manchester Univ., 1977, 1981; Visiting Critic: Thames Polytechnic; Bath Univ.; Oxford Polytechnic; Sheffield Univ. Architect: Fairlawn Sch., LCC, 1957; Nottingham Playhouse, 1964; alterations, Royal Opera House, Covent Garden, 1964; Birstall Sch., Leics, 1964; housing schemes, GLC and Southwark, 1967–80; theatre, Hull Univ., the Gulbenkian Centre, 1970; additions and alterations, Bristol Old Vic, 1972; theatre, New Univ. of Ulster, 1976; Plymouth Theatre Royal, 1982; Taliesin Theatre, UC Swansea, 1984. Sen. Pres., Assoc. of British Theatre Technicians (Founder Mem.); Member: Council, RIBA, 1967–73; Housing the Arts Cttee, Arts Council of GB, 1975–78. Governor, Ravensbourne Coll. of Art and Design, 1976–. Lectures in UK, Finland, Norway, Germany and Holland. Bronze Medal, RIBA, 1964; 4 Civic Trust Awards and Commendations; Heritage Award, 1975; Concrete Award, 1983. *Publications:* contribs to technical jls in UK, Germany, France, Italy, Portugal and Japan. *Address:* 20 Blackheath Park, SE3 9RP. *T:* 01–852 0250.

MORONY, Gen. Sir Thomas (Lovett), KCB 1981; OBE 1969; retired; UK Military Representative to NATO, 1983–86; Aide-de-Camp General to the Queen, 1984–86; *b* 23 Sept. 1926; *s* of late Thomas Henry Morony, CSI, CIE, and Evelyn Myra (*née* Lovett); *m* 1961, Elizabeth, *d* of G. W. N. Clark; two *s. Educ:* Eton (KS). Commissioned, 1947. BM, King's African Rifles, 1958–61; GSO1 (DS) at Camberley and RMCS, 1963–65; GSO1, HQ Northern Army Gp, 1966–67; commanded 22 Light Air Defence Regt, RA, 1968–69; Comdr, 1st Artillery Bde, 1970–72; Dep. Comdt, Staff Coll., Camberley, 1973–75; Director RA, 1975–78; Comdt, RMCS, 1978–80; Vice Chief of the General Staff, 1980–83. Col Commandant: RA, 1978–; RHA, 1983–; Master Gunner, St James's Park, 1983–. Vice-Chm., Bd of Governors, Sherborne Sch. *Recreations:* gardening, music. *Address:* c/o Bank of Scotland, 8 Morningside Road, Edinburgh EH10 4DD. *Club:* Army and Navy.

MORPETH, Viscount; George William Beaumont Howard; Master of Ruthven; *b* 15 Feb. 1949; *s* and *heir* of 12th Earl of Carlisle, *qv. Educ:* Eton Coll.; Balliol Coll., Oxford. 9th/12th Royal Lancers, 1967–; Lieut 1970, Captain 1974, Major 1981. *Recreations:* reading, travel. *Address:* The Gate House, Naworth Castle, Brampton, Cumbria; 34 Epirus Road, SW6. *Clubs:* Beefsteak, Brooks's.

MORPETH, Sir Douglas (Spottiswoode), Kt 1981; TD 1959; FCA; Partner, Touche Ross & Co., Chartered Accountants, 1958–85; Senior Partner, Touche Ross, 1977–85; *b* 6 June 1924; *s* of Robert Spottiswoode Morpeth and Louise Rankine Morpeth (*née* Dobson); *m* 1951, Anne Rutherford, *yr d* of Ian C. Bell, OBE, MC, Edinburgh; two *s* two *d. Educ:* George Watson's Coll., Edinburgh; Edinburgh Univ. (BCom). Commissioned RA; served 1943–47, India, Burma, Malaya. Qualified as Mem. of Inst. of Chartered Accountants in England and Wales, 1952, Fellow, 1957 (Council of Inst., 1964–84, Vice-Pres., 1970, Dep. Pres., 1971, Pres., 1972). Dir, Clerical Medical and General Life Assurance Soc., 1973– (Dep. Chm., 1974; Chm., 1978–); Dir, Brixton Estate plc, 1977– (Dep. Chm., 1983–); Chm. of Trustees, British Telecom Staff Superannuation Scheme, 1983–. Mem., Investment Grants Advisory Cttee, 1968–71; Chm., Inflation Accounting Steering Gp, 1976–80; Vice-Chm., Accounting Standards Cttee, 1970–82. Chm., Taxation Cttee, CBI, 1973–76. Honourable Artillery Company: Member, 1949–; commanded 'B' Battery, 1958–61; Lt-Col, comdg 1st Regt RHA, 1964–66; Master Gunner within the Tower of London, 1966–69. Master, Co. of Chartered Accountants in England and Wales, 1977–78. *Recreations:* golf, tennis, gardening. *Address:* Summerden House, Shamley Green, near Guildford, Surrey. *T:* Guildford 892689. *Clubs:* Athenæum, City Livery, Royal Automobile.

MORPHET, David Ian; Under-Secretary, Atomic Energy Division, Department of Energy, since 1985; *b* 24 Jan. 1940; *s* of late A. Morphet and of Sarah Elizabeth Morphet; *m* 1968, Sarah Gillian Sedgwick; two *s* one *d. Educ:* King James's Grammar Sch., Almondbury, Yorks; St John's Coll., Cambridge (History Schol.; English Tripos, class I, Pts I and II). Foreign Office, 1961; Vice Consul, Taiz, 1963; Doha, 1963–64; Arabian Dept, FO, 1964–66; Asst Private Sec. to Foreign Secretary, 1966–68; First Sec., Madrid, 1969–72; Diplomatic Service Observer, CS Selection Board, 1972–74; transf. to Dept of Energy, 1974; Asst Sec., 1975; Dep. Chm., Midlands Electricity Board (on secondment), 1978–79; Under-Secretary: Electricity Div., 1979–83; Energy Policy Div., 1983–85. Dir,

BICC Cables Ltd, 1981–. *Recreations:* music, theatre, reading, walking. *Address:* c/o Department of Energy, Millbank, SW1.

MORPURGO, Jack Eric; Professor of American Literature, University of Leeds, 1969–83, now Emeritus; author; *b* 26 April 1918; *s* of late Mark Morpurgo, Islington; *m* 1946, Catherine Noel Kippe, *d* of late Prof. Emile Cammaerts; three *s* one *d*. *Educ:* Christ's Hosp.; Univ. of New Brunswick; Coll. of William and Mary, USA (BA); Durham Univ. Enlisted RA, 1939; served as regimental and staff officer in India, Middle East, Greece and Italy; GSO 2, Public Relations Directorate, War Office. Editorial Staff, Penguin Books, 1946–49; Editor Penguin Parade; General Editor, Pelican Histories, 1949–67; Asst Dir, Nuffield Foundation, 1950–54; Dir-Gen., Nat. Book League, 1955–69, Dep. Chm., 1969–71, Vice-Pres., 1971–; Prof. of American Studies, Univ. of Geneva, 1968–70; Visiting Professor: Michigan State Univ., 1950; George Washington Univ., 1970; Vanderbilt Univ., 1981; Schol.-in-residence, Rockefeller Res. Center, Italy, 1974; Vis. Fellow, ANU, 1975, 1977; has lectured in USA, Canada, Germany, India, Burma, etc. Dir of Unesco Seminar on Production of Reading Materials, Rangoon, 1957, Madras, 1959. Almoner, Christ's Hospital (Dep. Chm., 1980–84); Chm. Working Pty on Medical Libraries; Dir, William and Mary Historical Project, 1970–76. Director: Sexton Press Ltd, 1984–; P. and M. Youngman Carter Ltd, 1985–. Phi Beta Kappa, 1948; Hon. Fellow, Coll. of William and Mary, 1949. Hon. LitD Maine, 1961; Hon. DLitt Elmira, 1966; Hon. DHL William and Mary, 1970; Hon. DHL Idaho, 1984. Yorkshire Post Special Literary Award, 1980. *Publications:* American Excursion, 1949; Charles Lamb and Elia, 1949; The Road to Athens, 1963; Barnes Wallis, 1972; Treason at West Point, 1975; Their Majesties Royall Colledge, 1976; Allen Lane: King Penguin, 1979; Verses Humorous and Post-Humorous, 1981; contributor to: The Impact of America, 1951; joint author of: History of The United States (with Russel B. Nye), 1955; Venice (with Martin Hürlimann), 1964; (with G. A. T. Allan) Christ's Hospital, 1984; edited: Leigh Hunt: Autobiography, 1949; E. J. Trelawny: Last Days of Shelley and Byron, 1952; Poems of John Keats, 1953; Rugby Football: An Anthology (with Kenneth Pelmear), 1958; Cobbett: a year's residence in USA, 1964; Cooper: The Spy, 1968; Cobbett's America, 1985. *Recreation:* watching Rugby football. *Address:* 12 Laurence Mews, W12 9AT. *Clubs:* Army and Navy, Pilgrims.

MORPURGO DAVIES, Anna Elbina; *see* Davies, A. E.

MORRAH, Ruth, (Mrs Dermot Morrah), JP; Chairman, Metropolitan Juvenile Courts, 1945–64; *b* 21 Aug. 1899; *d* of Willmott Houselander; *m* 1923, Dermot Michael Macgregor Morrah (*d* 1974); two *d*. *Educ:* convent schs; St Anne's Coll., Oxford. JP 1944. Pro Ecclesia et Pontifice, 1964. *Recreations:* travelling, needlework. *Address:* 29 Tite Street, SW3. *T:* 01–352 0267.

See also T. E. Utley.

MORRELL, Frances Maine; Leader, Inner London Education Authority, since 1983 (Deputy Leader, 1981–83); Member for Islington South and Finsbury, Greater London Council, 1981–86; *b* 28 Dec. 1937; *d* of Frank and Beatrice Galleway; *m* 1964, Brian Morrell; one *d*. *Educ:* Queen Anne Grammar Sch., York; Hull Univ. BA (Hons) English Lang. and Lit. Secondary Sch. Teacher, 1960–69; Press Officer, Fabian Soc. and NUS, 1970–72; Research into MPs' constituency role, 1973; Special Adviser to Tony Benn, as Sec. of State for Industry, then as Sec. of State for Energy, 1974–79. Member: Oakes Cttee, Enquiry into Payment and Collection Methods for Gas and Electricity Bills (report publ. 1976); Exec., Campaign for Labour Party Democracy, 1979–; Women's Action Cttee, 1980–. Contested (Lab) Chelmsford, Feb. 1974. *Publications:* (with Tony Benn and Francis Cripps) A Ten Year Industrial Strategy for Britain, 1975; (with Francis Cripps) The Case for a Planned Energy Policy, 1976; From the Electors of Bristol: the record of a year's correspondence between constituents and their Member of Parliament, 1977; (jtly) Manifesto—a radical strategy for Britain's future, 1981. *Recreations:* reading, cooking, gardening. *Address:* c/o County Hall, SE1 7PB. *T:* 01–633 3330.

MORRELL, Col (Herbert) William (James), OBE 1954; MC 1944; TD; MA Oxon; DL; JP; *b* 1 Aug. 1915; *er s* of James Herbert Morrell, MA, Headington Hill, Oxford; *m* 1947, Pamela Vivien Eleanor, *d* of Richard Stubbs, Willaston, Cheshire; one *s* two *d*. *Educ:* Eton; Magdalen Coll., Oxford. 2nd Lt RA, 1936; served War of 1939–45 (France, Madagascar, Burma); retired 1948. DL 1961, JP 1959, High Sheriff 1960, Oxon. *Recreations:* hunting, sailing. *Address:* Caphill, Sandford St Martin, Oxon. *T:* Great Tew 291.

MORRELL, James George; Founder Director, Henley Centre for Forecasting, 1974–79; author and business forecaster; *b* 1923; *s* of late Frederick Morrell and Violet (*née* Smart); *m* 1st, 1944, Elizabeth Bristow (marr. diss. 1970); one *s* two *d*; 2nd, 1972, Margaret Helen Nickolls. *Educ:* Christ's Hospital; Ruskin and Wadham Colls, Oxford. MA Oxon 1953. Served RAF, 1941–46. Ford Motor Co., 1955; Phillips & Drew, 1957; Charterhouse Group, 1964; founded James Morrell & Associates, 1967. Visiting Professor, Univ. of Bradford, 1970–73; Associate Fellow, Oxford Centre for Management Studies, 1981–84. *Publications:* Business Forecasting for Finance and Industry, 1969; Business Decisions and the Role of Forecasting, 1972; Inflation and Business Management, 1974; 2002: Britain plus 25, 1977; The Regeneration of British Industry, 1979; Britain through the 1980s, 1980; The Future of the Dollar and the World Reserve System, 1981; Employment in Tourism, 1982, 2nd edn 1985; Business Forecasts for the Housing Market, 1985; The Impact of Tourism on London, 1985. *Recreations:* canals, Samuel Pepys, stock market. *Address:* 81 Speed House, Barbican, EC2Y 8AU.

MORRELL, Rt. Rev. James Herbert Lloyd; Canon and Prebend of Heathfield in Chichester Cathedral, 1959–82, Canon Emeritus since 1982; Provost of Lancing (Southern Division Woodard Schools), 1961–82; *b* 12 Aug. 1907; *s* of George Henry and Helen Adela Morrell. *Educ:* Dulwich Coll.; King's Coll., London; Ely Theological Coll. Deacon, 1931; Priest, 1932; Curate of St Alphage, Hendon, 1931–35; Curate of St Michael and All Angels, Brighton, 1935–39; Bishop of Chichester's Chaplain for men, 1939–41; Lecturer for The Church of England Moral Welfare Council, 1941–44; Vicar of Roffey, 1944–46; Archdeacon of Lewes, 1946–59; Bishop Suffragan of Lewes, 1959–77; Asst Bishop, Diocese of Chichester, 1978–85. Fellow of King's Coll., London, 1960. *Publications:* Four Words (broadcast talks to the Forces), 1941; The Heart of a Priest, 1958; A Priest's Notebook of Prayer, 1961; The Catholic Faith Today, 1964. *Recreations:* walking, photography. *Address:* 83 Davigdor Road, Hove BN3 1RA. *T:* Brighton 733971.

MORRELL, Leslie James, OBE 1986; JP; Chairman, Northern Ireland Water Council, since 1982; *b* 26 Dec. 1931; *s* of James Morrell; *m* 1958, Anne Wallace, BSc; two *s* one *d*. *Educ:* Portora Royal Sch., Enniskillen; Queen's Univ., Belfast. BAgric 1955. Member: Londonderry CC, 1969–73; Coleraine Bor. Council, 1973–77; Mem. (U) for Londonderry, NI Assembly, 1973–75; Minister of Agriculture, NI Exec., 1973–74; Dep. Leader, Unionist Party of NI, 1974–80. Mem., BBC Gen. Adv. Cttee, 1980–86; Chm., BBC NI Agricl Adv. Cttee, 1986–. Chm., NI Fedn of Housing Assocs, 1978–80; Hon. Secretary: James Butcher Housing Assoc. (NI), 1981– (Chm., 1976–81); James Butcher Retirement Homes Ltd, 1985 . Mem. Exec., Assoc. of Governing Bodies of Voluntary Grammar Schs, 1978–84; Chm., Virus Tested Stem Cutting Potato Growers Assoc., 1977–. JP Londonderry, 1966. *Address:* Dunboe House, Castlerock, Coleraine BT51 4UB. *T:* Castlerock 848352.

MORRELL, Col William; *see* Morrell, Col H. W. J.

MORRICE, Norman; choreographer; Director of the Royal Ballet, 1977–86; *b* Mexico, of British parents. *Educ:* Rambert School of Ballet. Joined the Ballet Rambert in early 1950s as a dancer; notably danced Dr Coppélius, in Coppélia, and subseq. also choreographer; first considerable success with his ballet, Two Brothers, in America, and at first London perf., Sept. 1958; première of his 2nd ballet, Hazaña, Sadler's Wells Theatre, 1958; the New Ballet Rambert Company was formed in 1966 and he was Co-Director with Marie Rambert, to create new works by unknown and established choreographers; his ballet, Hazard, was danced at Bath Festival, 1967; he composed 10 new ballets by 1968 and had taken his place with leading choreographers; *ballets include:* 1–2–3, Them and Us and Pastorale Variée, which were staged at the Jeanetta Cochrane Theatre, 1968–69; Ladies, Ladies!, perf. by Ballet Rambert at Young Vic, 1972; Spindrift, at Round House, 1974, etc. Has danced frequently overseas.

MORRIS; *see* Temple-Morris.

MORRIS, family name of **Barons Killanin, Morris, Morris of Grasmere** and **Morris of Kenwood.**

MORRIS, 3rd Baron *cr* 1918; **Michael David Morris;** *b* 9 Dec. 1937; *s* of 2nd Baron Morris and of Jean Beatrice (now Lady Salmon), *d* of late Lt-Col D. Maitland-Makgill-Crichton; *S* father, 1975; *m* 1st, 1959, Denise Eleanor (marr. diss. 1962), *o d* of Morley Richards; 2nd, 1962, Jennifer (marr. diss. 1969), *o d* of Squadron Leader Tristram Gilbert; two *d*; *m* 1980, Juliet, twin *d* of Anthony Buckingham; two *s* one *d*. *Educ:* Downside. FCA. *Heir:* *s* Hon. Thomas Anthony Salmon Morris, *b* 2 July 1982. *Address:* House of Lords, SW1A 0PW.

MORRIS OF GRASMERE, Baron *cr* 1967 (Life Peer), of Grasmere; **Charles Richard Morris,** KCMG 1963; Kt 1953; MA Oxon; Hon. LLD: Manchester, 1951; Aberdeen, 1963; Leeds, 1964; Malta, 1964; Hull, 1965; Hon. DLitt: Sydney, 1954; Lancaster, 1967; Hon. DTech Bradford, 1970; *b* 25 Jan. 1898; *s* of M. C. Morris, Sutton Valence, Kent; *m* 1923, Mary de Selincourt; one *s* one *d*. *Educ:* Tonbridge Sch.; Trinity Coll., Oxford. Lt RGA 1916–19; Fellow and Tutor of Balliol Coll., 1921–43; for one year, 1926–27 (while on leave of absence from Balliol), Prof. of Philosophy, Univ. of Michigan, USA; Senior Proctor, 1937–38; Mem. of Council of Girls Public Day Sch. Trust, 1933–38; Oxford City Councillor, 1939–41; Ministry of Supply, 1939–42; Under-Sec., Min. of Production, 1942–43; Head Master, King Edward's Sch., Birmingham, 1941–48; Chm., Cttee of Vice-Chancellors and Principals, 1952–55; Central Joint Adv. Cttee on Tutorial Classes, 1948–58; Commonwealth Univ. Interchange Cttee and Recruitment Sub-Cttee of British Council, 1951; Sch. Broadcasting Council, 1954–64; Inter-Univ. Council for Higher Education Overseas, 1957–64; Independent Chm., Jt Adv. Cttee for Wool Textile Industry, 1952; Pres., Council of Coll. of Preceptors, 1954–63. Vice-Chancellor of Leeds Univ., 1948–63; Pro-Chancellor, Univ. of Bradford, 1966–69. Member: Royal Commn on Local Govt in Greater London, 1957; Cttee of Inquiry on Australian Univs, 1957; Chairman: Adv. Bd Of Univs Quarterly, 1960; Local Govt Training Bd, 1967–75; President: Brit. Student Tuberculosis Foundn, 1960; Assoc. of Teachers in Colls and Depts of Educn, 1961–64. *Publications:* A History of Political Ideas (with Mary Morris), 1924; Locke, Berkeley, Hume, 1931; Idealistic Logic, 1933; In Defence of Democracy (with J. S. Fulton), 1936; British Democracy, 1939; various essays and papers to learned societies. *Recreation:* fell walking. *Address:* Ladywood, White Moss, Ambleside, Cumbria LA22 9SF. *T:* 286. *Club:* Athenæum.

MORRIS OF KENWOOD, 2nd Baron *cr* 1950, of Kenwood; **Philip Geoffrey Morris,** JP; Company Director; *b* 18 June 1928; *s* of 1st Baron Morris of Kenwood, and Florence (*d* 1982), *d* of Henry Isaacs, Leeds; *S* father, 1954; *m* 1958, Ruth, *o d* of late Baron Janner and of Lady Janner, *qv*; one *s* three *d*. *Educ:* Loughborough Coll., Leics. Served RAF, Nov. 1946–Feb. 1949; July 1951–Oct. 1955. JP Inner London, 1967. *Recreations:* tennis, golf, ski-ing. *Heir:* *s* Hon. Jonathan David Morris, *b* 5 Aug. 1968. *Address:* Lawn Cottage, Orchard Rise, Kingston, Surrey KT2 7EY. *T:* 01–942 6321.

MORRIS, Air Marshal Sir Alec, KBE 1982; CB 1979; Executive, British Aerospace Plc, since 1983; *b* 11 March 1926; *s* of late Harry Morris; *m* 1946, Moyna Patricia, *d* of late Norman Boyle; one *s* one *d* (twins). *Educ:* King Edward VI Sch., East Retford; King's Coll., Univ. of London; Univ. of Southampton. Commnd RAF, 1945; radar duties, No 90 (Signals) Gp, 1945–50; Guided Weapons Dept, RAE, 1953–56; exchange duty, HQ USAF, 1958–60; space res., Min. of Supply, 1960–63; DS, RAF Staff Coll., 1963–65; OC Eng, No 2 Flying Trng Sch., Syerston, 1966–68; Asst Dir, Guided Weapons R&D, Min. of Tech., 1968–70; OC RAF Central Servicing Develt Estabt, Swanton Morley, 1970–72; SASO, HQ No 90 (Signals) Gp, 1972–74; RCDS, 1974; Dir of Signals (Air), MoD, 1975–76; Dir Gen. Strategic Electronic Systems, MoD (PE), 1976–79; Air Officer Engineering, RAF Strike Command, 1979–81; Chief Engineer, RAF, 1981–83, retired. *Recreations:* tennis, gardening. *Address:* 6 Liverpool Road, Kingston-upon-Thames, Surrey KT2 7SZ. *Club:* Royal Air Force.

MORRIS, Rt. Hon. Alfred; PC 1979; MP (Lab and Co-op) Manchester (Wythenshawe) since 1964; Opposition Front Bench Spokesman on Social Services, specialising in the problems of disabled people, 1970–74 and since 1979; *b* 23 March 1928; *s* of late George Henry Morris and Jessie Morris (*née* Murphy); *m* 1950, Irene (*née* Jones); two *s* two *d*. *Educ:* elem. and evening schs, Manchester; Ruskin Coll., Oxford; St Catherine's, Univ. of Oxford (MA); Univ. of Manchester (Postgrad. certif. in Educn). Employed in office of a Manchester brewing firm from age 14 (HM Forces, 1946–48); Teacher and Lectr, Manchester, 1954–56; Industrial Relations Officer, The Electricity Coun., London, 1956–64. Nat. Chm., Labour League of Youth, 1950–52; contested Liverpool (Garston), Gen. Elec. 1951; Observer, Coun. of Europe, 1952–53; PPS to Minister of Agric., Fisheries and Food, 1964–67, and to Lord President of the Council and Leader of House of Commons, 1968–70; Parly Under-Sec. of State, DHSS, as Britain's first-ever Minister for the Disabled, 1974–79. Treasurer, British Gp, IPU, 1971–74; Mem., UK Parly Delegn to UN Gen. Assembly, 1966; Chm., Food and Agriculture Gp of Parly Lab. Party, 1971–74; Representative of Privy Council on Council of RCVS, 1969–74; promoted Chronically Sick and Disabled Persons Act, 1970, Food and Drugs (Milk) Act, 1970, Police Act, 1972, as a Private Member; Parly Adviser to the Police Fedn, 1971–74; Chm., Co-operative Parly Group, 1971–72 and 1983–85; Vice-Chm., All-Party Parly Retail Trade Gp, 1972–74; Chairman: Managing Trustees, Parly Pensions Fund, 1983– (Man. Trustee, 1980–83); Managing Trustees, H of C Members' Fund, 1983–; Anzac Gp of MPs and Peers, 1982–; Jt Treasurer, British-Amer. Parly Gp, 1983–. Mem., Gen. Adv. Council, BBC, 1968–74, 1983–; Patron: Disablement Income Group, 1970–; Motability, 1978–; Mem., Exec. Cttee, Nat. Fund for Research into Crippling Diseases, 1970–74. Chm., World Cttee apptd to draft "Charter for the 1980's" for disabled people worldwide, 1980–81; Pres., N of England Regional Assoc. for the Deaf, 1980–; Trustee, Crisis at Christmas, 1982–. Field Marshal Lord Harding Award, 1971, for services to the disabled;

Grimshaw Meml Award of Nat. Fedn of the Blind, 1971. *Publications:* Value Added Tax: a tax on the consumer, 1970; The Growth of Parliamentary Scrutiny by Committee, 1970; (with A. Butler) No Feet to Drag, 1972; Ed. lectures (Human Relations in Industry), 1958; Ed. Jl (Jt Consultation) publ. Nat. Jt Adv. Coun. Elec. Supply Ind., 1959–61. *Recreations:* gardening, tennis, snooker, chess. *Address:* House of Commons, SW1A 0AA.

MORRIS, Alfred Cosier; Director, Bristol Polytechnic, since 1986; *b* 12 Nov. 1941; *s* of late Stanley Bernard Morris, Anlaby, E Yorks, and Jennie Fletcher; *m* 1970, Annette, *er d* of Eamonn and May Donovan, Cork, Eire; one *d*. *Educ:* Hymers Coll., Hull (E Riding Scholar); Univ. of Lancaster (MA Financial Control 1970). FCA; FSS. Articled clerk to Oliver Mackrill & Co., 1958–63; Company Sec., Financial Controller and Dir, several cos, 1963–71; Sen. Leverhulme Res. Fellow in Univ. Planning and Orgn, Univ. of Sussex, 1971–74; Vis. Lectr in Financial Management, Univ. of Warwick, 1973; Group Management Accountant, Arthur Guinness Ltd, 1974–76; Management Consultant, Deloitte Haskins & Sells, 1976–77; Financial Adviser, subsids of Arthur Guinness, 1977–80; Dep. Dir, Polytechnic of the South Bank, 1980–85, Acting Dir, 1985–86. Adviser to H of C Select Cttee on Educn, Sci. and Arts, 1979–83. *Publications:* (ed jtly and contrib.) Resources and Higher Education, 1982; articles and contribs to jls on higher educn. *Recreations:* sailing, wind-surfing. *Address:* Bristol Polytechnic, Coldharbour Lane, Frenchay, Bristol BS16 1QY. *Club:* Little Ship.

MORRIS, Air Marshal Sir (Arnold) Alec; *see* Morris, Air Marshal Sir Alec.

MORRIS, Prof. Benjamin Stephen; Professor of Education, University of Bristol, 1956–75, now Emeritus; *b* 25 May 1910; *s* of Rev. B. S. Morris, Sherborne, Dorset, and Annie McNicol Duncan, Rothesay, Bute; *m* 1938, Margaret, *d* of Mr and Mrs Lamont, Glasgow; two *s* one *d*. *Educ:* Rothesay Academy; Glasgow Univ. BSc 1933, MEd 1937 (Glasgow). Trained as teacher, Jordanhill Training Coll., Glasgow; teacher, primary and secondary schs, 1936–39; Lecturer: in Psychology, Logic and Ethics, Jordanhill Trng Coll., 1939–40; in Educn, Univ. of Glasgow, 1940–46. Temp. Civil Servant, Min. of Food, 1941; Army Psychologist, 1942–46; Sen. Psychologist (WOSB), 1945–46; Hon. Lt-Col 1946. Student at Inst. of Psychoanalysis, London, 1946–50; Senior staff, Tavistock Institute of Human Relations, 1946–50 (Chm. Management Cttee, 1947–49); Dir Nat. Foundation for Educl Research in England and Wales, 1950–56. Vis. Prof. of Education, Harvard Univ., 1969–70. *Publications:* Objectives and Perspectives in Education, 1972; Some Aspects of Professional Freedom of Teachers, 1977; contributed to: The Function of Teaching, 1959; How and Why Do We Learn?, 1965; Study of Education, 1966; Higher Education, Demand and Response, 1969; Towards a Policy for the Education of Teachers, 1969; Towards Community Mental Health, 1971; The Sciences, The Humanities and the Technological Threat, 1975; articles in educational and psychological jls. *Recreation:* living in the country. *Address:* 7 Howcroft, Churchdown, Gloucester GL3 2EP.

MORRIS, Prof. Brian Robert, MA, DPhil; Principal, St David's University College, Lampeter, since 1980; *b* 4 Dec. 1930; *o s* of William Robert Morris and Ellen Elizabeth Morris (*née* Shelley); *m* 1955, Sandra Mary James, JP; one *s* one *d*. *Educ:* Cardiff High School; Worcester Coll., Oxford (MA, DPhil). National service with Welch Regt, 1949–51. Fellow of Shakespeare Inst., Univ. of Birmingham, 1956–58; Asst Lectr 1958–60, Lectr 1960–65, Univ. of Reading; Lectr 1965–67, Sen. Lectr 1967–71, Univ. of York; Prof. of English Literature, Univ. of Sheffield, 1971–80. Gen. Editor: New Mermaid Dramatists, 1964–; New Arden Shakespeare, 1974–82. Member: Council, Yorkshire Arts Assoc., 1973–81 (Chm. Literature Panel, 1973–77); Welsh Arts Council, 1983–86 (Mem. Lit. Cttee, 1978–); Archbishops' Council on Evangelism, 1971–75; Yr Academi Gymreig, 1979–; British Library Bd, 1980–; Council, Poetry Soc., 1980–; Council, Nat. Library of Wales, 1981–; Chm., Museums and Galls Comm, 1985– (Mem., 1975– (formerly Standing Commn on Museums and Galls)). Vice President: Council for Nat. Parks, 1985–; Museums Assoc., 1985–. Trustee: Nat. Portrait Gall., 1977–; Nat. Heritage Meml Fund, 1980–; Welsh Adv. Cttee, British Council, 1983–. Broadcaster, scriptwriter and presenter of television programmes. *Publications:* John Cleveland: a Bibliography of his Poems, 1967; (with Eleanor Withington) The Poems of John Cleveland, 1967; (ed) New Mermaid Critical Commentaries I–III, 1969–72; Mary Quant's London, 1973; (ed) Ritual Murder, 1980; *edited plays:* Ford's The Broken Heart, 1965, and 'Tis Pity She's a Whore, 1968; (with Roma Gill) Tourneur's The Atheist's Tragedy, 1976; Shakespeare's The Taming of the Shrew, 1981; *poetry:* Tide Race, 1976; Stones in the Brook, 1978; contribs to journals. *Recreations:* music, mountains, and museums. *Address:* Bryn, North Road, Lampeter, Dyfed SA48 7HZ. *T:* Lampeter 422335. *Clubs:* Athenæum, Beefsteak.

MORRIS, Rt. Hon. Charles Richard; PC 1978; DL; *b* 14 Dec. 1926; *s* of George Henry Morris, Newton Heath, Manchester; *m* 1950, Pauline, *d* of Albert Dunn, Manchester; two *d*. *Educ:* Brookdale Park Sch., Manchester. Served with Royal Engineers, 1945–48. Pres., Clayton Labour Party, 1950–52. Mem. of Manchester Corporation, 1954–64; Chm. of Transport Cttee, 1959–62; Dep. Chm. of Establishment Cttee, 1963–64. Mem., Post Office Workers Union (Mem. Nat. Exec. Council, 1959–63). Contested (Lab) Cheadle Div. of Cheshire, 1959. MP (Lab) Manchester, Openshaw, Dec. 1963–1983; PPS to the Postmaster-General, 1964; Govt Asst Whip, 1966–67; Vice-Chamberlain, HM Household, 1967–69; Treasurer, HM Household (Deputy Chief Whip), 1969–70; PPS to Rt Hon. H. Wilson, MP, 1970–74; Minister of State: DoE, March–Oct. 1974; CSD, 1974–79; Dep. Shadow Leader of the House, 1980–83. Sec., NW Gp of Labour MPs, 1979–83. Chm., Oldham–Rochdale Groundwork Trust, 1984–. DL Greater Manchester, 1985. *Address:* 24 Buxton Road West, Disley, Stockport, Cheshire. *T:* Disley 2450.

MORRIS, Rev. Dr Colin; Head of Religious Broadcasting, BBC, since 1979 (Deputy Head, 1978–79), and Head of Religious Programmes, BBC Television, 1978–84; Special Adviser to the Director-General, BBC, since 1986; *b* 13 Jan. 1929; *o s* of Daniel Manley Morris and Mary Alice Morris, Bolton, Lancs. *Educ:* Bolton County Grammar Sch.; Univs of Oxford and Manchester. Served RM, 1947–49. Student, Nuffield Coll., Oxford, 1953–56; Missionary, Northern Rhodesia, 1956–60; President: United Church of Central Africa, 1960–64; United Church of Zambia, 1965–68; Minister of Wesley's Chapel, London, 1969–73; Gen. Sec., Overseas Div., Methodist Church, 1973–78; Pres. of the Methodist Conference, 1976–77. Chm., Community and Race Relations Unit, BCC, 1974–76. Lectures: Willson, Univ. of Nebraska, 1968; Cousland, Univ. of Toronto, 1972; Voigt, S Illinois Conf. United Methodist Church, 1973; Hickman, Duke University, North Carolina, 1974; Palmer, Pacific NW Univ., 1976; Heslington, Univ. of York, 1983; Hibbert, BBC Radio 4, 1986; William Barclay Meml, Glasgow, 1986; Select Preacher, Univ. of Cambridge, 1975, Oxford, 1976; holds several hon. degrees. Officer-Companion, Order of Freedom (Zambia), 1966. *Publications:* Black Government (with President K. D. Kaunda), 1960; Hour After Midnight, 1961; Out of Africa's Crucible, 1961; End of the Missionary, 1961; Church and Challenge in a New Africa, 1965; Humanist in Africa (with President K. D. Kaunda), 1966; Include Me Out, 1968; Unyoung, Uncoloured, Unpoor, 1969; What the Papers Didn't Say, 1971; Mankind My Church, 1971; The Hammer of the Lord, 1973; Epistles to the Apostle, 1974; The Word and the Words, 1975; Bugles in the Afternoon, 1977; Get Through Till Nightfall, 1979;

(ed) Kaunda on Violence, 1980; God-in-a-Box: Christian strategy in the TV age, 1984; A Week in the Life of God, 1986; Raising the Dead: a preacher's notebook, 1987; *relevant publication:* Spark in the Stubble, by T. L. Charlton, 1969. *Recreations:* writing, walking, music. *Address:* c/o BBC TV, Wood Lane, W12 7RJ. *T:* 01–576 1478.

MORRIS, David Edward; Chief Scientist, Civil Aviation Authority, 1972–78, retired; *b* 23 July 1915; *m* 1950, Heather Anne Court; one *s* two *d*. *Educ:* University Coll. of North Wales, Bangor; Trinity Coll., Cambridge. Aerodynamics Dept, RAE, 1938–56; Chief Supt, A&AEE, 1956–59; Chief Supt, RAE, Bedford, 1959–61; Dir-General, Development (RAF), Min. of Aviation, 1961–65; Dir-Gen., Civil Aircraft and Gen. Services Research and Develt, 1965–69; Scientific Adviser (Civil Aviation), BoT, later DTI, 1969–72. FRAeS 1956. *Publications:* various reports and memoranda. *Recreations:* walking, bridge. *Address:* 38 Days Lane, Biddenham, Bedford. *T:* 66644.

MORRIS, David Elwyn; Registrar of the Principal Registry of the Family Division of the High Court of Justice, since 1976; *b* 22 May 1920; *s* of Rev. S. M. Morris and K. W. Morris; *m* 1st, 1947, Joyce Hellyer (*d* 1977); one *s* one *d*; 2nd, 1978, Gwendolen Pearce, *widow* of Dr John Pearce. *Educ:* Mill Hill Sch.; Brasenose Coll., Oxford (Hulme Exhibnr; MA). With Friends' Ambulance Unit in China, 1942–44; served British Army in India, 1944–46. Called to Bar, Inner Temple, 1949; admitted Solicitor of the Supreme Court, 1955; Mem., Matrimonial Causes Rule Cttee, 1967–75. Partner, Jaques & Co. until 1975. Adv. Editor, Atkin's Encyclopaedia of Court Forms in Civil Proceedings, 1982–. *Publications:* China Changed My Mind, 1948; The End of Marriage, 1971; contrib. Marriage For and Against, 1972; Pilgrim through this Barren Land, 1974. *Recreation:* reading. *Address:* 8 Rodney House, Pembridge Crescent, W11 3DY. *T:* 01–727 7975.

MORRIS, David Griffiths; barrister; a Recorder, since 1984; *b* 10 March 1940; *s* of Thomas Griffiths Morris and Margaret Eileen Morris; *m* 1971, Carolyn Mary (*née* Miller); one *s* one *d*. *Educ:* Abingdon Sch.; King's Coll., Univ. of London (LLB Hons). Called to the Bar, Lincoln's Inn, 1965. Pupillage in London (Temple and Lincoln's Inn), 1965–67; Tenant in London Chambers (Temple), 1967–72; Tenant in Cardiff Chambers, 1972–; Asst Recorder, 1979–84; Local Junior for Cardiff Bar, 1981–; Head of Chambers, June 1984. Founder Member: Llantwit Major Round Table and 41 Clubs; Llantwit Major Rotary Club (Pres., 1984–85); Llanmaes Community Council, 1982–84. *Recreations:* Rugby Union football, cricket, swimming, theatre, drinking beer, talking, family. *Address:* 30 Park Place, Cardiff CF1 3BA. *T:* Cardiff 398421. *Club:* Cardiff and County (Cardiff).

MORRIS, Prof. David William, PhD; FRAgS; dairy and sheep farmer, since 1983; Agricultural Consultant, Midland Bank, since 1984; *b* 7 Dec. 1937; *s* of late David William Morris and Mary Olwen Ann Lewis; *m* 1966, Cynthia Cooper; one *s* one *d*. *Educ:* Ardwyn Grammar Sch.; UC of Wales (BSc Agric.); Univ. of Newcastle upon Tyne (PhD). FRAgS 1974. Develt Officer, Agric. Div., ICI, 1963–64; Asst Dir, Cockle Park Exptl Farm, Newcastle upon Tyne Univ., 1964–68; Farms Manager for Marquis of Lansdowne, Bowood, Wilts, 1968–70; Principal, Welsh Agric. Coll., Aberystwyth, 1970–83; Prof. of Agric., UC Wales, Aberystwyth, 1979–83. Churchill Fellowship, 1973. *Publications:* Practical Milk Production, 1976, 3rd edn 1977; (with M. M. Cooper) Grass Farming, 5th edn 1984. *Recreation:* farming. *Address:* Wern Berni Farm, Llanboidy, Whitland, Dyfed. *T:* Llanboidy 214. *Club:* Farmers'.

MORRIS, Denis Edward, OBE 1958; Head, and ultimately Controller of Light Programme, BBC, 1960–67; *b* 29 June 1907; *s* of Philip and Edith Morris; *m* 1st, 1931, Angela Moore (marr. diss., 1942); one *s*; 2nd, 1943, Catharine Garrett (*née* Anderton); one *s*. *Educ:* Tonbridge Sch. BBC Talks Producer, 1936; BBC Midland Public Relations Officer, 1938; BBC Empire Public Relations Officer, 1939; MOI Dir, Midland Region, 1940–42; BBC Midland Regional Programme Dir, 1943–48; Head of Midland Regional Programmes, 1948–60. Leicester City Council, 1933–36; Chm., Findon Parish Council, 1971–74; Chm., Lord Mayor of Birmingham's War Relief Fund Publicity and Appeals Cttee, 1942–48; Pres., Shoreham Cons. Assoc., 1976–79 and 1983–86 (Chm., 1971–75); Member: Hosp. Management Cttee, St Francis Hosp. and Lady Chichester Hosp., 1966–71; Exec. Cttee, Nat. Cricket Assoc., 1969–74 (Chm., Public Relations Standing Cttee, 1969–72); Dep. Chm., Lord's Taverners' Council, 1963–65 (Mem., 1962–67); Public Relations Advisor to MCC and the Counties, 1967–68; Mem., Public Relations and Promotion Sub-Cttee, TCCB, 1968–75. *Publications:* Poultry-Keeping for Profit, 1949; The French Vineyards, 1958; A Guide to the Pleasures of Wine-Drinking, 1972; ABC of Wine, 1977. *Recreations:* swimming, golf, drinking wine and writing about it (for Daily Telegraph). *Clubs:* MCC; Incogniti CC; Sussex Martlets CC; Gentlemen of Leicestershire CC; Blackheath Rugby Football; Sussex Rugby Football.
See also T. D. Morris.

MORRIS, Derek James, MA, DPhil; Fellow and Tutor, Oriel College, Oxford; *b* 23 Dec. 1945; *s* of Denis William and Olive Margaret Morris; *m* 1975, Susan Mary Whittles; two *s*. *Educ:* Harrow County Grammar Sch.; St Edmund Hall, Oxford; Nuffield Coll., Oxford. MA (Oxon); DPhil. Research Fellow, Centre for Business and Industrial Studies, Warwick Univ., 1969–70; Fellow and Tutor in Economics, Oriel Coll., Oxford, 1970–; Tutor and Sen. Tutor, Oxford University Business Summer Sch., 1970–78; Visiting Fellow, Oxford Centre for Management Studies, 1977–; Economic Dir, Nat. Economic Develt Office, 1981–84. Chm., Oxford Economic Forecasting, 1984–; Editorial Board: Oxford Economic Papers, 1984–; Annual Register of World Events, 1985–; Asst Editor, Jl of Industrial Economics, 1984–; Associate Editor, Oxford Review of Economic Policy, 1985–. *Publications:* (ed) The Economic System in the UK, 1977, 3rd edn 1985; (with D. Hay) Industrial Economics, Theory and Evidence, 1979; (with D. Hay) Unquoted Companies, 1984; articles on unemployment, trade policy and performance, productivity growth, industrial policy, exchange rates and profitability. *Recreations:* skiing, rugby, reading history. *Club:* Reform.

MORRIS, Desmond John, DPhil; writer on animal and human behaviour; *b* 24 Jan. 1928; *s* of Capt. Harry Howe Morris and Dorothy Marjorie Fuller Morris (*née* Hunt); *m* 1952, Ramona Baulch; one *s*. *Educ:* Dauntsey's Sch.; Birmingham Univ. (BSc); Magdalen Coll., Oxford (DPhil). Postdoctoral research in Animal Behaviour, Dept of Zoology, Oxford Univ., 1954–56; Head of Granada TV and Film Unit at Zool. Soc. of London, 1956–59; Curator of Mammals, Zool. Soc. of London, 1959–67; Dir, Inst. of Contemp. Arts, London, 1967–68; Research Fellow, Wolfson Coll., Oxford, 1973–81. Chm. of TV programmes: Zootime (weekly), 1956–67; Life (fortnightly), 1965–68; TV series: The Human Race, 1982. *Publications:* (Jt Ed.) International Zoo Yearbook, 1959–62; The Biology of Art, 1962; The Mammals: A Guide to the Living Species, 1965; (with Ramona Morris) Men and Snakes, 1965; (with Ramona Morris) Men and Apes, 1966; (with Ramona Morris) Men and Pandas, 1966; The Naked Ape, 1967; (ed) Primate Ethology, 1967; The Human Zoo, 1969; Patterns of Reproductive Behaviour, 1970; Intimate Behaviour, 1971; Manwatching: a field guide to human behaviour, 1977; (jtly) Gestures: their origins and distribution, 1979; Animal Days (autobiog.), 1979; The Giant Panda, 1981; The Soccer Tribe, 1981; Inrock (novel), 1983; The Book of Ages, 1983; The Art of Ancient Cyprus, 1985; Bodywatching: a field guide to the human species, 1985; The

Illustrated Naked Ape, 1986; Catwatching, 1986; Dogwatching, 1986; numerous papers in zoological jls. *Recreations:* painting, archæology. *Address:* c/o Jonathan Cape, 32 Bedford Square, WC1.

MORRIS, Desmond Victor; HM Diplomatic Service, retired; *b* 26 June 1926; *s* of late John Walter Morris and Bessie (*née* Mason); *m* 1st, 1951, Peggy Iris Mumford; two *d* 2nd, 1961, Patricia Irene Ward, *d* of Charles Daniel and Emma Camwell; one *d*. *Educ:* Portsmouth Southern Secondary Sch. for Boys; Durham Univ. Served RAF, 1945–48 (Actg Corporal). Joined HM Diplomatic Service, 1948; served at Seattle, Budapest, Saigon, Addis Ababa, Berne, Ankara and Pretoria; Dep High Comr, Georgetown, 1973–78; Dep. Head of Accommodation and Services Dept, FCO, 1979–82; Consul-Gen. and Counsellor (Administration), Washington, 1982–86. *Recreations:* gardening and the other fine arts. *Address:* Grayshott, Green Lane, Axminster, Devon EX13 5TD.

MORRIS, Air Marshal Sir Douglas (Griffith), KCB 1962 (CB 1954); CBE 1945; DSO 1945; DFC 1941; AOC-in-C, RAF Fighter Command, 1962–66; *b* 3 Dec. 1908; 2nd *s* of D. G. Morris, late of Natal, South Africa; *m* 1936, Audrey Beryl Heard; one *s* one *d*. *Educ:* St John's Coll., Johannesburg, South Africa. Commissioned RAF, 1930; trained as pilot, 1930–31; No. 40 (B) Sqdn, 1931–32; Fleet Air Arm, 1932–34; qualified as Flying Instructor, Central Flying Sch., 1934; on instructor duties, 1934–40; RAF Staff Coll., 1940; Air Ministry, 1940–41; on night fighting ops, 1941–42; Comdg No. 406 RCAF Sqdn, 1941–42, as Wing Comdr; Comd RAF North Weald, as Group Capt., 1942–43; on staff of Allied Exped. Air HQ, 1943–44; Comd No. 132 (F) Wing, 1944–45, in Normandy, Belgium, Holland; SASO No 84 Gp HQ, as Air Cdre, Feb.-Nov. 1945; in W Africa, Nov. 1945–46; Jt Planning staff, Min. of Defence, 1946–47; Nat. War Coll., Washington, 1947–48; on staff of Brit. Jt Services Mission, Washington, DC, 1948–50; Sector Comdr, Southern Sector, 1950–52; Sector Comdr, Metropolitan Sector, Fighter Comd, 1952–53; idc 1954; Air Vice-Marshal, 1955, and SASO, 2nd TAF; ACAS (Air Defence), Air Ministry, 1957–59; Chief of Staff, Allied Air Forces, Central Europe, 1960–62. Comdr Order of St Olav, 1945; Comdr Order of Orange-Nassau, 1947; ADC to King George VI, 1949–52; ADC to the Queen, 1952. Retired, 1966. Mem. Council, St Dunstan's, 1968–85. *Recreations:* golf, ski-ing. *Address:* Friar's Côte, Northiam, Rye, East Sussex. *Club:* Royal Air Force.

MORRIS, Edward Allan, CMG 1967; OBE 1961; *b* 8 Sept. 1910; *s* of late John Morris, Twickenham; *m* 1937, Phyllis, *d* of late Francis Guise, Twickenham; one *d* (one *s* decd). *Educ:* Hampton Grammar Sch.; Univ. of London (BCom). Entered Crown Agents' Office, 1928. RAFVR, 1942–46; Sqdn Leader (King's Commendation, 1946). Crown Agents' Office: Asst Head of Dept, 1956; Head of Dept, 1958; Asst Crown Agent, 1964; Crown Agent for Oversea Governments and Administrations, 1968–71. *Recreations:* cricket, Rugby Union football, church bells and change-ringing, preserving the riverside area of Twickenham. *Address:* 56 Lebanon Park, Twickenham, Mddx. *T:* 01–892 5856. *Clubs:* Royal Air Force, MCC, Corona (Hon. Treas.); Harlequin Football.

MORRIS, Air Commodore Edward James, CB 1966; CBE 1959; DSO 1942; DFC 1944; RAF, retired 1968; *b* 6 April 1915; *s* of late D. G. Morris, and late Mrs E. Morris, Bulawayo, Southern Rhodesia; *m* 1945, Alison Joan, *d* of Sir Charles Henderson, KBE; two *s*. *Educ:* Michaelhouse, Natal, S Africa. Commnd, 1937; Fighter Comd, 1938–41; Desert Air Force, 1941–45; Staff Coll., 1945–46; BAFO Germany, 1946–49; Old Sarum, 1949–52; Caledonian Sector, Fighter Command, 1952–53; RAF Flying Coll., 1953–54; Exchange Posting with USAF, Florida, 1954–56; SASO HQ 12 Group, 1956–58; OC Wattisham, 1958–59; HQ Fighter Command, 1959–60; Air Ministry, 1960–64; Chief of Staff, Headquarters Middle East Command, 1964–66; AOC Air Cadets, and Comdt Air Training Corps, 1966–68. American DFC 1945. *Recreations:* golf, fishing. *Address:* PO Box 85, Underberg, Natal, 4590, South Africa.

MORRIS, Gareth; *see* Morris, J. G.

MORRIS, Gareth (Charles Walter); flautist; Professor of the Flute, Royal Academy of Music, 1945–85; *b* Clevedon, Som, 13 May 1920, *e s* of late Walter and Enid Morris; *m* 1954; one *d*; *m* 1975, Patricia Mary, *y d* of Neil and Sheila Murray, Romsey, Hampshire; one *s* two *d*. *Educ:* Bristol Cathedral Sch.; Royal Academy of Music, London. First studied the flute at age of twelve under Robert Murchie and later won a scholarship to RAM. Career since then has been as soloist, chamber music and symphonic player, teacher and lecturer; Principal Flautist, 1949–72, Chm., 1966–72, Philharmonia Orch. Has been mem. Arts Council Music Panel, and Warden of Incorporated Soc. of Musicians Soloists Section; Adjudicator, International Flute playing Competitions, Geneva, 1973, 1978, Munich, 1974, Leeds, 1977, 1980, Ancona, 1978, 1979, 1984. Played at Her Majesty's Coronation in Westminster Abbey in 1953. ARAM 1945; FRAM 1950; FRSA 1967 (Mem. Council, 1977–83; Chm., Music Cttee, 1981–83). *Recreations:* reading and collecting books, astronomy, antiquarian horology. *Address:* 4 West Mall, Clifton, Bristol BS8 4BH. *T:* Bristol 734966.

MORRIS, Prof. Howard Redfern; Professor of Biological Chemistry, since 1980 and Head of Department of Biochemistry, since 1985, Imperial College, University of London; *b* 4 Aug. 1946; *s* of Marion Elizabeth and Herbert Morris, Bolton, Lancs; *m* 1969, Lene Verny Jensen; two *d*. *Educ:* Univ. of Leeds (BSc 1967; PhD 1970). SRC Fellow, Cambridge, 1970–72; Scientific Staff, MRC Lab. of Molecular Biol., Cambridge, 1972–75; Imperial College: Lectr, Dept of Biochem, 1975–78; Reader in Protein Chem., 1978–80; Chm., Div. of Life Sciences, 1985–. Founder Chm., M-Scan Ltd, analytical chem. consultants, 1979–. Visiting Professor: Univ. of Virginia, 1978; Soviet Acad. of Scis, 1982; Univ. of Naples, 1983; Life Scis Div., E. I. Dupont, USA, 1984–85. Mem., EMBO, 1979–. BDH Gold Medal and Prize for analytical biochem., Biochem. Soc., 1978; Medal and Prize for macromolecules and polymers, RSC, 1982. *Publications:* (ed) Soft Ionisation Biological Mass Spectrometry, 1981; numerous contribs to learned jls, on enkephalin, SRS-A leukotrienes, interleukin, calcitonin gene related peptide, mass spectrometry, protein and glycoprotein structure elucidation. *Recreations:* fell walking, gardening, guitar. *Address:* Department of Biochemistry, Imperial College, Exhibition Road, SW7 2AZ. *T:* 01–589 5111.

MORRIS, Ivor Gray, CMG 1974; Former Chairman and Managing Director, Morris Woollen Mills (Ipswich) Pty Ltd; Chairman Queensland Export Advisory Committee; *b* 28 March 1911; *s* of John and Annie Morris, Talybont, Cards, and Ipswich, Qld; *m* 1944, Jessie Josephine Halley; two *d*. *Educ:* Scotch Coll., Melbourne; Scots Coll., Warwick, Qld; Ipswich Grammar Sch., Qld; Leeds Univ. Founded Morris Woollen Mills (Ipswich) Pty Ltd, 1934. Former Mem. Exec., Wool Textile Manufrs Assoc. of Australia; Life Mem., Nuclear Physics Foundn; Former Mem., Trade Develt Council, Canberra. Former Chm. of Trustees, Ipswich Grammar Sch.; Vice-Pres., Qld Museum Trust, 1970–; Patron, St David's Welsh Soc.; Foundn Mem. and District Governor, Ipswich Apex Club (1st Apex Club formed in Austr.), 1938. *Recreations:* music, reading. *Address:* River Road, Redbank, Queensland 4301, Australia. *T:* 88–29–35. *Clubs:* Tattersall's (Brisbane); Ipswich, Ipswich North Rotary (Ipswich, Qld).

MORRIS, James; *see* Morris, Jan.

MORRIS, James Peter; Secretary General, National Cold Storage Federation, since 1977; *b* 17 Sept. 1926; *s* of Frank Morris and Annie (*née* Collindridge) *m* 1st, Peggy Giles (marr. diss.); 2nd, Margaret Law. *Educ:* Barnsley Grammar Sch.; Manchester Univ. (BA, Teaching Dip.). Served RAF, 1945–48; Research Dept, Labour Party, 1952–59; Govt Information Services, 1960–73; Dir of Information, GLC, 1973–77. Sen. Treas. and Travel Bd, NUS, 1952–56; Borough Councillor, 1956–59; Nat. Exec., IPCS, 1964–73. *Publication:* Road Safety: a Study of Cost Benefit in Public Service Advertising, 1972. *Recreation:* painting. *Address:* 88 Ridgmount Gardens, WC1E 7AY. *T:* 01–637 2141. *Clubs:* MCC, Reform.

MORRIS, (James) Richard (Samuel), CBE 1985; FEng; Chairman and Managing Director, Brown and Root (UK) Ltd, since 1980; *b* 20 Nov. 1925; *o s* of James John Morris and Kathleen Mary Morris (*née* McNaughton); *m* 1958, Marion Reid Sinclair; two *s* two *d*. *Educ:* Ardingly Coll.; Birmingham Univ. BSc, 1st cl. hons Chem. Engrg; Vice-Chancellor's Prize, 1955; FEng, FIChemE. Captain Welsh Guards, 1944–48. Courtaulds Ltd, 1950–78: Man. Dir, National Plastics Ltd, 1959–64; Dep. Chm., British Cellophane Ltd, 1967–70; Chm., British Celanese Ltd, 1970–72; Chm., Northgate Gp Ltd, 1971–76; Chm., Meridian Ltd, 1972–76; Dir, 1967–78, Gp Technical Dir, 1976–78, Courtaulds Ltd; Dir, British Nuclear Fuels Ltd, 1971–85. Vis. Prof. of Chem. Engrg, Univ. of Strathclyde, 1979–86; Pro-Chancellor, 1982–86, Sen. Pro-Chancellor and Chm. of Council, 1986– Loughborough Univ. Member: Nuclear Power Adv. Bd, 1973; Adv. Council for Energy Conservation, 1974–80; Adv. Bd for Res. Councils, 1981–; Dep. Chm., NEB, 1978–79; Industrial Adviser to Barclays Bank, 1980–85. Mem. Council, 1974, Vice-Pres., 1976, Pres., 1977, IChemE; Vice-Pres., Soc. of Chem. Industry, 1978–81; Hon. Sec., 1979–82, Hon. Sec. for Educn and Training, 1984–, Fellowship of Engineering; Pres., Pipeline Industries Guild, 1983–85. FRSA 1986. Hon. DSc: Leeds, 1981; Bath, 1981; Birmingham, 1985. *Recreations:* ski-ing, gardening, music. *Address:* Breadsall Manor, Derby DE7 6AL. *T:* Derby 831368. *Club:* Athenæum.

MORRIS, James Shepherd, ALI; ARSA; RIBA, FRIAS; Partner, Morris & Steedman, Architects and Landscape Architects; *b* 22 Aug. 1931; *s* of Thomas Shepherd Morris and Johanna Sime Malcolm; *m* 1959, Eleanor Kenner Smith; two *s* one *d*. *Educ:* Daniel Stewart's Coll.; Edinburgh Sch. of Architecture (DipArch); Univ. of Pennsylvania (MLA). *Architectural works:* Edinburgh Univ., Strathclyde Univ., Princess Margaret Rose Hosp., Countryside Commn for Scotland. Member, Arts Council of Gt Britain, 1973–80; Vice-Chm., Scottish Arts Council, 1976–80 (Chm., Art Cttee, 1976–80); Mem., Enquiry into Community Arts, 1974); Past Member: Council, RIAS and Edinburgh AA, 1969–71; Council of Cockburn Assoc., Edinburgh; Cttee of Management, Traverse Theatre, Edinburgh. Convenor, Fellowship Cttee, RIAS, 1985–. Trustee, Nat. Mus. of Antiquities, 1980–. RIBA Award, 1974; 9 Civic Trust Awards, 1962–75; British Steel Award, 1971; European Architectural Heritage Award, 1975; European Heritage Business & Industry Award, 1975. *Publications:* contribs to RIBA Jl. *Recreations:* golf, tennis, skiing, painting. *Address:* (office) 38 Young Street Lane North, Edinburgh EH2 4JE. *T:* (office) 031–226 6563. *Clubs:* New (Edinburgh); Scottish Arts (Edinburgh); Philadelphia Cricket (Philadelphia).

MORRIS, Jan, FRSL; writer; *b* 2 Oct. 1926. Commonwealth Fellow, USA, 1953; Editorial Staff, The Times, 1951–56; Editorial Staff, The Guardian, 1957–62. Mem., Yr Academi Gymreig. *Publications* (as James Morris until 1973, subseq. as Jan Morris): Coast to Coast, 1956, rev. edn 1962; Sultan in Oman, 1957, rev. edn 1983; The Market of Seleukia, 1957; Coronation Everest, 1958; South African Winter, 1958; The Hashemite Kings, 1959; Venice, 1960, 2nd rev. edn, 1983; The Upstairs Donkey, 1962 (for children); The World Bank, 1963; Cities, 1963; The Presence of Spain, 1964, rev. edns (as Spain), 1979, 1982; Oxford, 1965, 2nd edn 1986; Pax Britannica, 1968; The Great Port, 1970, rev. edn 1985; Places, 1972; Heaven's Command, 1973; Conundrum, 1974; Travels, 1976; Farewell the Trumpets, 1978; The Oxford Book of Oxford, 1978; Destinations, 1980; My Favourite Stories of Wales, 1980; The Venetian Empire, 1980; The Small Oxford Book of Wales, 1982; A Venetian Bestiary, 1982; The Spectacle of Empire, 1982; (with Paul Wakefield) Wales, The First Place, 1982; (with Simon Winchester) Stones of Empire, 1983; The Matter of Wales, 1984; Journeys, 1984; Among the Cities, 1985; Last Letters from Hav, 1985; (with Paul Wakefield) Scotland, The Place of Visions, 1986; Manhattan '45, 1987. *Address:* Trefan Morys, Llanystumdwy, Cricieth, Gwynedd, Wales. *T:* Cricieth 2222.

MORRIS, Prof. Jeremy Noah, CBE 1972; FRCP; Professor of Community Health, University of London, at London School of Hygiene and Tropical Medicine, 1967–78; *b* 6 May 1910; *s* of Nathan and Annie Morris; *m* 1939, Galina Schuchalter; one *s* one *d*. *Educ:* Hutcheson's Grammar Sch., Glasgow; Univ. of Glasgow; University Coll. Hosp., London; London School of Hygiene and Tropical Medicine (Hon. Fellow 1979). MA, DSc, DPH. Qual., 1934; hosp. residencies, 1934–37; general practice, 1937–38; Asst MOH, Hendon and Harrow, 1939–41; Med. Spec., RAMC, 1941–46 (Lt-Col 1944–46); Rockefeller Fellow, Prev. Med., 1946–47; Dir, MRC Social Med. Unit, 1948–75; Prof., Social Med., London Hosp., 1959–67; Visiting Professor: Yale, 1957; Berkeley, 1963; Jerusalem, 1968, 1980; Adelaide, 1983. Lectures: Ernestine Henry, RCP London; Gibson, RCP Edinburgh; Fleming, RCPS Glasgow; Carey Coombs, Univ. of Bristol; Brontë Stewart, Univ. of Glasgow; St Cyres, Nat. Heart Hosp.; Alumnus, Yale; Delamar, Johns Hopkins Univ.; Wade Hampton Frost, APHA; George Clarke, Univ. of Nottingham. Member: Royal Commission on Penal Reform; Cttee, Personal Social Services, Working Party Med. Admin, 1964–72; Health Educn Council, 1978–80; Chairman: Nat. Adv. Cttee on Nutrition Educn, 1979–83; Fitness and Health Adv. Gp, Sports Council, and Health Educn Council, 1980–. Hon. Member: Amer. Epid. Soc., 1976; Soc. for Social Medicine, 1978; British Cardiac Soc., 1982; Swedish Soc. for Sports Medicine, 1984. Hon. FFCM, 1977. Hon. MD Edinburgh, 1974; Hon. DSc Hull, 1982. Bisset Hawkins Medal, RCP, 1980; Honor Award, Amer. Coll. of Sports Medicine, 1985. *Publications:* Uses of Epidemiology, 1957, 3rd edn 1975 (trans. Japanese, Spanish); papers on coronary disease and exercise, and on health and prevention. *Recreations:* walking, swimming, piano music. *Address:* 3 Briardale Gardens, NW3. *T:* 01–435 5024.

MORRIS, Rt. Hon. John, PC 1970; QC 1973; MP (Lab) Aberavon Division of Glamorgan since Oct. 1959; a Recorder of the Crown Court, since 1982; Opposition Spokesman on Legal Affairs and Shadow Attorney General, since 1983; *b* Nov. 1931; *s* of late D. W. Morris, Penywern, Talybont, Cardiganshire; *m* 1959, Margaret M. Morris, JP, *d* of late Edward Lewis, OBE, JP, of Llandysul, three *d*. *Educ:* Ardwyn, Aberystwyth; University Coll. of Wales, Aberystwyth; Gonville and Caius Coll., Cambridge (LLM); Academy of International Law, The Hague; Holker Senior Exhibitioner, Gray's Inn. Commissioned Royal Welch Fusiliers and Welch Regt. Called to the Bar, Gray's Inn, 1954, Bencher, 1985. Parly Sec., Min. of Power, 1964–66; Jt Parly Sec., Min. of Transport, 1966–68; Minister of Defence (Equipment), 1968–70; Sec. of State for Wales, 1974–79. Dep. Gen. Sec. and Legal Adviser, Farmers' Union of Wales, 1956–58. Member: UK Delegn Consultative Assembly Council of Europe and Western European Union, 1963–64, 1982–83; N Atlantic Assembly, 1970–74. Chairman: Nat. Pneumoconiosis Jt Cttee, 1964–66; Joint Review of Finances and Management, British Railways, 1966–67; Nat. Road Safety Advisory Council, 1967; Mem. Courts of University Colls, Aberystwyth, Swansea and Cardiff. Hon. LLD Wales, 1983. *Address:* House of Commons, SW1.

MORRIS, Maj.-Gen. John Edward Longworth, CB 1963; CBE 1956; DSO 1945; Director of Recruiting, War Office, 1960–64, retired; *b* 1 June 1909; *s* of Col A. E. Morris and M. E. Stanyon; *m* 1939, Pamela Gresley Ball; two *d*. *Educ:* Cheltenham Coll. Commissioned Regular Army, 1929; served War of 1939–45: India, Middle East and NW Europe, Col Comdt, RA, 1966–74. *Recreations:* sailing, model railways, electronics. *Address:* Garden House, Garden Road, Burley, Hants. *Clubs:* Royal Ocean Racing, Royal Artillery Yacht (Admiral, 1972–78).

MORRIS, John Evan A.; *see* Artro Morris.

MORRIS, Prof. (John) Gareth, FIBiol; Professor of Microbiology, University College of Wales, Aberystwyth, since 1971; *b* 25 Nov. 1932; *s* of Edwin Morris and Evelyn Amanda Morris (*née* Griffiths); *m* 1962, Áine Mary Kehoe; one *s* one *d* *Educ:* Bridgend Grammar Sch.; Univ. of Leeds; Trinity Coll., Oxford. DPhil; FIBiol 1971. Guinness Res. Fellow, Univ. of Oxford, 1957–61; Rockefeller Fellow, Univ. of Calif at Berkeley, 1959–60; Tutor in Biochem., Balliol Coll., Oxford, 1960–61; Lectr, subseq. Sen. Lectr, Univ. of Leicester, 1961–71. Vis. Associate Prof., Purdue Univ., USA, 1965. Mem., UGC, 1981–. *Publications:* A Biologist's Physical Chemistry, 1968, 2nd edn 1974; contribs on microbial biochemistry and physiology. *Recreations:* gardening, walking. *Address:* Cilgwyn, 16 Lôn Tyllwyd, Llanfarian, Aberystwyth, Dyfed SY23 4UH. *T:* Aberystwyth 612502.

MORRIS, Rev. (John) Marcus (Harston), OBE 1983; Editorial Director, 1960–64, Managing Director, 1964–82, Deputy Chairman, 1979–84, The National Magazine Co. Ltd; *b* 25 April 1915; *er s* of late Rev. Canon W. E. H. Morris and Edith (*née* Nield); *m* 1941, Jessica *d* of late John Hamlet Dunning and Alice (*née* Hunt-Jones); one *s* three *d*. *Educ:* Dean Close Sch., Cheltenham; Brasenose Coll., Oxford (Colquitt Exhibnr; BA Lit. Hum. 1937); Wycliffe Hall, Oxford (BA Theol. 1939, MA 1947). Deacon 1939, priest 1940. Curate: St Bartholomew's, Roby, 1939–40; Great Yarmouth, 1940–41; Chaplain, RAFVR, 1941–43; Rector of Weeley, 1943–45; Vicar of St James's, Birkdale, 1945–50; Editor, The Anvil, 1946–50; Founder and Editor, Eagle, Girl, Swift, and Robin, 1950–59; Man. Editor, Housewife, 1954–59. Hon. Chaplain, St Bride's, Fleet Street, 1952–83. *Publications:* Stories of the Old Testament, 1961; Stories of the New Testament, 1961; (ed) The Best of Eagle, 1977. *Recreation:* salmon and trout fishing. *Address:* The Mill House, Midford, near Bath, Avon BA2 7DE. *T:* Combe Down 833939. *Club:* Savile.

MORRIS, Keith Elliot Hedley; HM Diplomatic Service; Head of Personnel Policy Department, Foreign and Commonwealth Office, 1984–86; *b* 24 Oct. 1934; *m* Maria del Carmen Carratala; two *s* two *d*. Entered Foreign Office, 1959; served Dakar, Algiers, Paris, Bogota; First Sec., FCO, 1971–76; Counsellor (Commercial), Warsaw, 1976–79; Minister, Mexico City, 1979–84. *Address:* c/o Foreign and Commonwealth Office, SW1.

MORRIS, Rev. Marcus; *see* Morris, Rev. J. M. H.

MORRIS, Max; educational propagandist and reformer; pioneer of the Comprehensive School; Headmaster, Willesden High School, 1967–78, retired; *b* 15 Aug. 1913; *s* of Nathan and Annie Morris; *m* 1961, Margaret Saunders (*née* Howard), historian. *Educ:* Hutcheson's, Glasgow; Kilburn Grammar Sch., Mddx; University Coll., Univ. of London (BA 1st cl. Hons History); Inst. of Education, Univ. of London (DipEd); LSE. Began teaching, 1936, in Willesden. Served War, 1941–46, demobilised as Captain RASC. Sen. Lectr, Colls of Education, 1946–50; Dep. Head, Tottenham, 1960, after nine years of political discrimination in Middlesex; Headmaster, Chamberlayne Wood Secondary Sch., Willesden, 1962–67. NUT: Mem. Exec., 1966–79; Pres., 1973–74; Chm. Action Cttee, 1976–79. Chairman: Mddx Regional Examining Bd, 1975–79; London Regional Examining Bd, 1979–; Vice-Chm., Centre for Information and Advice on Educnl Disadvantage, 1975–80; Member: Schools Council Cttees, 1967–84; Burnham Cttee, 1970–79; Board of NFER, 1970–80; CLEA/School Teachers Cttee, 1972–79; Schools Broadcasting Council, 1972–80; Nat. Adv. Cttee on Supply and Trng of Teachers, 1973–78; Sub-Cttee on Educn, Labour Party NEC, 1978–83; Council, Inst. of Educn; Jt Council, GCE and CSE Boards. Mem. (Lab) Haringey Borough Council, 1984–86. *Publications:* The People's Schools, 1939; From Cobbett to the Chartists, 1948; Your Children's Future, 1953; (with Jack Jones) An A to Z of Trade Unionism and Industrial Relations, 1982; contribs on educnl and historical subjects in newspapers, weeklies and jls. *Recreations:* baiting the Dept of Education and Science; ridiculing Trotskyists and trendies; tasting malt whiskey. *Address:* 44 Coolhurst Road, N8. *T:* 01–348 3980.

MORRIS, Michael Sachs; Director-General, British Insurance Brokers' Association, 1980–85; *b* 12 June 1924; *s* of late Prof. Noah Morris, MD, DSc, and Hattie Michaelis; *m* 1952, Vera Leonie, *er d* of Paul and Lona Heller; one *s* one *d*. *Educ:* Glasgow Acad.; St Catharine's Coll., Cambridge. Wrangler, 1948. Scientific Officer, Admty Signals Estabt, 1943–46; Asst Principal, BoT, 1948; idc 1970; Under Secretary: Insurance Div., DoT, 1973; Shipping Policy Div., DoT, 1978–80. Chm., Consultative Shipping Gp, 1979–80. Mem., Barnet Health Authy, 1985–. *Recreation:* sitting in the sun. *Address:* 5 Sunrise View, The Rise, Mill Hill, NW7 2LL. *T:* 01–959 0837. *Club:* United Oxford & Cambridge University.

MORRIS, Michael Wolfgang Laurence; MP (C) Northampton South since Feb. 1974; Proprietor, A. M. International, communication consultancy, since 1980; *b* 25 Nov. 1936; *m* 1960, Dr Ann Appleby (Dr Ann Morris, MB, BS, MRCS, MRCP); two *s* one *d*. *Educ:* Bedford Sch.; St Catharine's Coll., Cambridge (MA). BA Hons Econs, MIPA, MInstM. Management Trainee to Marketing Manager, UK, India and Ceylon, Reckitt & Colman Gp, 1960–63; Service Advertising Ltd, 1964–68; Marketing Exec. to Account Supervisor, Horniblow Cox-Freeman Ltd, 1968–71, Dir 1969–71; Dir, Benton & Bowles Ltd, 1971–81. Contested (C) Islington North, 1966. Islington Council: Councillor, 1968–70; Alderman, 1970–74; Chm. of Housing, 1968; Leader, 1969–71. PPS to Minister of State, NI Office, 1979–81; Member: Public Accounts Cttee, 1979–; Select Cttee on Energy, 1982–85; Chairman's Panel, 1984–; Mem. Council, Europe and Western European Union, 1983–; Chairman: British Sri Lanka Cttee, 1979–; British Singapore Cttee, 1985–; Vice-Chm., British Indonesia Cttee; Treas., British Asean and Thai Cttees; Secretary: British Malaysia and Burma Cttees; Cons. Housing and Local Govt Cttee, 1974–76; Cons Trade Cttee, 1974–76; Cons. Environment Cttee, 1977–79; Vice-Chm., Cons. Energy Cttee, 1981–; Vice Captain, Parly Golf Soc. Governor, Bedford Sch., 1982–. *Publications:* (jtly) Helping the Exporter, 1967; (contrib.) Marketing below the Line: Studies in Management, 1972; The Disaster of Direct Labour, 1978. *Recreations:* restoration work, clocks, cricket, tennis, golf. *Address:* Caesar's Camp, Sandy, Beds. *T:* Sandy 80388. *Clubs:* Carlton; George Row, Conservative, Whitworth, Billing Road, St George's (Northampton).

MORRIS, Nigel Godfrey, CMG 1955; LVO 1966; QPM 1954; *b* 11 Nov. 1908; 2nd *s* of late Lt-Col G. M. Morris, 2/8th Gurkha Rifles and late Mrs Morris; *m* 1st, 1941, Mrs G. E. Baughan, *widow* (*d* 1982), *e d* of late J. C. Sidebottom; one *d* and one step *d*; 2nd, 1984, Mrs M. C. Berkeley-Owen (*née* Mullally). *Educ:* Wellington Coll. Asst Superintendent SS Police, 1928; Chinese language course, Amoy, China, 1929; Asst Supt of Police, Singapore CID 1931; Special Branch, 1935; Asst Supt of Police, Town Penang, 1939; interned by Japanese, 1942; repatriated to UK, 1945; Asst Dir, Malayan Security Service, 1946; Dir, Special Branch, Singapore, 1948; Dep. Commissioner, CID, Singapore, 1950, Comr, 1952; Deputy Inspector-General of Colonial Police, Colonial Office, 1957–63; Commissioner of Police, Bahamas, 1963–68, retired. Colonial Police Medal, 1949. *Recreation:* golf. *Address:* 118 Cranmer Court, SW3. *T:* 01–584 9875; 21 Whitelock House, Phyllis Court Drive, Henley-on-Thames, Oxon RG9 2HU. *T:* Henley-on-Thames 573853. *Club:* Phyllis Court (Henley).

MORRIS, Prof. Norman Frederick, MD, FRCOG; Professor of Obstetrics and Gynæcology, University of London, Charing Cross and Westminster Medical School (formerly Charing Cross Hospital Medical School), 1958–85, now Emeritus; Dean, Faculty of Medicine, University of London, 1971–76; Deputy Vice-Chancellor, University of London, 1976–80; *b* Luton, 26 Feb. 1920; *s* of F. W. Morris, Luton; *m* 1944, Lucia Xenia Rivlin; two *s* two *d*. *Educ:* Dunstable Sch., Dunstable; St Mary's Hospital Medical Sch. MRCS, LRCP 1943; MRCOG 1949; MB, BS (London) 1943; MD (London) 1949; FRCOG 1959. House appts St Mary's Hosp., Paddington and Amersham, 1944–46; Res. Obstetrician and Surg. Officer, East Ham Memorial Hosp., E6; Surg. Specialist RAF (Sqdn Ldr), 1946–48; Registrar, St Mary's Hosp., W2, and East End Maternity Hosp., E1, 1948–50; Sen. Registrar (Obst. and Gynæcol.), Hammersmith Hosp., 1950–52; First Asst, Obstetric Unit, Univ. Coll. Hosp., WC1, 1953–56; Reader, Univ. of London in Obst. and Gynæcol., Inst. of Obstetrics and Gynæcology, 1956–58. Dep. Chm., NW Thames RHA, 1974–80; Chm., NW Thames Reg. Res. Cttee, 1981–. External Examiner, Univs of Sheffield, Leeds, Dundee and Liverpool. President: Internat. Soc. of Psychosomatic Obstetrics and Gynaecology, 1972–80; Section of Obstetrics and Gynaecology, RSocMed, 1978–79. Chm., Assoc. of Profs of Obstets and Gynaecol. of UK, 1981–; Mem., Academic Forum, DHSS, 1981–84. Mem., Hammersmith and Fulham HA, 1983–84. Mem. Ct and Senate, Univ. of London, 1972–80; Governor: Wye Coll., 1973–80; St Paul's Sch., 1976–. Fellow, Soc. Gyn. et Obst., Italy, 1970–. Formerly Chairman: Assoc. of University Clinical Academic Staff; 3rd World Congress of Psychosomatic Medicine in Obst. and Gynæcol. (Editor, Proceedings, 1972). Editor, Midwife and Health Visitor Jl. *Publications:* Sterilisation, 1976; Contemporary Attitudes to Care in Labour (The Psychosomatic Approach); articles in medical jls related to obstetric problems, 1952–. *Recreations:* travelling, collecting glass, music. *Address:* 16 Provost Road, NW3. *T:* 01–722 4244. *Clubs:* Athenæum, 1942.

MORRIS, Owen Humphrey, CB 1977; CMG 1967; Deputy Under-Secretary of State, Welsh Office, 1974–81, retired; *b* 15 June 1921; *o c* of late David Humphreys Morris, Ton Pentre, Rhondda, Glam., and Mrs Amy Ann Morris (*née* Jones); *m* 1972, Mair Annetta Evans, *d* of late Capt. Daniel Evans, DSC, Tynllys, Morfa Nefyn. *Educ:* Public Elem. Schs; King's Coll. Sch., Wimbledon (Schol.); Balliol Coll., Oxford (Schol.; MA). Served War of 1939–45: The Welch Regt and King's African Rifles, 1941–45 (Capt.). Asst Princ., Colonial Office, 1946; seconded Sierra Leone Administration, 1952–53; Asst Sec., 1955; Dept of Techn. Cooperation, 1962; Min. of Overseas Development, 1964; Min. of Housing and Local Govt, 1966; Welsh Office, 1969; Asst Under-Sec., 1970; Dep. Sec., 1974. Chm., Gwynedd Archaeol Trust, 1984–. *Address:* Taltreuddyn Fawr, Dyffryn Ardudwy, Gwynedd.

MORRIS, Peter Christopher West; barrister; *b* 24 Dec. 1937; *s* of C. T. R. and L. B. Morris; *m* 1959, Joy; two *s* one *d*. *Educ:* Seaford Coll.; Christ's Coll., Cambridge, 1958–61 (MA, LLB). Hockey Blue, 1959, 1960, 1961; Hockey for Wales, 1962–65. National Service, 1956–58. Admitted Solicitor, 1965; Partner with Wild Hewitson & Shaw, 1967; a Recorder of the Crown Court, 1980; voluntary removal from Roll of Solicitors, 1982; called to the Bar, Middle Temple, 1982. *Recreations:* golf, cricket, squash, photography. *Address:* 234 Milton Road, Cambridge CB4 1LQ. *T:* Cambridge 68761. *Clubs:* Flyfishers'; Hawks (Cambridge); Royal Worlington and Newmarket Golf.

MORRIS, Prof. Peter John; Nuffield Professor of Surgery, Oxford University, since 1974; Fellow of Balliol College, since 1974; *b* 17 April 1934; *s* of Stanley Henry and Mary Lois Morris; *m* 1960, Mary Jocelyn Gorman; three *s* two *d*. *Educ:* Xavier Coll., Melbourne; Univ. of Melbourne (MB, BS, PhD). FRCS, FRACS, FACS. Jun. surg. appts at St Vincent's Hosp., Melbourne, Postgrad. Med. Sch., London, Southampton Gen. Hosp. and MGH Boston, 1958–64; Research Fellow, Harvard Med. Sch., 1965–66; Asst Prof. in Surgery, Med. Coll. of Virginia, 1967; 2nd Asst in Surgery, Univ. of Melbourne, 1968–69, 1st Asst 1970–71; Reader in Surgery, Univ. of Melbourne, 1972–74. WHO Consultant, 1970–84; Cons. to Walter and Eliza Hall Inst. of Med. Res., 1969–74. Pres., Transplantation Soc., 1984–; Mem., MRC, 1983–. Selwyn Smith Prize, Univ. of Melbourne, 1971. Hunterian Prof., RCS, 1972. USA Nat. Kidney Foundn Prof., 1986. Hon. Fellow, Amer. Surgical Assoc.; Hon. FACS 1986. *Publications:* Kidney Transplantation: principles and practice, 1979, 2nd edn 1984; Tissue Transplantation, 1982; Transient Ischaemic Attacks, 1982; Progress in Transplantation, Vol. 1 1984, Vol. 2 1985, Vol. 3 1986; numerous sci. articles and chapters in books concerned mainly with transplantation and surgery. *Recreations:* golf, tennis, cricket. *Address:* 19 Lucerne Road, Oxford OX2 7QB. *Clubs:* United Oxford & Cambridge University, MCC; Oxford University Croquet and Lawn Tennis, Frilford Heath Golf (Oxford); St Cyprien Golf (France); Melbourne Cricket (Melbourne).

MORRIS, Rex G.; *see* Goring-Morris.

MORRIS, Richard; *see* Morris, J. R. S.

MORRIS, Sir Robert (Byng), 10th Bt *cr* 1806, of Clasemont, Glamorganshire; *b* 25 Feb. 1913; *s* of Percy Byng Morris (*d* 1957) (*g s* of 2nd Bt), and Ethel Maud (*d* 1923), *d* of William Morley Glascott, Melbourne; *S* cousin, 1982; *m* 1947, Christina Kathleen, *d* of Archibald Field, Toddington, Glos; one *s* three *d*. *Heir:* *s* Allan Lindsay Morris, *b* 27 Nov. 1961. *Address:* Norton Creek Stables, RR5, St Chrysostome, Quebec, Canada.

MORRIS, Robert Matthew; Assistant Under Secretary of State, Fire and Emergency Planning Department, Home Office, since 1983; *b* 11 Oct. 1937; *s* of late William Alexander Morris and of Mary Morris (*née* Bryant); *m* 1965, Janet Elizabeth Gillingham; two *s* one *d*. *Educ:* Handsworth Grammar Sch.; Christ's Coll., Cambridge. Joined Home Office, 1961; Asst Private Sec. to Home Sec., 1964–66; CSD, 1969–71; Principal Private Sec. to Home Sec., 1976–78; Sec. to UK Prison Services Inquiry (May Cttee), 1978–79; Head of Crime Policy Planning Unit, 1979–81. *Address:* c/o Home Office, 50 Queen Anne's Gate, SW1H 9AP.

MORRIS, Rear-Adm. Roger Oliver, FRICS, FRGS; Hydrographer of the Navy, since 1985; *b* 1 Sept. 1932; *s* of Dr Oliver N. Morris and H. S. (Mollie) Morris (*née* Hudson). *Educ:* Mount House School, Tavistock; Royal Naval College, Dartmouth. Entered Royal Navy, 1946, commissioned 1952; specialized in Hydrographic Surveying, 1956; commanded HM Ships Medusa, Beagle, Hydra, Fawn, Hecla, Hydra, 1964–80; RCDS 1978; Director of Hydrographic Plans and Surveys, 1980–81; Asst Hydrographer, 1982–84. *Recreations:* heraldry, opera, bird watching. *Address:* Hydrographic Department, Ministry of Defence, Taunton, Somerset. *T:* Taunton 87900. *Club:* Royal Commonwealth Society.

MORRIS, Air Vice-Marshal Ronald James Arthur, CB 1974; retired; *b* 27 Nov. 1915; *s* of late Dr James Arthur Morris, Ladybank, Fife; *m* 1945, Mary Kerr Mitchell; one *s* two *d*. *Educ:* Madras Coll., St Andrews; St Andrews Univ. MB, ChB 1939; DPH Edinburgh, 1953; MFCM 1972. Commnd RAF, 1939; served on Fighter Comd Stns, 1940–41; India and Burma Campaign, 1941–45; HQ Techn. Trng Comd, 1946–48; SMO, HQ Air Forces Western Europe, 1948–50; Sen. Trng Officer and Comdt Med. Trng Estabt, 1950–52; Exchange Officer, Sch. of Aviation Medicine (USAF), 1955–56; Dept MA7, Air Min., 1956–60; OC RAF Chessington, 1960–61; OC RAF Hosp. Wroughton, 1961–63; PMO, Signals Comd, 1963–65; Dep. PMO, Far East Air Forces, 1965–69, PMO, Maintenance Comd, 1969–70; DDGMS (RAF), 1971–73; PMO, RAF Strike Comd, 1974–75. QHS, 1971–75. CStJ 1974. *Recreations:* golf, fishing. *Address:* 2 Cairnsden Gardens, St Andrews, Fife KY16 8SQ. *T:* St Andrews 75326.

MORRIS, Prof. Terence Patrick, JP; Professor of Social Institutions, University of London, since 1981; *b* 8 June 1931; *s* of Albert and Norah Avis Morris; *m* 1954, Pauline Jeannette Peake (*née* Morris) (marr. diss. 1973); one *d*; *m* 1973, Penelope Jane, *y d* of Stanley and Alexandra Tomlinson. *Educ:* John Ruskin Grammar Sch., Croydon; LSE, Univ. of London (Leverhulme Schol.). BSc (Soc) 1953, PhD (Econ) 1955. Lectr in Sociology, LSE, 1955–63; Reader, 1963–69, Prof., 1969–81, Sociology (with special ref. to Criminology), London Univ. Vis. Prof. of Criminology, Univ. of California, 1964–65. Mem., Adv. Mission on Treatment of Offenders (Western Pacific, British Honduras, Bahamas), 1966. Member: Magistrates' Assoc. Treatment of Offenders Cttee (co-opted), 1969–77; Council, Inst. for Study of Drug Dependence. Man. Editor, British Jl of Sociology, 1965–74. JP Inner London, 1967. *Publications:* The Criminal Area, 1957; (with Pauline Morris) Pentonville: a sociological study of an English prison, 1963; (with L. J. Blom-Cooper) A Calendar of Murder, 1964; Deviance and Control: the secular heresy, 1976; contribs to Brit. Jl Criminology, Brit. Jl Sociology, Encycl. Britannica. *Recreations:* sailing and maintenance of small boats, cycling, photography. *Address:* c/o London School of Economics, Houghton Street, WC2A 2AE. *Club:* Cyclists' Touring.

MORRIS, Most Rev. Thomas; *see* Cashel and Emly, Archbishop of, (RC).

MORRIS, Timothy Denis, DL; Chairman: The Birmingham Post & Mail Ltd, since 1982 (Director, since 1967); London & Westminster Newspapers Ltd, since 1984 (Director, since 1977); South Hams Newspapers Ltd, since 1985; *b* 15 Feb. 1935; *s* of D. E. Morris, OBE, *qv*, and Mrs P. H. Skey; *m* 1959, Caroline Wynn; one *s* one *d*. *Educ:* Tonbridge Sch.; Pembroke Coll., Cambridge (MA). Managing Director, Coventry Newspapers Ltd, 1970–77 (Dir, 1985–); Director: British Transfer Printing Co. Ltd, 1970–; BPM Holdings plc, 1977–; Cambridge Newspapers Ltd, 1970–77, 1985–; Dillons Newsagents Ltd, 1977–; Press Association Ltd, 1980– (Chm., 1985–86); Burton Daily Mail Ltd, 1983–; Yattendon Investment Trust Ltd, 1985–. Chm., Birmingham Civic Soc., 1979–83; Dir, Birmingham Hippodrome Theatre Trust, 1980–; President: W Midlands Newspaper Soc., 1975–76; Newspaper Soc., 1984–85; Coventry Chamber of Commerce, 1976–77. County Comr, Warwickshire Scouts, 1974–77. DL West Midlands, 1975. *Recreations:* golf, philately. *Address:* c/o The Birmingham Post & Mail Ltd, 28 Colmore Circus, Queensway, Birmingham B4 6AX. *Club:* Naval.

MORRIS, Trefor Alfred, QPM 1985; Chief Constable, Hertfordshire Constabulary, since 1984; *b* 22 Dec. 1934; *s* of Kenneth Alfred Morris and Amy Ursula (*née* Burgess); *m* 1958, Martha Margaret (*née* Wroe); two *d*. *Educ:* Ducie Technical High School, Manchester; Manchester University (Dip. Criminology); Nat. Exec. Inst., USA. Constable to Chief Superintendent, Manchester City Police, Manchester and Salford Police, Greater Manchester Police, 1955–76; Asst Chief Constable, Greater Manchester Police, 1976–79; Dep. Chief Constable, Herts, 1979–84. CBIM 1986. OStJ. *Recreations:* squash, golf, wine, walking, gardening. *Address:* Police HQ, Hertfordshire Constabulary, Stanborough Road, Welwyn Garden City, Herts. *T:* Welwyn Garden City 31177.

MORRIS, Walter Frederick; LLB London; ACII; FBIM; Consultant, Morris, Scott & Co., Solicitors, Highcliffe, Christchurch, Dorset; *b* 15 Oct. 1914; *s* of late Captain Frederick James Morris and Elsie Eleanor (*née* Williams); *m* 1945, Marjorie Vaughan, *o d* of late Thomas Vaughan Phillips and Eleanor Mirren (*née* Jones); one *s* one *d*. *Educ:* Cardiff High Sch.; University Coll., Cardiff (Law Prizeman), Legal practice, 1936–39; Served RA (TA), 1939–45: GHQ Home Forces (Intelligence); WO Sch. of Military Administration; Certificate of Merit, Western Comd; GSO1 (Lt-Col), HQ 21st Army Gp, BLA (later BAOR); commanded Legal Aid Organisation, which provided legal assistance to all British Army and RAF personnel in Europe; legal practice (and Hon. District Army Welfare Officer), 1945–47; entered Administrative Home Civil Service, 1947; Min. of Social Security, 1947–68 (Prin. Dep. Chief Insce Off., Asst Sec.); Admin. Staff Coll., Henley, 1953; on loan to Export Credits Guarantee Dept, 1955–57; Manchester Business Sch., 1968; trans. to HM Diplomatic Service, 1968; HM Consul-Gen., Cairo, 1968–70; ME Centre for Arab Studies, Shemlan, Lebanon, 1969; Head of Claims Dept, FCO, 1970–72; Dep. High Comr, later Consul-Gen., Lahore, 1972–73; retired from HM Diplomatic Service, 1973. Mem., Law Soc. Liveryman, City of London Solicitor's Co. *Recreations:* yachting, golf, travel. *Address:* 17 Camden Hurst, Pless Road, Milford-on-Sea, Lymington, Hants SO4 0WL. *T:* Lymington 43551; 548 Canebières, 83490 Le Muy, Var, France. *T:* (94) 45–07–46; 46900 State Road 74, Unit 334, Punta Gorda, Fla 33950–9725, USA. *T:* 813–639–6668. *Clubs:* Royal Lymington Yacht; Barton-on-Sea Golf; Punjab (Lahore).

MORRIS, William; Deputy General Secretary, Transport and General Workers Union, since 1986; *b* 19 Oct. 1938; *s* of William and Una Morris; *m* 1957, Minetta; two *s*. *Educ:* Jamaica. TGWU: Dist Officer, Nottingham, 1973; Dist Sec., Northampton, 1976; Nat. Sec., Passenger Services, 1979–85. Mem., Commn for Racial Equality, 1977–. *Recreations:* walking, gardening, watching sports. *Address:* 156 St Agnells Lane, Grove Hill, Hemel Hempstead, Herts HP2 6EG. *T:* Hemel Hempstead 63110.

MORRIS, Prof. William Ian Clinch; Professor of Obstetrics and Gynaecology, University of Manchester, 1949–72, Professor Emeritus since 1972; *b* 10 May 1907; *s* of Dr J. M. Morris, Neath; *m* 1938, Mary Farquharson (*d* 1976); one *d*. *Educ:* Royal High Sch., Edinburgh; Edinburgh Univ. Obstetrician to Ayr County Council, 1937–46; Sen. Lectr in Obstetrics and Gynaecology, Univ. of Edinburgh, 1946–49. RAMC (TA) 1935; war service, 1939–43. *Publications:* (jointly) A Combined Text-book of Obstetrics and Gynaecology, 1950; contribs to Jl of Obstetrics and Gynaecology of British Commonwealth, Lancet, Edinburgh Med. Jl, etc. *Address:* Edenfield House, Springfield, by Cupar, Fife KY15 5RT.

MORRIS, Rev. William James, JP; Minister of Glasgow Cathedral, since 1967; a Chaplain to the Queen in Scotland, since 1969; *b* Cardiff, 22 Aug. 1925; *o s* of William John Morris and Eliza Cecilia Cameron Johnson; *m* 1952, Jean Daveena Ogilvy Howie, MBE, *o c* of Rev. David Porter Howie and Veena Christie, Kilmarnock; one *s*. *Educ:* Cardiff High Sch.; Univ. of Wales; Edinburgh Univ. BA 1946, BD 1949, Wales; PhD Edinburgh, 1954. Ordained, 1951. Asst, Canongate Kirk, Edinburgh, 1949–51; Minister, Presbyterian Church of Wales, Cadoxton and Barry Is, 1951–53; Buckhaven (Fife): St David's, 1953–57; Peterhead Old Parish, 1957–67; Chaplain to the Lord High Comr to the General Assembly of the Church of Scotland, 1975–76; Chaplain: Peterhead Prison, 1963–67; Glasgow DC, 1967–; Trades House of Glasgow, 1967–; W of Scotland Engrs Assoc., 1967–; The High Sch. of Glasgow, 1974–76, 1983–; Glasgow Acad., 1976–; Strathclyde Police, 1977–; Hon. Chaplain, The Royal Scottish Automobile Club; Moderator, Presbytery of Deer, 1965–66; Convener Adv. Bd, Church of Scotland, 1977–80; Vice-Chm., Bd of Nomination to Church Chairs, Church of Scotland, 1978–81. Mem. IBA, 1979–84 (Chm. Scottish Adv. Cttee). President: Rotary Club of Peterhead, 1965–66; Peterhead and Dist Professional and Business Club, 1967; Chairman: Iona Cath. Trust, 1976 (Trustee, 1967); Council, Soc. of Friends of Glasgow Cath., 1967; Club Service Cttee, Dist 101, RIBI, 1964–66; Prison Chaplaincies Bd (Church of Scotland Home Bd), 1969–83; Vice-Pres., St Andrew's Soc., Glasgow, 1967–82; Member: Scottish Cttee, British Sailors' Soc., 1967–83; Bd of Management, W of Scotland Convalescent Home, 1967–; Gen. Convocation, Strathclyde Univ., 1967–; Council of Management, Quarriers' Homes, 1968–; Bd of Management, Glasgow YMCA, 1973–; Scottish Council on Crime, 1974–76; Church of Scotland Bd of Practice and Procedure, 1981–85; Bd of Governors, Jordanhill Coll. of Educn, Glasgow, 1983–; Hon. Mem., Scottish Ambulance Assoc., 1981. JP: Co. of Aberdeen, 1963–71; Co. of City of Glasgow, 1971. SubChapStJ 1978. Hon. LLD Strathclyde, 1974; Hon. DD Glasgow, 1979; FRCPS(Hon.) 1983. *Publication:* A Walk Around Glasgow Cathedral, 1986. *Recreations:* fishing, gardening. *Address:* 94 St Andrews Drive, Glasgow G41 4RX. *T:* 041–427 2757. *Clubs:* New (Edinburgh); RNVR (Scotland) (Hon.); University of Strathclyde Staff (Hon.); Rotary of Dennistoun (Hon.); Rotary of Glasgow (Hon.).

MORRIS, Wyn, FRAM; Chief Conductor and Musical Director of Symphonica of London; *b* 14 Feb. 1929; *s* of Haydn Morris and Sarah Eluned Phillips; *m* 1962, Ruth Marie McDowell; one *s* one *d*. *Educ:* Llanelli Grammar Sch.; Royal Academy of Music; Mozarteum, Salzburg. August Mann's Prize, 1950; Apprentice Conductor, Yorkshire Symph. Orch., 1950–51; Musical Dir, 17th Trg Regt, RA Band, 1951–53; Founder and Conductor of Welsh Symph. Orch., 1954–57; Koussevitsky Memorial Prize, Boston Symph. Orch., 1957; (on invitation George Szell) Observer, Cleveland Symph. Orch., 1957–60; Conductor: Ohio Bell Chorus, Cleveland Orpheus Choir and Cleveland Chamber Orch., 1958–60; Choir of Royal National Eisteddfod of Wales, 1960–62; London debut, Royal Festival Hall, with Royal Philharmonic Orch., 1963; Conductor: Royal Choral Society, 1968–70; Huddersfield Choral Soc., 1969–74; Ceremony for Investiture of Prince Charles as Prince of Wales, 1969; Royal Choral Soc. tour of USA, 1969. FRAM 1964. Specialises in conducting of Mahler; has recorded Des Knaben Wunderhorn (with Dame Janet Baker and Sir Geraint Evans), Das Klagende Lied, Symphonies 1, 2, 5, 8 and 10 in Deryck Cooke's final performing version. Mahler Memorial Medal (of Bruckner and Mahler Soc. of Amer.), 1968. *Recreations:* chess, Rugby football, climbing, cynghanedd and telling Welsh stories.

MORRIS-JONES, Prof. Huw, CBE 1983; Professor, University College of North Wales, Bangor, 1966–79; Head of Department of Social Theory and Institutions, University College, 1966–79; *b* 1 May 1912; *s* of William Oliver Jones and Margaret Jones; *m* 1942, Gwladys Evans; one *s* one *d*. *Educ:* Alun Grammar Sch., Mold, Flintshire; University Coll. of North Wales, Bangor; Oriel Coll., Oxford. Educn Officer, S Wales Council of Social Service, 1937–39; Tutor and Lectr, Dept of Extra-Mural Studies, Univ. of Nottingham, 1939–42; Lectr, Sen. Lectr and Prof., Bangor, 1942–79. Member: Aves Cttee of Inquiry into Voluntary Workers in Social Services, 1966–69; Welsh Hosp. Bd, 1967–70; Prince of Wales Cttee for Wales, 1967–70; Welsh Economic Council (Chm., Environmental Panel), 1967–71; Broadcasting Council for Wales, 1957–60; IBA (Chm., Welsh Adv. Cttee), 1976–82; Welsh Fourth TV Channel Auth., 1981–82. Chm., Caernarfon Borough, later Jt Caernarfon-Gwyrfai, Magistrates' Ct, 1949–82; Mem. Council, Magistrates' Assoc., 1950– (Chm., Gwynedd Br., 1952–). *Publications:* Y Gelfyddyd Lenyddol yng Nghymru, 1957; (contrib.) Aesthetics in the Modern World (ed Osborne), 1968; Emile Durkheim, 1983; Philosophy, Jl of Royal Inst. Philosophy, Monist, Efrydiau Athronyddol. *Address:* Ceredigion, Pentraeth Road, Menai Bridge, N Wales. *T:* Menai Bridge 712522. *Club:* United Oxford & Cambridge University.

MORRIS-JONES, Ifor Henry, QC 1969; **His Honour Judge Morris-Jones;** a Circuit Judge, since 1977; *b* 5 March 1922; *s* of late Rev. Prof. and Mrs D. Morris-Jones; *m* 1950, Anne Diana, *d* of late S. E. Ferris, OBE, Blundellsands; one *s* two *d*. *Educ:* Taunton Sch.; Sidney Sussex Coll., Cambridge. Called to the Bar, Lincoln's Inn, 1947. Joined Northern Circuit, 1947; Assistant Recorder, Carlisle, 1962; Dep. Chm., Cumberland Sessions, 1969; a Recorder, 1972–76. Mem., Bar Council, 1972. *Recreation:* golf. *Address:* 3 Paddock Close, Blundellsands, Liverpool L23 8UX. *T:* 051–924 4848. *Club:* Artists' (Liverpool).

MORRIS-JONES, Prof. Wyndraeth Humphreys; Emeritus Professor of University of London and Leverhulme Emeritus Fellow; *b* 1 Aug. 1918; *s* of late William James Jones, Carmarthen, and Annie Mary Jones (*née* Morris); *m* 1953, Graziella Bianca Genre; one *s* two *d*. *Educ:* University Coll. Sch., Hampstead; London Sch. of Economics (BSc(Econ.) First Class, 1938; Leverhulme Research Grant, 1939; Hon. Fellow, 1980); Christ's Coll., Cambridge Research Schol., 1940. Indian Army, 1941–46 (Lt-Col, Public Relations Directorate, 1944); Constitutional Adviser to Viceroy of India, 1947; Lecturer in Political Science, London Sch. of Economics, 1946–55; Prof. of Political Theory and Instns, Univ. of Durham, 1955–65; Prof. of Commonwealth Affairs and Dir, Inst. of Commonwealth Studies, Univ. of London, 1966–83. Rockefeller Travel Grants, 1954, 1960 and 1967. Vis. Prof. of Commonwealth Hist. and Instns, Indian Sch. of Internat. Studies, New Delhi, 1960; Visiting Professor: Univ. of Chicago, 1962; Univ. of California, Berkeley, 1964–65. Editor, Jl of Commonwealth and Comparative Politics (formerly Commonwealth Polit. Studies), 1964–80. *Publications:* Parliament in India, 1957; Government and Politics of India, 1964, 3rd edn, 1971; (with Biplab Dasgupta) Patterns and Trends in Indian Politics, 1976; Politics Mainly Indian, 1978; articles in Polit. Studies, Asian Survey, Modern Asian Studies, etc. *Address:* 95 Ridgway, SW19 4SX.

MORRIS WILLIAMS, Christine Margaret; *see* Puxon, C. M.

MORRISH, John Edwin, (Jack); Councillor (Lab), Deputy Leader, and Chairman, Education Committee, Northamptonshire County Council, 1981–85; Hon. Treasurer, United Kingdom Reading Association (World Congress Local Arrangements Committee), 1985–86; *b* 23 Sept. 1915; *s* of Henry Edwin Morrish and Ada Minnie (*née* Tapping); *m* 1st, 1937, Norah Lake; one *d*; 2nd, 1944, Violet Saunders (marr. diss.); one *s* one *d*; 3rd, 1984, Betty Lupton (*née* Wear). *Educ:* Fleet Road, Hampstead, Elem. Sch.; University Coll. Sch.; Northampton Polytechnic, London; various work-faces. Post Office Techn. Officer, 1932–54; coalminer, 1944–45. Trade Union Official: Civil Service Union, 1954–72; Soc. of Civil and Public Servants, 1972–76 (Gen. Sec., Customs and Excise Gp). Administrator, Northants Rural Community Council, 1979. Census Officer, 1980–81. Vice-Chm., E Midlands Further Educn Council, 1982–85; Member: Adv. Cttee, Supply and Educn of Teachers; Assoc. of County Councils, 1981–85; Hon. Chm., Northants Child Poverty Action Gp, 1980–84. Chm., Nene Coll. Governors, 1981–85. *Publications:* The Future of Forestry, 1971; contrib. Trade Union jls. *Recreations:* thinking, pursuit of justice, music, talking. *Address:* 23 Marshworth, Tinkers Bridge, Milton Keynes. *T:* Milton Keynes 670142; 2 Weavers Close, Isleworth, Middx TW7 6EH. *T:* 01–647 3364.

MORRISON, family name of **Viscount Dunrossil** and of **Barons Margadale** and **Morrison.**

MORRISON, 2nd Baron *cr* 1945, of Tottenham; **Dennis Morrison;** Manufacturing Executive with The Metal Box Co. Ltd, 1957–72, retired; *b* 21 June 1914; *e* and *o* surv. *s* of 1st Baron Morrison, PC, and Grace, *d* of late Thomas Glossop; *S* father 1953; *m* 1940, Florence Alice Helena (marr. diss. 1958), *d* of late Augustus Hennes, Tottenham; *m* 1959, Joan (marr. diss. 1975), *d* of late W. R. Meech. *Educ:* Tottenham County Sch. Employed by The Metal Box Co. Ltd on research work, 1937–51; Quality Controller, 1952–57. Lord Lieutenant's Representative for Tottenham, 1955–. FSS 1953–57. Vice-Pres., Acton Chamber of Commerce, 1972 (Mem., Exec. Cttee, 1962). Hon. President: Robert Browning Settlement, 1967–; 5th Acton Scout Group, 1969. *Recreation:* gardening. *Heir:* none. *Address:* 7 Ullswater Avenue, Felixstowe, Suffolk. *T:* Felixstowe 77405.

MORRISON, Maj.-Gen. (retd) Albert Edward, CB 1956; OBE 1942; *b* 17 March 1901; *s* of late Major A. Morrison; *m* 1926, Esther May Lacey. *Educ:* Dover Coll.; RMA Woolwich. Royal Artillery, 1922–26; Royal Signals, 1926–57. Retired as Chief Signal Officer, AFHQ, March 1957. Col Commandant, Royal Corps of Signals, 1959–. Legion of Merit (US), 1946; Order of Rafidain (Iraq), 1940. *Recreation:* golf. *Address:* Wesley House, 68 Fairways, Ferndown, Wimborne, Dorset BH22 8BB.

MORRISON, Alexander John Henderson; His Honour Judge Morrison; a Circuit Judge, since 1980; *b* 16 Nov. 1927; *yr s* of late Dr Alexander Morrison and Mrs A. Morrison; *m* 1978, Hon. Philippa, *y d* of 1st Baron Hives. *Educ:* Derby Sch.; Emmanuel Coll., Cambridge. MA, LLB. Called to the Bar, Gray's Inn, 1951. Mem. of Midland Circuit; Dep. Chm., Derbyshire QS, 1964–71; Regional Chm. of Industrial Tribunals, Sheffield, 1971–80; a Recorder of the Crown Court, 1971–80. Pres., Derbys Union of Golf Clubs, 1977–79. *Recreations:* golf, music. *Address:* 17 Eastwood Drive, Littleover, Derby. *T:* Derby 45376.

MORRISON, Hon. Charles Andrew; MP (C) Devizes since May 1964; *b* 25 June 1932; 2nd *s* of 1st Baron Margadale, *qv*; *m* 1st, 1954, Hon. Sara Long (*see* Hon. Sara Morrison) (marr. diss. 1984); one *s* one *d*; 2nd, 1984, Mrs Rosalind Ward. *Educ:* Eton. Nat. Service in The Life Guards, 1950–52; Royal Wilts Yeo. (TA), 1952–66. County Councillor, Wilts, 1958–65 (Chm., Educn Cttee, 1963–64). Chm., Nat. Cttee for Electoral Reform, 1985–; Mem. Bd of Dirs, Global Cttee of Parliamentarians on Population and Develt, 1984–. Chairman: South West Regional Sports Council, 1966–68; Young Volunteer Force Foundn, 1971–74; British Trust for Conservation Volunteers, 1973–78; Member: Council, Salmon and Trout Assoc.; Game Conservancy (Vice-Chm.). A Vice-Chm., 1922 Cttee, 1974–83 (Mem. Exec., 1972–). *Recreations:* gardening, shooting, fishing. *Address:* House of Commons, SW1A 0AA; Brook House, Luckington, Chippenham, Wilts. *Clubs:* White's, Pratt's.

See also Hon. J. I. Morrison, Hon. M. A. Morrison, Hon. P. H. Morrison.

MORRISON, Donald Alexander Campbell; Assistant Under-Secretary of State, Home Office, 1972–76; *b* 30 Nov. 1916; *s* of late George Alexander Morrison, sometime MP for Scottish Univs, and late Rachel Brown Morrison (*née* Campbell); *m* 1st, 1951, Elma Margaret Craig (*d* 1970); two *s* one *d*; 2nd, 1973, Jane Margaret Montgomery; one step *s*. *Educ:* Fettes Coll.; Christ Church, Oxford (BA). Home Office, 1939; Asst Sec., 1955. A Senior Clerk (acting), House of Commons, 1976–81. War Service, 1940–45: 79th (Scottish Horse) Medium Regt, RA, 1942–45. *Recreation:* music. *Address:* 27 High Street, Wingham, near Canterbury, Kent CT3 1AW. *T:* Canterbury 720774.

MORRISON, Air Vice-Marshal Ian Gordon, CB 1965; CBE 1957 (OBE 1946); RNZAF (retired); Deputy Chairman, Wm Scollay & Co., since 1980; *b* 16 March 1914; *s* of W. G. Morrison; *m* 1938, Dorothy, *d* of W. H. Franks; one *s* two *d*. *Educ:* Christchurch Boys' High Sch., NZ. RAF 1935; RNZAF 1939; No 75 Sqdn, UK, 1939; Comd RNZAF, Omaka, 1941; Comd RNZAF, Gisborne, 1942; SASO, Islands Gp, 1943; Comd No 3 BR Sqdn Pacific, 1944–45; jssc, UK, 1950; Comd RNZAF, Ohakea, 1952; Air Mem. for Supply, 1954; idc, 1958; AOC, RNZAF, HQ London, 1959–60; Air Mem. for Personnel, 1961–62; Chief of the Air Staff, Royal New Zealand Air Force, 1962–66. Develt Dir, A. S. Cornish Gp, 1970–80. Nat. Pres., Scout Assoc. of NZ, 1967–79. *Recreations:* golf and angling. *Address:* 2 Taungata Road, York Bay, Eastbourne, New Zealand. *T:* Wellington 683367. *Clubs:* Wellington (Pres., 1978–82), Wellington Golf (both in NZ).

MORRISON, Prof. James, OBE 1963; BSc, NDA; Professor of Crop and Animal Husbandry, The Queen's University of Belfast, 1944–65, also Director, Agricultural Research Institute, Hillsborough, NI, 1934–65; retired; *b* 11 Aug. 1900; *m* 1934, Grace F. Stockdale, Clogher, Co. Tyrone; three *d*. *Educ:* Fordyce Academy, Banffshire, Scotland; Marischal Coll., Aberdeen Univ. Instructor in Agriculture, Co. Tyrone and Co. Down, 1925 and 1926; Sec. and Agric. Organiser, Co. Armagh, 1927–30; Inspector, Min. of Agric. for N Ireland, 1931–33; Lectr in Crop and Animal Husbandry, QUB, 1934. *Recreation:* gardening. *Address:* Loxwood, 35 Lisburn Road, Hillsborough, Co. Down BT26 6HW. *T:* Hillsborough (Co. Down) 682208.

MORRISON, Hon. James Ian, TD, DL; director of companies; farmer; *b* 17 July 1930; *e s* and *heir* of Baron Margadale, *qv*; *m* 1952, Clare Barclay; two *s* one *d*. *Educ:* Eton Coll.; Royal Agricultural Coll., Cirencester. 2nd Lieut, Life Guards, 1949–50; Major, Royal Wilts Yeo., 1960–68; Hon. Colonel: A (RWY) Sqn Royal Yeomanry RAC TA, and B (RWY) Sqn Royal Wessex Yeomanry, 1982–; Royal Wessex Yeomanry RAC TA, 1984–. Member, Queen's Body Guard for Scotland, 1960–. County Councillor, Wilts, 1955 and 1973–77, County Alderman, 1969; Chairman, W Wilts Conservative Assoc., 1967–71, Pres., 1972–84; Chm., Wilts CLA, 1978–81. Chm., Tattersalls Cttee, 1969–80. DL 1977–, High Sheriff 1971, Wiltshire. *Recreations:* racing, shooting, hunting. *Address:* Hawking Down, Hindon, Salisbury, Wilts SP3 6DN; Islay Estate Office, Bridgend, Islay, Argyll PA44 7PA. *Clubs:* White's, Jockey.

See also Hon. C. A. Morrison, Hon. M. A. Morrison, Hon. P. H. Morrison, Viscount Trenchard.

MORRISON, James Victor, CB 1979; TD 1950; *b* 13 Sept. 1917; *s* of Frederick Armand Morrison, Mountstewart, Co. Down, and Hannah Maria Snow, Kells, Co. Meath; *m* 1944, Sophie Winifred Ives; one *s* two *d*. *Educ:* Regent House. Entered NICS, 1937; War service, 1939–46: BEF, France; SE Asia; TA Service, 1947–57; comd 245 (Ulster) Light Air Defence Regt. NI Industrial Develt Rep., New York, 1957–60; Chief Administrative Officer, Police Authority for NI, 1970–74; Dep. Sec., NICS, seconded to NI Office, 1974–79. Mem., Police Authy for NI, 1979–85. *Recreations:* gardening, hi-fi, reading, walking. *Address:* 49 Castlehill Road, Belfast BT4 3GP. *T:* Belfast 63344.

MORRISON, John Lamb Murray, CBE 1957; DSc; FEng; FIMechE; Formerly Professor of Mechanical Engineering, University of Bristol, Emeritus 1971; *b* 22 May 1906; *s* of late Latto A. Morrison, Biggar, Lanarkshire; *m* 1936, Olga, *d* of late M. Nierenstein, DSc; two *s*. *Educ:* Biggar High Sch.; Univ. of Glasgow (DSc 1939). Lecturer in Mechanical Engineering; Reader in Mechanical Engineering, Univ. of Bristol. Pres., IMechE, 1970–71. Hon. DSc Salford, 1972. *Publications:* An Introduction to the Mechanics of Machines, 1964; various papers on strength of materials and design of machines. *Recreations:* gardening, golf. *Address:* Dreva, Rayleigh Road, Bristol BS9 2AU. *T:* 681193.

MORRISON, John Sinclair; President, Wolfson College (formerly University College), Cambridge, 1966–80; *b* 15 June 1913; *s* of Sinclair Morrison (and *g s* of William Morrison, NY and Stagbury, Chipstead, Surrey) and Maria Elsie, *d* of William Lamaison, Salmons, Kenley, Surrey; *m* 1942, Elizabeth Helen, *d* of S. W. Sulman, Bexhill, Sussex; three *s* two *d*. *Educ:* Charterhouse; Trinity Coll., Cambridge. Fellow Trinity College, Cambridge, 1937–45; Asst Lecturer Manchester University, 1937–39; Editor of Cambridge Review, 1939–40. Ordinary Seaman (Volunteer), 1940–41. In service of British Council, Cairo, Zagazig, Baghdad, 1941–42; British Council Rep. in Palestine and Transjordan, 1942–45; Pres. Jerusalem Rotary Club, 1945; Prof. of Greek and Head of Dept of Classics and Ancient History at the Durham Colls of Univ. of Durham, 1945–50; Fellow Tutor and Senior Tutor of Trinity Coll., Cambridge, 1950–60; Vice-Master and Sen. Tutor of Churchill Coll., Cambridge, 1960–65, now Hon. Fellow. Leverhulme Fellow, 1965. Mellon Prof., 1976–77, Kenan Prof., 1981–82, Reed Coll., Oregon, USA; Leverhulme Emeritus Fellow, 1984–85. Member: Sierra Leone Educn Commission, 1954; Annan Cttee on Teaching of Russian, 1961; Hale Cttee on University Teaching Methods, 1961; Schools Council, 1965–67; Jt Working Party on 6th Form Curriculum and Examinations, 1968–72; Governing Bodies Assoc., 1965; Governor: Bradfield Coll., 1963–83; Wellington Coll., 1963–83; Charterhouse Sch., 1970–83. Jt Editor, Classical Review, 1968–75. Trustee, National Maritime Museum, 1975–82; Chm., Trireme Trust, 1984–. *Publications:* (with R. T. Williams) Greek Oared Ships, 1968; Long Ships and Round Ships, 1980; (with J. F. Coates) The Athenian Trireme, 1986. *Address:* Granhams, Granhams Road, Great Shelford, Cambridge.

MORRISON, Hon. Mary Anne, DCVO 1982 (CVO 1970); Woman of the Bedchamber to the Queen since 1960; *b* 17 May 1937; *o d* of Baron Margadale, *qv*. *Educ:* Heathfield School. *Address:* Fonthill House, Tisbury, Wilts. *T:* Tisbury 870202; Eallabus, Bridgend, Isle of Islay, Argyllshire. *T:* Bowmore 223.

See also Hon. C. A. Morrison, Hon. J. I. Morrison, Hon. P. H. Morrison.

MORRISON, Hon. Peter Hugh; MP (C) City of Chester since Feb. 1974; a Deputy Chairman of the Conservative Parly, since 1986; *b* 2 June 1944; 3rd *s* of 1st Baron Margadale, *qv*. *Educ:* Eton; Keble Coll., Oxford (Hons Law). Personal Asst to Rt Hon. P. Walker, MP, 1966–67; Investment Manager, 1968–70; independent business, 1970–74. Sec., NW Cons. Members' Gp, 1974–76; Jt Sec., Cons. Smaller Businesses Cttee, 1974–76. An Opposition Whip, 1976–79; a Lord Comr of HM Treasury, and Govt Pairing Whip, 1979–81; Parly Under-Sec. of State, 1981–83, Minister of State, 1983–85, Dept of Employment; Minister of State, DTI, 1985–86. *Address:* 81 Cambridge Street, SW1V 4PS; The Stable House, Puddington, Chester. *Clubs:* White's, Pratt's.

See also Hon. C. A. Morrison, Hon. J. I. Morrison, Hon. M. A. Morrison.

MORRISON, Maj.-Gen. Reginald Joseph Gordon, CB 1969; CBE 1959; MD, FRCP; retired; Physician, The Royal Hospital, Chelsea, 1969–79; Director of Medicine, Ministry of Defence (Army), and Consulting Physician to the Army, 1965–68; *b* 29 March 1909; *s* of R. Morrison; *m* 1947, Norma Jacqueline Nicholson; two *s*. *Educ:* Dulwich Coll.; St Joseph's Coll., SE19; St Bartholomew's Hosp. House Phys., St Bart's Hosp., 1934; Res. MO, Hove Gen. Hosp. Commnd RAMC, 1936; served as Med. Specialist, RAMC. Adviser in Medicine, EA Command, 1947–50; OC, Med. Div., QA Mil. Hosp., 1950–56; Cons. Phys., Far East, 1956–59; Prof. of Trop. Med., Royal Army Medical College, 1959–65. QHP 1963–68. *Publications:* (with W. H. Hargreaves) The Practice of Tropical Medicine, 1965; chapter in: Exploration Medicine, 1965; Medicine in the Tropics, 1974; various articles in Lancet, BMJ, Proc. RSM, etc. *Recreations:* rose growing, golf. *Address:* Flat 2, Highclere, Old Hill, Chislehurst, Kent.

MORRISON, Hon. Sara Antoinette Sibell Frances, (Hon. Mrs Sara Morrison); *b* 9 Aug. 1934; *d* of 2nd Viscount Long and of Laura, Duchess of Marlborough; *m* 1954, Hon. Charles Andrew Morrison, *qv* (marr. diss. 1984); one *s* one *d*. *Educ:* in England and France. Gen. Electric Co., 1975– (Dir 1980–); Director: Abbey Nat. Building Soc., 1979–86; Imperial Group Ltd, 1981–86. Chairman: Nat. Council for Voluntary Orgns (formerly Nat. Council of Social Service), 1977–81; Nat. Adv. Council on Employment of Disabled People, 1981–84. County Councillor, then Alderman, Wilts, 1961–71; Chairman: Wilts Assoc. of Youth Clubs, 1958–63; Wilts Community Council, 1965–70; Vice-Chairman: Nat. Assoc. Youth Clubs, 1969–71; Conservative Party Organisation, 1971–75; Member: Governing Bd, Volunteer Centre, 1972–77; Annan Cttee of Enquiry into Broadcasting, 1974–77; Nat. Consumer Council, 1975–77; Bd, Fourth Channel TV Co., 1980–85. *Address:* Wyndham's Farm, Wedhampton, Devizes, Wilts. *T:* Chirton 221; 16 Groom Place, SW1. *T:* 01–245 6553.

MORRISON, Dr Stuart Love; Professor of Community Medicine, University of Edinburgh, 1964–75, retired; *b* 25 Nov. 1922; *o s* of late William James Morrison, Ironfounder, Glasgow and late Isabella Murdoch, Edinburgh; *m* 1947, Dr Audrey Butler Lornie, *yr d* of late Lt-Col W. S. Lornie, MC, TD, MRCVS, Perth; one *d*. *Educ:* Glasgow Acad.; Dundee High Sch.; St Andrews and London Univs. MB, ChB (St Andrews) 1951; DPH (London) 1954; MRCP Edinburgh, 1966; FRCP Edinburgh, 1968; FFCM 1975. Served in RAF, 1939–46; Hosp. and gen. practice, 1951–53; Public Health appts, 1954–56; Mem., Scientific Staff, MRC Social Medicine Research Unit, 1956–62; Vis. Fellow, Epidemiology and Statistics, Univ. of N Carolina, 1961–62; Sen. Lectr in Social Med., Univ. of Edinburgh, 1962–64; Professorial Fellow in Community Medicine, 1976–82 and Dir of Centre for Med. Res., 1979–82, Univ. of Sussex; Vis. Prof. of Community Medicine, LSHTM, 1982–84; Prof. of Community Medicine, Univ. of Malta, 1984–86. *Publications:* (jtly) The Image and the Reality, 1978; contribs to med. jls on epidemiology, organisation of medical care and medical administration. *Recreation:* book collecting. *Address:* The Bower House, Roselands, Sidmouth, Devon EX10 8PB.

MORRISON, William Charles Carnegie, CA; UK Managing Partner, KMG Thomson McLintock (formerly Thomson McLintock & Co.), Chartered Accountants, since 1980; Partner, Klynveld Main Goerdeler, since 1979, Member International Management Committee, since 1985; Visiting Professor in Accountancy, University of Strathclyde, since 1983; *b* 10 Feb. 1938; *s* of late William and Grace Morrison; *m* 1st; two *d*; 2nd, 1977, Joceline Mary (*née* Saint). *Educ:* Kelvinside Acad., Lathallan; Merchiston Castle Sch. Thomson McLintock & Co.: qual. CA (with distinction), 1961; Partner, 1966; Jt Sen. Partner, Glasgow and Edinburgh, 1974–80. Director: Thomas Cook & Son Ltd, 1971–72; Scottish Amicable Life Assurance Soc., 1973–; Securities Trust of Scotland, 1976–80; Brownlee & Co., 1978–80. Pres., Inst. of Chartered Accountants of Scotland, 1984–85 (Vice-Pres., 1982–84). Vice Pres., Scottish Council (Develt and Industry), 1982– (mem. various cttees); Member: Scottish Telecommunications Bd, 1978–80; Scottish Cttee, Design Council, 1978–81. Governor, Kelvinside Acad., 1967–80 (Chm. of Governors, 1975–80); Hon. Treasurer, Transport Trust, 1982–. *Publications:* occasional professional papers. *Recreations:* vintage transport, model railways. *Address:* 87 Campden Hill Court, Holland Street, W8 7HW. *T:* 01–937 2972. *Clubs:* Caledonian; Royal Scottish Automobile (Glasgow).

MORRISON-BELL, Sir William (Hollin Dayrell), 4th Bt *cr* 1905; *b* 21 June 1956; *s* of Sir Charles Reginald Francis Morrison-Bell, 3rd Bt and of Prudence Caroline, *d* of late Lt-Col W. D. Davies, 60th Rifles (she *m* 2nd, Peter Gillbanks); *S* father, 1967; *m* 1984, Cynthia Hélène Marie White; one *s*. *Educ:* Eton; St Edmund Hall, Oxford. *Heir:* *s* Thomas Charles Edward Morrison-Bell, *b* 13 Feb. 1985. *Address:* Highgreen, Tarset, Hexham, Northumberland. *T:* Greenhaugh 223; 106 Bishops Road, SW6. *T:* 01–736 4940.

MORRISON-LOW, Sir James; *see* Low.

MORRISON-SCOTT, Sir Terence Charles Stuart, Kt 1965; DSC 1944; DSc; DL; Director, British Museum (Natural History), 1960–68 (Director, Science Museum, 1956–60); *b* Paris, 24 Oct. 1908; *o s* of late R. C. S. Morrison-Scott, DSO, and Douairière Jhr. R. Quarles van Ufford; *m* 1935, Rita, 4th *d* of late E. J. Layton. *Educ:* Eton; Christ Church (MA of the House, 1947), Oxford; Royal College of Science (1st Class Hons Zoology, BSc, ARCS 1935, MSc 1939); FLS 1937; DSc London, 1952. Asst Master, Eton, 1935; Scientific Staff, Brit. Museum (Natural Hist.) in charge of Mammal Room, 1936–39, 1945–55 and part of 1956. Served War of 1939–45, with Royal Navy (DSC). Lt-Comdr RNVR. Treas., Zoological Soc. of London, 1950–76; Treas., XVth Internat. Congress of Zoology, 1958. Trustee, Imp. War Museum, 1956–60; Dir, Arundel Castle Trustees Ltd, 1976–. Governor, Imperial Coll. of Science and Technology, 1956–76 (Fellow, 1963); Mem., Standing Commn on Museums and Galleries, 1973–76; National Trust: Mem., Properties Cttee, 1968–83; Chm., Nature Cons. Panel, 1970–81; Chm., Architectural Panel, 1973–82. Goodwood Flying Sch. (solo), 1975. DL West Sussex, 1982. *Publications:* Palaearctic and Indian Mammals (with J. R. E.), 1951; Southern African Mammals (with J. R. E. and R. W. H.), 1953; papers in scientific jls on taxonomy of mammals. *Address:* Upperfold House, Fernhurst, Haslemere, Surrey GU27 3JH. *Clubs:* Athenæum, Brooks's; Vincent's (Oxford); Leander.

MORRITT, (Robert) Andrew, QC 1977; *b* 5 Feb. 1938; *s* of Robert Augustus Morritt and Margaret Mary Morritt (*née* Tyldesley Jones); *m* 1962, Sarah Simonetta Merton, *d* of John Ralph Merton, *qv*; two *s*. *Educ:* Eton Coll.; Magdalene Coll., Cambridge (BA 1961). 2nd Lieut Scots Guards, 1956–58. Called to the Bar, Lincoln's Inn, 1962, Bencher, 1984; Mem., Gen. Council of the Bar, 1969–73. Junior Counsel: to Sec. of State for Trade in Chancery Matters, 1970–77; to Attorney-Gen. in Charity Matters, 1972–77; Attorney General to HRH The Prince of Wales, 1978–. Member: Adv. Cttee on Legal Educn, 1972–76; Top Salaries Review Body, 1982–. *Recreations:* fishing, shooting. *Address:* 7 Stone Buildings, Lincoln's Inn, WC2A 3SZ. *T:* 01–405 3886. *Club:* Garrick.

MORROCCO, Alberto, RSA 1963 (ARSA 1952); RP 1977; RGI; Head of School of Painting, Duncan of Jordanstone College of Art, Dundee, 1950–82; *b* 14 Dec. 1917; *m* 1941, Vera Cockburn Mercer; two *s* one *d*. *Educ:* Gray's Sch. of Art, Aberdeen. Carnegie Schol., 1937; Brough Schol., 1938. In the Army, 1940–46. Guthrie Award, 1943; San Vito Prize, Rome, 1959. Pictures in: Scottish Modern Arts Coll.; Contemporary Arts Soc.; Scottish Arts Council Coll.; Hull, Aberdeen, Glasgow, Perth, Dundee and Edinburgh City Art Galleries and Scottish Gall. of Modern Art. Mem., Royal Fine Art Commn for Scotland, 1978–. Hon. LLD Dundee, 1980. *Recreations:* travel, swimming, eating. *Address:* Binrock, 456 Perth Road, Dundee. *T:* Dundee 69319. *Club:* Scottish Arts.

MORROGH, Henton, CBE 1969; FRS 1964; FEng 1979; Director, BCIRA (formerly British Cast Iron Research Association), 1959–85; *b* 29 Sept. 1917; *s* of Clifford and Amy Morrogh; *m* 1949, Olive Joyce Ramsay; one *d*. Distinguished for his work on the microstructure and solidification of cast iron and for the development of ductile cast iron. Visiting Prof., Dept of Industrial Engineering and Management Univ. of Technology, Loughborough, 1967–72. President: Instn of Metallurgists, 1967–68; Inst. of British Foundrymen, 1972–73; Internat. Cttee of Foundry Technical Assocs, 1978. Hon. Mem., Japanese Foundrymen's Soc., 1984. DSc (*hc*), Univ. of Birmingham, 1965; Iron and Steel Inst. Andrew Carnegie Gold Medal, 1946; E. J. Fox Medal Inst. of Brit. Foundrymen, 1951; McFadden Gold Medal, Amer. Foundrymen's Soc., 1952; Robert Hadfield Medal, Iron & Steel Inst., 1956; Gold Medal, Amer. Gray Iron Founders' Soc., 1961; Bessemer Gold Medal, Metals Soc., 1977. *Address:* Cedarwood, Penn Lane, Tanworth-in-Arden, Warwicks B94 5HH. *T:* Tanworth-in-Arden 2414.

MORROW, Sir Ian (Thomas), Kt 1973; CA; FCMA, JDipMA, FBIM; CompIEE; Chairman: The Laird Group plc (Director, since 1973); MAI (formerly Mills and Allen International) plc (Director, since 1974); Mills & Allen Money Brokers Ltd; International Harvester Co. of Great Britain Ltd (Director, 1974–85); Harlow Meyer Savage Ltd (Director, since 1980); Strong & Fisher (Holdings) PLC (Director, since 1981); Additional Underwriting Agencies (No 3) Ltd, since 1985; Efamol plc, since 1986; Deputy Chairman, Hambros PLC, since 1972; Director, Hambros Industrial Management Ltd, since 1965; *b* 8 June 1912; *er s* of late Thomas George Morrow and Jamesina Hunter, Pilmour Links, St Andrews; *m* 1940, Elizabeth Mary Thackray (marr. diss. 1967); one *s* one *d*; *m* 1967, Sylvia Jane Taylor; one *d*. *Educ:* Dollar Academy, Dollar. Chartered Accountant 1935; FCMA 1945; Asst Accountant, Brocklehurst-Whiston Amalgamated Ltd, 1937–40; Partner, Robson, Morrow & Co., 1942–51; Financial Dir, 1951–52, Dep. Man. Dir, 1952–56, Joint Man. Dir, 1956–57, Man. Dir, 1957–58, The Brush Electrical Engineering Co. Ltd (now The Brush Group Ltd); Jt Man. Dir, H. Clarkson & Co. Ltd, 1961–72; Chairman: Associated Fire Alarms Ltd, 1965–70; Rowe Bros & Co. (Holdings) Ltd, 1960–70; Kenwood Manufacturing Co. Ltd, 1961–68; Crane Fruehauf Trailers Ltd, 1969–71; Collett, Dickenson, Pearce Internat. Ltd, 1979–83; Scotia DAF Trucks Ltd, 1979–83; Agricultural Holdings Co. Ltd, 1981–84; UKO International plc (formerly UK Optical & Industrial Holdings Ltd), 1979–86 (former Man. Dir and Chm. of subsidiary cos); former Chairman and Director: W. M. Still & Sons Ltd; Martin-Black PLC; Pearl & Dean Ltd (Hong Kong); Hugh Paul Holdings Ltd; Deputy Chairman, Rolls Royce Ltd, 1970–71, Rolls Royce (1971) Ltd, 1971–73 (Man. Dir, 1971–72); Director: DAF Trucks (GB), 1977–83; Zeus Management Ltd, 1985–; Harlow Veda Savage (Holdings) Ltd, 1985–. Led Anglo-American Council on Productivity Team on Management Accounting to US, 1950. Council Member: British Electrical & Allied Manufacturers' Assoc., 1957–58; British Internal Combustion Engine Manufacturers' Assoc., 1957–58; Member: Grand Council, FBI, 1953–58; Council, Production Engineering Research Assoc., 1955–58; Council, Inst. of Cost and Works Accountants (now Inst. of Cost and Management Accountants), 1952–70 (Pres. 1956–67, Gold Medallist 1961); Performing Right Tribunal, 1968–74; Council, Inst. of Chartered Accountants of Scotland, 1968–72, 1979–82 (Vice-Pres. 1970–72, 1979–80, 1980–81, Pres., 1981–82); Inflation Accounting Steering Gp, 1976–79; Lay Member, Press Council, 1974–80; Freeman, City of London; Liveryman, Worshipful Co. of Spectaclemakers. DUniv. Stirling, 1979; Hon. DLitt Heriot-Watt, 1982. *Publications:* papers and addresses on professional and management subjects. *Recreations:* reading, music, golf, ski-ing. *Address:* 2 Albert Terrace Mews, NW1 7TA. *T:* 01–722 7110. *Clubs:* National Liberal, Royal Automobile; Royal and Ancient (St Andrews).

MORROW, Martin S.; Stipendiary Magistrate, Glasgow, since 1972; *b* 16 Nov. 1923; *s* of late Thomas Morrow and Mary Lavery; *m* 1952, Nancy May, BMus, LRAM; one *s* two *d*. *Educ:* St Aloysius' Coll., Glasgow; Glasgow Univ. Solicitor. Private practice, 1951–56; Asst Procurator Fiscal, 1956–72. *Recreations:* music, golf, reading. *Address:* 68 Lauderdale Gardens, Glasgow G12 9QW. *T:* 041–334 1324. *Club:* St Mungo (Glasgow).

MORSE, Sir Christopher Jeremy, KCMG 1975; Chairman: Lloyds Bank, since 1977 (Deputy Chairman, 1975–77); Lloyds Merchant Bank Holdings, since 1985; City Communications Centre, since 1985; Director: Legal & General Assurance Society Ltd; ICI plc; Deputy Chairman, Business in the Community; President, British Bankers' Association, since 1984; *b* 10 Dec. 1928; *s* of late Francis John Morse and Kinbarra (*née* Armfield-Marrow); *m* 1955, Belinda Marianne, *d* of Lt-Col R. B. Y. Mills; three *s* one *d* (and one *d* decd). *Educ:* Winchester; New Coll., Oxford. 1st Class Lit. Hum. 1953. 2nd Lt KRRC, 1948–49. Trained in banking at Glyn, Mills & Co., and made a director in 1964; Executive Dir, Bank of England, 1965–72; Lloyds Bank International: Chm., 1979–80; Dep. Chm., 1975–77 and 1980–85; Alternate Governor for UK of IMF, 1966–72; Chm. of Deputies of Cttee of Twenty, IMF, 1972–74; Chm., Cttee of London Clearing Bankers, 1980–82 (Dep. Chm., 1978–80); President: Institut Internat. d'Etudes Bancaires, 1982–83; British Overseas Bankers' Club, 1983–84; Internat. Monetary Conf., 1985–86. Mem., NEDC, 1977–81. Dir, Alexanders Discount Co. Ltd, 1975–84. Governor, Henley Management Coll., 1966–85; Pres., London Forex Assoc., 1978–. Freeman, City of London, 1978; Chm., City Arts Trust, 1976–79. Fellow: All Souls Coll., Oxford, 1953–68, 1983–; Winchester Coll., 1966–82; Hon. Fellow, New Coll., Oxford, 1979–; Hon. DLitt City, 1977. FIDE Internat. Judge for chess compositions, 1975–; Pres., British Chess Problem Soc., 1977–79. *Recreations:* poetry, problems and puzzles, coarse gardening, golf. *Address:* 102a Drayton Gardens, SW10. *T:* 01–370 2265. *Club:* Athenæum.

MORSE, David A.; partner, law firm of Jones, Day, Reavis & Pogue (Washington DC, California, New York City, Texas, Paris, London and Riyadh); *b* New York City, 31 May 1907; *m* 1937, Mildred H. Hockstader. *Educ:* Somerville Public Schs, NJ; Rutgers Coll., NJ; Harvard Law Sch. LittB (Rutgers), 1929, LLB (Harvard), 1932. Admitted to New Jersey Bar, 1932, NY Bar, Washington DC Bar; Chief Counsel Petroleum Labor Policy Bd, Dept of Interior, 1934–35. US Dept of Interior; Special Asst to US Attorney-Gen., 1934–35; Regional Attorney, National Labor Relations Bd (Second Region), 1935–38. Impartial Chm., Milk Industry Metropolitan Area of New York, 1940–42, when entered Army. Lectr on Labor Relations, Labor Law, Administrative Law, various colleges and law schools, 1938–47. Gustav Pollak Lectr on Research in Govt, Harvard Univ., 1955–56. Formerly: Perm. US Govt Mem. on Governing Body of Internat. Labor Office; US Govt Deleg. to Internat. Labor Confs; Statutory Mem. Bd of Foreign Service; Dep. Chm. Interdepartmental Cttee on Internat. Social Policy; Mem., Cttee for Conservation of Manpower in War Industry, State of NJ; served in N Africa, Sicily and Italy, 1943–44 (Chief of Labor Div., Allied Mil. Govt); arrived in England, 1944. Major, 1944; Chief of Labor Section, US Group Control Council for Germany and prepared Labor Policy and Program for Germany; also advised and assisted SHAEF in preparation of Labor Policy and Program for France, Belgium, Holland, etc; Lt-Col and Dir Labor for Mil. Govt Group, 1945; returned to US; Gen. Counsel, Nat. Labor Relations Bd, 1945–46; Asst Sec. of Labor, 1946–47; Under-Sec. of Labor, 1947–48; Actg Sec. of Labor, June-Aug. 1948; Dir-Gen., Internat. Labor Office, Geneva, 1948–70; Adviser to Administrator, UN Develt Programme. Member: Amer. Bar Assoc.; Council on Foreign Relations; World Rehabilitation Fund; Albert and Mary Lasker Foundn; Nat. Council of UN Assoc. of USA; Amer. Arbitration Assoc.; American Legion; Impartial Chm., Coat and Suit Ind. of Metropolitan Area of NY, 1970. Hon. LLD: Rutgers, 1957; Geneva, 1962; Strasbourg, 1968; Hon. DSc, Laval, Quebec, 1969; Hon. DHL Brandeis Univ., 1971. Sidney Hillman Foundn Award, 1969; Rutgers Univ. Alumni Award, 1970; Internat. League for Rights of Man Award, 1970; Three Bronze Battle Stars; Legion of Merit; Officier de l'Etoile Equatoriale (Gabon); Ordre de la valeur (Cameroon); Order of Merit of Labour (Brazil); Grand Officer, Simon Bolivar, (Columbia), 1970; Grand Officer, Order of Merit (Italy), 1971; Grand Officer, French Legion of Honour, 1971; Orden El Sol (Peru), 1972; Grand Officer, Ordre National du Lion (Senegal), 1978. *Address:* 575 Park Avenue, New York, NY 10021, USA. *Clubs:* Metropolitan (Washington DC); Century Association (New York); Interalliée (Paris).

MORSE, Sir Jeremy; *see* Morse, Sir C. J.

MORSON, Basil Clifford, VRD 1963; MA, DM Oxon; FRCS; FRCPath; FRCP; Civilian Consultant in Pathology to the Royal Navy, since 1976; Consultant Pathologist to St Mark's Hospital since 1956; Director of the Research Department, since 1958; Director, WHO International Reference Centre for Gastrointestinal Cancer, since 1969; *b* 13 Nov. 1921; *s* of late A. Clifford Morson, OBE, FRCS; *m* 1st, 1950, Pamela Elizabeth Gilbert (marr. diss. 1982); one *s* two *d*; 2nd, 1983, Sylvia Dutton, MBE. *Educ:* Beaumont Coll.; Wadham Coll., Oxford; Middlesex Hosp. Medical Sch. House Surg., Middlesex Hosp., 1949; House Surg., Central Middlesex Hosp., 1950; Asst Pathologist, Bland-Sutton Institute of Pathology, Middlesex Hosp., 1950. Sub-Lt RNVR, 1943–46; Surgeon-Comdr RNR (London Div.), retd 1972. President: Sect. of Proctology, RSocMed, 1973–74; British Soc. of Gastroenterology, 1979–80; British Div., Internat. Acad. of Pathology, 1978–; Treas., RCPath, 1983– (Vice-Pres., 1978–81). Vis. Prof. of Pathology, Univ. of Chicago, 1959; Sir Henry Wade Vis. Prof., RCSE, 1970; Vis. Prof of Pathology, Univ. of Texas System Cancer Center, 1980 (Joanne Vandenberg Hill Award); Lectures: Lettsomian, Med. Soc., 1970; Sir Arthur Hurst Meml, British Soc. of Gastroenterology, 1970; Richardson, Massachusetts Gen. Hosp., Boston, 1970; Skinner, RCR, 1983; Shelley Meml, Johns Hopkins Univ., 1983. FRCS 1972; FRCP 1979 (MRCP 1973); Hon. Fellow: Amer. Soc. of Colon and Rectal Surgeons, 1974; Amer. Coll. of Gastroenterology, 1978; French Nat. Soc. of Gastroenterology, 1982. *Publications:* section, Pathology of Alimentary Tract, in Systemic Pathology, ed G. Payling Wright and W. St C. Symmers, 1966, 2nd edn 1978, chapter on Pathology of Alimentary Tract, 3rd edn 1987; (ed) Diseases of the Colon, Rectum and Anus, 1969; Textbook of Gastrointestinal Pathology, 1972, 2nd edn 1979; Histological Typing of Intestinal Tumours, 1976; The Pathogenesis of Colorectal Cancer, 1978; Pathology in Surgical Practice, 1985; Atlas on Pre-cancerous Lesions of the Gastrointestinal Tract, 1987; numerous articles in medical journals. *Recreations:* gardening, ornithology, travel. *Address:* 52 Gordon Place, W8. *T:* 01–937 7101.

MORT, Rt. Rev. John Ernest Llewelyn, CBE 1965; Canon Residentiary and Treasurer of Leicester Cathedral, since 1970; Assistant Bishop, Diocese of Leicester, since 1972; *b* 13 April 1915; *s* of late Trevor Ll. Mort, JP, and Ethel Mary Mort; *m* 1953, Barbara Gifford. *Educ:* Malvern Coll.; St Catharine's Coll., Cambridge (BA Hist. Tripos 1938; MA 1942); Westcott House, Cambridge. Asst Curate, Dudley, 1940–44; Worcester Diocesan Youth Organiser, 1944–48; Private Chaplain to Bishop of Worcester, 1943–52; Vicar of St John in Bedwardine, Worcester, 1948–52; Bishop of N Nigeria, 1952–69. Hon. LLD Ahmadu Bello Univ., 1970. *Address:* 7 St Martin's East, Leicester LE1 5FX. *T:* Leicester 530580.

MORTIMER, Chapman; *see* Chapman-Mortimer, W. C.

MORTIMER, Clifford Hiley, DSc, DrPhil; FRS 1958; Distinguished Professor in Zoology, University of Wisconsin-Milwaukee, 1966–81, now Distinguished Professor

Emeritus; *b* Whitchurch, Som, 27 Feb. 1911; *er s* of Walter Herbert and Bessie Russell; *m* 1936, Ingeborg Margarete Closs, Stuttgart, Germany; two *d*. *Educ:* Sibford and Sidcot Schs; Univ. of Manchester. BSc (Manchester) 1932, DSc (Manchester) 1946; Dr Phil (Berlin) 1935. Served on scientific staff of Freshwater Biological Assoc., 1935–41 and 1946–56. Seconded to Admiralty scientific service, 1941–46. Sec. and Dir, Scottish Marine Biological Assoc., 1956–66; Dir, Center for Great Lakes Studies, Univ. of Wisconsin-Milwaukee, 1966–79. Hon. DSc Wisconsin–Milwaukee, 1985. *Publications:* scientific papers on lakes and the physical and chemical conditions which control life in them. *Recreations:* music, travel. *Address:* 2501 E Menlo Boulevard, Shorewood, Wisconsin 53211, USA.

MORTIMER, Gerald James, CBE 1979 (MBE (mil.) 1944); FEng; Councillor, since 1973, Chairman, Policy Committee, since 1986, Surrey County Council; *b* 2 Sept. 1918; *s* of late Rev. Fernley Mortimer and Grace Mortimer (*née* Whiting); *m* 1942, Connie (*née* Dodd); two *s* two *d*. *Educ:* Caterham Sch.; Royal School of Mines, London Univ. (BSc (mining engrg), ARSM). Served War, Major, RE, UK and NW Europe, 1939–46. Mining official on Witwatersrand gold mines, S Africa, and in E Africa, 1946–55; Consolidated Gold Fields Ltd: Management staff, London, 1955–63; Exec. Dir, 1963–78; Dep. Chm., 1969–78; Gp Chief Exec., 1976–78; non. exec. Dir, 1978–80; Consultant, 1978–83; Dir, other Gp cos, 1957–79; in charge Goldsworthy iron ore project, W Australia, 1964–65; Exec. Chm., Amey Roadstone Corp. Ltd, 1967–75. President: Overseas Mining Assoc., 1972–73; Instn of Mining and Metallurgy, 1977–78; Inst. of Quarrying, 1980–81; Board Mem., 1978–83, Vice-Chm., 1981–82, Chm., 1982–83, CEI. Hon. Treas., Fellowship of Engrg, 1981–84. President: Old Caterhamians Assoc., 1970–71; RSM Assoc., 1976–77. Chm., E Surrey Cons. Assoc., 1980–82, Treasurer, 1982–83. FRSA; Hon. FIMM; Hon. FIQ. *Recreations:* history, politics. *Address:* 40 Harestone Valley Road, Caterham, Surrey CR3 6HD. *T:* Caterham 44853.

MORTIMER, James Edward; General Secretary of the Labour Party, 1982–85; *b* 12 Jan. 1921; *m*; two *s* one *d*. *Educ:* Junior Techn. Sch., Portsmouth; Ruskin Coll., Oxford; London Sch. of Economics. Worked in Shipbuilding and Engrg Industries as Ship Fitter Apprentice, Machinist and Planning Engr; TUC Schol., Oxford, 1945–46; TUC Economic Dept, 1946–48; full-time Trade Union Official, Draughtsmen's and Allied Technicians' Assoc., 1948–68. Dir, London Co-operative Soc., 1968–71. Mem., NBPI, 1968–71; LTE, 1971–74. Chm., ACAS (formerly Conciliation and Arbitration Service), 1974–81. Member: Wilberforce Ct of Inquiry into the power dispute, 1970; Armed Forces Pay Review Body, 1971–74; EDC for Chemical Industry, 1973–74; Chm. EDC for Mechanical and Electrical Engineering Construction, 1974–82. Vis. Fellow, Admin. Staff Coll., Henley, 1976–82; Sen. Vis. Fellow, Bradford Univ., 1977–82; Vis. Prof., Imperial Coll. of Sci. and Technol., London Univ., 1981–83; Ward-Perkins Res. Fellow, Pembroke Coll., Oxford, 1981. Hon. DLitt Bradford, 1982. *Publications:* A History of Association of Engineering and Shipbuilding Draughtsmen, 1960; (with Clive Jenkins) British Trade Unions Today, 1965; (with Clive Jenkins) The Kind of Laws the Unions Ought to Want, 1968; Industrial Relations, 1968; Trade Unions and Technological Change, 1971; History of the Boilermakers' Society, vol. 1, 1973; (with Valerie Ellis) A Professional Union: the evolution of the Institution of Professional Civil Servants, 1980. *Recreation:* camping. *Address:* 31 Charleston Street, SE17 1RL. *T:* 01–708 4415.

MORTIMER, Hon. John Barry; Hon. Mr Justice Mortimer; a Judge of the Supreme Court of Hong Kong, since 1985; *b* 7 Aug. 1931; *s* of John William Mortimer and Maud (*née* Snarr) Mortimer; *m* 1958, Judith Mary (*née* Page); two *s* two *d*. *Educ:* St Peters' School, York, (Headmasters' Exhibitioner 1945); Emmanuel College, Cambridge; BA 1955, MA 1959. Commissioned into 4 RTR, 1951; served in Egypt, 1951–52; 45/51 RTR (TA), 1952–57. Called to the Bar, Middle Temple, 1956 (Bencher 1980); Harmsworth Law Scholar 1957; Prosecuting Counsel on NE Circuit: to Post Office, 1965–69; to Inland Revenue, 1969–71; QC 1971; a Recorder, 1972–85. Chancellor, Dio. of Ripon, 1971–85. Member: Bar Council, 1970–75; Senate, 1979–85. *Recreations:* reading, shooting, cricket. *Address:* Supreme Court, Queensway, Hong Kong. *T:* 5–821 4325; The Grange, Staveley, Knaresborough, N Yorks HG5 9LD. *Clubs:* Travellers'; Durham; Hong Kong.

MORTIMER, John (Clifford), CBE 1986; QC 1966; barrister; playwright and author; *b* 21 April 1923; *s* of Clifford Mortimer and Kathleen May (*née* Smith); *m* 1st, 1949, Penelope Ruth Fletcher; one *s* one *d*; 2nd, Penelope (*née* Gollop); two *d*. *Educ:* Harrow; Brasenose Coll., Oxford. Called to the Bar, 1948; Master of the Bench, Inner Temple, 1975. Mem. Nat. Theatre Bd, 1968–. Pres., Berks, Bucks and Oxon Naturalists' Trust, 1984–. Hon. DLitt Susquehanna Univ., 1985; Hon. LLD Exeter, 1986. Won the Italia Prize with short play, The Dock Brief, 1958; another short play What Shall We Tell Caroline, 1958. Full-length plays: The Wrong Side of the Park, 1960; Two Stars for Comfort, 1962; (trans.) A Flea in Her Ear, 1966; The Judge, 1967; (trans.) Cat Among the Pigeons, 1969; Come as You Are, 1970; A Voyage Round My Father, 1970 (filmed, 1982); (trans.) The Captain of Köpenick, 1971; I, Claudius (adapted from Robert Graves), 1972; Collaborators, 1973; Mr Luby's Fear of Heaven (radio), 1976; Heaven and Hell, 1976; The Bells of Hell, 1977; (trans.) The Lady from Maxim's, 1977; (trans.) A Little Hotel on the Side, 1984. Film Scripts: John and Mary, 1970; Brideshead Revisited (TV), 1981; Edwin (TV), 1984. British Acad. Writers Award, 1979. *Publications: novels:* Charade, 1947; Rumming Park, 1948; Answer Yes or No, 1950; Like Men Betrayed, 1953; Three Winters, 1956; Will Shakespeare: an entertainment, 1977; Rumpole of the Bailey, 1978 (televised; BAFTA Writer of the Year Award, 1980); The Trials of Rumpole, 1979; Rumpole's Return, 1980 (televised); Regina v Rumpole, 1981; Paradise Postponed, 1985 (televised 1986); *travel:* (in collab. with P. R. Mortimer) With Love and Lizards, 1957; *plays:* The Dock Brief and Other Plays, 1959; The Wrong Side of the Park, 1960; Lunch Hour and Other Plays, 1960; Two Stars for Comfort, 1962; (trans.) A Flea in Her Ear, 1965; A Voyage Round My Father, 1970; (trans.) The Captain of Köpenick, 1971; Five Plays, 1971; Collaborators, 1973; Edwin and Other Plays, 1984; *autobiography:* Clinging to the Wreckage (Book of the Year Award, Yorkshire Post), 1982; writes TV plays (incl. three Rumpole series); contribs to periodicals. *Recreations:* working, gardening, going to opera. *Address:* Turville Heath Cottage, Henley on Thames, Oxon. *Club:* Garrick.

MORTIMER, Katharine Mary Hope; Director of Policy, Securities and Investment Board, since 1985; *b* 28 May 1946; *d* of Robert Cecil Mortimer and Mary Hope (*née* Walker); *m* 1973, John Noel Nicholson (marr. diss. 1986); one *s*. *Educ:* School of SS Mary and Anne, Abbots Bromley; Somerville Coll., Oxford. MA, BPhil Oxon. World Bank, 1969–72; Central Policy Review Staff, 1972–78; N. M. Rothschild Asset Management Ltd, 1978–84; Director, N. M. Rothschild & Sons Ltd (International Corporate Finance), 1984–. Mem., ESRC, 1983–86; Non-Executive Director: National Bus Company, 1979–; Inst. of Development Studies, 1983–; Mem. Governing Body, Centre for Economic Policy Res., 1986–. *Address:* 73 Ravenscourt Road, W6 0UJ.

MORTIMER, Penelope (Ruth), FRSL; writer; *b* 19 Sept. 1918; *d* of Rev. A. F. G. and Amy Caroline Fletcher; *m* 1st, 1937, Charles Dimont (marr. diss. 1949); four *d*; 2nd, 1949, John Clifford Mortimer, QC (marr. diss. 1972); one *s* one *d*. *Educ:* Croydon High Sch.; New Sch., Streatham; Blencathra, Rhyl; Garden Sch., Lane End; St Elphin's Sch. for Daughters of Clergy; Central Educnl Bureau for Women; University Coll., London. *Publications:* Johanna (as Penelope Dimont), 1947; A Villa in Summer, 1954; The Bright Prison, 1956; (with John Mortimer) With Love and Lizards, 1957; Daddy's Gone A-Hunting, 1958; Saturday Lunch with the Brownings, 1960; The Pumpkin Eater, 1962; My Friend Says It's Bulletproof, 1967; The Home, 1971; Long Distance, 1974; About Time (autobiog.), 1979 (Whitbread Prize); The Handyman, 1983; Queen Elizabeth: a life of the Queen Mother, 1986. *Address:* The Old Post Office, Chastleton, Moreton-in-Marsh, Glos. *T:* Barton-on-the-Heath 242.

MORTIMER, Air Vice-Marshal Roger, CBE 1972; Officer Commanding RAF Institute of Pathology and Tropical Medicine and Consultant Adviser in Pathology and Tropical Medicine, 1969–76; Dean of Air Force Medicine, 1975–76; *b* 2 Nov. 1914; *s* of Henry Roger Mortimer, tea planter, Dooars, India and Lily Rose (*née* Collier); *m* 1942, Agnes Emily Balfour (*d* 1985); two *d*. *Educ:* Uppingham; St Mary's Hosp. Med. School. MB, BS London, FRCPath, DCP, DTM&H. Joined RAF, 1942; Sqdn Med. Officer to Nos 23 and 85 Sqdns, 1942–44; Service Narrator and Editor to Official RAF Medical History of the War, 1944–47; specialised in Pathology and Tropical Medicine from 1947. Founder Mem. RCPath; Assoc. Editor and Council Mem., British Div. of Internat. Academy of Pathology, 1967–73; Editor, International Pathology, 1970–73; Mem. Council, Royal Soc. Trop. Med. and Hygiene, 1970–73. QHS 1973–76. *Publications:* papers on approved laboratory methods, practical disinfection, blood transfusion and infusion. *Recreations:* cars, anything mechanical, do-it-yourself, laboratory design. *Address:* 13 Welclose Street, St Albans, Herts AL3 4QD. *T:* St Albans 64247.

MORTIMER, William Charles C.; *see* Chapman-Mortimer.

MORTLOCK, Herbert Norman; Civil Service, retired; *b* 1926. Ministry of Defence: Superintendent, Royal Armament Research & Development Estabt, 1964–71; Asst Director, Procurement Executive, 1971–73; Dep. Dir., Chemical Defence Estabt, 1973–78; Dep. Dir, 1978–79, Dir, 1979–84, Materials Quality Assurance Directorate; Dir, Quality Assurance (Technical Support), 1984.

MORTON, family name of **Baron Morton of Shuna**.

MORTON, 22nd Earl of, *cr* 1458 (*de facto* 21st Earl, 22nd but for the Attainder); **John Charles Sholto Douglas;** Lord Aberdour, 1458; Lord-Lieutenant of West Lothian, since 1985; *b* 19 March 1927; *s* of Hon. Charles William Sholto Douglas (*d* 1960) (2nd *s* of 19th Earl) and Florence (*d* 1985), *er d* of late Major Henry Thomas Timson; *S* cousin, 1976; *m* 1949, Sheila Mary, *d* of late Rev. Canon John Stanley Gibbs, MC, Didmarton House, Badminton, Glos; two *s* one *d*. DL West Lothian, 1982. *Recreation:* polo. *Heir: s* Lord Aberdour, *qv*. *Address:* Dalmahoy, Kirknewton, Midlothian. *Clubs:* Farmers'; Edinburgh Polo, Dalmahoy Country.

MORTON OF SHUNA, Baron *cr* 1985 (Life Peer), of Stockbridge in the District of the City of Edinburgh; **Hugh Drennan Baird Morton;** QC 1974; *b* 10 April 1930; *s* of late Rev. T. R. Morton, DD, and J. M. M. Morton (*née* Baird); *m* 1956, Muriel Miller; three *s*. *Educ:* Glasgow Academy; Glasgow Univ. (BL). Admitted Faculty of Advocates, 1965. *Address:* 25 Royal Circus, Edinburgh EH3 6TL. *T:* 031–225 5139.
See also G. M. Morton.

MORTON, Alastair; *see* Morton, R. A. N.

MORTON, Alastair; *see* Morton, S. A.

MORTON, Rev. Andrew Queen; Minister of Culross Abbey since 1959; *b* 4 June 1919; *s* of Alexander Morton and Janet Queen; *m* 1948, Jean, *e d* of George Singleton and late Jean Wands; one *s* two *d*. *Educ:* Glasgow Univ. MA 1942, BD 1947, BSc 1948. Minister of St Andrews, Fraserburgh, 1949–59. Dept of Computer Science, Univ. of Edinburgh, 1965–. FRSE 1973. *Publications:* The Structure of the Fourth Gospel, 1961; Authorship and Integrity in the New Testament, 1963; (with G. H. C. Macgregor) The Structure of Luke and Acts, 1965; Paul the Man and the Myth, 1965; (with S. Michaelson) The Computer in Literary Research, 1973; Literary Detection, 1979; (with S. Michaelson and N. Hamilton-Smith) Justice for Helander, 1979; (with James McLeman) The Genesis of John, 1980. *Recreations:* thinking, talking. *Address:* The Abbey Manse, Culross, Dunfermline, Fife KY12 8JD. *T:* Newmills 880231.

MORTON, Admiral Sir Anthony (Storrs), GBE 1982; KCB 1978; King of Arms, Order of the British Empire, since 1983; *b* 6 Nov. 1923; *s* of late Dr Harold Morton. *Educ:* Loretto School. Joined RN 1941; war service in Atlantic, Mediterranean and Far East (despatches, HMS Wrangler, 1945); Commander 1956; Comd HMS Appleton and 100th MSS 1957–58; HMS Undine 1960; HMS Rocket 1960–62; Captain 1964; Captain (F) 20th Frigate Squadron, 1964–66; Chief Staff Officer, Plans and Policy, to Commander Far East Fleet, 1966–68; Senior Naval Officer, Northern Ireland, 1968–70; Senior Naval Mem., RCDS, 1971–72; ACDS (Policy), 1973–75; Flag Officer, First Flotilla, 1975–77; Vice-Chief of Defence Staff, 1977–78; Vice-Chief of Naval Staff, 1978–80; UK Mil. Rep. to NATO, 1980–83. Chairman: Govs, Royal Star and Garter Home, 1986–; Trustees, RN Museum, Portsmouth, 1985–; King George's Fund for Sailors, 1986–. *Recreations:* fishing, sailing, shooting, watching Association football. *Address:* c/o Barclays Bank, Alresford, Hants. *Clubs:* Army and Navy, Royal Cruising; Royal Yacht Squadron; Irish Cruising.

MORTON, Rev. Arthur, CVO 1979; OBE 1961; Director, National Society for the Prevention of Cruelty to Children, 1954–79; *b* 29 June 1915; *s* of Arthur Morton and Kate Floyd Morton; *m* 1940, Medora Gertrude Harrison; two *d*. *Educ:* Imperial Service Coll., Windsor; Jesus Coll., Cambridge (MA); Wycliffe Hall, Oxford (GOE). Curate, St Catherine's, Neasden, NW2, 1938–41; Chaplain, Missions to Seamen, Manchester, 1941–51. Asst Dir, NSPCC, 1951–54. Member, Adv. Council in Child Care and of Central Trng Council, 1956–71; frequent broadcasts on work of NSPCC. Mem., Glaziers Co., 1976–. *Publication:* (with Anne Allen) This is Your Child: the story of the NSPCC, 1961. *Recreations:* golf, fishing, reading, gardening. *Address:* 25 Cottes Way, Hill Head, Fareham, Hants PO14 3NF. *T:* Stubbington 663511.

MORTON, Sir Brian, Kt 1973; FRICS; Chairman, Harland & Wolff, 1975–80; *b* 24 Jan. 1912; *s* of Alfred Oscar Morton and Margaret Osborne Hennessy; *m* 1937, Hilda Evelyn Elsie Hillis; one *s* (and one *s* decd). *Educ:* Campbell Coll., Belfast. Estate Agency, Brian Morton & Co., Belfast, 1936; retired, 1964. Elected Councillor (U) Cromac Ward, Belfast Corp., 1967; apptd Mem. Craigavon Development Commn, 1968; Chm., Londonderry Develt Commn, 1969–73. *Recreations:* golf, sailing, landscape painting, fishing. *Address:* Rolly Island, Comber, Co. Down, N Ireland. *Clubs:* Royal Automobile; Ulster Reform (Belfast); Royal County Down Golf (Newcastle).

MORTON, Air Commodore Crichton Charles, CBE 1945; Command Electronics Officer, HQ Bomber Command, 1962–66, retired; *b* 26 July 1912; *s* of late Charles Crichton Morton, Ramsey, IOM; *m* 1956, Diana Yvonne, *d* of late Maj.-Gen. R. C. Priest, CB, RMS and *widow* of Group Captain N. D. Gilbart-Smith, RAF; no *c*. *Educ:* King

William's Coll., IOM; RAF Coll., Cranwell. Various flying duties, 1932–36; RAF Officers Long Signals Course, Cranwell, 1936–37; signals duties, 1937–39; radar duties at HQ Fighter Comd, No 5 Signals Wing France, HQ 60 Signals Gp, Air HQ Iceland, HQ Air Comd SE Asia, 1939–45; Dir of Radar and Dep. Dir of Signals, Air Min., 1945–49; jssc Latimer, 1949–50; OC No 3 Radio Sch., RAF Compton Bassett, 1950–52; OC Communications Gp, Allied Air Forces Central Europe, 1952–55; Inspector of Radio Services, 1955–58; Dep. Chief Signals Office, HQ, SHAPE, 1958–60; Chm. of Brit. Jt Communications Electronics Board, Ministry of Defence, 1960–62. AMIEE 1955; AFRAeS 1965; MIERE 1965; CEng 1966. *Recreation:* researching Visigothic remains. *Address:* Apartamento 102, Torre Tramontana, Apartado 50, Playa de Aro, Gerona, Spain.

MORTON, Prof. Frank, CBE 1976 (OBE 1968); DSc 1952, PhD 1936 (Manchester); MSc Tech; FIChemE; Professor of Chemical Engineering, University of Manchester, 1956–73, now Professor Emeritus; a Pro-Vice-Chancellor, 1968–72; *b* Sheffield, 11 Aug. 1906; *s* of late Joseph Morton, Manchester; *m* 1936, Hilda May, *d* of John W. Seaston, Withington, Manchester; one *s*. *Educ:* Manchester Univ. Demonstrator in Chemical Technology, 1931–36; Research Chemist, Trinidad Leaseholds Ltd, 1936–40; Superintendent of Research and Development, Trinidad Leaseholds, Trinidad, 1940–45; Chief Chemist, Trinidad Leaseholds Ltd, UK, 1945–49; Prof. of Chemical Engineering, Univ. of Birmingham, 1949–56. Actg Principal, Manchester Coll. of Science and Technology, 1964–65; Dep. Principal, Univ. of Manchester Inst. of Science and Technology, 1966–71. Member: Council, Manchester Business Sch., 1964–72; Chemical and Allied Products Training Board, 1968–71; European Fedn of Chemical Engineering, 1968–72. Pres., IChemE, 1963–64 (Hon. FIChemE 1983). Society of Chemical Industry: Vice-Pres., 1967–; Jubilee Memorial Lectr, 1967; Medal, 1969. Hon. Fellow, UMIST, 1978. *Publications:* Report of Inquiry into the Safety of Natural Gas as a Fuel (Ministry of Technology), 1970; various papers on petroleum, organic chemistry, chemical engineering and allied subjects. *Recreation:* golf. *Address:* 47 Penrhyn Beach East, Llandudno, Gwynedd. *T:* Llandudno 48037. *Club:* Savage.

MORTON, George Martin; Secretary, Tameside and Glossop Community Health Council, since 1984; *b* 11 Feb. 1940; *s* of Rev. Thomas Ralph Morton, DD, and Janet Maclay MacGregor Morton (*née* Baird). *Educ:* Fettes Coll Edinburgh; Edinburgh Coll. of Art; Glasgow Univ. RIBA. Member: Manchester City Council, 1971–74; Greater Manchester Council, 1973–77. MP (Lab) Manchester, Moss Side, July 1978– 1983; an Opposition Whip, 1979–83. *Address:* 4 St Anne's Road, Manchester M21 2TG. *T:* 061–881 8195.

See also Baron Morton of Shuna.

MORTON, Rev. Harry Osborne; Methodist Minister, supernumerary 1981, due to ill-health; *b* 28 June 1925; *s* of John William Morton and Alice Morton (*née* Betteridge); *m* 1954, Patricia Mary McGrath; two *s* two *d* (and one *d* decd). *Educ:* The King's Sch., Pontefract, Yorks; King's Coll., Cambridge (MA Cantab); Hartley Victoria Methodist Theological Coll., Manchester. Marconi's Wireless Telegraph Co. Ltd, 1945; Gen. Sec., Order of Christian Witness, 1947; entered Methodist Ministry, 1949; ordained Deacon, Church of South India, 1954, Presbyter, 1955; Sec. for Scholarships, World Council of Churches, Geneva, 1960; Sec. for East and Central Africa, Methodist Missionary Soc., 1963, Gen. Sec. 1972–73; Gen. Sec., BCC, 1973–80; Superintendent Minister, London Mission (East Ham) Circuit, 1980–81. Pres., Methodist Conf., 1972. Select Preacher, Cambridge Univ., 1972 and 1975. *Recreation:* music. *Address:* 34B Campbell Road, Bow, E3 4DT. *T:* 01–980 9460.

MORTON, Prof. Keith William; Professor of Numerical Analysis, and Professorial Fellow of Balliol College, Oxford University, since 1983; *b* 28 May 1930; *s* of Keith Harvey Morton and Muriel Violet (*née* Hubbard); *m* 1952, Patricia Mary Pearson; two *s* two *d*. *Educ:* Sudbury Grammar Sch.; Corpus Christi Coll., Oxford (BA 1952; MA 1954); New York Univ. (PhD 1964). Theoretical Physics Div., AERE, Harwell, 1952–59; Res. Scientist, Courant Inst. of Mathematical Sci., NY Univ., 1959–64; Head of Computing and Applied Maths, Culham Lab., UKAEA, 1964–72; Prof. of Applied Maths, Reading Univ., 1972–83. *Publications:* (with R. D. Richtmyer) Difference Methods for Initial-value Problems, 1967; (ed with M. J. Baines) Numerical Methods for Fluid Dynamics, 1982; numerous articles on numerical analysis and applied maths in learned jls. *Recreations:* reading, tennis, walking, gardening, listening to music. *Address:* 23 Erleigh Road, Reading RG1 5LR. *T:* Reading 64197; Oxford University Computing Laboratory, 8–11 Keble Road, Oxford OX1 3QD. *T:* Oxford 54141, ext. 316.

MORTON, Kenneth Valentine Freeland, CIE 1947; OBE 1971; Secretary East Anglian Regional Hospital Board, 1947–72, retired; *b* 13 May 1907; *s* of Kenneth John Morton; *m* 1936, Mary Hadwin Hargreaves; four *s* one *d*. *Educ:* Edinburgh Academy; University Coll., Oxford. Joined ICS, 1930; Under-Sec. (Political) Punjab Govt, 1934–36; Deputy Commissioner, 1936–39; Colonisation Officer, 1939–43; Deputy Sec., Development Dept, 1943–46; Sec. Electricity and Industries Depts, 1946–47; retired, 1947. *Address:* Temple End House, 27 Temple End, Great Wilbraham, Cambridge CB1 5JF. *T:* Cambridge 880691. *Club:* East India, Devonshire, Sports and Public Schools.

MORTON, Sir Ralph (John), Kt 1960; CMG 1954; OBE 1947; MC 1918; Judge of High Court of Southern Rhodesia, 1949–59; *b* 2 Aug. 1896; *yr s* of John Morton, Wotton-under-Edge, Glos; *m* 1923, Cato Marie van den Berg (*d* 1975); one *d*. *Educ:* Bishop's Stortford; Cambridge Univ. Served European War, RFA, 1915–19. Southern Rhodesia: Solicitor General, 1934; Attorney General, 1944. *Address:* 3 Dundalk Avenue, Parkview, Johannesburg, 2193, South Africa.

MORTON, (Robert) Alastair (Newton); Chief Executive, Guinness Peat Group, since 1982; Chairman, Guinness Mahon, since 1986; *b* 11 Jan. 1938; *s* of late Harry Newton Morton and Elizabeth Martino; *m* 1964, Sara Bridget Stephens; one *s* one *d*. *Educ:* St John's Coll. and Witwatersrand Univ., Johannesburg (BA); Worcester Coll., Oxford (MA). Special grad. student, MIT, 1964. Anglo American Corp. of SA (mining finance), London and Central Africa, 1959–63; Internat. Finance Corp., Washington, 1964–67; Industrial Reorganisation Corp., 1967–70; Exec. Dir, 117 Group of investment trusts, 1970–72; Chm., Draymont Securities, 1972–76. Chm. or Dir, various public engineering groups, 1970–76; Man. Dir, BNOC, 1976–80. Non-Exec. Member: Royal Ordnance Factories Bd, 1974–76; British Steel Corp., 1979–82. Mem., City and East London AHA, 1974–77; Governor: London Hosp., Whitechapel, 1971–74 (Special Trustee, 1974–77); St Peter's Hosps, 1973–76. *Recreation:* sailing. *Address:* 115 Clifton Hill, NW8.

MORTON, (Stephen) Alastair, TD 1949; JP; **His Honour Judge Morton;** a Circuit Judge (formerly Deputy Chairman, Greater London Quarter Sessions), since 1971; *b* 28 July 1913; *o s* of Philip Morton, Dune Gate, Dorchester; *m* 1939, Lily Yarrow Eveline, *o d* of J. S. P. Griffith-Jones, Drews, Beaconsfield, Bucks; one *s* one *d*. *Educ:* private sch.; Trinity Hall, Cambridge. Commnd Dorset Heavy Bde, RA, TA, 1932; served War of 1939–45, Royal Artillery. Called to the Bar, Middle Temple, 1938; Western Circuit, 1938; Master of the Bench, 1964. Counsel to the Crown at County of London Sessions, 1954–59; Central Criminal Court: First Junior Treasury Counsel, 1959–64; Senior Treasury Counsel, 1964–71; Recorder of Devizes, 1957–71; Dep.-Chm. Quarter Sessions: Dorset, 1957–71; Norfolk, 1969–71. JP Dorset, 1957. *Recreation:* painting. *Address:* 53 Eaton Terrace, SW1. *T:* 01–730 7730; Cringles, Overy Staithe, near King's Lynn, Norfolk. *T:* Fakenham 738339. *Clubs:* White's, Pratt's.

MORTON BOYD, John; *see* Boyd, J. M.

MORTON JACK, David; His Honour Judge Morton Jack; a Circuit Judge, since 1986; *b* 5 Nov. 1935; *o s* of late Col W. A. Morton Jack, OBE, and late Mrs Morton Jack (*née* Happell); *m* 1972, Rosemary, *o d* of F. G. Rentoul; four *s*. *Educ:* Stowe (scholar); Trinity Coll., Oxford (Cholmeley Schol., MA). 2nd Lieut, RIF, 1955–57. Called to the Bar, Lincoln's Inn, 1962; a Recorder of the Crown Court, 1979–86. *Recreations:* country pursuits, sheep-keeping, reading, music, gardens. *Address:* 1 Harcourt Buildings, Temple, EC4Y 9DA.

MORTON-SANER, Robert, CVO 1966; CBE 1962 (OBE 1946; MBE 1941); HM Diplomatic Service, retired; *b* 30 December 1911; *o s* of late Major A. E. Saner; *m* 1943, Katharine Mary Gordon (*d* 1981); two *d*. *Educ:* Westminster Sch.; Christ Church, Oxford. ICS, 1935; served in United Provinces; Under Sec., Defence Department, Government of India, 1940; Deputy Secretary and Chief Administrative Officer, General Headquarters, New Delhi, 1943–45; served with Resettlement Directorate, 1945–47. Retired from Indian Civil Service and entered Foreign (subseq. Diplomatic) Service, 1947. Served in Madras, 1947–50; Foreign Office, 1950–52; Budapest, 1953–55; NATO Defence College, 1955; Counsellor and Consul-General, Djakarta, 1955–59; Counsellor, Buenos Aires, 1960–64; Consul-General, Antwerp, 1964–70. Acted as Chargé d'Affaires, 1953, 1954, 1956, 1958, 1959, 1960. Member, Skinners' Company. Commander, Order of Leopold II (Belgium). *Recreations:* gardening, old churches. *Address:* Hethe Cottage, Hethe, Oxon. *Club:* Anglo-Belgian.

MOSDELL, Lionel Patrick; Judge of the High Court of Kenya, 1966–72, Tanganyika, 1960–64; part time Chairman, Pensions Appeal Tribunals, since 1976; *b* 29 Aug. 1912; *s* of late William George Mosdell and late Sarah Ellen Mosdell (*née* Gardiner); *m* 1945, Muriel Jean Sillem; one *s* one *d*. *Educ:* Abingdon Sch.; St Edmund Hall, Oxford (MA). Solicitor, England, 1938. Served War of 1939–45, Gunner, Sussex Yeomanry RA, 1939–41; Commnd Rifle Bde, 1941; Libyan Arab Force; Force 133; No 1 Special Force; Egypt, Cyrenaica, Eritrea, Abyssinia, Italy (Capt.). Registrar of Lands and Deeds, N Rhodesia, 1946; Resident Magistrate, 1950; Senior Resident Magistrate, 1956; Barrister, Gray's Inn, 1952; Asst Solicitor, Law Soc., 1964–66. Part-time Chairman: Surrey and Sussex Rent Assessment Panel, 1972–82; Nat. Insce Local Tribunal, London S Region, 1974–84; Immigration Appeal Tribunal, 1975–84. *Recreations:* walking, cycling. *Address:* 10 Orpen Road, Hove, East Sussex BN3 6NJ. *Clubs:* Special Forces, Royal Commonwealth Society.

MOSELEY, Sir George (Walker), KCB 1982 (CB 1978); Chairman: Cement Makers Federation; Ancient Monuments Advisory Committee; Member, Historic Buildings and Monuments Commission for England; *b* 7 Feb. 1925; *o c* of late William Moseley, MBE, and Bella Moseley; *m* 1950, Anne Mercer; one *s* one *d*. *Educ:* High Sch., Glasgow; St Bees Sch., Cumberland; Wadham Coll., Oxford (MA). Pilot Officer, RAF Levies, Iraq, 1943–48. Asst Principal, Min. of Town and Country Planning, 1950; Asst Private Sec. to Minister of Housing and Local Govt, 1951–52; Private Sec. to Parly Sec., 1952–54; Principal Private Sec. to Minister of Housing and Local Govt, 1963–65; Asst Sec. 1965; Under-Sec. 1970–76; Dep. Sec., DoE, 1976–78, CSD, 1978–80; Second Permanent Sec., DoE, 1980–81, Perm. Sec., 1981–85. *Recreations:* listening to music, gardening, watching sport. *Address:* 41 Ormond Avenue, Hampton, Mddx.

MOSELEY, (Thomas) Hywel; QC 1985; barrister; a Recorder of the Crown Court, since 1981; *b* 27 Sept. 1936; *s* of Rev. Luther Moseley and late Megan Eiluned Moseley; *m* 1960, Monique Germaine Thérèse Drufin; three *d*. *Educ:* Caterham Sch.; Queens' Coll., Cambridge (LLB, MA). Called to the Bar, Gray's Inn, 1964; in private practice, Cardiff, 1965–, and London, 1977–. Lectr in Law, 1960–65, Prof. of Law, 1970–82, UCW, Aberystwyth. *Publication:* (with B. Rudden) Outline of the Law of Mortgages, 4th edn 1967. *Recreation:* bee-keeping. *Address:* Nantceiro, Llanbadarn Fawr, Aberystwyth, Dyfed SY23 3HW. *T:* Aberystwyth 3532. *Club:* Reform.

MOSER, Sir Claus (Adolf), KCB 1973; CBE 1965; FBA 1969; Warden, Wadham College, Oxford, since 1984; Chancellor, University of Keele, since 1986; Director: N. M. Rothschild & Sons, since 1978 (Vice-Chairman, 1978–84); The Economist Newspaper, since 1979; Chairman of the Royal Opera House, since 1974; *b* Berlin, 24 Nov. 1922; *s* of late Dr Ernest Moser and Lotte Moser; *m* 1949, Mary Oxlin; one *s* two *d*. *Educ:* Frensham Heights Sch.; LSE, Univ. of London. RAF, 1943–46. London Sch. of Economics: Asst Lectr in Statistics, 1946–49; Lectr, 1949–55; Reader in Social Statistics, 1955–61; Prof. of Social Statistics, 1961–70; Vis. Prof. of Social Statistics, 1970–75; Vis. Fellow, Nuffield Coll., Oxford, 1972–80. Dir, Central Statistical Office and Hd of Govt Statistical Service, 1967–78. Statistical Adviser, Cttee on Higher Educn, 1961–64. Chm., Economist Intelligence Unit, 1979–83; Director: Equity & Law Life Assurance Soc., 1980–; International Medical Statistics Inc., 1982–; Octopus Books Ltd, 1982–; Property & Reversionary Investments plc, 1983–86. Member: Governing Body, Royal Academy of Music, 1967–79; BBC Music Adv. Cttee, 1971–83; Court of Governors, Royal Shakespeare Theatre, 1982–; British Amer. Arts Assoc., 1982–; Pilgrim Trust, 1982–. Pres., Royal Statistical Soc., 1978–80. Hon. FRAM, 1970. Hon. Fellow, LSE, 1976; Hon. DSocSci Southampton, 1975; Hon. DSc: Leeds, 1977; City, 1977; Sussex, 1980; DUniv: Surrey, 1977; Keele, 1979; York, 1980; Hon. DTech Brunel, 1981. Comdr de l'Ordre National du Mérite (France), 1976; Commander's Cross, Order of Merit (FRG), 1985. *Publications:* Measurement of Levels of Living, 1957; Survey Methods in Social Investigation, 1958; (jtly) Social Conditions in England and Wales, 1958; (jtly) British Towns, 1961; papers in statistical jls. *Recreation:* music. *Address:* 3 Regent's Park Terrace, NW1 7EE. *T:* 01–485 1619; Wadham College, Oxford OX1 3PN. *Club:* Garrick.

MOSES, Sir Charles (Joseph Alfred), Kt 1961; CBE 1954; Hon. Councillor, Asian Broadcasting Union, since 1977 (Secretary-General, 1965–77); General Manager, Australian Broadcasting Commission, 1935–65; Company Director; *b* 21 Jan. 1900; *s* of Joseph Moses and Lily (*née* Henderson); *m* 1922, Kathleen, *d* of Patrick O'Sullivan, Bruree, Co. Limerick; one *s* (one *d* decd). *Educ:* Oswestry Grammar Sch.; RMC Sandhurst. Lt 2nd Border Regt, 1918–22, serving in Germany and Ireland; fruitgrower, Bendigo, Australia, 1922–24; in motor business in Melbourne, 1924–30; in radio, ABC: Announcer/Commentator, 1930–32; Talks and Sporting Editor, Sydney, 1933–34; Federal Talks Controller, 1934–35. War of 1939–45 (despatches): AIF in Malaya and Singapore, Major, 1941–42, in New Guinea, Lt-Col, 1942–43. Leader of Austr. Delegn to UNESCO Annual Gen. Conf., Paris, 1952; Chm. Commonwealth Jubilee Arts Cttee, 1951; Vice-President: Royal Agricultural Society of NSW, 1951–; Elizabethan Theatre Trust, 1954–84; Royal NSW Instn for Deaf and Blind Children, 1965–; Pres., Remembrance Driveway (NSW), 1953–. Hon. Dir, Postgraduate Med. Foundn (NSW). Mem., Internat. Inst. of Communications, London, 1965–; Vice-Chm., Asian Mass Communications and Inf. Centre, Singapore, 1969–83. Pres., 1944–69, Patron, 1969–, Eastern Suburbs Rugby Club; Pres., Athletic Assoc. of NSW, 1946–67. *Publication:*

Diverse Unity: a history of the Asia-Pacific Broadcasting Union 1957–77, 1978. *Recreations:* reading, music. *Address:* 56/28 Curagul Road, North Turramurra, NSW 2074, Australia. *T:* 32 4224. *Clubs:* Australian, Tattersall's, Rugby Union (Sydney).

MOSES, Eric George Rufus, CB 1973; Solicitor of Inland Revenue, 1970–79; *b* 6 April 1914; *s* of Michael and Emily Moses; *m* 1940, Pearl Lipton; one *s*. *Educ:* University Coll. Sch., London; Oriel Coll., Oxford. Called to Bar, Middle Temple, 1938, Hon. Bencher, 1979. Served Royal Artillery, 1940–46 (Major). Asst Solicitor, Inland Revenue, 1953–65, Principal Asst Solicitor, 1965–70. *Recreations:* walking, opera. *Address:* Broome Cottage, Castle Hill, Nether Stowey, Bridgwater, Somerset.

MOSES, Very Rev. John Henry, PhD; Provost of Chelmsford; *b* 12 Jan. 1938; *s* of late Henry William Moses and of Ada Elizabeth Moses; *m* 1964, Susan Elizabeth (*née* Wainwright); one *s* two *d*. *Educ:* Ealing Grammar School; Nottingham Univ. (Gladstone Meml Prize 1958, BA History 1959, PhD 1965); Trinity Hall and Dept of Education, Cambridge (Cert. in Education 1960); Lincoln Theological Coll. Deacon 1964, priest 1965; Asst Curate, St Andrew, Bedford, 1964–70; Rector of Coventry East Team Ministry, 1970–77; Examining Chaplain to Bishop of Coventry, 1972–77; Rural Dean of Coventry East, 1973–77; Archdeacon of Southend, 1977–82. Vis. Fellow, Wolfson Coll., Cambridge, 1987. *Address:* The Provost's House, 3 Harlings Grove, Waterloo Lane, Chelmsford, Essex CM1 1YQ. *T:* Chelmsford 354318.

MOSES, Kenneth, FEng 1985; Board Member (Technical), National Coal Board, since 1986; *b* 29 Nov. 1931; *s* of Thomas and Mary Moses; *m* 1949, Mary Price; one *s* two *d*. *Educ:* Cowley Boys Grammar Sch., St Helens; Wigan Mining Coll. (Dip. in Mining; 1st Cl. Cert., Mines and Quarries Act). Mineworker, 1954; Management Trainee, 1960; Undermanager, 1962; Dep. Manager, 1964; Colliery Manager, 1967; Mem. Directing Staff, NCB Staff Coll., 1971; National Coal Board: Chief Mining Engr, N Yorks, 1974; Dir of Planning, 1978; Dir, N Derbys, 1981. Laurence Holland Medal, IMinE, 1961; Douglas Hay Medal, 1982. *Publications:* contribs to learned journals. *Recreations:* gardening, walking, swimming, reading. *Address:* Oaktrees, 6 Heath Avenue, Mansfield NG18 3EU. *T:* Mansfield 653843; Ennismore Gardens, SW7. *T:* 01–584 3165.

MOSHINSKY, Elijah; Associate Producer, Royal Opera House, since 1979; *b* 8 Jan. 1946; *s* of Abraham and Eva Moshinsky; *m* 1970, Ruth Dyttman; two *s*. *Educ:* Melbourne Univ. (BA); St Antony's Coll., Oxford. Apptd to Royal Opera House, 1973; work includes original productions of: Peter Grimes, 1975; Lohengrin, 1978; The Rake's Progress, 1979; Macbeth, 1981; Samson et Dalila, 1981; other opera productions include: Wozzeck, 1976; A Midsummer Night's Dream, 1978; Boris Godunov, 1980; Un Ballo in Maschera, Met. Opera, New York, 1980; Il Trovatore, Australian Opera, 1983; Samson, Met. Opera, NY; I Vespri Siciliani, Grand Théâtre, Geneva; Les Dialogues des Carmélites, Australian Opera; Die Meistersinger von Nürnberg, Holland Fest.; for ENO: Le Grand Macabre, 1982; The Mastersingers of Nuremberg, 1984; The Bartered Bride, 1985, 1986; for Royal Opera: Tannhäuser, 1984; Samson, 1985. Productions at National Theatre: Troilus and Cressida, 1976; The Force of Habit, 1976; productions for the BBC: All's Well that Ends Well, 1980; A Midsummer Night's Dream, 1981; Cymbeline, 1982; Coriolanus, 1984; Love's Labour's Lost, 1985; Ibsen's Ghosts; The Rivals. *Recreations:* painting, conversation. *Address:* 28 Kidbrooke Grove, SE3. *T:* 01–858 4179. *Club:* Garrick.

MOSIMANN, Anton; Maître Chef des Cuisines, Dorchester Hotel, since 1976; *b* 23 Feb. 1947; *s* of Otto and Olga Mosimann; *m* 1973, Kathrin Roth; two *s*. *Educ:* private school in Switzerland; youngest Chef to be awarded Chef de Cuisine Diplome; 3 degrees. Served apprenticeship in Hotel Baeren, Twann; worked in Canada, France, Italy, Japan, Sweden, Belgium, Switzerland, 1962–; cuisinier at: Villa Lorraine, Brussels; Les Près d'Eugénie, Eugénie-les-Bains; des Frères Troisgros, Roanne; Paul Bocuse, Collonges au Mont d'Or; Moulin de Mougins; joined Dorchester Hotel, 1975. Hon. Mem., Chefs' Assoc., Canada, Japan, Switzerland, S Africa. Numerous Gold Medals in Internat. Cookery Competitions; Chef Award, Caterer and Hotelkeeper, 1985; Personnalité de l'année award, 1986; Glenfiddich Awards Trophy, 1986. *Publications:* Cuisine à la Carte, 1981; A New Style of Cooking: the art of Anton Mosimann, 1983; Cuisine Naturelle, 1985. *Recreations:* jogging, travelling, collecting art. *Address:* 46 Abingdon Villas, W8. *T:* 01–937 4383. *Club:* Garrick.

MOSLEY, family name of **Baron Ravensdale.**

MOSLEY, Nicholas; *see* Ravensdale, 3rd Baron.

MOSS, Dr Alfred Allinson; Keeper of Minerals, British Museum (Natural History), 1968–74; *b* 30 Dec. 1912; *o s* of Frank Allinson and Alice Moss; *m* 1938, Sheila Mary, *o d* of Charles H. Sendell; two *d*. *Educ:* Ilfracombe Grammar Sch.; University Coll., Exeter. BSc London; PhD London. Chemist: War Dept, 1936; Govt Laboratory, 1937–39; Asst Keeper, Brit. Mus., 1939–40; Chemist, Chief Chemical Inspectorate, Min. of Supply, 1940–45; Asst Keeper, Brit. Mus., 1945–49; Principal Scientific Officer: Brit. Mus., 1949–53; Brit. Mus. (Nat. Hist.), 1953–59; Dep. Keeper of Minerals, Brit. Mus. (Nat. Hist.), 1959; Keeper, 1968. Treas., Mineralogical Soc., 1966–73. *Publications:* papers on archaeological and mineralogical subjects in various jls. *Recreations:* horology, chess, photography. *Address:* 12 Somerfields, Lyme Regis, Dorset DT7 3EZ. *T:* Lyme Regis 3443.

MOSS, Very Rev. Basil Stanley; Provost of Birmingham Cathedral, 1973–85; Rector, Cathedral parish of St Philip, 1973–85; *b* 7 Oct. 1918; *e s* of Canon Harry George Moss and Daisy Violet (*née* Jolly); *m* 1950, Rachel Margaret, *d* of Dr Cyril Bailey and Gemma (*née* Creighton); three *d*. *Educ:* Canon Slade Grammar Sch., Bolton; The Queen's Coll., Oxford. Asst Curate, Leigh Parish Church, 1943–45; Sub-Warden, Lincoln Theological Coll., 1946–51; Sen. Tutor, St Catharine's Cumberland Lodge, Windsor Gt Pk, 1951–53; Vicar of St Nathanael with St Katharine, Bristol, 1953–60; Dir, Ordination Training, Bristol Dioc., 1956–66; Residentiary Canon of Bristol Cath., 1960–66, Hon. Canon, 1966–72; Chief Secretary, Advisory Council for the Church's Ministry, 1966–72; Chaplain to Church House, Westminster, 1966–72; Examining Chaplain to Bishop of Bristol, 1956–72, to Bishop of Birmingham, 1985–. Chm., Birmingham Community Relations Council, 1973–81. *Publications:* Clergy Training Today, 1964; (ed) Crisis for Baptism, 1966; (contrib.) Living the Faith, 1980. *Recreations:* walking, music. *Address:* 25 Castle Grove, Old Swinford, Stourbridge DY8 2HH. *T:* Stourbridge 378799. *Club:* Stourbridge Rotary.

MOSS, Charles James, CBE 1977; Director, National Institute of Agricultural Engineering, 1964–77; *b* 18 Nov. 1917; *s* of James and Elizabeth Moss; *m* 1939, Joan Bernice Smith; two *d*. *Educ:* Queen Mary Coll., London Univ. (BSc). CEng, FIMechE. Rotol Ltd, Gloucester, 1939–43; RAE Farnborough, 1943–45; CIBA Ltd, Cambridge, 1945–51; ICI Ltd, Billingham, 1951–58; Central Engineering Estabt, NCB, Stanhope Bretby, 1958–61; Process Develt Dept, NCB, London, 1961–63; Vis. Prof., Dept of Agric. Engrg, Univ. of Newcastle upon Tyne, 1972–75; Head of Agr. Engineering Dept, Internat. Rice Res. Inst., Philippines, 1977–80; Liaison scientist and agr. engineer, Internat. Rice Res. Inst., Cairo, 1980–81. *Publications:* papers in learned jls, confs., etc. *Recreations:* gardening, walking. *Address:* Windrush, 13 Woodlands Drive, Colsterworth, near Grantham, Lincs NG33 5NH.

MOSS, David Francis; JP; Assistant Chief Executive, Dockyards, Ministry of Defence, Bath, 1981–82, retired; *b* 11 July 1927; *s* of Frank William and Dorothy May Moss; *m* 1950, Beryl Eloïse (*née* Horsley); one *s* one *d*. *Educ:* Manchester Grammar Sch.; Manchester Univ. (BSc Hons MechEng); RNC Greenwich (Naval Architecture Cert.). Devonport Dockyard, 1952; Director General Ships, Bath, 1956; HM Dockyards: Gibraltar, 1961; Devonport, 1964; Singapore, 1967; Rosyth, 1969; Chatham, 1973; Rosyth, 1975; Portsmouth, 1979. JP Bath 1983. *Recreations:* hill walking, handiwork; material and philosophical aspects of early Mediterranean sea power. *Address:* 16 Beaufort West, Grosvenor, Bath BA1 6QB.

MOSS, David Joseph; HM Diplomatic Service; Counsellor, Head of Chancery and Deputy Permanent Representative, UK Mission, Geneva, since 1983; *b* 6 Nov. 1938; *s* of Herbert Joseph and Irene Gertrude Moss; *m* 1961, Joan Lillian Moss; one *s* one *d*. *Educ:* Hampton Grammar Sch. CS Commn, 1956; FO, 1957; RAF, 1957–59; FO, 1959–62; Third Sec., Bangkok, 1962–65; FO, 1966–69; First Sec., La Paz, 1969–70; FCO, 1970–73; First Sec. and Head of Chancery, The Hague, 1974–77; First Sec., FCO, 1978–79, Counsellor, 1979; Head, Perm. Under-Sec.'s Dept, FCO, 1981–83. *Recreations:* squash, reading, listening to music. *Address:* c/o Foreign and Commonwealth Office, SW1. *T:* 01–233 3000.

MOSS, Edward Herbert St George; Under-Secretary, University Grants Committee, 1971–78; *b* 18 May 1918; *s* of late Sir George Moss, KBE, HM Consular Service in China, and late Lady (Gladys Lucy) Moss; *m* 1948, Shirley Evelyn Baskett; two *s* one *d*. *Educ:* Marlborough; Pembroke Coll., Cambridge. PhD Surrey, 1984. Army Service in UK and Middle East, 1940–45; entered HM Foreign (subseq. Diplomatic) Service, 1945; served in Japan, FO, Belgrade (Head of Chancery 1951–55), St Louis, Detroit, FO; transf. to Home Civil Service (MoD), 1960; Asst Sec. 1961; Dept of Educn and Science, 1969. *Publication:* (with Rev. Robert Llewelyn) Fire from a Flint: daily readings with William Law, 1986. *Recreations:* writing, gardening. *Address:* Prospect, 29 Guildown Avenue, Guildford, Surrey. *T:* Guildford 66984.

MOSS, Elaine Dora; Children's Books Adviser to The Good Book Guide, since 1980; *b* 8 March 1924; *d* of Percy Philip Levy and Maude Agnes Levy (*née* Simmons); *m* 1950, John Edward Moss, FRICS, FAI; two *d*. *Educ:* St Paul's Girls' Sch.; Bedford Coll. for Women (BA Hons); Univ. of London Inst. of Educn (DipEd); University College London Sch. of Librarianship (ALA). Teacher, Stoatley Rough Sch., Haslemere, 1945–47; Asst Librarian, Bedford Coll., 1947–50; freelance journalist and broadcaster (Women's Hour, The Times, TES, TLS, The Spectator, Signal, etc.), 1956–; Editor and Selector, NBL's Children's Books of the Year, 1970–79; Librarian, Fleet Primary Sch., ILEA, 1976–82. Eleanor Farjeon Award, 1976. *Publications:* texts for several picture books, incl. Polar, 1976; catalogues for Children's Books of the Year, 1970–79; Picture Books for Young People 9–13, 1981, 2nd edn 1985; Part of the Pattern: a personal journey through the world of children's books 1960–1985, 1986. *Recreations:* walking, art galleries, reading, ballet. *Address:* 3 The Mount, Heath Street, NW3 6SZ. *T:* 01–435 3184.

MOSS, James Richard Frederick, OBE 1955; FRINA; RCNC; Founder, and Chairman, Polynous, Cambridge, since 1978; Chief Executive, Balaena Structures (North Sea), 1974–77, retired; *b* 26 March 1916; *s* of late Lt-Cdr J. G. Moss, RN, and late Kathleen Moss (*née* Steinberg); *m* 1941, Celia Florence Lucas; three *d*. *Educ:* Marlborough College; Trinity Coll., Cambridge (1st Cl. Hons Mech. Sci. Tripos and Maths Pt I); RCNC, 1941; Constructor Comdr to C-in-C, Far East Fleet, 1949–52; Chief Constructor, HM Dockyard, Singapore, 1955–58; Supt, Naval Construction Research Estab., Dunfermline, 1965–68; Dir, Naval Ship Production, 1968–74. *Recreations:* yachting and dinghies, music. *Address:* 25 Church Street, Stapleford, Cambridge CB2 5DS. *T:* Cambridge 843108. *Clubs:* Royal Naval Sailing Association, Cruising Association.

MOSS, Jane Hope; *see* Bown, J. H.

MOSS, Sir John H. T. E.; *see* Edwards-Moss.

MOSS, (John) Michael; Assistant Under-Secretary of State (Air), Procurement Executive, Ministry of Defence, since 1984; *b* 21 April 1936; *s* of Ernest and Mary Moss. *Educ:* Accrington Grammar Sch.; King's Coll., Cambridge (Foundn Scholar; MA Math. Tripos, Pt I Cl. I, Pt II Wrangler, Pt III Hons with Dist.). National Service, RAF Educn Branch: Pilot Officer 1958; Flying Officer 1959; Flt Lieut 1960; RAF Technical Coll., Henlow, 1959–60. Asst Principal, Air Min., 1960–63; Private Sec. to Air Member for Supply and Orgn, 1962–63; Principal, Air Min., 1963–64, and MoD, 1964–70; Private Sec. to Parly Under- Sec. of State for Defence for the RAF, 1969–70; Asst Sec., MoD, 1971–72; Estab. Officer, Cabinet Office, 1972–75; Sec., Radcliffe Cttee of Privy Counsellors on Ministerial Memoirs, 1975; returned to MoD as Asst Sec., 1976–83; RCDS, 1983. Cantoris Bass, St Bartholomew-the-Great, Smithfield, 1968–. *Recreations:* travel, photography, choral singing. *Address:* c/o Ministry of Defence, Main Building, Whitehall, SW1A 2HB. *Clubs:* Royal Air Force, United Oxford & Cambridge University.

MOSS, John Ringer, CB 1972; Deputy Secretary, Ministry of Agriculture, Fisheries and Food, 1970–80; *b* 15 Feb. 1920; 2nd *s* of late James Moss and Louisa Moss; *m* 1946, Edith Bland Wheeler; two *s* one *d*. *Educ:* Manchester Gram. Sch.; Brasenose Coll., Oxford (MA). War Service, mainly India and Burma, 1940–46; Capt., RE, attached Royal Bombay Sappers and Miners. Entered Civil Service (Min. of Agric., Fisheries and Food) as Asst Princ., 1947; Princ. Private Sec. to Minister of Agric., Fisheries and Food, 1959–61; Asst Sec., 1961; Under-Sec., Gen. Agricultural Policy Gp, Min. of Agric., Fisheries and Food, 1967–70. Mem., Economic Develt Cttee for Agriculture, 1969–70. Chm. Council, RVC, 1983– (Mem., 1980–). Adviser to companies in Associated British Foods Gp, 1980–; Specialist Adviser to House of Lords' Select Cttee on European Communities, 1982–. *Recreations:* music, travel. *Address:* 16 Upper Hollis, Great Missenden, Bucks. *T:* Great Missenden 2676.

MOSS, Martin Grenville, CBE 1975; Director of National Trust Enterprises Ltd, since 1985; *b* 17 July 1923; *s* of late Horace Grenville Moss and Gladys Ethel (*née* Wootton); *m* 1953, Jane Hope Bown, *qv*; two *s* one *d*. *Educ:* Lancing Coll. Served RAF, 1942–46 (Sqdn Ldr, pilot). Managing Director: Woollands Knightsbridge, 1953–66; Debenham & Freebody, 1964–66; Simpson (Piccadilly) Ltd, 1966–73, 1981–85; Chm. and Chief Exec. Officer, May Department Stores Internat., USA, 1974–80. Member: Export Council of Europe, 1960–64; Design Council, 1964–75 (Dep. Chm., 1971–75); Council, RCA, 1953–58; Royal Fine Art Commn, 1982–84; Council, RSA (Chm., 1983–85). Formerly Governor: Sevenoaks Sch.; Ravensbourne Coll. of Art and Design; W Surrey Coll. of Art and Design. Order of the Finnish Lion, 1970. *Recreations:* gardening, painting, classic cars. *Address:* Lasham House, Lasham, near Alton, Hants GU34 5SD. *T:* Herriard 216. *Club:* Royal Air Force.

MOSS, Michael; *see* Moss, J. M.

MOSS, Norman J.; *see* Jordan-Moss.

MOSS, Ronald Trevor; Metropolitan Stipendiary Magistrate, since 1984; *b* 1 Oct. 1942; *s* of Maurice and Sarah Moss; *m* 1971, Cindy (*née* Fiddleman); one *s* one *d*. *Educ:* Hendon County Grammar School; Nottingham University (Upper Second BA; Hons Law). Admitted Solicitor, 1968; Partner, Moss Beachley, solicitors, 1973–84; Mem., Cttee of London Criminal Courts Solicitors' Assoc., 1982–84. *Recreations:* golf, Watford Football Club, lawn tennis. *Address:* c/o Highbury Corner Magistrates' Court, 51 Holloway Road, N7 8JA. *Clubs:* St James's; Moor Park Golf.

MOSS, Rosalind Louisa Beaufort, FSA; Editor of Porter-Moss Topographical Bibliography of Ancient Egyptian Hieroglyphic Texts, Reliefs, and Paintings, 1924–72, retired; *b* 21 Sept. 1890; *d* of Rev. H. W. Moss, Headmaster of Shrewsbury Sch., 1866–1908. *Educ:* Heathfield Sch., Ascot; St Anne's Coll., Oxford. Diploma in Anthropology (distinction), 1917, BSc Oxon 1922. Took up Egyptology, 1917. FSA 1949. Hon. DLitt Oxon, 1961. Hon. Fellow, St Anne's Coll., Oxford, 1967. *Publications:* Life after Death in Oceania, 1925; Topographical Bibliography (see above); articles in Journal of Egyptian Archæology, etc. *Recreation:* travel. *Address:* 51 Yew Tree Bottom Road, Epsom, Surrey KT17 3NQ.

MOSS, Stirling, OBE 1959; FIE; Racing Motorist, 1947–62, retired; Managing Director, Stirling Moss Ltd; Director: Designs Unlimited Ltd; SM Design & Interior Decorating Co.; Hankoe Stove Enamelling Ltd; Motoring Editor: Harpers & Queen Magazine; Saga Magazine; *b* 17 Sept. 1929; *m* 1st, 1957, Kathleen Stuart (marr. diss. 1963), *y d* of F. Stuart Moison, Montreal, Canada; 2nd, 1964, Elaine (marr. diss. 1968), 2nd *d* of A. Barbarino, New York; one *d*; 3rd, 1980, Susan, *y d* of Stuart Paine, London; one *s*. *Educ:* Haileybury and Imperial Service Coll. Brit. Nat. Champion, 1950, 1951, 1952, 1954, 1955, 1956, 1957, 1958, 1959, 1961; Tourist Trophy, 1950, 1951, 1955, 1958, 1959, 1960, 1961; Coupe des Alpes, 1952, 1953, 1954; Alpine Gold Cup (three consecutive wins), 1954. Only Englishman to win Italian Mille Miglia, 1955. Competed in 494 races, rallies, sprints, land speed records and endurance runs, and won 222 of these. Successes include Targa Florio, 1955; Brit. Grand Prix, 1955, 1957; Ital. GP, 1956, 1957, 1959; NZ GP, 1956, 1959; Monaco GP, 1956, 1960, 1961; Leguna Seca GP, 1960, 1961; US GP, 1959, 1960; Aust. GP, 1956; Bari GP, 1956; Pescara GP, 1957; Swedish GP, 1957; Dutch GP, 1958; Argentine GP, 1958; Morocco GP, 1958; Buenos Aires GP, 1958; Melbourne GP, 1958; Villareal GP, 1958; Caen GP, 1958; Portuguese GP, 1959; S African GP, 1960; Cuban GP, 1960; Austrian GP, 1960; Cape GP, 1960; Watkins Glen GP, 1960; German GP, 1961; Modena GP, 1961. Twice voted Driver of the Year, 1954 and 1961. *Publications:* Stirling Moss's Book of Motor Sport, 1955; In the Track of Speed, 1957; Stirling Moss's Second Book of Motor Sport, 1958; Le Mans, 1959; My Favourite Car Stories, 1960; A Turn at the Wheel, 1961; All But My Life, 1963; Design and Behaviour of the Racing Car, 1964; How to Watch Motor Racing, 1975; *relevant publication:* Stirling Moss, by Robert Raymond, 1953. *Recreations:* snow-ski-ing, water ski-ing, dancing, spear-fishing, model making, the theatre, and designing. *Address:* (business) Stirling Moss Ltd, 46 Shepherd Street, W1; (residence) 44 Shepherd Street, W1. *Clubs:* White Elephant; British Racing Drivers', British Automobile Racing, British Racing and Sports Car, Road Racing Drivers of America, 200 mph, Lord's Taverners, Royal Automobile; Internationale des Anciens Pilotes des Grand Prix; Chm. or Pres. of 36 motoring clubs.

MOSS, Trevor Simpson, PhD; FInstP; Editor: Journal of Infra Red Physics, since 1961; Journal of Progress in Quantum Electronics, since 1978; *b* 28 Jan. 1921; *s* of William Moss and Florence Elizabeth (*née* Simpson); *m* 1948, Audrey (*née* Nelson). *Educ:* Alleynes, Uttoxeter; Downing Coll., Cambridge. MA, PhD, ScD Cantab. Research on radar, Royal Aircraft Establishment, 1941–43; research on radar and semiconductors, Telecommunications Research Estabt, 1943–53; RAE, 1953–78; Dep. Dir, Royal Signals and Radar Estabt, 1978–81. Mem., Lloyd's. Various hon. commissions in RAF, 1942–45. Max Born Medal, German and British Physical Societies, 1975. *Publications:* Photoconductivity, 1952; Optical Properties of Semiconductors, 1959; Semiconductor Optoelectronics, 1973; Handbook of Semiconductors, 4 vols, 1980–82; approx. 100 res. papers in internat. physics jls. *Address:* 2 Shelsley Meadow, Colwall, Malvern, Worcs. *T:* Colwall 40079.

MÖSSBAUER, Rudolf L., PhD; Professor of Experimental Physics, Technische Universität München, since 1964; *b* Munich, 31 Jan. 1929; *m*; one *s* two *d*. *Educ:* High Sch. and Technische Hochschule, München (equiv. Bachelor's and Master's degrees). PhD (München) 1958. Thesis work, Max Planck Inst., Heidelberg, 1955–57; Research Fellow: Technische Hochschule, München, 1958–60, and at Caltech, 1960–61; Prof. of Physics, CIT, 1962–64; Prof. of Experimental Physics, München, 1964; Dir, Institut Max von Laue-Paul Langevin, and French-German-British High-Flux-Reactor at Grenoble, 1972–77. Member: Bavarian Acad. of Sci.; Amer. Acad. of Sci.; Amer. Acad. of Arts and Scis; Pontifical Acad.; Soviet Acad. of Sci.; Acad. Leopoldina, etc. Hon. degrees Oxon, Leuwen, Madrid, Grenoble, etc. Nobel Prize for Physics, 1961, and numerous other awards. Bavarian Order of Merit, 1962. *Publications:* on gamma resonance spectroscopy (Mössbauer effect) and on neutrino physics. *Recreations:* photography, music, mountaineering. *Address:* Technische Universität München, Physik-Department E 15, James-Franck-Strasse, 8046 Garching, Federal Republic of Germany.

MOSSELMANS, Carel Maurits, TD 1961; Chairman, Sedgwick Group plc, since 1984; *b* 9 March 1929; *s* of Adriaan Willem Mosselmans and Nancy Henriette Mosselmans (*née* van der Wyck); *m* 1962, Hon. Prudence Fiona McCorquodale, *d* of 1st Baron McCorquodale of Newton, KCVO, PC; two *s*. *Educ:* Stowe; Trinity Coll. Cambridge (MA Modern Langs and Hist.). Queen's Bays 2nd Dragoon Guards, 1947–49; City of London Yeomanry (Rough Riders), TA, 1949; Inns of Court and City Yeomanry, 1961; Lt-Col comdg Regt, 1963. Joined Sedgwick Collins & Co., 1952; Dir, 1964– (Sedgwick Forbes 1973, Sedgwick Forbes Bland Payne 1979, Sedgwick Group 1981); Dep. Chm., Sedgwick Group, 1982; Chairman: Sedgwick Forbes (Lloyd's Underwriting Agents), 1975–86; Sedgwick Lloyd's Underwriting Agents, 1986–; The Sumitomo Marine & Fire Insurance Co. (Europe), 1981–; Dir, Coutts & Co., 1981–. *Recreations:* shooting, fishing, golf, tennis, music. *Address:* 15 Chelsea Square, SW3. *T:* 01–352 0621. *Clubs:* White's, Cavalry and Guards.

MOSTYN, 5th Baron, *cr* 1831; **Roger Edward Lloyd Lloyd-Mostyn,** Bt 1778; MC 1943; *b* 17 April 1920; *e s* of 4th Baron Mostyn; *S* father, 1965; *m* 1943, Yvonne Margaret Stuart (marr. diss., 1957), *y d* of A. Stuart Johnston, Henshall Hall, Congleton, Cheshire; one *s* one *d*; 2nd, 1957, Mrs Sheila Edmondson Shaw, DL, *o c* of Major Reginald Fairweather, Stockwell Manor, Silverton, Devon, and of Mrs Fairweather, Yew Tree Cottage, Fordcombe, Kent. *Educ:* Eton; Royal Military College, Sandhurst. 2nd Lt, 9th Queen's Royal Lancers, 1939. Served War 1939–45, France, North Africa, and Italy (wounded, despatches, MC). Temp. Major, 1946. *Heir:* *s* Hon. Llewellyn Roger Lloyd Lloyd-Mostyn [*b* 26 Sept. 1948; *m* 1974, Denise Suzanne, *d* of Roger Duvanel; one *s* one *d*. *Educ:* Eton. Called to the Bar, Middle Temple, 1973]. *Address:* Mostyn Hall, Mostyn, Clwyd, North Wales. *T:* Mostyn 222.

MOSTYN, Lt-Gen. Sir David; *see* Mostyn, Lt-Gen. Sir J. D. F.

MOSTYN, Sir Jeremy (John Anthony), 14th Bt *cr* 1670; Consultant to Hampton & Sons, since 1986; *b* 24 Nov. 1933; *s* of Sir Basil Anthony Trevor Mostyn, 13th Bt and Anita Mary, *d* of late Lt-Col Rowland Charles Feilding, DSO; *S* father 1956; *m* 1963, Cristina, *o d* of Marchese Orengo, Turin; one *s* two *d*. *Educ:* Rhodesia and Downside. Contested: Ealing South (L) General Election, 1959; Cities of London and Westminster, LCC Elections, 1960. Green Staff Officer, Investiture of the Prince of Wales, 1969. FRSA; AMRSH. Kt of Honour and Devotion, SMO Malta. *Recreation:* saving and restoring old houses. *Heir:* *s* William Basil John Mostyn, *b* 15 Oct 1975. *Address:* The Manor House, Lower Heyford, Oxon.

MOSTYN, Gen. Sir (Joseph) David Frederick, KCB 1984; CBE 1974 (MBE 1962); Adjutant General, since 1986; *b* 28 Nov. 1928; *s* of late J. P. Mostyn, Arundel, and of Mrs J. D. S. Keenan, Farnham; *m* 1952, Diana Patricia Sheridan; four *s* two *d*. *Educ:* Downside; RMA Sandhurst; psc, rcds. Commnd Oxf. and Bucks LI, 1948; served BAOR, Greece, Cyprus, UK, 1948–58; Canadian Army Staff Coll., 1958; WO, 1959–61; Coy Comdr 1st Green Jackets, Malaya, Brunei, Borneo, 1962–63 (despatches); Instructor, Staff Coll., Camberley, 1964–67; MoD, 1967–69; CO 2 RGJ, BAOR and NI, 1969–71; Comdt Officers' Wing, Sch. of Infantry, 1972; Comdr 8 Inf. Bde, NI, 1972–74; Dep. Dir Army Training, 1974–75; RCDS 1976; BGS, HQ BAOR, 1977; Dir Personnel Services (Army), 1978–80; GOC Berlin and Comdt British Sector, 1980–83; Military Sec., 1983–86. Col Commandant: The Light Div., 1983–86; Army Legal Corps, 1983–. Kt SMO Malta, 1974. *Publications:* articles in mil. and RUSI jls. *Recreations:* maintaining a home for the family; all field sports. *Address:* c/o Lloyds Bank Plc, 6 Pall Mall, SW1. *Club:* Army and Navy.

MOTE, Harold Trevor, JP, DL; Member for Harrow East, Greater London Council, 1965–86; company director, company consultant and engineer, retired; *b* 28 Oct. 1919; *s* of late Harold Roland Mote; *m* 1944, Amplias Pamela, *d* of late Harold Johnson, Oswestry; three *s* one *d*. *Educ:* Upper Latymer Sch.; St Paul's Sch.; Regent Street Polytechnic; Army Staff Coll. RE, TA, 1935; served War, Royal Signals, 1940–46 (Lt-Col); Royal Signals, TA, 1948–54. Councillor, Harrow, 1953–67, Alderman 1967; 1st Mayor, London Bor. of Harrow, 1965–66; Opposition Leader, Harrow Council, 1971–73, Leader, 1973–77, resigned 1978. Greater London Council, 1965–86: Member, Leader's Cttee, 1977–78, 1979–81 (formerly with special responsibility for Law and Order); Dep. Leader, Planning and Communications Policy Cttee, 1977–78, 1980–81; Chm., 1978–79; Chm., London Transport Cttee, 1979–81; Opposition Spokesman on Transport, 1981–82; Technical Services, 1985–86; Member: Staff Cttee, 1981–82; Planning Cttee, 1981–86; Shadow Leaders Cttee, 1981–82 and 1985–86; formerly: Chm., Scrutiny Cttee; Vice-Chm., Public Services Cttee; Member: Policy and Resources Cttee; West and North Area Planning Bds; Opposition Leader, Fire Bde Cttee; Chm., W Area Planning and Transportation Sub-Cttee; Member: Finance and Estabt Cttee; Public Services and Safety Cttee. Mem., Thames Water Authority, 1973–83 (Chm., Personnel Sub-Cttee, 1973–83; Nat. Rep. on Personnel Matters, 1973–83). JP Mddx 1965; DL Greater London 1967; Rep. DL Harrow 1969. *Address:* Mercury, 48A High Street, Pinner, Middlesex. *T:* 01–866 8500.

MOTHERWELL, Bishop of, (RC), since 1983; **Rt. Rev. Joseph Devine;** *b* 7 Aug. 1937; *s* of Joseph Devine and Christina Murphy. *Educ:* Blairs Coll., Aberdeen; St Peter's Coll., Dumbarton; Scots Coll., Rome. Ordained priest in Glasgow, 1960; postgraduate work in Rome (PhD), 1960–64; Private Sec. to Archbishop of Glasgow, 1964–65; Assistant Priest in a Glasgow parish, 1965–67; Lecturer in Philosophy, St Peter's Coll., Dumbarton, 1967–74; a Chaplain to Catholic Students in Glasgow Univ., 1974–77; Titular Bishop of Voli and Auxiliary to Archbishop of Glasgow, 1977–83. Papal Bene Merenti Medal, 1962. *Recreations:* general reading, music, Association football. *Address:* 17 Viewpark Road, Motherwell ML1 3ER. *T:* Motherwell 63715.

MOTION, Andrew; Poetry Editor, since 1983 and Editorial Director, since 1985, Chatto & Windus; *b* 26 Oct. 1952; *s* of Andrew Richard Motion and Catherine Gillian Motion; *m* 1973, Joanna Jane Powell (marr. diss. 1983); *m* 1985, Janet Elisabeth Dalley; one *s*. *Educ:* Radley Coll.; University Coll., Oxford (BA 1st Cl. Hons, MLitt). Lectr in English, Univ. of Hull, 1977–81; Editor of Poetry Review, 1981–83. *Publications: poetry:* The Pleasure Steamers, 1978, 3rd edn 1983; Independence, 1981; The Penguin Book of Contemporary British Poetry (anthology), 1982; Secret Narratives, 1983; Dangerous Play, 1984 (Rhys Meml Prize); *criticism:* The Poetry of Edward Thomas, 1981; Philip Larkin, 1982; *biography:* The Lamberts, 1986. *Recreation:* cinema.

MOTT, Gregory George Sidney, CBE 1979; self-employed consultant; Managing Director, Vickers Shipbuilding and Engineering Ltd, 1979–84; *b* 11 Feb. 1925; *s* of Sidney Cyril George Mott and Elizabeth Rolinda Mott; *m* 1949, Jean Metcalfe. *Educ:* Univ. of Melbourne (BMechE Hons). Trainee Manager, Vickers Armstrong Ltd Naval Yard, 1948–49; Supervising Engr, A. E. Turner and John Coates, London, 1950–52; Sen. Draughtsman, Melbourne Harbour Trust Comrs, 1952–56; joined Vickers Armstrong Ltd, Barrow, trng on submarine construction, 1956; seconded to Naval Section Harwell, for shielding design DS/MP1 (specialised in computer technol.), 1957–59; returned to Barrow as Project Manager, Dreadnought, 1959–61; Technical Manager, Nuclear, 1961–64; Projects Controller, 1964–67; Local Dir, Vickers Ltd Shipbuilding Gp, 1966; responsible for Special Projects Div., incl. Oceanics Dept, 1968–72; Man. Dir, Vickers Oceanics Ltd, on formation of company, 1972–75; Dir, Vickers Ltd Shipbuilding Gp, and Gen. Manager, Barrow Shipbuilding Works (retained directorship, Vickers Oceanics Ltd, resigned later), 1975–77; Dir, Vickers Shipbuilding Gp Ltd, 1977; Gen. Manager and Dir, Barrow Engrg Works, Vickers Shipbuilding Gp Ltd, 1978.

MOTT, John Charles Spencer, FEng, FICE, FIStructE; CBIM; Chairman, May Gurney Holdings Ltd, since 1986; *b* Beckenham, Kent, 18 Dec. 1926; *m* 1953, Patricia Mary (*née* Fowler); two *s*. *Educ:* Balgowan Central Sch., Beckenham, Kent; Brixton Sch. of Building; Battersea Polytechnic; Rutherford Coll. of Technology, Newcastle upon Tyne. Served war, Lieut, Royal Marines, 1943–46. Indentured as Engr with L. G. Mouchel & Partners, 1949–52; joined Kier Ltd, 1952; Agent on heavy civil engrg contracts, 1952–63; Chm., French Kier Holdings plc, 1974–86 (Dir, on merger, 1973, Chief Exec., 1974–84). Director: Kier Ltd, 1963; J. L. Kier & Co. Ltd (Holding Co.), 1968; RMC plc, 1986–. Mem. Council, Fellowship of Engrg, 1983–86; Past Member: Council, Instn Civil Engrs; Bragg Cttee of Falsework. *Address:* (home) 91 Long Road, Cambridge; (office) May Gurney Holdings Ltd, Trowse, Norwich NR14 8SZ. *T:* Norwich 627281. *Club:* Danish.

MOTT, Sir John (Harmar), 3rd Bt, *cr* 1930; Regional Medical Officer, Department of Health and Social Security, 1969–84; *b* 21 July 1922; *s* of 2nd Bt and Mary Katherine (*d* 1972) *d* of late Rev. A. H. Stanton; *S* father, 1964; *m* 1950, Elizabeth (*née* Carson); one *s* two *d*. *Educ:* Radley Coll.; New Coll., Oxford. MA Oxford, 1948; BM, BCh, 1951. Served War of 1939–45: Pilot, Royal Air Force, 1943–46. Middlesex Hospital: House Physician, 1951; House Surgeon, 1952. Mem., RCGP. *Recreations:* sailing, photography. *Heir:* *s* David Hugh Mott [*b* 1 May 1952; *m* 1980, Amanda Jane, *d* of Lt-Comdr D. W. P. Fryer, RN; one *s*]. *Address:* Staniford, Brookside, Kingsley, Cheshire WA6 8BG. *T:* Kingsley 88123.

MOTT, Michael Duncan; His Honour Judge Mott; a Circuit Judge, since 1985; *b* 8 Dec. 1940; *s* of Francis J. Mott and Gwendolen Mott; *m* 1970, Phyllis Ann Gavin; two *s*. *Educ:* Rugby Sch.; Caius Coll., Cambridge (Exhibnr, MA). Called to Bar, Inner Temple, 1963; practised Midland and Oxford Circuit, 1964–69; Resident Magistrate, Kenya, 1969–71; resumed practice, Midland and Oxford Circuit, 1972; a Deputy Circuit Judge, 1976–80; a Recorder, 1980–85. *Recreations:* tennis, ski-ing, travel, music. *Address:* c/o Circuit Administrator, Midland and Oxford Circuit, 2 Newton Street, Birmingham B4 7LU. *Clubs:* Cambridge Union Society; Union and County (Worcester).

MOTT, Sir Nevill (Francis), Kt 1962; FRS 1936; MA Cantab; Cavendish Professor of Physics, Cambridge University, 1954–71; Senior Research Fellow, Imperial College, London, 1971–73, Fellow, 1978; *b* 30 Sept. 1905; *s* of C. F. Mott, late Dir of Educn, Liverpool, and Lilian Mary Reynolds; *m* 1930, Ruth Horder; two *d*. *Educ:* Clifton Coll.; St John's Coll., Cambridge. Lecturer at Manchester Univ., 1929–30; Fellow and Lecturer, Gonville and Caius Coll., Cambridge, 1930–33; Melville Wills Prof. of Theoretical Physics in the Univ. of Bristol, 1933–48; Henry Overton Wills Prof. and Dir of the Henry Herbert Wills Physical Laboratories, Univ. of Bristol, 1948–54. Master of Gonville and Caius Coll., Univ. of Cambridge, 1959–66. Corr. mem., Amer. Acad. of Arts and Sciences, 1954; Pres., International Union of Physics, 1951–57; Pres., Mod. Languages Assoc., 1955; Pres., Physical Soc., 1956–58; Mem. Governing Board of Nat. Inst. for Research in Nuclear Science, 1957–60; Mem. Central Advisory Council for Education for England, 1956–59; Mem. Academic Planning Cttee and Council of University Coll. of Sussex; Chm. Ministry of Education's Standing Cttee on Supply of Teachers, 1959–62; Chairman: Nuffield Foundation's Cttee on Physics Education, 1961–73; Physics Education Cttee (Royal Society and Inst. of Physics), 1965–71. Chairman, Taylor & Francis, Scientific Publishers, 1970–75, Pres., 1976–. Foreign Associate, Nat. Acad. of Sciences of USA, 1957; Hon. Member: Akademie der Naturforscher Leopoldina, 1964; Société Française de Physique, 1970; Inst. of Metals, Japan, 1975; Sociedad Real Española de Fisica y Quimica, 1980; European Physical Soc., 1985; Hon. Fellow: St John's Coll., Cambridge, 1971; UMIST, 1975; Darwin Coll., Cambridge, 1977; For. Fellow, Indian Nat. Science Acad., 1982. Hon. DSc: Louvain, Grenoble, Paris, Poitiers, Bristol, Ottawa, Liverpool, Reading, Sheffield, London, Warwick, Lancaster, Heriot-Watt, Oxon, East Anglia, Bordeaux, St Andrews, Essex, William and Mary, Stuttgart, Sussex, Marburg, Bar Ilan, Lille, Rome, Lisbon; Hon. Doctorate of Technology, Linköping, Sweden. Hon. FInstP 1972. Hughes Medal of Royal Society, 1941; Royal Medal, 1953; Grande Médaille de la Société Française de Métallurgie, 1970; Copley Medal, 1972; Faraday Medal, IEE, 1973; (jtly) Nobel Prize for Physics, 1977. Chevalier, Ordre Nat. du Mérite, France, 1977. *Publications:* An Outline of Wave Mechanics, 1930; The Theory of Atomic Collisions (with H. S. W. Massey), 1933; The Theory of the Properties of Metals and Alloys (with H. Jones), 1936; Electronic Processes in Ionic Crystals (with R. W. Gurney), 1940; Wave Mechanics and its Applications (with I. N. Snedden), 1948; Elements of Wave Mechanics, 1952; Atomic Structure and the Strength of Metals, 1956; Electronic Processes in Non-Crystalline Materials (with E. A. Davis), 1971, 2nd edn 1979; Elementary Quantum Mechanics, 1972; Metal-Insulator Transitions, 1974; Conduction in Non-crystalline Materials, 1986; A Life in Science (autobiog.), 1986; various contribs to scientific periodicals about Atomic Physics, Metals, Semi-conductors and Photographic Emulsions and Glasses. *Recreation:* photography. *Address:* The Cavendish Laboratory, Madingley Road, Cambridge CB3 0HE; 63 Mount Pleasant, Aspley Guise, Milton Keynes MK17 8JX. *Club:* Athenæum.

MOTT, Norman Gilbert, CMG 1962; retired, 1969; *b* 7 Sept. 1910; *s* of late Albert Norman Mott and late Ada Emily Kilby; *m* 1941, Betty Mary, *d* of late Sidney Hugh Breeze; two *s*. *Educ:* Christ's Coll., Finchley. Served in HM Forces (Intelligence Corps), 1940–47. Joined HM Diplomatic Service, 1948; served since in Foreign Office and at Trieste. *Recreations:* gardening, photography. *Address:* 34 Ferndale Road, Chichester, West Sussex. *T:* Chichester 527960.

MOTT-RADCLYFFE, Sir Charles (Edward), Kt 1957; DL; Captain Rifle Brigade, Reserve of Officers; *b* 1911; *o s* of Lt-Col C. E. Radclyffe, DSO, Rifle Brigade (killed in action 1915), Little Park, Wickham, Hants, and Theresa Caroline, *o d* of John Stanley Mott, JP, Barningham Hall, Norfolk; *m* 1940, Diana (*d* 1955), *d* of late Lt-Col W. Gibbs, CVO, 7th Hussars; three *d*; *m* 1956, Stella, *d* of late Lionel Harrisson, Caynham Cottage, Ludlow, Salop. *Educ:* Eton; Balliol Coll., Oxford. Hon. Attaché Diplomatic Service, Athens and Rome, 1936–38; Mem. Military Mission to Greece, 1940–41; served as Liaison Officer in Syria, 1941, and with Rifle Brigade in Middle East and Italy, 1943–44; MP (C) Windsor, 1942–70; Parliamentary Private Sec. to Sec. of State for India (Rt Hon. L. S. Amery), Dec. 1944–May 1945; Junior Lord of the Treasury, May-July 1945; Conservative Whip, Aug. 1945–Feb. 1946; Chm. Conservative Parly Foreign Affairs Cttee, 1951–59. Mem., Plowden Commn on Overseas Representational Services, 1963–64. A Governor of Gresham's Sch., Holt, 1957–; Mem., Historic Buildings Council for England, 1962–70; President: Country Landowners Assoc. (Norfolk Branch), 1972–; Norfolk CCC, 1972–74 (Chm., 1976–); Royal Norfolk Show, 1979. High Sheriff, 1974, DL 1977, of Norfolk. Comdr, Order of Phoenix (Greece). *Publication:* Foreign Body in the Eye (a memoir of the Foreign Service), 1975. *Recreations:* cricket (Captain, Lords and Commons Cricket, 1952–70), shooting. *Address:* Barningham Hall, Matlaske, Norfolk. *T:* Matlaske 250; Flat 1, 38 Cadogan Square, SW1. *T:* 01–584 5834. *Clubs:* Turf, Buck's, Pratt's, MCC.

MOTTELSON, Prof. Ben R., PhD; Danish physicist; Professor, Nordic Institute for Theoretical Atomic Physics, Copenhagen, since 1957; *b* Chicago, Ill, USA, 9 July 1926; *s* of Goodman Mottelson and Georgia Mottelson (*née* Blum); *m* 1948, Nancy Jane Reno; three *c*; became a Danish citizen, 1971. *Educ:* High Sch., La Grange, Ill; Purdue Univ. (officers' trng, USN, V12 program; BSc 1947); Harvard Univ. (grad. studies, PhD 1950). Sheldon Trav. Fellowship from Harvard at Inst. of Theoretical Physics, Copenhagen (later, the Niels Bohr Inst.), 1950–51. His Fellowship from US Atomic Energy Commn permitted continuation of work in Copenhagen for two more years, after which he held research position in CERN (European Organization for Nuclear Research) theoretical study group, formed in Copenhagen. Visiting Prof., Univ. of Calif at Berkeley, Spring term, 1959. Nobel Prize for Physics (jtly), 1975; awarded for work on theory of Atomic Nucleus, with Dr Aage Bohr (3 papers publ. 1952–53). *Publications:* Nuclear Structure, vol. I, 1969; vol. II, 1975 (with A. Bohr); contrib. Rev. Mod. Phys (jt), etc. *Address:* Nordita, Copenhagen, Denmark.

MOTTERSHEAD, Frank William, CB 1957; Deputy Secretary, Department of Health and Social Security (formerly Ministry of Health), 1965–71; *b* 7 Sept. 1911; *o s* of late Thomas Hastings and Adeline Mottershead; unmarried. *Educ:* King Edward's Sch., Birmingham; St John's Coll., Cambridge. BA 1933, MA 1973. Entered Secretary's Dept of Admiralty, 1934; Principal Private Sec. to First Lord, 1944–46; idc 1949; Under Sec., 1950; Transferred to Ministry of Defence, 1956; Deputy Sec., 1958; Deputy Under-Sec. of State, 1964. *Address:* Old Warden, Grevel Lane, Chipping Campden, Glos. *T:* Evesham 840548. *Club:* United Oxford & Cambridge University.

MOTTISTONE, 4th Baron, *cr* 1933, of Mottistone; **David Peter Seely,** CBE 1984; Lord Lieutenant for Isle of Wight, since 1986; *b* 16 Dec. 1920; 4th *s* of 1st Baron Mottistone; *S* half brother, 1966; *m* 1944, Anthea, *er d* of T. V. W. McMullan, Bangor, Co. Down, N Ireland; two *s* two *d* (and one *d* decd). *Educ:* RN Coll., Dartmouth. Convoy escorting, Atlantic and Mediterranean, 1941–44; qualified in Communications, 1944; Served in Pacific, 1945; in comd HMS Cossack, FE Flt, 1958–59; in comd HMS Ajax and 24th Escort Sqdn, FE Flt (offensive ops against Indonesian confrontation) (despatches), 1963–65; Naval Advr to UK High Comr, Ottawa, 1965–66; retired at own request as a Captain, 1967. Dir of Personnel and Training, Radio Rentals Gp, 1967–69; Dir, Distributive Industry Trng Bd, 1969–75; Dir, Cake and Biscuit Alliance, 1975–81; Export Secretary: Cake and Biscuit Alliance, 1981–83; Cocoa, Chocolate and Confectionary Alliance, 1981–83. Chm., Westminster Industrial Brief Ltd, 1981–. FIERE; FIPM; FBIM. DL Isle of Wight, 1981. *Recreation:* yachting. *Heir:* *s* Hon. Peter John Philip Seely [*b* 29 Oct. 1949; *m* 1st, 1972, Joyce Cairns (marr. diss. 1975); one *s*; 2nd, 1982, Linda, *d* of W. Swain, Bulphan Fen, Essex; one *d*]. *Address:* The Old Parsonage, Mottistone, Isle of Wight. *Clubs:* Royal Commonwealth Society; Royal Yacht Squadron, Royal Cruising, Island Sailing, Royal Navy Sailing Association.

MOTTRAM, Maj.-Gen. John Frederick, CB 1983; LVO 1976; OBE 1969; Director General, Fertiliser Manufacturers Association, since 1983; *b* 9 June 1930; *s* of Frederick Mottram and Margaret Mottram (*née* Butcher); *m* 1956, Jennifer Thomas; one *s* one *d*. *Educ:* Enfield Central Sch.; Enfield Technical Coll. Joined RM, 1948; 42 Commando, Malaya, ME, 1951–54; Special Boat Squadron, 1955–56; HMS Loch Lomond, Persian Gulf, 1957–58; Adjutant, Commando Trng Centre, 1959–62; Student, Army Staff Coll., 1963; Staff of CGRM and RM Equerry to HRH The Duke of Edinburgh, 1964–65; Bde Major, 3 Commando Bde, Far East, 1966–68; Directing Staff, Army Staff Coll., 1969–71; CO, 40 Commando, NI and Plymouth, 1972–74 (mentioned in Despatches, 1973); Student, Naval War Coll., 1974; Jt Warfare Attaché, British Embassy, Washington DC, 1974–77; Col GS, DCGRM and RM ADC to HM The Queen, 1978–80; Maj.-Gen., 1980; Maj.-Gen. Training and Reserve Forces, RM, 1980–83, retd. *Recreation:* fishing. *Address:* c/o Fertiliser Manufacturers Association, 90 Cowcross Street, EC1M 6BH. *Clubs:* Army and Navy, Farmers.

MOTTRAM, Richard Clive; Assistant Under Secretary, Ministry of Defence, since 1986; *b* 23 April 1946; *s* of John Mottram and Florence Yates; *m* 1971, Fiona Margaret Erskine; three *s* one *d*. *Educ:* King Edward VI Camphill Sch., Birmingham; Univ. of Keele (1st Cl. Hons Internat. Relns). Entered Home Civil Service by open competition, 1968, assigned to Ministry of Defence: Asst Private Sec. to Sec. of State for Defence, 1971–72; Principal, Naval Programme and Budget, 1973; Cabinet Office, 1975–77; Ministry of Defence: Private Sec. to Perm. Under Sec., 1979–81; Asst Sec., Manpower Control and Audit, Procurement Exec., 1981; Private Sec. to Sec. of State for Defence, 1982–86. *Recreations:* cinema, tennis. *Address:* c/o Ministry of Defence, Whitehall, SW1A 2HB. *T:* 01–218 9000.

MOTYER, Rev. John Alexander; Minister of Christ Church, Westbourne, Bournemouth, since 1981; *b* 30 Aug. 1924; *s* of Robert Shankey and Elizabeth Maud Motyer; *m* 1948, Beryl Grace Mays; two *s* one *d*. *Educ:* High Sch., Dublin; Dublin Univ. (MA, BD); Wycliffe Hall, Oxford. Curate: St Philip, Penn Fields, Wolverhampton, 1947–50; Holy Trinity, Old Market, Bristol, 1950–54; Tutor, Clifton Theol Coll., Bristol, 1950–54, Vice-Principal, 1954–65; Vicar, St Luke's, Hampstead, 1965–70; Dep. Principal, Tyndale Hall, Bristol, 1970–71; Principal and Dean of College, Trinity Coll., Bristol, 1971–81. *Publications:* The Revelation of the Divine Name, 1959; After Death, 1965; The Richness of Christ (Epistle to the Philippians), 1966; The Tests of Faith (Epistle of James), 1970, 2nd edn 1975; (Old Testament Editor) New Bible Commentary Revised, 1970; The Day of the Lion (Amos), 1975; The Image of God: Law and Liberty in Biblical Ethics (Laing Lecture), 1976; The Message of Philippians, 1984; The Message of James, 1985; contributor: New Bible Dictionary; Expositor's Bible Commentary; Law and Life (monograph); New International Dictionary of New Testament Theology; Evangelical Dictionary of Theology. *Recreations:* reading, odd-jobbing. *Address:* Christ Church Vicarage, 43 Branksome Dene Road, Bournemouth BH4 8JW. *T:* Bournemouth 762164.

MOTZ, Prof. Hans; Professor of Engineering, University of Oxford, 1972–77, now Emeritus; Emeritus Fellow of St John's College, Oxford and St Catherine's College, Oxford; Honorary Professor, Technical University, Vienna, since 1980; Hon. Consultant, Culham Laboratory, United Kingdom Atomic Energy Authority; *b* 1 Oct. 1909; *s* of Karl and Paula Motz; *m* 1959, Lotte Norwood-Edlis; one *d*. *Educ:* Technische Hochschule, Vienna; Besançon Univ. (Schol.); Trinity Coll., Dublin (Schol.). Dipl. Ing 1932, Dr Techn. Sc. 1935, MSc TCD, MA Oxon; FInstP. Research Engr, Standard Telephones & Cables, 1939–41; Demonstrator, Dept of Engrg Science, Oxford, 1941; Lectr in Engrg Physics, Sheffield Univ., 1946–48; Research Assoc., Microwave Lab., Stanford Univ., 1949; Donald Pollock Reader in Engrg Science, Oxford, 1954; Professorial Fellow, St Catherine's Coll., Oxford, 1963. Internat. Fellow, Stanford Res. Inst., 1956; Guest Prof., Paris Univ. (Saclay), 1964; Visiting Professor: Brown Univ., 1959; Brooklyn Polytech., 1965; Innsbruck Univ., 1967; Tech. Univ., Vienna, 1979–80 (permanent Hon. Prof., 1980). Ehrenkreuz für Wissenschaft und Kunst, 1st class (Austria), 1980. *Publications:* Problems of Microwave Theory, 1951; The Physics of Laser Fusion, 1979; many papers in sci. jls, including Neuroscience. *Recreations:* ski-ing, yachting, silversmith, and enamel work. *Address:* 16 Bedford Street, Oxford. *T:* Oxford 241895.

MOULE, Rev. Prof. Charles Francis Digby, CBE 1985; FBA 1966; Lady Margaret's Professor of Divinity in the University of Cambridge, 1951–76; Fellow of Clare College, Cambridge, since 1944; Canon Theologian (non-residentiary) of Leicester, 1955–76, Canon Emeritus, since 1976; Honorary Member of Staff, Ridley Hall, Cambridge, 1976–80; *b* 3 Dec. 1908; *s* of late Rev. Henry William Moule and Laura Clements Pope; unmarried. *Educ:* Weymouth Coll., Dorset; Emmanuel Coll., Cambridge (scholar) (Hon. Fellow 1972); Ridley Hall, Cambridge. 1st Cl. Classical Tripos Part I, 1929; BA (1st Cl. Classical Tripos Part II), 1931; Evans Prize, 1931; Jeremie Septuagint Prize, 1932; Crosse Scholarship, 1933; MA 1934. Deacon, 1933, priest, 1934; Curate, St Mark's, Cambridge, and Tutor of Ridley Hall, 1933–34; Curate, St Andrew's, Rugby, 1934–36; Vice-Principal, Ridley Hall, 1936–44, and Curate of St Mary the Great, Cambridge, 1936–40. Dean of Clare Coll., Cambridge, 1944–51; Faculty Asst Lecturer in Divinity in the Univ. of Cambridge, 1944–47; Univ. Lecturer, 1947–51. Burkitt Medal for Biblical Studies, British Acad., 1970. Hon. DD Univ. of St Andrews, 1958. *Publications:* An Idiom Book of New Testament Greek, 1953; The Meaning of Hope, 1953; The Sacrifice of Christ, 1956; Colossians and Philemon (Cambridge Greek Testament Commentary), 1957; Worship in the New Testament, 1961; The Birth of the New Testament, 1962, 3rd edn 1981; The Phenomenon of the New Testament, 1967; (co-editor) Christian History and Interpretation, 1968; The Origin of Christology, 1977 (Collins Theological Book Prize, 1977); The Holy Spirit, 1978; Essays in New Testament Interpretation, 1982; (co-editor) Jesus and the Politics of His Day, 1984; contrib., Encyclopædia Britannica, Interpreter's Dictionary of the Bible, Biblisch-Historisches Handwörterbuch. *Address:* 1 King's Houses, Pevensey, East Sussex.

MOULE-EVANS, David, DMus Oxon; Composer; Conductor; Professor of Harmony, Counterpoint and Composition, Royal College of Music, 1945–74; *b* 21 Nov. 1905; *s* of

John Evans, MA Cantab, and Emily Blanche Evans (*née* Cookson); *m* 1935, Monica Warden Evans, *d* of Richardson Evans, ICS; no *c*. *Educ:* The Judd Sch.; Royal College of Music. Mem. of Queen's Coll., Oxford. Open Scholarship in Composition, RCM, 1925 (Senior Composition Scholar); Mendelssohn Scholarship, 1928; DMus Oxford, 1930. Carnegie Publication Award (for Concerto for String Orchestra), 1928. Symphony in G Major awarded £1,000 Prize offered by Australian Govt, 1952. Examiner, Associated Bd, Royal Schs of Music, 1945–74. Many public and broadcast performances of orchestral and other works; has written music for many documentary films, including British Council commissions. *Publications: published orchestral works include:* Overture: The Spirit of London, 1947; Vienna Rhapsody, 1948; The Haunted Place (for String Orchestra), 1949, Old Tupper's Dance, 1951; chamber works: instrumental pieces and songs. *Recreations:* reading and studying subjects other than music. *Address:* Bracken, 44 Deepdene Avenue, Dorking, Surrey RH5 4AE. *T:* Dorking 880294.

MOULTON, Alexander Eric, CBE 1976; RDI; FEng; Managing Director, Moulton Developments Ltd, since 1956; *b* 9 April 1920; *s* of John Coney Moulton, DSc, The Hall, Bradford-on-Avon, and Beryl Latimer Moulton. *Educ:* Marlborough Coll.; King's Coll., Cambridge (MA). Bristol Aeroplane Co., 1939–44: Engine Research Dept; George Spencer, Moulton & Co. Ltd, 1945–56; became Techn. Dir; estab. Research Dept (originated work on rubber suspensions for vehicles, incl. own design Flexitor); formed Moulton Developments Ltd, 1956 to do develt work on own designs of rubber suspensions for BLMC incl. Hydrolastic and Hydragas (Queen's Award to Industry, 1967); formed Moulton Bicycles Ltd to produce own design Moulton Bicycle, 1962 (Design Centre Award, 1964); designer of Moulton Coach, 1968–70; launched Alex Moulton Bicycle, 1983. Dir, SW Regional Bd, National Westminster Bank, 1982–. RDI 1968 (Master, 1982–83); FRSA 1968; FEng 1980. Hon. Dr, RCA, 1967; Hon. DSc Bath, 1971. SIAD Design Medal, 1976; (jointly): James Clayton Prize, Crompton-Lanchester Medal, and Thomas Hawksley Gold Medal, IMechE, 1979. *Publications:* numerous articles and papers on engineering and education. *Recreations:* cycling, canoeing, steam boating, shooting. *Address:* The Hall, Bradford-on-Avon, Wilts. *T:* Bradford-on-Avon 2991. *Clubs:* Brooks's; Royal Southern Yacht (Hamble).

MOULTON, Maj.-Gen. James Louis, CB 1956; DSO 1944; OBE 1950; retired; *b* 3 June 1906; *s* of Capt. J. D. Moulton, RN; *m* 1937, Barbara Aline (*née* Coode); one *s* one *d*. *Educ:* Sutton Valence Sch. Joined Royal Marines, 1924; Pilot, Fleet Air Arm, 1930; Staff Coll., Camberley, 1938; served War of 1939–45: GSO3 GHQ, BEF, 1940; GSO1, Force 121 (Madagascar), 1942; Commanding Officer, 48 Commando, NW Europe, 1944–45 (DSO); Comd 4th Commando Bde, NW Europe, 1945 (despatches); CO Commando Sch., 1947–49; Comd 3rd Commando Bde, Middle East, 1952–54; Maj.-Gen. Royal Marines, Portsmouth, 1954–57; Chief of Amphibious Warfare, 1957–61. Rep. Col Comdt RM, 1971–72. Naval Editor, 1964–69, Editor, 1969–73, Brassey's Annual. *Publications:* Haste to the Battle, 1963; Defence in a Changing World, 1964; The Norwegian Campaign of 1940, 1966; British Maritime Strategy in the 1970s, 1969; The Royal Marines, 1972, 2nd rev. and enl. edn 1981; Battle for Antwerp, 1978. *Address:* Fairmile, Woodham Road, Woking, Surrey GU21 4DN. *T:* Woking 5174.

MOULTON, Air Vice-Marshal Leslie Howard, CB 1971; DFC 1941; with The Plessey Co., 1971–82, retired; *b* 3 Dec. 1915; *s* of late Peter Moulton, Nantwich, Cheshire; *m* Lesley, *d* of late P. C. Clarke, Ilford; two *s* two *d*. *Educ:* Nantwich and Acton School. Joined RAF, 1932; served War of 1939–45, Pilot; Operations with 14 Sqdn in Africa, 1940–42; CFS, 1942–44; specialised in Signals, 1945; Staff Coll., 1950; USAF, Strategic Air Comd, 1954–56; Dep. Dir Radio, Air Min., 1958–61; Comdt RAF Cosford, 1961–63; CSO Fighter Comd, 1963–65; Min. of Technology, 1965–68. Wing Comdr 1955; Gp Captain 1959; Air Cdre 1964; Air Vice-Marshal 1969; AOC No 90 (Signals) Group, RAF, 1969–71; retired 1971. FIERE, CEng, 1959; FRSA, 1974. *Recreations:* gardening, golf, hill walking. *Address:* Hill Top, Reeth, near Richmond, N Yorks. *T:* Richmond 84320. *Club:* Royal Air Force.

MOUND, Laurence Alfred, DSc; FRES; Keeper of Entomology, British Museum (Natural History), since 1981; *b* 22 April 1934; *s* of John Henry Mound and Laura May Cape; *m* 1958, Agnes Jean Solari; one *s* two *d*. *Educ:* Warwick Sch.; Sir John Cass Coll., London; Imperial Coll., London (DIC); DSc London; Imperial Coll. of Tropical Agriculture, Trinidad (DipTropAgric). Nigerian Federal Dept of Agricl Research, 1959–61; Empire Cotton Growing Corp., Republic of Sudan, 1961–64; Sen. Scientific Officer, BM (NH), 1964–69; Australian CSIRO Research Award, 1967–68; PSO, 1969–75, Dep. Keeper, Dept of Entomology, BM (NH), 1975–81. Sec., Council for Internat. Congresses of Entomology, 1976–; Consultant Dir, Commonwealth Inst. of Entomology, 1981–. Editor, Jl of Royal Entomological Soc. of London, 1973–81 (Vice-Pres., RES, 1975–76). Numerous expedns studying thrips in tropical countries. *Publications:* over 80 technical books and papers on biology of thrips and whitefly, particularly in Bull. of BM (NH), incl. Whitefly of the World (with S. H. Halsey). *Recreations:* thrips with everything. *Address:* c/o British Museum (Natural History), Cromwell Road, SW7. *T:* 01–589 6323.

MOUND, Trevor Ernest John, OBE 1977; HM Diplomatic Service; Consul General, Shanghai, since 1985; *b* 27 July 1930; *e s* of late Harvey Mound and late Margaret Webb; *m* 1955, Patricia Kathleen de Burgh (marr. diss. 1972); two *s*. *Educ:* Royal Grammar Sch., Worcester; RMA Sandhurst; Univs of London and Hong Kong. Enlisted Coldstream Gds; 2nd Lt, Worcs Regt (Malayan Campaign), 1951–54; Parachute Regt (ME), 1954–56; Adjutant, Airborne Forces, 1956–58; GSO 3, 16 Parachute Bde (ME), 1958–60; MoD, 1965–67; retired 1967; joined HM Diplomatic Service, 1967; First Secretary and Head of Chancery: Luxembourg, 1969–71; Calcutta, 1971–73; FCO, 1973–76; Beirut, 1976–77; Counsellor (Commercial), Peking, 1978–81; Counsellor (Econ.), Oslo, 1981–83; Counsellor (Hong Kong negotiations), FCO, 1984. *Recreation:* yoga. *Address:* c/o Foreign and Commonwealth Office, SW1A 2AH.

MOUNSEY, John Patrick David, MA, MD, FRCP; Provost, Welsh National School of Medicine, 1969–79, retired; *b* 1 Feb. 1914; *s* of late John Edward Mounsey and late Christine Frances Trail Robertson; *m* 1947, Vera Madeline Sara King; one *s* one *d*. *Educ:* Eton Coll.; King's Coll., Cambridge; King's Coll. Hosp., London. Sherbrook Res. Fellow, Cardiac Dept, London Hosp., 1951; Royal Postgraduate Medical School: Lectr, 1960; Sen. Lectr and Sub-Dean, 1962; Cons. Cardiologist, Hammersmith Hosp., 1960; Dep. Dir, British Postgrad. Med. Fedn, 1967; Member: GMC, 1970–79; GDC, 1973–79; Council, St David's University Coll., Lampeter, 1975–83; South Glamorgan AHA (T); British Cardiac Soc.; Assoc. of Physicians; Soc. of Physicians in Wales. Corresp. Mem., Australasian Cardiac Soc.; late Asst Ed., British Heart Jl. Hon. LLD Wales, 1980. *Publications:* articles on cardiology mainly in British Heart Jl. *Recreations:* painting, gardening, music. *Address:* Esk House, Coombe Terrace, Wotton-under-Edge, Glos GL12 7NA. *T:* Wotton-under-Edge 2792. *Club:* Athenæum.

MOUNT, Air Cdre Christopher John, CBE 1956; DSO 1943; DFC 1940; DL; retired; *b* 14 Dec. 1913; *s* of Capt. F. Mount; *m* 1947, Audrey Mabel Clarke; two *s*. *Educ:* Eton; Trinity Coll., Oxford. Royal Auxiliary Air Force, 1935; Royal Air Force, 1938. Consultant, Wrights (formerly C. R. Thomas & Son), Solicitors, Maidenhead (partner, 1970–79). DL Berks, 1984. *Address:* Garden House, Bagshot Road, Sunninghill, Ascot, Berks.

MOUNT, Ferdinand; *see* Mount, W. R. F.

MOUNT, Sir James (William Spencer), Kt 1979; CBE 1965; BEM 1946; VMH; *b* 8 Nov. 1908; *s* of Spencer William Mount and Kathleen Mount (*née* Ashenden) *m* 1931, Margaret Geikie (*d* 1973); one *s* three *d*; *m* 1975, Jane Mount. *Educ:* Tonbridge School. Chairman and Director, S. W. Mount & Sons Ltd, 1944–. Chairman: Horticultural Advisory Cttee, MAFF, 1963–69; National Fruit Trials Advisory Cttee, MAFF, 1973–78; Governing Body, E Malling Res. Station, 1960–80. VMH 1982. *Recreations:* fishing, gardening. *Address:* Woolton Farm, Bekesbourne, Canterbury, Kent. *T:* Canterbury 830202. *Club:* Farmers'.

MOUNT, Sir William (Malcolm), 2nd Bt, *cr* 1921; Lieutenant-Colonel Reconnaissance Corps; *b* 28 Dec. 1904; *s* of Sir William Mount, 1st Bt, CBE, and Hilda Lucy Adelaide (*d* 1950), OBE, *y d* of late Malcolm Low of Clatto, Fife; *S* father, 1930; *m* 1929, Elizabeth Nance, *o d* of Owen John Llewellyn, Badminton Vicarage, Glos; three *d*. *Educ:* Eton; New Coll., Oxford. Berkshire: DL 1946; High Sheriff, 1947–48; Vice-Lieutenant, 1960–76. *Recreation:* fishing. *Heir: nephew* William Robert Ferdinand Mount, *qv*. *Address:* Wasing Place, Aldermaston, Berks.

See also Sir W. S. Dugdale, Bt.

MOUNT, (William Robert) Ferdinand; journalist; *b* 2 July 1939; *s* of late Robin and Lady Julia Mount; *heir pres.* to Sir William Mount, *qv*; *m* 1968, Julia Margaret, *d* of late Archibald Julian and Hon. Mrs Lucas; two *s* one *d* (and one *s* decd). *Educ:* Eton; Christ Church, Oxford. Has worked for Sunday Telegraph, Conservative Research Dept, Daily Sketch, National Review, Daily Mail, The Times; Political Columnist: The Spectator, 1977–82 and 1985–; The Standard, 1980–82; Daily Telegraph, 1984–; Head of Prime Minister's Policy Unit, 1982–83. *Publications:* Very Like a Whale, 1967; The Theatre of Politics, 1972; The Man Who Rode Ampersand, 1975; The Clique, 1978; The Subversive Family, 1982. *Address:* 17 Ripplevale Grove, N1. *T:* 01–607 5398.

MOUNT CHARLES, Earl of; Henry Vivian Pierpoint Conyngham; *b* 23 May 1951; *s* and *heir* of 7th Marquess Conyngham, *qv*; *m* 1st, 1971, Juliet Ann, *yr d* of Robert Kitson (marr. diss. 1985); one *s* one *d*; 2nd, 1985, Lady Iona Grimston, *yr d* of 6th Earl of Verulam. *Educ:* Harrow; Harvard Univ. Irish Rep., 1976–78, Consultant, 1978–84, Sotheby's; Chairman: Slane Castle Ltd; Slane Castle Productions. Dir, Grapevine Arts Centre, Dublin. Trustee, Irish Youth Foundn. *Heir: s* Viscount Slane, *qv*. *Address:* Slane Castle, Co. Meath, Eire. *Club:* Kildare Street and University (Dublin).

MOUNT EDGCUMBE, 8th Earl of, *cr* 1789; **Robert Charles Edgcumbe;** Baron Edgcumbe, 1742; Viscount Mount Edgcumbe and Valletort, 1781; Farm Manager, for Lands and Survey, New Zealand, 1975–84; *b* 1 June 1939; *s* of George Aubrey Valletort Edgcumbe (*d* 1977) and of Meta Blucher, *d* of late Robert Charles Lhoyer; *S* uncle, 1982; *m* 1960, Joan Ivy Wall; five *d*. *Educ:* Nelson College. Career from farm worker to farm manager, managing first farm, 1960; taking up family seat in Cornwall, 1984. *Recreations:* hunting game, restoring classic cars. *Heir: half-b* Piers Valletort Edgcumbe, *b* 23 Oct. 1946. *Address:* Mount Edgcumbe House, Plymouth, Devon PL10 1HZ.

MOUNTAIN, Sir Denis Mortimer, 3rd Bt *cr* 1922; Chairman and Managing Director: Eagle Star Insurance Co. Ltd, 1974–85; Eagle Star Holdings plc, 1979–85, Hon. President, since 1985; Chairman, Eagle Star Insurance Co. of America, 1978–85; *b* 2 June 1929; *er s* of Sir Brian Edward Stanley Mountain, 2nd Bt, and of Doris Elsie, *e d* of late E. C. E. Lamb; *S* father, 1977; *m* 1958, Hélène Fleur Mary Kirwan-Taylor; two *s* one *d*. *Educ:* Eton. Late Lieut, Royal Horse Guards. Chairman: Australian Eagle Insurance Co. Ltd, 1977–85; South African Eagle Insurance Co. Ltd, 1977–85, and other companies both in UK and overseas; Pres., Compagnie de Bruxelles Risques Divers SA d'Assurances (Belgium), 1977–85; Director: Rank Organisation PLC, 1968–; Grovewood Securities Ltd, 1969–85 (Dep. Chm.); Philip Hill Investment Trust plc, 1967–; Bank of Nova Scotia (Toronto), 1978–; BAT Industries plc, 1984–85; Allied London Properties, 1986–, and other UK and overseas companies. *Recreations:* fishing, shooting. *Heir: s* Edward Brian Stanford Mountain, *b* 19 March 1961. *Address:* Shawford Park, Shawford, near Winchester, Hants. *T:* Twyford 712289; 12 Queens Elm Square, Old Church Street, Chelsea, SW3 6ED. *T:* 01–352 4331.

MOUNTBATTEN, family name of **Marquess of Milford Haven.**

MOUNTBATTEN OF BURMA, Countess (2nd in line) *cr* 1947; **Patricia Edwina Victoria Knatchbull,** CD; JP; Viscountess Mountbatten of Burma, 1946; Baroness Romsey, 1947; Vice Lord-Lieutenant of Kent, since 1984; *b* 14 Feb. 1924; *er d* of Admiral of the Fleet 1st Earl Mountbatten of Burma, KG, GCB, OM, GCSI, GCIE, GCVO, DSO, PC, FRS, and Countess Mountbatten of Burma, CI, GBE, DCVO, LLD (*d* 1960) (Hon. Edwina Cynthia Annette Ashley, *e d* of 1st Baron Mount Temple, PC); *S* father, 1979; *m* 1946, Baron Brabourne, *qv*; four *s* two *d* (and one *s* decd). *Educ:* Malta, England and New York City. Served War in WRNS, 1943–46. Colonel-in-Chief, Princess Patricia's Canadian Light Infantry. Vice-Pres., BRCS; Dep. Vice-Chm., NSPCC; Chm., Sir Ernest Cassel Educational Trust. President: WES/PNEU; SOS Children's Villages (UK); Friends of Cassel Hosp.; Friends of William Harvey Hosp.; Kent Branches of NSPCC, Save the Children Fund and Marriage Guidance Council. Vice-President: FPA; Nat. Childbirth Trust; SSAFA; RLSS; Shaftesbury Soc.; Shaftesbury Homes and Arethusa; Nat. Soc. for Cancer Relief; Kent Voluntary Service Council; The Aidis Trust; RCN. Hon. President: Soc. for Nautical Research; British Maritime Charitable Foundn; Patron: Commando Assoc.; HMS Cavalier Trust; Legion of Frontiersmen of the Commonwealth; Foudroyant Trust; HMS Kelly Reunion Assoc.; Nuclear Weapons Freeze; VADs (RN); Compassionate Friends; Vice-Patron, Burma Star Assoc. Governor: Ashford School, Kent; Caldecott Community, Kent. JP 1971 and DL 1973, Kent. DStJ 1981. *Heir: s* Lord Romsey, *qv*. *Address:* Newhouse, Mersham, Ashford, Kent TN25 6NQ. *T:* Ashford 23466; 39 Montpelier Walk, SW7 1JH. *T:* 01–589 8829.

MOUNTEVANS, 3rd Baron *cr* 1945, of Chelsea; **Edward Patrick Broke Evans;** Assistant Marketing Manager, British Tourist Authority, since 1982; *b* 1 Feb. 1943; *s* of 2nd Baron Mountevans and of Deirdre Grace, *d* of John O'Connell, Cork; *S* father, 1974; *m* 1973, Johanna Keyzer, *d* of late Antonius Franciscus Keyzer, The Hague. *Educ:* Rugby; Trinity Coll., Oxford. Reserve Army Service, 1961–66; 74 MC Regt RCT, AER; Lt 1964. Joined management of Consolidated Gold Fields Ltd, 1966; British Tourist Authority, 1972: Manager, Sweden and Finland, 1973; Head of Promotion Services, 1976. *Heir: b* Hon. Jeffrey de Corban Richard Evans [*b* 13 May 1948; *m* 1972, Hon. Juliet, *d* of Baron Moran, *qv*; two *s*]. *Address:* c/o House of Lords, SW1A 0PW.

MOUNTFIELD, Peter; Under Secretary, HM Treasury, since 1980; *b* 2 April 1935; *s* of late Alexander Stuart Mountfield, and of Agnes Elizabeth (*née* Gurney); *m* 1958, Evelyn Margaret Smithies; three *s*. *Educ:* Merchant Taylors' Sch., Crosby; Trinity Coll., Cambridge (BA); Graduate Sch. of Public Admin, Harvard. RN, 1953–55. Asst Principal,

HM Treasury, 1958; Principal, 1963; Asst Sec., 1970; Under Sec., Cabinet Office, 1977. *Recreations:* reading, walking, looking at buildings. *Address:* 42 Lambardes, New Ash Green, near Dartford, Kent DA3 8HX. *T:* Ash Green 873677.
See also R. Mountfield.

MOUNTFIELD, Robin; Deputy Secretary, Department of Trade and Industry, since 1984; *b* 16 Oct. 1939; *s* of late Alexander Stuart Mountfield, and of Agnes Elizabeth (*née* Gurney); *m* 1963, Anne Newsham; two *s* one *d*. *Educ:* Merchant Taylors' Sch., Crosby; Magdalen Coll., Oxford (BA). Assistant Principal, Ministry of Power, 1961, Principal, 1965; Private Sec. to Minister for Industry, 1973–74; Asst Sec., Dept of Industry, 1974, seconded to Stock Exchange, 1977–78; Under Sec., DoI, later, DTI, 1980–84. *Address:* Department of Trade and Industry, Ashdown House, 123 Victoria Street, SW1E 6RB. *T:* 01-212 6904.
See also P. Mountfield.

MOUNTFORD, Arnold Robert, CBE 1984; MA; FSA; FMA; Director, City Museum and Art Gallery, Stoke-on-Trent, since 1962; *b* 14 Dec. 1922; *s* of Ernest Gerald and Dorothy Gwendoline Mountford; *m* 1943, Joan (*née* Gray); one *s*. *Educ:* Hanley High School; Univ. of Keele (MA History). FMA 1963; FSA 1973. Royal Artillery, seconded to Special Liaison Unit and Special Communications Unit, 1942–47; demobilized 1947 (Captain). Joined staff of City Museum and Art Gallery, Stoke-on-Trent, specializing in archaeology and ceramics, 1949. Editor, Jl of Ceramic History, 1968–83. *Publications:* The Illustrated Guide to Staffordshire Saltglazed Stoneware, 1971; contribs to Transactions of English Ceramic Circle. *Recreations:* touring inland waterways, gardening. *Address:* City Museum and Art Gallery, Stoke-on-Trent, Staffs. *T:* Stoke-on-Trent 273173.

MOUNTFORT, Guy Reginald, OBE 1970; retired as Director, Ogilvy & Mather International Inc., New York (1964–66); and as Managing Director, Ogilvy and Mather Ltd, London (1964–66); *b* 4 Dec. 1905; *s* of late Arnold George Mountfort, artist, and late Alice Edith (*née* Hughes); *m* 1931, Joan Hartley (*née* Pink); two *d*. *Educ:* Grammar Sch. General Motors Corporation (France), 1928–38. War service, 1939–46, 12 Regt HAC and British Army Staff (Washington) Lt-Col; service in N Africa, Italy, Burma, Pacific, Germany. Procter & Gamble Inc., USA, 1946–47; Mather & Crowther Ltd, 1947, Dir, 1949; Vice-Chm., Dollar Exports Bd Advertising Cttee, 1948–49. Hon. Sec., Brit. Ornithologists' Union, 1952–62, Pres. 1970–75 (Union Medal, 1967); Leader of scientific expedns to Coto Doñana, 1952, 1955, 1956; Bulgaria, 1960; Hungary, 1961; Jordan, 1963, 1965; Pakistan, 1966, 1967. Vice Pres., World Wildlife Fund (Gold Medal, 1978); Scientific FZS (Stamford Raffles Award, 1969). Medal of Société d'Acclimatation, 1936. Commander, Order of the Golden Ark, Netherlands, 1980. *Publications:* A Field Guide to the Birds of Europe (co-author), 1954; The Hawfinch, 1957; Portrait of a Wilderness, 1958; Portrait of a River, 1962; Portrait of a Desert, 1965; The Vanishing Jungle, 1969; Tigers, 1973; So Small a World, 1974; Back from the Brink, 1977; Saving the Tiger, 1981; Wild India, 1985; contribs to ornithological and other scientific jls; television and radio broadcasts on ornithology and exploration. *Recreations:* ornithology, gardening, photography, travel. *Address:* Hurst Oak, Sandy Lane, Lyndhurst, Hants SO4 7DN. *T:* Lyndhurst 2462.

MOUNTGARRET, 17th Viscount (Ireland) *cr* 1550; Baron (UK) *cr* 1911; **Richard Henry Piers Butler;** *b* 8 Nov. 1936; *s* of 16th Viscount; *S* father, 1966; *heir-pres.* to earldoms of Marquess of Ormonde, *qv*; *m* 1st, 1960, Gillian Margaret (marr. diss. 1970), *o d* of Cyril Francis Stuart Buckley, London, SW3; two *s* one *d*; 2nd, 1970, Mrs Jennifer Susan Melville Fattorini (marr. diss. 1983), *yr d* of Captain D. M. Wills, Barley Wood, Wrington, near Bristol; 3rd 1983, Mrs Angela Ruth Waddington, *e d* of T. G. Porter, The Croft, Church Fenton, Tadcaster. *Educ:* Eton; RMA, Sandhurst. Commissioned, Irish Guards, 1957; retd rank Capt., 1964. *Recreations:* shooting, stalking, cricket, golf. *Heir: s* Hon Piers James Richard Butler, *b* 15 April 1961. *Address:* Stainley House, South Stainley, Harrogate, Yorks. *T:* Harrogate 770087. *Clubs:* White's, Pratt's; Yorks CC (Pres., 1984–).

MOURANT, Arthur Ernest, DM, FRCP; FRS 1966; formerly Director, Serological Population Genetics Laboratory; Conseiller Scientifique Etranger, Institut d'Hématologie, Immunologie et Génétique Humaine, Toulouse, since 1974; *b* 11 April 1904; *er s* of Ernest Charles Mourant and Emily Gertrude (*née* Bray); *m* 1978, Mrs Jean E. C. Shimell. *Educ:* Victoria Coll., Jersey; Exeter Coll., Oxford; St Bartholomew's Hosp. Medical Coll. London. BA 1925, DPhil (Geol.) 1931, MA 1931, BM, BCh 1943, DM 1948, Oxford; FRCP 1960; FRCPath 1963. 1st cl. hons Chem., 1926; Sen. King Charles I Schol., Exeter Coll., Oxford, 1926; Burdett-Coutts Schol., Oxford Univ., 1926. Demonstrator in Geology, Univ. of Leeds, 1928–29; Geol Survey of Gt Brit., 1929–31; teaching posts, 1931–34; Dir, Jersey Pathological Lab., 1935–38; Med. Student, 1939–43; House med. appts, 1943–44; Med. Off., Nat. Blood Transfusion Service, 1944–45; Med. Off., Galton Lab. Serum Unit, Cambridge, 1945–46; Dir, Blood Gp Reference Lab., Min. of Health and MRC, 1946–65 (Internat. Blood Gp Reference Lab., WHO, 1952–65); Hon. Adviser, Nuffield Blood Gp Centre, 1952–65; Hon. Sen. Lectr in Haematology, St Bartholomew's Hospital Medical Coll., 1965–77. Visiting Professor: Columbia Univ., 1953; Collège de France, 1978–79. Marett Meml Lectr, Exeter Coll., Oxford, 1978. Pres., Section H (Anthropology), Brit. Assoc., 1956; Vice-Pres., Mineralogical Soc., 1971–73; Mem. Hon., Société Jersiaise (Vice-Pres., 1977–80, 1984–); Corresp. Mem., Académie des Sciences, Inscriptions et Belles-Lettres, Toulouse; Honorary Member: Internat. Soc. of Blood Transfusion; British Soc. for Haematology; Peruvian Pathological Soc.; Soc. for Study of Human Biol. (Vice-Pres., 1960–63). Past or present Mem. Ed. Bd of eight British, foreign and internat. scientific jls. Hon. Citizen, Toulouse, 1985. Oliver Meml Award, 1953; Huxley Memorial Medal, Royal Anthropological Institute, 1961; Landsteiner Meml Award, Amer. Assoc. of Blood Banks, 1973; Osler Meml Medal, Univ. of Oxford, 1980; R. H. Worth Prize, Geolog. Soc., 1982. *Publications:* The Distribution of the Human Blood Groups, 1954, (jtly) 2nd edn, 1976; (jtly) The ABO Blood Groups: Comprehensive Tables and Maps of World Distribution, 1958; (ed jtly) Man and Cattle, 1963; (jtly) Blood Groups and Diseases, 1978; (jtly) The Genetics of the Jews, 1978; Blood Relations, 1983; numerous papers in scientific jls on blood groups and other biol subjects, geology and archæology. *Recreations:* photography, geology, archæology, travel, reading in sciences other than own, alpine gardening. *Address:* The Dower House, Maison de Haut, Longueville, St Saviour, Jersey, Channel Islands. *T:* Jersey 52280.

MOVERLEY, Rt. Rev. Gerald; *see* Hallam, Bishop of, (RC).

MOWAT, John Stuart; Sheriff of Glasgow and Strathkelvin (formerly Lanark and Glasgow), since 1974; *b* 30 Jan. 1923; *s* of George Mowat and Annie Barlow; *m* 1956, Anne Cameron Renfrew; two *s* two *d*. *Educ:* Glasgow High Sch.; Belmont House; Merchiston Castle Sch.; Glasgow Univ. (MA, LLB). Served RAF Transport Comd, 1941–46; Flt-Lt 1944. Journalist, 1947–52; Advocate, 1952; Sheriff-Substitute, then Sheriff, of Fife and Kinross at Dunfermline, 1960–72; Sheriff of Fife and Kinross at Cupar and Kinross, 1972–74. Contested (L) Caithness and Sutherland, 1955; Office-bearer, Scottish Liberal Party, 1954–58; Life Trustee: Carnegie Dunfermline Trust, 1967–73; Carnegie UK Trust, 1971–73. *Recreations:* golf, curling, watching football. *Address:* 31 Westbourne Gardens, Glasgow G12 9PF. *T:* 041-334 3743.

MOWBRAY (26th Baron *cr* 1283), **SEGRAVE** (27th Baron *cr* 1283), **AND STOURTON,** of Stourton, Co. Wilts (23rd Baron *cr* 1448); **Charles Edward Stourton,** CBE 1982; *b* 11 March 1923; *s* of William Marmaduke Stourton, 25th Baron Mowbray, 26th Baron Segrave and 22nd Baron Stourton, MC, and Sheila (*d* 1975), *er d* of Hon. Edward Gully, CB; *S* father, 1965; *m* 1952, Hon. Jane de Yarburgh Bateson, *o c* of 5th Baron Deramore, and of Nina Lady Deramore, OBE, *d* of Alastair Macpherson-Grant; two *s*. *Educ:* Ampleforth; Christ Church, Oxford. Joined Army, 1942; Commissioned Gren. Guards, 1943; served with 2nd Armd Bn Gren. Gds, as Lt, 1943–44 (wounded, France, 1944; loss of eye and invalided, 1945). Mem. of Lloyd's 1952; Mem. Securicor, 1961–64; Director: Securicor (Scotland) Ltd, 1964–70; Economic International Resources Corporation Ltd, Jersey, 1980–; GDC Ltd, Ghana, 1980–; EIRC, Ghana, Ltd, 1982–; EIRC (Suisse) SA, 1983–; EIRC, Canada, Inc., 1983–. Mem., Nidderdale RDC, 1954–58. A Conservative Whip in House of Lords, 1967–70, 1974–78; a Lord in Waiting (Govt Whip), and spokesman for DoE, 1970–74; Dep. Chief Opposition Whip in House of Lords, 1978–79; a Lord in Waiting (Govt Whip), and spokesman for the arts, envt and transport, 1979–80. Chm., Govt Picture Buying Cttee, 1972–74; Trustee, College of Arms Trust, 1975–. Chancellor, Primrose League, 1974–80, 1981–. Hon. Pres., Safety Glazing Assoc., 1975–78. Bicentennial Year Award of Baronial Order of Magna Charta, USA, 1976. Kt of Hon. and Devotion, SMO Malta, 1947; Kt Gr. Cross, Mil. Order of St Lazarus, 1970. *Recreations:* reading, shooting, gardening. *Heir: s* Hon. Edward William Stephen Stourton [*b* 17 April 1953; *m* 1980, Penelope, *e d* of Dr Peter Brunet; two *d*]. *Address:* Marcus, by Forfar, Angus DD8 3QH. *T:* Finavon 219; 23 Warwick Square, SW1V 2AB. *Clubs:* Turf, White's, Pratt's, Beefsteak, Pilgrims.
See also F. P. Crowder, Hon. J. J. Stourton.

MOWBRAY, Sir John, Kt 1983; Chairman: Development Finance Corporation of New Zealand, since 1976; Motor Holdings Ltd, since 1978; GEC New Zealand Ltd, since 1976; DIC Ltd, since 1982; *b* 23 Sept. 1916; *s* of Harry Logan Campbell Mowbray and Therese Josephine Mowbray; *m* 1946, Audrey Burt Steel; two *s* one *d*. *Educ:* King's Coll., Auckland; Auckland University Coll. BCom, Dip. in Banking, Univ. of NZ; FCA NZ 1973. Served War, 2nd NZ Div. Field Artillery, ME, 1940–46 (Lieut). Joined staff of The National Bank of New Zealand, 1934; Gen. Man.'s Asst, 1957; Asst Gen. Man., 1961; Gen. Man. and Chief Exec., 1966–76. Chairman: NZ Bankers' Assoc., 1966, 1972 and 1975; Higher Salaries Cttee in the State Services, 1972–78; Bd of Trustees, NZ Inst. of Econ. Res., 1978–; formerly Chairman: Japan/NZ Businessmen's Conf.; NZ Cttee, Pacific Basin Econ. Council; Life Member: NZ Admin. Staff Coll. (formerly Chm.); Arthritis and Rheumatism Foundn of NZ. FNZIM 1974; Hon. Fellow, NZ Inst. of Bankers, 1975; FRSA 1970. *Recreations:* golf, bridge, gardening. *Address:* 167 Karori Road, Karori, Wellington 5, New Zealand. *T:* 766–334. *Clubs:* Wellington, United Services Officers (Wellington); Northern (Auckland); Wellington Golf.

MOWBRAY, Sir John Robert, 6th Bt *cr* 1880; *b* 1 March 1932; *s* of Sir George Robert Mowbray, 5th Bt, KBE, and of Diana Margaret, *d* of Sir Robert Heywood Hughes, 12th Bt; *S* father, 1969; *m* 1957, Lavinia Mary, *d* of late Lt-Col Francis Edgar Hugonin, OBE, Stainton House, Stainton in Cleveland, Yorks; three *d*. *Educ:* Eton; New College, Oxford. *Address:* Hunts Park, Great Thurlow, Suffolk. *T:* Thurlow 232.

MOWBRAY, William John, QC 1974; *b* 3 Sept. 1928; *s* of James Nathan Mowbray, sugar manufr and E. Ethel Mowbray; *m* 1960, Shirley Mary Neilan; one *s* three *d*. *Educ:* Upper Canada Coll.; Mill Hill Sch.; New Coll., Oxford. BA 1952. Called to Bar, Lincoln's Inn, 1953 (Bencher, 1983); called to Bahamian Bar, 1971. Chairman: Chancery Bar Assoc., 1985–; Westminster Assoc. for Mental Health, 1981–; Westminster Christian Council, 1986 (Vice-Chm., 1984–85). *Publications:* Lewin on Trusts, 16th edn, 1964; Estate Duty on Settled Property, 1969; articles in jls. *Recreations:* music, observing nature in Sussex garden. *Address:* 12 New Square, Lincoln's Inn, WC2A 3SW. *T:* 01–405 3808/9, 01–405 0988/9. *Club:* Travellers'.

MOWER, Brian Leonard; Director of Information, Home Office, since 1982; *b* 24 Aug. 1934; *s* of Samuel William and Nellie Elizabeth Rachel Mower; *m* 1960, Margaret Ann Wildman; one *s* one *d*. *Educ:* Hemel Hempstead Grammar Sch. Royal Air Force, 1954–56. Executive, Service Advertising Co., 1956–66; entered Civil Service, Sen. Information Officer, HM Treasury, 1966; Principal Information Officer, Central Statistical Office, 1969; Dep. Head of Information, HM Treasury, 1978; Head of Information, Dept of Employment, 1980; Dep. Press Sec. to Prime Minister, 1982. *Recreations:* bridge, walking. *Address:* 34 Wrensfield, Hemel Hempstead, Herts HP1 1RP. *T:* Hemel Hempstead 52277.

MOWLL, Christopher Martyn; Clerk to The Clothworkers' Company of the City of London and Secretary to The Clothworkers' Foundation, since 1978; *b* 14 Aug. 1932; *s* of late Christopher Kilvinton Mowll and Doris Ellen (*née* Hutchinson) *m* 1958, Margaret Frances (*née* Laird); four *s*. *Educ:* Epsom Coll.; Gonville and Caius Coll., Cambridge (MA). Admitted Solicitor, 1956. Member: Council, National Library for the Blind, 1964–79; Council, Metropolitan Society for the Blind, 1964– (Treas., 1965–79; Vice-Chm., 1971–79; Chm., 1979–); Exec. Council, RNIB, 1982–; Britain-Australia Bicentennial Cttee, 1984–. *Address:* Clothworkers' Hall, Dunster Court, Mincing Lane, EC3R 7AH. *T:* 01–623 7041.

MOXON, Prof. (Edward) Richard; Professor and Head of the Department of Paediatrics, University of Oxford, since 1984; *b* 16 July 1941; *s* of late Gerald Richard Moxon and of Margaret Forster Mohun; *m* 1973, Marianne Graham; one *s* one *d*. *Educ:* Shrewsbury Sch.; St John's Coll., Cambridge (BA 1963; MB, BChir 1966). MA Oxon 1984. FRCP 1984 (MRCP 1968). House Physician, Peace Meml Hosp., Watford, 1966; Sen. House Officer and Res. Pathologist, St Thomas' Hosp., 1967; Sen. House Officer in Paediatrics: Whittington Hosp., 1968; Hosp. for Sick Children, Gt Ormond St, 1969; Children's Hosp. Medical Center, Boston, Mass, USA: Asst Resident in Pediatrics, 1970; Res. Fellow in Infectious Diseases Div., 1971–74; Johns Hopkins Hosp., Baltimore, Md, USA: Asst Prof. in Paediatrics, 1974–80; Associate Prof. in Paediatrics, 1980–84; Chief, Eudowood Div. of Paediatric Infectious Diseases, 1982–84. *Publications:* (contrib.) Barnett's Textbook of Paediatrics; (contrib.) Mandell's Textbook of Principles and Practice of Infectious Diseases, 2nd edn, 1984; articles in Jl of Infectious Diseases, Proc. National Acad. of Sciences, and Lancet. *Recreations:* squash, tennis, music, literature. *Address:* 17 Moreton Road, Oxford OX2 7AX. *T:* Oxford 55344.

MOYA, (John) Hidalgo, CBE 1966; RIBA 1956; architect; *b* Los Gatos, Calif, 5 May 1920; *s* of Hidalgo Moya; *m* 1947, Janiffer Innes Mary Hall; one *s* two *d*. *Educ:* Oundle Sch.; Royal West of England Coll. of Art; AA Sch. of Architecture; AA Dip., 1943. Partner, Powell and Moya, 1946, Powell Moya and Partners, 1976–. Major works include: Churchill Gardens Flats, Westminster, 1948–62; Houses at Chichester, 1950; Toys Hill, 1954; Mayfield Sch., Putney, 1955; Plumstead Manor Sch., Woolwich, 1970; Chichester Festival Theatre, 1962; Public Swimming Baths, Putney, 1967; British Nat. Pavilion, Expo 1970, Osaka; Dining Rooms, Bath Acad. of Art, 1970, Eton Coll., 1974; Psychiatric Hosp. extensions at Fairmile, 1957 and Borocourt, 1965; Brasenose Coll., 1961 and Corpus Christi Coll., 1969, Oxford extensions; Christ Church Coll., Oxford Picture Gall. and undergraduate rooms, 1967; St. John's Coll., 1967 and Queens' Coll.,

1978, Cambridge, new buildings; Wolfson Coll., Oxford, 1974; General Hosps at Swindon, Slough, High Wycombe, Wythenshawe, Woolwich and Maidstone; new headquarters for London & Manchester Assurance Co., near Exeter, 1978; extensions for Schools for Advanced Urban Studies and of Extra Mural Studies, Univ. of Bristol, 1980; Nat. West. Bank, Shaftesbury Ave, London, 1982. Pimlico Housing Scheme, Winning Design in Open Competition, 1946; Skylon, Festival of Britain Winning Design, 1950 (Award, 1951); Mohlg Good Design in Housing Award, 1954; RIBA Bronze Medal, 1958, 1961 (Bucks, Berks, Oxon); Civic Trust Awards (Class I and II), 1961; Architectural Design Project Award, 1965; RIBA Architectural Award, (London and SE Regions), 1967; Royal Gold Medal for Architecture, RIBA, 1974. *Address:* Powell, Moya and Partners, Architects, 21 Upper Cheyne Row, SW3 5JW. *T:* 01-351 3882.

MOYERS, Bill D., BJ, BD; journalist; Senior News Analyst, CBS Evening News, since 1981; *b* 5 June 1934; *s* of John Henry Moyers and Ruby Moyers (*née* Johnson); *m* 1954, Judith Suzanne Davidson; two *s* one *d*. *Educ:* High Sch., Marshall, Texas; Univ. of Texas; Univ. of Edinburgh; Southwestern Theological Seminary. BJ 1956; BD 1959. Personal Asst to Senator Lyndon B. Johnson, 1959–60; Executive Asst, 1960; US Peace Corps: Associate Dir, 1961–63; Dep. Dir, 1963. Special Asst to President Johnson, 1963–66; Press Sec., 1965–67; Publisher of Newsday, Long Island, 1967–70; Exec. Ed., Bill Moyers' Jl, Public Broadcasting Service, 1971–76, 1978–81; editor and chief reporter, CBS Reports, 1976–79. Contributing Editor, Newsweek Magazine. Eleven Emmy Awards, incl. most outstanding broadcaster, 1974; Lowell Medal, 1975; ABA Gavel Award for distinguished service to American system of law, 1974; ABA Cert. of Merit, 1975; Peabody Award, 1977; Awards for The Fire Next Door: Monte Carlo TV Festival Grand Prize, Jurors Prize and Nymph Award, 1977; Robert F. Kennedy Journalism Grand Prize, 1978; Christopher Award, 1978; Sidney Hillman Prize for Distinguished Service, 1978, 1981; Distinguished Urban Journalism Award, Nat. Urban Coalition, 1978; George Polk Award, 1981; Columbia—Du Pont Award, 1981; Peabody Award, 1981, 1986; Overseas Press Award, 1986. *Publication:* Listening to America, 1971. *Address:* 76 Fourth Street, Garden City, Long Island, New York 11530, USA.

MOYES, Lt-Comdr Kenneth Jack, MBE (mil.) 1960; RN retd; Under-Secretary, Department of Health and Social Security, 1975–78; *b* 13 June 1918; *s* of Charles Wilfrid and Daisy Hilda Moyes; *m* 1943, Norma Ellen Outred Hillier; one *s* two *d*. *Educ:* Portsmouth Northern Grammar Sch. FCIS. Royal Navy, 1939–63. Principal, Dept of Health and Social Security, 1963; Asst Secretary, 1970. *Recreations:* gardening, tennis, squash, bridge. *Address:* Garden House, Darwin Road, Birchington, Kent CT7 9JL. *T:* Thanet 42015.

MOYLAN, John David FitzGerald; His Honour Judge Moylan; a Circuit Judge (formerly Judge of the County Courts), since 1967; *b* 8 Oct. 1915; *s* of late Sir John FitzGerald Moylan, CB, CBE, and late Lady Moylan (*née* FitzGerald); *m* 1946, Jean, *d* of late F. C. Marno-Edwards, Lavenham, Suffolk; one *s* two *d*. *Educ:* Charterhouse; Christ Church, Oxford. Served War of 1939–45, with Royal Marines. Inner Temple, 1946; practised on the Western Circuit. *Recreations:* travel and music. *Address:* Ufford Hall, Fressingfield, Diss, Norfolk IP21 5TA.

MOYLE, Rt. Hon. Roland (Dunstan); PC 1978; barrister-at-law; Joint Deputy Chairman, Police Complaints Authority, since 1985; *b* 12 March 1928; *s* of late Baron Moyle, CBE; *m* 1956, Shelagh Patricia Hogan; one *s* one *d*. *Educ:* Infants' and Jun. Elem. Schs, Bexleyheath, Kent; County Sch., Llanidloes, Mont.; UCW Aberystwyth (LLB); Trinity Hall, Cambridge (MA, LLM). Called to the Bar, Gray's Inn, 1954. Commnd in Royal Welch Fusiliers, 1949–51. Legal Dept, Wales Gas Bd, 1953–56; Industrial Relations Executive with Gas Industry, 1956–62, and Electricity Supply Industry, 1962–66. MP (Lab) Lewisham N, 1966–74, Lewisham E, 1974–83; PPS to Chief Secretary to the Treasury, 1966–69, to Home Secretary, 1969–70; opposition spokesman on higher educn and science, 1972–74; Parly Sec., MAFF, 1974; Min. of State, NI Dept, 1974–76; Min. of State for the Health Service, 1976–79; opposition spokesman on health, 1979–80; deputy foreign affairs spokesman, 1980–83; opposition spokesman on defence and disarmament, 1983. Mem., Select Cttee on Race Relations and Immigration, 1968–72; Vice-Chm., PLP Defence Group, 1968–72; Sec., 1971–74, Mem. Exec. Cttee, 1968–83, British Amer. Parly Gp. *Recreations:* gardening, motoring, swimming, reading. *Address:* 19 Montpelier Row, Blackheath, SE3 0RL.

MOYNE, 2nd Baron, *cr* 1932, of Bury St Edmunds; **Bryan Walter Guinness,** MA; FRSL; poet, novelist and playwright; Vice-Chairman of Arthur Guinness, Son and Co., 1949–79, retired (Director, 1934–79); Trustee: Iveagh (Housing) Trust, Dublin; Guinness (Housing) Trust, London; Barrister-at-Law; *b* 27 Oct. 1905; *e s* of 1st Baron Moyne (3rd *s* of 1st Earl of Iveagh) and Lady Evelyn Erskine (*d* 1939), 3rd *d* of 14th Earl of Buchan; *S* father 1944; *m* 1st, 1929, Diana Freeman-Mitford (marr. diss. 1934); two *s*; 2nd, 1936, Elisabeth Nelson; three *s* five *d* (and one *s* decd). *Educ:* Eton; Christ Church, Oxford. Called to Bar, 1930. Capt., Royal Sussex Regiment, 1943. A Governor National Gallery of Ireland, 1955; Mem., Irish Acad. of Letters, 1968. Hon. FTCD 1979. Hon. LLD: TCD, 1958; NUI, 1961. *Publications:* (as Bryan Guinness): 23 Poems, 1931; Singing out of Tune, 1933; Landscape with Figures, 1934; Under the Eyelid, 1935; Johnny and Jemima, 1936; A Week by the Sea, 1936; Lady Crushwell's Companion, 1938; The Children in the Desert, 1947; Reflexions, 1947; The Animals' Breakfast, 1950; Story of a Nutcracker, 1953; Collected Poems, 1956; A Fugue of Cinderellas, 1956; Catriona and the Grasshopper, 1957; Priscilla and the Prawn, 1960; Leo and Rosabelle, 1961; The Giant's Eye, 1964; The Rose in the Tree, 1964; The Girl with the Flower, 1966; The Engagement, 1969; The Clock, 1973; Dairy Not Kept, 1975; Hellenic Flirtation, 1978; Potpourri from the Thirties, 1982; Personal Patchwork, 1986; *plays:* The Fragrant Concubine, 1938; A Riverside Charade, 1954. *Recreation:* travelling. *Heir:* *s* Hon. Jonathan Bryan Guinness, *qv*. *Address:* Biddesden House, Andover, Hants. *T:* Andover 790237; Knockmaroon, Castleknock, Co. Dublin. *Clubs:* Athenæum, Carlton; Kildare Street and University (Dublin).

See also Hon. D. W. Guinness.

MOYNIHAN, family name of **Baron Moynihan.**

MOYNIHAN, 3rd Baron, *cr* 1929; **Antony Patrick Andrew Cairnes Berkeley Moynihan;** Bt 1922; *b* 2 Feb. 1936; *s* of 2nd Baron Moynihan, OBE, TD, and of Ierne Helen Candy; *S* father 1965; *m* 1st, 1955, Ann Herbert (marr. diss., 1958); 2nd, 1958, Shirin Roshan Berry (marr. diss., 1967); one *d*; 3rd, 1968, Luthgarda Maria Fernandez (marr. diss. 1979); three *d*; 4th, Editha. *Educ:* Stowe. Late 2nd Lt Coldstream Guards. *Recreation:* dog breeding. *Heir:* *half-b* Hon. Colin Berkeley Moynihan, *qv*.

MOYNIHAN, Hon. Colin Berkeley; MP (C) Lewisham East, since 1983; Vice-Chairman, Ridgways Tea and Coffee Merchants, since 1983 (Chief Executive, 1982–83); *b* 13 Sept. 1955; *s* of 2nd Baron Moynihan, OBE, TD, and of June Elizabeth (who *m* 1965, N. B. Hayman), *d* of Arthur Stanley Hopkins; *half-brother* and *heir* of 3rd Baron Moynihan, *qv*. *Educ:* Monmouth Sch. (Music Scholar); University Coll., Oxford (BA PPE 1977, MA 1982). Pres., Oxford Union Soc., 1976. Personal Asst to Chm., Tate & Lyle Ltd, 1978–80; Manager, Tate & Lyle Agribusiness, resp. for marketing strategy and develt finance, 1980–82; external consultant, Tate & Lyle PLC, 1983–. Director: Corporate Pensions Analysts, 1986; Demerger Corp. PLC. Political Asst to the Foreign Sec., 1983; PPS to Minister of Health, 1985, to Paymaster General, 1985–. Chm., All-Party Parly Gp on Afghanistan, 1986; Vice Chm., Cons. Food and Drinks Sub-Cttee, 1983–85; Sec. Cons. Foreign and Commonwealth Affairs Cttee, 1983–85. Member: Paddington Conservative Management Cttee, 1980–81; Bow Group, 1978– (Mem., Industry Cttee, 1978–79; Chm. Trade & Industry Standing Cttee, 1983–). Hon. Sec., Friends of British Council. Patron, Land & City Families Trust. Gov., Feltonfleet Sch. Member: Sports Council, 1982–85; Major Spectator Sports Cttee, CCPR, 1979–82; CCPR Enquiry into Sponsorship of Sport, 1982–83; Steward, British Boxing Bd of Control, 1979–; Trustee: Oxford Univ. Boat Club, 1980–; Sports Aid Trust, 1983–; Governor, Sports Aid Foundn (London and SE), 1980–82. Oxford Double Blue, Rowing and Boxing, 1976 and 1977; World Gold Medal for Lightweight Rowing, Internat. Rowing Fedn, 1978; Olympic Silver Medal for Rowing, 1980; World Silver Medal for Rowing, 1981. Freeman, City of London, 1978; Liveryman, Worshipful Co. of Haberdashers, 1981. *Recreations:* reading The Economist, collecting Nonesuch Books, music, sport. *Address:* Flat 42, Buckingham Court, Buckingham Gate, SW1. *Clubs:* Brooks's, Royal Commonwealth Society (Mem. Council, 1980–82); Royal Mid-Surrey (Richmond); Vincent's (Oxford).

MOYNIHAN, Senator Daniel Patrick; US Senator from New York State, since 1977; *b* Tulsa, Oklahoma, 16 March 1927; *s* of John Henry and Margaret Ann Phipps Moynihan; *m* 1955, Elizabeth Therese Brennan; two *s* one *d*. *Educ:* City Coll., NY; Tufts Univ.; Fletcher Sch. of Law and Diplomacy. MA, PhD. Gunnery Officer, US Navy, 1944–47. Dir of Public Relations, Internat. Rescue Commn, 1954; successively Asst to Sec., Asst Sec., Acting Sec., to Governor of NY State, 1955–58; Mem., NY Tenure Commn, 1959–60; Dir, NY State Govt Res. Project, Syracuse Univ., 1959–61; Special Asst to Sec. of Labor, 1961–62; Exec. Asst to Sec., 1962–63, Asst Sec. of Labor, 1963–65; Dir, Jt Center Urban Studies, MIT and Harvard Univ., 1966–69; Prof. of Govt, 1972–77 and Senior Mem., 1966–77, Harvard (Prof. of Education and Urban Politics, 1966–73). Asst to Pres. of USA for Urban Affairs, 1969–70; Counsellor to Pres. (with Cabinet rank), 1969–70; Consultant to Pres., 1971–73; US Ambassador to India, 1973–75; US Permanent Rep. to the UN and Mem. of Cabinet, 1975–76. Democratic Candidate for the Senate, NY, 1976. Mem., US delegn 26th Gen. Assembly, UN, 1971. Fellow, Amer. Acad. Arts and Scis; Member: Amer. Philosophical Soc.; AAAS (formerly Vice-Pres.); Nat. Acad. Public Admin; President's Sci. Adv. Cttee, 1971–73. Hon. Fellow, London Sch. of Economics, 1970. Holds numerous hon. degrees. Britannica Award, 1986. *Publications:* (co-author) Beyond the Melting Pot, 1963; (ed) The Defenses of Freedom, 1966; (ed) On Understanding Poverty, 1969; Maximum Feasible Misunderstanding, 1969; (ed) Toward a National Urban Policy, 1970; (jt ed) On Equality of Educational Opportunity, 1972, The Politics of a Guaranteed Income, 1973; Coping: On the Practice of Government, 1974; (jt ed) Ethnicity: Theory and Experience, 1975; A Dangerous Place, 1979; Counting Our Blessings, 1980; Loyalties, 1984; Family and Nation, 1986. *Address:* Senate Office Building, Washington, DC 20510, USA. *Clubs:* Century, Harvard (NYC); Federal City (Washington).

MOYNIHAN, Martin John, CMG 1972; MC; HM Diplomatic Service, retired; *b* 17 Feb. 1916; *e s* of late William John Moynihan and Phoebe Alexander; *m* 1946, Monica Hopwood; one *s* one *d*. *Educ:* Birkenhead Sch.; Magdalen Coll., Oxford (MA). India Office, 1939. War of 1939–45: Indian Army, 1940; QVO Corps of Guides; served with Punjab Frontier Force Regt, N-W Frontier and Burma (MC); Commonwealth Service: Delhi, Madras, Bombay and London, 1946–54; Deputy High Commissioner: Peshawar, 1954–56; Lahore, 1956–58; Kuala Lumpur, 1961–63; Port of Spain, 1964–66; HM Consul-General, Philadelphia, 1966–70; Ambassador to Liberia, 1970–73; High Comr in Lesotho, 1973–76. Administering Officer, Kennedy Meml Trust, 1977–79. Member: Council, Hakluyt Soc., 1976–81 and 1985–; Charles Williams Soc., 1977; Pres., Lesotho Diocesan Assoc., 1976–83. Fellow: Internat. Scotist Congress, Padua, 1976; Internat. Arthurian Congress, Regensburg, 1979; inaugural session of Inklings-Gesellschaft, Aachen, 1983; Associate Mem. in S African Studies, Clare Hall, Cambridge, 1977–78. Hon. Knight Grand Band of Humane Order of African Redemption (Liberia), 1973. *Publications:* The Strangers, 1946; South of Fort Hertz, 1956. *Address:* The Gatehouse, 5 The Green, Wimbledon Common, SW19 5AZ. *T:* 01–946 7964. *Clubs:* Athenæum, Travellers'.

MOYNIHAN, Sir Noël (Henry), Kt 1979; MA, MB, BCh; FRCGP; *b* 24 Dec. 1916; *o s* of Dr Edward B. Moynihan and Ellen (*née* Shea), Cork, Ireland; *m* 1941, Margaret Mary Lovelace, JP, *d* of William John Lovelace, barrister-at-law, and Mary Lovelace, JP, Claygate, Surrey; two *s* two *d*. *Educ:* Ratcliffe; Downing Coll., Cambridge (BA English Tripos 1940, MA 1946; Pres., Downing Coll. Assoc., 1985–; Associate Fellow, 1986–) (represented Cambridge in athletics (mile) and cross country, v Oxford, 1939, 1940); MB 1956, BChir 1955 London; MRCS, LRCP 1954, MRCGP 1965, FRCGP 1981. Served War, RAF, Sqdn Ldr, 1940–46 (despatches twice). Medically qual., St Thomas' Hosp., 1954; Newsholme Public Health Prize, 1954; Sutton Sams Prize (Obstet. and Gynaecol.), 1954. Upjohn Travelling Fellow, RCGP, 1967; Leverhulme Travelling Res. Fellow, 1974. Co-Founder, Med. Council on Alcoholism, 1963 (Mem. Council, 1963–79; Hon. Vice-Pres., 1972–85); Mem. Bd, S London Faculty, RCGP, 1958–73; Chm., Public Relations and Fund Raising Cttee, African Med. and Res. Foundn, 1959–64; President: Harveian Soc. of London, 1967 (Mem. Council, 1963–68, 1978–79); Chelsea Clinical Soc., 1978 (Mem. Council, 1969–78); Mem. Council, 1972–86, Vice-Chm., 1972–77, Chm., 1977–82, Save the Children Fund; Hon. Sec., Council, 1981–82, Vice-Pres., 1982–85, Med. Soc. of London. Mem. Exec. Cttee, St Francis Leper Guild, 1964–85 (Vice-Pres., 1981). Mem. Bd, Royal Med. Benevolent Fund, 1973–77. Editor, St Thomas' Hosp. Gazette, 1952–54. Mem., Inner Temple, 1948; Yeoman, Worshipful Soc. of Apothecaries, 1956, Liveryman, 1959; Mem., Cttee of Liverymen, 1984–; Freeman, City of London, 1959. CStJ 1971; Kt SMO Malta 1958 (Officer of Merit, 1964; Comdr of Merit, 1979); KSG 1966. *Publications:* The Light in the West, 1978; Rock Art of the Sahara, 1979; contribs to med. jls, 1953–78. *Recreations:* Save The Children Fund, rock art of the Sahara. *Address:* 25–27 Sloane Court West, Chelsea, SW3 4TD. *T:* 01–730 1828; Herstmonceux Place, Flowers Green, near Hailsham, East Sussex. *T:* Herstmonceux 832017. *Clubs:* Brooks's, Carlton, MCC; Hawks (Cambridge), Achilles.

MOYNIHAN, Rodrigo, CBE 1953, RA 1954 (ARA 1944); artist; lately Professor of Painting at the Royal College of Art; *b* 17 Oct. 1910; *s* of Herbert James Moynihan and late Maria de la Puerta; *m* 1931, Elinor Bellingham Smith; one *s*; *m* 1960, Anne, *d* of Sir James Hamet Dunn, 1st Bt; one *s*. *Educ:* UCS, London, and in USA. Slade Sch., 1928–31; Mem. of London Group, 1933; one-man shows at: Redfern Gall., 1940, 1958, 1961; Leicester Gallery, 1946; Hanover Gallery, 1963, 1967; Fischer Fine Art, 1973, 1982; Royal Academy (major retrospective), 1978; Galerie Claude Bernard, Paris, 1984; New York: Egan Gallery, 1966; Tibor de Nagy, 1968; Robert Miller Gall., 1980, 1983. Vis. Prof., Slade Sch., 1980–84. Army Service, 1940–43; Official War Artist, 1943–44. Pictures purchased by Chantrey Bequest, Tate Gallery, Contemporary Art Soc., War Artists' Advisory Cttee, Nat. Portrait Gallery, Hirschhorn Coll., Washington. Hon. Dr RCA 1969; Fellow UCL, 1970–. Editor (jtly with wife), Art and Literature, 1963–68.

Publication: Goya, 1951. *Address*: c/o Royal Academy, Piccadilly, W1V 0DS. *Club*: Buck's.

MOYOLA, Baron *cr* 1971 (Life Peer), of Castledawson; **James Dawson Chichester-Clark,** PC (Northern Ireland) 1966; DL; *b* 12 Feb. 1923; *s* of late Capt. J. L. C. Chichester-Clark, DSO and bar, DL, MP, and Mrs C. E. Brackenbury; *m* 1959, Moyra Maud Haughton (*née* Morris); two *d* one step *s*. *Educ*: Eton. Entered Army, 1942; 2nd Lieut Irish Guards, Dec. 1942; wounded, Italy, 1944; ADC to Governor-General of Canada (Field-Marshal Earl Alexander of Tunis), 1947–49; attended Staff Coll., Camberley, 1956; retired as Major, 1960. MP (U), S Derry, NI Parlt, 1960–72; Asst Whip, March 1963; Chief Whip, 1963–67; Leader of the House, 1966–67; Min. of Agriculture, 1967–69; Prime Minister, 1969–71. DL Co. Derry, 1954. *Recreations*: shooting, fishing, ski-ing. *Address*: Moyola Park, Castledawson, Co. Derry, N Ireland.
See also Sir R. Chichester-Clark.

MPUCHANE, Samuel Akuna; Permanent Secretary for External Affairs, Botswana, since 1986; *b* 15 Dec. 1943; *s* of Chiminya Thompson Mpuchane and Motshidiemang Phologolo; *m* Sisai Felicity Mokgokong; two *s* one *d*. *Educ*: Univ. of Botswana, Lesotho and Swaziland (BA Govt and Hist.); Southampton Univ. (MSc Internat. Affairs). External Affairs Officer, 1969–70; First Secretary: Botswana Mission to UN, 1970–71; Botswana Embassy, Washington, 1971–74; Under Sec., External Affairs, 1974–76; on study leave, 1976–77; Dep. Perm. Sec., Min. of Mineral Resources and Water Affairs, 1977–79; Admin. Sec., Office of Pres., 1979–80; Perm. Sec., Min. of Local Govt and Lands, 1980–81; High Comr for Botswana in UK, 1982–85. *Recreations*: playing and watching tennis, watching soccer. *Address*: c/o Ministry of External Affairs, Private Bag 1, Gaborone, Botswana.

MTEKATEKA, Rt. Rev. Josiah; *b* 1903; *s* of Village Headman; *m* 1st, 1925, Maude Mwere Nambote (*d* 1940); one *s* four *d*; 2nd, 1944, Alice Monica Chitanda; six *s* two *d* (and five *c* decd). *Educ*: Likoma Island School; S Michael's Teachers' Training Coll., Likoma; St Andrew's Theological Coll., Likoma. Deacon, 1939; Priest, 1943. Asst Priest, Nkhotakota, Nyasaland Dio., 1943–45; Chiulu, Tanganyika, 1945–50; Priest, Mlangali, Tanganyika, Nyasaland Dio., 1950–52; Mlangali, SW Tanganyika Dio., 1952–60; rep. SW Tanganyika Dio. at UMCA Centenary Celebrations in England, 1957; Canon of SW Tanganyika Dio., 1959; Priest-in-charge, Manda, 1960–64, Njombe, 1964–65, SW Tanganyika Dio.; Archdeacon of Njombe, 1962–65; Suffragan Bishop, Nkhotakota, Dio. Malawi, 1965–71; Bishop of Lake Malaŵi, 1971–77. *Address*: Madimba 1, PO Box 5, Likoma Island, Malaŵi.

MUDD, (William) David; MP (C) Falmouth and Camborne, since 1970; *b* 2 June 1933; *o s* of Capt. W. N. Mudd and Mrs T. E. Mudd; *m* 1965, Helyn Irvine Smith; one *s* one *d* (and one step *d*). *Educ*: Truro Cathedral Sch. Journalist, Broadcaster, TV Commentator; work on BBC and ITV (Westward Television). Editor of The Cornish Echo, 1952; Staff Reporter: Western Morning News, 1952–53 and 1959–62; Tavistock Gazette, 1963. Mem., Tavistock UDC, 1963–65. Secretary: Conservative West Country Cttee, 1973–76; Conservative Party Fisheries Sub-Cttee, 1974–75, 1981–82. PPS, Dept of Energy, 1979–81; Mem., Transport Select Cttee, 1982–. *Publications*: Cornishmen and True, 1971; Murder in the West Country, 1975; Facets of Crime, 1975; The Innovators, 1976; Down Along Camborne and Redruth, 1978; The Falmouth Packets, 1978; Cornish Sea Lights, 1978; Cornwall and Scilly Peculiar, 1979; About the City, 1979; Home Along Falmouth and Penryn, 1980; Around and About the Roseland, 1980; The Cruel Cornish Sea, 1981; The Cornish Edwardians, 1982; Cornwall in Uproar, 1983. *Recreations*: jigsaw puzzles, boating, photography. *Address*: c/o House of Commons, SW1A 0AA. *Clubs*: Athenæum (Falmouth); Royal Cornwall Yacht (Falmouth).

MUELLER, Anne Elisabeth, CB 1980; Second Permanent Secretary, Management and Personnel Office, since 1984; *b* 15 Oct. 1930; *d* of late Herbert Constantin Mueller and Phoebe Ann Beevers; *m* 1958, James Hugh Robertson (marr. diss. 1978). *Educ*: Wakefield Girls' High Sch.; Somerville Coll., Oxford (Hon. Fellow, 1984). Entered Min. of Labour and Nat. Service, 1953; served with Orgn for European Econ. Co-op., 1955–56; Treasury, 1962; Dept of Economic Affairs, 1964; Min. of Technology, 1969; DTI 1970; Under-Sec., DTI, later DoI, 1972–77; Dep. Sec., DoI, later DTI, 1977–84. Dir, EIB, 1978–84. Mem. Bd, Business in the Community, 1984–; Mem. Council: Inst. of Manpower Studies, 1981–; Templeton Coll., Oxford, 1985–; Manchester Business Sch., 1985–; Trustee, Whitechapel Art Gall., 1985–. Hon. DLitt Warwick, 1985. *Address*: c/o Cabinet Office, Great George Street, SW1P 3AL. *T*: 01–233 5009.

MUFF, family name of **Baron Calverley.**

MUGABE, Robert Gabriel; Prime Minister, since 1980 and First Secretary of Politburo, since 1984, Zimbabwe; also Minister of Defence since 1980, Minister of Public Service, since 1981, and Minister of Industry and Technology, since 1984; President (Co-Founder, 1963), Zimbabwe African National Union (ZANU), since 1977; *b* Kutama, 1924; *m* Sarah Mugabe. *Educ*: Kutama and Empanden Mission School; Fort Hare Univ. (BA (Educ), BSc (Econ)); London Univ. (by correspondence: BSc(Econ); BEd; LLB; LLM; MSc(Econ)); Univ. of S Africa (by correspondence BAdm). Teacher, 1942–58: Kutama, Mapanzure, Shabani, Empandeni Mission, Hope Fountain Mission, Driefontein Mission, South Africa; Mbizi Govt Sch., Mambo Sch., Chalimbana Trng Coll., Zambia; St Mary's Teacher Trng Coll., Ghana. Publ. Sec. of Nat. Dem. Party, 1960–61; Publicity Sec. and acting Sec.-Gen., Zimbabwe African People's Union, 1961–62. Political detention, 1962, escaped to Tanzania, 1963; became Sec.-Gen. ZANU, Aug. 1963, but in detention in Rhodesia, 1964–74; resident in Mozambique, 1975–79. Jt Leader (with Joshua Nkomo) of the Patriotic Front, Oct. 1976. Attended Confs: Geneva Constitutional Conf. on Rhodesia, 1976; Malta Conf., 1978; London Conf., 1979. Hon. LLD Ahmadu Bello. *Address*: Office of the Prime Minister, Harare, Zimbabwe.

MUGGERIDGE, Malcolm; *b* 24 March 1903; *s* of late H. T. Muggeridge; *m* 1927, Katherine, *d* of G. C. Dobbs; two *s* one *d* (and one *s* decd). *Educ*: Selhurst Grammar Sch.; Selwyn Coll., Cambridge. Lecturer at Egyptian Univ., Cairo, 1927–30; Editorial Staff, Manchester Guardian, 1930–32; Manchester Guardian correspondent, Moscow, 1932–33; Asst Editor, Calcutta Statesman, 1934–35; Editorial staff, Evening Standard, 1935–36. Served in War of 1939–45, in East Africa, North Africa, Italy and France, Intelligence Corps, Major (Legion of Hon., Croix de Guerre with Palm, Médaille de la Reconnaissance Française). Daily Telegraph Washington Correspondent, 1946–47; Dep. Editor Daily Telegraph, 1950–52; Editor of Punch, Jan. 1953–Oct. 1957. Rector, Edinburgh Univ., 1967–68. *Television*: Muggeridge Ancient and Modern (series), 1981. *Publications*: Three Flats, produced by the Stage Society, 1931; Autumnal Face, 1931; Winter in Moscow, 1933; The Earnest Atheist, a life of Samuel Butler, 1936; In A Valley of this Restless Mind, 1938, new edn, 1978; The Thirties, 1940; edited English edn Ciano's Diary, 1947; Ciano's Papers, 1948; Affairs of the Heart, 1949; Tread Softly for you Tread on my Jokes, 1966; London à la Mode (with Paul Hogarth), 1966; Muggeridge through the Microphone (Edited by C. Ralling); Jesus Rediscovered, 1969; Something Beautiful for God, 1971; Paul: envoy extraordinary (with A. R. Vidler), 1972; Chronicles of Wasted Time (autobiog.), vol. 1, 1972, vol. 2, 1973; Malcolm's Choice, 1972; Jesus: the man who lives, 1975; A Third Testament, 1977; A Twentieth-Century Testimony, 1979; Like It Was (diaries), 1981. *Recreation*: walking. *Address*: Park Cottage, Robertsbridge, East Sussex.

MUGNOZZA, Carlo S.; *see* Scarascia-Mugnozza.

MUIR, Alec Andrew, CBE 1968; QPM 1961; DL; Chief Constable of Durham Constabulary, 1967–70; *b* 21 Aug. 1909; *s* of Dr Robert Douglas Muir, MD, and Edith Muir, The Limes, New Cross, SE14; *m* 1948, Hon. Helen (who *m* 1st, 1935, Wm Farr; marr. diss., 1948), *er d* of Baron du Parcq (*d* 1949); one *s* one *d* (and one step *s* one step *d*). *Educ*: Christ's Hosp.; Wadham Coll., Oxford (MA). Receivers' Office, Metropolitan Police, 1933; Metropolitan Police Coll., 1934; Supt, 1948; Chief Constable, Durham Co. Constabulary, 1950. DL, Co. Durham, 1964. OStJ 1957. *Recreations*: cricket, bowls, squash, sailing. *Address*: 7 Newcombe Court, 300 Woodstock Road, Oxford. *T*: Oxford 512518. *Clubs*: United Oxford & Cambridge University; County (Durham).

MUIR, Dr Alexander Laird, MD; FRCPE, FRCR; Reader in Medicine, University of Edinburgh, since 1981; Honorary Consultant Physician, Edinburgh Royal Infirmary, since 1974; Physician to the Queen in Scotland, since 1985; Honorary Physician to the Army in Scotland, since 1986; *b* 12 April 1937; *s* of Andrew Muir and Helena Bauld; *m* 1968, Berenice Barker Snelgrove, FRCR; one *s* one *d*. *Educ*: Morrisons Acad.; Fettes Coll.; Univ. of Edinburgh. MB ChB; MD 1970; FRCPE 1975 (MRCPE 1967); FRCR 1986. MO, British Antarctic Survey, 1963–65; MRC Fellow, McGill Univ., 1970–71; Consultant Physician, Manchester Royal Infirmary, 1973–74; Sen. Lectr in Medicine, Univ. of Edinburgh, 1974. Canadian MRC Vis. Scientist, Univ. of British Columbia, 1982. Mem., Admin of Radioactive Substances Adv. Cttee, 1986–. Member Editorial Board: Thorax, 1981–; British Heart Jl, 1986–. *Publications*: contribs on physiology and diseases of heart and lungs to medical books, symposia and jls. *Recreations*: gardening, reading, ski-ing, sailboarding. *Address*: 45 Cluny Drive, Edinburgh EH10 6DU. *T*: 031–447 2652. *Club*: Edinburgh University Staff (Edinburgh).

MUIR, (Charles) Augustus; author and journalist; Regimental Historian, The Royal Scots; *b* Carluke, Ontario, Canada, 15 Nov. 1892; *s* of late Rev. Walter Muir and Elizabeth Carlow; *m* Jean Murray Dow Walker (*d* 1972); *m* 1975, Mair Davies. *Educ*: George Heriot's Sch. and Edinburgh Univ.; contributor to various dailies, weeklies, and monthlies; Asst Editor and subsequently Editor, the World; served 1914–19 in Royal Scots, King's Own Scottish Borderers, and on Staff. *Publications*: The Third Warning, 1925; The Black Pavilion, 1926; The Blue Bonnet, 1926; The Shadow on the Left, 1928; The Silent Partner, 1929; Birds of the Night, 1930; Beginning the Adventure, 1932; The House of Lies, 1932; The Green Lantern, 1933; The Riddle of Garth, 1933; Scotland's Road of Romance, 1934; Raphael MD, 1935; The Crimson Crescent, 1935; Satyr Mask, 1936; The Bronze Door, 1936; The Red Carnation, 1937; The Man Who Stole the Crown Jewels, 1937; Castles in the Air, 1938; The Sands of Fear, 1939; The Intimate Thoughts of John Baxter, Bookseller, 1942; Joey and the Greenwings, 1943; Heather-Track and High Road, 1944; (ed jtly) The Saintsbury Memorial Volume, 1945; Scottish Portrait, 1948; (ed jtly) A Last Vintage: Essays by George Saintsbury, 1950; The Story of Jesus, 1953; The Fife Coal Company, 1953; (ed) How to Choose and Enjoy Wine, 1953; The History of the Shotts Iron Company, 1954; Candlelight in Avalon, A Spiritual Pilgrimage, 1954; Nairns of Kirkcaldy, 1956; 75 Years of Progress: The History of Smith's Stamping Works (Coventry) Ltd and Smith-Clayton Forge, Lincoln, 1958; The Life of the Very Rev. Dr John White, CH, 1958; The First of Foot: the History of The Royal Scots (The Royal Regiment), 1961; Andersons of Islington, The History of C. F. Anderson & Son Ltd, 1963; Churchill & Sim Ltd, 1963; Blyth, Greene, Jourdain & Co. Ltd, Merchant Bankers, 1963; The Kenyon Tradition, 1964; The History of Baker Perkins Ltd, 1968; In Blackburne Valley: The History of Bowers Mills, 1969; The History of the British Paper and Board Makers Association, 1972; The Vintner of Nazareth, a study of the early life of Christ, 1972; (with Mair Davies) A Victorian Shipowner: A Portrait of Sir Charles Cayzer Baronet, of Gartmore, 1978. *Address*: 26 Bentfield Road, Stansted-Mountfitchet, Essex. *T*: Bishops Stortford 812289. *Clubs*: Savage, Saintsbury; Royal Scots (Edinburgh).

MUIR, Frank, CBE 1980; writer and broadcaster; *b* 5 Feb. 1920; *s* of Charles James Muir and Margaret Harding; *m* 1949, Polly McIrvine; one *s* one *d*. *Educ*: Chatham House, Ramsgate; Leyton County High Sch. Served RAF, 1940–46. Wrote radio comedy-series and compered TV progs, 1946. With Denis Norden, 1947–64; collaborated for 17 years writing comedy scripts, including: (for radio): Take it from Here, 1947–58; Bedtime with Braden, 1950–54; (for TV): And so to Bentley, 1956; Whack-O,! 1958–60; The Seven Faces of Jim, 1961, and other series with Jimmy Edwards; resident in TV and radio panel-games; collaborated in film scripts, television commercials, and revues (Prince of Wales, 1951; Adelphi, 1952); joint Advisors and Consultants to BBC Television Light Entertainment Dept, 1960–64; jointly received Screenwriters Guild Award for Best Contribution to Light Entertainment, 1961; together on panel-games My Word!, 1956–, and My Music, 1967–. Asst Head of BBC Light Entertainment Gp, 1964–67; Head of Entertainment, London Weekend Television, 1968–69, resigned 1969, and reverted to being self-unemployed; resumed TV series Call My Bluff, 1970; began radio series Frank Muir Goes Into . . ., 1971; The Frank Muir Version, 1976. Pres., Johnson Soc., Lichfield, 1975–76. Rector, Univ. of St Andrews, 1977–79. (With Simon Brett) Writers' Guild Award for Best Radio Feature Script, 1973; (with Denis Norden) Variety Club of GB Award for Best Radio Personality of 1977; Radio Personality of the Year, Radio Industries Club, 1977; Sony Gold Award, 1983. Hon. LLD St Andrews, 1978; Hon. DLitt Kent, 1982. *Publications*: (with Patrick Campbell) Call My Bluff, 1972; (with Denis Norden) You Can't Have Your Kayak and Heat It, 1973; (with Denis Norden) Upon My Word!, 1974; Christmas Customs and Traditions, 1975; The Frank Muir Book: an irreverant companion to social history, 1976; What-a-Mess, 1977; (with Denis Norden) Take My Word for It, 1978; (with Simon Brett) Frank Muir Goes Into . . ., 1978; What-a-Mess the Good, 1978; (with Denis Norden) The Glums, 1979; (with Simon Brett) The Second Frank Muir Goes Into . . ., 1979; Prince What-a-Mess, 1979; Super What-a-Mess, 1980; (with Simon Brett) The Third Frank Muir Goes Into . . ., 1980; (with Simon Brett) Frank Muir on Children, 1980; (with Denis Norden) Oh, My Word!, 1980; What-a-Mess and the Cat-Next-Door, 1981; (with Simon Brett) The Fourth Frank Muir Goes Into . . ., 1981; (with Polly Muir) The Big Dipper, 1981; A Book at Bathtime, 1982; What-a-Mess in Spring, What-a-Mess in Summer, What-a-Mess in Autumn, What-a-Mess in Winter, 1982; (with Simon Brett) The Book of Comedy Sketches, 1982; What-a-Mess at the Seaside, 1983; (with Denis Norden) The Complete and Utter "My Word!" Collection, 1983; What-a-Mess goes to School, 1984; What-a-Mess has Breakfast, 1986; What-a-Mess has Lunch, 1986; What-a-Mess has Tea, 1986; What-a-Mess has Dinner, 1986. *Recreations*: book collecting, staring silently into space. *Address*: Anners, Thorpe, Egham, Surrey TW20 8UE. *T*: Chertsey 62759. *Clubs*: Garrick, Savile.

MUIR, (Isabella) Helen (Mary), CBE 1981; MA, DPhil, DSc; FRS 1977; Director, since 1977, and Head of Division of Biochemistry, since 1966, Kennedy Institute of Rheumatology, London; *b* 20 Aug. 1920; *d* of late G. B. F. Muir, ICS, and Gwladys Muir (*née* Stack). *Educ*: Downe House, Newbury; Somerville Coll., Oxford (Hon. Fellow, 1978). MA 1944, DPhil (Oxon) 1947, DSc (Oxon) 1973. Research Fellow, Dunn's Sch. of

Pathology, Oxford, 1947–48; Scientific Staff, Nat. Inst. for Med. Research, 1948–54; Empire Rheumatism Council Fellow, St Mary's Hosp., London, 1954–58; Pearl Research Fellow, St Mary's Hosp., 1959–66; Vis. Prof., Queen Elizabeth Coll., Univ. of London, 1981–. Scientific Mem. Council, Med. Research Council (first woman to serve), Oct. 1973–Sept. 1977. Member, Editorial Board: Biochemical Jl, 1964–69; Annals of the Rheumatic Diseases, 1971–. Trustee, Wellcome Trust, 1982–. Heberden Orator, London, 1976; Bunim Lectr, New Orleans, 1978. Hon. Mem., Amer. Soc. of Biological Chemists, 1982. Hon. DSc: Edinburgh, 1982; Strathclyde, 1983. Feldberg Foundn Award, 1977; Neil Hamilton Fairley Medal, RCP, 1981; Ciba Medal, Biochem. Soc., 1981; Steindler Award, Orthop. Soc., USA, 1982. *Publications:* many scientific papers, mainly on biochem. of connective tissues in reln to arthritis and inherited diseases in Biochem. Jl, Biochim. et Biophys. Acta, Nature, etc; contribs to several specialist books. *Recreations:* gardening, music, horses, natural history and science in general. *Address:* Mathilda and Terence Kennedy Institute of Rheumatology, Bute Gardens, W6 7DW. *T:* 01–748 9966.

MUIR, Jean Elizabeth, (Mrs Harry Leuckert), CBE 1984; RDI; FSIAD; Designer-Director and Co-Owner, Jean Muir Ltd, since 1967; *d* of Cyril Muir and Phyllis Coy; *m* 1955, Harry Leuckert. *Educ:* Dame Harper Sch., Bedford. Selling/sketching, Liberty & Co., 1950; Designer, Jaeger Ltd, 1956, then Jane & Jane; with Harry Leuckert as co-director, formed own company, 1966. Member: Art & Design Cttee, TEC, 1978–83; BTEC Bd for Design and Art, 1983–; Design Council, 1983–; Adv. Council, V&A Museum, 1979–83; Trustee, V&A Museum, 1984–. Awards: Dress of the Year, British Fashion Writers' Gp, 1964; Ambassador Award for Achievement, 1965; Harpers Bazaar Trophy, 1965; Maison Blanche Rex Internat. Fashion Award, New Orleans, 1967, 1968 and 1974 (also Hon. Citizen of New Orleans); Churchman's Award as Fashion Designer of the Year, 1970; Neiman Marcus Award, Dallas, Texas, 1973; British Fashion Industry Award for Services to the Industry, 1984. Hon. DLit Newcastle, 1985. RDI 1972; FRSA 1973; FSIAD 1978; Hon. Dr RCA, 1981. *Address:* 59/61 Farringdon Road, EC1M 3HD. *T:* 01–831 0691.

MUIR, John Gerald Grainger, CBE 1975; DSC 1944; bee-keeper; *b* 19 Jan. 1918; *s* of George Basil Muir, ICS and Gladys Stack; *m* 1945, Lionella Maria Terni; three *d. Educ:* Rugby Sch.; Corpus Christi Coll., Oxford (MA). Bd of Educn Studentship, 1938. RN, Norway, Medit., Channel and Germany, 1939–46. British Council: Italy, 1946–49; Asst, Leeds, 1949–50; Asst Rep., Syria, 1950–55; Representative: Arab Gulf, 1955–60; Portugal, 1960–64; Iraq, 1964–67; Dep. Controller, Educn, 1968–72; Rep., Spain, 1972–76; Controller, Overseas Div. (Europe), 1976–78, retired. *Publications:* contribs to Mariner's Mirror, Bull. SOAS, and Soc. de Geographia, Lisbon. *Recreations:* music, nautical research, sailing, travel, flowers. *Address:* c/o Lloyds Bank, 6 Pall Mall, SW1Y 5NH. *Club:* Naval.

MUIR, Sir John (Harling), 3rd Bt, *cr* 1892; TD; DL; Director, James Finlay & Co. Ltd, 1946–81 (Chairman, 1961–75); Member, Queen's Body Guard for Scotland (The Royal Company of Archers); *b* 7 Nov. 1910; *s* of James Finlay Muir (*d* 1948), Braco Castle, Perthshire, and of Charlotte Escudier, *d* of J. Harling Turner, CBE; *S* uncle 1951; *m* 1936, Elizabeth Mary, *e d* of late Frederick James Dundas, Dale Cottage, Cawthorne, near Barnsley; five *s* two *d. Educ:* Stowe. With James Finlay & Co. Ltd, in India, 1932–40. Served War of 1939–45: joined 3rd Carabiniers, Sept. 1940, Lieut; transferred 25th Dragoons, 1941, Capt.; Major, 1942; transferred RAC Depot, Poona, i/c Sqdn, 1942; transferred to Staff, HQ 109 L of C Area, Bangalore; held various Staff appointments terminating as AA and QMG with actg rank of Lt-Col; demobilised, 1946, with rank of Major. DL, Perthshire, 1966. *Recreations:* shooting, fishing, gardening. *Heir:* *s* Richard James Kay Muir [*b* 25 May 1939; *m* 1965, Susan Elizabeth (marr. diss.), *d* of G. A. Gardner, Leamington Spa; two *d*; *m* 1975, Lady Linda Mary Cole, *d* of 6th Earl of Enniskillen, *qv*; two *d*]. *Address:* Bankhead, Blair Drummond, by Stirling, Perthshire. *T:* Doune 841207. *Clubs:* Oriental; Tollygunge (Calcutta).

See also Sir G. J. Aird, Bt.

MUIR, Prof. Kenneth, FBA 1970; King Alfred Professor of English Literature, University of Liverpool, 1951–74, now Professor Emeritus; *b* 5 May 1907; *s* of Dr R. D. Muir; *m* 1936, Mary Ewen; one *s* one *d. Educ:* Epsom Coll.; St Edmund Hall, Oxford. Lectr in English, St John's Coll., York, 1930–37; Lectr in English Literature, Leeds Univ., 1937–51; Liverpool University: Public Orator, 1961–65; Dean of the Faculty of Arts, 1958–61. Visiting Professor: Univ. of Pittsburgh, 1962–63; Univ. of Connecticut, 1973; Univ. of Pennsylvania, 1977. Editor, Shakespeare Survey, 1965–80; Vice-Pres., Internat. Shakespeare Assoc., 1986–– (Chm., 1974–85). Leeds City Councillor, 1945–47, 1950–51; Chm. of Leeds Fabian Soc., 1941–46; Pres., Leeds Labour Party, 1951; Birkenhead Borough Councillor, 1954–57. FRSL 1978. Docteur de l'Université: de Rouen, 1967; de Dijon, 1976. *Publications:* The Nettle and the Flower, 1933; Jonah in the Whale, 1935; (with Sean O'Loughlin) The Voyage to Illyria, 1937; English Poetry, 1938; Collected Poems of Sir Thomas Wyatt, 1949; Arden edn Macbeth, 1951; King Lear, 1952; Elizabethan Lyrics, 1953; (ed) Wilkins' Painful Adventures of Pericles, 1953; John Milton, 1955; The Pelican Book of English Prose I, 1956; Shakespeare's Sources, 1957; (ed with F. P. Wilson) The Life and Death of Jack Straw, 1957; (ed) John Keats, 1958; Shakespeare and the Tragic Pattern, 1959; trans. Five Plays of Jean Racine, 1960; Shakespeare as Collaborator, 1960; editor Unpublished Poems by Sir Thomas Wyatt, 1961; Last Periods, 1961; (ed) U. Ellis-Fermor's Shakespeare the Dramatist, 1961; (ed) Richard II, 1963; Life and Letters of Sir Thomas Wyatt, 1963; Shakespeare: Hamlet, 1963; (ed) Shakespeare: The Comedies, 1965; Introduction to Elizabethan Literature, 1967; (ed) Othello, 1968; (ed) The Winter's Tale, 1968; (ed with Patricia Thomson) Collected Poems of Sir Thomas Wyatt, 1969; The Comedy of Manners, 1970; (ed) The Rivals, 1970; (ed) Double Falsehood, 1970; (ed with S. Schoenbaum) A New Companion to Shakespeare Studies, 1971; Shakespeare's Tragic Sequence, 1972; Shakespeare the Professional, 1973; (ed) Essays and Studies, 1974; (ed) Three Plays of Thomas Middleton, 1975; The Singularity of Shakespeare, 1977; The Sources of Shakespeare's Plays, 1977; Shakespeare's Comic Sequence, 1979; Shakespeare's Sonnets, 1979; (trans.) Four Comedies of Calderón, 1980; (ed) U. Ellis-Fermor's Shakespeare's Drama, 1980; (ed with S. Wells) Aspects of the Problem Plays, 1982; (ed with M. Allen) Shakespeare's Plays in Quarto, 1982; (ed) Troilus and Cressida, 1982; (ed with S. Wells) Aspects of King Lear, 1982; (ed with J. Halio and D. Palmer) Shakespeare: man of the theater, 1983; Shakespeare's Didactic Art, 1984; (ed) King Lear: Critical Essays, 1984; (ed) Interpretations of Shakespeare, 1985; Shakespeare: contrasts and controversies, 1985; (trans. with A. L. Mackenzie) Three Comedies of Calderón, 1985; King Lear: a critical study, 1986; Antony and Cleopatra: a critical study, 1987. *Recreations:* acting, producing plays, local government. *Address:* 6 Chetwynd Road, Oxton, Birkenhead, Merseyside. *T:* 051–652 3301.

MUIR, Sir Laurence (Macdonald), Kt 1981; VRD 1954; company director; Chairman, Canberra Development Board, since 1979; *b* 3 March 1925; *s* of Andrew Muir and Agnes Campbell Macdonald; *m* 1948, Ruth Richardson; two *s* two *d. Educ:* Yallourn State Sch.; Scotch Coll., Melbourne; Univ. of Melbourne (LLB). Served RAN, 1942–46 (Lieut); Lt-Comdr, RANR, 1949–65. Admitted Barrister and Solicitor, Supreme Court of Victoria, 1950. Sharebroker, 1949–80; Mem., Stock Exchange of Melbourne, 1960–80; Partner,

1962–80, Sen. Partner, 1976–80, Potter Partners. Director: ANZ Banking Gp, 1980–; ACI Internat. Ltd (formerly ACI Ltd), 1980–; Nat. Commercial Union Assce Co. of Aust. Ltd (formerly Commercial Union Assce Co. of Aust.), 1979–; Wormald Internat. Ltd, 1980–; Herald and Weekly Times Ltd, 1982–; ANZ Pensions Ltd, 1982–; Alcoa of Australia Ltd, 1982–; Chairman: Aust. Biomedical Corp. Ltd, 1983–; Liquid Air Australia Ltd; Elders Austral Chartering Pty Ltd. Fellow: Securities Inst. of Australia, 1962; Australian Inst. of Dirs, 1967; FAIM 1965. Chairman: John Curtin Sch. of Medical Res. Adv. Bd, 1982–; Baker Medical Res. Inst, and its Develt Council; Microsurgery Foundn; Vic. Appeals Cttee, Anti-Cancer Council; Member: Parlt House Construction Authority; Board, Alfred Hosp., Council; Gen. Motors, Aust.; L'Air Liquide Internat. Adv. Council. Trustee and Board Member: Sir Robert Menzies Meml Trust; Earthwatch Australia. Mem. Exec. Cttee, World Athletic Cup 1985; Council Mem., HRH Duke of Edinburgh's 6th Commonwealth Study Conf. (Chm., Aust. Finance Cttee). *Recreations:* gardening, fishing. *Address:* 9/5 Grand View Grove, Hawthorn, Vic 3123, Australia; Meadow End, Kyla Park, Tuross Head, NSW 2537, Australia. *Clubs:* Melbourne, Melbourne Cricket, Lawn Tennis Association of Victoria (Melbourne).

MUIR, Richard John Sutherland; HM Diplomatic Service; Foreign and Commonwealth Office, since 1985; *b* 25 Aug. 1942; *s* of John Muir and Edna (*née* Hodges); *m* 1966, Caroline Simpson; one *s* one *d. Educ:* The Stationers' Co.'s Sch.; Univ. of Reading (BA Hons). Entered HM Diplomatic Service, 1964; FO, 1964–65; MECAS, Lebanon, 1965–67; Third, then Second Sec. (Commercial), Jedda, 1967–70; Second Sec., Tunis, 1970–72; FCO, 1972–75; First Sec., Washington, 1975–79; seconded to Dept of Energy, 1979–81; First Sec., Jedda, 1981–82; Counsellor, Jedda and Dir-Gen., British Liaison Office, Riyadh, 1983–85. *Address:* c/o Foreign and Commonwealth Office, SW1.

MUIR BEDDALL, Hugh Richard; see Beddall.

MUIR MACKENZIE, Sir Alexander (Alwyne Henry Charles Brinton), 7th Bt *cr* 1805; *b* 8 Dec. 1955; *s* of Sir Robert Henry Muir Mackenzie, 6th Bt and Charmian Cecil de Vere (*d* 1962), *o d* of Col Cecil Charles Brinton; *S* father, 1970; *m* 1984, Susan Carolyn, *d* of John David Henzel Hayter. *Educ:* Eton; Trinity Coll., Cambridge. *Address:* Buckshaw House, Holwell, near Sherborne, Dorset.

MUIR WOOD, Sir Alan (Marshall), Kt 1982; FRS 1980; FEng; FICE; Consultant, Sir William Halcrow & Partners (Partner, 1964–84, Senior Partner, 1979–84); *b* 8 Aug. 1921; *s* of Edward Stephen Wood and Dorothy (*née* Webb); *m* 1943, Winifred Leyton Lanagan; three *s. Educ:* Abbotsholme Sch.; Peterhouse, Cambridge Univ. (MA; Hon. Fellow 1982). FICE 1957; Fellow, Fellowship of Engrg, 1977, a Vice-Pres., 1984–. Engr Officer, RN, 1942–46. Asst Engr, British Rail, Southern Reg., 1946–50; Res. Asst, Docks and Inland Waterways Exec., 1950–52; Asst Engr, then Sen. Engr, Sir William Halcrow & Partners, 1952–64. Principally concerned with studies and works in fields of tunnelling, geotechnics, coastal engrg, energy, roads and railways; major projects include: (Proj. Engr) Clyde Tunnel and Potters Bar railway tunnels; (Partner) Cargo Tunnel at Heathrow Airport, and Cuilfail Tunnel, Lewes; studies and works for Channel Tunnel (intermittently from 1958); Dir, Orange-Fish Consultants, resp. for 80 km irrigation tunnel. Mem., SERC, 1981–84. Member: Adv. Council on Applied R & D, 1980–84; Governing Body, Inst. of Development Studies, 1981–; Council, ITDG, 1981–84. Mem. Council, Royal Soc., 1983–84, a Vice-Pres., 1983–84; President: (first), Internat. Tunnelling Assoc., 1975–77; ICE, 1977–78. Fellow, Imperial Coll., 1981; Foreign Fellow, Royal Swedish Acad. of Engrg Sci., 1980; Hon. Fellow, Portsmouth Polytech., 1984. Hon. DSc: City, 1978; Southampton, 1986; Hon. LLD Dundee, 1985. Telford Medal, ICE, 1976; James Alfred Ewing Medal, ICE and Royal Soc., 1984. *Publications:* Coastal Hydraulics, 1969, (with C. A. Fleming) 2nd edn 1981; papers, mainly on tunnelling and coastal engrg, in Proc. ICE, and Geotechnique. *Address:* Franklands, Bere Court Road, Pangbourne, Berks. *T:* Pangbourne 2833. *Club:* Athenæum.

MUIRHEAD, Sir David (Francis), KCMG 1976 (CMG 1964); CVO 1957; HM Diplomatic Service, retired; *b* 30 Dec. 1918; *s* of late David Muirhead, Kippen, Stirlingshire; *m* 1942, Hon. Elspeth Hope-Morley, *d* of 2nd Baron Hollenden, and of Hon. Mary Gardner, *d* of 1st Baron Burghclere; two *s* one *d. Educ:* Cranbrook Sch. Commissioned Artists Rifles (Rifle Brigade), 1937; passed Officers Exam., RMC Sandhurst; apptd to Bedfs and Herts Regt, 1939; served War of 1939–45 in France, Belgium and SE Asia. Hon. Attaché, Brit. Embassy, Madrid, 1941. Passed Foreign Service Exam., 1946; appointed to Foreign Office, 1947; La Paz, 1948; Buenos Aires, 1949; Brussels, 1950; Foreign Office, 1953; Washington, 1955; Foreign Office, 1959; Under-Sec., Foreign Office, 1966–67; HM Ambassador: Peru, 1967–70; Portugal, 1970–74; Belgium, 1974–78. Mem. Council, St Dunstan's, 1981–; Comr, Commonwealth War Graves Commn, 1981–86. Grand Cross, Military Order of Christ (Portugal); Grand Cross, Order of Distinguished Service (Peru). *Recreation:* tennis. *Address:* 16 Pitt Street, W8. *T:* 01–937 2443. *Club:* Travellers'.

MUIRSHIEL, 1st Viscount, *cr* 1964, of Kilmacolm; **John Scott Maclay,** KT 1973; CH 1962; CMG 1944; PC 1952; DL; Lord-Lieutenant of Renfrewshire, 1967–80; *b* 26 Oct. 1905; *s* of 1st Baron Maclay, PC; *m* 1930, Betty L'Estrange Astley (*d* 1974). *Educ:* Winchester; Trinity Coll., Cambridge. MP (Nat. L and C) for Montrose Burghs, 1940–50, for Renfrewshire West, 1950–64. Head of Brit. Merchant Shipping Mission, Washington, 1944; Parliamentary Sec., Min. of Production, May-July 1945; Minister of Transport and Civil Aviation, 1951–52; Minister of State for Colonial Affairs, Oct. 1956–Jan. 1957; Sec. of State for Scotland, Jan. 1957–July 1962. Pres., Assembly of WEU, 1955–56. Pres., National Liberal Council, 1957–67; Chm., Joint Exchequer Board for Northern Ireland, 1965–72. Dir, Clydesdale Bank, 1970–82. DL Renfrewshire, 1981. Hon. LLD: Edinburgh, 1963; Strathclyde, 1966; Glasgow, 1970. *Heir:* none. *Address:* Knapps, Kilmacolm, Renfrewshire. *T:* Kilmacolm 2770. *Clubs:* Boodle's; Western (Glasgow); Royal Yacht Squadron.

MUKHERJEE, Pranab Kumar; Member, since 1969, and Leader, since 1980, Rajya Sabha; Finance Minister, India, 1982–84; *b* 11 Dec. 1935; *s* of Kamda Kinkar Mukherjee, of an illustrious family which was involved actively in the Freedom Movement of India; *m* 1957, Suvra Mukherjee; two *s* one *d. Educ:* Vidyasagar Coll., Suri; Calcutta Univ. (MA (Hist. and Pol Sci.); LLB). Dep. Minister, Mins of Industrial Develt and of Shipping and Transport, 1973–74; Minister of State, Finance Min., 1974–77; Cabinet Minister i/c of Mins of Commerce, Steel and Mines, 1980–82; became youngest Minister to hold Finance Portfolio in Independent India, 1982. *Publications:* Crisis in Democracy; An Aspect of Constitutional Problems in Bengal, 1967; Mid-Term Poll, 1969. *Recreations:* music, gardening, reading. *Address:* 2 Jantar Mantar Road, New Delhi 110001, India. *T:* (home) 382875, 381328; (office) 372810.

MUKHERJEE, Tara Kumar, FLIA; Senior Sales Manager, Save & Prosper Group, since 1984; Branch Manager, Guardian Royal Exchange PFM Ltd, since 1985; President, Confederation of Indian Organisations (UK), since 1975; *b* 20 Dec. 1923; *s* of Sushil Chandra Mukherjee and Sova Moyee Mukherjee; *m* 1951, Betty Patricia Mukherjee; one *s* one *d. Educ:* Scottish Church Collegiate Sch., Calcutta, India; Calcutta Univ. (matriculated 1939). Shop Manager, Bata Shoe Co. Ltd, India, 1941–44; Buyer, Brevitt Shoes, Leicester,

1951–56; Sundries Buyer, British Shoe Corp., 1956–66; Prodn Administrator, Priestley Footwear Ltd, Great Harwood, 1966–68; Head Stores Manager, Brit. Shoe Corp., 1968–70; Save & Prosper Group: Dist Manager, 1970–78; Br. Manager, 1978–84. Pres., India Film Soc., Leicester. Chm., Leicester Community Centre Project; Member: Brit. Europ. Movement, London; Exec. Council, Leics Europ. Movement; Council of Management, Coronary Prevention Gp, 1986–; Trustees, Haymarket Theatre, Leicester. *Recreation:* cricket (1st Cl. cricketer; played for Bihar, Ranji Trophy, 1941; 2nd XI, Leics CCC, 1949). *Address:* Tallah, 1 Park Avenue, Hutton, Brentwood, Essex CM13 2QL. *T:* Brentwood 215438. *Club:* (Gen. Sec.) Indian National (Leicester).

MULCAHY, Geoffrey John; Chief Executive, Woolworth Holdings plc, since 1986 (Group Managing Director, 1984–86); Chairman and Chief Executive, F. W. Woolworth plc, since 1984; *b* 7 Feb. 1942; *s* of Maurice Frederick Mulcahy and Kathleen Love Mulcahy; *m* 1965, Valerie Elizabeth; one *s* one *d. Educ:* King's Sch., Worcester; Manchester Univ. (BSc); Harvard Univ. (MBA). Esso Petroleum, 1964–74; Norton Co., 1974–77; British Sugar, 1977–83; Woolworth Holdings, 1983–. *Recreations:* sailing, squash. *Address:* 75 Alleyn Road, Dulwich, SE21 8AD. *T:* 01–670 1420. *Club:* Lansdowne.

MULDOON, Rt. Hon. Sir Robert (David), GCMG 1984; CH 1977; PC 1976; MP Tamaki, since 1960; Shadow Minister of Foreign Affairs, since 1986; Prime Minister, and Minister of Finance, New Zealand, 1975–84; Leader of the National Party, 1974–84; *b* 25 Sept. 1921; *s* of James Henry and Mamie R. Muldoon; *m* 1951, Thea Dale Flyger; one *s* two *d. Educ:* Mt Albert Grammar School. FCANZ, CMANZ, FCIS, FCMA. Chartered Accountant. Pres., NZ Inst. of Cost Accountants, 1956. Parly Under-Sec. to Minister of Finance, 1963–66; Minister of Tourism, 1967; Minister of Finance, 1967–72; Dep. Prime Minister, Feb.-Nov. 1972; Dep. Leader, National Party and Dep. Leader of the Opposition, 1972–74; Leader of the Opposition, 1974–75 and 1984. Chm., Bd of Governors, IMF and World Bank, 1979–80; Chm., Ministerial Council, OECD, 1982. *Publications:* The Rise and Fall of a Young Turk, 1974; Muldoon, 1977; My Way, 1981; The New Zealand Economy: a personal view, 1985; No 38, 1986. *Recreation:* horticulture. *Address:* 7 Homewood Place, Birkenhead, Auckland 10, New Zealand. *Clubs:* Wellington, Professional (New Zealand).

MULDOWNEY, Dominic John; Music Director, National Theatre, since 1976; *b* 19 July 1952; *s* of William and Barbara Muldowney. *Educ:* Taunton's Grammar School, Southampton; York University. BA, BPhil. Composer in residence, Southern Arts Association, 1974–76; composer of chamber, choral, orchestral works, including work for theatre and TV; *music published:* Piano Concerto, 1983; The Duration of Exile, 1984; Saxophone Concerto, 1985. *Recreation:* France.

MULGRAVE, Earl of; Constantine Edmund Walter Phipps; *b* 24 Feb. 1954; *s* and *heir* of 4th Marquis of Normanby, *qv. Educ:* Eton (Oppidan Scholar); Worcester Coll., Oxford. *Publication:* Careful with the Sharks, 1985. *Address:* Mulgrave Castle, Whitby, N Yorks.

MULHOLLAND, family name of **Baron Dunleath.**

MULHOLLAND, Major Sir Michael (Henry), 2nd Bt *cr* 1945; retired; *b* 15 Oct. 1915; *s* of Rt Hon. Sir Henry George Hill Mulholland, 1st Bt, and Sheelah (*d* 1982), *d* of Sir Douglas Brooke, 4th Bt; *S* father, 1971; *cousin* and *heir-pres.* to 4th Baron Dunleath, *qv*; *m* 1st, 1942, Rosemary Ker (marr. diss. 1948); 2nd, 1949, Elizabeth, *d* of Laurence B. Hyde; one *s. Educ:* Eton; Pembroke College, Cambridge (BA). Regular Army Commission, 1937, Oxford and Bucks Light Infantry; retired, 1951, with rank of Major. *Heir: s* Brian Henry Mulholland [*b* 25 Sept. 1950; *m* 1976, Mary Joana, *y d* of Major R. J. F. Whistler; two *s* one *d*]. *Address:* Storbrooke, Massey Avenue, Belfast BT4 2JT. *T:* Belfast 63394. *Clubs:* Light Infantry (Shrewsbury); Green Jackets (Winchester).

MULKEARNS, Most Rev. Ronald Austin; *see* Ballarat, Bishop of, (RC).

MULKERN, John, FCIT; Managing Director and Member of Board, BAA plc (formerly British Airports Authority), since 1977; *b* 15 Jan. 1931; *s* of late Thomas Mulkern and Annie Tennant; *m* 1954, May Egerton (*née* Peters); one *s* three *d. Educ:* Stretford Grammar Sch. Dip. in Govt Admin. Harvard Business Sch. AMP, 1977. FCIT 1973 (Mem. Council, 1979–82). Ministries of Supply and Aviation, Civil Service, 1949–65: Exec. Officer, finally Principal, Audit, Purchasing, Finance, Personnel and Legislation branches; British Airports Authority, 1965–: Dep. Gen. Man., Heathrow Airport, 1970–73; Dir, Gatwick Airport, 1973–77. Chm., British Airports International Ltd, 1978–82; Board Mem., Airport Operators Council Internat., 1978–81; President: Western European Airports' Assoc., 1981–83; Internat. Civil Airports Assoc. (Europe), 1986–; Chm., Co-ordinating Council, Airports Assocs, 1982. CBIM 1981; FInstD 1982. *Recreations:* family pursuits, opera, classical recorded music, destructive gardening. *Club:* Royal Automobile.

MULLALY, Terence Frederick Stanley; Art Critic of The Daily Telegraph since 1958; *b* 14 Nov. 1927; *s* of late Col B. R. Mullaly (4th *s* of Maj.-Gen. Sir Herbert Mullaly, KCMG, CB, CSI) and Eileen Dorothy (*née* Stanley); *m* 1949, Elizabeth Helen (*née* Burkitt). *Educ:* in India, England, Japan and Canada; Downing Coll., Cambridge (MA). FSA 1977; FRNS 1981. Archæological studies in Tripolitania, 1948, and Sicily, 1949; has specialised in study of Italian art, particularly Venetian and Veronese painting of 16th and 17th centuries; lecturer and broadcaster. Pres. Brit. Section, Internat. Assoc. of Art Critics, 1967–73; Chm., British Art Medal Soc., 1986– (Vice Chm., 1982–86); Mem., Adv. Cttee: Cracow Art Festival, 1974; Palermo Art Festival, 1976; Mem. UK Delgn, Budapest Cultural Forum, 1985; Mem. Council: Attingham Summer Sch. Trust, 1984–; Derby Porcelain Internat. Soc., 1985–; Artistic Adviser, Grand Tours; Dir, Special tours. FRSA 1969; Commendatore, Order Al Merito, Italy, 1974 (Cavaliere Ufficiale, 1964); l'Ordre du Mérite Culturel, Poland, 1974; Order of Merit of Poland (Silver Medal), 1978; Bulgarian 1300th Anniversary Medal, 1981; Sacro Militare Ordine Costantiniano di S Giorgio (Silver Medal), 1982; Premio Pietro Torta per il restauro di Venezia, 1983. *Publications:* Ruskin a Verona, 1966; catalogue of exhibition, Disegni veronesi del Cinquecento, 1971; contrib. to catalogue of exhibition Cinquant' anni di pittura veronese: 1580–1630, 1974; ed and contrib. to catalogue of exhibition, Modern Hungarian Medal, 1984; contribs on history of art, to Burlington Magazine, Master Drawings, Arte Illustrata, Antologia di Belle Arti, The Minneapolis Inst. of Arts Bulletin, Jl of British Art Medal Soc., etc. *Recreations:* collecting and travel. *Address:* Waterside House, Pulborough, Sussex. *T:* Pulborough 2104.

MULLAN, Charles Heron, CBE 1979; VRD 1950; DL; Resident Magistrate, 1960–82, retired; Lieutenant-Commander RNVR; retired, 1951; *b* 17 Feb. 1912; *s* of Frederick Heron Mullan, BA, DL, Solicitor, Newry, Co. Down, and Minnie Mullan, formerly of Stow Longa, Huntingdonshire; *m* 1940, Marcella Elizabeth Sharpe, *er d* of J. A. McCullagh, Ballycastle, Co. Antrim; one *s. Educ:* Castle Park, Dalkey, Co. Dublin; Rossall Sch., Fleetwood; Clare Coll., Cambridge. Hons Degree Law, Cambridge, 1934; MA 1939. Joined Ulster Div. RNVR, 1936; called up for active service with Royal Navy, Aug. 1939; served throughout the war, HMS Rodney 1939–40; destroyers and escort vessels, Channel, North Sea, North Atlantic, etc, 1940–44 (with Royal Norwegian Navy, 1941–43); King Haakon VII War Decoration 1944. MP (UU) Co. Down, 1946–50, Westminster Parlt; contested S Down, 1945, for NI Parlt. Mem. Ulster Unionist Council, 1946–60. Solicitor 1948; JP 1960; Chm., Belfast Juvenile Courts, 1964–79. Member: N Ireland Section of British Delegn to 3rd UN Congress on Prevention of Crime and Treatment of Offenders, Stockholm, 1965; initial N Ireland Legal Aid Adv. Cttee, 1967–75; Mem. Exec. Cttee, British Juvenile Courts Soc., 1973–79; Vice-Pres., NI Juvenile Courts Assoc., 1980–; NI Rep. to 9th Congress of Internat. Assoc. of Youth Magistrates, Oxford, 1974; Adviser, Internat. Assoc. of Youth Magistrates, 1974–82. Hon. Governor, South Down Hospitals Gp, 1965–73; Vice-Pres., Rossallian Club, 1974. DL Co. Down, 1974. *Recreations:* ornithology, walking, boating. *Address:* Casanbarra, Carrickmore Road, Ballycastle, Co. Antrim, Northern Ireland BT54 6QS. *T:* 62323.

MULLENS, Maj.-Gen. Anthony Richard Guy, OBE 1979 (MBE 1973); Commander 1st Armoured Division, since 1985; *b* 10 May 1936; *s* of late Brig. Guy John de Wette Mullens, OBE, and of Gwendoline Joan Maclean; *m* 1964, Dawn Elizabeth Hermione Pease. *Educ:* Eton; RMA Sandhurst. Commnd 4th/7th Royal Dragoon Guards, 1956; regtl service, BAOR, 1956–58; ADC to Comdr 1st British Corps, 1958–60; Adjt 1962–65; sc 1967, psc; MA to VCGS, MoD, 1968–70; regtl service, 1970–72; Bde Major, 1972–73; Directing Staff, Staff Coll., 1973–76; CO 4/7 DG, BAOR, 1976–78; HQ BAOR, 1978–80; Comdr 7th Armd Bde, 1980–82; MoD (DMS(A)), 1982–85. Niedersachsen Verdienstkreuz, 1982. *Recreations:* travel, riding, shooting, ski-ing. *Address:* c/o Lloyds Bank, 6 Pall Mall, SW1. *Clubs:* Cavalry and Guards, Hurlingham.

MULLER, Franz Joseph; QC 1978; a Recorder of the Crown Court, since 1977; *b* England, 19 Nov. 1938; *yr s* of late Wilhelm Muller and Anne Maria (*née* Ravens); *m* 1985, Helena, *y d* of Mieczyslaw Bartosz. *Educ:* Mount St Mary's Coll.; Univ. of Sheffield (LLB). Called to the Bar, Gray's Inn, 1961; called to NI Bar, 1982. Graduate Apprentice, United Steel Cos, 1960–61; Commercial Asst, Workington Iron and Steel Co. Ltd, 1961–63. Commenced practice at the Bar, 1964. Non-Executive Director: Richards of Sheffield (Holdings) PLC, 1969–77; Satinsteel Ltd, 1970–77; Joseph Rodgers and Son Ltd and Rodgers Wostenholm Ltd, 1975–77. Mem., Sen. Common Room, UC Durham, 1981. *Recreations:* squash, fell walking, being in Greece, listening to music. *Address:* 13 Taptonville Road, Sheffield S10 5BQ; 11 King's Bench Walk, Temple, EC4Y 7EQ. *T:* 01–353 3337.

MULLER, Mrs Robert; *see* Whitelaw, Billie.

MULLETT, Aidan Anthony (Tony), QPM 1982; Chief Constable, West Mercia Constabulary, since 1985; *b* 24 May 1933; *s* of Bartholomew Joseph and Mary Kate Mullett; *m* 1957, Monica Elizabeth Coney; one *s* one *d. Educ:* Moat Boys' Sch., Leicester. Served Royal Air Force, 1950–56; joined Leicester City Police, 1957; Leicestershire and Rutland Constabulary, 1966, Chief Superitendent, 1973; Asst Chief Constable, W Mercia Constabulary, 1975–82; Dep. Chief Constable, Dyfed Powys Police, 1982–85. *Recreations:* golf, swimming. *Address:* West Mercia Police Headquarters, Hindlip Hall, Worcester WR3 8SP. *T:* Worcester 27188.

MULLETT, Leslie Baden; consultant; Visiting Professor, University of Reading, since 1982; *b* 22 Aug. 1920; *s* of Joseph and Edith Mullett; *m* 1st, 1946, Katherine Lear (marr. diss. 1968); no *c*; 2nd, 1971, Gillian Pettit. *Educ:* Gram. Sch., Hales Owen, Worcs; Birmingham Univ. BSc (Hons Physics) 1941. Telecommunications Research Estab., 1941–46; AEA, 1946–60 (Head of Accelerator Div., 1958); Asst Dir, Rutherford High Energy Lab., SRC, 1960–68; on secondment to Res. Gp, Min. of Technology, 1966–68; CSO, Min. of Transport, 1968; CSO, Res. Requirements, DoE, 1970–74; Dep. Dir, Transport and Road Res. Lab., DoE/Dept of Transport, 1974–80. *Publications:* A Guide to Transport for Disabled People, 1982; papers in learned jls on particle accelerators and solar energy. *Recreation:* fishing. *Address:* 22 Wellington Court, Spencers Wood, Reading, Berks. *T:* (business). Reading 875123.

MULLETT, Tony; *see* Mullett, A. A.

MULLEY, family name of **Baron Mulley.**

MULLEY, Baron *cr* 1984 (Life Peer), of Manor Park in the City of Sheffield; **Frederick William Mulley;** PC 1964; barrister-at-law and economist; *b* 3 July 1918; *er s* of late William and M. A. Mulley, Leamington Spa; *m* 1948, Joan D., *d* of Alexander and Betty Phillips; two *d. Educ:* Bath Place Church of England Sch.; Warwick Sch. (Schol.); Christ Church, Oxford (Adult Scholar, 1945). 1st Class Hons Philosophy, Politics and Economics, 1947; Research Studentship, Nuffield Coll., Oxford, 1947; Fellowship (Economics), St Catharine's Coll., Cambridge, 1948–50. Called to Bar, Inner Temple, 1954. Son of general labourer; clerk, National Health Insurance Cttee, Warwicks; joined Labour Party and Nat. Union of Clerks, 1936. Served War of 1939–45, Worcs Regt; Lance-Sgt 1940 (prisoner of war in Germany, 1940–45, meanwhile obtaining BSc (Econ.) and becoming Chartered Sec.). Contested (Lab) Sutton Coldfield Division of Warwicks, 1945. MP (Lab) Sheffield, Park, 1950–83; PPS to Minister of Works, 1951; Deputy Defence Sec. and Minister for the Army, 1964–65; Minister of Aviation, Dec. 1965–Jan. 1967; Jt Minister of State, FCO (formerly FO), 1967–69; Minister for Disarmament, 1967–69; Minister of Transport, 1969–70; Minister for Transport, DoE, 1974–75; Sec. of State for Educn and Science, 1975–76; Sec. of State for Defence, 1976–79. Parly deleg. to Germany, 1951, to Kenya, 1957; deleg. to Council of Europe and WEU, 1958–61 and 1979–83; WEU Assembly: Vice-Pres., 1960 (also Vice-Pres., Econ. Cttee); Pres., 1980–83. Mem., Labour Party NEC, 1957–58, 1960–64, 1965–80; Chm., Labour Party, 1974–75. Director: Radio Hallam, Sheffield, 1980–; Brassey's Defence Publications, 1983–. Chm., London Conf. for Overseas Students, 1984–. *Publications:* The Politics of Western Defence, 1962; articles on economic, defence and socialist subjects. *Address:* House of Lords, SW1A 0PW.

MULLIGAN, Andrew Armstrong; President: Mulligan Communications Inc., since 1983; Television Services International Inc.; Anglovision Ltd, since 1985; *b* 4 Feb. 1936; *s* of Col Hugh Waddell Mulligan, CMG, MD, DSc and Rita Aimee Armstrong; *m* 1964, Pia Ursula Schioler; two *s* two *d. Educ:* Magdalene Coll., Cambridge (Geog. and Anthropol Tripos (Hons). Personal Asst to Man. Dir, De La Rue Co., London, 1958–60; special assignment to Australia and NZ for Irish Export Bd, 1961–62; Foreign Correspondent: Daily Telegraph and London Observer in Paris, 1962–68; Independent Television News at Ten, 1968; Producer and reporter, BBC's Panorama, 1969–73; Head of General Reports Div., EEC, Brussels, 1973–74; Dir of Press and Information, Delegn of Commn of European Communities to the US, 1975–83. Dir, Ireland Fund of the US, 1976–. Publisher, Europe magazine, 1975–82. *Publications:* Ouvert l'Après Midi, 1963; The All Blacks, 1964. *Recreations:* rugby, tennis, skiing, sailing, landscape painting. *Address:* 1855 Shepherd Street, Washington, DC 20011, USA. *Clubs:* Annabel's; Hawks (Cambridge); Kildare Street and University (Dublin); Anglo-American Press Association (Paris); National Press (Washington, DC).

MULLIGAN, Most Rev. Patrick; *b* 9 June 1912; *s* of James and Mary Martin. *Educ:* St Macartan's, Monaghan; Maynooth. Prof., St Macartan's, 1938; Bishop's Sec., 1943; Headmaster, Clones, 1948; Headmaster, St Michael's, Enniskillen, 1957; Parish Priest of Machaire Rois and Vicar General and Archdeacon, 1966; Bishop of Clogher, 1970–79.

Publications: contribs to IER, JLAS, Seanchas Clochair. *Address:* 2 Clones Road, Monaghan, Ireland.

MULLIGAN, Prof. William, FRSE; Professor of Veterinary Physiology since 1963, and Vice-Principal, 1980–83, University of Glasgow; *b* 18 Nov. 1921; *s* of John Mulligan and Mary Mulligan (*née* Kelly); *m* 1948, Norah Mary Cooper one *s* two *d. Educ:* Banbridge Academy; Queen's Univ. of Belfast (BSc). PhD London. Assistant, Dept of Chemistry, QUB, 1943–45; Demonstrator/Lectr, St Bartholomew's Med. Coll., London, 1945–51; Sen. Lectr, Veterinary Biochemistry, Univ. of Glasgow, 1951–63; McMaster Fellow, McMaster Animal Health Laboratory, Sydney, Aust., 1958–60; Dean of Faculty of Veterinary Medicine, Univ. of Glasgow, 1977–80. Dr. med. vet. *hc* Copenhagen, 1983. *Publications:* (jtly) Isotopic Tracers, 1954, 2nd edn 1959; numerous contribs to scientific jls on immunology and use of radiation and radioisotopes in animal science. *Recreations:* golf, tennis, gardening, pigeon racing, theatre. *Address:* Brooks House, Cardross, Dunbartonshire G82 5HD. *T:* Cardross 841269. *Club:* Royal Commonwealth Society.

MULLIKEN, Prof. Robert S., PhD; Professor of Physics and Chemistry, University of Chicago, Emeritus, 1983; *b* Newburyport, Mass, 7 June 1896; *s* of Samuel Parsons Mulliken, Prof. of Organic Chemistry, and Katherine (*née* Mulliken); *m* 1929, Mary Helen Noé (decd); two *d. Educ:* Massachusetts Inst. of Technology; Univ. of Chicago. BS (MIT), 1917; PhD (Chicago), 1921. Nat. Research Coun. Fellow, Univ. of Chicago, and Harvard Univ., 1921–25; Guggenheim Fellow, Europe, 1930 and 1932–33; Fulbright Scholar, Oxford Univ., 1952–53; Vis. Fellow, St John's Coll., Oxford, 1952–53. Jun. Chem. Engr, Bureau of Mines, US Dept of Interior, Washington, 1917–18; Chemical Warfare Service, US Army, 1918 (Pte First-Class); Asst in Rubber Research, New Jersey Zinc Co., Penn., 1919; Asst Prof. of Physics, Washington Sq. Coll., New York Univ., 1926–28; Univ. of Chicago: Assoc. Prof. of Physics, 1928–31; Prof. of Physics, 1931–61 and Chemistry, 1961–83; Ernest de Witt Burton Distinguished Service Prof., 1956–61; Distinguished Service Prof. of Physics and Chemistry, 1961–83; Distinguished Research Prof. of Chemical Physics, Florida State Univ., (Jan.-March) 1965–72. Dir, Editorial Work and Information, Plutonium Project, Univ. of Chicago, 1942–45; Scientific Attaché, US Embassy, London, 1955. Baker Lectr, Cornell Univ., 1960; Silliman Lectr, Yale Univ., 1965; Visiting Professor: Bombay, 1962; Kanpur, 1962; Jan van Geuns Vis. Prof., Amsterdam Univ., 1965. Member: Amer. Acad. of Arts and Sciences; Nat. Acad. of Sciences; Amer. Philosophical Soc.; Amer. Chem. Soc.; Fellow: Amer. Physical Soc.; Amer. Acad. for Advancement of Science; Internat. Acad. of Quantum Molecular Science; Hon. Fellow: Chem. Soc. of Gt Britain; Indian Nat. Acad. of Science; Foreign Mem., Royal Soc.; Hon. Member: Soc. de Chimie Physique, Paris; Chem. Soc., Japan; Corresp. Mem., Soc. Royale des Sciences de Liège. Hon. Mem., Royal Irish Acad.; Hon. ScD: Columbia, 1939; Marquette, 1966; Cantab, 1966; Hon. PhD Stockholm, 1960. Nobel Prize for Chemistry, 1966; other medals and awards. *Publications:* (with Willis B. Person) Molecular Complexes, 1969; Selected Papers, 1975; (with Walter C. Ermler) Diatomic Molecules: results of ab initio calculations, 1977; (with Walter C. Ermler) Polyatomic Molecules: results of ab initio calculations, 1981; over 200 contributions (1919–; in recent years dealing extensively with structure and spectra of molecular complexes) to various American and foreign journals including: Jl Am. Chem. Soc.; Jl Chem. Phys; Rev. Mod. Phys; Phys Rev.; Chem. Rev.; Nature; also contributions: Proc. Nat. Acad. Sci.; Trans Faraday Soc. *Recreations:* driving a car, Oriental rugs, art. *Address:* 4000 North 25th Place, Arlington, Va 22207–5103, USA. *Club:* Cosmos (Washington).

MULLIN, Christopher John, (Chris); journalist and author; Editor, Tribune, 1982–84; *b* 12 Dec. 1947; *s* of Leslie and Teresa Mullin. *Educ:* Univ. of Hull (LLB). Freelance journalist, travelled extensively in Indo-China and China; sub editor, BBC World Service, 1974–78. Executive Member: Campaign for Labour Party Democracy, 1975–; Labour Co-ordinating Cttee, 1978–82. Contested (Lab): Devon N, 1970; Kingston upon Thames, Feb. 1974; Prosp. Parly Cand. (Lab) Sunderland South. Editor: Arguments for Socialism, by Tony Benn, 1979; Arguments for Democracy, by Tony Benn, 1981. *Publications:* A Very British Coup (novel), 1982; The Last Man Out of Saigon, 1986; Error of Judgement—the truth about the Birmingham pub bombings, 1986; pamphlets: How to Select or Reselect your MP, 1981; The Tibetans, 1981. *Address:* c/o Tribune, 308 Gray's Inn Road, WC1X 8DY. *T:* 01–278 0911.

MULLIN, Prof. John William, DSc, PhD, FRSC, FEng, FIChemE; Ramsay Memorial Professor of Chemical Engineering, since 1985 (Professor, 1969–85), Vice-Provost, since 1980, University College London; *b* Rock Ferry, Cheshire, 22 Aug. 1925; *er s* of late Frederick Mullin and Kathleen Nellie Mullin (*née* Oppy); *m* 1952, Averil Margaret Davies, Carmarthen; one *s* one *d. Educ:* Hawarden County Sch.; UCW Cardiff (Fellow, 1981); University Coll. London (Fellow, 1981). 8 yrs in organic fine chemicals industry; Lectr 1956, Reader 1961, Dean, Faculty of Engrg, 1975–77, University Coll. London; Dean, Faculty of Engrg, London Univ., 1979–85. Vis. Prof., Univ. New Brunswick, 1967. Chm. Bd of Staff Examrs, Chem. Eng. Univ. London, 1965–70. Hon. Librarian, IChemE, 1965–77, Mem. Council, 1973–76; Mem., European Space Agency Cttee, 1977–81; Founder Mem., Brit. Assoc. for Crystal Growth. Member: Cttee of Management, Inst. of Child Health, 1970–83; Court of Governors, University Coll., Cardiff, 1982–; Council, Sch. of Pharmacy, Univ. of London, 1983–. Chm., BS and ISO Cttees on industrial screens, sieves, particle sizing, etc. Moulton Medal, IChemE, 1970. *Publications:* Crystallization, 1961, 2nd edn 1972; (ed) Industrial Crystallization, 1976; papers in Trans IChemE, Chem. Engrg Sci., Jl Crystal Growth, etc. *Address:* 4 Milton Road, Ickenham, Mddx UB10 8NQ. *Club:* Athenæum.

MULLINS, Brian Percival, PhD; Director of Research and Laboratory Services and Head of Safety in Mines Research Establishment, Health and Safety Executive, (Under-Secretary), 1975–80; *b* 5 Aug. 1920; *s* of Thomas Percival Mullins and Lillian May Mullins; *m* 1944, Margaret Fiona Howell, MA; one *s* one *d. Educ:* Shooters' Hill Sch., London; Woolwich Polytechnic Evening Inst. BSc Nat. Sciences (London), 1940; PhD Fuel Techn. (Extern. London), 1951; BA Modern and Classical Chinese (London) 1984. Clerical Officer, Air Ministry, 1937–40; Research Scientist, Engine Dept, Royal Aircraft Estabt, 1941–42; seconded to Univ. of Cambridge for high vacuum gas analysis research, 1943; fuels, combustion and aero-engine research at Power Jets (R&D) Ltd and at Nat. Gas Turbine Estabt, 1944–60; Head of Chemistry Dept, RAE, 1960–62; Head of Chemistry, Physics and Metallurgy Dept, RAE, 1962–65; idc (seconded), 1966; Head of Structures Dept, RAE, 1967–74. Chm., Combustion Panel, AGARD-NATO, 1954–57; Sen. UK Mem., Structures and Materials Panel, AGARD-NATO, 1967–74. *Publications:* Spontaneous Ignition of Liquid Fuels, 1955; (jtly) Explosions, Detonations, Flammability and Ignition, 1959; numerous scientific research papers. *Recreation:* oriental languages. *Address:* 1 St Michael's Road, Farnborough, Hants GU14 8ND. *T:* Farnborough (Hants) 542137.

MULLINS, Rt. Rev. Daniel Joseph; Titular Bishop of Stowe, and Area Bishop in Swansea (RC); *b* 10 July 1929; *s* of Timothy Mullins. *Educ:* Mount Melleray; St Mary's, Aberystwyth; Oscott Coll.; UC of S Wales and Mon, Cardiff (Fellow, University Coll., Cardiff). Priest, 1953. Curate at: Barry, 1953–56; Newbridge, 1956; Bargoed, 1956–57; Maesteg, 1957–60; Asst Chaplain to UC Cardiff, 1960–64; Sec. to Archbp of Cardiff,

1964–68; Vicar General of Archdiocese of Cardiff, 1968; Auxiliary Bishop, 1970. Pres., Catholic Record Soc.; Chairman: Cttee for Catholics in Higher Educn; Council of Bds of Religious Studies; Assoc. of Voluntary Colls. Member of Court: UC Cardiff; UWIST; Governor, Digby Stuart Coll. *Recreations:* golf, walking. *Address:* Bishop's House, Maesgwyn, 63 Margam Road, Port Talbot, W Glam SA13 2HR. *T:* Port Talbot 883323.

MULLINS, Edwin Brandt; free-lance author, journalist and film-maker; *b* 14 Sept. 1933; *s* of Claud and Gwendolen Mullins; *m* 1st, 1960, Gillian Brydone (*d* 1982); one *s* two *d;* 2nd, 1984, Anne Kelleher. *Educ:* Midhurst Grammar Sch.; Merton Coll., Oxford (BA Hons, MA). Co-editor, Two Cities, 1957–58; Sub-editor and Art Correspondent, Illustrated London News, 1958–62; Art Critic: Sunday Telegraph, 1962–69; Telegraph Sunday Magazine, 1964–; contributor on arts subjects, 1962–, to The Guardian, Financial Times, Director, Apollo, Art and Artists, Studio, Radio Times. Regular broadcaster on radio and television; scriptwriter and presenter of numerous BBC and Channel 4 TV documentaries, incl. 100 Great Paintings, The Pilgrimage of Everyman, Gustave Courbet, Fake?, Prison, The Great Art Collection, A Love Affair with Nature. *Publications:* Souza, 1962; Alfred Wallis, 1967; Josef Herman, 1967; Braque, 1968; The Art of Elisabeth Frink, 1972; The Pilgrimage to Santiago, 1974; Angels on the Point of a Pin (novel), 1979; (ed) Great Paintings, 1981; Sirens (novel), 1983; (ed) The Arts of Britain, 1983; The Painted Witch, 1985; A Love Affair with Nature, 1985. *Recreations:* everything except football. *Address:* 7 Lower Common South, SW15 1BP. *T:* 01–789 2553.

MULLINS, Leonard, CMG 1976; PhD, DSc; Director of Research, Malaysian Rubber Producers' Research Association, Brickendonbury, Hertford, 1962–83; *b* 21 May 1918; *s* of Robert and Eugenie Alice Mullins; *m* 1943, Freda Elaine Churchouse; two *d. Educ:* Eltham Coll.; University Coll., London; Inst. of Educn, London. BSc (Hons), PhD, DSc. CPhys; FInstP; FPRI. Experimental Officer, Min. of Supply, 1940–44; Scientific Officer, finally Head of Physics Gp, Research Assoc. of British Rubber Manufrs, 1944–49; Malaysian (previously British) Rubber Producers' Research Assoc., 1950–83; Foundn Lectr, Instn of Rubber Industry, 1968. Pres., Plastics and Rubber Inst., 1981–83 (Chm., 1976–77; Vice-Pres., 1977–81); Chm., Adv. Cttee, Nat. Coll. of Rubber Technology, 1976–; Vice-Pres., Rubber and Plastic's Research Assoc., 1983–. Member: Court, Cranfield Inst. of Technology; Adv. Bd, Inst. of Technol., Loughborough Univ.; Council, Rubber and Plastics Res. Assoc. Discovered Mullins Effect, relating to elastic behaviour of rubber. Moore Meml Lecture, Bradford Univ., 1982. Governor of local schools. Colwyn Medal, IRI, 1966; Médaille de la Ville de Paris, 1982; Charles Goodyear Medal Award, Rubber Div., American Chem. Soc., 1986. Comdr, Malaysian Order of Chivalry, JMN, 1975. *Publications:* numerous original scientific papers in field of rubber physics. *Address:* 32 Sherrardspark Road, Welwyn Garden City, Herts AL8 7JS. *T:* Welwyn Garden 323633. *Club:* Athenæum.

MULRONEY, Rt. Hon. (Martin) Brian, PC 1984; MP (Progressive Conservative) Manicouagan, since 1984; Prime Minister of Canada, since 1984; *b* 20 March 1939; *s* of Benedict Mulroney and Irene O'Shea; *m* 1973, Mila Pivnicki; three *s* one *d. Educ:* St Francis Xavier Univ. (BA); Université Laval (LLL). Partner, Ogilvy, Renault (Montreal law firm), 1965–76; Pres., Iron Ore Co. of Canada, 1976–83. Leader of the Opposition, 1983–84. Royal Comr, Cliche Commn investigating violence in Quebec construction industry, 1974. Hon. LLD: St Francis Xavier Univ., 1979; Meml Univ., 1980. *Publication:* Where I Stand, 1983. *Recreations:* tennis, swimming. *Address:* 24 Sussex Drive, Ottawa, Ont K1M 1M4, Canada. *Clubs:* Mount Royal (Montreal); Albany (Toronto); Garrison (Quebec).

MULVANEY, Prof. Derek John, CMG 1982; Professor of Prehistory, Australian National University, 1971–85, now Emeritus; *b* 26 Oct. 1925; *s* of Richard and Frances Mulvaney; *m* 1954, Jean Campbell; four *s* two *d. Educ:* Univ. of Melbourne (MA); Clare Coll., Univ. of Cambridge (BA, MA 1959, PhD 1970). FAHA 1970, FSA 1977, corr. FBA 1983. Navigator, RAAF, 1943–46 (Flying Officer); Lectr and Senior Lectr in History, Univ. of Melbourne, 1954–64; Senior Fellow, ANU, 1965–70; Vis. Prof., Cambridge, 1976–77; Chair of Australian Studies, Harvard, 1984–85; Mem. Council, Aust. Inst. of Aboriginal Studies, 1964–80 (Chm., 1982–84); Australian Heritage Commissioner, 1976–82; Mem., Cttee of Inquiry, Museums and National Collections, 1974–75. *Publications:* Cricket Walkabout, 1967; The Prehistory of Australia, 1969, 2nd edn 1975; numerous excavation reports and historical articles. *Recreation:* gardening. *Address:* 128 Schlich Street, Yarralumla, ACT 2600, Australia. *T:* Canberra 812352.

MUMFORD, Sir Albert (Henry), KBE 1963 (OBE 1946); CEng, Hon. FIEE; Engineer-in-Chief, GPO, 1960–65, retd; *b* 16 April 1903; *s* of late George Mumford; *m* 1927, Eileen Berry; two *s* two *d. Educ:* Bancroft's Sch.; Queen Mary Coll., Univ. of London. BSc (Eng) 1st Class Hons (London) 1923. Entered GPO Engineering Dept, 1924; Staff Engineer radio branch, 1938; Imperial Defence Coll., 1948; Asst Engineer-in-Chief, 1951; Dep. Engineer-in-Chief, 1954. Treasurer, Instn of Electrical Engineers, 1969–72 (Chm. Radio Section, 1945–46; Vice-Pres. 1958–63; Pres. 1963–64; Hon. Fellow, 1980); Pres. Assoc. Supervising Electrical Engineers, 1964–66; Treas., Instn of Electrical and Electronic Incorporated Engineers, 1967– (Hon. Fellow 1978). Fellow, Queen Mary Coll., 1962; Hon. Fellow, Polytechnic of the South Bank, 1982; Hon. Mem., City and Guilds of London Inst. *Publications:* many scientific papers. *Address:* 27 Grendon Gardens, Wembley Park, Mddx. *T:* 01–904 2360.

MUMFORD, Prof. Enid; Professor of Organizational Behaviour, Manchester Business School, since 1979; *d* of Arthur McFarland and Dorothy Evans; *m* 1947, Jim Mumford; one *s* one *d. Educ:* Wallasey High Sch.; Liverpool Univ. (BA, MA); Manchester Univ. (PhD). CIPM; FBCS. Personnel Officer, Rotol Ltd, 1946–47; Production Supervisor, J. D. Francis Ltd, 1947–48; Research Associate: Dept of Social Science, Liverpool Univ., 1948–56; Bureau of Public Health Economics, Univ. of Michigan, USA, 1956–57; Res. Lectr, Dept of Social Science, Liverpool Univ., 1957–65; Lectr, then Sen. Lectr and Reader, Manchester Business Sch., 1966–79. *Publications:* Chester Royal Infirmary 1856–1956, 1956; Living with a Computer, 1964; Computers Planning and Personnel Management, 1969; Systems Design for People, 1971; Job Satisfaction: a study of computer specialists, 1972; (with others) Coal and Conflict, 1963; (with O. Banks) The Computer and the Clerk, 1967; (with T. B. Ward) Computers: planning for people, 1968; (with E. Pettigrew) Implementing Strategic Decisions, 1975; (ed, with H. Sackman) Human Choice and Computers, 1975; (ed, with K. Legge) Designing Organizations for Efficiency and Satisfaction, 1978; (with D. Henshall) A Participative Approach to Computer Systems Design, 1978; (with M. Weir) Computer Systems in Work Design, 1979; (ed. with C. Cooper) The Quality of Working Life, 1979; (with others) The Impact of Systems Change in Organizations, 1980; Values, Technology and Work, 1980; Designing Secretaries, 1983; Designing Human Systems for New Technology, 1983; Using Computers for Business Success, 1986; contribs to books and journals. *Address:* Manchester Business School, Booth Street West, Manchester M15 6PB. *T:* 061–273 8228.

MUMFORD, Lewis; writer; *b* 19 Oct. 1895; *s* of Lewis Mack and Elvina Conradina Baron; *m* 1921, Sophia Wittenberg; (one son killed in action 1944) one *d. Educ:* Coll. of the City of New York, Columbia Univ. Radio operator (USN) 1918; Associate editor

Fortnightly Dial, 1919; Acting Editor Sociological Review (London), 1920; Co-editor American Caravan, 1927–36. Member: National Inst. of Arts and Letters 1930–; Amer. Academy of Arts and Letters, 1956– (Pres., 1962–65); Amer. Philosophical Soc., Amer. Academy of Arts and Sciences; Bd of Higher Educn, City of New York, 1935–37; Commn on Teacher Educn, Amer. Council on Educn, 1938–44; Prof. of Humanities, Stanford Univ., 1942–44. Hon. LLD Edinburgh 1965; Hon. Dr Arch., Rome, 1967. Hon. Phi Beta Kappa, 1957; Hon. Fellow, Stanford Univ., 1941. Hon. FRIBA (Hon. ARIBA, 1942); Hon. MRTPI (Hon. Mem. TPI, 1946); Hon. Member: Amer. Inst. of Architects, 1951; Town Planning Inst. of Canada, 1960; Amer. Inst. of Planners, 1955; Colegio del Arquitectas del Peru; Prof. of City Planning, Univ. of Pennsylvania, 1951–56; Vis. Prof., MIT, 1957–60; Ford Prof., Univ. of Pennsylvania, 1959–60; Univ. of Calif., 1961; Fellow, Wesleyan Univ. Center for Advanced Studies, 1963; MIT: Vis. Lectr, 1973–74; Charles Abrams Prof., 1975. Co-chairman Wenner-Gren Foundation Conf. on Man's Use of the Earth, 1955. Made six documentary films on City for National Film Board, Canada, 1964. Hon. Fellow, Royal Inst. of Architects of Ireland. Townsend Harris Medal, 1939; Ebenezer Howard Memorial Medal, 1946; Medal of Honour, Fairmount Park Art Assoc., 1953; TPI (later RTPI) Gold Medal, 1957; RIBA Royal Gold Medal for Architecture, 1961; Presidential Medal of Freedom, 1964; Emerson-Thoreau Medal, Amer. Acad. of Arts and Sciences, 1965; Gold Medal, Belles Lettres, Nat. Inst. of Arts and Letters, 1970; Leonardo da Vinci Medal, Soc. for Hist. of Technology, 1969; Hodgkins Medal, Smithsonian Instn, 1971; Thomas Jefferson Meml Foundn Medal, 1972; Nat. Medal for Literature, 1972; Prix Mondial del Duca, 1976; Benjamin Franklin Medal, RSA, 1983. Hon. KBE 1975. *Publications:* The Story of Utopias, 1922; Sticks and Stones, 1924; The Golden Day, 1926; Herman Melville, 1929; The Brown Decades, 1931; Technics and Civilization, 1934; The Culture of Cities, 1938; Whither Honolulu?, 1938; Men Must Act, 1939; Faith for Living, 1940; The South in Architecture, 1941; The Condition of Man, 1944; City Development, 1945; Values for Survival, 1946 (Programme for Survival (Eng.), 1946); Green Memories: The Story of Geddes Mumford, 1947; The Conduct of Life, 1951; Art and Technics, 1952; In the Name of Sanity, 1954; The Human Prospect, 1955; From the Ground Up, 1956; The Transformations of Man, 1956; The City in History, 1961; Highway and City, 1962; Herman Melville (rev. edn), 1963; The Myth of the Machine, 1967; The Urban Prospect, 1968; The Van Wyck Brooks-Lewis Mumford Letters, 1970; The Pentagon of Power, 1971; The Letters of Lewis Mumford and Frederic J. Osborn, 1971; Interpretations and Forecasts, 1973; Findings and Keepings: analects for an autobiography, 1975; Architecture as a Home for Man, 1975; My Works and Days: a personal chronicle, 1979; Sketches from Life: the early years, 1982. *Address:* Amenia, New York 12501, USA.

MUMFORD, Rt. Rev. Peter; *see* Truro, Bishop of.

MUMFORD, William Frederick; Assistant Under-Secretary of State, Ministry of Defence, since 1980; *b* 23 Jan. 1930; *s* of late Frederick Charles Mumford and Hester Leonora Mumford; *m* 1958, Elizabeth Marion, *d* of Nowell Hall; three *s* one *d*. *Educ:* St Albans Sch.; Lincoln Coll., Oxford (MA PPE). Nat. Service commission, Royal Artillery, 1949–50. Appointed to Home Civil Service, 1953; Asst Principal, 1953–58, Principal, 1958–60, Air Ministry; First Secretary, UK Delegn to NATO, Paris, 1960–65; Principal, 1965–67, Asst Sec., 1967–73, Defence Secretariat, MoD; Dep. Head of UK Delegn to MBFR Exploratory Talks, Vienna, 1973; Principal Private Sec. to Secretaries of State for Defence: Rt Hon. Lord Carrington, 1973–74, Rt Hon. Ian Gilmour, MP and Rt Hon. Roy Mason, MP, 1974–75; Under-Sec., Machinery of Govt Div., CSD, 1975–76; Asst Sec.-Gen. for Defence Planning and Policy, NATO, Brussels, 1976–80. *Recreations:* antique book collecting, music, swimming. *Address:* c/o Barclays Bank, 366 Strand, WC2R 0JQ.

MUMMERY; *see* Lockhart-Mummery.

MUMMERY, John Frank; Treasury Junior Counsel (Chancery), since 1981; *b* 5 Sept. 1938; *s* of Frank Stanley Mummery and Ruth Mummery (*née* Coleman) Coldred, Kent; *m* 1967, Elizabeth Anne Lamond Lackie, *d* of Dr D. G. L. Lackie and Ellen Lackie (*née* Easterbrook), Edinburgh; one *s* one *d*. *Educ:* Oakleigh House, Dover; Dover County Grammar Sch.; Pembroke Coll., Oxford, 1959–63 (MA, BCL; Winter Williams Prize in Law). National Service, The Border Regt and RAEC, 1957–59. Called to Bar, Gray's Inn (Atkin Schol.), 1964, Bencher, 1985. Mem., Justice Cttee on Privacy and the Law, 1967–70; Treasury Junior Counsel in Charity Matters, 1977–81. Member, Senate of Inns of Court and Bar, 1978–81. Mem., Art Registration Cttee, 1969–. *Publication:* (co-ed) Copinger and Skone James on Copyright, 12th edn. *Recreation:* long walks with family, friends and alone. *Address:* (chambers) 5 New Square, Lincoln's Inn, WC2. *T:* 01–404 0404; (home) 5 Canonbury Grove, N1. *T:* 01–226 4140.

MUNFORD, William Arthur, MBE 1946; PhD; FLA; Librarian Emeritus, National Library for the Blind; *b* 27 April 1911; *s* of late Ernest Charles Munford and Florence Margaret Munford; *m* 1934, Hazel Despard Wilmer; two *s* one *d*. *Educ:* Hornsey County Sch.; LSE (BScEcon, PhD). Asst, Hornsey Public Libraries, 1927–31; Chief Asst, Ilford Public Libraries, 1931–34; Borough Librarian, Dover, 1934–45 (Food Exec. Officer, 1939–45); City Librarian, Cambridge, 1945–53; Dir-Gen., Nat. Library for the Blind, 1954–82. Hon. Sec., Library Assoc., 1952–55, Hon. Fellow 1977. Trustee, Ulverscroft Foundn. *Publications:* Books for Basic Stock, 1939; Penny Rate: aspects of British public library history, 1951; William Ewart, MP, 1960; Edward Edwards, 1963; (with W. G. Fry) Louis Stanley Jast, 1966; James Duff Brown, 1968; A History of the Library Association, 1877–1977, 1976; (with S. Godbolt) The Incomparable Mac (biog. of Sir J. Y. W. MacAlister), 1983; contribs to Librarianship jls, 1933–. *Recreations:* reading, rough gardening, wood sawing, cycling, serendipity. *Address:* 11 Manor Court, Pinehurst, Grange Road, Cambridge CB3 9BE. *T:* Cambridge 62962. *Club:* National Liberal.

MUNIR, Ashley Edward; Under Secretary, Ministry of Agriculture, Fisheries and Food, since 1982; *b* 14 Feb. 1934; *s* of late Hon. Sir Mehmed Munir Bey, Kt, CBE, and late Lady (Vessime) Munir; *m* 1960, Sureyya S. V. Dormen; one *s*. *Educ:* Brentwood Sch.; St John's Coll., Cambridge (MA). Called to the Bar, Gray's Inn, 1956. Practised as barrister, 1956–60; Crown Counsel, 1960–64; entered Govt Legal Service, 1964; Asst Solicitor, MAFF, 1975–82. *Publication:* Perinatal Rights, 1983. *Recreations:* walking, playing the double-bass, listening to music. *Address:* Grassdale, 31 Kingwell Road, Hadley Wood, Herts EN4 0HZ. *T:* (office) 01–233 7599; L'Acapulco, Appt 506, Avenue du Casino, 34280 La Grande Motte, France. *Club:* United Oxford & Cambridge University.

MUNN, Sir James, Kt 1985; OBE 1976; MA; Chairman, Manpower Services Committee for Scotland, since 1984; *b* 27 July 1920; *s* of Douglas H. Munn and Margaret G. Dunn; *m* 1946, Muriel Jean Millar Moles; one *d*. *Educ:* Stirling High Sch.; Glasgow Univ. (MA (Hons)). Entered Indian Civil Service, 1941; served in Bihar, 1942–47. Taught in various schools in Glasgow, 1949–57; Principal Teacher of Modern Languages, Falkirk High Sch., 1957–62, Depute Rector, 1962–66; Rector: Rutherglen Acad., 1966–70; Cathkin High Sch., Cambuslang, Glasgow, 1970–83. Member: Consultative Cttee on Curriculum, 1968–80, Chm., 1980–; University Grants Cttee, 1973–82; Chm., Cttee to review structure of curriculum at SIII and SIV, 1975–77. Mem. Court, Strathclyde Univ., 1983–. Chevalier des Palmes Académiques, 1967. DUniv Stirling, 1978. *Recreations:* reading, bridge. *Address:* 4 Kincath Avenue, High Burnside, Glasgow G73 4RP. *T:* 041–634 4654.

MUNN, Rear-Adm. William James, CB 1962; DSO 1941; OBE 1946; *b* 15 July 1911; *s* of late Col R. G. Munn, CMG, FRGS, and late Mrs R. G. Munn; *m* 1940, Susan Astle Sperling, Teviot Bank, Hawick, Scotland; two *s*. *Educ:* Britannia Royal Naval College, Dartmouth. Cadet and Midshipman in HMS Nelson, 1929–31. Flag Lt (Battle Cruiser Sqdn during Spanish Civil War); served War of 1939–45 (despatches, DSO): First Lt Destroyer HMS Mohawk; Comd Destroyer HMS Hereward (Battle of Matapan, evacuation of Crete), 1941. POW in Italy and Germany, 1941–45. Comd HMS Venus (Mediterranean during Palestine trouble, OBE), 1945–47; Comdr 1946; psc 1949; Exec. Officer, Cruiser HMS Kenya (Far East Station, Korean War, despatches), 1949–51; Capt., 1951; Capt. of the Britannia Royal Naval College, Dartmouth, 1956–58; Capt. of HMS Gambia, Nov. 1958–Dec. 1960; Rear-Adm. 1960; Chief of Staff to the Comdr-in-Chief, Home Fleet, 1961–63, retd. *Recreation:* golf. *Address:* The Old Rectory, Langham, near Bury St Edmunds, Suffolk. *T:* Walsham-le-Willows 234. *Clubs:* Royal Worlington Golf, North Berwick Golf, Gullane Golf.

MUNNS, Victor George; Counsellor (Labour), Washington, 1983–86; *b* 17 June 1926; *s* of Frederick William Munns and Lilian Munns; *m* 1952, Pamela Ruth Wyatt; two *s*. *Educ:* Haberdashers' Aske's, Hatcham; University Coll., London (BA). Served HM Forces (Army Intell.), 1945–48. Min. of Labour Employment Service, 1951–61; ILO, Trinidad and Belize, 1962–63; Sec., Shipbldg Industry Trng Bd, 1964–66; Res. Staff, Royal Commn on Trade Unions, 1966; Principal, Dept of Employment (Indust. Trng and Indust. Relations), 1967–72; Dep. Chief Officer, Race Relations Bd, 1973–74; Sec., Health and Safety Commn, 1974–77; Asst Sec., Health and Safety Exec., 1977–82. *Club:* Royal Over-Seas League.

MUNRO, Alan Gordon, CMG 1984; HM Diplomatic Service; Ambassador to Algeria, since 1984; *b* 17 Aug. 1935; *s* of late Sir Gordon Munro, KCMG, MC and Lilian Muriel Beit; *m* 1962, Rosemary Grania Bacon; twin *s* two *d*. *Educ:* Wellington Coll.; Clare Coll., Cambridge (MA). MIPM. Mil. Service, 4/7 Dragoon Guards, 1953–55; Middle East Centre for Arab Studies, 1958–60; British Embassy, Beirut, 1960–62; Kuwait, 1961; FO, 1963–65; Head of Chancery, Benghazi, 1965–66 and Tripoli, 1966–68; FO, 1968–73; Consul (Commercial), 1973–74, Consul-Gen., 1974–77, Rio de Janeiro; Head of E African Dept, FCO, 1977–78; Head of Middle East Dept, FCO, 1979; Head of Personnel Ops Dept, FCO, 1979–81; Regl Marketing Dir (ME), MoD, 1981–83. *Recreations:* historic buildings, gardening, music, history. *Address:* c/o Foreign and Commonwealth Office, SW1A 2AL. *Club:* Travellers'.

MUNRO of Lindertis, Sir Alasdair (Thomas Ian), 6th Bt *cr* 1825; Marketing Consultant; Chairman, Munro, Jennings & Doig, since 1983; *b* 6 July 1927; *s* of Sir Thomas Torquil Alfonso Munro, 5th Bt and Beatrice Maude (*d* 1974), *d* of Robert Sanderson Whitaker; *S* father, 1985; *m* 1954, Marguerite Lillian, *d* of late Franklin R. Loy, Dayton, Ohio, USA; one *s* one *d*. *Educ:* Georgetown Univ., Washington, DC (BSS 1946); Univ. of Pennsylvania (MBA 1951); IMEDE, Lausanne. 2nd Lieut, USAF (previously US Army), 1946–53. Senior Vice-Pres., McCann-Erickson, New York, 1952–69; Pres., Jennings Real Estate, Waitsfield, Vermont, 1970–83. Founder, Dir (and Past Pres.), St Andrew's Soc. of Vermont, 1972–; Vice-Chm., Assoc. Bd of Directors, Howard Bank, Waitsfield, 1974–84; Founder, sometime Dir and Pres., Valley Area Assoc., Waitsfield, 1972–80. *Recreations:* gardening, travel, Scottish heritage matters. *Heir:* *s* Keith Gordon Munro, *b* 3 May 1959. *Address:* River Ridge, Waitsfield, Vermont 05673, USA; Ruthven Mill, Meigle, Perthshire, Scotland.

MUNRO, Dame Alison, DBE 1985 (CBE 1964); Chairman: Chichester Health Authority, since 1982; Code Monitoring Committee on Infant Formulae, since 1985; *d* of late John Donald, MD; *m* 1939, Alan Lamont Munro (killed on active service, 1941); one *s*. *Educ:* Queen's Coll., Harley Street; Wynberg Girls' High Sch., South Africa; St Paul's Girls' Sch.; St Hilda's Coll., Oxford (MA). Ministry of Aircraft Production, 1942–45; Principal, Ministry of Civil Aviation, 1945; Asst Sec., 1949; Under-Sec., Ministry of Transport and Civil Aviation, 1958; Under-Sec., Ministry of Aviation, 1960; High Mistress, St Paul's Girls' Sch. Hammersmith, 1964–74. Chm., Merton, Sutton and Wandsworth AHA(T), 1974–82. Chairman: Training Council for Teachers of the Mentally Handicapped, 1966–69; Cttee of Inquiry into Children's Footwear, 1972; Central Transport Consultative Cttee, 1980–85; Maternity Services Adv. Cttee, 1981–85; Member: Board, BEA, 1966–73; Board, British Library, 1973–79; British Tourist Authority, 1973–81. Governor, Charing Cross Group of Hospitals, 1967–74. *Recreations:* gardening, tennis, sailing, Scottish dancing. *Address:* Harbour Way, Ellanore Lane, West Wittering, West Sussex PO20 8AN. *T:* Birdham 513274. *Club:* Royal Commonwealth Society.

MUNRO, Charles Rowcliffe; *b* 6 Nov. 1902; *s* of Charles John Munro, CA, Edinburgh, Hon. Sheriff Substitute, County of Selkirk, and of Edith Rowcliffe; *m* 1942, Moira Rennie Ainslie, *d* of Dr Alexander Cruickshank Ainslie; two *s*. *Educ:* Merchiston Castle Sch., Edinburgh. Hon. Treasurer W Edinburgh Unionist Assoc., 1945–61, Hon. Treas. Scottish Nat. Cttee English-Speaking Union of the Commonwealth 1952–64; Pres. Edinburgh Union of Boys' Clubs, 1957–66. *Recreation:* fishing. *Address:* 17 Succoth Place, Edinburgh EH12 6BJ. *T:* 031–337 2139.

MUNRO, Colin William Gordon R.; *see* Ross-Munro.

MUNRO, Ian Arthur Hoyle, MB, FRCP; Editor of The Lancet, since 1976; *b* 5 Nov. 1923; *o s* of Gordon Alexander and Muriel Rebecca Munro; *m* 1948, Olive Isabel, MRCS, LRCP, *o d* of Ernest and Isabella Jackson; three *s* two *d*. *Educ:* Huddersfield Coll.; Paston Sch., North Walsham; Royal Liberty Sch., Romford; Guy's Hosp. (MB 1946). FRCP 1984 (MRCP 1980). Served with RAMC, 1947–50. Joined staff of The Lancet, 1951, Dep. Editor, 1965–76. Regents' Lectr, UCLA, 1982. *Recreations:* cricket, crosswords. *Address:* Oakwood, Bayley's Hill, Sevenoaks, Kent TN14 6HS. *T:* Sevenoaks 454993. *Clubs:* Athenæum; Yorkshire CC.

MUNRO of Foulis-Obsdale, Sir Ian Talbot, 15th Bt *cr* 1634; *b* 28 Dec. 1929; *s* of Robert Hector Munro (*d* 1965) (*n* of 12th and 13th Bts) and Ethel Amy Edith, *d* of Harry Hudson; *S* cousin, Sir Arthur Herman Munro, 14th Bt, 1972. *Heir:* *uncle* Malcolm Munro [*b* 24 Feb. 1901; *m* 1931, Constance, *d* of William Carter; one *d* (one *s* decd)]. *Address:* 38 Clarence Gate Gardens, NW1.

MUNRO, John Bennet Lorimer, CB 1959; CMG 1953; *b* 20 May 1905; *s* of late Rev. J. L. Munro; *m* 1st, 1929, Gladys Maie Forbes Simmons (*d* 1965); three *s*; 2nd, 1965, Margaret Deacy Ozanne, *d* of John Deacy, Blackfort House, Foxford, County Mayo. *Educ:* Edinburgh Academy; Edinburgh University; Corpus Christi Coll., Oxford (MA). ICS: entered, 1928; Under-Sec. Public Dept, Fort St George, 1934; HM Treasury, 1939; Min. of Supply, 1943; idc, 1949; Div. of Atomic Energy Production, 1950; Chief Administrative Officer, UK High Commission for Germany, 1951; Under-Sec.: Min. of Supply, 1953; Bd of Trade, 1955–62; Export Credits Guarantee Dept, 1962–65; Consultant, Export

Council for Europe, 1966–67. *Address*: 77 Shirley Drive, Hove, Sussex BN3 6UE. *T*: Brighton 556705.

MUNRO OF FOULIS, Captain Patrick, TD 1958; DL 1949; 30th Chief of Clan Munro; landowner and farmer; Vice-Lieutenant of Ross and Cromarty, 1968–77; *b* 30 Aug. 1912; *e s* of late Col C. H. O. Gascoigne, DSO, Seaforth Highlanders, and Eva Marion, *d* of Sir Hector Munro of Foulis, 11th Bt; assumed arms and designation of Munro of Foulis on death of his grandfather; *m* 1947, Eleanor Mary, *d* of Capt. Hon. William French, French Park, Co. Roscommon, Eire; three *s* one *d*. *Educ*: Imperial Service Coll., Windsor; RMC Sandhurst. 2nd Lt Seaforth Highlanders, 1933; Capt. 1939. Served War of 1939–45, France (POW). Mem. Ross and Cromarty T&AFA, 1938. Hon. Sheriff of Ross and Cromarty, 1973. *Address*: Foulis Castle, Evanton, Ross-shire. *T*: Evanton 212. *Club*: MCC.

MUNRO, Sir Robert (Lindsay), Kt 1977; CBE 1962; President of the Senate, Fiji, 1970–82; *b* NZ, 2 April 1907; *s* of Colin Robert Munro and Marie Caroline Munro; *m* 1937, Lucie Ragnhilde Mee; two *s* one *d*. *Educ*: Auckland Grammar Sch.; Auckland University Coll. (LLB). Barrister and Solicitor, 1929. Served War, 1940–46: 1st Lieut, FMF. Founder Chairman, Fiji: Town Planning Bd, 1946–53; Broadcasting Commn, 1953–61. Member: Educn Bd and Educn Adv. Council, 1943–70; Legislative Council, 1945–46; Nat. Health Adv. Cttee, 1976–. President: Law Soc., 1960–62 and 1967–69; Family Planning Assoc. of Fiji, 1963–. Internat. Planned Parenthood Federation: formerly Mem., Governing Body; Regional Vice-Pres., 1973–. Govt Representative: Bangkok reg. pre-consultation World Population Conf., ECAFE, 1974; World Pop. Conf., Bucharest, 1974; E Asian and Pacific Copyright Seminar, Sydney, 1976. Order of St Olav, Norway, 1966. Rifle shooting Blue; Captain, NZ Hockey Team, 1932. *Recreations*: literature, garden, music. *Address*: Foulis, 6 Milne Road, Suva, Fiji. *T*: 22166. *Club*: Fiji (Suva).

MUNRO, Sir Sydney Douglas G.; *see* Gun-Munro, S. D.

MUNRO, William, QC (Scotland) 1959; *b* 19 April 1900; *s* of William Munro, JP, Kilmarnock, and Janet Thomson Munro; *m* 1950, Christine Frances, *d* of W. B. Robertson, MC, DL, Colton, Dunfermline; three *d*. *Educ*: Glasgow High Sch.; Glasgow Univ. (MA, LLB). Called to Scottish Bar, 1925; called to Bar of Straits Settlements, 1927; Johore, 1927. Practised in Singapore and Malaya, 1927–57; Partner, Allen & Gledhill, Singapore. 1933–57 (Prisoner of war, Feb. 1942–Aug. 1945). Resumed practice Scottish Bar, 1958. *Recreation*: reading. *Address*: 9 The Hawthorns, Muirfield Park, Gullane EH31 2DZ. *T*: Gullane 84 2398. *Clubs*: New (Edinburgh); Hon. Company of Edinburgh Golfers.

MUNROW, Roger Davis; Chief Master of the Supreme Court of Judicature (Chancery Division), since 1986 (Master, 1985–86); *b* 20 March 1929; *s* of late William Davis Munrow, CBE and Constance Caroline Munrow (*née* Moorcroft); *m* 1957, Marie Jane Beresford; three *d*. *Educ*: Bryanston School; Oriel College, Oxford. MA; Solicitor. Entered Treasury Solicitor's Dept as Legal Assistant, 1959; Senior Legal Assistant, 1965; Assistant Treasury Solicitor, 1973; Principal Asst Treasury Solicitor, 1981. *Recreations*: swimming, cycling, tennis. *Address*: 20 Monahan Avenue, Purley, Surrey CR2 3BA. *T*: 01–660 1872.

MUNSTER, 7th Earl of, *cr* 1831; **Anthony Charles FitzClarence;** Viscount FitzClarence, Baron Tewkesbury, 1831; stained glass conservator for Chapel Studio, Hertfordshire, since 1983; *b* 21 March 1926; *s* of 6th Earl of Munster, and Monica Shiela Harrington (*d* 1958), *d* of Lt-Col Sir Henry Mulleneux Grayson, 1st Bt, KBE; *S* father, 1983; *m* 1st, 1949, Diane Delvigne (marr. diss. 1966); two *d*; 2nd, 1966, Pamela Hyde (marr. diss. 1979); one *d*; 3rd, 1979, Alexa Maxwell. *Educ*: St Edward's School, Oxford. Served RN, 1942–46, Mediterranean, Far East, Pacific. Graphic Designer: Daily Mirror Newspapers, 1957–66; IPC Newspapers Division (Sun), 1966–69; freelance 1971–79; stained glass conservator for Burrell collection, 1979–83. *Recreations*: field sports, carpentry. *Heir*: none. *Address*: 78 Bushey Hall Road, Bushey, Herts. *Club*: Chelsea Arts.

MURCHIE, John Ivor; His Honour Judge Murchie; a Circuit Judge, since 1974; *b* 4 June 1928; *s* of Captain Peter Archibald Murchie, OBE, RD, RNR; *m* 1953, Jenifer Rosalie Luard; one *s* two *d*. *Educ*: Edinburgh Academy; Rossall Sch.; Exeter Coll., Oxford (MA). Called to the Bar, Middle Temple, 1953; Harmsworth Scholarship, 1956. Dep. Chm., Berkshire QS, 1969–71; a Recorder of the Crown Court, 1972–74. Chm. Council, Rossall Sch., 1979–. *Recreations*: versifying and diversifying. *Address*: Brook House, Warren Row, Wargrave, Reading RG10 8QS.

MURDOCH, Dame Elisabeth (Joy), DBE 1963 (CBE 1961); *b* 1909; *d* of Rupert Greene and Marie (*née* de Lancey Forth); *m* 1928, Sir Keith (Arthur) Murdoch (*d* 1952); one *s* three *d*. *Educ*: Clyde Sch., Woodend, Victoria. Pres., Royal Children's Hospital, Melbourne, Victoria, Australia, 1953–65. Trustee, National Gallery, Victoria, 1968–76. Hon. LLD Melbourne, 1982. *Recreation*: gardening. *Address*: Cruden Farm, Langwarrin, Victoria 3910, Australia. *Clubs*: Alexandra, Lyceum (Melbourne).
See also K. R. Murdoch.

MURDOCH, Iris; *see* Murdoch, J. I.

MURDOCH, (Jean) Iris, (Mrs J. O. Bayley), CBE 1976; novelist and philosopher; Fellow of St Anne's College, Oxford, since 1948. Hon. Fellow, 1963; *b* Dublin, 15 July 1919; *d* of Wills John Hughes Murdoch and Irene Alice Richardson; *m* 1956, John Oliver Bayley, *qv*. *Educ*: Froebel Educational Inst., London; Badminton Sch., Bristol; Somerville Coll., Oxford (Lit. Hum. 1st Class 1942). Hon. Fellow 1977. Asst Principal, Treasury, 1942–44; Administrative Officer with UNRRA, working in London, Belgium, Austria, 1944–46; Sarah Smithson studentship in philosophy, Newnham Coll., Cambridge, 1947–48; Lectr, RCA, 1963–67. Mem., Irish Academy, 1970; Hon. Member: Amer. Acad. of Arts and Letters, 1975; Amer. Acad. of Arts and Sciences, 1982. Hon. Fellow, Newnham Coll., Cambridge, 1986. *Publications*: Sartre, Romantic Rationalist, 1953; Under the Net, 1954; The Flight from the Enchanter, 1955; The Sandcastle, 1957; The Bell, 1958; A Severed Head, 1961 (play, Criterion, 1963); An Unofficial Rose, 1962; The Unicorn, 1963; The Italian Girl, 1964 (play, Criterion, 1967); The Red and the Green, 1965; The Time of The Angels, 1966; The Nice and the Good, 1968; Bruno's Dream, 1969; A Fairly Honourable Defeat, 1970; The Sovereignty of Good, 1970; An Accidental Man, 1971; The Black Prince, 1973 (James Tait Black Meml Prize); The Sacred and Profane Love Machine, 1974 (Whitbread Prize); A Word Child, 1975; Henry and Cato, 1976; The Fire and the Sun, 1977; The Sea, the Sea, 1978 (Booker Prize, 1978); Nuns and Soldiers, 1980; The Philosopher's Pupil, 1983; The Good Apprentice, 1985; Acastos, 1986; *plays*: The Servants and the Snow (Greenwich), 1970; The Three Arrows (Arts, Cambridge), 1972; Art and Eros (Nat. Theatre), 1980; *poems*: A Year of Birds, 1978; papers in Proc. Aristotelian Soc., etc. *Recreation*: learning languages.

MURDOCH, (Keith) Rupert, AC 1984; Publisher; Group Chief Executive, The News Corporation Ltd, Australia; Chairman and Chief Executive (formerly Managing Director), News International plc, UK; Chairman and President, News America Publishing Inc.; Chairman, Times Newspapers Holdings Ltd, since 1982; *b* 11 March 1931; *s* of late Sir Keith Murdoch and of Dame Elisabeth (Joy) Murdoch, *qv*; *m* 1967,

Anna Torv; two *s* two *d*. *Address*: New York Post, 210 South Street, New York, NY 10002, USA; 1 Virginia Street, E1 9XN.

MURDOCH, Richard Bernard; Actor (stage, films, broadcasting, television); *b* Keston, Kent; *s* of late Bernard Murdoch and late Amy Florence Scott, both of Tunbridge Wells; *m* 1932, Peggy Rawlings; one *s* two *d*. *Educ*: Charterhouse; Pembroke Coll., Cambridge. Commenced theatrical career in chorus of musical comedies, after which played dancing, light comedy and juvenile rôles in musical comedy and revue. Productions include: The Blue Train; Oh, Kay; That's a Good Girl; The Five O'Clock Girl; C. B. Cochran's 1930 Revue; Stand Up and Sing; Ballyhoo; various Charlot revues; Over She Goes. The advent of broadcasting brought firstly several appearances as an early television star and then the famous partnership with Arthur Askey. At outbreak of War, 1939, was playing in Band Waggon at London Palladium and also making films; these include; The Terror; Over She Goes; Band Waggon; Charlie's Big-Hearted Aunt; The Ghost Train; I Thank You. In Jan. 1941 joined RAF as Pilot-Officer in Admin. and Special Duties Branch; one year at Bomber Command HQ (Intelligence Br.) and subs. Intelligence Officer at various stations all over the country; towards end of War became Sqdn Ldr under Wing-Comdr Kenneth Horne in Directorate of Administrative Plans, Air Ministry. In off-duty hours at Air Ministry during this period Much-Binding-in-the-Marsh was evolved with Kenneth Horne. Released from RAF Oct. 1945; went on tour with George Black's revue, Strike a New Note. Dame in Emile Littler's Pantomime, Little Miss Muffet, London Casino, Dec. 1949. 20 weeks in Australia for ABC recordings, 1954. Other films include: Three Men and a Girl. BBC radio series: Men from the Ministry, 1961–77; A Slight Case of Murdoch, 1986. Season with Shaw Festival of Canada and tour of USA, 1973. TV appearances include: Hazell; The Avengers; Owner Occupied; In the Looking Glass; This is Your Life; Rumpole of the Bailey; Doctor's Daughters; Churchill: The Wilderness Years, etc. *Recreations*: sailing, golf. *Address*: 2 Priory Close, Harrow Road West, Dorking, Surrey RH4 3BG. *Clubs*: Royal Automobile; Walton Heath Golf.

MURDOCH, Robert, (Robin Murdoch), TD 1946; MD; FRCSGlas, FRCOG; Consultant Obstetrician and Gynaecologist, Royal Maternity and Royal Samaritan Hospitals, Glasgow, 1946–76; *b* 31 July 1911; *s* of late James Bowman Young Murdoch and Christina Buntin Murdoch (*née* Wood); *m* 1941, Nora Beryl (*née* Woolley); two *s* (and one *s* decd). *Educ*: Hillhead High Sch., Glasgow; Glasgow Univ. MB ChB 1934, MD 1955; MRCOG 1940; FRCSGlas 1959; FRCOG 1961. Pres., Glasgow Univ. Union, 1933. Served War, 1939–45; Major RAMC. Examiner in Obstetrics and Gynaecology, Univs of Glasgow and Cambridge. Royal College of Gynaecologists: Examiner; Mem. Council, 1954–60, 1968–74; Jun. Vice-Pres., 1974–75; Sen. Vice-Pres., 1975–77. Pres., Scottish AAA, 1956; Mem., British Amateur Athletic Bd, 1956. *Publications*: contribs to medical jls. *Recreations*: angling, golf, gardening, athletics (rep. Scotland (British Empire Games, 1934), and GB (1931, 1933, 1934, 1935, 1938) in 220 yds). *Address*: Carrick Arden, Torwoodhill Road, Rhu, Helensburgh G84 8LE. *T*: Helensburgh 820481. *Clubs*: Oriental; Royal Scottish Automobile (Glasgow).

MURDOCH, Rupert; *see* Murdoch, K. R.

MURDOCH, William Ridley Morton, CBE 1963; DSC 1940 and Bar, 1942; VRD 1949; Sheriff of Grampian, Highland and Islands (formerly Ross and Cromarty), at Dingwall and Tain, 1971–78; *b* 17 May 1917; *s* of William Ridley Carr Murdoch and Margaret Pauline Mackinnon; *m* 1941, Sylvia Maud Pearson; one *s* one *d*. *Educ*: Kelvinside Academy, Glasgow; Glasgow Univ. (MA, LLB). War Service in Navy, 1939–45; Captain, RNR, 1959. Solicitor in private practice, 1947–71; Dir, Glasgow Chamber of Commerce, 1955–71; Dean, Royal Faculty of Procurators in Glasgow, 1968–71. DL, County of City of Glasgow, 1963–75. OStJ 1976. *Recreations*: sailing, gardening. *Address*: Aird House, Gairloch, Ross-shire. *T*: Badachro 243.

MURERWA, Dr Herbert Muchemwa; High Commissioner for Zimbabwe, since 1984; *b* 31 May 1941; *m* 1969, Ruth Chipo; one *s* four *d*. *Educ*: Harvard University. EdD (Educational Planning). Economic Affairs Officer, UN Economic Commission for Africa, Addis Ababa, 1978–80; Permanent Sec., Min. of Manpower Planning, 1980–81; Permanent Sec., Min. of Labour and Social Services, 1982–84. *Address*: Zimbabwe House, 429 Strand, WC2 0SA. *T*: 01–836 7755.

MURGATROYD, Prof. Walter, PhD; Professor of Thermal Power, Imperial College of Science and Technology, since 1968; Rockefeller International Fellow, Princeton University, 1979; *b* 15 Aug. 1921; *s* of Harry G. Murgatroyd and Martha W. Strachan; *m* 1952, Denise Geneviève, *d* of late Robert Adolphe Schlumberger, Paris and Bénouville; one *s* one *d* (and one *s* decd). *Educ*: St Catharine's Coll., Cambridge. BA 1946, PhD 1952. Hawker Aircraft Ltd, 1942–44; Rolls Royce Ltd, 1944–46; Univ. of Cambridge (Liquid Metal and Reactor heat transfer research), 1947–54; UK Atomic Energy Authority, Harwell, 1954–56; Head of Dept of Nuclear Engineering, Queen Mary Coll., Univ. of London, 1956–67, and Dean of Engineering, 1966–67. Member: British-Greek Mixed Commn, 1963–78; British-Belgian Mixed Commn, 1964–78; British-Austrian Mixed Commn, 1965–78. Specialist Adviser to H of C Select Cttee on Energy, 1980–. *Publications*: contrib. to various scientific and technical journals. *Recreation*: music. *Address*: 3 Helme Close, SW19 7EB. *T*: 01–946 0415.

MURLESS, Sir (Charles Francis) Noel, Kt 1977; Trainer of racehorses, Newmarket, 1953–76; Owner: Woodditton Stud, Cambridgeshire; Cliff Stud, Yorkshire; *b* 1910; *m* 1940, Gwen Carlow; one *d*. Leading Trainer on the flat for ninth year at end of British flat racing season, 1973 (former years being 1948, 1957, 1959, 1960, 1961, 1967, 1968, 1970); The Queen's trainer until flat racing season of 1969. He made a new record in earnings ('256,899) for his patrons, 1967; over '2,500,000 in winning stakes; has trained the winners of 19 Classic races: Two Thousand Guineas (2); One Thousand Guineas (6); Derby (3) (Crepello, 1957; St Paddy, 1960; Royal Palace, 1967); Oaks (5); St Leger (3); other major races: King George VI and Queen Elizabeth (3); Eclipse (5); Coronation Cup (5); Champion Stakes (3). Mem., Jockey Club, 1977–. *Address*: The Bungalow, Woodditton, Newmarket, Suffolk.
See also H. R. A. Cecil.

MURLEY, John Tregarthen, DPhil; *b* 22 Aug. 1928; *s* of John Murley and Dorothea Birch; *m* 1954, Jean Patricia Harris; one *d*. *Educ*: University College, London (BA 1st Cl. Hons History); St Antony's Coll., Oxford (DPhil). Entered FO, 1955; Counsellor, Washington, 1976–80. *Publication*: The Origin and Outbreak of the Anglo-French War of 1793, 1959. *Recreations*: tennis, squash, piano.

MURLEY, Sir Reginald (Sydney), KBE 1979; TD 1946; FRCS; President, Royal College of Surgeons, 1977–80; *b* 2 Aug. 1916; *s* of Sydney Herbert Murley and Beatrice Maud Baylis; *m* 1947, Daphne, 2nd *d* of Ralph E. and Rowena Garrod; three *s* two *d* and one step *d*. *Educ*: Dulwich Coll.; Univ. of London; St Bartholomew's Hosp. (MB, BS Hons 1939, MS 1948). MRCS, LRCP 1939; FRCS 1946. Served War, RAMC, 1939–45: ME, E Africa, N Africa, Sicily, Italy and NW Europe; regtl and fld ambulance MO; Surgical Specialist, No 1 and 2 Maxillo-Facial Units and Fld Surg. Units; Major. St Bartholomew's Hospital: Jun. Scholarship, 1935; Sen. Schol., and Sir William Dunn

Exhibn in Anat., Univ. of London, 1936; House Surg., 1939; Anat. Demonstrator, 1946; Surg. Chief Asst, 1946–49; Cattlin Res. Fellow and Mackenzie Mackinnon Res. Fellow, RCP and RCS, 1950–51; Surgeon: St Albans Hosp., 1947; Royal Northern Hosp., London, 1953; Hon. Consultant Surgeon, St Bartholomew's Hosp., 1979. Chm., Med. Council on Alcoholism, 1980. Royal Coll. of Surgeons: formerly Tutor and Reg. Adviser; Examiner, primary FRCS, 1966–72; Mem. Council, 1970–82; Hunterian Orator, 1981; Bradshaw Lectr, 1981; Mem. Ct of Patrons, 1981–. Vis. Prof., Cleveland Clinic, USA, 1979 and 1982. Mitchiner Lectr, RAMC, 1981. FRSM; Fellow, Assoc. of Surgeons of GB and Ireland. Member: Hunterian Soc. (Pres., 1970–71; Orator, 1978); Med. Soc. of London (former Mem. Council; Pres., 1982); Harveian Soc. (former Mem. Council; Pres., 1983); BMA (former Councillor); Exec. Cttee, Soc. Internat. de Chirurgie, 1979–83 (Vice-Pres., 1985–86); European and internat. cardiovascular socs. Hon. Vice-Pres., Nat. Stroke Campaign, 1985; Hon. Member: Brit. Assoc. of Plastic Surgs, 1983; Brit. Assoc. of Clinical Anatomists, 1983; Reading Path. Soc., 1985. Sundry eponymous lectures and orations; Hon. FRACS and Syme Orator, 1979; Hon. FCSSA 1979; Hon. FRCSI 1980; Hon. FDSRCS 1981; Hon. Fellow: Italian Soc. Surg., 1979; Polish Assoc. of Surgeons, 1983. President: Sir John Charnley Trust, 1983–; Alleyn Club, 1983; Fellowship for Freedom in Medicine 1972–; Mem. Council, Freedom Assoc., 1982–; Patron, Jagiellonian Trust, 1984–; Sponsor, 1984, Trustee, 1986, Youth & Family Concern (The Responsible Soc.). *Publications:* (contrib.) Financing Medical Care, 1962; contrib. surg. textbooks; articles in med. literature on breast, thyroid and vascular diseases; articles on med. politics and econs. *Recreations:* golf, swimming, gardening, music, reading history and economics. *Address:* (home) Cobden Hill House, Radlett, Herts. *T:* 01–779 6532; (office) Consulting Suite, Wellington Hospital, Wellington Place, NW8 9LE. *T:* 01–586 5959. *Clubs:* Royal Automobile; Fountain (St Bart's Hospital).

MURPHY, Rear-Adm. Anthony Albert, CBE 1976; Special Project Executive, Ministry of Defence, 1977–82; retired, 1983; *b* 19 May 1924; *s* of Albert Edward Murphy and Jennie (*née* Giles); *m* 1954, Antonia Theresa (*née* Rayner); four *s*. *Educ:* Sir George Monoux Grammar Sch. National Provincial Bank, 1940–42; joined RN, 1942; commnd, 1944; Western Approaches, 1944–45; HMS Vanguard (Royal Tour of S Africa), 1945–49; HMS Bulwark (Suez); Comdr 1960; HMS Yarmouth/6th Frigate Sqdn, Kuwait, 1961–63; HMS Eagle, 1965–67; Captain 1967; Dir, Naval Guided Weapons, 1970–73; in comd HMS Collingwood, 1973–76; Rear-Adm. 1977; Vice-Pres., and Senior Naval Mem., Ordnance Board, 1977. *Recreations:* cricket, soccer (Chm. RNFA, 1973–76), country activities.

MURPHY, Mrs Brian Taunton; *see* Hufton, Prof. Olwen.

MURPHY, Christopher Philip Yorke; MP (C) Welwyn/Hatfield, since 1979; *b* 20 April 1947; *s* of Philip John and Dorothy Betty Murphy; *m* 1969, Sandra Gillian Ashton. *Educ:* Devonport High Sch.; Queen's Coll., Oxford (MA). Formerly Associate Dir, D'Arcy MacManus & Masius. President, Oxford Univ. Conservative Assoc., 1967; held number of Conservative Party offices, 1968–72. Contested (C): Bethnal Green and Bow, Feb. 1974, Oct. 1974. Vice-Chairman: Parly Urban and New Town Affairs Cttee, 1980–; Parly Arts and Heritage Cttee, 1981–; Mem., Select Cttee on Statutory Instruments, 1980–; UK Delegate to Council of Europe/WEU, 1983–. Nat. Cttee for 900th Anniversary of Domesday Book, 1986. Parish Councillor, Windlesham, Surrey, 1972–76. FRSA. Freeman, City of London, 1984. *Recreations:* walking, theatre, music, reading. *Address:* House of Commons, SW1. *Clubs:* Carlton; Hatfield Conservative; Oxford Union Society.

MURPHY, Cornelius McCaffrey, (Neil Murphy), MBE 1982; MA; Editor-in-Chief of Building Magazine, since 1983 (Editor 1974–83); Managing Director, Building (Publishers) Ltd, since 1981; Director, The Builder Group Ltd, since 1979; *b* 31 May 1936; 2nd *s* of Edward and Annie Murphy, Glasgow; *m* 1963, Joan Anne, *o d* of William Tytler, master carpenter, retd; two *d*. *Educ:* Holyrood Sch.; Univ. of Glasgow (MA 1958). Joined The Builder Group, 1962, following spells of teaching and management trng. Dep. Chm., Periodical Trng Trust Ltd (ptt), 1983–85. Mem., Worshipful Co. of Tylers and Bricklayers. *Recreations:* reading, racing, golf. *Address:* 42 St John's Park, Blackheath, SE3 7JH. *T:* 01–853 2625. *Club:* Royal Automobile.

MURPHY, Dervla; *b* 28 Nov. 1931; *d* of Fergus Murphy and Kathleen Rochfort-Dowling; one *d*. *Educ:* Ursuline Convent, Waterford. American Irish Foundn Literary Award, 1975; Christopher Ewart-Biggs Meml Prize, 1978; Irish Amer. Cultural Inst. Literary Award, 1985. *Publications:* Full Tilt, 1965, 7th edn 1984; Tibetan Foothold, 1966, 3rd edn 1968; The Waiting Land, 1967, 3rd edn 1969; In Ethiopia with a Mule, 1968, 4th edn 1985; On a Shoe String to Coorg, 1976, 3rd edn 1985; Where the Indus is Young, 1977, 2nd edn 1984; A Place Apart, 1978, 5th edn 1984; Wheels Within Wheels, 1979, 5th edn 1984; Race to the Finish?, 1981; Eight Feet in the Andes, 1983, 2nd edn 1985; Muddling Through in Madagascar, 1985; Ireland, 1985. *Recreations:* reading, music, cycling, swimming, walking. *Address:* Lismore, Co. Waterford, Ireland.

MURPHY, Rev. Canon Gervase; *see* Murphy, Rev. Canon J. G. M. W.

MURPHY, Sheriff James Patrick; Sheriff of North Strathclyde, since 1976; *b* 24 Jan. 1932; *s* of Henry Francis Murphy and Alice (*née* Rooney); *m* 1956, Maureen Coyne; two *s* one *d*. *Educ:* Notre Dame Convent; St Aloysius' Coll., Glasgow; Univ. of Glasgow (BL 1953). Admitted Solicitor, 1953; assumed partner, R. Maguire Cook & Co., Glasgow, 1959; founded firm of Ross Harper & Murphy, Glasgow, 1961. President: Glasgow Juridical Soc., 1962–63; Glasgow Bar Assoc., 1966–67; Mem. Council, Law Soc. of Scotland, 1974–76. Governor, St Aloysius' Coll., Glasgow, 1978–. *Recreations:* photography, canoeing, cycling, books, the history of writing. *Address:* 84 Kelvin Court, Glasgow, G12 0AH.

MURPHY, Most Rev. John A., DD; Archbishop Emeritus of Cardiff, (RC) (Archbishop, 1961–83); *b* Birkenhead, 21 Dec. 1905; *s* of John and Elizabeth Murphy. *Educ:* The English Coll., Lisbon. Ordained 1931; consecrated as Bishop of Appia and Coadjutor Bishop of Shrewsbury, 1948; Bishop of Shrewsbury, 1949–61. ChStJ 1974. *Address:* Ty Mair, St Joseph's Nursing Home, Malpas, Newport, Gwent NP9 6ZE.

MURPHY, Rev. Canon (John) Gervase (Maurice Walker), MA; Domestic Chaplain to the Queen, Rector of Sandringham and Leader of Sandringham Group of Parishes, since 1979; Rural Dean of Heacham and Rising, since 1985; Hon. Canon of Norwich Cathedral, since 1986; *b* 20 Aug. 1926; *s* of William Stafford and Yvonne Iris Murphy; *m* 1957, Joy Hilda Miriam Livermore; five *d*. *Educ:* Methodist Coll., Belfast; Trinity Coll., Dublin (BA 1952, MA 1955; Rugby football team, 1947–52 (Capt., 1951–52); cricket colours). Guardsman, Irish Guards, 1944–45; commissioned Royal Ulster Rifles, 1945–47. TCD, 1947–52 and Divinity Sch., TCD, 1949–52. Ordained, 1952; Curate, Shankill Parish, Lurgan, 1952–55. Royal Army Chaplains' Dept, 1955; served: Korea, 1955–57; Woolwich, 1957–59; Aden, 1959–62; Infantry Junior Leaders, Oswestry, 1962–64; Bagshot, 1964–65; Worthy Down, 1965; Commonwealth Bde Sen. Chaplain, 1965–67; Sen. Chaplain, Guards Depot, Pirbright, 1967–69; DACG, Rhine Area, 1969–72; Sen. Chaplain, RMA Sandhurst, 1972–74; Asst Chaplain General: BAOR, 1974–75; South East, 1975–77. Vicar of Ranworth and RD of Blofield, 1977–79; Chaplain for Holidaymakers on Norfolk Broads, 1977–79. Played: Internat. Rugby football for Ireland, 1952, 1954 and 1958; Rugby football for British Army 1957, and for Barbarians, 1958. *Recreations:* people; sport, walking, gardening, interior decorating, wood chopping! *Address:* Sandringham Rectory, Norfolk PE35 6EH. *T:* Dersingham 40587. *Clubs:* British Sportsman's, London Irish RFC, Public School Wanderers RFC; Leprechauns Cricket (Ireland); Mid-Ulster Cricket.

MURPHY, Sir Leslie (Frederick), Kt 1978; Chairman: Petroleum Economics Ltd, since 1980; National Enterprise Board, 1977–79 (Deputy Chairman, 1975–77); *b* 17 Nov. 1915; *s* of Frederick Charles and Lillian Annie Murphy; *m* 1940, Marjorie Iris Cowell; one *s* one *d*. *Educ:* Southall Grammar Sch.; Birkbeck Coll., Univ. of London. Principal Private Sec. to Minister of Fuel and Power, 1947–49; Asst Sec., Min. of Fuel and Power, 1949–52; Chm., Mobil Supply Co. Ltd and Mobil Shipping Co. Ltd, 1955–59; Finance Dir, Iraq Petroleum Co. Ltd, 1959–64; Dir, J. Henry Schroder Wagg & Co. Ltd, 1964–75 (Dep. Chm. 1972–73); Dep. Chm., Schroders Ltd, 1973–75, Dir, 1979–; Director: Unigate Ltd, 1968–75; Simon Engrg Ltd, 1980–85; Folksam International Insurance (UK) Ltd, 1980–. Mem., NEDC, 1977–79. Mem. Royal Commn on Distribution of Income and Wealth, 1974–76; Board Mem., Church Army, 1964–; Chm., Church Army Housing Ltd, 1973–82, Pres., 1982–84. Trustee, SDP, 1981–. *Recreations:* music, golf. *Address:* Hedgerley, Barton Common Road, Barton-on-Sea, Hants.

MURPHY, Neil; *see* Murphy, C. McC.

MURPHY, Patrick James, CMG 1985; HM Diplomatic Service; Counsellor, Foreign and Commonwealth Office, since 1981; *b* 11 March 1931; *e s* of late Dr James Murphy and Cicely Mary (*née* Crowley); *m* 1st, 1959, Barbara May Healey-Purse (marr. diss. 1969); two *s*; 2nd, 1974, Jutta Ulrike Oehlmann; one *s*. *Educ:* Cranbrook School; Gonville and Caius College, Cambridge (BA; Geography Tripos). Oxford and Cambridge Far Eastern Expedition, 1955–56; BBC Gen. Overseas Service, 1956; Joined FO, 1957; Frankfurt, 1958; Berlin, 1959; FO, 1962; Second Sec. (Commercial), Warsaw, 1962; First Sec., FO, 1965; First Sec. (Commercial) and Consul, Phnom Penh, 1966; Consul, Düsseldorf, 1969; Consul, Hamburg, 1971; FCO, 1974; First Sec., Vienna, 1977. *Recreations:* history, travel, wine, boating, skiing. *Address:* c/o Foreign and Commonwealth Office, SW1; c/o Lloyds Bank, 6 Pall Mall, SW1. *Club:* Royal Air Force.

MURPHY, Patrick Wallace; Under Secretary, Ministry of Agriculture, Fisheries and Food, since 1986; *b* 16 Aug. 1944; *s* of Lawrence Vincent Murphy and Agnes Dunn; *m* 1972, Denise Lillieth Fullarton-Fullarton; two *s*. *Educ:* St Chad's College, Wolverhampton; Trinity Hall, Cambridge (BA Hons). Joined MAFF, 1966; Asst Private Sec. to Minister of Agriculture, Fisheries and Food, 1970; First Sec. (Agriculture and Commercial), British Embassy, Washington, 1974–78; Controller of Plant Variety Rights, 1978–82; Head, Land Use and Tenure Div., MAFF, 1982–86. Non-Exec. Dir, IDV (UK), 1985–. *Recreations:* cricket, gardening. *Address:* Moors Cottage, Elstead, Surrey. *T:* Elstead 703151.

MURPHY, Richard Holmes; Chairman, Industrial Tribunals, 1972–84; *b* 9 July 1915; *o s* of Harold Lawson Murphy, KC, and Elsie, 4th *d* of Rt Hon. Lord Justice Holmes; *m* 1967, Irene Sybil, *e d* of Reginald and Elizabeth Swift. *Educ:* Charterhouse; Emmanuel Coll., Cambridge (MA, LLB). Called to Bar, Inner Temple, 1939. Enlisted Inns of Court Regt, 1939; Commissioned 3rd County of London Yeomanry, 1940; served Middle East and Italy, 1941–45; Judge Advocate-Gen.'s Dept, WO, 1945–46; released, rank of Major. Resident Magistrate, Tanganyika, 1948; Chief Registrar, Gold Coast Supreme Ct and Registrar of W African Ct of Appeal, 1951; Sen. Magistrate, Gold Coast, 1955; Puisne Judge, Ghana, 1957–60; Judge of High Court, Tanganyika, 1960–64; Senior Lectr in Law, Polytechnic of Central London (formerly Holborn Coll.), 1965–72. *Address:* 3 Abingdon Court, Abingdon Villas, W8 6BS. *T:* 01–937 4540.

MURPHY, Stephen Dunlop; Chief Assistant (Television), Independent Broadcasting Authority, 1982–85; *b* Glasgow, 28 Aug. 1921; *s* of Stephen Dunlop Murphy and Jean Irwin; *m* 1944, Jean Marian Smith, Burnley; two *s* one *d*. *Educ:* Royal Grammar Sch., Newcastle upon Tyne; Manchester Grammar Sch.; Balliol Coll., Oxford (BA). Asst Master, Manchester Grammar Sch., 1943; BBC Educn Officer, 1951; BBC Producer, 1955; ITA Regional Officer North, 1961; Senior Programme Officer, ITA, 1966; Secretary, British Bd of Film Censors, 1971–75; Programme Officer, IBA, 1976–82. *Address:* 16 Selwyn Court, Church Road, Richmond, Surrey.

MURPHY, Thomas A(quinas); Director, General Motors Corporation (Chairman, 1974–80); *b* Hornell, NY, 10 Dec. 1915; *s* of John Joseph Murphy and Alma (*née* O'Grady); *m* 1941, Catherine Rita Maguire; one two *d*. *Educ:* Leo High Sch., Chicago; Univ. of Illinois. US Naval Reserve, 1943–46. Joined General Motors Corporation, 1938; Asst Treas., 1959; Comptroller, 1967; Treas., 1968–70; Vice-Pres. and Gp Exec., Car and Truck Div., 1970–72; Vice-Chm., 1972–74. *Address:* c/o General Motors Corporation, General Motors Building, Detroit, Mich 48202, USA.

MURPHY, William Parry, AB, MD; Lecturer on Medicine, Harvard Medical School, 1948–58, Lecturer Emeritus, 1958; Senior Associate in Medicine, Peter Bent Brigham Hospital, 1935–58, Senior Associate Emeritus in Medicine and Consultant in Hematology since 1958; Consultant Hematologist: Melrose Hospital, Melrose, Mass; Quincy City Hospital, Quincy, Mass; Emerson Hospital, Concord, Mass; Consultant in Internal Medicine, Delaware State Hospital, Farnhurst, Delaware; *b* 6 Feb. 1892; *s* of Thomas Francis Murphy and Rose Anna Parry; *m* 1919, Pearl Harriett Adams; one *s* (one *d* decd). *Educ:* Univ. of Oregon (AB); Harvard Med. Sch. (MD). Army, enlisted Medical Reserve, 1917–18; acted as House Officer at the Rhode Island Hosp., 1920–22; as Asst Resident Physician, 1922–23; Junior Associate in Medicine, 1923–28; Associate in Medicine, 1928–35 at Peter Bent Brigham Hospital; Asst in Medicine, 1923–28; Instructor in Medicine, 1928–35; Associate in Medicine, Harvard Medical Sch., 1935–48; has been engaged in the practice of Medicine since 1923, and carried on research at the Peter Bent Brigham Hospital in Boston; Diplomate in Internal Medicine, 1937. Mem. Bd of Dirs, Cordis Corp., 1960–70. Mem. many American and foreign medical and scientific socs; co-discoverer of the liver treatment for pernicious anemia; Cameron Prize in Medicine, Univ. of Edinburgh Medical Faculty, 1930; Bronze Medal, American Medical Association, 1934; Nobel Prize in Physiology or Medicine, 1934; Paul Harris Fellow Award, Brookline Rotary Club, 1980. Hon. Dr of Science, Gustavus Adolphus Coll., 1963; Hon. Member: Univ. of Oregon Med. Alumni Assoc., 1964; Internat. Soc. for Research on Civilisation Diseases and Vital Substances, 1969. Commander of the first rank, Order of the White Rose, Finland, 1934; gold medal, Mass Humane Soc., 1935; National Order of Merit, Carlos J. Finlay, Official, Havana, Cuba, 1952; Dist. Achievement Award, City of Boston, 1965; Internat. Bicentenial Symposium Award, Boston, 1972; Gold Badge, Mass Med. Soc. 50th Anniv., 1973. *Publications:* Anemia in Practice: Pernicious Anemia, 1939; about 75 papers published in medical journals, especially on diseases of the blood. *Recreation:* collector of rare old firearms. *Address:* 97 Sewall Avenue, Brookline, Mass 02146, USA. *Clubs:* Sigma xi (Harvard); Harvard (Boston); Rotary (Brookline, Mass).

MURPHY-O'CONNOR, Rt. Rev. Cormac; *see* Arundel and Brighton, Bishop of, (RC).

MURRAY; *see* Erskine-Murray.

MURRAY, family name of **Duke of Atholl,** of **Earl of Dunmore,** of **Earl of Mansfield and Mansfield** and of **Barons Murray of Epping Forest** and **Murray of Newhaven.**

MURRAY, Rt. Hon. Lord; Ronald King Murray, PC 1974; a Senator of the College of Justice in Scotland, since 1979; *b* 15 June 1922; *s* of James King Murray, MIEE, and Muriel (*née* Aitken), Glasgow; *m* 1950, Sheila Winifred Gaml one *s* one *d*. *Educ:* George Watson's Coll., Edinburgh; Univ. of Edinburgh; Jesus Coll., Oxford. MA (1st cl. hons Phil) Edinburgh, 1948; LLB Edinburgh, 1952. Served HM Forces, 1941–46; commnd in REME, 1942; India and SEAC, 1943–46. Asst in Moral Philosophy, Edinburgh Univ., 1949; called to Scottish Bar, 1953; QC (Scotland) 1967; Standing Jun. Counsel to BoT (Scotland), 1961–64; Advocate-Depute, 1964–67; Senior Advocate-Depute, 1967–70. MP (Lab) Leith, Edinburgh, 1970–79; Lord Advocate, 1974–79. Assessor, Edinburgh Univ. Court, 1981–. *Publications:* articles in various jls. *Recreation:* boating. *Address:* 31 Boswall Road, Edinburgh EH5 3RP. *T:* 031–552 5602. *Clubs:* Royal Forth Yacht, Forth Corinthian Yacht.

MURRAY, Bishop of The, since 1970; **Rt. Rev. Robert George Porter,** OBE 1952; *b* 7 Jan. 1924; *s* of Herbert James and Eileen Kathleen Porter; *m* 1954, Elizabeth Mary Williams; two *d*. *Educ:* Canterbury Boys' High School; St John's Theological Coll., Morpeth, NSW; Moore College, Sydney (ThL Hons). Served with AIF, 1942–44. Deacon 1947, priest 1948; Assistant Curate, Christ Church Cathedral, Ballarat, Victoria, 1947–49; Assistant Curate, St Paul's, Burwood, Sydney, 1949–50; Priest in charge of Isivita and Agenehambo, Diocese of New Guinea, 1950–57; Archdeacon of Ballarat, 1957–70; Assistant Bishop of Ballarat, 1967–70. *Recreations:* gardening, reading. *Address:* 48 Eleanor Terrace, Murray Bridge, SA 5253, Australia. *T:* 32 2240.

MURRAY OF EPPING FOREST, Baron *cr* 1985 (Life Peer), of Telford in the County of Shropshire; **Lionel Murray,** OBE 1966; PC 1976; General Secretary of the Trades Union Congress, 1973–84; *b* 2 Aug. 1922; *m* 1945, Heather Woolf; two *s* two *d*. *Educ:* Wellington (Salop) Gram. Sch.; Univ. of London, 1940–41; NCLC; New Coll., Oxford, 1945–47 (Hon. Fellow, 1975). Economic Dept, TUC, 1947, Head of Dept, 1954–69; Asst Gen. Sec., TUC, 1969–73. Mem., NEDC, 1973–84; Vice-President: ICFTU, 1973; European Trade Union Confedn, 1974. Vice-President: Nat. Children's Home; Hearing and Speech Trust; Luton Industrial Coll.; Ironbridge Mus. Trust. Trustee: Carnegie UK Trust; Anglo-German Foundn; Crisis at Christmas; Prison Service Trust. Governor: NIESR; LSE; Ditchley Foundn; Nat. Youth Theatre, etc. Vis. Fellow, Nuffield Coll., Oxford, 1974. Hon. Fellow, Sheffield City Polytechnic, 1979. Hon. DSc: Aston, 1977; Salford, 1978; Hon. LLD: St Andrews, 1979; Leeds, 1985. *Publication:* Contrib. to Economics and Technical Change. *Address:* 29 The Crescent, Loughton, Essex. *T:* 01–508 4425.

MURRAY OF NEWHAVEN, Baron *cr* 1964 (Life Peer); **Keith Anderson Hope Murray,** KCB 1963; Kt 1955; Chancellor, Southampton University, 1964–74; Visitor, Loughborough University of Technology, 1968–78; *b* 28 July 1903; 2nd surv. *s* of late Rt Hon. Lord Murray, PC, CMG, LLD. *Educ:* Edinburgh Academy; Edinburgh Univ. (BSc); Ministry of Agriculture, 1925–26; Commonwealth Fund Fellowship, 1926–29, at Cornell Univ., New York (PhD); Oriel Coll. and Agricultural Economics Research Institute, 1929–32, University of Oxford (BLitt and MA); Research Officer, 1932–39; Fellow and Bursar, Lincoln Coll., 1937–53, and Rector, 1944–53; Chm., Univ. Grants Cttee, 1953–63. Oxford City Council, 1938–40; Min. of Food, 1939–40; RAFVR 1941–42; Dir of Food and Agriculture, Middle East Supply Centre, GHQ, MEF, 1942–45; Oxfordshire Education Cttee, 1946–49; JP, City of Oxford, 1950–53; Chm., Vice-Chancellor's Commission of Enquiry on Halls of Residence, 1947; Mem. of Commission of Enquiry into Disturbances in the Gold Coast, 1948; Development Commissioner, 1948–53; Chairman: Advisory Cttee on Colonial Colleges of Arts, Science and Technology, 1949–53, RAF Education Advisory Cttee, 1947–53; National Council of Social Service, 1947–53. Advisory Cttees on Agricultural Colls, 1954–60, Harkness Fellowship Cttee of Award, 1957–63, Cttee on Provincial Agricultural Economics Service, 1949–57, Cttee on Australian Univs, 1957; World Univ. Service, 1957–62; Dartmouth Review Cttee, 1958; Pres. Agric. Economics Soc., 1959–60; Pres. Agricultural History Soc., 1959–62; Chairman: Colonial Univ. Grants Cttee, 1964–66; London Conf. on Overseas Students, 1963–67; Academic Adv. Cttee for Stirling Univ., 1967–75. Vice-Pres., Wellington Coll., 1966–69; Governor, The Charterhouse, 1957–69. Mem. Bd, Wellcome Trustees, 1965–73; Dir, Leverhulme Trust Fund, 1964–72; Hon. Pres., Nat. 1.wUnion of Students, 1967–70. Chairman: Cttee of Enquiry into Governance of London Univ., 1970–72; Royal Commn for Exhibition of 1851, 1962–71. Director: Bristol Aeroplane Co., 1963–67; Metal Box Co., 1964–68. Hon. Fellow: Downing Coll., Cambridge; Oriel Coll., Oxford; Lincoln Coll., Oxford; Birkbeck Coll., London. Hon. LLD: Western Australia and of Bristol, 1963; Cambridge, Hull, Edinburgh, Southampton, Liverpool and Leicester, 1964; Calif., 1966; London and Strathclyde, 1973; Hon. DCL Oxford, 1964; Hon. DLitt Keele, 1966; Hon. DUniv. Stirling, 1968; Hon. DU Essex, 1971; Hon. FDSRCS, 1964; Hon. FUMIST, 1965. *Address:* 224 Ashley Gardens, SW1. *T:* 01–828 4113. *Club:* United Oxford & Cambridge University.

MURRAY, Dame (Alice) Rosemary, DBE 1977; MA, DPhil; JP; DL; President, New Hall, Cambridge, 1964–81 (Tutor in Charge, 1954–64); Vice-Chancellor, Cambridge University, 1975–77; *b* 28 July 1913; *d* of late Adm. A. J. L. Murray and Ellen Maxwell Spooner. *Educ:* Downe House, Newbury; Lady Margaret Hall, Oxford (Hon. Fellow, 1968). MA (Oxon and Cantab); BSc, DPhil (Oxon). Lecturer in chemistry: Royal Holloway Coll., 1938–41; Sheffield Univ., 1941–42. Served War of 1939–45, Experimental Officer, Admiralty Signals Establishment, 1941; WRNS, 1942–46, successively Wren, 3rd, 2nd, 1st and Chief Officer. Lectr in Chemistry, Girton Coll., Cambridge, 1946–54, Fellow, 1949, Tutor, 1951, Hon. Fellow, 1976; Demonstrator in Chemistry, Univ. of Cambridge, 1947–52. Dir, Midland Bank Ltd, 1978–84; Independent Dir, The Observer, 1981–. Member: Lockwood Cttee on Higher Educn in NI, 1963–65; Wages Councils, 1968–; Council, GPDST, 1969–; Armed Forces Pay Review Body, 1971–81; Pres., Nat. Assoc. of Adult Educn, 1977–80, Vice-Pres., 1980–83. Governor and Chm., Keswick Coll. of Education, 1953–83; Mem. Delegacy, Goldsmiths' Coll., London Univ., 1986–. Mem. Council, Toynbee Hall, 1983–. Liveryman, Goldsmiths' Co., 1978–. JP City of Cambridge, 1953–83; DL Cambs, 1982. Hon. Fellow: LMH, Oxford, 1970; Girton Coll., Cambridge, 1975; New Hall, Cambridge, 1981; Robinson Coll., Cambridge, 1985. Hon. DSc: New Univ. of Ulster, 1972; Leeds, 1975; Pennsylvania, 1975; Wellesley Coll., 1976; Hon. DCL Oxon, 1976; Hon. DL Univ. Southern California, 1976; Hon. LLD Sheffield, 1977. *Recreations:* foreign travel, gardening, book binding and restoring. *Address:* 9 Grange Court, Cambridge CB3 9BD. *Club:* University Women's.

MURRAY, Andrew Robin; HM Diplomatic Service; Counsellor, UK Mission to the United Nations, since 1984; *b* 21 Sept. 1941; *s* of Robert Alexander Murray and Jean Agnes Murray (*née* Burnett); *m* 1965, Irene Dorothy Foy; one *s* one *d*. *Educ:* Trinity Coll., Glenalmond; Edinburgh Univ. (MA Hons 1965). Economist with Govt of Ontario, Canada, 1966; investment analyst, ICFC, 1969; joined HM Diplomatic Service, 1973; First Sec., Islamabad, 1975–78; Head of Chancery, Buenos Aires, 1979–81; FCO, 1982–84. *Recreation:* sporadic sport. *Address:* c/o Foreign and Commonwealth Office, SW1.

MURRAY, Athol Laverick, PhD; FRHistS; Keeper of the Records of Scotland, since 1985; *b* Tynemouth, Northumberland, 8 Nov. 1930; *s* of late George Murray and Margery Laverick; *m* 1958, Irene Joyce Cairns; one *s* one *d*. *Educ:* Royal Grammar Sch., Lancaster; Jesus Coll., Cambridge (BA, MA); Univ. of Edinburgh (LLB, PhD). Research Assistant, Foreign Office, 1953; Assistant Keeper, Scottish Record Office, 1953–83; Deputy Keeper, 1983–84. FRHistS 1971. *Publications:* The Royal Grammar School, Lancaster, 1951; articles in Scottish Historical Review, etc. *Address:* 33 Inverleith Gardens, Edinburgh EH3 5PR. *T:* 031–556 4465. *Club:* Royal Commonwealth Society.

MURRAY, Brian; Under Secretary, Minerals and Metals Division, Department of Trade and Industry, since 1983; *b* 7 Feb. 1933; *s* of Sidney Franklin Murray and Marjorie Manton Murray; *m* 1958, Pamela Anne Woodward (marr. diss. 1982); one *s* two *d*. *Educ:* Queen Mary College, London. BSc Chem. Central Research Labs, Bowater Corp., 1957–64; Dept. of Scientific and Industrial Research, 1964–66; Min. of Technology, 1967–70; Cabinet Office, 1971–74; DTI 1974. *Recreations:* skiing, hill walking, running. *Address:* 8 Deepdale Avenue, Bromley, Kent. *T:* 01–464 6261.

MURRAY, Rear-Adm. Sir Brian (Stewart), KCMG 1982; AO 1978; Governor of Victoria, 1982–85; *b* 26 Dec. 1921; *s* of Alan Stewart Murray and Lily Astria (*née* Fenton); *m* 1st, 1954, Elizabeth Malcolmson (*d* 1962); one *s* two *d*; 2nd, 1973, Janette, *d* of Mr and Mrs J. J. Paris. *Educ:* Hampton High Sch., Vic; Royal Naval Coll., Dartmouth. Joined RAN, 1939; served War, 1939–45: cruisers and destroyers in Pacific, Indian and Atlantic Oceans, North Sea and China Sea; served Korean War, 1952–53: Sen. Air Direction Officer, HMAS Sydney (despatches); CO HMAS, Condamine, 1954–55; Staff course, RNC Greenwich, 1958–59; CO HMAS: Queenborough, 1961–62; Parramatta, 1963; Dir of Plans, Navy Office, 1964–65; IDC, London, 1966; CO HMAS Supply, 1967; Aust. Services Attaché, Tokyo, 1968–70; served Vietnam War, 1970: CO HMAS Sydney (troop transport); Hon. ADC to the Queen, 1971–72; Dir, Jt Ops and Plans, Dept of Defence, 1971, Dir of Jt Policy, 1972–73; Naval Officer i/c, Vic, 1974–75; Dep. Chief of Naval Staff, 1975–78; retd RAN, 1978. Operator of small vineyard and winery at Murrumbateman, on southern tablelands of NSW, 1978–. *Recreations:* golf, tennis, horse racing. *Address:* Doonkuna, Murrumbateman, NSW 2582, Australia.

MURRAY, Cecil James Boyd, MS; FRCS; Emeritus Consultant Surgeon, Middlesex Hospital, since 1975 (Surgeon, 1946–75); Surgeon, Royal Masonic Hospital, London, 1958–75; *b* 8 Jan. 1910; *s* of Richard Murray, MIEE; *m* 1940, Bona (*d* 1974), *o d* of Rev. William Askwith, MA, Ripon; two *s*. *Educ:* Warriston Sch., Moffat; King's Sch., Canterbury; Middlesex Hospital Medical Sch. MB, BS, 1935; MS 1936; MRCS, LRCP, 1933, FRCS 1936. Formerly: Surgeon, King Edward Memorial Hospital, Ealing; Lecturer in Operative Surgery, Middlesex Hospital Medical Sch. Served War of 1939–45 (despatches), temp. Lt-Col RAMC. Mem., Court of Examiners, Royal College of Surgeons of England; Fellow, Assoc. of Surgeons of Great Britain; FRSocMed. *Publications:* papers in medical journals. *Recreation:* fly-fishing. *Address:* Conifera, Comrie, Perthshire PH6 2LT. *T:* Comrie 70395. *Clubs:* Flyfishers', MCC.

MURRAY, Charles Henry; Chairman, Northern Bank (Ireland) Ltd, since 1986; Director, Northern Bank, since 1982; Deputy Chairman, Co-operation North, since 1983; *b* 1917; *s* of Charles and Teresa Murray; *m* 1942, Margaret Ryan; one *s* four *d*. *Educ:* Christian Brothers Sch., Synge Street, Dublin; London Univ. (BCom). Asst Secretary, Dept of Finance (Ireland), 1961, Secretary, 1969–76; Dir, 1969–76, Governor, 1976–81, Central Bank of Ireland. Hon. LLD, NUI, 1977. *Recreations:* reading, theatre, golf. *Address:* 6 Washington Park, Dublin 14. *T:* 947781.

MURRAY, Hon. Donald Bruce; Hon. Mr Justice Murray; Judge of the High Court of Justice in Northern Ireland, since 1975; *b* 24 Jan. 1923; *y s* of late Charles Benjamin Murray and late Agnes Mary Murray, Belfast; *m* 1953, Rhoda Margaret, *o c* of late Thomas and Anna Parke, Londonderry; two *s* one *d*. *Educ:* Belfast Royal Acad.; Queen's Univ. Belfast (LLB Hons); Trinity Coll. Dublin (BA). 1st Cl., Certif. of Honour, Gray's Inn Prize, English Bar Final Exam., 1944; Called to Bar, Gray's Inn, 1945. Asst Parly Draftsman to Govt of NI, 1945–51; Asst Lectr, Faculty of Law, QUB, 1951–53. Called to NI Bar, 1953, and to Inner Bar, NI, 1964; Bencher, Inn of Court, NI, 1971; Chm., Gen. Council of Bar of NI, 1972–75. Dep. Chm., Boundary Commn for NI, 1976–84. Mem. 1971, Chm. 1974, Incorporated Council of Law Reporting for NI; Dir, NI Legal Quarterly; Member: UK Delegn to Commn Consultative des Barreaux des Pays des Communautés Européennes, 1972–75; Jt Standing Cttee of Bars of UK and Bar of Ireland, 1972–75; Deptl Cttee on Registration of Title to Land in N Ireland. Chm., Deptl Cttee on Reform of Company Law in NI; Inspector apptd to report on siting of new prison in NI. Mem., Legal Adv. Cttee of Standing Cttee of General Synod of Church of Ireland. Governor, Belfast Royal Academy. *Publications:* articles in various legal periodicals. *Recreations:* playing the piano, DXing. *Address:* 40 Cadogan Park, Belfast, N Ireland.

MURRAY, Sir Donald (Frederick), KCVO 1983; CMG 1973; HM Diplomatic Service, retired; *b* 14 June 1924; *s* of A. T. Murray and F. M. Murray (*née* Byfield); *m* 1949, Marjorie Culverwell; three *s* one *d*. *Educ:* Colfe's Grammar Sch.; King's Sch., Canterbury (King's and Entrance Schols); Worcester Coll., Oxford. Royal Marines, 1943–46 (41 (RM) Commando). Entered Foreign Office, 1948; Third Sec., Warsaw, 1948; FO 1951; Second Sec., Vienna, 1953; First Sec., Political Office, ME Forces, 1956; FO, 1957; First Sec. (Comm.), Stockholm, 1958; Head of Chancery, Saigon, 1962; FO 1964; Counsellor, 1965; Head of SE Asia Dept, 1966; Counsellor, Tehran, 1969–72; RCDS, 1973; Ambassador to Libya, 1974–76; Asst Under-Sec. of State, FCO, 1977–80; Ambassador to Sweden, 1980–84. Assessor Chm., CS Selection Bd, 1984–. Dir, Goodlass Wall and Co., 1985–. Kent County Chm., SSAFA, 1985–. Grand Cross, Order of North Star (Sweden), 1983. *Publication:* Article in Seaford House Papers, 1973. *Recreations:* gentle sports (Oxford v Cambridge cross-country, 1942; athletics, 1943; small-bore shooting, 1947), gardening, music. *Address:* Oxney House, Wittersham, Kent TN30 7ED.

MURRAY, George Raymond B.; *see* Beasley-Murray.

MURRAY, George Sargent; Forestry Commissioner, 1981–84; *b* 2 Oct. 1924; *s* of James and Helen Murray; *m* 1951, Anita Garden Fraser; two *s*. *Educ:* Buckie High School. Inland Revenue, 1941–43; Royal Navy, 1943–46; Inland Revenue, 1946–49; Dept of Agriculture and Fisheries for Scotland, 1949–67; Scottish Development Dept, 1967–71; Scottish Economic Planning Dept, Scottish Office, 1971–76; Dept of Agriculture and Fisheries for Scotland, 1976–81. *Recreations:* golf, lapidary work. *Address:* 30 Easter Currie Terrace, Currie, Midlothian EH14 5LE. *T:* 031–449 2538.

MURRAY, Gen. Sir Horatius, GCB 1962 (CB 1945); KBE 1956; DSO 1943; Colonel of The Cameronians (Scottish Rifles), 1958–64, now retired; *b* 18 April 1903; *s* of late Charles Murray; *m* 1953, Beatrice (*d* 1983), artist, *y d* of Frederick Cuthbert, Upwood Park. *Educ:* Peter Symonds Sch., Winchester; RMC, Sandhurst. Gazetted to Cameronians, 1923; transferred to Camerons, 1935. Served War of 1939–45, North Africa, Sicily, Italy,

France (DSO, CB); GOC 6 Armoured Division, 1944–45; Dir of Personal Services, War Office, 1946–47; GOC 1st Infantry Division, 1947–50; GOC Northumbrian District, 1951–53; Commander, Commonwealth Division in Korea, 1953–54; GOC-in-C, Scottish Command and Governor of Edinburgh Castle, 1955–58; Commander-in-Chief, Allied Forces, Northern Europe, 1958–61, retired. Commander Legion of Merit (US); Knight of the Sword (Sweden). *Recreations:* golf, cricket. *Address:* 3 Duneaves, Mount Park Road, Harrow-on-the-Hill, Mddx HA1 3JS.

MURRAY, Sir James, KCMG 1978 (CMG 1966); HM Diplomatic Service, retired; Ambassador and Permanent UK Representative to UN and other International Organisations at Geneva, 1978–79; *b* 3 Aug. 1919; *er s* of late James Hamilton Murray, King's Cross, Isle of Arran, and Hester Macneill Buie; *m* 1982, Mrs Jill Charmian Chapuisat, *d* of Maj.-Gen. Frederick William Gordon-Hall, *qv;* two step *d. Educ:* Bellahouston Acad.; Glasgow Univ. Royal Regt of Artillery, 1939; served India and Burma, 1943–45; Staff Coll., Quetta, 1945; Bde Major (RA) 19 Ind. Div.; GSO II (RA) ALFSEA; GSO II War Office. HM Foreign (subseq. Diplomatic) Service, 1947; Foreign Office, 1947–49; First Sec. (Information), HM Embassy, Cairo, 1949–54; Foreign Office, 1954–56; attached National Defence Coll. of Can., 1956–57; First Sec., HM Embassy, Paris, 1957–61; HM Consul in Ruanda-Urundi, 1961–62; Special Ambassador for Independence celebrations in Ruanda, July 1962, and in Burundi, Sept. 1962; Ambassador to Rwanda and Burundi, 1962–63; Deputy Head of UK Delegation to European Communities, 1963–65; Counsellor, Djakarta, 1965–67; Head of Far Eastern Dept, FCO, 1967–70; Consul-Gen., San Francisco, 1970–73; Asst Under-Sec. of State, FCO, 1973–74; Dep. Perm. Representative to UN, 1974–78 (Ambassador, 1976). Special Envoy of 5 Western Govts for negotiations on Namibia, 1979–80; Advr, Trade Policy Res. Centre, London, 1981–; Hanson Industries, NY, 1983–. *Recreations:* horses, lawn tennis. *Address:* 220 Columbia Heights, Brooklyn Heights, New York, NY 11201, USA. *T:* (718) 852.3320. *Clubs:* Brooks's, Beefsteak, Pratt's; River (New York).

MURRAY, Prof. James Dickson, FRS 1985; FRSE 1979; Professor of Mathematical Biology, since 1986, Director, Centre for Mathematical Biology, since 1983, and Senior Research Fellow, Corpus Christi College, since 1985, University of Oxford; *b* 2 Jan. 1931; *s* of Peter and Sarah Murray; *m* 1959, Sheila Todd Murray; one *s* one *d. Educ:* Dumfries Acad.; Univ. of St Andrews (BSc 1953; Carstairs Medal; Miller Prize; PhD 1956); Univ. of Oxford (MA 1961; DSc 1968). Lectr, Applied Maths, Kings Coll., Durham Univ., 1955–56; Gordon MacKay Lectr and Res. Fellow, Tutor in Applied Maths, Leverett House, Harvard, 1956–59; Lectr, Applied Maths, UCL, 1959–61; Fellow and Tutor in Maths, Hertford College, Oxford, 1961–63; Res. Associate, Harvard, 1963–64; Prof. of Engineering Mechanics, Univ. of Michigan, 1964–67; Prof. of Maths, New York Univ., 1967–70; Fellow and Tutor in Maths, Corpus Christi Coll., Oxford, 1970–85; Reader in Maths, Univ. of Oxford, 1972–86. Vis. Fellow, St Catherine's Coll., Oxford, 1967; Guggenheim Fellow, Pasteur Inst., Paris, 1968; Vis. Professor: Nat. Tsing Hua Univ., 1975; Univ. of Florence, 1976; MIT, 1979; Winegard Prof., Univ. of Iowa, 1979; Univ. of Utah, 1979, 1985; Ida Beam Prof., Univ. of Guelph, 1980; Univ. of Heidelberg, 1980; CIT, 1983; Scott Hawkins Lectr, Southern Methodist Univ., Dallas, 1984; Stan Ulam Vis. Schol., Univ. of Calif. Berkeley's Los Alamos Nat. Lab., 1985. Member Editorial Boards: Jl Theor. Biol.; Jl Math. Biol.; Jl Maths Applied in Medicine and Biol.; Lecture Notes in Biomaths; Biomaths Series. *Publications:* Asymptotic Analysis, 1974, 2nd edn 1984; Nonlinear Differential Equation Models in Biology, 1977 (Russian trans. 1983); (ed with S. Brenner and L. Wolpert) Theories of Biological Pattern Formation, 1981; (ed with W. Jäger) Modelling of Patterns in Space and Time, 1984; numerous articles in learned jls. *Address:* Centre for Mathematical Biology, Mathematical Institute, 24–29 St Giles', Oxford OX1 3LB. *T:* Oxford 54295.

MURRAY, Prof. James Greig; Professor of Surgery, University of London, 1964–80, retired; Hon. Consultant Surgeon, King's College Hospital, London; *b* 1 April 1919; *s* of J. A. F. Murray and Christina (*née* Davidson); *m* 1946, Cecilia (*née* Mitchell Park); one *s* one *d. Educ:* Peterhead Acad.; Aberdeen Univ. MB, ChB 1942; FRCS Edinburgh 1950; ChM (Aberdeen) 1961; FRCS 1964. Surg.-Lt, RNVR, 1943–46. Lectr in Anatomy Dept, Univ. Coll., London, 1950–54; Clinical Research Fellow, MRC, RCS of England, 1954–56; Sen. Lectr in Surgery, Univ. of Aberdeen, 1958–59. Member: Senate of Univ. of London, 1973–77; SE Thames RHA, 1977–80. Chm., Cancer Res. Campaign Study on Breast Cancer. *Publications:* Scientific Basis of Surgery, 1965; Gastric Secretion: Mechanism and Control, 1965; After Vagotomy, 1969; articles in scientific and clinical jls on composition of vagus nerves, regeneration of nerves, physiology of gastric secretion and treatment of peptic ulceration, cancer of the breast, etc. *Recreations:* fishing, golf. *Address:* Pitearn, Alves by Forres, Moray, Scotland IV36 ORB. *T:* Alves 616.

MURRAY, James Patrick, CMG 1958; *b* 1906; *m* 1934, Margaret Ruth Buchanan; three *s. Educ:* St Edward's Sch., Oxford; Christ Church, Oxford. Cadet, Northern Rhodesia, 1929; District Officer, Northern Rhodesia, 1931; Provincial Commissioner, Northern Rhodesia, 1950; Senior Provincial Commissioner, Northern Rhodesia, 1955; Commissioner for Northern Rhodesia in London, 1961–64 (Country became Independent, as Zambia, 1964). *Address:* Trewen, Shaftesbury Road, Woking, Surrey. *T:* Woking 61988. *Club:* Royal Commonwealth Society.

MURRAY, John, QC (Scotland) 1974; *b* 8 July 1935; *o s* of J. H. Murray, farmer, Stranraer; *m* 1960, Bridget Jane, *d* of Sir William Godfrey, 7th Bt, and of Lady Godfrey; three *s. Educ:* Cairnryan Sch.; Park Sch., Stranraer; Stranraer High Sch.; Edinburgh Academy; Corpus Christi Coll., Oxford; Edinburgh Univ. BA Oxon 1959, LLB Edinburgh 1962. Advocate, 1962. Mem., Scottish Law Commn, 1979–. Chairman: Scottish Lawyers' European Gp, 1975–78; Scottish Council of Law Reporting, 1978–; Scottish Cttee on Law of Arbitration, 1986–; Vice-Pres., Agricultural Law Assoc., 1985– (Chm., 1979–85). *Publications:* (contrib.) Festschrift für Dr Pikalo, 1979; (contrib.) Mélanges offert à Jean Megret, 1985; (contrib.) Encyclopedia of Scots Law, 1987; articles in legal and ornithological jls. *Recreations:* farming, gardening, birdwatching, opera, field sports. *Address:* 4 Moray Place, Edinburgh EH3 6DS. *T:* 031–225 1881; Fell Cottage, Craigcaffie, Stranraer. *T:* Stranraer 3356; Wood of Dervaird Farm, Glenluce. *T:* Glenluce 222. *Clubs:* New, Puffins (Edinburgh).

MURRAY, John (Arnaud Robin Grey), CBE 1975 (MBE 1945); FSA; FRSL; Senior Director of Publishing House of John Murray since 1968; *o s* of late Thomas Robinson Grey and Dorothy Evelyn Murray; *m* 1939, Diana Mary, 3rd *d* of late Col Bernard Ramsden James and Hon. Angela Kay-Shuttleworth; two *s* two *d. Educ:* Eton; Magdalen Coll., Oxford (BA Hist). Joined publishing firm of John Murray, 1930; Asst Editor, Cornhill Magazine, 1931; Asst Editor, Quarterly Review, 1933. Served with Royal Artillery and Army-Air Support, War Office, 1940–45. Relaunched Cornhill Magazine with Peter Quennell, 1945. Member: Council, Publishers' Assoc., to 1976; Council, RGS, to 1978; Pres., English Assoc., 1976. *Publication:* (editor, with Peter Quennell) Byron: A Self-Portrait, 1950. *Recreations:* Byron, archives, forestry, music. *Address:* (office) 50 Albemarle Street, W1X 4BD. *T:* 01–493 4361; (home) Cannon Lodge, 12 Cannon Place, NW3. *T:* 01–435 6537. *Clubs:* Pratt's, Beefsteak, Brooks's; Roxburghe.

See also Viscount Mersey.

MURRAY, Katherine Maud Elisabeth, MA, BLitt, FSA; Principal, Bishop Otter College, Chichester, 1948–70; *b* 3 Dec. 1909; *d* of Harold J. R. Murray (former HMI of Schools) and Kate M. Crosthwaite. *Educ:* Colchester County High Sch.; Somerville Coll., Oxford. Tutor and Librarian, Ashburne Hall, Manchester, 1935–37; Mary Somerville Research Fellow, Somerville Coll., Oxford, 1937–38; Asst Tutor and Registrar, 1938–44, Domestic Bursar, 1942–44, and Junior Bursar, 1944–48, Girton Coll., Cambridge. Chairman of Council, Sussex Archæological Soc., 1964–77, Pres., 1977–80. Mem., Chichester District Council, 1973– (Chm. Planning Cttee, 1979–82, Vice-Chm., 1976–79, 1983–85). Hon. DLitt: Sussex, 1978; Coll. of Wooster, Ohio, 1979. *Publications:* The Constitutional History of the Cinque Ports, 1935; Register of Daniel Rough, Kent Record Soc., 1945; Caught in the Web of Words: James A. H. Murray and the Oxford English Dictionary, 1977; articles in Sussex Notes and Queries, Transactions of the Royal Historical Society, Archæologia Cantiana, English Historical Review. *Recreations:* walking, archæology. *Address:* Upper Cranmore, Heyshott, Midhurst, West Sussex. *T:* Midhurst 2325.

MURRAY, Prof. Kenneth, PhD; FRS 1979; Professor of Molecular Biology, University of Edinburgh, since 1976; *b* 1930; *yr s* of Allen and Elizabeth Ann Murray; *m* 1958, Noreen Elizabeth Parker (*see* N. E. Murray). *Educ:* Birmingham. Dept of Molecular Biology, Univ. of Edinburgh: Sen. Lecturer, 1967–73; Reader, 1973–76; Prof., 1976–. Member: Biochemical Soc.; European Molecular Organisation; British Biophysical Soc. *Publications:* papers on nucleic acid biochem. and molecular genetics. *Address:* Department of Molecular Biology, University of Edinburgh, Edinburgh EH9 3JR.

MURRAY, Kenneth Alexander George, CB 1977; MA, EdB; Special Adviser to the Home Office on Police Service, Prison Service, and Fire Service selection, 1977–80; Director, Civil Service Selection Board, and Civil Service Commissioner, 1964–77; *b* 16 June 1916; *s* of late George Dickie Murray and Isabella Murray; *m* 1942, Elizabeth Ward Simpson; one *d. Educ:* Skene Street and Central Schools, Aberdeen; Aberdeen Univ. (MA English (1st Cl. Hons), EdB Psychol. (1st Cl. Hons)). RAMC and War Office Selection Bd, 1940–45, Captain. Psychological Adviser, Govt of India, 1945–47; Lectr in Psychology, Univ. of Hull, 1948–50; Principal Psychologist and Chief Psychologist, CS Selection Bd, 1951–63. Adviser to Police Service in high-grade selection, 1963–, also to Fire and Prison Services, to Church of Scotland and C of E; Adviser (earlier) to Govts of Pakistan and Western Nigeria through their Public Service Commns. FBPs S 1984. *Recreations:* reading, walking, bridge, watching cricket and Rugby League. *Address:* 15 Melvinshaw, Leatherhead, Surrey KT22 8SX. *T:* Leatherhead 372995. *Clubs:* MCC, Royal Commonwealth Society.

MURRAY of Blackbarony, Sir Nigel Andrew Digby, 15th Bt *cr* 1628; farmer; *b* 15 Aug. 1944; *s* of Sir Alan John Digby Murray of Blackbarony, 14th Bt, and of Mabel Elisabeth, *d* of late Arthur Bernard Schiele, Arias, Argentina; *S* father, 1978; *m* 1980, Diana Margaret, *yr d* of Robert C. Bray, Olivos, Buenos Aires; one *s* one *d. Educ:* St Paul's School, Argentina; Salesian Agricl Sch., Argentina; Royal Agricultural Coll., Cirencester. Farms dairy cattle, store cattle, crops and bees. Holds a private pilot's licence. *Heir: s* Alexander Nigel Robert Murray, *b* 1 July 1981. *Address:* Establecimiento Tinamú, cc 115, 2624 Arias, Provincia de Córdoba, Argentina. *Clubs:* Venado Tuerto Polo and Athletic; Tigre Boat.

MURRAY, Noreen Elizabeth, PhD, FRS 1982; Reader, Department of Molecular Biology, University of Edinburgh, since 1978; *b* 26 Feb. 1935; *d* of John and Lillian Grace Parker; *m* 1958, Kenneth Murray, *qv. Educ:* King's College London (BSc); Univ. of Birmingham (PhD). Research Associate: Stanford Univ., California, 1960–64; Univ. of Cambridge, 1964–67; Mem., MRC Molecular Genetics Unit, Edinburgh, 1968–74; Lectr, 1974, later Sen. Lectr, Dept. of Molecular Biology, Univ. of Edinburgh; scientist in European Molecular Biol. Lab., Heidelberg, 1980–82. Member: EMBO; Genetical Soc.; Genetics Soc., USA. *Publications:* original research papers and reviews in field of genetics and molecular biology. *Recreation:* gardening. *Address:* Department of Molecular Biology, University of Edinburgh, Mayfield Road, Edinburgh. *T:* 031–667 1081.

MURRAY, Sir Patrick (Ian Keith), 12th Bt *cr* 1673; *b* 22 March 1965; *s* of Sir William Patrick Keith Murray, 11th Bt, and of Susan Elizabeth (who *m* 1976, J. C. Hudson, PhD), *d* of Stacey Jones; *S* father, 1977. *Educ:* Christ College, Brecon, Powys; LAMDA. *Heir: kinsman* Major Peter Keith-Murray, Canadian Forces [*b* July 1935; *m* 1960, Judith Anne, *d* of late Andrew Tinsley; one *s* one *d*]. *Address:* Sheephouse, Hay-on-Wye, Powys.

MURRAY, Peter, CMG 1959; HM Diplomatic Service, retired; *b* 18 July 1915; *m* 1960, E. M. Batchelor. *Educ:* Portsmouth Gram. Sch.; Merton Coll., Oxford. Burma Commission, 1937–49, Foreign Service, 1947; HM Ambassador to Cambodia, 1961–64; Ambassador to Ivory Coast, Upper Volta and Niger, 1970–72. *Address:* Brae Cottage, Lion Lane, Haslemere GU27 1JR. *Club:* East India.

MURRAY, Peter (John), PhD (London), FSA; Professor of the History of Art at Birkbeck College, University of London, 1967–80, now Emeritus; *b* 23 April 1920; *er s* of John Knowles Murray and Dorothy Catton; *m* 1947, Linda Bramley. *Educ:* King Edward VI Sch., Birmingham; Robert Gordon's Coll., Aberdeen; Gray's Sch. of Art, Aberdeen; Slade Sch. and Courtauld Inst., Univ. of London. Sen. Research Fellow, Warburg Inst., 1961. Trustee, British Architectural Library, 1979–83. Pres., Soc. of Architectural Historians of GB, 1969–72; Chm., Walpole Soc., 1978–81. Rhind Lecturer, Edinburgh, 1967; Vis. Prof., Univ. of Victoria, BC, 1981. *Publications:* Watteau, 1948; Index of Attributions . . . before Vasari, 1959; Dictionary of Art and Artists (with Linda Murray), 1959 (5th edn 1983); History of English Architecture (with P. Kidson), 1962 (with P. Kidson and P. Thomson), 1965; The Art of the Renaissance (with L. Murray), 1963; The Architecture of the Italian Renaissance, 1963, 3rd edn 1986; Renaissance Architecture, 1971; The Dulwich Picture Gallery, a Catalogue, 1980; (ed) J. Burckhardt, The Architecture of the Italian Renaissance, 1985; contribs to New Cambridge Mod. Hist., Encycl. Britannica, etc.; translations; articles in Warburg and Courtauld Jl, Burlington Mag., Apollo, foreign jls. *Address:* The Old Rectory, Farnborough, Banbury OX17 1DZ.

MURRAY, Robin MacGregor, MD; Dean, Institute of Psychiatry, since 1982; *b* 31 Jan. 1944; *s* of James Alistair Campbell Murray and Helen Murray; *m* 1970, Shelagh Harris; one *s* one *d. Educ:* Royal High Sch., Edinburgh; Glasgow Univ. (MB, ChB 1968; MD 1974). MRCP 1971; MRCPsych 1976; MPhil London, 1976. Registrar, Dept of Medicine, Univ. of Glasgow/Western Infirmary, 1971; Sen. House Officer, successively Registrar and Sen. Registrar, Maudsley Hosp., 1972–76; Vis. Fellow, National Inst. of Health, Washington, DC, 1977; Sen. Lectr, Inst. of Psych., 1978–82. *Publications:* (jtly) Essentials of Postgraduate Psychiatry, 1979; (jtly) Misuse of Psychotropic Drugs, 1981; articles on analgesic and alcohol abuse, schizophrenia, psychiatric illness in doctors, and psychiatric genetics.

MURRAY, Roger; President, Cargill Europe Ltd, since 1982; Chairman, Cargill UK Ltd, since 1982; *b* 8 June 1936; *s* of Donald Murray and Nancy (*née* Rons); *m* 1960, Anthea Mary (*née* Turnbull); one *s* three *d. Educ:* Uppingham Sch.; Brasenose Coll., Oxford (MA). RNVR (Sub-Lieut), 1954–56. Joined Cargill Inc., Minneapolis, 1959; various positions in Hull and Geneva, 1960–70; Pres., Cargill Canada, 1973. Mem., Management Cttee, Cargill Inc., 1986–. Canadian and British citizen. *Recreations:* sailing, ski-ing. *Address:* 11 Pembridge Place, W2 4XB. *T:* 01-243 0026.

MURRAY, Rt. Hon. Ronald King; *see* Murray, Rt Hon. Lord.

MURRAY, Dr Ronald Ormiston, MBE (mil.) 1945; MD; FRCPE, DMR, FRCR; Consulting Radiologist: Royal National Orthopaedic Hospital, since 1977 (Consultant Radiologist, 1956–77); Lord Mayor Treloar's Orthopaedic Hospital, Alton, and Heatherwood Hospital, Ascot, since 1977 (Consultant Radiologist, 1951–77); *b* 14 Nov. 1912; *y s* of late John Murray and Elizabeth Ormiston Murray (*née* MacGibbon); *m* 1st, 1940, Catherine Joan Suzette Gauvain, FFCM (*d* 1980), *d* of late Sir Henry Gauvain, MD, FRCS, and Laura Louise Butler; one *s* two *d*; 2nd, 1981, Jane (*née* Tierney), *widow* of Dr J. G. Mathewson. *Educ:* Glasgow Acad.; Loretto Sch.; St John's Coll., Cambridge (MA); St Thomas's Hosp. Med. Sch. Casualty Officer and Ho. Surg., St Thomas' Hosp., 1938–39; RAMC (TA), 1939–45, MO 2nd Bn The London Scottish, Hon. Lt-Col. Associate Prof., Radiology, Amer. Univ. Hosp., Beirut, 1954–56. Sen. Lectr in Orthopaedic Radiology, Inst. of Orthopaedics, London Univ., 1963–77; Robert Jones Lectr, RCS, 1973; Baker Travelling Prof. in Radiology, Australasia, 1974; Caldwell Lectr, Amer. Roentgen Ray Soc., 1975, also Corresp. Mem. of the Soc., 1973–; Skinner Lectr, RCR, 1979; other eponymous lectures. Associate Editor, Brit. Jl of Radiology, 1959–71. Founder Vice-Pres., Internat. Skeletal Soc., 1973, Pres., 1977–78. Fellow: Brit. Orthopaedic Assoc.; RSocMed (Pres., Sect. of Radiol., 1978–79); Hon. Fellow: Amer. Coll. of Radiology, 1969; Royal Australasian Coll. of Radiol., 1979; Fac. Radiol., RCSI, 1981; Hon. Member: Mexican and Peruvian Rad. Socs, 1968; Rad. Soc. of N Amer., 1975; GETROA, France, 1976. *Publications:* chapters in: Modern Trends in Diagnostic Radiology, 1970; D. Sutton's Textbook of Radiology, 1969, 2nd edn 1975; (jtly) Radiology of Skeletal Disorders: exercises in diagnosis, 1971, 2nd edn 1977; (jtly) Orthopaedic Diagnosis, 1984; papers in med. jls, mainly concerning radiological aspects of orthopaedics. *Recreations:* golf; formerly: Rugby football (Cambridge XV 1934–35, Scotland XV 1935), swimming (Cambridge Univ. Team 1933–34, British Univs Team, Turin, 1934). *Address:* Little Court, The Bury, Odiham, Hants RG25 1LY. *T:* Odiham 2982. *Clubs:* United Oxford & Cambridge University; Hawks (Cambridge), Berkshire Golf, Rye Golf.

MURRAY, Dame Rosemary; *see* Murray, Dame A. R.

MURRAY, Sir Rowland William Patrick, 14th Bt *cr* 1630; retired hotel general manager; *b* 26 Oct. 1910; *s* of late Rowland William Murray, 2nd *s* of 12th Bt, and Gertrude Frances McCabe; *S* uncle 1958; *m* 1944, Josephine Margaret Murphy; four *s* two *d*. Served in US Army during War of 1939–45. Captain. *Heir: s* Rowland William Murray, [*b* 22 Sept. 1947; *m* 1970, Nancy Diane, *d* of George C. Newberry; two *s*].

MURRELL, Geoffrey David George; HM Diplomatic Service; Counsellor, Moscow, since 1983; *b* 19 Dec. 1934; *s* of Stanley Hector Murrell and Kathleen Murrell (Martin); *m* 1962, Kathleen Ruth Berton; one *s* three *d*. *Educ:* Minchenden Grammar School, Southgate; Oxford Univ. BA French and Russian. FCO Research Dept, 1959–61; Moscow, 1961–64; FCO, 1964–68; Moscow, 1968–70; Head, Soviet Section, FCO Research Dept, 1970–75; First Sec., Belgrade, 1975–78; Regional Dir, Soviet and East European Region, Research Dept, 1978–83. *Recreations:* tennis, guitar. *Address:* c/o Foreign and Commonwealth Office, SW1A 2AH.

MURRELL, Prof. John Norman, PhD; FRSC; Professor of Chemistry since 1965, and Pro-Vice-Chancellor (Science), since 1985,University of Sussex; *b* London, 1932. *Educ:* Univ. of London (BSc); Univ. of Cambridge (PhD). University of Sussex: Dean, Sch. of Molecular Scis, 1979–84; Acad. Dir of Univ. Computing, 1984–85. Chm., Science Bd Computing Cttee, SERC, 1981–84. *Publications:* Theory of Electronic Spectra of Organic Molecules, 1960; (jointly): Valence Theory, 1965; Semi-empirical Self-consistent-field-molecular Theory of Molecules, 1971; Chemical Bond, 1978; Properties of Liquids and Solutions, 1982; Molecular Potential Energy Surfaces, 1985. *Address:* School of Molecular Sciences, University of Sussex, Falmer, Brighton BN1 9QJ.

MURRIE, Sir William (Stuart), GCB 1964 (CB 1946); KBE 1952; Permanent Under-Secretary of State for Scotland, 1959–64, retired; *b* Dundee, 19 Dec. 1903; *s* of Thomas Murrie and Catherine Burgh; *m* 1932, Eleanore Boswell (*d* 1966). *Educ:* S America; Harris Acad., Dundee; Edinburgh Univ.; Balliol Coll., Oxford. Entered Scottish Office, 1927; transferred to Dept of Health for Scotland, 1935; Under-Sec., Offices of War Cabinet, 1944; Deputy Sec. (Civil), Cabinet Office, 1947; Deputy Under-Sec. of State, Home Office, 1948–52; Sec. to the Scottish Education Dept, 1952–57; Sec., Scottish Home Dept, 1957–59. Chm., Board of Trustees for Nat. Galls of Scotland, 1972–75; Member: Council on Tribunals, 1965–77; Adv. Cttee on Rhodesian Travel Restrictions, 1968–79 (Chm., 1979). General Council Assessor, Edinburgh Univ. Court, 1967–75. Hon. LLD, Dundee Univ., 1968. *Address:* 7 Cumin Place, Edinburgh EH9 2JX. *T:* 031-667 2612.

MURSELL, Sir Peter, Kt 1969; MBE 1941; Vice-Lord-Lieutenant, West Sussex, since 1974; *b* 20 Jan. 1913; *m* 1938, Cicely, *d* of late Mr and Mrs M. F. North; two *s* two *d*. *Educ:* Bedales Sch.; Downing Coll. Cambridge. Fruit growing, 1934. War Service: Air Transport Auxiliary, 1940–44, Sen. Comdr. West Sussex County Council: Mem., 1947–74; Chm., 1962–67 and 1969–74. Member: Cttee on Management in Local Govt, 1965–66; Royal Commn on Local Govt in England, 1966–69; Water Space Amenity Commn, 1973–76; Inland Waterways Amenity Adv. Council, 1974–77. DL West Sussex, 1962. *Recreations:* sailing, mountain walking, skiing, squash, canal cruising. *Address:* Dounhurst Farm, Wisborough Green, Billingshurst, West Sussex. *T:* Kirdford 501. *Club:* Farmers'.

MURTA, Prof. Kenneth Hall, FRIBA; Professor of Architecture, University of Sheffield, since 1974; Dean, Faculty of Architectural Studies, 1973–76 and since 1984; *b* 24 Sept. 1929; *s* of John Henry Murta and Florence (*née* Hall); *m* 1955, Joan Wilson; two *s* one *d*. *Educ:* King's Coll., Univ. of Durham (BArch, DipArch). Architect in private practice and public service, 1954–59; Sen. Lectr, Nigerian Coll. of Arts, Science and Technology, then Amadhu Bello Univ., 1959–62; Lectr, then Sen. Lectr, Univ. of Sheffield, 1962–74. *Publications:* contribs to Architectural Rev., Ecclesiologist, Trans RIBA, Architects' Jl. *Recreations:* cricket, soccer, churchwatching, travel. *Address:* Underedge, Back Lane, Hathersage, Derbyshire S30 1AR. *T:* Hope Valley 50833.

MURTAGH, Miss Marion; Managing Director, Stats (MR) Ltd; Chairman, CSB Data Processing Ltd. *Educ:* Waverley Gram. Sch., Birmingham. Qualified as: Certified Accountant, 1947; Chartered Secretary, 1948. Proprietor, The Calculating Bureau, 1938–51, Joint Owner, 1951–61. Member: Anglo-Thai Soc.; West Midlands Bridge Club (Pres.). *Recreation:* bridge. *Address:* 116 Chessetts Wood Road, Lapworth, Solihull, West Midlands B94 6EL. *T:* Lapworth 2089.

MURTON, family name of **Baron Murton of Lindisfarne.**

MURTON OF LINDISFARNE, Baron *cr* 1979 (Life Peer), of Hexham in the County of Northumberland; **(Henry) Oscar Murton,** PC 1976; OBE 1946; TD 1947 (Clasp 1951); JP; a Deputy Chairman of Committees, since 1981 and a Deputy Speaker, since 1983, House of Lords; *b* 8 May 1914; *o s* of late H. E. C. Murton, and of E. M. Murton (*née* Renton), Hexham, Northumberland; *m* 1st, 1939, Constance Frances (*d* 1977), *e d* of late F. O'L. Connell; one *s* one *d*; 2nd, 1979, Pauline Teresa (Freeman, City of London, 1980; Chevalier, Nat. Order of Merit, France, 1976), *y d* of late Thomas Keenan. *Educ:* Uppingham Sch. Commissioned, TA, 1934; Staff Coll., Camberley, 1939; tsc; active service, Royal Northumberland Fusiliers, 1939–46; Lt-Col, Gen. Staff, 1942–46. Managing Dir, Henry A. Murton Ltd, Departmental Stores, Newcastle-upon-Tyne and Sunderland, 1949–57. MP (C) Poole, 1964–79; Sec., Cons. Parly Cttee for Housing, Local Government and Land, 1964–67, Vice-Chm., 1967–70; Chm., Cons. Parly Cttee for Public Building and Works, 1970; PPS to Minister of Local Government and Development, 1970–71; an Asst Govt Whip, 1971–72; a Lord Comr, HM Treasury, 1972–73; Second Dep. Chm., 1973–74, First Dep. Chm., 1974–76, Dep. Speaker and Chm. of Ways and Means, House of Commons, 1976–79. Member: Exec. Cttee, Inter-Parliamentary Union British Group, 1970–71; Panel of Chairmen of Standing Cttees, 1970–71; a former Vice-Pres., Assoc. of Municipal Corporations; Mem. Herrison (Dorchester) Hosp. Group Management Cttee, 1963–74. Governor, Canford Sch., 1972–76. Freeman, City of London, 1977; Freeman, Wax Chandlers' Co., 1978; Liveryman, 1979, a Warden, 1986, Clockmakers' Co. JP, Poole, 1963. *Recreations:* sailing, painting, military history. *Address:* 49 Carlisle Mansions, Carlisle Place, SW1P 1HY. *T:* 01-834 8226.

MUSCROFT, Harold Colin; barrister; *b* Leeds, 12 June 1924; *s* of Harold and Meta Catrina Muscroft; *m* 1958; three *d*. *Educ:* Dept of Navigation, Southampton Univ.; home; Exeter Coll., Oxford (MA). Volunteer, Royal Corps of Signals, 1942; commnd RA, 1943; served in India, Burma (wounded), Malay and Java; demobilised 1947 (Captain). Oxford, 1947–51. Called to Bar, Inner Temple, 1953; practised NE Circuit; a Recorder of the Crown Court, 1972–82. Called to Hong Kong Bar, 1982. Huddersfield Town Councillor, 1958–59. *Recreation:* writing. *Address:* 11 Chelmsford Road, Harrogate, North Yorks. *T:* Harrogate 503344; (chambers) 1201/2 Princes Building, Chater Road, Hong Kong.

MUSGRAVE, Sir Christopher (Patrick Charles), 15th Bt *cr* 1611; *b* 14 April 1949; *s* of Sir Charles Musgrave, 14th Bt and of Olive Louise Avril, *o d* of Patrick Cringle, Norfolk; *S* father, 1970; *m* 1978, Megan, *d* of Walter Inman, Hull; one *d*. *Recreations:* sailing, tennis, table-tennis, painting. *Heir: b* Julian Nigel Chardin Musgrave, *b* 8 Dec. 1951. *Address:* c/o Royal Bank of Scotland, Silver Street, Hull.

MUSGRAVE, Dennis Charles, FICE; Director, British Water Industries Group, since 1981; *b* 10 Feb. 1921; *s* of Frederick Charles Musgrave and Jane Elizabeth (*née* Gulliver); *m* 1942, Marjorie Cynthia (*née* Chaston); one *s*. *Educ:* privately. MIStructE, FIWES. Engineering Assistant: Howard Humphreys and Sons, Consulting Engrs; Coode and Partners, Cons. Engrs, 1938–45; Asst Port Engr, Lagos, Nigeria, 1945–47; Engrg Asst, Borough of Willesden, 1947–49; Agent, Ruddock and Meighan, Civil Engrg Contractors, 1949–56; Associate Partner, Sandford, Fawcett and Partners, Cons. Engrs, in Canada, 1956–63, in Westminster, 1963–66. Engineering Inspector, Min. of Housing and Local Govt, 1966, Sen. Inspector, 1971; Asst Dir, DoE, 1974; Chief Water Engr, DoE, 1977–82. *Publications:* various technical papers. *Recreations:* music, literature. *Address:* Gaywoods, Ringshall Road, Little Gaddesden, near Berkhamstead, Herts HP4 1PE. *T:* Little Gaddesden 3501.

MUSGRAVE, Sir Richard James, 7th Bt, *cr* 1782; *b* 10 Feb. 1922; *s* of Sir Christopher Norman Musgrave, 6th Bt, OBE, and Kathleen (*d* 1967), 3rd *d* of late Robert Chapman, Co. Tyrone; *S* father 1956; *m* 1958, Maria, *d* of late Col M. Cambanis, and Mrs Cambanis, Athens, Greece; two *s* four *d*. *Educ:* Stowe. Capt., The Poona Horse (17th Queen Victoria's Own Cavalry), 1940–45. *Recreation:* shooting. *Heir: s* Christopher John Shane Musgrave, *b* 23 Oct. 1959. *Address:* Riverstown, Tara, Co. Meath. *T:* Drogheda 25121; Komitu, Syros, Greece. *Club:* Kildare Street and University (Dublin).

MUSGRAVE, Thea; composer; *b* 1928; *d* of James P. Musgrave and Joan Musgrave (*née* Hacking); *m* 1971, Peter, *s* of Irving Mark, NY. *Educ:* Moreton Hall, Oswestry; Edinburgh Univ.; Paris Conservatoire; privately with Nadia Boulanger. *Works include:* Cantata for a summer's day, 1954; The Abbot of Drimock (Chamber opera), 1955; Triptych for Tenor and orch., 1959; Colloquy for violin and piano, 1960; The Phoenix and the Turtle for chorus and orch., 1962; The Five Ages of Man for chorus and orch., 1963; The Decision (opera), 1964–65; Nocturnes and arias for orch., 1966; Chamber Concerto No. 2, in homage to Charles Ives, 1966; Chamber Concerto No 3 (Octet), 1966; Concerto for orchestra, 1967; Music for Horn and Piano, 1967; Clarinet Concerto, 1968; Beauty and the Beast (ballet), 1968; Night Music, 1969; Memento Vitae, a concerto in homage to Beethoven, 1970; Horn concerto, 1971; From One to Another, 1972; Viola Concerto, 1973; The Voice of Ariadne (opera), 1972–73; Rorate Coeli, for chorus, 1974; Space Play, 1974; Orfeo I and Orfeo II, 1975; Mary, Queen of Scots (opera), 1976–77; Christmas Carol (opera), 1979; An Occurrence at Owl Creek Bridge (radio opera), 1981; Peripeteia (orchestral), 1981; Harriet, the Woman called Moses (opera), 1984; Black Tambourine for women's chorus and piano, 1985; Pierrot, 1985; For the Time Being for chorus, 1986. Performances and broadcasts: UK, France, Germany, Switzerland, Scandinavia, USA, USSR, etc., Edinburgh, Cheltenham, Aldeburgh, Zagreb, Venice and Warsaw Festivals. Hon. MusDoc, CNAA. *Address:* c/o Novello & Co. Ltd, Borough Green, Kent.

MUSGRAVE, Prof. William Kenneth Rodgerson, PhD, DSc (Birmingham); Professor of Organic Chemistry, 1960–81, now Emeritus, and Head of Department of Chemistry, 1968–71, 1974–77, 1980–81, University of Durham; *b* 16 Sept. 1918; *s* of late Charles Musgrave and late Sarah Alice Musgrave; *m* 1944, Joyce Cadman; two *s*. *Educ:* Stanley Grammar Sch., Co. Durham; Univ. of Birmingham. British-Canadian Atomic Energy Project, 1944–45; Univ. of Durham: Lecturer in Chemistry, 1945–56; Senior Lecturer, 1956–60; Personal Readership in Organic Chem., 1960; Second Pro-Vice-Chancellor, 1970–73; Pro-Vice-Chancellor and Sub-Warden, 1973–78; Acting Vice-Chancellor, 1979. *Publications:* (joint) Advances in Fluorine Chemistry, Vol. I, edited by Stacey, Tatlow and Sharpe, 1960; Rodd's Chemistry of Carbon Compounds, vols Ia and IIIa, edited by Coffey; scientific papers in chemical journals. *Recreations:* gardening, rough shooting. *Address:* The Orchard, Potter's Bank, Durham City. *T:* Durham 43196.

MUSGROVE, Prof. Frank, DLitt; Sarah Fielden Professor of Education, University of Manchester, 1970–82, now Emeritus; Dean of the Faculty of Education, 1976–78; *b* 16 Dec. 1922; *e s* of late Thomas and Fanny Musgrove; *m* Dorothy Ellen (*née* Nicholls); one *d*. *Educ:* Henry Mellish Grammar Sch., Nottingham; Magdalen Coll., Oxford; Univ. of Nottingham. MA Oxon, PhD Nottingham, MEd Manchester. Served War, RAFVR, 1941–45; Navigator, Bomber Command (commnd), Ops 149 Sqdn (tour of bombing missions completed 1944). Educational appts in England and in the Colonial Educn Service, E Africa, 1947–57; Lectureships in Univs of Leicester and Leeds, 1957–65; Foundn Chair of Research in Educn, Univ. of Bradford, 1965–70. Visiting Professor: of Educn, Univ. of BC, 1965; of Sociology, Univ. of California (Davis), 1969; Guest lectr, Inst. of Sociology, Univ. of Utrecht, 1968; The Chancellor's Lectr, Univ. of Wellington,

NZ, 1970; British Council Lectr, Univs of Grenoble, Aix-en-Provence, Nice, Paris, 1972; Raymond Priestley Lectr, Univ. of Birmingham, 1975. Hon. Prof., Univ. of Hull, 1985–. Co-editor, Research in Education, 1971–76. FRAI 1952; FRSA 1971. DLitt Open, 1982. *Publications:* The Migratory Elite, 1963; Youth and the Social Order, 1964; The Family, Education and Society, 1966; Society and the Teacher's Role (with P. H. Taylor), 1969; Patterns of Power and Authority in English Education, 1971; Ecstasy and Holiness: counter culture and the open society, 1974; Margins of the Mind, 1977; School and the Social Order, 1979; Education and Anthropology, 1982; research papers in: Africa; Sociological Review; Brit. Jl of Sociology; Brit. Jl of Educational Psychology; Economic History Review; Brit. Jl of Social and Clinical Psychology, etc. *Recreations:* fell walking, fly fishing. *Address:* Dibscar, The Cedar Grove, Beverley, N Humberside HU17 7EP. *T:* Hull 868799.

MUSGROVE, Harold John; Chairman and Chief Executive, Austin Rover Group, 1982–86; *b* 19 Nov. 1930; *s* of Harold Musgrove; *m* 1959, Jacquelin Mary Hobbs; two *s* two *d*. *Educ:* King Edward Grammar Sch., Birmingham; Birmingham Tech. Coll. Nat. Cert. of Mech. Eng. Apprentice, Austin Motor Co., 1945; held various positions, incl. Chief Material Controller (Commission as Navigator, RAF, during this period); Senior Management, Truck and Bus Group, Leyland Motor Corp., 1963–78; Austin Morris: Dir of Manufacturing, 1978–79; Man. Dir, 1979–80; Chm. and Man. Dir, 1980–81; Chm., Light Medium Cars Group, 1981–82. Midlander of the Year Award, 1980; IProdE Internat. Award, 1981; Soc. of Engineers Churchill Medal, 1982. *Recreations:* golf, cricket. *Address:* Cherry Trees, Honiley Road, Sen End, near Kenilworth, Warwicks.

MUSGROVE, Prof. John, RIBA; Haden Pilkington Professor of Environmental Design and Engineering, University of London at University College, 1978–85; Head of the Bartlett School of Architecture and Planning, University College London, 1980–85; *b* 20 June 1920; *s* of James Musgrove and Betsy (*née* Jones); *m* 1941, Gladys Mary Webb; three *s*. *Educ:* Univ. of Durham (King's Coll.) (BArch, 1st Cl. Hons). Asst to late Baron Holford, RA, 1952–53; Research Architect, Nuffield Foundn, 1953–60; Sen. Lectr and Reader in Architecture, University Coll. London, 1960–70, Prof., 1970–78. Hon. Fellow, Inst. of Architects, Sri Lanka, 1972. *Publications:* (jtly) The Function and Design of Hospitals, 1955; (jtly) The Design of Research Laboratories, 1960; numerous articles and papers in Architects' Jl, RIBA Jl, and reviews. *Recreations:* painting in oils, gardening. *Address:* Netherby, Green End Road, Boxmoor, Hemel Hempstead, Herts HP1 1QW.

MUSHIN, Prof. William W(oolf), CBE 1971; MA Oxon, 1946; MB, BS (Hons) London, 1933; FRCS 1966; FFARCS 1948; Professor and Director of Anaesthetics, Welsh National School of Medicine, University of Wales, 1947–75, now Emeritus; *b* London, Sept. 1910; *y s* of Moses Mushin and Jesse (*née* Kalmenson); *m* 1939, Betty Hannah Goldberg; one *s* three *d*. *Educ:* Davenant Sch.; London Hosp. Med. Sch. (Buxton Prize in Anatomy, Anderson Prize in Clinical Medicine). Various resident hosp. posts; formerly: Anaesthetist, Royal Dental Hosp.; first Asst, Nuffield Dept of Anaesthetists, Univ. of Oxford. Lectures: Clover, RCS, 1955; Kellogg, George Washington Univ., 1950; Guedel, Univ. of Calif, 1957; John Snow, 1964; Baxter Travenol, Internat. Anaesth. Research Soc., 1970; Macgregor, Univ. of Birmingham, 1972; Rovenstine, Amer. Soc. of Anesthesiol., 1973; Crawford Long, Emory Univ., USA, 1981. Visiting Professor or Consultant to univs, academic and other bodies in USA, Argentine, Uruguay, Brazil, Denmark, NZ, Australia, India, Germany, Ghana, Kenya, S Africa, and Holland. Examiner: Univ. of Oxford for MD and PhD; FFARCS, 1953–73; FRCSI, 1962–67. Welsh Regional Hospital Board: Cons. Adviser in Anaesthetics, 1948–74; Mem., 1961–74. Member: Central Health Services Council, 1962–72; Safety of Drugs Cttee, Dept of Health and Social Security, 1964–76; Medicines Commn, 1976–83; Assoc. of Anaesthetists, 1936– (Mem. Council, 1946–59 and 1961–73; Vice-Pres., 1953–56); Anaesthetists Group Cttee, BMA, 1950–69; Bd of Governors, United Cardiff Hosps, 1956–65; Court, Univ. of Wales, 1957–58; Commonwealth Scholarships Commn, 1969–78. Welsh National School of Medicine: Mem. Senate, 1947–75; Mem. Council, 1957–58; Vice-Provost, 1958–60; Royal College of Surgeons: Mem. Bd, Faculty of Anaesthetists, 1954–71; Mem. Council, 1961–64; Dean, Faculty of Anaesthetists, 1961–64. Mem. Bd of Management and Consulting Editor, British Jl of Anaesthesia, 1947–75. Hon. Mem., various societies of anaesthetists. Hon. FFARACS 1959; Hon. FFA(SA) 1962; Hon. FFARCSI 1962; Hon. DSc Wales, 1982. John Snow Silver Medal, 1974; Henry Hill Hickman Medal, RSocMed, 1978. *Publications:* Anaesthesia for the Poor Risk, 1948; (with Sir R. Macintosh) Local Analgesia: Brachial Plexus, 1954, 4th edn 1967; Physics for the Anaesthetist, 1946, 4th edn 1986; Automatic Ventilation of Lungs, 1959, 3rd edn 1980; (ed) Thoracic Anaesthesia, 1963. Numerous papers on anaesthesia and allied subjects in British and foreign jls. *Address:* 30 Bettws-y-Coed Road, Cardiff CF2 6PL. *T:* Cardiff 751002.

MUSKER, Sir John, Kt 1952; Banker; Director, Cater, Ryder & Co., Ltd, Bankers, 1960–79 (Chairman, 1960–71); *b* 25 Jan. 1906; *o s* of late Capt. Harold Musker, JP, Snarehill Hall, Thetford, Norfolk; *m* 1st, 1932, Elizabeth (decd), *d* of Captain Loeffler, 51 Grosvenor Square, W1; two *d*; 2nd, 1955, Mrs Rosemary Pugh (*d* 1980), *d* of late Maj.-Gen. Merton Beckwith-Smith; 3rd 1982, Hon. Audrey Elizabeth Paget, *d* of 1st Baron Queenborough, GBE. *Educ:* privately; St John's Coll., Cambridge (BA). Mem. LCC for City of London, 1944–49. Lt, RNVR, 1940. Hon. Treas., London Municipal Soc., 1936–46. *Address:* Shadwell Park, Thetford, Norfolk. *T:* Thetford 3257; 4 Cliveden Place, SW1. *Club:* White's.

MUSKERRY, 8th Baron (Ireland), *cr* 1781; **Hastings Fitzmaurice Tilson Deane;** 13th Bt (Ireland), *cr* 1710; Radiologist to Regional Health Authority, Limerick, 1961–77; *b* 12 March 1907; 3rd and *o surv. s* of 7th Baron Muskerry and Mabel Kathleen Vivienne (*d* 1954), *d* of Charles Henry Robinson, MD, FRCSI; *S* father, 1966; *m* 1944, Betty Fairbridge, *e d* of George Wilfred Reckless Palmer, South Africa; one *s* one *d*. *Educ:* Sandford Park Sch., Dublin; Trinity Coll., Dublin; MA, MB, BCh, BAO; DMR London. Served War of 1939–45, S African Army (Western Desert; seconded RAMC, Italy, Greece). Specialised in Radiology, London Univ., 1946–48; Consultant Radiologist to Transvaal Administration, 1949–57. *Heir:* *s* Hon. Robert Fitzmaurice Deane, BA, BAI [*b* 26 March 1948; *m* 1975, Rita Brink, Pietermaritzburg. *Educ:* Sandford Park Sch., Dublin; Trinity Coll. Dublin]. *Address:* Springfield Castle, Drumcollogher, Co. Limerick. *T:* Drumcollogher 5.

MUSKIE, Edmund Sixtus; Secretary of State, USA, 1980–81; lawyer and politician; *b* Rumford, Maine, 28 March 1914; *s* of Stephen Muskie and Josephine Czarnecki; *m* 1948, Jane Frances Gray; two *s* three *d*. *Educ:* Bates Coll., Maine (AB); Cornell Law Sch., Ithaca, New York (LLB). Served War, Lt USNR, 1942–45. Admitted to Bar: Massachusetts, 1939; Maine, 1940, and practised at Waterville, Maine, 1940 and 1945–55; Federal District Court, 1941. Mem., Maine House of Reps, 1947–51; Democratic Floor Leader, 1949–51; Dist. Dir for Maine, Office of Price Stabilisation, 1951–52; City Solicitor, Waterville, Maine, 1954–55; Governor of State of Maine, 1955–59; US Senator from Maine, 1959–80; Senate Assistant Majority Whip, 1966–80; Chm., Senate Budget Cttee, 1974–80. Cand. for Vice-Presidency of US, 1968. Mem., Senate Foreign Relations Cttee, 1970–74, 1979–80; Former Chm., and Mem. *ex officio*, Democratic Senatorial Campaign Cttee; Chairman, Senate Sub-Cttees on: Environmental Pollution, Senate Environment and Public Wks Cttee; Intergovtl Relations, Senate Governmental Affairs Cttee, 1959–78; Former Member: Special Cttee on Aging; Exec. Cttee, Nat. Governors' Conf.; Chm., Roosevelt Campobello Internat. Park Commn. Mem, Amer. Acad. of Arts and Sciences. Has numerous hon. doctorates. Phi Beta Kappa; Phi Alpha Delta. Presidential Medal of Freedom, 1981; Notre Dame Laetare Medal, 1981; Distinguished Service Award, Former Members of Congress Assoc., 1981. *Publication:* Journeys, 1972. *Address:* Chadbourne, Parke, Whiteside & Wolff, 1101 Vermont Ave, NW, Washington, DC 20005, USA.

MUSSON, Maj.-Gen. Alfred Henry, CB 1958; CBE 1956; pac; late RA; President, Ordnance Board, 1957–58, retired (Vice-President, 1955–57); *b* 14 Aug. 1900; *s* of Dr A. W. Musson, Clitheroe, Lancs; *m* 1932, Joan Wright Taylor; three *s*. *Educ:* Tonbridge Sch.; RMA Woolwich. Served War of 1939–45. *Address:* Lyndon, The Ridgeway, Tonbridge, Kent TN10 4NH. *T:* Tonbridge 364978.

MUSSON, Gen. Sir Geoffrey (Randolph Dixon), GCB 1970 (KCB 1965; CB 1959); CBE 1945; DSO 1944; BA; *b* 9 June 1910; *s* of late Robert Dixon Musson, Yockleton, Shrewsbury; *m* 1939, Hon. Elspeth L. Bailey, *d* of late Hon. Herbert Crawshay Bailey; one *s* (one *d* decd). *Educ:* Shrewsbury; Trinity Hall, Cambridge. 2nd Lt KSLI, 1930. Served War of 1939–45, North Africa and Italy; Comdr 2nd Bn DCLI, 1943–44; Comdr 36th Infantry Bde, 1944–46. Comdr Commonwealth Forces in Korea, 1954–55; Comdt Sch. of Infantry, 1956–58, Comdr 7th Armoured Div., BAOR, 1958; Maj.-Gen. 1958; Comdr, 5th Div., 1958–59. Chief of Staff, GHQ, Near East Land Forces, 1959–62; Vice-Adjutant-Gen., War Office, subseq. Min. of Defence, 1963–64; GOC-in-C, N Command, 1964–67; Adjutant-General, 1967–70, retired. Colonel: King's Shropshire Light Infantry, 1963–68; The Light Infantry, 1968–72. A Vice-Chm., Nat. Savings Cttee, 1970–78; Chairman: HM Forces Savings Cttee, 1970–78; Regular Forces Employment Assoc., 1978–80; Vice-Pres., Royal Patriotic Fund Corporation, 1974–83; Pres., Victory Services Club, 1970–80. *Address:* Barn Cottage, Hurstbourne Tarrant, Andover, Hants SP11 0BD. *T:* Hurstbourne Tarrant 354. *Club:* Army and Navy.

MUSSON, John Nicholas Whitaker; Warden of Glenalmond College, 1972–Sept. 1987; *b* 2 Oct. 1927; *s* of late Dr J. P. T. Musson, OBE and Gwendoline Musson (*née* Whitaker); *m* 1953, Ann Priest; one *s* three *d*. *Educ:* Clifton; Brasenose Coll., Oxford (MA). Served with Welsh Guards and Lancs Fusiliers, 1945–48 (commnd); BA Hons Mod. Hist., Oxford, 1951; HM Colonial Admin. Service, 1951–59; District and Provincial Administration, N Nigeria; Lectr, Inst. of Administration, N Nigeria; Staff Dept, British Petroleum, London, 1959–60; Asst Master and Housemaster, Canford Sch., 1961–72. Chm., Scottish Div. HMC, 1981–83. *Recreations:* hill walking, history, fine arts. *Address:* (until Sept. 1987) The Warden's House, Glenalmond College, Perthshire PH1 3RY. *T:* Glenalmond 205; The Farmhouse, Tarrant Keyneston, Blandford, Dorset DT11 9JE. *Clubs:* East India, Lansdowne; New (Edinburgh).

MUSSON, Samuel Dixon, CB 1963; MBE 1943; Chief Registrar of Friendly Societies and Industrial Assurance Commissioner, 1963–72; *b* 1 April 1908; *e s* of late R. Dixon Musson, Yockleton, Salop; *m* 1949, Joan I. S., 2nd *d* of late Col D. Davies-Evans, DSO, Penylan, Carmarthenshire. *Educ:* Shrewsbury Sch.; Trinity Hall, Cambridge. Called to Bar (Inner Temple), 1930; practised as Barrister, 1930–46; commnd, Pilot Officer, RAFVR, 1941; served Egypt, N Africa, Italy, 1942–45 (despatches). Ministry of Health: Senior Legal Asst, 1946; Asst Solicitor, 1952; Principal Asst Solicitor, 1957. Vice-Pres., Building Socs Assoc., 1972–77; Mem., Trustee Savings Bank Inspection Cttee. *Recreations:* golf, country pursuits. *Address:* Prospect Hill Farm, Headley, Bordon, Hants. *T:* Headley Down 713183. *Club:* Savile.

MUSTAFA, Nasr El-Din; Medal of Merit, First Class, 1972; Order of the Dedicated Son of Sudan, 1978; Order of the Two Niles, First Class, 1979; Ambassador of the Democratic Republic of Sudan to the Court of St James's, 1982–83; *b* 10 Oct. 1930; *m* 1962, Raga Yousif Sukkar; three *s* three *d*. *Educ:* University Coll. Khartoum. BSc(Eng), London; FICE. Sudan Railways (Civil Engrg), 1956–68; Messrs Goode & Partners, Consulting Engrs, UK, 1958–60; Sudanese Estate Bank, 1968–69; Sudanese People's Armed Forces, 1969–74; Chm., Sea Ports Corp., 1974–76; Minister of State for Planning, 1976–77; Minister of Nat. Planning, 1977–81 (and as such Governor for Sudan in IBRD, Arab Fund for Socio-Econ. Develt, IDB, ADB/F, and Nat. Authorising Officer, EDF); Dep. Pres., Ministerial Cttee for Economic Sector, 1979–81. Mem., Sudan Railway Bd of Dirs, 1973–76; Chm., Bd of Dirs, Khartoum Polytechnic, 1976–79. *Recreations:* reading, swimming. *Address:* c/o Ministry of Foreign Affairs, Khartoum, Sudan. *Club:* Royal Automobile.

MUSTILL, Rt. Hon. Sir Michael (John), Kt 1978; PC 1985; **Rt. Hon. Lord Justice Mustill;** a Lord Justice of Appeal, since 1985; *b* 10 May 1931; *o s* of Clement William and late Marion Mustill; *m* 1st, Beryl Reid Davies (marr. diss.); 2nd, Caroline Phillips; two *s* and one step *d*. *Educ:* Oundle Sch.; St John's Coll., Cambridge. Royal Artillery, 1949–51 (commissioned, 1950). Called to Bar, Gray's Inn, 1955, Bencher, 1976. QC 1968. Dep. Chm., Hants QS, 1971; a Recorder of the Crown Court, 1972–78; Judge of High Court, QBD, 1978–85. Presiding Judge, NE Circuit, 1981–84. Chairman: Civil Service Appeal Tribunal, 1971–78; Judicial Studies Board, 1985–; Deptl Cttee on Law of Arbitration, 1985–. *Publications:* The Law and Practice of Commercial Arbitration in England (with S. C. Boyd, QC), 1982; Joint Editor: Scrutton on Charterparties and Bills of Lading; Arnould on Marine Insurance; articles in legal periodicals. *Recreations:* visiting France, reading, music, active sports. *Address:* Royal Courts of Justice, Strand, WC2.

MUSTOE, Mrs Anne, MA; Headmistress, St Felix School, Southwold, since 1978; *b* 24 May 1933; *d* of H.W. Revill; *m* 1960, Nelson Edwin Mustoe, QC (*d* 1976). *Educ:* Girton Coll., Cambridge (BA Classical Tripos 1955, MA 1958). DipIPM 1959. Guest, Keen & Nettlefolds Ltd, 1956–60; Head of Classics, Francis Holland School, NW1, 1965–69; independent travel agent, 1969–73; Dep. Headmistress, Cobham Hall, Kent, 1975–78. Chm., ISIS, 1986–; President, Girls' Schools Assoc., 1984–85; Mem., Board of Managers of Girls' Common Entrance Examinations, 1983–. JP Suffolk, 1981–85. *Recreations:* travel, cycling. *Address:* Craigmyle House, St Felix School, Southwold, Suffolk IP18 6SD. *T:* Southwold 722175.

MUSTON, Rt. Rev. Gerald Bruce; *see* Australia, North-West, Bishop of.

MUTI, Riccardo; Principal Conductor and Music Director, Philadelphia Orchestra, since 1980; Conductor Laureate, Philharmonia Orchestra, since 1982; Music Director, La Scala, Milan, since 1986; *b* 28 July 1941; *m* 1969, Cristina Mazzavillani; two *s* one *d*. *Educ:* Diploma in pianoforte, Conservatorio di Napoli; Diploma in conducting and composition, Milan. Principal Conductor, 1973–82, Music Dir, 1979–82, New Philharmonia, later Philharmonia Orchestra; Principal Conductor, Orchestra Maggio Musicale Fiorentino, 1969–81; Principal Guest Conductor, Philadelphia Orchestra, 1977–80. Concert tours in USA: with Boston, Chicago, and Philadelphia orchestras; concerts at Salzburg, Edinburgh, Lucerne, Flanders and Vienna Festivals; concerts with Berlin Philharmonic, Vienna Philharmonic, Concertgebouw Amsterdam; opera in Florence, Salzburg, Vienna, Munich, Covent Garden, Milan. Recording prizes from France, Germany, Italy and Japan. Accademico: dell'Accademia di Santa Cecilia, Rome; dell'Accademia Luigi Cherubini,

Florence. Verdienstkreuz, 1st class (Germany), 1976. *Address:* Via Corti alle Mura 25, Ravenna, Italy.

MWANZA, Dr Jacob Mumbi; Vice-Chancellor, University of Zambia, since 1976; *b* 2 Feb. 1937; *m* 1964, Elizabeth Maria; three *d*. *Educ:* Univ. of Munster, W Germany (MA Econ. 1968); Cornell Univ., USA (PhD 1973). Lectr, then Sen. Lectr, 1968–74, Head of Econs Dept, 1973–74, Univ. of Zambia. Man. Dir, Zambia Energy Corp., 1974–76. Mem., UN Cttee for Develt Planning; Vice-Chm., Senate, UN Inst. for Namibia, 1980–; Pres., Council for Develt of Economic and Social Research in Africa, 1982–. Mem. Council, Univ. of Dar es Salaam. *Publications:* Orienting Economics Teaching to Development Needs, in The Teaching of Economics in African Universities, 1973; The Operation of Public Enterprises in Zambia, 1978; contrib. Developing Economies. *Recreations:* fishing, tennis. *Address:* (home) Hawndsworth Park, Lumubashi Road 1–5, Lusaka, Zambia; (office) Box 302811, Lusaka, Zambia. *Clubs:* Flying, Economics (Lusaka).

MWENDWA, Hon. Maluki Kitili; MP Kitui West, Kenya, since 1984; Chairman: United Nations Association, Kenya; Chania Enterprises Ltd; ExpoAfrica Ltd; Fad Investments Ltd; Export Promotion Services; Inter Continental Holdings Ltd; Kenya Advertising Corporation Ltd; Kenya Allied Travel Enterprises Ltd; Kenya Pisci-Culture Ltd; Mugie Ltd; Pasha Club Ltd; Housing Finance Company of Kenya; Ranching and Agricultural Consultants Ltd; Research, Editorial and Design Services Ltd; Wendo Ltd; Consultant General, Private Sector; *b* 24 Dec. 1929; *s* of Senior Chief M. Kitavi Mwendwa and Mrs Kathuka Mwendwa; *m* 1964, Winifred Nyiva Mangole (Hon. Mrs Winifred Mwendwa, MP Kitui West; one of first four Kenya women MPs, Oct. 1974); one *s* three *d*. *Educ:* Alliance High Sch., Kenya; Nabumali High Sch., Uganda; Makerere University Coll.; London Univ.; Exeter Univ.; St Catherine's Coll., Oxford. DipEd 1950; LLB 1955 (Sir Archibald Bodkin Prize for Criminal Law, 1953); DPA 1956; BA 1959, MA 1963. President: Cosmos Soc., 1959; Jowett Soc., 1959; St Catherine's Debating Soc., 1959, Oxford. Called to the Bar, Lincoln's Inn, 1961. Lectr Kagumo Teacher Training Coll., 1951. Asst Sec., Min. of Commerce and Industry, 1962, Min. of Works and Communications, 1962; Sen. Asst Sec., Min. of Tourism, Forests and Wild Life, 1962–63; Perm. Sec., Min. of Social Services, 1963, and Min. of Home Affairs, 1963–64; Solicitor Gen., 1964–68 (acting Attorney Gen., 1967); Chief Justice of Kenya, 1968–71. Leader, Kenya Delegn: Commonwealth and Empire Law Conf., Sydney, 1965; World Peace through Law Conf., Washington, 1965; Conf. on Intellectual Property, Stockholm, 1967 (Vice-Pres. of Conf.); UN Special Cttee on Friendly Relations, Geneva, 1967; Conf. on Law of Treaties, Vienna, 1968; Kenya Rep. on 6th Cttee, 21st Session, and on 2nd and 6th Cttees (Vice-Chm. of 6th Cttee), 22nd Session, UN Gen. Assembly; Ambassador to 22nd Session, UN Gen. Assembly, 1967 (Vice-Chm., Kenya Delegn to April/May 1967 Special Session); Mem., UN Internat. Trade Law Commn, 1967–74; Chm., Business Premises Rent Tribunal, 1983; Mem., Executive Council: African Inst. of Internat. Law, Lagos; Kenya Farmers' Assoc.; Donovan Maule Theatre, Nairobi; Agricultural Soc. of Kenya, Nairobi, 1970–73 (Life Governor, 1978); African Automobile Assoc., Nairobi. Chm., Bd of Governors: Ngara Sch., 1965–73; Parklands Sch., 1967–73; Kitui Sch., 1972–74. *Publication:* Constitutional Contrasts in the East African Territories, 1965. *Recreations:* hunting, swimming, cycling, walking. *Address:* c/o Gigiri House, Gigiri Crescent, PO Box 40198, Nairobi, Kenya. *T:* Nairobi 23450. *Clubs:* Pasha (Nairobi), Mount Kenya Safari (Nanyuki).

MWINYI, Ndugu Ali Hassan; President, United Republic of Tanzania, since 1985; *b* 8 May 1925; *s* of late Hassan Mwinyi Chande and Asha Mwinyishehe; *m* 1960, Siti A. Mwinyi (*née* Abdulla); five *s* four *d*. *Educ:* Mangapwani Sch. and Dole Sch., Zanzibar; Teachers' Training Coll., Zanzibar; Durham Univ. Inst. of Education. Primary sch. teacher, head teacher, Tutor, Principal, Zanzibar, 1945–64; Acting Principal Sec., Min. of Educn, 1964–65; Dep. Gen. Manager, State Trading Corp., 1965–70; Minister of State, President's Office, Dar es Salaam, 1970–72; Minister for Health, 1972–75; Minister for Home Affairs, 1975–77; Ambassador to Egypt, 1977–81; Minister for Natural Resources and Tourism, 1982–83; Minister of State, Vice-President's Office, 1983; Vice-Pres., Union Govt, 1984. Chama cha Mapinduzi (Revolutionary Party): Member, 1977; Nat. Exec. Cttee, 1982; Central Cttee, 1984; Vice-Chm., 1984–; Mem., Afro-Shirazi Party, 1964. Chairman: Zanzibar Film Censorship Bd, 1964–65; E African Currency Bd, Zanzibar, 1964–67; Nat. Kiswahili Council, 1964–77; Tanzania Food and Nutrition Council, 1974–76. Mem.,Univ. Council of Dar es Salaam, 1964–65. *Address:* State House, Dar es Salaam, United Republic of Tanzania.

MYDDELTON, Lt-Col Ririd, MVO 1945; JP; Extra Equerry to The Queen since 1952; Vice-Lieutenant of Denbighshire, 1968–74; *b* 25 Feb. 1902; *e s* of late Col Robert Edward Myddelton, TD, DL, JP, Chirk Castle, and late Lady Violet, *d* of 1st Marquess of Abergavenny; *m* 1931, Margaret Elizabeth Mercer Nairne (now Lady Margaret Elizabeth Myddelton; granted rank as *d* of a Marquess, 1946), *d* of late Lord Charles Mercer Nairne; two *s* one *d*. *Educ:* Eton; RMC Sandhurst. 2nd Lt Coldstream Guards, 1923; Adjutant, 3rd Bn, 1928–31; Staff Capt., London District, 1934–37; seconded as Dep. Master of the Household to King George VI, 1937–39; DAAG London District, 1939–40; Staff Coll., Camberley, War Course, 1942; Commanded: 1st (Armd) Bn, Coldstream Guards, 1942–44 (Normandy); retired, 1946. JP 1948, DL 1949, High Sheriff, 1951–52, Denbigh. KStJ 1961. *Recreations:* hunting, fishing. *Address:* Chirk Castle, North Wales. *T:* Chirk 772460. *Club:* Turf.

See also Captain Sir A. S. Aird.

MYER, Sidney Baillieu, MA Cantab; Chairman, Myer Emporium Ltd, since 1978 (Director, since 1955); Deputy Chairman, Coles Myer Ltd, since 1986; *b* 11 Jan. 1926; *s* of late Sidney Myer and late Dame (Margery) Merlyn Baillieu Myer, DBE; *m* 1955, Sarah J., *d* of late S. Hordern; two *s* one *d*. *Educ:* Geelong Grammar Sch.; Pembroke Coll., Cambridge (MA). Sub-Lieut, RANVR, 1944–46. Joined Myer Emporium, 1953; Vice-Pres., Myer Foundn, 1959–. Director: Elders IXL Ltd, 1972–82 and 1986–; Cadbury Schweppes Aust. Ltd, 1976–82; Nat. Mutual Life Assoc. of Australasia, 1978–86; Commonwealth Banking Corp., 1979–83; Network Ten Holdings Ltd and associated Cos, 1985–. Part-time Mem. Executive, CSIRO, 1981–85. Pres., French Chamber of Commerce (Vic), 1962–64; Rep. Chm., Aust.-Japan Foundn, 1976–81; Member: Consultative Cttee on Relations with Japan, 1978–81; Aust.-China Council, 1979–81; Nat. Bicentennial Sci. Centre Adv. Cttee, 1986–. Councillor: Aust. Conservation Foundn, 1964–73; Vic. Coll. of Arts, 1973–78; Chm., Art Foundn of Vic., 1986–; Vice-Pres., Nat. Gall. Soc. of Vic., 1964–68; Trustee, Nat. Gall. of Vic., 1973–83 (Vice-Pres., 1977–83); Chm., Commonwealth Research Centres of Excellence Cttee, 1981–82. *Address:* 250 Elizabeth Street, Melbourne, Victoria 3000, Australia.

MYERS, Dr David Milton, CMG 1974; Vice-Chancellor, La Trobe University, Melbourne, 1965–76; *b* 5 June 1911; *s* of W. H. Myers, Sydney; *m* 1937, Beverley A. H., *d* of Dr T. D. Delprat; three *s*. *Educ:* Univs of Sydney and Oxford. BSc, BE, DScEng; FIE Aust., FIEE, FInstP. 1st Chief of Div. of Electrotechnology, CSIR, 1939–49; P. N. Russell Prof. of Elec. Engrg, Univ. of Sydney, 1949–59; Dean, Faculty of Applied Science, and Prof. of Elec. Engrg, Univ. of British Columbia, 1960 65. Mem. Adv. Council, CSIRO, 1949–55; Mem. Nat. Res. Council of Canada, 1965; Chairman: Cttee on Overseas Professional Qualifications, 1969–84; Inquiry into Unemployment Benefits, for Aust. Govt, 1977; Cttee of Inquiry into fluoridation of Victorian water supplies, 1979–80; Consultative Council on Victorian Mental Health Act, 1981. Pres., Aust. Inst. of Engineers, 1958. Kernot Meml Medal, 1974; P. N. Russell Meml Medal, 1977. *Publications:* various research papers in sci. jls. *Recreations:* golf, tennis, music. *Address:* 76 Glenard Drive, Heidelberg, Vic. 3084, Australia. *T:* 459 9629. *Club:* Melbourne (Melbourne).

MYERS, Brig. (Retired) Edmund Charles Wolf, CBE 1944; DSO 1943; BA Cantab; MICE; *b* 12 Oct. 1906; *er s* of late Dr C. S. Myers, CBE, FRS; *m* 1943, Louisa, *er d* of late Aldred Bickham Sweet-Escott; one *d*. *Educ:* Haileybury; Royal Military Academy, Woolwich; Caius Coll., Cambridge. Commissioned into Royal Engineers, 1926. Served Palestine, 1936 (despatches); War of 1939–45; Comdr, British Mil. Mission to Greek Resistance Forces, 1942–43; Middle East, including Balkans, until 1944 (African Star, Italy Star, DSO, CBE); North-West Europe, 1944–45 (France and Germany Star, Dutch Bronze Lion, Norwegian Liberty Medal); Far East, 1945; Korea, 1951–52 (despatches, American Legion of Merit). Chief Engineer, British Troops in Egypt, 1955–56; Dep. Dir, Personnel Administration in the War Office, 1956–59; retired 1959. Chief Civil Engineer Cleveland Bridge & Engineering Co. Ltd, 1959–64. Construction Manager, Power Gas Corp. Ltd, Davy-Ashmore Group, 1964–67. Regional Sec., British Field Sports Soc., 1968–71. *Publication:* Greek Entanglement, 1955. *Recreations:* horse training and riding, sailing, flying (1st Sec. RE Flying Club, 1934–35), fishing. *Address:* Wheatsheaf House, Broadwell, Moreton-in-Marsh, Glos GL56 0TY. *T:* Cotswold 30183. *Clubs:* Army and Navy, Special Forces.

MYERS, Geoffrey, CBE 1984; CEng; FCIT; Vice-Chairman, British Railways Board, since 1985 (Member, since 1980); *b* 12 July 1930; *s* of Ernest and Annie Myers; *m* 1959, Patricia Mary (*née* Hall); two *s*. *Educ:* Belle Vue Grammar Sch.; Bradford Technical Coll. (BScEng London). CEng, MICE 1963; FCIT 1973. RE, 1955–57. British Rail: civil engrg positions, 1957–64; Planning Officer, N Eastern Reg., 1964–66; Divl Movements Manager, Leeds Div., 1966–68; Dir of Studies, British Transport Staff Coll., 1968–70; Divl Man., Sheffield, 1970–76; Dep. Gen. Man., Eastern Reg., 1976–77, Gen. Man., 1977–78; Dir of Strategic Develt, 1978–80; Dep. Chief Exec. (Railways), 1983; Jt Managing Dir (Railways), 1984–85. Mem., Carmen's Co., 1983. OStJ 1979. *Recreations:* golf, walking. *Address:* The Spinney, Lands Lane, Knaresborough, N Yorks. *T:* Harrogate 863719.

MYERS, Geoffrey Morris Price; Under-Secretary, Agricultural and Food Research Council, 1973–May 1987; *b* 8 May 1927. *Educ:* Reigate Grammar Sch.; King's Coll., London. Civil Service, 1950; UKAEA, 1959–67, Private Sec. to Chm.; Nat. Econ. Develt Office, 1967–69; Agric. Research Council, 1970. *Address:* 42 Bardsley Close, Croydon CR0 5PT. *T:* 01-680 0827.

MYERS, Gordon Elliot, CMG 1979; Under-Secretary, Arable Crops, Pigs and Poultry Group, Ministry of Agriculture, Fisheries and Food, since 1986; *b* 4 July 1929; *s* of William Lionel Myers and Yvonne (*née* Arthur); *m* 1963, Wendy Jane Lambert; two *s* one *d* *Educ:* Kilburn Grammar Sch.; University Coll., Oxford (BA 1st Cl. Hons Modern History). Asst Principal, MAFF, 1951; Principal, 1958; Asst Sec., 1966; Head successively of Land Drainage Div., Sugar and Tropical Foods Div., and EEC Div., 1966–74; Under-Sec., MAFF, 1975; Minister (Agriculture), Office of UK Perm. Rep. to EEC, 1975–79; Under-Sec., Food Policy Gp, 1980–85, Cereals and Sugar Gp, 1985–86, MAFF. *Address:* Woodlands, Nugents Park, Hatch End, Pinner, Mddx. *Club:* United Oxford & Cambridge University.

MYERS, Harry Eric, QC 1967; QC Gibraltar 1977; *b* 10 Jan. 1914; *s* of Harry Moss Myers and Alice Muriel Serjeant; *m* 1951, Lorna Babette Kitson (*née* Blackburn); no *c*. *Educ:* Bedford Sch. Admitted Solicitor of Supreme Court, 1936; called to Bar, Middle Temple, 1945. Prosecuting Counsel to Bd of Inland Revenue on SE Circuit, 1965. *Address:* 202 Beatty House, Dolphin Square, SW1V 3PH.

MYERS, John David; Chairman of Industrial Tribunals, since 1982; *b* 30 Oct. 1937; *s* of Frank and Monica Myers; *m* 1974, Anne McGeough (*née* Purcell), *widow* of J. T. McGeough; one *s*. *Educ:* Marist College, Hull; Hull University. LLB Hons. Called to the Bar, Gray's Inn, 1968. Schoolmaster, 1958–64; University, 1964–67; pupillage with J. D. Walker (later Judge Walker); practice at Hull, 1969–82 (Junior, NE Circuit, 1975–76). *Recreations:* cooking, oenology, singing with Hull Choral Union. *Address:* 120 Newland Park, Hull. *T:* Hull 42342. *Club:* Hull and East Riding (Hull).

MYERS, Sir Kenneth (Ben), Kt 1977; MBE 1944; FCA; retired; *b* 5 March 1907; *s* of Hon. Sir Arthur Myers and Lady (Vera) Myers (*née* Levy); *m* 1933, Margaret Blair Pirie one *s* two *d*. *Educ:* Marlborough Coll.; Gonville and Caius Coll., Cambridge (BA 1928). FCA 1933. Returned to NZ, 1933; served War with 2nd NZEF, ME and Italy, 1940–45. *Recreation:* looking after my family. *Address:* 21 Upland Road, Auckland 5, New Zealand. *T:* Auckland 545499. *Clubs:* Boodle's; Northern (Auckland).

MYERS, His Honour Mark; QC 1977; a Circuit Judge, 1984–85; *b* 22 July 1930; *s* of late Lewis Myers and Hannah Myers; *m* 1964, Katherine Ellen Desormeaux Waldram; one *s* one *d*. *Educ:* King's Sch., Ely; Trinity Coll., Cambridge (Exhibnr; MA). Called to the Bar, Gray's Inn, 1954; Recorder, 1979–84. Sublector in Law, Trinity Coll., Cambridge, 1954–61; Part-time Lectr in Law, Southampton Univ., 1959–61. Mem., Consumers Cttee for England and Wales, and Consumers Cttee for GB, 1974–85. *Publications:* articles in legal jls. *Recreations:* music and country life. *Address:* 73 Cholmeley Crescent, Highgate, N6 5EX. *T:* 01–340 7623.

MYERS, Sir Philip (Alan), Kt 1985; OBE 1977; QPM 1972; DL; one of Her Majesty's Inspectors of Constabulary, since 1982; *b* 7 Feb. 1931; *s* of John and Catherine Myers; *m* 1951, Hazel Gittings; two *s*. *Educ:* Grove Park, Wrexham. RAF, 1949–50. Shropshire Constabulary, 1950–67; West Mercia Police, 1967–68; Dep. Chief Constable, Gwynedd Constabulary, 1968–70; Chief Constable, North Wales Police, 1970–81. OStJ 1972. DL Clwyd, 1983.

MYERS, Sir Rupert (Horace), KBE 1981 (CBE 1976); FTS 1979; Professor Emeritus; Chairman, New South Wales State Pollution Control Commission, since 1971; *b* 21 Feb. 1921; *s* of Horace Alexander Myers and Dorothy (*née* Harris); *m* 1944, Io Edwina King; one *s* three *d*. *Educ:* Melbourne High Sch.; Univ. of Melbourne. BSc 1942; MSc 1943; PhD 1947; CEng, FIM, FRACI; FAIM; FIDA; MAusIMM. Commonwealth Res. Fellow, Univ. of Melbourne, 1942–47; Principal Res. Officer, CSIRO, AERE Harwell, 1947–52; Univ. of New South Wales: Foundn Prof. of Metallurgy, 1952–81; Dean, Faculty of Applied Science, 1956–61; Pro-Vice-Chancellor, 1961–69; Vice-Chancellor and Principal, 1969–81. Chairman: Aust. Vice-Chancellors' Cttee, 1977–79; Cttee of Inquiry into Technol Change in Australia, 1979–80; Commonwealth Cttee of Review of Nat. Capital Develt Commn, 1982–83; Consultative Cttee for Nat. Conservation Strategy for Australia, 1983–85; Coastal Council of NSW, 1982–85; Director: CSR Ltd, 1982–; Energy Resources of Australia Ltd, 1982–; Chm. of Directors: Technoproduct Resources Pty Ltd, 1982–; Technoproduct Holdings Ltd, 1985–; Member: Nat. Energy Adv. Cttee, 1980–82; Australian Manufacturing Council, 1980–82. Mem., Sydney Opera House

Trust, 1976–83; Foundn Pres., Friends of Royal Botanic Gdns, Sydney, 1982–85. Hon. LLD Strathclyde, 1973; Hon. DSc Wollongong, 1976; Hon. DEng Newcastle, 1981; Hon. DLitt NSW, 1981. *Publications:* Technological Change in Australia, 1980; numerous on metallurgy and atomic energy (also patents). *Recreations:* tennis, bowls, music, working with silver. *Address:* 135 Neerim Road, Castlecove, NSW 2069, Australia. *Club:* Australian (Sydney).

MYERSON, Arthur Levey, QC 1974; **His Honour Judge Myerson;** a Circuit Judge, since 1978; *b* 25 July 1928; *o s* of Bernard and Eda Myerson; *m* 1960, Elaine Shirley Harris; two *s. Educ:* Blackpool Grammar Sch.; Queens' Coll., Cambridge. BA 1950, LLB 1951; BA (Open Univ.) 1985. Called to the Bar, 1952. A Recorder of the Crown Court, 1972–78. RAF, 1946–48. *Recreations:* reading, sailing. *Address:* 25 Sandmoor Drive, Leeds LS17 2RE. *T:* Leeds 684169. *Clubs:* Royal Commonwealth Society; Moor Allerton Golf (Leeds).

MYERSON, Aubrey Selwyn, QC 1967; a Recorder of the Crown Court, since 1972; *b* Johannesburg, S Africa, 10 Dec. 1926; *o s* of late Michael Colman Myerson, MRCSI, LRCPI, and late Lee Myerson; *m* 1955, Helen Margaret, *d* of late Hedley Lavis, Adelaide, S Austr.; one *s* one *d. Educ:* Cardiff High Sch.; University Coll., Cardiff (Fellow, 1981). Called to Bar, Lincoln's Inn, 1950, Bencher, 1975. Leader, Wales and Chester Circuit, 1981–83. Mem., Criminal Injuries Compensation Bd, 1985–. *Recreations:* competing aggressively at all pursuits. *Address:* 8 Sloane Court East, Chelsea, SW3. *T:* 01–730 4707; 1 Dr Johnson's Buildings, Temple, EC4. *T:* 01–353 9328. *Clubs:* Western (Glasgow); Bristol Channel Yacht.

MYINT, Prof. Hla; Professor of Economics, London School of Economics, 1966–85, now Professor Emeritus; *b* Bassein, Burma, 20 March 1920; *m* 1944, Joan (*née* Morris); no *c. Educ:* Rangoon Univ.; London Sch. of Economics. Prof. of Econs, Rangoon Univ., and Econ. Adviser to Govt of Burma, 1946–49; Univ. Lectr in Econs of Underdeveloped Countries, Oxford Univ., 1950–65; Rector of Rangoon Univ., 1958–61. Vis. Prof., Univs of Yale, Cornell and Wisconsin; has served on UN Expert Cttees; Hon. DLitt, Rangoon, 1961. Order of Sithu (Burma), 1961. *Publications:* Theories of Welfare Economics, 1948; The Economics of the Developing Countries, 1964; Economic Theory and the Underdeveloped Countries, 1971; Southeast Asia's Economy: development policies in the 1970s, 1972; many papers in learned jls. *Recreations:* walking, garden watching. *Address:* 12 Willow Drive, Barnet, Herts. *T:* 01–449 3028.

MYLAND, Howard David; Deputy Comptroller and Auditor General, National Audit Office, since 1984; *b* 23 June 1929; *s* of John Tarrant and Frances Grace Myland; *m* 1951, Barbara Pearl Mills; two *s* one *d. Educ:* Queen Mary's Sch.; Basingstoke. Served Intelligence Corps, 1948–50. Entered Exchequer and Audit Dept, 1948; Dep. Dir of Audit, 1972; Dir of Audit, 1977; Dep. Sec. of Dept, 1979; an Asst Auditor Gen., National Audit Office, 1984. Member: Basingstoke Round Table, 1962–70; Basingstoke Ex-Tablers, 1970–. *Recreations:* travel, caravanning, contract bridge. *Address:* 20 Wallis Road, Basingstoke, Hants RG21 3DN. *T:* Basingstoke 464347.

MYLES, David Fairlie; tenant hill farmer; *b* 30 May 1925; *s* of Robert C. Myles and Mary Anne S. (*née* Fairlie); *m* 1951, Janet I. (*née* Gall); two *s* two *d. Educ:* Edzell Primary Sch.; Brechin High Sch. National Farmers Union of Scotland: Mem. Council, 1970–79; Convenor of Organisation and Publicity Cttee, 1976–79. MP (C) Banff, 1979–83; Sec., Cons. backbench Cttees on European Affairs and on Agriculture, Fisheries and Food (Jt Sec.); Mem., Select Cttees on Agriculture and on European Legislation. Contested (C) Orkney and Shetland, 1983. Councillor, Angus DC, 1984–. Chm., Dairy Produce Quota Tribunal for Scotland, 1984–; Member: North of Scotland Hydro-Electric Bd, 1985–; Extra-Parly Panel (Scotland), 1986–. *Recreations:* curling, Scottish fiddle music. *Address:* Dalbog, Edzell, Brechin, Angus DD9 7UU; (home) The Gorse, Dunlappie Road, Edzell, Brechin, Angus DD9 7UB. *Clubs:* Farmers'; Brechin Rotary.

MYLLENT, Peter; *see* Hamylton Jones, K.

MYLNE, Nigel James; QC 1984; a Recorder, since 1985; *b* 11 June 1939; *s* of late Harold James Mylne and of Dorothy Evelyn Mylne (now D. E. Hogg); *m* 1st, 1967, Julie Phillpotts (marr. diss. 1977); two *s* one *d;* 2nd, 1979, Judith Hamilton; one *s. Educ:* Eton College. National Service, 10th Royal Hussars, 1957–59. Called to the Bar, Middle Temple, 1963. *Recreation:* beekeeping. *Address:* 10 Guildford Road, SW8. *T:* 01–720 6741. *Clubs:* White's, Pratt's, Garrick.

MYNORS, Sir Humphrey (Charles Baskerville), 1st Bt, *cr* 1964; *b* 28 July 1903; 2nd *s* of Rev. A. B. Mynors, Rector of Langley Burrell, Wilts; *m* 1939, Lydia Marian, *d* of late Sir Ellis Minns, LittD, FSA, FBA; one *s* four *d. Educ:* Marlborough; Corpus Christi Coll., Cambridge. Fellow of Corpus Christi Coll., Cambridge, 1926–33; Hon. Fellow, 1953. Entered the service of the Bank of England, 1933; a Dir, 1949–54; Dep. Governor, 1954–64. Chm., Panel on Take-overs and Mergers, 1968–69; Dep. Chm., 1969–70. Hon. DCL Durham. *Heir: s* Richard Baskerville Mynors [*b* 5 May 1947; *m* 1970, Fiona Bridget, *d* of Rt Rev. G. E. Reindorp, *qv;* three *d*]. *Address:* Treago, St Weonards, Hereford HR2 8QB. *T:* St Weonards 208.

MYNORS, Sir Roger (Aubrey Baskerville), Kt 1963; FBA 1944; *b* 28 July 1903; *s* of Rev. A. B. Mynors, Rector of Langley Burrell, Wilts; *m* 1945, Lavinia Sybil, *d* of late Very Rev. C. A. Alington, DD. *Educ:* Eton; Balliol College, Oxford. Fellow and Classical Tutor of Balliol, 1926–44 (Hon. Fellow 1963); Kennedy Prof. of Latin in the Univ. of Cambridge and Fellow of Pembroke Coll., 1944–53 (Hon. Fellow, 1965); Corpus Christi Prof. of Latin Language and Literature, Oxford, 1953–70 (Hon. Fellow, Corpus Christi Coll., 1970). Vis. Lectr, Harvard, 1938. Temp. Principal, HM Treasury, 1940. Longman Vis. Fellow, Leeds Univ., 1974. Pres., Classical Assoc., 1966. Hon. DLitt: Edinburgh; Durham; Hon. LittD: Cambridge; Sheffield; Hon. LLD Toronto. Hon. Fellow, Warburg Inst.; Hon. Member: Amer. Acad. of Arts and Sciences; Amer. Philosophical Soc.; Istituto di Studi Romani. *Publications:* Cassiodori Senatoris Institutiones, 1937; Durham Cathedral MSS before 1200, 1939; Catulli Carmina, 1958; Catalogue of Balliol MSS, 1963; Plinii Epistulae, 1963; Panegyrici Latini, 1964; Vergilii Opera, 1969. *Address:* Treago, St Weonards, Hereford HR2 8QB. *T:* St Weonards 208.

MYRDAL, Prof. (Karl) Gunnar; Swedish economist; *b* 6 Dec. 1898; *s* of Carl Adolf Pettersson and Anna Sofia Carlsdotter; *m* 1924, Alva Reimer (*d* 1986); one *s* two *d. Educ:* Stockholm Univ. Studied in Germany and Britain, 1925–29; Rockefeller Fellow, US, 1929–30; Assoc. Prof., Post-Grad. Inst. of Internat. Studies, Geneva; Lars Hierta Prof. of Polit. Econ. and Public Finance, Stockholm Univ., 1933; Mem. Swedish Senate (Social Democrat), 1934; directed study of Amer. Negro problem for Carnegie Corp., NY, 1938; returned to Sweden, 1942, re-elected to Senate, Mem. Bd of Bank of Sweden, Chm. Post-War Planning Commn; Minister of Commerce, 1945–47; Exec. Sec., UN Econ. Commn for Europe, 1947–57; directed study of econ. trends and policies in S Asian countries for Twentieth Century Fund, 1957–67; Prof. of Internat. Econs, Stockholm Univ., 1961; founded Inst. for Internat. Econ. Studies, Stockholm Univ., 1961; past Chm., Bd of Stockholm Internat. Peace Research Inst. (Mem. Bd); Vis. Res. Fellow, Center for Study of Democratic Instns, Santa Barbara, 1973–74; Distinguished Vis. Prof., New York City Univ., 1974–75; Regents' Prof., Univ. of California, Irvine, Spring 1977; Dist. Vis. Prof., Univ. of Madison, Autumn 1977; Jt Slick Prof. of Peace, L. B. Johnson Sch. of Public Affairs, Univ. of Texas, 1978. Member: British Acad.; Amer. Acad. of Arts and Scis; Royal Swedish Acad. of Scis; Hungarian Acad. of Scis; Fellow, Econometric Soc.; Hon. Mem., Amer. Econ. Assoc. Holds numerous hon. degrees and has received many awards, incl. Nitti Prize, 1976; Nobel Prize for Economics (jtly), 1974; Nehru Award, 1982. *Publications:* numerous sci. works, incl: The Cost of Living in Sweden 1830–1930, 1933; Monetary Equilibrium, 1939; An American Dilemma: The Negro Problem and Modern Democracy, 1944; The Political Element in the Development of Economic Theory, 1953; An International Economy: Problems and Prospects, 1956; Economic Theory and Underdeveloped Regions, 1957; Value in Social Theory, 1958; Beyond the Welfare State: Economic Planning and its International Implications, 1960; Challenge to Affluence, 1963; Asian Drama: An Inquiry into the Poverty of Nations, 1968; Objectivity in Social Research, 1969; The Challenge of World Poverty: A World Anti-Poverty Program in Outline, 1970; Against the Stream: Critical Essays on Economics, 1973. *Address:* Svalnäs Allé 12B, 18263 Djursholm, Sweden.

MYRES, John Nowell Linton, CBE 1972; LLD, DLitt, DLit, MA; FBA 1966; FSA; President, Society of Antiquaries, 1970–75 (Vice-President, 1959–63; Director, 1966–70), now Hon. Vice-President; Bodley's Librarian, University of Oxford, 1947–65; Hon. Student of Christ Church, 1971 (Student 1928–70), and Fellow of Winchester College, 1951–77; *b* 27 Dec. 1902; *yr s* of late Emeritus Prof. Sir John Linton Myres, OBE; *m* 1929, Joan Mary Lovell, *o d* of late G. L. Stevens, Jersey; two *s. Educ:* Winchester Coll. (Scholar); New Coll., Oxford (Scholar), Hon. Fellow, 1973. 1st Class Lit Hum., 1924; 1st Class Modern History, 1926; BA 1924; MA 1928; Lecturer, 1926, Student and Tutor, 1928–48, Librarian, 1938–48, of Christ Church; Univ. Lectr in Early English History, 1935–47; served in Min. of Food, 1940–45 (Head of Fruit and Veg. Products Div., 1943–45); mem. of Council of St Hilda's Coll., Oxford, 1937–52; Pres. Oxford Architectural and Historical Soc., 1946–49. Mem. Institute for Advanced Study, Princeton, 1956; Pres. Council for British Archæology, 1959–61; Member: Ancient Monuments Board (England), 1959–76; Royal Commn on Historical Monuments (England), 1969–74; Chm. Standing Conference of National and Univ. Libraries, 1959–61. Pres: Library Assoc., 1963; Soc. for Medieval Archæology, 1963–66. Lectures: Ford's, in English History, 1958–59; O'Donnell, Edinburgh Univ., 1961; Oxford 1966–67; Rhind, Edinburgh, 1964–65; Raleigh, British Acad., 1970. Hon. Mem., Deutsches Archäologisches Institut. Hon. LLD Toronto, 1954; Hon. DLitt: Reading, 1964; Durham, 1983; Hon. DLit Belfast, 1965. Has supervised excavations at Caerleon Amphitheatre, 1926, St Catharine's Hill, Winchester, 1925–28, Colchester, 1930, Butley Priory, 1931–33, Aldborough, 1934–35 and elsewhere. Gold Medal, Soc. of Antiquaries, 1976. Hon. Foreign Corresp. Mem. Grolier Club, New York. *Publications:* part-author: St Catharine's Hill, Winchester, 1930; Anglo-Saxon Pottery and the Settlement of England, 1969; A Corpus of Anglo-Saxon Pottery, 1977; (contrib.) Oxford History of England, Vol. I, (with R. G. Collingwood) Roman Britain and the English Settlements, 1936, pt revd as Vol. IB, The English Settlements, 1986; articles and reviews in learned periodicals. *Recreations:* growing of vegetables and fruit; bibliophily, study of antiquities. *Address:* Manor House, Kennington, Oxford. *T:* Oxford 735353.

N

NAAS, Lord; Charles Diarmuidh John Bourke; *b* 11 June 1953; *e s* and *heir* of 10th Earl of Mayo, *qv*; *m* 1975, Marie Antoinette Cronnelly; one *d*. *Educ*: St Aubyn's, Rottingdean; Portora Royal Sch., Enniskillen; QUB; Bolton Street Coll. of Technology, Dublin. *Address*: Doon House, Maam, Co. Galway, Eire.

NABARRO, Prof. Frank Reginald Nunes, MBE 1946; FRS 1971; Professor of Physics, University of the Witwatersrand, 1953–84, now Hon. Professorial Research Fellow; *b* 7 March 1916; *s* of late Stanley Nunes Nabarro and Leah Nabarro; *m* 1948, Margaret Constance, *d* of late James Dalziel, ARAM; three *s* two *d*. *Educ*: Nottingham High Sch.; New Coll., Oxford (MA, BSc). DSc Birmingham. Sen. Exper. Officer, Min. of Supply, 1941–45; Royal Soc. Warren Research Fellow, Univ. of Bristol, 1945–49; Lectr in Metallurgy, Univ. of Birmingham, 1949–53; University of Witwatersrand: Prof. and Head of Dept of Physics, 1953–77, City of Johannesburg Prof. of Physics, 1970–77; Dean, Faculty of Science, 1968–70; Representative of Senate on Council, 1967–77; Deputy Vice-Chancellor, 1978–80. Vis. Prof., Nat. Research Council, Ottawa, 1956; Vice-Pres., S African Inst. of Physics, 1956–57; Republic Steel Vis. Prof., Dept of Metallurgy, Case Inst. of Techn., Cleveland, Ohio, 1964–65; Overseas Fellow of Churchill Coll., Cambridge, 1966–67; Gauss Prof., Akademie der Wissenschaften, Göttingen, 1970; Professeur-associé, Univ. Paris-Sud, 1971, Montpellier II, 1973; Vis. Prof. Dept of Material Science, Univ. of Calif., Berkeley, 1977; Vis. Fellow, Robinson Coll., Cambridge, 1981; Vis. Prof., Dept of Materials Engrg, Technion, Haifa, 1983. Hon. FRSSAf 1973. Beilby Memorial Award, 1950; South Africa Medal, 1972; De Beers Gold Medal, 1980; Claude Harris Leon Foundn Award of Merit, 1983. *Publications*: Theory of Crystal Dislocations, 1967; scientific papers, mainly on solid state physics. *Recreation*: gardening. *Address*: 32 Cookham Road, Auckland Park, Johannesburg, South Africa. *T*: (011) 726–7745.

NABARRO, Sir John (David Nunes), Kt 1983; MD; FRCP; Consultant Physician, The Middlesex Hospital, London, 1954–81, now Emeritus Consultant Physician; Hon. Research Associate, Departments of Medicine and Biochemistry, Middlesex Hospital Medical School, since 1981; Director, Cobbold Laboratories, Middlesex Hospital Medical School, 1970–81; Hon. Consultant Physician, Royal Prince Alfred Hospital, Sidney, since 1959; *b* 21 Dec. 1915; *s* of David Nunes Nabarro and Florence Nora Nabarro (*née* Webster); *m* 1948, Joan Margaret Cockrell; two *s* two *d*. *Educ*: Oundle Sch.; University Coll., London (Howard Cluff Meml Prize 1935; Fellow, UCL, 1963); University Coll. Hosp. Med. Sch. (Magrath Schol., Atkinson Morley Schol., Atchison Schol., 1938). MD London. Medical Specialist, OC Med. Div., RAMC, 1939–45: served in Iraq; 8th Army, Italy (Salerno Anzio); Middle East (despatches). UCH: House Phys., 1939; Med. Registrar, 1945–47; Res. Asst Phys., 1948–49; First Asst, Med. Unit, UCH Med. Sch., 1950–54; WHO Travelling Fellowship, 1952. Hon. Cons. Endocrinologist to Army, 1965–81. Examiner in Medicine, Univs of Cambridge, London and Sheffield. Chm., Jt Consultants Cttee, 1979–84. Mem., Assoc. of Physicians of GB and Ire., 1952; Pres., Sect. of Endocrinology, RSM, 1968–70; Chm., Med. and Sci. Sects, 1975–77, Chm. Council, 1986–, Brit. Diabetic Assoc. RCP: Mem. Council, 1954–55; Oliver Sharpey Lectr, 1960; Joseph Senior White Fellow, 1960; Examiner for MRCP, 1964–81; Procensor, 1973; Censor, 1974; Croonian Lectr, 1976; Sen. Censor and First Vice-Pres., 1977. William McIlwrath Guest Prof., Royal Prince Alfred Hosp., Sidney, 1959; John Mathison Shaw Lectr, RCPE, 1963; Guest Visitor, St Vincent's Hosp., Sidney, 1963; Guest Lectr, Postgrad. Cttee, Christchurch Hosps, NZ, 1973; Banting Meml Lectr, Brit. Diabetic Assoc., 1978; Best Meml Lectr, Toronto Diabetes Assoc., 1984. *Publications*: Biochemical Investigations in Diagnosis and Treatment, 1954, 3rd edn, 1962; papers on endocrinology and diabetes in med. jls. *Recreation*: gardening. *Address*: 33 Woodside Avenue, N12. *T*: 01–445 7925; 121 Harley Street, W1. *T*: 01–935 7200.

NADER, Ralph; author, lecturer, lawyer; *b* Winsted, Conn, USA, 27 Feb. 1934; *s* of Nadra Nader and Rose (*née* Bouziane). *Educ*: Gilbert Sch., Winsted; Woodrow Wilson Sch. of Public and Internat. Affairs, Princeton Univ. (AB *magna cum laude*); Harvard Univ. Law Sch. (LLB). Admitted to: Bar of Conn, 1958; Bar of Mass, 1959; US Supreme Court Bar, 1963. Served US Army, 1959. Law practice in Hartford, Conn, 1959–; Lectr in History and Govt, Univ. of Hartford, 1961–63; Lectr, Princeton Univ., 1967–68. Member: Amer. Bar Assoc., 1959–; AAAS, 1964–; Phi Beta Kappa. Has pursued actively better consumer protection and improvement in the lot of the American Indian; lobbied in Washington for safer food, drugs, air, water and against nuclear reactors; played very important role in work for passing of: National Traffic and Motor Vehicle Safety Act, 1966; Wholesome Meat Act, 1967; Occupational Safety and Health Act, 1970; Safe Drinking Water Act, 1974; Freedom of Information Act, 1974. Niemen Fellows Award, 1965–66; named one of the Ten Outstanding Young Men of the Year by US Jun. Chamber of Commerce, 1967. *Publications*: Unsafe at Any Speed: the designed-in dangers of the American automobile, 1965, rev. edn 1972; (jtly) What to do with Your Bad Car, 1971, Working on the System: a manual for citizen's access to federal agencies, 1972; (jtly) Action for a Change, 1972; (jtly) Whistleblowing, 1972; (jtly) You and Your Pension, 1973; (ed) The Consumer and Corporate Accountability, 1973; (co-ed) Corporate Power in America, 1973; (jtly) Taming the Giant Corporation, 1976; (co-ed) Verdicts on Lawyers, 1976; (jtly) Menace of Atomic Energy, 1977; (co-ed) Who's Poisoning America?, 1981; (jtly) The Big Boys: power and position in American business, 1986; contrib. articles to many magazines; has weekly syndicated newspaper column. *Address*: PO Box 19367, Washington, DC 20036, USA.

NADESAN, Pararajasingam, CMG 1955; OBE 1954; Governor, Rotary International, District 321; Member, Legislative Council, Rotary International; Director: Cargills (Ceylon) Ltd; Associated Hotels Co. Ltd; Past Chairman: Low Country Products Association; Air Ceylon; *b* 20 Dec. 1917; *s* of Sir Sangarapillai Pararajasingam, *qv*; *m* 1st, 1941, Gauri Nair (decd); one *s* one *d*; 2nd, 1953, Kamala Nair; three *d*. *Educ*: Royal College, and Ceylon Univ. Coll.; Univ. of London (BA Hons). Tutor, Ceylon Univ. Coll., 1940; entered Ceylon Civil Service, 1941; held various appts in sphere of provincial administration, 1941–47; Asst Permanent Sec., Min. of Transport and Works, 1948–53; Dir of Civil Aviation in addition to duties as Asst Sec. Min. of Transport and Works, 1954–56; Sec. to the Prime Minister and Information Officer, Ceylon, 1954–56; Member: Ceylon Delegation to the Bandung Conf.; Commonwealth Prime Minister's Conf.; ICAO Gen. Assembly; ILO Cttee on Plantations. Past Mem., Nat. Planning Council. Pres. Emeritus and Life Mem., Ceylon Hotels Assoc.; FHCIMA. FCIT. President: Orchid Circle of Ceylon; Sri Lanka Horticultural Soc. Officer Order of Merit (Italy), 1954; Knight Comdr Order of the Crown, Thailand, 1955; Comdr Order of Orange Nassau, Netherlands, 1955; Defence Medal, 1947; Coronation Medal, 1953; Ceylon Armed Services Inauguration Medal, 1956. *Recreations*: golf, tennis, gardening, collecting antiques, stamps and coins. *Clubs*: Colombo, Orient, Rotary (Colombo); Gymkhana.

NAGDA, Kanti; Manager, Community Centre; *b* 1 May 1946; *s* of Vershi Bhoja Nagda and Zaviben Nagda; *m* 1972, Bhagwati Desai; two *s*. *Educ*: City High Sch., Kampala, Uganda; Coll. of Further Educn, Chippenham, Wilts; E African Univ., Uganda. Sec.-Gen., Confedn of Indian Organisations (UK), 1975–. Exec. Cttee Member: Harrow Community Relations Council, 1974–76; Gujarati Literary Acad. (GB), 1976–82. Mem., European Movement. President: Uganda Art Circle, 1968–71; Anglo Indian Circle, 1973–82 and 1985–; Indian Cricket Club, Harrow, 1976–80. Representative: Harrow Youth Council; Brent Youth Council; Harrow Arts Council. Hon. Editorial Consultant, International Asian Guide & Who's Who, 1975–; Asst Editor, Oswal News, 1977–84. *Publications*: Muratiyo Ke Nokar (Gujarati novel), Kenya 1967; stories and articles in newspapers and jls. *Recreations*: cricket, photography. *Address*: 11 North Avenue, Harrow, Mddx HA2 7AE. *T*: 01–427 0696. *Club*: Indian National.

NAGEON de LESTANG, Sir (Marie Charles Emmanuel) Clement, Kt 1960; *b* 20 Oct. 1910; *e s* of late M. F. C. Nageon de Lestang, Solicitor and Simone Savy; *m* 1933, Danielle Sauvage; one *s* three *d* (and one *s* decd). *Educ*: St Louis' Coll., Seychelles; King's Coll., London. LLB (Hons) London, 1931. Called to the Bar, Middle Temple, 1931. Private practice, Seychelles, 1932–35; Legal Adviser and Crown Prosecutor to Govt of Seychelles, 1936–39; Actg Chief Justice, Seychelles, 1939–44; Resident Magistrate, Kenya, 1944–47; Puisne Judge, Kenya, 1947–56; Federal Justice, Federal Supreme Court of Nigeria, 1956–58; Chief Justice of the High Court of Lagos, 1958–64, and of the Southern Cameroons, 1958–60; Justice of Appeal, Court of Appeal for Eastern Africa, 1964, Vice-Pres., 1966–69. *Recreations*: yachting, fishing. *Address*: Pennies, Court Drive, Shillingford, Oxon.

NAGY, János L.; *see* Lörincz-Nagy, J.

NAILOR, Prof. Peter; Professor of History, Royal Naval College, Greenwich, since 1977; Dean of the College, 1982–84 and since 1986; *b* 16 Dec. 1928; *o s* of Leslie Nailor and Lily Matilda (*née* Jones). *Educ*: Mercers' Sch.; Wadham Coll., Oxford (BA 1952, MA 1955). Home Civil Service, 1952; Asst Principal, Admiralty, 1952; First Lord's Representative on Admiralty Interview Bd, 1960–62; Polaris Executive, 1962–67; Asst Sec., MoD, 1967–69; Professor of Politics, Univ. of Lancaster, 1969–77. Visiting research appts and professorships in Canada, Australia and India; Member: Political Science Cttee, SSRC, 1975–81; FCO adv. panel on arms control and disarmament, 1975; MoD adv. panel on historical records, 1979; Chairman, British International Studies Assoc., 1983–86. Freeman and Liveryman, Mercers' Co., 1969. *Publications*: articles in learned jls, pamphlets. *Recreations*: cooking, gardening, reading. *Address*: Royal Naval College, Greenwich, SE10 9NN. *T*: 01–858 2154.

NAIPAUL, Vidiadhar Surajprasad; author; *b* 17 Aug. 1932; *m* 1955, Patricia Ann Hale. *Educ*: Queen's Royal Coll., Trinidad; University Coll., Oxford (Hon. Fellow, 1983). Hon. Dr Letters Columbia Univ., NY, 1981; Hon. LittD Cambridge, 1983. *Publications*: The Middle Passage, 1962; An Area of Darkness, 1964; The Loss of El Dorado, 1969; The Overcrowded Barracoon, and other articles, 1972; India: a wounded civilization, 1977; The Return of Eva Perón, 1980; Among the Believers, 1981; Finding the Centre, 1984; *novels*: The Mystic Masseur, 1957 (John Llewelyn Rhys Memorial Prize, 1958); The Suffrage of Elvira, 1958; Miguel Street, 1959 (Somerset Maugham Award, 1961); A House for Mr Biswas, 1961; Mr Stone and the Knights Companion, 1963 (Hawthornden Prize, 1964); The Mimic Men, 1967 (W. H. Smith Award, 1968); A Flag on the Island, 1967; In a Free State, 1971 (Booker Prize, 1971); Guerrillas, 1975; A Bend in the River, 1979; The Enigma of Arrival, 1987. *Address*: c/o Aitken & Stone Ltd, 29 Fernshaw Road, SW10.

NAIR, Chengara Veetil Devan; President of Singapore, 1981–85; *b* Malacca, Malaysia, 5 Aug. 1923; *s* of Karunakaran Illath Vayalakkara and Devaki Chengara Veetil Nair; *m* 1953, Avadai Dhanam Lakshimi; three *s* one *d*. *Educ*: Victoria Sch., Singapore. Teacher, St Andrew's Sch., 1949–51; Gen. Sec., Singapore Teachers' Union, 1949–51; Convenor, and Mem. Central Exec. Cttee, People's Action Party, 1954–56; Political Sec., Min. of Education, 1959–60; Chm., Singapore Adult Educn Bd, 1961–64; National Trades Union Congress: Sec. Gen., 1962–65, 1969–79; Dir, Res. Unit, 1969–81; Pres., 1979–81; Pres., Asian Regl Orgn, ICFTU, 1976–81. MP Malaysia, 1964–69, Singapore, 1979–81; first Sec. Gen., Democratic Action Party, Malaysia, 1964–69. Member: Nat. Wages Council, 1972–81; Housing and Develt Bd, 1975–81; Presidential Council for Minority Rights, 1979–81; Chm., Singapore Labour Foundn, 1977–81. Mem. Council, Nat. Univ. of Singapore, 1980–81; Chm., Hindu Adv. Bd, 1981. Life Member: Singapore Cancer Soc.; Ramakrishna Mission; Sri Aurobindo Soc. Hon. DLitt Nat. Univ. of Singapore, 1976.

Publications: (ed) Who Lives if Malaysia Dies?, 1969; (ed) Singapore: Socialism that Works, 1976; (ed) Tomorrow: the peril and the promise, 1976; (ed) Asian Labour and the Dynamics of Change, 1977; (ed) Not by Wages Alone, 1982. *Address:* 7 Brookvale Drive, #01–09, Singapore 2159.

NAIRN, Air Vice-Marshal Kenneth Gordon, CB 1945; chartered accountant; *b* 9 Nov. 1898; *m* 1920, Mary Fleming Martin; two *s* one *d. Educ:* George Watson's Coll., Edinburgh; Univ. of Manitoba. Lived in Edinburgh till 1911; proceeded to Canada; service in Strathcona Horse and transferred to RFC 1916–19; Pilot, rank Lt; moved to Vancouver from Winnipeg, 1921; retired. Hon. Wing Commander of 111 Aux. Squadron RCAF 1933; Active Service, 1939–45; on Air Council as Air Mem. Accounts and Finance till Oct. 1944, then Special Adviser to Minister for Air on Finance. Hon. ADC for Province of BC to the Governor-General, Viscount Alexander, 1947. Norwegian Cross of Liberation, 1948. *Recreations:* golf, fishing, yachting. *Address:* 1611 Drummond Drive, Vancouver, BC. *T:* 224–1500. *Clubs:* Royal Air Force; Vancouver, Royal Vancouver Yacht (Vancouver).

NAIRN, Margaret, RGN, SCM; Chief Area Nursing Officer, Greater Glasgow Health Board, 1974–84; *b* 20 July 1924; *d* of James R. Nairn and Anne G. Nairn. *Educ:* Aberdeen Academy. Nurse Training: general: Aberdeen Royal Infirmary, to 1945 (RGN); midwifery: Aberdeen Maternity Hosp., until 1948 (State Certified Midwife); Health Visitors: Aberdeen Coll. for Health Visitors, until 1952 (Health Visitors Cert.); administrative: Royal Coll. of Nursing, London, to 1959 (Nursing Admin. Cert.); 6 months study in USA as British Commonwealth and Empire Nurses Scholar, 1956. Ward Sister and Night Supt, Aberdeen Maternity Hosp., 1945–52; Director of Nursing Services in Aberdeen and Glasgow, 1952–74. *Publications:* articles in medical and nursing press: A Study of 283 Families with Rent Arrears; Liaison Services between Hospital and Community Nursing Services; Health Visitors in General Practice. *Recreations:* reading, gardening, swimming. *Address:* 12 Countesswells Terrace, Aberdeen AB1 8LQ.

NAIRN, Sir Michael, 4th Bt *cr* 1904; *b* 1 July 1938; *s* of Sir Michael George Nairn, 3rd Bt, TD, and of Helen Louise, *yr d* of Major E. J. W. Bruce, Melbourne, Aust.; *S* father, 1984; *m* 1972, Diana (*d* 1982), *er d* of Leonard Bligh, NSW; two *s* one *d; m* 1986, Mrs Sally Straker, *d* of Major W. P. S. Hastings. *Educ:* Eton; INSEAD. *Heir: s* Michael Andrew Nairn, *b* 2 Nov. 1973. *Address:* 39 Ann Street, Edinburgh EH4 1PL. *Club:* Caledonian.

NAIRN, Sir Robert Arnold S.; *see* Spencer-Nairn.

NAIRNE, Lady (12th in line, of the Lordship *cr* 1681); **Katherine Evelyn Constance Bigham;** *b* 22 June 1912; *d* of 6th Marquess of Lansdowne and Elizabeth (she *m* 2nd, Lord Colum Crichton-Stuart, who *d* 1957; she *d* 1964); *S* to brother's Lordship of Nairne, 1944; *m* 1933, Hon. Edward Bigham (later 3rd Viscount Mersey, who *d* 1979); three *s. Heir: s* Viscount Mersey, *qv. Address:* Bignor Park, Pulborough, W Sussex. *T:* Sutton (Sussex) 214.

NAIRNE, Rt. Hon. Sir Patrick (Dalmahoy), GCB 1981 (KCB 1975; CB 1971); MC 1943; PC 1982; Master, St Catherine's College, Oxford, since 1981; Chancellor, Essex University, since 1983; *b* 15 Aug. 1921; *s* of late Lt-Col C. S. and Mrs E. D. Nairne; *m* 1948, Penelope Chauncy Bridges, *d* of Lt-Col R. F. and Mrs L. C. Bridges; three *s* three *d. Educ:* Radley Coll.; University Coll., Oxford (Exhibr; Hon. Fellow, 1981). Seaforth Highlanders, 1941–45 (Capt.). 1st cl. hons Mod. Hist. (Oxon), 1947. Entered Civil Service and joined Admty, Dec. 1947; Private Sec. to First Lord of Admty, 1958–60; Asst Sec., 1960; Private Sec. to Sec. of State for Defence, 1965–67; Assistant Under-Sec. of State (Logistics), MoD, 1967–70; Dep. Under-Sec. of State, MoD, 1970–73; Second Perm. Sec., Cabinet Office, 1973–75; Perm. Sec., DHSS, 1975–81. Mem., Falkland Isles Review Cttee, 1982; Govt Monitor, Hong Kong, 1984. Dep. Chm., W Midlands Bd, Central Indep. TV, 1986–. Chm., Soc. of Italic Handwriting, 1981–; Trustee: Nat. Maritime Museum, 1981–; Rowntree Meml Trust; Member: VSO Council; Council, RCA; President: Radleian Soc., 1980–83; Seamen's Hosp. Soc. FRSA 1978. Hon. LLD: Leicester, 1980; St Andrews, 1984; DU Essex, 1983. *Recreations:* watercolour painting, calligraphy. *Address:* Master's Lodgings, St Catherine's College, Oxford. *Club:* United Oxford & Cambridge University.

NAIROBI, Archbishop of, (RC), since 1971; **HE Cardinal Maurice Otunga;** *b* Jan. 1923. Priest, 1950; Titular Bishop of Tacape, 1957; Bishop of Kisii, 1960; Titular Archbishop of Bomarzo, 1969; Cardinal 1973. *Address:* Archbishop's House, PO Box 14231, Nairobi, Kenya.

NAKASONE, Yasuhiro; Prime Minister of Japan, since 1982; *b* 27 May 1918; 2nd *s* of Matsugoroh Nakasone; *m* 1945, Tsutako Kobayashi; one *s* two *d. Educ:* Faculty of Law, Imperial Univ. (graduate). Joined Min. of Home Affairs, 1941; commd as Lt-Comdr, 1945. Elected to House of Representatives (first of 15 consecutive times), 1947; Minister of State, Dir-Gen. of Science and Technology Agency, 1959–60; Minister of Transport, 1967–68; Minister of State, Dir-Gen. of Defence Agency, 1970–71; Minister of Internat. Trade and Industry, 1972–74; Minister of State for Admin. Management Agency, 1980–82. Chm. Exec. Council, 1971–72, Sec. Gen., 1974–76, Liberal Democratic Party. Hon. DHL, Johns Hopkins, 1984. Médaille de la Chancellerie, Univs of Paris. *Publications:* The Ideals of Youth, 1947; Japan Speaks, 1954; The New Conservatism, 1978; Human Cities—a proposal for the 21st century, 1980. *Address:* (official residence) Nagatachyo 2-3-1, Chiyoda-ku, Tokyo 101, Japan.

NALDER, Hon. Sir Crawford David, Kt 1974; farmer; active in voluntary and charitable organisations; *b* Katanning, WA, 14 Feb. 1910; *s* of H. A. Nalder, Wagin; *m* 1st, 1934, Olive May (*d* 1973), *d* of S. Irvin; one *s* two *d;* 2nd, 1974, Brenda Wade. *Educ:* State Sch., Wagin; Wesley Coll., Perth, WA. Sheep, wheat and pig farmer, 1934–; Country rep. for Perth butchers. Entered parliament, 1947; MLA (CP) for Katanning, Parliament of Western Australia, 1950–73 (for Wagin, 1947–50); Dep. Leader, Country Party, 1956; Minister: for War Service Land Settlement, 1959–66; for Agriculture, 1959–71; for Electricity, 1962–71; Leader, Parly Country Party, 1962–73. Chm., Girls College Council. Knighted for services to the state and in local govt. *Recreations:* tennis, gardening. *Address:* 7 Morriett Street, Attadale, WA 6156, Australia.

NALL, Sir Michael (Joseph), 2nd Bt *cr* 1954; DL; *b* 6 Oct. 1921; *er s* of Colonel Sir Joseph Nall, 1st Bt; *S* father, 1958; *m* 1951, Angela Loveday Hanbury, *e d* of Air Chief Marshal Sir Alec Coryton, KCB, KBE, MVO, DFC; two *s. Educ:* Wellington College, Berks. Joined Royal Navy, 1939. Served War of 1939–45 (at sea); psc(mil.) 1949; Lt-Comdr, 1950–61, retired. General Manager, Guide Dogs for the Blind Association, 1961–64. Pres., Nottingham Chamber of Commerce and Industry, 1972–74. DL Notts, 1970–; High Sheriff, Notts, 1971. Chm., Notts Scout Assoc., 1968– (Silver Acorn, 1979). *Recreations:* field sports, flying. *Heir: s* Edward William Joseph Nall, *b* 24 Oct. 1952. *Address:* Hoveringham Hall, Nottingham NG14 7JR. *T:* Nottingham 663634.

NALL-CAIN, family name of **Baron Brocket.**

NANCE, Francis James, LLM; **His Honour Judge Nance;** a Circuit Judge (formerly a Judge of County Courts and Commissioner, Liverpool and Manchester Crown Courts), since 1966; *b* 5 Sept. 1915; *s* of late Herbert James Nance, South Africa, and Margaret Ann Nance, New Brighton; *m* 1943, Margaret Gertrude Roe (*d* 1978); two *s. Educ:* St Francis Xavier's College, Liverpool; University of Liverpool (LLM 1938). Called to the Bar, Gray's Inn, 1936. Served War of 1939–45, Royal Corps of Signals (Captain): Normandy invasion, NW Europe (despatches). Practised on Northern Circuit, 1936–66. Deputy Chairman, Lancashire QS, 1963–71; Pres., HM Council of Circuit Judges, 1984. *Recreation:* chess. *Address:* c/o Queen Elizabeth II Law Courts, Liverpool, Merseyside. *Club:* Athenæum (Liverpool).

NANDY, Dipak; Chief Executive, Intermediate Technology Development Group, since 1986; *b* 21 May 1936; *s* of B. C. Nandy and Leela Nandy; *m* 1st, 1964, Margaret Gracie (decd); 2nd, 1972, Hon. Luise Byers; two *d. Educ:* St Xavier's Coll., Calcutta; Univ. of Leeds BA 1st Cl. Hons English Literature, 1960; C. E. Vaughan Research Fellowship, 1960–62. Lectr, English Literature, Univ. of Leicester, 1962–66; Lectr and Fellow of Rutherford College, Univ. of Kent at Canterbury, 1966–68; founder-Director, The Runnymede Trust, 1968–73; Vis. Fellow, Adlai Stevenson Inst. of International Affairs, Chicago, 1970–73; Research Fellow, Social and Community Planning Research, 1973–75; Dep. Chief Exec., Equal Opportunities Commn, 1976–86. Member: Cttee of Inquiry into Future of Broadcasting, 1974–77; Council, Nat. Assoc. Citizens' Advice Bureaux, 1983–; BBC: Chm., Asian Programmes Adv. Cttee, 1983–; Mem., General Adv. Council. Mem. Council, Northern Chamber Orch., 1980–84. Governor, BFI, 1984–. Trustee, CSV, 1981–. Hon. Liaison, Employment and Labour Law Sect., Amer. Bar Assoc., 1980–. *Publications:* numerous essays in books, periodicals and newspapers on literature, political thought, race relations, urban problems, equality for women, broadcasting policy and development issues. *Recreations:* collecting records, opera, computing. *Address:* c/o Intermediate Technology Development Group, Myson House, Railway Terrace, Rugby CV21 3HD. *T:* Rugby 60631. *Club:* National Liberal.

NANKIVELL, Owen; JP; economic and business consultant; Executive Director, Hinksey Centre, since 1982; *b* 6 April 1927; *s* of John Hamilton Nankivell and Sarah Ann Mares; *m* 1956, Mary Burman Earnshaw; one *s* two *d. Educ:* Torquay Grammar Sch.; Univ. of Manchester. BA (Econ) 1951, MA (Econ) 1963. FRSS. Admty, 1951–52; Colonial Office, 1952–55; Central Statistical Office, 1955–65; DEA, 1965–69; HM Treasury, 1969–72; Asst Dir, Central Statistical Office, 1972–79; Gp Chief Economist, Lucas Industries, 1979–82. JP Worcester, 1984. *Publication:* All Good Gifts, 1978. *Recreations:* Christian, tennis, choral music, singing. *Address:* 12 Whittington Road, Worcester WR5 2JU. *T:* Worcester 352948.

NAPIER, family name of **Lord Napier and Ettrick** and **Baron Napier of Magdala.**

NAPIER, 14th Lord, *cr* 1627 (Scotland), **AND ETTRICK,** 5th Baron, *cr* 1872 (UK); **Francis Nigel Napier,** CVO 1985 (LVO 1980); DL; a Bt of Nova Scotia, 1666, 11th Bt of Thirlestane; Major, Scots Guards (Reserve of Officers); Private Secretary, Comptroller and Equerry to HRH the Princess Margaret, Countess of Snowdon, since 1973; *b* 5 Dec. 1930; *e s* of 13th Baron Napier and 4th Ettrick, TD, and Muir, *e d* of Sir Percy Newson, Bt; *S* father 1954; *m* 1958, Delia Mary, *yr d* of A. D. B. Pearson; two *s* two *d. Educ:* Eton; RMA, Sandhurst. Commissioned, 1950; served Malaya, 1950–51 (invalided); Adjt 1st Bn Scots Guards, 1955–57. Equerry to His late Royal Highness The Duke of Gloucester, 1958–60, retd, 1960. Deputy Ceremonial and Protocol Secretary, CRO, 1962–66; Purple Staff Officer at State Funeral of Sir Winston Churchill, 1966. A Cons. Whip, House of Lords, 1970–71; handed over Instruments of Independence to Tuvalu (formerly Ellice Is) on behalf of The Queen, 1978. Mem. Royal Co. of Archers (Queen's Body Guard for Scotland), 1953–. Pres., St John Ambulance Assoc. and Brigade for County of London, 1975–83. DL Selkirkshire, 1974, Ettrick and Lauderdale, 1975–. Freeman, City of London; Liveryman, Worshipful Company of Grocers. OStJ 1982. *Heir: s* Master of Napier, *qv. Address:* Forest Lodge, The Great Park, Windsor SL4 2BU. *T:* Windsor 861262; Apartment 2, St James's Palace, SW1A 1BA. *T:* 01–930 0242; (seat) Thirlestane, Ettrick, Selkirkshire. *Clubs:* White's, Pratt's; Royal Caledonian Hunt (Edinburgh).

NAPIER OF MAGDALA, 5th Baron (UK), *cr* 1868; **Robert John Napier,** OBE 1944; MICE; late Royal Engineers; Brigadier, Chief Engineer, HQ, Scottish Command, retd; *b* 16 June 1904; *o s* of 4th Baron and Florence Martha (*d* 1946), *d* of Gen. John Maxwell Perceval, CB; *S* father, 1948; *m* 1939, Elizabeth Marian, *y d* of E. H. Hunt, FRCS; three *s* two *d. Educ:* Wellington. Served Waziristan, 1936–37 (despatches); War of 1939–45, Sicily (OBE). *Heir: s* Hon. Robert Alan Napier [*b* 6 Sept. 1940; *m* 1964, Frances Clare, *er d* of late A. F. Skinner, Monks Close, Woolpit, Suffolk; one *s* one *d*]. *Address:* 8 Mortonhall Road, Edinburgh EH9 2HW.

NAPIER, Master of; Hon. Francis David Charles Napier; *b* 3 Nov. 1962; *s* and *heir* of 14th Lord Napier (and 5th Baron Ettrick), *qv. Educ:* Stanbridge Earls School. With a Lloyd's agency. *Address:* Forest Lodge, The Great Park, Windsor. *Club:* Turf.

NAPIER, Barbara Langmuir, OBE 1975; Senior Tutor to Women Students in the University of Glasgow, 1964–74; Member, the Industrial Arbitration Board (formerly Industrial Court), 1963–76; *b* 21 Feb. 1914; *y c* of late James Langmuir Napier, Consultant Engineer, and late Siblie Agnes Mowat. *Educ:* Hillhead High Sch., Glasgow; Univ. of Glasgow (MA); Glasgow and West of Scotland Coll. of Domestic Science. Org. Sec. Redlands Hosp., Glasgow, 1937–41; Univ. of Glasgow: Warden, Queen Margaret Hall, 1941–44; Gen. Adv. to Women Students, 1942–64; Appts Officer (Women), 1942–65. Founder Mem. Assoc. of Principals, Wardens and Advisers to Univ. Women Students, 1942, Hon. Mem., 1977– (Pres. 1965–68); Local Rep. and later Mem. Coun., Women's Migration and Overseas Appts Soc., 1946–64; Winifred Cullis Lecture Fellowship (midwest USA) of Brit. Amer. Associates, 1950. Founder Dir, West of Scotland Sch. Co. Ltd, 1976–77. Member, Tribunal under National Insurance Acts, 1954–60; President, Standing Conference of Women's Organisations (Glasgow), 1955–57; Member: Scottish Committee, ITA, 1957–64; Executive Cttee, Nat. Advisory Centre on Careers for Women, (formerly Women's Employment Fedn), 1963–68, 1972–77; Indep. Member: Flax and Hemp Wages Council (GB), 1962–70 (Dep. Chm. 1964–70); Hat, Cap and Millinery Wages Council (GB), 1963–70; Laundry Wages Council (GB), 1968–70. Governor: Westbourne Sch., Glasgow, 1951–77 (Chm., 1969–77; Hon. Governor, 1981); Notre Dame Coll. of Educn, Glasgow, 1959–64. Admitted as Burgess and Guild Sister (*qua* Hammerman) of Glasgow, and Mem., Grand Antiquity Soc. of Glasgow, 1956. JP Glasgow 1955–75, Stirling 1975–80. *Publications:* (with S. Nisbet) Promise and Progress, 1970; contrib. The College Courant, etc. *Recreations:* reading, travel, gardening, painting, being with cats. *Address:* 67 Brisbane Street, Largs, Ayrshire KA30 8QP. *T:* Largs 675495. *Club:* College (Glasgow).

NAPIER, John; stage designer; *b* 1 March 1944; *s* of James Edward Thomas Napier and Laurie Napier (*née* Godbold); *m* 1st, Andreane Neofitou; one *s* one *d;* 2nd, Douna King, one *s. Educ:* Hornsey Coll. of Art; Central Sch. of Arts and Crafts. Designed 1st production, A Penny for a Song, Pheonix, Leicester, 1967; London productions: Fortune and Men's Eyes, 1968; The Ruling Class, The Fun War, Muzeeka, George Frederick (ballet), La

Turista, 1969; Cancer, Isabel's a Jezebel, 1970; Mister, The Foursome, The Lovers of Viorne, Lear, 1971; Jump, Sam Sam, Big Wolf, 1972; The Devils (ENO), Equus, The Party, 1973; Knuckle, 1974; Kings and Clowns, The Travelling Music Show, 1978; The Devils of Loudon, Lohengrin (Covent Garden); King John, Richard II, Cymbeline, Macbeth, Richard III, 1974; Hedda Gabler, 1975; Much Ado About Nothing, The Comedy of Errors, King Lear, 1976; A Midsummer Night's Dream, As You Like It, 1977; The Merry Wives of Windsor, Twelfth Night, Three Sisters, Once in a Lifetime, 1979; The Greeks, Nicholas Nickleby (SWET award, Tony Award), 1980; Cats (Tony award), 1981; Henry IV Parts I and II, Peter Pan, 1982; Idomeneo (Glyndebourne), 1983; Macbeth (Covent Garden), 1983; Starlight Express, 1984; Les Misérables, 1985; Time, 1986; numerous designs for stage productions in Europe, Africa, USA and for TV and film. *Recreation:* photography. *Address:* c/o MLR, 200 Fulham Road, SW10.

NAPIER, Sir Joseph William Lennox, 4th Bt, *cr* 1867; OBE 1944; *b* 1 Aug. 1895; *s* of 3rd Bt and Mabel Edith Geraldine (*d* 1955), *d* of late Rev. Charles Thornton Forster; *S* father (killed in action, Gallipoli), 1915; *m* 1931, Isabel Muriel, *yr d* of late Maj. Siward Surtees, DL, JP, Redworth Hall, Co Durham; two *s*. *Educ:* Rugby; Jesus College, Cambridge. Served European War, 1914–18, in South Wales Borderers, Gallipoli and Mesopotamia (wounded three times; POW, Turkey). Joined 57 Home Counties Bde RFA (TF), 1920; re-employed 1939, Lt-Col (AQMG (Movt)) HQ Staff, Eastern Command and Italy (OBE mil.). Mem., Lloyds, 1921–73. Former Dir of public companies and Mem., Council of Inst. of Directors. Gold Staff Officer, Coronations 1937 and 1953. *Recreations:* painting, fishing. *Heir: s* Robert Surtees Napier [*b* 5 March 1932; *m* 1971, Jennifer Beryl, *d* of late H. Warwick Daw; one *s*]. *Address:* 17 Cheyne Gardens, Chelsea, SW3. *Clubs:* Alpine, Hurlingham; Swinley Forest Golf.

See also Brigadier V. J. L. Napier.

NAPIER, Maj.-Gen. Lennox Alexander Hawkins, CB 1983; OBE 1970; MC 1957; DL; General Officer Commanding Wales, 1980–83, retired; Chairman, Central Transport Consultative Committee, since 1985; *b* 28 June 1928; *s* of Major Charles McNaughton Napier and D. C. Napier; *m* 1959, Jennifer Dawn Wilson; one *s* two *d*. *Educ:* Radley; RMA Sandhurst. Joined Army, 1946; commnd into South Wales Borderers, 1948; commanded 1st Bn S Wales Borderers and 1st Bn Royal Regt of Wales, 1967–70; Instructor, JSSC, 1970–72; served Min. of Defence, 1972–74; Brigade Commander, Berlin Infantry Bde, 1974–76; Prince of Wales's Division: Divisional Brigadier, 1976–80; Col Commandant, 1980–83; Col, The Royal Regt of Wales, 1983–; Hon. Col, Cardiff Univ. OTC, 1985–. DL Gwent 1983. *Recreations:* shooting, riding. *Address:* Osbaston Farm, Monmouth, Gwent. *Club:* Lansdowne.

NAPIER, Sir Oliver John, Kt 1985; Councillor for East Belfast, Belfast City Council, since 1977; *b* 11 July 1935; *e s* of James J. and Sheila Napier; *m* 1962, Brigid (*née* Barnes); three *s* five *d* (and one *s* decd). *Educ:* Ballycruttle Public Elem. Sch., Downpatrick; St Malachy's Coll., Belfast; Queen's Univ., Belfast (LLB). Qual. Solicitor, NI, 1959; Lectr and Mem. Bd of Examrs, Incorp. Law Soc. of NI, 1965–71. Mem. Exec., Ulster Liberal Party, 1962–69; Founder Mem., New Ulster Movt, 1969; Founder Mem., Alliance Party, 1970, Leader 1973–84. Mem. (Alliance), E Belfast, NI Assembly, 1973–75; Minister of Legal Affairs, NI Executive, Jan.-May 1974; Mem. (Alliance), N Ireland Constitutional Convention for E Belfast, 1975–76; Mem. (Alliance) Belfast E, NI Assembly, 1982–86. Contested (Alliance), E Belfast, 1979, 1983. *Recreations:* many and varied. *Address:* 83 Victoria Road, Holywood, Co. Down.

NAPIER, Brigadier Vivian John Lennox, MC 1918; late S Wales Borderers; Vice-Lieutenant, Brecknock, 1964–74; *b* 13 July 1898; 3rd *s* of Sir William Lennox Napier, 3rd Bt; *m* 1958, Marion Avis, OBE, *d* of late Sir John and Lady Lloyd. *Educ:* Uppingham; RMC. Served European War, 1914–18: France and Belgium (wounded, MC); served War of 1939–45: HQ Cairo Bde and 1 Bn Welch Regt, North Africa (despatches, prisoner). Brig. Comdg Mombasa Area, 1948–49; Dep. Comdr S-W District, UK, 1949–51; retd, 1952. Commissioner, St John Ambulance, Breconshire, 1957–62. DL Brecknock, 1958. Order of Leopold (Belgium), 1925; OStJ 1959. *Recreation:* fishing. *Address:* Ty Nant, Groesffordd, Brecon, Powys.

See also Sir Joseph Napier, Bt.

NAPIER, Sir William Archibald, 13th Bt, of Merchiston, *cr* 1627; *b* 19 July 1915; *s* of Sir Robert Archibald Napier, 12th Bt and Violet Payn; *S* father 1965; *m* 1942, Kathleen Mabel, *d* of late Reginald Greaves, Tafelberg, CP; one *s*. *Educ:* Cheam School; Stowe. Captain S African Engineers, Middle East, 1939–45. Mechanical Engineer. AM Inst. of (SA) Mech. Engineers; AM Inst. of Cert. Engineers (Works); Fellow, Inst. of Matériel Handling. *Recreations:* golf, squash. *Heir: s* John Archibald Lennox Napier [*b* 6 Dec. 1946; *m* 1969, Erica, *d* of late Kurt Kingsfield; one *s* one *d*]. *Address:* Merchiston Croft, PO Box 65177, Benmore, Transvaal, 2010, S Africa. *T:* 7832651. *Clubs:* Rand, Johannesburg Country, Wanderers' (Johannesburg).

NAPLEY, Sir David, Kt 1977; Solicitor; Senior Partner in Kingsley Napley; President of the Law Society, 1976–77 (Vice-President, 1975–76); *b* 25 July 1915; *s* of late Joseph and Raie Napley; *m* 1940, Leah Rose, *d* of Thomas Reginald Saturley; two *d*. *Educ:* Burlington College. Solicitor, 1937. Served with Queen's Royal (W Surrey) Regt, 1940; commnd 1942; Indian Army, 1942; Captain 1942; invalided 1945. Contested (C): Rowley Regis and Tipton, 1951; Gloucester, 1955. Pres., London (Criminal Courts) Solicitors Assoc., 1960–63; Chm. Exec. Council, British Academy of Forensic Sciences, 1960–74 (Pres. 1967; Director, 1974–); Mem. Council, Law Soc., 1962–; Mem. Judicial Exchange with USA, 1963–64; Chm., Law Soc's Standing Cttee on Criminal Law, 1963–76; Pres., City of Westminster Law Soc., 1967–68; Mem. Editorial Bd, Criminal Law Review, 1967–; Chairman: Contentious Business, Law Soc., 1972–75; Legal Aid Cttee, 1969–72; Exam. Bd, Incorp. Soc. of Valuers and Auctioneers, 1981–84; Mem. Home Office Law Revision Cttee, 1971–. Mem. Council and Trustee, Imperial Soc. of Kts Bachelor, 1981–. Chm., Mario & Franco Restaurants Ltd, 1968–77. Trustee, W Ham Boys' Club, 1979–, Pres., 1981–. *Publications:* Law on the Remuneration of Auctioneers and Estate Agents, 1947; (ed) Bateman's Law of Auctions, 1954; The Law of Auctioneers and Estate Agents Commission, 1957; Crime and Criminal Procedure, 1963; Guide to Law and Practice under the Criminal Justice Act, 1967; The Technique of Persuasion, 1970, 3rd edn 1984; Not without Prejudice, 1982; a section, Halsbury's Laws of England; contrib. legal and forensic scientific jls, press, legal discussions on radio and TV. *Recreations:* painting, reading, writing, music, eating. *Address:* 107–115 Long Acre, WC2E 9PT. *T:* 01–240 2411. *Club:* Garrick.

NAPOLITAN, Leonard, CB 1970; Director of Economics and Statistics, Ministry of Agriculture, Fisheries and Food, 1965–77; *b* 9 April 1919; *s* of late Domenic and Rose G. Napolitan; *m* 1945, Dorothy Laycock; two *d*. *Educ:* Univ. of London (BSc Econ. 1944); LSE (MSc Econ. 1946). Asst Agric. Economist, Univ. of Bristol, 1947–48; joined Min. of Agric. and Fisheries as Agric. Economist, 1948. Pres., Agric. Econs Soc., 1974–75. FRSA 1984. *Address:* 4 Rectory Gardens, Burway Road, Church Stretton, Shropshire SY6 6DP.

NAPPER, John Pelham; painter; *b* London, 17 Sept. 1916; *e s* of late John Mortimer Napper and late Dorothy Charlotte (*née* Hill); *m* 1st, 1935, Hedvig Sophie Armour; 2nd, 1945, Pauline Davidson. *Educ:* Frensham Heights, Surrey and privately; Dundee Sch. of Art; Royal Acad. Schs of Art. Served War of 1939–45: commnd RA, 1941; Ceylon, 1942, War Artist to Ceylon comd, 1943–44; seconded to RNVR, 1944, E Africa, 1944; demobilised, 1945. Lived in France, 1957–70. One-man exhibitions: Leicester Galleries, London, 1949, 1961, 1962; The Adams Gallery, London, 1957 and 1959; La Maison de la Pensée Française, Paris, 1960; Galerie Lahumière, Paris, 1963; Galleries Hervé and Lahumière, Paris, 1965; Larcada Gallery, New York, 1968, 1970, 1972, 1975, 1977; Browse and Darby Gall., 1978, 1980; Ludlow Fest., 1985; Thos Agnew and Sons, 1986. retrospective exhibitions: Walker Art Gall., Liverpool, 1959; Oldham Art Gall., 1984; represented in many public and private collections. Vis. Prof. of Fine Arts, Southern Illinois Univ., USA, 1968–69. Awarded prize at International Exhibition of Fine Arts, Moscow, 1957; Awarded International Assoc. of Art Critics Prize, 1961. *Address:* Steadvallets Farm, Bromfield, Ludlow, Salop. *T:* Bromfield 247.

NARAIN, Sase, OR 1976; CMG 1969; SC (Guyana) 1985; JP (Guyana); solicitor; Speaker of the National Assembly, Guyana, since 1971; Chairman: Berger Paints (Guyana) Ltd; National Bank of Industry and Commerce (Guyana), since 1986; *b* 27 Jan. 1925; *s* of Oudit and Sookdai Naraine; *m* 1952, Shamshun Narain (*née* Rayman); four *s*. *Educ:* Modern Educational Inst.; Gibson and Weldon Law Tutors. Solicitor, admitted in England and Guyana, 1957. Town Councillor, City of Georgetown, 1962–70; Member: History and Arts Council, 1969–; Republic Cttee of Guyana, 1969; Pres., Guyana Sanatan Dharma Maha Sabha, 1963–. Comr for Oaths to Affidavits, 1961; Notary Public, 1968. Dep. Chm., Public Service Commn, Guyana, 1966–71; Mem., Police Service Commn, 1961–71. Member: Nat. Awards Cttee of Guyana; Bd of Governors, President's Coll., Guyana, 1985–. JP 1962. *Recreations:* golf, cricket, swimming. *Address:* 217 South Street, Lacytown, Georgetown, Demerara, Guyana. *T:* 66611. *Clubs:* Georgetown, Georgetown Cricket, Everest Cricket (Guyana).

NARAIN, Sir Sathi, KBE 1980 (MBE 1971); Managing Director, Narain Construction Co. Ltd, since 1945; *b* 26 Sept. 1919; *s* of Suramma and Appalsamy Narain; *m* 1969, Hannah Shakuntla (*née* Pratap); three *s*. *Educ:* Suva, Fiji. Government apprentice carpenter, 1933–44; Man. Dir, Narain Construction Co. Ltd, 1945–, and of subsidiary companies (hotels, land development, road development, shipping), 1950–; Director: Burns Philps South Sea Co. Ltd; Queensland Insurance Co. Ltd. Suva City Councillor, 1956–59; Member of Parliament, 1963–67. Mem., CPA, 1970. Hon. Architect, Fiji Assoc. of Architects, 1983. *Recreations:* golf, bowling. *Address:* (business) Narain Construction Co. Ltd, Box 412, Suva, Fiji. *T:* 23873; (residence) 20 Narain Place, Tamavua, Suva, Fiji. *T:* 381027. *Clubs:* Defence, Royal Yacht, Fiji (Suva, Fiji); Tattersall (Sydney, Aust.).

NARASIMHAN, Chakravarthi Vijayaraghava; Senior Fellow, UN Institute for Training and Research, since 1978; *b* 21 May 1915; *s* of Chakravarthi V. and Janaki Vijayaraghavachari; *m* 1938, Janaki, *d* of Dr M. T. Chari; two *d*. *Educ:* University of Madras (BA); Oxford (MA). Indian Civil Service, 1936; Dep. Sec., Development Dept, Government of Madras, 1945–48; Min. of Agriculture, Govt of India, 1950–53; Joint Sec., Economic Affairs Dept, Ministry of Finance, 1953–56; Executive Sec., UN Economic Commission for Asia and Far East, 1956–59; Under-Sec. for Special Political Affairs, UN, 1959–62; Chef de Cabinet of the Sec.-Gen., UN, 1961–73; Under-Sec., 1962–67, Under-Sec.-Gen. 1967–69, for Gen. Assembly Affairs, UN; Dep. Administrator, UN Develt Prog., 1969–72; Under-Sec.-Gen. for Inter-Agency Affairs and Co-ordination, UN, 1973–78; Organizing Exec. Sec., Cotton Develt Internat., UN Develt Programme, 1979–81. Hon. Doctor of Laws, Williams Coll. Williamstown, Mass, 1960; Hon. Dr of Humane Letters, Colgate Univ., 1966. *Recreations:* Sanskrit literature, South Indian classical music, tennis. *Address:* 210 East 47th Street, New York, NY 10017, USA. *T:* (212) 355–2092.

NARAYAN, R. K., (Rasipuram Krishnaswamy); Author; *b* Madras, 10 Oct. 1906. *Educ:* Maharaja's College, Mysore, India. Padma Bushan award for distinguished services to literature. Hon. LittD Leeds, 1967. *Publications: novels:* Swami and Friends, 1935; The Bachelor of Arts, 1937; The Dark Room, 1939; The English Teacher, 1945; Mr Sampath, 1947; The Financial Expert, 1952; Waiting for the Mahatma, 1955; The Guide, 1958; The Man-Eater of Malgudi, 1961; Gods, Demons and Others, 1964; The Sweet Vendor, 1967; The Painter of Signs, 1977; A Tiger for Malgudi, 1983; (ed) The Ramayana, 1973; (ed) The Mahabharata, 1978; *autobiography:* My Days, 1975; *short stories:* An Astrologer's Day; The Lawley Road; A Horse and Two Goats, 1970; Under the Banyan Tree and Other Stories, 1985, etc; *essays:* Next Sunday, 1955 (India); My Dateless Diary, 1960 (India). *Address:* c/o Anthony Sheil Associates, 43 Doughty Street, WC1N 2LF; Yadavagiri, Mysore 2, India.

NARAYAN, Rudy; barrister; *b* Guyana, 11 May 1938; *s* of Sase Narayan and Taijbertie (*née* Sawh); *m* 1969, Dr Naseem Akbar; two *d*. *Educ:* Lincoln's Inn. Came to UK, 1953; served HM Forces, BAOR and HQ MELF, 1958–65. Lincoln's Inn: Founder/1st Pres., Students Union, 1966; Chm. of Debates, and Captain of Cricket, 1967; called to the Bar, 1968. Vice-Chm., Lambeth Council for Community Relations 1974; Founder Chm., Lambeth Law Centre; Councillor, Lambeth, 1974–76. Co-Chm., Black Rights (UK); Founder/Chm., Soc. of Asian Lawyers; Legal Adviser: Caribbean Times, Asian Times, African Times (London). Formerly: Mem., Race Relations Bd; Legal Officer, W Indian Standing Conf.; Founder/Sec., Soc. of Black Lawyers. *Publications:* Black Community on Trial, 1976; Black England, 1977; Barrister for the Defence, 1985; Black Silk, 1985; From Trinidad with Love (novel), 1986. *Recreations:* cricket, debating, theatre, ballet, opera. *Address:* 23 Woodbourne Avenue, SW16. *T:* 01–769 4307. *Club:* Wig and Pen.

NARJES, Karl-Heinz; Vice-President, Commission of the European Communities, since 1985 (Member, since 1981); *b* 30 Jan. 1924; *s* of Heinrich Narjes; *m* 1951, Eva-Maria Rahe; one *s* one *d*. *Educ:* Hamburg Univ. Entered Foreign Service, 1953; Chef du Cabinet, Pres. of EEC, 1963; Dir-Gen., Press and Inf. Directorate, EEC, 1968–69; Minister of Econs and of Transport, Schleswig-Holstein, 1969–73. Mem., Bundestag, 1972–; Mem., For. Affairs Cttee, 1976–80; Pres., Econ. Affairs Cttee, 1972–76, 1980–. *Address:* 200 rue de la Loi, 1049 Brussels, Belgium.

NARUEPUT, Owart S.; *see* Suthiwart-Narueput.

NASH, (Denis Frederic) Ellison, OBE 1982; AE; FRCS; Consulting Surgeon, St Bartholomew's Hospital; *b* 10 Feb. 1913; *m* 1938, Joan Mary Andrew; two *s* two *d*. *Educ:* Dulwich College; St Bartholomew's Medical College. MRCS, LRCP, 1935; FRCS 1938. Served war of 1939–45, RAFVR, Wing-Comdr (Air Efficiency Award, 1943). Hunterian Professor, 1949 and 1956. Arris and Gale Lecturer, 1950. Consultant Surgeon: St Bartholomew's Hosp., 1947–78; Chailey Heritage Hosp., 1952–78; Dean, St Bartholomew's Hospital Medical College, 1957–62; Special Trustee, St Bartholomew's Hosp., 1974–78; Regional Postgraduate Dean, and Asst Dir, British Postgraduate Medical Fedn, Univ. of London, 1948–74. Special interest in the education and care of the physically handicapped; Hon. Med. Adviser: Shaftesbury Soc.; John Groom's Assoc. for Disabled. Senior Member, British Assoc. of Urological Surgeons. Senior Fellow, British Orthopædic Assoc.; Fellow, Assoc. of Surgeons of GB. Hon. Fellow, Med. Artists Assoc. Chm., Dulwich Coll. Preparatory Sch. Trust. *Publications:* The Principles and Practice of

Surgery for Nurses and Allied Professions, 1955, 7th revised edn, 1980; scientific papers in medical journals particularly concerned with surgery of childhood. *Recreations:* photography, fuchsias. *Address:* 28 Hawthorne Road, Bickley, Bromley, Kent BR1 2HH. *T:* 01–467 1142. *Club:* City of London Guild of Freemen.

NASH, John Edward; Director, S. G. Warburg & Co. Ltd, since 1977; Chairman, S. G. Warburg Bank AG, Zürich, since 1980 (Director, since 1977, Deputy Chairman, 1977–80); Director: Reckitt & Colman plc, 1966–73 and since 1977; Ailsa Investment Trust plc, since 1981; Chairman: Mercury Money Market Trust Ltd, since 1979; Mercury Far Eastern Trust Ltd, since 1980; *b* 25 June 1925; *s* of Joseph and Madeleine Nash; *m* 1947, Ralda Everard Herring; two *s* two *d. Educ:* Univ. of Sydney (BEc); Balliol Coll., Oxford (BPhil). Teaching Fellow in Economics, Sydney Univ., 1947. Exec. Dir, Samuel Montagu & Co. Ltd, 1956; also Director, 1960–73: British Australian Investment Trust; Montagu Trust Ltd; Midland Montagu Industrial Finance Ltd; Capel Court Corp. (in Melb.); resigned all directorships on appt to Brussels, 1973; Dir of Monetary Affairs, EEC, 1973–77. Dir, Oxford Univ. Business Summer Sch., 1965; Research Fellow, Nuffield Coll., Oxford (part-time), 1966–69. Hon. Treasurer, PEP, 1964–73. Mem. Bd of Trustees, WWF Internat., 1979–. *Recreations:* golf, skiing, horse-racing, music. *Address:* Chalet Gstelli, 3781 Gsteig bei Gstaad, Switzerland. *T:* (030) 51162. *Clubs:* Turf, Buck's, MCC, University (Sydney).

NASH, Philip; Commissioner of Customs and Excise, since 1986; *b* 14 March 1930; *s* of late John Hollett Nash and of Edith Grace Knee; *m* 1953, Barbara Elizabeth Bangs; one *s. Educ:* Watford Grammar School. National Service, RAF, 1949–50. HM Customs and Excise, 1950–; on loan to Civil Service College, 1970–73; Asst Sec. and Head of Management Services, 1978–81; Asst Sec., Customs Directorate, 1981–86; Director, Customs, 1986–. *Recreation:* collecting things. *Address:* 149 Merryhill Road, Bushey, Watford, Herts WD2 1DF. *T:* 01–950 1048. *Club:* Civil Service.

NASH, Thomas Arthur Manly, CMG 1959; OBE 1944; Dr (Science); retired; *b* 18 June 1905; *s* of late Col L. T. Nash, CMG, RAMC; *m* 1930, Marjorie Wenda Wayte; (one *s* decd). *Educ:* Wellington Coll.; Royal Coll. of Science. Entomologist, Dept Tsetse Research and Reclamation, Tanganyika Territory, 1927; Entomologist, Sleeping Sickness Service, Med. Dept, Nigeria, 1933. Doctorate of Science, 1933. In charge Anchau Rural Development Scheme, 1937–44; seconded as Chief Entomologist, W African Institute for Trypanosomiasis Research, 1948; Deputy Director, WAITR, 1953; Director, 1954–59; Dir, Tsetse Research Lab., Univ. of Bristol, Veterinary Field Station, Langford, 1962–71. *Publications:* Tsetse Flies in British West Africa, 1948; Africa's Bane, The Tsetse Fly, 1969; A Zoo without Bars, 1984; numerous scientific publications on tsetse and trypanosomiasis. *Recreation:* fishing. *Address:* Spring Head Farm, Upper Langford, near Bristol. *T:* Churchill 852321.

NASH, Ven. Trevor Gifford, Archdeacon of Basingstoke, since 1982; *b* 3 May 1930; *s* of Frederick Walter Gifford Nash and Elsie Violet Louise Nash; *m* 1957, Wanda Elizabeth (*née* Freeston); four *d. Educ:* Haileybury College, Hertford; Clare Coll., Cambridge (MA); Cuddesdon Coll., Oxford. Curate: Cheshunt, 1955–57; Kingston-upon-Thames, 1957–61; Priest-in-Charge, Stevenage, 1961–63; Vicar, Leagrave, Luton, 1963–67; Senior Chaplain, St George's Hosp., London, 1967–73; Rector, St Lawrence with St Swithun, Winchester, 1973–82; Priest-in-Charge, Holy Trinity, Winchester, 1977–82; RD of Winchester, 1978–82; Bishop's Adviser for Ministry of Healing, 1973–; Hon. Canon of Winchester, 1980–. RAChD (TA), 1956–67. *Recreations:* clay modelling, music, walking. *Address:* 3 Crossborough Hill, Basingstoke, Hants RG21 2AG. *T:* Basingstoke 28572.

NASIR, Rt. Rev. Eric Samuel; *b* 7 Dec. 1916. *Educ:* St Stephen's College, Delhi (MA); St Xavier's College, Calcutta (BT); Westcott House, Cambridge; Bishop's College, Calcutta. Warden, St Paul's Hostel, Delhi, 1942–45, 1951–52, 1956–62; Principal, Delhi United Christian School, 1956–62. Vicar: St Andrew's Church, Rewari, 1942–47; St Mary's Church, Ajmer, 1947–49; St James' Church, Delhi, 1949–51; St Thomas' Church, New Delhi, 1953–56; Holy Trinity Church, Delhi, 1952. Chaplain, St Stephen's College, Delhi, 1945–47. Bishop of Delhi, 1970–81; Moderator, Church of N India, 1971–81. Member, Central Committee, World Council of Churches, 1968–81. *Address:* c/o Bishop's House, 1 Church Lane, New Delhi 1, India. *T:* 387471.

NASMITH; *see* Dunbar-Nasmith.

NASON, Justin Patrick Pearse, OBE 1980; HM Diplomatic Service; Deputy High Commissioner, Colombo, since 1982; *b* 29 March 1937; *s* of John Lawrence Nason and Catherine Agnes (*née* McFadden). *Educ:* Ampleforth; University Coll., Oxford. National Service, RAF, 1956–58. BICC, 1962–63; entered HM Foreign Service, 1963; FO, 1964–65; Prague, 1965–67; FCO, 1967–71; First Sec., Pretoria and Cape Town, 1971–74; Head of Chancery, Saigon, 1974–75; FCO, 1975–79; Head of Chancery, Kampala, 1979–81; Nat. Defence Coll. of Canada, 1981–82. *Recreation:* golf. *Address:* c/o Foreign and Commonwealth Office, SW1. *Club:* United Oxford & Cambridge University.

NATAL, Bishop of, since 1982; **Rt. Rev. Michael Nuttall;** *b* 3 April 1934; *s* of Neville and Lucy Nuttall; *m* 1959, Dorris Marion Meyer; two *s* one *d. Educ:* Maritzburg Coll. (matric. 1951); Univ. of Natal (BA 1955); Rhodes Univ. (BA Hons in History 1956). MA (Cantab), MA, DipEd (Oxon), BD Hons (London). Teacher at Westville High Sch., Natal, 1958; Lectr in History, Rhodes Univ., 1959–62; Theological Student, St Paul's Coll., Grahamstown, 1963–64; ordained deacon, 1964, priest 1965; Assistant Priest, Cathedral of St Michael and St George, Grahamstown, 1965–68; Lectr in Ecclesiastical History, Rhodes Univ., 1969–74; Dean of Grahamstown, 1975; Bishop of Pretoria, 1975–81. *Publications:* a chapter on Raymond Raynes in Better Than They Knew, Volume 2 (ed R. M. de Villiers); articles in Dictionary of S African Biography. *Recreations:* walking, trout fishing. *Address:* Bishop's House, 5 Chaceley Place, Morningside, Durban 4001, South Africa.

NATALI, Lorenzo; politician and lawyer, Italy; a Vice-President, Commission of the European Communities, since 1977; *b* 2 Oct. 1922. *Educ:* Collegio d'Abruzzo dei Padri Gesuiti; Univ. of Florence. MP (Christian Democrat); Under-Secretary of State: for the Press and Information, 1955–57; Min. of Finance, 1957–59; Treasury, 1960–64; Minister: for Merchant Marine, 1966–68; of Public Works, 1968; of Tourism and Entertainments, 1968–69; of Agriculture, 1970–73. *Recreation:* sport. *Address:* 200 rue de la Loi, 1049 Brussels, Belgium; (home) Via Nibby 18, Rome, Italy.

NATH, Dhurma Gian; High Commissioner for Mauritius in the UK, since 1983; *b* 29 May 1934; *s* of Anmole Facknath, OBE and Mrs B. Facknath; *m* 1961, Chitralekha, *d* of Dr and Mrs Chiranji Lal Sud; two *s* one *d. Educ:* Delhi Univ. (BA Hons English 1960, MA 1962). Postgrad. Inst. of Internat. Affairs, New Delhi. Educn Officer, John Kennedy Coll., Mauritius, 1963–66 (Head of Dept of English, 1965–66); entered Diplomatic Service, Mauritius, as trainee, 1966; apptd to Mauritius High Commn, London, 1968; Head of Chancery, 1969; Counsellor, Mauritius Mission to EEC, 1971–76; Dep. High Comr, London, 1976–82; Ambassador in Cairo, 1982–83. Sec., OAU Gp, London, 1973–82. Mem., Television Bd, Mauritius Broadcasting Corp., 1965–66. Representative

of Mauritius at various internat. meetings. *Recreations:* bridge, history of World War II, table tennis. *Address:* 32/33 Elvaston Place, SW7 5NW. *T:* 01–589 0791.

NATHAN, family name of **Baron Nathan.**

NATHAN, 2nd Baron, *cr* 1940; **Roger Carol Michael Nathan;** *b* 5 Dec. 1922; *s* of 1st Baron Nathan, PC, TD, and Eleanor Joan Clara (*d* 1972), *d* of C. Stettauer; *S* father, 1963; *m* 1950, Philippa Gertrude, *d* of Major J. B. Solomon, MC; one *s* two *d. Educ:* Stowe Sch.; New Coll., Oxford (MA). Served War of 1939–45: Capt., 17/21 Lancers (despatches, wounded twice). Admitted Solicitor (Hons), 1950. Associate Member: Bar Assoc. of City of New York; NY County Lawyers' Assoc.; FSA; FRSA; FRGS. Pres., Jewish Welfare Board, 1967–71; Chm., Central British Fund for Jewish Relief and Rehabilitation, 1971–77; Chm. Exec. Cttee, British Empire Cancer Campaign, 1970–75, Hon. Treasurer, 1979–; a Vice-Pres., The Jewish Museum; Chm., Working Party on Energy and the Environment (reported 1974); Vice Chm., Cttee on Charity Law and Practice (reported 1976); Mem., Royal Commn on Environmental Pollution, 1979–. Mem., House of Lords Select Cttee on European Communities, 1983– (Chm., Sub-Cttee G (Environment), 1983–). Chm., RSA, 1975–77. Vice-Pres., 1977–. Chm., City Festival of Flowers, 1964; Master, Worshipful Company of Gardeners, 1963–64. *Heir:* s Hon. Rupert Harry Bernard Nathan, *b* 26 May 1957. *Address:* 20 Copthall Avenue, EC2. *T:* 01–628 9611. *TA:* Client, London; Collyers Farm, Lickfold, Petworth, West Sussex. *T:* Lodsworth 284. *TA:* Ronath, Lodsworth. *Clubs:* Athenæum, Cavalry and Guards.
See also Hon. Lady Waley-Cohen.

NATHANS, Prof. Daniel; Professor of Molecular Biology and Genetics, The Johns Hopkins University School of Medicine, since 1980; Senior Investigator, Howard Hughes Medical Institute, since 1982; *b* 30 Oct. 1928; *s* of Samuel Nathans and Sarah Nathans (*née* Levitan); *m* 1956, Joanne Gomberg; three *s. Educ:* Univ. of Delaware, Newark, Del (BS Chemistry); Washington Univ., St Louis, Mo (MD). Intern, 1954–55, and resident, 1957–59, in Medicine, Columbia-Presbyterian Medical Center, NYC; Clinical Associate, Nat. Cancer Inst., Bethesda, Md, 1955–57; Guest Investigator, Rockefeller Inst., NYC, 1959–62; Prof. of Microbiology, 1962 and Faculty Mem., Johns Hopkins Univ. Sch. of Medicine, Baltimore, Md, 1962–. Nobel Prize in Physiology or Medicine, 1978. *Address:* 2227 Crest Road, Baltimore, Md 21209, USA.

NATWAR-SINGH, Kanwar; Padma Bhushan, 1984; Union Minister of State for Steel, India, since 1984; *b* 16 May 1931; *s* of Govind Singh and Prayag Kaur; *m* 1967, Princess Heminder Kumari, *e d* of late Maharaja Yadvindra Singhji of Patiala; one *s* one *d. Educ:* St Stephen's Coll., Delhi Univ.; 1st cl. hons History Delhi. Joined Indian Foreign Service, 1953; 3rd Sec., Peking, 1956–58; Under Sec., Ministry of External Affairs, and Private Sec. to Sec. General, 1958–61; Adviser, Indian Delegn to UN, NY, 1961–66; Rapporteur, UN Cttee on Decolonisation, 1962–66; Rapporteur, UN Trusteeship Council, 1965; Alt. Deleg. of India to UN Session for 1962; Rep. of India on Exec. Bd of UNICEF, NY, 1962–66; Dep. Sec. to Prime Minister of India, 1966–67; Dir, Prime Minister's Secretariat, New Delhi, 1967–70; Jt Sec. to Prime Minister, 1970–71; Ambassador to Poland, 1971–73; Dep. High Comr in London, 1973–77; High Comr for India in Zambia and Botswana, 1977–80; Ambassador to Pakistan, 1980–82; Sec., Min. of External Affairs, India, 1982–84. Attended Commonwealth Heads of Govt Meetings: Jamaica, 1975; Lusaka, 1979; Member: Commonwealth Cyprus Cttee, 1977; Indian Deleg. to Zimbabwe Indep. Celebrations, 1980; Sec.-Gen., 7th Non-Aligned Summit, New Delhi, 1983; Chief Co-ordinator, Commonwealth Heads of State and Govt Meeting, New Delhi, 1983. Dir, Air India, 1982–84. Exec. Trustee, UNITAR, 1981–. Hon. Res. Fellow, UCL. *Publications:* E. M. Forster: A Tribute, 1964; The Legacy of Nehru, 1965; Tales from Modern India, 1966; Stories from India, 1971; Maharaja Suraj Mal, 1707–1763, 1981; Curtain Raisers, 1984; writes and reviews for national and international papers. *Recreations:* tennis, reading, writing, walking, good conversations followed by prolonged periods of reflective uninterrupted silence. *Address:* Union Minister of State for Steel, Udyog Bhavan, New Delhi 110 011, India. *Clubs:* Garrick, Royal Over-Seas League (Life Mem.); India International Centre (Life Mem.); Gymkhana (Life Mem; Pres., 1984) (Delhi).

NAUNTON MORGAN, Sir Clifford; *see* Morgan, Sir C. N.

NAVARRETE, Jorge Eduardo; Mexican Ambassador to the Court of St James's, since 1986; *b* 29 April 1940; *s* of Gabriel Navarrete and late Lucrecia López; *m* 1st, 1962, María Antonieta Linares (marr. diss. 1973); one *s*; 2nd, 1976, María de Navarrete (*d* 1985). *Educ:* Nat. Sch. of Economics, Nat. Autonomous Univ. of Mexico (equivalent BA Econ.); post-graduate studies in internat. economy. Center for Latin American Monetary Studies, Mexico, 1963–65; Nat. Foreign Trade Bank, Mexico, 1966–72; joined Mexican Foreign Service, 1972; Ambassador to: Venezuela, 1972–75; Austria, 1976–77; Yugoslavia, 1977–79; Dep. Perm Rep. to UN, NY, 1979; Under Sec. (Economics), Min. of Foreign Affairs, Mexico, 1979–85. Holds decorations from Argentina, Brazil, Ecuador, Federal Republic of Germany, Italy, Panama, Poland, Sweden, Venezuela. *Publications:* The International Transfer of Technology (with G. Bueno and M. S. Wionczeck), 1969; Mexico's Economic Policy, 2 vols, 1971, 1972; Cancun 1981: the international meeting on co-operation and development, 1982; numerous essays on Mexican and Latin American economic issues, in Mexican and foreign jls. *Recreation:* chess. *Address:* Mexican Embassy, 48 Belgrave Square, SW1X 7DW. *T:* 01–235 6515.

NAYLOR, Rev. Canon Charles Basil; Chancellor and Canon Residentiary of Liverpool Cathedral, 1956–81, retired 1982; Canon Emeritus, Diocese of Liverpool, since 1981; *b* 29 Oct. 1911; *s* of Charles Henry Naylor and Eva Garforth Naylor. *Educ:* Rugby School; Keble College, Oxford. BA 2nd class Lit. Hum., 1934; MA 1939. Deacon, 1939, priest, 1940, Liverpool; Asst Master, Llandovery Coll., 1935–39; Asst Master, Chaplain and Housemaster, Liverpool College, 1939–43; Chaplain RNVR, 1943–46, East Indies Station and Fleet. Curate, St Peter le Bailey Oxford, 1946–56; Chaplain of St Peter's Coll., 1946–56, Dean, 1946–52, Fellow, 1950–56; Tutor in Theology, 1952–56. Examining Chaplain: to Bishop of Blackburn, 1951–; and to Bishop of Liverpool, 1954–; Senior Proctor of Univ. of Oxford, 1952–53. Exchanged duties with Dean of Christchurch, New Zealand, Dec. 1960–April 1961. Dir of Ordination Candidates and Dir of Post-Ordination Training, Liverpool dio., 1956–72; Dir of In-service Trng, Liverpool dio., 1973–81. Librarian, Radcliffe Library, Liverpool Cathedral, 1958–81. Mem., Liturgical Commn, 1962–66. Trustee, St Peter's Coll., Oxford, 1971–. *Publications:* Why Prayer Book Revision at all, 1964; contrib. Theological Collections: The Eucharist Then and Now, 1968; Ground for Hope, 1968; contrib. Arias of J. S. Bach, 1977; (ed) Front Line Praying, 1981. *Recreations:* music, walking. *Address:* 50 Park Road, Rugby, Warwickshire CV21 2QH. *Clubs:* National Liberal; Athenæum (Liverpool).

NAYLOR, (Charles) John; National Secretary, National Council of YMCAs, since 1982; Vice-Chairman, National Council for Voluntary Youth Services, since 1985; *b* 17 Aug. 1943; *s* of late Arthur Edgar Naylor, MBE and of Elizabeth Mary Naylor; *m* 1968, Margery Veronica Thomson; two *s. Educ:* Royal Grammar Sch., Newcastle upon Tyne; Haberdashers' Aske's Sch., Elstree; Clare Coll., Cambridge (MA History). Jun. and sen. exec. posts in industry, 1965–75; Dir, YMCA National Centre, Lakeside, Cumbria, 1975–80; Dep. National Sec., National Council of YMCAs, 1980–82. Mem., Nat. Adv.

Council for Youth Service. *Publications*: contribs on outdoor educn to DES and MSC pubns; articles in national and internat. YMCA pubns. *Recreations*: running, the outdoors (partic. the mountains), theatre, church, a growing family. *Address*: National Council of YMCAs, 640 Forest Road, E17 3DZ. *T*: 01–520 5599.

NAYLOR, Prof. Ernest, PhD, DSc; FIBiol; Lloyd Roberts Professor of Zoology, University College of North Wales, Bangor, since 1982; *b* 19 May 1931; *s* of Joseph and Evelyn Naylor; *m* 1956, Carol Gillian Bruce; two *d*. *Educ*: Univ. of Sheffield (BSc); Univ. of Liverpool (PhD, DSc). FIBiol 1972. Successively Asst Lectr, Lectr, Sen. Lectr and Reader in Zoology, University Coll. of Swansea, Wales, 1956–71; Prof. of Marine Biology, Univ. of Liverpool, 1971–82. Vis. Professor: Duke Univ., USA, 1969, 1970; Univ. of Otago, NZ, 1982. *Publications*: British Marine Isopods, 1972; (co-ed with R. G. Hartnoll) Cyclic Phenomena in Marine Plants and Animals, 1979; over 70 papers in learned jls. *Recreations*: gardening, theatre. *Address*: School of Animal Biology, University College of North Wales, Bangor, Gwynedd LL57 2DG. *T*: Bangor 351151.

NAYLOR, (Gordon) Keith, TD 1973; **His Honour Judge Naylor;** a Circuit Judge, since 1985; *b* 26 Feb. 1933; *yr s* of late Henry and Elizabeth Naylor, Hoylake; *m* 1962, Anthea Laverock, *d* of late G. E. Shaw and Mrs Elizabeth Douglas; two *s*. *Educ*: Wallasey Grammar Sch.; Univ. of Liverpool (Grotius Prize, 1953; LLB 1955). Called to the Bar, Gray's Inn, 1957; in practice on Northern Circuit, 1957–85; a Recorder, 1980–85. National Service, Cheshire Regt, 1955–57 (commnd, 1956); served TA, 4th and 4th/7th Bns Cheshire Regt, 1957–70; Lt-Col, comd Liverpool Univ. OTC, 1975–78 (Jubilee Medal); TA Col, HQ NW Dist, 1979–80. *Publications*: book revs and articles in legal pubns. *Address*: Queen Elizabeth II Law Courts, Derby Square, Liverpool L2 1XA; Hantsport, Lightfoot Lane, Gayton, Wirral, Merseyside L60 2TP. *T*: 051–342 6739. *Clubs*: Athenæum (Liverpool); Border and County (Carlisle).

NAYLOR, John; *see* Naylor, C. J.

NAYLOR, Prof. Malcolm Neville, RD 1967; BSc, BDS, PhD; FDSRCS; Professor of Preventive Dentistry, University of London, since 1970; Head of Department of Periodontology and Preventive Dentistry, Guy's Hospital Dental School, since 1980; *b* 30 Jan. 1926; *er s* of late Roland B. Naylor, MBE and Mabel L. (*née* Neville), Walsall, Staffs; *m* 1956, Doreen Mary, *d* of late H. E. Jackson, CBE; one *s*. *Educ*: Queen Mary's Grammar Sch., Walsall; Univ. of Glasgow; Univ. of Birmingham (BSc 1951, BDS 1955; Nuffield Scholar, 1949–51); Univ. of London (PhD 1963). FDSRCS 1958. Hosp. appts, Birmingham and Dundee, 1955–59; Guy's Hosp. Dental School: Res. Fellow, 1959–62; Sen. Lectr in Preventive Dentistry, 1962–66; Reader in Preventive Dentistry, 1966–70; Hon. Consultant Dental Surgeon, Guy's Hosp., 1966–. William Waldorf Astor Fellow, USA, 1963. Hon. Treasurer, British Div., IADR, 1975–; Pres., Odontol Sect., RSocMed, 1984–85. Served RNVR and RNR, retiring as Surg. Captain (D), 1943–76; Hon. Dental Surgeon to the Queen, 1976; Hon. Col, Univ. of London OTC, 1979–; Sec., 1978–82, Chm., 1982–, COMEC; Chairman: Mil. Educn Cttee, Univ. of London, 1979–; Sea Cadet Assoc., Sports Council, 1976–. Governor: Roehampton Inst. for Higher Educn, 1978–; Whitelands Coll., 1975–; Bacons Sch., Bermondsey, 1979– (Vice Chm., 1981–). Lay Reader, C of E, 1974–. Mem., Southwark Diocesan Synod, 1983–. Freeman, City of London, 1983; Liveryman, Bakers' Co., 1983–. *Publications*: papers and articles in prof. and scientific jls. *Recreations*: sailing, music, restoring church organs. *Address*: Carrick Lodge, Roehampton, SW15 5BN. *T*: 01–788 5045. *Clubs*: Royal Society of Medicine; Royal Solent Yacht, Royal Naval Sailing Assoc.

NAYLOR, Maurice; *see* Naylor, W. M.

NAYLOR, Peter Brian; Representative, British Council, Greece, 1983–86; *b* 10 July 1933; *s* of Eric Sydney Naylor and Phyllis Marian Jolly; *m* 1958, Barbara Pearson; three *s* one *d*. *Educ*: Grange High Sch., Bradford; Selwyn Coll., Cambridge (Open Exhibnr; BA 1957). Wool Top Salesman, Hirsch, Son & Rhodes, Bradford, 1957; British Council: Asst Rep., Bangkok, 1959; Courses Dept and E Europe Dept, London, 1962; Asst Rep., Warsaw, 1967; Reg. Rep., Dacca, E Pakistan, 1969; Actg Rep., Athens, 1971; Rep., Argentina, 1972, Brazil, 1975; Controller, European Div., 1978–83. *Recreations*: painting, music, books, games. *Address*: 3 Farmadine Court, Saffron Walden, Essex CB11 3HT. *T*: Saffron Walden 27708.

NAYLOR, (William) Maurice, CBE 1973; FHSM; JP; Director, National Association of Health Authorities, 1981–84; *b* 1920; *s* of late Thomas Naylor; *m* 1948, Maureen Ann, *d* of John Walsh; one *s* two *d*. *Educ*: St Joseph's Coll., Market Drayton; Manchester Univ. (BA Admin). FHSM 1956. Sec., Sheffield Regional Hosp. Bd, 1963–73; Regional Administrator, Trent RHA, 1973–81. Pres., IHSM, 1975–76 (Chm., Educn Cttee, 1980–). Hon. MBA Sheffield, 1982. *Address*: 8 Middlefield Croft, Dore, Sheffield S17 3AS. *T*: Sheffield 350778.

NAYLOR-LEYLAND, Sir Vivyan (Edward), 3rd Bt, *cr* 1895; *b* 5 March 1924; *e s* of Sir Edward Naylor-Leyland, 2nd Bt, and Marguerite Helene (*d* 1945), 2nd *d* of late Baron de Belabre; *S* father 1952; *m* 1st, 1952, Elizabeth Anne (marr. diss. 1960), *yr d* of 2nd Viscount FitzAlan of Derwent, OBE; one *s*; 2nd, 1967, Starr Anker-Simmons (marr. diss. 1975); one *d*; 3rd, 1980, Jameina F. Reid, *d* of James Freeman Reid, High Park, Co. Offaly, Eire; one *d*. *Educ*: Eton; Christ Church, Oxford; Royal Agricultural Coll., Cirencester. Grenadier Guards, 1942–47. **Heir:** *s* Philip Vyvyan Naylor-Leyland [*b* 9 August 1953; *m* 1980, Lady Isabella Lambton, *d* of Viscount Lambton, *qv*; one *s* one *d*]. *Address*: Le Neuf Chemin, St Saviour, Guernsey, Channel Islands. *T*: Guernsey 65708. *Clubs*: White's (overseas mem.), MCC.

NEAL, Prof. Bernard George, MA, PhD, ScD; FEng 1980; Emeritus Professor, since 1982 and Fellow, since 1986, Imperial College of Science and Technology, London University (Professor of Applied Science, 1961–72, of Engineering Structures, 1972–81, of Civil Engineering, 1981–82, and Head of Civil Engineering Department, 1976–82); *b* 29 March 1922; *s* of late Horace Bernard Neal, Wembley, and Hilda Annie Webb; *m* 1948, Elizabeth Ann, *d* of late William George Toller, Woodbridge, and Bertha Catharine Toller; one *s* one *d*. *Educ*: Merchant Taylors'; Trinity College, Cambridge (Schol.). MA Cantab, 1947; PhD Cantab 1948; ScD Cantab 1965; FInstCE 1960; FIStructE 1966. Temp. Experimental Officer, Admiralty, 1942–45; Research Student, Univ. of Cambridge, 1945–48; Research Associate, Brown University, USA, 1948–49; Demonstrator, 1949–51, Lecturer, 1951–54, Univ. of Cambridge; Research Fellow, 1947–50, Staff Fellow, 1950–54, Trinity Hall, Cambridge; Prof. of Civil Engineering, University Coll. of Swansea, 1954–61. Pro-Rector, Imperial Coll., London, 1972–74. Dean of City and Guilds Coll., 1964–67; Visiting Prof., Brown Univ., USA, 1959–60. Underwriting Mem. of Lloyd's, 1977. Telford Premium, 1951, Manby Premium, 1952, Instn Civil Engineers. *Publications*: The Plastic Methods of Structural Analysis, 1956; Structural Theorems and their Applications, 1964; technical papers on theory of structures, strength of materials. *Recreations*: lawn tennis, croquet. *Address*: Imperial College of Science and Technology, South Kensington, SW7. *T*: 01–589 5111.

NEAL, Sir Eric (James), Kt 1982; Director, since 1972, Chief Executive, since 1973 and Managing Director, since 1982, Boral Ltd; *b* 3 June 1924; *s* of James and May Neal; *m*

1950, Thelma Joan, *d* of R. E. Bowden; two *s*. *Educ*: South Australian Sch. of Mines. CEng; HFIE(Aust), FIGasE, FAIE, FAIM. Chm., Oil Co. of Australia NL; Director: Westpac Banking Corp.; Atlas Copco Australia Pty Ltd. Mem., Cttee apptd by Fed. Govt to advise on Higher Defence Orgn, 1982. Member: Amer. Bureau of Shipping; Aust. Gas Assoc. (former Mem. Bd); Inst. of Dirs. Chm. Exec. Cttee, Duke of Edinburgh's Sixth Commonwealth Study Conf. 1986; Nat. Co-ordinator, Duke of Edinburgh's Award Scheme in Australia. *Recreations*: naval history, travel, reading, shipping. *Address*: 30 Powell Street, Killara, NSW 2071, Australia. *T*: (02) 498 3425. *Clubs*: Union, American National, Elanora Country, Australian Jockey, Australasian Pioneers (Sydney).

NEAL, Frederick Albert, FIL; UK Representative on Council of International Civil Aviation Organization, Montreal, since 1983; *b* 22 Dec. 1932; *s* of Frederick William George Neal and Frances Elizabeth (*née* Duke); *m* 1958, Gloria Maria Moirano. *Educ*: Royal Grammar Sch., High Wycombe; Birkbeck Coll., London (BA). FIL 1965. Min. of Supply, 1953; Asst Defence Supply Attaché, Bonn, 1958–64; Principal, Min. of Technology (subseq. DTI), 1967; Asst Sec., DTI, 1974; Counsellor (Economic and Commercial), Ottawa, 1975–80; Asst Sec., Dept of Trade, 1980–83. *Recreations*: golf, bridge, music. *Address*: International Civil Aviation Organization, Suite 928, 1000 Sherbrooke Street West, Montreal, Canada. *Clubs*: Naval and Military, Royal Over-Seas League; South Herts Golf, Royal Montreal Golf.

NEAL, Harry Morton, FIC; Managing Director, since 1963, and Chairman, since 1985, Harry Neal Ltd; *b* 21 Nov. 1931; *s* of late Godfrey French Neal and Janet Bryce Morton; *m* 1954, Cecilia Elizabeth Crawford, *d* of late Col M. Crawford, DSO; one *s* three *d*. *Educ*: Uppingham Sch.; London Univ. (BSc(Eng)); City and Guilds Coll. (ACGI). Flying Officer, RAF, 1953. Chm., Connaught Hotel Ltd, 1980–; Dir, Savoy Hotel Ltd, 1982–. Member of Lloyd's. Chm., City and Guilds of London Inst., 1979–; Member: Technician Educn Council, 1982–83; Business and Technician Educn Council, 1983–; Bd of Governors, Willesden Tech. Coll., 1983–; Management Cttee, Courtauld Inst. of Art, 1983–. Pres., Greater London NW County Scout Council, 1983. Liveryman, Carpenters' Co., 1955–. FCIOB, FRSA; FCGI 1983. Chevalier de Tastevin, 1981. *Recreations*: gardening, shooting. *Address*: Great Sarratt Hall, Sarratt, near Rickmansworth, Herts.

NEAL, Sir Leonard (Francis), Kt 1974; CBE 1971; FCIT; CIPM; Industrial Relations Consultant to number of industrial and commercial companies; *b* 27 Aug. 1913; *s* of Arthur Henry Neal and Mary Neal; *m* 1939, Mary Lilian Puttock; one *s* one *d*. *Educ*: London School of Economics; Trinity College, Cambridge (MA). Labour Manager, Esso, 1956; Employee Relations Manager, Fawley Refinery, 1961; Labour Relations Adviser, Esso Europe Inc. Mem., British Railways Board, 1967–71; Chm., Commn on Industrial Relations, 1971–74. Prof. (part-time) of Industrial Relations, UMIST, 1970–76; Chairman: MAT Transport International Gp Ltd, 1974–; Employment Conditions Abroad Ltd, 1977–84; Dir (non-exec.), Pilkington Bros, 1976–83; Dir (non-exec.), Rosgill Holdings Ltd, 1980–84. *Publication*: (with A. Robertson) The Managers Guide to Industrial Relations. *Recreations*: reading, gardening, motoring. *Address*: Brightling, Sussex. *Club*: Institute of Directors.

NEAL, Michael David, Headmaster, Cranborne Chase School, 1969–83; *b* 27 Jan. 1927; *s* of David Neal, FCA; *m* 1952, Barbara Lisette, *d* of late Harold Carter, MA; two *s* two *d*. *Educ*: Winchester; University Coll., Oxford (BA). Rifle Bde, 1945–48 (Captain); Asst Master, RNC Dartmouth, 1952–54; Eton Coll., 1954–69 (Housemaster, 1963–69). Mem., Eton UDC, 1960–63. *Address*: Wegnall's Mill, Presteigne, Powys LD8 2LD. *T*: Presteigne 267012.

NEALE, Sir Alan (Derrett), KCB 1972 (CB 1968); MBE 1945; Member, 1981–86, and a Deputy Chairman, 1982–86, Monopolies and Mergers Commission; *b* 24 Oct. 1918; *o s* of late W. A. Neale; *m* 1956, Joan, *o d* of late Harry Frost, Wisbech; one *s*. *Educ*: Highgate School; St John's College, Oxford. War Service, Intelligence Corps, 1940–45. Board of Trade, 1946–68; Second Sec., 1967; Dep. Sec., Treasury, 1968–71, Second Permanent Sec., 1971–72; Perm. Sec., MAFF, 1973–78. Commonwealth Fund Fellowship, USA, 1952–53; Fellow of Center for Internat. Affairs, Harvard Univ., 1960–61. *Publications*: The Anti-Trust Laws of the USA, 1960; The Flow of Resources from Rich to Poor, 1961. *Recreations*: music, bridge. *Address*: 95 Swains Lane, N6 6PJ. *T*: 01–340 5236. *Club*: Reform.

NEALE, Gerrard Anthony; MP (C) North Cornwall, since 1979; *b* 25 June 1941; *s* of Charles Woodhouse Neale and Phyllis Muriel Neale; *m* 1965, Deirdre Elizabeth McCann; one *s* two *d*. *Educ*: Bedford Sch. Articled to solicitors, Bedford, 1961; admitted 1966; established Gerrard Neale Fennemore & Co., Solicitors, Milton Keynes, 1966. Dir, Telephone Rentals, 1979–. Councillor, Borough of Milton Keynes, 1973–79, Mayor, 1976–77. Chm., Buckingham Constituency Cons. Assoc., 1974–76. Contested (C) N Cornwall, Oct. 1974; PPS to Minister for Consumer Affairs, 1981–82, to Minister of State for Trade, 1981–83, to Sec. of State for Transport, 1985–86, to Sec. of State for the Environment, 1986–. *Recreations*: sailing, tennis. *Address*: House of Commons, SW1A 0AA.

NEALE, Rt. Rev. John Robert Geoffrey; *see* Ramsbury, Area Bishop of.

NEALE, Kenneth James, OBE 1959; FSA; consultant; author and lecturer; Assistant Under Secretary of State, Home Office, 1976–82; *b* 9 June 1922; *s* of late James Edward and Elsie Neale; *m* 1943, Dorothy Willett; three *s* one *d*. *Educ*: Hackney Downs (Grocers') Sch., London. Entered Civil Service as Clerical Officer, Tithe Redemption Commn, 1939. Lieut, RNVR, 1941–46. Exec. Officer, Min. of Nat. Insce, 1947–51; Asst Princ., 1951–55, Principal, 1955–64, Colonial Office; Sec. for Interior and Local Govt, Cyprus, 1957; Dep. Admin Sec., Cyprus, 1958–59; Central African Office, 1962–64; Asst Sec., Commonwealth Office, Diplomatic Service, 1964–67; Home Office: Asst Sec., 1967–70; Dir, Industries and Supply, 1970–75; Controller, Planning and Develt, 1976–80; Dir, Regimes and Services, 1980–82. Member: Prisons Bd, 1967–69, 1976–82; European Cttee on Crime Problems, 1976–84; Chairman: Council of Europe Select Cttee on Standard Minimum Rules for Treatment of Prisoners, 1978–80; Council of Europe Cttee for Co-operation in Prison Affairs, 1981–84; Consultant to Council of Europe, 1984–. Chairman: Essex Archaeol and Historical Congress, 1984–; Friends of Historic Essex, 1986–; Mem. Council, Essex Soc. for Archaeol. and Hist. (formerly Essex Archaeol Soc.), 1984–. *Publications*: Discovering Essex in London, 1970; Victorian Horsham, 1975; Work in Penal Institutions, 1976; Essex in History, 1977; Her Majesty's Commissioners, 1978; various articles and papers on local history, natural history, penology. *Recreations*: reading, local history, natural history. *Address*: Honeysuckle Cottage, Great Sampford, Saffron Walden, Essex. *T*: Great Sampford 304.

NEALE, Michael Cooper, CEng, FIMechE, FRAeS; Director General Engines (Procurement Executive), Ministry of Defence, since 1980; *b* 2 Dec. 1929; *s* of Frank and Edith Kathleen Neale; *m* 1956, Thelma Weare; one *s* two *d*. *Educ*: West Bridgford Grammar Sch., Nottingham; Queen Mary Coll., Univ. of London (BScEng, MScEng). Postgraduate research on fuel injection in diesel engines, 1951–53; Engr Officer, Royal Air Force, 1953–56; joined Civil Service, 1956; Aeroplane and Armament Experimental

Estabt, Boscombe Down, 1956–58; joined Nat. Gas Turbine Estabt, Pyestock, 1958; Asst Director of Engine Develt, MoD Headquarters, 1971; Dep. Director (R&D), Nat. Gas Turbine Estabt, 1973–80. *Publications:* papers in Aeronautical Research Council reports and memoranda series and elsewhere in the technical press, mainly concerning engines. *Recreations:* old railways, cricket. *Address:* 108 Wargrave Road, Twyford, Reading, Berks RG10 9PJ. *T:* Twyford 341759.

NEALON, Dr Catherina Theresa, (Rina), CBE 1979; JP; Chairman, Lothian Health Board, 1973–81; *d* of John and Margaret O'Reilly, Glasgow; *m* 1940, James Patrick Nealon; one *s. Educ:* Convent of Mercy, Garnethill, Glasgow. Mem., Edinburgh Town Council for Pilton Ward, 1949–74; served as Magistrate, 1954–57; Licensing Court, 1954–57; Judge of Police, 1957–62; Chm., Health Cttee, 1972–73. Member: Educn Cttee, Civil Defence Commn, 1949–73; Royal Infirmary and Associated Hosp's Bd of Management, 1952–56; NHS Exec. Council for City of Edinburgh, 1953–74 (Vice-Chm., May 1966–74); Exec. Cttee of Scottish Assoc. of Exec. Councils, 1967–74 (Vice-Pres., 1971, Pres., 1972); SE Regional Hosp. Bd, Scotland, 1966–74 (Chm., 1969–74); Med. Educn Cttee, 1969–74 (Chm., 1972–74); Livingston New Town Jt Health Service Adv. Cttee, 1969–73; Scottish Health Service Planning Council, 1974–81; Common Services Agency, Management Cttee, and Convenor, Estabt and Accommodation Sub-Cttee, Scottish Health Service, 1974–77; Univ. Liaison Cttee, 1974– (Chm., 1978–81); Edinburgh and SE District Cttee, Scottish Gas Consultative Council, 1967–74 (Chm., 1970–74; Mem. Council, 1969–74); Clean Air Council for Scotland, 1966–75; Nat. Soc. for Clean Air, Scottish Div., 1963– (Vice-Pres., 1970–72, Pres., 1972–74); A&C Whitley Council, 1973–81 (Vice-Chm., 1975–81); Nat. Negotiating Cttee; Ambulance Officers' Negotiating Cttee (Management Side Chm., 1979–81); Gen. Whitley Council (Mem., Gen. Purposes Cttee and Jt Negotiating Cttee, 1980–81); Nat. Appeals Panel; SE Dist Cttee, Gas Consumers' Council, 1981–; Chm., Scottish Hosp. Supplies Steering Cttee, 1972–74. Former Member: Edin. and Lothian Probation Cttee; Animal Disease Res. Assoc.; Edin. Coll. of Art; Royal Blind Asylum and Sch.; Scottish Accident Prevention Council; Marriage Guidance Council; Nat. Assoc. for Maternal and Child Welfare; Nat. Council on recruitment of Nurses and Midwives; Scottish Assoc. for Mental Health; Assoc. of Sea and Airport Authorities; Edin. and Lothians Tourist Assoc.; Youth Employment Cttee; Extra-Mural Cttee, Edin. Univ., 1960–65; Mem. Bd of Governors: Napier Coll. of Science and Technology, 1964–73 (Vice-Chm., 1971–73); Telford Coll. for Further Education, 1969–72; Moray House Coll. of Educn; Wellington Farm Approved Sch.; Dr Guthrie's Girls' Sch. JP Edinburgh, 1957; Mem. Justices Cttee, 1975; Justice on District Court, 1975–83; Mem. Extra-Parliamentary Panel, 1976–86. Attended 25th Anniv. Meeting, President's Cttee on Employment of Handicapped, Washington, 1972. Travelled to many countries with Internat. Hosp. Fedn study tours. Member, Church of Scotland. Dr *hc* Edinburgh, 1977. *Recreations:* dancing, dressmaking. *Address:* 34 Learmonth Crescent, Edinburgh EH4 1DE.

NEAME, Captain Douglas Mortimer Lewes, DSO 1940, Bar 1942; RN retired; *b* Oct. 1901; *s* of late Douglas John Neame; *m* 1937, Elizabeth Ogilvy Carnegy; one *s* two *d. Educ:* RN Colleges, Osborne and Dartmouth. Served European War, 1917–19; Fleet Air Arm, 1927–31; Commander, 1936; Capt. 1940. Commanded HM Ships Carlisle and Vengeance in War of 1939–45; Commodore 2nd Class, 1947–50; retd 1950. Member of Olympic Team, Amsterdam, 1928, British Empire Games, Canada, 1930. Vice-Patron AAA; Vice-Pres. LAC. *Address:* Cradock House, Salisbury, Wilts. *Clubs:* Naval; Milocarian, London Athletic.

NEAME, Robert Harry Beale; Chairman, Shepherd Neame Brewers, since 1971; *b* 25 Feb. 1934; *s* of Jasper Beale Neame and Violet Evelyn Neame; *m* 1st, Sally Elizabeth Corben; one *s* two *d* (and one *s* decd); 2nd, 1974, Yvonne Mary Mackenzie; one *d. Educ:* Harrow (Head of School). Joined Shepherd Neame, 1956; Dir., 1957–. Local Dir, Royal Insurance Co., 1971–; SE Regl Dir, National Westminster Bank, 1982–. Chm., SE England Tourist Bd, 1979–. Mem. (C) for Faversham, Kent CC, 1965– (Leader, 1982–84). *Recreations:* cricket, squash, rackets (Army Rackets Champion, 1954), golf, shooting. *Address:* Dane Court Farmhouse, Kits Hill, Selling, Faversham, Kent ME13 9QP. *T:* Selling 284. *Clubs:* Press; MCC, Free Foresters, I Zingari, Band of Brothers, Butterflies; Escorts, Jesters; Royal St George's Golf (Sandwich).

NEAME, Ronald; film producer and director; *b* 23 Apr. 1911; *s* of Elwin Neame and Ivy Close; *m* 1933, Beryl Yolanda Heanly; one *s. Educ:* University College School; Hurstpierpoint College. Entered film industry, 1928; became Chief Cameraman, 1934. In charge of production on: In Which We Serve, This Happy Breed, Blithe Spirit, Brief Encounter, 1942–45; produced: Great Expectations, Oliver Twist, The Magic Box; directed: Take My Life, The Card, 1945–51; The Million Pound Note, 1953; The Man Who Never Was, 1954; Windom's Way, 1957; The Horse's Mouth, 1958; Tunes of Glory, 1960; I Could Go On Singing, 1962; The Chalk Garden, 1963; Mr Moses, 1964; Gambit, 1966; The Prime of Miss Jean Brodie, 1968; Scrooge, 1970; The Poseidon Adventure, 1972; Odessa File, 1973; Meteor, 1978; Hopscotch, 1979; First Monday in October, 1980. *Address:* c/o Hutton Management Ltd, 200 Fulham Road, SW10 9PN. *Club:* Savile.

NEARS, Colin Gray; Producer, BBC Television, Music and Arts, since 1967; Member of Council, and Chairman of Advisory Panel on Dance, Arts Council of Great Britain, since 1982; *b* 19 March 1933; *s* of William Charles Nears and Winifred Mildred Nears (*née* Gray). *Educ:* Ipswich Sch.; King's Coll., Cambridge (MA). Admin. Asst, RIBA, 1956; BBC, 1958–; Producer, Schools Television, 1960. Author and director of programmes on literature, the visual arts, music and dance. Editor, Review, 1971–72. BAFTA award for Best Specialised Programme, 1973; Prix Italia music prize, 1982. *Recreations:* reading, gardening, painting, swimming. *Address:* 16 Ashchurch Terrace, W12 9SL. *T:* 01–749 3615.

NEARY, Martin Gerard James; Organist and Master of Music, Winchester Cathedral, since 1972; Organ Recitalist and Conductor; Founder and Conductor, Martin Neary Singers, since 1972; Conductor, Waynflete Singers, since 1972; President, Cathedral Organists' Association, since 1985; *b* 28 March 1940; *s* of Leonard Walter Neary and Jeanne Marguerite (*née* Thébault); *m* 1967, Penelope Jane, *d* of Sir Brian Warren, *qv*, and Dame A. J. M. T. Barnes, *qv*; one *s* two *d. Educ:* HM Chapels Royal, St James's Palace; City of London Sch.; Gonville and Caius Coll., Cambridge (Organ Schol., MA). FRCO. St Margaret's, Westminster: Asst Organist, 1963–65; Organist and Master of Music, 1965–71; Prof. of Organ, Trinity Coll., London, 1963–72. Organ Advr to dio. of Winchester, 1975–. Conductor, Twickenham Musical Soc., 1966–72; Founder and Conductor, St Margaret's Westminster Singers, 1967–71; Dir, Southern Cathedrals Festival, 1972, 1975, 1978, 1981, 1984, 1987. Mem. Council, RCO, 1982–. Many organ recitals and broadcasts in UK, incl. Royal Festival Hall and music festivals; has conducted many premières of music by British composers incl. John Tavener's Ultimos Ritos, 1979, Jonathan Harvey's Hymn, 1979, and Passion and Resurrection, 1981; with Martin Neary Singers perf. madrigals and graces at 10 Downing Street, 1970–74. Toured US and Canada, 1963, 1968, 1971, 1973, 1975, 1977, 1979, 1982, 1984, 1986; BBC Promenade Concerts, 1979, 1982; sometime Conductor with: ECO; LSO; Bournemouth SO and

Sinfonietta; Acad. of Ancient Music; Winchester Baroque Ensemble; many European tours; many recordings, incl. Lloyd Webber's Requiem (Golden Disc). Hon. FTCL, 1969. Hon. Citizen of Texas, 1971. Prizewinner, St Alban's Internat. Organ Festival, 1963; Conducting Scholarship, Berkshire Music Center, USA, 1963; Diploma, J. S. Bach Competn, Leipzig, 1968; UK/USA Bicentennial Fellow, 1979–80; Artist-in-residence, Univ. of California at Davis, 1984. *Publications:* edns of early organ music; contribs to organ jls. *Recreation:* watching cricket. *Address:* 10 The Close, Winchester, Hants. *T:* Winchester 54392.

NEAVE, Sir Arundell Thomas Clifton, 6th Bt, *cr* 1795; JP; late Major Welsh Guards; *b* 31 May 1916; *e s* of Col Sir Thomas Lewis Hughes Neave, 5th Bt, and Dorina (*d* 1955) (author of 26 years on the Bosphorus, Remembering Kut, 1937, Romance of the Bosphorus, 1950), *d* of late George H. Clifton; *S* father, 1940; *m* 1946, Richenda, *o c* of Sir Robert J. Paul, 5th Bt; two *s* two *d. Educ:* Eton. Served in 1939–45 war, Welsh Guards (Major); Dunkirk, 1940, retired 1947. JP for Anglesey, 1950. *Heir: s* Paul Arundell Neave [*b* 13 December 1948; *m* 1976, Coralie Jane Louise, *e d* of Sir Robert Kinahan, *qv*; two *s*]. *Address:* Greatham Moor, Liss, Hants. *Clubs:* Carlton, Pratt's.
See also Sir Richard Williams-Bulkeley.

NEAVE, Julius Arthur Sheffield, CBE 1978 (MBE (mil.) 1948); JP; DL; General Manager, since 1966, Director since 1977, Mercantile & General Reinsurance Co. Ltd (Managing Director, 1980–82); Director, Prudential Corporation plc, since 1982; *b* 17 July 1919; *s* of Col Richard Neave and Helen Mary Elizabeth (*née* Miller); *m* 1951, Helen Margery, *d* of Col P. M. Acton-Adams, DSO, Clarence Reserve, Marlborough, NZ; three *d. Educ:* Sherborne School. Joined Mercantile & General Reinsurance Co. Ltd, 1938. Served War, 1939–46: called as Territorial, commnd 13th/18th Royal Hussars, Adjt 3 years, final rank Major (despatches 1945). Returned to Mercantile & General, 1946; Asst Gen. Manager, 1964. (First) Chairman, Reinsurance Offices Assoc., 1969–74, Hon. Pres., 1974–82; Chm., Reinsurance Panel, British Insce Assoc., 1971–82; representative, Gt Britain: Cttee, annual internat. meeting of reinsurers, Monte Carlo, 1969–82; Vice-Pres., Assoc. Internat. pour l'Etude de l'Assurance, Geneva, 1976–83, Pres., 1983. Dir and Governor, Internat. Insce Seminars, 1977–82 (Founder's Gold Medal, 1977); President: Insce Inst. of London, 1976–77, 1983–84; Chartered Insce Inst., 1983–84 (Mem. Council, 1975–); Mem. Court, Insurers' Co., 1979– (Master, 1984–85). Hon. Fellow, RSA, 1975. JP (Brentwood) Essex, 1975, DL Essex, 1983. *Publications:* Speaking of Reinsurance, 1980; Still Speaking of Reinsurance, 1983. *Recreations:* shooting, fishing, golf, tennis. *Address:* Mill Green Park, Ingatestone, Essex CM4 0JB. *T:* Ingatestone 353036. *Club:* Cavalry and Guards.

NEAVE AIREY, family name of **Baroness Airey of Abingdon.**

NEDD, Sir (Robert) Archibald, Kt 1985; Chief Justice of Grenada, since 1979; *b* 7 Aug. 1916; *s* of late Robert and Ruth Nedd; *m* 1941, Annis (*née* McDowall); two *s* one *d. Educ:* King's Coll. London (LLB). Called to the Bar, Inner Temple, 1938. Registrar of High Court, and Addtl Magistrate, St Vincent, 1940–41, Dominica, 1941–43; Magistrate, St Lucia, 1943–44 (acted Crown Attorney); Crown Attorney, Dominica, 1944–49 (Officer administering Govt of Dominica, March 1945–Nov. 1946); Magistrate, full powers, Nigeria, 1949–53; private practice, Nigeria, 1953–70; Principal State Counsel, Rivers State, Nigeria, 1970–71 (exercising functions of legal draftsman); Legal draftsman, Rivers State, Nigeria, 1971–74 (occasionally perf. functions of Solicitor-Gen.); Puisne Judge of Supreme Court of Associated States of W Indies and Grenada, at Antigua, 1974–75, at Grenada, 1975–79. *Recreation:* reading. *Address:* Upper Lucas Street, St George's, Grenada, West Indies. *T:* 809–440–2391.

NEEDHAM, family name of **Earl of Kilmorey.**

NEEDHAM, Dorothy Mary Moyle, ScD Cantab; FRS 1948; Research Worker, Biochemical Laboratory, Cambridge, 1920–63; Foundation Fellow, Lucy Cavendish Collegiate Society, University of Cambridge, 1965, Emeritus Fellow, 1966; *b* London, 22 Sept. 1896; *d* of John Moyle and Ellen Daves; *m* 1924, Joseph Needham, *qv*; no *c. Educ:* Claremont Coll., Stockport; Girton Coll., Cambridge (Hon. Fellow, 1976). Research for DSIR, 1920–24; Gamble Prize, 1924; Beit Meml Research Fellow, 1925–28. Specialised in biochemistry of muscle, carbohydrate metabolism and phosphorylations; carried out research and teaching at Cambridge and in laboratories in USA, France, Germany, Belgium, etc., 1928–40; Research Worker for Ministry of Supply (Chemical Defence), 1940–43; Chemical Adviser and Acting Director, Sino-British Science Cooperation Office, Chungking, China, 1944–45; Research Worker for MRC 1946–52; Research grant from Broodbank Fund, Univ. of Cambridge, 1952–55; Research Worker for ARC, 1955–62; Foulerton Gift Donation, Royal Society, 1961–62; Leverhulme Award, 1963. Hon. Fellow, Gonville and Caius Coll., Cambridge, 1979. *Publications:* Biochemistry of Muscle, 1932; Science Outpost (ed jtly), 1948; Machina Carnis: the biochemistry of muscle contraction in its historical development, 1971; Source-Book in the History of Biochemistry 1740 to 1940, 1985; numerous original papers in biochemical journals and Proc. Royal Soc. *Address:* 42 Grange Road, Cambridge CB3 9DG. *T:* Cambridge 352183.

NEEDHAM, Prof. John, MA (Sheffield); FRIBA, DipArch (Leeds); Professor of Architecture, The University, Sheffield, 1957–72, now Professor Emeritus; *b* 2 April 1909; British; *s* of P. Needham; *m* 1934, Bessie Grange; three *d. Educ:* Belle Vue Grammar School, Bradford; Leeds School of Architecture. Diploma in Architecture, Leeds, 1931; ARIBA 1931, FRIBA 1948; RIBA; Alfred Bossom Silver Medal, 1937; Alfred Bossom Gold Medal, 1938; Soane Medal, 1938; Athens Bursar, 1949. Head, Dundee School of Architecture, 1938–57. 1st Premium in Open Architectural Competition for new County Buildings, Cupar, Fife, 1947. Mem. Amenity Cttee set up by Sec. of State for Scotland under Hydro Electric (Scotland) Development Acts, 1956–81. Hon. Editor, Quarterly Jl of Royal Incorporation of Architects in Scotland, 1946–50. *Address:* 16 Ferndene Court, Moor Road South, Gosforth, Newcastle upon Tyne NE3 1NN.

NEEDHAM, Joseph, MA, PhD, ScD (Cantab); FRS 1941; FBA 1971; Director, East Asian History of Science Library, Cambridge, since 1976; Master of Gonville and Caius College, 1966–76; Hon. Counsellor, UNESCO; *b* 1900; *s* of late Joseph Needham, MD, of Harley Street and Clapham Park, and Alicia A. Needham; *m* 1924, Dorothy Mary (see D. M. M. Needham), *d* of John Moyle, Babbacombe, Devon. *Educ:* Oundle School. Fellow Gonville and Caius Coll., 1924–66, 1976– (Librarian, 1959–60, Pres., 1959–66); Univ. Demonstrator in Biochem., 1928–33; Sir William Dunn Reader in Biochemistry, 1933–66, now Emeritus; Vis. Prof. of Biochem. at Stanford Univ., California, USA, 1929; Hitchcock Prof., Univ. of California, 1950; Visiting Professor: Univ. of Lyon, 1951; Univ. of Kyoto, 1971; Collège de France, Paris, 1973; Univ. of British Columbia, Vancouver, 1975; Hon. Professor: Inst. of History of Science, Acad. Sinica, Peking, 1980–; Chinese Acad. of Soc. Sci., 1983–. Lectures: Terry and Carmalt, Yale Univ.; Goldwin-Smith, Cornell Univ.; Mead-Swing, Oberlin College, Ohio, USA, 1935; Oliver Sharpey, RCP, 1935–36; Herbert Spencer, Oxford, 1936–37; for Polskie Towarzystwo Biologicznej in the Universities of Warsaw, Lwów, Kraków and Wilno, 1937; Comte Memorial, London, 1940; Conway Memorial, London, 1947; Boyle, Oxford, 1948; Noguchi, Johns Hopkins Univ., 1950; Hobhouse, London Univ., 1950; Dickinson, Newcomen Soc.,

1956; Colombo, Singapore, Peking and Jaipur Universities, 1958; Wilkins, Royal Society, 1958; Wilde, Manchester, 1959; Earl Grey, Newcastle upon Tyne, 1960–61; Henry Myers, Royal Anthropological Institute, 1964; Harveian, London, 1970; Rapkine, Paris, 1971; Bernal, London, 1971; Ballard Matthews, Bangor, 1971; Fremantle, Oxford, 1971; Irvine, St Andrews, 1973; Dressler, Leeds, 1973; Carr-Saunders, London, Gerald Walters, Bath, First John Caius, Padua, 1974; Bowra, Oxford, 1975; Danz, Seattle, 1977; Harris, Northwestern, 1978; First Wickramasinghe, Colombo, 1978; Ch'ien Mu and Huang Chan, Hong Kong, 1979; Creighton, London, 1979; Radhakrishnan, Oxford, 1980; Priestley, London, 1982; First E Asian Hist. of Sci. Foundn, Hongkong, 1983. Head of the British Scientific Mission in China and Scientific Counsellor, British Embassy, Chungking, and Adviser to the Chinese National Resources Commission, Chinese Army Medical Administration and Chinese Air Force Research Bureau, 1942–46; Director of the Dept of Natural Sciences, UNESCO, 1946–48. Chm. Ceylon Government University Policy Commission, 1958. Pres., Internat. Union of Hist. of Science, 1972–75. Foreign Member: Nat. Acad. of Science, USA; Amer. Acad. Arts and Sciences; Amer. Hist. Assoc.; National Academy of China (Academia Sinica); Mem. Internat. Academies of Hist. of Science and of Med.; Hon. Member Yale Chapter of Sigma Xi. Hon. Fellow, UMIST. Hon. FRCP 1984. Hon. DSc, Brussels, Norwich, Chinese Univ. of Hong Kong; Hon. LLD Toronto and Salford; Hon. LittD Cambridge, Hongkong, Newcastle upon Tyne, Hull, Chicago and Wilmington, NC; DUniv Surrey; Hon. PhD Uppsala. Sir William Jones Medallist, Asiatic Society of Bengal, 1963; George Sarton Medallist, Soc. for History of Science, 1968; Leonardo da Vinci Medallist, Soc. for History of Technology, 1968; Dexter Award for History of Chemistry, 1979; Science Award (1st cl.), Nat. Sci. Commn of China, 1984. Order of the Brilliant Star, 3rd cl. with sash (China). *Publications:* Science, Religion and Reality (ed), 1925; Man a Machine, 1927; The Sceptical Biologist, 1929; Chemical Embryology (3 vols), 1931; The Great Amphibium, 1932; A History of Embryology, 1934; Order and Life, 1935; Christianity and the Social Revolution (ed), 1935; Adventures before Birth (tr.), 1936; Perspectives in Biochemistry (Hopkins Presentation Volume; ed), 1937; Background to Modern Science (ed), 1938; Biochemistry and Morphogenesis, 1942; The Teacher of Nations, addresses and essays in commemoration of John Amos Comenius (ed), 1942; Time, the Refreshing River, 1943; History is on Our Side, 1945; Chinese Science, 1946; Science Outpost, 1948; Hopkins and Biochemistry (ed), 1949; Science and Civilisation in China (7 vols, 20 parts; jtly), 1954–: vol. I, Introductory Orientations, 1954; vol. II, History of Scientific Thought, 1956; vol III, Mathematics and the Sciences of the Heavens and the Earth, 1959; vol. IV, Physics and Physical Technology, part 1, Physics, 1962, part 2, Mechanical Engineering, 1965, part 3, Civil Engineering and Nautics, 1971; vol. V, Chemistry and Chemical Technology, part 2, Spagyrical Discovery and Invention, 1974, part 3, History of Alchemy, 1976, part 4, Apparatus, Theory and Comparative Macrobiotics, 1980, part 5, Physiological Alchemy, 1983, part 7, The Gunpowder Epic, 1985; vol. VI, part 1, Botany, 1985; The Development of Iron and Steel Technology in China, 1958; Heavenly Clockwork, 1960, rev. edn 1986; Within the Four Seas, 1970; The Grand Titration, 1970; Clerks and Craftsmen in China and the West (jtly), 1970; The Chemistry of Life (ed), 1970; Moulds of Understanding, 1976; Celestial Lancets, a history and rationale of Acupuncture and Moxa (jtly), 1980; The Hall of Heavenly Records: Korean astronomical instruments and clocks 1380–1780 (jtly), 1986; Trans-Pacific Echoes and Resonances, Listening Once Again (jtly), 1986. Chart to illustrate the History of Physiology and Biochemistry, 1926; original papers in scientific, philosophical and sinological journals. *Address:* 42 Grange Road, Cambridge; East Asian History of Science Library, 16 Brooklands Avenue at Clarendon Road, Cambridge. *T:* Cambridge 311545. *Club:* United Oxford & Cambridge University.

NEEDHAM, N. J. T. M.; *see* Needham, Joseph.

NEEDHAM, Richard Francis; (6th Earl of Kilmorey, but does not use the title); MP (C) Wiltshire North, since 1983 (Chippenham, 1979–83); Parliamentary Under-Secretary of State, Northern Ireland Office, since 1985; *b* 29 Jan. 1942; *e s* of 5th Earl of Kilmorey (*d* 1977), and of Helen (who *m* 2nd, 1978, Harold William Elliott, *qv*), *y d* of Sir Lionel Faudel-Phillips, 3rd Bt; *m* 1965, Sigrid Juliane Thiessen-Gairdner, *o d* of late Ernst Thiessen and of Mrs John Gairdner, Hamburg; two *s* one *d*. *Educ:* Eton College. Former Chairman, R. G. M. Print Holdings Ltd. CC Somerset, 1967–74. Contested (C): Pontefract and Castleford, Feb. 1974; Gravesend, Oct. 1974; Personal Asst to Rt Hon. James Prior, MP, 1974–79. PPS: to Sec. of State for NI, 1983–84; to Sec. of State for the Environment, 1984–85. Cons. Vice-Chm., Employment Cttee, 1981–83; Mem., Public Accts Cttee, 1982–83. Founder Mem., Anglo-Japanese 2000 Gp. *Publication:* Honourable Member, 1983. *Heir: s* Viscount Newry and Morne, *qv*. *Address:* House of Commons, SW1.

NEEDHAM, Prof. Roger Michael, FRS 1985; Professor of Computer Systems, since 1981, Head of Computer Laboratory, since 1980, and Fellow of Wolfson College, since 1967, University of Cambridge; *b* 9 Feb. 1935; *s* of Leonard William Needham and Phyllis Mary Needham; *m* 1958, Karen Ida Boalth Spärck Jones. *Educ:* Cambridge Univ. (MA, PhD). FBCS. Cambridge University: Sen. Asst in Research, Computer Lab., 1963–64; Asst Dir of Research, 1964–73; Reader in Computer Systems, 1973–81. Mem., UGC, 1985–. Member: Chesterton RDC, 1971–74; South Cambs DC, 1974–86. Hon. DSc Kent, 1983. *Publications:* (with M. V. Wilkes) The Cambridge CAP Computer and its operating system, 1979; (with A. J. Herbert) The Cambridge Distributed Computing System, 1982; contribs to publications on computer operating systems, communications, security and protection. *Recreations:* sailing, politics. *Address:* 7 Brook Lane, Coton, Cambridge CB3 7PY. *T:* Madingley 210366; (work) Cambridge 334607. *Clubs:* Naval; Royal Harwich Yacht.

NÉEL, Prof. Louis Eugène Félix, Grand Croix de la Légion d'Honneur; Croix de Guerre avec Palme; Président d'Honneur, Institut National Polytechnique de Grenoble; *b* Lyon, 22 Nov. 1904; *m* 1931, Hélène Hourticq; one *s* two *d*. *Educ:* Ecole Normale Supérieure. Agrégé de l'Université; Dr Sc. Prof., Univ. Strasbourg, 1937–45. Dir, Centre d'Etudes Nucléaires, Grenoble, 1956–71, and Delegate of High Comr for Atomic Energy at the centre, 1971–76; rep. France at Scientific Council, NATO, 1960–83; Prés., Conseil Sup. Sûreté Nucléaire. Mem., Acad. of Science, Paris, 1953; For. Member: Acad. of Science, USSR, 1959, Rumania, 1965, Poland, 1975; Royal Netherlands Acad., 1959; Deutsche Akademie der Naturforscher Leopoldina, 1964; Royal Society, 1966; Amer. Acad. of Arts and Sciences, 1966; Pres., Internat. Union of Pure and Applied Physics, 1963–66. Gold Medal, CNRS, 1965; Nobel Prize for Physics, 1970. Hon. Dr: Graz, 1948; Nottingham, 1951; Oxford, 1958; Louvain, 1965; Newcastle, 1965; Coïmbra, 1966; Sherbrooke, 1967; Madrid, 1978. *Publications:* numerous on magnetism. *Address:* 15 rue Marcel-Allégot, 92190 Meudon-Bellevue, France. *T:* 45 34 36 51.

NEELY, Air Vice-Marshal John Conrad, CB 1957; CBE 1952; DM; FRCS; retired; Senior Consultant, 1955, and Consultant in Ophthalmology, RAF Central Medical Establishment, 1950–59; *b* 29 Mar. 1901; *s* of late William Neely; *m* 1st, 1938, Marjorie Monica (*d* 1964), *d* of Dr Ernest Bramley, Eastbourne; 2nd, 1966, Roma, *widow* of Group Capt. Neil McKechnie, GC. *Educ:* Stonyhurst; Oxford Univ.; Guy's Hosp. MRCS, LRCP, 1927; MA, BM, BCh, 1928, DO (Oxon) 1935, DM 1945, Oxford; DOMS London, 1933. Joined RAF 1928; served War of 1939–45; Middle East (despatches); RAF Hosp., Halton. KHS 1951. Wing Comdr, 1940; Air Cdre, 1950; Air Vice-Marshal, 1955; retired, 1959. FRCS 1958. CStJ 1955.

NEGARA BRUNEI DARUSSALAM, HM Sultan of; Hassanal Bolkiah Mu'izzaddin Waddaulah, DKMB, DK, PSSUB, DPKG, DPKT, PSPNB, PSNB, PSLJ, SPMB, PANB; Hon. GCMG; DMN, DK (Kelantan), DK (Johor), DK (Negeri Sembilan), DK (Pahang); Ruler of Negara Brunei Darussalam (formerly Brunei), since 1967; Prime Minister, Finance and Home Affairs Minister, Negara Brunei Darussalam, since its independence, Jan, 1984; *b* 15 July 1946; *s* of Sultan Sir Muda Omar 'Ali Saifuddien Sa'adul Khairi Waddien, DKMB, DK, GCVO, KCMG, PSSUB, PHBS, PBLI (*d* 1986). *Educ:* Victoria Inst., Kuala Lumpur; RMA Sandhurst (Hon. Captain, Coldstream Guards, 1968; Hon. General 1984). Collar of the Supreme Order of the Chrysanthemum; Grand Order of Mugunghwa. *Address:* Istana Nurul Iman, Bandar Seri Begawan, Negara Brunei Darussalam.

NEGUS, Norma Florence, (Mrs D. J. Turner-Samuels); a Metropolitan Stipendiary Magistrate, since 1984; *b* 31 July 1932; *d* of late George David Shellabear and Kate (*née* Calvert); *m* 1st, 1956, Richard Negus (marr. diss. 1960); 2nd, 1976, David Jessel Turner-Samuels, *qv*. *Educ:* Malvern Girls' Coll., Malvern, Worcs. Fashion promotion and advertising in UK, Canada and USA, 1950–61; Merchandise Editor, Harper's Bazaar, 1962–63; Asst Promotion Manager, Vogue and House & Garden, 1963–65; Unit Manager, Trends Merchandising and Fashion Promotion Unit, 1965–67; Export Marketing Manager and Advertising Manager, Glenoit (UK) Ltd, 1967–68. Called to the Bar, Gray's Inn, 1970; Mem., Middle Temple, 1984. In practice on SE Circuit, 1971–84. Mem., Central Criminal Court Bar Mess, 1978–84. *Recreations:* cooking, reading, listening to music, travel, swimming. *Address:* New Court, Temple, EC4Y 9BE. *T:* 01–353 7613; Cherry Tree Cottage, Petworth Road, near Haslemere, Surrey GU27 3BG. *T:* Haslemere 51970.

NEGUS, Richard; consultant designer; Senior Partner, Negus & Negus, since 1967; *b* 29 August 1927; *s* of Bertie and Kate Negus; *m* 1949, Pamela Wheatcroft-Hancock; two *s* one *d*. *Educ:* Battersea Grammar Sch.; Camberwell Sch. of Arts and Crafts. PPSIAD, FSTD. Staff designer, Festival of Britain, 1948–51; Partner, Negus & Sharland, 1951–67; Lecturer, Central Sch. of Art, 1951–53. Consultant to: Cotton Board Design Centre, 1960–67; BNEC, 1969–75; British Airways, 1973–84, 1985–; Pakistan Airlines, 1975–; Rank Organisation, 1979–; City of Westminster, 1973–75; National Exhibition Centre, 1974–77; Lloyds Bank, 1972–75; Godfrey Davis, 1971–80; John Laing, 1970–73; Andry Montgomery, 1967–; Celltech, 1980–83; Vickers Ltd, 1980–; SDP, 1981–; Historic Buildings and Monuments Commn, 1984–; Nat. Maritime Mus., 1984–; Royal Armouries, 1984–; The Emirates (Airline), 1985–; Tower of London, 1986–; Northern Foods, 1986–. Member: Design Council Poster Awards Cttee, 1970–72; PO Stamps Adv. Cttee, 1977–; CNAA, 1980–; Design Council, 1981–; Art and Design Cttee, Technician Educn Council, 1981–. Advisor, Norwich Sch. of Art, 1969–71; External Assessor, Birmingham and Bradford Colls of Art, 1969–73; Governor: Camberwell Sch. of Art, 1964–78; Chelsea Sch. of Art, 1977–; Mem. Court, RCA, 1979–82. Pres., SIAD, 1977–79, Vice Pres. 1966–68. *Publications:* Designing for Export Printing, 1972; contribs to: Design Mag., The Designer, Graphis, Gebrauchgraphick, Architectural Review, Rolls Royce Mag., Creative Review, Art and Artists. *Address:* Myddelton Cottage, Canonbury Park South, N1. *T:* 01–226 2381; Little Gravenhurst, Bolney, Sussex. *Club:* Reform.

NEHRU, Braj Kumar; Governor of Gujarat, 1984–86; *b* Allahabad, 4 Sept. 1909; *s* of Brijlal and Rameshawri Nehru; *m* 1935, Magdalena Friedmann; three *s*. *Educ:* Allahabad Univ.; LSE (Fellow); Balliol Coll., Oxford. BSc; BSc(Econ.). Called to Bar, Inner Temple. Joined ICS, 1934; Asst Comr, 1934–39; Under-Sec., Dept of Education, Health and Lands, 1939; Mem., Indian Legislative Assembly, 1939; Officer on special duty, Reserve Bank of India, and Under-Sec., Finance Dept, 1940; Jt Sec., 1947; Exec. Dir, IBRD (World Bank), and Minister, Indian Embassy, Washington, 1949–54 and 1958–62; Sec., Dept of Econ. Affairs, 1957–58; Comr-Gen. for Econ. Affairs, Min. of Finance, 1958–61; Ambassador to USA, 1961–68; Governor: Assam and Nagaland, 1968–73; Meghalaya, Manipur and Tripura, 1972–73; Jammu and Kashmir, 1981–84; High Comr in London, 1973–77. Rep. of India: Reparations Conf., 1945; Commonwealth Finance Ministers Confs, UN Gen. Assembly, 1949–52, and 1960; FAO Confs, 1949–50; Sterling Balance Confs, 1947–49; Bandung Conf., 1955; deputed to enquire into Australian Fed. Finance, 1946; Mem., UN Adv. Cttee on Admin and Budgetry Questions, 1951–53; Advr to Sudan Govt, 1955; Mem., UN Investments Cttee, 1962– (Chm., 1977–). Hon. LLD Mo Valley Coll.; Hon. LittD Jacksonville; Hon. DLitt Punjab. *Publications:* Australian Federal Finance, 1947; Speaking of India, 1966; Thoughts on the Present Discontents, 1986. *Recreations:* bridge, reading, conversation. *Address:* 1 Western Avenue, Maharani Bagh, New Delhi 110065, India. *Club:* Gymkhana (Delhi).

NEIDPATH, Lord; Hon. James Donald Charteris, Lord Douglas of Neidpath; *b* 22 June 1948; *s* and *heir* of 12th Earl of Wemyss and March, *qv*; *m* 1983, Catherine Ingrid, *d* of Hon. Jonathan Guinness, *qv*, and of Mrs Paul Channon; one *s*. *Educ:* Eton; University College, Oxford (BA 1969, MA 1974); St Antony's Coll., Oxford (DPhil 1975); Royal Agricultural Coll., Cirencester (Diploma, 1978); ARICS 1983. Page of Honour to HM Queen Elizabeth the Queen Mother, 1962–64. Mem., Royal Co. of Archers (Queen's Body Guard for Scotland), 1978–. *Publication:* The Singapore Naval Base and the Defence of Britain's Eastern Empire 1919–42, 1981. *Heir: s* Hon. Francis Richard Percy Charteris, *b* 15 Sept. 1984. *Address:* Stanway, Cheltenham, Glos. *Clubs:* Brooks's, Pratt's, Ognisko Polskie; Puffin's (Edinburgh).

NEIGHBOUR, Oliver Wray, FBA 1982; Music Librarian, Reference Division of the British Library, 1976–85; *b* 1 April 1923; *s* of Sydney William Neighbour, OBE, TD, and Gwenydd Joyce (*née* Prentis). *Educ:* Eastbourne Coll.; Birkbeck Coll., London (BA 1950). Entered Dept of Printed Books, BM, 1946; Asst Keeper in Music Room, 1951; Dep. Keeper, 1976. *Publications:* (with Alan Tyson) English Music Publishers' Plate Numbers, 1965; The Consort and Keyboard Music of William Byrd, 1978; (ed) Music and Bibliography: essays in honour of Alec Hyatt King, 1980; article on Schoenberg in New Grove Dictionary of Music and Musicians, 1980; editor of first publications of works by Schumann, Schoenberg and Byrd. *Recreations:* walking, ornithology. *Address:* 12 Treborough House, 1 Nottingham Place, W1M 3FP. *T:* 01–935 1772.

NEIL, Andrew Ferguson; Editor, The Sunday Times, since 1983; *b* Paisley, 21 May 1949; *s* of James and Mary Neil; unmarried. *Educ:* Paisley Grammar Sch.; Univ. of Glasgow (MA Hons Politics and Economics, 1971). Conservative Res. Dept, 1971–72; joined The Economist, 1973; Reporter, Ulster, 1973–74; Lobby Correspondent, 1974–75; Labour Corresp., 1975–78; Amer. Corresp., 1979–82; UK Editor, 1982–83. Sen. Consultant to National Econ. Res. Assocs, 1982–83. Formerly Presenter of BBC TV's The Risk Business, ITV's Look Here, and BBC Scotland's Public Account; regular appearances on Nationwide, Today and Weekend World. *Publication:* The Cable Revolution, 1982. *Recreations:* dining out in New York and Aspen, Colorado. *Address:* The Sunday Times, 1 Pennington Street, E1. *Club:* Royal Automobile.

NEIL, Prof. Eric; John Astor Professor of Physiology in the University of London, at the Middlesex Hospital Medical School, 1956–84, now Emeritus Professor; *b* 15 Feb. 1918; *s* of George Neil, MC, and Florence Neil; *m* 1946, Anne Baron, *d* of late T. J. M. B. Parker and of Evelyn Maud Parker; two *d*. *Educ:* Heath Grammar School; University of Leeds. BSc Hons (Physiology) (Leeds), 1939; MB, ChB, 1942; MD (Dist.), 1944 and DSc, 1953 (Leeds); FRCP 1978. Demonstrator and Lecturer in Physiology, Univ. of Leeds, 1942–50; Sen. Lecturer and later Reader in Physiology, Middx Hosp. Med. School., 1950–56. Hon. Treas., Physiological Soc.; Chm., European Editorial Bd of Physiological Reviews, 1960–67; Mem., Brit. Nat. Cttee of Physiological Sciences, 1960–80; Pres., Internat. Union of Physiological Sciences, 1974–77, 1977–84 (Treasurer, 1968–74). Hon. For. Mem., Royal Acad. of Medicine, Belgium, 1978. Examiner in Physiology, Univs of London, Oxford, Cambridge, Birmingham, Trinity Coll., Dublin. Hon. MD Ghent, 1977. Queen's Silver Jubilee Medal, 1977. *Publications:* (with Prof. C. Heymans) Reflexogenic Areas in the Cardiovascular System, 1958; (with Prof. C. A. Keele) Samson Wright's Applied Physiology, 10th edn 1961, 13th edn 1982; (with Prof. B. Folkow) Circulation, 1971; The Mammalian Circulation, 1974, 2nd edn, 1978; The Life and Work of William Harvey, 1975; papers on physiological topics in British and foreign med. scientific jls. *Recreations:* pianoforte, Venetian painting. *Address:* 53 Talbot Road, Highgate, N6. *T:* 01–340 0543.

NEIL, Matthew, CBE 1976; Secretary and Chief Executive, Glasgow Chamber of Commerce, 1954–83; *b* 19 Dec. 1917; *er s* of John Neil and Jean Wallace. *Educ:* John Neilson High Sch., Paisley; Glasgow Univ. (MA, LLB). Served War, 1939–46: Far East, ME, Mediterranean and Western Europe; RHA, RA and Air Observation Post; RAuxAF, 1950–57. Admitted solicitor, 1947. Mem., British Overseas Trade Adv. Council, 1975–82. Hon. LLD Glasgow, 1983. *Recreations:* skiing, golf, music. *Address:* 39 Arkleston Road, Paisley PA1 3TH. *T:* 041–889 4975. *Clubs:* East India, Devonshire, Sports and Public Schools; Lamlash Golf, Prestwick Golf.

NEIL, Thomas, CMG 1962; TD 1951; Director, Thomson Foundation, 1963–79; *b* 23 December 1913; *s* of late W. R. Neil; *m* 1939, Phyllis Selina Gertrude Sargeant; one *d*. *Educ:* King's College, University of Durham (now University of Newcastle upon Tyne) (BSc, NDA). Lectr in Agriculture, Devon County Council, 1936–39; Chief Technical Officer, 1946. Colonial Service: District Officer, Kenya, 1947; Assistant Chief Secretary, 1957; Permanent Secretary, 1957; Permanent Secretary, Ministry of State, Kenya, 1959–63. Director, Kenya Famine Relief, 1961–63. Lay Mem., Immigration Appeal Tribunal, 1971–84. Directed Africanisation of CS. Served War of 1939–45 with Devonshire Regiment (TA), Lieutenant-Colonel, in UK, E Africa, Middle East. *Recreation:* country life. *Address:* Summerhill, Bourne End, Bucks. *T:* Bourne End 20403.

NEILD, Prof. Robert Ralph; Professor of Economics, University of Cambridge, 1971–84, now Emeritus; Fellow of Trinity College, Cambridge; *b* 10 Sept. 1924; *o s* of Ralph and Josephine Neild, Letchmore Heath, Hertfordshire; *m* 1st, 1957, Nora Clemens Sayre (marr. diss. 1961); 2nd, 1962, Elizabeth Walton Griffiths; one *s* four *d* (incl. twin *d*). *Educ:* Charterhouse; Trinity Coll., Cambridge. Royal Air Force, 1943–44; Operational Research, 1944–45. Secretariat of United Nations Economic Commission for Europe, Geneva, 1947–51; Economic Section, Cabinet Office and Treasury, 1951–56; Lecturer in Economics, and Fellow, Trinity College, Cambridge, 1956–58; National Institute of Economic and Social Research: at first as Editor of its Quarterly Economic Review; then as Deputy Director of the Institute, 1958–64; MIT Center for International Studies, India Project, New Delhi, 1962–63; Economic Adviser to HM Treasury, 1964–67; Dir, Stockholm Internat. Peace Research Inst., 1967–71. Vis. Fulbright Prof., Hampshire Coll. and Five Colls, Amherst, Mass, USA, 1985. Mem., Fulton Cttee on Reform of CS, 1966–68; Vice-Chm., Armstrong Cttee on Budgetary Reform in UK, Inst. for Fiscal Studies, 1979–80. Director: Nat. Mutual Life Assce Soc., 1959–64; Investing in Success Equities Ltd, 1961–64, 1972–. *Publications:* Pricing and Employment in the Trade Cycle, 1964; (with T. S. Ward) The Measurement and Reform of Budgetary Policy, 1978; How to Make Up Your Mind about the Bomb, 1981; various articles. *Address:* Trinity College, Cambridge CB2 1TQ.

NEILL, Rt. Hon. Sir Brian (Thomas), Kt 1978; PC 1985; **Rt. Hon. Lord Justice Neill;** a Lord Justice of Appeal, since 1985; *b* 2 Aug. 1923; *s* of late Sir Thomas Neill and Lady (Annie Strachan) Neill (*née* Bishop); *m* 1956, Sally Margaret, *d* of late Sydney Eric Backus and late Marguerite Backus; three *s*. *Educ:* Highgate Sch.; Corpus Christi Coll., Oxford (Hon. Fellow 1986). Rifle Brigade, 1942–46 (Capt.). MA Oxford. Called to the Bar, Inner Temple, 1949, Bencher, 1976. QC 1968; a Recorder of the Crown Court, 1972–78; a Judge of the High Court, Queen's Bench Div., 1978–84. A Judge of the Commercial and Admiralty Courts, 1980–84; a Judge of Employment Appeal Tribunal, 1981–84. Mem., Departmental Cttee to examine operation of Section 2 of Official Secrets Act, 1971; Chairman: Adv. Cttee on Rhodesia Travel Restrictions, 1973–78; IT and the Courts Cttee, 1985–; Supreme Court Procedure Cttee, 1986–. Mem., Ct of Assts, 1972–, Master, 1980–81, Turners' Co. Governor, Highgate Sch., 1969–. *Publication:* (with Colin Duncan) Defamation, 1978, 2nd edn (ed with R. Rampton), 1984. *Address:* c/o Royal Courts of Justice, Strand, WC2. *Clubs:* MCC, Hurlingham.
See also Sir F. P. Neill.

NEILL, Prof. Derrick James, DFC 1943; Professor of Prosthetic Dentistry, University of London, since 1969; Sub-Dean of Dental Studies, Guy's Hospital Dental School, 1969–76; Consultant Dental Surgeon, Guy's Hospital, since 1960; *b* 14 March 1922; *s* of Jameson Leonard Neill, MBE, and Lynn Moyle; *m* 1st, 1952, Iris Jordan (*d* 1970); one *s* one *d*; 2nd, 1971, Catherine Mary Daughtry. *Educ:* East Sheen County Grammar Sch.; Guy's Hosp. Dental Sch., Univ. of London. LDSRCS 1952; FDSRCS 1955; MDS London, 1966. Served RAFVR, 1941–46, 150 Sqdn, Bomber Comd (Sqdn Ldr). Dept of Dental Prosthetics, Guy's Hosp. Dental School: Lectr, 1954; Sen. Lectr, 1959; Univ. Reader in Dental Prosthetics, 1967. Examr, Univs of London, Glasgow, Belfast, Nairobi and Hong Kong. Council Member, Odontological Section, Royal Soc. of Medicine, 1966–73; Past Pres., British Soc. for Study of Prosthetic Dentistry. Mem. Council of Governors: Guy's Hosp. Med. Sch., 1980–82; United Med. Schs of Guy's and St Thomas's Hosps, 1982–. *Publications:* (jtly) Complete Dentures, 1968; Partial Denture Construction, 1976; Restoration of the Partially Dentate Mouth, 1984; numerous papers in dental jls. *Recreations:* golf, music. *Address:* Hurst, Clenches Farm Road, Kippington, Sevenoaks, Kent. *T:* Sevenoaks 452374. *Club:* Royal Automobile.

NEILL, Sir (Francis) Patrick, Kt 1983; QC 1966; Vice-Chancellor, Oxford University, since 1985; Warden of All Souls College, Oxford, since 1977; a Judge of the Courts of Appeal of Jersey and Guernsey, since 1977; *b* 8 Aug. 1926; *s* of late Sir Thomas Neill, JP, and Lady (Annie Strachan) Neill (*née* Bishop); *m* 1954, Caroline Susan, *d* of late Sir Piers Debenham, 2nd Bt, and Lady (Angela) Debenham; four *s* two *d*. *Educ:* Highgate Sch.; Magdalen College, Oxford. Gibbs Law Scholar, 1949; Eldon Law Scholar, 1950. BA 1950; BCL 1951; MA 1972. Served Rifle Brigade, 1944–47 (Captain); GSO III (Training), British Troops Egypt, 1947. Fellow of All Souls, 1950–77, Sub-Warden 1972–74; Lectr in Air Law, LSE, 1955–58. Called to the Bar, Gray's Inn, 1951; Bencher, 1971; Member, Bar Council, 1967–71, Vice-Chm., 1973–74, Chm., 1974–75; Chm., Senate of the Inns of Court and the Bar, 1974–75; a Recorder of the Crown Court, 1975–78. Chm., Justice—All Souls Cttee for Rev. of Admin. Law, 1978–86. Chairman: Press Council, 1978–83; Cttee of Inquiry into Regulatory Arrangements at Lloyd's, 1986; first Chm., Council for the Securities Industry, 1978–85. Hon. Prof. of Legal Ethics, Birmingham Univ., 1983–84. Hon. LLD Hull. *Recreations:* music and forestry. *Address:* All Souls College, Oxford OX1 4AL. *T:* Oxford 722251. *Clubs:* Athenæum, Garrick, Beefsteak.
See also Rt Hon. Sir Brian Neill.

NEILL, Hugh; *see* Neill, J. H.

NEILL, Major Rt. Hon. Sir Ivan, Kt 1973; PC (N Ireland) 1950; DL; *b* Belfast 1 July 1906; *m* 1928, Margaret Helena Allen. *Educ:* Ravenscroft Nat. Sch., Belfast; Shaftesbury House Tutorial Coll., Belfast; Queen's Univ., Belfast (BSc Econ). FRGS. Served War of 1939–45: RE in UK and FE, 1939–46; Major. MP Ballynafeigh Div. of Belfast, Parlt of Northern Ireland, 1949–73; Government of Northern Ireland: Minister of Labour and National Insurance, 1950–62; Minister of Home Affairs, Aug.-Oct. 1952; Minister of Education, 1962–64; Minister of Finance, 1964–65; Leader of House of Commons, Oct. 1964; resigned from Govt, April 1965; Minister of Develt, Dec. 1968–March 1969; Speaker of House of Commons, 1969–73. Represented N Ireland at Internat. Labour Confs, 1950–61. Councillor and Alderman in Belfast Corp., 1946–50 (specialised in educn, housing and youth welfare). DL Belfast, 1966. *Address:* Greenlaw, Ballywilliam, Donaghadee, Co. Down, Northern Ireland.

NEILL, Very Rev. Ivan Delacherois, CB 1963; OBE 1958; Provost of Sheffield and Vicar of the Cathedral Church of St Peter and St Paul, 1966–74, now Emeritus; Chaplain to the Queen, 1962–66; *b* 10 July 1912; *s* of Rev. Robert Richard Neill and Bessie Montrose (*née* Purdon); *m* 1938, Enid Eyre Godson (*née* Bartholomew); one *s* one *d*. *Educ:* St Dunstan's College; Jesus College, Cambridge (MA); London College of Divinity. Curate: St Mary, West Kensington, 1936–38; Christ Church, Crouch End, 1938–39. CF 4th Cl., Chatham; served BEF and UK with 3rd Div., Orkneys, Sandhurst, 1941–43; Sen. Chaplain, N Aldershot, 1943; 43rd (Wessex) Div., 1943–45 (despatches); DACG, 1st British Corps, 1945–46; Sen. Chaplain, Guards Depot, Caterham, 1947–50; DACG, N Canal, Egypt, 1950–53; Catterick, 1953; Warden, Royal Army Chaplains Dept Trg Centre Depot, 1954–57; Sen. Chaplain, SHAPE 1957–58; Asst Chaplain-Gen., Middle East Land Forces, 1958–60; QHC 1960; Chaplain General to HM Forces, 1960–66. Chairman of Governors, Monkton Combe Sch., Bath, 1969–81; Pres. of Foundn, St Paul's and St Mary's C of E Coll. of Educn, Cheltenham, 1978–. Knight Officer, Order of Orange Nassau (with Swords) 1946. *Address:* Rodborough Crest, Rodborough Common, Stroud, Glos GL5 5BT. *T:* Amberley 3224; Churchtown, Broadway, Co. Wexford, Republic of Ireland. *T:* Wexford 31221. *Club:* National.

NEILL, (James) Hugh, CBE 1969; TD 1950; JP; Lord-Lieutenant for South Yorkshire, since 1985; Chairman, James Neill Holdings Ltd, since 1963; *b* 29 March 1921; *o s* of Col Sir Frederick Neill, CBE, DSO, TD, DL, JP, and Lady (Winifred Margaret) Neill (*née* Colver); *m* 1st, 1943, Jane Margaret Shuttleworth (*d* 1980); two *d*; 2nd, 1982, Anne O'Leary. *Educ:* Rugby School. War service with RE and Royal Bombay Sappers and Miners, UK, Norway, India, Burma and Germany, 1939–46 (despatches, Burma, 1945). Mem., British Overseas Trade Bd, 1973–78; Pres., European Tool Cttee, 1972–76; Mem., Trent Regional Health Authority, 1974–80; Chm. Exec. Cttee, Sheffield Council for Voluntary Service, 1953–; Mem. Council, CBI, 1965–83; Chm., E and W Ridings Regional Council, FBI, 1962–64; Pres., Nat. Fedn of Engrs Tool Manufrs, 1963–65; Pres., Fedn of British Hand Tool Manufrs, 1960–61; Vice-Pres., Inst. of Export. Pres., Sheffield Chamber of Commerce, 1984–85. FBIM. Hon. Fellow, Sheffield City Polytechnic, 1978; Hon. LLD Sheffield, 1982. Master Cutler of Hallamshire, 1958; High Sheriff of Hallamshire, 1971; DL South Yorkshire, 1974, JP 1985. KStJ 1986. *Recreations:* golf, horse trials, racing, shooting. *Address:* Barn Cottage, Lindrick Common, near Worksop S81 8BA. *T:* Dinnington 562806. *Clubs:* East India; Sheffield (Sheffield); Lindrick (Worksop); Royal and Ancient (St Andrews).

NEILL, Rt. Rev. John Robert Winder; *see* Tuam, Killala and Achonry, Bishop of.

NEILL, Sir Patrick; *see* Neill, Sir F. P.

NEILSON, Ian (Godfrey), DFC 1944; TD 1951; *b* 4 Dec. 1918; *er s* of James Wilson Neilson, solicitor, Glasgow; *m* 1945, D. Alison St Clair Aytoun, Ashintully; one *s* one *d*. *Educ:* Glasgow Acad.; Glasgow Univ. (BL). Legal Trng, Glasgow, 1935–39; Territorial Army, 1938; War Service, 1939–45: Field Artillery; Air Observation Post, 1941; RA Staff, 1944; Lt-Col comdg War Crimes Investigation Unit, Germany, 1945–46; formed and commanded No 666 (Scottish) Sqdn, RAuxAF, 1948–53. Enrolled Solicitor, 1946. Royal Institution of Chartered Surveyors: Scottish Sec., Edinburgh, 1946–53; Asst Sec., London, 1953–61; Under-Sec., 1961–65; The Boys' Brigade: Brigade Sec., 1966–74; Officer, 5th Mid-Surrey Co., 1972–78; Nat. Hon. Vice-Pres., 1982–; Hon. Vice-Pres., W of England Dist, 1983–; Hon. Vice-Pres., Wilts Bn, 1985–. Clerk to Governors of the Cripplegate Foundn, Cripplegate Educnl Foundn, Trustees of St Giles and St Luke's Jt Parochial Charities, and Governors of the Cripplegate Schs Foundn, 1974–81. Hon. Treasurer, Thames Youth Venture Adv. Council (City Parochial Foundn), 1968–76. Vice-Chm., British Council of Churches Youth Dept, 1971–74; Trustee: St George's Chapel, London Airport, 1978– (Chm., 1983–); Douglas Haig Meml Homes, 1979–; Mem., Nat. Council for Voluntary Youth Services, 1966–74; Pres., London Br., Glasgow Academical Club, 1977–79; Chm. of Governors, Lucas-Tooth Leadership Training Fund for Boys, 1976–83; Governor, Kingsway-Princeton Coll. of Further Educn, 1977–83. Elder, United Reformed Church, St Andrew's, Cheam, 1972–83; Lay Mem., Provincial Ministerial Cttee, URC, 1974–83; Dir and Asst Sec., URC Trust, 1982–; Mem. Council: Christchurch, Marlborough, 1984–; St Peter's and St Paul's Trust, Marlborough, 1985–. BIM: Hon. Sec., City of London Branch, 1976–79, Chm., 1979–81, Vice Pres., 1981–; Chm., Inner London Branches Area Cttee, 1981–83; FBIM 1980. Sen. Instr, Royal Yachting Assoc., 1977–; Vice-Pres., Air Observation Post Officers Assoc., 1978–; Chm., Epsom Choral Soc., 1977–81. Freeman, Guild of Air Pilots and Air Navigators, 1976–78, Liveryman, 1978; Freeman, City of London, 1975; Chm., Queenhithe Ward Club, 1977–78. Hon. Editor, Tower and Town, Marlborough, 1984–. *Recreations:* golf, music, gardening, sailing. *Address:* The Paddock, Kingsbury Street, Marlborough, Wilts SN8 1HZ. *T:* Marlborough 55114. *Clubs:* Athenæum, Little Ship; Marlborough Golf; St Mawes Sailing.

NEILSON, Nigel Fraser, MC 1943; Chairman, Neilson McCarthy, since 1962; Director, Phoenix Lloyd Limited, since 1982; *b* 12 Dec. 1919; *s* of Lt-Col W. Neilson, DSO, 4th Hussars and Maud Alice Francis Anson; *m* 1949, Pamela Catherine Georgina Sheppard; one *s* one *d*. *Educ:* Hereworth Sch.; Christ's Coll., New Zealand; RADA. Inns of Court Regt; commnd Staffs Yeomanry, 1939; seconded Cavalry Regt, Transjordanian Frontier Force; served Syrian Campaign; returned Staffs Yeo., Seventh Armoured Div., GSO 111 Ops; served desert and Italy; Staff Coll., 1944; served in Germany, Holland and France; C of S, Bergen area, Norway; served with SAS and French SAS. On demobilisation worked in theatre, cabaret, films, London, USA and NZ; joined J. Walter Thompson, 1951; became personal rep. to Aristotle Onassis, 1955, later consultant to his daughter,

Christina; founded Neilson McCarthy Internat. Public Relations Consultants in UK, USA, Australia, NZ and SE Asia, 1962. Past Pres., NZ Soc., 1978–79. Chevalier de la Légion d'Honneur 1946, Croix de Guerre avec Palme 1946. *Recreations:* riding, shooting, music, theatre. *Address:* Woolfield Farm, Froxfield, Hants; Hulton House, 161/166 Fleet Street, EC4. *T:* 01-353 7781. *Club:* Buck's.

NEILSON, Richard Alvin, LVO 1968; HM Diplomatic Service; Head of Southern European Department, Foreign and Commonwealth Office, since 1984; *b* 9 July 1937; *s* of Robert and Ethel Neilson; *m* 1961, Olive Tyler; one *s*. *Educ:* Burnley Grammar Sch.; Leeds Univ. (BA Hons 1958, MA 1960). Fulbright Fellow, Univ. of Wisconsin, 1959–60; Asst Lectr, Univ. of Edinburgh, 1960–61; joined FO, 1961; Third (later Second) Sec., Kinshasa, 1963–65; Treasury Centre for Admin. Studies, 1965; Second (later First) Sec. (Information), Santiago, 1966–69; First Sec., Canberra, 1969–73; FCO, 1973–77; Counsellor, seconded to NI Office as Head of Political Affairs Div., 1977–79; Dep. High Comr, Lusaka, 1979–80, Acting High Comr, Nov. 1979–June 1980; Dep. Governor and Political Advr, Gibraltar, 1981–84. *Publications:* contribs to geomorphological literature. *Address:* c/o Foreign and Commonwealth Office, SW1A 2AH; Maynes Hill Farm, Hoggeston, Buckingham, Bucks. *T:* Winslow 2308. *Club:* Royal Commonwealth Society.

NEILSON, Hon. William Arthur, AC 1978; Premier of Tasmania, 1975–77; Agent-General for Tasmania, in London, 1978–81; *b* 27 Aug. 1925; *s* of late Arthur R. Neilson; *m* 1948, Jill, *d* of A. H. Benjamin; one *s* three *d*. *Educ:* Ogilvie Commercial High Sch., Hobart. When first elected to Tasmanian Parlt in 1946, aged 21, youngest MP in British Commonwealth and youngest member ever elected to any Australian parlt. Re-elected, 1948, 1950, 1955, 1956, 1959, 1964, 1969 and 1972, resigned 1977. Labor Party Whip, Dec. 1946–Feb. 1955; Minister for Tourists and Immigration and Forests, Oct. 1956–Aug. 1958; Attorney-Gen. and Minister for Educn, Aug.-Oct 1958; Minister for Educn, until April 1959, then Treasurer and Minister for Educn, April-May 1959; Minister for Educn, 1959–69 and May 1972–March 1974; Attorney-Gen., also Dep. Premier, Minister for Environment and Minister administering Police Dept and Licensing Act, April 1974–March 1975; Treasurer, 1975–77. *Recreations:* reading, writing, chess, Australian Rules football, amateur theatre. *Address:* 7 Amarina Court, Kingston Beach, Hobart, Tasmania 7151, Australia.

NELDER, John Ashworth, DSc; FRS 1981; Head of Statistics Department, 1968–84, and of Division of Biomathematics, Jan-Oct. 1984, Rothamsted Experimental Station; Visiting Professor, Imperial College of Science and Technology, since 1971; *b* 8 Oct. 1924; *s* of Reginald Charles and Edith May Ashworth Nelder; *m* 1955, Mary Hawkes; one *s* one *d*. *Educ:* Blundell's Sch., Tiverton; Cambridge Univ. (MA); DSc Birmingham. Head, Statistics Section, National Vegetable Research Station, 1950–68. Pres., Royal Statistical Soc., 1985–86. Hon. DSc Paul Sabatier, Toulouse, 1981. *Publications:* Computers in Biology, 1974; (with P. McCullagh) Generalized Linear Models, 1983; responsible for statistical programs (computer), Genstat and GLIM; numerous papers in statistical and biological jls. *Recreations:* piano-playing, music, natural history. *Address:* Cumberland Cottage, 33 Crown Street, Redbourn, St Albans, Herts AL3 7JX. *T:* Redbourn 2907.

NELIGAN, Desmond West Edmund, OBE 1961; National Insurance Commissioner, 1961–76, retired; *b* 20 June 1906; *s* of late Rt Rev. M. R. Neligan, DD (one time Bishop of Auckland, NZ), and Mary, *d* of Edmund Macrory, QC; *m* 1st, 1936, Penelope Ann, *d* of Henry Mason (marr. diss., 1946); two *s*; 2nd, 1947, Margaret Elizabeth, *d* of late Captain Snook, RN; one step *d*. *Educ:* Bradfield Coll.; Jesus Coll., Cambridge. BA Cantab, 1929; Barrister, Middle Temple, 1940. Practising Barrister until 1961. Appointed Umpire under National Service Acts, Nov. 1955. Dep. Comr for National Insurance, 1955–61. Served War of 1939–45, in 2 NZ Division, in Greece, Crete and Western Desert. *Publications:* (ed) 6th, 7th and 8th Editions Dumsday's Parish Councils Handbook; (with Sir A. Safford, QC) Town and Country Planning Act, 1944, and *ibid*, 1947; Social Security Case Law: digest of Commissioners' decisions, 1979; Lawful Lyrics and Cautionary Tales for Lawyers, 1984. *Recreations:* formerly: hockey, cricket (Mem. MCC), tennis and hunting. *Address:* Frobishers, Danhill Cross Roads, West Chiltington, Pulborough, West Sussex. *T:* Coolham 434.

NELLIST, David; MP (Lab) Coventry South East, since 1983; *b* July 1952. Mem., AUEW-TASS. Mem., W Midlands CC, 1982–86. *Address:* House of Commons, SW1A 0AA. *T:* 01-219 4214.

NELSON, family name of **Earl Nelson** and **Baron Nelson of Stafford.**

NELSON, 9th Earl *cr* 1805, of Trafalgar and of Merton; **Peter John Horatio Nelson;** Baron Nelson of the Nile and of Hilborough, Norfolk, 1801; Viscount Merton, 1805; Detective Sergeant, Hertfordshire Police Force; *b* 9 Oct. 1941; *s* of Captain Hon. John Marie Joseph Horatio Nelson (*d* 1970) (*y s* of 5th Earl) and of Kathleen Mary, *d* of William Burr, Torquay; *S* uncle, 1981; *m* 1969, Maureen Diana, *d* of Edward Patrick Quinn, Kilkenny; one *s* one *d*. President: Royal Naval Commando Assoc.; Nelson Soc.; Vice-Pres., Jubilee Sailing Trust; Mem. Council, Friends of Nat. Maritime Mus.; Hon. Life Member: Royal Naval Assoc.; Royal Naval Museum. *Heir: s* Viscount Merton, *qv*. *Address:* c/o Hertfordshire Police Headquarters, Stanborough Road, Welwyn Garden City, Herts AL8 6XF. *Club:* St James's.

NELSON OF STAFFORD, 2nd Baron, *cr* 1960; **Henry George Nelson,** Bt 1955; MA, FEng, FICE, Hon. FIMechE, Hon. FIEE, FRAeS; Director: The General Electric Company plc, since 1968 (Chairman, 1968–83); Bank of England, since 1961; International Nickel Company of Canada, 1966–74, and since 1975; Enserch Corp., since 1984; *b* Manchester, 2 Jan. 1917; *s* of 1st Baron Nelson of Stafford and late Florence Mabel, *o d* of late Henry Howe, JP; *S* father, 1962; *m* 1940, Pamela Roy Bird, *yr d* of late Ernest Roy Bird, formerly MP for Skipton, Yorks; two *s* two *d*. *Educ:* Oundle; King's Coll., Cambridge. Exhibnr 1935; Mechanical Sciences Tripos, 1937. Practical experience in England, France and Switzerland, 1937–39. Joined the English Electric Co. Ltd, 1939; Supt, Preston Works, 1939–40; Asst Works Man., Preston, 1940–41; Dep. Works Man., Preston, 1941–42; Man. Dir, D. Napier & Son Ltd, 1942–49; Exec. Dir, The Marconi Co. Ltd, 1946–58; Dep. Man. Dir, 1949–56, Man. Dir, 1956–62, Chm. and Chief Exec., 1962–68, The English Electric Co. Ltd. Dep. Chm., British Aircraft Corp., 1960–77; Chm., Royal Worcester Ltd, 1978–84; Director: ICL, 1968–74; Nat. Bank of Australasia Ltd (London Bd of Advice), 1950–81. Outside Lectr, Univ. of Cambridge (Mech. Sciences Tripos course on Industrial Management), 1947–49. Chancellor of Aston Univ., 1966–79. Member: Govt. Adv. Council on Scientific Policy, 1955–58; Adv. Council on Middle East Trade, 1958–63 (Industrial Leader and Vice-Chm., 1959–63); Civil Service Commn (Part time Mem. Final Selection and Interview Bds), 1956–61; Engrg Adv. Council, 1958–61; Council, Inst. Electrical Engineers, 1959–76 (Vice-Pres. 1957–62 and 1965–70, Pres., 1970–71); Middle East Assoc. (Vice-Pres., 1962–); Gen. Bd of NPL, 1959–66; Council, SBAC, 1943–64 (Pres. 1961–62); Council Foundn on Automation and Employment Ltd, 1963–68; Council, BEAMA, 1964– (Pres., 1966); Adv. Council, Min. of Technology, 1964–70; Engineering Industries Council, 1975–84; H of L Select Cttee on Sci. and Technology, 1984–. World Power Conference: Mem., British Nat. Cttee, 1954–, Chm., 1971–74. Mem., Nat. Def. Industries Council, 1969–77 (Chm., 1971–77); President: Locomotive and Allied Manufacturers Assoc., 1964–66; British Electrical Power Convention, 1965–67; Orgalime (Organisme de Liaison des Industries Métalliques Européennes), 1968–70; Sino-British Trade Council, 1973–83. Liveryman: Worshipful Co. of Coachmakers and Coach Harness Makers of London, 1944; Worshipful Co. of Goldsmiths, 1961 (Prime Warden, 1983–84). Lord High Steward of Borough of Stafford, 1966–71. Hon. DSc: Aston, 1966; Keele, 1967; Cranfield, 1972; Hon. LLD Strathclyde, 1971; Fellow, Imp. Coll. of Science and Technology, 1969. Benjamin Franklin Medal, RSA, 1959. *Recreations:* shooting, tennis, ski-ing. *Heir: s* Hon. Henry Roy George Nelson [*b* 26 Oct. 1943; *m* 1968, Dorothy, *yr d* of Leslie Caley, Tibthorpe Manor, Driffield, Yorks; one *s* one *d*]. *Address:* 8 Carlton Lodge, 37 Lowndes Street, SW1X 9HX. *T:* 01-235 6551. *Clubs:* Carlton, Hurlingham.

NELSON, NZ, Bishop of, since 1965; **Rt. Rev. Peter (Eves) Sutton;** Senior Anglican Bishop, since 1979; Acting Primate, New Zealand, 1985–86; *b* Wellington, NZ, 7 June 1923; *m* 1956, Pamela Cherrington, *e d* of R. A. Dalley, Patin House, Kidderminster; one *s* one *d*. *Educ:* Wellesley Coll.; Nelson Coll.; University of New Zealand. BA 1945; MA 1947; LTh 1948. Deacon, 1947; Priest, 1948 (Wellington); Curate of Wanganui, New Zealand, 1947–50; St John the Evangelist, Bethnal Green, 1950–51; Bishops Hatfield, Diocese of St Albans (England), 1951–52; Vicar of St Cuthberts, Berhampore (NZ), 1952–58; Whangarei, Diocese of Auckland, New Zealand, 1958–64; Archdeacon of Waimate, 1962–64; Dean of Dunedin and Vicar of St Paul's Cathedral, Dunedin, 1964–65. ChStJ 1986. *Publication:* Freedom for Convictions, 1971. *Recreations:* golf (Canterbury Univ. Blue), tennis. *Address:* Bishopdale, Nelson, New Zealand.

NELSON, Anthony; *see* Nelson, R. A.

NELSON, Bertram James, OBE 1984; HM Diplomatic Service, retired; Consul-General, Antwerp, 1983–85; *b* 7 Dec. 1925; *s* of Herbert James Nelson and Adelaide Mabel Nelson (*née* Newton); *m* 1958, Constance Dangerfield; one *s* one *d*. *Educ:* North Kensington Central School. Grenadier Guards, 1944–47; Post Office and Cable and Wireless, 1947–54; Foreign Office, 1954; served Cairo, Budapest, Athens, Asunción, Zagreb, DSAO, 1966–69; Vice-Consul, Tokyo, 1969–71; Vice-Consul, Tehran, 1972–75; FCO, 1975–79; First Sec. and Consul, Brussels, 1979–83. *Recreations:* gardening, amateur dramatics, ballet, theatre, cinema. *Address:* 11 Sefton Road, Petts Wood, Orpington, Kent BR5 1RG.

NELSON, Campbell Louis; Chairman, 1971–80, and Managing Director, 1960–80, Ultramar plc (Director, since 1947; Executive Director, 1947–60); *b* 14 Dec. 1910; *s* of George Francis Nelson and Kate Nelson (*née* Wilson); *m* 1939, Pauline Frances Blundell (*d* 1978); one *s* one *d*. *Educ:* Seaford Coll.; King's Coll., London Univ. FCA. Partner of Limebeer & Co., Chartered Accountants, 1933–41. Served War, KRRC (Motor Bns), 1941–44. Sen. Partner, Limebeer & Co., 1951–74 (retd); Exec. Dir, 1948–85, Chm., 1957–85, British-Borneo Petroleum Syndicate Ltd (retd); Dir, 1970–81, Chm., 1976–81, Gellatly Hankey & Co. Ltd (retd); Chm., 1975–85, Scottish Offshore Investors Ltd (retd); Dir, Harrisons (Clyde) Ltd, 1981–. Councillor: Maritime Trust, 1979–; Indonesian Assoc., 1980–; Patron, St James and St Vedast Schools, 1980–. *Recreations:* golf, bridge. *Address:* 2 Chelsea House, 26 Lowndes Street, SW1X 9JD. *T:* 01-235 8260; Queenshill, Sunningdale, Berks. *T:* Ascot 20088. *Clubs:* City of London; Royal and Ancient Golf (St Andrews), Sunningdale Golf.

NELSON, Air Cdre Eric Douglas Mackinlay, CB 1952; DL; retired, Sept. 1963; *b* 2 Jan. 1912; *e s* of late Rear-Adm. R. D. Nelson, CBE, and the late Ethel Nelson (*née* MacKinlay); *m* 1939, Margaret Yvonne Taylor; one *s* one *d*. *Educ:* Dover Coll.; RAF Coll., Cranwell. Commissioned RAF, 1932; served War of 1939–45 (despatches); CO 103 (HB) Sqdn Elsham Wolds, 1943–44; Group Capt., 1944; ADC to the Queen, 1953–57; Air Commodore, 1956; Commandant, RAF, Halton, 1956–58; Commandant, Royal Air Force Staff College, Andover, 1958–60; AOA Transport Command, 1960–61; Air Officer Commanding and Commandant, Royal Air Force College, Cranwell, 1961–63. DL Lincs, 1966. *Recreations:* sailing, beagling. *Address:* (permanent) Jasmine Cottage, Carlton-le-Moorland, Lincoln. *T:* Bassingham 309. *Club:* Royal Air Force.

NELSON, Eric Victor, LVO 1975; HM Diplomatic Service; Consul-General, Bordeaux, since 1984; *b* 11 Jan. 1927; *s* of Victor H. H. and E. Vera B. Nelson (*née* Collingwood); *m* 1960, Maria Teresa (Marité) Paul; two *d*. *Educ:* Western High School; George Washington University, Washington DC. Royal Air Force, 1945–48. Board of Trade, 1949; served FO, later FCO: Athens, Belgrade, Haiphong, Caracas; First Sec., Saigon, 1962; First Sec. and Consul, Bujumbura, 1964 (Chargé d'Affaires *ai*, 1966–67); FO 1968; First Sec. and Consul, Asunçión, 1971; First Sec., Mexico City, 1974; FCO, 1978; seconded to Brunei Govt Service as Special Adviser to HM Sultan of Brunei, for Establishment of Brunei Diplomatic Service, 1981–84. Order of the Aztec Eagle, Mexico, 1975. *Recreations:* photography, giving illustrated talks, tourism, cartooning, sculpture. *Address:* c/o Foreign and Commonwealth Office, King Charles Street, SW1A 2AH. *Club:* Travellers'.

NELSON, Maj.-Gen. Sir (Eustace) John (Blois), KCVO 1966 (MVO 1953); CB 1965; DSO 1944; OBE 1948; MC 1943; *b* 15 June 1912; *s* of late Roland Hugh Nelson and late Hylda Letitia Blois; *m* 1936, the Lady Jane FitzRoy (granted rank and precedence of *d* of a duke, 1931), *er d* of (William Henry Alfred FitzRoy) Viscount Ipswich; two *d*. *Educ:* Eton; Trinity College, Cambridge. BA (Hons) History, MA 1983. Commissioned Grenadier Guards, Sept. 1933; served 1939–45 with 3rd and 5th Bns, Belgium, N Africa, Italy (wounded three times, despatches); comd 3rd Bn Grenadier Guards, 1944–45, Italy. Contested (C) Whitechapel, 1945. Comd 1st Guards Parachute Bn, 1946–48, Palestine; comd 1st Bn Gren. Gds, 1950–52, Tripoli, N Africa. Planning Staff Standing Group, Washington, DC, 1954–56, Imperial Defence College, 1958; comd 4th Guards Bde, 1959–61, Germany; GOC London District, and Maj.-Gen. comdg Household Brigade 1962–65; GOC Berlin (British Sector), 1966–68. Chm., Christian Youth Challenge Trust; Vice-Pres., Nat. Playing Fields Assoc. (Gen. Sec. 1969–72). Silver Star (USA), 1944. *Recreations:* the countryside, sailing. *Address:* Tigh Bhaan, Appin, Argyll. *T:* Appin 252.

NELSON, Michael Edward; General Manager since 1976, and Deputy Managing Director since 1981, Reuters Ltd; Chairman, Visnews, since 1985; *b* 30 April 1929; *s* of Thomas Alfred Nelson and Dorothy Pretoria Nelson; *m* 1960, Helga Johanna (*née* den Ouden); two *s* one *d*. *Educ:* Latymer Upper School; Magdalen College, Oxford (MA). Joined Reuters, London, as trainee financial journalist, 1952; assignments Asia, 1954–57; returned to London; Manager, Reuters Economic Services, 1962. *Recreations:* walking, music, photography. *Address:* Reuters Ltd, 85 Fleet Street, EC4P 4AJ. *T:* 01-250 1122. *Club:* Garrick.

NELSON, Air Marshal Sir Richard; *see* Nelson, Air Marshal Sir S. R. C.

NELSON, (Richard) Anthony; MP (C) Chichester, since Oct. 1974; *b* 11 June 1948; *o s* of late Gp Captain R. G. Nelson, BSc, CEng, FRAeS, MICE, and of Mrs J. M. Nelson; *m* 1974, Caroline Victoria Butler; one *s* one *d*. *Educ:* Harrow Sch.; Christ's Coll., Cambridge (MA (Hons) Economics and Law). State Scholarship to Harrow, 1961; Head of School, 1966; Rothschild Scholar, 1966. N. M. Rothschild & Sons Ltd, 1969–73. Founder Mem., Nat. Victims Assoc., 1972; Mem., Bow Gp Council, 1973. Dir, Chichester Fest. Th.,

1983–. Contested (C) E Leeds, Feb. 1974. Mem., Select Cttee on Science and Technology, 1975–79; PPS to Minister for Housing and Construction, 1979–83, to Minister of State for the Armed Forces, 1983–85. FRSA 1979. *Recreations:* music, rugby. *Address:* The Old Vicarage, Easebourne, Midhurst, West Sussex.

NELSON, Robert Franklyn; QC 1985; a Recorder, since 1986; *b* 19 Sept. 1942; *s* of Clarence William and Lucie Margaret Nelson; *m* 1968, Anne-Marie Sabina Hall; two *s*. *Educ:* Repton; St John's Coll., Cambridge (MA). Called to the Bar, Middle Temple, 1965 (Harmsworth Entrance Exhibn, 1963). *Recreations:* cricket, opera, golf. *Address:* 1 Paper Buildings, Temple, EC4. *T:* 01–583 7355.

NELSON, St Elmo Dudley, CMG 1964; Permanent Secretary, Military Governor's Office, Kano, 1968–76; Acting Secretary to Military Government, and Head of Kano State Civil Service, 1970, 1973 and 1975; *b* 18 March 1919; *s* of Dudley Nelson and Dorothy Maida (*née* Browne), Highton, Victoria, Australia; *m* 1958, Lynette Margaret, *o d* of late Phillip Anthony Browne, Yarram and Frankston, Victoria, Australia. *Educ:* privately; Geelong School; Oxford University; Sorbonne. Served War of 1939–45 (despatches): 2/7 Australian Infantry Bn (Major); campaigns N Africa, Greece, Crete, New Guinea; Instructor Staff Coll., Cabalah, 1944. Joined HM Colonial Administrative Service. Nigeria: Cadet 1947; Administrative Officer (Class II), 1957; Resident, Plateau Province, 1961; Resident and Provincial Sec., Kabba Province, 1962; Provincial Sec., Kano Province, 1963–67, Sokoto, 1967–68. Chm., Cttee which divided assets of Northern Region between the six Northern States, 1967. Election supervisor, Rhodesian independence elecns, 1980. Gen. Tax Comr, S Wilts, 1980–. *Recreations:* fishing, polo, squash. *Address:* Burcombe Manor, Burcombe, near Salisbury, Wilts SP2 0EJ. *Club:* MCC.

NELSON, Air Marshal Sir (Sidney) Richard (Carlyle), KCB 1963 (CB 1962); OBE 1949; Director-General, Royal Air Force Medical Services, 1962–67; Director of Research and Medical Services, Aspro-Nicholas Ltd, 1967–72; *b* Ponoka, Alberta, Canada, 14 Nov. 1907; *s* of M. O. Nelson, BA; *m* 1939, Christina Elizabeth Powell; two *s*. *Educ:* University of Alberta (MD). Commissioned in RAF, 1935; served: England 1935–36; Egypt and Western Desert, 1936–42; Fighter Command, 1943; UK Delegation (Canada), 1943–44; British Jt Services Mission (Washington), 1945–48; RAF Staff Coll., 1949; Air Ministry, 1949–52; Comd RAF Hosp., Nocton Hall, 1953–55; SMO British Forces, Arabian Peninsula, 1956–57; PMO Technical Training Comd, 1957–59; Bomber Comd, 1959–62, QHP 1961–67. *Recreations:* fishing, golf. *Address:* Caffyn's Copse, Shappen Hill Lane, Burley, Hants. *T:* Burley 3308. *Clubs:* Royal Air Force; Royal Lymington Yacht.

NELSON, Sir William Vernon Hope, 3rd Bt, *cr* 1912; OBE 1952; Major (retired) late 8th Hussars; *b* 25 May 1914; *s* of late William Hope Nelson (2nd *s* of 1st Bt); *S* uncle, Sir James Hope Nelson, 2nd Bt, 1960; *m* 1945, Elizabeth Ann Bevil, *er d* of 14th Viscount Falkland; three *s* three *d*. *Educ:* Beaumont; Royal Military College, Sandhurst. Commissioned 2nd Lt, 8th Hussars, 1934. Served in Palestine, 1936–39 (despatches, medal with clasp). Served War of 1939–45; served Korea, 1950–51 (OBE). *Heir:* *s* Jamie Charles Vernon Hope Nelson [*b* 23 Oct. 1949; *m* 1983, Marilyn Hodges; one *s*]. *Address:* c/o Hoare & Co., 16 Waterloo Place, SW1.

NEMETZ, Hon. Nathaniel Theodore; Hon. Chief Justice Nemetz; Canada Medal 1967; Chief Justice of British Columbia and Administrator of the Province of British Columbia, since 1979; *b* 8 Sept. 1913; *s* of Samuel and Rebecca (*née* Birch); *m* 1935, Bel Newman; one *s*. *Educ:* Univ. of British Columbia (BA (1st Cl. Hons)). Called to the Bar, 1937; KC (Canada) 1950. Justice, Supreme Court of BC, 1963–68; Justice, Court of Appeal of BC, 1968–73; Chief Justice, Supreme Court of BC, 1973–78. Special counsel to: City of Vancouver, City of New Westminster and Municipality of Burnaby; Electrical Assoc.; BC Hosp. Assoc.; Public Utilities Commn of BC; Royal Commission on: Expropriation, 1961; Fishing, 1964; Election Regulations, 1965; Forest Industry, 1966. Chm., Educational Delegn to People's Republic of China, 1974; Advisor to Canadian Govt Delegn, ILO, Geneva, 1973. University of British Columbia: Chm., Bd of Governors, 1965–68; Chancellor, 1972–75; Pres., Alumni Assoc., 1957; Mem., Bd of Governors, Canadian Inst. for Advanced Legal Studies, Cambridge, England. Hon. Fellow, Hebrew Univ., Jerusalem, 1976. Hon. LLD: Notre Dame (Nelson), 1972; Simon Fraser, 1975; British Columbia, 1975; Victoria, 1976. Silver Jubilee Medal, 1977. *Publications:* Swedish Labour Law and Practice, 1967; Judicial Administration and Judicial Independence, 1976; The Jury and the Citizen, 1985; The Concept of the Independence of the Judiciary, 1985. *Recreations:* swimming, billiards. *Address:* 5688 Newton Wynd, Vancouver, BC V6T 1H5, Canada. *T:* (604) 224–5383; (office) (604) 660–2710. *Clubs:* Vancouver, University, Faculty of University of British Columbia (all Vancouver).

NEPEAN, Lt-Col Sir Evan Yorke, 6th Bt, *cr* 1802; late Royal Signals; *b* 23 Nov. 1909; *s* of Sir Charles Evan Molyneux Yorke Nepean, 5th Bt, and Mary Winifred, *o d* of Rev. William John Swayne, formerly Vicar of Heytesbury, Wilts, and Custos of St John's Hospital, Heytesbury; *S* father 1953; *m* 1940, (Georgiana) Cicely, *o d* of late Major Noel Edward Grey Willoughby, Middlesex Regiment, of Chancel End House, Heytesbury, Wilts; three *d*. *Educ:* Winchester; Downing College, Cambridge. BA 1931, MA 1946. North West Frontier of India (Mohmand), 1935. Served War of 1939–45: GSO3, War Office, 1939–40; with Royal Signals (Lt-Col 1943), UK, and Middle East, Major 1946; on Staff Southern Command, 1947; GSO1 Royal Signals, Ministry of Defence, 1950–53; Lt-Col 1952; Cmdg 11 Air Formation Signal Regt, BAOR, 1955–56, retired. Civil Servant, 1957–59; CSO's branch at HQ Southern Command (Retired Officers' Staff appt), 1959–73. CEng; MIEE. *Recreations:* sailing, amateur radio. *Heir:* none. *Address:* Goldens, Teffont, Salisbury, Wilts. *T:* Teffont 275. *Club:* Royal Lymington Yacht.

NERINA, Nadia; (*née* Nadine Judd); Prima Ballerina; Ballerina with Royal Ballet, 1951–69; *b* Cape Town, Oct. 1927; *m* 1955, Charles Gordon. Joined Sadler's Wells Sch., 1946; after two months joined Sadler's Wells Theatre Ballet; transferred Sadler's Wells Ballet, Royal Opera House (now Royal Ballet), as soloist, 1967. *Rôles:* Princess Aurora in The Sleeping Beauty; Ondine; Odette-Odile in Swan Lake; Swanhilda in Coppelia; Sylvia; Giselle; Cinderella; Firebird; Can Can Dancer in La Boutique Fantasque; Ballerina in Petrushka; Colombine in Carnaval; Mazurka, Little Waltz, Prelude, in Les Sylphides; Mam'zelle Angot; Ballet Imperial; Scènes de Ballet; Flower Festival of Genzano; Les Rendezvous; Polka in Façade; The Girl in Spectre de la Rose; Casse Noisette; Laurentia; Khadra; Vagabonds; The Bride in A Wedding Bouquet; *creations:* Circus Dancer in Mardi Gras; Fairy Spring in Cinderella; Queen of the Earth in Homage to the Queen; Faded Beauty in Noctambules; Variation on a Theme; Birthday Offering; Lise in La Fille Mal Gardée; Electra; The Girl in Home; Clorinda in Tancredi. Appeared with Royal Ballet: Europe; South Africa; USA; Canada; USSR; Bulgaria; Romania. Recital Tours with Alexis Rassine: South Africa, 1952–55; England, 1956–57; concert performances, Royal Albert Hall and Royal Festival Hall, 1958–60. *Guest appearances include:* Turkish Nat. Ballet, 1957; Bolshoi Ballet, Kirov Ballet, 1960; Munich Ballet, 1963; Nat. Finnish Ballet, Royal Danish Ballet, 1964; Stuttgart Ballet, 1965; Ballet Theatre, Opera House Chicago, 1967; Royal Command Variety Performances, 1963–66. Mounted, dir. and prod three Charity Gala performances, London Palladium, 1969, 1971, 1972. Many TV appearances, UK and USA. Hon. Consultant on Ballet, Ohio Univ., 1967–69. British Jury Member, 3rd Internat. Ballet Competition, Moscow, 1977. Fellow, 1959, Patron, 1964, Cecchetti Soc. Mem. Council, RSPCA, 1969–74. *Publications:* contrib.: La Fille Mal Gardée, 1960; Ballet and Modern Dance, 1974; *relevant publication:* Ballerina, ed Clement Crisp, 1975. *Address:* c/o Royal Opera House, Covent Garden, WC2.

NESS, Air Marshal Sir Charles, KCB 1980 (CB 1978); CBE 1967 (OBE 1959); Military Adviser, International Computers Ltd, since 1983; *s* of late Charles W. Ness and Jessica Ness; *m* 1951, Audrey, *d* of late Roy and Phyllis Parker; one *s*. *Educ:* George Heriot's Sch.; Edinburgh Univ. CBIM, MIPM. Joined RAF, 1943; flying and staff appts in Bomber Comd and with USAF, 1944–62; Commander, British Skybolt Trials Force, Florida, 1962–63; Station Commander, Royal Air Force, Steamer Point, Aden, 1965–67; Air Comdr, Gibraltar, 1971–73; Director of Organisation and Administrative Plans (RAF), MoD, 1974–75; Comdr, Southern Maritime Air Region, 1975–76; Dir Gen., Personnel Management (RAF), 1976–80; Air Mem. for Personnel, 1980–83. *Address:* Perseverance Cottage, Wentworth, near Ely, Cambs. *T:* Ely 778968. *Club:* Royal Air Force.

NETHERTHORPE, 3rd Baron *cr* 1959, of Anston, W Riding; **James Frederick Turner;** student; *b* 7 Jan. 1964; *s* of 2nd Baron Netherthorpe, and of Belinda, *d* of F. Hedley Nicholson; *S* father, 1982. *Educ:* Heatherdown Prep. School; Harrow School. *Heir:* *b* Hon. Patrick Andrew Turner, *b* 4 June 1971. *Address:* Boothby Hall, Boothby Pagnell, Grantham, Lincs. *T:* Ingoldsby 374.

NEUBERGER, Albert, CBE 1964; PhD (London), MD (Würzburg); FRCP; FRS 1951; FRSC; Professor of Chemical Pathology, St Mary's Hospital, University of London, 1955–73, now Emeritus Professor; *b* 15 April 1908; *s* of late Max Neuberger and Bertha Neuberger; *m* 1943, Lilian Ida, *d* of late Edmund Dreyfus and Marguerite Dreyfus, London; four *s* (one *d* decd). *Educ:* Gymnasium, Würzburg; Univs of Würzburg and London. Beit Memorial Research Fellow, 1936–40; Research at the Biochemistry Department, Cambridge, 1939–42; Mem. of Scientific Staff, Medical Research Council, 1943; Adviser to GHQ, Delhi (Medical Directorate), 1945; Head of Biochemistry Dept, Nat. Inst. for Medical Research, 1950–55; Principal of the Wright Fleming Institute of Microbiology, 1958–62. Visiting Lectr on Medicine, 1960, on Biol Chemistry, 1964, Harvard Univ., and Physician-in-Chief (*Pro Tem.*), Peter Bent Brigham Hosp., Boston. Mem. of Editorial Bd, Biochemical Jl, 1947–55, Chm., 1952–55; Associate Man. Editor, Biochimica et Biophysica Acta, 1968–81. Member: MRC, 1962–66; Council of Scientific Policy, 1968–69; ARC, 1969–79; Indep. Cttee on Smoking and Health, 1973–82; Chm., Jt ARC/MRC Cttee on Food and Nutrition Res., 1971–73; Chairman: Governing Body, Lister Inst., 1971– (Mem., 1968–); Advisory Board, Beit Memorial Fellowships, 1967–73; Biochemical Soc., 1967–69 (Hon. Mem., Biochemical Soc., 1973); Dep. Chm., Bd of Governors, Hebrew Univ., Jerusalem. Pres., Assoc. of Clinical Biochemists, 1972–73; Hon. Pres., British Nutrition Foundn, 1982–. For. Hon. Mem., Amer. Acad. Arts and Sciences, 1972. FRCPath 1964; FRCP 1966. William Julius Mickle Fellowship of Univ. of London, 1946–47; Heberden Medal, 1959; Frederick Gowland Hopkins Medal, 1960; Kaplun Prize, 1973. Hon. LLD, Aberdeen, 1967; Hon. PhD, Jerusalem, 1968; Hon. DSc Hull, 1981. *Publications:* papers in Biochemical Jl, Proceedings of Royal Society and other learned journals. *Address:* 37 Eton Court, Eton Avenue, NW3 3HJ. *T:* 01–586 5470; Lister Institute of Preventive Medicine, Charing Cross Hospital Medical School, St Dunstan's Road, W6 8RP. *Club:* Athenæum.

NEUBERT, Michael Jon; MP (C) Romford, since Feb. 1974; a Lord Commissioner of HM Treasury, since 1986 (an Assistant Government Whip, 1983–86); *b* 3 Sept. 1933; *s* of Frederick Henry and Mathilda Marie Louise Neubert; *m* 1959, Sally Felicity Bilger; one *s*. *Educ:* Queen Elizabeth's Sch., Barnet; Bromley Grammar Sch.; Royal Coll. of Music; Downing Coll., Cambridge. MA (Cantab) Modern and Medieval Langs. Travel and industrial consultant. Councillor, Borough of Bromley, 1960–63; London Borough of Bromley: Councillor, 1964–68; Alderman, 1968–74; Leader of the Council, 1967–70; Mayor, 1972–73. Contested (C): N Hammersmith, 1966; Romford, 1970. PPS to: Minister for Social Security and for the Disabled, 1980; Ministers of State, NI Office, 1981; Minister of State for Employment, 1981–82; Sec. of State for Trade, 1982–83. Chm., Bromley Conservative Assoc., 1968–69. *Publication:* Running Your Own Society, 1967. *Recreations:* music, literature, cinema, theatre, the countryside. *Address:* 12 Greatwood, Chislehurst, Kent BR7 5HU. *T:* 01–467 0040. *Club:* Romford Conservative and Constitutional.

NEUMANN, Prof. Bernhard Hermann, FACE 1970; FAA 1964; FRS 1959; Honorary Research Fellow, CSIRO Division of Mathematics and Statistics, since 1978; *b* Berlin-Charlottenburg, 15 Oct. 1909; *s* of late Richard Neumann and late Else (*née* Aronstein); *m* 1st, 1938, Hanna Neumann (*née* von Caemmerer) (*d* 1971), DPhil, DSc, FAA, formerly Prof. and Head of Dept of Pure Mathematics, Sch. of Gen. Studies, ANU; three *s* two *d*; 2nd, 1973, Dorothea Neumann (*née* Zeim), MA, PhD. *Educ:* Herderschule, Berlin; Univs of Freiburg, Berlin, Cambridge. Dr phil Berlin, 1932; PhD Cambridge 1935; DSc Manchester 1954. Asst Lectr, University Coll, Cardiff, 1937–40. Army Service, 1940–45. Lectr, University Coll., Hull, 1946–48; Lectr, Senior Lectr, Reader, Univ. of Manchester, 1948–61; Prof. and Hd of Dept of Maths, Inst. of Advanced Studies, ANU, Canberra, 1962–74, Emeritus Prof., 1975–; Sen. Res. Fellow, CSIRO Div. of Maths and Stats, 1975–77. Visiting Lecturer: Australian Univs, 1959; Univ. of Cambridge, 1970; Monash Univ., 1980; Visiting Professor: Tata Inst. of Fundamental Research, Bombay, 1959; New York Univ., 1961–62; Univ. of Wisconsin, 1966–67; Vanderbilt Univ., 1969–70; G. A. Miller Vis. Prof., Univ. of Illinois at Urbana-Champaign, 1975; Univ. of Manitoba, 1979; Vis. Fellow, Fitzwilliam Coll., Cambridge, 1970; SERC Vis. Fellow, Univ. of Glasgow, 1985. Wiskundig Genootschap te Amsterdam Prize, 1949; Adams Prize, Univ. of Cambridge, 1952–53. Mem., Aust. Subcommn, Internat. Commn Math. Instruct., 1967–75 (Chm.), and 1979–83; Mem.-at-large, Internat. Commn Math. Instruct., 1975–82, Mem. Exec. Cttee, 1979–82; Mem., Programme Adv. Cttee, Congress Math. Educn, Karlsruhe, 1976, Berkeley, Calif., 1980, Adelaide, Australia, 1984. Member Council: London Math. Society, 1954–61 (Vice-Pres., 1957–59); Aust. Math. Society, 1963–79 (Vice-Pres., 1963–64, 1966–68, 1971–73, Pres., 1964–66; Hon. Mem. 1981–); Aust. Acad. of Science, 1968–71 (a Vice-Pres., 1969–71). Mem. Aust. Nat. Cttee for Mathematics, 1963–75 (Chm., 1966–75); (Foundation) Pres., Aust. Assoc. Math. Teachers, 1966–68, Vice-Pres., 1968–69, Hon. Mem., 1975–; (Foundn) Pres., Canberra Math. Assoc., 1963–65, Vice-Pres., 1965–66, Hon. Mem., 1975–; Hon. Mem., NZ Math. Soc., 1975–; Mem., Acad. Adv. Council, RAN Coll., 1978–. Chairman: Internat. Math. Olympiad Site Cttee, 1981–83; Aust. Math. Olympiad Cttee, 1980–86. Hon. DSc: Univ. of Newcastle, NSW, 1974; Monash Univ., 1982; Hon. DMath Univ. of Waterloo, 1986. Non-res. Fellow (Tutor), Bruce Hall, ANU, 1963–; Hon. Fellow, Dept of Maths, Inst. of Advanced Studies, ANU, 1975–. Pres., Amateur Sinfonia of Canberra Inc., 1978–80, Vice-Pres., 1980–81, 1983–84, Hon. Mem., 1984–; Vice-Pres., Friends of the Canberra Sch. of Music, 1983–. Hon. Editor, Proc. London Math. Soc., 1959–61; Assoc. Editor, Pacific Jl Math., 1964–; (Foundation) Editor, Bulletin of Aust. Math. Soc., 1969–79, Hon. Editor, 1979–; Member Editorial Board: Communications in Algebra, 1973–84; Houston Math. Jl, 1974–; Indian Jl Math. Educn, 1974–; Mem., Adv. Bd, Zentralblatt Didaktik

Math. 1970–84; Founder Editor and Publisher, IMU Canberra Circular, 1972–; Mem. and Regional Chm., IMU Exchange Commn, 1975–78. *Publications:* Appendix to German and Hungarian translations of A. G. Kuroš: Teoriya Grupp, 1953, 1955: Topics in the Theory of Infinite Groups, Bombay, 1961; Special Topics in Algebra, Vol. I: Universal Algebra, Vol. II: Order Techniques, New York, 1962; papers, mainly on theory of groups, in various mathematical journals. *Recreations:* chess, cycling, music. *Address:* 20 Talbot Street, Forrest, ACT 2603, Australia. *T:* (062) Canberra 733447.

NEVE, David Lewis; President, Immigration Appeal Tribunal, since 1978; *b* 7 Oct. 1920; *s* of Eric Read Neve, QC, and Nellie Victorine Neve (*née* Uridge); *m* 1948, Betsy Davida Bannerman; one *s* (decd). *Educ:* Repton; Emmanuel Coll., Cambridge (BA). Served war, Royal Artillery, 1940–46. Called to Bar, Middle Temple, 1947; Resident Magistrate, Uganda, 1952–59; Sen. Resident Magistrate, Uganda, 1959–62; Acting Judge, Uganda, 1962. Immigration Appeals Adjudicator, 1970; Vice-Pres., Immigration Appeals Tribunal, 1976. *Recreations:* sailing, music, reading. *Address:* Deans, Lewes Road, Ditchling, Hassocks, East Sussex.

NEVILE, Henry Nicholas; Lord-Lieutenant of Lincolnshire, since 1975; High Steward, Lincoln Cathedral, since 1985; *b* 1920; *e s* of Charles Joseph Nevile, Wellingore, Lincoln and Muriel (*née* O'Conor), *m* 1944, Jean Rosita Mary, MBE 1984, *d* of Cyril James Winceslas Torr and Maude (*née* Walpole); two *s* three *d*. *Educ:* Ampleforth; Trinity Coll., Cambridge. Served war, Scots Guards, in NW Europe, 1940–46 (despatches). Member: Upper Witham IDB, 1952–83 (Chm., 1964–76); Lincs River Bd and Authy, 1962–82; Kesteven CC, 1964–72. Liveryman, Farmers' Co., 1975–. JP 1950, DL 1962, High Sheriff, 1963, Lincolnshire. Hon. Col, Lincs ACF. KStJ. *Address:* Aubourn Hall, Lincoln. *T:* Bassingham 270. *Club:* Brooks's.

NEVILL, family name of **Marquess of Abergavenny.**

NEVILL, Prof. Bernard Richard, FSIAD; designer; Professor of Textile Design, since 1984, and Fellow, since 1985, Royal College of Art; *b* 24 Sept. 1934; *s* of R. G. Nevill. *Educ:* privately; St Martin's Sch. of Art; Royal Coll. of Art. FSIA 1970. Designed exhibn, Opera and Ballet, for Cotton Bd, Manchester, 1950; lectured in art, fashion, history of costume, textile design and fashion drawing, Shoreditch Coll., 1954–56 (resp. for first dress show staged at GLC Chm's annual reception, County Hall); Lectr, St Martin's Sch. of Art and RCA, 1959–74 (liaised between Fashion and Textile Schs, devising projs and themes for finale to RCA annual diploma show); lectured in theatre design and book illustration, Central Sch. of Art and Design, 1957–60; freelance illustrator, Good Housekeeping, Woman's Jl, Vogue, Harper's Bazaar, incl. covers for Queen and Sketch, 1956–60; freelance journalist, Vogue, Sketch and textile and fashion periodicals, 1956–66; Art Critic, Vogue, 1965–66; Designer (later Design Dir), Liberty Prints, 1961: for next decade, produced collections which became fashion landmarks and re-estabd Liberty's as major source of fashion textiles worldwide; collections designed: Islamic, 1963 (anticipated Eastern revival in fashion); Jazz, 1964 (first re-appraisal of Art Deco); Tango, 1966; Renaissance, 1967; Chameleon, 1969 (co-ordinated prints); Designer and Design Dir, Ten Cate, Holland, 1969–71; Design Consultant in dress fabrics to Cantoni (founders of cotton industry in Italy), 1971–: printed velvets and cottons have placed Cantoni in fore-front of internat. ready-to-wear; designed printed sheet collection for Cantoni Casa, 1977. Designed: two collections for Internat. Wool Secretariat, 1975–77; English Country House Collection for Sekers Internat., 1981–82 (collection used when redesigned Long Gall., Lutyen's British Embassy, Washington); English Gardens and Botanic Collections for Romanex de Boussac, France, 1982–85. Designed costumes: films: Genevieve, 1953; Next To No Time, 1955; The Admirable Crichton, 1957; musical: Marigold, 1958; opera: Cosi fan tutte (Glyndebourne), 1962. Mem., Adv. Panel, National Dip. of Design, 1964–66; Governor, Croydon Coll. of Art, 1966–67. FRSA 1967, resigned 1977. Illustrated articles on his work have appeared in the Press. *Recreations:* looking at large well-built walls and buildings; passionate conservationist and environmentalist, collector, bibliophil; tree-worship, chamber music. *Address:* West House, 35 Glebe Place, SW3; Fonthill Abbey, Fonthill Gifford, near Salisbury, Wilts.

NEVILL, Maj.-Gen. Cosmo Alexander Richard, CB 1958; CBE 1954; DSO 1944; War Office, 1958–60; Colonel, Royal Fusiliers, 1959–63, retired; *b* 14 July 1907; *s* of late Maj. Cosmo Charles Richard Nevill, DSO, OBE, Eccleston, Leamington Spa; *m* 1934, Grania, *d* of late Maj. G. V. Goodliffe, MC, Birdstown, co. Donegal; one *s* one *d*. *Educ:* Harrow; Royal Military College. Commissioned as Second Lieutenant, Royal Fusiliers, 1927; served War of 1939–45 (DSO, OBE): on staff, India; commanded 2nd battalion Devonshire Regiment, Normandy; Lieutenant-Colonel, 1944. A General Staff Officer, Military Staff Committee, United Nations, New York, 1946–48; commanded 1st battalion Royal Fusiliers, 1950–51; temporary Brigadier, 1951; a Brigade Commander, 1951–54; Commandant School of Infantry, 1954–56; Major-General 1957; GOC 2nd Infantry Division, 1956–58. CC West Suffolk, 1962–67. Lay Canon, St Edmundsbury Cathedral, 1979–85. *Address:* Holt, Edwardstone, Boxford, Suffolk CO6 5PJ. *T:* Boxford 210428. *Club:* Army and Navy.

NEVILLE, family name of **Baron Braybrooke.**

NEVILLE, Prof. Adam Matthew, MC 1944; TD 1963; FEng 1986; FRSE 1979; Principal and Vice-Chancellor, University of Dundee, since 1978; consultant on concrete and structural design and failures; *b* 5 Feb. 1923; *m* 1952, Mary Hallam Cousins; one *s* one *d*. BSc 1st cl. Hons, MSc, PhD, DSc (Eng) London; DSc Leeds; FICE, FIStructE, FAmSCE, MSocCE (France), FCIArb. Lectr, Southampton Univ., 1950–51; Engr, Min. of Works, NZ, 1951–54; Lectr, Manchester Univ., 1955–60; Prof. of Civil Engrg, Nigerian Coll. of Technology, 1960–62; Dean of Engrg, Calgary Univ., 1963–67, also Dean of Graduate Studies, 1965–66; Vis. Prof., Swiss Federal Inst. of Technology, 1967–68; Prof. and Head of Dept of Civil Engineering, Univ. of Leeds, 1968–78. Former Chm., Permanent Concrete Commn, RILEM (Internat. Union of Testing and Res. Labs for Materials and Structures); Dir, Petroleum Recovery Res. Inst.; Advr to Canadian Govt on management of concrete research. Member Council: Concrete Soc., 1968–77, Pres., 1974–75; IStructE, 1976–79; Faculty of Building, 1976–80; Open University, 1979–; Council of Europe Standing Conference on Univ. Problems, 1980– (Pres., 1984–86); Member: Bd, Architectural Educn, ARC, 1980–; Exec. Cttee, IUPC, 1979– (Vice-Chm., 1983–85). Mem. Editorial Boards of various technical jls. Fellow, Amer. Concrete Inst., 1973, Hon. Mem., 1986; Hon. Fellow, Inst. of Concrete Technologists, 1976; For. Mem., Académie Royale des Sciences d'Outre-Mer, Belgium, 1974. IStructE Research Award, 1960; Reinforced Concrete Assoc. Medal, 1961; Senior Research Fellowship, Nat. Research Council of Canada, 1967. Stanton Walker Award (US) 1968; Medal of Univ. of Liège (Belgium), 1970; Arthur R. Anderson Award, Amer. Concrete Inst., 1972; President's Medal, Soc. of Engrs, 1985. OStJ 1983. *Publications:* Properties of Concrete, 1963, 3 edns, trans. into 9 languages; (with J. B. Kennedy) Basic Statistical Methods, 1964, 3 edns; Creep of Concrete: plain, reinforced and prestressed, 1970; (with A. Ghali) Structural Analysis: a unified classical and matrix approach, 1971, 2 edns, trans. into Chinese; Hardened Concrete: physical and mechanical aspects, 1971; High Alumina Cement Concrete, 1975; (with W. H. Dilger and J. J. Brooks) Creep of Plain and Structural Concrete, 1983; numerous research papers on concrete and concrete structures. *Recreations:* ski-ing, travel. *Address:* The University, Dundee. *Clubs:* Athenæum, Caledonian.

NEVILLE, Prof. (Alexander) Munro, MD; FRCPath; Research Administrator, Ludwig Institute for Cancer Research, since 1985; *b* 24 March 1935; *s* of Alexander Munro and Georgina Neville; *m* 1961, Anne Margaret Stroyan Black; one *s* one *d*. *Educ:* Hillhead High Sch.; Univ. of Glasgow (MB ChB 1959; PhD 1965; MD 1969); Harvard Med. Sch.; DSc London, 1985. MRCPath 1969, FRCPath 1981. Med. appts, Glasgow Royal and Victoria Infirmaries, 1960–65; Res. Fellow, Harvard Med. Sch., 1965–67; Sen. Lectr in Pathology, Univ. of Glasgow, 1967–70; Hon. Consultant Pathologist, Royal Marsden Hosp., 1970–85; Prof. of Experimental Pathology, Univ. of London, 1972–85; Dean, Inst. of Cancer Research, 1982–84; Dir, Ludwig Inst. for Cancer Research, London Branch, 1975–85. *Publications:* The Human Adrenal Cortex, 1982; numerous papers on oncology and pathology in primary jls. *Recreations:* golf, gardening. *Address:* Feldblumenstrasse 125, 8136 Adliswil, Switzerland. *T:* 01–710 9409; Flat 6, 42 Eagle Street, WC1R 4AP. *T:* 01–405 9005. *Club:* Banstead Downs.

NEVILLE, (Eric) Graham; His Honour Judge Neville; a Circuit Judge, since 1980; *b* 12 Nov. 1933; *s* of late Frederick Thomas Neville and Doris Winifred (*née* Toye); *m* 1966, Jacqueline Catherine, *d* of late Major Francis Whalley and Alexandrina Whalley (*née* MacLeod). *Educ:* Kelly Coll.; Sidney Sussex Coll., Cambridge. Served Royal Air Force, General Duties. Called to Bar, Middle Temple, 1958. A Recorder of the Crown Court, 1975–80. *Recreations:* sailing, fishing. *Address:* Trillow House, Nadderwater, Exeter EX4 2LD. *T:* Exeter 54403. *Clubs:* Royal Western Yacht (Plymouth); Royal Fowey; Valletta Yacht.

NEVILLE, John, OBE 1965; actor, stage and film; Hon. Professor in Drama, Nottingham University, since 1967; Artistic Director, Festival Theatre, Stratford, Ontario, since 1985; *b* Willesden, 2 May 1925; *s* of Reginald Daniel Neville and Mabel Lillian (*née* Fry); *m* 1949, Caroline Hooper; three *s* three *d*. *Educ:* Willesden and Chiswick County Schools; Royal Academy of Dramatic Art. Worked as a stores clerk before studying at RADA. First appearance on stage, walking-on part in Richard II; subseq. parts at Open Air Theatre, in repertory at Lowestoft, and with Birmingham Repertory Co.; Bristol Old Vic Co., 1950–53; Old Vic Co., London, 1953–61; Nottingham Playhouse, 1961–63; Theatre Director, Nottingham Playhouse, 1963–68; Dir, Park Theatre Co., Fortune, 1969; Theatre Director: Citadel Theatre, Edmonton, Canada, 1973–78; Neptune Theatre, Halifax, NS, 1978–83. Parts with Old Vic include: Ferdinand in The Tempest, Macduff, Richard II, Orlando in As You Like It, Henry Percy in Henry IV, Part I, Mark Antony; during Old Vic tour of Europe, 1958, Hamlet, Sir Andrew Aguecheek. Played lead in Irma La Douce, Lyric, 1959–60; produced Henry V, Old Vic, 1960; The Lady From the Sea, Queen's, 1961; The School for Scandal, Haymarket, 1962; Alfie, Mermaid and Duchess, 1963. Acted in: The Chichester Festival Theatre, 1962; Beware of the Dog, St Martin's, 1967; Iago in Othello, Nottingham Playhouse, 1967; Mr and Mrs, Palace, 1968; The Apple Cart, Mermaid, 1970; The Beggar's Opera, The Doctor's Dilemma, Chichester, 1972; Sherlock Holmes, NY, 1975; Happy Days, Nat. Theatre, 1977; Grand Theatre, London, Ontario: acted in Dear Antoine and Arsenic and Old Lace, directed Hamlet, 1983; Stratford, Ontario: acted in Loves Labours' Lost, 1983, Merchant of Venice, 1984. Tour W Africa (Jt Dir and acting), 1963. *Films:* Oscar Wilde; Topaze; Billy Budd; A Study in Terror. Has appeared on television, incl. The First Churchills, series for BBC 2. Hon. Dr Dramatic Arts Lethbridge Univ., 1979; Hon. DFA Nova Scotia Coll. of Art and Design, 1981. *Address:* 99 Norman Street, Stratford, Ont N5A 5R8, Canada; c/o Larry Dalzell Associates, 3 Goodwin's Court, St Martin's Lane, WC2.

NEVILLE, (John) Oliver, MA, PhD; Principal, Royal Academy of Dramatic Art, since 1984; *b* 14 Aug. 1929; *s* of Frederick and Ethel Neville; *m* 1st, 1952, Shirley Hall; one *s* one *d*; 2nd, 1964, Pat Heywood. *Educ:* Price's Sch., Fareham; King's Coll., Cambridge (Le Bas Student; BA Eng. Lit., MA, PhD). After National Service, engaged in following with ultimate aim of becoming a theatre director: studied theatre design under Reginald Leefe, 1949–51; joined Old Vic Co., walking on in Tyrone Guthrie's Tamburlaine, with Donald Wolfit, 1951; studied singing with Clive Carey and Frank Titterton; seasons of rep. at York, Scarborough, Worthing, Bristol, Birmingham and Manchester, 1952–58; re-joined Old Vic Co., 1958 (roles included Warwick in Henry VI Trilogy and Claudius in Hamlet); toured America, Poland, Russia, India, Pakistan, Ceylon, with Old Vic and Bristol Old Vic, as stage dir, actor and dir; Associate Dir, Old Vic Co., 1960–62 (directed Macbeth and The Tempest); Director: Library Theatre, Manchester, 1963–66; Arts Theatre, Ipswich, 1966–69; Mature Student, Cambridge, 1969–76 (PhD on Ben Jonson's Masques and Poetry); Caroline Spurgeon Res. Fellow, Bedford Coll., London, 1977–79; Sen. Lectr in Drama, Univ. of Bristol, 1979–84. *Recreations:* mediaeval church architecture and stained-glass, gardening. *Address:* Royal Academy of Dramatic Art, 62–64 Gower Street, WC1E 6ED. *T:* 01–636 7076.

NEVILLE, Munro; *see* Neville, A. M.

NEVILLE, Sir Richard (Lionel John Baines), 3rd Bt *cr* 1927; *b* 15 July 1921; *s* of Sir Reginald James Neville Neville, 1st Bt (*d* 1950), and Violet Sophia Mary (*d* 1972), *widow* of Captain Richard Jocelyn Hunter, Rifle Bde and *d* of Lt-Col Cuthbert Johnson Baines, Gloucester Regt, The Lawn, Shirehampton, Glos; *S* half-brother, 1982; unmarried. *Educ:* Eton; Trinity Coll., Cambridge (BA 1941, MA 1948). Served War of 1939–45: joined Army, 1941; Captain, Oxford and Bucks Light Infantry; seconded Royal West African Frontier Force (1st Gold Coast Regt), Burma Campaign, 1944–45. Journalist and Director of English Broadcasts of Radio-Télévision Française (RTF), Indochina, 1953–55; Dir of Foreign Broadcasts, RTF (English, Spanish and Portuguese), French Equatorial Africa (Congo), 1956–57; Algeria, 1957–60. Master, Worshipful Co. of Bowyers, 1972–74. *Recreations:* history, genealogy, heraldry and supporting lost causes. *Heir:* none. *Address:* Sloley Hall, Norwich NR12 8HA. *T:* Swanton Abbott 236.

NEVILLE, Maj.-Gen. Sir Robert Arthur Ross, KCMG 1952; CBE 1948; late RM; *b* 17 Dec. 1896; *s* of late Col William Neville, DSO, Cheshire Regt; *m* 1943, Doris Marie (*d* 1977), *y d* of late Capt. Philip Collen, 14th Sikh Regiment; one *s* one *d*. *Educ:* Cheltenham College. Joined Royal Marines, 1914, served European War, 1914–18, Grand Fleet and France (despatches); Lt-Col, 1940; served War of 1939–45, Admlty, as Asst Dir of Naval Intelligence, Combined Ops, and in Mediterranean; Colonel, 1945; ADC to the King, 1946–48; Maj.-Gen., 1948. Governor and C-in-C, Bahamas, 1950–Dec. 1953. Dir, Epsylon Industries Ltd, 1954–61; Chm., Vectron Electronics, 1961–66. *Address:* Townsend Wood, Sutton Mandeville, Salisbury, Wiltshire. *Club:* White's.

NEVILLE, Royce Robert; Agent-General for Tasmania, in London, 1971–78; Governing Director, Neville Constructions Pty Ltd, Burnie; *b* 5 Oct. 1914; *s* of R. P. Neville, Launceston, Tasmania; *m* 1941, Joan, *d* of G. A. Scott; two *s* one *d*. *Educ:* Launceston Technical Coll. Served War, Sqdn Ldr (OC Flying, Chief Flying Instr, Gen Reconnaissance Sqdn), RAAF, 1941–45. OC Air Trg Corps, Burnie, 1947. Past President: Air Force Assoc., 1947; Tas. Apex, 1948; Tas. Master Builders' Assoc., 1965–67; Master Builders' Fedn of Aust., 1965–66; Comr of Oaths for Tasmania, 1971; Mem., Australia Soc.,

London; Life Mem., Tasmanian Master Builders' Assoc. FInstD, FRAIB, AFAIM, Fellow, Inst. of Dirs, Aust., 1971; MIEx 1973; FFB 1976; FIArb 1977. Freeman, City of London, 1975; Freeman, Guild of Air Pilots and Air Navigators, 1976. JP 1974. *Recreations:* boating, fishing, water skiing, painting, tennis. *Address:* 29 Seaview Avenue, Burnie, Tasmania 7320, Australia. *Clubs:* Wig and Pen; Naval, Military and Air Force (Hobart).

NEVILLE-JONES, (Lilian) Pauline; HM Diplomatic Service; Head of Planning Staff, Foreign and Commonwealth Office, since 1983; *b* 2 Nov. 1939; *d* of Roland Neville-Jones and Cecilia Emily Millicent Rath. *Educ:* Leeds Girls' High Sch.; Lady Margaret Hall, Oxford (BA Hons Mod. History). Harkness Fellow of Commonwealth Fund, USA, 1961–63; joined FO, 1963; Third Sec., Salisbury, Rhodesia, 1964–65; Third, later Second Sec., Singapore, 1965–68; FCO, 1968–71; First Sec., Washington, 1971–75; FCO, 1975–77; Mem. Cabinet, later Chef de Cabinet to Christopher Tugendhat, European Comr for Budget, Financial Control, Financial Instns and Taxation, 1977–82; Vis. Fellow, RIIA, and Inst. français des relations internationales, 1982–83. FRSA. *Recreations:* antiques, cooking, gardening. *Address:* 3 Donne Place, SW3. *T:* 01–581 3274.

NEVIN, His Honour (Thomas) Richard, TD 1949 (and Bar); JP; LLB; retired 1984, as senior Circuit Judge on NE Circuit; a Judge of County Courts, later a Circuit Judge, 1967–84; a Deputy High Court Judge, 1974–84; Hon. Life Member, Council of HM Circuit Judges; *b* 9 Dec. 1916; *e s* of late Thomas Nevin, JP, and Phyllis (*née* Strickland), Ebchester Hall and Mirfield; *m* 1955, Brenda Micaela (marr. diss. 1979), *e d* of Dr B. C. Andrade-Thompson, MC, Scarborough; one *s* (and one *s* decd). *Educ:* Bilton Grange; Shrewsbury School; Leeds University. LLB 1939. 2nd Lt, W Yorks Regt (Leeds Rifles) TA, 1935. Served London Bombardment, India and Burma, 1939–46; Indian Artillery, Lt-Col 1944 (despatches), SEAC; DJAG, XII Army, 1945. Major, TARO, 1951. WR Special Constab., 1938–66. Articled Clerk to Sir A. M. Ramsden, CB, Solicitor, 1935. Called to Bar, Inner Temple, 1948; practised 19 years on NE Circuit (Junior, 1951); Law Lectr, Leeds Coll. of Commerce, 1949–51; Asst Recorder of Leeds, 1961–64; Recorder of Doncaster, 1964–67; Dep. Chm., Quarter Sessions: W Riding, 1965–71; E Riding, 1968–71, Yorkshire; Chm., Northern Agricultural Land Tribunal, 1963–67 (Dep. Chm. 1961–63); a special Divorce Comr, 1967–72; Mem., County Court Rule Cttee, 1974–80; Chm., Lord Chancellor's Adv. Cttee on JP's, Hull, 1968–74; Founder Chm., Leeds Family Mediation Service, 1979–84. Director, Bowishott Estates Ltd; Member: Leeds Gp Hospital Management Cttee, 1965–67; Thoresby Soc.; Yorks Archæological Soc.; President, Yorks Numismatic Soc., 1968; Life Member: Guild of Freemen of London; British Numismatic Soc.; Vice-Pres. Leeds Univ. Law Graduates; Mem., Leeds Univ. Adv. Cttee on Law. FRNS; FRSA; FCIArb. Freeman of City of London. JP West Yorks 1965–. *Publications:* Hon. Editor, Yorkshire Numismatic Soc.; and various articles. *Recreations:* coinage, our past, gardening, and rest therefrom. *Address:* The Court House, 1 Oxford Row, Leeds; 11 King's Bench Walk, Temple, EC4.

NEW, Maj.-Gen. Laurence Anthony Wallis, CB 1986; CBE 1980; Lieutenant Governor of the Isle of Man, since 1985; *b* 25 Feb. 1932; *s* of Lt-Col S. W. New, MBE and Mrs C. M. New; *m* 1956, Anna Doreen Verity; two *s* two *d. Educ:* King William's College, Isle of Man; RMA Sandhurst. RMA, 1950–52; commissioned, RTR, 1952; service in Hong Kong, Germany, Malaya, Borneo; CO 4 RTR, 1971–73; Bde Major, 20th Armd Bde, 1969–70; Sec., Defence Policy Staff, 1970–71; Defence and Military Attaché, Tel Aviv, 1974–77; Col GS, MoD, 1977–79; Brig. GS, MoD, 1981–82; ACGS (Op. Reqs), 1983–84; ACDS (Land Systems), MoD, 1985; graduate Staff Coll., JSSC, RCDS. Col Comdt, RTR, 1986–. Licenced Reader, C of E; Church Warden, St Peter upon Cornhill, 1986. Pres., Soldiers' and Airmen's Scripture Readers Assoc., 1985–; Chm., Officers' Christian Union, 1981–83. County Pres., St John Ambulance Brigade and Assoc., 1985; Pres., Manx Music Fest., 1985; Chairman: Bishop Barrow's Trustees, 1985; Prince's Trust (IoM), 1986. Pres., White House School, Wokingham, 1985–. Freeman, City of London, 1985; Liveryman, Glass Sellers' Co., 1985. FBIM 1979; CBIM 1986. KStJ 1986. *Recreations:* music, walking, family tennis, sailing. *Address:* Government House, Isle of Man. *Club:* Army and Navy.

NEW WESTMINSTER, Archbishop of, since 1981; **Most Rev. Douglas Walter Hambidge,** DD; Metropolitan of the Ecclesiastical Province of British Columbia, since 1981; *b* London, England, 6 March 1927; *s* of Douglas Hambidge and Florence (*née* Driscoll); *m* 1956, Denise Colvill Lown; two *s* one *d. Educ:* London Univ.; London Coll. of Divinity. BD, ALCD; DD, Anglican Theol. Coll. of BC, 1970. Asst Curate, St Mark's, Dalston, 1953–56; Rector: All Saints, Cassiar, BC, 1956–58; St James, Smithers, BC, 1958–64; Vicar, St Martin, Fort St John, BC, 1964–69; Canon, St Andrew's Cathedral, Caledonia, 1965–69; Bishop of Caledonia, 1969–80; Bishop of New Westminster, 1980. Pres., Missions to Seamen, 1980–; Mem. Bd of Governors, Vancouver Sch. of Theology, 1981–86. *Address:* #302–814 Richards Street, Vancouver, BC V6B 3A7, Canada. *T:* (604) 684–6306. *Clubs:* University, Arbutus (Vancouver).

NEW ZEALAND, Primate and Archbishop of, since 1986; **Most Rev. Brian Newton Davis;** Bishop of Wellington, since 1986; *b* 28 Oct. 1934; *s* of Leonard Lancelot and Ethel May Davis; *m* 1961, Marie Lynette Waters: four *d. Educ:* Stratford Primary and Technical High School; Ardmore Teachers' Training Coll., Auckland; Victoria Univ. of Wellington (MA 1st class Hons Geog.); Christchurch Theol Coll. (LTh). Teacher, Stratford Primary School, 1954; Laboratory Asst, Victoria Univ., 1958. Deacon 1960, priest 1961; Assistant Curate: St Mark's, Wellington, 1960–62; Parish of Karori and Makara, 1962–64; Vicar: Makara and Karori West, 1964–67; Dannevirke, 1967–73; Cathedral Parish of St John the Evangelist and Dean of Waiapu, 1973; Vicar General of Waiapu, 1979–80; Bishop of Waikato, 1980–86. *Publication:* (contrib.) An Encyclopaedia of New Zealand, 1966. *Recreations:* tennis, wood carving and turning, water colour painting. *Address:* Bishopscourt, 28 Eccleston Hill, Wellington, New Zealand.

NEWALL, family name of **Baron Newall.**

NEWALL, 2nd Baron, *cr* 1946; **Francis Storer Eaton Newall;** company director and Chairman of several companies; Chairman, British Greyhound Racing Board, since 1985; *b* 23 June 1930; *o s* of 1st Baron (Marshal of the RAF Lord) Newall, GCB, OM, GCMG, CBE, AM; *S* father, 1963; *m* 1956, Pamela Elizabeth, *e d* of E. H. L. Rowcliffe, Pinkney Park, Malmesbury, Wilts; two *s* one *d. Educ:* Eton College; RMA Sandhurst. Commissioned into 11th Hussars (Prince Albert's Own), 1950; served in: Germany, 1950–53; Malaya, 1953–55; on staff of GHQ FarELF, Singapore, 1955–56; Adjt Royal Gloucestershire Hussars, 1956–58; retired 1961. Introduced Farriers Registration Acts and Betting Gaming and Lotteries Amendment Acts (Greyhound Racing) in House of Lords. Cons. Whip and front bench spokesman, 1976–79; Founder Mem., House of Lords all party Defence Study Group; official visits to NATO, SHAPE, Norway, Morocco, Bonn, Cyprus, BAOR, Qatar, Oman, Bahrain; Deleg. to Council of Europe and WEU, 1983. Mem., Select Cttee on Laboratory Animals Protection Bill. Hon. Pres., Corp. of Insurance and Financial Advisors (formerly Corp. of Mortgage Brokers). Mem., Merchant Taylors' Co (Master, 1985–86). *Recreations:* shooting, travel, meeting people. *Heir: s* Hon. Richard Hugh Eaton Newall, *b* 19 Feb. 1961. *Address:* 18 Lennox Gardens, SW1X 0DG; Wotton Underwood, near Aylesbury, Bucks. *Club:* Cavalry and Guards.

NEWARK, Archdeacon of; *see* Leaning, Ven. D.

NEWBIGGING, David Kennedy, OBE 1982; Deputy Chairman, Provincial Group PLC (formerly Provincial Insurance PLC), since 1985 (Director, since 1984); Director: Rentokil Group PLC, since 1986; PACCAR (UK) Ltd, since 1986; Mason Best International, since 1986; International Financial Markets Trading Ltd, since 1986; Member, National Coal Board (trading as British Coal), since 1984; *b* 19 Jan. 1934; *s* of late David Locke Newbigging, CBE, MC, and Lucy Margaret; *m* 1968, Carolyn Susan (*née* Band); one *s* two *d. Educ:* in Canada; Oundle Sch., Northants. Joined Jardine, Matheson & Co. Ltd, Hong Kong, 1954; Man. Dir, 1970; Sen. Man. Dir, 1975–83; Chairman: Hongkong & Kowloon Wharf & Godown Co. Ltd, 1970–80; Jardine Matheson & Co. Ltd, 1975–83; Jardine Fleming & Co. Ltd, 1975–83; Hongkong Land Co. Ltd, 1975–83; Hongkong Electric Holdings Ltd, 1982–83 (Dir, 1975–83); Director: Hongkong & Shanghai Banking Corp., 1975–83; Hong Kong Telephone Co., 1975–83; Safmarine and Rennies Holdings (formerly Rennies Consolidated Holdings), 1975–85. Mem., Internat. Council, Morgan Guaranty Trust Co. of NY, 1977–85. Member: Hong Kong Exec. Council, 1980–84; Hong Kong Legislative Council, 1978–82. Chairman: Hong Kong Tourist Assoc., 1977–82; Hong Kong Gen. Chamber of Commerce, 1980–82; Steward, Royal Hong Kong Jockey Club, 1975–84. JP (unofficial) Hong Kong, 1971. *Recreations:* most outdoor sports; Chinese art. *Address:* 103 Mount Street, W1Y 5HE. *T:* 01–499 7526. *Clubs:* Boodle's, Turf, Hurlingham; Hongkong (Hong Kong).

NEWBIGIN, Rt. Rev. (James Edward) Lesslie, CBE 1974; DD; Minister, United Reformed Church, Winson Green, since 1980; *b* 8 Dec. 1909; *s* of Edward Richmond Newbigin, Shipowner, Newcastle, and Annie Ellen Newbigin (*née* Affleck); *m* 1936, Helen Stewart, *d* of Rev. Robert Henderson; one *s* three *d. Educ:* Leighton Park Sch.; Queens' Coll., Cambridge; Westminster Coll., Cambridge. Intercollegiate Secretary, Student Christian Movement, Glasgow, 1931–33. Ordained by Presbytery of Edinburgh and appointed to Madras Mission of Church of Scotland, 1936; served as missionary in Chingleput and Kancheepuram, 1936–46; Bishop in Madura and Ramnad, Church of South India, 1947. Chairman, Advisory Cttee on Main Theme for Second Assembly, World Council of Churches, 1954; Vice-Chairman, Commission on Faith and Order, 1956; Chairman, International Missionary Council, 1958. Resigned from See of Madura, 1959. General Secretary, International Missionary Council, 1959; Associate General Secretary, World Council of Churches, 1959–65; Bishop in Madras, 1965–74; Lectr in Theology, Selly Oak Colls, Birmingham, 1974–79. Moderator, Gen. Assembly of URC, 1978. Hon. DD: Chicago Theological Seminary, 1954; St Andrews Univ., 1958; Hamburg, 1960; Basel, 1965; Hull, 1975; Newcastle, 1981. *Publications:* Christian Freedom in the Modern World, 1937; The Reunion of the Church, 1948; South India Diary, 1951; The Household of God, 1953; Sin and Salvation, 1956; A Faith for This One World?, 1962; Honest Religion for Secular Man, 1966; The Finality of Christ, 1969; The Good Shepherd, 1977; The Open Secret, 1978; The Light has come, 1982; The Other Side of 1984, 1983; Unfinished Agenda, 1985; Foolishness to the Greeks, 1986. *Recreations:* music, walking. *Address:* 15 Fox Hill, Birmingham B29 4AG.

NEWBOLD, Sir Charles Demorée, KBE 1970; Kt 1966; CMG 1957; QC (Jamaica) 1947; President, Court of Appeal for East Africa, 1966–70; *b* 11 June 1909; *s* of late Charles Etches and Laura May Newbold; *m* 1936, Ruth, *d* of Arthur L. Vaughan; two *d. Educ:* The Lodge Sch., Barbados; Keble Coll., Oxford (BA). Called to Bar, Gray's Inn, 1931. Private practice at the Bar, Trinidad, 1931–35; joined Colonial Legal Service, 1936, as Principal Officer, Supreme Court Registry, Trinidad; Magistrate, Trinidad, 1937; Legal Draftsman, Jamaica, 1941; Solicitor-General Jamaica, 1943; Member of Commission of Enquiry into Land Taxation, Jamaica, 1942–43; represented Jamaica at Quarantine Conf. in Trinidad, 1943; at US Bases Conf. in Trinidad, 1944; at Washington, USA, for labour contracts, 1945; Actg Attorney-Gen., 1946; Legal Secretary, East Africa High Commn, 1948–61. Mem. of East Africa Central Legislative Assembly, 1948–61 (Chm. of Committee of Supply, 1948–61); Commissioner for Revision of High Commn Laws, 1951; Vice-Chm. Governing Council of Royal Technical Coll., 1954–59; Justice of Appeal, Court of Appeal for Eastern Africa, 1961–65; Vice-Pres., 1965–66. Star of Africa (Liberia). *Publications:* Joint Editor of Trinidad Law Reports, 1928–33; Editor of East African Tax Cases Reports, 1948–61. *Recreations:* cricket, tennis, croquet, reading. *Address:* Low Water, Harbour Way, Bosham, W Sussex.

NEWBOROUGH, 7th Baron, *cr* 1776; **Robert Charles Michael Vaughan Wynn,** Bt 1742; DSC 1942; *b* 24 April 1917; *er s* of 6th Baron Newborough, OBE, JP, DL, and Ruby Irene (*d* 1960), 3rd *d* of Edmund Wigley Severne, of Thenford, Northamptonshire and Wallop, Shropshire; *S* father, 1965; *m* 1st, 1945, Rosamund Lavington Barbour (marr. diss. 1971); one *s* two *d*; 2nd, 1971, Jennifer, *y d* of late Captain C. C. A. Allen, RN, and Lady Morgan. *Educ:* Oundle. Served as 2nd Lt, SR, 1935–39, with 9th Lancers, 5th Inniskilling Dragoon Guards, then as Lt with 16th/5th Lancers after 6 months attachment with Royal Dragoon Guards; invalided out of Army, 1940. Took command of vessel attached to Fleet Air Arm, 1940, as civilian, and took part in Dunkirk evacuation; then joined RNVR as Sub Lieut; later had command of MTB 74 and took part in St Nazaire raid, 1942 (wounded, despatches, DSC, POW, escaped from Colditz 1944). High Sheriff of Merionethshire, 1963. *Recreation:* yachting. *Heir: s* Hon. Robert Vaughan Wynn [*b* 11 Aug. 1949; *m* 1981, Sheila Christine, *d* of William A. Massey; one *d*]. *Address:* Rhug, Corwen, Clwyd, North Wales. *T:* Corwen 2510. *Clubs:* Goat, Naval and Military.

NEWBURGH, 12th Earl of, *cr* 1660 (Scot.); **Don Filippo Giambattista Francesco Aldo Maria Rospigliosi;** Viscount Kynnaird, Baron Levingston, 1660; 11th Prince Rospigliosi (Holy Roman Empire), 11th Duke of Zagarolo, 14th Prince of Castiglione, Marquis of Giuliana, Count of Chiusa, Baron of La Miraglia and Valcorrente, Lord of Aidone, Burgio, Contessa and Trappeto, and Conscript Roman Noble, Patrician of Venice, Genoa and Pistoia; *b* 4 July 1942; *s* of 11th Earl of Newburgh and of Donna Giulia, *d* of Don Guido Carlo dei Duchi, Visconti di Mondrone, Count of Lonate Pozzolo; *S* father, 1986; *m* 1972, Baronessa Donna Luisa, *d* of Count Annibale Caccia Dominioni; one *d.* *Heir: d* Princess Donna Benedetta Francesca Maria Rospigliosi, *b* 4 June 1974. *Address:* Piazza Sant'Ambrogio 16, 20123 Milan, Italy.

NEWBY, (George) Eric, MC 1945; FRSL 1972; FRGS 1975; writer; *b* 6 Dec. 1919; *o s* of George Arthur Newby and Hilda Pomeroy, London; *m* 1946, Wanda, *d* of Viktor Skof and Gisella Urdih, Trieste; one *s* one *d. Educ:* St Paul's School. With Dorland Advertising, London, 1936–38; apprentice and ord. seaman, 4-masted Finnish barque, Moshulu, 1938–39; served War of 1939–45, The Black Watch and Special Boat Section, POW 1942–45; Women's Fashion Business, 1946–56 (with Worth Paquin, 1955–56); explored in Nuristan and made unsuccessful attempt to climb Mir Samir, Afghan Hindu Kush, 1956; with Secker & Warburg, 1956–59; with John Lewis Partnership (Central Buyer, Model Dresses), 1959–63; descended Ganges with wife, 1963. Travel Editor, The Observer, and Gen. Editor, Time Off Books, 1964–73. Mem., Assoc. of Cape Horners. *Publications:* The Last Grain Race, 1956; A Short Walk in the Hindu Kush, 1958; Something Wholesale, 1962; Slowly Down the Ganges, 1966; Time Off in Southern Italy, 1966; Grain Race: Pictures of Life Before the Mast in a Windjammer, 1968; (jointly) The Wonders of Britain, 1968; (jointly) The Wonders of Ireland, 1969; Love and War in the Apennines, 1971; (jointly) The World of Evelyn Waugh, 1973; Ganga (with photographs by Raghubir Singh), 1973; World Atlas of Exploration, 1975; Great Ascents, 1977; The Big Red Train Ride, 1978; A Traveller's Life, 1982; On the Shores of the Mediterranean, 1984; A Book of Travellers' Tales, 1985. *Recreations:* walking, running, cycling, gardening. *Address:* West Bucknowle House, Bucknowle, Wareham, Dorset BH20 5PQ. *T:* Corfe Castle 480374. *Club:* Garrick.

NEWBY, (Percy) Howard, CBE 1972; novelist; *b* 25 June 1918; *o s* of Percy Newby and Isabel Clutsam Newby (*née* Bryant); *m* 1945, Joan Thompson; two *d*. *Educ:* Hanley Castle Grammar Sch., Worcester; St Paul's Coll., Cheltenham. Served War of 1939 45, RAMC, 1939–42; BEF, France, 1939–40; MEF, 1941–42; seconded as Lecturer in English Literature, Fouad 1st University, Cairo, 1942–46. Joined BBC, 1949; Controller: Third Programme, 1958–69; Radio Three, 1969–71; Dir of Programmes, Radio, 1971–75; Man. Dir, BBC Radio, 1975–78. Chm., English Stage Co., 1978–84. Atlantic Award, 1946; Somerset Maugham Prize, 1948; Yorkshire Post Fiction Award, 1968; Booker Prize, 1969 (first recipient). *Publications:* A Journey to the Interior, 1945; Agents and Witnesses, 1947; The Spirit of Jem, 1947; Mariner Dances, 1948; The Snow Pasture, 1949; The Loot Runners, 1949; Maria Edgeworth, 1950; The Young May Moon, 1950; The Novel, 1945–50, 1951; A Season in England, 1951; A Step to Silence, 1952; The Retreat, 1953; The Picnic at Sakkara, 1955; Revolution and Roses, 1957; Ten Miles from Anywhere, 1958; A Guest and his Going, 1959; The Barbary Light, 1962; One of the Founders, 1965; Something to Answer For, 1968; A Lot to Ask, 1973; Kith, 1977; (with F. Maroon) The Egypt Story, 1979; Warrior Pharaohs, 1980; Feelings Have Changed, 1981; Saladin in his Time, 1984; Leaning in the Wind, 1986. *Address:* Garsington House, Garsington, Oxford OX9 9AB. *T:* Garsington 420.

NEWCASTLE, 9th Duke of, *cr* 1756; **Henry Edward Hugh Pelham-Clinton-Hope,** OBE 1945; Earl of Lincoln, 1572; Wing Comdr, retd; *b* 8 April 1907; *o s* of 8th Duke and Olive Muriel (*d* 1912), *d* of George Horatio Thompson, banker, Melbourne, formerly wife of Richard Owen; *S* father 1941; *m* 1st, 1931, Jean (from whom he obtained a divorce 1940), *d* of D. Banks, Park Avenue, New York; 2nd, 1946, Lady Mary Diana Montagu-Stuart-Wortley (marr. diss., 1959), 2nd *d* of 3rd Earl of Wharncliffe; two *d*; 3rd, 1959, Mrs Sally Ann Wemyss Hope (Jamal), *d* of Brig. John Henry Anstice, DSO. *Educ:* Eton; Cambridge. Sqdn Ldr Comdg No 616 Sqdn, 1938–39; served War of 1939–45 in RAF at home and overseas. *Heir:* cousin Edward Charles Pelham-Clinton, *b* 18 Aug. 1920. *Address:* 5 Quay Hill, Lymington, Hants SO4 9AB.

NEWCASTLE, Bishop of, since 1981; **Rt. Rev. Andrew Alexander Kenny Graham;** *b* 7 Aug. 1929; *o s* of late Andrew Harrison and Magdalene Graham; unmarried. *Educ:* Tonbridge Sch.; St John's Coll., Oxford; Ely Theological College. Curate of Hove Parish Church, 1955–58; Chaplain and Lectr in Theology, Worcester Coll., Oxford, 1958–70; Fellow and Tutor, 1960–70, Hon. Fellow, 1981; Warden of Lincoln Theological Coll., 1970–77; Canon and Prebendary of Lincoln Cathedral, 1970–77. Examining Chaplain to: Bishop of Carlisle, 1967–77; Bishop of Bradford, 1972–77; Bishop of Lincoln, 1973–77; Bishop Suffragan of Bedford, 1977–81. Chm., ACCM, 1984–. *Recreation:* hill walking. *Address:* Bishop's House, 29 Moor Road South, Newcastle upon Tyne NE3 1PA. *T:* Tyneside 2852220. *Club:* United Oxford & Cambridge University.

NEWCASTLE, Provost of; *see* Spafford, Very Rev. C. G. H.

NEWCASTLE, NSW, Bishop of, since 1978; **Rt. Rev. Alfred Charles Holland;** *b* 23 Feb. 1927; *s* of Alfred Charles Holland and Maud Allison; *m* 1954, Joyce Marion Embling; three *s* one *d*. *Educ:* Raine's Sch., London; Univ. of Durham (BA 1950, DipTh 1952). RNVR, 1945–47; Univ. of Durham, 1948–52; Assistant Priest, West Hackney, London, 1952–54; Rector of Scarborough, WA, 1955–70; Asst Bishop, Dio. Perth, WA, 1970–77. Life Member: Stirling Rugby Football Club, 1969; Durham Univ. Society, 1984. *Publication:* Luke Through Lent, 1980. *Recreations:* reading, painting. *Address:* Bishopscourt, Newcastle, NSW 2300, Australia. *T:* (office) 263733, (home) 262767. *Clubs:* Australian (Sydney); Newcastle (NSW).

NEWDEGATE, Francis Humphrey Maurice F.; *see* FitzRoy Newdegate.

NEWE, Rt. Hon. Gerard Benedict, PC (N Ireland) 1971; CBE 1977 (OBE 1961); Chairman, Personal Social Services Advisory Committee for Northern Ireland, 1974–81; *b* 5 Feb. 1907; *s* of Patrick Newe and Catherine Newe (*née* McCanny); unmarried. *Educ:* St Malachy's Coll., Belfast; Belcamp Coll., Dublin. Editor, The Ulster Farmer, 1931–67. Area Admin. Officer, Min. of Health and Local Govt, NI, 1941–48; Regional Officer and Dir, NI Council of Social Service, 1948–72. First Roman Catholic Minister of State, Govt of NI, 1971–72. Last Minister to be appointed to HM Privy Council in Northern Ireland. Chief Welfare Officer, Civil Defence, Belfast, 1951–68; Member: BBC's NI Agr. Adv. Cttee, 1954–58; BBC's NI Appeals Adv. Cttee, 1956–59; ITA NI Cttee, 1960–66; Nat. Trust Cttee for NI, 1962–71; NI Indust. Trng Council, 1964–73 (Chm., Res. Cttee); NI Cttee, Nuffield Provincial Hosps Trust, 1954–63; First Bd of Governors, Rupert Stanley Coll. of Further Educn, Belfast, 1964–72; NI Legal Aid Adv. Cttee, 1967–75; NI Adv. Cttee, Council for Trng in Social Work, 1966–70; N Area Health and Social Services Bd, 1973–77 (Chm., Personal Social Services Cttee); Founder Member: Ulster Folklife Soc. (Vice-Pres.); PACE (and co-Patron); NIACRO (a Vice-Pres.); The Assissi Fellowship (Chm.). Council of Europe Fellow, 1970. Hon. MA The Queen's Univ. of Belfast, 1967; Hon. DLitt New Univ. of Ulster, Coleraine, 1971. *Publications:* The Catholic in the Community, 1958, 2nd edn 1965; The Story of the Northern Ireland Council of Social Service, 1963; contribs to Tablet, The Furrow, Christus Rex, Aquarius. *Recreations:* reading, trying to be lazy. *Address:* Prospect House, 28 Coast Road, Cushendall, Ballymena, Co. Antrim BT44 0RY. *T:* Cushendall 219.

NEWELL, Prof. Kenneth Wyatt, MD; Middlemass Hunt Professor of Tropical Community Health and Head of Department of International Community Health, Liverpool School of Tropical Medicine, since 1984; *b* 7 Nov. 1925; *s* of Herbert William and Mary Irene Newell; *m* 1977, Priscilla Jane Watts; four *s*. *Educ:* Univ. of New Zealand; MB, ChB; DPH (distinction) London, MD Tulane, USA, MCCM (NZ), FFCM. Epidemiologist, PHLS, Colindale, 1954–56; Lectr, Social and Preventive Medicine, QUB, 1956–58; WHO Epidemiologist, Indonesia, 1958–60; Field Dir, ICMRT Cali, Colombia, 1960–67; William Hamilton Watkins Professor of Epidemiology, Tulane Univ., USA, 1960 67; Dir, WHO, Geneva, 1967–77; Prof. of Community Health, Univ. of Otago, NZ, 1977–83. *Publication:* (ed) Health by the People, 1975. *Recreations:* fishing, gardening, opera. *Address:* Five Oaks, Street Hey Lane, Willaston, South Wirral, Cheshire L64 1SS. *T:* 051–327 4057.

NEWELL, Philip Staniforth, CB 1961; *b* 1903; *m* 1927, Sylvia May Webb (*d* 1982); two *s* one *d*. *Educ:* Uppingham; Emmanuel College, Cambridge (Scholar). First Class Part I, Mathematical Tripos, First Class Mechanical Sciences Tripos; Assistant Master at Uppingham; Chief Mathematical Master, Repton; Headmaster of Gresham's School, Holt, 1935–44; Admiralty, 1944–64; Imperial Defence College, 1955; Under-Secretary, 1956, Principal Finance Officer, 1961–64, Director, Greenwich Hosp., 1964–69; a Maths Master, Pierrepont Sch., Surrey, 1969–72. *Publication:* Greenwich Hospital, a Royal

Foundation 1692–1983, 1984. *Address:* Dawson's, Tilford, Surrey. *T:* Frensham 2787. *Club:* Athenæum.

NEWELL, Rt. Rev. Phillip Keith; *see* Tasmania, Bishop of.

NEWENS, (Arthur) Stanley; Member (Lab) London Central, European Parliament, since 1984; Chairman, British Labour Group, since 1985; *b* 4 Feb. 1930; *s* of Arthur Ernest and Celia Jenny Newens, Bethnal Green; *m* 1st, 1954, Ann (*d* 1962), *d* of J. B. Sherratt, Stoke-on-Trent; two *d*; 2nd, 1966, Sandra Christina, *d* of J. A. Frith, Chingford; two *d*. *Educ:* Buckhurst Hill County High Sch.; University Coll., London (BA Hons History); Westminster Training Coll. (Post-Graduate Certificate of Education). Coal face worker in N Staffs mines, 1952–55. Secondary Sch. Teacher, 1956–65, 1970–74. MP (Lab) Epping, 1964–70 (NUT sponsored); MP (Lab and Co-op) Harlow, Feb. 1974–1983. Contested (Lab) Harlow, 1983. Chairman: Eastern Area Gp of Lab. MPs, 1974–83; Tribune Gp of MPs, 1982–83 (Vice-Chm., 1981–82); PLP Foreign Affairs Gp, 1982–83 (Vice-Chm., 1976–77); British Lab. Gp of MEPs, 1985–; Vice-Chairman: E Reg. Council, Lab. Party; Labour Action for Peace. Active Member: Labour Party, holding numerous offices, 1949–; NUM, 1952–55; NUT, 1956–. Chm., Liberation (Movement for Colonial Freedom), 1967–. Dir, London Co-operative Soc., 1971–77 (Pres., 1977–81); Mem., Central Exec., Co-op. Union, 1974–80. Sec., Harlow Council for Voluntary Service, 1983–84. *Publications:* The Case Against NATO (pamphlet), 1972; Nicolae Ceausescu, 1972; Third World: change or chaos, 1977; A History of North Weald Bassett and its People, 1985; pamphlets and articles. *Recreations:* local historical research, family, reading. *Address:* The Leys, 18 Park Hill, Harlow, Essex. *T:* Harlow 20108.

NEWEY, John Henry Richard, QC 1970; **His Honour Judge Newey;** a Circuit Judge appointed to perform Official Referee duties in London, since 1980; Commissary General of the City and Diocese of Canterbury, since 1971; *b* 20 Oct. 1923; *s* of late Lt-Col T. H. Newey, ED and of Mrs I. K. M. Newey (*née* Webb); *m* 1953, Mollie Patricia (*née* Chalk), JP; three *s* two *d*. *Educ:* Dudley Grammar Sch.; Ellesmere Coll.; Queens' Coll., Cambridge (MA, LLM (1st class); Foundn Scholar). Served Central India Horse, Indian Army, 1942–47 in India, Middle East, Italy and Greece, Captain (US Bronze Star, 1944). Called to Bar, Middle Temple, 1948, Bencher 1977. Prosecuting Counsel to Post Office, South Eastern Circuit, 1963–64; Standing Counsel to Post Office at Common Law, 1964–70; Personal Injuries Junior to Treasury, 1968–70; Dep. Chm., Kent County QS, 1970–71; a Recorder of the Crown Court, 1972–80. Legal Assessor, GMC and GDC, 1973–80; an Advr to the Home Sec. under Prevention of Terrorism Act, 1978–80; Parly Boundary Comr for England, 1980–. Chm., Cheshire Structure Plan Exam., 1977; Inspector: Calder Valley Motorway Inquiry, 1978; Gatwick Air Port Inquiry, 1980. Legal Mem., Rhodesian Travel Facilities Cttee, 1978–80. Lectr, (part-time), Coll. of Estate Mgt, Univ. of London, 1951–59. Contested (C and L) Cannock Div. of Staffs, 1955. Alternate Chm., Burnham and other Teachers' Remuneration Cttees, 1969–80. Chairman: Sevenoaks Preservation Soc., 1962–65; Sevenoaks Div. Conservative Assoc., 1965–68. *Recreations:* history, excursions. *Address:* St David's, 68 The Drive, Sevenoaks, Kent TN13 3AF. *T:* Sevenoaks 454597.

NEWEY, Sidney Brian; General Manager, Western Region, British Rail, since 1985; *b* 8 Jan. 1937; *s* of Sidney Frank Newey and Edith Mary Newey; *m* 1967, Margaret Mary Stevens; one *s*. *Educ:* Burton upon Trent Grammar Sch.; Worcester Coll., Oxford (MA Mod. History). MCIT. British Rail: Traffic apprentice, Western Region, 1960; Stationmaster, Southall, Mddx, 1964; Freight Marketing Manager, Western Region, 1971; Divl Manager, Birmingham, 1978; Dep. General Manager, London Midland Region, 1980. *Recreations:* fell walking, history, reading, carpentry. *Address:* Chestnut Cottage, The Green South, Warborough, Oxon OX9 8DN. *T:* Warborough 8322.

NEWFOUNDLAND, CENTRAL, Bishop of, since 1976; **Rt. Rev. Mark Genge;** *b* 18 March 1927; *s* of Lambert and Lily Genge; *m* 1959, Maxine Clara (*née* Major); five *d*. *Educ:* Queen's Coll. and Memorial Univ., Newfoundland; Univ. of Durham (MA); BD Gen. Synod of Canada. Deacon, Corner Brook, Newfoundland, 1951; priest, Stephenville, 1952; Durham, 1953–55; Vice-Principal, Queen's Coll., St John's, Newfoundland, 1955–57; Curate, St Mary's Church, St John's, 1957–59; Rector: Foxtrap, 1959–64; Mary's Harbour, 1964–65; Burgeo, 1965–69; Curate, Marbleton, PQ, 1969–71; Rector, South River, Port-de-Grave, 1971–73; District Sec., Canadian Bible Soc., 1973–76. *Recreations:* badminton, swimming. *Address:* (home) 35 Airport Boulevard, Gander, Newfoundland A1V 1K7, Canada; (office) 34 Fraser Road, Gander, Newfoundland A1V 2E8.

NEWFOUNDLAND, EASTERN, AND LABRADOR, Bishop of, since 1980; **Rt. Rev. Martin Mate;** *b* 12 Nov. 1929; *s* of John Mate and Hilda Mate (*née* Toope); *m* 1962, Florence Hooper, Registered Nurse; two *s* three *d*. *Educ:* Meml Univ. of Newfoundland and Queen's Coll., St John's, Newfoundland (LTh); Bishop's Univ., Lennoxville, PQ. BA (1st Cl. Hons), MA. Deacon 1952, priest 1953; Curate, Cathedral of St John the Baptist, St John's, Newfoundland, 1952–53; Deacon-in-charge and Rector, Parish of Pushthrough, 1953–58; Incumbent, Mission of St Anthony, 1958–64; Rural Dean, St Barbe, 1958–64; Rector of Cookshire, Quebec, 1964–67; Rector of Catalina, Newfoundland, 1967–72; RD of Bonavista Bay, 1970–72; Rector of Pouch Cove/Torbay, 1972–76; Treasurer, Diocesan Synod of E Newfoundland and Labrador, 1976–80. *Publication:* Pentateuchal Criticism, 1967. *Recreations:* carpentry, hunting, fishing, camping. *Address:* 19 King's Bridge Road, St John's, Newfoundland A1C 3K4, Canada.

NEWFOUNDLAND, WESTERN, Bishop of, since 1978; **Rt. Rev. Sidney Stewart Payne;** *b* 6 June 1932; *s* of Albert and Hilda Payne; *m* 1962, Selma Carlson Penney, St Anthony, Newfoundland; two *s* two *d*. *Educ:* Elementary and High School, Fogo, Newfoundland; Memorial Univ. of Newfoundland (BA); Queen's Coll., Newfoundland (LTh); BD(General Synod). Incumbent of Mission of Happy Valley, 1957–65; Rector, Parish of Bay Roberts, 1965–70; Rector, Parish of St Anthony, 1970–78. DD *hc* Univ. of King's Coll., Halifax, NS, 1981. *Address:* 13 Cobb Lane, Corner Brook, Newfoundland A2H 2V3, Canada. *T:* 709–639–9987.

NEWHOUSE, Ven. Robert John Darrell; Archdeacon of Totnes and Canon Residentiary of Exeter Cathedral, 1966–76, now Archdeacon Emeritus and Canon Emeritus; Treasurer of Exeter Cathedral, 1970–76; *b* 11 May 1911; *s* of Rev. R. L. C. Newhouse; *m* 1938, Winifred (*née* Elton); two *s*. *Educ:* St Edward's Sch.; Worcester Coll., Oxford; Cuddesdon College. Ordained, 1936. Curate of: St John's, Peterborough, 1936–40; St Giles, Cambridge, 1940–46; Chaplain, RNVR, 1941–46; Rector of Ashwater, Devon, 1946–56; Rural Dean of Holsworthy, 1954–56; Vicar of Littleham-cum-Exmouth, 1956–66; Rural Dean of Aylesbeare, 1965–66. *Recreation:* gardening. *Address:* Pound Cottage, Northlew, Okehampton, Devon. *T:* Beaworthy 532.

NEWING, Rt. Rev. Kenneth Albert; *see* Plymouth, Bishop Suffragan of.

NEWINGTON, Michael John, CMG 1982; HM Diplomatic Service; Ambassador to Venezuela and concurrently (non-resident) to Dominican Republic, since 1985; *b* 10 July 1932; *er s* of J. T. Newington, Spalding, Lincs; *m* 1956, Nina Gordon-Jones; one *s* one *d*. *Educ:* Stamford Sch.; St John's Coll., Oxford. MA. RAF, 1951–52, Pilot Officer. Joined

Foreign Office, 1955; Economic Survey Section, Hong Kong, 1957–58; resigned 1958. ICI, 1959–60. Rejoined FO, 1960; Second, later First Sec. (Economic), Bonn, 1961–65; First Sec., Lagos, 1965–68; Asst Head of Science and Technology Dept, FCO, 1968–72; Counsellor (Scientific), Bonn, 1972–75; Counsellor and Consul-Gen., Tel Aviv, 1975–78; Head of Republic of Ireland Dept, FCO, 1978–81; Consul-Gen., Düsseldorf, 1981–85. *Recreations:* ski-ing, golf, gardening. *Address:* c/o Foreign and Commonwealth Office, SW1.

NEWIS, Kenneth, CB 1967; CVO 1970 (MVO 1958); *b* 9 Nov. 1916; *o s* of late H. T. and G. Newis, Manchester; *m* 1943, Kathleen, *o d* of late John Barrow, Davenport, Cheshire; two *d. Educ:* Manchester Grammar Sch.; St John's Coll., Cambridge (Scholar). BA 1938, MA 1942. Entered HM Office of Works, 1938; Private Sec. to Minister of Works (Rt Hon. C. W. Key), 1948–49; Asst Sec., 1949; Under-Sec., 1959; Dir of Management Services, MPBW, 1969–70; Under-Sec., Scottish Develt Dept, 1970–73, Sec., 1973–76. Chairman: Queen's Hall (Edinburgh) Ltd; Budget Cttee, Methodist Church of GB, 1979–; MHA Housing Assoc. Member: Historic Buildings Council for Scotland, 1978–; Cockburn Conservation Trust; Bd, Methodist Homes for the Aged; Scottish Baroque Ensemble Ltd; Bd, RSAMD; Scottish Churches' Council, 1984– (Chm., Friends of Scottish Churches' Council, 1984–). Conservator of Wimbledon and Putney Commons, 1963–70. Governor: Farrington's School, 1964–70; Richmond College, 1964–70. *Recreation:* music. *Address:* 11 Abbotsford Park, Edinburgh EH10 5DZ. *Club:* New (Edinburgh).

NEWLAND, Prof. David Edward, MA; ScD; FEng 1982; FIMechE; Professor of Engineering (1875), University of Cambridge, since 1976; Fellow, Selwyn College, Cambridge, since 1976; consulting engineer (part-time), since 1963; *b* 8 May 1936; *s* of late Robert W. Newland and of Marion A. Newland (*née* Dearman); *m* 1959, Patricia Frances Mayne; two *s. Educ:* Alleyne's Sch., Stevenage; Selwyn Coll., Cambridge (Lyttleton Scholar, 1956); Mech. Sciences Tripos: Rex Moir Prize, 1956, Ricardo Prize, 1957; MA]; Massachusetts Inst. of Technol. (ScD thesis on nonlinear vibrations, 1963). English Electric Co., 1957–61; Instr and Asst Prof. of Mech. Engrg, MIT, 1961–64; Lectr and Sen. Lectr, Imperial Coll. of Science and Technol., 1964–67; Prof. of Mech. Engrg, Sheffield Univ., 1967–76. Past or present mem., cttees of IMechE, Dept of Industry, BSI, SERC, Design Council and Fellowship of Engineering, including: Mem., Editorial Panel, 1968–82 and Consultant Editor, 1983–, Jl Mech. Engrg Sci., Proc. IMechE, Part C; Member: SRC Transport Cttee, 1969–72; Mech. Engrg and Machine Tools Requirements Bd, 1977, 1978; Engrg Awards Panel, Design Council, 1977–79; Council, Fellowship of Engrg, 1985–; Chm., BSI Tech. Cttee on bellows expansion jts, 1976–85. Technical witness, Flixborough Inquiry, 1974–75, and other legal cases; Mem., Royal Commn on Environmental Pollution, 1984–. Governor, St Paul's Schs, 1978–; Churchwarden, Ickleton, 1979–87. *Publications:* An Introduction to Random Vibrations and Spectral Analysis, 1975, 2nd edn 1984; technical papers, mostly in British and Amer. engrg jls. *Recreations:* gardening, cycling, engineering memorabilia. *Address:* c/o University Engineering Department, Trumpington Street, Cambridge CB2 1PZ. *T:* Cambridge 66466. *Club:* Athenæum.

NEWLEY, Edward Frank, CBE 1960; consultant; *b* 9 June 1913; *s* of Frederick Percy Newley; *m* 1946, Sybil Madge Alvis; two *s* one *d. Educ:* King's Coll., London. 1st class hons BSc; MSc. GPO Engrg Dept, Radio Research Br, 1937–44; GPO Factories Dept, 1944–49; Royal Naval Scientific Service, 1949–55; joined UKAEA, 1955; Dep. Dir, AWRE, 1959; Dir, Atomic Weapons Establishment, Aldermaston, 1965–76. *Publications:* sundry scientific and technical papers. *Address:* Rosapenna, Leigh Woods, Bristol BS8 3PX.

NEWLEY, (George) Anthony; actor since 1946; author, composer; *b* 24 Sept. 1931; *m* 1956, Ann Lynn; *m* 1963, Joan Collins; one *s* one *d; m* Dareth Rich; one *s* one *d. Educ:* Mandeville Street Sch., Clapton, E5. Appeared on West End stage in: Cranks, 1955; Stop the World, I Want to Get Off (co-author and co-composer, with Leslie Bricusse), 1961–62; subseq. starred in New York production, 1962–63; The Good Old Bad Old Days (co-author and co-composer with Leslie Bricusse), 1972; The Roar of the Greasepaint-the Smell of the Crowd (co-author and composer, with Leslie Bricusse, star and director); New York, 1965; Chaplin, Los Angeles, 1983. Has acted in over 40 films in last 17 years. *Films include:* Adventures of Dusty Bates; Oliver Twist; Up To His Neck; Cockleshell Heroes; High Flight; Idle on Parade; Jazz Boat; The Small World of Sammy Lee; Dr Doolittle; Sweet November; (wrote, produced and acted) Can Heironymus Merkin ever forget Mercy Humppe and find True Happiness?; (directed) Summertree, 1970; (score) Willy Wonka and the Chocolate Factory (Academy Award nomination, 1972); Quilp, 1974; It Seemed Like a Good Idea at the Time, 1974. *TV appearances include:* Anthony Newley Shows; The Strange World of Gurney Slade, 1960–61; Johnny Darling Show, 1962; Lucy in London, 1966; appears on TV and stars in leading night clubs and theatres in US. He is also a successful recording star. *Recreations:* photography, painting, fishing. *Address:* c/o Raymond Katz Enterprises Inc., Suite 1115, 9255 Sunset Boulevard, Los Angeles, Calif 90069, USA.

NEWMAN, Dr Barry Hilton; consultant; Director, Propellants, Explosives and Rocket Motor Establishment, and Head of Rocket Motor Executive, Ministry of Defence, 1980–84, retired; *b* 16 Sept. 1926; *s* of Charles Ernest Newman and Kathleen (*née* Hilton); *m* 1950, Dorothy Ashworth Truesdale; one *s* one *d. Educ:* Bishop Vesey's Grammar Sch., Sutton Coldfield; Univ. of Birmingham (BSc (Hons) 1947, PhD 1950). Joined Scientific Civil Service, 1950; Explosives R&D Estabt, 1950–63; Defence Research Staff, Washington, 1963–66; Supt Explosives Br., Royal Armament R&D Estabt, 1966–71; Asst Dir, Directorate General Weapons (Army), 1971–72; Dir, Research Armaments, 1972–74; RCDS 1975; Head of Terminal Effects Dept, RARDE, 1976–77; Dep. Dir, RARDE, 1977–80. *Publications:* official reports. *Recreations:* cricket, bridge, reading, music. *Address:* Chevy Chase, St Mary's Drive, Riverhead, Sevenoaks, Kent TN13 2AR. *T:* Sevenoaks 454809.

NEWMAN, Charles, CBE 1965; MD (Cantab); FRCP; retired; Emeritus Dean, Postgraduate Medical School (now Royal Postgraduate Medical School); Harveian Librarian, 1962–79, Royal College of Physicians; *b* 16 March 1900; *s* of Charles Arnold Newman and Kate Beck; *m* 1st, 1952, Phyllis (*d* 1965), *d* of I. Bloomfield; 2nd, 1971, Anne (*d* 1982), *d* of F. W. Stallard. *Educ:* Shrewsbury Sch.; Magdalene Coll., Cambridge (Scholar); King's College Hospital (Scholar; Fellow of Med. School, 1980). Murchison Scholar RCP, 1926; FRCP 1932; FKC 1982. Volunteer Asst to Prof. Aschoff, Univ. of Freiburg i B. 1930; Hon. Treas., RSocMed, 1946–50; Fellow Medical Society of London (Orator, 1961); Hon. Member Assoc. of Physicians, 1965. Hon. Secretary, 1942–47. Hon. Treasurer, 1948–58; Mem., British Gastro-enterological Soc. (Pres., 1964); Governor, St Clement Dane's Sch., 1955–76, Vice-Chm., 1958–76; Mem. Cttee of Management of Conjoint Board in England, 1958–68 (Chm., 1965–68). Goulstonian Lectr, 1933; FitzPatrick Lectr, 1954, 1955 and 1968; Linacre Fellow, 1966; Harveian Orator, 1973; Assistant Registrar, RCP, 1933–38; Sub-Editor, EMS, Official Medical History of the War, 1942–47; late Physician, Medical Tutor and Vice-Dean, King's College Hospital and Asst Physician, Belgrave Hospital for Children. *Publications:* Medical Emergencies,

1932, 3rd edn 1946, repr. 1948; Evolution of Medical Education in the Nineteenth Century, 1957; articles in medical text-books and encyclopædias; papers on diseases of the liver and gall-bladder, medical history and education. *Address:* Basset, South Road, Oundle, Peterborough, Northants. *T:* Oundle 73310. *Club:* Athenæum.

NEWMAN, Cyril Wilfred Francis, QC 1982; His Honour Judge Newman; a Circuit Judge, since 1986; *b* 2 July 1937; *s* of late Wilfred James Newman and Cecilia Beatrice Lily Newman; *m* 1966, Winifred de Kok; two *s* one *d. Educ:* Sacred Heart Coll., Droitwich; Lewes County Grammar Sch. for Boys; Merton Coll., Oxford (BA 1959, MA 1964). President: OU Law Soc., 1959; OU Middle Temple Soc., 1959. Blackstone Entrance Scholar, Blackstone Pupillage Prize, and Harmsworth Major Scholar, Middle Temple, 1958–60; called to the Bar, Middle Temple, 1960; a Recorder, 1982–86. Asst Comr, Boundary Commn for England, 1976; Mem., Criminal Injuries Compensation Bd, 1985–. Hon. Treasurer, 1973–, Rear-Cdre 1985–, Bar Yacht Club. *Recreations:* sailing, ski-ing, beagling, swimming, opera, church music. *Address:* 3 Gray's Inn Place, Gray's Inn, WC1R 5EA. *T:* 01–831 8441; Orlestone Grange, Orlestone, near Ham Street, Kent TN26 2EB. *T:* Ham Street 2306. *Clubs:* Western (Glasgow); Bar Yacht.

NEWMAN, Edward; Member (Lab) Greater Manchester Central, European Parliament, since 1984; *b* 14 May 1953. Formerly in light engineering, cable making; postal worker, Manchester. *Address:* Flat 2, 30 Delalunays Road, Crumpsall, Manchester M8 6QS.

NEWMAN, Frederick Edward Fry, CBE 1986; MC 1945; Chairman: Dan-Air Services, since 1953; Davies & Newman Holdings, since 1971; *b* 14 July 1916; *s* of Frank Newman and Katharine Newman; *m* 1947, Margaret Helen (*née* Blackstone); two *s* one *d. Educ:* The Leys School, Cambridge. Joined Davies & Newman, 1937; served HAC and 9th Field Regt, RA, 1939–46; formed Dan-Air Services, 1953. *Recreation:* golf. *Address:* Cranstone, Hook Heath Road, Woking, Surrey. *T:* Woking 72605.

NEWMAN, Sir Geoffrey (Robert), 6th Bt, *cr* 1836; *b* 2 June 1947; *s* of Sir Ralph Alured Newman, 5th Bt, and of Hon. Ann Rosemary Hope, *d* of late Hon. Claude Hope-Morley; *S* father, 1968; *m* 1980, Mary, *y d* of Colonel Martin St John Valentine Gibbs, *qv*; one *s* one *d. Educ:* Heatherdown, Ascot; Kelly Coll., Tavistock. 1st Bn, Grenadier Guards, 1967–70. FRGS. *Recreations:* sub-aqua, sailing, all sports. *Heir:* *s* Robert Melvil Newman, *b* 4 Oct. 1985. *Address:* Blackpool House, Dartmouth, Devon.

NEWMAN, George Michael; QC 1981; a Recorder, since 1985; *b* 4 July 1941; *s* of Wilfred James Newman and Cecilia Beatrice Lily Newman; *m* 1966, Hilary Alice Gibbs (*née* Chandler); two *s* one *d. Educ:* Lewes County Grammar Sch.; St Catharine's Coll., Cambridge (BA Hons Law). Called to the Bar, Middle Temple, 1965. *Recreations:* tennis, skiing, alpine walking, the countryside. *Address:* 1 Crown Office Row, Temple, EC4Y 7HH. *T:* 01–583 9292.

NEWMAN, Sir Gerard (Robert Henry Sigismund), 3rd Bt, *cr* 1912; *b* 19 July 1927; *s* of Sir Cecil Gustavus Jacques Newman, 2nd Bt, and Joan Florence Mary, CBE (*d* 1969), *e d* of late Rev. Canon Hon. Robert Grimston; *S* father, 1955; *m* 1960, Caroline Philippa, *d* of late Brig. Alfred Geoffrey Neville, CBE, MC; three *s* one *d. Educ:* Eton; Jesus Coll., Oxford (BA 1951). Dir, APL Engineering Ltd, 1951–53; Asst to Man. Dir, Enfield Rolling Mills Ltd, 1953–56; Director: Enfield Zinc Products Ltd, 1953–56; The Rom River Co. Ltd, 1954–72 (Chm., 1955); Galloway (Mechanical Services) Ltd, Dundee, 1973– (Chm., 1980); Chairman: Seven Seas Engineering Ltd, Glasgow, 1975–78; Woodcote Grove Estate Ltd, 1975–. Dep. Traffic Comr for the Metropolitan Area, 1972–85. Governor, Wellesley House & St Peter's Court Schs Trust, 1963–86; Pres., Friends of Royston and District Hosp., 1975–; Chm., Cambridge Symphony Orchestra Trust, 1982– (Trustee, 1979–). Farmer, 1969–; Pres., Herts Agricl Soc., 1983. High Sheriff, Herts, 1981–82. *Recreations:* travel and pursuits of the countryside. *Heir:* *s* Francis Hugh Cecil Newman, *b* 12 June 1963. *Address:* Burloes, Royston, Herts. *T:* Royston 42150; 27 Bloomfield Terrace, SW1. *T:* 01–730 7540. *Club:* Boodle's.

NEWMAN, Graham Reginald, FICS; Chairman, Tatham Bromage (Holdings) Ltd and group of companies, since 1953; *b* 26 July 1924; *s* of late A. H. G. Newman and Ethel (*née* Wadey); *m* 1952, Joycelyn Helen Newman, MB, ChB, DPH (*née* Sandison). *Educ:* Canford Sch.; Hertford Coll., Oxford. War service, Royal Signals, India and Far East, 1941–46, retd Captain. Director, Tatham Bromage & Co. Ltd, 1945. Elected to Baltic Exchange, 1947; Dir, 1967; Chm., 1977–79; Chm., Baltic Exchange Clerks' Pension Fund, 1966–68. Pres., Baltic Charitable Soc., 1982–84. Mem. Cttee of Management, RNLI and sub-cttees, 1977–. Mem. Ct of Assistants, Shipwrights' Co. *Recreations:* golf, sailing. *Address:* 46 St Mary Axe, EC3A 8EY. *Club:* Highgate Golf.

NEWMAN, Sir Jack, Kt 1977; CBE 1963; FCIT 1955; JP; Founder, 1938, President, 1981, Newman Group Ltd (formerly TNL), Nelson, New Zealand; *b* 3 July, 1902; *s* of Thomas Newman and Christina Thomson; *m* 1926, Myrtle O. A. Thomas; four *d. Educ:* Nelson Coll. for Boys, NZ. Joined Newman Bros Ltd (family business), 1922; Manager, 1927; Managing Director, 1935. Dir, L & M Mining (NZ) Ltd. Past President and Life Member: NZ Cricket Council; NZ Travel Assoc.; NZ Passenger Transport Fedn; former Dir, Pacific Area Travel Assoc. Represented: NZ, at cricket, 1931–33; Nelson, Canterbury and Wellington, at cricket; Nelson, at Rugby football, golf, and lawn bowls. JP Nelson, 1950. *Recreation:* lawn bowls. *Address:* (home) 36 Brougham Street, Nelson, New Zealand; (office) Newman Group Ltd, PO Box 48, Nelson, NZ. *Clubs:* MCC; Wellesley (Wellington); Nelson (Nelson).

NEWMAN, Karl Max, CB 1979; Second Counsel to the Chairman of Committees and Legal Adviser to the European Communities Committee, House of Lords, since 1982; *b* 26 March 1919; *s* of Karl Neumann, DrJur, and Licie Neumann; *m* 1952, Annette, *d* of late Ronald Cross Sheen; one *s* one *d. Educ:* Ottershaw Coll., Surrey; Christ Church, Oxford (MA). Bacon Scholar of Gray's Inn, 1939. Served War in Army, 1940–42. Called to Bar, Gray's Inn, 1946; joined Lord Chancellor's Office, 1949; Asst Solicitor, 1962; Under-Sec., 1972–82; part-time Legal Adviser to European Unit of Cabinet Office, 1972–82; Head of Delegn negotiating UK accession to EEC Convention on Jurisdiction and Judgments, 1972–78. Member: UK delegns to Internat. Diplomatic Confs on Nuclear Liability, 1962–63; expert Cttees of Council of Europe, 1961–68; 10th and 11th Session of Hague Conf. on Private Internat. Law, 1964–68. Mem., EEC expert cttees, 1972–82. *Publications:* Das Englisch-Amerikanische Beweisrecht, 1949 (Heidelberg); contribs to legal publications on internat. jurisdiction and recognition of judgments. *Recreations:* philately, looking at paintings. *Address:* 17 Marryat Road, Wimbledon, SW19 5BB. *Club:* United Oxford & Cambridge University.

NEWMAN, Sir Kenneth (Leslie), Kt 1978; QPM 1982; Commissioner of the Metropolitan Police, since 1982; *s* of John William Newman and Florence Newman; *m* 1949, Eileen Lilian. *Educ:* London Univ. (LLB Hons). Served War, RAF, 1942–46. Palestine Police, 1946–48; Metropolitan Police, 1948–73; Comdr, New Scotland Yard, 1972; Royal Ulster Constab., 1973–79; Sen. Dep. Chief Constable, 1973; Chief Constable, 1976–79; Comdt, Police Staff Coll., and HM Inspector of Constabulary, 1980–82. CBIM (FBIM 1977). Freeman of the City of London, 1983. CStJ 1984. Communicator of the

Year, BAIE, 1984. *Recreation:* riding. *Address:* c/o Metropolitan Police, New Scotland Yard, Broadway, SW1H 0BG.

NEWMAN, Dr Lotte Therese, (Mrs N. E. Aronsohn), FRCGP; general practitioner since 1958; Member, General Medical Council, since 1984; *b* 22 Jan. 1929; *d* of Dr George Newman and Dr Tilly Newman; *m* 1959, Norman Edward Aronsohn; three *s* one *d. Educ:* North London Collegiate Sch.; Univ. of Birmingham; King's College London and Westminster Hosp. Med. Schs. BSc 1951, MB BS 1957; LRCP, MRCS 1957; FRCGP 1977; FRSM 1977. Casualty Officer, Westminster Hosp.; Paediatric House Officer, Westminster Children's Hosp.; gen. medicine, St Stephen's Hosp. Hon. Sec., Medical Women's Fedn, 1981–; Dir, Private Patients Plan, 1983–. Member: Council, RCGP, 1980– (former Provost, NE London Faculty; formerly examr, RCGP); Council, BMA, 1985–; Central Ethical Cttee, BMA; General Med. Services Cttee, 1983–; Vice-Chm., Camden and Islington Local Med. Cttee, 1983–; Chm., Regional Co-ordinating Cttee of Area Local Med. Cttees, 1985–; Lectr, Royal Army Med. Coll., 1976–; temp. Adviser, WHO; formerly UK rep., OECD and Mem., Expert Cttees studying Primary Health Care in Germany, Switzerland, Sweden. Member: Hunterian Soc.; Hampstead Medical Soc. Freeman, City of London; Yeoman, Apothecaries' Soc. of London. *Publications:* papers on: multidisciplinary training and courses of Primary Health Care Team; breast feeding; ENT conditions and management of mental health handicap in gen. practice. *Recreations:* listening, music, boating. *Address:* Abbey Medical Centre, 87–89 Abbey Road, NW8 0AG. *T:* 01–624 9383. *Clubs:* Royal Automobile, City Livery, Little Ship.

NEWMAN, Nanette, (Mrs Bryan Forbes); actress and writer; *b* 29 May 1939; *d* of Sidney and Ruby Newman; *m* 1958, Bryan Forbes, *qv;* two *d. Educ:* Sternhold Coll., London; Italia Conti Stage Sch.; RADA. Appeared as a child in various films for Children's Film Foundn; other film appearances include: The L-Shaped Room, 1962; The Wrong Arm of the Law, 1962; Seance on a Wet Afternoon, 1963; The Wrong Box, 1965; The Whisperers, 1966; Deadfall, 1967; The Madwoman of Chaillot, 1968; The Raging Moon, 1971 (Variety Club Best Film Actress Award); The Stepford Wives, 1974; International Velvet, 1978 (Evening News Best Film Actress Award); *television:* Call My Bluff, What's My Line, The Fun Food Factory (own series), London Scene, Stay with me till Morning (Yorkshire), Jessie (title role, BBC TV), Let There Be Love (Thames series), A Breath of Fresh Air (TSW). *Publications:* God Bless Love, 1972 (repr. 16 times); Lots of Love, 1973 (repr. 7 times); Vote for Love, 1976 (repr. 4 times); All Our Love, 1978; Fun Food Factory, 1976 (repr. twice); Fun Food Feast, 1978; The Root Children, 1978; The Pig Who Never Was, 1979; Amy Rainbow, 1980; The Facts of Love, 1980; That Dog, 1980; Reflections, 1981; The Dog Lovers Coffee Table Book, 1982; The Cat Lovers Coffee Table Book, 1983; My Granny was a Frightful Bore, 1983; A Cat and Mouse Love Story, 1984; Nanette Newman's Christmas Cook Book, 1984; Pigalev, 1985; The Facts of Love, 1985; The Summer Cookbook, 1986; Archie, 1986. *Recreation:* needlepoint. *Address:* c/o The Bookshop, Virginia Water, Surrey. *T:* Wentworth 2463.

NEWMAN, Philip Harker, CBE 1976; DSO 1940; MC; FRCS; FCS(SA); formerly Consulting Orthopædic Surgeon, Middlesex Hospital, Royal National Orthopædic Hospital, King Edward VII's Hospital for Officers, W1, retired; *b* 22 June 1911; *s* of John Harker Newman, Mannofield, Ingatestone, Essex; *m* 1943, Elizabeth Anne, *er d* of Rev. G. H. Basset, Turners, Belchamp St Paul, Suffolk; two *s* one *d. Educ:* Cranleigh; Middlesex Hospital Medical School (Senior Broderip Scholar and 2nd Year Exhibitioner), MRCS, LRCP, 1934; FRCS, 1938; Hunterian Prof., RCS, 1954; late Lt-Col RAMC; Served War of 1939–45 (DSO, MC); FRSM (formerly Pres., Section of Orthopaedics); Fellow Brit. Orthopædic Assoc. (Pres., 1975–76); Chm., British Editorial Soc. of Bone and Joint Surgery, 1973–75; Chm., Medical Br., St John, 1976–82; Member British Medical Association. Corresp. Member: Amer. Orthopaedic Assoc.; S African Orthopaedic Assoc. *Publications:* The Prisoner of War Mentality, 1944; Early Treatment of Wounds of the Knee Joint, 1945; The Etiology of Spondylolisthesis, 1962; The Spine, the Wood and the Trees, 1968; Spinal Fusion, Operative Surgery, 1969; Safer than a Known Way, 1983; Orthopædic Surgery, Medical Encyclopædia, 1956; (contrib.) Total Hip Replacement, 1971; The Scientific Basis of Medicine, Annual Review, 1973. *Recreations:* sailing, golf. *Address:* 72A Saxmundham Road, Aldeburgh, Suffolk. *T:* Aldeburgh 3373. *Club:* Army and Navy.

NEWMAN, Ronald William; HM Diplomatic Service, retired; *b* 6 April 1921; *s* of William James Newman and Louisa Ellen Taylor; *m* 1943, Victoria Brady; three *d. Educ:* Wandsworth Sch. Served War, RAF, 1940–46. Min. of Agriculture and Fisheries, later MAFF, 1946–58; Statistical Org. Adviser to Central Bureau of Statistics, Jerusalem, 1958; O&M Adviser to Basutoland, Bechuanaland and Swaziland, 1959–61; MAFF, 1962–65; CRO, 1965–67; First Secretary: (Econs), Accra, 1967; (Capital Aid), Nairobi, 1968–72; (Econs), Islamabad, 1973–75; Counsellor, Khartoum, 1975–76; Consul General, Casablanca, 1977. *Recreations:* squash, swimming, diving, flying. *Address:* 20 Cranley Close, Guildford, Surrey GU1 2JN. *T:* Guildford 576728.

NEWMAN, Sydney Cecil, OC 1981; film and television producer and executive; President, Sydney Newman Enterprises; *b* Toronto, 1 April 1917; *m* 1944, Margaret Elizabeth (*d* 1981), *d* of Rev. Duncan McRae, DD; three *d. Educ:* Ogden Public School and Central Technical School, Toronto. Painter, stage, industrial and interior designer; still and cinema photographer, 1935–41. Joined National Film Board of Canada under John Grierson as splicer-boy, 1941. Editor and Director of Armed Forces training films and war information shorts, 1942. Producer of Canada Carries On, 1945. Exec. Producer in charge of all films for cinemas, including short films, newsreels, films for children and travel, 1947–52. Over 300 documentaries, including: Suffer Little Children (UN), It's Fun to Sing (Venice Award), Ski Skill, After Prison What? (Canada Award). For Canadian Govt to NBC in New York to report on American television techniques, 1949–50. Joined Canadian Broadcasting Corporation as Television Director of Features and Outside Broadcasts, 1953. Supervisor of Drama and Producer of General Motors Theatre, On Camera, Ford Theatre, Graphic, 1954. Supervisor of Drama and Producer Armchair Theatre, ABC Television, England, 1958–62 (devised, The Avengers, 1961); Head of Drama Group, TV, BBC, 1963–67 (devised Dr Who, 1963, and Adam Adamant Lives!, 1966); Producer, Associated British Productions Ltd, Elstree, 1968–69; Special Advisor to Chm. and Dir, Broadcast Programmes Branch, Canadian Radio and Television Commn, 1970; Canadian Govt Film Comr and Chm., Nat. Film Bd of Canada, 1970–75; Special Advisor on Film to Sec. of State for Canada, 1975–77; Chief Creative Consultant, Canadian Film Develt Corp., 1978–84 (Dir, Montreal, 1970–75). Dir, Canadian Broadcasting Corp., 1972–75. Producer: Stephen D, 1963; The Rise and Fall of the City of Mahagonny, 1965; The Tea Party, 1965; Britten's The Little Sweep, 1987. Produced first plays by Arthur Hailey, inc. Flight into Danger, Course for Collision; commissioned and prod. first on-air plays of Alun Owen, Harold Pinter, Angus Wilson, Robert Muller, Peter Luke; also plays by Clive Exton, David Perry and Hugh Leonard. Trustee, Nat. Arts Center, Ottawa, 1970–75; Governor, Canadian Conf. of the Arts; Member: New Western Film and TV Foundn; BAFTA; RTS. FRSA 1970; Fellow Soc. of Film and Television Arts. Ohio State Award for Religious Drama; Liberty Award, Best Drama

Series; Desmond Davis Award, 1967, Soc. of Film and Television Arts; President's Award, 1969, and Zeta Award, 1970, Writers Guild of Great Britain; Canadian Picture Pioneers Special Award, 1973; Special Recognition Award, SMPTE, 1975. Kt of Mark Twain, USA. *Address:* c/o Holmes Associates, 10/16 Rathbone Street, W1P 1AH.

NEWNHAM, Captain Ian Frederick Montague, CBE 1955; RN Retired; *b* 20 Feb. 1911; *s* of late John Montague Newnham, OBE, DL, JP, and Hilda Newnham; *m* 1947, Marjorie Warden; no *c. Educ:* RN College, Dartmouth. Served War of 1939–45 (despatches). Captain, 1952; retd 1961. Lent to Indian Navy as Chief of Material, 1952–55; Chief of Staff to Admiral, British Joint Service Mission, and Naval Attaché, Washington, 1959–61. Gen. Manager, Precision Engineering Div., Short Brothers and Harland, Belfast, 1961–68. *Recreations:* golf, fishing. *Address:* The Lodge, Mill Lane, Stedham, Midhurst, West Sussex GU29 0PS. *T:* Midhurst 3663.

NEWNS, Sir (Alfred) Foley (Francis Polden), KCMG 1963 (CMG 1957); CVO 1961; MA Cantab; *b* 30 Jan. 1909; *s* of late Rev. Alfred Newns, AKC; *m* 1936, Jean (*d* 1984), *d* of late A. H. Bateman, MB, BS; one *s* one *d. Educ:* Christ's Hospital; St Catharine's College, Cambridge. Colonial Administrative Service, Nigeria, 1932; served E Reg. and Colony; Enugu Secretariat, 1947; Lagos Secretariat, 1949; attached Cabinet Office, London, 1951; Resident, 1951; Secretary to Council of Ministers, 1951; Secretary to Governor-General and the Council of Ministers, Federation of Nigeria, 1955–59; Dep. Governor, Sierra Leone, 1960–61; Acting Gov. during 1960; Adviser to the Government of Sierra Leone after Independence, 1961–63; Sec. to Cabinet, Govt of the Bahamas, 1963–71. FRSA 1969. *Publications:* various papers on Cabinet procedure and government machinery, circulated in Commonwealth. *Recreations:* astronomy, natural history, gardening. *Address:* Cedar House, Caxton Lane, Foxton, Cambridge CB2 6SR. *T:* Cambridge 870629.
  See also J. Ounsted.

NEWPORT, Viscount; Alexander Michael Orlando Bridgeman; *b* 6 Sept. 1980; *s* and *heir* of 7th Earl of Bradford, *qv.*

NEWRY AND MORNE, Viscount; Robert Francis John Needham; student; *b* 30 May 1966; *s* and *heir* to Earl of Kilmorey (*see* R. F. Needham). *Educ:* Sherborne Prep. School; Eton College; Lady Margaret Hall, Oxford. *Recreations:* playing for football 1st XI and squash 1st V in college teams. *Address:* The Croft House, Somerford Keynes, near Cirencester, Glos GL7 6DW. *T:* Cirencester 861333.

NEWSAM, Peter Anthony; Chairman, Commission for Racial Equality, since 1982; *b* 2 Nov. 1928; *s* of late W. O. Newsam and of Mrs D. E. Newsam; *m* 1953, Elizabeth Joy Greg; four *s* one *d. Educ:* Clifton Coll.; Queen's Coll., Oxford (MA, DipEd). Asst Principal, BoT, 1952–55; teacher, 1956–63; Asst Educn Officer, N Riding of Yorks, 1963–66; Asst Dir of Educn, Cumberland, 1966–70; Dep. Educn Officer: W Riding of Yorks, 1970–72; ILEA, 1972–76; Educn Officer, ILEA, 1977–82. Vis. Fellow, Nuffield Coll., Oxford, 1982–. *Address:* 18 Grenville Road, N19.

NEWSOM, George Harold, QC 1956; Chancellor: Diocese of St Albans, since 1958; Diocese of London, since 1971; Diocese of Bath and Wells, since 1971; *b* 29 Dec. 1909; *e s* of late Rev. G. E. Newsom, Master of Selwyn Coll., Cambridge; *m* 1939, Margaret Amy, *d* of L. A. Allen, OBE; two *s* one *d. Educ:* Marlborough; Merton College, Oxford. 2nd Class Lit Hum, 1931; 1st Class Jurisprudence, 1932; Harmsworth Senior Scholar; Merton College, 1932; Cholmeley Student, 1933, called to Bar, 1934, Lincoln's Inn; Bencher, 1962; Treasurer, 1980; practised at Chancery Bar, 1934–79. Min. of Economic Warfare, 1939–40; Trading with the Enemy Dept, Treasury and Bd of Trade, 1940–45; Junior Counsel to Charity Comrs, 1947–56; Conveyancing Counsel to PO, 1947–56; Dep. Chm., Wilts QS, 1964–71; a Recorder of the Crown Court, 1972–74. Member Gen. Council of the Bar, 1952–56. Vis. Prof. in Law, Auckland Univ., NZ, 1971. *Publications:* Restrictive Covenants affecting freehold land, 1st edn (with late C. H. S. Preston), 1940, 7th edn 1982; Limitation of Actions, 1st edn (with late C. H. S. Preston), 1939, 2nd edn 1943, 3rd edn (with L. Abel-Smith), 1953; The Discharge and Modification of Restrictive Covenants, 1957; (with J. G. Sherratt) Water Pollution, 1972. *Recreations:* wine, walking. *Address:* The Old Vicarage, Bishop's Cannings, Devizes, Wilts. *T:* Cannings 660. *Club:* Athenæum.

NEWSOM-DAVIS, Prof. John Michael, MD, FRCP; Medical Research Council Clinical Research Professor of Neurology, Royal Free Hospital Medical School and Institute of Neurology, 1980–Oct. 1987; Action Research Professor of Clinical Neurology, University of Oxford, from Oct. 1987; *b* 18 Oct. 1932; *s* of John Kenneth and Dorothy Eileen Newsom-Davis; *m* 1963, Rosemary Elisabeth (*née* Schmid); one *s* two *d. Educ:* Sherborne Sch.; Pembroke Coll., Cambridge (BA 1957 Nat. Scis); Middlesex Hosp. Med. Sch. (MB BChir 1960, MD 1966); FRCP 1973. RAF, 1951–53 (Pilot); Academic Registrar, Inst. of Neurology, 1964–65; Lectr, Univ. Dept of Clinical Neurology, Nat. Hosp. for Nervous Diseases, 1967–69; Neurological Research Fellow, Cornell Med. Center, New York Hosp., 1969–70; Consultant Neurologist, Royal Free Hosp. and Nat. Hosp. for Nervous Diseases, 1970–80, Hon. Consultant, 1980–; Mem., Medical Research Council, 1983– (Mem., Neurosciences Grants Cttee, 1978–80; Neurosciences Bd Mem., 1980–83, Chm., 1983–85); Pres., Biomedical Section, BAAS, 1982–83; Hon. Sec., Assoc. of British Neurologists, 1981–84; Hon. Mem., Aust. Assoc. of Neurologists; corr. Mem., Amer. Acad. of Neurology; Mem. Editorial Bds of Brain, Jl of Neurological Sci., Jl of Neuroimmunology. *Publications:* Respiratory Muscles: mechanics and neural control (with E. J. M. Campbell and E. Agostoni), 1970; numerous papers in Neurol. and Immunol. jls. *Recreations:* music and France. *Address:* (until Oct. 1987) Department of Neurological Science, Royal Free Hospital, NW3 2QG. *T:* 01–794 0500; Department of Neurology, Radcliffe Infirmary, Oxford.

NEWSOME, David Hay, MA; LittD Cantab 1976; FRSL 1981; Master of Wellington College, since 1980; *b* 15 June 1929; *s* of Captain C. T. Newsome, OBE; *m* 1955, Joan Florence, *d* of Lt-Col L. H. Trist, DSO, MC; four *d. Educ:* Rossall Sch., Fleetwood; Emmanuel Coll., Cambridge (Scholar). First Cl. in Hist. Tripos Parts I and II, 1952, 1953. Asst Master, Wellington Coll., 1954–59 (Head of History Dept, 1956–59); Fellow of Emmanuel Coll., Cambridge, 1959–70; Asst Lectr in Ecclesiastical History, Univ. of Cambridge, 1961–66; Univ. Lectr, 1966–70; Sen. Tutor, Emmanuel Coll., Cambridge, 1965–70; Headmaster of Christ's Hospital, 1970–79. Lectures: Gore Memorial, Westminster Abbey, 1965; Bishop Westcott Memorial, Cambridge, 1968; Birkbeck, Univ. of Cambridge, 1972. Council of: Ardingly Coll., 1965–69; Eastbourne Coll., 1966–70; Epsom Coll., 1966–70. FRHistS, 1970. *Publications:* A History of Wellington College, 1859–1959, 1959; Godliness and Good Learning, Four Studies in a Victorian Ideal, 1961; The Parting of Friends, a study of the Wilberforces and Henry Manning, 1966; Bishop Westcott and the Platonic Tradition, 1969; Two Classes of Men: Platonism and English Romantic Thought, 1974; On the Edge of Paradise: A. C. Benson the Diarist, 1980 (Whitbread Book of the Year Award); (ed) Edwardian Excursions, 1981; articles in Jl of Theological Studies, Jl of Ecclesiastical History, Theology, History Today, Historical Jl. *Recreations:* music, fell-walking. *Address:* Wellington College, Crowthorne, Berks RG11 7PU. *T:* Crowthorne 772261; The Retreat, Thornthwaite, Keswick, Cumbria. *T:* Braithwaite 372. *Clubs:* Athenæum, MCC.

NEWSOME, William Antony; Director-General, Association of British Chambers of Commerce, 1974–84; *b* 8 Nov. 1919; *s* of William F. Newsome and Elizabeth (*née* Thompson); *m* 1951, Estella Ann (*née* Cope); one *s*. *Educ:* King Henry VIII Sch., Coventry; Bedford Modern Sch. Student Engineer, W. H. Allen, Sons & Co. Ltd, Bedford, 1937–40. Served War, Royal Engineers: N Africa, Sicily, Italy campaigns, 1940–47. Engrg Dept, Crown Agents for Oversea Governments and Administrations, 1949–61; Principal: Home Office, 1961–64; Min. of Technology, 1964–70; Dept of Trade and Industry, 1970–71; Asst Sec., Dept of Trade, 1971–74. Member: SITPRO, 1972–84; Production Statistics Adv. Cttee, 1975–84; Home Office Standing Cttee on Crime Prevention, 1978–84. *Recreations:* photography, swimming, golf. *Address:* Bourdon Lacey, Old Woking Road, Woking, Surrey GU22 8HR. *T:* Woking 62237.

NEWSON-SMITH, Sir John (Kenneth), 2nd Bt *cr* 1944; DL; Member of HM Commission of Lieutenancy for City of London, since 1947; *b* 9 Jan. 1911; *s* of Sir Frank Newson-Smith, 1st Bt and Dorothy (*d* 1955), *d* of late Sir Henry Tozer; *S* father, 1971; *m* 1st, 1945, Vera Margaret Allt (marr. diss. 1971); one *s* two *d*; 2nd, 1972, Anne, *d* of late Harold Burns. *Educ:* Dover Coll.; Jesus Coll., Cambridge (MA). Joined Newson-Smith & Co, 1933, Partner 1938. Served War, Royal Navy, 1939–40; RNVR 1940. Rejoined Newson-Smith & Co, 1946 (which subseq. became Fielding Newson-Smith & Co.). Master of Turners Co., 1969–70; Liveryman: Merchant Taylors' Co.; Spectaclemakers' Co. Court of Common Council, 1945–78; Deputy, Ward of Bassishaw, 1961–76. DL City of London, 1947. *Recreations:* travelling, gardening. *Heir:* *s* Peter Frank Graham Newson-Smith [*b* 8 May 1947; *m* 1974, Mrs Mary-Ann Owens, *o d* of Cyril C. Collins; one *s* one *d*]. *Address:* Orchard Cottage, Babcary, Somerton, Somerset. *T:* Charlton Mackrell 3547. *Club:* City Livery.

NEWTH, Prof. David Richmond; Regius Professor of Zoology, University of Glasgow, 1965–81; *b* 10 Oct. 1921; *s* of late Herbert Greenway Newth and Annie Munroe (*née* Fraser); *m* 1946, Jean Winifred (*née* Haddon); two *s* one *d*. *Educ:* King Edward VI High Sch., Birmingham. Entered University Coll., London, 1938; graduated in Zoology, 1942. Served War of 1939–45, REME, commnd 1943. Asst Lectr in Zoology at University Coll., London, 1947; Lectr, 1949; Prof. of Biology as Applied to Medicine in the Univ. of London, at the Middlesex Hospital Medical Sch., 1960–65. Mem., Nature Conservancy Council, 1978–81. President: Scottish Marine Biol. Assoc., 1973–79; British Soc. for Developmental Biology, 1979–83. FRSE 1966. Editor, Journal of Embryology and Experimental Morphology, 1960–69. *Publications:* Animal Growth and Development, 1970; original articles in scientific journals, translations, and contrib. (popular) scientific works. *Recreation:* resting. *Address:* Monevechadan, Lochgoilhead, Cairndow, Argyll PA24 8AN. *T:* Lochgoilhead 287.

NEWTON, 4th Baron, *cr* 1892; **Peter Richard Legh;** *b* 6 April 1915; *er s* of 3rd Baron Newton, TD, DL, JP, and Hon. Helen Meysey-Thompson (*d* 1958); *S* father 1960; *m* 1948, Priscilla, *yr d* of late Capt. John Egerton-Warburton and *widow* of William Matthew Palmer, Visc. Wolmer; two *s*. *Educ:* Eton; Christ Church, Oxford (MA). 2nd Lt, Grenadier Guards (SR), 1937; Captain, 1941; Major, 1945. JP 1951; CC Hampshire, 1949–52 and 1954–55. Chairman East Hampshire Young Conservatives, 1949–50. MP (C) Petersfield Division of Hants, Oct. 1951–June 1960; PPS to Fin. Sec. to Treasury, 1952–53; Asst Govt Whip, 1953–55; a Lord Comr of Treasury, 1955–57; Vice-Chamberlain of the Household, 1957–59; Treasurer of the Household, 1959–60; Capt. Yeomen of the Guard and Govt Asst Chief Whip, 1960–62; (Joint) Parly Sec., Min. of Health, 1962–64; Min. of State for Education and Science, April-Oct. 1964. *Recreations:* photography, clock repairing, making gadgets. *Heir:* *s* Hon. Richard Thomas Legh [*b* 11 Jan. 1950; *m* 1978, Rosemary Whitfoot Clarke, *yr d* of Herbert Clarke, Eastbourne; one *s* one *d*]. *Address:* Vernon Hill House, Bishop's Waltham, Hampshire. *T:* Bishop's Waltham 2301. *Clubs:* Carlton, St Stephen's Constitutional, Pratt's; Hampshire (Winchester).
See also Earl of Selborne.

NEWTON, Antony Harold, OBE 1972; MP (C) Braintree since Feb. 1974; Minister of State (Minister for Health), Department of Health and Social Security, since 1986; Chairman, National Health Service Management Board, since 1986; economist; *b* Aug. 1937; *m*; two *c*. *Educ:* Friends' Sch., Saffron Walden; Trinity Coll., Oxford. Hons PPE. President: OU Conservative Assoc., 1958; Oxford Union, 1959. Formerly Sec. and Research Sec., Bow Group. Head of Conservative Research Dept's Economic Section, 1965–70; Asst Dir, Conservative Research Dept, 1970–74. Chm. Coningsby Club, 1965–66. Contested (C) Sheffield, Brightside, 1970. An Asst Govt Whip, 1979–81; a Lord Comr of HM Treasury, 1981–82; Parly Under-Sec. of State for Social Security, 1982–84, and Minister for the Disabled, 1983–84, Minister of State (Minister for Social Security and the Disabled), 1984–86, DHSS. Vice-Chm., Fedn of Univ. Conservative and Unionist Assocs. Governor: City Literary Inst.; Felsted Sch. Interested in taxation and social services. *Address:* House of Commons, SW1A 0AA.

NEWTON, Air Vice-Marshal Barry Hamilton, OBE 1975; Commandant, Joint Service Defence College, since 1986; *b* 1 April 1932; *s* of late Bernard Hamilton Newton, FCA and Dorothy Mary Newton; *m* 1959, Constance Lavinia, *d* of late Col J. J. Aitken, CMG, DSO, OBE; one *s* one *d*. *Educ:* Highgate; RAF College Cranwell. Commissioned 1953; 109 Sqn, 1954; 76 Sqn, Australia and Christmas Island, 1956; Flying Instr, RAF Coll. and No 6 Flying Trng Sch., 1959–63; HQ Flying Trng Comd, 1964; Staff Coll., Bracknell, 1966; Personal Staff Officer to Comdr, Second Allied Tactical Air Force, 1967; OC Ops Wing, RAF Cottesmore, 1969; Air Warfare Course, 1971; Defence Policy Staff, 1972; Cabinet Office, 1975; Asst Dir, Defence Policy, 1978; Cabinet Office, 1979; Air Cdre Flying Trng, HQ RAF Support Comd, 1982; Sen. Directing Staff (Air), RCDS, 1984. ADC to the Queen, 1983. *Recreations:* game-shooting, philately, reading. *Address:* c/o National Westminster Bank, Blue Boar Row, Salisbury, Wilts. *Club:* Royal Air Force.

NEWTON, Clive Trevor; Under Secretary, Head of Consumer Affairs Division, Department of Trade and Industry, since 1986; *b* 26 Aug. 1931; *s* of Frederick Norman and Phyllis Laura Newton; *m* 1961, Elizabeth Waugh Plowman; one *s* one *d*. *Educ:* Hove Grammar School for Boys. LLB London; called to Bar, Middle Temple, 1969; certified accountant. Examiner, Insolvency Service, Board of Trade, 1952, Sen. Examiner, 1963, Asst Official Receiver, 1967; Principal, Marine Div., BoT, 1969; Sen. Principal, Marine Div., Dept of Trade, 1973; Asst Director of Consumer Credit, Office of Fair Trading, 1974; Asst Sec., Regional Development Grants Div., Dept of Industry, 1978; Dir of Consumer Affairs, OFT, 1980. *Recreations:* golf, watching cricket and football. *Address:* 115 Hangleton Way, Hove, Sussex BN3 8AF. *T:* Brighton 416048. *Clubs:* Sussex County Cricket; East Brighton Golf; West Hove Golf.

NEWTON, Derek Henry; Chairman, C. E. Heath plc, since 1984; *b* 14 March 1933; *s* of Sidney Wellington Newton and Sylvia May Newton (*née* Peacock); *m* 1957, Judith Ann, *d* of Roland Hart, Kingston, Surrey; two *d*. *Educ:* Emanuel School. FCII. Commissioned Royal Artillery, 1952–54 (Lieut). Clerical, Medical & General Life Assurance Society, 1954–58; C. E. Heath Urquhart (Life & Pensions), 1958–83, Chm., 1971–84; Dir. C. E. Heath, 1975, Dep. Chm., 1983–84; Director: Glaxo Insurance (Bermuda), 1980–; Glaxo Trustees, 1980–; Clarges Pharmaceutical Trustees, 1985. Governor, BUPA Med. R&D, 1981–; Dir, British Aviation Insurance Co., 1986–; Alternate Dir, Trade Indemnity Co., 1984–. *Recreations:* cricket, golf. *Address:* Cuthbert Heath House, 150 Minories, EC3N 1NR. *T:* 01–488 2488; Pantiles, Meadway, Oxshott, Surrey. *T:* Oxshott 2273. *Clubs:* Surrey County Cricket (Chm. 1979–), MCC.

NEWTON, Douglas Anthony, CB 1976; Senior Registrar, Principal Registry, Family Division of High Court, 1972–75, retired; *b* 21 Dec. 1915; *s* of John and Janet May Newton; *m* 1946, Barbara Sutherland; one *s* one *d*. *Educ:* Westminster Sch. Joined Civil Service, 1934. Served War, British and Indian Armies, 1940–46. Apptd Registrar, 1959; Sen. Registrar, 1972. *Recreations:* beer, boats, building.

NEWTON, Sir Gordon; *see* Newton, Sir L. G.

NEWTON, Sir (Harry) Michael (Rex), 3rd Bt, *cr* 1900; Director Thos Parsons & Sons Ltd; *b* 7 Feb. 1923; 2nd and *e* surv. *s* of Sir Harry K. Newton, 2nd Bt, OBE, DL, and Myrtle Irene (*d* 1977), *e d* of W. W. Grantham, Balneath Manor, Lewes; *S* father, 1951; *m* 1958, Pauline Jane, *o d* of late R. J. F. Howgill, CBE; one *s*; three adopted *d*. *Educ:* Eastbourne College. Served War of 1939–45, with KRRC, in 8th Army and Middle East, 1941–46 (wounded). Master, Girdlers' Company, 1975–76; Freeman of City of London. *Recreations:* shooting, sailing (winner of 1953 Fastnet Race), ski-ing, fencing. *Heir:* *s* George Peter Howgill Newton, *b* 26 March 1962. *Address:* Weycroft Hall, near Axminster, Devon. *T:* 3169. *Club:* Royal Ocean Racing.

NEWTON, Sir Hubert, Kt 1968; President, Britannia Building Society, since 1985 (Chairman, 1976–85); *b* 2 Sept. 1904; *s* of Joe Newton and Gertrude Eliza Newton; *m* 1931, Elsie (*née* Wilson); one *d*. *Educ:* Burnley Gram. School. Burnley Building Soc., 1918–23; Mortgage Dept Controller, Northampton Town Building Soc., 1923–26; Controller of Investment Dept, Leeds Perm. Building Soc., 1926–30; Asst Sec., Bristol & West Building Soc., 1930–33; Leek and Moorlands Building Soc.: Sec., 1933–40; Gen. Man., 1940–63; Chm. and Man. Dir, 1963–66, when Leek and Moorlands amalgamated with Westbourne Park Building Soc. to form Leek and Westbourne Building Soc.; Man. Dir, 1966–69, Chm., 1966–74, Leek and Westbourne Building Soc.; on further amalgamation, Jt Dep. Chm., Leek Westbourne and Eastern Counties Building Soc. (name changed to Britannia Building Soc., 1975), 1974–76, 1978–84. Local Dir, N Staffs, Royal Insce Co. Ltd. Former Member Council: Building Socs Assoc. of Gt Britain (Chm., 1952–54); and Mem., Exec. Cttee, Internat. Union of Building Socs and Savings Assocs (Dep. Pres., Washington Congress, 1962; Pres., London Congress, 1965); Vice-President: Chartered Building Socs Inst., 1962; Building Socs Assoc. of Jamaica Ltd, 1967; President: Midland Assoc. of Building Socs, 1979; N Staffs Chamber of Commerce, 1964–65. Former Mem., Skelmersdale Develt Corp. Past Mem., Central Housing Adv. Cttee; Mem. Council, Nat. House-Building Council (Vice-Pres.). Founder Pres., Rotary Club, Leek, 1937; Pres., Stoke City FC, 1983–. Liveryman, Gold and Silver Wyre Drawers' Company. Hon. MA Keele, 1971. Coronation Medal, 1953. *Publications:* contribs to Building Socs Gazette. *Recreations:* golf, travel. *Address:* Birchall, Leek, Staffs ST13 5RA. *T:* Leek 382397. *Club:* English-Speaking Union.

NEWTON, Rev. Dr John Anthony; Chairman of the Liverpool District of the Methodist Church, since 1986; *b* 28 Sept. 1930; *s* of late Charles Victor Newton and of Kathleen Marchant; *m* 1963, Rachel, *d* of late Rev. Maurice H. Giddings and of Hilda Giddings, Louth, Lincs; four *s*. *Educ:* Grammar School, Boston, Lincs; University Coll., Hull; London Univ.; Wesley House, Cambridge. BA, PhD (Lond), MA (Cantab). Jun. Research Fellow, Inst. of Historical Research, London Univ., 1953–55; Housemaster and actg Chaplain, Kent Coll., Canterbury, 1955–56; trained for Methodist Ministry, Wesley House, 1956–58; Asst Tutor, Richmond Coll., Surrey, 1958–61, having been ordained, 1960; Circuit Minister at Louth, Lincs, 1961–64, and Stockton-on-Tees, 1964–65; Tutor at Didsbury Coll. (from 1967, Wesley Coll.), Bristol, 1965–72; taught Church History, St Paul's United Theolog. Coll., Limuru, Kenya, and Univ. of Nairobi, 1972–73; Principal of Wesley Coll., Bristol, 1973–78; Superintendent Minister, London Mission (W London) Circuit, 1978–86. President of the Methodist Conference, 1981–82. Chm. of Governors, Westminster Coll., Oxford, 1979–; Trustee, Wesley House, Cambridge, 1979–. Governor, Rydal School, Colwyn Bay, 1986–. Hon. DLitt Hull, 1982. *Publications:* Methodism and the Puritans, 1964; Susanna Wesley and the Puritan Tradition in Methodism, 1968; The Palestine Problem, 1972; Search for a Saint: Edward King, 1977; The Fruit of the Spirit in the Lives of Great Christians, 1979; A Man for All Churches: Marcus Ward, 1984. *Recreations:* music, gardening, walking, book-collecting. *Address:* 49 Queen's Drive, Mossley Hill, Liverpool L18 2DT. *T:* 051–722 1219.

NEWTON, John David; a Recorder of the Crown Court, since 1983; *b* 4 April 1921; *s* of late Giffard and Mary Newton; *m* 1942, Mary Bevan; one *s* one *d*. *Educ:* Berkhamsted School; University College London. LLB 1947. Served war of 1939–45 in Royal Artillery and Indian Army (Major); called to the Bar, Middle Temple, 1948; Lectr in Law, University College, Hull, 1948–51; Lectr then Senior Lectr in Law, Liverpool University, 1951–82. *Publication:* (ed) Halsbury's Laws of England, 4th edn, 1982, Vol. 39, Rent Charges and Annuities. *Recreations:* fishing, golf. *Address:* 10 Rose Mount, Oxton, Birkenhead, Merseyside L43 5SW. *T:* 051–652 4675. *Clubs:* Athenæum (Liverpool); Royal Liverpool Golf.

NEWTON, Prof. John Michael; Professor of Pharmaceutics, School of Pharmacy, University of London, since 1984; *b* 26 Dec. 1935; *s* of Richard and Dora Newton; *m* 1959, Janet Hinninghan (marr. diss. 1986); one *s* two *d*. *Educ:* Leigh Grammar Sch., Lancs; Sch. of Pharmacy, Univ. of London (BPharm); Univ. of Nottingham (PhD). FPS. Apprentice pharmacist, Royal Albert Edward Infirmary, Wigan, 1953–55; Demonstrator, Univ. of Nottingham, 1958–62; Sen. Lectr, Sunderland Polytechnic, 1962–64; Lectr, Univ. of Manchester, 1964–67; Sen. Scientist, Lilly Research Centre Ltd, 1968–71; Lectr, Univ. of Nottingham, 1972–78; Prof. of Pharmaceutics, Univ. of London, at Chelsea College, 1978–83. *Publications:* numerous articles in sci. jls associated with pharmaceutical technology. *Recreations:* fell walking, long distance running, gardening. *Address:* 16 Britten House, Britten Street, SW3 3BU. *T:* 01–352 1748.

NEWTON, Sir Kenneth (Garnar), 3rd Bt *cr* 1924; OBE 1970 (MBE 1944); TD; Executive Chairman, Garnar Booth plc, since 1972 (Managing Director, 1961–83); *b* 4 June 1918; *s* of Sir Edgar Henry Newton, 2nd Bt, and Gladys Maud (*d* 1966), *d* of late Sir James Garnar; *S* father, 1971; *m* 1st, 1944, Margaret Isabel (*d* 1979), *d* of Rev. Dr George Blair, Dundee; two *s*; 2nd, 1980, Mrs Pamela S. Wilson. *Educ:* Wellington College, Berks. Served War of 1939–45 (MBE); Lt-Col, RASC (TA). General Commissioner for Income Tax, 1961–. Pres., Internat. Council of Tanners, 1972–78; Past President, British Leather Federation (1968–69); Liveryman and Member of Court of Assistants, Leathersellers' Company (Master, 1977–78) and Feltmakers' Company (Master, 1983–84). *Heir:* *s* John Garnar Newton [*b* 10 July 1945; *m* 1972, Jacynth A. K. Miller; three *s*]. *Address:* Wildways, High Broom Lane, Crowborough, Sussex TN6 3SP. *T:* Crowborough 61089.

NEWTON, Sir (Leslie) Gordon, Kt 1966; Editor of The Financial Times, 1950–72, Director 1967–72; *b* 1907; *s* of John and Edith Newton; *m* 1935, Peggy Ellen Warren; (one *s* decd). *Educ:* Blundell's School; Sidney Sussex College, Cambridge. Chm., LBC,

1974–77; Director: Trust Houses Forte Ltd, 1973–80; Mills & Allen (Internat.) Ltd, 1974–81. Hannen Swaffer Award for Journalist of the Year, 1966; Granada Television special award, 1970. *Address:* Little Basing, Vicarage Walk, Bray-on-Thames, Berks.

NEWTON, Margaret; Schools Officer, Diocese of Oxford, since 1984; *b* 20 Dec. 1927; 2nd *d* of F. L. Newton, KStJ, MB, ChB, and Mrs A. C. Newton, MBE, BA. *Educ:* Sherborne School for Girls; St Andrews Univ.; Oxford University. MA Hons St Andrews, 1950; Educn Dip. Oxon 1951. Asst Mistress, King Edward VI Grammar School, Handsworth, Birmingham, 1951–54; Classics Mistress, Queen Margaret's Sch., York, 1954–60 (House Mistress, 1957); House Mistress, Malvern Girls' College, 1960–64 (Head of Classics Dept, 1962); Headmistress, Westonbirt Sch., 1965–80; Gen. Sec., Friends of the Elderly, 1981–83. *Address:* The Comedy, Sherborne Street, Lechlade, Glos.

NEWTON, Sir Michael; *see* Newton, Sir H. M. R.

NEWTON-CLARE, Herbert Mitchell, (Bill), CBE 1976; MC 1943; Chairman and Managing Director, NC Advisory Services Ltd, since 1978; Chairman and Chief Executive: Mervyn Hughes (International) Ltd, since 1984; Lansdowne International Services Ltd, since 1984; ORS Hospital Projects Ltd, since 1984; Chairman, Albemarle Securities Ltd, since 1986; *b* 5 May 1922; *s* of Herbert John and Eileen Margaret Newton-Clare; *m* 1970, Maureen Mary Thorp; three *d. Educ:* Cheltenham Coll. TA, Middlesex Regt, 1938; served War of 1939–45: mobilised, 1939; commnd, Wiltshire Regt, 1941; wounded, Normandy, 1944; demobilised, 1945 (Major). Joined Bowyers (Wiltshire) Ltd, as trainee, 1945; Factory Manager, 1955, Gen. Manager, 1957, Man. Dir, 1960, Chm., 1966; following take-over by Unigate of Scot Bowyers (formerly Bowyers (Wiltshire) Ltd), became Director of Unigate, 1973, Vice-Chm., 1974–76; Dir, FMC Ltd, and ancillary cos, 1976–77; Director: Aidaco (Finance) Ltd, 1980–; Hilliers Bacon Curing Co. Ltd, 1980–82. Chm., Meat Manufrs Assoc., 1970–82; Member: Exec. and Council, Food Manufrs Fedn, 1970–82; Food and Drink Industries Fedn, 1970–82; Exec. Centre de Liaison des Industries Transformatrice de Viandes de la Commune Européenne, 1970–82. *Recreations:* golf, tennis, swimming, fishing. *Address:* 4A Walham Grove, SW6 1QP. *T:* 01–381 0131. *Club:* Sunningdale Golf.

NEWTON DUNN, William Francis; Member (C) Lincolnshire, European Parliament, since 1979; *b* 3 Oct. 1941; *s* of Lt-Col Owen Newton Dunn, OBE, and Barbara (*née* Brooke); *m* 1970, Anna Terez Arki; one *s* one *d. Educ:* Marlborough Coll. (scholar); Gonville and Caius Coll., Cambridge (MA); INSEAD Business Sch., Fontainebleau (MBA). With Fisons Ltd (Fertilizer Division), 1974–79. European Parliament: Cons. Spokesman on Transport, 1984–; Chm., 1979 Cttee (Cons. backbench MEPs), 1983–. Contested (C): general elections: Carmarthen, Feb. 1974; Cardiff West, Oct. 1974. *Publication:* Greater in Europe, 1986. *Recreation:* spending time with his children. *Address:* 10 Church Lane, Navenby, Lincoln LN5 0EG. *T:* Lincoln 810812.

NGAIZA, Christopher Pastor; Chairman and Managing Director, PES Consultants Ltd, Tanzania; *b* 29 March 1930; parents decd; *m* 1952, Thereza; three *s* two *d* (and one *s* decd). *Educ:* Makerere University Coll.; Loughborough Co-operative College. Local Courts Magistrate, 1952–53; Secretary/Manager, Bahaya Co-operative Consumer Stores, 1955–57; Loughborough Co-operative Coll., 1957–59; Auctioneer and Representative of Bukoba Native Co-operative Union, Mombasa, 1959–61; Foreign Service, 1961–; Counsellor, Mission to UN, 1961–62; Counsellor, Tanganyika High Commn, London, 1962–63; High Commissioner for United Republic of Tanganyika and Zanzibar in London, 1964–65; Tanzanian Ambassador: to Netherlands, 1965–67, to Arab Republic of Egypt, 1972–77; Mem., E African Common Market Tribunal, 1968–69; Tanzania's first High Comr to Zambia, 1969–72; Special Personal Assistant to Pres. of Tanzania, 1977–85; Comr for Kagera River Basin Orgn, 1977. *Recreations:* music, tennis. *Address:* PES Consultants Ltd, PO Box 23113, Dar-es-Salaam, Tanzania.

NGATA, Sir Henare Kohere, KBE 1982 (OBE); chartered accountant, Gregory Chambers, Gisborne, New Zealand; *b* Waiomatatini, 19 Dec. 1917; *s* of Sir Apirana Ngata and Arihia, *d* of Tuta Tamati; *m* 1940, Rora Lorna, *d* of Maihi Rangipo Mete Kingi; one *s. Educ:* Waiomatatini Sch.; Te Aute Coll., Victoria Univ. of Wellington, BA; BCom; FCA (NZ Soc. of Accountants). Served 28th Maori Bn, 1939–45: POW, Greece; Germany, 1941–45. Chm., Mangatu 1, 3 & 4 Blocks Incorp., 1959–; Director: Fieldair Ltd, 1960–79; Gisborne Sheepfarmers Mercantile Co. Ltd; Gisborne Sheepfarmers Freezing Co. Ltd. Member: Gisborne Reg. Commn, NZ Historic Places Trust, 1962–70; NZ Maori Council, 1962–; C of E Provincial Commn on Maori Schs, 1964–; Gisborne/East Coast Regional Develt Council, 1973–78; Finance Cttee, Bishopric of Aotearoa. Nat. Pres., 28th Maori Bn Assoc., 1964–66. Vice-Pres., NZ Nat. Party, 1967–69. Hon. LLD, Victoria Univ. of Wellington, 1979. *Address:* Grant Road, Gisborne, New Zealand; Gregory Chambers, Derby Street, Gisborne, New Zealand.

NG'ETHE NJOROGE; businessman; High Commissioner for Kenya in London, 1970–78; *m* 1972, Dr Njeri Ng'ethe Njoroge; one *s. Educ:* Kenya and Uganda (Cambridge Sch. Cert., 1949); United States: Central State Coll., Wilberforce, Ohio (BSc (Gen. Sci.) 1955); Univ. of Dayton, Dayton, Ohio (Sociology, 1955–56); Boston Univ. (MSc (Pol. Sci. and Journalism) 1962). Began as journalist, Patriot Ledger, Quincy, Mass; subseq., Kenya Govt: Asst Sec. (Admin), in Min. of Lands and Settlement, and Min. of Works, 1963–64; Min. of Foreign Affairs, 1964; Head of Africa Div., 1964–67; Counsellor, Kenya Embassy, Bonn, 1968–70. Delegate: Commonwealth Conf., 1965, 1966, 1971; Organization of African Unity Confs, 1964–67; UN Gen. Assembly, 1964, 1965, 1966. *Recreations:* music (collector of jazz and classical records), photography (colour slides), reading; interest in current public and international issues. *Address:* PO Box 30384, Nairobi, Kenya.

NGONDA, Putteho Muketoi; Zambian Ambassador to USA, Peru, Brazil and Venezuela, since 1977; *b* 16 Aug. 1936; *m* 1965, Lungowe Mulala; three *s. Educ:* Mongu and Munali Secondary Schs, Zambia; UC of Rhodesia and Nyasaland, Salisbury. BScEcon (Hons). District Officer, 1963–64; 2nd Sec., Zambia Perm. Mission to UN, 1964–65; 1st Sec., Zambian Embassy, Washington, 1967–68; Asst Sec. (Political), Min. of Foreign Affairs, 1968–70; Under-Sec., Min. of Foreign Affairs, 1970–72; Ambassador to Ethiopia, 1972–74; High Comr to UK, 1974–75; Perm. Sec., Ministry of Foreign Affairs, 1975–77. *Recreation:* mainly tennis. *Address:* Embassy of the Republic of Zambia, 2419 Massachusetts Avenue, NW, Washington, DC 20008, USA.

NIAGARA, Archbishop of, since 1985; **Most Rev. John Charles Bothwell,** DD; Metropolitan of Ontario, since 1985; Bishop of Niagara, 1973; *b* 29 June 1926; *s* of William Alexander Bothwell and Anne Bothwell (*née* Campbell); *m* 1951, Joan Cowan; three *s* two *d. Educ:* Runnymede Public School; Humberside Coll. Inst., Toronto; Trinity Coll., Univ. of Toronto (BA 1948, LTh 1951, BD 1952; DD 1972). Asst Priest, St James' Cathedral, Toronto, 1951–53; Sen. Assistant at Christ Church Cathedral, Vancouver, 1953–56; Rector: St Aidan's, Oakville, Ont, 1956–60; St James' Church, Dundas, Ont, 1960–65; Canon of Christ Church Cathedral, Hamilton, Ont, 1963; Dir of Programs for Niagara Diocese, 1965–69; Exec. Dir of Program, Nat. HQ of Anglican Church of Canada, Toronto, 1969–71; Bishop Coadjutor of Niagara, 1971–73. *Publication:* Taking Risks and Keeping Faith, 1985. *Recreations:* golf, cross-country ski-ing, swimming. *Address:* (office) 67 Victoria Avenue South, Hamilton, Ontario L8N 2S8, Canada. *T:* 416/527–1117; (home) 838 Glenwood Avenue, Burlington, Ont L7T 2J9, Canada. *T:* 416/634–8649. *Clubs:* Dundas Valley Golf and Country (Dundas, Ont); Hamilton Chamber of Commerce (Hamilton, Ont).

NIALL, Sir Horace Lionel Richard, Kt 1974; CBE 1957 (MBE 1943); Civil Servant (retd); *b* 14 Oct. 1904; *s* of late Alfred George Niall and Jane Phyllis Niall; *m* 1965, Una Lesley Niall (*née* de Salis); one *d. Educ:* Mudgee High Sch., NSW; Sydney Univ., NSW. Served War of 1939–45: with AIF, four yrs in New Guinea, rank Major, No NGX 373, all campaigns in New Guinea. NSW Public Service (Water Conservation Commn), 1923–27. Public Service of Papua, New Guinea, 1927–64: joined as a Cadet and retd as Dist Comr; rep. PNG at South Pacific Commn, 1954, and UN Trusteeship Council, 1957; Mem. for Morobe in first House of Assembly and Speaker First House, 1964. *Recreations:* golf, surfing. *Address:* 9 Commodore, 50 Palm Beach Road, Palm Beach, NSW 2108, Australia. *T:* 919 5462. *Clubs:* Palm Beach Golf, RSL Palm Beach (NSW).

NIARCHOS, Stavros Spyros; Grand Cross of Order of the Phœnix (Greece), 1957; Commander of Order of George I of Greece, 1954; Commander of Order of St George and St Constantine (Greece), 1964; Head of Niarchos Group of Shipping Companies which controls over 5.75 million tons of shipping (operational and building); *b* 3 July 1909; *s* of late Spyros Niarchos and of Eugenie Niarchos; *m* 1st, 1939, Melpomene Capparis (marr. diss., 1947); no *c*; 2nd, 1947, Eugenie Livanos (*d* 1970); three *s* one *d*; 3rd, 1965, Charlotte Ford (marr. diss., 1967); one *d*; 4th, 1971, Mrs Athina Livanos (*d* 1974). *Educ:* Univ. of Athens (Dr of Laws). On leaving Univ. joined family grain and shipping business; started independent shipping concern, 1939. Joined Royal Hellenic Navy Volunteer Reserve, 1941; served on destroyer engaged in North Atlantic convoy work (despatches). Demobilised, 1945, with rank of Lieut-Comdr. Returned to Shipping business. Pioneered super-tankers. *Recreations:* yachting, ski-ing. *Address:* c/o Niarchos (London) Ltd, 41/43 Park Street, W1. *T:* 01–629 8400. *Clubs:* Athenian, Royal Yacht Club of Greece (both in Athens).

NIBLETT, Prof. William Roy, CBE 1970; BA, MLitt; Professor of Higher Education, University of London, 1967–73, Professor Emeritus, 1973; *b* 25 July 1906; *m* 1938, Sheila Margaret, OBE 1975, *d* of A. C. Taylor, Peterborough; one *s* one *d. Educ:* Cotham Sch., Bristol; University of Bristol (1st cl. hons English; John Stewart Schol.); St Edmund Hall, Oxford. Lectr in Educn, King's Coll., Newcastle, 1934–45 (Registrar of Univ. Durham, 1940–44); Prof. of Educn, University Coll., Hull, 1945–47; Prof. of Education, and Dir, Inst. of Education, Univ. of Leeds, 1947–59; Dean, Univ. of London Inst. of Education, 1960–68. Hibbert Lectr, 1965; Fulbright Schol. (Harvard) and Kellogg International Fellow, 1954; sometime Visiting Professor, Universities of California, Melbourne, Otago and Univs of Japan. Mem., UGC, 1949–59; Chairman: UGC Sub-Cttee on Halls of Residence, 1956 (Report 1957); Educn Dept, BCC, 1965–71; Higher Educn Policy Gp, 1969–72; President: European Assoc. for Res. in Higher Educn, 1972; Higher Educn Foundn, 1984– (Chm. Trustees, 1980–81). Vice-President: World Univ. Service (UK), 1963–; Soc. for Res. in Higher Educn, 1978–; Gloucestershire Historic Churches Preservation Trust, 1981–. Member: Nat. Advisory Coun. on Trng and Supply of Teachers, 1950–61; Adv. Council on Army Educn, 1961–70; Council, Royal Holloway College, 1963–76; Council, Cheltenham Ladies' College, 1967–79; Trustee, Westhill Coll., Birmingham. Chm., Editorial Bd, Studies in Higher Education, 1975–82. FRSA. *Publications:* Education and the Modern Mind, 1954; Christian Education in a Secular Society, 1960; (ed) Moral Education in a Changing Society, 1963; (ed) Higher Education: Demand and Response, 1969; (ed with R. F. Butts) World Year Book of Education, 1972–73; Universities Between Two Worlds, 1974; (with D. Humphreys and J. Fairhurst) The University Connection, 1975; (ed) The Sciences, The Humanities and the Technological Threat, 1975; (contrib.) International Encyclopedia of Higher Education, 1977; (contrib.) The Study of Education, 1980; (contrib.) Validation in Higher Education, 1983. *Address:* 7 Blenheim Road, Bristol BS6 7JL. *T:* Bristol 735891.

NIBLOCK, Henry, (Pat), OBE 1972; HM Diplomatic Service, retired; HM Consul-General, Strasbourg, 1968–72; *b* 25 Nov. 1911; *s* of Joseph and Isabella Niblock, Belfast; *m* 1940, Barbara Mary Davies, *d* of late Captain R. W. Davies, Air Ministry; two *s.* Vice-Consul: Bremen, 1947–50; Bordeaux, 1951; Second Sec. (Commercial), Copenhagen, 1951–53; Consul, Frankfurt-on-Main, 1954–57; First Sec. and Consul, Monrovia, 1957–58; Consul, Houston, 1959–62; Chargé d'Affaires, Port-au-Prince, 1962–63; First Sec. and Consul, Brussels, 1964; Consul (Commercial), Cape Town, 1964–67. *Recreations:* walking, photography. *Address:* 10 Clifton House, 2 Park Avenue, Eastbourne, East Sussex BN22 9QN. *T:* Eastbourne 505695. *Club:* Civil Service.

NICCOL, Kathleen Agnes; *see* Leo, Dame Sister M.

NICHOL, Duncan Kirkbride; Regional General Manager, Mersey Regional Health Authority, since 1984; Member, NHS Management Board, since 1985; *b* 30 May 1941; *s* of James and Mabel Nichol; *m* 1972, Elizabeth Wilkinson; one *s* one *d. Educ:* Bradford Grammar Sch.; St Andrews Univ. (MA Hons). AHA 1967. Asst Gp Sec. and Hosp. Sec. to Manchester Royal Infirmary, 1969–73; Dep. Gp Sec. and Actg Gp Sec., Univ. Hosp. Management Cttee of S Manchester, 1973–74; Dist Administrator, Manchester S Dist, 1974–77; Area Administrator, Salford AHA(T), 1977–81; Regional Administrator, Mersey RHA, 1981–84. Hon. Lectr, Dept of Social Admin, Manchester Univ., 1977–. Member: Central Health Services Council, 1980–81; NHS Training Authy, 1983–85; Nat. Council, Inst. of Health Services Management, 1976– (Vice-Chm., 1982–83; Chm., 1983–84; Pres., 1984–85); Educn Cttee, King Edward's Hosp. Fund for London, 1981–. *Publications:* contributed: Health Care in the United Kingdom, 1982; Management for Clinicians, 1982; Working with People, 1983. *Recreations:* walking, golf, squash. *Address:* 1 Pipers Close, Heswall, Wirral, Merseyside L60 9LJ. *T:* 051–342 2699.

NICHOL, Mrs Muriel Edith; JP; *e d* of late R. C. Wallhead, MP Merthyr Tydfil, 1922–34; *m* James Nichol, MA; one *s.* Counsellor, Welwyn Garden City UDC, 1937–45 (Chm. 1943–44); formerly Dep. Chm., Welwyn Magistrates' Court. MP (Lab) North Bradford, 1945–50; Mem. Parly Delegation to India, Jan.-Feb. 1946; Mem. "Curtis" Cttee (Home Office) on Care of Children, 1945–46. JP Herts, 1944. *Recreations:* local government, social welfare, education.

NICHOLAS, (Angela) Jane (Udale); Dance Director, Arts Council of Great Britain, since 1979; *b* 14 June 1929; *d* of late Bernard Alexander Royle Shore, CBE; *m* 1964, William Alan Nicholas. *Educ:* Norland Place Sch.; Rambert Sch. of Ballet; Arts Educnl Trust; Sadler's Wells Ballet Sch. Founder Mem., Sadler's Wells Theatre Ballet, 1946–50; Mem., Sadler's Wells Ballet at Royal Opera House, 1950–52; freelance dancer, singer, actress, 1952–60; British Council Drama Officer, 1961–70; Arts Council of Great Britain: Dance Officer, 1970–75; Asst Dance Dir, 1975–79. *Recreations:* pruning, weeding, collecting cracked porcelain. *Address:* 21 Stamford Brook Road, W6 0XJ. *T:* 01–741 3035.

NICHOLAS, Barry; *see* Nicholas, J. K. B. M.

NICHOLAS, David, CBE 1982; Editor and Chief Executive, Independent Television News, since 1977; *b* 25 Jan. 1930; *m* 1952, Juliet Davies; one *s* one *d*. *Educ:* Neath Grammar School; University Coll. of Wales, Aberystwyth. BA (Hons) English. National Service, 1951–53. Journalist with Yorkshire Post, Daily Telegraph, Observer; joined ITN, 1960; Deputy Editor, 1963–77. Produced ITN General Election Results, Apollo coverage, and ITN special programmes, 1963–77. Fellow, Royal Television Soc., 1980. Producers' Guild Award 1967, on return of Sir Francis Chichester; Cyril Bennett Award, RTS, 1985. *Recreations:* walking, sailing. *Address:* ITN, 48 Wells Street, W1. *Club:* Reform.

NICHOLAS, Sir Harry; *see* Nicholas, Sir Herbert Richard.

NICHOLAS, Prof. Herbert George, FBA 1969; Rhodes Professor of American History and Institutions, Oxford University, 1969–78; Fellow of New College, Oxford, 1951–78, Emeritus 1978–80, Honorary Fellow since 1980; *b* 8 June 1911; *s* of late Rev. W. D. Nicholas. *Educ:* Mill Hill Sch.; New Coll., Oxford. Commonwealth Fund Fellow in Modern History, Yale, 1935–37; MA Oxon, 1938; Exeter College, Oxford: Lectr, 1938, Fellow, 1946–51; Amer. Div., Min. of Information, and HM Embassy, Washington, 1941–46; Faculty Fellow, Nuffield Coll., Oxford, 1948–57; Nuffield Reader in the Comparative Study of Institutions at Oxford Univ., 1956–69. Chm., British Assoc. for American Studies, 1960–62; Vice-Pres., British Academy, 1975–76. Vis. Prof., Brookings Instn, Washington, 1960; Albert Shaw Lectr in Diplomatic History, Johns Hopkins, 1961; Vis. Fellow, Inst. of Advanced Studies, Princeton, 1964; Vis. Faculty Fellow, Inst. of Politics, Harvard, 1968. Hon. DCL Pittsburgh, 1968. *Publications:* The American Union, 1948; The British General Election of 1950, 1951; To the Hustings, 1956; The United Nations as a Political Institution, 1959, 5th edn 1975; (ed) Tocqueville's De la Démocratie en Amérique, 1961; Britain and the United States, 1963; The American Past and The American Present, 1971; The United States and Britain, 1975; The Nature of American Politics, 1980, 2nd edn 1986; (ed) Washington Despatches, 1941–45, 1981; La Naturaleza de la Política Norteamericana, 1985; articles. *Recreations:* gardening, listening to music. *Address:* 3 William Orchard Close, Old Headington, Oxford. *T:* Oxford 63135. *Club:* Athenæum.

NICHOLAS, Sir Herbert Richard, (Sir Harry Nicholas), Kt 1970; OBE 1949; General Secretary of the Labour Party, 1968–72; *b* 13 March 1905; *s* of Richard Henry and Rosina Nicholas; *m* 1932, Rosina Grace Brown. *Educ:* Elementary sch., Avonmouth, Bristol; Evening Classes; Correspondence Courses. Clerk, Port of Bristol Authority, 1919–36. Transport and Gen. Workers Union: District Officer, Gloucester, 1936–38; Regional Officer, Bristol, 1938–40; National Officer, London: Commercial Road Transport Group, 1940–42; Chemical Section, 1942–44; Metal and Engineering Group, 1944–56; Asst Gen. Sec., 1956–68 (Acting Gen. Sec., Oct. 1964–July 66). Mem., TUC General Council, 1964–67. Mem., Labour Party Nat. Exec. Cttee, 1956–64, 1967–; Treasurer, Labour Party, 1960–64. *Publications:* occasional articles in press on Industrial Relations subjects. *Recreations:* Rugby football, fishing, reading, gardening. *Address:* 33 Madeira Road, Streatham, SW16. *T:* 01–769 7989.

NICHOLAS, Jane; *see* Nicholas, A. J. U.

NICHOLAS, (John Keiran) Barry (Moylan); Principal of Brasenose College, Oxford, since 1978 (Fellow, 1947–78); *b* 6 July 1919; *s* of Archibald John Nicholas and Rose (*née* Moylan); *m* 1948, Hildegart, *d* of Prof. Hans Cloos, Bonn; one *s* one *d*. *Educ:* Downside; Brasenose Coll., Oxford (Scholar). 1st cl. Class. Mods, 1939 and Jurisprudence, 1946. Royal Signals, 1939–45: Middle East, 1941–45; Major, 1943. Called to Bar, Inner Temple, 1950, Hon. Bencher, 1984. Tutor, 1947–71 and Vice-Principal, 1960–63, Brasenose Coll.; All Souls Reader in Roman Law, Oxford Univ., 1949–71; Prof. of Comparative Law, Oxford, 1971–78. Vis. Prof.: Tulane Univ., 1960; Univ. of Rome Inst. of Comparative Law, 1964; Fordham Univ., 1968, 1985. *Publications:* Introduction to Roman Law, 1962; Jolowicz's Historical Introduction to Roman Law, 3rd edn, 1972; French Law of Contract, 1982. *Address:* Brasenose College, Oxford. *T:* Oxford 248641. *Club:* United Oxford & Cambridge University.

NICHOLAS, Sir John (William), KCVO 1981; CMG 1979; HM Diplomatic Service, retired; *b* 13 Dec. 1924; *m* 1947, Rita (*née* Jones); two *s*. *Educ:* Birmingham Univ. Served 7th Rajput Regt, Indian Army, 1944–47; joined Home Civil Service, 1949; War Office, 1949–57; transf. to CRO 1957; First Sec., Brit. High Commn, Kuala Lumpur, 1957–61; Economic Div., CRO, 1961–63; Dep. High Comr in Malawi, 1964–66; Diplomatic Service Inspector, 1967–69; Dep. High Comr and Counsellor (Commercial), Ceylon, 1970–71; Dir, Establishments and Finance Div., Commonwealth Secretariat, 1971–73; Hd of Pacific Dependent Territories Dept, FCO, 1973–74; Dep. High Comr, Calcutta, 1974–76; Consul Gen., Melbourne, 1976–79; High Comr to Sri Lanka and (non-resident) to Republic of the Maldives, 1979–84. *Address:* Constant Spring, Whitmore Vale Road, Hindhead, Surrey. *Club:* Royal Over-Seas League.

NICHOLAS, William Ford, OBE 1954; Director, London Chamber of Commerce and Industry, 1974–84; *b* 17 March 1923; *s* of William and Emma Nicholas; *m* 1954, Isobel Sybil Kennedy; two *s*. *Educ:* Stockport Grammar School. Called to Bar, Middle Temple, 1965. Joined S Rhodesia Civil Service, 1947; Private Sec. to Prime Minister, S Rhodesia, 1950; Private Sec. to Prime Minister, Fedn of Rhodesia and Nyasaland, 1953; Counsellor, High Comr's Office, London, 1960; retd 1963. Dir, UK Cttee, Fedn of Commonwealth Chambers of Commerce, 1964; Dep. Dir, London Chamber of Commerce, 1966. *Address:* 2 Lime Close, Frant, Tunbridge Wells, Kent. *T:* Frant 428.

NICHOLL, Anthony John David; a Recorder of the Crown Court, since 1978; barrister-at-law; *b* 3 May 1935; *s* of late Brig. and Mrs D. W. D. Nicholl; *m* 1961, Hermione Mary Landon; one *s* two *d*. *Educ:* Eton; Pembroke Coll., Oxford. Called to Bar, Lincoln's Inn, 1958. Practising in Birmingham, 1961–. *Recreations:* history, gardening and other rural pursuits. *Address:* 2 Fountain Court, Steelhouse Lane, Birmingham B4 6DR. *T:* 021–236 3882.

NICHOLLS; *see* Harmar-Nicholls.

NICHOLLS, Brian; Director: John Brown Engineering Ltd, since 1979; John Brown Engineering Gas Turbines Ltd, since 1979; *b* 1928; *s* of Ralph and Kathleen Nicholls; *m* 1961, Mary Elizabeth Harley; one *s* two *d*. *Educ:* Haberdashers' Aske's Sch., Hampstead; London Univ. (BSc Econ); Harvard Business Sch. George Wimpey & Co., 1951–55; Constructors John Brown Ltd, 1955–75; Director: CJB Projects Ltd, 1972–75; CJB Pipelines Ltd, 1974–75; Industrial Adviser, Dept of Trade, 1975–78; Dep. Chm., CJB Mohandessi Iran Ltd, 1974–75. Member: Council, British Rly Industry Export Gp, 1976–78; Overseas Projects Bd, 1976–78; BOTB, 1978. Member: Council, British Chemical Engineering Contractors Assoc., 1973–75; Trade and Industry Cttee, British Algerian Soc., 1974–75; Scottish Council for Develt and Industry, 1983–. *Recreations:* writing, walking, music. *Address:* Croy, Shandon, by Helensburgh, Dunbartonshire. *T:* Rhu 820388. *Club:* Royal Northern and Clyde Yacht (Rhu).

NICHOLLS, Clive Victor, QC 1982; a Recorder, since 1984; *b* 29 Aug. 1932; twin *s* of Alfred Charles Victor Nicholls and Lilian Mary (*née* May); *m* 1960, Alison Virginia, *d* of late Arthur and Dorothy Oliver; three *s* three *d*. *Educ:* Brighton Coll.; Trinity Coll., Dublin (MA, LLB); Sidney Sussex Coll., Cambridge (BA *ad eund*); LLB. Called to the Bar, Gray's Inn, 1957. *Recreations:* sailing, fishing. *Address:* Queen Elizabeth Building, Temple, EC4Y 9BS. *T:* 01–583 9744.

See also C. A. A. Nicholls.

NICHOLLS, Colin Alfred Arthur, QC 1981; a Recorder, since 1984; *b* 29 Aug. 1932; twin *s* of Alfred Charles Victor Nicholls and Lilian Mary (*née* May); *m* 1976, Clarissa Allison Spenlove, *d* of late Clive and of Theo Dixon; two *s*. *Educ:* Brighton Coll.; Trinity Coll., Dublin. MA, LLB. Called to the Bar, Gray's Inn, 1957 (Albion Richardson Schol.). Auditor, 1956, and Hon. Mem., 1958–, TCD Historical Soc. *Recreations:* painting (exhib. RHA), sailing. *Address:* Queen Elizabeth Building, Temple, EC4Y 9BS. *T:* 01–583 9744.

See also C. V. Nicholls.

NICHOLLS, David Alan, CMG 1984; Deputy Under Secretary of State (Policy), Ministry of Defence, since 1984; *s* of Thomas Edward and Beatrice Winifred Nicholls; *m* 1955, Margaret (*née* Lewis); two *d*. *Educ:* Cheshunt Grammar School; St John's Coll., Cambridge (Schol., Wright's Prizeman 1952, 1953; BA Hons 1954). Served RAF (Flying Officer), 1950–51. Admiralty, 1954–64; Asst Principal, 1954; Private Sec. to Parliamentary Sec., 1958–59; Principal, 1959; MoD, 1964–75; Private Sec. to Minister of Defence for Admin, 1968–69; Asst Sec., 1969; Cabinet Office, 1975–77; Asst Under-Sec. of State, MoD, 1977–80; Asst Sec., Gen. for Defence Planning and Policy, NATO, 1980–84. *Recreations:* sketching, printmaking. *Address:* c/o Midland Bank, Church Stretton, Shropshire.

NICHOLLS, Rt. Hon. Sir Donald (James), Kt 1983; PC 1986; **Rt. Hon. Lord Justice Nicholls;** a Lord Justice of Appeal, since 1986; *b* 25 Jan. 1933; *yr s* of William Greenhow Nicholls and late Eleanor Jane; *m* 1960, Jennifer Mary, *yr d* of late W. E. C. Thomas, MB, BCh, MRCOG, JP; two *s* one *d*. *Educ:* Birkenhead Sch.; Liverpool Univ.; Trinity Hall, Cambridge (Foundn Schol.). LLB 1st cl. hons Liverpool, BA 1st cl. hons with dist., Pt II Law Tripos Cantab, LLB 1st cl. hons with dist. Cantab. Certif. of Honour, Bar Final, 1958; called to Bar, Middle Temple, 1958, Bencher, 1981; in practice, Chancery Bar, 1958–83; QC 1974; Judge of High Court of Justice, Chancery Div., 1983–86. Mem., Senate of Inns of Court and the Bar, 1974–76. *Recreations:* gardening, history, music. *Address:* Royal Courts of Justice, Strand, WC2A 2LL. *Club:* Athenæum.

NICHOLLS, Pastor Sir Douglas (Ralph), KCVO 1977; Kt 1972; OBE 1968; Governor of South Australia, 1976–77; *b* Cummeragunja, NSW, 9 Dec. 1906; *s* of H. Nicholls, Cummeragunja; *m* 1942, Gladys (*d* 1981), *d* of M. Bux; one *s* one *d*. *Educ:* at Cummeragunja. Formerly one of the best-known aborigines of Australia in the field of athletics and football; Pastor, Churches of Christ Aborigines' Mission, Fitzroy, Victoria; Dir, Aborigines Advancement League, 1969–76. KStJ 1977. *Publications:* contribs AAL quarterly magazines. *Recreations:* formerly running (won Nyah Gift and Warracknabeal Gift, 4th Melbourne Thousand, 1929); football (rep. Vic. in interstate matches).

NICHOLLS, Rear-Adm. (Francis) Brian (Price) B.; *see* Brayne-Nicholls.

NICHOLLS, Air Marshal Sir John (Moreton), KCB 1978; CBE 1970; DFC 1953; AFC 1965; Director in Charge, British Aircraft Co. (British Aerospace), Saudi Arabia, 1980–82; *b* 5 July 1926; *s* of Alfred Nicholls and Elsie (*née* French); *m* 1st, 1945, Enid Jean Marjorie Rose (*d* 1975); two *d*; 2nd, 1977, Shelagh Joyce Hall (*née* Strong). *Educ:* Liverpool Collegiate; St Edmund Hall, Oxford. RAF Coll., 1945–46; No 28 Sqdn, 1947–49; No 257 Sqdn, 1949–52; 335th Ftr Sqdn USAF, Korea, 1952; Fighter Leader Sch., 1953–56; 435th and 83rd Ftr Sqdns USAF, 1956–58; attached British Aircraft Co., Lightning Project, 1959–61; psa 1961; Comd, Air Fighting Develt Sqdn, 1962–64; jssc 1964; MoD, 1964–67; comd RAF Leuchars, 1967–70; idc 1970; SASO 11 Gp, 1971; Principal Staff Officer to CDS, 1971–73; SASO, Strike Comd, 1973–75; ACAS (Op. Requirements), 1976–77; Air Mem. for Supply and Orgn, 1977–79; Vice-Chief of the Air Staff, 1979–80. CBIM. Pres., Bourne Dist British Legion. DFC (USA) and Air Medal (USA), 1953. *Address:* Morton, Bourne, Lincs. *Club:* Royal Air Force.

NICHOLLS, Nigel Hamilton, CBE 1982; Under Secretary, Cabinet Office, since 1986; *b* 19 Feb. 1938; *s* of late Bernard Cecil Hamilton Nicholls and Enid Kathleen Nicholls (*née* Gwynne); *m* 1967, Isobel Judith, *d* of Rev. Canon Maurice Dean; two *s*. *Educ:* King's School, Canterbury; St John's College, Oxford (Exhibr). BA 1962; MA 1966. Asst Principal, Admiralty, 1962, MoD, 1964; Asst Private Sec. to Minister of Defence for RN, 1965–66; Principal, 1966; Directing Staff, RCDS, 1971–73; Asst Private Sec. to Sec. of State for Defence, 1973–74; Asst Sec., 1974; Defence Counsellor, UK Delegation to MBFR Talks, Vienna, 1977–80; Asst Under-Sec. of State, MoD, 1984. *Recreations:* choral singing, genealogy. *Address:* Cabinet Office, 70 Whitehall, SW1. *Club:* United Oxford & Cambridge University.

NICHOLLS, Patrick Charles Martyn; MP (C) Teignbridge, since 1983; *b* 14 Nov. 1948; *s* of late Douglas Charles Martyn Nicholls and Margaret Josephine Nicholls; *m* 1976, Bridget Elizabeth Fergus Owens; one *s* two *d*. *Educ:* Redrice College, Andover. Qualified solicitor, 1974. Partner, Dunn & Baker, 1976, Partner, Dunn & Baker in association with Roger M. L. Williams & Co., 1979–. Mem., E Devon District Council, 1980–84. PPS to Ministers of State, Home Office, 1984–. Steward, British Boxing Bd of Control, 1985–. *Recreations:* theatre, opera, historical research, ski-ing. *Address:* Luchana, Woodway Road, Teignmouth, Devon TQ14 8PZ. *T:* Teignmouth 79490. *Club:* Carlton.

NICHOLLS, Philip, CB 1976; *b* 30 Aug. 1914; *yr s* of late W. H. Nicholls, Radlett; *m* 1955, Sue, *yr d* of late W. E. Shipton; two *s*. *Educ:* Malvern; Pembroke Coll., Cambridge. Asst Master, Malvern, 1936; Sen. Classical Master, 1939; resigned, 1947. Served in Army, 1940–46: 8th Bn, The Worcestershire Regt; HQ, East Africa Command; Allied Commn for Austria. Foreign Office (German Section), 1947; HM Treasury, 1949; a Forestry Commissioner (Finance and Administration), 1970–75, retired. Mem. Council, Malvern Coll. (Vice-Chm., 1963). *Address:* Barnards Green House, Barnards Green, Malvern, Worcs. *T:* Malvern 4446.

NICHOLLS, Robert Michael; District General Manager, Southmead District Health Authority, since 1985; *b* 28 July 1939; *s* of late Herbert Edgar Nicholls and of Bennetta L'Estrange (*née* Burges); *m* 1961, Dr Deirín Deirdre (*née* O'Sullivan); four *s*. *Educ:* Hampton Sch.; University Coll. of Wales (BA 1961); Univ. of Manchester (DSA 1962). AHA 1963. Asst Sec., Torbay Hosp., 1964; House Governor, St Stephen's Hosp., Chelsea, 1966; Asst Clerk to the Governors, St Thomas' Hosp., 1968; Dep. Gp Sec., Southampton Univ. Hosp. Management Cttee, 1972; Dist Administrator, Southampton and SW Hampshire Health Dist, 1974; Area Administrator, Newcastle upon Tyne AHA(T), 1977; Regl Administrator, SW RHA, 1981. Mem., Health Educn Council, 1984–. National Council, Inst. of Health Service Administrators: Mem., 1976–86; Hon. Treasurer, 1980–81; Vice Chm., 1981–82; Chm., 1982–83; Pres., 1983–84. Mem., Education Cttee, King Edward's Hosp. Fund for London, 1975–81. *Publications:* (contrib.) Resources in Medicine, 1970; (contrib.) Working with People, 1983; contrib. Hosp. and Health Services Rev., Health and Soc. Services Jl and The Health Services. *Recreations:*

bird-watching, jazz, opera, sport. *Address:* 47 Woodhill Road, Portishead, Bristol BS20 9EY. *T:* Bristol 848215.

NICHOLLS, Rt. Rev. Vernon Sampson; Hon. Assistant Bishop of Coventry, since 1983; *b* 3 Sept. 1917; *s* of Ernest C. Nicholls, Truro, Cornwall; *m* 1943, Phyllis, *d* of Edwin Potter, Stratford-on-Avon; one *s* one *d. Educ:* Truro Sch.; Univ. of Durham and Clifton Theological Coll., Bristol. Curate: St Oswald Bedminster Down, Bristol, 1941–42; Liskeard, Cornwall, 1942–43. CF, 1944–46 (Hon. CF 1946). Vicar of Meopham, 1946–56; Rural Dean of Cobham, 1953–56; Mem., Strood RDC, 1948–56; Vicar and Rural Dean of Walsall, and Chaplain to Walsall Gen. Hosp., 1956–67; Preb. of Curborough, Lichfield Cath., 1964–67, Archdeacon of Birmingham, 1967–74; Diocesan Planning Officer and Co-ordinating Officer for Christian Stewardship, 1967–74; Bishop of Sodor and Man, 1974–83; Dean of St German's Cathedral, Peel, 1974–83. MLC, Tynwald, IoM, 1974–83; Member: IoM Bd of Educn, 1974–83; Bd of Social Security, 1974–81; IoM Health Services Bd, 1981–83; Founder Chm., IoM Council on Alcoholism, 1979. JP, IoM, 1974–83. *Recreations:* meeting people, gardening, motoring. *Address:* 4 Winston Close, Hathaway Park, Shottery, Stratford-upon-Avon, Warwickshire CV37 9ER. *T:* Stratford-upon-Avon 294478.

NICHOLS, Clement Roy, CMG 1970; OBE 1956; Chairman, Alpha Spinning Mills Pty Ltd; *b* 4 Jan. 1909; *s* of C. J. Nichols, Melbourne; *m* 1933, Margareta, *d* of A. C. Pearse, Melbourne; one *s* one *d. Educ:* Scotch Coll., Melbourne. CText; ATI. Lifetime in wool worsted manufacturing. Past Pres., Wool Textile Mfrs of Australia; Vice-Pres., Internat. Wool Textile Organisation, 1970–75; President: Victorian Chamber of Mfrs, 1970–72, 1977–78; Associated Chambers of Mfrs of Australia, 1971–74. Mem., World Scouts' Cttee, 1959–65, 1967–73; Chm., Asia Pacific Region, 1962–64; Chief Comr, Scout Assoc., 1963–66; Chief Comr, Victorian Br., 1952–58; Nat. Chm., 1973–79; Vice-Pres., Scout Assoc. of Australia, 1979–. *Address:* 82 Studley Park Road, Kew, Victoria 3101, Australia. *Clubs:* Australian (Melbourne); Rotary (Heidelberg).

NICHOLS, Sir Edward (Henry), Kt 1972; TD; Town Clerk of City of London, 1954–74; *b* 27 Sept. 1911; *o s* of Henry James and Agnes Annie Nichols, Notts; *m* 1941, Gwendoline Hetty, *d* of late Robert Elgar, Leeds; one *s. Educ:* Queen Elizabeth's Gram. Sch., Mansfield; Selwyn Coll., Cambridge (BA, LLB). Articled Town Clerk, Mansfield, 1933; Asst Solicitor, Derby, 1936–40. Served War of 1939–45, Hon. Lt-Col RA. Dep. Town Clerk, Derby, 1940–48, Leicester, 1948–49; Town Clerk and Clerk of the Peace, Derby, 1949–53. Hon. DLitt City Univ., 1974. Chevalier, Order of N Star of Sweden; holds other foreign orders. *Address:* 35A The Avenue, Claygate, Surrey KT10 0RX. *T:* Esher 65102. *Club:* City Livery.

NICHOLS, John; *see* Nichols, K. J. H.

NICHOLS, John Winfrith de Lisle, BSc (Eng); CEng; FIEE; retired; Director: National Maritime Institute, 1976–79; Computer Aided Design Centre, Cambridge, 1977–79; *b* 7 June 1919; *er s* of late John F. Nichols, MC, PhD, FRHistS, FSA, Godalming; *m* 1942, Catherine Lilian (*d* 1984), *er d* of Capt. A. V. Grantham, RNR, Essex; two *s* two *d. Educ:* Sir Walter St John's Sch., Battersea; London Univ. Royal Navy, 1940–46; GPO, Dollis Hill, 1946–47; RN Scientific Service, 1947–55; Chief Research Officer, Corp. of Trinity House, 1955–59; UKAEA, 1959–65; Min. of Technology, later DTI and Dept of Industry, 1965–; Under-Sec., and Chm., Requirement Bd for Computers, Systems and Electronics, 1972–74; Under Sec., Research Contractors Div., DoI, 1974–76. *Recreations:* gardening, sailing, caravanning. *Address:* Leybourne End, Wormley, Godalming, Surrey. *T:* Wormley 3252.

NICHOLS, (Kenneth) John (Heastey); Metropolitan Stipendiary Magistrate, since 1972; *b* 6 Sept. 1923; *s* of Sidney Kenneth Nichols, MC and Dorothy Jennie Heastey Richardson; *m* 1st, 1946, Audrey Heather Powell; one *d*; 2nd, 1966, Pamela Marjorie Long, *qv. Educ:* Westminster School. Served War of 1939–45: 60th Rifles, 1941–43; Parachute Regt, NW Europe, SE Asia Comd, 1943–46 (Captain). Admitted Solicitor, 1949; Partner, Speechly, Mumford & Soames (Craig), 1949–69. Mem., Inner London Probation Service Cttee, 1975–. Mem. Council of Law Soc., 1959–68. Pres., Newheels, 1980–86; Vice-Pres., David Isaacs Fund, 1982–86. *Recreations:* cricket, music, walking. *Address:* Marlborough Street Magistrates' Court, Great Marlborough Street, W1. *Club:* MCC.

NICHOLS, Pamela Marjorie, (Mrs John Nichols); *see* Long, P. M.

NICHOLS, Peter, OBE 1982; Rome Correspondent of The Times, since 1957; *b* 15 Feb. 1928; *s* of Walter and Beatrice Nichols; *m* 1974, Paola Rosi; one *s* (and four *c* by a previous marriage). *Educ:* Portsmouth Grammar Sch.; Oxford Univ. BA (Mod. Hist.). Correspondent, The Times, London, Berlin, Bonn, Rome, 1954–. Peripheral activities include BBC TV documentaries, radio and television programmes for Italian broadcasting corporation. Internat. prize for journalism, Città di Roma, 1973. *Publications:* Piedmont and the English, 1967; Politics of the Vatican, 1968; Italia, Italia, 1973 (Book of the Year Prize, 1976, for Italian edn); Italian Decision, 1977; Ruffo in Calabria, 1977; The Pope's Divisions, The Roman Catholic Church Today, 1981; contrib. Foreign Affairs, etc. *Recreation:* relaxing. *Address:* 45 Via degli Spagnoli, Rome, Italy. *T:* Rome 6541076.

NICHOLS, Peter Richard, FRSL 1983; playwright since 1959; *b* 31 July 1927; *s* of late Richard George Nichols and Violet Annie Poole; *m* 1960, Thelma Reed; one *s* two *d* (and one *d* decd). *Educ:* Bristol Grammar Sch.; Bristol Old Vic Sch.; Trent Park Trng College. Actor, mostly in repertory, 1950–55; worked as teacher in primary and secondary schs, 1958–60. Mem., Arts Council Drama Panel, 1973–75. Playwright in residence, Guthrie Theatre, Minneapolis, 1976. *TV plays:* Walk on the Grass, 1959; Promenade, 1960; Ben Spray, 1961; The Reception, 1961; The Big Boys, 1961; Continuity Man, 1963; Ben Again, 1963; The Heart of the Country, 1963; The Hooded Terror, 1963; The Brick Umbrella, 1964; When the Wind Blows, 1964 (later adapted for radio); Daddy Kiss It Better, 1968; The Gorge, 1968; Hearts and Flowers, 1971; The Common, 1973; See Me (in 5 parts), 1984; *films:* Catch Us If You Can, 1965; Georgy Girl, 1967; Joe Egg, 1971; The National Health, 1973; Privates on Parade, 1983; Changing Places, 1984; *stage plays:* A Day in The Death of Joe Egg, 1967 (Evening Standard Award, Best Play; Tony Award, Best Revival, 1985); The National Health, 1969 (Evening Standard Award, Best Play); Forget-me-not Lane, 1971; Chez Nous, 1973; The Freeway, 1974; Privates on Parade, 1977 (Evening Standard Best Comedy, Soc. of West End Theatres Best Comedy and Ivor Novello Best Musical Awards); Born in the Gardens, 1979 (televised 1986); Passion Play, 1980 (Standard Best Play award, 1981); A Piece of My Mind, 1986; *musical:* Poppy, 1982 (SWET Best Musical Award). *Publications:* Feeling You're Behind (autobiog.), 1984; some TV plays in anthologies; all above stage plays published. *Recreations:* listening to jazz, looking at cities. *Address:* Margaret Ramsay Ltd, 14 Goodwin's Court, WC2. *T:* 01–240 0691.

NICHOLS, Rt. Rev. Mgr Vincent Gerard; General Secretary, Roman Catholic Bishops' Conference of England and Wales, since 1984; *b* 8 Nov. 1945; *s* of Henry Joseph Nichols and Mary Nichols (*née* Russell). *Educ:* St Mary's College, Crosby; Gregorian Univ., Rome (STL PhL); Manchester Univ. (MA Theol); Loyola Univ., Chicago (MEd). Chaplain, St John Rigby VI Form College, Wigan, 1972–77; Priest, inner city of Liverpool, 1978–81; Director, Upholland Northern Inst., with responsibility for in service training of clergy and for adult Christian educn, 1981–84. Advr to Cardinal Hume and Archbishop Worlock, Internat. Synods of Bishops, 1980, 1983. *Publications:* articles in The Clergy Review. *Address:* Bishops' Conference Secretariat, 39 Eccleston Square, SW1V 1PD. *T:* 01–630 8220.

NICHOLS, William Henry, CB 1974; *b* 25 March 1913; *s* of William and Clara Nichols. *Educ:* Owens School. Entered Inland Revenue, 1930; Exchequer and Audit Dept, 1935, Secretary, 1973–75, retired. *Address:* 17 Park House, Winchmore Hill Road, N21 1QL. *T:* 01–886 4321; 11 Old Street, Haughley, Stowmarket, Suffolk IP14 3NT.

NICHOLS, William Reginald, CBE 1975; TD; MA; Clerk of the Worshipful Company of Salters, 1946–75, Master, 1978–79; *b* 23 July 1912; *s* of late Reginald H. Nichols, JP, FSA, Barrister-at-Law; *m* 1946, Imogen, *d* of late Rev. Percy Dearmer, DD, Canon of Westminster, and late Nancy (who *m* 1946, Sir John Sykes, KCB; he died, 1952); one *s* one *d. Educ:* Harrow; Gonville and Caius Coll., Cambridge (Sayer Classical Scholar). MA 1938. Called to the Bar, Gray's Inn, 1937. Served War of 1939–45 with Hertfordshire Regt (despatches) and on staff 21st Army Group. Former Jt Hon. Sec., CGLI; Governor of Christ's Hospital; former Governor of Grey Coat Hospital Foundation. *Address:* The Farriers Cottage, St Nicholas-at-Wade, Birchington, Kent CT7 0NR.

NICHOLSON, Air Commodore Angus Archibald Norman, CBE 1961; AE 1945; Deputy Secretary-General, International Shipping Secretariat, 1971–80; *b* 8 March 1919; *s* of Major Norman Nicholson and Alice Frances Nicholson (*née* Salvidge), Hoylake, Cheshire; *m* 1943, Joan Mary, *d* of Ernest Beaumont, MRCVS, DVSM; one *s* one *d. Educ:* Eton; King's Coll., Cambridge. Cambridge Univ. Air Sqn, 1938–39; commissioned, 1939. Served War 1939–45: flying duties in Bomber Command and Middle East. Air Cdre, 1966; Dir of Defence Plans (Air), Min. of Defence, 1966–67; Defence Adviser to British High Comr in Canada and Head of British Defence Liaison Staff, 1968–70; retired from RAF, 1970. MBIM 1967, FBIM 1980. *Recreations:* sailing, golf, music. *Address:* 12 Captain's Row, Lymington, Hants. *Clubs:* Army and Navy; Leander (Henley); Royal Lymington Yacht.

NICHOLSON, Anthony Thomas Cuthbertson; a Recorder of the Crown Court, 1980–84; *b* 17 May 1929; *s* of Thomas and Emma Cuthbertson Nicholson, Stratford, E; *m* 1955, Sheila Rose, *er d* of Albert and Rose Pigram, Laindon, Essex; two *s* one *d. Educ:* St Bonaventure's Grammar Sch., Forest Gate, E7. Journalist, 1944–62. Served Army, 1947–49, RAF, 1950–53. Called to the Bar, Gray's Inn, 1962. *Publications:* (play) Van Call, 1954; Esprit de Law, 1973. *Recreation:* wildfowling. *Address:* The Old Vicarage, Southminster, Essex CM0 7ES; 3 Hare Court, Temple, EC4.

NICHOLSON, Bryan Hubert; Chairman, Manpower Services Commission, since 1984; *b* 6 June 1932; *s* of late Reginald Hubert and Clara Nicholson; *m* 1956, Mary Elizabeth, *er d* of A. C. Harrison of Oxford; one *s* one *d* (and one *s* decd). *Educ:* Palmers School, Grays, Essex; Oriel College, Oxford (MA PPE). 2nd Lieut, RASC, 1950–52; Unilever Management Trainee, 1955–58; Dist. Manager, Van den Berghs, 1958–59; Sales Manager, Three Hands/Jeyes Group, 1960–64; Sperry Rand: Sales Dir, UK, Remington Div., 1964–66; Gen. Manager, Australia, Remington Div., 1966–69; Managing Dir, UK and France, Remington Div., 1969–72; Dir., Ops, Rank Xerox (UK), 1972–76; Dir, Overseas Subsidiaries, Rank Xerox, 1976; Exec. Main Bd Dir, Rank Xerox, 1976–84; Chm., Rank Xerox (UK) and Chm., Rank Xerox GmbH, 1979–84; Non-executive Director: Rank Xerox, 1984–; Baker Perkins Holdings, 1982–84; Evode, 1981–84. Mem., NEDC, 1985–; Vice-Pres., Re-Solv (Soc. for Prevention of Solvent Abuse), 1985–; Mem. Council, Inst. of Manpower Studies, 1985–. UK Hon. Rep., W Berlin, 1983–84. CBIM 1985; FRSA 1985. *Recreations:* tennis, bridge, political history. *Address:* Point Piper, Lilley Drive, Kingswood, Surrey KT20 6JA. *T:* Mogador 832208. *Club:* United Oxford & Cambridge University.

NICHOLSON, Sheriff (Charles) Gordon (Brown); QC (Scot.) 1982; Member, Scottish Law Commission, since 1982; *b* 11 Sept. 1935; *s* of William Addison Nicholson, former Director, Scottish Tourist Board, and late Jean Brown; *m* 1963, Hazel Mary Nixon; two *s. Educ:* George Watson's Coll., Edinburgh; Edinburgh Univ. MA Hons (English Lit.) 1956, LLB 1958. 2nd Lieut Queen's Own Cameron Highlanders, 1958–60. Admitted Faculty of Advocates, Edinburgh, 1961; in practice at Bar; Standing Junior Counsel, Registrar of Restrictive Trading Agreements, 1968; Advocate-Depute, 1968–70; Sheriff of: South Strathclyde, Dumfries and Galloway, 1970–76; Lothian and Borders, 1976–82. Vice-Pres., Sheriffs' Assoc., 1979–82 (Sec., 1975–79). Member: Scottish Council on Crime, 1972–75; Dunpark Cttee on Reparation by Offenders, 1974–77; May Cttee of Inquiry into UK Prison Service, 1978–79; Hon. Vice-Pres., Scottish Assoc. for Study of Delinquency, 1982– (Chm., 1974–79); Chm., Edinburgh CAB, 1979–82. *Publication:* The Law and Practice of Sentencing in Scotland, 1981. *Recreations:* music, philately. *Address:* 1A Abbotsford Park, Edinburgh EH10 5DX. *T:* 031–447 4300. *Club:* New (Edinburgh).

NICHOLSON, Hon. Sir David (Eric), Kt 1972; Speaker of the Legislative Assembly of Queensland, 1960–72 (record term); MLA (CP) for Murrumba, 1950–72; *b* 26 May 1904; *s* of J. A. Nicholson; *m* 1934, Cecile F., *d* of M. E. Smith; two *s* two *d. Recreations:* bowls, swimming, gardening. *Address:* 8/178 Bowen Terrace, New Farm, Qld 4005, Australia. *Clubs:* Redcliffe Trotting (Life Mem.), Redcliffe Agricl, Horticultural and Industrial Soc. (Life Mem.); Returned Servicemen's (Caboolture) (Life Mem.); New Farm Bowls.

NICHOLSON, (Edward) Max, CB 1948; CVO 1971; Chairman, Land Use Consultants, since 1966; *b* 1904; *m* 1st, 1932, Eleanor Mary Crawford (marr. diss., 1964); two *s*; 2nd, Marie Antoinette Mauerhofer; one *s. Educ:* Sedbergh; Hertford Coll., Oxford. Head of Allocation of Tonnage Division, Ministry of War Transport, 1942–45; Secretary of Office of The Lord President of the Council, 1945–52. Member Advisory Council on Scientific Policy, 1948–64; Dir-Gen., Nature Conservancy, 1952–66; Convener, Conservation Section, Internat. Biological Programme, 1963–74; Secretary, Duke of Edinburgh's Study Conference on the Countryside in 1970, 1963; Albright Lecturer, Univ. of California, 1964; a Dir and Managing Editor, Environmental Data Services Ltd, 1978–80. President: RSPB, 1980–85; Simon Population Trust, 1985–; Vice-President: RSA, 1978–82; PSI (formerly PEP); Wildfowl Trust; WWF, UK; Trustee, Fair Isle Bird Observatory; Member: Council, Internat. Inst. of Environment and Develt; Bd and Editorial Cttee, Birds of the Western Palearctic, 1965–; Internat. Council, WWF, 1983–. Chairman: Environmental Cttee, London Celebrations for the Queen's Silver Jubilee, 1976–77; London Looks Forward Conf., 1977; Ecological Parks Trust, 1977–; UK Standing Cttee for World Conservation Strategy Prog., 1981–83; Common Ground Internat., 1981–. Hon. Member: IUCN; World Wildlife Fund; RTPI. Scientific FZS; Corr. Fellow, American Ornithologists' Union. Hon. Fellow RIBA; Hon. LLD Aberdeen, 1964; Hon. Dr, RCA, 1970; Hon. DL Birmingham, 1983. John C. Phillips Medallist International Union for Conservation of Nature and Natural Resources, 1963; Europa Preis für Landespflege, 1972. Comdr, Order of Golden Ark, Netherlands, 1973. *Publications:* Birds in England, 1926; How Birds Live, 1927; Birds and Men, 1951; Britain's Nature Reserves, 1958; The System, 1967; The Environmental Revolution, 1970 (Premio Europeo Cortina-Ulisse, 1971); The Big Change, 1973; and other books, scientific papers and articles. *Address:* 13 Upper Cheyne Row, SW3 5JW. *Club:* Athenæum.

NICHOLSON, (Edward) Rupert, FCA; Partner, Peat Marwick Mitchell & Co. (UK), 1949–77; *b* 17 Sept. 1909; *s* of late Alfred Edward Nicholson and late Elise (*née* Dobson); *m* 1935, Mary Elley (*d* 1983); one *s* one *d. Educ:* Whitgift Sch., Croydon. Articled to father, 1928–33; joined Peat Marwick Mitchell & Co., 1933. Apptd by BoT, jointly, Inspector of Majestic Insurance Co. Ltd and two others, 1961; apptd Liquidator, Davies Investments Ltd, 1967; apptd Receiver, Rolls-Royce Ltd, 1971; Receiver, Northern Developments (Holdings), 1975. Chm., Techn. Adv. Cttee, Inst. Chartered Accountants, 1969–70; Liquidator, Court Line Ltd, 1974; Mem., Post Office Review Cttee, 1976. Chm., Croydon Business Venture, 1983–. Governor, Whitgift Foundn, 1976, Chm., 1978–. Master, Horners' Co., 1984–85. *Publications:* articles in learned jls. *Address:* Grey Wings, The Warren, Ashtead, Surrey. *T:* Ashtead 72655. *Club:* Caledonian.

NICHOLSON, Emma Harriet; Vice-Chairman, Conservative Party, since 1983; *b* 16 Oct. 1941; *d* of Sir Godfrey Nicholson, Bt, *qv. Educ:* St Mary's School, Wantage; Royal Academy of Music. LRAM, ARCM. Computer Programmer, Programming Instructor, Systems Analyst, ICL, 1963–66; computer consultant, John Tyzack, 1967–69; gen. management consultant and computer consultant, McLintock Mann and Whinney Murray, 1969–73; joined Save the Children Fund, Dir of Fund Raising, 1977–85. Dep. Chm., Duke of Edinburgh Award 30th Anniv. Tribute Project for 1986; fundraising consultant to World Association of Girl Guides and Girl Scouts; Bd Mem. (England), and Mem., Comité d'Honneur, Sauvé Les Enfants (France). Prospective Parly candidate (C), Torridge and West Devon, 1985–. *Recreations:* walking, cross country ski-ing, swimming. *Address:* c/o Conservative & Unionist Central Office, 32 Smith Square, SW1P 3HH. *T:* 01-222 9000. *Club:* Royal Commonwealth Society.

NICHOLSON, Rev. Prof. Ernest Wilson, DD; Oriel Professor of the Interpretation of Holy Scripture and Fellow of Oriel College, Oxford University, since 1979; *b* 26 Sept. 1938; *s* of Ernest Tedford Nicholson and Veronica Muriel Nicholson; *m* 1962, Hazel (*née* Jackson); one *s* three *d. Educ:* Portadown Coll.; Trinity Coll., Dublin (Scholar, BA 1960, MA 1964); Glasgow Univ. (PhD 1964). MA (by incorporation) 1967, BD 1971, DD 1978, Cambridge; DD Oxford (by incorporation) 1979. Lectr in Hebrew and Semitic Languages, TCD, 1962–67; Univ. Lectr in Divinity, Cambridge Univ., 1967–79; Fellow: University Coll. (now Wolfson Coll.), Cambridge, 1967–69; Pembroke Coll., Cambridge, 1969–79; Chaplain, Pembroke Coll., Cambridge, 1969–73, Dean, 1973–79. Guest Lecturer at universities and colleges in Scandinavia, USA, and Australia. *Publications:* Deuteronomy and Tradition, 1967; Preaching to the Exiles, 1971; Exodus and Sinai in History and Tradition, 1973; (with J. Baker) The Commentary of Rabbi David Kimḥi on Psalms 120–150, 1973; Commentary on Jeremiah 1–25, 1973; Commentary on Jeremiah 26–52, 1975; God and His People: covenant and theology in the Old Testament, 1986; articles in biblical and Semitic jls. *Recreations:* music, the English countryside. *Address:* 19 Five Mile Drive, Oxford OX2 8HT. *T:* Oxford 58759.

NICHOLSON, Sir Godfrey, 1st Bt, *cr* 1958; Distiller; *b* 9 Dec. 1901; *s* of late Richard Francis Nicholson of Woodcott, Hants, and late Helen Violet Portal; *m* 1936, Lady Katharine Constance Lindsay (*d* 1972), 5th *d* of 27th Earl of Crawford; four *d. Educ:* Winchester; Christ Church, Oxford. MP (Nat. C) Morpeth, 1931–35; Royal Fusiliers, 1939–42; MP (C) Farnham Division of Surrey, 1937–66; retired. Chairman, Estimates Cttee, 1961–64. Pres., British Assoc. of Parascending Clubs, 1973–81. Chm., St Birinus Hosp. Gp (Psychiatric), 1966–74. Chm., Friends of Friendless Churches, 1962–. FSA. *Address:* Bussock Hill House, Newbury, Berks. *T:* Chieveley 248260. *Clubs:* Athenæum, Pratt's.

See also Rt Hon. R. N. Luce, Sir J. C. F. Montgomery Cuninghame, E. H. Nicholson.

NICHOLSON, Gordon; *see* Nicholson, C. G. B.

NICHOLSON, Dr Howard, FRCP; Physician, University College Hospital, since 1948; Physician, Brompton Hospital, 1952–77, retired; Fellow of University College, London, since 1959; *b* 1 Feb. 1912; *s* of Frederick and Sara Nicholson; *m* 1941, Winifrid Madeline Piercy. *Educ:* University Coll., London, and University Coll. Hospital. MB, BS, London, 1935; MD London 1938; MRCP 1938, FRCP 1949. House appointments and Registrarship, UCH, 1935–38; House Physician at Brompton Hosp., 1938. Served War, 1940–45, RAMC; Physician to Chest Surgical Team and Officer i/c Medical Div. (Lt-Col). Registrar, Brompton Hosp., and Chief Asst, Inst. of Diseases of Chest, 1945–48. Goulstonian Lecturer, RCP, 1950. *Publications:* sections on Diseases of Chest in The Practice of Medicine (ed J. S. Richardson), 1961, and in Progress in Clinical Medicine, 1961; articles in Thorax, Lancet, etc. *Recreations:* reading, going to the opera. *Address:* Chelwood, Laughton, Lewes, E Sussex BN8 6BE.

NICHOLSON, James Frederick; farmer; MP (OU) Newry and Armagh, 1983–85; *b* 29 Jan. 1945; *s* of Thomas and Matilda Nicholson; *m* 1968, Elizabeth Gibson; six *s. Educ:* Aghavilly Primary Sch. Member: Armagh Dist Council, 1975–; Southern Health and Social Services Bd, 1977–. Mem. (OU) Newry and Armagh, NI Assembly, 1982–86.

NICHOLSON, (John) Leonard, DSc(Econ); formerly Chief Economic Adviser to Department of Health and Social Security; Chairman, Michael Karolyi Memorial Trust; *b* 18 Feb. 1916; *er s* of late Percy Merwyn Nicholson and late Jane Winifred Nicholson (*née* Morris). *Educ:* Stowe; Institute of Actuaries; London School of Economics. MSc (Econ); DSc (Econ) London (Bowley and Frances Wood Meml Prizes). With Oxford University Inst. of Statistics, 1940–47; Ministry of Home Security, 1943–44; Central Statistical Office, 1947–68; Simon Research Fellow, Manchester Univ., 1962–63; Chief Economic Advr to DHSS and to successive Secretaries of State for Social Services, 1968–76; Assoc. Prof. of Quantitative Econs, Brunel Univ., 1972–74; Sen. Fellow, PSI, 1977–83. *Publications:* The Beveridge Plan for Social Security (jtly), 1943; Variations in Working Class Family Expenditure, 1949; The Interim Index of Industrial Production, 1949; Redistribution of Income in the United Kingdom, 1965; The Arithmetic of the Welfare State, 1986; contrib. to: D. Wedderburn, Poverty, Inequality and Class Structure, 1974; A. B. Atkinson, The Personal Distribution of Incomes, 1976; V. Halberstadt and A. J. Culyer, Public Economics and Human Resources, 1977; DHSS Social Security Research, 1977; DHSS Definition and Measurement of Poverty, 1979; P. Streeten and H. Maier, Human Resources, Employment and Development, vol. 2, 1983; various articles concerned with national income, family expenditure, economic welfare and statistics in academic journals. *Recreations:* music, painting, real tennis, skiing. *Address:* 53 Frognal, NW3 6YA. *Clubs:* MCC, Queen's.

NICHOLSON, Sir John (Norris), 2nd Bt, *cr* 1912; KBE 1971; CIE 1946; JP; Lord-Lieutenant, 1980–86, and Keeper of the Rolls, 1974–86, of the Isle of Wight; *b* 19 Feb. 1911; *o c* of late Captain George Crosfield Norris Nicholson, RFC, and Hon. Evelyn Izme Murray, *y d* of 10th Baron and 1st Viscount Elibank (she *m* 2nd 1st Baron Mottistone, PC); *S* grandfather, 1918; *m* 1938, Vittoria Vivien, *y d* of late Percy Trewhella, Villa Sant' Andrea, Taormina; two *s* two *d. Educ:* Winchester Coll., Trinity Coll., Cambridge. Captain 4th Cheshires (TA), 1939–41. BEF Flanders 1940 (despatches). Min. of War Transport, India and SE Asia, 1942–46. Chairman: Ocean Steam Ship Co. Ltd, 1957–71; Liverpool Port Employers Assoc., 1957–61; Martins Bank Ltd, 1962–64 (Dep. Chm., 1959–62); Management Cttee, HMS Conway, 1958–65; British Liner Cttee, 1963–67; Cttee, European Nat. Shipowners' Assoc., 1965–69; IoW Develt Bd, 1986–; Mem., Shipping Advisory Panel, 1962–64; Pres., Chamber of Shipping of the UK, 1970–71; Mem., Economic and Social Cttee, EEC, 1973–74. Director: Barclays Bank Ltd, 1969–81; Royal Insurance Co. Ltd, 1955–81. Pres., E Wessex TA&VRA, 1982–84. Governor, IoW Technical Coll. Vice Lord-Lieutenant, IoW, 1974–80. Silver Jubilee Medal, 1977. *Heir: s* Charles Christian Nicholson [*b* 15 Dec. 1941; *m* 1975, Martie, *widow* of Niall Anstruther-Gough-Calthorpe and *d* of Stuart Don]. *Address:* Mottistone Manor, Isle of Wight. *T:* Brighstone 740322. *Clubs:* Army and Navy; Royal Yacht Squadron (Commodore, 1980–86).

NICHOLSON, Leonard; *see* Nicholson, J. L.

NICHOLSON, Lewis Frederick, CB 1963; *b* 1 May 1918; *s* of Harold and May Nicholson; *m* 1947, Diana Rosalind Fear; one *s* two *d. Educ:* Taunton Sch.; King's Coll., Cambridge. Research Laboratories of GEC, 1939; Royal Aircraft Establishment, 1939–59; Head of Aerodynamics Dept, RAE, 1953–59; Imperial Defence Coll., 1956; Director-General of Scientific Research (Air), Ministry of Aviation, 1959–63; Dep. Director (Air) Royal Aircraft Establishment, 1963–66; Chief Scientist, RAF, 1966–69; Vice Controller Aircraft, MoD (PE), 1969–78, retired. *Publications:* (Joint) Compressible Airflow-Tables; Compressible Airflow-Graphs; papers on aerodynamic subjects. *Address:* 15 Silver Birches Way, Elstead, Godalming, Surrey GU8 6JA. *T:* Elstead 702362.

NICHOLSON, Max; *see* Nicholson, E. M.

NICHOLSON, Michael Constantine; a Recorder of the Crown Court, since 1980; *b* 3 Feb. 1932; *m* 1960, Kathleen Mary Strong; two *d. Educ:* Wycliffe Coll., Stonehouse; University Coll. of Wales, Aberystwyth (LLB). Called to the Bar, Gray's Inn, 1957; Crown Counsel, Nyasaland, 1960–63; Wales and Chester circuit, 1963–. *Recreations:* cinema, theatre. *Address:* (home) 11 The Rise, Cardiff. *T:* Cardiff 756212; (chambers) 33 Park Place, Cardiff. *T:* Cardiff 33313. *Club:* Cardiff Golf.

NICHOLSON, Norman Cornthwaite, OBE 1981; poet and critic; *b* Millom, Cumberland, 8 Jan. 1914; *s* of Joseph and Edith Nicholson; *m* 1956, Yvonne Edith Gardener (*d* 1982). *Educ:* local schools. Literary criticism in weekly press. FRSL 1945; Hon. Fellow, Manchester Polytechnic, 1979. MA (Hon.): Manchester Univ., 1959; Open Univ., 1975; Hon. DLitt Liverpool, 1980; Hon. LittD Lancaster, 1984. Cholmondley Award for Poetry, 1967; Soc. of Authors Travelling Award, 1972; Queen's Medal for Poetry, 1977. *Publications: poetry:* Five Rivers, 1944 (Heinemann Prize, 1945); Rock Face, 1948; The Pot Geranium, 1954; Selected Poems, 1966; A Local Habitation, 1973; Sea to the West, 1981; Selected Poems 1940–1982, 1982; *verse drama:* The Old Man of the Mountains (produced Mercury Theatre), 1946; A Match for the Devil, 1955; Birth by Drowning, 1960; *criticism:* Man and Literature, 1943; William Cowper, 1951; *topography:* Cumberland and Westmorland, 1949; The Lakers, 1955; Provincial Pleasures, 1959; Portrait of the Lakes, 1963; Greater Lakeland, 1969; *autobiography:* Wednesday Early Closing, 1975; *anthology:* The Pelican Anthology of Modern Religious Verse, 1943; A Choice of Cowper's Verse, 1975; The Lake District, 1977. *Address:* 14 St George's Terrace, Millom, Cumbria. *T:* Millom 2024.

NICHOLSON, Paul Douglas, DL; Chairman and Managing Director, Vaux Group, since 1976; *b* 7 March 1938; *s* of late Douglas Nicholson, TD and Pauline Nicholson; *m* 1970, Sarah, *y d* of Sir Edmund Bacon, Bt, KG, KBE, TD; one *d. Educ:* Harrow; Clare College, Cambridge (MA). FCA. Lieut, Coldstream Guards, 1956–58; joined Vaux Breweries, 1965. Mem., N Regional Bd, Lloyds Bank, 1982–; Chm., Northern Investors Co., 1984–; Director: Tyne Tees Television, 1981–; NE Electricity Bd, 1985–; Northern Development Co. Ltd, 1986–. Chm., N Region, CBI, 1977–79; Chm., N Regional Bd, British Technology Group, 1979–84. High Sheriff, Co. Durham, 1980–81; DL Co. Durham, 1980. *Recreations:* deerstalking, driving horses, flying. *Address:* Quarry Hill, Brancepeth, Durham DH7 8DW. *T:* Durham 780275. *Clubs:* Boodle's; Northern Counties (Newcastle upon Tyne).

NICHOLSON, Ralph Lambton Robb; Secretary, United Kingdom Atomic Energy Authority, 1984–86; *b* 26 Sept. 1924; *s* of Ralph Adam Nicholson and Kathleen Mary Nicholson (*née* Robb); *m* 1951, Mary Kennard; one *s* two *d. Educ:* Sherborne School; Cambridge Univ.; Imperial College, London (BSc; ACGI). FIChemE. Royal Engineers, 1943–47. Chemical engineer, Distillers Co., 1950–51; Wellcome Foundation, 1951–54; Fisons, 1954–58; planning and commercial manager, UKAEA, 1958–67; Dir, Min. of Technology Programmes Analysis Unit, 1967–71; Principal Programmes and Finance Officer, UKAEA, 1971–84. *Publications:* contribs to energy and management jls. *Recreations:* gardening, music, canals. *Address:* The Garth, Midgham, Reading, Berks. *T:* Woolhampton 712211. *Club:* United Oxford & Cambridge University.

NICHOLSON, Robert; publisher, designer, artist, writer; *b* Sydney, Australia, 8 April 1920; *m* 1951; one *s* one *d. Educ:* Troy Town Elementary Sch., Rochester; Rochester Tech. Sch.; Medway Sch. of Art. Served 1939–45, RAMC (mainly pathology in Middle East). Responsible with brother for major design projects during post-war design boom, 1945–55, including Festival of Britain Exhibition in Edinburgh, 1951 and Design Centre, London, 1956. Writer and publisher of guide books including: Nicholson's London Guide; Street Finder; Guide to Great Britain, guides to the Thames, the canals, etc. Benjamin Franklin medal, 1960. Exhibns of landscape painting in London, 1976, Madrid, 1982, and annually in Kent and Sussex. Lives in Kent.

NICHOLSON, Sir Robin (Buchanan), Kt 1985; PhD; FRS 1978; FEng 1980; Director, Pilkington Brothers plc, since 1986; *b* 12 Aug. 1934; *s* of Carroll and Nancy Nicholson; *m* 1958, Elizabeth Mary, *d* of late Sir Sydney Caffyn; one *s* two *d. Educ:* Oundle Sch.; St Catharine's Coll., Cambridge. BA 1956, PhD 1959, MA 1960. FIM; MInstP; CBIM. University of Cambridge: Demonstrator in Metallurgy, 1960; Lectr in Metallurgy, 1964; Fellow of Christ's Coll., 1962–66, Hon. Fellow 1984; Prof. of Metallurgy, Univ. of Manchester, 1966. Inco Europe Ltd: Dir of Research Lab., 1972; Dir, 1975; Man. Dir, 1976–81; Co-Chm., Biogen NV, 1979–81. Chief Scientific Advr to Cabinet Office, 1983–85 (Central Policy Review Staff, 1981–83). Chief Exec., Electro-Optical Div., Pilkington Gp, 1986; Dir, Rolls-Royce plc, 1986–. Mem., SERC (formerly SRC), 1978–81. Mem. Council, Royal Soc., 1983–85. Foreign Associate, Nat. Acad. of Engrg, USA, 1983. Hon. FIChemE; Hon. DSc: Cranfield, 1983; Aston, 1983; Manchester, 1985; Hon. DMet Sheffield, 1984; Hon. DEng Birmingham, 1986. Rosenhain Medallist, Inst. of Metals, 1971; Platinum Medal, Metals Soc., 1982. *Publications:* Precipitation Hardening (with A. Kelly), 1962; (jtly) Electron Microscopy of Thin Crystals, 1965; (ed and contrib. with A. Kelly) Strengthening Methods in Crystals, 1971; numerous papers to learned jls. *Recreations:* family life, gardening, music. *Address:* Whittington House, 8 Fisherwick

Road, Whittington, near Lichfield, Staffs WS14 9LH. *T:* Whittington 432081. *Club:* MCC.

NICHOLSON, Rupert; *see* Nicholson, E. R.

NICKELL, Prof. Stephen John; Professor of Economics, Director of the Institute of Economics and Statistics and Fellow of Nuffield College, University of Oxford, since 1984; *b* 25 April 1944; *s* of John Edward Hilary Nickell and Phyllis Nickell; *m* 1976, Susan Elizabeth (*née* Pegden); one *s* one *d*. *Educ:* Merchant Taylors' Sch.; Pembroke Coll., Cambridge (BA); LSE (MSc). Maths teacher, Hendon County Sch., 1965–68; London School of Economics: Lectr, 1970–77; Reader, 1977–79; Prof. of Economics, 1979–84. *Publications:* The Investment Decisions of Firms, 1978; articles in learned jls. *Recreations:* jogging, riding, cooking. *Address:* Cedar Cottage, North Side, Steeple Aston, Oxon OX5 3SE.

NICKERSON, Albert Lindsay; retired as Chairman and Chief Executive Officer, Mobil Oil Corporation; *b* 17 Jan. 1911; *s* of Albert Lindsay Nickerson and Christine (*née* Atkinson); *m* 1936, Elizabeth Perkins; one *s* three *d*. *Educ:* Noble and Greenough Sch., Mass; Harvard. Joined Socony-Vacuum Oil Co. Inc. as Service Stn Attendant, 1933; Dist. Man., 1940; Div. Manager, 1941; Asst General Manager, Eastern Marketing Div., 1944; Director, 1946; name of company changed to Socony Mobil Oil Co. Inc., 1955; President, 1955–61; Chairman Exec. Cttee and Chief Exec. Officer, 1958–69; Chm. Bd, 1961–69; name of company changed to Mobil Oil Corporation, 1966. Chairman, Vacuum Oil Co. Ltd, London (later Mobil Oil Co. Ltd), 1946. Director, Placement Bureau War Manpower Commission, Washington, 1943. Chm., Federal Reserve Bank of NY, and Federal Reserve Agent, 1969–71; Mem., The Business Council (Chm. 1967–69). Director: American Management Assoc., NY, 1948–51, 1953–56, 1958–61; Federal Reserve Board of NY, 1964–67; Metrop. Life Insurance Co., 1965–81; Mobil Oil Corp., 1946–75; Raytheon Co.; State Street Investment Corp.; State Street Growth Fund Inc.; Harvard Management Co., 1974–84; Transportation Assoc. of America, 1969; State Street Exchange Fund; Trustee: International House, NY City, 1952–62; Cttee for Economic Development, NY, 1961–65; Brigham and Women's Hosp., Boston; Rockefeller Univ.; (Emeritus) Boston Symphony Orch.; American Museum of Natural History, 1958–62, 1964–69; Mem. Emeritus, Corp. of Woods Hole Oceanographic Instn, Mass; former Director and Treas., American Petroleum Institute; former Member: Council on Foreign Relations; National Petroleum Council; Harvard Corp., 1965; Fellow, Harvard Univ., 1965–75; Overseer Harvard Univ., 1959–65. Hon. LLD: Hofstra Univ., 1964; Harvard Univ., 1976. Comdr, Order of Vasa (Sweden), 1963; Grand Cross of the Republic (Italy), 1968. *Recreations:* golfing, fishing, sailing, camping. *Address:* (office) Room 20E202, 150 East 42nd Street, New York, NY 10017, USA. *T:* 212 883–5225; (home) Lexington Road, Lincoln, Mass 01773, USA. *T:* (617) 259–9664. *Clubs:* Thames Rowing; Harvard Varsity, Cambridge Boat (Cambridge, Mass); Country (Brookline, Mass); Harvard (NY City); Harvard (Boston); 25 Year Club of Petroleum Industry.

NICKLAUS, Jack William; golfer; *b* 21 Jan. 1940; *s* of Louis Charles Nicklaus and Helen (*née* Schoener); *m* 1960, Barbara Jean Bash; four *s* one *d*. *Educ:* Upper Arlington High Sch.; Ohio State Univ. Won US Amateur golf championship, 1959, 1961; became professional golfer, 1961; designs golf courses in USA, Europe, and Far East; Chm., Golden Bear Inc. Captained US team which won 25th Ryder Cup, 1983. *Major wins include:* US Open, 1962, 1967, 1972, 1980; US Masters, 1963, 1965, 1966, 1972, 1975, 1986; US Professional Golfers' Assoc., 1963, 1971, 1973, 1974, 1975, 1980; Colonial National Invitation Tournament, 1982; British Open, 1966, 1970, 1978, and many other championships in USA, Europe, Australia and Far East. Hon. Dr Athletic Arts Ohio State, 1972; Hon. LLD St Andrews, 1984. *Publications:* My 55 Ways to Lower Your Golf Score, 1962; Take a Tip from Me, 1964; The Greatest Game of All, 1969; Golf My Way, 1974; The Best Way to Better Your Golf, vols 1–3, 1974; Jack Nicklaus' Playing Lessons, 1976; Total Golf Techniques, 1977; On and Off the Fairway, 1979; The Full Swing, 1982. *Address:* (office) 11760 US Highway #1, North Palm Beach, Florida 33408, USA.

NICKOLS, Herbert Arthur; Headmaster, Westonbirt School, Tetbury, Gloucestershire, 1981–86; *b* 17 Jan. 1926; *s* of Herbert and Henrietta Elizabeth Nickols; *m* 1953, Joyce Peake; two *s* one *d*. *Educ:* Imperial Coll., Univ. of London (BSc). ACGI. Res. Demonstrator, Imperial Coll., 1947–49; Housemaster, Sen. Science Master and later Dep. Headmaster, St Edmund's Sch., Canterbury, Kent, 1949–81. *Recreations:* music, travel, cricket. *Address:* 146 New Dover Road, Canterbury, Kent. *T:* Canterbury 52605.

NICKSON, David Wigley, CBE 1981; DL; CBIM; Chairman, Scottish & Newcastle Breweries plc, since 1983 (Director, since 1981; Deputy Chairman, 1982–83); President, Confederation of British Industry, since 1986 (Deputy President, 1985–86); *b* 27 Nov. 1929; *s* of late Geoffrey Wigley Nickson and of Janet Mary Nickson; *m* 1952, Helen Louise Cockcraft; three *d*. *Educ:* Eton; RMA, Sandhurst. Commnd Coldstream Guards, 1949–54. Joined Wm Collins, 1954; Dir, 1961–85; Jt Man. Dir, 1967; Vice Chm., 1976–83; Gp Man. Dir, 1979–82; Chm., Pan Books, 1982. Director: Scottish United Investors plc, 1970–83; General Accident Fire and Life Assurance Corp. plc, 1971–; Clydesdale Bank plc, 1981–; Radio Clyde PLC, 1982–85; Edinburgh Investment Trust plc, 1983–. Member: Scottish Indust. Develt Adv. Bd, 1975–80; Scottish Econ. Council, 1980–; NEDC, 1985–; Scottish Cttee, Design Council, 1978–81. Chm., Countryside Commn for Scotland, 1983–85. Chm., CBI in Scotland, 1979–81; CBIM 1980. Mem. Management Cttee, Atlantic Salmon Trust, 1982–, Vice-Chm., 1985–. Mem., Queen's Body Guard for Scotland, Royal Co. of Archers. DL Stirling and Falkirk, 1982. *Recreations:* fishing, bird watching, the countryside. *Address:* Renagour, Aberfoyle, Stirling FK8 3TF. *Clubs:* Boodle's, Flyfishers', MCC; Western (Glasgow).

NICKSON, Francis; Chief Executive and Town Clerk, London Borough of Camden, since 1977; *b* 9 Sept. 1929; *s* of Francis and Kathleen Nickson; *m* 1957, Helena (*née* Towers). *Educ:* Preston Catholic College; Liverpool Univ. (LLB). LMRTPI. Admitted Solicitor (Hons), 1953; Asst Solicitor, Newcastle-under-Lyme, 1953–56; Senior Asst Solicitor, Wood Green, 1956–60; Assistant Town Clerk, Enfield, 1960–71; Deputy Town Clerk, Camden, 1971–77. Hon. Clerk, Housing and Works Cttee, London Boroughs Assoc., 1979–84; Hon. Sec., London Boroughs Children's Regional Planning Cttee, 1977–. FRSA. *Recreations:* listening to music, country walking. *Address:* 14 Waggon Road, Hadley Wood, Barnet, Herts EN4 0HL. *T:* 01–449 9390.

NICOL, family name of **Baroness Nicol.**

NICOL, Baroness *cr* 1982 (Life Peer), of Newnham in the County of Cambridgeshire; **Olive Mary Wendy Nicol;** JP; Opposition Whip, House of Lords, since 1983; *b* 21 March 1923; *d* of James and Harriet Rowe-Hunter; *m* 1947, Alexander Douglas Ian Nicol (CBE 1985); two *s* one *d*. Civil Service, 1943–48. Trustee, Cambridge United Charities, 1967–86; Director, Cambridge and District Co-operative Soc., 1975–81, Pres. 1981–85; Member: Supplementary Benefits Tribunal, 1976–78; Cambridge City Council, 1972–82; Assoc. of District Councils, Cambridge Branch, 1974–76 and 1980–82; various school Governing Bodies, 1974–80; Council, Granta Housing Soc., 1975–; Careers Service Consultative Group, 1978–81. JP Cambridge City, 1972–. *Recreations:* reading, walking. *Address:* 39 Grantchester Road, Cambridge CB3 9ED.

NICOL, Angus Sebastian Torquil Eyers; barrister; a Recorder of the Crown Court, since 1982; *b* 11 April 1933; *s* of Henry James Nicol and Phyllis Mary Eyers; *m* 1968, Eleanor Denise Brodrick; two *d*. *Educ:* RNC, Dartmouth. Served RN, 1947–56. Called to the Bar, Middle Temple, 1963. Dir, 1981–84, Jt Sec., 1984–, Highland Soc. of London; Fearcathrach, Comunn na Foghlvim Gaidhlig an Lunnainn, 1984–. FSA (Scot.). *Recreations:* music, Gaelic language and literature, shooting, fishing, sailing, gastronomy. *Address:* 32 Elm Park Road, SW3. *T:* 01–352 4702; 5 Paper Buildings, Temple, EC4Y 7HB. *T:* 01–353 8494. *Clubs:* Flyfishers', Wig and Pen.

NICOL, Davidson Sylvester Hector Willoughby, CMG 1964; MA, MD, PhD (Cantab); FRCPath; President, World Federation of United Nations Associations, since 1983; Under-Secretary-General of the United Nations and Executive Director, United Nations Institute for Training and Research (UNITAR), 1972–82; Hon. Special Fellow, UNITAR, 1983; Hon. Consultant Pathologist, Sierra Leone Government; *b* 14 Sept. 1924, of African parentage; *m*; three *s* two *d*. *Educ:* Schools in Nigeria and Sierra Leone; Cambridge and London Univs. Science Master, Prince of Wales Sch., Sierra Leone, 1941–43. Cambridge: Foundation Schol., Prizeman, 1943–47, Fellow and Supervisor in Nat. Sciences and Med., 1957–59, Christ's Coll. (Hon. Fellow, 1972); BA 1946; 1st Cl. Hons (Nat. Sciences), 1947; Beit Meml Fellow for Medical Research, 1954; Benn Levy Univ. Studentship, Cambridge, 1956; Univ. Schol., House Physician (Medical Unit and Clinical Pathology), Receiving Room Officer, and Research Asst (Physiology), London Hosp., 1947–52; Univ. Lectr, Medical School, Ibadan, Nigeria, 1952–54; Visiting Lecturer: Univs of Toronto, California (Berkeley), Mayo Clinic, 1958; Aggrey-Fraser-Guggisberg Meml Lectr, Univ. of Ghana, 1963; Danforth Fellowship Lectr in African Affairs, Assoc. of Amer. Colls, USA, 1968–71. Sen. Pathologist, Sierra Leone, 1958–60; Principal, Fourah Bay Coll., Sierra Leone, 1960–68, and first Vice-Chancellor, Univ. of Sierra Leone, 1966–68; Perm. Rep. and Ambassador for Sierra Leone to UN, 1969–71 (Security Council, 1970–71, Pres. Sept. 1970; Chm., Cttee of 24 (Decolonisation); Mem., Economic and Social Council, 1969–70); High Comr for Sierra Leone in London, and Ambassador to Norway, Sweden and Denmark, 1971–72. Margaret Wrong Prize and Medal for Literature in Africa, 1952; Chm., Sierra Leone Nat. Library Bd, 1959–65; Member: Governing Body, Kumasi Univ., Ghana; Public Service Commn, Sierra Leone, 1960–68; W African Council for Medical Research, 1959–62; Exec. Council, Assoc. of Univs of British Commonwealth, 1960 and 1966; Commn for proposed Univ. of Ghana, 1960; Chm., Univ. of E Africa Visiting Cttee, 1962; Chm., UN Mission to Angola, July 1976. Director: Central Bank of Sierra Leone; Consolidated African Selection Trust Ltd (London); Davesme Corp. President: W African Science Assoc., 1964–66; Sierra Leone Red Cross Soc., 1962–66; Chm., W African Exams Council, 1964–69. Consultant, Ford Foundn, NY. Member, Board of Trustees: African-Amer. Inst., NY; Fund for Peace, NY. Conference Delegate to: WHO Assembly, 1960; UNESCO Higher Educn Conf., Tananarive, 1963; Commonwealth Prime Ministers' Conf., London, 1965 and 1969, Singapore 1971. Guest Scholar: Woodrow Wilson Internat. Center, Washington, 1983; Hoover Instn, Stanford Univ., 1984; Vis. Fellow, Johns Hopkins Sch. of Advanced Internat. Studies, Washington, 1983. Hon. Fellow, Ghana Acad. of Scis. Hon. LLD: Leeds; Barat, Ill; Univ. of West Indies (St Augustine), 1981; Tuskegee, Ala, 1981; Hon. DSc: Newcastle upon Tyne; Kalamazoo, Mich; Laurentian, Ont; Hon. DLitt Davis and Elkins Coll., W Va. Independence Medal, Sierra Leone, 1961. Grand Commander: Order of Rokel, Sierra Leone, 1974; Star of Africa, Liberia, 1974. *Publications:* Africa, A Subjective View, 1964; contribs to: Malnutrition in African Mothers and Children, 1954; HRH the Duke of Edinburgh's Study Conference, Vol. 2, 1958; The Mechanism of Action of Insulin, 1960; The Structure of Human Insulin, 1960; Africanus Horton and Black Nationalism (1867), 1969; New and Modern Rôles for Commonwealth and Empire, 1976; The United Nations and Decision Making: the role of women, 1978; Nigeria and the Future of Africa, 1980; (ed) Paths to Peace, 1981; (ed) Essays on the UN Security Council and its Presidency, 1981; (ed) Regionalism and the New International Economic Order, 1981; The United Nations Security Council: towards greater effectiveness, 1981; Creative Women, 1982; also to Jl Trop. Med., Biochem. Jl, Nature, Jl of Royal African Soc., Times, Guardian, New Statesman, Encounter, West Africa, etc. *Recreation:* creative writing. *Address:* Christ's College, Cambridge. *Clubs:* United Oxford & Cambridge University, Royal Commonwealth Society; Senior Dinner (Freetown).

NICOL, Prof. Donald MacGillivray, FBA 1981; FKC 1980; Koraës Professor of Modern Greek and Byzantine History, Language and Literature, University of London, King's College, since 1970; Vice Principal, King's College, 1980–81 (Assistant Principal, 1977–80); *b* 4 Feb. 1923; *s* of late Rev. George Manson Nicol and Mary Patterson (*née* MacGillivray); *m* 1950, Joan Mary Campbell, *d* of Sir Walter Campbell, KCIE; three *s*. *Educ:* King Edward VII Sch., Sheffield; St Paul's Sch., London; Pembroke Coll., Cambridge (MA, PhD). Friends' Ambulance Unit, 1942–46; Scholar at British Sch. of Archæology, Athens, 1949–50; Lectr in Classics, University Coll., Dublin, 1952–64; Vis. Fellow, Dumbarton Oaks, Washington, DC, 1964–65; Vis. Prof. of Byzantine History, Indiana Univ., 1965–66; Sen. Lectr and Reader in Byzantine History, Univ. of Edinburgh, 1966–70. Birkbeck Lectr, Cambridge, 1976–77. Pres., Ecclesiastical Hist. Soc., 1975–76. MRIA 1960; FRHistS 1971. Editor, Byzantine and Modern Greek Studies, 1973–83. *Publications:* The Despotate of Epiros, 1957; Meteora, the Rock Monasteries of Thessaly, 1963, rev. edn, 1975; The Byzantine Family of Kantakouzenos (Cantacuzenus) ca 1100–1460: a genealogical and prosopographical study, 1968; The Last Centuries of Byzantium, 1261–1453, 1972; Byzantium: Its Ecclesiastical History and Relations with the Western World, 1972; Church and Society in the Last Centuries of Byzantium, 1979; The End of the Byzantine Empire, 1979; The Despotate of Epiros 1267–1479: a contribution to the history of Greece in the middle ages, 1984; articles in Byzantine, classical and historical jls. *Recreation:* bookbinding. *Address:* 19 Highshore Road, SE15 5AA. *T:* 01–732 6164. *Club:* Athenæum.

NICOL, Dr Joseph Arthur Colin, FRS 1967; Professor of Zoology, University of Texas Institute of Marine Science, 1967–80, now Professor Emeritus; *b* 5 Dec. 1915; *s* of George Nicol and Noele Petrie; *m* 1941, Helen Wilhelmina Cameron; one *d*. *Educ:* Universities of McGill, Western Ontario and Oxford. BSc (hons Zool.) 1938, McGill; MA 1940, Western Ontario; DPhil 1947, DSc 1961, Oxford. Canadian Army, RCCS, 1941–45. Asst Professor in Zoology, University of British Columbia, 1947–49; Experimental Zoologist, Marine Biological Assoc., UK, 1949 (research on marine animals, comparative physiology, luminescence, vision, at Plymouth Laboratory, 1949–66). Guggenheim Fellow, Scripps Inst. Oceanography, 1953–54. Vis. Prof., Univ. of Texas, 1966–67. *Publications:* Biology of Marine Animals, 1960; papers on comparative physiology and anatomy in Jl Marine Biol. Assoc. UK, Proc. Royal Soc, Jl Exp. Biol., Biol. Review, etc. *Recreation:* English literature. *Address:* Ribby, Lerryn, Lostwithiel, Cornwall PL22 0PG. *T:* Bodmin 872319.

NICOL, William Allardyce, CA, FCIS; Director, Eagle Star Insurance Co. Ltd (Isle of Man), since 1975; Deputy Chairman, Eagle Star (International Life), since 1982; Chairman, Isle of Man Assurance Group, since 1976; *s* of William Nicol and Mary Wilson Gilmour;

m 1st, 1933, Elizabeth (*d* 1967), *d* of James Miller; one *s* one *d*; 2nd, 1970, Sally Philippa, *d* of Robert Patrick Vernon Brettell; one *s* one *d*. *Educ:* Glasgow University. Guest, Keen & Nettlefolds: Asst to Man. Dir, 1939–48; Group Sec., 1948–60; Dir, 1958–77; full-time Exec. Admin. Dir, 1960–68; Dep. Chm., Eagle Star Insurance Co. Ltd, 1968–75; Director: Powell Duffryn Ltd, 1968–75; Barclays Bank Ltd (Birmingham Bd), 1961–75; Stait Carding Gp Ltd (Chm., 1973–75); Chm., John Stait Gp, 1972–75. Chm., Assoc. Scottish Chartered Accountants in Midlands, 1953–68; Mem. Grand Council, CBI, 1965–67. *Recreations:* golf, fishing, music. *Address:* Longmead, Ballakillowey, Colby, Isle of Man. *T:* Port Erin 832005.

NICOLL, Douglas Robertson, CB 1980; retired; *b* 12 May 1920; *s* of James George Nicoll and Mabel Nicoll (*née* Styles); *m* 1949, Winifred Campion; two *s*. *Educ:* Merchant Taylors' School; St John's College, Oxford (MA 1946). FCO (GCHQ), 1946–80; Joint Services' Staff College, 1953; Under Secretary, 1977–80. *Address:* c/o National Westminster Bank, 31 The Promenade, Cheltenham, Glos GL50 1LH. *Club:* Travellers'.

NICOLL, Prof. Ronald Ewart, MSc, FRTPI, FRICS; Professor of Urban and Regional Planning, University of Strathclyde, 1966–80; Partner, 1980–85, Consultant, since 1985, PEIDA; *b* 8 May 1921; *s* of William Ewart Nicoll and Edith May Choat; *m* 1943, Isabel Christina McNab; one *s* one *d*. *Educ:* Southend Municipal Coll.; Hammersmith Sch. of Architecture and Building; Royal College of Science and Technology, Glasgow. Served War, Royal Navy, 1939–46. Planning Asst, 1949–53: Southend CB; Derbyshire CC; Northamptonshire CC. Dep. Dir of Planning, Glasgow City, 1953–64; Chief Planning Officer, Scottish Development Dept, 1964–66. Consultant to UN and WHO. Member: Scottish Social Advisory Council, 1970; Scottish Council on Crime, 1971; Scottish Council (Develt and Industry), 1971; Glasgow Chamber of Commerce, 1971; Royal Commn on Environmental Pollution, 1973–79. RICS Gold Medal, 1975. FRSA. *Publications:* Oceanspan, 1970; Energy and the Environment, 1975; contribs to: The Future of Development Plans, 1965 (HMSO); How Do You Want to Live?, 1972 (HMSO); A Future for Scotland, 1973. *Recreations:* travel, photography, hill walking. *Address:* 78 Victoria Park Drive North, Glasgow G14 9PJ. *T:* 041–959 7854. *Clubs:* Royal Commonwealth Society; Carrick (Glasgow).

NICOLL, William, CMG 1974; a Director General, Secretariat of the Council of Ministers of the European Communities, since 1982; *b* 28 June 1927; *s* of Ralph Nicoll and Christina Mowbray Nicoll (*née* Melville); *m* 1954, Helen Morison Martin; two *d*. *Educ:* Morgan Acad., Dundee; St Andrews Univ. Entered BoT, 1949; British Trade Comr, India, 1955–59; Private Sec. to Pres. of BoT, 1964–67; Commercial Inspector, FCO, 1967–69; DTI, 1969–72; Office of UK Perm. Rep. to European Communities, 1972–75; Under Sec., Dept of Prices and Consumer Protection, 1975–77; Dep. UK Rep. to EEC, 1977–82. Hon. LLD Dundee, 1983. *Publications:* (contrib.) Government and Industry, 1986; contribs to various jls on European subjects. *Address:* Council of the European Communities, 170 Rue de la Loi, 1048 Brussels, Belgium.

NICOLSON, family name of **Baron Carnock.**

NICOLSON, Sir David (Lancaster), Kt 1975; FEng 1977; Chairman: Wertheim and Co. (UK), since 1984; German Securities & Investment Trust plc, since 1985; Northern Telecom plc, since 1986; VSEL Consortium, since 1986; *b* 20 Sept. 1922; *s* of Charles Tupper Nicolson, consulting engineer, and Margaret Lancaster Nicolson; *m* 1945, Joan Eileen, *d* of Major W. H. Griffiths, RA; one *s* two *d*. *Educ:* Haileybury; Imperial Coll., London Univ. (BSc; Hon. Fellow 1971). FCGI, FIMechE, FIProdE; FIAM; FBIM; FRSA. Constructor Lt, Royal Corps Naval Constructors, 1942–45; served N Atlantic and Normandy, 1944 (despatches). Management Consultant, Production-Engineering Ltd, 1946–50; Production Manager, Bucyrus-Erie Co., Milwaukee, 1950–52; Manager, later Dir, Production-Engineering Ltd, 1953–62; Chairman: P-E Consulting Gp, 1963–68; Associated British Maltsters Ltd, 1965–71; Howden Gp Ltd, 1971–72; British Airways Board, 1971–75; BTR plc, 1969–84 (Dep. Chm., 1965–69, Dir, 1984–); Rothmans International plc, 1975–84; Farmer Stedall plc, 1982–; Selincourt plc, 1982–85; Co-Chm., European Channel Tunnel Gp, 1980–84. Director: Delta Metal Co., 1967–79; Bank of Montreal, 1970–; Richard Costain, 1970–78; MEPC, 1976–80; Todd Shipyards Corp., 1976–; Alfred Dunhill, 1976–; Drayton Consolidated Trust Ltd, 1977–83; CIBA-Geigy (UK), 1978–; Carling O'Keefe, 1978–; Confederation Life Insce Co., 1981–; Titech Internat., 1981–; GKN, 1984–; London & Scottish Marine Oil, 1983–; European Adviser, NY Stock Exchange, 1985–. Mem. (C) London Central, European Parlt, 1979–84. Mem. Council: CBI, 1972– (Chm., Environment Cttee, 1976–79); Inst. of Directors, 1971–76; Brit. Inst. of Management, 1964–69; Inst. of Production Engrs, 1966–68; City and Guilds of London Inst., 1968–76; Member: SRC, 1970–71; SRC Engineering Bd, 1969–71; Chm. Management Consultants Assoc., 1964; Mem. Brit. Shipbuilding Mission to India, 1957; Chairman: Cttee for Hosiery and Knitwear, NEDC, 1966–68; BNEC Cttee for Canada, 1967–71. Industrial Advr, European Democratic Gp, 1980–. Founder Chm., Amer. European Community Assoc., 1981–; Chm., European Movement, 1986–. President: Westminster for Europe, 1980–; ABCC, 1983–86. Mem. Council, Templeton Coll. (formerly Oxford Centre for Management Studies), 1982–; Governor: Imperial Coll., London Univ., 1966–77; Cranleigh Sch., 1979–. *Publications:* contribs to technical jls; lectures and broadcasts on management subjects in UK, USA, Australia, etc. *Recreation:* sailing. *Address:* Berkeley Square House, Berkeley Square, W1X 5PE. *T:* 01–493 7358; 10 Fordie House, Sloane Street, SW1; Howicks, Dunsfold, Surrey. *Clubs:* Carlton; Royal Thames Yacht.

NICOLSON, Malise Allen, MC 1945; Chairman, McConnell Salmon (formerly Highland Trout) Ltd, since 1980; Director: Bangor-on-Dee Steeplechases Ltd, since 1972 (Chairman, since 1984); The Race Course Association Ltd, since 1984; *b* 31 Oct. 1921; *e s* of late Sir Kenneth Nicolson, MC; *m* 1946, Vivien Bridget, *y d* of late Arthur Hilton Ridley, CBE; one *s* two *d*. *Educ:* Eton. Served War, Probyn's Horse, 1940–45 (MC; Burma); served 1st Royal Dragoons, 1946–47. Gladstone, Lyall Ltd, Calcutta, 1948–55; joined Booker McConnell, 1956; Dir, 1968–83; Chairman: Booker Line, 1968–83 (Dir, 1957–83); Coe Metcalf Shipping, 1977–83; Govt 'A' Dir, Mersey Docks and Harbour Co., 1974–80. Chairman: Liverpool Steam Ship Owners, 1971–72; Employers Assoc., Port of Liverpool, 1972–74; Vice-Chm., British Shipping Fedn, 1968–71; Pres., Gen. Council of British Shipping, 1982–83; Mem., Nat. Dock Labour Bd, 1986–. *Recreation:* country sports. *Address:* Frog Hall, Tilston, Malpas, Cheshire SY14 7HB. *T:* Tilston 320. *Club:* Cavalry and Guards.

NICOLSON, Nigel, MBE 1945; FSA; FRSL; author; Director of Weidenfeld and Nicolson Ltd since 1947; *b* 19 Jan. 1917; 2nd *s* of late Hon. Sir Harold Nicolson, KCVO, CMG and Hon. V. Sackville-West, CH; *heir-pres.* to 4th Baron Carnock, *qv*; *m* 1953, Philippa Janet (marr. diss. 1970), *d* of Sir Gervais Tennyson d'Eyncourt, 2nd Bt; one *s* two *d*. *Educ:* Eton Coll.; Balliol Coll., Oxford. Capt. Grenadier Guards. Served War of 1939–45 in Tunisian and Italian Campaigns (MBE). Contested (C) NW Leicester, 1950, and Falmouth and Camborne, 1951; MP (C) Bournemouth East and Christchurch, Feb. 1952–Sept. 1959. Chm. Exec. Cttee, UNA, 1961–66. *Publications:* The Grenadier Guards, 1939–45, 1949 (official history); People and Parliament, 1958; Lord of the Isles, 1960; Great Houses of Britain, 1965, revd edn 1978; (editor) Harold Nicolson: Diaries and Letters, 3 vols, 1966–68; Great Houses, 1968; Alex (FM Alexander of Tunis), 1973; Portrait of a Marriage, 1973; (ed) Letters of Virginia Woolf, 1975–80 (6 vols); The Himalayas, 1975; Mary Curzon, 1977 (Whitbread Award); Napoleon: 1812, 1985. *Recreation:* archæology. *Address:* Sissinghurst Castle, Kent. *T:* Cranbrook 714239. *Club:* Beefsteak.

NIEDUSZYŃSKI, Anthony John; Head of Radio Regulatory Division, Department of Trade and Industry, since 1985; *b* 7 Jan. 1939; *er s* of Tadeusz Adolf Antoni Nieduszyński, LLD and Madaleine Gladys Lilian (*née* Huggler); *m* 1980, Frances, *yr d* of Wing Comdr Max Oxford, OBE; one *d*. *Educ:* St Paul's School (Foundation Scholar); Merton College, Oxford (Postmaster; 1st cl. Hon. Mods 1959; 1st cl. Lit Hum 1961; MA). Board of Trade, 1964; Private Sec. to Pres. of BoT, 1967–68; Principal Private Sec. to Minister for Trade and Consumer Affairs, 1972–74 and to Sec. of State for Trade, 1974; Asst Sec., Dept of Prices and Consumer Protection, 1974, Dept of Industry, 1977, Home Office, 1982; Under Sec., DTI, 1985–. *Recreations:* gardening, riding, skating, linguistics, opera. *Address:* 8 Walpole Gardens, Twickenham, Middx TW2 5SJ. *T:* 01–894 3738.

NIELD, Sir Basil Edward, Kt 1957; CBE 1956 (MBE 1945); DL; Judge of High Court of Justice, Queen's Bench Division, 1960–78; *b* 7 May 1903; *yr s* of late Charles Edwin Nield, JP, and Mrs F. E. L. Nield, MBE, LLA, Upton-by-Chester. *Educ:* Harrow Sch.; Magdalen Coll., Oxford (MA). Officers Emergency Reserve, 1938; served War of 1939–45: commnd Captain, 1940; 1941; GHQ MEF (Major), HQs E Africa Force, Abyssinia, Palestine and Syria; Pres., Palestine Military Courts in Jerusalem; 1942; HQs Eritrea and 8th Army; 1943: HQ Persia and Iraq; Asst Dep. Judge Advocate-Gen., ME (Lt-Col; despatches); Home Estab.; 1944: 21 Army Gp; HQ Lines of Communication, BLA, Normandy; HQ 2nd Army, France, Belgium, Holland and Germany (MBE); Home Estab., 1945; RARO until 1948. Called to Bar, Inner Temple, 1925, Reader, 1976, Treasurer, 1977; Northern Circuit, Chambers in Liverpool; KC 1945; Recorder of Salford, 1948–56; Recorder and first permanent Judge of Crown Court at Manchester, 1956–60. MP (C) City of Chester, 1940–56; sponsored as Private Member's Bill the Adoption of Children Act, 1949; Hon. Parly Chm., Dock and Harbour Authorities Assoc., 1944–50; Mem., Special Cttee under Reorganisation Areas Measure for Province of York, 1944. Mem., Gen. Council of Bar, 1951; Master of Bench of Inner Temple, 1952–. Member: Magistrates' Rules Cttee, 1952–56; Legal Bd, Church Assembly, 1952–56; Home Secretary's Adv. Cttee on Treatment of Offenders, 1957. Chancellor, Diocese of Liverpool, 1948–56. Vice-President: Nat. Chamber of Trade, 1948–56; Graduate Teachers Assoc., 1950–56; Corp. of Secretaries, 1950; Assoc. of Managers of Approved Schools, 1956; Cheshire Soc. in London; Spastics Soc., Manchester. Chm., Chester Conservative Assoc., 1930–40. Member: Court, Liverpool Univ., 1948–56; Adv. Council, E-SU, 1951; Oxford Soc.; Imperial Soc. of Knights Bachelor; Life Mem., Royal Soc. of St George. Governor, Harrow Sch., 1961–71. FAMS. JP Co. Lancaster, 1956; DL County Palatine of Chester, 1962–. Freeman, City of London, 1963. *Publication:* Farewell to the Assizes, 1972. *Address:* 7 King's Bench Walk, Temple, EC4. *T:* 01–353 3868. *Clubs:* Carlton; City, Grosvenor (Chester).

NIELD, Sir William (Alan), GCMG 1972; KCB 1968 (CB 1966); Deputy Chairman, Rolls Royce (1971) Ltd, 1973–76; *b* 21 Sept. 1913; *s* of William Herbert Nield, Stockport, Cheshire, and Ada Nield; *m* 1937, Gwyneth Marion Davies; two *s* two *d*. *Educ:* Stockport Gram. Sch.; St Edmund Hall, Oxford. Research and Policy Dept of Labour Party, 1937–39; K-H News Letter Service, 1939. Served Royal Air Force and Royal Canadian Air Force, 1939–46 (despatches, 1944); demobilised as Wing Comdr, 1946. Min. of Food, 1946–47; HM Treasury, 1947–49; Min. of Food and Min. of Agric., Fisheries and Food, 1949–64 (Under-Sec., 1959–64); Dept of Economic Affairs: Under-Sec., 1964–65; Dep. Under-Sec. of State, 1965–66; a Dep. Sec., Cabinet Office, 1966–68; Permanent Under-Sec. of State, DEA, 1968–69; Permanent Secretary: Cabinet Office, 1969–72; NI Office, 1972–73. Pres., St Edmund Hall Assoc., 1981–83. *Address:* South Nevay, Stubbs Wood, Chesham Bois, Bucks. *T:* Amersham 3869. *Club:* Farmers'.

NIELSEN, Aksel Christopher W.; *see* Wiin-Nielsen.

NIELSEN, Hon. Erik H., DFC; PC 1984; QC 1962; MP (Progressive Conservative Party) for Yukon, since 1957; Deputy Prime Minister of Canada, 1984–86; Minister of Defence, 1985–86; *b* 24 Feb. 1924; *m* 1st, Pamela Hall (*d* 1969); three *c*; 2nd, 1983, Shelley Coxford. *Educ:* Dalhousie Univ. (LLB). Royal Canadian Air Force, 1942–51; flew Lancaster bombers, War of 1939–45. Called to the Bar of Nova Scotia, 1951; legal practice in Whitehorse, Yukon, 1952–. Minister of Public Works, 1979; Dep. House Leader, 1980–81; Opposition appts, 1981–83. Member: Canadian Bar Assoc; Yukon Law Soc.; Hon. Member: Internat. Union of Mine, Mill and Smelter Workers; Whitehorse Chamber of Commerce. Vice-Pres., Dawson City Museum and Hist. Soc. *Address:* House of Commons, Ottawa, Ont K1A 0A3, Canada.

NIEMEYER, Oscar; architect; *b* Rio de Janeiro, 15 Dec. 1907; *s* of Oscar Niemeyer Soares; *m* Anita Niemeyer; one *d*. *Educ:* Escola Nacional de Beles Artes, Univ. of Brazil. Joined office of Lúcio Costa, 1935; worked on Min. of Education and Health Building, Rio de Janeiro, Brazilian Pavilion, NY World Fair, etc., 1936–41. Major projects include: Pamphulha, Belo Horizonte, 1941–43; also Quintandinha, Petrópolis; Exhibition Hall, São Paulo, 1953; Brasilia (Dir of Architecture), 1957–. Brazilian Rep., UN Bd of Design Consultants, 1947. Lenin Peace Prize, 1963; Prix Internat. de l'Architecture Aujourd'hui, 1966. *Address:* 3940 avenida Atlântica, Rio de Janeiro, Brazil.

NIGERIA, Archbishop of, since 1979; **Most Rev. Timothy Olufosoye,** OON 1964; Bishop of Ibadan; *b* 31 March 1918; *s* of Chief D. K. Olufosoye and Felecia O. Olufosoye; *m* 1947; one *s* three *d*. *Educ:* St Andrew's Coll., Oyo, Nigeria; Vancouver School of Theology, Univ. of BC (STh). Headmaster, 1942–44; deacon 1946, priest 1947; appointments in Ondo, Lagos, and overseas in St Helens, Lancs, Sheffield Cathedral, Yorks, and Christ Church Cathedral, Vancouver, BC; Canon, 1955; Provost, St Stephen's Cathedral, Ondo, 1959; Vicar-Gen., 1963; Bishop of Gambia and Rio Pongas, 1965–70. Member: World Council of Churches; Gen. and Exec. Cttee, All Africa Conf. of Churches. Hon. DD, St Paul's Univ., Tokyo, 1958. Knight Comdr, Humane Order of African Redemption, Republic of Liberia. *Publications:* Egbogi fun Ibanuje, 1967; editor of The Beacon, Ibadan Ecclesia Anglicana, The Rubric. *Recreation:* poultry farming. *Address:* Bishopscourt, Arigidi Street, Bodija Estate, PO Box 3075, Ibadan, Nigeria. *T:* 022/411331 Ibadan. *Club:* Ibadan Dining.

NIGHTINGALE, Sir Charles (Manners Gamaliel), 17th Bt *cr* 1628; Higher Executive Officer, Department of Health and Social Security, since 1977; *b* 21 Feb. 1947; *s* of Sir Charles Athelstan Nightingale, 16th Bt, and of Evelyn Nadine Frances, *d* of late Charles Arthur Diggens; *S* father, 1977. *Educ:* St Paul's School. BA Open Univ., 1983. Entered DHSS as Executive Officer, 1969; Higher Executive Officer, 1977. *Heir:* *cousin* Edward Lacy George Nightingale, *b* 11 May 1938. *Address:* 14 Frensham Court, 27 Highbury New Park, N5 2ES.

NIGHTINGALE, Edward Humphrey, CMG 1955; Farmer in Kenya since 1954; *b* 19 Aug. 1904; *s* of Rev. Edward Charles Nightingale and Ada Mary Nightingale; *m* 1944, Evelyn Mary Ray; three *s* one *d*. *Educ:* Rugby Sch.; Emmanuel Coll., Cambridge. Joined Sudan Political Service, 1926; Dep. Civil Sec., Sudan Government, 1951–52; Gov., Equatoria Province, Sudan, 1952–54. Order of the Nile, 4th Class, 1940. *Recreations:* polo, photography. *Address:* Nunjoro Farm, PO Box 100, Naivasha, Kenya. *T:* Kerati, Naivasha 2Y1. *Clubs:* Rift Valley Sports (Nakuru); Muthaiga Country (Nairobi).

NIGHTINGALE, Sir John (Cyprian), Kt 1975; CBE 1970; BEM 1941; QPM 1965; DL; Chief Constable, Essex, 1962–69 and 1974–78, retired (Essex and Southend-on-Sea Joint Constabulary, 1969–74); *b* 16 Sept. 1913; *s* of Herbert Paul Nightingale, Sydenham, London; *m* 1947, Patricia Mary, *d* of Norman Maclaren, Glasgow University. *Educ:* Cardinal Vaughan Sch., Kensington; University Coll., London. Joined Metropolitan Police, 1935; Asst Chief Constable, Essex, 1958. Chm., Police Council, 1976–78; Mem., Parole Bd, 1978–82. Served with RNVR, 1943–45. DL Essex 1975. *Publications:* various police pubns. *Address:* Great Whitman's Farm, Purleigh, Essex.

NIGHTINGALE of Cromarty, Michael David, OBE 1960; BSc; BLitt; FSA; Baron of Cromarty; Chairman, The Chillington Corporation PLC; Esquire Bedell, University of London, since 1953; *b* 6 Dec. 1927; *s* of late Victor Russell John Nightingale, Wormshill, Kent; *m* 1956, Hilary Marion Olwen, *d* of late John Eric Jones, Swansea; two *s* three *d*. *Educ:* Winchester; Wye Coll.; Magdalen Coll., Oxford. Organised Exhibition from Kent Village Churches, Canterbury, 1951; Asst to Investment Manager, Anglo-Iranian Oil Co., 1951–53; Investment Adviser, Univ. of London, 1954–66; Dir, Charterhouse Japhet Ltd, 1965–70. Secretary: Museums Assoc. (and Editor of Museums Jl), 1954–60; Museum Cttee, Carnegie UK Trust, 1954–60; Member: Advisory Council on Export of Works of Art, 1954–60; British Cttee of International Council of Museums, 1956–60; Canterbury Diocesan Advisory Cttee, 1964–79; Exec. Cttee, SE Arts Assoc., 1974–77; Area Archaeol. Adv. Cttee for SE England, 1975–79; Investment Cttee, Univs Superannuation Scheme, 1977–84; Mem. Bd, Commonwealth Develt Corp., 1985–. Mem., Gen. Synod of C of E, 1979–85 (Panel of Chairmen, 1984–85). Member: Kent CC, 1973–77; Maidstone Borough Council, 1973– (Chm., Planning Cttee, 1973–77; Leader, 1976–77; Mayor, 1984–85). Vice-Pres., North Downs Soc.; Chm., Churches Cttee, Kent Archaeological Soc. Dep. Steward, Royal Manor of Wye, 1954–; Asst of Rochester Bridge. *Publications:* articles on agrarian and museum subjects. *Address:* Wormshill Court, Sittingbourne, Kent. *T:* Wormshill 235; Perceval House, 21 Dartmouth Row, Greenwich, SE10. *T:* 01–692 6033; Cromarty House, Ross and Cromarty. *T:* Cromarty 265. *Club:* Athenæum.

NIKLASSON, Frau Bertil; *see* Nilsson, Birgit.

NIKLAUS, Prof. Robert, BA, PhD London; LèsL Lille; DrUniv Rennes *hc* 1963; Hon. DLitt Exon 1981; Officier de l'Ordre National du Mérite, 1972; Professor of French, 1956–75, now Emeritus, also Head of Department of French and Spanish, 1958–64, French and Italian, 1964–75, University of Exeter; *b* 18 July 1910; *s* of late Jean Rodolphe and Elizabeth Niklaus; *m* 1st, 1935, Thelma (*née* Jones) (*d* 1970); two *s* one *d*; 2nd, 1973, Kathleen (*née* Folta). *Educ:* Lycée Français de Londres; University Coll., London; Univ. of Lille. Sen. Tutor, Toynbee Hall, London, 1931–32; Asst and Asst Lecturer at University Coll., 1932–38; Asst Lecturer, Lecturer, Univ. of Manchester, 1938–52; Prof. of French, UC of the SW, 1952–56. Dean of the Faculty of Arts, Exeter, 1959–62; Dep. Vice-Chancellor, 1965–67. Visiting Professor: Univ. of Calif., Berkeley, 1963–64; Univ. of British Columbia, 1975–76; Hd of Dept of Langs, Univ. of Nigeria, Nsukka, 1977–78. Pres., Assoc. of Univ. Teachers, 1954–55, Mem. Executive Cttee, 1948–62; Pres. Internat. Assoc. of Univ. Profs and Lecturers, 1960–64 (Vice-Pres., 1958–60, 1964–66); Member: Cttee of Modern Humanities Research Association, 1956–71; Cttee, Soc. for French Studies, 1965–72 (Vice-Pres., 1967–68 and 1970–71, Pres. 1968–70); Pres., British Soc. for XVIIIth Century Studies, 1970–72; Treasurer, Internat. Soc. for Eighteenth-century Studies, 1969–79; Post-graduate Awards Cttee of Min. of Education, 1956–61; Management Cttee, British Inst., Paris, 1965–67. Gen. Editor, Textes Français Classiques et Modernes, Univ. of London Press. *Publications:* Jean Moréas, Poète Lyrique, 1936; The Nineteenth Century (Post-Romantic) and After (in The Year's Work in Modern Language Studies, VII-XIII), 1937–52; Diderot and Drama, 1942; Beaumarchais, Le Barbier de Séville, 1968; A Literary History of France, the Eighteenth Century, 1970; Beaumarchais, Le Mariage de Figaro, 1983; critical editions of: J.-J. Rousseau, Les Rêveries du Promeneur Solitaire, 1942; Denis Diderot, Pensées Philosophiques, 1950; Denis Diderot, Lettre sur les Aveugles, 1951; Marivaux, Arlequin poli par l'Amour, 1959 (in collab. with Thelma Niklaus); Sedaine, La Gageure imprévue, 1970; (contrib.) Diderot: Œuvres Complètes, vol. II, 1975, vol. IV, 1979; articles in Encyclopaediæ and learned journals; textbooks for schools and universities. *Recreations:* aviculture, the theatre, the cinema. *Address:* 17 Elm Grove Road, Topsham, Exeter, Devon. *T:* Topsham 3627.

NIKOLAYEVA-TERESHKOVA, Valentina Vladimirovna; Hero of the Soviet Union; Order of Lenin; Gold Star Medal; Order of October Revolution; Joliot-Curie Peace Medal; Soviet cosmonaut; *b* Maslennikovo, 6 March 1937; *d* of late Vladimir and of Elena Fyodorovna Tereshkova; *m* 1963, Andrian Nikolayev; one *d*. Formerly textile worker, Krasny Perekop mill, Yaroslavl; served on cttees; Sec. of local branch, Young Communist league, 1960; Member: CPSU, 1962–; Central Cttee, CPSU, 1971; Deputy, 1966, Mem. of Presidium, 1970, Supreme Soviet of Russia; Pres., Soviet Women's Cttee, 1968. Joined Yaroslavl Air Sports Club, 1959, and started parachute jumping; joined Cosmonaut Training Unit, 1962; became first woman in the world to enter space when she made 48 orbital flights of the earth in spaceship Vostok VI, 16–19 June 1963. Nile Collar (Egypt), 1971; holds honours and citations from other countries. *Address:* Soviet Women's Committee, 6 Nemirovich-Danchenko Street, 103009 Moscow, USSR.

NILSSON, Birgit, (Fru Bertil Niklasson); Swedish operatic soprano; *b* Karup, Kristianstadslaen, 1922. *Educ:* Stockholm Royal Academy of Music. Debut as singer, 1946; with Stockholm Opera, 1947–51. Has sung at Glyndebourne, 1951; Bayreuth, 1953, 1954, 1957–70; Munich, 1954–58; Hollywood Bowl, Buenos Aires, Florence, 1956; La Scala, Milan, 1958–; Covent Garden, 1957, 1960, 1962, 1963, 1973 and 1977; Edinburgh, 1959; Metropolitan, New York, 1959–; Moscow, 1964; also in most leading opera houses and festivals of the world. Particularly well-known for her Wagnerian rôles. Austrian Kammersängerin, 1968; Bavarian Kammersängerin, 1970. Hon. RAM, 1970. Hon. Dr: Andover Univ., Mass, 1970; Manhattan Sch. of Music, NY, 1982; East Lansing Univ. of Fine Arts, Mich, 1982. Swedish Royal Acad. of Music's Medal for Promotion of Art of Music, 1968; Swedish Golden Medal (cl. 18 *illis quorum*) (only lady to be so honoured). Comdr of the Vasa Order (1st cl.), Sweden, 1974.

NIMMO, Derek Robert; actor and producer; *b* 19 Sept. 1932; *s* of Harry Nimmo and Marjorie Sudbury (Hardy); *m* 1955, Patricia Sybil Ann Brown; two *s* one *d*. *Educ:* Quarry School, Liverpool. *Stage:* First appearance, Hippodrome, Bolton, as Ensign Blades in Quality Street, 1952; repertory and variety; Waltz of the Toreadors, Criterion, 1957; Duel of Angels, Apollo, 1958; How Say You?, Aldwych, 1959; The Amorous Prawn, Saville, 1959; The Irregular Verb to Love, Criterion, 1961; See How They Run, Vaudeville, 1964; Charlie Girl, Adelphi, 1965–71 and overseas, 1971–72; Babes in the Wood, Palladium, 1972; Why Not Stay for Breakfast?, Apollo, 1973, and overseas tours; Same Time Next Year, Prince of Wales, 1978; Shut Your Eyes and Think of England, Australia, 1979; See How They Run, Shaftesbury, 1984; A Friend Indeed, Shaftesbury, 1984; produced and appeared in numerous plays and countries for Intercontinental Entertainment, 1976–; *television: series include:* All Gas and Gaiters; Oh Brother; Oh Father; Sorry I'm Single; The Bed Sit Girl; My Honorable Mrs; The World of Wooster; Blandings Castle; Life Begins at Forty; Third Time Lucky; Hell's Bells; *interview series:* If it's Saturday it must be Nimmo; Just a Nimmo; numerous other appearances; *films include:* Casino Royale; The Amorous Prawn; The Bargee, Joey Boy; A Talent for Loving; The Liquidator; Tamahine; One of our Dinosaurs is Missing. RTS Silver Medal, 1970; Variety Club Show Business Personality of the Year, 1971. *Publications:* Derek Nimmo's Drinking Companion, 1979; Shaken and Stirred, 1984. *Recreations:* sailing, collecting English 17th and 18th century walnut furniture and Derby porcelain. *Address:* c/o Barry Burnett Ltd, Suite 42, 2 Golden Square, W1. *Clubs:* Garrick; Athenæum (Liverpool).

NIMMO, Hon. Sir John (Angus), Kt 1972; CBE 1970; Justice of the Federal Court of Australia, 1977–80; Justice of Australian Industrial Court, 1969–80; *b* 15 Jan. 1909; *s* of John James Nimmo and Grace Nimmo (*née* Mann); *m* 1st, 1935, Teanie Rose Galloway (*d* 1984); two *s*; 2nd, 1985, Maude Pearce. *Educ:* Univ. of Melbourne. Admitted to practise at Victorian Bar, 1933. QC 1957. Mem., Commonwealth Taxation Bd of Review No 2, 1947–54; Actg Supreme Court Justice, Victoria, 1963; Dep. Pres., Commonwealth Conciliation and Arbitration Commn, 1964–69; Chm., Health Insce Cttee of Enquiry, 1968–69. Dep. Pres., Trade Practices Tribunal, 1966–73, also a Justice of Supreme Courts of ACT and NT, 1966–74; on secondment as Chief Justice of Fiji, 1972–74. Royal Comr into future of Norfolk Is, 1975–76; Chm., Commonwealth Legal Aid Commn, 1978–79; Mem., Cttee on Overseas Professional Qualifications, 1978–82. OStJ 1945. *Recreations:* reading, bowls, walking. *Address:* 2/15 Dalsten Grove, Mount Eliza, Victoria 3930, Australia. *T:* 787–6266.

NIMMO SMITH, William Austin, QC (Scot.) 1982; *b* 6 Nov. 1942; *s* of Dr Robert Herman Nimmo Smith and Mrs Ann Nimmo Smith; *m* 1968, Jennifer Main; one *s* one *d*. *Educ:* Eton Coll. (King's Scholar, 1956); Balliol Coll., Oxford (BA 1965); Edinburgh Univ. (LLB 1967). Admitted to Faculty of Advocates, 1969; Standing Junior Counsel to Dept of Employment, 1977–82; Advocate-Depute, 1983–86. *Recreations:* hill-walking, music. *Address:* 29 Ann Street, Edinburgh EH4 1PL. *Club:* New (Edinburgh).

NIND, Philip Frederick, OBE 1979; TD 1946; Director, Foundation for Management Education, 1968–83; Secretary, Council of Industry for Management Education, 1969–83; *b* 2 Jan. 1918; *s* of W. W. Nind, CIE; *m* 1944, Fay Allardice Crofton (*née* Errington); two *d*. *Educ:* Blundell's Sch.; Balliol Coll., Oxford (MA). War service, 1939–46, incl. Special Ops in Greece and Albania (despatches), 1943–44, Mil. Govt Berlin, 1945–46 (Major). Shell Gp of Cos in Venezuela, Cyprus, Lebanon, Jordan and London, 1939–68. Educn and Trng Cttee, CBI (formerly FBI), 1961–68; OECD Working Gp on Management Educn, 1966–69; Nat. Adv. Council on Educn for Industry and Commerce, 1967–70; UGC Management Studies Cttee, 1968–83; NEDO Management Educn Trng and Develt Cttee, 1968–83; Chm., NEDO Management Teacher Panel, 1969–72; Member: Council for Techn. Educn and Trng for Overseas Countries, 1970–75; CNAA Management Studies Bd, 1971–83; Vice-Pres., European Foundn for Management Develt, 1978–83. Member: Oxford Univ. Appts Cttee, 1967–83; Exec. Cttee, Royal Academy of Dancing, 1970–; Governor: Univ. of Keele, 1961–; Bedford Coll., London Univ., 1967–85. FRSA. Chevalier, Order of Cedars of Lebanon, 1959; Grand Cross, Orders of St Mark and Holy Sepulchre, 1959. *Publications:* (jtly) Management Education and Training Needs of Industry, 1963; Fourth Stockton Lecture, 1973; A Firm Foundation, 1985; articles in various jls. *Address:* c/o Lloyds Bank, F Section, 6 Pall Mall, SW1. *Club:* Special Forces.

NINEHAM, Rev. Prof. Dennis Eric, DD (Oxon); BD (Cantab); Hon. DD (Birmingham); Hon. DD (BDS Yale); Professor of Theology and Head of Theology Department, Bristol University, 1980–86, now Emeritus; Honorary Canon of Bristol Cathedral, since 1980; *b* 27 Sept. 1921; *o c* of Stanley Martin and Bessie Edith Nineham, Shirley, Southampton; *m* 1946, Ruth Corfield, *d* of Rev. A. P. Miller; two *s* two *d*. *Educ:* King Edward VI Sch., Southampton; Queen's Coll., Oxford. Asst Chaplain of Queen's Coll., 1944; Chaplain, 1945; Fellow and Praelector, 1946; Tutor, 1949; Prof. of Biblical and Historical Theology, Univ. of London (King's Coll.), 1954–58; Prof. of Divinity, Univ. of London, 1958–64; Regius Prof. of Divinity, Cambridge Univ., and Fellow, Emmanuel Coll., 1964–69; Warden of Keble Coll., Oxford, 1969–79, Hon. Fellow, 1980. FKC 1963. Examining Chaplain: to Archbishop of York and to Bishop of Ripon; to Bishop of Sheffield, 1947–54; to Bishop of Norwich, 1964–73; to Bishop of Bristol, 1981–. Select Preacher to Univ. of Oxford, 1954–56, 1971, and to Univ. of Cambridge, 1959; Proctor in Convocation of Canterbury: for London Univ., 1955–64; for Cambridge Univ., 1965–69. Mem. General Synod of Church of England for Oxford Univ., 1970–76; Mem., C of E Doctrine Commn, 1968–76. Roian Fleck Resident-in-Religion, Bryn Mawr Coll., Pa, 1974. Governor of Haileybury, 1966–. *Publications:* The Study of Divinity, 1960; A New Way of Looking at the Gospels, 1962; Commentary on St Mark's Gospel, 1963; The Use and Abuse of the Bible, 1976; Explorations in Theology, no 1, 1977; (Editor) Studies in the Gospels: Essays in Honour of R. H. Lightfoot, 1955; The Church's Use of the Bible, 1963; The New English Bible Reviewed, 1965; contrib. to: Studies in Ephesians (editor F. L. Cross), 1956; On the Authority of the Bible, 1960; Religious Education, 1944–1984, 1966; Theologians of Our Time, 1966; Christian History and Interpretation, 1967; Christ for us To-day, 1968; Christian Believing, 1976; The Myth of God Incarnate, 1977; Imagination and the Future, 1980. *Recreation:* reading. *Address:* 4 Wootten Drive, Iffley Turn, Oxford OX4 4DS. *T:* Oxford 715941.

See also Rev. J. H. Drury.

NINIS, Ven. Richard Betts; Archdeacon of Lichfield (formerly Stafford) and Treasurer of Lichfield Cathedral, since 1974; *b* 25 Oct. 1931; *s* of late George Woodward Ninis and of Mary Gertrude Ninis; *m* 1967, Penelope Jane Harwood; two *s* one *d*. *Educ:* Lincoln Coll., Oxford (MA); Bishop's Hostel, Lincoln (GOE). Curate, All Saints, Poplar, 1955–62; Vicar of: St Martins, Hereford, 1962–71; Bullinghope and Dewsall with Callow, 1966–71. Diocesan Missioner for Hereford, 1971–74. *Recreations:* gardening, viticulture, travel. *Address:* 24 The Close, Lichfield, Staffs. *T:* Lichfield 258813.

NIRENBERG, Dr Marshall Warren; Research Biochemist; Chief, Laboratory of Biochemical Genetics, National Heart, Lung and Blood Institute, National Institutes of Health, Bethesda, Md, since 1966; *b* New York, 10 April 1927; *m* 1961, Perola Zaltzman; no *c*. *Educ:* Univs of Florida (BS, MS) and Michigan (PhD). Univ. of Florida: Teaching Asst, Zoology Dept, 1945–50; Res. Associate, Nutrition Lab., 1950–52; Univ. of Michigan: Teaching and Res. Fellow, Biol Chemistry Dept, 1952–57; Nat. Insts of Health, Bethesda: Postdoctoral Fellow of Amer. Cancer Soc., Nat. Inst. Arthritis and Metabolic Diseases, 1957–59, and of Public Health Service, Section of Metabolic Enzymes, 1959–60; Research Biochemist, Section of Metabolic Enzymes, 1960–62 and Section of Biochem. Genetics, 1962–66. Member: Amer. Soc. Biol Chemists, Amer. Chem. Soc.; Amer. Acad. Arts and Sciences; Biophys. Soc.; Nat. Acad. Sciences; Washington Acad. Sciences; Sigma

Xi; Soc. for Study of Development and Growth; (Hon.) Harvey Soc.; Leopoldina Deutsche Akademie der Naturforscher; Neurosciences Research Program, MIT; NY Acad. Sciences; Pontifical Acad. Science, 1974. Robbins Lectr, Pomona Coll., 1967; Remsden Mem. Lectr, Johns Hopkins Univ., 1967. Numerous awards and prizes, including Nobel Prize in Medicine or Physiology (jtly), 1968. Hon. Dr Science: Michigan, Yale, and Chicago, 1965; Windsor, 1966; Harvard Med. Sch., 1968; Hon. PhD, Weitzmann Inst. of Science, Israel, 1978. *Publications:* numerous contribs to learned jls and chapters in symposia. *Address:* Laboratory of Biochemical Genetics, National Heart, Lung and Blood Institute, Bethesda, Md 20014, USA; 7001 Orkney Parkway, Bethesda, Maryland, USA.

NISBET, Prof. Hugh Barr; Professor of Modern Languages, University of Cambridge, since 1982; Professorial Fellow, Sidney Sussex College, since 1982; *b* 24 Aug. 1940; *s* of Thomas Nisbet and Lucy Mary Hainsworth; *m* 1962, Monika Luise Ingeborg Uecker; two *s*. *Educ:* Dollar Acad.; Univ. of Edinburgh. MA, PhD 1965. University of Bristol: Asst Lectr in German, 1965–67; Lectr, 1967–72; Reader, 1972–73; Prof. of German Lang. and Lit., Univ. of St Andrews, 1974–81. Mem., Gen. Teaching Council for Scotland, 1978–81. Governor, Dollar Acad., 1978–81. Jt Editor, Cambridge Studies in German, 1983–; Germanic Editor, 1973–80, Gen. Editor, 1981–84, Modern Language Rev. *Publications:* Herder and the Philosophy and History of Science, 1970; (ed with Hans Reiss) Goethe's Die Wahlverwandtschaften, 1971; Goethe and the Scientific Tradition, 1972; (ed) German Aesthetic and Literary Criticism: Winckelmann to Goethe, 1985; *translations:* Kant, Political Writings, 1970, 2nd edn 1977; Hegel, Lectures on the Philosophy of World History, 1975, 2nd edn 1980; articles and reviews on German literature and thought. *Recreations:* music, art history, cycling. *Address:* Sidney Sussex College, Cambridge CB2 3HU. *T:* Cambridge 61501.

NISBET, Prof. John Donald, OBE 1981; MA, BEd, PhD; FEIS; FRSA; Professor of Education, Aberdeen University, since 1963; *b* 17 Oct. 1922; *s* of James Love Nisbet and Isabella Donald; *m* 1952, Brenda Sugden; one *s* one *d*. *Educ:* Dunfermline High Sch.; Edinburgh Univ. (MA, BEd); PhD (Aberdeen); Teacher's Certif. (London). FEIS 1975; FRSA 1982. Royal Air Force, 1943–46. Teacher, Fife, 1946–48; Lectr, Aberdeen Univ., 1949–63. Editor: British Jl of Educnl Psychology, 1967–74; Studies in Higher Education, 1979–84; Chairman: Educnl Research Bd, SSRC, 1972–75; Cttee on Primary Educn, 1974–80; Scottish Council for Research in Educn, 1975–78; Pres., British Educnl Research Assoc., 1975. *Publications:* Family Environment, 1953; Age of Transfer to Secondary Education, 1966; Transition to Secondary Education, 1969; Scottish Education Looks Ahead, 1969; Educational Research Methods, 1970; Educational Research in Action, 1972; Impact of Research, 1980; Towards Community Education, 1980; (ed) World Yearbook of Education, 1985; Learning Strategies, 1986; papers in jls on educnl psychology and curriculum develt. *Recreations:* golf, orienteering. *Address:* 5 The Chanonry, Aberdeen AB2 1RP. *T:* Aberdeen 44375.
See also S. D. Nisbet.

NISBET, Prof. Robin George Murdoch, FBA 1967; Corpus Christi Professor of Latin, Oxford, since 1970; *b* 21 May 1925; *s* of R. G. Nisbet, Univ. Lecturer, and A. T. Husband; *m* 1969, Anne, *d* of Dr J. A. Wood. *Educ:* Glasgow Academy; Glasgow Univ.; Balliol Coll., Oxford (Snell Exhibitioner). Fellow and Tutor in Classics, Corpus Christi College, Oxford, 1952–70. *Publications:* Commentary on Cicero, *in Pisonem*, 1961; (with M. Hubbard) on Horace, *Odes I*, 1970; *Odes II*, 1978; articles and reviews on Latin subjects. *Recreation:* 20th century history. *Address:* 80 Abingdon Road, Cumnor, Oxford. *T:* Oxford 862482.

NISBET, Prof. Stanley Donald; Professor of Education, University of Glasgow, 1951–78; *b* 26 July 1912; *s* of Dr J. L. and Isabella Nisbet; *m* 1942, Helen Alison Smith; one *s* one *d*. *Educ:* Dunfermline High Sch., Edinburgh Univ. MA (1st Cl. Hons Classics), 1934; Diploma in Education, 1935; BEd (with distinction in Education and Psychology), 1940. Taught in Moray House Demonstration Sch., Edinburgh, 1935–39. Served War in RAF, 1940–46; research officer at Air Ministry, 1944–46. Lecturer in Education, Univ. of Manchester, Feb.-Sept. 1946; Prof. of Education, Queen's Univ. of Belfast, 1946–51. FRSE 1955; FEIS 1976. *Publications:* Purpose in the Curriculum, 1957; (with B. L. Napier) Promise and Progress, 1970; articles in psychological and educational journals. *Recreations:* walking, sailing. *Address:* 6 Victoria Park Corner, Glasgow G14 9NZ.
See also J. D. Nisbet.

NISBET-SMITH, Dugal; Director, Newspaper Society, since 1983; *b* 6 March 1935; *s* of David and Margaret Homeward Nisbet-Smith; *m* 1959, Dr Ann Patricia Taylor; one *s* two *d*. *Educ:* Southland Boys' High Sch., Invercargill, NZ. Journalist on Southland Daily News, NZ, 1952–56; Features writer and reporter, Beaverbrook Newspapers, London, 1956–60; variously Asst Editor, Gen. Manager and Man. Dir, Barbados Advocate Co., Barbados, WI, Gen. Manager, Sierra Leone Daily Mail Ltd, W Africa, Dep. Gen. Manager, Trinidad Mirror Co., 1960–66; Sen. Industrial Relations Manager, Mirror Gp Newspapers, London, 1966–68; Develt Manager, 1969–71, Production Dir, 1971–73, Man. Dir, 1974–78, Scottish Daily Record and Sunday Mail Ltd, Glasgow; joined Bd, Mirror Gp Newspapers, 1976; Dir/General Manager, 1978–80, Man. Dir, 1980–81, Times Newspapers Ltd; Publishing Advr to HH the Aga Khan, Aiglemont, France, 1981–83. *Recreations:* travel, sculpture, painting. *Address:* 19 Highgate Close, Hampstead Lane, N6. *T:* 01-340 9457. *Club:* Royal Automobile.

NISSAN, Prof. Alfred Heskel, PhD, DSc (Chem. Eng, Birmingham), FIChemE, FAIChE, FACS; Member Sigma XI; Consultant to WESTVACO (formerly West Virginia Pulp and Paper), New York (Vice-President, 1967–79, and Corporate Director of Research, 1962–79); Professor, College of Environmental Science and Forestry, Syracuse, New York, since 1979; *b* 14 Feb. 1914; *s* of Heskel and Farha Nissan, Baghdad, Iraq; *m* 1940, Zena Gladys Phyllis, *o d* of late Phillip and Lillian Frances Pursehouse-Ahmed, Birmingham; one *d*. *Educ:* The American Sch. for Boys, Baghdad, Iraq; Univ. of Birmingham. Instn of Petroleum Scholarship, 1936; first cl. Hons BSc 1937; Sir John Cadman Medal, 1937; Instn of Petroleum Medal and Prize and Burgess Prize, 1937; Research Fellow, 1937, Lectr, 1940, Univ. of Birmingham; Head of Central Research Laboratories, Bowater Paper Corporation Ltd, 1947; Technical Director in charge of Research, Bowaters Development and Research Ltd, 1950; Research Prof. of Wool Textile Engineering, the Univ. of Leeds, 1953; Prof. of Chemical Engineering, Rensselaer Polytechnic Inst., Troy, NY, USA, 1957. Hon. Vis. Prof., Uppsala Univ., 1974. Schwarz Memorial Lectr, Amer. Soc. of Mech. Engrs, 1967. Member: Adv. Council for Advancement of Industrial R&D, State of NY, 1965–; Board of Directors: Technical Assoc. of Pulp & Paper Industry, 1968–71 (R&D Div. Award, 1976); Industrial Res. Inst., 1973–77. Alexander Mitscheslich Medal, Zellcheming, W Germany, 1980; Gold Medal, Technical Assoc. of Pulp and Paper Industry, 1982. *Publications:* (ed) Textile Engineering Processes, 1959; (ed) Future Technical Needs and Trends in the Paper Industry, 1973; Lectures on Fiber Science in Paper, 1977; papers on physical chemistry and chemical engineering problems of petroleum, paper and textile technology in scientific jls. *Address:* 6A Dickel Road, Scarsdale, NY 10583, USA.

NISSEN, George Maitland; Director, Morgan Grenfell Holdings Ltd, since 1984; *b* 29 March 1930; *s* of Col Peter Norman Nissen, DSO, and Lauretta Maitland; *m* 1956, Jane Edmunds, *d* of late S. Curtis Bird, New York; two *s* two *d*. *Educ:* Eton; Trinity Coll., Cambridge (MA). National Service, KRRC, 1949–50, 2/Lieut. Sen. Partner, Pember & Boyle, Stockbrokers, 1982–86. Mem., Stock Exchange, 1956– (Dep. Chm., 1978–81; Mem. Council, 1973–); Chm., Gilt-Edged Market Makers Assoc., 1986–; Mem., Inflation Accounting Steering Gp, 1976–80. Governor: Reed's Sch., Cobham; St Paul's Girls' Prep. Sch., Hammersmith. *Recreations:* railways, music. *Address:* Swan House, Chiswick Mall, W4 2PS. *T:* 01-994 8203.

NISSEN, Karl Iversen, MD, FRCS; retired Surgeon, Royal National Orthopædic Hospital, W1, 1946–71; Orthopædic Surgeon: Harrow Hospital 1946–71; Peace Memorial Hospital, Watford, 1948–71; *b* 4 April 1906; *s* of Christian and Caroline Nissen; *m* 1935, Margaret Mary Honor Schofield (*d* 1981); one *s* one *d*. *Educ:* Otago Boys' High Sch., Dunedin, NZ; Univ. of Otago, NZ. BSc (NZ) 1927; MB, ChB (NZ) 1932; MD (NZ) 1934; FRCS 1936. Served as Orthopædic Specialist, RNVR, 1943–46. Corresp. mem. Belgian, French, Swiss, German, Scandinavian, Norwegian, Finnish, Danish Socs of Orthopædics. Writes articles and gives talks on primary osteoarthrosis of the hip, Morton's metatarsalgia, and the carpal tunnel syndrome. *Recreation:* French. *Address:* Prospect House, The Avenue, Sherborne, Dorset. *T:* Sherborne 813539. *Club:* Naval.

NIVEN, Sir (Cecil) Rex, Kt 1960; CMG 1953; MC 1918; *b* 20 Nov. 1898; *o s* of late Rev. Dr G. C. and Jeanne Niven, Torquay, Devon; *m* 1st, 1925, Dorothy Marshall (*d* 1977), *e d* of late D. M. Mason, formerly MP (Coventry and E Edinburgh); one *d* (and one *d* decd); 2nd, 1980, Mrs Pamela Beerbohm, *d* of late G. C. Leach, ICS, Sibton Park, Lyminge, Kent, and Mrs Leach, and *widow* of Dr O. H. B. Beerbohm. *Educ:* Blundell's Sch., Tiverton; Balliol Coll. Oxford (MA Hons). Served RFA 1917–19, France and Italy. Colonial Service Nigeria, 1921–54; served Secretariats, and Provinces; PRO, Nigeria, 1943–45; Senior Resident, 1947; twice admin. Northern Govt; Mem. N House of Assembly, 1947–59 (Pres. 1952–58; Speaker, 1958–59); Mem., N Executive Council, 1951–54; Comr for Special Duties in N Nigeria, 1959–62; Dep. Sec., Southwark Dio. Bd of Finance, 1962–68. Life Mem., BRCS; Member: Council, RSA, 1963–69; Council, N Euboea Foundation; Council, Imp. Soc. of Knights Bachelor, 1969–; Gen. Synod of C of E, 1975–80; St Charles's (formerly Paddington) Group Hosp. Management Cttee, 1963–72. FRGS. *Publications:* A Short History of Nigeria, 1937, 12th edn 1971; Nigeria's Story, 1939; Nigeria: the Outline of a Colony, 1946; How Nigeria is Governed, 1950; West Africa, 1958; Short History of the Yoruba Peoples, 1958; You and Your Government, 1958; Nine Great Africans, 1964; Nigeria (in Benn's Nations of the Modern World), 1967; The War of Nigerian Unity, 1970; (collab.) My Life, by late Sardauna of Sokoto, 1962; A Nigerian Kaleidoscope, 1982. *Recreations:* walking, architecture, philately. *Address:* 12 Archery Square, Walmer, Kent CT14 7HP. *T:* Deal (0304) 361863. *Club:* Royal Over-Seas League.

NIVEN, Ian; *see* Niven, J. R.

NIVEN, John Robertson, (Ian Niven); Under-Secretary, Department of the Environment, formerly Ministry of Housing and Local Government, 1974–79; *b* 11 May 1919; *s* of Robert Niven and Amelia Mary Hill; *m* 1946, Jane Bicknell; three *s*. *Educ:* Glasgow Academy; Jesus Coll., Oxford. Entered Min. of Town and Country Planning, 1946; Sec., Royal Commn on Local Govt in Greater London, 1957–60. *Address:* White Gates, Parham, Woodbridge, Suffolk.

NIVEN, Margaret Graeme, ROI 1936; Landscape and Portrait Painter; *b* Marlow, 1906; *yr d* of William Niven, FSA, ARE, JP, Marlow Place, Marlow, Bucks, and Eliza Mary Niven. *Educ:* Prior's Field, Godalming. Studied at Winchester Sch. of Art, Heatherley Sch. of Fine Art, and under Bernard Adams, RP, ROI; Mem. of National Soc. Painters, Sculptors, and Engravers, 1932. Exhibitor at Royal Academy and Royal Soc. of Portrait Painters. Works purchased by Bradford Art Gallery, The Ministry of Works, Homerton Coll., Cambridge, and Bedford Coll., London. Served with WRNS, 1940–45. *Address:* Broomhill, Sandhills, Wormley, near Godalming, Surrey.

NIVEN, Sir Rex; *see* Niven, Sir C. R.

NIVEN, Col Thomas Murray, CB 1964; TD 1941; FICE (retired); FIMechE (retired); *b* 20 Aug. 1900; *s* of Thomas Ogilvie Niven, Civil Engineer, Glasgow. *Educ:* Glasgow Academy; Glasgow Univ. Served War of 1939–45 with Royal Signals: comdg 52 (Lowland) Div. Signals, 1938–40; comdg Royal Signals Mobilisation Centre, 1941–43; Dep. Chief Signal Officer, Northern Command, 1944. Comdg 6 Glasgow Home Guard Bn, 1952–56; Hon. Col 52 (Lowland) Signal Regt (TA), 1950–66; Chm., Glasgow T & AFA, 1959–62. Formerly Dir of Mechans Ltd, Engineers, Scotstoun Iron Works, Glasgow. DL Glasgow, 1949–75. *Recreation:* walking. *Clubs:* Naval and Military; Royal Channel Islands Yacht (Guernsey).

NIVISON, family name of **Baron Glendyne.**

NIX, Prof. John Sydney; Professor of Farm Business Management, since 1982, and Head, Farm Business Unit, since 1974, Wye College, University of London; *b* 27 July 1927; *s* of John William Nix and Eleanor Elizabeth (*née* Stears); *m* 1950, Mavis Marian (*née* Cooper); one *s* two *d*. *Educ:* Brockley County Sch.; University Coll. of the South-West. BSc Econ (London), MA Cantab. Instr Lieut, RN, 1948–51. Farm Economics Branch, Sch. of Agriculture, Univ. of Cambridge, 1951–61; Wye College: Farm Management Liaison Officer and Lectr, 1961–70; Sen. Tutor, 1970–72; Sen. Lectr, 1972–75; Reader, 1975–82; apptd to personal chair, the first in Farm Business Management in UK, 1982. Founder Mem., Farm Management Assoc., 1965; Member: Study Groups etc. for Natural Resources (Tech.) Cttee; Agric. Adv. Council; ARC Tech. Cttee; ADAS Exptl and Develt Cttee; Meat and Livestock Commn; Countryside Commn. Programme Advr, Southern Television, 1966–81. British Inst. of Management: Chm., Jl Cttee of Centre of Management of Agric., 1971–; Chm., Bd of Farm Management, 1979–81; Nat. Award for outstanding and continuing contrib. to advancement of management in agric. industry, 1982 (1st recipient); CBIM 1983. FRSA 1984; FRAgS 1985. *Publications:* Farm Management Pocketbook, 1967, 17th edn 1986; (with C. S. Barnard) Farm Planning and Control, 1973, 2nd edn 1979, Spanish edn 1984; (with W. Butterworth) Farm Mechanisation for Profit, 1983; (with G. P. Hill and N. T. Williams) Land and Estate Management, 1986; articles in Jl of Agricl Econs, Jl of RASE, Farm Management, etc. *Recreations:* theatre, cinema, travel, rugby, cricket. *Address:* Keynton, Cherry Garden Lane, Wye, Ashford, Kent TN25 5AR. *T:* Wye 812274. *Club:* Farmers'.

NIXON, Sir Edwin (Ronald), Kt 1984; CBE 1974; non-executive Chairman, IBM United Kingdom Holdings Ltd and its subsidiaries, since 1986 (Managing Director, 1965–86; Chairman and Chief Executive, 1979–86); *b* 21 June 1925; *s* of William Archdale Nixon and Ethel (*née* Corrigan); *m* 1952, Joan Lilian (*née* Hill); one *s* one *d*. *Educ:* Alderman Newton's Sch., Leicester; Selwyn Coll., Cambridge (MA; Hon. Fellow 1983). Dexion Ltd, 1950–55; IBM United Kingdom Ltd, 1955–; Director: National Westminster Bank PLC, 1975–; Royal Insurance PLC, 1980–. Mem. Council: Foundn for Automation and Employment, 1967–77; Electronic Engineering Assoc., 1965–76; CBI, 1971– (Chm. Standing Cttee on Marketing and Consumer Affairs, 1971–78; Mem., Cttee on Industrial Policy, 1978–); Foundn for Management Educn, 1973–84. Member:

British Cttee of Awards for Harkness Fellowships, 1976–82; Adv. Council, Business Graduates Assoc., 1976–; Board of Governors, United World Coll. of Atlantic, 1977–; Member Council: Manchester Business Sch., 1974– (Chm., 1979–); Business in the Community, 1981–; Westfield Coll., London, 1969–82 (Vice Chm., 1980–82; Hon. Fellow 1983); William Temple Coll., Manchester, 1972–80; Oxford Centre for Management Studies, 1973–83; Mem. Adv. Council, CS Staff Coll., Sunningdale, 1979–. Trustee, Inst. of Econ. Affairs, 1986–. Pres., Nat. Assoc. for Gifted Children, 1980–; Vice-Pres., Opportunities for the Disabled, 1980–; Chm., Jt Bd for Pre-Vocational Educn, 1983–; Mem., Study Commn on the Family, 1979–83. Chm. of Bd of Trustees and a Dir, Royal Opera House, Covent Garden, 1984– (Trustee, 1980–); Trustee, Monteverdi Choir and Orch., 1980–. Patron, Assoc. Internationale des Etudiantes en Sciences Economiques et Commercials, 1980–. Hon. Fellow Inst. of Marketing, 1982 (Hon. Vice-Pres., 1980–). Hon. DSc Aston, 1985; DUniv Stirling, 1985; Hon. DTech Brunel, 1986. *Recreations:* music, tennis, golf, sailing. *Address:* Starkes Heath, Rogate, Petersfield, Hants. *T:* Rogate 504. *Clubs:* Athenæum, Reform.

NIXON, Rev. Sir Kenneth Michael John Basil, SJ; 4th Bt *cr* 1906; Teaching Member of the Jesuit Community at St George's College, Harare, since 1954; *b* 22 Feb. 1919; *s* of Sir Christopher William Nixon, 2nd Bt, DSO, and Louise (*d* 1949), *d* of Robert Clery, JP, The Glebe, Athlacca, Limerick; *S* brother, 1978. *Educ:* Beaumont College; Heythrop College, Oxon. Catholic priest and member of the Society of Jesus; ordained, 1952. *Recreation:* cricket. *Heir:* *b* Major Cecil Dominic Henry Joseph Nixon, MC [*b* 5 Feb. 1920; *m* 1953, Brenda, *d* of late Samuel Lycett Lewis and *widow* of Major M. F. McWhor; three *s* one *d*]. *Address:* St George's College, PB 7727, Causeway, Zimbabwe. *T:* Harare 724650.

NIXON, Richard M.; President of the United States of America, 1969–74, resigned 10 Aug. 1974; *b* 9 Jan. 1913; *s* of Francis A. and Hannah Milhous Nixon; *m* 1940, Patricia Ryan; two *d*. *Educ:* Whittier Coll., Whittier, California (AB); Duke University Law Sch., Durham, North Carolina (LLB). Lawyer, Whittier, California, 1937–42; Office of Price Administration, 1942; Active duty, US Navy, 1942–46. Member 80th, 81st Congresses, 1947–50; US Senator from California, 1950–53. Vice-President of the USA, 1953–61; Republican candidate for the Presidency of the USA, 1960. Lawyer, Los Angeles, 1961–63, NY, 1963–68. Republican Candidate for Governor of California, 1962. Member: Board of Trustees, Whittier Coll., 1939–68; Society of Friends; Order of Coif. *Publications:* Six Crises, 1962; Memoirs, 1978; The Real War, 1980; Leaders, 1982; Real Peace: a strategy for the West, 1983; No More Vietnams, 1986. *Address:* 26 Federal Plaza, New York, NY 10278, USA.

NOAD, Sir Kenneth (Beeson), Kt 1970; Consulting Physician, 1931–84; Patron, Australian Postgraduate Federation in Medicine; *b* 25 March 1900; *s* of James Beeson and Mary Jane Noad; *m* 1935, Eileen Mary Ryan; no *c*. *Educ:* Maitland, NSW; Sydney University. MB, ChM 1924, MD 1953, Sydney; MRCP 1929; FRCP 1948; Foundn FRACP 1938 (PRACP 1962–64). Hon FACP 1964; Hon. FRCPE 1968. Served War of 1939–45, Palestine, Egypt, Greece, Crete, New Guinea; Lt-Col Comdr Medical Div. of an Australian General Hospital. Hon. DLitt and Hon. AM Singapore. *Publications:* papers in Brain, Med. Jl of Australia. *Recreations:* walking, music. *Address:* 22 Billyard Avenue, Elizabeth Bay, NSW 2011, Australia. *Clubs:* Australian (Sydney); Royal Sydney Golf.

NOAKES, Col Geoffrey William, OBE 1958; TD 1948; JP; DL; Past Managing Director, William Timpson Ltd, Footwear Retailers; Member, Industrial Tribunals, Manchester, since 1975; *b* Manor House, Basingstoke, Hants, 19 Nov. 1913; *s* of Charles William Noakes; *m* 1936, Annie, *d* of Albert Hough, Peel Green; two *s* two *d*. *Educ:* Wyggeston Sch. Commissioned RA, 1936. Served War: in France, 1940; Burma, 1940–46 (despatches); Staff Coll., Quetta, 1944; AQMG, Fourteenth Army, 1944–45. In command 252 Field Regt RA, 1951–57; DCRA, 42 Div., 1957–62. Past Pres., Multiple Shoe Retailers' Assoc.; Past Pres. and Chm., Footwear Distributors' Fedn; Past Leader and Sec., Employer's side, Boot and Shoe Repairing Wages Council; Past Pres., Nat. Assoc. of Shoe Repair Factories. Past Chm., Publicity and Recruiting Cttee, and Vice-Chm., NW of England and IOM TAVR Assoc.; Pres., Burma Star Assoc., Altrincham; Past Mem., Bd of Examiners, Sch. of Business Studies, Manchester Polytechnic; Mem. Exec. Cttee, Manchester and Dist Boys' Clubs; Governor, Manchester Univ.; formerly Rep. Col Comdt, RA Uniformed Staff; Vice-President: Cholmondeley Cons. Assoc.; Cholmondeley FC; Chm., Border Castles Driving Club. JP Manchester, 1963; DL Lancs 1974. FBIM, FIWM, MIPM, ABSI. *Recreations:* hunting, shooting, fishing (Pres. Altrincham Angling Club), golf. *Address:* The Mill House, Bickley, near Malpas, Cheshire SY14 8EG. *T:* Hampton Heath 309. *Club:* Army and Navy.

See also P. R. Noakes.

NOAKES, Rt. Rev. George; *see* St Davids, Bishop of.

NOAKES, Michael, PPROI, RP; portrait and landscape painter; *b* 28 Oct. 1933; *s* of late Basil and of Mary Noakes; *m* 1960, Vivien Noakes (*née* Langley), writer; two *s* one *d*. *Educ:* Downside; Royal Academy Schs, London. Nat. Dipl. in Design, 1954; Certificate of Royal Academy Schools, 1960. Commnd: National Service, 1954–56. Has broadcast and appeared on TV on art subjects in UK and USA; Art Correspondent, BBC TV programme Town and Around, 1964–68; subject (with Eric Morley) of BBC film, Portrait, 1977, 1978. Member Council: ROI, 1964–78 (Vice-Pres. 1968–72; Pres., 1972–78; Hon. Mem. Council, 1978–); RP, 1969–71, 1972–74, 1978–80; NS, 1962–76 (Hon. Mem., 1976–); Chm., Contemp. Portrait Soc., 1971; Dir, Fedn of British Artists, 1981–83 (Governor, 1972–83). *Exhibited:* Royal Acad.; Royal Inst. Oil Painters; Royal Soc. Portrait Painters; Contemp. Portrait Soc.; Nat. Society; Young Contemporaries, Grosvenor Galleries, Upper Grosvenor Galls, Woodstock Galls, Royal Glasgow Inst. of Fine Arts, Nat. Portrait Gall.; Roy. Soc. of British Artists; Grafton Gall.; New Grafton Galls; Art Exhibitions Bureau, touring widely in Britain, USA and Canada. Judge, Miss World Contest, 1976. Platinum disc, 1977 (record sleeve design Portrait of Sinatra). *Portraits include:* The Queen (unveiled Silver Jubilee year, for Manchester; Queen's Lancs Regt); Queen Elizabeth The Queen Mother (as Chancellor, Univ. of London; as Patron, RADAR); Prince of Wales (for 2nd KEO Gurkhas); Princess Anne (for Saddlers' Co.; Royal Signals); Lord Aberconway; Lord Aldington; Lord Amory; Princess Ashraf; Lord Benson; Lord Barnetson; Lord Boothby; Lord Bowden; Lord Boyd; FM Lord Carver; Lord Chuter-Ede; Lord Denning; Paul Dirac; Abbot of Downside; Lord Elwyn-Jones; Archbishop Lord Fisher; Lord Fulton; Sir Alec Guinness; Gen. Sir John Hackett, Gilbert Harding; Robert Hardy; Sir Alan Hodgkin; Cardinal Hume; Amb. John J. Louis, USA; Lord Selwyn-Lloyd; Cliff Michelmore; Eric Morley; Robert Morley; Malcolm Muggeridge; Sir Gerald Nabarro; Sir David Napley; Valerie Profumo; J. B. Priestley; Francis Pym; Sir Ralph Richardson; Edmund de Rothschild; Archbishop Runcie; Dame Margaret Rutherford; Very Rev. M. Sullivan; Lord Todd; Dennis Wheatley; Sir Mortimer Wheeler; Lord Wolfenden; Sir Donald Wolfit; *major group portraits:* Royal Family, with Lord and Lady Mayoress, for Guildhall; Members and Officers, Metropolitan Water Board (47 figures); Lords of Appeal in Ordinary (for Middle Temple); Queen Elizabeth the Queen Mother opening Overlord Embroidery to public view, with Princess Alice, Lord Mountbatten, Duke of Norfolk, etc. *Represented in collections:* The Prince of Wales; British Mus.; Nat. Portrait Gall. (Hugill Fund Purchase, RA, 1972); numerous Oxford and Cambridge colleges; County Hall, Westminster; various livery companies and Inns of Court; House of Commons; Univs of London, Nottingham, East Anglia; City Univ.; Frank Sinatra. *Publications:* A Professional Approach to Oil Painting, 1968; contributions to various art journals. *Recreation:* idling. *Address:* 146 Hamilton Terrace, St John's Wood, NW8 9UX. *T:* 01–328 6754.

NOAKES, Philip Reuben, OBE 1962; HM Diplomatic Service, retired; *b* 12 Aug. 1915; *y s* of late Charles William and Elizabeth Farey Noakes; *m* 1940, Moragh Jean Dickson; two *s*. *Educ:* Wyggeston Grammar Sch.; Wycliffe Coll.; Queens' Coll., Cambridge (Open Schol.). Mod. Langs Tripos Part I, Hist. Tripos Part II; BA 1937; MA 1945; Pres., Cambridge Union Soc., 1937. Served War, 1940–46; Capt.-Adjt 2nd Fife and Forfar Yeomanry, RAC (despatches). Public Relations Officer, Royal Over-Seas League, 1947–48; Sen. Information Officer, Colonial Office, 1948; Prin. Information Officer, CO, 1953; Information Adviser to Governor of Malta, 1960–61; Chief Information Officer, CO, 1963–66; Commonwealth Office, 1967; Counsellor (Information), Ottawa, 1967–72; Consul-Gen., Seattle, 1973–75. *Recreations:* bird-watching, fishing, ski-ing. *Address:* Little St Mary's, Uplyme, Lyme Regis, Dorset DT7 3XH. *T:* Axminster 33371. *Club:* Royal Over-Seas League.

See also G. W. Noakes.

NOAKES, His Honour Sidney Henry; a Circuit Judge (formerly County Court Judge), 1968–77; *b* 6 Jan. 1905; *s* of Thomas Frederick Noakes (Civil Servant) and Ada Noakes. *Educ:* Merchant Taylors' Sch.; St John's Coll., Oxford (MA). Called to Bar, Lincoln's Inn, 1928; SE Circuit; Bencher, 1963. War Service, Lt-Col., Intelligence Corps, England and NW Europe. Deputy Chairman: Surrey QS, 1963; Herts QS, 1964; Recorder of Margate, 1965–68. *Publication:* Fire Insurance, 1947. *Recreations:* regretfully now only walking and gardening. *Address:* 14 Meadway Crescent, Hove, E Sussex BN3 7NL. *T:* Brighton 736143.

NOBAY, Prof. (Avelino) Robert, PhD; Brunner Professor of Economic Science, University of Liverpool, since 1980; *b* 11 July 1942; *s* of Theodore Anastasio Nobay and Anna Gracia D'Silva; *m* 1965, Susan Clare Saunders; two *s*. *Educ:* Univ. of Leicester (BA); Univ. of Chicago; PhD Southampton. Jun. Economist, Electricity Council, London, 1964–66; Res. Officer, NIESR, 1966–70; Sen. Lectr, Univ. of Southampton, 1970–80. Vis. Associate Prof., Univ. of Chicago, 1977–79. *Publications:* (with H. G. Johnson) The Current Inflation; (with H. G. Johnson) Issues in Monetary Economics. *Recreations:* sailing, golf, music. *Address:* Springfield, 28 Knowsley Road, Cressington Park, Liverpool L19 0PG. *T:* 051–427 2093.

NOBES, (Charles) Patrick; Headmaster, St Francis' College, Letchworth, since 1986; *b* 17 March 1933; *o c* of Alderman Alfred Robert Nobes, OBE, JP, and Marguerite Violet Vivian (*née* Fathers), Gosport, Hants; *m* 1958, Patricia Jean (*nee* Brand); three *s*. *Educ:* Price's Sch., Fareham, Hants; University Coll., Oxford. MA. With The Times, reporting and editorial, 1956–57; Head of English Dept, King Edward VI Grammar Sch., Bury St Edmunds, 1959–64; Head of English and General Studies and Sixth Form Master, Ashlyns Comprehensive Sch., Berkhamsted, 1964–69; Headmaster: The Ward Freman Sch., Buntingford, Herts, 1969–74; Bedales Sch., 1974–81; Weymouth Grammar Sch., 1981–85, later The Budmouth Sch., 1985–86. Chairman: HMC Co-ed Schs Gp, 1976–80; Soc. of Headmasters of Independent Schs, 1978–80; Mem., SHA Council, 1985–86. General Editor and adapter, Bulls-Eye Books (series for adults and young adults with reading difficulties), 1972–. *Recreations:* cricket and hockey, King Arthur, Hampshire, music, First World War. *Address:* The Headmaster's House, St Francis' College, Letchworth, Herts SG6 3PJ.

NOBLE, Adrian Keith; Associate Director, Royal Shakespeare Company, since 1982; *b* 19 July 1950; *s* of William John Noble and Violet Ena (*née* Wells). *Educ:* Chichester High Sch. for Boys; Bristol Univ. (BA); Drama Centre, London. Associate Dir, Bristol Old Vic, 1976–79; Resident Dir, RSC, 1980–82; Guest Dir, Royal Exchange Theatre, Manchester, 1980–81. *Stage productions include:* Ubu Rex, A Man's A Man, 1977; A View from the Bridge, Titus Andronicus, The Changeling, 1978; Love for Love, Timon of Athens, Recruiting Officer (Edinburgh Fest.), 1979; Duchess of Malfi, 1980; Dr Faustus, The Forest, A Doll's House, 1981; King Lear, Antony and Cleopatra, 1982; A New Way to Pay Old Debts, Comedy of Errors, Measure for Measure, 1983; Henry V, The Winter's Tale, The Desert Air, 1984; As You Like It, 1985; Mephisto, The Art of Success, 1986; *opera:* Don Giovanni, Kent Opera, 1983. *Address:* Barbican Theatre, EC2.

NOBLE, Sir Andrew Napier, 2nd Bt, *cr* 1923; KCMG 1954 (CMG 1947); *b* 16 Sept. 1904; *s* of Sir John Henry Brunel Noble, 1st Bt, and Amie (*d* 1973), *d* of S. A. Walker Waters; *S* father, 1938; *m* 1934, Sigrid, 2nd *d* of M. Michelet, of Royal Norwegian Diplomatic Service; two *s* one *d*. *Educ:* Eton; Balliol Coll., Oxford. Counsellor of the British Embassy, Buenos Aires, 1945–47; Assistant Under-Secretary of State, Foreign Office, 1949; HM Minister at Helsinki, 1951–54; HM Ambassador: Warsaw, 1954–56; Mexico, 1956–60; Netherlands, 1960–64, retired. *Publications:* (jt author) Centenary History, OURFC, 1969; History of the Nobles of Ardmore and of Ardkinglas, 1971. *Heir:* *s* Iain Andrew Noble, *qv*. *Address:* 11 Cedar House, Marloes Road, W8 5LA. *T:* 01–937 7952. *Club:* Boodle's.

NOBLE, Barrie Paul; HM Diplomatic Service; Counsellor, Foreign and Commonwealth Office, since 1984; *b* 17 Oct. 1938; *s* of late Major F. A. Noble and Mrs Henrietta Noble; *m* 1965, Alexandra Helene Giddings; one *s*. *Educ:* Hele's, Exeter; New Coll., Oxford (BA Jurisprudence); Univ. of Dakar. RAF, 1957–59. Joined HM Diplomatic Service, 1962; Third, later Second Sec., (Leopoldville) Kinshasa, 1965–67; Second Sec. (Commercial), Kaduna, 1967–69; FCO, 1969–72; First Sec., 1972–75 and Head of Chancery, 1975, Warsaw; FCO, 1976–80; Counsellor, UK Mission to UN, Geneva, 1980–84. *Publication:* Droit Coutumier, Annales Africaines, 1965. *Recreations:* grass cutting, bridge, skiing. *Address:* c/o Foreign and Commonwealth Office, SW1. *Clubs:* Royal Air Force, Ski Club of Great Britain.

NOBLE, David, WS, JP; Sheriff of North Strathclyde at Oban, Campbeltown and Fort William, since 1983; *b* 11 Feb. 1923; *s* of late Donald Noble, Solicitor, Inverness, and Helen Kirk Lynn Melville or Noble; *m* 1947, Marjorie Scott Smith or Noble; two *s* one *d*. *Educ:* Inverness Royal Academy; Edinburgh Univ. (MA, LLB *summa cum laude*). Royal Air Force Bomber Command, 1942–46. Partner in Miller Thomson & Robertson, WS, Edinburgh, 1953–82. JP Midlothian, 1970. *Address:* Woodhouselee, North Connel, Argyll PA37 1QZ. *T:* Connel 678.

NOBLE, David; Under Secretary and Head of Administrative Division, Medical Research Council, since 1981; *b* 12 June 1929; *s* of late William Ernest Noble and of Maggie (*née* Watt); *m* 1969, Margaret Patricia Segal. *Educ:* Buckhurst Hill County High Sch., Essex; University Coll., Oxford (BA Hons English, 1952). Admin. Assistant, UCH, 1952–58; Mem., Operational Res. Unit, Nuffield Provincial Hosps Trust, 1958–61; Project Sec., Northwick Park Hosp. and Clinical Res. Centre, NW Thames RHA and MRC, 1961–68; Medical Research Council: Principal, 1968–72; Asst Sec., 1972–81. *Publications:* contribs to literature on operation and design of hosps and res. labs. *Recreations:* music, reading, travel. *Address:* 173 Bittacy Hill, NW7 1RT. *T:* 01–346 8005.

NOBLE, Prof. Denis, FRS 1979; Burdon Sanderson Professor of Cardiovascular Physiology, Oxford University, since 1984; Tutorial Fellow, 1963–84, Professorial Fellow, since 1984, Balliol College, Oxford; *b* 16 Nov. 1936; *s* of George and Ethel Noble; *m* 1965, Susan Jennifer Barfield, BSc, DPhil; one *s* one *d. Educ:* Emanuel Sch., London; University Coll. London (BSc, MA, PhD; Fellow 1985). Asst Lectr, UCL, 1961–63; Tutor in Physiology, Balliol Coll., and Univ. Lectr, Oxford Univ., 1963–84; Vice-Master, Balliol Coll., 1983–85. Vis. Prof., Alberta, 1969–70; Foreign Correspondent, Royal Acad. of Medicine, Belgium, 1985. Editor, Progress in Biophysics, 1967–. Praefectus of Holywell Manor (Balliol Graduate Centre), 1971–. Hon. Sec., 1974–80, Foreign Sec., 1986–, Physiol Soc. Darwin Lectr, British Assoc., 1966; Nahum Lectr, Yale, 1977; Bottazzi Lectr, Pisa, 1985; Veda Lectr, Tokyo, 1985. Scientific Medal, Zoolog. Soc., 1970; Gold Medal, British Heart Foundn, 1985. *Publications:* Initiation of the Heartbeat, 1975, 2nd edn, 1979; Electric Current Flow in Excitable Cells, 1975; papers mostly in Jl of Physiology. *Recreations:* Indian and French cooking, Occitan, classical guitar. *Address:* Holywell Manor, Manor Road, Oxford OX1 3UH. *T:* Oxford 248738.

NOBLE, Sir Fraser; *see* Noble, Sir T. A. F.

NOBLE, Iain Andrew; Proprietor since 1972, and Chairman, Fearann Eilean Iarmain, Isle of Skye; Chairman, Noble & Co. Ltd, since 1980; *b* 8 Sept. 1935; *s* and *heir* of Sir Andrew Napier Noble, Bt, *qv. Educ:* China, Argentina and England. University College, Oxford (MA 1959). Matthews Wrightson, 1959–64; Scottish Council (Develt and Industry), 1964–69; Founder and Jt Man. Dir, Noble Grossart, 1969–72; Jt Founder and Chm., Seaforth Maritime, 1972–78; Chm., Lennox Oil Co., 1980–85; Dir, Adam & Co., 1983–; Dir of other cos in Scotland. Dir and Dep. Chm., Traverse Theatre Co., 1966–68; Trustee: Sabhal Mor Ostaig, 1974–84; Nat. Museums of Scotland, 1986–. Mem., Edinburgh Univ. Court, 1970–73. *Publication:* Sources of Finance, 1968. *Recreations:* Comhradh, Ceol is Ceilidh a measg deagh chompanaich. *Address:* An Laimrig, Eilean Iarmain, An t-Eilean Sgitheanach, IV43 8QR. *T:* (office) Isle Ornsay 266; 031–225 9677. *Club:* New (Edinburgh).

NOBLE, Kenneth Albert, CBE 1975; Member, Price Commission, 1973–77 (Deputy Chairman, 1973–76); Director, 1954–73, Vice-Chairman, 1966–73, Co-operative Wholesale Society Ltd; Director of associated organisations and subsidiaries. Member: CoID, 1957–65; Post Office Users Nat. Council, 1965–73; Monopolies Commn, 1969–73; London VAT Tribunals Panel, 1977–82. Served War, 1940–46 (despatches); Major RASC. *Publication:* (jtly) Financial Management Handbook, 1977, 2nd edn 1980. *Address:* Flat 1, York Mansions, Kings Parade, Holland-on-Sea, near Clacton-on-Sea, Essex CO15 5JP.

NOBLE, Major Sir Marc (Brunel), 5th Bt, *cr* 1902; *b* 8 Jan. 1927; *er s* of Sir Humphrey Brunel Noble, 4th Bt, MBE, MC, and Celia (*d* 1982), *d* of late Captain Stewart Weigall, RN; *S* father, 1968; *m* 1956, Jennifer Lorna, *yr d* of late John Mein-Austin, Flint Hill, West Haddon, Northants; two *s* one *d* (and one *d* decd). *Educ:* Eton. Commissioned into King's Dragoon Guards as 2nd Lieut, 1947; on amalgamation, transferred Royal Dragoons, 1958. Training Major and Adjutant, Kent and County of London Yeomanry (Sharpshooters), 1963–64; retired 1966. Commonwealth Comr, 1972, Chm., Cttee of Council, 1979–80, Scout Assoc. High Sheriff, Kent, 1985. *Heir: er s* David Brunel Noble, *b* 25 Dec. 1961. *Address:* Deerleap House, Knockholt, Sevenoaks, Kent TN14 7NP. *T:* Knockholt 33222. *Club:* Cavalry and Guards.

NOBLE, Sir Peter (Scott), Kt 1967; Principal of King's College, University of London, 1952–July 1968; *b* 17 Oct. 1899; *s* of Andrew Noble and Margaret Trail; *m* 1928, Mary Stephen (*d* 1983); two *s* one *d. Educ:* Aberdeen Univ.; St John's Coll., Cambridge. First Bursar at Aberdeen Univ., 1916, MA, with 1st Class Honours in Classics 1921, Simpson Prize and Robbie Gold Medal in Greek, Seafield Medal and Dr Black prize in Latin, Jenkyns Prize in Comparative Philology, Liddell Prize in Greek Verse, Fullerton Scholarship in Classics, 1921, Croom Robertson Fellow (1923–26); Scholar of St John's Coll., Cambridge; 1st class Classical Tripos Part I (1922) Part II (1923), 1st Class Oriental Langs Tripos Part I (1924) Part II (1925), Bendall Sanskrit Exhibition (1924), (1925), Hutchison Student (1925); Lecturer in Latin at Liverpool Univ., 1926–30; Professor of Latin Language and Literature in the University of Leeds, 1930–37; Fellow of St John's Coll., Cambridge, 1928–31; Regius Professor of Humanity, University of Aberdeen, 1938–52; Member of University Grants Cttee, 1943–53; Vice-Chancellor, University of London, 1961–64; Member of General Dental Council, 1955; Member of Educational Trust, English-Speaking Union, 1958; Governor of St Thomas' Hospital, 1960. Hon. LLD Aberdeen, 1955. *Publications:* Joint editor of Kharosthi Inscriptions Vol. III; reviews, etc, classical journals. *Address:* 17 Glenorchy Terrace, Edinburgh EH9 2DQ.

NOBLE, Sir (Thomas Alexander) Fraser, Kt 1971; MBE 1947; Principal and Vice-Chancellor, University of Aberdeen, 1976–81; *b* 29 April 1918; *s* of late Simon Noble, Grantown-on-Spey and Jeanie Graham, Largs, Ayrshire; *m* 1945, Barbara A. M. Sinclair, Nairn; one *s* one *d. Educ:* Nairn Acad; Univ. of Aberdeen. After military service with Black Watch (RHR), entered Indian Civil Service, 1940. Served in NW Frontier Province, 1941–47, successively as Asst Comr, Hazara; Asst Polit. Agent, N Waziristan; Controller of Rationing, Peshawar; Under-Sec., Food Dept and Develt Dept; Sec., Home Dept; Joint Dep. Comr, Peshawar; Civil Aide to Referendum Comr. Lectr in Political Economy, Univ. of Aberdeen, 1948–57; Sec. and Treas., Carnegie Trust for Univs of Scotland, 1957–62; Vice-Chancellor, Leicester Univ., 1962–76. Mem. and Vice-Chm., Bd of Management, Aberdeen Mental Hosp. Group, 1953–57. Sec., Scottish Economic Soc., 1954–58; Vice-Pres., 1962–. Chm., Scottish Standing Conf. of Voluntary Youth Organisations, 1958–62; Vice-Chm., Standing Consultative Council on Youth Service in Scotland, 1959–62. Mem., Departmental Cttee on Probation Service, 1959–62; Chairman: Probation Advisory and Training Board, 1962–65; Television Research Cttee, 1963–69; Advisory Council on Probation and After-Care, 1965–70; Univs Council for Adult Education, 1965–69; Min. of Defence Cttee for Univ. Assistance to Adult Educn in HM Forces, 1965–70; Advisory Board, Overseas Students' Special Fund, 1967–71, Fees Awards Scheme, 1968–75; Cttee of Vice-Chancellors and Principals of Univs of UK, 1970–72; British Council Cttee on Exchanges between UK and USSR, 1973–78; Scottish Council for Community Educn, 1979–80. Member: Academic Advisory Cttee, Univs of St Andrews and Dundee, 1964–66; E Midlands Economic Planning Council, 1965–68; Council, Assoc. Commonwealth Univs, 1970–79; Exec. Cttee, Inter-Univ. Council for Higher Educn Overseas, 1972–79; Exec. Cttee, British Council, 1973–79; British Council Cttee for Commonwealth Univ. Interchange, 1973–79; US-UK Educnl Commn, 1973–76. Hon. LLD: Aberdeen, 1968; Leicester, 1976; Glasgow, 1981; Washington Coll., Maryland, 1981. *Publications:* articles in economic journals and on education. *Recreation:* golf. *Address:* Hedgerley, Victoria Street, Nairn. *Clubs:* Athenæum; Royal Northern and University (Aberdeen); Royal Aberdeen Golf, Nairn Golf.

NOCK, Rt. Rev. Frank Foley, DD; *b* 27 Feb. 1916; *s* of David Nock and Esther Hambidge; *m* 1942, Elizabeth Hope Adams; one *s* one *d. Educ:* Trinity Coll., Toronto (BA, BD). Curate, St Matthew's, Toronto, 1940–42; Incumbent, Christ Church, Korah, Sault Ste Marie, 1942–45; Rector: Bracebridge, St Thomas', 1945–48; Church of the Epiphany, Sudbury, 1948–57; St Luke's Cathedral, 1957–74; Dean of Algoma, 1957–74; Bishop of Algoma, 1975–83; Priest in Charge, St John the Divine, Arva, Ont, 1983–86. Chancellor, Thorneloe Univ., Sudbury, 1974–83; Director: Sault Ste Marie & Dist Gp Health Assoc.; Community Concerts Assoc.; Mem., Sault Ste Marie Rotary Club. Hon. DD Toronto, 1957; Hon. STD Thorneloe, 1980. *Recreations:* music, golfing, cross country skiing. *Address:* Apt 1002, Harbour View Apts, 89 Pine Street, Sault Ste Marie, Ont P6A 6M6, Canada.

NOCK, Sir Norman (Lindfield), Kt 1939; Director, Nock & Kirby Holdings Ltd, Sydney (Chairman, 1926–79); *s* of Thomas Nock, Stanhope Road, Killara, Sydney; *m* 1927, Ethel Evelina Bradford; one *s. Educ:* Sydney Church of England Grammar Sch. Alderman for Gipps Ward, City of Sydney, 1933–41; Lord Mayor of Sydney, 1938–39; Chairman, Federal Australian Comforts Fund, 1939–43; Chairman, Australian Comforts Fund, NSW Division, 1939–45; President of the National Roads and Motorists Association, 1954–69; Chairman Royal North Shore Hospital of Sydney, 1940–69; Member National Health and Medical Research Council, 1946–69. JP for New South Wales. *Recreations:* golf, sailing and motoring. *Address:* 5–11 Thornton Street, Darling Point, NSW 2027, Australia. *Club:* Royal Sydney Golf (Sydney).

NOCKOLDS, Stephen Robert, FRS 1959; PhD; Reader in Geochemistry in the University of Cambridge, 1957–72, now Emeritus Reader; *b* 10 May 1909; *s* of Dr Stephen and Hilda May Nockolds; *m* 1st, 1932, Hilda Jackson (*d* 1976); 2nd, 1978, Patricia, *d* of late Flying Officer F. Horsley; one step *s* two step *d. Educ:* Felsted; University of Manchester (BSc); University of Cambridge (PhD). Fellow of Trinity Coll. and formerly Lectr in Petrology, Univ. of Cambridge. Murchison Medal, Geol Soc., 1972. Hon. Fellow, Geol. Soc. of India. *Publications:* (jtly) Petrology for Students, 1978; various papers in mineralogical and geological journals. *Recreation:* gardening. *Address:* Elm Lodge, Station Road, Keyingham, North Humberside HU12 9TB.

NODDER, Timothy Edward, CB 1982; Development Worker, Tower Hamlets Inter-Agency Group for Alcohol Services, since 1985; *b* 18 June 1930; *s* of Edward Nodder. *Educ:* St Paul's Sch.; Christ's Coll., Cambridge. Under-Sec., 1972, Dep. Sec., 1978–84, DHSS. *Recreation:* natural history. *Address:* 10 Frognal Lane, NW3.

NOEL, family name of **Earl of Gainsborough.**

NOËL, Sir Claude; *see* Noël, Sir M. E. C.

NOEL, Rear-Adm. Gambier John Byng, CB 1969; retired; *b* 16 July 1914; *s* of late G. B. E. Noel; *m* 1936, Miss Joan Stevens; four *d. Educ:* Royal Naval Coll., Dartmouth. Joined Royal Navy, 1931; Served in War of 1939–45, HMS Aurora and HMS Norfolk (despatches twice). Captain 1959; Imperial Defence Coll., 1962; Staff of Commander Far East Fleet, 1964–67; Rear-Admiral 1967; Chief Staff Officer (Technical) to C-in-C, Western Fleet, 1967–69. *Recreations:* gardening, golf. *Address:* Woodpeckers, Church Lane, Haslemere, Surrey. *T:* Haslemere 3824. *Club:* Anglo-Belgian.

NOEL, Geoffrey Lindsay James; Metropolitan Stipendiary Magistrate, since 1975; *b* 19 April 1923; *s* of Major James Noel and Maud Noel; *m* 1st, 1947; two *d*; 2nd, 1966, Eileen Pickering (*née* Cooper); two step *s. Educ:* Crewkerne Sch., Somerset. Enlisted Royal Regt of Artillery, 1941; commnd, 1942; attached 9th Para Bn, 6 Airborne Div., 1944, Captain; regular commn, 1946; Major 1957; retd 1960. Called to Bar, Middle Temple, 1962; practised London and SE circuit. Chm., Juvenile Courts, 1977–79; Dep. Circuit Judge, 1980–82. *Recreation:* gardening. *Address:* c/o 1 Garden Court, Temple, EC4.

NOEL, Hon. Gerard Eyre Wriothesley; author, publisher and journalist; Editor, Catholic Herald, 1971–76 and 1982–84, Editorial Director, since 1984; *b* 20 Nov. 1926; *s* of 4th Earl of Gainsborough, OBE, TD, and Alice (*née* Eyre); *m* 1958, Adele Julie Patricia, *d* of Major V. N. B. Were; two *s* one *d. Educ:* Georgetown, USA; Exeter Coll., Oxford (MA, Modern History). Called to Bar, Inner Temple, 1952. Director: Herder Book Co., 1959–66; Search Press Ltd, 1972–. Literary Editor, Catholic Times, 1958–61; Catholic Herald: Asst Editor, 1968; Editorial Dir, 1976–81. Mem. Exec. Cttee, 1974–, Hon. Treasurer, 1979–81, Council of Christians and Jews. Contested (L) Argyll, 1959. Liveryman, Co. of Stationers and Newspapermakers. Freeman, City of London. *Publications:* Paul VI, 1963; Harold Wilson, 1964; Goldwater, 1964; The New Britain, 1966; The Path from Rome, 1968; Princess Alice: Queen Victoria's Forgotten Daughter, 1974; contrib. The Prime Ministers, 1974; The Great Lock-Out of 1926, 1976; The Anatomy of the Roman Catholic Church, 1980; Ena: Spain's English Queen, 1984; Cardinal Basil Hume, 1984; *translations:* The Way to Unity after the Council, 1967; The Holy See and the War in Europe (Official Documents), 1968; articles in: Church Times, Catholic Times, Jewish Chronicle, Baptist Times, Catholic Herald, Universe. *Recreations:* walking, travel, exploring London. *Address:* 105 Cadogan Gardens, SW3. *T:* 01–730 8734; Westington Mill, Chipping Campden, Glos. *T:* Evesham 840240. *Clubs:* Beefsteak, Garrick.

NOËL, Sir (Martial Ernest) Claude, Kt 1976; CMG 1973; Director and Chairman of sugar and other companies; *b* 1 Feb. 1912; *m* 1937, Héléne Fromet de Rosnay; three *s* three *d. Educ:* College du St Esprit, Mauritius. Maths teacher, 1930; joined sugar industry, 1931; Manager sugar estate, 1939–. Chairman: Central Cttee of Estate Managers on several occasions; Mauritius Sugar Producers; Mauritius Employers Fedn, 1962–63. Membre d'Honneur, Mauritius Chamber of Agriculture, 1980 (Chm., 1971–72, Pres., 1974–). Citoyen d'Honneur Escalier Village. *Address:* Floréal, Mauritius. *T:* Curepipe 2235. *Clubs:* Dodo, Mauritius Turf (Mauritius).

NOEL-BAKER, Hon. Francis Edward; Director: North Euboean Enterprises Ltd, since 1973; Fini Fisheries, Cyprus, since 1976; *b* 7 Jan. 1920; *o s* of late Baron Noel-Baker, PC, and late Irene, *o d* of Frank Noel, British landowner, of Achmetaga, Greece; *m* 1957, Barbara Christina, *yr d* of late Joseph Sonander, Sweden; four *s* one *d. Educ:* Westminster Sch.; King's Coll., Cambridge (Exhibitioner; 1st cl. hons History). Founder and Chm., CU Lab. Club, 1939; left Cambridge to join Army, summer 1940, as Trooper, Royal Tank Regt; Commissioned in Intelligence Corps and served in UK, Force 133, Middle East (despatches); returned to fight Brentford and Chiswick Div.; MP (Lab) Brentford and Chiswick Div. of Mddx, 1945–50; Editor, United Nations World/World Horizon, 1945–47, Go! magazine, 1947–48; PPS Admiralty, 1949–50; BBC European Service, 1950–54; MP (Lab) Swindon, 1955–68, resigned from Labour Party, 1969; Sec., 1955–64, Chm., 1964–68, UN Parly Cttee; Vice-Chm., Lab. Cttee for Europe, 1976–78; Member: SDP 1981–83; Conservative Party, 1984–; NUJ, 1946–81. Chm., Advertising Inquiry Council, 1951–68. Chairman: North Euboean Foundation Ltd, 1965–; Candili Craft Centre, Philip Noel-Baker Centre, Euboea, 1983–; European Council for Villages and Small Towns, 1984–; Pres., Internat. Campaign for Environmental Health, 1985; Hon. Pres., Union of Forest Owners of Greece, 1968–. Member: Parochial Church Council, St Martin in the Fields, 1960–68; Freedom from Hunger Campaign UK Cttee Exec. Cttee, 1961; Ecology Party, 1978–; Soil Assoc., 1979–. Governor, Campion Sch., Athens, 1973–78. *Publications:* Greece, the Whole Story, 1946; Spanish Summary, 1948; The Spy

Web, 1954; Land and People of Greece, 1957; Nansen, 1958; Looking at Greece, 1967; My Cyprus File, 1985. *Recreation:* gardening. *Address:* Achmetaga Estate, 340–04 Procopi, Greece. *T:* 0227 41204; *Greece Telex:* 214716. 5 Cresswell Gardens, SW7 0BJ. *T:* 01–373 6345; (office) 27 Bryanston Square, W1H 7LS. *T:* 01–723 9405; *London Telex:* 917506. *Clubs:* Travellers', Special Forces; Athens.

NOEL-BUXTON, family name of **Baron Noel-Buxton.**

NOEL-BUXTON, 3rd Baron *cr* 1930; **Martin Connal Noel-Buxton;** *b* 8 Dec. 1940; *s* of 2nd Baron Noel-Buxton and Helen Nancy (*d* 1949), *yr d* of late Col K. H. M. Connal, CB, OBE, TD; *S* father, 1980; *m* 1st, 1964, Miranda Mary (marr. diss. 1968), *er d* of H. A. Chisenhale-Marsh; 2nd, 1972, Sarah Margaret Surridge (marr. diss. 1982), *o d* of N. C. W. Barrett, TD; one *s* one *d*. *Educ:* Bryanston School; Balliol College, Oxford (MA). Admitted a Solicitor, 1966. *Heir:* *s* Hon. Charles Connal Noel-Buxton, *b* 17 April 1975.

NOEL-PATON, family name of **Baron Ferrier.**

NOGUEIRA, Albano Pires Fernandes; Ambassador of Portugal; *b* 8 Nov. 1911; *m* 1937, Alda Maria Marques Xavier da Cunha. *Educ:* Univ. of Coimbra. 3rd Sec., Washington, 1944; 2nd Sec., Pretoria, 1945; 1st Sec., Pretoria, 1948; Head of Mission, Tokyo, 1950; Counsellor, London, 1953; Consul-Gen., Bombay, 1955; Consul-Gen., NY, 1955; Asst Perm. Rep. UN, NY, 1955; Asst Dir-Gen., Econ. Affairs, Lisbon, 1959; Dir Gen., Econ. Affairs, Lisbon, 1961; Ambassador to: European Communities, Brussels, 1964; NATO, 1970; Court of St James's, 1974–76; Sec.-Gen., Ministry for Foreign Affairs, 1977. Vis. Prof., Univ. of Minho, Braga, 1979, 1980. Mem., Internat. Assoc. of Literary Critics, 1981–. Grand Cross: Merito Civil (Spain), 1961; Order of Infante Dom Henrique (Portugal), 1964; Isabel la Católica (Spain), 1977; Merit (Germany), 1977; St Olav (Norway), 1978; Christ (Portugal), 1981; the Flag with golden palm (Yugoslavia), 1978; Grand Officer: Cruzeiro do Sul (Brazil), 1959; White Elephant (Thailand), 1960. *Publications:* Imagens em espelho Côncavo (essays); Portugal na Arte Japonesa (essay); Uma Agulha no Céu (novel); The Pull of the Continent—Portugal opts for a European as well as an Atlantic role; contrib. leading Portuguese papers and reviews. *Recreations:* reading, writing. *Address:* Avenue Gaspar Corte-Real 18, Apt 4D, 2750 Cascais, Portugal. *T:* 2868264; 5 Rua Alberto de Oliveira, 5–3, 3000 Coimbra, Portugal. *T:* 715035. *Clubs:* Grémio Literário, Automóvel de Portugal (Lisbon).

NOLAN, Brig. Eileen Joan, CB 1976; Director, Women's Royal Army Corps, 1973–77; *b* 19 June 1920; *d* of late James John and Ethel Mary Nolan. *Educ:* King's Norton Grammar Sch. for Girls. Joined ATS, Nov. 1942; commissioned, 1945. Lt-Col, 1967; Col, 1970; Brig., 1973. Hon. ADC to the Queen, 1973–77; Chm., NATO Senior Women Officers' Cttee, 1975–77; Dep. Controller Comdt, WRAC, 1977–84. *Address:* c/o Barclays Bank, High Street, Crowthorne, Berkshire.

NOLAN, Hon. Sir Michael (Patrick), Kt 1982; **Hon. Mr Justice Nolan;** a Judge of the High Court of Justice, Queen's Bench Division, since 1982; Presiding Judge, Western Circuit, since 1985; *b* 10 Sept. 1928; *yr s* of James Thomas Nolan and Jane (*née* Walsh); *m* 1953, Margaret, *yr d* of Alfred Noyes, CBE, and Mary (*née* Mayne); one *s* four *d*. *Educ:* Ampleforth; Wadham Coll., Oxford. Served RA, 1947–49; TA, 1949–55. Called to Bar, Middle Temple, 1953 (Bencher, 1975); QC 1968; called to Bar, NI, 1974; QC (NI) 1974; a Recorder of the Crown Court, 1975–82. Member: Bar Council, 1973–74; Senate of Inns of Court and Bar, 1974–81 (Treasurer, 1977–79). Mem., Sandilands Cttee on Inflation Accounting, 1973–75. Mem. Governing Body, Convent of the Sacred Heart, Woldingham, 1973–83; Governor, Combe Bank Sch., 1974–83. *Recreation:* fishing. *Address:* c/o Royal Courts of Justice, WC2. *Club:* MCC.

NOLAN, Sir Sidney (Robert), OM 1983; Kt 1981; CBE 1963; artist; *b* Melbourne, 22 April 1917; *s* of late Sidney Henry Nolan; *m* 1939, Elizabeth Patterson (marr. diss. 1942); *m* 1948, Cynthia Hansen (*d* 1974); *m* 1977, Mary Elizabeth à Beckett Perceval. *Educ:* State and technical schools, Melbourne; National Art Gallery Sch., Victoria. Italian Government Scholar, 1956; Commonwealth Fund Fellow, to USA, 1958; Fellow: ANU, 1965 (Hon. LLD, 1968); York Univ., 1971; Bavarian Academy, 1971. Hon. DLit London, 1971. Exhibited: Paris, 1948, 1961; New Delhi, 1953; Pittsburgh International, 1953, 1954, 1955, 1964, 1967, 1970; Venice Biennale, 1954; Rome, 1954; Pacific Loan Exhibition, 1956; Brussels International Exhibition, 1958; Documenta II, Kassel, 1959; Retrospective, Art Gallery of New South Wales, Sydney, 1967; Retrospective, Darmstadt, 1971; Ashmolean Museum, Oxford, 1971; Retrospective, Royal Dublin Soc., 1973; Perth Festival, 1982. Exhibits Tate Gallery, Marlborough New London Gallery, Marlborough Gallery, New York. Ballet Designs for Icare, Sydney, 1941; Orphée (Cocteau), Sydney, 1948; The Guide, Oxford, 1961; Rite of Spring, Covent Garden, 1962; The Display, Adelaide Festival, 1964; opera designs for: Samson et Delilah, Covent Garden, 1981; Il Trovatore, Sydney Op. House, 1983; mural for Victorian Cultural Centre Concert Hall, 1982. Works in Tate Gallery, Museum of Modern Art, New York, Australian national galleries, Contemporary Art Society and Arts Council of Great Britain, etc. Film, Nolan at 60, BBC and ABC, 1977. Hon. DLitt Sydney, 1977. *Publication:* Paradise Garden (poems, drawings and paintings), 1972; *Illustrated:* Near the Ocean, by Robert Lowell, 1966; The Voyage, by Baudelaire, trans. Lowell, 1968; Children's Crusade, by Benjamin Britten, 1973; *Relevant publications:* Kenneth Clark, Colin MacInnes, Bryan Robertson: Nolan, 1961; Robert Melville: Ned Kelly, 1964; Elwyn Lynn: Sydney Nolan: Myth and Imagery, 1967; Melville and Lynn: The Darkening Ecliptic: Ern Malley Poems, Sidney Nolan Paintings, 1974; Cynthia Nolan: Open Negative, 1967; Sight of China, 1969; Paradise, and yet, 1971. *Address:* c/o Marlborough Fine Art Ltd, 6 Albemarle Street, W1. *Clubs:* Athenæum, Garrick.

NONWEILER, Prof. Terence Reginald Forbes, BSc; PhD; CEng; FRAeS; FIMA; Professor of Mathematics, Victoria University of Wellington, since 1975; *b* 8 Feb. 1925; *s* of Ernest James Nonweiler and Lilian Violet Amalie Nonweiler (*née* Holfert); *m* 1949, Patricia Hilda Frances (*née* Neame); four *s* two *d*. *Educ:* Bethany Sch., Goudhurst, Kent; University of Manchester, BSc 1944, PhD 1960. Scientific Officer, Royal Aircraft Establishment, Farnborough, Hants, 1944–50; Scientific Officer, Scientific Advisor's Dept, Air Ministry, 1950–51; Senior Lecturer in Aerodynamics, College of Aeronautics, Cranfield, Beds, 1951–57; Senior Lecturer in Aeronautical Engineering, The Queen's Univ. of Belfast, 1957–61; Mechan Prof. of Aeronautics and Fluid Mechanics, Glasgow Univ., 1961–75. Consultant: to Admiralty, 1951; to Ministry of Aviation, 1959; to Ministry of Agriculture, 1966; to Wellington City Corp., 1977. Member, International Academy of Astronautics. *Publications:* Jets and Rockets, 1959; Computational Mathematics, 1984; numerous technical papers on aeronautics, space flight, and submarine motion. *Recreations:* acting and stage production. *Address:* Victoria University, Private Bag, Wellington, New Zealand.

NOONE, Dr Paul; Consultant Medical Microbiologist, Royal Free Hospital, NW3, since 1972; *b* 4 March 1939; *s* of Michael John Noone and Florence Miriam Noone (*née* Knox); *m* 1st, 1963, Ahilya Nehaul (marr. diss.); two *s*; 2nd, 1982, Malila Perera (*née* Tambimuttu); one step *s* three step *d*. *Educ:* Darlington Grammar Sch.; Christ Church, Oxford (BA, 1st Class Hons Animal Physiology, 1960; BM BCh, 1965); Middlesex Hosp. Med. Sch. FRCPath 1983 (MRCPath 1971). Various house officer jobs in London; Lectr in Pathology, Bland Sutton Inst. of Pathology, 1967; Sen. Registrar in Bacteriology, Central Middx Hosp., 1969; Lectr in Bacteriology, Middx Hosp., 1970. Specialises in diagnosis and management of infection, especially treatment of life-threatening hospital-acquired infection; lectures extensively on various aspects of antibiotics and infection throughout Britain, also Europe, USA, Saudi Arabia, Sri Lanka, Thailand, Malaysia, Indonesia, Turkey, Australia and Hong Kong. Engaged in junior hospital doctors' campaign for improved conditions and trng; Mem., ASTMS delegn to TUC Annual Congress, 1971 and 1972. Founder, 1977, and Chm. 1978–86, NHS Consultants Assoc. *Publications:* A Clinician's Guide to Antibiotic Therapy, 1977, 2nd edn 1979 (also Italian edn 1978, Spanish 1983); Some Poems: 1958–1982, 1983; over ninety articles in Lancet, BMJ and many other specialist medical jls on antibiotics, infections and related subjects. *Recreations:* spending time with family and friends. *Address:* 39 Wykeham Hill, Wembley, Middx HA9 9RY.

NORBURY, 6th Earl of, *cr* 1827; **Noel Terence Graham-Toler;** Baron Norwood, 1797; Baron Norbury, 1800; Viscount Glandine, 1827; *b* 1 Jan. 1939; *s* of 5th Earl and Margaret Greenhalgh (*d* 1984); *S* father 1955; *m* 1965, Anne Mathew; one *s* one *d*. *Heir:* *s* Viscount Glandine, *qv*. *Address:* Stock Exchange, EC2.

NORBURY, Brian Martin; Head of Schools Branch 1, Department of Education and Science, since 1984; *b* 2 March 1938; *s* of Robert Sidney Norbury and Doris Lilian (*née* Broughton). *Educ:* Churcher's Coll., Petersfield; King's Coll., London (BA; AKC 1959). National Service, RAEC, 1959–61. Asst Principal, WO, 1961; Private Sec. to Under Sec. of State for War, 1962; Asst Private Sec. to Dep. Sec. of State for Defence, 1964; Principal, MoD, 1965, Cabinet Office, 1969; Private Sec. to Sec. of the Cabinet, 1970–73; Asst Sec., MoD, 1973; Private Sec. to Sec. of State for Def., 1979–81; Under Sec., MoD, 1981, DES, 1984–. *Address:* 63 Aberdeen Road, N5. *Club:* Reform.

NORCROSS, Lawrence John Charles, OBE 1986; Headmaster, Highbury Grove School, since 1975; *b* 14 April 1927; *s* of Frederick Marshall Norcross and Florence Kate (*née* Hedges); *m* 1958, Margaret Wallace; three *s* one *d*. *Educ:* Ruskin Coll., Oxford; Univ. of Leeds (BA Hons English). Training Ship, Arethusa, 1941–42; RN, 1942–49 (E Indies Fleet, 1944–45); clerical asst, 1949–52; Asst Teacher: Singlegate Sch., 1957–61; Abbey Wood Sch., 1961–63; Housemaster, Battersea County Sch., 1963–74; Dep. Headmaster, Highbury Grove Sch., 1974–75. Member: Secondary Heads' Assoc.; NAS/UWT; HMC; Trustee and Mem. Exec. Cttee, Nat. Council for Educnl Standards; Trustee, Educnl Res. Trust; Member: Educn Study Gp, Centre for Policy Studies; Univ. Entrance and Schs Examinations Council, Univ. of London, 1980–84; Steering Cttee, Campaign for a Gen. Teaching Council. Founder and Hon. Sec., John Ireland Soc.; former Chm., Contemp. Concerts Co-ordination. Occasional broadcasts and television appearances. *Publications:* (with F. Naylor) The ILEA: a case for reform, 1981; (with F. Naylor and J. McIntosh) The ILEA after the Abolition of the GLC, 1983; (contrib.) The Wayward Curriculum, 1986; occasional articles. *Recreations:* talking to friends, playing bridge badly, watching cricket, listening to music. *Address:* 3 St Nicholas Mansions, 6–8 Trinity Crescent, SW17. *T:* 01–767 4299; Crockwell Cottage, Crockwell Street, Long Compton, Warwicks. *T:* Long Compton 662. *Club:* Surrey County Cricket.

NORDEN, Denis, CBE 1980; scriptwriter and broadcaster; *b* 6 Feb. 1922; *s* of George Norden and Jenny Lubell; *m* 1943, Avril Rosen; one *s* one *d*. *Educ:* Craven Park Sch., London; City of London Sch. Theatre Manager, 1939–42; served RAF, 1942–45; staff-writer in Variety Agency, 1945–47. With Frank Muir, 1947–64: collaborated for 17 years writing comedy scripts, including: (for radio): Take it from Here, 1947–58; Bedtime with Braden, 1950–54; (for TV): And so to Bentley, 1956; Whack-O!, 1958–60; The Seven Faces of Jim, 1961, and other series with Jimmy Edwards; resident in TV and radio panel-games; collaborated in film scripts, television commercials, and revues; joint Advisors and Consultants to BBC Television Light Entertainment Dept, 1960–64; jointly received Screenwriters Guild Award for Best Contribution to Light Entertainment, 1961; together on panel-games My Word!, 1956–, and My Music, 1967–. Since 1964, solo writer for television and films; Chm., Looks Familiar (Thames TV), 1973–; It'll Be Alright on the Night (LWT), 1977, 1979, 1980, 1984; It'll be Alright on the Day, 1983. Film Credits include: The Bliss of Mrs Blossom; Buona Sera, Mrs Campbell; The Best House in London; Every Home Should Have One; Twelve Plus One; The Statue; The Water Babies. Variety Club of GB Award for Best Radio Personality (with Frank Muir), 1978; Male TV Personality of the Year, 1980. *Publications:* (with Frank Muir): You Can't Have Your Kayak and Heat It, 1973; Upon My Word!, 1974; Take My Word for It, 1978; The Glums, 1979; Oh, My Word!, 1980; The Complete and Utter My Word Stories, 1983; Coming to You Live! behind-the-screen memories of Forties and Fifties Television, 1986. *Recreations:* reading, loitering. *Address:* 8/20 Short's Gardens, WC2H 9AU. *Club:* Saturday Morning Odeon.

NORDMEYER, Hon. Sir Arnold (Henry), KCMG 1975 (CMG 1970); JP; Leader of the Opposition (Labour), New Zealand, 1963–65; *b* Dunedin, New Zealand, 7 Feb. 1901; *s* of Arnold and Martha Nordmeyer; *m* 1931, Frances Maria Kernahan; one *s* one *d*. *Educ:* Waitaki Boys' High Sch.; Otago Univ. (BA, DipSocSci.). Presbyterian Minister for 10 years. Entered New Zealand Parliament, 1935; MP for Oamaru, 1935–49, for Brooklyn, 1951–54, for Island Bay, 1954–69; Minister of: Health, 1941–47; Industries and Commerce, 1947–49; Finance, 1957–60. JP 1970. Hon. LLD Otago, 1970. *Recreations:* shooting, fishing. *Address:* 53 Milne Terrace, Wellington, New Zealand.

NORELL, Dr Jacob Solomon, (Jack), FRCGP; general medical practitioner, since 1956; *b* 3 March 1927; *s* of Henry (formerly Habib) Norell and Malka Norell; *m* 1948, Brenda Honeywell (marr. diss. 1973); three *s*. *Educ:* South Devon Technical Coll.; Guy's Hosp. Med. Sch. (MB, BS 1953). MRCS, LRCP 1953; LMSSA 1952; MRCGP 1972, FRCGP 1982. Principal in general practice, 1956–. Dean of Studies, RCGP, 1974–81; Exec. Officer, Jt Cttee on Postgrad. Educn for Gen. Practice, 1976–81. Pres., Balint Soc., 1984–. William Pickles Lectr, RCGP, 1984. Editor, The Practitioner, 1982–83. *Publications:* (co-ed) Six Minutes for the Patient, 1973; Entering General Practice, 1981; papers and chapters on general practice topics: consultation, practice orgn, postgrad. educn, women doctors, measuring quality of med. care, professional self-regulation, doctor-patient relationship. *Recreations:* rural walks, driving open-topped cars, spotting unclad emperors. *Address:* 50 Nottingham Terrace, York Gate, Regent's Park, NW1 2QD. *T:* 01–486 2979.

NORFOLK, 17th Duke of, *cr* 1483; **Miles Francis Stapleton Fitzalan-Howard,** KG 1983; GCVO 1986; CB 1966; CBE 1960; MC 1944; DL; Earl of Arundel, 1139; Baron Beaumont, 1309; Baron Maltravers, 1330, Earl of Surrey, 1483; Baron FitzAlan, Clun, and Oswaldestre, 1627; Earl of Norfolk, 1644; Baron Howard of Glossop, 1869; Earl Marshal and Hereditary Marshal and Chief Butler of England; Premier Duke and Earl; *b* 21 July 1915; *s* of 3rd Baron Howard of Glossop, MBE, and Baroness Beaumont (11th in line), OBE; *S* to barony of mother, 1971, and of father, 1972, and to dukedom of cousin, 1975; *m* 1949, Anne Mary Teresa, *e d* of late Wing Commander Gerald Joseph Constable Maxwell, MC, DFC, AFC; two *s* three *d*. *Educ:* Ampleforth Coll.; Christ Church, Oxford

(MA; Hon. Student, 1983). 2nd Lieut, Grenadier Guards, 1937. Served War of 1939–45, France, North Africa, Sicily, Italy (despatches, MC), NW Europe. Appointed Head of British Military Mission to Russian Forces in Germany, 1957; Commanded 70 Bde KAR, 1961–63; GOC, 1 Div., 1963–65 (Maj.-Gen.); Dir, Management and Support Intelligence, MoD, 1965–66; Director, Service Intelligence, MoD, 1966–67; retd 1967. Chm., Arundel Castle Trustees, Ltd, 1976–. Pres., Building Socs Assoc., 1982–86. Prime Warden, Fishmongers' Co., 1985–86. Hon. Fellow, St Edmund's House, Cambridge, 1983; Hon. Bencher, Inner Temple, 1984. DL West Sussex, 1977. Knight of the Sovereign Order of Malta. *Heir: s* Earl of Arundel and Surrey, *qv*. *Address:* Arundel Castle, Sussex BN18 9AB. *T:* Arundel 882173; Carlton Towers, Goole, North Humberside DN14 9LZ. *T:* Goole 860 243; Bacres House, Hambleden, Henley-on-Thames, Oxfordshire RG9 6RY. *T:* Henley-on-Thames 571350. *Club:* Pratt's.

See also Lord Michael Fitzalan-Howard, D. P. Frost.

NORFOLK, Lavinia Duchess of; Lavinia Mary Fitzalan-Howard, CBE 1971; Lord-Lieutenant of West Sussex, since 1975; *b* 22 March 1916; *d* of 3rd Baron Belper and of Eva, Countess of Rosebery, DBE; *m* 1937, 16th Duke of Norfolk, KG, PC, GCVO, GBE, TD (*d* 1975); four *d*. *Educ:* Abbotshill, Hemel Hempstead, Herts. President: Nat. Canine Defence League, 1969–; Pony Riding for the Disabled Trust, Chigwell, 1964–; BHS, 1980–82. Vice-President: ASBAH, 1970–; Spastic Soc., 1969–; NSPCC, 1967–. Patron, Riding for the Disabled, 1986– (Pres., 1970–86). Chairman, King Edward VII Hosp., Midhurst, 1975–. Steward, Goodwood, 1976–78. BRCS Certificate of Honour and Badge, Class 1, 1969. Silver Jubilee Medal, 1977. *Address:* Arundel Park, Sussex. *T:* Arundel 882041.

See also Earl of Ancram, Lady Herries of Terregles.

NORFOLK, Archdeacon of; *see* Dawson, Ven. Peter.

NORFOLK, Ven. Edward Matheson; Archdeacon of St Albans, since 1982; *b* 29 Sept. 1921; *s* of Edward and Chrissie Mary Wilson Norfolk; *m* 1947, Mary Louisa Oates; one *s* one *d* (and one *s* decd). *Educ:* Latymer Upper School; Leeds Univ. (BA); College of the Resurrection, Mirfield. Deacon, 1946; priest, 1947; Assistant Curate: Greenford, 1946–47; King Charles the Martyr, South Mymms, 1947–50; Bushey, 1950–53; Vicar: Waltham Cross, 1953–59; Welwyn Garden City, 1959–69; Rector, Great Berkhamsted, 1969–81; Vicar, King's Langley, 1981–82. Hon. Canon of St Albans, 1972–82. *Recreations:* walking, bird-watching. *Address:* 6 Sopwell Lane, St Albans, Herts AL1 1RR. *T:* St Albans 57973.

NORFOLK, Leslie William, CBE 1973 (OBE 1944); TD 1946; CEng; engineering consultant; *b* 8 April 1911; *e s* of late Robert and Edith Norfolk, Nottingham; *m* 1944, A. I. E. W. (Nancy) Watson (then WRNS), *d* of late Sir Hugh Watson, IFS (retd); two *s* one *d*. *Educ:* Southwell Minster Grammar Sch., Notts; University Coll., Nottingham (BSc). MICE; MIMechE; MIEE. Assistant and later Partner, E. G. Phillips, Son & Norfolk, consulting engineers, Nottingham, 1932–39. 2nd Lieut 1931, 5 Foresters TA, transferred and served with RE, France, Gibraltar, Home Forces, 1939–45, Lt-Col. Engineer, Dyestuffs Div., ICI Ltd, 1945–53; Resident Engineer, ICI of Canada, Kingston, Ont., 1953–55; Asst Chief Engr, Metals Div., ICI Ltd, 1955–57; Engineering Manager, Severnside Works, ICI Ltd, 1957–59; Engineering Director, Industrias Quimicas Argentinas Duperial SAIC, Buenos Aires, 1959–65; Director, Heavy Organic Chemicals Div., ICI Ltd, 1965–68; retired from ICI, 1968; Chief Exec., Royal Dockyards, MoD, 1969–72. *Recreations:* home workshop, industrial archaeology. *Address:* Beechwoods, Beechwood Road, Combe Down, Bath, Avon. *T:* Combe Down 832104. *Club:* Bath & County (Bath).

NORGARD, John Davey, AO 1982; Chairman, Australian Broadcasting Commission, 1976–81; retired as Executive General Manager, Operations, BHP Co. Ltd, and as Chairman, Associated Tin Smelters, 1970; *b* 3 Feb. 1914; *s* of John Henry and Ida Elizabeth Norgard; *m* 1943, Irena Mary Doffkont; one *s* three *d*. *Educ:* Adelaide Univ. (BE); SA Sch. of Mines (FSASM). Part-time Chm., Metric Conversion Bd, Australia, 1970–81; Chairman: Commonwealth Employment Service Review, 1976–77; Pipeline Authority, 1976–81; Mem., Nat. Energy Adv. Cttee, 1977–80. Dep. Chancellor, La Trobe Univ., 1972–75. Chm., Grad. Careers Council of Australia, 1979–. *Recreation:* golf. *Address:* 29 Montalto Avenue, Toorak, Victoria 3142, Australia. *T:* (03) 2414937. *Clubs:* Australian, Royal Melbourne Golf, Sciences (all Melbourne); Newcastle (NSW).

NORLAND, Otto Realf; London representative, Deutsche Schiffahrtsbank AG, since 1984; *b* 24 Feb. 1930; *s* of Realph I. O. Norland and Aasta S. Sæther; *m* 1955, Gerd Ellen Andenæs; one *s* two *d*. *Educ:* Norwegian University College of Economics and Business Administration, Bergen. FIB. Hambros Bank Ltd, 1953–84: Manager, 1963; Dir, 1964–84; Advr, 1984–. Director: Alcoa of Great Britain Ltd, 1968–84 (Chm., 1978–84); Norsk Alcoa, 1978–84; Platou Investment, Oslo, 1981–86; Øivind Lorentzen, Oslo, 1983–84; IKO (UK) Ltd, 1984– (Chm., 1984–); Data-Ship (UK) Ltd, 1984–; Oslo Partners Ltd, 1985– (Chm.). Dir, Aluminium Fedn, 1979–84 (Pres., 1982). *Recreations:* tennis, skiing, books (polar explorations). *Address:* Grocers' Hall, Princes Street, EC2. *T:* 01–726 8726. *Clubs:* Den Norske; Norske Selskab (Oslo).

NORMAN, Baroness (Priscilla), CBE 1963; JP; *b* 1899; *o d* of late Major Robert Reyntiens and late Lady Alice Bertie; *m* 1st, 1921, Alexander Koch de Gooreynd (marr. diss. 1929); two *s*; 2nd, 1933, 1st Baron Norman, PC, DSO (*d* 1950). Member: London County Council, 1925–33; Chelsea Borough Council, 1928–31; Bethlem Royal and the Maudsley Hospital Board, 1951–75; South-East Metropolitan Regional Board, 1951–74; Hon. Pres., World Fedn for Mental Health, 1972. Vice-Chm., Women's Voluntary Services for Civil Defence, 1938–41; Vice-Pres., Royal College of Nursing. JP 1944. *Publication:* In the Way of Understanding, 1983. *Address:* Aubrey Lodge, Aubrey Road, W8 7JJ.

See also S. P. E. C. W. Towneley, P. G. Worsthorne.

NORMAN, (Alexander) Vesey (Bethune); Master of the Armouries, The Royal Armouries, HM Tower of London, since 1977; *b* 10 Feb. 1930; *s* of Lt-Col A. M. B. Norman and Sheila M. Maxwell; *m* 1954, Catherine Margaret Barne; one *s*. *Educ:* Alford Sch.; Trinity Coll., Glenalmond; London Univ. (BA Gen.). FSA; FSAScot. Asst Curator, Scottish United Services Museum, Edinburgh Castle, 1957; Hon. Curator of Arms and Armour, Abbotsford, 1957; Asst to Dir, Wallace Collection, 1963; Inspector of Armouries, 1977. Vice-Pres., NADFAS, 1984–. Liveryman, Gunmakers' Co., 1981–. *Publications:* Arms & Armour, 1964 (also foreign edns); (with Don Pottinger) Warrior to Soldier, 449–1660, 1966 (USA edn as A History of War and Weapons, 449–1660, reprinted as English Weapons and Warfare, 449–1660, 1979); Small Swords and Military Swords, 1967; The Medieval Soldier, 1971 (also USA); Arms and Armour in the Royal Scottish Museum, 1972; A Catalogue of Ceramics, Wallace Collection, Pt I, 1976; (with C. M. Barne) The Rapier and Small-Sword, 1460–1820, 1980; articles in learned jls. *Recreation:* study of arms and armour. *Address:* The Royal Armouries, HM Tower of London, EC3N 4AB.

NORMAN, Rear-Adm. Anthony Mansfeldt; Director General, Naval Personal Services, Ministry of Defence (Navy), since 1986; *b* 16 Dec. 1934; *s* of Cecil and Jean Norman; *m* 1961, Judith Pye; one *s* one *d*. *Educ:* Royal Naval Coll., Dartmouth. Graduate ndc. Various sea/shore appts, 1952–73; Staff of Dir Underwater Weapons, 1973–74; student ndc, 1974–75; CO HM Ships Argonaut and Mohawk, 1975–76; Fleet Anti-Submarine Warfare Officer, 1976–78; CO (Captain), HMS Broadsword, 1978–80; Asst Dir Naval Plans, MoD, 1980–83; Captain: 2nd Frigate Sqdn, HMS Broadsword, 1983–85; Sch. of Maritime Ops, HMS Dryad, 1985–86. *Recreations:* tennis, squash, hill walking, travel. *Address:* c/o National Westminster Bank, 208 Piccadilly, W1A 2DG.

NORMAN, Archibald Percy, MBE 1945; FRCP; MD; Medical Adviser, Tadworth Court Hospital Trust, since 1983; Hon. Medical Adviser, Tadworth Court Children's Hospital, since 1984; Physician, Hospital for Sick Children, 1950–77, now Hon. Physician; Paediatrician, Queen Charlotte's Maternity Hospital, 1951–77, now Hon. Paediatrician; *b* 19 July 1912; *s* of Dr George Percy Norman and Mary Margaret MacCallum; *m* 1950, Aleida Elisabeth M. M. R. Bisschop; five *s*. *Educ:* Charterhouse; Emmanuel Coll., Cambridge. Served War of 1939–45, in Army, 1940–45. Chm., Med. and Res. Cttee, Cystic Fibrosis Res. Trust, 1976–84; Mem., Attendance Allowance Appeals Bd, 1978–84. *Publications:* (ed) Congenital Abnormalities, 1962, 2nd edn 1971; (ed) Moncrieff's Nursing and Diseases of Sick Children, 1966; (ed) Cystic Fibrosis, 1983; contributions to medical journals. *Address:* White Lodge, Heather Close, Kingswood, Surrey. *T:* Mogador 832626.

NORMAN, Sir Arthur (Gordon), KBE 1969 (CBE 1966); DFC 1943; and Bar 1944; Chairman, The De La Rue Company, since 1964 (Chief Executive, 1972–77); Vice-Chairman, Sun Life Assurance Society, 1984–May 1987 (Director, 1966–84); *b* N Petherton, Som, 18 Feb. 1917; *m* 1944, Margaret Doreen Harrington (*d* 1982); three *s* two *d*. *Educ:* Blundell's Sch. Joined Thomas De La Rue & Co., 1934. RAF 1939–45 (DFC and Bar); Wing-Comdr, 1943. Rejoined Thomas De La Rue & Co., 1946; Director, 1951; Managing Director, 1953. Director: SKF (UK) Ltd, 1970–; Kleinwort, Benson, Lonsdale plc, 1985– . Pres., CBI, 1968–70. Bd mem., Internat. Inst. for Environment and Develt; Chairman: World Wildlife Fund, UK, 1977–84; UK Centre for Economic and Environmental Develt (CEED), 1984–; Mem., Nature Conservancy Council, 1980–86. Trustee: RAF Museum; King Mahendra Trust for Nature Conservation (Nepal). *Recreations:* tennis, golf, country life. *Address:* De La Rue House, 3/5 Burlington Gardens, W1A 1DL. *T:* 01–734 8020.

NORMAN, Barry (Leslie); author, journalist and broadcaster; *b* 21 Aug. 1933; *s* of Leslie and Elizabeth Norman; *m* 1957, Diana, *o d* of late A. H. and C. A. Narracott; two *d*. *Educ:* Highgate Sch. Entertainments Editor, Daily Mail, 1969–71, then made redundant; Writer and Presenter of Film, 1973–81, and Film 1983–86, BBC1; Presenter of: Today, Radio 4, 1974–76; Going Places, Radio 4, 1977–81; Breakaway, Radio 4, 1979–80; Omnibus, BBC1, 1982; The Chip Shop, Radio 4, 1984; Writer and Presenter of: The Hollywood Greats, BBC1, 1977–79, 1984, 1985; The British Greats, 1980. Weekly columnist, The Guardian, 1971–80. Richard Dimbleby Award, BAFTA, 1981. *Publications:* The Matter of Mandrake, 1967; The Hounds of Sparta, 1968; Tales of the Redundance Kid, 1975; End Product, 1975; A Series of Defeats, 1977; To Nick a Good Body, 1978; The Hollywood Greats, 1979; The Movie Greats, 1981; Have a Nice Day, 1981; Sticky Wicket, 1984; The Film Greats, 1985. *Recreation:* playing village cricket. *Address:* c/o Curtis Brown Ltd, 162–168 Regent Street, W1.

NORMAN, Desmond; *see* Norman, N. D.

NORMAN, Rt. Rev. Edward Kinsella, KBE 1984; DSO 1945; MC 1943; Assistant Bishop, Diocese of Lichfield, since 1986; *b* 1916; *m* 1941, Margaret Edith Wilson; four *d*. *Educ:* Univ. of New Zealand (BA 1939); St John's Coll., Auckland; Westcott House, Cambridge. Served War of 1939–45 (despatches, MC, DSO). Deacon 1947, priest 1948, Newcastle upon Tyne; Curate of Berwick-on-Tweed, 1947–49; Vicar of Waiwhetu, 1949–52; Levin, 1952–59; Tauranga, 1959–65; Karori, 1965–73; Chaplain to Samuel Marsden Coll. Sch., 1965–73; Chaplain to RNZNVR, 1966–73; Archdeacon of Wellington, 1969–73; Bishop of Wellington, 1973–86; Senior Anglican Chaplain to NZ Forces, 1979–86. Legion of Merit (US), 1945. *Address:* 14 The Close, Lichfield, Staffs WS13 7LD. *Clubs:* Wellington, United Services Officers' (Wellington).

NORMAN, Rev. Dr Edward Robert; Dean of Peterhouse, Cambridge, since 1971; Lecturer in History, University of Cambridge, since 1965; *b* 22 Nov. 1938; *o s* of Ernest Edward Norman and Yvonne Louise Norman. *Educ:* Chatham House Sch.; Monoux Sch.; Selwyn Coll., Cambridge (MA, PhD, DD). FRHistS. Lincoln Theological Coll., 1965. Deacon, 1965; Priest, 1971. Asst Master, Beaconsfield Sec. Mod. Sch., Walthamstow, 1957–58; Fellow of Selwyn Coll., Cambridge, 1962–64; Fellow of Jesus Coll., Cambridge, 1964–71; Wilkinson Prof. of Church History, Wycliffe Coll., Univ. of Toronto, 1981–82. NATO Res. Fellow, 1966–68. Asst Chaplain, Addenbrooke's Hosp., Cambridge, 1971–78. Reith Lectr, 1978; Prideaux Lectr, 1980; Suntory-Toyota Lectr, LSE, 1984. Six Preacher in Canterbury Cathedral, 1984–. *Publications:* The Catholic Church and Ireland, 1965; The Conscience of the State in North America, 1968; Anti-Catholicism in Victorian England, 1968; The Early Development of Irish Society, 1969; A History of Modern Ireland, 1971; Church and Society in Modern England, 1976; Christianity and the World Order, 1979; Christianity in the Southern Hemisphere, 1981; The English Catholic Church in the Nineteenth Century, 1983; Roman Catholicism in England, 1985; The Victorian Christian Socialists, 1987. *Recreation:* watching television. *Address:* Peterhouse, Cambridge. *T:* Cambridge 50256. *Club:* Athenæum.

NORMAN, Vice-Adm. Sir Geoffrey; *see* Norman, Vice-Adm. Sir H. G.

NORMAN, Geoffrey; JP; Assistant Secretary of Commissions (Training), The Magistrates' Association, since 1986 (Secretary, 1977–86); *b* 25 March 1935; *s* of late William Frederick Trafalgar Norman and of Vera May Norman (*née* Goodfellow); *m* 1958, Dorothy Frances King (*d* 1978); two *s* two *d*. *Educ:* Harrow County Sch.; Brasenose Coll., Oxford (MA). Admitted Solicitor, 1959. Deputy Clerk to the Justices, Uxbridge, 1961–66; Clerk to the Justices, N Hertfordshire and Stevenage, 1966–77. Mem., Duty Solicitor Scheme-making Cttee, 1984–86. JP Inner London, 1982. Freeman, City of London, 1981; Liveryman, Curriers' Co., 1983. *Publications:* articles on magistrates' courts and related subjects. *Recreations:* painting, badminton. *Address:* Easter Cottage, Gosmore, Hitchin, Herts SG4 7QH. *T:* Hitchin 50783.

NORMAN, George Alfred B.; *see* Bathurst Norman.

NORMAN, Vice-Admiral Sir (Horace) Geoffrey, KCVO 1963; CB 1949; CBE 1943; *b* 25 May 1896; *m* 1924, Noreen Frances, *o d* of late Brig.-General S. Geoghegan; one *s* one *d*. *Educ:* Trent Coll.; RN Coll., Keyham. HMS Queen Elizabeth and destroyers, 1914–18; Long Gunnery Course, 1921; passed RN Staff Coll., 1929; Commander, 1932; Captain, 1938; idc 1939; Rear-Admiral, 1947; Chief of Staff to C-in-C, Mediterranean Station, 1948–50; Admiralty, 1950; Vice-Admiral (retired), 1951. Sec., Nat. Playing Fields Assoc., 1953–63. *Recreations:* fishing and outdoor sports. *Address:* Chantry Cottage, Wickham, Hants PO17 6JA. *T:* Wickham 832248.

NORMAN, Jessye; soprano, concert and opera singer; *b* Augusta, Ga, USA, 15 Sept. 1945; *d* of late Silas Norman and of Janie King. *Educ:* Howard Univ., Washington, DC (BM *cum laude*). Peabody Conservatory, 1967; Univ. of Michigan, 1967–68 (MMus). Operatic début, Deutsche Oper, Berlin, 1969; La Scala, Milan, 1972; Royal Opera House, Covent Garden, 1972; NY Metropolitan Opera, 1983; American début, Hollywood Bowl, 1972; Lincoln Centre, NYC, 1973; first Covent Garden recital, 1980; début at Barbican, 1983. Tours include North and South America, Europe, Middle East, Australia, Israel. Many international festivals, including Aix-en-Provence, Aldeburgh, Berlin, Edinburgh, Flanders, Helsinki, Lucerne, Salzburg, Tanglewood, Spoleto, Hollywood, Ravinia. Hon. DMus: Howard, 1982; Univ. of the South, Sewanee, 1984; Boston Conservatory, 1984. Musician of the Year, Musical America, 1982; prizes include: Grand Prix du Disque (Acad. du Disque Français), 1973, 1976, 1977, 1982, 1984; Grand Prix du Disque (Acad. Charles Cros), 1983; Deutscher Schallplattenpreis, 1975, 1981. Commandeur de l'Ordre des Arts et des Lettres, France, 1984. *Address:* c/o Shaw Concerts Incorporated, 1995 Broadway, New York, NY 10023, USA.

NORMAN, Kenneth Roy, FBA 1985; Reader in Indian Studies, University of Cambridge, since 1978; *b* 21 July 1925; *s* of Clement and Peggy Norman; *m* 1953, Pamela Raymont; one *s* one *d*. *Educ:* Taunton School; Downing College, Cambridge (MA 1954). Fellow and Tutor, Downing College, Cambridge, 1952–64; Lectr in Indian Studies (Prakrit), Univ. of Cambridge, 1955–78. Foreign Mem., Royal Danish Acad. of Sciences and Letters, 1983. *Publications:* Elders' Verses I (Theragāthā), 1969; Elders' Verses II (Therīgāthā), 1971; (trans.) Jain Cosmology, 1981; Pāli Literature, 1983; The Group of Discourses (Sutta-nipāta), 1984; (ed) Pāli Tipiṭakaṁ Concordance, Vol. II 4–9, 1963–73; (ed) Critical Pāli Dictionary Vol. II 11–13, 1981–85. *Recreations:* reading, walking. *Address:* Faculty of Oriental Studies, Sidgwick Avenue, Cambridge CB3 9DA. *T:* Cambridge 335133.

NORMAN, Air Cdre Sir Mark (Annesley), 3rd Bt, *cr* 1915; DL; Chairman, IU Europe Ltd; Director, Gotaas-Larsen Shipping Corporation, and other companies; *b* 8 Feb. 1927; *s* of Sir Nigel Norman, 2nd Bt, CBE, and Patricia Moyra (who *m* 2nd, 1944, Sir Robert Perkins, *qv*), *e d* of late Colonel J. H. A. Annesley, CMG, DSO; *S* father, 1943; *m* Joanna Camilla, *d* of late Lt-Col I. J. Kilgour, Bampton, Oxon; two *s* one *d*. *Educ:* Winchester Coll. Coldstream Guards, 1945–47; Flying Officer, 601 (County of London) Sqdn, RAuxAF, 1953–56. Hon. Air Cdre, No 4624 (County of Oxford) Movements Sqdn, RAuxAF; Air Cdre RAuxAF, 1984. Chm., Anglo-US Cttee, RAF Upper Heyford, 1984–. Chm., St Luke's, Oxford, 1986–. Patron and Churchwarden, St Peter's, Wilcote, 1972–. High Sheriff, 1983–84, DL 1985, Oxon. *Recreations:* gardening, workshop, the building of minor follies. *Heir:* *s* Nigel James Norman, late Major 13/18th Royal Hussars (Queen Mary's Own) [*b* 5 Feb. 1956; *m* 1985, Joanna, *d* of Captain Michael Naylor-Leyland, MC]. *Address:* Wilcote Manor, Charlbury, Oxon. *T:* Ramsden 357; c/o 12 Chesterfield Hill, W1. *T:* 01–499 4624. *Clubs:* White's, Pratt's, Royal Air Force, MCC; St Moritz Tobogganing.

See also N. D. Norman, W. R. Norman.

NORMAN, Mark Richard, CBE 1977 (OBE 1945); Managing Director of Lazard Brothers & Co. Ltd, 1960–75; Chairman, Gallaher Ltd, 1963–75; Director of other public companies, 1947–75; Deputy Chairman, National Trust, 1977–80 (Chairman, Finance Committee, 1969–80); *b* 3 April 1910; *s* of late Ronald C. Norman; *m* 1933, Helen, *d* of late Thomas Pinckney Bryan, Richmond, Virginia; two *s* three *d*. *Educ:* Eton; Magdalen Coll., Oxford. With Gallaher Ltd, 1930–32; Lazard Brothers & Co. Ltd, 1932–39. Served War of 1939–45: Hertfordshire Yeomanry; wounded Greece, 1941; an Asst Military Secretary, War Cabinet Offices, 1942–45 (Lieut-Colonel). Partner Edward de Stein & Co., 1946–60. *Address:* Garden House, Moor Place, Much Hadham, Herts. *T:* Much Hadham 2703. *Club:* Brooks's.

NORMAN, (Nigel) Desmond, CBE 1970; CEng; FRAeS; Deputy Chairman and Managing Director, The Norman Aeroplane Co. Ltd, (formerly NDN Aircraft Ltd, Isle of Wight), since 1979; Managing Director, NDN Aeroculture Ltd, since 1979; *b* 13 Aug. 1929; 2nd *s* of Sir Nigel Norman, 2nd Bt (*d* 1943), CBE, and Patricia Moyra (who *m* 2nd, 1944, Sir Robert Perkins, *qv*); *m* 1st, Anne Fogg-Elliott; two *s*; 2nd, 1965, Mrs. Boel Elizabeth Holmsen; two *s* two *d*. *Educ:* Eton; De Havilland Aeronautical Technical Sch. (1946–49). RAF GD Pilot, thereafter 601 Sqdn, RAuxAF Fighter Sqdn, until disbandment, 1948–57. Export Asst at SBAC, 1951–53; Founder of Britten-Norman Ltd with F. R. J. Britten, 1954, Jt Man. Dir, 1954–71. Non-Exec. Director: Bridport Aviation Products Ltd, 1980–; Bridport-Gundry plc, 1981–. *Recreations:* aviation, sailing, shooting. *Address:* Norman Aeroplane Co. Ltd, Cardiff Wales Airport, Rhoose Road, Rhoose, S Glamorgan CF6 9AY. *T:* Rhoose 711884; The Old Vicarage, Llantwit Major, S Glamorgan. *Clubs:* Royal Air Force, Royal Yacht Squadron.

See also Sir Mark Norman, Bt, W. R. Norman.

NORMAN, Prof. Richard Oswald Chandler, DSc; FRS 1977; CChem, FRSC; Chief Scientific Adviser, Ministry of Defence, since 1983, on secondment; Professor of Chemistry, University of York, since 1965; *b* 27 April 1932; *s* of Oswald George Norman and Violet Maud Chandler; *m* 1982, Jennifer Margaret Tope. *Educ:* St Paul's Sch.; Balliol Coll., Oxford (MA, DSc). CChem; FRIC 1963. Jun. Res. Fellow, Merton Coll., Oxford, 1956–58, Fellow and Tutor, 1958–65; Univ. Lectr in Chemistry, Oxford, 1958–65. Mem., SERC, 1983–. President: RIC, 1978–80; RSC, 1984–86; Dir, Salters' Inst. of Indust. Chemistry, 1975–. Tilden Lectr, Chemical Soc., 1976. Meldola Medal, RIC, 1961; Corday-Morgan Medal, Chemical Soc., 1967. *Publications:* Principles of Organic Synthesis, 1968; (with D. J. Waddington) Modern Organic Chemistry, 1972; papers in Jl Chem. Soc. *Recreations:* cricket, music, gardening. *Address:* 129 The Mount, York YO2 2DA. *T:* York 53900. *Club:* Athenæum.

NORMAN, Sir Robert (Wentworth), Kt 1970; JP; *b* 10 April 1912; *s* of William Henry Norman and Minnie Esther Brown; *m* 1942, Grace Hebden, *d* of Sidney Percy Hebden; one *s* one *d*. *Educ:* Sydney Grammar Sch. Served Army 1940–46: Captain, AIF. Joined Bank of New South Wales, 1928; Manager, Head Office, 1961; Dep. Gen. Manager, 1962; Chief Gen. Manager, 1964–77; Dir, 1977–84. Councillor: Science Foundn for Physics within Univ. of Sydney; Inst. of Public Affairs; Senator and Life Mem., Junior Chamber Internat. FAIM. JP NSW, 1956. 3rd Order of the Rising Sun (Japan), 1983. *Recreations:* bowls, reading. *Address:* 432 Edgecliff Road, Edgecliff, NSW 2027, Australia. *T:* 32 1900. *Clubs:* Union, Royal Sydney Golf, Australian Jockey (Sydney).

NORMAN, Vesey; *see* Norman, A. V. B.

NORMAN, Willoughby Rollo; Hon. President, The Boots Co. Ltd, since 1972 (Chairman, 1961–72); Deputy Chairman, English China Clays Ltd; 2nd *s* of Major Rt Hon. Sir Henry Norman, 1st Bt; *m* 1st, 1934, Hon. Barbara Jacqueline Boot, *er d* of 2nd and last Baron Trent, KBE; one *s* two *d*; 2nd, 1973, Caroline Haskard, *d* of William Greville and Lady Diana Worthington. *Educ:* Eton; Magdalen Coll., Oxford. Served War of 1939–45, Major, Grenadier Guards. Director: National Westminster Bank (Chm. Eastern Region), 1963–79; Sheepbridge Engineering Ltd, 1979; Guardian Royal Exchange Assurance, 1961–79. Vice-Chairman Boots Pure Drug Co. Ltd, 1954–61. High Sheriff of Leicestershire, 1960. *Recreations:* shooting, farming, gardening. *Address:* The Grange, South Harting, Petersfield, Hants; 28 Ranelagh House, Elystan Place, SW3. *T:* 01–584 9410. *Clubs:* White's, Pratt's.

See also Sir Mark Norman, Bt, N. D. Norman.

NORMANBY, 4th Marquis of, *cr* 1838; **Oswald Constantine John Phipps,** KG 1985; CBE 1974 (MBE (mil.) 1943); Baron Mulgrave (Ireland), 1767; Baron Mulgrave (Great Britain), 1794; Earl of Mulgrave and Viscount Normanby, 1812; Lord-Lieutenant of North Yorkshire, since 1974 (of North Riding of Yorkshire, 1965–74); *b* 29 July 1912; *o s* of Rev. the 3rd Marquess and Gertrude Stansfeld, OBE, DGStJ (*d* 1948), *d* of Johnston J. Foster of Moor Park, Ludlow; *S* father, 1932; *m* 1951, Hon. Grania Maeve Rosaura Guinness, *d* of 1st Baron Moyne; two *s* five *d*. *Educ:* Eton; Christ Church, Oxford. Served War of 1939–45, The Green Howards (wounded, prisoner, repatriated). PPS to Sec. of State for Dominion Affairs, 1944–45, to Lord President of the Council, 1945; a Lord-in-Waiting to the King, 1945. High Steward of York Minster, 1980–. Mem., Council of St John for N Yorks (formerly NR of Yorks), 1948– (Chm., 1948–77; Pres., 1977–); Chairman: KCH, 1948–74; Nat. Art-Collections Fund, 1981–86; Pres., Nat. Library for the Blind, 1977–; Vice-President: St Dunstans; RNLI, 1984– (Mem. Cttee of Management, 1972–84); Member: Gen. Council, King Edward's Hosp. Fund; Chapter-Gen., OStJ. Hon. Col Comdt, The Green Howards, 1970–82; Dep. Hon. Col, 2nd Bn Yorks Volunteers, 1971–72; President: TA&VRA for N of England, 1971–74 (Vice-Pres., 1968–71); TA&VRA N Yorks and Humberside, 1980–83. KStJ. Hon. DCL: Durham Univ; York Univ. *Heir:* *s* Earl of Mulgrave, *qv*. *Address:* Mulgrave Castle, Whitby, N Yorks YO21 3RJ; Argyll House, 211 King's Road, SW3. *T:* 01–352 5154. *Club:* Yorkshire (York).

NORMANTON, 6th Earl of, *cr* 1806; **Shaun James Christian Welbore Ellis Agar;** Baron Mendip, 1794; Baron Somerton, 1795; Viscount Somerton, 1800; Baron Somerton (UK), 1873; Royal Horse Guards, 1965; Blues and Royals, 1969; left Army, 1972, Captain; *b* 21 Aug. 1945; *er s* of 5th Earl of Normanton; *S* father, 1967; *m* 1970, Victoria Susan, *o d* of J. H. C. Beard, Turmer House, Somerley, Ringwood, Hants; one *s* two *d*. *Educ:* Eton. *Recreations:* shooting, skiing, motor boating. *Heir:* *s* Viscount Somerton, *qv*. *Address:* Somerley, Ringwood, Hants BH24 3PL. *T:* Ringwood 3253. *Clubs:* White's; Royal Yacht Squadron.

NORMANTON, Tom, TD; BA (Com); MP (C) Cheadle since 1970; Member (C) European Parliament, since 1973, elected for Cheshire East, 1979; chairman of a group of companies; *b* 12 March 1917; *m* 1942, Annabel Bettine (*née* Yates); two *s* one *d*. *Educ:* Manchester Grammar Sch.; Manchester Univ. (BA (Com); Chm., Cons. Assoc., 1937–38; Vice-Pres. Students' Union, 1938). Joined family group of textile cos, 1938. Served War of 1939–45: Army (commnd TA 1937) Europe and N Africa; GS appts, GHQ BEF, HQ First and Eighth Armies; HQ 21 Army Gp (wounded, Calais, 1940; despatches, 1944); demob., rank Major, 1946. Chm., Rochdale YC, 1948; Mem. Rochdale CB Council, 1950–53; contested (C) Rochdale, 1959 and 1964. Hon. Sec., Cons. Backbencher Industry Cttee, 1972–74; Mem., Expenditure Cttee, 1972–73; opposition front bench spokesman on energy, 1975–79; European Parliament: Member: Cttee on Energy and Research, 1973–79 (Vice-Chm., 1976–79 and (as elected Member), 1979–); Cttee on Economic and Monetary Affairs, 1973–79; Jt Africa, Caribbean, Pacific States Standing Conf., 1975–79; spokesman on Competition Policy, 1975; Deleg. to US Congress, 1975–78; Mem. European Cons. Gp, resp. Indust. Policy; special interests energy and defence; Chm., European All-Party Gp Friends with Israel, 1979–; Vice-Pres., Par European Union eV, 1980. Mem. Supervisory Bd, European Inst. for Security. Manager, Lancashire Fusiliers Compassionate Fund, 1964–; Trustee, Cotton Industry War Memorial Fund, 1965; apptd Employer panel, NBPI, 1966–68; Member: Council, British Employers Confedn, 1959–64; Council, CBI, 1964–76 (Mem. Europe Cttee, 1964, and Econ. Policy Cttee, 1964–70), 1979– (co-opted); Stockport Chamber of Commerce, 1970–; Central Training Council, 1968–74; Exec., UK Automation Council, 1966– (Vice-Chm., 1970–73); Cotton and Allied Textiles Ind. Trng Bd, 1966–70; Exec. Council, British Textile Confederation, 1972–76; Vice-Chm. Manchester Br. of Inst. of Dirs, 1969–71; Chm., European Textile Industries Cttee; President: British Textile Employers Assoc., 1970–71; Internat. Fedn of Cotton & Allied Textiles Industries, 1976– (Vice-Pres., 1972–76, Pres., 1976–78). Director: Industrial Training Services Ltd, 1972–; N Reg. Bd, Commercial Union Assurance Ltd, 1974–; Manchester Chamber of Commerce, 1970–. Consultant, Midland Bank Gp, EEC, Brussels, 1979–. Mem. Cttee, Anglo-Austrian Soc.; Patron, Assoc. for Free Russia, Speaks French and German. AMBIM. *Recreations:* sailing, walking, gardening. *Address:* Bollin Court, Macclesfield Road, Wilmslow, Cheshire. *T:* Wilmslow 524930. *Clubs:* Beefsteak, House of Commons Yacht (Hon. Treasurer, 1972–74, Commodore, 1976); St James's (Manchester).

NORREYS, Lord; Henry Mark Willoughby Bertie; *b* 6 June 1958; *s* and *heir* of the Earl of Lindsey (14th) and Abingdon (9th), *qv*. *Educ:* Eton; Univ. of Edinburgh. *Address:* Gilmilnscroft, Sorn, Mauchline, Ayrshire KA5 6ND. *Club:* Puffin's (Edinburgh).

NORRIE, family name of **Baron Norrie.**

NORRIE, 2nd Baron, *cr* 1957; **George Willoughby Moke Norrie;** Director: Fairfield Nurseries (Hermitage) Ltd; International Garden Centre (British Group) Ltd, 1984; *b* 27 April 1936; *s* of 1st Baron Norrie, GCMG, GCVO, CB, DSO, MC, and Jocelyn Helen (*d* 1938), *d* of late R. H. Gosling; *S* father, 1977; *m* 1964, Celia Marguerite, JP, *d* of John Pelham Mann, MC; one *s* two *d*. *Educ:* Eton College; RMA Sandhurst. Commissioned 11th Hussars, 1956; ADC to C-in-C Middle East Comd, 1960–61; GSO 3 (Int.) 4th Guards Brigade, 1967–69; retired, 1970. Pres. Royal British Legion (Newbury Branch). *Recreations:* skiing, tennis. *Heir:* *s* Hon. Mark Willoughby John Norrie, *b* 31 March 1972. *Address:* Henwick Old Farm, Newbury, Berks RG16 9EP. *T:* Thatcham 62808. *Clubs:* Cavalry and Guards, MCC.

NORRIE, Marian Farrow, (Mrs W. G. Walker); Her Honour Judge Norrie; a Circuit Judge, since 1986; *b* 25 April 1940; *d* of Arthur and Edith Jackson; *m* 1st, 1964; two *d*; 2nd, 1983, William Guy Walker; one step *s* two step *d*. *Educ:* Manchester High Sch. for Girls; Nottingham Univ. (LLB). Admitted Solicitor of Supreme Court, 1965; a Recorder, 1979–86. Consultant, Norrie, Bowler & Wrigley, Solicitors, Sheffield, 1983–86 (Sen. Partner, 1968–83). Member: Parole Bd, 1983–85; Appts Commn, Press Council, 1985–. *Address:* Croydon Crown Court, Barclay Road, Croydon CR9 3NE.

NORRINGTON, Roger Arthur Carver, OBE 1980; Principal Conductor, Bournemouth Sinfonietta, since 1985; Chief Guest Conductor, Jerusalem Symphony Orchestra, since 1986; Musical Director: London Classical Players, since 1978; Schütz Choir of London, since 1962; *b* 16 March 1934; *s* of late Sir Arthur Norrington and Edith Joyce, *d* of William Moberly Carver; *m* 1964, Susan Elizabeth McLean May (marr. diss. 1982); one *s* one *d*; *m* 1986, Karalyn Mary Lawrence. *Educ:* Dragon Sch., Oxford; Westminster; Clare Coll., Cambridge (BA); Royal Coll. of Music. Freelance singer, 1962–72. Principal Conductor, Kent Opera, 1966–84. Musical Dir, Early Opera Project, 1984–; co-Dir, Historic Arts, 1986–. Guest conducts many British and European orchestras, appears at Proms, City of London, Bath, Aldeburgh, Edinburgh and Harrogate festivals; broadcasts regularly at home and abroad. Debuts: British, 1962; BBC Radio, 1964; TV 1967; Germany, Austria, Denmark, Finland, 1966; Portugal, 1970; Italy, 1971; France and Belgium, 1972; USA, 1974; Holland, 1975; Switzerland, 1976. Many gramophone recordings. Cavaliere, Order al Merito della Repubblica Italiana, 1981.

Publications: occasional articles in various musical journals. *Recreations:* reading, walking, sailing.

NORRIS, Dame Ada (May), DBE 1976 (OBE 1954); CMG 1969; *b* 28 July 1901; *d* of Allan Herbert Bickford and Alice Hannah (*née* Baggs); *m* 1929, Hon. Sir John Gerald Norris, *qv*; two *d. Educ:* Melbourne High Sch.; Melbourne Univ. (MA, DipEd). Teacher, 1925–29. Vice-Chm., Victorian Council on the Ageing, 1951–80; Member-at-Large, Aust. Council on the Ageing; Vice-Pres., Victorian Soc. for Crippled Children and Adults, 1951–; President: Australian Adv. Council for the Physically Handicapped, 1955–57; Children's Book Council of Victoria, 1954–60, of Aust., 1960; Member: Commonwealth Immigration Adv. Council, 1950–71 (Dep. Chm., 1968–71); Exec. Cttee. Internat. Council of Women, 1950–79; Life-Vice-Pres., Nat. Council of Women of Australia (Pres., 1967–70); Chairman: Nat. Cttee for Internat. Women's Year, 1974–76; UNAA Nat. Cttee for Status of Women and Decade for Women, 1976–; Mem. Exec. Cttee, Melbourne Internat. Centenary Exhbn 1980, 1979–. Australian Rep., UN Commn on Status of Women, 1961–63. Chm., Appeal Cttee, Hall of Residence for Women Students, Univ. of Papua New Guinea, 1969–73. Hon. LLD Melbourne, 1980. UN Peace Medal, 1975. *Publications:* The Society: history of the Victorian Society for Crippled Children and Adults, 1974; Champions of the Impossible, 1978; papers on status of women and social welfare matters. *Recreations:* gardening, travel. *Address:* 10 Winifred Crescent, Toorak, Vic 3142, Australia. *T:* Melbourne (03) 2415166. *Club:* Lyceum.

NORRIS, Sir Alfred (Henry), KBE 1961 (OBE 1950; MBE 1938); *b* 27 April 1894; *s* of late Alfred James Norris, Hornchurch, Essex, and Charlotte Norris; *m* 1925, Betty K. R. Davidson (decd); *m* 1936, Winifred Gladys, *d* of late Archibald Henry Butler; three *s. Educ:* Cranbrook Sch., Kent. Served War of 1914–18, King's Own Royal (Lancaster) Regt. Retired Company Director and Chartered Accountant; formerly of Brazil. *Recreations:* social work, gardening. *Address:* 11 Abbey Close, Elmbridge, Cranleigh, Surrey. *Clubs:* Canning; Royal British (Lisbon).

NORRIS, Vice-Adm. Sir Charles (Fred Wivell), KBE 1956; CB 1952; DSO 1944; *b* 16 Dec. 1900; *m* 1924, Violet Cremer; one *s. Educ:* RNC Osborne and Dartmouth. Comdr, 1934; RN Staff Course, 1935; commanded HMS Aberdeen, 1936–39; Captain, 1941; commanded HMS Bellona, 1943–45; commanded HMS Dryad (Navigation and Direction School), 1945–46; Imperial Defence Coll., 1947; Captain of the Fleet, Home Fleet, 1948–50; Rear-Admiral, 1950; Director of Naval Training, and Deputy Chief of Naval Personnel, 1950–52; Vice-Admiral, 1953; Flag Officer (Flotilla), Mediterranean, 1953–54. Commander-in-Chief, East Indies Station, 1954–56, retired, 1956. Director of the British Productivity Council, 1957–65. *Address:* Clouds, 56 Shepherds Way, Liphook, Hants GU30 7HH. *T:* Liphook 722456.

NORRIS, Air Chief Marshal Sir Christopher Neil F.; *see* Foxley-Norris.

NORRIS, Rt. Rev. Mgr David Joseph; Prelate of Honour to the Pope; Vicar General of Westminster Diocese, since 1972; General Secretary to RC Bishops' Conference of England and Wales, 1967–83; *b* 17 Aug. 1922; *s* of David William and Anne Norris. *Educ:* Salesian Coll., Battersea; St Edmund's Coll., Ware; Christ's Coll., Cambridge (MA). Priest, 1947; teaching at St Edmund's Coll., Ware, 1948–53; Cambridge, 1953–56; Private Secretary to Cardinal Godfrey, 1956–64; National Chaplain to Catholic Overseas Students, 1964–65; Private Secretary to Cardinal Heenan, 1965–72. *Recreations:* reading, music, sport. *Address:* Archbishop's House, Westminster, SW1P 1QJ. *T:* 01–834 4717.

NORRIS, Sir Eric (George), KCMG 1969 (CMG 1963); HM Diplomatic Service, retired; Director: Inchcape & Co., since 1977 (Deputy Chairman, 1981–86); London Sumatra Plantations Ltd; Gray Mackenzie Ltd; *b* 14 March 1918; *s* of late H. F. Norris, Bengeo, Hertford; *m* 1941, Pamela Crane; three *d. Educ:* Hertford Grammar Sch.; St Catharine's Coll., Cambridge. Served Royal Corps of Signals, 1940–46 (Major). Entered Dominions Office, 1946. Served in British Embassy, Dublin, 1948–50; UK High Commission in Pakistan, 1952–55; UK High Commission in Delhi, 1956–57; Dep. High Commissioner for the UK, Bombay, 1957–60; IDC 1961; British Dep. High Comr, Calcutta, 1962–65; Commonwealth Office, 1966–68; High Comr, Kenya, 1968–72; Dep. Under Sec. of State, FCO, 1972–73; High Comr, Malaysia, 1974–77. PMN (Malaysia), 1974. *Address:* Homestead, Great Amwell, Herts. *T:* Ware 870739. *Clubs:* East India, Royal Commonwealth Society (Chm. 1980–84).

NORRIS, Gilbert Frank; Chief Road Engineer, Scottish Development Department, 1969–76; *b* 29 May 1916; *s* of Ernest Frank Norris and Ada Norris; *m* 1941, Joan Margaret Catherine Thompson; one *s. Educ:* Bemrose Sch., Derby; UC Nottingham. FICE. Served with Notts, Bucks and Lindsey County Councils, 1934–39; Royal Engineers, 1939–46; Min. of Transport: Highways Engr in Nottingham, Edinburgh and Leeds, 1946–63; Asst Chief Engr, 1963–67; Dep. Chief Engr, 1967; Dir, NE Road Construction Unit, 1967–69. *Recreations:* motoring, photography. *Address:* Woodhead Lee, Lamlash, Isle of Arran KA27 8JU. *T:* Lamlash 323.

NORRIS, Col Graham Alexander, OBE (mil.) 1945; JP; company director; Vice Lord-Lieutenant of County of Greater Manchester, since 1975; *b* 14 April 1913; *er s* of late John O. H. Norris and Beatrice H. Norris (*née* Vlies), Manchester; *m* 1st, 1938, Frances Cicely, *d* of late Walter Gorton, Minchinhampton, Glos; one *d*; 2nd, 1955, Muriel, *d* of late John Corris, Manchester. *Educ:* William Hulme's Grammar Sch.; Coll. of Technology, Manchester; Regent St Polytechnic, London; Merchant Venturers Techn. Coll., Bristol. CEng, FIMechE. Trng as automobile engr, Rolls Royce Ltd, Bristol Motor Co. Ltd; Joseph Cockshoot & Co. Ltd: Works Man., 1937, Works Dir 1946, Jt. Man. Dir 1964, Chm. and Man. Dir, 1968; Dir, Lex Garages Ltd, 1968–70; Dir, Red Garages (N Wales) Ltd, 1973–. War service, RAOC and REME, UK, ME and Italy, 1940–46 (Lt-Col); Comdr REME 22 (W) Corps Tps (TA), 1947–51; Hon. Col, 1957–61. Mem., NEDC for Motor Vehicle Distrib. and Repair, 1966–74; Pres., Motor Agents Assoc., 1967–68; Vice-Pres., Inst. of Motor Industry, 1973–76; Mem., Industrial Tribunal Panel, 1976–82. Pres., Manchester and Dist Fedn of Boys' Clubs, 1968–74; Vice-Pres., NABC, 1972–; Chm. Council, UMIST, 1971–83; Member Court: Univ. of Manchester; UMIST. Master, Worshipful Co. of Coachmakers and Coach Harness Makers, 1961–62; Freeman, City of London, 1938. JP, Lancashire 1963; DL Co. Palatine of Lancaster, 1962. *Recreations:* gardening, walking, social service activities. *Address:* 5 Brook Court, Brook Road, Windermere, Cumbria LA23 2LA.

NORRIS, Herbert Walter; Regional Director, South East Region, National Westminster Bank Ltd, 1969–73; Deputy Chief General Manager, 1962–65, Director, 1965–68, Westminster Bank Ltd; *b* 9 Dec. 1904; *s* of Walter Norris, Farnworth, Widnes, Lancs; *m* 1935, Laura Phyllis Tardif, *d* of A. Tardif, St Martin's, Guernsey; no *c. Educ:* Liverpool Collegiate School. Joined Westminster Bank, Liverpool Office, 1921; Joint General Manager, Westminster Bank Ltd, 1949. FIB (Mem. Council, Inst. of Bankers, 1952–65; Dep. Chairman, 1959–61). Master of Coopers' Company, 1973–74. *Recreations:* reading, music. *Address:* 53 Chancellor House, Tunbridge Wells, Kent.

NORRIS, Hon. Sir John (Gerald), Kt 1982; ED 1945; Judge of the Supreme Court of Victoria, 1972–75, retired; *b* 12 June 1903; *s* of John Alexander Norris, CMG and Mary Ellen (*née* Heffernan); *m* 1929, Ada May Bickford (*see* Dame Ada Norris); two *d. Educ:* Camberwell State Sch.; Melbourne High Sch.; Univ. of Melbourne (LLM); (jtly) Supreme Court Prize, 1924). Called to the Victorian Bar, 1925; KC 1950. Served War, 1939–45: Australia and New Guinea; Lt-Col. Actg County Court Judge, 1950; County Court Judge, 1955–72; Actg Supreme Court Judge for periods during 1968–72. Royal Comr on admin of law relating to prostitution in WA, 1975–76; Chm., Victorian Govt Cttee to consider recommendations of Bd of Inquiry into allegations against Victorian Police, 1976–78; reviewed law relating to coroners for Victorian Govt, 1979–80; conducted inquiry into concentration of ownership and control of press in Vic, 1980–81. Univ. of Melbourne: Lectr in Commercial Law, 1932–52; Mem., Standing Cttee of Convocation, 1952–62; Warden of Convocation, 1962–65; Mem. Council, 1965–81. Chm., Sir Edmund Herring Meml Cttee, 1983–. Pres., Baden Powell Scout Guild of Australia, 1979–81. Hon. Col, 4th/19th Prince of Wales's Light Horse, 1964–72; Patron, Vic Br., Royal Aust. Armoured Corps Assoc., 1975–. Hon. LLD Melb., 1980. *Publications:* The Financial Emergency Acts, 1932; articles in legal jls. *Recreations:* gardening, walking, reading. *Address:* 10 Winifred Crescent, Toorak, Vic 3142, Australia. *T:* 241 5166. *Clubs:* Australian, Royal Automobile of Victoria (Melbourne); Toorak Services.

NORRIS, John Robert, PhD; Director, Group Research, Cadbury Schweppes Ltd, since 1979; *b* 4 March 1932; *s* of Albert Norris and Winifred May Perry; *m* 1956, Barbara Jean Pinder; two *s* one *d* (and one *s* decd). *Educ:* Depts of Bacteriology and Agriculture, Univ. of Leeds (BSc 1st Cl. Hons 1954, PhD 1957). Lectr in Bacteriology, Univ. of Glasgow, 1957–63; Microbiologist, Shell Research Ltd, 1963–73 (Dir, Borden Microbiol Lab., 1970–73); Dir, Agr. Res. Council's Meat Res. Inst., 1973–79. Editor, Methods in Microbiology, 1969–. *Publications:* papers in microbiol jls. *Recreations:* walking, wood carving, Yoga. *Address:* 32 Redland Grove, Bristol BS6 6PR. *T:* Bristol 47175. *Club:* Farmers'.

NORRIS, Steven John; MP (C) Oxford East, since 1983; *b* 24 May 1945; *s* of John Francis Birkett Norris and Eileen Winifred (*née* Walsh); *m* 1969, Peta Veronica (*née* Cecil-Gibson); two *s. Educ:* Liverpool Institute; Worcester College, Oxford. MA. Private company posts, 1967–82; Chm., Steve Norris Ltd, 1982–. Mem., Berks CC, 1977–85; Dep. Leader, Cons. Group, 1983–85. Mem., Berks AHA, 1979–82; Vice-Chm., W Berks District HA, 1982–85. PPS to Minister for Local Govt, DoE, 1985–. Mem., Select Cttee on Social Services, 1984–85. Chm. of Governors, The Downs School, Compton, 1981–85; Governor, Mary Hare School for the Deaf, 1979–. Freeman, City of London; Liveryman, Coachmakers' Co. *Recreations:* reading, not walking. *Address:* House of Commons, SW1A 0AA. *T:* 01–219 6384. *Clubs:* Carlton, United and Cecil.

NORRIS, Sydney George; Assistant Under Secretary of State, Director of Operational Policy, Prison Department, Home Office, since 1985; *b* 22 Aug. 1937; *s* of late George Samuel Norris, FCA and of Agnes Rosa Norris; *m* 1965, Brigid Molyneux FitzGibbon; two *s* one *d. Educ:* Liverpool Inst. High Sch. for Boys; University Coll., Oxford (MA); Trinity Hall and Inst. of Criminology, Cambridge (Dip. in Criminology); Univ. of California, Berkeley (MCrim). Intelligence Corps, 1956–58; Home Office, 1963; Private Sec. to Parly Under Sec. of State, 1966; Harkness Fellow, 1968–70; Sec., Adv. Council on Penal System, 1970–73; Principal Private Sec. to Home Sec., 1973–74; Asst Sec., 1974; seconded to HM Treasury, 1979–81; Asst Under Sec. of State, 1982; seconded to NI Office as Principal Estabt and Finance Officer, 1982–85. *Recreations:* running, fell walking, garden maintenance, DIY, piano. *Address:* Home Office, SW1. *Club:* Thames Hare and Hounds.

NORSTAD, Gen. Lauris, DSM (US) with Oak Leaf Cluster and Silver Star; Legion of Merit (US) with Cluster; Air Medal; United States Air Forces, retired; Hon. Chairman (formerly Chairman and Chief Executive Officer, 1967–72), Owens-Corning Fiberglas Corporation (President, Owens-Corning Fiberglas International, January-December 1963); *b* Minneapolis, USA, 24 March 1907; *s* of Martin Norstad; *m* 1935, Isabelle Helen Jenkins; one *d. Educ:* US Military Academy (BS). 2nd Lieut, Cavalry, 1930; graduated, Air Corps Sch., 1931. Served in various branches of Air Force; duty at GHQ Air Force, Langley Field, Va., 1940; Assistant Chief of Staff for Operations, 12th Air Force, 1942, served with 12th Air Force, England and Algiers; Director of Operations, Allied Air Forces, Mediterranean, Dec. 1943; Chief of Staff, 20th Air Force, Washington, 1944; Asst Chief of Staff for Plans, Army Air Force HQ, 1945; Director of Plans and Operations Div., War Dept, Washington, 1946; Dep. Chief of Staff for Operations, USAF, 1947; Acting Vice Chief of Staff, Air Force, May 1950; C-in-C US Air Forces in Europe and C-in-C Allied Air Forces Central Europe, 1951; Deputy (Air) to Supreme Allied Commander, Europe, 1953; C-in-C, US European Comd, 1956–62, and Supreme Allied Commander, Europe, 1956–62; retired, 1963. Has several hon. degrees. Hon. CBE (GB). Holds other foreign orders. *Address:* (business) 717 Fifth Avenue, New York, NY 10022, USA.

NORTH, family name of **Earl of Guilford.**

NORTH, Lord; Piers Edward Brownlow North; *b* 9 March 1971; *s* and *heir* of Earl of Guilford, *qv.*

NORTH, John Joseph; Senior Visiting Fellow, Department of Land Economy, University of Cambridge, since 1985; *b* 7 Nov. 1926; *s* of Frederick James North and Annie Elizabeth North (*née* Matthews); *m* 1958, Sheila Barbara Mercer; two *s. Educ:* Rendcomb College; Univ. of Reading (BSc, DipAgric); Univ. of California (MS). FIBiol 1972. Agricultural Adviser, Nat. Agricultural Advisory Service, 1951; Kellogg Fellowship, USA, 1954–55; Regional Agricultural Officer, Cambridge, 1972; Senior Agricultural Officer, 1976; Chief Agricl Officer, ADAS, MAFF, 1979. *Recreations:* golf, gardening. *Address:* 28 Hauxton Road, Little Shelford, Cambridge. *T:* Cambridge 843369.

NORTH, Sir Jonathan; *see* North, Sir W. J. F.

NORTH, Dr Peter Machin, DCL; Principal of Jesus College, Oxford, since 1984; *b* Nottingham, 30 Aug. 1936; *o s* of late Geoffrey Machin North and Freda Brunt (*née* Smith); *m* 1960, Stephanie Mary, *e d* of T. L. Chadwick; two *s* one *d. Educ:* Oakham Sch.; Keble Coll., Oxford (BA 1959, BCL 1960, MA 1963, DCL 1976). National Service, Royal Leics Regt, 2nd Lieut, 1955–56. Teaching Associate, Northwestern Univ. Sch. of Law, Chicago, 1960–61; Lecturer: University Coll. of Wales, Aberystwyth, 1961–63; Univ. of Nottingham, 1963–65; Tutor in Law, 1965–76, Fellow, 1965–84, Hon. Fellow, 1984, Keble Coll., Oxford; Mem., Hebdomadal Council, 1985–. A Law Comr, 1976–84. Vis. Professor: Univ. of Auckland, 1969; Univ. of BC, 1975–76; Dir of Studies, Hague Acad. of Internat. Law, 1970; Lectures: Hague Acad. of Internat. Law, 1980; Horace Read Meml, Dalhousie Univ., 1980; Colston, Bristol Univ., 1984; Frances Moran Meml, TCD, 1984; Philip James, Leeds Univ., 1985. Chairman: Road Traffic Law Review, 1985–; Conciliation Project Adv. Cttee, 1985–; Management Cttee, Oxford CAB, 1985–; Member: Lord Chancellor's Adv. Cttee on Legal Educn, 1973–75; Social Scis and the Law Cttee, ESRC (formerly SSRC), 1982–85; Govt and Law Cttee, ESRC, 1985–;

Council, British Inst. of Internat. and Comparative Law, 1986– (Chm., Private Internat. Law Section, Adv. Bd, 1986–). Associate Mem., Inst. of Internat. Law, 1985. Mem., Editorial Cttee, British Yearbook of Internat. Law, 1983–; General Editor, Oxford Jl of Legal Studies, 1987–. *Publications:* (ed jtly) Chitty on Contracts, 23rd edn 1968 - 25th edn 1982; Occupiers' Liability, 1971; The Modern Law of Animals, 1972; Private International Law of Matrimonial Causes, 1977; Cheshire and North's Private International Law, 11th edn 1987; Contract Conflicts, 1982; (with J. H. C. Morris) Cases and Materials on Private International Law, 1984; articles and notes in legal jls. *Recreations:* children, gardening, cricket (both playing and sleeping through). *Address:* Jesus College, Oxford. *T:* Oxford 279701. *Club:* United Oxford & Cambridge University.

NORTH, Robert, (Robert North Dodson); dancer and choreographer; Artistic Director, Ballet Rambert, 1981–86; *b* 1 June 1945; *s* of Charles Dodson and Elizabeth Thompson; *m* 1978, Janet Smith. *Educ:* Pierrepont Sch. (A levels in Maths, Physics and Art); Central Sch. of Art; Royal Ballet Sch. Dancer and choreographer, London Contemporary Dance Co., 1966–81; seasons with Martha Graham Dance Co., 1967 and 1968; Teacher of Modern Dance, Royal Ballet Sch., 1979–81. Has choreographed about 30 ballets, including: Troy Game; Death and the Maiden; The Annunciation; Running Figures; Pribaoutki; Colour Moves; Entre dos Aguas; choreography for other cos, including: Royal Ballet; Dance Theatre of Harlem; Royal Danish Ballet; San Francisco Ballet; Oakland Ballet; Helsinki Ballet; Batsheva; Janet Smith and Dancers; also choreography for films, television, theatre and musicals (incl. For My Daughter).

NORTH, Sir Thomas (Lindsay), Kt 1982; FAIM, FRMIA; Chairman, G. J. Coles & Coy Limited, Melbourne, Australia, 1979–83, Hon. Chairman, 1983–84; *b* 11 Dec. 1919; *s* of John North and Jane (*née* Irwin); *m* 1944, Kathleen Jefferis; two *d*. *Educ:* Rutherglen, Vic. FAIM 1972. Joined G. J. Coles & Co. Ltd, 1938; Gen. Man., 1966; Dep. Man. Dir, 1969; Man. Dir, 1975–79; Dir, various G. J. Coles subsid. cos. Dep. Chm., KMart (Australia) Ltd, 1975–; Chm., Island Cooler Pty Ltd, 1985–. *Recreations:* horse racing, swimming. *Address:* 31 Power Street, Toorak, Vic 3142, Australia. *T:* 03.203161. *Clubs:* Athenæum, Royal Automobile Club of Victoria (Melbourne); Australian, Australian Armoured Corps (Sydney); Victorian Amateur Turf (Mem. Cttee), Victorian Racing Club, Moonee Valley Race; Melbourne Cricket, Sydney Cricket.

NORTH, Sir (William) Jonathan (Frederick), 2nd Bt, *cr* 1920; *b* 6 Feb. 1931; *s* of Muriel Norton (2nd *d* of 1st Bt) and Hon. John Montagu William North (who *m* 2nd, 1939, Marion Dyer Chase, Boston, Mass); *g s* of Sir William Hicking, 1st Bt; *S* grandfather, 1947 (under special remainder); *m* 1956, Sara Virginia, *d* of Air Chief Marshal Sir Donald Hardman, GBE, KCB, DFC; one *s* two *d*. *Educ:* Marlborough Coll. *Heir: s* Jeremy William Francis North [*b* 5 May 1960; *m* 1986, Lucy, *d* of G. A. van der Meulen, Kasama, Zambia]. *Address:* Frogmore, Weston-under-Penyard, Herefordshire.

NORTHAMPTON, 7th Marquess of, *cr* 1812; **Spencer Douglas David Compton;** DL; Earl of Northampton, 1618; Earl Compton, Baron Wilmington, 1812; *b* 2 April 1946; *s* of 6th Marquess of Northampton, DSO, and of Virginia, *d* of Lt-Col David Heaton, DSO; *S* father, 1978; *m* 1st, 1967, Henriette Luisa Maria (marr. diss. 1973), *o d* of late Baron Bentinck; one *s* one *d*; 2nd, 1974, Annette Marie (marr. diss. 1977), *er d* of C. A. R. Smallwood; 3rd, 1977, Hon. Mrs Rosemary Dawson-Damer (marr. diss. 1983); one *d*; 4th, 1985, Hon. Mrs Michael Pearson; one *d*. *Educ:* Eton. DL Northants 1979. *Heir: s* Earl Compton, *qv*. *Address:* Compton Wynyates, Tysoe, Warwicks CV35 0UD. *T:* Tysoe 629. *Club:* Turf.

NORTHAMPTON, Bishop of, (RC), since 1982; **Rt. Rev. Francis Gerard Thomas;** Prelate of Honour, 1969; *b* 29 May 1930; *s* of Edward James and Elizabeth May Thomas. *Educ:* St Dominic's Primary School, Stone, Staffs; Cotton College, Staffs; Oscott College, Sutton Coldfield. Priest, 1955; Curate at St Peter's, Leamington Spa, 1955–56; further study in theology, Gregorian Univ., Rome, 1956–59; Lectr in Theology, Oscott Coll., 1959; Rector of the College, 1968–79; Chapter Canon and Vicar General, Archdiocese of Birmingham, 1979–82; Parish Priest of Holy Trinity, Newcastle-under-Lyme, 1979–82. Assistant Editor of Liturgy and Music. *Address:* Bishop's House, Marriott Street, Northampton NN2 6AW. *T:* Northampton 715635.

NORTHAMPTON, Archdeacon of; *see* Marsh, Ven. Bazil Roland.

NORTHARD, John Henry, OBE 1979; FEng 1983; FIMinE; Operations Director, British Coal, since 1985, and Board Member, National Coal Board, since 1986; *b* 23 Dec. 1926; *s* of William Henry Northard and Nellie Northard; *m* 1952, Marian Josephine Lay; two *s* two *d*. *Educ:* St Bede's Grammar School, Bradford; Barnsley Mining and Technical College (Certificated Colliery Manager, first class). Colliery Manager, Yorks, 1955–57, Leics, 1957–63; Group Manager, Leics Collieries, 1963–65; Dep. Chief Mining Engineer, Staffs Collieries, 1965–70; Area Dep. Dir (Mining), NCB, N Derbyshire Area, 1970–73; Area Dir, NCB, N Derbyshire Area, 1973–81, Western Area, 1981–85. Pres., IMinE, 1982. SBStJ 1981. *Publications:* contribs to mining engineering instns and tech. jls. *Recreation:* piloting light aircraft. *Address:* Rydal, 196 Ashgate Road, Chesterfield, Derbyshire. *T:* Chesterfield 32260.

NORTHBOURNE, 5th Baron *cr* 1884; **Christopher George Walter James;** Bt 1791; FRICS; Chairman, Betteshanger Farms Ltd, since 1975; Chief Executive, Kent Salads Ltd, since 1981; Director, Chillington Corporation PLC; Regional Director, Lloyds Bank plc, since 1986; *b* 18 Feb. 1926; *s* of 4th Baron Northbourne and Katherine Louise (*d* 1980), *d* of late George A. Nickerson, Boston, Mass; *S* father, 1982; *m* 1959, Aliki Louise Hélène Marie Sygne, *e d* of Henri Claudel, Chatou-sur-Seine, and *g d* of late Paul Claudel; three *s* one *d*. *Educ:* Eton; Magdalen Coll., Oxford (MA). *Heir: s* Hon. Charles Walter Henri James, *b* 14 June 1960. *Address:* 11 Eaton Place, SW1. *T:* 01-235 6790; Coldharbour, Northbourne, Deal, Kent. *T:* Sandwich 611277. *Clubs:* Brooks's, Farmers'.

NORTHBROOK, 5th Baron, *cr* 1866; **Francis John Baring,** Bt 1793; DL; Chairman, Winchester District Health Authority, since 1981; *b* 31 May 1915; *s* of 4th Baron Northbrook and Evelyn Gladys Isabel (*d* 1919), *d* of J. G. Charles; *S* father 1947; *m* 1951, Rowena Margaret, 2nd *d* of late Brig-General Sir William Manning, and of Lady Manning, Hampton Court Palace; one *s* three *d*. *Educ:* Winchester; Trinity Coll., Oxford. Chm., Hants AHA, 1978–81. JP 1955, DL 1972, Hants. *Heir: s* Hon. Francis Thomas Baring, *b* 21 Feb. 1954. *Address:* East Stratton House, East Stratton, Winchester, Hants.

NORTHCOTE, family name of **Earl of Iddesleigh.**

NORTHCOTE, Prof. Donald Henry, FRS 1968; Master of Sidney Sussex College, Cambridge, since 1976; Professor of Plant Biochemistry, University of Cambridge, since 1972 (Reader, 1965–72); *b* 27 Dec. 1921; *m* Eva Marjorie Mayo; two *d*. *Educ:* Sir George Monoux Grammar Sch., London; London Univ.; Cambridge Univ. Fellow, St John's College, Cambridge, 1960–76. Hon. Fellow, Downing Coll., Cambridge, 1976. Mem. Governing Council, John Innes Inst., 1980–. *Publication:* Differentiation in Higher Plants, 1974, 2nd edn 1980. *Recreations:* sitting and chatting; strolling about. *Address:* The Master's Lodge, Sidney Sussex College, Cambridge. *T:* Cambridge 355860. *Club:* United Oxford & Cambridge University.

NORTHCOTE, Peter Colston; His Honour Judge Northcote; a Circuit Judge since 1973; *b* 23 Oct. 1920; *s* of late William George Northcote and late Edith Mary Northcote; *m* 1947, Patricia Bickley; two *s*. *Educ:* Ellesmere Coll.; Bristol Univ. Called to Bar, Inner Temple, 1948. Chm., Nat. Insce Tribunal; Chm., W Midland Rent Tribunal; Dep. Chm., Agric. Land Tribunal. Commnd KSLI, 1940; served 7th Rajput Regt, Far East (Major). *Recreations:* music, travel, ski-ing. *Address:* Wroxeter Grange, Wroxeter, Shrewsbury, Salop. *T:* Cross Houses 279. *Club:* Army and Navy.

NORTHCOTE-GREEN, Roger James, MC 1944; TD 1950; JP; Headmaster, Worksop College, Notts, 1952–70; *b* 25 July 1912; *s* of Rev. Edward Joseph Northcote-Green and Mary Louisa Catt; *m* 1947, Joan, *d* of Ernest Greswell and Grace Lillian (*née* Egerton); three *s* one *d*. *Educ:* St Edward's Sch. and The Queen's Coll., Oxford (MA). Served with Oxford and Bucks Light Infantry, 1939–44, in India and Burma; Staff Coll., Quetta, 1944–45; Bde Major, 53rd Ind. Inf. Bde, Malaya, 1945. Assistant Master, St Edward's Sch., 1936–39, 1946–52; Housemaster, 1947. Representative OURFC on RU Cttee, 1946–52. S Western Sec., Independent Schs Careers Orgn, 1970–77. JP Nottinghamshire, 1964. *Recreations:* gardening, poultry. *Address:* Manor Cottage, Woolston, Williton, Som. *T:* Williton 32445. *Clubs:* East India, Devonshire, Sports and Public Schools, MCC; Vincent's (Oxford).

NORTHCOTT, Rev. Cecil; *see* Northcott, Rev. (William) C.

NORTHCOTT, Prof. Douglas Geoffrey, MA, PhD, Cambridge; FRS 1961; Town Trust Professor of Mathematics, University of Sheffield, 1952–82, now Emeritus; *b* London, 1916; *m* 1949, Rose Hilda Austin, Twickenham, Middlesex; two *d*. *Educ:* Christ's Hospital; St John's Coll., Cambridge; Princeton Univ., USA. *Publications:* Ideal Theory, 1953; An Introduction to Homological Algebra, 1960; Lessons on Rings, Modules and Multiplicities, 1968; A First Course of Homological Algebra, 1973; Finite Free Resolutions, 1976; Affine Sets and Affine Groups, 1980; Multilinear Algebra, 1984. *Address:* 25 Parkhead Road, Ecclesall, Sheffield S11 9RA.

NORTHCOTT, Rev. (William) Cecil, MA; PhD; Churches Correspondent, Daily Telegraph, 1967–79; Editorial Secretary United Society for Christian Literature and Editor, Lutterworth Press, 1952–72; Editor-at-large, Christian Century of USA, 1945–70; *b* Buckfast, Devon, 5 April 1902; *s* of William Ashplant Northcott; *m* 1930, Jessie Morton, MA, 2nd *d* of J. L. Morton, MD, Hampstead and Colyford, Devon; one *s* one *d*. *Educ:* Hele's Sch., Exeter; Fitzwilliam Coll., and Cheshunt Coll., Cambridge. PhD London Univ. (School of Oriental and African Studies), 1961. Three years social work East End of London; Member Cambridge delegation to League of Nations, Geneva, 1926; Joint Proprietor and Editor The Granta, 1927–28; Congregational Church, St Helens, 1929–32; Minister Duckworth Street Congregational Church, Darwen, Lancs, 1932–35; Home Secretary and Literary Superintendent London Missionary Society, 1935–50; General Secretary and Editor United Council for Missionary Education (Edinburgh House Press), 1950–52; Chairman, London Missionary Society, 1954–55 (World Conferences, Amsterdam, 1948, Willingen, 1952, Evanston, 1954, New Delhi, 1961, Uppsala, 1968, Nairobi, 1975). Member, World Council of Churches Information Cttee, 1954–61; Member, British Council of Churches Christian Aid Cttee, 1946–64. Select Preacher, Cambridge, 1958; Danforth Foundation Lecturer, USA, 1961; Visiting Lecturer, Garrett Theological Seminary, USA, 1965, 1967, 1969, 1971. British Information Services, USA, 1944; editor, Congregational Monthly, 1953–58. Leverhulme Research Award, 1958. *Publications:* Time to Spare (Collab. BBC Talks), 1935; Southward Ho!, 1936; Guinea Gold, 1937; Who Claims the World?, 1938; John Williams Sails On, 1939; Change Here for Britain, 1942; Glorious Company, 1945; Whose Dominion?, 1946; Religious Liberty, 1948; Venturers of Faith, 1950; Voice Out of Africa, 1952; Robert Moffat: Pioneer in Africa, 1961; Christianity in Africa, 1963; David Livingstone: his triumph, decline and fall, 1973; Slavery's Martyr, 1976; ed Encyclopedia of the Bible for Children, 1964; People of the Bible, 1967. *Recreation:* old books. *Club:* Royal Commonwealth Society.

NORTHERN ARGENTINA, Bishop of, since 1980; **Rt. Rev. David Leake;** Presiding Bishop, Province of the Anglican Church of the Southern Cone of America, since 1983; *b* 26 June 1935; *s* of Rev. Canon William Alfred Leake and Dorothy Violet Leake; *m* 1961, Rachel Yarham; two *s* one *d*. *Educ:* St Alban's Coll., Buenos Aires; London Coll. of Divinity. ALCD 1959 (LTh). Deacon 1959, priest 1960; Assistant Bishop: Paraguay and N Argentina, 1969–73; N Argentina, 1973–80. *Recreations:* observing people's behaviour at airports, railway stations and bus terminals. *Address:* Casilla 187, 4400 Salta, Argentina. *T:* (087) 221247.

NORTHERN TERRITORY (AUSTRALIA), Bishop of the, since 1983; **Rt. Rev. Clyde Maurice Wood,** BA, ThL; *b* 7 Jan. 1936; *s* of Maurice O. Wood and Helen M. Wood; *m* 1957, Margaret Joan Burls; two *s* one *d*. *Educ:* Perry Hall, Melbourne (ThL 1964); Monash Univ. (BA 1974). Deacon 1965, priest 1965; Curate: St John's, Bentleigh, 1965–66; St Paul's, Ringwood, 1966–67; in Dept of Evangelism and Extension, 1967–70; Curate-in-Charge: St Philip's, Mount Waverley, 1967–70; Armadale/Hawksburn, 1970–72; Rector and Canon Res., Christ Church Cathedral, Darwin, 1974, Dean 1978–83. On leave, Rector St Timothy's Episcopal Church, Indianapolis, USA, 1981. OStJ 1980; ChStJ 1985. *Recreations:* golf, sailing. *Address:* PO Box 39352, Winnellie, NT 5789, Australia. *T:* (office) (089) 85 2790; 5 Rankin Street, Nightcliff, NT 5792, Australia. *T:* (089) 85 3099.

NORTHESK, 13th Earl of, *cr* 1647; **Robert Andrew Carnegie;** Lord Rosehill and Inglismaldie, 1639; Landowner, Farmer; *b* 24 June 1926; *yr s* of 12th Earl of Northesk and Dorothy Mary (*d* 1967), *er d* of late Col Sir William Robert Campion, KCMG, DSO; *S* father, 1975; *m* 1949, Jean Margaret, *yr d* of Captain (John) Duncan George MacRae, Ballimore, Otter Ferry, Argyll; one *s* two *d* (and one *s* decd). *Educ:* Pangbourne RNR Coll.; Tabor Naval Acad., USA. Served with Royal Navy, 1942–45. Mem., Council, Fédération Internationale des Assocs d'éléveurs de la race bovine Charolaise; Council, Game Research Assoc., 1955–57; Council, British Charolais Cattle Soc., 1972–74. Chm. Bd, Chandler, Hargreaves Whittal IoM Ltd, 1980–; Dir, NEL Britannia International Assurance Ltd, 1984–; Member: Bd of Dirs, IoM Bank, 1980–; IoM Br., CPA; Bd of Governors, Buchan Sch., IoM, until 1986. President: Save the Children Fund, Douglas, IoM, 1977; Friends of the Physically Disabled, IoM, 1985. Trustee, Pain Relief Foundn, 1985–. Midhurst RDC, 1968–75 (Chm., 1972–74). *Heir: s* Lord Rosehill, *qv*. *Address:* Springwaters, Ballamodha, Isle of Man.

See also Baron Fisher.

NORTHFIELD, Baron *cr* 1975 (Life Peer), of Telford, Salop; **(William) Donald Chapman;** Chairman: Telford Development Corporation, since 1975; Consortium Developments Ltd, since 1986; *b* 25 Nov. 1923; *s* of Wm H. and Norah F. E. Chapman, Barnsley. *Educ:* Barnsley Grammar Sch.; Emmanuel Coll., Cambridge, MA (1st Cl. Hons) Economics, also degree in Agriculture; Senior Scholar of Emmanuel Coll. Research in Agric. Economics, Cambridge, 1943–46. Cambridge City Councillor, 1945–47; Sec., Trades Council and Labour Party, 1945–57; MP (Lab) Birmingham (Northfield), 1951–70. Research Sec. of the Fabian Soc., 1948–49, Gen. Sec., 1949–53. Gwilym Gibbon Fellow, Nuffield Coll., Oxford, 1971–73; Vis. Fellow, Centre for Contemporary European

Studies, Sussex Univ., 1973–79. Special Adviser to EEC Commn, 1978–; Chairman: Develt Commn, 1974–80; Inquiry into recent trends in acquisition and occupancy of agric. land, 1977–79. *Publications:* The European Parliament: the years ahead, 1973; The Road to European Union, 1975; articles and Fabian pamphlets. *Recreation:* travel. *Address:* Priorslee Hall, Telford TF2 9NT. *T:* Telford 613131.

NORTHOLT, Archdeacon of; *see* Shirras, Ven. E. S.

NORTHROP, Filmer S(tuart) C(uckow), PhD, LittD, LLD; Sterling Professor of Philosophy and Law Emeritus, the Law School and the School of Graduate Studies, Yale University, USA, since 1962; *b* 27 Nov. 1893; *s* of Marshall Ellsworth Northrop and Ruth Cuckow; *m* 1st, 1919, Christine Johnston; two *s*; 2nd, 1969, Marjorie Carey. *Educ:* Beloit Coll. (BA 1915, LittD 1946); Yale (MA 1919); Harvard (MA 1922, PhD 1924); Imperial Coll. of Science and Technology, London; Trinity Coll., Cambridge. Instr. at Yale, 1923–26; Asst Prof., Yale, 1926–29; Associate Prof., Yale, 1929–32, Prof., 1932–47; Master of Silliman Coll., 1940–47; Sterling Prof. of Philosophy and Law, Yale, 1947–62; Visiting Prof., summer session, Univ. of Iowa, 1926; Univ. of Michigan, 1932; Univ. of Virginia, 1931–32; Visiting Prof. and Mem. of East-West Conf. on Philosophy at Univ. of Hawaii, 1939; Prof. Extraordinario, La Universidad Nacional Autonoma de Mexico, 1949; Fellow: American Acad. of Arts and Sciences, 1951; American Acad. of Political and Social Science, 1957; Pres., American Philosophical Assoc. (Eastern Div.), 1952. Hon. Founder: Macy Foundn Conferences, 1944–53; Amer. Soc. of Cybernetics, 1964; Mem., SEATO Round Table, Bangkok, 1958. Hon. LLD: Univ. of Hawaii, 1949, Rollins Coll., 1955; Hon. LittD: Beloit Coll., 1946; Pratt Inst., 1961. Order of the Aztec Eagle (Mexican), 1946. *Publications:* Science and First Principles, 1931; The Meeting of East and West, 1946; The Logic of the Sciences and the Humanities, 1947; The Taming of the Nations, A Study of the Cultural Bases of International Policy, 1952 (Wilkie Memorial Building Award, 1953); European Union and United States Foreign Policy, 1954; The Complexity of Legal and Ethical Experience, 1959; Philosophical Anthropology and Practical Politics, 1960; Man, Nature and God, 1962; Co-Editor, Cross-cultural Understanding: Epistemology in Anthropology, 1964; Chapter 5 in Contemporary American Philosophy, second series, 1970; (with J. Sinões da Fonseca) Interpersonal Relations in Neuropsychological and Legal Science, 1975; ed, Ideological Differences and World Order, 1949; Prolegomena to a Philosophia Naturales, 1985. *Recreations:* travel, baseball. *Address:* 8 Hampton Road, Exeter, NH 03833, USA. *Clubs:* Century (New York); Beaumont, Berzilius, Elizabethan, Graduates, Mory's (New Haven); American Academy of Arts and Sciences (Philosophy Section) (Boston).

NORTHROP, John Howard; Member Rockefeller University (formerly Institute), 1924, Emeritus 1962; Visiting Professor of Bacteriology, University of California, 1949, Emeritus, 1959; Professor Biophysics, 1958, Emeritus 1959; Research Biophysicist, Donner Laboratory, 1958; *b* Yonkers, NY, 5 July 1891; *s* of Dr John I. Northrop, of Department of Zoology, Columbia Univ., and Alice Rich Northrop, of Dept of Botany, Hunter Coll., NY City; *m* 1917, Louise Walker, NY City; one *s* one *d*. *Educ:* Columbia Univ. BS 1912; AM 1913; PhD 1915; W. B. Cutting Travelling Fellow, Columbia Univ. (year in Jacques Loeb's laboratory at Rockefeller Inst.), 1915; on staff of Rockefeller Inst. 1916; Member, 1924; Stevens prize, Coll. of Physicians and Surgeons, Columbia Univ., 1931; Captain, Chemical Warfare Service, 1917–18; discovered and worked on fermentation process for manufacturing acetone; ScD Harvard 1936, Columbia 1937, Yale 1937, Princeton 1940, Rutgers 1941; LLD, University of California, 1939; Chandler Medal, Columbia Univ., 1937; DeLamar Lectr, Sch. of Hygiene and Public Health, Johns Hopkins, 1937; Jesup Lectr, Columbia Univ., 1938; Hitchcock Lectr, Univ. of California, 1939; Thayer Lectr, Johns Hopkins, 1940; Daniel Giraud Elliot Medal for 1939 of National Acad. of Science, 1944; Consultant, OSRD, 1941–45. Shared Nobel Prize in Chemistry, 1946. Certificate of Merit, USA, 1948. Alex. Hamilton Medal, Columbia Univ., 1961. Member: Sons of the American Revolution; Delta Kappa Epsilon fraternity, Sigma Xi, Phi Lambda Upsilon; American Society of Biological Chemists; National Acad. of Sciences, Halle Akademie der Naturforscher; Société Philomathique (Paris); American Philosophical Society; Society of General Physiologists; Chemical Society (Hon. Fellow); Fellow World Academy; Benjamin Franklin Fellow, RSA. *Publications:* Crystalline Enzymes, 1939; numerous papers on physical chemistry of proteins, agglutination of bacteria, kinetics of enzyme reactions, and isolation and chemical nature of enzymes; editorial board of Journal of General Physiology, Experimental Biology Monographs; Contrib. Editor, Funk & Wagnell's Encyclopedia. *Recreations:* field shooting, salmon fishing. *Address:* PO Box 1387, Wickenburg, Arizona 85358, USA. *Club:* Century Association (New York).

NORTHUMBERLAND, 10th Duke of, *cr* 1766; **Hugh Algernon Percy,** KG 1959; GCVO 1981; TD 1961; PC 1973; JP; FRS 1970; Earl of Northumberland, Baron Warkworth, 1749; Earl Percy, 1776; Earl of Beverly, 1790; Lord Lovaine, Baron of Alnwick, 1784; Bt, *cr* 1660; Baron Percy (by writ), 1722; Lord Steward of HM Household, since 1973; Lord-Lieutenant and Custos Rotulorum of Northumberland 1956–84; Chancellor of University of Newcastle since 1964; *b* 6 April 1914; 2nd *s* of 8th Duke of Northumberland, KG, CBE, MVO (*d* 1930), and Lady Helen Gordon-Lennox (Helen, Dowager Duchess of Northumberland, who *d* 1965), *y d* of 7th Duke of Richmond and Gordon; *S* brother (killed in action), 1940; *m* 1946, Lady Elizabeth Diana Montagu-Douglas-Scott, *er d* of 8th Duke of Buccleuch and Queensberry, KT, PC, GCVO; three *s* three *d*. *Educ:* Eton; Oxford. Lieut, Northumberland Hussars, 1936; RA, 1940; Captain, 1941; Captain, Northumberland Hussars, 1947; TARO, 1949–64; Chm., T&AFA, 1950–56; Pres., Northumberland T&AFA, 1956–68; Pres., TA&VR Assoc. for North of England, 1968–71; Hon. Colonel: 7th Bn, Royal Northumberland Fusiliers, 1948–70; The Northumbrian Volunteers, 1971–75; 6th (V) Bn, Royal Regt of Fusiliers, T&AVR, 1975–. A Lord in Waiting, May-July 1945. Mem., Northumberland CC, 1944–55, Alderman, 1955–67. President: Northern Area, British Legion; Northumberland Boy Scouts' Assoc., 1946–; Northumb. Assoc. of Boys' Clubs, 1942–; British Horse Soc., 1950; North of England Shipowners' Assoc., 1952–78; Hunters Improvement and Light Horse Breeding Soc., 1954; Royal Agricultural Soc. of England, 1956, 1962; BSJA, 1959; The Wildfowl Trust, 1968–72. Chairman: Departmental Cttee on Slaughter of Horses, 1952; Court of Durham Univ., 1956–64; Border Forest Park Cttee, 1956–68; ARC, 1958–68; Departmental Cttee for Recruitment of Veterinary Surgeons, 1964; Cttee of Enquiry on Foot-and-Mouth Disease, 1968–69; MRC, 1969–77; Agricultural EDC, 1971–78. Member: Agricultural Improvement Council, 1953–62; National Forestry Cttee for England and Wales, 1954–60; Hill Farming Advisory Cttee for England and Wales, 1946–60; County Agricultural Exec. Cttee, 1948–59; Royal Commn on Historical Manuscripts, 1973–. Chm. Council, RASE, 1971–74. Hon. Treasurer, RNLI; Associate, RCVS, 1967. Master of Percy Foxhounds, 1940–. KStJ 1957. Hon. DCL Durham, 1958. *Heir:* *s* Earl Percy, *qv*. *Address:* Alnwick Castle, Northumberland NE66 1NG. *T:* Alnwick 602456; Syon House, Brentford, Middx TW8 8JF. *T:* 01–560 2353; Clive Lodge, Albury, Guildford. *T:* Shere 2695. *Clubs:* Boodle's, Northern Counties, Turf.

See also Duke of Hamilton and Brandon, Sir Aymer Maxwell, Bt, Lord Richard Percy, Duke of Sutherland.

NORTHUMBERLAND, Archdeacon of; *see* Thomas, Ven. W. J.

NORTHWAY, Eileen Mary, RRC 1982 (ARRC 1969); Matron-in-Chief, Queen Alexandra's Royal Naval Nursing Service, since 1986; *b* 22 July 1931; *d* of Ernest and Margaret Northway. *Educ:* St Michael's Convent, Newton Abbot. SRN 1952, SCM 1954; joined QARNNS 1956. OStJ 1985. *Recreations:* gardening, reading. *Address:* 16 Fairthorne Gardens, Alverstoke, Gosport, Hants. *T:* Gosport 583511.

NORTON; *see* Hill-Norton.

NORTON, family name of **Barons Grantley** and **Rathcreedan.**

NORTON, 7th Baron, *cr* 1878; **John Arden Adderley,** OBE 1964; *b* 24 Nov. 1915; *s* of 6th Baron Norton; *S* father, 1961; *m* 1946, Betty Margaret, *o d* of late James McKee Hannah; two *s*. *Educ:* Radley; Magdalen Coll., Oxford (BA). Oxford University Greenland Expedition, 1938; Assistant Master, Oundle School, 1938–39. Served War, 1940–45 (despatches); RE (N Africa, Europe). Major, 1944. Asst Secretary, Country Landowners Assoc., 1947–59. *Recreations:* mountaineering, shooting, heraldry and genealogy. *Heir:* *s* Hon. James Nigel Arden Adderley [*b* 2 June 1947; *m* 1971, Jacqueline Julie Willett, *e d* of Guy W. Willett, Woking, Surrey; one *s* one *d*]. *Address:* Fillongley Hall, Coventry, West Midlands. *T:* Fillongley 40303.

NORTON, Sir Clifford John, KCMG 1946 (CMG 1933); CVO 1937; *b* 17 July 1891; *o surv. s* of late Rev. George Norton and Clara, *d* of late John Dewey; *m* 1927, Noel Evelyn (*d* 1972), *d* of late Sir Walter Charleton Hughes, CIE, MInstCE; no *c*. *Educ:* Rugby Sch.; Queen's Coll., Oxford, MA 1915. Suffolk Regt, 1914, Gallipoli, Palestine; Captain, General Staff EEF, 1917; Political Officer, Damascus, Deraa, Haifa, 1919–20; entered Diplomatic Service, 1921; Private Secretary to the Permanent Under-Secretary of State for Foreign Affairs, 1930–37; First Secretary, 1933; Counsellor British Embassy, Warsaw, 1937–39; Foreign Office, 1939–42; Minister, Berne, 1942–46; HM Ambassador in Athens, 1946–51; retired, 1951; Hon. Citizen of Athens, 1951. UK Delegate (alternate) to United Nations Assembly, 1952 and 1953. Past President, Anglo-Swiss Society. Hon. Fellow, Queen's Coll., Oxford, 1963. *Address:* 21a Carlyle Square, SW3.

NORTON, Donald; Regional Administrator, Oxford Regional Health Authority, 1973–80, retired; *b* 2 May 1920; *s* of Thomas Henry Norton and Dora May Norton (*née* Prentice); *m* 1945, Miriam Joyce, *d* of Herbert and Florence Mann; two *s* one *d*. *Educ:* Nether Edge Grammar Sch., Sheffield; Univs of Sheffield and London. LLB, DPA; FHA. Senior Administrator Sheffield Regional Hosp. Bd, 1948–51; Sec. Supt, Jessop Hosp. for Women and Charles Clifford Dental Hosp., Sheffield, 1951–57; Dep. Sec., Archway Gp of Hosps, London, 1957–60; Gp Sec., Dudley Road Gp of Hosps, Birmingham 1960–70; Sec., Oxford Regional Hosp. Bd, 1970–73. *Recreations:* marriage, golf, gardening. *Address:* The Squirrels, 14 Pullens Field, Headington, Oxford OX3 0BU. *T:* Oxford 67291. *Clubs:* Victory; Clarendon (Oxford); Frilford Heath.

NORTON, Captain Gerard Ross, VC 1944; MM; 1/4th Hampshire Regiment; *b* S Africa, 7 Sept. 1915; *m* 1942, Lilia Morris, East London, S Africa; one *d*. *Educ:* Selborne Coll., East London, S Africa. Bank clerk. *Recreations:* Rugger-provincial, tennis, cricket. *Address:* Minnehaha, PO Raffingora, Zimbabwe.

NORTON, Mary; children's writer; *b* 10 Dec. 1903; *d* of Reginald Spencer Pearson and Minnie Savile Hughes; *m* 1st, 1926, Robert Charles Norton; two *s* two *d*; 2nd, 1970, Lionel Bonsey. *Educ:* St Margaret's Convent, East Grinstead. Old Vic Co. under Lilian Baylis, 1925–26; domiciled family home in Portugal, 1926–39; war job and acting for BBC, 1940; war job, British Purchasing Commn, New York, 1941; returned to London, 1942, caring for own children and acting for H. M. Tennant. *Publications:* Bonfires and Broomsticks, 1947; The Borrowers, 1952 (Library Assoc. Carnegie Medal, 1952; Hans Christian Anderson Honours Award); The Borrowers Afield, 1955; The Borrowers Afloat, 1959; The Borrowers Aloft, 1961; Poor Stainless, 1971; Are All the Giants Dead?, 1975; The Borrowers Avenged, 1982. *Recreations:* (formerly) swimming and training for show-jumping. *Address:* The Old Rectory, Kilcoe, Aughadown, Ballydehob, West Cork, Ireland. *T:* Skibbereen 38150. *Club:* Lansdowne.

NORTON-GRIFFITHS, Sir John, 3rd Bt *cr* 1922; FCA; President and Chief Executive Officer, Main Street Data Services Inc.; *b* 4 Oct. 1938; *s* of Sir Peter Norton-Griffiths, 2nd Bt, and Kathryn (*d* 1980), *e d* of late George F. Schrafft; *S* father, 1983; *m* 1964, Marilyn Margaret, *er d* of Norman Grimley. *Educ:* Eton. FCA 1966. Lately Sub Lieutenant RN. *Heir:* *b* Michael Norton-Griffiths [*b* 11 Jan. 1941; *m* 1965, Ann, *o d* of late Group Captain Blair Alexander Fraser; one *s*]. *Address:* 17 Royal Drive, Bricktown, NJ 08723, USA.

NORWICH, 2nd Viscount, *cr* 1952, of Aldwick; **John Julius Cooper,** FRSL, FRGS; writer and broadcaster; *b* 15 Sept. 1929; *s* of 1st Viscount Norwich, PC, GCMG, DSO, and Lady Diana Cooper (*d* 1986), *d* of 8th Duke of Rutland; *S* father, 1954; *m* 1952, Anne (Frances May) (marr. diss. 1985), *e d* of late Hon. Sir Bede Clifford, GCMG, CB, MVO; one *s* one *d*. *Educ:* Upper Canada Coll., Toronto, Canada; Eton; University of Strasbourg; New Coll., Oxford. Served 1947–49 as Writer, Royal Navy. Entered Foreign Office, 1952; Third Secretary, British Embassy, Belgrade, 1955–57; Second Secretary, British Embassy, Beirut, 1957–60; worked in Foreign Office (First Secretary from 1961) and in British Delegation to Disarmament Conference, Geneva, from 1960 until resignation from Foreign Service 1964. Chairman: Venice in Peril Fund; British Theatre Museum, 1966–71; Member: Exec. Cttee, National Trust, 1969– (Properties Cttee, 1970–); Franco-British Council, 1972–79; Bd, English Nat. Opera, 1977–81. Has made some thirty documentary films for television, mostly on history and architecture. Chm., Serenissima Travel Ltd. Commendatore, Ordine al Merito della Repubblica Italiana. *Publications:* *as John Julius Norwich:* Mount Athos (with Reresby Sitwell), 1966; The Normans in the South (as The Other Conquest, US), 1967; Sahara, 1968; The Kingdom in The Sun, 1970; Gen. Editor, Great Architecture of the World, 1975; A History of Venice, vol. I, The Rise to Empire, 1977, vol. II, The Greatness and the Fall, 1981; Christmas Crackers, 1980; Gen. Editor, Britain's Heritage, 1982; (ed) The Italian World: history, art and the genius of a people, 1983; The Architecture of Southern England, 1985; Glyndebourne, 1985; A Taste for Travel, 1985. *Recreations:* sight-seeing, walking at night through Venice. *Heir:* *s* Hon. Jason Charles Duff Bede Cooper, *b* 27 Oct. 1959. *Address:* 24 Blomfield Road, W9. *T:* 01–286 5050. *Clubs:* Beefsteak, Garrick.

NORWICH, Bishop of, since 1985; **Rt. Rev. Peter John Nott;** *b* 30 Dec. 1933; *s* of Cecil Frederick Wilder Nott and Rosina Mabel Bailey; *m* 1961, Elizabeth May Maingot; one *s* three *d*. *Educ:* Bristol Grammar School; Dulwich Coll.; RMA Sandhurst; Fitzwilliam House, Cambridge; Westcott House, Cambridge (MA). Curate of Harpenden, 1961–64; Chaplain of Fitzwilliam Coll., Cambridge, 1964–69; Fellow of Fitzwilliam Coll., 1967–69; Chaplain of New Hall, Cambridge, 1966–69; Rector of Beaconsfield, 1969–77; Bishop Suffragan of Taunton, 1977–85. Archbishop's Adviser to HMC, 1980–85; President: SW Region, Mencap, 1978–84; Somerset Rural Music Sch., 1981–85. *Address:* Bishop's House, Norwich NR3 1SB. *T:* Norwich 629001.

NORWICH, Dean of; *see* Burbridge, Very Rev. J. P.

NORWICH, Archdeacon of; *see* Handley, Ven. A. M.

NORWOOD, Suzanne Freda, (Mrs John Lexden Stewart); Her Honour Judge Norwood; a Circuit Judge, since 1973; *b* 24 March 1926; *d* of late Frederic Francis Norwood and of Marianne Freda Norwood (*née* Thomas); *m* 1954, John Lexden Stewart (*d* 1972); one *s*. *Educ:* Lowther Coll., Bodelwyddan; St Andrews Univ. MA English, MA Hons History. Called to Bar, Gray's Inn, 1951; practised at Bar, SE Circuit. Mem., Parole Bd, 1976–78; Mental Health Review Tribunal, 1983. Member: Greenwich and Bexley AHA, 1979–82; Greenwich DHA, 1982–85; Bexley DHA, 1985. *Recreations:* walking, housekeeping, opera. *Address:* 69 Lee Road, SE3. *T:* 01–852 1954.

NORWOOD, Sir Walter (Neville), Kt 1971; Hon. President, New Zealand Motor Corporation; *b* 14 July 1907; *s* of late Sir Charles Norwood; *m* 1935, Rana Muriel, *d* of David Redpath; two *s* one *d*. *Educ:* Wellington and Wanganui. Trustee: Nuffield Trust for Crippled Children; Laura Fergusson Trust for Disabled Persons; C. J. B. Norwood Crippled Children's Trust; Norwood Cricket Trust. Past President: Wellington Rotary Club; Wellington Racing Club. *Recreations:* racing, farming, sailing. *Address:* Hillcrest, 24 Mataroa Avenue, Wellington, New Zealand. *Clubs:* Wellesley, Wellington (Wellington, NZ).

NOSS, John Bramble; HM Diplomatic Service; High Commissioner to Solomon Islands, since 1986; *b* 20 Dec. 1935; *s* of John Noss and Vera Ethel (*née* Mattingly); *m* 1957, Shirley May Andrews; two *s* one *d*. *Educ:* Portsmouth Grammar School. Foreign Office, 1954; RAF, 1955–57; served FO, Beirut, Copenhagen, FCO; Russian language training, 1965; Moscow, 1965–68; Santiago, 1968–70; FCO, 1970–73; First Sec. (Economic), Pretoria, 1974–77; First Sec. (Commercial), Moscow, 1977–78; FCO, 1978–81; Consul (Inward Investment), New York, 1981–85. *Recreations:* photography, reading, running. *Address:* c/o Foreign and Commonwealth Office, SW1A 2AH.

NOSSAL, Sir Gustav (Joseph Victor), Kt 1977; CBE 1970; FRS 1982; FAA; Director, The Walter and Eliza Hall Institute of Medical Research, Melbourne, since 1965; Professor of Medical Biology, University of Melbourne, since 1965; *b* Austria, 4 June 1931; *m* 1955, Lyn B. Dunnicliff; two *s* two *d*. *Educ:* Sydney Univ. (1st Cl. Hons BScMed (Bacteriology), 1952; 1st Cl. Hons MB, BS 1954 (Mills Prize)); Melbourne Univ. (PhD 1960). FAA 1967; FRACP 1967; Hon. FRCPA 1971; FRACMA 1971; FRCP 1980; FTS 1981; Hon. FRSE 1983. Jun., then Sen. Resident Officer, Royal Prince Alfred Hosp., Sydney, 1955–56; Res. Fellow, Walter and Eliza Hall Inst. of Med. Res., 1957–59; Asst Prof., Dept of Genetics, Stanford Univ. Sch. of Medicine, Calif, 1959–61; Dep. Dir (Immunology), Walter and Eliza Hall Inst. of Med. Res., 1961–65. Vis. scientist and vis. professor to several univs and res. insts; has given many lectures to learned societies, assocs and univs. Dir, CRA Ltd, 1977–. World Health Organisation: Member: Expert Adv. Panel on Immunology, 1967; Adv. Cttee Med. Res., 1973–80; Special Consultant, Tropical Disease Res. Prog., 1976. Chm., West Pac Adv. Co. Med. Res., 1976–80; Member: Aust. Science and Technol. Council, 1975–83; Adv. Bd, John Curtin Sch. of Med. Res., 1981–; Centre for Recombinant DNA Res., Res. Sch. of Biol Sciences, ANU, 1981– (Founder Mem.); Baker Med. Res. Inst., 1982–; Scientific Adv. Cttee, Centenary Res. Inst. of Cancer Medicine and Cell Biol., Sydney, 1983–; Aust. Industrial Res. Develt Incentives Bd, 1983–. Mem., Aust. Soc. of Immunology; Hon. Mem., Amer. (1975), French (1979), Indian (1976), Soc. of Immunology; Foreign Hon. Mem., Amer. Acad. of Arts and Scis, 1974. For. Associate, US Nat. Acad. of Scis, 1979; Fellow, New York Acad. of Scis, 1977; For. Fellow, Indian Nat. Sci. Acad., 1980. Hon. MD Johannes Gutenberg Univ., Mainz, 1981. Emil von Behring Prize, Philipps Univ., Marburg, Germany, 1971; Rabbi Shai Shacknai Memorial Prize, Univ. of Jerusalem, 1973; Ciba Foundn Gold Medal, 1978; Burnet Medal, Aust. Acad. of Sci., 1979. Mem. Editorial Bd of several med. jls. *Publications:* Antibodies & Immunity, 1968 (rev. edn 1977); Antigens Lymphoid Cells & The Immune Response, 1971; Medical Science & Human Goals, 1975; Nature's Defences (Boyer Lectures), 1978; Reshaping Life: key issues in genetic engineering, 1984. *Recreations:* golf, literature. *Address:* 46 Fellows Street, Kew, Vic 3101, Australia. *T:* 861 8256. *Clubs:* Melbourne (Melbourne); Rosebud Country.

NOSSITER, Bernard Daniel; journalist; *b* 10 April 1926; *s* of Murry and Rose (Weingarten) Nossiter; *m* 1950, Jacqueline Robinson; four *s*. *Educ:* Dartmouth Coll., Hanover, NH (BA); Harvard Univ., Cambridge, Mass. (MA Econ). Washington Post: Nat. Econs Corresp., 1955–62; European Econs Corresp., 1964–67; S Asia Corresp., 1967–68; Nat. Bureau Reporter, 1968–71; London Corresp., 1971–79; UN Bureau Chief, NY Times, 1979–83. Nieman Fellow, Harvard, 1962–63. *Publications:* The Mythmakers, 1964; Soft State, 1970; Britain: a future that works, 1978; The Global Struggle for More, 1987; contribs to Amer. Econ. Rev., Harvard Business Rev., Annals Amer. Acad. Pol. Sci. *Address:* 108 East 38th Street, New York, NY 10016, USA. *T:* 679–9685.

NOSWORTHY, Harold George, CMG 1965; *b* 15 March 1908; *m* 1941, Marjorie Anjelique; two *d*. *Educ:* Kingston Technical High Sch.; private tuition. Entered Jamaica Civil Service, 1929; 2nd class Clerk, 1938; Examiner of Accounts, 1943; Asst Commissioner, Income Tax, 1947; Asst Trade Administrator, 1950; Trade Administrator and Chairman Trade Control Board, 1953; Principal Asst Secretary, Ministry of Finance, 1955; Auditor-General, 1957–66; Dir, Internal Audit Service, UN, 1966–68. Queen's Coronation Medal, 1953; Jamaica Independence Medal, 1962. *Recreations:* reading, billiards, bridge, swimming. *Address:* 18 Hyperion Avenue, PO Box 127, Kingston 6, Jamaica. *T:* 9279889. *Club:* Kingston Cricket (Jamaica).

NOTT, Charles Robert Harley, CMG 1959; OBE 1952; retired, New Zealand; *b* 24 Oct. 1904; *e s* of late John Harley Nott, JP, Leominster, Herefordshire and late Mrs Nott, formerly of Bodenham Hall, Herefordshire; *m* 1935, Marion (*née* Macfarlane), Auckland, NZ; one *s* one *d*. *Educ:* Marlborough; Christ's Coll., Cambridge (MA). Colonial Administrative Service: Fiji, 1926; Administrative Officer (Grade II), 1938, (Grade I), 1945. Member of the Legislative Council, Fiji, 1950; HBM's Agent and Consul, Tonga, 1954–57; Sec. for Fijian Affairs, 1957–59; MLC, MEC, retired, 1960. *Recreation:* trout fishing. *Address:* PO Box 106, Havelock North, New Zealand.

NOTT, Rt. Hon. Sir John (William Frederic), KCB 1983; PC 1979; Chairman and Chief Executive, Lazard Brothers & Co. Ltd, since 1985 (Director, since 1983); a Deputy Chairman, Royal Insurance PLC, since 1986 (Director, since 1985); *b* 1 Feb. 1932; *s* of Richard William Kandahar Nott, Bideford, Devon, and late Phyllis (*née* Francis); *m* 1959, Miloska Sekol, Maribor, Yugoslavia; two *s* one *d*. *Educ:* King's Mead, Seaford; Bradfield Coll.; Trinity Coll., Cambridge. Lieut, 2nd Gurkha Rifles (regular officer), Malayan emergency, 1952–56; Trinity Coll., Cambridge, 1957–59 (BA Hons Law and Econs); Pres., Cambridge Union, 1959; called to the Bar, Inner Temple, 1959; Gen. Manager, S. G. Warburg & Co. Ltd, Merchant Bankers, 1960–66. MP (C) Cornwall, St Ives, 1966–83; Sec., Cons. Parly Finance Cttee, 1969–70; Minister of State, HM Treasury, 1972–74; Cons. front bench spokesman on: Treasury and Economic Affairs, 1975–76; Trade, 1976–79; Sec. of State for Trade, 1979–81, for Defence, 1981–83. *Address:* 21 Moorfields, EC2. *T:* 01–588 2721.

NOTT, Kathleen Cecilia, FRSL; author, broadcaster, lecturer and journalist; *d* of Philip and Ellen Nott; *m* Christopher Bailey (marr. diss.). *Educ:* Mary Datchelor Sch., London; Somerville Coll., Oxford (BA Hons, PPE); King's Coll., London. FRSL 1977. President: Progressive League, 1959–61; English PEN, 1974–75. Editor, PEN International (formerly Internat. PEN Bulletin of Selected Books), 1960–. *Publications: poetry:* Landscapes and Departures, 1947; Poems from the North, 1956; Creatures and Emblems, 1960; Elegies and Other Poems, 1980; *novels:* Mile End, 1938; The Dry Deluge, 1947; Private Fires, 1960; An Elderly Retired Man, 1963; *criticism and philosophy:* The Emperor's Clothes, 1954; A Soul in the Quad, 1969; Philosophy and Human Nature, 1970; The Good Want Power, 1977; *general:* A Clean Well-lighted Place, 1961 (Sweden); contribs to collections of essays, and to periodicals. *Recreations:* playing the piano, gardening. *Clubs:* University Womens', PEN, Society of Authors.

NOTT, Very Rev. Michael John, BD; FKC; Provost of Portsmouth, 1972–82; Hon. Officiating Chaplain, Royal Navy, since 1978; *b* 9 Nov. 1916; *s* of Frank and Ann Nott; *m* 1942, Elisabeth Margaret Edwards; one *s* one *d*. *Educ:* St Paul's; King's Coll., London, FKC 1972; Lincoln Theological Coll. Curate of: Abington, Northampton, 1939–45; St Mary, Reading, 1945–46; Vicar of St Andrew, Kettering, 1946–54; Rural Dean of Kettering, 1952–54; Warden and Chaplain, Heritage Craft Sch. and Hospital, Chailey; Vicar of Seaford, 1957–64; Rural Dean of Seaford, 1961–64; Senior Chaplain to Archbishop of Canterbury, 1964–65; Archdeacon of Maidstone, 1965–67; Archdeacon of Canterbury, 1967–72; Canon Residentiary of Canterbury Cathedral, 1965–72. *Recreations:* reading, walking, travel. *Address:* 9 Clarence Parade, Southsea, Hants. *Club:* Royal Naval (Portsmouth).

NOTT, Rt. Rev. Peter John; *see* Norwich, Bishop of.

NOTTAGE, Raymond Frederick Tritton, CMG 1964; Deputy Chairman, Association of Lloyd's Members; Treasurer, Arkwright Arts Trust, Hampstead, since 1975; *b* 1 Aug. 1916; *s* of Frederick and Frances Nottage; *m* 1941, Joyce Evelyn, *d* of Sidney and Edith Philpot; three *d*. *Educ:* Hackney Downs Secondary Sch. Civil servant, Post Office Headquarters, 1936–49; Editor of Civil Service Opinion, and Member Exec. Cttee, Soc. of Civil Servants, 1944–49; Dir-Gen., RIPA, 1949–78. Mem. Hornsey Borough Council, 1945–47. Mem. Cttee on Training in Public Admin. for Overseas Countries, 1961–63; Vice-Pres. Internat. Inst. of Admin. Sciences, 1962–68; Mem. Governing Body, Inst. of Development Studies, Univ. of Sussex, 1966–76; travelled abroad as Consultant and Lectr. *Publications:* Sources of Local Revenue (with S. H. H. Hildersley), 1968; Financing Public Sector Pensions, 1975; (with Gerald Rhodes) Pensions: a plan for the future, 1986; articles in Public Administration and similar jls. *Recreations:* enjoying music, taking exercise. *Address:* 36e Arkwright Road, NW3. *T:* 01–794 7129.

NOTTINGHAM, Bishop of, (RC), since 1974; **Rt. Rev. James Joseph McGuinness;** *b* 2 Oct. 1925; *s* of Michael and Margaret McGuinness. *Educ:* St Columb's College, Derry; St Patrick's College, Carlow; Oscott College, Birmingham. Ordained, 1950; Curate of St Mary's, Derby, 1950–53; Secretary to Bishop Ellis, 1953–56; Parish Priest, Corpus Christi Parish, Clifton, Nottingham, 1956–72; Vicar General of Nottingham Diocese, 1969; Coadjutor Bishop of Nottingham and Titular Bishop of St Germans, 1972–74. *Recreations:* gardening, golf. *Address:* Bishop's House, 27 Cavendish Road East, The Park, Nottingham NG7 1BB.

NOTTINGHAM, Archdeacon of; *see* Handford, Ven. G. C.

NOULTON, John David; Under Secretary, Department of Transport, since 1985; *b* 5 Jan. 1939; *s* of John Noulton and Kathleen (*née* Sheehan); *m* 1961, Anne Elizabeth Byrne; three *s* one *d*. *Educ:* Clapham Coll. MCIT. Asst Principal, Dept of Transport, 1970–72; Principal, DoE, 1972–78; Pvte Sec. to Minister of State, DoE, 1976–78; Asst Sec., Depts of the Environment and of Transport, 1978–85. *Recreations:* boating, swimming, walking, reading. *Address:* 7 Rydal Road, SW16 1QF. *T:* 01–769 4793.

NOURSE, Rt. Hon. Sir Martin (Charles), PC 1985; Kt 1980; **Rt. Hon. Lord Justice Nourse;** a Lord Justice of Appeal, since 1985; *b* 3 April 1932; *yr s* of late Henry Edward Nourse, MD, MRCP, of Cambridge, and Ethel Millicent, *d* of Rt Hon. Sir Charles Henry Sargant, Lord Justice of Appeal; *m* 1972, Lavinia, *yr d* of late Comdr D. W. Malim; one *s* one *d*. *Educ:* Winchester; Corpus Christi Coll., Cambridge. National Service as 2nd Lieut, Rifle Bde, 1951–52; Lieut, London Rifle Bde Rangers (TA), 1952–55. Called to Bar, Lincoln's Inn, 1956; Bencher, 1978; Mem., General Council of the Bar, 1964–68; a Junior Counsel to BoT in Chancery matters, 1967–70; QC 1970; Attorney Gen., Duchy of Lancaster, 1976–80; a Judge of the Courts of Appeal of Jersey and Guernsey, 1977–80; Judge of the High Court of Justice, Chancery Div., 1980–85. *Address:* Royal Courts of Justice, Strand, WC2. *Club:* Cambridge County (Cambridge).

See also Sir Edmund Sargant.

NOVA SCOTIA, Bishop of, since 1984; **Rt. Rev. Arthur Gordon Peters;** *b* 21 Dec. 1935; *s* of William Peters and Charlotte Peters (*née* Symes); *m* 1962, Elizabeth Baert; one *s* two *d*. *Educ:* High School, North Sydney, NS; Univ. of King's College, Halifax, NS (BA 1960, BST 1963, BD 1973). Student, Parish of Waverley, 1961–63; deacon 1962, priest 1963, Nova Scotia; Morris Scholar, 1963, at Canterbury (Eng.), Geneva, Jerusalem, Norton (dio. Durham, Eng.); Rector: Weymouth, NS, 1964–68; Annapolis-Granville, NS, 1968–73; Christ Church, Sydney, NS, 1973–82; Bishop Coadjutor of Nova Scotia, 1982–84. Hon. DD Univ. of King's College, 1982. *Recreations:* swimming, ski-ing, reading, skating, photography. *Address:* 5732 College Street, Halifax, NS B3H 1X3, Canada. *T:* 423–8301.

NOVE, Prof. Alexander, FRSE 1982; FBA 1978; Professor of Economics, University of Glasgow, 1963–82, now Emeritus; Hon. Senior Research Fellow, Glasgow University, since 1982; *b* Leningrad, 24 Nov. 1915; *s* of Jacob Novakovsky; *m* 1951, Irene MacPherson; three *s*. *Educ:* King Alfred Sch., London; London Sch. of Economics (Hon. Fellow, 1982). BSc (Econ) 1936. Army, 1939–46. Civil Service (mainly BoT), 1947–58; Reader in Russian Social and Economic Studies, Univ. of London, 1958–63. Hon. Dr.agr Giessen, 1977. *Publications:* The Soviet Economy, 1961; (with J. A. Newth) The Soviet Middle East, 1965; Was Stalin Really Necessary?, 1965; Economic History of the USSR, 1969; (ed, with D. M. Nuti) Socialist Economics, 1972; Efficiency Criteria for Nationalised Industries, 1973; Stalinism and After, 1976; The Soviet Economic System, 1977, 3rd edn 1986; Political Economy and Soviet Socialism, 1979; The Economics of Feasible Socialism, 1983; Socialism, Economics and Development, 1986. *Recreations:* walking in Scottish hills, travel, music, theatre, exotic dishes. *Address:* 55 Hamilton Drive, Glasgow G12 8DP. *T:* 041–339 1053. *Club:* Royal Commonwealth Society.

NOWAR, Maj.-Gen. Ma'an Abu, Jordanian Star 1st Class; Minister of Tourism and Antiquities, and of Culture and Youth, Hashemite Kingdom of Jordan, since 1981; *b* 26 July 1928; *m* Vivian Ann Richards; two *s* seven *d*; *m* 1976, Susan Ann Coombs, Bath, Som; one *d*. *Educ:* London Univ. (Dip. World Affairs, 1963). Joined Jordanian Armed Forces, 1943; comd Regt, 1956; comd Bde, 1957; Counsellor, Jordan Embassy, London, 1963; Dir of Civil Defence, 1964; Dir of Public Security, 1967; Asst Chief of Staff, Jordan Armed Forces, 1969; Minister of Culture and Information, 1972–73; Ambassador of Jordan to the Court of St James's, 1973–76; Mayor of Amman, 1976–80; Minister of Public Works, 1980–81. *Publications:* The Battle of Karameh, 1968; For Jerusalem, 1969;

40 Armoured Brigade, 1970; The State in War and Peace, 1971; History of the Jordan Army, 1972; The Olympic Games Old and Modern, 1983. *Recreation:* swimming. *Address:* Ministry of Tourism and Antiquities, Amman, Jordan.

NOWELL-SMITH, Prof. Patrick Horace, AM (Harvard); MA (Oxon); Professor of Philosophy, York University, Toronto, 1969–85, now Emeritus; *b* 17 Aug. 1914; *s* of Nowell Charles Smith; *m* 1st, 1946, Perilla Thyme (marr. diss. 1968), *d* of Sir Richard Vynne Southwell; three *s* one *d*; 2nd, 1968, Felicity Margret (marr. diss. 1986), *d* of Dr Richard Leonard Ward; two *d*. *Educ:* Winchester Coll.; New College, Oxford. Commonwealth Fellow, Harvard Univ., 1937–39. Served War of 1939–45, in Army, 1939–45. Fellow and Lecturer, Trinity Coll., Oxford, 1946–57, Estates Bursar, 1951–57; Professor of Philosophy: University of Leicester, 1957–64; University of Kent, 1964–69. *Publications:* Ethics, 1954; articles in Mind, Proc. Aristotelian Soc., Theoria, etc. *Address:* Ty Isaf, Taliaris, Llandeilo, Dyfed.

See also S. H. Nowell-Smith, Sir S. S. T. Young.

NOWELL-SMITH, Simon Harcourt, FSA; *b* 5 Jan. 1909; *s* of late Nowell Charles Smith, sometime Headmaster of Sherborne; *m* 1st, 1938, Marion Sinclair (*d* 1977), *d* of late W. S. Crichton, Liverpool; two *s* one *d*; 2nd, 1986, Judith Adams, *d* of Frederick B. Adams, *qv*. *Educ:* Sherborne; New Coll., Oxford (MA). Editorial Staff of The Times, 1932–44; Assistant Editor, Times Literary Supplement, 1937–39; attached to Intelligence Division, Naval Staff, 1940–45; Secretary and Librarian, The London Library, 1950–56; Secretary, Hospital Library Services Survey, 1958–59; President, Bibliographical Society, 1962–64; Lyell Reader in Bibliography, Oxford Univ., 1965–66. Pres., Oxford Bibliographical Soc., 1972–76. Trustee, Dove Cottage Trust, 1974–82. OStJ. *Publications:* Mark Rutherford, a bibliography, 1930; The Legend of the Master (Henry James), 1947; The House of Cassell, 1958; (ed) Edwardian England, 1964; Letters to Macmillan, 1967; International Copyright Law and the Publisher, 1968; Postscript to Autobiography of William Plomer, 1975. *Address:* 7 Beaumont Road, Headington, Oxford OX3 8JN.

See also Prof. P. H. Nowell-Smith.

NSEKELA, Amon James; Chairman and Managing Director, National Bank of Commerce, 1967–74 and since 1981; *b* 4 Jan. 1930; *s* of Ngonile Reuben Nsekela and Anyambilile Nsekela (*née* Kalinga); *m* 1957, Christina Matilda Nsekela; two *s*. *Educ:* Rungwe Dist Sch.; Malangali Secondary Sch.; Tabora Govt Sen. Sec. Sch.; Makerere UC (DipEd); Univ. of Pacific (Scholar, MA). Entered Civil Service as DO, Moshi, 1960; Perm. Sec., Min. of External Affairs and Defence, 1963; Perm. Sec. to Min. of Commerce, 1964; Prin. Sec. to Treasury, 1966–67. MP 1973–75, and Mem. E African Legis. Assembly, 1967–70. High Comr, UK, 1974–81, and Ambassador Extraordinary and Plenipotentiary to Ireland, 1979–81. Chm. or Dir of many cos and corporations, 1967–, incl.: Chm., Nat. Insurance Corp. of Tanzania, 1967–72; Director: Nat. Develt Corp. (past Chm. when Tanganyika Develt Corp.); Bd of Internal Trade; E African Airways Corp.; Bd, African Medical Res. Fund, 1986–. Mem./Sec., Presidential Commn on Estabt of Democratic One-Party State in Tanzania; Mem., Internat. Council of Trustees, Internat. Defence and Aid Fund for Southern Africa, 1985–. Chairman: Council, Inst. of Finance Management, 1971–; Public Service Salaries Review Commn, 1985–86. Pres., Tanzania Soc. for Internat. Develt; Past Pres., Economic Assoc. of Tanzania; Vice-Chm., Britain–Tanzania Soc., 1982–. Chm. Council, Univ. of Dar es Salaam. *Publications:* Minara ya Historia ya Tanganyika: Tanganyika hadi Tanzania, 1965, new edns 1966 and 1971; Demokrasi Tanzania, 1973; (with A. L. Nhonoli) The Development of Health Services in Mainland Tanzania: Tumetoka Mbali, 1973; Socialism and Social Accountability in a Developing Nation, 1977; Towards Rational Alternatives, 1985; A Time to Act, 1985; contribs to Jl of Administration Overseas (ODM), African Review, Development Dialogue. *Address:* Box 1863, Dar-es-Salaam, Tanzania.

NTIWANE, Nkomeni Douglas; Group Personnel, Training and Localisation Manager, Swaki Group of Companies, since 1980; *b* 16 Feb. 1933; *s* of Isaiah Myotha and Jane Dlamini; *m* 1st, 1960, Sophia Pulane Kali (*d* 1981); three *s*; 2nd, 1983, Phindile T. Mamba. *Educ:* DOT Coll., Middelburg, Transvaal, SA; Columbia Univ. (1967–68; Carnegie Fellow in Dipl.). Certificate Teacher: Mbekelweni Sch., 1962–63; Mhlume Central Sch., 1964–66; Lozitha Central Sch., Jan.-Sept. 1967. High Commissioner for Swaziland in London, 1968–71; Ambassador: Federal Republic of Germany, March 1969; Republic of France, April 1969. Permanent Secretary: Dept of Foreign Affairs, Swaziland, 1971–72; Ministry of Health, 1972–77; Ministry of Commerce, Industry, Mines and Tourism, 1977–80; retired from Civil Service, 1980. Swaziland Independence Medal, 1968; Meritorious Service Medal, Royal Swaziland Umbutfo Defence Force, 1978. *Publication:* Asive Ngwane (siSwati poetry). *Address:* Emangweni, PO Box 41, Malkerns, Swaziland.

NUGEE, Edward George, TD 1964; QC 1977; *b* 9 Aug. 1928; *o s* of late Brig. George Travers Nugee, CBE, DSO, MC, RA, and of Violet Mary (*née* Richards, now Brooks); *m* 1955, Rachel Elizabeth Makower (*see* R. E. Nugee); four *s*. *Educ:* Brambletye; Radley Coll. (Open Scholar); Worcester Coll., Oxford (Open Exhibnr; Law Mods, Distinction, 1950; 1st Cl. Hons Jurisprudence, 1952; Eldon Law Scholar, 1953; MA 1956). National Service, RA, 1947–49 (Office of COS, GHQ, FARELF); service with 100 Army Photographic Interpretation Unit, TA, 1950–64 (retd Captain, Intell. Corps, 1964). Read as pupil with Lord Templeman and Lord Brightman; called to the Bar, Inner Temple, 1955, Bencher 1976; *ad eundem* Lincoln's Inn, 1968. Jun. Counsel to Land Commn (Chancery and Conveyancing), 1967–71; Counsel for litigation under Commons Registration Act, 1965, 1968–77; Conveyancing Counsel to Treasury, WO, MAFF, Forestry Commn, MoD (Admiralty), and DoE, 1972–77; Conveyancing Counsel of Court, 1976–77. Poor Man's Lawyer, Lewisham CAB, 1954–72. Member: CAB Adv. Cttee, Family Welfare Assoc., 1969–72; Management Cttee, Greater London Citizens Advice Bureaux Service Ltd, 1972–74; Man. Cttee, Forest Hill Advice Centre, 1972–76; Bar Council, 1962–66 (Mem., External Relations Cttee, 1966–71); Council of Legal Educn, 1967– (Vice-Chm. 1976–82, and Chm. of Bd of Studies, 1976–82); Adv. Cttee on Legal Educn, 1971–; Common Professional Exam. Bd, 1976– (Chm., 1981–); Lord Chancellor's Law Reform Cttee, 1973–; various working parties and consultative groups of Law Commn, 1966–; Inst. of Conveyancers, 1971– (Pres., 1986–87); Chm., Cttee of Inquiry into Management Problems of Privately Owned Blocks of Flats, 1984–85. Chm. Governors, Brambletye Sch., 1972–77; Mem. Council, Radley Coll., 1975–. *Publications:* (jtly) Nathan on the Charities Act 1960, 1962; (ed jtly) Halsbury's Laws of England, titles Landlord and Tenant (3rd edn 1958), Real Property (3rd edn 1960, 4th edn 1982); contribs to legal jls. *Recreations:* travel, cooking, the family. *Address:* 3 New Square, Lincoln's Inn, WC2A 3RS. *T:* 01–405 5296; 10 Heath Hurst Road, Hampstead, NW3 2RX. *T:* 01–435 9204.

NUGEE, Rachel Elizabeth, JP, MA; *b* 15 Aug. 1926; *d* of John Moritz Makower and Adelaide Gertrude Leonaura Makower (*née* Franklin); *m* 1955, Edward George Nugee, *qv*; four *s*. *Educ:* Roedean Sch., Brighton; Lady Margaret Hall, Oxford; MA (EngLang and Lit); Reading Univ. (Dip. Soc. Studies). Joined Mothers' Union, 1956; Diocesan Pres., London Dio., 1974–76; Central Pres., 1977–82; Vice Chairman: Central Publications Cttee, 1971–74; Social Concern Cttee, 1983–85; MU rep. on Women's Nat. Commn, 1983–. Member: Royal Free Hosp. (Hampstead Gen. Hosp.) House Cttee and Patients' Services Cttee, 1961–72; London Diocesan Bd for Social Responsibility, 1984–85. Trustee, Marriage Res. Fund, 1984–. JP Inner London (Thames), 1971, Dep. Chm. of Bench, 1985–. *Publications:* several religious articles and booklets. *Recreations:* active support of Church and family life; reading, especially history; visiting friends. *Address:* 10 Heath Hurst Road, Hampstead, NW3 2RX. *T:* 01–435 9204.

NUGENT, family name of **Earl of Westmeath** and **Baron Nugent of Guildford.**

NUGENT OF GUILDFORD, Baron, *cr* 1966 (Life Peer), of Dunsfold; **George Richard Hodges Nugent;** Bt 1960; PC 1962; *b* 6 June 1907; *s* of late Colonel George H. Nugent, RA; *m* 1937, Ruth, *d* of late Hugh G. Stafford, Tilford, Surrey. *Educ:* Imperial Service Coll., Windsor; RMA, Woolwich. Commissioned RA, 1926–29. MP (C) Guildford Division of Surrey, 1950–66. Parliamentary Secretary: Ministry of Agriculture, Fisheries and Food, 1951–57; Min. of Transport, 1957–Oct. 1959. A Dep. Speaker, House of Lords. JP Surrey; CC and sometime Alderman, Surrey, 1944–51. Member: Exec. Council, NFU, 1945–51; Agricl Improvement Council, 1947–51; Vice-Chairman: Nat. Fedn of Young Farmers, 1948–51; Wye Agricl Coll., 1946–51; Harper Adams Agricl Coll., 1947–51; Chairman: Thames Conservancy Board, 1960–74; Nat. Water Council, 1973–78; House of Commons Select Cttee for Nationalised Industries, 1961–64; Agricultural Market Development Cttee, 1962–68; Animal Virus Research Institute, 1964–77; Standing Conf. on London and SE Regional Planning, 1962–81; Defence Lands Cttee, 1971–73; President, Assoc. of River Authorities, 1965–74; Mem., Guildford Diocesan Synod, 1970–. Pres., RoSPA, 1980–82. FRSA 1962. Hon. FIPHE; Hon. FIWES. DUniv Surrey, 1968. Hon. Freeman, Borough of Guildford, 1985. *Address:* Blacknest Cottage, Dunsfold, Godalming, Surrey GU8 4PE. *Club:* Royal Automobile (Vice-Pres., 1974).

NUGENT of Bellême, David James Douglas, (Prince HSH, title of Austrian Empire, *cr* 1816; also 7th Baron Nugent, Austrian title *cr* 1859 and confirmed by Royal Warrant of Edward VII, 1908); *b* 24 Nov. 1917; 2nd *s* of Albert Beauchamp Cecil Nugent (HSH Prince Nugent, and 5th Baron) and Frances Every Douglas, niece of 3rd Baron Blythswood, KCB, CVO; *S* brother, 1944; *m* 1968, Mary Louise (*d* 1975), *er d* of William Henry Wroth, Bigbury Court, Devonshire; *m* 1979, Evelyn Diana, *er d* of late Lt-Col Francis Noel, OBE, and *widow* of Sir Hector Lethbridge, 6th Bt. *Educ:* Lancing Coll. Director, Book Guild, Lewes, Sussex. *Recreation:* historical research. *Address:* Gresham Hall Cottage, Gresham Hall, Gresham, near Norwich NR11 8AW. *Club:* Norfolk (Norwich).

NUGENT, Sir John (Edwin Lavallin), 7th Bt *cr* 1795; JP; Chairman, Lambourn Holdings Ltd, since 1980; *b* 16 March 1933; *s* of Sir Hugh Charles Nugent, 6th Bt, and of Margaret Mary Lavallin, *er d* of late Rev. Herbert Lavallin Puxley; *S* father, 1983; *m* 1959, Penelope Anne, *d* of late Brig. Richard Nigel Hanbury, CBE, TD; one *s* one *d*. *Educ:* Eton. Short service commn, Irish Guards, Lieut, 1953–56. PA to William Geoffrey Rootes (later 2nd Baron Rootes), Chm. of Rootes Gp, 1957–59; joined board of Lambourn group of cos, 1959. High Sheriff of Berks, 1981–82; JP Berks, 1962. *Recreations:* garden and fishing. *Heir:* *s* Nicholas Myles John Nugent, *b* 17 Feb. 1967. *Address:* Limes Farm, Upper Lambourn, Newbury, Berks RG16 7RG. *T:* Lambourn 71369, (office) 71011. *Club:* Kildare Street and University (Dublin).

NUGENT, Sir Peter Walter James, 5th Bt, *cr* 1831; *b* 26 Jan. 1920; *s* of Sir Walter Richard Nugent, 4th Bt and of Aileen Gladys, *y d* of late Middleton Moore O'Malley, JP, Ross, Westport, Co. Mayo; *S* father, 1955; *m* 1947, Anne Judith, *o d* of Major Robert Smyth, Gaybrook, Mullingar, Co. Westmeath; two *s* two *d*. *Educ:* Downside. Served War of 1939–45; 2nd Lieut, Hampshire Regt, 1941; Major, 1945. *Heir:* *s* Walter Richard Middleton Nugent, *b* 15 Nov. 1947. *Address:* Bay Bush, Straffan, Co. Kildare, Eire.

NUGENT, Sir Robin (George Colborne), 5th Bt *cr* 1806; *b* 11 July 1925; *s* of Sir Guy Nugent, 4th Bt and of Maisie, Lady Nugent, *d* of J. A. Bigsby; *S* father, 1970; *m* 1st, 1947, Ursula Mary (marr. diss. 1967), *d* of late Lt-Gen. Sir Herbert Fothergill Cooke, KCB, KBE, CSI, DSO; two *s* one *d*; 2nd, 1967, Victoria Anna Irmgard, *d* of late Dr Peter Cartellieri. *Educ:* Eton; RWA School of Architecture. Lt Grenadier Guards, 1943–48; served Italy, 1944–45. ARIBA 1959. *Recreation:* fishing. *Heir:* *s* Christopher George Ridley Nugent, *b* 5 Oct. 1949. *Address:* Bannerdown House, Batheaston, Bath, Avon. *T:* Bath 858481.

NUNAN, Manus; lecturer; *b* 26 March 1926; *s* of Manus Timothy Nunan, Dist Justice, and Nan (*née* FitzGerald); *m* 1960, Anne Monique Fradin; one *s* one *d*. *Educ:* St Mary's Coll., Dublin; Trinity Coll., Dublin (BA, LLB). Called to the Irish Bar, King's Inns, 1950; called to the English Bar, Gray's Inn, 1956, retired from practice, 1985. Asst d'Anglais, Lycée Masséna, Nice, 1949–50; practised at Irish Bar, 1950–53; Crown Counsel, Nigeria, 1953–62; Solicitor-Gen., Northern Nigeria, 1962–64; Minister of Govt, Northern Nigeria, 1962; QC (Nigeria) 1962; a Recorder, 1978–84; since 1985 has lectured throughout Australia and North America on the life and trials of Oscar Wilde. *Address:* 2B Mosslea Park, Liverpool L18 8DS. *T:* 051–724 5373. *Clubs:* Racquet (Liverpool); Kildare Street and University (Dublin).

NUNBURNHOLME, 4th Baron *cr* 1906; **Ben Charles Wilson;** Major, Royal Horse Guards, retired; *b* 16 July 1928; *s* of 3rd Baron Nunburnholme, and Lady Mary Thynne, *y d* of 5th Marquess of Bath, KG, PC, CB; *S* father, 1974; *m* 1958, Ines Dolores Jeanne, *d* of Gerard Walravens, Brussels; four *d* (including twin *d*). *Educ:* Eton. *Heir:* *b* Hon. Charles Thomas Wilson [*b* 27 May 1935; *m* 1969, Linda Kay, *d* of Cyril James Stephens; one *s* one *d*]. *Address:* Shillinglee Park, Chiddingfold, Surrey. *T:* Northchapel 461.

NUNN, John Francis, PhD; MD; FRCS; FFARCS; Head of Division of Anaesthesia, Medical Research Council Clinical Research Centre, since 1968; *b* 7 Nov. 1925; *s* of late Francis Nunn, Colwyn Bay; *m* 1949, Sheila, *d* of late E. C. Doubleday; one *s* two *d*. *Educ:* Wrekin Coll.; Birmingham Univ. MO, Birmingham Univ. Spitzbergen Expedition, 1948; Colonial Med. Service, Malaya, 1949–53; University Research Fellow, Birmingham, 1955–56; Leverhulme Research Fellow, RCS, 1957–64; Part-time Lectr, Postgrad. Med. Sch., Univ. of London, 1959–64; Consultant Anæsth., Hammersmith Hosp., 1959–64; Prof. of Anaesthesia, Univ. of Leeds, 1964–68. Member: Council, RCS, 1977–82 (Mem. Board, Faculty of Anaesthetists, Vice-Dean, 1977–79, Dean, 1979–82); Council, Assoc. of Anaesthetists, 1973–76; Pres., Sect. Anaesthesia, RSM, 1984–85. Hunterian Professor, RCS, 1960; Visiting Professor to various American Universities, 1960–; British Council Lecturer: Switzerland, 1962; USSR, 1963; Czechoslovakia, 1969; China, 1974. Joseph Clover Lectr, RCS, 1968. Mem., Egypt Exploration Soc. Hon. FFARACS; Hon. FFARCSI. *Publications:* Applied Respiratory Physiology, 1969, 2nd edn 1977; Jt Editor, General Anaesthesia, 3rd edn, 1971, 4th edn 1980; several chapters in medical text-books, and publications in Journal Appl. Physiol., Lancet, Nature, British Journal Anæsth., etc. *Recreations:* archaeology, model engineering, ski-ing. *Address:* MRC Clinical Research Centre, Northwick Park, Harrow, Middx; 3 Russell Road, Moor Park, Northwood, Mddx. *T:* Northwood 26363.

NUNN, Rear-Adm. John Richard Danford, CB 1980; Bursar and Official Fellow, Exeter College, Oxford, since 1981; *b* 12 April 1925; *s* of Surg. Captain Gerald Nunn and Edith Florence (*née* Brown); *m* 1951, Katharine Mary (*née* Paris); three *d*. *Educ:* Epsom Coll. CEng, FIMechE; MPhil Cantab, 1981; MA Oxon, 1982. Entered RN, 1943; RN

Engrg Coll., Keyham, 1943–47; HMS Devonshire, Second Cruiser Sqdn, 1945; HMS Vengeance, 1947; Advanced Engineering Course, RNC Greenwich, 1949–51. HMS Amethyst, Korea, 1952–53; HMS Tiger, 1957–59; Commander, 1960; HMS Glamorgan, 1967–68; Captain, 1969; Sea Dart and Seaslug Chief Engineer, 1970–72; Cabinet Office, 1973–74; Staff of SACLANT, 1975–77; Rear-Adm., 1978; Port Adm., Rosyth, 1977–80. Fellow Commoner, Downing Coll., Cambridge, 1980–. Editor, The Naval Review, 1980–83. *Recreations:* sailing, tennis, gliding, travel. *Address:* Warner's Cottage, Corhampton, Hants SO3 1LL; 2 Sadler Walk, St Ebbes, Oxford. *Clubs:* Naval; Automobile Association; Royal Naval Sailing Association (Portsmouth).

NUNN, Trevor Robert, CBE 1978; Joint Artistic Director, Royal Shakespeare Company, since 1978 (Artistic Director, 1968–78; Chief Executive, until 1986); *b* 14 Jan. 1940; *s* of Robert Alexander Nunn and Dorothy May (*née* Piper); *m* 1969, Janet Suzman, *qv* (marr. diss. 1986); one *s*. *Educ:* Northgate Grammar Sch., Ipswich; Downing Coll., Cambridge (BA). Producer, Belgrade Theatre, Coventry; subseq. Associate Dir, Royal Shakespeare Company. Hon. MA: Newcastle upon Tyne, 1982; Warwick. *Address:* c/o Barbican Centre, Silk Street, EC2.

NUNNELEY, John Hewlett, FCIT; Managing Director, British Transport Advertising Ltd, since 1969; *b* Sydney, NSW, 26 Nov. 1922; *o s* of late Wilfrid Alexander Nunneley and Audrey Mary (*née* Tebbitt); *m* 1945, Lucia, *e d* of Enrico Ceruti, Milan, Italy; one *s* one *d*. *Educ:* Lawrence Sheriff Sch., Rugby. Served War of 1939–45: Somerset LI, seconded KAR; Abyssinia, Brit. Somaliland, 1942; Burma campaign, 1944 (wounded, despatches); Captain and Adjt. Various management posts in aircraft, shipping, printing and publishing industries, 1946–55. Exec., Beaverbrook Newspapers, 1955–62; joined BTC, 1962: Chief Publicity Officer, 1962–63; Chief Development Officer (Passenger) BR Bd, 1963–64; Chief Passenger Manager, 1964–69; Pres. and Chm., BR-Internat. Inc., New York, USA, 1966–69. Principal Advertising Consultant, Hong Kong Govt, 1981–83. Member: Passenger Co-ordination Cttee for London, 1964–69; Outdoor Advertising Council, 1969–. Pres., European Fedn of Outdoor Advertising (FEPE), 1984–. Introduced BR Corporate Identity, 1964 and Inter-City concept, 1965. FRSA. City of Paris Medal. *Publications:* numerous articles on aviation, transport and advertising subjects. *Recreation:* gliding (FAI Gold C and Two Diamonds). *Address:* 6 Ashfield Close, Petersham, Surrey TW10 7AF.

NUREYEV, Rudolf Hametovich; ballet dancer and choreographer; Directeur Artistique de la Danse, Théâtre National de l'Opéra, Paris, since 1983; *b* Ufa, E Siberia, 1939, of a farming family. Joined Kirov Ballet School and at age 17 appeared with the Company in 1959; when on tour, in Paris, sought political asylum, May 1961. Joined Le Grand Ballet du Marquis de Cuevas Company and has made frequent appearances abroad; London debut at Royal Academy of Dancing Gala Matinée, organised by Dame Margot Fonteyn, Dec. 1961; debut at Covent Garden in Giselle with Margot Fonteyn, Feb. 1962; Choreographic productions include: La Bayadère, Raymonda, Swan Lake, Tancredi, Sleeping Beauty, Nutcracker, Don Quixote, Romeo and Juliet, Manfred, The Tempest, Washington Square; guest artist in England and America in wide variety of rôles. Has danced in many countries of the world. Gold Star, Paris, 1963. *Films:* Romeo and Juliet, 1965; I am a Dancer, 1972; Don Quixote, 1974; Valentino, 1977; Exposed, 1983. *Publication:* Nureyev, 1962. *Recreations:* listening to and playing music. *Address:* c/o S. A. Gorlinsky Ltd, 33 Dover Street, W1X 4NJ.

NURJADIN, Air Chief Marshal Roesmin; Minister of Communications, Indonesia, since 1983 (of Transport, Communications and Tourism, 1978–83); *b* 31 May 1930; *m* 1962, Surjati Subali; two *s* one *d*. *Educ:* Indonesian Air Force Academy; Techn. Coll., Univ. Gadjahmada. Student Army, 1945–50. Comdr 3rd Fighter Sqdn, 1953; RAF CFS, England, 1954; Law Sch., 1956; Instructor, Jet Sqdn, 1957–59; Junior Staff Sch., 1959; Defence Services Staff Coll., Wellington, India, 1960–61; Dir Operation AF HQ, 1961–62; Dep. Comdr Operational Comd, Chief of Staff Air Defence Comd, 1962–64; Air Attaché: Bangkok, 1964–65; Moscow, 1965–66; Minister/C-in-C/Chief of Staff, Indonesian Air Force, 1966–70; Ambassador to the UK, 1970–74, to the USA, 1974–78. *Recreations:* golf, swimming. *Address:* Ministry of Communications, Jl Merdeka Barat 8, Jakarta, Indonesia. *Clubs:* Highgate Golf; Djakarta Golf.

NURSAW, James, CB 1983; Legal Adviser to the Home Office and the Northern Ireland Office, since 1983; *b* 18 Oct. 1932; *s* of William George Nursaw, *qv*; *m* 1959, Eira, *yr d* of late E. W. Caryl-Thomas, MD, BSc, Barrister-at-law; two *d*. *Educ:* Bancroft's School; Christ's Coll., Cambridge (Schol.; MA, LLB). Called to Bar, Middle Temple, 1955 (Blackstone Entrance Schol. and Prize, Harmsworth Schol.). Senior Research Officer, Cambridge Univ. Dept of Criminal Science, 1958. Joined Legal Adviser's Branch, Home Office, 1959; Principal Asst Legal Advr, HO and NI Office, 1977–80; Legal Secretary, Law Officers' Dept, 1980–83. Liveryman, Loriners' Co. *Address:* Legal Adviser's Office, Home Office, 50 Queen Anne's Gate, SW1H 9AT. *Clubs:* United Oxford & Cambridge University, MCC.

NURSAW, William George; investment consultant since 1961; financial writer and company director; *b* 5 Sept. 1903; *s* of George Edward Nursaw and Amy Elizabeth (*née* Davis); *m* 1931, Lilian May (*née* Howell); one *s* two *d*. *Educ:* Rushmore Road LCC Primary Sch.; Holloway Grammar Sch. (Schol.). Insurance, 1920–61: Trustee Man., Atlas Assce Co.; subseq. Dir Throgmorton Management (Man. Dir, 1962–71) and Hogg Robinson Gardner Mountain Pensions Management (Chm., 1963–71); Hon. Financial Adviser, RAF Escapers Soc., 1964–83, and National Birthday Trust, 1947– (and Hon. Treas.); Co-founder and Dep. Chm., Covenanters Educational Trust and Perry Foundn, 1945–; Freeman, City of London; Past Warden, Loriners' Co.; Deacon, Chingford Congregational Church, 1944–62; Youth Leader, 1942–67; Chm., Chingford and Waltham Forest Playing Fields Assoc., 1959–79 (this completed 51 yrs as an hon. officer for the dist); Exec., Essex County Playing Fields Assoc., then Greater London Playing Fields, 1948–85. Civil Defence (Post Warden), 1938–65. FSS; ACII; FCIS (Mem. Council, 1962–70, Chm., London, 1968–69); FCIArb (Mem. Council, 1968–74); Associate, Soc. of Investment Analysts. Mem., Royal Soc. of St George. *Publications:* Investment in Trust: problems and policies, 1961; Art and Practice of Investment, 1962, 4th edn 1974; Purposeful Investment, 1965; Principles of Pension Fund Investment, 1966, 2nd edn 1976; Investment for All, 1972; articles for national press on investment and insurance, incl. over 200 articles for The Guardian, Observer, etc. *Recreations:* rose-growing, cricket (Pres. and Captain, Chingford Park CC), writing, portrait painting, playing-fields movement, 1934–85 (Duke of Edinburgh award). *Address:* 603 Mountjoy House, Barbican, EC2Y 8BP. *T:* 01–628 7638; 6 Carlton Road East, Westgate, Kent. *T:* Thanet 32105. *Clubs:* City Livery, Aldersgate Ward, MCC, Pen International.

See also James Nursaw.

NURSTEN, Prof. Harry Erwin, PhD, DSc; CChem, FRSC; FIFST; Professor, since 1976, and Head of Department of Food Science and Technology, since 1986, Reading University; *s* of Sergius Nursten and Helene Nursten; *m* 1950, Jean Patricia Frobisher. *Educ:* Ilkley Grammar Sch.; Leeds Univ. (BSc 1st Cl. Hons Colour Chemistry, 1947; PhD 1949; DSc 1973). FRIC 1957; FIFST 1972. Bradford Dyers Assoc. Res. Fellow, Dept of Colour Chem. and Dyeing, Leeds Univ., 1949–52; Lectr in Textile Chem. and Dyeing, Nottingham and Dist Tech. Coll., 1952–54; Lectr 1955–65, Sen. Lectr 1965–70, and Reader 1970–76, Procter Dept of Food and Leather Science, Leeds Univ.; Head of Dept of Food Sci., Reading Univ., 1976–86. Res. Associate, Dept of Nutrition, Food Science and Technol., MIT, 1961–62; Vis. Prof., Dept of Food Science and Technol., Univ. of Calif, Davis, 1966. Chief Examiner, Mastership in Food Control, 1982. Pres., Soc. of Leather Technologists and Chemists, 1974–76. Bill Littlejohn Memorial Medallion Lectr, Brit. Soc. of Flavourists, 1974. *Publications:* (ed jtly) Progress in Flavour Research, 1979; papers in Jl Sci. Food Agric., Jl Soc. Leather Technol. Chem., and Jl Chem. Soc. *Address:* Department of Food Science and Technology, University of Reading, Whiteknights, PO Box 226, Reading, Berks RG6 2AP. *T:* Reading 875123.

NUTMAN, Dr Phillip Sadler, FRS 1968; Head of Department of Soil Microbiology, Rothamsted Experimental Station, Harpenden, 1957–79; *b* 10 Oct. 1914; *s* of John William Nutman and Elizabeth Hester Nutman (*née* Hughes); *m* 1940, Mary Meta Stanbury; two *s* one *d*. *Educ:* Teignmouth Grammar Sch.; Imperial Coll., London Univ. Research Asst, Rothamsted Experimental Station, 1940; Senior Research Fellow, Canberra, Australia, 1953–56; Rothamsted, 1956–79; Hannaford Res. Fellow, Waite Inst., Adelaide, 1980. Huxley Medal, 1959. *Publications:* research papers in plant physiological, genetical and microbiological journals. *Recreations:* music, woodworking. *Address:* Great Hackworthy Cottage, Tedburn St Mary, Exeter EX6 6DW. *T:* Tedburn St Mary 364.

NUTTALL, Rev. Derek; Director, Cruse, the National Organisation for the Widowed and their Children, since 1978 (National Organiser, 1974–78); *b* 23 Sept. 1937; *s* of Charles William Nuttall and Doris Nuttall; *m* 1965, Margaret Hathaway Brown; two *s* one *d*. *Educ:* Ironville Sch.; Somercotes Sch.; Overdale Coll., Selly Oak (Diploma). Semi-skilled worker in industry, 1953–60; office clerk, 1960–61; college, 1961–65; ministry in Falkirk, 1965–67; ordained, 1967; ministry and community work in Aberfan, 1967–74: Gen. Sec., Community Assoc.; mem., church and community cttees. Member: Exec., Internat. Fedn of Widow/Widower Orgns, 1980–; Internat. Workgroup on Death and Dying, 1980–. *Publications:* The Early Days of Grieving, 1986; articles and papers on bereavement and on needs of widows, widowers and bereaved children. *Recreations:* music, reading, sport (mainly spectating), keeping up with the family's activities. *Address:* Cruse House, 126 Sheen Road, Richmond, Surrey TW9 1UR. *T:* 01–940 4818; 51 Spinney Hill, Addlestone, Surrey. *T:* Weybridge 46897. *Club:* Royal Society of Medicine.

NUTTALL, Dr Geoffrey Fillingham; Ecclesiastical historian, retired; Visiting Professor, King's College, London, 1977–80; *b* Colwyn Bay, Wales, 8 Nov. 1911; *s* of Harold Nuttall and Muriel Fillingham (*née* Hodgson); *m* 1944, Mary (*née* Preston) (*d* 1982), *widow* of George Philip Powley. *Educ:* Bootham Sch., York; Balliol Coll., Oxford (MA 1936); Mansfield Coll., Oxford (BD 1938, DD 1945). Ordained Congregational Minister, 1938; Warminster, Wilts, 1938–43; Fellow, Woodbrooke, Selly Oak Colls, Birmingham, 1943–45; Lectr in Church Hist., New Coll. (Sch. of Divinity), London Univ., 1945–77; Chm., Bd of Studies in Theol., Univ. of London, 1957–59; Dean, Faculty of Theol., 1960–64; FKC 1977. University Preacher: Leeds, 1950; Cambridge, 1958; London, 1968; Oxford, 1972, 1980. Lectures: Friends of Dr Williams's Library, 1951; Drew, New Coll., London, 1956; Hibbert, 1962; W. M. Llewelyn, Memorial Coll., Swansea, 1966; Charles Gore, Westminster Abbey, 1968; Owen Evans, Aberystwyth, 1968; F. D. Maurice, King's Coll., London, 1970; R. T. Jenkins, Bangor, 1976; Ethel M. Wood, London, 1978; Dr Williams Meml, Swansea, 1978. External Examiner: Belfast, Birmingham, Cambridge, Canterbury, Durham, Edinburgh, Leeds, McMaster, Manchester, Nottingham, Oxford, Salford, St Andrews, Wales. President: Friends' Hist. Soc., 1953; Congregational Hist. Soc., 1965–72; London Soc. for Study of Religion, 1966; Eccles. History Soc., 1972; United Reformed Church History Soc., 1972–77. Trustee, Dr Daniel Williams's Charity. A Vice-Pres., Hon. Soc. of Cymmrodorion, 1978–. Mem., Adv. Editorial Bd, Jl of Eccles. History, 1950–. For. Hon. Mem., Kerkhistorisch Gezelschap, 1981–. Hon. DD Wales, 1969. *Publications:* (ed) Letters of John Pinney 1679–1699, 1939; The Holy Spirit in Puritan Faith and Experience, 1946 (2nd edn 1947); The Holy Spirit and Ourselves, 1947 (2nd edn 1966); Studies in Christian Enthusiasm illustrated from Early Quakerism, 1948; (ed) Philip Doddridge 1702–1751: his contribution to English religion, 1951; Richard Baxter and Philip Doddridge: a study in a tradition, 1951; The Reality of Heaven, 1951; James Nayler: a fresh approach, 1954; (contrib.) Studies in Christian Social Commitment, 1954; Visible Saints: the Congregational Way 1640–1660, 1957; The Welsh Saints 1640–1660: Walter Cradock, Vavasor Powell, Morgan Llwyd, 1957; Christian Pacifism in History, 1958 (2nd edn 1971); (ed with Owen Chadwick) From Uniformity to Unity 1662–1962, 1962; Better Than Life: the lovingkindness of God, 1962; (contrib.) Man's Faith and Freedom: the theological influence of Jacobus Arminius, 1962; (contrib.) The Beginnings of Nonconformity, 1964; (contrib.) Choose your Weapons, 1964; Richard Baxter (Leaders of Religion), 1965; Howel Harris 1714–1773: the last enthusiast, 1965; The Puritan Spirit: essays and addresses, 1967; Congregationalists and Creeds, 1967; (contrib.) A Declaration of Faith (Congregational Church in England and Wales), 1967; The Significance of Trevecca College 1768–91, 1969; The Faith of Dante Alighieri, 1969; Christianity and Violence, 1972; (contrib.) Violence and Oppression: a Quaker Response, 1973; (contrib.) Christian Spirituality: essays in honour of Gordon Rupp, 1975; (contrib.) Der Pietismus in Gestalten und Wirkungen: Martin Schmidt zum 65 Geburtstag, 1975; New College, London and its Library, 1977; The Moment of Recognition: Luke as story-teller, 1978; contrib. Studies in Church History: Vol. VII, 1971; Vol. X, 1973; (contrib.) Pietismus und Réveil, 1978; (ed) Calendar of the Correspondence of Philip Doddridge, DD 1702–1751, 1979; (contrib.) Reformation Principle and Practice: essays in honour of A. G. Dickens, 1980; (contrib.) Philip Doddridge, Nonconformity and Northampton, 1981; Handlist of the Correspondence of Mercy Doddridge 1751–1790, 1984; (with J. van den Berg) Philip Doddridge and the Netherlands, 1986; contrib. Dict. of Nat. Biog., Encyc. Brit., Dict. d'Histoire et de Géog. Ecclés., Evang. Kirchenlexikon; articles and revs in Jl Eccles. History and Jl Theol Studies; *Festschrift:* Reformation, Conformity and Dissent: essays in honour of Geoffrey Nuttall, 1977. *Recreations:* walking, genealogy, motoring (as passenger), languages. *Address:* 35 Queen Mother Court, 151 Selly Wood Road, Birmingham B30 1TH. *T:* 021–472 2320. *Club:* Penn.

NUTTALL, Rt. Rev. Michael; *see* Natal, Bishop of.

NUTTALL, Sir Nicholas Keith Lillington, 3rd Bt, *cr* 1922; *b* 21 Sept. 1933; *s* of Lieut-Colonel Sir E. Keith Nuttall, 2nd Bt, RE (who died on active service, Aug. 1941), and Gytha Primrose Harrison (*d* 1967), *e d* of Sidney H. Burgess, of Heathfield, Bowdon, Cheshire; *S* father, 1941; *m* 1st, 1960, Rosemary Caroline (marr. diss. 1971), *e d* of Christopher York, *qv*; one *s* one *d*; 2nd, 1971, Julia Jill Beresford (marr. diss. 1975), *d* of Thomas Williamson; 3rd, 1975, Miranda, *d* of Richard St John Quarry and of Lady Mancroft; three *d*; 4th, 1983, Eugenie Marie Alicia, *e d* of William Thomas McWeeney; one *s*. *Educ:* Eton; Royal Military Academy, Sandhurst. Commissioned Royal Horse Guards, 1953; Captain, 1959; Major 1966; retd 1968. *Heir: s* Harry Nuttall, *b* 2 Jan. 1963. *Address:* Lyford Cay, PO Box N7776, Nassau, Bahamas. *Club:* White's.

NUTTER, Most Rev. Harold Lee; *see* Fredericton, Archbishop of.

NUTTGENS, Patrick John, CBE 1983; Director, Leeds Polytechnic, 1969–86; *b* 2 March 1930; 2nd *s* of late Joseph Edward Nuttgens, stained glass artist, and of Kathleen Mary Nuttgens (*née* Clarke); *m* 1954, Bridget Ann Badenoch; five *s* three *d. Educ*: Ratcliffe Coll., Leicester; Univ. of Edinburgh; Edinburgh Coll. of Art. MA, PhD, DA(Edin), ARIBA. Lectr, Dept of Architecture, Univ. of Edinburgh, 1956–61; Dir, Inst. of Advanced Architectural Studies, Univ. of York, 1962–68; Prof. of Architecture, Univ. of York, 1968–69; Hoffman Wood Prof. of Architecture, Univ. of Leeds, 1968–70. Member: Royal Commn on Ancient and Historical Monuments of Scotland, 1967–76; Ancient Monuments Bd, 1975–78; Royal Fine Art Commn, 1983–. Chairman: BBC North Region Adv. Council, 1970–75; BBC Continuing Educn Adv. Council, 1977–82; CNAA Cttee for Art and Design, 1981–84. Hon. Prof., York Univ., 1986–. Hon. Fellow, Leeds Polytechnic. DUniv: York, 1986; Open, 1986. *Publications*: Reginald Fairlie, a Scottish Architect, 1959; York, City Building Series, 1971; The Landscape of Ideas, 1972; (contrib.) Spirit of the Age, 1975; York: the continuing city, 1976; Leeds, Old and New, 1976; Leeds, 1979; Yorkshire section, Shell Book of English Villages, 1980; Pocket Guide to Architecture, 1980; (Gen. Editor) World's Great Architecture, 1980; (contrib.) Study Service, 1982; The Story of Architecture, 1983; regular contributor to jls on architecture, planning, education and environmental studies. *Recreations*: drawing, painting. *Address*: Roselea Cottage, Terrington, York YO6 4PP.

NUTTING, Rt. Hon. Sir (Harold) Anthony, 3rd Bt *cr* 1902; PC 1954; *b* 11 Jan. 1920; 3rd and *y s* of Sir Harold Stansmore Nutting, 2nd Bt, and Enid Hester Nina (*d* 1961), *d* of F. B. Homan-Mulock; *S* father, 1972; *m* 1st, 1941, Gillian Leonora (marr. diss., 1959), *d* of Edward J. Strutt, Hatfield Peverel, Essex; two *s* one *d*; 2nd, 1961, Anne Gunning, *d* of Arnold Parker, Cuckfield, Sussex. *Educ*: Eton; Trinity College, Cambridge. Leics. Yeo., 1939; invalided, 1940. In HM Foreign Service on special duties, 1940–45; MP (C) Melton Division of Leics, 1945–56, resigned. Chairman: Young Conservative and Unionist Movement, 1946; National Union of Conservative and Unionist Associations, 1950; Conservative National Executive Cttee, 1951. Parliamentary Under-Secretary of State for Foreign Affairs, 1951–54; Minister of State for Foreign Affairs, 1954–56, resigned. Leader, UK Delegn to UN General Assembly and to UN Disarmament Commn, 1954–56. *Publications*: I Saw for Myself, 1958; Disarmament, 1959; Europe Will Not Wait, 1960; Lawrence of Arabia, 1961; The Arabs, 1964; Gordon, Martyr and Misfit, 1966; No End of a Lesson, 1967; Scramble for Africa: the Great Trek to The Boer War, 1970; Nasser, 1972. *Recreation*: fishing. *Heir*: *s* John Grenfell Nutting [*b* 28 Aug. 1942; *m* 1973, Diane Countess Beatty; one *s* one *d*]. *Club*: Boodle's.

NUTTING, Prof. Jack, MA, ScD, PhD; FEng, FIM; Professor of Metallurgy, Houldsworth School of Applied Science, University of Leeds, since 1960; *b* 8 June 1924; *o s* of Edgar and Ethel Nutting, Mirfield, Yorks; *m* 1950, Thelma Kippax, *y d* of Tom and Florence Kippax, Morecambe, Lancs; one *s* two *d. Educ*: Mirfield Grammar School, Yorks; Univ. of Leeds. BSc Leeds, 1945; PhD Leeds, 1948; MA Cantab, 1952; ScD Cantab, 1967. Research at Cavendish Laboratory, Cambridge, 1948–49; University Demonstrator, 1949–54, University Lecturer, 1954–60, Department of Metallurgy, Cambridge University. President: Metals Soc., 1977–78; Instn of Metallurgists, 1980–81; Historical Metallurgy Soc., 1984–86. Awarded Beilby medal and prize, 1961; Hadfield medal and prize, 1964. Hon. DSc: Acad. of Mining and Metallurgy, Cracow, 1969; Moratuwa Univ., Sri Lanka, 1981. *Publications*: numerous papers in Jls of Iron and Steel Inst., Inst. of Metals and Metals Soc. *Recreations*: foreign travel, mountain walking. *Address*: St Mary's, 57 Weetwood Lane, Headingley, Leeds LS16 5NP. *T*: Leeds 751400.

NYAKYI, Anthony Balthazar; High Commissioner for Tanzania in London, since 1981; *b* 8 June 1936; *m* 1969, Margaret Nyakyi; two *s* two *d. Educ*: Makerere Coll., Univ. of E Africa (BA Gen.). Admin. Office, Prime Minister's Office and Min. of Educn, 1962–63; Head of Political Div., Foreign Service Office, 1963–68; Ambassador: to the Netherlands, 1968–70; to Fed. Republic of Germany, 1970–72; Principal Sec., Foreign Affairs, 1972–78; Principal Sec., Defence, 1978–80; High Comr to Zimbabwe, 1980–81. *Address*: Tanzania High Commission, 43 Hertford Street, W1Y 7TF. *T*: 01–499 8951.

NYE, Prof. John Frederick, FRS 1976; Melville Wills Professor of Physics, University of Bristol, since 1985 (Professor of Physics, since 1969); *b* 26 Feb. 1923; *s* of Haydn Percival Nye and Jessie Mary, *d* of Anderson Hague, painter; *m* 1953, Georgiana Wiebenson; one *s* two *d. Educ*: Stowe; King's Coll., Cambridge (Maj. Schol.; MA, PhD 1948). Research, Cavendish Laboratory, Cambridge, 1944–49; Univ. Demonstrator in Mineralogy and Petrology, Cambridge, 1949–51; Bell Telephone Laboratories, NJ, USA, 1952–53; Lectr, 1953, Reader, 1965, Univ. of Bristol; Visiting Professor: in Glaciology, California Inst. of Technol., 1959; of Applied Sciences, Yale Univ., 1964; of Geophysics, Univ. of Washington, 1973. President: Internat. Glaciological Soc., 1966–69; Internat. Commn of

Snow and Ice, 1971–75. For. Mem., Royal Swedish Acad. of Scis, 1977. Kirk Bryan Award, Geol. Soc. of Amer., 1961; Seligman Crystal, Internat. Glaciol Soc., 1969; Antarctic Service Medal, USA, 1974. *Publications*: Physical Properties of Crystals, 1957, rev. edn 1985; papers on physics of crystals, glaciology, and applications of catastrophe theory in scientific jls. *Address*: 45 Canynge Road, Bristol BS8 3LH. *T*: Bristol 733769.
See also P. H. Nye.

NYE, Ven. Nathaniel Kemp; retired; *b* 4 Nov. 1914; *s* of Charles Frederick and Evelyn Nye; *m* 1941, Rosa Jackson; two *s* one *d. Educ*: Merchant Taylors' Sch.; King's College London (AKC 1935); Cuddesdon College, Oxford. Ordained 1937 to St Peter's, St Helier Estate, Morden, Surrey; Chaplain RAF, 1940–46 (POW 1941–43; escaped from Italy at liberation); Rector, Holy Trinity, Clapham, 1946–54; Vicar, St Peter's, St Helier Estate, 1954–60; Vicar, All Saints, Maidstone (Parish Church), Canon, and Rural Dean, 1960–66; Tait Missioner, Canterbury Diocese, 1966–72; Archdeacon of Maidstone, 1972–79. Hon. Canon of Canterbury, 1960; Canon Emeritus, 1979; Archdeacon Emeritus, dio. Canterbury, 1982. *Recreations*: woodcraft, sailing, travel; family life! *Address*: Lees Cottage, Boughton Lees, Ashford, Kent. *T*: Ashford 26175.

NYE, Peter Hague; Reader in Soil Science, University of Oxford, since 1961; Fellow of St Cross College, since 1966 (Senior Fellow, 1982–83); *b* 16 Sept. 1921; *s* of Haydn Percival Nye and Jessie Mary (*née* Hague); *m* 1953, Phyllis Mary Quenault; one *s* two *d. Educ*: Charterhouse; Balliol Coll., Oxford (MA, BSc (Domus Exhibnr)); Christ's Coll., Cambridge. Agricl Chemist, Gold Coast, 1947–50; Lectr in Soil Science, University Coll. of Ibadan, Nigeria, 1950–52; Sen. Lectr in Soil Science, Univ. of Ghana, 1952–60; Res. Officer, Internat. Atomic Energy Agency, Vienna, 1960–61; Vis. Professor, Cornell Univ., 1974, 1981; Commonwealth Vis. Prof., Univ. of Western Aust., 1979. Pres., British Soc. Soil Science, 1968–69; Mem. Council, Internat. Soc. Soil Science, 1968–74. Governor, Nat. Vegetable Res. Station, 1972–. *Publications*: The Soil under Shifting Cultivation, 1961; Solute Movement in the Soil-Root System, 1977; articles, mainly in Jl of Soil Science, Plant and Soil, Jl of Agricl Science. *Recreations*: gardening; formerly cricket, tennis, squash. *Address*: Hewel Barn, Common Road, Beckley, Oxon OX3 9UR.
See also J. F. Nye.

NYE, Robert; writer; *b* 15 March 1939; *s* of Oswald William Nye and Frances Dorothy Weller; *m* 1st, 1959, Judith Pratt (marr. diss. 1967); three *s*; 2nd, 1968, Aileen Campbell; one *d. Educ*: Southend High School, Essex. Freelance writer, 1961–. FRSL 1977. *Publications*: poetry: Juvenilia 1, 1961; Juvenilia 2, 1963 (Eric Gregory Award, 1963); Darker Ends, 1969; Divisions on a Ground, 1976; fiction: Doubtfire, 1967; Tales I Told My Mother, 1969; Falstaff, 1976 (The Guardian Fiction Prize, 1976; Hawthornden Prize, 1977); Merlin, 1978; Faust, 1980; The Voyage of the Destiny, 1982; The Facts of Life and Other Fictions, 1983; plays: (with Bill Watson) Sawney Bean, 1970; The Seven Deadly Sins: A Mask, 1974; Penthesilea, Fugue and Sisters, 1976; children's fiction: Taliesin, 1966; March Has Horse's Ears, 1966; Wishing Gold, 1970; Poor Pumpkin, 1971; Out of the World and Back Again, 1977; Once Upon Three Times, 1978; The Bird of the Golden Land, 1980; Harry Pay the Pirate, 1981; Three Tales, 1983; translation: Beowulf, 1968; editions: A Choice of Sir Walter Ralegh's Verse, 1972; William Barnes: Selected Poems, 1973; A Choice of Swinburne's Verse, 1973; The English Sermon 1750–1850, 1976; The Faber Book of Sonnets, 1976; PEN New Poetry 1, 1986; contribs to British and American periodicals. *Recreation*: gambling. *Address*: 2 Westbury Crescent, Wilton, Cork, Ireland.

NYERERE, Julius Kambarage; President, United Republic of Tanzania (formerly Tanganyika and Zanzibar), 1964–85; President, Tanganyika African National Union, since 1954; Chairman, Chama cha Mapinduzi (The Revolutionary Party) (born of merger between mainland's TANU and Zanzibar Afro-Shiraz Party), since 1977; Chancellor, University of Dar es Salaam, since 1970; *b* 1922; *m* 1953, Maria Magige; five *s* two *d. Educ*: Tabora Secondary School; Makerere University College; Edinburgh University (MA). Began as Teacher; became President African Association, Dar es Salaam, 1953; formed Tanganyika African National Union, left teaching and campaigned for Nationalist Movement, 1954; addressed Trusteeship Council, 1955, and Cttee of UN Gen. Assembly, 1956. MLC Tanganyika, July-Dec. 1957, resigned in protest; elected Mem. for E Prov. in first elections, 1958, for Dar es Salaam, 1960; Chief Minister, 1960; Prime Minister of Tanganyika, 1961–62; President, Tanganyika Republic, 1962–64. Chm., OAU, 1984–. First Chancellor, Univ. of East Africa, 1963–70. Holds hon. degrees. *Publications*: Freedom and Unity-Uhuru Na Umoja, 1966; Freedom and Socialism-Uhuru na Ujamaa, 1969; Essays on Socialism, 1969; Freedom and Development, 1973; Swahili trans of Julius Caesar and The Merchant of Venice, 1969. *Address*: c/o State House, Dar es Salaam, United Republic of Tanzania.

O

OAKELEY, Sir (Edward) Atholl, 7th Bt *cr* 1790; author; *b* 31 May 1900; *s* of late Major E. F. Oakeley, South Lancashire Regiment, and late Everilde A. Oakeley, *d* of Henry Beaumont; *S* cousin (Sir Charles Richard Andrew Oakeley, 6th Bt), 1959; *m* 1st, 1922, Ethyl Felice O'Coffey (marr. diss.); 2nd, (Patricia) Mabel Mary (*née* Birtchnell) (marr. diss.); one *s*; 3rd, Doreen (*née* Wells) (marr. diss.); 4th, 1960, Shirley Church; one *d*. *Educ:* Clifton and Sandhurst. Lieutenant, Oxfordshire and Buckinghamshire Light Infantry, 1919–23; then Chief Contact to late Sir Charles Higham in Advertising; Captain, Amateur International Wrestling Team, 1928–29; Heavyweight Wrestling Champion of Europe, 1932; Heavyweight Wrestling Champion of Gt Britain, 1930–35; Manager to World Heavyweight Wrestling Champion, Jack Sherry, 1935–39; Promoter of Championship Wrestling, Harringay Arena, 1949–54. Hon. Mem., Mark Twain Soc. of America, 1977; Hon. Chm., Anglo-American Lorna Doone Soc.,1985. *Publications:* The Facts on which R. D. Blackmore based Lorna Doone, 1969; Blue Blood on the Mat, 1971. *Recreations:* cricket; hunting; athletics; sailing; wrestling; boxing; weight-lifting. *Heir: s* John Digby Atholl Oakeley [*b* 27 Nov. 1932; *m* 1958, Maureen, *d* of John and Helen Cox, Hamble, Hants; one *s* one *d*]. *Address:* Nomad, Lynton, Devon.

See also M. Oakeley.

OAKELEY, Mary, MA Oxon; Headmistress, St Felix School, Southwold, 1958–78; *b* 2 April 1913; *d* of Maj. Edward Francis Oakeley, S Lancs Regt, and Everilde Anne (*née* Beaumont). *Educ:* St John's Bexhill-on-Sea; St Hilda's Coll., Oxford. MA Hons History. Asst Mistress: St James's, West Malvern, 1935–38; St George's, Ascot, 1938–39; Headmistress, Craighead Diocesan Sch., Timaru, NZ, 1940–55; Head of American Section, La Châtelainie, St Blaise, Switzerland, 1956–58. *Recreations:* gardening, embroidery. *Address:* 8 Newland Close, Eynsham, Oxon. *T:* Oxford 880759. *Club:* Royal Over-Seas League.

See also Sir Atholl Oakeley, Bt.

OAKES, Sir Christopher, 3rd Bt, *cr* 1939; *b* 10 July 1949; *s* of Sir Sydney Oakes, 2nd Bt, and Greta (*d* 1977), *yr d* of Gunnar Victor Hartmann, Copenhagen, Denmark; *S* father, 1966; *m* 1978, Julie Dawn, *d* of Donovan Franklin Cowan, Regina, Canada; one *s* one *d*. *Educ:* Bredon, Tewkesbury; Georgia Mil. Acad., USA. *Heir: s* Victor Oakes, *b* 6 March 1983.

OAKES, Rt. Hon. Gordon James; PC 1979; MP (Lab) Halton, since 1983 (Widnes, Sept. 1971–1983); *b* 22 June 1931; *o s* of late James Oakes and Florence (*née* Hewitt), Widnes, Lancs; *m* 1952, Esther O'Neill, *e d* of late Councillor Joseph O'Neill; three *s*. *Educ:* Wade Deacon Gram. Sch., Widnes; Univ. of Liverpool. BA (Hon.) English, 1952; Admitted Solicitor, 1956. Entered Widnes Borough Council, 1952 (Mayor, 1964–65). Chm. Widnes Constituency Labour Party, 1953–58; contested (Lab): Bebington, 1959; Moss Side (Manchester) by-election, 1961; MP (Lab) Bolton West, 1964–70; PPS, Home Office, 1966–67, DES, 1967–70; Front Bench Opposition spokesman on local govt and the environment, 1970–74; Parly Under-Secretary of State: DoE, 1974–76; Dept of Energy, 1976; Minister of State, DES, 1976–79; Front Bench Opposition spokesman on Environment, 1979–83. British Deleg., NATO Parliamentarians, 1967–70; Member: Select Cttee on Race Relations, 1969–70; Executive, NW Region of Labour Party, 1971–73; Exec. Cttee, CPA, 1979–; Chm., All-Party Energy Efficiency Gp, 1980–; Vice-Chm., All-Party Chem. Industry Gp, 1982–; Jt Chm., All-Party Gp for the Licensing Trade, 1986–. Vice-President: Rural District Councils Assoc., 1972–74; County Councils Assoc., 1982–; Environmental Officers' Assoc. (formerly Inst. of Public Health Inspectors), 1973–; Building Societies Assoc., 1984–; Jt Chm., Nat. Waste Management Adv. Council, 1974–76. *Publications:* The Management of Higher Education in the Maintained Sector, 1978; various articles. *Recreations:* conversation, motoring with the family, caravanning, maps. *Address:* Upton Bridle Path, Widnes, Cheshire.

OAKES, Joseph Stewart; barrister-at-law; *b* 7 Jan. 1919; *s* of Laban Oakes and Mary Jane Oakes; *m* 1950, Irene May Peasnall. *Educ:* Royal Masonic Sch., Bushey; Stretford Grammar Sch.; Manchester Univ., 1937–40 (BA Hons). Royal Signals, 1940–48, Captain. Called to Bar, Inner Temple, 1948; practised on Northern Circuit, 1948–; a Recorder, 1975–82. *Recreations:* horticulture, photography, music. *Address:* 38 Langley Road, Sale, Greater Manchester M33 5AY. *T:* 061–962 2068; 28 St John Street, Manchester M3 4DJ. *T:* 061–834 8418.

OAKESHOTT, Michael Joseph, FBA 1966; MA; Professor Emeritus, University of London, 1969; Fellow of Gonville and Caius College, Cambridge, since 1925; *b* 11 Dec. 1901; *s* of Joseph Francis Oakeshott and Frances Maude Hellicar. *Educ:* St George's School, Harpenden; Gonville and Caius College, Cambridge. Fellow, Nuffield College, Oxford, 1949–50; University Prof. of Political Science at LSE, Univ. of London, 1951–69. Served in British Army, 1940–45. Muirhead Lecturer, Univ. of Birmingham, 1953. *Publications:* Experience and its Modes, 1933, repr. 1986; A Guide to the Classics (with G. T. Griffith), 1936, 1947; Social and Political Doctrines of Contemporary Europe, 1939; Hobbes's Leviathan, 1946; The Voice of Poetry in the Conversation of Mankind, 1959; Rationalism in Politics and other Essays, 1962; Hobbes on Civil Association, 1975; On Human Conduct, 1975; On History, 1983. *Address:* Victoria Cottage, Acton, Langton Matravers, Swanage, Dorset.

OAKESHOTT, Sir Walter (Fraser), Kt 1980; MA; FBA 1971; FSA; Hon. LLD (St Andrews); Hon. DLitt (East Anglia); Rector of Lincoln College, Oxford, 1953–72, Hon. Fellow, 1972; *b* 11 Nov. 1903; *s* of Walter Field Oakeshott, MD, and Kathleen Fraser; *m* 1928, Noël Rose (*d* 1976), *d* of R. O. Moon, MD, FRCP; twin *s* two *d*. *Educ:* Tonbridge; Balliol Coll., Oxford. Class. Mods 1924; Lit. Hum. 1926; Hon. Fellow, 1974. Assistant Master, Bec School, SW17, 1926–27; Assistant Master Merchant Taylors', 1927–30; Kent Education Office, 1930–31; Assistant Master Winchester College, 1931–38; released for 15 months (1936–37) for membership of Pilgrim Trust Unemployment Enquiry; High Master of St Paul's School, 1939–46; Headmaster of Winchester College, 1946–54. Vice-Chancellor, Oxford University, 1962–64; Pro-Vice-Chancellor, 1964–66. President, Bibliographical Society, 1966–68. Trustee, Pilgrim Trust, 1949–76. Rhind Lecturer, Edinburgh Univ., 1956. Master, Skinners' Co., 1960–61. *Publications:* Men Without Work (joint), 1938; The Artists of the Winchester Bible, 1945; The Mosaics of Rome, Fourth to Fourteenth Centuries, 1967; Sigena Wall Paintings, 1972; The Two Winchester Bibles, 1981; various semi-popular books on literature and medieval art. *Recreations:* pictures, books. *Address:* The Old School House, Eynsham, Oxford. *Club:* Roxburghe.

OAKHAM, Archdeacon of; *see* Fernyhough, Ven. B.

OAKLEY, Brian Wynne, CBE 1981; Deputy Secretary, Department of Trade and Industry, and Director, Alvey Programme, since 1983; *b* 10 Oct. 1927; *s* of Bernard and Edna Oakley; *m* 1953, Marian Elizabeth (*née* Woolley); one *s* three *d*. *Educ:* Exeter Coll., Oxford. MA. FInstP, FBCS. Telecommunication Res. Establishment, 1950; Head, Industrial Applications Unit, RRE, 1966–69; Head, Computer Systems Branch, Min. of Technology, 1969–72; Head, Res. Requirements Div., DTI, 1972–78; Sec., SRC, later SERC, 1978–83. *Recreations:* theatre, sailing. *Address:* 120 Reigate Road, Ewell, Epsom, Surrey KT17 3BX. *T:* 01–393 4096.

OAKLEY, Christopher John; Editor, Liverpool Echo, since 1983; Director, Liverpool Daily Post and Echo Ltd, since 1984; *b* 11 Nov. 1941; *s* of late Ronald Oakley and of Joyce Oakley; *m* 1962, Linda Margaret Viney; one *s* two *d*. *Educ:* Skinners' School, Tunbridge Wells. Kent and Sussex Courier, 1959; Bromley and Kentish Times, 1963; Kent and Sussex Courier, 1963; Evening Argus, Brighton, 1966; Evening Echo, Basildon, 1969; Evening Post, Leeds, 1970; Dep. Editor, Yorkshire Post, 1976; Editor, Lancashire Evening Post, 1981; Dir, Lancashire Evening Post, 1981–83. *Recreations:* farming, learning about wine, driving too fast.

OAKLEY, John Davidson, CBE 1981; DFC 1944; Chairman: Grosvenor Development Capital, since 1981; Robert Jenkins (Holdings) Ltd, since 1983 (Deputy Chairman, 1978–83); Grosvenor Technology Ltd, 1986; Director: Ionian Securities Ltd, since 1978; Gardners Transformers Ltd, since 1982 (Deputy Chairman, since 1984); Member, British Overseas Trade Advisory Council, since 1977; *b* 15 June 1921; *s* of Richard Oakley and Nancy Davidson; *m* 1943, Georgina Mary Hare; two *s*. *Educ:* Green Lane Sch. Joined Briggs Motor Bodies Ltd, 1937. Served War in RAF, 1941–46: commissioned 1942; Flt Lt 1943; actg Sqdn Leader 1944; apptd to Air Min. Directorate Staff, 1945. Engrg Buyer, Briggs Motor Bodies Ltd, 1946–53; Dep. Purchase Manager, Body Div., Ford Motor Co. Ltd, 1953–56; Production Dir/General Manager, Standard Triumph (Liverpool) Ltd, until 1962; Managing Director: Copeland & Jenkins Ltd, 1963–71; R. Woolf & Co. Ltd, 1964–67; Gp Man. Dir, L. Sterne & Co., 1967–69; Chairman: General Electric & Mechanical Systems Ltd, 1970–73; Berwick Timpo Ltd, 1970–82; Edgar Allen Balfour Ltd, 1974–79; Australian British Trade Assoc., 1977–81 (Vice-Pres., British Council, 1981–); BOTB Adv. Gp Australia and NZ, 1977–81; Director: Blairs Ltd, 1976–82; Eagle & Globe Steel Ltd, NSW, 1978–79; Nexos Office Systems Ltd, 1981–82; Isis Industrial Services plc, 1982–; Beau Brummel Ltd, 1972–85. Oxford Univ. Business Summer School: Dir for 1978; Mem., Steering Cttee, 1981–, Chm., 1984–. Cons. Mem., Essex CC, 1982–85. Member: Glovers' Co.; Cutlers' Co. in Hallamshire; Inst. of British Carriage & Automobile Manufacturers. CBIM; FIPS. FRSA. *Recreations:* golf, tennis, walking, bridge. *Address:* 25 Manor Links, Bishop's Stortford, Herts CM23 5RA. *T:* Bishop's Stortford 507552. *Clubs:* Reform, Royal Air Force; Bishop's Stortford Golf (Bishop's Stortford, Herts).

OAKLEY, Wilfrid George, MD, FRCP; Hon. Consulting Physician, King's College Hospital, since 1971; Vice President, British Diabetic Association, since 1971; *b* 23 Aug. 1905; *s* of late Rev. Canon G. D. Oakley and Mrs Oakley; *m* 1931, Hermione Violet Wingate-Saul; one *s*. *Educ:* Durham School; Gonville and Caius College, Cambridge; St Bartholomew's Hospital. Tancred studentship in Physic, Gonville and Caius Coll., 1923; Bentley Prize and Baly Research Schol., St Bart's Hosp., 1933. Formerly Physician i/c Diabetic Dept, King's College Hosp., 1957–70. Examr, Cambridge and Glasgow Univs. MD (Hon. Mention) Cantab 1934; FRCP 1942. FRSocMed; Pres., Med. Soc., London, 1962; Mem. Assoc. of Physicians of Great Britain; Vice-Pres., British Diabetic Assoc., 1971. *Publications:* (jtly) Clinical Diabetes and its Biochemical Basis, 1968; Diabetes and its Management, 1973, 3rd edn 1978; scientific articles and chapters in various text-books on diabetes. *Address:* 149 Harley Street, W1. *T:* 01–935 4444.

OAKSEY, 2nd Baron *cr* 1947 (properly **TREVETHIN,** 4th Baron *cr* 1921, **AND OAKSEY); John Geoffrey Tristram Lawrence,** OBE 1985; JP; Racing Correspondent to Daily Telegraph since 1957, to Horse and Hound since 1959 and to Sunday Telegraph since 1960; racing commentator for ITV, since 1970; Director, HTV, since 1980; *b* 21 March 1929; *o s* of 1st Baron Oaksey and 3rd Baron Trevethin and Marjorie (*d* 1984), *d* of late Commander Charles N. Robinson, RN; *S* father, 1971; *m* 1959, Victoria Mary, *d* of late Major John Dennistoun, MBE; one *s* one *d*. *Educ:* Horris Hill; Eton; New College, Oxford (BA); Yale Law School. JP Malmesbury, 1978. *Publications:* History of Steeplechasing (jointly), 1967; The Story of Mill Reef, 1974. *Recreations:* skiing, riding. *Heir: s* Hon. Patrick John Tristram Lawrence, *b* 29 June 1960. *Address:* Hill Farm, Oaksey, Malmesbury, Wilts SN16 9HS. *T:* Crudwell 303; 20 Aldebert Terrace, SW8. *T:* 01–582 7502. *Club:* Brooks's.

See also H. S. L. Dundas.

OAKSHOTT, Hon. Sir Anthony (Hendrie), 2nd Bt *cr* 1959; *b* 10 Oct. 1929; *s* of Baron Oakshott, MBE (Life Peer), and Joan (*d* 1986), *d* of Marsden Withington; *S* to baronetcy of father, 1975; *m* 1965, Mrs Valerie de Pret-Roose (marr. diss. 1981), *d* of Jack Vlasto. *Educ:* Rugby. *Heir: b* Hon. Michael Arthur John Oakshott [*b* 12 April 1932; *m* 1957, Christina Rose Methuen, *d* of late Thomas Banks; three *s*]. *Address:* 42 Eaton Square, SW1. *T:* 01-235 2107. *Club:* White's.

OATES, Prof. (Edward Ernest) David (Michael), FSA; FBA 1974; Professor of Western Asiatic Archaeology, University of London, 1969–82; *b* 25 Feb. 1927; *s* of Thomas Oates and Dora B. Strike; *m* 1956, Joan Louise Lines; one *s* two *d. Educ:* Callington County Sch.; Oundle Sch.; Trinity Coll., Cambridge (BA, MA). Fellow of Trinity Coll., Cambridge, 1951–65; Director, British School of Archaeology in Iraq, 1965–69. Director, British Archaeological Expedition to Tell Brak, Syria, 1976–. FSA 1954. *Publications:* Studies in the Ancient History of N Iraq, 1968; (with J. Oates) The Rise of Civilisation, 1976; contribs to The Dark Ages, ed D. Talbot Rice, 1965; Papers of the British School at Rome, Iraq, etc. *Recreations:* history, carpentry. *Address:* 86 High Street, Barton, Cambridge CB3 7BG. *T:* Comberton 2273.
See also Sir Thomas Oates.

OATES, Rev. Canon John; Rector of St Bride's Church, Fleet Street, since 1984; *b* 14 May 1930; *s* of John and Ethel Oates; *m* 1962, Sylvia Mary, *d* of Herbert Charles and Ada Harris; three *s* one *d. Educ:* Queen Elizabeth School, Wakefield; SSM, Kelham. Curate, Eton College Mission, Hackney Wick, 1957–60; Development Officer, C of E Youth Council and mem. staff, Bd of Education, 1960–64; Development Sec., C of E Council for Commonwealth Settlement, 1964–65, Gen. Sec. 1965–70; Sec., C of E Cttee on Migration and Internat. Affairs, Bd for Social Responsibility, 1968–71; Vicar of Richmond, Surrey, 1970–84; RD, Richmond and Barnes, 1979–84. Commissary: of Archbishop of Perth and Bishop of NW Australia, 1968–; to Archbishop of Jerusalem, 1969–75; to Bishop of Bunbury, 1969–. Hon. Canon, Bunbury, 1969–. Chaplain: Inst. of Journalists, 1984–; Inst. of Public Relations, 1984–. Freeman, City of London, 1985. *Recreations:* walking, exploring, squash. *Address:* St Bride's Rectory, Fleet Street, EC4Y 8AU. *T:* 01-353 1301. *Clubs:* Royal Commonwealth Society, Publicity (Hon. Chaplain), Duffers.

OATES, John Claud Trewinard, FBA 1976; Emeritus Reader in Historical Bibliography, University of Cambridge; Emeritus Fellow of Darwin College, Cambridge; *b* 24 June 1912; *s* of Claud Albert Oates and Clarissa Alberta Wakeham; *m* 1960, Helen Cooke (*née* Lister). *Educ:* Crypt Sch., Gloucester; Trinity Coll., Cambridge (BA 1935, MA 1938). Sch. of Tank Technol., Mil. Coll. of Science, 1941–46. Univ. of Cambridge: Walston Student, 1935; Asst Under-Librarian, 1936, Under-Librarian, 1949, Dep. Librarian, 1975, Acting Librarian, 1979–80, Univ. Library; Sandars Reader in Bibliography, 1952, 1965. Pres., Bibliograph. Soc., 1970–72; Pres., Cambridge Bibliograph. Soc., 1978–81; Trustee, Laurence Sterne Trust, 1968–. Editor, The Library (Trans Bibliograph. Soc.), 1953–60. *Publications:* A Catalogue of the Fifteenth-Century Printed Books in the University Library, Cambridge, 1954; (contrib.) The English Library before 1700 (ed F. Wormald and C. E. Wright), 1958; Shandyism and Sentiment 1760–1800 (bicentenary lecture), 1968; Cambridge University Library: a history from the beginnings to the Copyright Act of Queen Anne, 1986; contrib. bibliograph. jls. *Recreation:* walking the dog. *Address:* 144 Thornton Road, Cambridge. *T:* Cambridge 276653.

OATES, Sir Thomas, Kt 1972; CMG 1962; OBE 1958 (MBE 1946); Governor and Commander-in-Chief of St Helena, 1971–76; *b* 5 November 1917; *er s* of late Thomas Oates, Wadebridge, Cornwall; unmarried. *Educ:* Callington Grammar School, Cornwall; Trinity College, Cambridge (MA). Mathematical Tripos (Wrangler). Admiralty Scientific Staff, 1940–46; HMS Vernon, Minesweeping Section, 1940–42; British Admiralty Delegn, Washington, DC, 1942–46; Temp. Lieut, RNVR. Colonial Administrative Service, Nigeria, 1948–55; seconded to HM Treasury, 1953–55; Adviser to UK Delegn to UN Gen. Assembly, 1954. Financial Sec. to Govt of: British Honduras, 1955–59, Aden, 1959–63; Dep. High Comr, Aden, 1963–67; Permanent Sec., Gibraltar, 1968–69; Dep. Governor, Gibraltar, 1969–71. *Recreations:* photography, walking. *Address:* Tristan, Trevone, Padstow, Cornwall. *Clubs:* East India, Devonshire, Sports and Public Schools, Royal Commonwealth Society.
See also E. E. D. M. Oates.

OATLEY, Brian; County Education Officer, Kent, since 1984; *b* 1 June 1935; *s* of Arnold and Vivian Oatley. *Educ:* Bolton School; King's College, Cambridge. BA, PGCE. Teacher, North Manchester Grammar School, 1959–64; Assistant, Senior Assistant and Deputy County Education Officer, Kent County Council, 1964–84. Member: RHS; Kent Trust for Nature Conservation; Weald Singers, Maidstone. *Recreations:* music, travel, gardening. *Address:* Kent County Education Offices, Springfield, Maidstone, Kent.

OATLEY, Sir Charles (William), Kt 1974; OBE 1956; MA; FRS 1969, FEng, FIEE, FIEEE; Professor of Electrical Engineering, University of Cambridge, 1960–71, now Emeritus; Fellow of Trinity College, Cambridge, since 1945; *b* 14 Feb. 1904; *s* of William Oatley and Ada Mary Dorrington; *m* 1930, (Dorothy) Enid West; two *s. Educ:* Bedford Modern Sch.; St John's Coll., Cambridge. Demonstrator, later lecturer, Dept of Physics, KCL, 1927–39. Min. of Supply, Radar Research and Development Establishment, 1939–45. Actg Superintendent in charge of scientific work, 1944–45. Lecturer, later Reader, Dept of Engineering, Cambridge Univ., 1945–60. Director, English Electric Valve Company, 1966–85. Member: Council, Inst. of Electrical Engineers, 1954–56, 1961–64 (Chm. of Radio Section, 1954–55); Council, Royal Society, 1970–72. FEng 1976. Hon. Fellow, Royal Microscopical Soc., 1970; FKC 1976; Foreign Associate, Nat. Acad. of Engineering, USA, 1979. Hon. DSc: Heriot-Watt, 1974; Bath, 1977. Achievement Award, Worshipful Co. of Scientific Instrument Makers, 1966; Duddell Medal, Inst. of Physics and Physical Soc., 1969; Royal Medal, Royal Soc., 1969; Faraday Medal, IEE, 1970; Mullard Award, Royal Soc., 1973; James Alfred Ewing Medal, ICE, 1981; Distinguished Scientist Award, Electron Microscopy Soc. of America, 1984. *Publications:* Wireless Receivers, 1932; The Scanning Electron Microscope, 1972; Electric and Magnetic Fields, 1976; papers in scientific and technical journals. *Recreation:* gardening. *Address:* 16 Porson Road, Cambridge. *T:* Cambridge 356194. *Club:* Athenæum.
See also M. C. Oatley.

OATLEY, Michael Charles, OBE 1975; HM Diplomatic Service; Counsellor, Foreign and Commonwealth Office, since 1984; *b* 18 Oct. 1935; *s* of Sir Charles Oatley, *qv* and Lady Oatley (*née* Enid West); *m* 1965, Pippa Howden; two *s* one *d. Educ:* The Leys Sch.; Trinity Coll., Cambridge. FO, 1959–61; seconded to CO, Nairobi and Kampala, 1961–62; FO, 1962–63; Lome, 1963–65; FO, 1965–66; Kampala, 1966–68; Accra, 1968–69; FCO, 1969–73; seconded to NI Office, Belfast, 1973–75; Hong Kong, 1975–77; FCO, 1977–81; Counsellor, Harare (formerly Salisbury), 1981–84. *Address:* c/o Foreign and Commonwealth Office, SW1A 2AH.

OBASANJO, Gen. Olusegun; Nigerian Head of State, Head of the Federal Military Government and Commander-in-Chief of the Armed Forces, Nigeria, 1976–79; Member, Advisory Council of State, since 1979; farmer; *b* Abeokuta, Ogun State, Nigeria, 5 March 1937; *m*; two *s* three *d. Educ:* Abeokuta Baptist High Sch.; Mons Officers' Cadet Sch., England. Entered Nigerian Army, 1958; commission, 1959; served in Zaire (then, the Congo), 1960. Comdr, Engrg Corps, 1963; Comdr of 2nd (Rear) Div. at Ibadan; GOC 3rd Inf. Div., 1969; Comdr, 3rd Marine Commando Div.; took surrender of forces of Biafra, in Nigerian Civil War, 1969–70; Comdr Engrg Corps, 1970–75. Political post as Federal Comr for Works and Housing, Jan.-July 1975. Chief of Staff, Supreme HQ, July 1975–Feb. 1976. Mem., Internat. Indep. Commn on Disarmament and Security. Part-time Associate, Univ. of Ibadan. *Publication:* My Command (autobiog.), 1980. *Recreations:* squash, table tennis, billiards, snooker. *Address:* PO Box 2286, Abeokuta, Nigeria.

OBASI, Godwin Olu Patrick; Secretary-General, World Meteorological Organization, since 1984; *b* 24 Dec. 1933; *s* of Albert B. Patrick Obasi and Rhoda A. Akande; *m* 1967, Winifred O. Akande; one *s* five *d. Educ:* McGill Univ., Canada (BSc Hons Maths and Physics); Massachusetts Inst. of Technology (MSc, DSc Meteorology). Mem., Inst. of Statisticians. University of Nairobi: WMO/UNDP Expert and Sen. Lectr, 1967–74; Acting Head of Dept of Meteorology, 1972–73; Dean, Faculty of Science, Prof. of Meteorology and Chm., Dept of Meteorology, 1974–76; Adviser in Meteorology to Nigerian Govt and Head of Nigerian Inst. for Met. Res. and Training, 1976–78; Dir, Educn and Training Dept, WMO, 1978–83. Gold plaque merit award medal, Czechoslovakian Acad. of Sciences, 1986. *Publications:* numerous contribs to learned jls. *Recreations:* tennis, gardening. *Address:* Chemin en Vuaracaux, 1297 Founex, Vaud, Switzerland. *T:* (022) 76 28 25.

OBEEGADOO, (Louis) Claude; High Commissioner for Mauritius in UK, 1982–83; *b* 12 June 1928; *m* 1955, Primerose Moutousamy; two *s. Educ:* London University. BSc 1955. Teacher, 1948–73, Manager, 1952–82, Trinity College Group, Mauritius. *Publication:* The Pupil and the Total Environment, 1977. *Recreations:* community service, reading, yoga. *Address:* Royal Road, Moka, Mauritius. *Club:* Rotary (Port Louis, Mauritius).

O'BEIRNE, Cornelius Banahan, CBE 1964; QC; consultant, since 1986; Assistant Director (Commonwealth), British Institute of International and Comparative Law, since 1978; *b* 9 September 1915; *e s* of late Captain C. B. O'Beirne, OBE; *m* 1949, Ivanka, *d* of Miloc Tupanjanin, Belgrade; one *s* one *d. Educ:* Stonyhurst Coll. Solicitor (Eng.), 1940. Served War, 1940–46; Maj. RA, Eur., Mid. E; Polit. Adviser's Office, Brit. Emb., Athens, 1945–46. Colonial Office, 1947–48. Called to Bar, Lincoln's Inn, 1952. Crown Counsel: Nigeria, 1949–53; High Commn Territories, SA, 1953–59; Solicitor-Gen., 1959; Attorney-General, High Commission Territories, South Africa, 1961–64; Counsellor (Legal), British Embassy, SA, 1964–65; Senior Legal Asst, Lord Chancellor's Office, 1966–71 (seconded as Attorney-Gen., Gibraltar, 1966–70); Council on Tribunals, 1971–78. QC: Basutoland, Bechuanaland and Swaziland, 1962; Gibraltar, 1967. Member: RIIA; Justice; Plowden Soc.; Commonwealth Parly Assoc. *Publications:* Laws of Gibraltar, rev. edn 1968; contribs to jls. *Recreations:* reading, photography. *Address:* Nanhoran Cottage, Claremont Lane, Esher, Surrey.

O'BEIRNE RANELAGH, John, (John Ranelagh), PhD; Commissioning Editor, Channel Four Television Company, since 1981 (Secretary to the Board, 1981–83); *b* 3 Nov. 1947; *o s* of James O'Beirne Ranelagh and Elaine Lambert O'Beirne Ranelagh; *m* 1974, Elizabeth Grenville, *y d* of Sir William Hawthorne, *qv. Educ:* St Christopher's Sch.; Cambridgeshire Coll. of Arts and Technology; Christ Church, Oxford (MA); Eliot Coll., Univ. of Kent (PhD). Chase Manhattan Bank, 1970; Campaign Dir, Outset Housing Assoc., 1971; Univ. of Kent Studentship, 1972–74; BBC TV, 1974; Conservative Res. Dept, 1975–79; Associate Producer, Ireland: a television history, BBC TV, 1979–81. Member: Political Cttee, UNA, 1978–; Exec. Cttee, Broadcasting Research Unit, 1984–. Governor, Daneford Sch., 1977–81. *Publications:* Science, Education and Industry, 1978; (with Richard Luce) Human Rights and Foreign Policy, 1978; Ireland: an illustrated history, 1981; A Short History of Ireland, 1983; The Agency: the rise and decline of the CIA, 1986. *Recreations:* old Bentley motor cars, quarter horses, Ireland. *Address:* The Garner Cottages, Mill Way, Grantchester, Cambridge. *Club:* Travellers'.

OBOLENSKY, Sir Dimitri, Kt 1984; MA, PhD, DLitt; FBA 1974; FSA; FRHistS; Emeritus Professor, University of Oxford (Professor of Russian and Balkan History, 1961–85, and Student of Christ Church, 1950–85); *b* Petrograd, 1 April 1918; *s* of late Prince Dimitri Obolensky and late Countess Mary Shuvalov; *m* 1947, Elisabeth Lopukhin. *Educ:* Lycée Pasteur, Paris; Trinity College, Cambridge. Cambridge: 1st Class Modern and Medieval Langs Tripos Parts I and II; Amy Mary Preston Read and Allen Schol.; Fellow of Trinity Coll., 1942–48; Faculty Asst Lecturer, 1944; Lecturer, Trinity Coll., 1945; Univ. Lecturer in Slavonic Studies, 1946; Reader in Russian and Balkan Medieval History in Univ. of Oxford, 1949–61. Vis. Schol., Dumbarton Oaks Center for Byzantine Studies, Harvard Univ., 1952, 1964, 1977, Vis. Fellow, 1981–82; Vis. Prof. of Russian History, Yale Univ., 1957; Vis. Prof. of European Hist., Univ. of California, Berkeley, 1973; Davis Prof. in Slavic Studies, Wellesley Coll., Mass, 1982; Vis. Mellon Prof., Inst. for Advanced Study, Princeton, 1985–86; Birkbeck Lecturer in Ecclesiastical History, Trinity Coll., Cambridge, 1961; Raleigh Lectr, British Acad., 1981. Vice-Pres., British Acad., 1983–85. Gen. Sec. Thirteenth Internat. Congress of Byzantine Studies, Oxford, 1966; British Co-Chairman: Anglo-Bulgarian Conf. of Historians, 1973; Anglo-Romanian Conf. of Historians, 1975. Corresp. Mem., Acad. of Athens. Hon. Dr Univ. Paris, Sorbonne, 1980. *Publications:* The Bogomils, A Study in Balkan Neo-Manichaeism, 1948; (ed) The Penguin Book of Russian Verse, 1962; (jointly) The Christian Centuries, vol. 2: The Middle Ages, 1969; Byzantium and the Slavs, 1971; The Byzantine Commonwealth, 1971; (ed jtly) Companion to Russian Studies, 3 vols, 1976–80; The Byzantine Inheritance of Eastern Europe, 1982. *Address:* 29 Belsyre Court, Woodstock Road, Oxford. *T:* Oxford 56496. *Club:* Athenæum.

OBOTE, Dr (Apollo) Milton; President of Uganda and Minister of Foreign Affairs, 1980–85; former Leader, Uganda People's Congress Party; *b* 1924; *m*; three *s.* Migrated to Kenya and worked as labourer, clerk and salesman, 1950–55; Founder Mem., Kenya Africa Union. Mem., Uganda Nat. Congress, 1952–60; Mem., Uganda Legislative Council, 1957–71; Founder and Mem., Uganda People's Congress, 1960–71; Leader of the Opposition, 1961–62; Prime Minister, 1962–66; Minister of Defence and Foreign Affairs, 1963–65; President of Uganda, 1966–71 (deposed by military coup); in exile in Tanzania, 1971–80; returned to Uganda, 1980.

Ó BRIAIN, Hon. Barra, MSM; President of the Circuit Court and, *ex officio,* Judge of High Court in Ireland 1959–73 (seconded as President of the High Court of Justice, Cyprus, 1960–62); *b* 19 September 1901; *s* of Dr Christopher Michael and Mary Theresa Ó Briain, Merrion Square, Dublin; *m* 1928, Anna Flood, Terenure, Dublin (*d* 1968); three *s* eight *d. Educ:* Belvedere College; University Coll., Dublin; Paris University. Served in IRA in Irish War of Independence, 1920–21; National Army, 1922–27; Mil. Sec. to Chief of Staff, 1926–27. Called to Irish Bar, 1926; Hon. Bencher, King's Inns, 1974. Sen. Counsel, 1940; Circuit Judge, 1943 (S Western Circuit). Mem., Cttee of Inquiry into operation of Courts in Ireland, 1962; Chm., Cttee to recommend safeguards for persons in police custody, 1977. *Publication:* The Irish Constitution, 1927. *Recreations:* fishing, gardening, walking. *Address:* Dún Árd, Islington Avenue, Sandycove, Co. Dublin.

O'BRIEN, family name of **Barons Inchiquin** and **O'Brien of Lothbury.**

O'BRIEN OF LOTHBURY, Baron *cr* 1973 (Life Peer), of the City of London; **Leslie Kenneth O'Brien,** PC 1970; GBE 1967; President, British Bankers' Association, 1973–80; *b* 8 Feb. 1908; *e s* of late Charles John Grimes O'Brien; *m* Isabelle Gertrude Pickett; one *s*. *Educ:* Wandsworth School. Entered Bank of England, 1927; Deputy Chief Cashier, 1951; Chief Cashier, 1955; Executive Director, 1962–64; Deputy Governor, 1964–66; Governor, 1966–73; Director: Commonwealth Develt Finance Co. Ltd, 1962–64; The Prudential Assurance Co. Ltd, 1973–80; The Prudential Corp. Ltd, 1979–83; The Rank Organisation, 1974–78; Bank for International Settlements, 1966–73, 1974–83 (Vice-Chm., 1979–83); Saudi Internat. Bank, 1975–84; Vice-Chm., Banque Belge, 1981–; Mem., Adv. Bd, Unilever Ltd, 1973–78; Consultant to J. P. Morgan & Co., 1973–79; Chm., Internat. Council of Morgan Guaranty Trust Co., NY, 1974–78; Mem. Internat. Adv. Council, Morgan Grenfell & Co. Ltd, 1974–. Chm., Cttee of Inquiry into export of animals for slaughter, 1973. Member: Finance and Appeal Cttee, RCS, 1973–85; Council, RCM, 1973–; Bd of National Theatre, 1973–78; Council, Marie Curie Meml Foundn, 1963–78; Investment Adv. Cttee, Mercers' Co., 1973–; City of London Savings Cttee, 1966–78. A Trustee of Glyndebourne Arts Trust, 1974–78; Hon. Treasurer and Mem. Exec. Cttee, Royal Opera House Develt Appeal, 1977–. Pres., United Banks' Lawn Tennis Assoc., 1958–81; Vice-Pres., Squash Rackets Assoc., 1972–78. One of HM Lieutenants for City of London, 1966–73; Freeman, City of London in Co. of Mercers; Hon. Liveryman, Leathersellers Co. Hon. DSc City Univ., 1969; Hon. LLD Univ. of Wales, 1973. FRCM 1979. Hon. Fellow, Inst. of Bankers. Cavaliere di Gran Croce al Merito della Repubblica Italiana, 1975; Grand Officier, Ordre de la Couronne (Belgium), 1976. *Address:* 23 Burghley House, Somerset Road, SW19 5JB. *T:* 01–946 7749. *Clubs:* Athenæum, Boodle's, Grillions, MCC, All England Lawn Tennis.

O'BRIEN, Brian Murrough Fergus; Special Commissioner of Income Tax since 1981; *b* 18 July 1931; *s* of Charles Murrough O'Brien, MB, BCh and Elizabeth Joyce O'Brien (*née* Peacocke). *Educ:* Bedford Sch.; University Coll., Oxford (BA 1954, MA 1959). Nat. Service, Royal Inniskilling Fusiliers, 1949–50. Called to the Bar, Lincoln's Inn, 1955; Office of Solicitor of Inland Revenue, 1956–70; Asst Solicitor, Law Commn, 1970–80; Secretary, Law Commn, 1980–81. Mem., Senate of Inns of Court and Bar Council, 1977–80; Hon. Gen. Sec., 1962–67 and Chm., 1974–76, CS Legal Soc.; Chm., Assoc. of First Div. Civil Servants, 1979–81. Lay Chm., Westminster (St Margaret's) Deanery Synod, 1978–82. Chm., Trustees, St Mary's, Bourne St, 1968–. *Recreations:* music, travel, light-hearted bridge. *Address:* 20 Manchester Street, W1. *T:* 01–935 4285. *Clubs:* Reform; Kildare Street and University (Dublin).

O'BRIEN, Charles Michael, MA; FIA, FPMI; General Manager (formerly Manager), and Actuary, 1955–84, Council Member, since 1984, Royal National Pension Fund for Nurses; *b* 17 Jan. 1919; *s* of late Richard Alfred O'Brien, CBE, MD, and Nora McKay; *m* 1950, Joy, *d* of late Rupert Henry Prebble and Phyllis Mary Langdon; two *s*. *Educ:* Westminster Sch.; Christ Church, Oxford (MA). Commissioned, Royal Artillery, 1940 (despatches, 1945). Asst Actuary, Equitable Life Assce Soc., 1950; Royal National Pension Fund for Nurses: Asst Manager, 1953; Manager and Actuary, 1955. Dir, M & G Assurance Gp plc, 1984–. Institute of Actuaries: Fellow, 1949; Hon. Sec., 1961–62; Vice-Pres., 1965–68; Pres., 1976–78. Mem., Governing Body, Westminster Sch. *Recreation:* training gundogs. *Address:* The Boundary, Goodley Stock, Crockham Hill, Edenbridge, Kent TN8 6TA. *T:* Edenbridge 866349.

O'BRIEN, Conor Cruise; Contributing Editor, The Atlantic, Boston; Editor-in-Chief, The Observer, 1979–81; Pro-Chancellor, University of Dublin, since 1973; *b* 3 November 1917; *s* of Francis Cruise O'Brien and Katherine Sheehy; *m* 1st, 1939, Christine Foster (marr. diss. 1962); one *s* two *d*; 2nd, 1962, Máire Mac Entee; one adopted *s* one adopted *d*. *Educ:* Sandford Park School, Dublin; Trinity College, Dublin (BA, PhD). Entered Department of External Affairs of Ireland, 1944; Counsellor, Paris, 1955–56; Head of UN section and Member of Irish Delegation to UN, 1956–60; Asst Sec., Dept of External Affairs, 1960; Rep. of Sec.-Gen. of UN in Katanga, May-Dec. 1961; resigned from UN and Irish service, Dec. 1961. Vice-Chancellor, Univ. of Ghana, 1962–65; Albert Schweitzer Prof. of Humanities, New York Univ., 1965–69. TD (Lab) Dublin North-East, 1969–77; Minister for Posts and Telegraphs, 1973–77. Mem. Senate, Republic of Ireland, 1977–79. Vis. Fellow, Nuffield Coll., Oxford, 1973–75; Fellow, St Catherine's Coll., Oxford, 1978–81; Vis. Prof., Dartmouth Coll., USA, 1984–85. Member: Royal Irish Acad.; Royal Soc. of Literature. Hon. DLitt: Bradford, 1971; Ghana, 1974; Edinburgh, 1976; Nice, 1978; Coleraine, 1981. Valiant for Truth Media Award, 1979. *Publications:* Maria Cross (under pseud. Donat O'Donnell), 1952 (reprinted under own name, 1963); Parnell and his Party, 1957; (ed) The Shaping of Modern Ireland, 1959; To Katanga and Back, 1962; Conflicting Concepts of the UN, 1964; Writers and Politics, 1965; The United Nations: Sacred Drama, 1967 (with drawings by Felix Topolski); Murderous Angels, 1968; (ed) Power and Consciousness, 1969; Conor Cruise O'Brien Introduces Ireland, 1969; (ed) Edmund Burke, Reflections on the Revolution in France, 1969; Camus, 1969; A Concise History of Ireland, 1972; (with Máire Cruise O'Brien) The Suspecting Glance, 1972; States of Ireland, 1972; Herod, 1978; Neighbours: the Ewart-Biggs memorial lectures 1978–79, 1980; The Siege: the saga of Israel and Zionism, 1986. *Recreation:* travelling. *Address:* Whitewater, Howth Summit, Dublin, Ireland. *T:* Dublin 322474. *Club:* Athenæum.

O'BRIEN, Dermod Patrick; QC 1983; a Recorder of the Crown Court, since 1978; *b* 23 Nov. 1939; *s* of Lieut D. D. O'Brien, RN, and Mrs O'Brien (*née* O'Connor); *m* 1974, Zoë Susan Norris; two *s*. *Educ:* Ampleforth Coll., York; St Catherine's Coll., Oxford. BA (Jurisprudence); MA. Called to Bar, Inner Temple, 1962; joined Western Circuit, 1963. *Recreations:* fishing, shooting, skiing. *Address:* Little Daux Farm, Billingshurst, West Sussex RH14 9DB. *T:* Billingshurst 4800; (chambers) 2 Temple Gardens, Temple, EC4Y 9AY. *T:* 01–583 6041.

O'BRIEN, Edna; writer; *b* Ireland; marr. diss.; two *s*. *Educ:* Irish convents; Pharmaceutical Coll. of Ireland. Yorkshire Post Novel Award, 1971. *Publications:* The Country Girls, 1960 (screenplay for film, 1983); The Lonely Girl, 1962; Girls in Their Married Bliss, 1963; August is a Wicked Month, 1964; Casualties of Peace, 1966; The Love Object, 1968; A Pagan Place, 1970; (play) A Pagan Place, 1971; Night, 1972; (short stories) A Scandalous Woman, 1974; Mother Ireland, 1976; Johnnie I hardly knew you, 1977; Mrs Reinhardt and other stories, 1978; Virginia (play), 1979; The Dazzle, 1981; Returning, 1982; A Christmas Treat, 1982; A Fanatic Heart (selected stories), 1985; Flesh and Blood (play), 1987; Madame Bovary (play), 1987. *Recreations:* reading, writing, remembering. *Address:* c/o Douglas Rae Ltd, 28 Charing Cross Road, WC2H 0DB.

O'BRIEN, Sir Frederick (William Fitzgerald), Kt 1984; QC (Scotland) 1960; Sheriff Principal of Lothian and Borders, since 1978; Sheriff of Chancery in Scotland, since 1978; *b* 19 July 1917; *s* of Dr Charles Henry Fitzgerald O'Brien and Helen Jane; *m* 1950, Audrey Muriel Owen; two *s* one *d*. *Educ:* Royal High Sch., Univ. of Edinburgh; MA 1938; LLB 1940. Admitted Faculty of Advocates, 1947. Comr, Mental Welfare Commission of Scotland, 1962–65; Home Advocate Depute, 1964–65; Sheriff-Principal of Caithness, Sutherland, Orkney and Shetland, 1965–75; Interim Sheriff-Principal of Aberdeen, Kincardine and Banff, 1969–71; Sheriff Principal of N Strathclyde, 1975–78; Interim Sheriff Principal of S Strathclyde, 1981. Member: Scottish Medical Practices Cttee, 1973–76; Scottish Records Adv. Council, 1974–83; Convener of Sheriffs Principal, 1972–; Chm., Sheriff Court Rules Council, 1975–81. Chm., Northern Lighthouse Bd, 1983–84 and 1986–87. Convener, Gen. Council Business Cttee, Edinburgh Univ., 1980–84. Hon. Pres., Royal High Sch. Former Pupils Club, 1982 (Pres. 1975–76). Mem., Inst. of Advanced Motorists. *Recreations:* golf, music. *Address:* 22 Arboretum Road, Edinburgh EH3 5PN. *T:* 031–552 1923. *Clubs:* New (Edinburgh); Bruntsfield Golf, Scottish Arts.

O'BRIEN, Rt. Rev. James Joseph; Auxiliary Bishop of Westminster (Bishop in Hertfordshire) (RC), and Titular Bishop of Manaccenser, since 1977; *s* of John and Mary Elizabeth O'Brien. *Educ:* St Ignatius College, Stamford Hill; St Edmund's Coll., Ware. Priest, 1954; Assistant, St Lawrence's, Feltham, 1954–62; Catholic Missionary Society, 1962–68; Director of Catholic Enquiry Centre, 1967–68; Rector of Allen Hall, 1968–77. Chm., Dept for Internat. Affairs, Bishops' Conf. of England and Wales, 1984–. Prelate of Honour, 1969. *Address:* The Farm Cottage, All Saints Pastoral Centre, London Colney, St Albans, Herts AL2 1AQ. *T:* Bowmansgreen 24664.

O'BRIEN, Prof. John W., PhD; Rector Emeritus, Concordia University (incorporating Loyola College and Sir George Williams University, Montreal), since 1984 (Rector and Vice-Chancellor, 1969–84); Professor of Economics, since 1965; *b* 4 Aug. 1931; *s* of Wilfred Edmond O'Brien and Audrey Swain; *m* 1956, Joyce Helen Bennett; two *d*. *Educ:* McGill Univ., Montreal, Que. BA 1953, MA 1955, PhD 1962. Sir George Williams Univ.: Lectr in Economics, 1954; Asst Prof. of Economics, 1957; Associate Prof. of Economics and Asst Dean, 1961; Dean, Faculty of Arts, 1963; Vice-Principal (Academic), 1968–69. Hon. DCL Bishop's Univ., 1976; Hon. LLD McGill Univ., 1976. *Publication:* Canadian Money and Banking, 1964 (2nd edn, with G. Lermer, 1969). *Address:* Concordia University, 1455 de Maisonneuve Boulevard West, Montreal, Que H3G 1M8, Canada. *T:* (514) 848–2424.

O'BRIEN, Most Rev. Keith Michael Patrick; *see* St Andrews and Edinburgh, Archbishop of, (RC).

O'BRIEN, Rt. Rev. Kevin; *see* O'Brien, Rt Rev. T. K.

O'BRIEN, (Michael) Vincent; trainer of horses for flat and National Hunt racing, England and Ireland; *b* 9 April 1917; *s* of Daniel P. O'Brien and Kathleen (*née* Toomey); *m* 1951, Jacqueline (*née* Wittenoom), Perth, Australia; two *s* three *d*. *Educ:* Mungret Coll., Ireland. Started training in Co. Cork, 1944; moved to Co. Tipperary, 1951. Won all principal English and Irish steeple-chases, incl. 3 consecutive Grand Nationals, Gold Cups and Champion Hurdles. From 1959 has concentrated on flat racing and has trained winners of 16 English classics, incl. 6 Derbys; trainer of Nijinsky, first triple crown winner since 1935; also 6 Irish Derbys, 1 French Derby, 3 Prix de l'Arc de Triomphe and Washington International. Hon. LLD NUI, 1983. *Recreations:* fishing, golf. *Address:* Ballydoyle House, Cashel, Co. Tipperary, Ireland. *T:* 062–61222; Telex 28214.

O'BRIEN, Oswald; Director, Workplace Services, Alcohol Concern (national charity) (Director, Education Division, 1984); freelance lecturer, since 1983; *b* 6 April 1928; *s* of Thomas and Elizabeth O'Brien; *m* 1950, Freda Rosina Pascoe; one *s*. *Educ:* St Mary's Grammar Sch., Darlington; Fircroft Coll., Birmingham; Durham Univ. BA Hons Politics and Economics. Royal Navy, 1945–48; various posts in industry, 1948–59; College and University, 1959–63; Tutor, WEA, 1963–64; Staff Tutor, Durham Univ., 1964–78; Senior Industrial Relations Officer, Commn on Indust. Relations, 1970–72 (secondment); Dir of Studies and Vice-Principal, Co-operative Coll., 1978–83. Dept of Employment and ACAS Arbitrator in Shipbuilding, 1968–78; Indust. Relations Adviser to various statutary bodies, 1965–78; Chm., Soc. of Indust. Tutors, 1978–82. MP (Lab) Darlington, March-June 1983. FBIM. *Publications:* (jtly) Going Comprehensive, 1970; various papers, reports and case studies. *Recreations:* reading, talking, dancing, singing, swimming. *Address:* 6 Hillclose Avenue, Darlington, Co. Durham DL3 8BH. *T:* Darlington 51440.

O'BRIEN, Owen; Joint General Secretary, Society of Graphical and Allied Trades 1982 (SOGAT 82), 1982–83; *b* Stepney, 22 June 1920; *m*; two *s* two *d*. *Educ:* Tower Hill Sch., E1. Entered printing industry, 1934. Served War: Merchant Navy, 1939–41; RAF, 1941–46. Elected: Asst Sec., London Machine Br. of NATSOPA, Dec. 1951; (unopposed) Sec. of Br., Nov. 1952; Sec. of Union's London Jt Branches, 1952–63; Nat. Asst Sec., 1964–75; Gen. Sec., 1975–82. Mem., Employment Appeal Tribunal, 1984–. Past Mem., local Labour Party and London Labour Party; Mem., Stepney Borough Council, 1947–50; Chm., Printing and Publishing Industry Training Board, 1977– (Mem. Exec. Cttee and Chm., Levy and Grant Cttee from Bd's constitution, 1968–77); Mem. Council, Industrial Soc. Governor, London Coll. of Printing, 1964– (Chm., Governors, 1969, 1977). *Recreations:* walking, reading, swimming. *Address:* 58 Hurst Road, Sidcup, Kent DA15 9AA.

O'BRIEN, Raymond Francis; DL; Chief Executive and Board Member, Severn-Trent Water Authority, since 1986; *b* 13 Feb. 1936; *s* of Ignatius and Anne O'Brien; *m* 1959, Mary Agnes (Wendy) Alcock; two *s* two *d*. *Educ:* St Mary's Coll., Great Crosby, Liverpool; St Edmund Hall, Oxford. BA Hons 1959, MA 1962; IPFA. Accountant, Cheshire CC, 1959–65; Head of Data Processing, Staffs CC, 1965–67; Asst County Treas., Notts CC, 1967–70; Dep. Clerk, Notts CC, 1970–73; Clerk of CC and Chief Executive, Notts, 1973–77; Chief Exec., Merseyside MCC, 1978–86. Mem., Merseyside Area Bd, MSC, 1980–86; Director: Merseyside Economic Development Co. Ltd, 1981–86; Merseyside Cablevision Ltd, 1982–86; Anfield Foundation, 1983–. DL Merseyside, 1980. *Recreations:* cricket, rugby, gardening, topiary, music, reading. *Address:* The Conifers, 153 Hampton Lane, Solihull, West Midlands B91 2RS. *T:* 021–704 4925.

O'BRIEN, Sir Richard, Kt 1980; DSO 1944, MC 1942 (Bar 1944); Chairman, Manpower Services Commission, 1976–82; *b* 15 Feb. 1920; *s* of late Dr Charles O'Brien and of Marjorie Maude O'Brien; *m* 1951, Elizabeth M. D. Craig; two *s* three *d*. *Educ:* Oundle Sch.; Clare Coll., Cambridge (MA). Served, 1940–45, with Sherwood Foresters and Leicesters, N Africa, ME, Italy and Greece; Personal Asst to Field Marshal Montgomery, 1945–46. Develt Officer, Nat. Assoc. of Boys' Clubs, 1946–48; Richard Sutcliffe Ltd, Wakefield (latterly Prodn Dir), 1948–58; Dir and Gen. Man., Head Wrightson Mineral Engrg Ltd, 1958–61; Dir, Industrial Relns, British Motor Corp., 1961–66; Industrial Adviser (Manpower), DEA, 1966–68; Delta Metal Co. Ltd (subseq. Dir of Manpower, and Dir 1972–76), 1968–76. Chairman: CBI Employment Policy Cttee, 1971–76; Crown Appointments Commn, 1979; Concordia (Youth Service Volunteers), 1981–; Engineering Industry Trng Bd, 1982–85; Archbishop's Commn on Urban Priority Areas, 1983–85; Industrial Participation Assoc., 1983–86; Policy Studies Inst., 1984–; Employment Inst. and Charter for Jobs, 1985–; AMARC/TES Ltd, 1986–. Member: NEDC, 1977–82; Engrg Council, 1985–; President: British Inst. of Industrial Therapy, 1982–; Inst. of Trng and Develt, 1983–84; Nat. Assoc. of Colls of Further and Higher Educn, 1983–85. Member Council: Industrial Soc., 1962–86; Univ. of Birmingham, 1969–; Mem. Ct of Governors, ASC, 1977–83. Hon. DSc Aston, 1979; Hon. LLD: Bath, 1981; Liverpool, 1981; Birmingham, 1982; Hon. DLitt Warwick, 1983; Hon. Fellow Sheffield City Polytech., 1980. JP Wakefield, 1955–61. *Publications*: contrib: Conflict at Work (BBC pubn), 1971; Montgomery at Close Quarters, 1985; Seekers and Finders, 1985; articles in various jls. *Recreation*: reading. *Address*: 24 Argyll Road, W8. *T*: 01–937 8944.

O'BRIEN, (Robert) Stephen; Chief Executive, Business in the Community, since 1983; *b* 14 Aug. 1936; *s* of Robert Henry and Clare Winifred O'Brien; *m* 1958, Zoë T. O'Brien; two *s* two *d*. *Educ*: Sherborne Sch., Dorset. Joined Charles Fulton & Co. Ltd, 1956; Dir, 1964; Chm., 1970–82. Chairman: Foreign Exchange and Currency Deposit Brokers Assoc., 1968–72; Project Fullemploy Ltd, 1973–; Home Sec.'s Adv. Bd on Community Radio, 1985–; Dir, Kirkland-Whittaker Co. Ltd, 1981–82. Ordained Deacon, 1971; Hon. Curate, St Lawrence Jewry, 1973–82; Chm., Christian Action, 1976–. Pres., Esher Assoc. for Prevention of Addiction, 1979–. Mem., Administrative Council, Royal Jubilee Trusts, 1984–. *Recreations*: causes, gentle gardening, tennis. *Address*: 13 Tredegar Square, E3. *T*: 01–980 1435. *Club*: Island Cruising (Salcombe, Devon).

O'BRIEN, Terence John, CMG 1971; MC 1945; HM Diplomatic Service, retired; *b* 13 Oct. 1921; *s* of Joseph O'Brien; *m* 1950, Phyllis Mitchell (*d* 1952); *m* 1953, Rita Emily Drake Reynolds; one *s* two *d*. *Educ*: Gresham's Sch., Holt; Merton Coll., Oxford. Ayrshire Yeo., 1942–45. Dominions Office, 1947; CRO, 1947–49; British High Comr's Office, Ceylon, 1950–52; Princ., Treasury, 1953–56; 1st Sec. (Financial), Canberra, 1956–58; Planning Officer, CRO, 1958–60; 1st Sec., Kuala Lumpur, 1960–62; Sec. to Inter-Governmental Cttee, Jesselton, 1962–63; Head of Chancery, New Delhi, 1963–66; Imp. Def. Coll., 1967; Counsellor, FCO (formerly FO), 1968–70; Ambassador: Nepal, 1970–74; Burma, 1974–78; Indonesia, 1978–81. *Address*: Beaufort House, Woodcutts, Dorset.

O'BRIEN, Rt. Rev. (Thomas) Kevin; Auxiliary Bishop of Middlesbrough, (RC), and Titular Bishop of Ard Carna, since 1981; *b* Cork City, Republic of Ireland, 18 Feb. 1923; *s* of Jack and Mary O'Brien. *Educ*: Christian Brothers Coll., Cork. Ordained, All Hallows College, Dublin, 1948; Curate at Batley, Yorks, 1948–51, and St Anne's Cathedral, Leeds, 1951–56; Catholic Missionary Society, 1956–71, Superior 1960–71; Vicar General, Diocese of Leeds, 1971–81; Parish Priest: St Patrick's, Huddersfield, 1971–79; St Francis, Bradford, 1979–81. *Address*: St Charles Rectory, Jarratt Street, Hull HU1 3HB.

O'BRIEN, Timothy Brian; designer; *b* 8 March 1929; *s* of Brian Palliser Tiegue O'Brien and Elinor Laura (*née* Mackenzie). *Educ*: Wellington Coll.; Corpus Christi, Cambridge (MA); Yale Univ. Design Dept, BBC TV, 1954; Designer, Associated Rediffusion, 1955–56; Head of Design, ABC Television, 1956–66 (The Flying Dutchman, 1958); partnership in stage design with Tazeena Firth estabd 1961; output incl.: The Bartered Bride, The Girl of the Golden West, 1962; West End prodns of new plays, 1963–64; London scene of Shakespeare Exhibn, 1964; Tango, Days in the Trees, Staircase, RSC, and Trafalgar at Madame Tussaud's, 1966; All's Well that Ends Well, As You Like It, Romeo and Juliet, RSC, 1967; The Merry Wives of Windsor, Troilus and Cressida (also Nat. Theatre, 1976), The Latent Heterosexual, RSC, 1968; Pericles (also Comédie Française, 1974), Women Beware Women, Bartholomew Fair, RSC, 1969; 1970: Measure for Measure, RSC; Madame Tussaud's in Amsterdam; The Knot Garden, Royal Opera; 1971: Enemies, Man of Mode, RSC; 1972: La Cenerentola, Oslo; Lower Depths, The Island of the Mighty, RSC; As You Like It, OCSC; 1973: Richard II, Love's Labour's Lost, RSC; 1974: Next of Kin, NT; Summerfolk, RSC; The Bassarids, ENO; 1975: John Gabriel Borkman, NT; Peter Grimes, Royal Opera (later in Göteborg, Paris); The Marrying of Ann Leete, RSC; 1976: Wozzeck, Adelaide Fest.; The Zykovs, RSC; The Force of Habit, NT; 1977: Tales from the Vienna Woods, Bedroom Farce, NT; Falstaff, Berlin Opera; 1978: The Cunning Little Vixen, Göteborg; Evita, London (later in Australia, Austria, USA); A Midsummer Night's Dream, Sydney Opera House; 1979: The Rake's Progress, Royal Opera; 1981: Lulu, Royal Opera; 1982: La Ronde, RSC; Le Grand Macabre, ENO; 1983: Turandot, Vienna State Opera; 1984: The Mastersingers of Nuremberg, ENO; Tannhäuser, Royal Opera; 1985: Samson, Royal Opera; Sicilian Vespers, Grande Théâtre, Geneva; Old Times, Haymarket; Lucia di Lammermoor, Köln Opera; 1986: The Threepenny Opera, NT; Die Meistersinger von Nürnberg, Netherlands Opera. (Jtly) Gold Medal for Set Design, Prague Quadriennale, 1975. *Recreation*: sailing. *Address*: 33 Lansdowne Gardens, SW8 2EQ. *T*: 01–622 5384.

O'BRIEN, Sir Timothy John, 7th Bt *cr* 1849; *b* 6 July 1958; *s* of John David O'Brien (*d* 1980) and of Sheila Winifred, *o d* of Sir Charles Arland Maitland Freake, 4th Bt; *S* grandfather, 1982. *Heir*: *b* James Patrick O'Brien, *b* 22 Dec. 1964.

O'BRIEN, Turlough Aubrey, CBE 1959; Public Relations Consultant, since 1972; *b* 30 Sept. 1907; *er s* of late Lieut-Colonel A. J. O'Brien, CIE, CBE; *m* 1945, Phyllis Mary (*d* 1986), twin *d* of late E. G. Tew; two *s* one *d*. *Educ*: Charterhouse; Christ Church, Oxford. Assistant to Director of Public Relations, Board of Trade, 1946–49; Public Relations Officer: Home Office, 1949–53; Post Office, 1953–64; Chief Public Relations Officer, 1964–66; Director, Public Relations, 1966–68; Public Relations Manager, Bank of London and South America, 1968–72. President, Institute of Public Relations, 1965. *Recreation*: fishing. *Address*: Claremount, 11 Kiln Gardens, Hartley Wintney, Basingstoke, Hants RG27 8RG. *Club*: United Oxford & Cambridge University.

O'BRIEN, Vincent; *see* O'Brien, M. V.

O'BRIEN, William, JP; MP (Lab) Normanton, since 1983; *b* 25 Jan. 1929; *m* Jean; three *d*. *Educ*: state schools; Leeds Univ. Coalminer, 1945–83. Wakefield DC: Mem., 1973–83; former Dep. Leader and Chm., Finance and Gen. Purposes Cttee. Mem., NUM, 1945–; Local Branch Official, 1956–83. Member: Public Accounts Cttee, 1983–; Energy Select Cttee, 1986–. JP Wakefield, 1979. *Recreations*: reading, organising. *Address*: House of Commons, SW1A 0AA. *T*: 01–219 3000; 4 Elizabeth Drive, Ferrybridge, Knottingley WF11 8PB.

O'BRIEN, Adm. Sir William (Donough), KCB 1969 (CB 1966); DSC 1942; Commander-in-Chief, Western Fleet, Feb. 1970–Sept. 71, retd Nov. 1971; Vice-Admiral of the United Kingdom and Lieutenant of the Admiralty, 1984–86; *b* 13 Nov. 1916; *s* of late Major W. D. O'Brien, Connaught Rangers and I. R. Caroe (*née* Parnis); *m* 1943, Rita Micallef, Sliema, Malta; one *s* two *d*. *Educ*: Royal Naval Coll., Dartmouth. Served War of 1939–45: HM Ships Garland, Wolsey, Witherington, Offa, 1939–42; Cottesmore i/c, 1943–44; Arakan Coast, 1945. HMS Venus i/c, 1948–49; Commander 1949; HMS Ceylon, 1952; Admiralty, 1953–55; Captain, 1955; Captain (D) 8th DS in HMS Cheviot, 1958–59; HMS Hermes i/c, 1961–64; Rear-Admiral 1964; Naval Secretary, 1964–66; Flag Officer, Aircraft Carriers, 1966–67; Comdr, Far East Fleet, 1967–69; Admiral 1969. Rear-Admiral of the UK, 1979–84. Chairman: Kennet and Avon Canal Trust, 1974–; King George's Fund for Sailors, 1974–86. Pres., Assoc. of RN Officers, 1973. *Address*: The Black Barn, Steeple Ashton, Trowbridge, Wilts. *T*: Keevil 870496. *Club*: Army and Navy.

O'CATHAIN, Detta, (Mrs William Bishop), OBE 1983; Managing Director, Milk Marketing Board, since 1985; *b* 3 Feb. 1938; *d* of Caoimhghin O'Cathain and late Margaret O'Cathain; *m* 1968, William Bishop. *Educ*: Laurel Hill, Limerick; University College, Dublin (BA). Aer Lingus, Dublin, 1961–66; Group Economist, Tarmac, 1966–69; Economic Advr, Rootes Motors, 1969–72; Sen. Economist, Carrington Vyella, 1972–73; Economic Advr, British Leyland, 1973–74; Dir, Market Planning, Leyland Cars, 1974–76; Corporate Planning Exec., Unigate, 1976–81; Head of Strategic Planning, MMB, 1981–83; Dir and Gen. Manager, 1984. Advr on Agricl Marketing to Minister of Agriculture, 1979–83. Director: Midland Bank, 1984–; Channel 4, 1985–86; Tesco, 1985–. *Recreations*: music, tennis, reading, getting and hoping to keep fit. *Address*: The Old Malthouse, Queen Street, Arundel, West Sussex BN18 9JG. *T*: Arundel 883775.

OCHOA, Dr Severo; Distinguished Member, Roche Institute of Molecular Biology, New Jersey, since 1974; *b* Luarca, Spain, 24 Sept. 1905; *s* of Severo Ochoa and Carmen (*née* Albornoz); *m* 1931, Carmen G. Coblan. *Educ*: Malaga Coll.; University of Madrid. AB, Malaga, 1921; MD, Madrid, 1929. Lecturer in Physiology, University of Madrid Medical School, 1931–35; Head of Physiology Div., Institute for Medical Research, 1935–36; Guest Research Asst, Kaiser Wilhelm Inst., Heidelberg, 1936–37; Marine Biological Lab., Plymouth, July-Dec. 1937; Demonstrator and Nuffield Research Assistant in Biochemistry, University of Oxford Medical School, 1938–41; Instructor and Research Assoc. in Pharmacology, Washington Univ. School of Medicine, St Louis, 1941–42; New York University School of Medicine: Research Assoc. in Medicine, 1942–45; Asst Professor of Biochemistry, 1945–46; Professor of Pharmacology, and Chairman of Dept of Pharmacology, 1946–54; Prof. of Biochemistry, and Chm. of Dept of Biochemistry, 1954–74. Carlos Jimenez Diaz lectr, Madrid Univ., 1969. Pres., Internat. Union of Biochemistry, 1961–67. Member: US National Academy of Sciences; American Academy of Arts and Sciences; American Philosophical Society; Deutsche Akademie der Naturforscher (Leopoldina), etc. Nobel Prize (joint) in Physiology and Medicine, 1959. Hon. degrees from universities and colleges in Argentina, Brazil, Chile, England, Italy, Peru, Philippines, Scotland, Spain and USA. Foreign Member: Royal Society, 1965; USSR Academy of Science, 1966; Polish Acad. of Science; Acad. of Science, DDR, 1977; Acad. of Med. Scis, Argentina, 1977; Chilean Acad. of Scis, 1977; Indian Nat. Sci. Acad., 1977. Hon. Mem., Royal Acad. Med., Sevilla, 1971. Gold Medal, Madrid Univ., 1969; Quevedo Gold Medal, Madrid, 1969; Albert Gallatin Medal, NY Univ., 1970. Order of Rising Sun, 2nd class, 1967. *Publications*: papers on biochemistry and molecular biology. *Recreations*: colour photography and swimming. *Address*: 530 East 72nd Street, New York, NY 10021, USA. *T*: 879–1480.

O'CONNELL, John Eugene Anthony, MS (London), FRCS; Consulting Neurological Surgeon, St Bartholomew's Hospital; *b* 16 Sept. 1906; *s* of Thomas Henry and Catherine Mary O'Connell; *m* Marjorie Hutchinson Cook, MBE (*d* 1986). *Educ*: Clongowes Wood and Wimbledon Colleges; St Bartholomew's Hospital. Held posts of House Surgeon, Senior Demonstrator of Anatomy, and Surgical Chief Assistant, St Bartholomew's Hospital, 1931–39; Studied at Universities of Michigan and Chicago on Rockefeller Foundation Travelling Fellowship, 1935–36; Surgeon in charge of an EMS Neurosurgical Unit, 1941–46; Surgeon i/c Dept of Neurol Surgery, St Bartholomew's Hosp., 1946–71; Hunterian Professor, Royal College of Surgeons, 1943 and 1950. Emeritus Mem., Soc. of Brit. Neurol Surgeons (ex-Pres.); FRSM (ex-Vice-Pres.); Hon. Member: Neurosurgical Soc. Australasia; Deutsche Gesellschaft für Neurochirurgie; Corresp. Mem., Amer. Assoc. Neurol Surgeons. *Publications*: papers in neurological, surgical and other journals and books. *Recreations*: fly-fishing, bird watching. *Address*: Fishing Cottage, Itchen Abbas, Winchester, Hants. *T*: Itchen Abbas 227. *Club*: Athenæum.

O'CONNELL, Sir Morgan (Donal Conail), 6th Bt, *cr* 1869; *b* 29 Jan. 1923; *o s* of Captain Sir Maurice James Arthur O'Connell, 5th Bt, KM, MC, and Margaret Mary, *d* of late Matthew J. Purcell, Burton Park, Buttevant; *S* father, 1949; *m* 1953, Elizabeth, *o d* of late Major and Mrs John MacCarthy O'Leary, Lavenders, West Malling, Kent; two *s* four *d*. *Educ*: The Abbey School, Fort Augustus, Scotland. Served War of 1939–45, in Royal Corps of Signals, 1943–46; BLA, 1944–46. *Recreations*: fishing and shooting. *Heir*: *s* Maurice James Donagh MacCarthy O'Connell, *b* 10 June 1958. *Address*: Lakeview, Killarney, Co. Kerry. *T*: 31845.

O'CONNOR, Surgeon Rear-Adm. Anthony, LVO 1967; Director, Red Cross Blood Transfusion Service, Western Australia, 1981–84 (Deputy Director, 1975–81); *b* 8 Nov. 1917; *s* of Armel John O'Connor and Lucy Violet O'Connor (*née* Bullock-Webster); *m* 1946, Catherine Jane (*née* Hayes); three *d*. *Educ*: Kings Coll., Strand, London; Westminster Hosp. Med. Sch. MRCS, LRCP, MB, BS, FFARCS, MFCM. Qualified Medical Practitioner, 1941; joined Royal Navy (RNVR), 1942; Permanent Commn, 1945; Dep. Medical Director General (Naval), 1969; MO i/c, Inst. of Naval Med. and Dean of Naval Med., 1972–75. QHP 1970–75. *Recreations*: gardening, photography. *Address*: c/o Lloyds Bank, Ludlow, Shropshire.

O'CONNOR, Rt. Rev. Cormac Murphy; *see* Murphy-O'Connor.

O'CONNOR, Professor Daniel John; Professor of Philosophy, University of Exeter, 1957–79, now Emeritus; *b* 2 April 1914; *m* 1948, Kathleen Kemsley; no *c*. *Educ*: Birkbeck Coll., University of London. Entered Civil Service, 1933; Commonwealth Fund Fellow in Philosophy, University of Chicago, 1946–47; Professor of Philosophy, University of Natal, SA, 1949–51; Professor of Philosophy, University of the Witwatersrand, Johannesburg, 1951–52; Lecturer in Philosophy, Univ. Coll. of North Staffordshire, 1952–54; Professor of Philosophy, University of Liverpool, 1954–57. Visiting Professor, University of Pennsylvania, 1961–62. *Publications*: John Locke, 1952; Introduction to Symbolic Logic (with A. H. Basson), 1953; Introduction to the Philosophy of Education, 1957; A Critical History of Western Philosophy (ed), 1964; Aquinas and Natural Law, 1968; Free Will, 1971; (ed jtly) New Essays in the Philosophy of Education, 1973; The Correspondence Theory of Truth, 1975; various papers in philosophical journals. *Address*: c/o Department of Philosophy, University of Exeter, Queen's Building, The Queen's Drive, Exeter EX4 4QH.

O'CONNOR, Lt-Gen. Sir Denis (Stuart Scott), KBE 1963 (CBE 1949; OBE 1946); CB 1959; DL; *b* Simla, 2 July 1907; *s* of Lieut-Colonel Malcolm Scott O'Connor and Edith Annie (*née* Rees); *m* 1936, Martha Neill Algie (*née* Johnston), Donaghadee, Co. Down; two *s* one *d*. *Educ*: Glengorse, Eastbourne; Harrow School; RMA Woolwich. Commnd 2nd Lieut, Royal Artillery, 1927; India, 1929–35; France, 1939, Captain; Student Staff Coll., 1940; Major Instructor, Staff Coll., 1941, Lieut-Colonel GSO 1, 11th Armoured Division, 1942–44; N.W. Europe, CO Artillery Regt, 1944 (despatches); Colonel, 14th Army, 1945; Brigadier, Director of Plans, Supreme Allied Commander, South East Asia, 1945–46; Middle East, BGS, 1946–49; Student, IDC 1950; School of Artillery, 1951–52; CRA, 11th Armoured Division, BAOR, 1953–54; Director of Plans, War Office, 1955–56; Maj.-General, Commander, 6th Armoured Division, BAOR, 1957–58; Chief Army Instructor, Imperial Defence Coll., London, 1958–60; GOC, Aldershot District, 1960–62; Vice Chief of Defence Staff, Ministry of Defence, 1962–64; Commander British Forces, Hong Kong, 1964–66, retired. Colonel Commandant, RA,

1963–72. Member of Administrative Board of Governors, Corps of Commissionaires, 1964–75, Life Governor, 1975. HQ Staff, Army Benevolent Fund, 1967–75. DL Surrey, 1968. *Recreations:* shooting, fishing, golf. *Address:* Springfield Lodge, Camberley, Surrey.

O'CONNOR, Gillian Rose; Editor, Investors Chronicle, since 1982; *b* 11 Aug. 1941; *d* of Thomas McDougall O'Connor and Kathleen Joan O'Connor (*née* Parnell). *Educ:* Sutton High School for Girls; St Hilda's College, Oxford. *Address:* Investors Chronicle, Greystoke Place, Fetter Lane, EC4A 1ND. *T:* 01–405 6969.

O'CONNOR, Rt. Rev. Kevin, JCL; Titular Bishop of Glastonbury and an Auxiliary Bishop of Liverpool, (RC), since 1979; *b* 20 May 1929. *Educ:* St Francis Xavier, Liverpool; Junior and Senior Seminaries, Upholland; Gregorian Univ., Rome. Priest, 1954; Member, Archdiocesan Marriage Tribunal; Parish Priest, St Anne's and Chancellor of Archdiocese of Liverpool, 1977. *Address:* 12 Richmond Close, Eccleston, St Helens WA10 5JE.

O'CONNOR, Air Vice-Marshal Patrick Joseph, CB 1976; OBE 1943; MD; FRCPE, FRCPsych; Civil Consultant in Neuropsychiatry, Royal Air Force, since 1978; Consultant in Neurology and Psychiatry to Civil Aviation Authority, British Airways and British Caledonian Airways, since 1978; *b* 21 Aug. 1914; *s* of Charles O'Connor, Straffan, Co. Kildare, Eire, farmer; *m* 1946, Elsie, *o d* of David Craven, Leeds, Yorks; one *s* two *d* (and one *d* decd). *Educ:* Roscrea Coll.; University of Dublin. MB, BCh 1938. Joined RAF, 1940; Air Cdre 1966; Air Vice-Marshal 1971; Consultant Adviser in Neurology and Psychiatry to RAF, 1964–78; Senior Consultant to RAF at Central Medical Establishment, 1975–78, retired. MD 1950; MRCPE 1950; DPM 1953; FRCPE 1960; MRCP 1960; FRCPsych 1970. QHP 1967–78. Member: Med. Council to Migraine Trust; Med. Council on Alcoholism; The EEG Soc.; Assoc. of British Neurologists; Internat. Acad. of Aviation and Space Med., 1977; Internat. League against Epilepsy; Flying Personnel Res. Cttee. Fellow, Aerospace Med. Assoc; FRSM. *Publications:* contrib.: Journal Neurology, Psychiatry and Neurosurgery; British Journal Psychiatry; BMJ. *Recreations:* gardening, shooting. *Address:* 108 Harley Street, W1. *T:* 01–935 8033; St Benedicts, Bacombe Lane, Wendover, Bucks. *T:* Aylesbury 623329. *Club:* Royal Air Force.

O'CONNOR, Rt. Hon. Sir Patrick McCarthy, Kt 1966; PC 1980; **Rt. Hon. Lord Justice O'Connor;** a Lord Justice of Appeal, since 1980; *b* 28 Dec. 1914; *s* of late William Patrick O'Connor; *m* 1938, Mary Garland (*d* 1984), *d* of William Martin Griffin, KC, of Vancouver, BC; two *s* two *d*. *Educ:* Downside; Merton Coll., Oxford. Called to the Bar, Inner Temple, 1940; Master of the Bench, 1966. Junior Counsel to the Post Office, 1954–60; QC 1960; Recorder: of King's Lynn, 1959–61; of Southend, 1961–66; a Judge of the High Ct of Justice, QBD, 1966–80; Dep. Chairman, IoW QS, 1957–71. Vice-Chm., Parole Bd, 1974–75. A Governor of Guy's Hospital, 1956–60. *Recreation:* golf. *Address:* Royal Courts of Justice, Strand, WC2; 210 Rivermead Court, Ranelagh Gardens, SW6 3SG. *T:* 01–731 3563. *Club:* Huntercombe.

O'CONNOR, Rory; Hon. Mr Justice O'Connor; Judge of the High Court of Hong Kong, since 1977; *b* Co. Down, 26 Nov. 1925; *s* of late James O'Connor and Mary (*née* Savage); *m* 1963, Elizabeth, *d* of late Frederick Dew; one *s* two *d*. *Educ:* Blackrock Coll., Dublin; Univ. Coll., Dublin (BCom). Called to Irish Bar, King's Inns, 1949. Resident Magistrate, Kenya, 1956–62; Hong Kong: Magistrate, 1962–70; District Judge, 1970–77. *Address:* Courts of Justice, Hong Kong. *Clubs:* Royal Hong Kong Jockey, United Services Recreation, Ladies Recreation (Hong Kong).

O'CONNOR, Sandra Day; Associate Justice of the Supreme Court of the United States, since 1981; *b* 26 March 1930; *d* of Harry and Ada Mae Day; *m* 1952, John Jay O'Connor III; three *s*. *Educ:* Stanford Univ. (BA 1950; LLB 1952). Legal appts in Calif and Frankfurt, 1952–57; in private practice, 1959–65; Asst Attorney-Gen., Arizona, 1965–69; Judge: Maricopa County Superior Ct, 1974–79; Arizona Ct of Appeals, 1979–81. Mem. Senate, Arizona, 1969–74 (majority leader, 1973–74). Director: Nat. Bank of Arizona, Phoenix, 1971–74; Blue Cross/Blue Shield, Arizona, 1975–79. Chm., Maricopa County Juvenile Detention Home, 1966–68; Pres., Heard Museum, Phoenix, 1979–81; Mem. Nat. Bd, Smithsonian Assocs, 1981–82. Trustee, Stanford Univ., 1976–80. Hon. Bencher, Gray's Inn, 1982. *Address:* Supreme Court Building, 1 First Street NE, Washington, DC 20543, USA.

O'CONNOR HOWE, Mrs Josephine Mary; HM Diplomatic Service, retired; *b* 25 March 1924; *d* of late Gerald Frank Claridge and late Dulcie Agnes Claridge (*née* Waldegrave); *m* 1947, John O'Connor Howe (decd); one *d*. *Educ:* Wychwood Sch., Oxford; Triangle Coll. (course in journalism). Inter-Allied Information Cttee, later, United Nations Information Office, 1942–45; Foreign Office: The Hague, 1945–46; Internat. News Service and freelance, 1946–50; FO, 1952; Counsellor, FCO, 1974–1979. Reader's Digest, 1979–83; Dir, Council for Arms Control, 1983–84; Freelance Editor, Inst. for the Study of Conflict, 1985–. *Publication:* (ed) Armed Peace—the search for world security, 1984. *Recreations:* theatre, gardening, grandchildren. *Address:* Dering Cottage, Little Chart, Ashford, Kent TN27 0PT. *T:* Pluckley 328. *Club:* Royal Commonwealth Society.

ODDIE, Christopher Ripley; His Honour Judge Oddie; a Circuit Judge, since 1974; *b* Derby, 24 Feb. 1929; *o s* of Dr and Mrs J. R. Oddie, Uttoxeter, Staffs; *m* 1957, Margaret Anne, *d* of Mr and Mrs J. W. Timmis; one *s* three *d*. *Educ:* Giggleswick Sch.; Oriel Coll., Oxford (MA). Called to Bar, Middle Temple, 1954, Oxford Circuit. Contested (L) Ludlow, Gen. Election, 1970. A Recorder of the Crown Court, 1972–74. Chm., County Court Rule Cttee, 1985– (Mem., 1981–). Mem. Council, St Mary's Hosp. Med. Sch., 1980–. *Recreations:* reading, gossip, opera, fishing. *Address:* 89 The Vineyard, Richmond, Surrey. *T:* 01–940 4135; Woodside Cottage, Clun, Craven Arms, Salop.

ODDIE, Prof. Guy Barrie, BArch, DipTP; architect and designer; Robert Adam Professor of Architecture, 1968–82, now Emeritus, and Head of Department of Architecture, 1968–80, University of Edinburgh; *b* 1 Jan. 1922; *o s* of Edward Oddie and Eleanor Pinkney; *m* 1952, Mabel Mary Smith; no *c*. *Educ:* Hookergate Grammar Sch.; Univ. of Newcastle upon Tyne. Demonstrator, Univ. of Newcastle upon Tyne, 1944; Sen. Lectr, Birmingham Sch. of Architecture, 1950–52; Research Architect, Building Res. Stn, 1947–50; Develt Gp, Min. of Educn, 1952–58; Staff architect, UGC, 1958–63; Consultant to OECD, 1963–66; Dir, Laboratories Investigation Unit, DES, 1966–68. Sen. Advr to OECD Prog. on Educnl Bldg, 1972–84. *Publications:* School Building Resources and their Effective Use, 1966; Development and Economy in Educational Building, 1968; Industrialised Building for Schools, 1975; contrib. Architects Jl, Architectural Rev., RIBA Jl. *Recreations:* dry-fly fishing, gardening. *Address:* The Causeway, Edinburgh EH15 3QA. *T:* 031–661 5492.

ODDY, Revel, FSA; Keeper, Department of Art and Archaeology, Royal Scottish Museum, Edinburgh, 1974–83; *b* 11 April 1922; *s* of Sidney Oddy and Muriel Barnfather; *m* 1949, Ariadne Margaret, *d* of late Sir Andrew Gourlay Clow, KCSI, CIE; two *s* two *d*. *Educ:* Worksop Coll.; Pembroke Coll., Cambridge (MA). FSA 1982. Served War, Loyal Regt and King's African Rifles, 1941–46. Mod. langs master, Dr Challoner's Grammar Sch., Amersham, 1949; Res. Asst, V&A Mus., London, 1950–55; Asst Keeper, Royal Scottish Mus., Edinburgh, 1955–74. *Recreations:* mild gardening, reading. *Address:* 44 Findhorn Place, Edinburgh EH9 2NT. *T:* 031–667 5815. *Clubs:* Civil Service; University of Edinburgh Staff (Edinburgh).

O'DEA, Sir Patrick Jerad, KCVO 1974; retired public servant, New Zealand; public affairs consultant; Extra Gentleman Usher to the Queen, since 1981; *b* 18 April 1918; 2nd *s* of late Patrick O'Dea; *m* 1945, Jean Mary, *d* of Hugh Mulholland; one *s* three *d*. *Educ:* St Paul's Coll. and Univ. of Otago, Dunedin, NZ; Victoria Univ., Wellington, NZ. Joined NZ Public Service, 1936; served in Agriculture Dept, 1936–47. Served War in Royal New Zealand Artillery of 2 NZEF, 1941–45. With Industries and Commerce Dept, 1947–49; subseq. served with Dept of Internal Affairs in various posts interrupted by 2 years' full-time study at Victoria Univ. of Wellington (DPA). Group Exec. Officer, Local Govt, 1959–64; Dep. Sec., 1964–67; Sec. for Internal Affairs, NZ, 1967–78; formerly Sec. for: Local Govt; Civil Defence; Sec. of Recreation and Sport; Clerk of the Writs; NZ Sec. to the Queen, 1969–78, reapptd 1981, for visit of Queen and Duke of Edinburgh to NZ. Pres., Keep NZ Beautiful Inc.; Chairman: Nat. Parks Centennial Commn; Dorothy Daniels Foundn; Vice-Chm., NZ Ballet Co.; Chm., NZ Sch. of Dance Bd; Nat. Co-ordinator, Duke of Edinburgh's Award Scheme in NZ; Mem., Vicentian Foundn. Dep. Chm., NZ Racing Authority. *Publications:* several papers on local govt in New Zealand. *Recreations:* gardening, golf, bowls. *Address:* 1 Tensing Place, Khandallah, Wellington, New Zealand. *T:* Wellington 792–424. *Clubs:* Shandon Golf (Petone, NZ); Khandallah Bowling (Khandallah, NZ); Wellesley (Wellington).

ODELL, John William, (Jack), OBE 1969; Joint Vice-Chairman, Lesney Products & Co. Ltd, Diecasting Engineers, London E9, 1981–82 (Joint Managing Director, 1947–73; Deputy Chairman, 1973–81); Chairman, Lledo (London) Ltd.

O'DELL, Mrs June Patricia; Deputy Chairman, Equal Opportunities Commission, since 1986; *b* 9 June 1929; *d* of Leonard Vickery, RN and Myra Vickery; *m* 1951 (marr. diss. 1963); one *s* two *d*. *Educ:* Edgehill Girls College; Plymouth Technical College. Estate Agent with own practice, 1965–. Nat. Pres., Fedn of Business and Professional Women, 1983–85; Chm., Employment Cttee, Internat. Fedn of Business and Professional Women, 1985–; Mem., Women's Nat. Commn, 1983–85. *Publication:* The Impact of New Technology on Employment of Women (Report), 1982–83. *Recreations:* music, particularly opera and choral; writing, literature, the countryside, equestrian events. *Address:* Fir Tree Cottage, Buslins Lane, Chartridge, Bucks HP5 2SN. *Club:* University Women's.

ODELL, Prof. Noel Ewart; geological research worker, since retirement from last professorship in 1962; *b* 25 Dec. 1890; *s* of Rev. R. W. Odell and M. M. Odell (*née* Ewart); *m* 1917, Gwladys Jones; one *s*. *Educ:* Brighton College; Imperial Coll. of Science and Technology (ARSM); Clare Coll., Cambridge (PhD; Hon. Fellow, 1983). MIMM, FGS, FRSE, FRGS. Served RE: 1915–19 (wounded three times); 1940–42, British and Indian Armies (Major, Bengal Sappers and Miners). Staff Lectr, Council for Adult Educn in Forces, 1942–47. Geologist, Anglo Persian Oil Co. Ltd, 1922–25; cons. geologist and mining engineer, Canada, 1927–30; Univ. Lectr in Geology and Tutor, Harvard Univ., 1928–30; Research Student and Univ. Lectr, Cambridge, 1931–40 (Fellow Commoner and Supervisor of Studies, Clare Coll.); Leverhulme Fellowships, 1934 and 1938; Lectr, McGill Univ. and Vis. Prof., Univ. of BC, Canada, 1948–49; Prof. of Geology and Head of Dept, Univ. of Otago, NZ, 1950–56, Peshawar Univ., Pakistan, 1960–62. British Council Lectr, Scandinavian univs 1946, 1959, Swiss univs 1947; Vis. Lectr, Göttingen Univ., Germany, 1985. Foreign expeditions: geologist to Oxford Univ. Spitsbergen expedn, 1921; geologist and leader, Merton Coll. Arctic expedn, 1923; Mt Everest 1924 (geologist, to 27,500 ft without oxygen, search for Mallory and Irvine) (private audience of HM King George V at Buckingham Palace, Nov. 1924); Mt Everest 1938, to 25,000 ft; Norway 1929 and British Columbia 1930, geological research; mountaineering and exploration in Canadian Rockies, 1927–47; Nanda Devi, 26,640 ft, first ascent with H. W. Tilman, 1936 (for 14 years highest peak climbed to summit); geol exploration in N Labrador, 1931; NE Greenland, 1933; Lloyd George Mts, Rockies, 1947; St Elias Mts, Yukon, Alaska, 1949 and 1977. Star in constellation Lyra named after N. E. Odell, Internat. Star Register, 1925. *Publications:* chapters in: Norton: The Fight for Everest, 1925; Tilman: Everest, 1938; Granites of Himalaya, Karakorum and Hindu Kush, ed Prof. F. A. Shams; contribs to journals, scientific *et al. Recreations:* fell-walking, watching Rugby football, listening to music. *Address:* Clare College, Cambridge CB2 1TL; 5 Dean Court, Cambridge. *T:* Cambridge 247701. *Clubs:* (Hon. Mem.) Alpine, Himalayan, and many foreign alpine and mountaineering clubs in Canada, NZ, SA, USA, Switzerland, Norway, Japan, inc. Arctic (former Pres.), and Arctic Inst. of N America.

ODELL, Prof. Peter Randon; Director, Centre for International Energy Studies, Erasmus University, Rotterdam, since 1981; *b* 1 July 1930; *s* of late Frank James Odell and late Grace Edna Odell; *m* 1957, Jean Mary McKintosh; two *s* two *d*. *Educ:* County Grammar Sch., Coalville; Univ. of Birmingham (BA, PhD); Fletcher Sch. of Law and Diplomacy, Cambridge, Mass (AM). FInstPet. RAF 1954–57. Economist, Shell International Petroleum Co., 1958–61; Lectr, LSE, 1961–65; Sen. Lectr, LSE, 1965–68; Prof. of Economic Geography, Erasmus Univ., 1968–81. Visiting Professor: LSE, 1983–; College of Europe, Bruges, 1983–; Scholar in Residence, Rockefeller Centre, Bellagio, 1984. Stamp Meml Lectr, London Univ., 1975. Canadian Council Fellow, 1978. Adviser, Dept of Energy, 1977–78. FRSA 1983. *Publications:* An Economic Geography of Oil, 1963; Natural Gas in Western Europe, 1969; Oil and World Power, 1970, 8th edn 1986; (with D. A. Preston) Economics and Societies in Latin America, 1973, 2nd edn 1978; Energy: Needs and Resources, 1974, 2nd edn 1977; (with K. E. Rosing) The North Sea Oil Province, 1975; The West European Energy Economy: the case for self-sufficiency, 1976; (with K. E. Rosing) The Optimal Development of the North Sea Oilfields, 1976; (with L. Vallenilla) The Pressures of Oil: a strategy for economic revival, 1978; British Oil Policy: a Radical Alternative, 1980; (with K. E. Rosing) The Future of Oil, 1980–2080, 1980, 2nd edn 1983. *Address:* De Lairesselaan 191, 3062 PH Rotterdam, The Netherlands. *T:* Rotterdam 4525341.

ODELL, Sir Stanley (John), Kt 1986; farmer and landowner; *b* 20 Nov. 1929; *s* of George Frederick Odell and Florence May Odell; *m* 1952, Eileen Grace Stuart; four *d*. *Educ:* Bedford Modern School. Chairman: Mid Beds Young Conservatives, 1953–59; Mid Beds Cons. Assoc., 1964–69; Beds Cons. European Constituency Council, 1979; E of England Provincial Council, Cons. Party, 1983 ; Vice-Chm., Nat. Union of Cons. and Unionist Assocs, 1986–. *Recreations:* politics, shooting. *Address:* Woodhall Farm, Campton, Shefford, Beds SG17 5PB. *T:* Hitchin 813230. *Club:* Farmers'.

ODGERS, Graeme David William; Deputy Chairman and Chief Finance Officer, British Telecommunications, since 1986; *b* 10 March 1934; *s* of William Arthur Odgers and Elizabeth Minty (*née* Rennie); *m* 1957, Diana Patricia Berge; one *s* two *d* (and one *d* decd). *Educ:* St John's Coll., Johannesburg; Gonville and Caius Coll., Cambridge (Mech. Scis Tripos); Harvard Business Sch. (MBA, Baker Scholar). Investment Officer, Internat. Finance Corp., Washington DC, 1959–62; Management Consultant, Urwick Orr and Partners Ltd, 1962–64; Investment Executive, Hambros Bank Ltd, 1964–65; Director: Keith Shipton and Co. Ltd, 1965–72; C. T. Bowring (Insurance) Holdings Ltd, 1972–74;

Chm., Odgers and Co. Ltd (Management Consultants), 1970–74; Dir, Industrial Develt Unit, DoI, 1974–77; Assoc. Dir (Finance), General Electric Co., 1977–78; Gp Finance Dir, 1979–86, Gp Man. Dir, 1983–86, Tarmac. Govt Dir, British Telecom, 1984–86 (pt-time Mem. Bd, 1983–86). *Recreations:* tennis, golf, wind surfing. *Address:* The Old Rectory, Eaton Constantine, Shrewsbury, Shropshire. *T:* Cressage 295. *Club:* Lansdowne.

ODGERS, Paul Randell, CB 1970; MBE 1945; TD 1949; Deputy Secretary, Department of Education and Science, 1971–75; *b* 30 July 1915; *e s* of late Dr P. N. B. Odgers and Mrs M. A. Odgers (*née* Higgins); *m* 1944, Diana, *d* of late R. E. F. Fawkes, CBE; one *s* one *d*. *Educ:* Rugby; New Coll., Oxford. Entered CS, Board of Education, 1937. Army Service, 1939–45 (despatches three times); Asst Secretary: Min. of Educn, 1948; Cabinet Office, 1956; Under-Secretary: Min. of Educn, 1958; Office of First Secretary of State, 1967; Office of Lord President of the Council, 1968; Office of Sec. of State for Social Services, 1968; Cabinet Office, 1970. Vice-Pres., Soc. for Promotion of Roman Studies; Mem. Council, GPDST. *Address:* Stone Walls, Aston Road, Haddenham, Bucks. *T:* Haddenham 291830. *Club:* United Oxford & Cambridge University.
See also C. D. Compston.

ODLING, Thomas George, CB 1974; *b* 18 Sept. 1911; *yr s* of late Major W. A. Odling, Paxford, Glos and late Mary Bennett Odling (*née* Case); *m* 1st, Camilla Haldane Paterson (marr. diss.); two *s*; 2nd, Hilary Katharine, *d* of late W. J. Palgrave-Ker, Lilliput, Dorset. *Educ:* Temple Grove; Rugby Sch.; New Coll., Oxford (MA). House of Commons: Asst Clerk, 1935; Clerk of Private Bills, Examr of Petitions for Private Bills and Taxing Officer, 1961–73; Clerk of Select Cttee on Parly Comr for Admin, 1969–73; Clerk of Committees, 1974–76, retired 1976. Temp. attached to Consultative Assembly of Council of Europe during 1949 and later sessions. *Recreations:* music, gardening. *Address:* Paxford, Campden, Glos. *Clubs:* Athenæum, MCC.
See also Maj.-Gen. W. Odling.

ODLING, Maj.-Gen. William, CB 1963; OBE 1951; MC; DL; President, English-Speaking Union (Eastern Counties); Chairman: Roman River (Colchester) Conservation Zone; Friends of Essex Churches; Member, Fingringhoe Parish Council, Vice-Chairman of School, and Chairman of Hall; Treasurer/Secretary, Fingringhoe Ancient Charities; *b* 8 June 1909; *s* of late Major and Mrs W. A. Odling, Paxford, Campden, Glos; *m* 1939, Margaret Marshall (*née* Gardner); one *s* two *d*. *Educ:* Temple Grove; Wellington Coll.; RMA, Woolwich. Subaltern RHA and RA, chiefly in India until 1938; Captain, 1938; Major, 1946; Lieut-Colonel, 1951; Colonel, 1953; Brigadier 1957; Maj.-General, 1961; Adjutant, TA, 1939; CRA, Madagascar Force, 1942 (MC); GSO 1, RA, COSSAC, Planning Staff for Operation Overlord, 1943; NW Europe Campaign (despatches), 1944; GSO 1, War Office, 1945; GSO 1, Training, GHQMELF, 1948; AQMG, MELF, 1950; AAG Colonel, War Office, 1953; CRA E Anglian Div., 1957; Brig. AQ, HQ E Comd, 1959; Maj.-Gen. i/c Admin, GHQ FELF, 1961–62; COS GHQ FELF 1962–64. DL Essex, 1975. *Recreations:* sailing (Cdre, Atalanta (Yacht) Owners Assoc.), print collecting, gardening, brick building, economising. *Address:* Gun House, Fingringhoe, Colchester CO5 7AL. *T:* Peldon 320. *Club:* Army and Navy.
See also T. G. Odling.

ODLING-SMEE, John Charles; Under-Secretary, HM Treasury, since 1982; *b* 13 April 1943; *s* of Charles William Odling-Smee and Katharine Hamilton Odling-Smee (*née* Aitchison). *Educ:* Durham School; St John's College, Cambridge. BA Cantab 1964, MA Oxon 1966. Junior Research Officer, Dept of Applied Economics, Cambridge, 1964–65; Asst Research Officer, Inst. of Economics and Statistics, Oxford, 1965–66; Fellow in Economics, Oriel College, Oxford, 1966–70; Research Officer, Inst. of Economics and Statistics, Oxford, 1968–71 and 1972–73; Economic Research Officer, Govt of Ghana, 1971–72; Senior Research Officer, Centre for Urban Economics, LSE, 1973–75; Economic Adviser, Central Policy Review Staff, Cabinet Office, 1975–77; Senior Economic Adviser, HM Treasury, 1977–80; Senior Economist, IMF, 1981–82. *Publications:* (with A. Grey and N. P. Hepworth) Housing Rents, Costs and Subsidies, 1978, 2nd edn 1981; (with R. C. O. Matthews and C. H. Feinstein) British Economic Growth 1856–1973, 1982; articles in books and learned jls. *Address:* 107 Clapham Manor Street, SW4 6DR. *T:* 01–720 5167.

O'DONNELL, Dr Michael; author and broadcaster; *b* 20 Oct. 1928; *o s* of late James Michael O'Donnell and Nora (*née* O'Sullivan); *m* 1953, Catherine Dorrington Ward; one *s* two *d*. *Educ:* Stonyhurst; Trinity Hall, Cambridge (Lane Harrington Schol.); St Thomas's Hosp. Med. Sch., London (MB, BChir). Editor, Cambridge Writing, 1948; Scriptwriter, BBC Radio, 1949–52. General Medical Practitioner, 1954–64. Editor, World Medicine, 1966–82. Member: General Medical Council, 1971–; Longman Editorial Adv. Bd, 1978–82. Inaugural lecture, Green Coll., Oxford, 1981. Scientific Adviser: O Lucky Man (film), 1972; Inside Medicine (BBC TV), 1974; Don't Ask Me (Yorkshire TV), 1977; Don't Just Sit There (Yorkshire TV), 1979–80; Where There's Life (Yorkshire TV), 1981–83. *Television plays:* Suggestion of Sabotage, 1963; Dangerous Reunion, 1964; Resolution, 1964; *television documentaries:* You'll Never Believe It, 1962; Cross Your Heart and Hope to Live, 1975; The Presidential Race, 1976; From Europe to the Coast, 1976; Chasing the Dragon, 1979; Second Opinion, 1980; Judgement on Las Vegas, 1981; Is Your Brain Really Necessary, 1982; Plague of Hearts, 1983; Medical Express, 1984; Can You Avoid Cancer?, 1984; O'Donnell Investigates . . . booze, 1985; O'Donnell Investigates . . . food, 1985; O'Donnell Investigates . . . the food business, 1986; *radio:* contributor to Stop the Week (BBC), 1976–; Chm., My Word (BBC), 1983–. Medical Journalists Assoc. Award, 1971 and 1982; British Science Writers' Award, 1979. *Publications:* Cambridge Anthology, 1952; The Europe We Want, 1971; My Medical School, 1978; The Devil's Prison, 1982; Doctor! Doctor! an insider's guide to the games doctors play, 1986; contrib. Punch, New Scientist, Vogue, The Times, Sunday Times, Daily Telegraph, Daily Mail. *Recreations:* golf, listening to music, loitering (with and without intent). *Address:* Cedar Tree House, Weybridge Park, Weybridge, Surrey KT13 8SJ. *T:* Weybridge 46095. *Club:* Garrick.

O'DONNELL, Rt. Hon. Turlough; PC 1979; **Rt. Hon. Lord Justice O'Donnell;** Lord Justice of Appeal, Supreme Court of Northern Ireland, since 1979; *b* 5 Aug. 1924; *e s* of Charles and Eileen O'Donnell; *m* 1954, Eileen McKinley; two *s* two *d*. *Educ:* Abbey Grammar Sch., Newry; Queen's Univ., Belfast (LLB). Called to Bar of Northern Ireland, 1947; called to Inner Bar, 1964; Puisne Judge, NI, 1971–79. Chairman: NI Bar Council, 1970–71, Council of Legal Educn, NI, 1980–. *Recreations:* golf, folk music. *Address:* 155 Glen Road, Belfast BT11 8BS. *T:* 613965; Royal Courts of Justice (Ulster), Belfast BT1 3JF.

O'DONOGHUE, Michael; His Honour Judge O'Donoghue; a Circuit Judge, since 1982; *b* 10 June 1929; *s* of late Dr James O'Donoghue, MB, ChB and Vera O'Donoghue. *Educ:* Rhyl County School; Univ. of Liverpool. LLB (Hons) 1950. Called to the Bar, Gray's Inn, 1951; National Service as Flying Officer, RAF, 1951–53; practised at the Chancery Bar, 1954–82; Lectr in Law (part time), Univ. of Liverpool, 1966–82. *Recreations:* music, sailing, photography. *Address:* 21 Princes Park Mansions, Liverpool L8

3SA; Helen View, 29 Rhes Segontiwm, Caernarfon, Gwynedd LL55 2PH. *Clubs:* Athenæum (Liverpool); Royal Welsh Yacht (Caernarfon) (Commodore, 1980–82).

O'DONOGHUE, Philip Nicholas, CBiol, FIBiol; General Secretary, Institute of Biology, since 1982; *b* 9 Oct. 1929; *s* of Terence Frederick O'Donoghue and Ellen Mary (*née* Haynes); *m* 1955, Veronica Florence Campbell; two *d*. *Educ:* East Barnet Grammar Sch.; Univ. of Nottingham (BSc; MSc 1959). FIBiol 1975. Experimental Officer, ARC's Field Stn, Compton, 1952–55 and Inst. of Animal Physiology, Babraham, 1955–61; Scientific Officer, National Inst. for Res. in Dairying, Shinfield, 1962–66; Lectr in Exptl Vet. Science and later Sen. Lectr in Lab. Animal Science, Royal Postgrad. Med. Sch., Univ. of London, 1966–82. Vice-Pres., Inst. of Animal Technicians, 1969–; Hon. Sec., Inst. of Biology, 1972–76; Member: TEC, 1973–79 (Chm., Life Sciences Cttee, 1973–80); Council, Section of Comparative Medicine, RSM, 1983– (Pres., 1985–86). Editor, Laboratory Animals, 1967–82. *Publications:* editor of books and author of articles chiefly on the law relating to and the effective use and proper care of laboratory animals. *Recreations:* music, local history, talking. *Address:* 21 Holyrood Road, New Barnet, Herts EN5 1DQ. *T:* 01–449 3692. *Clubs:* Athenæum, Royal Society of Medicine.

O'DONOVAN, Rev. Canon Oliver Michael Timothy, DPhil; Regius Professor of Moral and Pastoral Theology, University of Oxford, since 1982; Canon of Christ Church, Oxford, since 1982; *b* 28 June 1945; *s* of Michael and Joan M. O'Donovan; *m* 1978, Joan Elizabeth Lockwood; two *s*. *Educ:* University Coll. Sch., Hampstead; Balliol Coll., Oxford (MA, DPhil); Wycliffe Hall, Oxford; Princeton Univ. Ordained deacon 1972, priest 1973, dio. of Oxford. Tutor, Wycliffe Hall, Oxford, 1972–77; Prof. of Systematic Theology, Wycliffe Coll., Toronto, 1977–82. Member: C of E Bd for Social Responsibility, 1976–77, 1982–85; Anglican-Roman Catholic Internat. Commn, 1985–; Anglican-Orthodox Jt Doctrinal Discussions, 1982–84. *Publications:* The Problem of Self-Love in Saint Augustine, 1980; Begotten or Made?, 1984; Resurrection and Moral Order, 1986; contrib. Jl of Theol Studies and Jl of Religious Ethics. *Address:* Christ Church, Oxford OX1 1DP.

OEHLERS, Maj.-Gen. Gordon Richard; Assistant Chief of Defence Staff (Command, Control, Communications and Information Systems), since 1984; *b* 19 April 1933; *s* of late Dr Roderic Clarke Oehlers and Hazel Ethne Oehlers (*née* Van Geyzel); *m* 1956, Doreen Gallant; one *s* one *d*. *Educ:* St Andrews School, Singapore. CEng, FIEE, MIERE. Commissioned Royal Corps of Signals, 1958; UK and Middle East, 1958–64; Adjutant, 4th Div. Signals Regt, 1964–66; Instructor, School of Signals, 1966–68; OC 7th Armd Bde HQ and Signals Sqdn, 1968–70; GSO2 (Weapons), 1970–72; CO 7th Signal Regt, 1973–76; Commander Corps Royal Signals, 1st (British) Corps, 1977–79; Dir, Op. Requirements 4 (Army), 1979–84. Pres., British Wireless Dinner Club, 1986–. *Recreations:* interested in all games esp. badminton (Captain Warwicks County Badminton Team, 1954–56), lawn tennis (Chm., Army Lawn Tennis Assoc., 1980–). *Address:* c/o National Westminster Bank, 4 High Street, Petersfield, Hants GU32 3JF.

OESTREICHER, Rev. Canon Paul; Director of the International Ministry of Coventry Cathedral, since 1986; Canon Residentiary of Coventry Cathedral, since 1986; Member of the Society of Friends (Quakers), since 1982; journalist; *b* Germany, 29 Sept. 1931; *s* of Paul Oestreicher and Emma (*née* Schnaus); *m* 1958, Lore Feind; two *s* two *d*. *Educ:* King's High Sch., Dunedin; Otago and Victoria Univs, NZ; Bonn Univ. (Humboldt Res. Fellow); Lincoln Theol College. BA Mod. Langs Otago 1953; MA Hons Polit. Sci. Victoria 1955. Ordained 1959. Fled to NZ with refugee parents, 1939; returned to Europe, 1955. Fraternal worker with German Lutheran Church at Rüsselsheim, trng in problems of industrial soc. (Opel, Gen. Motors), 1958–59; Curate, Dalston, E London, 1959–61; Producer, Relig. Dept, BBC Radio, 1961–64; Assoc. Sec., Dept of Internat. Affairs, Brit. Council of Churches with special resp. for East-West Relations, 1964–69; Vicar, Church of the Ascension, Blackheath, 1968–81; Asst Gen. Sec. and Sec. for Internat. Affairs, BCC, 1981–86; Dir of (Lay) Trng, Dio. Southwark, 1969–72; Hon. Chaplain to Bp of Southwark, 1975–81; Public Preacher in Dio. Southwark, 1981–86; Hon. Canon of Southwark Cathedral, 1978–83, Canon Emeritus 1983–86. Mem. Gen. Synod of C of E, 1970–86. Member: Brit. Council of Churches working parties on Southern Africa and Eastern Europe; Anglican Pacifist Fellowship (sometime exec. mem.), 1960–; Exec. Mem., Christian Concern for Southern Africa, 1978–81; Chm., of Trustees, Christian Inst. (of Southern Africa) Fund, 1984–; Chm., British Section, Amnesty International, 1974–79. Mem. Council, Keston Coll. (Centre for the Study of Religion and Communism), 1976–82. Vice-Chm., Campaign for Nuclear Disarmament, 1980–81, Vice-Pres. 1983–; Mem. Alternative Defence Commn, 1981–; Vice-Chm., Ecumenical Commn for Church and Society in W Europe (Brussels), 1982–86. Editor, Critic (Otago Univ. newspaper), 1952–53; subseq. free-lance journalist and broadcaster. *Publications:* (ed English edn) Helmut Gollwitzer, The Demands of Freedom, 1965; (trans.) H. J. Schultz, Conversion to the World, 1967; (ed, with J. Klugmann) What Kind of Revolution: A Christian-Communist Dialogue, 1968; (ed) The Christian Marxist Dialogue, 1969; (jtly) The Church and the Bomb, 1983. *Address:* Coventry Cathedral Office, 7 Priory Row, Coventry, W Midlands CV1 5EX. *T:* Coventry 27597; 20 Styvechale Avenue, Coventry CV5 6DX. *T:* Coventry 73704.

O'FAOLAIN, Sean; writer. *Publications:* Midsummer Night Madness, 1932; A Nest of Simple Folk, 1933; Constance Markievicz: a biography, 1934; Bird Alone, 1936; A Purse of Coppers, 1937; King of the Beggars: a biography, 1938; She Had to Do Something (play), 1938; An Irish Journey, 1940; Come Back to Erin, 1940; The Great O'Neill: a biography, 1942; Teresa, 1946; The Short Story, 1948; Summer in Italy, 1949; Newman's Way, 1952; South to Sicily, 1953; The Vanishing Hero, 1956; The Stories of Sean O'Faolain, 1958; I Remember! I Remember!, 1962; Vive Moi!, 1965; The Heat of the Sun, 1966; The Talking Trees, 1970; Foreign Affairs and Other Stories, 1976; Selected Stories of Sean O'Faolain, 1978; And Again?, 1979; The Collected Stories, vol. I, 1980, vol. II, 1981, vol. III, 1982. *Address:* 17 Rosmeen Park, Dunlaoire, Dublin.

O'FERRALL, Very Rev. Basil Arthur, CB 1979; MA; Dean of Jersey, and Rector of St Helier, Jersey, since 1985; Hon. Canon of Winchester, since 1986; *b* 25 Aug. 1924; *s* of Basil James and Mabel Violet O'Ferrall, Dublin; *m* 1952, Joyce Forbes (*née* Taylor); one *s* two *d*. *Educ:* St Patrick's Cathedral Gram. Sch., Dublin; Trinity Coll., Dublin (BA 1948, MA 1966). Curate Assistant, St Patrick's, Coleraine, 1948; Chaplain RN, 1951; served: HMS Victory, 1951; Ganges, 1952; Gambia, 1952–54; Curlew, 1955; Daedalus, 1956; Amphibious Warfare Sqdn, 1956–58; HMS Adamant, 1958–60; 40 Commando, RM, 1960–62; RN Hosp., Bighi, 1962; HMS Victorious, 1963–64; Condor, 1964–66; Maidstone, 1966–68; St Vincent, 1968; Commando Training Centre, RM, 1969–71; HM Naval Base, Portsmouth, 1971–74; CTC, RM, 1975; Chaplain of the Fleet and Archdeacon of the Royal Navy, 1975–80; Vicar of Ranworth wih Panxworth and Woodbastwick (Norwich) and Bishop's Chaplain for the Broads, 1980–85; Chaplain to the Queen, 1980–85. Hon. Canon of Gibraltar, 1977–80. QHC 1975–80. *Recreations:* sailing, ornithology. *Address:* The Deanery, Jersey, CI.

OFFALY, Earl of; Thomas FitzGerald; *b* 12 Jan. 1974; *s* of Marquess of Kildare, *qv*.

OFFICER, Maj.-Gen. William James, CB 1962; CBE 1959 (OBE 1945); MB, ChB; late RAMC; *b* 24 August 1903; *s* of John Liddell Officer, OBE, WS, Edinburgh; *m* 1934, Doris, *d* of William Charles Mattinson, Keswick, Cumberland; three *d*. *Educ:* Edinburgh Acad.; Durham School; Edinburgh University. MB, ChB, Edin., 1927. Commissioned 7/9 (Highland) Bn, The Royal Scots (TA), 1920; joined RAMC, 1929; Major, 1939; Commanding Officer British Military Hosp., Deolali, and Officer-in-Charge RAMC Records, India and Burma, 1939–41; Served War of 1939–45 (despatches twice); in Burma, 1941–45; ADMS, 17th Indian Division and 2nd British Division; DDMS, Chindits Special Force and 33rd Indian Corps. Lt-Col, 1946; Asst Commandant, RAMC Depot and Training Establishment; Commanding Officer, British Military Hospital, Fayid (T/Col), 1949; Col 1951; ADMS, Hannover Dist, 1952; ADMS, N Midland Dist, 1954; DDMS (Actg Brig.), 2 (Br) Corps (Suez), 1956; Brig., 1957; Dir of Medical Services (temp. Maj.-Gen.), Middle East Land Forces, 1957–60; Maj.-Gen., 1960; Dir of Medical Services, Far East Land Forces, 1960–63; QHS 1961–63, retired 1963. *Address:* c/o Royal Bank of Scotland, Kirkland House, SW1. *Club:* Naval and Military.

OFFLER, Prof. Hilary Seton, MA; FBA 1974; Professor of Medieval History in the University of Durham, 1956–78, now Professor Emeritus; *b* 3 Feb. 1913; *s* of Horace Offler and late Jenny Whebby; *m* 1951, Betty Elfreda, *d* of late Archibald Jackson, Sawbridgeworth; two *s*. *Educ:* Hereford High School; Emmanuel College, Cambridge. 1st Cl. Historical Tripos Pt I, 1932, Part II, 1933, Theological Tripos Pt II, 1934; Lightfoot Schol., Cambridge, 1934; Research Fellow, Emmanuel Coll., 1936–40. Served with RA in N Africa, Sicily and NW Europe, 1940–46. Lecturer, Univ. of Bristol, 1946; Reader in Medieval History, Univ. of Durham, 1947. Pres., Surtees Society, 1980– (Sec., 1950–66). *Publications:* edited: Ockham, Opera politica, vol. i (jtly) 1940, *ed. altera* 1974; vol. ii (jtly) 1963; vol. iii 1956; (with E. Bonjour and G. R. Potter) A Short History of Switzerland, 1952; Medieval Historians of Durham, 1958; Durham Episcopal Charters 1071–1152, 1968; articles in English and foreign hist. jls. *Address:* 28 Old Elvet, Durham. *T:* Durham 46219.

OFFORD, Albert Cyril, DSc London; PhD Cantab; FRS 1952; FRSE; Emeritus Professor of Mathematics, University of London; Professor, 1966–73, Hon. Fellow, 1978, London School of Economics and Political Science; *b* 9 June 1906; *s* of Albert Edwin and Hester Louise Offord; *m* 1945, Marguerite Yvonne Pickard; one *d*. *Educ:* Hackney Downs School, London; University Coll. London (Fellow, 1969); St John's Coll., Cambridge. Fellow of St John's Coll., Cambridge, 1937–40; Lectr, UC N Wales, Bangor, 1940–41; Lectr, King's Coll., Newcastle upon Tyne, 1941–45; Professor: King's College, Newcastle upon Tyne, 1945–48; Birkbeck Coll., Univ. of London, 1948–66. *Publications:* papers in various mathematical journals. *Recreation:* early, especially Renaissance, music. *Address:* West Cottage, 24A Norham Gardens, Oxford OX2 6QD. *T:* Oxford 513703.

O'FIAICH, His Eminence Cardinal Tomás Séamus; *see* Armagh, Archbishop of, (RC).

O'FLAHERTY, Dr Coleman Anthony; Director and Principal (formerly Principal), Tasmanian State Institute of Technology (formerly Tasmanian College of Advanced Education), Australia, since 1978; *b* 8 Feb. 1933; *s* of Michael and Agnes O'Flaherty; *m* 1957, Nuala Rose Silke. *Educ:* Nat. Univ. of Ireland (BE); Iowa State Univ. (MS, PhD). FICE; FIE(Aust); FIHT; FRSA; FAIM; FCIT. Engineer: Galway Co. Council, Ireland, 1954–55; Canadian Pacific Railway Co., Montreal, 1955–56; M. W. Kellogg Co., USA, 1956–57; Asst Prof., Iowa State Univ., 1957–62; Leeds University: Lectr, 1962–66; Prof. of Transport Engineering, Inst. for Transport Studies and Dept of Civil Engineering, 1966–74; First Asst Comr (Engineering), Nat. Capital Develt Commn, Canberra, 1974–78. Vis. Prof., Univ. of Melbourne, 1973. *Publications:* Highways, 1967, 2nd edn 1974, vol. I of 3rd edn (Traffic Planning and Engineering), 1986; (jtly) Passenger Conveyors, 1972; (jtly) Introduction to Hovercraft and Hoverports, 1975; contribs to professional jls. *Recreation:* walking. *Address:* Tasmanian State Institute of Technology, PO Box 1214, Launceston, Tasmania 7250, Australia. *T:* (003) 260531. *Club:* Launceston.

O'FLYNN, Hon. Francis Duncan; QC 1968; MP (Lab) Island Bay, since 1978; Minister of State and Defence, New Zealand, since 1984; *b* 1918; *s* of Hon. Francis E. O'Flynn, MLC; *m* 1942, Sylvia Elizabeth Hefford; one *s* three *d*. *Educ:* Christchurch Boys' High School; Victoria University of Wellington (BA, LLM). Flight Lieut, RNZAF, 1942–46; Flying Instructor, NZ and 6 Flying Boat Sqdn, Pacific. Barrister and Solicitor, 1948; in practice on own account, 1954–. MP for Kapiti, 1972–75. Member: Otaki Borough Council, 1968–71; Wellington City Council, 1977–83. Mem. Council, Wellington District Law Soc., 1970–74. *Recreations:* golf, bowls. *Address:* 105 Grant Road, Thorndon, New Zealand. *T:* (04) 720344.

of MAR, family name of **Countess of Mar.**

OGDEN, (Edward) Michael, QC 1968; Barrister since 1950; a Recorder (formerly Recorder of Hastings), since 1971; *b* 9 Apr. 1926; *er s* of late Edward Cannon Ogden and Daisy (*née* Paris); *m* 1951, Joan Kathleen, *er d* of late Pius Charles Brodrick and Kathleen (*née* Moran); two *s* two *d*. *Educ:* Downside Sch.; Jesus Coll., Cambridge (MA). Served in RAC (Royal Glos Hussars and 16th/5th Lancers), 1944–47 (Capt.); Inns of Court Regt (TA) 1950–56. Jesus Coll., Cambridge, 1948–49; called to Bar, Lincoln's Inn, 1950; Bencher, 1977. Mem. Bar Council, 1960–64, 1966–70, 1971–78 (responsible for fee negotiations, 1968–72, Treas., 1972–74, Chm., Internat. Relns Cttee, 1974–75); Mem. Senate of the Inns of Court, 1966–70, 1972–78. Leader, SE Circuit, 1975–78. Member: Council of Union Internationale des Avocats, 1962–83; Council of Legal Educn, 1969–74; Council, Internat. Bar Assoc., 1983–. Chairman: Criminal Injuries Compensation Bd, 1975– (Mem., 1968–); Inter-Professional Wkg Party publishing Actuarial Tables for Personal Injury and Fatal Accident Cases, 1982–84; Mem., Lord Chancellor's Adv. on Legal Education, 1972–74. Dir, Internat. Assoc. of Crime Victim Compensation Bds, 1978– (Co-Chm. 1983–). Assessor for Home Sec. of compensation for persons wrongly convicted, 1978–. *Address:* 2 Crown Office Row, Temple, EC4Y 7HJ. *T:* 01–353 9337.

OGDEN, Eric; *b* 23 Aug. 1923; *s* of Robert and Jane Lillian Ogden, Rhodes, Co. Lancaster; *m*; one *s*; *m* Marjorie (*née* Smith); two *s* two step *d*. *Educ:* Queen Elizabeth's Grammar School, Middleton, Lancs; Leigh Tech. Coll.; Wigan Mining and Tech. Coll. Merchant Service, 1942–46. Textiles, 1946–52; NCB, 1952–64. Mem., Nat. Union of Mineworkers. Councillor, Borough of Middleton, 1958–65. NUM sponsored candidate, West Derby, Liverpool, 1962. MP (Lab 1964–81, SDP 1981–83) Liverpool, Derby W, 1964–83; contested (SDP) Liverpool, Derby W, 1983. Dir, Ogden's, Fotografica & Fulcrum Ltd. Mem., PO Stamps Adv. Cttee. Chairman: Falkland Islands Assoc.; UK Falkland Islands Cttee. *Recreations:* gardening, photography, motoring. *Club:* Europe House.

OGDEN, Frank Collinge, CBE 1956; FRGS; *b* 30 Mar. 1907; *s* of Paul and Nora Ogden; *m* 1944, Margaret, *o d* of Fred and Elizabeth Greenwood; one *s* two *d* (and one *d* decd). *Educ:* Manchester Grammar School; King's College, Cambridge. Entered Levant Consular Service, 1930; served in Cairo, Alexandria, Bagdad and Damascus; served War, 1941–42; Min. of Information, 1942; Tabriz, 1942; 1st Sec., Bogotá, 1944, Chargé d'Affaires, 1945; Consul, Shiraz, 1947; transferred to Seattle, 1949; Consul-General, Seattle, 1952; Basra, 1953; Gothenburg, 1955; Couns., Brit. Emb. in Libya, 1958; Chargé d'Affaires, 1958, 1959; Counsellor and Consul-General, Brit. Emb., Buenos Aires, 1960–65; retired. *Recreations:* swimming, motoring. *Address:* Yellow Sands, Thorney Drive, Selsey, Chichester, West Sussex. *Club:* Royal Automobile.

OGDEN, Michael; *see* Ogden, E. M.

OGDON, John (Andrew Howard); Pianist, Composer; *b* Mansfield Woodhouse, Notts, 27 Jan. 1937; *m* 1960, Brenda Mary Lucas; one *s* one *d*. *Educ:* Manchester Gram. Sch.; Royal Manchester Coll. of Music. Concert Appearances include: Michelangeli Festival, Brescia, 1966; Festivals of Spoleto, Edinburgh, Prague Spring, Zagreb Biennale, Cheltenham. Founded Cardiff Festival (with Alun Hoddinott), 1967, Jt Artistic Dir. Two-piano recitals with Brenda Lucas; concert appearances, USA, USSR, Australia, Far East, European capitals. Prof. in Music Dept, Univ. of Indiana, Bloomington, 1977–80. Awards: Liverpool, 1959; Liszt Prize, 1961; Tchaikovsky Prize (*ex aequo* with Vladimir Ashkenazy), Moscow, 1962; Harriet Cohen International Award. *Compositions:* large and small, mainly for piano. *Recreations:* history, literature, especially P. G. Wodehouse. *Address:* c/o Basil Douglas Ltd, 8 St George's Terrace, Regent's Park Road, NW1 8XJ.

OGILVIE, Sir Alec (Drummond), Kt 1965; Chairman, Powell Duffryn Ltd, 1969–78 (Deputy Chairman, 1967–69); *b* 17 May 1913; *s* of late Sir George Drummond Ogilvie, KCIE, CSI; *m* 1945, Lesley Constance, *d* of E. B. Woollan; two *s*. *Educ:* Cheltenham College. Served War of 1939–45; 2/2nd Gurkha Rifles (Indian Army), 1940–45; Captain 1941; PoW, Singapore, 1942–45. Joined Andrew Yule & Co. Ltd, Calcutta, 1935, Man. Dir, 1956, and Chm., 1962–65. Director: Westinghouse Brake & Signal Co. Ltd, 1966–79; Lindustries Ltd, 1973–79; J. Lyons & Co. Ltd, 1977–78. Pres., Bengal Chamber of Commerce and Industry, 1964–65; Pres., Associated Chambers of Commerce and Industry of India, 1964–65. Member: Council, King Edward VII Hosp. for Officers, 1967– (Vice-Pres., 1979–); Council, Cheltenham Coll., 1973–85 (Dep. Pres., 1983–85). *Recreations:* golf, walking. *Address:* Townlands, High Street, Lindfield, West Sussex RH16 2HT. *T:* Lindfield 3953. *Clubs:* Oriental, MCC; Bengal (Calcutta).

OGILVIE, Lady, (Mary Helen); Principal of St Anne's College, Oxford, 1953–66; *b* 22 March 1900; *e d* of late Rev. Professor A. B. Macaulay, DD, of Glasgow; *m* 1922, (Sir) Frederick Wolff Ogilvie, LLD (*d* 1949), Principal of Jesus College, Oxford, 1945–49; one *s* (and two *s* decd). *Educ:* St George's, Edinburgh; Somerville College, Oxford (Hon. Fellow, 1978). BA Hon. Sch. of Mod. Hist., Oxford, 1922, MA 1937. Member: Royal Commission on Population, 1944–49; Archbp's Commn on Church and State, 1967–70. Tutor of Women Students, University of Leeds, 1949–53. Member of Arts Council of Great Britain, 1953–58; on Governing Board of Cheltenham Ladies' College, 1951–75; Governing Board of Clifton College, 1960–72. Hon. LLD: Wilson College, Pa, 1956, QUB 1960; Leeds Univ., 1962; Trent Univ., Ont, 1972; Hon. DCL Stirling, 1973. Hon. Fellow: St Anne's College, Oxford, 1966; Lucy Cavendish Collegiate Soc., 1971. *Recreation:* travel.

OGILVIE-GRANT, family name of **Earl of Seafield.**

OGILVIE THOMPSON, Julian; Deputy Chairman, Anglo American Corporation of SA Ltd, since 1983; Chairman, De Beers Consolidated Mines Ltd, since 1985 (Deputy Chairman, 1982–85); *b* 27 Jan. 1934; *s* of Hon. N. Ogilvie Thompson, formerly Chief Justice of S Africa, and Eve Ogilvie Thompson; *m* 1956, Hon. Tessa Mary Brand, *yr* surv. *d* of 4th Viscount Hampden, CMG and Leila, Viscountess Hampden; two *s* two *d*. *Educ:* Diocesan Coll., Rondebosch; Univ. of Cape Town; Worcester Coll., Oxford. MA. Diocesan Coll. Rhodes Scholar, 1953. Joined Anglo American Corp. of SA Ltd, 1956; Dir, 1970; Exec. Dir, 1971–82; Chairman: Anglo American Gold Investment Co. Ltd, 1976–; Minerals and Resources Corp. Ltd, 1982–; Vice Chm., Barclays Nat. Bank Ltd, 1977–. *Recreations:* shooting, fishing, golf. *Address:* Froome, Froome Street, Athol Extension 3, Sandton, Transvaal, S Africa. *T:* 884–3925. *Clubs:* White's; Rand (Johannesburg); Kimberley (Cape Province); The Brook (NY).
See also Baroness Dacre.

OGILVY, family name of **Earl of Airlie.**

OGILVY, Lord; David John Ogilvy; *b* 9 March 1958; *s* and *heir* of 13th Earl of Airlie, *qv*; *m* 1981, Hon. Geraldine Harmsworth, *d* of Viscount Rothermere, *qv*; one *d*. *Educ:* Eton and Oxford (MA). *Address:* 13 St Leonards Terrace, Chelsea, SW3. *T:* 01–730 8741.

OGILVY, Hon. Angus James Bruce; *b* 14 Sept. 1928; *s* of 12th (*de facto* 9th) Earl of Airlie, KT, GCVO, MC; *m* 1963, HRH Princess Alexandra of Kent; one *s* one *d*. *Educ:* Eton Coll.; Trinity Coll., Oxford (MA). Scots Guards, 1946–48; Mem., HM Body Guard for Scotland (The Royal Company of Archers). President: Imperial Cancer Res. Fund, 1964–; NAYC, 1969– (Chm. 1964–69); Carr-Gomn Soc., 1983–; Vice-Pres., Friends of the Elderly & Gentlefolk's Help, 1969– (Treasurer, 1952–63; Chm. 1963–69); Chairman, Council: Nat. Youth Enterprise Scheme, 1983–86; Fairbridge/YES, 1986– (Chm. Trustees, Fairbridge/YES Foundn (formerly YES Foundn), 1983–); Patron: Nat. Assoc. of Ladies' Circles, 1973–82; Arthritis Care (formerly British Rheumatism and Arthritis Soc.), 1978– (Chm. 1963–69; Pres., 1969–78); Inst. for Complementary Medicine, 1982–; Scottish Wildlife Trust, 1974 (Pres., 1969–74); Vice-Patron: TocH, 1963–83; Nat. Children's Homes, 1986–; Member: Governing Council, SPCK, 1984–; Council, City of London Business in the Community, 1983–; Governing Council, Business in the Community, 1984–. Trustee: Leeds Castle Foundn, 1975–; GB-Sasakawa Foundn, 1985–. Director of various public cos. *Recreations:* architecture, reading, music. *Address:* Thatched House Lodge, Richmond, Surrey. *T:* 01–546 8833. *Club:* White's.
See also under Royal Family.

OGILVY, Sir David (John Wilfrid), 13th Bt, *cr* 1626; DL; farmer and landowner; *b* 3 February 1914; *e s* of Gilbert Francis Molyneux Ogilvy (*d* 1953) (4th *s* of 10th Bt) and Marjory Katharine, *d* of late M. B. Clive, Whitfield, Herefordshire; *S* uncle, Sir Herbert Kinnaird Ogilvy, 12th Bt, 1956; *m* 1966, Penelope Mary Ursula, *d* of Arthur Lafone Frank Hills, White Court, Kent; one *s*. *Educ:* Eton; Trinity College, Oxford. Served in the RNVR in War of 1939–45. JP 1957, DL 1971, East Lothian. *Heir: s* Francis Gilbert Arthur Ogilvy, *b* 22 April 1969. *Address:* Winton House, Pencaitland, East Lothian EH34 5AT. *T:* Pencaitland 340222. *Club:* New (Edinburgh).

OGILVY, David Mackenzie, CBE 1967; Founder, Ogilvy and Mather, 1948, Chairman to 1973; *b* 23 June 1911; *s* of Francis John Longley Ogilvy and Dorothy Fairfield; *m* 1973, Herta Lans; one *s*. *Educ:* Fettes College, Edinburgh; Christ Church, Oxford (Scholar). British Security Coordination, 1942–45. Dir, NY Philharmonic, 1957–67. Chm., Utd Negro Coll. Fund, 1968. Trustee and Mem. of Honor, World Wildlife Fund. Dr of letters (*hc*), Adelphi Univ., USA, 1977. *Publications:* Confessions of an Advertising Man, 1963; Blood, Brains and Beer (autobiog.), 1978; Ogilvy On Advertising, 1983. *Recreation:* gardening. *Address:* Château de Touffou, 86300 Bonnes, France. *Club:* Brook (NY).

OGILVY-WEDDERBURN, Sir Andrew John Alexander, 13th and 7th Bt *cr* 1704 and 1803; Major, The Black Watch (Royal Highland Regiment); *b* 4 Aug. 1952; *s* of Sir

(John) Peter Ogilvy-Wedderburn, 12th and 6th Bt, and of Elizabeth Katharine, *e d* of late John A. Cox, Drumkilbo; *S* father, 1977; *m* 1984, Gillian Meade, *yr d* of Richard Adderley, Pickering, N Yorks; one *d. Educ:* Gordonstoun. *Heir: cousin* Caryl Eustace Wedderburn Ogilvy, ARIBA [*b* 10 Dec. 1925; *m* 1953, Katharine Mary, *o d* of William Steele; one *s* two *d*]. *Address:* Silvie, Alyth, Perthshire.

OGLE-SKAN, Peter Henry, CVO 1972; TD 1948; Director, Scottish Services, Department of the Environment, 1970–75; *b* 4 July 1915; 2nd *s* of Dr H. W. Ogle-Skan, Hendon; *m* 1941, Pamela Moira Heslop; one *s* one *d. Educ:* Merchant Taylors' Sch., London. Clerk with Arbuthnot-Latham & Co. Ltd, London, 1933–39. Commnd into Royal Engineers (TA), 1936; War Service, 1939–46; England, 1939–42; India, 1942–45. Min. of Works: Temp. Principal, 1946; Principal, 1948; Asst Sec., 1955; Under-Sec., Scottish HQ, MPBW, 1966–70. *Recreations:* golf, walking, photography. *Address:* 44 Ravelston Garden, Edinburgh EH4 3LF. *T:* 031–337 6834.

OGLESBY, Peter Rogerson, CB 1982; Director, Regency Life Assurance Co. (formerly Transinternational Life Insurance Co. Ltd), since 1983; *b* 15 July 1922; *s* of late Leonard William Oglesby and late Jessie Oglesby (*née* Rogerson); *m* 1947, Doreen Hilda Hudson; three *d. Educ:* Woodhouse Grove Sch., Apperley Bridge. Clerical Officer, Admlty, 1939–47; Exec. Officer, Min. of Nat. Ins., 1947–56; Higher Exec. Officer, MPNI, 1956–62, Principal 1962–64; Principal Private Secretary: to Chancellor of Duchy of Lancaster, 1964–66; to Minister without Portfolio, 1966; to First Sec. of State, 1966–68; to Lord President, 1968; Asst Sec., Cabinet Office, 1968–70, Asst Sec., DHSS, 1970–73; Sec., Occupational Pensions Bd, 1973–74; Under Sec., 1974–79; Dep. Sec., 1979–82, DHSS. *Address:* 41 Draycot Road, Wanstead, E11 2NX. *T:* 01–989 5526.

OGMORE, 2nd Baron *cr* 1950, of Bridgend; **Gwilym Rees Rees-Williams;** *b* 5 May 1931; *er s* of 1st Baron Ogmore, PC, TD, and of Constance, *er d* of W. R. Wills; *S* father, 1976; *m* 1967, Gillian Mavis, *d* of M. K. Slack; two *d. Educ:* Mill Hill School; St Luke's Coll., Exeter. *Heir: b* Hon. Morgan Rees-Williams [*b* 19 Dec. 1937; *m* 1964, Patricia (marr. diss. 1970), *o d* of C. Paris Jones; *m* 1972, Roberta (marr. diss. 1976), *d* of Captain Alec Cunningham-Reid, DFC]. *Address:* 4 Foster Road, Chiswick, W4 4NY. *Club:* London Welsh Rugby Football.

OGNALL, Sir Harry Henry, Kt 1986; **Hon. Mr Justice Ognall;** a Judge of the High Court of Justice, Queen's Bench Division, since 1986; *b* 9 Jan. 1934; *s* of Leo and Cecilia Ognall; *m* 1977, Elizabeth Young; two step *s* and two *s* one *d* of former marriage. *Educ:* Leeds Grammar Sch.; Lincoln Coll., Oxford (MA (Hons)); Univ. of Virginia, USA (LLM). Called to Bar (Gray's Inn), 1958; Bencher, 1983. Joined NE Circuit; a Recorder, 1972–86; QC 1973. Member: Criminal Injuries Compensation Bd, 1976; Planning Cttee, Senate of Inns of Court and Bar, 1980–83; Professional Conduct Cttee, 1985; Judicial Studies Bd (Chm., Criminal Cttee), 1986–. Arbitrator, Motor Insurers' Bureau Agreement, 1979–85. *Recreations:* photography, music, travel. *Address:* Royal Courts of Justice, Strand, WC2A 2LL.

O'GORMAN, Rev. Brian Stapleton; President of the Methodist Conference, 1969–70; *b* 4 March 1910; *s* of William Thomas and Annie Maria O'Gorman; *m* 1939, Margaret, *d* of William and Margaret Huggon, Carlisle; two *d. Educ:* Bowdon College, Cheshire; Handsworth Theological College, Birmingham. Porlock, 1931–32; Handsworth College, 1932–35; Manchester Mission, 1935–40; Islington Mission, London, 1940–43; Longton Mission, Stoke on Trent, 1943–50; Sheffield Mission, 1950–57; Chm., Wolverhampton and Shrewsbury Dist of Methodist Church, 1957–75. *Address:* 9 Trysull Gardens, Wolverhampton WV3 7LD. *T:* Wolverhampton 762167.

O'GRADY, Prof. Francis William, CBE 1984; TD 1970; MD; FRCP, FRCPath; Foundation Professor of Microbiology, University of Nottingham, since 1974; Hon. Consultant Microbiologist: Public Health Laboratory Service and Nottingham Health Authority, since 1974; to the Army, since 1982; *b* 7 Nov. 1925; *s* of Francis Joseph O'Grady and Lilian Maud Hitchcock; *m* 1951, Madeleine Marie-Thérèse Becquart; three *d. Educ:* Middlesex Hosp. Med. Sch., London (BSc 1st Cl. Hons; MB, BS Hons; MSc; MD). FRCP 1976; FRCPath 1972. House Physician, Mddx and North Mddx Hosps, 1951; Asst Pathologist, Bland-Sutton Inst. of Pathol., Mddx Hosp., 1952–53, 1956–58 and 1961–62; Pathologist, RAMC, 1954–55, AER, 1956–72; Asst Prof. of Environmental Medicine, Johns Hopkins Univ., Baltimore, 1959–60; Reader, 1962–66, and Prof. of Bacteriology, 1967–74, Univ. of London; Bacteriologist, St Bartholomew's Hosp., 1962–74. Mem., MRC, 1980–84; Chm., MRC Physiol Systems and Disorders Bd, 1980–82 (Mem., 1977–80; Mem., Grants Cttee, 1975–76); Chm., MRC Cttee on Hosp. Infection, 1977–80 (Mem., 1967–77). Member: Antibiotics Panel, Cttee on Med. Aspects of Food Policy, 1968–72; Sub-Cttee on Toxicity, Clin. Trials and Therapeutic Efficacy, 1971–75, and Sub-Cttee on Biol Substances, 1971–81, Cttee on Safety of Medicines; Jt Sub-Cttee on Antimicrobial Substances, Cttee on Safety of Medicines and Vet. Products Cttee, 1973–80; Cttee on Rev. of Medicines, 1975–81; Public Health Lab. Service Bd, 1980–; Nat. Biological Standards Bd, 1983–. William N. Creasy Vis. Prof. of Clin. Pharmacology, Duke Univ., NC, 1979. Erasmus Wilson Demonstrator, RCS, 1967; Foundn Lectr, Univ. of Hong Kong, 1974; Sydney Watson Smith Lectr, RCPE, 1975; Jacobson Vis. Lectr, Univ. of Newcastle upon Tyne, 1979; Berk Lectr, British Assoc. of Urol Surgeons, 1980; Garrod Lectr, British Soc. for Antimicrobial Chemotherapy, 1983. Pres. Council, British Jl of Exper. Pathol., 1980– (Mem., 1968–80); Mem. Editorial Boards: Jl of Med. Microbiol., 1970–75; Pathologie Biologie, 1973–78; British Jl of Clin. Pharmacol., 1974–84; Drugs, 1976–; Gut, 1977–83; Jl of Infection, 1978–; Revs of Infectious Diseases, 1979–. *Publications:* Airborne Infection: transmission and control, 1968; Antibiotic and Chemotherapy, 1968, 5th edn 1981; (ed) Urinary Tract Infection, 1968; (ed) Microbial Perturbation of Host Defences, 1981; papers on clin. and exper. infections and on antimicrobial chemotherapy. *Recreations:* admiring other people's furniture, houses and gardens; occasionally restoring my own. *Address:* Department of Microbiology, University Hospital, Queen's Medical Centre, Nottingham NG7 2UH. *T:* Nottingham 700111, ext. 3523.

OGSTON, Alexander George, MA, DSc; FRS 1955; President of Trinity College, Oxford, 1970–78, Hon. Fellow 1978; Fellow, 1937, and Bedford Lecturer, 1950, Balliol College; *b* 30 January 1911; *s* of late Walter Henry Ogston and late Josephine Elizabeth Ogston (*née* Carter); *m* 1934, Elizabeth Wicksteed; one *s* three *d. Educ:* Eton College (King's Scholar); Balliol College, Oxford. DPhil 1936, MA 1937, DSc 1970. Demonstrator, Balliol College, 1933; Freedom Research Fellow, London Hospital, 1935; Departmental Demonstrator (Biochemistry), 1938; University Demonstrator, 1944, Oxford; Reader in Biochemistry, University of Oxford, 1955–59; Prof. of Physical Biochemistry, John Curtin School of Medical Research, ANU, 1959–70, Prof. Emeritus, 1970. Vis. Fellow, Inst. for Cancer Research, Philadelphia, Nov. 1978–Jan. 1979 and March-June 1981; Silver Jubilee Vis. Fellow, University House, ANU, March-Aug. 1979. Chairman, Editorial Bd, Biochemical Journal, 1955–59 (Member of Board, 1951–55). Chm., Central Council, Selly Oak Colleges, Birmingham, 1980–84 (Vice-Chm., 1976–80). Fellow, Australian Acad. of Science, 1962; Hon. Fellow: Balliol Coll., Oxford, 1969; Univ. of York, 1980; Selly Oak Colls, 1984; Hon. Mem. American Soc. of Biological Chemists,

1965; Hon. DMed Uppsala, 1977. Davy Medal, Royal Soc., 1986. *Publications:* scientific papers on physical chemistry and biochemistry. *Address:* 6 Dewsbury Terrace, York YO1 1HA.

OGSTON, Prof. Derek, MD, PhD, DSc; FRCP; FRSE 1982; Professor of Medicine, since 1983, and Dean, Faculty of Medicine, since 1984, University of Aberdeen; *b* 31 May 1932; *s* of Frederick John Ogston and Ellen Mary Ogston; *m* 1963, Cecilia Marie Clark; one *s* two *d. Educ:* King's Coll. Sch., Wimbledon; Univ. of Aberdeen (MA, MD, PhD, DSc). FRCP Edin 1973; FRCP 1977. Univ. of Aberdeen: Res. Fellow, 1959–62; Lectr in Medicine, 1962–69; Sen. Lectr in Med., 1969–75; Reader in Med., 1975–76; Regius Prof. of Physiology, 1977–83. MRC Trav. Fellow, 1967–68. Mem., GMC, 1984–. *Publications:* Physiology of Hemostasis, 1983; Antifibrinolytic Drugs, 1984; scientific papers on haemostasis. *Recreation:* home maintenance. *Address:* 64 Rubislaw Den South, Aberdeen AB2 6AX. *T:* Aberdeen 36587.

O'HAGAN, 4th Baron, *cr* 1870; **Charles Towneley Strachey;** Member (C) Devon, European Parliament, since 1979; *b* 6 Sept. 1945; *s* of Hon. Thomas Anthony Edward Towneley Strachey (*d* 1955; having assumed by deed poll, 1938, the additional Christian name of Towneley, and his mother's maiden name of Strachey, in lieu of his patronymic) and of Lady Mary (who *m* 1981, St John Gore), *d* of 3rd Earl of Selborne, PC, CH; *S* grandfather, 1961; *m* 1967, Princess Tamara Imeretinsky (marr. diss. 1984); one *d*; *m* 1985, Mrs Mary Claire Parsons (*née* Roose-Francis); one *d. Educ:* Eton; (Exhibitioner) New College, Oxford. Page to HM the Queen, 1959–62. Independent Member, European Parliament, 1973–75; Junior Opposition Whip, House of Lords, 1977–79. *Heir: b* Hon. Richard Towneley Strachey, *b* 29 Dec. 1950. *Clubs:* Beefsteak, Pratt's.

O'HAGAN, Desmond, CMG 1957; *b* 4 Mar. 1909; *s* of Captain Claud O'Hagan, Nyeri, Kenya and Eva O'Hagan (*née* Napier Magill); *m* 1942, Pamela, *d* of Major A. H. Symes-Thompson, DSO, Kiambu, Kenya; one *s* two *d. Educ:* Wellington Coll.; Clare Coll., Cambridge. Entered Colonial Administrative Service, Kenya, 1931. Called to Bar, Inner Temple, 1935. Private Secretary to British Resident, Zanzibar, 1937; served with E African Forces in N Province, Kenya, 1940–42; Native Courts Adviser, 1948–51; Provincial Commissioner, Coast Province, Kenya, 1952–59; Chairman, Transport Licensing Authority, Tanganyika, 1959–63. *Recreations:* bridge, golf. *Address:* Kianjibbi, Kiambu, Kenya. *Clubs:* East India, Devonshire, Sports and Public Schools; Muthaiga (Nairobi).

O'HALLORAN, Sir Charles (Ernest), Kt 1982; Chairman, Irvine Development Corporation, 1983–85; *b* 26 May 1924; *s* of Charles and Lily O'Halloran; *m* 1943, Annie Rowan; one *s* two *d. Educ:* Conway St Central Sch., Birkenhead. Telegraphist, RN, 1942–46. Elected Ayr Town Council, 1953; Provost of Ayr, 1964–67; Mem., Strathclyde Regional Council, 1974–82 (Convener, 1978–82). Freeman of Ayr Burgh, 1975. Parly Cand. (Lab) Ayr Burghs, 1966. Dir, Radio Clyde, 1980–; Mem., BRB(Scot.), 1981–85. *Recreations:* politics, golf, soccer spectating. *Address:* 40 Savoy Park, Ayr. *T:* Ayr 266234. *Clubs:* Royal Scottish Automobile (Glasgow); Labour, Ex-Servicemen's (Ayr).

O'HALLORAN, Michael Joseph; Building and Construction Works Manager; *b* 20 Aug. 1933; British; *m* 1956, Stella Beatrice McDonald; three *d* (one *s* decd). *Educ:* Clohanes National School, Eire; self-educated. Railway worker, 1948–63; building works manager, 1963–69. MP (Lab 1969–81, SDP 1981–82, Ind. Lab 1983) Islington N, Oct. 1969–1983; contested (Ind. Lab) Islington N, 1983. *Recreations:* boxing, football. *Address:* 40 Tytherton Road, N19 4QA.

O'HARA, Bill; National Governor of the BBC for Northern Ireland, 1973–78; *b* 26 Feb. 1929; *s* of William P. O'Hara and Susanna Agnes O'Hara (*née* Gill); *m* 1953, Anne Marie Finn; two *s* two *d. Address:* Ashvale, 14 Raglan Road, Bangor, Co. Down, N Ireland. *T:* Bangor 60869. *Clubs:* Royal Ulster Yacht, Royal Belfast Golf, Sunnyland Beagles.

O'HARA, Air Vice-Marshal Derek Ive, CB 1981; Military Advisor, Cray Electronics Holdings PLC, since 1983; *b* 14 Feb. 1928; *s* of late William Edward O'Hara and Daisy Bathurst O'Hara (*née* Ive); *m* 1953, Angela Elizabeth (*née* Marchand); two *s* one *d. Educ:* Ardingly Coll., Sussex; RAF Coll., Cranwell. Commnd RAF Coll., 1950; RAF Horsham St Faith and Tuddenham, 1950–54; Egypt, 1954–56; HQ Bomber Comd, 1956–59; Instructor, RAF Coll., 1959–61; RAF Staff Coll., Andover, 1961; Jt Planning HQ ME, Aden, 1962–64; OC Supply, RAF Finningley, 1964; Manchester Univ., 1965; OC Supply, 14 MU RAF Carlisle, 1966–68; Directing Staff, RAF Staff Coll., Andover, 1968–70; Comd of RAF Stafford, 1970–72; Dep. Dir, Supply Management, MoD Harrogate, 1972; RCDS, 1973; Air Commodore Supply and Movements, HQ Strike Comd, 1974–75; Dir, Engrg and Supply Policy, 1975–79; Dir Gen. of Supply, RAF, 1979–82. *Recreations:* sailing, fishing, gardening. *Club:* Royal Air Force.

O'HARA, Prof. Michael John, PhD; FRS 1981; FRSE 1969; Professor of Geology and Head of Geology Department, University College of Wales, Aberystwyth, since 1978; *b* 22 Feb. 1933; *s* of Michael Patrick O'Hara, OBE, and Winifred Dorothy O'Hara; *m* 1st, 1962, Janet Tibbits; one *s* two *d*; 2nd, 1977, Susan Howells; two *s* one *d. Educ:* Dulwich Coll. Prep. Sch.; Cranleigh; Peterhouse, Cambridge (MA, PhD). Asst, Lectr, Reader and Prof. (1971), Edinburgh Univ., 1958–78; Principal Investigator, NASA Lunar Science Prog., 1968–75. Sherman-Fairchild Vis. Scholar, Calif Inst. of Technology, 1984–85. Mem., NERC, 1986–. Associate Mem., Geol Soc. of France. Murchison Medal, Geol Soc., 1983; Volcanology, Geochemistry and Petrology Award, Amer. Geophys. Union, 1984. *Publications:* numerous in learned jls. *Recreation:* mountaineering. *Address:* Geology Department, University College of Wales, Aberystwyth, Dyfed SY23 3DB. *T:* Aberystwyth 3111.

O'HIGGINS, Prof. Paul; Regius Professor of Laws, Trinity College, Dublin, since 1984; *b* 5 Oct. 1927; *s* of Richard Leo O'Higgins, MC, MRCVS and Elizabeth O'Higgins, MA (*née* Deane); *m* 1952, Rachel Elizabeth Bush; one *s* three *d. Educ:* St Ignatius' Coll., Galway; St Columba's Coll., Rathfarnham; Trinity Coll., Dublin. MA, LLB; MA, PhD Cantab. MRIA 1986. Called to the Bar, King's Inns, 1957, and Lincoln's Inn, 1959. University of Cambridge: Fellow, Christ's College, 1959–; Dir of Studies in Law, Peterhouse, 1960–74; Steward, Christ's Coll., 1964–68; Tutor for Advanced Students, Christ's, 1970–79; University Lectr, 1965–79; Reader in Labour Law, 1979–84. Co-founder, Cambridge Law Surgery, 1969. Lectr in Labour Law, Inns of Court Sch. of Law, 1976–84; Vis. Prof., Univ. of Kent at Canterbury, 1973–74; Mem. Bureau, European Inst. of Social Security, 1970–; Mem., Staff Side Panel, Civil Service Arbitration Tribunal, 1972–84; Vice-Pres., Inst. of Shops, Health and Safety Acts Admin, 1973–; Chm., Irish Soc. for Labour Law, 1985–. Patron, Cambridge Univ. Graduate Union, 1973–84; Trustee, Cambridge Union Soc., 1973–84; Gilbert Murray Prize (jt), 1968; Hon. Mem., Grotian Soc., 1968. Grand Consul honorifique du consulat de la Vinée de Bergerac, 1983. *Publications:* Bibliography of Periodical Literature relating to Irish Law, 1966, 2nd supp. 1983; (with B. A. Hepple) Public Employee Trade Unionism in the UK: the legal framework, 1971; (with B. A. Hepple) Employment Law, 1971, 4th edn 1981; Censorship in Britain, 1972; Workers' Rights, 1976, 2nd edn 1986; Cases and Materials on Civil Liberties, 1980; Bibliography of Irish Trials, 1986; (with M. Partington) Bibliography of Social Security Law, 1986;

British and Irish Labour Law, 1979–85: a bibliography, 1986; (with A. D. Dubbins and J. Gennard) Fairness at Work: even-handed industrial relations, 1986. *Recreations:* talking and travelling, particularly in France and Italy. *Address:* Trinity College, Dublin 2, Ireland; Christ's College, Cambridge CB2 3BU. *T:* Cambridge 67641. *Club:* Royal Dublin Society (Dublin).

O'HIGGINS, Hon. Thomas Francis, SC (Ireland) 1954; a Judge of the European Court of Justice, since 1985; *b* 23 July 1916; *e s* of Dr Thomas F. O'Higgins and Agnes McCarthy; *m* 1948, Thérese Keane; five *s* two *d. Educ:* St Mary's Coll., Rathmines, Clongowes Wood Coll.; University Coll., Dublin (BA); King's Inns, Dublin (BL). Called to Irish Bar, 1938; Bencher of King's Inns, 1967; Judge of High Court, 1973; Chief Justice of Ireland, 1974–85. Elected to Dail Eireann, 1948; Minister for Health, 1954; contested Presidency, 1966 and 1973. *Recreations:* fishing, golf. *Address:* European Court of Justice, L-2920 Luxembourg; Jerpoint, Elton Park, Sandycove, Co. Dublin. *T:* 803605. *Clubs:* Stephen's Green, Miltown Golf.

OHLSON, Sir Brian (Eric Christopher), 3rd Bt *cr* 1920; money broker; *b* 27 July 1936; *s* of Sir Eric James Ohlson, 2nd Bt, and of Marjorie Joan, *d* of late C. H. Roosmale-Cocq; *S* father, 1983. *Educ:* Harrow School; RMA Sandhurst. Commissioned into Coldstream Guards, 1956–61. Started money broking, 1961; *Recreations:* sport of kings, cricket, squash, bridge. *Heir: b* Peter Michael Ohlson [*b* 18 May 1939; *m* 1968, Sarah, *o d* of Maj.-Gen. Thomas Brodie, *qv*]. *Address:* 1 Courtfield Gardens, SW5. *Clubs:* MCC, Naval and Military, Hurlingham, Cavalry and Guards.

OISTRAKH, Igor Davidovich; Soviet Violinist; *b* Odessa, 27 April 1931; *s* of late David Oistrakh. *Educ:* Music Sch. and State Conservatoire, Moscow. Many foreign tours (USSR, Europe, South America, Japan); many gramophone records; many concerts with father. 1st prize, Violin Competition, Budapest, 1952, Wieniawski Competition, Poznan, 1952; Honoured Artist of RSFSR. *Address:* State Conservatoire, 13 Ulitsa Herzen, Moscow, USSR.

OKA, Prof. Takeshi, PhD; FRS 1984; FRSC 1977; Professor of Chemistry and Professor of Astronomy and Astrophysics, University of Chicago, since 1981; *b* 10 June 1932; *s* of Shumpei and Chiyoko Oka; *m* 1960, Keiko Nukui; two *s* two *d. Educ:* University of Tokyo. BSc, PhD. Fellow, Japanese Soc. for Promotion of Science, 1960–63; National Research Council of Canada: Postdoctorate Fellow, 1963–65; Asst Research Physicist, 1965–68; Associate Research Physicist, 1968–71; Senior Research Physicist, 1971–75; Herzberg Inst. of Astrophysics, 1975–81. Centenary Lectr, Royal Soc., 1982; Steacie Prize, Steacie Fund, NRSC, 1972; Earle K. Plyler Prize, Amer. Physical Soc., 1982. *Recreation:* running. *Address:* 1463 East Park Place, Chicago, Illinois 60637, USA. *T:* (312)-752–5963.

O'KEEFE, John Harold; TV consultant; Director, Abracadabra Films; *b* 25 Dec. 1938; *s* of Terence Harold O'Keefe and Christian Frances (*née* Foot); *m* 1959, Valerie Anne Atkins; two *s* two *d. Educ:* Acton County Grammar School. Dir, Newspaper Publishers Assoc., 1974; Hd of Industrial Relations, 1974–81, Production Dir, Central London, 1981, Thames TV; Man. Dir, Limehouse Studios, 1982–86. *Address:* Flat 2, 2 West Grove, Greenwich, SE10 8QT.

O'KEEFFE, (Peter) Laurence, CMG 1983; CVO 1974; HM Diplomatic Service; Head of British Delegation to Conference on Security and Co-operation in Europe Review Conference, Vienna, since 1986; *b* 9 July 1931; *s* of Richard O'Keeffe and Alice (*née* Chase); *m* 1954, Suzanne Marie Jousse; three *d. Educ:* St Francis Xavier's Coll., Liverpool; University Coll., Oxford (schol.). HM Customs and Excise, 1953–62; 2nd, later 1st Sec. (Economic), Bangkok, 1962–65; FO, 1965–68; 1st Sec. and Head of Chancery, Athens, 1968–72; Commercial Counsellor, Jakarta, 1972–75; Head of Hong Kong and Indian Ocean Dept, FCO, 1975–76; Dir.-Gen., British Information Services, and Dep. Consul General (Information), New York, 1976–78; Counsellor, Nicosia, 1978–81; Research Associate, Inst. for the Study of Diplomacy, Georgetown Univ., Washington, DC, 1981–82; Ambassador to Senegal, 1982–85, and concurrently (non-resident) to Guinea, Guinea-Bissau, Mali, Mauritania and Cape Verde, 1982–85; Diplomatic Service Chm., CSSB, 1985–86. *Publications:* (as Laurence Halley): Simultaneous Equations (novel), 1975; Ancient Affections, 1985; Abiding City (novel), 1986. *Recreations:* photography, music. *Address:* c/o Foreign and Commonwealth Office, SW1.

O'KELLY, Surgeon Rear-Adm. Francis Joseph, OBE 1965; Royal Navy, retired 1980; Occupational Health Consultant, Medical and Health Department, Government of Hong Kong, 1980–86; *b* 24 Dec. 1921; *s* of Francis John O'Kelly and Elizabeth Mary O'Kelly (*née* Rogan); *m* 1954, Winifred Mary Teresa Henry; one *s* three *d. Educ:* St Patrick's Coll., Cavan; University Coll., Dublin. MB, BCh 1945; FFCM, FFOM (RCPI), MFOM (RCPE); Hon. FACOM; DPH, DIH. Hosp. appts in Dublin, 1946–48; joined RN 1948; served with RM Commandos, Middle and Far East, 1948–52; HM Ships Unicorn, St Bride's Bay and Centaur, RNB Chatham and RN Air Station, Brawdy, 1952–63; Naval MOH appts, Far East Fleet, Scotland and NI Comd, Portsmouth and Chatham Comd, 1963–72; Dep. Dir, Health and Research, 1972–74; MO i/c RN Hosp. Gibraltar, 1974–77; Surgeon Rear-Adm. (Ships and Establishments), 1977–78; Surg. Rear-Adm. (Naval Hosps), 1978–80; QHP 1977–80. Adviser in Preventive and Industrial Medicine to Med. Dir Gen. (Naval), 1972–77, in Community Medicine, 1977–80. Fellow, RSM. *Publications:* articles in med jls. *Recreations:* reading and travel. *Address:* Breffni, 38 Seamead, Stubbington, Fareham, Hants PO14 2NG.

O'KENNEDY, Michael E.; TD (Fianna Fáil) Tipperary North, 1969–80 and since 1982; *b* Nenagh, Co. Tipperary, 21 Feb. 1936; *s* of Éamonn and Helena O'Kennedy; *m* 1965, Breda, *d* of late Andrew Heavey and of Mary Heavey; one *s* two *d. Educ:* St Flannan's College, Ennis, Co. Clare; Univ. Coll., Dublin. MA 1957. Called to Irish Bar, 1961; Senior Counsel 1973. Elected to Seanad Éireann, 1965; Mem., Oireachtas Select Constitutional Cttee, 1966. Parly Sec. to Minister for Educn, 1970–72; Minister without Portfolio, Dec. 1972–Jan. 1973; Minister for Transport and Power, Jan.-March 1973; Opposition spokesman on Foreign Affairs, 1973–77; Minister for Foreign Affairs, 1977–79; Pres., Council of Ministers of the European Communities, July-Dec. 1979; Minister for Finance, 1979–81; opposition spokesman on finance, 1983–. Mem., Commn of the European Communities, 1981–82. Member: All-Party Cttee on Irish Relns, 1973–77; Dáil and Seanad Jt Cttee on Secondary Legislation of the European Communities, 1973–77; Chm., Inter-Party Cttee on Implications of Irish Unity, 1972–73. *Address:* Gortlandroe, Nenagh, Co. Tipperary, Ireland.

OKEOVER, Sir Peter Ralph Leopold W.; *see* Walker-Okeover.

OKOGIE, Most Rev. Anthony Olubunmi; *see* Lagos, Archbishop of, (RC).

OKOTH, Most Rev. Yona; *see* Uganda, Archbishop of.

OLAGBEGI II, The Olowo of Owo, (Sir Olateru), Kt 1960; Oba Alaiyeluwa, Olagbegi II, Olowo of Owo, since 1941; Minister of State, Western Region (now Western Provinces) of Nigeria, 1952; President of the House of Chiefs, Western Region (now Western Provinces), 1965; *b* 1910; *s* of Oba Alaiyeluwa, Olagbegi I, Olowo of Owo;

married; many *s* and *d* (some decd). *Educ:* Owo Government School. A Teacher in 1934; Treasury Clerk in Owo Native Administration, 1935–41. Queen's Medal, 1957. *Recreations:* lawn tennis, squash racquets. *Address:* PO Box 1, Afin Oba Olowo, Owo, Western Provinces of Nigeria. *T:* Owo 1.

OLANG', Most Rev. Festo Habakkuk; *b* 11 Nov. 1914; *m* 1937, Eseri D. Olang'; four *s* eight *d. Educ:* Alliance High School. Teacher, 1936–43; ordained 1945; consecrated Assistant Bishop of Mombasa in Namirembe Cathedral, by Archbishop of Canterbury, 1955; Bishop of Maseno, 1961; Bishop of Nairobi, 1970; Archbishop of Kenya, 1970–79. Hon. DD Univ. of the South Sewanee, USA. *Address:* PO Box 1, Maseno, Kenya.

OLDENBOURG-IDALIE, Zoë; Chevalier, Légion d'Honneur, 1980; Officier du Mérite des Arts et des Lettres, 1978; writer (as Zoë Oldenbourg); *b* 31 March 1916; *d* of Sergius Oldenbourg, writer and historicist, and of Ada (*née* Starynkevitch); *m* 1948, Heinric Idalie; one *s* one *d. Educ:* Lycée Molière and Sorbonne, Paris. Prix Fémina, 1953. *Publications:* Argile et cendres, 1946 (The World is Not Enough, 1949); La Pierre angulaire, 1953 (The Cornerstone, 1954); Réveillés de la Vie, 1956 (The Awakened, trans. E. Hyams, 1957); Les Irréductibles, 1958 (The Chains of Love, 1959); Bûcher de Montségur, 1959 (Massacre at Montségur, 1962); Les Brûlés, 1961 (Destiny of Fire, trans. P. Green, 1961); Les Cités charnelles, 1961 (Cities of the Flesh, 1963); Les Croisades: un essai historique, 1963 (The Crusades, trans. Anne Carter, 1966); Catherine de Russie, 1965 (Catherine the Great, 1965); Saint Bernard, 1969; La Joie des pauvres, 1970 (The Heirs of the Kingdom, trans. Anne Carter, 1972); L'Epopée des cathédrales, 1973; Que vous a donc fait Israël?, 1974; Visages d'un autoportrait (autobiog.), 1977; La Joie-Souffrance, 1980; Le Procès du Rêve, 1982; Que nous est Hécube?, 1984. *Recreation:* painting. *Address:* c/o Victor Gollancz Ltd, 14 Henrietta Street, WC2; 4 rue de Montmorency, 92100 Boulogne, France.

OLDFIELD, Bruce; designer; *b* 14 July 1950; parents unknown; brought up by Dr Barnado's, Ripon, Yorks. *Educ:* Ripon Grammar School; Sheffield City Polytechnic; Ravensbourne College of Art; St Martin's College of Art. Established fashion house, 1975; produced designer collections of high fashion clothes for UK and overseas; began exporting clothes worldwide, 1975; began making couture clothes for individual clients, 1981; opened first Bruce Oldfield retail shop, selling ready to wear and couture to international clientèle, 1984. British Design Exhibn, Vienna. Lectures: Fashion Inst., NY, 1977; Los Angeles County Museum, 1983; Internat. Design Conf., Aspen, Colorado, 1986 (Speaker and show). Designed for films: Jackpot, 1974; The Sentinel, 1976. *Recreations:* music, reading, driving, working. *Address:* 27 Beauchamp Place, SW3. *T:* 01–584 1363.

OLDFIELD, John Richard Anthony; *b* July 1900; *s* of late Major H. E. Oldfield; *m* 1953, Jonnet Elizabeth, *d* of late Maj. H. M. Richards, DL, JP. *Educ:* Eton; Trinity College, Cambridge; Served in: Coldstream Guards, 1918–20; RN, 1939–45. MP (Lab) South-East Essex, 1929–31; Parliamentary Private Secretary to Sec. of State for Air, 1929–30. Mem. LCC, 1931–58 (Vice-Chairman, 1953); CC (C) Kent, 1965–81. *Address:* Doddington Place, near Sittingbourne, Kent.

OLDFIELD, Michael Gordon, (Mike); musician and composer; *b* 15 May 1953; *s* of Dr Raymond Henry Oldfield and Maureen Bernadine Liston; one *s* one *d* by Sally A. Cooper. *Educ:* St Edward's, Reading; Presentation Coll., Reading. Records include: Tubular Bells, 1973 (over 10 million copies sold to date); Hergest Ridge; Ommadawn; Incantations; Platinum; QE2, 1980; Five Miles Out, 1982; Crises, 1983; Discovery, 1984; The Killing Fields (film sound track), 1984. Extensive world wide concert tours, 1979–. Mem., Assoc. of Professional Composers. Freeman, City of London, 1982. Hon. Pict. *Recreations:* helicopter pilot, squash, ski-ing, cricket. *Address:* Regency House, 1/4 Warwick Street, W1. *Club:* Jacobs Larder (Ealing).

OLDFIELD-DAVIES, Alun Bennett, CBE 1955; MA; Controller, Wales, British Broadcasting Corporation, 1945–67; *b* 1905; *s* of Rev. J. Oldfield-Davies, Wallasey, Cheshire; *m* 1931, Lilian M. Lewis, BA. *Educ:* Porth County Sch., Rhondda; University College, Aberystwyth. Schoolmaster and Lecturer to University Extension Classes in Ammanford, Carmarthenshire, and Cardiff, 1926–37. British Broadcasting Corporation: Schools Asst, 1937–40; Welsh Executive, 1940–44; Overseas Services Establishment Officer, 1944–45. Mem., Court, Univ. of Wales; Vice-Pres., University Coll., Cardiff; President: Nat. Museum of Wales, 1972–77; Welsh Council for Education in World Citizenship. Formerly Warden, University of Wales Guild of Graduates. Hon. LLD, Univ. of Wales, 1967. *Address:* Ty Gwyn, Llantrisant Road, Llandaff, Cardiff. *T:* 565920.

OLDHAM, Rev. Canon Arthur Charles Godolphin; *b* 5 Apr. 1905; *s* of late Sidney Godolphin and Lilian Emma Oldham; *m* 1934, Ursula Finch Wigham Richardson (*d* 1984), *d* of late George and Isabel Richardson, Newcastle upon Tyne; one *s* two *d. Educ:* King's College School; King's College, London. Business, music and journalism to 1930. Ordained, to Witley, Surrey, 1933; Vicar of Brockham Green, 1936; Rector of Merrow, 1943; Rural Dean of Guildford, 1949; Vicar of Godalming, 1950; Rural Dean of Godalming, 1957; Director of Ordination Training, and Bishop's Examining Chaplain, 1958; Hon. Canon of Guildford, 1959; Canon Residentiary of Guildford Cathedral, 1961–71, retired. *Recreations:* music, sketching. *Address:* Dora Cottage, Beech Hill, Hambledon, Surrey. *T:* Wormley 2087.

OLDMAN, Col Sir Hugh (Richard Deare), KBE 1974 (OBE 1960); MC 1942; retired; *b* 24 June 1914; *s* of late Maj.-Gen. R. D. F. Oldman, CB, CMG, DSO, and Mrs Helen Marie Oldman (*née* Pigot); *m* 1947, Agnes Fielding Murray Oldman (*née* Bayles) (*d* 1978); *m* 1979, Susan V. Oldman (*née* Vance). *Educ:* Wellington Coll.; RMC Sandhurst. CO 8th Bn Durham LI, 1944–45; psc 1945; Chief Instructor, Quetta Staff Coll.; comd Bn, Aden Protectorate Levies, 1957–60; comd Sultan's Armed Forces, Oman, 1961–64; Staff, HQ Allied Forces Southern Europe (NATO), 1965–67; retd from Army, 1967; subseq. Sec. for Defence, Sultanate of Oman. Croix de Guerre (Palme), 1944; Order of Merit 1st cl., Oman, 1972. *Recreations:* yachting, golf. *Address:* PO Box 73, White Marsh, Va 23183, USA. *Clubs:* Liphook Golf; Ware River Yacht (Gloucester Co., Va); Muthaiga Country (Kenya).

O'LEARY, Michael; barrister; TD (FG) for Dublin South West, since 1982 (TD (Lab), Dublin North Central, 1965–82); *b* 8 May 1936; *s* of John O'Leary and Margaret McCarthy; unmarried. *Educ:* Presentation Coll., Cork; University Coll., Cork; Columbia Univ., NY. Called to the Bar, King's Inns, Dublin, 1979. Educn Officer, Irish TUC, 1962–65. Minister for Labour, 1973–77; Dep. Leader, Labour Party, 1977–81, Leader, 1981–82 (resigned); Tánaiste (Dep. Prime Minister) and Minister for Industry and Energy, 1981–82; joined Fine Gael, 1982. President, ILO, 1976. Mem. for Ireland, European Parlt, 1979–81. *Address:* Leinster House, Kildare Street, Dublin 2, Ireland. *T:* Dublin 789911.

O'LEARY, Patrick; *see* Guerisse, A. M. E.

O'LEARY, Peter Leslie; Under-Secretary, Inland Revenue, 1978–84; *b* 12 June 1929; *s* of Archibald and Edna O'Leary; *m* 1960, Margaret Elizabeth Debney; four *d. Educ:* Portsmouth Southern Grammar Sch.; University Coll., London (BA). Joined Inland

Revenue as Inspector, 1952; Sen. Principal Inspector, 1974. *Recreations:* horology, gardening, wine-making. *Address:* Windy Ridge, 38 Seven Ash Green, Chelmsford CM1 5SE. *T:* Chelmsford 50072.

O'LEARY, Terence Daniel, CMG 1982; MA; HM Diplomatic Service; High Commissioner in New Zealand and concurrently to Western Samoa, and Governor of Pitcairn, since 1984; *b* 18 Aug. 1928; 2nd *s* of late Daniel O'Leary; *m* 1960, Janet Douglas Berney, *d* of Dr H. B. Berney, Masterton, NZ; twin *s* one *d*. *Educ:* Dulwich; St John's Coll., Cambridge. BA 1950. Army, commnd Queen's Royal Regt, 1946–48. Commerce, 1951–53; Asst Principal, CRO, 1953; 2nd Sec., British High Commn, Wellington, 1956–58; Principal, PSO's Dept, CRO, 1958; 1st Sec., New Delhi, 1960–63; 1st Sec., Dar es Salaam, 1963–64; CRO, 1964–65; 1st Sec. and Defence Sec., Canberra, 1965–68; Actg Head, S Asia Dept, FCO, 1969; Asst Sec., Cabinet Office, 1970–72; Counsellor, Pretoria/Cape Town, 1972–74; Dep. High Comr, Wellington, 1974–78; Senior Civil Mem., Directing Staff, Nat. Defence Coll., 1978–81; High Comr in Sierra Leone, 1981–84. *Recreations:* cutting grass, tennis, Pacific history. *Address:* c/o Foreign and Commonwealth Office, SW1; The Old Rectory, Petworth, W Sussex. *T:* Petworth 43335. *Clubs:* Travellers'; Wellington (Wellington).

OLINS, Wally, MA Oxon; FSIAD; Chairman, Wolff Olins Ltd; *b* 19 Dec. 1930; *s* of Alfred Olins and Rachel (*née* Muscovitch); *m* 1957, Maria Renate Olga Laura Steinert; two *s* one *d*. *Educ:* Highgate Sch.; St Peter's Coll., Oxford (Hons History, MA). National Service, Army, in Germany, 1950–51. S. H. Benson Ltd, London, 1954–57; Benson, India, 1957–62; Caps Design Group, London, 1962–65; Wolff Olins, London, 1965–. Vis. Lectr, Design Management, London Business Sch., 1984–. Vice-Pres., SIAD, 1982–85. *Publications:* The Corporate Personality, 1978; The Wolff Olins Guide to Corporate Identity, 1983; The Wolff Olins Guide to Design Management, 1985; numerous articles in Design and Management publications. *Recreations:* looking at buildings, theatre, reading, old cars. *Address:* Wolff Olins Ltd, 22 Dukes Road, WC1H 9AB. *T:* 01–387 0891.

OLIPHANT, Air Vice-Marshal David Nigel Kington B.; *see* Blair-Oliphant.

OLIPHANT, Sir Mark, (Marcus Laurence Elwin), AC 1977; KBE 1959; FRS 1937; FAA 1954; FTS 1976; Governor of South Australia, 1971–76; *b* Adelaide, 8 Oct. 1901; *e s* of H. G. Oliphant; *m* 1925, Rosa Wilbraham, Adelaide, S Australia; one *s* one *d*. *Educ:* Unley and Adelaide High Schools; University of Adelaide; Trinity Coll., Cambridge (1851 Exhibitioner, Overseas 1927, Senior 1929; PhD 1929). Messel Research Fellow of Royal Society, 1931; Fellow and Lecturer St John's Coll., 1934. Hon. Fellow, 1952; Assistant Director of Research, Cavendish Laboratory, Cambridge, 1935, Poynting Professor of Physics, University of Birmingham, 1937–50; Dir, Research Sch. of Physical Sciences, ANU, Canberra, 1950–63; Prof. of Physics of Ionised Gases, Inst. of Advanced Studies, ANU, 1964–67, now Professor Emeritus. Pres., Aust. Acad. of Sciences, 1954–57. Hon. DSc (Toronto, Belfast, Melbourne, Birmingham, New South Wales, ANU, Adelaide, Flinders); Hon. LLD (St Andrews). KStJ 1972. *Publications:* Rutherford: recollections of the Cambridge days, 1972; various papers on electricity in gases, surface properties and nuclear physics. *Address:* 4/33 Buxton Street, North Adelaide, SA 5006, Australia. *Club:* Adelaide (Adelaide).

OLIVER, family name of **Baron Oliver of Aylmerton.**

OLIVER OF AYLMERTON, Baron *cr* 1986 (Life Peer), of Aylmerton in the County of Norfolk; **Peter Raymond Oliver;** Kt 1974; PC 1980; a Lord of Appeal in Ordinary, since 1986; *b* 7 March 1921; *s* of David Thomas Oliver, Fellow of Trinity Hall, Cambridge, and Alice Maud Oliver; *m* 1945, Mary Chichester Rideal (*d* 1985), *d* of Sir Eric Keightley Rideal, MBE, FRS; one *s* one *d*. *Educ:* The Leys, Cambridge; Trinity Hall, Cambridge (Hon. Fellow, 1980). Military Service, 1941–45, 12th Bn RTR (despatches). Called to Bar, Lincoln's Inn, 1948, Bencher 1973; QC 1965; Judge of the High Ct of Justice, Chancery Div., 1974–80; a Lord Justice of Appeal, 1980–86. Mem., Restrictive Practices Court, 1976–80; Chm., Review Body on Chancery Div. of High Court, 1979–81. *Recreations:* gardening, music. *Address:* House of Lords, SW1.

See also Hon. D. K. R. Oliver.

OLIVER, Benjamin Rhys; Stipendiary Magistrate for Mid-Glamorgan, since 1983; a Recorder of the Crown Court, since 1972; *b* 8 June 1928; *m* 1955; one *s* one *d*. *Educ:* Llandovery and Aberystwyth. Called to the Bar, Inner Temple, 1954. *Recreation:* golf.

OLIVER, Hon. David Keightley Rideal; QC 1986; *b* 4 June 1949; *o s* of Baron Oliver of Aylmerton, *qv*. *Educ:* Westminster School; Trinity Hall, Cambridge; Institut d'Etudes Européennes, Brussels. Called to the Bar, Lincoln's Inn, 1972; Junior Counsel to Dir-Gen. of Fair Trading, 1980–86. *Recreations:* gardening, bird watching, shooting. *Address:* 13 Old Square, Lincoln's Inn, WC2A 3UA. *T:* 01–404 4800. *Club:* Garrick.

OLIVER, Dennis Stanley, CBE 1981; PhD, FEng, FIM, FInstP; Director, Pilkington Brothers plc, 1977–86; *b* 19 Sept. 1926; *s* of late James Thomas Oliver and Lilian Mabel Oliver (*née* Bunn); *m* 1952, Enid Jessie Newcombe. *Educ:* Deacon's School, Peterborough; Birmingham Univ. BSc, PhD. Research Fellowship, Univ. of Bristol, 1949–52; Senior Scientific Officer, UKAEA, Culcheth, 1952–55; Head of Metallurgy Div., UKAEA, Dounreay, 1955–63; Chief R & D Officer, Richard Thomas & Baldwin Ltd, 1963–68; Group R & D Dir, Pilkington Brothers plc, 1968–77. Member: Board, British Technology Gp (Member: NEB, 1981; NRDC, 1981); Court and Council, Cranfield Inst. of Technology, 1976–. Vis. Prof., Cranfield Inst. of Technology, 1984–. Director: Anglo-American Venture Fund Ltd, 1980–84; Monotype Corp., 1985–. Chm., Industrial Experience Projects Ltd, 1981–; Pres., European Industrial Res. Management Assoc., 1977–81. Patron, Science and Technology Educn on Merseyside, 1982– (Pres., 1978–81); Governor: Liverpool Inst. of Higher Educn, 1979–85; Christ's and Notre Dame Coll., Liverpool, 1979–; Royal Nat. Coll. for the Blind, 1981–85; Dir, L'Ecole Supérieure du Verre, Belgium, 1971–; Governor, Community of St Helens Trust Ltd, 1978–; Founder Trustee, Anfield Foundn, 1983–. Freeman of City of London; Liveryman: Spectaclemakers Co. (Court of Assts, 1985–); Co. of Engrs, 1984. FBIM. KSG 1980. *Publications:* The Use of Glass in Engineering, 1975; Glass for Construction Purposes, 1977; various publications on technical subjects and technology transfer. *Recreations:* music, poetry, travel. *Address:* Castell Bach, Bodfari, Denbigh, Clwyd LL16 4HT. *T:* Bodfari 354. *Clubs:* Athenæum, Institute of Directors.

OLIVER, Sir (Frederick) Ernest, Kt 1962; CBE 1955; TD 1942; DL; Chairman, George Oliver (Footwear) Ltd, 1950–73; *b* 31 Oct. 1900; *s* of late Colonel Sir Frederick Oliver and late Lady Oliver, CBE; *m* 1928, Mary Margaret (*d* 1978), *d* of late H. Simpson; two *d* (one *s* decd). *Educ:* Rugby School. Member Leicester City Council, 1933–73, Lord Mayor, 1950. Officer, Territorial Army, 1922–48. Served UK and Burma, 1939–45. President: Multiple Shoe Retailers' Assoc., 1964–65; Leicester YMCA, 1955–76; Leicester Conservative Assoc., 1952–66. Leicester: DL 1950; Hon. Freeman, 1971. *Address:* 6 Westminster Road, Leicester. *T:* 705310. *Club:* Leicestershire (Leicester).

OLIVER, Brig. James Alexander, CB 1957; CBE 1945; DSO 1942 (and Bar to DSO 1943); TD; DL; solicitor; Vice-Lieutenant, County of Angus, 1967–81; *b* 19 March 1906; *s* of Adam Oliver, Arbroath, Angus; *m* 1932, Margaret Whytock Scott; no *c*. *Educ:* Trinity Coll., Glenalmond. Commanded: 7th Black Watch, 1942; 152 Infantry Bde (Highland Div.), 1943; 154 Infantry Bde (Highland Div.), 1944; served War of 1939–45 with 51st Highland Div. in N Africa, Sicily and NW Europe (despatches). ADC to the Queen, 1953–63; Hon. Colonel, 6/7th Black Watch, 1960–67; Hon. Colonel, 51st Highland Volunteers, 1967–70. Member, Angus and Dundee T&AFA, 1938–59 (Chairman, 1945–59). Chm., 1972–73, Vice-Pres., 1973, The Earl Haig Fund, Scotland. Hon. LLD Dundee, 1967. DL Angus, 1948. *Address:* West Newton, Arbroath, Angus, Scotland. *T:* Arbroath 72579. *Club:* Naval and Military.

OLIVER, Dr John Andrew, CB 1968; *b* 25 Oct. 1913; *s* of Robert John Oliver, Limavady, Co. Londonderry and Martha Sherrard, Magilligan, Co. Londonderry; *m* 1943, Stella Ritson; five *s*. *Educ:* Royal Belfast Academical Institution; Queen's Univ., Belfast; Bonn Univ.; Königsberg Univ.; Zimmern School of International Studies, Geneva; Imperial Defence Coll., London. BA 1936; DrPhil, 1951; IDC, 1954. Ministry of Development, NI: Second Sec., 1964–71; Permanent Sec., 1971–74; Permanent Sec., Housing, Local Govt and Planning, NI, 1974–75; Chief Adviser, NI Constitutional Convention, 1975–76. Hon. Sec., Assoc. of Governing Bodies of Voluntary Grammar Schs in NI, 1964–77; Chm., Bd of Governors, Royal Belfast Academical Instn, 1970–77. UK Election Supervisor, Que Que, Rhodesia, 1980. Chm. Management Review, Royal Victoria Hosp. Gp, Belfast, 1981–82. Chm., S Lakeland Council for Voluntary Action, 1980; Vice-Chm., Voluntary Action Cumbria, 1980–. Proposer and interim Governor, new Dallam Schs, Cumbria, 1983–84. Retired deliberately from all cttees and exec. positions on reaching 70, to make way for younger people. Hon. MRTPI, 1964; Hon. Member, Assoc. for Housing and Town Planning, W Germany, 1966. Rhodesia Medal, 1980; Zimbabwe Independence Medal, 1980. *Publications:* Ulster Today and Tomorrow, 1978; Working at Stormont, 1978. *Recreations:* walking, maps, languages, family history. *Address:* Laundry Cottage, Hale, Milnthorpe, Cumbria LA7 7BL. *T:* Milnthorpe 2698. *Club:* Royal Over-Seas League.

OLIVER, Ven. John Keith; Archdeacon of Sherborne, since 1985; *b* 14 April 1935; *s* of Walter Keith and Ivy Oliver; *m* 1961, Meriel Moore; two *s* one *d*. *Educ:* Westminster School; Gonville and Caius Coll., Cambridge (MA, MLitt); Westcott House. Asst Curate, Hilborough Group of Parishes, Norfolk, 1964–68; Chaplain and Asst Master, Eton College, 1968–72; Team Rector: South Molton Group of Parishes, Devon, 1973–82; Parish of Central Exeter, 1982–85. *Publications:* The Church and Social Order, 1968; contribs to Theology, Crucible. *Recreations:* railways, music, architecture, fencing. *Address:* West Stafford Rectory, Dorchester, Dorset DT2 8AB. *T:* Dorchester 64637.

OLIVER, John Laurence; Journalist; *b* 14 Sept. 1910; *s* of late Harold and Teresa Oliver; *m* 1946, Renée Mary Webb; two *s*. *Educ:* Haberdashers' Aske's Hampstead School. Publicity Manager, The Book Society, 1934; Art Editor, The Bystander, 1935–39. War of 1939–45: served in the Field Security Corps; commissioned 1941, The Suffolk Regt (transferred The Cambridgeshire Regt). Joined staff of The Sphere, 1946; Art Editor, 1947; Assistant Editor, 1956; Editor, 1960–64; Editor, The Tatler, 1961–65. *Publications:* Saint John's Wood Church (with Rev. Peter Bradshaw), 1955; occasional short stories and articles. *Recreations:* reading, theatre going, watching cricket. *Address:* 10 Wellington Place, NW8 9JA. *T:* 01–286 5891. *Clubs:* Garrick, MCC.

OLIVER, Group Captain John Oliver William, CB 1950; DSO 1940; DFC 1940; RAF retired; *b* 1911; *e s* of William and Cicely Oliver; *m* 1935 (marr. diss., 1951); one *s* two *d*; *m* 1962, Anne Fraser Porteous; one *s* two *d* (of whom *s* and *yr d* are twins). *Educ:* Christ's Hospital; Cranwell. Commissioned from Cranwell, General Duties Pilot Branch permanent commn, 1931; served 43 (F) Squadron and 55 (B) Squadron, Iraq; qualified CFS. Served War of 1939–45 (despatches thrice); commanded 85 (F) Squadron, 1940; Fighter Command and Tactical Air Force; Wing Commander, 1940; Group Captain, 1942. Assistant Commandant, RAF Coll., Cranwell, 1948–50; ACOS Ops, Allied Forces Northern Europe, 1958–60; retired, 1961. Personnel Officer, ENV (Engineering) Ltd, 1961; Staff Institute Personnel Management, 1962; Personnel Manager, Humber Ltd, 1963; Manager, Training and Administrative Service, Rootes, Coventry, 1965; Senior Training Officer, Engineering Industry Training Board, 1968; Personnel and Trng Manager, Thorn Gp, 1970–76, retired. *Recreation:* sailing. *Address:* 9 Magdala Road, Hayling Island, Hants PO11 0BH. *Club:* Hayling Island Sailing.

OLIVER, Leslie Claremont, FRCS; FACS; Consulting Neurosurgeon: Charing Cross Hospital; Westminster Hospital; West London Hospital; Royal Northern Hospital; Founder, Neurosurgical Centre, Oldchurch Hospital, Romford. *Educ:* Latymer Sch.; Guy's Hospital. LRCP, MRCS, 1933; MB, BS, London, 1953; FRCS England, 1935; FACS 1957. Formerly: 1st Assistant and Registrar, Dept of Neurosurgery, London Hospital; Resident Asst Surgeon, W London Hospital; Surgical Registrar and Teacher in Surgery, Bristol General Hospital. Member Society British Neurological Surgeons; Corr. Member Soc. de Neurochirurgie de Langue Française. Formerly Chm. Court of Examiners, RCS. *Publications:* Essentials of Neurosurgery, 1952; Parkinson's Disease and its Surgical Treatment, 1953; (ed and contrib.) Basic Surgery, 1958; Parkinson's Disease, 1967; Removable Intracranial Tumours, 1969; Le Français Pratique. *Recreation:* travel. *Address:* Flat 6, 20 Harley Street, W1. *T:* 01–580 4855. *Clubs:* Royal Society of Medicine, Hurlingham.

OLIVER, Martin Hugh, PhD, CEng; Director General, Research Electronics, Procurement Executive, Ministry of Defence, 1972–76; *b* 9 July 1916; *s* of late Thomas Frederick Oliver and late Jessie Oliver (*née* Gibson), Peterborough; *m* 1963, Barbara Rivcah, *d* of late Richard Burgis Blakeley, Worcester; one *d*. *Educ:* King's Sch., Peterborough; Imperial Coll. (City and Guilds Coll.), Univ. of London. BSc (Eng) 1937, PhD (Eng) 1939; ACGI, DIC, MIEE. Metropolitan Vickers Electrical Co. Ltd, Manchester, 1938–41; National Physical Laboratory, Teddington, 1941–43; RRE, Malvern, 1943–65; Head of Radio Dept, RAE, Farnborough, 1965–68; Dir, Services Electronics Res. Lab., MoD, 1968–72.

OLIVER, Prof. Michael Francis, CBE 1985; MD, FRCP, PRCPEd, FFCM; Duke of Edinburgh Professor of Cardiology, University of Edinburgh, since 1979; *b* 3 July 1925; *s* of late Captain Wilfrid Francis Lenn Oliver, MC (DLI), and Cecilia Beatrice Oliver (*née* Daniel); *m* 1st, Margaret Yool Abbey (marr. diss.); two *s* one *d* (and one *s* decd); 2nd, Helen Louise Daniel. *Educ:* Marlborough Coll.; Univ. of Edinburgh. MB, ChB 1947, MD (Gold Medal) 1957. Consultant Physician, Royal Infirmary and Sen. Lectr in Medicine, Univ. of Edinburgh, 1961; Reader in Medicine, 1973 and Personal Prof. of Cardiology, 1977, Univ. of Edinburgh. Mem., Cardiovascular Panel, Govt Cttee on Medical Aspects of Food Policy, 1971–74, 1982–84; UK Rep. Mem., Adv. Panel for Cardiovascular Disease, WHO, 1972–; Chm., BBC-Medical Adv. Gp in Scotland, 1975–81; Mem. Scientific Bd, Internat. Soc. of Cardiology, 1968–78 (Chm., Council on Atherosclerosis and Ischaemic Heart Disease, 1968–75); Chairman: Brit. Atherosclerosis Gp, 1970–75; Science Cttee, Fondation Cardiologique Princess Lilian, Belgium, 1976–85; MoT Panel on driving and cardiovascular disease, 1985–. Convener, Cardiology Cttee,

Scottish Royal Colls, 1978–81; Council Mem., Brit. Heart Foundn, 1976–85. President: British Cardiac Soc., 1981–85; RCPEd, 1986–. Hon. Fellow, Amer. Coll. of Cardiology, 1973. Hon. MD: Karolinska Inst., Stockholm, 1980; Univ. Bologna, 1985. Purkinje Medal, 1981; Polish Cardiac Soc. Medal, 1984. *Publications:* Acute Myocardial Infarction, 1966; Intensive Coronary Care, 1970, 2nd edn 1974; Effect of Acute Ischaemia on Myocardial Function, 1972; Modern Trends in Cardiology, 1975; High-Density Lipoproteins and Atherosclerosis, 1978; Coronary Heart Disease in Young Women, 1978; Strategy for Screening of Coronary Heart Disease, 1986; contribs to sci. and med. jls on causes of coronary heart disease, biochemistry of fats, myocardial metabolism, mechanisms of sudden death, clinical trials of drugs, and population studies of vascular diseases. *Recreations:* work, questioning, talking. *Address:* Barley Mill House, Pencaitland, East Lothian EH34 5EP. *T:* Pencaitland 340433; 28 Chalcot Road, NW1. *T:* 01–722 4460. *Clubs:* Athenæum; New (Edinburgh).

OLIVER, Peter Richard, CMG 1965; HM Diplomatic Service, retired; Ambassador to Uruguay, 1972–77; *b* 3 June 1917; *yr s* of William Henry Oliver and Muriel Daisy Elisabeth Oliver (*née* Widdicombe); *m* 1940, Freda Evelyn Gwyther; two *s* two *d*. *Educ:* Felsted Sch.; Hanover; Berlin; Trinity Hall, Cambridge. Indian Civil Service, 1939–47; served in Punjab and Bahawalpur State. Transferred to HM Foreign (subsequently Diplomatic) Service, 1947; served in Karachi, 1947–49; Foreign Office, 1949–52; The Hague, 1952–56; Havana, 1956–59; Foreign Office, 1959–61; Djakarta, 1961–64; Bonn, 1965–69; Dep. High Comr, Lahore, 1969–72. *Recreations:* gardening, Bumbloclasm. *Address:* Bridge Cottage, Little Petherick, Wadebridge, Cornwall PL27 7QT. *T:* Rumford 540358. *Clubs:* Royal Commonwealth Society; Hawks (Cambridge); Union (Cambridge).

OLIVER, Prof. Emeritus Richard Alexander Cavaye; Professor of Education and Director of the Department of Education in the University of Manchester, 1938–70; Dean of Faculty of Education, 1938–48, 1962–65; Dean of Faculty of Music, 1952–62, 1966–70; *b* 9 Jan. 1904; *s* of Charles Oliver and Elizabeth Smith; *m* 1929, Annabella Margaret White, MA Edin, MA Oxon; one *s* one *d*. *Educ:* George Heriot's Sch.; University of Edinburgh; Stanford Univ., California, USA. Held Commonwealth Fund Fellowship at Stanford Univ., 1927–29; research educational psychologist in Kenya, 1929–32; Asst Master Abbotsholme Sch. and in Edinburgh, 1933–34; University Extension Lecturer, 1933–34; Asst Director of Education, Wilts Education Cttee, 1934–36; Dep. Secretary, Devon Education Cttee, 1936–38. Director, University of Manchester School of Education, 1947–51; Pro Vice-Chancellor, 1953–57 and 1960–61; Presenter of Hon. Graduands, 1959–64, 1966. Member National Advisory Council on Training and Supply of Teachers, 1949–59; Member, Northern Universities Joint Matriculation Board, 1942–70 (Chm., 1952–55); Member Secondary School Examinations Council, 1958–64. FBPsS. Hon. Research Fellow, Princeton Univ., 1961. Hon. LLD Manchester, 1981. *Publications:* (with others) The Educational Guidance of the School Child, 1936; Research in Education, 1946; The Content of Sixth Form General Studies, 1974; Joint Matriculation Board Occasional Publications; contrib. to East Africa Medical Journal, Africa, British Journal of Psychology, Yearbook of Education, Universities Quarterly, Research in Education, etc. *Recreations:* gardening, painting, cookery. *Address:* Waingap, Crook, Kendal, Cumbria LA8 9HT. *T:* Kendal 821277.

See also H. A. Hetherington.

OLIVER, Prof. Roland Anthony, MA, PhD (Cantab); Professor of the History of Africa, London University, 1963–86; *b* Srinagar, Kashmir, 30 March 1923; *s* of late Major D. G. Oliver and of Lorimer Janet (*née* Donaldson); *m* 1947, Caroline Florence (*d* 1983), *d* of late Judge John Linehan, KC; one *d*. *Educ:* Stowe; King's Coll., Cambridge. Attached to Foreign Office, 1942–45; R. J. Smith Research Studentship, King's Coll., Cambridge, 1946–48; Lecturer, School of Oriental and African Studies, 1948–58; Reader in African History, University of London, 1958–63; Francqui Prof., University of Brussels, 1961; Visiting Professor: Northwestern Univ., Illinois, 1962; Harvard Univ., 1967; travelled in Africa, 1949–50 and 1957–58; org. international Conferences on African History and Archæology, 1953–61; Haile Selassie Prize Trust Award, 1966. President: African Studies Assoc., 1967–68; British Inst. in Eastern Africa, 1981–. Member: Perm. Bureau, Internat. Congress of Africanists, 1973–78; Council, Royal African Society; Chm., Minority Rights Group. Corresp. Member, Académie Royale des Sciences d'Outremer, Brussels. Editor (with J. D. Fage) Jl of African History, 1960–73. *Publications:* The Missionary Factor in East Africa, 1952; Sir Harry Johnston and the Scramble for Africa, 1957; (ed) The Dawn of African History, 1961; A Short History of Africa (with J. D. Fage), 1962; A History of East Africa (ed with Gervase Mathew), 1963; Africa since 1800 (with A. E. Atmore), 1967; (ed) The Middle Age of African History, 1967; (with B. M. Fagan) Africa in the Iron Age, 1975; (with A. E. Atmore) The African Middle Ages, 1981; Gen. Editor (with J. D. Fage), Cambridge History of Africa, 8 vols, 1975–86. *Address:* Frilsham Woodhouse, Newbury, Berks. *T:* Hermitage 201407.

OLIVER, Dr Ronald Martin, RD 1973; Deputy Chief Medical Officer (Deputy Secretary), Department of Health and Social Security, since 1985; *b* 28 May 1929; *s* of late Cuthbert Hanson Oliver and Cecilia Oliver; *m* 1957, Susanna Treves Blackwell; three *s* one *d*. *Educ:* King's Coll. Sch., Wimbledon; King's Coll., London; St George's Hosp. Med. Sch. (MB, BS 1952). MRCS, LRCP 1952; DCH 1954; DPH 1960; DIH 1961; MD London 1965; MFOM 1978. Served RNR: Surg. Lieut, 1953–55; Surg. Lt-Comdr, retd 1974. St George's Hosp., London: House Surgeon and Physician, 1952–53; Resident Clin. Pathologist, 1955–56; trainee asst, gen. practice, 1956–57; Asst County MO, Surrey CC, 1957–59; MO, London Transport Exec., 1959–62; MO, later SMO, Treasury Med. Service (later CS Med. Adv. Service), 1962–74; seconded Diplomatic Service as Physician, British Embassy, Moscow, 1964–66; SMO, 1974–79, SPMO, 1979–85, DHSS; Chief Med. Advr, ODA, 1983–85. *Publications:* papers in med. jls on epidemiology of heart disease, public health, toxicology, and health service admin. *Recreations:* golf, sailing, gardening, bad bridge. *Address:* Greenhill House, Beech Avenue, Effingham, Surrey KT24 5PH. *T:* Bookham 52887. *Club:* Effingham Golf.

OLIVER, Stephen John Lindsay, QC 1980; barrister-at-law; *b* 14 Nov. 1938; *s* of Philip Daniel Oliver and Audrey Mary Oliver; *m* 1967, Anne Dawn Harrison Taylor; one *s* two *d*. *Educ:* Rugby Sch.; Oriel Coll., Oxford (MA Jurisprudence). National Service, RN, 1957–59: served submarines; Temp. Sub-Lieut. Called to the Bar, Middle Temple, 1963. Asst Boundary Comr, Parly Boundary Commn, 1977. *Recreations:* music, sailing. *Address:* 4 Pump Court, Temple, EC4Y 7AN. *T:* 01–583 9770; 14 Eliot Place, Blackheath, SE3 0QL. *T:* 01–852 2727.

OLIVIER, family name of **Baron Olivier.**

OLIVIER, Baron *cr* 1970 (Life Peer), of Brighton; **Laurence Kerr Olivier,** OM 1981; Kt 1947; Actor; Director, 1962–73, Associate Director, 1973–74, National Theatre; Member, South Bank Theatre Board, since 1967 (South Bank Theatre and Opera House Board, 1962–67; Olivier Theatre opened, 1976, in presence of the Queen); *b* 22 May 1907; *s* of late Rev. G. K. Olivier and Agnes Louise Crookenden; *m* 1st, 1930, Jill Esmond (marr. diss., 1940); one *s*; 2nd, 1940, Vivien Leigh (marr. diss., 1961; she *d* 1967); 3rd, 1961, Joan Plowright, *qv*; one *s* two *d*. *Educ:* St Edward's Sch., Oxford. MA Hon. Tufts, Mass, 1946; Hon. DLitt: Oxon, 1957; Manchester, 1968; Sussex, 1978; Hon. LLD Edinburgh 1964; Hon. DLitt London, 1968; Fellow, BAFTA, 1976. Sonning Prize, Denmark, 1966; Gold Medallion, Swedish Acad. of Literature, 1968; Special Award for directorship of Nat. Theatre, Evening Standard, 1973; Albert Medal, RSA, 1976; Hon. Oscar, 1979, for lifetime's contrib. to films; SWET Awards renamed Laurence Olivier Awards, 1984. Commander, Order Dannebrog, 1949; Officier Legion d'Honneur, 1953; Grande Ufficiale dell' Ordino al Merito della Repubblica (Italian), 1953; Order of Yugoslav Flag with Golden Wreath, 1971. First appeared in 1922 at Shakespeare Festival, Stratford-on-Avon special boys' performance, as Katherine in Taming of the Shrew; played in Byron, King Henry IV, toured in sketch Unfailing Instinct, with Ruby Miller, Season with Lena Ashwell, King Henry VIII, 1924–25; under management of Dame Sybil Thorndike, played with Birmingham Repertory Company till 1928; Stanhope in Journey's End, for Stage Society; Beau Geste; Circle of Chalk, Paris Bound, The Stranger Within; went to America, 1929; returned 1930 and played in The Last Enemy, After All and in Private Lives; New York, 1931, played Private Lives, 1933; Rats of Norway, London; Green Bay Tree, New York; returned London, 1934, Biography, Queen of Scots, Theatre Royal; Ringmaster under his own management, Golden Arrow, Romeo and Juliet, 1935; Bees on the Boat Deck and Hamlet at Old Vic, 1936; Sir Toby Belch in Twelfth Night, and Henry V, Hamlet at Kronborg, Elsinore, Denmark, 1937; Macbeth, 1937; Iago in Othello, King of Nowhere, and Coriolanus, 1938; No Time for Comedy, New York, 1939; under his own management produced and played Romeo and Juliet with Vivien Leigh. Lieut (A) RNVR until released from Fleet Air Arm, 1944, to co-direct The Old Vic Theatre Company with Joan Burrell and Ralph Richardson, at New Theatre; played in Old Vic, 1944–45 Season; Peer Gynt, Arms and the Man, Richard III, Uncle Vanya; toured Continent in May 1945 with Peer Gynt, Arms and the Man, Richard III; Old Vic Season, 1945–46; Henry IV, Parts I and II, Oedipus, The Critic, Uncle Vanya, Arms and the Man; six weeks' season in New York with Henry IV, Parts I and II, Oedipus, The Critic and Uncle Vanya; Old Vic, 1946–47 Season, produced and played King Lear. Made a tour of Australia and New Zealand, 1948, with Old Vic Company, in Richard III, School for Scandal, Skin of our Teeth, Old Vic, 1949 Season, Richard III, The School for Scandal, Antigone. Directed A Street Car Named Desire, Aldwych, 1949; St James's, 1950–51; produced and acted in Venus Observed, under own management, produced Captain Carvallo, 1950, Antony in Antony and Cleopatra, Caesar in Caeser and Cleopatra, 1951; also in US, 1951–52; The Sleeping Prince, Phoenix, 1953; Stratford Season, 1955; Macbeth, Malvolio in Twelfth Night, Titus in Titus Andronicus; Archie Rice in The Entertainer, Royal Court Theatre, 1957; presented The Summer of the Seventeenth Doll, 1957; toured Europe in Titus Andronicus, 1957; Titus in Titus Andronicus, Stoll, 1957; Archie Rice in The Entertainer (revival), Palace Theatre, 1957, and New York, 1958; Coriolanus in Coriolanus, Stratford, 1959, directed The Tumbler, New York; Berenger in Rhinoceros, Royal Court Theatre and Strand Theatre, 1960; Becket in Becket, New York, 1960; Henry II in Becket, US Tour and New York, 1961; Fred Midway in Semi-Detached, Saville Theatre, 1962. Apptd Dir of National Theatre (first, as Old Vic): 1963: (produced) Hamlet; 1963–64; acted in Uncle Vanya and in The Recruiting Officer, 1964; acted in Othello and in The Master Builder, 1964–65. Chichester Festival: first Director, also acted, 1962 (Uncle Vanya; The Broken Heart; also Director, The Chances), 1963 (Uncle Vanya, also Director); National Theatre (produced) The Crucible; in Love for Love, Moscow and London, 1965; Othello, Moscow and London, 1965; Othello, Love for Love, (dir.) Juno and the Paycock, 1966; Edgar in The Dance of Death, Othello, Love for Love (dir.) Three Sisters, National Theatre, 1967; A Flea in Her Ear, 1968; Home and Beauty, Three Sisters (directed and played Chebutikin), 1968–69; Shylock in Merchant of Venice, 1970, Long Day's Journey into Night, 1971, 1972; Saturday, Sunday, Monday, 1973; The Party, 1974; (dir.) Eden End, 1974; (appearance on film as Akash) Time, Dominion, 1986; *films:* Potiphar's Wife, The Yellow Passport, Perfect Understanding, No Funny Business, Moscow Nights, Fire Over England, As You Like It, The First and the Last, Divorce of Lady X, Wuthering Heights, Rebecca, Pride and Prejudice, Lady Hamilton, 49th Parallel, Demi-Paradise; produced, directed, played Henry V; produced, directed, played Hamlet (International Grand Prix, 1948, Oscar award, 1949); Carrie (Hollywood), 1950; Macheath in film The Beggar's Opera, 1953; produced, directed, played Richard III (British Film Academy's Award), 1956; produced, directed and played in The Prince and the Showgirl, 1957; General Burgoyne in The Devil's Disciple, 1959; The Entertainer; Spartacus; Term of Trial; Bunny Lake is Missing; Othello; Khartoum; The Power and The Glory, 1961, (TV) USA; Dance of Death; Shoes of the Fisherman; Oh! What a Lovely War; Battle of Britain; David Copperfield; directed and played Chebutikin in Three Sisters; Nicholas and Alexandra; Lady Caroline Lamb; Sleuth (NY Film Critics Award, Best Actor, 1972); Seven-per-cent Solution; Marathon Man (Variety Club of GB Award, 1977); A Bridge Too Far; The Betsy; Boys from Brazil; A Little Romance; Dracula; Clash of the Titans; Inchon; The Jazz Singer; The Jigsaw Man; The Bounty; Wild Geese II; Peter the Great; *television:* John Gabriel Borkmann, 1959; Long Day's Journey Into Night, 1972 (Emmy Award, 1973); The Merchant of Venice, 1973; Love Among The Ruins, USA, 1974 (Emmy Award, 1975); Jesus of Nazareth, 1976; The Collection, 1976; Cat on a Hot Tin Roof, 1976; Hindle Wakes, 1976; Come Back Little Sheba, Daphne Laureola, Saturday Sunday Monday, 1977; Brideshead Revisited, 1981; A Voyage Round My Father, 1982; King Lear, 1983; The Ebony Tower, 1984. Narrated World at War (TV), 1963. *Publications:* Confessions of an Actor (autobiog.), 1982; On Acting, 1986. *Recreations:* tennis, swimming, motoring, flying, gardening. *Address:* 33–34 Chancery Lane, WC2A 1EW. *Clubs:* Garrick, Green Room, MCC.

OLIVIER, Henry, CMG 1954; DScEng, PhD London, DEng; FICE, FASCE, Beit Fellow; FRSA; specialist consulting engineer in water resources engineering, Henry Olivier & Associates, since 1973; *b* 25 Jan. 1914; *s* of J. Olivier, Umtali, S Rhodesia; *m* 1st, 1940, Lorna Renée Collier; one *d* (one *s* decd); 2nd, 1979, Johanna Cecilia van der Merwe. *Educ:* Umtali High Sch.; Cape Town Univ. (BSc 1936; MSc 1947); University College, London (PhD 1953); DEng Witwatersrand, 1967. Beit Engineering Schol., 1932–38; Beit Fellow for two Rhodesias, 1939. Engineering post-grad. training with F. E. Kanthack & Partners, Consulting Engineers, Johannesburg, 1937; Sir Alex. Gibb & Partners, Cons. Engineers, London: training 1938, Asst Engineer, 1939. Experience covers design and construction of steam-electric power-stations, hydro-electric, floating harbour, irrigation, and water resources development schemes in UK, Africa, Middle East, and USA; Chief Engineer in charge civil engineering contracts, Owen Falls Hydro-Electric Scheme, Uganda, 1950–54; Partner in firm of Sir Alexander Gibb and Partners (Africa), 1954–55; Resident Director and Chief Engineer (Rhodesia), in firm of Gibb, Coyne & Sogei (Kariba), 1955–60; Consultant (mainly in connection with Indus Basin Project in Pakistan) to Sir Alexander Gibb and Partners, London, 1960–69 (Sen. Consultant, 1967); Partner, Gibb Hawkins and Partners, Johannesburg, 1963–69, associated with design and construction of Hendrik Verwoerd and P. K. le Roux dams on Orange River, RSA; Chm. LTA Ltd and LTA Engineering Ltd, 1969–73. Mem., Exec. Cttee, SA Nat. Cttee on Large Dams, 1972–81; Pres., SA Inst. of Civil Engineers, 1979. Hon. DSc: Cape, 1968; Rhodesia, 1977. *Publications:* Irrigation and Climate, 1960; Irrigation and Water Resources Engineering, 1972, Damit, 1975; Great Dams in Southern Africa, 1977; Papers to Institution Civil Engineering Journal; Int. Commn on Irrigation and Drainage; Water for Peace Conference, Washington, DC. *Recreation:* tennis. *Address:* Henry Olivier and Associates, PO Box 6844, Johannesburg, South Africa. *Club:* Country (Johannesburg).

OLIVIER, Lady, (Joan); *see* Plowright, Joan.

OLLARD, Richard Laurence, FRSL, FSA; author and editor; *b* 9 Nov. 1923; *s* of Rev. Dr S. L. Ollard and Mary Ollard (*née* Ward); *m* 1954, Mary Buchanan-Riddell; two *s* one *d*. *Educ:* Eton College; New College, Oxford. MA. Lectr in History and English, Royal Naval College, Greenwich, 1948–59; Senior Editor, Collins, 1960–83. *Publications:* The Escape of Charles II, 1966; Man of War: Sir Robert Holmes and the Restoration Navy, 1969; Pepys: a biography, 1974, new edn 1984; This War Without an Enemy, 1976; The Image of the King: Charles I and II, 1979; An English Education: a perspective of Eton, 1982; (ed jtly) For Veronica Wedgwood These Studies in Seventeenth-Century History, 1986. *Address:* Norchard Farmhouse, Morcombelake, Bridport, Dorset DT6 6ET. *T:* Chideock 263; c/o Curtis Brown Ltd, 162–168 Regent Street, W1. *Club:* Brooks's.

OLLERENSHAW, Dame Kathleen (Mary), DBE 1971; MA, DPhil; FIMA, FCP; Freeman of the City of Manchester, 1984; Chairman: Court, Royal Northern College of Music, Manchester, since 1968 (Companion, 1978); Council for St John Ambulance in Greater Manchester, since 1974; Member, Manchester City Council, 1956–80, Leader of Conservative Opposition, 1977–79; Alderman, 1970–74, Hon. Alderman since 1980; Lord Mayor, 1975–76, Deputy Lord Mayor, 1976–77; *b* 1 Oct. 1912; *d* of late Charles Timpson, JP, and late Mary Elizabeth Timpson (*née* Stops); *m* 1939, Robert Ollerenshaw; one *s* (one *d* decd). *Educ:* Ladybarn House Sch., Manchester; St Leonards Sch., St Andrews; (open schol. in maths) Somerville Coll., Oxford (Hon. Fellow, 1978). BA (Hons) 1934, MA 1943, DPhil 1945; Foundation Fellow, Institute of Mathematics and its Applications (FIMA), 1964 (Mem. Council, 1973–75, Vice-Pres., 1976–77, Pres., 1978–79; Hon. Fellow 1986). Research Assistant, Shirley Institute, Didsbury, 1937–40. Chairman: Educn Cttee, Assoc. of Municipal Corporations, 1968–71; Assoc. of Governing Bodies of Girls' Public Schs, 1963–69; Manchester Educn Cttee, 1967–70 (Co-opted Mem., 1954–56); Manchester Coll. of Commerce, 1964–69; Council, Science and Technology Insts, 1980–81; Member: Central Adv. Council on Educn in England, 1960–63; CNAA, 1964–74; SSRC, 1971–75; Tech. Educn Council, 1973–75; (Vice-Pres.,) British Assoc. for Commercial and Industrial Educn (Mem. Delegn to USSR, 1963); Exec., Assoc. of Educn Cttees, 1967–71; Nat. Adv. Council on Educn for Industry and Commerce, 1963–70; Gen. Adv. Council of BBC, 1966–72; Schools Council, 1968–71; Management Panel, Burnham Cttee, 1968–71; Nat. Foundn of Educnl Res., 1968–71; Layfield Cttee of Inquiry into Local Govt Finance, 1974–76; Council of Univ. of Salford, 1967– (a Pro-Chancellor, 1983–); Court, Univ. of Manchester, 1964–; Manchester Polytechnic, 1968–86 (Chm., 1969–72; Dep.-Chm., 1972–75; Hon. Fellow, 1979); Court, UMIST, 1971– (Vice-Pres., 1976–86); Council, Lancaster Univ., 1975– (Dep. Pro-Chancellor, 1978–); Council, CGLI, 1972– (Hon. Fellow, 1978; Vice-Pres., 1979–84); Sen. Res. Fellow (part-time), 1972–75, Hon. Res. Fellow, 1975–77, Lancaster Univ.; a Pro-Chancellor, Univ. of Salford, 1983–; Rep. Governor, Royal Coll. of Advanced Technol., Salford, 1959–67; Governor: St Leonards Sch., St Andrews, 1950–72 (Pres., 1980–); Manchester High Sch. for Girls, 1959–69; Ladies Coll., Cheltenham, 1966–68; Chethams Hosp. Sch., Manchester, 1967–77; Further Educn Staff Coll., Blagdon, 1960–74; Mem., Manchester Statistical Soc., 1950– (Mem. Council, 1977–; Vice-Pres., 1977, Pres., 1981–83); Hon. Member: Manchester Technology Assoc., 1976– (Pres., 1982); Manchester Literary and Philosophical Soc., 1981–; Hon. Col, Manchester and Salford Univs OTC, 1977–81. Dir, Greater Manchester Independent Radio, Ltd, 1972–83. Winifred Cullis Lecture Fellow to USA, 1965; Fourth Cockroft Lecture, UMIST and Manchester Tech. Assoc., 1977. DStJ 1983 (CStJ 1978) (Mem., Chapter Gen., 1974–). Hon. LLD CNAA, 1975; Hon. DSc Salford, 1975; Hon LLD Manchester, 1976. Mancunian of the Year, Jnr Chamber of Commerce, 1977. *Publications:* Education of Girls, 1958; Education for Girls, 1961; The Girls' Schools, 1967; Returning to Teaching, 1974; The Lord Mayor's Party, 1976; First Citizen, 1977; papers in mathematical journals, 1945–54 and 1977–, incl. Proc. RI 1981 (on form and pattern), Phil. Trans Royal Soc. 1982 (on magic squares), and Proc. Royal Soc. 1986 (on pandiagonal magic squares); articles on education and local govt in national and educational press. *Address:* 2 Pine Road, Didsbury, Manchester M20 0UY. *T:* 061–445 2948. *Club:* English-Speaking Union.

OLLIS, Prof. William David, BSc, PhD; FRS 1972; Professor of Organic Chemistry, University of Sheffield, since 1963 (Head of Department of Chemistry, 1973–75); *b* 22 Dec. 1924; *s* of Albert George and Beatrice Charlotte Ollis; *m* 1951, Sonia Dorothy Mary Weekes; two *d*. *Educ:* Cotham Grammar Sch., Bristol; University of Bristol. Assistant Lecturer in Organic Chemistry, University of Bristol, 1946–49, Lecturer, 1949–62, Reader, 1962–63. Visiting Research Fellow, Harvard, 1952–53; Visiting Professor: University of California, Los Angeles, 1962; University of Texas, 1966; Nat. Science Foundn Sen. Fellowship, 1970–71; Hon. Prof., Universidade Federal Rural do Rio de Janeiro, Brasil, 1969. Robert Gnehm Lecture, 1965; Chemical Soc. Tilden Lectr, 1969. *Publications:* Recent Developments in the Chemistry of Natural Phenolic Compounds, 1961; scientific papers mainly in Journal of Chemical Society. *Address:* Department of Chemistry, University of Sheffield, Sheffield S3 7HF. *Club:* Athenæum.

O'LOGHLEN, Sir Colman (Michael), 6th Bt, *cr* 1838; *b* 6 April 1916; *s* of Henry Ross O'Loghlen (*d* 1944; 6th *s* of 3rd Bt) and of Doris Irene, *d* of late Major Percival Horne, RA; *S* uncle 1951; *m* 1939, Margaret, *d* of Francis O'Halloran, Melbourne, Victoria; six *s* two *d*. *Educ:* Xavier Coll., Melbourne; Melbourne Univ. (LLB). Formerly Captain AIF. Sometime Magistrate and Judge of Supreme Court, PNG. *Heir:* *s* Michael O'Loghlen, *b* 21 May 1945. *Address:* 98 Williamsons Road, Doncaster, Victoria 3108, Australia.

OLSSON, Curt Gunnar; Chairman, Skandinaviska Enskilda Banken, since 1984; *b* 20 Aug. 1927; *s* of N. E. and Anna Olsson; *m* 1954, Asta Engblom; two *d*. *Educ:* Stockholm Sch. of Econs (BSc Econs 1950). Managing Director, Stockholm Group: Skandinaviska Banken, 1970–72; Skandinaviska Enskilda Banken, 1972–76; Man. Dir and Chief Exec., Head Office, 1976–82, and first Dep. Chm., 1982–84, Skandinaviska Enskilda Banken. Chairman: Bowater Svenska AB, 1977–; Esselte AB, 1983–; Svenska Dagbladets AB, 1984–; Scandinavian Bank Ltd, London, 1984–; Banque Scandinave en Suisse, Geneva, 1984–; Director: Atlas Copco AB, 1976–; Försäkrings AB Skandia, 1978–; Dillon, Read & Co. Inc., NY, 1979–; Fastighets AB Hufvudstaden, 1983–. Chairman: Finnish-Swedish Chamber of Commerce, 1982–; Swedish Bankers' Assoc., 1984–. Kt Order of Vasa, Sweden, 1976; King Carl XVI Gustaf's Gold Medal, Sweden, 1982; Comdr, Royal Norwegian Order of Merit, 1985. *Address:* Skandinaviska Enskilda Banken, S-106 40 Stockholm, Sweden. *T:* 22 19 00.

OLUFOSOYE, Most Rev. Timothy; *see* Nigeria, Archbishop of.

OLVER, Sir Stephen (John Linley), KBE 1975 (MBE 1947); CMG 1965; HM Diplomatic Service, retired; *b* 16 June 1916; *s* of late Rev. S. E. L. Olver and Mrs Madeleine Olver (*née* Stratton); *m* 1953, Maria Morena, Gubbio, Italy; one *s*. *Educ:* Stowe. Indian Police, 1935–44; Indian Political Service, Delhi, Quetta, Sikkim and Bahrain, 1944–47; Pakistan Foreign Service, Aug.-Oct. 1947; Foreign Service, Karachi, 1947–50; Foreign Office, 1950–53; Berlin, 1953–56; Bangkok, 1956–58; Foreign Office, 1958–61; Washington, 1961–64; Foreign Office, 1964–66; The Hague, 1967–69; High Comr, Freetown, 1969–72; High Comr, Nicosia, 1973–75. *Recreations:* golf, photography, painting. *Address:* 7 Seymour Square, Brighton, Sussex. *Club:* MCC.

OLYOTT, Ven. Leonard Eric; Archdeacon of Taunton and Prebendary of Milverton, since 1977; *b* 11 Jan. 1926; *s* of Thomas Olyott and Maude Ann Olyott (*née* Purser); *m* 1951, Yvonne Winifred Kate Keele; two *s* one *d*. *Educ:* Colchester Royal Grammar School; London Univ. (BA 1950); Westcott House, Cambridge. Served RNVR, 1944–47; commissioned, 1945. Asst Curate, St George, Camberwell, 1952–55; Priest-in-Charge, St Michael and All Angels, Birchwood, Hatfield, Herts, 1955–60; Vicar of Chipperfield, Herts, 1960–68; Vicar of Crewkerne, 1968–71; Rector of Crewkerne with Wayford, 1971–77; Rural Dean of Crewkerne, 1972–77; Prebendary of Timberscombe, 1976. Hospital Chaplains Adviser to Bishop of Bath and Wells, 1983–. *Recreations:* sailing, gardening, elkhounds, music. *Address:* Summerhayes, Higher Street, Curry Mallet, Taunton, Somerset. *T:* Hatch Beauchamp 480758.

O'MALLEY, Stephen Keppel; a Recorder of the Crown Court, Western Circuit, since 1978; *b* 21 July 1940; *s* of late D. K. C. O'Malley and Mrs R. O'Malley; *m* 1963, Frances Mary, *e d* of James Stewart Ryan, *qv*; four *s* two *d*. *Educ:* Ampleforth Coll.; Wadham Coll., Oxford (MA). Called to Bar, Inner Temple, 1962; Mem. Bar Council, 1968–72; Co-Founder, Bar European Gp, 1977. Wine Treasurer, Western Circuit, 1986–. *Publications:* Legal London, a Pictorial History, 1971; Manual of European Practice, 1987. *Address:* 24 Montague Road, Richmond, Surrey TW10 6QW. *T:* 01–940 2727.

OMAN, Julia Trevelyan, (Lady Strong), CBE 1986; RDI 1977; designer; Director, Oman Productions Ltd; *b* 11 July 1930; *d* of late Charles Chichele Oman and Joan Trevelyan; *m* 1971, Sir Roy Colin Strong, *qv*. *Educ:* Royal College of Art, London. Royal Scholar, 1953 and Silver Medal, 1955, RCA. Designer: BBC Television, 1955–67; Mefistofele, WNO, 1957; Alice in Wonderland, BBC TV Film, 1966; Brief Lives, London and New York, 1967; Country Dance, London and Edinburgh, 1967; Art Director (England), The Charge of the Light Brigade, 1967; Art Director, Laughter in the Dark, 1968; Designer: 40 Years On, 1968; (Production designer) Julius Caesar, 1969; The Merchant of Venice, National Theatre, 1970; Eugene Onegin, Covent Garden, 1971; The Straw Dogs (film), 1971; Othello, Stratford, 1971; Samuel Pepys Exhibn, Nat. Portrait Gall., 1971; Getting On, Queen's, 1971; Othello, RSC, Aldwych, 1972; Un Ballo in Maschera, Hamburgische Staatsoper, 1973; La Bohème, Covent Garden, 1974; The Importance of Being Earnest, Burgtheater, Vienna, 1976; Die Fledermaus, Covent Garden, 1977; Mme Tussaud's hist. tableaux, 1979; Danish TV, 1979; Hay Fever and The Wild Duck, Lyric, Hammersmith, 1980; The Shoemakers' Holiday, Nat. Theatre, 1981; The Bear's Quest for Ragged Staff, Warwick, 1981; Die Csardasfürstin, Kassel, 1982; Separate Tables, 1982; Otello, Stockholm, 1983; Arabella, Glyndebourne, 1984, 1985; The Consul, Connecticut Grand Opera, USA, 1985; *ballet:* Enigma Variations, 1968; A Month in the Country, 1976; Sospiri, 1980; Swan Lake, 1981; The Nutcracker, 1984. Mem., DES Vis. Cttee for RCA, 1981–85. DesRCA (1st class), 1955; FSIAD. Designer of the Year Award for Alice in Wonderland, 1967; Award for Cable Excellence, for Best Art Direction, NCTA, 1983. *Publications:* Street Children (photographs by Julia Trevelyan Oman; text by B. S. Johnson), 1964; (with Roy Strong) Elizabeth R, 1971; (with Roy Strong) Mary Queen of Scots, 1972; introd. The Merchant of Venice, Folio Soc. edn, 1975; (with Roy Strong) The English Year, 1982; contrib. Architectural Review (photographs), Vogue (text and photographs). *Address:* c/o Curtis Brown, 162–168 Regent Street, W1R 5TA. *T:* 01–437 9700.

OMOLODUN, John Olatunji, (Chief), The Ottun-Balogun of Awe (Oyo State, Nigeria); Director, Department of Asian and Pacific Affairs, Ministry of External Affairs, Lagos, 1981–82; *b* 24 June 1935; *s* of of late Chief Omolodun and Mrs Emmanuel Owolabi Omolodun; *S* father, 1965; *m* 1959, Risikatu Fowoshere; two *s* three *d*. *Educ:* King's Coll., Lagos; Univ. of London (LLB); Council of Legal Educn. Called to the Bar, Lincoln's Inn, 1959. Barrister and Solicitor, Supreme Court of Nigeria, 1960–65; Chm., Tax Appeal Bd, W Reg. Nigeria, 1963–65; Director: Nat. Bank of Nigeria, 1964–65; Wrought Iron Co. of Nigeria, 1964–65; Councillor, Oyo Div. Council, 1964–65; Agent-General for Western Reg. of Nigeria, UK, 1965–66; Actg High Commissioner of Nigeria: Pakistan, 1966–67; Sierra Leone, 1967–70; Chargé d'Affaires, Ivory Coast, 1971–73; Dep. Dir of African Affairs Dept, Min. of Ext. Affairs, Lagos, 1973–75; Actg High Comr, UK, 1976–77; High Comr, India, with concurrent accreditation to Sri Lanka, Burma, Thailand and Bangladesh, 1977. Order of Grand Star of Africa, Liberia, 1971. Sec.-Gen., UN Assoc. of Nigeria, 1960–63; Vice-Pres., World Fedn of UN Assocs, 1963–64. *Publications:* Economic Prospects in Sub-Saharan Africa, 1978; Nigeria, Africa and the World, 1981; pamphlet on overseas students in UK, and paper on International Court of Justice. *Recreations:* cricket, golf, cycling, table tennis. *Heir:* *s* Folarin Owolabi Omolodun, *b* 13 March 1968. *Address:* PO Box 3159, General Post Office, Marina, Lagos, Nigeria. *Clubs:* Royal Over-Seas League (Hon. Mem); Yoruba Tennis, Island (Lagos).

O'MORCHOE, David Nial Creagh, CB 1979; MBE 1967; (The O'Morchoe); Chief of O'Morchoe of Oulartleigh and Monamolin; sheep farmer; *b* 17 May 1928; *s* of Nial Creagh O'Morchoe and Jessie Elizabeth, *d* of late Charles Jasper Joly, FRS, FRIS, MRIA, Astronomer Royal of Ireland; *S* father as Chief of the Name (O'Morchoe), 1970; *m* 1954, Margaret Jane, 3rd *d* of George Francis Brewitt, Cork; two *s* one *d*. *Educ:* St Columba's Coll., Dublin (Fellow 1983); RMA Sandhurst. Commissioned Royal Irish Fusiliers, 1948; served in Egypt, Jordan, Gibraltar, Germany, Kenya, Cyprus, Oman; psc 1958, jssc 1966; CO 1st Bn RIrF, later 3rd Bn Royal Irish Rangers, 1967–68; Directing Staff, Staff Coll., Camberley, 1969–71; RCDS 1972; Brigade Comdr, 1973–75; Brig. GS, BAOR, 1975–76; Maj.-Gen. 1977; Comdr, Sultan of Oman's Land Forces, 1977–79, retired. Dep. Col, 1971–76, Col 1977–79, The Royal Irish Rangers. Mem. Council: Concern, Dublin, 1984–; Irish Grassland and Animal Prodn Assoc., 1985–. *Recreations:* sailing and most sports. *Heir:* *s* Dermot Arthur O'Morchoe, *b* 11 Aug. 1956. *Address:* c/o Ulster Bank, Patrick Street, Cork. *Clubs:* Friendly Brothers (Dublin); Irish Cruising.

O'NEIL, Most Rev. Alexander Henry, MA, DD; *m* 1931, Marguerite (*née* Roe); one *s*. *Educ:* Univ. of W Ontario; BA 1928, BD 1936, MA 1943; Huron Coll., London, Ont; LTh 1929. Deacon, 1929; Priest, 1930; Principal, Huron Coll., London, Ont, 1941–52; Gen. Sec., British and Foreign Bible Soc. in Canada, 1952–57; Bishop of Fredericton, 1957–63; Archbishop of Fredericton and Metropolitan of the Province of Canada, 1963–71. Hon. DD: Univ. of W Ontario, 1945; Wycliffe Coll., Toronto, 1954; King's Coll., Halifax, 1958; Hon. LLD: W Ontario, 1962; St Thomas Univ., Fredericton, 1970; Hon. DCL Bishop's Univ., Lennoxville, 1964. *Address:* Apt 807 Grosvenor Gates, 1 Grosvenor Street, London, Ont N6A 1Y2, Canada.

O'NEIL, Hon. Sir Desmond (Henry), Kt 1980; Chairman: Western Australia Lotteries Commission, 1981–84; Western Australia Greyhound Racing Association, 1981–84; *b* 27 Sept. 1920; *s* of late Henry McLelland O'Neil and Lilian Francis O'Neil; *m* 1944, Nancy Jean Culver; two *d*. *Educ:* Aquinas Coll., Perth; Claremont Teachers Coll., WA.

Served War, Australian Army, 1939–46: Captain, Aust. Corps of Signals. Educn Dept, WA, 1939–58; Mem., Legislative Assembly, WA, 1959–80; Govt Whip, 1962–65; Minister for Housing and Labour, 1965–71; Dep. Leader of Opposition, 1972–73; Minister for: Works and Housing, 1974–75; Works, Housing and the North-West, 1975–77; Dep. Premier, Chief Sec., Minister for Police and Traffic, Minister for Regional Admin and the NW, Western Australia, 1977–80. Col Comdt, Royal Aust. Corps of Signals 5 Mil. Dist, 1980–82. *Recreations:* power boating, fishing. *Address:* 42 Godwin Avenue, South Como, WA 6152, Australia. *T:* 450–4682. *Clubs:* South of Perth Yacht; Mt Pleasant Bowling (Patron).

O'NEILL, family name of **Barons O'Neill, O'Neill of the Maine,** and **Rathcavan.**

O'NEILL, 4th Baron *cr* 1868; **Raymond Arthur Clanaboy O'Neill,** TD 1970; DL; *b* 1 Sept. 1933; *s* of 3rd Baron and Anne Geraldine (she *m* 2nd, 1945, 2nd Viscount Rothermere, and 3rd, 1952, late Ian Fleming, and *d* 1981), *e d* of Hon. Guy Charteris; *S* father, 1944; *m* 1963, Georgina Mary, *er d* of Lord George Montagu Douglas Scott; three *s. Educ:* Eton; Royal Agricultural Coll. 2nd Lieut, 11th Hussars, Prince Albert's Own; Major, North Irish Horse, AVR; Lt-Col, RARO, Hon. Col D, 1986–. Chm., Ulster Countryside Cttee, 1971–75. Trustee, Ulster Folk and Transport Mus., 1969–; Member: NI Tourist Bd, 1973–80 (Chm., 1975–80); NI Nat. Trust Cttee, 1980– (Chm., 1981–); President: NI Assoc. of Youth Clubs, 1965–; Royal Ulster Agricl Soc., 1984–86 (Chm. Finance Cttee, 1974–83). DL Co. Antrim. *Recreations:* vintage motoring, railways, gardening. *Heir: s* Hon. Shane Sebastian Clanaboy O'Neill, *b* 25 July 1965. *Address:* Shane's Castle, Antrim, N Ireland. *T:* Antrim 63264. *Club:* Turf.
See also J. A. L. Morgan.

O'NEILL OF THE MAINE, Baron *cr* 1970 (Life Peer), of Ahoghill, Co. Antrim; **Terence Marne O'Neill,** PC (N Ireland) 1956; DL; *b* 10 Sept. 1914; *s* of Capt. Hon. Arthur O'Neill, MP (killed in action, 1914; *s* of 2nd Baron O'Neill, Shane's Castle, Antrim) and of late Lady Annabel Crewe-Milnes, *e d* of 1st and last Marquis of Crewe, KG; *m* 1944, Katherine Jean, *y d* of late W. I. Whitaker, Pylewell Park, Lymington, Hants; one *s* one *d. Educ:* Eton. Served, 1939–45, Irish Guards. MP (Unionist) Bannside, Parlt of N Ireland, 1946–70; Parly Sec., Min. of Health, 1948; Deputy Speaker and Chairman of Ways and Means, 1953; Joint Parly Sec., Home Affairs and Health, 1955; Minister: Home Affairs, 1956; Finance, 1956; Prime Minister of N Ireland, 1963–69. Mem., Hansard Soc. Commn on Electoral Reform, 1975–76. Director: Warburg International Holdings Ltd, 1970–83; Phoenix Assurance, 1969–84. Trustee, Winston Churchill Meml Trust; Governor, Nat. Gall. of Ireland. DL Co. Antrim, 1948; High Sheriff County Antrim, 1953. Hon. LLD, Queen's Univ., Belfast, 1967. *Publications:* Ulster at the Crossroads, 1969; The Autobiography of Terence O'Neill, 1972. *Address:* Lisle Court, Lymington, Hants. *Club:* Brooks's.

O'NEILL, Alan Albert; Clerk to the Drapers' Company, 1973–80, Member, Court of Assistants, since 1981; *b* 11 Jan. 1916; *o s* of late Albert George O'Neill; *m* 1939, Betty Dolbey; one *s. Educ:* Sir George Monoux Grammar Sch., Walthamstow. Joined staff Drapers' Co., 1933, Dep. Clerk 1967. Clerk to Governors, Bancroft's School, 1951–73, Governor, 1980–; Governor, Queen Mary Coll., 1973–80. Served War of 1939–45, Royal Navy: Telegraphist, RNV(W)R, 1939; DEMS Gunnery Officer, SS Aquitania and SS Nieuw Amsterdam; Lt-Comdr, RNVR, 1943; DEMS Staff Officer, Aberdeen and NE Coast Scotland, 1945. *Recreation:* gardening. *Address:* Wickenden, 36 Main Road, Sundridge, Sevenoaks, Kent TN14 6EP. *T:* Westerham 63530.

O'NEILL, Hon. Sir Con (Douglas Walter), GCMG 1972 (KCMG 1962; CMG 1953); *b* 3 June 1912; 2nd *s* of 1st Baron Rathcavan, PC and late Sylvia, *d* of Walter A. Sandeman, Morden House, Royston; *m* 1st, 1940, Rosemary (marriage dissolved 1954), *d* of late H. Pritchard, MD; one *s* one *d*; 2nd, 1954, Baroness Mady Marschall von Bieberstein (*d* 1960), *d* of late Baron von Holzing-Berstett; 3rd, 1961, Mrs Anne-Marie Lindberg, Helsinki. *Educ:* Eton College; Balliol Coll., Oxford (History Scholar). BA 1934 (1st Class, English), MA 1937; Fellow, All Souls College, Oxford, 1935–46; called to Bar, Inner Temple, 1936; entered Diplomatic Service, 1936; Third Secretary, Berlin, 1938; resigned from Service, 1939. Served War of 1939–45 in Army (Intelligence Corps), 1940–Nov. 1943; temp. employed in Foreign Office, 1943–46; Leader-writer on staff of Times, 1946–47; returned to Foreign Office, 1947; re-established in Foreign Service, 1948; served in Frankfurt and Bonn, 1948–53; Counsellor, HM Foreign Service, 1951; Imperial Defence College, 1953; Head of News Department, Foreign Office, 1954–55; Chargé d'Affaires, Peking, 1955–57; Asst Under-Sec., FO, 1957–60; Ambassador to Finland, 1961–63; Ambassador to the European Communities in Brussels, 1963–65; Dep. Under-Sec. of State, FO, 1965–68; Dir, Hill, Samuel & Co. Ltd, 1968–69; Dep. Under-Sec. of State, FCO, and Leader at official level of British delegn to negotiate entry to EEC, 1969–72; Chm., Intervention Bd for Agricl Produce, 1972–74; Dir, Unigate Ltd, 1974–83. Dir, Britain in Europe Campaign, 1974–75. *Publication:* Our European Future, 1972 (Stamp Meml Lecture). *Address:* 37 Flood Street, SW3.

O'NEILL, Martin (John); MP (Lab) Clackmannan, since 1983 (Stirlingshire, East and Clackmannan, 1979–83); *b* 6 Jan. 1945; *s* of John and Minnie O'Neill; *m* 1973, Elaine Marjorie Samuel; two *s. Educ:* Trinity Academy, Edinburgh; Heriot Watt Univ. (BA Econ.); Moray House Coll. of Education, Edinburgh. Insurance Clerk, Scottish Widows Fund, 1963–67; Asst Examiner, Estate Duty Office of Scotland, 1971–73; Teacher of Modern Studies, Boroughmuir High School, Edinburgh, 1974–77; Social Science Tutor, Craigmount High School, Edinburgh, 1977–79; Open Univ., 1976–79. Opposition spokesman on defence matters, 1984–. Mem., Select Cttee, Scottish Affairs, 1979–. Member: GMWU; MATSA; EIS. *Recreations:* watching football, playing squash, reading, listening to jazz, the cinema. *Address:* House of Commons, SW1. *T:* 01–219 4548.

O'NEILL, Most Rev. Michael Cornelius, OBE 1945; MM 1918; *b* 15 Feb. 1898; Irish Canadian. *Educ:* St Michael's College, University of Toronto; St Augustine's Seminary, Toronto. Overseas Service, Signaller, CFA, European War, 1916–19. St Joseph's Seminary, Edmonton; Professor, 1928–39; Rector, 1930–39. Overseas Service, Canadian Chaplain Services, War of 1939–45; Principal Chaplain (Army) Overseas, (RC), 1941–45; Principal Chaplain (Army), (RC), 1945–46. Archbishop of Regina, 1948–73. Hon. Chaplain, Saskatchewan Comd, Royal Canadian Legion, 1973. Nat. Lutheran Merit Award, 1974. Hon. LLD: Toronto, 1952; Univ. of Saskatchewan (Regina Campus), 1974; Hon. DD Univ. of St Michael's Coll., Toronto, 1977. *Address:* 67 Hudson Drive, Regina, Sask, Canada. *Club:* East India, Devonshire, Sports and Public Schools.

O'NEILL, Prof. Patrick Geoffrey, BA, PhD; Professor of Japanese, University of London, 1968–86; *b* 9 Aug. 1924; *m* 1951, Diana Howard; one *d. Educ:* Rutlish Sch., Merton; Sch. of Oriental and African Studies, Univ. of London. Lectr in Japanese, Sch. of Oriental and African Studies, Univ. of London, 1949. *Publications:* A Guide to Nō, 1954; Early Nō Drama, 1958; (with S. Yanada) Introduction to Written Japanese, 1963; A Programmed Course on Respect Language in Modern Japanese, 1966; Japanese Kana Workbook 1967; A Programmed Introduction to Literary-style Japanese, 1968; Japanese Names, 1972; Essential Kanji, 1973; (ed) Tradition and Modern Japan, 1982; (with H. Inagaki) A Dictionary of Japanese Buddhist Terms, 1984; A Reader of Handwritten Japanese, 1984. *Address:* School of Oriental and African Studies, London University, WC1E 7HP.

O'NEILL, Robert James, CMG 1978; HM Diplomatic Service; Ambassador at Vienna, since 1986; concurrently Head of UK Delegation to negotiations on mutual reduction of forces and armaments and associated measures in Central Europe, Vienna, since 1986; *b* 17 June 1932; *m* 1958, Helen Juniper; one *s* two *d. Educ:* King Edward VI Sch., Chelmsford; Trinity Coll., Cambridge (Schol.). 1st cl. English Tripos Pts I and II. Entered HM Foreign (now Diplomatic) Service, 1955; FO, 1955–57; British Embassy, Ankara, 1957–60; Dakar, 1961–63; FO, 1963–68, Private Sec. to Chancellor of Duchy of Lancaster, 1966, and to Minister of State for Foreign Affairs, 1967–68; British Embassy, Bonn, 1968–72; Counsellor Diplomatic Service, 1972; seconded to Cabinet Office as Asst Sec., 1972–75; FCO, 1975–78; Dep. Governor, Gibraltar, 1978–81; Under Sec., Cabinet Office, 1981–84; Asst Under-Sec. of State, FCO, 1984–86. *Recreation:* hill-walking. *Address:* c/o Foreign and Commonwealth Office, SW1A 2AH. *T:* Vienna 731575. *Club:* Travellers'.

O'NEILL, Dr Robert John; Director, International Institute for Strategic Studies, 1982–87; Chichele Professor of the History of War, University of Oxford, from Oct. 1987; Fellow, All Souls College, Oxford, from Oct. 1987; *b* 5 Nov. 1936; *s* of Joseph Henry and Janet Gibbon O'Neill; *m* 1965, Sally Margaret Burnard; two *d. Educ:* Scotch Coll., Melbourne; Royal Military Coll. of Australia; Univ. of Melbourne (BE); Brasenose Coll., Oxford (MA, DPhil 1965). Served Australian Army, 1955–68; Rhodes Scholar, Vic, 1961; Fifth Bn Royal Australian Regt, Vietnam, 1966–67 (mentioned in despatches); Major 1967; resigned 1968. Sen. Lectr in History, Royal Military Coll. of Australia, 1968–69; Australian National University: Sen. Fellow in Internat. Relations, 1969–77, Professorial Fellow, 1977–82; Head, Strategic and Defence Studies Centre, 1971–82. Official Australian Historian for the Korean War, 1969–82. Member: Council, IISS, 1977–82; Exec. Cttee, British Internat. Studies Assoc., 1983–; Commonwealth Sec.-Gen.'s Adv Gp on Small State Security, 1984–85. FASSA 1978; FIE(Aust) 1981. *Publications:* The German Army and the Nazi Party 1933–1939, 1966; Vietnam Task, 1968; General Giap: politician and strategist, 1969; (ed) The Strategic Nuclear Balance, 1975; (ed) The Defence of Australia: fundamental new aspects, 1977; (ed) Insecurity: the spread of weapons in the Indian and Pacific Oceans, 1978; (ed jtly) Australian Dictionary of Biography, Vols 7–9, 1891–1939, 1979–83; (ed with David Horner) New Directions in Strategic Thinking, 1981; Australia in the Korean War 1950–1953, Vol. 1, Strategy and Diplomacy, 1981, Vol. II, Combat Operations, 1985; (ed with David Horner) Australian Defence Policy for the 1980s, 1982; (ed) Security in East Asia, 1984; (ed) The Conduct of East-West Relations in the 1980s, 1985; (ed) New Technology and Western Security Policy, 1985; articles in many learned jls. *Recreations:* local history, walking. *Address:* International Institute for Strategic Studies, 23 Tavistock Street, WC2E 7NQ. *T:* 01–379 7676; (from Oct. 1987) All Souls College, Oxford OX1 4AL.

O'NEILL, Thomas P(hilip), Jr; Speaker, House of Representatives, USA, 1976–86; *b* Cambridge, Mass, 9 Dec. 1912; *s* of Thomas P. O'Neill and Rose Anne (*née* Tolan); *m* 1941, Mildred Anne Miller; three *s* two *d. Educ:* St John's High Sch.; Boston Coll., Mass. Grad. 1936. In business, insurance, in Cambridge, Mass. Mem., State Legislature, Mass, 1936–52: Minority Leader, 1947 and 1948; Speaker of the House, 1948–52. Member, Camb. Sch. Cttee, 1946, 1949. Member of Congresses: 83rd-87th, 11th Dist, Mass; 88th-99th, 8th Dist, Mass. Democrat: Majority Whip, 1971–73, Majority Leader, 1973–77. *Address:* c/o US Capitol, Washington, DC 20515, USA.

O'NIONS, Prof. Robert Keith, PhD; FRS 1983; Royal Society Research Professor, Cambridge University, since 1979; Official Fellow, Clare Hall, Cambridge, since 1980; *b* 26 Sept. 1944; *s* of William Henry O'Nions and Eva O'Nions; *m* 1967, Rita Margaret Bill; three *d. Educ:* Univ. of Nottingham (BSc 1966); Univ. of Alberta (PhD 1969). Post-doctoral Fellow, Oslo Univ., 1970; Demonstr in Petrology, Oxford Univ., 1971–72, Lectr in Geochem., 1972–75; Associate Prof., then Prof., Columbia Univ., NY, 1975–79. Mem., Norwegian Acad. of Sciences, 1980. Macelwane Award, Amer. Geophys. Union, 1979; Bigsby Medal, Geol. Soc. London, 1983. *Publications:* contrib. to jls related to earth and planetary sciences. *Address:* Department of Earth Sciences, Cambridge University, Cambridge. *T:* Cambridge 333400.

ONSLOW, family name of **Earl of Onslow.**

ONSLOW, 7th Earl of, *cr* 1801; **Michael William Coplestone Dillon Onslow,** Bt 1660; Baron Onslow, 1716; Baron Cranley, 1776; Viscount Cranley, 1801; *b* 28 Feb. 1938; *s* of 6th Earl of Onslow, KBE, MC, TD, and of Hon. Pamela Louisa Eleanor Dillon, *o d* of 19th Viscount Dillon, CMG, DSO; *S* father, 1971; *m* 1964, Robin Lindsay, *o d* of Major Robert Lee Bullard III, US Army, and of Lady Aberconway; one *s* two *d. Educ:* Eton; Sorbonne. Life Guards, 1956–60, served Arabian Peninsula. Farmer. Governor: University Coll. at Buckingham; Royal Grammar Sch., Guildford. High Steward of Guildford. *Heir: s* Viscount Cranley, *qv. Address:* Temple Court, Clandon Park, Guildford, Surrey. *Clubs:* White's, Beefsteak.
See also A. A. Waugh.

ONSLOW, Cranley Gordon Douglas; MP (C) Woking since 1964; *b* 8 June 1926; *s* of late F. R. D. Onslow and Mrs M. Onslow, Effingham House, Bexhill; *m* 1955, Lady June Hay, *yr d* of 13th Earl of Kinnoull; one *s* three *d. Educ:* Harrow; Oriel Coll., Oxford; Geneva Univ. Served in RAC, Lieut 7th QO Hussars, 1944–48, and 3rd/4th Co. of London Yeo. (Sharpshooters) (TA) as Captain, 1948–52. Joined HM Foreign Service, 1951; Third Sec. Br. Embassy, Rangoon, 1953–55; Consul at Maymyo, N Burma, 1955–56; resigned, 1960. Served on Dartford RDC, 1960–62, and Kent CC, 1961–64. Parly Under-Sec. of State, Aerospace and Shipping, DTI, 1972–74; an Opposition spokesman on health and social security, 1974–75, on defence, 1975–76; Minister of State, FCO, 1982–83. Chairman: Select Cttee on Defence, 1981–82; Cons. Aviation Cttee, 1970–72, 1979–82. Mem. Exec., 1922 Cttee, 1968–72, 1981–82, 1983–, Chm., 1984–. Mem., UK delegn to Council of Europe and WEU, 1977–81. Director: Argyll Group PLC, 1983–; Rediffusion PLC, 1985–. Chm., Nautical Museums Trust, 1983–. Council Member: Nat. Rifle Assoc.; Salmon & Trout Assoc.; Anglers' Co-operative Assoc.; Mem., British Field Sports Soc. Mem. Council, St John's Sch., Leatherhead. *Publication:* Asian Economic Development (ed), 1965. *Recreations:* fishing, shooting, watching cricket. *Address:* Highbuilding, Fernhurst, W Sussex. *Club:* English-Speaking Union.

ONSLOW, Sir John (Roger Wilmot), 8th Bt, *cr* 1797; Captain, Royal Yacht of Saudi Arabia; *b* 21 July 1932; *o s* of Sir Richard Wilmot Onslow, 7th Bt, TD, and Constance (*d* 1960), *o d* of Albert Parker; *S* father, 1963; *m* 1955, Catherine Zoia (marr. diss. 1973), *d* of Henry Atherton Greenway, The Manor, Compton Abdale, near Cheltenham, Gloucestershire; one *s* one *d*; *m* 1976, Susan Fay, *d* of E. M. Hughes, Frankston, Vic, Australia. *Educ:* Cheltenham College. *Heir: s* Richard Paul Atherton Onslow, *b* 16 Sept. 1958. *Address:* c/o Barclays Bank, Fowey, Cornwall.

ONTARIO, Metropolitan of; *see* Niagara, Archbishop of.

ONTARIO, Bishop of, since 1981; **Rt. Rev. Allan Alexander Read;** *b* 19 Sept. 1923; *s* of Alex P. Read and Lillice M. Matthews; *m* 1949, Mary Beverly Roberts; two *s* two *d*. *Educ:* Trinity Coll., Univ. of Toronto (BA, LTh). Incumbent, Mono East and Mono West, 1947–54; Rector, Trinity Church, Barrie, 1954–71; Canon of St James Cathedral, Toronto, 1957; Archdeacon of Simcoe, 1961–72; Bishop Suffragan of Toronto, 1972–81. Hon. DD: Trinity Coll., Toronto, 1972; Wycliffe Coll., Toronto, 1972; Hon. STD Thornloe Coll., Sudbury, 1982. Citizen of the Year, Barrie, 1969; Honorary Reeve, Black Creek, Toronto, 1980. *Publication:* Shepherds in Green Pastures, 1952. *Recreation:* organ music. *Address:* 90 Johnston Street, Kingston, Ont. K7L 1X7, Canada.

OPIE, Evelyn Arnold; Matron, King's College Hospital, SE5, 1947–60; *b* 21 Aug. 1905; *d* of George and Annie Opie. *Educ:* Wentworth School for Girls, Bournemouth. Westminster Sick Children's Hosp., 1924–26 (sick children's trng); Guy's Hosp., SE1, 1926–29; SRN Oct. 1929. Midwifery Trng SCM, 1930, Sister, 1930–32, Guy's Hosp.; private nursing, Bournemouth, 1932–33; Sister (Radium Dept and Children's Ward), 1933–39, Administrative Sister, Asst Matron, Dep. Matron, 1939–47, Guy's Hosp. Diploma in Nursing of London Univ., 1935. *Recreations:* music, gardening. *Address:* 29 Muir House, Beaulieu Road, Dibden Purlieu, Southampton SO4 5NY. *T:* Hythe 842232.

OPIE, Geoffrey James; Keeper, Education Department, Victoria and Albert Museum, since 1983; *b* 10 July 1939; *s* of Basil Irwin Opie and Florence Mabel Opie (*née* May); *m* 1st, 1964, Pamela Green; one *s* one *d*; 2nd, 1980, Jennifer Hawkins; one *s*. *Educ:* Humphry Davy Grammar School, Penzance; Falmouth Sch. of Art (NDD); Goldsmiths' Coll., London (ATC). Asst Designer, Leacock & Co., 1961; Curator, Nat. Mus. of Antiquities of Scotland, 1963; Designer, Leacock & Co., 1967; Curator, Victoria and Albert Mus., 1969, Educn Dept, 1978–. *Publications:* The Wireless Cabinet 1930–1956, 1979; contribs to various jls. *Recreations:* painting, literature, music, motorcycling. *Address:* 130 Kingston Road, Teddington, Middx TW11 9JA.

OPIE, Iona Margaret Balfour; folklorist; *b* 13 Oct. 1923; *d* of late Sir Robert Archibald, CMG, DSO, MD, and of Olive Cant; *m* 1943, Peter Mason Opie (*d* 1982); two *s* one *d*. *Educ:* Sandecotes Sch., Parkstone. Served 1941–43, WAAF meteorological section. Hon. Mem., Folklore Soc., 1974. Coote-Lake Medal (jtly with husband), 1960. Hon. MA Oxon, 1962. *Publications:* (all with Peter Opie): I Saw Esau, 1947; The Oxford Dictionary of Nursery Rhymes, 1951; The Oxford Nursery Rhyme Book, 1955; Christmas Party Games, 1957; The Lore and Language of Schoolchildren, 1959; Puffin Book of Nursery Rhymes, 1963 (European Prize City of Caorle); Children's Games in Street and Playground, 1969 (Chicago Folklore Prize); The Oxford Book of Children's Verse, 1973; Three Centuries of Nursery Rhymes and Poetry for Children (exhibition catalogue), 1973, enl. edn 1977; The Classic Fairy Tales, 1974; A Nursery Companion, 1980; The Oxford Book of Narrative Verse, 1983; The Singing Game, 1985. *Recreations:* reading, walking. *Address:* Westerfield House, West Liss, Hants.

OPIE, Roger Gilbert, CBE 1976; Fellow and Lecturer in Economics, New College, Oxford, since 1961; *b* Adelaide, SA, 23 Feb. 1927; *o s* of late Frank Gilbert Opie and late Fanny Irene Grace Opie (*née* Tregoning); *m* 1955, Norma Mary, *o d* of late Norman and late Mary Canter; two *s* one *d*. *Educ:* Prince Alfred Coll. and Adelaide Univ., SA; Christ Church and Nuffield Coll., Oxford. BA 1st Cl. Hons 1948, MA Adelaide 1950; SA Rhodes Schol., 1951; Boulter Exhibnr, 1952; George Webb Medley Jun. Schol., 1952, Sen. Schol., 1953; PPE 1st Cl. 1953; Nuffield Coll. Studentship, 1954; BPhil 1954. Tutor and Lectr, Adelaide Univ., 1949–51; Asst Lectr and Lectr, LSE, 1954–61; Econ. Adviser, Econ. Section, HM Treasury, 1958–60; Asst Dir, HM Treasury Centre for Administrative Studies, 1964; Asst Dir, Planning Div., Dept of Economic Affairs, 1964–66; Economic Adviser to Chm., NBPI, 1967–70; Special Univ. Lectr in Econs, Oxford, 1970–75; Tutor and Sen. Tutor, Oxford Univ. Business Summer Sch., 1974–79. Visiting Professor: Brunel Univ., 1975–77; Univ. of Strathclyde, 1984–. Member: Monopolies and Mergers Commn, 1968–81; Price Commn, 1977–80. Mem., ILO Mission to Ethiopia, 1982. City Councillor, Oxford, 1972–74; Oxford Dist Councillor, 1973–76. Economic Correspondent, New Statesman, 1967–71, 1974–76; Editor: The Bankers' Magazine, 1960–64; International Currency Review, 1970–71. Governor: Bryanston Sch.; Harpur Trust Schs, Bedford. FRSA 1980. *Publications:* co-author of a number of works in applied economics. *Recreations:* sailing, photography, hiding in Cornwall. *Address:* 8 New College Lane, Oxford OX1 3BL. *T:* Oxford 241769. *Club:* Lilliput Sailing (Dorset).

OPPÉ, Prof. Thomas Ernest, CBE 1984; FRCP; Professor of Paediatrics, University of London at St Mary's Hospital Medical School, since 1969; *b* 7 Feb. 1925; *s* of late Ernest Frederick Oppé and Ethel Nellie (*née* Rackstraw); *m* 1948, Margaret Mary Butcher; three *s* one *d*. *Educ:* University Coll. Sch., Hampstead; Guy's Hosp. Med. Sch. (MB BS, hons dist. in Medicine, 1947). DCH 1950; FRCP 1966. Sir Alfred Fripp Meml Fellow, Guy's Hosp., 1952; Milton Res. Fellow, Harvard Univ., 1954; Lectr in Child Health, Univ. of Bristol, 1956–60; Consultant Paediatrician, United Bristol Hosps, 1960; Asst Dir, 1960–64, Dir, 1964–69, Paediatric Unit, St Mary's Hosp. Med. Sch.; Consultant Paediatrician, St Mary's Hosp., 1960–. Consultant Adviser in Paediatrics, DHSS, 1971–86; Member, DHSS Committees: Safety of Medicines, 1974–79; Med. Aspects of Food Policy, 1966– (Chm., Panel on Child Nutrition); Child Health Services, 1973–76. Royal College of Physicians: Chm., Cttee on Paediatrics, 1970–74; Pro-Censor and Censor, 1975–77; Sen. Censor and Sen. Vice-Pres., 1983–84; University of London: Mem., Bd of Studies in Medicine, 1964– (Chm., 1978–80); elected Mem. of Senate, 1981–; Dean, Faculty of Medicine, 1984–86. Member: BMA (Dep. Chm., Bd of Sci. and Educn, 1974–82); British Paediatric Assoc. (Hon. Sec., 1960–63); European Soc. for Paediatric Res., 1969–; GMC, 1984–; sometime Mem., Governing Bodies, St Mary's Hosp., Inst. of Med. Ethics, Paddington Coll.; Examiner in Paediatrics, Univs of Glasgow, Leicester, Liverpool, London, Sheffield, Wales, Colombo, Singapore. *Publications:* Modern Textbook of Paediatrics for Nurses, 1961; Neurological Examination of Children (with R. Paine), 1966; chapters in books and papers on paediatrics and child health. *Address:* 8 Suffolk Road, Barnes, SW13 9NB. *T:* 01–748 3921.

OPPENHEIM, Tan Sri Sir Alexander, Kt 1961; OBE 1955; FRSE; MA, DSc (Oxon); PhD (Chicago); retired; Visiting Professor, University of Benin, Nigeria, 1973–77; Vice-Chancellor, University of Malaya, 1957–65 (Acting Vice-Chancellor, 1955); *b* 4 Feb. 1903; *o s* of late Rev. H. J. and Mrs F. Oppenheim; *m* 1930, Beatrice Templer (marr. diss. 1977), *y d* of Dr Otis B. Nesbit, Indiana, USA; one *d*; and two *s*. *Educ:* Manchester Grammar Sch.; Balliol Coll., Oxford (Scholar). Sen. Mathematical Schol., Oxf., 1926; Commonwealth Fund Fell., Chicago, 1927–30; Lectr, Edinburgh, 1930–31; Prof. of Mathematics, 1931–42, 1945–49; Dep. Principal, 1947, 1949, Raffles Coll., Singapore; Prof. of Mathematics, 1949–57; Dean, Faculty of Arts, 1949, 1951, 1953. Hon. degrees: DSc (Hong Kong) 1961; LLD: (Singapore) 1962; (Leeds) 1966; DLitt (Malaya) 1965. L/Bdr, SRA(V), POW (Singapore, Siam), 1942–45; Dean POW University, 1942; Pres. Malayan Mathematical Soc., 1951–55, 1957. Pres. Singapore Chess Club, 1956–60; Pres., Amer. Univs. Club, 1956. Chm. Bd of Management, Tropical Fish Culture Research Institute (Malacca), 1962; Member: Unesco-International Assoc. of Universities Study of Higher Education in Development of Countries of SE Asia, 1962; Academic Adv. Cttee, Univ. of Cape Coast, 1972. Visiting Professor: Univ. of Reading, in Dept of Mathematics, 1965–68; Univ. of Ghana, 1968–73. Alumni Medal, Univ. of Chicago Alumni Assoc., 1977. Panglima Mangku Negara (Fedn of Malaya), 1962; FWA, 1963. *Publications:* papers on mathematics in various periodicals. *Recreations:* chess, bridge. *Address:* Matson House, Remenham, Henley-on-Thames RG9 3HB. *T:* Henley-on-Thames 572049. *Clubs:* Royal Over-Seas League; Selangor (Kuala Lumpur).

OPPENHEIM, Sir Duncan (Morris), Kt 1960; Adviser to British-American Tobacco Co. Ltd, 1972–74 (Chairman 1953–66, President, 1966–72); Chairman, Tobacco Securities Trust Co. Ltd, 1969–74; Deputy Chairman, Commonwealth Development Finance Co., 1968–74; *b* 6 Aug. 1904; *s* of Watkin Oppenheim, BA, TD, and Helen, 3rd *d* of Duncan McKechnie; *m* 1st, 1932, Joyce Mary (*d* 1933), *d* of Stanley Mitcheson; no *c*; 2nd, 1936, Susan May (*d* 1964), *e d* of Brig.-Gen. E. B. Macnaghten, CMG, DSO; one *s* one *d*. *Educ:* Repton Sch. Admitted Solicitor of the Supreme Court, 1929; Messrs Linklaters & Paines, London, Assistant Solicitor, 1929–34; joined British-American Tobacco Ltd group as a Solicitor, 1934; Director: British-American Tobacco Co. Ltd, 1943; Lloyds Bank Ltd, 1956–75; Equity and Law Life Assurance Society, 1966–80. Chairman: Council, Royal College of Art, 1956–72; Council of Industrial Design, 1960–72 (Mem. 1959); British Nat. Cttee of Internat. Chamber of Commerce, 1963–74; Overseas Investment Cttee CBI, 1964–74; RIIA (Chatham House), 1966–71; Member: Adv. Council, V&A Mus., 1967–79 (Chm. V&A Associates, 1976–81); Crafts Council (formerly Crafts Adv. Cttee), 1972–83 (acting Chm., 1977; Dep. Chm., 1978); Governing Body of Repton School, 1959–79; Chm. Court of Governors, Admin. Staff Coll., 1963–71. Hon. Dr and Senior Fellow, Royal College of Art; Hon. FSIAD 1972. Bicentenary Medal, RSA, 1969. *Recreations:* painting, sailing. *Address:* 43 Edwardes Square, Kensington, W8. *T:* 01–603 7431. *Clubs:* Athenæum; Royal Yacht Squadron.

OPPENHEIM, Phillip Anthony Charles Lawrence; MP (C) Amber Valley, since 1983; *b* 20 March 1956; *s* of late Henry Oppenheim and of Rt Hon. Sally Oppenheim-Barnes, *qv*. *Educ:* Harrow; Oriel College, Oxford. BA Hons. Company director, farmer, journalist, author. Mem. Council, Parly IT Cttee, 1984–; Vice Pres., Videotex Industry Assoc., 1985–. Co-editor, What to Buy for Business, 1980–. *Publications:* A Handbook of New Office Technology, 1982; Telecommunications: a user's handbook, 1983; A Word Processing Handbook, 1984. *Recreations:* Rugby, tennis, travel, skiing. *Address:* House of Commons, SW1A 0AA.

OPPENHEIM-BARNES, Rt. Hon. Sally; PC 1979; MP (C) Gloucester since 1970; *b* 26 July 1930; *d* of Mark and Jeanette Viner; *m* 1st, 1949, Henry M. Oppenheim (*d* 1980); one *s* two *d*; 2nd, 1984, John Barnes. *Educ:* Sheffield High Sch.; Lowther Coll., N Wales. Formerly: Exec. Dir, Industrial & Investment Services Ltd; Social Worker, School Care Dept, ILEA. Trustee, Clergy Rest House Trust. Vice Chm., 1971–73, Chm., 1973–74, Cons. Party Parly Prices and Consumer Protection Cttee; Opposition Spokesman on Prices and Consumer Protection, 1974–79; Mem. Shadow Cabinet, 1975–79; Min. of State (Consumer Affairs), Dept of Trade, 1979–82. Non-exec. Dir and Mem., Main Bd, Boots Co. plc, 1982–. Formerly Nat. Vice-Pres., Nat. Union of Townswomen's Guilds; Pres., Glos Dist Br., BRCS. *Recreations:* tennis, bridge. *Address:* House of Commons, SW1. *Club:* (Pres.) Conservative (Gloucester).

See also P. A. C. L. Oppenheim.

OPPENHEIMER, Harry Frederick; Chairman: Anglo-American Corporation of SA Ltd, 1957–82 (Director, 1934–82); De Beers Consolidated Mines, Ltd, 1934–85; formerly Director, Metals and Resources Corporation Ltd, and other companies in Anglo American and De Beers Groups; *b* Kimberley, S Africa, 28 Oct. 1908; *s* of late Sir Ernest Oppenheimer, DCL, LLD; *m* 1943, Bridget, *d* of late Foster McCall; one *s* one *d*. *Educ:* Charterhouse; Christ Church, Oxford (MA; Hon. Student). MP (SA) Kimberley City, 1948–58. Served 4th SA Armoured Car Regt 1940–45. Chancellor, Univ. of Cape Town; Hon. DEcon, Univ. of Natal; Hon. DLaws, Univs of Leeds, Rhodes and Witwatersrand. Instn MM Gold Medal, 1965. *Recreations:* horse breeding and racing. *Address:* Brenthurst, Parktown, Johannesburg, South Africa. *Clubs:* Brooks's; Rand, Inanda (Johannesburg); Kimberley (SA); Harare (Zimbabwe).

OPPENHEIMER, Sir Michael (Bernard Grenville), 3rd Bt, *cr* 1921; BLitt, MA; *b* 27 May 1924; *s* of Sir Michael Oppenheimer, 2nd Bt, and Caroline Magdalen (who *m* 2nd, 1935, late Sir Ernest Oppenheimer), *d* of Sir Robert G. Harvey, 2nd Bt; *S* father, 1933; *m* 1947, Laetitia Helen, BPhil, MA, *er d* of Sir Hugh Munro-Lucas-Tooth of Teananich, 1st Bt; three *d*. *Educ:* Charterhouse; Christ Church, Oxford. Served with South African Artillery, 1942–45. Lecturer in Politics: Lincoln Coll., Oxford, 1955–68; Magdalen Coll., Oxford, 1966–68. *Heir:* none. *Address:* L'Aiguillon, Rue des Cotils, Grouville, Jersey. *Clubs:* Victoria (Jersey); Kimberley (Kimberley).

OPPENHEIMER, Peter Morris; Student of Christ Church, Oxford, and University Lecturer in Economics, since 1967; on secondment as Chief Economist, Shell International Petroleum Co., 1985–Dec. 1986; *b* 16 April 1938; *s* of Friedrich Rudolf and Charlotte Oppenheimer; *m* 1964, Catherine, *er d* of late Dr Eliot Slater, CBE, FRCP, and of Dr Lydia Pasternak; two *s* one *d*. *Educ:* Haberdashers' Aske's Sch.; The Queen's Coll., Oxford (BA 1961). National Service, RN, 1956–58. Bank for International Settlements, Basle, 1961–64; Research Fellow, Nuffield Coll., Oxford, 1964–67; Vis. Prof., London Graduate Sch. of Business Studies, 1976–77. Director: Investing in Success Equities Ltd, 1975–; Target Hldgs, 1982–84; J. Rothschild Investment Management, 1982–. Mem., Royal Commn on Legal Services, 1976–79. Mem. Council, Trade Policy Research Centre, 1976–, and co-Editor, The World Economy, 1977–. Presenter: (BBC radio): File on 4, 1977–80; Third Opinion, 1983; Poles Apart, 1984; (BBC TV) Outlook, 1982–85. *Publications:* (ed) Issues in International Economics, 1980; contribs to symposia, conference procs, prof. jls, bank reviews, etc. *Recreations:* music, opera, amateur dramatics, swimming, skiing. *Address:* 8 Lathbury Road, Oxford OX2 7AU. *T:* Oxford 58226.

OPPENHEIMER, Sir Philip (Jack), Kt 1970; Chairman, The Diamond Trading Co. (Pty) Ltd; *b* 29 Oct. 1911; *s* of Otto and Beatrice Oppenheimer; *m* 1935, Pamela Fenn Stirling; one *s* one *d*. *Educ:* Harrow; Jesus Coll., Cambridge. Director: De Beers Consolidated Mines Ltd; Anglo American Corp. of SA Ltd. Bronze Cross of Holland, 1943; Commandeur, Ordre de Léopold, 1977. *Recreations:* golf, horse-racing and breeding. *Address:* (office) 17 Charterhouse Street, EC1N 6RA. *Clubs:* Jockey, Portland, White's.

OPPERMAN, Hon. Sir Hubert (Ferdinand), Kt 1968; OBE 1952; Australian High Commissioner in Malta, 1967–72; *b* 29 May 1904; Australian; *m* 1928, Mavys Paterson Craig; one *s* (one *d* decd). *Educ:* Armadale, Vic.; Bailieston, Vic. Served RAAF 1940–45; commissioned 1942. Commonwealth Public Service: PMG's Dept, 1918–20; Navigation Dept, Trade and Customs, 1920–22. Cyclist: Australian Road Champion, 1924, 1926, 1927, 1929; Winner French Bol d'Or, 1928, and Paris-Brest-Paris, 1931; holder, numerous world's track and road unpaced and motor paced cycling records. Director, Allied Bruce Small Pty Ltd, 1936–60. MHR for Corio, Vic., 1949–67; Mem. Australian Delegn to CPA Conf., Nairobi, 1954; Chief Govt Whip, 1955–60; Minister for Shipping and Transport, 1960–63; Minister for Immigration, 1963–66. Convenor, Commonwealth Jubilee Sporting Sub-Cttee, 1951; Nat. Patron, Aust. Sportsmen's Assoc., 1980–; Chm. Selection Cttee, Aust. Hall of Sporting Fame; Hon. Master of Sport, Confedn of Aust.

Sport, 1984. GCSJ 1980 (KSJ 1973); Bailiff Prior, Victoria, 1980–83; Bailiff, Aust. Grand Council, 1983–. Hon. Rotarian, St Kilda Rotary, 1984. Coronation Medal, 1953; Medals of City of Paris, 1971, Brest, 1971, Verona, 1972; Médaille Mérite, French Cycling Fedn, 1978. *Publication:* Pedals, Politics and People (autobiog.), 1977. *Recreations:* cycling, swimming. *Address:* Unit 52, Salford Park, 100 Harold Street, Wantirna, Vic. 3152, Australia. *T:* 221–4010. *Clubs:* USI, Air Force (Victoria).

ORAM, family name of **Baron Oram.**

ORAM, Baron *cr* 1975 (Life Peer), of Brighton, E Sussex; **Albert Edward Oram;** *b* 13 Aug. 1913; *s* of Henry and Ada Edith Oram; *m* Frances Joan, *d* of Charles and Dorothy Barber, Lewes; two *s. Educ:* Burgess Hill Element. Sch.; Brighton Grammar Sch.; University of London (London School of Economics and Institute of Education). Formerly a teacher. Served War 1942–45; Royal Artillery, Normandy and Belgium. Research Officer, Co-operative Party, 1946–55. MP (Lab and Co-op) East Ham South, 1955–Feb. 1974; Parly Secretary, ODM, 1964–69; a Lord in Waiting (Govt Whip), 1976–78. Chm., Co-op. Develt Agency, 1978–81. Co-ordinator, Develt Programmes, Internat. Co-operative Alliance, 1971–73; Develt Administrator, Intermediate Technol. Develt Gp. Mem., Commonwealth Develt Corp., 1975–76. *Recreations:* country walking, cricket, chess. *Address:* 19 Ridgeside Avenue, Patcham, Brighton BN1 8WD. *T:* Brighton 505333. *Club:* MCC.

ORAM, Rt. Rev. Kenneth Cyril; *see* Grahamstown, Bishop of.

ORAM, Samuel, MD (London); FRCP; Consultant Cardiologist and Emeritus Lecturer; former Senior Physician, and Director, Cardiac Department, King's College Hospital; Censor, Royal College of Physicians; Medical Adviser, Rio Tinto Zinc Corporation Ltd; *b* 11 July 1913; *s* of Samuel Henry Nathan Oram, London; *m* 1940, Ivy, *d* of Raffaele Amato; two *d. Educ:* King's College, London; King's College Hospital, London. Senior Scholar, KCH, London; Sambrooke Medical Registrar, KCH. Served War of 1939–45, as Lt-Col, RAMC. Examiner in Medicine for RCP and Univs of Cambridge and London; Examiner: in Pharmacology and Materia Medica, The Conjoint Bd; in Medicine, The Worshipful Soc. of Apothecaries. Member: Assoc. of Physicians; Br. Cardiac Society; American Heart Assoc.; Corresp. Member Australasian Cardiac Soc. *Publications:* Clinical Heart Disease (textbook), 1971, 2nd edn 1981; various cardiological and medical articles in Quart. Jl Med., British Heart Jl, BMJ, Brit. Encyclopaedia of Medical Practice, The Practitioner, etc. *Recreation:* golf (execrable). *Address:* 73 Harley Street, W1. *T:* 01–935 9942. *Club:* Athenæum.

ORANMORE and BROWNE, 4th Baron (Ireland), *cr* 1836; Baron Mereworth of Mereworth Castle (UK), *cr* 1926; **Dominick Geoffrey Edward Browne;** *b* 21 Oct. 1901; *e s* of 3rd Baron and Lady Olwen Verena Ponsonby (*d* 1927), *e d* of 8th Earl of Bessborough; *S* father, 1927; *m* 1st, 1925, Mildred Helen (who obtained a divorce, 1936; she *d* 1980), *e d* of Hon. Thomas Egerton; two *s* one *d* (and two *d* decd); 2nd, 1936, Oonagh (marr. diss., 1950), *d* of late Hon. Ernest Guinness; one *s* (and two *s* decd); 3rd, 1951, Sally Gray, 5b Mount Street, London, W. *Educ:* Eton; Christ Church, Oxford. *Heir: s* Hon. Dominick Geoffrey Thomas Browne [*b* 1 July 1929; *m* 1957, Sara Margaret (marr. diss. 1974), *d* of late Dr Herbert Wright, 59 Merrion Square, Dublin, and late Mrs C. A. West, Cross-in-Hand, Sussex]. *Address:* 52 Eaton Place, SW1.

See also Hon. M. A. R. Cayzer.

ORCHARD, Edward Eric, CBE 1966 (OBE 1959); *b* 12 Nov. 1920. *Educ:* King's Sch., Grantham; Jesus Coll., Oxford (MA). War Service, 1941–46; FO and HM Embassy, Moscow, 1948–51; Lectr in Russian, Oxford, 1951–52; HM Embassy Moscow and FCO, 1953–76 (Dir of Research, 1970–76). Mem., Waverley Borough Council, 1978–; Dep. Mayor, Haslemere. *Publications:* articles and reviews. *Recreations:* swimming, gardening, local government and welfare. *Address:* Sturt Meadow House, Haslemere, Surrey. *T:* Haslemere 3034.

ORCHARD, Peter Francis, CBE 1982; Chief Executive, The De La Rue Co. plc, since 1977, Director, since 1963; *b* 25 March 1927; *s* of Edward Henslowe Orchard and Agnes Marjory Willett; *m* 1955, Helen Sheridan; two *s* two *d. Educ:* Downside Sch., Bath; Magdalene Coll., Cambridge (MA). CBIM. Service, KRRC, 1944–48. Joined Thomas De La Rue & Co. Ltd, 1950; Managing Director: Thomas De La Rue (Brazil), 1959–61; Thomas De La Rue International, 1962–70. Dir, Delta Group plc, 1981–. Mem., Court of Assistants, Drapers' Co., 1974–, Master 1982. Hon. Col 71st (Yeomanry) Signal Regt, TA, 1984–. *Recreations:* gardening, swimming, building, cricket. *Address:* Willow Cottage, Little Hallingbury, Bishop's Stortford, Herts CM22 7PX. *T:* Bishop's Stortford 54101. *Clubs:* Travellers', MCC.

ORCHARD-LISLE, Aubrey Edwin, CBE 1973; Consultant Partner, Healey & Baker, Surveyors, London, Amsterdam, Paris, New York and Brussels (Senior Partner until 1973); *b* 12 March 1908; *s* of late Edwin Orchard-Lisle and late Lucy Ellen Lock; *m* 1934, Phyllis Muriel Viall (*d* 1981); one *s* one *d. Educ:* West Buckland Sch., N Devon; Coll. of Estate Management. FRICS. Joined Healey & Baker, 1926. Governor, Guy's Hosp. 1953–74; Vice-Chm. of Bd, 1963–74; Governor, Guy's Hosp. Med. Sch., 1964–84; Chm., Special Trustees, Guy's Hosp., 1974–84; Mem., Lambeth, Southwark, Lewisham, AHA (Teaching), 1974–79; Property Consultant, NCB Superannuation Schemes, 1953–; Mem. Bd, Gen. Practice Finance Corp., 1966–80; Chm., Adv. Panel for Institutional Finance in New Towns, 1969–80; part-time Mem., Nat. Bus Co., 1971–77 (Mem., Nat. Bus Co. Property Cttee, 1971–83, Dir, Nat. Bus Properties Ltd, 1983–; Mem., Investment Adv. Cttee, Nat. Bus Co. Pension Schemes (Best (Estates) Ltd), 1974–). *Recreations:* work, gardens, swimming. *Address:* 30 Mount Row, Grosvenor Square, W1Y 5DA. *T:* 01–499 6470; White Walls, Quarry Wood Road, Marlow, Bucks. *T:* Marlow 2573. *Clubs:* St Stephen's Constitutional, Naval and Military, Buck's, Lansdowne, MCC.

ORD, Andrew James B.; *see* Blackett-Ord.

ORDE, Alan C. C.; *see* Campbell Orde.

ORDE, Denis Alan; His Honour Judge Orde; a Circuit Judge, since 1979; *b* 28 Aug. 1932; *s* of John Orde, CBE, Littlehoughton Hall, Northumberland, and late Charlotte Lilian Orde, County Alderman; *m* 1961, Jennifer Jane, *d* of late Dr John Longworth, Masham, Yorks; two *d. Educ:* Oxford Univ. (MA). Served Army, 1950–52, 2nd Lieut 1951; TA, 1952–64 (RA). Pres., Oxford Univ. Conserv. Assoc., 1954; Mem. Cttee, Oxford Union, 1954–55; Vice-Chm., Fedn of Univ. Conserv. Assocs., 1955. Called to Bar, Inner Temple, 1956; Pupil Studentship, 1956; Profumo Prize, 1959. North-Eastern Circuit, 1958. Asst Recorder: Kingston upon Hull, 1970; Sheffield, 1970–71; a Recorder of the Crown Court, 1972–79. Contested (C): Consett, Gen. Elec. 1959, Newcastle upon Tyne West, Gen. Elec. 1966, Sunderland South, Gen. Elec. 1970. *Recreations:* listening to music; cricket, golf, painting. *Address:* Chollerton Grange, Chollerton, near Hexham, Northumberland NE46 4TT; 11 King's Bench Walk, Temple, EC4. *Clubs:* Carlton, Coningsby, United and Cecil; Northern Counties (Newcastle).

ORDE, Sir John (Alexander) Campbell-, 6th Bt *cr* 1790, of Morpeth; *b* 11 May 1943; *s* of Sir Simon Arthur Campbell-Orde, 5th Bt, TD, and of Eleanor, *e d* of Col Humphrey Watts, OBE, TD, Haslington Hall, Cheshire; *S* father, 1969; *m* 1973, Lacy Ralls, *d* of Grady Gallant, Nashville, USA; one *s* three *d. Educ:* Gordonstoun. *Heir: s* John Simon Arthur Campbell-Orde, *b* 15 Aug. 1981. *Address:* Bee's Wing Farm, Route 2, Box 199H, Kingston Road, Fairview, Tenn 37062, USA. *Clubs:* Caledonian, Lansdowne.

ORDE-POWLETT, family name of **Baron Bolton.**

O'REGAN, Hon. Sir (John) Barry; Kt 1984; Judge of the Court of Appeal, Fiji, since 1984; *b* 2 Dec. 1915; *s* of John O'Regan; *m* Catherine, *d* of John O'Donnell; four *s* one *d. Educ:* Sacred Heart College, Auckland; Victoria University, Wellington (LLB). Army service, 1941–45 (Captain). Partner, Bell O'Regan & Co., 1945–73; Judge of High Court, NZ, 1973–84. Chairman: Prisons Parole Bd, 1977–83; War Pensions Appeal Bd, 1984–. Member: Council, Wellington Law Soc., 1959–69 (Pres., 1968); Council, NZ Law Soc., 1967–69; Council of Legal Education, 1969–73; Legal Aid Board, 1970–73. Consul-Gen. for Ireland, 1965–73. Trustee, Victoria Univ. Halls of Residence Foundn, 1967–. *Address:* Apt A/4 Lincoln Courts, 1 Washington Avenue, Wellington 2, New Zealand.

O'REILLY, Dr Anthony John Francis, (Dr Tony O'Reilly); President and Chief Executive Officer, H. J. Heinz Co. Inc., since 1979; *b* Dublin, 7 May 1936; *o c* of J. P. O'Reilly, former Inspector-General of Customs; *m* 1962, Susan, *d* of Keith Cameron, Australia; three *s* three *d* (of whom two *s* one *d* are triplets). *Educ:* Belvedere Coll., Dublin; University Coll., Dublin (BCL 1958); Bradford Univ. (PhD 1980). Admitted Solicitor, 1958. Industrial Consultant, Weston Evans UK, 1958–60; PA to Chm., Suttons Ltd, Cork, 1960–62; Chief Exec. Officer, Irish Dairy Bd, 1962–66; Man. Dir, Irish Sugar Bd, 1966–69; Man. Dir, Erin Foods Ltd, 1966–69; Jt Man. Dir, Heinz-Erin, 1967–70; Man. Dir, H. J. Heinz Co. Ltd, UK, 1969–71; Sen. Vice-Pres., N America and Pacific, H. J. Heinz Co., 1971–72; Exec. Vice-Pres. and Chief Op. Off., 1972–73, Pres. and Chief Operating Officer, 1973–79, H. J. Heinz Co. Lectr in Business Management, UC Cork, 1960–62. Director: Robt McCowen & Sons Ltd, 1961–62; Agricl Credit Corp. Ltd, 1965–66; Nitrigin Eireann Teoranta, 1965–66; Allied Irish Investment Bank Ltd, 1968–71; Thyssen-Bornemisza Co., 1970–72; Independent Newspapers (Vice Chm., 1973–80; Chm., 1980–); Nat. Mine Service Co., 1973–76; Mobil, 1979–; Bankers Trust Co., 1980–; Allegheny Internat. Inc., 1982–; Chairman: Fitzwilliam Securities Ltd, 1971–77; Fitzwilton Ltd, 1978– (Dep. Chm., 1972–78); Atlantic Resources PLC, 1981–. Member: Incorp. Law Soc.; Council, Irish Management Inst.; Hon. LLD: Wheeling Coll., 1974; Rollins Coll., 1978; Trinity Coll., 1978; Allegheny Coll., 1983. *Publications:* Prospect, 1962; Developing Creative Management, 1970; The Conservative Consumer, 1971; Food for Thought, 1972. *Recreations:* Rugby (played for Ireland 29 times), tennis. *Address:* 835 Fox Chapel Road, Pittsburgh, Pa 15238, USA; Castlemartin, Kilcullen, Co. Kildare, Ireland. *Clubs:* Reform, Annabels, Les Ambassadeurs; Stephen's Green (Dublin); Union League (New York); Duquesne, Allegheny, Fox Chapel, Pittsburgh Golf (Pittsburgh); Carlton (Chicago); Rolling Rock (Ligonier); Lyford Cay (Bahamas).

O'REILLY, Most Rev. Colm; *see* Ardagh and Clonmacnoise, Bishop of, (RC).

O'REILLY, Francis Joseph; Chairman, Ulster Bank Ltd, since 1982 (Deputy Chairman, 1974–82); Director: National Westminster Bank, since 1982; Irish Distillers Group Ltd, since 1966 (Chairman, 1966–83); Chancellor, University of Dublin, Trinity College, since 1985 (Pro-Chancellor, 1983–85); *b* 15 Nov. 1922; *s* of Lt-Col Charles J. O'Reilly, DSO, MC, MB, KSG and Dorothy Mary Martin; *m* 1950, Teresa Mary, *e d* of Captain John Williams, MC; three *s* seven *d. Educ:* St Gerard's Sch., Bray; Ampleforth Coll., York; Trinity Coll., Dublin (BA, BAI). Served HM Forces, RE, 1943–46. John Power & Son, 1946–66 (Dir, 1952–66, Chm., 1955–66); Chm., Player & Wills (Ire.) Ltd, 1964–81; Dir, Ulster Bank Ltd, 1961–. President: Marketing Inst. of Ireland, 1983–85; Inst. of Bankers in Ireland, 1985–86. Pres., Equestrian Fedn of Ireland, 1963–79; Chm., Royal Dublin Soc., 1980– (Mem. Cttees, 1959–80). LLD *hc*: Univ. of Dublin, 1978; NUI, 1986. *Recreations:* fox-hunting, racing, gardening. *Address:* Rathmore, Naas, Co. Kildare, Ireland. *T:* Naas 62136. *Clubs:* Kildare Street and University (Dublin); Irish Turf (The Curragh, Co. Kildare).

O'REILLY, William John, CB 1981; OBE 1971; FASA; Commissioner of Taxation, Australian Taxation Office, 1976–84, retired; *b* 15 June 1919; *s* of William O'Reilly and Ruby (*née* McCrudden). *Educ:* Nudgee Coll., Brisbane, Qld; Univ. of Queensland (Associate in Accountancy). FASA 1983. Served RAAF, 1942–44. Joined Australian Public Service, 1946; Australian Taxation Office: Brisbane, 1946–55; Melbourne, 1955–61; Canberra, 1961–; Asst Comr of Taxation, 1963; First Asst Comr of Taxation, 1964; Second Comr of Taxation (Statutory Office), 1967. *Recreations:* reading, walking. *Address:* c/o Mrs L. C. Bennedick, 1240 Waterworks Road, The Gap, Qld 4061, Australia. *T:* 30–1607. *Clubs:* Commonwealth, Canberra (Canberra).

OREJA AGUIRRE, Marcelino; Grand Cross: Order of Charles III, 1980; Order of Isabella the Catholic, 1982; Secretary General, Council of Europe, since 1984; *b* 13 Feb. 1935; *m* 1967, Silvia Arburua; two *s. Educ:* Univ. of Madrid (LLD). Prof. of Internat. Affairs, Diplomatic Sch., Madrid, 1962–70; Dir of Internat. Service, Bank of Spain, 1970–74; Minister of Foreign Affairs, 1976–80; Governor-Gen., Basque Country, 1980–82. Grand Officier de la Légion d'Honneur (France), 1976; Grand Cross: Order of Christ (Portugal), 1978; Order of the Crown (Belgium); (1st Cl.), Order of Service (Austria); (1st Cl.), Order of Merit (Federal Republic of Germany); Order of Orange-Nassau (Netherlands); (1st Cl.) Order of Polar Star (Sweden); Order of Dannebrog (Denmark); Order of Merit (Italy); Order of the Oak Crown (Luxembourg). *Address:* Council of Europe, Box 431 R6, F-67006 Strasbourg, France. *T:* (88) 61.49.61.

ORESCANIN, Bogdan; Ambassador of Yugoslavia to the Court of St James's, 1973–76; *b* 27 Oct. 1916; *m* 1947, Sonja Dapcevic; no *c. Educ:* Faculty of Law, Zagreb; Higher Mil. Academy. Organised uprising in Croatia; i/c various mil. and polit. duties in Nat. Liberation Struggle, War of 1939–45; Asst, then DCGS and Asst Defence Sec. of State, Yugoslav People's Army (Col General); formerly Mem. Fed. Parlt, Mem. Council of Fedn, Chm. Parly Cttee for Nat. Defence, Mem. For. Affairs Cttee of Fed. Parlt and Mem. Exec. Bd, Yugoslav Gp of IPU; Mil. Attaché in Gt Britain, 1952–54; Yugoslav Ambassador, People's Republics of China, Korea and Vietnam, 1970–73. Holds various Yugoslav and foreign decorations. *Publications:* articles on military-political theory; (study) Military Aspects of the Struggle for World's Peace, National Independence and Socialism. *Address:* Federal Secretariat for Foreign Affairs, Kneza Milosa 24, 11000 Belgrade, Yugoslavia.

ORGAN, (Harold) Bryan; painter; *b* Leicester, 31 Aug. 1935; *o c* of late Harold Victor Organ and Helen Dorothy Organ; *m* (marr. diss. 1981); *m* 1982, Sandra Mary Mills. *Educ:* Wyggeston Sch., Leicester; Coll. of Art, Loughborough; Royal Academy Schs, London. Lectr in Drawing and Painting, Loughborough Coll. of Art, 1959–65. One-man exhibns: Leicester Museum and Art Gallery, 1959; Redfern Gallery, 1967, 1969, 1971, 1973, 1975, 1978, 1980; Leicester 1973, 1976; New York, 1976, 1977; Turin, 1981. Represented: Kunsthalle, Darmstadt, 1968; Mostra Mercatao d'Arte Contemporanea,

Florence, 1969; 3rd Internat. Exhibn of Drawing, Germany, 1970; Sao Paolo Museum of Art, Brazil; Baukunst Gallery, Cologne, 1977. Works in public and private collections in England, USA, Germany, France, Canada, Italy. Portraits include: Malcolm Muggeridge, 1966; Sir Michael Tippett, 1966; David Hicks, 1968; Mary Quant, 1969; Nadia Nerina, 1969; Princess Margaret, 1970; Dr Roy Strong, 1971; Elton John, 1973; Lester Piggott, 1973; Lord Ashby, 1975; Sir Rex Richards, 1977; Harold Macmillan, 1980; Prince of Wales, 1981; Lady Diana Spencer, 1981; Lord Denning, 1982; Jim Callaghan, 1982; Duke of Edinburgh, 1983. Hon. MA Loughborough, 1974; Hon. DLitt Leicester, 1985. *Address:* c/o Redfern Gallery, 20 Cork Street, W1. *T:* 01–734 1732.

ORGANE, Sir Geoffrey (Stephen William), Kt 1968; MD, FFARCS; FRCS; Emeritus Professor of Anæsthetics, University of London, Westminster Medical School; formerly: Civilian Consultant in Anæsthetics to Royal Navy; Consultant Adviser in Anæsthetics, Ministry of Health; *b* Madras, 25 Dec. 1908; *er s* of Rev. William Edward Hartland Organe, K-i-H, and Alice (*née* Williams); *m* 1935, Margaret Mary Bailey, *e d* of Rev. David Bailey Davies, MC; one *s* two *d*. *Educ:* Taunton Sch.; Christ's Coll., Cambridge; Westminster Med. Sch. MRCS, LRCP, 1933; DA, RCP&S, 1937; MA, MD Cantab 1941; FFARCS 1948; FRCS 1965. Various resident appointments and first Anæsthetic Registrar (1938–39), Westminster Hospital; two years in general practice. Hon. Secretary, Medical Research Council's Anæsthetics Sub-Committee of Committee on Traumatic Shock, 1941–47; formerly Hon. Sec. Anæsthetics Cttee, Cttee on Analgesia in Midwifery; Vice-Pres., BMA Sect. Anæsthetics, Harrogate, 1949, Toronto, 1955; Pres., World Fedn of Socs. of Anæsthesiologists, 1964–68 (Sec.-Treas., 1955–64); Mem. Coun., RCS, 1958–61, Joseph Clover Lectr, Fac. of Anæsthetics; Royal Society of Medicine: Mem. Council; Hon. Sec. 1953–58; Hon. Fellow, 1974; Pres. Sect. of Anæsthetics, 1949–50 (Hon. Mem.); Assoc. of Anæsthetists of Gt Brit. and Ire.: Hon. Sec. 1949–53; Vice-Pres. 1953–54; Mem. Council, 1957–59; Pres. 1954–57; Hon. Mem., 1974; John Snow Silver Medal, 1972; Mem. Cttee of Anæsthetists' Group of BMA (Chm. 1955–58); Pres. SW Metropolitan Soc. of Anæsthetists, 1957–59; Dean, Faculty of Anæsthetists, 1958–61; Examr in Anæsthetics, Conjoint Bd; Examiner for FFARCS. Visited Italy, Turkey, Greece, Syria, Lebanon for Brit. Council; Denmark, Norway for WHO; also Portugal, France, Switzerland, Spain, Belgium, Netherlands, Germany, Finland, USA, Canada, Argentina, Australia, Venezuela, Mexico, Uganda, Peru, Japan, Hong Kong, Philippines, Brazil, Ceylon, Egypt, India, Iran, Israel, Malaysia, Uruguay, Austria, Sweden, Poland, USSR, Bulgaria, Czechoslovakia, Malta. Hon. or Corr. Mem., Danish, Argentine, Australian, Austrian, Brazilian, Canadian, Greek, Portuguese, French, German, Italian, Philippine, Spanish, Venezuelan Societies of Anæsthetists; Hon. FFARACS 1957; Hon. FFARCS 1975. *Publications:* various articles and chapters in medical journals and textbooks. *Recreations:* travel, gardening, photography, competitive sports; (formerly Pres., Vice-Pres., Hon. Treas., Capt. 1933) United Hospitals Athletic Club. *Address:* March Hares, The Street, Cherhill, Calne, Wilts SN11 8XP.

ORGEL, Leslie Eleazer, DPhil Oxon, MA; FRS 1962; Senior Fellow, Salk Institute, La Jolla, California, USA, and Adjunct Professor, University of California, San Diego, Calif, since 1964; *b* 12 Jan. 1927; *s* of Simon Orgel; *m* 1950, Hassia Alice Levinson; two *s* one *d*. *Educ:* Dame Alice Owen's Sch., London. Reader, University Chemical Laboratory, Cambridge, 1963–64, and Fellow of Peterhouse, 1957–64. *Publication:* An Introduction to Transition-Metal Chemistry, Ligand-Field Theory, 1960; The Origins of Life: molecules and natural selection, 1973. *Address:* Salk Institute, PO Box 85800, San Diego, Calif 92138, USA.

ORIGO, Marchesa Iris, DBE 1977; FRSL; author; *b* Birdlip, Glos, 15 August 1902; *o d* of W. Bayard Cutting, Westbrook, Long Island, USA, and Lady Sybil Cuffe; *m* 1924, Marchese Antonio Origo (*d* 1976); two *d*. *Educ:* privately, mostly in Florence. Holds honorary doctorates from Smith College and Wheaton College, USA; Isabella d'Este medal for essays and historical studies, Mantua, Italy, 1966. Gold Medal, Italian Red Cross, 1944 (for relief work in villages destroyed during Second World War); DBE (for work for partisans and escaped British POWs during Second World War). *Publications:* Leopardi, a biography, 1935 (revised 1953); Allegra, 1935; Tribune of Rome, 1938; War in Val d'Orcia, 1947; Giovanna and Jane, 1948; The Last Attachment, 1949; The Merchant of Prato, 1957; A Measure of Love, 1957; The World of San Bernardino, 1963; Images and Shadows, Part of a Life, 1970; The Vagabond Path: an anthology, 1972; A Need to Testify, 1983; articles in Speculum, History Today, Atlantic Monthly, TLS. *Recreations:* travel, gardening. *Address:* La Foce, Chianciano Terme, 53042 Siena, Italy. *T:* Rome 6541324.

O'RIORDAN, Rear-Adm. John Patrick Bruce, CBE 1982; Military Deputy Commandant, NATO Defence College, Rome, since 1986; *b* 15 Jan. 1936; *yr s* of Surgeon Captain Timothy Joseph O'Riordan, RN and Bertha Carson O'Riordan (*née* Young); *m* 1959, Jane, *d* of John Alexander Mitchell; one *s* two *d*. *Educ:* Kelly College. Nat. Service and transfer to RN, 1954–59; served in submarines, Mediterranean, Home and Far East; HM Ships Porpoise (i/c) and Courageous, NDC, HMS Dreadnought (i/c), MoD, 1960–76; Captain (SM), Submarine Sea Training, 1976–78; RCDS, 1979; HMS Glasgow (i/c), 1980–81; ACOS (Policy), Saclant, USA, 1982–84; Dir, Naval Warfare, MoD, 1984–86. FBIM; AMINucE. *Recreations:* sailing, Rugby football, travel. *Address:* NATO Defence College, Rome, c/o UK National Support Unit, HQ AF South, Naples, BFPO 8. *Clubs:* Army and Navy, Royal Navy of 1765 and 1785; Royal Yacht Squadron, Royal Naval Sailing Association.

ORKNEY, 8th Earl of, *cr* 1696; **Cecil O'Bryen Fitz-Maurice;** Viscount of Kirkwall and Baron of Dechmont, 1696; *b* 3 July 1919; *s* of Douglas Frederick Harold FitzMaurice (*d* 1937; *g g s* of 5th Earl) and Dorothy Janette (who *m* 2nd, 1939, Commander E. T. Wiggins, DSC, RN), *d* of late Capt. Robert Dickie, RN; *S* kinsman 1951; *m* 1953, Rose Katharine Durk, *yr d* of late J. W. D. Silley, Brixham. Joined RASC, 1939; served in North Africa, Italy, France and Germany, 1939–46, and in Korea, 1950–51. Heir: kinsman Oliver Peter St John [*b* 27 Feb. 1938; *m* 1963, Mary Juliet, *d* of W. G. Scott-Brown, *qv*; one *s* four *d*]. *Address:* Summerlanes, Princes Road, Ferndown, Dorset.

ORLEBAR, Michael Keith Orlebar S.; *see* Simpson-Orlebar.

ORMAN, Stanley, PhD; Director General, Strategic Defence Initiative Project Office, Ministry of Defence, since 1986; *b* 6 Feb. 1935; *s* of Jacob and Ettie Orman; *m* 1960, Helen (*née* Hourman); one *s* two *d*. *Educ:* Hackney Downs Grammar School; King's College London. BSc (1st Cl. Hons) 1957; PhD (Organic Chem.) 1960. MICorrST; FRIC 1969. Research Fellowship, Brandeis Univ., 1960–61; AWRE Aldermaston, research in corrosion and mechano-chemical corrosion, 1961–74, project work, 1974–78; Director Missiles, 1978–81, Chief Weapon System Engineer Polaris, 1981–82, MoD; Minister-Counsellor, Hd of Defence Equip. Staff, British Embassy, Washington, 1982–84; Dep. Dir, AWRE, MoD, 1984–86. *Publications:* numerous papers on free radical chemistry, materials science and mechano-chemical corrosion, in learned jls. *Recreations:* sporting—originally athletics, now tennis and badminton. *Address:* 311 The Meadway, Reading, Berks RG3 4NS. *T:* Reading 424880.

ORME, Ion G.; *see* Garnett-Orme.

ORME, Rt. Hon. Stanley, PC 1974; MP (Lab) Salford East, since 1983 (Salford West, 1964–83); *b* 5 April 1923; *s* of Sherwood Orme, Sale, Cheshire; *m* 1951, Irene Mary, *d* of Vernon Fletcher Harris, Worsley, Lancashire. *Educ:* elementary and technical schools; National Council of Labour Colleges and Workers' Educational Association classes. Warrant Officer, Air-Bomber Navigator, Royal Air Force Bomber Command, 1942–47. Joined the Labour party, 1944; contested (Lab) Stockport South, 1959. Minister of State: NI Office, 1974–76; DHSS, 1976; Minister of State for Social Security, 1976–77, Minister for Social Security, and Mem. Cabinet, 1977–79; Opposition Spokesman on Health and Social Services, June 1979–Dec. 1980, on Industry, 1980–83, on Energy, 1983–. Member of Sale Borough Council, 1958–65; Member: AEU; District Committee, Manchester; shop steward. Hon. DSc Salford, 1985. *Address:* House of Commons, SW1; 47 Hope Road, Sale, Cheshire. *Clubs:* ASE (Altrincham); Ashfield Labour (Salford).

ORMESSON, Comte Jean d'; Chevalier des Palmes académiques 1962; Commandeur des Arts et Lettres 1973; Chevalier de la Légion d'honneur 1973; Officier de l'Ordre national du Mérite, 1978; Membre Académie française 1973; Secretary-General, International Council for Philosophy and Humanistic Studies (UNESCO), since 1971 (Deputy, 1950–71); writer and journalist; *b* 16 June 1925; 2nd *s* of Marquis d'Ormesson, French diplomat and Ambassador; *m* 1962, Françoise Béghin; one *d*. *Educ:* Ecole Normale Supérieure. MA (History), Agrégé de philosophie. Mem. French delegns to various internat. confs, 1945–48; Mem. staff of various Govt Ministers, 1958–66; Mem. Council ORTF, 1960–62; Mem. Control Cttee of Cinema, 1962–69; Mem. TV Programmes Cttee, ORTF, 1973–74. Mem., Brazilian Acad. of Letters, 1979. Diogenes: Dep. Editor, 1952–72; Mem. Managing Cttee, 1972–80; Editor, 1980–82; Editor-in-Chief, 1982–; Le Figaro: Dir, 1974–77; Editor-in-Chief, 1975–77. *Publications:* L'Amour est un plaisir, 1956; Du côté de chez Jean, 1959; Un amour pour rien, 1960; Au revoir et merci, 1966; Les Illusions de la mer, 1968; La Gloire de l'Empire, 1971 (Grand Prix du Roman de l'Académie française), Amer. edn (The Glory of the Empire), 1975, Eng. edn 1976; Au Plaisir de Dieu, 1974, Amer. edn (At God's Pleasure), 1977, Eng. edn 1978; Le Vagabond qui passe sous une ombrelle trouée, 1978; Dieu, sa vie, son œuvre, 1981; Mon dernier rêve sera pour vous, 1982; Jean qui grogne et Jean et Jean qui rit, 1984; Le Vent du soir, 1985; articles and essays, columns in Le Figaro, Le Monde, Le Point, La Revue des Deux Mondes, La Nouvelle Revue Française. *Recreation:* ski-navigation. *Address:* CIPSH-UNESCO, 1 rue Miollis, 75732 Paris Cedex 15, France. *T:* 568.26.85; (home) 10 avenue du Parc Saint-James, 92200 Neuilly-sur-Seine, France.

ORMOND, Sir John (Davies Wilder), Kt 1964; BEM 1940; JP; Chairman: Shipping Corporation of New Zealand Ltd, since 1973; Container Terminals Ltd, since 1975; Exports and Shipping Council, since 1964; *b* 8 Sept. 1905; *s* of J. D. Ormond and Gladys Wilder; *m* 1939, Judith Wall; four *s* one *d*. *Educ:* Christ's Coll., Christchurch, New Zealand. Chairman, Waipukurau Farmers Union, 1929; President, Waipukurau Jockey Club, 1950; Member, New Zealand Meat Producers Board, 1934–72, Chm., 1951–72. Active Service Overseas (Middle East), 1940. JP, NZ, 1945. DSc (*hc*), 1972. *Recreations:* tennis, polo, Rugby Union football. *Address:* Wallingford, Waipukurau, New Zealand. *T:* Waipukurau 542M. *Club:* Hawke's Bay (New Zealand).

ORMOND, Richard Louis; Director, National Maritime Museum, since 1986 (Head of Picture Department, 1983–86); *b* 16 Jan. 1939; *s* of Conrad Eric Ormond and Dorothea (*née* Gibbons); *m* 1963, Leonée Jasper; two *s*. *Educ:* Oxford University. MA. Assistant Keeper, 1965–75, Dep. Director, 1975–83, Nat. Portrait Gallery. *Publications:* J. S. Sargent, 1970; Catalogue of Early Victorian Portraits in the National Portrait Gallery, 1973; Lord Leighton, 1975; Sir Edwin Landseer, 1982. *Recreations:* cycling, opera, theatre. *Address:* 8 Holly Terrace, N6 6LX. *T:* 01–340 4684.

ORMONDE, 7th Marquess of, *cr* 1825; **James Hubert Theobald Charles Butler,** MBE 1921; Earl of Ormonde, 1328; Viscount Thurles, 1525; Earl of Ossory, 1527; Baron Ormonde (UK), 1821; 31st Hereditary Chief Butler of Ireland; retired; *b* 19 April 1899; *s* of Lord Theobald Butler (4th *s* of 2nd Marquess) and Annabella Brydon (*d* 1943), *o d* of Rev. Cosmo Reid Gordon, DD; *S* cousin, 1971; *m* 1st, 1935, Nan Gilpin (*d* 1973); two *d*; 2nd, 1976, Elizabeth Liles (*d* 1980). *Educ:* Haileybury College; RMC Sandhurst. Commissioned Dec. 1917, King's Royal Rifle Corps; resigned commission, May 1926 (Lieut). Various business connections in USA. *Heir:* (to earldoms of Ormonde and Ossory) Viscount Mountgarret, *qv*. *Address:* 10 N Washington, Apt 120, Hinsdale, Ill 60521, USA. *Club:* Naval and Military.

ORMROD, Rt. Hon. Sir Roger (Fray Greenwood), PC 1974; Kt 1961; a Lord Justice of Appeal, 1974–82; *b* 20 Oct. 1911; *s* of late Oliver Fray Ormrod and Edith Muriel (*née* Pim); *m* 1938, Anne, *d* of Charles Lush; no *c*. *Educ:* Shrewsbury Sch.; The Queen's Coll., Oxford. BA Oxon (Jurisprudence) 1935. Called to Bar, Inner Temple, 1936; QC 1958; Judge of High Court of Justice, Family Division (formerly Probate, Divorce and Admiralty Division), 1961–74. Hon. Fellow, Queen's Coll., Oxford, 1966. BM, BCh Oxon, 1941; FRCP 1969. House Physician, Radcliffe Infirmary, Oxford, 1941–42. Served in RAMC, 1942–45, with rank of Major. DADMS 8 Corps. Lecturer in Forensic Medicine, Oxford Medical Sch., 1950–59. Hon. Prof. of Legal Ethics, Univ. of Birmingham, 1973–74. Chairman: Lord Chancellor's Cttee on Legal Education, 1968; Notting Hill Housing Trust, 1968–. Pres., British Acad. of Forensic Science, 1970–71; Chm., Cttee of Management, Institute of Psychiatry, 1973–84. Visitor, Royal Postgrad. Med. Sch., 1975–; Chm., British Postgrad. Med. Fedn, 1980–86. Hon. Fellow, Manchester Polytechnic, 1972; Hon. FRCPsych 1975; Hon. LLD Leicester, 1978; Hon. FRCPath 1983. *Publications:* ed, (with E. H. Pearce) Dunstan's Law of Hire-Purchase, 1938; (with Harris Walker) National Health Service Act 1946, 1949. *Address:* 4 Aubrey Road, W8. *T:* 01–727 7876. *Club:* Garrick.

ORMSBY GORE, family name of **Baron Harlech.**

OROWAN, Egon, DrIng; FRS 1947; Professor of Mechanical Engineering, Massachusetts Institute of Technology, Cambridge, Massachusetts, USA, 1950–67, now Emeritus; Senior Lecturer, MIT, 1967–73; *b* Budapest, 2 Aug. 1902; *s* of Berthold Orowan and Josephine Ságvári; *m* 1941, Yolande Schonfeld; one *d*. *Educ:* University of Vienna; Technical Univ., Berlin-Charlottenburg. Demonstrator Technical Univ., Berlin-Charlottenburg, 1928; i/c Krypton Works, United Incandescent Lamp and Electrical Co. Ltd, Ujpest, Hungary, 1936; Research in Physics of Metals, Physics Dept, University of Birmingham, 1937, and Cavendish Laboratory, Cambridge, 1939; Reader in the Physics of Metals, University of Cambridge. Alcoa Vis. Prof., Univ. of Pittsburgh, 1972–73. Mem., Nat. Acad. of Sciences; Corresp. Mem., Akademie der Wissenschaften, Göttingen. Thomas Hawksley Gold Medal, MechE, 1944; Bingham Medal, Society of Rheology, 1959; Carl Friedrich Gauss Medal, Braunschweigische Wissenschaftliche Gesellschaft, 1968; Vincent Bendix Gold Medal, Amer. Soc. of Engrg Educn, 1971; Paul Bergsøe Medal, Dansk Metallurgisk Selskab, 1973. DrIng (*hc*) Technische Universität, Berlin, 1965. *Publications:* Papers in scientific and engineering journals. *Address:* 44 Payson Terrace, Belmont, Mass 02178, USA.

ORR, Rt. Hon. Sir Alan (Stewart), PC 1971; Kt 1965; OBE 1944; A Lord Justice of Appeal, 1971–80; *b* 21 Feb. 1911; *s* of late William Orr and Doris Kemsley, Great

Wakering, Essex; *m* 1933, Mariana Frances Lilian (*d* 1986), *d* of late Captain J. C. Lang, KOSB; four *s*. *Educ:* Fettes; Edinburgh Univ. (1st Class Hons Classics); Balliol Coll., Oxford (1st Class Hons Jurisprudence). Barrister Middle Temple, 1936 (Cert. Hon.); Master of the Bench, 1965; Barstow Law Scholar; Harmsworth Scholar. RAF, 1940–45 (despatches, OBE), Wing Comdr. Lectr in Laws (pt-time), UCL, 1948–50. Member of General Council of the Bar, 1953–57; Junior Counsel (Common Law) to Commissioners of Inland Revenue, 1957–63; QC 1963; Recorder of: New Windsor, 1958–65; Oxford, Jan.-Aug. 1965; Dep. Chairman, Oxford Quarter Sessions, 1964–71; Judge of High Court of Justice, Probate, Divorce and Admiralty Division, 1965–71; Presiding Judge, North-Eastern Circuit, 1970–71. Mem., Chancellor's Law Reform Cttee, 1966–80 (Chm., 1973–80). Chm., Court of Governors, Mill Hill Sch., 1976–79. *Recreation:* golf. *Address:* The Steps, Ratley, Banbury, Oxon OX15 6DT. *T:* Edge Hill 704. *Club:* United Oxford & Cambridge University.

ORR, Sir David (Alexander), Kt 1977; MC and bar 1945; LLB; Chairman, British Council, since 1985; Deputy Chairman, Inchcape PLC, since 1986 (Chairman, 1983–86); Director: Shell Transport & Trading Co., since 1982; Rio Tinto-Zinc Corporation PLC, since 1981; Bank of Ireland, Dublin, since 1982; *b* 10 May 1922; *s* of late Canon Adrian William Fielder Orr and Grace (*née* Robinson); *m* 1949, Phoebe Rosaleen Davis; three *d*. *Educ:* High Sch., Dublin; Trinity Coll., Dublin (Hon. LLD 1978). Served Royal Engineers attached QVO Madras Sappers and Miners, 1941–46. With various Unilever companies, 1948–82; Hindustan Lever, 1955–60; Mem. Overseas Cttee, Unilever, 1960–63; Lever Bros Co., New York, 1963, Pres. 1965–67; Dir, 1967–82, Vice-Chm. 1970–74, Chm., 1974–82, Unilever Ltd; Vice-Chm., Unilever NV, 1974–82. Chm., Leverhulme Trust, 1982–; Jt Chm., Anglo-Irish Encounter, 1983–. Pres., Liverpool Sch. of Tropical Medicine, 1981–. Governor, LSE, 1980–. FRSA. Hon. LLD TCD, 1978; DUniv Surrey, 1981. Comdr, Order of Oranje Nassau, 1979. *Recreations:* golf, Rugby, travel. *Address:* 81 Lyall Mews West, SW1; Home Farm House, Shackleford, near Godalming, Surrey. *Club:* Sunningdale Golf.

ORR, James Bernard Vivian, CVO 1968 (MVO 1962); Secretary, Medical Commission on Accident Prevention, 1970–82; *b* 19 Nov. 1917; *s* of Dr Vivian Bernard Orr and Gladys Constance Orr (*née* Power); unmarried. *Educ:* Harrow; Gordonstoun; RMC, Sandhurst. British South Africa Police, Southern Rhodesia, 1939–46. Attached occupied Enemy Territory Administration in Ethiopia and Eritrea Police Forces, 1941–49; Kenya Police, 1954–57. Private Secretary to HRH The Duke of Edinburgh, 1957–70, an Extra Equerry, 1970–. *Recreations:* horse racing, watching cricket. *Address:* 10 Mulberry Trees, Shepperton, Mddx. *T:* Walton-on-Thames 245274.

ORR, Dr James Henry; Consultant in forensic psychiatry, since 1982; *b* 2 Feb. 1927; *s* of Hubert Orr and Ethel Maggs; *m* 1950, Valerie Elizabeth Yates; two *s* one *d*. *Educ:* Bristol Grammar Sch.; Bristol Univ. (MB, ChB 1955). DPM; FRCPsych. Enlisted, 1944; commnd RE, 1947; demobilised, 1949. Hosp. appts, 1955–56; gen. practice, 1956–58; Medical Officer, HM Prison: Leeds, 1958; Winchester, 1962; Lincoln, 1966; SMO, Leeds, 1967; Asst Dir, Prison Med. Services, 1973; Dir, Prison Med. Services, and Mem., Prisons Bd, 1976–82; Mem., Parole Bd, 1983–86. *Recreation:* gardening. *Address:* Newton Lodge, Regional Centre for Forensic Psychiatry, Wakefield, W Yorks WF1 3SP. *T:* Wakefield 375217.

ORR, Jean Fergus Henderson; Director, Office of Manpower Economics, 1973–80; *b* 3 April 1920; *yr d* of late Peter Orr, OBE and Janet Muir Orr (*née* Henderson). *Educ:* privately; University Coll., London (BA; Fellow, 1982). Min. of Aircraft Prodn, temp. Asst Principal, 1942; Min. of Supply: Asst Principal, 1946; Principal, 1949; HM Treasury, 1954: Principal, Official Side Sec. to Civil Service Nat. Whitley Council negotiations on Report of Royal Commn on Civil Service, 1953–55; Asst Sec. 1961; on loan to Office of Manpower Econs as Sec. to Top Salaries Review Body, 1971. *Recreations:* music, travel, natural history. *Address:* 21 Bathwick Hill, Bath, Avon BA2 6EW. *T:* Bath 63664. *Club:* United Oxford & Cambridge University.

ORR, Sir John Henry, Kt 1979; OBE 1972; QPM 1977; Chief Constable, Lothian and Borders Police, 1975–83; *b* 13 June 1918; *m* 1942, Isobel Margaret Campbell; one *s* one *d*. *Educ:* George Heriot's Sch., Edinburgh. Edinburgh City Police, 1937; served in RAF 1943–45 (Flying Officer; Defence and War Medals); Chief Constable: of Dundee, 1960; of Lothians and Peebles, 1968. Hon. Sec., Assoc. of Chief Police Officers (Scotland), 1974–83. Mem., divnl bd for Scotland, Nationwide Building Soc., 1983–. FBIM 1978. Coronation Medal, 1953; Police Long Service and Good Conduct Medal, 1959; Jubilee Medal, 1977; OStJ, 1975. Comdr, Polar Star, class III, Sweden, 1975; Legion of Honour, France, 1976. *Recreations:* Rugby (capped for Scotland; Past Pres., Scottish Rugby Union); golf. *Address:* 12 Lanark Road West, Currie, Midlothian EH14 5ET.

ORR, Captain Lawrence Percy Story; Director, Associated Leisure Ltd, 1972–84; *b* 16 Sept. 1918; *s* of late Very Rev. W. R. M. Orr, MA, LLD, sometime Dean of Dromore; *m* 1939, (separated 1952; marr. diss. 1976); four *s* (one *d* decd). *Educ:* Campbell Coll., Belfast; Trinity Coll., Dublin. Served with East Lancashire Regt, Royal Armoured Corps, and Life Guards, 1939–46. MP (UU) South Down, 1950–Sept. 1974. Mem. Exec., British Chamber of Commerce, 1951–56. Dir, Pye (Scottish) Telecommunications, 1952–62. Vice-Chairman, Conservative Broadcasting Cttee, 1959–62; Leader, Ulster Unionist Parly Party, 1964–74; Vice-Pres., Ulster Unionist Council. Imperial Grand Master, Orange Order, 1964–73. *Recreations:* fishing, painting, chess. *Address:* The Lodge, Honeywood House, Lydiard Millicent, Swindon, Wilts.

ORR, Prof. Robin, (Robert Kemsley Orr), CBE 1972; MA, MusD (Cantab); FRCM; Hon. RAM; Hon. FRSAM; Hon. DMus, Hon. LLD; Composer; Professor of Music, Cambridge University, and Fellow of St John's College, 1965–76, now Professor Emeritus; *b* Brechin, Scotland, 2 June 1909; *s* of Robert Workman Orr and Florence Mary Kemsley; *m* 1st, 1937, Margaret (marr. diss. 1979), *er d* of A. C. Mace; one *s* two *d*; 2nd, 1979, Doris Winny-Meyer, *d* of Leo Meyer-Bechtler, Zürich. *Educ:* Loretto Sch.; Royal Coll. of Music; Pembroke Coll., Cambridge (Organ Scholar); Accademia Musicale Chigiana, Siena. Studied privately with Casella and Nadia Boulanger. Dir of Music, Sidcot Sch., Somerset, 1933–36; Asst Lecturer in Music, Univ. of Leeds, 1936–38. Served War of 1939–45, RAFVR, Photographic Intelligence (Flight Lieut). Organist and Dir of Studies in Music, St John's Coll., 1938–51, and Fellow, 1948–56, Univ. Lecturer in Music, 1947–56, Cambridge; Prof. of Theory and Composition, RCM, 1950–56; Gardiner Prof. of Music, Univ. of Glasgow, 1956–65. Mem., Carl Rosa Trust, 1953–; Chm., Scottish Opera, 1962–76; Director: Arts Theatre, Cambridge, 1970–75; Welsh Nat. Opera, 1977–83. Compositions include: Sonatina for violin and piano, 1941; Three Chinese Songs, 1943; Sonata for viola and piano, 1947; Winter's Tale (Incidental Music), BBC, 1947; Overture, The Prospect of Whitby, 1948; Oedipus at Colonus (Cambridge Univ. Greek Play), 1950; Four Romantic Songs (for Peter Pears), 1950; Festival Te Deum, 1950; Three Pastorals for soprano, flute, viola and piano, 1951; Deirdre of the Sorrows (Incidental Music), BBC, 1951; Italian Overture, 1952; Te Deum and Jubilate in C, 1953; Motet, I was glad, 1955; Spring Cantata, 1955; Sonata for violin and clavier, 1956; Rhapsody for string orchestra; Antigone (Bradfield College Greek Play), 1961; Symphony in one movement, 1963; Full Circle (Opera), 1967; From the Book of Philip Sparrow, 1969; Journeys and Places (mezzo-sop. and strings), 1971; Symphony No 2, 1971; Hermiston (Opera), 1975; Symphony No 3, 1978; Versus from Ogden Nash for medium voice and strings, 1978; Songs of Zion (choir), 1978; ed, The Kelvin Series of Scots Songs. Hon. DMus Glasgow, 1972; Hon. LLD Dundee, 1976. *Recreations:* gardening, mountain walks. *Address:* 16 Cranmer Road, Cambridge CB3 9BL. *T:* Cambridge 352858.

ORR-EWING, family name of **Baron Orr-Ewing.**

ORR-EWING, Baron *cr* 1971 (Life Peer), of Little Berkhamsted; **(Charles) Ian Orr-Ewing,** OBE 1945, 1st Bt *cr* 1963; Consultant and Director various companies; Chairman, Metrication Board, 1972–77; *b* 10 Feb. 1912; *s* of Archibald Ian Orr Ewing and Gertrude (*née* Runge); *m* 1939, Joan McMinnies; four *s*. *Educ:* Harrow; Trinity Coll., Oxford. MA (Physics). Graduate apprentice, EMI, Hayes, 1934–37; BBC Television Service, 1938–39, 1946–49. Served RAFVR, 1939–46, N Africa, Italy, France and Germany, Wing Comdr, 1941; Chief Radar Officer, Air Staff, SHAEF, 1945 (despatches twice); BBC Television Outside Broadcasts Manager, 1946–48. MP (C) North Hendon, 1950–70; Joint Secretary, Parliamentary Scientific Cttee, 1950; Vice-Chm., Civil Air Cttee, 1955–57; Vice-Pres., Parliamentary and Scientific Cttee, 1965–68; Vice-Chm., 1922 Cttee, 1966–70 (Secretary, 1956); Vice-Chairman, Defence Cttee, 1966–70. PPS to Sir Walter Monckton, Minister of Labour and National Service, Nov. 1951–1955; Parliamentary Under-Secretary of State, for Air, Air Ministry, 1957–59; Parliamentary and Financial Secretary to Admiralty, 1959; Civil Lord of the Admiralty, 1959–63. Dep. Chm., Assoc. of Cons. Peers, 1980–. Mem., Royal Commn on Standards of Conduct in Public Life, 1975–76. Pres. and Chm. of Council, Electronic Engineering Assoc., 1969–70. Pres., Nat. Ski Fedn of GB, 1972–76. FIEE. *Recreations:* tennis, light-hearted cricket and ski-ing. *Heir* (to baronetcy only): *s* (Alistair) Simon Orr-Ewing [*b* 10 June 1940; *m* 1968, Victoria, *er d* of late Keith Cameron, Fifield House, Milton-under-Wychwood, Oxon; two *s* one *d*]. *Address:* 9 Cheyne Gardens, SW3 5QU. *Clubs:* Boodle's, MCC; Vincent's (Oxford).

ORR-EWING, Hamish; Chairman, Rank Xerox Ltd, 1980–86; Director, Tricentrol PLC, since 1975; *b* 17 Aug. 1924; *o s* of Hugh Eric Douglas Orr-Ewing and Esme Victoria (*née* Stewart), Strathgarry, Killiecrankie, Perthshire; *m* 1st, 1947, Morar Margaret Kennedy; one *s* (one *d* decd); 2nd, 1954, Ann Mary Teresa Terry. *Educ:* Heatherdown, Ascot; Eton. Served War, Captain Black Watch. Salesman, EMI, 1950; Ford Motor Co., 1954; Ford Light Car Planning Manager, 1959–63; Leyland Motor Corp. Ltd, 1963–65; joined Rank Xerox, 1965; apptd to Bd as Dir of Product Planning, 1968; Dir of Personnel, 1970; Man. Dir, Rank Xerox (UK) Ltd, 1971; Reg. Dir for Rank Xerox Ops in UK, France, Holland, Sweden and Belgium, 1977; Chm., Jaguar plc, 1984–85. Mem., MSC, 1983–85; Chairman: Work and Society, 1982–; European Govt Business Relations Council, 1980–84; Mem., Engrg Council, 1984–. CBI: Member: Bd, Educn Foundn (UBI), 1982–; Council, 1985–; Chm., Educn and Trng Cttee, 1985–. Trustee, Shaw Trust, 1985–. Governor: Interphil, 1985–; New Coll., Swindon, 1984–. CBIM 1981. *Recreations:* anything mechanical, country life, the Roman Empire. *Address:* Fox Mill, Purton, near Swindon, Wilts SN5 9EF. *T:* Swindon 770496.

ORR EWING, Major Sir Ronald Archibald, 5th Bt, *cr* 1886; Major (retired) Scots Guards; *b* 14 May 1912; *e s* of Sir Norman Orr Ewing, 4th Bt, CB, DSO, and Lady Orr Ewing (*née* Robarts), Tile House, Buckingham; *S* father, 1960; *m* 1938, Marion Hester, *yr d* of late Colonel Sir Donald Walter Cameron of Lochiel, KT, CMG, and of Lady Hermione Cameron of Lochiel, *d* of 5th Duke of Montrose, KT; two *s* two *d*. *Educ:* Eton; RMC, Sandhurst. Scots Guards, 1932–53, Major. Served War of 1939–45, Middle East (POW 1942). JP Perthshire, 1956; DL Perthshire, 1963. Grand Master Mason of Scotland, 1965–69. *Recreation:* shooting. *Heir:* *s* Archibald Donald Orr Ewing [*b* 20 Dec. 1938; *m* 1st, 1965, Venetia Elizabeth (marr. diss. 1972), *y d* of Major and Mrs Richard Turner, Co. Dublin; 2nd, 1972, Nicola Jean-Anne, *d* of Reginald Baron Black, Fovant, near Salisbury; one *s*]. *Address:* Cardross, Port of Menteith, Kippen, Stirling FK8 3JY. *T:* Port of Menteith 220. *Club:* New (Edinburgh).

ORREGO-VICUÑA, Prof. Francisco; Professor of International Law, School of Law and Institute of International Studies, University of Chile, since 1969; *b* 12 April 1942; *s* of Fernando Orrego Vicuña and Raquel Vicuña Viel; *m* 1965, Soledad Bauzá; one *s* two *d*. *Educ:* Univ. of Chile (Degree in Law). Admitted to legal practice, 1965. Sen. Legal Advisor, OAS, 1965–69 and 1972–74; Dir, Inst. of Internat. Studies, Univ. of Chile, 1974–83; Ambassador of Chile to UK, 1983–85. Advisor on legal matters to Min. of Foreign Affairs, 1974–83. *Publications:* Derecho de la Integraciòn Latinoamericana, 1969; Los Fondos Marinos, 1976; Antarctic Resources Policy, 1983; The Exclusive Economic Zone, 1984; contrib. Amer. Jl of Internat. Law and Annuaire Français de Droit Internat. *Recreations:* golf, skiing. *Address:* Institute of International Studies, University of Chile, PO Box 14187, Suc. 21, Santiago 9, Chile. *T:* 740–730. *Club:* Athenæum.

ORSON, Rasin Ward, CBE 1985; CompIEE; Member, The Electricity Council, since 1976; Director, Chloride Silent Power Ltd, since 1974; *b* 16 April 1927; *s* of Rasin Nelson Orson and Blanche Hyre; *m* 1st, 1950, Marie Goodenough; two *s*; 2nd, 1979, Lesley Jean Vallance. *Educ:* Stratford Grammar Sch.; London School of Economics (BScEcon 1948). Asst Statistician, Min. of Civil Aviation, 1948, Statistician, 1953; Electricity Council: Head of Economics and Forecasting Branch, 1963; Dep. Commercial Adviser, 1968; Commercial Adviser, 1972. *Recreations:* music, photography. *Address:* 128 De Beauvoir Road, N1. *T:* 01–254 7784.

ORTIZ DE ROZAS, Carlos; Argentine Ambassador to France, since 1984; *b* 26 April 1926; *m* 1952, María del Carmen Sarobe. *Educ:* School of Diplomacy, Min. of Foreign Affairs, Buenos Aires (grad. 1949). Lawyer, Faculty of Law, Univ. of Buenos Aires, 1950. Entered Argentine Foreign Service, 1948; served Bulgaria, Greece, UAR and UK (Minister); Ambassador to Austria, 1967–70; Permanent Rep. to UN, 1970–77; Pres. UN Security Council, 1971–72; Chairman: First (Polit. and Security) Cttee of 29th Gen. Assembly, 1974; Preparatory Cttee of Special Session on Disarmament, 1977–78; Cttee on Disarmament, Geneva, 1979; Mem. Adv. Bd on Disarmament Studies, New York, 1978–81; Ambassador to UK, 1980–82; Head, Argentine Special Mission to the Holy See, 1982–83. Universidad del Salvador, Buenos Aires: Prof. of History and Constitutional Law, 1958, Prof. of Political Science, 1958–, Faculty of Law; Prof. of Internat. Relations, School of Political Sciences, 1962–, and at School of Diplomacy, 1962–. Holds many foreign decorations incl. Grand Cross, Order of Pius IX, 1985, and Commandeur, Légion d'Honneur, 1985. *Address:* 6 rue Cimarosa, 75116 Paris, France. *Clubs:* Jockey, Círculo de Armas (Buenos Aires); Cercle de l'Union Interalliée (Paris); Doubles (New York).

ORTOLI, François-Xavier; Président Directeur Général, Total Compagnie Française des Pétroles, since 1984; *b* 16 Feb. 1925. *Educ:* Hanoi Faculty of Law; Ecole Nationale d'Administration. Inspector of Finances, 1948–51; Tech. Adv., Office of Minister of Econ. Affairs and Information, 1951–53; Asst Dir to Sec. of State for Econ. Affairs and Sec.-Gen., Franco-Italian Cttee of EEC, 1955; Head, Commercial Politics Service of Sec. of State for Econ. Affairs, 1957; Dir-Gen., Internal Market Div., EEC, 1958; Sec.-Gen., Inter-Ministerial Cttee for Questions of European Econ. Co-operation, Paris, 1961–; Dir of

Cabinet to Prime Minister, 1962–66; Comr-Gen. of the Plan, 1966–67; Minister: of Works, 1967–68; of Educn, 1968; of Finance, 1968–69; of Industrial and Scientific Develt, 1969–72; Pres., EEC, 1973–76, a Vice-Pres., with responsibility for econ. and financial affairs, 1977–84. Hon. DCL Oxon, 1975; Hon Dr Sch. of Political Scis, Athens, 1975. Officier de la Légion d'Honneur; Médaille Militaire; Croix de Guerre, 1945; Médaille de la Résistance. *Address:* 18 rue de Bourgogne, 75007 Paris, France.

OSBORN, Frederic Adrian, (Derek Osborn); Under Secretary, Finance, Department of the Environment, since 1982; *b* 14 Jan. 1941; *s* of Rev. George R. Osborn and E.M. Osborn; *m* 1971, Caroline Niebuhr Tod; one *d* one *s*. *Educ:* Leys School, Cambridge; Balliol College, Oxford. BA Maths 1963, BPhil 1965. Asst Principal, Min. of Housing and Local Govt, 1965; Private Sec. to Minister of State and Perm. Sec., 1967; Royal Commn on Standards of Conduct in Public Life, 1974; Dept of Transport, 1975–77; Dept of the Environment, 1977. *Recreations:* music, reading, chess. *Address:* 48 Talbot Road, N6 4QP. *T:* 01–340 7560.

OSBORN, Sir John (Holbrook), Kt 1983; MP (C) (NL and U, 1959–64), Hallam Division of Sheffield, since 1959; *b* 14 Dec. 1922; *s* of Samuel Eric Osborn and Aileen Decima, *d* of Colonel Sir Arthur Holbrook, KBE, MP; *m* 1st, 1952, Molly Suzanne (*née* Marten) (marr. diss.); two *d*; 2nd, 1976, Joan Mary MacDermot (*née* Wilkinson). *Educ:* Rugby; Trinity Hall, Cambridge. MA Cantab; Part 2 Tripos in Metallurgy; Diploma in Foundry Technology, National Foundry Coll., 1949. Served in Royal Corps of Signals, 1943–47 (West Africa, 1944–46; Captain); served in RA (TA) Sheffield, 1948–55, Major. Joined 1947, and Dir, 1951–79, Samuel Osborn & Co. Ltd, and associated companies. Chairman, Hillsborough Divisional Young Conservative and Liberal Association, 1949–53. PPS to the Secretary of State for Commonwealth Relations and for the Colonies, 1963–64. Chairman: Cons. Parly Transport Cttee, 1970–74; Parly Gp for Energy Studies, 1985– (Vice-Chm., Cons. Parly Energy Gp, 1979–81); Anglo-Swiss Parly Gp, 1981–; (or Vice-Chm.) Anglo-Soviet Parly Gp, 1968–; Vice Chm., Parly and Scientific Cttee, 1963–66, 1982 (Officer, 1959–); Member: Science and Technol. Select Cttee, 1970–73; Educn, Science and Arts Select Cttee, 1979–83; Chm., All Party Channel Tunnel Gp, 1985–. Mem., UK Delegn to Council of Europe and WEU, 1972–75, 1980–; Council of Europe: Vice Chm., Science and Technol. Cttee, 1981–; Chm., Eur. Scientific Contact Gp, 1982; Chm., Econ. Affairs and Develt Sub-Cttee (North/South: Europe's role), 1985–. Mem., European Parlt, 1975–79; an Hon. Sec., 1922 Cttee, 1968–; Mem. Exec., British Br., IPU, 1968–75, 1979–83. Freeman (Searcher), Co. of Cutlers in Hallamshire, 1950–. Fellow, Institute of British Foundrymen, 1948–72 (Member Council, Sheffield Branch, 1954–64); Fellow, Institute of Directors; Member Council: Sheffield Chamber of Commerce, 1956–; Assocs British Chambers of Commerce Council, 1960–62 (Hon. Secretary, 1962–64); British Iron and Steel Res. Association, 1965–68; CBI and Yorks and WR Br., CBI, 1968–79; Member: Inst. of Metals; Council, Industrial Soc. (Life Mem.); Court and Cttee of Sheffield Univ., 1951–; Pres., Sheffield Inst. of Advanced Motorists, 1960–; Chm., H of C Motor Club, 1979–84. Travels widely in business and politics. *Recreations:* golf, tennis, photography, gardening, skiing. *Address:* Folds Head Close, Calver, Sheffield S30 1XJ. *T:* Sheffield 369759; Flat 13, 102 Rochester Row, SW1. *T:* 01–219 4108. *Clubs:* Carlton; Sheffield.

OSBORN, Sir Richard (Henry Danvers), 9th Bt *cr* 1662, of Chicksands Priory, Co. Bedford; *b* 12 Aug. 1958; surv. *s* of Sir Danvers Lionel Rouse Osborn, 8th Bt, and of Lady Osborn (Constance Violette, JP, SSStJ, *d* of late Major Leonard Frank Rooke, KOSB and RFC); *S* father, 1983. *Educ:* Eton. Career in fine arts. *Recreations:* cricket, tennis, squash, horse racing. *Heir: kinsman* William Danvers Osborn [*b* 4 June 1909; *m* 1939, Jean Burns, *d* of R. B. Hutchinson, Vancouver; one *d*]. *Address:* The Dower House, Moor Park, Farnham, Surrey GU10 1QX. *Club:* MCC.

OSBORNE, Sir Basil, Kt 1967; CBE 1962; Lord Mayor of Hobart, Tasmania, 1959–70, Alderman, 1952–76; Chairman, Metropolitan Transport Trust, 1971–78; business consultant; *b* 19 April 1907; *s* of late Alderman W. W. Osborne, MBE; *m* 1934, Esma (*d* 1983), *d* of late T. Green; one *s*. *Educ:* Metropolitan Business Coll. Mem. Gen. Cttee, Savings Bank of Tas, 1969–85. Dir, Australian Brain Foundn (formerly Aust. Neurol Foundn), 1970–. Chm., Board of Management, Royal Hobart Hospital, 1968–81 (Vice-Chairman, 1952–68); President: St John's Ambulance Assoc., 1960–76; Asia–Pacific Life Saving Council, 1984–; Australian Pres., RLSS, 1979– (Life Governor, Commonwealth Vice Pres., 1982–, Commonwealth Council). Life Member: City of Hobart Eisteddfod Soc., 1972; (first), Asthma Foundn, 1984; Hon. Life Member: Hobart Orpheus Club, 1977; Hospital Public Relns Officers' Assoc. of Australia, 1977. Hon. Fellow: Australian Marketing Inst., 1967; Inst. of Ambulance Officers (Aust.), 1975. OStJ 1972. *Recreations:* music, sport. *Address:* 6 Myella Drive, Chigwell, Tasmania 7011, Australia. *Club:* Royal Autocar (Tasmania).

OSBORNE, Charles (Thomas); author; *b* 24 Nov. 1927; *s* of Vincent Lloyd Osborne and Elsa Louise Osborne; *m* 1970, Marie Korbelářová (marr. diss. 1975). *Educ:* Brisbane State High Sch. Studied piano and voice, Brisbane and Melbourne; acted in and directed plays, 1944–53; wrote poetry and criticism, published in Aust. and NZ magazines; co-owner, Ballad Bookshop, Brisbane, 1947–51; actor, London, provincial rep. and on tour, also TV and films, 1953–57; Asst Editor, London Magazine, 1958–66; Asst Lit. Dir, Arts Council of GB, 1966–71, Lit. Dir, 1971–86. Broadcaster, musical and literary progs, BBC, 1957–; Dir, Poetry International, 1967–74; Sec., Poetry Book Soc., 1971–84. Mem. Editorial Board: Opera, 1970–; Annual Register, 1971–. *Publications:* (ed) Australian Stories of Today, 1961; (ed) Opera 66, 1966; (with Brigid Brophy and Michael Levey) Fifty Works of English Literature We Could Do Without, 1967 (USA 1968); Kafka, 1967; Swansong (poems), 1968; The Complete Operas of Verdi, 1969 (USA 1970; Italian trans. 1975); Ned Kelly, 1970; (ed) Australia, New Zealand and the South Pacific, 1970; (ed) Letters of Giuseppe Verdi, 1971 (USA 1972); (ed) The Bram Stoker Bedside Companion, 1973 (USA 1974); (ed) Stories and Essays by Richard Wagner, 1973 (USA 1974); The Concert Song Companion, 1974 (USA 1985); Masterpieces of Nolan, 1976; Masterpieces of Drysdale, 1976; Masterpieces of Dobell, 1976; Wagner and his World, 1977 (USA 1977; trans. Spanish 1985); Verdi, 1977 (trans. Spanish 1985); (ed) Dictionary of Composers, 1977; The Complete Operas of Mozart, 1978 (USA 1978, trans. Ital. 1982); (ed) Masterworks of Opera: Rigoletto, 1979; The Opera House Album, 1979 (USA 1979, trans. Dutch 1981); W. H. Auden: the Life of a Poet, 1980 (USA 1979); (ed with Kenneth Thomson) Klemperer Stories, 1980 (trans. German 1981); The Complete Operas of Puccini, 1981 (USA 1981); The Life and Crimes of Agatha Christie, 1982 (USA 1982); The World Theatre of Wagner, 1982 (USA 1982); How to Enjoy Opera, 1983 (trans. Spanish 1985); The Dictionary of Opera, 1983 (USA 1983; trans. Finnish 1984); Letter to W. H. Auden and Other Poems, 1984; Schubert and his Vienna, 1985 (USA 1985; trans. German 1986); Giving It Away (memoirs), 1986; (ed) The Oxford Book of Best-Loved Verse, 1986; Verdi: a life in the theatre, 1987; The Complete Operas of Richard Strauss, 1987; poems in: The Oxford Book of Australian Verse, 1956; Australian Poetry, 1951–52, etc; The Queensland Centenary Anthology, 1959; Australian Writing Today, 1968; various jls; contrib.: TLS, Observer, Sunday Times, Times, Guardian, New Statesman, Spectator, London Mag., Encounter, Opera, Chambers Encyc. Yearbook, and Enciclopedia dello spettacolo; also cassettes. *Recreations:* travelling, planning future projects. *Address:* 26 Evelyn Mansions, Carlisle Place, SW1P 1NH.

OSBORNE, Maj.-Gen. the Rev. Coles Alexander, CIE 1945; Indian Army, retired; *b* 29 July 1896; *s* of late W. E. Osborne, formerly of Dover, Kent; *m* 1930, Joyce, *o d* of late R. H. Meares of Forbes and Sydney, NSW, Australia; two *d*. *Educ:* Dover County Sch. European War, 1914–18: served with HAC, Royal West Kent Regt, and RFC (wounded); transferred to 15th Sikhs, 1918; served in Afghan War 1919 and in NW Frontier Operations 1920–22 and 1939; Palestine 1938; Middle East 1940. Tactics Instructor at Royal Military Coll., Duntroon, Australia, 1928–30; Bt Major 1933; General Staff (Operations), War Office, 1934–38; Bt Lieut-Col 1936; Comd 1 Bombay Grenadiers, 1940; Deputy Director Military Training, India, 1940; Colonel, 1940; Commandant, Staff Coll., Quetta, 1941–42; Brigadier, 1941; Director Military Operations, GHQ, India and Burma, 1942–43; Temp. Maj.-Gen. 1942; Comd Kohat District, 1943–45; retired 1946. Student at Moore Theological Coll., Sydney, 1947; ordained, 1947; Hon. Asst Minister St Andrew's Cathedral, Sydney, Australia, 1947–53; Hon. Asst Minister, St Mark's Church, Darling Point, 1953–66; Personal Chaplain to Anglican Archbishop of Sydney, 1959–66. Director, Television Corp., 1956–75. Fellow of St Paul's Coll., Sydney Univ., 1953–69. Chairman, Freedom from Hunger Campaign, NSW, 1970–72. *Address:* 11 Charles Street, Warner's Bay, NSW 2282, Australia. *Club:* Australian (Sydney).

OSBORNE, Helena; *see* Moore, G. M.

OSBORNE, John (James); dramatist and actor; Director of Woodfall Films; *b* 12 Dec. 1929; *s* of Thomas Godfrey Osborne and Nellie Beatrice Grove; *m* 1st, 1951, Pamela Elizabeth Lane (marr. diss. 1957); 2nd, 1957, Mary Ure (marr. diss. 1963, she *d* 1975); 3rd, 1963, Penelope Gilliatt, *qv* (marr. diss. 1968); one *d*; 4th, 1968, Jill Bennett, *qv* (marr. diss. 1977); 5th, 1978, Helen Dawson. *Educ:* Belmont Coll., Devon. First stage appearance at Lyceum, Sheffield, in No Room at the Inn, 1948; toured and in seasons at: Ilfracombe, Bridgwater, Camberwell, Kidderminster, Derby, etc; English Stage Company season at Royal Court: appeared in Death of Satan, Cards of Identity, Good Woman of Setzuan, The Making of Moo, A Cuckoo in the Nest; directed Meals on Wheels, 1965; appeared in: The Parachute (BBC TV), 1967; First Night of Pygmalion (TV), 1969; First Love (film, as Maidanov), 1970; Get Carter (film), 1971; Lady Charlotte (TV), 1977; Tomorrow Never Comes (film), 1978. First play produced, 1949, at Theatre Royal, Huddersfield; other plays include: Personal Enemy, Opera House, Harrogate, 1955; The Blood of the Bambergs, 1962; Under Plain Cover, 1962; The Right Prospectus (TV), 1969. *Plays filmed:* Look Back in Anger, 1958; The Entertainer, 1959, 1975; Inadmissible Evidence, 1965; Luther, 1971. *Film:* Tom Jones, 1964 (Oscar for best screenplay). Hon. Dr RCA, 1970. *Publications:* Look Back in Anger (play), 1957 (produced 1956); The Entertainer (play), 1957 (also produced); Epitaph for George Dillon (with A. Creighton), 1958 (produced 1957); The World of Paul Slickey (comedy of manners with music), 1959 (produced 1959); Luther (play), 1960 (produced 1961, New York, 1964); A Subject of Scandal and Concern (TV play), 1960; Plays for England, 1963; Inadmissible Evidence (play), 1964 (produced 1965); A Patriot for Me (play), 1964 (produced 1965, 1983); A Bond Honoured, 1966 (produced 1966); The Hotel in Amsterdam, 1967 (produced 1968); Time Present, 1967 (produced 1968); Hedda Gabler (adaptation), 1970 (produced 1972); The Right Prospectus and Very Like a Whale (TV plays), 1971; West of Suez, 1971 (produced 1971); The Gift of Friendship (TV play), 1971; A Sense of Detachment, 1972 (produced 1972); A Place Calling Itself Rome, 1972; The Picture of Dorian Gray (play), 1973; The Gift of Friendship (TV play), 1974; Jill and Jack (TV play), 1974; The End of Me Old Cigar (play), 1975; Watch it come down (play), 1975; You're Not Watching Me, Mummy and Try a Little Tenderness (TV plays), 1978; A Better Class of Person (autobiog.), 1981 (televised, 1985); God Rot Tunbridge Wells! (TV play), 1985; contrib. to Declaration (a symposium), 1957; various newspapers, journals. *Address:* c/o Fraser and Dunlop, 91 Regent Street, W1. *Clubs:* Garrick; Portscatho Social.

OSBORNE, Kenneth Hilton; QC (Scot.) 1976; *b* 9 July 1937; *s* of Kenneth Osborne and Evelyn Alice (*née* Hilton); *m* 1964, Clare Ann Louise Lewis; one *s* one *d*. *Educ:* Larchfield Sch., Helensburgh; Merchiston Castle Sch., Edinburgh; Edinburgh Univ. (MA, LLB). Admitted to Faculty of Advocates in Scotland, 1962; Standing Junior Counsel to Min. of Defence (Navy) in Scotland, 1974–76; Advocate-Depute, 1982–84. Chairman: Disciplinary Cttee, Potato Marketing Bd, 1975–; (part-time), VAT Tribunals, 1985–; Mem., Lands Tribunal for Scotland, 1985–. *Recreations:* skiing, fishing, gardening, music, cooking. *Address:* 42 India Street, Edinburgh EH3 6HB. *T:* 031–225 3094; Primrose Cottage, Bridgend of Lintrathen, by Kirriemuir, Angus. *T:* Lintrathen 316. *Club:* New (Edinburgh).

OSBORNE, Surgeon Rear-Admiral (D) Leslie Bartlet, CB 1956; *b* 16 Sept. 1900; *s* of late Rev. Joseph Osborne, MA, and of Miriam Duke James; *m* 1929; two *s* one *d*; *m* 1955, Joan Mary Williams (*née* Parnell). *Educ:* Caterham Sch.; Guy's Hospital. LDS, RCS England 1923; FDS, RCS (Edinburgh) 1955. Dental House Surgeon, Guy's Hospital, 1923. Entered Royal Navy, Surgeon Lieutenant (D), 1923; Surgeon Commander (D), 1936; Surgeon Captain (D), 1948; Surgeon Rear-Admiral (D), 1954; Deputy Director-General for Dental Services in the Royal Navy, 1954–57, retired. Served War of 1939–45. KHDS 1951; QHDS 1953–58. *Recreations:* Rugby Football (rep. RN, Sussex and Devonport Services; Hon. Manager British Isles Rugby Union Team to New Zealand and Australia, 1950; Chairman Rugby Football Union Selection Cttee, 1949–51; President, Rugby Football Union, 1956); gardening. *Address:* 4 Westbourne Court, Cooden Drive, Cooden Beach, Bexhill-on-Sea, East Sussex TN39 3AA. *T:* Cooden 4431.

OSBORNE, Sir Peter (George), 17th Bt, *cr* 1629; Chairman and Managing Director, Osborne & Little plc (design company); *b* 29 June 1943; *s* of Lt-Col Sir George Osborne, 16th Bt, MC, and Mary (Grace), *d* of C. Horn; *S* father, 1960; *m* 1968, Felicity, *d* of Grantley Loxton-Peacock; four *s*. *Educ:* Wellington Coll., Berks; Christ Church Coll., Oxford. *Heir:* *s* Gideon Oliver Osborne, *b* 23 May 1971. *Address:* 36 Porchester Terrace, W2. *T:* 01–402 3903.

O'SHEA, Alexander Paterson, CMG 1962; North American Director, New Zealand Meat Producers' Board, USA, 1964–68, retired, 1968; *b* 29 Dec. 1902; *s* of John O'Shea; *m* 1935; one *d*. *Educ:* Otago Boys' High Sch.; Victoria University College (now Victoria Univ. of Wellington) (BCom). Farming, 1919–27. Wellington City Corporation, 1928–35; Secretary, Farmers' Union, 1935–46 (later Federated Farmers of NZ Inc.); General Secretary, Federated Farmers of New Zealand Inc., Wellington, NZ, 1946–64. Fellow (Chartered Accountant) New Zealand Society of Accountants. *Publication:* The Public Be Damned, 1946. *Recreation:* onlooker, Rugby football. *Address:* 8 Riverview Road, Kerikeri, RD2, Northland, New Zealand. *Clubs:* Civil Service, Wellesley (Wellington, NZ).

O'SHEA, David Michael; Solicitor to the Metropolitan Police, since 1982; *b* 27 Jan. 1927; *s* of late Francis Edward O'Shea and Helen O'Shea; *m* 1953, Sheila Winifred; two *s*. *Educ:* St Ignatius Coll., London; King's Coll., London Univ. (LLB). Served RN, 1946–48. Articled H. C. L. Hanne & Co., London, 1949–52; admitted solicitor, 1952; in practice with H. C. L. Hanne & Co., 1952–56; joined Solicitor's Dept, Metropolitan Police Office,

1956; Dep. Solicitor, 1976–82. *Recreation:* travel. *Address:* New Scotland Yard, SW1. *T:* 01–230 7353.

OSIFELO, Sir Frederick (Aubarua), Kt 1977; MBE 1972; Speaker of Legislative Assembly, Solomon Islands, 1974–78; Chairman: Public Service Commission, since 1975; Police and Prison Service Commission, since 1977; Member, Judicial and Legal Service Commission, since 1977; *b* 15 Oct. 1928; *s* of late Paul Iromea and Joy Ngangale Iromea; *m* 1949, Margaret Tanai; three *s* three *d*. *Educ:* Torquay Technical Coll., England (Dip. Public Admin). Office cleaner, 1945; clerk, 1950; 1st Cl. Magistrate, 1967; Admin. Officer, Cl. B, 1967; Admin. Officer, Cl. A, 1972; District Comr, Eastern Solomons, 1972; Sen. Sec., 1973; Comr of Lands, 1974. Chairman: Cttee of Prerogative of Mercy, 1979; ad hoc cttee on Solomon Islands Honours and Awards, 1979. Pres., Amateur Sports Assoc., 1975–. Lay Canon, 1977. *Address:* PO Box 548, Honiara, Solomon Islands. *T:* (office) 23111, ext. 25, (home) 22018.

OSLEY, Arthur Sidney, PhD; Consultant to Engineering Council, since 1983; *b* 21 Jan. 1917; *s* of Sidney Charles Osley and Emily Elizabeth Osley (*née* Fearn); *m* 1st, 1941, Betty Doreen Laird; two *s*; 2nd, 1955, Sheila Patricia Branigan. *Educ:* Peter Symonds School, Winchester; University College London (BA 1st Cl. Hons Classics 1938; DipEd 1940; PhD 1943). Admiralty, 1940–66; IDC 1961; MoD, 1966–74; Under Sec., Price Commn, 1976–78; Council of Engineering Instns, 1978–83. Set up Glade Press, 1969. Member: Art Workers' Guild; Double Crown Club. Hon. Mem., Vereniging Mercator, Holland. Editor, Jl of Soc. for Italic Handwriting, 1962–. *Publications:* Calligraphy and Palaeography: essays presented to Alfred Fairbank (ed), 1965; Mercator, 1969; Luminario: an introduction to the Italian Writing-Books of the sixteenth and seventeenth centuries, 1972; Scribes and Sources: handbook of the Chancery hand in the sixteenth century, 1980; contribs to learned jls. *Recreation:* printing, bookbinding, research into handwriting and calligraphy, chess, gardening, reading. *Address:* The Glade, Brook Road, Wormley, Godalming GU8 5UR. *T:* Wormley 2474.

OSMAN, Sir (Abdool) Raman (Mahomed), GCMG 1973; CBE 1963; Governor-General of Mauritius, 1972–77; *b* 29 Aug. 1902, of Mauritian parents; unmarried. *Educ:* Royal College, Mauritius; Inns of Court, London. District Magistrate, Mauritius, 1930–38; Additional Substitute Procureur and Advocate General, 1938–50; Actg Procureur and Advocate-General, 1950–51; Actg Chief Justice, Apr.-Nov. 1958; Puisne Judge, Supreme Court of Mauritius, 1950–59, Sen. Puisne Judge, 1959–60, retired. Hon. DCL Mauritius, 1975. *Address:* Le Goulet Terrace, Tombeau Bay, Mauritius. *Club:* Port Louis Gymkhana.

OSMAN, Louis, BA (Arch.); FRIBA; architect, artist, medallist, goldsmith; *b* 30 January 1914; *s* of Charles Osman, Exeter; *m* 1940, Dilys Roberts, *d* of Richard Roberts, Rotherfield, Sussex; one *d*. *Educ:* Hele's School, Exeter; London University (Fellow, UCL, 1984–). Open exhibn at Bartlett School of Architecture, University Coll. London, 1931, and at Slade School; Donaldson Medallist of RIBA, 1935. With British Museum and British School of Archæology Expeditions to Syria, 1936, 1937; designed private and public buildings, 1937–39. Served War of 1939–45, Major in Intelligence Corps: Combined Ops HQ and Special Air Service as specialist in Air Photography, Beach Reconnaissance Cttee, prior to invasion of Europe. Resumed practice in London, 1945, designed buildings, furniture, tapestries, glass, etc; work in Westminster Abbey, Lincoln, Ely and Exeter Cathedrals; Staunton Harold for National Trust; Bridge, Cavendish Square, with Jacob Epstein; Newnham Coll., Cambridge; factory buildings for Cambridge Instrument Co., aluminium Big Top for Billy Smart's Circus, two villages on Dartmoor, etc; consultant architect to British Aluminium Co.; executed commissions as goldsmith and jeweller, 1956–; commissioned by De Beers for 1st Internat. Jewellery Exhibn, 1961; designed and made Prince of Wales' crown for investiture, 1969; British Bicentennial Gift to America housing Magna Carta, 1976; Verulam Medal for Metals Soc., 1975; EAHY Medal, 1975; Olympic Medal, 1976; work in precious metals exhibited GB, Denmark, Holland, Germany, American, S Africa, Australia, Japan, etc; one-man retrospective exhibn, Goldsmiths' Hall, 1971. Mem. Exec. Cttee: The Georgian Group, 1952–56; City Music Soc., 1960–70. *Publications:* reviews and contributions to learned jls. *Recreation:* music. *Address:* Byford Court, Hereford HR4 7LD. *T:* Bridge Sollars 248.

OSMAN, Dr Mohammad Kheir; Member of Foundation Committee since 1981, and Professor and Dean of Students since 1985, Sultan Qaboos University, Muscat, Sultanate of Oman; *b* Gedarif, Sudan, 1928; *s* of Osman Khalifa Taha and Khadija Al Shareef; *m* 1953, Sara Ahmed. *Educ:* Khartoum Univ. (BA); London Univ. (PGCE; AcDip; MA); Univ. of California, LA (PhD). Director: Educational Research and Planning, 1970–71; Sudan/ILO Productivity Centre, Khartoum, 1972; Minister of Education, 1972–75; Mem., Sudan Nat. Assembly, 1972–75; Ambassador to UK, 1975–76; Manager, UNDP/UNESCO Educnl Project, Oman, 1977–84; Adviser to Min. of Educn, Oman, 1984–85. Professional interests include Western educnl experience and indigenous Afro/Arab conditions, and the problems of change through institutional educnl systems. Constitution Award, 1973; Two-Niles Decoration for Public Service, 1979. *Address:* Sultan Qaboos University, PO Box 6281, Ruwi, Sultanate of Oman. *Club:* Athenæum.

OSMAN, Sir Raman; *see* Osman, Sir A. R. M.

OSMOND, Prof. Charles Barry, PhD; FRS 1984; FAA; Professor of Biology, Department of Environmental Biology, Australian National University, Canberra, since 1978; Executive Director, Biological Sciences Center, Desert Research Institute, Reno, since 1982; *b* 20 Sept. 1939; *s* of Edmund Charles Osmond and Joyce Daphne (*née* Krauss); *m* 1st, 1962, Suzanne Alice Ward; two *s* one *d* (and one *s* decd); 2nd, 1983, Ulla Maria Cornelia Gauhl (*née* Büchen). *Educ:* Morisset Central Sch.; Wyong High Sch.; Univ. of New England, Armidale (University Medal in Botany, 1961; BSc 1961, MSc 1963); Univ. of Adelaide (PhD 1965). FAA 1978. Post-doctoral Res. Associate, Botanical Sciences Dept, Univ. of Calif, LA, 1965; Royal Commn for Exhibn of 1851 and CSIRO Fellow, Botany Sch., Cambridge Univ., 1966; successively Res. Fellow, Fellow and Sen. Fellow, Dept of Environmental Biol., ANU, Canberra, 1967–78. Fulbright Sen. Scholar, Univ. of Calif, Santa Cruz, 1973–74; Carnegie Instn Fellow (Plant Biol.), Stanford, 1973–74; Richard Mereton Guest Prof., Technical Univ., Munich, 1974; Overseas Fellow, Churchill Coll., Cambridge, 1980. Goldacre Award, Aust. Soc. of Plant Physiologists, 1972; Edgeworth David Medal, Royal Soc. of NSW, 1974. *Publications:* (ed jtly) Photosynthesis and Photorespiration, 1971; (ed jtly) Photorespiration in Marine Plants, 1976; (jtly) Physiological Processes in Plant Ecology, 1980; (ed jtly) Encyclopedia of Plant Physiology, Vols 12 A-D, Physiological Plant Ecology, 1981–83; articles on plant metabolic biology and its ecological implications in learned jls. *Recreations:* biological research, social cricket, music of romantic composers, confections of Continental Europe. *Address:* Department of Environmental Biology, Research School of Biological Sciences, Australian National University, Box 475, Canberra City, ACT 2601, Australia. *T:* (062) 492–406/473–628.

OSMOND, Sir Douglas, Kt 1971; CBE 1968 (OBE 1958); QPM 1962; DL; Chief Constable, Shropshire, 1946–62, Hampshire, 1962–77; *b* 27 June 1914. *Educ:* University Coll., London. Metropolitan Police Coll., Metropolitan Police, RN, Control Commn for Germany (Public Safety Branch); Dep. Asst Inspector Gen., 1944–46. Pres., Assoc. of Chief Police Officers of England and Wales, 1967–69; Chm., Police Council for UK, 1972, 1974; Provincial Police Representative, Interpol, 1968–70; Member: Inter-Deptl Cttee on Death Certification and Coroners, 1964–71; Bd of Governors, Police Coll., 1968–72 (Adv. Cttee, 1959–77); Royal Commn on Criminal Procedure, 1978–81. DL Hants, 1981. OStJ 1971. *Address:* Woodbine Cottage, Ovington, Alresford, Hants SO24 0RF.

OSMOND, Mervyn Victor, OBE 1978; Secretary, Council for the Protection of Rural England, 1966–77 (Assistant Secretary, 1946; Deputy Secretary 1963); *b* 2 July 1912; *s* of Albion Victor Osmond and Florence Isabel (*née* Edwards), Bristol; *m* 1940, Aimée Margaret Moir; one *d*. *Educ:* Clifton Coll. (Schol.); Exeter Coll., Oxford (Schol.). 1st cl. Hon. Class. Mods; 2nd cl. Lit. Hum.; 2nd cl. Jurisprudence; Poland Prizeman (Criminal Law), 1937; called to Bar (Inner Temple), 1938; MA 1939. Practising Barrister, Western Circuit, 1938–40. Joined Gloucestershire Regt, TA, 1931; served war of 1939–45; Royal Fusiliers; DAAG (Major) 352 L of C Sub-Area and 303 L of C Area (Calcutta). *Recreations:* reading, enjoying rural England. *Address:* 39 Stonehill Road, East Sheen, SW14 8RR. *T:* 01–876 7138.

OSMOND, Michael William Massy, CB 1977; Solicitor to the Department of Health and Social Security, and to the Office of Population Censuses and Surveys, and the General Register Office, 1974–78; *b* 1918; *s* of late Brig. W. R. F. Osmond, CBE, and Mrs C. R. E. Osmond; *m* 1943, Jill Ramsden; one *s* one *d*. *Educ:* Winchester; Christ Church, Oxford. 2nd Lieut Coldstream Guards, 1939–40. Called to Bar, Inner Temple, 1941; Asst Principal, Min. of Production, 1941–43; Housemaster, HM Borstal Instn, Usk, 1943–45; Legal Asst, Min. of Nat. Insce, 1946; Sen. Legal Asst, 1948; Asst Solicitor, Min. of Pensions and Nat. Insce, 1958; Principal Asst Solicitor, DHSS, 1969. *Recreations:* music, fishing. *Address:* Waylands, Long Newnton, near Tetbury, Glos. *T:* Tetbury 53308. *Club:* United Oxford & Cambridge University.

OSMOND, Sir (Stanley) Paul, Kt 1980; CB 1966; *b* 13 May 1917; *o s* of late Stanley C. and Susan Osmond; *m* 1942, Olivia Sybil, JP, *yr d* of late Ernest E. Wells, JP, Kegworth, Leicestershire; two *s*. *Educ:* Bristol Grammar School; Jesus College, Oxford. Served War of 1939–45, in Army (Gloucestershire Regiment and staff), 1940–46. Home Civil Service, 1939–75: Ministry of Education, 1946–48; Private Secretary to Prime Minister, 1948–51; Admiralty, 1951, Asst Secretary, 1954; Under-Secretary, 1959; HM Treasury, 1962, Third Secretary, 1965; Deputy Secretary: Civil Service Dept, 1968–70; Office of the Lord Chancellor, 1970–72; DHSS, 1972–75. Sec. to the Church Commissioners, 1975–80. Member: Lord Chancellor's Cttee on Public Records, 1978–80; Adv. Council on Public Records, 1983–. Royal Institution: a Manager, 1966–69, 1970–73; Hon. Treas. and Vice-Pres., 1981–86. Chm., Nat. Marriage Guidance Council, 1982–. Mem., Clergy Orphan Corp., 1980–; Hon. Treasurer, Central London YMCA, 1982–85; Governor, Bristol Grammar Sch., 1972– (Vice-Chm., 1984–); Chm., Lingfield Hosp. Sch., 1981–. CBIM 1978. *Recreations:* theatre, travel, gardening. *Address:* 20 Beckenham Grove, Bromley, Kent BR2 0JU. *T:* 01–460 2026. *Club:* Athenæum.

OSMOND-CLARKE, Sir Henry, KCVO 1969; CBE 1947; FRCS; Consulting Orthopædic Surgeon: London Hospital, E1 (Orthopædic Surgeon, 1946–70); Robert Jones and Agnes Hunt Orthopædic Hospital, Oswestry (Senior Visiting Surgeon, 1930–70); Hon. Civilian Consultant in Orthopædics, RAF, since 1946; Orthopædic Surgeon to the Queen, 1965–73; *e s* of W. J. Clarke, Brookeborough, Co. Fermanagh, NI; *m* Freda, *e d* of Richard Hutchinson, Bury, Lancs; two *d*. *Educ:* Clones High School; Trinity College, Dublin University; Vienna, Bologna, New York, Boston, London. BA 1925; MB, BCh (stip. cond.) 1926; FRCSIre 1930; FRCS 1932; Surgical Travelling Prize, TCD 1930. Consultant Orthopædic Surgeon, Oldchurch, Black Notley, Tilbury and East Grinstead Hosps; Orthopædic Surgeon, King Edward VII Hosp. for Officers, London; Cons. King Edward VII Convalescent Home for Officers, Osborne; Hunterian Prof. RCS, 1936. Service Cons. in Orthop. Surg., Air Cdre, RAF, 1941–46; Mayo Clinic Foundation Lecturer, 1948; Orthop. Mem. WHO Mission to Israel, 1951, to India, 1953, to Persia, 1957. Past President, British Orthop. Assoc. (former Editorial Sec. and Acting Sec.); FRSocMed and several Brit. Med. Socs. Formerly: Clinical Tutor in Orthop. Surg., Manchester Roy. Infirmary and Lecturer in Surg. Pathology (Orthop.), Univ. of Manchester; Orthop. Surg., Crumpsall Hosp., Manchester, and Biddulph Grange Orthop. Hosp., Stoke-on-Trent; Sen. Ho. Surg. and Orthop. Ho. Surg. Ancoats Hosp., Manchester, and Royal Nat. Orthop. Hospital, London. Mem. Council, RCS, 1959–75, Vice-Pres. 1970–72. Chm. Accident Services Review Cttee of Great Britain and Ireland, 1960. Hon. Mem. American Orthop. Assoc.; American Acad. of Orthopædic Surgery; Australian, New Zealand and Canadian Orthopædic Assocs; Corresp. Mem., French Orthopædic Society and Surg. Soc. of Lyon; Mem. International Soc. of Orthopædics and Traumatology. *Publications:* papers on surgical and orthopædic subjects in leading surgical text-books and med. jls, including Half a Century of Orthopædic Progress in Great Britain, 1951. *Recreations:* travel, reading, fishing. *Address:* 46 Harley House, Marylebone Road, NW1 5HJ. *T:* 01–486 9975. *Club:* Royal Air Force.

OSMOTHERLY, Edward Benjamin Crofton; Under Secretary, Director of Personnel Management and Training, Departments of the Environment and Transport, since 1985; *b* 1 Aug. 1942; *s* of Crofton and Elsie Osmotherly; *m* 1970, Valerie (*née* Mustill); one *d* one *s*. *Educ:* East Ham Grammar School; Fitzwilliam College, Cambridge (MA). Asst Principal, Ministry of Housing and Local Govt, 1963–68 (Private Sec. to Parly Sec., 1966–67, to Minister of State, 1967–68); Principal, 1968–76; Harkness Fellow, 1972–73 (Guest Scholar, Brookings Instn, Washington DC; Exec. Fellow, Univ. of California at Berkeley); Asst Sec., DoE, 1976–79; seconded to British Railways Bd, 1979; Head of Machinery of Govt Div., CSD, 1980–81; Under Sec. (Railways), Dept of Transport, 1982–85; Sec., Serpell Cttee on Railway Finances, 1982. *Recreation:* reading. *Address:* 63 Grove Avenue, N10 2AL. *T:* 01–883 3724.

OSOLA, (Victor) John, (Väinö Juhani), CBE 1980; FEng, FIMechE; Chairman, John Osola & Associates Ltd, since 1983; Secretary, Fellowship of Engineering, since 1983; *b* 24 Jan. 1926; *s* of Väinö Kaarlo Osola and Violet Agenoria (*née* Jones); *m* 1948, Brenda Lilian Davison; two *s* one *d*. *Educ:* Hymers Coll., Hull; Sunderland Technical Coll., Univ. of Durham (BSc). FEng 1979; FIMechE 1966; Fellow ASME; MInstE. Technical Commn, RE, 1945–48. Gas Turbine Res. Engr, C. A. Parsons & Co. Ltd, 1951–52; Sen. Proj. Design Engr, Procter & Gamble Ltd, 1952–57; Chief Engr, Lankro Chemicals Ltd, 1957–65; Technical Director: Fibreglass Ltd, 1965–72; Triplex Safety Glass Co. Ltd, 1972–79; Chm., Fibreglass Pilkington Ltd, Bombay, 1967–72; Director: Triplex Ireland Ltd, 1976–79; Triclover Safety Glass Co. Ltd, 1976–79; (non-exec.) Kongsberg Systems Technology Ltd, 1983–85; Mem., Pilkington Brothers European Safety Glass Bd, 1977–79; Group Chief Exec., Redman Heenan Internat. plc, 1979–82, non-exec. Dir, 1982–84. Pres., IMechE, 1982–83; Ind. Mem., Mech. Engrg and Machine Tool Requirements Bd, Dept of Industry, 1974–77, Chm. 1977–79; Chm., NEDO Adv. Manufacturing Systems Cttee, 1983–; Member: Court of Cranfield Inst. of Technol., 1979–; Policy Bd, Cranfield Product Engrg Centre, 1980–. Associate, St George's House, Windsor, 1980–; Governor, Malvern Coll., 1981–. FRSA 1976. MacRobert Award, 1978. *Publications:* papers in specialised engrg jls. *Recreations:* offshore sailing (BoT yachtmaster), music, theatre. *Address:* Whiddon End, Yarhampton Cross, near Stourport-on-Severn, Worcs DY13 0UY. *T:* Great Witley 293. *Clubs:* Army and Navy; Royal Dee Yacht (Cheshire); Royal Irish Yacht (Dublin); North West Venturers Yacht (Beaumaris).

OSTLERE, Dr Gordon; *see* Gordon, Richard.

O'SULLEVAN, Peter John, OBE 1977; Racing Correspondent: Daily Express, 1950–86; Today, since 1986; BBC Television Commentator; *b* 3 March 1918; *o s* of late Col John Joseph O'Sullevan, DSO, formerly Resident Magistrate, Killarney, and Vera, *o d* of Sir John Henry, DL, JP; *m* 1951, Patricia, *o d* of Frank Duckworth, Winnipeg, Manitoba, Canada. *Educ:* Hawtreys; Charterhouse; Collège Alpin, Switzerland. Specialised in ill-health in early life and not accepted for fighting forces in 1939–45 war, during which attached to Chelsea Rescue Services. Subsequently worked for John Lane, the Bodley Head, on editorial work and MSS reading. Joined Press Assoc. as Racing Correspondent, 1945, until appointed Daily Express, 1950, in similar capacity. Race-broadcasting 1946– (incl. Australia, S Africa, Italy, France, USA); in 1953 became first regular BBC TV and horse-racing commentator to operate without a race-reader; commentated: first television Grand National, 1960; world's first televised electronic horse race from Atlas computer at Univ. of London, transmitted by BBC TV Grandstand, 1967; first horse race transmitted live via satellite, from NY, to invited audience in London, 1980. Director: Internat. Racing Bureau, 1979–; Racing Post Ltd, 1985–. (With late Clive Graham) Derby Award for Racing Journalist of the Year, 1971; Racehorse Owner of the Year Award, Horserace Writers' Assoc., 1974; Timeform Racing Personality, 1974; Clive Graham Meml Award for services to racing, Press Club, 1978, 1985; Evening News Sports Commentator of the Year, 1978; William Hill Golden Spurs for services to racing, 1985. *Recreations:* racehorse owning, in minor way (happiest broadcasting experience commentating success of own horses, Be Friendly, 1966–67, and Attivo, 1974); travel, reading, art, food and wine. *Address:* 37 Cranmer Court, SW3 3HW. *T:* 01–584 2781.

O'SULLIVAN, (Carrol Austin) John (Naish), CB 1973; LLB (London); Public Trustee, 1971–75; *b* 24 Jan. 1915; *s* of late Dr Carrol Naish O'Sullivan and late Stephanie O'Sullivan (*née* Manning); *m* 1939, Lillian Mary, *y d* of Walter Frank Yate Molineux, Ulverston; one *s* one *d*. *Educ:* Mayfield College. Admitted Solicitor, 1936. Served War of 1939–45, Gordon Highlanders and HQ Special Force SEAC (Captain). Joined Public Trustee Office, 1945; Chief Administrative Officer, 1963–66; Asst Public Trustee, 1966–71. Pres., Holborn Law Soc., 1965–66. Chm. of Governors of St Thomas More High Sch. for Boys, Westcliff-on-Sea, 1964–66. *Publications:* articles in legal jls; short stories. *Recreations:* cathedrals, cricket, etymology, gadgets, whodunnits, and the hobby of the moment. *Address:* 3 The Leeway, Hopping Jack's Lane, Danbury, Essex CM3 4PS. *T:* Danbury 3829. *Club:* National Liberal.

O'SULLIVAN, Rt. Rev. Mgr. James, CBE 1973 (MBE 1963); Officiating Chaplain (RC), RAMC Depot and Training Centre, since 1973; *b* 2 Aug. 1917; *s* of Richard O'Sullivan and Ellen (*née* Ahern). *Educ:* St Finnbarr's Coll., Cork; All Hallows Coll., Dublin. Ordained, 1941; joined Royal Army Chaplain's Dept, 1942; 49 Infantry Div., Normandy, 1944; Senior RC Chaplain, Malaya, 1952–54 (despatches 1953); Chaplain Irish Guards, 1954–56; Senior RC Chaplain, Berlin, 1956–59; Staff Chaplain (RC), War Office, 1959–64; Senior RC Chaplain, BAOR, 1965–69; Principal RC Chaplain (Army), 1969–73. *Recreation:* golf. *Address:* Osgil, Vicarage Lane, Ropley, Alresford, Hants.

O'SULLIVAN, John; *see* O'Sullivan, C. A. J. N.

OSWALD, Vice-Adm. John Julian Robertson; Flag Officer, Third Flotilla, and Commander, Anti-Submarine Warfare, Striking Fleet, since 1985; *b* 11 Aug. 1933; *s* of George Hamilton Oswald and Margaret Elliot Oswald (*née* Robertson), Newmore, Invergordon; *m* 1958, Veronica Therese Dorette Thompson; two *s* three *d*. *Educ:* Beaudesert Park, Minchinhampton; Britannia RNC, Dartmouth. Junior Officer, 1951; served in HM Ships Devonshire, Vanguard, Verulam, Newfoundland, Jewel, Victorious, Naiad; specialised in Gunnery, 1960; Commanded HMS Yarnton, 1962–63, HMS Bacchante, 1971–72; MoD, 1972–75; RCDS, 1976; Commanded HMS Newcastle, 1977–79; RN Presentation Team, 1979–80; Captain, Britannia RNC, 1980–82; ACDS (Progs), 1982–84; ACDS (Policy and Nuclear), 1985. *Address:* c/o Naval Secretary, Old Admiralty Building, Whitehall, SW1.

OSWALD, Maj.-Gen. Marshall St John, CB 1965; CBE 1961; DSO 1945; MC 1943; retired as Director of Management and Support Intelligence, Ministry of Defence, 1966; *b* 13 Sept. 1911; *s* of William Whitehead Oswald and Katharine Ray Oswald; *m* 1st, 1938, Mary Georgina Baker (*d* 1970); one *s* two *d*; 2nd, 1974, Mrs Barbara Rickards. *Educ:* Rugby Sch.; RMA, Woolwich. Commissioned RA, 1931; served in RHA and Field Artillery, UK and India, 1931–39. Served War of 1939–45 (despatches, MC, DSO): Battery Comdr 4 RHA and Staff Officer in Egypt and Western Desert, 1939–42; GSO1, Tactical HQ, 8th Army, 1942–43; 2nd in Comd Field Regt, Italy, 1943–44; CO South Notts Hussars, Western Europe, 1944–45; Col on staff of HQ 21 Army Group, 1945. Mil. Govt Comdr (Col) of Cologne Area, 1946–47; Staff Officer, War Office (Lt-Col) 1948–49; Instructor (Col) Staff Coll., Camberley 1950–52; CO 19 Field Regt, Germany/Korea, 1953–55; GHQ, MELF (Col), 1955–56 (despatches 1957); IDC 1958; CCRA and Chief of Staff (Brig.) 1st Corps in Germany, 1959–62; DMI, War Office, 1962–64, Min. of Defence (Army), 1964–65. *Recreations:* fishing, shooting, ski-ing. *Address:* Eastfield House, Longparish, near Andover, Hants. *T:* Longparish 228. *Club:* Army and Navy.

OSWALD, Dr Neville Christopher, TD 1946; MD Cantab 1946; FRCP 1947; retired 1975; formerly: Consultant Physician: St Bartholomew's Hospital; Brompton Hospital; King Edward VII's Hospital for Officers, London; King Edward VII's Hospital, Midhurst; *b* 1 Aug. 1910; *s* of late Col Christopher Percy Oswald, CMG; *m* 1st, 1941, Patricia Rosemary Joyce Cooke (*d* 1947); one *s* one *d*; 2nd, 1948, Marjorie Mary Sinclair; one *d*. *Educ:* Clifton Coll.; Queens' Coll., Cambridge. Research Fellow, USA, 1938–39. Royal Army Medical Corps, 1939–45. Hon. Physician to the Queen, 1956–58; Hon. Consultant in Diseases of the Chest to the Army, 1972–75. Hon. Col, 17th (London) General Hospital RAMC (TA), 1963–70, 217 (Eastern) General Hospital RAMC (V), 1967–70. President: British Tuberculosis Assoc., 1965–67; Thoracic Soc., 1974. DL Greater London, 1973–78. RCP: Mitchell Lectr; Tudor Edwards Lectr. *Publications:* Recent Trends in Chronic Bronchitis, 1958; Diseases of the Respiratory System, 1962; many articles upon respiratory diseases. *Recreations:* travel, golf. *Address:* 2 The Old Rectory, Thurlestone, South Devon. *T:* Kingsbridge 560555.

OSWALD, Thomas; *b* 1 May 1904; *s* of John Oswald and Agnes Love, Leith; *m* 1933, Colina MacAskill, *d* of Archibald MacAlpin and Margaret MacAskill, Ballachulish, Argyllshire; three *s* one *d*. *Educ:* Yardheads and Bonnington Elementary Schools. Shipyard worker, transport worker. Official of Transport and General Workers' Union; Scottish Regional Trade Group Secretary, 1941–69. Contested (Lab) West Aberdeenshire, 1950. MP (Lab) Edinburgh Central, 1951–Feb. 1974; PPS to Secretary of State for Scotland, 1967–70. Sec. Treasurer, Scottish Parly Lab. Group, 1953–64; Sec., Members' Parly Cttee, 1956–66. Dir, St Andrew Animal Fund; Mem. Cttee, Scottish Soc. for Prevention of Vivisection; Nat. Pres., Scottish Old Age Pensions Assoc. *Recreations:* student economic and industrial history; swimming, camping, etc. *Address:* 46 Seaview Crescent, Joppa, Edinburgh EH15 2HD. *T:* 031–669 5569.

O'TOOLE, (Seamus) Peter; actor; *b* 1932; *s* of Patrick Joseph O'Toole; *m* Sian Phillips, *qv* (marr. diss.); two *d*. *Educ:* Royal Academy of Dramatic Art. With Bristol Old Vic Company, 1955–58; first appearance on London stage as Peter Shirley in Major Barbara, Old Vic, 1956. Associate Dir, Old Vic Co., 1980. *Plays include:* Oh, My Papa!, Garrick, 1957; The Long and the Short and the Tall, Royal Court and New, 1959; season with Shakespeare Memorial Theatre Company, Stratford-on-Avon, 1960; Baal, Phœnix, 1963; Hamlet, National Theatre, 1963; Ride a Cock Horse, Piccadilly, 1965; Juno and the Paycock, Man and Superman, Pictures in the Hallway, Gaiety, Dublin, 1966; Waiting for Godot, Happy Days (dir.), Abbey, Dublin, 1969; Uncle Vanya, Plunder, The Apple Cart, Judgement, Bristol Old Vic, 1973; Uncle Vanya, Present Laughter, Chicago, 1978; Macbeth, Old Vic, 1980; Man and Superman, Haymarket, 1982; Pygmalion, Shaftesbury, 1984; The Apple Cart, Haymarket, 1986. *Films include:* Kidnapped, 1959; The Day They Robbed the Bank of England, 1959; The Savage Innocents, 1960; Lawrence of Arabia, 1962; Becket, 1963; Lord Jim, 1964; What's New, Pussycat, 1965; How to Steal a Million, 1966; The Bible . . . in the Beginning, 1966; The Night of the Generals, 1967; Great Catherine, 1968; The Lion in Winter, 1968; Goodbye Mr Chips, 1969; Brotherly Love, 1970; Murphy's War, 1971; Under Milk Wood, 1971; The Ruling Class, 1972; Man of La Mancha, 1972; Rosebud, 1975; Man Friday, 1975; Foxtrot, 1975; The Stunt Man, 1977; Coup d'Etat, 1977; Zulu Dawn, 1978; Power Play, 1978; The Antagonists, 1981; My Favorite Year, 1981; Supergirl, 1983; Creator, 1984; Club Paradise; *television:* Rogue Male, BBC, 1976; Strumpet City, RTE, 1979; Masada, ABC, 1981; Svengali, CBS, 1982; Pygmalion, 20th Century Fox TV, 1983; Kim, ABC, 1983; Banshee. *Club:* Garrick.

OTTAWA, Archbishop of, (RC), since 1967; **Most Rev. Joseph Aurèle Plourde;** *b* 12 Jan. 1915; *s* of Antoine Plourde and Suzanne Albert. *Educ:* Bathurst Coll.; Bourget Coll., Rigaud; Major Seminary of Halifax; Inst. Catholique, Paris; Gregorian Univ., Rome. Auxiliary Bishop of Alexandria, Ont., 1964. Hon. DEducn, Moncton Univ., 1969. *Address:* Archbishop's Residence, 145 Saint Patrick Street, Ottawa, Ont K1N 5K1, Canada. *T:* 237–4540.

OTTAWA, Bishop of, since 1981; **Rt. Rev. Edwin Keith Lackey.** *Educ:* Bishop's Univ., Lennoxville (BA 1953). Deacon 1953, priest 1954, Ottawa; Curate of Cornwall, 1953–55; Incumbent of Russell, 1955–60, Vankleek Hill, 1960–63; Rector of St Michael and All Angels, Ottawa, 1963–72; Director of Programme, dio. Ottawa, 1972–78; Hon. Canon, 1972–78; Archdeacon of the Diocese, 1978–81. *Address:* Bishop's Office, 71 Bronson Avenue, Ottawa, Ontario K1R 6G6, Canada.

OTTAWAY, Richard Geoffrey James; MP (C) Nottingham North, since 1983; *b* 24 May 1945; *s* of late Professor Christopher Ottaway, PhD, FRCVS and of Grace Ottaway; *m* 1982, Nicola E. Kisch. *Educ:* Backwell Secondary Modern School, Somerset; Bristol University. LLB (Hons). Entered RN as an Artificer apprentice, 1961; commissioned and entered RNC, Dartmouth, 1966; served with Western Fleet, HM Ships Beechampton, Nubian and Eagle, 1967–70; Bristol Univ., 1971–74; articled to Norton Rose Botterell & Roche, 1974; admitted Solicitor, 1977; Partner, William A. Crump & Son, 1981–; specialist in marine law. PPS to Ministers of State, FCO, 1985–. *Publications:* papers on combating internat. maritime fraud and on financial matters. *Recreations:* sailing, jazz, conservation. *Address:* House of Commons, SW1A 0AA. *Clubs:* Island Sailing, Royal Corinthian Yacht.

OTTER, Air Vice-Marshal Victor Charles, CBE 1967 (OBE 1945); Air Officer Engineering, Air Support Command Royal Air Force, 1966–69, retired; *b* 9 February 1914; *s* of Robert and Ada Annie Otter; *m* 1943, Iris Louise Dykes; no *c*. *Educ:* Weymouth Gram. School. RAF Aircraft Apprentice, 1929–32; flying duties, 1935–37; commissioned Engr. Br., 1940; SO (Techn) Controller Research and Development (MAP), 1942–47; Asst Air Attaché, Budapest, 1947–48; Officer Comdg Central Servicing Develt Establt, 1953–55; Chief Engrg Officer, Bomber Comd, 1956–59; OC No 32 Maintenance Unit, 1959–61; STSO Flying Trng Comd, 1961–63; Project Dir, P1154/P1127, 1963–66. CEng, FRAeS, psc. *Address:* Harpenden, 21 Keats Avenue, Littleover, Derby DE3 7EE. *T:* Derby 512048. *Club:* Royal Air Force.

OTTEWILL, Prof. Ronald Harry, PhD; FRS 1982; FRSC; Leverhulme Professor of Physical Chemistry, University of Bristol, since 1982; *b* 8 Feb. 1927; *m* Ingrid Geraldine Roe; one *s* one *d*. *Educ:* Southall Grammar Sch.; Queen Mary Coll., London (BSc 1948; PhD 1951); Fitzwilliam Coll., Cambridge (MA 1955; PhD 1956). Sen. Asst in Res., 1955–58, Asst Dir of Res., 1958–63, Dept of Colloid Sci., Cambridge Univ.; Bristol University: Lectr, 1964–66; Reader, 1966–70; Prof. of Colloid Science, 1970–82; Head of Dept of Physical Chem., 1973. Chm., SERC Neutron Beam Res. Cttee, 1982–85. Hon. Treas., Faraday Soc. Lectures: A. E. Alexander, RACI, 1982; Liversidge, RSC, 1985–86. Medal for Surface and Colloid Chemistry, RSC, 1972; Wolfgang Ostwald Medal, Kolloid Gesellschaft, W Germany, 1979. *Publications:* contribs to learned jls. *Address:* School of Chemistry, The University, Bristol BS8 1TS.

OTTLEY, Agnes May; retired as Principal, S Katharine's College, Tottenham, N17, Dec. 1959; *b* 29 June 1899; *d* of late Rev. Canon Robert Lawrence Ottley, Professor of Moral and Pastoral Theology, Oxford. *Educ:* privately; Society of Oxford Home Students. Final Honours School of Modern History, Oxford, 1921; MA Oxon; Assistant Mistress at S Felix School, Southwold, 1925; Lecturer in History, Avery Hill Training College, 1927. *Address:* St Ann's Court, Nizell's Avenue, Hove, East Sussex BN3 1LP. *T:* Brighton 733958.

OTTON, Sir Geoffrey (John), KCB 1981 (CB 1978); Second Permanent Secretary, Department of Health and Social Security, 1979–86, retired; *b* 10 June 1927; *s* of late John Alfred Otton and Constance Alma Otton; *m* 1952, Hazel Lomas (*née* White); one *s* one *d*. *Educ:* Christ's Hosp.; St John's Coll., Cambridge (MA). Home Office, 1950–71: (seconded to Cabinet Office, 1959–61; Principal Private Sec. to Home Sec., 1963–65); Dept of Health and Social Security, 1971–86 (Chief Advr to Supplementary Benefits Commn, 1976–79). *Recreation:* music. *Address:* 72 Cumberland Road, Bromley, Kent. *T:* 01–460 9610.

OTTON, Hon. Sir Philip (Howard), Kt 1983; **Hon. Mr Justice Otton;** a Judge of the High Court of Justice, Queen's Bench Division, since 1983; Presiding Judge, Midland and Oxford Circuit, since 1986; *b* 28 May 1933; *o s* of late Henry Albert Otton, Kenilworth and of Leah Otton; *m* 1965, Helen Margaret, *d* of late P. W. Bates, Stourbridge; two *s* one *d*. *Educ:* Bablake School, Coventry; Birmingham Univ. LLB 1954. 3rd Dragoon Guards, 1955–57. Called to the Bar, Gray's Inn, 1955, Bencher 1983; QC 1975. Dep. Chm., Beds QS, 1970–72; Junior Counsel to the Treasury (Personal Injuries), 1970–75; a Recorder of the Crown Court, 1972–83. Governor, Nat. Heart and Chest Hosps, 1979–85. Hon. Mem., Amer. Bar Assoc. *Recreations:* theatre, opera, music. *Address:* Royal Courts of Justice, Strand, WC2A 2LL. *Clubs:* Garrick, Pilgrims, Roehampton.

OTUNGA, HE Cardinal Maurice; *see* Nairobi, Archbishop of, (RC).

OULTON, Sir (Antony) Derek (Maxwell), KCB 1984 (CB 1979); QC 1985; MA, PhD; Permanent Secretary, Lord Chancellor's Office, and Clerk of the Crown in Chancery, since 1982; barrister-at-law; *b* 14 Oct. 1927; *y s* of late Charles Cameron Courtenay Oulton and Elizabeth, *d* of T. H. Maxwell, KC; *m* 1955, Margaret Geraldine, *d* of late Lt-Col G. S. Oxley, MC, 60th Rifles; one *s* three *d*. *Educ:* St Edward's Sch., Oxford; King's Coll., Cambridge (scholar; BA (1st Cl.), MA; PhD 1974). Called to Bar, Gray's Inn, 1952, Bencher, 1982; in private practice, Kenya, 1952–60; Private Sec. to Lord Chancellor, 1961–65; Sec., Royal Commn on Assizes and Quarter Sessions, 1966–69; Asst Solicitor, 1969–75. Dep. Sec., 1976–82, and Dep. Clerk of the Crown in Chancery, 1977–82, Lord Chancellor's Office. *Publication:* (jtly) Legal Aid and Advice, 1971. *Address:* 35 St John's Wood Terrace, NW8 6JL. *T:* 01 586 1555.

OULTON, Air Vice-Marshal Wilfrid Ewart, CB 1958; CBE 1953; DSO 1943; DFC 1943; FEng; FRIN; FIERE; Chairman, Medsales Executive Ltd, since 1982; *b* 27 July 1911; *s* of Llewellin Oulton, Monks Coppenhall, Cheshire; *m* 1935, Sarah, *d* of Rev. E. Davies, Pitsea, Essex; three *s*. *Educ:* University Coll., Cardiff; Cranwell. Commissioned, 1931; Director, Joint Anti-Submarine School, 1946–48; Joint Services Staff College, 1948–50; Air Attaché, Buenos Aires, Montevideo, Asuncion, 1950–53; idc 1954; Director of Operations, Air Ministry, 1954–56; commanded Joint Task Force "Grapple" for first British megaton weapon tests in the Pacific, 1956–58; Senior Air Staff Officer, RAF Coastal Command, HQ, 1958–60; retd. *Recreations:* music, squash, golf, travel. *Address:* Farthings, Hollywood Lane, Lymington, Hants. *T:* Lymington 73498. *Clubs:* Royal Air Force; Royal Lymington Yacht.

OUNSTED, John, MA Cantab; HM Inspector of Schools, 1971–81, retired; *b* London, 24 May 1919; *e s* of late Rev. Laurence J. Ounsted, Dorchester Abbey, Oxon (ordained 1965; formerly with Sun Life Assurance); *m* 1940, Irene, 3rd *d* of late Rev. Alfred Newns; one *s* four *d*. *Educ:* Winchester (Scholar); Trinity College, Cambridge (Major Scholar). Math. Tripos Part I, 1st Class; Science Tripos Part II, 1st Class; Senior Scholarship, Trinity College. Assistant Master, King Edward's School, Birmingham, 1940–48; Headmaster, Leighton Park School, 1948–70. First layman ever to be Select Preacher, Oxford Univ., 1964. Page Scholarship to visit USA, 1965. Liveryman, Worshipful Company of Mercers. *Publications:* verses from various languages in the 2 vols of Translation, 1945 and 1947; contributions to Watsonia, The Proceedings of the Botanical Society of the British Isles, and various other educational and botanical periodicals. *Recreations:* botany, camping, being overtaken when motoring. *Address:* Apple Tree Cottage, Woodgreen Common, Fordingbridge, Hants. *T:* Downton 22271.

See also Sir A. Foley Newns.

OUTERBRIDGE, Col Hon. Sir Leonard Cecil, Kt 1946; CC (Canada) 1967; CBE 1926; DSO 1919; CD 1954; Director, Harvey & Co., Ltd, and other Cos, St John's, Newfoundland; *b* 1888; *s* of late Sir Joseph Outerbridge; *m* 1915, Dorothy Winifred (*d* 1972), *d* of late John Alexander Strathy, Barrie, Ontario. *Educ:* Marlborough; Toronto Univ. (BA, LLB; Hon. LLD, 1950); Hon. LLD: Laval Univ., 1952; Memorial Univ. of Newfoundland, 1961. Solicitor and Barrister, Ontario, 1914; President, Newfoundland Board of Trade, 1923–24; Chairman, Newfoundland Committee arranging Exhibits at British Empire Exhibition (1924 and 1925) (CBE); served European War, 1914–19 (despatches twice, DSO). Hon. Private Sec. to the Governor of Newfoundland, 1931–44; Director of Civil Defence, 1942–45; Lieutenant-Governor of Newfoundland, 1949–57. Hon. Col, Royal Newfoundland Regt, 1950–75. KStJ 1951. *Address:* Littlefield, 3 Pringle Place, St John's, Newfoundland, Canada.

OUTERIÑO, Felix C.; *see* Candela Outeriño.

OUTRAM, Sir Alan James, 5th Bt, *cr* 1858; MA; Housemaster, Harrow School; *b* 15 May 1937; *s* of late James Ian Outram and late Evelyn Mary Littlehales; *S* great-uncle, 1945; *m* 1976, Victoria Jean, *d* of late George Dickson Paton, Bexhill-on-Sea; one *s* one *d*. *Educ:* Spyway, Langton Matravers, Swanage; Marlborough College, Wilts; St Edmund Hall, Oxford. Lt-Col TAVR. *Recreations:* golf, tennis, bridge. *Heir: s* Douglas Benjamin James Outram, *b* 15 March 1979. *Address:* Druries, Harrow-on-the-Hill HA1 3HR.

OVENDEN, John Frederick; engineer; County Councillor, Kent; *b* 17 Aug. 1942; *s* of late Richard Ovenden and Margaret Louise Ovenden (*née* Lucas); *m* 1963, Maureen (*née* White); one *d*. *Educ:* Salmestone County Primary Sch., Margate; Chatham House Grammar Sch., Ramsgate. Asst Exec. Engr, Post Office, 1961–74. MP (Lab) Gravesend, Feb. 1974–1979. Contested (Lab) Gravesham, 1983. *Recreations:* football (as a spectator), cricket (Kent), theatre, books. *Clubs:* Gillingham Labour (Gillingham); Gravesend Trades Hall (Gravesend).

OVENS, Maj.-Gen. Patrick John, OBE 1968; MC 1951; Commandant, Joint Warfare Establishment, 1976–79; retired; *b* 4 Nov. 1922; *s* of late Edward Alec Ovens and late Mary Linsell Ovens, Cirencester; *m* 1952, Margaret Mary White; one *s* two *d*. *Educ:* King's Sch., Bruton. Commnd into Royal Marines, 1941; HMS Illustrious, 1942–43; 46 Commando, 1945; HQ 3rd Commando Bde, 1946–48; 41 Indep. Commando, Korea, 1950–52; HQ Portsmouth Gp, 1952–55; psa 1955–56; Staff of CGRM, 1959–61; Amphibious Warfare Sqdn, 1961–62; 41 Commando, 1963–65, CO 1965–67; C-in-C Fleet Staff, 1968–69; Comdr 3 Commando Bde, 1970–72; RCDS 1973; COS to Comdt Gen., RM, MoD, 1974–76. *Recreations:* sailing, music, gardening. *Address:* Virginia House, Netherhampton, Salisbury, Wilts SP2 8PU. *T:* Salisbury 743113.

OVERALL, Sir John (Wallace), Kt 1968; CBE 1962; MC and Bar; architect, town planner and company director; *b* 15 July 1913; *s* of late W. Overall, Sydney; *m* 1943, Margaret J., *d* of C. W. Goodman; four *s*. *Educ:* Sydney Techn. College. AIF, 1940–45: CO, 1 Aust. Para. Bn (Lt-Col). Chief Architect, S Australian Housing Trust, 1946–48; private practice, Architect and Town Planner, 1949–52; Dir of Architecture, Commonwealth Dept of Works, 1952–57; Comr, Nat. Capital Develt Commn, 1958–72; Chm., Nat. Capital Planning Cttee, 1958–72; Comr, Cities Commn (Chm., Adv. Cttee), 1972–73; Principal, John Overall and Partners, 1973–81; Director: Land Lease Corp. Ltd, 1973–83; General Property Trust, 1975–83; Alliance Holdings Ltd, 1975–83 (Chm., 1980–83); CSR Ltd, 1973–85. Mem., Parliament House Construction Authority (Commonwealth Govt of Australia), 1979–85; Chm. Assessors, Parlt House Design Competition, 1979–80. Chm. of Olympic Fine Arts Architecture and Sculpture Exhibn, Melb., 1956. Life Fellow, RAIA and API; Hon. Fellow, AIA, 1984; Pres., Austr. Inst. of Urban Studies, 1970–71. Past Pres., Canberra Legacy Club. Sydney Luker Meml Medal, 1970; Sir James Barrett Medal, 1970; Gold Medal, RAIA, 1982. *Publications:* Observations on Redevelopment Western Side of Sydney Cove, 1967; sundry papers to professional jls. *Recreations:* golf, tennis. *Address:* 3a Vancouver Street, Red Hill, Canberra, ACT 2603, Australia. *Clubs:* Commonwealth (Canberra); Royal Sydney Golf.

OVEREND, Prof. William George; Professor of Chemistry in the University of London, 1957–Sept. 1987, then Professor Emeritus; Master, Birkbeck College, 1979–Sept. 1987 (Vice-Master, 1974–79); *b* 16 Nov. 1921; *e s* of late Harold George Overend, Shrewsbury, Shropshire; *m* 1949, Gina Olava, *y d* of late Horace Bertie Cadman, Birmingham; two *s* one *d*. *Educ:* Priory School, Shrewsbury; Univ. of Birmingham. BSc (Hons) 1943, PhD 1946, DSc 1954, Birmingham; CChem; FRSC (FRIC 1955). Asst Lecturer, Univ. Coll., Nottingham, 1946–47; Research Chemist with Dunlop Rubber Co. Ltd and subsequently British Rubber Producers' Assoc., 1947–49; Hon. Research Fellow, 1947–49, Lecturer in Chemistry, 1949–55, Univ. of Birmingham; Vis. Associate Prof., Pennsylvania State Univ., 1951–52; Reader in Organic Chemistry, Univ. of London, 1955–57; Hd of Dept of Chem., Birkbeck Coll., London, 1957–79. Univ. of London: Mem., Academic Council, 1963–67, 1976–79 and 1984–; Mem., Collegiate Council, 1979–; Mem., University Entrance and Schools Examination Council, 1966–67 and 1985–; Mem., F and GP Cttee, 1976–; Mem., External Cttee, 1984–; Chm., Bd of Studies in Chemistry, 1974–76; Mem., Senate, 1976–; Mem., Jt Cttee of Court and Senate for collective planning, 1976–79; Dean, Faculty of Science, 1978–79; Chm., Acad. Adv. Bd in Sci., 1978–79; Mem., Extra-Mural Council, 1979–, Chm., 1983–84; Chm., Cttee for Extra-Mural Studies, 1984–. Mem. Council: Inst. of Educn, 1979–82; National Inst. of Adult Continuing Educn, 1983–; London and E Anglian Gp for GCSE, 1986–; Mem. Chem. Bd, 1981–84, Mem. Adv. Bd on Credit Accumulation and Transfer, 1986–, CNAA. Rep. of South Bank Poly, Assoc. of Colls of Further and Higher Educn, 1981–. Royal Institute of Chemistry: Examiner, 1958–62; Assessor, 1959–72; Mem., Institutions and Examinations Cttee, 1969–75 (Chm., 1976–85); Mem. Council, 1977–80; Mem. Qual. and Admissions Cttee, 1977–80; Mem. Qual. and Exam. Bd, RSC, 1980–85; Chemical Society (subseq. Royal Society of Chemistry): Mem. Council, 1967–70, 1972–77; Mem. Publications Bd, 1967–78; Hon. Sec. and Hon. Treasurer, Perkin Div., 1972–75; Vice-Pres., 1975–77; Mem., Interdivisional Council, 1972–75; Mem., Educn and Trng Bd, 1972–78; Soc. of Chemical Industry: Mem., Council, 1955–65; Mem., Finance Committee, 1956–65; Mem., Publications Cttee, 1955–65 (Hon. Sec. for publications and Chairman of Publications Committee, 1958–65); Member: Brit. Nat. Cttee for Chemistry, 1961–66, 1973–78; Brit. Nat. Cttee for Biochemistry, 1975–81; Chemical Council, 1960–63 and 1964–69 (Vice-Chm. 1964–69); European Cttee for Carbohydrate Chemists, 1970–85 (Chm.); Hon. Sec., Internat. Cttee for Carbohydrate Chemistry, 1972–75 (Pres., 1978–80); Mem., Jt IUPAC-IUB Commn on Carbohydrate Nomenclature, 1971–. Jubilee Memorial Lecturer, Society of Chemical Industry, 1959–60; Lampitt Medallist, Society of Chemical Industry, 1965; Member: Pharmacopœia Commission, 1963–81; Home Office Poisons Board, 1973–. Governor: Polytechnic of the South Bank, 1970– (Chm., 1980–); Thomas Huxley Coll., 1971–77; Mem., Council of Governors, Queen Elizabeth Coll., Univ. of London, 1983–85. Mem., Cttee of Management, Inst. of Archaeology, 1980–86. Hon. FCollP 1986. *Publications:* The Use of Tracer Elements in Biology, 1951; papers in Nature, and Jl of Chemical Soc. *Recreation:* gardening. *Address:* (until Sept. 1987) Master's Office, Birkbeck College, Malet Street, WC1E 7HX. *T:* 01–580 6622; The Retreat, Nightingales Lane, Chalfont St Giles, Bucks HP8 4SR. *Club:* Athenæum.

OVERTON, Sir Hugh (Thomas Arnold), KCMG 1983 (CMG 1975); HM Diplomatic Service, retired; Member of Council, Dr Barnardo's, since 1985; *b* 2 April 1923; *e s* of late Sir Arnold Overton, KCB, KCMG, MC; *m* 1948, Claire-Marie Binet; one *s* two *d*. *Educ:* Dragon Sch., Oxford; Winchester; Clare Coll., Cambridge. Royal Signals, 1942–45. HM Diplomatic Service, 1947–83; served: Budapest; UK Delegn to UN, New York; Cairo; Beirut; Disarmament Delegn, Geneva; Warsaw; Bonn; Canadian Nat. Defence Coll.; Head of N America Dept, FCO, 1971–74; Consul-Gen., Düsseldorf, 1974–75; Minister (Econ.), Bonn, 1975–80; Consul-Gen., New York, and Dir-Gen., British Trade Develt in USA, 1980–83. Mem., RIIA. *Recreations:* reading, handwork, sailing, fishing. *Address:* c/o Barclays Bank, 276 Kensington High Street, W8. *Club:* Royal Automobile.

OWEN, (Alfred) David; Chairman and Group Chairman, Rubery Owen Holdings Ltd, since 1975; *b* 26 Sept. 1936; *m* 1966, Ethne (*née* Sowman); two *s* one *d*. *Educ:* Brocksford Hall; Oundle; Emmanuel Coll., Cambridge Univ. (MA). Joined Rubery Owen Gp, 1960; Gen. Man., Rubery Owen Motor Div., 1962–67; Dep. Man. Dir, Rubery Owen & Co. Ltd, 1967; Acting Chm. and Man. Dir, Rubery Owen Holdings Ltd, 1969. Dir, W Midlands Bd, Central Indep. Television, 1986–. Trustee, Community Projects Foundn, 1978–; Member: Council, Univ. of Aston, 1981–; Bd, British Library, 1982–; Bd, Nat. Exhibn Centre, 1982–. *Recreations:* squash, photography, music, industrial archaeology, local history, collecting books. *Address:* Mill Dam House, Mill Lane, Aldridge, Walsall, West Midlands. *T:* 021–353 1221. *Clubs:* National, Royal Automobile.

OWEN, Alun, MC 1945; retired; Under-Secretary, Land Use Planning Group, Welsh Office, 1975–79; *b* 14 March 1919; *s* of late Evan Thomas Owen and of Gwladys (*née* David); *m* 1946, Rhona Evelyn Griffiths; one *s* four *d*. *Educ:* West Monmouth Grammar Sch.; Bridgend Grammar Sch.; LSE (BScEcon). Mil. Service, 1939–46: Ches. Regt, 1940–46 (Captain) (despatches, Normandy, 1944); Civil Service, Cadet Officer, Min. of Labour NW Region, 1946–48; Asst Principal, Min. of Fuel and Power, 1948–50; Customs and Excise, 1950–59, Principal 1951; Welsh Office, Min. of Housing and Local Govt, 1959–62; Admin. Mem., Welsh Bd of Health, 1962–69; Welsh Office: Asst Sec., hosp., health and social work services, 1969–72; Estabt Officer, 1972–73; Under-Sec., Health Services, 1974–75. *Address:* 41 Rest Bay Close, Porthcawl, Mid Glam.

OWEN, Alun (Davies); writer since 1957; *b* 24 Nov. 1925; *s* of Sidney Owen and Ruth (*née* Davies); *m* 1942, (Theodora) Mary O'Keeffe; two *s*. *Educ:* Cardigan County School, Wales; Oulton High School, Liverpool. Worked as Stage Manager, Director and Actor, in theatre, TV and films, 1942–59. Awards: Screenwriters and Producers Script of the Year, 1960; Screenwriters Guild, 1961; Daily Mirror, 1961; Golden Star, 1967. *Acted in: stage:* Birmingham Rep., 1943–44; Humoresque, 1948; Snow White and the Seven Dwarfs, 1951; Old Vic season, 1953; Tamburlaine the Great, As You Like It, King Lear, Twelfth Night, The Merchant of Venice, Macbeth, The Wandering Jew, The Taming of the Shrew, 1957; Royal Court Season, 1957; Man with a Guitar, The Waiting of Lester Abbs, The Samson Riddle, 1972; The Ladies, 1977; *films:* Every Day Except Christmas, 1957; I'm All Right Jack, 1959; The Servant, 1963; *television:* Glas y Dorlan, BBC Wales. *Author of productions: stage:* The Rough and Ready Lot, 1959 (Radio 1958), publ. 1960; Progress to the Park, 1959 (Radio 1958), publ. 1962; The Rose Affair, 1966 (TV 1961), publ. 1962; A Little Winter Love, 1963, publ. 1964; Maggie May, 1964; The Game, 1965; The Goose, 1967; Shelter, 1971 (TV 1967), publ. 1968; There'll Be Some Changes Made, 1969; Norma, 1969 (extended version, Nat. Theatre, 1983); We Who Are About To (later title Mixed Doubles), 1969, publ. 1970; The Male of the Species, 1974 (TV 1969), publ. 1972; Lucia, 1982; *screen:* The Criminal, 1960; A Hard Day's Night, 1964 (Oscar nomination); Caribbean Idyll, 1970; *radio:* Two Sons, 1957; It Looks Like Rain, 1959; Earwig (series), 1984; *television:* No Trams to Lime Street, 1959, After the Funeral, 1960, Lena, Oh My Lena, 1960, publ. as Three TV Plays, 1961; The Ruffians, 1960; The Ways of Love, 1961; Dare to be a Daniel, 1962, publ. in Eight Plays, Book 1, 1965; The Hard Knock, You Can't Wind 'em All, 1962; The Strain, Let's Imagine Series, The Stag, A Local Boy, 1963; The Other Fella, The Making of Jericho, 1966; The Wake, 1967, publ. in A Collection of Modern Short Plays, 1972; George's Room, 1967, publ. 1968; The Winner, The Loser, The Fantasist, Stella, Thief, 1967; Charlie, Gareth, Tennyson, Ah There You Are, Alexander, Minding the Shop, Time for the Funny Walk, 1968; Doreen, 1969, publ. in The Best Short Plays, 1971; The Ladies, Joan, Spare Time, Park People, You'll Be the Death of Me, Male of the Species, 1969; Hilda, And a Willow Tree, Just the

Job, Female of the Species, Joy, 1970; Ruth, Funny, Pal, Giants and Ogres, The Piano Player, 1971; The Web, 1972; Ronnie Barker Show (3 scripts), Buttons, Flight, 1973; Lucky, Norma, 1974; Left, 1975; Forget Me Not (6 plays), 1976; The Look, 1978; Passing Through, publ. 1979; The Runner, 1980; Sealink, 1980; Lancaster Gate End, 1982; Cafe Society, 1982; Kish-Kisch, 1982; Colleagues, 1982; Soft Impeachment, 1983; Tiger (musical drama), 1984; (adap.) Lovers of the Lake, 1984 (Banff award, 1985); Widowers, 1985. *Recreations:* languages and history. *Address:* c/o Julian Friedmann, Blake Friedmann Literary Agency, 37–41 Gower Street, WC1E 6HH.

OWEN, Aron, PhD; **His Honour Judge Owen;** a Circuit Judge, since 1980; *b* 16 Feb. 1919; *m* 1946, Rose (*née* Fishman), JP; one *s* two *d. Educ:* Tredegar County Grammar Sch.; Univ. of Wales (BA Hons, PhD). Called to the Bar, Inner Temple, 1948. Freeman, City of London, 1963. *Recreations:* travel, gardening. *Address:* 44 Brampton Grove, Hendon, NW4 4AQ. *T:* 01–202 8151.

OWEN, Bernard Laurence; a Chairman of Industrial Tribunals, since 1982; *b* 8 Aug. 1925; *s* of Albert Victor Paschal Owen and Dorothy May Owen; *m* 1950, Elsie Yarnold; one *s* two *d. Educ:* King Edward's School, Birmingham; solicitor. Commissioned Royal Warwickshire Regt, 1945, service in Sudan, Eritrea, Egypt; staff appts in GHQs Middle East and Palestine, 1946–47; retired 1947 (Major); qualified as solicitor, 1950; a Senior Partner, C. Upfill Jagger Son & Tilley, 1952–82. *Recreations:* gardening, photography, bird watching.

OWEN, David; *see* Owen, A. D.

OWEN, Rt. Hon. David Anthony Llewellyn, PC 1976; MP Plymouth, Devonport, since 1974 (Plymouth, Sutton, 1966–74) (Lab, 1966–81, SDP since 1981); Leader, Social Democratic Party, since 1983; *b* Plympton, South Devon, 2 July 1938; *s* of Dr John William Morris Owen and Mary Llewellyn; *m* 1968, Deborah Schabert; two *s* one *d. Educ:* Bradfield College; Sidney Sussex College, Cambridge (Hon. Fellow, 1977); St Thomas' Hospital. BA 1959; MB, BChir 1962; MA 1963. St Thomas' Hospital: house appts, 1962–64; Neurological and Psychiatric Registrar, 1964–66; Research Fellow, Medical Unit, 1966–68. Contested (Lab) Torrington, 1964. PPS to Minister of Defence, Administration, 1967; Parly Under-Sec. of State for Defence, for RN, 1968–70; Opposition Defence Spokesman, 1970–72, resigned over EEC, 1972; Parly Under-Sec. of State, DHSS, 1974; Minister of State: DHSS, 1974–76; FCO, 1976–77; Sec. of State for Foreign and Commonwealth Affairs, 1977–79; Opposition spokesman on energy, 1979–80. Sponsored 1973 Children's Bill; ministerially responsible for 1975 Children's Act. Co-founder, SDP, 1981; Chm., Parly Cttee, SDP, 1981–82; Dep. Leader, SDP, 1982–83. Chm., Decision Technology Internat., 1970–72. Member: Independent Commn on Disarmament and Security Issues, 1980–; Ind. Commn on Internat. Humanitarian Issues, 1983–. Governor of Charing Cross Hospital, 1966–68; Patron, Disablement Income Group, 1968–. Chairman of SW Regional Sports Council, 1967–71. *Publications:* (ed) A Unified Health Service, 1968; The Politics of Defence, 1972; In Sickness and in Health, 1976; Human Rights, 1978; Face the Future, 1981; A Future That Will Work, 1984; A United Kingdom, 1986; contrib. to Social Services for All, 1968; articles in Lancet, Neurology, Clinical Science, and Economic Affairs. *Recreation:* sailing. *Address:* 78 Narrow Street, Limehouse, E14. *T:* 01–987 5441; Trevean, George Lane, Plympton, Plymouth, Devon. *T:* Plymouth 336130; House of Commons, SW1. *T:* 01–219 5531.

OWEN, Dr David Elystan, CBE 1972; Director, Manchester Museum, 1957–76; *b* 27 Feb. 1912; *s* of Dr John Griffith Owen, Kingston-on-Thames, and Mrs Gertrude Owen (*née* Heaton); *m* 1936, Pearl Jennings, Leicester; one *s* one *d. Educ:* The Leys Sch., Cambridge; King's Coll., London Univ. 1st cl. hons BSc 1933, PhD 1935. Keeper, Dept of Geology, Liverpool Museum, 1935–47; War Service, 1939–45 in Artillery (Major, RA); Dir, Leeds City Museums, 1947–57. Treas. 1956–61, Pres. 1968–69, Museums Assoc. *Publications:* The Story of Mersey and Deeside Rocks, 1939; A History of Kirkstall Abbey, 1955; Water Highways, 1967; Water Rallies, 1969; Water Byways, 1973; Canals to Manchester, 1977; Cheshire Waterways, 1979; The Manchester Ship Canal, 1982; Exploring England by Canal, 1986; Staffordshire Waterways, 1986; numerous palaeontological papers in Palaeontology, Geological Jl, etc. *Recreation:* cruising the British canal and river system. *Address:* 9 Carleton Road, Higher Poynton, Cheshire. *T:* Poynton 872924.

OWEN, David Harold Owen; Registrar of the Privy Council, since 1983; *b* 24 May 1933; *er* twin *s* of late Lloyd Owen Owen and Margaret Glyn Owen, Machynlleth, Powys; *m* 1961, Ailsa Ransome Wallis; three *d. Educ:* Harrow Sch.; Gonville and Caius Coll., Cambridge. Called to the Bar, Gray's Inn, 1958. Served Royal Welch Fusiliers, 1951–53 (2nd Lieut). Campbell's Soups Ltd, King's Lynn, 1958–68; Lord Chancellor's Dept, 1969–80 (Private Sec. to Lord Chancellor, 1971–75); Chief Clerk, Judicial Cttee of Privy Council, 1980–83. *Recreations:* music, travel. *Address:* Judicial Committee of the Privy Council, Downing Street, SW1. *T:* 01–233 4846. *Club:* Reform.

OWEN, Maj.-Gen. David Lanyon Ll.; *see* Lloyd Owen.

OWEN, Rt. Rev. Edwin, MA; *b* 3 Nov. 1910; *s* of late William Rowland Owen; *m* 1940, Margaret Mary Williams, BA; one *s* one *d. Educ:* Royal School, Armagh; Trinity College, Dublin (MA). Deacon 1934, priest 1935, Dublin; Curate of Glenageary, 1934–36; Christ Church, Leeson Park, Dublin, 1936–38; Minor Canon of St Patrick's Cathedral, Dublin, 1935–36; Chancellor's Vicar, 1936–38; Succentor, 1938–42; Incumbent of Birr with Eglish, 1942–57; Canon, Killaloe Cathedral, 1954–57; Rector of Killaloe and Dean of Killaloe Cathedral, 1957–72; Diocesan Secretary of Killaloe and Kilfenora, 1957–72; Bishop of Killaloe, Kilfenora, Clonfert and Kilmacduagh, 1972–76, when diocese amalgamated with Limerick, Ardfert and Aghadoe, and Emly; Bishop of Limerick and Killaloe, 1976–81. *Recreation:* classical music. *Address:* 5 Frankfort Avenue, Rathgar, Dublin 6.

OWEN, Eric Hamilton; retired; *b* 4 Aug. 1903; *s* of Harold Edwin Owen and Hilda Guernsey; *m* 1937, Margaret Jeannie Slipper. Served Artists' Rifles, 1921–39; RASC, 8th Army, 1940–45; 21st SAS Regt (Artists), 1946–48 (despatches). Formerly: Chm., Charterhouse Investment Trust; Dep. Chm., Charterhouse Gp Ltd and Grindlays Bank Ltd. Dir, Gabbitas-Thring Educational Trust Ltd. Member Board of Trade Mission to Ghana, 1959. CBIM. *Recreations:* photography, travel. *Address:* 11 Broom Hall, Oxshott, Surrey. *Club:* Army and Navy.

OWEN, Dr Gareth, DSc; MRIA; FIBiol; Principal, University College of Wales, Aberystwyth, since 1979; Vice-Chancellor, University of Wales, 1985–Aug. 1987; *b* 4 Oct. 1922; *s* of J. R. and B. M. Owen; *m* 1953, Beti Jones; one *s* two *d. Educ:* Pontypridd Boys' Grammar Sch.; University Coll., Cardiff (BSc 1950; Fellow, 1982). DSc Glasgow, 1959. FIBiol 1964. Served War, RAF Pilot, 1942–47. Lectr in Zoology, Univ. of Glasgow, 1950–64; Prof. of Zool., 1964–79, and Pro-Vice-Chancellor, 1974–79, Queen's Univ. of Belfast. Welsh Supernumerary, Jesus Coll., Oxford, 1981–82 and 1986–87. Mem., Nature Conservancy Council, 1984– (Chm., Adv. Cttee for Wales, 1985–). MRIA 1976. Hon. Fellow, UCW, Cardiff, 1982; Hon. Mem. of the Gorsedd, 1983. Hon. DSc QUB, 1982. *Publications:* contrib. Trans Royal Soc., Proc. Malacol. Soc. London, Jl Mar. Biol. Soc., and

Qly Jl Micro. Sci. *Recreation:* photography. *Address:* Plas Penglais, Aberystwyth, Dyfed SY23 3DF. *T:* Aberystwyth 3583. *Club:* Royal Commonwealth Society.

OWEN, Gerald Victor; QC 1969; a Recorder of the Crown Court, since 1979; *b* London, 29 Nov. 1922; *m* 1946, Phyllis (*née* Ladsky); one *s* one *d. Educ:* Kilburn Grammar Sch.; St Catharine's Coll., Cambridge. Exhibr, St Catharine's Coll., Cambridge, 1940; Drapers' Company Science Schol., Queen Mary Coll., London, 1940. 1st cl. Maths Tripos I, 1941; Senior Optimes Tripos II, 1942; BA 1943, MA 1946, Cantab; Royal Statistical Soc. Certif., 1947; LLB London (Hons) 1949. Research Ballistics, Min. of Supply, 1942–45; Statistical Officer, LCC, 1945–49. Called to Bar, Gray's Inn, 1949; *ad eundem* Inner Temple, 1969. A Dep. Circuit Judge, 1971. Chairman: Dairy Produce Quota Tribunal, 1984–85; Medical Appeals Tribunal, 1984–. Member, Cttees of Justice on: Legal Aid in Criminal Cases; Complaints against Lawyers, 1970; False Witness, the problem of perjury, 1973. *Address:* 3 Paper Buildings, Temple, EC4. *T:* 01–353 1182. *Club:* Maccabaeans.

OWEN, Maj.-Gen. Harry, CB 1972; Chairman, Medical Appeal Tribunal, 1972–84; *b* 17 July 1911; *m* 1952, Maureen (*née* Summers); one *s* one *d. Educ:* University Coll., Bangor. BA Hons Philosophy, 1934. Solicitor of Supreme Court, 1939. Commissioned in Queen's Own Cameron Highlanders, 1940–43; joined Mil. Dept of Office of Judge Advocate General, 1943; served in: W Africa, 1945–46; Middle East, 1947–50; Austria, 1952–53; Dep. Dir of Army Legal Services: Far East, 1960–62; HQ, BAOR, 1962–67; Brig. Legal Staff, 1968–69; Maj.-Gen. 1969; Dir, Army Legal Services, 1969–71, retd. *Recreations:* philosophy, history of art, walking, gardening. *Address:* Clavering, 40 North Park, Gerrards Cross, Bucks. *T:* Gerrards Cross 886777.

OWEN, Sir Hugh (Bernard Pilkington), 5th Bt *cr* 1813; *b* 28 March 1915; *s* of Sir John Arthur Owen, 4th Bt and Lucy Fletcher (*d* 1985), *e d* of F. W. Pilkington; *S* father, 1973. *Educ:* Chillon Coll., Switzerland. *Heir:* *b* John William Owen [*b* 7 June 1917; *m* 1963, Gwenllian Mary, *er d* of late E. B. Phillips]. *Address:* 63 Dudsbury Road, Ferndown, Dorset.

OWEN, Sir Hugo Dudley C.; *see* Cunliffe-Owen.

OWEN, Idris Wyn; a director of a company in the construction industry; *b* 1912; *m. Educ:* Stockport Sch. and Coll. of Technology; Manchester Sch. of Commerce. Contested (C): Manchester Exchange, 1951; Stalybridge and Hyde, 1955; Stockport North 1966; MP (C) Stockport North, 1970–Feb. 1974; contested (C) Stockport North, Oct. 1974. Member, Stockport Borough Council, 1946; Mayor, 1962–63. Vice-Pres., Nat. Fedn of Building Trades Employers, 1965. FIOB. *Address:* Gawsworth Old Rectory, Cheshire.

OWEN, Hon. Sir John Arthur Dalziel, Kt 1986; **Hon. and Rt. Worshipful Mr Justice John Owen;** a Judge of the High Court of Justice, Queen's Bench Division, since 1986; Dean of the Arches Court of Canterbury and Auditor of the Chancery Court of York, since 1980; *b* 22 Nov. 1925; *s* of late R. J. Owen and Mrs O. B. Owen; *m* 1952, Valerie, *d* of W. Ethell; one *s* one *d. Educ:* Solihull Sch.; Brasenose Coll., Oxford. MA, BCL 1949. Commnd 2nd King Edward VII's Own Gurkha Rifles, 1944. Called to Bar, Gray's Inn, 1951, Bencher, 1980. Dep. Chm., Warwickshire QS, 1967–71; QC 1970; a Recorder, 1972–84; Dep. Leader, Midland and Oxford Circuit, 1980–84; a Circuit Judge, 1984–86. Mem. Senate of the Inns of Court and the Bar, 1977–80. Chm., West Midlands Area Mental Health Review Tribunal, 1972–80. Mem., General Synod of Church of England, Dio. Coventry, 1970–80; Chancellor, Dio. Derby, 1973–80, Dio. Coventry, 1973–80, Dio. Southwell, 1979–80. *Address:* Royal Courts of Justice, Strand, WC2; Lansdowne House, Shipston-on-Stour, Warwicks. *T:* Shipston-on-Stour 61521; 1 Verulam Buildings, Gray's Inn, WC1R 5LQ. *Club:* Garrick.

See also Dame J. A. D. Seccombe.

OWEN, Prof. John Benjamin Brynmor, DSc (Oxon), MSc (Wales); CEng; John William Hughes Professor of Civil Engineering, University of Liverpool, 1950–77, now Emeritus Professor; *b* 2 Sept. 1910; *s* of David Owen, (Degwyl), and Mary Alice Owen; *m* 1938, Beatrice Pearn (*née* Clark); two *d. Educ:* Universities of Oxford and Wales. Drapers Company Scholar, Page Prize and Medal, University College, Cardiff, 1928–31 (Fellow, 1981); Meyricke Scholar, Jesus Coll., Oxford, 1931–32; British Cotton Industry Research Association, 1933–35; Messrs A. V. Roe, Manchester, 1935–36; Royal Aircraft Establishment, Farnborough, 1936–48; Naval Construction Research Establishment, 1948–50. *Publications:* Light Structures, 1965; many contributions to learned journals on design of structures, on helicopters and on investigation of aircraft accidents. *Address:* Department of Civil Engineering, The University of Liverpool, PO Box 147, Brownlow Street, Liverpool L69 3BX. *T:* 051–709 6022.

OWEN, Col John Edward; Deputy Receiver, Metropolitan Police, since 1986; *b* 21 Aug. 1928; *s* of John and Mary Owen; *m* 1951, Jean Pendlebury; one *s* two *d. Educ:* Aberdare Grammar Sch.; Woolwich Polytechnic. CEng, FIEE, FIERE; FMS; FBIM; CDipAF. Commnd, REME, 1950; OC 6 Infantry Workshop, 1964–66; Commander: REME Sch. of Artillery, 1966–69; REME 1st Div., BAOR, 1969–71; Asst Dir, HQ DEME, 1971–72; Metropolitan Police: Dep. Chief Engr, 1972–76; Dir, Management Services, 1976; Chief Engr, 1976–86. *Recreations:* gardening, reading. *Address:* 9 St Catherine's Drive, Guildford GU2 5HE.

OWEN, John Gethin M.; *see* Morgan-Owen.

OWEN, John Halliwell, OBE 1975; HM Diplomatic Service; Counsellor, Foreign and Commonwealth Office, since 1986; *b* 16 June 1935; *e s* of late Arthur Llewellyn Owen, OBE and Doris Spencer (*née* Halliwell); *m* 1st, 1963 (marr. diss. 1971); one *s* one *d*; 2nd, 1972, Dianne Elizabeth (*née* Lowry); one *d. Educ:* Sedbergh School; The Queen's Coll., Oxford (Hastings Scholar). MA. 2nd Lieut, RA, 1954–56; HMOCS, Tanganyika Govt Service, 1960; Dist Officer, Provincial Administration, 1960–61; Dist Comr, 1962; Dist Magistrate and Regional Local Courts Officer, 1963–65; HM Foreign Service, 1966; Second Sec., Dar-es-Salaam, 1968–70; FCO, 1970–73; First Sec., Dacca, 1973–75; FCO 1976; First Sec., Accra, 1976–80; FCO, 1980–82; Counsellor, Pretoria, 1982–86. *Recreations:* music, travel, ornithology, conchology. *Address:* c/o Foreign and Commonwealth Office, SW1A 2AH. *Club:* Dar-es-Salaam Yacht.

OWEN, Maj.-Gen. John Ivor Headon, OBE 1963; UK Partnership Secretary to KMG Thomson McLintock, Chartered Accountants, since 1974 (the British Member of KMG, Klynveld Main Goerdeler, since 1979); *b* 22 Oct. 1922; *s* of Major William H. Owen; *m* 1948, Margaret Jean Hayes; three *d. Educ:* St Edmund's Sch., Canterbury. FBIM; psm, jssc, idc. Joined Royal Marines (as Marine), 1942; temp. 2nd Lieut RM, 1942; 44 Commando RM, Far East, 1942–46; demobilised 1946 (Captain RM); Constable, Metropolitan Police, 1946–47; rejoined Royal Marines as Lieut, 1947; regimental service, 1948–55; Staff Coll., Camberley, 1956; Bde Major, HQ 3 Cdo Bde, 1959–62; Naval Plans, Admty/MoD, 1962–64; 42 Cdo RM, 1964–66; Instructor, Jt Services Staff Coll., 1966–67; CO 45 Cdo RM, 1967–68 (despatches); Col GS, Staff of CGRM, 1969–70; Royal Coll. of Defence Studies, 1971–72; Maj.-Gen., Commando Forces RM, Plymouth, 1972–73. Lt-Col 1966; Col 1970; Maj.-Gen. 1972; Col Comdt, RM, 1983–84, Rep. Col Comdt, 1985–86. Chm. Exec. Cttee, Bowles Outdoor Pursuits Centre, 1984–; Treas., Clergy Orphan Corp.,

1980–; Mem., Ct of Assistants, Sons of the Clergy, 1981–; Chairman of Governors: St Edmund's Sch., Canterbury, 1980–; St Margaret's Sch., Bushey, 1980–. Editor, Current Military Literature, 1983–. *Publications:* Brassey's Infantry Weapons of the World, 1975; contrib. Seaford House Papers, 1971; articles in Contemporary Review and the press. *Recreations:* woodworking, gardening. *Address:* c/o Midland Bank, 89 Queen Victoria Street, EC4V 4AQ. *Club:* Army and Navy.

OWEN, John Simpson, OBE 1956; conservationist; *b* 1912; *s* of late Archdeacon Walter Edwin Owen and late Lucy Olive (*née* Walton); *m* 1946, May Patricia, *d* of late Francis Gilbert Burns and late May (*née* Malone); three *d. Educ:* Christ's Hospital; Brasenose Coll., Oxford. Sudan Political Service, 1936–55; Director of National Parks, Tanzania, 1960–70, Asst to Director, 1971; Consultant on National Parks in Eastern and Central Africa, 1972–74; Woodrow Wilson Internat. Centre for Scholars, Washington, DC, 1973; Council of the Fauna Preservation Soc., 1975–80. Hon. DSc (Oxon) 1971; World Wildlife Fund Gold Medal, 1971. *Publications:* papers and articles on National Parks and African Zoology. *Address:* 5 Calverley Park Crescent, Tunbridge Wells TN1 2NB. *T:* Tunbridge Wells 29485.

OWEN, Prof. John V.; *see* Vallance-Owen.

OWEN, Joslyn Grey, CBE 1979; Chief Education Officer, Devon, since 1972; *b* 23 Aug. 1928; *s* of W. R. Owen, (Bodwyn), and Nell Evans Owen; *m* 1961, Mary Patricia Brooks; three *s. Educ:* Cardiff High Sch.; Worcester Coll., Oxford (MA). Asst Master, Chigwell Sch., and King's Sch., Canterbury, 1952–58; Asst Educn Officer, Croydon, 1959–62, and Somerset, 1962–66; Jt Sec., Schs Council, 1966–68; Dep. Chief Educn Officer, Devon, 1968–72. Adviser, ACC and Council of Local Educn Authorities, 1977–. Pres., BAAS Educn Section, 1978–79; Chairman: Further Educn Unit, 1982–; IBA Educnl Adv. Council, 1982–86 (Vice-Chm., 1980–82); County Educn Officers' Soc., 1980–81; Member: Assessment of Perf. Unit Consultative Cttee, 1974–80; NFER Management Cttee, 1973–86; Council of Educnl Technol., 1972–82; Gulbenkian Working Party, Arts in the Curriculum, 1978–81; Macfarlane Working Party, 16–19 Educn, 1979–80; Educnl Research Board of SSRC, 1976–82; Nat. Adv. Bd for Local Auth. Higher Educn, 1982–; Nat. Joint Council, Further Education, 1980–84; Cttee for Academic Policy, CNAA, 1981–84. Mem. Council, Univ. of Exeter, 1976–. FRSA 1977; Hon. FCP 1979; Hon. Fellow Plymouth Polytechnic, 1981. OStJ 1985. *Publications:* The Management of Curriculum Development, 1973; chapters in edited works, papers and contribs to jls. *Recreation:* learning to garden. *Address:* 4 The Quadrant, Exeter, Devon EX2 4LE. *T:* Exeter 74326. *Club:* Reform.

OWEN, Prof. Paul Robert, CBE 1974; FRS 1971; FEng; Zaharoff Professor of Aviation, London University, at Imperial College of Science and Technology, 1963–84, now Emeritus Professor; *b* 24 Jan. 1920; *s* of Joseph and Deborah Owen; *m* 1958, Margaret Ann, *d* of Herbert and Dr Lily Baron; two *s* two *d. Educ:* Queen Mary Coll., London Univ. BSc (London) 1940, MSc (Manchester), FRAeS, FRMetS. Aerodynamics Dept, RAE, Farnborough, 1941–53; Reader and Director of Fluid Motion Laboratory, Manchester Univ., 1953–56; Professor of the Mechanics of Fluids and Director of the Laboratory, Manchester Univ., 1956–62. Vis. Prof., Univ. of Colorado, 1985–86. Member: ARC, 1964–67, 1969–80 (Chm., 1971–79); Safety in Mines Research Adv. Bd, 1956–73; Environmental Design Res. Cttee, DoE (Chm., 1973–); British Nat. Cttee for Theoretical and Applied Mechanics, 1971–78 (Chm., 1973–78); Construction and Housing Res. Adv. Council, 1976–80; Anglo-French Mixed Commn on Cultural Exchange, 1976–; Anglo-Italian Mixed Commn on Cultural Exchange, 1983–. Fellow, Queen Mary Coll., 1967. Founder Fellow, Fellowship of Engineering, 1976; Hon. FCGI 1983. Hon. Dr Aix-Marseille, 1976. *Publications:* papers on Aerodynamics in R & M series of Aeronautical Research Council, Journal of Fluid Mechanics, etc. *Recreations:* music, theatre. *Address:* 1 Stanley Lodge, 25 Stanley Crescent, W11 2NA. *T:* 01–229 5111.

OWEN, Peter Francis; Deputy Secretary, Housing and Construction, Department of the Environment, since 1986; *b* 4 Sept. 1940; *s* of Arthur Owen and Violet (*née* Morris); *m* 1963, Ann Preece; one *s* one *d. Educ:* The Liverpool Inst.; Liverpool Univ. (BA French). Joined MPBW, 1964; Cabinet Office, 1971–72; Private Sec. to successive Ministers of Housing and Construction, 1972–74; Asst Sec., Housing Policy Review, 1975–77, Local Govt Finance, 1977–80; Under Sec. and Regional Dir of Northern Yorks and Humberside Regs, Depts of the Environment and of Transport, 1980–82; Under Secretary: Rural Affairs, DoE, 1983; Local Govt Finance Policy, DoE, 1984–86. *Recreations:* reading, gardening, French language and literature. *Address:* Oakmead, The Avenue, Hampton, Mddx TW12 3RS. *T:* 01–979 3586.

OWEN, Philip Loscombe Wintringham, TD 1950; QC 1963; JP; *b* 10 Jan. 1920; *er s* of Rt Hon. Sir Wintringham Stable, MC, and late Lucie Haden (*née* Freeman); assumed surname of Owen in lieu of Stable by deed poll, 1942; *m* 1949, Elizabeth Jane, *d* of late Lewis Trelawny Widdicombe, Effingham, Surrey; three *s* two *d. Educ:* Winchester; Christ Church, Oxford (MA). Served War of 1939–45, Royal Welch Fusiliers: W Africa, India, Ceylon, Burma, 1939–47; Major TARO. Received into Roman Catholic Church, 1943. Called to Bar, Middle Temple, 1949; Bencher, 1969; Mem., Gen. Council of the Bar of England and Wales, 1971–77; a Deputy Chairman of Quarter Sessions: Montgomeryshire, 1959–71; Cheshire, 1961–71; Recorder of Merthyr Tydfil, 1971; a Recorder of the Crown Court, 1972–82; Leader, Wales and Chester Circuit, 1975–77. Chm., Adv. Bd constituted under Misuse of Drugs Act, 1974–. Legal Assessor to: Gen. Med. Council, 1970–; Gen. Dental Council, 1970–; RICS, 1970–. Contested (C) Montgomeryshire, 1945. JP Montgomeryshire, 1959; JP Cheshire, 1961. Vice-Pres., Montgomeryshire Cons. and Unionist Assoc.; Pres., Montgomeryshire Soc., 1974–75. Dir, Swansea City AFC Ltd. *Recreations:* shooting, fishing, forestry, music, Association football. *Address:* 1 Brick Court, Temple, EC4Y 9BY. *T:* 01–583 0777; Plas Llwyn Owen, Llanbrynmair, Powys SY19 7BE. *T:* Llanbrynmair 229. *Clubs:* Carlton, Pratt's; Cardiff and County; Welshpool and District Conservative; Bristol Channel Yacht (Mumbles).

See also R. O. C. Stable.

OWEN, Rear-Adm. Richard Arthur James, CB 1963; *b* 26 Aug. 1910; *s* of late Captain Leonard E. Owen, OBE, JP; *m* 1941, Jean Sophia (*née* Bluett); one *s* two *d. Educ:* Sevenoaks Sch. Joined RN, 1927; Commander (S) 1945; Captain, 1954; Rear-Admiral, 1961; Director-General, Personal Services, Admiralty, 1962–64; retired. *Address:* High Bank, Martin, near Fordingbridge, Hants. *T:* Martin Cross 295.

OWEN, Robert Davies, CBE 1962; FRCS; FRCSE; Senior Ear and Throat Surgeon, Cardiff Royal Infirmary, 1928–64, retired; Lecturer in Oto-Laryngology, Welsh National School of Medicine, 1929–64, retired; *b* 8 May 1898; 2nd *s* of late Capt. Griffith Owen and late Mrs Jane Owen; *m* 1928, Janet Miles, Llantrisant; two *d. Educ:* Towyn Grammar Sch. Cadet, Harrison Line, Liverpool, 1916–18; University College, Cardiff, 1918–21; Guy's Hospital, London, 1921–27. BSc (Wales) 1921. MRCS, LRCP 1923; FRCS 1930; FRCSEd 1926. *Publications:* contrib. BMJ, Lancet, Proc. Royal Society of Medicine. *Recreations:* shooting, fishing. *Address:* 1 The Mount, Cardiff Road, Llandaff, Cardiff. *T:* Cardiff 568739. *Club:* Cardiff and County.

OWEN, Robert Penrhyn; Director and Secretary, The Water Companies' Association, 1974–83, retired; *b* 17 Dec. 1918; *s* of late Captain Richard Owen; *m* 1949, Suzanne, *d* of late L. H. West; one *s* one *d. Educ:* Friar's School. War service in Royal Welch Fusiliers, 1939–46, in Madagascar, India, The Arakan and North and Central Burma. Admitted Solicitor, 1947. Asst Solicitor: Berks CC, 1948–50; Leics CC, 1950–54; Chief Asst Solicitor, Lancs CC, 1954–60; 2nd Dep. Clerk and 2nd Dep. Clerk of the Peace, Lancs CC, 1960–63; Gen. Manager, Telford Develt Corp. (New Town), 1963–69; Sec., Chief Exec. Officer and Solicitor, Thames Conservancy, 1969–74. *Recreations:* all sport, gardening, reading. *Address:* Pilgrims Wood, Fawley Green, Henley-on-Thames, Oxon RG9 6JF. *T:* Henley-on-Thames 572994. *Clubs:* MCC; Phyllis Court (Henley-on-Thames).

OWEN, Sir Ronald (Hugh), Kt 1980; Director, Prudential Assurance Co. Ltd, 1974–80 (Chairman, 1975–80); President, Prudential Corporation plc, since 1985 (Director, 1978–85; Chairman, 1978–80); *b* 2 June 1910; *er s* of late Owen Hugh Owen and late Jane Tegwedd Owen; *m* 1939, Claire May Tully; one *s. Educ:* King's College Sch., Wimbledon. FIA 1936. Served War of 1939–45: 52 Field Regt, RA (Major); Bde Major RA, 8 Ind. Division, Middle East and Italy. Joined Prudential, 1929: India, 1936–39; Dep. General Manager, 1959–67; Chief General Manager, 1968–73. Dep. Chm., British Insurance Assoc., 1971–72. Member, Governing Body, King's College Sch., Wimbledon (Chm., Finance Cttee, 1966–85). *Recreation:* golf. *Address:* 110 Rivermead Court, Hurlingham, SW6. *T:* 01–736 4842. *Clubs:* MCC, Hurlingham; Royal Wimbledon Golf.

OWEN, Rowland Hubert, CMG 1948; Deputy Controller, HM Stationery Office, 1959–64, retired; *b* 3 June 1903; *s* of William R. and Jessie M. Owen, Armagh, NI; *m* 1st, 1930, Kathleen Margaret Evaline Scott (*d* 1965); no *c*; 2nd, 1966, Shelagh Myrle Nicholson. *Educ:* Royal Sch., Armagh; Trinity Coll., Dublin (BA, LLB). Entered Dept of Overseas Trade, 1926; Private Secretary to Comptroller-General, 1930; Secretary Gorell Cttee on Art and Industry, 1931; idc, 1934; Commercial Secretary, Residency, Cairo, 1935; Ministry of Economic Warfare, 1939; Rep. of Ministry in Middle East, 1942; Director of Combined (Anglo-American) Economic Warfare Agencies, AFHQ, Mediterranean, 1943; transferred to Board of Trade and appointed Senior UK Trade Commissioner in India, Burma and Ceylon, 1944; Economic Adviser to UK High Commissioner in India, 1946; Adviser to UK Delegation at International Trade Conf., Geneva, 1947. Comptroller-General, Export Credits Guarantee Dept, 1953–58; Member Managing Cttee, Union d'Assureurs des Crédits Internationaux, 1954–58. Staff, NPFA, 1964–68. Vice-Chm., Haslemere Br., British Heart Foundn Appeal. Vice-President, Tilford Bach Society, 1962–69; Organist: St Mary's, Bramshott, 1964–70; St John the Evangelist, Farncombe, 1970–75; St Luke's, Grayshott, 1975–; Pres., Surrey Organists' Assoc., 1976, Secretary, 1977–83. US Medal of Freedom. *Publications:* Economic Surveys of India, 1949 and 1952; Insurance Aspects of Children's Playground Management, 1966; Children's Recreation: Statutes and Constitutions, 1967; miscellaneous church music miniatures. *Recreations:* music, theatre, gardening. *Address:* Oak Tree Cottage, Holdfast Lane, Haslemere, Surrey.

OWEN, Samuel Griffith, CBE 1977; MD, FRCP; Second Secretary, Medical Research Council, 1968–82, retired; *b* 3 Sept. 1925; *e s* of late Rev. Evan Lewis Owen and of Marjorie Lawton; *m* 1954, Ruth, *e d* of late Merle W. Tate, Philadelphia, Pa, USA; two *s* two *d. Educ:* Dame Allen's Sch.; Durham Univ. MB, BS Dunelm 1948; MRCP 1951; MD Dunelm 1954; FRCP 1965; clinical and research appts at Royal Victoria Infirmary, Newcastle upon Tyne, 1948–49 and 1950–53; RAMC, SMO, HM Troopships, 1949–50; Med. Registrar, Nat. Heart Hosp., 1953–54; Instr in Pharmacology, Univ. of Pennsylvania Sch. of Med., 1954–56; Reader in Med., Univ. of Newcastle upon Tyne, 1964–68 (First Asst, 1956, Lectr, 1960, Sen. Lectr, 1961); Hon. Cons. Physician, Royal Victoria Infirmary, Newcastle upon Tyne, 1960–68; Clin. Sub-Dean of Med. Sch., Univ. of Newcastle upon Tyne, 1966–68 (Academic Sub-Dean, 1964–66); Examr in Med., Univ. of Liverpool, 1966–68; Examr in Membership, RCP, 1967–68 and Mem., Research Cttee, RCP, 1968–76; Member: Brit. Cardiac Soc., 1962–82; Assoc. of Physicians of GB, 1965–; European Molec. Biol. Conf., 1971–82; European Molec. Biol. Lab., 1974–82; Exec. Council, European Science Foundn, 1974–78; Comité de la Recherche Médicale et de la Santé Publique, EEC, 1977–82; Scientific Coordinating Cttee, Arthritis and Rheumatism Council, 1978–82; NW Thames RHA, 1978–82. Consultant to WHO, SE Asia, 1966 and 1967–68; Commonwealth Fund Fellow, Univ. of Illinois, 1966; Fellow, Hunterian Soc., 1978. Chm., Feldberg Foundn, 1974–78; Governor, Queen Charlotte's Hosp. for Women, 1979–82. Liveryman, Soc. of Apothecaries, 1976–. *Publications:* Essentials of Cardiology, 1961 (2nd edn 1968); Electrocardiography, 1966 (2nd edn 1973); contribs to med. jls on heart disease, cerebral circulation, thyroid disease, med. research, etc. *Recreations:* chess, gastronomy. *Address:* 60 Bath Road, Chiswick, W4. *T:* 01–995 3228. *Club:* Royal Society of Medicine.

OWEN, Thomas Arfon; Director, Welsh Arts Council, since 1984; *b* 7 June 1933; *s* of late Hywel Peris Owen and Jennie Owen; *m* 1955, Joy (*née* Phillips); three *s* one *d. Educ:* Ystalyfera Grammar School; Magdalen College, Oxford. MA Oxon, MA Wales. Deputy Registrar, 1959, Registrar 1967, UCW Aberystwyth; Chm., Mid-Wales Hosp. Management Cttee, 1972–74; Member: East Dyfed Health Authy, 1982–84; S Glam Health Authy, 1984–; Consumers' Cttee for GB, 1975–; Vice-Chm., Coleg Harlech, 1984–. Vice-Pres., Llangollen Internat. Eisteddfod, 1984–; Mem., Gorsedd of Bards, Royal National Eisteddfod, 1984–. High Sheriff, Dyfed, 1976–77. *Publications:* articles in educ. jls. *Recreations:* the arts, crossword puzzles. *Address:* Welsh Arts Council, Museum Place, Cardiff CF1 3NX. *T:* Cardiff 394711. *Club:* Cardiff and County (Cardiff).

OWEN, Thomas Joseph, DL; Town Clerk, Nottingham, 1951–66; *b* 3 Nov. 1903; *s* of late Richard Owen, Sarn, Caernarvonshire; *m* 1935, Marjorie Ethel Tilbury (*d* 1985). Articled to late Sir Hugh Vincent, 1921–26; admitted a Solicitor, 1926; Asst Solicitor with Town Clerk, Stoke-on-Trent, 1926–27; Asst Solicitor, Leeds, 1927–30; Asst Solicitor, Brighton, 1930–36; Deputy Town Clerk, Nottingham, 1936–50. President: Nottinghamshire Law Society, 1957–58; Commn of Income Tax for Nottingham Dist. Trustee: Nottingham Roosevelt Travelling Scholarship Fund; Holbrook Trust (Painting and Sculpture). DL Notts, 1966. *Recreations:* watching Rugby football and cricket; travel abroad, reading. *Address:* Woodlands, Sherwood, Nottingham. *T:* Nottingham 61767. *Club:* United Services (Nottingham).

OWEN, Trevor Bryan; Managing Director, Remploy Ltd, since 1978; *b* 3 April 1928; *s* of Leonard Owen, CIE and Dilys (*née* Davies Bryan); *m* 1955, (Jennifer) Gaie (*née* Houston); one *s* one *d. Educ:* Rugby Sch.; Trinity Coll., Oxford (Scholar; MA). CBIM 1981; CIPM 1982. Sch. Student, British Sch. of Archaeology, Athens, 1953–54; ICI, 1955–78: wide range of jobs culminating in, successively: Chm., J. P. MacDougall Ltd; Dir, Paints, Agricl and Plastics Divs; Co. Personnel Manager. Member: Higher Educn Review Gp, Govt of NI, 1979–81; CNAA, 1973–79; Continuing Educn Adv. Council, BBC, 1977–85; Council, CBI, 1982–87; Council, Industrial Soc., 1967–; Council, Inst. of Manpower Studies, 1975–; Chm., Bd of Governors, Nat. Inst. for Social Work, 1985– (Mem., 1982–; Mem., Working Party on Role and Tasks of Social Workers, 1981–82).

Publications: Business School Programmes—the requirements of British manufacturing industry (with D. Casey and N. Huskisson), 1971; Making Organisations Work, 1978; The Manager and Industrial Relations, 1979; articles in jls. *Address:* 9 Rochester Terrace, NW1 9JN.

OWEN, Prof. Walter Shepherd, PhD, DEng; Professor of Physical Metallurgy, Emeritus, Massachusetts Institute of Technology; *b* 13 March 1920; *s* of Walter Lloyd and Dorothea Elizabeth Owen; *m*; one *d. Educ:* Alsop High Sch.; University of Liverpool. Metallurgist, D. Napier and Sons and English Electric Co., 1940–46; Asst Lecturer and Lecturer in Metallurgy, Univ. of Liverpool, 1946–54; Commonwealth Fund Fellow, Metallurgy Dept, Mass Inst. of Technol., 1951–52; on research staff, 1954–57, and Henry Bell Wortley Professor of Metallurgy, 1957–66, Univ. of Liverpool; Thomas R. Briggs Prof. of Engineering and Dir of Materials Science and Engineering, Cornell Univ., 1966–70; Dean of Technological Inst., Northwestern Univ., 1970–71; Vice Pres. for Science and Research, Northwestern Univ., 1971–73; Head of Dept, 1973–82, and Prof. of Physical Metallurgy, 1973–85, Mass Inst. of Technol. Mem., Nat. Acad. of Engineering, USA, 1977. *Publications:* papers in British and American journals on aspects of physical metallurgy. *Recreation:* sailing. *Address:* 16 Portview, Box 569A, Kennebunkport, Maine 04046, USA. *Club:* St Botolph (Boston).

OWEN-JONES, John Eryl, CBE 1969; JP; DL; Clerk of Caernarvonshire County Council, 1956–74, and Clerk of Lieutenancy; *b* 19 Jan. 1912; *s* of late John Owen-Jones, Rhydwenfa, Old Colwyn; *m* 1944, Mabel Clara, *d* of Grant McIlvride, Ajmer, Rajputana; one *s* one *d. Educ:* Portmadoc Grammar Sch.; University Coll. of Wales, Aberystwyth; Gonville and Caius Coll., Cambridge. LLB Wales 1933; MA Cantab 1939. Admitted Solicitor, 1938; Asst Solicitor, Chester Corp., 1939. Sqdn Ldr, RAFVR, 1945; Legal Staff Officer, Judge Advocate General's Dept, Mediterranean. Dep. Clerk, Caernarvonshire CC, 1946; Clerk of the Peace, Caernarvonshire, 1956–71; formerly: Sec., N Wales Combined Probation and After-Care Cttee; Dep. Clerk, Snowdonia Jt Adv. Cttee; Dep. Clerk, Gwynedd Police Authority, 1967. Member: Central Council, Magistrates' Cts Cttees, 1980–82; Bd, Civic Trust for Wales, 1982–. Hon. Sec., Caernarvonshire Historical Soc. Mem., Gorsedd of Royal National Eisteddfod of Wales. DL Caernarvonshire, 1971; JP 1974, DL 1974, Gwynedd. *Recreations:* music, gardening, photography. *Address:* Rhiw Dafnau, Caernarvon, Gwynedd. *T:* Caernarvon 3370. *Club:* National Liberal.

OWENS, Bernard Charles; Member, Monopolies and Mergers Commission, since 1981; Chairman and Managing Director, Bernard Owens & Partners Ltd, since 1962; *b* 20 March 1928; *s* of Charles A. Owens and late Sheila (*née* O'Higgins); *m* 1954, Barbara Madeline Murphy; two *s* four *d. Educ:* Solihull Sch.; London Sch. of Econs and Pol Science. Commnd 2nd Lieut, RASC, 1947; transf. RARO, 1949 (Lieut). Managing Director: Stanley Bros, 1962–67; Coronet Industrial Securities, 1965–67; Chairman: Unochrome Industries, 1964–79; Silverthorne Group, 1972–79; Director: Hobbs Savill & Bradford, 1957–62; Trinidad Sugar Estates, 1965–67; Local Dir, Alexander Stenhouse UK (formerly Reed Stenhouse UK), 1980–. Mem. of Lloyd's, 1978–. Dep. Chm., Metal Finishing Assoc., 1985– (Chm., 1982–85); Member: Cttee, Nat. Clayware Fedn, 1962–67; Council, British Jewellery and Giftware Fedn, 1981–. Mem., Solihull Council, 1953–63 (Chm., Finance Cttee, 1957–63); contested (C) Birmingham, Small Heath, 1959 and March 1961. Freeman, City of London, 1981; Liveryman, Worshipful Co. of Gardeners, 1982; Mem., HAC, 1984–. Governor, RNLI, 1984–. FRSA 1972; FRGS 1980; FZS 1980. Mem., SMO Malta, 1979. *Recreations:* painting, globe trotting, tennis, gardening. *Address:* The Vatch House, Stroud, Glos GL6 7JY. *T:* Stroud 3402. *Clubs:* Carlton, Wig and Pen, City Livery, City Livery Yacht, MCC; Stroud Rugby Football.

OWENS, Frank Arthur Robert, CBE 1971; Editor, Birmingham Evening Mail, 1956–74; Director, Birmingham Post & Mail Ltd, 1964–75; *b* 31 Dec. 1912; *s* of Arthur Oakes Owens; *m* 1st, 1936, Ruby Lilian Long; two *s*; 2nd, Olwen Evans, BSc; one *s* one *d. Educ:* Hereford Cathedral School. Served with RAF, 1940–46 (despatches). Member: Defence, Press and Broadcasting Cttee, 1964–75; Deptl Cttee on Official Secrets Act 1911, 1970–71; West Midlands Econ. Planning Council, 1975–77; Press Council, 1976–79. Pres., Guild of British Newspaper Editors, 1974–75. Hon. Mem., Mark Twain Soc. *Address:* 31 The Dreel, Edgbaston, Birmingham B15 3NS.

OWENS, Richard Hugh M.; *see* Mills-Owens.

OWER, Dr David Cheyne, TD 1975; Senior Principal Medical Officer, Department of Health and Social Security, since 1976; *b* 29 July 1931; *s* of Ernest Ower and Helen Edith Cheyne (*née* Irvine); *m* 1954, June Harris; two *s* two *d. Educ:* King's Coll. Sch., Wimbledon; King's Coll., London; King's Coll. Hosp. Med. Sch. (MB, BS 1954). DObstRCOG 1959; FFCM 1983 (MFCM 1976). Jun. hosp. appts, King's Coll. Hosp. and Kingston Hosp., 1955; RAF Med. Br., 1956–58; gen. practice, 1959–64; DHSS (formerly Min. of Health) Med. Staff, 1965–. T&AVR, and RAMC(V), 1962–; Lt-Col RAMC(V); CO 221 (Surrey) Field Amb., 1973–75. *Recreations:* music, bridge, thinking about playing golf. *Address:* Merlewood, 94 Coombe Lane West, Kingston-upon-Thames, Surrey. *T:* 01–942 8552.

OWO, The Olowo of; *see* Olagbegi II.

OXBURGH, Prof. Ernest Ronald, PhD; FRS 1978; Professor of Mineralogy and Petrology, University of Cambridge, since 1978; Head of Department of Earth Sciences, since 1980; President, Queens' College, Cambridge, since 1982; *b* 2 Nov. 1934; *m* Ursula Mary Brown; one *s* two *d. Educ:* Liverpool Inst.; Univ. of Oxford (BA 1957, MA 1960); Univ. of Princeton (PhD 1960). Departmental Demonstrator, 1960–61, Lectr in Geology, 1962–78, Univ. of Oxford; Fellow of St Edmund Hall, Oxford, 1964–78, Emeritus Fellow, 1978, Hon. Fellow, 1986; Fellow of Trinity Hall, Cambridge, 1978–82, Hon. Fellow, 1983. Vis. Professor: CIT, 1967–68; Stanford and Cornell Univs, 1973–74; Sherman Fairchild Distinguished Vis. Scholar, CIT, 1985–86. Pres., Eur. Union of Geosciences, 1985–. FGS; Fellow: Geol. Soc. of America; Amer. Geophys. Union. Hon. Mem., Geologists' Assoc.; Foreign Corresp., Geologische Bundesanstalt, Austria and of Geological Soc. of Vienna. Hon. Fellow, Univ. Coll., Oxford, 1983. Bigsby Medal, Geol Soc., 1979. *Publications:* The Geology of the Eastern Alps, 1968; (ed and contrib.) Structural, Metamorphic and Geochronological Studies in the Eastern Alps, 1971; contribs to Nature, Jl Geophys Res. *Recreations:* mountaineering, reading, theatre. *Address:* Department of Earth Sciences, Downing Street, Cambridge CB2 3EQ. *T:* Cambridge 333400.

OXBURY, Harold Frederick, CMG 1961; Deputy Director-General, British Council, 1962–66 (Assistant Director-General, 1959); *b* 11 Nov. 1903; *s* of Fredric Thomas Oxbury; *m* 1st, 1928, Violet Bennets (*d* 1954); one *s* one *d*; 2nd, 1954, Helen Shipley (*d* 1975), *d* of Amos Perry, FLS, VMH. *Educ:* Norwich Sch.; Trinity Coll., Cambridge (Senior Scholar). Entered Indian Civil Service, 1928; Chief Collector of Customs, Burma, 1940; Government of Burma Representative, Burma Office, 1942–44; Dep. Controller Finance (Colonel), Military Administration, Burma, 1945; Finance Secretary, Government of Burma, 1946; British Council: Director, Colonies Dept, 1947; Controller Finance, 1956. *Publications:* (ed) Concise Dictionary of National Biography 1901–1970, 1982; Great Britons: twentieth century lives, 1985; contribs to biographical works. *Recreations:* gardening, writing, painting. *Address:* Huntersmoon, Horton-cum-Studley, Oxon. *Club:* East India and Sports.

OXFORD, Bishop of; *no appointment at time of going to press.*

OXFORD, Archdeacon of; *see* Weston, Ven. F. V.

OXFORD AND ASQUITH, 2nd Earl of, *cr* 1925; **Julian Edward George Asquith,** KCMG 1964 (CMG 1961); Viscount Asquith, *cr* 1925; Governor and Commander-in-Chief, Seychelles, 1962–67; Commissioner, British Indian Ocean Territory, 1965–67; *b* 22 April 1916; *o s* of late Raymond Asquith and Katharine Frances (*d* 1976), *d* of late Sir John Horner, KCVO; *S* grandfather, 1928; *m* 1947, Anne Mary Celestine, CStJ, *d* of late Sir Michael Palairet, KCMG; two *s* three *d. Educ:* Ampleforth; Balliol Coll., Oxford (Scholar), 1st Class Lit. Hum., 1938. Lieut, RE, 1941; Assistant District Commissioner, Palestine, 1942–48; Dep. Chief Secretary, British Administration, Tripolitania, 1949; Director of the Interior, Government of Tripolitania, 1951; Adviser to Prime Minister of Libya, 1952; Administrative Secretary, Zanzibar, 1955; Administrator of St Lucia, WI, 1958. KStJ. *Heir: s* Viscount Asquith, *qv. Address:* The Manor House, Mells, Frome, Somerset. *T:* Mells 812324. *Club:* Naval and Military.
See also Baron Hylton.

OXFORD, Kenneth Gordon, CBE 1981; QPM 1976; Chief Constable, Merseyside Police, since 1976; *b* Lambeth, 25 June 1924; *s* of Ernest George Oxford and late Gladys Violet (*née* Seaman); *m* 1954, Muriel (*née* Panton). *Educ:* Caldecot Sch., Lambeth. RAF, Bomber Comd, SEAC, 1942–47. Metropolitan Police, 1947–69, with final rank Det. Ch. Supt, following Intermed. Comd Course, 1966, Sen. Staff Course, 1968, The Police Coll., Bramshill; Asst Chief Constable (Crime), Northumberland Constabulary, 1969; Northumbria Police, 1974; Dep. Chief Constable, Merseyside Police, 1974–75. Member: Forensic Science Soc., 1970; Medico-Legal Soc., 1975; Chairman: Crime Cttee, Assoc. of Chief Police Officers of Eng., Wales and NI, 1977–83; Jt Standing Cttee on Police Use of Firearms, 1979–; Anti-Terrorist Cttee, 1982–; Rep., ICPO (Interpol), 1983–86; President: NW Police Benevolent Fund, 1978–; Assoc. of Chief Police Officers of England, Wales and NI, 1982–83. Pres., Merseyside Br., BIM, 1983– (Chm., 1978–81; Vice-Chm., 1975–78); CBIM 1980. Merseyside County Dir, St John Ambulance Assoc., 1976–84 (Vice Pres., 1985). Freeman, City of London, 1983. FRSA 1983. OStJ 1977. *Publications:* contrib. articles and papers to prof. papers on crime and kindred matters. *Recreations:* shooting, cricket, music, books, roses. *Address:* Chief Constable's Office, PO Box 59, Liverpool L69 1JD. *T:* 051–709 6010. *Clubs:* Royal Commonwealth Society; Surrey CC, Lancashire CC, Liverpool St Helens Rugby Football.

OXFUIRD, 13th Viscount of, *cr* 1651; **George Hubbard Makgill;** Bt 1627; Lord Macgill of Cousland, 1651; *b* 7 Jan. 1934; *s* of Richard James Robert Haldane Makgill, RNZAF (*d* 1948) (*yr s* of 11th Bt) and Elizabeth Lyman (*d* 1981), *d* of Gorham Hubbard, Boston, USA; *S* uncle, 1986; *m* 1st, 1967, Alison Campbell (marr. diss. 1977), *er d* of late Neils Max Jensen, Randers, Denmark; three *s* (inc. twin *s*); 2nd, 1980, Valerie Cunitia Mary, *o d* of Major Charles Anthony Steward, Crondall, Farnham, Surrey; one *s. Educ:* St Peter's School, Cambridge, NZ; Wanganui Collegiate School. Commissioned RAF, 1955–58. *Recreations:* fishing, gardening, shooting. *Heir: s* Master of Oxfuird, *qv. Address:* Hill House, St Mary Bourne, Andover, Hants. *Club:* Caledonian.

OXFUIRD, Master of; Hon. Ian Arthur Alexander Makgill; *b* 14 Oct. 1969; *s* and *heir* of 13th Viscount of Oxfuird, *qv.*

OXLADE, Zena Elsie, CBE 1984; SRN, RNT; Regional Nursing Officer, East Anglian Regional Health Authority, since 1981; *b* 26 April 1929; *d* of James and Beatrice May Oxlade. *Educ:* Latymer Grammar Sch., N9. SRN 1950; RNT (London Univ.). Ward Sister, 1952; Theatre Sister 1953; Night Sister, 1954; Sister Tutor, 1956; Principal Tutor, 1963; Principal Nursing Officer, 1969; Chief Nursing Officer, 1973; District Nursing Officer, 1974; Area Nursing Officer, Suffolk AHA, 1978–81. Chm., GNC, 1977–83 (Mem., 1975–83); Mem., UK Council for Nurses, Midwives and Health Visitors, 1983–. *Publication:* Ear, Nose and Throat Nursing, 1972. *Recreations:* motoring, reading, handicrafts. *Address:* (home) 5 Morgan Court, Old Ipswich Road, Claydon, Suffolk IP6 0AB. *T:* Ipswich 831895; (office) East Anglian Regional Health Authority, Union Lane, Chesterton, Cambridge CB4 1RF. *T:* Cambridge 61212.

OXLEY, Humphrey Leslie Malcolm, CMG 1966; OBE 1956; HM Diplomatic Service, retired; *b* 9 Oct. 1909; *s* of W. H. F. Oxley, MRCS, LRCP, FRCOG, and Lily Malcolm; *m* 1945, Frances Olga, *d* of George Bowden, San Jose, Costa Rica; twin *s. Educ:* Epsom Coll. Admitted Solicitor, 1933; Junior Legal Assistant, India Office, 1933; Commissioner for Oaths, 1934; Assistant Solicitor, 1944; Commonwealth Relations Office, 1947; Assistant Legal Adviser, 1961; Legal Counsellor, Commonwealth Office, 1965–67; HM Diplomatic Service, 1967; Dep. Legal Adviser, FCO, 1967–69. Legal Consultant to HM Comr, Magistrate, various legal appts, Anguilla, 1971–72. *Recreations:* sailing, gardening. *Address:* Sandpipers, Crooked Lane, Birdham, Chichester, West Sussex. *Club:* Civil Service.

OXLEY, James Keith R.; *see* Rice-Oxley.

OXMANTOWN, Lord; Laurence Patrick Parsons; *b* 31 March 1969; *s* and *heir* of Earl of Rosse, *qv.*

OZAWA, Seiji; Japanese conductor; Music Director, Boston Symphony Orchestra, since 1973; *b* Shenyang, China, 1 Sept. 1935; 3rd *s* of Kaisaku and Sakura Ozawa; *m* 1st, Kyoko Edo; 2nd, Vera Ilyan; one *s* one *d. Educ:* Toho School of Music, Tokyo; studied with Hideo Saito, Eugène Bigot, Herbert von Karajan, Leonard Bernstein. Won Besançon Internat. Comp., 1959, Koussevitsky Meml Scholarship, 1960. Asst Conductor, NY Philharmonic Orch., 1961–62 and 1964–65; music dir, Ravinia Fest., Chicago, 1964–69; conductor, Toronto Symph. Orch., 1965–69; music dir, San Francisco Symph. Orch., 1970–76, music advisor, 1976–77; Artistic Dir, Tanglewood Fest., 1970–73. Tours with Boston Symphony Orchestra: Europe, 1976 and 1982; Japan, 1978; China (musical and cultural exchange), 1979; European music festivals, 1979 and 1984; 14 USA cities (orchestra's hundredth birthday), 1982; Japan, 1982 and 1986. Guest conductor with major orchestras in Canada, Europe, Far East and USA. Opera highlights: La Scala, Milan; Covent Garden, London; Paris Opera (incl. world première of Messiaen's Saint François d'Assise); many recordings (awards). *Address:* c/o Ronald A. Wilford, Columbia Artists Management Inc. Conductors Division, 165 West 57th Street, New York, USA; c/o Harold Holt Ltd, 31 Sinclair Road, W14.

P

PÄCHT, Otto Ernst, MA, DPhil; FBA 1956; Professor in the History of Art, and Director of the Kunsthistorisches Institut, Vienna University, 1963–72, now Professor Emeritus; *b* Vienna, 7 Sept. 1902; *s* of David and Josephine Pächt; *m* 1940, Jeanne Michalopulo (*d* 1971); one *s*. *Educ:* Vienna and Berlin Universities. Lecturer in History of Art: Heidelberg Univ., 1933; Oriel Coll., Oxford, 1945. Senior Lecturer in Medieval Art, 1952, Reader, 1962, Oxford Univ. Lyell Reader, Oxford, 1971. Membre de la Société Archéologique française. Wirkl. Mitgl. Oesterr. Akad. d. Wissenschaft, 1967. Hon. DLitt Oxon, 1971. *Publications:* Oesterreichische Tafelmalerei der Gotik, 1929; Master of Mary of Burgundy, 1948; The St Albans Psalter, 1960; The Rise of Pictorial Narrative in Twelfth-century England, 1962; Vita Sancti Simperti, 1964; (ed with J. J. G. Alexander) Illuminated Manuscripts in the Bodleian Library, 1973; (ed with D. Thoss) Illuminated Manuscripts in the Austrian National Library, French School, 1974–77; (ed with U. Jenni) Illuminated Manuscripts in the Austrian National Library, Dutch School, 1975; Methodisches zur kunsthistorischen Praxis, 1977; (ed with U. Jenni and D. Thoss) Illuminated Manuscripts in the Austrian National Library, Flemish School I, 1983; contribs to Kritische Berichte, Kunstwissenschaftliche Forschungen, Burlington Magazine, Journal of the Warburg Institute, Revue des Arts, Jahrbuch der Kunsthistorischen Sammlungen Wien, Pantheon, Revue de l'Art, Gazette des Beaux-Arts. *Address:* Pötzleinsdorferstrasse 66, 1180 Vienna, Austria.

PACK, Prof. Donald Cecil, CBE 1978 (OBE 1969); MA, DSc, FIMA, FEIS, FRSE; Professor of Mathematics, University of Strathclyde, Glasgow, 1953–82, Hon. Professor, 1982–86, Professor Emeritus, 1986 (Vice-Principal, 1968–72); *b* 14 April 1920; *s* of late John Cecil and late Minnie Pack, Higham Ferrers; *m* 1947, Constance Mary Gillam; two *s* one *d*. *Educ:* Wellingborough School; New Coll., Oxford. Lecturer in Mathematics, University College, Dundee, University of St Andrews, 1947–52; Visiting Research Associate, University of Maryland, 1951–52; Lecturer in Mathematics, University of Manchester, 1952–53. Guest Professor: Technische Universität, Berlin, 1967; Bologna Univ. and Politenico Milano, 1980; Technische Hochschule Darmstadt, 1981; other vis. appts at Warsaw Univ., 1977, Kaiserslautern, 1980, 1984. Member: Dunbartonshire Educn Cttee, 1960–66; Gen. Teaching Council for Scotland, 1966–73; Chairman: Scottish Certificate of Educn Examn Bd, 1969–77; Cttee of Inquiry into Truancy and Indiscipline in Schools in Scotland, 1974–77; Member: various Govt Scientific Cttees, 1952–84; British Nat. Cttee for Theoretical and Applied Mechanics, 1973–78; Council, Gesellschaft für Angewandte Mathematik und Mechanik, 1977–83; Council, RSE, 1960–63; Scottish Arts Council, 1980–85; Founder Chm., NYO of Scotland, 1978–; Mem., European Music Year UK Cttee (Chm., Scottish Sub-Cttee), 1982–86; First Hon. Treasurer, IMA, 1964–72; Governor, Hamilton Coll. of Education, 1977–81; Pres., Milngavie Music Club, 1983–. *Publications:* papers on fluid dynamics. *Recreations:* music, gardening, golf. *Address:* 18 Buchanan Drive, Bearsden, Glasgow. *T:* 041–942 5764.

PACKARD, Lt-Gen. Sir (Charles) Douglas, KBE 1957 (CBE 1945; OBE 1942); CB 1949; DSO 1943; retired as GOC-in-C Northern Ireland Command, 1958–61; *b* 17 May 1903; *s* of late Capt. C. T. Packard, MC, Copdock, near Ipswich; *m* 1st, 1937, Marion Lochhead (*d* 1981); one *s* two *d*; 2nd, 1982, Mrs Patricia Miles Sharp. *Educ:* Winchester; Royal Military Academy, Woolwich. 2nd Lieut, RA, 1923; served War of 1939–45, in Middle East and Italy (despatches, OBE, DSO, CBE); Dep.-Chief of Staff, 15th Army Group, 1944–45; Temp. Maj.-Gen. and Chief of Staff, Allied Commission for Austria (British Element), 1945–46; Director of Military Intelligence, WO, 1948–49; Commander British Military Mission in Greece, 1949–51; Chief of Staff, GHQ, MELF, 1951–53; Vice-Quarter-Master-General War Office, 1953–56; Military Adviser to the West African Governments, 1956–58. Lt-Gen. 1957. Col Comdt, RA, 1957–62. Officer Legion of Merit (USA). *Recreations:* sailing, bird-watching. *Address:* Park Side, Lower Road, Ufford, Woodbridge, Suffolk IP13 6DL. *T:* Eyke 460418.

PACKARD, Vance (Oakley); Author; *b* 22 May 1914; *s* of Philip and Mabel Packard; *m* 1938, Mamie Virginia Mathews; two *s* one *d*. *Educ:* Pennsylvania State Univ.; Columbia Univ. Reporter, The Boston Record, 1938; Feature Editor, The Associated Press, 1939–42; Editor and Staff Writer, The American Magazine, 1942–56; Staff writer, Colliers, 1956; Distinguished Alumni Award, Pennsylvania State University, 1961; Outstanding Alumni Award, Columbia University Graduate School of Journalism, 1963. LittD Monmouth Coll., 1974. *Publications:* (books on social criticism): The Hidden Persuaders, 1957; The Status Seekers, 1959; The Waste Makers, 1960; The Pyramid Climbers, 1962; The Naked Society, 1964; The Sexual Wilderness, 1968; A Nation of Strangers, 1972; The People Shapers, 1977; Our Endangered Children, 1983; numerous articles for The Atlantic Monthly. *Recreations:* reading, boating. *Address:* Mill Road, New Canaan, Conn 06840, USA. *T:* WO 6–1707.

PACKER, Kerry Francis Bullmore, AC 1983; Chairman and Managing Director: Consolidated Press Holdings Ltd, since 1974; Publishing and Broadcasting Ltd, since 1974; Chairman, Australian Consolidated Press Ltd, since 1974; Director, General Television Corporation Ltd, since 1974; *b* 17 Dec. 1937; *s* of late Sir Douglas Frank Hewson Packer, KBE, and Lady (Gretel Joyce) Packer (*née* Bullmore); *m* 1963, Roslyn Redman Weedon; one *s* one *d*. *Educ:* Cranbrook Sch., Sydney, NSW; Geelong C of E Grammar Sch., Vic. Trainee Exec., Aust. Consolidated Press and Conpress Printing, 1955. *Recreations:* golf, tennis, shooting, cricket. *Address:* 54 Park Street, Sydney, NSW 2000, Australia. *T:* (02) 268–0666. *Clubs:* Athenæum (Melbourne); Royal Sydney Golf, Australian Golf, Elanora Country, Tattersall's (NSW).

PACKER, Richard John; Under Secretary, Food, Drink, Marketing Policy Group, Ministry of Agriculture, Fisheries and Food, since 1985; *b* 18 Aug. 1944; *s* of George Charles Packer and Dorothy May Packer (*née* Reynolds); *m* 1st, Alison Mary Sellwood; two *s* one *d*; 2nd, Lucy Jeanne Blackett-Ord (*née* Neville-Rolfe); two *s*. *Educ:* City of London School; Manchester Univ. (BSc 1965, MSc 1966). MAFF, 1967; 1st Sec., Office of Perm Rep. to EEC, 1973–76; Principal Private Sec. to Minister, 1976–78; Asst Sec., 1979. Non-exec. Dir, ABM Chemicals (Stockport), 1985–. *Recreation:* living intensely. *Address:* Ministry of Agriculture, Fisheries and Food, Whitehall Place, SW1. *T:* 01–233 4420.

PADMORE, Elaine Marguirite; Artistic Director, Wexford Festival Opera, since 1982; Announcer, Radio 3, since 1982; *b* Haworth, Yorks, 3 Feb. 1947; *d* of Alfred and Florence Padmore. *Educ:* Newland High Sch., Hull; Arnold Sch., Blackpool; Birmingham Univ. (MA; BMus); Guildhall Sch. of Music; LTCL. Liberal Studies Lectr, Croydon and Kingston Colls of Art, 1968–70; Books Editor, OUP Music Dept, 1970–71; Producer, BBC Music Div., 1971–76. Major BBC Radio 3 series include: Parade, Music of Tchaikovsky's Russia, England's Pleasant Land, Journal de mes Mélodies; Presenter of numerous programmes, incl. Festival Comment, Edinburgh Fest., 1973–81; Chief Producer, Opera, BBC Radio, 1976–83: series incl. complete operas of Richard Strauss and first performances of works by Delius and Havergal Brian; active as professional singer (soprano), particularly of opera; Lectr in Opera, RAM, 1979–83. Hon. ARAM. Hungarian Radio Pro Musica Award for prog. Summertime on Bredon, 1973; Prix Musical de Radio Brno for prog. The English Renaissance, 1974; Sunday Independent Award for services to music in Ireland, 1985. *Publications:* Wagner (Great Composers' Series), 1970; Music in the Modern Age: chapter on Germany, 1973; contributor to: New Grove Dict. of Music, Proc. of Royal Musical Assoc., Music and Letters, The Listener. *Recreations:* gardening, travel, art exhibitions. *Address:* 11 Lancaster Avenue, Hadley Wood, Barnet, Herts EN4 0EP. *T:* 01–449 5369.

PADMORE, Sir Thomas, GCB 1965 (KCB 1953; CB 1947); MA; FCIT; *b* 23 April 1909; *e s* of Thomas William Padmore, Sheffield; *m* 1st, 1934, Alice (*d* 1963), *d* of Robert Alcock, Ormskirk; two *d* (one *s* decd); 2nd, 1964, Rosalind Culhane, *qv*. *Educ:* Central Sch., Sheffield; Queens' Coll., Cambridge (Foundation Scholar; Hon. Fellow, 1961). Secretaries' Office, Board of Inland Revenue, 1931–34; transferred to Treasury, 1934; Principal Private Secretary to Chancellor of Exchequer, 1943–45; Second Secretary, 1952–62; Permanent Sec., Min. of Transport, 1962–68. Dir, Laird Gp Ltd, 1970–79; Dep. Chm., Metropolitan Cammell Ltd, 1969–80. Chairman: Rehearsal Orchestra, 1961–71; Handel Opera Soc., 1963–86. Hon. Treas., Inst. of Cancer Res., 1973–81. *Address:* 39 Cholmeley Crescent, Highgate, N6. *T:* 01–340 6587. *Club:* Reform.

PADMORE, Lady (Thomas); *see* Culhane, Rosalind.

PADOVAN, John Mario Faskally; Head of Corporate Finance, Barclays de Zoete Wedd Ltd, since 1986; *b* 7 May 1938; *s* of Umberto Mario Padovan and Mary Nina Liddon Padovan; *m* 1984, Sally Kay (*née* Anderson); three *s*. *Educ:* St George's College, Weybridge; King's College London (LLB); Keble College, Oxford (BCL). FCA. County Bank, 1970–84: Dir, 1971; Dep. Chief Exec., 1974; Chief Exec., 1976; Chm., 1984; Dep. Chm., Hambros Bank and Dir, Hambros, 1984–86. Director: Tesco, 1982–; M. S. Instruments, 1985–. *Recreations:* golf, squash, walking. *Address:* White House, Church Road, Milford, Surrey GU8 5JB. *T:* Godalming 5728. *Club:* West Surrey Golf.

PAFFARD, Rear-Admiral (retired) Ronald Wilson, CB 1960; CBE 1943; *b* Ludlow, 14 Feb. 1904; 4th *s* of Murray Paffard and Fanny (*née* Wilson); *m* 1933, Nancy Brenda Malim; one *s* one *d*. *Educ:* Maidstone Grammar Sch. Paymaster Cadetship in RN, 1922; Paymaster Commander, 1940; Captain (S), 1951; Rear-Admiral, 1957. Secretary to Adm. of the Fleet Lord Tovey in all his Flag appointments, including those throughout the War of 1939–45; Supply Officer of HMS Vengeance, 1946–48; Portsmouth Division, Reserve Fleet, 1948–50; HMS Eagle, 1950–51; Asst Director-General, Supply and Secretarial Branch, 1952–54; Commanding Officer, HMS Ceres, 1954–56; Chief Staff Officer (Administration) on staff of Commander-in-Chief, Portsmouth, 1957–60, retired. *Recreations:* painting, golf. *Address:* 2 Little Green Orchard, Alverstoke, Hants PO12 2EY.

PAFFORD, John Henry Pyle, MA, DLit (London); FSA; FLA; Goldsmiths' Librarian of the University of London, 1945–67; *b* 6 March 1900; *s* of John Pafford and Bessie (*née* Pyle); *m* 1941, Elizabeth Ford, *d* of R. Charles Ford and Margaret Harvey; one *d* (and one *d* decd). *Educ:* Trowbridge High Sch.; University Coll., London (Fellow, 1956). Library Asst, University College, London, 1923–25; Librarian, and Tutor, Selly Oak Colleges, 1925–31 (Hon. Fellow 1985); Sub-Librarian, National Central Library, 1931–45; Lecturer at University of London School of Librarianship, 1937–61. Editor, Year's Work in Librarianship, 1935–38 (jointly), and 1939–46; Library Adviser, Inter-Univ. Council for Higher Education Overseas, 1960–68. *Publications:* Bale's King Johan, 1931, and The Sodder'd Citizen, 1936 (Malone Society); Library Co-operation in Europe, 1935; Accounts of Parliamentary Garrisons of Great Chalfield and Malmesbury, 1645–46, 1940; Books and Army Education, 1946; W. P. Ker, A Bibliography, 1950; The Winter's Tale (Arden Shakespeare), 1963; Watts's Divine Songs for Children, 1971; L. Bryskett's Literary Works, 1972; (with E. R. Pafford) Employer and Employed, 1974. *Address:* Hillside, Allington Park, Bridport, Dorset DT6 5DD. *T:* Bridport 22829.

PAGE, family name of **Baron Whaddon.**

PAGE, Sir Alexander Warren, (Sir Alex Page), Kt 1977; MBE 1943; Chairman: Paine & Co. Ltd, since 1981; PFC International Portfolio Fund Ltd, since 1985; *b* 1 July 1914; *s* of Sydney E. Page and Phyllis (*née* Spencer); *m* 1st, 1940, Anne Lewis Hickman (marr. diss.); two *s* one *d*; 2nd, 1981, Mrs Andrea Mary Wharton. *Educ:* Tonbridge; Clare Coll., Cambridge (MA). Served REME, with Guards Armoured Div., 1940–45, Lt-Col REME. Joined The Metal Box Co. Ltd, 1936; joined board as Sales Dir, 1957; Man. Dir 1966;

Dep. Chm. 1969; Chief Exec., 1970–77; Chm., 1970–79. Director: J. Lyons & Co. Ltd, Feb.-Oct. 1978; C. Shippam Ltd, 1979–85; Chairman: Electrolux, 1978–82; G. T. Pension Services Ltd, 1981–85. Mem., IBA (formerly ITA), 1970–76; Mem., Food Science and Technology Bd, 1973–. Pres., BFMIRA, 1980. FIMechE; CBIM. Governor, Colfe's Grammar Sch., Lewisham, 1977–. *Recreations:* golf, tennis. *Address:* 2 Montagu Square, W1. *T:* 01–935 9894; Merton Place, Dunsfold, Godalming, Surrey. *T:* Dunsfold 211.

PAGE, Ven. Alfred Charles; Archdeacon of Leeds, 1969–81, now Archdeacon Emeritus; *b* 24 Dec. 1912; *s* of late Henry Page, Homersfield, Suffolk; *m* 1944, Margaret Stevenson, *d* of late Surtees Foster Dodd, Sunderland, Co. Durham. *Educ:* Bungay Grammar Sch.; Corpus Christi Coll., Cambridge (MA); Wycliffe Hall, Oxford. Curate: Wortley-de-Leeds, 1936; Leeds Parish Church, 1940 (Sen. Curate and Priest-in-charge of S Mary, Quarry Hill, 1941); Vicar: St Mark, Woodhouse, Leeds, 1944; Rothwell, Yorks, 1955. Rural Dean of Whitkirk, 1961–69; Surrogate, 1963; Hon. Canon of Ripon, 1966; Vicar of Arthington, 1969–73. *Recreation:* photography. *Address:* 602 King Lane, Alwoodley Park, Leeds LS17 7AN. *T:* Leeds 696458.

PAGE, Col Alfred John, CB 1964; TD 1945; DL; Chairman, TA&VR Association for Greater London, 1968–71 (Chairman, County of London T&AFA, 1957–68); *b* 3 January 1912; *s* of Harry Gould Page, Surbiton, Surrey; *m* 1941, Sheila Margaret Aileen (marr. diss. 1966), *d* of Charles Skinner Wilson, Ugley, Essex; one *s* two *d*; *m* 1969, Margaret Mary Juliet Driver (*d* 1985), *widow* of Harold Driver. *Educ:* Westminster School. 2nd Lt 19th London Regt (TA), 1931. Served 1939–45 with RA in AA Comd. Brevet Colonel 1952; ADC (TA) to the Queen, 1961–66; Hon. Col, Greater London Regt RA (Territorials), 1967–71; Dep. Hon. Col, 6th Bn, Queen's Regt, T&AVR, 1971–72. Master, Worshipful Co. of Pattenmakers, 1973–74. DL Co. of London, 1951; DL Greater London, 1965. *Address:* 66 Iverna Court, W8. *T:* 01–937 2590. *Club:* Army and Navy.

PAGE, Annette, (Mrs Ronald Hynd); Ballerina of the Royal Ballet until retirement, 1967; Ballet Mistress, Ballet of the Bayerischestaatsoper, Munich, 1984–86; *b* 18 Dec. 1932; *d* of James Lees and Margaret Page; *m* 1957, Ronald Hynd, *qv*; one *d*. *Educ:* Royal Ballet School. Audition and award of scholarship to Roy. Ballet Sch., 1944. Entry into touring company of Royal Ballet (then Sadler's Wells Theatre Ballet), 1950; promotion to major Royal Ballet Co. (Sadler's Wells Ballet), 1955. Mem., Arts Council of GB, 1976–79. *Roles included:* The Firebird, Princess Aurora in Sleeping Beauty, Odette-Odile in Swan Lake, Giselle, Lise in La Fille Mal Gardée, Juliet in Romeo and Juliet, Cinderella. *Recreations:* music, books, gardening.

PAGE, Anthony (Frederick Montague); *b* India, 21 Sept. 1935; *s* of Brig. F. G. C. Page, DSO, OBE, and P. V. M. Page. *Educ:* Oakley Hall, Cirencester; Winchester Coll. (Schol.); Magdalen Coll., Oxford (Schol., BA); Neighborhood Playhouse Sch. of the Theater, NY. Asst, Royal Court Theatre, 1958: co-directed Live Like Pigs, directed The Room; Artistic Dir, Dundee Repertory Theatre, 1962; The Caretaker, Oxford and Salisbury; Women Beware Women, and Nil Carborundum, Royal Shakespeare Co., 1963; BBC Directors' Course, then several episodes of Z-Cars, Horror of Darkness and 1st TV prodn Stephen D; Jt Artistic Dir, Royal Court, 1964–65; directed Inadmissible Evidence (later Broadway and film), A Patriot for Me, 1st revival of Waiting for Godot, Cuckoo in the Nest; Diary of a Madman, Duchess, 1966; Artistic Dir, two seasons at Royal Court: Uncle Vanya, 1970; Alpha Beta (also film); Hedda Gabler; Krapp's Last Tape; Not I; Cromwell; other plays transf. from Royal Court to West End: Time Present; Hotel in Amsterdam; revival, Look Back in Anger; West of Suez; directed Hamlet, Nottingham, 1970; Rules of the Game, National Theatre; King Lear, Amer. Shakespeare Fest., 1975; Cowardice, Ambassadors, 1983; Heartbreak House, Broadway, 1984 (televised); Mrs Warren's Profession, Nat. Theatre, 1985; *television:* The Parachute; Emlyn; Hotel in Amsterdam; Speaking of Murder; You're Free; Pueblo (nominated for Emmy award); The Changeling; Headmaster; Missiles of October (nominated for Emmy award); Scott Fitzgerald in Hollywood; Adam's Chronicle; Sheppey; Patricia Neal Story; in USA: FDR's Last Year; (with Mickey Rooney) Bill (Golden Globe Award); Johnny Belinda; Grace Kelly Story; Bill on His Own; *Films:* I Never Promised You a Rose Garden; Absolution; The Lady Vanishes; Forbidden. Directors' and Producers' Award for TV Dir of Year, 1966. *Recreations:* movies, reading, riding, travelling. *Address:* 68 Ladbroke Grove, W11.

PAGE, Sir (Arthur) John, Kt 1984; MP (C) Harrow West since March 1960; *b* 16 Sept. 1919; *s* of Sir Arthur Page, QC (late Chief Justice of Burma), and Lady Page, KiH; *m* 1950, Anne, *d* of Charles Micklem, DSO, JP, DL, Longcross House, Surrey; four *s*. *Educ:* Harrow, Magdalene College, Cambridge. Joined RA as Gunner, 1939, commissioned, 1940; served War of 1939–45, Western Desert (wounded), France, Germany; demobilised as Major, comdg 258 Battery Norfolk Yeomanry, 1945; various positions in industry and commerce, 1946–63. Chm. Bethnal Green and E London Housing Assoc., 1957–70; contested (C) Eton and Slough, Gen. Election, 1959. PPS to Parly Under-Sec. of State, Home Office, 1961–63; Conservative Parly Labour Affairs Cttee: Sec., 1960–61, 1964–, Vice-Chm., 1964–69, Chm., 1970–74; Sec., Conservative Broadcasting Cttee, 1974–76. Pres., Cons. Trade Unionists Nat. Adv. Council, 1967–69; Member: Parly Select Cttee on Race Relations and Immigration, 1970–71; British Delegn to Council of Europe and WEU, 1972– (Chm. Budget Cttee, 1973–74, Social and Health Cttee, 1975–78). Mem. Exec., IPU, British Gp, 1970 (Treasurer, 1974–77; Vice-Chm., 1977–79; Chm., 1979–82); Acting Internat. Pres., IPU, 1984 (Dep. Internat. Pres., 1982–84). Vice-Pres., British Insurance Brokers Assoc., 1980–; President: Water Companies Assoc., 1986– (Dep. Pres., 1984–86); Independent Schools Assoc., 1971–78; Chm., Council for Indep. Educn, 1974–80. *Recreations:* painting and politics. *Address:* Hitcham Lodge, Taplow, Bucks. *T:* Burnham 5056. *Clubs:* Brooks's, MCC.

PAGE, Bertram Samuel; University Librarian and Keeper of the Brotherton Collection, University of Leeds, 1947–69, Emeritus Librarian, since 1969; *b* 1 Sept. 1904; *s* of Samuel and Catherine Page; *m* 1933, Olga Ethel, *d* of E. W. Mason. *Educ:* King Charles I School Kidderminster; University of Birmingham. BA 1924, MA 1926. Asst Librarian (later Sub-Librarian), Univ. of Birmingham, 1931–36; Librarian, King's College, Newcastle upon Tyne, 1936–47. Pres. Library Assoc., 1960 (Hon. Fellow, 1961); Chairman: Standing Conf. of Nat. and Univ. Libraries, 1961–63; Exec. Cttee, Nat. Central Library, 1962–72 (Trustee, 1963–75); Librarianship Bd, Council for Nat. Academic Awards, 1966–71. Mem. Court of Univ. of Birmingham, 1954–69. Hon. DUniv. York, 1968. *Publications:* contrib. to Stephen MacKenna's trans. of Plotinus, vol. 5, 1930 (revised whole trans. for 2nd, 3rd, 4th edns, 1958, 1962, 1969); A Manual of University and College Library Practice (jt ed.), 1940; articles and reviews in classical and library jls. *Address:* 24 St Anne's Road, Headington, Oxford. *T:* Oxford 65981.

PAGE, Bruce; journalist; Managing Director, Pagemakers Ltd (formerly Executive Producers Ltd), since 1983; *b* 1 Dec. 1936; *s* of Roger and Beatrice Page; *m* 1969, Anne Louise Darnborough; one *s* one *d*. *Educ:* Melbourne High Sch.; Melbourne Univ. The Herald, Melbourne, 1956–60; Evening Standard, 1960–62; Daily Herald, 1962–64; Sunday Times, 1964–76; Daily Express, 1977; Editor, The New Statesman, 1978–82. *Publications:* (jtly) Philby, 1968, 3rd edn 1977; (jtly) An American Melodrama, 1969; (jtly) Do You Sincerely Want to be Rich?, 1971; (jtly) Destination Disaster, 1976; contrib. Ulster, 1972; The Yom Kippur War, 1974; The British Press, 1978. *Recreations:* sailing, reading. *Address:* 35 Duncan Terrace, N1 8AL. *T:* 01–359 1000.

PAGE, Maj.-Gen. Charles Edward, CB 1974; MBE 1944; DL; Independent Telecommunications Consultant; *b* 23 Aug. 1920; *s* of late Sir (Charles) Max Page, KBE, CB, DSO, FRCS and Lady (Helen) Page; *m* 1948, Elizabeth Marion, *d* of late Sir William Smith Crawford, KBE; two *s* one *d*. *Educ:* Marlborough Coll.; Trinity Coll., Cambridge. BSc (Eng) London 1949; CEng, FIEE 1968. Commissioned 2nd Lieut Royal Signals from TA, 1941; regimental appts Guards Armd Divisional Signals, 1941–45; CO 19 Indian Div. Signals, 1945–46; psc 1951; GSO2 Staff Coll., 1955–58; GSO1 Combat Develt Directorate, WO, 1960–63; CO 1st Div. Signal Regt, 1963–65; CCR Signals 1 (BR) Corps, 1966–68; Sec., NATO Mil. Cttee, Brussels, 1968–70; DCD(A) MoD, 1971–74; retired 1974. Col Comdt, Royal Corps of Signals, 1974–80. Hon. Col, Women's Transport Service (FANY), 1976. DL W Sussex, 1986. *Recreations:* shooting, golf, fishing. *Address:* Church Farm House, Old Bosham, Chichester, W Sussex PO18 8HL. *T:* Chichester 573191. *Clubs:* Army and Navy; Royal and Ancient (St Andrews).

PAGE, Cyril Leslie, OBE 1965; Controller, Personnel, Television, BBC Television Service, 1971–76, retired; *b* 20 Oct. 1916; *s* of Cyril Herbert Page and Rosamund Clara Page; *m* 1939, Barbara Mary Rowland; one *s* one *d*. *Educ:* Sherborne Sch. Royal Air Force, 1936–46 (Wing Comdr). British Broadcasting Corporation, 1946–: Asst, Appts Dept, 1947; Asst Admin. Officer, Overseas Services, 1949; Asst Head of TV Admin., 1951; Estabt Officer, TV, 1958; Head of TV Estabt Dept, 1961; Asst Controller, TV Admin., 1964. Member: Council, Royal Postgrad. Med. Sch., 1975; Cttee of Management, Inst. of Obstetrics and Gynaecology, 1973. *Recreations:* reading, gardening. *Address:* 95 Fountain Gardens, Windsor, Berks SL4 3SU.

PAGE, Rt. Rev. Dennis Fountain; *b* 1 Dec. 1919; *s* of Prebendary Martin Fountain Page and Lilla Fountain Page; *m* 1946; Margaret Bettine Clayton; two *s* one *d*. *Educ:* Shrewsbury Sch.; Gonville and Caius Coll., Cambridge (MA); Lincoln Theological Coll. Curate, Rugby Parish Church, 1943; Priest-in-Charge, St George's Church, Hillmorton, Rugby, 1945; Rector of Hockwold, Vicar of Wilton and Rector of Weeting, Norfolk, 1949; Archdeacon of Huntingdon and Vicar of Yaxley, 1965–75; Hon. Canon of Ely Cathedral, 1968; Bishop Suffragan of Lancaster, 1975–85. *Publication:* Reflections on the Reading for Holy Communion in the Alternative Service Book 1980, 1983. *Recreations:* music, carpentry, gardening. *Address:* Larkrise, Hartest Hill, Hartest, Bury St Edmunds, Suffolk IP29 4ES.

PAGE, Brig. (Edwin) Kenneth, CBE 1951 (OBE 1946); DSO 1945; MC 1918; *b* 23 Jan. 1898; *s* of G. E. Page, Baldock, Herts; *m* 1921, Kate Mildred (*d* 1975), *d* of G. H. Arthur, Yorkshire, Barbados, BWI; two *s*. *Educ:* Haileybury College; RMA, Woolwich. 2nd Lt, RFA, 1916; BEF, France, 1916–18. Adjt TA, 1924–27; Staff College, Camberley, 1928–29; Staff Captain, India, 1931–35; GSO2, War Office, 1936–39; Lt-Col, 1939; served War of 1939–45: BEF, France, 1940; Col, 1945; Brig., 1946; Dep. Director, WO, 1946–48; Commander, Caribbean Area, 1948–51; employed War Office, 1951; retired pay, 1952. CC 1961–74, CA 1968–74, Dorset. *Address:* 1 Eastfields Gardens, East Mill Lane, Sherborne, Dorset DT9 3DP. *T:* Sherborne 813819. *Club:* Army and Navy.

See also Prof. J. K. Page.

PAGE, Ewan Stafford, PhD, MA, BSc; Vice-Chancellor, University of Reading, since 1979; *b* 17 Aug. 1928; *s* of late Joseph William Page and Lucy Quayle (*née* Stafford); *m* 1955, Sheila Margaret Smith; three *s* one *d*. *Educ:* Wyggeston Grammar Sch., Leicester; Christ's Coll., Cambridge (MA, PhD, Raleigh Prize 1952); Univ. of London (BSc). Instr, RAF Techn. Coll., 1949–51; Lectr in Statistics, Durham Colls, 1954–57; Director: Durham Univ. Computing Lab., 1957–63; Newcastle Univ. Computing Lab., 1963–78; Visiting Prof., Univ. of N Carolina, Chapel Hill, USA, 1962–63; University of Newcastle upon Tyne: Prof. of Computing and Data Processing, 1965–78; Pro-Vice Chancellor, 1972–78 (Actg Vice-Chancellor, 1976–77). Mem. Bd, Aycliffe and Peterlee Develt Corp., 1969–78. Pres., British Computer Soc., 1984–85 (Dep. Pres., 1983–84); Mem., Gen. Optical Council, 1984–; Hon. Treasurer, Royal Statistical Soc., 1983–. Hon. Fellow, Amer. Statistical Assoc., 1974; Hon. FBCS, 1976; Hon. Fellow, Newcastle upon Tyne Polytechnic, 1979. *Publications:* (jtly) Information Representation and Manipulation in a Computer, 1973, 2nd edn 1978; (jtly) Introduction to Computational Combinatorics, 1978; papers in statistical and computing jls. *Recreations:* golf, music, reading, vegetable gardening, country wine and beer making. *Address:* University of Reading, Whiteknights, Reading, Berks RG6 2AH. *T:* Reading 875123.

PAGE, Sir Frederick (William), Kt 1979; CBE 1961; FRS 1978; FEng, Hon. FRAeS; Member of the Board, British Aerospace PLC, 1977–83; Chairman and Chief Executive, Aircraft Group of British Aerospace PLC, 1977–82; retired 1983; *b* 20 Feb. 1917; *s* of Richard Page and Ellen Potter; *m* 1940, Kathleen Edith de Courcy; three *s* one *d*. *Educ:* Rutlish Sch., Merton; St Catharine's Coll., Cambridge (MA). Hawker Aircraft Co., 1938; English Electric, 1945; Chief Engr, 1950, and Dir and Chief Exec. (Aircraft), English Electric Aviation, 1959; Managing Dir, Mil. Aircraft Div. of BAC, 1965–72, Chm., 1967; apptd Managing Dir (Aircraft), BAC, and Chm., Commercial Aircraft Div., 1972. Jt Chm. of SEPECAT, the Anglo-French co. formed for management of Jaguar programme, 1966–73; apptd to Bd of Panavia Aircraft GmbH, 1969, Chm. 1977; apptd Chm. BAC Ltd (a co. of Brit. Aerospace), 1977. Mem. Council, Soc. of Brit. Aerospace Cos Ltd; apptd to Bd of BAC (Operating) Ltd, 1963; Dir, BAC (USA) Inc., 1975–77. FRAeS, 1951–80, Hon. FRAeS, 1980 (Gold Medal, 1974); Fellow, Fellowship of Engrg, 1977. Hon. Fellow, UMIST, 1970. Hon. DSc Cranfield, 1979. British Gold Medal for Aeronautics, 1962. *Recreation:* gardening. *Address:* Renvyle, 60 Waverley Lane, Farnham, Surrey GU9 8BN. *T:* Farnham 714999. *Club:* United Oxford & Cambridge University.

PAGE, Sir John; *see* Page, Sir A. J.

PAGE, John Brangwyn; Chairman, Agricultural Mortgage Corporation, 1982–85; Director: Standard Chartered Bank, since 1982; Nationwide Building Society, since 1982; *b* 23 Aug. 1923; *s* of late Sidney John Page, CB, MC; *m* 1948, Gloria Vail; one *s* one *d*. *Educ:* Highgate Sch. (Foundation Schol.); King's Coll., Cambridge (BA). RAF, 1942–46; Cambridge, 1946–48; Bank of England, 1948; seconded to IMF, 1953; Chief Cashier, 1970–80; Exec. Dir, 1980–82. FIB; CBIM; FRSA. *Recreations:* gardening, music, travel.

PAGE, Maj.-Gen. John Humphrey, CB 1977; OBE 1967; MC 1952; Director of the London Law Trust, since 1979; a non-executive Director, RBM (Holdings), since 1980; *b* 5 March 1923; *s* of late Captain W. J. Page, JP, Devizes and late Alice Mary Page (*née* Richards); *m* 1956, Angela Mary Bunting; three *s* one *d*. *Educ:* Stonyhurst. Commnd into RE, 1942; served in NW Europe, India, Korea, Middle East and UK, 1942–60; Instr, Staff Coll., Camberley, 1960–62; comd 32 Armd Engr Regt, 1964–67; idc 1968; CCRE 1st Br. Corps, 1969–70; Asst Comdt, RMA Sandhurst, 1971–74; Dir of Personal Services (Army), MoD, 1974–78, retd. Col Comdt, RE, 1980–85. Mem. Council, Officers' Pension Soc.; Vice-Chm., SSAFA, 1983–. Chm. Trustees, Home-Start Consultancy, 1982–. *Address:* Vanner's Farm House, Stour Provost, Gillingham, Dorset.

PAGE, Sir John (Joseph Joffre), Kt 1979; OBE 1959; Chairman, North Western Regional Health Authority, since 1982; *b* 7 Jan. 1915; 2nd *s* of late William Joseph and Frances Page; *m* 1939, Cynthia Maynard, *d* of late L. M. Swan, CBE; two *s*. *Educ:* Emanuel School. FCIT. RAF, 1933–38 and 1939–46 (despatches, 1943); Group Captain. Iraq Petroleum Group of Cos, 1938–39 and 1946–70; served in Palestine, Jordan, Lebanon, Syria, Iraq, Qatar, Bahrain and Abu Dhabi; Head Office, London, 1958–61; Gen. Man., 1955–58; Chief Representative, 1961–70. Chm., 1972–77 and 1980–84, Chief Exec., 1975–77, Mersey Docks and Harbour Co.; Dep. Chm., British Ports Assoc., 1974–77; Chm., Nat. Ports Council, 1977–80. Chm., Chester DHA, 1981–82. *Recreations:* photography, fishing, music. *Address:* Springhill, Hill Road North, Helsby, Cheshire WA6 9AG. *T:* Helsby 2994. *Clubs:* Oriental, Royal Air Force, MCC.

PAGE, Prof. John Kenneth; Professor of Building Science, University of Sheffield, 1960–84; *b* 3 Nov. 1924; *s* of Brig. E. K. Page, *qv*; *m* 1954, Anita Bell Lovell; two *s* two *d*. *Educ:* Haileybury College; Pembroke College, Cambridge. Served War of 1939–45, Royal Artillery, 1943–47. Asst Industrial Officer, Council of Industrial Design, 1950–51; taught Westminster School, 1952–53; Sen. Scientific Officer, Tropical Liaison Section, Building Research Station, 1953–56; Chief Research Officer, Nuffield Div. for Architectural Studies, 1956–57; Lecturer, Dept. of Building Science, Univ. of Liverpool, 1957–60. Former Chm., Environmental Gp, and Mem., Econ. Planning Council, Yorks and Humberside Region, 1965–78. Former Chm., UK Section, Internat. Solar Energy Soc. Mem., UN Technical Panel on Solar Energy for New and Renewable Sources of Energy. *Publications:* 200 papers on Energy policy, Environmental Design and Planning, Building Climatology and Solar Energy. *Address:* c/o Division of Economic Studies, University of Sheffield, Sheffield S10 2TN. *T:* Sheffield 78555.

PAGE, Kenneth; *see* Page, Edwin Kenneth.

PAGE, Prof. Raymond Ian, LittD; Elrington and Bosworth Professor of Anglo-Saxon, University of Cambridge, since 1984; Fellow since 1962, and Librarian since 1965, Corpus Christi College, Cambridge; *b* 25 Sept. 1924; *s* of Reginald Howard Page and Emily Louise Page; *m* 1953, Elin Benedicte Hustad, *d* of Tormod Kristoffer Hustad and Anne Margarethe Hustad, Oslo; two *d* (one *s* decd). *Educ:* King Edward VII Sch., Sheffield; Rotherham Technical Coll,; Univ. of Sheffield. LittD Cambridge 1974. Assistant Lecturer and Lecturer, Univ. of Nottingham, 1951–61; successively Lectr, Reader and Professor, Dept of Anglo-Saxon, Norse and Celtic, Cambridge, 1961–. *Address:* Ashton House, Newnham Road, Cambridge.

PAGE, Richard Lewis; MP (C) Hertfordshire South West, since Dec. 1979; Director of family company, since 1964; *b* 22 Feb. 1941; *s* of Victor Charles and Kathleen Page; *m* 1964, Madeleine Ann Brown; one *s* one *d*. *Educ:* Hurstpierpoint Coll.; Luton Technical Coll. Apprenticeship, Vauxhall Motors, 1959–64; HNC Mech. Engineering. Young Conservatives, 1964–66; Councillor, Banstead UDC, 1968–71; contested (C) Workington, Feb. and Oct. 1974; MP (C) Workington, Nov. 1976–1979; PPS: to Sec. of State for Trade, 1981–82; to Leader of the House, 1982–. *Recreation:* most sport. *Address:* House of Commons, SW1A 0AA.

PAGE, Simon Richard; Registrar, Guildford, Epsom and Reigate County Courts, and District Registrar, High Court of Justice, since 1980; a Recorder of the Crown Court, since 1980; *b* 7 March 1934; *s* of Eric Rowland Page and Vera (*née* Fenton); *m* 1st, 1963, (marr. diss. 1977); three *s* one *d*; 2nd, 1984. *Educ:* Lancing; LSE (LLB External, 1956). Admitted solicitor (hons), 1957. National Service, Second Lieut RA, 1957–59. Private practice as solicitor, 1959–75; Pres., West Surrey Law Soc., 1972–73; Registrar, Croydon County Court, 1975–80; Pres., Assoc. of County Court and District Registrars, 1983–84. *Recreations:* squash racquets, cricket, bridge. *Address:* c/o The Law Courts, Mary Road, Guildford. *Club:* County (Guildford).

PAGE WOOD, Sir Anthony John, 8th Bt, *cr* 1837; *b* 6 Feb. 1951; *s* of Sir David (John Hatherley) Page Wood, 7th Bt and Evelyn Hazel Rosemary, *d* of late Captain George Ernest Bellville; *S* father 1955. *Heir: uncle,* Matthew Page Wood [*b* 13 Aug. 1924; *m* 1947; two *d*]. *Address:* 22 Godfrey Street, SW3 3TA.

PAGET, family name of **Marquess of Anglesey** and **Baron Paget of Northampton.**

PAGET OF NORTHAMPTON, Baron *cr* 1974 (Life Peer), of Lubenham, Leics; **Reginald Thomas Paget,** QC 1947; *b* 2 Sept. 1908; *m* 1931. *Educ:* Eton; Trinity College, Cambridge. Barrister, 1934. Lt RNVR, 1940–43 (invalided). Contested Northampton, 1935; MP (Lab) Northampton, 1945–Feb. 1974. Hon. Sec., UK Council of European Movement, 1954. Master, Pytchley Hounds, 1958–71. *Publications:* Manstein-Campaigns and Trial, 1951; (with late S. S. Silverman, MP) Hanged—and Innocent?, 1958; The Human Journey, 1979. *Address:* 9 Grosvenor Cottages, SW1. *T:* 01–730 4034.

PAGET, Sir John (Starr), 3rd Bt *cr* 1886; CEng, FIMechE; Chairman, Somerset Fruit Machinery Ltd, since 1986; Proprietor, Sir John Paget Woodworker; Senior Partner, Haygrass Cider Orchards; *b* 24 Nov. 1914; *s* of Sir Richard Paget, 2nd Bt and Lady Muriel Paget, CBE; *S* father 1955; *m* 1944, Nancy Mary Parish, JP, *d* of late Lieutenant-Colonel Francis Parish, DSO, MC; two *s* five *d*. *Educ:* Oundle; Chateau D'Oex; Trinity College, Cambridge (MA). Joined English Electric Co. Ltd, 1936; Asst Works Supt, English Electric, Preston, 1941; Joined D. Napier & Son Ltd, 1943; Assistant Manager, D. Napier & Son Ltd, Liverpool, 1945; Manager, D. Napier & Son Ltd, London Group, 1946; Works Director, Napier Aero Engines, 1961–62 (Dir and Gen. Man. D. Napier & Son Ltd, 1959–61). Director: Thermal Syndicate Ltd, Wallsend, 1939–84 (Chm., 1973–80; Chm. Emeritus, 1980–84); Glacier Metal Group, 1963–65; Hilger & Watts, 1965–68; Rank Precision Industries Ltd, 1968–70. Hon. DTech Brunel, 1976. Silver Medal, Instn of Production Engineers, 1950. *Recreations:* music, cooking. *Heir: s* Richard Herbert Paget [*b* 17 February 1957; *m* 1985, Richenda, *d* of Rev. J. T. C. B. Collins; one *d*]. *Address:* Haygrass House, Taunton, Somerset. *T:* Taunton 81779. *Club:* Athenæum.

PAGET, Lt-Col Sir Julian (Tolver), 4th Bt *cr* 1871; CVO 1984; Gentleman Usher to the Queen, since 1971; author; *b* 11 July 1921; *s* of General Sir Bernard Paget, GCB, DSO, MC (*d* 1961) (*g s* of 1st Bt), and of Winifred, *d* of Sir John Paget, 2nd Bt; *S* uncle, Sir James Francis Paget, 3rd Bt, 1972; *m* 1954, Diana Frances, *d* of late F. S. H. Farmer; one *s* one *d*. *Educ:* Radley College; Christ Church, Oxford (MA). Joined Coldstream Guards, 1940; served North West Europe, 1944–45; retired as Lt-Col, 1968. *Publications:* Counter-Insurgency Campaigning, 1967; Last Post: Aden, 1964–67, 1969; The Story of the Guards, 1976; The Pageantry of Britain, 1979; Yeoman of the Guard, 1984. *Recreations:* fishing, shooting, travel, writing. *Heir: s* Henry James Paget, *b* 2 Feb. 1959. *Address:* 4 Trevor Street, SW7. *T:* 01–584 3524. *Clubs:* Cavalry and Guards, Pratt's, Flyfishers'.

PAGNAMENTA, Peter John; Head of Current Affairs, BBC Television, since 1985; *b* 12 April 1941; *s* of Charles Francis Pagnamenta and Daphne Pagnamenta; *m* 1966, Sybil Healy; one *s* one *d*. *Educ:* Shrewsbury Sch.; Trinity Hall, Cambridge (BA). Joined BBC, 1965 (scriptwriter, radio and television news); Prodn Asst, Tonight and 24 Hours, 1965–67; Asst Editor, 24 Hours, 1967; New York office, 1968–71 (Producer, US Election coverage and Apollo flights); Editor: 24 Hours, 1971; Midweek, 1972–75; Panorama, 1975–77; Dir of News and Current Affairs, Thames Television, 1977–80; Exec. Producer, Documentary Dept, BBC, 1981–85; Exec. Producer, All Our Working Lives (eleven part series), BBC2, 1984; Editor, Real Lives (documentary strand), BBC 1, 1984–85. *Publication:* (with Richard Overy) All Our Working Lives, 1984. *Recreations:* walking, fishing. *Address:* BBC, Lime Grove Studios, W12 7RJ. *T:* 01–743 8000.

PAIBA, Denis Anthony; His Honour Judge Paiba; a Circuit Judge, since 1982; *b* 10 Dec. 1926; *e s* of late Geoffrey Paiba and Geraldine Paiba; *m* 1955, Lesley Patricia Dresden; two *s*. *Educ:* University Coll. Sch. (Junior); Magdalen Coll. Sch., Oxford; Jesus Coll., Cambridge. 44 Royal Marine Commando, 1945–47. Financial Times, 1957–58. Called to the Bar, Gray's Inn, 1958; a Recorder of the Crown Court, 1980–82. *Recreations:* theatre, music, gardening, archery, watching rugby and cricket, wining and dining. *Address:* Roehampton, SW15; 3 Temple Gardens, Temple, EC4Y 5BG. *T:* 01–353 3102.

PAICE, Karlo Bruce; Assistant Under-Secretary of State, Home Office, 1955–66; *b* 18 August 1906; *s* of H. B. Paice, Horsham, Sussex; *m* 1st, 1935, Islay (*d* 1965), *d* of late Paymaster Comdr Duncan Cook; four *s*; 2nd, 1966, Mrs Gwen Morris (*née* Kenyon). *Educ:* Collyer's School, Horsham; Jesus Coll., Cambridge (MA). Second Clerk, Metropolitan Police Courts, 1928; Assistant Principal, Home Office, 1929; Asst Sec. to the Poisons Bd, 1933–35; Private Sec. to successive Parliamentary Under-Secretaries of State for Home Affairs, 1935–39. Principal, 1936; Assistant Secretary, 1941, serving in London Civil Defence Region, Fire Service Department, and Aliens Department. Secretary to the Prison Commission and a Prison Commissioner, 1949–55. *Recreations:* walking, history, music. *Address:* Flat 5, Windsor Lodge, Third Avenue, Hove, East Sussex. *T:* Brighton 733194. *Clubs:* Athenæum; Hove.

PAIGE, Prof. Edward George Sydney, PhD; FRS 1983; Professor of Electrical Engineering, University of Oxford, since 1977; *b* 18 July 1930; *s* of Sydney and Maude Paige; *m* 1953, Helen Gill; two *s* two *d*. *Educ:* Reading University (BSc, PhD). FInstP; FIEE. Junior Research Fellow to DCSO, Royal Radar Establishment, Malvern, 1955–77. *Address:* Department of Engineering Science, University of Oxford, Parks Road, Oxford. *T:* Oxford 59988.

PAIGE, Rear-Adm. Richard Collings, CB 1967; *b* 4 October 1911; *s* of Herbert Collings Paige and Harriet Pering Paige; *m* 1937, Sheila Brambles Ward, *d* of late Dr Ernest Ward, Paignton; two *s*. *Educ:* Blundell's School, Tiverton; RNE College, Keyham. Joined Navy, 1929. Served in HMS Neptune, Curaçao, Maori, King George V, Superb, Eagle (despatches twice); Captain, 1957; Commanding Officer, RNE College, 1960–62; Commodore Supt, HM Naval Base, Singapore, 1963–65; Admiral Supt HM Dockyard, Portsmouth, 1966–68. Rear-Adm. 1965.

PAIGE, Victor Grellier, CBE 1978; Chairman, National Health Service Management Board, and Second Permanent Secretary, Department of Health and Social Security, 1985–86; *b* 5 June 1925; *s* of Victor Paige and Alice (*née* Grellier); *m* 1948, Kathleen Winifred, 3rd *d* of Arthur and Daisy Harris; one *s* one *d*. *Educ:* East Ham Grammar Sch.; Univ. of Nottingham. CIPM, FCIT, CBIM, FAIM. Roosevelt Mem. Schol. 1954. Dep. Personnel Manager, Boots Pure Drug Co. Ltd, 1957–67; Controller of Personnel Services, CWS Ltd, 1967–70; Dir of Manpower and Organisation, 1970–74, Exec. Vice-Chm. (Admin), 1974–77, Nat. Freight Corp.; Dep. Chm., Nat. Freight Corp., later Nat. Freight Co., 1977–82; Dir and Dep. Chm., 1982–85, and non-exec. Dir, 1985–, Nat. Freight Consortium. Chm., Iveco (UK), 1984–85. Chm., PLA, 1980–85; Member: Manpower Services Commn, 1974–80; Thames Water Authy, 1983–85. Member: Notts Educn Cttee, 1957–63; Secondary Schs Examn Council, 1960–63; UK Adv. Council for Educn in Management, 1962–65; Careers Adv. Bd, Univ. of Nottingham, 1975–81; Chairman: Regional Adv. Council for Further Educn, E Mids, 1967; Exec. Council, British Assoc. for Commercial and Industrial Educn, 1974 (Vice-Pres. 1980) Pres., Inst. of Admin. Management, 1984–; Vice-Pres., Chartered Inst. of Transport, 1984–85 (Mem. Council, 1976–79); Mem. Council, CBI, 1983–85 (Chm., Educn and Trng Cttee, 1983–85). Vice-Pres., London Fedn of Boys' Clubs. Freeman, Co. of Watermen and Lightermen of the River Thames; Freeman, City of London, 1981. Commander, Order of Orange Nassau, The Netherlands, 1982. *Publications:* contrib. techn. press on management. *Recreations:* reading, sport generally, athletics in particular (Pres. Notts Athletic Club, 1962–67). *Address:* Queen's Wood, Frithsden, Berkhamsted, Herts. *T:* Berkhamsted 5030. *Clubs:* Athenæum, MCC.

PAIN, Barry Newton, CBE 1979; QPM 1976; Commandant, Police Staff College, Bramshill, and HM Inspector of Constabulary, since 1982; *b* 25 Feb. 1931; *s* of Godfrey William Pain and Annie Newton; *m* 1952, Marguerite Agnes King; one *s* one *d*. *Educ:* Waverley Grammar Sch., Birmingham. Clerk to Prosecuting Solicitor, Birmingham, 1947–51; 2nd Lieut (Actg Captain) RASC, Kenya, 1949–51. Birmingham City Police, 1951–68; Staff Officer to HM Inspector of Constabulary, Birmingham, 1966–68; Asst Chief Constable, Staffordshire and Stoke-on-Trent Constabulary, 1968–74; Chief Constable of Kent, 1974–82; JSSC 1970. Adviser to Turkish Govt on Reorganization of Police, 1972. Pres., Assoc. of Chief Police Officers, 1981–82. *Recreations:* golf, shooting, boating. *Address:* Police Staff College, Bramshill House, near Hartley Wintney, Hants.

PAIN, Lt-Gen. Sir (Horace) Rollo (Squarey), KCB 1975 (CB 1974); MC 1945; farmer; late 4th/7th Royal Dragoon Guards; Head of British Defence Staff, Washington, 1975–78, retired; *b* 11 May 1921; *s* of late Horace Davy Pain, Levenside, Haverthwaite, Ulverston, and late Audrey Pain (*née* Hampson); *m* 1950, Denys Sophia (*née* Chaine-Nickson); one *s* two *d*. Commissioned into Reconnaissance Corps during War of 1939–45: served NW Europe (MC). After War, served for two years in E Africa and Brit. Somaliland before joining 4th/7th Royal Dragoon Gds in Palestine, 1947; attended Staff Coll., Camberley, 1951; subseq. served in Mil. Ops Directorate, in War Office; served with his Regt in BAOR, 1955–56; Mem. Directing Staff, Staff Coll., Camberley, 1957; GSO1, Brit. Army Staff, Washington, DC, 1960; commanded his Regt in BAOR, 1962; commanded one of the three divs, Staff Coll., Camberley, 1964; commanded 5 Inf. Bde in Borneo, 1965; IDC, 1968; ADC to the Queen, 1969; BGS, HQ, BAOR, 1969–70; GOC 2nd Div., 1970–72; Dir of Army Training, MoD, 1972–75; Col Comdt, Mil. Provost Staff Corps, 1974–83; Col. 4th/7th Royal Dragoon Guards, 1979–83. *Recreation:* hunting. *Address:* Eddlethorpe Hall, Malton, North Yorkshire. *T:* Burythorpe 218. *Club:* Cavalry and Guards.

PAIN, Hon. Sir Peter (Richard), Kt 1975; **Hon. Mr Justice Pain;** a Judge of the High Court of Justice, Queen's Bench Division, since 1975; *b* 6 Sept. 1913; *s* of Arthur Richard Pain and Elizabeth Irene Pain (*née* Benn); *m* 1941, Barbara Florence Maude Riggs; two *s*. *Educ:* Westminster; Christ Church, Oxford. Called to the Bar, Lincoln's Inn, 1936, Bencher 1972. QC 1965. Chairman: Race Relations Board Conciliation Cttee for Greater London, 1968–71; South Metropolitan Conciliation Cttee, 1971–73; Mem., Parole Bd, 1978–80. Pres., Holiday Fellowship, 1977–83. *Publications:* Manual of Fire Service Law, 1951; The Law Relating to the Motor Trade (with K. C. Johnson-Davies), 1955. *Recreations:* forestry, cricket, mountain walking. *Address:* Loen, St Catherine's Road, Frimley, Surrey. *T:* Deepcut 835639.

PAIN, Sir Rollo; see Pain, Sir H. R. S.

PAINE, George, CB 1974; DFC 1944; *b* 14 Apr. 1918; 3rd *s* of late Jack Paine and Helen Margaret (*née* Hadow), East Sutton; *m* 1969, Hilary (*née* Garrod), *widow* of Dr A. C. Frazer. *Educ*: Bradfield Coll.; Peterhouse, Cambridge. External Ballistics Dept, Ordnance Bd, 1941; RAF, 1942–46; Min. of Agriculture, 1948; Inland Revenue, 1949; Central Statistical Office, 1954; Board of Trade, 1957; Dir of Statistics and Intelligence, Bd of Inland Revenue, 1957–72; Dir, OPCS and Registrar Gen. for Eng. and Wales, 1972–78. Hon. Treasurer, Royal Statistical Soc., 1974–78. *Recreations*: fruit growing, beekeeping. *Address*: Springfield House, Broad Town, near Swindon, Wilts SN4 7RU. *T*: Broad Hinton 377.

PAINE, Peter Stanley, CBE 1981; DFC 1944; Chairman, Oracle Teletext Ltd, since 1984; *b* 19 June 1921; *s* of Arthur Bertram Paine and Dorothy Helen Paine; *m* 1942, Sheila Mary, *d* of Frederick Wigglesworth, MA; two *s* two *d*. *Educ*: King's Sch., Canterbury. Served 1940–46, 2 Gp RAF (Flt-Lt). Worked in Punch Publishing Office, 1945–47; Sales Promotion Man., Newnes Pearson, 1948–52, Odhams Press, then Sales Dir and Dir of Tyne Tees Television, 1958–67; Sales Dir and Dir of Yorkshire Television, 1967–74; Managing Director: Tyne Tees Television, 1974–83; Tyne Tees Television Holdings, 1981–84. Director: Trident Television, 1970–81; Independent Television News Ltd, 1982–83; Independent Television Publications Ltd, 1977–83; Broadcasters Audience Res. Bd, 1980–86; Member: Council, Independent Television Companies Assoc., 1974–83 (4 yrs Chm. Marketing Cttee); Cable Authority, 1984–. *Recreations*: golf, fishing, theatre, music, reading. *Address*: Briarfield, Ashwood Road, Woking, Surrey GU22 7JW. *T*: Woking 73183. *Clubs*: Thirty; Worplesdon Golf.

PAINE, Dr Thomas Otten; Chairman, Thomas Paine Associates, Los Angeles, since 1982; *b* 9 Nov. 1921; *s* of George Thomas Paine, Cdre, USN retd and Ada Louise Otten; *m* 1946, Barbara Helen Taunton Pearse; two *s* two *d*. *Educ*: Maury High, Norfolk, Va; Brown Univ.; Stanford Univ. Served War of 1939–45 (US Navy Commendation Ribbon 1944; Submarine Combat Award with two stars, 1943–45). Research Associate: Stanford Univ., 1947–49; General Electric Res. Lab., Schenectady, 1949–50; Manager, TEMPO, GE Center for Advanced Studies, Santa Barbara, 1963–67; Dep. Administrator, US Nat. Aeronautics and Space Admin., Washington, 1968, Administrator 1968–70; Group Executive, GE, Power Generation Group, 1970–73, Sen. Vice-Pres., GE, 1974–76; Pres. and Chief Operating Officer, Northrop Corp., 1976–82. Member, Board of Directors: Eastern Air Lines, 1981–; Quotron Systems, Inc., 1982–; RCA, 1982–; NBC, 1982–; Director: Arthur D. Little Inc., 1982–; NIKE Inc., 1982–. Chairman: Pacific Forum, 1980–; US National Commn on Space, 1985–. MInstMet; Member: Newcomen Soc.; Nat. Acad. of Engineering; Acad. of Sciences, NY; Sigma Xi; Trustee: Occidental Coll.; Brown Univ.; Asian Inst. Tech.; Harvey Mudd Coll. Outstanding Contribution to Industrial Science Award, AAS, 1956; NASA DSM, 1970; Washington Award, Western Soc. of Engrs, 1972; John Fritz Medal, United Engrg Soc., 1976; Faraday Medal, IEE, 1976. Hon. Dr of Science: Brown, 1969; Clarkson Coll. of Tech., 1969; Nebraska Wesleyan, 1970; New Brunswick, 1970; Oklahoma City, 1970; Hon. Dr Engrg: Worcester Polytechnic Inst., 1970; Cheng Kung Univ., 1978. Grand Ufficiale della Ordine Al Merito della Repubblica Italiana, 1972. *Publications*: various technical papers and patents. *Recreations*: sailing, beachcombing, skin diving, photography, book collecting, oil painting. *Address*: (office) Thomas Paine Associates, 10880 Wilshire Boulevard, Suite 2011, Los Angeles, Calif 90024, USA; (home) 765 Bonhill Road, Los Angeles, Calif 90049. *Clubs*: Sky, Lotos, Explorers (New York); Army and Navy, Space, Cosmos (Washington); California, Regency (Los Angeles).

PAINTAL, Prof. Autar Singh, Padma Vibhushan; MD, PhD, DSc; FRS 1981; FRSE; Professor of Physiology and Director, Vallabhbhai Patel Chest Institute, Delhi University, since 1964 (Assistant Director, 1954–56); *b* 24 Sept. 1925; *s* of Dr Man Singh and Rajwans Kaur; one *s* two *d*. *Educ*: SSBS Khalsa High Sch., Lahore; Forman Christian Coll., Lahore; Lucknow Univ. (MB, BS, MD); Edinburgh Univ. (PhD, DSc). Lectr in Physiol., King George's Med. Coll., Lucknow Univ., 1949; Rockefeller Fellow, 1950; Lectr in Physiol., Edinburgh Univ., 1951; Control Officer, Technical Develt Estabt Labs, Min. of Defence, Kanpur, 1952–54; Prof. of Physiology, All-India Inst. of Med. Sciences, New Delhi, 1958–64; Dean, Faculty of Med. Sciences, Delhi Univ., 1966–77. Associate Prof., Albert Einstein Coll. of Medicine, New York, 1956; Vis. Associate Prof. of Physiol., Univ. of Utah, 1957; Commonwealth Vis. Prof.; St Bartholomew's Hosp. Med. Sch., London, 1966. FRSE 1966; Fellow: Indian Acad. of Med. Sciences, 1966; Indian National Science Acad., 1971 (Vice Pres., 1981–83); President: Nat. Coll. of Chest Physicians, 1981–86; Indian Sci. Congress, 1984–85; Member: Physiol Soc., UK, 1953; Ergonomics Res. Soc., UK, 1954. B. C. Roy Orator, New Delhi, 1973; Sharpey-Schafer Lectr, Univ. of Edin., 1981; Dr Zakir Husain Meml Lectr, Jawaharlal Nehru Univ., 1984. Hon. DSc: Benares Hindu Univ., 1982; Delhi Univ., 1984; Aligarh Muslim Univ., 1986. Basanti Devi Amir Chand Prize, 1967; Silver Jubilee Res. Award, 1978; Barclay Medal, Asiatic Soc., 1982; R. D. Birla Award, 1982; Nehru Sci. Award, 1983; Maharishi Dayanand Centenary Gold Medal, 1983; Acharya J. C. Bose Medal, 1985. *Publications*: (ed) Morphology and Mechanisms of Chemoreceptors, 1976; (ed) Respiratory Adaptations, Capillary Exchange and Reflex Mechanisms, 1977; papers in Jl of Physiol. and in other physiol jls. *Recreations*: swimming, rowing, bird watching. *Address*: Vallabhbhai Patel Chest Institute, Delhi University, PO Box 2101, Delhi 110007, India. *T*: Delhi 2523856 and 231749. *Club*: Roshanara (Delhi).

PAINTER, George Duncan, OBE 1974; Biographer and Incunabulist; Assistant Keeper in charge of fifteenth-century printed books, British Museum, 1954–74; *b* Birmingham, 5 June 1914; *s* of George Charles Painter and Minnie Rosendale (*née* Taylor); *m* 1942, Isabel Joan, *d* of Samuel Morley Britton, Bristol; two *d*. *Educ*: King Edward's Sch., Birmingham; Trinity Coll., Cambridge (Schol.). Bell Exhibr; John Stewart of Rannoch Schol.; Porson Schol.; Waddington Schol.; 1st cl. hons Class. Tripos pts I and II; Craven Student; 2nd Chancellor's Class. Medallist, 1936; MA Cantab 1945. Asst Lectr in Latin, Univ. of Liverpool, 1937; joined staff of Dept of Printed Books, BM, 1938. FRSL 1965. Hon. DLitt Edinburgh, 1979. *Publications*: André Gide, A Critical Biography, 1951, rev. edn 1968; The Road to Sinodun, Poems, 1951; André Gide, Marshlands and Prometheus Misbound (trans.), 1953; Marcel Proust, Letters to his Mother (trans.), 1956; Marcel Proust, A Biography, vol. 1, 1959, vol. 2, 1965 (Duff Cooper Memorial Prize); The Vinland Map and the Tartar Relation (with R. A. Skelton and T. E. Marston), 1965; André Maurois, The Chelsea Way (trans.), 1966; William Caxton, a Quincentenary Biography, 1976; Chateaubriand, A Biography, vol. 1, The Longed-for Tempests, 1977 (James Tait Black Meml Prize); Studies in Fifteenth-Century Printing, 1984; articles on fifteenth-century printing in The Library, Book Collector, Gutenberg-Jahrbuch. *Recreations*: family life, walking, gardening, music. *Address*: 10 Mansfield Road, Hove, East Sussex. *T*: Brighton 416008.

PAINTER, Terence James; a Deputy Chairman, Board of Inland Revenue, since 1986; *b* 28 Nov. 1935; *s* of late Edward Lawrence Painter and Ethel Violet (*née* Butler); *m* 1959, Margaret Janet Blackburn; two *s* two *d*. *Educ*: City of Norwich Sch.; Downing Coll., Cambridge (BA (History)). Nat. Service Commn, Royal Norfolk Regt, 1958–59. Entered

Inland Revenue as Asst Principal, 1959; Principal, 1962; seconded to Civil Service Selection Bd, 1967–68; Asst Sec., 1969; seconded to HM Treasury, 1973–75; Under-Sec., 1975–86. *Recreations*: music, books. *Address*: 9 Grant Gardens, Harpenden, Herts AL5 4QD. *T*: Harpenden 60269.

PAISH, Frank Walter, MC 1918; MA; Professor Emeritus, University of London; *b* 15 January 1898; *e s* of late Sir George Paish; *m* 1927, Beatrice Marie, *d* of late G. C. Eckhard; two *s* one *d*. *Educ*: Winchester College; Trinity College, Cambridge. Served European War (RFA), 1916–19. Employed by Standard Bank of South Africa, Ltd, in London and South Africa, 1921–32. Lecturer, London School of Economics, 1932–38; Reader, 1938–49; Professor of Economics (with special reference to Business Finance), 1949–65; Hon. Fellow, 1970. Secretary, London and Cambridge Economic Service, 1932–41 and 1945–49; Editor, 1947–49. Deputy-Director of Programmes, Ministry of Aircraft Production, 1941–45. Consultant on Economic Affairs, Lloyds Bank Ltd, 1965–70. *Publications*: (with G. L. Schwartz) Insurance Funds and their Investment, 1934; The Post-War Financial Problem and Other Essays, 1950; Business Finance, 1953; Studies in an Inflationary Economy, 1962; Long-term and Short-term Interest Rates in the United Kingdom, 1966; (ed) Benham's Economics, 8th edn, 1967, (with A. J. Culyer) 9th edn, 1973; How the Economy Works and Other Essays, 1970; The Rise and Fall of Incomes Policy, 1969; articles in The Economic Journal, Economica, London and Cambridge Bulletin, etc. *Address*: The Old Rectory Cottage, Kentchurch, Hereford.

PAISLEY, Bishop of, (RC), since 1968; **Rt. Rev. Stephen McGill;** *b* Glasgow, 4 Jan. 1912; *s* of Peter McGill and Charlotte Connolly. *Educ*: St Aloysius', Glasgow; Blairs College, Aberdeen; Coutances, France; Institut Catholique, Paris. Ordained Priest of St Sulpice, 1936. STL Paris. St Mary's College, Blairs, Aberdeen: Spiritual Director, 1940–51; Rector, 1951–60. Bishop of Argyll and the Isles, 1960–68. *Address*: Bishop's House, Porterfield Road, Kilmacolm, Renfrewshire.

PAISLEY, Rev. Ian Richard Kyle; MP (Democratic Unionist) North Antrim, since 1974 (ProtU 1970–74) (resigned seat Dec. 1985 in protest against Anglo-Irish Agreement; re-elected Jan. 1986); Member (DemU) Northern Ireland, European Parliament, since 1979; Minister, Martyrs Memorial Free Presbyterian Church, Belfast, since 1946; *b* 6 April 1926; 2nd *s* of late Rev. J. Kyle Paisley and Mrs Isabella Paisley; *m* 1956, Eileen Emily Cassells; two *s* three *d* (incl. twin *s*). *Educ*: Ballymena Model Sch.; Ballymena Techn. High Sch.; S Wales Bible Coll.; Reformed Presbyterian Theol. Coll., Belfast. Ordained, 1946. Moderator, Free Presbyterian Church of Ulster, 1951; Pres., Whitefield Coll. of the Bible, 1979–. Commenced publishing The Protestant Telegraph, 1966. Contested (Prot U) Bannside, NI Parlt, 1969; MP (Prot U), Bannside, Co. Antrim, NI Parlt, 1970–72; Leader of Opposition, 1972; Chm., Public Accounts Cttee, 1972. Co-Founder, Democratic Unionist Party, NI, 1972. Mem. (Democratic Unionist), N Antrim, NI Assembly, 1973–75; Mem. (UUUC), N Antrim, NI Constitutional Convention, 1975–76; Mem. (DemU) N Antrim, NI Assembly, 1982–86. Hon. DD Bob Jones Univ., SC. FRGS. Mem., Internat. Cultural Soc., Korea, 1977. *Publications*: History of the 1859 Revival, 1959; Christian Foundations, 1960; Ravenhill Pulpit, Vol. 1, 1966, Vol. 2, 1967; Exposition of the Epistle to the Romans, 1968; Billy Graham and the Church of Rome, 1970; The Massacre of St Bartholomew, 1972; America's Debt to Ulster, 1976; (jtly) Ulster—the facts, 1981; No Pope Here, 1982; Dr Kidd, 1982; Those Flaming Tennents, 1983. *Address*: House of Commons, SW1; The Parsonage, 17 Cyprus Avenue, Belfast BT5 5NT.

PAISLEY, John Lawrence, CB 1970; MBE 1946; Consultant with L. G. Mouchel & Partners, Consulting Engineers, 1971–82, retired; *b* Manchester, 4 Sept. 1909; *e s* of J. R. and Mrs E. W. Paisley; *m* 1937, Angela Dorothy Catliff; three *d*. *Educ*: King George V Sch., Southport; Univ. of Liverpool. BEng 1930, MEng 1935. Asst Engineer: Siemens Bros & Co. Ltd, North Delta Transmission Lines, Egypt, 1930–34; Howard Humphreys & Sons, Cons. Engrs, Tunnels and Viaduct on A55, in N Wales, 1934–35; W Sussex CC, 1935–37; Asst Engr in Scotland, Min. of Transport, 1937–39. War Service with Royal Engineers, 1939–46: took part in Dunkirk evacuation and finally as Major, RE (now Hon. Major), commanded 804 Road Construction Co. in UK, France and Germany (MBE). Ministry of Transport: Engr in Scotland, 1946–52; Senr Engr in HQ, London, 1952–60; Divl Rd Engr, NW Div. at Manchester, 1960–64; Dep. Chief Engr, HQ, London, 1964–66; Chief Highway Engr, Min. of Transport, 1966–70. Hon. Vice-Pres., Permanent Internat. Assoc. of Road Congresses. FICE; FInstHE. *Publications*: contribs Proc. Instn of Civil Engrs, Proc. Instn of Highway Engrs. *Recreation*: fell walking. *Address*: Weybrook, Warren Road, Guildford, Surrey. *T*: Guildford 62798. *Clubs*: Civil Service, Victory; Rucksack (Manchester).

PAISLEY, Robert, OBE 1977; Board Member, since 1983, and Team Consultant, since 1985, Liverpool Football Club (Manager, 1974–83); *b* 23 Jan. 1919; *s* of Samuel and Emily Paisley; *m* 1946, Jessie Chandler; two *s* one *d*. *Educ*: Eppleton Sen. Mixed Sch., Tyne and Wear. Apprentice bricklayer, 1934; also Hetton Juniors Amateur FC, 1934–37; Bishop Auckland Amateur FC, 1937–39; signed as professional for Liverpool FC, 1939; Army Service, RA, 1939–46; Liverpool FC: 2nd Team Trainer, 1954–59; 1st Team Trainer, 1959–70; Asst Manager, 1970–74. Successes since becoming manager: UEFA Cup, 1976; League Championship, 1976, 1977, 1979, 1980, 1982, 1983; European Cup, 1977, 1978, 1981; League Cup (now known as Milk Cup), 1981, 1982, 1983. Manager of the Year Award, 1976, 1977, 1979, 1980, 1982, 1983; Special Merit Award, PFA Award, 1983. Hon. MSc Liverpool, 1983. Freeman, City of Liverpool, 1983. *Publications*: Bob Paisley's Liverpool Scrap Book, 1979; Bob Paisley: an autobiography, 1983. *Recreations*: all types of sport. *Address*: 29 Bower Road, Woolton, Liverpool L25 4RG.

PAKENHAM, family name of **Earl of Longford.**

PAKENHAM, Elizabeth; see Longford, Countess of.

PAKENHAM, Henry Desmond Verner, CBE 1964; HM Diplomatic Service, retired; *b* 5 Nov. 1911; *s* of Hamilton Richard Pakenham and Emilie Willis Stringer; *m* 1st, 1946, Crystal Elizabeth Brooksbank (marr. diss., 1960); one *s* one *d* (and one *s* decd); 2nd, 1963, Venetia Maude; one *s* one *d*. *Educ*: Monkton Combe; St John Baptist College, Oxford. Taught modern languages at Sevenoaks School, 1933–40. Served in HM Forces, 1940–45. Entered Foreign Service, 1946; served in Madrid, Djakarta, Havana, Singapore, Tel Aviv, Buenos Aires and Sydney; retired 1971. Chm., Suffolk Preservation Soc., 1979–82. Asst Editor, Satow's Guide to Diplomatic Practice, 5th edn, 1979. *Address*: Rose Farm, Brettenham, Suffolk.

PAKENHAM, Hon. Michael Aidan; HM Diplomatic Service; Head of Arms Control and Disarmament Department, Foreign and Commonwealth Office, since 1983; *b* 3 Nov. 1943; *s* of 7th Earl of Longford, *qv* and Countess of Longford, *qv*; *m* 1980, Meta (Mimi) Landreth Doak, *d* of William Conway Doak of Maryland, USA; two *d* two step *d*. *Educ*: Ampleforth College; Trinity College, Cambridge (MA Classics); Rice University, Texas. Washington Post, 1965; Foreign Office, 1965; Nairobi, 1966; Warsaw, 1967; FCO, 1970; Asst Private Sec., later Private Sec. to Chancellor of Duchy of Lancaster (European Community Affairs), on secondment to Cabinet Office, 1971–74; Geneva (CSCE), 1974;

New Delhi, 1974; Washington, 1978. *Recreations:* tennis, golf, bridge, reading history, museums. *Address:* 23 Sutherland Place, W2 5BZ. *T:* 01–229 8812; Bernhurst, Hurst Green, E Sussex. *T:* Hurst Green 494. *Clubs:* MCC; Delhi Golf.

PAKENHAM, Thomas (Frank Dermot); writer; *b* 14 Aug. 1933; *e s* of 7th Earl of Longford, *qv* and of Countess of Longford, *qv*; (does not use courtesy title); *m* 1964, Valerie, *d* of Major R. G. McNair Scott; two *s* two *d. Educ:* Dragon School, Oxford; Belvedere Coll., Dublin; Ampleforth Coll., York; Magdalen Coll., Oxford (BA Greats 1955). Travelled, Near East and Ethiopia, 1955–56 (discovered unrecorded medieval Ethiopian church at Bethlehem, Begemdir, 1956). Free-lance writing, 1956–58. Editorial staff: Times Educational Supplement, 1958–60, Sunday Telegraph, 1961; The Observer, 1961–64. Founder Mem. 1958, and Member Cttee 1958–64, Victorian Soc.; Founder Mem., and Mem. Cttee 1968–72, Historic Irish Tourist Houses and Gardens Assoc. (HITHA); Treas., British-Irish Assoc., 1972–; Sec. (co-founder), Christopher Ewart-Biggs Memorial Trust, 1976–. Research Fellow, St Antony's Coll., Oxford, 1979–81. *Publications:* The Mountains of Rasselas: An Ethiopian Adventure, 1959; The Year of Liberty: The Story of the Great Irish Rebellion of 1798, 1969; The Boer War, 1979 (Cheltenham Prize, 1980). *Recreation:* water. *Address:* 111 Elgin Crescent, W11. *T:* 01–727 7624; Tullynally, Castlepollard, Westmeath, Ireland. *T:* Mullingar 61159. *Clubs:* Beefsteak, Brooks's; Stephen's Green (Dublin).

PAKENHAM-WALSH, John, CB 1986; Principal Assistant Legal Adviser to the Home Office, since 1980; *b* 7 Aug. 1928; *s* of late Rev. W. P. Pakenham-Walsh, formerly ICS, and Guendolen (*née* Elliott); *m* 1951, Deryn, *er d* of Group Captain R. E. G. Fulljames, MC, and Mrs Muriel Fulljames; one *s* four *d. Educ:* Bradfield Coll.; University Coll., Oxford (MA). Called to the Bar, Lincoln's Inn, 1951. Crown Counsel, Hong Kong, 1953–57; Parly Counsel, Fedn of Nigeria, 1958–61; joined Legal Adviser's Br., Home Office, 1961; seconded to Law Officers Dept, 1971–73; Asst Legal Adviser, Home Office, 1973–80. *Address:* Home Office, Queen Anne's Gate, SW1H 9AT. *Clubs:* United Oxford & Cambridge University; Liphook Golf (Hants).

PAKES, Ernest John, CBE 1954; Under-writing Member of Lloyd's, since 1956; *b* 28 Jan. 1899; *s* of Ernest William Pakes; *m* 1st, 1928, Emilie Pickering (*d* 1981); one *s*; 2nd, 1984, Mrs Margarita Eileen Gilmore. *Educ:* Hampton Gram. Sch. Served with London Scottish Regt, 1917–19; Ceylon Defence Force, 1940–44; Min. of War Transport, Karachi, 1945–46. Employed in shipping industry, P&O Group, 1916–62 including: Mackinnon Mackenzie & Co., India, Ceylon etc., 1921–54 (Chm., 1951–54); British India Steam Navigation Co. Ltd, 1954–62 (Chm., 1960–62); Director: Allahabad Bank, India, 1947–54 (Chm., 1951–54); Chartered Bank, London, 1958–62. Chm., Karachi Chamber of Commerce, 1946–47; Pres., Bengal Chamber of Commerce and Assocd Chambers of Commerce of India, 1953–54. Liveryman, Worshipful Co. of Shipwrights. *Recreation:* golf. *Address:* Staneway, Tyrrells Wood, Leatherhead, Surrey. *T:* Leatherhead 373243. *Clubs:* Oriental; Walton Heath.

PAKINGTON, family name of **Baron Hampton.**

PAL, Dr Benjamin Peary, Padma Shri 1958; Padma Bhushan 1968; FRS 1972; Chairman, National Committee on Environmental Planning and Coordination, 1977–81; *b* 26 May 1906; *s* of Dr R. R. Pal; unmarried. *Educ:* Rangoon Univ.; Downing Coll., Cambridge University. MSc hons, PhD Cantab. 2nd Economic Botanist, Imperial Agric. Research Inst., 1933; Imperial Economic Botanist, 1937; Dir, Indian Agric. Res. Inst., 1950; Dir-Gen., Indian Council of Agric. Research, 1965–72, Scientist Emeritus 1972. Hon. DSc: Punjab Agric. Univ.; Sardar Patel Univ.; UP Agric. Univ.; Haryana Agric. Univ.; Orissa Agric. Univ.; Foreign Mem., All Union Lenin Acad. of Agric. Sciences; Hon. Member: Japan Acad.; Acad. d'Agriculture de France; Fellow: Linnean Soc. of London; Indian Nat. Science Acad. (Pres., 1975–76). *Publications:* Beautiful Climbers of India, 1960; Wheat, 1966; Charophyta, The Rose in India, 1966; Flowering Shrubs, 1967; All About Roses, 1973; Bougainvilleas, 1974. *Recreations:* rose gardening, painting. *Address:* P11, Hauz Khas Enclave, New Delhi 110016, India. *T:* 660245.

PALADE, Prof. George Emil; scientist, USA; Senior Research Scientist, Department of Cell Biology, Yale University, since 1983; *b* Iassy, Roumania, 19 Nov. 1912; *s* of Emil Palade and Constanta Cantemir; *m* 1st, 1941, Irina Malaxa (decd); one *s* one *d*; 2nd, 1970, Dr Marilyn Farquhar. *Educ:* Liceul Al. Hasdeu, Buzau, Roumania; Med. Sch., Univ. of Bucharest (MD). Arrived in US, 1946; naturalized US citizen, 1952. Instructor, Asst Prof., then Lectr in Anatomy, Sch. of Med., Univ. of Bucharest, 1940–45; Visiting Investigator, Rockefeller Inst. for Med. Research, 1946–48; continuing as an Assistant (later the Inst. became Rockefeller Univ., NYC); promoted to Associate, 1951, and Associate Mem., 1953; Prof. of Cell Biology, Rockefeller Univ. and full Member of Rockefeller Inst., 1956. Fellow, Amer. Acad. of Arts and Sciences; Member: Nat. Acad. of Sciences; Pontifical Acad. of Sciences; Amer. Soc. Cell Biology; Amer. Assoc. for the Advancement of Science; For. Mem., Royal Soc., 1984. Awards include: Albert Lasker Basic Research, 1966; Gairdner Award, 1967; Hurwitz Prize, 1970; Nobel Prize for Medicine, 1974; Nat. Medal of Science, USA, 1986. *Publications:* Editor: Jl of Cell Biology (co-founder); Jl of Membrane Biology; numerous contribs med. and sci. jls. *Address:* Department of Cell Biology, Yale University School of Medicine, 333 Cedar Street, PO Box 3333, New Haven, Conn. 06510, USA. *T:* (203) 436–2376.

PALAMOUNTAIN, Edgar William Irwin; Director, Esmée Fairbairn Trust, since 1980 (Trustee, 1966–80); *m* 1948, Eleanor, *d* of Maj.-Gen. Sir Richard Lewis, KCMG, CB, CBE; one *s* two *d. Educ:* Charterhouse; St John's Coll., Oxford (MA). Served War of 1939–45, RHA and staff (mentioned in despatches) Major 1945, Actg Lt-Col 1946; Allied Commn for Austria, 1945–47. Anglo-Iranian Oil Co., London and Tehran, 1948–51; Tootal Ltd, 1952–56 (Personal Asst to Chm.; Prodn Manager); M & G Group, 1957–79: Exec. Dir, 1962; Man. Dir, 1968; Chm., 1977. Dir of various cos. Chairman: Unit Trust Assoc., 1977–79; Institutional Shareholders Cttee, 1978–79; Wider Share Ownership Council, 1967–; Money Management Council, 1985–. Trustee: Nat. Assoc. of Almshouses, 1963–80; Thames Help Trust, 1980–; Social Affairs Unit, 1982–. Patron, Inst. of Economic Affairs, 1972–; Governor, NIESR, 1981–; Mem. Bd, Adam Smith Inst., 1982–; Mem. Council, Univ. of Buckingham (formerly UC, Buckingham), 1975–(Chm., 1979–84). Mem. Cttee, London Voluntary Service Council, 1969–. FRSA. DUniv. *Publication:* Taurus Pursuant: a history of the Eleventh Armoured Division, 1945. *Recreations:* lawn tennis, golf, stalking. *Address:* Duns Tew Manor, Oxford; 35 Chelsea Towers, SW3. *Clubs:* Boodle's, City of London, MCC.

PALETHORPE-TODD, Richard Andrew; *see* Todd, Richard.

PALETTE, John, OBE 1986; Director of Personnel, British Rail, since 1982; *b* 19 May 1928; *s* of Arthur and Beatrice Palette; *m* 1950, Pamela Mabel Palmer; three *s. Educ:* Alexandra Sch., Hampstead. MCIT. Gen. Railway Admin, 1942–69; Divl Manager, Bristol, 1969–72; Asst Gen. Manager, Western Region, 1972–74; Divl Manager, Manchester, 1974–76; Gen. Manager, Scottish Region, 1976–77, Southern Region, 1977–82, British Railways. Chm., British Transport Ship Management (Scotland) Ltd, 1976–. *Recreations:* walking, reading, gardening, watching sport. *Address:* 90 Wargrave Road, Twyford, Reading, Berks. *T:* Twyford (Berks) 340965.

PALIN, Michael Edward; freelance writer and actor; *b* 5 May 1943; *s* of Edward and Mary Palin; *m* 1966, Helen M. Gibbins; two *s* one *d. Educ:* Birkdale Sch., Sheffield; Shrewsbury; Brasenose Coll., Oxford (BA 2nd Cl. Hons Mod. Hist.). Chm., Transport 2,000, 1986. Actor and writer: Monty Python's Flying Circus, BBC TV, 1969–74; Ripping Yarns, BBC TV, 1976–80; writer, East of Ipswich, BBC TV, 1986. *Films:* actor and jt author: And Now for Something Completely different, 1970; Monty Python and the Holy Grail, 1974; Monty Python's Life of Brian, 1978; Time Bandits, 1980; Monty Python's "The Meaning of Life," 1982; actor, writer and co-producer: The Missionary, 1982; actor: Jabberwocky, 1976; A Private Function, 1984; Brazil, 1985. Contributor, Great Railway Journeys of the World, BBC TV, 1980. *Publications:* Monty Python's Big Red Book, 1970; Monty Python's Brand New Bok, 1973; Dr Fegg's Encyclopaedia of *All* World Knowledge, 1984; Limericks, 1985; *for children:* Small Harry and the Toothache Pills, 1981; The Mirrorstone, 1986; The Cyril Stories, 1986. *Recreations:* reading, running, railways—preferably all three in a foreign country. *Address:* 6 Cambridge Gate, NW1 4JR. *T:* 01–487 4487. *Club:* Turf.

PALING, Helen Elizabeth, (Mrs W. J. S. Kershaw); Her Honour Judge Paling; a Circuit Judge, since 1985; *b* 25 April 1933; *o d* of A. Dale Paling and Mabel Eleanor Thomas; *m* 1961, William John Stanley Kershaw, PhD; one *s* three *d. Educ:* Prince Henry's Grammar Sch., Otley; London Sch. of Economics. LLB London 1954. Called to Bar, Lincoln's Inn, 1955; a Recorder, 1972–85. *Address:* 46 Grainger Street, Newcastle upon Tyne. *T:* Newcastle upon Tyne 21980, 22392.

PALING, William Thomas; *b* 28 Oct. 1892; *s* of George Thomas Paling, Sutton-in-Ashfield, Notts; *m* 1919, Gladys Nellie, MBE, *d* of William Frith, James Street, Nuncar Gate, Nottinghamshire; one *s* one *d.* MP (Lab) Dewsbury, 1945–59, retired. *Address:* 3 Lancaster Close, Tickhill, near Doncaster, South Yorks. *T:* Doncaster 742875.

PALLEY, Dr Claire Dorothea Taylor; Principal of St Anne's College, Oxford, since 1984; *b* 17 Feb. 1931; *d* of Arthur Aubrey Swait, Durban; *m* 1952, Ahrn Palley (marr. diss. 1985); five *s. Educ:* Durban Girls' Coll.; Univs of Cape Town and London. BA 1950, LLB 1952, Cape Town; PhD London 1965; MA Oxon 1984. Called to Bar, Middle Temple; Advocate, S Africa and Rhodesia. Lecturer: Cape Town Univ., 1953–55; UC Rhodesia and Nyasaland, 1960–65; QUB, 1966–67; Reader, QUB, 1967–70, Prof. of Public Law, 1970–73, and Dean of Faculty of Law, 1971–73; Prof. of Law, 1973–84, and Master of Darwin Coll., 1974–82, Univ. of Kent. Chm., SE Area Cttee, Nat. Assoc. of Citizens' Advice Bureaux, 1974–79; Member: Council, Minority Rights Group, 1975–; Commonwealth Scholarships Commn, 1980–82; UK Nat. Commn for UNESCO, 1984–. Constitutional Adviser to: African Nat. Council at Const. Talks on Rhodesia, 1976; Govt of Republic of Cyprus, 1980–. *Publications:* The Constitutional History and Law of Southern Rhodesia, 1966; contrib. learned jls. *Address:* St Anne's College, Oxford.

PALLISER, Rt. Hon. Sir (Arthur) Michael, GCMG 1977 (KCMG 1973; CMG 1966); PC 1983; HM Diplomatic Service, retired; Chairman, Council of the International Institute for Strategic Studies, since 1983; Chairman, Samuel Montagu & Co. (Holdings) Ltd, since 1984 (Director, since 1983); Director, since 1983: Samuel Montagu & Co. Ltd (Vice Chairman, 1984; Chairman, 1984–85); BAT Industries plc; Booker McConnell plc; Eagle Star Holdings; Shell Transport & Trading Co. plc; United Biscuits (Holdings); Director, Arbor Acres Farm Inc., since 1985; Member, Security Commission, since 1983; *b* 9 Apr. 1922; *s* of late Admiral Sir Arthur Palliser, KCB, DSC, and of Lady Palliser (*née* Margaret Eva King-Salter); *m* 1948, Marie Marguerite, *d* of late Paul-Henri Spaak; three *s. Educ:* Wellington Coll.; Merton Coll., Oxford. Served with Coldstream Guards, 1942–47; Capt. 1944. Entered HM Diplomatic Service, 1947; SE Asia Dept, Foreign Office, 1947–49; Athens, 1949–51; Second Sec., 1950; Foreign Office: German Finance Dept, 1951–52; Central Dept, 1952–54; Private Sec. to Perm. Under-Sec., 1954–56; First Sec., 1955; Paris, 1956–60; Head of Chancery, Dakar, 1960–62 (Chargé d'Affaires in 1960, 1961 and 1962); Counsellor, and seconded to Imperial Defence College, 1963; Head of Planning Staff, Foreign Office, 1964; a Private Sec. to PM, 1966; Minister, Paris, 1969; Ambassador and Head of UK Deleg. to European Communities, Brussels, 1971; Ambassador and UK Permanent Representative to European Communities, 1973–75; Permanent Under-Sec. of State, FCO and Head of Diplomatic Service, 1975–82. Pres., Internat. Social Service of GB, 1982–; Governor, Wellington Coll., 1982–. Chevalier, Order of Orange Nassau, 1944; Chevalier, Légion d'Honneur, 1957. *Address:* 12b Wedderburn Road, NW3 5QG. *Club:* Buck's.

PALLOT, Arthur Keith, CB 1981; CMG 1966; Secretary and Director-General, Commonwealth War Graves Commission, 1975–82 (Director of Finance and Establishments, 1956–75); *b* 25 Sept. 1918; *s* of Harold Pallot, La Tourelle, Jersey; *m* 1945, Marjorie, *d* of J. T. Smith, Rugby; two *d. Educ:* Newton College. Royal Navy, 1936; retired as Lt-Comdr, 1947. Commonwealth War Graves Commission, 1947. Awarded the Queen's Commendation for brave conduct, 1958. *Recreations:* walking, squash, cricket, golf. *Address:* Northways, Stubbles Lane, Cookham Dean, Berks. *T:* Marlow 6529.

PALMAR, Sir Derek (James), Kt 1986; FCA; CBIM; Chairman: Bass, since 1976 (Chairman and Chief Executive, 1976–84; Director, 1970–76); Rush & Tompkins Group, since 1974; Yorkshire Television, since 1982; Vice President, Brewers' Society, since 1982 (Chairman, 1980–82); *b* 25 July 1919; *o s* of late Lt-Col F. J. Palmar; *m* 1946, Edith Brewster; one *s* one *d. Educ:* Dover College. FCA 1957 (ACA 1947). Served RA and Staff, 1941–46; psc; Lt-Col 1945. Peat, Marwick, Mitchell & Co., 1937–57; Dir, Hill Samuel Group, 1957–70. Adviser, Dept of Economic Affairs, 1965–67; Mem., British Railways Bd, 1969–72; Chm., BR Southern Regional Adv. Bd, 1972–79. Director: Grindlays Bank, 1970–85; Drayton Consolidated Trust; Consolidated Venture Trust; City Merchants Holdings; United Newspapers, 1986–; Centre for Policy Studies. Chairman: Zool Soc. of London Develt Trust, 1986–; Leeds Univ. Foundn, 1986–; Member: Accounting Standards Cttee, 1982–84; Alcohol Educn and Res. Council; Ct, Brewers' Co. Trustee, Civic Trust. Freeman, City of London. *Recreations:* shooting, gardening. *Address:* 30 Portland Place, W1N 3DF. *T:* 01–637 5499. *Club:* Boodle's.

PALMER, family name of **Earl of Selborne, Baron Palmer** and **Baroness Lucas of Crudwell.**

PALMER, 3rd Baron, *cr* 1933, of Reading; **Raymond Cecil Palmer,** OBE 1968; Bt *cr* 1916; former Director, Associated Biscuit Manufacturers Ltd, retired 1980; Chairman: Huntley & Palmers Ltd, 1969–80; Huntley Boorne & Stevens Ltd, Reading, 1956–80 (Deputy Chairman, 1948); *b* 24 June 1916; *er s* of 2nd Baron Palmer and Marguerite (*d* 1959), *d* of William McKinley Osborne, USA, Consul-General to Great Britain; *S* father 1950; *m* 1941, Victoria Ellen, (CBE 1984), *o c* of late Captain J. A. R. Weston-Stevens, Maidenhead; two *d* (and one *d* decd). *Educ:* Harrow; University Coll., Oxford. Joined Huntley & Palmers Ltd, 1938, Dep. Chm., 1966–69, Man. Dir, 1967–69. Served War of 1939–45 in Grenadier Guards as Lieut, in UK and North Africa, 1940–43 (invalided).

Mem., Southern Electricity Bd, 1965–77. Pres., Berks CCC. *Recreations:* music, gardening. *Heir: b* Col Hon. Gordon William Nottage Palmer, *qv*. *Address:* Farley Hill House, Farley Hill, Reading, Berkshire. *T:* Eversley 732260. *Club:* Cavalry and Guards.

See also Lord Wodehouse.

PALMER, Andrew Eustace, CVO 1981; HM Diplomatic Service; Ambassador to Cuba, since 1986; *b* 30 Sept. 1937; *s* of Lt-Col Rodney Howell Palmer, MC, and Mrs Frances Pauline Ainsworth (*née* Gordon-Duff); *m* 1962, Davina, *d* of Sir Roderick Barclay, *qv*; two *s* one *d*. *Educ:* Winchester Coll.; Pembroke Coll., Cambridge (MA). Second Lieut. Rifle Bde, 1956–58. Joined HM Foreign (later Diplomatic) Service, 1961; American Dept, FO, 1962–63; Third, later Second, Secretary (Commercial), La Paz, 1963–65; Second Sec., Ottawa, 1965–67; Treasury Centre for Administrative Studies, 1967–68; Central Dept, FO, later Southern European Dept, FCO, 1968–72; First Sec. (Information), Paris, 1972–76; Asst Head of Defence Dept, FCO, 1976–77; RCDS 1978; Counsellor, Head of Chancery and Consul-Gen., Oslo, 1979–82; Hd, Falkland Is Dept, FCO, 1982–85; Fellow, Harvard Center for Internat. Affairs, 1985–86. *Recreations:* fishing, tennis, following most other sports, photography. *Address:* c/o Foreign and Commonwealth Office, SW1. *Clubs:* Brooks's, MCC.

PALMER, Anthony Wheeler, QC 1979; a Recorder of the Crown Court, since 1980; *b* 30 Dec. 1936; *s* of late Philip Palmer and of Doris Palmer; *m* Jacqueline, *d* of Reginald Fortnum, Taunton; one *s* two *d*. *Educ:* Wrekin Coll., Salop. Called to the Bar, Gray's Inn, 1962. *Address:* 17 Warwick Avenue, Coventry CV5 6DJ. *T:* Coventry 75340.

PALMER, Arnold Daniel; professional golfer since 1954; golf course designer; *b* 10 Sept. 1929; *s* of Milfred J. and Doris Palmer; *m* 1954, Winifred Walzer; two *d*. *Educ:* Wake Forest Univ. Winner of numerous tournament titles, including: British Open Championship, 1961, 1962; US Open Championship, 1960; Masters Championship, 1958, 1960, 1962, 1964; Spanish Open Championship, 1975; Professional Golfers' Assoc. Championship, 1975; Canadian PGA, 1980; USA Seniors' Championship, 1981. Hon. Dr of Laws: Wake Forest; Nat. Coll. of Educn; Hon. Dr Hum: Thiel Coll.; Florida Southern College. Hon. Member: Royal and Ancient Golf Club, 1979; Troon Golf Club, 1982; Royal Birkdale Golf Club, 1983. *Publications:* (all jointly) Arnold Palmer Golf Book, 1961; Portrait of a Professional Golfer, 1964; My Game and Yours, 1965; Situation Golf, 1970; Go for Broke, 1973; Arnold Palmer's Best 54 Golf Holes, 1977; Arnold Palmer's Complete Book of Putting, 1986. *Recreations:* aviation (speed record for flying round world in twin-engine jet, 1976), bridge, hunting, fishing. *Address:* PO Box 52, Youngstown, Pa 15696, USA. *T:* (412) 537–7751. *Clubs:* (Owner and Pres.) Latrobe Country; (Pres. and Part-Owner) Bay Hill and Isleworth (Orlando, Fla); (Tournament Professional) Laurel Valley Golf; numerous other country, city, golf.

PALMER, Arthur Montague Frank, CEng, FIEE, FInstE; *b* 4 Aug. 1912; *s* of late Frank Palmer, Northam, Devon; *m* 1939, Dr Marion Ethel Frances Woollaston, medical consultant; two *d*. *Educ:* Ashford Gram. Sch.; Brunel Technical College (now Brunel Univ.). Is a Chartered Engineer and a Chartered Fuel Technologist. Studied electrical supply engineering, 1932–35, in London; Member technical staff of London Power Co., 1936–45; former Staff Mem., Electrical Power Engineers Assoc. Member Brentford and Chiswick Town Council, 1937–45. MP (Lab) for Wimbledon, 1945–50; MP (Lab and Co-op): Cleveland Div. of Yorks, Oct. 1952–Sept. 1959; Bristol Central, 1964–74; Bristol NE, 1974–83; Frontbench Opposition Spokesman on fuel and power, 1957–59; Chairman: Parly and Scientific Cttee, 1965–68; House of Commons Select Cttee on Science and Technology, 1966–70, 1974–79; Co-operative party Parly Gp, 1970–73; Vice-Chm., Select Cttee on Energy, 1979–83. *Publications:* The Future of Electricity Supply, 1943; Modern Norway, 1950; Law and the Power Engineer, 1959; Nuclear Power: the reason why, 1984; Energy Policy in the Community, 1985; articles on political, industrial, and economic subjects. *Recreations:* walking, motoring, gardening, reading novels, history and politics. *Address:* Manton Thatch, Manton, Marlborough, Wilts SN8 4HR. *T:* Marlborough 53313. *Club:* Athenæum.

PALMER, Bernard Harold Michael, MA; Editor of the Church Times since 1968; *b* 8 Sept. 1929; *e s* of late Christopher Harold Palmer; *m* 1954, Jane Margaret, *d* of late E. L. Skinner; one *s* one *d*. *Educ:* St Edmund's School, Hindhead; Eton (King's Scholar); King's College, Cambridge. BA 1952; MA 1956. Member of editorial staff, Church Times, 1952–; Managing Director, 1957–; Editor-in-Chief, 1960–68; Chm., 1962–. *Recreations:* cycling, penmanship. *Address:* 143 Bradbourne Vale Road, Sevenoaks, Kent. *T:* Sevenoaks 53327. *Club:* Royal Commonwealth Society.

PALMER, Brian Desmond; Under Secretary, Northern Ireland Office, since 1981; *b* 1 May 1939; *m* 1964, Hilary Eileen Latimer; one *s* one *d*. *Educ:* Royal Belfast Academical Instn; Queen's Univ. of Belfast (LLB 1962). Northern Ireland Civil Service, 1957–: Estate Duty Office, 1957–62; Min. of Home Affairs, 1962–65; Dept of the Environment, 1965–77; Head of Central Secretariat, 1977–81. *Recreation:* golf. *Address:* Northern Ireland Office, Dundonald House, Belfast BT4 3SU. *T:* Belfast 63255.

PALMER, Charles Alan Salier, CBE 1969; DSO 1945; Chairman, Associated Biscuit Manufacturers Ltd, 1969–72 (Vice-Chm., 1963); *b* 23 Oct. 1913; *s* of late Sir (Charles) Eric Palmer, Shinfield Grange, near Reading; *m* 1939, Auriol Mary, *d* of late Brig.-Gen. Cyril R. Harbord, CB, CMG, DSO. *Educ:* Harrow; Exeter Coll., Oxford. Joined Huntley & Palmer's, 1934 (Bd, 1938; Dep.-Chm. 1955; Chm., Huntley & Palmer's, 1963). Served War of 1939–45: with Berks Yeo., Adjt, 1939–41; GSO3, HQ 61 Div., 1941–42; GSO2, HQ III Corps, 1942–43; Lt-Col; commanded SOE mission, Albania, 1943–45 (despatches). Pres., Reading Conservative Assoc., 1946–86. Chm., Cake & Biscuit Alliance, 1967–70; Mem. Council, CBI 1967–70; Mem. British Productivity Council, 1970–73. *Recreations:* shooting, fishing, tropical agriculture. *Address:* Forest Edge, Farley Hill, Reading, Berks. *T:* Arborfield Cross 760223.

PALMER, Sir (Charles) Mark, 5th Bt, *cr* 1886; *b* 21 Nov. 1941; *s* of Sir Anthony Frederick Mark Palmer, 4th Bt, and of Henriette (*see* Lady Abel Smith); *S* father 1941; *m* 1976, Hon. Catherine Elizabeth Tennant, *y d* of 2nd Baron Glenconner; one *s* one *d*. *Heir:* *s* Arthur Morris Palmer, *b* 9 March 1981. *Address:* Mill Hill Farm, Sherborne, Northleach, Glos. *T:* Windrush 395.

PALMER, Lt-Gen. (Charles) Patrick (Ralph), CBE 1982 (OBE 1974); Military Secretary, Ministry of Defence, since 1986; head of a review of officer career structure, Ministry of Defence, 1986; *b* 29 April 1933; *s* of late Charles Dudley Palmer and Catherine Anne (*née* Hughes-Buller); *m* 1st, 1960, Sonia Hardy Wigglesworth (*d* 1965); one *s*; 2nd, 1966, Joanna Grace Baines; two *d*. *Educ:* Marlborough Coll. psc 1963. Commnd Argyll and Sutherland Highlanders, 1953; served British Guiana, Berlin, Suez Operation and Cyprus; Instructor, RMA Sandhurst, 1961–62; BM 153(H) Inf. Bde, 1964–65; 1 Argyll and Sutherland Highlanders, Borneo, Singapore and Aden, 1965–68; MA to Dep. CDS (Intell.), MoD, 1968–70; Instructor, Staff Coll., 1970–72; reformed and commanded 1st Bn Argyll and Sutherland Highlanders, 1972–74; Chief of Staff to Comd British Forces Hong Kong, 1974–76; RCDS, 1977; Comd 7th Armoured Bde, 1977–78; Dep. Comd 1 Armoured Div., 1978–80; Comd British Mil. Adv. and Training Team, Zimbabwe, 1980–82; GOC NE Dist, 1982 and Comd 2nd Inf. Div., 1983; Comdt, Staff Coll., Camberley, 1984–86. Col of the Argyll and Sutherland Highlanders, 1982–. *Recreations:* travel, outdoor interests. *Address:* c/o Royal Bank of Scotland, Comrie, Perthshire PH6 2DW. *Club:* Army and Navy.

PALMER, Charles Stuart William, OBE 1973; Chairman, British Olympic Association, since 1983 (Vice-Chairman, 1977–83); President, British Judo Association, since 1977 (Chairman, 1962–85); *b* London, 15 April 1930; *s* of Charles Edward Palmer and Emma Byrne. *Educ:* Drayton Manor County Sch. Represented GB in internat. judo comps, 1949–59; studied judo in Japan, 1951–55; obtained 1st Dan 1948, 4th Dan 1955, 8th Dan 1980; Mem. 1957, Capt. 1958, 1959, European Judo Champs winning team. Pres., Internat. Judo Fedn, 1965–79 (Hon. Life Pres., 1979–); Vice-Pres., British Schs Judo Assoc., 1967–; Chm., British Univs Judo Assoc., 1968–75. Sec.-Gen., Gen. Assoc of Internat. Sports Fedns, 1975–84; Member: IOC Tripartite Commn, 1974–81; Sports Council, 1983–; Exec. Council, Assoc. of European Nat. Olympic Cttees, 1985–; Exec. Cttee, CCPR, 1975– (Chm., Games and Sports Div., 1980–). Governor, Sports Aid Foundn, 1979–. Manning Award, Sports Writers' Assoc., 1976. Olympic Order (silver), 1980; Gold Medal, European Judo Union, 1982. Key of City of Taipei, 1974, Key of City of Seoul, 1981; Diploma and Bronze Medal, City of Bordeaux, 1970; Distinguished Service Gold Medal (China), 1974; Merito Deportivo Gold Medal (Spain), 1976. *Publications:* technical papers and articles on judo and sports politics. *Recreations:* judo, skiing, sport generally, flying light aircraft, orchestral music, opera, languages. *Address:* 4 Hollywood Road, SW10 9HY. *T:* 01–352 6238.

PALMER, David Vereker; Chairman and Chief Executive, Willis Faber plc; *b* 9 Dec. 1926; *s* of late Brig. Julian W. Palmer and Lena Elizabeth (*née* Vereker); *m* 1950, Mildred Elaine O'Neal Palmer; three *d*. *Educ:* Stowe. ACII 1950. Commnd The Life Guards, 1944; served as regular officer in Europe and ME, 1944–49; joined Edward Lumley & Sons, 1949; Manager, New York office, 1953–59; joined Willis, Faber & Dumas Ltd, 1959; Dir, 1961; Partner, 1965; Dep. Chm., 1972. Mem. Lloyd's, 1953. Dep. Chm., British Insurance Brokers Assoc., 1984–; Pres., Insurance Inst. of London, 1985–86. Commissioner, Royal Hosp. Chelsea, 1982–. Master, Worshipful Co. of Insurers, 1982. *Recreations:* farming, shooting. *Address:* Burrow Farm, Hambleden, near Henley-on-Thames, Oxon RG9 6LT. *T:* Henley 571256. *Clubs:* City of London; Swinley Forest Golf.

PALMER, Rev. Canon Derek George; Home Secretary, Board for Mission and Unity of the Church of England, since 1983; *b* 24 Jan. 1928; *s* of late George Palmer, MBE and Edna Palmer; *m* 1952, June Cecilie Goddard; two *s* two *d*. *Educ:* Clifton Coll.; Selwyn Coll., Cambridge (MA); Wells Theological Coll. Deacon 1952, priest 1953; Priest in Charge, Good Shepherd, Bristol, 1954–58; first Vicar of Hartcliffe, 1958–68; Vicar of Christ Church, Swindon, 1968–77; Archdeacon of Rochester and Canon Residentiary of Rochester Cathedral, 1977–83. Mem., General Synod, 1971–81. Hon. Canon of Rochester Cathedral, 1983–. *Publications:* All Things New, 1963; Quest, 1971. *Recreation:* canals. *Address:* 54 Oakhill Road, Putney, SW15. *T:* 01–870 1504.

PALMER, Edward Hurry, CB 1972; retired Civil Servant; *b* 23 Sept. 1912; *s* of late Harold G. Palmer and late Ada S. Palmer; *m* 1940, Phyllis Eagle; no *c*. *Educ:* Haileybury. Dep. Chief Surveyor of Lands, Admty, 1942; Chief Surveyor of Lands, Admty, 1950; Chief Surveyor of Defence Lands, MoD, 1964; Comptroller of Defence Lands and Claims, MoD, 1968–72; Property Services Agency, DoE: Dir, Defence Lands Services, 1972–73; Dir, Estate Surveying Services, 1973–74. *Recreations:* gardening, walking. *Address:* 49 Paines Lane, Pinner, Middlesex. *T:* 01–866 5961.

PALMER, Felicity Joan; mezzo-soprano; *b* 6 April 1944. *Educ:* Erith Grammar Sch.; Guildhall Sch. of Music and Drama. AGSM (Teacher/Performer), FGSM. Kathleen Ferrier Meml Prize, 1970; major appearances at concerts in Britain, America, Belgium, France, Germany, Italy, Russia and Spain; operatic début, Marriage of Figaro, Houston, USA, Oct. 1973; ENO: The Magic Flute, 1975; Don Giovanni, 1976; Tristan und Isolde, 1981; Rienzi, 1983; Mazeppa, 1984; Alcina, Bern, 1977; Julius Caesar, Frankfurt, 1978; Idomeneo, Zürich, 1980; Orfeo, Opera North, 1984; King Priam, Royal Opera, 1985; Albert Herring, Glyndebourne, 1985; Tamburlaine, Opera North, 1985; Katya Kabanova, Chicago Lyric Opera, 1986; recitals in Amsterdam, Paris, Vienna, 1976–77; concert tours with BBC SO, Europe, 1973, 1977 and 1984, Australasia, Far East and Eastern Europe, 1977–; ABC tour of Australia, 1978. Recordings include: Poèmes pour Mi, with Pierre Boulez; Holst Choral Symphony, with Sir Adrian Boult; title role in Gluck's Armide; Elektra in Idomeneo, with Nikolaus Harnoncourt; The Music Makers; Sea Pictures; Britten's Phaedra; recitals, with John Constable, of songs by Poulenc, Ravel and Fauré, and of Victorian ballads. *Address:* 27 Fielding Road, W4 1HP.

PALMER, Rev. Preb. Francis Harvey; Diocesan Missioner, Diocese of Lichfield, since 1980; Prebendary of Sawley in Lichfield Cathedral, since 1986; *b* 13 Jan. 1930; *s* of Harry Hereward North Palmer and Ada Wilhelmina Annie Utting; *m* 1955, Mary Susan Lockhart; three *d*. *Educ:* Nottingham High Sch.; Jesus Coll., Cambridge (Exhibr); Wycliffe Hall, Oxford. MA. Deacon, 1955; Priest, 1956. Asst Curate: Knotty Ash, Liverpool, 1955–57; St Mary, Southgate, Crawley, 1958–60; Chaplain, Fitzwilliam House, Cambridge, 1960–64; Vicar of Holy Trinity, Cambridge and Chaplain to Cambridge Pastorate, 1964–71; Principal, Ridley Hall, Cambridge, 1971–72; Rector of Worplesdon, Surrey, 1972–80; Diocesan Ecumenical Officer, Guildford, 1974–80. *Publication:* (contrib.) New Bible Dictionary, 1959. *Recreation:* stamp collecting. *Address:* 14 Gorway Gardens, Walsall WS1 3BJ.

PALMER, Prof. Frank Robert, FBA 1975; Professor and Head of Department of Linguistic Science, University of Reading, since 1965; *b* 9 April 1922; *s* of George Samuel Palmer and Gertrude Lilian (*née* Newman); *m* 1948, Jean Elisabeth Moore; three *s* two *d*. *Educ:* Bristol Grammar Sch.; New Coll., Oxford (Ella Stephens Schol., State Schol.) 1942–43 and 1945–48; Merton Coll., Oxford (Harmsworth Sen. Schol.) 1948–49. MA Oxon 1948; Craven Fellow, 1948. Served war, E Africa, 1943–45. Lectr in Linguistics, Sch. of Oriental and African Studies, Univ. of London, 1950–60 (study leave in Ethiopia, 1952–53); Prof. of Linguistics, University Coll. of N Wales, Bangor, 1960–65; Dean of Faculty of Letters and Social Sciences, Univ. of Reading, 1969–72; Linguistic Soc. of America Prof., Buffalo, 1971; Distinguished Visiting Professor: Foreign Languages Inst., Beijung, 1981; Univ. of Delaware, 1983. Professional visits to Canada, USA, Mexico, Venezuela, Peru, Chile, Argentine, Uruguay, Brazil, India, China, Indonesia, Morocco, Tunisia, Uganda, Kuwait and most countries of Europe. *Publications:* The Morphology of the Tigre Noun, 1962; A Linguistic Study of the English Verb, 1965; (ed) Selected Papers of J. R. Firth, 1968; (ed) Prosodic Analysis, 1970; Grammar, 1971, 2nd edn 1984; The English Verb, 1974; Semantics, 1976, 2nd edn 1981; Modality and the English Modals, 1979; Mood and Modality, 1986; articles and reviews on Ethiopian langs, English and linguistic theory, in learned jls. *Recreations:* gardening, crosswords. *Address:* Whitethorns, Roundabout Lane, Winnersh, Wokingham, Berks RG11 5AD. *T:* Wokingham 786214.

PALMER, Sir Geoffrey (Christopher John), 12th Bt, *cr* 1660; *b* 30 June 1936; *er s* of Lieutenant-Colonel Sir Geoffrey Frederick Neill Palmer, 11th Bt, and Cicely Katherine (who *m* 1952, Robert W. B. Newton), *o d* of late Arthur Radmall, Clifton, nr Watford; *S* father 1951; *m* 1957, Clarissa Mary, *er d* of Stephen Villiers-Smith, Knockholt, Kent; four *d*. *Educ:* Eton. *Recreations:* squash, racquets, cricket, shooting. *Heir:* *b* Jeremy Charles Palmer [*b* 16 May 1939; *m* 1968, Antonia, *d* of late Ashley Dutton; two *s*]. *Address:* Carlton Curlieu Hall, Leicestershire. *T:* Great Glen 2656. *Clubs:* Boodle's; MCC, I Zingari, Free Foresters, Eton Ramblers, Butterflies, Gentlemen of Leicestershire, Lincolnshire Gentlemen's Cricket, Derbyshire Friars, Oakham Cricket, XL, Frogs, Pedagogues, Market Harborough CC, Stoneygate, Old Etonian Golfing Society, Old Etonian Racquets and Tennis, Langtons CC, Northants Amateurs' CC, Knockturnes CC.

PALMER, Rt. Hon. Geoffrey Winston Russell, PC 1985; MP (Lab) Christchurch Central, since 1979; Deputy Prime Minister, Minister of Justice and Attorney General, New Zealand, since 1984; *b* 21 April 1942; *s* of Leonard Russell and Jessie Patricia Palmer; *m* 1963, Margaret Eleanor Hinchcliff; one *s* one *d*. *Educ:* Nelson Coll.; Victoria Univ. of Wellington (BA; LLB); Univ. of Chicago (JD). Barrister and Solicitor, High Court of New Zealand. Professor of Law: Univs of Iowa and of Virginia, 1969–73; Victoria Univ., Wellington, 1974–79. *Publications:* Unbridled Power? - an interpretation of New Zealand's constitution and government, 1979; Compensation for Incapacity - a study of law and social change in Australia and New Zealand, 1979. *Recreations:* cricket, golf, playing the trumpet. *Address:* 288 Bealey Avenue, Christchurch, New Zealand. *T:* 892584.

PALMER, Col Hon. Gordon William Nottage, OBE 1957 (MBE 1944); TD 1950; Lord-Lieutenant of Berkshire, since 1978; *b* 18 July 1918; *yr s* of 2nd Baron Palmer and Marguerite Osborne, USA; *heir-pres.* to 3rd Baron Palmer, *qv*; *m* 1950, Lorna Eveline Hope, *d* of Major C. W. H. Bailie; two *s*. *Educ:* Eton Coll.; Christ Church, Oxford. Served War of 1939–45, with Berks Yeo., 1939–41; staff Capt. RA, HQ 61 Div., 1941; DAQMG, Malta, 1942: GSO2, Ops, GHQ Middle East, 1943–44; GSO2, HQ 5 Div., 1944–45; Lt-Col, Instructor Staff College, Camberley, 1945; Comd Berkshire Yeo., TA, 1954–56. Hon. Colonel: Berkshire and Westminster Dragoons, 1966–67; Royal Yeomanry, 1972–75; 2nd Bn The Wessex Regt (V), 1983–85. Dir, Huntley, Boorne & Stevens Ltd, 1948–69; Chm. Cake and Biscuit Alliance, 1957–59; Man. Dir, Huntley & Palmer Ltd, 1959–65; Chm. and Man. Dir, Associated Biscuits Ltd, 1978–83; Chm., Huntley & Palmer Foods plc (formerly Associated Biscuit Manufacturers), 1978–83. Vice-Chm., Morlands Brewery (Abingdon). Mem., British National Export Council, 1966–69. Dir, S Midlands Regional Bd, Lloyds Bank Ltd. Pres., Council, Reading Univ., 1973–75 (Mem. 1954–, Treas., 1955–59, Vice-Pres., 1966–73; Hon. LLD, 1975); Chm. Council, Royal Coll. of Music, 1973–; FRCM 1965; FRAM 1983; Mem. Council, Bradfield College (Warden, 1984–); DL Berks, 1960; JP 1956; High Sheriff, 1965; Vice Lord-Lieutenant, 1976; Chairman, Berkshire T&AFA, 1961–68. KStJ. *Recreation:* gardening. *Address:* Harris House, Mortimer, Berkshire. *T:* Mortimer 332317; Edrom Newton, Duns, Berwickshire. *T:* Chirnside 292. *Club:* Cavalry and Guards.

PALMER, John, CB 1986; a Deputy Secretary, Department of Transport, since 1982; *b* 13 Nov. 1928; 2nd *s* of late William Nathaniel Palmer and Grace Dorothy May Palmer (*née* Procter); *m* 1958, Lyliane Marthe Jeanjean, *o d* of René Jeanjean and Jeanne Jeanjean (*née* Larrouy); two *d*. *Educ:* Heath Grammar Sch., Halifax; The Queen's Coll., Oxford (Lit. Hum.) (MA). Entered Min. of Housing and Local Govt, 1952; Cabinet Office, 1963–65; Asst Sec., 1965; Under Secretary: DoE, 1971; Dept of Transport, 1976–82. *Address:* 2 The Hermitage, Richmond, Surrey. *Club:* United Oxford & Cambridge University.

PALMER, Sir John (Chance), Kt 1979; DL; solicitor; Consultant, Ashford Sparkes and Harward, Tiverton, Exeter and Crediton; *b* 21 March 1920; *s* of Ernest Clephan Palmer and Claudine Pattie Sapey; *m* 1945, Mary Winifred Ellyatt; four *s*. *Educ:* St Paul's Sch.; St Edmund Hall, Oxford (MA). Served War, RNVR, Atlantic and Mediterranean, 1939–46. Admitted a Solicitor, 1948; Elected Council of Law Society, 1963, President, 1978–79; Member: Criminal Injuries Compensation Board, 1981–; SW Region Mental Health Tribunal, 1983–. Governor, Coll. of Law, 1965–83; Pres., Devon and Exeter Law Society, 1972; Pres., S Western Law Societies, 1973; Chm., Governors of Blundells Sch.; Chm. Trustees, London Sailing Project. Mem. Council, Exeter Univ. Hon. Member: Amer. Bar Assoc.; Canadian Bar Assoc. DL Devon, 1984. Hon. LLD Exeter, 1980. *Recreations:* gardening, sailing. *Address:* Hensleigh, Tiverton, Devon EX16 5NJ. *T:* Tiverton 252959. *Clubs:* Royal Over-Seas League, Naval; Western (Glasgow); Royal Yacht Squadron.

PALMER, Sir John (Edward Somerset), 8th Bt, *cr* 1791; Consultant; Director, Atkins Land and Water Management, since 1979; *b* 27 Oct. 1926; *e s* of Sir John A. Palmer, 7th Bt; *S* father, 1963; *m* 1956, Dione Catharine Skinner; one *s* one *d*. *Educ:* Canford School; Cambridge Univ. (MA); Durham Univ. (MSc). Colonial Service, Northern Nigeria, 1952–61. R. A. Lister & Co. Ltd, Dursley, Glos, 1962–63; Min. Overseas Develt, 1964–68. *Heir:* *s* Robert John Hudson Palmer, *b* 20 Dec. 1960. *Address:* Gayton House, Gayton, Northampton NN7 3EZ. *T:* Northampton 858336; 43 Bermuda Terrace, Cambridge. *T:* Cambridge 323600. *Clubs:* Institute of Directors; Rock Sailing.

PALMER, Maj.-Gen. Sir (Joseph) Michael, KCVO 1985; Director, Alexanders, Laing & Cruickshank Service Co.; Chairman, Copley Marshall & Co. Ltd; *b* 17 Oct. 1928; *s* of late Lt-Col William Robert Palmer, DSO, and late Joan Audrey Palmer (*née* Smith); *m* 1953, Jillean Monica Sherston; two *s* one *d*. *Educ:* Wellington College. Commissioned 14th/20th King's Hussars, 1948; Adjutant 14th/20th King's Hussars, 1953–55; Adjutant Duke of Lancaster's Own Yeomanry, 1956–59; psc 1960; jssc 1965; CO 14th/20th King's Hussars, 1969–72; Comdr RAC 1st (BR) Corps, 1974–76; Asst Chief of Staff, Allied Forces Central Europe, 1976–78; Director, Royal Armoured Corps, 1978–81; Defence Services Sec., 1982–85. Col, 14th/20th King's Hussars, 1981–. Chm. of Governors, Sandroyd Sch., 1984–. Liveryman, Salters' Co., 1965. FBIM. *Recreations:* riding, shooting, music, reading. *Club:* Cavalry and Guards.

PALMER, Leslie Robert, CBE 1964; Director-General, Defence Accounts, Ministry of Defence, 1969–72; *b* 21 Aug. 1910; *s* of Robert Palmer; *m* 1937, Mary Crick; two *s* one *d*. *Educ:* Battersea Grammar School; London University. Entered Admiralty Service, 1929; Assistant Dir of Victualling, 1941; Dep. Dir of Victualling, 1954; Dir of Victualling, Admiralty, 1959–61; Principal Dir of Accounts, Admiralty, 1961–64; Principal Dir of Accounts (Navy) MoD, 1964–68. Hon. Treasurer and Chm., Finance and Admin Dept, United Reformed Church, 1973–79; Hon. Treasurer, BCC, 1980–82. *Recreation:* music. *Address:* 3 Trossachs Drive, Bath BA2 6RP. *T:* Bath 61981.

PALMER, Sir Mark; *see* Palmer, Sir C. M.

PALMER, Maj.-Gen. Sir Michael; *see* Palmer, Maj.-Gen. Sir J. M.

PALMER, Monroe Edward, OBE 1982; FCA; Partner, Palmer Marshall, Chartered Accountants, London; *b* 30 Nov. 1938; *s* of William and Sybil Polikoff; *m* 1962, Susette Sandra (*née* Cardash); two *s* one *d*. *Educ:* Orange Hill Grammar Sch. FCA 1963. Chm., Hendon Citizens Advice Bureau, 1981–83; Treasurer: Disablement Assoc., London Borough of Barnet, 1971–; Liberal Parly Party, 1977–83; Jt Treasurer, Liberal Party, 1977–83. Councillor (L) London Borough of Barnet, 1986–. Contested (L) Hendon South, 1979, 1983. *Recreations:* politics, archery. *Address:* 31 The Vale, NW11 8SE. *T:* 01–455 5140. *Club:* National Liberal.

PALMER, Most Rev. Norman Kitchener; *see* Melanesia, Archbishop of.

PALMER, Maj.-Gen. Patrick; *see* Palmer, Maj.-Gen. C. P. R.

PALMER, Maj.-Gen. (Retd) Philip Francis, CB 1957; OBE 1945; Major-General late Royal Army Medical Corps; *b* 8 Aug. 1903. MB, BCh, BAO, Dublin, 1926; DPH 1936. Served North West Frontier of India, 1930–31 (medal and clasp). Adjutant Territorial Army, 1932–36. War of 1939–45 (OBE). Director of Medical Services, Middle East Land Forces, Dec. 1955; QHS, 1956–60, retired. Col Comdt, RAMC, 1963–67. *Address:* c/o Royal Bank of Scotland, Whitehall, SW1.

PALMER, Robert Henry Stephen; His Honour Judge Palmer; a Circuit Judge, since 1978; *b* 13 Nov. 1927; *s* of Henry Alleyn Palmer and Maud (*née* Obbard); *m* 1955, Geraldine Elizabeth Anne Evens; one *s* two *d*. *Educ:* Charterhouse; University Coll., Oxford. Called to the Bar, 1950. Dep. Chm., Berks QS, 1970. A Recorder of the Crown Court, 1972–78. *Publications:* Harris's Criminal Law, 1960; Guide to Divorce, 1965. *Recreation:* self-sufficiency. *Address:* 44 Staveley Road, Chiswick, W4 3ES. *T:* 01–994 3394.

PALMER, Sidney John, CB 1972; OBE 1953; Deputy Director General, Ships, and Head of Royal Corps of Naval Constructors, 1968–73; *b* 28 Nov. 1913; *m* 1941, Mavis Beatrice Blennerhassett Hallett; four *s*. *Educ:* RNC Greenwich. WhSch 1937. Admty Experiment Works, Haslar, 1938; Portsmouth Dockyard, 1942; Chief Constructor, Sydney, 1945; Constructor Comdr, Hong Kong, 1946; Chief Constructor Aircraft Carriers, 1948; Prof. of Naval Architecture, RNC Greenwich, 1952; Asst Dir Dreadnought Project, 1959; Dep. Dir Polaris Programme, 1963; Dir Naval Ship Production, 1966; Dep. Dir General Ships, 1968. Mem. Council, RINA, 1960; Liveryman, Shipwrights' Co., 1968; Hon. Research Fellow, UCL, 1968. Mem., Cttee of Management, RNLI, 1974–78. *Address:* Bloomfield Avenue, Bath, Avon. *T:* Bath 312592.

PALMER, Thomas Joseph; Group Chief Executive, Legal & General Group, plc, since 1984; *b* 11 Sept. 1931; *m* 1955, Hilary Westrup; two *s* two *d*. *Educ:* King's School, Bruton; Trinity College, Cambridge. MA. Asst Gen. Man. (Planning), Legal and General Assurance Soc., 1969–72, Dir and Gen. Man. (Admin.), 1972–78; Dir and Gen. Man. (Internat.), Legal & General Group plc, 1978–83. Chm., London Business Sch. Assoc., 1974–78; Pres., Insurance Inst. of London, 1982–83. *Recreations:* tennis, gardening, long-distance walking, skiing. *Address:* 30 Colcokes Road, Banstead, Surrey. *T:* Burgh Heath 53215.

PALMER, Maj.-Gen. Tony Brian, CB 1984; CEng, FIMechE; conducting a study on maintenance philosophy and organisation in the Army, 1986; *b* 5 Nov. 1930; *s* of Sidney Bernard Palmer and Ann (*née* Watkins); *m* 1953, Hazel Doris Robinson; two *s*. *Educ:* Wolverton Technical College; Luton College of Technology; General Motors Inst. of Technology, USA. General Motors UK, 1948–51 and 1953–54; commissioned REME 1954; RMCS, 1960–62; Tank Gunnery Trials, Infantry Workshop, staff duties MoD, JSSC, Ops and Plans MoD, 1962–70; Head, DG FVE Secretariat, 1970–72; Comdr REME, 3 Div., 1972–74; Head, Tech. Intell. (Army), 1974–76; Dir, Elect. and Mech. Engineering (Organisation and Training), 1977–79; Comdt, REME Training Centre, 1979–83; Dir-Gen. of Elect. and Mech. Engrg, MoD (Army), 1983–85. Col Comdt, REME, 1986–. Vice-Pres., S Region, British Sports Assoc. for Disabled, 1980–. MBIM. *Recreations:* history, gardening, bird watching. *Address:* c/o Barclays Bank, 6 Market Place, Newbury, Berks. *Club:* Army and Navy.

PALMER, William John, CBE 1973; Judge of Her Majesty's Chief Court for the Persian Gulf, 1967–72; Member, Court of Appeal for Anguilla, 1973–81; *b* 25 April 1909; *o s* of late William Palmer and late Mary Louisa Palmer (*née* Dibb), Suffolk House, Cheltenham; *m* 1st, 1935, Zenaida Nicolaevna (*d* 1944), *d* of late Nicolai Maropoulo, Yalta, Russia; 2nd, 1949, Vanda Ianthe Millicent, *d* of late William Matthew Cowton, Kelvin Grove, Queensland; one *s* two *d*. *Educ:* Pate's Grammar School, Cheltenham; Christ's College, Cambridge (Lady Margaret Scholar). Barrister, Gray's Inn. Joined Indian Civil Service, 1932; Deputy Commissioner, Jalpaiguri, 1943, Chief Presidency Magistrate, Calcutta, 1945; retired from ICS, 1949. Joined Colonial Legal Service as Magistrate, Nigeria, 1950; Chief Registrar, High Court, Eastern Region, 1956; Judge, 1958; Acting Chief Justice of Eastern Nigeria, Oct.-Dec. 1963 and Aug.-Nov. 1965. Judge of HM's Court for Bahrain and Assistant Judge of the Chief Court for the Persian Gulf, 1965–67. A part-time Chm. of Industrial Tribunals, 1975–78. *Recreations:* swimming, travel, history. *Address:* Guys Farm, Icomb, Glos GL54 1JD. *T:* Cotswold 30219. *Clubs:* East India, Devonshire, Sports and Public Schools; Union (Sydney, NSW).

PALMES, Peter Manfred Jerome; Principal Assistant Director, Public Prosecutions Department, 1979–81; *b* 28 Feb. 1920; *s* of Manfred Palmes and Gwendoline Robb; *m* 1st, 1945, Sylvia Theodor (decd); 2nd, 1969, Brenda Laban; one step *d*. *Educ:* Charterhouse; Worcester Coll., Oxford. Served War of 1939–45: Oxford and Bucks LI and 1/8th Gurkha Rifles, 1940–45. Called to Bar, Inner Temple, 1948. Public Prosecutions Dept: Legal Assistant, 1948; Sen. Legal Asst, 1958; Asst Solicitor, 1969; Asst Director, 1977. Jubilee Medal, 1977. *Address:* 4/12 Queen Anne's Gate, SW1. *T:* 01–213 3440.

PALUMBO, Peter Garth, MA; *b* 20 July 1935; *s* of Rudolph and Elsie Palumbo; *m* 1959, Denia (*d* 1986), *d* of late Major Lionel Wigram; one *s* two *d*. *Educ:* Eton College; Worcester College, Oxford. MA Hons Law. Governor, London School of Economics and Political Science, 1976–; Chairman: Tate Gallery Foundn, 1986–; Painshill Park Trust Appeal, 1986–; Trustee: Mies van der Rohe Archive, 1977–; Tate Gallery, 1978–85; Whitechapel Art Gallery Foundation, 1981–; Trustee and Hon. Treas., Writers and Scholars Educnl Trust, 1984–. Hon. FRIBA. *Recreations:* music, travel and reading. *Address:* Bagnor Manor, Bagnor, Newbury, Berks RG16 8AG. *T:* Newbury 40930. *Clubs:* White's, Turf.

PANAYIDES, Tasos Christou; High Commissioner of Cyprus in the UK, and Ambassador to Sweden, Norway, Denmark, and Iceland, since 1979; *b* 9 April 1934; *s* of Christos Panayides and Efrosini Panayides; *m* 1969, Pandora Constantinides; two *s* one *d*. *Educ:* Paphos Gymnasium; Teachers' Training Coll.; Univ. of London (Diploma in Education); Univ. of Indiana, USA (MA Political Science, Diploma in Public Administration). Teacher, 1954–59; First sec. to Pres., 1960–68; Director President's Office, 1969; Ambassador of Cyprus to Federal Republic of Germany, Switzerland, Austria, and Atomic Energy organisation, Vienna, 1969–78. Chairman: Commonwealth Foundn Grants Cttee, 1985–87; Commonwealth Fund Tech. Co-operation Bd of Reps, 1986–87. Hon. Fellow, Ealing Coll. of Higher Educn, 1983. Freeman, City of London, 1984. 1st Cl., Grand Order and Grand Cross with Star and Sash, Federal Republic of Germany, 1978; Grand Cross in Gold with Star and Sash, Austria, 1979; Golden Cross of the Archdiocese of Thyateira and Great Britain, 1981; Grand Cross in Gold of Patriarchate of Antioch, 1984. *Publications:* articles in newspapers and magazines. *Recreations:* swimming, reading books. *Address:* 5 Cheyne Walk, SW3. *T:* 01–351 3989.

PANCKRIDGE, Surg. Vice-Adm. Sir (William) Robert (Silvester), KBE 1962; CB 1960; Medical Director-General of the Navy, 1960–63, retired; *b* 11 Sept. 1901; *s* of W. P. Panckridge, OBE, MB, MRCS, LRCP, and Mrs Panckridge; *m* 1932, Edith Muriel, *d* of Sir John and Lady Crosbie, St John, Newfoundland; one *d. Educ:* Tonbridge School; Middlesex Hospital. FRSM 1955; QHP 1958. PMO, RN Coll., Dartmouth, 1948; Medical Officer-in-Charge; RN Hosp., Hong Kong, 1952; RN Hosp., Chatham, 1958; Surgeon Captain, 1952; Surgeon Rear-Admiral, 1958; Surgeon Vice-Admiral, 1960. QHP, 1958–63. CStJ 1959. *Recreations:* shooting, fishing, gardening. *Address:* Waterfall Lodge, Oughterard, Co. Galway. *T:* Galway 82168.

PANDEY, Ishwari Raj, Hon. GCVO; Prasiddha Prabala Gorakha-Dakshina Bahu, 1982; Vikhyata Trishakti-Patta, 1974; Ambassador of the Kingdom of Nepal to the Court of St James's, since 1983; concurrently Ambassador to Denmark, Finland, Norway, Iceland and Sweden; *b* 15 Aug. 1934; *s* of Rajguru Sri Hem Raj Panditgue and Nayab Bada Guruma Khaga Kumari Pandit; *m* 1953, Gita Rajya Laxmi Devi Rana; three *s* two *d. Educ:* Bombay Univ. (MA); Univ. of Pittsburgh (MPIA). Planning Officer, Min. of Planning and Develt, 1959; Under Sec., Min. of Finance (Foreign Aid Co-ordination), 1961; Dir, Dept of Industries, 1964; Head of Section for Econ. Relations, Min. of Foreign Affairs, 1966; First Secretary: Royal Nepalese Embassy, London, 1968; Perm. Mission of Kingdom of Nepal to UN, New York, 1972; Head of Section for Neighbouring Countries, Min. of For. Affairs, 1974; Chargé d'Affaires (Counsellor), Royal Nepalese Embassy, Tehran, 1975; Jt Sec., Div for Europe and the Americas, Min. of For. Affairs, 1979; Minister, Royal Nepalese Embassy, New Delhi, 1980. Coronation Medal, Bhutan, 1975. *Publications:* The Economic Impact of the Tourist Industry (with special reference to Puerto Rico and Nepal), 1961 (Univ. of Pittsburgh); contrib. to many jls. *Recreations:* reading, travelling. *Address:* Royal Nepalese Embassy, 12A Kensington Palace Gardens, W8 4QU. *T:* 01–229 1594; Bharatee Bhawan, Dhokatole, Kathmandu, Nepal. *T:* 211297. *Club:* Hurlingham.

PANDIT, Vijaya Lakshmi, (Mrs Ranjit S. Pandit); Padma Vibhusan, India, 1962; *b* 18 August 1900; *d* of Motilal Nehru and Sarup Rani Nehru; *m* 1921, Ranjit S. Pandit; three *d. Educ:* privately. Member Municipal Board, Allahabad, and Chm. Education Cttee, 1935; MLA, UP, and Minister of Local Govt and Health in Congress Cabinet of UP, 1937–39, and 1946–47. Leader India delegation to UN General Assembly, 1946, 1947, 1948; Ambassador to Moscow, 1947–49; Ambassador of India to the USA and Mexico, 1949–51; Member of Indian Parliament, 1952–54; High Commissioner for India in London, and Indian Ambassador to Ireland, 1954–61, concurrently Indian Ambassador to Spain, 1958–61; Governor of Maharashtra, 1962–64; MP, Phulpur, UP, 1964–69. Imprisoned three times for participation in national movement, 1932, 1941, 1942. President of the United Nations Assembly, 1953–54, Mem. Indian Delegn to UN, 1963. Trustee, Mountbatten Meml Trust, 1980–. Hon. DCL, Oxford, 1964, and numerous other Hon. degrees from Universities and Colleges. *Publications:* The Evolution of India (Whidden Lectures), 1958; The Scope of Happiness: a personal memoir, 1979. *Address:* 181B Rajpur Road, Dehra Dun, Uttar Pradesh, India.

PANK, Maj.-Gen. John David Graham; Director General of Personal Services, Army, since 1985; *b* 2 May 1935; *s* of Edward Graham Pank and Margaret Sheelah Osborne Pank; *m* 1963, Julia Letitia Matheson; two *s* one *d. Educ:* Uppingham Sch. Commnd KSLI, 1958; served in Germany, Borneo, Singapore and Malaya; commanded: 1st Bn The Light Infantry, 1974–76; 33rd Armoured Bde, 1979–81. *Recreations:* racing, fishing, cricket. *Address:* c/o Royal Bank of Scotland, Holt's Branch, Whitehall, SW1A 2EB. *Clubs:* Army and Navy; Mounted Infantry (Chm.); Free Foresters, I Zingari, Mount Cricket (Pres.).

PANKHURST, Air Vice-Marshal (Retd) Leonard Thomas, CB 1955; CBE 1944; *b* 26 August 1902; *s* of late Thomas William Pankhurst, Teddington, Middlesex; *m* 1939, Ruth, *d* of late Alexander Phillips, Cromer, Norfolk; one *s* two *d. Educ:* Hampton Grammar School. Joined Royal Air Force, 1925; Group Captain, 1942; Air Commodore, 1947; Actg Air Vice-Marshal, 1954. Served War of 1939–45 (despatches, CBE); Directorate of War Organisation, Air Ministry, 1938–41; Coastal Command, 1941–42; Mediterranean Air Forces, 1942–45. Air Officer Commanding 44 Group Transport Command, 1945–46; Asst Comdt RAF Staff Coll., 1946; idc, 1947; Dir Staff Trg, Air Ministry, 1948–50; Air Officer Commanding RAF E Africa, 1950–52; Dir of Postings, Air Ministry, 1953–54; Director-General of Personnel (I), Air Ministry, 1954–57. *Address:* Earl's Eye House, 8 Sandy Lane, Chester CH3 5UL. *T:* Chester 20993.

PANNETT, Juliet Kathleen, (Mrs M. R. D. Pannett), PS; FRSA; Portrait Painter; Free Lance Artist to The Times, Daily Telegraph, Radio Times, etc; Special Artist to Illustrated London News, 1958–65; *b* Hove; 2nd *d* of Charles Somers and May Brice; *m* 1938, Major M. R. D. Pannett (*d* 1980), late the Devonshire Regt; one *s* one *d. Educ:* Wistons Sch., Brighton; Brighton College of Art. *Exhibitions:* Royal Festival Hall, 1957, 1958; Qantas Gallery, 1959; New York, 1960; Cleveland, Ohio, 1960; Cooling Gallery, 1961; Coventry Cathedral Festival, 1962; Gloucester Three Choirs Festival, 1962; Brighton Corporation Gallery, Rottingdean, 1967; Arun Art Centre, 1967, 1969, 1972; Fine Art Gall., 1969; Mignon Gall., Bath, 1970; Brotherton Gall., 1980; Pacific Club, Hong Kong, 1986. Exhibitor: Royal Academy; Royal Society of Portrait Painters; Royal Inst. of Painters in Watercolours, etc. Official Artist on Qantas Inaugural Jet Flight, London to Sydney, 1959, London to Hong Kong, 1964; Air Canada Inaugural Flight, London to Vancouver, 1968. Freeman: City of London; Painter Stainers' Company. *Work in Permanent Collections:* portraits in: National Portrait Gall.; Brighton Art Gall.; Hove Art Gall.; Worthing Art Gall.; Cambridge Colleges; Oxford Colleges; Bodleian Library; Maudsley Hospital; Army Phys. Training Sch., Aldershot; Painter Stainers' Hall, London; Edinburgh Univ.; Portraits, many for official bodies, include: HRH Princess Alexandra: HRH Prince Andrew, HRH Prince Edward, for HM The Queen; HRH Princess Marina, Duchess of Kent, 1968; Lord Annan; Field-Marshal Sir Claude Auchinleck; Lord Ashby; Sir Alfred Ayer; Lord Baden-Powell; Lady Baden-Powell; Group Captain Sir Douglas Bader; Sir Adrian Boult; Lord George-Brown; Sir Arthur Bryant; Lord Butler; Lord Caldecote; Lord David Cecil; Group Captain Leonard Cheshire; Canon Collins; Dame Margery Corbett Ashby; Lord Dacre; Lord Denning; Sir Theodore Fox; Lord Fulton; Lt-Gen. Sir John Glubb; Lord Goodman; Rear-Adm. Sir Alexander Gordon Lennox; Lord Hailsham; Field Marshal Lord Harding; Rt Hon. Edward Heath; Ivon Hitchens; Lt-Gen. Sir Brian Horrocks; Bishop Huddleston; Malcolm Innes of Edingight, Lord Lyon King of Arms; Gen. Sir Charles Jones; Col 'H' Jones, VC; Sir John Kendrew; Sir Bernard Lovell; Lord McLeod; Sir William McTaggart; Bishop Marshall; Dr Quett Masire, President of Botswana; Lord Montagu; Lady Montagu; Patrick Moore; Sir Nevill Mott; Lord Mountbatten of Burma; Sir David Napley; Lavinia Duchess of Norfolk; Sir Leon Radzinowicz; Dame Marie Rambert; Bishop Roberts; Lord Salmon; Dame Evelyn Sharp; Lord Shawcross; Gilbert Spencer; Michael Stancliffe, Dean of Winchester; Rt Hon. Margaret Thatcher; Lord Tonypandy; Lord Todd; Sir Barnes Wallis; Lord Widgery; Rt Hon. Sir Harold Wilson; R. E. S. Wyatt; Lord Wemyss; Lady Wemyss; Prof. Yigael Yadin. Commemorative Stained Glass Window, Garrison church, Münster, 1967. *Publications:* Illustr. articles in The Artist; Leisure Painter; Illustr. for article in The Lancet; cover portraits: Gerald Pawle's The War and Colonel Warden; Law Guardian; Guardian Gazette; frontispieces, etc. *Recreations:* watercolour landscape, travel, music. *Address:* Pound House, Angmering Village, Sussex BN16 4AL. *T:* Rustington 784446.

PANT, Apasaheb Balasaheb; Padma Shri 1954; retired 1975; *b* 11 Sept. 1912; *s* of Pratinidhis of Aundh; *m* 1942, Nalini Pant, MB, BS, FRCS; two *s* one *d. Educ:* Univ. of Bombay (BA); Univ. of Oxford (MA). Barrister-at-Law, Lincoln's Inn. Educn Minister, Aundh State; Prime Minister, 1944–48 (when State was merged into Bombay State). Member, AICC, 1948; an alternate Deleg., of India, at UN, 1951 and 1952; Comr for Govt of India in Brit. E Africa, 1948–54; apptd Consul-Gen. for Belgian Congo and Ruanda-Urundi, Nov. 1950, and Comr for Central Africa and Nyasaland, Dec. 1950; Officer on Special Duty, Min. of Ext. Affairs, 1954–55; Polit. Officer in Sikkim and Bhutan with control over Indian Missions in Tibet, 1955–61; Ambassador of India: to Indonesia, Oct. 1961–June 1964; to Norway, 1964–66; to UAR, 1966–69; High Comr in London, 1969–72; Ambassador to Italy, 1972–75. *Publications:* Tensions and Tolerance, 1965; Aggression and Violence: Gandhian experiments to fight them, 1968; Yoga, 1968 (Arabic edn); Surya Namaskar, 1969 (Italian edn; Marathi edn, 1985); Mahatma Gandhi; A Moment in Time, 1973; Mandala, An Awakening, 1976; Progress, Power, Peace and India, 1978; Survival of the Individual, 1981; A Different Kind of a King, 1985 (Marathi edn); Un-Diplomatic Incidents, 1985; Story of the Pants: an extended family and fellow pilgrims, 1985; Energy: Intelligence: Love, 1986. *Recreations:* photography, yoga, tennis, ski-ing, gliding. *Address:* Pant Niwas, Bhandarkar Road, Deccan Gymkhana, Poona 4, India. *T:* 58615.

PANTCHEFF, Theodore Xenophon Henry, CMG 1977; HM Diplomatic Service, retired; *b* 29 Dec. 1920; *s* of Sophocles Xenophon Pantcheff and Ella Jessie, *d* of Dr S. H. Ramsbotham, Leeds; *m* 1954, Patricia Mary Tully; two *s. Educ:* Merchant Taylors' Sch.; Gonville and Caius Coll., Cambridge (MA). HM Forces, 1941–47; Control Commn for Germany, 1948–51; joined Foreign Office, 1951; Vice-Consul, Munich, 1954–56; 1st Sec., Lagos, 1958–60; 1st Sec., Leopoldville, 1961–63; seconded MoD, 1969–71; Counsellor, FCO, 1971–77. Jurat of the Court of Alderney, 1979. *Publication:* Alderney: fortress island, 1981. *Recreations:* reading and conversation. *Address:* Butes Cottage, Alderney. *Clubs:* Carlton; Alderney Society (Alderney).

PANTER-DOWNES, Mollie Patricia, (Mrs Clare Robinson); London Correspondent, The New Yorker, since 1939; *b* 25 Aug. 1906; *o c* of late Major Edward Panter-Downes, Royal Irish Regt; *m* 1927, Clare, 3rd *s* of late Aubrey Robinson; two *d. Educ:* mostly private. Wrote novel, The Shoreless Sea, at age of 16 (published John Murray, 1924); wrote in various English and American publications. *Publications:* Letter from England, 1940; Watling Green (children's book), 1943; One Fine Day, 1947; Ooty Preserved, 1967; At the Pines, 1971; London War Notes, 1972; contributed to The New Yorker Book of War Pieces, 1947. *Address:* Roppelegh's, near Haslemere, Surrey.
See also J. M. F. Baer.

PANTIN, Most Rev. Anthony; *see* Port of Spain, Archbishop of.

PANTON, Air Cdre Alastair Dyson, CB 1969; OBE 1950; DFC 1939; Provost Marshal and Director of RAF Security, 1968–71; retired; *Educ:* Bedford School; RAF Coll., Cranwell. Pilot Officer, No 53 Sqdn RAF, 1937; POW 1940–45; OC, Nos 58 and 540 Sqdns, 1946–47; Air Staff, Hong Kong, 1948–50; Wing Comdr Flying, RAF Coningsby, 1951–53; Staff Coll., 1953–54; Air Ministry, 1954–57; Station Comdr, RAF Cranwell, 1957–60, RAF Bircham Newton, 1961–62, RAF Tern Hill, 1963–64; HQ Far East Air Force, 1965–67. *Recreations:* gardening, poetry, Tchaikovsky.

PANTON, Dr Francis Harry, MBE 1948; Consultant, Cabinet Office, since 1985; Director, Royal Armament Research and Development Establishment, Ministry of Defence, 1980–83; *b* 25 May 1923; 3rd *s* of George Emerson Panton and Annie Panton; *m* 1952, Audrey Mary (*née* Lane); two *s. Educ:* City Sch., Lincoln; University College and Univ. of Nottingham. PhD Nottingham 1952. Served War of 1939–45: commissioned, Bomb Disposal, Royal Eng., 1943–47. Pres., Univ. of Nottingham Union, 1950–51; Vice-Pres., Nat. Union of Students, 1952–54; Technical Officer, ICI, Billingham, 1952–53; Permanent Under-Secretary's Dept, FO, 1953–55; Office of Political Adviser, Berlin, 1955–57; Dep. Head, Technical Research Unit, MoD, 1957–58; Attaché, British Embassy, Washington, DC, 1958–59; Technical Adviser, UK Delegn to Conf. on Discontinuance of Nuclear Tests, Geneva, 1959–61; Permanent Under-Secretary's Dept, FO, 1961–63; Counsellor (Defence), British Embassy, Washington, DC, 1963–66; Head of Defence Science 6, MoD, 1966–68; Asst Chief Scientific Adviser (Nuclear), MoD, 1969–76; Dir Gen., Estabs, Resources and Programmes (B), MoD, April-Sept. 1976; Dir, Propellants, Explosives and Rocket Motor Estabt, and Head, Rocket Motor Exec., MoD, 1976–80. FRSC (FRIC 1961); FRSA 1973; FRAeS 1982. *Recreations:* bridge, reading local history. *Address:* Cantis House, 1 St Peter's Lane, Canterbury, Kent. *T:* Canterbury 52902. *Club:* Reform.

PANTRIDGE, Prof. (James) Frank, CBE 1978; MC 1942; MD, FRCP, FACC; *b* 3 Oct. 1916. *Educ:* Queen's Univ., Belfast (MD). FRCP 1957; FACC 1967. Research Fellow, Univ. of Mich, 1948–49; Dir, Regional Medical Cardiology Centre, NI, 1977–82; Hon. Prof. of Cardiol., QUB. Canadian Heart Foundn Orator; St Cyres Orator, National Heart Hosp., London. Chm., British Cardiac Soc., 1978. Developer (with J. S. Geddes) of the Portable Defibrillator and initiator of pre-hospital coronary care. Hon. FRCPI. DUniv Open, 1981; Hon. DSc NUU, 1981. *Publication:* The Acute Coronary Attack, 1975. *Recreation:* fishing. *Address:* Hillsborough, Co. Down, N Ireland. *T:* Hillsborough 682911. *Club:* Athenæum.

PANUFNIK, Andrzej; composer and conductor; *b* 24 Sept. 1914; 2nd *s* of Tomasz Panufnik and Mathilda Thonnes Panufnik; *m* 1963, Camilla Ruth Jessel, FRPS, *yr d* of Commander R. F. Jessel, DSO, OBE, DSC, RN (retired); one *s* one *d. Educ:* Warsaw State Conservatoire; Vienna State Acad. for Music (under Professor Felix von Weingartner). Diploma with distinction, Warsaw Conservatoire, 1936. Conductor of the Cracow Philharmonic, 1945–46; Director and Conductor of the Warsaw Philharmonic Orchestra, 1946–47. Conducting leading European orchestras such as L'Orchestre National, Paris, Berliner Philharmonisches Orchester, L'Orchestre de la Suisse Romande, Geneva, and all principal British orchestras, 1947–. Polish decorations: Standard of Labor 1st class (1949), twice State Laureate (1951, 1952). Left Poland and settled in England, 1954; naturalized British subject, 1961. Vice-Chairman of International Music Council of UNESCO, Paris, 1950–53; Musical Director and Conductor, City of Birmingham Symphony Orchestra, 1957–59. Hon. Member of International Mark Twain Society (USA), 1954; Knight of Mark Twain, 1966; Hon. RAM 1984. Doctor of Philosophy *hc*, Polish Univ. in Exile, London, 1985. The Sibelius Centenary Medal, 1965; Prix de composition musical Prince Pierre de Monaco, 1983. *Ballets:* Elegy, NY, 1967; Cain and Abel, Berlin, 1968; Miss Julie, Stuttgart, 1970; Homage to Chopin (SW Royal Ballet), 1980; Adieu (Royal Ballet), 1980; Polonia (SW Royal Ballet), 1980; Dances of the Golden Hall (Martha Graham), NY, 1982. *Compositions:* Piano Trio, 1934; Five Polish Peasant Songs, 1940; Tragic Overture, 1942; Twelve Miniature Studies for piano, 1947; Nocturne for orchestra, 1947; Lullaby for 29 stringed instruments and 2 harps, 1947; Sinfonia Rustica, 1948; Hommage à Chopin-Five vocalises for soprano and piano, 1949; Old Polish Suite for strings, 1950; Concerto in modo antico, 1951; Heroic Overture, 1952; Rhapsody for orchestra, 1956; Sinfonia Elegiaca, 1957; Polonia-Suite for Orchestra, 1959; Piano Concerto, 1961; Autumn Music, 1962; Landscape, 1962; Two Lyric Pieces, 1963; Sinfonia Sacra, 1963 (first prize, Prix de Composition Musicale Prince Rainier III de Monaco, 1963); Song to the Virgin Mary, 1964; Katyn Epitaph, 1966; Jagiellonian Triptych, 1966; Reflections for piano, 1967; The Universal Prayer, 1969; Thames Pageant, 1969; Violin Concerto, 1971; Triangles, 1972; Winter Solstice, 1972; Sinfonia Concertante, 1973; Sinfonia di Sfere, 1974; String Quartet No 1, 1976, No 2, 1980; Dreamscape, 1976; Sinfonia Mistica, 1977; Metasinfonia, 1978; Concerto Festivo, 1979; Concertino, 1980; Sinfonia Votiva, 1981; A Procession for Peace, 1982; Arbor Cosmica, 1984; Pentasonata, 1985; Bassoon Concerto, 1985. *Address:* Riverside House, Twickenham, Middlesex TW1 3DJ. *Club:* Garrick.

See also O. R. Jessel, T. F. H. Jessel.

PAO, Sir Yue-Kong, Kt 1978; CBE 1976; JP; LLD; Chairman, World-Wide Shipping Group, since 1974; Deputy Chairman, Standard Chartered Bank, since 1986; *b* Chekiang, China, 10 Nov. 1918; *s* of late Sui-Loong Pao and Chung Sau-Gin Pao; *m* 1940, Sue-Ing Haung; four *d. Educ:* Shanghai, China. Banking career in China until went to Hong Kong, 1949; engaged in import and export trade; shipowner, 1955–. Chairman: World International (Holdings) Ltd; Hong Kong and Kowloon Wharf and Godown Co. Ltd; Eastern Asia Navigation Co. Ltd; Wheelock Marden Gp; Hong Kong Dragon Airlines Ltd; China Capital Partners Ltd; Director: Hang Seng Bank Ltd; Inchcape Far East Ltd. Adviser, Indust. Bank of Japan. Chm., E Asia Cttee, Lloyd's Register of Shipping; Hon. Chairman: Hong Kong Cttee, Nippon Kaiji Kyokai of Japan; IBJ Asia Ltd. Member: Internat. Gen. Cttee, Bureau Veritas of France; Asia/Pacific Adv. Council, Amer. Telephone & Telegraph Internat.; Internat. Adv. Cttee, Chase Manhattan Bank of New York; Pacific Adv. Council, Utd Technologies Corp., USA; (Life), Court of Univ. of Hong Kong; Rockefeller Univ. Council, New York; Hon. Mem., INTERTANKO. Hon. Vice-Pres., Maritime Trust. Overseas Hon. Trustee, Westminster Abbey Trust. Trustee, Hong Kong Arts Centre. Hon. LLD: Univ. of Hong Kong, 1975; Chinese Univ. of Hong Kong, 1977. JP Hong Kong, 1971. Commander: National Order of Cruzeiro do Sul, Brazil, 1977; Order of the Crown, Belgium, 1982; Vasquo Nunez de Balboa, Panama, 1982. *Recreations:* swimming, golf. *Address:* World-Wide Shipping Agency Ltd, Wheelock House, 6/F, 20 Pedder Street, Hong Kong. *T:* 5–8423888. *Clubs:* Royal Automobile; Woking Golf (Surrey); Royal and Ancient Golf (St Andrews, Fife); Sunningdale Golf (Berks).

PAOLOZZI, Eduardo Luigi, CBE 1968; RA 1979 (ARA 1972); Sculptor; Tutor in Ceramics, Royal College of Art, since 1968; Professor of Sculpture at Akademie der Bildenden Künste, Munich, since 1981; HM Sculptor in Ordinary for Scotland, since 1986; *b* 7 March 1924; *s* of Rudolpho Antonio Paolozzi and Carmella (*née* Rossi), both Italian; *m* 1951, Freda Elliott; three *d. Educ.* Edinburgh School of Art; Slade Sch. Worked in Paris, 1947–50; Instructor, Central School of Arts and Crafts, London, 1950–55; Lecturer, St Martin's School of Art, 1955–56; Prof. of Ceramics at Fachhochschule, Cologne, 1977–81. Fellow, UCL, 1986. Hon. Dr RCA, 1979; Hon. DLitt Glasgow, 1980. British Critics Prize, 1953; David E. Bright Foundn Award, 1960; Watson F. Blaire Prize, 1961; Purchase Prize, Internat. Sculpture Exhibn at Solomon R. Guggenheim Mus., 1967; First Prize for Sculpture, Carnegie Internat. Exhibn, 1967; Sculpture Prize, European Patent Office, Munich, 1978; First Prize, Rhinegarten Cologne comp., 1981; Grand Prix d'Honneur, Print Biennale at Ljubljana, Yugoslavia, 1983. *One-man exhibitions:* first in London, Mayor Gallery, 1947; first in New York, Betty Parsons Gallery, 1960, also 1962; Tate Gallery, 1971; V&A Mus., 1973, 1977 (print retrospective); Nationalgal., W Berlin, 1975; Fruit Market Gall., Edinburgh, 1976; Marlborough Fine Art Gallery, 1976; Anthony d'Offay Gall., 1977; Kassel, Germany, 1978; Glasgow League of Artists, 1979; Edinburgh Univ., 1979; Cologne, Germany, 1979; Museum for Künste und Gewerbe, Hamburg, 1982; Aedes Gall., Berlin, 1983; Invited artist, 6th Internat. Drawing Biennale, Cleveland (UK), 1983; Wissenschaftskolleg zu Berlin, 1983; Architectural Assoc., London; Royal Scottish Acad., Stadische Galerie im Lenbachhaus, Munich; New Metropole Arts Centre, Folkstone, 1984; Mus. Ludwig, Cologne; De Beyerd Mus., Breda, Holland; Contemporary Art Centre, Lyon, France; Ivan Dougherty Gall., Sydney, Aust., 1985; Cork, Ireland, 1985; Mus. of Mankind, 1986; RA, 1986. *Group exhibitions include:* Whitechapel Gall., 1981; Ashmolean Mus., 1982; Museo Municipal of Madrid, 1983; Mus. of Contemp. Art, LA, 1984; designed: glass mosaics for Tottenham Ct Road Underground Station, London; film sets for Percy Adlon's Herschel and the Music of the Stars, 1984–85. Work in permanent collections: Tate Gallery; Contemporary Art Society; Museum of Modern Art, New York, etc. Work exhibited in: British Pavilion, Venice Biennale, 1952; Documenta 2, Kassel, 1959; New Images of Man, New York, 1959; British Pavilion, 30th Venice Biennale; International Exhibition of Sculpture, Boymans Museum, Rotterdam; Open Air Sculpture, Battersea Park, London; Critics Choice, Tooths Gallery, London; City Art Gallery, Manchester, Oct. 1960; British Sculpture in the Sixties, Tate Gallery, March 1965; Chelsea School of Art, 1965; Hanover Gallery, 1967; Tate Gall., 1971. Hon. Mem., AA, 1980. *Relevant publications:* Eduardo Paolozzi, by Winfried Konnertz, 1984. *Recreation:* music. *Address:* 107 Dovehouse Street, SW3. *Club:* Athenæum.

PAPADOPOULOS, Achilles Symeon, CMG 1980; LVO 1972; MBE 1954; HM Diplomatic Service, retired; High Commissioner in the Bahamas, 1981–83; *b* 16 Aug. 1923; *s* of late Symeon Papadopoulos and of Polyxene Papadopoulos; *m* 1954, Joyce Martin (*née* Stark); one *s* two *d. Educ:* The English School, Nicosia, Cyprus. British Mil. Admin, Eritrea, 1943; HMOCS: Cyprus, 1953; Dar es Salaam, 1959; Malta, 1961; HM Diplomatic Service: Malta, 1965; Nairobi, 1965; FCO, 1968; Colombo, 1971; Washington, 1974; Havana, 1974; Ambassador to El Salvador, 1977–79, to Mozambique, 1979–80; attached UK Mission to UN, Sept.-Dec. 1980. *Recreations:* golf, bridge. *Address:* 14 Mill Close, Great Bookham, Leatherhead, Surrey KT23 3JX. *Club:* Royal Commonwealth Society.

PAPE, Hon. Sir George (Augustus), Kt 1968; Judge of Supreme Court of Victoria, 1957–75, retired; *b* 29 Jan. 1903; *s* of George Frederick Pape and Minnie Maud Pape (*née* Bryan); *m* 1952, Mabel (*d* 1983), *d* of Alfred Lloyd; no *c. Educ:* All Saints Grammar Sch., St Kilda; University of Melbourne (LLB). QC 1955. RAAF, 1940–46. *Recreation:* golf. *Address:* 146 Kooyong Road, Toorak, Victoria 3142, Australia. *T:* 20–6158. *Club:* Australian (Melbourne).

PAPE, (Jonathan) Hector (Carruthers), OBE 1980; FCIT; Advocate; International Port/Dock Labour Consultant; Chief General Manager, National Dock Labour Board, 1975–82 (General Manager and Secretary, 1970–75); *b* 8 March 1918; *er s* of Jonathan Pape, MA and Florence Muriel Myrtle; *m* 1944, Mary Sullins (*née* Jeffries) (*d* 1985); one *s. Educ:* Merchant Taylors' Sch., Crosby. Mercantile Marine, 1934–46; Master Mariner (FG), 1944 (Liverpool Qualif.). Manager, Master Stevedoring Co., Liverpool, 1947–51; National Dock Labour Board: Dep. Port Manager, London, 1952–57; Asst Gen. Manager, Bd HQ, 1957–69; Dep. Gen. Manager and Secretary, Bd HQ, 1969. Mem., Honourable Co. of Master Mariners, 1965. Freeman, City of London. *Recreations:* swimming, gardening, and riding at anchor in what spare time is left. *Address:* Apartment 42, Homedane House, Denmark Place, Hastings, East Sussex TN34 1PF. *Club:* Wig and Pen.

PAPUA NEW GUINEA, Archbishop of, since 1983; **Most Rev. George Somboba Ambo,** OBE 1978; Bishop of Popondetta, since 1977; *b* Gona, Nov. 1925; *s* of late J. O. Ambo, Gona; *m* 1946, Marcella O., *d* of Karau; two *s* two *d. Educ:* St Aidan's College, Dogura; Newton Theological Coll., Dogura. Deacon, 1955; Priest, 1958. Curate of: Menapi, 1955–57; Dogura, 1957–58; Priest in charge of Boianai, Diocese of New Guinea, 1958–63; Missionary at Wamira, 1963–69; an Asst Bishop of Papua New Guinea, 1960 (first Papuan-born Anglican Bishop). *Publication:* St John's Gospel in Ewage. *Recreations:* reading, carpentry. *Address:* PO Box 26, Popondetta, Papua New Guinea.

PAQUET, Dr Jean-Guy, OC 1984; FRSC; Rector, Université Laval, Québec, Canada, since 1977; *b* Montmagny, Qué, 5 Jan. 1938; *s* of Laurent W. Paquet and Louisianne Coulombe. *Educ:* Université Laval (BSc Engrg Physics, 1959; DSc Elec. Engrg, 1963); Ecole Nat. Sup. de l'Aéronautique, Paris (MSc Aeronautics, 1960). FRSC 1978; FAAAS 1981. Université Laval: Asst Prof. of Elec. Engrg, 1962; Associate Prof., 1967; Head, Elec. Engrg Dept, 1967–69; Vice-Dean (Research), Faculty of Science, 1969–72; Prof. of Elec. Engrg, 1971; Vice-Rector (Academic), 1972–77. Fellowships: French Govt, 1959; NATO, 1962; Nat. Science Foundn, 1964; Québec Govt, 1965. Def. Res. Bd of Canada Grant, 1965–76. National Research Council of Canada: Fellowship, 1961; Grant, 1964–77; Mem., Associate Cttee on Automatic Control, 1964–70; Special Asst to Vice-Pres. (Scientific), 1971–72. Pres., Conf. of Rectors and Principals of Univs of Prov. of Québec, 1979–81. Member: Council, Univs of Prov. of Qué, 1973–77; Bd, Assoc. of Scientific, Engrg and Technol Community of Canada, 1970–77 (Pres., 1975–76); Bd, French Canadian Assoc. for Advancement of Science, 1969–71; Canadian Assoc. of Univ. Res. Administrators; Special Task Force on Res. and Develt, Science Council of Canada, 1976; Order of Engrs, Qué; Amer. Soc. for Engrg Educn; New York Acad. of Science, 1980–; Amer. Management Assoc., 1980–; Soc. for Res. Administrators. Member Board: Hockey Canada, 1980–; Interamerican Univs Assoc., 1980–; Assoc. des universités partiellement ou entièrement de langue française, 1981– (Vice-Pres., 1983–); Assoc. of Commonwealth Univs, 1981–; Social Sciences and Humanities Res. Council of Canada, 1982–; Inst. of Canadian Bankers, 1980–; Founding Mem., Corporate Higher Educn Forum. Pres., Selection Cttee, Outstanding Achievement Awards, Canada, 1984. DSc *hc* McGill Univ., 1982; DLaw *hc*, York Univ., 1983. *Publications:* (with P. A. Roy) Rapport d'études bibliographiques: l'automation dans la production et la distribution de l'énergie électrique, 1968; (with J. F. Le Maître) Méthodes pratiques d'étude des oscillations non-linéaires: application aux systèmes par plus-ou-moins, 1970; more than fifty pubns in scientific jls, on control systems engrg; articles on research, develt and scientific policy. *Recreations:* jogging, travels, golf. *Address:* Université Laval, Québec G1K 7P4, Canada. *Clubs:* Cercle de la Garnison de Québec, Club de Golf Cap-Rouge (Qué).

PARARAJASINGAM, Sir Sangarapillai, Kt 1955; Senator, Ceylon, 1954–59; Chairman, Board of Directors, Colonial Motors Ltd, 1961–74; former Member, Board of Trustees, Ceylon Social Service League; *b* 25 June 1896; *s* of late W. Sangarapillai, social worker and philanthropist; *m* 1916, Padmavati, *d* of Sir Ponnambalam Arunachalam; one *s* one *d. Educ:* St Thomas' Coll., Mt Lavinia. Past President, Board of Directors, Manipay Hindu Coll., Manager, 1929–61; Past President Ceylon Poultry Club; Member National Savings Cttee; Past Chairman, Board Governors, Ceylon Inst. of Scientific and Industrial Research. Formerly Chairman: Board of Directors, Agricultural and Industrial Credit Corporation of Ceylon; Education Cttee, Ceylon Social Service League; Low Country Products Assoc., 1943–44 and 1944–45; Ceylon Coconut Board; Coconut Commn; Past Member: Textile Tribunal; Land Advisory Cttee; Ceylon Tea Propaganda Board; Coconut Research Scheme; Radio Advisory Board; Excise Advisory Cttee; Central Board of Agriculture; Income Tax Board of Review; Rice Advisory Board; Services Standing Wages Board; Board for Approval of Credit Agencies; Commn on Broadcasting; Past President Vivekananda Society; Rotary Club of Colombo; Governor, Rotary Internat. District 320, 1951–52; formerly Trustee and Hon. Treasurer, Ceylon Society of Arts; formerly Manager, all Schools managed by Ceylon Social Service League. JP Ceylon 1923. Travelled widely in the UK, Europe, USA, India, Far East. Coronation Medals, 1937 and 1953. *Recreations:* gardening, agriculture and farming. *Address:* No 50, Pathmalaya, Flower Road, Colombo 7, Sri Lanka. *T:* 23159.

See also P. Nadesan.

PARAYRE, Jean-Paul Christophe; Officier, l'Ordre National du Mérite, 1978; Member, Supervisory Board, Peugeot SA, since 1984; General Manager, Dumez SA, since 1984 (Director, since 1974); *b* 5 July 1937; *s* of Louis Parayre and Jehanne Malarde; *m* 1962, Marie-Françoise Chaufour; two *s* two *d. Educ:* Lycées de Casablanca et Versailles; Ecole Polytechnique, Paris; Ecole Nationale des Ponts et Chaussées. Engr, Dept of Highways, 1963–67; Technical Adviser: Min. of Social Affairs, 1967; Min. of Economy and Finance, 1968; Min. of Industry and Res., 1969; Dir of Mech. Industries, Min. of Industry and Res., 1970–74; Chief Adviser to Chm. and Gen. Management, Banque Vernes et Commerciale de Paris, 1974; Chief Attaché to Gen. Management of Peugeot SA, 1974; Manager of Automobile Planning, Peugeot, 1975; Manager, Automobile Div., Peugeot-Citroen, 1976; Mem. Exec. Cttee, PSA Peugeot-Citroen, 1977; Président, Peugeot SA, 1977–84. Mem., Board of Directors: Crédit National, 1978–; Framatome; Scoa; Valeo. *Recreation:* tennis. *Address:* 3 Rond-Point Saint-James, 92200 Neuilly-sur-Seine, France. *Club:* Polo de Paris.

PARBO, Sir Arvi (Hillar), Kt 1978; Executive Chairman, Western Mining Corporation Ltd, since 1986 (Chairman and Managing Director, 1974–86); Chairman, Alcoa of Australia Ltd, since 1978; *b* 10 Feb. 1926; *s* of Aado and Hilda Parbo; *m* 1953, Saima Soots; two *s* one *d. Educ:* Clausthal Mining Acad., Germany; Univ. of Adelaide (BE Hons). Western Mining Corporation: Underground Surveyor, 1956; Techn. Asst to Managing Dir, 1960; Dep. Gen. Supt, WA, 1964; Gen. Manager, 1968; Dep. Managing Dir, 1971; Managing Director, 1971. Director: Aluminium Co. of America, 1980–; Hoechst Australian Investments Pty Ltd, 1981–; Chase AMP Bank Ltd, 1985–; Chairman: Munich Reinsurance Company of Australia Ltd, 1984 (Dir, 1983–); Zurich Insurance Australian Group, 1985–. Comdr, Order of Merit, Germany, 1979. *Recreations:* reading, carpentry. *Address:* Western Mining Corporation Ltd, 360 Collins Street, Melbourne, Vic 3000, Australia; GPO Box 860K, Melbourne, Vic 3001. *T:* 602 0300. *Clubs:* Melbourne, Australian (both Melbourne); Weld (Perth); Commonwealth (Canberra); Hannans (Kalgoorlie).

PARBURY, George Mark, CB 1980; Chief Registrar of the High Court of Justice in Bankruptcy, 1975–80; *b* 27 April 1908; *s* of late Norman Cecil Parbury and Ellen Parbury; *m* 1942, Roma Constance, *d* of late James Robert Raw, JP, New Zealand, and Clare Raw. *Educ:* Geelong, Australia; Jesus Coll., Cambridge. Called to Bar, Lincoln's Inn, 1934. Practised at Chancery Bar, 1934–39. Served War of 1939–45, 1940–45, Temp. Lt-Col, 1944; AAG, AG3e War Office, Mil. Govt 21 Army Group. Again practised at Chancery Bar, 1946–65; Mem. Bar Council, 1961–62. Registrar, High Court of Justice in Bankruptcy, 1965–75. *Recreations:* walking on the Downs; gardening. *Address:* 5 Bolsover Court, Bolsover Road, Eastbourne, East Sussex. *T:* Eastbourne 639343.

PARDOE, Dr Geoffrey Keith Charles, PhD; CEng, FRAeS; Chairman and Managing Director, General Technology Systems Ltd, since 1973; Chairman, General Technology Systems (Scandinavia) A/S, since 1985; President, General Technology Systems SA, Belgium, since 1979; Managing Director, Surrey Satellite Technology Ltd, since 1985; *b* 2 Nov. 1928; *s* of James Charles Pardoe and Ada Violet Pardoe; *m* 1953, Dorothy Patricia Gutteridge; one *s* one *d*. *Educ:* Wanstead County High Sch., London; London Univ. (BScEng Hons); Loughborough Coll. (DLC Hons Aeronautics); PhD (Astronautics) Loughborough Univ., 1984). CEng, FRAeS 1968. Sen. Aerodynamicist, Armstrong Whitworth Ltd, 1949–51; Chief Aerodynamicist, Guided Weapons, De Havilland Props Ltd, 1951–56, Proj. Manager, Blue Streak, 1956–60; Chief Engr, Weapons and Space Research, De Havilland Aircraft, 1960–63; Chief Proj. Engr, Space Div., Hawker Siddeley Dynamics Ltd, 1963–69, Sales Exec., 1969–73; Exec. Dir, British Space Develt Co. Ltd, 1960–74. Chm., Procogen Computer Systems Ltd, 1981–; Director: Philip A. Lapp Ltd, Canada, 1973–; Gen. Technology Systems (Netherlands) BV, Den Haag, 1982–; Eurosat SA, Switzerland, 1971–83; Eurotech Develts Ltd, 1981–83. Vice Pres., Eurospace (Paris), 1961–73; Pres., RAeS, 1984–85 (Vice-Pres., 1981–83). Dep. Chm., 1981–86, Chm., 1986–, Watt Cttee on Energy. FBIS; MInstD. *Publications:* The Challenge of Space, 1964; Integration of Payload and Stages of Space Carrier Vehicles, 1964; Project Apollo: The way to the Moon, 1969, 2nd edn 1970; The Future for Space Technology, 1984; over 50 main pubns in learned society pubns and jls; about 100 articles. *Recreations:* skiing, flying, badminton, photography, wind-surfing. *Address:* 23 Stewart Road, Harpenden, Herts AL5 4QE. *T:* Harpenden 4719. *Clubs:* Royal Air Force, Institute of Directors, Ski of GB.

PARDOE, John George Magrath, CBE 1975; FRAeS; Director-General, Airworthiness, Civil Aviation Authority, 1972–79. *Educ:* Coll. of Aeronautical Engineering. Entered design work in Aircraft Industry, 1935; joined Accidents Inspection Br. of Air Ministry, 1942; joined Staff, Air Registration Bd, 1945; Chief Technical Officer, 1969. Médaille de l'aéronautique, 1980.

PARDOE, John Wentworth; Managing Director, Sight and Sound Education Ltd; Senior Research Fellow of Policy Studies Institute; *b* 27 July 1934; *s* of Cuthbert B. Pardoe and Marjorie E. W. (*née* Taylor); *m* 1958, Joyce R. Peerman; two *s* one *d*. *Educ:* Sherborne; Corpus Christi Coll., Cambridge (MA). Television Audience Measurement Ltd, 1958–60; Osborne Peacock Co. Ltd, 1960–61; Liberal News, 1961–66. MP (L) Cornwall N, 1966–79; Treasurer of the Liberal Party, 1968–69. Presenter, Look Here, LWT, 1979–81. Consultant to Nat. Assoc. of Schoolmasters, 1967–73. Director: William Schlackman Ltd, 1968–71; Gerald Metals, 1972–83; Mem. London Metal Exchange, 1973–83. Mem., Youth Trng Bd, 1985–. *Recreations:* cricket, walking, singing. *Address:* 18 New End Square, NW3.

PARE, Rev. Philip Norris; *b* 13 May 1910; *s* of Frederick William and Florence May Pare; *m* 1943, Nancy Eileen, *d* of late Canon C. Patteson; two *s* two *d*. *Educ:* Nottingham High Sch.; King's Coll., Cambridge; Cuddesdon Theological Coll. Curate, All Saints, W Dulwich, 1934–37; Chaplain and Vice-Principal, Bishops Coll., Cheshunt, 1937–39; Curate, St Mary the Less, Cambridge, 1939–40. Chaplain RNVR, 1940–46. Vicar of Cheshunt, Herts, 1946–57; Rural Dean of Ware, 1949–56; Examining Chaplain to Bishop of St Albans, 1952–56; Missioner Canon Stipendiary, Diocese of Wakefield, 1957–62; Diocesan Adviser for Christian Stewardship, 1959–68; Provost, and Vicar of Cathedral Church of All Saints, Wakefield, 1962–71; Vicar of Cholsey, dio. Oxford, 1973–82. A Church Commissioner, 1968–71; Member Board of Ecclesiastical Insurance Office, 1966–83; Provost of Woodard Schools (Northern Div.), 1977–82; Trustee, Ely Stained Glass Museum, 1980–. *Publications:* Eric Milner-White, A Memoir (with Donald Harris), 1965; Re-Thinking Our Worship, 1967; God Made the Devil?: a ministry of healing, 1985; articles in Theology, The Reader, etc. *Recreations:* modern stained glass and architecture; railways, motor cars; church music. *Address:* 73 Oakland Drive, Ledbury, Herefordshire HR8 2EX. *T:* Ledbury 3619.

PAREKH, Prof. Bhikhu Chhotalal; Professor of Political Theory, University of Hull, since 1982; a Deputy Chairman, Commission for Racial Equality, since 1985; *b* 4 Jan. 1935; *s* of Chhotalal Parekh and Gajaraben Parekh; *m* 1959, Pramila (*née* Dalal); three *s*. *Educ:* Univ. of Bombay (BA 1954, MA 1956); Univ. of London (PhD 1966). Tutor, LSE, 1962–63; Asst Lectr, Univ. of Glasgow, 1963–64; Univ. of Hull: Lectr, Sen. Lectr and Reader, 1964–82. Vice-Chancellor, Univ. of Baroda, 1982–84. *Publications:* Politics and Experience, 1968; Dissent and Disorder, 1971; The Morality of Politics, 1972; Knowledge and Belief in Politics, 1973; Bentham's Political Thought, 1973; Jeremy Bentham: ten critical essays, 1974; The Concept of Socialism, 1975; Hannah Arendt and the Search for a New Political Philosophy, 1981; Karl Marx's Theory of Ideology, 1982; Contemporary Political Thinkers, 1982. *Recreations:* reading, music. *Address:* 211 Victoria Avenue, Hull HU5 3EF.

PARES, Peter; *b* 6 Sept. 1908; 2nd *s* of late Sir Bernard Pares, KBE, DCL, and late Margaret Pares (*née* Dixon); unmarried. *Educ:* Lancing Coll.; Jesus Coll., Cambridge (Scholar). Entered Consular Service, 1930; served in Philadelphia, 1930; Havana, 1932; Consul, Liberec and Bratislava, Czechslovakia, 1936–39; Budapest, 1939; Cluj, Rumania, 1940; New York, 1941; Washington, as First Secretary, 1944; Control Commission for Germany, 1946; Foreign Office, 1949; Casablanca, 1952; Strasbourg, 1956; Deputy Consul-General, Frankfurt, 1957; Consul-General, Asmara, Eritrea, 1957–59; Head of Education and Cultural Relations Dept, CRO, 1960–63. *Address:* 17 Beechwood Crescent, Eastbourne, East Sussex.

PARFIT, Derek Antony, FBA 1986; Senior Research Fellow, All Souls College, Oxford, since 1984; *b* 11 Dec. 1942; *s* of Norman and Jessie Parfit. *Educ:* Eton; Balliol College, Oxford. BA Modern History, 1964. Fellow of All Souls, 1967–. *Publication:* Reasons and Persons, 1984. *Recreation:* architectural photography. *Address:* All Souls College, Oxford. *T:* Oxford 722251.

PARGETER, Edith; *b* 28 Sept. 1913; 3rd *c* of Edmund Valentine Pargeter and Edith Hordley; unmarried. *Educ:* Dawley C of E Elementary Sch.; County High School for Girls, Coalbrookdale. Worked as a chemist's assistant, and at twenty succeeded in finding a publisher for first-and unsuccessful-book. WRNS Aug. 1940, teleprinter operator (BEM 1944); dispersed from the Service, Aug. 1945. FIIAL 1962. Gold Medal and Ribbon, Czechoslovak Society for International Relations, 1968. *Publications:* Hortensius, Friend of Nero, Iron Bound, 1936; The City Lies Foursquare, 1939; Ordinary People, 1941; She Goes to War, 1942; The Eighth Champion of Christendom, 1945; Reluctant Odyssey, 1946; Warfare Accomplished, 1947; By Firelight, 1948; The Fair Young Phoenix, 1948; The Coast of Bohemia, 1949; Lost Children, 1950; Fallen Into the Pit, 1951; Holiday with Violence, 1952; This Rough Magic, 1953; Most Loving Mere Folly, 1953; The Soldier at the Door, 1954; A Means of Grace, 1956; Tales of the Little Quarter (trans. from the Czech of Jan Neruda), 1957; Don Juan (trans. from the Czech of Josef Toman), 1958; Assize of the Dying, 1958; The Heaven Tree, 1960; The Green Branch 1962; The Scarlet Seed, 1963; The Terezín Requiem (trans. from the Czech of Josef Bor), 1963; The Lily Hand and other stories, 1965; Close Watch on the Trains (trans from the Czech of Bohumil Hrabal), 1968; Report on my Husband (trans. from the Czech of Josefa Slánská), 1969; A Bloody Field by Shrewsbury, 1972; Sunrise in the West, 1974; The Dragon at Noonday, 1975; The Hounds of Sunset, 1976; Afterglow and Nightfall, 1977; The Marriage of Meggotta, 1979; *as Ellis Peters:* 22 crime and mystery novels including: Monk's-hood, 1980 (Silver Dagger, Crime Writers Assoc.); Saint Peter's Fair, 1981; The Leper of Saint Giles, 1981; The Virgin in the Ice, 1982; The Sanctuary Sparrow, 1982; The Devil's Novice, 1983; Dead Man's Ransom, 1984; The Pilgrim of Hate, 1984; An Excellent Mystery, 1985; The Raven in the Foregate, 1986. *Recreations:* collecting gramophone records, particularly of voice; reading anything and everything; theatre. *Address:* Parkville, Park Lane, Madeley, Telford, Salop TF7 5HF. *T:* Telford 585178.

PARHAM, Adm. Sir Frederick Robertson, GBE 1959 (CBE 1949); KCB 1955 (CB 1951); DSO 1944; *b* 9 Jan. 1901; *s* of late Frederick James Parham, Bath, and late Jessie Esther Brooks Parham (*née* Robertson), Cheltenham; *m* 1st, 1926, Kathleen Dobrée, (*d* 1973), *d* of Eugene Edward Carey, Guernsey; one *s*; 2nd, 1978, Mrs Joan Saunders (*née* Charig). *Educ:* RN Colleges, Osborne and Dartmouth. Joined HMS Malaya as Midshipman, 1917; specialised in gunnery, 1925; Commander, 1934. Commanded HMS Shikari, 1937, HMS Gurkha, 1938–40. Captain, 1939. Commanded HMS Belfast, 1942–44 (despatches), HMS Vanguard, 1947–49; Dep. Chief, Naval Personnel, 1949–51; Rear-Admiral, 1949; Vice-Admiral, 1952; Flag Officer (Flotillas) and 2nd in command, Mediterranean, 1951–52; a Lord Commissioner of the Admiralty, Fourth Sea Lord and Chief of Supplies and Transport, 1954–55, Commander-in-Chief, The Nore, 1955–58; retired list, 1959. Member British Waterways Board, Jan. 1963–1967, Vice-Chairman (part-time) Aug. 1963–1967. Naval ADC to the King, 1949. Grand Cross of Military Order of Avis (Portugal), 1955; Order of Al Rafidain (Class II, Mil., conferred by the King of Iraq), 1956; Ordine al merito della Repubblica, Grande Ufficiale (Italy) 1958. *Address:* The Coach House, Church Road, West Lavington, Midhurst, West Sussex GU29 0EH. *T:* Midhurst 3183.

PARIKIAN, Manoug; violinist; Professor of Violin, Royal Academy of Music, since 1959; *b* Mersin, Turkey, 15 Sept. 1920, of Armenian parentage; *s* of late Stepan Parikian and Vanouhi (*née* Bedelian); *m* 1957, Diana Margaret (*née* Carbutt); two *s*. *Educ:* Trinity College of Music, London (Fellow). Leader: Liverpool Philharmonic Orchestra, 1947–48; Philharmonia Orchestra, London, 1949, until resignation, 1957; has appeared in all European countries as solo violinist. Introduced Shostakovitch Violin Concerto to Scandinavia (Stockholm), 1956; first public performance of works by Iain Hamilton, Rawsthorne, Musgrave, Alexander Goehr, Elizabeth Maconchy, Gordon Crosse and Hugh Wood. Toured: USSR, April-May 1961, and Nov. 1965; Latin America, July-Aug. 1974. Dir, Yorkshire Sinfonia, 1976–78; Musical Dir, Manchester Camerata, 1980–84; Artistic Dir, Giggleswick Summer Music Fest., 1981. Formed trio with Amaryllis Fleming ('cello) and Bernard Roberts (piano), 1977 (Roberts replaced by Hamish Milne, 1984). Sir Robert Mayer Vis. Lectr, Leeds Univ., 1974–75. Member Jury: Tchaikovsky Violin Competition, Moscow, 1970; Carl Flesch Internat. Competition, 1984. Hon. RAM, 1963. *Recreations:* collecting early printed books in Armenian; backgammon. *Address:* The Old Rectory, Waterstock, Oxford. *T:* Ickford 603.

PARIS, Archbishop of; *see* Lustiger, His Eminence Cardinal J.-M.

PARISH, Sir David (Elmer) W.; *see* Woodbine Parish.

PARK, Andrew Edward Wilson, QC 1978; *b* 27 Jan. 1939; *s* of late Dennis Edward Park and of Margaret Alison Park; *m* 1962, Ann Margaret Woodhead; two *s* one *d* (and one *s* decd). *Educ:* Leeds Grammar Sch.; University Coll., Oxford. Winter Williams Law Schol., 1959; BA (Jurisp.) 1960, MA 1964. Various academic posts in UK and abroad, 1960–68. Called to the Bar, Lincoln's Inn, 1964, Bencher, 1986; practice at Revenue Bar, 1965–; Chm., Taxation and Retirement Benefits Cttee of the Bar Council, 1978–82; Treasurer, Senate of the Inns of Court and Bar, 1982–85. *Publications:* The Sources of Nigerian Law, 1963; various articles, notes and reviews in legal periodicals, mainly concerning taxation. *Recreations:* squash, tennis. *Address:* Blandford Cottage, Weston Green Road, Thames Ditton, Surrey KT7 0HX. *T:* 01–398 5349.

PARK, Daphne Margaret Sybil Désirée, CMG 1971; OBE 1960; HM Diplomatic Service, retired; Principal of Somerville College, Oxford, since 1980; *b* England, 1 Sept. 1921; British parents; unmarried. *Educ:* Rosa Bassett Sch.; Somerville Coll., Oxford. WTS (FANY), 1943–47 (Allied Commn for Austria, 1946–48). FO, 1948; UK Delegn to NATO, 1952; 2nd Sec., Moscow, 1954; FO, 1956; Consul and 1st Sec., Leopoldville, 1959; FO, 1961; Lusaka, 1964; FO, 1967; Consul-Gen., Hanoi, 1969–70; Hon. Res. Fellow, Univ. of Kent, 1971–72, on sabbatical leave from FCO; Chargé d'Affaires *ai*, Ulan Bator, Apr.-June 1972; FCO, 1973–79. Chm., Legal Aid Adv. Cttee to the Lord Chancellor, 1985–. Member: British Library Bd; RIIA; Royal Asiatic Soc.; Mem. Council, VSO, 1981–84. Governor, BBC, 1982–. Pro-Vice-Chancellor, Univ. of Oxford, 1985–. *Recreations:* good talk, politics, and difficult places. *Address:* Somerville College, Oxford OX2 6HD. *Clubs:* United Oxford & Cambridge University, Naval and Military, Royal Commonwealth Society, Special Forces.

PARK, George Maclean; MP (Lab) Coventry North East since Feb. 1974; *b* 27 Sept. 1914; *s* of James McKenzie Park and Mary Gorman Park; *m* 1941, Joyce, *d* of Robert Holt Stead and Gertrude Stead; one *d*. *Educ:* Onslow Drive Sch., Glasgow; Coventry Techn. College. Sen. AEU Shop Steward, Chrysler UK Ltd, Ryton, 1968–73. Coventry City Councillor, 1961–74; Coventry District Councillor, 1973–74; Leader of Council Labour Gp, 1967–74; W Mids Metropolitan CC, 1973–77; Chm. Coventry and District Disablement Adv. Cttee, 1960–74; Leader, Coventry City and District Councils, 1972–74; Chm. Policy Adv. Cttee, 1972–74. PPS to Dr J. Gilbert, Minister for Transport, 1975–76; PPS to E. Varley, Sec. of State for Industry, 1976–79. Chm., W Midland Regional Council of the Labour Party, 1983–. Chm. Belgrade Theatre Trust, 1972–74. JP Coventry, 1961–84. AEU Award of Merit, 1967. *Recreations:* reading, walking. *Address:* 170 Binley Road, Coventry CV3 1HG. *T:* Coventry 458589.

PARK, Hon. Sir Hugh (Eames), Kt 1965; Judge of the High Court of Justice, Queen's Bench Division, 1973–85 (Family Division, 1965–73); *b* 24 April 1910; *er s* of late William Robert and Helen Beatrice Park; *m* 1938, Beryl Josephine, *d* of late Joseph and Margery Coombe; three *d*. *Educ:* Blundell's; Sidney Sussex Coll., Cambridge (Hon. Fellow, 1968). Called to the Bar, Middle Temple, 1936; QC 1960; Bencher, 1965. Member Western Circuit. Served War, 1940–45; Sqdn Leader, 1945. Recorder of Penzance, 1959–60; of Exeter, 1960–64; of Southampton, 1964–65. Member, Court of Exeter Univ., 1961; Member, Board of Governors, Blundell's Sch., 1961–81. Commn of Assize, North East Circuit, 1963; Judge of the Courts of Appeal, Channel Islands, 1964–65; Chairman, County of Devon Quarter Sessions, 1964–71; Deputy Chairman, Cornwall County Quarter Sessions, 1959–71; Presiding Judge, Western Circuit, 1970–75. Hon. LLD Exeter, 1984. *Recreation:* fishing. *Address:* 34 Ordnance Hill, St John's Wood, NW8. *T:* 01–586 0417; Gorran Haven, Cornwall. *T:* Mevagissey 842333.

PARK, Ian Grahame; Managing Director, Northcliffe Newspapers Group Ltd, since 1982; Director, Associated Newspaper Holdings plc, since 1983; *b* 15 May 1935; *s* of William Park and Christina (*née* Scott); *m* 1965, Anne Turner; one *s*. *Educ:* Lancaster

Royal Grammar Sch.; Queens' Coll., Cambridge. 1st Bn Manchester Regt, Berlin (Nat. Service Commn), 1954–56. Trainee Journalist, Press and Journal, Aberdeen, 1959; Asst Lit. Editor, Sunday Times, 1960–63; various management posts, Thomson Newspapers, 1963–65; Liverpool Daily Post and Echo, 1965–, Man. Dir and Editor in Chief, 1972–82. Mem. Council, Newspaper Soc., 1967– (Pres., 1980–81); Dir, Press Assoc., 1973–83 (Chm., 1978–79 and 1979–80); Dir, Reuters, 1978–82. Mem. Newspaper Panel, Monopolies and Mergers Commn, 1986–. Dir, Radio City (Sound of Merseyside Ltd), 1973–82; Dir, Liverpool Playhouse, 1973–80; Trustee, Blue Coat Soc. of Arts, Liverpool, 1973–82. FRSA. *Recreations:* reading, theatre, visiting galleries. *Address:* 6 Cheyne Row, SW3. *Club:* Reform.

PARK, (Ian) Michael (Scott), CBE 1982; Partner, Paull & Williamsons, Advocates, Aberdeen, since 1964; *b* 7 April 1938; *m* 1964, Elizabeth Mary Lamberton Struthers; two *s. Educ:* Aberdeen Grammar Sch.; Aberdeen Univ. (MA, LLB). Admitted Mem. Soc. of Advocates, Aberdeen, 1962. Law Society of Scotland: Mem. Council, 1974–85; Vice-Pres., 1979–80; Pres., 1980–81. Chm., Aberdeen Citizens Advice Bureau, 1976–; Mem., Criminal Injuries Compensation Bd, 1983–. Trustee, Petroleum Law Educn Trust, 1983–. Frequent broadcaster on legal topics. *Recreations:* golf, gardening. *Address:* Beechwood, 46 Rubislaw Den South, Aberdeen AB2 6AX. *T:* Aberdeen 33799. *Club:* New (Edinburgh).

PARK, Dame Kiri; *see* Te Kanawa, Dame K.

PARK, Dame Merle (Florence), (Dame Merle Bloch), DBE 1986 (CBE 1974); Principal, Royal Ballet; Director, Royal Ballet School, since 1983; *b* Salisbury, S Rhodesia, 8 Oct. 1937; *d* of P. J. Park, Eastlea, Salisbury, S Rhodesia, C Africa; *m* 1st, 1965, James Monahan, CBE (marr. diss. 1970; he *d* 1985); one *s*; 2nd, 1971, Sidney Bloch. *Educ:* Elmhurst Ballet Sch. Founder, Ballet Sch., St Peter's Sq., W6, 1977–83. Joined Sadler's Wells Ballet, 1955; first rôle, a Mouse (Sleeping Beauty prologue); first solo, Milkmaid (Façzce); principal soloist, 1959. First danced: Blue Bird (Act III, Sleeping Beauty), 1956; Swanhilda (Coppelia), Mamzelle Angot (Mamzelle Angot), 1958; Lise (Fille Mal Gardée), 1960; Cinderella, 1962; Juliet (Romeo and Juliet), 1965; Giselle, Celestial (Shadow Play), 1967; Clara (Nutcracker), Aurora (Sleeping Beauty), 1968; Odette (Swan Lake), 1971; A Walk to Paradise Garden, 1972; Firebird, Odette/Odile (Swan Lake), Dances at a Gathering, 1973; Manon, Emilia (The Moor's Pavane), Aureole, Terpsichore (Apollo), Elite Syncopations, 1974; Lulu, 1976; Kate (The Taming of the Shrew), La Bayadère, Tuesday's Child (Jazz Calendar), Triad, Symphonic Variations, Waltzes of Spring (in Royal Opera Fledermaus), Le Papillon, 1977; Countess Larisch (Mayerling), 1978; La Fin du Jour, 1979; Mary Vetsera (Mayerling), Natalia (A Month in the Country), Adieu, 1980; Chloë (Daphnis and Chloë), Isadora, 1981; Raymonda, 1983. Queen Elizabeth Award, Royal Acad. of Dancing, 1982. *Recreations:* gardening, reading. *Address:* c/o Royal Ballet School, 144 Talgarth Road, W14.

PARK, Michael; *see* Park, I. M. S.

PARK, Trevor; Lecturer in Industrial Relations, since 1972 and Senior Fellow, since 1983, Department of Adult Education and Extramural Studies, University of Leeds; *b* 12 Dec. 1927; *s* of late Stephen Clifford Park and Annie Park (*née* Jackson); *m* 1953, Barbara Black; no *c. Educ:* Bury Grammar Sch.; Manchester Univ. (MA). History Master, Bacup and Rawtenstall Grammar Sch., 1949–56; WEA, Tutor and Organiser (NW District), 1956–60; Lecturer, Extramural Dept, Univ. of Sheffield (politics and internat. relations), 1960–64; WEA Tutor and Organiser, Manchester, 1970–72. Parliamentary Labour Candidate: Altrincham and Sale, General Election, 1955; Darwen, General Election, 1959; MP (Lab) South East Derbyshire, 1964–70. Mem. (Lab) Leeds CC, 1979– (Chairman: Mun. Services Cttee, 1980–83; Planning and Develt Cttee, 1983–). Member: TGWU; Select Cttees on Nationalised Industries, 1966–68, and on Education and Science, 1968–70; Yorkshire and Humberside Economic Planning Council, 1977–79. Chm. ATAE, 1972–75. *Recreation:* walking. *Address:* Department of Adult Education and Extramural Studies, The University, Leeds LS2 9JT.

PARKE, Prof. Dennis Vernon William, PhD, DSc; CChem, FRSC, FIBiol, FRCPath; (first) Professor and Head of Department of Biochemistry, University of Surrey, since 1967; *b* London, 15 Nov. 1922; *e s* of William Parke and Florence Parke; *m* 1943, Doreen Joan Dunn; two *s* one *d. Educ:* West Ham Municipal Secondary Sch. (Gurney Scholar); Chelsea and University Colls, Univ. of London 1940–48; St Mary's Hosp. Med. Sch., London (PhD DSc). War Service, RA RAMC, 1942–47. Head, Dept of Microbiol Chem., Glaxo Labs Ltd, 1948–49; St Mary's Hosp. Med. Sch., Univ. of London: Res. Asst to Prof. R. T. Williams, FRS, 1949–52; Lectr in Biochem., 1952–58, Sen. Lectr, 1958–62; Reader in Biochem., 1962–67; Dean, Faculty of Biol and Chem. Sciences, Univ. of Surrey, 1971–75. Sometime Examnr, Univs of Dublin (Trinity), Edinburgh, Glasgow, Liverpool, London, Newcastle upon Tyne, Reading, Strathclyde, Wales, Auckland, Ibadan, Nairobi, Singapore, Sydney and Wellington. Sigma Xi Lectr, Univ. of Calif (Davis), 1978. Member: Cttee on Safety of Drugs, 1968–70; Cttee on Safety of Medicines, 1970–83; Cttee on Med. Aspects of Chemicals in Food and Environment, DHSS, 1972–; Food Additives and Contaminants Cttee, MAFF, 1972–80; WHO Expert Panel on Food Additives, 1975–; WHO Sci. Gp on Toxicity Evaluation of Chemicals, 1975; WHO Cons. in Indust. Toxicol., 1974, 1979, 1981, 1983; Sci. Dir, NATO Workshop on Ecotoxicology, July-Aug. 1977. Mem., Internat. Acad. of Environmental Safety. Hon. MRCP 1985; Hon. Mem., Polish Soc. of Toxicology, 1984; Hon. Fellow, Polish Soc. of Occupational Medicine, 1984. Editor, Xenobiotica, 1970–. *Publications:* The Biochemistry of Foreign Compounds, 1968; (ed) Enzyme Induction, 1975; chapters in books and res. papers in biochem., pharm. and med. jls. *Recreations:* landscape gardening, music. *Address:* Trevelen, Poyle Road, Guildford, Surrey. *T:* Guildford 573667. *Club:* Athenæum.

PARKE, Dr Mary, FRS 1972; Senior Phycologist, Marine Biological Association, Plymouth, 1947–73, retired; *b* 23 March 1908. *Educ:* Notre Dame Convent, Everton Valley; Univ. of Liverpool. DSc, PhD; FLS, FIBiol. Isaac Roberts Research Schol. in Biology, 1929; Phycologist, Marine Biological Stn, Port Erin, IoM, 1930–40; research on algae for Develt Commn and Min. of Supply, 1941–46. Corresp. Mem., Royal Botanical Soc. of Netherlands, 1970; Mem., Norwegian Acad. of Science and Letters, 1971. Hon. DSc Liverpool, 1986. *Publications:* (with M. Knight) Manx Algae, 1931; papers in Jl of Marine Biol Assoc., Plymouth, etc. *Address:* 6 Alfred Street, Plymouth PL1 2RP. *T:* Plymouth 668609.

PARKER, family name of **Earls of Macclesfield** and **Morley.**

PARKER, Viscount; Richard Timothy George Parker; *b* 31 May 1943; *s* and *heir* of 8th Earl of Macclesfield, *qv*; *m* 1967, Tatiana Cleone, *d* of Major Craig Wheaton-Smith; three *d* (including twins); *m* 1986, Mrs Sandra Hope Mead. *Educ:* Stowe; Worcester Coll., Oxford. *Address:* Portobello Farm, Shirburn, Watlington, Oxon.

PARKER, A(gnes) Miller, RE; Artist and Wood-engraver; *b* Irvine, Ayrshire, 25 March 1895; *d* of William McCall and Agnes Mitchell Parker; *m* 1918, William McCance, Artist (marr. diss. 1963, and she legally assumed maiden name); no *c. Educ:* Glasgow School of Art (Diploma, Haldane Scholar). Instructress, Glasgow School of Art, 1918–20; Art Mistress, Maltmans Green School, Gerrards Cross, 1920–28; Art Mistress, Clapham High School and Training Coll., 1928–30; Walter Brewster Prize, 1st International Exhibition of Engraving and Lithography, Chicago, 1929; Wood-engraver to Gregynog Press, Newtown, Montgomeryshire, 1930–33. *Publications:* Chief Illustrated Editions; Esopes Fables by Caxton, 1931; Daisy Matthews and three other tales by Rhys Davies, 1932; XXI Welsh Gypsy Folk-Tales, collected by John Sampson, 1933; The House with the Apricot by H. E. Bates, 1933; Forest Giant-translated from the French by J. H. Ross (Colonel T. E. Lawrence), 1935; Through the Woods by H. E. Bates, 1936; Down the River by H. E. Bates, 1937; Gray's Elegy written in a Country Church-yard (Limited Editions Club of NY), 1938; Richard II-Shakespeare (Limited Editions Club of NY), 1940; A Shropshire Lad by A. E. Housman, 1940; The Return of the Native by Thomas Hardy (Limited Editions Club of NY), 1942; Essays in Russet by Herbert Furst, 1944; Spring of the Year by Richard Jefferies, 1946; The Life of the Fields, 1947, Field and Hedgerow, 1948, The Open Air, 1948, The Old House at Coate, 1948, by Richard Jefferies; Animals Under the Rainbow by Aloysius Roche, 1952; The Faerie Queene by Edmund Spenser, vols I and II, 1953; Lucifer by J. C. Powys, 1956; Tess of the D'Urbervilles, 1956, and Far From the Madding Crowd, 1958, by Thomas Hardy (New York); The Tragedies of Shakespeare (New York), 1959; The Mayor of Casterbridge by Thomas Hardy (Limited Editions Club of NY), 1964; Poems of Shakespeare (Limited Editions Club of NY), 1967; Jude the Obscure by Thomas Hardy (Limited Editions Club of NY), 1969. *Recreations:* fishing and cats.

PARKER, Sir Alan; *see* Parker, Sir W. A.

PARKER, Alan William; film director and writer; *b* 14 Feb. 1944; *s* of William and Elsie Parker; *m* 1966, Annie Inglis; three *s* one *d. Educ:* Owen's Sch., Islington. Advertising Copywriter, 1965–67; Television Commercials Director, 1968–78. Wrote screenplay, Melody, 1969; wrote and directed: No Hard Feelings, 1972; Our Cissy, 1973; Footsteps, 1973; Bugsy Malone, 1975; directed: The Evacuees, 1974; Midnight Express, 1977; Fame, 1979; Shoot the Moon, 1981; The Wall, 1982; Birdy, 1984. Vice-Chm., Directors Guild of Great Britain, 1982–; Chm., Producers/Directors section, ACTT, 1983–84; Member: Council, BAFTA, 1983–84; British Screen Adv. Council, 1985–. *Publications: novels:* Bugsy Malone, 1976; Puddles in the Lane, 1977; *cartoon:* Hares in the Gate, 1983. *Address:* Pinewood Studios, Iver Heath, Bucks SL0 0NH. *T:* Iver 655052.

PARKER, Prof. Alexander Augustine, MA, LittD; Professor of Spanish Literature, University of Texas at Austin, 1970–78, now Emeritus; *b* Montevideo, 1908; *er s* of Arthur Parker and Laura Bustamante; *m* 1941, Frances Ludwig; two *s* two *d. Educ:* Hawkesyard School (later Blackfriars School, Laxton); Gonville and Caius Coll., Cambridge (Exhibn. and scholar; 1st Class Mod. and Medieval Langs Tripos, Part I 1928, Part II 1930; Gibson Schol., 1931; LittD 1968). Fellow of Gonville and Caius Coll., 1933–39, Hon. Fellow 1985. Lecturer and Head of Dept of Spanish, University of Aberdeen, 1939–49; Reader in Spanish, University of Aberdeen, 1949–53; Cervantes Professor of Spanish, University of London (King's Coll.), 1953–63; Prof. of Hispanic Studies, Univ. of Edinburgh, 1963–69. Seconded to University College of the West Indies as Prof. of Modern Languages, 1960–61; Andrew Mellon Visiting Prof., University of Pittsburgh, 1964, 1968, 1969–70. Corresponding Member: Royal Acad. of Letters of Seville, 1958; Hispanic Society of America, 1960 (Member, 1976); Royal Spanish Academy, 1964. Hon. DLitt: Durham, 1975; St Andrews, 1978; Hon. LittD Liverpool, 1978. Commander of the Order of Isabel la Católica, 1956. *Publications:* The Allegorical Drama of Calderón, An Introduction to the Autos Sacramentales, 1943; (ed) No hay más Fortuna que Dios, by Calderón, 1949; Literature and the Delinquent: the Picaresque Novel in Spain and Europe (1599–1753), 1967; Luis de Góngora, Fable of Polyphemus and Galatea: a study of a baroque poem, 1977; The Philosophy of Love in Spanish Literature (1480–1680), 1985; papers and articles in literary and academic journals. *Recreations:* opera, horticulture and lepidoptera. *Address:* 9 West Castle Road, Edinburgh EH10 5AT. *T:* 031–229 1632.

PARKER, Cameron Holdsworth; Managing Director, Lithgows Ltd; Chairman: Campbeltown Shipyard Ltd; J. Fleming Engineering Ltd; Glasgow Iron & Steel Co. Ltd; Landcatch Ltd; Lithgow Electronics Ltd; Malakoff & Wm Moore Ltd; McKinlay & Blair Ltd; Prosper Engineering Ltd; Director: Lithgows Pty Ltd; Stokes Castings Ltd; *b* 14 April 1932; *s* of George Cameron Parker and Mary Stevenson Parker; *m* 1st, 1957, Elizabeth Margaret Thomson (*d* 1985); three *s*; 2nd, 1986, Marlyne Honeyman, Mem. Stock Exchange. *Educ:* Morrison's Acad., Crieff; Glasgow Univ. (BSc Hons). John G. Kincaid & Co. Ltd, Greenock: Asst Manager, 1958; Asst Gen. Man., 1961; Dir, 1963; Man. Dir, 1967; Chm., 1976; Chm. and Chief Exec., Scott Lithgow Ltd, Port Glasgow, 1980–83. Bd Mem., British Shipbuilders, 1977–80, 1981–83. *Recreation:* golf. *Address:* Heath House, Rowantreehill Road, Kilmacolm, Renfrewshire PA13 4PE. *T:* Kilmacolm 3197. *Club:* Caledonian.

PARKER, Christopher William Oxley, MA; JP; DL; *b* 28 May 1920; *s* of late Lieut-Col John Oxley Parker, TD, and Mary Monica (*née* Hills); *m* 1947, Jocelyn Frances Adeline, *d* of late Colonel C. G. Arkwright, Southern Rhodesia; one *s* two *d. Educ:* Eton; Trinity Coll., Oxford. Director: Strutt and Parker (Farms) Ltd; Lord Rayleighs Farm Inc.; Local Dir, Chelmsford Bd, Barclays Bank, 1951–83. Served War of 1939–45, with 147th Field Regt (Essex Yeomanry) Royal Artillery, 1939–42. JP Essex, 1952; High Sheriff of Essex, 1961; DL Essex 1972. *Recreations:* shooting, tennis, golf; estate management. *Address:* Faulkbourne Hall, Witham, Essex. *T:* Witham 513385. *Clubs:* Boodle's, MCC.

PARKER, Clifford Frederick, MA, LLB Cantab; JP; Bracton Professor of Law at the University of Exeter, 1957–85 (Deputy Vice-Chancellor, 1963–65, Public Orator, 1977–81); *b* 6 March 1920; *yr s* of late Frederick James Parker and Bertha Isabella (*née* Kemp), Cardiff; *m* 1945, Christine Alice (*née* Knowles); two *d. Educ:* Cardiff High Sch.; Gonville and Caius Coll., Cambridge. Royal Air Force, 1940–43. Solicitor of Supreme Court, 1947. Lecturer in Common Law, University of Birmingham, 1951–57; Senior Tutor and Asst Director of Legal Studies, Faculty of Law, University of Birmingham, 1956–57. Pres., Soc. of Public Teachers of Law, 1974–75. Chm., Exeter Area, Supplementary Benefit Appeal Tribunal, 1978–. JP Devon, 1969. *Publications:* contrib. to legal periodicals. *Recreation:* touring. *Address:* Lynwood, Exton, Exeter EX3 0PR. *T:* Topsham 4051.

PARKER, Sir Douglas D.; *see* Dodds-Parker.

PARKER, Rear-Adm. Douglas Granger, CB 1971; DSO 1945; DSC 1945; AFC 1952; Assistant Chief of Naval Staff (Operations and Air), 1969–71, retired; *b* 21 Nov. 1919; *s* of R. K. Parker; *m* 1953, Margaret Susan, *d* of late Col W. Cooper; one *s* one *d. Educ:* W Hartlepool Technical Coll. Joined Royal Navy, 1940; Command Fleet Air Arm Fighter Squadrons, 1948–51; Commanded: HMS Cavendish, 1961–62; RN Air Station, Lossiemouth, 1965–67; HMS Hermes, 1967–69. Captain 1959; Rear-Adm. 1969. *Address:* High Meadow, Walhampton, Lymington, Hants. *T:* Lymington 3259. *Club:* Royal Lymington Yacht.

PARKER, Sir Douglas William Leigh, Kt 1966; OBE 1954; retired as Director of Orthopædic Services, Tasmanian Government Health Dept, 1966; *b* 12 July 1900; *m* 1933, Hilary Secretan; two *s* one *d*. *Educ:* University of Sydney; University of Liverpool. MB, ChM (Sydney), 1923; FRCSEd 1925; MChOrth (Liverpool), 1930; FRACS, 1935. War of 1939–45: Surgeon, 2/9 AGH, 1940–42, 111 AGH, 1942–46. Senior Orthopædic Surgeon, Royal Hobart Hospital. Comr St John Ambulance Bde, Tasmania. Member Legacy, Hobart. OStJ. *Address:* 30 Fisher's Avenue, Lower Sandy Bay, Hobart, Tasmania 7005, Australia. *Clubs:* Tasmanian, Naval and Military and Air Force (Hobart).

PARKER, Eric Wilson, FCA; Group Chief Executive, Trafalgar House PLC, since 1983; *b* 8 June 1933; *s* of Wilson Parker and Edith Gladys (*née* Wellings); *m* 1955, Marlene Teresa (*née* Neale); two *s* two *d*. *Educ:* The Priory Grammar Sch. for Boys, Shrewsbury. FCA 1967 (ACA 1956); CBIM 1983. Articled Clerk with Wheeler, Whittingham & Kent, Shrewsbury, 1950–55; National Service, Pay Corps, 1956–58; Taylor Woodrow Gp, 1958–64; Trafalgar House Gp, 1965–: Finance/Admin Dir, 1969; Dep. Man. Dir, 1973; Gp Man. Dir, 1977; Dir, Associated Container Transportation (Aust.), 1983–. Dir, John Brown PLC, 1985–; Non-Executive Director: Sealink UK Ltd, 1979–81; British Rail Investments Ltd, 1980–84; Evening Standard Co. Ltd, 1982–85; Touche Remnant Hldgs Ltd, 1985–; European Assets Trust NV, 1972–85; The Automobile Pty Ltd, 1986–; Metal Box plc, 1985–. FRSA 1983; CBIM. *Recreations:* sports (including golf and horseracing), wines. *Address:* Trafalgar House, 1 Berkeley Street, W1A 1BY; Nower Hayes, The Drive, Tyrrell's Wood, Leatherhead, Surrey KT22 8QW. *Clubs:* Royal Automobile, MCC; Tyrrell's Wood Golf (Leatherhead).

PARKER, Geoffrey; *see* Parker, N. G.

PARKER, Geoffrey John, CBE 1985; Managing Director, Atlantic Steam Navigation Co. Ltd, since 1974; Chairman: European Ferries Group Plc, since 1986 (Director, since 1979); Felixstowe Dock & Railway Co., since 1983 (Managing Director, 1976–86); Larne Harbour Board, since 1983; Member, National Bus Co. Ltd, since 1980; *b* 20 March 1937; *s* of Stanley John Parker and Alice Ellen Parker; *m* 1957, Hazel Mary Miall; two *s* two *d*. *Educ:* County Grammar Sch., Hendon. Commercial Dir, Townsend Car Ferries Ltd, 1972–74. FCIT 1982. *Recreation:* golf. *Address:* 101 Valley Road, Ipswich, Suffolk IP1 4NF. *T:* Ipswich 216003. *Clubs:* Ipswich Golf (Purdis Heath, Ipswich); Felixstowe Master Mariners.

PARKER, Herbert John Harvey; *see* Parker, John.

PARKER, Hugh; Director: Business International Inc., since 1984; Lewis and Peat Holdings Ltd, since 1983; DPCE Ltd, since 1983; Norman Magnetics Ltd, since 1986; Albemarle International Ltd, since 1984; *b* 12 June 1919; *s* of Ross Parker and Ruth Baker Parker; *m* 1957, Elsa del Carmen Mijares Osorio; one *s* one *d*. *Educ:* Tabor Academy; Trinity Hall, Cambridge; Massachusetts Inst. of Technology. North Carolina Shipbuilding Co., 1941–43; General Electric Co., 1945–46; Ludlow Manufacturing Co., 1947–50; McKinsey & Co. Inc., 1951–84 (Sen. Dir, 1974–84). Pres., American Chamber of Commerce (UK), 1976–79. Pres., MIT Alumni Club of GB, 1962–84. Governor, Ditchley Foundn. *Publications:* Letters to a New Chairman, 1979; numerous articles on management. *Recreations:* reading, sculling, cooking. *Address:* 9 Cheyne Walk, SW3. *T:* 01–352 9592. *Clubs:* The Pilgrims, United Oxford & Cambridge University; Leander; Racquet and Tennis (New York); Eastern Yacht (Mass).

PARKER, James Geoffrey; High Master, Manchester Grammar School, since 1985; *b* 27 March 1933; *s* of late Ian Sutherland Parker and Kathleen Lilian Parker; *m* 1956, Ruth Major; two *d*. *Educ:* Alderman Newton's Sch., Leicester; Christ's Coll., Cambridge (Exhibnr); Wadham Coll., Oxford. National Service, RA, 1954–56. Asst Master, Bedford Modern Sch., 1957–66; Head of History Dept, Tonbridge Sch., 1966–75; Headmaster, Queen Elizabeth Grammar Sch., Wakefield, 1975–85. *Recreation:* sailing. *Address:* 143 Old Hall Lane, Manchester M14 6HL. *T:* 061–224 3929.

PARKER, James Mavin, (Jim Parker); composer and conductor; *b* Hartlepool, 18 Dec. 1934; *s* of James Robertson Parker and Margaret Mavin; *m* 1969, Pauline George; two *d*; one *d* by a previous marriage. *Educ:* various grammar schools; Guildhall Sch. of Music (AGSM 1959; Silver Medal). LRAM 1959. Professional oboeist, 1959; joined the Barrow Poets, 1963. Wrote musical settings of Sir John Betjeman's poems, Banana Blush, 1973 (recorded these and subsequent settings with Sir John as speaker); wrote music for Chichester Theatre, 1974–77; music for television and films, 1977–, includes: Credo; Another Six English Towns; Good Behaviour; Wynne and Penkovsky; Mapp and Lucia; Time After Time; Betjeman's Britain; Late Flowering Love. *Compositions* include: (with William Bealby-Wright) Moonshine Rock, 1972; (with William Bealby-Wright) Mister Skillicorn Dances, 1974; (with Cicely Herbert) Mayhew's London, 1978; (with John Betjeman) Poems (ballet), 1981; In The Gold Room (words by Oscar Wilde), 1983. Recordings with Barrow Poets, Keith Michell, Peter Sellers, Harry Secombe, Twiggy, etc. *Publications:* (with Wally K. Daly) Follow the Star, 1975; (with Jeremy Lloyd) Captain Beaky, 1977; (with Tom Stanier) The Shepherd King, 1979; (with Tom Stanier) The Burning Bush, 1980; (with Tom Stanier) All Aboard, 1983; A Londoner in New York (suite for brass), 1986; (with Tom Stanier) Blast Off, 1986. *Recreations:* tennis, literature, 20th Century art. *Address:* 19 Laurel Road, Barnes, SW13 0EE. *T:* 01–876 8571.

PARKER, James Roland Walter, CMG 1978; OBE 1968; HM Diplomatic Service, retired; Governor and Commander-in-Chief, Falkland Islands and Dependencies, and High Commissioner, British Antarctic Territory, 1976–80; *b* 20 Dec. 1919; *s* of late Alexander Roland Parker, ISM; *m* 1941, Deirdre Mary Ward. Served War of 1939–45: 1st London Scottish, 1940–41. Ministry of Labour, 1938–57; Labour Attaché, Tel Aviv, 1957–60; Labour Adviser: Accra, 1960–62; Lagos, 1962–64; seconded to Foreign Office, 1965–66; Dep. High Comr, Enugu, 1966–67; Commonwealth Office (later FCO), 1968–70; Head of Chancery, Suva, Fiji, 1970–71; High Comr in The Gambia, 1972–75; Consul-Gen., Durban, 1976. *Address:* Crockers Hill, Yarlington, Somerset BA9 8DJ; 1 St Edmund's Court, NW8 7QL.

PARKER, John, CBE 1965; President, Fabian Society, since 1980 (Vice-President, 1972–80); *b* 15 July 1906; *s* of H. A. M. Parker, schoolmaster; *m* 1943, Zena Mimardiere; one *s*. *Educ:* Marlborough; St John's College, Oxford. Chm., Oxford Univ. Labour Club, 1928; Asst to Director, Social Survey of Merseyside (Liverpool Univ.), 1929–32; Gen. Sec., New Fabian Res. Bureau, 1933–39; Fabian Society: Gen. Sec., 1939–45; Vice-Chm., 1946–50; Chm., 1950–53. Contested (Lab) Holland with Boston, 1931; MP (Lab): Romford, Essex, 1935–45; Dagenham, 1945–83; PPS to Miss Ellen Wilkinson, Min. of Home Security, 1940–42; Parly Under-Sec. of State, Dominions Office, 1945–46; Member: Speaker's Conferences, 1944, 1965–67, 1973–74; Procedure Cttee, 1966–73; Parly Delegation to USSR, 1945; National Executive Labour Party, 1943–44; Executive London Labour Party, 1942–47; Select Cttee Parliamentary Disqualifications, 1956; Parly Delegations to Italy, 1957, Ethiopia, 1964, Forestry Delegation, Yugoslavia, 1971; Leader, Delegation to Windward Islands, 1965; Chm., British-Yugoslav Parly Gp, 1960–83; Father of the House of Commons, 1979–83; Chairman: History of Parlt Trust, 1979–83; H of C Pensions Fund, 1969–83. Hon. Sec., Webb Trustees; Governor, LSE, 1949–81; Member: Court, Essex Univ., 1968–; Exec. Cttee, Nat. Trust, 1969–81; Historic Buildings Council, 1974–84; Inland Waterways Amenity Council, 1968–83. Mem., TGWU. Yugoslav Red Star, 1975. *Publications:* The Independent Worker and Small Family Business, 1931; Public Enterprise (Forestry Commission), 1937; Democratic Sweden (Political Parties); Modern Turkey, 1940; 42 Days in the Soviet Union, 1946; Labour Marches On, 1947; Newfoundland, 1950; (ed) Modern Yugoslav Novels (English edn), 1958–64; (comp. and ed) biographies, inc. Harold Wilson and Willy Brandt, 1964; Father of the House: 50 Years in Politics, 1982. *Recreations:* architecture and gardening. *Address:* 4 Essex Court, Temple, EC4. *T:* 01–353 8521.

PARKER, John; *see* Parker, T. J.

PARKER, Sir John; *see* Parker, Sir W. J.

PARKER, Comdr (John) Michael (Avison), CVO 1957 (MVO 1953); RN (retired); Director, Leo Burnett-Australia; *b* 23 June 1920; *s* of late Capt. C. A. Parker, CBE, Royal Australian Navy, Melbourne; *m* 1st, 1943, Eileen Margaret Anne (*née* Allan) (marr. diss. 1958); one *s* one *d*; 2nd, 1962, Carol (marr. diss.; she *d* 1977); one *s* one *d*; 3rd, 1976, Mrs Jean Lavinia Grice Ramsay. *Educ:* Xavier College, Melbourne, Australia. Royal Navy, 1938–47. Equerry-in-Waiting to Princess Elizabeth and the Duke of Edinburgh, 1947–52; Private Sec. to Duke of Edinburgh, 1947–57. Dir, Leo Burnett P/L. Member: Aust.-Britain Soc. (Vice-Pres.); Navy League; RSL; Australian Ballet Trust; Trustee: Victorian Conservation Trust; World Wildlife Australia. Chairman: Sail Training Cttee, Aust; Plain English Speaking Award, Aust. *Recreations:* painting, tennis and sailing. *Address:* Santosa, 33 Albany Road, Toorak, Vic 3142, Australia. *Clubs:* Melbourne; Royal South Yarra Tennis, Sandringham Yacht (Melbourne).

PARKER, Jonathan Frederic; QC 1979; *b* 8 Dec. 1937; *s* of late Sir (Walter) Edmund Parker, CBE and late Elizabeth Mary Butterfield; *m* 1967, Maria-Belen Burns; three *s* one *d*. *Educ:* Winchester College; Magdalene College, Cambridge (MA). Called to Bar, Inner Temple, 1962, Bencher, 1985; practising member of the Bar, 1962–. *Recreations:* painting, gardening. *Address:* The Grange, Radwinter, Saffron Walden, Essex. *T:* Radwinter 375; 11 Old Square, Lincoln's Inn, WC2A 3TS. *T:* 01–430 0341. *Club:* Garrick.

PARKER, Sir Karl (Theodore), Kt 1960; CBE 1954; MA, PhD; FBA 1950; Hon. DLitt Oxon, 1972; Hon. Antiquary to the Royal Academy, 1963; Hon. Fellow, Oriel College, Oxford; Trustee, National Gallery, 1962–69; Keeper of the Ashmolean Museum, Oxford, 1945–62 (retired); Keeper of the Department of Fine Art, Ashmolean Museum, and of the Hope Collection of Engraved Portraits, 1934–62; *b* 1895; *s* of late R. W. Parker, FRCS, and Marie Luling; *m* Audrey (*d* 1976), *d* of late Henry Ashworth James, of Hurstmonceux Place; two *d*. *Educ:* Bedford; Paris; Zürich. Studied art at most continental centres and at the British Museum; edited Old Master Drawings, a Quarterly Magazine for Students and Collectors, since its inception, 1926; late Asst Keeper, Dept of Prints and Drawings, British Museum. *Publications:* North Italian Drawings of the Quattrocento; Drawings of the Early German Schools; Alsatian Drawings of the XV and XVI Centuries; Drawings of Antoine Watteau; Catalogue of Drawings in the Ashmolean Museum, Vol. I, 1938, Vol. II, 1956; Catalogue of Holbein's Drawings at Windsor Castle, 1945; The Drawings of Antonio Canaletto at Windsor Castle, 1948; Antoine Watteau: Catalogue Complet de son œuvre Dessiné, Vol. I (with J. Mathey), 1957, Vol. II, 1958; and articles, mostly on Old Master drawings, in various English and continental periodicals. *Address:* 4 Saffrons Court, Compton Place Road, Eastbourne.

PARKER, Keith John; Editor, Express and Star, Wolverhampton, since 1977; *b* 30 Dec. 1940; *s* of Sydney John Parker and Phyllis Mary Parker; *m* 1962, Marilyn Ann Edwards; one *s*. Various editorial appointments; Editor, Shropshire Star, 1972–77. Member: Guild of British Newspaper Editors; Assoc. of British Editors. *Recreations:* reading, travel. *Address:* 94 Wrottesley Road, Tettenhall, Wolverhampton, West Midlands. *T:* Wolverhampton 758595.

PARKER, Kenneth Alfred Lamport; CB 1959; Receiver for the Metropolitan Police District, 1967–74; *b* 1 April 1912; *e s* of A. E. A. and Ada Mary Parker; *m* 1938, Freda Silcock (OBE 1975); one *s* one *d*. *Educ:* Tottenham Grammar Sch.; St John's College, Cambridge. Home Office, 1934; London Civil Defence Region, 1938–45; (Assistant Secretary, 1942, Deputy Chief Administrative Officer, 1943); Assistant Under-Secretary of State, Home Office, 1955–67 (Head of Police Dept, 1961–66). Imperial Defence College, 1947. Mem., Chairman's Panel, CS Selection Bd, 1974–82. *Publications:* articles on police matters. *Recreations:* garden, cellar, library. *Address:* 18 Lichfield Road, Kew, Surrey. *T:* 01–940 4595. *Club:* United Oxford & Cambridge University.

PARKER, Margaret Annette McCrie Johnston, (Margaret Johnston); actress; *d* of James and Emily Dalrymple Johnston; *m* 1946, Albert E. W. Parker (*d* 1974). *Educ:* North Sydney and Neutral Bay High School; Sydney University, Australia. Student, RADA; studied with Dr Stefan Hock; in repertory and acted as understudies. *Plays:* Murder without Crime, 1943; Fifth Column, 1944; Last of Summer, 1944; Time of Your Life, 1946; Shouting Dies, 1946; Barretts of Wimpole Street, 1947; Always Afternoon, 1949; Summer and Smoke, 1950; Second Threshold, 1951; The Dark is Light Enough, 1954; Sugar in the Morning, 1959; The Ring of Truth, 1959; Masterpiece, 1961. Stratford Memorial Theatre, 1956 season: Othello, The Merchant of Venice, Measure for Measure; Chichester Festival Theatre, 1966 Season: Lady Macbeth. *Films:* Rake's Progress, 1945; Man About the House, 1946; Portrait of Clare, 1949; Magic Box, 1951; Knave of Hearts, 1953; Touch and Go, 1955; Nose on her Face; Life at the Top, 1965; Psychopath; Sebastian. Television plays. *Address:* c/o Al Parker Ltd, 55 Park Lane, W1.

PARKER, Dame Marjorie Alice Collett, DBE 1977; welfare worker, Tasmania; Deputy-Chairman, Australian National Council of Women, 1960–64 (Life Member, since 1974); *b* Ballarat; *d* of W. Shoppee, Ballarat, Vic; *m* 1926, Max Parker; one *s*. *Educ:* Ballarat State Sch. Announcer and Dir Women's Interests, Radio Launceston, 1941–69; Public Relations Adviser for Girl Guide Assoc., 1954–68; Pres. and Org., Red Cross Meals on Wheels, Launceston, Tas., 1961–71; State Exec. and Public Relations Officer, Good Neighbour Council, Tas., 1964–70; N Regional Pres., Aust. Red Cross Soc., Tas. Div., 1965–68; Pres., Victoria League, Launceston, 1966–69; Exec. Mem., Soc. for Care of Crippled Children (Life Mem. 1973). Past Pres., N Tas. Branch, Royal Commonwealth Soc. Vice-Pres., United Nations Assoc., Launceston, 1964–68. *Recreation:* gardening. *Address:* Apsley, 5 Croydon Grove, Cypress Street, Launceston, Tasmania 7250, Australia. *Clubs:* Soroptimist (Pres. 1951), Royal Commonwealth Soc. (Launceston, Tas).

PARKER, Comdr Michael; *see* Parker, Comdr (J.) M. (A.).

PARKER, Michael Clynes, QC 1973; **His Honour Judge Parker;** a Circuit Judge, since 1978; *b* 2 Nov. 1924; *s* of Herbert Parker and Elsie Vera Parker (sometime Pres., NUT); *m* 1950, Molly Leila Franklin; one *s* two *d*. *Educ:* City of London Sch.; Pembroke Coll., Cambridge (BA, LLB). Sec., Cambridge Union, 1943. Flt-Sgt/Air Gunner, RAF, 1943–47. Called to Bar, Gray's Inn, 1949; practised in London and SE Circuit. A Recorder of the Crown Court, 1972–78. Contested (Lab) S Kensington, 1951. *Recreations:* theatre, watching cricket. *Address:* 17 Courtnell Street, W2. *Club:* United Oxford & Cambridge University.

See also B. Tizard.

PARKER, Michael Joseph Bennett; Managing Director since 1970, and Chairman since 1980, Favor Parker Ltd; *b* 22 June 1931; *s* of Henry Gordon Parker and Alice Rose Parker; *m* 1960, Tania Henrietta Tiarks; two *s* one *d*. *Educ:* Eton; Magdalene Coll., Cambridge (BA Agric., MA). Chm., Sovereign Chicken Gp, 1977–. Chm., Land Settlement Assoc., 1982–85; Mem., UKAEA, 1985–. *Recreations:* country sports, windsurfing, lying in the sun. *Address:* Gooderstone Manor, King's Lynn, Norfolk. *T:* Gooderstone 255.

PARKER, Michael St J.; *see* St John Parker.

PARKER, Prof. (Noel) Geoffrey, PhD, LittD; FBA 1984; Charles E. Nowell Professor of History, University of Illinois at Champaign-Urbana, since 1986; *b* 25 Dec. 1943; *s* of Derek Geoffrey Parker and late Kathleen Betsy Symon; *m* 1965, Angela Maureen Chapman (marr. diss. 1980); one *s* one *d*; *m* 1986, Jane Helen Ohlmeyer. *Educ:* Nottingham High Sch.; Christ's Coll., Cambridge (BA 1965; MA; PhD 1968; LittD 1980). Fellow of Christ's Coll., Cambridge, 1968–72; Lectr in Mod. Hist., 1972–78, Reader in Mod. Hist., 1978–82, and Prof. of Early Mod. Hist., 1982–86, St Andrews Univ. British Acad. Exchange Fellow, Newberry Library, Chicago, 1981; Visiting Professor: Vrije Universiteit, Brussels, 1975; Univ. of BC, Vancouver, Canada, 1979–80; Keio Univ., Tokyo, 1984. Lees Knowles Lectr in Mil. Hist., Univ. of Cambridge, 1984. Television scripts and broadcasts. *Publications:* The Army of Flanders and the Spanish Road 1567–1659, 1972, 2nd edn 1975; The Dutch Revolt, 1977, 3rd edn 1985; Philip II, 1978; Europe in Crisis 1598–1648, 1979; Spain and the Netherlands 1559–1659, 1979; The Thirty Years' War, 1984; The World: an illustrated history, 1986; edited numerous other works; articles and reviews. *Recreations:* travel, archaeology, golf. *Address:* Department of History, University of Illinois, 309 Gregory Hall, 810 South Wright Street, Urbana, Ill 61801, USA. *T:* (217) 333–4193.

PARKER, Sir Peter, Kt 1978; LVO 1957; Chairman: Rockware Group, 1971–76, and since 1983 (Director, since 1976); Mitsubishi Electric (UK), since 1984; Whitehead Mann, since 1984; Target Group, since 1984; Oakland Development Capital Fund, since 1985; *b* 30 Aug. 1924; *s* of late Tom and Dorothy S. Parker; *m* 1951, Gillian Rowe-Dutton, *d* of late Sir Ernest Rowe-Dutton, KCMG, CB, and of Lady Rowe-Dutton; three *s* one *d*. *Educ:* Bedford Sch.; London Univ.; Lincoln Coll., Oxford (Hon. Fellow, 1980). Major, Intelligence Corps, 1943–47. Commonwealth Fund Fellowship to Cornell and Harvard, 1950–51. Contested (Lab) Bedford, 1951. Phillips Electrical, 1951–53; Head of Overseas Dept, Industrial Soc. 1953–54; Sec., Duke of Edinburgh's Study Conf. on Human Problems of Industry, 1954–56; joined Booker McConnell Ltd, 1956; Chairman: Bookers Engineering & Industrial Holdings Ltd, 1966–70; Associated British Maltsters Ltd, 1971–73; Curtis Brown Ltd, 1971–76; Victoria Deep Water Terminal Ltd, 1971–76; Dawnay Day Group, 1971–76; Vice-Chm., H. Clarkson & Co. (Hldgs), 1984– (Dir, 1976–; Chm., 1975–76); Director: Booker Bros McConnell & Co. Ltd, 1960–70; Renold Group Ltd; Group 4 Securitas, 1984–; Chm., BRB, 1976–83. Chm.-designate, Nat. Ports Authority, 1970; Chm., Clothing EDC, 1971–78; Member: BSC, 1967–70; British Tourist Authy Bd, 1969–75; British Airways Bd, 1971–81; Nat. Theatre Bd, 1986; Ct of London Univ. (Dep. Chm. 1970–); Political and Econ. Plannning Exec. (Vice-Chm., 1969–70; Hon. Treasurer, 1973–78); Council, BIM (Chm., 1984–86); Foundn on Automation & Human Develt, 1971–; Engineering Industries Council, 1975–76; NEDC, 1980–83; Honeywell Adv. Council, 1984–. Founder Mem., Council of Foundn for Management Educn; Chairman: Westfield College, 1969–76 (Hon. Fellow, 1979); Adv. Council, Business Graduates Assoc. Vis. Fellow, Nuffield Coll., Oxford, 1980 (Hon. Fellow, 1980). Mem. Council, Oxford Mus. of Modern Art, 1984–; Trustee: Conran Foundn Boilerhouse Proj., 1980–; British Architecture Library Trust, 1984. Dimbleby Lecture, BBC TV, 1984. Hon. Fellow, SIAD. Hon. LLD: London, 1981; Manchester Polytechnic, 1981; Bath, 1983. Communicator of the Year Award, British Assoc. of Indust. Editors, 1981. CStJ 1983. *Recreations:* Rugby (played for Bedford and E Mids); swimming, browsing. *Address:* Rockware Group, 12 Camomile Street, EC3A 7BP.

PARKER, Rev. Reginald Boden; *b* Wallasey, Cheshire, 4 June 1901; *s* of Joseph William and Ada Parker. *Educ:* Wallasey Grammar School; St Catherine's College, Oxford University; Ripon Hall, Oxford. BSc (London), 1923; MA (Oxon), 1938. Assistant Master, Ashton Gram. Sch., Lancs, 1925–30; Asst Master, Newton Gram. Sch., Lancs, 1930–32; Curate, Childwall, Liverpool, 1935–37; Curate, St Margaret's, Westminster, 1937–39; Asst Master and Chaplain, Oundle School, 1940–48; Headmaster, Igbobi College, Lagos, 1948–58; Bishop's Chaplain in Liverpool University, 1958–61; Residentiary Canon, Liverpool Cathedral, 1958–61; Precentor, Liverpool Cathedral, 1959–61; Asst Master, Wellington Coll., 1961–64; Rector of Bentham, dio. of Bradford, 1964–72. Hon. Lecturer in Hellenistic Greek, Liverpool University, 1959; Select Preacher, Oxford University, 1960. Member of Headmasters' Conference, 1950. *Publications:* (with J. P. Hodges): The Master and the Disciple, 1938 (SPCK); The King and the Kingdom, 1939 (SPCK); The Holy Spirit and The Kingdom, 1941 (SPCK). *Address:* 3 Yew Tree Cottages, Sheepscombe, Stroud, Glos GL6 7RB. *T:* Painswick 812650.

PARKER, Sir Richard (William) Hyde, 12th Bt, *cr* 1681; *b* 5 April 1937; *o s* of Sir William Stephen Hyde Parker, 11th Bt, and Ulla Ditlef, *o d* of C. Ditlef Nielsen, Dr of Philosophy, Copenhagen; *S* father 1951; *m* 1972, Jean, *d* of late Sir Lindores Leslie, 9th Bt; one *s* three *d* (incl. twin *d*). *Educ:* Millfield; Royal Agricultural College. *Heir: s* William John Hyde Parker, *b* 10 June 1983. *Address:* Melford Hall, Long Melford, Suffolk.

PARKER, Rt. Hon. Sir Roger (Jocelyn), Kt 1977; PC 1983; **Rt. Hon. Lord Justice Parker;** a Lord Justice of Appeal, since 1983; *b* 25 Feb. 1923; *s* of Captain Hon. T. T. Parker, DSC, RN (Retired) and Marie Louise Leonie (*née* Kleinwort); *m* 1948, Ann Elizabeth Frederika (*née* White); one *s* three *d*. *Educ:* Eton; King's Coll., Cambridge. Served Rifle Bde, 1941–46. Called to Bar, Lincoln's Inn, 1948, QC 1961; Bencher, 1969. Dep. Chm., Herts QS, 1969–71; Judge of the Courts of Appeal, Jersey and Guernsey, 1974–83; a Judge of the High Court, QBD, 1977–83. Member, Bar Council, 1968–69, Vice-Chm., 1970–72, Chm., 1972–73. Vice-Pres., Senate of Four Inns of Court, 1972–73. Conducted Windscale Nuclear Fuel Reprocessing Inquiry, 1977. Chm., Court of Inquiry into Flixborough Explosion, 1974. *Clubs:* Lansdowne; Leander.

PARKER, Ronald William, CBE 1959; JP; *b* 21 Aug. 1909; *s* of late Ernest Edward Parker, MBE, Accountant of Court, and Margaret Parker (*née* Henderson); *m* 1937, Phyllis Mary (*née* Sherren); two *s*. *Educ:* Royal High School, Edinburgh. Chartered Accountant, 1933. Secretary, later Dir, Weston Group of Companies, 1935; Asst Dir of Finance, Ministry of Fuel and Power, 1942; Partner, J. Aikman, Smith & Wells, CA, 1946. National Coal Board: Finance Dir, Scottish Division, 1947; Dep. Chm., North Western Division, 1954; Chm., Scottish Division, 1955–67; Regional Chm., Scottish Region, 1967–68; Chm., Scottish Gas Region (formerly Scottish Gas Bd), 1968–74. JP City and County of Edinburgh, 1972. *Recreations:* golf, gardening, fishing. *Address:* Claremont, 3 South Lauder Road, Edinburgh EH9 2LL. *T:* 031–667 7666. *Club:* New (Edinburgh).

PARKER, (Thomas) John, FEng; Chairman and Chief Executive, Harland and Wolff, since 1983; *b* 8 April 1942; *s* of Robert Parker and Margaret Elizabeth Parker (*née* Bell); *m* 1967, Emma Elizabeth (*née* Blair); one *s* one *d*. *Educ:* Belfast Coll. of Technology. FEng 1983; FRINA; FIMarE; MNECInst. Harland & Wolff Ltd, Belfast: Student Apprentice Naval Architect, 1958–63; Ship Design Staff, 1963–69 (Nat. Physical Lab. (Ship Hydrodynamics), on secondment, 1964); Numerical Applications Manager, 1969–71; Prodn Drawing Office Manager, 1971–72; Gen. Manager, Sales and Projects, 1972–74; Man. Dir, Austin-Pickersgill Ltd, Sunderland, 1974–78; British Shipbuilders: Dir of Marketing, 1977–78; Bd Mem. for Shipbuilding, 1978–83; Dep. Chief Exec., 1980–83, with responsibility for: Technology; Trng, Educn and Safety Ltd; Merchant Shipbuilding Div.; Engrg Div. Member: Council, RINA, 1978–80, 1982–; Cttee, Sunderland RNLI, 1980–83; Bd of Governors, Sunderland Polytechnic, 1976–81; Internat. Cttee, Bureau Veritas, Paris, 1979–83; Gen. Cttee, Lloyd's Register of Shipping, 1983–; Industrial Develt Bd of NI, 1983–. Hon. DSc (Eng) Queen's Univ. Belfast, 1986. *Publications:* papers to Trans IES, RINA. *Recreations:* reading, motoring in the countryside, music, family pursuits, ships. *Address:* Harland and Wolff Ltd, Queen's Island, Belfast BT3 9DU. *T:* Belfast 58456.

PARKER, Vice-Adm. Sir (Wilfred) John, KBE 1969 (OBE 1953); CB 1965; DSC 1943; *b* 12 Oct. 1915; *s* of Henry Edmond Parker and Ida Mary (*née* Cole); *m* 1943, Marjorie Stuart Jones, Halifax, NS, Canada; two *d*. *Educ:* RN College, Dartmouth. Joined Royal Navy, 1929; War Service in N Atlantic, N Russia, Mediterranean, Pacific, Korea (OBE); sunk in HMS Edinburgh and HMS Trinidad; mined in HMS Sheffield; torpedoed in HMS Newfoundland; DSC (Capture of Sicily); twice mentioned in despatches (HMS Edinburgh on N Russian convoys, and destruction of an Italian convoy, HMS Aurora 1942); Imperial Defence College, 1957; Commodore West Indies, 1958–60; Captain RNC Dartmouth, 1961–63; an Asst Chief of Defence Staff, Min. of Defence, 1963–66; Flag Officer, Medway, and Adm. Supt HM Dockyard, Chatham, 1966–69, retd 1969. *Recreations:* 6 grandchildren (3 Mayo, 3 Panton); tennis, ski-ing, sailing. *Address:* Flint Cottage, East Harting, Petersfield, Hants GU31 5LT. *Club:* Royal Navy.

PARKER, Sir (William) Alan, 4th Bt *cr* 1844; *b* 20 March 1916; *er s* of Sir William Lorenzo Parker, 3rd Bt, OBE, and late Lady Parker; *S* father, 1971; *m* 1946, Sheelagh Mary, *o d* of late Dr Sinclair Stevenson; one *s* one *d*. *Educ:* Eton; New College, Oxford. Served War of 1939–45, RE (Captain); Middle East, 1941–45. *Heir: s* William Peter Brian Parker, FCA [*b* 30 Nov. 1950; *m* 1976, Patricia Ann, *d* of R. Filtness; one *s* one *d*]. *Address:* Apricot Hall, Sutton-cum-Beckingham, Lincoln LN5 0RE. *T:* Fenton Claypole 322.

PARKER BOWLES, Dame Ann, DCVO 1977; CBE 1972; Chief Commissioner, Girl Guides, 1966–75; *b* 14 July 1918; *d* of Sir Humphrey de Trafford, 4th Bt, MC; *m* 1939, Derek Henry Parker Bowles (*d* 1977); three *s* one *d*. County Comr, Girl Guides (Berkshire), 1959–64; Dep. Chief Comr, Girl Guides, 1962–66. *Recreation:* horse racing. *Address:* Forty Hill, Highclere, Newbury, Berkshire. *T:* Highclere 253735.

PARKER-JERVIS, Roger, DL; Deputy Chairman, CGA plc, since 1982; *b* 11 Sept. 1931; *s* of George Parker-Jervis and Ruth, *d* of C. E. Farmer; *m* 1958, Diana, *d* of R. St V. Parker-Jervis; two *s* one *d*. *Educ:* Eton; Magdalene College, Cambridge. Served Rifle Brigade, 1950–51, Queen Victoria Rifles, 1951–54; ADC to Governor of Tasmania, 1954–56. Bucks County Council: Mem., 1967; Chm., Planning and Transp. Cttee, 1974; Chm., Policy and Resources Cttee, 1977; Vice-Chm. Council, 1979; Chm. Council, 1981–85. Mem., Milton Keynes Develt Corp., 1976–; Pres., Timber Growers of England and Wales, 1981–83; Vice-Chm., Forestry Cttee of GB, 1981–83. High Sheriff of Bucks, 1973–74, DL Bucks, 1982. *Recreations:* painting, shooting. *Address:* The Gardeners Cottage, Great Hampden, Great Missenden, Bucks HP16 9RJ. *T:* Hampden Row 531. *Clubs:* Farmers', Naval and Military, Greenjackets.

PARKES, Sir Alan (Sterling), Kt 1968; CBE 1956; FRS 1933; MA, PhD, DSc, ScD; Fellow of Christ's College, Cambridge, 1961–69, Hon. Fellow 1970; Fellow of University College, London; Chairman, Galton Foundation, 1969–85; *b* 1900; *y s* of E. T. Parkes, Purley; *m* 1933, Ruth, *d* of Edward Deanesly, FRCS, Cheltenham; one *s* two *d*. *Educ:* Willaston School; Christ's College, Cambridge; BA Cantab, 1921, ScD 1931; PhD Manchester, 1923; Sharpey Scholar, University College, London, 1923–24; Beit Memorial Research Fellow, 1924–30; MA Cantab 1925; Schäfer Prize in Physiology, 1926; DSc London 1927; Julius Mickle Fellowship, University of London, 1929; Hon. Lecturer, University College, London, 1929–31; Member of the Staff of the National Institute for Medical Research, London, 1932–61; Mary Marshall Prof. of the Physiology of Reproduction, Univ. of Cambridge, 1961–67, Professor Emeritus 1968. Consultant, Cayman Turtle Farm Ltd, Grand Cayman, BWI, 1973–80. Foulerton Student of the Royal Society, 1930–34. Mem., Biol. and Med. Cttee, Royal Commn on Population, 1944–46. Lectures: Sidney Ringer, University College Hospital, 1934; Ingleby, Univ. of Birmingham, 1940; Galton, Eugenics Society, 1950; Addison, Guy's Hospital, 1957; Darwin, Inst. of Biology; Robert J. Terry, Washington Univ., Sch. of Medicine, 1963; Ayerst, Amer. Fertility Soc., 1965; Dale, Soc. for Endocrinology, 1965; Dick, Univ. of Edinburgh, 1969; Cosgrave, Amer. Coll. of Obstetricians and Gynaecologists, 1970; Tracy and Ruth Storer, Univ. of Calif, Davis, 1973. President: Section of Endocrinology, Roy. Soc. Med., 1949–50, Section of Comparative Medicine, 1962–63; Section D Brit. Assoc. for the Advancement of Science, 1958; Eugenics Soc., 1968–70; Inst. of Biology, 1959–61; Assoc. of Scientific Workers, 1960–62. Chairman: Soc. for Endocrinology, 1944–51; Soc. for Study of Fertility, 1950–52, 1963–66; Nuffield Unit of Tropical Animal Ecology, 1966–69; Breeding Policy Cttee, Zool Soc. of London, 1960–67; Scientific Adv. Cttee, Brit. Egg Mkting Bd, 1961–70. Mem. Adv. Cttee on Med. Research of the WHO, 1968–71. Executive Editor, Jl Biosocial Science, 1969–78; Sec., Jls of Reproduction & Fertility Ltd, 1960–76. Consultant, IPPF, 1969–79. Cameron Prize, 1962; Sir Henry Dale Medal, Soc. for Endocrinology, 1965; John Scott Award (jtly with Dr A. U. Smith and Dr C. Polge), City of Philadelphia, 1969; Marshall Medal, Soc. Stud. Fert., 1970; Oliver Bird Medal, FPA, 1970. *Publications:* The Internal Secretions of the Ovary, 1929; Sex, Science and Society, 1966; Patterns of Sexuality and Reproduction, 1976; Off-beat Biologist, 1985; papers on the Physiology of Reproduction, on Endocrinology and on the behaviour of living cells at low temperatures in Jl of Physiology, Proc. Royal Society, and other scientific jls. Ed. Marshall's Physiology of Reproduction, 3rd edn, 1952, consultant 4th edn (in preparation). *Address:* 1 The Bramleys, Shepreth, Royston, Hertfordshire SG8 6PY.

PARKES, Sir Basil (Arthur), Kt 1971; OBE 1966; *b* 20 Feb. 1907; *s* of late Sir Fred Parkes, Boston, Lincs, and Blackpool, Lancs, and late Gertrude Mary Parkes (*née* Bailey); *m* 1933, May Lewis McNeill; two *s* one *d*. *Educ:* Boston Grammar Sch., Lincs. Joined family trawler owning Co., 1924 (Dir, 1928; Man. Dir, 1946). Pres., North British Maritime Gp Ltd (formerly United Towing Ltd), 1960–. Hon. Brother, Hull Trinity House. Mem., Worshipful Co. of Fishmongers; Mem., Worshipful Co. of Poulters; Officier de l'ordre du Mérite National Français, 1973; Ordre de la Couronne, Belgium, 1979. *Recreations:* golf, shooting. *Address:* Loghan-y-Yuiy, The Garey, Lezayre, near Ramsey, Isle of Man. *T:* Ramsey 815449. *Clubs:* City Livery, St Stephen's Constitutional.

PARKES, Sir Edward (Walter), Kt 1983; FEng; Vice-Chancellor, University of Leeds, since 1983; *b* 19 May 1926; *o s* of Walter Frederick Parkes; *m* 1950, Margaret Parr (*see* Margaret Parkes); one *s* one *d*. *Educ:* King Edward's, Birmingham; St John's College, Cambridge; Scholar; 1st cl. hons Mech. Sci. Tripos, 1945; MA, PhD, ScD; FIMechE. At RAE and in the aircraft industry, 1945–48; research student and subsequently Univ. Lecturer, Cambridge, 1948–59; Fellow and Tutor of Gonville and Caius College; Vis. Prof., Stanford Univ., 1959–60; Head of the Department of Engineering, Univ. of Leicester, 1960–65; Prof. of Mechanics, Cambridge, and Professorial Fellow, Gonville and Caius Coll., 1965–74 (Mem. Gen. Bd, Dep. head of Dept of Engineering); Vice-Chancellor, City Univ., 1974–78; Chm., UGC, 1978–83. Member: Brynmor Jones Cttee, 1964–65; Adv. Bd for Res. Councils, 1974–83; University and Polytechnic Grants Cttee for Hong Kong, 1974–; Vice-Chm., Cttee of Vice-Chancellors and Principals, 1985–. Chm., Adv. Panel on Limestone Workings in the W Midlands, 1983–. Hon. DTech Loughborough, 1984; Hon. DSc Leicester, 1984; Hon. LLD Wales, 1984. *Publications:* Braced Frameworks, 1965, 2nd edn 1974; papers on elasticity, dynamic plasticity or thermal effects on structures in Proc. and Phil. Trans. Royal Society and other jls. *Address:* University of Leeds, Leeds LS2 9JT. *Club:* Athenæum.

PARKES, John Hubert, CB 1984; Permanent Secretary, Department of Education, Northern Ireland, since 1979; *b* 1 Oct. 1930; 2nd *s* of Frank Hubert Parkes and Mary Edith (*née* Barnes), Birmingham; *m* 1956, Elsie Griffiths Henderson; two *s*. *Educ:* George Dixon Sch., Birmingham; Magdalen Coll., Oxford (MA). Joined NI Civil Service, 1953; Asst Sec. 1966; RCDS 1972; Dep. Sec., 1973. *Address:* c/o Department of Education, Rathgael House, Balloo Road, Bangor, Co. Down, Northern Ireland. *Club:* United Oxford & Cambridge University.

PARKES, Margaret, (Lady Parkes), JP; a Governor of the BBC, since 1984; Member: Secondary Examinations Council, since 1983; Voluntary Sector Consultative Council, since 1984; *b* 26 Sept. 1925; *d* of John and Dorothy Parr; *m* 1950, Sir Edward Walter Parkes, *qv*; one *s* one *d*. *Educ:* Perse School for Girls, Cambridge; Leicester Univ. (MEd). Homerton Coll., Cambridge, 1965–74. Chairman: London and Southwark Diocesan Cttee for Personal Relationships, 1976–81; London Diocesan Bd of Educn, 1976–80; London Diocesan Family Educn Cttee, 1981–83; Colleges Adv. Cttee, Gen. Synod Bd of Educn, 1982–; Radio London Adv. Council, 1979–83; Mem., Press Council, 1978–84. Chm. of Governors, Whitelands Coll., London, 1981–. JP Inner London 1977. *Address:* The Vice-Chancellor's Lodge, Grosvenor Road, Leeds LS6 2DZ.

PARKES, Norman James, CBE 1976 (OBE 1960); Clerk of the Australian House of Representatives, 1971–76, retired; *b* 29 July 1912; *s* of Ernest William Parkes; *m* 1937, Maida Cleave, *d* of James Nicholas Silk; two *s*. *Educ:* Victorian State Schools. AASA. Parliamentary officer, 1934: with Reporting Staff, 1934–37; with House of Representatives, 1937–76. *Recreation:* bowls. *Address:* 3/3 Nuyts Street, Red Hill, Canberra, ACT 2603, Australia. *T:* Canberra 957320. *Clubs:* Canberra Bowling, National Press (Canberra).

PARKHOUSE, James, MD, FFARCS; Director, Medical Careers Research Group, Oxford, since 1984; *b* 30 March 1927; *s* of Charles Frederick Parkhouse and Mary Alice Sumner; *m* 1952, Hilda Florence Rimmer; three *s* two *d*. *Educ:* Merchant Taylors' Sch., Great Crosby; Liverpool Univ. (MD 1955). MB ChB, 1950; MA Oxon 1960; MSc Manchester 1974. DA; FFARCS 1952. Anaesthetist, RAF Med. Br., 1953–55. Sen. Resident Anaesth., Mayo Clinic, 1957–58; First Asst, Nuffield Dept of Anaesths, Oxford, and Hon. Cons. Anaesth., United Oxford Hosps, 1958–66; Prof. and Head of Dept of Anaesths, Univ. of Manitoba, and Chief Anaesth., Winnipeg Gen. Hosp., 1967–68; Postgrad. Dean, Faculty of Med., Sheffield Univ., and Hon. Cons. Anaesth., United Sheffield Hosps, 1969–70; Prof. of Anaesths, Manchester Univ., and Hon. Cons. Anaesth., Manchester and Salford AHAs (Teaching), 1970–80; Prof. of Postgraduate Med. Educn, Univ. of Newcastle upon Tyne, and Postgrad. Dean and Dir, Northern Postgrad. Inst. for Medicine and Dentistry, 1980–84. Consultant, postgrad. med. trng, WHO, 1969–; Specialist Adviser, H of C Social Services Cttee, 1980–. Member: Sheffield Reg. Hosp. Bd, 1969–70; Bd, Faculty of Anaesthetists, 1971–82; Neurosciences Bd, MRC, 1977–80; GMC, 1979–; Nat. Trng Council, NHS, 1981–84; North Tyneside HA, 1982–84. *Publications:* A New Look at Anaesthetics, 1965; Medical Manpower in Britain, 1979; contrib. to The Lancet, BMJ and specialist jls. *Recreations:* music, golf. *Address:* Churchill Hospital, Headington, Oxford OX3 7LJ; 145 Cumnor Hill, Oxford OX2 9JA.

PARKHOUSE, Peter; Under Secretary, Ministry of Agriculture, Fisheries and Food, 1973 and 1979–84; *b* 22 July 1927; *s* of late William Richard Parkhouse, MBE, and late Alice Vera Parkhouse (*née* Clarke); *m* 1950, Mary Alison Holland; one *s* one *d*. *Educ:* Blundell's Sch.; Peterhouse, Cambridge (organist, 1944–45); Cologne Univ. BA 1947, MA 1950. Instr Lieut, RN, 1947–50; Asst Master, Uppingham Sch., 1951–52; Asst Principal, Min. of Food, 1952; transf. to MAFF, 1955; served in private office of successive Ministers and Parly Secs, 1954–58; Principal 1958; Principal Private Sec. to Minister, 1966–67; Asst Sec. 1967; Under-Sec. 1973; Dir in Directorate-Gen. for Agriculture, Commn of European Communities, 1973–79; Under Sec., 1979–84. Mem., EDC for Agriculture, 1982–84. *Recreations:* music (sub-organist of Tetbury Parish Church), fishing. *Address:* Stafford House, The Chipping, Tetbury, Glos GL8 8ET. *T:* Tetbury 52540. *Club:* United Oxford & Cambridge University.

PARKHURST, Raymond Thurston, BSc(Agr), MSc, PhD; Director of South Central Poultry Research Laboratory, State University, Mississippi, 1960–68, retired; *b* Everett, Massachusetts, USA, 24 April 1898; *o s* of Fred Lincoln and Celeste Elizabeth Parkhurst; *m* 1922; one *s* one *d*; *m* 1985, Christine Jennings. *Educ:* Fitchburg (Massachusetts) High School; Universities of Massachusetts, Idaho and Edinburgh. Extension Poultryman, Iowa State College, 1919–21; Professor of Poultry Husbandry, Experiment Station Poultry Husbandman, and Head, Dept of Poultry Husbandry, University of Idaho, 1921–27; Director, Brit. Nat. Institute of Poultry Husbandry, 1927–32; Head, Department Agricultural Research, National Oil Products Co., 1932–38; Head, Dept of Poultry Husbandry, University of Massachusetts, Amherst, 1938–44; Director, Nutrition and Research, Flory Milling Co., Bangor, Pa, 1944–49; Director of Nutrition and Research, Lindsey-Robinson and Company, Roanoke, Va, USA, 1949–60; Member: Amer. Poultry Science Assoc.; Amer. Assoc. of Retired Persons; Nat. Assoc. of Retired Persons, etc.; First President of British Poultry Education Association. *Publications:* Vitamin E in relation to Poultry; The Comparative Value of various Protein Feeds for Laying Hens; Factors Affecting Egg Size; Mixed Protein Foods for Layers; Ricketts and Perosis in Growing Chickens; Rexing the Rabbit; Corn Distillers By-Products in Poultry Rations; Calcium and Manganese in Poultry Nutrition; Crabmeal and Fishmeal in Poultry Nutrition; Commercial Broiler Raising; Gumboro Disease, etc. *Recreations:* roses, bridge, stamps, coins. *Address:* 119 Kirk Side, Starkville, Miss 39759, USA. *Club:* Kiwanis International.

PARKIN, John Mackintosh; Administrator, Royal Courts of Justice, 1982–85, retired; *b* 18 June 1920; *s* of Thomas and Emily Cecilia Parkin; *m* Biancamaria Giuganino, Rome; two *d*. *Educ:* Nottingham High Sch.; Emmanuel Coll., Cambridge (Sen. Schol.; MA). Royal Artillery, 1939–46 (Captain). Asst Principal, WO, 1949; Registrar, RMCS, 1957–60; Principal Private Sec. to Sec. of State for War, 1960–62; Asst Sec. 1962; Sen. Fellow, Harvard Univ., 1966–67; Comd Sec., BAOR, 1967–70; Asst Under-Sec. of State, MoD, 1974–80. Mem., Royal Patriotic Fund Corpn, 1977–80. *Recreation:* history of architecture and art. *Address:* 35 Little Bornes, Dulwich, SE21 8SD. *T:* 01-670 5564.

PARKINSON, Rt. Hon. Cecil Edward, PC 1981; MP (C) Hertsmere, since 1983 (Enfield West, Nov. 1970–1974; Hertfordshire South, 1974–83); *b* 1 Sept. 1931; *s* of Sidney Parkinson, Carnforth, Lancs; *m* 1957, Ann Mary, *d* of F. A. Jarvis, Harpenden, Herts; three *d*. *Educ:* Royal Lancaster Grammar Sch., Lancaster; Emmanuel Coll., Cambridge. BA 1955, MA 1961. Joined Metal Box Company as a Management Trainee; joined West, Wake, Price, Chartered Accountants, 1956; qualified 1959; Partner, 1961–71; founded Parkinson Hart Securities Ltd, 1967; Director of several cos, 1965–79, 1984–. Constituency Chm., Hemel Hempstead Conservative Assoc.; Chm., Herts 100 Club, 1968–69; contested (C) Northampton, 1970. PPS to Minister for Aerospace and Shipping, DTI, 1972–74; an Asst Govt Whip, 1974; an Opposition Whip, 1974–76; Opposition Spokesman on trade, 1976–79; Minister for Trade, Dept of Trade, 1979–81; Paymaster General, 1981–83; Chancellor, Duchy of Lancaster, 1982–83; Sec. of State for Trade and Industry, June-Oct. 1983. Chm. of Cons. Party, 1981–83. Sec., Cons. Parly Finance Cttee, 1971–72; Chm., Anglo-Swiss Parly Gp, 1979–82; Pres., Anglo-Polish Cons. Soc., 1986–. *Recreations:* reading, golf, skiing; ran for combined Oxford and Cambridge team against Amer. Univs, 1954 and 1955; ran for Cambridge against Oxford, 1954 and 1955. *Address:* House of Commons, SW1A 0AA. *Clubs:* Carlton; Hawks (Cambridge).

PARKINSON, Cyril Northcote, MA, PhD, FRHistS; author, historian and journalist; Seigneur of Anneville, Mauxmarquis and Beavoir; Professor Emeritus and Hon. President, Troy State University, Alabama, since 1970; *b* 30 July 1909; *yr s* of late W. Edward Parkinson, ARCA and late Rose Emily Mary Curnow; *m* 1st, 1943, Ethelwyn Edith Graves (marr. diss.); one *s* one *d*; 2nd, 1952, Elizabeth Ann Fry (*d* 1983); two *s* one *d*; 3rd, 1985, Iris Hilda Waters. *Educ:* St Peter's School, York; Emmanuel College, Cambridge; King's College, London. Fellow of Emmanuel Coll., Cambridge, 1935; Sen. History Master, Blundell's Sch., Tiverton, 1938; Master, RNC, Dartmouth, 1939. Commissioned as Captain, Queen's Roy. Regt, 1940; Instructor in 166 OCTU; attached RAF, 1942–43; Major, 1943; trans. as GSO2 to War Office (General Staff), 1944; demobilised, 1945; Lectr in History, Univ. of Liverpool, 1946; Raffles Professor of History, University of Malaya, Singapore, 1950–58. Visiting Professor: Univ. of Harvard, 1958; Univs of Illinois and California, 1959–60. Mem. French Académie de Marine and US Naval Inst.; Mem. Archives Commission of Govt of India. Hon. LLD Maryland, 1974; Hon. DLitt Troy State, 1976. *Plays:* Helier Bonamy, Guernsey, 1967; The Royalist, Guernsey, 1969. *Publications:* many books including: Edward Pellew Viscount Exmouth, 1934; Trade in the Eastern Seas, 1937; (ed.) The Trade Winds, 1948; The Rise of the Port of Liverpool, 1952; War in the Eastern Seas, 1954; Britain in the Far East, 1955; Parkinson's Law, the Pursuit of Progress, 1958; The Evolution of Political Thought, 1958; British Intervention in Malaya, 1867–1877, 1960; The Law and the Profits, 1960; In-laws and Outlaws, 1962; East and West, 1963; Ponies Plot, 1965; A Law unto Themselves, 1966; Left Luggage, 1967; Mrs Parkinson's Law, 1968; The Law of Delay, 1970; The Life and Times of Horatio Hornblower, 1970; Big Business, 1974; Gunpowder, Treason and Plot, 1977; Britannia Rules, 1977; The Rise of Big Business, 1977; (with Nigel Rowe) Communicate, 1977; Jeeves: a Gentleman's Personal Gentleman, 1979; (with H. Le Compte) The Law of Longer Life, 1980; *novels:* Devil to Pay, 1973; The Fireship, 1975; Touch and Go, 1977; Dead Reckoning, 1978; So Near So Far, 1981; The Guernseyman, 1982; The Fur-Lined Mousetrap, 1984; contribs to Encyclopædia Britannica, Economist, Guardian, New York Times, Fortune, Saturday Evening Post, Punch and Foreign Policy. *Recreations:* painting, travel, sailing. *Address:* 45 Howe Road, Onchan, Douglas, Ise of Man. *Club:* Army and Navy.

PARKINSON, Dr David Hardress; science writer and consultant; formerly Director General, Establishments Resources and Programmes, A, Ministry of Defence (1973–77); *b* Liverpool, 9 March 1918; *s* of E. R. H. Parkinson; *m* 1st, 1944, Muriel Gwendoline Patricia (*d* 1971), *d* of Captain P. W. Newenham; two *s*; 2nd, 1974, Daphne Margaret Scott-Gall (marr. diss. 1978). *Educ:* Gravesend County Grammar Sch.; Wadham Coll., Oxford (MA, DPhil). CPhys, FInstP. Royal Artillery, 1939–45 (Major); Oxford Univ., 1937–39 and 1945–49; Civil Service: TRE, Malvern, 1949; Supt Low Temp. and Magnetics Div., RRE, Malvern, 1956–63; Head Physics Gp, RRE, 1963–68; Head Physics and Electronics Dept, RRE and Dep. Dir, 1968–72. Hon. Prof. Physics, Birmingham Univ., 1966–73. Chm. Midland Br., Inst. Physics, 1968–70; Vice-Pres. (Exhibns), Inst. Physics, 1973–78; Mem., European Physical Soc., 1982– (Chm. Adv. Cttee on Physics and Society). *Publications:* (with B. Mulhall) Generation High Magnetic Fields, 1967; many scientific papers and articles. *Recreations:* antiques, silversmithing. *Address:* South Bank, 47 Abbey Road, Great Malvern, Worcs WR14 3HH. *T:* Malvern 5423. *Club:* Royal Commonwealth Society.

PARKINSON, Desmond Frederick, CMG 1975; HM Diplomatic Service, retired; *b* 26 Oct. 1920; *m* 1977, Patricia Jean Campbell Taylor; two *s* two *d* of former *m*. HM Forces, 1939–49; served FO, 1949–51; Rangoon, 1951–53; Jakarta, 1954–55; FO, 1955–57; Rabat, 1957–60; Lagos, 1960–61; FO, 1961–63; Singapore, 1963–65; Delhi, 1965–67; FCO, 1967–78. *Address:* Woodrow, Silchester, near Reading. *T:* Reading 700257. *Club:* Huntercombe Golf.

PARKINSON, Desmond John, OBE 1950; Under-Secretary, Agricultural Research Council, 1971–73; *b* 8 March 1913; *s* of late Frederick A. Parkinson, Rio de Janeiro; *m* 1st, 1940, Leonor Hughes (marr. diss. 1954); 2nd, 1955, Lorna Mary Britton (*née* Wood); no *c*. *Educ:* Hereford Cathedral Sch.; St John's Coll., Cambridge; Brasenose Coll., Oxford. BA Cantab 1935; Colonial Admin. Service, 1936–60 (Gold Coast, Colonial Office, British Guiana, Nigeria); UK MAFF, 1960–63; ARC, 1963–73. *Recreation:* gardening. *Address:* Glebe House, North Cadbury, Yeovil, Somerset BA22 7DW. *T:* North Cadbury 40181. *Clubs:* United Oxford & Cambridge University; Bath and County.

PARKINSON, Ewart West, BSc, DPA, CEng, FICE, PPRTPI, FIMunE; OStJ; development adviser; Director of Environment and County Engineer, County of South Glamorgan, 1973–85; *b* 9 July 1926; *s* of Thomas Edward Parkinson and Esther Lilian West; *m* 1948, Patricia Joan Wood; two *s* one *d*. *Educ:* Wyggeston Sch., Leicester; Coll. of Technology, Leicester (BSc, DPA). Miller Prize (bridge design), Instn CE, 1953. After working with Leicester, Wakefield, Bristol and Dover Councils, he became Dep. Borough Engr, Chelmsford, 1957–60; Dep. City Surveyor Plymouth, 1960–64; City Planning Officer, Cardiff, 1964–73. Mem. Council, RTPI, 1971–83 (Vice-Pres., 1973–75, Pres., 1975–76, Chm. Internat. Affairs Bd, 1975–80); Member: Sports Council for Wales, 1966–78 (Chm., Facilities Cttee); Internat. Soc. of City and Regional Planners, 1972; Govt Deleg. to UN Conf. on Human Settlements, 1976; Watt Cttee for Energy, 1977–83 (Chm., Working Gp on Energy and Envt, 1980–83); UK mem., Internat. Wkg Party on Urban Land Policy, Internat. Fedn for Housing and Planning, 1979–85; Chairman:

Internat. Wkg Party on Energy and the Environment, Internat. Fedn for Housing and Planning, 1982–85 (Life Mem. 1986); Wkg Party on Land Policy, Royal Town Planning Inst., 1983–85; led Study Tours to Soviet Union, 1977, India and Bangladesh, 1979, China, 1980, Kenya, Zimbabwe and Tanzania, 1981; study visit, People's Republic of China at invitation of State Admin of Urban Construction, 1982, 1986. Chairman: STAR Community Trust Ltd, 1979–; Intervol, 1985–; Dir, CEDA, 1986–; Vice-Pres., Wales Council for the Disabled, 1982–. Diamond Jubilee Silver Medal, Nat. Housing and Town Planning Council, 1978. OStJ 1980 (S Glamorgan Council, 1975–). *Publications:* The Land Question, 1974; And Who is my Neighbour?, 1976; articles in prof. jls on land policy, energy and the environment, and public participation. *Recreations:* working, travelling, being with family, talking with friends. *Address:* 42 South Rise, Llanishen, Cardiff. *T:* Cardiff 756 394.

PARKINSON, Graham Edward; Metropolitan Stipendiary Magistrate, since 1982; *b* 13 Oct. 1937; *s* of Norman Edward Parkinson and Phyllis (*née* Jaquiss); *m* 1963, Dinah Mary Pyper; one *s* one *d. Educ:* Loughborough Grammar Sch. Admitted Solicitor of the Supreme Court, 1961. Articled to J. Tempest Bouskell, Leicester, 1955–60; Asst Solicitor: Slaughter & May, 1961–63; Amery Parkes & Co., 1963–67; Partner, Darlington and Parkinson, Ealing, 1967–82. Pres., Central and S Mddx Law Soc., 1978–79; Vice Chm. Exec. Cttee, Soc. of Conservative Lawyers, 1978–82; Mem. Cttee, London Criminal Courts Solicitors Assoc., 1978–80. *Recreations:* going to the opera, reading, piano playing, listening to music. *Address:* Highbury Corner Magistrates' Court, 51 Holloway Road, N7 8JA.

PARKINSON, Dr James Christopher, MBE 1963; TD 1962; Deputy Director, Brighton Polytechnic, 1970–83, retired; *b* 15 Aug. 1920; *s* of late Charles Myers Parkinson, Pharmacist, Blackburn, Lancs; *m* 1950, Gwyneth Margot, *d* of late Rev. John Raymond Harrison, Macclesfield, Ches; three *s. Educ:* Queen Elizabeth's Gram. Sch., Blackburn; Univ. Coll., Nottingham. BPharm, PhD (London), FPS. Served in Mediterranean area, Parachute Regt, 1943–46; Parachute Regt TA: 16 AB Div. and 44 Parachute Bde, 1949–63 (Major). Lectr, Sch. of Pharmacy, Univ. of London, 1948–54; Head of Sch. of Pharmacy, Brighton Coll. of Technology, 1954–64; Dep. Sec., Pharmaceutical Soc. of Gt Britain, 1964–67; Principal, Brighton Coll. of Technology, 1967–70. Mem. various pharmaceutical cttees of British Pharmacopœia, British Pharmaceutical Codex and British Veterinary Codex, 1956–64; Examr, Pharmaceutical Soc. of Gt Britain, 1954–64; Mem. Bds of Studies in Pharmacy and Librarianship, CNAA, 1965–75. Member, Gen. Synod of Church of England, 1970–85. *Publications:* research papers on applied microbiology in Jl Appl. Bact. and Jl Pharm. (London) and on pharmaceutical education in Pharm. Jl. *Recreation:* do-it-yourself. *Address:* 92 Wickham Hill, Hurstpierpoint, West Sussex BN6 9NR. *T:* Hurstpierpoint 833369.

PARKINSON, Michael; interviewer, television presenter, writer; *b* 28 March 1935; *m* Mary Heneghan; three *s. Educ:* Barnsley Grammar School. Journalist on local paper; The Guardian; Daily Express; columnist on Sunday Times; radio work; has written for Punch, The Listener, New Statesman; columnist for Daily Mirror, 1986–; Producer and interviewer: Granada's Scene; Granada in the North; World in Action; What the Papers Say; reporter on 24 Hours (BBC); Exec. producer and presenter, London Weekend Television, 1968; Presenter: Cinema, 1969–70; Tea Break, Where in the World, The Movie Quiz, 1971; host of own chat show, Parkinson, 1971–82; TV-am, 1983–84; Parkinson in Australia, 1979–84; Give Us a Clue, 1984–; All Star Secrets, 1984–; The Skag Kids, 1985; Desert Island Discs, BBC Radio 4, 1986–. Founder-Director, Pavilion Books, 1980–. *Publications:* Football Daft, 1968; Cricket Mad, 1969; (with Clyde Jeavons) Pictorial History of Westerns, 1972; Sporting Fever, 1974; (with Willis Hall) Football Classified, 1974; George Best: an intimate biography, 1975; (with Willis Hall) A-Z of Soccer, 1975; Bats in the Pavilion, 1977; The Woofits, 1980; Parkinson's Lore, 1981; The Best of Parkinson, 1982. *Address:* c/o Michael Parkinson Enterprises Ltd, 58 Queen Anne Street, W1M 0DX.

PARKINSON, Sir Nicholas (Fancourt), Kt 1980; Consultant in Australia, Sears World Trade Inc.; *b* 5 Dec. 1925; *s* of late Rev. C. T. Parkinson, MA Oxon, and Dorothy Fancourt (*née* Mitchell); *m* 1952, Roslyn Sheena Campbell; two *d. Educ:* King's Sch., Parramatta, NSW; Univ. of Sydney (BA). Entered Aust. Foreign Service, 1951; Third Sec., Cairo, 1953–56; First Sec., Hong Kong, 1958–61; Counsellor, Moscow, Wellington, Kuala Lumpur, 1963–67; Chm., Jt Intell. Cttee, Dept of Defence, Canberra, 1967–70; High Comr, Singapore, 1970–74; Dep. Sec., Dept of For. Affairs, Canberra, 1974–76; Ambassador to the US, 1976–77 and 1979–82; Sec., Dept of For. Affairs, Canberra, 1977–79. *Recreation:* bridge. *Address:* 19 Beagle Street, Red Hill, ACT 2603, Australia. *T:* Canberra 953893. *Club:* Commonwealth (Canberra).

PARKINSON, Norman, CBE 1981; photographer; *b* 21 April 1913; *m* 1945, Wenda (*née* Rogerson); one *s. Educ:* Westminster School. Always a photographer of people old and young, horses, birds, still-life, active life, fashion, reportage and travel. Has recently photographed, together and separately, all members of the Royal Family (in particular 21st Birthday and Engagement pictures of HRH The Princess Anne, and official 80th and 85th Birthday photographs of Queen Elizabeth, the Queen Mother, incl. the stamp issued to mark the 80th birthday occasion). Retrospective Exhibn, Fifty Years of Portraits and Fashion, National Portrait Gall., 1981; comprehensive exhibn of photographs, Sotheby Parke Bernet Gall., NY, 1983. Hon. FRPS; Hon. FIIP. Lifetime Achievement Award, Amer. Magazine Photographers Assoc., 1983. *Publications:* Life, Look Magazines, (USA); continually contributing to all the Vogues; his photographs have appeared in almost all the world's periodicals, in particular Town and Country, 1977–; Sisters Under the Skin (photographs, with text by leading authors), 1978; Photographs by Norman Parkinson, 1981; Lifework (collected works), 1983 (Fifty Years of Style and Fashion, US, 1983); Would You Let Your Daughter . . .?, 1985. *Recreations:* pig farming (manufactures the famous Porkinson banger in Tobago); sun worshipping, bird watching, breeding Creole racehorses. *Address:* Tobago, West Indies. *T:* none fortunately. *Clubs:* Annabel's; Union (Trinidad); Turf (Tobago).

PARKINSON, Ronald Dennis; Assistant Keeper, Education Department, Victoria and Albert Museum, since 1978; *b* 27 April 1945; *s* of Albert Edward Parkinson and Jennie Caroline Clara Meager. *Educ:* St Dunstan's Coll.; Clare Coll., Cambridge (MA). Res. Assistant: Paul Mellon Foundn for British Art, 1971–72; V&A Mus., 1972–74; Asst Keeper, Tate Gall., 1974–78. *Publications:* articles in Apollo, Burlington Mag., Cambridge Res., Connoisseur, Country Life, Times Higher Educn Sup. *Recreations:* reading, shopping. *Address:* Victoria and Albert Museum, South Kensington, SW7 2RL. *T:* 01–589 6371. *Club:* Algonquin.

PARKINSON, Thomas Harry, CBE 1972; DL; Town Clerk, 1960–72, Clerk of the Peace, 1970–72, Birmingham; *b* Bilston, 25 June 1907; *y s* of G. R. J. Parkinson; *m* 1936, Joan Catherine, *d* of C. J. Douglas-Osborn; two *s* one *d. Educ:* Bromsgrove; Birmingham University. LLB Hons 1929. Admitted Solicitor, 1930. RAF, 1939–45. Asst Solicitor, Birmingham Corp., 1936–49; Dep. Town Clerk, Birmingham, 1949–60. Pres., Birmingham Law Soc., 1969–70. Sec., W Midlands Passenger Transport Authority, 1969–72; Member: Water Services Staff Adv. Commn, 1973–78; W Midlands Rent Assessment Panel, 1972–78; Sec., Nat Exhibn Centre Ltd, 1972–78; Hon. Member: Birmingham Assoc. of Mech. Engrs; Inst. of Housing. DL Warwickshire, 1970. Hon. DSc Aston, 1972. *Recreations:* walking, sailing, gardening. *Address:* Stuart House, Middlefield Lane, Hagley, Worcs. *T:* Hagley 882422.

PARKYN, Brian (Stewart); General Manager, Training Services, British Caledonian Airways Ltd, since 1981; Director, Hunting Industrial Plastics Ltd, since 1979; *b* 28 April 1923; *o s* of Leslie and Gwen Parkyn, Whetstone, N20; *m* 1951, Janet Anne, *o d* of Charles and Jessie Stormer, Eastbourne; one *s* one *d. Educ:* King Edward VI Sch., Chelmsford; technical colleges. Principal, Glacier Inst. of Management (Associated Engineering Ltd), 1976–80. Dir, Scott Bader Co. Ltd, 1953–83; British Plastics Federation: Chm., Reinforced Plastics Gp, 1961–63; Mem. Council, 1959–75. Vice Pres., Rubber and Plastics Inst., 1972–75. Has travelled widely and lectured in N and S America, Africa, Australasia, India, Japan, USSR and China, etc.; Plastics Lectr, Worshipful Co. of Horners, 1967. Contested (Lab) Bedford, 1964; MP (Lab) Bedford, 1966–70; Mem., Select Cttee on Science and Technology, 1967–70; Chm., Sub-Cttee on Carbon Fibres, 1969; contested (Lab) Bedford, Oct. 1974. Member: Council, Cranfield Inst. of Technology, 1971–; Council, RSA, 1976–82 (Hon. Treas., 1977–82). FPRI. *Publications:* Democracy, Accountability and Participation in Industry, 1979; various papers and books on polyester resins and reinforced plastics. *Recreations:* writing, industrial democracy. *Address:* 9 Clarendon Square, Leamington Spa, Warwicks CV32 5QJ. *T:* Leamington 30066.

PARMOOR, 4th Baron *cr* 1914; **Milo Cripps;** *b* 18 June 1929; *s* of 3rd Baron Parmoor, DSO, TD, DL, and Violet Mary Geraldine, *d* of Sir William Nelson, 1st Bt; *S* father, 1977. *Educ:* Ampleforth; Corpus Christi College, Oxford. *Heir:* *cousin* (Matthew) Anthony Leonard Cripps, *qv. Address:* Manor House, Sutton Veny, Wilts.

PARNELL, family name of **Baron Congleton.**

PARNIS, Alexander Edward Libor, CBE 1973; *b* 25 Aug. 1911; *s* of Alexander T. J. Parnis and Hetty Parnis (*née* Dams). *Educ:* Malvern Coll.; London Univ. BSc(Econ); MA (Cantab). Entered HM Consular Service, 1933: Acting British Vice-Consul, Paris, 1933–34; transferred to HM Treasury, 1937; Finance Officer, Friends' Ambulance Unit, 1941–45; returned to HM Treasury, 1945. Sec., Gowers Cttee on Houses of Outstanding Historic or Architectural Interest, 1950; Sec., Waverley Cttee on Export of Works of Art, etc., 1952; Treasurer, Univ. of Cambridge, 1953–62; Fellow, King's Coll., Cambridge, 1959–62; Asst Sec., Univ. Grants Cttee, 1962–72. Sec., Church's Main Cttee, 1973–81. *Recreations:* music, travel, cycling, walking. *Address:* 26 Ardilaun Road, N5 2QR. *T:* 01–226 2688. *Clubs:* Reform; The Casino (1852) (Malta).

PARR, Thomas Donald, CBE 1986; Chairman, William Baird PLC, since 1981; *b* 3 Sept. 1930; *s* of Thomas and Elizabeth Parr; *m* 1954, Gwendoline Mary Chaplin; three *s* one *d. Educ:* Burnage Grammar Sch. Own business, 1953–64; Chm., Thomas Marshall Investments Ltd, 1964–76; Dir, William Baird PLC, 1976–; NW Regional Dir, Lloyds Bank Plc, 1978–. Member: NW Industrial Develt Bd, 1975–; Ct of Governors, UMIST, 1984–. *Recreation:* sailing. *Address:* Homestead, Homestead Road, Disley, Stockport, Cheshire SK12 2JP. *T:* Disley 5211. *Clubs:* Royal Ocean Racing (Past Commodore); Royal Yacht Squadron (Cowes).

PARRINDER, Prof. (Edward) Geoffrey (Simons); Professor of Comparative Study of Religions, University of London, at King's College, 1970–77, Professor Emeritus, 1977; *b* 30 April 1910; *s* of William Patrick and Florence Mary Parrinder; *m* 1936, Esther Mary Burt; two *s* one *d. Educ:* private sch.; Richmond Coll., London Univ.; Faculté libre de théologie protestante, Montpellier. MA, PhD, DD London. Minister of Methodist Church, Dahomey and Ivory Coast, 1933; ordained 1936; Principal, Séminaire Protestant, Dahomey, 1936–40, 1945–46; Methodist Church: Redruth, 1940; Dahomey, 1943; Guernsey, 1946; Lectr in Religious Studies, 1949, Sen. Lectr, 1950–58, UC Ibadan; Reader in Comparative Study of Religions, Univ. of London, 1958–70; Dean, Faculty of Theology, KCL, 1972–74. Mem. Editorial Bd of Religious Studies and Jl of Religion in Africa. Hon. Sec., Internat. Assoc. for History of Religions, British Br., 1960–72, Pres., 1972–77. Pres., London Soc. for Study of Religion, 1980–82; Pres., London Soc. of Jews and Christians, 1981–. Lectures: Charles Strong (Australian Church), 1964; Wilde, in Natural and Comparative Religion, Oxford Univ., 1966–69; Teape, Delhi, Madras, 1973. Vis. Prof., Internat. Christian Univ., Tokyo, 1977–78; Vis. Lectr, Surrey Univ., 1978–83. FKC 1972; Hon. DLitt Lancaster, 1975. *Publications:* West African Religion, 1949; Bible and Polygamy, 1950; West African Psychology, 1951; Religion in an African City, 1953; African Traditional Religion, 1954; Story of Ketu, 1956; Introduction to Asian Religions, 1957; Witchcraft, 1958; (ed) African Ideas of God, 1961; Worship in the World's Religions, 1961; Comparative Religion, 1962; Upanishads, Gītā and Bible, 1962; What World Religions Teach, 1963; The Christian Debate, 1964; The World's Living Religions, 1965; A Book of World Religions, 1965; Jesus in the Qur'ān, 1965; African Mythology, 1967; Religion in Africa, 1969 repr. as Africa's Three Religions, 1976; Avatar and Incarnation, 1970; Dictionary of Non-Christian Religions, 1971; (ed) Man and his Gods, 1971, repr. as Illustrated History of the World's Religions, 1983; The Indestructible Soul, 1973; Themes for Living, 1973; The Bhagavad Gita, a Verse Translation, 1974; Something after Death?, 1974; The Wisdom of the Forest, 1975; Mysticism in the World's Religions, 1976; The Wisdom of the Early Buddhists, 1977; Sex in the World's Religions, 1980; Storia Universale delle Religioni, 1984; articles and reviews in Times Lit. and Educnl Supplements, and jls of theology, African and Asian religions and Annual Register, 1958–. *Recreations:* travel, gardening, literature. *Address:* 31 Charterhouse Road, Orpington, Kent. *T:* Orpington 23887.

See also D. M. Boston.

PARRIS, Matthew Francis; Presenter, Weekend World, London Weekend Television, since 1986; *b* 7 Aug. 1949; *s* of Leslie Francis Parris and Theresa Eunice Parris (*née* Littler). *Educ:* Waterford School, Swaziland; Clare Coll., Cambridge (BA Hons); Yale Univ., USA (Paul Mellon Fellowship). Foreign Office, 1974–76; Conservative Research Dept, 1976–79; MP (C) West Derbyshire, 1979–86. *Recreation:* distance running. *Address:* 41 Bramfield Road, SW11 6RA.

PARRISH, Alfred Sherwen; Chief Constable, Derbyshire, 1981–85; *b* 21 Feb. 1931; *s* of Claude Tunstall Parrish and Georgena Parrish (*née* Sherwen); *m* 1953, Amy Johnston; one *s* one *d. Educ:* Whitehaven (West Cumberland) Grammar School. FBIM. Joined Cumberland and Westmorland Constabulary, 1953; Police Constable, Traffic, CID; Det/Sgt 1964; transf. to E Riding of Yorkshire, Det/Inspector 1966; Head of CID, 1967; York and NE Yorks Police, 1968, Supt; West Mercia Police, 1973, Chief Supt; Director, Police Staff Coll., Bramshill, Hants, 1976; Asst Chief Constable (Operations), N Yorkshire Police, 1976–79; Dep. Chief Constable, Derbyshire, 1979. FBIM. OStJ 1984. *Recreations:* music, photography, golf. *Address:* c/o Police Headquarters, Butterley Hall, Ripley, Derbyshire DE5 3RS. *T:* Ripley 43551. *Club:* Special Forces.

PARRY, family name of **Baron Parry.**

PARRY, Baron *cr* 1975 (Life Peer), of Neyland, Dyfed; **Gordon Samuel David Parry;** Chairman: Wales Tourist Board, 1978–84; Milford Docks Company, since 1984; *b* 30 Nov. 1925; *s* of Thomas Lewis Parry and Anne Parry (*née* Evans); *m* 1948, Glenys Parry (*née* Incledon); one *d*. *Educ:* Neyland Board Sch.; Pembroke County Intermediate Sch.; Trinity Coll., Carmarthen; Univ. of Liverpool (Dipl. Advanced Educn). Teacher: Coronation Sch., Pembroke Dock, 1945–46; Llanstadwell Voluntary Primary Sch., Neyland, 1946–47; Barn St Voluntary Sch., Haverfordwest, 1947; County Primary Sch., Neyland, 1947–52; Librarian, Housemaster, County Sec. Sch., Haverfordwest, 1952–62 and 1963–68; Inst. of Educn, Univ. of Liverpool, 1962–63; Warden, Pembs Teachers' Centre, 1969–78. Former member: Welsh Develt Authority; Gen. Adv. Council, IBA; Welsh Arts Council; Schs Council Cttee for Wales; Member: Fac. of Educn, Univ. Coll. of Wales Aberystwyth; Council, Open Univ. (Chm., Adv. Cttee on Studies in Educn, 1978–83); British Tourist Authority, 1978–84; President: Pembs Br., Multiple Sclerosis Soc.; Pembs Spastics Soc.; Spastics Soc., Wales; Commonwealth Games Appeal Cttee for Wales, 1979; Keep Wales Tidy Cttee, 1979– (Chm., 1979–86); BICSc, 1981–; Chairman: British Cleaning Council, 1983–; Keep Britain Tidy, 1986–; Keep Britain Tidy Gp and Keep Britain Beautiful Campaign, 1986–; Vice President: Nat. Chamber of Trade, 1980; Internat. Year of Disabled People in Wales, 1979; Nat. Soc. for Mentally Handicapped Children, S Wales Region; Soc. of Handicapped Drivers in Wales; Welsh Nat. Council of YMCAs. Contested (Lab) Monmouth 1959, Pembroke 1970, and Feb. and Oct. 1974. Writer, broadcaster, and TV panel Chm. FRSA; Fellow: Tourism Soc.; BICSc; HCIMA. *Recreations:* travel; watching Welsh Rugby XV win the Grand Slam; reading. *Address:* Willowmead, 52 Port Lion, Llangwm, Haverfordwest, Pembrokeshire, Dyfed SA62 4JT. *T:* Neyland 600667.

PARRY, Anthony Joseph; County Fire Officer, Greater Manchester, since 1985; *b* 20 May 1935; *s* of Henry Joseph Parry and Mary Elizabeth McShane; *m* 1959, Elizabeth Therese Collins; three *s* one *d*. *Educ:* St Francis Xavier's Coll., Liverpool. MIFireE. Liverpool Fire Bde, 1958; Fire Service Technical Coll., 1967; Gloucestershire Fire Service, 1969; Avon Fire Service, 1974; Lancashire County Fire Service, 1975. Long Service and Good Conduct Medal, 1978. *Address:* Greater Manchester County Fire Service, Bolton Road, Swinton, Greater Manchester.

PARRY, Emyr Owen; solicitor; a Recorder of the Crown Court, since 1979; *b* 26 May 1933; *s* of Ebenezer Owen Parry and Ellen Parry; *m* 1959, Enid Griffiths; one *s* one *d*. *Educ:* Caernarfon Grammar Sch.; University Coll. of Wales, Aberystwyth (LLB Hons Wales, 1954). Admitted solicitor, 1957. Estabd own practice in Llangefni, Anglesey, 1958; formed partnership (Emyr Parry & Davies) with Mrs Elinor C. Davies, 1964; Dep. Circuit Judge, 1975. Chm., National Insurance Appeals Tribunal, Holyhead Area, 1969–; Solicitor Mem., Lord Chancellor's County Court Rule Cttee, 1975–80. *Recreations:* cricket, music. *Clubs:* Llangefni Cricket (Chm., Life Mem.); Anglesey County Cricket (Vice Pres.).

PARRY, Sir Ernest J.; *see* Jones-Parry.

PARRY, Sir Hugh (Nigel), Kt 1963; CBE 1954; *b* 26 Aug. 1911; *s* of Charles Frank Parry and Lilian Maud Parry (*née* Powell); *m* 1945, Ann Maureen Forshaw; two *d*. *Educ:* Cheltenham Coll.; Balliol Coll., Oxford. Entered Colonial Administrative Service, 1939. Chief Secretary, Central African Council, Salisbury, S Rhodesia, 1951–53; Secretary, Office of Prime Minister and External Affairs, Federal Government of Rhodesia and Nyasaland, 1953–63; Ministry of Overseas Development, 1965; Acting Head, Middle East Develt Div., 1969–71, retd 1971. *Recreations:* sailing, motoring. *Address:* c/o Grindlays Bank, 13 St James's Square, SW1.

PARRY, John Alderson, CBE 1985; President, Royal College of Veterinary Surgeons, July 1986–87; *b* 3 Jan. 1934; *s* of Albert Parry and Mary Parry (*née* Alderson); *m* 1959, Joan Rathbone; one *s* one *d*. *Educ:* Leighton Park, Reading; Christ's College, Cambridge (MA, Vet MB). MRCVS. Veterinary practice, Brecon, 1958–. Mem., Agricl Adv. Council, 1969–73; Chairman: Hill Farming Res. Orgn, 1981– (Mem., 1971–); Welsh Agricl Adv. Cttee, BBC, 1978–85; Welsh Office Hydatid Control Steering Cttee, 1981–; Member: Sec. of State for Wales' Agricl Adv. Cttee, 1978–; AFRC, 1982– (Chm., Animals Res. Cttee, 1983–); Develt Bd for Rural Wales, 1985–; Council, Royal Welsh Agricl Soc., 1986–; Pres., BVA, 1976–77. *Recreations:* field sports. *Address:* Watergate Mill, Brecon, Powys LD3 9AN. *T:* Brecon 2113. *Clubs:* United Oxford & Cambridge University, Farmers'; Hawks (Cambridge); Cardiff & County (Cardiff).

PARRY, Mrs Margaret Joan; Headmistress of Heathfield School, Ascot, 1973–82; *b* 27 Nov. 1919; *d* of W. J. Tamplin, Llantrisant, Glamorgan; *m* 1946, Raymond Howard Parry; two *s* one *d*. *Educ:* Howell's Sch., Llandaff, Cardiff; Univ. of Wales. Hons English Cl I. Married to a schoolmaster at Eton; taught and coached interesting people from time to time; Examiner for: Civil Service, LCC, Schools Examination Boards. Patron, Univ. of Buckingham, 1983. *Recreations:* books, music, tapestry. *Address:* Carreg Gwaun, 23a Murray Court, Ascot, Berks SL5 9BP. *T:* Ascot 26299.

PARRY, Robert; MP (Lab) Liverpool, Riverside, since 1983 (Liverpool Exchange, 1970–74; Liverpool, Scotland Exchange, 1974–83); *b* 8 Jan. 1933; *s* of Robert and Sarah Parry (*née* Joyce); *m* 1956, Marie (*née* Hesdon). *Educ:* Bishop Goss RC School, Liverpool. Became a building trade worker. Full-time organizer for National Union of Public Employees, 1960–67; now sponsored Member, Transport and General Workers' Union. Member of Co-operative Party. Member, Liverpool City Council, 1963–74. Chm., Merseyside Gp of Labour MPs, 1976–. Patron: UNA Hong Kong, 1977–; Rotunda Boxing Club, 1975–; KIND (Kids in Need and Distress); President: Liverpool and Dist Sunday Football League (largest in Europe), 1973–; Assoc. for Democracy in Hong Kong, 1980–; Liverpool Transport Boxing and Sporting Club, 1982–. Special interests: human rights, civil liberties, foreign affairs, particularly Central and SE Asia, overseas aid and the third world. *Address:* House of Commons, SW1A 0AA. *Club:* Riverside Labour.

PARRY, Victor Thomas Henry, MA Oxon; FLA; Director of Central Library Services and Goldsmiths' Librarian, University of London, since 1983; *b* 20 Nov. 1927; *s* of Thomas and Daisy Parry; *m* 1959, Mavis K. Russull; two *s* one *d*. *Educ:* St Julian's High Sch., Newport; St Edmund Hall, Oxford (MA); University College, London (DipLib). FLA 1959. Manchester Public Libraries, 1950–56; Colonial Office and CRO Library, 1956–60; Librarian, Nature Conservancy, 1960–63; British Museum (Natural History), 1963–74; Chief Librarian and Archivist, Royal Botanic Gdns, Kew, 1974–78; Librarian, SOAS, Univ. of London, 1978–83. Chm., Circle of State Librarians, 1966–68; Mem., Adv. Cttee, British Library Reference Div., 1983–; Council Member: Sir Anthony Panizzi Foundn, 1983–; London Soc., 1984–. FRSA. *Publications:* contrib. prof. books and jls. *Recreations:* ball games, books, railways. *Address:* Senate House, University of London, Malet Street, WC1E 7HU; 69 Redway Drive, Twickenham TW2 7NN. *T:* 01–894 0742.

PARRY, Prof. William, PhD; FRS 1984; Professor of Mathematics, University of Warwick, since 1970; *b* 3 July 1934; *s* of late Richard Parry and of Violet Irene Parry; *m* 1958, Benita (*née* Teper); one *d*. *Educ:* University Coll. London (BSc 1956); Univ. of Liverpool (MSc 1957); Imperial Coll. of Science and Technol., London (PhD 1960). Lectr, Univ. of Birmingham, 1960–65; Sen. Lectr, Univ. of Sussex, 1965–68; Reader, Univ. of Warwick, 1968– 70. Member: Labour Party; NCCL. *Publications:* Entropy and Generators in Ergodic Theory, 1969; Topics in Ergodic Theory, 1981; (with S. Tuncel) Classification Problems in Ergodic Theory, 1982; articles in Trans Amer. Math. Soc., Amer. Jl of Maths, and Annals of Maths. *Recreations:* theatre, concerts, walking. *Address:* Manor House, High Street, Marton CV23 9RR. *T:* Marton 632501.

PARRY BROWN, Arthur Ivor; *see* Brown, A. I. P.

PARRY-EVANS, Air Marshal Sir David, KCB 1985; CBE 1978; C-in-C RAF Germany and Commander, Second Allied Tactical Air Force, since 1985; *b* 19 July 1935; *s* of late Group Captain John Parry-Evans, MRCS, LRCP, DLO, and of Dorothy Parry-Evans; *m* 1960, Ann, 2nd *d* of late Charles Reynolds and of Gertrude Reynolds; two *s*. *Educ:* Berkhamsted School. Joined RAF, 1956; served FEAF, Coastal Command, United States Navy, RN Staff Coll., 1958–70; Headquarters Strike Command, 1970–74; OC 214 Sqn, 1974–75; OC RAF Marham, 1975–77; MoD, 1977–81 (Director of Defence Policy, 1979–81); Comdt, RAF Staff Coll., 1981–82; AOC Nos 1 and 38 Groups, RAF Strike Comd, 1982–85. *Recreation:* Rugby (Chairman, RAFRU, 1978–83). *Address:* c/o National Westminster Bank, 26 Spring Street, W2. *Club:* Royal Air Force.

PARRY EVANS, Mary Alethea, (Lady Hallinan); a Recorder of the Crown Court, since 1978; *b* 31 Oct. 1929; *o c* of Dr Evan Parry Evans, MD, JP, and Dr Lilian Evans; *m* 1955, Sir Adrian Lincoln Hallinan, *qv*; two *s* two *d*. *Educ:* Malvern Girls' Coll.; Somerville Coll., Oxford (BCL, MA). Called to Bar, Inner Temple, 1953; Wales and Chester Circuit. Member: Cardiff City Council, 1961–70; S Glamorgan CC, 1972–81; S Glamorgan Health Authority, 1977–. Lady Mayoress of Cardiff, 1969–70. *Address:* (chambers) 33 Park Place, Cardiff. *T:* Cardiff 33313.

PARSLOE, Prof. Phyllida; Professor of Social Work, Bristol University, since 1978; *b* 25 Dec. 1930; *d* of late Charles Guy Parsloe and of Mary Zirphie (*née* Munro). *Educ:* Bristol Univ. (BA, PhD); London Univ. (Cert. in Mental Health). Probation Officer, Devon CC, 1954–59; Psychiatric Social Worker, St George's Hospital, 1959–65; Lectr, London Sch. of Economics, 1965–70; Associate Prof., Sch. of Law, Indiana Univ., 1970–73; Prof. of Social Work, Univ. of Aberdeen, 1973–78. *Publications:* The Work of the Probation and After Care Officer, 1967; Juvenile Justice in Britain and America, 1978; (with Prof. O. Stevenson) Social Service Teams: the practitioner's view, 1978; Social Service Area Teams, 1981; contribs to: British Jl of Social Work, Community Care, Social Work Today, British Jl Criminology. *Recreations:* hill walking, crafts, gardening, squash. *Address:* 15 Elliston Road, Bristol BS6 6QG.

PARSONS, family name of **Earl of Rosse.**

PARSONS, Adrian; *see* Parsons, C. A. H.

PARSONS, Alan; *see* Parsons, T. A.

PARSONS, Alfred Roy, AO 1986; High Commissioner for Australia in UK, since 1984; *b* 24 May 1925; *s* of W. G. R. Parsons and R. E. Parsons; *m* 1958, Gillian Tryce Pigot; two *s* one *d*. *Educ:* Hobart High School; Univ. of Tasmania (postgraduate research; BCom); Canberra University College. Dept of Foreign Affairs, 1947; Djakarta, 1950–53, Rangoon, 1956–58, Berlin, 1961–62; Aust. Mission to UN, NY, 1962–64; Counsellor, Djakarta, 1964–66; High Comr, Singapore, 1967–70; First Asst Sec., Canberra, 1970–73; High Comr, Kuala Lumpur, 1973–76; Dep. Sec., periodically Acting Sec., Dept of Foreign Affairs, 1978–83; Member: Australia Japan Foundn, 1978–83; Australia China Council. *Recreations:* golf, reading. *Address:* Australian High Commission, Australia House, Strand, WC2B 4LA. *T:* 01–438 8209. *Clubs:* Royal Canberra Golf, Canberra Wine and Food.

PARSONS, Sir Anthony (Derrick), GCMG 1982 (KCMG 1975; CMG 1969); LVO 1965; MC 1945; HM Diplomatic Service, retired; Research Fellow and Lecturer, University of Exeter, since 1984; *b* 9 Sept. 1922; *s* of late Col H. A. J. Parsons, MC; *m* 1948, Sheila Emily Baird; two *s* two *d*. *Educ:* King's Sch., Canterbury; Balliol Coll., Oxford (Hon. Fellow 1984). HM Forces, 1940–54; Asst Mil. Attaché, Baghdad, 1952–54; Foreign Office, 1954–55; HM Embassy: Ankara, 1955–59; Amman, 1959–60; Cairo, 1960–61; FO, 1961–64; HM Embassy, Khartoum, 1964–65; Political Agent, Bahrain, 1965–69; Counsellor, UK Mission to UN, NY, 1969–71; Under-Sec., FCO, 1971–74; Ambassador to Iran, 1974–79; FCO, 1979; UK Perm. Rep. to UN, 1979–82; Special Advr to PM on foreign affairs, 1982–83. Bd Mem., British Council, 1982–86. Order of the Two Niles (Sudan), 1965. *Publications:* The Pride and the Fall, 1984; They Say the Lion, 1986. *Recreations:* gardening, golf, tennis. *Address:* Highgrove, Ashburton, South Devon. *Clubs:* MCC, Royal Over-Seas League.

PARSONS, (Charles) Adrian (Haythorne); Charity Commissioner since 1974; *b* 15 June 1929; *s* of Dr R. A. Parsons and Mrs W. S. Parsons (*née* Haythorne); *m* 1951, Hilary Sharpe; one *d*. *Educ:* Bembridge Sch.; Wadham Coll., Oxford. Called to Bar, Gray's Inn, 1964. Coutts & Co., Bankers, 1952–64; joined Charity Commn, 1964; Dep. Comr, 1972. *Address:* c/o Charity Commission, 14 Ryder Street, St James's, SW1Y 6AH. *Club:* United Oxford & Cambridge University.

See also Sir R. E. C. F. Parsons.

PARSONS, Geoffrey Penwill, OBE 1977; concert accompanist; *b* 15 June 1929; *s* of Francis Hedley Parsons and Edith Vera Buckland. *Educ:* Canterbury High Sch., Sydney; State Conservatorium of Music (with Winifred Burston), Sydney. Winner ABC Concerto Competition, 1947; first tour of Australia, 1948; arrived England, 1950; made 25th tour of Australia, 1983; has accompanied many of world's greatest singers and instrumentalists, incl. Elisabeth Schwarzkopf, Victoria de los Angeles, Janet Baker, Jessye Norman, Margaret Price, in 40 countries of world on all six continents. Master Classes: South Bank Summer Festival, 1977 and 1978; Sweden, 1984, 1985; Austria 1985; Geoffrey Parsons and Friends, internat. song recital series, Barbican Concert Hall opening season 1982, 1983, 1984. Harriet Cohen Internat. Music Award, 1968. Hon. RAM, 1975; Hon. GSM, 1983. *Address:* 176 Iverson Road, NW6 2HL. *T:* 01–624 0957.

PARSONS, John Christopher; Assistant Treasurer to HM the Queen, since 1985; *b* 21 May 1946; *s* of Arthur Christopher Parsons and Veronica Parsons; *m* 1982, Hon. Anne Manningham-Buller, *d* of 1st Viscount Dilhorne, PC; two *s*. *Educ:* Harrow; Trinity College, Cambridge. BA (Mech. Scis) 1968. FCA, MIMC. Dowty Group Ltd, 1968–72; Peat, Marwick, Mitchell & Co., 1972–85. *Address:* 19 Melrose Gardens, W6 7RN. *T:* 01–602 3035.

PARSONS, Mrs J. D.; *see* Beer, Patricia.

PARSONS, Sir (John) Michael, Kt 1970; Deputy Chairman and Chief Executive, 1979–81, Senior Managing Director, 1976–81, Director, 1971–81, Inchcape & Co. Ltd; *b* 29 Oct. 1915; *s* of late Rt Rev. Richard Godfrey Parsons, DD, Bishop of Hereford; *m* 1st, 1946, Hilda Mary Frewen (marr. diss. 1964); one *s* two *d*; 2nd, 1964, Caroline Inagh

Margaret Frewen. *Educ:* Rossall Sch.; University Coll., Oxford. Barry & Co., Calcutta, 1937. Served in Royal Garhwal Rifles (Indian Army), 1939–45: Bde Major, 1942; POW, Singapore, 1942. Macneill & Barry Ltd, Calcutta, 1946–70; Chm. & Managing Dir, 1964–70; Chm., Macdonald Hamilton & Co. Pty Ltd, 1970–72; Chairman and Director: Assam Investments, 1976–81; Paxall Investments Ltd, 1982–84; Dep. Chm. and Dir, Inchcape Insurance Hldgs Ltd, 1979–83; Dir, Commonwealth Develt Finance Co. Ltd, 1973–86. Vice-Chm., Indian Jute Mills Assoc., 1960–61; President: Bengal Chamber of Commerce, 1968–69; Associated Chambers of Commerce of India, 1969; Chm., UK Cttee, Fedn of Commonwealth Chambers of Commerce, 1974; Mem., Advisory Council on Trade, Bd of Trade, India, 1968–69. Chm. Council, Royal Commonwealth Soc., 1976–80, Vice Pres., 1980 ; Pres., India, Pakistan and Bangladesh Assoc., 1973–78, Vice Pres., 1978. Dep. Chm., Internat. Bd, United World Colls, 1981–. *Recreation:* golf. *Address:* Tall Trees, Warren Hill Lane, Aldeburgh, Suffolk IP15 5QB. *T:* Aldeburgh 2917. *Clubs:* Oriental; Bengal, Tollygunge (Calcutta); Union (Sydney).

PARSONS, Kenneth Charles, CMG 1970; OBE 1962; HM Diplomatic Service, retired; Counsellor, Foreign and Commonwealth Office, 1972–80; *b* 9 Jan. 1921; *m* 1st, 1949, Monica (*née* Howell) (decd); two *d*; 2nd, 1977, Mary Woolhouse. *Educ:* Haverfordwest Grammar Sch.; Exeter Coll., Oxford. Served War of 1939–45: with Oxfordshire and Buckinghamshire LI, 1941–46. 1st Class Hons, Mod. Langs (at Oxford), 1948. Joined Diplomatic Service, 1949; served FO, Moscow, Tokyo, Rangoon and Athens, 1951–72; FCO, 1972–77; Counsellor, with British Forces, Hong Kong, 1977–79. *Recreations:* rowing, swimming, walking. *Address:* 2 Ashfield Cottages, Rectory Road, Crickhowell, Powys NP8 1DW. *T:* Crickhowell 810332 *Club:* Carlton.

PARSONS, Sir Michael; see Parsons, Sir J. M.

PARSONS, Peter John, FBA 1977; Lecturer in Papyrology, University of Oxford, since 1965; Student of Christ Church, Oxford, since 1964; *b* 24 Sept. 1936; *s* of Robert John Parsons and Ethel Ada (*née* Frary). *Educ:* Raynes Park County Grammar Sch.; Christ Church, Oxford (MA 1961). Oxford University: Craven Scholar, 1955; 1st Cl. Hons Mods and de Paravicini Scholar, 1956; Chancellor's Prize for Latin Verse and Gaisford Prize for Greek Verse, 1st Cl. Lit. Hum., Derby Scholar, Dixon and Sen. Scholar of Christ Church, 1958; Passmore Edwards Scholar, 1959; Lectr in Documentary Papyrology, 1960–65; J. H. Gray Lectr, Univ. of Cambridge, 1982. Hon. PhD Bern, 1985. *Publications:* (jtly) The Oxyrhynchus Papyri XXXI, 1966, XXXIII and XXXIV, 1968; The Oxyrhynchus Papyri XLII, 1973; (with H. Lloyd-Jones) Supplementum Hellenisticum, 1983; articles in learned jls. *Recreations:* music, cinema, cooking and eating. *Address:* Christ Church, Oxford OX1 1DP. *T:* Oxford 243979.

PARSONS, Sir Richard (Edmund Clement Fownes), KCMG 1982 (CMG 1977); HM Diplomatic Service; Ambassador to Sweden, since 1984; *b* 14 March 1928; *s* of Dr R. A. Parsons, *m* 1960, Jenifer Jane Mathews (*d* 1981); three *s. Educ:* Bembridge Sch.; Brasenose Coll., Oxford. Served in Army, 1949–51; joined HM Foreign (subseq. Diplomatic) Service, 1951; FO, 1951–53; 3rd Sec., Washington, 1953–56; 2nd Sec., Vientiane, 1956–58; FO, 1958–60; 1st Sec., Buenos Aires, 1960–63; FO, 1963–65; 1st Sec., Ankara, 1965–67; FO, 1967–69; Counsellor, Lagos, 1969–72; Head of Personnel Ops Dept, FCO, 1972–76; Ambassador to: Hungary, 1976–79; Spain, 1980–84. *Recreations:* reading, writing, music, travel. *Address:* c/o Foreign and Commonwealth Office, King Charles Street, SW1. *Club:* Travellers'.

See also C. A. H. Parsons.

PARSONS, Roger, PhD, DSc; FRS 1980; FRSC; Professor of Chemistry, University of Southampton, since 1985; *b* 31 Oct. 1926; *s* of Robert Harry Ashby Parsons and Ethel Fenton; *m* 1953, Ruby Millicent Turner; three *s* one *d. Educ:* King Alfred Sch., Hampstead; Strathcona High Sch., Edmonton, Alta; Imperial Coll. of Science and Technol., (BSc, PhD). DSc Bristol 1962; ARCS 1946; FRIC 1962. Asst Lectr, Imp. Coll. of Science and Technol., 1948–50; Deedes Fellow, Dundee Univ., 1950–54; Lectr, then Reader in Electrochem., Bristol Univ., 1954–79; Dir, Lab. d'Electrochimie Interfaciale, Centre Nat. de la Recherche Scientifique, Meudon, France, 1977–84. Unesco Specialist, Buenos Aires, 1961; Vis. Prof., Calif Inst. of Technol., 1966–67. Hon. Fellow, Polish Chem. Soc., 1981. Palladium Medal, US Electrochem. Soc., 1979. Editor, Jl of Electroanal. Chem., 1962–. *Publications:* Electrochemical Data, 1956; (with J. Lyklema) Electrical Properties of Interfaces; (ed jtly) Standard Potentials in Aqueous Solution, 1985; (ed with R. Kalvoda) Electrochemistry in Research and Development, 1985; circa 150 papers in scientific jls. *Recreations:* listening to music, going to the opera. *Address:* Department of Chemistry, The University, Southampton SO9 5NH.

PARSONS, (Thomas) Alan, CB 1984; LLB; Chief Adjudication Officer, Department of Health and Social Security, 1983–86; *b* 25 Nov. 1924; *s* of late Arthur and Laura Parsons; *m* 1st, 1947, Valerie Vambeck; one *s*; 2nd, 1957, Muriel Lewis; two *s. Educ:* Clifton Coll.; Bristol Univ. (LLB). Called to the Bar, Middle Temple, 1950. Served, Royal Marines, 1943–46. Legal Asst, Min. of Nat. Insurance, 1950; Sen. Legal Asst, Min. of Pensions and Nat. Insurance, 1955; Asst Solicitor, 1968, Principal Asst Solicitor, 1977, DHSS. *Recreations:* walking, listening to music. *Address:* 11 Northiam Street, Pennethorne Place, E9. *T:* 01-986 0930. *Club:* University Women's (Dining Mem.).

PARSONS-SMITH, Basil Gerald, OBE 1945; MA, MD, FRCP; Hon. Consulting Neurologist, Charing Cross Hospital; Hon. Consulting Physician, St Mary's Hospital Group; Teacher in Medicine, London University; *b* 19 Nov. 1911; *s* of late Dr Basil Parsons-Smith, FRCP, and Marguerite, *d* of Sir David Burnett, 1st Bt; *m* 1939, Aurea Mary, *d* of late William Stewart Johnston, Sunningdale; two *s* one *d. Educ:* Harrow; Trinity Coll., Cambridge. St George's Hospital: Entrance Exhib., 1933; Brackenbury Prize in Medicine, 1936; House Surgeon, House Physician, Med. Registrar. Physician: Western Ophthalmic Hospital (St Mary's), 1938–60; Electro Encephalograph Dept, Middlesex Hospital Medical Sch., 1950–55; Dept of Neurology, West London and Charing Cross Hosps, 1950–77; Graylingwell Hosp., Chichester, 1950; West End Hosp. for Neurology, 1951–72; Neurologist, Florence Nightingale Hosp., 1955. MRCP 1939. Served War of 1939–45, as Blood Transfusion Officer, Chelsea EMS, then as medical specialist i/c medical divisions in RAF Hospitals in ME; Sqdn Leader RAFVR (despatches, OBE). MD (Cantab) 1949, Prox. Acc. Raymond Horton-Smith Prize; FRCP 1955. Examiner, RCP. FRSocMed. Member: Med. Appeals Trib., 1966–83; Vaccine Damage Tribunal, 1979–83; Association of British Neurologists; Ophthalmic Society of UK. Liveryman, Society of Apothecaries. Appeared in Hospital 1922, BBC TV, 1972. *Publications:* EEG of Brain Tumours, 1949; Sir Gordon Holmes, in Historical Aspects of the Neurosciences, 1982; 58 contribs to medical, neurological and ophthalmic jls mostly on the immediate treatment of acute stroke of the brain (1979) and eye (1952). *Recreation:* managing wife's equitation centre. *Address:* Roughets House, Bletchingley, Surrey RH1 4QX. *T:* Caterham 43929. *Clubs:* Royal Society of Medicine; Pitt (Cambridge).

PART, Sir Antony (Alexander), GCB 1974 (KCB 1966; CB 1959); MBE 1943; Chairman, Orion Insurance Company, 1976–June 1987; Director: Life Association of Scotland; Lucas Industries; Savoy Hotel Group; *b* 28 June 1916; *s* of late Alexander Francis Part and late Una Margaret Reynolds (*née* Snowdon); *m* 1940, Isabella Bennett;

no *c. Educ:* Wellesley House, Broadstairs; Harrow; Trinity Coll., Cambridge. First Class Hons Modern and Mediæval Langs Tripos. Entered Board of Education, 1937; Asst Private Secretary to successive Ministers of Supply, 1939–40. Served War of 1939–45 (despatches); Army Service, 1940–44; Lt-Col GS(1), 21 Army Group, 1944. Principal Private Secretary to successive Ministers of Education, 1945–46; Home Civil Service Commonwealth Fund Fellow to USA, 1950–51; Under-Secretary, Ministry of Education, 1954–60; Deputy Secretary: Ministry of Education, 1960–63; MPBW, 1963–65; Permanent Secretary: MPBW, 1965–68; BoT, 1968–70; DTI, 1970–74; DoI, 1974–76. Director: Debenhams, 1976–80; EMI, 1976–80; Metal Box, 1976–86. Chairman: Cttee on N Sea Oil Taxation, 1981; Adv. Panel on tech. transmission standards for UK services of direct broadcasting by satellite, 1982; Mem. Council, Regular Forces Employment Assoc., 1982–86. Governor, Administrative Staff Coll., 1968–; Governor, LSE, 1968– (Vice-Chm. of Governors, 1979–84). Hon. Fellow, LSE, 1984. Hon DTech Brunel, 1966; Hon. DSc: Aston, 1974; Cranfield, 1976. CBIM. *Recreation:* travel. *Address:* Flat 5, 71 Elm Park Gardens, SW10 9QE. *T:* 01-352 2950. *Clubs:* MCC, United Oxford & Cambridge University.

PARTON, Prof. John Edwin; Professor of Electrical Engineering, University of Nottingham, 1954–78, now Emeritus; *b* Kingswinford, Staffordshire, 26 Dec. 1912; *s* of Edwin and Elizabeth Parton; *m* 1940, Gertrude Brown; one *s* one *d. Educ:* Huntington Church of England Sch.; Cannock Chase Mining Coll.; University of Birmingham. BSc (1st Class Hons), 1936, PhD, 1938, Birmingham; DSc Glasgow, 1971. Training: Littleton Collieries, 1934; Electrical Construction Co., 1935; Asst Engineer, PO Engineering Dept, Dollis Hill Research Station, 1938–39; Part-time Lecturer: Cannock Chase Mining Coll., 1931–38; Northampton Polytechnic, 1938–39. Served RNVR Electrical Branch, Sub-Lt, 1939, to Lt-Comdr, 1943–45. Sen. Sci. Officer, British Iron and Steel Research Assoc., 1946; Lecturer, 1946–54, Senior Lecturer, 1954, University of Glasgow. Sen. Vis. Scientist, Nat. Sci. Foundn at Univ. of Tennessee, 1965–66; Vis. Prof., Univ. of W Indies, Trinidad, 1979, 1980. Chairman, East Midland Centre Institution of Electrical Engineers, 1961–62. FIEE 1966; Sen. Mem. IEEE 1966; FIMechE 1967. *Publications:* Applied Electromagnetics (jtly), 1975; papers in Proc. IEE, Trans. IEEE, Trans. IES, Instrument Practice, International Journal of Electrical Engineering Education, etc. *Recreations:* golf, gardening, bowls, bridge. *Address:* 93 Parkside, Wollaton, Nottingham NG8 2NQ. *T:* Nottingham 286693.

PARTRIDGE, Bernard B.; see Brook-Partridge.

PARTRIDGE, Derek William; HM Diplomatic Service; High Commissioner to Sierra Leone, since 1986; *b* 15 May 1931; *o s* of late Ernest and Ethel Elizabeth Partridge (*née* Buckingham), Wembley. *Educ:* Preston Manor County Grammar Sch., Wembley. Entered Foreign Service (later Diplomatic Service), 1949 Royal Air Force, 1949 51. Served: Foreign Office, 1951–54; Oslo, 1954–56; Jedda, 1956; Khartoum, 1957–60; Sofia, 1960–62; Bangkok, 1962; Manila, 1962–65; Djakarta, 1965–67; FCO, 1967–70; Diplomatic Service Inspectorate, 1970–72; British Consul-General, Brisbane, 1972–74; First Sec. (Economic and Commercial), Colombo, 1974–77; FCO, 1977–86: Counsellor and Head of Migration and Visa Dept, 1981–83; Counsellor and Head of Nationality and Treaty Dept, 1983–86. *Address:* c/o Foreign and Commonwealth Office, SW1.

PARTRIDGE, Harry Cowderoy; Chairman, Caviapen Investments Ltd, since 1985 (Non-executive Chairman, 1983–85); *b* 29 Aug. 1925; *y s* of late Harry Ewart Partridge and Edith Cowderoy; *m* 1st, 1950, Margaret Neill Cadzow (*d* 1967), *o d* of Charles J. M. Cadzow, OBE; two *s* one *d*; 2nd, 1973, Jeanne Margaret Henderson; one *s* one *d. Educ:* George Watson's Coll., Edinburgh; Edinburgh Univ. CA. Air-gunner, RAF, 1943–47. Company Accountant, McGrouther Ltd, 1955–59; Plant Controller, IBM UK Ltd, 1959–63; Sec., George Kent Ltd, 1963, Financial Dir 1965–71; Civil Aviation Authority: Controller of Finance and Planning, 1972; Mem. Bd, 1974–85; Gp Dir, Finance and Central Services, 1977. Director: Charterhouse Japhet Venture Fund Management Ltd, 1984–; German Smaller Cos Investment Trust PLC, 1985–; Automated Microbiology Systems Inc., San Diego, Calif. *Recreations:* house and garden. *Address:* Rushey Ford House, Box End, Kempston, Beds. *T:* Bedford 851594. *Club:* Savile.

PARTRIDGE, Ian (Harold); concert singer (tenor); *b* 12 June 1938; *s* of Harold Partridge and Ena Stinson; *m* 1959, Ann Glover; two *s. Educ:* New Coll., Oxford (chorister); Clifton Coll. (music scholar); Royal Coll. of Music; Guildhall Sch. of Music (LGSM, singing and teaching). Began as piano accompanist, although sang tenor in Westminster Cath. Choir, 1958–62; full-time concert singer, 1963–; performs in England and all over the world, both in recitals (with sister Jennifer) and in concerts; has worked with many leading conductors, incl. Stokowski, Boult, Giulini, Boulez and Colin Davis. Opera debut at Covent Garden as Iopas in Berlioz, Les Troyens, 1969. Title role, Britten's St Nicolas, Thames Television (Prix Italia, 1977). Over 100 records, *including:* Schubert, Die Schöne Müllerin; Schumann, Dichterliebe; Beethoven, An die ferne Geliebte; Vaughan-Williams, On Wenlock Edge; Warlock, The Curlew; Fauré and Duparc Songs; Britten, Serenade and Winter Words. Innumerable radio broadcasts, many TV appearances. Governor, Clifton Coll., 1981–. *Recreations:* bridge, horse racing, theatre, cricket. *Address:* 127 Pepys Road, SW20 8NP.

PARTRIDGE, John Albert, CBE 1981; ARA; FRIBA; architect in private practice; a Senior and Founder Partner, Howell, Killick, Partridge & Amis (HKPA), since 1959; *b* 26 Aug. 1924; *s* of George and Gladys Partridge; *m* 1953, Doris (*née* Foreman); one *s* one *d. Educ:* Shooter's Hill Grammar Sch., Woolwich; Polytechnic School of Architecture, Regent Street. FRIBA 1966 (ARIBA 1951); ARA 1980. London County Council Housing Architects Dept, 1951–59; Design Tutor, Architectural Assoc., 1958–61. The work of HKPA includes universities, colleges, public buildings and housing; principal commissions include: Wolfson, Rayne and Gatehouse building, St Anne's Coll., Oxford; New Hall and Common Room building, St Antony's Coll., Oxford; Wells Hall, Reading Univ.; Middlesex Polytechnic College of Art, Cat Hill; Medway Magistrates Court; The Albany, Deptford; Hall of Justice, Trinidad and Tobago, Warrington Court House. RIBA: Vice-Pres., 1977–79; Hon. Librarian, 1977–81; Chm. Res. Steering Gp, 1977–84. Vice-Pres., Concrete Soc., 1979–81. External Examiner in Architecture: Bath Univ., 1975–78; Thames Polytechnic, 1978–86; Cambridge Univ., 1979–81; Manchester Univ., 1982–; South Bank Polytechnic, 1982–86. Governor, Building Centre Trust, 1982–; Chm., Assoc. of Consultant Architects, 1983–85. NEDO Construction Res. Strategy Cttee, 1983–86; Architect Mem., FCO Adv. Bd on the Diplomatic Estate, 1985–. *Publications:* articles in technical press. *Recreations:* looking at buildings, travel, sketching and taking photographs. *Address:* Cudham Court, Cudham, near Sevenoaks, Kent TN14 7QF. *T:* Biggin Hill 71294.

PARTRIDGE, Michael John Anthony, CB 1983; Deputy Under-Secretary of State, Home Office, since 1983; *b* 29 Sept. 1935; *s* of late Dr John Henry Partridge, DSc, PhD, and of Ethel Green; *m* 1968, Joan Elizabeth Hughes; two *s* one *d. Educ:* Merchant Taylors'; St John's Coll., Oxford. BA (1st Cl. Hons Mods and Lit Hum) 1960, MA 1963. Entered Home Civil Service (Min. of Pensions and Nat. Insce), 1960; Private Sec. to Permanent Sec., 1962–64; Principal, 1964–71 (MPNI, Min. of Social Security and DHSS); DHSS:

Asst Sec., 1971–76; Under Sec., 1976–81; Dep. Sec., 1981–83. Senior Treasurer, Methodist Ch. Finance Div., 1980–. *Recreations:* Do-it-Yourself, Greece, reading, skiing. *Address:* 27 High View, Pinner, HA5 3NZ. *T:* 01–868 0657. *Club:* United Oxford & Cambridge University.

PARTRIDGE, Prof. (Stanley) Miles, FRS 1970; Professor of Biochemistry, University of Bristol, since 1976; *b* Whangarei, NZ, 2 Aug. 1913; *s* of Ernest Joseph Partridge and Eve Partridge (later Eve McCarthy) (*d* 1977); *m* 1940, Ruth Dowling; four *d. Educ:* Harrow County Sch.; Battersea Coll. of Technology. PhD Chemistry 1937; MA 1946, ScD 1964, Cantab. Beit Memorial Fellow, Lister Inst. of Preventive Medicine, 1940; Techn. Adviser, Govt of India, 1944; returned to Low Temperature Stn, Cambridge, 1946; Principal Scientific Officer 1952; Dep. Chief Scientific Officer, ARC, 1964; Head of Dept of Biochem. and Physiol., ARC Meat Research Inst., 1968–78. Member: Biochemical Soc. Cttee, 1957–61; Nuffield Foundn Rheumatism Cttee, 1965–77. Fourth Tanner Lectr and Award, Inst. of Food Technologists, Chicago, 1964. Hon. DSc Reading, 1984. Laurea ad Honorem in Medicine and Surgery, Padua, 1986. *Publications:* scientific papers, mainly in Biochemical Jl. *Recreation:* gardening. *Address:* Millstream House, St Andrew's Road, Cheddar, Somerset. *T:* Cheddar 742130.

PARTRIDGE, Rt. Rev. William Arthur; Assistant Bishop of Hereford, 1963–75; Prebendary Emeritus, Hereford Cathedral, since 1977; *b* 12 Feb. 1912; *s* of Alfred and Sarah Partridge; *m* 1945, Annie Eliza Joan Strangwood (*d* 1984); one *s. Educ:* Alcester Grammar Sch.; Birmingham Univ.; Scholæ Cancellarii, Lincoln. Curate of Lye, Worcs, 1935; SPG Studentship at Birmingham Univ. Education Dept, 1938–39; Educational Missionary, Dio. Madras, 1939–43; Chaplain, RAFVR, 1943–46; Lecturer Meston Training Coll., Madras, 1947–51; Metropolitan's Commissary and Vicar-General in Nandyal, 1951; Asst Bishop of Calcutta (Bishop in Nandyal), 1953–63; Vicar of Ludford, 1963–69. *Publication:* The Way in India, 1962. *Recreation:* the organ. *Address:* Flat 3, Capel Court, The Burgage, Prestbury, Cheltenham, Glos GL52 3EL. *T:* Cheltenham 576505.

PASCO, Richard Edward, CBE 1977; actor; Associate Artist, Royal Shakespeare Company; *b* 18 July 1926; *s* of Cecil George Pasco and Phyllis Irene Pasco; *m* 1st, Greta (*née* Watson) (marr. diss.); one *s*; 2nd, 1967, Barbara (*née* Leigh-Hunt). *Educ:* Colet Court; King's Coll. Sch., Wimbledon. Served HM Forces, 1944–48. 1st stage appearance, She Stoops to Conquer, 1943; 1st London appearance, Zero Hour, Lyric, 1944; 1st New York appearance, The Entertainer, 1958. London appearances include: leading roles, English Stage Co., Royal Court, 1957; The Entertainer, Palace, 1957; The Lady from the Sea, Queen's, 1961; Teresa of Avila, Vaudeville, 1961; Look Homeward, Angel, Phoenix, 1962; The New Men, Strand, 1962; The Private Ear and the Public Eye, Globe, 1963; Bristol Old Vic: Henry V (title role), Berowne in Love's Labour's Lost, 1964; Peer Gynt (title role), Angelo in Measure for Measure, Hamlet (title role), 1966 (and world tour); Ivanov, Phoenix, 1965; The Italian Girl, Wyndham's, 1968. Joined RSC, 1969; leading roles include: Becket, Murder in the Cathedral, Aldwych, 1972; (alternated with Ian Richardson) Richard and Bolingbroke in Richard II, Stratford-on-Avon, 1973, and Stratford and Aldwych, 1974; tour of Amer. univs; Jack Tanner in Man and Superman, Malvern Festival, tour and Savoy, 1977; Timon in Timon of Athens, Clarence in Richard III, Arkady Schatslivtses in The Forest, Stratford, 1980–81; La Ronde, Aldwych, 1982. Many foreign tours; accompanied HSH Princess Grace of Monaco at Edinburgh, Stratford and Aldeburgh Festivals and on tour of USA, 1977–78. Frequent appearances at Aldeburgh, Brighton, Windsor and Harrogate festivals, Stratford-upon-Avon Poetry Festival etc. Recent films: A Watcher in the Woods; Wagner. Countless TV and radio appearances; recent television: Disraeli; Sorrell & Son; Love and Marriage; Pythons on the Mountain; Drummonds. Many recordings of poems, plays, recitals, etc. *Recreations:* music, gardening, reading. *Address:* c/o Michael Whitehall Ltd, 125 Gloucester Road, SW7 4TE. *Club:* Garrick.

PASCO, Rowanne; Editor, The Universe, since 1981 (Deputy Editor, 1979–81); *b* 7 Oct. 1938; *d* of John and Ann Pasco. *Educ:* Dominican Convent, Chingford; Ursuline Convent, Ilford; Open Univ. (BA). Reporter, 1956–57, Editor, 1957–58, Chingford Express; Publicity Officer, NFU, 1958–59; Account Exec., Leslie Frewin PR, 1959–60; Travel Rep., Horizon Holidays, 1960–64; Publicity Asst, Paramount Pictures Corp., Hollywood, 1964–66; Publicity Officer, Religious Progs, Radio and TV, BBC, 1966–71; Reporter, BBC Radio London, 1971–72; TV Editor, Ariel, BBC Staff Newspaper, 1972–74; Radio 4 Reporter, 1974–76; Researcher, Religious Progs, BBC TV, 1976–77; Producer and Presenter, Religious Progs, BBC Radio, 1977–78. *Recreations:* gardening, Italian, creative cooking. *Address:* (office) 33/39 Bowling Green Lane, EC1R 0AB. *T:* 01–278 7321.

PASCOE, Alan Peter, MBE 1975; Managing Director, Alan Pascoe Associates Ltd, since 1983 (Director, 1976–83); *b* 11 Oct. 1947; *s* of Ernest George Frank Pascoe and Joan Rosina Pascoe; *m* 1970, Della Patricia (*née* James); one *s* one *d. Educ:* Portsmouth Southern Grammar Sch.; Borough Road Coll. (Cert. in Educn); London Univ. (Hons degree in Educn). Master, Dulwich Coll., 1971–74; Lectr in Physical Educn, Borough Road Coll., Isleworth, 1974–80. Member: Sports Council, 1974–80; Minister for Sport's Working Party on Centres of Sporting Excellence; BBC Adv. Council, 1975–79. European Indoor Champion, 50m Hurdles, 1969; Europ. Games Silver Medallist, 110m Hurdles, 1971; Silver Medal, Olympic Games, Munich, 4 × 400m Relay, 1972; Europa Gold Cup Medallist, 400m Hurdles, 1973; Commonwealth Games Gold Medal, 400m Hurdles, and Silver Medal, 4 × 400m Relay, 1974; Europ. Champion and Gold Medallist in both 400m Hurdles and 4 × 400m Relay, 1974; Europa Cup Gold Medallist, 400m Hurdles, 1975; Olympic Finalist (injured), Montreal, 1976; Europe's Rep., World Cup Event, 1977. *Publication:* An Autobiography, 1979. *Recreation:* gardening. *Address:* c/o Alan Pascoe Associates Ltd, Durham House, Durham House Street, WC2N 6HG. *T:* 01–930 6332.

PASCOE, Dr Michael William; Head of Science, Camberwell School of Arts and Crafts, since 1981; *b* 16 June 1930; *s* of Canon W. J. T. Pascoe and Mrs D. Pascoe; *m* 1st, 1956, Janet Clark (marr. diss. 1977); three *d*; 2nd, 1977, Brenda Hale Reed; one *d. Educ:* St John's, Leatherhead; Selwyn Coll., Cambridge (BA, PhD). MInstP. Res. Student (Tribology), Cambridge, 1951–55; Physicist: Mount Vernon Hosp., Northwood, 1956–57; British Nylon Spinners Ltd, 1957–60; Chemist/Physicist, ICI Paints Div., 1960–67; Lectr (Polymer Science), Brunel Univ., 1967–77; Principal Scientific Officer, 1976–79, Keeper of Conservation and Technical Services, 1979–81, British Museum. Tutor and Counsellor, Open Univ., 1971–76. Consultant to: Royal Acad. of Arts; Mary Rose Trust; Council for the Care of Churches; Public Record Office. FRSA. *Publications:* contrib. to books on polymer tribol. and technol.; articles in scientific, engrg and conservation jls on tribol., materials technol. and on conservation methods. *Recreations:* painting and drawing *inter alia*. *Address:* Camberwell School of Arts and Crafts, Peckham Road, SE5. *T:* 01–703 0987.

PASCOE, Nigel Spencer Knight; a Recorder of the Crown Court, since 1979; *b* 18 Aug. 1940; *er s* of late Ernest Sydney Pascoe and of Cynthia Pascoe; *m* 1964, Elizabeth Anne Walter; two *s* four *d. Educ:* Epsom Coll. Called to the Bar, Inner Temple, 1966. County Councillor for Lyndhurst, Hants, 1979–84. Founder and Editor, All England Qly Law Cassettes, 1976–85. *Publications:* The Trial of Penn and Mead, 1985; articles in legal jls. *Recreations:* theatre, devising legal anthologies, cricket, writing. *Address:* 3 Pump Court, Temple, EC4 7AJ. *T:* 01–353 0711. *Clubs:* Garrick; Hampshire (Winchester).

PASCOE, Lt-Gen. Sir Robert (Alan), KCB 1985; MBE 1968; General Officer Commanding Northern Ireland, since 1985; *b* 21 Feb. 1932; *er s* of late C. and Edith Mary Pascoe; *m* 1955, Pauline (*née* Myers); one *s* three *d. Educ:* Tavistock Grammar Sch.; RMA, Sandhurst. rcds, psc. Commissioned Oxford and Bucks LI, 1952; served with 1 Oxf. Bucks, 1 DLI and 4 Oxf. Bucks (TA), 1953–57; Middle East Centre for Arab Studies, Lebanon, 1958–59; 1st Cl. Interpretership (Arabic); GSO2 Land Forces Persian Gulf, 1960–62; sc Camberley, 1963; Co. Comd 2RGJ, UK and Malaysia, 1964–66 (despatches (Borneo) 1966); GSO2 HQ 2 Div. BAOR, 1967–68; Co. Comd 1RGJ, UK and UNFICYP, 1968–69; Second in Comd 2RGJ, BAOR, 1969; MA to QMG, 1970–71; Comd 1RGJ, 1971–74, BAOR and NI (despatches (NI) 1974); Col General Staff HQ UKLF, 1974–76; Comd 5 Field Force BAOR, 1976–79; rcds 1979; Asst Chief of Gen. Staff (Operational Requirements), MoD, 1980–83; Chief of Staff, HQ, UKLF, 1983–85. Col Comdt, 1st Bn Royal Green Jackets, 1986–. Governor, Royal Sch. for Daughters of Officers of the Army, 1981–. Pres., Army LTA, 1986. *Recreations:* gardening, golf, fishing, tennis, windsurfing, ski-ing. *Address:* c/o Lloyds Bank, Cox's & King's Branch, 6 Pall Mall, SW1. *Club:* Army and Navy.

PASHLEY, Prof. Donald William, FRS 1968; Professor of Materials and Head of Department of Metallurgy and Materials Science, since 1979, and Dean, Royal School of Mines, since 1986, Imperial College of Science and Technology; *b* 21 Apr. 1927; *s* of late Harold William Pashley and Louise Pashley (*née* Clarke); *m* 1954, Glenys Margaret Ball; one *s* one *d. Educ:* Henry Thornton Sch., London; Imperial Coll., London (BSc). 1st cl. hons Physics, 1947; PhD 1950. Research Fellow, Imp. Coll., 1950–55; TI Res. Labs, Hinxton Hall: Res. Scientist, 1956–61; Gp Leader and Div. Head, 1962–67; Asst Dir, 1967–68; Dir, 1968–79 (also Dir of Research, TI Ltd, 1976–79). Mem. Governing Body, Imp. Coll. of Sci. and Technology, 1986–. Mem. Council, Royal Soc., 1981–83. Rosenhain Medal, Inst. of Metals, 1968. *Publications:* (jtly) Electron Microscopy of Thin Crystals, 1965; numerous papers on electron microscopy and diffraction, thin films and epitaxy in Phil. Mag., Proc. Roy. Soc., etc. *Address:* 50 Exeter House, Putney Heath, SW15 3SX. *T:* 01–788 4800; Department of Metallurgy and Materials Science, Imperial College, SW7 2AZ.

PASLEY, Sir (John) Malcolm (Sabine), 5th Bt *cr* 1794; Fellow and Tutor, Magdalen College, Oxford, 1958–86; *b* 5 April 1926; *s* of Sir Rodney Marshall Sabine Pasley, 4th Bt, and Aldyth Werge Hamber (*d* 1983); *S* father, 1982; *m* 1965, Virginia Killigrew Wait; two *s. Educ:* Sherborne Sch.; Trinity Coll., Oxford (MA). War service, Royal Navy, 1944–46. Laming Travelling Fellow, Queen's Coll., Oxford, 1949–50; Lectr in German, Brasenose and Magdalen Colls, 1950–58; Vice-Pres., Magdalen Coll., 1979–80. Mem., Deutsche Akademie für Sprache und Dichtung, 1983–. *Publications:* (co-author) Kafka-Symposion, 1965; (ed) Germany: A Companion to German Studies, 1972, 2nd edn 1982; (trans.) Kafka Shorter Works, vol. 1, 1973; (ed) Nietzsche: Imagery and Thought, 1978; (ed) Franz Kafka, Das Schloss, 1982. *Heir: s* Robert Killigrew Sabine Pasley, *b* 23 Oct. 1965. *Address:* 25 Lathbury Road, Oxford.

PASMORE, (Edwin John) Victor, CH 1981; CBE 1959; RA 1984; Artist; *b* Chelsham, Surrey, 3 Dec. 1908; *s* of late E. S. Pasmore, MD; *m* 1940, Wendy Blood; one *s* one *d. Educ:* Harrow; attended evening classes, LCC Central School of Arts & Crafts. Local government service, LCC County Hall, 1927–37; joined the London Artists' Assoc., 1932–34, and the London Group, 1932–52. Associated with the formation of the Euston Road School, 1937–39, and the first post-war exhibitions of abstract art, 1948–53; joined the Penwith Society, St Ives, 1951–53. Visiting teacher, LCC Camberwell School of Art, 1945–49; Central School of Arts and Crafts, 1949–53. Master of Painting, Durham University, 1954–61; consultant urban and architectural designer, South West Area, Peterlee New Town, 1955–77. Trustee, Tate Gall., 1963–66. Hon. degrees from Newcastle-upon-Tyne, 1967; Surrey, 1969; RCA; Warwick, 1985. *Retrospective exhibitions:* Venice Biennale, 1960; Musée des Arts Décoratifs, Paris, 1961; Stedelijk Museum, Amsterdam, 1961; Palais des Beaux Arts, Brussels, 1961; Louisiana Museum, Copenhagen, 1962; Kestner-Gesellschaft, Hanover, 1962; Kunsthalle, Berne, 1963; Tate Gallery, 1965; São Paolo Biennale, 1965; Cartwright Hall, Bradford, 1980; Royal Acad., London, 1980; Musée des Beaux Arts, Calais, 1985; Marlborough Galleries, London, Rome, NY, Zurich and Toronto. *Retrospective graphic exhibitions:* Marlborough Gallery, Tate Gallery, Galleria 2RC, Rome, Milan, Lubjlana, Messina, Oslo, Osaka. Stage backcloth designs for Young Apollo, Royal Ballet, Covent Gdn, 1984. Works represented in: Tate Gallery and other public collections in Gt Britain, Canada, Australia, Holland, Italy, Austria, Switzerland, France and the USA. Carnegie Prize for painting, Pittsburgh International, 1964. Grand Prix d'Honneur, International Graphics Biennale, Lubjlana, 1977; Charles Wollaston Award, Royal Acad., 1983. *Publication:* Monograph and Catalogue Raisonnée, 1980. *Address:* Dar Gamri, Gudja, Malta; 12 St Germans Place, Blackheath, SE3. *Club:* Arts.

PASQUILL, Frank, DSc; FRS 1977; retired from Meteorological Office, 1974; *b* 8 Sept. 1914; *s* of late Joseph Pasquill and Elizabeth Pasquill (*née* Rudd), both of Atherton, Lancs; *m* 1937, Margaret Alice Turnbull, West Rainton, Co. Durham; two *d. Educ:* Henry Smith Sch., Hartlepool; Durham Univ. BSc (1st Cl. Hons Physics) 1935, MSc, 1949, DSc 1950. Meteorological Office, 1937–74, with posts at Chem. Defence Res. Estabt, Porton, 1937–46 (incl. overseas service in Australia); Sch. of Agric., Cambridge Univ., 1946–49; Atomic Energy Res. Estabt, Harwell, 1949–54; Chem. Defence Res. Estabt, Porton, 1954–61; Meteorological Office HQ Bracknell, 1961–74 (finally Dep. Chief Scientific Officer, and Head of Boundary Layer Research Br.). Visiting Prof., Pennsylvania State Univ., Autumn, 1974, N Carolina State Univ., Spring, 1975; Visiting Scientist, Penn. State Univ., 1975, Winter, 1976, Winter, 1977, Savannah River Lab., S Carolina, Winter, 1976. Royal Meteorological Society: Editor, 1961–64; Pres., 1970–72; Hon. Mem., 1978; Chm., Aero Res. Council's Gust Res. Cttee, 1963–68; Chm., CEGB's Adv. Panel on Environmental Res., 1962–80. Symons Medal, RMetS, 1983. *Publications:* Atmospheric Diffusion, 1962, 3rd edn (with F. B. Smith) 1983; papers on atmospheric turbulence and diffusion in various jls. *Address:* Woodwell, 37 Arbor Lane, Winnersh, Wokingham, Berks RG11 5JE.

PASTERFIELD, Rt. Rev. Philip John; an Assistant Bishop, Diocese of Exeter, since 1984; *b* 1920; *s* of Bertie James Pasterfield and Lilian Bishop Pasterfield (*née* Flinn); *m* 1948, Eleanor Maureen, *d* of William John Symons; three *s* one *d. Educ:* Denstone Coll., Staffs; Trinity Hall, Cambridge (MA); Cuddesdon Coll., Oxford. Army Service, 1940–46; commnd in Somerset Light Infantry. Deacon 1951, Priest 1952. Curate of Streatham, 1951–54; Vicar of West Lavington, Sussex, and Chaplain, King Edward VII Hosp., Midhurst, 1954–60; Rector of Woolbeding, 1955–60; Vicar of Oxton, Birkenhead, 1960–68; Rural Dean of Birkenhead, 1966–68; Canon Residentiary and Sub Dean of St Albans, 1968–74; Rural Dean of St Albans, 1972–74; Bishop Suffragan of Crediton, 1974–84. *Recreations:* ornithology, music. *Address:* Wesley House, Harberton, near Totnes, Devon TQ9 7SW. *T:* Totnes 865093.

PASTINEN, Ilkka, KCMG (Hon.) 1976; Finnish Ambassador to the Court of St James's, since 1983; *b* 17 March 1928; *s* of Martti and Ilmi Pastinen; *m* 1950, Eeva Marja Viitanen; two *d.* Entered Diplomatic Service, 1952; served Stockholm, 1955; Perm. Mission to UN, 1957–60; Peking, 1962–64; London, 1966–69; Ambassador and Dep. Representative of Finland to UN, 1969–71; Special Representative of Sec. Gen. of UN to Cttee of Disarmament, 1971–75; Ambassador and Perm. Representative of Finland at UN, NY, 1977–83. Kt Comdr of Order of Lion of Finland, 1978. *Address:* 14 Kensington Palace Gardens, W8. *T:* 01–221 4433; Finnish Embassy, 38 Chesham Place, SW1. *T:* 235 9531. *Clubs:* Athenæum, Travellers'; Swinley Forest Golf.

PASTON-BEDINGFELD, Sir Edmund George Felix, 9th Bt, *cr* 1661; Major late Welsh Guards; Managing Director, Handley Walker (Europe) Ltd, 1969–80; *b* 2 June 1915; *s* of 8th Bt and Sybil (*d* 1985), *e d* of late H. Lyne Stephens of Grove House, Roehampton; *S* father, 1941; *m* 1st, 1942, Joan Lynette (*née* Rees) (*d* 1965); one *s* one *d*; 2nd, 1957, Agnes Kathleen (*d* 1974), *d* of late Miklos Gluck, Budapest; 3rd, 1975, Mrs Peggy Hannaford-Hill, Fort Victoria, Rhodesia. *Educ:* Oratory School; New College, Oxford. Under-Sec., Head of Agricultural Div., RICS, 1966–69. *Heir: s* Henry Edgar Paston-Bedingfeld, *qv*. *Address:* Arundell House, Brettenham, Ipswich. *T:* Rattlesden 607.

PASTON-BEDINGFELD, Henry Edgar; Rouge Croix Pursuivant of Arms, since 1983; *b* 7 Dec. 1943; *s* and *heir* of Sir Edmund Paston-Bedingfeld, Bt, *qv*; *m* 1968, Mary Kathleen, *d* of Brig. R.D. Ambrose, CIE, OBE, MC; two *s* two *d*. *Educ:* Ampleforth College, York. Chartered Surveyor. Founder Chairman, Norfolk Heraldry Soc., 1975–80, Vice-Pres. 1980–; Mem. Council, Heraldry Soc., 1976–; Secretary, Standing Council of the Baronetage, 1984–. Freeman of the City of London, 1985. Kt of Sovereign Mil. Order of Malta. *Publication:* Oxburgh Hall, The First 500 Years, 1982. *Address:* The College of Arms, Queen Victoria Street, EC4. *T:* 01–236 6420; Oxburgh Hall, King's Lynn, Norfolk. *T:* Gooderstone 269. *Club:* Norfolk (Norwich).

PASTON BROWN, Dame Beryl, DBE 1967; *b* 7 March 1909; *d* of Paston Charles Brown and Florence May (*née* Henson). *Educ:* Streatham Hill High School; Newnham Coll., Cambridge (MA); London Day Training College. Lecturer: Portsmouth Training Coll., 1933–37; Goldsmiths' Coll., Univ. of London, 1937–44 and 1946–51. Temp. Asst Lecturer, Newnham Coll., 1944–46. Principal of City of Leicester Training Coll., 1952–61; Principal, Homerton College, Cambridge, 1961–71. Chairman, Assoc. of Teachers in Colleges and Depts of Educn, 1965–66. *Address:* 21 Keere Street, Lewes, East Sussex. *T:* Lewes 473608.

PATCH, Air Chief Marshal Sir Hubert (Leonard), KCB 1957 (CB 1952); CBE 1942; *b* 16 Dec. 1904; *s* of late Captain Leonard W. Patch, RN (retd), St Margarets-on-Thames; *m* 1960, Claude Renée, *d* of Major Jean-Marie Botéculet (Légion d'Honneur, Croix de Guerre, Médaille Militaire, MC (British), killed in action in Morocco, 1925). *Educ:* Stonyhurst; RAF Coll., Cranwell, Lincs. Joined RAF, 1925; Acting Group Captain, 1942; Group Captain, 1946; Air Cdre, 1947; Air Vice-Marshal, 1951. Served 1939–44 (despatches, CBE). Senior Air Staff Officer, HQ Far East Air Force, 1952–53; AOC No 11 Gp, Fighter Comd, Nov. 1953–Jan. 1956; Air Officer Commanding-in-Chief (Temp.), Fighter Command, Jan.-Aug. 1956; Commander-in-Chief, Middle East Air Force, 1956–58; Air Member for Personnel April-Sept. 1959; Commander-in-Chief, British Forces, Arabian Peninsula, October 1959–May 1960; Acting Air Marshal, 1956; Air Marshal, 1957; Air Chief Marshal, 1959. Retired from Royal Air Force, 1961. Representative of British Aircraft Corporation to the NATO countries, 1961–63. *Address:* Loma de Rio Verde, Marbella, Spain; c/o Barclays Bank, Colchester, Essex. *Club:* Royal Air Force.

PATCHETT, Terry; MP (Lab) Barnsley East, since 1983; *b* 11 July 1940; *s* of Wilfred and Kathleen Patchett; *m* 1961, Glenys Veal; one *s* two *d*. *Educ:* State schools; Sheffield University (Economics and Politics). Miner; NUM Houghton Main Branch Delegate, 1966–83; Mem., Yorkshire Miners' Exec., 1976–83; former Member: Appeals Tribunals; Community Health Council. Mem., Wombwell UDC, 1969–73. Mem., H of C Expenditure Cttee (Social Services Sub-Cttee), 1985–. *Recreations:* walking, gardening, golf. *Address:* 71 Upperwood Road, Darfield, near Barnsley, S Yorks. *T:* Barnsley 757684. *Clubs:* Darfield Working Men's, Mitchell and Darfield Miners' Welfare.

PATE, Prof. John Stewart, FRS 1985; FAA 1980; Professor of Botany, University of Western Australia, since 1974; *b* 15 Jan. 1932; *s* of Henry Stewart Pate and Muriel Margaret Pate; *m* 1959, Elizabeth Lyons Sloan, BSc; three *s*. *Educ:* Campbell College; Queen's Univ., Belfast (BSc, MSc, PhD, DSc). Lectr, Sydney Univ., 1956–60; Lectr, Reader, Personal Chair in Plant Physiology, Queen's Univ. Belfast, 1960–73. Vis. Fellow, Univ. of Cape Town, 1973. *Publications:* (ed with J. F. Sutcliffe) Physiology of the Garden Pea, 1977; (ed with A. J. McComb) Biology of Australian Plants, 1981; (with K. W. Dixon) Tuberous, Cormous and Bulbous Plants, 1983; (ed with J. S. Beard) Kwongan: plant life of the sandplain, 1984. *Recreations:* music, nature study, rugby football, jogging. *Address:* 83 Circe Circle, Dalkeith, WA 6009, Australia. *T:* 3866070 (Perth, WA).

PATEL, Ambalal Bhailalbhai, CMG 1949; *b* 1 May 1898; *e s* of late Bhailalbhai Dharamdas Patel, Changa, Gujarat; *m* Gangalaxmi Patel (decd); three *s* one *d* (and one *s* decd). *Educ:* Petlad High School; Baroda Coll. (BA); Bombay University (LLB). Barrister-at-Law, Lincoln's Inn, 1923. Advocate, Supreme Court of Kenya, 1924; as Kenya Indian Deleg. gave evidence before Joint Parl. Committee on Closer Union, London, 1931. Pres. E African Indian National Congress, 1938–42, and 1945–46; Pres. Kenya Indian Conf., 1942; Mem. standing and exec. Cttees of EAIN Congress, 1924–56; Chm. Indian Elected Members Organization, 1941–48; Hon. Sec. Coast Elected Members Organization, 1949–56; Mem. Makerere Coll. Assembly, 1938–48. Chm. Central Indian Advisory Man-Power Cttee and Indian E Dist Man-Power Cttee during War of 1939–45. Chm. Indian and Arab Land Settlement Bd, 1946–54; attended African Conf. in London, 1948; Mem. E African Central Legislative Assembly, 1948–52; Minister without Portfolio, Govt of Kenya, 1954–56, retired. MLC 1938–56, MEC Kenya, 1941–56. Mem. Royal Technical College Council, Nairobi, and Makerere University Coll. Council, 1954–56. Gen. Sec. and Treasurer, World Union, 1964–; Member: Emergency Council for World Govt, World Union Movement (Hesbjerg, Denmark), 1974–83; World Federal Authority Cttee (Geneva), 1975–81; Co-pres., World Constitution and Parliament Assoc., 1977–83, Hon. Pres., 1983; First signatory, Constitution for Fedn of Earth, 1977; elected Speaker, 1st Provisional World Parliament, Brighton, Sept. 1982. Pres. or trustee various political, social and cultural institutions at different times. Coronation Medal, 1953. *Publications:* Toward a New World Order, 1974; Earth an Evolutionary Planet, 1986. *Address:* c/o Sri Aurobindo Ashram, Pondicherry-605002 (via Madras), India. *T:* 4834.

PATEL, Indraprasad Gordhanbhai, PhD; Director, London School of Economics and Political Science, since 1984; *b* 11 Nov. 1924; *s* of F. Patel Gordhanbhai Tulsibhai and M. Patel Kashiben Jivabhai; *m* 1958, Alaknanda Dasgupta; one *d*. *Educ:* Bombay Univ. (BA Hons); King's Coll., Cambridge (BA, PhD). Prof. of Economics, Maharaja Sayajirao Univ. of Baroda, 1949; Economist, later Asst Chief, IMF, 1950–54; Dep. Economic Adviser, Min. of Finance, India, 1954–58; Alternate Exec. Dir for India, IMF, 1958–61; Chief Economic Adviser, Min. of Finance and Planning Commn, 1962–64, 1965–67; Special Sec. and Sec., Dept of Economic Affairs, 1967–72; Dep. Administrator, UN Develt Programme, 1972–77; Governor, Reserve Bank of India, 1977–82; Dir, Indian Inst. of Management, Ahmedabad, 1982–84. Vis. Prof., Delhi Univ., 1964. Hon. DLitt Sardar Patel Univ. *Publications:* articles in IMF staff papers etc. on inflation, monetary policy, internat. trade. *Recreations:* music, reading, watching cricket. *Address:* London School of Economics and Political Science, Houghton Street, Aldwych, WC2A 2AE. *T:* 01–405 7686 ext. 728. *Club:* Athenæum.

PATEL, Praful Raojibhai Chaturbhai; Company Director; Investment Adviser in UK, since 1962; Hon. Secretary, All-Party Parliamentary Committee on UK Citizenship, since 1968; *b* Jinja, Uganda, 7 March 1939; *s* of Raojibhai Chaturbhai Patel, Sojitra, Gujarat, India, and Maniben Jivabhai Lalaji Patel, Dharmaj, Gujarat; unmarried. *Educ:* Government Sec. Sch., Jinja, Uganda; London Inst. of World Affairs, attached to University Coll., London (Extra Mural Dept). Sec., Uganda Students Union, 1956–58; Deleg. to Internat. Youth Assembly, New Delhi, 1958; awarded two travel bursaries for visits to E, Central and S Africa, and Middle East, to study and lecture on politics and economics; arrived in Britain as student, then commenced commercial activities, 1962; increasingly involved in industrial, cultural and educational projects affecting immigrants in Britain. Spokesman for Asians in UK following restriction of immigration resulting from Commonwealth Immigrants Act 1968; Council Mem., UK Immigrants Advisory Service, 1970–; Mem., Uganda Resettlement Bd, 1972–74; Hon. Sec., Uganda Evacuees Resettlement Advisory Trust, 1974–; Pres., Nava Kala India Socio-Cultural Centre, London, 1962–75; Chm. Bd of Trustees, Swaminarayan Hindu Mission, UK, 1970–76; Jt Convener, Asian Action Cttee, 1976; Convener, Manava Trust, 1979–. *Publications:* articles in newspapers and journals regarding immigration and race relations. *Recreations:* cricket; campaigning and lobbying; current affairs; and inter-faith co-operation. *Address:* 60 Bedford Court Mansions, Bedford Avenue, Bedford Square, WC1B 3AD. *T:* 01–580 0897. *Club:* Royal Commonwealth Society.

PATEMAN, Jack Edward, CBE 1970; FEng; Deputy Chairman: GEC Avionics, since 1986; Marconi Co., since 1986; Director: General Electric Co. plc, since 1986; GEC Computers Ltd, since 1971 (Chairman 1978–82); Canadian Marconi Co., since 1971; Elliott Bros (London) Ltd, since 1979; GEC Avionics Projects Ltd, since 1980; Marconi Electronic Devices Ltd, since 1980; GEC Avionics Projects (UK) Ltd, since 1984; *b* 29 Nov. 1921; *s* of William Edward Pateman and Lucy Varley (*née* Jetten); *m* 1949, Cicely Hope Turner; one *s* one *d*. *Educ:* Gt Yarmouth Grammar Sch. Served War of 1939–45, RAF, 1940–46. Research Engineer: Belling & Lee, 1946–48; Elliott Bros (London) Ltd, 1948–51; formed Aviation Div. of EBL at Borehamwood, 1951–62; Dep. Chm. and Jt Man. Dir, Elliott Flight Automation Ltd, 1962–71; Man. Dir, GEC Avionics, 1971–86; Dir, GEC Information Systems, 1982–86. British Gold Medal, RAeS, 1981. *Recreation:* sailing. *Address:* Spindles, Ivy Hatch, Sevenoaks, Kent. *T:* Plaxtol 810364.

PATEMAN, Prof. John Arthur Joseph, FRS 1978; FRSE 1974; Professor and Head of Department of Genetics, since 1979, and Executive Director of the Centre for Recombinant DNA Research, since 1982, Australian National University; *b* 18 May 1926; *s* of John and Isobel May Pateman; *m* 1952, Mary Phelps; one *s* two *d*. *Educ:* Clacton County High Sch., Essex; University Coll., Leicester. BSc, PhD(Lond); MA(Cantab). Lectr, Univ. of Sheffield, 1954–58; Sen. Lectr, Univ. of Melbourne, Australia, 1958–60; Lectr, Univ. of Cambridge, 1960–67; Prof., Flinders Univ., S Australia, 1967–70; Prof. of Genetics, Univ. of Glasgow, 1970–79. Fellow, Churchill Coll., Cambridge, 1961–67. *Publications:* scientific papers in genetical, biochemical and microbiological jls. *Recreations:* reading, music, walking. *Address:* 46 Amaroo Street, Reid, ACT 2601, Australia. *T:* 48–8327.

PATER, John Edward, CB 1953; PhD; Under Secretary, Ministry of Health and Department of Health and Social Security, 1947–73 (retired); *b* 15 March 1911; *s* of Edward Rhodes and Lilian Pater; *m* 1938, Margaret Anderson, *yr d* of M. C. Furtado; two *s* one *d*. *Educ:* King Edward VI School, Retford; Queens' College, Cambridge. Foundation Scholar, Queens' College; BA 1933, MA 1935, PhD 1982. Assistant Principal, Ministry of Health, 1933; Principal, 1938; Assistant Secretary, 1943; Principal Assistant Secretary, 1945; Director of Establishments and Organisation, 1960–65. Treasurer: Methodist Church Dept of Connexional Funds and Finance Bd, 1959–73; Div. of Finance, 1973–84; Central Finance Bd, 1968–74. Governor, Kingswood Sch., 1973–85. *Publication:* The Making of the National Health Service, 1981. *Recreations:* reading, archæology, walking (preferably on hills). *Address:* 1B Croham Mount, South Croydon CR2 0BR. *T:* 01–651 1601.

See also R. A. Furtado.

PATERSON, Alexander Craig, (Alastair), FEng 1983; Senior Partner, Bullen and Partners, Consulting Engineers, since 1969 (Partner 1960); *b* 15 Jan. 1924; *s* of Duncan McKellar Paterson and Lavinia (*née* Craig); *m* 1947, Betty Hannah Burley; two *s* two *d*. *Educ:* Glasgow High Sch.; Royal Coll. of Science and Technol. (ARCST); Glasgow Univ. (BSc); Mil. Coll. of Science. FICE 1963; FIMechE 1964; FIStructE 1970; FCIArb 1968. Commd REME, 1944; served India and Burma, attached Indian Army, 1944–47. Engineer: with Merz and McLellan, 1947–58; with Taylor Woodrow, 1958–60. Mem., Overseas Projects Bd, 1984–. Institution of Structural Engineers: Mem. Council, 1976–; Vice Pres., 1981–84; Pres., 1984–85; Institution of Civil Engineers: Mem. Council, 1978–81 and 1982–; Vice-Pres., 1985–. Pres., British Section, Société des Ingénieurs et Scientifiques de France, 1980; Chm., British Consultants Bureau, 1978–80; Member: Council for Environmental Science and Engrg, 1981–85; Comité des Bureaux d'Ingénerie, 1978–80; Council, British Bd of Agrément, 1982–; Court, Cranfield Inst. of Technol., 1970–80. *Publications:* professional and technical papers in engrg jls. *Recreations:* sailing, gardening. *Address:* Willows, The Byeway, West Wittering, Chichester, West Sussex PO20 8LU. *T:* Birdham 514199. *Club:* Caledonian.

PATERSON, Dame Betty (Fraser Ross), DBE 1981 (CBE 1973); JP; DL; Chairman: NW Thames Regional Health Authority, 1973–84; National Staff Advisory Committee for England and Wales (Nurses and Midwives), 1975–84; *b* 14 March 1916; *d* of Robert Ross Russell and Elsie Marian Russell (*née* Fraser); *m* 1940, Ian Douglas Paterson; one *s* one *d*. *Educ:* Harrogate Coll.; Western Infirmary, Glasgow. Mem. Chartered Soc. of Physiotherapy (MCSP). County Comr, Herts Girl Guides, 1950–57. Member: Herts CC, 1952–74 (Alderman 1959–74; Chm., 1969–73); NE Metropolitan Regional Hosp. Bd, 1960–74; Governing Body, Royal Hosp. of St Bartholomew, 1960–74; Commn for the New Towns, England and Wales, 1961–75 (Dep. Chm., 1971–75); Governing Body, Bishop's Stortford Coll., 1967–81; Central Health Services Council, 1969–74; Gen. Council, King Edward's Hosp. Fund for London, 1975–84 (Management Cttee, 1975–80); Pres., Herts Assoc. of Local Councils, 1980–. JP Herts, 1950 (Chm. Bishop's Stortford Bench, 1978–86); DL Herts, 1980. *Recreations:* music, cooking, foreign travel. *Address:* Twyford Bury, Bishop's Stortford, Herts. *T:* Bishop's Stortford 53184.

PATERSON, Sir Dennis (Craig), Kt 1976; MB, BS 1953, MD 1983; FRCS, FRACS; Director and Chief Orthopaedic Surgeon, Adelaide Children's Hospital, since 1970; Consultant Orthopaedic Surgeon: Royal Adelaide Hospital, since 1964; Queen Victoria Hospital, since 1968; *b* 14 Oct. 1930; *s* of Gilbert Charles Paterson and Thelma Drysdale

Paterson; *m* 1955, Mary, *d* of Frederick Mansell Hardy; one *s* three *d*. *Educ:* Collegiate Sch. of St Peter; Univ. of Adelaide (MB, BS 1953). FRCS 1958, FRACS 1961. Res. Med. Officer: Royal Adelaide Hosp., 1954; Adelaide Children's Hosp., 1956; Registrar, Robert Jones & Agnes Hunt Orthop. Hosp., Oswestry, Shropshire, 1958–60; Sen. Registrar, Royal Adelaide Hosp., 1960–62; Cons. Orthop. Surg., Repatriation Gen. Hosp., Adelaide, 1962–70; Adelaide Children's Hospital: Asst Hon. Orthop. Surg., 1964–66; Sen. Hon. Orthop. Surg., 1966–70; Mem. Bd of Management, 1976–84; Chm., Med. Adv. Cttee, 1976–84; Chm., Med. Staff Cttee, 1976–84. Amer./British/Canadian Trav. Prof., 1966. Royal Australasian Coll. of Surgeons: Mem., Bd of Orthop. Surg., 1974–82, 1984– (Chm., 1977–82); Mem., Court of Examnrs, 1974–84; Mem., SA Cttee, 1974–78; Fellow: British Orthopaedic Assoc.; RSocMed; Member: Aust. Orthopaedic Assoc. (Censor-in-Chief, 1976–80; Dir, Continuing Educn, 1982–85); AMA; Internat. Scoliosis Res. Soc.; SICOT (Aust. Nat. Delegate, 1975–84, First Vice-Pres., 1984–87); Paediatric Orthopaedic Soc.; W Pacific Orthopaedic Soc.; Hon. Mem., American Acad. of Orthopaedic Surgeons, 1981. Pres., Crippled Children's Assoc. of South Australia Inc., 1970–84 (Mem. Council, 1966–70). Life Mem., S Aust. Cricket Assoc. Queen's Jubilee Medal, 1977. *Publications:* over 60 articles in Jl of Bone and Joint Surg., Clin. Orthopaedics and Related Res., Aust. and NZ Jl of Surg., Med. Jl of Aust., Western Pacific Jl of Orthop. Surg. *Recreations:* tennis, golf, gardening. *Address:* 31 Myall Avenue, Kensington Gardens, SA 5068, Australia. *T:* 08 3323364. *Clubs:* Adelaide, Royal Adelaide Golf, Kooyonga Golf (Adelaide).

PATERSON, Francis, (Frank), FCIT; General Manager, Eastern Region, British Rail, York, 1978–85; Member, British Railways (Eastern) Board, 1978–85; *b* 5 April 1930; *s* of Francis William Paterson and Cecilia Eliza Reid Brownie; *m* 1950, Grace Robertson; two *s* two *d*. *Educ:* Robert Gordon's Coll., Aberdeen. Joined LNER as Junior Clerk, 1946; clerical and supervisory positions in NE Scotland; management training, Scotland, 1956–59; various man-management, operating and marketing posts, Scotland, Lincs and Yorks, 1960–66; Operating Supt, Glasgow North, 1967–68; Sales Manager, Edinburgh, 1968; Asst Divl Manager, S Wales, 1968–70; Dir, United Welsh Transport, 1968–70; Harbour Comr, Newport Harbour, 1968–70; Divl Manager, Central Div., Southern Region, 1970–75; Director: Southdown Motor Services Ltd, 1970–73; Brighton, Hove & District Omnibus Co., 1970–73; Dep. Gen. Man., Southern Region, 1975–77; Chief Freight Manager, British Railways Bd, 1977–78. Vice-Chm., Nat. Railway Mus. Cttee, 1984– (Mem., 1978–); Member: CBI Southern Regional Council, 1975–77; CBI Transport Policy Cttee, 1977–78; Council, CIT, 1979–84. FCIT 1978. Mem. Court, Univ. of York, 1981–. Officer Brother of St John. *Publications:* papers to transport societies. *Recreations:* transport, travel, hill walking, country pursuits, Scottish culture, enjoying grandchildren. *Address:* Alligin, 97 Main Street, Askham Bryan, York YO2 3QS. *T:* York 708478.

PATERSON, Frank David; His Honour Judge Paterson; a Circuit Judge (formerly County Court Judge), since 1968; *b* 10 July 1918; *yr s* of late David Paterson and Dora Paterson, Liverpool; *m* 1953, Barbara Mary, 2nd *d* of late Oswald Ward Gillow and Alice Gillow, Formby; one *s* two *d*. *Educ:* Calderstones Preparatory Sch. and Quarry Bank High Sch., Liverpool; Univ. of Liverpool (LLB). Called to Bar, Gray's Inn, 1941; Warden, Unity Boys' Club, Liverpool, 1941; Asst Warden, Florence Inst. for Boys, Liverpool, 1943. Practised on Northern Circuit. Chairman: Min. of Pensions and Nat. Insce Tribunal, Liverpool, 1957; Mental Health Review Tribunal for SW Lancashire and Cheshire, 1963. Asst Dep. Coroner, City of Liverpool, 1960. *Address:* Vailima, 2 West Lane, Formby, Liverpool L37 7BA. *T:* Formby 74345. *Club:* Athenæum (Liverpool).

PATERSON, Sir George (Mutlow), Kt 1959; OBE 1946; QC (Sierra Leone) 1950; Chairman, Industrial Tribunals, 1965–79; *b* 3 Dec. 1906; *e s* of late Dr G. W. Paterson; *m* 1935, Audrey Anita, *d* of late Major C. C. B. Morris, CBE, MC; one *s* two *d*. *Educ:* Grenada Boys' School; St John's College, Cambridge. Appointed to Nigerian Administrative Service, 1929. Called to the Bar, Inner Temple, 1933. Magistrate, Nigeria, 1936; Crown Counsel, Tanganyika, 1938. War of 1939–45: served with the King's African Rifles, 1939 (wounded 1940); Occupied Enemy Territories Admin., 1941; Lieutenant-Colonel 1945. Solicitor-General, Tanganyika, 1946; Attorney-General, Sierra Leone, 1949, Ghana, 1954–57; Chief Justice of Northern Rhodesia, 1957–61, retired 1961; appointed to hold an inquiry into proposed amendments to the Potato Marketing Scheme, 1962; appointed legal chairman (part-time), Pensions Appeal Tribunals, 1962; appointed chairman Industrial Tribunals, South Western Region, 1965. *Recreations:* shooting, gardening, genealogy. *Address:* St George's, Westbury, Sherborne, Dorset. *T:* Sherborne 814003. *Club:* Bath and County (Bath).
See also T. P. P. Clifford.

PATERSON, Sqdn-Ldr Ian Veitch, CBE 1969; DL; JP; Deputy Chairman, Local Government Boundary Commission for Scotland, 1974–80; *b* 17 Aug. 1911; *s* of Andrew Wilson Paterson; *m* 1940, Anne Weir, *d* of Thomas Brown; two *s* one *d*. *Educ:* Lanark Grammar School; Glasgow University. Served RAF, 1940–45. Entered local govt service, Lanark, 1928; Principal Legal Asst, Aberdeen CC; Lanarkshire: Dep. County Clerk, 1949; County Clerk, 1956, resigned 1974. Chm., Working Party who produced The New Scottish Local Authorities Organisation and Management structures, 1973. DL Lanarkshire (Strathclyde), 1963; JP Hamilton (formerly Lanarkshire). *Address:* 35 Stewarton Drive, Cambuslang, Glasgow.

PATERSON, (James Edmund) Neil, MA; Author; *b* 31 Dec. 1915; *s* of late James Donaldson Paterson, MA, BL; *m* 1939, Rosabelle, MA, 3rd *d* of late David MacKenzie, MC, MA; two *s* one *d*. *Educ:* Banff Academy; Edinburgh Univ. Served in minesweepers, War of 1939–45, Lieut RNVR, 1940–46. Director: Grampian Television; Scottish Film Production Trust; Consultant, Films of Scotland (Mem., 1954–76; Dir, 1976–78); Member: Scottish Arts Council, 1967–76 (Vice-Chm., 1974–76); Arts Council of Great Britain, 1974–76; Governor: Nat. Film Sch., 1970–80; Pitlochry Festival Theatre, 1966–76; British Film Institute, 1958–60; Atlantic Award in Literature, 1946; Award of American Academy of Motion Picture Arts and Sciences, 1960. *Publications:* The China Run, 1948; Behold Thy Daughter, 1950; And Delilah, 1951; Man on the Tight Rope, 1953; The Kidnappers, 1957; film stories and screen plays. *Recreations:* golf, fishing. *Address:* St Ronans, Crieff, Perthshire. *T:* 2615.

PATERSON, James Rupert; HM Diplomatic Service; Consul-General, Istanbul, since 1985; *b* 7 Aug. 1932; *s* of late Major Robert Paterson, MC, Seaforth Highlanders and Mrs Josephine Paterson; *m* 1956, Kay Dineen; two *s* two *d*. *Educ:* Nautical Coll., Pangbourne; RMA, Sandhurst. Commnd RA, 1953 (Tombs Meml Prize); Staff Coll., Camberley, 1963; retd from Army with rank of Major, 1970; joined FCO, 1970; First Sec., Pakistan, 1972; Dep. High Comr, Trinidad and Tobago, 1975; Ambassador to the Mongolian People's Republic, 1982. *Recreations:* letter-writing, ballet, golf. *Address:* c/o Foreign and Commonwealth Office, King Charles Street, SW1A 2AH; c/o Barclays Bank, Carshalton Beeches, Surrey SM5 3LA.

PATERSON, James Veitch; Sheriff of the Lothian and Borders (formerly Roxburgh, Berwick and Selkirk) at Jedburgh, Selkirk and Duns, since 1963; *b* 16 April 1928; *s* of John Robert Paterson, ophthalmic surgeon, and Jeanie Gouinlock; *m* 1956, Ailie, *o d* of Lt-Comdr Sir (George) Ian Clark Hutchison, *qv*; one *s* one *d*. *Educ:* Peebles High School; Edinburgh Academy; Lincoln College, Oxford; Edinburgh University. Admitted to Faculty of Advocates, 1953. *Recreations:* fishing, shooting, gardening. *Address:* Sunnyside, Melrose, Roxburghshire. *T:* Melrose 2502. *Club:* New (Edinburgh).

PATERSON, John Allan; Agent-General in London and Deputy Minister Abroad for Province of New Brunswick, 1968–75; *b* Montreal, 20 May 1909; *s* of William A. and M. Ethel Paterson; *m* 1935, Elizabeth Stewart Messenger; four *s*. *Educ:* Westmount, Quebec; Mount Allison Univ. (BSc 1932); Queen's Univ. Prudential Insurance Co. of America, 1934–46; RCAF 1941–45 (Sqdn Ldr); New Brunswick Dept of Industry, 1946–68 (Deputy Minister, 1956); Provincial Co-ordinator of Civil Defence, 1950–55; Bd of Comrs, Oromocto, 1956–63; Chm., Provincial Govts of Canada Trade and Industry Council, 1956–57, 1961–62, 1964–65 and 1966–67. Mem. Bd of Regents, Mount Allison Univ., 1959–63; Pres. Oromocto Develt Corp., 1963–68. *Publication:* (co-author) The New Brunswick Economy, Past Present and Future, 1955. *Recreations:* golf, motoring, fishing. *Address:* The Coach House, Back Lane, Great Malvern, Worcs.

PATERSON, John Mower Alexander, OBE 1985; JP; Vice Lord-Lieutenant of Buckinghamshire, since 1984; Chairman, BETEC PLC (formerly Bifurcated Engineering), Aylesbury, 1960–85 (Director); *b* 9 Nov. 1920; *s* of Leslie Martin Paterson and Olive Hariette Mower; *m* 1944, Daisy Miriam Ballanger Marshall; one *s* two *d*. *Educ:* Oundle; Queens' Coll., Cambridge (MA Hons). Served War, RE, 1941–46. Cincinnati Milling Machines, Birmingham, 1946–48; Dir and Works Man., Bifurcated & Tubular Rivet Co. Ltd, Aylesbury, 1948–60; Dep. Chm., Rickmansworth Water Co., 1986– (Dir, 1984–). Member: Southern Regional Council, CBI, 1971–85 (Chm., 1974–76); Grand Council, CBI, 1971–84. Gen. Comr of Taxes, Aylesbury Div., 1959–. Mem., Lloyd's, 1960–. Pres., Aylesbury Divl Cons. and Unionist Assoc., 1984–85; Chairman: Bucks Council for Voluntary Youth Services, 1978–; Council, Order of St John in Buckinghamshire, 1981– (Mem., 1980–); Member: Management Cttee, Waddesdon Manor (NT), 1980–; Governing Body, Aylesbury Coll. of Further Educn, 1961– (Chm., 1977–); Governing Body, Aylesbury GS, 1974– (Chm., 1984–). JP 1962, High Sheriff 1978, DL 1982, Bucks. CStJ 1986. *Recreations:* sailing, veteran cars, gardening. *Address:* Park Hill, Potter Row, Great Missenden, Bucks HP16 9LT. *T:* Great Missenden 2995. *Clubs:* Royal Ocean Racing; Royal Yacht Squadron (Cowes); Royal Lymington Yacht (Cdre, 1973–76).

PATERSON, Very Rev. John Munn Kirk; Minister of St Paul's Parish Church, Milngavie, since 1970; Moderator of the General Assembly of the Church of Scotland, 1984–85; *b* 8 Oct. 1922; *s* of George Kirk Paterson and Sarah Ferguson Paterson (*née* Wilson); *m* 1946, Geraldine Lilian Parker; two *s* one *d*. *Educ:* Hillhead High School, Glasgow; Edinburgh Univ. MA, BD. RAF, 1942–46 (Defence and Victory medals, Italy Star, 1945). Insurance Official, 1940–58 (ACII 1951); Assistant Minister, 1958–64; Ordained Minister of Church of Scotland, 1964–. Hon. DD Aberdeen, 1986. *Recreations:* fishing, hill walking. *Address:* 8 Buchanan Street, Milngavie, Glasgow G62 8DD. *T:* 041–956 1043. *Clubs:* New, Caledonian, Royal Over-Seas League (Edinburgh).

PATERSON, Sir John (Valentine) J.; *see* Jardine Paterson.

PATERSON, Neil; *see* Paterson, James Edmund N.

PATERSON, Robert Lancelot, OBE 1980; MC 1945; ERD 1957; part-time Adjudicator, Home Office Immigration Appeals, 1970–83; Director, Merseyside Chamber of Commerce and Industry, 1967–81; *b* 16 May 1918; *e s* of Lancelot Wilson and Sarah Annie Paterson; *m* 1940, Charlotte Orpha, *d* of James and Elizabeth Nicholas; three *s*. *Educ:* Monmouth Sch.; University Coll. of Wales, Aberystwyth (BA); London School of Economics. Commissioned into Border Regt, SR, Dec. 1937; served War of 1939–45, 4th Bn, Border Regt, France, ME, Syria, Tobruk, Burma and India (Chindits, 1943–44); Asst Chief Instr 164 (Inf.), OCTU, 1946. Entered Colonial Admin. Service, Tanganyika, 1947; Dist Officer, 1947–60; Principal Asst Sec., Min. of Home Affairs, 1960–62; prematurely retired on attainment of Independence by Tanganyika. Dep. Sec., Liverpool Chamber of Commerce, 1963–67; Member, Nat. Council, Assoc. of Brit. Chambers of Commerce, 1969–81; Pres., Brit. Chambers of Commerce Executives, 1977–79; Governor, Liverpool Coll. of Commerce, 1967–71; Mem., Liverpool Univ. Appts Bd, 1968–72; *Recreations:* archaeology, gardening. *Address:* 4 Belle Vue Road, Henley-on-Thames, Oxon RG9 1JG.

PATEY, Very Rev. Edward Henry; Dean of Liverpool, 1964–82, now Dean Emeritus; *b* 12 Aug. 1915; *s* of Walter Patey, MD, and Dorothy Patey; *m* 1942, Margaret Ruth Olivia Abbott; one *s* three *d*. *Educ:* Marlborough College; Hertford College, Oxford; Westcott House, Cambridge. Assistant Curate, St Mary-at-the-Walls, Colchester, 1939; MA (Oxon) 1941; Assistant Curate Bishopwearmouth Parish Church, Sunderland, 1942; Youth Chaplain to the Bishop of Durham, 1946; Vicar of Oldland, with Longwell Green, Bristol, 1950; Secretary, Youth Department, The British Council of Churches, 1952; Assistant Gen. Secretary, The British Council of Churches, 1955; Canon Residentiary of Coventry Cathedral, 1958. Hon. LLD Liverpool, 1980. *Publications:* Religion in the Club, 1956; Boys and Girls Growing Up, 1957; Worship in the Club, 1961; A Doctor's Life of Jesus, 1962; Young People Now, 1964; Enquire Within, 1966; Look out for the Church, 1969; Burning Questions, 1971; Don't Just Sit There, 1974; Christian Lifestyle, 1975; All in Good Faith, 1978; Open the Doors, 1978; Open the Book, 1981; I Give You This Ring, 1982; My Liverpool Life, 1983; Becoming An Anglican, 1985; Preaching on Special Occasions, 1985; Questions For Today, 1986. *Recreations:* reading, listening to music, walking. *Address:* 139 High Street, Malmesbury, Wilts.

PATON; *see* Noel-Paton, family name of **Baron Ferrier.**

PATON, Major Adrian Gerard Nigel H.; *see* Hadden-Paton.

PATON, Alan (Stewart); writer; was National President of the South African Liberal Party until it was made an illegal organisation in 1968; living at Botha's Hill, Natal; *b* Pietermaritzburg, 11 Jan. 1903; *s* of James Paton; *m* 1st, 1928, Doris Olive (*d* 1967), *d* of George Francis; two *s*; 2nd, 1969, Anne Hopkins. *Educ:* Natal Univ. (BSc, BEd). Formerly Principal Diepkloof Reformatory, 1935–48. Chubb Fellow, Yale Univ., 1973. Hon. LHD, Yale, 1954; Hon. DLitt: Kenyon Coll., 1962; Univ. of Natal, 1968; Trent Univ., 1971; Harvard, 1971; Rhodes, 1972; Williamette Univ., 1974; Michigan, 1977; Univ. of Durban-Westville; Hon. DD Edinburgh, 1971; Hon. LLB Univ. of Witwatersrand, 1975. Freedom House Award (USA), 1960. *Publications:* Cry, the Beloved Country, 1948; Too Late the Phalarope, 1953; Land and People of South Africa, 1955; South Africa in Transition (with Dan Weiner), 1956; Debbie Go Home (short stories), 1961; Hofmeyr (biography), 1965; Instrument of Thy Peace, 1968; The Long View, 1969; Kontakion For You Departed, 1969; Apartheid and the Archbishop, 1973; Knocking on the Door, 1975; Towards the Mountain (autobiog.), 1981; Ah, But Your Land is Beautiful, 1981. *Address:* PO Box 278, Hillcrest, Natal 3650, South Africa.

PATON, Sir Angus; *see* Paton, Sir T. A. L.

PATON, Rev. Canon David Macdonald; Chaplain to the Queen, 1972–83; Rector of St Mary de Crypt and St John the Baptist, Gloucester, 1970–81; Vicar of Christ Church, Gloucester, 1979–81; Hon. Canon of Canterbury Cathedral, 1966–80 (now Canon Emeritus); *b* 9 Sept. 1913; *e s* of late Rev. William Paton, DD and Grace Mackenzie Paton (*née* Macdonald); *m* 1946, Alison Georgina Stewart; three *s*. *Educ*: Repton; Brasenose Coll., Oxford. BA 1936, MA 1939. SCM Sec., Birmingham, 1936–39; Deacon 1939, Priest 1941; Missionary in China, 1940–44 and 1947–50; Chaplain and Librarian, Westcott House, Cambridge, 1945–46; Vicar of Yardley Wood, Birmingham, 1952–56; Editor, SCM Press, 1956–59; Sec., Council for Ecumenical Co-operation of Church Assembly, 1959–63; Sec., Missionary and Ecumenical Council of Church Assembly, 1964–69; Chairman: Churches' China Study Project, 1972–79; Gloucester Civic Trust, 1972–77. Hon. Fellow, Selly Oak Colls, 1981. *Publications*: Christian Missions and the Judgment of God, 1953; (with John T. Martin) Paragraphs for Sundays and Holy Days, 1957; (ed) Essays in Anglican Self-Criticism, 1958; (ed) The Ministry of the Spirit, 1960; Anglicans and Unity, 1962; (ed) Reform of the Ministry, 1968; (ed) Breaking Barriers (Report of WCC 5th Assembly, Nairobi, 1975), 1976; (ed with C.H. Long) The Compulsion of the Spirit, 1983; (ed) The 1483 Gloucester Charter in History, 1983; R.O.: The Life and Times of Bishop Ronald Hall of Hong Kong, 1985. *Address*: 37A Cromwell Street, Gloucester GL1 1RE. *T*: Gloucester 422051.

See also Bishop of Birmingham, Ven. M. J. M. Paton, Prof. Sir W. D. M. Paton.

PATON, Douglas Shaw F.; *see* Forrester-Paton.

PATON, Maj.-Gen. Douglas Stuart, CBE 1983 (MBE 1961); FFCM; Commander Medical HQ BAOR, 1983–85; *b* 3 March 1926; *s* of Stuart Paton and Helen Kathleen Paton (*née* Hooke); *m* 1957, Jennifer Joan Land; two *d*. *Educ*: Sherborne; Bristol University. MB ChB 1951; FFCM 1982. Commissioned RAMC, 1952; served Middle East (Canal Zone), Malaya, Hong Kong and UK, 1952–61; 16 Para Bde, 1961–66; jssc 1966; CO BMH Terendak, Malaysia, 1967–70; MoD, 1970–73; CO Cambridge Mil. Hosp., Aldershot, 1973–76; rcds 1977; DDMS HQ 1 (BR) Corps, 1978–81; Dep. Dir-Gen., Army Med. Services, MoD, 1981–83. QHP 1981. CStJ 1986. *Publications*: contribs to Jl RAMC. *Recreations*: golf, skiing, travel, opera, gardening. *Address*: Brampton, Springfield Road, Camberley, Surrey GU15 1AB.

PATON, Ven. Michael John Macdonald; Archdeacon of Sheffield, since 1978; *b* 25 Nov. 1922; *s* of late Rev. William Paton, DD, and Grace Mackenzie Paton (*née* Macdonald); *m* 1952, Isobel Margaret Hogarth; one *s* four *d*. *Educ*: Repton School; Magdalen Coll., Oxford (MA). Indian Army, 1942–46; HM Foreign Service, 1948–52; Lincoln Theological Coll., 1952–54; Deacon 1954, priest 1955; Curate, All Saints', Gosforth, Newcastle upon Tyne, 1954–57; Vicar, St Chad's, Sheffield, 1957–67; Chaplain, United Sheffield Hosps, 1967–70; Vicar, St Mark's, Broomhill, Sheffield, 1970–78. *Publications*: contrib. to: Essays in Anglican Self-criticism, 1958; Religion and Medicine, 1976. *Recreations*: hill walking, music. *Address*: 62 Kingfield Road, Sheffield S11 9AU. *T*: Sheffield 557782.

See also Bishop of Birmingham, Rev. Canon D. M. Paton, Prof. Sir W. D. M. Paton.

PATON, Sir Stuart (Henry), KCVO 1965; CBE 1945; Captain RN, retired; *b* 9 July 1900; *s* of William Henry Paton and Winifred Powell, Norwood; *m* 1925, Dorothy Morgan (*d* 1984), Shrewsbury; two *s* two *d*. *Educ*: Hillside, Godalming; RN Colleges, Osborne and Dartmouth. Served European War: Midshipman, HMS Marlborough, Grand Fleet, 1916; Sub-Lt, HMS Orcadia, English Channel, 1918. Specialised as Torpedo Officer; posts Lieut to Commander: Mediterranean and Home Fleets, Admiralty Plans Division, and New Zealand. War of 1939–45: HMS Vernon, Captain, 1940; Admiralty, Joint Intelligence Staff, 1941; Comd HMS Curacoa, E. Coast Convoys, 1942; Comd HMS Nigeria, Home Fleet and Eastern Fleet, 1942–44 (despatches Malta Convoy); Admiralty and served as a Dep.-Director, Admin. Planning, 1945–46; student, IDC, 1947; Comd HMS Newcastle, Mediterranean Fleet, 1948–49; Appointed ADC to King George VI, 1949; retired, 1950; General Secretary to King George's Fund for Sailors, 1950–65. *Recreations*: gardening, photography. *Address*: Bernard Sunley Nursing Home, College Road, Maybury Hill, Woking, Surrey GU22 8BT. *T*: Woking 24964.

See also Sir J. E. C. Kennon.

PATON, Sir (Thomas) Angus (Lyall), Kt 1973; CMG 1960; FRS 1969; FEng; Consulting Civil Engineer, since 1984; *b* 10 May 1905; *s* of Thomas Lyall Paton and Janet (*née* Gibb); *m* 1932, Eleanor Joan Delmé-Murray (*d* 1964); two *s* two *d*. *Educ*: Cheltenham Coll.; University College, London. Fellow of University College. Joined Sir Alexander Gibb & Partners as pupil, 1925; after experience in UK, Canada, Burma and Turkey on harbour works, hydro-electric projects and industrial development schemes, was taken into partnership, 1938; Senior Partner, 1955–77; Senior Consultant, 1977–84. Responsible for design and supervision of construction of many large industrial factories and for major hydro-electric and irrigation projects, including Owen Falls and Kariba Schemes, and for overall supervision of Indus Basin Project in W. Pakistan; also for economic surveys in Middle East and Africa on behalf of Dominion and Foreign Governments. Member UK Trade Mission to: Arab States, 1953; Egypt, Sudan and Ethiopia, 1955. Mem. NERC, 1969–72. Pres. ICE, 1970–71; Chm., Council of Engineering Instns, 1973; Past Chairman Assoc. of Consulting Engineers. FICE (Hon. FICE, 1975); FIStructE, Fellow Amer. Soc. of Civil Engineers, Past Pres., British Section, Soc. of Civil Engineers (France); a Vice-Pres., Royal Soc., 1977–78; For. Associate, Nat. Acad. of Engineering, USA, 1979. Founder Fellow, Fellowship of Engineering, 1976; FRSA. Fellow, Imperial Coll., London, 1978. Hon. DSc: London, 1977; Bristol, 1981. *Publications*: Power from Water, 1960; technical articles on engineering subjects. *Address*: L'Epervier, Route Orange, St Brelade, Jersey. *T*: 45619. *Club*: Athenæum.

PATON, Prof. Sir William (Drummond Macdonald), Kt 1979; CBE 1968; MA, DM; FRS 1956; FRCP 1969; JP; Professor of Pharmacology in the University of Oxford, and Fellow of Balliol College, 1959–84, now Emeritus Professor and Emeritus Fellow; Honorary Director, Wellcome Institute for History of Medicine, since 1983; *b* 5 May 1917; 3rd *s* of late Rev. William Paton, DD, and Grace Mackenzie Paton; *m* 1942, Phoebe Margaret, *d* of Thomas Rooke and Elizabeth Frances (*née* Pearce); no *c*. *Educ*: Winchester House Sch., Brackley; Repton Sch.; New Coll., Oxford (Scholar; Hon. Fellow, 1980); University College Hospital Medical Sch. BA (Oxon) Natural Sciences, Physiology, 1st class hons, 1938; Scholarships: Theodore Williams (Physiology), 1938; Christopher Welch, 1939; Jesse Theresa Rowden, 1939; Demonstrator in Physiology, Oxford, 1938–39; Goldsmid Exhibition, UCH Medical Sch., 1939; Ed. UCH Magazine, 1941; Fellowes Gold Medal in Clinical Med., 1941; BM, BCh Oxon, 1942; House physician, UCH Med. Unit, 1942. Pathologist King Edward VII Sanatorium, 1943–44; Member scientific staff, National Institute for Medical Research, 1944–52; MA 1948. Reader in Pharmacology, University College and UCH Med. Sch., 1952–54; DM 1953; Professor of Pharmacology, RCS, 1954–59. Delegate, Clarendon Press, 1967–72; Rhodes Trustee, 1968– (Chm., 1978–82). Chm., Cttee for Suppression of Doping, 1970–71; Member: Pharmacological Soc. (Chm. Edtl Bd, 1969–74, Hon. Mem., 1981); Physiological Soc. (Hon. Sec. 1951–57; Hon. Mem., 1985); British Toxicological Soc., 1980– (Chm., 1982–83); MRC, 1963–67; Council, Royal Society, 1967–69; British Nat. Cttee for

History of Science, 1972– (Chm., 1980–85); Council, Inst. Study of Drug Dependence, 1969–75; Central Adv. Council for Science and Technology, 1970; DHSS Independent Cttee on Smoking, 1978–83; Adv. Cttee on Animal Experiments, 1980–85; Advr, HO Breath-alcohol Survey, 1984–85. Pres., Inst. of Animal Technicians, 1969–75, Vice-Pres., 1976–; Chm., Research Defence Soc., 1972–78 (Paget Lectr, 1978). Wellcome Trustee, 1978–. Consultant, RN (Diving), 1978–82. Hon. Member: Soc. Franc. d'Allergie; Australian Acad. Forensic Sci.; Corresp. Mem., German Pharmacological Soc.; Hon. Lectr, St Mary's Hosp. Med. Sch., 1950; Visiting Lecturer: Swedish Univs, 1953; Brussels, 1956. Robert Campbell Oration, 1957; Lectures: Clover, 1958; Bertram Louis Abrahams, RCP, 1962; Ivison Macadam, RCSE, 1973; Osler, RCP, 1978; Cass, Dundee, 1981; Scheuler, Tulane, 1981; Hope Winch, Sunderland, 1982. Editor with R. V. Jones, Notes and Records of Royal Soc., 1971–. FRSA 1973; Hon. FFARCS 1975; Hon. FRSM 1982. JP St Albans, 1956. Hon. DSc London, 1985; DUniv Surrey, 1986. Bengue Meml Prize, 1952; Cameron Prize, 1956; Gairdner Foundn Award, 1959; Gold Medal, Soc. of Apothecaries, 1976; Baly Medal, RCP, 1983; Osler Meml Medal, Univ. of Oxford, 1986. *Publications*: Pharmacological Principles and Practice (with J. P. Payne), 1968; Man and Mouse: animals in medical research, 1984; papers on diving, caisson disease, histamine, synaptic transmission, drug action and drug dependence in physiological and pharmacological journals. *Recreations*: music, old books. *Address*: 13 Staverton Road, Oxford. *Club*: Athenæum.

See also Bishop of Birmingham, Rev. Canon D. M. Paton, Ven. M. J. M. Paton, Dr J. F. Stokes.

PATRICK, Graham McIntosh, CMG 1968; CVO 1981; DSC 1943; Under Secretary, Department of the Environment, 1971–81, retired; *b* 17 Oct. 1921; *m* 1945, Barbara Worboys; two *s*. *Educ*: Dundee High Sch.; St Andrews Univ. RNVR (Air Branch), 1940–46. Entered Ministry of Works, 1946; Regional Director: Middle East Region, 1965–67; South West Region, DoE, 1971–75; Chm., South West Economic Planning Bd, 1971–75; Dir, Scottish Services, PSA, 1975–81. *Address*: 3 Blueberry Downs, Coastguard Road, Budleigh Salterton, Devon EX9 6NW. *Club*: New (Edinburgh).

PATRICK, (James) McIntosh, ROI 1949; ARE; RSA 1957 (ARSA 1949); Painter and Etcher; *b* 1907; *s* of Andrew G. Patrick and Helen Anderson; *m* 1933, Janet (*d* 1983), *d* of W. Arnot Watterston; one *s* one *d*. *Educ*: Morgan Academy, Dundee; Glasgow School of Art. Awarded Guthrie Award RSA, 1935; painting Winter in Angus purchased under the terms of the Chantrey Bequest, 1935; paintings purchased for Scottish Nat. Gall. of Modern Art; National Gallery, Millbank; National Gallery of South Africa, Cape Town; National Gallery of South Australia; Scottish Contemp. Art Assoc.; and Municipal collections Manchester, Aberdeen, Hull, Dundee, Liverpool, Glasgow, Greenock, Perth, Southport, Newport (Mon.), Arbroath, also for Lady Leverhulme Art Gallery, etc.; etchings in British Museum and other print collections. Served War of 1939–46, North Africa and Italy; Captain (General List). Hon. LLD Dundee, 1973. *Recreations*: gardening, music. *Address*: c/o Fine Art Society, 148 New Bond Street, W1; The Shrubbery, Magdalen Yard Road, Dundee. *T*: Dundee 68561. *Club*: Scottish Arts (Edinburgh).

PATRICK, John Bowman; Sheriff of North Strathclyde (formerly Renfrew and Argyll) at Greenock, 1968–83; *b* 29 Feb. 1916; *s* of late John Bowman Patrick, Boot and Shoe maker, Greenock, and late Barbara Patrick (*née* James); *m* 1945, Sheina Struthers McCrea; one *d*. *Educ*: Greenock Academy; Edinburgh Univ.; Glasgow Univ. MA Edinburgh, 1937. Served War in Royal Navy, Dec. 1940–Dec. 1945; conscripted as Ordinary Seaman, finally Lieut RNVR. LLB Glasgow 1946. Admitted as a Solicitor in Scotland, June 1947; admitted to Faculty of Advocates, July 1956. Sheriff of Inverness, Moray, Nairn, Ross and Cromarty at Fort William and Portree (Skye), 1961–68. *Address*: 77 Union Street, Greenock, Renfrewshire PA16 8BG. *T*: Greenock 20712.

PATRICK, Margaret Kathleen, OBE 1976; District/Superintendent Physiotherapist, Central Birmingham Health Authority (Teaching) (formerly United Birmingham Hospitals Hospital Management Committee), since 1951; *b* 5 June 1923; *d* of late Roy and Rose Patrick. *Educ*: Godolphin and Latymer Sch., London; Guy's Hosp. Sch. of Physiotherapy. BA, Open Univ., 1980. MCSP. Chm. Physio. Adv. Cttee, and Mem. Health Care Planning for Elderly, Birmingham AHA (T). Member: Exec., Whitley Council PTA, 1960–75 (Chm., PTA Cttee C, 1960–75); Tunbridge Cttee on Rehab. Services, 1971–72; Hosp. Adv. Service on Geriatrics, 1972; DHSS Working Party on Stat. Data in Physio., 1969–76; Council, Chartered Soc. of Physio., 1953–75 (Exec. Mem., 1960–75; Vice Chm., 1971–75); Birmingham AHA (Teaching), 1979–82; Vice-Chm., Bromsgrove and Redditch HA, 1982–. Assoc. of Supt Chartered Physiotherapists: Chm., 1964–75; Pres., 1971–72. *Publications*: Ultrasound Therapy: a textbook for physiotherapists, 1965; (contrib.) Physiotherapy in some Surgical Conditions, ed Joan Cash, 1977, 2nd edn 1979; contrib. Physiotherapy, and articles on ultrasound therapy, geriatric care, and paediatrics. *Recreation*: gardening. *Address*: General Hospital, Birmingham B4 6NH.

PATTEN, Brian; poet; *b* 7 Feb. 1946. Regents Lectr, Univ. of Calif (San Diego), 1985. *Publications*: poetry: Penguin Modern Poets, 1967; Little Johnny's Confession, 1967; Notes to the Hurrying Man, 1969; The Irrelevant Song, 1971; The Unreliable Nightingale, 1973; Vanishing Trick, 1976; The Shabby Angel, 1978; Grave Gossip, 1979; Love Poems, 1981; Clare's Countryside: a book on John Clare, 1982; New Volume, 1983; novel: Mr Moon's Last Case, 1975 (Mystery Writers of Amer. Award, 1976); for younger readers: The Elephant and the Flower, 1969; Jumping Mouse; 1971; Emma's Doll, 1976; The Sly Cormorant and the Fish: adaptations of The Aesop Fables, 1977; (ed) Gangsters, Ghosts and Dragonflies, 1981; Gargling with Jelly, 1985; plays: The Pig And The Junkle, 1975; (with Roger McGough) The Mouth Trap, 1982; Blind Love, 1983; records: Brian Patten Reading His Own Poetry, 1969; British Poets Of Our Time, 1974; Vanishing Trick, 1976; The Sly Cormorant, 1977. *Address*: c/o Allen and Unwin Ltd, Publishers, 40 Museum Street, WC1. *Club*: Chelsea Arts.

PATTEN, Christopher Francis, MP (C) Bath, since 1979; Minister of State (Minister for Overseas Development), Foreign and Commonwealth Office, since 1986; *b* 12 May 1944; *s* of late Francis Joseph Patten and Joan McCarthy; *m* 1971, Mary Lavender St Leger Thornton; three *d*. *Educ*: St Benedict's School, Ealing; Balliol College, Oxford. Conservative Research Dept, 1966–70; Cabinet Office, 1970–72; Home Office, 1972; Personal Asst to Chairman of Conservative Party, 1972–74; Director, Conservative Research Dept, 1974–79; PPS to Chancellor of Duchy of Lancaster and Leader of House of Commons, 1979–81; to Secretary of State for Social Services, 1981; Parly Under-Sec. of State, NI Office, 1983–1985; Minister of State, DES, 1985–86. Vice Chm., Cons. Parly Finance Cttee, 1981–83; Mem., Select Cttees on Defence and Procedure, 1982–83. *Publication*: The Tory Case, 1983. *Recreations*: reading, gardening, travelling in France. *Address*: 47 Morpeth Mansions, Morpeth Terrace, SW1. *T*: 01–828 3082; Cromwell's Rest, 207 Conkwell, near Winsley, Wilts. *T*: Limpley Stoke 3378. *Club*: Beefsteak.

PATTEN, John Haggitt Charles; MP (C) Oxford West and Abingdon, since 1983 (City of Oxford, 1979–83); Minister of State for Housing, Urban Affairs and Construction, Department of the Environment, since 1985; Fellow of Hertford College, Oxford, since

1972; *b* 17 July 1945; *s* of Jack Patten and late Maria Olga (*née* Sikora); *m* 1978, Louise Alexandra Virginia, 2nd *d* of late John Rowe, Norfolk, and of Claire Rowe, London; one *d*. *Educ:* Wimbledon Coll.; Sidney Sussex Coll., Cambridge (PhD 1972). University Lectr, Univ. of Oxford, 1969–79. Oxford City Councillor, 1973–76. PPS to Mr Leon Brittan and Mr Tim Raison, Ministers of State at the Home Office, 1980–81; Parliamentary Under-Secretary of State: NI Office, 1981–83; DHSS, 1983–85. Editor, Journal of Historical Geography, 1975–80. Mem. Council, Univ. of Reading. *Publications:* The Conservative Opportunity (with Lord Blake), 1976; English Towns, 1500–1700, 1978; Pre-Industrial England, 1979; (ed) The Expanding City, 1983; (with Paul Coones) The Penguin Guide to the Landscape of England and Wales, 1986; articles on economic, regional and envl matters. *Recreation:* talking to my wife. *Address:* House of Commons, SW1; Hertford College, Oxford. *Clubs:* Beefsteak; Clarendon (Oxford).

PATTEN, Prof. Tom, CBE 1981; PhD; FEng 1986; FIMechE; FRSE; consultant; Director, Pict Petroleum plc, since 1981; Professor and Head of Department of Mechanical Engineering, Heriot-Watt University, 1967–82, now Emeritus; *b* 1 Jan. 1926; *s* of late William Patten and of Isabella (*née* Hall); *m* 1950, Jacqueline McLachlan (*née* Wright); one *s* two *d*. *Educ:* Leith Acad.; Edinburgh Univ. (BSc, PhD). CEng, FIMechE 1965; FRSE 1967. Captain REME, 1946–48: served Palestine and Greece. Barry Ostlere & Shepherd Ltd, Kirkcaldy, 1949; Asst Lectr, Lectr and Sen. Lectr, Dept of Engrg, Univ. of Edinburgh, 1950–67; Dir, Inst. of Offshore Engineering, Heriot-Watt Univ., 1972–79; Vice-Principal, Heriot-Watt Univ., 1978–80, Acting Principal, 1980–81. Vis. Res. Fellow, McGill Univ., Canada, 1958. Researches in heat transfer, 1950–83; British and foreign patents for heat exchange and fluid separation devices. Man. Dir, Compact Heat Exchange Ltd, 1970–; Director: Melville Street Investments (Edinburgh) Ltd, 1983–; New Darien Oil Trust plc, 1985–; Seaboard Lloyd Ltd, 1986–; Brown Brothers & Co. Ltd, 1986–; Chm., Environment and Resource Technology Ltd, 1982–. Member: Council, IMechE, 1971–73 and 1975–; Oil Develt Council for Scotland, 1973–78; Offshore Technol. Bd, Dept of Energy, 1985–; SRC Marine Technol. Task Force, 1975–76; Design Council (Scottish Cttee), 1979–82; Council, RSE, 1969–79 (Vice-Pres. RSE, 1976–79); Pres., Soc. for Underwater Technol., 1985–. *Publications:* technical and scientific papers in field of heat transfer in Proc. IMechE, and Internat. Heat Transfer Conf. Proc.; also papers on offshore engineering. *Recreations:* squash, gardening, music. *Address:* 15 Frogston Road West, Edinburgh EH10 7AB. *T:* 031–445 1464. *Clubs:* Caledonian; New (Edinburgh).

PATTERSON, Arthur, CMG 1951; Assistant Secretary, Department of Health and Social Security, 1968–71; *b* 24 June 1906; 2nd *s* of late Alexander Patterson; *m* 1942, Mary Ann Stocks, *er d* of late J. L. Stocks; two *s* one *d*. *Educ:* Methodist Coll., Belfast; Queen's Univ., Belfast; St John's Coll., Cambridge. Entered Ministry of Labour, 1929; Assistant Secretary, 1941; transferred to Ministry of National Insurance, 1945; lent to Cyprus, 1953; Malta, 1956; Jamaica, 1963; Kuwait, 1971. *Address:* 42 Campden Hill Square, W8 7JR. *T:* 01–229 3894.

PATTERSON, Maj.-Gen. Arthur Gordon, CB 1969; DSO 1964; OBE 1961; MC 1945; Director of Army Training, 1969–72; retired; *b* 24 July 1917; *s* of late Arthur Abbey Patterson, Indian Civil Service; *m* 1949, Jean Mary Grant; two *s* one *d*. *Educ:* Tonbridge Sch.; RMC Sandhurst. Commnd, 1938; India and Burma, 1939–45; Staff Coll., Camberley, 1949; jssc 1955; CO 2nd 6th Queen Elizabeth's Own Gurkha Rifles, 1959–61; Comdr 99 Gurkha Inf. Brigade, 1962–64; idc 1965; GOC 17 Div. and Maj.-Gen., Bde of Gurkhas, 1965–69. Col, 6th Queen's Own Gurkha Rifles, 1969–73. *Address:* Burnt House, Benenden, Cranbrook, Kent. *Club:* Naval and Military.

PATTERSON, Ben; *see* Patterson, G.B.

PATTERSON, Rt. Rev. Cecil John, CMG 1958; CBE 1954; DD (Lambeth), 1963; DD (University of Nigeria, Nsukka), 1963; Commander of the Federal Republic (CFR) (Nigeria), 1965; *b* 9 Jan. 1908. *Educ:* St Paul's School; St Catharine's Coll., Cambridge; Bishop's Coll., Cheshunt. London Curacy, 1931–34; Missionary in S Nigeria, 1934–41; Asst Bishop on the Niger, 1942–45; Bishop on the Niger, 1945–69; Archbishop of West Africa, 1961–69; Representative for the Archbishops of Canterbury and York for Community Relations, 1970–72; Hon. Asst Bishop, Diocese of London, 1970–76. Hon. Fellow, St Catharine's Coll., Cambridge, 1963. *Address:* 6 High Park Road, Kew, Surrey TW9 4BH. *T:* 01–876 1697.

PATTERSON, (Constance) Marie, (Mrs Barrie Devney), CBE 1978 (OBE 1973); National Officer, Transport and General Workers' Union, 1976–84 (National Woman Officer, 1963–76); Member of General Council of TUC 1963–84 (Chairman, 1974–75 and 1977); *b* 1 April 1934; *d* of Dr Richard Swanton Abraham; *m* 1st, 1960, Thomas Michael Valentine Patterson (marr. diss. 1976); 2nd, 1984, Barrie Devney. *Educ:* Pendleton High Sch.; Bedford Coll., Univ. of London (BA). Member: Exec., Confedn of Shipbuilding and Engrg Unions, 1966–84 (Pres., 1977–78); Hotel and Catering Trng Bd, 1966–; Equal Opportunities Commn, 1975–84; Central Arbitration Commn, 1976–. Dir of Remploy, 1966–. Lay Mem., Press Council, 1964–70. Hon. DSc Salford, 1975. *Recreations:* cooking, sight-seeing. *Address:* 15 Mackeson Road, NW3. *T:* 01–267 1820.

PATTERSON, Eric, MBE 1970; HM Diplomatic Service; Consul-General, Auckland, since 1982, and Director for Trade Promotion in New Zealand, since 1983; *b* 2 May 1930; *s* of Richard and Elizabeth Patterson; *m* 1953, Doris (*née* Mason); two *s*. *Educ:* Hookergate Grammar Sch., Co. Durham. Served Royal Signals, 1948–50. Local govt service, 1947–50; Lord Chancellor's Dept, 1950–52; BoT, 1952–62; Asst Trade Comr, Halifax, NS, 1962–67; Second Sec. (Commercial), Khartoum, 1967–70; First Sec. (Commercial), The Hague, 1970–74; FCO, 1974–76; First Sec. (Commercial), Warsaw, 1976–80; FCO, 1980–82. *Recreations:* golf, sailing, photography, fly-fishing. *Address:* 20 Dudley Road, Auckland, New Zealand; c/o Foreign and Commonwealth Office, SW1. *Clubs:* Civil Service; Royal Over-Seas League, Northern, Auckland, Auckland Golf, Remuera Golf, Royal New Zealand Yacht Squadron (Auckland).

PATTERSON, George Benjamin, (Ben); Member (C) Kent West, European Parliament, since 1979; *b* 21 April 1939; *s* of late Eric James Patterson and of Ethel Patterson; *m* 1970, Felicity Barbara Anne Raybould; one *s* one *d*. *Educ:* Westminster Sch.; Trinity Coll., Cambridge (MA); London Sch. of Economics. Lecturer, Swinton Conservative Coll., 1961–65; Editor (at Conservative Political Centre), CPC Monthly Report, 1965–74; Dep. Head, London Office of European Parlt, 1974–79. *Publications:* The Character of Conservatism, 1973; Direct Elections to the European Parliament, 1974; Europe and Employment, 1984; Vredeling and All That, 1984. *Recreations:* squash, reading science fiction. *Address:* 84 London Road, Tunbridge Wells, Kent TN1 1ED. *T:* Tunbridge Wells 22582; Elm Hill House, Hawkhurst, Kent TN18 4XU. *Club:* Institute of Directors.

PATTERSON, Harry; novelist; *b* 27 July 1929; *s* of Henry Patterson and Rita Higgins Bell; *m* 1st, 1958, Amy Margaret Hewitt (marr. diss. 1984); one *s* three *d*; 2nd, 1985, Denise Lesley Anne Palmer. *Educ:* Roundhay Sch., Leeds; Beckett Park Coll. for Teachers; London Sch. of Economics as external student (BSc(Hons) Sociology). FRSA. NCO, The Blues, 1947–50. 1950–58: tried everything from being a clerk to a circus tent-hand; 1958–72: variously a schoolmaster, Lectr in Liberal Studies, Leeds Polytechnic, Sen. Lectr in Education, James Graham Coll. and Tutor in Sch. Practice, Leeds Univ.; since age of 41, engaged in full-time writing career. Dual citizenship, British/Irish. *Publications include:* (as Jack Higgins) Prayer for the Dying, 1973 (filmed 1985); The Eagle has Landed, 1975 (filmed 1976); Storm Warning, 1976; Day of Judgement, 1978; Solo, 1980; Luciano's Luck, 1981; Touch the Devil, 1982; Exocet, 1983; Confessional, 1985 (filmed 1985); (as Harry Patterson) The Valhalla Exchange, 1978; To Catch a King, 1979 (filmed 1983); Dillinger, 1983; and many others (including The Violent Enemy, filmed 1969, and The Wrath of God, filmed 1972) under pseudonyms (Martin Fallon, Hugh Marlowe, Henry Patterson); some books trans. into 42 languages. *Recreations:* tennis, old movies. *Address:* c/o Higham Associates Ltd, 5/8 Lower John Street, Golden Square, W1R 4HA. *T:* 01–437 7888.

PATTERSON, Hugh Foggan, MA; Secretary, King's College London, 1977–83; *b* 8 Nov. 1924; *s* of late Sir John Robert Patterson, KBE, CMG, and late Esther Margaret Patterson; *m* 1956, Joan Philippa Abdy Collins; one *s* two *d*. *Educ:* Royal Grammar Sch., Newcastle upon Tyne; King's Coll., Cambridge (MA). Served War, Royal Artillery, 1943–47. HMOCS, Nigeria, 1950–61; Universities of: Birmingham, 1962–63; Warwick, 1964–69; London, 1969–83 (Clerk of the Senate, 1976–77). *Recreations:* music, golf, tennis. *Address:* Lower Beechcroft, Chesham Road, Berkhamsted HP4 3AB. *T:* Berkhamsted 4353.

PATTERSON, John Allan; Director of Savings and Head of Department for National Savings, since 1986; *b* 10 Oct. 1931; *s* of William Gilchrist Patterson and May (*née* Eggie); *m* 1956, Anne Marie Lasson; one *s* two *d*. *Educ:* Epsom Coll.; Clare Coll., Cambridge (Major Scholar in Classics, Stewart of Rannoch Scholar; BA 1954). HM Diplomatic Service, 1954–65: served in Bangkok, 1957–61 and in Rome, 1961–64 (Private Sec. to the Ambassador); HM Treasury, 1965–81 (on loan to Cabinet Office, 1974–78); Dep. Dir of Savings, Dept for Nat. Savings, 1981–86. *Recreations:* gardening, walking, languages, church. *Address:* 5 Nelson Gardens, Guildford, Surrey GU1 2NZ. *T:* Guildford 64369.

PATTERSON, Marie; *see* Patterson, C. M.

PATTERSON, Dr Mark Lister; *b* 2 March 1934; *s* of Alfred Patterson and Frederica Georgina Mary Lister Nicholson; *m* 1958, Jane Teresa Scott Stokes; one *s* two *d*. *Educ:* privately; St Bartholomew's Hosp. Med. Coll., Univ. of London (MB 1959). MRCP. Jun. hosp. appts at St Bartholomew's Hosp., Royal Postgrad. Med. Sch., and MRC Exptl Haematol. Unit; Consultant Haematologist to Nat. Heart and Chest Hosps, 1967–84. Mem., GLC, 1970–73 and 1977–81; Parly Candidate (C) Ealing N, 1974. *Recreations:* medicine, politics. *Address:* Wolverton Manor, Shorwell, Newport, Isle of Wight. *T:* Brighstone 740609. *Club:* Carlton.

PATTERSON, Paul Leslie; composer; Professor of Composition, since 1970, Head of Composition and Twentieth Century Music, since 1985, Royal Academy of Music; formed The Patterson Quintet, 1982; *b* 15 June 1947; *s* of Leslie and Lilian Patterson; *m* 1981, Hazel Wilson; one *s* one *d*. *Educ:* Royal Academy of Music. FRAM 1980. Freelance composer, 1968–; Arts Council Composer in Association, English Sinfonia, 1969–70; Director, Contemporary Music, Warwick Univ., 1974–80; Composer in Residence: SE Arts Assoc., 1980–82; Bedford School, 1984–85. Member: Exec. Cttee, Composers Guild, 1972–75; Council, SPNM, 1975–81, 1985–; Adv. Council, BBC Radio London, 1986–; Adv. Cttee, Arts Council's Recordings Panel, 1986–. Performances world wide by leading orchestras and soloists and ensembles; also film and TV music. *Publications:* Rebecca, 1968; Trumpet Concerto, 1969; Time Piece, 1972; Kyrie, 1972; Requiem, 1973; Comedy for Five Winds, 1973; Requiem, 1974; Fluorescences, 1974; Clarinet Concerto, 1976; Cracowian Counterpoints, 1977; Voices of Sleep, 1979; Concerto for Orchestra, 1981; Canterbury Psalms, 1981; Sinfonia, 1982; Mass of the Sea, 1983; Deception Pass, 1983; Duologue, 1984; Mean Time, 1984; Europhony, 1985; Missa Brevis, 1985; Stabat Mater, 1986; String Quartet, 1986; Magnificat and Nunc Dimittis, 1986. *Recreations:* sailing, croquet *Address:* 31 Cromwell Avenue, Highgate, N6 5HN. *T:* 01–348 3711.

PATTERSON, Very Rev. William James; Dean of Ely since 1984; *b* 25 Sept. 1930; *s* of William Moscrop and Alice Patterson; *m* 1955, Elisabeth Roederer; one *s* two *d*. *Educ:* Haileybury; Balliol College, Oxon. MA. Asst Curate of St John Baptist, Newcastle upon Tyne, 1955–58; Priest-in-Charge, Rio Claro with Mayaro, Dio. Trinidad, 1958–65; Rector of Esher, 1965–72; RD of Emly, 1968–72; Rector of Little Downham, 1972–80; Priest-in-Charge of Coveney, 1978–80; Archdeacon of Wisbech, 1979–84; Vicar of Wisbech St Mary, 1980–84. *Recreation:* cycling. *Address:* The Deanery, Ely, Cambs CB7 4DN. *T:* Ely 2432.

PATTIE, Geoffrey Edwin; MP (C) Chertsey and Walton since Feb. 1974; Minister of State, Department of Trade and Industry (Minister for Information Technology), since 1984; *b* 17 Jan. 1936; *s* of late Alfred Edwin Pattie and Ada Clive (*née* Carr); *m* 1960, Tuëma Caroline (*née* Eyre-Maunsell); one *s* (one *d* decd). *Educ:* Durham Sch.; St Catharine's Coll., Cambridge (MA). BA Cantab 1959. Called to Bar, Gray's Inn, 1964. Served: Queen Victoria's Rifles (TA), 1959–61; (on amalgamation) Queen's Royal Rifles (TA), now 4th Royal Green Jackets, 1961–65; Captain, 1964. Mem. GLC, Lambeth, 1967–70; Chm. ILEA Finance Cttee, 1968–70. Chm. of Governors, London Coll. of Printing, 1968–69. Contested (C) Barking, 1966 and 1970. Sec., Cons. Parly Aviation Cttee, 1974–75, 1975–76, Vice Chm., 1976–77, 1977–78; Jt Sec., Cons. Parly Defence Cttee, 1975–76, 1976–77, 1977–78, Vice Chm., 1978–79; Mem., Cttee of Public Accounts, 1976–79; Vice-Chm., All Party Cttee on Mental Health, 1977–79. Parly Under Sec. of State for Defence for the RAF, 1979–81, for Defence Procurement, 1981–83; Minister of State for Defence Procurement, 1983–84. Mem. General Synod of Church of England, 1970–75. *Publications:* Towards a New Defence Policy, 1976; (with James Bellini) A New World Role for the Medium Power: the British Opportunity, 1977. *Recreations:* travel, opera, cricket. *Address:* c/o House of Commons, SW1A 0AA. *Club:* Royal Green Jacket.

PATTINSON, Hon. Sir Baden, KBE 1962; LLB; Member, legal firm Pattinson, McLaughlin & Reid Smith; *b* 22 Dec. 1899; *m* 1926, Florence, *d* of T. A. Doman. Mayor of Maitland, 1928–30, and 1933; Mayor of Glenelg, 1944–47; MHA, South Australia: for Yorke Peninsula, 1930–38; for Glenelg, 1947–65; Minister of Education, SA, 1953–65. *Recreations:* horse riding, reading. *Address:* 12 Maturin Road, Glenelg, Adelaide, SA 5045, Australia.

PATTINSON, Derek; *see* Pattinson, W. D.

PATTINSON, John Mellor, CBE 1943; MA; *b* 1899; *s* of late J. P. Pattinson, JP, Mobberley, Cheshire; *m* 1927, Wilhelmina (*d* 1983), *d* of late W. J. Newth, Cheltenham; two *s*. *Educ:* Rugby Sch.; RMA; Cambridge Univ. RFA with BEF, 1918–19. Anglo-Iranian Oil Co., South Iran, 1922–45, General Manager, 1937–45. Director until 1969: British Petroleum Co. of Canada Ltd; Triad Oil Co. Ltd; BP Germany AG; Dep. Chm. 1960–65, and Man. Dir 1952–65, British Petroleum Co. Ltd; Dir, Chartered Bank, 1965–73. *Recreations:* gardening, travel. *Address:* Oakhurst, West Byfleet, Surrey. *Club:* East India, Devonshire, Sports and Public Schools.

PATTINSON, Peter L. F.; *see* Foden-Pattinson, P. L.

PATTINSON, (William) Derek; Secretary-General, General Synod of Church of England, since 1972; *b* 31 March 1930; *s* of late Thomas William and Elizabeth Pattinson. *Educ:* Whitehaven Grammar Sch.; Queen's Coll., Oxford (Stanhope Historical Essay Prize, 1951). BA 1952; MA 1956. Entered Home Civil Service, 1952; Inland Revenue Dept, 1952–62 and 1965–68; HM Treasury, 1962–65 and 1968–70; Assoc. Sec. -Gen., General Synod, 1970–72. Chm., William Temple Assoc., 1966–70; Member: Archbishops' Commn on Church and State, 1966–70; British Council of Churches; London Diocesan Synod. Vice-Chm., Grosvenor Chapel Cttee, 1973–81; Vice-Pres., SPCK; Chm. of Governors, Liddon House, 1972–; Chm., English Friends of Anglican Centre in Rome; Governor: Sir John Cass Foundn; Greycoat Foundn. Freeman, City of London, 1973; Master, Parish Clerks' Co.; Mem., Woolmens' Co. *Address:* 4 Tufton Street, SW1P 3QY. *T:* 01–222 6307. *Club:* Athenæum.

PATTISON, Prof. Bruce; Professor of Education, University of London Institute of Education, 1948–76, now Emeritus; *b* 13 Nov. 1908; *s* of Matthew and Catherine Pattison; *m* 1937, Dorothy Graham (*d* 1979). *Educ:* Gateshead Grammar Sch.; King's Coll., Newcastle upon Tyne; Fitzwilliam House, Cambridge. Henry Mellish Sch., Nottingham, 1933–35; Hymers Coll., Hull, 1935–36; Lecturer in English, University College, London, 1936–48 (Reader, 1948). Board of Trade, 1941–43; Ministry of Supply, 1943–45. *Publications:* Music and Poetry of the English Renaissance, 1948, 2nd edn 1970; Special Relations, 1984. *Address:* 62 The Vale, Coulsdon, Surrey CR3 2AW. *T:* 01–660 2991. *Clubs:* Athenæum, National Liberal.

PATTISON, David Arnold, PhD; Principal Management Consultant, Arthur Young Group, since 1985; *b* 9 Feb. 1941; *s* of David Pattison and Christina Russell Bone; *m* 1967, Anne Ross Wilson; two *s* one *d*. *Educ:* Glasgow Univ. (BSc 1st Cl. Hons, PhD). Planning Assistant, Dunbarton County Council, 1966–67; Lecturer, Strathclyde Univ., 1967–70; Head of Tourism Division, Highlands and Islands Development Board, 1970–81; Chief Exec., Scottish Tourist Board, 1981–85. *Publications:* Tourism Development Plans for: Argyll, Bute, Ayrshire, Burgh of Ayr, Ulster. *Recreations:* reading, watching soccer and Rugby, golf, gardening. *Address:* 7 Cramond Glebe Gardens, Cramond, Edinburgh EH4 6NZ.

PATTISON, Michael Ambrose; Secretary General, Royal Institution of Chartered Surveyors, since 1985; Director, Surveyors Holdings Ltd; *b* 14 July 1946; *s* of Osmond John Pattison and Eileen Susanna Pattison (*née* Cullen); *m* 1975, Beverley Jean, *d* of Genevieve and Hugh Webber, Florida, USA; one *d*. *Educ:* Sedbergh School; University of Sussex (BA Hons 1968). Min. of Overseas Develt, 1968; Asst Private Sec. to Minister, 1970; seconded to HM Diplomatic Service as First Sec., Perm. Mission to UN, New York, 1974; ODA, 1977; Private Sec. to successive Prime Ministers, 1979–82; ODA, 1982, Establishment Officer, 1983–85. *Recreations:* countryside, cricket, real tennis. *Address:* Royal Institution of Chartered Surveyors, 12 Great George Street, SW1P 3AD. *T:* 01–222 7000; 1 Church Houses, Kineton, Warwicks CV35 0JT. *T:* Kineton 640498. *Club:* Warwickshire CC.

PATTON, Joseph Alexander, CBE 1982; farmer; *b* 17 Jan. 1936; *s* of Marshall Lyons and Bessie Robinson Patton; *m* 1967, Mary Morton Kirkpatrick; one *s* two *d*. Member: Milk Marketing Board, NI, 1982–; Council, Food From Britain, 1983–; Broadcasting Council of NI, 1982–84. President: Young Farmers' Clubs of Ulster, 1969–71; Ulster Farmers' Union, 1980–81. *Address:* Roseyards, 107 Kirk Road, Ballymoney, Co. Antrim, Northern Ireland BT53 8HN. *T:* Dervock 41263.

PATTON, Thomas William Saunderson, OBE 1985; Lord Mayor of Belfast, 1982–83; *b* 27 July 1914; *s* of Florence and Robert Patton; *m* 1940, Alice Glover; three *s* three *d* (and one *d* decd). *Educ:* Templemore Avenue School, Belfast. Harland and Wolff Ltd, 1932–61; Ulster Folk and Transport Museum, 1962–82. *Recreations:* gardening, football. *Address:* 89 Park Avenue, Belfast BT4 1JJ. *T:* Belfast 658645.

PATTULLO, (David) Bruce; Treasurer and General Manager (Chief Executive), Bank of Scotland, since 1979 (Deputy Treasurer and General Manager, 1978); *b* 2 Jan. 1938; *s* of Colin Arthur Pattullo and Elizabeth Mary Bruce; *m* 1962, Fiona Jane Nicholson; three *s* one *d*. *Educ:* Rugby Sch.; Hertford Coll., Oxford (MA). FIB (Scot.). Commnd Royal Scots and seconded to Queen's Own Nigeria Regt. Gen. Man., Bank of Scotland Finance Co. Ltd, 1975–77; Dir, 1977–, Chief Exec., 1977–78, British Linen Bank Ltd. Director: Bank of Scotland, 1980–; Melville Street Investments (Edinburgh) Ltd, 1973–. Chm., Cttee, Scottish Clearing Bankers, 1981–83; a Vice-Pres., Inst. of Bankers in Scotland, 1977–. First Prizeman (Bilsland Prize), Inst. of Bankers in Scotland, 1964. *Recreation:* tennis. *Address:* 6 Cammo Road, Edinburgh EH4 8EB. *T:* 031–339 6012. *Clubs:* Caledonian; New (Edinburgh).

PAUK, György; international concert violinist; Professor at Guildhall School of Music and Drama; *b* 26 Oct. 1936; *s* of Imre and Magda Pauk; *m* 1959, Susanne Mautner; one *s* one *d*. *Educ:* Franz Liszt Acad. of Music, Budapest. Toured E Europe while still a student; won three internat. violin competitions, Genoa 1956, Munich 1957, Paris 1959; soon after leaving Hungary, settled in London, 1961, and became a British citizen. London début, 1961; seasonal appearances there and in the provinces, with orchestra, in recital and chamber music; also plays at Bath, Cheltenham and Edinburgh Fests and London Promenade Concerts; performs in major European music venues; US début, under Sir George Solti, with Chicago Symph. Orch., 1970, followed by further visits to USA and Canada to appear with major orchs; holds master classes, in Colo; plays regularly in Hungary following return in 1973; overseas tours to Australia, NZ, S America, S Africa, Middle and Far East; many performances for BBC, incl. Berg and Bartók concertos, with Boulez. As conductor/soloist, has worked with the English, Scottish and Franz Liszt chamber orchs and London Mozart Players; guest dir, Acad. of St Martin-in-the-Fields. Has made many recordings including: Bartok Sonatas (among top records in US, 1982); Tippett Concerto (Best Gramophone Record Award, 1983); Berg Concerto (Caecilia Prize, Belgium, 1983). With Peter Frankl and Ralph Kirshbaum, formed chamber music trio, 1973; performances at major fests; public concerts in Gt Britain have incl. complete Brahms and Beethoven Cycles; the trio has also made many broadcasts for the BBC; first perf. of Penderecki's Violin Concerto, Japan, 1979, UK, 1980; first perf. of Tippett's Triple Concerto, London, 1980; first British, Dutch and Hungarian perfs of Lutosławski's Chain 2, with composer conducting, 1986–87. Hon. Mem., Guildhall Sch. of Music, 1980. *Address:* c/o Ibbs & Tillett Ltd, 450 Edgware Road, W2 1EG. *T:* 01–226 2864.

PAUL, Dr David Manuel; HM Coroner: City of London, since 1966; Northern District of London, since 1968; *b* 8 June 1927; *s* of Kenneth and Rachael Paul; *m* 1948, Gladys Audrey Garton, MCSP; two *d*. *Educ:* Selhurst Grammar Sch. for Boys, Croydon; St Bartholomew's Hosp. Med. Coll.; The London Hosp. Med. Coll. MRCS, LRCP 1953; DRCOG 1962; DA 1962; DMJ (Clin.) 1965. Served Manchester Regt, 1946–49 (Lieut). House Surgeon, Beckenham Hosp., 1954; Obstetric House Surgeon, Luton and Dunstable Hosp., 1955; gen. practice, Drs Duncan & Partners, Croydon, 1955–67; Clin. Asst Anaesthetist, Croydon Gp of Hosps, 1956–68; GP Obstetrician, Purley Hosp., 1958–68; Divl Surgeon, Z Div., Met. Police, 1956–68. Hon. Lectr, Court Practice and Clin. Forensic Medicine, Guy's Hosp. Med. Sch., 1966–; Hon. Consultant, Clin. Forensic Medicine, Surrey Constab., 1967–. Chm., Med. Section, 1973–76, and Chm., Exec. Council, 1979–83, British Acad. of Forensic Sciences. *Publications:* contrib. medico-legal jls and text books on forensic medicine. *Recreations:* travel, equitation, fishing, photography. *Address:* Cobhambury Farm, Edenbridge, Kent TN8 5NG. *T:* Edenbridge 863280; The Coroner's Court, Milton Court, Moor Lane, EC2Y 9BL. *T:* 01–606 3030; The Coroner's Court, Myddelton Road, Hornsey, N8 7PY. *T:* 01–348 4411.

PAUL, Geoffrey David; Editor, Jewish Chronicle, since 1977; *b* 26 March 1929; *s* of Reuben Goldstein and Anne Goldstein; *m* 1st, 1952, Joy Stirling (marr. diss. 1972); one *d*; 2nd, 1974, Rachel Mann; one *s*. *Educ:* Liverpool, Kendal, Dublin. Weekly newspaper and news agency reporter, 1947–57; asst editor, Jewish Observer and Middle East Review, 1957–62; Jewish Chronicle, 1962–: successively sub-editor, foreign editor, Israel corresp., deputy editor. *Publication:* Living in Jerusalem, 1981. *Address:* 25 Furnival Street, EC4A 1JT. *T:* 01–405 9252.

PAUL, Air Cdre Gerard John Christopher, CB 1956; DFC 1944; MA; FRAeS; *b* 31 Oct. 1907; *s* of E. W. Paul, FRCS; *m* 1937, Rosemary (*d* 1975), *d* of Rear-Admiral H. G. E. Lane, CB; two *s* one *d*. *Educ:* Cheltenham Coll.; St John's Coll., Cambridge. Entered Royal Air Force, 1929; Fleet Air Arm, 1931–36; served War of 1939–45 in England and N.W. Europe; Commandant, Central Flying School, 1954–56; retired, 1958. Secretary-General of the Air League, 1958–71. Life Vice-Pres., RAF Gliding and Soaring Assoc.; Pres., Popular Flying Assoc., 1969–78. Croix de Guerre avec Palme (Belgium), 1944; Military Cross (Czechoslovakia), 1945. *Recreations:* dogs, garden. *Address:* Wearne House, Old Alresford, Hants SO24 9DH. *Club:* Royal Air Force.

PAUL, Hugh Glencairn B.; *see* Balfour-Paul.

PAUL, Sir John (Warburton), GCMG 1965 (KCMG 1962); OBE 1959; MC 1940; Director, Overseas Relations, St John Ambulance, since 1981; *b* 29 March 1916; 2nd *s* of Walter George Paul and Phoebe (*née* Bull), Weymouth; *m* 1946, Kathleen Audrey, CStJ 1962, *d* of Dr A. D. Weeden, Weymouth; three *d*. *Educ:* Weymouth Coll., Dorset; Selwyn Coll., Cambridge (MA; Hon. Fellow, 1982). Secretary, Maddermarket Theatre, Norwich, 1936. Commissioned Royal Tank Regt (Suppl. Res.), 1937; regular commission, RTR, 1938; BEF 1940 (despatches, prisoner-of-war); ADC and Private Secretary to Governor of Sierra Leone, 1945 (seconded). Called to the Bar, Inner Temple, 1947. Colonial Administrative Service, Sierra Leone, 1947; District Commissioner, 1952; Permanent Secretary, 1956; Provincial Commissioner, 1959; Secretary to the Cabinet, 1960; Governor and C-in-C, The Gambia, 1962–65; Governor-General of The Gambia, 1965–66; Governor and C-in-C: British Honduras, 1966–72; The Bahamas, 1972–73; Governor-General, The Bahamas, July-Oct. 1973; Lt Governor, Isle of Man, 1974–80. Member Board, West African Airways Corporation, 1954–56. Chm., St Christopher Motorists' Security Assoc., and associated cos, 1980–. A Patron, Pain Relief Foundn, 1980–. Mem., Bd of Governors, Pangbourne Coll., 1981–86. KStJ 1962. *Recreation:* painting. *Address:* Sherrens Mead, Sherfield-on-Loddon, Hampshire. *Clubs:* Athenæum, MCC.

PAUL, Noël Strange, CBE 1978; Director, Press Council, 1976–79 (Assistant Secretary, 1964, Secretary, 1968–76), retired; *b* 1914; *y s* of late S. Evan Paul, SSC, and Susan, *d* of Dr Henry Habgood; *m* 1950, Mary, *yr d* of Philip J. Bone, FRSA, MRST, Luton. *Educ:* Kingston Grammar School. Journalist, Press Assoc., 1932; served War of 1939–45, Iran and Italy, Major seconded RAF (despatches). Home Counties Newspapers, 1949; Liverpool Daily Post, 1958. Mem., Steering Cttee on the Mass Media, Council of Europe, 1976–82; Governor, English-Speaking Union, 1980–82. *Publications:* Self-regulation of the Press, 1982; Principles for the Press, 1985. *Recreations:* sailing, photography. *Address:* The Lodge, St Catherine's, Strachur, Argyllshire PA25 8AZ. *T:* Inveraray 2208.

PAUL, Air Vice-Marshal Ronald Ian S.; *see* Stuart-Paul.

PAUL, Swraj; Padma Bhushan; Chairman: Caparo Group Ltd, since 1978; Caparo Industries Plc, since 1981; Barton Tubes, Ltd, Canada, since 1983; Fidelity PLC, since 1984; United Merchant Bar PLC, since 1985; *b* 18 Feb. 1931; *s* of Payare and Mongwati Paul; *m* 1956, Aruna Vij; three *s* one *d* (and one *d* decd). *Educ:* Punjab Univ. (BSc); Mass Inst. of Technol. (BSc, MSc (Mech. Engrg)); Harvard Business Sch. (Company Management Course). Began work as Partner in family-owned Apeejay Surrendra Gp, India, 1953; came to UK in 1966 and estabd first business, Natural Gas Tubes Ltd; Caparo Group Ltd formed in 1978 as holding co. for UK businesses involved in engrg, hotel and property develt, investment, oil exploration, tea, shipping and electronics; Caparo Industries Plc (engrg, metals and electronics) formed in 1981; Caparo Properties Plc (property co.) acquired 1983, now Egerton Trust PLC; Fidelity PLC acquired 1984; Utd Merchant Bar PLC (Scunthorpe) formed 1985. Founder Chm., Indo-British Assoc., 1975–; Mem., World Business Council, USA, 1980–. FRSA. Padma Bhushan (equivalent to British Peerage), 1983. Hon. PhD Amer. Coll. of Switzerland, Leysin, 1986. Spec. Award for Outstanding Entrepreneurship and Promotion of Art and Culture of India, Convention of Asian Indians in N America, 1984. *Publication:* Indira Gandhi, 1984, 2nd edn 1985. *Address:* 6 Ambika House, 9a Portland Place, W1N 3AA. *T:* 01–637 5525. *Clubs:* MCC, Oriental, Royal Automobile; Royal Calcutta Turf, Royal Calcutta Golf (Calcutta); Cricket of India (Bombay).

PAULET, family name of **Marquess of Winchester.**

PAULING, Linus (Carl); Research Professor, Linus Pauling Institute of Science and Medicine, since 1974; *b* 28 Feb. 1901; *s* of Herman William Pauling and Lucy Isabelle Darling; *m* 1923, Ava Helen Miller (*d* 1981); three *s* one *d*. *Educ:* Oregon State Coll.; California Institute of Technology. BS Oregon State Coll., 1922; PhD California Inst. of Technology, 1925; Hon. DSc: Oregon State Coll., 1933; Univ. of Chicago, 1941; Princeton Univ., 1946; Yale, 1947; Cambridge, 1947; London, 1947; Oxford, 1948; Brooklyn Polytechnic Inst., 1955; Humboldt Univ. (Berlin), 1959; Melbourne, 1964; York (Toronto), 1966; LLD Reed Coll., 1959; LHD Tampa, 1949; Dr *hc*: Paris, 1948; Toulouse, 1949; Liège, 1955; Montpellier, 1958; Warsaw, 1969; Lyon, 1970; UJD, NB, 1950; DFA, Chouinard Art Inst., 1958. Asst in Chemistry and in Mechanics and Materials, Oregon State Coll., 1919–22; Graduate Asst, California Inst. Technology, 1922–23; Teaching Fellow, 1923–25; Research Associate, 1925–26; Nat. Res. Fellow in Chemistry, 1925–26; Fellow of John Simon Guggenheim Meml Foundn, 1926–27 (Univs of Munich, Zürich, Copenhagen); Asst Prof., California Inst. of Technology, 1927–29; Associate Prof., 1929–31; Prof. of Chemistry, 1931–63; Dir of Gates and Crellin Labs of Chemistry, and Chm., Div. of Chemistry and Chemical Engrg, 1936–58; Prof. of Chemistry, Stanford Univ., 1969–74. George Fisher Baker Lectr in Chemistry, Cornell Univ., Sept. 1937–Feb. 1938; George Eastman Prof., Oxford Univ., Jan.-June 1948, etc. Amer. Chem. Soc. Award in Pure Chemistry, 1931; William H. Nichols Medal, 1941; J. Willard Gibbs Medal, 1946; Theodore William Richards Medal, 1947; Davy Medal of Royal Society, 1947; Presidential Medal for Merit, 1948; Gilbert Newton Lewis Medal, 1951; Thomas Addis Medal, 1955; Amedeo Avogadro Medal, 1956; Pierre Fermat Medal, Paul Sabatier Medal, 1957; International Grotius Medal, 1957; Nobel Prize for Chemistry, 1954;

Nobel Peace Prize for 1962, 1963; Linus Pauling Medal, 1966; Internat. Lenin Peace Prize, 1971; 1st Martin Luther King Jr Medical Award, 1972; Nat. Medal of Science, 1975; Lomonosov Gold Medal, Soviet Acad. of Scis, 1978. Member: Nat. Acad. of Sciences; Amer. Phil. Soc.; Amer. Acad. of Arts and Sciences, etc.; Hon. Fellow: Chemical Society (London), Royal Institution, etc.; For. Member: Royal Society, Akademia Nauk, USSR, etc.; Associé étranger, Acad. des Sciences, 1966. War of 1939–45, Official Investigator for projects of National Defense Research Cttee on Medical Research, and Office of Scientific Research and Development. Grand Officer, Order of Merit, Italian Republic. *Publications:* The Structure of Line Spectra (with S. Goudsmit), 1930; Introduction to Quantum Mechanics (with E. B. Wilson, Jun), 1935; The Nature of the Chemical Bond, 1939 (3rd ed., 1960); General Chemistry, 1947 (2nd ed., 1953); College Chemistry, 1950 (3rd ed., 1964); No More War!, 1958 (revised edn, 1962); The Architecture of Molecules (with Roger Hayward), 1964; The Chemical Bond, 1967; Vitamin C and the Common Cold, 1971; (with Peter Pauling) Chemistry, 1975; Vitamin C, the Common Cold and the Flu, 1976; (with Ewan Cameron) Cancer and Vitamin C, 1979; How to Live Longer and Feel Better, 1986; also numerous scientific articles in the fields of chemistry, physics, and biology including the structure of crystals, quantum mechanics, nature of the chemical bond, structure of gas molecules, structure of antibodies and nature of serological reactions, etc. *Address:* Linus Pauling Institute of Science and Medicine, 440 Page Mill Road, Palo Alto, California 94306, USA.

PAULSON, Godfrey Martin Ellis, CB 1966; CMG 1959; OBE (mil.) 1945; HM Diplomatic Service, retired 1970; *b* 6 July 1908; *s* of late Lt-Col P. Z. Paulson, OBE, Manchester Regt and Royal Signals, and late Mrs M. G. Paulson, *d* of late Dr W. H. Ellis, Shipley Hall, Bradford, Yorkshire; *m* 1936, Patricia Emma, *d* of late Sir Hugh Murray, KCIE, CBE, and late Lady Murray, Englefield Green House, Surrey; one *s* one *d*. *Educ:* Westminster and Peterhouse, Cambridge. BA (Hons), 1930, MA 1940. Colonial Service; Assistant District Commissioner, Gold Coast Colony, 1930–32. Admitted Solicitor, 1936; practised in City of London until outbreak of war, 1939. Served 1939–45, Manchester Regt and on General Staff in Africa, UK, and North West Europe, including Military Mission to Free French; Lt-Col, 1945 (OBE 1945). Control Commn for Germany, 1945, for Austria, 1947–48. Joined Foreign Service, 1948, and served in Venice, Stockholm, Far East (Singapore), Beirut, Rome, Nice and Foreign Office. Member: British Sect., Franco-British Council, 1978–; Exec. Cttee, Franco-British Soc., 1972–85. Officer, Order of St Charles, Monaco, 1981. *Address:* Yew Tree Cottage, Church Street, Hampstead Norreys, near Newbury, Berks RG16 0TD. *T:* Hermitage 201572. *Clubs:* United Oxford & Cambridge University, Garrick, Special Forces, MCC.

PAULUSZ, Jan Gilbert; a Recorder of the Crown Court, since 1980; *b* 18 Nov. 1929; *s* of Jan Hendrik Olivier Paulusz and Edith (*née* Gilbert); *m* 1973, Luigia Maria Attanasio. *Educ:* The Leys Sch., Cambridge. Called to the Bar, Lincoln's Inn, 1957; South Eastern Circuit, 1959–. *Recreations:* mountain walking, photography. *Address:* 50 Royston Gardens, Redbridge, Ilford, Essex IG1 3SY.

PAUNCEFORT, Bernard Edward, OBE 1983; HM Diplomatic Service; retired; *b* 8 April 1926; *o s* of Frederick George Pauncefort and Eleanor May (*née* Jux); *m* 1956, Patricia Anne, *yr d* of Charles Ernest Leah and Alice (*née* Kendal-Banks). *Educ:* Wandsworth School. RAFVR 1943–44; Royal Fusiliers, 1944–48. Metropolitan Police Civil Staff, 1948–53; HM Colonial Service, 1953; Malaya, 1953–56; Tanganyika, 1956–63; CRO, 1963–67; First Sec., Zambia, 1967–68; Consul, Cape Town, 1969–72; Lord Pearce's staff, Rhodesia, 1971–72; Head of Chancery, Madagascar, 1972–73; FCO, 1973–76; Head of Chancery, Burma, 1976–78; Dir, British Inf. Services, S Africa, 1978–80; Lord Soames' staff, Rhodesia-Zimbabwe, 1979–80; Administrator, Ascension Island, 1980–82; FCO, 1982–83; Counsellor and Chief Sec., Falkland Is, 1983–85; Counsellor, FCO, 1985–86. Zimbabwa Medal, 1980. *Recreations:* dogs, showing and breeding; birds, waterways. *Address:* New Church Road, Uphill, Weston-super-Mare, Avon.

PAUNCEFORT-DUNCOMBE, Sir Philip; *see* Duncombe.

PAVITT, Laurence Anstice; MP (Lab and Co-op) Brent South, since 1974 (Willesden West, Oct. 1959–1974); *b* 1 Feb. 1914; *s* of George Anstice Pavitt and May (*née* Brooshooft); *m* 1937, Rosina (*née* Walton); one *s* one *d*. *Educ:* Elementary and Central Sch., West Ham. National Organising Secretary, British Fedn of Young Co-operators, 1942–46; Gen. Secretary, Anglo Chinese Development Soc., 1946–52; Regional Education Officer, Co-operative Union, 1947–52; UN Technical Assistance Programme, Asian Co-operative Field Mission, 1952–55; National Organiser, Medical Practitioners' Union, 1956–59. PPS to: Secretary for Education and Science, 1964–65; Secretary of State for Foreign Affairs, 1965–66; Secretary of State for Economic Affairs, 1966–67; an Asst Govt Whip, 1974–76. Vice-Chairman: Parly Labour Party's Health Gp, 1977–80 (Chm., 1964–77); British China All Party Gp, 1978– (Chm., 1974–78); Chm., All Party Gp on Action on Smoking and Health, 1974–78; Member: Select Cttee on Overseas Aid, 1969–71; Exec. Cttee, Inter-Parly Union, 1967–81, 1984–; Exec. Cttee, Commonwealth Parly Assoc., 1969–82; UK Delegn to Council of Europe, 1980–84; UK Delegn to WEU, 1980–84; Nat. Exec., Cooperative Party (Chm. Parly Gp), 1980–81. Vice-President: Brit. Assoc. for the Hard of Hearing; Royal Coll. of Nursing; Member: Hearing Aid Council, 1968–74; MRC, 1969–72. *Recreations:* reading, walking. *Address:* House of Commons, SW1. *T:* 01-219 5225.

PAWSEY, James Francis; MP (C) Rugby and Kenilworth, since 1983 (Rugby, 1979–83); *b* 21 Aug. 1933; *s* of William Pawsey and Mary Mumford; *m* 1956, Cynthia Margaret Francis; six *s* (including twins twice). *Educ:* Coventry Tech. School; Coventry Tech. Coll. Dir, Autobar Group Ltd. Parliamentary Private Secretary: DES, 1982–83; DHSS, 1983–84; to Minister of State for NI, 1984–86. Member: Select Cttee on the Environment, 1981–82; Parly Scientific Cttee, 1982–; Select Cttee of Parly Comr for Admin, 1983–; Select Cttee for Energy, 1986–; Exec., IPU, 1984–; Chm., Cons Parly Educn Cttee, 1985–; Secretary: British Solidarity with Poland Campaign, 1982–; British/Greek Parly Gp, 1982–; British Portuguese Parly Gp, 1984–; Cons. Back Bench Social Services and Educn Cttees, 1982–83; Treasurer: Parly Assoc. for Euro/Arab Co-operation; British/Bangladesh Parly Gp, 1984–; CTU Teachers Gp, 1983–85. Member: Rugby RDC, 1965–73; Rugby Borough Council, 1973–75; Warwickshire CC, 1974–79; former Chm. and Pres., Warwickshire Assoc. of Parish Councils. MInstD. KLJ. *Publication:* The Tringo Phenomenon, 1983. *Address:* Shilton House, Shilton, Coventry, Warwickshire. *T:* Coventry 612922; (office) Rugby and Kenilworth Conservative Association, Albert Buildings, Albert Street, Rugby. *T:* Rugby 69556. *Club:* Carlton.

PAXTON, John; author, also writing as Jack Cherrill; Editor, The Statesman's Year-Book, since 1969; *b* 23 Aug. 1923; *m* 1950, Joan Thorne; one *s* one *d*. Head of Economics department, Millfield, 1952–63. Asst Editor, 1964–68, and Dep. Editor, 1968, of The Statesman's Year-Book; Consultant Editor, The New Illustrated Everyman's Encyclopaedia, 1981–84. *Publications:* (with A. E. Walsh) Trade in the Common Market Countries, 1965; (with A. E. Walsh) The Structure and Development of the Common Market, 1968; (with A. E. Walsh) Trade and Industrial Resources of the Common Market and Efta Countries, 1970; (with John Wroughton) Smuggling, 1971; (with A. E. Walsh) Into Europe, 1972; (ed) Everyman's Dictionary of Abbreviations, 1974, 2nd edn, 1986; World Legislatures, 1974; (with C. Cook) European Political Facts 1918–1973, 1975, 2nd edn, European Political Facts 1918–84, 1986; The Statesman's Year-Book World Gazetteer, 1975, 3rd edn, 1986; (with A. E. Walsh) Competition Policy: European and International Trends and Practices, 1975; The Developing Common Market, 1976; (with C. Cook) European Political Facts 1848–1918, 1977; A Dictionary of the European Economic Community, 1977, 2nd edn, A Dictionary of the European Communities, 1982 (commended, McColvin Medal Cttee); (with C. Cook) Commonwealth Political Facts, 1979; (with S. Fairfield) Calendar of Creative Man, 1980; (with C. Cook) European Political Facts 1789–1848, 1981; Companion to Russian History, 1984; Companion to the French Revolution, 1987; contrib. to Keesing's Contemporary Archives, TLS. *Address:* Moss Cottage, Hardway, Bruton, Somerset BA10 0LN. *T:* Bruton 813423. *Clubs:* National, Royal Over-Seas League, PEN.

PAXTON, Peter James, FCIS; FCCA; FIB; Chief Executive, Don Ridgway Associates, since 1986; Founder, Peter Paxton Marketing, 1986; *b* 27 April 1923; *m* 1947, Betty Jane Madden (marr. diss. 1980); one *s* one *d*; *m* 1985, Sylvia June Stock. *Educ:* Lawrence Sherriff Sch., Rugby. Served RAF, 1941–46. Accountant, Rugby Co-operative Society Ltd, 1949–55; Chief Accountant, 1955, Chief Exec. Officer, 1972–86, Cambridge and District Co-operative Society Ltd; Chairman: CWS, 1980–86; Co-operative Bank, 1980–86; First Co-op. Finance, 1980–86; Co-op. City Investments, 1983–86; Dep. Chm., Co-op. Insce Soc., 1983–86. *Address:* Harvest Home, 37 Green End, Fen Ditton, Cambridge CB5 8SX.

PAYE, Jean-Claude; Chevalier de la Légion d'Honneur; Officier de l'Ordre National du Mérite; Chevalier de l'Ordre National du Mérite agricole; Croix de la Valeur militaire; Secretary-General, OECD, since 1984; *b* 26 Aug. 1934; *s* of late Lucien Paye and of Suzanne Paye (*née* Guignard); *m* 1963, Laurence Hélène Marianne Jeanneney; two *s* two *d*. *Educ:* Lycée Bugeaud, Algiers; Lycée Carnot, Tunis; Faculté de droit, Tunis; Institut d'Etudes Politiques, Paris; Ecole Nationale d'Administration. Government service, 1961–64; Technical Adviser to: Sec. of State for Scientific Research, 1965; Minister of Social Affairs, 1966; Chief Adviser to Vice-Pres., EEC, 1967–73; Adviser, Embassy, Bonn, 1973; Asst Principal Private Sec. to Minister of Foreign Affairs, 1974–76; Diplomatic Advr to Prime Minister, 1976–79; Head of Economic and Financial Affairs, Ministry of Foreign Affairs, 1979–84; Pres., Exec. Cttee in special Session, OECD, 1979–84. *Address:* OECD, 2 rue André-Pascal, Château de la Muette, 75016 Paris, France.

PAYKEL, Prof. Eugene Stern, FRCP; FRCPE; FRCPsych; Professor of Psychiatry and Head of Department, University of Cambridge, since 1985; Professorial Fellow, Gonville and Caius College, Cambridge, since 1985; *b* 9 Sept. 1934; *s* of late Joshua Paykel and Eva Stern Paykel; *m* 1969, Margaret, *d* of late John Melrose and Joan Melrose; two *s*. *Educ:* Auckland Grammar Sch.; Univ. of Otago (MB ChB, MD; Stuart Prize, Joseph Pullar Schol., 1956); DPM London. Maudsley Hosp., 1962–65; Asst Prof. of Psychiatry and Co-Dir/Dir, Depression Res. Unit, Yale Univ., 1966–71; Consultant and Sen. Lectr, 1971–75, Reader, 1975–77, Prof. of Psychiatry, 1977–85, St George's Hosp. Med. Sch., Univ. of London. Chm., Social and Community Psych. Section, RCPsych, 1984– (Mem. Council, Exec. and Finance, Public Policy, Research Cttees, 1984–); Chief Scientist's Adviser and Mem., Mental Illness Res. Liaison Gp, DHSS, 1984–; previously examiner Univs of Edinburgh, Nottingham, Manchester, London, and RCPsych; Mem., Res. Cttee, Mental Health Foundn. Pres., British Assoc. for Psychopharmacology, 1982–84 (Hon. Sec., 1979–82); Mem., Neurosciences Bd, MRC, 1981–85. Foundations Fund Prize for Res. in Psychiatry, 1978; BMA Film Competition Bronze Award, 1981; Anna Monika Stiftung 2nd Prize, 1985. Jt Editor in Chief, Jl of Affective Disorders, 1979–; Member, Editorial Board: Social Psychiatry; Psychopharmacology; Jl of Psychosomatic Research. *Publications:* The Depressed Woman, 1974; Psychopharmacology of Affective Disorders, 1979; Monoamine Oxidase Inhibitors: the state of the art, 1981; Handbook of Affective Disorders, 1982; Community Psychiatric Nursing for Neurotic Patients, 1983; papers on depression, psychopharmacology, social psychiatry, life events, evaluation of treatment. *Recreations:* opera, music, theatre. *Address:* Department of Psychiatry, University of Cambridge Clinical School, Addenbrooke's Hospital, Hills Road, Cambridge CB2 2QQ. *T:* Cambridge 244014. *Club:* Athenæum.

PAYNE, Alan Jeffrey; HM Diplomatic Service; Consul-General, Lyons, since 1982; *b* 11 May 1933; *s* of Sydney Ellis Payne and Lydia Payne; *m* 1959, Letitia Freeman; three *s*. *Educ:* Enfield Grammar Sch.; Queens' Coll., Cambridge (Exhibnr). RN, 1955–57. EMI, London, later Paris, 1957–62; Secretariat, NATO, Paris, 1962–64; joined Diplomatic Service, 1965; Commonwealth Relations Office (later FCO), 1965–67; British High Commn, Kuala Lumpur, 1967–70; FCO, 1970–72; British Embassy, Budapest, 1972–75; Counsellor, Mexico City, 1975–79; FCO, 1979–82. *Recreations:* music, theatre. *Address:* c/o Foreign and Commonwealth Office, King Charles Street, SW1A 2AH. *Clubs:* Royal Commonwealth Society; Cercle de l'Union (Lyons).

PAYNE, Anson; *see* Payne, J. A.

PAYNE, Arthur Stanley, OBE 1977; HM Diplomatic Service; Counsellor and Head of Commercial Department, British Embassy, Manila, since 1983; *b* 17 Nov. 1930; *s* of late Arthur and of Lilian Gertrude Payne; *m* 1964, Heather Elizabeth Cavaghan; one *d*. *Educ:* Chatham Tech. Sch.; Gillingham Grammar Sch.; Nat. Defence Coll. HM Forces, 1949–50. Joined BoT, 1949; Raw Materials Dept, Washington, 1951–52; Min. of Materials, London, 1953–55; British Trade Commns, New Delhi, Bombay, Port of Spain, and Georgetown (First Sec.), 1956–67; joined HM Diplomatic Service, 1965; First Sec. (Inf.), Auckland, 1967–70; FCO, 1971–74; Dacca, 1974–76; Bonn, 1976–78; FCO, 1978–79; Dep. High Comr and Head of Chancery, Gabarone, 1980–83. *Recreations:* bridge, golf, music. *Address:* c/o Foreign and Commonwealth Office, SW1A 2AL. *Club:* Royal Commonwealth Society.

PAYNE, Maj.-Gen. George Lefevre, CB 1966; CBE 1963; Director of Ordnance Services, Ministry of Defence, 1964–68; retired, 1968; *b* 23 June 1911; *s* of Dr E. L. Payne, MRCS, LRCP, Brunswick House, Kew, Surrey; *m* 1938, Betty Maud (*d* 1982), *d* of Surgeon Captain H. A. Kellond-Knight, RN, Eastbourne, Sussex; three *s*. *Educ:* The King's Sch., Canterbury; Roy. Mil. Coll., Sandhurst. Royal Leicestershire Regiment: England, Northern Ireland, 1931–33; India, 1933–37; Royal Army Ordnance Corps: England, 1938–39; France, 1939–40; England, 1941–. Deputy Director Ordnance Services: HQ, BAOR, 1952–54; War Office, 1955–57; Commandant, Central Ordnance Depot, Chilwell, 1957–59; Deputy Director Ordnance Services, War Office, 1959–63; Commander, Stores Organization, RAOC, 1963–64; Col Comdt, RAOC, 1968–72. *Recreations:* fishing, gardening. *Address:* 15 Lincoln House, Basil Street, SW3 1AN. *Clubs:* Army and Navy, Royal Commonwealth Society.

PAYNE, Maj.-Gen. Henry Salusbury Legh D.; *see* Dalzell-Payne.

PAYNE, Ian; barrister; *b* 15 July 1926; *s* of late Douglas Harold Payne and of Gertrude (*née* Buchanan); *m* 1st, 1951, Babette (marr. diss. 1975), *d* of late Comte Clarence de Chalus; four *s* two *d*; 2nd, 1977, Colette Eugénie, *d* of late Marinus Jacobus van der Eb,

Rotterdam. *Educ:* Wellington Coll. Commnd 60th Rifles, 1944–48. Called to the Bar, Lincoln's Inn, 1953, Hong Kong, 1981; Dep. Recorder of Derby, 1969–72; a Recorder, 1972–81. *Address:* 2 Crown Office Row, Temple, EC4; 603 Hang Chong Building, 5 Queen's Road C, Hong Kong. *T:* 5–212616. *Clubs:* Garrick; Hong Kong; Refreshers Cricket.

PAYNE, Prof. Jack Marsh; Director, AFRC Institute for Research on Animal Diseases, since 1973; *b* 9 March 1929; *m* 1952, Sylvia Bryant; two *s* two *d.* *Educ:* Royal Veterinary Coll., London; University Coll. Hosp. Med. Sch., London. PhD, BSc; MRCVS; FIBiol. Res. Fellowship under Sir Roy Cameron, FRS, 1952–57; apptd, 1957, to staff of IRAD, Compton, Newbury, Berks, where principal res. has involved investigation of metabolic disorders of dairy cattle; esp. interest has centred around the concept of prodn disease and the develt of the Compton Metabolic Profile Test; recent esp. interest in zoonoses. Head of Dept of Functional Pathology, IRAD, 1961–73. Member: British Veterinary Assoc.; Assoc. of Veterinary Teachers and Res. Workers; Pathological Soc. Chm., VETEC (round table of experts on vet. science in EEC), 1976. WHO adviser; Veterinary Advr, British Council, 1977. FRSA. G. Norman Hall Gold Medal, 1972; RASE: Res. Gold Medal, 1972; Bledisloe Trophy and Medal, 1981; Victory Medal, Central Vet. Assoc. London, 1984. Editor: British Veterinary Jl, 1984–; Zoonosis Data Base, 1984–. *Publications:* Metabolic Disorders in Farm Animals, 1977; numerous references in sci. jls, esp. on subject of metabolic disorders. *Recreations:* fell walking, music (especially collecting rare operas), painting. *Address:* University of Reading Department of Agriculture, PO Box 236, Reading, Berks RG6 2AT. *T:* Reading 875123. *Club:* Athenæum.

PAYNE, Rev. James Richmond, MBE 1982; ThL; JP; General Secretary, Bible Society in Australia, since 1968; Chairman, United Bible Societies World Executive Committee, since 1976; *b* 1 June 1921; *s* of late R. A. Payne, Sydney, New South Wales; *m* 1943, Joan, *d* of late C. S. Elliott; three *s.* *Educ:* Drummoyne High School; Metropolitan Business College, Moore Theological College, Sydney. Served War of 1939–45: AIF, 1941–44. Catechist, St Michael's, Surry Hills, NSW, 1944–47; Curate, St Andrew's, Lismore, NSW, 1947–50; Rector, St Mark's, Nimbin, NSW, 1950–52; Chaplain, RAAF, Malta and Amberley, Qld, 1952–57; Rector, St Stephen's, Coorparoo, Qld, 1957–62; Dean of Perth, Western Australia, 1962–68. JP, Queensland, 1960; JP, ACT, 1969. *Publications:* Around the World in Seventy Days, 1965; And Now for the Good News, 1982. *Recreations:* sport, walking, reading, family. *Address:* GPO Box 507, Canberra, ACT 2601, Australia. *T:* 485188. *Clubs:* Weld (Perth); Commonwealth (Canberra).

PAYNE, Jane Marian, (Mrs A. E. Payne); *see* Manning, J. M.

PAYNE, (John) Anson, OBE 1945; Chairman, FMC, 1974–75 (Executive Vice-Chairman, 1972–74); formerly Director: FMC (Meat); C. & T. Harris (Calne); Marsh and Baxter, and other cos; *b* 19 May 1917; *yr s* of late Major R. L. Payne, DSO and of Mrs L. M. Payne (*née* Duncan); *m* 1949, Deirdre Kelly; one *s* one *d.* *Educ:* St Lawrence Coll., Ramsgate; Trinity Hall, Cambridge (MA). Entered Civil Service as Assistant Principal, 1939. Served War of 1939–45 (despatches twice, OBE): RAFVR, 1940–45; Wing Commander, 1943. Principal Private Secretary to Minister of Agriculture and Fisheries, 1947–51; Asst Secretary, 1951; seconded to Treasury, 1953–54; Under-Secretary, Min. of Agriculture, 1960–68. *Address:* Sandpit Cottage, 4 High Street, Ditchling, Sussex BN6 8TA. *T:* Hassocks 2310.

PAYNE, Keith, VC 1969; *b* 30 Aug. 1933; *s* of Henry Thomas Payne and Remilda Payne (*née* Hussey); *m* 1954, Florence Catherine Payne (*née* Plaw); five *s.* *Educ:* State School, Ingham, North Queensland. Soldier, Department of Army, Aug. 1951–75; 1 RAR, Korea, 1952–53; 3 RAR, Malaya, 1963–65; Aust. Army Trng Team, Vietnam, 1969 (Warrant Officer); WO Instructor: RMC, Duntroon, ACT, 1970–72; 42 Bn, Royal Qld Regt, Mackay, 1973–75; Captain, Oman Army, 1975–76. Member: VC and GC Assoc.; Returned Services League; Korea and South East Asia Forces Assoc. Freeman City of Brisbane and of Shire of Hinchinbrook. Vietnamese Cross of Gallantry, with bronze star, 1969; US Meritorious Unit Citation; Vietnamese Unit Citation Cross of Gallantry with Palm. *Recreations:* football, fishing, hunting. *Address:* 11 Canberra Street, North Mackay, Qld 4740, Australia. *T:* (079) 578497.

PAYNE, Leonard Sidney, CBE 1983; Director, J. Sainsbury Ltd, 1974–86; Adviser on Distribution and Retailing, Coopers & Lybrand; *b* 16 Dec. 1925; *s* of Leonard Sydney Payne and Lillian May Leggatt; *m* 1944, Marjorie Vincent; two *s.* *Educ:* Woodhouse Grammar School. FCCA, CBIM, FCIT, MBCS, MIRTE. Asst Accountant, Peek Frean & Co. Ltd, 1949–52; Chief Accountant, Administrator of various factory units, head office appts, Philips Electrical Industries, 1952–62; Dep. Gp Comptroller, Morgan Crucible Co. Ltd, 1962–64; British Road Services Ltd: Finance Dir, 1964–67; Asst Man. Dir, 1967–69; Man. Dir, 1969–71; Dir of Techn. Services and Develt, Nat. Freight Corp., 1971–74, Vice-Chm. Executive 1974; Pres., Freight Transport Assoc., 1980–82; Pres., Chartered Inst. of Transport, 1983–84. Chm., CBI Transport Policy Cttee, 1980–. *Recreations:* gardening, swimming, squash, chess. *Address:* Wisley, Gills Hill Lane, Radlett, Herts WD7 8DD.

PAYNE, Sir Norman (John), Kt 1985; CBE 1976 (OBE 1956; MBE (mil.) 1944); FEng; Chairman, BAA plc (formerly British Airports Authority), since 1977 (Chief Executive, 1972–77); *b* 9 Oct. 1921; *s* of late F. Payne, Folkestone; *m* 1946, Pamela Vivien Wallis; four *s* one *d.* *Educ:* Lower Sch. of John Lyon, Harrow; City and Guilds Coll., London. BSc Eng Hons; FCGI, FICE, MIHE, FCIT, FEng, MSocCE (France); Mem. Architectural Assoc. Royal Engrs (Captain), 1939–45 (despatches twice); Imperial Coll. of Science and Technology London (Civil), 1946–49; Sir Frederick Snow & Partners, 1949, Partner 1955; British Airports Authority: Dir of Engrg, 1965; Dir of Planning, 1969, and Mem. Bd 1971. Pres., West European Airports Assoc., 1975–77; Chairman: Airports Assoc. Co-ordinating Council, 1976; Aerodrome Owners' Assoc., 1983–84. Chm., British Sect., Centre for European Public Enterprise, 1979–82. Chm., NICG, 1982–83; Comr, Manpower Services Commn, 1983–85. Pres., CIT, 1984–85. CBIM (FBIM 1975). Hon. DTech Loughborough, 1985. *Publications:* various papers on airports and air transport. *Recreation:* travel. *Address:* BAA plc, Corporate Office, 130 Wilton Road, SW1V 1LQ. *T:* 01–834 9449. *Clubs:* Reform, RAC.

PAYNE, Peter Charles John, PhD; MSc(AgrEng); agricultural consultant, arbitrator and farmer, since 1975; *b* 8 Feb. 1928; *s* of late C. J. Payne, China Clay Merchant, and Mrs F. M. Payne; *m* 1961, Margaret Grover; two *s* one *d.* *Educ:* Plymouth Coll.; Teignmouth Grammar School; Reading University. BSc Reading 1948; Min. of Agriculture Scholar, Durham Univ., MSc(AgrEng) 1950; Scientific Officer, Nat. Institute of Agricultural Engineering, 1950–55; PhD Reading 1954; Lecturer in Farm Mechanisation, Wye College, London Univ., 1955–60; Lecturer in Agricultural Engineering, Durham Univ., 1960–61; Principal, Nat. Coll. of Agricultural Engineering, Silsoe, 1962–75; Visiting Professor: Univ. of Reading, 1969–75; Cranfield Inst. of Technology, 1975–80. Chm., Agricl Panel, Intermed. Technol. Develt Gp, 1979–; Mem., British Inst. of Agricl Consultants, 1978. Vice-Pres., Section III, Commn Internationale du Génie Rural, 1969. FIAgrE 1968; FRAgSs 1971; CEng 1980; ACIArb 1986. *Publications:* various papers in agricultural and engineering journals. *Recreation:* sailing. *Address:* Garlidna Farm, Porkellis, Helston TR13 0JX. *T:* Falmouth 40301. *Club:* Farmers'.

PAYNE, Rt. Rev. Sidney Stewart; *see* Newfoundland, Western, Bishop of.

PAYNE, (Trevor) Ian; *see* Payne, I.

PAYNE-BUTLER, George William; County Treasurer, Surrey County Council, 1973–79 (Assistant, 1962; Deputy, 1970); *b* 7 Oct. 1919; *s* of late George and Letitia Rachel Payne; *m* 1947, Joyce Louise Cockburn; one *s* two *d.* *Educ:* Woking Sch. for Boys. Joined Surrey CC, 1937. Served War, RAF, 1940–45. Chartered Municipal Treasurer, 1950 (CIPFA). *Recreations:* gardening, handicraft work in wood, reading. *Address:* Janston, Hillier Road, Guildford, Surrey GU1 2JQ. *T:* Guildford 65337.

PAYNE-GALLWEY, Sir Philip (Frankland), 6th Bt, *cr* 1812; Director, British Bloodstock Agency plc, since 1968; *b* 15 March 1935; *s* of late Lt-Col Lowry Philip Payne-Gallwey, OBE, MC and of Janet, *d* of late Albert Philip Payne-Gallwey; *S* cousin, 1964. *Educ:* Eton; Royal Military Academy, Sandhurst. Lieut, 11th Hussars, 1957. *Recreations:* hunting, shooting, golf. *Heir:* none. *Address:* The Little House, Boxford, Newbury, Berks. *T:* Boxford 315; British Bloodstock Agency plc, 16/17 Pall Mall, SW1Y 5LU. *T:* 01–839 3393. *Club:* Cavalry and Guards.

PAYNTER, Prof. John Frederick, OBE 1985; Professor of Music Education and Head of Department of Music, University of York; *b* 17 July 1931; *s* of late Frederick Albert Paynter and late Rose Alice Paynter; *m* 1956, Elizabeth Hill; one *d.* *Educ:* Emanuel Sch., London; Trinity Coll. of Music, London (GTCL 1952). DPhil York, 1971. Teaching appts, primary and secondary schs, 1954–62; Lectr in Music, City of Liverpool C. F. Mott Coll. of Educn, 1962–65; Principal Lectr (Head of Dept of Music), Bishop Otter Coll., Chichester, 1965–69; Lectr, Dept of Music, Univ. of York, 1969, Sen. Lectr, 1974–82. Composer and writer on music-educn. Dir, Schs Council Proj., Music in the Secondary School Curriculum, 1973–82. Gen. Editor, series, Resources of Music; Jt Editor, British Jl of Music Educn. Hon. GSM 1985. *Publications:* Sound and Silence (with Peter Aston), 1970; Hear and Now, 1972; (with Elizabeth Paynter) The Dance and the Drum, 1974; All Kinds of Music, vols 1–3, 1976, vol. 4, 1979; Sound Tracks, 1978; Music in the Secondary School Curriculum: trends and developments in class music teaching, 1982; articles and revs in Music in Educn, Music Teacher, Times Educnl Sup., Music Now (Aust. Contemp. Music Qtly), Music Educn Rev., Canadian Music Educator, Muziek en Onderwijs, beQuadro, Kreativ Musik Undervining, Muzikale vorming, Proposte di musica creativa nella scuola, Investigating Music (Australian Broadcasting Commn); scripts and commentaries for schs broadcasts and TV; *musical compositions:* choral and instrumental works including: Landscapes, 1972; The Windhover, 1972; May Magnificat, 1973; God's Grandeur, 1975; Sacraments of Summer, 1975; Galaxies for Orchestra, 1977; The Voyage of Brendan, 1978; The Visionary Hermit, 1979; The Inviolable Voice, 1980; String Quartet, 1981; Cantata for the Waking of Lazarus, 1981; The Laughing Stone, 1982; Contrasts for Orchestra, 1982; Variations for Orchestra and Audience, 1983; Conclaves, 1984; solo vocal and instrumental works and music-theatre works for children. *Recreation:* walking. *Address:* Westfield House, Newton upon Derwent, York YO4 5DA.

PAYNTER, Air Cdre Noel Stephen, CB 1946; DL; retired; *b* 26 Dec. 1898; *s* of late Canon F. S. Paynter, sometime Rector of Springfield, Essex; *m* 1925, Barbara Grace Haagensen; one *s* one *d.* *Educ:* Haileybury; RMC, Sandhurst. Flying Brevet, 1917; France and Russia, 1918–19 (St Anne 3rd Class); North-West Frontier, 1919–21; North-West Frontier, 1925–30; Malta, 1934; Directorate of Intelligence, Air Ministry, 1936–39; Chief Intelligence Officer, Middle East, 1939–42 (despatches); Chief Intelligence Officer, Bomber Command, 1942–45 (CB); Directorate of Intelligence, Air Ministry, 1946. Chm. Buckinghamshire Playing Fields Assoc., 1958–65; Chm. Bucks Army Cadet Force (TA), 1962–65. High Sheriff, Bucks, 1965. DL Buckinghamshire, 1963. *Address:* Lawn House, Edgcott, near Aylesbury, Bucks. *T:* Grendon Underwood 238.

PAYTON, Stanley Walden, CMG 1965; Chief of Overseas Department, Bank of England, 1975–80, retired; *b* 29 May 1921; *s* of late Archibald Walden Payton and late Ethel May Payton (*née* Kirtland); *m* 1941, Joan (*née* Starmer); one *s* one *d.* *Educ:* Monoux School. Fleet Air Arm, 1940–46; Entered Bank of England, 1946; UK Alternate on Managing Board of European Payments Union, Paris, 1957–59; First Governor of Bank of Jamaica, 1960–64.

PAYTON, Rev. Wilfred Ernest Granville, CB 1965; Vicar of Abingdon, 1969–79; Rural Dean of Abingdon, 1976–79; *b* 27 Dec. 1913; *s* of Wilfred Richard Daniel Payton and Alice Payton (*née* Lewin); *m* 1946, Nita Mary Barber; one *s* one *d.* *Educ:* Nottingham High School; Emmanuel College, Cambridge (MA); Ridley Hall, Cambridge. Ordained, 1938; Chaplain, RAF, 1941; Asst Chaplain-in-Chief, 1959; Chaplain-in-Chief, 1965–69; Archdeacon, Prebendary and Canon of St Botolph, Lincoln Cathedral, 1965–69. Hon. Chaplain to the Queen, 1965–69. *Recreations:* cricket (Cambridge Univ. 1937), hockey (Notts 1938–39), tennis. *Address:* Westwood, Nailsworth, Gloucester GL6 0AW. *Clubs:* MCC; Hawks (Cambridge).

PAZ, Octavio; Mexican author; poet; Director, Revista Vuelta; *b* Mexico City, 31 March 1914; *s* of Octavio Paz and Josefina Lozano; *m* Marie José Tramini; one *d.* *Educ:* National Univ. of Mexico. Founded and directed Mexican literary reviews: Barandal, 1931; Taller, 1938; El Hijo Pródigo, 1943. Guggenheim Fellowship, USA, 1944. Sec., Mexican Embassy, Paris, 1946; New Delhi, 1952; Chargé d'Affaires *ad interim*, Japan, 1952; posted to Secretariat for External Affairs México, 1953–58; Extraordinary and Plenipotentiary Minister to Mexican Embassy, Paris, 1959–62; Ambassador to India, 1962–68; in Oct. 1968 resigned in protest at bloody students' repression in Tlatelolco. Simon Bolivar Prof. of Latin-American Studies, Cambridge, 1970; Vis. Prof. of Spanish American Lit., Univ. of Texas, Austin, and Pittsburgh Univ., 1968–70; Charles Eliot Norton Prof. of Poetry, Harvard Univ., 1971–72. Editor, Plural, Mexico City, 1971–75. Prizes include: Internat. Poetry Grand Prix, 1963; Nat. Prize for Literature, Mexico, 1977; Jerusalem Prize, 1977; Critics' Prize, Spain, 1977; Golden Eagle, Nice, 1978; Ollin Yoliztli, Mexico, 1980; Cervantes, Spain, 1982; Neustadt Internat. Prize for Literature, US, 1982. *Publications: poetry:* Luna Silvestre, 1933; Bajo tu Clara Sombra y otras poemas sobre España, 1937; Raiz del Hombre, 1937; Entre la Piedra y la Flor, 1941; A la Orilla del Mundo, 1942; Libertad bajo Palabra, 1949; Aguila o Sol?, 1951; Semillas para un Himno, 1956; Piedra de Sol, 1957 (trans. as Sun Stone, 1960); La Estación Violenta, 1958; Libertad bajo Palabra (poetical works 1935–57), 1960; Salamandra (poetical works 1958–61), 1962; Viento Entero, 1965; Blanco, 1967; Discos Visuales, 1968; Ladera Este, 1969; La Centena, 1969; Topoemas, 1971; Renga, 1971; New Poetry of Mexico (Anthol.), 1972; Pasado en Claro, 1975; Vuelta, 1976; Poemas 1935–1975, 1979; *in English:* Early Poems (1935–57), 1963; Eagle or Sun?, 1970; Configurations, 1971; A Draft of Shadows and Other Poems, 1979; Airborn/Hijos del Aire, 1981; Selected Poems, 1984; *prose:* El Laberinto de la soledad, 1950 (trans. as Labyrinth of Solitude, 1961); El Arco y la Lira, 1956 (trans. as The Bow and The Lyre, 1975); Las Peras del Olmo, 1957; Cuadrivio, 1965; Los Signos en Rotación, 1965; Piertas al campo, 1966; Corriente Alterna, 1967 (trans. as Alternating Current, 1972); Claude Levi-Strauss o el Nuevo Festín de Esopo, 1967 (trans. as On Levi-Strauss,

1970); Marcel Duchamp o El Castillo de la Pureza, 1968 (trans. as Marcel Duchamp or the Castle of Purity, 1970); Conjunciones y Disyunciones (essay), 1969 (trans. as Conjunctions and Disjunctions, 1974); Postdata, 1970 (trans. as The Other Mexico, 1972); El Mono Gramático, 1971 (trans. as The Monkey Grammarian, 1981); Las Cosas en su Sitio, 1971; Traducción: Literatura y Literalidad, 1971; El Signo y el Garabato, 1973; Los Hijos del Limo, 1974 (trans. as Children of the Mire, 1974); Marcel Duchamp: Apariencia Desnuda, 1978 (trans. as Marcel Duchamp: Appearance Stripped Bare, 1981); Xavier Villaurrutia en Persona y en Obra, 1978; El Ogro Filantrópico, 1979; In mediaciones, 1979; *translations:* Versiones y Diversiones, 1974. *Address:* c/o Revista Vuelta, Leonardo da Vinci 17, México 03910, DF México.

PEACH, Captain Charles Lindsay K.; *see* Keighly-Peach.

PEACH, Denis Alan, CB 1985; Chief Charity Commissioner, since 1982; *b* 10 Jan. 1928; *s* of late Richard Peach and Alice Ellen Peach; *m* 1957, Audrey Hazel Chamberlain. *Educ:* Selhurst Grammar Sch., Croydon. Home Office, 1946–82: Asst Principal, 1951; Private Sec. to Perm. Under Sec of State, 1956; Principal, 1957; Sec. to Anglo-Egyptian Resettlement Bd, 1957–58; Prison Commn, 1958–62; Asst Sec., 1967; Asst Under Sec. of State, 1974–82 (Prin. Finance Officer, 1974–80). *Recreations:* painting, gardening. *Address:* 10 Morkyns Walk, Alleyn Park, SE21 8BG. *T:* 01–670 5574. *Club:* Reform.

PEACOCK, Prof. Alan Turner, DSC 1945; MA; FBA 1979; Research Professor in Public Finance, Heriot-Watt University, since 1985; Chairman, Scottish Arts Council, since 1986; *b* 26 June 1922; *s* of late Professor A. D. Peacock, FRSE and of Clara Mary (*née* Turner); *m* 1944, Margaret Martha Astell Burt; two *s* one *d. Educ:* Dundee High School; University of St Andrews (1939–42, 1945–47). Royal Navy, 1942–45 (Lieut RNVR). Lecturer in Economics: Univ. of St Andrews, 1947–48; London Sch. of Economics, 1948–51 (Hon. Fellow, 1980); Reader in Public Finance, Univ. of London, 1951–56; Prof. of Economic Science, Univ. of Edinburgh, 1957–62; Prof. of Economics, Univ. of York, 1962–78; Prof. of Economics, and Principal-designate, University Coll. at Buckingham, 1978–80, Principal, 1980–83; Vice-Chancellor, Univ. of Buckingham, 1983–84, Professor Emeritus, 1985–. Seconded from Univ. of York as Chief Economic Adviser, Depts of Industry and Trade, 1973–76. Visiting Prof. of Economics, Johns Hopkins Univ., 1958. Member: Commission of Enquiry into land and population problems of Fiji, 1959; Adv. Council, Inst. Economic Affairs, 1959–; Departmental Committee on Electricity in Scotland, 1961; Council, REconS, 1961–78; Cttee of Enquiry on impact of rates, 1964; Commn on the Constitution, 1970–73; SSRC, 1972–73; Cttee of Inquiry on Retirement Provision, 1984; Arts Council, 1986–; Pres., Internat. Inst. of Public Finance, 1966–69; Chairman: Arts Council Enquiry on Orchestral Resources, 1969–70; Council, London Philharmonic Orch., 1975–79; Cttee on Financing the BBC, 1985–86. Non-exec. Dir, Economist Intelligence Unit Ltd, 1977–84. DUniv Stirling, 1974; Hon. DEcon Zürich, 1984; Hon. DSc Buckingham, 1986. *Publications:* Economics of National Insurance, 1952; (ed) Income Redistribution and Social Policy 1954; National Income and Social Accounting (with H. C. Edey), 1954, 3rd imp. 1967; The National Income of Tanganyika (1952–54) (with D. G. M. Dosser), 1958; The Growth of Public Expenditure in the UK, 1890–1955 (with J. Wiseman), 1961; Economic Theory of Fiscal Policy (with G. K. Shaw), 1971, 2nd edn, 1976; The Composer in the Market Place (with R. Weir), 1975; Welfare Economics: a liberal re-interpretation (with C. K. Rowley), 1975; Economic Analysis of Government, 1979; (ed and contrib.) Structural Economic Policies in West Germany and the UK, 1980; (ed jtly) Political Economy of Taxation, 1981; (ed and contrib.) The Regulation Game, 1984; articles on applied economics in Economic Jl, Economica and other journals. *Recreations:* trying to write music, wine spotting. *Address:* 8 Gilmour Road, Edinburgh EH16 5NF. *T:* 031–667 0544. *Clubs:* Reform, Naval; Scottish Arts.

PEACOCK, Hon. Andrew Sharp; MP (L) Kooyong, Australia, since 1966; *b* 13 Feb. 1939; *s* of late A. S. Peacock and Iris Peacock; *m* 1983, Margaret St George. *Educ:* Scotch Coll., Melbourne, Vic; Melbourne Univ. (LLB). Former Partner, Rigby & Fielding, Solicitors; Chm., Peacock and Smith Pty Ltd, 1962–69. CMF Reserve (Captain), 1966. Pres., Victorian Liberal Party, 1965–66; Minister for Army and Minister assisting Prime Minister, 1969–71; Minister for Army and Minister asstg Treasurer, 1971–72; Minister for External Territories, Feb.-Dec. 1972; Mem., Opposition Exec., 1973–75; Oppos. Shadow Minister for For. Affairs, 1973–75, 1985–; Minister for: Foreign Affairs, 1975–80; Industrial Relns, 1980–81; Industry and Commerce, 1982–83; Leader of the Parly Liberal Party, and of the Opposition, 1983–85. *Recreations:* horse racing, sailboarding, Australian Rules football. *Address:* 400 Flinders Street, Melbourne, Vic 3000, Australia. *T:* 622521. *Clubs:* Melbourne, Melbourne Cricket (Melbourne).

PEACOCK, Elizabeth Joan, JP; MP (C) Batley and Spen, since 1983; *b* 4 Sept. 1937; *d* of late John Gates and of Dorothy Gates; *m* 1963, Brian D. Peacock; two *s. Educ:* St Monica's Convent, Skipton. Asst to Exec. Dir, York Community Council, 1979–83; Administrator, four charitable trusts, York, 1979–83. County Councillor, N Yorks, 1981–84. Mem., Select Cttee on Employment, 1983–. Sec., Yorks Cons. MPs, 1983–; Vice Chm., Cons. Back Bench Party Organisation Cttee, 1985–. Vice President: Yorks Area Young Conservatives, 1984–; Nat. Assoc. of Approved Driving Instructors, 1984–. JP Macclesfield, 1975–79, Bulmer East 1983. *Recreations:* dressmaking, motoring. *Address:* House of Commons, SW1A 0AA. *T:* 01–219 4092; (constituency office) 11 Providence Street, Scholes, Cleckheaton, West Yorks. *T:* Cleckheaton 872968.

PEACOCK, Sir Geoffrey (Arden), Kt 1981; CVO 1977; MA; Remembrancer, City of London, 1968–81; *b* 7 Feb. 1920; *s* of Warren Turner Peacock and Elsie (*née* Naylor); *m* 1949, Mary Gillian Drew, *d* of Dr Harold Drew Lander, Rock, Cornwall; two *d. Educ:* Wellington Coll.; Jesus Coll., Cambridge. Served in War, 1939–46; RA and Roy. Lincs. Regt; Lt-Col 1945; Pres. of War Crimes Court, Singapore. Called to the Bar, Inner Temple. Legal Asst, Treasury Solicitor's Dept, 1949; Princ., HM Treasury, 1954; Sen. Legal Asst, Treasury Solicitor's Dept, 1958. Hon. Steward, Westminster Abbey, 1981–. Master: Pewterers Co., 1985 and 1986; Co. of Watermen and Lightermen, 1986. Chm., Brighton and Storrington Beagles, 1970–73. Various foreign decorations. *Recreations:* beagling, sailing, rowing. *Address:* Haymarsh, Duncton, Petworth, West Sussex GU28 0JY. *T:* Petworth 42793. *Clubs:* Cruising Association, London Rowing, City Livery, Leander.

PEACOCK, (Ian) Michael; Managing Director, Dumbarton Films Ltd (formerly Video Arts Television Ltd), since 1978; Chairman, Monitor Enterprises Ltd, since 1970; Director: Video Arts Ltd; Greater Manchester Independent Radio Ltd; *b* 14 Sept. 1929; *e s* of Norman Henry and Sara Barbara Peacock; *m* 1956, Daphne Lee; two *s* one *d. Educ:* Kimball Union Academy, USA; Welwyn Garden City Grammar School; London School of Economics (BSc Econ.). BBC Television: Producer, 1952–56; Producer Panorama, 1956–58; Asst Head of Television Outside Broadcasts, 1958–59; Editor, Panorama, 1959–61; Editor, BBC Television News, 1961–63; Chief of Programmes, BBC-2, 1963–65; Controller, BBC-1, BBC Television Service, 1965–67; Managing Dir, London Weekend Television Ltd, 1967–69; Man. Dir, Warner Bros TV Ltd, 1972–74; Exec. Vice-Pres., Warner Bros Television Inc., 1974–76. Pres., Video Arts Inc., 1976–78. IPPA: First Chm., 1981–82; Mem. Council, 1983–85. Member: Council, Counsel and Care for the Elderly, 1986–; Ct of Governors, LSE, 1982–. *Recreations:* sailing, theatre, cinema, concerts, gardening. *Address:* 21 Woodlands Road, Barnes, SW13. *T:* 01–876 2025. *Clubs:* Savile, Royal Ocean Racing; Royal Southern Yacht.

PEACOCK, Prof. Joseph Henry, MD, FRCS; Professor of Surgical Science, University of Bristol, 1969–84, now Emeritus; *b* 22 Oct. 1918; *s* of Harry James Peacock and Florence Peacock; *m* 1950, Gillian Frances Pinckney; one *s* one *d. Educ:* Bristol Grammar Sch.; Univ. of Birmingham (MB, ChB 1941, ChM 1957, MD 1963). MRCS, LRCP 1941, FRCS 1949. House appts, 1942; served RAMC, 1942–47: surgical and orthopaedic specialist, England and Far East; Hon. Major; Demonstr in Anat., Univ. of Birmingham, 1947; Surg. Registrar, 1948–51, and Sen. Surg. Registrar, 1952–53, United Bristol Hosp.; Rockefeller Fellow, Ann Arbor, 1951; Lectr in Surgery, 1953, and Reader in Surg., 1965, Univ. of Bristol; Consultant Surgeon: United Bristol Hosp., 1955; SW Reg. Hosp. Bd, 1960. Member: GMC, 1975–85 (Chm., Sub-cttee F, 1980–85); SW RHA, 1975–84 (Chm., Res. Cttee, 1981–84); Vascular Surgical Soc. of GB (also Pres.); Founder Member: Surgical Res. Soc.; European Soc. of Surg. Res.; Fellow, Assoc. of Surgeons of GB. Royal Coll. of Surgeons of England: Jacksonian Prize, 1954 and 1967; Hunterian Prof., 1956; Arris and Gale Lectr, 1960; Examr, LDS, 1958–63, and primary FRCS, 1965–71; Mem., Ct of Examrs, 1976–82 (Chm., 1982). Examr in Surg., Univs of Bristol, Birmingham, London, Wales, Ghana, Sudan and Liverpool. *Publications:* Raynaud's Disease: British surgical practice, 1960; scientific pubns on vascular surgery and liver transplantation. *Recreations:* short wave radio, gardening. *Address:* The Old Manor, Ubley, near Bristol BS18 6PJ. *T:* Blagdon 62733. *Club:* Army and Navy.

PEACOCK, Michael; *see* Peacock, I. M.

PEACOCK, Ronald, MA, LittD (Leeds), MA (Manchester), DrPhil (Marburg); Professor of German, Bedford College, University of London, 1962–75, now Emeritus Professor; Fellow of Bedford College, 1980; *b* 22 Nov. 1907; *s* of Arthur Lorenzo and Elizabeth Peacock; *m* 1933, Ilse Gertrud Eva, *d* of Geheimer Oberregierungsrat Paul Freiwald; no *c. Educ:* Leeds Modern Sch.; Universities of Leeds, Berlin, Innsbruck, Marburg. Assistant Lecturer in German, University of Leeds, 1931–38; Lecturer, 1938–39; Professor, 1939–45; Henry Simon Professor of German Language and Literature, University of Manchester, 1945–62; Dean of the Faculty of Arts, 1954–56; Pro-Vice-Chancellor, 1958–62; Visiting Professor of German Literature, Cornell Univ. (USA), 1949; Visiting Professor of German Literature and Comparative Literature, University of Heidelberg, 1960–61; Professor of Modern German Literature, University of Freiburg, 1965, 1967–68. Pres., MHRA, 1983. Hon. LittD Manchester, 1977. *Publications:* The Great War in German Lyrical Poetry, 1934; Das Leitmotiv bei Thomas Mann, 1934; Hölderlin, 1938; The Poet in the Theatre, 1946 (reprinted with additional essays, 1960); The Art of Drama, 1957; Goethe's Major Plays, 1959; Criticism and Personal Taste, 1972; various articles on literature contributed to reviews and periodicals. *Recreations:* music, theatre, travel. *Address:* Greenshade, Woodhill Avenue, Gerrards Cross, Bucks.

PEACOCK, Dr William James, BSc, PhD; FRS 1982; FAA; Chief, Division of Plant Industry, Commonwealth Scientific and Industrial Research Organization, since 1978; *b* 14 Dec. 1937; *m* 1961, Margaret Woodward; one *s* two *d. Educ:* Katoomba High Sch.; Univ. of Sydney (BSc, PhD). FAA 1976. CSIRO Postdoctoral Fellow, 1963 and Vis. Associate Prof. of Biology, 1964–65, Univ. of Oregon; Res. Consultant, Oak Ridge National Lab., USA, 1965; res. staff, Div. of Plant Industry, CSIRO, 1965–. Adjunct Prof. of Biology, Univ. of Calif, San Diego, 1969; Vis. Professor: of Biochem., Stanford Univ., 1970; of Molecular Biol., Univ. of Calif, LA, 1977. Edgeworth David Medal, Royal Soc. of NSW, 1967; Lemberg Medal, Aust. Biochem. Soc., 1978. *Publications:* editor of 5 books on genetics and molecular biology; approx. 120 papers. *Recreations:* squash, sailing, bush-walking. *Address:* 16 Brassey Street, Deakin, ACT 2600, Australia. *T:* (home) (062) 814485, (office) (062) 465250.

PEACOCKE, Rev. Dr Arthur Robert, DSc, ScD, DD; Director, Ian Ramsey Centre, St Cross College, Oxford, since 1985; Fellow of St Cross College; *b* 29 Nov. 1924; *s* of Arthur Charles Peacocke and Rose Elizabeth (*née* Lilly); *m* 1948, Rosemary Winifred Mann; one *s* one *d. Educ:* Watford Grammar Sch.; Exeter Coll., Oxford (Scholar; BA Chem., BSc 1946; MA, DPhil 1948). DSc Oxon, 1962; ScD Cantab (incorp.), 1973; DD Oxon, 1982. DipTh 1960, BD 1971, Birmingham. Asst Lectr, Lectr and Sen. Lectr in Biophys. Chemistry, Univ. of Birmingham, 1948–59; Lectr in Biochem., Oxford Univ., and Fellow and Tutor in Chem., subseq. in Biochem., St Peter's Coll., 1959–73; Lectr in Chem., Mansfield Coll., Oxford, 1964–73; Dean and Fellow, Clare Coll., Cambridge, 1973–84. Rockefeller Fellow, Univ. of Calif at Berkeley, and Univ. of Wis, 1951–52; Vis. Fellow, Weizmann Inst., Israel, 1956; Bishop Williams Meml Lectr, Rikkyo (St Paul's) Univ., Japan, 1981; Shann Lectr, Univ. of Hong Kong, 1982; Mendenhall Lectr, DePauw Univ., Indiana, 1983; Prof. of Judeo-Christian Studies, Tulane Univ., 1984; McNair Lectr, Univ. of N Carolina, 1984; J. K. Russell Fellow in Religion and Science, Center for Theology and Natural Sci., Berkeley, 1986; Nina Booth Bricker Meml Lectr, Tulane Univ., 1986; Norton Lectr, Southern Baptist Seminary, Louisville, 1986. Lay Reader, Oxford Dio., 1960–71; ordained, 1971; Mem., Archbps' Commn on Christian Doctrine, 1969–76 (Mem. sub-gp on Man and Nature, 1972–74); Chm., Science and Religion Forum, 1972–78, Vice-Pres., 1981–; Vice-Pres., Inst. of Religion in an Age of Science, USA, 1984–. Select Preacher, Oxford Univ., 1973, 1985; Hulsean Preacher, Cambridge Univ., 1976; Bampton Lectr, Oxford Univ., 1978; Judge, Templeton Foundn Prize, 1979–82. Meetings Sec., Sec. and Chm., Brit. Biophys. Soc., 1965–69. Hon. DSc DePauw Univ., Indiana, 1983; Mem. Editorial Bd, Biochem. Jl, and Biopolymers, 1966–71, Zygon, 1973–. Editor, Monographs in Physical Biochemistry (OUP), 1967–. Lecomte du Noüy Prize, 1973. *Publications:* Molecular Basis of Heredity (with J. B. Drysdale), 1965 (repr. 1967); Science and the Christian Experiment, 1971; (with M. P. Tombs) Osmotic Pressure of Biological Macromolecules, 1974; (with J. Dominian) From Cosmos to Love, 1977; Creation and the World of Science, 1979; (ed) The Sciences and Theology in the Twentieth Century, 1982; The Physical Chemistry of Biological Organization, 1983; Intimations of Reality, 1984; (ed) Reductionism in Academic Disciplines, 1985; God and the New Biology, 1986; articles and papers in scientific and theol jls, and symposia vols. *Recreations:* piano, music, mountain walking, churches. *Address:* Ian Ramsey Centre, St Cross College, Oxford; 55 St John Street, Oxford.

PEACOCKE, Rt. Rev. Cuthbert Irvine, TD; MA; *b* 26 April 1903; *er s* of late Rt Rev. Joseph Irvine Peacocke, DD; *m* 1931, Helen Louise Gaussen; one *s* one *d. Educ:* St Columba's Coll., Dublin; Trinity Coll., Dublin; Curate, Seapatrick Parish, 1926–30; Head of Southern Mission, 1930–33; Rector, Derriaghy, 1933–35; Rector, St Mark's, Dundela, 1935–56; CF, 1939–45; Archdeacon of Down, 1950–56; Dean of St Anne's Cathedral, Belfast, 1956–69; Bishop of Derry and Raphoe, 1970–75. *Publication:* The Young Parson, 1936. *Recreations:* games, garden and reading. *Address:* Culmore House West, Culmore Point, Londonderry.

PEAKE, family name of **Viscount Ingleby.**

PEAKE, Air Cdre (retired) Dame Felicity (Hyde), (Lady Peake), DBE 1949 (MBE 1941); AE; *b* 1 May 1913; *d* of late Colonel Humphrey Watts, OBE, TD, and Mrs Simon Orde; *m* 1st, 1935, John Charles Mackenzie Hanbury (killed on active service, 1939); no *c*; 2nd, 1952, Sir Harald Peake, AE (*d* 1978); one *s*. *Educ:* St Winifreds, Eastbourne; Les Grands Huguenots, Vaucresson, Seine et Oise, France. Joined ATS Company of the RAF, April 1939; commissioned in the WAAF, Aug. 1939; served at home and in the Middle East; Director, Women's Auxiliary Air Force, 1946–49; Director Women's Royal Air Force, from its inception, 1949, until her retirement, 1950. Member Advisory Cttee, Recruitment for the Forces, 1958. Trustee, Imperial War Museum, 1963–85; Governor, London House, 1958–76, 1978–; Mem. Council, RAF Benevolent Fund (a Vice-Pres., 1978–); Mem. Council, Union Jack Club, 1950–78. Hon. ADC to King George VI, 1949–50.

PEAKE, John Fordyce; Keeper of Zoology, British Museum (Natural History), since 1985; *b* 4 June 1933; *s* of late William Joseph Peake and of Helena (*née* Fordyce); *m* 1963, Pamela Joyce Hollis; two *d*. *Educ:* City of Norwich Grammar Sch.; University Coll. London (BSc). National Trust, 1955–56; Norwich Technical Coll., 1956–58; Nature Conservancy Studentship, 1958–59; British Museum (Natural History): Research Fellow, 1959–61; Sen. Scientific Officer, 1961–69; PSO, 1969–71; Dep. Keeper, 1971–85. Hon. Research Associate, Bernice P. Bishop Mus., Honolulu, 1972–. Royal Society: Member: Aldabra Research Cttee, 1972–77; Southern Zones Cttee, 1982–; Unitas Malacologica: Treas. 1962–63, Mem. Council, 1963–75; Vice Pres., Malacological Soc. of London, 1976–78; Council Mem., Zoological Soc. of London, 1985–. *Publications:* (editor and contributor with Dr V. Fretter) Pulmonates, 3 vols, 1975–79; papers on taxonomy, biogeography and ecology of terrestrial molluscs in sci. jls. *Recreation:* gardening. *Address:* Spring Cottage, Trycewell Lane, Ightham, Sevenoaks, Kent TN15 9HN. *T:* Borough Green 882423.

PEAKER, Prof. Malcolm, PhD; FZS, FIBiol, FRSE; Director, Hannah Research Institute, Ayr, since 1981; Hannah Professor of Dairy Science, University of Glasgow, since 1981; *b* 21 Aug. 1943; *s* of Ronald Smith Peaker and Marian (*née* Tomasin); *m* 1965, Stephanie Jane Large; three *s*. *Educ:* Henry Mellish Grammar Sch., Nottingham; Univ. of Sheffield (BSc Zoology); Univ. of Hong Kong (SRC NATO Scholar; PhD). FZS 1969; FIBiol 1979; FRSE 1983. Inst. of Animal Physiology, ARC, 1968–78; Head, Dept of Physiol., Hannah Res. Inst., 1978–81. Mem. Editorial Board: Jl of Dairy Science, 1975–78; Internat. Zoo Yearbook, 1978–82; Jl of Endocrinology, 1981–; Editor: British Jl of Herpetology, 1977–81; Internat. Circle of Dairy Research Leaders, 1982–. *Publications:* Salt Glands in Birds and Reptiles, 1975; (ed) Avian Physiology, 1975; (ed) Comparative Aspects of Lactation, 1977; (ed jtly) Physiological Strategies in Lactation, 1984; papers in physiol, endocrinol, zool, biochem., vet. and agricl science jls. *Recreations:* vertebrate zoology, natural history, golf, grumbling about bureaucrats. *Address:* 13 Upper Crofts, Alloway, Ayr KA7 4QX. *T:* Alloway 43999. *Club:* Farmers'.

PEARCE, family name of **Baron Pearce.**

PEARCE, Baron (Life Peer) *cr* 1962, of Sweethaws; **Edward Holroyd Pearce,** PC 1957; Kt 1948; RBA 1940; Chairman of the Press Council, 1969–74; Chairman, Appeals Committee, Take-over Panel, 1969–76; *b* 9 Feb. 1901; *s* of late John W. E. Pearce and Irene, *d* of Holroyd Chaplin; *m* 1927, Erica (*d* 1985), *d* of late Bertram Priestman, RA; one *s* (and one *s* decd). *Educ:* Charterhouse; Corpus Christi Coll., Oxford. Hon. Fellow, Corpus Christi Coll., 1950. Called to Bar, 1925; QC 1945; Bencher, Hon. Society of Lincoln's Inn, 1948; Treasurer, 1966. Deputy Chairman, East Sussex Quarter Sessions, 1947–48; Judge of High Court of Justice, Probate, Divorce and Admiralty Division, 1948–54, Queen's Bench Division, 1954–57; a Lord Justice of Appeal, 1957–62; a Lord of Appeal in Ordinary, 1962–69. Chairman, Cttee on Shipbuilding Costs, 1947–49; Mem., Royal Commission on Marriage and Divorce, 1951; Chairman: Commn to test Rhodesian approval of proposed British-Rhodesian settlements, 1971–72; Cttee on the organisation of Bar and Inns of Court, 1971–73 (Hon. Mem. Senate, Four Inns of Court, 1974); Indep. Chm., Press discussions on Charter of Press Freedom, 1976–77. Mem., Governing Body, Charterhouse Sch., 1943–64; Governor: Tonbridge Sch., 1945–78; Sutton's Hospital in Charterhouse; Fedn of British Artists, 1970–73. Prof. of Law, Royal Acad. of Arts, 1971–. Past Master and past Member of Court of Company of Skinners; President, Artists League of GB, 1950–74; Trustee, Chantrey Bequest; Hon. FRBS. One-man show of landscapes at The Mall Galleries, 1971 and (with wife) 1973, 1976; also in provinces; one-man show of Alpine landscapes at Chur, Switzerland, 1977 and at Alpine Gall., London, 1983. *Recreations:* painting and pictures. *Address:* House of Lords, SW1; Sweethaws, Crowborough. *T:* 61520. *Club:* Athenæum.
See also Hon. R. B. H. Pearce.

PEARCE, Andrew; Member (C) Cheshire West, European Parliament, since 1979; *b* 1 Dec. 1937; *s* of late Henry Pearce, Liverpool cotton broker, and Evelyn Pearce; *m* 1966, Myra Whelan; three *s* one *d*. *Educ:* Rydal School, Colwyn Bay; University of Durham. BA. Formerly in construction industry; in Customs Dept, EEC, Brussels, 1974–79. Contested (C) Islington North, 1969 and 1970; Founder and Vice-Pres., British Cons. Assoc. in Belgium; Vice-Pres., Consultative Assembly of Lomé Convention, 1980–. Governor: Woodchurch High Sch., Birkenhead, 1985; Archway Comprehensive School, 1967–70. *Address:* (office) 30 Grange Road, West Kirby, Wirral. *T:* 051–625 1896.

PEARCE, (Ann) Philippa, (Mrs M. J. G. Christie); freelance writer of children's fiction, since 1967; *d* of Ernest Alexander Pearce and Gertrude Alice (*née* Ramsden); *m* 1963, Martin James Graham Christie (decd); one *d*. *Educ:* Perse Girls' Sch., Cambridge; Girton Coll., Cambridge (MA Hons English Pt I, History Pt II). Temp. civil servant, 1942–45; Producer/Scriptwriter, Sch. Broadcasting, BBC Radio, 1945–58; Editor, Educn Dept, Clarendon Press, 1958–60; Children's Editor, André Deutsch Ltd, 1960–67. Also lectures. *Publications:* Minnow on the Say, 1955 (3rd edn 1974); Tom's Midnight Garden, 1958 (3rd edn 1976; Carnegie Medal, 1959); Mrs Cockle's Cat, 1961 (2nd edn 1974); A Dog So Small, 1962 (2nd edn 1964); (with Sir Harold Scott) From Inside Scotland Yard, 1963; The Strange Sunflower, 1966; (with Sir Brian Fairfax-Lucy) The Children of the House, 1968 (2nd edn 1970); The Elm Street Lot, 1969 (enlarged edn, 1979); The Squirrel Wife, 1971; What the Neighbours Did and other stories, 1972 (2nd edn 1974); (ed) Stories from Hans Christian Andersen, 1972; Beauty and the Beast (re-telling), 1972; The Shadow Cage and other stories of the supernatural, 1977; The Battle of Bubble and Squeak, 1978 (Whitbread Award, 1978); Wings of Courage (trans. and adapted from George Sand's story), 1982; The Way to Sattin Shore, 1983; Lion at School and other stories, 1985; Who's Afraid? and other strange stories, 1986; reviews in TLS and Guardian. *Address:* c/o Viking-Kestrel Books, 536 King's Road, SW10 0UH. *T:* 01–351 2393.

PEARCE, Sir Austin (William), Kt 1980; CBE 1974; PhD; Chairman, British Aerospace, since 1980; *b* 1 Sept. 1921; *s* of William Thomas and Florence Annie Pearce; *m* 1st, 1947, Maglona Winifred Twinn (*d* 1975); three *d*; 2nd, 1979, Dr F. Patricia Grice (*née* Forsythe). *Educ:* Devonport High Sch. for Boys; Univ. of Birmingham. BSc (Hons) 1943, PhD 1945; Cadman Medallist. Joined Agwi Petroleum Corp., 1945 (later Esso Petroleum Co., Ltd): Asst Refinery Manager, 1954–56; Gen. Manager Refining, 1956–62; Dir, 1963; Man. Dir, 1968–71; Chm., 1972–80; Director: Esso Europe Inc., 1972–80; Esso Africa Inc., 1972–80; Pres., Esso Holding Co. UK Inc., 1971–80; Chairman: Esso Pension Trust Ltd, 1972–80; Irish Refining Co. Ltd, 1965–71; Director: Williams & Glyn's Bank, 1974–85 (a Dep. Chm., 1980–83; Chm., 1983–85); Royal Bank of Scotland Gp (formerly Nat. & Commercial Banking Gp), 1978–, a Vice-Chm., 1985–; Pearl Assurance PLC, 1985–; Jaguar PLC, 1986. Part-time Mem., NRDC, 1973–76; Member: Adv. Council for Energy Conservation, 1974–79; Energy Commn, 1977–79; British Aerospace, 1977– (Mem., Organising Cttee, 1976); Standing Commn on Energy and the Environment, 1978–81; Chm., UK Petroleum Industry Adv. Cttee, 1977–80; Pres., UK Petroleum Industry Assoc. Ltd, 1979–80; CBI: Chm., Industrial Policy Cttee, 1982–; Chm., Industrial Steering Policy Gp. President: Inst. of Petroleum, 1968–70; The Pipeline Industries Guild, 1973–75; Oil Industries Club, 1975–77; Pres., SBAC, 1982–83 Mem., Bd of Governors, English-Speaking Union, 1974–80; Chm., Bd of Trustees, Science Museum, 1986–. Mem. Council, Surrey Univ., 1981– (Pro-Chancellor, 1986). Hon. DSc: Southampton, 1978; Exeter, 1985. Hon. DEng Birmingham, 1986. *Recreations:* golf, woodwork. *Address:* British Aerospace PLC, 100 Pall Mall, SW1Y 5HR. *T:* 01–930 1020. *Clubs:* Athenæum; Royal Wimbledon Golf.

PEARCE, (Daniel Norton) Idris, CBE 1982; TD 1972; Managing Partner, Richard Ellis, Chartered Surveyors and International Property Consultants, since 1985; Property Adviser to National Health Service Management Board, since 1985; *b* 28 Nov. 1933; *s* of Lemuel George Douglas Pearce and Evelyn Mary Pearce; *m* 1963, Ursula Helene Langley; two *d*. *Educ:* West Buckland Sch.; College of Estate Management. FRICS. Commnd RE, 1958; comd 135 Field Survey Sqdn, RE(TA), 1970–73. Joined Richard Ellis 1959, Partner 1961, Chm. Management and Policy Cttees, 1985–. Royal Instn of Chartered Surveyors: Member: Gen. Council, 1980–; Exec. Cttee, 1984–; Chm., Parly and Public Affairs Cttee, 1984–; Vice Pres., 1986–. Chm., Internat. Assets Valuation Standards Cttee, 1981–86. Member: Adv. Panel for Instnl Finance in New Towns, 1974–80; Sec. of State for Health and Social Security Inquiry into Surplus Land in the NHS, 1982; PSA Adv. Bd, 1981–86; FCO Adv. Panel on Diplomatic Estate, 1985–. Chm., Works and Bldgs Sub-Cttee, Greater London TA&VRA, 1983– (Mem. 1970–). Chm. Governors, Stanway Sch., Dorking, 1982–85. Contested (C) Neath, 1959. *Publications:* various articles on valuation and property matters. *Recreations:* reading, opera, ballet, travel. *Address:* Mickleham Cottage, Mickleham, near Dorking, Surrey RH5 6EQ. *T:* Leatherhead 373319. *Clubs:* Brooks's, Carlton, City of London.

PEARCE, Sir Eric (Herbert), Kt 1979; OBE 1970; Director of Community Affairs, General Television Corporation, Channel Nine, Melbourne, Australia, since 1979; *b* 5 March 1905; *s* of Herbert Clement Pearce and Louise Mary Pearce; *m* 1956, Betty Constance Ham; one *d*. *Educ:* Raynes Sch., Hants. Served War, FO RAAF, 1942–44. Studio Manager/Chief Announcer, Radio Stn 3DB, Melbourne, 1944–50; Gen. Man., Radio Stns 5KA-AO-RM, SA, 1950–55; Dir of Progs, major broadcasting network, Australia, 1955–56; Chief Announcer/Sen. Newsreader, General TV, Channel Nine, 1957–79. *Recreations:* walking, swimming, golf. *Address:* 48 Lansell Road, Toorak, Vic 3142, Australia. *Clubs:* Athenæum, Toorak Services (Melbourne).

PEARCE, Most Rev. George; former Archbishop of Suva; *b* 9 Jan. 1921; *s* of George H. Pearce and Marie Louise Duval. *Educ:* Marist Coll. and Seminary, Framingham Center, Mass, USA. Entered Seminary, 1940; Priest, 1947; taught in secondary sch. in New England, USA, 1948–49; assigned as missionary to Samoa, 1949; consecrated Vicar Apostolic of Samoa, 1956; first Bishop of Apia, 1966; Archbishop of Suva, 1967–76, retired 1976. *Address:* Cathedral Rectory, 30 Fenner Street, Providence, RI 02903, USA. *T:* (401) 331–2434.

PEARCE, Howard Spencer; Director for Wales, Property Services Agency, Department of Environment, 1977–85; *b* 23 Sept. 1924; *m* 1951, Enid Norma Richards; one *s*. *Educ:* Barry County Sch.; College of Estate Management. ARICS. Armed Services, Major RE, 1943–47. Ministry of Works: Cardiff, 1953–61; Salisbury Plain, 1961–64; Ministry of Public Building and Works: Hong Kong, 1964–67; Abingdon, 1967–70; Area Officer, Abingdon, 1970–72; Regional Works Officer, SW Region, Bristol, PSA, Dept of Environment, 1972–77. *Recreations:* music, playing golf and watching Rugby football. *Address:* 2 Longhouse Close, Lisvane, Cardiff CF4 5XR. *T:* Cardiff 762029. *Clubs:* Civil Service; Cardiff Golf.

PEARCE, Idris; *see* Pearce, D. N. I.

PEARCE, John Brian; *b* 25 Sept. 1935; *s* of late George Frederic Pearce and Constance Josephine Pearce; *m* 1960, Michelle Etcheverry; four *s*. *Educ:* Queen Elizabeth Grammar Sch., Wakefield; Brasenose Coll., Oxford (BA). Asst Principal: Min. of Power, 1959; Colonial Office, 1960; Private Sec. to Parly Under-Sec. of State, 1963; Principal: Colonial Office, 1964; Dept of Economic Affairs, 1967; Principal Private Sec. to Sec. of State for Economic Affairs, 1968–69; Asst Sec., Civil Service Dept, 1969, Under-Sec., 1976; Under-Sec., HM Treasury, 1981–86, retd. *Recreations:* comparative theology, music, architecture. *Address:* 124 Court Lane, SE21 7EA.

PEARCE, John Dalziel Wyndham, MA, MD, FRCP, FRCPEd, FRCPsych, DPM, FBPsS; Consulting Psychiatrist: St Mary's Hospital; Queen Elizabeth Hospital for Children; *b* 21 Feb. 1904; *s* of John Alfred Wyndham Pearce and Mary Logan Dalziel; *m* 1929, Grace Fowler (marr. diss., 1964), no *c*; *m* 1964, Ellinor Elizabeth Nancy Draper. *Educ:* George Watson's Coll.; Edinburgh Univ. Formerly: Physician-in-charge, Depts of Psychiatry, St Mary's Hosp. and Queen Elizabeth Hosp. for Children; Cons. Psychiatrist, Royal Masonic Hosp.; Hon. physician, Tavistock Clinic and West End Hospital for Nervous Diseases; Medical co-director Portman Clinic, Institute for Study and Treatment of Delinquency (ISTD); medico-psychologist, LCC remand homes; Mem. Academic Boards, Inst. of Child Health, and St Mary's Hosp. Med. Sch. (Univ. of London); Examiner in Medicine: RCP; Univ. of London; Royal Coll. of Psychiatrists; Chm., Adv. Cttee on delinquent and maladjusted children, Internat. Union for Child Welfare; Mem., Army Psychiatry Adv. Cttee; Lt-Col, RAMC; adviser in psychiatry, Allied Force HQ, CMF (despatches). Member: Council, National Assoc. for Mental Health; Home Sec's Adv. Council on Treatment of Offenders. *Publications:* Juvenile Delinquency, 1952; technical papers in scientific journals. *Recreations:* golf, painting. *Address:* Stamford House, 4 Hampstead Square, NW3 1AB. *T:* 01–435 1387. *Club:* Caledonian.

PEARCE, John Trevor Archdall, CMG 1964; *b* 7 May 1916; *s* of late Rev. W. T. L. A. Pearce, Seven Hills, NSW, Australia, and late N. B. Pearce, Prahran, Victoria, Australia; *m* 1st, 1948, Isabel Bundey Rankine(*d* 1983), Hindmarsh Island, S Australia; no *c*; 2nd, 1984, Judith Burland Kingsley-Strack, Sydney, NSW. *Educ:* The King's Sch., Parramatta, Australia; Keble Coll., Oxford. MA. District Officer, Tanganyika, 1939. War Service: Kenya, Abyssinia, Ceylon, India, Burma, 1940–46, Major RE. Tanganyika: District Commissioner, 1950; Provincial Commissioner, 1959; Permanent Secretary (Admin), Office of the Vice-President, 1961; Chairman, Public Service Commn, Basutoland, 1963, Swaziland, 1965; Registrar, Papua and New Guinea Univ. of Technology, 1969–73. *Recreations:* golf, piano music, solitude, travel in remote places. *Address:* Clippings, 14 Golf Street, Buderim, Qld 4556, Australia.

PEARCE, Kenneth Leslie; retired as Chairman, East Midlands Gas Region (formerly East Midlands Gas Board), 1968–74; *b* 2 May 1910; *s* of late George Benjamin Pearce and Eliza Jane Pearce; *m* 1940, Evlyn Sarah Preedy (*d* 1957); two *s*. *Educ:* Dudley Grammar Sch.; Birmingham Central Techn. Coll. Engr and Man., Bilston Gas Light & Coke Co., 1939–48; Engr and Man., City of Leicester Gas Dept, 1948–49; East Midlands Gas Board: Divisional Gen. Man., Leicester and Northants, 1949–50; Divisional Gen. Man., Notts and Derby, 1950–62; Chief Distribution Engr, 1962–67; Dep. Chairman, 1967–68. *Recreations:* fishing, gardening. *Address:* Stoneridge, Coppice Lane, The Wergs, Wolverhampton WV6 9BS. *T:* Wolverhampton 755260.

PEARCE, Maj.-Gen. Leslie Arthur, CB 1973; CBE 1971 (OBE 1964; MBE 1956); Chief of General Staff, NZ Army, 1971–73, retd; *b* 22 Jan. 1918; British parents; *m* 1944, Fay Mattocks, Auckland, NZ; two *s* one *d*. *Educ:* in New Zealand. Joined Army, 1937; served War: Greece, Western Desert, Italy, 1939–45. Staff Coll., Camberley, 1948. Directing Staff, Australia Staff Coll., 1958–59; Commandant, Army Schools, NZ, 1960; Comdg Officer, 1 NZ Regt, in NZ and Malaysia, 1961–64; Dep. QMG, NZ Army, 1964–65; Dir of Staff Duties, NZ Army, 1966; IDC, 1967; QMG, 1968–69; Dep. Chief of Defence Staff, 1970. Chm., Vocational Training Council, 1975–81. Company director. Dep. Chm., NZ Council for Educnl Res., 1983–85 (Mem., 1977–85). *Recreations:* golf, fishing, gardening; Provincial and Services Rugby representative, in youth. *Address:* 1064A Beach Road, Torbay, Auckland, New Zealand.

PEARCE, Neville John Lewis; Chief Executive, Avon County Council, since 1982; *b* 27 Feb. 1933; *s* of John and Ethel Pearce; *m* 1958, Eileen Frances Potter; two *d*. *Educ:* Queen Elizabeth's Hosp., Bristol; Silcoates Sch., Wakefield; Univ. of Leeds (LLB Hons 1953, LLM 1954). Asst Solicitor: Wakefield CBC, 1957–59; Darlington CBC, 1959–61; Chief Asst Solicitor, Grimsby CBC, 1961–63, Dep. Town Clerk, 1963–65; Dep. Town Clerk, Blackpool CBC, 1965–66; Town Clerk, Bath CBC, 1967–73; Dir of Admin and County Solicitor, Avon CC, 1973–82. *Recreations:* home, family, Anglican and ecumenical church affairs. *Address:* Penshurst, Weston Lane, Bath BA1 4AB. *T:* (home) Bath 26925, (office) Bristol 290777.

PEARCE, Philippa; *see* Pearce, A. P.

PEARCE, Hon. Richard Bruce Holroyd; QC 1969; **His Honour Judge Pearce;** a Circuit Judge, since 1982; *b* 12 May 1930; *s* of Lord Pearce, *qv*, and Erica, *d* of late Bertram Priestman, RA; *m* 1958, Dornie Smith-Pert; one *s* one *d*. *Educ:* Charterhouse; Corpus Christi Coll., Oxford (MA). Served HM Forces, 1949–56: RE and E African Engrs, 1949–50; 119 Field Engr Regt RE, TA, 1950–56. Called to Bar, Lincoln's Inn, 1955, Bencher, 1977; *ad eund.* Mem., Middle Temple, 1958; a Recorder of the Crown Court, 1972–82. A Legal Assessor to GMC, 1974–82, GDC, 1974–82, GNC, 1975–82. Master, Skinner's Co., 1976–77. Governor, Tonbridge School. *Club:* Beefsteak.

PEARD, Rear-Admiral Sir Kenyon (Harry Terrell), KBE 1958 (CBE 1951); retired; *b* 1902; *s* of Henry T. Peard; *m* 1935, Mercy Leila Bone; one *s* one *d*. *Educ:* RN Colleges, Osborne and Dartmouth. Went to sea, 1919; Torpedo Specialist, 1929; transferred to Electrical Branch, 1946, Director, Naval Electrical Dept, Admiralty, 1955–58; retired 1958. *Address:* Finstead, Shorefield Crescent, Milford-on-Sea, Hants.

PEARL, Valerie Louise, DPhil; President, New Hall, Cambridge, since 1981; *b* 31 Dec. 1926; *d* of Cyril R. Bence, *qv*, and late Florence Bence; *m* 1949, Morris Leonard Pearl; one *d*. *Educ:* King Edward VI High Sch., Birmingham; St Anne's Coll., Oxford (Exhibnr). BA Hons Mod. History; MA, DPhil (Oxon). Allen Research Studentship, St Hugh's Coll., Oxford, 1951; Eileen Power Studentship, 1952; Sen. Research Studentship, Westfield Coll., London, 1962; Leverhulme Research Award, 1962; Graham Res. Fellow and Lectr in History, Somerville Coll., Oxford, 1965; Reader in History of London, 1968–81, Prof. of History of London, 1976–81, University College London. Convenor of confs to found The London Journal, Chm. of Editorial Bd, Editor-in-Chief, 1973–77; McBride Vis. Prof., Cities Program, Bryn Mawr Coll., Pennsylvania, 1974; Woodward Lectr, Yale Univ., New Haven, 1974; Lectr, Indian Council for Soc. Sci., Calcutta, Research on Indian Cities, New Delhi, 1977; John Stow Commem. Lectr, City of London, 1979; James Ford Special Lectr, Oxford, 1980; Sir Lionel Denny Lectr, Barber Surgeons' Co., 1981. Literary Dir, Royal Historical Soc., 1975–77 (Mem. Studies in History Bd, 1976–82); Pres., London and Mddx Archaeol. Soc., 1980–82; Governor, Museum of London, 1978–; Member: Royal Commn on Historical MSS, 1983–; Syndic: Cambridge Univ. Library, 1982–; Cambridge Univ. Press, 1984–. FSA 1976. *Publications:* London and the Outbreak of the Puritan Revolution, 1625–43, 1961; (ed jtly) History and Imagination: essays for Hugh Trevor-Roper, 1981; contribs to: Nuove Questione (ed L. Bulferetti), 1965; Studies in London History (ed W. Kellaway, A. Hollaender), 1969; The Interregnum (ed G. Aylmer), 1972; Puritans and Revolutionaries (ed K. Thomas, D. Pennington), 1978; also to learned jls and other works, including Trans Royal Hist. Soc., Eng. Historical Review, History of English Speaking Peoples, Past and Present, Archives, Economic Hist. Review, History, Jl of Eccles. History, Times Literary Supplement, The London Journal, London Review of Books, Listener, BBC. *Recreations:* walking and swimming. *Address:* New Hall, Cambridge. *T:* Cambridge 351721.

PEARLMAN, Valerie Anne; Her Honour Judge Pearlman; a Circuit Judge, since 1985; *b* 6 Aug. 1936; *d* of Sidney and Marjorie Pearlman; *m* 1972; one *s* one *d*. *Educ:* Wycombe Abbey Sch. Called to the Bar, Lincoln's Inn, 1958; a Recorder, 1982–85. *Recreations:* gardening, painting, reading. *Address:* Lamb Building, Temple, EC4Y 7AS. *T:* 01–353 0774. *Club:* English-Speaking Union.

PEARMAN, Sir James (Eugene), Kt 1973; CBE 1960; Senior Partner, Conyers, Dill & Pearman; *b* 24 Nov. 1904; *o s* of Eugene Charles Pearman and Kate Trott; *m* 1st, 1929, Prudence Tucker Appleby (*d* 1976); two *s*; 2nd, 1977, Mrs Antoinette Trott, *d* of Dr and Mrs James Aiguier, Philadelphia, Pa. *Educ:* Saltus Grammar Sch., Bermuda; Bromsgrove Sch., Worcs; Merton Coll., Oxford; Middle Temple. Law partnership with N. B. Dill, 1927–29; law partnership with Sir Reginald Conyers and N. B. Dill, 1929 and still continuing as firm of Conyers, Dill & Pearman. Member Colonial Parlt, Bermuda, 1943–72; MEC, 1955–63 and 1968–72; MLC, 1972–. Hon. Consul for Bolivia. *Recreations:* deep-sea fishing, bridge. *Address:* Tideway, Point Shares, Pembroke, Bermuda. *T:* 21125. *Clubs:* Carlton; Anglers' (New York); Rod and Reel (Miami); Royal Bermuda Yacht.

PEARS, David Francis, FBA 1970; Student of Christ Church, Oxford, since 1960; Professor of Philosophy, Oxford University, since 1985; *b* 8 Aug. 1921; *s* of Robert and late Gladys Pears; *m* 1963, Anne Drew; one *s* one *d*. *Educ:* Westminster Sch.; Balliol Coll., Oxford. Research Lecturer, Christ Church, 1948–50; Univ. Lectr, Oxford, 1950–72, Reader, 1972–85; Fellow and Tutor, Corpus Christi Coll., 1950–60. Visiting Professor: Harvard, 1959; Univ. of Calif, Berkeley, 1964; Rockefeller Univ., 1967; Los Angeles, 1979; Hill Prof., Univ. of Minnesota, 1970; Humanities Council Res. Fellow, Princeton, 1966. Mem., l'Inst. Internat. de Philosophie, 1978–. Governor, Westminster Sch., 1976. *Publications:* (trans. with B. McGuinness), Wittgenstein, Tractatus Logico-Philosophicus, 1961, repr. 1975; Bertrand Russell and the British Tradition in Philosophy, 1967, 2nd edn 1972; Ludwig Wittgenstein, 1971; What is Knowledge?, 1971; (ed) Russell's Logical Atomism, 1973; Some Questions in the Philosophy of Mind, 1975; Motivated Irrationality, 1984. *Address:* 31 Northmoor Road, Oxford. *T:* Oxford 54767.

PEARSE, Prof. Anthony Guy Everson, MA, MD (Cantab); FRCP, FRCPath; DCP (London); Professor of Histochemistry, University of London, Royal Postgraduate Medical School, 1965–81, now Emeritus; *b* 9 Aug. 1916; *o s* of Captain R. G. Pearse, DSO, MC, Modbury, Devon, and Constance Evelyn Steels, Pocklington, Yorks; *m* 1947, Elizabeth Himmelhoch, MB, BS (Sydney), DCP (London); one *s* three *d*. *Educ:* Sherborne Sch.; Trinity Coll., Cambridge. Kitchener Scholar, Raymond Horton-Smith prizeman, 1949–50. Posts, St Bart's Hospital, 1940–41; Surg.-Lt, RNVR, 1941–45. Registrar, Edgware General Hospital, 1946; Asst Lecturer in Pathol., PG Med. School, London, 1947–51, Lecturer, 1951–57; Cons. Pathol., Hammersmith Hospital, 1951; Fulbright Fellow and Visiting Prof. of Path., University of Alabama, 1953–54; Guest Instructor in Histochemistry: University of Kansas, 1957, 1958; Vanderbilt Univ., 1967; Reader in Histochemistry, University of London, 1957–65; Middleton Goldsmith Lectr, NY Path. Soc., 1976; Feulgen Lectr, Deutsch Ges. Histochem., 1983. Member: Path. Society (GB), 1949; Biochem. Society (GB), 1957; European Gastro Club, 1969; Hon. Member or Member various foreign societies incl. Deutsche Akademie der Naturforscher Leopoldina, 1973 and Amer. Assoc. Endocrine Surgeons, 1981; Corresp. Mem., Deutsche Gesellschaft für Endokrinologie, 1978; Hon. Fellow, Royal Microscop. Society, 1964 (Vice-Pres., 1970–72; Pres., 1972–74). Hon. Mem., Mark Twain Soc., 1977. Hon. MD: Basel, 1960; Krakow, 1978. John Hunter Medal and Triennial Prize, RCS, 1976–78; Ernest Jung Prize for Medicine, 1979; Fred W. Stewart Medal and Prize, Sloan-Kettering Cancer Center, NY, 1979. Member Editorial Board: Histochemie, 1958–73; Histochemical Jl, 1968–; Histochemistry, 1974–; Progress in Histochem. Cytochem., 1973–; Acta Histochem., 1980–; Basic and Applied Histochem., 1979–; Jl Histochem. Cytochem., 1959–68; Enzymol. biol. clin., 1961–67; Brain Research, 1968–76; Cardiovascular Research, 1968–75; Virchow's Archiv 'B', 1968–; Jl of Royal Microscopical Soc., 1967–69; Jl Microscopy, 1969–81; Jl of Neuro-visceral Relations, 1969–73; Jl of Molecular and Cellular Cardiology, 1970–79; Scand. Jl Gastroenterol., 1971–; Jl Neural Transmission, 1973–76; Jl of Pathology, 1973–83; Mikroscopie, 1977–; Editor, Medical Biology, 1974–. *Publications:* Histochemistry Theoretical and Applied, 1953, 2nd edn, 1960; 3rd edn, vol. I, 1968, vol. II, 1972; 4th edn vol. I, 1980, vol. II, 1984, vol. III, 1987; numerous papers on theoretical and applied histochemistry, esp. endocrinology (Diffuse Neuroendocrine System). *Recreations:* horticulture (plant hybridization, Liliaceae, Asclepiadaceae); ship modelling, foreign touring. *Address:* 46 Muswell Hill Road, NW10; Gorwyn House, Cheriton Bishop, Exeter. *T:* Cheriton Bishop 231. *Club:* Naval.

PEARSE, Rear-Adm. John Roger Southey G.; *see* Gerard-Pearse.

PEARSON, family name of **Viscount Cowdray.**

PEARSON, Brig. Alastair Stevenson, CB 1958; DSO; OBE 1953; MC; TD; Farmer; Lord Lieutenant of Dunbartonshire, since 1979; Keeper of Dumbarton Castle, since 1981; *b* 1 June 1915; *m* 1944, Mrs Joan Morgan Weld-Smith; three *d*. *Educ:* Kelvinside Acad.; Sedbergh. Co. Director, 1936–39; served War of 1939–45 (MC, DSO, and three Bars); embodied 6th Bn Highland LI, TA, 1939; transferred to Parachute Regt, 1941; Lt-Col 1942; CO 1st and 8th Para Bns, 1942–45, CO 15th (Scottish) Bn The Parachute Regt (TA), 1947–53; Dep. Comd 46 Parachute Bde (TA), 1953–59. Comd Scotland Army Cadet Force, Brigadier, 1967–81. ADC to the Queen, 1956–61. Hon. Colonel: 15th (Scottish) Bn The Parachute Regt (TA), 1963–77 and 1983–85; Renfrew and Bute Bn ACF, 1981–. DL Glasgow, 1951, Dunbartonshire, 1975. KStJ 1980. *Address:* Tullochan, Gartocharn, By Alexandria, Dunbartonshire. *T:* Gartocharn 205.

PEARSON, David Compton Froome; Deputy Chairman, Robert Fleming Holdings Ltd, since 1986 (Director, since 1974); *b* 28 July 1931; *s* of late Compton Edwin Pearson, OBE and of Marjorie (*née* Froome); *m* 1966, Venetia Jane Lynn; two *d*. *Educ:* Haileybury; Downing Coll., Cambridge (MA). Linklaters & Paines, Solicitors, 1957–69 (Partner, 1961–69); Dir, Robert Fleming & Co. Ltd, 1969–; Chairman: The Fleming Property Unit Trust, 1971–; Gill & Duffus Group Plc, 1982–85 (Dir, 1973–85); Robert Fleming Securities, 1985–; Dep. Chm., Austin Reed Group Plc, 1977– (Dir, 1971–); Dir, Blue Circle Industries Plc, 1972–. Mem., Finance Act 1960 Tribunal, 1978–84. *Recreation:* gardening. *Address:* The Manor, Berwick St John, Shaftesbury, Dorset SP7 0EX. *T:* Donhead 363. *Club:* Brooks's.

PEARSON, Sir Denning; *see* Pearson, Sir J. D.

PEARSON, Derek Leslie, CB 1978; Deputy Secretary, Overseas Development Administration (formerly Ministry of Overseas Development), 1977–81; *b* 19 Dec. 1921; *s* of late George Frederick Pearson and Edith Maud Pearson (*née* Dent); *m* 1956, Diana Mary, *d* of late Sir Ralph Freeman; no *c*. *Educ:* William Ellis Sch.; London Sch. of Economics. BSc (Econ). Observer, FAA, 1941–45. Colonial Office: Asst Principal, 1947; Principal, 1949; seconded to Kenya, 1954–56; Principal Private Sec. to Sec. of State for Colonies, 1959–61; Dept of Technical Cooperation, 1961; Asst Sec., 1962; ODM, 1964; Under Secretary: CSD, 1970–72; Min. of Overseas Develt, 1972–75; Dep. Sec., Cabinet Office, 1975–77. *Address:* Langata, Little London Road, Horam, Heathfield, East Sussex TN21 0BG. *T:* Horam Road 2276. *Clubs:* Naval, Civil Service.

PEARSON, (Edward) John (David); Director, Fisheries Directorate-General, Commission of the European Communities, since 1981; *b* 1 March 1938; *s* of Sydney Pearson and Hilda Beaumont; *m* 1963, Hilary Stuttard; three *s* two *d*. *Educ:* Huddersfield Coll.; Emmanuel Coll., Cambridge (MA). Admin. Trainee, London Transport Exec., 1959; Asst Principal, MoT, 1960, Principal 1965; Sen. Principal, DoE, 1971; Head of Div., Transport Directorate-Gen., Commn of Eur. Communities, 1973. *Recreation:* orienteering (Pres., Belgian Orienteering Assoc., 1982–; Chm., Develt and Promotion Cttee, Internat. Orienteering Fedn, 1986–). *Address:* Rue du Repos 56, 1180 Brussels, Belgium. *T:* 375.11.82.

PEARSON, Sir Francis Fenwick, 1st Bt, *cr* 1964; MBE 1945; JP; DL; Chairman, Central Lancashire New Town Development Corporation, 1971–86; *b* 13 June 1911; *s* of Frank Pearson, solicitor, Kirby Lonsdale, and Susan Mary Pearson; *m* 1938, Katharine Mary Fraser, *d* of the Rev. D. Denholm Fraser, Sproughton, Roxburgh; one *s* one *d*. *Educ:* Uppingham; Trinity Hall, Cambridge. 1st Gurkha Rifles, 1932; ADC to Viceroy of India, 1934–36; Indian Political Service, 1936; Under-Secretary, Political Dept, 1942–45; Chief Minister, Manipur State, 1945–47; retired, 1947. MP (C) Clitheroe, Oct. 1959–1970; Assistant Whip (unpaid), 1960–62; a Lord Commissioner of the Treasury, 1962–63; PPS to Prime Minister, Nov. 1963–Oct. 1964. JP Lancs, 1952; DL Co. Palatine of Lancaster, 1971. *Recreation:* fishing. *Heir:* *s* Francis Nicholas Fraser Pearson [*b* 28 Aug. 1943; *m* 1978, Henrietta, *d* of Comdr Henry Pasley-Tyler]. *Address:* Beech Cottage, Borwick, Carnforth. *T:* Carnforth 4191. *Club:* Carlton.

PEARSON, Dr Graham Scott, CChem, FRSC; Director, Chemical Defence Establishment, Porton Down, since 1984; *b* 20 July 1935; *s* of Ernest Reginald Pearson and Alice (*née* Maclachlan); *m* 1960, Susan Elizabeth Meriton Benn; two *s*. *Educ:*

Woodhouse Grove Sch., Bradford; St Salvator's Coll., Univ. of St Andrews (BSc 1st Cl. Hons Chemistry, 1957; PhD 1960). Postdoctoral Fellow, Univ. of Rochester, NY, USA, 1960–62; joined Scientific Civil Service, 1962; Rocket Propulsion Estab., 1962–69; Def. Res. and Develt Staff, Washington, DC, 1969–72; PSO to Dir Gen. Res. Weapons, 1972–73; Asst Dir, Naval Ordnance Services/Scientific, 1973–76; Technical Adviser/Explosives, Materials and Safety (Polaris), 1976–79; Principal Supt, Propellants Explosives and Rocket Motor Estab., Westcott, 1979–80; Dep. Dir 1, 1980–82 and Dep. Dir 2, 1982–83, RARDE, Fort Halstead; Dir Gen., ROF (Res. and Develt), 1983–84. *Publications:* contrib. to: Advances in Photochemistry, vol. 3, 1964; Advances in Inorganic and Radio Chemistry, vol. 8, 1966; Oxidation and Combustion Reviews, vol. 3, 1968 and vol. 4, 1969; articles on combustion in scientific jls; official reports. *Recreations:* long distance walking, reading, gardening, badminton, bridge. *Address:* Chemical Defence Establishment, Porton Down, Salisbury, Wilts SP4 0JQ. *T:* Idmiston 610211.

PEARSON, Air Commodore Herbert Macdonald, CBE 1944; RAF retired; *b* Buenos Aires, Argentina, 17 Nov. 1908; *s* of John Charles Pearson; *m* 1st, 1939, Jane Leslie (*d* 1978); one *s* two *d*; 2nd, 1982, Elizabeth Griffiths, JP, *widow* of Dr E. P. Griffiths. *Educ:* Cheltenham Coll.; Cranwell. Left Cranwell, 1928; Malta, 1929–31; Central Flying Sch., 1932; Instructor, Cranwell, 1933–34; attached to Peruvian Government, 1935–36; Asst Air Attaché in Spain, 1936–38; comd No. 54 Sqdn, 1938–39. War of 1939–45, in Fighter Command; then France, Belgium and Germany; Air Attaché, Lima, Peru, 1946; Deputy Director Air Foreign Liaison, Air Ministry, 1949; Commanding Royal Air Force, Kai Tak, Hong Kong, 1951–53; Assistant Chief of Staff Intelligence, Headquarters of Allied Air Forces, Central Europe, 1953–55. Air Commodore, 1953; retired, 1955. *Address:* Mapleridge Barn, Horton, Chipping Sodbury, Bristol. *Club:* Naval and Military.

PEARSON, Sir (James) Denning, Kt 1963; JP; FEng 1976; Chairman and Chief Executive, Rolls-Royce Ltd, 1969–70; Chairman, Gamma Associates, 1972–80; *b* 8 Aug. 1908; *s* of James Pearson and Elizabeth Henderson; *m* 1932, Eluned Henry; two *d*. *Educ:* Canton Secondary Sch., Cardiff; Cardiff Technical Coll. Senior Wh. Scholarship; BSc Eng. Joined Rolls-Royce Ltd, 1932; Technical Production Engineer, Glasgow Factory, 1941; Chief Quality and Service Engineer (resident in Canada for one year), 1941–45; Gen. Man. Sales and Service, 1946–49; Director, 1949; Director and Gen. Man., Aero Engine Division, 1950; Managing Director (Aero Engine Div.), 1954–65; Chief Exec. and Dep. Chm., 1957–68. President, SBAC, 1963; Mem., NEDC, 1964–67. FRAeS, 1957–64, Hon. FRAeS, 1964; Hon. FIMechE; DrIngEh Brunswick Univ., 1962–86. Member: Council, Manchester Business Sch.; Governing Body, London Graduate Sch. of Business Studies, 1968–70; Governing Body, Admin. Staff Coll., Henley, 1968–73; Council, Voluntary Service Overseas. Fellow, Imperial Coll. of Science and Technology, 1968–; Hon. Fellow, Manchester Univ. Inst. of Science and Technology, 1969; Hon. DSc: Nottingham, 1966; Wales, 1968; Cranfield Inst. of Technology, 1970; Hon. DTech: Loughborough, 1968; CNAA, 1969. Gold Medal, Royal Aero Club, 1969; Benjamin Franklin Medal, RSA, 1970. FRSA 1970. *Recreations:* reading, golf, tennis, sailing. *Address:* Green Acres, Holbrook, Derbyshire. *T:* Derby 881137.

PEARSON, Prof. James Douglas; Emeritus Professor of Bibliography, with reference to Asia and Africa, School of Oriental and African Studies, University of London (Professor, 1972–79); *b* 17 Dec. 1911; *m* 1st, Rose Betty Burden (marr. diss.); one *s*; 2nd, Hilda M. Wilkinson; three *s*. *Educ:* Cambridge Univ. (MA). Asst Under-librarian, Cambridge Univ. Library, 1939–50; Librarian, Sch. of Oriental and African Studies, Univ. of London, 1950–72. Hon. FLA, 1976. *Publications:* Index Islamicus, 1958–82; Oriental and Asian Bibliography, 1966; Oriental Manuscripts in Europe and North America, 1971; (ed jtly) Arab Islamic Bibliography, 1977; (ed) South Asia Bibliography, 1978; Creswell's Bibliography of the Architecture, Arts and Crafts of Islam, Supplement II, 1984. *Recreations:* natural history, walking. *Address:* 79 Highsett, Hills Road, Cambridge CB2 1NZ.

PEARSON, John; *see* Pearson, E. J. D.

PEARSON, Captain John William, CBE 1981; Regional Administrator, Mersey Regional Health Authority, 1977–81; *b* 19 Sept. 1920; *s* of Walter and Margaret Jane Pearson; *m* 1945, Audrey Ethel Whitehead; two *s*. *Educ:* Holloway Sch. FCIS, FHA, FCCA, IPFA. Served War, RA (Field), 1939–46. Hospital Service, LCC, 1947–48; NW Metropolitan Regional Hosp. Bd, 1948–49; Northern Gp, HMC, Finance Officer, 1949–62; Treasurer: St Thomas' Bd of Governors, 1962–73; Mersey Regional Health Authority, 1973–77. Pres., Assoc. of Health Service Treasurers, 1970–71. *Recreations:* tennis, golf, gardening, snooker. *Address:* 20 Weare Gifford, Shoeburyness, Essex SS3 8AB. *T:* Southend 585039.

PEARSON, Keith Philip, MA; Headmaster, George Heriot's School, Edinburgh, since 1983; *b* 5 Aug. 1941; *s* of Fred G. and Phyllis Pearson; *m* 1965, Dorothy (*née* Atkinson); two *d*. *Educ:* Madrid Univ. (Dip. de Estudios Hispanicos); Univ. of Cambridge (MA; Cert. of Educn). Teacher, Rossall Sch., 1964–72 (Head of Mod. Langs, 1968–72); George Watson's College: Head of Mod. Langs, 1972–79; Dep. Principal, 1979–83. *Recreations:* sport, mountains, music, DIY. *Address:* 41 Morningside Park, Edinburgh EH10 5EZ. *T:* 031–447 5861.

PEARSON, Norman Charles, OBE 1944; TD 1944; *b* 12 Aug. 1909; *s* of late Max Pearson and Kate Pearson; *m* 1951, Olive May, *d* of late Kenneth Harper and Ruth Harper, Granston Manor, Co. Leix; one *s* one *d*. *Educ:* Harrow Sch. (Scholar); Gonville and Caius Coll., Cambridge (Sayer Scholar). Commnd Royal Signals (TA), 1932; Middx Yeomanry; served War of 1939–45, N Africa (despatches, OBE), Italy, Greece; Lt-Col, comd 6th Armd Div. Signals, 1942; 10 Corps Signals, 1944; Mil. Comd Athens Signals; 4th Div. Signals, 1945; subseq. re-formed 56 Div. Signals Regt (TA). Boots Pure Drug Co. Ltd, 1931–37; Borax (Holdings) Ltd, 1937–69, Director, 1951–69; Director: UK Provident Instn, 1965–80; Cincinnati Milacron Ltd, 1968–83 (Dep. Chm., 1972–83). Lay Mem., Restrictive Practices Court, 1968–86; Mem., Air Transport Licensing Bd, 1971–72. *Recreation:* gardening. *Address:* Copt Heath, Cold Ash, Newbury, Berks RG16 9JN. *Club:* Carlton.

PEARSON, Maj.-Gen. Ronald Matthew, CB 1985; MBE 1959; Director Army Dental Service, 1982–85, retired; *b* 25 Feb. 1925; *s* of Dr John Pearson and Sheila Pearson (*née* Brown); *m* 1956, Florence Eileen Jack; two *d*. *Educ:* Clifton Hall Sch., Ratho, Midlothian; Glasgow Acad.; Glasgow Univ./Glasgow Dental Hosp. LDS RFPS(Glas) 1948; FBIM 1979. Civilian Dental Practice, 1948–49. Commnd RADC, 1949; served: RWAFF, 1950–53; UK, 1953–57; BAOR, 1957–60; UK, 1961–67; CO No 1 Dental Gp, BAOR, 1967–70; CO Army Dental Centres, Cyprus, 1970–73; CO No 8 Dental Gp, UK, 1973–75; CO No 4 Dental Gp, UK, 1975–76; Dep. Dir Dental Service, UKLF, 1976–78; Dep. Dir Dental Service, BAOR, 1978–82. QHDS, 1978–85. CStJ 1983. *Recreations:* trout fishing, photography, gardening, caravanning. *Address:* c/o Royal Bank of Scotland, Holts Branch, Victoria Road, Farnborough, Hants.

PEARSON, Rt. Rev. Thomas Bernard; Bishop Auxiliary in the Diocese of Lancaster, 1952 62 and 1965 83; Episcopal Vicar for Cumbria (formerly Cumberland,

Westmorland and Furness), 1967–83; *b* Preston, Lancs, 18 January 1907; *s* of Joseph Pearson and Alice (*née* Cartmell). *Educ:* Upholland College; Ven. English College, Rome. Pontifical Gregorian University, Rome; PhD 1930; Bachelor of Canon Law, Licent. Sacred Theology, 1933. Priest, 1933; Assistant Priest, 1934–44; Parish Priest, St Cuthbert's, Blackpool, 1944–67; Titular Bishop of Sinda, 1949. Mem., Order of Discalced Carmelites, 1974. *Recreation:* mountaineering. *Address:* Howard Lodge, 90 Warwick Road, Carlisle CA1 1JU. *T:* Carlisle 24952. *Clubs:* Alpine, Fell and Rock, English Lake District; Achille Ratti Climbing (Founder President).

PEARSON, Gen. Sir Thomas (Cecil Hook), KCB 1967 (CB 1964); CBE 1959 (OBE 1953); DSO 1940, and Bar, 1943; DL; retired 1974; *b* 1 July 1914; *s* of late Vice-Admiral J. L. Pearson, CMG; *m* 1947, Aud, *d* of late Alf Skjelkvale, Oslo; two *s*. *Educ:* Charterhouse; Sandhurst. 2nd Lieutenant Rifle Bde, 1934. Served War of 1939–45, M East and Europe; CO 2nd Bn The Rifle Bde, 1942; Dep. Comdr 2nd Independent Parachute Bde Gp 1944; Dep. Comdr 1st Air-landing Bde 1945; GSO1 1st Airborne Div. 1945; CO 1st Bn The Parachute Regt 1946; CO 7th Bn The Parachute Regt 1947; GSO1 (Land Air Warfare), WO, 1948; JSSC, GSO1, HQ Malaya, 1950; GSO1 (Plans), FARELF, 1951; Directing Staff, JSSC, 1953; Comdr 45 Parachute Bde TA 1955; Nat. Defence Coll., Canada, 1956; Comdr 16 Indep. Parachute Bde 1957; Chief of Staff to Dir of Ops Cyprus, 1960; Head of Brit. Mil. Mission to Soviet Zone of Germany, 1960; Major-General Commanding 1st Division, BAOR, 1961–63; Chief of Staff, Northern Army Group, 1963–67; Comdr, FARELF, 1967–68; Military Sec., MoD, 1968–72; C-in-C, Allied Forces, Northern Europe, 1972–74; psc 1942; jssc 1950; ndc Canada 1957. ADC Gen. to the Queen, 1974. Col Comdt, the Royal Green Jackets, 1973–77. Fisheries Mem., Welsh Water Auth., 1980–83. DL Hereford and Worcester, 1983. Haakon VII Liberty Cross, 1948; Medal of Honour, Norwegian Defence Assoc., 1973. *Recreations:* field sports, yachting. *Address:* Streete House, Weston under Penyard, Ross on Wye, Herefordshire HR9 7NY. *Clubs:* Naval and Military; Island Sailing, Kongelig Norsk Seilforenning.

PEARSON, William Thomas Shipston; retired from Civil Service, 1980; *b* 21 Aug. 1917; *s* of William Pearson and Alice (*née* Shipston); *m* 1948, Pauline Daphne Scott (*née* Wilkinson); one *s* two *d*. *Educ:* High Pavement Sch., Nottingham; University Coll., Nottingham (BSc). MRAeS, CEng. Appts at RAE, 1939–45; Hon. Commn, Flying Officer, RAFVR, 1944; Blind Landing Experimental Unit, Martlesham Heath, 1945–47; RAF Transport Comd Develt Unit, 1947–50; TRE, 1950–52; seconded to Australian Scientific Service, Long Range Weapons Estab., 1952–56; RAE, Farnborough, 1956–62; Asst Dir, Air Armaments, Min. of Aviation, 1962–65; Div. Head, Weapons Dept, RAE (concerned with various projs), 1965–76; seconded to FCO, as Counsellor (Defence Res.), British High Commn, Canberra, and Head of British Defence Res. and Supply Staffs, Australia, 1977–79. *Publications:* official reports. *Recreation:* photography. *Address:* Cooinda, Pine Avenue, Camberley, Surrey GU15 2LY. *Club:* Royal Air Force.

PEART, family name of **Baron Peart**.

PEART, Baron *cr* 1976 (Life Peer), of Workington; **(Thomas) Frederick Peart,** PC 1964; Leader of the Opposition in the House of Lords, 1979–82; *b* 30 Apr. 1914; *m* 1945, Sarah Elizabeth Lewis; one *s*. *Educ:* Crook Council; Wolsingham Grammar; Henry Smith Secondary, Hartlepool; Bede Coll., Durham Univ. (BSc); Inner Temple, Inns of Court. Pres. Durham University Union Soc. Councillor Easington RDC, 1937–40. Became a Schoolmaster. Served War of 1939–45, commissioned Royal Artillery, served in North Africa and Italy. MP (Lab) Workington Div. of Cumberland, 1945–76; PPS to Minister of Agriculture, 1945–51; Minister of Agriculture, Fisheries and Food, 1964–68 and 1974–76; Leader of the House of Commons, 1968–70; Lord Privy Seal, April–Oct. 1968; Lord President of the Council, Oct. 1968–1970; Opposition Spokesman; House of Commons Matters, 1970–71; Agriculture, 1971–72; Defence, 1972–74; Lord Privy Seal and Leader of the House of Lords, 1976–79; British Delegate to Council of Europe, 1952–55 (Rep. Agriculture Cttee and Cttee for Culture and Science (Vice-Pres.)). Privy Council Rep. on Council of RCVS, Dir, FMC, 1971–74. Chairman: Adv. Council for Applied R&D, 1976–80; Retail Consortium, 1979–81. Hon. DSc Cranfield, 1977. *Address:* House of Lords, SW1.

PEART, Brian; Under-Secretary, Ministry of Agriculture, Fisheries and Food, 1976–85; *b* 17 Aug. 1925; *s* of late Joseph Garfield Peart and Frances Hannah Peart (*née* English); *m* 1952, Dorothy (*née* Thompson); one *s* one *d*. *Educ:* Wolsingham Grammar Sch.; Durham Univ. (BA). Served War, RAF, 1943–47. Agricultural Economist, Edinburgh Sch. of Agric., 1950–57; Sen. Agricultural Economist, 1957–64; Regional Farm Management Adviser, MAFF, West Midlands Region, 1964–67; Chief Farm Management Adviser, MAFF, 1967–71; Regional Manager, MAFF, Yorks/Lancs Region, 1971–74; Head of Intelligence and Trng Div., 1974–76; Chief Administrator, ADAS, 1976–80. *Recreations:* golf, bridge, The Times crossword. *Address:* 18 Derwent Close, Claygate, Surrey KT10 0RF. *Club:* Farmers'.

PEART, Prof. Sir (William) Stanley, Kt 1985; MD; FRS 1969; Professor of Medicine, University of London, at St Mary's Hospital Medical School, 1956–Sept. 1987; *b* 31 March 1922; *s* of J. G. and M. Peart; *m* 1947, Peggy Parkes; one *s* one *d*. *Educ:* King's College School, Wimbledon; Medical School, St Mary's Hospital. MB, BS (Hons), 1945; FRCP, 1959; MD (London), 1949. Lecturer in Medicine, St Mary's Hospital, 1950–56. Chm., Beit Fellowship Cttee. Trustee, Wellcome Trust, 1975–. Goulstonian Lectr, 1959, Croonian Lectr, 1979, RCP. Stouffer Prize, 1968. *Publications:* chapters in: Cecil-Loeb, Textbook of Medicine; Renal Disease; Biochemical Disorders in Human Disease; articles in Biochemical Journal, Journal of Physiology, Lancet. *Recreations:* reading, tennis. *Address:* 17 Highgate Close, N6 4SD; (until Sept. 1987) Medical Unit, St Mary's Hospital, Praed Street, W2 1NY. *T:* 01–262 1280.

PEASE, family name of **Barons Daryngton, Gainford,** and **Wardington**.

PEASE, Sir (Alfred) Vincent, 4th Bt *cr* 1882; *b* 2 April 1926; *s* of Sir Alfred (Edward) Pease, 2nd Bt (*d* 1939), and of his 3rd wife, Emily Elizabeth (Dowager Lady Pease, JP) (*d* 1979); *S* half-brother, 1963; unmarried. *Educ:* Bootham School, York. *Heir: b* Joseph Gurney Pease [*b* 16 Nov. 1927; *m* 1953, Shelagh Munro, *d* of C. G. Bulman; one *s* one *d*]. *Address:* Flat 13, Hamilton House, Belgrave Road, Seaford, East Sussex BN25 2EL.

PEASE, Dr Rendel Sebastian, FRS 1977; Programme Director for Fusion, UKAEA, since 1981; *b* 1922; *s* of Michael Stewart Pease and Helen Bowen (*née* Wedgwood); *m* 1952, Susan Spickernell; two *s* three *d*. *Educ:* Bedales Sch.; Trinity Coll., Cambridge (MA, ScD). Scientific Officer, Min. of Aircraft Prodn at ORS Unit, HQ, RAF Bomber Comd, 1942–46; research at AERE, Harwell, 1947–61; Div. Head, Culham Lab. for Plasma Physics and Nuclear Fusion, UKAEA, 1961–67; Vis. Scientist, Princeton Univ., 1964–65; Asst Dir, UKAEA Research Gp, 1967; Dir, Culham Lab., UKAEA, 1968–81. Gordon Godfrey Prof. of Theoretical Physics, Univ. NSW, 1984. Chairman: Adam Hilger Ltd, 1976–77; Plasma Physics Commn, Internat. Union of Pure and Applied Physics, 1975–78; Internat. Fusion Res. Council, Internat. Atomic Energy Agency, 1976–83. Member: Council, Royal Soc., 1985–86; Fabian Soc.; Inst. of Physics (Vice-Pres., 1973–77; Pres, 1978–80); Amer. Inst. of Physics; IEE. DUniv Surrey, 1973; Hon. DSc Aston, 1981.

Publications: articles in physics jls. *Recreation:* music. *Address:* The Poplars, West Ilsley, Newbury, Berks RG16 0AW.

PEASE, Sir Richard Thorn, 3rd Bt *cr* 1920; Director, Barclays Bank, since 1965; Chairman, Yorkshire Bank, since 1986 (Director, since 1977; Deputy Chairman, 1981–86); *b* 20 May 1922; *s* of Sir Richard Arthur Pease, 2nd Bt, and Jeannette Thorn (*d* 1957), *d* of late Gustav Edward Kissel, New York; *S* father, 1969; *m* 1956, Anne, *d* of late Lt-Col Reginald Francis Heyworth; one *s* two *d*. *Educ:* Eton. Served with 60th Rifles, Middle East, Italy and Greece, 1941–46 (Captain). Director: Owners of the Middlesbrough Estate Ltd, 1954–; Bank of Scotland, 1977–85; Vice-Chairman: Barclays Bank Ltd, 1970–82; Barclays Bank UK Management, 1971–82. *Heir: s* Richard Peter Pease, *b* 4 Sept. 1958. *Address:* Hindley House, Stocksfield-on-Tyne, Northumberland.

PEASE, Robert John Claude; HM Diplomatic Service, retired; Counsellor (Administration) and Consul-General, British Embassy, Moscow, 1977–80; *b* 24 April 1922; *s* of Frederick Robert Hellier Pease and Eileen Violet Pease (*née* Beer); *m* 1945, Claire Margaretta Whall; one *s* two *d*. *Educ:* Cattedown Road Sch., Plymouth; Sutton High Sch., Plymouth. Served War of 1939–45; Telegraphist, RN, 1942; commnd Sub Lt RNVR, 1944. Clerk, Lord Chancellor's Dept, Plymouth County Court, 1939, Truro County Court, 1946; Foreign Office, 1948; Moscow, 1952; HM Consul, Sarajevo, 1954; 2nd Sec., Bangkok, 1958; HM Consul, Gdynia, 1959, Düsseldorf, 1961; 1st Sec., Pretoria, 1964, Bombay, 1966; FCO, 1969; Dep. High Commissioner, Mauritius, 1973. *Recreations:* golf, opera. *Address:* 5 Springfield Road, Camberley, Surrey.

PEASE, Sir Vincent; *see* Pease, Sir A. V.

PEAT, Gerrard Charles, FCA; Partner, Peat, Marwick Mitchell & Co., Chartered Accountants, since 1956; Auditor to the Queen's Privy Purse, since 1980 (Assistant Auditor, 1969–80); *b* 14 June 1920; *s* of Charles Urie Peat, MC, FCA, and Ruth (*née* Pulley); *m* 1949, Margaret Josephine Collingwood; one *s*. *Educ:* Sedbergh Sch. FCA 1961. Served War, RAF and ATA (pilot), 1940–45 (Service Medals); Pilot, 600 City of London Auxiliary Sqdn, 1948–51. Underwriting Mem. of Lloyd's, 1973–; Mem. Cttee, Assoc. of Lloyd's Members, 1983–. Member: Corp. of City of London, 1973–78; Worshipful Co. of Turners, 1970–. Hon. Treasurer, Assoc. of Conservative Clubs, 1971–78. Jubilee Medal, 1977. *Recreations:* travel, shooting, fishing, golf, flying. *Address:* 1 Puddle Dock, Blackfriars, EC4V 3PD. *T:* 01-236 8000; Flat 10, 33/35 Pont Street, SW1X 0BB. *T:* 01-245 9736; Home Farm, Upper Basildon, Pangbourne, Berks RG8 8ND. *T:* Upper Basildon 671241. *Clubs:* Boodle's, City Livery.

PEAT, (William Wood) Watson, CBE 1972; JP; farmer; broadcaster; Scottish Governor of the BBC, since 1984; Chairman, Broadcasting Council for Scotland, since 1984; *b* 14 Dec. 1922; *o s* of William Peat and Margaret Hillhouse; *m* 1955, Jean Frew Paton McHarrie; two *s* one *d*. *Educ:* Denny Public School. Served with Royal Signals, Europe and India, 1941–46; Lieut 1944. Member: Nat. Council, Scottish Assoc. of Young Farmers' Clubs, 1949– (Chm., 1953–54; Vice-Pres., 1975; Pres., 1979); Stirling CC, 1959–74 (Vice-Convenor, 1967–70); Council, NFU Scotland, 1959–78 (Pres., 1966–67); Scottish River Purification Adv. Cttee, 1960–79; Bd of Management, Royal Scottish Nat. Hosp., 1962–72; Council, Hannah Research Inst., 1963–82; Council, Scottish Agricultural Organisation Soc. Ltd, 1963– (Pres., 1974–77); Bd of Management, British Farm Produce Council, 1964 (Vice-Chm., 1980–83); Agric. Marketing Develt Exec. Cttee, 1966–67; Central Council for Agric. and Horticultural Co-operation, 1967–; Food from Britain Co-operative Development Board, 1983–; Bd of Management, Oatridge Agric. Coll., 1967–75; Gen. Comr of Income Tax, 1962; Governor, West of Scotland Agric. Coll., 1964– (Vice Chm., 1975, Chm., 1983–); Chm. Council, Scottish Agricl Colls, 1984–; Dir, Agri-Finance (Scotland) Ltd, 1968–79; Chm., BBC Scottish Agric. Adv. Cttee, 1971–75; Chm., Scottish Adv. Cttee, Assoc. of Agriculture, 1974–79, Vice Pres., 1979–; Director: Fedn of Agricultural Co-operatives (UK) Ltd, 1974–77; FMC PLC, 1974–83; Mem., British Agricl Council, 1974–84. JP Stirlingshire, 1963. *Recreations:* amateur radio, flying. *Address:* Carbro, 61 Stirling Road, Larbert, Stirlingshire FK5 4SG. *T:* Larbert 562420. *Clubs:* Farmers'.

PECK, Antony Dilwyn, CB 1965; MBE 1945; Deputy Secretary, Department of Trade and Industry, 1970–73; retired; *b* 10 April 1914; *s* of late Sir James Peck, CB, and late Lady Peck; *m* 1st, 1939, Joan de Burgh Whyte (*d* 1955); one *s* one *d*; 2nd, 1956, Sylvia Glenister; one *s* two *d*. *Educ:* Eton; Trinity College, Oxford. Fellow of Trinity College, 1938–46. Served War of 1939–45, Army, 1940–46 (Major). Joined Treasury as Principal, 1946; Asst Secretary, 1950; Under-Secretary, 1959; Dep. Under-Sec. of State, MoD, 1963–68; Second Sec., BoT, 1968–70. *Recreation:* bridge. *Address:* Holly Tree House, Compton, Chichester, W Sussex PO18 9HD.

PECK, His Honour David (Edward); a Circuit Judge (formerly Judge of County Courts), 1969–85; *b* 6 April 1917; *m* 1st, 1950, Rosina Seton Glover Marshall (marr. diss.); one *s* three *d*; 2nd, 1973, Frances Deborah Redford (*née* Mackenzie) (marr. diss.); one *s*; 3rd, 1983, Elizabeth Charlotte Beale (*née* Boost). *Educ:* Charterhouse School; Balliol College, Oxford. Served Army (Cheshire Regiment), 1939–46. Called to Bar, Middle Temple, 1949. Mem., County Court Rule Cttee, 1978–84 (Chm., 1981–84); Jt Editor, County Court Practice, 1982–. *Address:* 8 New Square, Lincoln's Inn, WC2.

PECK, Sir Edward (Heywood), GCMG 1974 (KCMG 1966; CMG 1957); HM Diplomatic Service, retired; British Permanent Representative to North Atlantic Council, 1970–75; *b* 5 Oct. 1915; *s* of Lt-Col Edward Surman Peck, IMS, and Doris Louise Heywood; *m* 1948, Alison Mary MacInnes; one *s* two *d*. *Educ:* Clifton College; The Queen's College, Oxford. 1st Cl. Hons (Mod. Langs), 1937; Laming Travelling Fellow, 1937–38. Entered Consular Service, 1938; served in Barcelona, 1938–39; Foreign Office, 1939–40; Sofia, 1940; Ankara, 1940–44; Adana, 1944; Iskenderun, 1945; Salonica, 1945–47; with UK Deleg. to UN Special Commn on the Balkans, 1947; Foreign Office, 1947–50; seconded to UK High Commissioner's Office, Delhi, 1950–52; Counsellor, Foreign Office, 1952–55; Dep. Comdt, Brit. Sector, Berlin, 1955–58; on staff of UK Commissioner-General for S-E Asia, 1959–60; Assistant Under-Secretary of State, Foreign Office, 1961–66; British High Commissioner in Kenya, 1966–68; Dep. Under-Secretary of State, FCO, 1968–70. Dir, Outward Bound (Loch Eil), 1976–; Mem. Council, Nat. Trust for Scotland, 1982–. Hon. Vis. Fellow in Defence Studies, Aberdeen Univ., 1976–85. *Publications:* North-East Scotland (Bartholomew's Guides Series), 1981; Avonside Explored, 1983. *Recreations:* mountaineering, ski-ing; reading history and writing guide books. *Address:* Easter Torrans, Tomintoul, Banffshire AB3 9HJ. *Club:* Alpine.

PECK, Gregory; film actor, US, since 1943; *b* 5 April 1916; *s* of Gregory P. Peck and Bernice Ayres; *m* 1st, 1942, Greta Konen Rice (marr. diss. 1954); two *s* (and one *s* decd); 2nd, 1955, Veronique Passani; one *s* one *d*. *Educ:* Calif Public Schools; Univ. of Calif (BA). Broadway stage, 1941–43. *Films:* Days of Glory, 1943; Keys of the Kingdom, Valley of Decision, 1944; Spellbound, 1945; Duel in the Sun, The Yearling, 1946; The Macomber Affair, Gentlemen's Agreement, 1947; The Paradine Case, 1948; Yellow Sky, The Great Sinner, Twelve O'Clock High, 1949; The Gun Fighter, 1950; Only the Valiant, Captain Horatio Hornblower, David and Bathsheba, 1951; The World in his Arms, 1952; The Snows of Kilimanjaro, 1952; Roman Holiday, 1953; The Million Pound Note, 1953; Night People, 1954; The Purple Plain, 1954; The Man in the Grey Flannel Suit, 1956; Moby Dick, 1956; Designing Woman, 1957; The Bravados, 1958; The Big Country (co-producer), 1958; Pork Chop Hill, 1959; On the Beach, 1959; Guns of Navarone, 1960; Cape Fear, 1961; To Kill a Mocking Bird, 1962; Captain Newman, MD, 1963; Behold a Pale Horse, 1964; Mirage, 1965; Arabesque, 1965; Mackenna's Gold, 1967; The Chairman, 1968; The Stalking Moon, 1968; Marooned, 1970; I Walk the Line, 1971; Shoot Out, 1971; The Trial of the Catonsville Nine, 1972; Billy Two-Hats, 1974; The Boys From Brazil, 1978; The Sea Wolves, 1980; *television:* The Blue and the Gray, 1982; The Scarlet and the Black, 1983; *produced:* The Dove, 1974; The Omen, 1976; MacArthur, 1977. Nat. Chm., Amer. Cancer Soc., 1966. Mem., Nat. Council on Arts, 1965–67, 1968–; Pres., Acad. Motion Pictures Arts and Sciences, 1967–70; Chm., Board of Trustees, Amer. Film Inst., 1967–69. Medal of Freedom Award, 1969; Jean Hersholt Humanitarian Award, Acad. of Motion Picture Arts and Sciences, 1968. *Recreations:* riding, swimming, bicycling, gardening. *Club:* Players (New York).

PECK, Sir John (Howard), KCMG 1971 (CMG 1956); HM Diplomatic Service, retired; *b* Kuala Lumpur, 16 Feb. 1913; *o s* of late Howard and Dorothea Peck; *m* 1939, Mariska Caroline (*d* 1979), *e d* of Josef Somló; two *s*. *Educ:* Wellington College; CCC, Oxford. Assistant Private Secretary to First Lord of Admiralty, 1937–39; to Minister for Coordination of Defence, 1939–40; to the Prime Minister, 1940–46; transferred to Foreign Service, 1946; served in United Nations Dept, 1946–47; in The Hague, 1947–50; Counsellor and Head of Information Research Dept, 1951–54; Counsellor (Defence Liaison) and Head of Political Division, British Middle East Office, 1954–56; Director-General of British Information Services, New York, 1956–59; UK Permanent Representative to the Council of Europe, and Consul-General, Strasbourg, 1959–62; Ambassador to Senegal, 1962–66, and Mauritania, 1962–65; Asst Under-Sec. of State, FO, then FCO, 1966–70; Ambassador to the Republic of Ireland, 1970–73. *Publications:* Dublin from Downing Street (memoirs), 1978; various essays and light verse. *Recreations:* photography, gardening. *Address:* Stratford, Naval Park Road, Dalkay, Co. Dublin. *Club:* Stephen's Green (Dublin).

PECK, Stanley Edwards, CBE 1974; BEM 1954; QPM 1964; DL; HM Inspector of Constabulary, 1964–78; *b* 1916; *er s* of late Harold Edwards Peck, Edgbaston and Shanghai; *m* 1939, Yvonne Sydney Edwards, *er d* of late John Edwards Jessop, LDS; two *s* two *d*. *Educ:* Solihull School; Birmingham University. Served with RAF, 1941–45 (Flt-Lt). Joined Metropolitan Police, 1935; Chief Inspector and Supt, New Scotland Yard, 1950–54; Asst Chief Constable, Staffs, 1954–61; Chief Constable, Staffs, 1961–64. DL Staffs, 1962. Pres., Royal Life Saving Soc., UK, 1969–74 (Chm., East Midlands Region, RLSS, 1968–80). OStJ. *Recreations:* golf and dog walking. *Address:* Lodge Gardens, Walnut Grove, Radcliffe-on-Trent, Nottinghamshire. *Club:* Royal Air Force.

PECKFORD, Hon. (Alfred) Brian; MHA (Progressive C), Green Bay, Newfoundland, since 1972; Premier of the Province of Newfoundland and Labrador, since 1979; *b* Whitbourne, Newfoundland, 27 Aug. 1942; *s* of Ewart Peckford and Allison (*née* Young), St John's; *m* 1969, Marina, *d* of Raymond Dicks and Hope (*née* Adams), Halls Bay; two *d*. *Educ:* Lewisporte High Sch.; Memorial Univ. of Newfoundland (BAEd). Schoolmaster, 1962–63 and 1966–72. MHA Green Bay, 1972–; Special Asst to Premier, 1973; Minister: of Dept of Municipal Affairs and Housing, 1974; of Mines and Energy, 1976, also of Rural Development, 1978. Leader of Progressive Cons. Party, Newfoundland and Labrador, 1979–. *Recreations:* reading, sport, swimming. *Address:* Premier's Office, 8th Floor, Confederation Building, St John's, Newfoundland A1C 5T7, Canada.

PECKHAM, Arthur John; UK Permanent Representative, Food and Agriculture Organisation, Rome, 1977–80; *b* 22 Sept. 1920; *s* of Richard William Peckham and Agnes Mercy (*née* Parker); *m* 1949, Margaret Enid Quirk; two *s* one *d*. *Educ:* The Judd Sch., Tonbridge. RAF (Pilot), 1942–46, 59 Sqdn Coastal Command. Cadet, Min. of Labour and Nat. Service, 1948; Colonial Office: Asst Principal, 1950; Private Sec. to Perm. Under-Sec., 1952; Principal, 1954; Counsellor (Technical Assistance), Lagos, 1964; Asst Sec., Min. of Overseas Develt, 1966; Minister, FAO, Rome, 1977. *Recreations:* gardening, hill walking. *Address:* 7 Yardley Park Road, Tonbridge, Kent. *T:* Tonbridge 353735.

PECKHAM, Prof. Michael John, FRCP, FRCPGlas, FRCR; Director, British Postgraduate Medical Federation, since 1986; *b* 2 Aug. 1935; *s* of William Stuart Peckham and Gladys Mary Peckham; *m* 1958, Catherine Stevenson King; three *s*. *Educ:* St Catharine's Coll., Cambridge (MA); University College Hosp. Med. Sch., London (MD). MRC Clin. Res. Schol., Inst. Gustav Roussy, Paris, 1965–67; Lectr, Institute of Cancer Research, London: 1967–71; Sen. Lectr, 1971–74; Prof. of Radiotherapy, 1974–86; Dean, 1984–86. Consultant: Royal Marsden Hosp., 1971–86; to Royal Navy, 1974–. *Publications:* Management of Testicular Tumours, 1981; (jtly) The Biological Basis of Radiotherapy, 1983; (jtly) Primary Management of Early Breast Cancer, 1985. *Recreation:* painting (exhibitions: 1964, 1967, 1970, 1976, 1982, 1983). *Address:* 35 Brook Green, W6 7BL. *T:* 01-602 2347.

PEDDER, Vice-Adm. Sir Arthur (Reid), KBE 1959; CB 1956; retired as Commander, Allied Naval Forces, Northern Europe (1957–59); *b* 6 July 1904; *s* of late Sir John Pedder, KBE, CB; *m* 1934, Dulcie, *d* of O. L. Bickford; two *s*. *Educ:* Osborne and Dartmouth. Served in various ships, 1921–; qualified as Naval Observer, 1930; promoted Commander and appointed Admiralty, 1937–40; Executive Officer, HMS Mauritius, 1940–42; Admiralty Asst, Dir of Plans (Air), 1942–45; Capt. 1944; comd HM Ships Khedive and Phoebe, 1945–47; idc 1948; Admiralty (Dep. Dir of Plans), 1949–50; Fourth Naval Member of Australian Commonwealth Naval Board, 1950–52; Rear-Adm. 1953; Asst Chief of Naval Staff (Warfare), Admiralty, 1953–54; Flag Officer, Aircraft Carriers, December 1954–May 1956; Vice-Adm. 1956. *Recreation:* everything outdoors. *Address:* Langhurst Barn Cottage, Hascombe, Godalming, Surrey. *T:* Hascombe 294. *Club:* Athenæum.

PEDDER, Air Marshal Sir Ian (Maurice), KCB 1982; OBE 1963; DFC 1949; Deputy Chairman, Dan-Air Services, since 1986; *b* 2 May 1926; *s* of Maurice and Elsie Pedder; *m* 1949, Jean Mary (*née* Kellett); one *s* two *d*. *Educ:* Royal Grammar Sch., High Wycombe; Queen's Coll., Oxford. Service in Nos 28, 60, 81, 213 Sqdns, CFS, and with Burma Air Force, 1946–59; Staff Coll., Andover, and MoD, 1959–62; Far East, 1962–64; Staff appts, 1965–70; RCDS, 1971; Comdg RAF Chivenor, 1972–74; Nat. Air Traffic Services, 1974–84, Dep. Controller, 1977–81, Controller, 1981–84. *Publications:* contribs to Service jls, UK and US. *Recreations:* study of Victorian times, photography, riding (a bicycle). *Address:* Pilton, Barnstaple, North Devon. *Club:* Royal Air Force.

PEDDIE, Maj.-Gen. Graham, CB 1959; DSO 1945; MBE 1941; *b* 15 Oct. 1905; *s* of late Graham Peddie and of Mrs Peddie; *m* 1937, Dorothy Mary Humfress (decd); one *s* one *d*; *m* 1959, Alexandra Mavrojani. *Educ:* Sherborne School, Royal Military Academy, Woolwich. Commissioned into RA, 1926; served in UK, 1926–30, in Egypt and Sudan, 1930–36; Instructor, RMA, Woolwich, 1937–39. War of 1939–45, in UK and NW Europe; 1st AA Group (Dep. Comd), 1948–50; idc, 1950–51. BAOR 1953–56; Director of Manpower Planning, War Office, 1957–60; retired, 1960. *Address*: 19 Mullings Court, Dugdale Road, Cirencester, Glos GL7 2AW. *T*: Cirencester 3087.

PEDDIE, Robert Allan; Chairman, South Eastern Electricity Board, 1977–83; general management consultant since 1983; *b* 27 Oct. 1921; *s* of Robert Allan Peddie and Elizabeth Elsie (*née* Sharp); *m* 1946, Ilene Ivy Sillcock; one *d*. *Educ*: Nottingham Univ. (BSc Eng). Electricity Dept, Hull Corp., 1946; joined nationalised electricity supply industry, 1948, and held various appts: Supt, Bradwell Nuclear Power Stn, 1958; Asst Reg. Dir, NW Region, 1962; Dep. Reg. Dir, Mids Region, 1967; Dir-Gen., SE Region, 1970; Mem. CEGB, 1972–77; part-time Mem., UKAEA, 1972–77. *Recreations*: swimming, golf, walking. *Address*: Torness, The Mount Drive, Reigate, Surrey. *T*: Reigate 44996.

PEDDIE, Ronald, CBE 1971; JP; *b* 24 May 1905; *s* of Rev. James Peddie, BA and Elsie Mary, *d* of John Edward Corby; *m* 1931, Vera (*d* 1981), *d* of W. G. Nicklin, Guildford; three *s* one *d*. *Educ*: Glasgow Academy; Leys Sch., Cambridge; St John's Coll., Cambridge (MA). CA 1930; Jt Dipl. Management Accounting, 1967. McClelland Ker & Co., CA, Glasgow, 1926–31; Accountant and Asst Sec., C. & J. Clark Ltd, Street, Som, 1931–43; The United Steel Cos Ltd, 1943–67 (Sec. from 1946, later Dir Finance and Admin); British Steel Corp.: Dir, Finance and Admin, Midland Group, 1967–69; Man. Dir, Administration, 1969–71, retd. Dir, Iron Trades Employers' Insurance Assoc. Ltd, 1970–75. Sec., Trevelyan Scholarships, 1958–81; Governor, Ashorne Hill Management Coll., 1967–71. Past Mem., Cambridge and Leeds Univs Appt Bds. JP Sheffield, 1964. *Publications*: The United Steel Companies, 1918–1968: a History, 1968; The Trevelyan Scholarships, 1975; articles in Accountants Magazine and Accountancy. *Recreations*: gardening, reading, all games (now as a spectator). *Address*: Springwater Farm, Mudgley, Wedmore, Somerset BS28 4TY. *T*: Wedmore 713065.

PEDERSEN, (Knud) George, PhD; FCCT; FRSA; President, The University of Western Ontario, since 1985; *b* 13 June 1931; *s* of Hjalmar Nielsen Pedersen and Anna Marie (*nee* Jensen); *m* 1953, Joan Elaine Vanderwarker; one *s* one *d*. *Educ*: Vancouver Normal Sch. (Dip. in Teaching 1952); Univ. of BC (BA History and Geography, 1959); Univ. of Washington (MA 1964); Univ. of Chicago (PhD 1969). FCCT 1977; FRSA 1983. Schools in North Vancouver: Teacher, Highlands Elem. Sch., 1952–56; Vice-Principal, North Star Elem. Sch., 1956–59; Principal, Carisbrooke Elem. Sch., 1959–61; Vice-Principal, Handsworth Sec. Sch., 1961–63; Principal, Balmoral Sec. Sch., 1963–65; Univ. of Chicago: Teaching Intern, 1966; Staff Associate, Midwest Admin Center, 1965–66; Res. Associate (Asst Prof.), 1966–68; Asst Prof., Ontario Inst. for Studies in Educn and Univ. of Toronto, 1968–70; Asst Prof. and Associate Dir, Midwest Admin Center, Div. of Social Sciences, Univ. of Chicago, 1970–72; Faculty of Educn, Univ. of Victoria: Associate Prof., 1972–75; Dean, 1972–75; Vice-Pres. (Academic), and Prof., Univ. of Victoria, 1975–79; Pres. and Prof., Simon Fraser Univ., 1979–83; Pres., Univ. of British Columbia, 1983–85. Universities Council of British Columbia: Mem., Prog. Co-ordinating Cttee, 1975–78; Mem., Business Affairs Cttee, 1975–78; Mem., Long-range Planning Cttee, 1979–85. Chm., Adv. Cttee on Educnl Planning, Min. of Educn (Prov. of BC), 1977–78; Member: Jt Bd of Teacher Educn, Prov. of BC, 1972–75; Planning Cttee, Canadian Teachers' Fedn, 1974; Planning Cttee, 1973–74, and Bd of Dirs, 1974–75 and 1979–80, BC Council for Leadership in Educn; Interior Univ. Progs Bd, Min. of Educn, 1977–78. Member, Board of Directors: Assoc. of Univs and Colls of Canada, 1979–84 (Mem., Adv. Cttee, Office of Internat. Develt, 1979–); Inter-American Orgn for Higher Educn, 1979–85; Public Employers' Council of BC, 1979–84; Vancouver Bd of Trade, 1983–85; Pulp and Paper Res. Inst. of Canada, 1983. President: N Vancouver Teachers' Assoc., 1962–63; N Vancouver Principals' and Vice-Principals' Assoc., 1963–64; Sec.-Treasurer, Canadian Assoc. of Deans and Directors of Educn, 1972–73 and 1973–74. Member: Amer. Educnl Res. Assoc., 1965–; National Soc. for Study of Educn, 1965–; Canadian Assoc. of Sch. Administrators, 1968–; Canadian Educn Assoc., 1968–; Canadian Educnl Researchers' Assoc., 1968–; Canadian Soc. for Study of Educn, 1968–; Internat. Council on Educn for Teaching, 1968–; Canadian Bureau for Internat. Educn, 1970–; Canadian Foundn for Econ. Educn, 1970–; Canadian Soc. for Study of Higher Educn, 1975–; Inst. of Public Admin. of Canada, 1976–; Internat. Assoc. of Univ. Presidents, 1979–; Commonwealth Assoc. of Univs, 1979–; Comparative and Internat. Educn Soc., 1980–; Assoc. for Advancement of Scandinavian Studies in Canada, 1981–. Member: BoT, Vancouver, 1983–85; Nat. Council, Canadian Human Rights Foundn, 1984–. Mem., Board of Directors: Pulp and Paper Res. Inst. of Canada, 1983–; MacMillan Bloedel Ltd, 1984–86. Member, Board of Governors: Arts, Sciences and Technol. Centre, 1980–85; Leon and Thea Koerner Foundn, 1981–85; Mem., Bd of Trustees, Discovery Foundn, 1980–85. *Publications*: The Itinerant Schoolmaster: a socio-economic analysis of teacher turnover, 1973; chapters in books on educn; articles in Administrator's Notebook (Univ. of Chicago), Selected Articles for Elem. Sch. Prinicpals, Res. in Educn, Educn and Urban Soc., Educn Canada, Teacher Educn, Resources in Educn, Elem. Sch. Jl, Jl of Educnl Admin, and Canadian Jl of Univ. Continuing Educn; book reviews; proc. of confs and symposia; governmental and institutional studies and reports. *Address*: President's Office, Room 113, Stevenson-Lawson Building, The University of Western Ontario, London, Ontario N6A 5B8, Canada. *T*: (519) 661–3106; (home) Gibbons Lodge, 1836 Richmond Street, London, Ontario N6A 4B6, Canada. *T*: (519) 433–5062. *Clubs*: London Hunt and Country, London, University (London, Ont.).

PEDLER, Sir Frederick (Johnson), Kt 1969; *b* 10 July 1908; *s* of Charles Henry Pedler and Lucy Marian (*née* Johnson); *m* 1935, Esther Ruth Carling; two *s* one *d*. *Educ*: Watford Grammar School; Caius College, Cambridge (MA). Colonial Office, 1930; seconded to Tanganyika, 1934; Secretary to Commission on Higher Educn in E Africa and Sudan, 1937; Sec. to Lord Privy Seal, 1938; Sec. to Lord Hailey in Africa, 1939, Congo, 1940; Chief Brit. Econ. Representative, Dakar, 1942; Finance Dept, Colonial Office, 1944. Joined United Africa Co., 1947, Director, 1951, Deputy Chairman, 1965–68. Director: Unilever Ltd and NV, 1956–68; William Baird Ltd, 1969–75. Chm., Council for Technical Educn and Training for Overseas Countries, 1962–73. Chm., E Africa and Mauritius Assoc., 1966–68; Mem., Inter-University Council, 1967–73. Treas., SOAS, Univ. of London, 1969–81, Hon. Fellow, 1976. *Publications*: West Africa, 1951 (2nd edn 1959); Economic Geography of W Africa, 1955; The Lion and the Unicorn in Africa, 1974; Main Currents of West African History 1940–78, 1979. *Recreations*: languages, history. *Address*: 36 Russell Road, Moor Park, Northwood, Mddx HA6 2LR.

PEDLEY, Alan Sydney, DFC 1946; Lord Mayor of Leeds, 1975–1976; District Insurance Manager, 1974–82, retired; *b* 16 Aug. 1917; *s* of Herbert Leonard Pedley and Edith Mary (*née* Skipsey); *m* 1st, 1949, Evelyn Anderson (*née* Scott) (*d* 1977); 2nd, 1981, Shirley Elizabeth, *widow* of Reg Howard. *Educ*: Leeds Modern Sch. Entered Insurance, 1934; retd (Commercial Union), 1971; joined Barclays Insurance Services Co. Ltd, 1971. Member: Leeds City Council, 1951–81; W Yorkshire Metropolitan CC, 1973–81; Dep. Lord Mayor, 1971–72. FCII 1949. *Recreations*: cricket, Association football, Rugby League, music, theatre, the Arts, after dinner speaking. *Address*: Whitelea, 8 Bentcliffe Close, Leeds LS17 6QT. *T*: Leeds 685424. *Club*: Leeds Taverners.

PEDLEY, Rev. (Geoffrey) Stephen; Chaplain to the Queen, since 1984; Vicar of St Peter's, Stockton, since 1977; *b* 13 Sept. 1940; *s* of Geoffrey Heber Knight and Muriel

---

Pedley; *m* 1970, Mary Frances Macdonald; two *s* one *d*. *Educ*: Marlborough College; Queens' College, Cambridge (MA); Cuddesdon Theological College. Curate: Liverpool Parish Church, 1966; Holy Trinity, Coventry, 1969; Rector of Kitwe, Zambia, 1971–77. *Recreations*: architecture, English literature, travel. *Address*: St Peter's Vicarage, 77 Yarm Road, Stockton-on-Tees, Cleveland TS18 3PJ. *T*: Stockton-on-Tees 676625.

PEDLEY, Prof. Robin; Professor Emeritus, University of Southampton, since 1979; *b* 11 Aug. 1914; *s* of Edward and Martha Jane Pedley; *m* 1951, Jeanne Lesley Hitching, BA; one *s* one *d*. *Educ*: Richmond Sch., Yorks; Durham Univ. (MA, PhD, Teaching Dip.; Gibson Prize in Archaeology, Gladstone Meml Prize in Mod. Hist.). Research Fellow, Durham Univ., 1936–38; Teacher, Friends' Sch., Great Ayton, 1938–42, and Crossley and Porter Schs, Halifax, 1943–46. Lecturer: Coll. of St Mark and St John, Chelsea, 1946–47; Leicester Univ. Dept of Educn, 1947–63. Dir, Exeter Univ. Inst. of Educn, 1963–71; University of Southampton: Head of Sch. of Educn and Dean, Faculty of Educn, 1971–75; Head, Dept of Educn, 1976–79. *Publications*: Comprehensive Schools Today, 1955; Comprehensive Education: a new approach, 1956; The Comprehensive School, 1963, 3rd edn 1978; The Comprehensive School (with J. Orring, publ. in Hebrew, Jerusalem), 1966; Towards the Comprehensive University, 1977; many articles various educational jls. *Recreations*: sport, reading. *Address*: Annerley, Waters Green, Brockenhurst, Hants, SO4 7RG. *T*: Lymington 23001.

PEDLEY, Stephen; *see* Pedley, G. S.

PEEBLES, Prof. Phillip James Edwin, FRS 1982; Professor of Physics, since 1965, and Albert Einstein Professor of Science, since 1984, Princeton University; *b* Winnipeg, 25 April 1935; *s* of Andrew Charles Peebles and Ada Marian (*née* Green); *m* 1958, Jean Alison Peebles; three *d*. *Educ*: Univ. of Manitoba (BSc 1958); Princeton Univ. (Ma 1959; PhD 1962). Member: Amer. Phys. Soc.; Amer. Astron. Soc.; AAAS; Amer. Acad. of Arts and Scis; Internat. Astron. Union. Hon. DSc: Univ. of Toronto, 1986; Univ. of Chicago, 1986. *Publications*: Physical Cosmology, 1971; The Large Scale Structure of the Universe, 1979; (ed jtly) Objects of High Redshift, 1980. *Address*: 24 Markham Road, Princeton, NJ 08540, USA; Joseph Henry Laboratories, Physics Department, Princeton University, Princeton, NJ 08544, USA.

PEECH, Alan James; *b* 24 August 1905; *s* of late Albert Orlando Peech; *m* 1948, Betty Leese; no *c*. *Educ*: Wellington College; Magdalen College, Oxford (BA). Former Governor, Wellington College, retd 1975. Independent Chm., Cement Makers' Fedn, 1970–76; former Dep. Chm., Steetley Co. Ltd, retd 1976; Pres., British Iron and Steel Fedn, Jan.-June 1967; Jt Man. Dir, United Steel Cos Ltd, 1962–67, Chm., 1962–71; a Dep. Chm., BSC, 1967–70; Man. Dir, Midland Gp BSC, 1967–70. Hon. LLD Sheffield, 1966. *Recreations*: fishing and shooting. *Address*: High House, Blyth, Worksop, Notts. *T*: Blyth 255. *Club*: MCC.

PEECH, Neil Malcolm; President for life, Steetley PLC, since 1976 (Managing Director, 1935–68, Chairman, 1935–76); *b* 27 Jan. 1908; *s* of Albert Orlando Peech; *m* 1932, Margaret Josephine, *d* of late R. C. Smallwood, CBE, Worplesdon, Surrey; one *s* one *d*. *Educ*: Wellington College; Magdalen College, Oxford. Developed the production of magnesia from seawater and dolomite, 1939. Consul for Sweden, 1974–76 (Vice Consul, 1949–74). Underwriting member of Lloyd's, 1950–69; Director, Sheepbridge Engineering Ltd, 1949–79, and Albright & Wilson Ltd, 1958–79. Chairman, Ministry of Power Solid Smokeless Fuel Committee, 1959. High Sheriff of Yorkshire, 1959. Chevalier, Order of Vasa, Sweden, 1963. *Recreations*: fishing and shooting. *Address*: Park House, Firbeck, Worksop. *T*: Worksop 730338. *Club*: MCC.

PEEK, Sir Francis (Henry Grenville), 4th Bt, *cr* 1874; *b* 16 Sept. 1915; *o s* of 3rd Bt and Edwine Warner (*d* 1959), *d* of late W. H. Thornburgh, St Louis, USA; *S* father, 1927; *m* 1st, 1942, Ann (marr. diss., 1949), *d* of late Captain Gordon Duff and *widow* of Sir Charles Mappin, Bt (she *m* 1951, Sir William Rootes, later 1st Baron Rootes); 2nd, Marilyn (marr. diss., 1967; she *m* 1967, Peter Quennell), *d* of Dr Norman Kerr, London and Bahamas; one *s* decd; 3rd, Mrs Caroline Kirkwood, *d* of late Sir Robert Kirkwood, KCMG, OJ. *Educ*: Eton; Trinity College, Cambridge. ADC to Governor of Bahamas, 1938–39; served Irish Guards, 1939–46. *Heir*: *cousin* William Grenville Peek [*b* 15 Dec. 1919; *m* 1950, Lucy Jane, *d* of late Major Edward Dorrien-Smith, DSO; one *s* three *d*]. *Address*: 60 Grosvenor Close, Nassau, Bahamas. *Club*: White's.

PEEK, Vice-Adm. Sir Richard (Innes), KBE 1972 (OBE 1944); CB 1971; DSC 1945; pastoralist; *b* 30 July 1914; 2nd *s* of late James Norman and Kate Doughty Peek; *m* 1943, Margaret Seinor (*née* Kendall) (*d* 1946); one *s*; *m* 1952, Mary Catherine Tilley (*née* Stops); two *d*. *Educ*: Royal Australian Naval College. Joined RAN, 1928; served War of 1939–45 in HMS Revenge, HMAS Cerberus, Hobart, Australia, Navy Office; Korean War Service in HMAS Tobruk, 1951; Flag Officer Comdg HMA Fleet, 1967–68; Chief of Naval Staff, Australia, 1970–73. Legion of Merit (US), 1951. *Recreations*: gardening, golf. *Address*: Rothlyn, RMB, Monaro Highway, via Cooma, NSW 2630, Australia. *Clubs*: Imperial Service (Sydney); Royal Commonwealth Society (Canberra).

PEEL, family name of **Earl Peel**.

PEEL, 3rd Earl *cr* 1929; **William James Robert Peel**; Bt 1800; Viscount Peel, 1895; Viscount Clanfield, 1929; *b* 3 Oct. 1947; *s* of 2nd Earl Peel and Kathleen (*d* 1972), *d* of Michael McGrath; *S* father, 1969; *m* 1973, Veronica Naomi Livingston, *d* of Alastair Timpson; one *s* one *d*. *Educ*: Ampleforth; University of Tours; Cirencester Agric. Coll. *Heir*: *s* Viscount Clanfield, *qv*. *Address*: Gunnerside Lodge, Richmond, North Yorks. *Club*: Turf.

PEEL, Lady, (Beatrice); *see* Lillie, Beatrice.

PEEL, Prof. Edwin Arthur, DLit; Professor of Education, University of Birmingham, 1950–78, and Chairman of School of Education, 1965–70; *b* 11 March 1911; *s* of late Arthur Peel and Mary Ann Miller; *m* 1939, Nora Kathleen Yeadon; two *s* two *d*. *Educ*: Prince Henry's Grammar School, Otley, Yorks; Leeds University; London University. Teaching in various London Schools, 1933–38; LCC School of Building, 1938–41; MA London, 1938; Ministry of Supply, 1941–45; PhD London 1945; Part-time Lecturer London Univ. Institute of Education, 1945; Lecturer in Education, King's College, Newcastle, 1946; Reader in Psychology, Durham University, 1946–48; Professor of Educational Psychology, University of Durham, 1948–50. President British Psychological Society 1961–62. DLit, London, 1961. *Publications*: The Psychological Basis of Education, 1956; The Pupil's Thinking, 1960; The Nature of Adolescent Judgment, 1971; various in leading British and foreign journals of psychology; Editor and contrib., Educational Review. *Recreation*: painting. *Address*: 47 Innage Road, Birmingham B31 2DY. *T*: 021–475 2820.

See also J. D. Y. Peel.

PEEL, Jack Armitage, CBE 1972; DL; industrial relations consultant; *b* 8 Jan. 1921; *s* of Martha and George Henry Peel; *m* 1950, Dorothy Mabel Dobson; one *s* one *d*. *Educ*: elem. and modern sch.; Ruskin Coll., Oxford (Schol., Social Sci.), 1948–49. Railwayman,

1936–47. National Union of Dyers, Bleachers and Textile Workers: full-time Officer, 1950; Asst Gen.-Sec., 1957–66, Gen. Sec., 1966–73; Mem. Gen. Council of TUC, 1966–72; Dir, Industrial Relations, in the Social Affairs Directorate, EEC, 1973–79, Chief Adviser, 1979–81. Part-time Director: British Wool Marketing Board, 1968–73; NCB, 1969–73. Served on several courts of inquiry, incl. Rochdale Cttee of Inquiry into Merchant Navy; Special Adviser to Sec. of State for Transport on long term industrial relns strategy, May 1983 - Jan. 1984. Senior Vis. Fellow in Industrial Relns, Bradford Univ., 1984–. Hon. MA Bradford, 1979. DL West Yorks, 1971; JP Bradford, 1960–72. *Publication:* The Real Power Game, 1979. *Recreations:* cricket, painting, guitar music, swimming. *Address:* Timberleigh, 39 Old Newbridge Hill, Bath, Avon. *T:* Bath 23959.

PEEL, Sir John; *see* Peel, Sir W. J.

PEEL, John; *see* Ravenscroft, J. R. P.

PEEL, Prof. John David Yeadon; Charles Booth Professor of Sociology, since 1974, and Dean, Faculty of Social and Environmental Studies, since 1985, University of Liverpool; *b* 13 Nov. 1941; *e s* of Prof. Edwin Arthur Peel, *qv*; *m* 1969, Jennifer Christine Ferial, *d* of K. N. Pare, Leicester; three *s*. *Educ:* King Edward's Sch., Birmingham; Balliol Coll., Oxford (Scholar; BA 1963, MA 1966); LSE (PhD 1966). Asst Lectr, then Lectr in Sociology, Nottingham Univ., 1965–70; Lectr in Sociology, LSE, 1970–73. Vis. Reader in Sociology and Anthropology, Univ of Ife, Nigeria, 1973–75; Vis. Prof. in Anthropology and Sociology, Univ. of Chicago, 1982–83. Associate, Inst. of Develt Studies, 1973–; Mem. Council, African Studies Assoc. of UK, 1978–81. Editor, Jl of Develt Studies, 1972–73; Consulting Editor, Amer. Jl of Sociology, 1978–80, 1986–; Editor, Africa, and Officer, Internat African Inst., 1979–86. Amaury Talbot Prize for African Anthropology, 1983; Herskovits Award, African Studies Assoc., USA, 1984. *Publications:* Aladura: a religious movement among the Yoruba, 1968; Herbert Spencer: the evolution of a sociologist, 1971; (ed) Herbert Spencer on Social Evolution, 1972; Ijeshas and Nigerians, 1983; articles in anthropological, sociological and Africanist jls. *Recreations:* gardening, old churches. *Address:* 23 Mount road, Upton, Wirral, Merseyside L49 6JA. *T:* 051–678 6783.

PEEL, Sir John (Harold), KCVO 1960; MA, BM, BCh; FRCP 1971; FRCS 1933; FRCOG 1944; Surgeon-Gynæcologist to the Queen, 1961–73; Consulting Obstetric and Gynæcological Surgeon, King's College Hospital, since 1969; Emeritus Consulting Gynæcologist, Princess Beatrice Hospital, since 1965; *b* 10 December 1904; *s* of Rev. J. E. Peel; *m* 1947, Freda Margaret Mellish; one *d*. *Educ:* Manchester Grammar Sch.; Queen's Coll., Oxford. MA, BM, BCh Oxon 1932. King's College Hospital Med. Sch., qualified 1930; MRCS, LRCP. Obstetric and Gynæcological Surgeon: King's Coll. Hosp., 1936–69; Princess Beatrice Hosp., 1937–65; Queen Victoria Hosp., East Grinstead, 1941–69; Surgeon EMS, 1939–45. Director of Clinical Studies, King's College Hospital Medical School, 1948–67. Mem., Economic and Social Cttee, EEC, 1973–78. Litchfield Lecturer, Oxford University, 1961 and 1969; Sir Kadar Nath Das Lecturer, Bengal O and G Soc., 1962; Sir A. Mudaliar Lecturer, Madras Univ., 1962; Vis. Prof., Cape Town Univ., 1963; Travelling Prof., S African Council, RCOG, 1968. Past Examiner, Universities of Oxford, Cambridge, London, Liverpool, Bristol, Glasgow, Newcastle, Nat. Univ. of Ireland, Birmingham, Dundee, Sheffield, Conjoint Board, RCOG and CMB. Nuffield visitor to Colonies, 1950 and 1953. President, RCOG, 1966–69 (Hon. Treasurer, 1959–66, Councillor, 1955–); President: Internat. Fedn of Obstetrics and Gynæcology, 1970–73; Chelsea Clinical Society, 1960; BMA 1970 (Chm., Bd of Science and Educn, 1972–76); Family Planning Assoc., 1971–74; Chm., DHSS Cttees of Enquiry: Domiciliary Midwifery and Bed Needs, 1971; The Use of Fetus and Fetal Material for Research, 1972. FKC 1980; Hon. Fellow: American Association of Obstetricians and Gynæcologists, 1962 (Joseph Price Oration, 1961); Edinburgh Obstetrical Soc., 1971; RSM, 1973; Hon. Member: Canadian Assoc. of O and G, 1955; Italian Assoc O and G, 1960; Hon. Treas., GMC, 1972–75; Hon. FRCS (Canada), 1967; Hon. FCOG (SA), 1968; Hon. MMSA 1970; Hon. FACS 1970; Hon. FACOG 1971; Hon. Fellow, American Gynæcological Soc., 1974. Hon. DSc Birmingham, 1972; Hon. DM Southampton, 1974; Hon. DCh Newcastle, 1980. *Publications:* Textbook of Gynæcology, 1943; Lives of the Fellows of Royal College of Obstetricians and Gynaecologists 1929–69, 1976; numerous contributions to Medical Journals. *Recreations:* fishing, golf, gardening. *Address:* Gean Trees, 78 Countess Road, Amesbury, Wilts SP4 7AT. *Club:* Naval and Military.

PEEL, Jonathan Sidney, MC 1957; Vice Lord-Lieutenant of Norfolk, since 1981; Director, Norwich Union Insurance Group, since 1973; *b* 21 June 1937; *s* of Major D. A. Peel (killed in action 1944) and Hon. Mrs David Peel (*née* Vanneck); *m* 1965, Jean Fulton Barnett, *d* of Air Chief Marshal Sir Denis Barnett, *qv*; one *s* four *d*. *Educ:* Norwich Sch.; Eton; St John's Coll., Cambridge (BA Land Economy; MA 1970). Commnd, Rifle Bde, Royal Green Jackets, 1956; served Malaya, 1956–57; UN forces, Congo (Zaire), 1960–61; Cyprus, 1962–63; resigned, 1966. Chm., Pleasureworld Ltd, 1986. Vice Pres., Norfolk Naturalists Trust, 1984– (Mem., 1980–); National Trust: Mem. Exec. Cttee, 1982–; Mem. Council, 1984–; Chm., Cttee for East Anglia, 1982–. Chairman: Norfolk Police Authority, 1983–; The Broads Authority, 1985–; Norwich Sch., 1985–. Mem., Norfolk CC, 1973–. JP North Walsham, 1973–86. High Sheriff, Norfolk, 1984. *Publication:* (with M. J. Sayer) Towards a Rural Policy for Norfolk, 1973. *Recreations:* forestry, music. *Address:* Barton Hall, Barton Turf, Norwich NR12 8AU. *T:* Smallburgh 250, and 298. *Clubs:* Boodle's; Norfolk (Norwich).

PEEL, Sir (William) John, Kt 1973; *b* 16 June 1912; *s* of late Sir William Peel, KCMG, KBE, and Violet Mary Drake, *er d* of W. D. Laing; *m* 1936, Rosemary Mia Minka, *er d* of Robert Readhead; one *s* three *d*. *Educ:* Wellington College; Queens' College, Cambridge. Colonial Administrative Service, 1933–51; on active service, 1941–45; British Resident, Brunei, 1946–48; Res. Comr, Gilbert and Ellice Is Colony, 1949–51. Personal Asst to Man. Dirs of Rugby Portland Cement Co. Ltd, 1952–54. Contested (C) Meriden Division of Warwickshire, 1955; MP (C) Leicester SE, 1957–Feb. 1974; Parliamentary Private Secretary to: Economic Secretary to the Treasury, 1958–59; Minister of State, Board of Trade, 1959–60; Asst Govt Whip (unpaid), 1960–61; a Lord Comr of the Treasury, Nov. 1961–Oct. 1964. Parly Delegate to: Assemblies of Council of Europe, 1961–74; WEU 1961–74 (Vice-Pres., 1967, Pres. 1972, Chm., Defence and Armaments Cttee, 1970–72, WEU); N Atlantic Assembly, 1959–74 (Leader, 1970–74; Pres., N Atlantic Assembly, Nov. 1972); Mem., British Delegn to European Parlt, Strasbourg, 1973–74; Hon. Dir, Cons. Party Internat. Office, 1975–76. Member Council: Victoria League for Commonwealth Friendship, 1974–83 (Dep. Chm., 1976–81; Chm., 1982–83; Mem., Chairman's Adv. Cttee, 1983–); Royal Over-Seas League, 1980–86; British Atlantic Cttee; Chairman: Hospitality and Branches Cttee of Victoria League, 1974–78, Hospitality Cttee, 1978–81; Overseas Students Adv. Cttee, 1980–81; Jt Standing Cttee of Victoria League and Royal Commonwealth Soc., 1975–83; Westminster for Europe Branch, European Movement, 1974–77. Mem. Ct of Assistants, Framework Knitters' Co. (Master, 1983). Dato Seri Laila Jasa Brunei 1969; Dato Setia Negara Brunei 1971. *Recreations:* varied. *Address:* 51 Cambridge Street, SW1. *T:* 01–834 8762. *Clubs:* Carlton, Hurlingham, Royal Over-Seas League; Hawks (Cambridge).

PEELER, Joseph; Regional Director for the South-East Region, Departments of the Environment and Transport, and Chairman of Regional Board, 1979–86, retired; *b* 22 April 1930; *s* of late Edward Francis Peeler and Marjorie Cynthia Peeler; *m* 1958, Diana Helen (*née* Wynne); three *s* one *d*. *Educ:* King Edward VI Grammar Sch., Stratford-on-Avon; Wimbledon Coll.; Jesus Coll., Oxford (Scholar, 1948; BA 1st Cl. Hons Modern History, 1951; MA 1955). RAF, 1951–53. Entered Civil Service (Min. of Transport and Civil Aviation), 1953; Private Sec. to Parly Sec., 1956–58; Principal, 1958; seconded to Home Office, 1964–66; Asst Sec., 1966; Under Sec., 1978. *Recreations:* history, crosswords, bridge, walking. *Address:* Farthings, The Folly, Lightwater, Surrey. *T:* Bagshot 72228.

PEERS, Most Rev. Michael Geoffrey; Primate of the Anglican Church of Canada, since 1986; *b* 31 July 1934; *s* of Geoffrey Hugh Peers and Dorothy Enid Mantle; *m* 1963, Dorothy Elizabeth Bradley; two *s* one *d*. *Educ:* University of British Columbia (BA Hons); Universität Heidelberg (Zert. Dolm.-Interpreter's Certificate); Trinity Coll., Toronto (LTh). Deacon 1959, priest 1960; Curate: St Thomas', Ottawa, 1959–61; Trinity, Ottawa, 1961–65; University Chaplain, Diocese of Ottawa, 1961–66; Rector: St Bede's, Winnipeg, 1966–72; St Martin's, Winnipeg, with St Paul's Middlechurch, 1972–74; Archdeacon of Winnipeg, 1969–74; Rector, St Paul's Cathedral, Regina, 1974–77; Dean of Qu'Appelle, 1974–77; Bishop of Qu'Appelle, 1977–82; Archbishop of Qu'Appelle and Metropolitan of Rupert's Land, 1982–86. Hon. DD: Trinity Coll., Toronto, 1978; St John's Coll., Winnipeg, 1981. *Address:* 600 Jarvis Street, Toronto, Ontario M4Y 2J6, Canada. *T:* 416–924–9192.

PEET, Ronald Hugh, CBE 1974; Chairman, Stockley Plc, since 1984; Deputy Chairman, PWS International Plc, since 1986; *b* 12 July 1925; *s* of Henry Leonard and Stella Peet; *m* 1st, 1949, Winifred Joy Adamson (*d* 1979); two *s* two *d*; 2nd, 1981, Lynette Judy Burgess Kinsella. *Educ:* Doncaster Grammar Sch.; Queen's Coll., Oxford (MA). Served in HM Forces, Captain RA, 1944–47. Joined Legal and General Assurance Soc. Ltd, 1952; emigrated to Australia, 1955; Sec., Legal & General's Australian Branch, 1955–59; Asst Life Manager, 1959–65; Manager and Actuary for Australia, 1965–69; returned to UK as General Manager (Ops), 1969. Chairman: Aviation & General Insurance Co. Ltd, 1978–80; Legal & General Assce Soc., 1980–84 (Dir, 1969–84; Chief Exec., 1972–80); Howard Gp plc, 1985–86; Dir and Gp Chief Exec., Legal & General Gp, 1979–84; Dir, AMEC Plc, 1984–. Director: City Arts Trust Ltd, 1976– (Chm., 1980–); Royal Philharmonic Orchestra Ltd, 1977–; English National Opera, 1978–84. Chm., British Insurance Assoc., 1978–79. FIA. *Recreations:* music, opera. *Address:* 36 Shawfield Street, SW3. *Clubs:* Hurlingham, City of London.

PEGG, Michael Anstice, PhD; University Librarian and Director, John Rylands University Library, University of Manchester, since April 1981; *b* 3 Sept. 1931; *s* of Benjamin and Rose Pegg; *m* 1st, 1955, Jean Williams; three *s*; 2nd, 1986, Margaret Rae. *Educ:* Burton-on-Trent Grammar Sch.; Univ. of Southampton. BA (London); PhD (Southampton); MA (Manchester) 1985. Captain, Royal Army Education Corps, Educn Officer, SHAPE, Paris, 1958–61; Asst Keeper, Nat. Library of Scotland, Edinburgh, 1961–67; Sec. and Estabt Officer, Nat. Library of Scotland, Edinburgh, 1967–76; Librarian, Univ. of Birmingham, 1976–80. Member: British Library Bd, 1981–84; Standing Conference of Nat. and Univ. Libraries' Council, 1981–83. Vis. Fellow, Wolfson Coll., Oxford, 1986. *Publications:* Les Divers Rapports d'Eustorg de Beaulieu (édn critique), 1964 (Geneva); Catalogue of German Reformation Pamphlets in Libraries of Great Britain and Ireland, 1973 (Baden Baden); Catalogue of Sixteenth-century German Pamphlets in Collections in France and England, 1977 (Baden Baden); Catalogue of Reformation Pamphlets in Swiss Libraries, 1983; occasional papers to learned jls. *Recreations:* cricket, tennis, railway modelling. *Address:* John Rylands University Library, University of Manchester, Oxford Road, Manchester M13 9PP.

PEGGIE, Robert Galloway Emslie, CBE 1986; Commissioner for Local Administration (Ombudsman) in Scotland, since 1986; *b* 5 Jan. 1929; *s* of John and Euphemia Peggie; *m* 1955, Christine Jeanette Simpson; one *s* one *d*. *Educ:* Lasswade High Sch. Certified accountant; Accountancy apprenticeship, 1946–52; Accountant in industry, 1952–57; Public Service, Edinburgh City, 1957–74; Chief Exec., Lothian Regl Council, 1974–86. *Recreation:* golf. *Address:* 54 Liberton Drive, Edinburgh EH16 6NW. *T:* 031–664 1631.

PEGLER, Alfred Ernest, OBE 1978; DL; Councillor: Crawley Borough Council, since 1956; West Sussex County Council, since 1959; *b* 18 Jan. 1924; *s* of Frank Walter James Pegler and Violet Maud Pegler; *m* 1944, E. E. McDonald; one *s* one *d*. *Educ:* Cork Street Sch., Peckham; Oliver Goldsmith Sch., Peckham. Engrg apprentice, 1938–42; served War, RAF Air Crew, 1942–46; toolmaker, 1946–62; Civil Service Engrg Inspector, 1963–81. Chm., Crawley Council, 1959 and 1966; Chm. Housing Cttee, 1971–77. Leader, Labour Gp, W Sussex CC, 1977–. Mem., Crawley Cttee, New Towns Commn, 1962– (Chm., 1974–). Mayor, Crawley Borough Council, 1982–83, 1983–84. Mem., Sussex Police Authority, 1973–77. Parly Candidate (Labour): Horsham, 1959 and 1964; Gloucester, Feb. 1974. DL West Sussex, 1982. *Recreations:* gardening, politics. *Address:* 7 Priors Walk, Three Bridges, Crawley, West Sussex RH10 1NX. *T:* Crawley 27330.

PEGLER, James Basil Holmes, TD; BA; FIA, FSS, FIS, FIMA; Professor of Actuarial Science, City University, 1976–79, Visiting Professor, 1979–86; *b* 6 Aug. 1912; *s* of late Harold Holmes Pegler and late Dorothy Cecil (*née* Francis); *m* 1937, Enid Margaret Dell; one *s* three *d*. *Educ:* Charterhouse; Open Univ. Joined Clerical, Medical and Gen. Life Assce Soc., 1931; Gen. Man. and Actuary, 1950–69; Man. Dir, 1970–75; non-exec. Dir, 1975–83. War service, Queen's Royal Regt and RA, 1939–45 (Major). Inst. of Actuaries: Fellow, 1939; Hon. Sec., 1955–57; Pres., 1968–70. Chm., Life Offices' Assoc., 1959–61; Chm., Life Gp of Comité Européen des Assurances, 1964–70. *Publications:* contribs to Jl Inst. Actuaries. *Recreations:* mathematics, music, languages, squash rackets. *Address:* Dormers, Deepdene Wood, Dorking, Surrey RH5 4BQ. *T:* Dorking 885955. *Club:* Army and Navy.

PEIERLS, Sir Rudolf (Ernst), Kt 1968; CBE 1946; FRS 1945; MA Cantab; DSc Manchester, DPhil Leipzig; Wykeham Professor of Physics, Oxford University, and Fellow, New College, Oxford, 1963–74, now Emeritus Fellow (Hon. Fellow 1980); Professor of Physics (part-time), University of Washington, Seattle, 1974–77; *b* Berlin, 5 June 1907; *s* of H. Peierls; *m* 1931, Eugenia, *d* of late N. Kannegiesser; one *s* three *d*. *Educ:* Humboldt School, Oberschöneweide, Berlin; Universities of Berlin, Munich, Leipzig. Assistant, Federal Institute of Technology, Zürich, 1929–32; Rockefeller Fellow, 1932–33; Honorary Research Fellow, Manchester University, 1933–35; Assistant-in-Research, Royal Society Mond Laboratory, 1935–37; Professor of Mathematical Physics (formerly Applied Mathematics), University of Birmingham, 1937–63; worked on Atomic Energy Project in Birmingham, 1940–43, in USA, 1943–46. Royal Society: Royal Medal, 1959; Copley Medal, 1986; Lorentz Medal of Royal Netherlands Academy of Sciences, 1962; Max Planck Medal, Assoc. of German Physical Societies, 1963; Guthrie Medal, IPPS, 1968; first British recipient of Enrico Fermi Award, US Dept of Energy, 1980. FInstP 1973. Hon. DSc: Liverpool, 1960; Birmingham, 1967; Edinburgh, 1969; Sussex, 1978; Chicago, 1981. Foreign Hon. Mem., American Academy of Arts and Sciences, 1962; Hon. Associate, College of Advanced Technology, Birmingham, 1963; Foreign Associate:

Nat. Acad. of Sciences, USA, 1970; French Acad. of Sciences, 1984; Hon. Mem., French Phys. Soc., 1979; For. Mem., Royal Danish Acad., 1980; Mem., Leopoldina Acad., E Germany, 1981; Corres. Mem., Yugoslav Acad. of Arts and Sciences, 1983. *Publications:* Quantum Theory of Solids, 1955; The Laws of Nature, 1955; Surprises in Theoretical Physics, 1979; Bird of Passage, 1985; papers on Quantum Theory. *Address:* 2B Northmoor Road, Oxford OX2 6UP; Nuclear Physics Laboratory, Keble Road, Oxford. *Club:* Athenæum.

PEILE, Vice-Admiral Sir Lancelot Arthur Babington, KBE 1960; CB 1957; DSO 1941; MVO 1947; DL; retired; *b* 22 Jan. 1905; *s* of late Basil Wilson Peile and Katharine Rosamond (*née* Taylor); *m* 1928, Gertrude Margaret (*née* Tolcher); two *s. Educ:* RN Colleges, Osborne and Dartmouth. Commander (E) 1939; Captain (E), 1947; Rear-Admiral, 1955; Vice-Admiral, 1958. Asst Engineer-in-Chief, 1948; Command of RN Engineering College, 1951; idc 1954. Asst Director of Dockyards, 1955–57; Admiral Superintendent, Devonport Dockyard, 1957–60; retired, 1960. DL Devon, 1969. *Address:* Strawberry How, Thurlestone, Kingsbridge, Devon. *T:* Thurlestone 209.

PEIRIS, Dr Mahapitage Velin Peter, OBE 1956; *b* 28 July 1898; *s* of M. A. Peiris and H. D. Selestina, Panadura, Ceylon; *m* 1945, Edith Doreen Idona Carey, Negombo, Ceylon; three *s* one *d. Educ:* St John's Coll., Panadura; St Joseph's Coll., Colombo; Ceylon Medical Coll., Colombo. LMS Ceylon, 1926; MB, BS London, 1936; FRCS 1930; FICS 1957; FACS 1959. Served in Ceylon Army Med. Corps, 1930–45: Surg. to Mil. Hosps, Ceylon, 1940–45. Vis. Surgeon: Gen. Hosp., 1936–60; Children's Hosp., Colombo, 1951–60; Surg. to Orthop. Clinic, 1950–60; Cons. Orthop. Surg., Gen. Hosp., Colombo; Medico-Legal Adviser to Crown; Prof. of Surgery, Univ. of Ceylon, 1952–60. Senator, Ceylon Parlt, 1954–68: Minister of Health, 1960; Leader of Senate, and Minister of Commerce and Trade, 1965–68. Ambassador of Ceylon to USSR, 1968–69; High Comr for Ceylon in the UK, 1969–70. Mem. Coun., Univ. of Ceylon, 1960; President: Ceylon Med. Assoc., 1954; University Teachers' Assoc.; UNA of Ceylon, 1966–68. *Publications:* contribs to Indian and Ceylon medical jls. *Recreations:* swimming, photography. *Address:* 19 Beverley Court, Wellesley Road, W4 4LQ.

PEIRSE, Sir Henry G. de la P. B.; *see* Beresford-Peirse.

PEIRSE, Air Vice-Marshal Richard Charles Fairfax, CB 1984; Defence Service Secretary, since 1985; *b* 16 March 1931; *s* of late Air Chief Marshal Sir Richard Peirse, KCB, DSO, AFC and late Lady Peirse; *m* 1st, 1955, Karalie Grace Cox (marr. diss. 1963); two *d*; 2nd, 1963, Deirdre Mary O'Donovan (*d* 1976); one *s*; 3rd, 1977, Anna Jill Margaret Long (*née* Latey). *Educ:* Bradfield Coll.; RAF Coll., Cranwell. Commnd 1952; 2nd TAF No 266 Sqdn and HQ 2 Gp, 1952; Flying Instructor, Cranwell, 1956; Air Staff No 23 Gp, 1960; Staff Coll., 1962; Flt Comdr No 39 Sqdn and OC Ops Wg, Luqa, Malta, 1963; Air Sec.'s Dept, 1965; jssc 1968; OC No 51 Sqdn, 1968; Dep. Captain, The Queen's Flight, 1969; RCDS 1972; OC RAF Waddington, 1973; Dep. Dir, Op Requirements, 1976; Dir of Personnel (Air), 1977; Dir of Op Requirements, 1980; AOC and Comdt, RAF Coll. Cranwell, 1982. *Recreations:* squash, theatre, archaeology. *Address:* 10 Pembroke Road, W8. *T:* 01–602 5888. *Club:* Royal Air Force.

PELHAM, family name of **Earls of Chichester** and **Yarborough.**

PELHAM BURN, Angus Maitland; JP; farmer; Vice-Lord-Lieutenant for Kincardineshire, since 1978; Director, Bank of Scotland, since 1977 (Director, since 1973, Chairman, since 1977, Aberdeen Local Board); Director: Pelett Administration Ltd, since 1973 (Chairman); MacRobert Farms (Douneside) Ltd, since 1970 (Chairman); Jessfield Ltd, since 1970; Scottish Provident Institution, since 1975; Prime Space Design (Scotland) Ltd, since 1981; Member Accounts Commission, since 1980; Aberdeen Fund Managers, since 1985; Status Timber Systems, since 1986; *b* 13 Dec. 1931; *s* of late Brig. Gen. H. Pelham Burn, CMG, DSO, and Mrs K. E. S. Pelham Burn; *m* 1959, Anne R. Pelham Burn (*née* Forbes-Leith); four *d. Educ:* Harrow; N of Scotland Coll. of Agriculture. Hudson's Bay Co., 1951–58. Director: Aberdeen and Northern Marts Ltd, 1970–86 (former Chm.); Aberdeen Meat Marketing Co. Ltd, 1973–86 (former Chm.); Taw Meat Co., 1984–86 (former Chm.). Mem. Council, Winston Churchill Meml Trust, 1984–; Chm., Aberdeen Assoc. for Prevention of Cruelty to Animals, 1984– (Dir, 1975–). Member: Kincardine CC, 1967–75 (Vice Convener, 1973–75); Grampian Regional Council, 1974–. Member, Queen's Body Guard for Scotland (Royal Co. of Archers), 1968–. Liveryman, Farmers' Co. JP Kincardine and Deeside, 1984; DL Kincardineshire 1978. OStJ 1978. *Recreations:* fishing, vegetable gardening, photography, stalking. *Address:* Knappach, Banchory, Kincardineshire AB3 3JS. *T:* Crathes 555. *Clubs:* Caledonian; New (Edinburgh); Royal Northern (Aberdeen).

PELHAM-CLINTON-HOPE, family name of **Duke of Newcastle.**

PELIZA, Major Robert John, ED 1955; Leader of the Opposition, Gibraltar, 1972; Chief Minister, 1969–72; *b* 16 Nov. 1920; *s* of late Robert Peliza; *m* 1950, Irma Risso; three *s* four *d. Educ:* Christian Brothers' Coll., Gibraltar. Served in Gibraltar Defence Force (now Gibraltar Regt), 1939–61. Company Director, 1962–. Founder Mem., Integration with Britain Party (first leader), 1967; apptd Chief Minister, following Gen. Elections, 1969. *Recreations:* walking, painting, reading, rowing. *Address:* Buena Vista Cottage, Buena Vista Road, Gibraltar. *Club:* Royal Gibraltar Yacht.

PELLEREAU, Maj.-Gen. Peter John Mitchell, MA, CEng, FIMechE, FBIM; Secretary, Association of Consulting Engineers, since 1977; *b* Quetta, British India, 24 April 1921; *s* of late Col J. C. E. Pellereau, OBE and of Mrs A. N. V. Pellereau (*née* Betham), Penshurst; *m* 1949, Rosemary, *e d* of late S. R. Garnar; two *s. Educ:* Wellington Coll.; Trinity Coll., Cambridge. BA 1942, MA 1957. Commnd into Royal Engrs, 1942; War Service in NW Europe, 1944–45; OC 26 Armd Engr Sqdn, RE, 1946; ptsc, psc, 1950–51; Sec., Defence Research Policy Cttee, 1960; Asst Mil. Sec., WO, 1961; CO 131 Parachute Engr Regt RE TA, 1963; Mil. Dir of Studies, RMCS, 1965; Asst Dir RE Equipment Develt, 1967; Sen. Mil. Officer, Royal Armament R&D Estabt, 1970; Vice-Pres., 1973–75, Pres., 1975–76, Ordnance Board; retired 1976. Hon. Col, RE (Vol.) (Explosive Ordnance Disposal), 1980–86. Liveryman: Worshipful Co. of Plumbers, 1977; Worshipful Co. of Engineers, 1984. Mem., Smeatonian Soc. of Civil Engineers, 1981–. Vice-Pres., Surrey Hockey Umpires' Assoc., 1979–85; Pres., Oxted Hockey Club, 1975–84. *Recreation:* lawn tennis. *Address:* Woodmans Folly, Crockham Hill, Edenbridge, Kent. *T:* Edenbridge 866309.

PELLEW, family name of **Viscount Exmouth.**

PELLEW, Mark Edward, LVO 1980; HM Diplomatic Service; Counsellor, Washington, since 1983; *b* 28 Aug. 1942; *s* of Comdr Anthony Pownoll Pellew, RN retd, and Margaret Julia Critchley (*née* Cookson); *m* 1965, Jill Hosford Thistlethwaite; two *s. Educ:* Winchester; Trinity Coll., Oxford (BA). Entered HM Diplomatic Service, 1965; FO, 1965–67; Third Sec., Singapore, 1967–69; Second Sec., Saigon, 1969–70; FCO, 1970–76; First Sec., Rome, 1976–80; Asst Head of Personnel Ops Dept, FCO, 1981–83. *Recreations:* singing, playing the horn. *Address:* c/o Foreign and Commonwealth Office, King Charles Street, SW1A 2AH. *Club:* Hurlingham.

PELLING, Anthony Adair; Under Secretary, Construction Industry Directorate, Department of the Environment, since 1985; *b* 3 May 1934; *s* of Brian and Alice Pelling; *m* 1958, Margaret Lightfoot; one *s* one *d. Educ:* Purley Grammar Sch.; London Sch. of Economics. BSc (Econ); MIPM. National Coal Board, 1957–67: O & M Officer, W Midlands; Head of Manpower Planning, Industrial Relations Dept; entered MPBW as Principal, 1967; Asst Sec., 1970, Under Sec., 1981, DoE; seconded as Dep. Dir, Business in the Community, 1981–83; Under Sec., Highways, Contracts, Admin and Maintenance, Dept of Transport, 1983–85. Dir, Croydon Business Venture. *Recreations:* family, gardening. *Address:* Bishops Fold, Sprucedale Gardens, Pine Coombe, Croydon. *Club:* Reform.

PELLING, Henry Mathison; Fellow of St John's College, Cambridge, 1966–80 and since 1980; *b* 27 Aug. 1920; *s* of late D. L. Pelling, Prenton, Cheshire, and late Mrs M. M. Pelling; unmarried. *Educ:* Birkenhead School; St John's Coll., Cambridge. Class. Tripos Part I, 1941; History Tripos Part II, 1947 (MA 1945; PhD 1950; LittD 1975). Army service, 1941–45; Commnd RE, 1942; served NW Europe campaign, 1944–45. Fellow, Queen's Coll., Oxford, 1949–65; Tutor, 1950–65; Dean, 1963–64; Supernumerary Fellow, 1980; Asst Dir of Research (History), Cambridge, 1966–76; Reader in Recent British History, Cambridge, 1976–80. Smith-Mundt Schol., University of Wisconsin, USA, 1953–54; Fellow, Woodrow Wilson Center, Washington, DC, 1983. Hon. DHL New Sch. for Social Res., New York, 1983. *Publications:* Origins of the Labour Party, 1954; Challenge of Socialism, 1954; America and the British Left, 1956; British Communist Party, 1958; (with Frank Bealey) Labour and Politics, 1958; American Labor, 1960; Modern Britain, 1885–1955, 1960; Short History of the Labour Party, 1961, 8th edn 1985; History of British Trade Unionism, 1963, 4th edn 1987; Social Geography of British Elections, 1967; Popular Politics and Society in Late Victorian Britain, 1968, 2nd edn 1979; Britain and the Second World War, 1970; Winston Churchill, 1974; The Labour Governments 1945–51, 1984; articles and reviews in learned journals. *Recreations:* theatre, films. *Address:* St John's College, Cambridge CB2 1TP. *T:* Cambridge 61621. *Clubs:* National Liberal, Royal Commonwealth Society.

PELLY, Derek Roland, (Derk); Deputy Chairman, Barclays Bank PLC, since 1986; (Vice Chairman, 1984–85); Vice Chairman, Barclays International Ltd, since 1977; *b* 12 June 1929; *s* of late Arthur Roland Pelly and late Elsie Pelly; *m* 1953, Susan Roberts; one *s* two *d. Educ:* Marlborough; Trinity Coll., Cambridge. Served RA, 1947–49 (2nd Lieut). Entered Barclays Bank, 1952; Local Director: Chelmsford, 1959; Luton, 1969. Member: Milton Keynes Develt Corp., 1976–85; Council, ODI, 1984–. Governor, London House for Overseas Graduates, 1985–. *Recreation:* painting. *Address:* 11 Wallside, Monkwell Square, EC2Y 8BH. *T:* 01–588 0454. *Club:* Royal Commonwealth Society.

PELLY, Major Sir John (Alwyne), 6th Bt *cr* 1840; JP, DL; landowner and farmer; *b* 11 Sept. 1918; *s* of Sir (Harold) Alwyne Pelly, 5th Bt, MC, and Caroline (*d* 1976), *d* of late Richard Heywood Heywood-Jones; *S* father, 1981; *m* 1950, Elsie May, (Hazel), *d* of late L. Thomas Dechow, Rhodesia; one *d* (and two *d* decd). *Educ:* Canford; RMC Sandhurst; Royal Agricultural Coll. Commissioned Coldstream Guards, 1938; served War of 1939–45; Malaya, 1948–50; retired (Major), 1950. Rhodesia, 1950–61; Royal Agric. Coll., 1962–63 (Certificate of Merit). Mem., Lands Tribunal, 1981–. JP 1966, High Sheriff 1970–71, DL 1972, Hants. *Recreations:* ski-ing, shooting. *Heir: b* Richard Heywood Pelly [*b* 25 April 1920; *m* 1948, Mary Elizabeth, *d* of late John Luscombe; one *s* one *d*]. *Address:* Preshaw House, Upham, Hants SO3 1HP. *T:* Bishop's Waltham 2531. *Club:* Royal Over-Seas League.

PEMBERTON; *see* Leigh-Pemberton.

PEMBERTON, Sir Francis (Wingate William), Kt 1976; CBE 1970; DL; FRICS; *b* 1 Oct. 1916; *s* of late Dr William Warburton Wingate (assumed Arms of Pemberton, by Royal Licence, 1921) and Viola Patience Campbell Pemberton; *m* 1941, Diana Patricia, *e d* of late Reginald Salisbury Woods, MD, and Irene Woods, CBE, TD; two *s. Educ:* Eton; Trinity Coll., Cambridge (MA). Senior Consultant, Bidwells, Chartered Surveyors. Director: Agricultural Mortgage Corp. Ltd, 1969–; Barclays Bank UK Ltd, 1977–81. Hon. Dir, Royal Show, 1963–68; Royal Agricultural Society of England: Mem. Council, 1951– (Pres., 1974–75, Dep. Pres., 1975–76); Chm. Exec. Bd, 1969–71; Trustee, 1969–. Trustee, Robinson Coll., Cambridge, 1973–85. Member: Water Resources Board, 1964–74; Winston Churchill Meml Trust, 1965–80; Economic Planning Council for East Anglia, 1965–74; National Water Council, 1974–81; Water Authorities Superannuation Pension Fund (Dep. Chm, Fund Management and Policy Cttee, 1983–). High Sheriff, Cambridgeshire and Isle of Ely, 1965–66; DL Cambs, 1979. *Address:* Trumpington Hall, Cambridge. *T:* Cambridge 841941. *Club:* Farmers'.

PEMBERTON, Prof. John, MD London; FRCP, FFCM; DPH Leeds; Professor of Social and Preventive Medicine, The Queen's University, Belfast, 1958–76; *b* 18 Nov. 1912; British; *m* 1937, Winifred Ethel Gray; three *s. Educ:* Christ's Hospital; University College and UCH, London. House Physician and House Surgeon, University College Hospital, 1936–37; Rowett Research Institute under the late Lord Boyd Orr, 1937–39; Rockefeller Travelling Fellow in Medicine, Harvard, Mass., USA, 1954–55; Director of MRC Group for research on Respiratory Disease and Air Pollution, and Reader in Social Medicine, University of Sheffield, 1955–58. Mem., Health Educn Council, DHSS, 1973–76. Milroy Lectr, RCP, 1976. *Publications:* (with W. Hobson) The Health of the Elderly at Home, 1954; (ed) Recent Studies in Epidemiology, 1958; (ed) Epidemiology: Reports on Research and Teaching, 1963; Will Pickles of Wensleydale, 1970; articles in Lancet, BMJ, etc. *Recreations:* reading, TV, walking, visual arts. *Address:* Iona, Cannon Fields, Hathersage, Sheffield S30 1AG.

PEMBROKE, 17th Earl of, *cr* 1551, **AND MONTGOMERY,** 14th Earl of, *cr* 1605; **Henry George Charles Alexander Herbert;** Baron Herbert of Caerdiff, 1551; Baron Herbert of Shurland, 1605; Baron Herbert of Lea (UK), 1861; Hereditary Grand Visitor of Jesus College, Oxford; *b* 19 May 1939; *s* of 16th Earl of Pembroke and Montgomery, CVO, and of Mary Countess of Pembroke, *qv*; *S* father, 1969; *m* 1966, Claire Rose (marr. diss. 1981), *o d* of Douglas Pelly, Swaynes Hall, Widdington, Essex; one *s* three *d. Educ:* Eton Coll.; Oxford Univ. Royal Horse Guards, 1958–60 (National Service); Oxford University, 1960–63. *Recreations:* photography, gardening, horse racing. *Heir: s* Lord Herbert, *qv. Address:* Wilton House, Salisbury, Wilts. *T:* Salisbury 743211.

PEMBROKE, Mary Countess of; Mary Dorothea Herbert, CVO 1947; DL; Extra Lady-in-Waiting to Princess Marina, Duchess of Kent, 1950–68 (Lady-in-Waiting, 1934–50); *o d* of 1st Marquess of Linlithgow; *m* 1936, Lord Herbert (later 16th Earl of Pembroke and Montgomery, who *d* 1969); one *s* one *d*. DL Wilts, 1980. *Address:* The Old Rectory, Wilton, near Salisbury, Wilts SP2 0HT. *T:* Salisbury 743157.

PEÑA, Paco; musician; flamenco guitar player, since 1954; Professor of Flamenco, Rotterdam Conservatory, since 1985; *b* 1 June 1942; *s* of Antonio Peña and Rosario Perez; *m* 1982, Karin Vaessen; two *d. Educ:* Córdoba, Spain. London début, 1963; founded Paco Peña Flamenco Co., 1970; founded Centro Flamenco Paco Peña, Córdoba, 1981;

Ramón Montoya Prize, 1983. *Address:* c/o Hetherington Seelig, 28 Museum Street, WC1A 1LH. *T:* 01–637 5661.

PENDER, 3rd Baron, *cr* 1937; **John Willoughby Denison-Pender;** Joint Chairman, Bremar Trust Ltd, 1977–83; Chairman, J. J. L. D. Frost plc, 1983–84; *b* 6 May 1933; *s* of 2nd Baron and Camilla Lethbridge, *o d* of late Willoughby Arthur Pemberton; *S* father, 1965; *m* 1962, Julia, *yr d* of Richard Nevill Cannon; one *s* two *d. Educ:* Eton. Formerly Lieut, 10th Royal Hussars and Captain, City of London Yeomanry (TA). Dir, Globe Investment Trust Ltd, 1969–70. Steward, Folkestone Racecourse, 1985–. *Heir: s* Hon. Henry John Richard Denison-Pender, *b* 19 March 1968. *Address:* North Court, Tilmanstone, Kent. *T:* Sandwich 611726. *Clubs:* White's, Pratt's.

PENDERECKI, Krzysztof; Rector, State Academy of Music, Kraków, since 1972; Professor of Composition, School of Music, Yale University, New Haven, Conn, 1973–78; *b* Debica, Poland, 23 Nov. 1933; *s* of Tadeusz Penderecki and Zofia Penderecki; *m* 1965, Elzbieta Solecka; one *s* one *d. Educ:* State Acad. of Music, Kraków, Poland (Graduate 1958). Compositions include: Threnody to the Victims of Hiroshima, 1959–61 (52 strings); Passion According to St Luke, 1965–66 (oratorio); Utrenja, 1969–71 (oratorio); Devils of Loudun, 1969 (opera); Cello Concerto No 1, 1971–72; First Symphony, 1972; Magnificat, 1974 (oratorio); Awakening of Jacob, 1974 (orchestra); Paradise Lost, 1976–78 (rappresentazione for Chicago Lyric Opera; Milton libretto, Christopher Fry); Violin Concerto, 1977; Te Deum, 1979–80; (Christmas) Symphony No 2, 1980; Lacrimosa, 1980; Agnus Dei (for chorus a cappella), 1981; Cello Concerto No 2, 1982; Viola Concerto, 1983; Polish Requiem, 1983–84; Die schwarze Maske, 1986 (opera). Hon. Dr: Univ. of Rochester, NY; St Olaf Coll., Northfield, Minn; Katholieke Univ., Leuven; Univ. of Bordeaux; Georgetown Univ., Washington; Univ. of Belgrade. Member: RAM (Hon.); Akad. der Künste, Berlin (Extraordinary); Akad. der Künste der DDR, Berlin (Corresp.); Kungl. Musikaliska Akad., Stockholm; Accad. Nazionale di Santa Cecilia, Rome (Hon.); Acad. Nacional de Bellas Artes, Buenos Aires (Corresp.). Grosser Kunstpreis des Landes Nordrhein-Westfalen, 1966; Prix Italia, 1967/68; Gottfried von Herder Preis der Stiftung FvS zu Hamburg, 1977; Prix Arthur Honegger, 1978; Sibelius Prize, Wihouri Foundn, 1983; Premio Lorenzo Magnifico, 1985. *Publications:* all works published. *Recreation:* collecting old furniture, clocks and paintings. *Address:* Cisowa 22, 30229 Kraków, Poland. *T:* 225760; 324 Livingston Street, New Haven, Conn 06511, USA. *T:* 203–789 0354.

PENDLEBURY, Edward; Assistant Under Secretary of State (Sales Administration), Ministry of Defence, 1983–85, retired; *b* 5 March 1925; *s* of Thomas Cecil Pendlebury and Alice (*née* Sumner); *m* 1957, Joan Elizabeth Bell; one *s. Educ:* King George V Sch., Southport; Magdalen Coll., Oxford (MA). Served War, RNVR, 1943–46. Asst Principal, Min. of Food, 1949–53; Principal: MAFF, 1953–56; MoD (British Defence Staff, Washington), 1956–60; MAFF, 1960–66; Asst Secretary: DEA, 1966–70; MoD, 1970–80; Exec. Dir (Civilian Management), MoD, 1980–83. *Recreations:* gramophone, gardening, gazing. *Address:* Whitegates, Oakwood Road, Burgess Hill, W Sussex RH15 0HZ. *T:* Burgess Hill 6730.

PENDRY, Prof. John Brian, PhD; FRS 1984; Professor of Theoretical Solid State Physics, Department of Physics, Imperial College of Science and Technology, University of London, since 1981; *b* 4 July 1943; *s* of Frank Johnson Pendry and Kathleen (*née* Shaw); *m* 1977, Patricia Gard. *Educ:* Downing Coll., Cambridge (MA; PhD 1969). Res. Fellow in Physics, Downing Coll., Cambridge, 1969–72; Mem. of Technical Staff, Bell Labs, USA, 1972–73; Sen. Asst in Res., Cavendish Lab., Cambridge Univ., and Fellow in Physics and Praelector, Downing Coll., 1973–75; SPSO and Head of Theory Gp, Daresbury Lab., 1975–81. *Publications:* Low Energy Electron Diffraction, 1974; scientific papers. *Recreations:* music, gardening. *Address:* The Blackett Laboratory, Imperial College of Science and Technology, SW7 2BZ. *T:* 01–589 5111, ext. 6901.

PENDRY, Thomas; MP (Lab) Stalybridge and Hyde since 1970; *b* 10 June 1934; *m* 1966, Moira Anne Smith; one *s* one *d. Educ:* St Augustine's, Ramsgate; Oxford Univ. RAF, 1955–57. Full time official, Nat. Union of Public Employees, 1960–70; Mem., Paddington Borough Council, 1962–65; Chm., Derby Labour Party, 1966. An Opposition Whip, 1971–74; a Lord Comr of the Treasury and Govt Whip, 1974, resigned 1977; Parly Under-Sec. of State, NI Office, 1978–79; Opposition Spokesman on NI, 1979–, on overseas development, 1981–, on regional affairs and devolution, 1982–84. Chairman: All Party Football Cttee, 1980—; PLP Sports Cttee, 1984–. Member: Speaker's Conf., 1973; UK delegn to WEU and Council of Europe, 1973–75; Industrial Law Soc. Mem., Nat. Adv. Cttee, Duke of Edinburgh's Award Scheme. Pres., Stalybridge Public Band. *Recreations:* sport; football, cricket, boxing (sometime Middleweight Champion, Hong Kong; boxed for Oxford Univ.). *Address:* 6 St Mary's Court, Hollingworth, Hyde, Cheshire. *Clubs:* Reform; Manchester Press; Stalybridge and Hyde Labour.

PENFOLD, Maj.-Gen. Robert Bernard, CB 1969; LVO 1957; *b* 19 Dec. 1916; *s* of late Bernard Hugh Penfold, Selsey, and late Ethel Ives Arnold; *m* 1940, Ursula, *d* of late Lt-Col E. H. Gray; two *d. Educ:* Wellington; RMC, Sandhurst. 2nd Lieut, Royal Leics Regt, 1936; commnd into 11th Sikh Regt, Indian Army, 1937; served in NWFP and during War of 1939–45 in Middle East, Central Mediterranean Forces; Instructor, Staff Coll., Quetta, 1946–47; transf. to British Army, RA, 1947; RN Staff Coll., 1953; Secretary, British Joint Services Mission, Washington, 1957–59; comdg 6 King's African Rifles, Tanganyika, 1959–61; Comdr 127 Inf. Bde (TA), 1962–64; Security Ops Adviser to High Commissioner, Aden, 1964–65; Imperial Defence Coll., 1966; Chief of Defence Staff, Kenya, 1966–69; GOC South East District, 1969–72. Gen. Manager, Royal Hong Kong Jockey Club, 1972–80. Chm., Horseracing Adv. Council, 1980–86. *Recreations:* shooting, golf, gardening. *Address:* Park House, Amport, Andover, Hants. *Club:* Army and Navy.

PENGELLY, Richard Anthony; Under Secretary, Welsh Office, 1977–85; *b* 18 Aug. 1925; *s* of Richard Francis Pengelly and Ivy Mildred Pengelly; *m* 1st, 1952, Phyllis Mary Rippon; one *s*; 2nd, 1972, Margaret Ruth Crossley; two *s* one *d. Educ:* Plymouth Coll.; School of Oriental and African Studies; London Sch. of Economics and Political Science (BScEcon). Served War: Monmouthshire Regt and Intell. Corps, 1943–47. Joined Min. of Supply as Asst Principal, 1950, Principal, 1954; NATO Defence Coll., 1960–61; Asst Sec., Min. of Aviation, 1964; RCDS 1971; Min. of Defence, 1972. *Recreations:* skiing, golf. *Address:* Byways, Wern Goch Road, Cyncoed, Cardiff, S Wales CF2 6SD. *T:* Cardiff 764418.

PENHALIGON, David Charles; MP (L) Truro since Oct. 1974; *b* 6 June 1944; *s* of late Robert Charles Penhaligon and of Sadie Jewell; *m* 1968, Annette Lidgey; one *s* one *d. Educ:* Truro Sch.; Cornwall Techn. College. CEng, MIMechE. R&D Engr, Holman Bros, Camborne, 1962–74. Liberal Party spokesman on employment, 1976–81, 1983–, on energy, 1979–82, on industry, 1981–83, and on the treasury, 1985–; Pres., Liberal Party, 1985–86. *Address:* 54 Daniell Road, Truro, Cornwall. *T:* Truro 70977. *Club:* National Liberal.

PENLEY, William Henry, CB 1967; CBE 1961; PhD; FEng; engineering consultant, since 1985; *b* 22 March 1917; *s* of late William Edward Penley and late Clara (*née* Dodgson), Wallasey, Cheshire; *m* 1st, 1943, Raymonde Evelyn (*d* 1975), *d* of late Frederick Richard Gough, Swanage, Dorset; two *s* one *d*; 2nd, 1977, Marion Claytor, *d* of late Joseph Enoch Airey, Swanage, Dorset. *Educ:* Wallasey Grammar Sch.; Liverpool Univ.; BEng, 1937; PhD, 1940. FIEE (MIEE 1964); FRAeS 1967; FRSA 1975; FEng 1978. Head of Guided Weapons Department, Royal Radar Establishment, 1953–61; Director, Royal Radar Establishment, 1961–62; Director-General of Electronics Research and Development, Ministry of Aviation, 1962–64; Deputy Controller of Electronics, Ministry of Aviation, then Ministry of Technology, 1964–67; Dir, Royal Armament R&D Establishment, 1967–70; Chief Scientist (Army), 1970–75, Dep. Controller, Establishments and Res. B, 1971–75, MoD; Controller, R&D Establishments, and Research, MoD, and Professional Head of Science Gp of the Civil Service, 1976–77; Chm., Appleton Lab. Establishment Cttee, 1977–79; Dep. Dir, Under Water Weapons, Marconi Space and Defence Systems Ltd, Stanmore, 1979–82; Engrg Dir, Marconi Underwater Systems Ltd, 1982–85. Silver Jubilee Medal, 1977. *Address:* 28 Walrond Road, Swanage, Dorset BH19 1PD. *T:* Swanage 425042. *Clubs:* Royal Commonwealth Society; Swanage Sailing.

PENLINGTON, Ross Grange, OBE (mil.) 1980; AE 1972 (Clasp 1979); **Hon. Mr Justice Penlington;** a Judge of the High Court of Hong Kong, since 1980; *b* 3 March 1931; *s* of Cedric Grange Penlington and Elsie May Penlington; *m* 1956, Valerie Ann Wacher; two *d. Educ:* Christ Coll., NZ; Univ. of Canterbury, NZ. LLB 1954. Barrister and Solicitor, Christchurch, NZ, 1954–59; Legal Officer, Magistrate and Attorney Gen., Western Samoa, 1959–64; Hong Kong: Crown Counsel, 1965–75; Dir of Public Prosecutions, 1976–77; District Court Judge, 1977–80. Commnd Hong Kong RAuxAF, 1964; Pilot's Brevet, 1965; CO (Wing Comdr), 1975–83; Hon. Air Cdre, 1983–. *Recreations:* flying, golf, tennis, fishing, racing. *Address:* 19 Peak Mansions, Hong Kong. *T:* 5–97106. *Clubs:* Royal Air Force; Hong Kong, Royal Hong Kong Jockey (Hong Kong); Canterbury (NZ).

PENMAN, Most Rev. David John; *see* Melbourne, Archbishop of.

PENMAN, Ian Dalgleish; Deputy Secretary, Central Services, Scottish Office, since 1984; *b* 1 Aug. 1931; *s* of late John B. Penman and of Dorothy Dalgleish; *m* 1963, Elisabeth Stewart Strachan; three *s. Educ:* Glasgow Univ. (MA Classics); Balliol Coll., Oxford (MA Lit. Hum.; Snell Exhibnr and Ferguson Scholar). National Service, RAF, 1955–57 (Educn Br.). Asst Principal, HM Treasury, 1957–58; Scottish Office, 1958–: Private Sec. to Parly Under-Sec. of State, 1960–62; Principal, Scottish Develt Dept, 1962–69; Asst Sec., Estab. Div., 1970–72; Asst Sec., Scottish Home and Health Dept, 1972–78; Under-Sec., Scottish Develt Dept, 1978–84. *Recreations:* walking, music, swimming. *Address:* 4 Wardie Avenue, Edinburgh EH5 2AB. *T:* 031–552 2180. *Club:* New (Edinburgh).

PENMAN, John, FRCP; Consulting Neurologist to The Royal Marsden Hospital; *b* 10 Feb. 1913; *er s* of late William Penman, FIA; *m* 1st, 1938, Joan, *d* of late Claude Johnson (marr. diss. 1975); one *s* two *d*; 2nd, 1975, Elisabeth Quin. *Educ:* Tonbridge Sch.; University College, Oxford (Senior Classical Scholar); Queen Mary Coll., E1; The London Hospital. MB, BS (London) 1944; MRCP 1948, FRCP 1969. Neurologist to The Royal Marsden Hospital, 1954–77. Member of Association of British Neurologists. *Publications:* The Epodes of Horace: a new English version, 1980; contributions to medical journals, mainly on tic douloureux and brain tumours; section on trigeminal injection, in Operative Surgery, 1957; chapters in Handbook of Clinical Neurology, 1968. *Recreations:* poetry; etymology; Japanese flower arrangement. *Address:* Forest View, Upper Chute, Andover, Hants. *Club:* Royal Automobile.

PENN, Lt-Col Sir Eric, GCVO 1981 (KCVO 1972; CVO 1965); OBE 1960; MC 1944; Extra Equerry to The Queen since 1963; *b* 9 Feb. 1916; *o s* of Capt. Eric F. Penn (killed in action 1915), Grenadier Guards, and late Gladys Ebden; *m* 1947, Prudence Stewart-Wilson, *d* of late Aubyn Wilson and late Muriel Stewart-Stevens, Balnakeilly, Pitlochry, Perthshire; two *s* one *d. Educ:* Eton; Magdalene Coll., Cambridge. Grenadier Guards, 1938–60. Assistant Comptroller, Lord Chamberlain's Office, 1960–64, Comptroller, 1964–81. *Address:* 6 Rosscourt Mansions, 4 Palace Street, SW1E 5HZ. *T:* 01–828 6262. *Clubs:* White's, Pratt's.

PENNANT; *see* Douglas-Pennant.

PENNANT, His Honour David Edward Thornton; a Circuit Judge (formerly County Court Judge), 1961–84; *b* 2 Aug. 1912; *s* of David Falconer Pennant, DL, JP, Barrister-at-law, late of Nantlys, St Asaph, N. Wales, and late Lilla Agnes Pennant; *m* 1938, Alice Catherine Stainer; three *s* one *d. Educ:* Charterhouse; Trinity Coll., Cambridge. Called to Bar, Inner Temple, 1935. Served, 1939–45, with Royal Signals (TA); OC, Signals Officers' Training Sch., Mhow, India, 1944–45. Chancellor, Dio. Monmouth, 1949–77. Governing and Representative Bodies, Church in Wales, 1946–83. Chm., Radnorshire QS, 1962–64; Deputy Chairman: Brecknockshire QS, 1956–64; Flintshire QS, 1962–71; Dorset QS, 1971. Joint Chairman, Medical Appeals Tribunal for Wales, 1957–61; Mem., County Court Rule Cttee, 1970–78. *Recreation:* gardening. *Address:* Parkbury, Balcombe Road, Branksome Park, Poole, Dorset. *T:* Bournemouth 765614.

PENNANT-REA, Rupert Lascelles; Editor, The Economist, since 1986; *b* 23 Jan. 1948; *s* of Peter Athelwold Pennant-Rea and Pauline Elizabeth Pennant-Rea; *m* 1st, 1970, Elizabeth Louise Greer (marr. diss. 1975); 2nd, 1979, Jane Trevelyan Hamilton; one *s* one *d. Educ:* Peterhouse, Zimbabwe; Trinity Coll., Dublin (BA); Manchester Univ. (MA). Confedn of Irish Industry, 1970–71; Gen. and Municipal Workers Union, 1972–73; Bank of England, 1973–77; The Economist, 1977–. *Publications:* Gold Foil, 1979; (jtly) Who Runs the Economy?, 1980; (jtly) The Pocket Economist, 1983; (jtly) The Economist Economics, 1986. *Recreations:* music, tennis, fishing, family. *Address:* (office) 25 St James's Street, SW1A 1HG. *T:* 01–839 9118. *Clubs:* MCC, Reform.

PENNELL, Rev. Canon (James Henry) Leslie, TD and Bar, 1949; Rector of Foxearth and Pentlow (Diocese of Chelmsford), 1965–72, and of Borley and Lyston (Diocese of Chelmsford), 1969–72; Hon. Canon, Inverness Cathedral, since 1965 (Provost, 1949–65); *b* 9 Feb. 1906; *s* of late J. H. L. Pennell and late Elizabeth Esmé Gordon Steel; *m* 1939, Ursula Mary, *d* of Rev. A. E. Gledhill; twin *s* and *d. Educ:* Edinburgh Academy; Edinburgh University (BL); Edinburgh Theological College. Precentor, Inverness Cathedral, 1929–32; Rector, St Mary's, Dunblane, and Offic. Chaplain to Queen Victoria School, 1932–49; Officiating Chaplain, Cameron Barracks, 1949–64. TA, 1934; BEF, 1940; SCF, 1943; DACG, 34th Ind. Corps, 1945; SCF Corps Troops, Scottish Comd, 1946–50. *Recreations:* reading and travel. *Address:* The Croft, Hundon, Clare, Suffolk. *T:* Hundon 221.

PENNEY, family name of **Baron Penney.**

PENNEY, Baron, *cr* 1967, of East Hendred (Life Peer); **William George Penney,** OM 1969; KBE 1952 (OBE 1946); MA; PhD; DSc; FRS 1946; Rector of the Imperial College of Science and Technology, 1967–73; *b* 24 June 1909; *s* of W. A. Penney, Sheerness, Kent; *m* 1st, 1935, Adele Minnie Elms (decd); two *s*; 2nd, 1945, Eleanor Joan Quennell. *Educ:*

Tech. School, Sheerness; Royal College of Science, London Univ. (BSc, PhD). Commonwealth Fund Fellowship. University of Wisconsin (MA), 1931–33; Senior Student of 1851 Exhibition, Trinity Coll., Cambridge, 1933–36; PhD (Cambridge), DSc (London), 1935; Stokes Student of Pembroke Coll., 1936; Assistant Professor of Mathematics at Imperial College of Science, London, 1936–45; on loan for scientific work to Ministry of Home Security and Admiralty, 1940–44; Principal Scientific Officer, DSIR, at Los Alamos Laboratory, New Mexico, 1944–45; Chief Superintendent, Armament Research, Ministry of Supply, 1946–52; Director Atomic Weapons Research Establishment, Aldermaston, 1953–59; Member for Weapons R&D, UKAEA, 1954–59; Member for Research, UKAEA, 1959–61; Dep. Chm., 1961–64; Chm., 1964–67. Director: Tube Investments, 1968–79; Standard Telephones and Cables, 1971–83. Treasurer, Royal Society, 1956–60 (Vice-President, 1957–60); Fellow, Imperial Coll.; Fellow, Winchester Coll., 1959; Supernumerary Fellow, St Catherine's Coll., Oxford, 1960; Hon. Fellow: Manchester College of Science and Technology, 1962; Trinity Coll., Cambridge, 1969; Pembroke Coll., Cambridge, 1970; Hon FRSE, 1970; For. Assoc., National Academy of Sciences, USA, 1962. Hon. DSc: Durham, 1957; Oxford, 1959; Bath University of Technology, 1966; Hon. LLD Melbourne, 1956. Rumford Medal, Royal Society, 1966; Glazebrook Medal and Prize, 1969; Kelvin Gold Medal, 1971. *Publications:* articles in scientific journals on theory of molecular structure. *Recreations:* golf, cricket. *Address:* Cat Street, East Hendred, Wantage, Oxford OX12 8JT. *Club:* Athenæum. ·

PENNEY, Most Rev. Alphonsus Liguori; *see* St John's (Newfoundland), Archbishop of, (RC).

PENNEY, Jennifer Beverly; Senior Principal, Royal Ballet; *b* 5 April 1946; *d* of Beverley Guy Penney and Gwen Penney. *Educ:* in Canada (grades 1–12). Entered Royal Ballet Sch., 1962; joined Royal Ballet, 1963; became soloist during 1967, principal dancer during 1970, and senior principal dancer during 1974. Evening Standard Award, 1980. *Recreation:* painting (water-colours). *Address:* 35A Cathcart Road, SW10.

PENNEY, Reginald John; Assistant Under-Secretary of State, Ministry of Defence, 1964–73, retired; *b* 22 May 1919; *s* of Herbert Penney and Charlotte Penney (née Affleck); *m* 1941, Eileen Gardiner; one *s* two *d. Educ:* Westminster School. War Service, Royal West Kent Regt, 1939–46. Civil Servant, Air Ministry, until 1964, including service with Far East Air Force, Singapore, 1960–63. Chm., Sherborne Soc., CPRE, 1976. *Recreation:* golf. *Address:* Rumbow Cottage, Acreman Street, Sherborne, Dorset.

PENNING-ROWSELL, Edmund Lionel; wine writer; Wine Correspondent: Country Life, since 1954; Financial Times, since 1964; Chairman, International Co-operative Wine Society, since 1964; *b* 16 March 1913; *s* of Edmund Penning-Rowsell and Marguerite Marie-Louise Penning-Rowsell (née Egan); *m* 1937, Margaret Wintringham; one *s* two *d. Educ:* Marlborough College. Journalist, Morning Post, 1930–35; Book Publisher, Frederick Muller Ltd, 1935–50; Sales Manager, B. T. Batsford, 1952–57; Dir, book publisher, Edward Hulton & Co./Studio-Vista, 1957–63; Manager, World Book Fair, Earl's Court, 1964. Mem. Cttee of Management, Internat. Exhibition Co-op. Wine Soc., 1959– (Chm., 1964); Founder Mem., William Morris Soc., 1954 (Vice-Pres.). Chevalier de l'Ordre du Mérite Agricole (France), 1971; Chevalier de l'Ordre du Mérite National (France), 1981. *Publications:* Red, White and Rosé, 1967; The Wines of Bordeaux, 1969, 5th edn 1985. *Recreation:* drinking wine, particularly claret. *Address:* Yew Trees House, Wootton, Woodstock, Oxford OX7 1EG. *T:* Woodstock 811281. *Club:* Travellers'.

PENNINGTON, Michael Vivian Fyfe; freelance actor and writer; *b* 7 June 1943; *s* of late Vivian Maynard Cecil Pennington and of Euphemia Willock (née Fyfe); *m* Katharine Ann Letitia Barker (marr. diss.); one *s. Educ:* Marlborough Coll.; Trinity Coll., Cambridge (BA English). RSC, 1964–65; BBC, ITV, Woodfall Films Ltd, West End Theatre, Royal Court Theatre, etc, 1966–74; RSC, 1974–81: roles included Berowne, Angelo and Hamlet; Crime and Punishment, Lyric Hammersmith, 1983; National Theatre: Strider, 1984; Venice Preserv'd, 1984; Anton Chekhov, 1984; The Real Thing, Aldwych, 1985; English Shakespeare Co.: Jt Artistic Dir, 1986–87, Prince Hal and Henry V. *Publication:* Rossya—A Journey Through Siberia, 1977. *Recreations:* music, literature. *Address:* c/o James Sharkey Associates Ltd, 15 Golden Square, W1R 3AG. *Club:* MCC.

PENNINGTON, Prof. Robert Roland; Professor of Commercial Law, Birmingham University, since 1968; *b* 22 April 1927; *s* of R. A. Pennington; *m* 1965, Patricia Irene; one *d. Educ:* Birmingham Univ. (LLB, LLD). Solicitor. Reader, Law Soc.'s Sch. of Law, 1951–62; Mem. Bd of Management, Coll. of Law, 1962; Sen. Lectr in Commercial Law, 1962–68 and Dean, Faculty of Law, Birmingham Univ., 1979–82. Govt Adviser on Company Legislation, Trinidad, 1967 and Seychelles, 1970; UN Adviser on Commercial Law, 1970–; Special Legal Adviser to EEC, 1972–79. Editor, European Commercial Law Library, 1974–. *Publications:* Company Law, 1959, 5th edn 1985; Companies in the Common Market, 1962, 3rd edn as Companies in the European Communities, 1982; The Investor and the Law, 1967; Stannary Law: A History of the Mining Law of Cornwall and Devon, 1973; Commercial Banking Law, 1978; Gesellschaftsrecht des Vereinigten Königreichs, 1981 (in Jura Europae: Gesellschaftsrecht); The Companies Acts 1980 and 1981: a practitioners' manual, 1983; Stock Exchange Listing: the new regulations, 1985. *Recreations:* travel, walking, history, archaeology. *Address:* Gryphon House, Langley Road, Claverdon, Warwicks.

PENNISON, Clifford Francis, CBE 1977; *b* 28 June 1913; *s* of Henry and Alice Pennison; *m* 1940, Joan Margaret Hopkins; three *d. Educ:* Taunton Sch.; Bristol Univ. (BA, 1st Cl. Hons, Hist.). Barrister-at-Law, Inner Temple, 1951. Appointed senior management trainee, Unilever Ltd, 1938. Field Security Officer, Army, 1940–46 (Captain). Principal, Home Civil Service, 1946; Assistant Secretary, and Director of Organisation and Methods, Ministry of Food, 1949; Ministry of Agriculture: Director of Statistics Div., 1953; Director of Public Relations Div., 1958; Director of External Relations Div., 1961; FAO: Permanent UK representative, 1963–66; Director, Economic Analysis Div., 1966–67; Asst Dir-Gen., Admin and Finance, 1967–74; Consultant, EEC/FAO relations, 1974–76; retired 1976. Diplôme, Lettres Modernes, and Diplôme, Langue allemande, Univ. of Nice, 1977–81; Final examination (French), Inst. of Linguists, 1984. *Recreations:* travel, reading, foreign languages, tennis. *Address:* 54 Clarendon Road, Sheffield S10 3TR. *Clubs:* Beaulieu Tennis (Alpes-Maritimes); Fulwood Tennis (Sheffield).

PENNOCK, family name of **Baron Pennock.**

PENNOCK, Baron *cr* 1982 (Life Peer), of Norton in the County of Cleveland; **Raymond William Pennock;** Kt 1978; Deputy Chairman, Plessey Co., since 1985 (Director, since 1979); Chairman, Channel Tunnel Group, since 1986; *b* 16 June 1920; *s* of Frederick Henry Pennock and Harriet Ann Pennock (née Mathison); *m* 1943, Lorna Pearse; one *s* two *d. Educ:* Coatham Sch.; Merton Coll., Oxford (Hon. Fellow, 1979). MA; 2nd cl. hons History, Dipl. Educn. Royal Artillery (Captain), 1941–46 (despatches 1945). Joined ICI Ltd, 1947; Personnel Management and Commercial duties, 1947–61; Commercial Dir, Billingham Div., 1961–64, Dep. Chm., Billingham Div., 1964–68; Chm., Agric. (formerly Billingham) Div. 1968–72; Director, ICI Ltd, 1972, Dep. Chm., 1975–80;

Chm., BICC plc, 1980–84. Director: Morgan Grenfell Holdings Ltd, 1984–; Willis Faber plc, 1985–. Dep. Pres., CBI, 1979–80, Pres., 1980–82 (Chm., Economic Situation Cttee, 1977–80); President: CIA, 1978–79; UNICE, 1984–86. Member: Standard Chartered Bank Bd, 1982–; NEDC, 1979–82. Mem. Nat. Council, Oxford Soc. *Recreations:* tennis, music, ballet, travel. *Address:* c/o House of Lords, Westminster, SW1. *Clubs:* Queen's, Royal Tennis Court.

PENNY, family name of **Viscount Marchwood.**

PENNY, (Francis) David, CBE 1982; FRSE; FEng 1980; consulting engineer; *b* 20 May 1918; *s* of late David Penny and Esther Colley; *m* 1949, Betty E. Smith, *d* of late Oswald C. Smith. *Educ:* Bromsgrove County High School; University Coll., London (BSc), Fellow 1973. Engineering Apprenticeship, Cadbury Bros Ltd, 1934–39; Armament Design Establishment, Ministry of Supply, 1939–53; Chief Development Engineer, Fuel Research Station, 1954–58; Dep. Dir, Nat. Engineering Laboratory, 1959–66, Dir, 1967–69; Man. Dir, Yarrow Public Ltd Co., 1979–83. Chairman: Control Systems Ltd, 1979–83; Automatic Revenue Controls Ltd, 1979–83. FIMarE; FIMechE; Member Council, IMechE, 1964– (a Vice-Pres., 1977–81, Pres., 1981–82); Chm., Quality Assurance Council, BSI, 1982–. *Publications:* various technical papers. *Recreations:* gardening, walking. *Address:* Forefaulds, East Kilbride, Glasgow. *T:* East Kilbride 20102.

PENNY, Joseph Noel Bailey, QC 1971; *b* 25 Dec. 1916; *s* of Joseph A. Penny, JP and Isabella Downie, JP; *m* 1st, 1947, Celia (*d* 1969), *d* of Mr and Mrs R. H. Roberts; three *s* one *d*; 2nd, 1972, Sara Margaret, *d* of Sir Arnold France, *qv*; one *d. Educ:* Worksop College; Christ Church, Oxford; MA (Oxon). Major, Royal Signals, 1939–46 (despatches). Called to Bar, Gray's Inn, 1948. A Social Security (formerly Nat. Ins.) Comr, 1977–. *Recreations:* wine and song, travel and amateur dramatics. *Address:* Fair Orchard, Lingfield, Surrey. *T:* Lingfield 832191.
See also N. B. Penny.

PENNY, Nicholas Beaver, MA, PhD; Keeper of Western Art, Ashmolean Museum, Oxford, and Professorial Fellow, Balliol College, Oxford University, since 1984; *b* 21 Dec. 1949; *s* of Joseph Noel Bailey Penny, *qv*; *m* 1971, Anne Philomel Udy; two *d. Educ:* Shrewsbury Sch.; St Catharine's Coll., Cambridge (BA, MA); Courtauld Inst., Univ. of London (MA, PhD). Leverhulme Fellow in the History of Western Art, Clare Hall, Cambridge, 1973–75; Lectr, History of Art Dept, Univ. of Manchester, 1975–82; Sen. Res. Fellow, History of Western Art, King's Coll., Cambridge, 1982–84; Slade Prof. of Fine Art, Univ. of Oxford, 1980–81. *Publications:* Church Monuments in Romantic England, 1977; Piranesi, 1978; (with Francis Haskell) Taste and the Antique, 1981; Mourning, 1981; (ed jtly) The Arrogant Connoisseur, 1982; (with Roger Jones) Raphael, 1983; (ed) Reynolds, 1986; reviews for London Review of Books; articles in Apollo, Burlington Magazine, Connoisseur, Jl of Warburg and Courtauld Insts, Past and Present, and elsewhere. *Address:* 1 Kineton Road, Grandpont, Oxford.

PENRHYN, 6th Baron *cr* 1866; **Malcolm Frank Douglas-Pennant,** DSO 1945; MBE 1943; *b* 11 July 1908; 2nd *s* of 5th Baron Penrhyn and Alice Nellie (*d* 1965), *o d* of Sir William Charles Cooper, 3rd Bt; *S* father 1967; *m* 1954, Elisabeth Rosemary, *d* of late Brig. Sir Percy Laurie, KCVO, CBE, DSO, JP; two *d. Educ:* Eton; RMC, Sandhurst. Colonel (retd), KRRC. *Heir:* *b* Hon. Nigel Douglas-Pennant [*b* 22 Dec. 1909; *m* 1st, 1935, Margaret Dorothy (*d* 1938), *d* of T. G. Kirkham; one *s*; 2nd, 1940, Eleanor Stewart, *d* of late Very Rev. H. N. Craig; one *s* one *d*]. *Address:* Littleton Manor, Winchester, Hants. *T:* Winchester 880205. *Clubs:* Naval and Military, Flyfishers'.
See also Sir Peter Troubridge, Bt.

PENRICE, Geoffrey, CB 1978; consultant, since 1981, including International Monetary Fund Adviser, Ministry of Finance, Thailand, since 1984; *b* Wakefield, 28 Feb. 1923; *s* of Harry and Jessie Penrice; *m* 1947, Janet Gillies Allardice; three *s. Educ:* Thornes House Grammar Sch.; London Sch. of Economics. Control Commn for Germany, 1947; Asst Lectr in Statistics, LSE, 1952; Statistician, Inland Revenue, 1956; Statistician and Chief Statistician, Central Statistical Office, 1964; Chief Statistician, Min. of Housing and Local Govt, 1968; Under-Sec., BoT, Min. of Technology, DTI, 1968–73; Principal Dir of Stats, DoE, later DoE and Dept of Transport, 1973–78; Dir of Stats, and Dep. Sec., DoE, 1978–81. Statistical Adviser to Cttee on Working of Monetary System, 1957–59; OECD Consultant, Turkey, 1981–83. *Publications:* articles on wages, earnings, financial statistics and housing statistics. *Address:* 10 Dartmouth Park Avenue, NW5. *T:* 01–267 2175. *Club:* Reform.

PENRITH, Bishop Suffragan of, since 1979; **Rt. Rev. George Lanyon Hacker;** *b* 27 Dec. 1928; *s* of Edward Sidney Hacker and Carla Lanyon; *m* 1969, June Margaret Erica Smart; one *s* one *d. Educ:* Kelly College, Tavistock; Exeter College, Oxford (BA 1952, MA 1956); Cuddesdon College, Oxford. Deacon 1954, priest 1955, Bristol; Curate of St Mary Redcliffe, Bristol, 1954–59; Chaplain, King's College London at St Boniface Coll., Warminster, 1959–64; Perpetual Curate, Church of the Good Shepherd, Bishopwearmouth, 1964–71; Rector of Tilehurst, Reading, 1971–79. *Recreations:* photography, boating. *Address:* Great Salkeld Rectory, Penrith, Cumbria CA11 9NA. *T:* Lazonby 273.

PENROSE, Prof. Edith Tilton; economic consultant; Associate Fellow, Oxford Centre of Management Studies (now Templeton College, Oxford), 1982–85; Professor, 1977–84, Associate Dean for Research and Development, 1982–84, Professor Emeritus, since 1984, Institut Européen d'Administration des Affaires, Fontainebleau; Professor of Economics (with reference to Asia), School of Oriental and African Studies, University of London, 1964–78, Professor Emeritus, since 1978; *b* 29 Nov. 1914; *d* of George Albert Tilton and Hazel Sparling Tilton; *m* 1st, 1934, David Burton Denhardt (*d* 1938); 2nd, 1944, Ernest F. Penrose (*d* 1984); three *s. Educ:* Univ. of California, Berkeley (AB); Johns Hopkins Univ. (MA, PhD). Research Assoc., ILO, Geneva and Montreal, 1939–41; Special Asst, US Ambassador, London, 1941–46; US Delegn to UN, NY, 1946–47; research at Johns Hopkins Univ., 1948–50; Lectr and Res. Assoc., Johns Hopkins Univ., 1950–60; Vis. Fellow, Australian Nat. Univ., 1955–56; Assoc. Prof. of Econs, Univ. Baghdad, 1957–59; Reader in Econs, Univ. of London (LSE and SOAS), 1960–64; Actg Head, Dept of Econs and Polit. Studies, 1961–64; Head, Dept of Econs, SOAS, 1964–69; Visiting Professor: Univ. Dar Es Salaam, 1971–72; Univ. of Toronto, 1977. Member: Sainsbury Cttee of Enquiry into Relationship of Pharmaceutical Industry with Nat. Health Service, 1965–67; SSRC, 1974–76 (Econ. Cttee, 1970–76, Chm., 1974–76); Medicines Commn, 1975–78; Dir, Commonwealth Develt Corp., 1975–78; Mem. Council, Royal Economic Soc., 1975–; Governor, NIESR, 1974–. Dr *hc* Uppsala, 1984. *Publications:* Food Control in Great Britain, 1940; Economics of the International Patent System, 1951 (trans. Japanese, Spanish); The Theory of the Growth of the Firm, 1959 (trans. Japanese, French, Spanish, Italian); The Large International Firm in Developing Countries: The International Petroleum Industry, 1968 (trans. Japanese); The Growth of Firms, Middle East Oil and Other Essays, 1971; contrib. Amer. Econ. Rev., Bus. Hist. Rev., Econ. Jl, Economica, Jl Dev. Studies, Jl Econ. History, Yearbook of World Affairs, Etudes Internationales, Mondes en Développement. *Recreations:* travel, theatre, gardening. *Address:* The Barn, 30A Station

Road, Waterbeach, Cambridge CB5 9HT. *T:* Cambridge 861618. *Club:* Royal Commonwealth Society.

PENROSE, George William, QC 1978; Procurator to General Assembly of the Church of Scotland, since 1984; *b* 2 June 1938; *s* of late George W. Penrose and Janet L. Penrose; *m* 1964, Wendy Margaret Cooper; one *s* two *d. Educ:* Glasgow Univ. (MA, LLB). CA Advocate, 1964. *Recreation:* walking. *Address:* 5 Cobden Road, Edinburgh EH9 2BJ. *T:* 031–667 1819.

PENROSE, Maj.-Gen. (retd) John Hubert, OBE 1956; MC 1944; *b* 24 Oct. 1916; *e s* of late Brig. John Penrose, MC and late Mrs M. C. Penrose (*née* Hendrick-Aylmer); *m* 1941, Pamela Elizabeth, *d* of late H. P. Lloyd, Neath, Glam.; four *d. Educ:* Winchester Coll.; RMA Woolwich, 2nd Lieut, RA, 1936; war service in European Theatre, BEF, 1939–40, and BLA, 1944; subseq. service in India, Germany, Malaya and UK; idc 1964; Defence Adviser to British High Comr, New Delhi, 1968–71; retired 1972. *Publication:* (with Brigitte Mitchell) Letters from Bath, 1766–1767, by the Rev. John Penrose, 1983. *Address:* West Hoe House, Bishop's Waltham, Southampton SO3 1DT. *T:* Bishop's Waltham 2363.

PENROSE, Prof. Roger, FRS 1972; Rouse Ball Professor of Mathematics, University of Oxford, since 1973; *b* Colchester, Essex, 8 Aug. 1931; *s* of Lionel Sharples Penrose, FRS; *m* 1959, Joan Isabel Wedge (marr. diss. 1981); three *s. Educ:* University Coll. Sch.; University Coll., Univ. of London (BSc spec. 1st cl. Mathematics), Fellow 1975; St John's Coll., Cambridge (PhD). NRDC (temp. post, Feb.–Aug. 1956); Asst Lectr (Pure Mathematics), Bedford Coll., London, 1956–57; Research Fellow, St John's Coll., Cambridge, 1957–60; NATO Research Fellow, Princeton Univ. and Syracuse Univ., 1959–61; Research Associate King's Coll., London, 1961–63; Visiting Associate Prof., Univ. of Texas, Austin, Texas, 1963–64; Reader, 1964–66, Prof. of Applied Mathematics, 1966–73, Birkbeck Coll., London. Visiting Prof., Yeshiva, Princeton, Cornell, 1966–67 and 1969; Lovett Prof., Rice Univ., Houston, 1983–. Adams Prize (Cambridge Univ.), 1966–67; Dannie Heineman Prize (Amer. Phys. Soc. and Amer. Inst. Physics), 1971; Eddington Medal (with S. W. Hawking), RAS, 1975; Royal Medal, Royal Soc., 1985. Member: London Mathematical Soc.; Cambridge Philosophical Soc.; Inst. for Mathematics and its Applications; International Soc. for General Relativity and Gravitation. *Publications:* Techniques of Differential Topology in Relativity, 1973; (with W. Rindler) Spinors and Space-time, Vol. 1, 1984, Vol. 2, 1986; many articles in scientific jls. *Recreations:* reading science fiction, 3 dimensional puzzles, miniature stone carving, doodling at the piano. *Address:* Mathematical Institute, 24–29 St Giles, Oxford OX1 3LB. *T:* Oxford 54295.

PENRUDDOCK, Sir Clement (Frederick), Kt 1973; CBE 1954; Consultant with Lawrance, Messer & Co., Solicitors (Senior Partner, 1947–81); *b* 30 Jan. 1905; *s* of Rev. Frederick Fitzpatrick Penruddock and Edith Florence Smith; *m* 1945, Philippa Mary Tolhurst; one *s* three *d. Educ:* Marlborough Coll.; Keble Coll., Oxford. BA 1927. Admitted Solicitor, 1931. Sec., Chequers Trust, 1941–72. Chairman: Channel Islands & Internat. Investment Trust Ltd, 1960–; Granville Investment Trust Ltd, 1963–; Paten & Co. (Peterborough) Ltd, 1967–; Director: Save & Prosper Group Ltd, 1947–80; The Steetley Co. Ltd, 1951–75; Ocean Wilsons (Holdings) Ltd, 1955–; Lancashire & London Investment Trust Ltd, 1963–; The Scottish & Mercantile PLC, 1978–. Scottish Cities Investment Trust PLC, 1982–; *Recreations:* golf, ski-ing. *Address:* Venars, Nutfield, Redhill, Surrey RH1 4HS. *T:* Nutfield Ridge 2218, (office) 01–606 7691. *Clubs:* City, United Oxford & Cambridge University.

PENTNEY, Richard George; employed by Kent Social Services Committee, since 1981; *b* 17 Aug. 1922; *s* of late Rev. A. F. Pentney, MC; *m* 1953, Elisabeth, *d* of Sir Eric Berthoud, *qv;* four *d. Educ:* Kingswood School, Bath; St John's Coll., Cambridge. Mem., Univ. Cricket and Hockey XIs. RNVR (Lieut), 1942–46. Asst Master, Sedbergh School, 1947–58; Headmaster, St Andrew's Coll., Minaki, Tanzania, 1958–64; Asst Master, Oundle School, 1964–65; Headmaster, King's Coll., Taunton, 1965–69; Sec. for Appeals, St Christopher's Fellowship, 1969–70; Commoner Fellow, St John's Coll., Cambridge, 1970; Dir, Attlee House, Toynbee Hall, 1970–73. *Recreations:* walking, water-colour painting. *Address:* Bellmead Cottage, Packham's Hill, Rotherfield, East Sussex. *T:* Rotherfield 2180.

PENZIAS, Dr Arno Allan; Vice-President, Research, AT&T Bell Laboratories, since 1981; *b* 26 April 1933; *s* of Karl and Justine Penzias; *m* 1954, Anne Barras Penzias; one *s* two *d. Educ:* City Coll. of New York (BS Physics, 1954); Columbia Univ. (MA Physics, 1958; PhD Physics, 1962). Bell Laboratories: Mem., Technical Staff, 1961–72; Head, Radio Physics Res., 1972–76; Dir, Radio Res. Lab., 1976–79; Exec. Dir, Research, Communications Sciences, 1979–81. Lectr, Princeton Univ., 1967–72, Vis. Prof., Astrophysical Scis Dept, 1972–85; Res. Associate, Harvard Univ., 1968–80; Adjunct Prof., State Univ. of NY, Stony Brook, 1974–84; Member: Sch. of Engrg and Applied Science (Bd Overseers), Univ. Pennsylvania, 1983–; Union Councils for Soviet Jews Adv. Bd, 1983–; NSF Industrial Panel on Science and Technology, 1982–; CIT Vis. Cttee, 1977–79; NSF Astronomy Adv. Panel, 1978–79; MNAS, 1975–; Wissenschaftliche Fachbeirat, Max-Planck Inst., Bonn, 1978–. Vice-Chm., Cttee of Concerned Scientists, 1976–85 (Mem., 1975–). Trustee, Trenton State Coll., 1977–79. Hon. degrees: Paris Observatory, 1976; Wilkes Coll., City Coll. of NY, Yeshiva Univ., and Rutgers Univ., 1979; Bar Ilan Univ., 1983; Monmouth Coll., 1984. Henry Draper Medal, National Acad. of Sciences, 1977; Herschel Medal, RAS, 1977; (jtly) Nobel Prize for Physics, 1978. Mem. Editorial Bd, Annual Revs of Astronomy and Astrophysics, 1974–78; Associate Editor, Astrophysical Jl Letters, 1978–82. *Publications:* 100 published articles, principally in Astrophysical Jl. *Address:* AT&T Bell Laboratories, 600 Mountain Avenue, Murray Hill, NJ 07974, USA. *T:* (201) 582–3361.

PEPLOE, Denis (Frederic Neil), RSA 1966 (ARSA 1956); former Teacher of drawing and painting at Edinburgh College of Art; *b* 25 March 1914; *s* of late Samuel John Peploe, RSA, and late Margaret Peploe (*née* Mackay); *m* 1957, Elizabeth Marion (*née* Barr); one *s* one *d. Educ:* Edinburgh Academy. Studied at Edinburgh College of Art and Académie André Lhote, 1931–37. Served War of 1939–45: Royal Artillery and Intelligence Corps. Lectr, Edinburgh College of Art, 1954–79, retd, Governor 1982–85. *Recreations:* hill-walking, mycology. *Address:* 18 Mayfield Gardens, Edinburgh EH9 2BZ. *T:* 031–667 6164.

PEPPARD, Nadine Sheila, CBE 1970; race relations consultant; *b* 16 Jan. 1922; *d* of late Joseph Anthony Peppard and May Peppard (*née* Barber). *Educ:* Macclesfield High Sch.; Manchester Univ. (BA, Teacher's Dip.). French Mistress, Maldon Grammar Sch., 1943–46; Spanish Editor, George G. Harrap & Co. Ltd, 1946–55; Trg Dept, Marks and Spencer, 1955–57; Dep. Gen.-Sec., London Council of Social Service, 1957–64; Nat. Advisory Officer for Commonwealth Immigrants, 1964–65; Gen. Sec., Nat. Cttee for Commonwealth Immigrants, 1965–68; Chief Officer, Community Relations Commn, 1968–72; Adviser on Race Relations, Home Office, 1972–83, retd. *Publications:* (trans.) Primitive India, 1954; (trans.) Toledo, 1955; various professional articles. *Recreations:*

cookery, writing. *Address:* 20 Park House, Park Place, Cheltenham, Glos. *T:* Cheltenham 42583.

PEPPER, Claude Denson; Member of United States House of Representatives, former United States Senator (Democrat); *b* Dudleyville, Alabama, USA, 8 Sept. 1900; *s* of Joseph Wheeler Pepper and Lena (*née* Talbot); *m* 1936, Irene Mildred Webster (*d* 1979), St Petersburg, Fla; no *c. Educ:* University of Alabama (AB); Harvard Law School (JD, Phi Beta Kappa). Served with Armed Forces, 1918. Instr in Law, Univ. of Arkansas, 1924–25. Admitted to Alabama Bar, 1924; Florida Bar, 1925; practised law at Perry, Fla, 1925–30; House Mem. Fla State Legislature, 1929; practised law, Tallahassee, Fla, 1930–37; Mem. State Bd of: Public Welfare, 1931–32; Law Examiners, 1933–34; US Senator from Fla, 1936–51; Mem., various cttees; Chm., Middle East Sub-Cttee of Senate Foreign Relations Cttee (12 yrs) etc.; Chm. Fla Delegation to Dem. Nat. Convention, 1940–44; subseq. alternate Delegate, 1948, 1952, 1956, 1960, 1964, Delegate, 1968. Elected to: 88th Congress, 1962; 89th Congress, 1964; 90th Congress, 1966 (without opposition); 91st Congress, 1968; 92nd Congress, 1970; 93rd Congress, 1972; 94th Congress, 1974; 95th Congress, 1976; 96th Congress, 1978; 97th Congress, 1980; 98th Congress, 1982; 99th Congress, 1984; Member: (88th Congress) House Cttee on Banking and Currency, and sub cttees on Domestic Finance, Internat. Trade, and Internat. Finance; (89th, 90th, 91st, 92nd, 93rd, 94th, 95th, 96th and 97th Congress) House Rules Cttee; Chm. (91st and 92nd Congress) House Select Cttee on Crime, Cttee on Internal Security; Chm. (95th, 96th and 97th Congress) House Select Cttee on Aging and Sub-Cttee on Health and Long Term Care. Member: Board of Directors, Washington Federal Savings & Loan Assoc.; American Bar Assoc.; International Bar Association, etc. Mary and Albert Lasker Public Service Award, 1967; various other awards. Holds hon. degrees. Member, American Legion; Baptist; Mason; Shriner; Elk; Moose, Kiwanian. *Publications:* contributor to periodicals. *Recreations:* hunting, golf, swimming. *Address:* (home) 2121 North Bayshore Drive, Miami, Florida 33137, USA; 4201 Cathedral Avenue, NW, Washington, DC 20016, USA; (offices) 2239 Rayburn House Office Building, Washington, DC 20515. *Clubs:* Harvard, Jefferson Island, Army-Navy, Columbia Country, Burning Tree, etc (Washington); Miami, Bankers (Miami); various country (Florida).

PEPPER, Gordon Terry; stockbroker; Chairman: Greenwell Montagu & Co., since 1986; Greenwell Montagu Gilt-Edged Ltd, since 1986; Director: Samuel Montagu & Co. Holdings, since 1985; Payton Pepper & Sons Ltd, since 1986; *b* 2 June 1934; *s* of Harold Terry Pepper and Jean Margaret Gordon Pepper (*née* Furness); *m* 1958, Gillian Clare Huelin; three *s* one *d. Educ:* Repton; Trinity College, Cambridge (MA); FIA, Fellow, Soc. of Investment Analysts. Equity & Law Life Assurance Soc., 1957–60; W. Greenwell & Co.: Partner, 1962; Joint Senior Partner, 1980–86. *Publications:* papers to Jl of Inst. of Actuaries. *Recreations:* sailing, tennis, ski-ing, family. *Address:* Staddleden, Sissinghurst, Cranbrook, Kent TN17 2AN. *T:* Cranbrook 712852. *Clubs:* Royal Ocean Racing; Royal Channel Islands Yacht.

PEPPER, Kenneth Bruce, CB 1965; Commissioner of HM Customs and Excise, 1957–73; *b* 11 March 1913; *s* of late E. E. Pepper; *m* 1945, Irene Evelyn Watts; two *s. Educ:* County High Sch., Ilford; London Sch. of Economics. Joined HM Customs and Excise, 1932; Asst Sec., 1949; Commissioner, 1957. Lieutenant, Intelligence Corps, 1944. *Address:* Fairfield, Cae Mair, Beaumaris, Gwynedd.

PEPPER, Michael, PhD; FRS 1983; Senior Research Fellow, General Electric Co., Hirst Research Centre, since 1982; Fellow of Trinity College, Cambridge, since 1982; *b* 10 Aug. 1942; *s* of Morris and Ruby Pepper; *m* 1973, Jeannette Denise Josse, MB, BS, MRCPsych; two *d. Educ:* St Marylebone Grammar Sch.; Reading Univ. (BSc Physics, 1963; PhD Physics, 1967). Res. Physicist, Mullard Ltd, 1967–69; res. in solid state physics, The Plessey Co., Allen Clark Res. Centre, 1969–73; res. at Cavendish Lab., 1973– (in association with The Plessey Co., 1973–82); Warren Res. Fellow of Royal Soc., Cavendish Lab., 1978–86. Vis. Prof., Bar-Ilan Univ., Israel, 1984; Inaugural Mott Lectr, Inst. of Physics, 1985. Past and present mem. of various cttees and panels of Inst. of Physics, Royal Soc. and SERC. Guthrie Prize and Medal, Inst. of Physics, 1985; Hewlett-Packard Prize, European Physical Soc., 1985. *Publications:* papers on semiconductors and solid state physics in jls. *Recreations:* whisky tasting, reading, travel, homework with two *d. Address:* 2 Grange Road, Cambridge CB3 9DU. *T:* Cambridge 311215.

PEPPITT, John Raymond, QC 1976; Barrister-at-law; a Recorder of the Crown Court, since 1976; *b* 22 Sept. 1931; *s* of late Reginald Peppitt and Phyllis Claire Peppitt; *m* 1960, Judith Penelope James; three *s. Educ:* St Paul's Sch.; Jesus Coll., Cambridge (BA Classical Tripos). Called to the Bar, Gray's Inn, 1958, Bencher, 1982. *Recreations:* collecting water-colours, shooting. *Address:* Chegworth Manor Farm, Chegworth, near Harrietsham, Kent ME17 1DD.

PEPYS, family name of **Earl of Cottenham.**

PEPYS, Lady (Mary) Rachel, DCVO 1968 (CVO 1954); Lady-in-Waiting to Princess Marina, Duchess of Kent, 1943–68; *b* 27 June 1905; *e d* of 15th Duke of Norfolk, KG, PC, CVO (*d* 1917); *m* 1st, 1939, as Lady Rachel Fitz-Alan Howard, Lieutenant-Colonel Colin Keppel Davidson, CIE, OBE, RA (killed in action, 1943), *s* of Col Leslie Davidson, CB, RHA, and Lady Theodora, *d* of 7th Earl of Albemarle; one *s* one *d;* 2nd, 1961, Brigadier Anthony Hilton Pepys, DSO (*d* 1967). *Address:* Highfield House, Crossbush, Arundel, W Sussex. *T:* Arundel 883158.

PERAHIA, Murray; pianist; co-artistic director, Aldeburgh Festival, since 1983; *b* New York, 19 April 1947; *s* of David and Flora Perahia; *m* 1980, Naomi Shohet (Ninette); one *s. Educ:* High Sch. of Performing Arts; Mannes College (MS); studied piano with Jeanette Haien, M. Horszowski, Arthur Balsam. Won Kosciusko Chopin Prize, 1965; début Carnegie Recital Hall, 1966; won Leeds Internat. Piano Festival, 1972; Avery Fisher Award, 1975; regular tours of Europe, Asia, USA; numerous recordings include complete Mozart Piano Concertos (records as conductor and pianist). *Address:* c/o Harold Holt, 31 Sinclair Road, W14.

PERCEVAL, family name of **Earl of Egmont.**

PERCEVAL, Viscount; Thomas Frederick Gerald Perceval; *b* 17 Aug. 1934; *e s* of 11th Earl of Egmont, *qv.*

PERCEVAL, Michael; HM Diplomatic Service; Counsellor (Commercial), Rome, since 1985; *b* 27 April 1936; *o s* of Hugh Perceval and late Guida Brind; *m* 1968, Alessandra Grandis; one *s* one *d. Educ:* Downside Sch.; Christ Church, Oxford (Schol.; 2nd Cl. Hons English Lit.). Served Royal Air Force, Nicosia, 1956–60; film production asst, Athens, 1960; freelance correspondent, Madrid, 1961–69. Joined FCO, 1970; First Sec. (Press), UK Rep. to EC, Brussels, 1972–74; First Sec. and subseq. Head of Chancery, British High Commission, Nicosia, 1974–78; Asst Head of Mexico and Caribbean Dept, FCO, 1978–79; Counsellor, Havana, 1980–82; Counsellor (Political and Economic) and Consul-Gen., Brasilia, 1982–85. *Publication:* The Spaniards, 1969, 2nd edn 1972. *Recreations:* music, walking, the Mediterranean. *Address:* c/o Foreign and Commonwealth Office, King Charles Street, Whitehall, SW1. *Club:* Royal Commonwealth Society.

PERCEVAL, Robert Westby, TD 1968; Clerk Assistant, House of Lords, 1964–74; retired; *b* 28 Aug. 1914; *m* 1948, Hon. J. I. L. Littleton, *er d* of 5th Baron Hatherton; two *s* two *d*. *Educ:* Ampleforth; Balliol College, Oxford. Joined Parliament Office, House of Lords, 1938. Royal Artillery, 1939–44; General Staff, War Office, 1944–45. *Address:* Pillaton Old Hall, Penkridge, Staffs ST19 5RZ. *Clubs:* Beefsteak, Turf.

PERCIVAL, Allen Dain, CBE 1975; Executive Chairman, Stainer & Bell Publishers, since 1978; *b* 23 April 1925; *s* of Charles and Gertrude Percival, Bradford; *m* 1952, Rachel Hay. *Educ:* Bradford Grammar Sch.; Magdalene Coll., Cambridge. MusB Cantab 1948. Served War of 1939–45, RNVR. Music Officer of British Council in France, 1948–50; Music Master, Haileybury and Imp. Service Coll., 1950–51; Dir of Music, Homerton Coll., Cambridge, 1951–62; Conductor, CUMS, 1954–58; Dir of Music Studies, GSM, 1962–65, Principal, GSMD, 1965–78; Gresham Prof. of Music, City Univ., 1980–85. Also professional continuo playing, broadcasting and conducting. FRCM; FGSM; Hon. RAM 1966; Hon. FTCL 1967; Fellow: Hong Kong Conservatory of Music, 1980; Curwen Inst., 1981. Hon. DMus City, 1978. *Publications:* The Orchestra, 1956; The Teach Yourself History of Music, 1961; Music at the Court of Elizabeth I, 1975; Galliard Book of Carols, 1980; English Love Songs, 1980; contribs to musical and educnl jls. *Recreation:* travel. *Address:* 30 Beaufort Place, Cambridge. *T:* 353953.

PERCIVAL, Sir Anthony (Edward), Kt 1966; CB 1954; Chairman, Gordon & Gotch Holdings Ltd, 1971–81; *b* 23 Sept. 1910; *m* 1935, Doris Cuff; one *d*. *Educ:* Manchester Gram. Sch.; Cambridge. Entered Board of Trade, 1933; Assistant Secretary, 1942; Commercial Counsellor, Washington, on secondment, 1946–49; Under-Secretary, Board of Trade, 1949–58; Sec., Export Credits Guarantee Dept, 1962–71. Formerly: Chm., Brameast Gotch; Director: Simon Engineering; Bank of Adelaide; Switzerland (General) Insurance Co.; Dir, Trade Indemnity Co., 1973–81. President: Berne Union of Export Credit Insurance Organisations, 1966–68; Export Credit Gp, OECD, Paris, 1967–70. *Address:* 16 Hayes Way, Beckenham, Kent. *T:* 01–650 2648.

PERCIVAL, Rt. Hon. Sir Ian, Kt 1979; PC 1983; QC 1963; MP (C) Southport since 1959; *b* 11 May 1921; *s* of Eldon and Chrystine Percival; *m* 1942, Madeline Buckingham Cooke; one *s* one *d*. *Educ:* Latymer Upper School; St Catharine's College, Cambridge (MA). Served HM Forces, 1940–46: 2nd Bn the Buffs, N Africa and Burma; Major. Called to the Bar, Inner Temple, 1948, Bencher, 1970. Recorder of Deal, later of the Crown Court, 1971–. Solicitor-General, 1979–83; Conservative Parly Legal Committee: Sec., 1964–68; Vice-Chm., 1968–70; Chm., 1970–74 and 1983–. Counsel to Sidley & Austin, US and Internat. Attorneys at Law, 1984–. Fellow, Inst. of Taxation (Chm., Parly Cttee, 1965–71); Mem., Royal Economic Soc.; FCIArb 1983. *Recreations:* golf, parachuting, windsurfing. *Address:* 9 King's Bench Walk, Temple, EC4. *T:* 01–583 2939; Oxenden, Stone-in-Oxney, near Tenterden, Kent. *Clubs:* Carlton, Beefsteak; Rye Golf.

PERCIVAL, Prof. Ian Colin, PhD; FRS 1985; Professor of Applied Mathematics, Queen Mary College, University of London, since 1974; *b* 27 July 1931; *m* 1955, Jill Cuff (*née* Herbert); two *s* one *d*. *Educ:* Ealing County Grammar Sch.; UCL (BSc, PhD). FRAS. Lectr in Physics, UCL, 1957–61; Reader in Applied Maths, QMC, 1961–67; Prof. of Theoret. Physics, Univ. of Stirling, 1967–74. Naylor Prize, London Mathematical Soc., 1985. *Publications:* (with Derek Richards) Introduction to Dynamics, 1983; (with Owen Greene and Irene Ridge) Nuclear Winter, 1985; papers in learned jls on scattering theory, atomic and molecular theory, statistical mechanics and classical dynamics. *Address:* Queen Mary College, Mile End Road, E1 4NS. *T:* 01–980 4811.

PERCIVAL, Robert Clarendon, FRCS, FRCOG; Consulting Obstetric Surgeon, The London Hospital; *b* 16 Sept. 1908; British; *m* 1st, 1944, Beryl Mary Ind (*d* 1967); one *d*; 2nd, 1972, Beatrice Myfanwy Evans, FFARCS. *Educ:* Barker College, NSW; Sydney University; The London Hospital (qualified 1933). Resident appointments: Poplar Hospital; Hosp. for Sick Children, Gt Ormond St; The London Hosp.; Southend Gen. Hosp. Obstetric and Gynæcological 1st Asst, The London Hosp., 1937–41; Surgeon-Lt-Comdr, RNVR, 1941–45 (Surgical Specialist); Obstetric Surgeon, The London Hospital, 1947–73, Director, Obstetric Unit, 1968–73. Chm., Obst. Adv. Cttee, NE Region Met. Hosp. Bd, 1967–73; President: Section of Obst. and Gyn., RSocMed, 1973–74; The London Hosp. Clubs' Union, 1965 (Treasurer, 1955–73); United Hosps RFC, 1969–72; London Hosp. Cricket Club, 1946–72. *Publications:* (jtly) Ten Teachers' Midwifery, 1958, new edition as Ten Teachers' Obstetrics, 1972; (jtly) Ten Teachers' Diseases of Women, 1965, new edition as Ten Teachers' Gynæcology, 1971; (jtly) British Obstetric Practice, 1963; (ed) Holland and Brews Obstetrics, 1969, 14th edn 1979; contribs to Lancet, British Jl of Obst. and Gynæcol. *Recreations:* fishing, golf. *Address:* Coker Wood Cottage, Pendomer, near Yeovil, Somerset BA22 9PD. *T:* Corscombe 328. *Club:* Gynaeological Travellers'.

PERCIVAL, Sir (Walter) Ian; *see* Percival, Sir Ian.

PERCIVAL-PRESCOTT, Westby William, FIIC; practising conservator and painter; *b* 22 Jan. 1923; *s* of William Percival-Prescott and Edith Percival; *m* 1948, Silvia Haswell Miller; one *s*. *Educ:* Edinburgh Coll. of Art (DA Hons). FIIC 1957. Andrew Grant Scholar, National Gall., 1945; restoration of Rubens Whitehall ceiling, 1947–51; Restorer i/c House of Lords frescos, 1953; worked in National Gall. Conservation Dept, 1954–56; directed restoration of Painted Hall, Greenwich, 1957–60; National Maritime Museum: estabd Picture Conservation Dept, 1961; Keeper and Head of Picture Dept, 1977–83; organised first internat. conf. on Comparative Lining Techniques, 1973 (Ottawa, 1974); produced and designed historical exhibitions: Idea and Illusion, 1960; Four Steps to Longitude, 1963; The Siege of Malta, 1970; Captain Cook and Mr Hodges, 1979; The Art of the Van de Veldes, 1982. Vis. Sen. Lectr, Dept of Fine Art, Univ. of Leeds, 1980. Internat. Council of Museums: Co-ordinator, Conservation Cttee, 1975–84; Mem., Directory Bd, Conservation Cttee, 1981–84. *Publications:* The Coronation Chair, 1957; The Lining Cycle, 1974, Swedish edn 1975; Handbook of Lining Terms, 1974; Thornhill at Greenwich, 1978; Micro X-Ray Techniques, 1978; Techniques of Suction Lining, 1981; The Art of the Van de Veldes, 1982; technical papers. *Recreations:* listening to music, travel. *Address:* 34 Compayne Gardens, NW6 3DP. *T:* 01–624 4577. *Club:* Chelsea Arts.

PERCY, family name of **Duke of Northumberland.**

PERCY, Earl; Henry Alan Walter Richard Percy; *b* 1 July 1953; *s* and *heir* of 10th Duke of Northumberland, *qv*. *Educ:* Eton; Christ Church, Oxford. *Recreations:* tennis, shooting, movies. *Address:* Alnwick Castle, Northumberland; Syon House, Brentford, Mddx.

PERCY, Lord Richard Charles; Former Lecturer, Department of Zoology, in the University of Newcastle upon Tyne, retired; *b* 11 February 1921; *s* of 8th Duke of Northumberland and Lady Helen Gordon-Lennox (who *d* 1965, as Dowager Duchess of Northumberland, GCVO, CBE); *m* 1st, 1966, Sarah Jane Elizabeth Norton (*d* 1978), *o d* of Mr and Mrs Petre Norton, La Charca, Coin, Malaga, Spain; two *s*; 2nd, 1979, Hon. Mrs Clayre Ridley, 2nd *d* of 4th Baron Stratheden and Campbell, CBE. *Educ:* Eton; Christ Church, Oxford; Durham University. BSc. Lieut-Colonel Comdg Northumberland Hussars, TA, 1959–61; late Capt. Gren. Guards. Served War, 1941–45. DL Northumberland, 1968. *Address:* Lesbury House, Alnwick, Northumberland NE66 3PT. *T:* Alnmouth 830330; 58 Woodsford Square, W14 8DS. *T:* 01–603 2220; 212 Lambeth Road, SE1. *T:* 01–928 3441. *Clubs:* Turf; Northern Counties (Newcastle upon Tyne).

PERCY, Rodney Algernon; His Honour Judge Percy; a Circuit Judge, since 1979; *b* 15 May 1924; 3rd *s* of late Hugh James Percy, Solicitor, Alnwick; *m* 1948, Mary Allen, *d* of late J. E. Benbow, Aberystwyth; one *s* three *d*. *Educ:* Uppingham; Brasenose Coll., Oxford (MA). Lieut, Royal Corps of Signals, 1942–46, served in Burma, India, Malaya, Java. Called to Bar, Middle Temple, 1950. Dep. Coroner, N Northumberland, 1957; Asst Recorder, Sheffield QS, 1964; Dep. Chm., Co. Durham QS, 1966–71; a Recorder of the Crown Court, 1972–79. Pres., Tyneside Marriage Guidance Council, 1983–86; Founder Mem., Conciliation Service for Northumberland and Tyneside, 1982–. *Publications:* (ed) Charlesworth on Negligence, 4th edn 1962, 5th edn 1971, 6th edn 1977, 7th edn (Charlesworth & Percy on Negligence) 1983; (contrib.) Atkin's Court Forms, 2nd edn, Vol. 20, 1982 (title Health and Safety at Work), and Vol. 29, 1983 (title Negligence). *Recreations:* golf, gardening, hill walking, King Charles Cavalier spaniels, beach-combing. *Address:* Brookside, Lesbury, Alnwick, Northumberland NE66 3AT. *T:* Alnwick 830326.

PERDUE, Rt. Rev. Richard Gordon; *b* 13 Feb. 1910; *s* of Richard Perdue; *m* 1943, Evelyn Ruth Curry, BA; two *d*. *Educ:* Trinity Coll., Dublin. BA 1931; MA and BD 1938. Deacon 1933, priest 1934, Dublin. Curate of Drumcondra with N Strand, 1933–36; Rathmines, 1936–40; Incumbent of Castledermot with Kinneagh, 1940–43; Roscrea, Diocese of Killaloe, 1943–54; Archdeacon of Killaloe and Kilfenora, 1951–54; Examining Chaplain to Bishop of Killaloe, 1951–54; Bishop of Killaloe, Kilfenora, Clonfert and Kilmacduagh, 1953–57; Bishop of Cork, Cloyne and Ross, 1957–78. *Address:* Castleconnor, Enniscrone, Co. Sligo, Ireland.

PEREGRINE, Gwilym Rhys, DL; Member: Independent Broadcasting Authority, since 1982 (Chairman, Welsh Advisory Committee, since 1982); Welsh Fourth Channel Authority, since 1982; *b* 30 Oct. 1924; *s* of Rev. and Mrs T. J. Peregrine; *m* 1958, Gwyneth Rosemary Williams; one *s* one *d*. *Educ:* Caterham Sch., Surrey; Gwendraeth Valley Grammar Sch.; Swansea Univ. Law Sch. Admitted Solicitor, 1949. Carmarthenshire County Council: Asst Solicitor, 1949–56; Dep. Clerk, 1956–72 (also Dep. Clerk of the Peace); Clerk and Chief Exec., 1972–74; Chief Exec., Dyfed CC, 1974–81. DL Dyfed, 1974. *Recreations:* golf, cricket, Rugby, music, reading. *Address:* Dôl-y-Coed, 37 Bronwydd Road, Carmarthen, Dyfed SA31 2AL. *Clubs:* Carmarthen Golf; Glamorgan Cricket, Bronwydd Cricket.

PEREIRA, Arthur Leonard, FRCS; Consulting Ear, Nose and Throat Surgeon to St George's Hospital, London; *b* 10 March 1906; British; *m* 1973, Mrs Jane Wilson (*née* Lapworth). *Educ:* Merchant Taylors' School. MRCS, LRCP 1929; MB, BS London 1931; FRCS 1936. Otologist to: the Metropolitan Hospital, E8, 1941–47; St George's Hospital, 1946–71. *Address:* Dormers, The Drive, Old Bosham, Sussex. *T:* Bosham 572086.

PEREIRA, Sir Charles; *see* Pereira, Sir H. C.

PEREIRA, Helio Gelli, DrMed; FRS 1973; FIBiol 1975; Head of Department of Epidemiology and of World Reference Centre for Foot-and-Mouth Disease, Animal Virus Research Institute, 1973–79; Consultant, Department of Virology, Fundação Oswaldo Cruz, Rio de Janeiro, since 1979; *b* 23 Sept. 1918; *s* of Raul Pereira and Maria G. Pereira; *m* 1946, Marguerite McDonald Scott (*see* Marguerite Pereira); one *s* one *d* (and one *d* decd). *Educ:* Faculdade Fluminense de Medicina, also Instituto Oswaldo Cruz, Rio de Janeiro, Brazil. British Council Scholarship, Dept of Bacteriology, Manchester Univ. and Div. of Bacteriology and Virus Research, Nat. Inst. for Med. Research, London, 1945–47; Rickettsia Laboratory, Instituto Oswaldo Cruz, 1948–51; Asst to Prof. of Microbiology, Faculdade Fluminense de Medicina, 1943–45 and 1948–51. Nat. Inst. for Med. Research, Mill Hill, London: Mem. Scientific Staff, 1951–73; Head of Div. of Virology, 1964–73; Dir, World Influenza Centre, 1961–70. *Publication:* (with C. H. Andrewes) Viruses of Vertebrates (3rd edn), 1972, 4th edn (with C. H. Andrewes and P. Wildy) 1978. *Recreations:* swimming, music. *Address:* 3 Ducks Walk, Twickenham, Mddx TW1 2DD. *T:* 01–892 4511; Fundação Oswaldo Cruz, Caixa Postal 926, 21040 Rio de Janeiro, Brazil.

PEREIRA, Sir (Herbert) Charles, Kt 1977; DSc; FRS 1969; Consultant, tropical agriculture research; *b* 12 May 1913; *s* of H. J. Pereira and Maud Edith (*née* Machin), both of London; *m* 1941, Irene Beatrice, *d* of David Sloan, Belfast; three *s* one *d*. *Educ:* Prince Albert Coll., Saskatchewan; St Albans Sch.; London Univ. Attached Rothamsted Expl Stn for PhD (London) 1941. Royal Engineers, 1941–46 (despatches). Colonial Agric. Service, Coffee Research Stn, Kenya, 1946–52; Colonial Research Service, established Physics Div. at East African Agriculture and Forestry Research Org., Kenya, 1952–61; DSc London 1961; Dir, ARC of Rhodesia and Nyasaland, 1961–63; Dir, ARC of Central Africa (Rhodesia, Zambia and Malawi), 1963–67; Dir, East Malling Research Station, 1969–72; Chief Scientist, MAFF, 1972–77. Member: Natural Environment Res. Council, 1971–77; ARC, 1973–77; ABRC, 1973–77; Chm., Sci. Panel, Commonwealth Develt Corp., 1978–. Mem. Bd of Trustees, Royal Botanic Gdns, Kew, 1983–. FInstBiol; FRASE 1977; CompICE, 1971; Hon. DSc Cranfield, 1977. Haile Selassie Prize for Research in Africa, 1966. *Publications:* (jtly) Hydrological Effects of Land Use Changes in East Africa, 1962; Land Use and Water Resources, 1973; papers in research jls; Founding Editor, Rhodesian Jl Agric. Research. *Recreations:* swimming, sailing. *Address:* Peartrees, Teston, Maidstone, Kent ME18 5AD. *T:* Maidstone 813333. *Clubs:* Athenæum; Harare (Zimbabwe).

PEREIRA, Margaret, CBE 1985; BSc; FIBiol; Controller, Home Office Forensic Science Service, since 1982; *b* 22 April 1928. *Educ:* La Sainte Union Convent, Bexley Heath; Dartford County Grammar School for Girls; Chelsea Coll. of Science and Technol. BSc 1953. Joined Metropolitan Police Forensic Science Lab., New Scotland Yard, 1947; Dep. Dir, Home Office Forensic Science Central Res. Estab., 1976; Director, Home Office Forensic Science Laboratory: Aldermaston, 1977; Chepstow, 1979. *Address:* c/o Home Office Forensic Science Service, Horseferry House, Dean Ryle Street, SW1P 2AW.

PEREIRA, Marguerite Scott, MD; Director, Virus Reference Laboratory, Public Health Laboratory Service, London, since 1970; *b* 29 July 1921; *d* of Dr William McDonald Scott and Alice Clotilde Mollard Scott; *m* 1946, Dr Helio Gelli Pereira, *qv*; one *s* one *d* (and one *d* decd). *Educ:* James Allens Girls' Sch., Dulwich; Univ. of Aberdeen (MB, ChB, MD). Bacteriologist, Univ. of Manchester, 1944–46; Clinical Pathologist, Rio de Janeiro, 1947–49; Dir, Public Health Laboratory, Salisbury, 1954–57; Sen. Bacteriologist, Virus Reference Lab., and Dir, WHO Nat. Influenza Centre for England and Wales, 1957–69; Co-Dir, WHO Collaborating Centre for Reference and Research on Influenza, 1975–. *Publications:* mostly on medical virology and epidemiology, espec. influenza and respiratory disease. *Recreation:* reading. *Address:* 3 Ducks Walk, Twickenham, Mddx. *T:* 01–892 4511.

PEREIRA-MENDOZA, Vivian, MScTech, CEng, FIEE; Director, Polytechnic of the South Bank, 1970–80; *b* 8 April 1917; *o s* of Rev. Joseph Pereira-Mendoza, Manchester;

m 1942, Marjorie, *y d* of Edward Lichtenstein; two *d. Educ:* Manchester Central High Sch.; Univ. of Manchester. Asst Lectr, Univ. of Manchester, 1939. Served War, 1940–45, in Royal Corps of Signals; Major, and GSO II (War Office). Sen. Lectr, Woolwich Polytechnic, 1948; Head of Dept: of Electrical Engrg, NW Kent Coll. of Technology, 1954; of Electrical Engrg and Physics, Borough Polytechnic, 1957; Vice-Principal, Borough Polytechnic, 1964; Principal, Borough Polytechnic, 1966–70. Mem. Council, Chelsea Coll., Univ. of London, 1972–85. Vice-Pres., Bd of Elders, Spanish and Portuguese Jews' Congregation, 1986–. *Address:* 183 Salmon Street, Kingsbury, NW9. *T:* 01–205 0200.

PERETZ, David Lindsay Corbett; Under Secretary, Monetary Group, Home Finance, HM Treasury, since 1986; Director, Ocean Transport and Trading plc, since 1985; *b* 29 May 1943; *s* of Michael and April Peretz; *m* 1966, Jane Wildman; one *s* one *d. Educ:* The Leys Sch., Cambridge; Exeter Coll., Oxford (MA). Asst Principal, Min. of Technol., 1965–69; Head of Public Policy and Institutional Studies, IBRO, 1969–76; HM Treasury: Principal, 1976–80; Asst Sec., External Finance, 1980–84; Principal Pvte Sec. to Chancellor of Exchequer, 1984–85; Under-Sec., Home Finance, 1985–86. *Recreations:* walking, sailboarding. listening to music. *Address:* 36 Laurier Road, NW5 1SJ. *T:* 01–485 6981.

PÉREZ DE CUÉLLAR, Javier; Secretary-General, United Nations, since 1982; *b* 19 Jan. 1920; *m*; two *c. Educ:* Law Faculty, Catholic Univ., Lima, Perú. Joined Peruvian Foreign Ministry, 1940; Diplomatic Service, 1944; Sec., Peruvian Embassies in France, UK, Bolivia and Brazil and Counsellor, Embassy, Brazil, 1944–60; Mem., Peruvian Delegn to First Session of Gen. Assembly, UN, 1946; Dir, Legal, Personnel, Admin, Protocol and Political Affairs Depts, Min. of Foreign Affairs, Perú, 1961–63; Peruvian Ambassador to Switzerland, 1964–66; Perm. Under-Sec. and Sec.-Gen. of Foreign Office, 1966–69; Ambassador of Perú to USSR and to Poland, 1969–71; Perm. Rep. of Perú to UN, 1971–75 (Rep. to UN Security Council, 1973–74); Special Rep. of UN Sec.-Gen. in Cyprus, 1975–77; Ambassador of Perú to Venezuela, 1978–79; UN Under-Sec.-Gen. for Special Political Affairs, 1979–81. Prof. of Diplomatic Law, Academia Diplomática del Perú, 1962–63; Prof. of Internat. Relations, Academia de Guerra Aérea del Perú, 1963–64. LLD *hc:* Univ. of Nice, France, 1983; Carleton Univ., Ottawa, 1985; *hc* degrees: Jagiellonian Univ., Poland, 1984; Charles Univ. Czechoslovakia, 1984; Sofia Univ., Bulgaria, 1984; Universidad Nacional Mayor de San Marcos, Perú, 1984; Vrije Universiteit Brussel, Belgium, 1984; Sorbonne Univ., Paris, 1985. Various internat. awards. *Publication:* Manual de Derecho Diplomático, 1964. *Address:* United Nations, New York, NY 10017, USA. *T:* (212) 754–5012. *Clubs:* Nacional, Ecuestre Huachipa, Villa, Jockey (Lima, Perú).

PÉREZ ESQUIVEL, Adolfo; sculptor; General Co-ordinator, Servicio de Paz y Justicia en América Latina, since 1974; *b* 26 Nov. 1931; *m* 1956, Amanda Guerreño; three *s. Educ:* Nat. Sch. of Fine Arts, Buenos Aires. Prof. of Art, Manuel Belgrano Nat. Sch. of Fine Arts, Buenos Aires, 1956–76; Prof., Faculty of Architecture and Urban Studies, Univ. Nacional de la Plata, 1969–73. Work in permanent collections: Buenos Aires Mus. of Modern Art; Mus. of Fine Arts, Córdoba; Fine Arts Mus., Rosario. Joined group dedicated to principles of militant non-violence, and engaged in projects to promote self-sufficiency in urban areas, 1971; founded Paz y Justicia magazine, 1973. Co-founder, Ecumenical Movement for Human Rights, Argentina; Pres., Permanent Assembly for Human Rights. Premio la Nación de Escultura; Pope John XXIII prize, Pax Christi Orgn, 1977; Nobel Peace Prize, 1980. *Address:* Servicio de Paz y Justicia, Calle México 479, Buenos Aires, Argentina.

PERHAM, Richard Nelson, ScD, FRS 1984; Reader in Biochemistry of Macromolecular Structures, since 1977, Head of Department of Biochemistry, since 1985, Cambridge University; President of St John's College, Cambridge, since 1983 (Fellow since 1964); *b* 27 April 1937; *s* of Cyril Richard William Perham and Helen Harrow Perham (*née* Thornton); *m* 1969, Nancy Jane, *d* of Temple Haviland Lane, Halifax, Nova Scotia; one *s* one *d. Educ:* Latymer Upper School; St John's College, Cambridge; BA 1961, MA 1965, PhD 1965, ScD 1976; Scholar; Slater Studentship, 1961–64; Henry Humphreys Prize, 1963. Nat. Service RN, 1956–58. MRC Scholar, Lab. of Molecular Biol., Cambridge, 1961–64; Univ. Demonstrator in Biochem., 1964–69, Lectr, 1969–77; Res. Fellow, St John's Coll., 1964–67, Tutor, 1967–77; Helen Hay Whitney Fellow, Dept of Molecular Biophysics, Yale Univ., 1966–67; EMBO Fellow, Max-Planck-Institut für Medizinische Forschung, Heidelberg, 1971; Drapers' Vis. Prof., Univ. of New South Wales, 1972; Biochem. Soc. Visitor, Aust. and NZ, 1979; Member: EMBO, 1983; SRC Enzyme Chem. and Tech. Cttee, 1973–75; Enzyme Panel, Biol. Scis Cttee, 1975–76; SERC Biol. Scis Cttee, 1983–85; SERC Science Bd, 1985–; Biochem. Soc. Cttee, 1980–84; British Nat. Cttee for Biochem., 1981–; Dir's Adv. Gp, AFRC Inst. of Animal Physiology, 1983–; Lectures: Aust. Biochem. Soc., 1979; Alberta Heritage Foundn for Med. Res., 1982; Philip E. Wilcox Meml, Univ. of Washington, Seattle, 1983. *Publications:* (ed) Instrumentation in Amino Acid Sequence Analysis, 1975; papers in sci. jls. *Recreations:* gardening, rowing (Lady Margaret BC), theatre, nosing around in antique shops. *Address:* Department of Biochemistry, Tennis Court Road, Cambridge CB2 1QW. *T:* Cambridge 351781; St John's College, Cambridge CB2 1TP. *T:* Cambridge 61621; 107 Barton Road, Cambridge CB3 9LL. *T:* Cambridge 63752. *Club:* Hawks (Cambridge).

PERINAT, Marqués de, Luis Guillermo; Senator, Spanish Senate, since 1983; *b* 27 Oct. 1923; *s* of Luis Perinat and Ana Maria, Marquesa de Campo Real; *m* 1955, Blanca Escriva de Romani, Marquesa de Alginet; two *s* one *d. Educ:* Univs of Salamanca and Valladolid. Barrister-at-law. Sec., Spanish Embassy, Cairo, 1949–51; Dep. Consul-Gen., New York, 1954–56; Counsellor, Spanish Embassy, Paris, 1962–65; Permanent Sec., Spanish-American Jt Defence Cttee, 1965–70; Dir-Gen., N American and Far Eastern Affairs, Min. of Foreign Affairs, Madrid, 1973–76; Spanish Ambassador: to the Court of St James's, 1976–81; to the Soviet Union, 1981–83. Grand Cross: Order of Civil Merit (Spain); Merito Militar (Spain); Kt Comdr: Order of Isabel La Católica (Spain); Order of Merito Aeronautico (Spain); also holds foreign decorations. *Heir: s* Guillermo Perinat y Escriva de Romani. *Address:* Calle del Prado 26, Madrid, Spain. *Clubs:* White's, Travellers'; Puerto de Hierro, Nuevo (Madrid).

PERKINS, Bernard James; Chairman, Harlow Development Corporation, 1972–79; *b* 25 Jan. 1928; *y s* of George and Rebecca Perkins; *m* 1956, Patricia (*née* Payne); three *d. Educ:* Strand School. Member: Lambeth Council, 1962–71 (Leader, 1968–71); Community Relations Commn, 1970–72; SE Econ. Planning Council, 1971–79; Alderman, GLC, 1971–73; Chm., GLC Housing Cttee, 1972–73. *Recreation:* social service. *Address:* 25 Croxted Road, West Dulwich, SE21 8SZ. *T:* 01–670 9056.

PERKINS, Surg. Vice-Adm. Sir Derek Duncombe S.; *see* Steele-Perkins.

PERKINS, Prof. Donald Hill, FRS 1966; Professor of Elementary Particle Physics, Oxford University, since 1965; *b* 15 Oct. 1925; *s* of George W. and Gertrude Perkins; *m* 1955, Dorothy Mary (*née* Maloney); two *d. Educ:* Malet Lambert High School, Hull. BSc London 1945; PhD London 1948; 1851 Senior Scholar, 1948–51. G. A. Wills Research Associate in Physics, Univ. of Bristol, 1951–55; Lawrence Radiation Lab., Univ. of California, 1955–56; Lectr in Physics, 1956–60, Reader in Physics, 1960–65, Univ. of Bristol. Mem., SERC, 1985–. Hon. DSc Sheffield, 1982. Guthrie Medal, Inst. of Physics, 1979. *Publications:* The Study of Elementary Particles by the Photographic Method (with C. F. Powell and P. H. Fowler), 1959; Introduction to High Energy Physics, 1972, 3rd edn 1986; about 50 papers and review articles in Nature, Physical Review, Philosophical Magazine, Physics Letters, Proc. Royal Soc., Nuovo Cimento, etc. *Recreations:* squash, tennis. *Address:* c/o Department of Nuclear Physics, Keble Road, Oxford.

PERKINS, Francis Layton, CBE 1977; DSC 1940; Chairman, Insurance Brokers' Registration Council, 1977–84; Solicitor since 1937; *b* 7 Feb. 1912; *s* of Montague Thornton and Madge Perkins; *m* 1st, 1941, Josephine Brice Miller (marr. diss. 1971); one *s* two *d*; 2nd, 1971, Jill Patricia Greenish. *Educ:* Charterhouse. Served War of 1939–45, Comdr RNVR, in command of minesweepers. Partner in Clifford Turner & Co., 1946, Consultant, 1983; Dir, Hogg Robinson & Capel-Cure Ltd, 1962; Chairman: Hogg Robinson and Gardner Mountain Ltd, 1967–74; Hogg Robinson Group Ltd (formerly Staplegreen Insurance Holdings Ltd), 1971–77; Dir, Transport Holding Co., 1971–73. Master of Skinners' Company, 1966; Dep. Pres., 1971, Pres., 1972–77, Corp. of Insurance Brokers; Chairman: UK Insurance Brokers European Cttee, 1973–80; British Insurance Brokers' Assoc., 1976–80; Common Mkt Cttee, Bureau International des Producteurs d'Assurances et de Réassurances, 1977–79; Dep. Chm., Cttee of Management, Inst. of Laryngology and Otology, 1976–78 (Mem., 1974–78); Mem. Council: Industrial Soc., 1976– (Treasurer, 1976–85); Common Law Inst. of Intellectual Property, 1983–. Governor and Chm. of Cttee, Tonbridge Sch.; Governor: Sutton's Hospital in Charterhouse, 1974–; Royal National Throat, Nose and Ear Hospital, 1974–80; Chairman: Fund Raising Cttee, St Bartholomew's Hosp., 1980; City of London and Thames Estuary Panel, Duke of Edinburgh's 1974 Commonwealth Conf.; Trustee, Barts Res. Develt Trust. *Recreations:* tennis, golf, fishing. *Address:* Flat 4, 34 Sloane Court West, SW3. *T:* 01–730 9775. *Clubs:* Boodle's, MCC, All England Lawn Tennis; Royal St George's Golf; Hon. Co. of Edinburgh Golfers.

PERKINS, Air Vice-Marshal Irwyn Morse, MBE 1957; Royal Air Force, retired; Medical Officer, Royal Military College of Science, since 1980; *b* 15 Dec. 1920; *s* of William Lewis Perkins and Gwenllian Perkins, Ystalyfera, Swansea; *m* 1948, Royce Villiers Thompson, *d* of William Stanley Thompson and Zöe Thompson, The Mountain, Tangier; one *s* one *d. Educ:* Pontardawe, Swansea; St Mary's Hospital, Paddington, W2. MRCS, LRCP 1945; MFCM 1973. Commnd RAF, 1946; SMO: RAF Gibraltar, 1946–49; several flying stations in UK; DGMS Dept, MoD, 1955–57; RAF Laarbruch, Germany, 1958–61; RAF Khormaksar, Aden, 1964–66; DPMO, Bomber and Strike Commands, 1966–69; CO RAF Hospital, Ely, Cambs, 1969–72; PMO RAF Germany, 1972–75; CO PMRAF Hospital, Halton, 1975–77; PMO, Support Comd, 1977–80. Hon. Surgeon to HM the Queen, 1975–80. *Recreations:* sporting shooting, bodging. *Address:* 5 Redlands Close, Highworth, Swindon, Wilts SN6 7SN. *T:* Highworth 765097. *Club:* Royal Air Force.

PERKINS, James Alfred, MA, PhD; Chairman and Chief Executive Officer, International Council for Educational Development, since 1970; *b* 11 Oct. 1911; *s* of H. Norman Perkins and Emily (*née* Taylor); *m* 1st, 1938, Jean Bredin (*d* 1970); two *s* three *d*; 2nd, 1971, Ruth B. Aall; one step *s* three step *d. Educ:* Swarthmore Coll., Pa (AB); Princeton Univ., NJ (MA, PhD). Instructor Polit. Sci., Princeton Univ., 1937–39; Asst Prof. and Asst Dir, Sch. of Public and Internat. Affairs, Princeton, 1939–41; Dir, Pulp and Paper Div., Office of Price Admin., 1941–43; Asst to Administrator, For. Econ. Admin., 1943–45; Vice-Pres. Swarthmore Coll., 1945–50; Exec. Associate, Carnegie Corp. of NY, 1950–51; Dep. Chm. (on leave) Res. and Develt Bd, Dept of Defense, 1951–52; Vice-Pres., Carnegie Corp. of NY, 1951–63; Pres., Cornell Univ., 1963–69. Carnegie Foundn for the Advancement of Teaching: Sec. 1954–55; Vice-Pres., 1955–63. Chm., Pres. Johnson's Gen. Adv. Cttee on Foreign Assistance Prog., 1965–68; Trustee: Rand Corp., 1961–71; United Negro Coll. Fund (Chm. of Bd), 1965–69; Educl Testing Service, 1964–68; Dir Emeritus, Council on Foreign Relations; Mem. Gen. Adv. Cttee of US Arms Control and Disarmament Agency, 1963–; Chm. NY Regents Adv. Cttee on Educational Leadership, 1963–67. Member: Bd of Directors, Chase Manhattan Bank, 1967–75; Stevenson Memorial Fund, 1966–; Trustee, Aspen Inst., 1973–; Director: Overseas Develt Council, 1969–; Center for Inter-Amer. Relations, 1969–; Inst. of Internat. Educn, 1981–; Vice Chm., Acad. for Educnl Develt. Chm., President Carter's Commn on Foreign Language and Internat. Studies, 1978–79. Mem. Society of Friends, Swarthmore, Pa. Hon. LLD and Hon. LHD various colls and univs. *Publications:* The University in Transition, 1966; Higher Education: from Autonomy to Systems, 1972; The University as an Organization, 1973; contrib. to: Public Admin. Review, Amer. Polit. Sci. Review, Educational Record, etc. *Address:* (home) 94 North Road, Princeton, NJ 08540, USA; (office) 680 Fifth Avenue, New York City, NY 10019, USA. *Clubs:* Century Association, Coffee House University (NYC).

PERKINS, Maj.-Gen. Kenneth, CB 1977; MBE 1955; DFC 1953; Defence Adviser, British Aerospace Dynamics Group, since 1982; *b* 15 Aug. 1926; *s* of George Samuel Perkins and Arabella Sarah Perkins (*née* Wise); *m* 1st, 1949, Anne Theresa Barry (marr. diss. 1984); three *d*; 2nd, 1985, Hon. Celia Sandys, *d* of Rt Hon. Lord Duncan-Sandys, *qv*, and late Mrs Diana Churchill; one *s. Educ:* Lewes County Sch. for Boys; New Coll., Oxford. Enlisted 1944; commnd RA 1946; various appts in Middle and Far East, BAOR and UK until 1965, incl. Korean War, Malayan Emergency, and Staff Coll. Quetta 1958; Instructor, Staff Coll. Camberley, 1965–66; CO 1st Regt Royal Horse Artillery, 1967–69; GSO 1 Singapore, 1970; Comdr 24 Bde, 1971–72; RCDS 1973; Central Staff, MoD, 1974; Maj.-Gen., 1975; Comdr, Sultan's Armed Forces, Oman, 1975–77 (successfully concluded Dhofar War); Asst Chief of Defence Staff (Ops), 1977–80; Dir, Military Assistance Office, MoD, 1980–82. Col Comdt, RA, 1980–85. Selangor Distinguished Conduct Medal (Malaya), 1955; Hashemite Order of Independence, first class, 1975; Order of Oman, 1977. *Publications:* articles in various Service jls. *Recreations:* painting, physical exercise. *Address:* c/o National Westminster Bank, Seaford, Sussex. *Club:* Army and Navy.

PERKINS, Sir Robert Dempster, Kt 1954; *b* 1903; *s* of late W. Frank Perkins; *m* 1944, Lady Norman, *widow* of Sir Nigel Norman, 2nd Bt. *Educ:* Eton; Trinity Coll., Cambridge, MA. Mechanical Engineer. MP (C) Stroud (by-election May), 1931–45; MP (C) Stroud and Thornbury Division of Gloucestershire, 1950–55; Parliamentary Secretary, Ministry of Civil Aviation, 1945. Vice-Pres., BALPA, 1937–73, Pres. 1973–76. *Recreations:* aviation and fishing. *Address:* The Manor House, Downton, Salisbury, Wilts SP5 3PU.

PERKINS, Sir Walter Robert Dempster; *see* Perkins, Sir R. D.

PERKS, His Honour (John) Clifford, MC 1944; TD; a Circuit Judge (formerly County Court Judge), 1970–85; *b* 20 March 1915; *s* of John Hyde Haslewood Perks and Frances Mary Perks; *m* 1940, Ruth Dyke Perks (*née* Appleby); two *s* (one *s* two *d* decd). *Educ:* Blundell's; Balliol Coll., Oxford. Called to Bar, Inner Temple, 1938; joined Western Circuit; Chancellor, diocese of Bristol, 1950–71; Dep. Chm., Devon QS, 1965–71. *Recreation:* castles. *Address:* 32 Melbury Close, Chislehurst, Kent.

PERLMAN, Itzhak; violinist; *b* Tel Aviv, 31 Aug. 1945; *s* of Chaim and Shoshana Perlman; *m* 1967, Toby Lynn Friedlander; two *s* three *d*. Studied at Tel Aviv Acad. of Music with Ryvka Goldgart, and at Juilliard Sch., NY, under Dorothy Delay and Ivan Galamian. First solo recital at age of 10 in Israel; New York début, 1958. Leventritt Meml Award, NY, 1964. Has toured extensively in USA and played with all major American symphony orchestras; recital tours of Canada, South America, Europe, Israel, Far East and Australia; recorded many standard works for violin. Has received numerous Grammy Awards. Hon. degrees: Harvard; Yale; Brandeis. *Recreation:* cooking. *Address:* c/o IMG Artists, 22 East 71st Street, New York, NY 10021, USA.

PEROWNE, Rear-Adm. Benjamin Cubitt, CB 1978; General Secretary, Royal United Kingdom Beneficent Association, since 1978; *b* 18 Feb. 1921; *s* of late Bernard Cubitt Perowne and of Gertrude Dorothy Perowne; *m* 1946, Phyllis Marjorie, *d* of late Cdre R. D. Peel, RNR, Southampton; two *s* one *d*. *Educ:* Culford Sch. Joined RN, 1939; Sec. to Adm. Sir Deric Holland-Martin, GCB, DSO, DSC, 1955–64; Acting Captain, 1957–64, Captain 1966; Staff, Chief of Personnel and Logistics, 1967–70; (Cdre, 1969–70); comd, HMS Cochrane, 1971–73; Dir of Defence Policy, 1973–75 (Cdre); Dir, Management and Support Intelligence, 1976–78, also Chief Naval Supply and Secretariat Officer, 1977–78. *Recreations:* shooting, gardening. *Address:* c/o Barclays Bank, Haslemere, Surrey. *Club:* Army and Navy.

PEROWNE, Dame Freya; *see* Stark, Dame Freya.

PEROWNE, Stewart Henry, OBE 1944; KStJ 1956; FSA; FRSA; Orientalist and Historian; Colonial Administrative Service (retired); *b* 17 June 1901; 3rd *s* of late Arthur William Thomson Perowne, DD, Bishop of Worcester, and late Helena Frances Oldnall-Russell; *m* 1947, Freya Madeline Stark (*see* Dame Freya Stark). *Educ:* Haileybury Coll. (champion sprinter); Corpus Christi Coll., Cambridge (Hon. Fellow, 1981); Harvard Univ., USA. BA 1923, MA 1931, Cambridge. Joined Palestine Government Education Service, 1927; Administrative Service, 1930 (Press Officer 1931); Asst District Commissioner, Galilee, 1934; Asst Secretary Malta, 1934 (pioneered Pasteurization); Political Officer, Aden Prot., 1937; recovered inscriptions and sculpture from Imadia and Beihan; Arabic Programme Organiser, BBC, 1938 (pioneered programme, English by Radio); Information Officer, Aden, 1939; Public Relations Attaché, British Embassy, Baghdad, 1941; Oriental Counsellor, 1944; Colonial Secretary, Barbados, 1947–51; seconded as Principal Adviser (Interior), Cyrenaica, 1950–51; retired 1951. Discovered ancient city of Aziris, 1951. Adviser, UK delegation to UN Assembly, Paris, Nov. 1951. Helped design stamps for Malta, 1936, Aden, 1938, Barbados, 1949, Libya, 1951; currency notes for W. Indies Federation, 1949, and Libya, 1951; Assistant to the Bishop in Jerusalem for Refugee work, 1952; designer and supervisor of Refugee model villages. FSA 1957. Coronation Medal, 1937; Iraq Coronation Medal, 1953; Metropolitan Police Mounted Officers certificate. Member, C. of E. Foreign Relations Council. *Publications:* The One Remains, 1954; Herod the Great, 1956; The Later Herods, 1958; Hadrian, 1960; Cæsars and Saints, 1962; The Pilgrim's Companion in Jerusalem and Bethlehem, 1964; The Pilgrim's Companion in Roman Rome, 1964; The Pilgrim's Companion in Athens, 1964; Jerusalem, 1965; The End of the Roman World, 1966; The Death of the Roman Republic: from 146 BC to the birth of the Roman Empire, 1969; Roman Mythology, 1968, rev. edn 1983; (contrib.) Ancient Cities of the Middle East, 1970; The Siege within the Walls: Malta 1940–43, 1970; Rome, 1971; The Journeys of St Paul, 1973; The Caesars' Wives, 1974; The Archaeology of Greece and the Aegean, 1974; Holy Places of Christendom, 1976; articles in Encyclopædia Britannica, The Times, History Today, etc. *Recreations:* horses, the arts, archæology. *Address:* Vicarage Gate House, Vicarage Gate, W8 4AQ. *T:* 01–229 7938. *Clubs:* Travellers'; Casino (1852) Malta; Savannah (Bridgetown); Phoenix-SK (Harvard).

PERRETT, Desmond Seymour; QC 1980; a Recorder of the Crown Court, since 1978; *b* 22 April 1937; *s* of His Honour John Perrett, *qv*; *m* 1961, Pauline Merriel, *yr d* of late Paul Robert Buchan May, ICS, and of Esme May; one *s* one *d*. *Educ:* Westminster Sch. National Service, RN, 1955–57: midshipman RNVR, 1955; Suez, 1956, and Cyprus, 1957. Called to the Bar, Gray's Inn, 1962; Oxford Circuit, 1963–72; Midland and Oxford Circuit, 1972–; Mem., Senate of the Inns of Court and of the Bar, 1983–. Chm. Disciplinary Appeals Cttee, Cricket Council, 1986–. Mem. Governing Body, Horris Hill Sch., 1986–. *Recreations:* cricket, fishing, shooting. *Address:* The Old Tap House, Upper Wootton, Basingstoke, Hants. *T:* Basingstoke 850027; 2 Crown Office Row, Temple, EC4Y 7HJ. *T:* 01–353 9337. *Club:* MCC.

PERRETT, His Honour John, JP; a Circuit Judge (formerly a Judge of County Courts), 1969–81; *b* 22 Oct. 1906; *er s* of late Joseph and Alice Perrett, Birmingham; *m* 1933, Elizabeth Mary, *y d* of late William Seymour, Nenagh, Co. Tipperary; two *s* two *d*. *Educ:* St Anne's RC and Stratford Road Schools, Birmingham; King's Coll., Strand, WC2. Entered office of Philip Baker & Co., Solicitors, Birmingham, 1922; joined late Alfred W. Fryzer, Solicitor, Arundel St, WC2, 1925; joined Herbert Baron & Co., Solicitors, Queen Victoria St, EC4, 1934. Served War of 1939–45: RAPC, 1939–45; RASC, 1945. Called to Bar, Gray's Inn, 1946; practised in London and on Midland Circuit; Dep. Chm., Warwicks QS, 1970–71; JP Warwicks, 1970. *Address:* 5B Vicar's Close, Lichfield, Staffs WS13 7LE. *T:* Lichfield 252320.

See also D. S. Perrett, G. H. Rooke.

PERRIN, John Henry; *b* 14 Jan. 1916; *s* of Walter William Perrin, Faringdon and Sonning, Berks, and Amelia (*née* Honey), Oxford; *m* 1940, Doris Winifred Barrington-Brider; two *s*. *Educ:* Minchenden Sch.; London Univ. HM Customs and Excise; Royal Navy, 1939–46; Min. of Agriculture, 1948–76: Principal Private Sec. to Minister (Lord Amory), 1955–57; Regional Controller, Eastern Region, 1957–68; Under Sec., 1968–76. Dir-Gen., British Agricl Export Council, 1976–77. Inspector, Public Inquiries, Depts of the Environment and Transport, 1978–84. *Clubs:* Naval, Civil Service, Royal Yachting; RNVR Yacht.

PERRIN, Sir Michael (Willcox), Kt 1967; CBE 1952 (OBE 1946); FRSC; Chairman, The Wellcome Foundation Ltd, 1953–70; Director: Inveresk Research International, 1961–74 (Chairman, 1971–73); Radiochemical Centre Ltd, 1971–75; *b* 13 Sept. 1905; *s* of late Bishop W. W. Perrin; *m* 1934, Nancy May, *d* of late Bishop C. E. Curzon; one *s* one *d*. *Educ:* Winchester; New Coll., Oxford (BA, BSc). Post-graduate research, Toronto Univ. (MA), 1928–29; Amsterdam Univ., 1929–33; ICI (Alkali) Research Dept, Northwich, 1933–38; Asst Director, Tube Alloys (Atomic Energy), DSIR, 1941–46; Dep. Controller, Atomic Energy (Technical Policy), Ministry of Supply, 1946–51; Research Adviser, ICI, 1951–52. Chm. (Treasurer) Bd of Governors, St Bartholomew's Hosp. and Pres., Med. Coll. of St Bartholomew's Hosp., 1960–69; Member: Council, Royal Veterinary Coll., London Univ., 1967–76 (Chm. 1967–72); Council, Sch. of Pharmacy, London Univ., 1963–76; Central Adv. Council for Science and Technology, 1969–70; Governing Body, British Postgrad. Med. Fedn, 1970–77 (Chm., 1972–77). Trustee, British Museum (Natural History), 1974–83. Chm. Council, Roedean Sch., 1974–79. Hon. DSc Univ. of British Columbia, 1969. *Publications:* papers in scientific and technical journals. *Address:* 14 Christchurch Hill, Hampstead, NW3 1LB. *T:* 01–794 3064. *Club:* Athenæum.

PERRIN, Air Vice-Marshal Norman Arthur; Director, Telecommunications Engineering and Manufacturing Association, since 1987; *b* 30 Sept. 1930; *s* of late Albert Arthur and Mona Victoria (*née* Stacey); *m* 1956, Marie (*née* Bannon), *d* of late Peter and Lucy Bannon; one *s*. *Educ:* Liverpool Collegiate School; Hertford College, Oxford; RAF Technical College. BA; CEng, FRAeS. Nat. Service commn, Airfield Construction Branch, RAF, Suez Canal Zone, 1951–53; perm. commn, Tech. Branch, 1953; Advanced GW course, 1956–57; Air Ministry, 1958–61; HQ 11 Group, 1961–62; Staff Coll., 1963; FEAF, 1964–65; OC Eng Wing, RAF Seletar, 1966–67; JSSC 1967; Op. Requirements, SAGW, 1967–70; Chief Instructor, Systems Engineering, RAF Coll., 1970–72; Group Captain Plans, HQ Maintenance Comd, 1972–75; C. Mech. Eng., HQ Strike Comd, 1975–78; RCDS 1979; Dir Air GW MoD (PE), 1980–83; Vice-Pres. (Air), Ordnance Board, 1983: Pres., Ordnance Board, 1984–86. *Recreations:* bridge, crosswords, Liverpool FC watching. *Address:* c/o Barclays Bank, 84 High Street, Princes Risborough, Aylesbury, Bucks. *Club:* Royal Air Force.

PERRING, Franklyn Hugh, PhD; FIBiol; General Secretary, Royal Society for Nature Conservation, since 1979; *b* 1 Aug. 1927; *s* of Frank Arthur and Avelyn Millicent Perring; *m* 1st, 1951, Yvonne Frances Maud Matthews (marr. diss. 1972); one *s*; 2nd, 1972, Margaret Dorothy Barrow; one *d*. *Educ:* Earls Colne Grammar Sch.; Queens' Coll., Cambridge (MA, PhD). FLS. Botanical Society of British Isles Distribution Maps Scheme: Hd, 1954–59; Dir, 1959–64; Hd, Biological Records Centre, Monks Wood Experimental Station, 1964–79; Botanical Sec., Linnean Soc. of London, 1973–78. *Publications:* (jtly) Atlas of the British Flora, 1962; (jtly) A Flora of Cambridgeshire, 1964; Critical Supplement to the Atlas of the British Flora, 1968; (ed) The Flora of a Changing Britain, 1970; (ed jtly) The British Oak, 1974; (jtly) English Names of Wild Flowers, 1974; (jtly) British Red Data Book of Vascular Plants, 1977; RSNC Guide to British Wild Flowers, 1984; (jtly) Ecological Flora of the Shropshire Region, 1985; sci. papers in Jl of Ecology, Watsonia, etc. *Recreations:* opera-going, poetry reading, plant photography, gardening. *Address:* 24 Glapthorn Road, Oundle, Peterborough PE8 4JQ. *T:* Oundle 73388.

PERRING, John Raymond, TD 1965; Chairman, Perring Furnishings Ltd, since 1981; *b* 7 July 1931; *e s* and *heir* of Sir Ralph Perring, Bt, *qv*; *m* 1961, Ella Christine, *e d* of late A. G. Pelham and Mrs Ann Pelham; two *s* two *d*. *Educ:* Stowe School. Nat. Service, then TA, RA, 1949–60; Royal Fusiliers (City of London), 1960–65. Joined family furnishing business, 1951, Dir 1957, Jt Man. Dir 1964, Vice-Chm., 1972. One of HM Lieutenants of City of London, 1963–; Mem. Ct of Assistants, Merchant Taylors' Co., 1980–; Master, Furniture Makers' Co., 1978; Nat. Pres., Nat. Assoc. of Retail Furnishers, 1971–73; Chm., Retail Alliance, 1973–75; Mem. Council, Retail Consortium, 1972–80; Mem. EDC (Distributive Trades), 1974–78. FRSA. *Recreations:* sailing, ski-ing, swimming, gardening. *Address:* 21 Somerset Road, Wimbledon, SW19. *T:* 01–946 8971. *Clubs:* City Livery, Royal Automobile; Royal Wimbledon Golf; Bembridge Sailing.

PERRING, Sir Ralph (Edgar), 1st Bt *cr* 1963; Kt 1960; Chairman, Perring Furnishings Ltd, 1948–81; *b* 23 March 1905; *yr s* of late Colonel Sir John Perring, DL, JP; *m* 1928, Ethel Mary, OStJ, *o d* of late Henry T. Johnson, Putney; two *s* (and one *s* decd). *Educ:* University College Sch., London. Lieut, RA (TA) 1938–40, invalided. Member Court of Common Council (Ward of Cripplegate), 1948–51; Alderman of City of London (Langbourn Ward), 1951–75, one of HM Lieutenants of the City of London, and Sheriff, 1958–59. Lord Mayor of London, 1962–63. Chairman, Spitalfields Market Cttee, 1951–52; JP County of London, 1943–; Member: LCC for Cities of London and Westminster, 1952–55; County of London Licensing Planning Cttee; New Guildford Cathedral Council; Consumer Advisory Council, BSI, 1955–59; Bd of Governors, E-SU, 1976–81. Governor: St Bartholomew's Hospital, 1964–69; Imperial College of Science and Technology, 1964–67; Christ's Hospital; Vice-Chairman, BNEC Cttee for Exports to Canada, 1964–67, Chairman, 1968–70; Dir, Confederation Life Insurance Co. of Canada, 1969–81. Vice-President, Royal Bridewell Hospital (King Edward's Sch., Witley, 1964–75); Trustee, Morden Coll., Blackheath, 1970–, Chm. 1979–. Master Worshipful Co. of Tin Plate Workers, 1944–45; Master, Worshipful Co. of Painters-Stainers, 1977–78; Sen. Past Master and Founder Mem., Worshipful Co. of Furniture Makers; Mem. Court, Farmers' Co.; President Langbourn Ward Club, 1951–75. FRSA 1975. KStJ. Grand Cross of Merit (Republic of Germany), 1959; Order of Homayoun (Iran), 1959; Grand Officer, Order of Leopold (Belgium), 1963; Knight Commander, Royal Order of George I (Greece), 1963; Commander de la Valeur Camerounaise, 1963. *Heir: s* John Raymond Perring, *qv*. *Address:* 15 Burghley House, Somerset Road, Wimbledon, SW19. *T:* 01–946 3433. *Clubs:* St Stephen's Constitutional, Royal Automobile, City Livery (President, 1951–52).

PERRINS, Wesley, MBE 1952; former official of Municipal and General Workers' Union, Birmingham District Secretary; Member, Worcestershire County Council until 1974 (formerly Alderman); formerly Member, West Midlands Economic Planning Council; *b* 21 Sept. 1905; *s* of Councillor Amos Perrins, Stourbridge; *m* 1932, Mary, *d* of Charles Evans; one *s* one *d*. *Educ:* Wollescote Council Sch.; Upper Standard Sch., Lye. MP (Lab) Yardley Division of Birmingham, 1945–50. Member of: Lye & Wollescote UDC, 1928–31; Stourbridge Borough Council, 1931–46, 1971. Mem., Court of Governors, Birmingham Univ., 1967–74. Hon. Alderman, Dudley MBC, 1982. *Address:* Cromlech Cottage, 19 Walker Avenue, Wollescote, Stourbridge, West Midlands. *T:* Stourbridge 4640.

PERRIS, Sir David (Arthur), Kt 1977; MBE 1970; JP; Secretary, Trades Union Congress West Midlands Regional Council, since 1974; *b* 25 May 1929; *s* of Arthur Perris; *m* 1955, Constance Parkes, BPharm, FPS; one *s* one *d*. *Educ:* Sparkhill Commercial Sch., Birmingham. Film distribution industry, 1944–61; Reed Paper Group, 1961–65; Vice-Chm., ATV Midlands Ltd, 1980–81; Dir, Central Independent Television plc, 1982–83 (Vice Chm., W Midlands Bd). Sec., Birmingham Trades Council, 1966–83; a Chm., Greater Birmingham Supplementary Benefits Appeal Tribunal, 1982–. Chairman: Birmingham Regional Hosp. Bd, 1970–74; West Midlands RHA, 1974–82; NHS National Trng Council, 1975–82; Mem. Bd of Governors, United Birmingham Hosps, 1965–74; Mem., Birmingham Children's Hosp. House Cttee, 1958–71 (Chm. 1967–71); Chm., Birmingham Hosp. Saturday Fund, 1985– (Vice-Chm., 1975–85). Member: W Mids Econ. Planning Council, 1968–70; Midlands Postal Bd, 1974–81; Life Governor, Univ. of Birmingham, 1972; Mem. Convocation, Univ. of Aston in Birmingham, 1975–; Pres., Public Service Announcements Assoc., 1983–; Chm. Magistrates' Assoc., Birmingham Br., 1975–. Hon. LLD Birmingham, 1981. JP Birmingham, 1961. *Recreations:* cinema, reading. *Address:* 24 Mayfield Road, Moseley, Birmingham B13 9HJ. *T:* 021–449 3652.

PERRIS, John Douglas; HM Diplomatic Service, retired; Counsellor (Administration), Bonn, 1982–86; *b* 28 March 1928; *s* of Frank William Perris and Alice Perris; *m* 1954, Kathleen Mary Lewington; one *s* two *d*. *Educ:* St Paul's, Knightsbridge; Westminster City Sch. Entered FO, 1945; Bahrain, 1951; Bucharest, 1953; Hamburg, 1955; FO, 1957;

Tehran, 1960; Second Sec. (Admin), Caracas, 1963; Second Sec. (Econ.), Berlin, 1966; First Sec. (Admin), Baghdad, 1969; FCO (Inspectorate), 1972; First Sec./Head of Chancery/Consul, Tegucigalpa, 1974; First Sec. (Consular and Immigration), New Delhi, 1976; FCO, 1979. *Recreations:* sport (non-active), reading (thrillers), bridge, DIY. *Address:* 128 Wakehurst Road, SW11 6BS. *T:* 01–228 0521.

PERROW, (Joseph) Howard; Chairman, Co-operative Union Ltd, 1975–83; Chief Executive Officer and Secretary, Greater Lancastria Co-operative Society Ltd, 1976–83; *b* 18 Nov. 1923; *s* of Joseph and Mary Elizabeth Perrow; *m* 1947, Lorraine Strick; two *s. Educ:* St Just, Penzance, Cornwall; Co-operative Coll., Stanford Hall, Leics (CSD). Joined Penzance Co-operative Soc., 1940. Served RAF, 1943–47. Various managerial positions in Co-operative Movement: in W Cornwall, with CRS N Devon, Carmarthen Soc., Silverdale (Staffs) and Burslem Socs; Mem., Co-operative Union Central Exec., 1966–83, Vice-Chm., 1973–75; Vice-Chm., NW Sectional Bd, 1970–75; Director: CWS, 1970–83; Nat. Co-operative Chemists, 1973–83; Greater Manchester Independent Radio, 1973–83; Mem., Central Cttee, Internat. Co-operative Alliance, 1975–83; Mem. Council (rep. Co-operative Union), Retail Consortium, 1976–83. President, Co-operative Congress, 1979. *Recreations:* football, cricket. *Address:* Blue Seas, Cliff Road, Mousehole, Penzance, Cornwall TR19 6QT. *T:* Penzance 731330. *Club:* Bolitho's (St Just).

PERRY, family name of **Baron Perry of Walton.**

PERRY OF WALTON, Baron *cr* 1979 (Life Peer), of Walton, Bucks; **Walter Laing Macdonald Perry,** Kt 1974; OBE 1957; FRS 1985; FRSE 1960; Vice-Chancellor, The Open University, 1969–80, Fellow, since 1981; *b* 16 June 1921; *s* of Fletcher S. Perry and Flora M. Macdonald; *m* 1st, 1946, Anne Elizabeth Grant (marr. diss. 1971); three *s*; 2nd, 1971, Catherine Hilda Crawley; two *s* one *d. Educ:* Ayr Acad.; Dundee High Sch. MB, ChB 1943, MD 1948, DSc 1958 (University of St Andrews); MRCP (Edinburgh), 1963; FRCPE 1967; FRCP 1978; Fellow, UCL, 1981–. Medical Officer, Colonial Medical Service (Nigeria), 1944–46; Medical Officer, RAF, 1946–47; Member of Staff, Medical Research Council, 1947–52; Director, Department of Biological Standards, National Institute for Medical Research, 1952–58. Prof. of Pharmacology, University of Edinburgh, 1958–68, Vice-Principal, 1967–68. Member, British Pharmacopœia Commission, 1952–68; Secretary, British Pharmacological Society, 1957–61. Chairman: Community Radio Milton Keynes, 1979–82; Living Tapes Ltd, 1980–; Research Defence Soc., 1979–82; Delegacy of Goldsmiths' Coll., 1981–84; Standing Cttee on Continuing Educn, UGC and NAB, 1985–. Dep. Leader, SDP peers in House of Lords, 1981–83. Hon. DSc Bradford, 1974; Hon. LLD Dundee, 1975; Hon. DHL: Maryland, 1978; State Univ. of NY, 1982; Hon. Dr Athabasca, 1979; DUniv: Stirling, 1980; Open, 1981; Hon. DLitt Deakin Univ., Australia, 1981. *Publications:* Open University, 1976; papers in Journal of Physiology, British Journal of Pharmacology and Chemo-therapy, etc. *Recreations:* making music and playing games. *Address:* International Centre for Distance Learning, Walton Hall, Milton Keynes MK7 6AA. *Club:* Savage.

PERRY, Alan Joseph; Assistant Secretary, HM Treasury, since 1980; *b* 17 Jan. 1930; *s* of late Joseph and Elsie Perry; *m* 1961, Vivien Anne Ball; two *s. Educ:* John Bright Grammar Sch., Llandudno; Dartford Grammar Sch. Served RE, 1948–50. HM Treasury, 1951–68 and 1970–78; CSD, 1968–70; Principal 1968, Asst Sec. 1976; Counsellor (Economic), Washington, 1978–80. Chm., Review of BBC External Services, 1984. *Address:* c/o HM Treasury, Parliament Street, SW1.
See also P. G. Perry.

PERRY, Charles Bruce; Professor of Medicine, University of Bristol, 1935–69, Emeritus since 1969; *b* 1903; *s* of Charles E. and Sarah Duthie Perry; *m* 1929, Mildred Bernice Harvey; three *d. Educ:* Bristol Grammar Sch.; University of Bristol, MB, ChB 1926, MD 1928; FRCP, 1936. Physician, Bristol Royal Hospital for Sick Children and Women, 1928; Physician, Winford Orthopædic Hospital, 1930; Buckston Browne Prize, Harveian Society of London, 1929; Markham Skeritt Memorial Prize, 1931; Asst Physician, Bristol General Hospital, 1933. Lectures: Long Fox Memorial, 1943; Bradshaw, RCP, 1944; Lumleian, RCP, 1969; Carey Coombs, Univ. of Bristol, 1969; Cyril Fernando Meml, Ceylon, 1971. Pro-Vice-Chancellor, University of Bristol, 1958–61 (Hon. Fellow, 1986); President Assoc. of Physicians of Great Britain and Ireland, 1961–62; Chairman, British Cardiac Society, 1961–62; Censor, RCP, 1962–64; Medical Mem., Pensions Appeals Tribunals, 1969–79; Trustee, Jenner Appeal, 1982–. *Publications:* Bacterial Endocarditis, 1936; The Bristol Royal Infirmary 1904–1974, 1981; various papers in the Medical Press dealing with research in Diseases of the Heart. *Address:* Beechfield, 54 Grove Road, Coombe Dingle, Bristol BS9 2RR. *T:* Bristol 682713.

PERRY, Sir David (Howard), KCB 1986; Chief of Defence Equipment Collaboration, Ministry of Defence, since 1985; *b* 13 April 1931; *s* of Howard Dace Perry and Annie Evelyn Perry; *m* 1961, Rosemary Grigg; one *s* two *d. Educ:* Berkhamsted Sch.; Pembroke Coll., Cambridge (MA). CEng, FRAeS. Joined Aero Dept, RAE, 1954; Aero Flt Div., 1954–66; Aero Projs Div., 1966–71; Head of Dynamics Div., 1971–73; RCDS, 1974; Head of Systems Assessment Dept, RAE, 1975–77; Ministry of Defence (Procurement Executive): Dir-Gen. Future Projects, 1978–80; Dir-Gen. Aircraft 1, 1980–81; Dep. Controller of Aircraft, 1981–82, Controller of Aircraft 1982; Chief of Defence Procurement, 1983–85. *Recreations:* gardening, painting. *Address:* Ministry of Defence, Horse Guards Avenue, Whitehall, SW1A 2HB.

PERRY, Sir David Norman; see Perry, Sir Norman.

PERRY, Ernest George; *b* 25 April 1908; British; *m* 1950, Edna Joyce Perks-Mankelow; one *s. Educ:* LCC secondary school. Textiles, 1923–33; Insurance, 1933–64. Member Battersea Borough Council, 1934–65 (Mayor of Battersea, 1955–56); Alderman, London Borough of Wandsworth, 1964–72. MP (Lab) Battersea S, 1964–74, Wandsworth, Battersea S, 1974–79; Asst Govt Whip, 1968–69; Lord Commissioner, HM Treasury, 1969–70; an Opposition Whip, 1970–74; an Asst Govt Whip, 1974–75. Served with Royal Artillery, 1939–46: Indian Army and Indian Artillery (Troop Sgt); Far East, 1942–45. *Recreations:* local government, sport, reading. *Address:* 6 Brinkley Road, Worcester Park, Surrey KT4 8JF. *T:* 01–337 4679.

PERRY, Frances Mary, (Mrs Roy Hay), MBE 1962; VMH 1971; horticulturist; *b* 19 Feb. 1907; *d* of Richard and Isabella Everett; *m* 1st, 1930, Gerald Amos Perry (*d* 1964); one *s* (and one *s* decd); 2nd, 1977, Robert Edwin Hay, *qv. Educ:* Enfield County Sch.; Swanley Horticultural Coll. (later Wye Coll.). Diploma in Horticulture. Organiser for Agricl and Horticultural Educn, Mddx CC, 1943; Principal, Norwood Hall Inst. and Coll. of Horticulture, 1953–67. Veitch Meml Medal in Gold, RHS, 1964; Sara Francis Chapman Medal, Garden Club of America, 1973. *Publications:* Water Gardening, 1938; The Herbaceous Border, 1949; The Garden Pool, 1954; The Woman Gardener, 1955; (as Charles Hewitt) Flower Arrangement, 1955; Guide to Border Plants, 1957; Making Things Grow, 1960; Shrubs and Trees for the Smaller Garden, 1961; Penguin Water Gardens, 1962; Colour in the Garden, 1964; Book of Flowering Bulbs, Corms and Tubers, 1966; Flowers of the World, 1972; Gardening in Colour, 1972; Plants & Flowers, 1974; Good Gardeners Guide, 1976; Beautiful Leaved Plants, 1979; Water Garden, 1981;

(with Roy Hay) Tropical and Subtropical Plants, 1982. *Recreations:* flower stamps, photography. *Address:* Bulls Cross Cottage, Enfield, Mddx EN2 9HE.

PERRY, George Henry; *b* 24 Aug. 1920; *s* of Arthur and Elizabeth Perry; *m* 1944, Ida Garner; two *d. Educ:* elementary sch. and technical college. Engineering Apprentice, 1934–41. Naval Artificer, 1941–46 (Atlantic and Italy Stars; 1939–45 Star). Railway Fitter, 1946–66. Derby Town Councillor, 1955–66. Chairman: Derby Water Cttee, 1957–61; S Derbys Water Board, 1961–66; Derby Labour Party, 1961–62; Secretary, Derby Trades Council, 1961–66. Contested (Lab) Harborough, 1964; MP (Lab) Nottingham South, 1966–70. *Recreation:* walking. *Address:* 123 Hawthorn Street, Derby. *T:* Derby 44687.

PERRY, Rev. John Neville; *b* 29 March 1920; *s* of Robert and Enid Perry; *m* 1946, Rita Dyson Rooke; four *s* four *d. Educ:* The Crypt Gram. Sch., Gloucester; Univ. of Leeds (BA 1941), College of the Resurrection, Mirfield. Asst Curate, All Saints', Poplar, 1943–50; Vicar, St Peter De Beauvoir Town, Hackney, 1950–63; Vicar, St Dunstan with St Catherine, Feltham, Mddx, 1963–75; Rural Dean of Hounslow, 1967–75; Archdeacon of Middlesex, 1975–82; Rector of Orlestone with Ruckinge and Warehorne, Kent, 1982–86. Mem. Latey Cttee on the Age of Majority, 1966–67. *Recreations:* D-I-Y handyman. *Address:* 73 Elizabeth Crescent, East Grinstead, West Sussex RH19 3JG.

PERRY, Ven. Michael Charles, MA; Archdeacon of Durham and Canon Residentiary of Durham Cathedral since 1970; *b* 5 June 1933; *o s* of late Charlie Perry; *m* 1963, Margaret, *o d* of late John Middleton Adshead; two *s* one *d. Educ:* Ashby-de-la-Zouch Boys' Grammar Sch.; Trinity Coll., Cambridge (Sen. Schol.); Westcott House, Cambridge. Asst Curate of Berkswich, Stafford, 1958–60; Chaplain, Ripon Hall, Oxford, 1961–63; Chief Asst for Home Publishing, SPCK, 1963–70; Examining Chaplain to Bishop of Lichfield, 1965–74. Sec., Archbishops' Commn on Christian Doctrine, 1967–70. Diocesan Chm., 1970–81, Mem. Council, 1975–81, USPG; Mem., 1981–, Vice-Chm., 1982–, Hosp. Chaplaincies Council, and Mem. Council for the Deaf, 1986–, Gen. Synod. Mem., Durham HA, 1982–. Trustee, 1970–, Chm., 1982–, Lord Crewe's Charity; Chm., Churches' Fellowship for Psychical and Spiritual Studies, 1986–. Lectures: Selwyn, NZ, 1976; Marshall Meml, Melbourne, 1976; Beard Meml, London, 1977; Maurice Elliott Meml, London, 1986. Editor, Church Quarterly, 1968–71; Editor, Christian Parapsychologist, 1977–. *Publications:* The Easter Enigma, 1959; The Pattern of Matins and Evensong, 1961; (co-author) The Churchman's Companion, 1963; Meet the Prayer Book, 1963; (contrib.) The Miracles and the Resurrection, 1964; (ed) Crisis for Confirmation, 1967; (co-author) Declaring The Faith: The Printed Word, 1969; Sharing in One Bread, 1973; The Resurrection of Man, 1975; The Paradox of Worship, 1977; A Handbook of Parish Worship, 1977; (contrib.) Yes to Women Priests, 1978; (co-author) A Handbook of Parish Finance, 1981; Psychic Studies: a Christian's view, 1984; Miracles Then & Now, 1986; (ed) Deliverance, 1987. *Address:* 7 The College, Durham DH1 3EQ. *T:* Durham 3861891. *Club:* Royal Commonwealth Society.

PERRY, Sir Norman, Kt 1977; MBE; Consultant: Whakatohea Maori Trust Board; Coast Resource Developments; Coast Biologicals Ltd. Knighthood awarded for services to the community and the Maori people, New Zealand. *Address:* Waiotahi, Opotiki, New Zealand; PO Box 162, Opotiki, New Zealand.

PERRY, Mrs Pauline; Chief Inspector, HM Inspectorate of Schools, since 1981; *b* 15 Oct. 1931; *d* of John George Embleton Welch and Elizabeth Welch; *m* 1952, George Walter Perry; three *s* one *d. Educ:* Girton Coll., Cambridge (MA). Teacher in English Secondary Sch., Canadian and American High Schs, 1953–54 and 1959–61; High School Evaluator, New England, USA, 1959–61; Research Fellow, Univ. of Manitoba, 1956–57; Lecturer in Philosophy (part-time): Univ. of Manitoba, 1957–59; Univ. of Massachusetts at Salem, 1960–62; Lectr in Education (part-time), Univ. of Exeter, 1962–66; Tutor for In-Service Trng, Berks, 1966–70; Part-time Lectr in Educn, Dept of Educational Studies, Oxford Univ., 1966–70; HM Inspector of Schools, 1970–; Staff Inspector, 1975. *Publications:* Case Studies in Teaching, 1969; Case Studies in Adolescence, 1970; Your Guide to the Opposite Sex, 1970; articles in various educnl jls; freelance journalism for radio and TV. *Recreations:* music, walking, cooking. *Address:* 35 Winsham Grove, SW11 0NB. *T:* 01–228 0434. *Club:* National Liberal.

PERRY, Peter George, CB 1983; JP; Under Secretary, Department of Health and Social Security, 1975–84; *b* 15 Dec. 1923; *s* of late Joseph and Elsie Perry; *m* 1957, Marjorie Margaret Stevens; no *c. Educ:* Dartford Grammar Sch.; London Univ. (LLB). Normandy with Northants Yeomanry, 1944. Joined Min. of Health, 1947; Private Sec. to Minister of State, 1968–70; Asst Sec., 1971. Mem., Industrial Tribunals, 1984–. JP City of London, 1974; Freeman, City of London, 1975. *Recreations:* sailing, squash, opera, wine. *Address:* 50 Great Brownings, College Road, Dulwich, SE21. *T:* 01–670 3387. *Club:* Little Ship.
See also A. J. Perry.

PERRY, Lt-Col Robert Stanley Grosvenor, DSO 1943; DL; *b* 1909; *s* of late Robert Grosvenor Perry, CBE, Barton House, Moreton-in-Marsh, Glos; *m* 1937, Margaret Louisa Elphinstone, *o c* of Horace Czarnikow; one *s. Educ:* Harrow; RMC, Sandhurst. 2nd Lieut, 9th Lancers, 1929, Major, 1941; Adjutant, Cheshire Yeomanry, 1938–40; Commanding: 2nd Lothians and Border Yeomanry, 1943; 9th Lancers, 1944–45; served War of 1939–45, Palestine, Western Desert, N Africa, Italy (despatches, wounded twice); Commandant, RACOCTU, 1945–48. One of HM Bodyguard of Hon. Corps of Gentlemen at Arms, 1959–79. High Sheriff of Dorset, 1961. DL Dorset, 1962. Member British Olympic Yachting Team, Helsinki, 1952, Melbourne (Silver Medal), 1956; Winner: Cup of Italy with Vision (5.5 Metre), 1956; One Ton Cup with Royal Thames (6 Metre), 1958. *Recreations:* yacht racing, foxhunting, National Hunt racing. *Address:* Crendle Court, Purse Caundle, Sherborne, Dorset. *T:* Milborne Port 250364. *Clubs:* Cavalry and Guards, Royal Yacht Squadron.

PERRY, Prof. Samuel Victor, BSc (Liverpool), PhD, ScD (Cantab); FRS 1974; Professor of Biochemistry, 1959–85, now Emeritus, and Head of Department of Biochemistry, 1968–85, University of Birmingham; *b* 16 July 1918; *s* of late Samuel and Margaret Perry; *m* 1948, Maureen Tregent Shaw; one *s* two *d. Educ:* King George V Sch., Southport; Liverpool Univ.; Trinity Coll., Cambridge. Served in War of 1939–45, home and N. Africa; Royal Artillery, 1940–46, Captain; POW 1942–45. Research Fellow, Trinity Coll., Cambridge, 1947–51; Commonwealth Fund Fellow, University of Rochester, USA, 1948–49; University Lecturer, Dept of Biochemistry, Cambridge, 1950–59. Member: Standing Cttee for Research on Animals, ARC, 1965–72; Biol Scis and Enzyme Cttees, SRC, 1968–71; Medical Res. Cttee, Muscular Dystrophy Gp of GB, 1970–; Systems Bd, MRC, 1974–77; Research Funds Cttee, British Heart Foundn, 1974–82; British Nat. Cttee for Biochemistry, 1978– (Chm., 1982–); Chairman: Cttee of Biochemical Soc., 1980–83; Adv. Bd, Meat Res. Inst., 1980–85. Croonian Lectr, Royal Soc., 1984. Hon. Mem., Amer. Soc. of Biol Chemists, 1978; Corresponding Mem., Société Royale des Sciences, Liège, 1978; Mem., Accad. Virgiliana, Mantova, 1979. CIBA Medal, Biochemical Soc., 1977. *Publications:* scientific papers in Biochemical Journal, Nature, Biochemica Biophysica Acta, etc. *Recreations:* gardening, building stone walls, Rugby football (Cambridge, 1946, 1947, England, 1947, 1948). *Address:* 64 Meadow Hill Road, King's Norton, Birmingham B38 8DA. *T:* 021–458 1511.

PERRY, William Arthur; Regional Marketing Director 2, Defence Sales Organisation, Ministry of Defence, since 1984; *b* 5 Aug. 1937; *s* of Arthur Perry and Elizabeth Grace (*née* Geller); *m* 1962, Anne Rosemary Dight; two *d. Educ:* St Dunstan's Coll. Min. of Aviation, 1960–61; Second Sec. (Defence Supply), Bonn, 1964–66; Min. of Technology, then MoD, 1966–74; First Sec., UK Delegn to NATO, 1974–77; Head, Defence Secretariat 8, MoD, 1978–80; Counsellor (Defence Supply), Bonn, 1980–84. *Recreations:* opera, gardening, philately, genealogy. *Address:* c/o Ministry of Defence, Stuart House, Soho Square, W1V 5FJ.

PERRY-KEENE, Air Vice-Marshal Allan Lancelot Addison, CB 1947; OBE 1940; RAF (retired); *b* 10 Nov. 1898; *s* of late L. H. A. and M. Perry-Keene; *m* 1923, K. L., *d* of late C. A. S. Silberrad, ICS; two *d. Educ:* Wolverley; King Edward's, Birmingham. Served European War, 1914–18; joined RFC, 1917; France, 1918–19; transferred RAF, 1918; Iraq, 1927–29; India, 1935–41; Burma and India, 1942; Director of Ground Training and Training Plans, Air Ministry, 1943–45; AOC 227 Group, India, and 3 (Indian) Group, 1946; Air Officer i/c Administration, Air HQ, India, 1946; Air Commander, Royal Pakistan Air Force, 1947–49. *Address:* Millway House, Weyhill, Andover, Hants SP11 8DE.

PERRYMAN, Francis Douglas; Corporate Commercial Director, British Telecommunications, since 1986; *b* 23 April 1930; *s* of Frank Smyth Perryman and Caroline Mary Anderson; *m* 1955, Margaret Mary Lamb; two *d. Educ:* West Hartlepool Grammar School; Durham Univ. BCom (Hons); FCA. Articled Clerk, 1951–55; Nat. Service, commnd RAPC, 1955–57; National Coal Board: Area Chief Accountant, Fife and Scottish South Areas, 1963–72; Finance Dir, Opencast Exec., 1972; Dir Gen. of Finance, 1978–81; Board Mem. for Finance, PO, 1981; Bd Mem., then Corporate Dir, for Finance, BT, 1981–86. FRSA. *Recreations:* golf, Rugby football, music, Francophile. *Address:* Long Mynd, 69 Copperkins Lane, Amersham, Bucks. *T:* Amersham 21611.

PERSSON, Rt. Rev. William Michael Dermot; *see* Doncaster, Bishop Suffragan of.

PERTH, 17th Earl of, *cr* 1605; **John David Drummond,** PC 1957; Baron Drummond of Cargill, 1488; Baron Maderty, 1609; Baron Drummond, 1686; Lord Drummond of Gilston, 1685; Lord Drummond of Rickertoun and Castlemaine, 1686; Viscount Strathallan, 1686; Hereditary Thane of Lennox, and Hereditary Steward of Menteith and Strathearn; Representative Peer for Scotland, 1952–63; First Crown Estate Commissioner, 1962–77; Chairman, Ditchley Foundation, 1963–66; *b* 13 May 1907; *o s* of 16th Earl of Perth, PC, GCMG, CB, and Hon. Angela Constable-Maxwell (*d* 1965), *y d* of 11th Baron Herries; *S* father 1951; *m* 1934, Nancy Seymour, *d* of Reginald Fincke, New York City; two *s. Educ:* Downside; Cambridge Univ. Lieut, Intelligence Corps, 1940; seconded to War Cabinet Offices, 1942–43, Ministry of Production, 1944–45; Minister of State for Colonial Affairs, 1957–62 (resigned). Chm., Reviewing Cttee on Export of Works of Art, 1972–76. Member: Court of St Andrews Univ., 1967–86; Adv. Council, V&A Museum, 1971–72; Trustee, Nat. Library of Scotland, 1968–. Hon. FRIBA 1978. Hon. LLD St Andrews, 1986. *Heir: s* Viscount Strathallan, *qv. Address:* 14 Hyde Park Gardens Mews, W2. *T:* 01–262 4667; Stobhall, by Perth.

PERTH, (St Ninian's Cathedral), Provost of; *see* Forbes, Very Rev. G. J. T.

PERTH (Australia), Archbishop of, and Metropolitan of Western Australia, since 1981; **Most Rev. Peter Frederick Carnley;** *b* 17 Oct. 1937; *s* of Frederick Carnley and Gweyenneth Lilian Carnley (*née* Read); *m* 1966, Carol Ann Dunstan; one *s* one *d. Educ:* St John's Coll., Morpeth, NSW (ThL 1st Cl., ACT, 1962); Univ. of Melbourne (BA, 1st Cl. Hons, 1966); Univ. of Cambridge (PhD 1969). Deacon 1962, priest 1964, Bath; Licence to Officiate, dio. Melbourne, 1963–65; Asst Curate of Parkes, 1966; Licence to Officiate, dio. Ely, 1966–69; Chaplain, Mitchell Coll. of Advanced Education, Bath, 1970–72; Research Fellow, St John's Coll., Cambridge, 1971–72; Warden, St John's College, St Lucia, Queensland, 1972–81; Residentiary Canon, St John's Cathedral, Brisbane, 1975–81; Examining Chaplain to Archbishop of Brisbane, 1975–81. DD *hc*, Gen. Theological Seminary, NY, 1984. ChStJ 1982. *Publications:* The Poverty of Historical Scepticism, in Christ, Faith and History (ed S. W. Sykes and J. P. Clayton), 1972; The Structure of Resurrection Belief, 1986. *Recreations:* gardening, swimming. *Address:* 52 Mount Street, Perth, WA 6000, Australia. *T:* 322 1777. *Clubs:* Weld, Western Australian (Perth); Royal Perth Yacht; St John's (Brisbane).

PERTH (Australia), Archbishop of, (RC), since 1983; **Most Rev. William J. Foley;** *b* 20 June 1931; *s* of Maurice and Augusta Foley. *Educ:* Christian Brothers' Coll., Perth, WA; St Charles Seminary, Guildford, WA; Brignole-Sale Coll., Genoa, Italy. Diocesan Director of Mission Aid Societies and Catholic Migration and Welfare Assoc., Perth, 1962–69; Diocesan Promoter of Vocations, Perth, 1969–71; Parish Priest, Maddington-Lynwood, 1971–76; Dean/Administrator, St Mary's Cathedral, 1976–81; Bishop of Geraldton, WA, 1981–83. Diocesan Priest Adviser to Christian Life Groups, Perth; State Chaplain, Knights of Southern Cross; Chm., Senate of Priests. Mem., Aust. Episcopal Cttees on Education, Mission, Liturgy. *Recreation:* golf. *Address:* St Mary's Cathedral, Victoria Square, Perth, WA 6000, Australia. *T:* 3259557.

PERTH (Australia), Assistant Bishops of; *see* Challen, Rt Rev. M. B.; Kyme, Rt Rev. B. R.

PERU, Bishop of, since 1978; **Rt. Rev. David Richard John Evans;** with delegated jurisdiction of Bolivia, since 1980; *b* 5 June 1938; *s* of William Henry Reginald Evans and Beatrix Catherine Mottram; *m* 1964, Dorothy Evelyn Parsons; one *s* two *d. Educ:* Caius College, Cambridge. Hons degree in Mod. Langs and Theology, 1963, MA 1966. Curate, Christ Church, Cockfosters, 1965–68; Missionary Pastor and Gen. Sec., Argentine Inter-Varsity Christian Fellowship, in Buenos Aires, Argentina, 1969–77; Chaplain, Good Shepherd Church, Lima, Peru, 1977–82. *Publication:* En Diálogo con Dios, 1976. *Recreations:* squash and philately. *Address:* Apartado 5152, Lima 18, Peru, S America. *T:* 45–3878.

PERUTZ, Max Ferdinand, CH 1975; CBE 1963; PhD; FRS 1954; Member, scientific staff, Medical Research Council Laboratory of Molecular Biology, 1979– (Chairman, 1962–79); *b* 19 May 1914; *s* of Hugo and Adèle Perutz; *m* 1942, Gisela Peiser; one *s* one *d. Educ:* Theresianum, Vienna; Univ. of Vienna; Univ. of Cambridge (PhD 1940). Hon. Fellow: Peterhouse, Cambridge, 1962; Darwin Coll., Cambridge, 1984. Dir, MRC Unit for Molecular Biology, 1947–62; Chm., European Molecular Biology Orgn, 1963–69. Reader, Davy Faraday Res. Lab., 1954–68, and Fullerian Prof. of Physiology, 1973–79, Royal Instn. Hon. FRSE, 1976; Hon. Member American Academy of Arts and Sciences, 1963; Corresp. Member, Austrian Acad. of Sciences, 1963; Mem., Akademie Leopoldina, Halle, 1964; Foreign Member: American Philosophical Society, 1968; Royal Netherlands Acad., 1972; French Acad. of Sciences, 1976; Bavarian Acad. of Sciences, 1983; National Acad. of Sciences, Rome, 1983; Accademia dei Lincei, Rome, 1984; Acad. of Science of DDR, 1985; For. Associate, Nat. Acad. of Sciences, USA, 1970; Mem., Pontifical Acad. of Sciences, Rome, 1981. Nobel Prize for Chemistry (jointly), 1962; Royal Medal, 1971, Copley Medal, 1979, Royal Soc. Actonian Prize, Royal Instn, 1984. Hon. degrees: in philosophy: Vienna, 1965; Salzburg, 1972; in science: Edinburgh, 1965; East Anglia, 1967; Cambridge, 1981. *Publications:* Proteins and Nucleic Acids, Structure and Function, 1962; (jtly) Atlas of Haemoglobin and Myoglobin, 1981; Ging's ohne Forschung besser?, 1982. *Address:* 42 Sedley Taylor Road, Cambridge; Laboratory of Molecular Biology, Hills Road, Cambridge.

PERY, family name of **Earl of Limerick.**

PESCOD, Prof. Mainwaring Bainbridge, OBE 1977; CEng, FICE, FIPHE, FIWES; Tyne and Wear Professor of Environmental Control Engineering, since 1976, and Head of Department of Civil Engineering and of School of Civil and Mining Engineering, since 1983, University of Newcastle upon Tyne; *b* 6 Jan. 1933; *s* of Bainbridge and Elizabeth Pescod; *m* 1957, Mary Lorenza (*née* Coyle); two *s. Educ:* Stanley Grammar Sch., Co. Durham; King's Coll., Univ. of Durham (BSc); MIT (SM). CEng 1973, FICE 1980; FIPHE 1971; FIWES 1983; MIWPC 1967; MRSH 1964; MInstWM 1985. Lectr in Engrg, Fourah Bay Coll, Freetown, Sierra Leone, 1957–61; Asst Engr, Babtie, Shaw & Morton, CCE, Glasgow, 1961–64; Asst and Associate Prof. of Environmental Engrg, 1964–72, Prof. and Head of Div. of Environmental Engrg, 1972–76, Asian Inst. of Technol., Bangkok, Thailand. *Publications:* (ed with D. A. Okun) Water Supply and Wastewater Disposal in Developing Countries, 1971; pubns on water supply, wastewater treatment, environmental pollution control and management in learned jls and conf. proc. *Recreations:* squash, reading, advisory assignments in developing countries. *Address:* Tall Trees, High Horse Close Wood, Rowlands Gill, Tyne and Wear NE39 1AN. *T:* Rowlands Gill 542104. *Clubs:* British, Royal Bangkok Sports (Bangkok, Thailand).

PESKETT, Stanley Victor, MA; Principal, Royal Belfast Academical Institution, 1959–78; *b* 9 May 1918; *o s* of late Sydney Timber and late Mary Havard Peskett; *m* 1948, Prudence Eileen, OBE 1974, *o d* of late C. R. A. Goatly, Calcutta; two *s* one *d* (and one *d* decd). *Educ:* Whitgift Sch.; St Edmund Hall, Oxford. Served War, 1939–46 (despatches) in Royal Marines, Norway, Shetland, Normandy, India and Java; Lt-Col, 1944; two Admiralty awards for inventions. Senior English Master, 1946–59, Housemaster 1954–59, The Leys School. Mem. Cttee, Headmasters' Conf., 1976; Mem. Council, Headmasters' Assoc., and Pres., Ulster Headmasters' Assoc., 1973–75; Chm., Northern Ireland Cttee, Voluntary Service Overseas, 1969–78; Founder Pres., Irish Schools Swimming Assoc., 1968–69 (Chm., Ulster Branch, 1968–78); Chm., NI Branch, School Library Assoc., 1964–73; Governor, Belfast Sch. of Music, 1974–77; Mem. Adv. Council, UDR, 1975–78. *Publications:* The Metfield Clock, 1980; (contrib.) People, Poverty and Protest in Hoxne Hundred 1780–1880, 1982; articles in educational jls. *Address:* Huntsman and Hounds Cottage, Metfield, Harleston, Norfolk IP20 0LB. *T:* Fressingfield 425.

PESTELL; *see* Wells-Pestell.

PESTELL, Catherine Eva, CMG 1984; HM Diplomatic Service; Minister (Economic), Bonn, since 1983; *b* 24 Sept. 1933; *d* of Edmund Ernest Pestell and Isabella Cummine Sangster. *Educ:* Leeds Girls' High Sch.; St Hilda's Coll., Oxford (MA). FO, 1956; Third Sec., The Hague, 1958; Second Sec., Bangkok, 1961; FO, 1964; First Sec., UK Delegn to OECD, Paris, 1969; FCO, 1971; St Antony's Coll., Oxford, 1974; Counsellor, East Berlin, 1975–78; Cabinet Office, 1978–80; Diplomatic Service Inspector, 1980–82. *Address:* c/o Foreign and Commonwealth Office, SW1A 2AH.
See also J. E. Pestell.

PESTELL, John Edmund; Assistant Under-Secretary of State, Ministry of Defence, since 1984; *b* 8 Dec. 1930; *s* of late Edmund Pestell and of Isabella (*née* Sangster); *m* 1958, Muriel Ada (*née* Whitby); three *s. Educ:* Roundhay Sch.; New Coll., Oxford (MA). National Service (Intell. Corps), 1949–50. Jt Intell. Bureau, 1953–57; Asst Principal, WO, 1957–60; Private Sec. to Parly Under Sec. of State for War, 1958–60; Principal, WO and MoD, 1960–70; Admin. Staff Coll., Henley, 1963; Private Sec. to Minister of Defence (Equipment), 1969–70; Asst Sec., MoD, 1970–72; Press Sec. (Co-ordination), Prime Minister's Office, 1972–74; Asst Sec., CSD, 1974–76, Under Sec., 1976–81; Under Sec., HM Treasury, 1981–84. Mem., CS Pay Res. Unit, 1978–80. Governor, Cranleigh Sch., 1975–. *Address:* New House, Bridge Road, Cranleigh, Surrey. *T:* Cranleigh 273489.
See also C. E. Pestell.

PESTELL, Sir John Richard, KCVO 1969; an Adjudicator, Immigration Appeals, Harmondsworth, since 1970; *b* 21 Nov. 1916; *s* of late Lt-Comdr Frank Lionel Pestell, RN, and Winifred Alice Pestell; *m* 1951, Betty Pestell (*née* Parish); three *d. Educ:* Portsmouth Northern Secondary Sch. Joined British South Africa Police, Southern Rhodesia, 1939; retired, 1965, with rank of Asst Commissioner. Served, 1944–47, Gen. List, MELF, in Cyrenaica Defence Force. Secretary/Controller to Governor of S Rhodesia, Rt Hon. Sir H. V. Gibbs, 1965–69. *Recreation:* walking. *Address:* Monks Walk, Ferry Lane, Medmenham, Marlow, Bucks.

PETCH, Barry Irvine, FCA; Vice President, Finance, IBM Europe, since 1983; *b* 12 Oct. 1933; *s* of Charles Reginald Petch and Anne (*née* Fryer); *m* 1966, Anne Elisabeth (*née* Johannessen); two *s* one *d. Educ:* Doncaster Grammar Sch. FCA 1967. IBM United Kingdom Ltd, 1959–80; Controller, IBM Europe, 1981–83. Part-time Mem., Price Commn, 1973–77. *Recreations:* tennis, sailing. *Address:* Les Moukelins, Chemin des Hauts de Grisy, 78860 St Nom La Breteche, France. *Club:* Reform.

PETCH, Prof. Norman James, FRS 1974; FEng; Professor of Metallurgy, University of Strathclyde, 1973–82, now Emeritus Professor; *b* 13 Feb. 1917; 3rd *s* of George and Jane Petch, Bearsden, Dunbartonshire; *m* 1st, 1942, Marion Blight (marr. diss. 1947); 2nd, 1949, Eileen Allen (*d* 1975); two *d*; 3rd, 1976, Marjorie Jackson. *Educ:* Queen Mary Coll., London; Sheffield Univ. Research at Cavendish Lab., Cambridge, 1939–42; Royal Aircraft Establishment, 1942–46; Cavendish Laboratory, 1946–48; British Iron and Steel Research Assoc., Sheffield, 1948–49; Reader in Metallurgy, Leeds Univ., 1949–56; First Professor of Metallurgy, Leeds Univ., 1956–59; Cochrane Prof. of Metallurgy, 1959–73, a Pro-Vice-Chancellor, 1968–71, Univ. of Newcastle upon Tyne. Former Member: Basic Properties of Metals Cttee, Interservice Metallurgical Res. Council; Ship Steels Cttee, Admiralty; Physics Cttee, Aeronautical Res. Council; Carbon Steel Cttee, BSC; Plasticity Div. Cttee, Nat. Engrg Lab.; former Regional Editor: Acta Metallurgica; Internat. Jl of Fracture. Royal Society: Mem. Council, 1979–81; Chm., Scientific Relief Cttee, 1983–. *Address:* Findon Cottage, Culbokie, Conon Bridge, Ross-shire IV7 8JJ. *T:* Culbokie 259.

PETERBOROUGH, Bishop of, since 1984; **Rt. Rev. William John Westwood;** *b* 28 Dec. 1925; *s* of Ernest and Charlotte Westwood; *m* 1954, Shirley Ann, *yr d* of Dr Norman Jennings; one *s* one *d. Educ:* Grove Park Grammar Sch., Wrexham; Emmanuel Coll. and Westcott House, Cambridge. MA Cantab. Soldier, 1944–47. Curate of Hull, 1952–57; Rector of Lowestoft, 1957–65; Vicar of S Peter Mancroft, Norwich, 1965–75; Hon. Canon, Norwich Cathedral, 1969–75; Rural Dean of Norwich, 1966–70, City Dean, 1970–73; Area Bishop of Edmonton, 1975–84. Member: General Synod, 1970–75 and 1977–; Archbishop's Commission on Church and State, 1966–70; Press Council, 1975–81; Church Commissioner, 1973–78 and 1985–; Chm., C of E Cttee for Communications,

1979–86; Member: IBA Panel of Religious Advisers, 1983–; Video Consultative Council, 1985–; broadcaster. Chm. Governors, Coll. of All Saints, Tottenham, 1976–78. Pres., Church Housing Assoc., 1985–. *Recreation:* modern poetry. *Address:* The Palace, Peterborough, Cambs PE1 1YA.

PETERBOROUGH, Dean of; *see* Wise, Very Rev. R. G.

PETERKEN, Laurence Edwin; General Manager, Greater Glasgow Health Board, since 1986; *b* 2 Oct. 1931; *s* of Edwin James Peterken and Constance Fanny (*née* Giffin); *m* 1st, 1955, Hanne Birgithe Von Der Recke (decd); one *s* one *d*; 2nd, 1970, Margaret Raynal Blair; one *s* one *d*. *Educ:* Harrow Sch. (Scholar); Peterhouse, Cambridge (Scholar); MA. Pilot Officer, RAF Regt, Adjt No 20 LAA Sqdn, 1950–52. Service Div. Manager, Hotpoint Ltd, 1961–63, Commercial Dir, 1963–66; Man. Dir, British Domestic Appliances Ltd, 1966–68; Dir, British Printing Corporation Ltd, 1969–73; Debenhams Ltd: Man. Dir, Fashion Multiple Div., 1974–76; Management Auditor, 1976–77; Controller, Operational Services, GLC, 1977–85. Chairman: Working Party on Disposal of Clinical Waste in London, 1982–83; GLC Chief Officers' Guild, 1983–85. Acting Dir, Royal Festival Hall, 1983–85, to implement open foyer policy. Churchwarden, Haslemere Parish Church, 1985–86. *Recreations:* opera, painting. *Address:* 25 Kingsborough Gardens, Glasgow G12. *Club:* Athenæum.

PETERKIEWICZ, Prof. Jerzy; novelist and poet; Professor of Polish Language and Literature, University of London, 1972–79; *b* 29 Sept. 1916; *s* of late Jan Pietrkiewicz and Antonina (*née* Politowska). *Educ:* Dlugosz Sch., Wloclawek; Univ. of Warsaw; Univ. of St Andrews (MA 1944); King's Coll., London (PhD 1947). Freelance writer until 1950; Reader (previously Lectr) in Polish Language and Literature, Sch. of Slavonic and East European Studies, Univ. of London, 1952–72, Head of Dept of E European Lang. and Lit., 1972–77. *Publications:* Prowincja, 1936; Wiersze i poematy, 1938; Pogrzeb Europy, 1946; The Knotted Cord, 1953; Loot and Loyalty, 1955; Polish Prose and Verse, 1956; Antologia liryki angielskiej, 1958; Future to Let, 1958; Isolation, 1959; (with Burns Singer) Five Centuries of Polish Poetry, 1960 (enlarged edn 1970); The Quick and the Dead, 1961; That Angel Burning at my Left Side, 1963; Poematy londynskie, 1965; Inner Circle, 1966; Green Flows the Bile, 1969; The Other Side of Silence (The Poet at the Limits of Language), 1970; The Third Adam, 1975; (ed and trans.) Easter Vigil and other Poems, by Karol Wojtyla (Pope John Paul II), 1979; Kula magiczna (Poems 1934–52), 1980; (ed and trans.) Collected Poems, by Karol Wojtyla (Pope John Paul II), 1982; Poezje wybrane (Selected Poems), 1986; essays, poems and articles in various periodicals. *Recreation:* travels, outward and inward. *Address:* 7 Lyndhurst Terrace, NW3.

PETERKIN, Sir Neville (Allan Mercer), Kt 1981; Chief Justice, West Indies Associated States, 1980–84; *b* 27 Oct. 1915; *s* of Joseph Allan Peterkin and Evelyn Peterkin; *m* 1942, Beryl Thompson; two *s* one *d*. *Educ:* Wellington Sch., Somerset, England. Called to Bar, Middle Temple, 1939. Registrar, St Lucia, 1943; Magistrate, Trinidad and Tobago, 1944; Resident Magistrate, Jamaica, 1954; High Court Judge: Trinidad, 1957; Associated States, 1967; Justice of Appeal, Associated States, 1975. *Recreations:* golf, bridge. *Address:* 16 Becune Point, Cap Estate, St Lucia, West Indies. *T:* 8447.

PETERS, Rt. Rev. Arthur Gordon; *see* Nova Scotia, Bishop of.

PETERS, Prof. David Keith, FRCP; Professor of Medicine, and Director of the Department of Medicine, Royal Postgraduate Medical School, Hammersmith Hospital, London, since 1977; *b* 26 July 1938; *s* of Herbert Lionel and Olive Peters; *m* 1st, 1961, Jean Mair Garfield (marr. diss. 1978); one *s* one *d*; 2nd, 1979, Pamela Wilson Ewan; one *s* one *d*. *Educ:* Welsh National Sch. of Medicine. MB, BCh, 1961; MRCP 1964; FRCP 1975. Junior posts in United Cardiff Hosps, 1961–65; Med. Research Council, Clinical Res. Fellowship, 1965–68; Lectr in Med., Welsh Nat. Sch. of Med., 1968–69; Royal Postgraduate Medical School: Lectr, 1969, Sen. Lectr, 1974, Reader in Med., 1975; Consultant Physician, Hammersmith Hosp., 1969–. Mem., MRC, 1984–. *Publications:* in various jls on immunology of renal disease. *Recreations:* tennis, chess. *Address:* 3 St Ann's Villas, W11 4RU. *T:* 01–603 1053. *Club:* Garrick.

PETERS, Ellis; *see* Pargeter, E.

PETERS, John; Assistant Under Secretary of State (Material Navy), Ministry of Defence, since 1984; *b* 5 Dec. 1929; *s* of Dr G. F. Peters and Mrs C. P. Peters; *m* 1955, Jane Catherine Mary Sheldon; one *s* two *d*. *Educ:* Downside Sch. (Scholar); Balliol Coll., Oxford (Exhibnr, MA). HM Forces, commissioned RAEC, 1948–49. Pres., Oxford Union Soc., 1953. Entered Administrative Class, Home Civil Service, Admiralty, 1953; PS to Civil Lord, 1956–59; Principal, 1959; PS to Navy Minister, 1964–67; PS to Minister of Defence (Equipment), 1967–68; Asst Sec., 1968; Dir of Naval Sales, 1968–72; Cabinet Office, 1974–75; Defence Counsellor, UK Delegn to NATO, Brussels, 1975–78; Asst Under Sec. of State (Air Staff), MoD, 1979–84. *Publication:* A Family from Flanders, 1985. *Address:* 60 Scotts Lane, Bromley, Kent. *T:* 01–650 0063. *Club:* United Oxford & Cambridge University.

PETERS, Kenneth Jamieson, CBE 1979; JP; DL; FSAScot; Director: Thomson North Sea Ltd, since 1981; Thomson Forestry Holdings Ltd, since 1982; Aberdeen Journals Ltd, since 1960 (Managing Director, 1960–80; Chairman, 1980–81); Member: Scottish Region Board, British Rail, since 1982; Girobank, Scotland Board, since 1984; *b* 17 Jan. 1923; *s* of William Jamieson Peters and Edna Rosa Peters (*née* Hayman); *m* 1951, Arunda Merle Jane Jones. *Educ:* Aberdeen Grammar Sch.; Aberdeen Univ. Served War of 1939–45: last rank Captain/Adjutant, 2nd Bn King's Own Scottish Borderers. Editorial staff, Daily Record and Evening News Ltd, 1947–51; Asst Editor: Evening Express, Aberdeen, 1951–52; Manchester Evening Chronicle, 1952–53; Editor: Evening Express, Aberdeen, 1953–56; The Press and Journal, Aberdeen, 1956–60; Pres., Scottish Daily Newspaper Soc., 1964–66 and 1974–76; Mem., Press Council, 1974–77; Director: Highland Printers Ltd (Inverness), 1968–83; Aberdeen Assoc. of Social Service, 1973–78; Thomson Regional Newspapers, 1974–80; Thomson Scottish Petroleum Ltd, 1981–86. Pres., Publicity Club of Aberdeen, 1972–; Member: Scottish Adv. Cttee of British Council, 1967–84; Cttee, Films of Scotland, 1970–82; Chm., NE Cttee, 1982–, Mem. Exec., 1982–, Scottish Council for Devlt and Industry; Mem., Peterhead Bay Harbour Authority Bd, 1983–; etc. FSAScot 1980; FBIM 1980; ACIT 1985. JP City of Aberdeen, 1961; DL Aberdeen, 1978. *Publications:* The Northern Lights, 1978; (ed) Great North Memories, vol. 1, 1978, vol. 2, 1981; Burgess of Guild, 1982. *Recreations:* cricket, Rugby football, walking. *Address:* 47 Abergeldie Road, Aberdeen AB1 6ED. *T:* Aberdeen 587647. *Clubs:* MCC; Royal Northern and University (Aberdeen).

PETERS, Mary Elizabeth, MBE 1973; self employed; Managing Director, Mary Peters Sports Ltd, since 1977; *b* 6 July 1939; *d* of Arthur Henry Peters and Hilda Mary Peters. *Educ:* Portadown Coll., Co. Armagh; Belfast Coll. of Domestic Science (DipDomSc). Represented Great Britain: Olympic Games: 4th place, Pentathlon, 1964; 1st, Pentathlon (world record), 1972; Commonwealth Games: 2nd, Shot, 1966; 1st, Shot, 1st Pentathlon, 1970; 1st, Pentathlon, 1974. Member: Sports Council, 1974–80; Northern Ireland Sports Council, 1974– (Vice-Chm., 1977–81); Ulster Games Foundn, 1984–; NI BBC Broadcasting Council, 1981–84. Dir, Churchill Foundn Fellowship Scholarship, Calif, 1972. Asst Sec., Multiple Sclerosis Soc., 1974–78; Pres., Old-Age Pensioners' Coal and Grocery Fund. Hon. Senior Athletic Coach, 1975–; BAAB Pentathlon Coach, 1976; Team Manager: GB women's athletic team, European Cup, 1979; GB women's athletic team, Moscow, 1980 and Los Angeles, 1984. Pres., NIWAAA, 1985–; Vice-President: Assoc. of Youth Clubs; NI Assoc. of Youth Clubs; Riding for the Disabled; Driving for the Disabled; Trustee, Ulster Sports Trust, 1972; Patron, NIAAA, 1981–. Awards: BBC Sports personality, 1972; Athletic Writers', 1972; Sports Writers', 1972; Elizabeth Arden Visible Difference, 1976; Athletics, Dublin (Texaco), 1970 and 1972. Hon. DSc, New Univ. of Ulster, 1974. *Publication:* Mary P., an autobiography, 1974. *Address:* Willowtree Cottage, River Road, Dunmurry, Belfast, N Ireland.

PETERS, Prof. Raymond Harry; Professor of Polymer and Fibre Science, University of Manchester, 1955–84, now Emeritus; *b* 19 Feb. 1918. *Educ:* County High Sch., Ilford; King's Coll., London Univ.; Manchester Univ. BSc (London) 1939, PhD (London), 1942, in Chemistry; BSc (Manchester), 1949, BSc (London), 1949, in Mathematics; DSc (London), 1968. Scientist at ICI Ltd, 1941–46 and 1949–55. Visiting Professor: UMIST, 1984–; Univ. of Strathclyde, 1984–. President, Society of Dyers and Colourists, 1967–68. *Publications:* Textile Chemistry: Vol. I, The Chemistry of Fibres, 1963; Vol. II, Impurities of Fibres: Purification of Fibres, 1967; Vol. III, Physical Chemistry of Dyeing, 1975; contributions to Journals of Chemical Society, Society of Dyers and Colourists, Textile Institute, British Journal of Applied Physics, etc. *Recreation:* gardening. *Address:* University of Manchester Institute of Science and Technology, Manchester M60 1QD. *T:* 061–236 3311.

PETERS, Prof. Richard Stanley, BA (Oxon), BA (London), PhD (London); Professor of the Philosophy of Education, University of London Institute of Education, 1962–82, now Emeritus Professor; Dean, Faculty of Education, London University, 1971–74; *b* 31 Oct. 1919; *s* of late Charles Robert and Mabel Georgina Peters; *m* 1943, Margaret Lee Duncan; one *s* two *d*. *Educ:* Clifton Coll., Bristol; Queen's Coll., Oxford; Birkbeck Coll., University of London. War service with Friends' Ambulance Unit and Friends' Relief Service in E. London, 1940–44. Classics Master, Sidcot School, Somerset, 1944–46; Birkbeck Coll., University of London: Studentship and part-time Lecturer in Philos. and Psychol., 1946–49; full-time Lecturer in Philos. and Psychol., 1949–58; Reader in Philosophy, 1958–62. Visiting Prof. of Education: Grad. School of Education, Harvard Univ., 1961; Univ. of Auckland, 1975; Visiting Fellow, Australian National Univ., 1969. Part-time lectureships, Bedford Coll., LSE; Tutor for University of London Tutorial Classes Cttee and Extension Cttee. Member, American National Academy of Education, 1966. *Publications:* (revised) Brett's History of Psychology, 1953; Hobbes, 1956; The Concept of Motivation, 1958; (with S. I. Benn) Social Principles and the Democratic State, 1959; Authority, Responsibility and Education, 1960; Ethics and Education, 1966; (ed) The Concept of Education, 1967; (ed) Perspectives on Plowden, 1969; (with P. H. Hirst) The Logic of Education, 1970; (ed with M. Cranston) Hobbes and Rousseau, 1971; (ed with R. F. Dearden and P. H. Hirst) Education and the Development of Reason, 1972; Reason and Compassion (Lindsay Meml Lectures), 1973; (ed) The Philosophy of Education, 1973; Psychology and Ethical Development, 1974; (ed) Nature and Conduct, 1975; (ed) The Role of the Head, 1976; Education and the Education of Teachers, 1977; (ed) John Dewey Reconsidered, 1977; Essays on Educators, 1981; Moral Development and Moral Education, 1981. *Address:* 16 Shepherd's Hill, N6.

PETERS, Theophilus, CMG 1967; HM Diplomatic Service, retired; Director, Theophilus Knapman & Co., since 1979; *b* 7 Aug. 1921; *er s* of late Mark Peters and Dorothy Knapman; *m* 1953, Lucy Bailey Summers, *d* of late Lionel Morgan Summers, Winter Park, Fla; two *s* three *d*. *Educ:* Exeter Sch., Exeter; St John's Coll., Cambridge (MA). Served War of 1939–45: 2nd Lieut, Intelligence Corps, 1942; Captain, 8 Corps HQ, 1944; Normandy, 1944; Holland, 1944–45 (despatches); Germany; Major. Entered HM Foreign (subseq. Diplomatic) Service; Vice-Consul/2nd Secretary, Peking, 1948; FO, 1951–52; Tripoli and Benghazi (Libya), 1953; FO, 1956; Dep. Secretary-General, Cento, 1960; Head of Chancery, Manila, 1962; Counsellor (Commercial), Peking, 1965; Dir, Diplomatic Service Language Centre, 1968–71, and Head of Training Dept, FCO, 1969–71; Counsellor and Consul-Gen., Buenos Aires, 1971–73; Consul-Gen., Antwerp, 1973–78. *Address:* c/o National Westminster Bank, Stamford, Lincs.

PETERS, Prof. Wallace, MD, DSc; FRCP; Professor of Medical Protozoology, London School of Hygiene and Tropical Medicine, University of London, since 1979; Joint Director, Malaria Reference Laboratory, Public Health Laboratory Service, since 1979; *b* 1 April 1924; *s* of Henry and Fanny Peters; *m* 1954, Ruth (*née* Scheidegger). *Educ:* Haberdashers' Aske's Sch.; St Bartholomew's Hosp., London. MB BS, 1947; MRCS, DTM&H. Served in RAMC, 1947–49; practised tropical medicine in West and East Africa, 1950–52; Staff Mem., WHO, Liberia and Nepal, 1952–55; Asst Dir (Malariology), Health Dept, Territory of Papua and New Guinea, 1956–61; Research Associate, CIBA, Basle, Switzerland, 1961–66; Walter Myers Prof. of Parasitology, Univ. of Liverpool, 1966–79. Dean, Liverpool Sch. of Tropical Medicine, 1975–78. Vice-Pres. and Pres., Brit. Soc. Parasit., 1972–76; Pres., Brit. Sect., Soc. Protozool., 1972–75; Vice-Pres., Royal Soc. of Trop. Medicine and Hygiene, 1982–83, 1985–. Chm., WHO Steering Cttee on Chemotherapy of Malaria, 1975–83; Member: Expert Adv. Panel, WHO, 1967–; WHO Steering Cttees on Leishmaniasis, 1979–; Editorial Bd, Ann. Trop. Med. Parasit., 1966–79; Trop. Med. Research Bd, MRC, 1973–77; Scientific Council, Inst. of Cellular and Molecular Path., 1981–84; Parasitol. Bd, Institut Pasteur, 1979–; Sec., European Fedn Parasit., 1979–84 (Vice-Pres., 1975–79). Rudolf Leuckart Medal, German Soc. of Parasitol., 1980; King Faisal Internat. Prize in Medicine, 1983. *Publications:* A Provisional Checklist of Butterflies of the Ethiopian Region, 1952; Chemotherapy and Drug Resistance in Malaria, 1970; (with H. M. Gilles) A Colour Atlas of Tropical Medicine and Parasitology, 1976, 2nd edn 1981; (with R. Killick-Kendrick) Rodent Malaria, 1978; (ed with W. H. G. Richards) Antimalarial Drugs, 2 vols, 1984; (ed with R. Killick-Kendrick) The Leishmaniases in Biology and Medicine, 1986; numerous papers in jls, on trop. med. and parasitology. *Recreation:* photography. *Address:* London School of Hygiene and Tropical Medicine, Keppel Street, WC1E 7HT. *T:* 01–636 8636.

PETERS, William, CMG 1981; LVO 1961; MBE 1959; HM Diplomatic Service, retired; Chairman, Executive Committee, Lepra, since 1984; *b* 28 Sept. 1923; *o s* of John William Peters and Louise (*née* Woodhouse), Morpeth, Northumberland; *m* 1944, Catherine B. Bailey; no *c*. *Educ:* King Edward VI Grammar Sch., Morpeth; Balliol Coll., Oxford. MA Lit. Hum. 1948. War Service, Queen's Royal Rifles, KOSB, and 9th Gurkha Rifles, 1942–46. Joined HMOCS as Asst District Comr, Gold Coast, 1950; served in Cape Coast, Bawku and Tamale; Dep. Sec., Regional Comr, Northern Region, 1958–59; joined CRO as Asst Prin., 1959; Prin., 1959; 1st Sec., Dacca, 1960–63; 1st Sec., Cyprus, 1963–67; Head of Zambia and Malawi Dept, CRO, 1967–68; Head of Central African Dept, FCO, 1968–69; Dir, Internat. Affairs Div., Commonwealth Secretariat, 1969–71; Counsellor and Head of Chancery, Canberra, 1971–73; Dep. High Comr, Bombay, 1974–77; Ambassador to Uruguay, 1977–80; High Comr in Malaŵi, 1980–83. Member: Soc. of Malaŵi, Blantyre; Royal African Soc. (Hon. Treas., 1983–85); Council, British-Uruguayan Soc.; S Atlantic Council, 1985–; Chm., Tibet Soc. of UK, 1985–; Pres.,

Downs Br., Royal British Legion. FBIM 1984. *Publications:* contribs to Jl of African Administration; Illustrated Weekly of India; Noticias (Uruguay); Army Qly and Defence Jl; Christian Aid; Diplomatic Service: Formation and Operation. *Recreations:* music, gardening, carpentry. *Address:* 12 Crown Court, Middle Street, Deal, Kent CT14 7AQ. *T:* 0304 362822; 12 The Hamlet, Champion Hill, SE5 8AW. *T:* 01–274 4376. *Clubs:* United Oxford & Cambridge University, Royal Commonwealth Society.

PETERSEN, Sir Jeffrey (Charles), KCMG 1978 (CMG 1968); HM Diplomatic Service, retired; *b* 20 July 1920; *s* of Charles Petersen and Ruby Petersen (*née* Waple); *m* 1962, Karin Kristina Hayward; two *s* four *d*. *Educ:* Westcliff High Sch.; London School of Economics. Served RN (Lieut, RNVR), 1939–46. Joined Foreign Office, 1948, 2nd Secretary, Madrid, 1949–50; 2nd Secretary, Ankara, 1951–52; 1st Secretary, Brussels, 1953–56; NATO Defence College, 1956–57; FO, 1957–62; 1st Secretary, Djakarta, 1962–64; Counsellor, Athens, 1964–68; Minister (Commercial), Rio de Janeiro, 1968–71; Ambassador to: Republic of Korea, 1971–74; Romania, 1975–77; Sweden, 1977–80. Chairman: British Materials Handling Bd; Anglo-Korean Soc.; Swedish Chamber of Commerce for UK. Knight Grand Cross, Order of Polar Star (Sweden), 1984; Order of Diplomatic Merit (Republic of Korea), 1985. *Recreations:* painting, entomology, sailing. *Address:* 32 Longmoore Street, SW1. *T:* 01–834 8262; Crofts Wood, Petham, Kent. *T:* Petham 537. *Clubs:* Travellers'; Kent and Canterbury.

PETERSEN, Hon. Sir Johannes B.; *see* Bjelke-Petersen.

PETERSHAM, Viscount; Charles Henry Leicester Stanhope; *b* 20 July 1945; *s* and *heir* of 11th Earl of Harrington, *qv*; *m* 1966, Virginia Alleyne Freeman Jackson, Mallow (marr. diss. 1983); one *s* one *d*; *m* 1984, Anita Countess of Suffolk and Berkshire. *Educ:* Eton. *Heir:* *s* Hon. William Henry Leicester Stanhope, *b* 14 Oct. 1967. *Address:* Flat 198, 7th Floor, Le Buckingham Palace, 11 Avenue St Michael, Monte Carlo, Monaco. *Club:* House of Lords Yacht.

PETERSON, Alexander Duncan Campbell, OBE 1946; Vice-President, International Council of United World Colleges, since 1980; *b* 13 Sept. 1908; 2nd *s* of late J. C. K. Peterson, CIE; *m* 1946, Corinna May, *d* of late Sir Arthur Cochrane, KCVO; two *s* one *d*. *Educ:* Radley; Balliol Coll., Oxford. Assistant master, Shrewsbury Sch., 1932–40; commissioned in MOI (SP), 1940; Deputy Director of Psychological Warfare, SEAC, 1944–46; Headmaster, Adams' Grammar Sch., 1946–52; Director-General of Information Services, Federation of Malaya, 1952–54; Headmaster, Dover College, 1954–57; Director: Dept of Educn, Oxford Univ., 1958–73; Internat. Baccalaureate Office, 1968–77. Contested (L) Oxford City, 1966. Chm., Army Educn Adv. Bd, 1959–66. Chairman: Farmington Trust, 1963–71; Internat. Council of United World Colls, 1978–80. Hon. DPed Univ. of Trieste, 1985. *Publications:* The Far East, 1948; 100 Years of Education, 1952; Educating our Rulers, 1957; The Techniques of Teaching (ed), 1965; The Future of Education, 1968; International Baccalaureate, 1972; The Future of the Sixth Form, 1973. *Address:* 107A Hamilton Terrace, NW8. *T:* 01–286 3995. *Clubs:* Travellers', Special Forces.

PETERSON, Colin Vyvyan, CVO 1982; Lay Assistant to Bishop of Winchester, since 1985; *b* 24 Oct. 1932; *s* of late Sir Maurice Drummond Peterson, GCMG; *m* 1966, Pamela Rosemary Barry; two *s* two *d*. *Educ:* Winchester Coll.; Magdalen Coll., Oxford. Joined HM Treasury, 1959; Sec. for Appointments to PM and Ecclesiastical Sec. to the Lord Chancellor, 1974–82; Under Sec., Cabinet Office (MPO), 1982–85. *Recreation:* fishing. *Address:* 87 Christchurch Road, Winchester, Hants. *T:* Winchester 53784.

PETERSON, Hon. David Robert; MLA Ontario, since 1975; Premier of Ontario, since 1985; *b* 29 Dec. 1943; *s* of Clarence Marwin Peterson and Laura Marie (*née* Scott); *m* 1974, Shelley Christine Matthews; two *s* one *d*. *Educ:* Univ. of Western Ontario (BA Phil./PolSci); Univ. of Toronto (LLB). MLA Ontario, 1975, re-elected 1977, 1981, 1985. *Address:* Parliament Buildings, Queen's Park, Toronto, Ontario M7A 1A1, Canada. *T:* (416) 965–1941. *Club:* London (Ontario) Hunt.

PETERSON, Rt. Rev. Leslie Ernest; *see* Algoma, Bishop of.

PETERSON, Oscar Emmanuel, CC (Canada) 1984 (OC 1972); concert jazz pianist; *b* 15 Aug. 1925; *s* of Daniel Peterson and Kathleen Peterson; *m* 1st, 1947, Lillian Alice Ann; two *s* three *d*; 2nd, 1966, Sandra Cythia, *d* of H. A. King; 3rd, Charlotte; one *s*. *Educ:* (academic) Montreal High Sch.; (music) private tutors. 1st prize, amateur show, 1940; Carnegie Hall debut, 1950; 1950–: numerous jazz awards; TV shows; composer and arranger; yearly concert tours in N America, Europe, GB and Japan; has performed also in S America, Mexico, WI, Australia, NZ and Russia. *Television series:* (Canada): Oscar Peterson Presents, 1974; Oscar Peterson and Friends, 1980; (BBC) Oscar Peterson's Piano Party, 1974. Faculty Member: Sch. of Jazz, Lenox, Mass.; Banff Centre, Toronto. Oscar Peterson scholarship established, Berklee Coll. of Mus., 1982. Grammy award, 1974, 1975, 1977. Hon. LLD: Carleton Univ., 1973; Queen's Univ., Kingston, 1976; Concardia, 1979; MacMaster, 1981; Victoria, 1981; York, 1982; Hon. DMus Sackville 1980. Civic Award of Merit, Toronto, 1972; Diplôme d'Honneur, Canadian Conf. of the Arts, 1974. *Publications:* Oscar Peterson New Piano Solos, 1965; Jazz Exercises and Pieces, 1965. *Recreations:* audio, photography, ham radio, sports. *Address:* 2421 Hammond Road, Mississauga, Ont, Canada. *T:* 416/255 5651.

PETHERBRIDGE, Edward; actor and director; Member, Royal Shakespeare Company, since 1978; Co-Director, McKellen Petherbridge Group, National Theatre, 1984–86; *b* 3 Aug. 1936; *s* of William and Hannah Petherbridge; *m* 1st, 1957, Louise Harris (marr. diss. 1980); one *s*; 2nd, 1981, Emily Richard, actress; one *d*. *Educ:* Grange Grammar Sch., Bradford; Northern Theatre Sch. Early experience in repertory and on tour; London début, Dumain in Love's Labours Lost and Demetrius in A Midsummer Night's Dream, Regent's Park Open Air Theatre, 1962; All in Good Time, Mermaid, and Phoenix, 1963; with Nat. Theatre Co. at Old Vic, 1964–70, chief appearances in: Trelawny of the Wells, Rosencrantz and Guildenstern are Dead, A Flea in her Ear, Love for Love, Volpone, The Advertisement, The Way of the World, The White Devil; Alceste in The Misanthrope, Nottingham, Lulu, Royal Court, and Apollo, 1970; John Bull's Other Island, Mermaid, Swansong, opening of Crucible, Sheffield, 1971; Founder Mem., Actors' Co., 1972; chief appearances at Edinburgh Fests, NY, and on tour, 1972–75: 'Tis Pity she's a Whore, Rooling the Roost, The Way of the World, Tartuffe, King Lear; also devised, dir. and appeared in Knots (from R. D. Laing's book), The Beanstalk, a wordless pantomime, and dir. The Bacchae; RSC tour of Australia and NZ, 1976; dir. Uncle Vanya, Cambridge Theatre Co., 1977; Chasuble in The Importance of Being Earnest, and dir., devised and appeared in Do You Love Me (from R. D. Laing's book), Actors' Co. tour and Round House, 1977; Crucifer of Blood, Haymarket, 1979; Royal Shakespeare Company: tour, 1978, Twelfth Night; Three Sisters, 1979; Suicide, Newman Noggs in Nicholas Nickleby (Best Supporting Actor, London Drama Critics' Award, 1981), No Limits to Love, 1980; Nicholas Nickleby, Broadway, 1981; Twelfth Night, British Council tour (Philippines, Singapore, Malaysia, China and Japan), followed by season at Warehouse, London, 1982; Peter Pan, Barbican, 1983; Strange Interlude, Duke of York's, 1984, Broadway, 1985 (Olivier Award, 1984); Love's Labours Lost, Stratford, 1984; National Theatre: The Rivals, 1983; Duchess of Malfi, The Cherry Orchard, The Real Inspector Hound, and The Critic, 1985, company appeared at Internat. Theatre Fests, Paris and Chicago, 1986. Numerous television appearances include: Vershinin in Three Sisters (from RSC prod.); Lytton Strachey in No Need to Lie; Newman Noggs in Nicholas Nickleby (from RSC prod.); Gower in Pericles; Lord Peter Wimsey. Member: Theatre Performers Working Group, Arts Council, 1978–; Specialist Allocations Bd, Arts Council, 1980–. *Recreations:* listening to music, photography, theatre history. *Address:* c/o Duncan Heath, 162/70 Wardour Street, W1V 5AT. *T:* 01–439 1471.

PETHICK, Brig. Geoffrey Loveston, CBE 1960; DSO 1944; *b* 25 Nov. 1907; *s* of late Captain E. E. Pethick, RN and May (*née* Brook); *m* 1st, 1939, Nancy Veronica Ferrand (*d* 1980); one *d*; 2nd, 1981, Mrs Paula Usborne. *Educ:* Newton College. Commissioned, Royal Artillery, 1927; RHA 1934; served War of 1939–45: Staff Coll., Camberley, 1940; CO, Field Regt, 1942; Far East, 1945; Jt Services Staff Coll., 1946; Chief Instructor, 1949; idc, 1950; Comdr 3 Army Group, RA, 1951; Comdr RA 3 Div. 1953; War Office, 1957; retired, 1960. Dir, British Paper Makers' Association, 1960–74. *Address:* Little Croft, Fireball Hill, Sunningdale, Ascot, Berks. *T:* Ascot 22018.

PETHYBRIDGE, Frank, CBE 1977; Regional Administrator, North Western Regional Health Authority, 1973–82, retired; Chairman, Lancashire Family Practitioner Committee, since 1985; *b* 19 Jan. 1924; *s* of Frank and Margaret Pethybridge; *m* 1947, Jean Ewing; one *s* one *d*. *Educ:* William Hulme's Grammar Sch., Manchester; Univ. of Manchester (BA Admin). FHSM, FRSH. Served with RAF, 1942–47 (Flt-Lt). Town Clerk's Dept, Manchester CBC, 1940–42 and 1947–62; Manchester Regional Hosp. Bd, 1962–73. *Recreations:* woodwork, walking, swimming. *Address:* 12 The Leylands, West Beach, Lytham St Annes FY8 5QS. *T:* Lytham 739854.

PETIT, Sir Dinshaw Manockjee, 4th Bt *cr* 1890; *b* 13 Aug. 1934; *s* of Sir Dinshaw Manockjee Petit, 3rd Bt and Sylla (*d* 1963), *d* of R. D. Tata; *S* father, 1983; *m* 1964, Nirmala Nanavatty; two *s*. *Heir:* *s* Jehangir Petit, *b* 21 Jan. 1965. *Address:* Petit Hall, Nepean Sea Road, Bombay 400 036, India.

PETIT, Roland; Chevalier de la Légion d'honneur; Chevalier des Arts et des Lettres; French choreographer and dancer; Artistic Director and Choreographer, Ballets de Marseille; *b* Villemomble, 13 Jan. 1924; *m* 1954, Renée (Zizi) Jeanmaire; one *s*. *Educ:* Ecole de Ballet de l'Opéra de Paris, studying under Ricaux and Lifar. Premier danseur, l'Opéra de Paris, 1940–44; founded Les Vendredis de la Danse, 1944, Les Ballets des Champs-Elysées, 1945, Les Ballets de Paris de Roland Petit, 1948. Choreographic works include: Les Forains, Le Jeune Homme et la Mort, Les Demoiselles de la nuit, Carmen, Deuil en 24 heures, Le Loup, L'éloge de la Folie, Les Chants de Maldoror, Notre Dame de Paris, Paradise Lost, Les Intermittences du coeur, La Symphonie fantastique, La Dame de Pique, Die Fledermaus, L'Arlésienne, Le Chat Botté, Coppelia, The Blue Angel, etc; choreographer and dancer: La Belle au Bois Dormant; Cyrano de Bergerac. Appeared in films Hans Christian Andersen; Un, Deux, Trois, Quatre (arr. ballets, for film, and danced in 3); 4 ballets, Black Tights. *Address:* Ballet National de Marseille Roland Petit, 1 place Auguste-Carli, 13001 Marseille, France.

PETO, Sir Henry (George Morton), 4th Bt *cr* 1855; consultant and company director; *b* 29 April 1920; *s* of Comdr Sir Henry Francis Morton Peto, 3rd Bt, RN, and Edith (*d* 1945), *d* of late George Berners Ruck Keene; *S* father, 1978; *m* 1947, Frances Jacqueline, JP, *d* of late Ralph Haldane Evers; two *s*. *Educ:* Sherborne; Corpus Christi College, Cambridge. Served War with Royal Artillery, 1939–46. Manufacturing industry, 1946–80. *Heir:* *s* Francis Michael Morton Peto [*b* 11 Jan. 1949; *m* 1974, Felicity Margaret, *d* of Lt-Col John Alan Burns; two *s*]. *Address:* Stream House, Selborne, Alton, Hants. *T:* Selborne 246.

PETO, Sir Michael (Henry Basil), 4th Bt *cr* 1927; *b* 6 April 1938; *s* of Brig. Sir Christopher Henry Maxwell Peto, 3rd Bt, DSO, and of Barbara, *yr d* of Edwyn Thomas Close; *S* father, 1980; *m* 1st, 1963, Sarah Susan (marr. diss. 1970), *y d* of Major Sir Dennis Stucley, 5th Bt; one *s* two *d*; 2nd, 1971, Lucinda Mary, *yr d* of Major Sir Charles Douglas Blackett, 9th Bt; two *s*. *Educ:* Eton; Christ Church, Oxford (MA). Called to the Bar, Inner Temple, 1960. Mem., Stock Exchange, 1965–; Dir, Barnett Consulting Gp, 1985–. *Heir:* *s* Henry Christopher Morton Bampfylde Peto, *b* 8 April 1967. *Address:* Lower Church Cottage, Cliddesden, near Basingstoke, Hants. *Club:* Pratt's.

PETRE, family name of **Baron Petre.**

PETRE, 17th Baron, *cr* 1603; **Joseph William Lionel Petre;** Captain Essex Regiment; *b* 5 June 1914; *s* of 16th Baron and Catherine (who *m* 2nd, 1921, Sir Frederic Carne Rasch, 2nd Bt, TD, *d* 1963) *d* of late Hon. John and late Lady Margaret Boscawen, Tregye, Falmouth, Cornwall; *S* father, 1915; *m* 1941, Marguerite, *d* of late Ion Wentworth Hamilton, Westwood, Nettlebed, Oxfordshire; one *s*. *Heir:* *s* Hon. John Patrick Lionel Petre [*b* 4 Aug. 1942; *m* 1965, Marcia Gwendolyn, *o d* of Alfred Plumpton; two *s* one *d*]. *Address:* Ingatestone Hall, Essex.

PETRE, Francis Herbert Loraine; His Honour Judge Petre; a Circuit Judge, since 1972; *b* 9 March 1927; *s* of late Maj.-Gen. R. L. Petre, CB, DSO, MC and Mrs Katherine Sophia Petre; *m* 1958, Mary Jane, *d* of Everard White, Masterton, NZ; three *s* one *d*. *Educ:* Downside; Clare Coll., Cambridge. Called to Bar, Lincoln's Inn, 1952; Dep. Chm., E Suffolk QS, 1970; Dep. Chm., Agricultural Lands Tribunal (Eastern Area), 1972; a Recorder, 1972; Regular Judge, Central Criminal Court, 1982. *Address:* c/o Central Criminal Court, EC4.

PETRIE, Cecilia, (Lady Petrie); *d* of late F. J. G. Mason, Kensington; *m* 1926, Sir Charles Petrie, 3rd Bt, CBE, FRHistS (*d* 1977); one *s*. Mem. Kensington Borough Council (Queen's Gate Ward), 1946–62; Alderman, 1965–71; Freeman, 1971; Mayor of the Royal Borough of Kensington, 1954–56. Member: (C) LCC, for S Kensington, 1949–65; Fulham & Kensington Hospital Management Committee, 1948–59 (Chairman, 1955–59); Chelsea and Kensington Hospital Management Cttee, 1959–72; Board of Governors, Charing Cross Hospital, 1959–68; Member Board of Governors of Hospital for Diseases of the Chest, 1951–73; Mem. Central Health Services Council, 1955–61; Dep.-Chm. of the London County Council, 1958–59; UK Delegate to United Nations Assembly, 14th Session, 1959; Member: SW Metropolitan Regional Hospital Board, 1959–65; London Exec. Council, Nat. Health Service, 1965–74; Family Practitioner Service, 1974–78; Whitley Council Committee C, 1949–71. *Recreation:* reading detective stories. *Address:* 31 Queen's Gate Terrace, SW7 5PP. *T:* 01–581 0112.

See also P. C. Petrie.

PETRIE, Sir (Charles) Richard (Borthwick), 4th Bt *cr* 1918; TD; MA(Oxon); Director, Richard Petrie Ltd Audio-Visual Programme Production; *b* 19 Oct. 1921; *s* of Sir Charles Alexander Petrie, 3rd Bt, CBE, and Ursula Gabrielle Borthwick (*d* 1962), *d* of late Judge Harold Chaloner Dowdall, QC; *S* father, 1977; *m* 1962, Jessie Ariana Borthwick, *d* of late Comdr Patrick Straton Campbell, RN. *Educ:* Radley College; Heidelberg Univ.; New Coll., Oxford. Served REME, 1942–47 and again (TA), 1949–67, Lt-Col; Commander REME, 43rd (Wessex) Inf. Div., TA, 1962–65. Member of Exec.

Cttee, Assoc. of Professional Recording Studios, 1968–75. *Publications:* Ghana: Portrait of a West African State, 1974; (contrib.) Sound Recording Practice, 1976. *Recreations:* music, shrub gardening. *Address:* 3 Northmoor Road, Oxford. *T:* Oxford 56081.

PETRIE, Joan Caroline, (Lady Bathurst); HM Diplomatic Service, retired 1972; *b* 2 Nov. 1920; *d* of late James Alexander Petrie, Barrister-at-law, and Adrienne Johanna (*née* van den Bergh); *m* 1968, Sir Maurice Edward Bathurst, *qv*; one step *s*. *Educ:* Wycombe Abbey Sch.; Newnham Coll., Cambridge (Mary Ewart Schol.). 1st cl. Med. and Mod. Langs Tripos, 1942, MA 1964. Entered HM Foreign Service, 1947: FO, 1947–48; 2nd Sec., The Hague, 1948–50; FO, 1950–54; 1st Sec., 1953; Bonn, 1954–58; FO (later FCO), 1958–71; Counsellor 1969; Head of European Communities Information Unit, FCO, 1969–71. Mem., UK Delegn to Colombo Plan Consultative Cttee, Jogjakarta, 1959. Adviser, British Group, Inter-Parly Union, 1962–68. Officer, Order of Leopold (Belgium), 1966. *Recreations:* music, genealogy. *Address:* Airlie, The Highlands, East Horsley, Surrey KT24 5BG. *T:* East Horsley 3269. *Club:* United Oxford & Cambridge University.

PETRIE, Peter Charles, CMG 1980; HM Diplomatic Service; Ambassador to Belgium, since 1985; *b* 7 March 1932; *s* of Sir Charles Petrie, 3rd Bt, CBE, FRHistS and of Lady (Cecilia) Petrie, *qv*; *b* and *heir presumptive* to Sir Richard Petrie, *qv*; *m* 1958, Countess Lydwine Maria Fortunata v. Oberndorff, *d* of Count v. Oberndorff, The Hague and Paris; two *s* one *d*. *Educ:* Westminster; Christ Church, Oxford. BA Lit. Hum., MA. 2nd Lieut Grenadier Guards, 1954–56. Entered HM Foreign Service, 1956; served in UK Delegn to NATO, Paris 1958–61; UK High Commn, New Delhi (seconded CRO), 1961–64; Chargé d'Affaires, Katmandu, 1963; Cabinet Office, 1965–67; UK Mission to UN, NY, 1969–73; Counsellor (Head of Chancery), Bonn, 1973–76; Head of European Integration Dept (Internal), FCO, 1976–79; Minister, Paris, 1979–85. *Recreations:* shooting, tennis. *Address:* 16A Cambridge Street, SW1V 4QH; 40 rue Lauriston, 75116 Paris, France; Le Hameau du Jardin, Lestre, 50300 Montebourg, France. *Clubs:* Brooks's; Jockey (Paris).

PETRIE, Sir Richard; *see* Petrie, Sir C. R. B.

PETTIFER, Julian; freelance writer and broadcaster; *b* 21 July 1935; *s* of Stephen Henry Pettifer and Diana Mary (*née* Burton); unmarried. *Educ:* Marlborough; St John's Coll., Cambridge. Television reporter, writer and presenter: Southern TV, 1958–62; Tonight, BBC, 1962–64; 24 Hours, BBC, 1964–69; Panorama, BBC, 1969–75; Presenter, Cuba—25 years of revolution (series), ITV, 1984; Host, Busman's Holiday, ITV, 1985–86. Numerous television documentaries, including: Vietnam, War without End, 1970; The World About Us, 1976; The Spirit of '76, 1976; Diamonds in the Sky, 1979; Nature Watch, 1981–82, 1985–86; Automania, 1984; The Living Isles, 1986. Reporter of the Year Award, Guild of Television Directors and Producers, 1968. *Publications:* (jtly) Diamonds in the Sky: a social history of air travel, 1979; (jtly) Nature Watch, 1981; (jtly) Automania, 1984. *Recreations:* travel, sport, cinema. *Address:* c/o Curtis Brown, 163–168 Regent Street, W1R 5TA. *T:* 01–437 9700. *Club:* Queen's.

PETTIGREW, Sir Russell (Hilton), Kt 1983; FInstD; FCIT; Deputy Chairman: New Zealand Forest Products Ltd, since 1980; Union Shipping Group & Union Steam Ship Company, since 1981; Chairman: AGC New Zealand Ltd, since 1984; NZ Maritime Holdings Ltd, since 1981; *b* 10 Sept. 1920; *s* of Albert and Bertha Pettigrew; *m* 1965, Glennis Olive Nicol; one *s* one *d*. *Educ:* Hangatiki Sch., King Country. Served War, Naval Service, 1941–45 (Service Medals). Hawkes Bay Motor Co., 1935–40; Pettigrews Transport, 1946–63; formed Allied Freightways (now Freightways Holdings Ltd), 1964. Director: Watties Industries Ltd; Rada Corp. Ltd; UEB Industries Ltd; FCIT 1972; Fellow, NZ Inst. of Dirs, 1972; Life Mem., NZ Road Transport Assoc., 1981. Knighthood for services to the Transport Industry. *Publication:* article in The Modern Freight Forwarder and the Road Carrier, 1971. *Recreations:* farming, deer farming, stud breeding (Herefords), Rugby, surfing, jogging, horse racing. *Address:* 8 Clyde Road, Napier, New Zealand. *T:* Napier 55–375. *Clubs:* Auckland, Hawkes Bay (New Zealand).

PETTINGELL, Sir William (Walter), Kt 1972; CBE 1965 (OBE 1959); Deputy Chairman, The Australian Gas Light Co. (General Manager, 1952–74); *b* Corrimal, NSW, 4 Sept. 1914; *s* of H. G. W. Pettingell, Cootamundra, NSW; *m* 1942, Thora M., *d* of J. Stokes; one *s* two *d*. *Educ:* Wollongong High Sch.; Univ. of Sydney. BSc (Sydney) 1st cl. hons, 1934. The Australian Gas Light Co.: Research Chemist, 1936; Production Engr, 1948; Works Manager, 1950; Asst Gen. Manager (Technical), 1951; Gen. Manager, 1952–74; Dir, 1974–. Chairman: Leighton Holdings Ltd; Indosuez Australia Ltd; Blackwood Hodge Ltd. Deputy Chairman: Australian Consolidated Industries; Sun Alliance Insurance; Director: Howard Smith Ltd; Coal and Allied Industries Ltd; Santos Ltd. FAIM, FIAM, FInstF, MInstGasE. *Recreation:* yachting (sails a 43 foot ocean racer and has taken part in annual Sydney to Hobart and other ocean yacht races). *Address:* 54 Linden Way, Castlecrag, NSW 2068, Australia. *T:* 95 1976. *Clubs:* Union, American, Royal Prince Alfred Yacht, Royal Sydney Yacht Squadron, Elanora Golf (all in NSW).

PETTIT, Sir Daniel (Eric Arthur), Kt 1974; Chairman, PosTel Investment Management (formerly Post Office Staff Superannuation Fund), 1979–83; *b* Liverpool, 19 Feb. 1915; *s* of Thomas Edgar Pettit and Pauline Elizabeth Pettit (*née* Kerr); *m* 1940, Winifred, *d* of William and Sarah Bibby; two *s*. *Educ:* Quarry Bank High Sch., Liverpool; Fitzwilliam Coll., Cambridge (MA; Hon. Fellow, 1985). School Master, 1938–40 and 1946–47; War Service, Africa, India, Burma, 1940–46 (Major, RA); Unilever: Management, 1948–57; Associated Company Dir and Chm., 1958–70. Chm., Nat. Freight Corp., 1971–78 (part-time Mem. Bd, 1968–70); Member: Freight Integration Council, 1971–78; National Ports Council, 1971–80; Bd, Foundn of Management Educn, 1973–; Waste Management Adv. Council, 1971–78; Chm., EDC for Distributive Trades, 1974–78. Chm., Incpen, 1979–; Director: Lloyds Bank Ltd, 1977–78 (Chm., Birmingham & W Midlands Bd, 1978–85); Lloyds Bank (UK) Ltd, 1979–85; Black Horse Life Assurance Co. Ltd, 1983–; Lloyds Bank Unit Trust Managers Ltd, 1981–; Bransford Farmers Ltd. Mem. Council, British Road Fedn Ltd. Hon. Col, 162 Regt RCT (V), 1978–80. Freeman, City of London, 1971; Liveryman, Worshipful Co. of Carmen, 1971. CBIM; FCIT (Pres. 1971–72); FRSA; MIPM. *Publications:* various papers on transport and management matters. *Recreations:* cricket, Association football (Olympic Games, 1936; Corinthian FC, 1935–); fly-fishing. *Address:* Bransford Court Farm, Worcester. *Clubs:* Farmers', MCC; Hawks (Cambridge).

PETTY, William Henry, CBE 1981; County Education Officer, Kent, 1973–84; *b* 7 Sept. 1921; *s* of Henry and Eveline Ann Petty, Bradford; *m* 1948, Margaret Elaine, *o d* of Edward and Lorna Bastow, Baildon, Yorks; one *s* two *d*. *Educ:* Bradford Grammar Sch.; Peterhouse, Cambridge; London Univ. MA 1950, BSc 1953. Served RA, India and Burma, 1941–45. Admin, teaching and lectrg in London, Doncaster and N R Yorks, 1946–57; Sen. Asst Educn Officer, W R Yorks CC 1957–64; Dep. County Educn Officer, Kent CC, 1964–73. Member: Council and Court, Univ. of Kent at Canterbury, 1974–84; Local Govt Trng Bd, Careers Service Trng Cttee, 1975–84; Careers Service Adv. Council, 1976–84; Trng and Further Educn Cons. Gp, 1977–83; Vital Skills Task Gp, 1977–78; Manpower Services Commn, SE Counties Area Bd, 1978–83; Bd of Dirs, Industrial Trng Service, 1978–; Exec. Mem. and Sec. for SE Reg., Soc. of Educn Officers, 1978–82; Pres., Soc. of Educn Officers, 1980–81; Chm., Assoc. of Educn Officers, 1979–80 (Vice-Chm., 1978–79); Member: JNC for Chief Officers, Officers' side, 1974–84 (Chm., 1981–84); C of E Bd of Educn, Schs Cttee, 1981–; County Educn Officers' Soc., 1974–84 (Chm., 1982–83); Youth Trng Task Gp, 1982; National Youth Trng Bd, 1983–84; Kent Area Manpower Bd, 1983–84; Consultant, Further Educn Unit, 1984–. Hon. DLitt Kent, 1983. Prizewinner: Cheltenham Fest. of Lit., 1968; Camden Fest. of Music and Arts, 1969. Greenwood Prize, 1978; Lake Aske Meml Award, 1980. *Publications:* No Bold Comfort, 1957; Conquest, 1967; (jtly) Educational Administration, 1980; contrib. educnl and lit. jls and anthologies. *Recreations:* literature, travel. *Address:* Godfrey House, Hollingbourne, Maidstone, Kent ME17 1TX. *T:* Hollingbourne 346. *Club:* United Oxford & Cambridge University.

PETTY-FITZMAURICE; *see* Mercer Nairne Petty-Fitzmaurice, family name of Marquess of Lansdowne.

PEYREFITTE, (Pierre-) Roger; French author; *b* 17 Aug. 1907; *o s* of Jean Peyrefitte, landowner, and Eugénie Jamme; unmarried. *Educ:* Collège St Benoit, Ardouane, Hérault (Lazarist); Collège du Caousou, Toulouse, Hte. Garonne (Jesuit); Lycée de Foix, Ariège; Université de Toulouse; Ecole libre des Sciences Politiques, Paris. Bachelier de l'enseignement secondaire; Diplôme d'études supérieures de langue et de littérature française; Diplômé de l'Ecole libre des Sciences Politiques (major de la section diplomatique). Concours diplomatique, 1931; attached to Ministry of Foreign Affairs, 1931–33; Secretary, French Embassy, Athens, 1933–38; attached to Ministry of Foreign Affairs, 1938–40 and 1943–45. *Publications:* Du Vésuve à l'Etna, 1952; Chevaliers de Malte, 1957; La Nature du Prince, 1963; Les Juifs, 1965; Notre Amour, 1967; Manouche, 1972; Un Musée de l'Amour, 1972; La Muse garçonnière, 1973; Catalogue de la collection de monnaies grecques et romaines de l'auteur, 1974; Tableaux de chasse, ou la vie extraordinaire de Fernand Legros, 1976; Propos secrets, 1977; La Jeunesse d'Alexandre, 1977; L'Enfant de coeur, 1978; Les Conquêtes d'Alexandre, 1980; Propos secrets 2, 1980; Alexandre le Grand, 1981; Henry de Montherlant-Roger Peyrefitte: Correspondence, 1983; Voltaire, Sa Jeunesse et son Temps, 1985; *novels:* Les Amitiés particulières, 1944 (Prix Théophraste Renaudot, 1945); Mademoiselle de Murville, 1947; L'Oracle, 1948; Les Amours singulières, 1949; La Mort d'une mère, 1950; Les Ambassades, 1951; La Fin des Ambassades, 1953; Les Clés de Saint Pierre, 1955; Jeunes proies, 1956; L'Exilé de Capri, 1959; Les Fils de la lumière, 1962; Les Américains, 1968; Des Français, 1970; La Coloquinte, 1971; Roy, 1979; L'Illustre écrivain, 1982; La Soutane rouge, 1983; *plays:* Le Prince des neiges, 1947; Le Spectateur nocturne, 1960; Les Ambassades (adaptation of A. P. Antoine), 1961. *Recreations:* travel, walks, collecting antiques. *Address:* 9 Avenue du Maréchal Maunoury, 75016 Paris, France.

PEYTON, family name of **Baron Peyton of Yeovil.**

PEYTON OF YEOVIL, Baron *cr* 1983 (Life Peer), of Yeovil in the County of Somerset; **John Wynne William Peyton;** PC 1970; Chairman, Texas Instruments Ltd, since 1974; *b* 13 Feb. 1919; *s* of late Ivor Eliot Peyton and Dorothy Helen Peyton; *m* 1947, Diana Clinch (marr. diss., 1966); one *s* one *d* (and one *s* decd); *m* 1966, Mrs Mary Cobbold. *Educ:* Eton; Trinity College, Oxford. Commissioned 15/19 Hussars, 1939; Prisoner of War, Germany, 1940–45. Called to the Bar, Inner Temple, 1945. MP (C) Yeovil, 1951–83; Parly Secretary, Ministry of Power, 1962–64; Minister of Transport, June-Oct. 1970; Minister for Transport Industries, DoE, 1970–74. *Address:* The Old Malt House, Hinton St George, Somerset. *T:* Crewkerne 73618; 6 Temple West Mews, West Square, SE11. *T:* 01–582 3611. *Club:* Boodle's.

PEYTON, Kathleen Wendy; writer (as K. M. Peyton); *b* 2 Aug. 1929; *d* of William Joseph Herald and Ivy Kathleen Herald; *m* 1950, Michael Peyton; two *d*. *Educ:* Wimbledon High Sch.; Manchester Sch. of Art (ATD). Taught art at Northampton High Sch., 1953–55; started writing seriously after birth of first child, although had already had 4 books published. *Publications: as Kathleen Herald:* Sabre, the Horse from the Sea, 1947, USA 1963; The Mandrake, 1949; Crab the Roan, 1953; *as K. M. Peyton:* North to Adventure, 1959, USA 1965; Stormcock Meets Trouble, 1961; The Hard Way Home, 1962; Windfall, 1963, USA (as Sea Fever), 1963; Brownsea Silver, 1964; The Maplin Bird, 1964, USA 1965 (New York Herald Tribune Award, 1965); The Plan for Birdsmarsh, 1965, USA 1966; Thunder in the Sky, 1966, USA 1967; Flambards Trilogy (Guardian Award, 1970): Flambards, 1967, USA 1968; The Edge of the Cloud, 1969, USA 1969 (Carnegie Medal, 1969); Flambards in Summer, 1969, USA 1970; Fly-by-Night, 1968, USA 1969; Pennington's Seventeenth Summer, 1970, USA (as Pennington's Last Term), 1971; The Beethoven Medal, 1971, USA 1972; The Pattern of Roses, 1972, USA 1973; Pennington's Heir, 1973, USA 1974; The Team, 1975; The Right-Hand Man, 1977; Prove Yourself a Hero, 1977, USA 1978; A Midsummer Night's Death, 1978, USA 1979; Marion's Angels, 1979, USA 1979; Flambards Divided, 1981; Dear Fred, 1981; Going Home, 1983, USA 1983; The Last Ditch, 1984, USA (as Free Rein), 1983; Froggett's Revenge, 1985; The Sound of Distant Cheering, 1986. *Recreations:* riding, walking, gardening. *Address:* Rookery Cottage, North Fambridge, Chelmsford, Essex CM3 6LP.

PFEIFFER, Alois; Member, Commission of the European Communities, since 1985; *b* 25 Sept. 1924. *Educ:* evening classes; Labour Acad., Frankfurt. Served War of 1939–45; PoW 1942–45. Horticultural, Agricultural and Forestry Workers' Union: Regl Dir, S Hessen, 1949–54; Land Dir, N Rhine-Westphalia, 1954–60; Mem. Nat. Exec., 1966–67; Dep. Pres., 1967–69; Pres., 1969–75. Member: Fed. Exec., Deutscher Gewerkschaftsbund, 1975–84; Exec., ETUC; Pres., European Fedn of Agricl Workers. *Address:* 200 rue de la Loi, 1049 Brussels, Belgium.

PFLIMLIN, Pierre; President, European Parliament, since 1984; *b* 5 Feb. 1907; *s* of Jules Pflimlin and Léonie Schwartz; *m* 1939, Marie-Odile Heinrich; one *s* two *d*. *Educ:* Mulhouse; University of Strasbourg. Dr of Laws, 1932. Mem. for Bas-Rhin Dept, French Parliament (Nat. Assembly), 1945–67; Under Sec. of State, Ministries for Public Health and for Economics, 1946; Minister: of Agriculture, 1947–49 and 1950–51; of Trade and External Economic Relations, 1951–52; of State in charge of relations with Council of Europe, 1952; for Overseas Territories, 1952–53; of Finance and Economics, 1955–56 and 1957–58; Prime Minister, May-June 1958; Minister of State in de Gaulle Govt, 1958–59; Minister of State for Co-operation with Overseas Countries, 1962. Mem., Consultative Assembly of Council of Europe (President, 1963–66) and of European Parliament, 1959–67; Vice-Pres., European Parlt, 1979–84. Mayor, City of Strasbourg, 1959–83. *Publications:* Industry in Mulhouse, 1932; The Economic Structure of the Third Reich, 1938; Alsace: destiny and will, 1963; The Europe of the Communities, 1966. *Address:* 24 avenue de la Paix, 67000 Strasbourg, France. *T:* 88/35–63–68.

PHALP, Geoffrey Anderson, CBE 1968; TD; Secretary, King Edward's Hospital Fund for London, 1968–80; *b* 8 July 1915; *s* of late Charles Anderson Phalp and late Sara Gertrude Phalp (*née* Wilkie); *m* 1946, Jeanne Margaret, OBE, JP, *d* of late Emeritus Prof. G. R. Goldsborough, CBE, FRS; one *s* one *d*. *Educ:* Durham Sch.; Univ. of Durham (BCom). Served with RA (despatches), 1939–46. Asst Registrar, Med. Sch., King's Coll., Newcastle upon Tyne, 1946–49; Dep. House Governor and Sec., United Newcastle upon Tyne Hosps, 1949–51; Sec. and Principal Admin. Officer, United Birmingham Hosps,

1951–68. Trustee, Child Accident Prevention Trust, 1982– (Chm., 1983). W. K. Kellogg Foundn Citation for contribn to develt of health admin, 1980. *Recreations:* fly fishing, gardening, music. *Address:* 19 Norfolk Road, Edgbaston, Birmingham B15 3PZ. *T:* 021–454 2616. *Club:* Savile.

PHAROAH, Prof. Peter Oswald Derrick, MD, FFCM; Professor of Community Health, University of Liverpool, since 1979; *b* 19 May 1934; *s* of Oswald Higgins Pharoah and Phyllis Christine Gahan; *m* 1960, Margaret Rose McMinn; three *s* one *d.* *Educ:* Lawrence Memorial Royal Military School, Lovedale, India; Palmers School, Grays, Essex; St Mary's Hospital Medical School. MD, MSc. Graduated, 1958; Med. House Officer and Med. Registrar appointments at various London Hosps, 1958–63, MO and Research MO, Dept of Public Health, Papua New Guinea, 1963–74; Sen. Lectr in Community Health, London School of Hygiene and Tropical Medicine, 1974–79. *Publication:* Endemic Cretinism, 1971. *Recreations:* squash, walking, philately. *Address:* 11 Fawley Road, Liverpool L18 9TE. *T:* 051–724 4896.

PHELAN, Andrew James; His Honour Judge Phelan; a Circuit Judge, since 1974; *b* 25 July 1923; *e s* of Cornelius Phelan, Clonmel, Eire; *m* 1950, Joan Robertson McLagan; one *s* two *d.* *Educ:* Clongoweswood, Co. Kildare; National Univ. of Ireland (MA); Trinity Coll., Cambridge. Called to: Irish Bar, King's Inn, 1945; English Bar, Gray's Inn, 1949. Jun. Fellow, Univ. of Bristol, 1948–50; in practice at English Bar, 1950–74. *Publication:* The Law for Small Boats, 2nd edn, 1970. *Recreations:* sailing, mountain walking. *Address:* 17 Hartington Road, Chiswick, W4 1PD. *T:* 01–994 6109. *Clubs:* Royal Cruising, Bar Yacht.

PHELPS, Anthony John, CB 1976; Deputy Chairman, Board of Customs and Excise, 1973–82; *b* 14 Oct. 1922; *s* of John Francis and Dorothy Phelps, Oxford; *m* 1st, 1949, Sheila Nan Rait (*d* 1967), *d* of late Colin Benton Rait, Edinburgh; one *s* two *d*; 2nd, 1971, Janet M. T., *d* of late Charles R. Dawson, Edinburgh. *Educ:* City of Oxford High Sch.; University Coll., Oxford. HM Treasury, 1946; Jun. Private Sec. to Chancellor of the Exchequer, 1949–50; Principal, 1950; Treasury Rep. in Far East, 1953–55; Private Sec. to the Prime Minister, 1958–61; Asst Sec., 1961; Under-Sec., 1968. Freeman, City of Oxford, 1971. *Recreations:* music, watching sport. *Address:* 1 Woodsyre, Sydenham Hill, SE26 6SS. *T:* 01–670 0735. *Clubs:* City Livery, MCC.

PHELPS, Charles Frederick, DPhil; Pro-Rector (External Affairs), Imperial College of Science and Technology, since 1984; *b* 18 Jan. 1934; *s* of Seth Phelps and Rigmor Kaae; *m* 1960, Joanna Lingeman; one *s* one *d.* *Educ:* Bromsgrove Sch.; Oxford Univ. (MA, DPhil). Lecturer, Univ. of Bristol: in Chemical Physiology, 1960–63; in Biochemistry, 1963–70; Reader in Biochemistry, Univ. of Bristol, 1970–74; Prof. of Biochemistry, Univ. of Lancaster, 1974–80; Principal, Chelsea Coll., London, 1981–84. Visiting Fellow, Univ. of Rome, 1968–69. Consultant, World Bank Educational Mission to China, 1980 and to Korea, 1982. Mem. Senate, 1980–84, Mem., F and GP Cttee, 1983–, Chm., Univ. Trng Cttee, 1984–, London Univ. Member: Cttee, Biochemical Soc., 1980–84; Cttee, British Biophysical Soc., 1974–84 (Chm., 1983–84); Research Cttee of Arthritis and Rheumatism Council, 1974–78. Mem. Council, Queen Elizabeth Coll., 1983–85; Governor: Furzedown Sch., 1980–; King Edward Sch., Witley, 1984–; Mill Hill Sch., 1985–. FKC 1985. Editorial Board: Biochim. Biophys. Acta, 1976–80, 1983–84; Internat. Research Communications Systems Jl of Med. Scis, 1980–. *Publications:* numerous papers in medical and science jls. *Recreations:* enjoying things Italian, 17th Century science, Brahms. *Address:* Brockhurst, The Green, Chiddingfold, near Guildford, Surrey GU8 4TU. *T:* Wormley 3092. *Club:* Athenæum.

PHELPS, Howard Thomas Henry Middleton; Director of Operations since 1979 and Board Member since 1973, British Airways Board; *b* 20 Oct. 1926; *s* of Ernest Henry Phelps, Gloucester, and Harriet (*née* Middleton); *m* 1949, Audrey (*née* Ellis); one *d.* *Educ:* Crypt Grammar Sch., Gloucester; Hatfield Coll.; Durham Univ. BA Hons Politics and Econs 1951. National Coal Board, Lancs, Durham and London, 1951–72, finally Dep. Dir-Gen. of Industrial Relations; Personnel Dir, BOAC, 1972; Gp Personnel Dir, BAB, 1972. FRAeS; FIPM; FCIT; CBIM. Chm., Alice Ruston Housing Assoc., 1973–84; Chm., Durham Univ. Soc., 1975–; Pres., Hatfield Assoc., 1983–. Mem. Council, Durham Univ. *Recreations:* gardening, musical appreciation. *Address:* Tall Trees, Chedworth, near Cheltenham, Glos. *T:* Fossebridge 324; 21 The Birches, Heathside Road, Woking, Surrey. *T:* Woking 62027. *Club:* Royal Over-Seas League.

PHELPS, Maj.-Gen. Leonard Thomas Herbert, CB 1973; OBE 1963; CBIM 1979; *b* 9 Sept. 1917; *s* of Abijah Phelps; *m* 1945, Jean Irene, *d* of R. Price Dixon; one *s* one *d.* CBIM 1980 (FBIM 1973). Served War, Hong Kong, 1940–41; India/Burma, 1941–47. Student, Staff Coll., Quetta, 1946; DAQMG, HQ Land Forces Hong Kong, 1951–53; Second in Command, 4th Trng Bn, RAOC, 1955–57; War Office: DAAG, 1957–59; ADOS, 1961–63; AA & QMG Singapore Mil. Forces, 1963; Chief of Staff and Dep Comdr, 4th Malaysian Inf. Bde, 1964; ADOS, WO, 1965–67; Chief Inspector, Land Service Ammunition, 1967–70; Comdr, Base Organisation, RAOC, 1970; Dir, Ordnance Services, MoD (Army), 1971–73; retired 1973; Col Comdt, RAOC, 1976–78. Man. Dir, The Warrior Gp, 1975–78; Director: Leon Davis & Co., 1975–82; Debenhams Business Systems Ltd, 1982–84. *Address:* South Port Cottage, Sutton Courtenay, Oxon.

PHELPS, Maurice Arthur; Board Member for Personnel and Industrial Relations, British Shipbuilders, since 1980; *b* 17 May 1935; *s* of H. T. Phelps; *m* 1960, Elizabeth Anne Hurley; two *s* one *d.* *Educ:* Wandsworth School; Corpus Christi College, Oxford Univ. BA Hons Modern History. Shell Chemical Co. Ltd, 1959–68; Group Personnel Planning Adviser, Pilkington Bros Ltd, 1968–70; Group Personnel Dir, Unicorn Industries Ltd, 1970–72; Dir of Labour and Staff Relations, W Midland Passenger Transport Exec., 1973–77; Dir of Personnel, Heavy Vehicle Div., Leyland Vehicles Ltd, 1977–80. *Address:* Abbotsfield, Goring Heath, S Oxon RG8 7SA.

PHELPS, Richard Wintour, CBE 1986; General Manager, Central Lancashire New Town Development Corporation, 1971–86; *b* 26 July 1925; *s* of Rev. H. Phelps; *m* 1955, Pamela Marie Lawson; two *d.* *Educ:* Kingswood Sch.; Merton Coll., Oxford (MA). 14th Punjab Regt, IA, 1944–46. Colonial Admin. Service, Northern Region and Fed. Govt. of Nigeria, 1948–57 and 1959–61; Prin., HM Treasury, 1957–59 and 1961–65; Sen. Administrator, Hants CC, 1965–67; Gen. Manager, Skelmersdale New Town Develt Corp., 1967–71. Winston Churchill Trust Travelling Fellowship, 1971. Trustee, British Motor Industry Heritage Trust, 1985. *Recreations:* reading, travel, music. *Address:* Fell Foot House, Newby Bridge, Ulverston, Cumbria LA12 8NL. *T:* Newby Bridge 31274. *Club:* Royal Commonwealth Society.

PHELPS BROWN, Sir Ernest Henry; *see* Brown, Sir E. H. P.

PHILBIN, Most Rev. William J., DD; *b* 26 Jan. 1907; *s* of late James Philbin and Brigid (*née* O Hora). *Educ:* St Nathy's Coll., Ballaghaderreen; St Patrick's, Maynooth. Priest, 1931; DD Maynooth, 1933. Curate, Eastbourne, 1933; Secondary teacher, Ballaghaderreen, 1934; Prof. of Dogmatic Theology, Maynooth, 1936; Bishop of Clonfert, 1953; Bishop of Down and Connor, 1962–82. *Publications:* Does Conscience Decide?, 1969; To You Simonides, 1973; The Bright Invisible, 1984; pamphlets on socio-moral questions; Irish translation of St Patrick's writings. Contributor to The Irish Theological Quarterly, Studies, The Irish Ecclesiastical Record. *Address:* 81 Highfield Road, Rathgar, Dublin 6, Ireland.

PHILIP, Alexander Morrison; QC (Scot) 1984; *b* 3 Aug. 1942; *s* of late Alexander Philip, OBE and of Isobel Thomson Morrison; *m* 1971, Shona Mary Macrae; three *s.* *Educ:* High School of Glasgow; St Andrews University (MA 1963); Glasgow University (LLB 1965). Solicitor, 1967–72; Advocate 1973; Standing Junior Counsel to Scottish Education Dept, 1982; Advocate-Depute, 1982–85. *Recreations:* golf, skiing. *Address:* 9 Rosebank Grove, Edinburgh. *T:* 031–552 8164. *Clubs:* Scottish Arts (Edinburgh); Royal Northern and University (Aberdeen).

PHILIP, John Robert, DSc; FRS 1974; FAA 1967; Chief, Division of Environmental Mechanics, Commonwealth Scientific and Industrial Research Organization, Australia, 1971–80 and since 1983; *b* 18 Jan. 1927; *e s* of Percival Norman Philip and late Ruth (*née* Osborne), formerly of Ballarat and Maldon, Vic., Australia; *m* 1949, Frances Julia, *o d* of E. Hilton Long; two *s* one *d.* *Educ:* Scotch Coll., Melbourne; Univ. of Melbourne (Queen's Coll.). BCE 1946, DSc 1960. Research Asst, Melb. Univ., 1947; Engr, Qld Irrig. Commn, 1948–51; Research Staff, CSIRO, 1951–; Sen. Princ. Res. Scientist, 1961–63; Chief Res. Scientist and Asst Chief, Div. of Plant Industry, 1963–71; Associate Mem., CSIRO Exec., 1978; Dir, Inst. of Physical Scis, 1980–83. Visiting Scientist, Cambridge Univ., 1954–55; Res. Fellow, Calif. Inst. Techn., 1957–58; Vis. Prof., Univ. of Illinois, 1958 and 1961; Nuffield Foundn Fellow, Cambridge Univ., 1961–62; Res. Fellow, Harvard Univ., 1966–67; Vis. Prof., Univ. of Florida, 1969; Vinton-Hayes Fellow, Harvard Univ., 1972; Vis. Res. Fellow, Cornell Univ., 1979. Horton Award, 1957, Horton Medal, 1982, Amer. Geophys. Union; David Rivett Medal, 1966; Thomas Ranken Lyle Medal, 1981. Mem. Council, Australian Acad. of Sci., 1972–78 (Biol. Sec., 1974–78); ANZAAS: Pres. Section 1 (Physics), 1970; Pres. Sect. 8 (Maths), 1971. FRMetS; Fellow, Amer. Geophys. Union, 1981. Hon. DEng Melbourne, 1983. *Publications:* papers in scientific jls on soil and porous medium physics, fluid mechanics, hydrology, micrometeorology, mathematical and physical aspects of physiology and ecology. *Recreations:* reading, writing, architecture. *Address:* CSIRO Division of Environmental Mechanics, GPO Box 821, Canberra, ACT 2601, Australia. *T:* (062) 46–5645; 42 Vasey Crescent, Campbell, ACT 2601. *T:* (062) 47–8958.

PHILIPPE, André J., Hon. GCVO 1972; Luxembourg Ambassador to the United Nations, New York, since 1984; *b* Luxembourg City, 28 June 1926. Dr-en-Droit. Barrister-at-Law, Luxembourg, 1951–52. Joined Luxembourg Diplomatic Service, 1952; Dep. to Dir of Polit. Affairs, Min. of Foreign Affairs, 1952–54; Dep. Perm. Rep. to NATO, 1954–61 and to OECD, 1959–61; Dir of Protocol and Legal Adviser, Min. of For. Affairs, 1961–68; Ambassador and Perm. Rep. to UN and Consul-Gen., New York, 1968–72 (Vice-Pres., 24th Session of Gen. Assembly of UN, 1969); Ambassador to UK, Perm. Rep. to Council of WEU, and concurrently Ambassador to Ireland and Iceland, 1972–78; Ambassador to France, 1978–84. Commander, Order of Adolphe Nassau and Order of Oaken Crown (Luxembourg); Commander, Légion d'Honneur (France); Grand Officer, Order of Merit (Luxembourg), 1983. *Address:* Luxembourg Mission to the United Nations, 801 Second Avenue, New York, NY 10017, USA. *T:* 370 9850.

PHILIPPS, family name of **Viscount St Davids** and **Baron Milford.**

PHILIPPS, Hon. Hanning; *see* Philipps, Hon. R. H.

PHILIPPS, Lady Marion (Violet), FRAgS; JP; farmer, since 1946; *b* 1 Feb. 1908; *d* of 12th Earl of Stair, KT, DSO; *m* 1930, Hon. Hanning Philipps, *qv*; one *s* one *d.* *Educ:* privately. FRAgS 1973. War Service: original Mem., WVS HQ Staff, i/c Canteen and Catering Information Services, 1938–41; Min. of Agriculture, 1942–45. Mem., Narberth Rural Dist Council, 1970–73. Chm., Picton Land & Investment Pty Ltd, WA. Trustee, Picton Castle Trust (Graham Sutherland Gallery), 1976–. Founder Mem., British Polled Hereford Soc., 1950– (also first Pres.); Member: Welsh Council, Historic Houses Assoc., 1975; Gardens Cttee, National Council of Historic Houses Assoc., 1975. Pres., Royal Welsh Agricultural Soc., 1978–. JP Dyfed (formerly Pembrokeshire), 1965. CStJ; Order of Mercy, 1926. *Recreation:* gardening. *Address:* Picton Castle, The Rhos, Haverfordwest, Dyfed SA62 4AS. *T:* Rhos 201.

PHILIPPS, Hon. (Richard) Hanning, MBE 1945; JP; Hon. Major Welsh Guards; Lord-Lieutenant of Dyfed, 1974–79 (HM Lieutenant of Pembrokeshire, 1958–74); *b* 14 Feb. 1904; 2nd *s* of 1st Baron and *b* of 2nd Baron Milford, *qv*; *m* 1930, Lady Marion Violet Dalrymple (*see* Lady Marion Philipps); one *s* one *d.* *Educ:* Eton. Contested (Nat) Brecon and Radnor, 1939. Served War of 1939–45, NW Europe, 1944–45 (MBE). Vice-Lieutenant of Pembrokeshire, 1957. Hon. Colonel Pembroke Yeomanry, 1959. Chairman: Milford Haven Conservancy Bd, 1963–75; Northern Securities Trust Ltd, 1950–80; Hon. Pres. (former Chm.) Schweppes Ltd; Dir, Picton Land and Investment Pty Ltd, W Australia; Trustee, Picton Castle Trust, Graham and Kathleen Sutherland Foundn. Pres., Order of St John, Pembrokeshire, 1958–. CStJ. *Recreations:* painting, forestry, gardening. *Address:* Picton Castle, Haverfordwest, Pembrokeshire, Dyfed SA62 4AS. *T:* Rhos 201. *Club:* Boodle's.

PHILIPS, Prof. Sir Cyril (Henry), Kt 1974; Professor of Oriental History, University of London, 1946–80; Director, School of Oriental and African Studies, London, 1957–76; Vice-Chancellor, University of London, 1972–76 (Deputy Vice-Chancellor, 1969–70); *b* Worcester, 27 Dec. 1912; *s* of William Henry Philips; *m* 1st, 1939, Dorcas (*d* 1974), *d* of John Rose, Wallasey; one *d* (one *s* decd); 2nd, 1975, Joan Rosemary, *d* of William George Marshall. *Educ:* Rock Ferry High School; Univs of Liverpool (MA) and London (PhD). Bishop Chavasse Prizeman; Gladstone Memorial Fellow. Frewen Lord Prizeman (Royal Empire Soc.), 1935; Alexander Prizeman (Royal Hist. Soc.), 1938; Sir Percy Sykes Meml Medal (RSAA), 1976; Asst Lectr, Sch. of Oriental Studies, 1936. Served in Suffolk Infantry, Army Education Corps, 1940–43; Col Commandant, Army School of Education, 1943. Chief Instructor, Dept of Training, HM Treasury, 1943–46. Colonial Office Mission on Community Development, Africa, 1947. Lectures: Montague Burton, Univ. of Leeds, 1966; Creighton, Univ. of London, 1972; James Smart, on Police, 1979; Home Office Bicentenary, 1982; Police, Univ. of Bristol, 1982; Dawtry Meml, Univ. of Leeds, 1983. Chairman: UGC Cttee on Oriental, African and Slavonic Studies, 1965–70; UGC Cttee on Latin American Studies, 1966–70; India Cttee of Inter-University Council and British Council, 1972–; Royal Commn on Criminal Procedure, 1978–80; Police Complaints Bd, 1980–85; Council on Tribunals, 1986–; Inst. of Archaeology, 1979–85, Inst. of Latin American Studies, 1978– (Univ. of London); Member: Social Development Cttee, Colonial Office, 1947–55; Colonial Office Research Council, 1955–57; University Grants Cttee, 1960–69; Commonwealth Education Commn, 1961–70; Postgraduate Awards Cttee (Min. of Education), 1962–64; Modern Languages Cttee (Min. of Education), 1964–67; Inter-Univ. Council, 1967–; Court, London Univ., 1970–; Governor: Chinese Univ. of Hong Kong, 1965–; Mill Hill Sch., 1980– (Chm., 1982); Governor and Trustee, Richmond Coll., 1979–. Pres., Royal Asiatic Soc., 1979–82, 1985–. Hon. DLitt: Warwick, 1967; Bristol, 1983; Hon. LLD Hong Kong, 1971. India Tagore Medal, 1968; Bombay Freedom Medal, 1977. *Publications:* The East India Company, 1940 (2nd edn 1961); India,

1949; Handbook of Oriental History, 1951 (2nd edn 1962); Correspondence of David Scott, 1951; Historians of India, Pakistan and Ceylon, 1961; The Evolution of India and Pakistan, 1962; Politics and Society in India, 1963; Fort William-India House Correspondence, 1964; History of the School of Oriental and African Studies, 1917–67, 1967; The Partition of India, 1970; The Correspondence of Lord William Bentinck, Governor General of India 1828–35, 1977. *Address:* School of Oriental and African Studies, Malet Street, WC1E 7HP. *T:* 01-637 2388. *Club:* Athenæum.

PHILIPSON, Garry, DFC 1944; Managing Director (formerly General Manager), Aycliffe and Peterlee Development Corporation, 1974–85; *b* 27 Nov. 1921; *s* of George and Marian Philipson; *m* 1949, June Mary Miller Somerville; one *d. Educ:* Stockton Grammar Sch.; Durham Univ. (BA(Hons)). Jubilee Prize, 1947. Local Govt, 1937–40. Served War, RAFVR (2 Gp Bomber Comd), 1940–46. Colonial Service and Overseas Civil Service, 1949–60. Various Dist and Secretariat posts, incl. Clerk, Exec. Council and Cabinet Sec., Sierra Leone; Principal, Scottish Develt Dept, 1961–66; Under Sec., RICS, 1966–67; Dir, Smith and Ritchie Ltd, 1967–70; Sec., New Towns Assoc., 1970–74; Vice-Chm. (NE), North Housing Assoc., 1985–. *Publications:* Press articles and contribs to various jls. *Recreations:* country pursuits, history, archaeology. *Address:* Tunstall Grange, Tunstall, Richmond, North Yorks. *T:* Richmond 833327. *Club:* Royal Air Force.

PHILIPSON, Oliphant James; *b* 9 Sept. 1905; 2nd *s* of late Hylton Philipson; *m* 1946, Helen Mabel (*d* 1976), *d* of David Fell. *Educ:* Eton. Served War of 1939–45, RNVR. *Address:* Manor House, Everton, near Lymington, Hampshire SO41 0HE. *Clubs:* Carlton; Royal Yacht Squadron.

PHILIPSON, Sir Robert James, (Sir Robin Philipson), Kt 1976; RA 1980 (ARA 1973); PRSA 1973 (RSA 1962; ARSA 1952); RSW 1954; Head of the School of Drawing and Painting, The College of Art, Edinburgh, 1960–82; President, Royal Scottish Academy, 1973–83 (Secretary, 1969–73); *b* 17 Dec. 1916; *s* of James Philipson; *m* 1949, Brenda Mark; *m* 1962, Thora Clyne (marr. diss. 1975); *m* 1976, Diana Mary Pollock; one adopted *s. Educ:* Whitehaven Secondary School; Dumfries Academy; Edinburgh College of Art, 1936–40. Served War of 1939–45: King's Own Scottish Borderers, 1942–46, in India and Burma; attached to RIASC. Member of teaching staff, Edinburgh College of Art, 1947. Exhibits with Browse & Darby Ltd, London, Scottish Gallery and Fine Art Soc., Edinburgh. Mem., Royal Fine Art Commn for Scotland, 1965–80. Hon. RA 1973; Hon. Mem., RHA 1979; Hon. Mem., RCA 1980. Commandeur de l'Ordre National du Mérite de la République Française, 1976. FRSA 1965; FRSE 1977. DUniv: Stirling, 1976; Heriot-Watt, 1985; Hon. LLD Aberdeen 1977. *Address:* 23 Crawfurd Road, Edinburgh EH16 5PQ. *T:* 031-667 2373. *Club:* Scottish Arts (Edinburgh).

PHILIPSON-STOW, Sir Christopher, 5th Bt *cr* 1907; DFC 1944; retired; *b* 13 Sept. 1920; *s* of Henry Matthew Philipson-Stow (*d* 1953) (3rd *s* of 1st Bt) and Elizabeth Willes (*d* 1979), *d* of Sir Thomas Willes Chitty, 1st Bt; *S* cousin, 1982; *m* 1952, Elizabeth Nairn, *d* of late James Dixon Trees and *widow* of Major F. G. McLaren, 48th Highlanders of Canada; two *s. Educ:* Winchester. *Heir: er s* Robert Matthew Philipson-Stow, *b* 29 Aug. 1953. *Address:* RR2, Port Carling, Ontario P0B 1J0, Canada. *T:* 705–765–3000.

PHILLIMORE, family name of **Baron Phillimore.**

PHILLIMORE, 3rd Baron, *cr* 1918, of Shiplake in County of Oxford; **Robert Godfrey Phillimore,** Bt, *cr* 1881; *b* 24 Sept. 1939; *s* of Capt. Hon. Anthony Francis Phillimore, 9th Queen's Royal Lancers (*e s* of 2nd Baron) and Anne, 2nd *d* of Maj.-Gen. Sir Cecil Pereira, KCB; *S* grandfather, 1947; *m* 1st, 1974, Amanda (marr. diss. 1982), *d* of Carlo Hugo Gonzales-Castillo; 2nd, 1983, Maria, *d* of Ilya Slonim. *Heir: u* Major Hon. Claud Stephen Phillimore [*b* 15 Jan. 1911; *m* 1944, Anne Elizabeth, *e d* of Maj. Arthur Algernon Dorrien-Smith, DSO; one *s* one *d*]. *Address:* Crumplehorn Barn, Corks Farm, Dunsden Green, near Reading, Berks.

PHILLIMORE, John Gore, CMG 1946; a Managing Director of Baring Brothers & Co. Ltd, 1949–72; *b* 16 April 1908; 2nd *s* of late Adm. Sir Richard and Lady Phillimore, Shedfield, Hants; *m* 1951, Jill, *d* of late Captain Mason Scott, Royal Navy retd, Buckland Manor, Broadway, Worcs, and of Hon. Mrs Scott; two *s* two *d. Educ:* Winchester College; Christ Church, Oxford. Partner of Roberts, Meynell & Co., Buenos Aires, 1936–48; Representative of HM Treasury and Bank of England in South America, 1940–45. Prime Warden, Fishmongers' Co., 1974–75. High Sheriff of Kent, 1975, DL Kent, 1979–84. Condor de los Andes (Bolivia), 1940; Commander, Orden de Mayo (Argentina), 1961. *Address:* Brooklyn House, Kingsclere, near Newbury, Berks. *T:* Newbury 298321. *Club:* White's.

PHILLIPS, family name of Baroness Phillips.

PHILLIPS, Baroness *cr* 1964 (Life Peer); **Norah Phillips,** JP; Director, Association for the Prevention of Theft in Shops; President (and former General Secretary), National Association of Women's Clubs; President: Institute of Shops, Health and Safety Acts Administration; Association for Research into Restricted Growth; Keep Fit Association; Industrial Catering Association; International Professional Security Association; Small Electrical Appliance Marketing Association; Pre-Retirement Association; Vice-President: National Chamber of Trade; Fair Play for Children; Chairman, Beatrice Webb House Trust; *d* of William and Catherine Lusher; *m* 1930, Morgan Phillips (*d* 1963); one *s* one *d* (*see* G. P. Dunwoody). *Educ:* Marist Convent; Hampton Training College. A Baroness in Waiting (Govt Whip), 1965–70. Lord-Lieutenant of Greater London, 1978–85. *Address:* 115 Rannoch Road, W6.

PHILLIPS, Adrian Alexander Christian; Director, The Countryside Commission, since 1981; *b* 11 Jan. 1940; *s* of Eric Lawrance Phillips, *qv*; *m* 1963, Cassandra Frances Elaïs Hubback; two *s. Educ:* The Hall, Hampstead; Westminster Sch.; Christ Church, Oxford (1st Cl. Hons MA Geography). MRTPI; FRSA. Planning Services, Min. of Housing and Local Govt, 1962–68; Sen. Research Officer and Asst Director, Countryside Commission, 1968–74; Special Asst, Executive Director, United Nations Environment Programme (UNEP), Nairobi, Kenya, 1974–75; Head, Programme Coordination Unit, UNEP, Nairobi, 1975–78; Director of Programmes, Internat. Union for Conservation of Nature and Natural Resources, Switzerland, 1978–81. *Publications:* articles on countryside planning and conservation in professional jls. *Recreations:* walking, skiing, stroking the cat. *Address:* c/o Countryside Commission, John Dower House, Crescent Place, Cheltenham, Glos GL50 3RA. *T:* Cheltenham 521381. *Club:* Royal Commonwealth Society.

PHILLIPS, Alan; *see* Phillips, D. A.

PHILLIPS, Arthur, OBE 1957; MA, PhD; JP; Barrister at Law (Middle Temple); Professor Emeritus, University of Southampton; *b* 29 May 1907; *e s* of Albert William Phillips and Agnes Phillips (*née* Edwards); *m* 1934, Kathleen Hudson; two *s* two *d. Educ:* Highgate School; Trinity College, Oxford. In chambers in Temple, 1929; joined Colonial Service, 1931, and served in Kenya: Dist Officer, 1931; Actg Resident Magistrate, 1933–35; Crown Counsel, 1936; Actg Solicitor-Gen., 1940 and 1946; Judicial Adviser, 1945; Mem. of Kenya Leg. Council, 1940. Served in Kenya Regt, Somaliland and Abyssinia, 1940–42; Chm. War Claims Commn, Br. Somaliland, 1942; retd from Colonial Service on medical grounds and practised at Bar, England, 1947–49. Reader in Law, LSE, Univ. of London, 1949–56; Prof. of English Law, Univ. of Southampton, 1956–67; Dean of Faculty of Law, 1956–62; Deputy Vice-Chancellor, 1961–63. Dep. Chm., Hants QS, 1960–71; a Recorder of the Crown Court, 1972–79. Director of Survey of African Marriage and Family Life, 1948–52. Chairman Milk and Dairies Tribunal, South-Eastern Region, 1961–79; Pres., Southern Rent Assessment Panel, 1965–72. JP Hants; Chairman Winchester County Magistrates' Court, 1956–61. Chancellor, dio. of Winchester, 1964–84. Member, Church Assembly, 1965–70. Former Lay Reader, Diocese of Winchester, and Counsellor to the Dean and Chapter of Winchester. *Publications:* Report on Native Tribunals (Kenya), 1945; (ed. and part-author) Survey of African Marriage and Family Life, 1953; (jt) Marriage Laws in Africa, 1971; principal contribr on Ecclesiastical Law, Halsbury's Laws of England, 1975. *Address:* 3 Oliver's Battery Crescent, Winchester, Hants. *T:* Winchester 69958. *Club:* Royal Commonwealth Society.

PHILLIPS, Prof. Calbert Inglis, FRCS, FRCSE; Professor of Ophthalmology, University of Edinburgh and Ophthalmic Surgeon, Royal Infirmary, Edinburgh, since 1972; *b* 20 March 1925; *o s* of Rev. David Horner Phillips and Margaret Calbert Phillips; *m* 1962, Christina Anne Fulton, MB, FRCSE; one *s. Educ:* Glasgow High Sch.; Robert Gordon's Coll., Aberdeen; Aberdeen Univ. MB, ChB Aberdeen 1946; DPH Edinburgh 1950; FRCS 1955; MD Aberdeen 1957; PhD Bristol 1961; MSc Manchester 1969; FRCSE 1973. Lieut and Captain, RAMC, 1947–49. House Surgeon: Aberdeen Royal Infirmary, 1946–47 (House Phys., 1951); Aberdeen Maternity Hosp., 1949; Glasgow Eye Infirmary, 1950–51; Asst, Anatomy Dept, Glasgow Univ., 1951–52; Resident Registrar, Moorfields Eye Hosp., 1953–54; Sen. Registrar, St Thomas' Hosp. and Moorfields Eye Hosp., and Res. Asst, Inst. of Ophthalmology, 1954–58; Consultant Surg., Bristol Eye Hosp., 1958–63; Alexander Piggott Wernher Trav. Fellow, Dept of Ophthal., Harvard Univ., 1960–61; Consultant Ophthalmic Surg., St George's Hosp., 1963–65; Prof. of Ophthal., Manchester Univ., and Hon. Consultant Ophthalmic Surg. to United Manchester Hosps, 1965–72. Hon. FBOA 1975. *Publications:* (ed jtly) Clinical Practice and Economics, 1977; Basic Clinical Ophthalmology, 1984; papers in Brit. and Amer. Jls of Ophthal., Nature, Brain, BMJ, etc, mainly on intra-ocular pressure and glaucoma, retinal detachments, ocular surgery and hereditary diseases. *Address:* Princess Alexandra Eye Pavilion, Chalmers Street, Edinburgh EH3 9HA. *T:* 031–229 2477.

PHILLIPS, Prof. Charles Garrett, FRS 1963; DM; FRCP; Dr Lee's Professor of Anatomy, University of Oxford, 1975–83, now Emeritus; Fellow of Hertford College, Oxford, 1975–83, now Emeritus; *b* 13 October 1916; *s* of Dr George Ramsey Phillips and Flora (*née* Green); *m* 1942, Cynthia Mary, *d* of L. R. Broster, OBE, FRCS; two *d. Educ:* Bradfield; Magdalen College, Oxford; St Bartholomew's Hospital. Captain, RAMC, 1943–46. Reader in Neurophysiology, 1962–66, Prof., 1966–75, Oxford Univ.; Fellow, Trinity Coll., 1946–75, Emeritus Fellow, 1975. Mem., MRC, 1980–84. Hon. Sec., Physiological Society, 1960–66; President: Sect. of Neurology, RSocMed, 1978–79; Assoc. of British Neurologists, 1980–81. Mem., Norwegian Acad. of Sci. and Letters, 1984; Hon. Member: Canadian Neurol Soc.; Belgian Soc. of Electromyography and Clin. Neurophysiology. Editor, Brain, 1975–81. Hon. DSc Monash, 1971. Lectures: Ferrier, 1968; Hughlings Jackson (and Medal), 1973; Victor Horsley Meml, 1981; Sherrington, Univ. of Liverpool, 1982. Feldberg Prize, 1970. *Publications:* Papers on neurophysiology in Jl of Physiology, etc. *Address:* Aubrey House, Horton-cum-Studley, Oxford OX9 1BU. *Club:* United Oxford & Cambridge University.

PHILLIPS, Prof. David; Wolfson Professor of Natural Philosophy since 1980, Deputy Director since 1986, Royal Institution of Great Britain; *b* 3 Dec. 1939; *s* of Stanley and Daphne Ivy Phillips; *m* 1970, Caroline Lucy Scoble; one *d. Educ:* South Shields Grammar-Technical Sch.; Univ. of Birmingham (BSc, PhD). Post doctoral Fellow, Univ. of Texas, 1964–66; Vis. Scientist, Inst. of Chemical Physics, Acad. of Scis of USSR, Moscow, 1966–67; Lectr 1967–73, Sen. Lectr 1973–76, Reader 1976–80, in Phys. Chem., Univ. of Southampton; Actg Dir, Royal Instn, Jan.–Oct. 1986. *Publications:* Time-Correlated Single-Photon Counting (jtly), 1984; Polymer Photophysics, 1985; over 200 res. papers and revs in sci. lit. on photochem., photophys. and lasers. *Recreations:* music, travel, tennis. *Address:* 195 Barnett Wood Lane, Ashtead, Surrey KT21 2LP. *T:* Ashtead 74385. *Club:* Athenæum.

PHILLIPS, (David) Alan; His Honour Judge Phillips; a Circuit Judge, since 1983; *b* 21 July 1926; *s* of Stephen Thomas Phillips, MC and Elizabeth Mary Phillips; *m* 1960, Jean Louise (*née* Godsell); two *s. Educ:* Llanelli Grammar Sch.; University Coll., Oxford (MA). Left school, 1944. Served War, Army, 1944; commnd, 1946, RWF; Captain (GS), 1947; demobilised, 1948. Oxford, 1948–51. Lectr, 1952–59. Called to Bar, Gray's Inn, 1960. Stipendiary Magistrate for Mid-Glamorgan, 1975–83; a Recorder of the Crown Court, 1974–83. *Recreations:* music, chess, swimming. *Address:* The Crown Court, The Castle, Chester.

PHILLIPS, Prof. Sir David (Chilton), Kt 1979; FRS 1967; BSc, PhD (Wales); FInstP; Professor of Molecular Biophysics and Fellow of Corpus Christi College, Oxford, since Oct. 1966; *b* 7 March 1924; *o s* of late Charles Harry Phillips and Edith Harriet Phillips (*née* Finney), Ellesmere, Shropshire; *m* 1960, Diana Kathleen (*née* Hutchinson); one *d. Educ:* Ellesmere C of E Schools; Oswestry Boys' High Sch.; UC, Cardiff. Radar Officer, RNVR, 1944–47. UC, Cardiff, 1942–44 and 1947–51. Post-doctoral Fellow, National Research Council of Canada, 1951–53; Research Officer, National Research Laboratories, Ottawa, 1953–55; Research Worker, Davy Faraday Research Lab., Royal Institution, London, 1955–66; Mem., MRC, 1974–78, Royal Soc. Assessor, 1978–83; Chm., Adv. Bd for the Research Councils, 1983–; Member: Adv. Council for Applied R&D, 1983–; Technology Requirements Bd, 1985–. UK Co-ordinator, Internat. Science Hall, Brussels Exhibition, 1958; Member, European Molecular Biology Organization (EMBO), 1964, Mem. Council, 1972–78; Royal Society: Vice-Pres., 1972–73, 1976–83; Biological Sec., 1976–83; Fullerian (Vis.) Prof. of Physiology, Royal Institution, 1979–85, Christmas lectures, 1980. For. Hon. Member, Amer. Academy of Arts and Sciences, 1968; Hon. Mem., Amer. Society of Biological Chemists, 1969 (Lecturer, 1965); For. Associate, Amer. Nat. Acad. of Science, 1985; Almroth Wright Memorial Lecturer, 1966; Plenary Lectures, Internat. Biochem. Congress, Tokyo, 1967, Hamburg, 1976, Internat. Crystallography Congress, Kyoto, 1972; Hassel Lecture, Oslo, 1968; Krebs Lecture and Medal, FEBS, 1971; Feldberg Prize, 1968; CIBA Medal, Biochem. Soc., 1971; Royal Medal, Royal Society, 1975; (jtly) Prix Charles Léopold Mayer, French Académie des Sciences, 1979. Hon. DSc: Leicester, 1974; Univ. of Wales, 1975; Chicago, 1978; Exeter, 1982; Warwick, 1982; Essex, 1983. Member, Ed. Board, Journal of Molecular Biology, 1966–76. *Publications:* papers in Acta Cryst. and other journals. *Address:* Molecular Biophysics Laboratory, Zoology Department, Rex Richards Building, South Parks Road, Oxford OX1 3QU. *T:* Oxford 50454; 3 Fairlawn End, Upper Wolvercote, Oxford OX2 8AR. *T:* Oxford 55828; Corpus Christi College, Oxford.

PHILLIPS, Prof. Dewi Zephaniah; Professor of Philosophy, University College, Swansea, since 1971; *b* 24 Nov. 1934; *s* of David Oakley Phillips and Alice Frances Phillips; *m* 1959, Margaret Monica Hanford; three *s. Educ:* Swansea Grammar Sch.; UC

Swansea (MA); St Catherine's Society, Oxford (BLitt). Asst Lectr, Queen's Coll., Dundee, Univ. of St Andrews, 1961–62; Lectr: at Queen's Coll., Dundee, 1962–63; UC Bangor, 1963–65; UC Swansea, 1965–67; Sen. Lectr, UC Swansea, 1967–71. Visiting Professor: Yale Univ., 1985; Claremont Graduate Sch., 1986. Hintz Meml Lectr, Univ. of Arizona, Tucson, 1975; Vis. Prof. and McMartin Lectr, Univ. of Carleton, 1976; Agnes Cuming Visitor, Univ. Coll. Dublin, 1982; William James Lectr, Lousiana State Univ., 1982; Marett Lectr, Oxford, 1983; Riddell Meml Lectr, 1986; Aquinas Lectr, Oxford, 1987. Editor, Philosophical Investigations, 1982–. *Publications:* The Concept of Prayer, 1965; (ed) Religion and Understanding, 1967; (ed) Saith Ysgrif Ar Grefydd, 1967; (with H. O. Mounce) Moral Practices, 1970; Death and Immortality, 1970; Faith and Philosophical Enquiry, 1970; (with Ilham Dilman) Sense and Delusion, 1971; Athronyddu Am Grefydd, 1974; Religion Without Explanation, 1976; (ed) John Anderson: Education and Inquiry, 1980; Through A Darkening Glass: Philosophy, Literature and Cultural Change, 1981; Dramau Gwenlyn Parry, 1981; Belief, Changes and Forms of Life, 1986; R. S. Thomas: poet of the hidden God, 1986; General Editor: Studies in Ethics and the Philosophy of Religion, 1968–74; Values and Philosophical Enquiry, 1976–86; papers in philosophical jls. *Recreations:* lawn tennis and supporting Swansea City AFC. *Address:* 45 Queen's Road, Sketty, Swansea. *T:* Swansea 203935.

PHILLIPS, Douglas Herbert Charles; HM Diplomatic Service, retired; Deputy High Commissioner, Sri Lanka, and Counsellor, Maldives, 1978–81; *b* 4 Nov. 1924; *s* of late Herbert Henry Phillips and Aida Phillips (*née* Gervasi); *m* 1st, 1950, Olwen Laverick (*d* 1971); one *d*; 2nd, 1972, Noreen Evelyn Mendelsohn; one step *s* one step *d*. *Educ:* Vaughan Sch., Kensington. RN, 1943–46; Min. of Civil Aviation, 1947; joined Commonwealth Service, 1948; served in Pakistan (Karachi and Peshawar), 1950–53; Second Sec., Calcutta, 1954–57; First Sec., Bombay, 1959–62; CRO, 1963–64; Diplomatic Service Admin., 1965–67; First Sec. (Commercial), Melbourne, 1967–72; FCO, 1972–75; First Sec. (Commercial), Singapore, 1975–78. *Address:* 7 Talbots Drive, Maidenhead, Berks. *T:* Maidenhead 35240. *Clubs:* Royal Colombo Golf; Warren (Singapore); Gymkhana (Bombay).

PHILLIPS, Edward Thomas John, CBE 1985; Controller, English Language and Literature Division, British Council, since 1985; *b* 5 Feb. 1930; *s* of late Edward Emery Kent Phillips and of Margaret Elsie Phillips; *m* 1952, Sheila May (*née* Abbott); two *s* two *d*. *Educ:* Exmouth Grammar Sch., University Coll. London; Inst. of Education, London; School of Oriental and African Studies London (BA Hons; postgraduate Cert. of Educn; Dip. in linguistics). RAF, 1948–49. HMOCS, Educn Officer, Nigeria, 1953–62; British Council: Head, Cultural and Educn Unit, Overseas Students' Dept, 1962–65; English Lang. Officer, Enugu, Nigeria, 1966–67; Sen. Lectr, Coll. of Educn, Lagos Univ., Nigeria, 1967–70; English Lang. Teaching Advr, Min. of Educn, Cyprus, 1970–72; Chief Inspector, English Teaching Div., London, 1972–75; Rep., Bangladesh, Dacca, 1975–77; Dir, Personnel Dept and Dep. Controller Personnel Staff Recruitment Div., 1977–80; Rep, Malaysia, 1980–85. *Publications:* (ed jtly) Organised English, Books I and II, 1973; contribs to English Language Teaching Jl. *Recreations:* music, theatre, tennis, golf, swiming. *Address:* 1 Bredune, Off Church Road, Kenley, Surrey. *T:* 01–660 1929.

PHILLIPS, Edwin William, MBE 1946; Chairman: Friends Provident Life Office, since 1968; United Kingdom Provident Institution, since 1986; Director, Lazard Bros & Co. Ltd, 1960–83; *b* 29 Jan. 1918; *s* of C. E. Phillips, Chiswick; *m* 1951, P. M. Matusch; two *s*. *Educ:* Latymer Upper Sch. Joined Edward de Stein & Co., Merchant Bankers, 1934. Army, 1939–46; Major, Sherwood Rangers Yeomanry. Rejoined Edward de Stein & Co., 1946, Partner, 1954; merged into Lazard Bros & Co. Ltd, 1960. Director: British Rail Property Bd, 1970; Phoenix Assurance, 1975–85; Woolwich Equitable Building Soc., 1977 (Vice-Chm., 1984–86; Sen. Vice-Chm., 1986–). *Recreation:* cricket. *Address:* Latymer House, Pennymead Rise, East Horsley, Surrey. *T:* East Horsley 4810. *Club:* MCC.

PHILLIPS, Eric Lawrance, CMG 1963; retired; *b* 23 July 1909; *s* of L. Stanley Phillips and Maudie Phillips (*née* Eekan), London, NW1; *m* 1938, Phyllis Bray, Artist; two *s* one step *d*. *Educ:* Haileybury Coll.; Balliol Coll., Oxford (Scholar, BA). With Erlangers Ltd, 1932–39. Served War of 1939–45, Captain, RA. Principal, Bd of Trade, 1945, Monopolies Commn, 1949; Asst Secretary, Monopolies Commn, 1951, Bd of Trade, 1952; Under-Sec., Bd of Trade, 1964–69; Sec., Monopolies Commn, 1969–74; consultant to Monopolies and Mergers Commn, 1974–75. Hon. Chm., Abbeyfield West London Soc., 1980–86. *Recreations:* looking at pictures, places and buildings. *Address:* 46 Platts Lane, NW3. *T:* 01–435 7873. *Club:* Royal Automobile.

See also A. A. C. Phillips.

PHILLIPS, Sir Fred (Albert), Kt 1967; CVO 1966; Senior Legal Adviser, Cable and Wireless (West Indies); *b* 14 May 1918; *s* of Wilbert A. Phillips, Brighton, St Vincent. *Educ:* London Univ. (LLB); Toronto Univ.; McGill Univ. (MCL); Hague Acad. of International Law. Called to the Bar, Middle Temple. Legal Clerk to Attorney-General of St Vincent, 1942–45; Principal Officer, Secretariat, 1945–47; Windward Island: Chief Clerk, Governor's Office, 1948–49; District Officer/Magistrate of District III, 1949–53; Magistrate, Grenada, and Comr of Carriacou, 1953–56; Asst Administrator and MEC, Grenada, 1957–58 (Officer Administrating the Govt, April 1958); Senior Asst Sec., Secretariat, Fedn of W Indies (dealing with constitutional development), 1958–60; Permanent Sec. (Sec. to Cabinet), 1960–62 (when Fedn dissolved); actg Administrator of Montserrat, 1961–62; Sen. Lectr, Univ. of W Indies and Sen. Resident Tutor, Dept of Extra-mural Studies, Barbados, 1962–63; Registrar, Coll. of Arts and Science, Univ. of W Indies, 1963–64; Sen. Res. Fellow, Faculty of Law and Centre for Developing Area Studies, McGill Univ., 1964–65; Guggenheim Fellow, 1965; Administrator of St Kitts, 1966–67; Governor, St Kitts/Nevis/Anguilla, 1967–69. Has attended numerous conferences as a Legal or Constitutional Adviser. KStJ 1968. *Publications:* Freedom in the Caribbean: a study in constitutional change, 1977; The Evolving Legal Profession in the Commonwealth, 1978; West Indian Constitutions: post-Independence reforms, 1985; papers in various jls. *Recreations:* reading, bridge. *Address:* Chambers, Kingstown, St Vincent, West Indies; PO Box 206, Bridgetown, Barbados.

PHILLIPS, (Gerald) Hayden; Deputy Secretary, Cabinet Office (Management and Personnel Office), since 1986; *b* 9 Feb. 1943; *s* of Gerald Phillips and Dorothy Phillips; *m* 1st, 1967, Dr Ann Watkins (marr. diss.); one *s* one *d*; 2nd, 1980, Hon. Laura Grenfell; two *d*. *Educ:* Cambridgeshire High Sch.; Clare Coll., Cambridge (MA); Yale Univ., USA (MA). Home Office: Asst Principal, 1967; Economic Adviser, 1970–72; Principal, 1972–74; Asst Sec., and Principal Private Sec. to Sec. of State for Home Dept, 1974–76; Dep. Chef de Cabinet to Pres., Commn of European Communities, 1977–79; Asst Sec., Home Office, 1979–81, Asst Under-Sec. of State, 1981–86. *Address:* c/o Cabinet Office (Management and Personnel Office), Great George Street, SW1P 3AL. *Club:* Brooks's.

PHILLIPS, Hayden; *see* Phillips, G. H.

PHILLIPS, Sir Henry (Ellis Isidore), Kt 1964; CMG 1960; MBE 1946; Director, SIFIDA Investment Co. (SA), since 1970, and other companies; Chairman, Ashley Industrial Trust plc, since 1986; *b* 30 Aug. 1914; *s* of late Harry J. Phillips, MBE; *m* 1st, 1941, Vivien Hyamson (marr. diss., 1965); two *s* one *d*; 2nd, 1966, Philippa Cohen. *Educ:* Haberdashers' Sch., Hampstead; University College, London. BA (London) 1936; MA 1939. Inst. of Historical Research, 1936–39. FRHistS. Commissioned in Beds and Herts Regt, 1939; served War of 1939–45, with 5th Bn, becoming Adjutant; POW, Singapore, 1942. Joined Colonial Administrative Service and appointed to Nyasaland, 1946 (until retirement in 1965); Development Secretary, 1952; seconded to Federal Treasury of Rhodesia and Nyasaland, 1953–57, Dep. Sec., 1956; Financial Sec., Nyasaland Govt, 1957–64, and Minister of Finance, 1961–64. Man. Dir, Standard Bank Finance and Development Corp., 1966–72. Dir, Nat. Bank of Malaŵi, 1983–. Mem., Civil Aviation Authority, 1975–80. Dep. Chm., Stonham Housing Assoc.; Hon. Treasurer, Stonham Meml Trust. *Address:* 34 Ross Court, Putney Hill, SW15. *T:* 01 789 1404. *Clubs:* MCC, Royal Commonwealth Society.

PHILLIPS, Herbert Moore, CMG 1949; MA; *b* 7 Feb. 1908; *s* of Herbert Phillips and Beatrice Moore; *m* 1934, Martha Löffler (marr. diss.); one *d*; *m* 1952, Doris Rushbrooke. *Educ:* St Olave's; Wadham Coll., Oxford (MA (Hons) Oxon 1931). Entered Min. of Labour, 1934; Asst Sec., Manpower Dept, 1942–45, Overseas Dept 1946; FO, 1946–49, as Counsellor for Econ. and Soc. Affairs in UK Delegn at seat of UN, Alternate UK Delegate to ECOSOC and Delegate to ECLA; Consultant, ECLA, 1950–51; UNESCO, 1952–68, as Head of Div. of Applied Social Sciences and Dir Analysis Office. Consultant, 1968–: OECD; UNESCO, UN, UNICEF, World Bank; Leader of World Bank Missions to Ethiopia, Taiwan and Turkey for preparation of educn loans; Mem., UN Family Planning Mission to Iran. *Publications:* Literacy and Development, 1970; Basic Education, a World Challenge, 1975; Educational Cooperation between Developed and Developing Countries, 1976. *Address:* Hameau du Plan, Plan de la Tour, 83120 Ste Maxime, France.

PHILLIPS, Sir Horace, KCMG 1973 (CMG 1963); HM Diplomatic Service, retired; Resident Representative, Taylor Woodrow International Ltd, in China (Peking), since 1985; *b* 31 May 1917; *s* of Samuel Phillips; *m* 1944, Idina Doreen Morgan; one *s* one *d*. *Educ:* Hillhead High Sch., Glasgow. Joined Board of Inland Revenue, 1935. Served War of 1939–45, Dorsetshire and 1st Punjab Regts, 1940–47. Transf. to FO, Oct. 1947; Acting Vice-Consul, Shiraz, Nov. 1947; Vice-Consul, Bushire, 1948 (Acting Consul, 1948); 1st Secretary and Consul, 1949; Kabul, Oct. 1949; Foreign Office, 1951; 1st Secretary, and Consul, Jedda, 1953; Counsellor, 1956; seconded to Colonial Office, Dec. 1956, as Protectorate Secretary, Aden, until Aug. 1960; Counsellor, British Embassy, Tehran, Oct. 1960; Deputy Political Resident in the Persian Gulf, at Bahrain, 1964–66; Ambassador to Indonesia, 1966–68; High Comr in Tanzania, 1968–72; Ambassador to Turkey, 1973–77. Resident Rep., Iran, 1978–79, Hong Kong, 1979–84, Bahrain, 1984–85, Taylor Woodrow Internat. Hon. LLD Glasgow, 1977. Order of the Taj (Iran), 1961. *Recreations:* swimming, languages, long-distance car driving. *Address:* 34a Sheridan Road, Merton Park, SW19 3HP. *T:* 01–542 3836, 1780. *Clubs:* Travellers'; Hong Kong (Hong Kong).

PHILLIPS, Ian, FCA; Director, Finance and Planning, British Railways Board, since 1985; *b* 16 July 1938; *s* of Wilfrid and Dorothy Phillips; *m* 1961, Fay Rosemary Stoner; two *s*. *Educ:* Whitgift Sch., South Croydon. Articled clerk, Hatfield Dixon Roberts Wright & Co., Accountants, 1955–61; Senior Asst, Robert J. Ward & Co., Accountants, 1961–65; Management Services Dept, John Lewis' Partnership, 1965–69; London Transport Executive: Director of Corporate Planning, 1969–75; Chief Business Planning Officer, 1975–78; Group Planning Director, 1978–80; Mem. Board, LTE, later LRT, 1980–84. *Recreations:* playing golf, watching any sport, the country, spending time with my family. *Address:* 113 Lower Camden, Chislehurst, Kent. *T:* 01–467 0529; Bakers Cottage, Church Road, Quenington, near Cirencester, Glos.

PHILLIPS, Jeremy Patrick Manfred, QC 1980; *b* 27 Feb. 1941; *s* of late Manfred Henry Phillips, CA, and late Irene Margaret (*née* Symondson); *m* 1968, Virginia Gwendoline (*née* Dwyer) (marr. diss. 1974); two *s*; *m* 1976, Judith Gaskell (*née* Hetherington); two *s* two *d*. *Educ:* St Edmund's Sch., Hindhead, Surrey; Charterhouse. Apprentice Accountant, Thomson McLintock & Co., 1957–61. Called to Bar, Gray's Inn, 1964; in practice, 1964–. Owner of Kentwell Hall, Long Melford, Suffolk, 1971–; organizer of Kentwell's Annual Historical Re-Creations of Tudor Domestic Life. *Publications:* contrib. Cooper's Students' Manual of Auditing, Cooper's Manual of Auditing and various pamphlets, papers, guides, etc, on Kentwell Hall and Tudor period. *Recreations:* Kentwell Hall, historic buildings, Tudor history and Tudor domestic life. *Address:* Kentwell Hall, Long Melford, Suffolk.

PHILLIPS, John, RIBA; architect in private practice, since 1955; *b* 25 Nov. 1926; *s* of John Tudor Phillips and Bessie Maud Phillips; *m* 1955, Eileen Margaret Fryer. *Educ:* Christ's Coll., Finchley; Northern Polytechnic, Holloway. ARIBA 1954. Studied under Romilly B. Craze, Architect, 1948–52. Surveyor to the Fabric: Truro Cathedral, 1961 (Consultant Architect, 1979–); Westminster Cathedral, 1976–; RIBA 1979–. Pres., Ecclesiastical Architects' and Surveyors' Assoc., 1982. *Recreations:* looking at churches, choral singing. *Address:* (home) 8 Friary Way, North Finchley, N12 9PH. *T:* 01–445 3414; (office) 55 Britton Street, EC1M 5NA. *T:* 01–253 4340.

PHILLIPS, John Fleetwood Stewart, CMG 1965; HM Diplomatic Service, retired; *b* 16 Dec. 1917; *e s* of late Major Herbert Stewart Phillips, 27th Light Cavalry, and Violet Gordon, *d* of late Sir Alexander Pinhey, KCSI; *m* 1948, Mary Gordon Shaw, MB, BS; two *s* two *d*. *Educ:* Brighton; Worcester Coll., Oxford (Open Exhibition in Classics, MA). Represented Univ. and County intermittently at Rugby football, 1938–39. Served with 1st Bn, Argyll and Sutherland Highlanders in N Africa and Crete (wounded and captured, 1941). Appointed to Sudan Political Service, 1945; served in Kordofan and Blue Nile Provinces. HM Diplomatic Service, 1955, served in Foreign Office; Oriental Secretary in Libya, 1957; Consul-General at Muscat, 1960–63; Counsellor, British Embassy, Amman, 1963–66; Imperial Defence Coll., 1967; Dep. High Comr, Cyprus, 1968; Ambassador to Southern Yemen, 1969–70, to Jordan, 1970–72, to Sudan, 1973–77. *Recreations:* gardening and feuding. *Address:* Southwood, Gordon Road, Horsham, Sussex. *T:* Horsham 52894. *Club:* Travellers'.

PHILLIPS, John Francis, CBE 1977 (OBE 1957); QC 1981; arbitrator; Chairman: London Court of International Arbitration, since 1984; Provident Association for Medical Care (Private Patients Plan), 1977–84, now President (Vice-Chairman, 1972–77; Director, since 1958); *b* 1911; *e s* of late F. W. Phillips and late Margaret (*née* Gillan); *m* 1937, Olive M. Royer; one *s* two *d*. *Educ:* Cardinal Vaughan Sch.; London Univ.; Trinity Hall, Cambridge. LLB (Hons) London; LLB (1st Cl. Hons), LLM Cantab. Barrister-at-law, Gray's Inn, 1944. Civil Servant (Lord Chancellor's Dept, Royal Courts of Justice), 1933–44; Parly Sec. and Asst Gen. Sec., Nat. Farmers' Union of England and Wales, 1945–57; Institute of Chartered Secretaries and Administrators: Sec. and Chief Exec., 1957–76; Mem. Council, 1976–81; Pres., 1977. Member: Council, Chartered Inst. of Arbitrators, 1969–83 (Vice-Pres., 1974–76; Pres., 1976–77); Gen. Cttee, Bar Assoc. for Commerce, Finance and Industry, 1967– (Vice-Chm., 1976–78 and 1980–81; Chm., 1978–80; Vice-Pres., 1982); Senate of the Inns of Court and the Bar; Bar Council; Cttees of Senate and Council, 1978–83; Council for Accreditation of Correspondence Colls, 1969–80 (Hon. Treas., 1969–74; Chm., 1975–80); British Egg Marketing Bd, 1969–71; Departmental Cttee of Enquiry into Fowl Pest, 1971; Vice-Chm. and Mem., Business

Educn Council, 1974–80; Chairman: Jt Cttee for Awards in Business Studies and Public Admin., 1968–75 (Mem. Jt Cttee for Awards, 1960–75); Associated Examining Bd, GCE, 1976– (Mem., 1958–; Vice-Chm., 1973–76); Houghton Poultry Res. Station, 1976–82 (Governor, 1973–82); Dep. Chm., Eggs Authority, 1971–80. Governor: Christ's Hospital, 1957–; Crossways Trust, 1959–71 (Financial Advisor, 1966–71); Nuffield Nursing Homes Trust, 1975–81 (Vice-Pres., 1981–84); Mem. Council and Exec. Cttee, Animal Health Trust, 1976–; Deleg. to Internat. Labour Conf., 1950–56. FCIS 1958; FCIArb (FIArb 1966); CBIM (Council of Inst., 1969–74). Master, Co. of Chartered Secretaries and Administrators, 1978; Founder Master, Worshipful Co. of Arbitrators, 1980–82; Master, Co. of Scriveners, 1982–83. OStJ. DCL City Univ., 1985. *Publications:* The Agriculture Act, 1947, 1948; Heywood and Massey's Lunacy Practice, 1939; many articles on aspects of law relating to land, agriculture and arbitration. *Recreation:* travel. *Address:* 17 Ossulton Way, Hampstead Garden Suburb, N2 0DT. *T:* 01–455 8460; (office) Private Patients Plan, Tavistock House, Tavistock Square, WC1H 9LJ; (chambers) 1 Verulam Buildings, Gray's Inn, WC1. *Clubs:* Athenæum, United Oxford & Cambridge University, City Livery.

PHILLIPS, Prof. John Guest, PhD, DSc; FRS 1981; Vice-Chancellor and Hon. Professor, Loughborough University of Technology, since 1986; *b* 13 June 1933; *s* of Owen Gwynne Phillips and Dorothy Constance Phillips; *m* 1961, Jacqueline Ann Myles-White; two *s*. *Educ:* Llanelli Grammar Sch. (County Major Scholar); Univ. of Liverpool (State Scholar, Univ. Studentship; ARC Studentship). BSc 1954, PhD 1957, Liverpool; DSc Hong Kong 1967; FIBiol; CBiol; FRSocMed. Vis. Scientist: Collège de France, 1955; CIBA Ag, Basel, 1956; Commonwealth Fund Fellow, Yale Univ., 1957–59; Fellow, Davenport Coll., Yale Univ., 1957–59; Lectr in Zoology, Univ. of Sheffield, 1959–62; Vis. Asst Prof., Univ. of BC, 1959; Milton Res. Assoc., Harvard Univ., 1960; Prof. of Zoology, Univ. of Hong Kong, 1962–67; Dir, Nuffield Unit, Univ. of Hong Kong, 1963–67; Dean of Faculty of Science, Hong Kong, 1965–66, acting Vice-Chancellor, 1966; Vis. Scientist, US Navy Namru 2, Manilla, 1963; University of Hull: Prof. and Head of Dept of Zoology, 1967–79; Dir, Wolfson Lab. for Res. in Gerontology, 1975–79; Dean, Faculty of Science, 1978–80; Wolfson Professor and Dir Wolfson Inst., 1979–85; Public Orator, 1970, 1972, 1976, 1979–81, 1983; Sen. Fellow, SERC (formerly SRC), 1979–83. Visiting Professor: Biology, Univ. of California, 1975; Pharmacology and Therapeutics, Univ. of Texas, 1979; Bengurion Univ., Israel, 1980; McKenzie Vis. Prof., Univ. of Alberta, 1986. Distinguished Visitor, La Trobe Univ., 1983; Vis. Fellow, Commonwealth Scholarship and Fellowship Plan to Australia, 1984. Member: Commonwealth Scholarships Commn, 1968–; Royal Commn for Exhibition of 1851, 1986–; Council, Marine Biological Assoc. of UK, 1969–71; Biology Cttee, SRC, 1975–78; Cttee of Soc. for Endocrinology, 1971–84; Treasurer, Soc. for Endocrinology, 1975–81, Chm., 1981–84; Chm., British Endocrine Socs, 1981–84. Chm., Hull DHA, 1981–84; Member: Humberside AHA, 1974–81 (Vice-Chm., 1979–81); Humberside Area Nurse Educn Adv. Cttee (Chm., 1976–82); Internat. Cttee for Comparative Endocrinology, 1974–; Humber Adv. Gp, 1975–80; Internat. Cttee for Endocrinology, 1976–84; Commonwealth Human Ecology Council, 1976–80; Exec. Cttee, British Soc. for Res. in Ageing, 1976– (Treas., 1980–83; Chm., 1983–87); Institute of Biology: Vice-Pres., 1983–84; Pres. Yorkshire Br., 1969–72; Mem. Council, 1979–84, Sec., 1982–84, Zool Soc. of London; Vice Pres., Soc. for Wildlife Art of the Nation. Chm., Editl Bd, Jl of Endocrinology, 1982–84 (Mem. 1971–84, Chm. 1981–84, Council of Management); Associate Editor, Procs of Royal Soc., 1982–; Mem., Editl Bd, Age and Ageing, 1983–. Fellow, Acad. of Zoology of India, 1966–. Trustee: Hull and E Riding Cardiac Trust, 1983–; Ferens Educnl Trust, 1983–; Chm. Bd of Trustees, Post Grad. Med. Educn Centre, Hull, 1983–. Governor: Endsleigh Coll. of Educn, Hull, 1967–77; St Anne's Special Sch., Hull, 1975–81 (Vice-Chm., 1978–81); Bridgeview Special Sch., 1977–81; Wold Special Sch., 1983–; Loughborough Endowed Schools. Assessor: Univ. of Malaya, 1979–; Univ. of Singapore, 1981–; British Council Visitor, Hungary, 1968, Singapore, 1982. Mem., Academic Adv. Council, 1978–84, Patron, 1984–, Univ. of Buckingham (formerly University Coll. of Buckingham). Annual Lecture, Biological Council, 1982; Colin Roscoe Lectr, Univ. of Manchester, 1984. Zoological Soc. of London Scientific Medal, 1970; Medal of Soc. for Endocrinology, 1971. *Publications:* Hormones and the Environment, 1971; Environmental Physiology, 1975; Physiological Strategies in Avian Biology, 1985; numerous papers in zoological, endocrinological and physiological jls. *Recreations:* gardening, music, travel. *Address:* Vice-Chancellor's Office, Loughborough University of Technology, Loughborough, Leics LE11 3TU. *T:* Loughborough 263171. *Club:* Royal Commonwealth Society.

PHILLIPS, Air Cdre Manfred Norman; retired, RAF Medical Branch; Consultant Radiologist, RAF Hospital, Ely, 1968–77; *b* 6 Nov. 1912; *s* of Lewis and Norah Phillips, Portsmouth; *m* 1942, Dorothy Ellen (*née* Green); two *s*. *Educ:* Liverpool Coll.; Liverpool Univ. Med. Sch.; Middlesex Hospital. MB, ChB 1936; DMRD 1954. *Publications:* articles in Brit. Jl Clinical Practice and Brit. Jl Radiology. *Recreations:* gardening, golf, walking. *Address:* Quaney, 83C Cambridge Road, Ely, Cambs. *T:* Ely 3539.

PHILLIPS, Marisa, DLitt; Principal Assistant Director of Public Prosecutions, since 1985; *b* 14 April 1932; *d* of Dr and Mrs J. Fargion; *m* 1956, Philip Harold Phillips; one *s* one *d*. *Educ:* Henrietta Barnet Sch., London; Rome Univ. (DLitt); Univ. of Redlands, California (Fulbright Schol.; BA Hons). Called to Bar, Lincoln's Inn, 1963. On return from Redlands Univ., worked for US Inf. Service, Rome, 1954–56; spent one year in Berlin, as husband then in Army; period of work with Penguin Books; read for the Bar, joining DPP as Legal Asst, 1964; Legal Adviser, Police Complaints Bd, 1977; returned to DPP, 1979; Asst Dir, DPP, 1981. *Recreations:* music, theatre, foreign travel. *Address:* Dane Court, 6 Kidderpore Avenue, NW3 7SP. *T:* 01–435 9293.

PHILLIPS, Captain Mark Anthony Peter, CVO 1974; ADC(P); *b* 22 Sept. 1948; *s* of P. W. G. Phillips, MC, and Anne Patricia (*née* Tiarks); *m* 1973, HRH The Princess Anne; one *s* one *d*. *Educ:* Marlborough Coll.; RMA Sandhurst. Joined 1st The Queen's Dragoon Guards, July 1969; Regimental duty, 1969–74; Company Instructor, RMA Sandhurst, 1974–77; Army Trng Directorate, MoD, 1977–78, retired. Personal ADC to HM the Queen, 1974–. Student, RAC Cirencester, 1978. In Three Day Equestrian Event, GB winning teams: Team Championships: World, 1970; European, 1971; Olympic Gold Medallists (Team), Olympic Games, Munich, 1972; Mem., Equestrian Team (Reserve), Olympic Games, Mexico, 1968 and Montreal, 1976. Winner, Badminton Three Day Event, 1971, 1972, 1974, 1981. Chm., Glos Youth Assoc.; Patron: BAFPA; Everyman Theatre, Cheltenham. Liveryman: Farriers' Co.; Farmers' Co; Carmen's Co.; Freeman: Loriners Co.; City of London; Yeoman, Saddlers' Co. *Recreations:* riding, Rugby football, athletics. *Address:* Buckingham Palace, SW1. *Club:* (Hon. Mem.) Buck's.

See also under Royal Family.

PHILLIPS, Max; Assistant Secretary, Ministry of Defence, since 1984; *b* 31 March 1924; *m* 1953, Patricia Moore; two *s* two *d*. *Educ:* Colston's Sch., Bristol; Christ's Hospital; Magdalene Coll., Cambridge (Schol.; 1st cl. Hist. Tripos, pts I and II; MA). Served War, RA, 1943–46. Appointed to Home Civil Service, 1949; Colonial Office, 1949–59; Sec., Nigeria Fiscal Commn, 1957–58; UKAEA, 1959–73; Procurement Exec., MoD, 1973–74; HM Treasury, 1974–77; Asst Under Sec. of State, MoD, 1977–84. Governor and Almoner, Christ's Hospital. *Recreations:* modern myths, exploring the imagination and the countryside. *Address:* 2 Wilderness Farmhouse, Onslow Village, Guildford, Surrey GU2 5QP. *T:* Guildford 61308.

PHILLIPS, Prof. Neville Crompton, CMG 1973; Vice-Chancellor and Rector, University of Canterbury, Christchurch, New Zealand 1966–77; retired; *b* 7 March 1916; 2nd *s* of Samuel and Clara Phillips, Christchurch, NZ; *m* 1940, Pauline Beatrice, 3rd *d* of Selby and Dorothy Palmer, Te Aratipi, Havelock North, NZ; one *s* two *d*. *Educ:* Dannevirke High Sch.; Palmerston North Boys' High Sch.; Canterbury University College; Merton Coll., Oxford. BA (NZ) 1936; MA 1938; Hon. LittD (Cantuar) 1977; NZ University Post-Grad. Schol. in Arts, Arnold Atkinson Prizeman, 1938; Journalist, Sun and Press, Christchurch, 1932–38; read PPE at Oxford, 1938–39; RA (Gunner, subseq. Major), 1939–46; service in Tunisia and Italy (despatches). Lecturer in History and Political Science, Canterbury University College, 1946–47; Senior Lecturer, 1948; Prof. of History and Political Science, 1949–62; Prof. of History, 1962–66; Emeritus Prof., 1966; presented with Festschrift, 1984. Chairman: Canterbury Centennial Provincial Historical Cttee, 1948–66; Management Cttee, Canterbury Archaeological Trust, Kent, 1980–83; 1st Pres., Canterbury Historical Assoc., 1953; Editorial Adviser, NZ War Histories, 1957–67; US Dept of State Leader Grantee, 1966; Member: Council, Canterbury Manufacturers' Assoc., 1967–77; Christchurch Teachers' Coll. Council, 1968–76; NZ Vice-Chancellors' Cttee, 1966–77 (Chm., 1973–74); Council, Assoc. of Commonwealth Univs, 1973–74; NZ Council Educational Research, 1973–77. *Publications:* Italy, vol. 1 (The Sangro to Cassino), 1957 (New Zealand War Histories); Yorkshire and English National Politics, 1783–84, 1961; The Role of the University in Professional Education, 1970; (ed) A History of the University of Canterbury, 1873–1973, 1973; articles, mainly on eighteenth-century English politics, in English and NZ jls. *Recreations:* walking, supermarket wine, watching cricket, things Italian. *Address:* Tyle House, Hackington Road, Tyler Hill, Canterbury, Kent CT2 9NF. *T:* Canterbury 471708.

PHILLIPS, Nicholas Addison, QC 1978; a Recorder of the Crown Court, since 1982; *b* 21 Jan. 1938; *m* 1972, Christylle Marie-Thérèse Rouffiac (*née* Doreau); two *d*, and one step *s* one step *d*. *Educ:* Bryanston Sch.; King's Coll., Cambridge (MA). Nat. Service with RN; commnd RNVR, 1956–58. Called to Bar, Middle Temple (Harmsworth Scholar), 1962, Bencher, 1984. In practice at Bar, 1962–. Jun. Counsel to Minister of Defence and to Treasury in Admiralty matters, 1973–78. Mem., Panel of Wreck Comrs, 1979. Governor, Bryanston Sch., 1975– (Chm. of Governors, 1981–). *Recreations:* sea and mountains. *Address:* 31 Hampstead Hill Gardens, NW3. *T:* 01–435 6180. *Club:* Brooks's.

PHILLIPS, Prof. Owen Martin, FRS 1968; Decker Professor of Science and Engineering, Johns Hopkins University, since 1975; *b* 30 Dec. 1930; *s* of Richard Keith Phillips and Madeline Lofts; *m* 1953, Merle Winifred Simons; two *s* two *d*. *Educ:* University of Sydney; Trinity Coll., Cambridge Univ. ICI Fellow, Cambridge, 1955–57; Fellow, St John's Coll., Cambridge, 1957–60; Asst Prof., 1957–60, Assoc. Prof., 1960–63, Johns Hopkins Univ.; Asst Director of Research, Cambridge, 1961–64; Prof. of Geophysical Mechanics, Johns Hopkins Univ., 1963–68, of Geophysics, 1968–75. Assoc. Editor Jl of Fluid Mechanics, 1964–; Mem. Council, Nat. Center of Atmospheric Research, Boulder, Colorado, 1964–68; Member: US Nat. Cttee Global Atmospheric Research Project, 1968; Res. Co-ord. Panel, Gas Research Inst., 1981–; Principal Staff, Applied Phys. Lab., 1982–. Mem.-at-large, Amer. Meteorol. Soc. Publications Commn, 1971–75; Pres., Maryland Acad. of Scis, 1979–85. Sec., Bd of Trustees, Chesapeake Res. Consortium, 1973–74 (Trustee, 1972–75). Adams Prize, Univ. of Cambridge, 1965; Sverdrup Gold Medal, Amer. Metereol. Soc., 1975. *Publications:* The Dynamics of the Upper Ocean, 1966, 3rd edn 1976, Russian edn 1968; The Heart of the Earth, 1968, Italian edns 1970, 1975; The Last Chance Energy Book, 1979; (ed) Wave Dynamics and Radio Probing of the Ocean Surface, 1985; various scientific papers in Jl Fluid Mechanics, Proc. Cambridge Philos. Soc., Jl Marine Research, Proc. Royal Society, Deep Sea Research, Journal Geophys. Research. *Address:* 23 Merrymount Road, Baltimore, Maryland 21210, USA. *T:* 433–7195. *Clubs:* Johns Hopkins (Baltimore), Hamilton Street (Baltimore); Quissett Yacht (Mass).

PHILLIPS, Reginald Arthur, CMG 1965; OBE 1951; Deputy Director-General, British Council, 1966–73, retired; *b* 31 Jan. 1913; *y s* of late James and Catherine Ann Phillips, Tredegar, Mon; *m* 1939, Doris Tate, *d* of William and Angelina Tate, São Paulo, Brazil; one *s* two *d*. *Educ:* Tredegar Grammar Sch.; Balliol Coll., Oxford (MA). Asst Master, St Paul's School, Brazil, 1936; Lecturer, Anglo-Brazilian Cultural Society, 1937–39. War of 1939–45: Intelligence Corps (Major), 1940–46. British Council: Latin America Dept, 1947; Home Div., 1948–54; Colonies Dept, 1954–57; Controller, Commonwealth Div., 1957–59; Controller, Finance Div., 1959–62; Assistant Director-General, 1962–66. *Recreations:* golf, walking, television, gardening. *Address:* 76 Chiltley Way, Liphook, Hants. *T:* Liphook 722610. *Club:* Athenæum.

PHILLIPS, Surgeon Rear-Adm. Rex Philip, CB 1972; OBE 1963; Medical Officer-in-Charge, Royal Naval Hospital, Plymouth, 1969–72, retired; *b* 17 May 1913; 2nd *s* of William John Phillips, late Consultant Anaesthetist at Royal Victoria Infirmary, Newcastle upon Tyne, and Nora Graham Phillips; *m* 1939, Gill Foley; two *s*. *Educ:* Epsom Coll.; Coll. of Med., Newcastle upon Tyne, Univ. of Durham (now Univ. of Newcastle upon Tyne). Qual. MB, BS 1937; Ho. Surg., Ingham Infirmary, S Shields, 1938. Joined RN, 1939; served War of 1939–45: HMS Rochester, 1939–41; Royal Marines, 1941–43; HMS Simba, 1943–45. HMS Excellent, 1945–47; qual. Dip. in Ophthalmology (London), 1948; HMS Implacable, Fleet MO, 1949–51; Specialist in Ophthalmology: HMS Ganges, 1951–53; Central Air Med. Bd, 1953–55; RN Hosp., Malta (Senior), 1955–57; Admty Adv. in Ophth. to Med. Dir-Gen., 1957–65; Surg. Captain 1963; SMO, RN Hosp., Malta, 1965–68; Staff MO to Flag Officer Submarines, 1968–69. QHS 1969–72. CStJ 1970. *Recreations:* golf, bridge. *Address:* Langstone House, 25 Langstone High Street, Havant, Hants PO9 1RY. *T:* Havant 484668.

PHILLIPS, Robin; actor and director; *b* 28 Feb. 1942; *s* of James William Phillips and Ellen Anne (*née* Barfoot). *Educ:* Midhurst Grammar School, Sussex. Trained as director, actor and designer, Bristol Old Vic Co.; first appearance, Bristol, as Mr Puff in The Critic, 1959; Associate Dir, Bristol Old Vic, 1960–61; played at Lyric, Hammersmith, 1961, Chichester Fest., 1962, and with Oxford Playhouse Co., 1964. Asst Dir, Timon of Athens and Hamlet, Royal Shakespeare Co., Stratford upon Avon, 1965; Dir or Associate Dir, Hampstead, Exeter, (Thorndike) Leatherhead, 1966–69; Artistic Dir, Stratford Festival, Canada, 1974–80; *London prodns include:* Tiny Alice, RSC, Aldwych, 1970; Abelard and Heloise, Wyndhams and Broadway; The Two Gentlemen of Verona, Stratford and Aldwych, 1970; Miss Julie, for RSC (also directed film); Virginia, Haymarket, 1981; *Chichester:* Caesar and Cleopatra and Dear Antoine, 1971; played Dubedat in The Doctor's Dilemma and directed The Lady's Not for Burning and The Beggar's Opera, 1972; The Jeweller's Shop, 1982; Antony and Cleopatra, 1985; *Greenwich:* formed Company Theatre and apptd Artistic Dir, 1973: plays directed include: The Three Sisters, Rosmerholm, Zorba; *Stratford Festival prodns incl.:* 1975: The Two Gentlemen of Verona and The Comedy of Errors (both also Nat. tour), Measure for Measure, Trumpets and Drums and The Importance of Being Earnest; 1976–78: Hamlet, The Tempest, Antony and Cleopatra, A Midsummer Night's Dream, The Way of the World, Richard III, The Guardsman, As You Like It, Macbeth, The Winter's Tale, Uncle Vanya, The Devils, Private Lives, Hay Fever, Judgement; 1979: Love's Labours Lost, The Importance of Being Earnest, King Lear; 1980: Virginia, Long Day's Journey into Night; Farther West, Theatre Calgary, 1982. Directorate, NY, 1978. *Films:* as actor: Decline and Fall, David Copperfield (title part), Tales from the Crypt. *TV:* Wilfred Desert in The Forsyte Saga, Constantin in The Seagull. *Address:* PO Box 51, Stratford, Ontario N5A 6S8, Canada.

PHILLIPS, Sir Robin Francis, 3rd Bt, *cr* 1912; with Radio Luxembourg, since 1983; *b* 29 July 1940; *s* of Sir Lionel Francis Phillips, 2nd Bt, and Camilla Mary, *er d* of late Hugh Parker, 22 Chapel Street, Belgrave Square, SW1; *S* father, 1944. *Educ:* Aiglon Coll., Switzerland. Chief Air Traffic Control Officer, Biggin Hill, 1970–78; Hazel Malaone Management, 1978–81; Devonair Radio, 1981–83. *Heir:* none. *Address:* 12 Manson Mews, Queens Gate, SW7.

PHILLIPS, Siân; actress; *d* of D. Phillips and Sally Phillips; *m* 1st, 1960, Peter O'Toole, *qv* (marr. diss. 1979); two *d;* 2nd, 1979, Robin Sachs. *Educ:* Pontardawe Grammar Sch.; Univ. of Wales (Cardiff Coll.) (BA Hons English; Fellow, 1982); RADA (Maggie Albanesi Scholarship, 1956; Bancroft Gold Medal, 1958). BBC Radio Wales, mid 1940s-, and BBC TV Wales, early 1950s-; Newsreader and Announcer, and Mem. Rep. Co., BBC, 1953–55; toured for Welsh Arts Council with National Theatre Co., 1953–55; Arts Council Bursary to study drama outside Wales, 1955. Arts Council Drama Cttee, 1970–75. Governor, St Davids Trust, 1970–73. London productions: Hedda Gabler, 1959; Ondine, and the Duchess of Malfi, 1960–61 (1st RSC season at Aldwych); The Lizard on the Rock, 1961; Gentle Jack, Maxibules, and The Night of the Iguana, 1964; Ride a Cock Horse, 1965; Man and Superman, and Man of Destiny, 1966; The Burglar, 1967; Epitaph for George Dillon, 1972; A Nightingale in Bloomsbury Square, 1973; The Gay Lord Quex, 1975; Spinechiller, 1978; You Never Can Tell, Lyric, Hammersmith, 1979; Pal Joey, Half Moon, 1980 and Albery, 1981; Dear Liar, Mermaid, 1982; Major Barbara, NT, 1982; Peg, Phoenix, 1984; Gigi, Lyric, Shaftesbury Ave., 1985. TV drama series include: Shoulder to Shoulder, 1974; How Green was my Valley, 1975; I, Claudius, 1976; Boudicca, and Off to Philadelphia in the Morning, 1977; The Oresteia of Aeschylus, 1978; Crime and Punishment, 1979; Sean O'Casey (RTE), 1980; Winston Churchill, The Wilderness Years, 1981; Language and Landscape (6 bilingual films, Welsh and English), 1985; TV films include: A Painful Case (RTE), 1985; Gigi, 1986. Films include: Becket, 1963; Goodbye Mr Chips, and Laughter in the Dark, 1968; Murphy's War, 1970; Under Milk Wood, 1971; The Clash of the Titans, 1979; Dune, 1984; Ewocks Again, and The Doctor and the Devils, 1985. Has made recordings, incl. Peg, Gigi, and I remember Mama. Critics Circle Award, New York Critics Award, and Famous 7 Critics Award, for Goodbye Mr Chips, 1969; BAFTA Award for How Green was my Valley and I, Claudius, 1978; Royal Television Soc. Award for I, Claudius (Best Performer), 1978. Mem., Gorsedd of Bards, 1960 (for services to drama in Wales). Hon. DLitt Wales, 1984. *Publications:* gen. journalism (Vogue, Cosmopolitan, Daily Mail, 3 years for Radio Times). *Recreations:* gardening, needlepoint. *Address:* c/o Saraband Ltd, 265 Liverpool Road, Barnsbury, N1 1HS.

PHILLIPS, Sydney William Charles, CB 1955; Second Civil Service Commissioner, 1968–70; *b* 1 Dec. 1908; *s* of late Frederick Charles and Elizabeth Phillips; *m* 1932, Phyllis, *d* of late James Spence; two *s*. *Educ:* Bridport Grammar Sch.; University College, London. Administrative Asst, University College, Hull, 1932–37; Asst Registrar, Liverpool Univ., 1937–45; seconded to Min. of Works, 1941–43; Min. of Town and Country Planning, 1943–51 (Principal Private Sec. to Minister, 1943–44); Asst Sec., 1944; Under-Sec., Min. of Housing and Local Govt, 1952–68, Dir of Establishments, 1963–68. Fellow, UCL, 1969. *Recreations:* walking and gardening. *Address:* Flat 2, 24 Box Ridge Avenue, Purley, Surrey. *T:* 01–660 8617. *Club:* Royal Commonwealth Society.

PHILLIPS, Tom, ARA 1984; painter, writer and composer; *b* 25 May 1937; *s* of David John Phillips and Margaret Agnes (*née* Arnold); *m* 1961, Jill Purdy; one *s* one *d*. *Educ:* St Catherine's College, Oxford (MA); Camberwell School of Art. NDD. One man shows: AIA Galleries, 1965; Angela Flowers Gall., 1970–71; Marlborough Fine Art, 1973–75; Dante Works, Waddington Galleries, 1983; retrospective exhibitions: Gemeente Museum, The Hague, 1975; Kunsthalle, Basel, 1975; Serpentine, 1975; work in collections: British Museum, Tate Gall., V&A, MOMA NY, Philadelphia Museum, Bibliothèque Nationale, Paris, Gemeente Museum, Boymans Museum, Rotterdam, Nat. Museum, Stockholm, Nat. Gall. of Australia; designed tapestries for St Catherine's, Oxford; music: first perf. opera Irma, 1973; York, 1974; ICA, 1983; recordings incl. Irma, 1980; Intervalles/Music of Tom Phillips 1982; television: collaborating on Dante series, 1984–; script for film: Tom Phillips (Grierson Award, BFI, 1976; Golden Palm Award, Chicago, 1976). Vice-Chm., British Copyright Council, 1984. Francis Williams Prize, V&A 1983. *Publications:* Trailer, 1971; A Humument, 1980; illustr. trans. Dante's Inferno, 1982; Works/Texts to 1974, 1975; Heart of a Humument, 1985. *Recreation:* collecting African sculpture. *Address:* 57 Talfourd Road, SE15. *T:* 01–701 3978. *Club:* Surrey County Cricket.

PHILLIPS GRIFFITHS, Allen; *see* Griffiths.

PHILLIS, Robert Weston; Managing Director, Central Independent Television plc, since 1981; *b* 3 Dec. 1945; *s* of Francis William Phillis and Gertrude Grace Phillis; *m* 1966, Jean (*née* Derham); three *s*. *Educ:* John Ruskin Grammar Sch.; Nottingham Univ. (BA Industrial Econs 1968). Apprentice, printing industry, 1961–65; Thomson Regional Newspapers Ltd, 1968–69; British Printing Corp. Ltd, 1969–71; Lectr in Industrial Relations, Edinburgh Univ. and Scottish Business Sch., 1971–75; Vis. Fellow, Univ. of Nairobi, 1974; Personnel Dir, later Man. Dir, Sun Printers Ltd, 1976–79; Man. Dir, Independent Television Publications Ltd, 1979–82. Chairman: ITV Network Programming Cttee, 1984–86; ITV Film Purchase Gp, 1985–. Director: Ind. Television Publications Ltd, 1979–; ITN Ltd, 1982–; Periodical Publishers Assoc., 1979–82; Ind. Television Cos Assoc., 1982–. *Recreations:* family, sport, art, theatre, gardening. *Address:* Central Independent Television plc, Central House, Broad Street, Birmingham B1 2JP. *T:* 021–643 9898.

PHILLPOTTS, (Mary) Adelaide Eden, (Mrs Nicholas Ross); writer; *b* Ealing, Middlesex; *d* of late Eden Phillpotts; *m* 1951, Nicholas Ross. *Publications: novels:* The Friend, 1923; Lodgers in London, 1926; Tomek, the Sculptor, 1927; A Marriage, 1928; The Atoning Years, 1929; Yellow Sands, 1930; The Youth of Jacob Ackner, 1931; The Founder of Shandon, 1932; The Growing World, 1934; Onward Journey, 1936; Broken Allegiance, 1937; What's Happened to Rankin?, 1938; The Gallant Heart, 1939; The Round of Life, 1940; Laugh with Me, 1941; Our Little Town, 1942; From Jane to John, 1943; The Adventurers, 1944; The Lodestar, 1946; The Fosterling, 1949; Stubborn Earth, 1951; *plays:* Arachne, 1920; Savitri the Faithful, 1923; Camillus and the Schoolmaster, 1923; Akhnaton, 1926; (with Eden Phillpotts) Yellow Sands, 1926; Laugh With Me, 1938; *poetry:* Illyrion, and other Poems, 1916; A Song of Man, 1959; *travel:* Panorama of the World, 1969; *miscellaneous:* Man, a Fable, 1922; (selected with Nicholas Ross) Letters to Nicholas Ross from J. C. Powys (ed A. Uphill), 1971; A Wild Flower Wreath, 1975; Reverie: An Autobiography, 1981. *Address:* Cobblestones, Kilkhampton, Bude, Cornwall.

PHILO, Gordon Charles George, CMG 1970; MC 1944; HM Diplomatic Service, retired; *b* 8 Jan. 1920; *s* of Charles Gilbert Philo and Nellie Philo (*née* Pinnock); *m* 1952, Mavis (Vicky) Ella (*d* 1986), *d* of John Ford Galsworthy and Sybel Victoria Galsworthy (*née* Strachan). *Educ:* Haberdashers' Aske's Hampstead Sch.; Wadham Coll., Oxford. Methuen Scholar in Modern History, Wadham Coll., 1938. Served War, HM Forces, 1940–46: Royal West African Frontier Force, 1942–43; Airborne Forces, Normandy and Europe, 1944–45; India 1945–46. Alexander Korda Scholar, The Sorbonne, 1948–49; Lectr in Modern History, Wadham Coll., 1949–50; Foundn Mem., St Antony's Coll., Oxford, 1950–51. Foreign Office, 1951; Russian course, Christ's Coll., Cambridge, 1952–53; Istanbul, Third Sec., 1954–57; Ankara, Second Sec., 1957–58; FO, 1958–63; Kuala Lumpur, First Sec., 1963–67; FO, 1968; Consul-Gen., Hanoi, 1968–69; FCO, 1969–78. Kesatria Mangku Negara (Hon.), Order of Malaysia, 1968. *Recreations:* travel, writing. *Club:* Athenæum.

PHILPOT, Oliver Lawrence Spurling, MC 1944; DFC 1941; Managing Director, Remploy Ltd, 1974–78; *b* Vancouver, BC, Canada, 6 March 1913; *s* of Lawrence Benjamin Philpot, London, and Catherine Barbara (*née* Spurling), Bedford; *m* 1st, 1938 (marr. diss. 1951); one *s* two *d;* 2nd, 1954, Rosl Widhalm, BA Hons History, PhD (Lond.), Vienna; one *s* one *d*. *Educ:* Queen Mary Sch., N Vancouver; Aymestrey Court, Worcester; Radley Coll.; Worcester Coll., Oxford (BA Hons PPE; MA). RAFVR: Pilot, 42 Torpedo/Bomber Sqdn, RAF Coastal Comd, 1940; shot down off Norway, 1941; 5 prison camps, Germany and Poland; escaped to Sweden and Scotland, as 3rd man in Wooden Horse, from Stalag Luft III at Sagan, Silesia, 1943; Sen. Scientific Officer, Air Min., 1944 (wrote 33 RAF Stations Manpower Survey, 1944). Management Trainee, Unilever Ltd, 1934; Asst (commercial) Sec., Unilever Home Margarine Exec., 1936; Exec., Maypole Dairy Ltd, 1946; Chm., Trufood Ltd, 1948; Office Manager, Unilever House, EC4, 1950; Gen. Manager (admin.), T. Walls & Sons Ltd, 1951; Coast-to-Coast Lecture Tour in N America on own book, Stolen Journey, with Peat Agency, Canadian Clubs and USAAF, 1952; Dir, Arthur Woollacott & Rappings Ltd, 1953; Chm. and Man. Dir, Spirella Co. of Great Britain Ltd, 1956; Man. Dir, Venesta (later Aluminium) Foils Ltd, 1959; Exec., Union International Ltd, 1962 (also Dep. Chm. and Chief Exec., Fropax Eskimo Frood Ltd, 1965–67), i/c Lonsdale & Thompson Ltd, John Layton Ltd, Merseyside Food Products Ltd, Union Distribution Co. Ltd, Weddel Pharmaceuticals Ltd, John Gardner (Printers) Ltd, and Union Internat. Res. Centre. Chairman: Royal Air Forces Escaping Soc., and RAFES Charitable Fund, 2 terms, 1963–69. Overseas Administrator, Help the Aged, 1979–82; Manager, St Bride Foundn Inst., 1982–; Mem., Nat. Adv. Council on Employment of Disabled People, 1978; Chm., London NW Area Cttee for Employment of Disabled People, 1981–86. Mem., Gen. Adv. Council, IBA, 1982–85. Supports European Community; fights local environmental battles. *Publication:* Stolen Journey, 1950 (5th edn 1951, repr. 1970; Swedish, Norwegian and Amer. edns, 1951–52; paperback 1954, repr. 4 times, 1962–66). *Recreations:* political activity incl. canvassing, sculling Boat Race course and return (No 452 in Head of the River Race for Scullers, 1986), talking, idling, listening to sermons, reading Financial Times and obituaries in Lancet. *Address:* 30 Abingdon Villas, Kensington, W8 6BX. *T:* 01–937 6013. *Clubs:* London Rowing, Ends of the Earth, Society of Authors, United Oxford & Cambridge University, Institute of Directors, Goldfish, Guild of St Bride, RAF Escaping Society, RAF ex-POW Association, Aircrew Association; Worcester College Society (London and Oxford).

PHILPOTT, Air Vice-Marshal Peter Theodore, CB 1966; CBE 1954 (OBE 1945); Director of Service Intelligence, Ministry of Defence, 1968–70, retired; *b* 20 March 1915; *s* of late Rev. and Mrs R. G. K. F. Philpott, Worcester; *m* 1942, Marie, *d* of Charles Griffin, Malvern; two *d*. *Educ:* Malvern Coll.; RAF Coll., Cranwell, 1933; No. 31 Sqn, India, 1936–41; Staff Coll., Quetta, 1941; Directorate of Op. Trg., Air Ministry, 1942–44; OC, RAF, Horsham St Faith, 1945–46; JSSC, 1947; HQ, Fighter Command, 1948–51; OC, RAF Deversoir, 1952–54; DD Policy, Air Ministry, 1954–56; IDC Student, 1957; Director of Policy and Plans, Air Ministry, 1958–61; Senior RAF Directing Staff, Imperial Defence Coll., 1961–63; AOC No. 23 Group, Flying Training Comd, 1963–65; Head of British Defence Liaison Staff, Canberra, 1965–68. *Address:* c/o Lloyds Bank, 19 Obelisk Way, Camberley, Surrey GU15 3SE. *Club:* Royal Air Force.

PHILPS, Dr Frank Richard, MBE 1946; retired; Consultant in Exfoliative Cytology, University College Hospital, WC1, 1960–73; Director, Joint Royal Free and University College Hospitals, Department of Cytology, 1972–73; *b* 9 March 1914; *s* of Francis John Philps and Matilda Ann Philps (*née* Healey); *m* 1941, Emma L. F. M. Schmidt; two *s* one *d*. *Educ:* Christ's Hospital, Horsham, Sussex. MRCS, LRCP, 1939; MB, BS, 1939; DPH 1947; MD London, 1952; FRCPath, 1966; Fellow, International Academy of Cytology, 1967. RAF Medical Service, 1940–46. Junior Hospital Appointments, UCH, 1950–54; Consultant Pathologist, Eastbourne, 1954–64; Research Asst, UCH, 1955–60. Hon. Cons. in Cytology, Royal Free Hosp., 1972–73. Producer, with wife, Wild Life Series of Educational Nature Films and films on pottery making, for Educational Foundation for Visual Aids; made BBC films, The Magic of a Dartmoor Stream, 1977, The Magic of a Dartmoor Wood, 1979. Exhibitor in the annual exhibition of the Royal Inst. of Painters in Watercolours, 1980–84. BBC Nature Film Prize, 1963; Council for Nature Film Prize, 1966. *Publications:* A Short Manual of Respiratory Cytology, 1964; Watching Wild Life, 1968, 3rd edn 1984; papers on Cytology to several medical journals, 1954–67. *Recreations:* living in the country; watching wild animals and filming them, painting. *Address:* Woodlands, Sydenham Wood, Lewdown, Okehampton EX20 4PP. *T:* Chillaton 347.

PHIPPS, family name of **Marquess of Normanby.**

PHIPPS, Colin Barry, PhD; Chairman: Clyde Petroleum plc, since 1983 (Deputy Chairman and Chief Executive, 1979–83); Tandata Holdings plc, since 1983; Phipps & Co. Ltd, since 1983; Mercia Petroleum Ltd, since 1984; *b* 23 July 1934; *s* of Edgar Reeves Phipps and Winifred Elsie Phipps (*née* Carroll); *m* 1956, Marion May Phipps (*née* Lawrey); two *s* two *d*. *Educ:* Townfield Elem. Sch., Hayes, Mddx; Acton County; Swansea Grammar; University Coll. London; Birmingham Univ. BSc, 1st cl. Hons Geol. London 1955; PhD, Geol. Birm. 1957. Royal Dutch/Shell Geologist: Holland, Venezuela, USA, 1957–64; Consultant Petroleum Geologist, 1964–79. Chm., Brindex (Assoc. of British Independent Oil Exploration Cos), 1983–. MP (Lab) Dudley W, Feb. 1974–1979. Contested: (Lab) Walthamstow E, 1969; (SDP/L Alliance) Worcester, 1983. Founder mem., SDP; Mem. SDP Nat. Cttee, 1984–. FGS 1956, FInstPet 1972; Mem. Instn of Geologists, 1978. Dir, English String Orch., 1985–. *Publications:* (co-ed) Energy and the Environment: democratic decision-making, 1978; What Future for the Falklands?, 1977 (Fabian tract 450); contrib.: Qly Jl Geol Sci., Geol. Mag., Geol. Jl, etc. *Recreations:* swimming, reading, collecting English water colours. *Address:* Mathon Court, Mathon, Malvern WR13 5NZ. *T:* Malvern 5606; 38 Cheyne Walk, SW3. *T:* 01–352 5381. *Clubs:* Reform, Chelsea Arts.

PHIPPS, Air Vice-Marshal Leslie William, CB 1983; AFC 1959; British Aerospace (Military Aircraft Division), since 1984; *b* 17 April 1930; *s* of late Frank Walter Phipps and Beatrice Kate (*née* Bearman). *Educ*: SS Philip and James Sch., Oxford. Commnd RAF, 1950; served, 1951–69: Fighter Sqdns; Stn Comdr, RAF Aqaba, Jordan; OC No 19 (F) Sqdn; Central Fighter Estab.; RN Staff Coll.; HQ 1 (British) Corps; Stn Comdr, RAF Labuan, Borneo; OC No 29 (F) Sqdn; Jt Services Staff Coll.; Dir, RAF Staff Coll., 1970–72; Comdr, Sultan of Oman's Air Force, 1973–74; RCDS, 1975; Comdr, UK Team to Kingdom of Saudi Arabia, 1976–78; Dir of Air Def. and Overseas Ops, 1978–79; Air Sec., (RAF), 1980–82; Sen. Directing Staff, RCDS, 1983; retired. *Recreations*: sailing, squash, music. *Address*: c/o Lloyds Bank, Cox's and King's Branch, 6 Pall Mall, SW1Y 5NH. *Clubs*: Royal Air Force; Royal Air Force Yacht (Hamble).

PHIPPS, Vice-Adm. Sir Peter, KBE 1964 (CBE 1962); DSC 1941 (Bar 1943); VRD 1945; retired, 1965; *b* 7 June 1909; *m* 1937, Jean Hutton; two *s* one *d*. *Educ*: Sumner Primary School; Christchurch Boys' High School. Joined staff of National Bank of NZ Ltd, 1927. Joined RNZNVR as Ord. Seaman, 1928; Sub-Lieut, 1930; Lieut, 1933. Served War of 1939–45 (American Navy Cross, 1943). Transferred to RNZN as Commander, 1945; Captain, 1952; Rear-Admiral, 1960. Chief of Naval Staff, NZ Naval Board, 1960–63; Chief of Defence Staff, New Zealand, 1963–65; Vice-Adm. 1964, retired 1965. *Recreations*: yachting, fishing, herpetology. *Address*: Picton, New Zealand. *Club*: Wellington (Wellington, NZ).

PHIPPS, Rt. Rev. Simon Wilton, MC 1945; *b* 6 July 1921; *s* of late Captain William Duncan Phipps, CVO, RN, and late Pamela May Ross; *m* 1973, Mary, *widow* of Rev. Dr James Welch and *d* of late Sir Charles Eric Palmer. *Educ*: Eton; Trinity Coll., Cambridge; Westcott House, Cambridge. Joined Coldstream Guards, 1940; commnd, 1941; Capt., 1944; ADC to GOC-in-C Northern Comd India, Nov. 1945; Mil. Asst to Adjt Gen. to the Forces, War Office, 1946; Major, 1946. BA (History) Cantab, 1948; MA 1953; Pres., Cambridge Univ. Footlights Club, 1949. Ordained 1950. Asst Curate, Huddersfield Parish Church, 1950; Chaplain, Trinity Coll., Cambridge, 1953; Industrial Chaplain, Coventry Dio., 1958; Hon. Canon, Coventry Cath., 1965; Bishop Suffragan of Horsham, 1968–74; Bishop of Lincoln, 1974–86. Member: Council, Industrial Soc.; Home Sec's Cttee of Inquiry into Liquor Licensing Laws, 1971–72. *Publication*: God on Monday, 1966. *Recreations*: walking, painting, cooking. *Address*: Sarsens, Shipley, W Sussex RH13 8PX. *Club*: Army and Navy.

PHIZACKERLEY, Ven. Gerald Robert; Archdeacon of Chesterfield, since 1978; Priest-in-charge of Ashford-in-the-Water with Sheldon, since 1978; *b* 3 Oct. 1929; *s* of John Dawson and Lilian Mabel Ruthven Phizackerley; *m* 1959, Annette Catherine Baker; one *s* one *d*. *Educ*: Queen Elizabeth Grammar School, Penrith; University Coll., Oxford (MA); Wells Theological Coll. Curate of St Barnabas Church, Carlisle, 1954–57; Chaplain of Abingdon School, 1957–64; Rector of Gaywood, Norfolk, 1964–78; Rural Dean of Lynn, 1968–78; Hon. Canon of Norwich Cathedral, 1975, of Derby Cathedral, 1978. Fellow, Woodard Corporation, 1981. JP Norfolk, 1972. *Address*: The Vicarage, Ashford-in-the-Water, Bakewell, Derbyshire. *T*: Bakewell 2298.

PHYSICK, John Frederick, CBE 1984; DrRCA; FSA; *b* 31 Dec. 1923; *s* of Nino William Physick and Gladys (*née* Elliott); *m* 1954, Eileen Mary Walsh; two *s* one *d*. *Educ*: Battersea Grammar Sch. Royal Navy, 1942–46 (Petty Officer Airman). Joined Victoria and Albert Museum, as Museum Asst, Dept of Engraving, Illustration and Design, 1948; Research Asst, 1949; Sen. Research Asst, 1965; Asst Keeper, Dept of Public Relations and Educn, 1967; Keeper, Dept of Museum Services, 1975–83; Sec. to Adv. Council, 1973–83; Asst to Dir, 1974–83; Dep. Dir, 1983. Leverhulme Trust Emeritus Fellow, 1984–86. Pres., Church Monument Soc., 1984–86; Member: Rochester Dio. Adv. Cttee for the Care of Churches, 1965–; RIBA Drawings Cttee, 1975; Cathedrals Adv. Cttee, 1977–81; Council for Care of Churches Monuments Sub-Cttee, 1978– (Chm., 1984–); Council for Care of Churches Conservation Cttee, 1984–; Council, British Archaeol Assoc., 1985–; Westminster Abbey Architectural Adv. Panel, 1985–. Trustee, London Scottish Regt, 1977–. FRSA. *Publications*: Catalogue of the Engravings of Eric Gill, 1963; (ed) Handbook to the Departments Prints and Drawings and Paintings, 1964; The Duke of Wellington in caricature, 1965; Designs for English Sculpture 1680–1860, 1969; The Wellington Monument, 1970; (jtly) Victorian Church Art, 1971; Five Monuments from Eastwell, 1973; (with M. D. Darby) Marble Halls, 1973; Photography and the South Kensington Museum, 1975; (with Sir Roy Strong) V&A Souvenir Guide, 1977; The Victoria and Albert Museum—the history of its building, 1982; (ed) V&A Album II, 1983; (ed) Sculpture in Britain 1530–1830, 2nd edn 1987; (contrib.) Change and Decay, the Future of our Churches, 1977; (contrib.) Westminster Abbey, 1986. *Recreations*: photography, looking at church monuments. *Address*: 49 New Road, Meopham, Kent DA13 0LS. *T*: Meopham 812301.

PICACHY, His Eminence Lawrence Trevor, Cardinal; *see* Calcutta, Archbishop of, (RC).

PICCARD, Dr Jacques; scientist; President, Foundation for the Study and Preservation of Seas and Lakes; *b* Belgium, 1922; Swiss Citizen; *s* of late Prof. Auguste Piccard (explorer of the stratosphere, in lighter-than-air craft, and of the ocean depths, in vehicles of his own design); *m* 1953, Marie Claude (*née* Maillard); two *s* one *d*. *Educ*: Brussels; Switzerland. Grad., Univ. of Geneva, 1946; Dip. from Grad. Inst. of Internat. Studies. Asst Prof., Univ. of Geneva, 1946–48. With his father, he participated in design and operation of the first deep diving vessels, which they named the bathyscaph (deep ship); this vessel, like its successor, operated independently of a mother ship; they first constructed the FNRS-2 (later turned over to the French Navy) then the Trieste (ultimately purchased by US Navy); Dr J. Piccard piloted the Trieste on 65 successive dives (the last, 23 Jan. 1960, was the record-breaking descent to 35,800 feet in the Marianas Trench, off Guam in the Pacific Ocean). He built in 1963, the mesoscaph Auguste Piccard, the first civilian submarine, which made, in 1964–65, over 1,100 dives carrying 33,000 people into the depths of Lake Geneva; built (with Grumman) 2nd mesoscaph, Ben Franklin, and in 1969 made 1.500 miles/30 days drift dive in Gulf Stream. Founded: Fondation pour l'Etude et la Protection de la Mer et des Lacs, 1966 (built research submersible, F. A.-FOREL, 1978); Institut International d'Ecologie, 1972. Hon. doctorate in Science, Amer. Internat. Coll., Springfield, Mass, 1962; Hon. DSc, Hofstra Univ., 1970. Holds Distinguished Public Service Award, etc. *Publications*: The Sun beneath the Sea, 1971; technical papers and a popularized account (trans. many langs) of the Trieste, Seven Miles Down (with Robert S. Dietz). *Address*: (home) 19 avenue de l'Avenir, 1012 Lausanne, Switzerland. *T*: (021) 28 80 83; (office) Fondation pour l'Etude et la Protection de la Mer et des Lacs, 1096 Cully, Switzerland. *T*: 021. 99 25 65.

PICK, Charles Samuel; Managing Director, Heinemann Group of Publishers, 1979–85; Founder, Charles Pick Consultancy, 1985; Consultant to: Octopus plc; Wilbur Smith; *b* 22 March 1917; *s* of Samuel and Ethel Pick; *m* 1938, Hilda Beryl Hobbs; one *s* one *d*. *Educ*: Masonic School, Bushey. Started in publishing with Victor Gollancz, 1933; founder member, Michael Joseph Ltd, 1935. Served War, 1939–46; commnd RA, AA Command; apptd Staff Captain; served ALFSEA, India, Ceylon and Singapore. Jt Man. Director, Michael Joseph Ltd, 1959; resigned, 1962; joined William Heinemann Ltd as Man. Director, 1962; Director, Heinemann Group of Publishers, 1962; Director, Pan Books, 1968–85; Chairman: Secker & Warburg, 1973–80; William Heinemann, 1973–80; William Heinemann, Australia and South Africa, 1973–80; William Heinemann International, 1979–85; Heinemann Educational Books International, 1979–85; Heinemann Inc., 1980–85; Heinemann Distribution Ltd, 1980–85; Chm. and Pres., Heinemann Holdings Inc., 1980–85. Mem. Council, Publishers' Assoc., 1980–83. *Recreations*: walking, reading, theatre. *Address*: Littlecot, Lindfield, Sussex RH16 2JZ *T*: 2218; 3 Bryanston Place, W1. *T*: 01–402 8043. *Clubs*: Savile, MCC.

PICKARD, Sir Cyril (Stanley), KCMG 1966 (CMG 1964); HM Diplomatic Service, retired; British High Commissioner in Nigeria, 1971–74; *b* 18 Sept. 1917; *s* of G. W. Pickard and Edith Pickard (*née* Humphrey), Sydenham; *m* 1st, 1941, Helen Elizabeth Strawson (*d* 1982); three *s* one *d* (and one *s* decd); 2nd, 1983, Mary Rosser (*née* Cozens-Hardy). *Educ*: Alleyn's Sch., Dulwich; New Coll. Oxford. 1st Class Hons Modern History, 1939. Asst Principal, Home Office, 1939. War of 1939–45: Royal Artillery, 1940–41, Captain; appointment in Office of Minister of State, Cairo, 1941–44 Principal, 1943; with UNRRA in Middle East and Germany, 1944–45; transf. to Commonwealth Relations Office, 1948; Office of UK High Comr in India, New Delhi, 1950; Local Asst Sec., Office of UK High Comr, Canberra, 1952–55; Commonwealth Relations Office, Head of South Asian Dept, 1955–58; Deputy High Commissioner for the UK in New Zealand, 1958–61; Asst Under Sec. of State, CRO, 1962–66 (Acting High Commissioner in Cyprus, 1964); British High Comr, Pakistan, 1966–71. *Recreation*: gardening. *Address*: 45 Blackwater Lane, Pound Hill, Crawley, West Sussex; 37A Brodrick Road, SW17.

PICKARD, Prof. Huia Masters, FDSRCS; Professor of Conservative Dentistry, University of London, 1963–74, now Emeritus; *b* 25 March 1909; *o s* of late Ernest Pickard and Sophie Elizabeth Robins; *m* 1945, Daphne Evelyn, *d* of Hugh F. Marriott; two *d*. *Educ*: Latymer Sch.; Royal Dental Hosp. of London Sch. of Dental Surgery; Charing Cross Hosp. MRCS, LRCP, FDSRCS. Private dental practice, pre-1940; EMS, East Grinstead, 1939. Served War, in RAMC, 8th Army (despatches), 1940–45. Dental practice and teaching, 1945; Dir, Dept of Conservative Dentistry, Royal Dental Hosp., and Consultant, 1955; Reader, London Univ., 1957–63; Dir of Dept of Restorative Dentistry, Royal Dental Hosp., 1965–74. Mem. Bd of Governors, St George's Hosp., 1969; First Pres., British Soc. for Restorative Dentistry, 1969; Pres., Odontological Section of Royal Soc. Med., 1971; Examr for Univs of London, Newcastle, Glasgow, Birmingham, Wales; also RCS. Governor, Latymer Sch., Edmonton, 1968–84 (Chm., 1980–83). Tomes Medal, BDA, 1983. *Publications*: Manual of Operative Dentistry, 1961, 5th edn 1983; contribs: Dental Record, Brit. Dental Jl, Internat. Dental Jl. *Recreations*: gardening, sailing. *Address*: The Nuttery, Newnham, Daventry, Northamptonshire. *T*: Daventry 703561.

PICKARD, Rt. Rev. Stanley Chapman, CBE 1968; retired; *b* 4 July 1910; *s* of John Chapman and Louisa Mary Pickard, Gloucester; unmarried. *Educ*: Grammar Sch., Birmingham. Studied pharmacy, 1928–32. Dorchester Theological College, 1933–36; Deacon, 1937; Priest, 1938; Curate St Catherine's, New Cross, SE14, 1937–39; joined UMCA, 1939; Kota Kota, Nyasaland, 1939–40; Likoma Island, Nyasaland, 1940–48; Archdeacon of Msumba, Portuguese East Africa, 1949–58; Bishop of Lebombo, 1958–68; Provincial Exec. Officer, Province of S Africa, 1968–71; Asst Bishop of Johannesburg, 1968–83; Rector of St John's, Belgravia, dio. Johannesburg, 1972–83; Chaplain to Anglicans of Jeppe Boys High School, 1972–83. *Recreations*: walking, bridge. *Address*: The Beauchamp Community, Newland, Malvern, Worcs WR13 5AX.

PICKAVANCE, Thomas Gerald, CBE 1965; MA, PhD; FRS 1976; Fellow, St Cross College, Oxford, 1967–84, now Emeritus; *b* 19 October 1915; *s* of William and Ethel Pickavance, Lancashire; *m* 1943, Alice Isobel (*née* Boulton); two *s* one *d*. *Educ*: Cowley School, St Helens; Univ. of Liverpool. BSc (Hons Phys) 1937; PhD 1940. Research Physicist, Tube Alloys Project, 1941–46; Lecturer in Physics, University of Liverpool, 1943–46; Atomic Energy Research Establishment, Harwell: Head of Cyclotron Group, 1946–54; Head of Accelerator Group, 1954–57; Deputy Head of General Physics Division, 1955–57; Dir, Rutherford High Energy Lab., SRC, 1957–69; Dir of Nuclear Physics, SRC, 1969–72. Chm., European Cttee for Future Accelerators, 1970–71. Hon. DSc, City Univ., 1969. *Publications*: papers and articles in learned journals on nuclear physics and particle accelerators. *Recreations*: motoring, travel, photography. *Address*: 3 Kingston Close, Abingdon, Oxon OX14 1ES. *T*: Abingdon 23934.

PICKEN, Dr Laurence Ernest Rowland, FBA 1973; Fellow of Jesus College, Cambridge, 1944–76, now Emeritus; *b* 1909. *Educ*: Oldknow Road and Waverley Road, Birmingham; Trinity Coll., Cambridge. BA 1931; PhD 1935; ScD 1952. Asst Dir of Research (Zoology), Cambridge Univ., 1946–66; Asst Dir of Research (Oriental Music), Cambridge Univ., 1966–76. FBA; FIBiol. Editor: Musica Asiatica, 1977–84; Music from the Tang Court, 1981–. *Publications*: The Organization of Cells and Other Organisms, 1960; Folk Musical Instruments of Turkey, 1975; contribs to many learned jls. *Address*: Jesus College, Cambridge.

PICKERILL, Dame Cecily (Mary Wise), DBE 1977 (OBE 1958); Retired Surgeon; *b* 9 Feb. 1903; *d* of Rev. Percy Wise Clarkson and Margaret Ann Clarkson; *m* 1934, Henry Percy Pickerill, CBE, MD, MDS (*d* 1956); one *d*. *Educ*: Diocesan High School for Girls, Auckland, NZ; Otago Univ. Medical School, Dunedin, NZ (MB, ChB). House Surg., Dunedin Hosp., 1926; Asst Plastic Surgeon in Sydney, Aust., 1927–35; Specialist Plastic Surgeon, Wellington, NZ, 1935–68; retired, 1968. Licencee, with late husband, and owner of Bassam Hosp., Lower Hutt, NZ—a "Rooming-In" hospital for mother nursing of infants and small children with congenital defects requiring plastic surgery. *Publications*: contribs to medical and nursing jls and NZ Education Jl, 1980. *Recreations*: travel, gardening, camping, nature conservation, great involvement with NZ Anglican Church. *Address*: Beech Dale, 50 Blue Mountains Road, Silverstream, New Zealand. *T*: Wellington 284542.

PICKERING, Derek; *see* Pickering, Frederick Derwent.

PICKERING, Sir Edward (Davies), Kt 1977; Executive Vice-Chairman, Times Newspapers Ltd, since 1982; *b* 4 May 1912; 3rd *s* of George and Louie Pickering; *m* 1st, 1936, Margaret Soutter (marr. diss., 1947); one *d*; 2nd, 1955, Rosemary Whitton; two *s* one *d*. *Educ*: Middlesbrough High Sch. Chief Sub-Editor Daily Mail, 1939. Served Royal Artillery 1940–44; Staff of Supreme Headquarters Allied Expeditionary Force, 1944–45. Managing Editor: Daily Mail, 1947–49; Daily Express, 1951–57; Editor, Daily Express, 1957–62; Dir, Beaverbrook Newspapers, 1956–64; Editorial Dir, The Daily Mirror Newspapers Ltd, 1964–68, Chm., 1968–70; Director: Scottish Daily Record and Sunday Mail Ltd, 1966–69; IPC, 1966–75; Times Newspapers Holdings Ltd, 1981–; William Collins Sons & Co. Ltd, 1981–; Chairman: International Publishing Corporation Newspaper Div., 1968–70; IPC Magazines, 1970–74; Mirror Group Newspapers, 1975–77. Member Press Council, 1964–69, 1970–82 (Vice-Chm., 1976–82). Treasurer, Fédération Internationale de la Presse Periodique, 1971–75; Chm. Council, Commonwealth Press Union, 1977–86. Freeman, Stationers' and Newspaper Makers' Co., 1985. Astor Award for distinguished service to Commonwealth Press, CPU, 1986.

Mem. Council, Royal Opera House, Covent Garden, 1978–. *Address:* Chatley House, Norton St Philip, Somerset. *Club:* Garrick.

PICKERING, Ven. Fred; Archdeacon of Hampstead, 1974–84; Archdeacon Emeritus since 1984; *b* 18 Nov. 1919; *s* of Arthur and Elizabeth Pickering; *m* 1948, Mabel Constance Threlfall; one *s* one *d. Educ:* Preston Grammar Sch.; St Peter's Coll., Oxford; St Aidan's Theol Coll., Birkenhead. BA 1941 (PPE), MA 1945. Curate: St Andrew's, Leyland, 1943–46; St Mary's, Islington, 1946–48; Organising Sec. for Church Pastoral Aid Soc. in NE England, 1948–51; Vicar: All Saints, Burton-on-Trent, 1951–56; St John's, Carlisle, 1956–63; St Cuthbert's, Wood Green, 1963–74; Rural Dean of East Haringey, 1968–73; Exam. Chaplain to Bp of Edmonton, 1973–84. *Address:* 23 Broadgate Way, Warmington, near Peterborough, Cambs PE8 6UN. *T:* Elton 548.

PICKERING, Frederick Derwent, (Derek Pickering), CBE 1974; DL; Chairman, Local Authorities Mutual Investment Trust, 1975–81; Member, Conference of Local and Regional Authorities of Europe, 1977–81; County Councillor, Berkshire, 1961–81; *b* 28 Nov. 1909; *s* of Frederick Owen Pickering and Emma Pickering; *m* 1935, Marjorie Champion (*née* Shotter) (*d* 1980), JP; one *s. Educ:* Bedford House Sch., Oxford. Employed in industry, 1927–43; Sudan CS, 1943–55; company dir, 1955–63. County Alderman, Berks, 1967–74; Chm., Berks CC, 1973–77; Vice-Chm., Exec. Council, ACC, 1976–78; Chm., Local Authorities Management Services and Computer Cttee, 1980–81. DL Berks, 1978. Hon. DLitt Reading, 1976. *Recreations:* cricket (now as spectator), politics (sometime Pres., Reading South, Windsor and Maidenhead Conservative Assocs). *Address:* Grimston Court, Hull Road, Dunnington, York YO1 5LE. *T:* York 489343.

PICKERING, Herbert Kitchener; Chief of Protocol, Government of Alberta, 1983–85; *b* 9 Feb. 1915; *s* of Herbert Pickering, Hull, and Ethel Bowman, Carlisle; *m* 1963, Florence Marion Carr; two *s* two *d. Educ:* Montreal; Bishop's Univ. (Business Admin); Cornell Univ. (Hotel Admin); Michigan State Univ. (Hotel and Business Admin). Canadian National Railways: Gen. Passenger Traffic Dept, Montreal, 1930; various cities in Canada and US; served War of 1939–45, RCAF; returned to CNR; assisted in creation and management of Maple Leaf Tour Dept, 1953–59; created Sales Dept for Canadian National Hotels in Western Canada and then for System, 1960–67; Man., Bessborough Hotel, Saskatoon, 1968; Gen. Man., Jasper Park Lodge, until 1973; Agent-Gen. for Alberta in London, 1973–80; opened Govt Office, Hong Kong, and served as Agent General, 1980–82; Senior Dir, International Operations, Edmonton, 1982–83. Charter Mem., Lion's International; Life Mem., Royal Canadian Legion, 1974 (Mem., 1946); Mem., Plaisters' Co., 1980–; Freeman, City of London, 1978. Hon. Mem., Wheelwrights' Co., 1979. *Recreations:* golf, ski-ing, swimming, philately. *Address:* 852 Hawthorne Road, Kelowna, British Columbia V1Z 1N6, Canada. *Clubs:* East India and Sports, MCC; Kelowna Canadian, International Skal.

PICKERING, Prof. John Frederick; Professor of Industrial Economics, University of Manchester Institute of Science and Technology, since 1975; *b* 26 Dec. 1939; *er s* of William Frederick and Jean Mary Pickering; *m* 1967, Jane Rosamund Day; two *d. Educ:* Slough Grammar Sch.; University Coll. London (BSc Econ; PhD; DSc Econ); MSc Manchester. In indust. market res., 1961–62; Lectr, Univ. of Durham, 1964–66, Univ. of Sussex, 1966–73; Sen. Directing Staff, Admin. Staff Coll., Henley, 1974–75. UMIST: Vice-Principal, 1983–85; Dep. Principal, 1984–85; Dean, 1985–. Mem., UGC Business and Management Studies sub-cttee, 1985–. Mem., Gen. Synod of Church of England, 1980–; Church Comr for England, 1983–; Mem., Archbishop's Commn on Urban Priority Areas, 1983–85; Pres., Bible Churchmen's Missionary Soc., 1986–. Member: Council of Management, Consumers' Assoc., 1969–73, 1980–83; Retail Prices Index Adv. Cttee, 1974–. *Publications:* Resale Price Maintenance in Practice, 1966; (jtly) The Small Firm in the Hotel and Catering Industry, 1971; Industrial Structure and Market Conduct, 1974; The Acquisition of Consumer Durables, 1977; (jtly) The Economic Management of the Firm, 1984; papers and articles in learned jls in economics and management. *Recreations:* family life, music, cricket. *Address:* c/o Department of Management Sciences, University of Manchester Institute of Science and Technology, PO Box 88, Manchester M60 1QD. *T:* 061–236 3311. *Club:* Royal Commonwealth Society.

PICKERING, His Honour John Robertson; a Circuit Judge, 1972–84; *b* 8 Jan. 1925; *s* of late J. W. H. Pickering and Sarah Lilian Pickering (*née* Dixon); *m* 1951, Hilde (*widow* of E. M. Wright); one *s* two step *s. Educ:* Winchester; Magdalene Coll., Cambridge. Degree in Classics (wartime) and Law, MA. Served War, Lieut RNVR, Russia, Europe and Far East, 1942–47. Called to Bar, Inner Temple, 1949. Subseq. with Nat. Coal Bd and Dyson Bell & Co (Parliamentary Agents). Mem. Parliamentary Bar. Dep. Chm. of Pneumoconiosis, Byssinosis and Miscellaneous Diseases Benefit Bd, and Workmen's Compensation (Supplementation) Bd, 1970; apptd Dep. Chm. NE London Quarter Sessions, 1971. *Address:* 35 Eaton Terrace, SW1. *T:* 01–730 4271. *Club:* MCC.

PICKERING, Richard Edward Ingram; His Honour Judge Richard Pickering; a Circuit Judge, since 1981; *b* 16 Aug. 1929; *s* of Richard and Dorothy Pickering; *m* 1962, Jean Margaret Eley; two *s. Educ:* Birkenhead Sch.; Magdalene Coll., Cambridge (MA). Called to the Bar, Lincoln's Inn, 1953; has practised on Northern Circuit, 1955–81; a Recorder of the Crown Court, 1977–81. Admitted as advocate in Manx Courts (Summerland Fire Inquiry), 1973–74. Councillor, Hoylake UDC, 1961–64; Legal Chm., Min. of Pensions and Nat. Insurance Tribunal, Liverpool, 1967–77; pt-time Chm., Liverpool Industrial Tribunal, 1977–79; Nominated Judicial Mem., Merseyside Mental Health Rev. Tribunal, 1984 (Legal Mem., 1967–79; Regional Chm., 1979–81). *Recreations:* walking, gardening, study of military history. *Address:* c/o The Crown Court, Liverpool. *Clubs:* United Oxford & Cambridge University; Athenæum (Liverpool); Union (Cambridge).

PICKETT, Thomas, CBE 1972; Senior Regional Chairman, North West Area, Industrial Tribunals (England and Wales), 1975–85 (Chairman for Manchester, 1972); *b* 22 November 1912; *s* of John Joseph Pickett and Caroline Pickett (*née* Brunt); *m* 1940, Winifred Irene Buckley, *yr d* of late Benjamin Buckley; no *c. Educ:* Glossop Grammar School; London University (LLB). Barrister-at-Law, Lincoln's Inn; called to Bar, 1948. Served in Army, 1939–50, retiring with permanent rank of Major. Dep. Asst Dir of Army Legal Services, 1948; Dist Magistrate, Gold Coast, 1950; Resident Magistrate, Northern Rhodesia 1955; Sen. Res. Magistrate, 1956; Acting Puisne Judge, 1960; Puisne Judge, High Courts of Northern Rhodesia, 1961–64, Zambia, 1964–69; Justice of Appeal, 1969–71, Acting Chief Justice, 1970, Judge President, Court of Appeal, 1971, Zambia. Chairman: Tribunal on Detainees, 1967; Electoral Commn (Supervisory); Delimitation Commn for Zambia, 1968; Referendum Commn, 1969; Local Govt Commn, 1970. *Recreations:* walking, swimming. *Address:* Bryn Awelon, Aber Place, Craigside, Llandudno, Gwynedd LL30 3AR. *T:* Llandudno 44244. *Clubs:* Royal Over-Seas League; Victoria, County (Llandudno).

PICKFORD, David Michael, FRICS; Chairman, Haslemere Estates plc, 1983–86; *b* 25 Aug. 1926; *s* of Aston Charles Corpe Pickford and Gladys Ethel Pickford; *m* 1956, Elizabeth Gwendoline Hooson; one *s* two *d. Educ:* Emanuel Sch., London; Coll. of Estate Management. FRICS 1953. Hillier Parker May & Rowden, 1943–46; LCC, 1946–48; London Investment & Mortgage Co., 1948–57; Haslemere Estates plc, 1957–86: Man. Dir, 1968–83. Pres., London Dist, The Boys' Bde, 1967–; Chm., Christian Union for the Estate Profession, 1978–. *Recreations:* sheep farming, youth work, gardening. *Address:* 33 Grosvenor Square, Mayfair, W1X 9LL; Elm Tree Farm, Mersham, near Ashford, Kent TN25 7HS. *T:* Aldington 200.

PICKFORD, Prof. (Lillian) Mary, DSc; FRS 1966; Professor, Department of Physiology, University of Edinburgh, 1966–72 (Reader in Physiology, 1952–66); retired 1972, now Emeritus Professor; *b* 14 Aug. 1902; *d* of Herbert Arthur Pickford and Lillian Alice Minnie Wintle. *Educ:* Wycombe Abbey Sch.; Bedford and University Colls, Univ. of London. BSc (1st cl., Gen.) 1924; BSc (2nd cl., Physiology Special) 1925; MSc (Physiology) 1926; MRCS, LRCP 1933; DSc London 1951. FRCPE 1977. House Physician and Casualty Officer, Stafford Gen. Infirmary, 1935; Jun. Beit Memorial Research Fellow, 1936–39; Lectr, Dept of Physiology, Univ. of Edinburgh, 1939; Personal Chair, Dept of Physiology, Univ. of Edinburgh, 1966. Special Prof. of Endocrinology, Nottingham Univ., 1973–83. Fellow, University Coll., London, 1968–. *Publications:* The Central Role of Hormones, 1969; papers in Jl Physiology, British Jl Pharmacology, Jl Endocrinology. *Recreations:* walking, travel, painting. *Address:* 12 Ormidale Terrace, Edinburgh EH12 6EQ.

PICKFORD, Prof. Mary; *see* Pickford, Prof. L. M.

PICKLES, James; His Honour Judge Pickles; a Circuit Judge, since 1976; *b* 18 March 1925. Practised at Bradford, 1949–76; a Recorder of the Crown Court, 1972–76. *Address:* c/o Leeds Crown Court, Leeds 1.

PICKTHORN, Sir Charles (William Richards), 2nd Bt *cr* 1959; *b* 3 March 1927; *s* of Rt Hon. Sir Kenneth William Murray Pickthorn, 1st Bt, and Nancy Catherine Lewis (*d* 1982), *d* of late Lewis Matthew Richards; *S* father, 1975; *m* 1951, Helen Antonia, *o d* of late Sir James Mann, KCVO; one *s* two *d. Educ:* Eton; Corpus Christi Coll., Cambridge (Major Schol., BA). Served RNVR, 1945–48. Called to the Bar, Middle Temple, 1952. Dir, J. Henry Schroder Wagg & Co. Ltd, 1971–79. Occasional journalism. Chm., R. S. Surtees Soc. *Recreations:* sailing, reading, smoking. *Heir: s* James Francis Mann Pickthorn, *b* 18 Feb. 1955. *Address:* Manor House, Nunney, near Frome, Somerset. *T:* Nunney 574; 3 Hobury Street, SW10. *T:* 01–352 2795.

PICKUP, Ronald Alfred; actor; *b* 7 June 1940; *s* of Eric and Daisy Pickup; *m* 1964, Lans Traverse, USA; one *s* one *d. Educ:* King's Sch., Chester; Leeds Univ. (BA); Royal Academy of Dramatic Art. Repertory, Leicester, 1964; Royal Court, 1964 and 1965–66; National Theatre, 1965, 1966–73, 1977: appearances include: Rosalind, in all-male As You Like It, 1967; Richard II, 1972; Edmund, in Long Day's Journey into Night, 1971; Cassius, in Julius Caesar, 1977; Philip Madras, in The Madras House, 1977; Norman, in Norman Conquests, Globe, 1974; Play, Royal Court, 1976; Hobson's Choice, Lyric, Hammersmith, 1981; Astrov, in Uncle Vanya, Haymarket, 1982; Allmers in Little Eyolf, Lyric, Hammersmith, 1985; *films:* Three Sisters, 1969; Day of the Jackal, 1972; Joseph Andrews, 1976; 39 Steps, Zulu Dawn, 1978; Nijinsky, 1979; Never Say Never Again, John Paul II, 1983; Eleni, Camille (remake), 1984; The Mission, 1985; The Fourth Protocol, 1986; *television:* Dragon's Opponent, 1973; Jennie, Fight Against Slavery, 1974; The Philanthropist, Ghost Trio, The Discretion of Dominic Ayres, 1977; Memories, Henry VIII, 1978; England's Green and Pleasant Land, Christ Hero, Tropic, 1979; Life of Giuseppe Verdi, The Letter, Ivanhoe, 1981; Wagner, 1982; Orwell on Jura, Life of Einstein, 1983; Moving, 1985. *Recreations:* listening to music, walking, painting.

PICOT, Jacques M. C. G.; *see* Georges-Picot.

PICTET, François-Charles; Ambassador of Switzerland to the Court of St James's, since 1984; *b* Geneva, 21 July 1929; *e s* of Charles Pictet, Geneva, and Elisabeth (*née* Decazes), France; *m* 1st, 1954, Elisabeth Choisy (*d* 1980), Geneva; three *s*; 2nd, 1983, Countess Marie-Thérèse Althann, Austria. *Educ:* College Calvin, Geneva; Univ. of Geneva (Faculty of Law). Called to the Swiss Bar, 1954. Joined Swiss Federal Dept of Foreign Affairs, 1956; Attaché, Vienna, 1957; Sec., Moscow, 1958–60; 1st Sec., Ankara, 1961–66; Dep. Dir, Internat. Orgns, Dept of For. Affairs, Berne, 1966–75; Minister Plenipotentiary, 1975; Ambassador to Canada and (non-resident) to the Bahamas, 1975–79; Ambassador, Perm. Rep. to Internat. Orgns in Geneva, 1980–84. *Address:* Swiss Embassy, 21 Bryanston Square, W1H 7FG. *T:* 01–723 0701.

PICTON, Jacob Glyndwr, (Glyn Picton), CBE 1972; Senior Lecturer in Industrial Economics, University of Birmingham, 1947–79; *b* Aberdare, 28 Feb. 1912; *s* of David Picton; *m* 1939, Rhiannon Mary James (Merch Megan), LRAM, ARCM (*d* 1978); one *s* one *d. Educ:* Aberdare Boys' County Sch.; Birmingham Univ. (MCom). Chance Bros Ltd, 1933–47, Asst Sec. 1945–47. Pres., W Midland Rent Assessment Panel, 1965–72 (Chm. Cttee 1973–81); Governor, United Birmingham Hosps, 1953–74; Chm., Children's Hosp., 1956–66; Teaching Hosps Rep. Professional and Techn. Whitley Council, 1955–61; Mem., Birmingham Regional Hosp. Bd, 1958–74 (Vice-Chm. 1971–74); Mem., NHS Nat. Staff Cttee, 1964–73 (Vice-Chm. 1968–73); Chm., Birmingham Hosp. Region Staff Cttee, 1964–74; Vice-Chm., W Mids RHA, 1973–79 (Mem., 1979–82); Vice-Chm., NHS Nat. Staff Cttee (Admin. and Clerical), 1973–82; NHS Nat. Assessor (Admin), 1973. Chm., Birmingham Industrial Therapy Assoc. Ltd, 1965–79 and W Bromwich Industrial Therapy Assoc. Ltd, 1969–79; Indep. Mem., Estate Agents Council, 1967–69; Chm. of Wages Councils, 1953–82; Dep. Chm., Commn of Inquiry concerning Sugar Confectionery and Food Preserving Wages Council, 1961; Chm., Commn of Inquiry concerning Licensed Residential Estabts and Restaurants Wages Council, 1963–64; sole Comr of Inquiry into S Wales Coalfield Dispute, 1965; Dep. Chm., Commn of Inquiry concerning Industrial and Staff Canteens Wages Council, 1975; Independent Arbitrator, Lock Industry, 1976–81. Has donated working papers on Picton family to Nat. Liby of Wales. *Publications:* various articles and official reports. *Recreations:* music, gardening, Pembrokeshire history. *Address:* 54 Chesterwood Road, Kings Heath, Birmingham B13 0QE. *T:* 021–444 3959.

PIDDINGTON, Philip Michael; HM Diplomatic Service; Counsellor (Administration) and Consul-General, British Embassy, Brussels, since 1983; *b* 27 March 1931; *s* of Percy Howard Piddington and Florence Emma (*née* Pearson); *m* 1955, Sylvia Mary Price; one *s* one *d. Educ:* Waverley Grammar Sch., Birmingham. Served HM Forces, 1949–51. Entered Min. of Works, 1947; FO, 1952; Jedda, 1956; Tokyo, 1962–66; First Sec., Lagos, 1969–71; Consul: NY, 1971–73; Istanbul, 1973–77; First Sec., FCO, 1978–83. *Recreations:* riding, walking, photography. *Address:* c/o Foreign and Commonwealth Office, SW1. *Club:* Cercle Gaulois (Brussels).

PIEŃKOWSKI, Jan Michal; designer and illustrator, since 1958; Art Director, Gallery Five Ltd, since 1961 (Founder Director, 1961); *b* 8 Aug. 1936; *s* of late Jerzy Dominik Pieńkowski and of Wanda Maria Pieńkowska. *Educ:* Cardinal Vaughan Sch., London; King's Coll., Cambridge (MA Classics and English). Art Director: J. Walter Thompson, London, 1958–59; William Collins, London, 1959–60; Art Editor, Time and Tide, London, 1960–61. Work includes graphics and surface design, posters and greeting cards, children's TV, and book illustration. Kate Greenaway Medal, Library Assoc., 1972 and

1979. *Publications:* illustrator: A Necklace of Raindrops, 1968; The Kingdom under the Sea, 1971; Meg and Mog series, 1973–87 (co-designed Meg and Mog Show, 1981, 1985); Tale of a One Way Street, 1978; The Jan Pieńkowski Fairy Tale Library, 1978; Ghosts and Bogles, 1985; Past Eight O'Clock, 1986, etc; illustrator/author: Nursery series, 1973–87; Haunted House, 1979; Robot, 1981; Dinner Time, 1981; Gossip, 1983; Christmas, 1984; Little Monsters, 1986. *Recreations:* movies, riding, skiing, gardening, collecting illustrated books. *Address:* Oakgates, 45 Lonsdale Road, Barnes, SW13 9JR. *T:* 01–748 6269. *Club:* Polish Hearth.

PIERCE, Francis William, MA (Belfast and Dublin); Hughes Professor of Spanish, University of Sheffield, 1953–80, now Emeritus Professor; Dean of the Faculty of Arts, 1964–67; *b* 21 Sept. 1915; *s* of late Robert Pierce, JP and Catherine Ismay Pierce; *m* 1944, Mary Charlotte Una, *o d* of late Rev. J. C. Black, Asyut, Upper Egypt; three *s. Educ:* Royal Belfast Academical Institution; Queen's University, Belfast. BA, 1st Cl. Hons, Spanish studies, QUB, 1938; Postgrad. Schol., Columbia Univ., New York, 1938–39; MA, QUB, 1939; Asst Lectr in Spanish, Univ. of Liverpool, 1939–40. Dep. to Prof. of Spanish, TCD, 1940–45; MA *jure officii*, Univ. of Dublin, 1943; Hughes Lectr in Spanish, Univ. of Sheffield, 1946. Visiting Professor: Brown Univ., Providence, RI, 1968; Case Western Reserve Univ., Cleveland, O, 1968. President: Anglo-Catalan Soc., 1955–57; Assoc. of Hispanists of GB and Ireland, 1971–73. *Publications:* The Heroic Poem of the Spanish Golden Age: Selections, chosen with Introduction and Notes, 1947; Hispanic Studies: Review and Revision, 1954; (ed) Hispanic Studies in Honour of I. González Llubera, 1959; La poesía épica del siglo de oro, 1961 (Madrid), 2nd edn 1968; The Historie of Aravcana, transcribed with introd. and notes, 1964; (ed with C. A. Jones) Actas del Primer Congreso Internacional de Hispanistas, 1964; (ed) Two Cervantes Short Novels, 1970, 2nd edn 1976; (ed) La Cristiada by Diego de Hojeda, 1971; (ed) Luís de Camões: Os Lusíadas, 1973, 2nd edn 1981; Amadís de Gaula, 1976; Alonso de Ercilla y Zúñiga, 1984; (ed) Repertorio de Hispanistas de Gran Bretaña e Irlanda, 1984; Asociación Internacional de Hispanistas: fundación e historia, 1986; articles and reviews in Hispanic Review, Mod. Language Review, Bulletin of Hispanic Studies, Bulletin Hispanique, Ocidente, Estudis Romànics, Quaderni Ibero-Americani. *Address:* 357 Fulwood Road, Sheffield S10 3BQ. *T:* Sheffield 664239.

PIERCE, Hugh Humphrey; *b* 13 Oct. 1931; *s* of Dr Gwilym Pierce, Abercynon, Glam; *m* 1958, Rachel Margaret Procter; two *s. Educ:* Clifton; King's Coll., Univ. of London. LLB Hons 1954; Pres. Faculty of Laws Soc.; Pres. Union. Called to Bar, Lincoln's Inn, 1955. Diploma Personnel Management, 1962; MIPM 1963. Army Service, 2nd Lieut Intell. Corps (Cyprus), 1955–57; Kodak Ltd, legal and personnel work, 1957–63; joined BBC, 1963, personnel and industrial relations; Admin. Officer, Local Radio, 1967–68; Local Radio Develt Manager, 1968–69; General Manager, Local Radio, 1970–74; Asst Controller, Staff Admin, 1974–78; Asst Controller, Employment Policy and Appts, 1978–80. Member: Justice; Amnesty; Exec. Cttee, Howard League; Treas., Prisoners' Advice and Law Service; Trustee: Community Develt Trust; Nat. Council for the Welfare of Prisoners Abroad. *Recreations:* chamber music, narrow boats. *Address:* 11 Wood Lane, Highgate, N6. *T:* 01–444 6001.

PIERCE, Rt. Rev. Reginald James, Hon. DD (Winnipeg), 1947; retired; *b* 1909; *s* of James Reginald Pierce and Clara (*née* Whitehand) Plymouth; *m* 1932, Ivy Bell, *d* of Edward and Lucy Jackson, Saskatoon, Canada; one *d. Educ:* University of Saskatchewan (BA 1931); Emmanuel Coll., Saskatoon (LTh 1932); Univ. of London (BD 1942). Deacon, 1932; priest, 1934; Curate of Colinton, 1932–33; Priest-in-charge, 1933–34; Rector and Rural Dean of Grande Prairie, 1934–38; Rector of South Saanich, 1938–41; Rector of St Barnabas, Calgary, 1941–43; Canon of St John's Cathedral, Winnipeg, and Warden of St John's Coll., 1943–50; Priest-in-charge of St Barnabas, Winnipeg, 1946–50; Bishop of Athabasca, 1950–74; Acting Rector: All Saints, Victoria, BC, 1975–76; St David's, Victoria, BC, 1976–78. Examining Chaplain: to Bishop of Athabasca, 1935–38; to Archbishop of Rupertsland, 1943–50.

PIERCE-GOULDING, Lt-Col Terence Leslie Crawford, MBE 1943; CD; Director, Commonwealth Press Union, since 1984 (Secretary, 1970–84); *b* 2 March 1918; *o s* of late Rev. Edward Pierce-Goulding and Christina; *m* 1964, Catherine Yvonne, *d* of John Welsh, Dunedin, NZ; one *s* one *d. Educ:* public and private schs, Edmonton, Alta. Enlisted British Army, 1940, 2nd Lieut Mddx Regt (DCO); Capt. Loyal Edmonton Regt, 1941–42; Staff Coll., 1943; GS03 (Ops), Canadian Planning Staff and HQ 1st Canadian Army, 1943–44; GSO2 (PR), HQ 21 Army Gp and BAOR, 1945–46; Sen. PRO, Central Comd HQ, 1947–48; Adviser to Perm. Canadian Delegn to UN, 1948–50; regtl and staff appts, Royal Canadian Regt and Army HQ, 1950–60; Chief Logistics Officer, UN Emergency Force (Middle East), 1962–63; Dir of Sen. Appts (Army), Canadian Forces HQ, 1963–66; Sen. Admin. Officer, Canadian Defence Liaison Staff (London), 1966–69, retd 1969. Canadian Internat. Development Agency, 1969–70. *Recreations:* golf, travel, photography, literature. *Address:* 20 Hill Rise, NW11. *T:* 01–455 2306. *Club:* Pathfinders.

PIERCY, family name of **Baron Piercy.**

PIERCY, 3rd Baron *cr* 1945, of Burford; **James William Piercy;** *b* 19 Jan. 1946; *s* of 2nd Baron Piercy and of Oonagh Lavinia, *d* of late Major Edward John Lake Baylay, DSO; *S* father, 1981. *Educ:* Shrewsbury; Edinburgh Univ. (BSc 1968). AMIEE; ACCA. *Heir:* b Hon. Mark Edward Pelham Piercy [*b* 30 June 1953; *m* 1979, Vivien Angela, *d* of His Honour Judge Evelyn Faithfull Monier-Williams, *qv*; two *d*]. *Address:* 13 Arnold Mansions, Queen's Club Gardens, W14 9RD.

PIERCY, Hon. Joanna Elizabeth; *see* Turner, Hon. J. E.

PIERCY, Hon. Penelope Katherine, CBE 1968; Under-Secretary, Ministry of Technology, 1965–68; *b* 15 Apr. 1916; *d* of 1st Baron Piercy, CBE. *Educ:* St Paul's Girls' School; Somerville College, Oxford. War of 1939–45, various appointments, Military Intelligence. Foreign Office, 1945–47; Economist, Colonial Development Corp., 1948–54; Department of Scientific and Industrial Research, 1955–65 (Sen. Prin. Scientific Officer, 1960). CIMechE. *Address:* Charlton Cottage, Tarrant Rushton, Blandford Forum, Dorset.

PIERRE, Abbé; (Henri Antoine Grouès); Officier de la Légion d'Honneur, 1980; French priest; Founder of the Companions of Emmaüs; *b* Lyon, 5 Aug. 1912; 5th *c* of Antoine Grouès, Soyeux. *Educ:* Collège des Jésuites, Lyon. Entered Capuchin Monastery, 1930; studied at Capuchin seminary, Crest, Drôme, and Faculté de Théologie, Lyon. Secular priest, St Joseph Basilica, Grenoble. Served war of 1939–45 (Officier de la Légion d'Honneur, Croix de Guerre, Médaille de la Résistance); Alsatian and Alpine fronts; Vicar of the Cathedral, Grenoble; assumed name of Abbé Pierre and joined resistance movement, 1942; Chaplain of French Navy at Casablanca, 1944; of whole Free French Navy, 1945. Elected (Indep.) to 1st Constituent Assembly of 4th French Republic, 1945; elected as candidate of Mouvement Républicain Populaire to 2nd Constituent Assembly; re-elected 1946; contested (Indep.), 1951. Président de l'Exécutif du Mouvement Universel pour une Confédération Mondiale, 1947–51. Founded the Companions of Emmaüs, a movement to provide a roof for the "sanslogis" of Paris. *Publications:* 23 Mois de Vie Clandestine; L'Abbé Pierre vous Parle; Vers l'Homme; Feuilles Eparses; Emmaüs ou Venger l'homme. *Address:* 2 Avenue de la Liberté, Charenton-Val de Marne, France. *T:* 368.62.44.

PIERS, Sir Charles Robert Fitzmaurice, 10th Bt, *cr* 1660; Lt-Comdr RCNVR; *b* 30 Aug. 1903; *s* of Sir Charles Piers, 9th Bt, and Hester Constance (Stella) (*d* 1936), *e d* of late S. R. Brewis of Ibstone House, Ibstone; *S* father, 1945; *m* 1936, Ann Blanche Scott (*d* 1975), *o d* of late Capt. Thomas Ferguson (The Royal Highlanders); one *s* one *d. Educ:* RN Colleges, Osborne and Dartmouth. Served European War, 1939–45. *Heir:* s James Desmond Piers, [*b* 24 July 1947; *m* 1975, Sandra Mae Dixon; one *s* one *d*]. *Address:* PO Box 748, Duncan, British Columbia V9L 3Y1, Canada.

PIERS, Rear-Adm. Desmond William, DSC 1943; CM 1982; CD; RCN, retd; Agent General of Nova Scotia in the United Kingdom and Europe, 1977–79; *b* 12 June 1913; *s* of William Harrington Piers and Florence Maud Piers (*née* O'Donnell), MD; *m* 1941, Janet, *d* of Dr and Mrs Murray Macneill, Halifax, NS; one step *d. Educ:* Halifax County Acad.; RMC of Canada; RN Staff Coll.; Nat. Defence Coll. of Canada. Joined RCN as cadet, 1932; CO, HMC Destroyer Restigouche, and Sen. Officer, Fourth Canadian Escort Gp on N Atlantic convoy routes, 1941–43 (DSC); CO, HMC Destroyer Algonquin with Brit. Home Fleet, Scapa Flow, and participated in invasion of Normandy and convoys to N Russia, 1944–45, Comdr 1945; Exec. Officer, HMC Aircraft Carrier Magnificent (Comdr), 1947–48; Dir, Naval Plans and Ops, Naval Headquarters, Ottawa (Captain), 1949–50; Asst COS (Personnel and Admin.) to SACLANT, 1952–53; CO, HMC Cruiser Quebec, 1955–56; Sen. Canadian Offr Afloat (Atlantic), 1956–57; Comdt, RMC Canada, and Hon. ADC to the Governor General (Cdre), 1957–60; Asst Chief of Naval Staff (Plans), Naval HQ, 1960–62; Chm., Can. Def. Liaison Staff, Washington DC, and Can. Rep. on NATO Mil. Cttee (Rear-Adm.), 1962–66; retd 1967. Hon. Life Mem., Nat. Trust for Scotland. Hon. DScMil, RMC of Canada, 1978. Freeman of City of London, 1978; KLJ 1969. *Recreations:* golf, tennis, figure skating, photography. *Address:* The Quarter Deck, Chester, Nova Scotia B0J 1J0, Canada. *T:* 902–275–4462. *Clubs:* Halifax (Halifax); Halifax Golf and Country, Chester Golf (all Nova Scotia).

PIGGOTT, Donald James; Director-General, British Red Cross Society, 1980–85; *b* 1 Sept. 1920; *s* of James Piggott and Edith Piggott (*née* Tempest); *m* 1974, Kathryn Courtenay-Evans. *Educ:* Bradford Grammar School; Christ's College, Cambridge (MA); London School of Economics. Served Army in NW Europe and India, 1941–46. PA to Finance and Supply Director, London Transport, 1947–50; Shell-Mex and BP Ltd, 1951–58; Manager Development Div., Marketing Dept, British Petroleum Co. Ltd, 1958–73; BRCS: Dir, Internat. Affairs, 1973; Head of Internat. Div., 1975; Asst Dir-Gen. International, 1980. Mem., Central Appeals Adv. Cttee, BBC and IBA, 1980–83. Mem., Open Sect., RSocMed, 1982–. OStJ 1983. *Recreations:* music, theatre. *Address:* 18 Elm Lodge, River Gardens, SW6. *T:* 01–385 5588; Beech Tree House, Tostock, Bury St Edmunds, Suffolk. *T:* Beyton 70589.

PIGGOTT, Maj.-Gen. Francis James Claude, CB 1963; CBE 1961; DSO 1945; *b* Tokyo, Japan, 11 Oct. 1910; *s* of late Maj.-Gen. F. S. G. Piggott, CB, DSO; *m* 1940, Muriel Joan, *d* of late Wilfred E. Cottam, Rotherham, Yorks; one *s* one *d. Educ:* Cheltenham; RMC Sandhurst. 2nd Lieut The Queen's Royal Regt, 1931; Language Officer, Japan, 1935–37; Captain, 1939; served 1939–45 in France (despatches), New Zealand, India and Burma (DSO); in Japan, UK and Egypt (OBE and Bt Lt-Col), 1946–52; attended 1st Course, Joint Services Staff Coll., 1947; Lt-Col comdg 1st Bn The Queen's Royal Regt, 1952, BAOR and Malaya; Colonel, War Office, 1954; Comd 161 Infantry Bde (TA), 1956; Dep. Director of Military Intelligence, War Office (Brigadier), 1958; Major-General, 1961; Assistant Chief of Staff (Intelligence), SHAPE, 1961–64; retired, 1964; served in Civil Service (Security), 1965–75. Col, The Queen's Royal Surrey Regt, 1964–66; Dep. Col (Surrey) The Queen's Regt, 1967–69. *Recreations:* cricket and foreign travel. *Address:* Ivy Cottage, Thorpe-le-Soken, Essex CO16 0HA. *T:* Clacton-on-Sea 861510. *Clubs:* Army and Navy, Free Foresters.

PIGGOTT, Lester Keith, OBE 1975; jockey, 1948–85; trainer, since 1985; *b* 5 Nov. 1935; *s* of Keith Piggott and Iris Rickaby; *m* 1960, Susan Armstrong; two *d.* Selection of races won: the Derby (9 times): 1954 (on Never Say Die); 1957 (on Crepello); 1960 (on St Paddy); 1968 (on Sir Ivor); 1970 (on Nijinsky); 1972 (on Roberto); 1976 (on Empery); 1977 (on The Minstrel); 1983 (on Teenoso); St Leger (8 times); The Oaks (6 times); 2,000 guineas (4 times); 1,000 guineas (twice). In many seasons 1955–85 he rode well over 100 winners a year, in this country alone; rode 4,000th winner in Britain, 14 Aug. 1982; Champion Jockey 11 times, 1960, 1964–71, 1981, 1982; rode frequently in France; won Prix de l'Arc de Triomphe on Rheingold, 1973, on Alleged, 1977 and 1978; won Washington, DC, International on Sir Ivor, 1968 (first time since 1922 an English Derby winner raced in USA), on Karabas, 1969, on Argument, 1980. *Relevant publication:* Lester, the Official Biography, by Dick Francis, 1986. *Recreations:* swimming, water skiing, golf. *Address:* Florizel, Newmarket, Suffolk. *T:* Newmarket 662584.

PIGGOTT, Prof. Stuart, CBE 1972; FBA 1953; Abercromby Professor of Prehistoric Archæology, University of Edinburgh, 1946–77; *b* 28 May 1910; *s* of G. H. O. Piggott. *Educ:* Churchers Coll., Petersfield; St John's Coll., Oxford (Hon. Fellow, 1979). On staff on Royal Commn on Ancient Monuments (Wales), 1929–34; Asst Dir of Avebury excavations, 1934–38; from 1939 in ranks and later as Intelligence Officer in Army in charge of military air photograph interpretation, South-East Asia. Conducted archæological excavations in southern England and carried out research on European prehistory up to 1942; in India, 1942–45; studied Oriental prehistory. FRSE; FSA (Gold Medal, 1983); Fellow, UCL, 1985. Mem. German Archæolog. Inst., 1953; Hon. Mem. Royal Irish Acad., 1956; Foreign Hon. Member American Academy of Arts and Sciences, 1960; advisory editor, Antiquity. Trustee, British Museum, 1968–74. Travelled in Europe and Asia. Hon. DLittHum, Columbia, 1954; Hon. DLitt Edinburgh, 1984. *Publications:* Some Ancient Cities of India, 1946; Fire Among the Ruins, 1948; British Prehistory, 1949; William Stukeley: an XVIII Century Antiquary, 1950; Prehistoric India, 1950; A Picture Book of Ancient British Art (with G. E. Daniel), 1951; Neolithic Cultures of British Isles, 1954; Scotland before History, 1958; Approach to Archæology, 1959; (ed) The Dawn of Civilization, 1961; The West Kennet Long Barrow, 1962; Ancient Europe, 1965; Prehistoric Societies (with J. G. D. Clark), 1965; The Druids, 1968; Introduction to Camden's Britannia of 1695, 1971; (ed jtly) France Before the Romans, 1974; Ruins in a Landscape, 1977; Antiquity Depicted, 1978; (ed and contrib.) Agrarian History of England and Wales Ii, 1981; The Earliest Wheeled Transport, 1983; numerous technical papers in archæological jls. *Recreations:* reading, cooking, travel. *Address:* The Cottage, West Challow, Wantage, Oxon. *Club:* United Oxford & Cambridge University.

PIGOT, Maj.-Gen. Sir Robert (Anthony), 7th Bt *cr* 1764; CB 1964; OBE 1959; DL; *b* 6 July 1915; *s* of George Douglas Hugh Pigot (*d* 1959) (2nd *s* of 5th Bt) and Hersey Elizabeth Pigot (*née* Maltby) (*d* 1970); *S* uncle, 1977; *m* 1942, Honor (*d* 1966), *d* of late Capt. Wilfred St Martin Gibbon; one *s* one *d*; *m* 1968, Sarah Anne Colville, *e d* of late David Colville and of Lady Joan Colville, The Old Vicarage, Dorton; one *s* one *d. Educ:* Stowe Sch. Commissioned into the Royal Marines, 1934; served War of 1939–45 (despatches): Regimental service in RM Div. and Special Service Group; Staff appts in 3rd

Commando Brigade in SE Asia; psc 1943–44; Directing Staff, Staff Coll., Camberley, 1946–47; Min. of Defence, 1953–54; Standing Group, NATO, Washington, 1954–57; Dep. Standing Gp Rep. with North Atlantic Council, Paris, 1958–59; Chief of Staff, Royal Marines, 1960–64; retd, Dec. 1964. Man. Director, Bone Brothers Ltd, 1964–66; Director: John Brown Plastics Machinery Ltd, 1965–66; Executive Appointments Ltd, 1968–70. Pres. and Mem. Cttee of Management, RNLI; Pres., Union Jack Club. High Sheriff, DL, Isle of Wight, 1978. *Recreations:* field sports and yachting. *Heir: s* George Hugh Pigot [*b* 28 Nov. 1946; *m* 1st, 1967, Judith (marr. diss. 1973), *er d* of late Major John Hele Sandeman-Allen, RA; one *d*; 2nd, 1980, Lucinda Jane, *yr d* of Donald Charles Spandler; two *s*]. *Address:* Yew Tree Lodge, Bembridge, Isle of Wight. *Clubs:* Royal Yacht Squadron; Bembridge Sailing; Royal Naval Sailing Association; Solent Cruising and Racing Association.

PIGOT, Thomas Herbert, QC 1967; **His Honour Judge Pigot;** a Circuit Judge, since 1972; Common Serjeant in the City of London, since 1984; Senior Judge (non-resident), Sovereign Base Area, Cyprus, since 1984 (Deputy Senior Judge, 1971–84); *b* 19 May 1921; *e s* of late Thomas Pigot and of Martha Ann Pigot; *m* 1950, Zena Marguerite, *yr d* of late Tom and Dorothy Gladys Wall; three *d. Educ:* Manchester Gram. Sch. (Schol.); Brasenose Coll., Oxford (Somerset Schol.). BA (1st cl. hons Jurisprudence) 1941; MA 1946; BCL 1947. Commissioned Welch Regt, 1942; served N Africa with Royal Lincs Regt; wounded and taken prisoner, 1943; released, 1945. Called to Bar, Inner Temple, 1947, Bencher, 1985; practised in Liverpool on Northern Circuit until 1967. Mem., Bar Council, 1970. One of HM Comrs of Lieutenancy, City of London. Hon. Liveryman, Cutlers' Co. *Recreation:* golf. *Address:* Central Criminal Court, EC4M 7EH. *Clubs:* MCC; Vincent's (Oxford); Royal Birkdale Golf; Huntercombe Golf; Harlequin FC.

PIGOTT, Sir (Berkeley) Henry (Sebastian), 5th Bt *cr* 1808; farmer; *b* 24 June 1925; *s* of Sir Berkeley Pigott, 4th Bt, and Christabel (*d* 1974), *d* of late Rev. F. H. Bowden-Smith; *S* father, 1982; *m* 1954, (Olive) Jean, *d* of John William Balls; two *s* one *d. Educ:* Ampleforth College. Served War with Royal Marines, 1944–45. *Recreation:* sailing (blue water). *Heir: er s* David John Berkeley Pigott [*b* 16 Aug. 1955; *m* 1981, Alison Fletcher (marr. diss.)]. *Address:* Brook Farm, Shobley, Ringwood, Hants. *T:* Ringwood 3268.

PIGOTT, Dr Christopher Donald; Director, University Botanic Garden, Cambridge, since 1984; *b* 7 April 1928; *s* of John Richards Pigott and Helen Constance Pigott (*née* Lee); *m* 1954, Margaret Elsie Beatson (*d* 1981); one *d*; *m* 1986, Sheila Lloyd (*née* Megaw). *Educ:* Mill Hill School; University of Cambridge. MA, PhD. Asst Lectr, and Lectr, Univ. of Sheffield, 1951–60; Univ. Lectr, Cambridge, 1960–64; Fellow of Emmanuel Coll., Cambridge, 1962–64; Prof. of Biology, Univ. of Lancaster, 1964–84; Professorial Fellow, Emmanuel Coll., Cambridge, 1984–; Member: Nature Conservancy, 1971–73; Nature Conservancy Council, 1979–82; Council, Nat. Trust, 1980–; Foreign Mem., Acad. d'Agriculture de France (Silviculture), 1982–. *Publications:* contribs to sci. jls (ecology and physiology of plants). *Recreations:* walking, travelling in Europe. *Address:* Emmanuel College, Cambridge CB2 3AP.

PIGOTT, Air Vice-Marshal Michael Joseph, CBE 1956; Director of Dental Services, RAF, 1954–58; retired, 1958; *b* 16 May 1904; *m* 1938, Ethel Norah, *d* of Alfred Sutherland Blackman; one *d. Educ:* Blackrock College, Dublin; Nat. Univ. of Ireland; Nat. Dental Hosp. of Ireland. BDS 1925; FDSRCS 1948. Joined RAF 1930. Served War of 1939–45, Bomber Command; Inspecting Dental Officer: MEAF, 1945–48, Flying Trng Comd, 1948–49, Tech. Trng Comd, 1949–50; Principal Dental Officer, Home Comd 1950–54; Air Vice-Marshal, 1955. QHDS, 1950–58. *Address:* 18 Duck Street, Cerne Abbas, Dorchester, Dorset DT2 7LA. *T:* Cerne Abbas 538.

PIGOTT-BROWN, Sir William Brian, 3rd Bt, *cr* 1902; *b* 20 Jan. 1941; *s* of Sir John Pigott-Brown, 2nd Bt (killed in action, 1942) and Helen (who *m* 1948, Capt. Charles Raymond Radclyffe), *o d* of Major Gilbert Egerton Cotton, Priestland, Tarporley, Cheshire; *S* father, 1942. *Heir:* none. *Address:* 25 Chapel Street, SW1.

PIHL, Brig. Hon. Dame Mary Mackenzie, (Fru Mary Pihl), DBE 1970 (MBE 1958); Director, Women's Royal Army Corps, 1967–Aug. 1970, retired; *b* 3 Feb. 1916; *d* of Sir John Anderson, later 1st Viscount Waverley, PC, GCB, OM, GCSI, GCIE, FRS, and Christina Mackenzie Anderson; *m* 1973, Frithjof Pihl. *Educ:* Sutton High Sch.; Villa Brillantmont, Lausanne. Joined Auxiliary Territorial Service, 1941; transferred to Women's Royal Army Corps, 1949. Hon. ADC to the Queen, 1967–70. *Address:* Engø, 3145 Tjøme, Norway. *Club:* English-Speaking Union.

PIKE, Baroness *cr* 1974 (Life Peer), of Melton, Leics; **Irene Mervyn Parnicott Pike,** DBE 1981; Chairman, Broadcasting Complaints Commission, 1981–85; *b* 16 Sept. 1918; *d* of I. S. Pike, Company Director, Okehampton, Devonshire. *Educ:* Hunmanby Hall; Reading University. BA Hons Economics and Psychology, 1941. Served WAAF, 1941–46. Mem., WRCC, 1955–57. Contested (C): Pontefract, 1951; Leek, Staffordshire, 1955. MP (C) Melton, Leics, Dec. 1956–Feb. 1974; Assistant Postmaster-General, 1959–63; Joint Parliamentary Under-Secretary of State, Home Office, 1963–64. Director: Watts, Blake, Bearne & Co. Ltd; Dunderdale Investments. Chairman: IBA Gen. Adv. Council, 1974–79; WRVS, 1974–81. *Recreations:* gardening, walking. *Address:* Hownam, near Kelso, Roxburgh TD5 8AL.

PIKE, Edward Roy, PhD; FRS 1981; Clerk Maxwell Professor of Theoretical Physics, King's College London, since 1986; Chief Scientific Officer, Royal Signals and Radar Establishment, Malvern, since 1984; *b* 4 Dec. 1929; *s* of Anthony Pike and Rosalind Irene Davies; *m* 1955, Pamela Sawtell; one *s* two *d. Educ:* Southfield Grammar Sch., Oxford; University Coll., Cardiff (BSc, PhD; Fellow, 1981). FInstP, FIMA. Served Royal Corps of Signals, 1948–50. Fulbright Schol., Physics Dept, MIT, 1958–60; Royal Signals and Radar Estabt Physics Group, 1960–: theoretical and experimental research condensed matter physics and optics; Individual Merit SPSO 1967, IM DCSO 1973. Vis. Prof. of Maths, Imperial Coll., London, 1985. Chm., Oval (114) Ltd, 1984–85; non-exec. Dir, Richard Clay plc, 1985–86. Govt assessor, SRC Physics Cttee, 1973–76. Mem. Council: Inst. of Physics, 1976–85; European Physical Soc., 1981–83; Vice-Pres. for Publications and Chm., Adam Hilger, 1981–85; Director, NATO Advanced Study Insts, 1973–77. Editor: Journal of Physics A, 1973–78; Optica Acta, 1978–83. Nat. Science Foundn Vis. Lectr, USA, 1959; Lectures: Univ. of Rome, 1976; Univ. of Bordeaux, 1977; Simon Fraser Univ., 1978; Univ. of Genoa, 1980. Royal Society Charles Parsons medal and lecture, 1975; MacRobert award (jtly) and lecture, 1977; Worshipful Co. of Scientific Instrument Makers Annual Achievement award (jtly), 1978; Committee on Awards to Inventors award, 1980; Confrérie St-Etienne, 1980–. *Publications:* (ed jtly) Photon Correlation and Light Beating Spectroscopy, 1974; (ed) High Power Gas Lasers, 1975; (ed jtly) Photon Correlation Spectroscopy and Velocimetry, 1977; (ed jtly) Frontiers in Quantum Optics, 1986; numerous papers in scientific jls. *Recreations:* music, languages, squash, woodwork. *Address:* 3a Golborne Mews, North Kensington, W10.

PIKE, Air Cdre James Maitland Nicholson, CB 1963; DSO 1942; DFC 1941; RAF, retired; with Ministry of Defence, 1969–78; *b* 8 Feb. 1916; *s* of late Frank Pike, Glendarary, Achill Island, Co. Mayo, Eire, and Daphne (*née* Kenyon Stow), Worcester; *m* 1st, 1942; one *d*; 2nd, 1955, Amber Pauline Bettesworth Hellard; one *s* one step *d*; 3rd, 1972, Dorothy May Dawson (*née* Holland); one step *d. Educ:* Stowe; RAF Coll., Cranwell. Commnd 1937; War Service: Aden, Middle East, UK (Coastal Command), Malta and Azores. Directing staff, RAF Staff Coll., 1945–47; Group Capt. 1955; Comd RAF Station, St Mawgan and RAF Station, Kinloss, 1955–57; SASO, RAF Malta, 1958–60; Air Cdre 1961; AOC, RAF Gibraltar, 1961–62; Imperial Defence College, 1963; Air Cdre Intelligence (B), Ministry of Defence, 1964; Dir of Security, RAF, 1965–69. *Recreations:* shooting, fishing.

PIKE, Michael Edmund, CMG 1984; HM Diplomatic Service; Minister and Deputy UK Permanent Representative to NATO, Brussels, since 1985; *b* 4 Oct. 1931; *s* of Henry Pike and Eleanor Pike; *m* 1962, Catherine (*née* Lim); one *s* two *d. Educ:* Wimbledon Coll.; London Sch. of Econs and Polit. Science; Brasenose Coll., Oxford (MA 1956). Service in HM Armed Forces, 1950–52. Editor, Cherwell, Oxford Univ., 1954; part-time News Reporter, Sunday Express, 1954–55; Feature Writer and Film Critic, Surrey Comet, 1955–56; joined HM Foreign (now Diplomatic) Service, 1956; Third Secretary: FO, 1956–57; Seoul, 1957–59; Second Secretary: Office of Comr Gen. for Singapore and SE Asia, 1960–62; Seoul, 1962–64; FO, 1964–68; First Sec., Warsaw, 1968–70; FCO, 1970–73; First Sec., Washington, 1973–75; Counsellor: Washington, 1975–78; Tel Aviv, 1978–82; RCDS, 1982; Ambassador to Vietnam, 1982–85. Pres., Union of Catholic Students of GB, 1955–56. *Recreations:* reading, running, contemplating London. *Address:* c/o Foreign and Commonwealth Office, SW1.

PIKE, Peter Leslie; MP (Lab) Burnley, since 1983; *b* 26 June 1937; *s* of Leslie Henry Pike and Gladys (*née* Cunliffe); *m* 1962, Sheila Lillian Bull; two *d. Educ:* Hinchley Wood County Secondary Sch. (Commercial Dept); Kingston Technical Coll. Pt 1 Exam., Inst. of Bankers. National Service, RM, 1956–58. Midland Bank, 1954–62; Twinings Tea, 1962–63; Organiser/Agent, Labour Party, 1963–73; Mullard (Simonstone) Ltd, 1973–83. Mem., GMBATU (Shop Steward, 1976–83). Member: Merton and Morden UDC, 1962–63; Burnley Bor. Council, 1976–84 (Leader, Labour Gp, 1980–83; Gp Sec., 1976–80). Mem., Environmental Select Cttee, 1985–. Mem., Nat. Trust, 1974–. *Recreation:* Burnley Football Club supporter. *Address:* 75 Ormerod Road, Burnley, Lancs BB11 2RU. *T:* Burnley 34719. *Clubs:* Burnley Labour; Byerden House Socialist; Mullard Sports and Social.

PIKE, Sir Philip Ernest Housden, Kt 1969; Chief Justice of Swaziland, 1970–72, retired; *b* 6 March 1914; *s* of Rev. Ernest Benjamin Pike and Dora Case Pike (*née* Lillie); *m* 2nd, 1959, Millicent Locke Staples; one *s* one *d* of 1st marriage. *Educ:* De Carteret School, and Munro Coll., Jamaica; Middle Temple, London. Barrister at Law, 1938. Crown Counsel, Jamaica, 1947–49; Legal Draftsman, Kenya, 1949–52; Solicitor General, Uganda, 1952–58; QC (Uganda) 1953; Attorney General, Sarawak, 1958–65; QC (Sarawak) 1958; Chief Justice, High Court in Borneo, 1965–68; Judge, High Court of Malawi, 1969–70, Actg Chief Justice, 1970. Coronation Medal, 1953. PNBS-Sarawak, 1965; Malaysia Commemorative Medal, 1967; PMN Malaysia 1968. *Recreations:* golf, gardening. *Address:* 3 Earlewood Court, Penhaligon Way, Robina Waters, Qld 4226, Australia.

PIKE, Rt. Rev. St John Surridge; DD *jure dig* 1958; Assistant Bishop, Diocese of Guildford, 1963–83; *b* 27 Dec. 1909; *s* of late Rev. Canon William Pike, Thurles, Co. Tipperary; *m* 1958, Clare, *d* of late William Henry Jones; one *s* one *d* (and one *s* decd). *Educ:* The Abbey, Tipperary; Bishop Foy School, Waterford; Trinity Coll., Dublin (MA). Deacon, 1932; Priest, 1934; Curate of Taney, 1932–37; Head of Southern Church Mission, Ballymacarrett, Belfast, 1937–47; SPG Missionary, Diocese of Gambia, 1947–52; Rector of St George's, Belfast, 1952–57; Commissary for Gambia in N Ireland, 1954–57; Bishop of Gambia and the Rio Pongas, 1958–63; Vicar of St Mary the Virgin, Ewshot, 1963–71; Vicar of Holy Trinity, Botleys and Lyne, and Christ Church, Longcross, 1971–83. *Address:* Box Cottage, Old Rectory Lane, Twyford, Hants. *T:* Twyford 712253.

See also Sir Theodore Pike.

PIKE, Sir Theodore (Ouseley), KCMG 1956 (CMG 1953); Chairman, Tricolor International, since 1984; *b* 1904; 3rd *s* of late Canon W. Pike, Thurles, Co. Tipperary; *m* 1934, Violet F., *d* of late Sir William Robinson, DL, JP; two *s* one *d. Educ:* The Abbey, Tipperary; Trinity Coll., Dublin; University Coll., Oxford. Irish Rugby International (8 caps), 1927–28. Colonial Administrative Service, Tanganyika, 1928–53. Governor, Somaliland Protectorate, 1953; Governor and Commander-in-Chief, Somaliland Protectorate, 1954–59. Hon. LLD (Dublin). *Address:* c/o Grindlay's Bank, 13 St James's Square, SW1. *Club:* Lansdowne (Hon. Mem.).

PIKE, Lt-Gen. Sir William (Gregory Huddleston), KCB 1961 (CB 1956); CBE 1952; DSO 1943; Chief Commander, St John Ambulance, 1969–75; b 24 June 1905; *s* of late Captain Sydney Royston Pike, RA, and Sarah Elizabeth Pike (*née* Huddleston); *m* 1939, Josephine Margaret, *er d* of late Maj.-Gen. R. H. D. Tompson, CB, CMG, DSO, and Mrs B. D. Tompson; one *s* two *d. Educ:* Bedford School; Marlborough Coll.; RMA Woolwich. Lieutenant RA, 20th and 24th Field Brigades, RA and "A" Field Brigade, Indian Artillery, 1925–36; Staff College, Camberley, 1937–38; Command and Staff Appointments in UK, France and Belgium, North Africa, USA and Far East, 1939–50; CRA, 1st Commonwealth Div., Korea, 1951–52; idc 1953; Director of Staff Duties, War Office, 1954–57; Chief of Staff, Far East Land Forces, Oct. 1957–60; Vice-Chief of the Imperial General Staff, 1960–63; Col Comdt RA, 1962–70. Lieutenant of HM Tower of London, 1963–66; Commissioner-in-Chief, St John Ambulance Brigade, 1967–73. Jt Hon. Pres., Anglo-Korean Society, 1963–69. Hon. Col 277 (Argyll and Sutherland Highlanders) Regt RA (TA), 1960–67; Hon. Col Lowland Regt RA (T), 1967–70. Member Honourable Artillery Company; Chm., Lord Mayor Treloar Trust, 1976–82; Corps of Commissionaires, 1964–81 (Mem. Administrative Bd). Officer, US Legion of Merit, 1953. GCStJ 1976. *Recreations:* field sports and gardening. *Address:* Ganwells, Bentley, Hants.

PILBROW, Richard Hugh; Chairman, Theatre Projects, since 1957; *b* 28 April 1933; *s* of Arthur Gordon Pilbrow and Marjorie Pilbrow; *m* 1st, 1958, Viki Brinton; one *s* one *d*; 2nd, 1974, Molly Friedel; one *d. Educ:* Cranbrook Sch.; Central Sch. of Speech and Drama. Stage Manager, Teahouse of the August Moon, 1954; founded Theatre Projects, 1957. Lighting Designer for over 200 prodns in London, New York, Paris and Moscow, incl.: Brand, 1959; Blitz, 1962; Zorba, 1968; Annie, 1978; Oklahoma!, 1980; The Little Foxes, Windy City, 1982; Singin' In the Rain, 1983; for Nat. Theatre Co., 1963–70, incl. Hamlet, 1963; Rosencrantz and Guildenstern are Dead, 1966; Heartbreak House, 1975; Love for Love, 1986. Theatrical Producer in London of prodns incl.: A Funny Thing Happened on the Way to the Forum, 1963, 1986; Cabaret, 1968; Company, 1972; A Little Night Music, 1975; West Side Story, 1984; The Mysteries, Lyceum, 1985; I'm Not Rappaport, 1986. Film Prod., Swallows and Amazons, 1973; TV Productions: All You Need is Love—the story of popular music, 1975; Swallows and Amazons for Ever, 1984; Dir, Mister, 1971. Theatre Projects Consultants have been consultants on many theatres incl. Nat. Theatre of GB, Barbican Theatre, Royal Opera House, and theatres and arts centres in Canada, Iran, Hong Kong, Saudi Arabia, Mexico, Iceland, Nigeria, Norway,

USA, etc. Vice President: Assoc. of British Theatre Technicians: Nat. Youth Theatre; Co-founder, Soc. of Brit. Theatre Designers, 1975; Mem., Assoc. of Lighting Designers (Chm., 1982–85); Member: Drama Panel, Arts Council of GB, 1968–70; Soc. of West End Theatre; Council, London Acad. of Music and Drama. FRSA. *Publication:* Stage Lighting, 1970, 2nd edn 1979. *Recreations:* The Hebrides, cooking, dogs. *Address:* Theatre Projects Ltd, 14 Langley Street, WC2H 9JU. *T:* 01–240 5411. *Club:* Garrick.

PILCHER, Sir (Charlie) Dennis, Kt 1974; CBE 1968; FRICS; Chairman, Commission for the New Towns, 1971–78; Consultant, late Senior Partner (Partner 1930), Graves, Son & Pilcher (Chartered Surveyors); Director, Save and Prosper Group Ltd, 1970–80; *b* 2 July 1906; *s* of Charlie Edwin Pilcher, Fareham, Hants; *m* 1929, Mary Allison Aumonier, *d* of William Aumonier, London; two *d. Educ:* Clayesmore Sch. Served War: Major, RA (despatches, Normandy), 1940–45. Hemel Hempstead Development Corp., 1949–56; Bracknell Development Corp., 1956–71 (Chm. 1968–71); Dir, Sun Life Assurance Soc. Ltd, 1968–77. Pres., RICS, 1963–64; Mem., Milner Holland Cttee on London Housing, 1963–64; Vice-Pres., London Rent Assessment Panel, 1966–70; Adviser to Business Rents Directorate of DoE, 1973–77. Mem. Council, Glyndebourne Fest. Opera, 1969–. *Recreations:* opera, golf, fishing. *Address:* Brambles, Batts Lane, Mare Hill, Pulborough, West Sussex. *T:* Pulborough 2126. *Club:* West Sussex Golf.
See also Earl of Strafford.

PILCHER, Sir John (Arthur), GCMG 1973 (KCMG 1966; CMG 1957); HM Diplomatic Service, retired; *b* 16 May 1912; *s* of late Lt-Col A. J. Pilcher; *m* 1942, Delia Margaret Taylor; one *d. Educ:* Shrewsbury; Clare Coll., Cambridge; France, Austria and Italy. Served in Japan, 1936–39; China, 1939–41; Ministry of Information and Foreign Office, 1941–48; Italy, 1948–51; Foreign Office, 1951–54; Spain (Counsellor, Madrid), 1954–59; Philippines (Ambassador), 1959–63; Assistant Under-Secretary, Foreign Office, 1963–65; Ambassador to: Austria, 1965–67; Japan, 1967–72. Dir, Foreign & Colonial Investment Trust, 1973–82; Chairman: Brazil Fund, 1975–82; Fleming Japan Fund, SA, 1976–85; Advisor on Far Eastern Affairs, Robert Fleming & Co., 1973–85. Member: Museums and Galleries Commn (formerly Standing Commission on Museums and Galleries), 1973–83; Cttee, Soc. for Protection of Ancient Buildings, 1974–82; Treasure Trove Reviewing Cttee, 1977–. Pres., Inst. of Linguists, 1982–84. Grand Cross (Gold) Austrian Decoration of Honour, 1966; Order of the Rising Sun, First Class, Japan, 1971; Grand Official of Order of Merit of the Italian Republic, 1977. *Address:* 33 The Terrace, SW13. *T:* 01–876 9710. *Club:* Brooks's.

PILCHER, Robin Sturtevant, MS, FRCS, FRCP; Emeritus Professor of Surgery, University of London; Professor of Surgery and Director of the Surgical Unit, University College Hospital, London, 1938–67; *b* 22 June 1902; *s* of Thorold and Helena Pilcher; *m* 1929, Mabel Pearks; one *s* one *d. Educ:* St Paul's Sch.; University Coll., London. Fellow University Coll., London. *Publications:* various surgical papers. *Address:* Swanbourne, 21 Church End, Haddenham, Bucks HP17 8AE. *T:* Haddenham 291048.

PILDITCH, James George Christopher, CBE 1983; Founder, AIDCOM International plc (Chairman, 1980–83); *b* 7 Aug. 1929; *s* of Frederick Henry Pilditch and Marie-Thérèse (*née* Priest); *m* 1st, 1952, Molly (marr. diss.); one *d*; 2nd, 1970, Anne Elisabeth W:son Johnson. *Educ:* Slough Grammar Sch.; Reading Univ. (Fine Arts); INSEAD. Nat. Service, commnd RA, 1950; Royal Canadian Artillery Reserve, 1953–56. Journalism in Canada including Maclean-Hunter Publishing Co., 1952–56; work in design offices, Orr Associates (Toronto), THM Partners (London), Jim Nash Assocs (New York), 1956–59; started Package Design Associates (later Allied International Designers), in London, 1959. Chairman: Design Bd, Business and Technician Educn Council, 1983–86; Furniture EDC, NEDO, 1985–; Design Working Party, NEDO, 1985–86; Member: Council, Marketing Gp of GB; Adv. panel, Design Management Unit, London Business School; Design Council, 1984–; Design Management Gp, SIAD, 1984–; Council, RSA; Council, Heritage of London Trust. FRSA; Hon. FSIAD 1985 (ASIAD 1968); First Hon. Fellow, Design Management Inst., USA. *Publications:* The Silent Salesman, 1961, 2nd edn 1973; (with Douglas Scott) The Business of Product Design, 1965; Communication By Design, 1970; Talk About Design, 1976; Hold Fast the Heritage, 1982. *Recreations:* real tennis, watching the Lord's Test, travel, writing, sketching. *Address:* 62 Cadogan Square, SW1. *T:* 01–584 9279; Brookhampton House, North Cadbury, Som. *T:* North Cadbury 40225. *Clubs:* Army and Navy, MCC.

PILDITCH, Sir Richard (Edward), 4th Bt, *cr* 1929; *b* 8 Sept. 1926; *s* of Sir Philip Harold Pilditch, 2nd Bt, and Frances Isabella, *d* of J. G. Weeks, JP, Bedlington, Northumberland; *S* brother (Sir Philip John Frederick Pilditch, 3rd Bt) 1954; *m* 1950, Pauline Elizabeth Smith; one *s* one *d. Educ:* Charterhouse. Served War of 1939–45, with Royal Navy, in India and Ceylon, 1944–45. *Recreations:* shooting, fishing. *Heir: s* John Richard Pilditch, *b* 24 Sept. 1955. *Address:* 4 Fishermans Bank, Mudeford, Christchurch, Dorset.

PILE, Colonel Sir Frederick (Devereux), 3rd Bt *cr* 1900; MC 1945; *b* 10 Dec. 1915; *s* of Gen. Sir Frederick Alfred Pile, 2nd Bt, GCB, DSO, MC; *S* father, 1976; *m* 1st, 1940, Pamela (*d* 1983), *d* of late Philip Henstock; two *d*; 2nd, 1984, Mrs Josephine Culverwell. *Educ:* Weymouth; RMC, Sandhurst. Joined Royal Tank Regt, 1935; served War of 1939–45, Egypt and NW Europe; commanded Leeds Rifles, 1955–56; Colonel GS, BJSM, Washington, DC, 1957–60; Commander, RAC Driving and Maintenance School, 1960–62. Secretary, Royal Soldiers' Daughters' School, 1965–71. *Recreations:* fishing, cricket, travelling. *Heir: nephew* Anthony John Devereux Pile [*b* 7 June 1947; *m* 1977, Jennifer Clare Youngman; two *s* one *d*]. *Address:* Brookfield House, Dallington, Sussex. *T:* Rushlake Green 830813. *Club:* MCC.

PILE, Sir William (Dennis), GCB 1978 (KCB 1971; CB 1968); MBE 1944; Chairman, Board of Inland Revenue, 1976–79; *b* 1 Dec. 1919; *s* of James Edward Pile and Jean Elizabeth Pile; *m* 1948, Joan Marguerite Crafter; one *s* two *d. Educ:* Royal Masonic School; St Catharine's College, Cambridge. Served Border Regt, 1940–45. Ministry of Education, 1947–50, 1951–66; Cabinet Office, 1950; Asst Under-Sec. of State: Dept of Education and Science, 1962; Ministry of Health, 1966; Dep. Under-Sec. of State, Home Office, 1967–70; Director-General, Prison Service, 1969–70; Permanent Under-Sec. of State, DES, 1970–76. Director: Nationwide Building Soc., 1980–; Distillers' Co. Ltd, 1980–. *Address:* The Manor House, Riverhead, near Sevenoaks, Kent. *T:* Sevenoaks 54498. *Clubs:* United Oxford & Cambridge University; Hawks (Cambridge).

PILKINGTON, Sir Alastair; *see* Pilkington, Sir L. A. B.

PILKINGTON, Antony Richard; Chairman, Pilkington Brothers plc, since 1980; *b* 20 June 1935; *s* of Arthur Cope Pilkington and Otilia Dolores Pilkington; *m* 1960, Alice Kirsty, *er d* of Sir Thomas Dundas, 7th Bt, MBE and of Lady Dundas; three *s* one *d. Educ:* Ampleforth Coll.; Trinity Coll., Cambridge (MA History). Coldstream Guards, 1953–55. Joined Pilkington Brothers, 1959; Dir, 1973–; Dep. Chm., 1979–80. Director: BSN Gervais Danone (France), 1975–80 (Mem., Internat. Consultative Cttee, 1982–); Pilkington ACI (Australia), 1981–; GKN, 1982–; National Westminster Bank, 1984–; Libbey-Owens-Ford Co. (USA), 1984–; Deputy Chairman: Flachglas AG, 1980–; Dahlbusch AG, 1980–. Chm., Community of St Helens Trust, 1978–. Mem. Council,

Liverpool Univ., 1977–79. *Recreations:* motor cars, ski-ing, sailing, squash. *Address:* Pilkington Brothers plc, Prescot Road, St Helens, Lancs WA10 3TT. *T:* St Helens 28882. *Club:* Pratt's.

PILKINGTON, Rev. Canon Evan Matthias, MA; Chaplain to the Queen since 1969; Canon Residentiary of St Paul's Cathedral, 1976–82, now Canon Emeritus; *b* 27 Dec. 1916; *s* of Rev. Matthias Pilkington; *m* 1946, Elsie (*née* Lashley); four *s. Educ:* Worksop Coll.; Keble Coll., Oxford; Cuddesdon Theol. College. Curate of: Bottesford and Ashby, Scunthorpe, 1940; Holy Trinity, Southall, 1942; St John the Divine, Kennington, 1944; Vicar of: East Kirkby and Miningsby, Lincs, 1946; Holy Trinity, Upper Tooting, 1952; Kingston upon Thames, 1961; Canon Residentiary, Bristol Cathedral, 1968–76. *Publication:* Learning to Pray, 1986. *Recreations:* walking, lettering. *Address:* 14 Park Close, Bladon, Oxford OX7 1RN. *T:* Woodstock 811122.

PILKINGTON, Godfrey; *see* Pilkington, R. G.

PILKINGTON, Lawrence Herbert Austin, CBE 1964; JP; Director, Pilkington Brothers Ltd, since 1935; *b* 13 Oct. 1911; 2nd *s* of Richard Austin and Hon. Hope Pilkington; *m* 1936, Norah Holden, Whitby, Ont., Canada; two *d. Educ:* Bromsgrove School; Magdalene College, Cambridge. Volunteer with Grenfell Mission, 1933–34. Joined Pilkington Brothers Limited, 1935. Chairman: Glass Delegacy, 1949–54; Glass Industry Research Assoc., 1954–58; British Coal Utilisation Research Assoc., 1963–68; Soc. of Acoustic Technology, 1963–; Member: Building Research Board, 1958–62; Wilson Cttee on Noise, 1960–63; Adv. Council on R&D for Fuel and Power, 1973–75. President, Soc. of Glass Technology, 1960–64. JP Lancs, 1942. Hon. LLD Sheffield, 1956; Hon. DSc Salford, 1970. *Publications:* mainly on glass in various technical jls. *Recreations:* sailing, climbing, amateur radio, shooting. *Address:* Coppice End, Colborne Road, St Peter Port, Guernsey, CI. *Club:* Royal Dee Yacht.

PILKINGTON, Sir Lionel Alexander Bethune, (Sir Alastair), Kt 1970; FRS 1969; President, Pilkington Brothers Ltd, St Helens, since 1985; Deputy Chairman, Chloride Group Ltd; Director, British Petroleum, since 1976; *b* 7 Jan. 1920; *yr s* of late Col L. G. Pilkington and Mrs L. G. Pilkington, Newbury, Berks; *m* 1945, Patricia Nicholls (*née* Elliott) (*d* 1977); one *s* one *d*; *m* 1978, Kathleen, *widow* of Eldridge Haynes. *Educ:* Sherborne School; Trinity Coll., Cambridge. War service, 1939–46. Joined Pilkington Brothers Ltd, Glass Manufacturers, St Helens, 1947: Production Manager and Asst Works Manager, Doncaster, 1949–51; Head Office, 1952; Sub-Director, 1953; Director, 1955–85; Dep. Chm., 1971–73; Chm., 1973–80. Dir, Bank of England, 1974–84. Member: Central Adv. Council for Science and Technology, 1970–; SRC, 1972–; British Railways Bd, 1973–76; Court of Governors, Administrative Staff Coll., 1973–; Chairman: Council for Business in the Community, 1982–; CNAA, 1984–; Pres., BAAS, 1983–. Pro-Chancellor, Lancaster Univ., 1980–. Hon. FUMIST, 1969; Hon. Fellow: Imperial Coll., 1974; LSE, 1980. FBIM 1971. Hon. DTech: Loughborough, 1968; CNAA, 1976; Hon. DEng Liverpool, 1971; Hon. LLD Bristol, 1979; Hon. DSc (Eng) London, 1979. Toledo Glass and Ceramic Award, 1963; Mullard Medal, Royal Soc., 1968; John Scott Medal, 1969; Wilhelm Exner Medal, 1970; Phoenix Award, 1981. *Recreations:* gardening, sailing, music. *Address:* Goldrill Cottage, Patterdale, near Penrith, Cumbria. *T:* Glenridding 263; 74 Eaton Place, SW1. *Club:* Athenæum.

PILKINGTON, Air Vice-Marshal Michael John, CBE 1982; Director-General of Training (Royal Air Force), since 1986; *b* 9 Oct. 1937; *s* of David and Mary Pilkington; *m* 1960, Janet Rayner; one *d. Educ:* Bromley Grammar Sch. psc rcds. Commnd Royal Air Force, 1956; Bomber Sqdns, No 35, No 83, No 27, 1959–70; RAF sc 1971; HQ Near East Air Force, 1972–73; CO No 230 Vulcan OCU, 1974–75; Defence Policy Staff, 1977–78; CO RAF Waddington, 1979–81; RCDS 1982; Branch Chief Policy, SHAPE, 1982–85. *Recreations:* golf, tennis, gardening, theatre, wine. *Address:* Sheene Manor, Meldreth, Royston, Herts SG8 6JP. *Club:* Royal Air Force.

PILKINGTON, Rev. Canon Peter; High Master of St Paul's School, since 1986; Hon. Canon of Canterbury Cathedral, since 1975; *b* 5 Sept. 1933; *s* of Frank and Doris Pilkington; *m* 1966, Helen, *d* of Charles and Maria Wilson; two *d. Educ:* Dame Allans Sch., Newcastle upon Tyne; Jesus Coll., Cambridge. BA 1955, MA 1958. Schoolmaster, St Joseph's Coll., Chidya, Tanganyika, 1955–57; ordained 1959; Curate in Bakewell, Derbs, 1959–62; Schoolmaster, Eton College, 1962–75, Master in College, 1965–75; Headmaster, King's Sch., Canterbury, 1975–86. *Address:* The High Master's House, St Paul's School, Lonsdale Road, Barnes, SW13 9JT. *T:* 01–748 9162. *Club:* Athenæum.

PILKINGTON, (Richard) Godfrey; Partner and Director, Piccadilly Gallery, since 1953; *b* 8 Nov. 1918; *e s* of Col Guy R. Pilkington, DSO and Margery (*née* Frost); *m* 1950, Evelyn Edith (Eve) Vincent; two *s* two *d. Educ:* Clifton; Trinity Coll., Cambridge (MA). Lieut, RA, N Africa and Central Mediterranean, 1940–46. Joined Frost & Reed, art dealers, 1947; edited Pictures and Prints, 1951–60; founded Piccadilly Gallery, 1953. Master, Fine Art Trade Guild, 1964–66; Chm., Soc. of London Art Dealers, 1974–77. *Publications:* numerous exhibn catalogues and magazine articles. *Recreations:* walking, boating, tennis, golf. *Address:* 45 Barons Court Road, W14 9DZ. *Clubs:* Athenæum, Hurlingham.

PILKINGTON, Dr Roger Windle; Author; *b* 17 Jan. 1915; 3rd *s* of Richard Austin Pilkington and Hon. Hope (*née* Cozens-Hardy); *m* 1937, Theodora Miriam Jaboor; one *s* one *d*; *m* 1973, Fru Ingrid Geijer, Stockholm. *Educ:* Rugby; Freiburg, Germany; Magdalene Coll., Cambridge (MA, PhD). Research, genetics, 1937; Chm., London Missionary Soc., 1962; Chm. of Trustees, Homerton Coll., Cambridge, 1962; Chm. of Govs, Hall Sch., 1962; jt author, Sex and Morality Report, Brit. Council of Churches, 1966; Vice-Pres., River Thames Soc., 1967; Master, Glass Sellers' Co., 1967. *Publications:* Males and Females, 1948; Stringer's Folly, Biology, Man and God, Sons and Daughters, 1951; How Your Life Began, 1953; Revelation Through Science, 1954; Jan's Treasure, In the Beginning, 1955; Thames Waters, The Facts of Life, 1956; Small Boat Through Belgium, The Chesterfield Gold, The Great South Sea, The Ways of the Sea, 1957; The Missing Panel, 1958; Small Boat Through Holland, Robert Boyle: Father of Chemistry, How Boats Go Uphill, 1959; Small Boat to the Skagerrak, World Without End, The Dahlia's Cargo, Don John's Ducats, 1960; Small Boat to Sweden, Small Boat to Alsace, The Ways of the Air, Who's Who and Why, 1961; Small Boat to Bavaria, Nepomuk of the River, Boats Overland, How Boats are Navigated, 1962; The River, (with Noel Streatfeild) Confirmation and After, Facts of Life for Parents, Small Boat to Germany, The Eisenbart Mystery, 1963; Heavens Alive, Small Boat Through France, 1964; Small Boat in Southern France, Glass, 1965; Small Boat on the Thames, The Boy from Stink Alley, 1966; Small Boat on the Meuse, Small Boat to Luxembourg, 1967; Small Boat on the Moselle, 1968; Small Boat to Elsinore, 1968; Small Boat in Northern Germany, 1969; Small Boat on the Lower Rhine, 1970; Small Boat on the Upper Rhine, 1971; Waterways in Europe, 1972; The Ormering Tide, 1974; The Face in the River, 1976; Geijer in England, 1983; Small Boat Down the Years, 1986; contribs to Guardian, Daily Telegraph, Times, Family Doctor, Yachting World, etc. *Recreations:* inland waterways, walking. *Address:* La Maison du Côti, Mont Arthur, St Aubin, Jersey, Channel Islands. *T:* Jersey 43760.

PILKINGTON, Sir Thomas Henry Milborne-Swinnerton-, 14th Bt, *cr* 1635; Chairman, Thos & James Harrison Ltd, since 1980 (Director, since 1963); Chairman, Charente Steamship Co. Ltd, since 1977; *b* 10 Mar. 1934; *s* of Sir Arthur W. Milborne-Swinnerton-Pilkington, 13th Bt and Elizabeth Mary (she *m* 1950, A. Burke), *d* of late Major J. F. Harrison, King's Walden Bury, Hitchin; *S* father 1952; *m* 1961, Susan, *e d* of N. S. R. Adamson, Durban, South Africa; one *s* two *d*. *Educ:* Eton College. *Recreations:* golf, racing. *Heir: s* Richard Arthur Milborne-Swinnerton-Pilkington, *b* 4 Sept. 1964. *Address:* King's Walden Bury, Hitchin, Herts. *Club:* White's.

PILL, Malcolm Thomas; QC 1978; a Recorder of the Crown Court, since 1976; *b* 11 March 1938; *s* of Reginald Thomas Pill and Anne Pill (*née* Wright); *m* 1966, Roisin Pill (*née* Riordan); two *s* one *d*. *Educ:* Whitchurch Grammar Sch.; Trinity Coll., Cambridge. MA, LLM, Dip. Hague Acad. of Internat. Law. Served RA, 1956–58; Glamorgan Yeomanry (TA), 1958–67. Called to Bar, Gray's Inn, 1962; Wales and Chester Circuit, 1963. 3rd Sec., Foreign Office, 1963–64. Chm., UNA (Welsh Centre) Trust, 1969–77, 1980–; Chm., Welsh Centre for Internat. Affairs, 1973–76. Chm., UK Cttee, Freedom from Hunger Campaign, 1978–. *Address:* 9 Westbourne Crescent, Whitchurch, Cardiff CF4 2BL. *T:* Cardiff 625961; Goldsmith Building, Temple, EC4Y 7BL. *T:* 01-353 7881. *Clubs:* Royal Commonwealth Society; Cardiff and County (Cardiff).

PILLAI, Sir (Narayana) Raghavan, KCIE 1946 (CIE 1939); CBE 1937; Padma Vibhushan, 1960; *b* 24 July 1898; *s* of M. C. Narayana Pillai, Trivandrum, S India; *m* 1928, Edith Minnie Arthurs (*d* 1976); two *s*. *Educ:* Madras Univ.; Trinity Hall, Cambridge (schol.). BA (Madras) 1st Cl. English, 1918; Natural Sciences Tripos Pt 1 (Cambridge), 1st Cl., 1921; Law Tripos Pt 2, 1st Cl., 1922; ICS 1921; various appointments under the Government of Central Provinces and the Government of India. Secretary General, Ministry of External Affairs, New Delhi, 1952–60. Hon. DLitt Kerala University, 1953. Hon. Fellow, Trinity Hall, Cambridge, 1970. *Recreation:* walking. *Address:* 26 Hans Place, SW1. *Clubs:* Oriental; Gymkhana (New Delhi).

PILLAR, Rt. Rev. Kenneth Harold; *see* Hertford, Bishop Suffragan of.

PILLAR, Adm. Sir William (Thomas), GBE 1983; KCB 1980; CEng, FIMechE; FIMarE; Lieutenant-Governor and Commander-in-Chief, Jersey, since 1985; *b* 24 Feb. 1924; *s* of William Pillar and Lily Pillar; *m* 1946, Ursula, *d* of Arthur B. Ransley, MC; three *s* one *d*. *Educ:* Blundells Sch., Tiverton; RNEC. FIMechE 1969, FIMarE 1972. Entered RN, 1942; HMS Illustrious, 1946–48; staff RNEC, 1948–51; HMS Alert, 1951–53; HM Dockyard, Gibraltar, 1954–57; HMS Corunna, 1957–59; BEO, HMS Lochinvar, 1959–61; staff of C-in-C, SASA, Cape Town, 1961–64; HMS Tiger, 1964–65; staff of Dir of Naval Officer Appts (Eng), 1965–67; Sowc 1967; Naval Ship Prodn Overseer, Scotland and NI, 1967–69, IDC 1970; Asst Dir, DG Ships, 1971–73; Captain RNEC, 1973–75; Port Adm., Rosyth, 1976–77; Asst Chief of Fleet Support, 1977–79; Chief of Fleet Support (Mem., Admiralty Bd of Defence Council), 1979–81; Comdt, RCDS, 1982–83. Cdre, RNSA, 1980–83. Member: Council, RUSI, 1984– (Vice Chm., 1986–); Man. Dir Bd, IMechE, 1984–. Past Pres., RN Modern Pentathlon Assoc. KStJ 1985. *Recreations:* sailing, rough gardening and fixing things. *Address:* Government House, Jersey, Channel Islands. *Clubs:* Army and Navy; Royal Yacht Squadron, Royal Naval Sailing Association (Portsmouth).

PILLING, Joseph Grant; Under Secretary, Department of Health and Social Security, since 1984; *b* 8 July 1945; *m* 1968, Ann Cheetham; two *s*. *Educ:* Rochdale Grammar Sch.; King's Coll., London; Harvard. Asst Principal, 1966, Pvte Sec. to Minister of State, 1970, Home Office; Asst. Pvte Sec. to Home Sec., 1970–71; NI Office, 1972; Home Office, 1974–78; Pvte Sec. to Sec. of State for NI, 1978–79; Home Office, 1979–84. *Address:* Department of Health and Social Security, Eileen House, 80–94 Newington Causeway, SE1 6EF. *Club:* Athenæum.

PIM, Captain Sir Richard (Pike), KBE 1960; Kt 1945; VRD; DL; Inspector-General, Royal Ulster Constabulary, retired; National Governor for Northern Ireland, BBC, 1962–67; Member of Council, Winston Churchill Memorial Trust, 1965–69; Member, Ulster Transport Authority, 1962–64, retired; *b* Dunmurry, Co. Antrim, 1900; *yr s* of late Cecil Pim; *m* 1925, Marjorie Angel, 3rd *d* of late John ff. Young, Dungiven, Londonderry; two *s*. *Educ:* Lancing Coll., Sussex; Trinity College, Dublin. Served in RNVR in European War, 1914–18; Royal Irish Constabulary, 1921. Appointed to Civil Service, N Ireland, 1922; Asst Secretary, Ministry of Home Affairs (N Ireland), 1935; Staff of Prime Minister, Northern Ireland, 1938; in charge of Mr Churchill's War Room at Admiralty, 1939, and later of Map Room at Downing St; Capt. RNVR. North African Campaign (despatches). DL City of Belfast, 1957. Order of Crown of Yugoslavia; Legion of Merit, USA. *Address:* Mullagh, Killyleagh, Co. Down, Northern Ireland. *T:* Killyleagh 828267.

PIMENTA, Most Rev. Simon Ignatius; *see* Bombay, Archbishop of, (RC).

PINA-CABRAL, Rt. Rev. Daniel (Pereira dos Santos) de; an Auxiliary Bishop, Diocese of Gibraltar in Europe, since 1976; *b* 27 Jan. 1924; *m* 1951, Ana Avelina Pina-Cabral; two *s* two *d*. *Educ:* University of Lisbon (Licentiate in Law). Archdeacon of the North in the Lusitanian Church, 1965; Suffragan Bishop of Lebombo (Mozambique), Church of the Province of Southern Africa, 1967; Diocesan Bishop of Lebombo, 1968; Canon of Gibraltar, 1976–. *Address:* Rua Fernão Lopes Castanheda, 51 4100 Porto, Portugal. *T:* Porto 677772.

PINAY, Antoine; Médiateur, French Republic, 1973–74; leather manufacturer; *b* Department of the Rhône, 30 Dec. 1891. *Educ:* Marist Fathers' Sch., St-Chamond. Joined a tannery business there; became Mayor, 1929–; later became gen. councillor, Dept of the Loire (Pres. 1949–). Was returned to Chamber of Deputies, 1936, Ind. Radical party; Senator, 1938; elected to 2nd Constituent Assembly, 1946; then to 1st Nat. Assembly; re-elected to Nat. Assembly as an associate of Ind. Republican group; Sec. of State for Economic Affairs, Sept. 1948–Oct. 1949; in several successive ministries, July 1950–Feb. 1952, he was Minister of Public Works, Transportation, and Tourism; Prime Minister of France, March-Dec. 1952; Minister of Foreign Affairs, 1955–56; Minister of Finance and Economic Affairs, 1958–60. Served European War, 1914–18, in artillery as non-commnd officer (Croix de Guerre, Médaille Militaire). *Address:* 17 avenue de Tourville, 75007 Paris, France.

PINCHAM, Roger James, CBE 1982; Chairman, Venture Consultants Ltd (formerly Roger Pincham (Consultants) Ltd), since 1980; Director, David Boddy PR Limited, since 1985; *b* 19 Oct. 1935; *y s* of Sam and Bessie Pincham; *m* 1965, Gisela von Ulardt (*d* 1974); one *s* two *d*. *Educ:* Kingston Grammar School. National Service, RAF, 1954–56. With Phillips & Drew, 1956–, Partner, 1967–76, consultant, 1976–. Contested (L) Leominster, 1970, Feb. and Oct. 1974, 1979, 1983. Liberal Party: Nat. Exec., 1974–75 and 1978–; Assembly Cttee, 1974–; Standing Cttee, 1975–83; Vice-Chm., 1977–80; Chm., 1980–82; Jt Negotiating Cttee with SDP, and signatory to A Fresh Start for Britain, 1981. Founder Chairman: Gladstone Club, 1973–; Centre for Commercial and Industrial Policy Studies, 1976–; First Chairman: Indep. Educnl Assoc., 1974–; St James and St Vedast Schools, 1974–; Treasurer, Roma Housing Soc., 1977–80; Pres., Kington Eisteddfod, 1978. Freeman, City of London. Liveryman: Barbers' Co.; Founders' Co.; Freeman, Co. of Watermen and Lightermen. *Publications:* (jtly) New Deal for Rural Britain, 1977; (ed) New Deal for British Farmers, 1978. *Recreations:* gardening, cricket, theatre. *Address:* 7 The Postern, Wood Street, Barbican, EC2Y 8BJ. *T:* 01-638 8154. *Clubs:* Reform, National Liberal, City of London, City Livery; Surrey County Cricket, Woolhope Naturalists' Field, Grange Cricket.

PINCHER, (Henry) Chapman; freelance journalist, novelist and business consultant; Assistant Editor, Daily Express, and Chief Defence Correspondent, Beaverbrook Newspapers, 1972–79; *b* Ambala, India, 29 March 1914; *s* of Major Richard Chapman Pincher, E Surrey Regt, and Helen (*née* Foster), Pontefract; *m* 1965, Constance Wolstenholme; one *s* one *d* (by previous *m*). *Educ:* Darlington Gram. Sch.; King's Coll., London (FKC 1979); Inst. Educn; Mil. Coll. of Science. Carter Medallist, London, 1934; BSc (hons Botany, Zoology), 1935. Staff Liverpool Inst., 1936–40. Joined Royal Armoured Corps, 1940; Techn SO, Rocket Div., Min. of Supply, 1943–46; Defence, Science and Medical Editor, Daily Express, 1946–73. Hon. DLitt Newcastle upon Tyne, 1979. Granada Award, Journalist of the Year, 1964; Reporter of the Decade, 1966. *Publications:* Breeding of Farm Animals, 1946; A Study of Fishes, 1947; Into the Atomic Age, 1947; Spotlight on Animals, 1950; Evolution, 1950; (with Bernard Wicksteed) It's Fun Finding Out, 1950; Sleep, and how to get more of it, 1954; Sex in Our Time, 1973; Inside Story, 1978; Their Trade is Treachery, 1981; Too Secret Too Long, 1984; The Secret Offensive, 1985; Traitors—the Labyrinths of Treason, 1987; *novels:* Not with a Bang, 1965; The Giantkiller, 1967; The Penthouse Conspirators, 1970; The Skeleton at the Villa Wolkonsky, 1975; The Eye of the Tornado, 1976; The Four Horses, 1978; Dirty Tricks, 1980; The Private World of St John Terrapin, 1982; original researches in genetics, numerous articles in scientific and agricultural jls. *Recreations:* fishing, shooting, natural history, country life; ferreting in Whitehall and bolting politicians. *Address:* The Church House, 16 Church Street, Kintbury, near Hungerford, Berks. *T:* Kintbury 58855.

PINCOTT, Leslie Rundell, CBE 1978; Vice-Chairman, Remploy Ltd, since 1979 (Director, since 1975); *b* 27 March 1923; *s* of Hubert George Pincott and Gertrude Elizabeth Rundell; *m* 1944, Mary Mae Tuffin; two *s* one *d*. *Educ:* Mercers' Sch., Holborn. Served War, Royal Navy, 1942–46. Broads Paterson & Co. (Chartered Accountants), 1946–50; joined Esso Petroleum Co. Ltd, 1950; Comptroller, 1958–61; Asst Gen. Manager (Marketing), 1961–65; Dir and Gen. Manager, Cleveland Petroleum Co. Ltd, 1966–68; Standard Oil Co. (NJ): Exec. Asst to Pres., and later, to Chm., 1968–70; Man. Dir, Esso Petroleum Co. Ltd, 1970–78; Chairman: Canada Permanent Trust Co. (UK) Ltd, 1978–80; Stone-Platt Industries, 1980–82; Edman Communications Gp, 1982–; Investment Cttee, London Development Capital Fund (Guinness Mahon), 1985–; BR Southern Region Bd, 1986– (Mem., 1977–86); Director: George Wimpey & Co.,Ltd, 1978–85; Highlands Fabricators Ltd, 1984–. A Dep. Chm., 1978–79, Chm., 1979–80, Price Commn; Chairman: Hundred Gp of Chartered Accountants, 1978–79; Oxford Univ. Business Summer Sch., 1975–78; Printing Industries EDC, NEDO, 1982–. Pres., District Heating Assoc., 1977–79. Vice-Pres., English Schs Athletics Assoc., 1977–; Mem. Council, ISCO, 1982–. Mem., The Pilgrims, 1971–. FCA, MInstM; CBIM. *Recreation:* tennis. *Address:* 6 Lambourne Avenue, Wimbledon, SW19 7DW. *Clubs:* Arts, Hurlingham.

PINDER, Ven. Charles; Archdeacon of Lambeth, since 1986; *b* 5 May 1921; *s* of Ernest and Gertrude Pinder; *m* 1943, Ethel, *d* of Albert and Emma Milke; four *d*. *Educ:* King's College London (AKC). Ordained, 1950; Curate, St Saviour, Raynes Park, 1950–53; Vicar: All Saints, Hatcham Park, 1953–60; St Laurence, Catford, 1960–73; Sub-Dean of Lewisham, 1968–73; Borough Dean of Lambeth, 1973–86. Hon. Chaplain to Bishop of Southwark, 1963–80; Hon. Canon of Southwark, 1973–86. Member of Parole Board, 1976–80; Chm., Brixton Prison Bd of Visitors, 1983–. *Recreations:* most outdoor sports and selective indoor games; listening to music. *Address:* 97 Kingsmead Road, Tulse Hill, SW2 3HZ. *T:* 01-674 6091.

PINDLING, Rt. Hon. Sir Lynden Oscar, KCMG 1983; PC 1976; Prime Minister and Minister of Economic Affairs of the Commonwealth of The Bahamas, since 1969; *b* 22 March 1930; *s* of Arnold Franklin and Viola Pindling; *m* 1956, Marguerite McKenzie; two *s* two *d*. *Educ:* Western Senior Sch., Nassau Govt High Sch.; London Univ. (LLB 1952; LLD 1970; DHL 1978). Called to the Bar, Middle Temple, 1953. Practised as Lawyer, 1952–67. Parly Leader of Progressive Liberal Party, 1956; elected to Bahamas House of Assembly, 1956, re-elected 1962, 1967, 1968, 1972 and 1977. Worked for human rights and self determination in the Bahamas; Mem., several delegns to Colonial Office, 1956–66; took part in Constitutional Conf., May 1963; Leader of Opposition, 1964; Mem., Delegns to UN Special Cttee of Twenty-four, 1965, 1966; Premier of the Bahamas and Minister of Tourism and Development, 1967; led Bahamian Delegn to Constitutional Conf., London, 1968; to Independence Conf., 1972 (first Prime Minister after Independence). Chm., Commonwealth Parly Assoc., 1968. *Recreations:* swimming, boating, travel. *Address:* Office of the Prime Minister, Rawson Square, Nassau, Bahamas.

PINE, John Bradley; *b* 2 Dec. 1913; *yr s* of late Percival William Pine and late Maud Mary Pine (*née* Bradley); *m* 1st, 1945, Elizabeth Mary (Jayne) Hallett (*d* 1948); one *s*; 2nd, 1952, Ann Carney (*d* 1984); one *s*. *Educ:* Douai School. Asst Solicitor, GWR, Eng., 1935–39; Mil. Service, Captain RAC, 1939–45; a Sen. Prosecutor, CCG, 1945–47; Resident Magistrate and Crown Counsel, N Rhodesia, 1947–49; Called to Bar, 1950; Asst Attorney Gen., Gibraltar, 1949–54; QC (Bermuda), 1955; Attorney Gen., Bermuda, 1955–57; Actg Governor of Bermuda, 1956; QC (Nyasaland), 1958; Solicitor Gen., Nyasaland, 1958–60; Minister of Justice and Attorney Gen., Nyasaland, 1960–62, when replaced by an Elected Minister under self-governing Constitution; Legal Adviser to Governor of Nyasaland, July 1963, until Independence, July 1964; Parly Draftsman, Govt of N Ireland, 1965–66; Sec., Ulster Tourist Develt Assoc., 1967; antique business, 1968–70. *Address:* 74 The Glebe, Lawshall, Bury St Edmunds, Suffolk IP29 4PW.

PINE, Leslie Gilbert; author and lecturer; Consultant, Burke's Peerage Ltd, since 1984; Editor, The National Message, 1977–80 (Assistant Editor, 1975–77); Chairman, Covenant Publishing Co. Ltd, 1978–79; *b* 22 Dec. 1907; *s* of Henry Moorshead Pine, Bristol, and Lilian Grace (*née* Beswetherick); *m* 1948, Grace V. Griffin; one *s*. *Educ:* Tellisford House Sch., Bristol; South-West London Coll., Barnes; London Univ. (BA). Asst Editor, Burke's Landed Gentry, 1935; subseq. Editor of Burke's Peerage and Landed Gentry and other reference books and then Managing Editor, The Shooting Times, 1960–64, and Shooting Times Library, 1962–64 (resigned as unable to agree with blood sports); Director L. & G. Pine & Co. Ltd, 1964–69; Man. Ed., Internat. Who's Who of the Arab World, 1975–76. Censorship and Air Min., 1940; Min. of Labour, 1941; RAF 1942; Sqn Ldr 1945–46; served in N Africa, Italy, Greece and India (Intel. Branch). Barrister-at-Law, Inner Temple, 1953; Freeman, City of London, Liveryman of the Glaziers' Company, 1954. Prospective Parly Candidate (C) Bristol Central, 1956; contested seat, 1959; re-adopted, 1960; resigned and joined Liberal Party, 1962; Prospective Parly Candidate (L), S Croydon, 1963, resigned candidature, June 1964, disagreeing profoundly with Liberalism. Dioc. Lay Reader, London, 1939, Canterbury, 1961, St Edmundsbury and Ipswich, 1975; received into Catholic Church, 1964; reconciled to C of E, 1971. Corr. Mem. Inst. Internacional de Genealogica y Heraldica (Madrid) and of Gen. Socs in Belgium, Chile and Brazil; Gov., St And. Sch., S Croydon, 1960–64. FSA Scot., 1940; MJI, 1947 (Mem. Council, 1953–61); FJI 1957; Associate, Zool. Soc., London, 1961; FRSA 1961; FRGS 1969; FRAS 1970; Fellow: Augustan Soc., 1967; Octavian Soc., 1982; Distinguished Fellow, Amer. Coll. of Heraldry, 1983. Member: RUSI; Royal Soc. St George. DLitt Central School of Religion, 1985. Has given over 1,000 lectures in Gt Britain, Ireland, Europe, Africa, etc, also series of tutorial lectures under WEA and Further Educn; Cambridge Univ. extra-mural lectures, 1986. Trustee and Reg. Org. Sec., Prayer Book Soc., 1976–. *Publications:* The Stuarts of Traquair, 1940; The House of Wavell, 1948; The Middle Sea, 1950, new edn, 1972; The Story of Heraldry, 1952 (4th edn 1968, Japan, USA); Trace Your Ancestors, 1953; The Golden Book of the Coronation, 1953; They Came with The Conqueror, 1954; The Story of the Peerage, 1956; Tales of the British Aristocracy, 1956; The House of Constantine, 1957; Teach Yourself Heraldry and Genealogy, 1957, 4th (enlarged) edn 1975; The Twilight of Monarchy, 1958; A Guide to Titles, 1959; Princes of Wales, 1959, new edn, 1970; American Origins, 1960, 1968; Your Family Tree, 1962; Ramshackledom, A Critical Appraisal of the Establishment, 1962; Heirs of the Conqueror, 1965; Heraldry, Ancestry and Titles, Questions and Answers, 1965; The Story of Surnames, 1965; After Their Blood, 1966; Tradition and Custom in Modern Britain, 1967; The Genealogist's Encyclopedia (USA and UK), 1969; The Story of Titles, 1969; International Heraldry, 1970; The Highland Clans, 1972; Sons of the Conqueror, 1972; The New Extinct Peerage, 1972; The History of Hunting, 1973; (contrib. to) World-wide Family Historian, 1982; A Dictionary of Mottoes, 1983; A Dictionary of Nicknames, 1984; Teach Yourself to Trace Family History, 1984; A Genealogy Workbook, 1986; contrib. Encyclopedia Britannica, 1974; Contributing Editor, The Augustan (USA). *Recreations:* reading, walking, gardening, travel, lecturing, contributing articles to press. *Address:* Hall Lodge Cottage, Brettenham, Ipswich, Suffolk IP7 7QP. *T:* Rattlesden 402. *Clubs:* City Livery, Press, Wig and Pen.

PINEAU, Christian Paul Francis, Commandeur, Légion d'Honneur; Compagnon de la Libération; Croix de Guerre (French), Médaille de la Résistance (Rosette); French Statesman and Writer; *b* Chaumont (Haute-Marne), 14 Oct. 1904; *m* 1962, Mlle Blanche Bloys; one *d* (and five *s* one *d* of previous marriages). Minister of Food and Supplies, June-Nov. 1945; General Rapporteur to Budget Commission 1945–46; Chm. Nat. Assembly Finance Commn, 1946–47; Minister of Public Works, Transport, and Tourism (Schuman Cabinet), 1947–48, also (Marie Cabinet) July-Aug. 1948, also (Queuille Cabinet), Sept. 1948, also (Bidault Cabinet), Oct. 1949; Minister of Finance and Economic Affairs (Schuman Cabinet), Aug. 1946; Chm. Nat. Defence Credits Control Commn, 1951–55; Designated Premier, Feb. 1955; Minister for Foreign Affairs, Feb. 1956–June 1957. Holds GCMG (Hon.) Great Britain, and numerous other foreign decorations. *Publications: books for children:* Contes de je ne sais quand; Plume et le saumon; L'Ourse aux pattons verts; Cornerousse le Mystérieux; Histoires de la forêt de Bercé; La Planète aux enfants perdus; La Marelle et le ballon; La Bête à bêtises; *other publications;* The SNCF and French Transport; Mon cher député; La simple verite, 1940–45; L'escalier des ombres; Khrouchtchev; 1956: Suez, 1976; economic and financial articles; contrib. to various papers. *Address:* 55 rue Vaneau, 75007 Paris, France.

PININFARINA, Sergio; Cavaliere del Lavoro, 1976; engineer; Member, European Parliament (Liberal and Democratic Group), since 1979; President, Pininfarina SpA; *b* 8 Sept. 1926; *s* of Battista Pininfarina and Rosa Copasso; *m* 1951, Giorgia Gianolio; two *s* one *d*. *Educ:* Polytechnic of Turin; graduated in Mech. Eng., 1950. Pres., Federpiemonte. Board Member: Confindustria; Ferrari; RIV SKF; Banca Passadore; Banca Popolare di Novara; Toro Assicurazioni. Légion d'Honneur, 1979. Hon. RDI 1983. *Recreation:* golf. *Address:* PO Box 295, 10100 Turin, Italy. *T:* 11–703232. *Clubs:* Società Whist Accademia Filarmonica, Rotary Torino; Circolo Golf Torino, Circolo I Roveri (Fiano Torinese).

PINKER, George Douglas, CVO 1983; FRCS Ed, FRCOG; Surgeon-Gynaecologist to the Queen, since 1973; Consulting Gynaecological Surgeon and Obstetrician, St Mary's Hospital, Paddington and Samaritan Hospital, since 1958; Consulting Gynaecological Surgeon, Middlesex and Soho Hospitals, since 1969; Consultant Gynæcologist, King Edward VII Hospital for Officers, since 1974; *b* 6 Dec. 1924; *s* of late Ronald Douglas Pinker and of Queenie Elizabeth Pinker (*née* Dix); *m* Dorothy Emma (*née* Russell); three *s* one *d* (incl. twin *s* and *d*). *Educ:* Reading Sch.; St Mary's Hosp., London Univ. MB BS London 1947; DObst 1949; MRCOG 1954; FRCS(Ed) 1957; FRCOG 1964. Late Cons. Gyn. Surg., Bolingbroke Hosp., and Res. Off., Nuffield Dept of Obst., Radcliffe Infirmary, Oxford; late Cons. Gyn. Surg., Queen Charlotte's Hosp. Arthur Wilson Orator and Turnbull Scholar, and Hon. Consultant Obstetrician and Gynaecologist, Royal Women's Hosp., Melbourne, 1972. Examiner in Obst. and Gynae.: Univs of Cambridge, Dundee, London, and FRCS Edinburgh; formerly also in RCOG, and Univs of Birmingham, Glasgow and Dublin. Sims Black Travelling Prof., RCOG, 1979; Vis. Prof., SA Regional Council, RCOG, 1980; Hon. Treas., 1970, Vice-Pres., 1980–, RCOG. Mem. Council, Winston Churchill Trust, 1979–. Mem., Editorial Bd, Modern Medicine (Obs. and Gynae.), 1976–. Mem., Blair Bell Research Soc.; FRSocMed. *Publications:* (all jtly) Ten Teachers Diseases of Women, 1964; Ten Teachers Obstetrics, 1966; A Short Textbook of Obstetrics and Gynaecology, 1967. *Recreations:* music, gardening, sailing, skiing, fell walking. *Address:* 96 Harley Street, W1N 1AF. *T:* 01–935 2292; Medley, Kingston Hill, Kingston-on-Thames, Surrey KT2 7IU.

PINKER, Prof. Robert Arthur; Pro-Director, since 1985 and Professor of Social Work Studies, since 1978, London School of Economics and Political Science; *b* 27 May 1931; *s* of Dora Elizabeth and Joseph Pinker; *m* 1955, Jennifer Farrington Boulton; two *d*. *Educ:* Holloway County Sch.; LSE (Cert. in Social Sci. and Admin. 1959; BSc Sociology 1962; MSc Econ 1965). University of London: Head of Sociology Dept, Goldsmiths' Coll., 1964–72; Lewisham Prof. of Social Admin, Goldsmiths' Coll. and Bedford Coll., 1972–74; Prof. of Social Studies, Chelsea Coll., 1974–78; Mem., Academic Council, 1986–. Chm., British Library Project on Family and Social Research, 1983–86; a Governor: Centre for Policies on Ageing; Richmond Fellowship, 1986–. Chairman, Editorial Board: Jl of Social Policy, 1981–86; Ageing and Society, 1981–; Editl Adviser to Community Care, 1983–. *Publications:* English Hospital Statistics 1861–1938, 1964; Social Theory and Social Policy, 1971; The Idea of Welfare, 1979. *Recreations:* reading, writing, travel, unskilled gardening. *Address:* 76 Coleraine Road, Blackheath, SE3 7PE. *Tel:* 01–858 5320.

PINKERTON, Prof. John Henry McKnight, CBE 1983; Professor of Midwifery and Gynæcology, Queen's University, Belfast, 1963–85, now Emeritus; formerly: Gynæcologist: Royal Victoria and City Hospitals, Belfast; Ulster Hospital for Women and Children; Surgeon, Royal Maternity Hospital, Belfast; *b* 5 June 1920; *s* of late William R. and Eva Pinkerton; *m* 1947, Florence McKinstry, MB, BCh, BAO; four *s*. *Educ:* Royal Belfast Academical Institution; Queen's Univ., Belfast. Hyndman Univ. Entrance Scholar, 1939; MB, BCh, BAO Hons; Magrath Scholar in Obstetrics and Gynæcology, 1943. Active service in HM Ships as Surg.-Lt, RNVR, 1945–47. MD 1948; MRCOG 1949; FRCOG 1960; FZS 1960; FRCPI 1977. Sen. Lectr in Obstetrics and Gynæcology, University Coll. of the West Indies, and Consultant Obstetrician and Gynæcologist to University Coll. Hosp. of the West Indies, 1953–59; Rockefeller Research Fellow at Harvard Medical Sch., 1956–57; Prof. of Obstetrics and Gynæcology, Univ. of London, at Queen Charlotte's and Chelsea Hosps and the Inst. of Obstetrics and Gynæcology, 1959–63; Obstetric Surgeon to Queen Charlotte's Hosp.; Surgeon to Chelsea Hosp. for Women. Vice-Pres., RCOG, 1977–80; Chm., Inst. of Obstetrics and Gynæcol., RCPI, 1984–. Hon. DSc NUI, 1986. *Publications:* various papers on obstetrical and gynæcological subjects. *Address:* 41c Sans Souci Park, Belfast BT9 5BZ. *T:* Belfast 682956.
See also W. R. Pinkerton.

PINKERTON, John Macpherson, QC (Scot) 1984; FSA (Scot); *b* 18 April 1941; *s* of John Cassels Pinkerton, CBE, MC, JP, BL, PPRICS and Mary Banks Macpherson, OBE, JP. *Educ:* Rugby School; Oxford Univ. (BA); Edinburgh Univ. (LLB). Advocate, 1966; Clerk of the Faculty of Advocates, 1971–77; Standing Junior Counsel: to Countryside Commn for Scotland; to HM Commissioners of Customs and Excise. Trustee, Nat. Library of Scotland. Chairman: Scottish Assoc. for Public Transport; Cockburn Assoc. *Publications:* (ed) Faculty of Advocates Minute Books, Vol. I, 1976, Vol. II, 1980; contribs to Macmillan Dictionary of Art, Stair Encyclopaedia of Scots Law. *Recreations:* conservation and collecting. *Address:* Arthur Lodge, 60 Dalkeith Road, Edinburgh EH16 5AD. *T:* 031–667 5163. *Club:* New (Edinburgh).

PINKERTON, William Ross, CBE 1977; JP; HM Nominee for Northern Ireland on General Medical Council, 1979–83, retired; a director of companies; *b* 10 April 1913; *s* of William Ross Pinkerton and Eva Pinkerton; *m* 1943, Anna Isobel Lyness; two *d*. Managing Director, H. Stevenson & Co. Ltd, Londonderry, 1941–76. Mem., Baking Wages Council (NI), 1957–74. Mem. later Chm, Londonderry/Gransha Psychiatric HMC, 1951–69; Vice-Chm., then Chm., North West HMC, 1969–72; Chm., Western Health and Social Services Board, 1972–79; Member: Central Services Agency (NI), 1972–79; NI Health and Social Services Council, 1975–79; Lay Mem., Health and Personal Social Services Tribunal, NI, 1978–. Member, New Ulster Univ. Court, 1973–85, Council, 1979–85. Hon. Life Governor: Altnagelvin, Gransha, Waterside, St Columb's, Roe Valley, Strabane, Foyle and Stradreagh Hosps. JP Co. Londonderry, 1965–84, Div. of Ards, 1984–. *Recreations:* yachting, fishing. *Address:* 2 Ard-Na-Ree, The Brae, Groomsport, Co. Down, N Ireland BT19 2JL. *T:* Bangor 464525. *Club:* Royal Highland Yacht (Oban).
See also J. H. McK. Pinkerton.

PINNER, Hayim; administrator, linguist, educator, lecturer, journalist, broadcaster; Secretary General, Board of Deputies of British Jews, since 1977; *b* London, 25 May 1925; *s* of late Simon Pinner and Annie Pinner (*née* Wagner); *m* 1956, Rita Reuben, Cape Town (marr. diss. 1980); one *s* one *d*. *Educ:* Davenant Foundation School; London University; Yeshivah Etz Hayim; Bet Berl College, Israel. Served RAOC, 1944–48; Editor, Jewish Vanguard, 1950–74; Exec. Dir, B'nai B'rith, 1957–77. Hon. Vice-Pres., Zionist Fedn of GB and Ireland, 1975– (Hon. Treasurer, 1971–75); Vice-Pres., Labour Zionist Movement; Member: Jewish Agency and World Zionist Orgn; Exec., Council of Christians and Jews; Adv. Council, World Congress of Faiths; Trades Adv. Council; Hillel Foundn; Jt Israel Appeal; Lab. Party Middle East Cttee; 'B' List of Parly Candidates; UNA. Freeman, City of London. Contribs to Radio 4, Radio London, London Broadcasting, BBC TV. *Publications:* contribs to UK and foreign periodicals, Isra-Kit. *Recreations:* travelling, swimming, reading, talking. *Address:* c/o Board of Deputies of British Jews, Woburn House, Tavistock Square, WC1. *T:* 01–387 3952.

PINNINGTON, Geoffrey Charles; Editor, Sunday People, 1972–82; *b* 21 March 1919; *s* of Charles and Beatrice Pinnington; *m* 1941, Beryl, *d* of Edward and Lilian Clark; two *d*. *Educ:* Harrow County Sch.; Rock Ferry High Sch., Birkenhead; King's Coll., Univ. of London. Served War as Air Navigator, RAF Bomber and Middle East Commands, 1940–45 (Sqdn Ldr, 1943). On staff of (successively): Middlesex Independent; Kensington Post (Editor); Daily Herald: Dep. News Editor, 1955; Northern Editor, 1957; Dep. Editor, 1958; Daily Mirror: Night Editor, 1961, Assistant Editor, 1964, Dep. Editor, 1968; Dir, Mirror Group Newspapers, 1976–82. Mem., Press Council, 1982–86 (Jt Vice-Chm., 1983–86). *Recreations:* his family, travel, reading, music, theatre and the arts, amateur cine-photography. *Address:* 23 Lauderdale Drive, Richmond, Surrey TW10 7BS.

PINNINGTON, Roger Adrian, TD 1967; Chief Executive, Royal Ordnance PLC, since 1986; *b* 27 Aug. 1932; *s* of William Austin Pinnington and Elsie Amy Pinnington; *m* 1974, Marjorie Ann Pearson; one *s* three *d*. *Educ:* Rydal Sch., Colwyn Bay; Lincoln Coll., Oxford (MA). Marketing Dir, Jonas Woodhead & Sons, 1963–74; 1975–82: Vice Pres., TRW Europe Inc.; Man. Dir, CAM Gears Ltd; Pres., TRW Italia SpA; Dir Gen., Gemmer France; Pres., Torfinasa; Dep. Chm. and Ch. Exec., UBM Group, 1982–85; Dir, Norcros, 1985–86. *Recreations:* gardening, arguing with Sally, collecting sad irons. *Address:* Robingate, Barrington Road, Letchworth, Herts SG6 3JY. *T:* Letchworth 670944. *Club:* Vincent's (Oxford).

PINNOCK, Comdr Harry James, RN retd; Director, Cement Makers' Federation, since 1979; *b* 6 April 1927; *s* of Frederick Walter Pinnock and Kate Ada (*née* Shepherd); *m* 1962, Fru Inger Connie Åhgren (*d* 1978); one *d*. *Educ:* Sutton Valence Sch. Joined RN, 1945; Midshipman, HMS Nelson, 1945–47; Sub-Lieut/Lieut, HMS Belfast, Far East, 1948–50; RN Rhine Flotilla, 1951–52; Staff of First Sea Lord, 1952–55; Lt-Comdr, Mediterranean Minesweepers, 1955–57; HMS Ceylon, E of Suez, 1957–59; Staff of C-in-C Plymouth, 1960–61; HQ Allied Naval Forces, Northern Europe, Oslo, 1961–63; Comdr, MoD, 1964–67, retd. Cement Makers' Fedn, 1970–. *Recreations:* ski-ing, gardening, travel. *Address:* Windy Ridge, Bells Lane, Tenterden, Kent TN30 6EX. *T:* Tenterden 3025. *Club:* Army and Navy.

PINNOCK, Trevor, ARCM; harpsichordist; conductor; Director, The English Concert, since 1973; *b* Canterbury, 16 Dec. 1946; *m* 1979, Florence de Courcel. *Educ:* Canterbury Cathedral Choir Sch.; Simon Langton Grammar Sch., Canterbury; Royal Coll. of Music, London (Foundn Scholar; Harpischord and Organ Prizes). ARCM Hons (organ) 1965. London début with Galliard Harpsichord Trio (Jt Founder with Stephen Preston, flute and Anthony Pleeth, 'cello), 1966; solo début, Purcell Room, London, 1968. Formed The English Concert for purpose of performing music of baroque period on instruments in original condition or good modern copies, 1972, making its London début in English Bach Festival, Purcell Room, 1973. Recordings of complete keyboard works of Rameau; Bach Tocatas, Partitas, Goldberg Variations, Concerti, Handel Suites, orchestral works of Bach, Handel, etc. *Address:* c/o Basil Douglas Artists' Management, 8 St George's Terrace, NW1 8XJ. *T:* 01–722 7142.

PINSENT, Sir Christopher (Roy), 3rd Bt *cr* 1938; Lecturer, Camberwell School of Art; *b* 2 Aug. 1922; *s* of Sir Roy Pinsent, 2nd Bt, and Mary Tirzah Pinsent (*d* 1951), *d* of Dr Edward Geoffrey Walls, Spilsby, Lincs; *S* father, 1978; *m* 1951, Susan Mary, *d* of John Norton Scorer, Fotheringhay; one *s* two *d*. *Educ:* Winchester College. *Heir: s* Thomas Benjamin Roy Pinsent, *b* 21 July 1967. *Address:* The Chestnuts, Castle Hill, Guildford, Surrey.

PINSENT, Roger Philip; HM Diplomatic Service, retired; *b* 30 Dec. 1916; *s* of late Sidney Hume Pinsent; *m* 1941, Suzanne Smalley; one *s* two *d*. *Educ:* Downside Sch.; Lausanne, London and Grenoble Univs. London Univ. French Scholar, 1938; BA Hons London, 1940. HM Forces, 1940–46; HM Diplomatic Service, May 1946; 1st Sec., HM Legation, Havana, 1948–50; HM Consul, Tangier, 1950–52; 1st Sec., HM Embassy, Madrid, 1952–53; FO, 1953–56; 1st Sec., Head of Chancery, HM Embassy, Lima (Chargé d'Affaires, 1958, 1959), 1956–59; Dep. Head of UK Delegation to the European Communities, Luxembourg, 1959–63; HM Ambassador to Nicaragua, 1963–67; Counsellor (Commercial), Ankara, 1967–70; Consul-Gen., São Paulo, 1970–73. Mem., Inst. of Linguists, 1976–79. *Recreations:* music, photography, book-binding, golf. *Address:* Cranfield Cottage, Maugersbury, Stow-on-the-Wold, Glos GL54 1HR. *T:* Cotswold 30992. *Clubs:* Canning; Broadway Golf; Stow on the Wold RFC.

PINSON, Barry, QC 1973; *b* 18 Dec. 1925; *s* of Thomas Alfred Pinson and Alice Cicily Pinson; *m* 1950, Miriam Mary; one *s* one *d*; *m* 1977, Anne Kathleen Golby. *Educ:* King Edward's Sch., Birmingham; Univ. of Birmingham. LLB Hons 1945. Fellow Inst. Taxation. Mil. Service, 1944–47. Called to Bar, Gray's Inn, 1949, Bencher 1981. Mem., Sadler's Wells Develt Capital Cttee, 1985–; Trustee, RAF Museums, 1980–. *Publications:* Revenue Law, 16 edns. *Recreations:* music, photography. *Address:* 11 New Square, Lincoln's Inn, WC2. *T:* 01–242 3981.

PINTER, Lady Antonia; *see* Fraser, Antonia.

PINTER, Harold, CBE 1966; actor, playwright and director; Associate Director, National Theatre, 1973–83; *b* 10 Oct. 1930; *s* of J. Pinter; *m* 1st, 1956, Vivien Merchant (marr. diss. 1980; she *d* 1982); one *s*; 2nd, 1980, Lady Antonia Fraser, *qv*. *Educ:* Hackney Downs Grammar Sch. Actor (mainly repertory), 1949–57. Directed: Exiles, Mermaid, 1970; Butley, 1971; Butley (film), 1973; Next of Kin, Nat. Theatre, 1974; Otherwise Engaged, Queen's, 1975, NY 1977; The Rear Column, Globe, 1978; Close of Play, Nat. Theatre, 1979; Quartermaine's Terms, Queen's, 1981; Incident at Tulse Hill, Hampstead, 1981; The Trojan War Will Not Take Place, Nat. Theatre, 1983; The Common Pursuit, Lyric Hammersmith, 1984; Sweet Bird of Youth, Haymarket, 1985; Circe and Bravo, Wyndham's, 1986. Shakespeare Prize, Hamburg, 1970; Austrian State Prize for European Literature, 1973; Pirandello Prize, 1980; Donatello Prize, 1982. Hon. DLitt: Reading, 1970; Birmingham, 1971; Glasgow, 1974; East Anglia, 1974; Stirling, 1979; Brown, 1982; Hull, 1986. *Plays:* The Room, The Birthday Party (filmed, 1968), The Dumb Waiter, 1957; The Hothouse, 1958 (stage 1980, television 1981); A Slight Ache (radio 1958, stage 1961); A Night Out (radio and television, 1961); The Caretaker (filmed 1963), 1960; Night School (television 1960); The Dwarfs (radio 1960, stage 1963); The Collection (television 1961, stage 1962); The Lover (television, stage 1963) (Italia Prize for TV); Tea Party (television 1964); The Homecoming, 1964; Landscape (radio 1968, stage 1969); Silence (stage 1969); Old Times (stage 1971); Monologue (television 1972); No Man's Land (stage 1975, television 1978); Betrayal (stage 1978 (SWET Award, 1979), filmed 1983); Family Voices (radio 1981 (Giles Cooper Award, 1982), stage 1982); Victoria Station, 1982; A Kind of Alaska, 1982; One for the Road, 1984 (television 1985). *Screenplays:* The Caretaker, The Servant, 1962; The Pumpkin Eater, 1963; The Quiller Memorandum, 1966; Accident, 1967; The Birthday Party, The Homecoming, 1968; The Go-Between, 1969; Langrishe, Go Down, 1970 (adapted for television, 1978); A la Recherche du Temps Perdu, 1972; The Last Tycoon, 1974; The French Lieutenant's Woman, 1981; Betrayal, 1981; Turtle Diary, 1985. *Publications:* The Caretaker, 1960; The Birthday Party, and other plays, 1960; A Slight Ache, 1961; The Collection, 1963; The Lover, 1963; The Homecoming, 1965; Tea Party, and, The Basement, 1967; (co-ed) PEN Anthology of New Poems, 1967; Mac, 1968; Jt Editor, New Poems 1967, 1968; Landscape, and, Silence, 1969; Five Screenplays, 1971; Old Times, 1971; Poems, 1971; No Man's Land, 1975; The Proust Screenplay: A la Recherche du Temps Perdu, 1978; Betrayal, 1978; I Know the Place, 1979; Family Voices, 1981; Other Places, 1982; One For The Road, 1984; Collected Poems and Prose, 1986; (co-ed) 100 Poems by 100 Poets, 1986. *Recreation:* cricket. *Address:* c/o Judy Daish Associates Ltd, 83 Eastbourne Mews, W2 6LQ.

PIPER, Bright Harold, (Peter Piper), CBE 1979; Director, 1970–84, Chief Executive, 1973–78, Lloyds Bank Group; *b* 22 Sept. 1918; 2nd *s* of Robert Harold Piper; *m* 1st, 1945, Marjorie Joyce, 2nd *d* of Captain George Arthur; one *s* one *d*; 2nd, 1979, Leonie Mary Lane, *d* of Major C. V. Lane. *Educ:* Maidstone Grammar School. Served with RN, 1939–46. Entered Lloyds Bank, 1935: Asst Gen. Man., 1963; Jt Gen. Man., 1965; Asst Chief Gen. Man., 1968; Dep. Chief Gen. Man., 1970; Chief Gen. Man., 1973. Director: Lewis' Bank, 1969–75; Lloyds and Scottish, 1970–75; Chm., Lloyds First Western (US), 1973–78. Freeman, City of London; Liveryman, Spectacle Makers' Company. *Recreation:* sailing. *Address:* Greenways, Hawkshill Close, Esher, Surrey. *Clubs:* Overseas Bankers, Australia.

PIPER, Sir David (Towry), Kt 1983; CBE 1969; MA, FSA; FRSL; Director, Ashmolean Museum, Oxford, 1973–85; Fellow of Worcester College, Oxford, 1973–85, now Emeritus; *b* 21 July 1918; *s* of late Prof. S. H. Piper; *m* 1945, Anne Horatia Richmond; one *s* three *d*. *Educ:* Clifton Coll.; St Catharine's Coll., Cambridge. Served War of 1939–45: Indian Army (9th Jat Regt); Japanese prisoner-of-war, 1942–45. National Portrait Gallery: Asst-Keeper, 1946–64; Dir, Keeper and Sec., 1964–67; Dir and Marlay Curator, Fitzwilliam Museum, Cambridge, 1967–73; Fellow, Christ's College, Cambridge, 1967–73. Slade Prof. of Fine Art, Oxford, 1966–67. Clark Lectr, Cambridge, 1977–78; Rede Lectr, Cambridge, 1983. Mem., Royal Fine Art Commn, 1970–. Trustee: Watts Gall., 1966–; Paul Mellon Foundn for British Art, 1969–70; Pilgrim Trust, 1973–; Leeds Castle Foundn, 1981–. Hon. Fellow, Royal Acad., 1985. Hon. DLitt Bristol, 1984. *Publications:* The English Face, 1957; Catalogue of the 17th Century Portraits in the National Portrait Gallery, 1963; The Royal College of Physicians; Portraits (ed G. Wolstenholme), 1964; (ed) Enjoying Paintings, 1964; The Companion Guide to London, 1964; Shades, 1970; London, 1971; (ed) The Genius of British Painting, 1975; The Treasures of Oxford, 1977; Kings and Queens of England and Scotland, 1980; (ed) Mitchell Beazley Library of Art, 1981; Artists' London, 1982; The Image of the Poet, 1982; (ed) Treasures of the Ashmolean Museum, 1985; *novels* (as Peter Towry) include: It's Warm Inside, 1953; Trial by Battle, 1959. *Address:* Overford Farm, Wytham, Oxford OX2 8QN. *T:* Oxford 247736. *Club:* United Oxford & Cambridge University.

PIPER, John Egerton Christmas, CH 1972; painter and writer; Member of the Oxford Diocesan Advisory Committee, since 1950; *b* 13 Dec. 1903; *s* of late C. A. Piper, Solicitor; *m* 1935, Mary Myfanwy Evans; two *s* two *d*. *Educ:* Epsom Coll.; Royal College of Art. Paintings, drawings, exhibited in London since 1925; Pictures bought by Tate Gallery, Contemporary Art Society, Victoria and Albert Museum, etc.; Series of watercolours of Windsor Castle commissioned by the Queen, 1941–42; windows for nave of Eton College Chapel commissioned 1958; windows and interior design, Nuffield College Chapel, Oxford, completed, 1961; window, Coventry Cathedral, completed, 1962; windows for King George VI Memorial Chapel, Windsor, 1969; windows for Robinson Coll., Cambridge, 1981. Designed Tapestry for High Altar, Chichester Cathedral, 1966, and for Civic Hall, Newcastle upon Tyne. Designer for opera and ballet. Mem., Royal Fine Art Commn, 1959–78; a Trustee: Tate Gallery, 1946–53, 1954–61, 1968–74; National Gallery, 1967–74, 1975–78; Arts Council art panel, 1952–57. Hon. Fellow, Robinson Coll., Cambridge, 1980. Hon. ARIBA, 1957, Hon. FRIBA 1971; Hon. ARCA 1959; Hon. DLitt: Leicester, 1960; Oxford, 1966; Sussex, 1974; Reading, 1977; Wales (Cardiff), 1981. *Publications:* Wind in the Trees (poems), 1921; 'Shell Guide' to Oxfordshire, 1938; Brighton Aquatints, 1939; British Romantic Painters, 1942; Buildings and Prospects, 1949; (ed with John Betjeman) Buckinghamshire Architectural Guide, 1948; Berkshire Architectural Guide, 1949; (illus.) The Castles on the Ground by J. M. Richards, 1973; (jtly) Lincolnshire Churches, 1976; (illus.) John Betjeman's Church Poems, 1981; (with Richard Ingrams) Piper's Places: John Piper in England and Wales, 1983. *Relevant publications:* John Piper: Paintings, Drawings and Theatre Designs, 1932–54 (arr. S. John Woods), 1955; John Piper, by Anthony West, 1979. *Address:* Fawley Bottom Farmhouse, near Henley-on-Thames, Oxon. *Club:* Athenæum.

PIPER, Peter; *see* Piper, Bright Harold.

PIPKIN, (Charles Harry) Broughton, CBE 1973; Chairman: BICC Ltd, 1977–80; Electrak International Ltd, 1982–84 (Director, 1982–85); *b* 29 Nov. 1913; *er s* of late Charles Pipkin and Charlotte Phyllis (*née* Viney), Lewisham; *m* 1941, Viola, *yr d* of Albert and Florence Byatt, Market Harborough; one *s* one *d*. *Educ:* Christ's Coll., Blackheath; Faraday House. CEng, FIEE; FBIM. Various appts with BICC, 1936–73, Dep. Chm. and Chief Exec., 1973–77. War service, 1940–46: Major REME, 14th Army (despatches). President: British Non-ferrous Metals Fedn, 1965–66; Electric Cable Makers' Fedn, 1967–68; BEAMA, 1975–76. *Recreations:* travel, reading, racing. *Address:* Pegler's Barn, Bledington, Oxon. *T:* Kingham 304. *Club:* City Livery.

PIPPARD, Prof. Sir (Alfred) Brian, Kt 1975; FRS 1956; Cavendish Professor of Physics, University of Cambridge, 1971–82, now Emeritus; *b* 7 Sept. 1920; *s* of late Prof. A. J. S. Pippard; *m* 1955, Charlotte Frances Dyer; three *d*. *Educ:* Clifton Coll.; Clare Coll., Cambridge (Hon. Fellow 1973). BA (Cantab) 1941, MA 1945. PhD 1949; ScD 1966. Scientific Officer, Radar Research and Development Establishment, Great Malvern, 1941–45; Stokes Student, Pembroke Coll., Cambridge, 1945–46; Demonstrator in Physics, University of Cambridge, 1946; Lecturer in Physics, 1950; Reader in Physics, 1959–60; John Humphrey Plummer Prof. of Physics, 1960–71; Pres., Clare Hall, Cambridge, 1966–73. Visiting Prof., Institute for the Study of Metals, University of Chicago, 1955–56. Fellow of Clare Coll., Cambridge, 1947–66. Cherwell-Simon Memorial Lectr, Oxford, 1968–69. Pres., Inst. of Physics, 1974–76. Hughes Medal of the Royal Soc., 1959; Holweck Medal, 1961; Dannie-Heineman Prize, 1969; Guthrie Prize, 1970. *Publications:* Elements of Classical Thermodynamics, 1957; Dynamics of Conduction Electrons, 1962; Forces and Particles, 1972; The Physics of Vibration, vol. 1, 1978, vol. 2, 1983; Response and Stability, 1985; papers in Proc. Royal Soc., etc. *Recreation:* music. *Address:* 30 Porson Road, Cambridge.

PIRATIN, Philip; *b* 15 May 1907; *m* 1929, Celia Fund; one *s* two *d*. *Educ:* Davenant Foundation Sch., London, E1. Was a Member of Stepney Borough Council, 1937–49; MP (Com) Mile End Division of Stepney, 1945–50.

PIRBHAI, Count Sir Eboo; *see* Eboo Pirbhai.

PIRIE, Group Captain Sir Gordon (Hamish Martin), Kt 1984; CBE 1946; JP; DL; Deputy High Bailiff of Westminster, since 1978; Member, Westminster City Council, 1949–82 (Mayor, 1959–60; Leader of Council, 1961–69; Alderman, 1963–78; Lord Mayor, 1974–75); Chairman, Services Sound and Vision Corporation, since 1979; Director, Parker Gallery; *b* 10 Feb. 1918; *s* of Harold Victor Campbell Pirie and Irene Gordon Hogarth; *m* 1st, 1953, Margaret Joan Bomford (*d* 1972); no *c*; 2nd, 1982, Joanna, *widow* of John C. Hugill. *Educ:* Eton (scholar); RAF Coll., Cranwell. Permanent Commission, RAF, 1938. Served War of 1939–45: Dir of Ops, RNZAF, Atlantic and Pacific (despatches, CBE); retired as Group Captain, 1946. Comr No 1 (POW) Dist SJAB, 1960–69; Comdr St John Ambulance, London, 1969–75; Chm., St John Council for London, 1975–85. A Governor of Westminster Sch., 1962–; Vice-Pres., Engineering Industries Assoc., 1966–69; Mem., Council of Royal Albert Hall, 1965– (a Vice-Pres., 1985–); a Trustee, RAF Museum, 1965–; Vice-Chm., London Boroughs Assoc., 1968–71; Pres., Conf. of Local and Regional Authorities of Europe, 1978–80 (Vice-Pres., 1974–75, 1977–78, 1980–82); Mem. Solicitors Disciplinary Tribunal, 1975–. Contested (LNat&U) Dundee West, 1955. DL, JP Co. of London, 1962; Mem., Inner London Adv. Cttee on appointment of Magistrates, 1969–; Chm., S Westminster PSD, 1974–77. Liveryman, Worshipful Company of Girdlers. KStJ 1969. Pro Merito Medal, Council of Europe, 1982. Comdr, Legion of Honour, 1960; Comdr, Cross of Merit, SMO Malta, 1971. JSM Malaysia, 1974. *Recreations:* motoring, bird-watching. *Address:* Cottage Row, Tarrant Gunville, Blandford, Dorset DT11 8JJ. *T:* Tarrant Hinton 212. *Clubs:* Carlton, Royal Air Force.

PIRIE, Henry Ward; crossword compiler, journalist and broadcaster; Sheriff (formerly Sheriff-Substitute) of Lanarkshire at Glasgow, 1955–74; *b* 13 Feb. 1922; *o* surv. *s* of late William Pirie, Merchant, Leith; *m* 1948, Jean Marion, *y d* of late Frank Jardine, sometime President of RCS of Edinburgh; four *s*. *Educ:* Watson's Coll., Edinburgh; Edinburgh Univ. MA 1944; LLB 1947. Served with Royal Scots; commnd Indian Army, 1944; Lieut, Bombay Grenadiers, 1944–46. Called to Scottish Bar, 1947. Sheriff-Substitute of Lanarkshire at Airdrie, 1954–55. OStJ 1967. *Recreations:* curling, golf, bridge. *Address:* 16 Poplar Drive, Lenzie, Kirkintilloch, Dunbartonshire. *T:* Kirkintilloch 2494.

PIRIE, Iain Gordon; Sheriff of Glasgow and Strathkelvin, since 1982; *b* 15 Jan. 1933; *s* of Charles Fox Pirie and Mary Ann Gordon; *m* 1960, Sheila Brown Forbes, MB, ChB; two *s* one *d*. *Educ:* Harris Acad., Dundee; St Andrews Univ. (MA, LLB). Legal Asst, Stirling, Eunson & Belford, Solicitors, Dunfermline, 1958–60; Depute Procurator Fiscal, Paisley, 1960–67; Sen. Depute Procurator Fiscal, Glasgow, 1967–71; Procurator Fiscal: Dumfries, 1971–76; Ayr, 1976–79; Sheriff of S Strathclyde, Dumfries and Galloway, 1979–82. *Recreations:* golf, tennis, reading, gardening, playing the violin. *Address:* 22 Dalziel Drive, Glasgow G41 4PU.

PIRIE, Norman Wingate, FRS 1949; *b* 1 July 1907; *yr s* of late Sir George Pirie, painter, Torrance, Stirlingshire; *m* 1931, Antoinette Patey; one *s*. *Educ:* Emmanuel Coll., Cambridge. Demonstrator in Biochemical Laboratory, Cambridge, 1932–40; Virus Physiologist, 1940–46, Head of Biochemistry Dept, 1947–73, Rothamsted Experimental Station, Harpenden. Vis. Prof., Indian Statistical Inst., Calcutta, 1971–. Copley Medal, 1971; Rank Prize for Nutrition, 1976. *Publications:* Food Resources: conventional and novel, 1969, 2nd edn 1976; Leaf Protein and other aspects of fodder fractionation, 1978, 2nd edn 1986; ed several works on world food supplies; scientific papers on various aspects of Biochemistry but especially on separation and properties of macromolecules; articles on viruses, the origins of life, biochemical engineering, and the need for greatly extended research on food production and contraception. *Address:* Rothamsted Experimental Station, Harpenden, Herts. *T:* Harpenden 63133.

PIRIE, Psyche; Consultant Design and Decoration Editor, Woman's Journal (IPC Magazines), 1979–84; *b* 6 Feb. 1918; *d* of late George Quarmby; *m* 1940, James Mansergh

Pirie; one *d. Educ:* Kensington High Sch.; Chelsea Sch. of Art. Air Ministry, 1940–44. Teaching, Ealing Sch. of Art and Willesden Sch. of Art, 1944–46; Indep. Interior Designer, 1946–56; Furnishing Editor, Homes and Gardens, 1956–68, Editor, 1968–78. *Recreations:* conversation, cinema, theatre, junk shops; or doing absolutely nothing. *Address:* 2 Chiswick Square, W4 2QG.

PIRZADA, Syed Sharifuddin, SPk 1964; Attorney-General of Pakistan, 1965–66, 1968–71 and since 1977; Adviser to the Chief Martial Law Administrator and Federal Minister, since 1978; Secretary-General, Organization of the Islamic Conference, since 1985; *b* 12 June 1923; *s* of Syed Vilayat Ali Pirzada; *m* 1960; two *s* two *d. Educ:* University of Bombay. LLB 1945. Secretary, Provincial Muslim League, 1946; Managing Editor, Morning Herald, 1946; Prof., Sind Muslim Law Coll., 1947–55; Advocate: Bombay High Court, 1946; Sind Chief Court, 1947; West Pakistan High Court, 1955; Supreme Court of Pakistan, 1961; Senior Advocate Supreme Court of Pakistan; Foreign Minister of Pakistan, 1966–68; Minister for Law and Parly Affairs, 1979–85. Represented Pakistan: before International Tribunal on Rann of Kutch, 1965; before Internat. Ct of Justice regarding Namibia, SW Africa, 1971; Pakistan Chief Counsel before ICAO Montreal in complaint concerning overflights over Indian territory; Leader of Pakistan delegations to Commonwealth Conf. and General Assembly of UN, 1966; Mem., UN Sub-Commn on Prevention of Discrimination and Protection of Minorities, 1972– (Chm., 1968). Hon. Advisor, Constitutional Commn, 1961; Chm., Pakistan Company Law Commn, 1962; Mem., Internat. River Cttee, 1961–68; President: Pakistan Br., Internat. Law Assoc., 1964–67; Karachi Bar Assoc., 1964; Pakistan Bar Council, 1966; Inst. of Internat. Affairs. Led Pakistan Delegn to Law of the Sea Conferences, NY, 1978 and 1979, and Geneva, 1980. Member: Pakistan Nat. Gp, Panel of the Permanent Ct of Arbitration; Panel of Arbitrators and Umpires, Council of Internat. Civil Aviation Organisation; Panel of Arbitrators, Internat. Centre for Settlement of Investment Disputes, Washington; Internat. Law Commn, 1981–. Chm., Cttee of Experts constituted by Organisation of Islamic Conf. for drafting statute of the Islamic Internat. Ct of Justice, 1980. *Publications:* Pakistan at a Glance, 1941; Jinnah on Pakistan, 1943; Leaders Correspondence with Jinnah, 1944, 3rd edn 1978; Evolution of Pakistan, 1962 (also published in Urdu and Arabic); Fundamental Rights and Constitutional Remedies in Pakistan, 1966; The Pakistan Resolution and the Historic Lahore Session, 1970; Foundations of Pakistan, vol. I, 1969, vol. II, 1970; Some Aspects of Quaid-i-Azam's Life, 1978; Collected Works of Quaid-i-Azam Mohammad Ali Jinnah, vol. I, 1985, vol. II, 1986. *Recreation:* bridge. *Address:* Organization of the Islamic Conference, PO Box 178, Jeddah 21411, Saudi Arabia; C-37, KDA Scheme No 1, Drigh Road, Karachi, Pakistan. *Clubs:* Sind (Karachi); Karachi Boat, Karachi Gymkhana.

PISANI, Edgard (Edouard Marie Victor); Chevalier de la Légion d'honneur; *b* Tunis, 9 Oct. 1918; *s* of François and Zoë Pisani; *m* Isola Chazereau (decd); three *s* one *d*; *m* 1984, Carmen Berndt. *Educ:* Lycée Carnot, Tunis; Lycée Louis-le-Grand, Paris. LèsL. War of 1939–45 (Croix de Guerre; Médaille de la Résistance). Chef du Cabinet, later Dir, Office of Prefect of Police, Paris, 1944; Dir, Office of Minister of Interior, 1946; Prefect: of Haute-Loire, 1946; of Haute-Marne, 1947; Senator (democratic left) from Haute-Marne, 1954; Minister of Agriculture, 1961; (first) Minister of Equipment, 1966; Deputy, Maine et Loire, 1967–68; Minister of Equipment and Housing, 1967; Conseiller Général, Maine et Loire, 1964–73; Mayor of Montreuil Bellay, 1965–75; Senator (socialist) from Haute-Marne, 1974–81; Mem., European Parlt, 1978–79 (Pres., Econ. and Monetary Affairs Cttee); Mem. for France, EEC, 1981–84; High Comr and Special Envoy to New Caledonia, 1984–85; Minister for New Caledonia, 1985–86. Mem., Commn on Develt Issues (Brandt Commn), 1978–80. Mem., Club of Rome, 1975. *Publications:* La région: pourquoi faire?, 1969; Le général indivis, 1974; Utopie foncière, 1977; Socialiste de raison, 1978; Défi du monde, campagne d'Europe, 1979; (contrib.) Pour la science, 1980; La main et l'outil, 1984. *Address:* (home) 225 rue du Faubourg St Honoré, 75008 Paris, France.

PITBLADO, Sir David (Bruce), KCB 1967 (CB 1955); CVO 1953; Chairman, Davies's Educational Trust, since 1979 (Member Council, since 1975); Comptroller and Auditor-General, 1971–76; *b* 18 Aug. 1912; *o s* of Robert Bruce and Mary Jane Pitblado; *m* 1941, Edith (*d* 1978), *yr d* of Captain J. T. and Mrs Rees Evans, Cardigan; one *s* one *d. Educ:* Strand Sch.; Emmanuel Coll., Cambridge (Hon. Fellow 1972); Middle Temple. Entered Dominions Office, 1935; Asst Private Secretary to Secretary of State, 1937–39; served in War Cabinet Office, 1942; transferred to Treasury, 1942; deleg. to UN Conf., San Francisco, 1945; Under-Secretary, Treasury, 1949; Principal Private Secretary to the Prime Minister (Mr Clement Attlee, Mr Winston Churchill, and Sir Anthony Eden), 1951–56; Vice Chm., Managing Bd, European Payments Union, 1958; Third Secretary, Treasury, 1960; Economic Minister and Head of Treasury Delegation, Washington, and Executive Dir for the UK, IMF and World Bank, 1961–63; Permanent Sec., Min. of Power, 1966–69, Permanent Sec. (Industry), Min. of Technology, 1969–70; Civil Service Dept, 1970–71. Advr on non-exec. directorships, Inst. of Dirs, 1977–81. Member: Data Protection Cttee, 1976–78; Victoria County Histories Cttee, 1974–; Finance Cttee, RPMS, 1980–; Council, SSAFA, 1976– (Hon. Treasurer). Jt Editor, The Shetland Report, 1978–. Companion Inst. of Fuel. *Address:* 23 Cadogan Street, SW3; Pengoitan, Borth, Dyfed. *Club:* Athenæum.

PITCHER, Desmond Henry, CEng, FIEE, FBCS; Group Chief Executive, and Board Member, The Littlewoods Organisation, since 1983; Chairman, Mersey Barrage Co., since 1986; *b* 23 March 1935; *s* of George Charles and Alice Marion Pitcher; *m*; two *s* twin *d. Educ:* Liverpool Coll. of Technology. MIEEE (USA). A. V. Roe & Co., Develt Engr, 1955; Automatic Telephone and Elec. Co. (now Plessey), Systems Engr, 1958; Univac Remington Rand (now Sperry Rand Ltd), Systems Engr, 1961; Sperry Univac: Dir, Systems, 1966; Managing Dir, 1971; Vice-Pres., 1974; Dir, Sperry Rand, 1971–78, Dep. Chm., 1974–78; Man. Dir, Leyland Vehicles Ltd, 1976–78; Dir, British Leyland, 1977–78; Man. Dir, Plessey Telecommunications and Office Systems, 1978–83; Dir, Plessey Co., 1979–83. Dir, CEI, 1979; Pres., TEMA, 1981–83. *Publications:* Institution of Electrical Engineers Faraday Lectures, 1974–75; various lectures on social implications of computers and micro-electronics. *Recreations:* golf, music. *Address:* Tudor Court, Selworthy Road, Birkdale, Southport, Merseyside. *T:* Southport 63531; Middle Dell, Bishopsgate Road, Englefield Green, Surrey. *T:* Egham 37645. *Clubs:* Brooks's; Royal Birkdale Golf; Royal Liverpool Golf; Camberley Heath Golf.

PITCHER, Prof. Wallace Spencer, PhD, DSc, DIC; George Herdman Professor of Geology, 1962–81, now Emeritus, and Leverhulme Emeritus Research Fellow, 1981–82, University of Liverpool; *b* 3 March 1919; *s* of Harry George and Irene Bertha Pitcher; *m* 1947, Stella Ann (*née* Scutt); two *s* two *d. Educ:* Acton Tech. Coll., Chelsea Coll. Asst Analytical Chemist, Geo. T. Holloway & Co., 1937–39. Served War, RAMC, 1939–44. Chelsea Coll., 1944–47; Imperial College: Demonstrator, 1947–48; Asst Lectr, 1948–50; Lectr, 1950–55; Reader in Geology, King's Coll., London, 1955–62. Geological Society London: Hon. Sec., 1970–73; Foreign Sec., 1974–75; Pres., 1976–77; Pres., Section C, British Assoc., 1979. Founder MIG; FIMM. Hon. MRIA 1977; Hon. Member: GA, 1972; Geol Soc. America, 1982. Hon. ScD Dublin, 1983. Lyell Fund, 1956, Bigsby Medal, 1963, Murchison Medal, 1979, Geol Soc. of London; Liverpool Geol Soc. Silver Medal, 1969; Aberconway Medal, Instn of Geologists, 1983. *Publications:* ed (with G. W. Flinn) Controls of Metamorphism, 1965; (with A. R. Berger) Geology of Donegal: a study of granite emplacement and unroofing, 1972; (with E. J. Cobbing) Geology of Western Cordillera of Northern Peru, 1981; (jtly) Magmatism at a Plate Edge: the Peruvian Andes, 1985; many papers on late Precambrian stratigraphy, tillites, Caledonian and Andean granites, structure of the Andes. *Address:* 14 Church Road, Upton, Wirral, Merseyside L49 6JZ. *T:* 051–677 6896.

PITCHERS, Christopher John; Barrister; a Recorder of the Crown Court, since 1981; *b* 2 Oct. 1942; *s* of Thomas and Melissa Pitchers; *m* 1965, Judith Stevenson; two *s. Educ:* Uppingham Sch.; Worcester Coll., Oxford. MA. Called to the Bar, Inner Temple, 1965. *Address:* The White House, Church Langton, Leics.

PITCHFORD; *see* Watkins-Pitchford.

PITCHFORD, Charles Neville; His Honour Judge Pitchford; a Circuit Judge, Wales and Chester Circuit, since 1972. Called to the Bar, Middle Temple, 1948. *Address:* Llanynant, Kennel Lane, Coed Morgan, Abergavenny, Gwent.

PITCHFORD, John Hereward, CBE 1971; FEng 1980; President, Ricardo Consulting Engineers Ltd, since 1976 (Chairman, 1962–76); *b* 30 Aug. 1904; *s* of John Pitchford and Elizabeth Anne Wilson; *m* 1930, Teresa Agnes Mary Pensotti; one *s* two *d. Educ:* Brighton Coll.; Christ's Coll., Cambridge (MA). FIMechE (Pres. 1962). Ricardo & Co. Engineers (1927) Ltd: Test Shop Asst, 1926; Asst Research Engr, 1929; Personal Asst to Man. Dir, 1935; Gen. Man., 1939; Dir and Gen. Man., 1941; Man. and Jt Techn. Dir, 1947; Chm. and Man. Dir, 1962; Chm. and Jt Man. Dir, 1965; Chm., 1967. Pres., Fédération Internationale des Sociétés d'Ingénieurs des Techniques de l'Automobile, 1961–63; Chm., Navy Dept Fuels and Lubricants Adv. Cttee, 1964–71. Hon. Mem., Associazione Tecnica Automobile, 1958. *Publications:* papers on all aspects of internal combustion engine. *Recreations:* music, sailing. *Address:* Byeways, Ditchling, East Sussex. *T:* Hassocks 2177. *Clubs:* Athenæum, Royal Automobile.

See also Sir J. H. G. Leahy.

PITCHFORTH, Harry; General Manager, Home Grown Cereals Authority, 1974–78, retired; *b* 17 Jan. 1917; *s* of John William Pitchforth and Alice Hollas; *m* 1941, Edna May Blakebrough; one *s* one *d. Educ:* Heath Sch., Halifax; Queen's Coll., Oxford. 1st class Hons, School of Modern History, Oxford, 1939. Served War, 1940–45, Captain, RASC, and later Education Officer, 5 Guards Brigade. Ministry of Food, 1945; Principal Private Secretary, to Minister, Major G. Lloyd-George, 1952–54; seconded to National Coal Board, 1955–58; Ministry of Agriculture, Fisheries and Food: Regional Controller, 1957–61; Director of Establishments and Organisation, 1961–65; Under-Sec., HM Treasury, 1965–67; Controller of HM Stationery Office and the Queen's Printer of Acts of Parliament, 1967–69; Chief Executive, Metropolitan Water Bd, 1969–74. *Recreations:* walking, music. *Address:* 93 George V Avenue, Pinner, Mddx. *T:* 01–863 1229.

PITFIELD, Hon. (Peter) Michael, CVO 1982; PC (Can.) 1984; QC (Can.) 1972; Senator, Canada, since Dec. 1982; *b* Montreal, 18 June 1937; *s* of Ward Chipman Pitfield and Grace Edith (*née* MacDougall); *m* 1971, Nancy Snow; one *s* two *d. Educ:* Lower Canada Coll., Montreal; Sedbergh Sch., Montebello; St Lawrence Univ. (BASc; Hon. DLitt 1979); McGill Univ. (BCL); Univ. of Ottawa (DESD). Lieut, RCNR. Read Law with Mathewson Lafleur & Brown, Montreal (associated with firm, 1958–59); called to Quebec Bar, 1962; QC (Fed.) 1972; Admin. Asst to Minister of Justice and Attorney-Gen. of Canada, 1959–61; Sec. and Exec. Dir, Royal Commn on Pubns, Ottawa, 1961–62; Attaché to Gov.-Gen. of Canada, 1962–65; Sec. and Res. Supervisor of Royal Commn on Taxation, 1963–66; entered Privy Council Office and Cabinet Secretariat of Govt of Canada, 1965; Asst Sec. to Cabinet, 1966; Dep. Sec. to Cabinet (Plans), and Dep. Clerk to Council, 1969; Dep. Minister, Consumer and Corporate Affairs, 1973; Clerk of Privy Council and Sec. to Cabinet, 1975–79 and 1980–Nov. 1982; Sen. Adviser to Privy Council Office, Nov.-Dec. 1982. Rep., UN Gen. Assembly, 1983; Chm., Senate Cttee on Security and Intelligence, 1983. Dir, Cadillac-Fairview Corp., Montreal. Fellow, Harvard Univ., 1974; Mackenzie King Vis. Prof., Kennedy Sch. of Govt, Harvard, 1979–80. Member: Canadian, Quebec and Montreal Bar Assocs; Can. Inst. of Public Admin; Can. Hist. Assoc.; Can. Polit. Sci. Assoc.; Amer. Soc. Polit. and Social Sci.; Internat. Commn of Jurists; Beta Theta Pi. Trustee, Twentieth Century Fund, NY; Mem. Council, IISS. *Recreations:* squash, ski-ing, reading. *Address:* (office) The Senate, Ottawa, Ont K1A 0K4, Canada. *Club:* University (Montreal).

PITMAN, Brian Ivor; Chief Executive and Director, Lloyds Bank Plc, since 1983; *b* 13 Dec. 1931; *s* of late Ronald Ivor Pitman and of Doris Ivy Pitman (*née* Short); *m* 1954, Barbara Mildred Ann (*née* Darby); two *s* one *d. Educ:* Cheltenham Grammar School. FIB. Entered Lloyds Bank, 1952, Jt Gen. Manager, 1975; Exec. Dir, Lloyds Bank International, 1976, Dep. Chief Exec., 1978; Dep. Group Chief Exec., Lloyds Bank Plc, 1982. Director: Lloyds Bank California, 1982–; Nat. Bank of New Zealand Ltd, 1982–; Lloyds and Scottish Plc, 1983; Lloyds Bank International Ltd, 1985–; Lloyds Merchant Bank Holdings Ltd, 1985–. *Recreations:* golf, cricket, music. *Address:* Lloyds Bank Plc, 71 Lombard Street, EC3P 3BS. *Clubs:* MCC, St George's Hill Golf.

PITMAN, Edwin James George, BSc, MA, FAA; Emeritus Professor of Mathematics, University of Tasmania (Professor, 1926; retired, Dec. 1962); *b* Melbourne, 29 Oct. 1897; of English parents; *s* of late Edwin Edward Major Pitman and Ann Ungley Pitman; *m* 1932, Edith Elinor Josephine, *y d* of late William Nevin Tatlow Hurst; two *s* two *d. Educ:* South Melbourne Coll.; Ormond Coll., University of Melbourne. Enlisted Australian Imperial Forces, 1918; returned from abroad, 1919; BA with First Class Honours, Dixson scholarship and Wyselaskie scholarship in Mathematics; acting-Professor of Mathematics at Canterbury Coll., University of New Zealand, 1922–23; Tutor in Mathematics and Physics at Trinity Coll. and Ormond Coll., University of Melbourne, 1924–25; Visiting Prof. of Mathematical Statistics at Columbia Univ., NY, Univ. of N Carolina, and Princeton Univ., 1948–49; Visiting Prof. of Statistics: Stanford Univ., Stanford, California, 1957; Johns Hopkins Univ., Baltimore, 1963–64; Chicago, 1968–69; Vis. Sen. Res. Fellow, Univ. of Dundee, 1973. Fellow, Inst. Math. Statistics, 1948; FAA 1954; Vice-Pres., 1960; Mem. International Statistical Institute, 1956; Pres., Australian Mathematical Soc., 1958–59; Hon. Fellow, Royal Statistical Soc., 1965; Hon. Life Member: Statistical Soc. of Australia, 1966 (first Pitman Medal, 1978, for contribs to theory of statistics and probability); Australian Mathematical Soc., 1968. Hon. DSc Tasmania, 1977. *Publication:* Some Basic Theory for Statistical Inference, 1979. *Address:* 301 Davey Street, Hobart, Tasmania 7000, Australia.

PITMAN, Jennifer Susan; professional racehorse trainer (National Hunt), since 1975; Director, Jenny Pitman Racing Ltd; *b* 11 June 1946; *d* of George and Mary Harvey; *m* 1965, Richard Pitman (marr. diss.); two *s. Educ:* Sarson Secondary Girls' School. Training of major race winners includes: Midlands National, 1977 (Watafella); Massey Ferguson Gold Cup, Cheltenham, 1980 (Bueche Giorod); Welsh National, 1982 (Corbiere), 1983 (Burrough Hill Lad); Grand National, 1983 (Corbiere); Cheltenham Gold Cup, 1984

(Burrough Hill Lad); King George VI Gold Cup, 1984 (Burrough Hill Lad); Hennessey Gold Cup, Newbury, 1984 (Burrough Hill Lad); Whitbread Trophy, 1985 (Smith's Man). Trainer of the Year, 1983/84. *Publication*: Glorious Uncertainty (autobiog.), 1984. *Address*: Weathercock House, Upper Lambourn, near Newbury, Berks. *T*: Lambourn 71714. *Club*: International Sporting.

PITOI, Sir Sere, Kt 1977; CBE 1975; MACE; Chairman, Public Services Commission of Papua New Guinea, since 1971; *b* Kapa Kapa Village, SE of Port Moresby, 11 Nov. 1935; *s* of Pitoi Sere and Laka Orira; *m* 1957, Daga Leva; two *s* three *d*. *Educ*: Sogeri (Teachers' Cert.); Queensland Univ. (Cert. in Diagnostic Testing and Remedial Teaching); Univ. of Birmingham, UK (Cert. for Headmasters and Administrators). Held a number of posts as teacher, 1955–57, and headmaster, 1958–68, in Port Moresby, the Gulf district of Papua, Eastern Highlands, New Britain. Apptd a District Inspector of Schools, 1968. Chm., Public Service Bd, Papua New Guinea, 1969–76. Fellow, PNG Inst. of Management. *Recreation*: fishing. *Address*: PO Box 6029, Boroko, Papua New Guinea. *Clubs*: Rotary (Port Moresby); Cheshire Home (PNG).

PITT, family name of **Baron Pitt of Hampstead.**

PITT OF HAMPSTEAD, Baron *cr* 1975 (Life Peer), of Hampstead, in Greater London and in Grenada; **David Thomas Pitt**, TC 1976; MB, ChB Edinburgh, DCH London; JP; General Practitioner, London, since 1947; *b* St David's, Grenada, WI, 3 Oct. 1913; *m* 1943, Dorothy Elaine Alleyne; one *s* two *d*. *Educ*: St David's RC Sch., Grenada, WI; Grenada Boys' Secondary Sch.; Edinburgh Univ. First Junior Pres., Student Rep. Council, Edinburgh Univ., 1936–37. Dist Med. Officer, St Vincent, WI, 1938–39; Ho. Phys., San Fernando Hosp., Trinidad, 1939–41; GP, San Fernando, 1941–47; Mem. of San Fernando BC, 1941–47; Dep. Mayor, San Fernando, 1946–47; Pres., West Indian Nat. Party (Trinidad), 1943–47. Mem. LCC, 1961–64, GLC 1964–77, for Hackney (Dep. Chm., 1969–70; Chm. 1974–75). Mem. Nat. Cttee for Commonwealth Immigrants, 1965–67; Chm., Campaign Against Racial Discrimination, 1965; Dep. Chm., Community Relations Commn, 1968–77, Chm. 1977; Mem., Standing Adv. Council on Race Relations, 1977–79. Mem. (part time), PO Bd, 1975–77. Chm., Shelter, 1979–. Pres., BMA, 1985–86. JP 1966. Contested (Lab): Hampstead, 1959; Clapham (Wandsworth), 1970. Hon. DSc Univ. of West Indies, 1975; Hon. DLitt Bradford, 1977; Hon. LLD: Bristol, 1977; Hull, 1983; Shaw Univ., N Carolina, 1985. *Recreations*: reading, watching television, watching cricket, listening to music, theatre. *Address*: 6 Heath Drive, NW3 7SY. *Clubs*: Royal Commonwealth Society, MCC.

PITT, Barrie (William Edward); author and editor of military histories; *b* Galway, 7 July 1918; *y s* of John Pitt and Ethel May Pitt (*née* Pennell); *m* 1st, 1943, Phyllis Kate (*née* Edwards); one *s* (decd); 2nd, 1953, Sonia Deirdre (*née* Hoskins) (marr. diss., 1971); 3rd, 1983, Frances Mary (*née* Moore). *Educ*: Portsmouth Southern Grammar Sch. Bank Clerk, 1935. Served War of 1939–45, in Army. Surveyor, 1946. Began writing, 1954. Information Officer, Atomic Energy Authority, 1961; Historical Consultant to BBC Series, The Great War, 1963; Editor, Purnell's History of the Second World War, 1964; Editor-in-Chief: Ballantine's Illustrated History of World War 2, 1967 (US Book Series); Ballantine's Illustrated History of the Violent Century, 1971; Editor: Purnell's History of the First World War, 1969; British History Illustrated, 1974–78. *Publications*: The Edge of Battle, 1958; Zeebrugge, St George's Day, 1918, 1958; Coronel and Falkland, 1960; 1918 The Last Act, 1962; The Battle of the Atlantic, 1977; The Crucible of War: Western Desert 1941, 1980; Churchill and the Generals, 1981; The Crucible of War: Year of Alamein 1942, 1982; Special Boat Squadron, 1983; contrib. to: Encyclopaedia Britannica; The Sunday Times. *Recreation*: golf. *Address*: FitzHead Court, Fitzhead, Taunton, Somerset TA4 3JP. *T*: Milverton 400923. *Club*: Savage.

PITT, Desmond Gordon; Commissioner of HM Customs and Excise, 1979–83; *b* 27 Dec. 1922; *s* of Archibald and Amy Pitt; *m* 1946, Barbara Irene; one *s* two *d*. *Educ*: Bournemouth Sch. FCCA, ACIS, AIB. Officer, HM Customs and Excise, 1947; Inspector, 1958; Asst Sec., 1973; Under Sec., 1979. Hon. Treasurer, Wessex Autistic Soc. *Recreations*: travel, sailing. *Address*: 4 Ken Road, Southbourne, Bournemouth, Dorset. *Club*: Thorpe Bay Yacht.

PITT, Rt. Rev. Mgr George Edward, CBE 1965; *b* 10 Oct. 1916; *s* of Francis Pitt and Anna Christina Oviedo. *Educ*: St Brendan's Coll., Bristol; Ven. English College, Rome. Priest, 1939; worked in Diocese of Clifton, 1940–43; joined Royal Navy as Chaplain, 1943; Principal Roman Catholic Chaplain, RN, 1963–69; Parish Priest, St Joseph's, Wroughton, Wilts, 1969–86. Nominated a Domestic Prelate, 1963. *Recreation*: music. *Address*: 5 West Mall, Bristol BS8 4BH. *T*: Bristol 733235.

PITT, Sir Harry (Raymond), Kt 1978; BA, PhD; FRS 1957; Vice-Chancellor, Reading University, 1964–79; *b* 3 June 1914; *s* of H. Pitt; *m* 1940, Clemency Catherine, *d* of H. C. E. Jacoby, MIEE; four *s*. *Educ*: King Edward's Sch., Stourbridge; Peterhouse, Cambridge. Bye-Fellow, Peterhouse, Cambridge, 1936–39; Choate Memorial Fellow, Harvard Univ., 1937–38; Univ. of Aberdeen, 1939–42. Air Min. and Min. of Aircraft Production, 1942–45. Prof. of Mathematics, Queen's Univ., Belfast, 1945–50; Deputy Vice-Chancellor, Univ. of Nottingham, 1959–62; Prof. of Pure Mathematics, Univ. of Nottingham, 1950–64. Visiting Prof., Yale Univ., 1962–63. Chm., Universities Central Council on Admissions, 1975–78. Pres., IMA, 1984–85. Hon. LLD: Aberdeen 1970; Nottingham 1970; Hon. DSc: Reading, 1978; Belfast, 1981. *Publications*: Tauberian Theorems, 1957; Measure, Integration and Probability, 1963; mathematical papers in scientific journals. *Address*: 46 Shinfield Road, Reading, Berks RG2 7BW. *T*: Reading 872962.

PITT, William Augustus Fitzgerald Lane F.; *see* Fox-Pitt.

PITT, William Henry; *b* 17 July 1937; *m* 1961, Janet Pitt (*née* Wearn). *Educ*: Heath Clark Sch., Croydon; London Nautical Sch.; Polytechnic of South Bank; Polytechnic of N London. Lighting Engineer, 1955–75; Housing Officer, Lambeth Borough Council, 1975–81. Chm., Lambeth Br., NALGO, 1979–81. Joined Liberal Party, 1959; contested (L) Croydon NW, Feb. and Oct. 1974, 1979, 1983. MP (L) Croydon NW, Oct. 1981–1983; first L and SDP alliance cand. to be elected MP. Chm., Classics Soc., Polytechnic of N London, 1985–. *Recreations*: photography, music, reading, walking. *Address*: 51 Edith Road, South Norwood, SE25 5PG. *Club*: National Liberal.

PITT-RIVERS, Dr Rosalind Venetia, FRS 1954; *b* 4 March 1907; *d* of late Hon. Anthony Morton Henley, CMG, DSO, and late Hon. Sylvia Laura Henley, OBE (*née* Stanley); *m* 1931, Captain George Henry Lane Fox Pitt-Rivers (*d* 1966); one *s*. *Educ*: Notting Hill High Sch.; Bedford Coll., University of London. MSc London 1931; PhD London, 1939. Head, Chemistry Division, Nat. Inst. for Medical Research, 1969–72. Hon. FRCP 1986. *Publications*: The Thyroid Hormones, 1959; The Chemistry of Thyroid Diseases, 1960; (with W. R. Trotter) The Thyroid Gland, 1964. *Address*: The Old Estate Office, Hinton St Mary, Sturminster Newton, Dorset DT10 1NA.

PITTAM, Robert Raymond; Assistant Under-Secretary of State, Home Office, 1972–79; *b* 14 June 1919; *e s* of Rev. R. G. Pittam and Elsie Emma Pittam (*née* Sale); *m* 1946, Gwendoline Lilian Brown; one *s* one *d*. *Educ*: Bootle Grammar Sch.; Pembroke Coll.,

Cambridge. MA; 1st Cl. Law Tripos. War of 1939–45: temp. Civil Servant, and service in RAOC, 1940–46. Home Office, 1946–66: Private Sec. to Home Secretary, 1955–57; Asst Sec., 1957; HM Treasury, 1966–68; CSD, 1968–72. Founder Chm., Home Office Retired Staff Assoc., 1982–. *Address*: 14 Devonshire Way, Shirley, Croydon, Surrey. *Club*: Civil Service.

PITTER, Ruth, CBE 1979; CLit 1974; poetess; *b* Ilford, Essex, 7 Nov. 1897; *d* of George Pitter, Elementary Schoolmaster. *Educ*: Elementary Sch.; Coborn Sch., Bow, E. Heinemann Foundation Award, 1954; Queen's Medal for Poetry, 1955. *Publications*: First Poems, 1920; First and Second Poems, 1927; Persephone in Hades (privately printed), 1931; A Mad Lady's Garland, 1934, A Trophy of Arms, 1936 (Hawthornden Prize, 1937); The Spirit Watches, 1939; The Rude Potato, 1941; The Bridge, 1945; Pitter on Cats, 1946; Urania, 1951; The Ermine, 1953; Still By Choice, 1966; Poems 1926–66, 1968; End of Drought, 1975. *Recreation*: gardening. *Address*: 71 Chilton Road, Long Crendon, near Aylesbury, Bucks. *T*: Long Crendon 208 373.

PITTOM, L(ois) Audrey, CB 1979; retired; Under Secretary, Health and Safety Executive, Department of Employment, 1975–78; *b* 4 July 1918; *d* of Thomas Pittom and Hylda (*née* Ashby). *Educ*: Laurels Sch., Wroxall Abbey, Warwick; St Anne's Coll., Oxford (BA Hons). Inspector of Factories, 1945; Superintending Inspector, Nottingham, 1967; Dep. Chief Inspector of Factories, 1970. *Recreations*: gardening, sight-seeing in Europe. *Address*: 1 Rectory Lane, Barby, Rugby, Warwicks. *T*: Rugby 890424.

PITTS, Sir Cyril (Alfred), Kt 1968; Chairman of Governors, Polytechnic of Central London, since 1985 (Governor, since 1984); *b* 21 March 1916; *m* 1942, Barbara; two *s* one *d*. *Educ*: St Olave's; Jesus Coll., Cambridge. Chairman of ICI Companies in India, 1964–68; Chm., ICI (Export) Ltd and Gen. Manager, Internat. Coordination, ICI Ltd, 1968–78; Dir, ICI Americas Ltd, 1974–77; Dep. Chm., Ozalid Gp Holdings Ltd, 1975–77. Chairman: Process Plant EDC, 1979–83; Peter Brotherhood, 1980–83. President: Bengal Chamber of Commerce and Industry, and Associated Chambers of Commerce and Industry of India, 1967–68; British and S Asian Trade Assoc., 1978–83. Councillor, RIIA, 1968–77. *Address*: 11 Middle Avenue, Farnham, Surrey GU9 8JL. *T*: Farnham 715864. *Clubs*: Oriental; Bengal (Calcutta).

PITTS CRICK, R.; *see* Crick, Ronald P.

PITTS-TUCKER, Robert St John, CBE 1975; *b* 24 June 1909; *e s* of Walter Greame Pitts-Tucker, Solicitor, and Frances Elsie Wallace; *m* 1942, Joan Margery, *d* of Frank Furnivall, Civil Engineer, India, and Louisa Cameron Lees; three *s* one *d*. *Educ*: Haileybury (Schol.); Clare Coll., Cambridge (Schol.). 1st cl. Class. Tripos, Pts I and II, 1930 and 1931. Asst Master, Shrewsbury Sch., 1931–44; Headmaster, Pocklington Sch., 1945–66; Dep. Sec. to HMC and HMA, 1966–69, Sec., 1970–74. Mem., House of Laity, Church Assembly, 1956–70; St Albans diocese: Reader; Vice-Pres. of Synod, 1976–79; Member: ER Yorks Educn Cttee, 1946–66; Herts Educn Cttee, 1974–85; Vice-Chm., Yorks Rural Community Council, 1949–65; Mem., Secondary Schools Examination Council, 1954–57. Governor: Mill Hill Sch.; Haileybury. Mem., GBA Exec. Cttee, 1975–80. *Recreations*: country walks, listening to music, gardening. *Address*: Hillside, Toms Hill Road, Aldbury, Tring, Herts HP23 5SA. *Clubs*: Royal Commonwealth Society, East India, Devonshire, Sports and Public Schools.

PIX WESTON, John; *see* Weston, J. P.

PIXLEY, Sir Neville (Drake), Kt 1976; MBE (mil.) 1944; VRD 1941; company director; *b* 21 Sept. 1905; *s* of Arthur and Florence Pixley; *m* 1938, Lorna, *d* of Llewellyn Stephens; three *d*. *Educ*: C of E Grammar Sch., Brisbane. FCIT. Served RANR, 1920–63; War Service, Comd Corvettes, 1939–46 (Comdr 1945). Macdonald, Hamilton & Co. (P&O agents), 1922–59, Managing Partner, 1949–59; Chm., P&O Lines of Australia, 1960–70; Director: Burns Philp & Co. Ltd, 1962–80; Mauri Brothers & Thomson Ltd, 1970–77; NSW Boards of Advice: Nat. Bank of Australasia Ltd, 1970–77; Elder Smith Goldsborough Mort Ltd, 1970–76. Chm. Australian Cttee, Lloyd's Register of Shipping, 1967–80. ADC to King George VI and to the Queen, 1951–54. Vice Chancellor, 1978–, and Receiver-Gen., 1963–, Order of St John in Australia; KStJ 1963; GCStJ 1984. Pres., Royal Humane Soc. of NSW. *Recreation*: tennis. *Address*: 23 Carlotta Road, Double Bay, Sydney, NSW 2028, Australia. *T*: 3275354. *Clubs*: Union, Australian (Sydney); Queensland (Qld).

See also N. S. Pixley.

PIXLEY, Norman Stewart, CMG 1970; MBE 1941; VRD 1927; retired company director; Dean of the Consular Corps of Queensland, 1965–72; Hon. Consul for the Netherlands, 1948–72; *b* Brisbane, 3 May 1898; 2nd *s* of Arthur and Florence Pixley; *m* 1931, Grace Josephine, *d* of Arthur and Grace Spencer; twin *s* one *d*. *Educ*: Bowen House Sch.; Brisbane Grammar School. Served in RANR, 1913–46; Comdr, RANR, retd. Councillor, National Trust of Queensland; Pres., Qld Lawn Tennis Assoc., 1948–52; Pres., Brisbane Chamber of Commerce, 1952–53; Leader of Aust. Delegn to British Commonwealth Chambers of Commerce Conf., 1951; founded Qld Div. of Navy League, 1953 (Pres. until 1969). FRHistSoc Qld 1965 (Pres. 1968–83). Kt, Order of Orange Nassau, 1964. *Publications*: papers on Australian history in Jl of Royal Hist. Soc. Qld, etc. *Recreations*: tennis, yachting, golf. *Address*: 1/16 Dovercourt Road, Toowong, Queensland 4066, Australia. *T*: 701150. *Clubs*: Queensland, United Service, Indooroopilly Golf (Qld).

See also Sir Neville Pixley.

PIZEY, Admiral Sir (Charles Thomas) Mark, GBE 1957 (KBE 1953); CB 1942; DSO 1942; idc; RN retired; DL; *b* 1899; *s* of late Rev. C. E. Pizey, Mark and Huntspill, Somerset; *m* Phyllis, *d* of Alfred D'Angibau; two *d*. Served European War, 1914–18, Midshipman, Revenge, 1916–18; Lieut, 1920; HMS Danae Special Service Squadron World Cruise, 1921–22; Flag Lieut to Vice-Admiral Sir Howard Kelly, 2nd in command Mediterranean Fleet, 1929–30; Destroyer Commands Mediterranean and Home Fleets, 1930–39; War of 1939–45: Captain, 1939; Commanded HMS Ausonia, Atlantic Patrol and Convoys, 1939–40. Captain (D) 21st Destoyer Flotilla in HMS Campbell, Nore Command, Channel and North Sea Operations, 1940–42 (CB, DSO, despatches twice); commanded HMS Tyne and Chief Staff Officer to Rear-Admiral Destroyers, Home Fleet, Russian convoys, 1942–43 (bar to DSO); Director of Operations (Home) Admiralty Naval Staff, 1944–45; Chief of Staff to C-in-C Home Fleet, 1946; Imperial Defence Coll., 1947; Rear-Admiral, 1948; Chief of UK Services Liaison Staff, Australia, 1948–49; Flag Officer Commanding First Cruiser Squadron, 1950–51; Vice-Admiral, 1951; Chief of Naval Staff and Commander-in-Chief, Indian Navy, 1951–55; Admiral, 1954; Commander-in-Chief, Plymouth, 1955–58, retired. DL County of Somerset, 1962. *Address*: 1 St Ann's Drive, Burnham on Sea, Somerset.

PIZZEY, Erin Patria Margaret; *see* Shapiro, E. P. M.

PLACE, Rear-Adm. (Basil Charles) Godfrey, VC 1944; CB 1970; DSC 1943; Lay Observer, 1975–78; *b* 19 July 1921; *s* of late Major C. G. M. Place, DSO, MC, and late Mrs Place; *m* 1943, Althea Annington, *d* of late Harry Tickler, Grimsby; one *s* two *d*.

Educ: The Grange, Folkestone; RNC, Dartmouth. Midshipman, 1939; 10th and 12th submarine flotillas, 1941–43; Lieut, 1942; Comdr, 1952; HMS Glory (801 Sqn), 1952–53; Comdg HMS Tumult, 1955–56; Exec. Officer, HMS Theseus, 1956–57; HMS Corunna, 1957–58; Captain, 1958; Chief SO to Flag Officer Aircraft Carriers, 1958–60; Deputy Director of Air Warfare, 1960–62; HMS Rothesay and Captain (D), 25th Escort Squadron, 1962–63; HMS Ganges, 1963–65; HMS Albion, 1966–67; Adm. Comdg Reserves, and Dir-Gen., Naval Recruiting, 1968–70. Chm., VC and GC Assoc., 1971–. Polish Cross of Valour, 1941. *Address:* The Old Bakery, Corton Denham, Sherborne, Dorset.

PLAIDY, Jean; *see* Hibbert, Eleanor.

PLAISTER, Sir Sydney, Kt 1980; CBE 1972; FRICS; chartered quantity surveyor, since 1930; *b* 15 Jan. 1909; *s* of Herbert Plaister; *m* 1937, Coralie Fraser Steele; one *s* one *d*. *Educ:* Acton and Chiswick Polytechnic; College of Estate Management. Partner, L. C. Wakeman & Partners, 1942, Consultant, 1977. Chairman, Solihull Conservative Assoc., 1951–53 and 1957; West Midlands Conservative Council: Hon. Treasurer, 1967–73; Chairman, 1973–76; President, 1980–83; Pres., Midlands Central Conservative Euro-constituency Council, 1985– (Chm., 1978–85); Mem. Exec. Cttee, Nat. Union of Conservative Associations, 1967–82. Freeman, City of London, 1981; Liveryman, Worshipful Co. of Glaziers, 1982. *Recreations:* gardening, music, travel. *Address:* Turnpike Close, Old Warwick Road, Lapworth, Warwickshire B94 6AP. *T:* Lapworth 2792.

PLASKETT, Maj.-Gen. Frederick Joseph, CB 1980; MBE 1966; FCIT; Director General and Chief Executive, Road Haulage Association, since 1981; *b* 23 Oct. 1926; *s* of Frederick Joseph Plaskett and Grace Mary Plaskett; *m* 1st, 1950, Heather (*née* Kington) (*d* 1982); four *d*; 2nd, 1984, Mrs Patricia Joan Healy. Commnd infantry, 1946; RASC, 1951; RCT, 1965; regimental and staff appts, India, Korea, Nigeria, Malaya, Germany and UK; Student, Staff Coll., Camberley, 1958; Jt Services Staff Coll., 1964; Instr, Staff Coll., Camberley, 1966–68; Management Coll., Henley, 1969; RCDS, 1975; Dir of Movements (Army), 1975–78; Dir Gen., Transport and Movements (Army), 1978–81, retired. Col Comdt, RCT, 1981–. Mem., British Railways Bd, London Midland Region, 1986–. Director: Foden Trucks (Paccar UK), 1981–; RHA Insce Services Ltd, 1982–; British Road Federation, 1982–. Comr, Royal Hosp., Chelsea, 1985–. *Recreations:* fishing, sailing, gardening. *Address:* c/o National Westminster Bank, Blue Boar Row, Salisbury, Wilts. *Clubs:* Army and Navy; Royal Automobile.

PLASTOW, Sir David (Arnold Stuart), Kt 1986; Managing Director and Chief Executive, Vickers PLC, since 1980 (Director, since 1975); *b* Grimsby, 9 May 1932; *s* of James Stuart Plastow and Marie Plastow; *m* 1954, Barbara Ann May; one *s* one *d*. *Educ:* Culford Sch., Bury St Edmunds. Apprentice, Vauxhall Motors Ltd, 1950; joined Rolls-Royce Ltd, Motor Car Div., Crewe, Sept. 1958; apptd Marketing Dir, Motor Car Div., 1967; Managing Director: Motor Car Div., 1971; Rolls-Royce Motors Ltd, 1972; Gp Man. Dir, 1974–80. Regional Dir, Lloyds Bank, 1974–76; non-executive Director: GKN, 1978–84; Legal & General Gp Plc, 1985–. Mem., European Adv. Council, Tenneco, 1984–86; Bd Mem., Tenneco Inc., 1985–. Vice-Pres., Inst. of Motor Industry; Pres., SMMT, 1976–77, 1977–78 (Dep. Pres., 1978–79, 1979–80); Pres., Motor Industry Res. Assoc., 1978–81; Chm., Grand Council, Motor and Cycle Trades Benevolent Fund, 1976–78. Patron, Coll. of Aeronautical and Automobile Engrg, 1972–79. Chm, Council, Industrial Soc., 1983– (Mem., 1981–83); Member: Council, CBI; BOTB, 1980–83; Engineering Council, 1980–83; Offshore Energy Technology Bd, 1985–; Bd of Companions, BIM (Pres. S Cheshire Br.); Council, Regular Forces Employment Assoc. Chm. Governors, Culford Sch., 1979–. Pres., Crewe Alexandra FC, 1975–82. Liveryman, Worshipful Co. of Coachmakers & Coach Harness Makers. FRSA. Young Business Man of the Year Award, The Guardian, 1976. Hon. DSc Cranfield, 1978. *Recreations:* golf, music. *Address:* Vickers PLC, Vickers House, Millbank Tower, Millbank, SW1P 4RA. *T:* 01–828 7777. *Club:* Royal and Ancient (St Andrews).

PLATER, Alan Frederick, FRSL 1985; freelance writer, since 1960; *b* 15 April 1935; *s* of Herbert Richard Plater and Isabella Scott Plater; *m* 1st, 1958, Shirley Johnson (marr. diss. 1985); two *s* one *d*; 2nd, 1986, Shirley Rubinstein; three step *s*. *Educ:* Pickering Road Jun. Sch., Hull; Kingston High Sch., Hull; King's Coll., Newcastle upon Tyne. ARIBA (now lapsed). Trained as architect and worked for short time in the profession before becoming full-time writer in 1960; has written extensively for radio, television, films and theatre; semi-regular contributor to Punch and has also written for The Guardian, Listener, New Statesman, etc. Works include: *theatre:* A Smashing Day (also televised); Close the Coalhouse Door (Writers' Guild Radio Award, 1972); And a Little Love Besides; Swallows on the Water; Trinity Tales; The Fosdyke Saga; Fosdyke Two; On Your Way, Riley!; Skyhooks; A Foot on the Earth; Prez; *films:* The Virgin and the Gypsy; It Shouldn't Happen to a Vet; Priest of Love; *television:* plays: So Long Charlie; See the Pretty Lights; To See How Far It Is (trilogy); Land of Green Ginger; Willow Cabins; The Party of the First Part; The Blacktoft Diaries; Thank You, Mrs Clinkscales; biographies: The Crystal Spirit; Pride of our Alley; Edward Lear—at the edge of the sand?; Coming Through; series and serials: Z Cars; Softly Softly; Shoulder to Shoulder; Trinity Tales; The Good Companions; The Consultant; The Beiderbecke Affair; *radio:* The Journal of Vasilije Bogdanovic (Sony Radio Award, 1983). Hon. Fellow, Humberside Coll. of Higher Educn, 1983; Hon. DLitt Hull, 1985. RTS Writer's Award, 1984/85. *Publications:* The Beiderbecke Affair, 1985; The Beiderbecke Tapes, 1986; plays and shorter pieces in various anthologies. *Recreations:* reading, theatre, snooker, jazz, dog-walking, talking and listening. *Address:* c/o Margaret Ramsay Ltd, 14A Goodwin's Court, St Martin's Lane, WC2N 4LL. *T:* 01–240 0691. *Clubs:* Dramatists', Connaught, Ronnie Scott's.

PLATT, family name of **Baroness Platt of Writtle.**

PLATT OF WRITTLE, Baroness *cr* 1981 (Life Peer), of Writtle in the County of Essex; **Beryl Catherine Platt,** CBE 1978; DL; Chairman, Equal Opportunities Commission, since 1983; *b* 18 April 1923; *d* of Ernest and Dorothy Myatt; *m* 1949, Stewart Sydney Platt; one *s* one *d*. *Educ:* Westcliff High School; Girton Coll., Cambridge (MA). CEng, FRAeS. Technical Assistant, Hawker Aircraft, 1943–46; BEA, 1946–49. Mem., Engineering Council, 1981–. Member, Chelmsford RDC, 1958–74. Member, Essex CC, 1965–85: Alderman, 1969–74; Vice-Chm., 1980–83; Chm., Education Cttee, 1971–80. Mem., Adv. Cttee on Women's Employment, 1984–. Vice-Chairman: Technician Education Council, 1979–81; London Regional Adv. Council for Technology Education, 1975–81. Member: CNAA, 1973–79; Council, CGLI, 1974–; Cambridge Univ. Appointments Bd, 1975–79; ACC Education Cttee, 1974–80; Council, Careers Research and Adv. Centre, 1983–; Council, RSA, 1983–; Court of Essex Univ., 1964–, and of City Univ., 1969–78. Trustee, Homerton Coll., 1970–81. Pres., Chelmsford Engineering Soc., 1979–80. DL Essex, 1983. FRSA. Hon. FIMechE 1984; Hon. FITD 1984. Hon. DSc: City, 1984; Salford, 1984; Cranfield, 1985; Hon. DUniv: Open Univ., 1985; Essex, 1985; Hon. DEng Bradford, 1985; Hon. DTech Brunel, 1986. *Recreations:* cooking, gardening, reading. *Address:* House of Lords, SW1; Equal Opportunities Commission, Overseas House, Quay Street, Manchester M3 3HN. *T:* 061–833 9244.

PLATT, Prof. Colin Peter Sherard; Professor of History, Southampton University, since 1983; *b* 11 Nov. 1934; twin *s* of James Westlake Platt and Veronica Norma Hope Arnold; *m* 1963, Valerie Ashforth; two *s* two *d*. *Educ:* Collyers Grammar School, Horsham; Balliol College, Oxford (BA 1st cl., MA); Leeds University (PhD). Research Assistant in Medieval Archaeology, Leeds Univ., 1960–62, Lectr, 1962–64; Lectr, Sen. Lectr and Reader in History, Southampton Univ., 1964–83. *Publications:* The Monastic Grange in Medieval England, 1969; Medieval Southampton: the port and trading community AD 1000–1600, 1973; (with Richard Coleman-Smith) Excavations in Medieval Southampton 1953–1969, 2 vols, 1975; The English Medieval Town, 1976; Medieval England: a social history and archaeology from the Conquest to 1600 AD, 1978; The Atlas of Medieval Man, 1979; The Parish Churches of Medieval England, 1981; The Castle in Medieval England and Wales, 1982; The Abbeys and Priories of Medieval England, 1984; Medieval Britain from the Air, 1984; The Traveller's Guide to Medieval England, 1985; The National Trust Guide to late Medieval and Renaissance Britain, 1986. *Recreations:* reading novels, visiting medieval antiquities. *Address:* Department of History, University of Southampton, Southampton SO9 5NH. *T:* Southampton 559122.

See also D. C. M. Platt.

PLATT, Prof. Desmond Christopher Martin; Professor of the History of Latin America, University of Oxford, since 1972; Fellow, since 1972, Senior Tutor, 1979–85, St Antony's College, Oxford; *b* 11 Nov. 1934; *s* of J. W. Platt, CBE; *m* 1st, 1958, Sarah Elizabeth Russell (marr. diss.); no *c*; 2nd, 1984, Sylvia Haanel Matthew. *Educ:* Collyer's Sch., Horsham; Balliol Coll., Oxford; Stanford Univ.; St Antony's Coll., Oxford. BA 1st cl. Hist. 1958, MA, DPhil 1962, Oxon; FRHistS. Asst Principal, Min. of Aviation, 1960–61; Asst Lectr, Edinburgh Univ., 1961–62; Lectr, Exeter Univ., 1962–68; Fellow, Queens' Coll., Cambridge and Univ. Lectr in Latin American History, 1969–72; Director: Centre of Latin Amer. Studies, Univ. of Cambridge, 1971–72; Latin American Centre, Univ. of Oxford, 1972–83. Chm., Soc. for Latin American Studies, 1973–75. *Publications:* Finance, Trade and Politics in British Foreign Policy 1815–1914, 1968; The Cinderella Service: British Consuls since 1825, 1971; Latin America and British Trade 1806–1914, 1972; (ed) Business Imperialism: an inquiry based on British experience in Latin America before 1930, 1977; Foreign Finance in Continental Europe and the USA 1815–1870, 1984; (ed) Argentina, Australia and Canada: studies in comparative development 1870–1965, 1985; (ed) The Political Economy of Argentina 1880–1946, 1986; Britain's Investment Overseas on the Eve of the First World War: the use and abuse of numbers, 1986; The Most Obliging Man in Europe: life and times of the Oxford Scout, 1986. *Address:* 23 Park Town, Oxford OX2 6SN. *T:* Oxford 54908.

See also C. P. S. Platt.

PLATT, Eleanor Frances, QC 1982; a Recorder of the Crown Court, since 1982; *b* 6 May 1938; *er d* of Dr Maurice Leon Platt and Sara Platt (*née* Stein), Hove, Sussex; *m* 1963; two *c*. *Educ:* Hove County School for Girls; University College London. LLB 1959. Called to the Bar, Gray's Inn, 1960. *Recreations:* the arts, travel, skiing. *Address:* 6 Pump Court, Temple, EC4. *T:* 01–583 6013.

PLATT, Sir Harry, 1st Bt, *cr* 1958; Kt 1948; MD (Victoria), MS (London), FRCS; Hon. FACS; Hon. FRCS (Canada); Hon. FRCSE; Hon. FDS; Professor of Orthopædic Surgery, University of Manchester, 1939–51, now Emeritus Professor; President, National Fund for Research into Crippling Diseases, since 1970; Hon. President: International Federation of Surgical Colleges (Pres., 1958–66); Société Internationale de Chirurgie Orthopédique et de Traumatologie; *b* Thornham, Lancashire, 7 Oct. 1886; *e s* of Ernest Platt; *m* 1916, Gertrude Sarah (*d* 1980), 2nd *d* of Richard Turney; one *s* four *d*. *Educ:* Victoria Univ. of Manchester. University Gold Medal. MB, BS (London), 1909; Gold Medal for thesis MD (Vic), 1921; Hunterian Prof. of Surgery and Pathology, RCS, 1921; post-graduate study in USA, 1913–14 (Boston, New York, etc). Captain RAMC (TF), 1915–19. Surgeon in charge of Special Military Surgical Centre (Orthopædic Hospital), Manchester. Consultant Adviser: Ministry of Health, 1940–63; Ministry of Labour, 1952–64. President: British Orthopædic Assoc., 1934–35; RCS, 1954–57; Central Council for the Disabled, 1969; Mem., Central Health Services Council, 1948–57. Hon. Degrees: DM Berne, 1954; Dr, Univ. of Paris, 1966; LLD: Univs of Manchester, 1955, Liverpool, 1955, Belfast, 1955, Leeds, 1965. KStJ 1972. *Publications:* monographs and articles on orthopædic surgery, medical education, hospital organisation, etc. *Recreations:* music, travel. *Heir:* *s* F(rank) Lindsey Platt, Barrister-at-Law [*b* 16 Jan. 1919; *m* 1951, Johanna Laenger]. *Address:* 14 Rusholme Gardens, Platt Lane, Manchester M14 5LS. *T:* 061–224 2427. *Clubs:* Travellers' (Life Mem.); St James's (Manchester).

See also Sir F. J. W. Williams, Bt.

PLATT, Norman, OBE 1985; Artistic Director of Kent Opera, since 1969; *b* 29 Aug. 1920; *s* of Edward Turner Platt and Emily Jane Platt; *m* 1st, 1942, Diana Franklin Clay; one *s* one *d*; 2nd, 1963, Johanna Sigrid Bishop; one *s* two *d*. *Educ:* Bury Grammar Sch.; King's Coll., Cambridge (BA). Principal: Sadler's Wells Opera, 1946–48; English Opera Group, 1948; Mem. Deller Consort, and freelance singer, actor, teacher and producer in Britain and Western Europe; founded Kent Opera, 1969. Hon. DCL Kent, 1981. *Publications:* translations of numerous songs and operas, incl. L'Incoronazione di Poppea, Don Giovanni and Fidelio; articles on musical subjects. *Recreations:* reading, looking at pictures. *Address:* Pembles Cross, Egerton, Ashford, Kent TN27 9EN. *T:* Egerton 406.

PLATT, Hon. Sir Peter, 2nd Bt *cr* 1959; Professor of Music, University of Sydney, since 1975; *b* 6 July 1924; *s* of Baron Platt (Life Peer), and of Margaret Irene, *d* of Arthur Charles Cannon; *S* to baronetcy of father, 1978; *m* 1948, Jean Halliday, *d* of late Charles Philip Brentnall, MC; one *s* two *d*. *Educ:* Abbotsholme School, Derbyshire; Magdalen Coll., Oxford; Royal College of Music. BMus 1950, MA, BLitt 1954, Oxon; FGSM 1973. Lectr and Sen. Lectr in Music, Univ. of Sydney, 1952–57; Professor of Music, Univ. of Otago, NZ, 1957–75. Served War of 1939–45 with RNVR (despatches). *Heir:* *s* Martin Philip Platt [*b* 9 March 1952; *m* 1971, Frances Corinne Moana, *d* of Trevor Samuel Conley; two *s* two *d*]. *Address:* 1 Ellison Place, Pymble, NSW 2073, Australia.

PLATT, Terence Charles; Assistant Under-Secretary of State and Director of Regimes and Services, Prison Department, Home Office, since 1982; *b* 22 Sept. 1936; *yr s* of Bertram Reginald Platt, QPM and Nina Platt; *m* 1959, Margaret Anne Cotmore; two *s*. *Educ:* St Olave's and St Saviour's Grammar School; Joint Services School for Linguists; Russian Interpreter. HM Immigration Officer, 1957; Asst Principal, Home Office, 1962; Principal, 1966; Cabinet Office, 1970; Principal Private Sec. to Sec. of State for NI (Rt Hon. William Whitelaw), 1972–73; Asst Sec., Home Office, 1973–81; Asst Under-Sec. of State and Princ. Estabt and Finance Officer, NI Office, 1981–82. *Publication:* New Directions in Prison Design (Wkg Party Report), 1985. *Recreations:* growing roses, photography, butterflies. *Address:* c/o Home Office, 50 Queen Anne's Gate, SW1H 9AT.

PLATT, Rev. William James; General Secretary, British and Foreign Bible Society, 1948–60; Consultant, 1960–61; retired, 1961; *b* 2 May 1893; *s* of James and Mary Platt; *m* 1921, Hilda Waterhouse (*d* 1975); one *d*. *Educ:* Rivington Grammar School; Didsbury Theological College, Manchester. Methodist Missionary in West Africa, 1916–30;

Chairman and General Superintendent, Methodist District of French West Africa, 1925–30; joined Bible Society Staff as Secretary for Equatorial Africa, 1930; since 1948 has travelled extensively as General Secretary of Bible Society. Chairman of Council, United Bible Societies, 1954–57. Hon. DD, Knox College, Toronto, Canada, 1954. Officer of the Order of Orange Nassau, 1954; Commander, National Order of the Ivory Coast Republic, 1985 (Officer, 1964). *Publications:* An African Prophet; From Fetish to Faith; Whose World?; Three Women in Central Asia; articles in religious and missionary publications. *Address:* Winton House, 51 Dedworth Road, Windsor, Berks SL4 5AZ. *T:* Windsor 840616. *Club:* Royal Commonwealth Society.

PLATTS-MILLS, John Faithful Fortescue, QC 1964; Barrister; *b* 4 Oct. 1906; *s* of John F. W. Mills and Dr Daisy Platts-Mills, Karori, Wellington, NZ; *m* 1936, Janet Katherine Cree; six *s*. *Educ:* Nelson College and Victoria University, NZ; Balliol College, Oxford (Rhodes Scholar). LLM (NZ), MA (1st Cl.), BCL Oxon. MP (Lab) Finsbury, 1945–48, (Lab Ind) 1948–50. Pilot Officer, RAF, 1940; "Bevin Boy", 1944; collier, 1945. Bencher, Inner Temple, 1970. Pres., Haldane Soc.; Vice-Pres., Internat. Assoc. of Democratic Lawyers; Mem. TGWU. *Address:* Cloisters, Temple, EC4. *T:* 01–583 9526; Terrible Down Farm, Halland, E Sussex. *T:* Halland 310. *Clubs:* Athenæum; Vincent's (Oxford); Leander.

PLAXTON, Ven. Cecil Andrew; Archdeacon of Wiltshire, 1951–74, now Archdeacon Emeritus of the Diocese of Salisbury; *b* 1902; *s* of Rev. J. W. Plaxton, Wells and Langport, Somerset; *m* 1929, Eleanor Joan Elisabeth Sowerby; one *s* (and one *d* decd). *Educ:* Magdalen College School, Oxford; St Edmund Hall, Oxford; Cuddesdon Theological College. BA 1924, MA 1928, Oxford; Deacon, 1926; Priest, 1927; Curate of Chard, 1926–28; Curate of St Martin, Salisbury, 1928–32; Vicar of Southbroom, Devizes, 1932–37; Vicar of Holy Trinity, Weymouth, 1937–51; Rural Dean of Weymouth, 1941–51; Rector of Pewsey, 1951–65; Canon of Salisbury and Prebend of Netheravon, 1949. Officiating Chaplain to the Forces, 1932–51. *Publication:* The Treasure of Salisbury: Life and Death of St Edmund of Abingdon, 1971, repr. 1980. *Recreations:* archæology and travelling, music. *Address:* 12 Castle Court, St John's Street, Devizes, Wilts. *T:* Devizes 3391.

PLAYER, Dr David Arnott, FRCPE, FRCPsych, FFCM; Director General, Health Education Council, since 1982; *b* 2 April 1927; *s* of John Player and Agnes Gray; *m* 1955, Anne Darragh; two *s*. *Educ:* Calder Street Sch.; Bellahouston Acad., Glasgow; Glasgow Univ. MB, ChB, DPH, DPM. House Surgeon, Dumfries and Galloway Royal Infirmary, 1950; Consultant in Dermatology and VD, RAMC (Far East), 1950–52; House Surgeon, Western Infirmary, Glasgow, 1952; House Physician, Bridge of Earn Hosp., 1952–53; House Surgeon (Obst., Gyn. and Paed.), Halifax Royal Infirmary, 1953–54; GP, W Cumberland and Dumfriesshire, 1954–59; Registrar (Infectious Diseases), Paisley Infectious Diseases Hosp., 1959–60; Asst MOH, Dumfriesshire, 1960–62; Registrar (Psychiatry), Crighton Royal Hosp., Dumfries, 1962–64; MOH, Dumfries Burgh, 1964–70; MO (Mental Health Div.), SHHD and Med. and Psych. Adviser to Sec. of State for Scotland on Scottish Prison and Borstal Service, 1970–73; Dir, Scottish Health Educn Group, 1973–82. Hon. Vis. Prof., Dept of Clinical Epidemiology and Gen. Practice, Royal Free Hosp. Sch. of Medicine, 1983–. *Publications:* articles in Health Bulletin, Internat. Jl of Health Educn, Scottish Trade Union Review. *Recreations:* golf, cycling. *Address:* c/o Health Education Council, 78 New Oxford Street, WC1A 1AH.

PLAYER, Denis Sydney, CBE 1967; Hon. President, Newall Engineering Group, 1973 (Chairman 1962–73; Deputy Chairman, 1955); Chairman, Newall Machine Tool Co. Ltd, 1964–73; *b* 13 Nov. 1913; *s* of Sydney Player and Minnie Emma Rowe; *m* 1940, Phyllis Ethel Holmes Brown (*d* 1975); three *d*. *Educ:* England; Worcester Acad., Mass. Apprenticed to Newall Engrg Co. Ltd, 1930; spent a year with Federal Produce Corp., RI, before rejoining Newall Engrg on Sales side; Man. Dir, Optical Measuring Tools, 1940; formed Sales Div. for whole of Newall Engrg Gp, 1945. Joined Royal Artillery, 1939; invalided out, 1940. CEng, FIProdE, FRSA. High Sheriff of Rutland, 1970–71. *Recreations:* yachting, fishing, shooting. *Address:* c/o National Westminster Bank, 8 Bennetts Hill, Birmingham B2 5RT. *Clubs:* Royal Automobile, Royal Ocean Racing; Royal Burnham Yacht.

PLAYER, Gary (Jim); professional golfer, since 1953; *b* Johannesburg, 1 Nov. 1935; *s* of Francis Harry Audley Player and late Muriel Marie Ferguson; *m* 1957, Vivienne, *d* of Jacob Wynand Verwey; two *s* four *d*. *Educ:* King Edward Sch., Johannesburg. Won first, Dunlop tournament, 1956; major championship wins include: British Open, 1959, 1968, 1974; US Masters, 1961, 1974, 1978; US PGA, 1962, 1972; US Open, 1965; S African Open, thirteen times, 1956–81; S African PGA, 1959, 1960, 1969, 1979, 1982; Australian Open, seven times, 1958–74; Tooth Gold Coast Classic, Australia, 1981; Johnnie Walker Trophy, Spain, 1984; World Match Play Tournament, 1965, 1966, 1968, 1971, 1973. *Address:* Mark McCormack Agency, 58 Queen Anne Street, W1M 0DX.

PLAYFAIR, Sir Edward (Wilder), KCB 1957 (CB 1949); *b* 17 May 1909; *s* of late Dr Ernest Playfair; *m* 1941, Dr Mary Lois Rae; three *d*. *Educ:* Eton; King's Coll., Cambridge (Hon. Fellow, 1986). Inland Revenue, 1931–34; HM Treasury, 1934–46 and 1947–56 (Control Office for Germany and Austria, 1946–47); Permanent Under-Secretary of State for War, 1956–59; Permanent Sec., Ministry of Defence, 1960–61. Chairman, International Computers and Tabulators Ltd, 1961–65; Director: National Westminster Bank Ltd, 1961–79; Glaxo Hldgs Ltd, 1961–79; Tunnel Holdings Ltd, 1966–80; Equity and Law Life Assce Soc. plc, 1968–83. Governor, Imperial Coll. of Science and Technology, 1958–83 (Fellow, 1972); College Cttee of UCL, 1961–77 (Hon. Fellow, UCL, 1969); Chm., National Gallery, 1972–74 (Trustee, 1967–74). Hon. FBCS. *Address:* 62 Coniger Road, Fulham, SW6 3TA. *T:* 01–736 3194. *Club:* Brooks's.

PLAYFORD, Jonathan Richard; QC 1982; a Recorder, since 1985; *b* 6 Aug. 1940; *s* of Cecil R. B. Playford and Euphrasia J. Playford; *m* 1978, Jill Margaret Dunlop; one *s* one *d*. *Educ:* Eton Coll.; London Univ. (LLB). Called to the Bar, Inner Temple, 1962. *Recreations:* music, country pursuits, golf. *Address:* 2 Harcourt Buildings, Temple, EC4Y 9DB. *T:* 01–583 9020. *Clubs:* Garrick, Royal Automobile; Huntercombe Golf (Henley).

PLEASENCE, Donald; actor; *b* 5 Oct. 1919; *s* of late Thomas Stanley and of Alice Pleasence; *m* 1st, 1940, Miriam Raymond; two *d*; 2nd, 1959, Josephine Crombie (marr. diss. 1970); two *d*; 3rd, 1970, Meira Shore; one *d*. *Educ:* The Grammar School, Ecclesfield, Yorkshire. Made first stage appearance at the Playhouse Theatre, Jersey, CI, May 1939; first London appearance, Twelfth Night, Arts Theatre, 1942. Served with RAF, 1942–46 (Flt Lieut); shot down and taken prisoner, 1944. Returned to stage in The Brothers Karamazov, Lyric, Hammersmith, 1946; Huis Clos, Arts Theatre; Birmingham Repertory Theatre, 1948–50; Bristol Old Vic, 1951; Right Side Up, and Saint's Day, Arts Theatre, 1951; Ziegfeld Theatre, New York (with L. Olivier Co.), 1951; played in own play, Ebb Tide, Edinburgh Festival and Royal Court Theatre, 1952; Stratford-on-Avon season, 1953. *Other London Appearances:* Hobson's Choice, 1952; Antony and Cleopatra, 1953; The Rules of the Game, 1955; The Lark, 1956; Misalliance, 1957; Restless Heart, 1960; The Caretaker, London, 1960, New York, 1961; Poor Bitos, London and New York; The Man in the Glass Booth, St Martin's, 1967 (London Variety Award for Stage Actor of the Year, 1968), New York, 1968–69; Tea Party, The Basement, London, 1970; Reflections, Theatre Royal, Haymarket, 1980; 1970; Wise Child, NY, 1972. Many television appearances, incl. The Barchester Chronicles, 1982, The Falklands Factor, 1983. Named Actor of the Year, 1958. *Films include:* The Beachcomber, Heart of a Child, Manuela, The Great Escape, Doctor Crippen, The Caretaker, The Greatest Story Ever Told, The Hallelujah Trail, Fantastic Voyage, Cul-de-Sac, The Night of the Generals, Eye of the Devil, Will Penny, The Mad Woman of Chaillot, Sleep is Lovely, Arthur! Arthur?, THX 1138, Outback, Soldier Blue, The Pied Piper, The Jerusalem File, Kidnapped, Innocent Bystanders, Death Line, Henry VIII, Wedding in White, The Rainbow Boys, Malachi's Cove, Mutations, Tales From Beyond the Grave, The Black Windmill, Escape to Witch Mountain, I Don't Want to be Born, Journey Into Fear, Hearts of the West, Trial by Combat, The Last Tycoon, The Passover Plot, The Eagle has Landed, Golden Rod, The Devil's Men, Tomorrow Never Comes, Telefon, Sgt Pepper's Lonely Hearts Club Band, Halloween, Power Play, Dracula, Halloween II, The Monster Club, Escape from New York, Race for the Yankee Zephyr, Frankenstein's Great Aunt Tilly, A Rare Breed, Warrior of the Lost World, Creepers, The Ambassador, The Corsican Brothers, Master of the Game, Arch of Triumph, Phenomenon, Honour Thy Father, Nothing Underneath. *Recreation:* talking too much. *Address:* 7 West Eaton Place Mews, SW1. *Clubs:* White Elephant, Burkes.

PLEASS, Sir Clement (John), KCMG 1955 (CMG 1950); KCVO 1956; KBE 1953; MA; retired as Governor; *b* 19 November 1901; *s* of J. W. A. Pleass, Tiverton, Devon; *m* 1927, Sybil, *d* of Alwyn Child, Gerrard's Cross; one *s*. *Educ:* Royal Masonic School; Selwyn College, Cambridge. Joined Colonial Administrative Service, Jan. 1924; served in Nigeria, 1924–56. Lieut-Governor, 1952–54, Governor, 1954–56, Eastern Region of Nigeria. Formerly Mem., Colonial Development Corporation. *Recreation:* golf. *Address:* Higher Barton, Malborough, near Kingsbridge, S Devon. *Club:* Royal Commonwealth Society.

PLENDERLEITH, Harold James, CBE 1959; MC 1918; BSc, PhD; FRSE; FBA 1973; FSA; FMA; Director, International Centre for the Study of the Preservation and Restoration of Cultural Property (created by UNESCO), 1959–71, now Emeritus; Vice-President, International Institute for the Conservation of Museum Objects, 1958 (President, 1965–67, Hon. Fellow 1971); Member, Directory Board of Museum Laboratories Committee, International Council of Museums; *b* 19 Sept. 1898; *s* of Robert James Plenderleith, FEIS; *m* 1926, Elizabeth K. S. Smyth (*d* 1982). *Educ:* Dundee Harris Acad.; St Andrews Univ. Scientific Asst, Dept of Scientific and Indust. Res., attached to British Museum, Bloomsbury, 1924; Asst Keeper, British Museum, 1927; Keeper, Research Lab., British Museum, 1949–59. Mem., Hon. Scientific Adv. Cttee, Nat. Gallery, 1935–81 (Chm., 1944–58); Professor of Chemistry, Royal Academy of Arts, London, 1936–58. Hon. Treas. Internat. Inst. for Conservation of Museum Objects, 1950–58. Rhind Lecturer (Edinburgh) 1954. Gold Medal, Society of Antiquaries of London, 1964; Gold Medal, Univ. of Young Nam, Tae Gu, Korea, 1970; Bronze Medal, UNESCO, 1971; Conservation Service Award, US Dept of the Interior, 1976; ICCROM International Oscar, Rome, 1979. Hon. LLD St Andrews. *Publications:* The Preservation of Antiquities, 1934; The Conservation of Prints, Drawings and Manuscripts, 1937; The Preservation of Leather Bookbindings, 1946; The Conservation of Antiquities and Works of Art, 1956 (2nd edn with A. E. A. Werner, 1971); papers on allied subjects and on technical examinations of museum specimens in museum and scientific journals. *Recreations:* art and music. *Address:* Riverside, 17 Rockfield Crescent, Dundee DD2 1JF. *T:* Dundee 641552. *Club:* Athenæum.

PLENDERLEITH, Thomas Donald, RE 1961 (ARE 1951); Senior Art Master, St Nicholas Grammar School, Northwood, since 1956; *b* 11 March 1921; *s* of James Plenderleith and Georgina Ellis; *m* 1949, Joyce Rogers; one *s*. *Educ:* St Clement Danes; Ealing Sch. of Art; Hornsey Sch. of Art. Pilot, Bomber Command, RAF, 1941–46. Art Master, Pinner County Grammar Sch., 1948–56. Art Teacher's Diploma, 1947. *Recreations:* cricket, badminton. *Address:* 46 Sylvia Avenue, Hatch End, Mddx. *T:* 01–428 5019.

PLEVEN, René Jean; French Statesman; Compagnon de la Libération, 1943; Commandeur du Mérite Maritime, 1945; Député des Côtes-du-Nord, 1945–73; Président du Conseil Général des Côtes-du-Nord, 1949; Président du Conseil Régional de Bretagne, 1974; *b* 15 April 1901; *s* of Colonel Jules Pleven; *m* 1924, Anne Bompard (*d* 1966); two *d*. *Educ:* Faculté de Droit de Paris (LLD); Ecole Libre des Sciences Politiques. Company Director. Deputy chief of French Air Mission to USA, 1939. French National Committee and Comité Français de Libération Nationale (Finances, Colonies, Foreign Affairs), 1941–44; Minister: of Colonies (Provisional Government), 1944; of Finances, 1944–46; of Defence, Nov. 1949 and 1952–54; Président du Conseil, July 1950, Aug. 1951–Jan. 1952; Vice-Président du Conseil, Feb. 1951; Ministre des Affaires Etrangères, 1958; Délégué à l'Assemblée parlementaire européenne, and Chm., Liberal Gp of this Assembly, 1956–69; Ministre de la Justice, et Garde des Sceaux, 1969–73. Grand Officer Order of Leopold, 1945; Grand Cross: Le Million d'éléphants, 1949; Etoile Polaire, 1950; Orange-Nassau, 1950; Dannebrog, 1950; Nicham Alaouite, 1950; Vietnam, 1951; Order of Merit of the Republic of Italy, 1972; National Order of Ivory Coast, 1972; Order of Central African Republic, 1972; Hon GBE, 1972. *Publications:* Les Ouvriers de l'agriculture anglaise depuis la guerre, 1925; Avenir de la Bretagne, 1962. *Recreation:* fishing. *Address:* 12 rue Chateaubriand, Dinan (Côtes-du-Nord), France.

PLEYDELL-BOUVERIE, family name of **Earl of Radnor.**

PLIATZKY, Sir Leo, KCB 1977 (CB 1972); Civil Service, 1947–80; *b* 1919; *m* 1948, Marian Jean Elias (*d* 1979); one *s* one *d*. *Educ:* Manchester Grammar Sch.; City of London Sch.; Corpus Christi Coll., Oxford (Hon. Fellow, 1980). First Cl. Classical Honour Mods, 1939. Served in RAOC and REME, 1940–45 (despatches). First Cl. Philosophy, Politics and Economics, 1946. Research Sec., Fabian Soc., 1946–47; Min. of Food, 1947–50; HM Treasury, 1950–77; Under-Sec., 1967; Dep. Sec., 1971; Second Permanent Sec., 1976; Permanent Sec., Dept of Trade, 1977; retired 1979, retained for special duties, 1979–80. Mem., British Airways Bd, 1980–84 (Non-exec. Dir, 1984–85); Director: Associated Communications Corporation Ltd, 1980–82; Central Independent Television plc, 1981–; Ultramar Co. plc, 1981–. Vis. Prof., City Univ., 1980–84; Associate Fellow, LSE, 1982–85; Sen. Res. Fellow, PSI, 1983–84. Trustee, History of Parliament Trust, 1982–, Treasurer 1983–. FRSA. Hon. DLitt Salford, 1986. *Publications:* Getting and Spending, 1982, rev. edn 1984; Paying and Choosing, 1985. *Address:* 27 River Court, Upper Ground, SE1. *T:* 01–928 3667. *Club:* Reform.

PLIMMER, Sir Clifford (Ulric), KBE 1967; *b* 25 July 1905; *s* of late Arthur Bloomfield Plimmer and Jessie Elizabeth (*née* Townsend); *m* 1935, Letha May (*née* Port); three *s* (and one *s* decd). *Educ:* Scots Coll., Wellington; Victoria Univ. of Wellington. Office Junior, 1922, Wright, Stephenson & Co. Ltd (stock and station agents, woolbrokers, gen. merchants, manufrs, car dealers, insurance agents, etc), retired as Chm. and Man. Dir, 1970. Director: McKechnie Bros. (NZ) Ltd; James Smith Ltd; Tradespan NZ Ltd; owns and operates a number of sheep and cattle farms in New Zealand. Nat. Patron, Intellectually Handicapped Children's Soc. Inc.; Member: Dr Barnardos in NZ; Wellington Med. Res.

Foundn. *Address:* PO Box 10218, Wellington, New Zealand. *Clubs:* Wellington; Northern, (Auckland); Hutt (Lower Hutt, NZ).

PLIMSOLL, Sir James, AC 1978; Kt 1962; CBE 1956; Governor of Tasmania, since 1982; *b* Sydney, New South Wales, 25 April 1917; *s* of late James E. and Jessie Plimsoll; unmarried. *Educ:* Sydney High School; University of Sydney. Economic Department, Bank of New South Wales, 1938–42; Australian Army, 1942–47. Australian Delegation, Far Eastern Commission, 1945–48; Australian Representative, United Nations Commission for the Unification and Rehabilitation of Korea, 1950–52; Assistant Secretary, Department of External Affairs, Canberra, 1953–59; Australian Permanent Representative at the United Nations, 1959–63; Australian High Commissioner to India and Ambassador to Nepal, 1963–65; Secretary of Dept of External Affairs, Australia, 1965–70; Australian Ambassador to USA, 1970–74, to the USSR and Mongolia, 1974–77, to Belgium, Luxembourg, and the European Communities, 1977–80; High Commissioner for Australia in UK, 1980–81; Australian Ambassador to Japan, 1981–82. Hon. DScEcon Sydney, 1984. KStJ 1982. *Address:* Government House, Hobart, Tasmania 7000, Australia.

PLOURDE, Most Rev. Joseph Aurèle; *see* Ottawa, Archbishop of, (RC).

PLOUVIEZ, Peter William; General Secretary, British Actors' Equity Association, since 1974; *b* 30 July 1931; *s* of Charles and Emma Plouviez; *m* 1978, Alison Dorothy Macrae; two *d* (by previous marr.). *Educ:* Sir George Monoux Grammar Sch.; Hastings Grammar Sch. Greater London Organiser, NUBE, 1955–60; Asst Sec., Equity, 1960, Asst Gen. Sec., Equity, 1964. Contested (Lab), St Marylebone bye-election, 1963; Councillor, St Pancras, 1962–65. Chairman: Radio and Television Safeguards Cttee, 1974–; Festival of British Theatre Ltd, 1983–; Sec., Fedn of Theatre Unions, 1974–; Vice-Pres., Confedn of Entertainment Unions, 1974–; Member: Cinematograph Films Council, 1974–; Cttee, Assoc. for Business Sponsorship of the Arts, 1977–; TUC Adv. Cttee on the Arts, Entertainment and Sports; British Screen Adv. Council, 1985–. Joint Secretary: London and Provincial Theatre Councils; Performers Alliance; Treasurer, Entertainment Charities Fund. Trustee: Theatres Trust, 1977–; Evelyn Norris Home; Dir, Carl Rosa Trust Ltd; Bd mem., Childrens Film and TV Foundn. *Recreations:* supporting (half-heartedly) Orient FC, (colour blind) painting. *Address:* 8 Harley Street, W1N 2AB. *T:* 01–637 9311. *Club:* Gerry's.

PLOW, Maj.-Gen. the Hon. Edward Chester, CBE 1945; DSO 1944; CD 1950; DCL; DScMil; Canadian Army (Retired); *b* St Albans, Vermont, 28 September 1904; *s* of late John Plow and Hortense Harlow Plow (*née* Locklin); *m* 1937, Mary Nichols, *d* of late Thomas E. G. Lynch and M. Edith Lynch (*née* Nichols), Digby, NS; one *d*. *Educ:* Montreal schools; RMC Kingston. Commnd in RCHA, 1925; served in Canada and UK until 1939. Served War of 1939–45 (despatches twice): Italy and NW Europe; Artillery Staff Officer and Comdr; during latter part of War was Senior Artillery Officer, Canadian Army. Following the War served in various appts in Germany, Canada and the UK, and was GOC Eastern Command, Canada, 1950–58. Lieut-Governor of the Province of Nova Scotia, 1958–63. Dir, Canadian Imperial Bank of Commerce, 1963–74. Member Board of Governors: Izaak Walton Killam Hosp. for Children, Halifax; Canadian Corps of Commissionaires. Life Mem., Royal Canadian Artillery Assoc. Patron, St John Ambulance Assoc. KStJ; Comdr, Order of Orange Nassau (Netherlands). Anglican. *Address:* Locklands, RR1, Brockville, Ont, Canada. *Club:* Brockville Country.

PLOWDEN, family name of **Baron Plowden.**

PLOWDEN, Baron, *cr* 1959, of Plowden (Life Peer); **Edwin Noel Plowden,** KCB 1951; KBE 1946; Chairman, Top Salaries Review Body, since 1981 (Member, since 1977); President of TI Group (formerly Tube Investments Ltd), since 1976 (Chairman, 1963–76); *b* 6 Jan. 1907; 4th *s* of late Roger H. Plowden; *m* 1933, Bridget Horatia (*see* Lady Plowden); two *s* two *d*. *Educ:* Switzerland; Pembroke College, Cambridge (Hon. Fellow, 1958). Temporary Civil Servant Ministry of Economic Warfare, 1939–40; Ministry of Aircraft Production, 1940–46; Chief Executive, and Member of Aircraft Supply Council, 1945–46; Vice-Chairman Temporary Council Cttee of NATO, 1951–52; Cabinet Office, 1947; Treasury, 1947–53, as Chief Planning Officer and Chairman of Economic Planning Board. Adviser on Atomic Energy Organization, 1953–54; Chairman, Atomic Energy Authority, 1954–59; Visiting Fellow, Nuffield College, 1956–64; Chm. Cttee of Enquiry: Treasury control of Public Expenditure, 1959–61; organisation of Representational Services Overseas, 1963–64; Aircraft Industry, 1964–65; Structure of Electricity Supply Industry in England and Wales, 1974–75; into CBI's aims and organisation, 1974–75; Dep. Chm., Cttee of Inquiry on Police, 1977–79; Chm., Police Complaints Bd, 1976–81; Independent Chm., Police Negotiating Bd, 1979–82. Director: Commercial Union Assurance Co. Ltd, 1946–78; National Westminster Bank Ltd, 1960–77; Chm., Equity Capital for Industry Ltd, 1976–82; Mem., Internat. Adv. Bd, Southeast Bank NA, 1982–. Chm., CBI Companies Cttee, 1976–80; Vice-Chm., CBI Pres.'s Cttee, 1977–80. Pres., London Graduate Sch. of Business Studies, 1976– (Chm. 1964–76); Chm., Standing Adv. Cttee on Pay of Higher Civil Service, 1968–70; Member: Civil Service Coll. Adv. Council, 1970–76; Engineering Industries Council, 1976; Ford European Adv. Council, 1976–83. Hon. DSc: Pennsylvania State Univ., 1958; Univ. of Aston, 1972; Hon. DLitt, Loughborough, 1976. *Address:* Martels Manor, Dunmow, Essex. *T:* Great Dunmow 2141; 11 Abingdon Gardens, Abingdon Villas, W8 6BY. *T:* 01–937 4238.
See also W. J. L. Plowden.

PLOWDEN, Lady, (Bridget Horatia), DBE 1972; Chairman, Independent Broadcasting Authority, 1975–80; 2nd *d* of late Admiral Sir H. W. Richmond, KCB, and of Lady Richmond (Elsa, *née* Bell); *m* 1933, Baron Plowden, *qv*; two *s* two *d*. *Educ:* Downe House. Dir, Trust Houses Forte Ltd, 1961–72. Chairman: Central Advisory Council for Education (England), 1963–66; Mary Feilding Guild (formerly Working Ladies Guild); Metropolitan Architectural Consortium for Educn, 1968–79; MSC Area Manpower Bd, N London, 1983–. A Governor and Vice-Chm., BBC, 1970–75; Mem., Nat. Theatre Bd, 1976–. Mem., Houghton Inquiry into Pay of Teachers, 1974; Chm. of Governors: Philippa Fawcett Coll. of Educn, 1967–76; Robert Montefiore Comp. Sch., 1968–78; Co-opted Mem., Educn Cttee, ILEA, 1967–73; Vice-Chm., ILEA Schools Sub-Cttee, 1967–70. Chm., Professional Classes Aid Council, 1958–73 (Pres., 1973–86); Vice-Pres., Pre-School Playgps Assoc., 1982– (Pres., 1972–82); President: Harding House Assoc.; Nat. Assoc. of Adult Continuing Educn, 1980–; Nat. Marriage Guidance Council, 1983–; Adv. Cttee for Educn of Romany and other Travellers. Liveryman, Goldsmiths' Co., 1979–. JP Inner London Area Juvenile Panel, 1962–71. FRTS 1980. Hon. FCP 1973 (Vice-Pres.). Hon. LLD: Leicester, 1968; Reading, 1970; London, 1976; Hon. DLitt Loughborough, 1976; DUniv Open, 1974. *Address:* Martels Manor, Dunmow, Essex. *T:* Great Dunmow 2141; 11 Abingdon Gardens, Abingdon Villas, W8 6BY. *T:* 01–937 4238.
See also W. J. L. Plowden.

PLOWDEN, William Julius Lowthian, PhD; Director-General, Royal Institute of Public Administration, since 1978; *b* 7 Feb. 1935; *s* of Lord and Lady Plowden, *qqv*; *m* 1960, Veronica Gascoigne; two *s* two *d*. *Educ:* Eton; King's Coll., Cambridge (BA, PhD); Univ. of Calif, Berkeley. Staff Writer, Economist, 1959–60; BoT, 1960–65; Lectr in Govt, LSE, 1965–71; Central Policy Review Staff, Cabinet Office, 1971–77; Under Sec., Dept of Industry, 1977–78. Hon. Prof., Dept of Politics, Univ. of Warwick, 1977–82; Vis. Prof. in Govt, LSE, 1982–. Mem., W Lambeth DHA, 1982–. *Publication:* The Motor Car and Politics in Britain, 1971. *Address:* 49 Stockwell Park Road, SW9. *T:* 01–274 4535.

PLOWDEN ROBERTS, Hugh Martin; Chairman, Dairy Crest Foods, since 1986; Director, Argyll Group plc, since 1983; *b* 6 Aug. 1932; *s* of Stanley and Joan Plowden Roberts; *m* 1956, Susan Jane Patrick; two *d*. *Educ:* St Edward's School, Oxford; St Edmund Hall, Oxford. BA 1954, MA 1956. FIGD 1980. Payne & Son Meat Group, 1954–60 (Dir, 1958); Asst Gen. Manager (Meat Group), Co-operative Wholesale Society, 1960–67; Allied Suppliers Ltd, 1967–82: Dir, 1971; Dep. Man. Dir, 1974; Man. Dir, 1978; Chm., 1980–82; Dir, Cavenham Ltd, 1979, Chm., 1981–82; Dep. Chm., Argyll Stores Ltd, 1983–85. Mem., MMB, 1983–. *Recreations:* country pursuits. *Address:* The Boxes, Ockham Lane, Hatchford, Cobham, Surrey KT11 1LN. *T:* Cobham (Surrey) (0932) 62669. *Club:* Farmers'.

PLOWMAN, Sir (John) Anthony, Kt 1961; Judge of the High Court of Justice (Chancery Division), 1961–76, Vice-Chancellor, 1974–76; *b* 27 Dec. 1905; *e s* of late John Tharp Plowman (solicitor); *m* 1933, Vernon, 3rd *d* of late A. O. Graham, Versailles; three *d*. *Educ:* Highgate School; Gonville and Caius Coll., Cambridge. Solicitors Final (John Mackrell Prize), 1927; LLB London, 1927; LLB Cantab (1st Cl.), 1929; LLM Cantab 1956. Called to Bar, Lincoln's Inn, 1931 (Tancred and Cholmeley studentships; Buchanan Prize); QC 1954; Bencher of Lincoln's Inn, 1961. Served, 1940–45, Squadron-Leader, RAF. Member of General Council of the Bar, 1956–60. *Address:* Lane End, High Wycombe, Bucks.

PLOWMAN, Hon. Sir John (Robin), Kt 1979; CBE 1970 (OBE 1949); Member of the Legislative Council, later Senator, Bermuda, 1966–82, Government Leader in the Senate, 1968–82; Minister of Government and Commercial Services, Bermuda, 1980–82; *b* Bermuda, 18 Sept. 1908; *s* of Owen and Elizabeth Plowman; *m* 1936, Marjorie Hardwick; two *s*. *Educ:* Bermuda and England. Member, Ealing Borough Council, 1931–35; returned to Bermuda, 1935; Bermuda Volunteer Engineers, 1939–42; Dep. Dir, Dir and later Chm. of Bermuda Supplies Commission, 1942–47; Man. Director of Holmes, Williams & Purvey Ltd, 1947–78, Chairman of Board, 1961–. Chm. or Mem. of various govt commns and bds, including Training and Employment, Ports Facilities, Transport Control and Civil Service; Minister of Organisation, 1968–77; Minister of Marine and Air Services, 1977–80. Attached to UK negotiating team for Bermuda II Civil Aviation agreement, 1977. Chm. Bd of Governors, Warwick Academy, 1946–73; Life Vice-Pres. Bermuda Olympic Assoc. and Bermuda Football Assoc. *Recreations:* golf, sports administration. *Address:* Chiswick, Paget, Bermuda. *Clubs:* Carlton; Royal Hamilton Dinghy and Mid-Ocean (Bermuda).

PLOWRIGHT, David Ernest; Managing Director, Granada Television Ltd, since 1981 (Joint Managing Director, 1975–81); Director: Granada International, since 1975; Granada Group, since 1981; Independent Television News, since 1981; *b* 11 Dec. 1930; *s* of late William Ernest Plowright and of Daisy Margaret Plowright; *m* 1953, Brenda Mary (*née* Key); one *s* two *d*. *Educ:* Scunthorpe Grammar Sch.; on local weekly newspaper and during National Service, Germany. Reporter, Scunthorpe Star, 1950; freelance corresp. and sports writer, 1952; Reporter, Feature Writer and briefly Equestrian Corresp., Yorkshire Post, 1954; Granada Television: News Editor, 1957; Producer, Current Affairs, 1960; Exec. Prod., Scene at 6.30, 1964; Exec. Prod., World in Action, 1966; Head of Current Affairs, 1968; Dir, 1968; Controller of Programmes, 1969–79. Chm., Network Programme Cttee, ITV, 1980–82. Chm., Independent Television Cos Assoc., 1984–86 (Dir, 1976–). Vice Pres., RTS, 1982–. Governor, Nat. Film Sch., 1981–. *Recreations:* television, theatre, watching sport, messing about in a boat, late interest in golf. *Address:* Granada TV Ltd, Manchester M60 9EA. *T:* 061–832 7211; Granada TV, 36 Golden Square, W1. *T:* 01–734 8080.
See also J. A. Plowright.

PLOWRIGHT, Joan Ann, (The Lady Olivier), CBE 1970; leading actress with the National Theatre, 1963–74; Member of the RADA Council; *b* 28 Oct. 1929; *d* of late William Ernest Plowright and of Daisy Margaret (*née* Burton); *m* 1st, 1953, Roger Gage (marr. diss.); 2nd, 1961, (as Sir Laurence Olivier) Baron Olivier, *qv*; one *s* two *d*. *Educ:* Scunthorpe Grammar School; Laban Art of Movement Studio; Old Vic Theatre School. First stage appearance in If Four Walls Told, Croydon Rep. Theatre, 1948; Bristol Old Vic and Mem. Old Vic Co., S Africa tour, 1952; first London appearance in The Duenna, Westminster, 1954; Moby Dick, Duke of York's, 1955; season of leading parts, Nottingham Playhouse, 1955–56; English Stage Co., Royal Court, 1956; The Crucible, Don Juan, The Death of Satan, Cards of Identity, The Good Woman of Setzuan, The Country Wife (transferred to Adelphi, 1957); The Chairs, The Making of Moo, Royal Court, 1957; The Entertainer, Palace, 1957; The Chairs, The Lesson, Phoenix, NY, 1958; The Entertainer, Royale, NY, 1958; The Chairs, The Lesson, Major Barbara, Royal Court, 1958; Hook, Line and Sinker, Piccadilly, 1958; Roots, Royal Court, Duke of York's, 1959; Rhinoceros, Royal Court, 1960; A Taste of Honey, Lyceum, NY, 1960 (Best Actress Tony Award); Rosmersholm, Greenwich, 1973; Saturday, Sunday, Monday, Queen's, 1974–75; The Sea Gull, Lyric, 1975; The Bed Before Yesterday, Lyric, 1975 (Variety Club of GB Award, 1977); Filumena, Lyric, 1977 (Soc. of West End Theatre Award, 1978); Enjoy, Vaudeville, 1980; The Cherry Orchard, Haymarket, 1983; Chichester Festival: Uncle Vanya, The Chances, 1962; St Joan (Best Actress Evening Standard Award), Uncle Vanya, 1963; The Doctor's Dilemma, The Taming of the Shrew, 1972; Cavell, 1982; The Way of the World, 1984; National Theatre: St Joan, Uncle Vanya, Hobson's Choice, opening season, 1963; The Master Builder, 1964; Much Ado About Nothing, 1967, 1968; Three Sisters, 1967, 1968; Tartuffe, 1967, 1968; The Advertisement, 1968; Love's Labour's Lost, 1968; The Merchant of Venice, 1970; A Woman Killed With Kindness, 1971; The Rules of the Game, 1971; Eden End, 1974; Mrs Warren's Profession, 1985. Directed, Rites, 1969; produced, The Travails of Sancho Panza, 1969; Dir, A Prayer for Wings, 1985. *Films include:* Moby Dick, The Entertainer, Three Sisters, The Merchant of Venice, Equus, Britannia Hospital, Brimstone and Treacle, Wagner, A Dedicated Man, Revolution. Appears on TV; Daphne Laureola, 1976. *Recreations:* reading, music, entertaining. *Address:* c/o 33–34 Chancery Lane, WC2A 1EN; ICM, 388 Oxford Street, W1N 9HE.
See also D. E. Plowright.

PLOWRIGHT, Rosalind Anne; soprano; *b* 21 May 1949; *d* of Robert Arthur Plowright and Celia Adelaide Plowright. *Educ:* Notre Dame High Sch., Wigan; Royal Northern Coll. of Music, Manchester. LRAM. London Opera Centre, 1974–75; Glyndebourne Chorus and Touring Co., 1974–77; début with ENO as the Page in Salome, 1975; Miss Jessel in Turn of the Screw, ENO, 1979 (SWET award); début at Covent Garden as Ortlinde in Die Walküre, 1980; with Bern Opera, 1980–81, Frankfurt Opera and Munich Opera, 1981; débuts: in USA (Philadelphia and San Diego), Paris, Madrid and Hamburg, 1982; at La Scala, Milan, Edinburgh Fest. (concert performance), San Francisco and New York (Carnegie Hall), 1983; with Deutsche Oper, Berlin, 1984; in Houston, Pittsburgh and Verona, 1985. Principal rôles include: Ariadne; Alceste; Desdemona in Otello;

Elizabeth I in Maria Stuarda; Elena in Sicilian Vespers; Manon Lescaut; Leonora in Il trovatore; Aida; Suor Angelica; Giorgetta in Il Tabarro; Violetta in La Traviata; Norma; Madama Butterfly; Médée; Amelia in Un Ballo in Maschera; Maddalena in Andrea Chénier; Leonora in La Forza del Destino. Has given recitals and concerts in UK, Europe and USA, and made opera recordings. First prize, 7th Internat. Comp. for Opera Singers, Sofia, 1979; Prix Fondation Fanny Heldy, Acad. Nat. du Disque Lyrique, 1985. *Recreations:* wind surfing, cliff climbing. *Address:* c/o Kaye Artists Management Ltd, Kingsmead House, 250 Kings Road, SW3 6NR. *T:* 01-352 4494.

PLOWRIGHT, Walter, CMG 1974; DVSc; FRCVS 1977; FRS 1981; *b* 20 July 1923; 2nd *s* of Jonathan and Mahala Plowright, Holbeach, Lincs; *m* 1959, Dorothy Joy (*née* Bell). *Educ:* Moulton and Spalding Grammar Schs; Royal Veterinary Coll., London. MRCVS 1944; DVSc (Pret.) 1964. Commissioned, RAVC, 1945–48; Colonial Service, 1950–64; Animal Virus Research Inst., Pirbright, 1964–71 (seconded E Africa, 1966–71); Prof. of Vet. Microbiology, RVC, 1971–78; Hd, Dept of Microbiology, ARC Inst. for Res. on Animal Disease, Compton, Berks, 1978–83. Hon. DSc Univ. of Nairobi, 1984. J. T. Edwards Memorial Prize, 1964; R. B. Bennett Commonwealth Prize of RSA, 1972; Bledisloe Vet. Award, RASE, 1979; King Baudouin Internat. Devclt Prize, 1984; Dalrymple-Champneys Cup, BVA, 1984. *Publications:* numerous contribs to scientific jls relating to virus diseases of animals. *Recreations:* gardening, travel. *Address:* Whitehill Lodge, Goring-on-Thames, Reading RG8 0LL. *T:* Goring 872891.

PLUM, Patrick; *see* McConville, M. A.

PLUMB, Sir (Charles) Henry, Kt 1973; DL; Member (C) The Cotswolds, European Parliament, since 1979 (Chairman, Agricultural Committee, 1979–82; Leader, European Democratic Group, since 1982); *b* 27 March 1925; *s* of Charles and Louise Plumb; *m* 1947, Marjorie Dorothy Dunn; one *s* two *d*. *Educ:* King Edward VI School, Nuneaton. National Farmers Union: Member Council, 1959; Vice-President, 1964, 1965; Deputy-President, 1966, 1967, 1968, 1969; President, 1970–79. Chm., British Agricl Council, 1975–79. Mem., Duke of Northumberland's Cttee of Enquiry on Foot and Mouth Disease, 1967–68; Member Council: CBI; Animal Health Trust. Pres., Royal Agric. Soc. of England, 1977, Dep. Pres. 1978; Pres., Internat. Fedn of Agricl Producers, 1979–82; Past Pres., Comité des Organisations Professionels Agricoles de la CEE (COPA). Pres., Nat. Fedn of Young Farmers' Clubs, 1976–; Patron, Warwicks Co. Fedn of YFC, 1974–; Hon. Pres., Ayrshire Cattle Soc. Director: United Biscuits Ltd; Lloyds Bank Ltd; Fisons Ltd. Liveryman, Farmers' Co. FRSA 1970; FRAgS 1974. DL Warwick 1977. Hon. DSc Cranfield, 1983. *Recreations:* shooting, fishing. *Address:* Southfields Farm, Coleshill, Birmingham, West Midlands B46 3EJ. *T:* Coleshill 63133; 2 Queen Anne's Gate, SW1H 9AA. *T:* 01-222 1720; 01-222 0411. *Clubs:* St Stephen's Constitutional, Farmers', Institute of Directors; Coleshill Rotary (Hon. Member).

PLUMB, Sir Henry; *see* Plumb, Sir C. H.

PLUMB, Sir John (Harold), Kt 1982; FBA 1968; historian; Master of Christ's College, Cambridge, 1978–82; Professor of Modern English History, University of Cambridge, 1966–74; *b* 20 Aug. 1911; 3rd *s* of late James Plumb, Leicester. *Educ:* Alderman Newton's Sch., Leicester; University Coll., Leicester; Christ's Coll., Cambridge. BA London, 1st Class Hons History, 1933; PhD Cambridge, 1936; LittD Cambridge, 1957. Ehrman Research Fellow, King's Coll., Cambridge, 1939–46; FO, 1940–45; Fellow of Christ's Coll., 1946–, Steward, 1948–50, Tutor, 1950–59. Vice-Master, 1964–68. Univ. Lectr in History, 1946–62; Reader in Modern English History, 1962–65; Chm. of History Faculty, 1966–68, Univ. of Cambridge. Trustee of National Portrait Gallery, 1961–82; Syndic of the Fitzwilliam Museum, 1960–77; Member: Wine Standards Bd, 1973–75; Council, British Acad., 1977–80; Chm., Centre of E Anglian Studies, 1979–82. FRHistS; FSA; FRSL 1969. Visiting Prof., Columbia Univ., 1960; Distinguished Vis. Prof., NYC Univ., 1971–72, 1976; Cecil and Ida Green Honors Chair, Texas Christian Univ., 1974; Dist. Vis. Prof., Washington Univ., 1977; Lectures: Ford's, Oxford Univ., 1965–66; Saposnekov, City College, NY, 1968; Guy Stanton Ford, Univ. of Minnesota, 1969; Stenton, Reading, 1972; George Rogers Clark, Soc. of the Cincinnati, 1977. Hon. For. Mem., Amer. Acad. for Arts and Sciences, 1970; Hon. Member: Soc. of Amer. Historians, 1976; Amer. Historical Assoc., 1981. Hon. DLitt: Leicester, 1968; East Anglia, 1973; Bowdoin Coll., 1974; S California, 1978; Westminster Coll., 1983; Washington Univ., St Louis, 1983. Editor, History of Human Society, 1959–; Sen. Editor to American Heritage Co. Historical Adviser, Penguin Books, 1960–; Editor, Pelican Social History of Britain, 1982–. *Publications:* England in the Eighteenth Century, 1950; (with C. Howard) West African Explorers, 1952; Chatham, 1953; (ed) Studies in Social History, 1955; Sir Robert Walpole, Vol. I, 1956, Vol. II, 1960, both vols repr. 1972; The First Four Georges, 1956; The Renaissance, 1961; Men and Places, 1962; Crisis in the Humanities, 1964; The Growth of Political Stability in England, 1675–1725, 1967; Death of the Past, 1969; In the Light of History, 1972; The Commercialisation of Leisure, 1974; Royal Heritage, 1977; New Light on the Tyrant, George III, 1978; Georgian Delights, 1980; Royal Heritage: The Reign of Elizabeth II, 1980; (with Neil McKendrick and John Brewer) The Birth of a Consumer Society, 1982; *contrib. to:* Man versus Society in Eighteenth Century Britain, 1968; Churchill Revised, 1969 (Churchill, the historian); *Festschrift:* Historical Perspectives: Essays in Honour of J. H. Plumb, 1974. *Address:* Christ's College, Cambridge. *T:* Cambridge 334900; The Old Rectory, Westhorpe, Stowmarket, Suffolk. *T:* Bacton 781235. *Clubs:* Brooks's, Beefsteak.

PLUME, John Trevor; Regional Chairman, Industrial Tribunals (London North), 1984–April 1987; *b* 5 Oct. 1914; *s* of William Thomas and Gertrude Plume; *m* 1948, Christine Mary Wells; one *d*. *Educ:* City of London School; Inns of Court School of Law. Called to the Bar, Gray's Inn, 1936, Bencher, 1979. Legal Associate Mem., Town Planning Inst., 1939; served Royal Artillery, 1940–46 (Captain). Practiced at Bar, specialising in property law, 1936–76; Chm., Industrial Tribunals, 1976–87. Liveryman, Clockmakers' Co. *Recreations:* beekeeping, carpentry, gardening, fishing. *Address:* Mulberry Cottage, Forest Side, Epping, Essex CM16 4ED. *T:* Epping 72389.

PLUMLEY, Rev. Prof. Jack Martin; Herbert Thompson Professor of Egyptology, University of Cambridge, 1957–77; Priest-in-Charge, Longstowe, Cambs, since 1981; *b* 2 Sept. 1910; *e s* of Arthur Henry Plumley and Lily Plumley (*née* Martin); *m* 1938, Gwendolen Alice Darling (*d* 1984); three *s*; *m* 1986, Ursula Clara Dowle. *Educ:* Merchant Taylors' Sch., London; St John's Coll., Durham (BA, Univ. Hebrew Schol., MLitt); King's Coll., Cambridge (MA). Deacon 1933; Priest 1934; Curacies, 1933–41; Vicar of Christ Church, Hoxton, 1942–45, of St Paul's, Tottenham, 1945–47; Rector and Vicar of All Saints', Milton, Cambridge, 1948–57. Acting Dean, Pembroke Coll., Cambridge, 1981–82. Associate Lectr in Coptic, Univ. of Cambridge, 1949–57; Fellow Selwyn Coll., 1957. Stephen Glanville Meml Lectr, Fitzwilliam Mus., Cambridge, 1982. Mem. Council of Senate, Cambridge, 1965–70. Dir of excavations on behalf of Egypt Exploration Soc. at Qasr Ibrim, Nubia, 1963, 1964, 1966, 1969, 1972, 1974, 1976; Chm., British Cttee of Internat. Critical Greek New Testament Project, 1963–. Pres., Internat. Soc. for Nubian Studies, 1978–82, Patron, 1982–. FSA 1966; Fellow, Inst. of Coptic Studies, United Egyptian Repub., 1966; Corresp. Mem., German Inst. of Archaeology, 1966. *Recreations:* music, rowing, photography, travel. *Address:* Selwyn College, Cambridge; 13 Lyndewode Road, Cambridge. *T:* Cambridge 350328.

PLUMMER, family name of **Baron Plummer of St Marylebone.**

PLUMMER OF ST MARYLEBONE, Baron *cr* 1981 (Life Peer), of the City of Westminster; **(Arthur) Desmond (Herne) Plummer;** Kt 1971; TD 1950; JP; DL; Chairman: Portman Building Society, since 1983 (Vice-Chairman, 1979–82); National Employers' Life, since 1983; *b* 25 May 1914; *s* of late Arthur Herne Plummer and Janet (*née* McCormick); *m* 1941, Pat Holloway (Pres., Cons. Women's Adv. Cttee, Greater London Area, 1967–71); one *d*. *Educ:* Hurstpierpoint Coll.; Coll. of Estate Management. Served 1939–46, Royal Engineers. Member: TA Sports Bd, 1953–79; London Electricity Consultative Council, 1955–66; St Marylebone Borough Council, 1952–65 (Mayor, 1958–59); LCC, for St Marylebone, 1960–65; Inner London Educn Authority, 1964–76. Greater London Council: Mem. for Cities of London and Westminster, 1964–73, for St Marylebone, 1973–76; Leader of Opposition, 1966–67 and 1973–74; Leader of Council, 1967–73. Member: South Bank Theatre Board, 1967–74; Standing Conf. on SE Planning, 1967–74; Transport Co-ordinating Council for London, 1967–69; Local Authorities Conditions of Service Adv. Bd, 1967–71; Exec. Cttee, British Section of Internat. Union of Local Authorities, 1967–74; St John Council for London, 1971–; Exec. Cttee, Nat. Union Cons. and Unionist Assocs, 1967–76; Chm., St Marylebone Conservative Assoc., 1965–66. Chm., Horserace Betting Levy Bd, 1974–82; Dep. Chm., Nat. Employers' Mutual Gen. Insurance Assoc., 1973–86; Pres., Met. Assoc. of Bldg Socs, 1983–. Member of Lloyd's. Mem. Court, Univ. of London, 1967–77. Chairman: Epsom and Walton Downs Trng Grounds Man. Bd, 1974–82; National Stud, 1975–82; President: London Anglers' Assoc., 1976–; Thames Angling Preservation Soc., 1970–. Liveryman, Worshipful Co. of Tin Plateworkers. FAI 1948; FRICS 1970; FRSA 1974; Hon. FFAS 1966. JP, Co. London, 1958; DL Greater London, 1970. Comdr (Brother) KStJ 1986. *Publications:* Time for Change in Greater London, 1966; Report to London, 1970; Planning and Participation, 1973. *Recreations:* swimming (Capt. Otter Swimming Club, 1952–53); growing things, relaxing. *Address:* 4 The Lane, St Johns Wood, NW8 0PN. *Clubs:* Carlton (Chm., Political Cttee, 1979–84; Pres., 1984–), Royal Automobile, MCC.

PLUMMER, (Arthur) Christopher (Orme), CC (Canada) 1968; actor; *b* Toronto, 13 Dec. 1929; *m* 1st, 1956, Tammy Lee Grimes; one *d*; 2nd, 1962, Patricia Audrey Lewis (marr. diss. 1966); 3rd, 1970, Elaine Regina Taylor. *Educ:* public and private schs, Montreal. French and English radio, Canada, 1949–52; Ottawa Rep. Theatre; Broadway: Starcross Story, 1951–52; Home is the Hero, 1953; The Dark is Light Enough, 1954 (Theatre World Award); The Lark, 1955; J. B., 1958 (Tony nomination); Arturo Ui, 1963; Royal Hunt of the Sun, 1965–66; Stratford, Conn, 1955: Mark Antony, Ferdinand; leading actor, Stratford Festival, Canada, 1956–67: Henry V, The Bastard, Hamlet, Leontes, Mercutio, Macbeth, Cyrano de Bergerac, Benedic, Aguecheek, Antony; Royal Shakespeare Co., Stratford-on-Avon, 1961–62: Benedic, Richard III; London debut as Henry II in Becket, Aldwych and Globe, 1961 (Evening Standard Best Actor Award, 1961); National Theatre, 1971–72: Amphytrion 38, Danton's Death; Broadway musical, Cyrano, 1973 (Outer Critics Circle Award and Tony Award for Best Actor in a Musical, NY Drama Desk Award); The Good Doctor, NY, 1974; Iago in Othello, NY, 1982 (Drama Desk Award). *Films:* Stage-Struck, 1956; Across the Everglades, 1957; The Fall of the Roman Empire, 1963; The Sound of Music, 1964 (Golden Badge of Honour, Austria); Daisy Clover, 1964; Triple Cross, 1966; Oedipus Rex, 1967; The Battle of Britain, 1968; Royal Hunt of the Sun, 1969; The Pyx, 1973; The Man Who Would Be King, 1975; Aces High, 1976; The Moneychangers, 1976 (Emmy Award); International Velvet, 1978; The Silent Partner, 1978; Hanover Street, 1979; Murder by Decree, 1980 (Genie Award, Canada); The Disappearance, 1981; The Janitor, 1981; The Amateur, 1982; Dreamscape, 1984; Playing for Keeps, 1985; Lily in Love, 1985, and others. TV appearances, Britain, Denmark, and major N American networks, incl. Hamlet at Elsinore, BBC and Danish TV, 1964 (4 Emmy Award nominations). First entertainer to win Maple Leaf Award (Arts and Letters), 1982. *Recreations:* tennis, ski-ing, piano. *Clubs:* Hurlingham; Players, River (New York).

PLUMMER, Christopher; *see* Plummer, A. C. O.

PLUMMER, Maj.-Gen. Leo Heathcote, CBE 1974; retired 1979; *b* 11 June 1923; *s* of Lt-Col Edmund Waller Plummer and Mary Dorothy Brookesmith; *m* 1955, Judyth Ann Dolby; three *d*. *Educ:* Canford Sch.; Queens' Coll., Cambridge. Commnd RA, 1943; War Service, N Africa, Sicily, Italy, 1943–45 (mentioned in despatches, 1945); Adjt, TA, 1947–49; Staff Coll., Camberley, 1952, Directing Staff, 1961–63; Comdt, Sudan Staff Coll., 1963–65; CO, 20 Heavy Regt, 1965–67; Col, Gen. Staff, MoD, 1967; Brig., 1967; Comdr, 1st Artillery Bde, 1967–70; Dep. Dir Manning (Army), 1971–74; Asst Chief of Staff Ops, HQ Northern Army Gp, 1974–76; Chief, Jt Service Liaison Orgn, Bonn, 1976–78. ADC to HM The Queen, 1974–76; Col Comdt, RA, 1981–86. Chm., Civil Service Commn Selection Bd, 1983–. *Recreation:* gardening. *Address:* High Street, Wingham, Canterbury, Kent CT3 1AY. *Club:* Army and Navy.

PLUMMER, Peter Edward; Deputy Director, Department for National Savings, 1972–79; *b* 4 Nov. 1919; *s* of Arthur William John and Ethel May Plummer; *m* 1949, Pauline Wheelwright; one *s* one *d*. *Educ:* Watford Grammar Sch. Served War, REME, 1941–46. Customs and Excise, 1936–38; Dept for National Savings, 1938–79; Principal, 1956; Assistant Sec., 1964; seconded to Nat. Giro, 1970–71; Under-Sec., 1972. *Recreations:* gardening, photography. *Address:* Old Timbers, Farm Lane, Nutbourne, Chichester, W Sussex. *T:* Emsworth 77450.

PLUMPTON, Alan, CBE 1980; BSc, CEng, FIEE; FCIBS; CBIM; FRSA; Chairman, Ewbank Preece Group, since 1986; Director, Schlumberger (UK), since 1986; Chairman, Manx Electricity Authority; *b* 24 Nov. 1926; *s* of late John Plumpton and of Doris Plumpton; *m* 1950, Audrey Smith; one *s* one *d*. *Educ:* Sunderland Technical Sch.; Durham Univ. (BSc Elec. Eng). Pupil Engr, Sunderland Corp. Elec. Undertaking, 1942; various engrg and commercial appts, NEEB, 1948–61; Dist Manager, E Monmouthshire Dist, S Wales Electricity Bd, 1961–64. Admin. Staff Coll., Henley, 1963; Dep. Chief Commercial Engr, S Wales Elec. Bd, 1964–67; Chief Commercial Engr, S Wales Elec. Bd, 1967–72; Dep. Chm., London Elec. Bd, 1972–76, Chm., 1976–81; Dep. Chm., Electricity Council, 1981–86. Liveryman, Gardeners' Co. JP Mon, 1971–72. *Recreations:* golf, gardening. *Address:* Lockhill, Stubbs Wood, Amersham, Bucks HP6 6EX. *T:* Amersham 3791. *Clubs:* City Livery, Harewood Downs Golf.

PLUMPTRE, family name of **Baron Fitzwalter.**

PLUMTREE, Air Vice-Marshal Eric, CB 1974; OBE 1946; DFC 1940; Co-ordinator of Anglo-American Relations, Ministry of Defence (Air), 1977–84; *b* 9 March 1919; *s* of William Plumtree, Plumbley Farm, Mosborough, Derbys, and Minnie Plumtree (*née* Wheatley); *m* 1942, Dorothy Patricia (*née* Lyall); two *s* (and one *s* decd). *Educ:* Eckington Grammar Sch. Served War of 1939–45: No 53 Army Co-op. Sqdn, 1940–41; No 241 FR Sqdn, 1942; OC No 169 FR Sqdn, 1943; Chief Instr, No 41, OTU, 1944; HQ, Fighter Command, 1945; Staff Coll., Haifa, 1946; Personal Staff Officer to C-in-C, MEAF,

1947–49; OC, No 54 (F) Sqdn, 1949–52; PSO to Chief of Air Staff, 1953–56; OC Flying Wing, Oldenburg, 1957–58; OC, Admin. Wing, Jever, 1958; JSSC, Latimer, 1959; OC, RAF Leuchars, 1959–61; Dep. Dir, Joint Planning Staff, 1962–63; IDC, 1964; Air Adviser to UK High Comr and Head of BDLS (Air), Ottawa, 1965–67; Air Cdre 1966; Dir, Air Plans, MoD (Air), 1968–69; AOC 22 Group RAF, 1970–71; Air Vice-Marshal 1971; Comdr, Southern Maritime Air Region, 1971–73; Economy Project Officer (RAF), MoD, 1973–74. Mem. Council, Ardingly Coll., 1976–. *Recreations:* gardening, most sports. *Address:* Wings Cottage, Ditchling, Sussex. *T:* Hassocks 5539. *Club:* Royal Air Force.

PLUNKET, family name of **Baron Plunket.**

PLUNKET, 8th Baron *cr* 1827; **Robin Rathmore Plunket;** *b* 3 Dec. 1925; *s* of 6th Baron Plunket (*d* 1938) and Dorothé Mabel (*d* 1938), *d* of late Joseph Lewis and *widow* of Captain Jack Barnato, RAF; *S brother*, 1975; *m* 1951, Jennifer, *d* of late Bailey Southwell, Olivenhoutpoort, S Africa. *Educ:* Eton. Formerly Captain, Rifle Brigade. *Heir: b* Hon. Shaun Albert Frederick Sheridan Plunket [*b* 5 April 1931; *m* 1961, Judith Ann, *e d* of late G. P. Power; one *s* one *d; m* 1980, Mrs Elizabeth de Sancha (*d* 1986)]. *Address:* Rathmore, Chimanimani, Zimbabwe; 39 Lansdowne Gardens, SW8.

PLUNKET GREENE, Mary, (Mrs Alexander Plunket Greene); *see* Quant, Mary.

PLUNKETT, family name of **Baron Dunsany,** and of **Baron Louth.**

PLUNKETT, Brig. James Joseph, CBE 1945; Colonel Commandant, Royal Army Veterinary Corps, 1953–59; *b* 1893; *m* 1951, Mrs Rachel Kelly, *d* of Eustace H. Bent, Lelant, Cornwall. *Educ:* Royal Dick Veterinary College. Commissioned, 1914; continuous military service; mentioned in despatches: War of 1914–18 (twice); Waziristan Campaign (once); War of 1939–45 (twice). Director Army Veterinary and Remount Services, 1947–51; retired pay, 1951. *Address:* Templeshanbo, near Enniscorthy, Co. Wexford, Eire. *Club:* Naval and Military.

PLUNKETT, William Joseph; Valuer and Estates Surveyor, Greater London Council, 1977–81; *b* 8 Nov. 1921; *s* of John Joseph Archer and Marjorie Martin Plunkett; *m* 1949, Gwendoline Innes Barron; two *s* five *d. Educ:* Finchley Catholic Grammar Sch.; Coll. of Estate Management. BSc(Est. Man.). FRICS. RN, 1941–46; commnd, 1942; Lt RNVR. Dep. County Valuer, Middlesex CC, 1962–65; Asst Valuer, Valuation and Estates Dept, GLC, 1965–73; Dep. Valuer and Estates Surveyor, GLC, 1973–74; Dir of Valuation and Estates Dept, GLC, 1974–77. Mem., South Bank Polytechnic Adv. Cttee on Estate Management, 1973–76; Chm., Covent Garden Officers' Steering Gp, 1977–81. Mem. General Council, RICS, 1978–80 (Pres. Planning and Develt Div., 1978–79; Chm., S London Br. Cttee, 1976–77); Pres., Assoc. of Local Authority Valuers and Estate Surveyors, 1980–81. *Publications:* articles on Compensation, Valuation and Development. *Address:* 63 Radnor Cliff, Folkestone, Kent CT20 2JL. *T:* Folkestone 38868.

PLYMOUTH, 3rd Earl of, *cr* 1905; **Other Robert Ivor Windsor-Clive;** Viscount Windsor (UK 1905); 15th Baron Windsor (England, *cr* 1529); DL; FRSA 1953; *b* 9 October 1923; *e s* of 2nd Earl and Lady Irene Charteris, *d* of 11th Earl of Wemyss; *S father*, 1943; *m* 1950, Caroline Helen, *o d* of Edward Rice, Dane Court, Eastry, Kent; three *s* one *d. Educ:* Eton. Mem., Museums and Galls Commn (formerly Standing Commn on Museums and Galls), 1972–82; Chm., Reviewing Cttee on Export of Works of Art, 1982–85. DL County of Salop, 1961. *Heir: s* Viscount Windsor, *qv. Address:* Oakly Park, Ludlow, Salop.
See also Dr Alan Glyn.

PLYMOUTH, Bishop of, (RC), since 1986; **Rt. Rev. Mgr. Hugh Christopher Budd;** *b* 27 May 1937; *s* of John Alfred and Phyllis Mary Budd. *Educ:* St Mary's Primary School, Hornchurch, Essex; Salesian Coll., Chertsey, Surrey; Cotton Coll., North Staffs; English Coll., Rome. PhL; STD. Ordained Priest, 1962; post-ordination studies, 1963–65; Tutor, English Coll., Rome, 1965–71; Lectr at Newman Coll., Birmingham and part-time Asst Priest, Northfield, Birmingham, 1971–76; Head of Training, Catholic Marriage Advisory Council, National HQ, London, 1976–79; Rector, St John's Seminary, Wonersh, Surrey, 1979–85; Administrator, Brentwood Cathedral, Essex, Nov. 1985–Jan. 1986. *Recreations:* walking, cricket (watching), music (listening). *Address:* Vescourt, Hartley Road, Plymouth PL3 5LR. *T:* Plymouth 772950.

PLYMOUTH, Bishop Suffragan of, since 1982; **Rt. Rev. Kenneth Albert Newing;** *b* 29 Aug. 1923; *s* of Albert James Pittock Newing and Nellie Louise Maude Newing; unmarried. *Educ:* Dover Grammar School; Selwyn College, Cambridge (MA); Theological College, Mirfield, Yorks. Assistant Curate, Plymstock, 1955–63; Rector of Plympton S Maurice, Plymouth, 1963–82; Archdeacon of Plymouth, 1978–82. *Address:* 38 Huxhams Cross, Dartington, Totnes, Devon TQ9 6NT. *T:* Staverton 263.

PLYMOUTH, Archdeacon of; *see* Ellis, Ven. R. G.

POANANGA, Maj.-Gen. Brian Matauru, CB 1980; CBE 1977 (OBE 1967; MBE 1962); Chief of General Staff, New Zealand Army, 1978–81, retired; *b* 2 Dec. 1924; *s* of Henare and Atareta Poananga; *m* 1949, Doreen Mary Porter (formerly QAIMNS/R); two *s* one *d. Educ:* Royal Military College, Duntroon, Australia. Graduated RMC, 1946; served BCOF, Japan, 1947–48; Commonwealth Div., Korea, 1952–53; (mentioned in despatches, 1952); Staff Coll., Camberley, 1957; 28 Commonwealth Inf. Bde, Malaya, 1959–61; Jt Services Staff Coll., Latimer, 1964; CO 1RNZIR, Malaysia, 1965–67 (mentioned in despatches, Sarawak, 1966); Dir of Army Training, 1968–69; Dir of Services Intelligence, 1969–70; Comdr Army Training Gp, 1970–72; RCDS, 1973; Comdr 1st (NZ) Inf. Bde Gp, 1974; NZ High Commissioner to Papua New Guinea, 1974–76; Deputy Chief of General Staff, 1977–78. *Recreations:* golf and fishing. *Address:* PO Box 397, Taupo, New Zealand. *T:* Taupo 48296. *Club:* Taupo (NZ).

POCHIN, Sir Edward (Eric), Kt 1975; CBE 1959; MA, MD, FRCP; *b* 22 Sept. 1909; *s* of Charles Davenport Pochin; *m* 1940, Constance Margaret Julia (*d* 1971), *d* of T. H. Tilly; one *s* one *d. Educ:* Repton; St John's Coll., Cambridge. Natural Science Tripos, Part I, 1st 1930, Part II (Physiology) 1st, 1931; Michael Foster Student, Strathcona Student, 1931–32; MA 1935; MD 1945 (Horton Smith Prize); FRCP 1946. Mem. of Scientific Staff of MRC, 1941; Dir, Dept of Clinical Research, UCH Med. Sch., 1946–74. Lectures: Oliver Sharpey, London, 1950; Robert Campbell Oration, Belfast, 1953; Mackenzie Davidson, London, 1959; Skinner, London, 1966; Ringer, London, 1968; Hevesy, 1970; Lauriston Taylor, Washington, 1978; Douglas Lee, Bristol, 1979; Antoine Béclère, Paris, 1979; Sievert, IRPA, W Berlin, 1984. Mem., International Commn on Radiological Protection, 1959, Chm., 1962–69, Emeritus Mem., 1977; Member: Nat. Radiological Protection Bd, 1971–82; Physiological Soc., Assoc. of Physicians, Internat. Radiation Protection Assoc.; British Inst. of Radiology; Medical Research Soc.; Hon. Fellow: Royal Coll. of Radiologists; Hon. Member: British Radiological Protection Assoc.; Nippon Soc. Radiologica; British Nuclear Med. Soc.; Hospital Physicists' Assoc.; Amer. Thyroid Assoc. UK Representative, UN Scientific Cttee on Effects of Atomic Radiation, 1956–82. Gifford-Edmunds Prize, Ophthalmol Soc., 1940. *Publications:* Nuclear Radiation: risks and benefits, 1984; articles on thyroid disease, radiation protection and risk estimation in

scientific journals. *Recreations:* trivial painting, fell walking. *Address:* c/o National Radiological Protection Board, Chilton, Didcot, Oxon. *Clubs:* Athenæum, Oriental.

POCOCK, Air Vice-Marshal Donald Arthur, CBE 1975 (OBE 1957); Director, British Metallurgical Plant Constructors Association, 1980–85; *b* 5 July 1920; *s* of late A. Pocock and of E. Broad; *m* 1947, Dorothy Monica Griffiths; two *s* three *d. Educ:* Crouch End. Served War of 1939–45: commissioned, 1941; Middle East, 1941–48. Transport Command, 1948–50; commanded RAF Regt Sqdn, 1950–52; Staff Coll., 1953; Staff Officer, HQ 2nd Allied TAF, 1954–57; comd RAF Regt Wing, 1957–58; MoD, 1958–59; HQ Allied Air Forces Central Europe, 1959–62; Sen. Ground Defence SO, NEAF, 1962–63; MoD, 1963–66; Sen. Ground Defence SO, FEAF, 1966–68; ADC to the Queen, 1967; Commandant, RAF Catterick, 1968–69; Dir of Ground Defence, 1970–73; Comdt-Gen. RAF Regt, 1973–75. Gen. Man., Iran, British Aerospace Dynamics Gp, 1976–79. *Recreations:* shooting, equitation. *Address:* Brincliffe, Dence Park, Herne Bay, Kent CT6 6BQ. *T:* Herne Bay 374773. *Club:* Royal Air Force.

POCOCK, Gordon James; Director, Communications Educational Services Ltd, since 1983; *b* 27 March 1933; *s* of Leslie Pocock and Elizabeth Maud Pocock; *m* 1959, Audrey Singleton. *Educ:* Royal Liberty Sch., Romford; Keble Coll., Oxford. Joined PO, 1954; Private Sec. to Dir Gen., 1958–59; Principal, 1960–68; Asst Sec., 1968–72; Dep. Dir, 1972–76; Dir, Ext. Telecommns, 1976–79; Dir, Telecommns Marketing, 1979, Sen. Dir, 1979–81; Chief Exec., Merlin Business Systems, BT, 1981–84. Fellow, Nolan Norton & Co., 1985. *Publications:* Corneille and Racine, 1973; Boileau and the Nature of Neo-Classicism, 1980. *Recreations:* travel, theatre, local history. *Address:* Friars Lodge, Friars Lane, Richmond, Surrey TW9 1NL. *T:* 01–940 7118.

POCOCK, Hugh Shellshear; formerly: Director, Associated Iliffe Press Ltd; Chairman of Iliffe Electrical Publications Ltd; Managing Editor, The Electrical Review; (formerly Editor) of The Wireless World; retired Dec. 1962; *b* 6 May 1894; 3rd *s* of late Lexden Lewis Pocock, artist; *m* 1920, Mayda, *d* of late Serab Sévian. *Educ:* Privately. Served European War, 1914–18: commissioned RE, 1915; served in Egypt, Mesopotamia, Persia, on wireless and intelligence work with rank of Capt. (despatches). Assisted in organisation of first short wave amateur transatlantic tests, 1921–22; organised first transatlantic broadcasting trials, 1923; proposed Empire Broadcasting on short wave in 1926, and urged its adoption in face of BBC opposition. Promoted and organised the National Wireless Register of technical personnel 1938, under Service auspices; CEng, FIEE; Life Senior Member of the Institute of Electrical and Electronics Engineers. Hon. Mem., British Record Soc.; Member of Honour, Union Internationale de la Presse Radiotechnique et Electronique. *Publications:* numerous articles relating to radio and electrical progress, technical and general. *Recreations:* genealogy and local history research. *Address:* 103 Boydell Court, St Johns Wood, NW8 6NH. *Clubs:* 25, Dynamicables.

POCOCK, Kenneth Walter; *b* 20 June 1913; *s* of Walter Dunsdon Pocock and Emily Marion Pocock; *m* 1939, Anne Tidmarsh; one *s* one *d. Educ:* Canford School. United Dairies (London) Ltd, 1930; Armed Forces, 1942–46; Man. Dir, Edinburgh and Dumfriesshire Dairy Co. Ltd, 1946; Dir, United Dairies Ltd, 1948; Pres., Scottish Milk Trade Fedn, 1956–59; Dir, Unigate Ltd, 1959; Man. Dir, Unigate Ltd and United Dairies Ltd, 1963; Chm. of Milk Div., Unigate Ltd, 1968; Dep. Chm., Unigate Ltd, 1970–75; Pres., Unigate Long Service Corps (40 years), 1971–. Governor, Nat. Dairymen's Benevolent Instn (Chm., 1977–81). *Recreations:* motoring, shooting, photography, gardening. *Address:* Cedar Lodge, Marsham Lane, Gerrards Cross, Bucks SL9 8HD. *T:* Gerrards Cross 889278.

POCOCK, Leslie Frederick, CBE 1985; Chairman, Liverpool Health Authority, 1982–86; *b* 22 June 1918; *s* of Frederick Pocock and Alice Helena Pocock; *m* 1946, Eileen Horton; two *s. Educ:* Emanuel School. FCCA. Chief Accountant: London & Lancashire Insurance Co. Ltd, 1959; Royal Insurance Co. Ltd, 1966; Chief Accountant and Taxation Manager, 1971, Dep. Gp Comptroller, 1974, Royal Insurance Gp; retired 1981. Pres., Assoc. of Certified Accountants, 1977–78. Mem., UK Central Council for Nursing, Midwifery and Health Visiting, 1983–. *Recreations:* countryside, golf. *Address:* Farnley, Croft Drive West, Caldy, Wirral, Merseyside. *T:* 051–625 5320.

PODDAR, Prof. Ramendra Kumar, PhD; Professor of Biophysics, Calcutta University, since 1973; Member, Rajya Sabha, since 1985; *b* 9 Nov. 1930; *m* 1955, Srimati Jharna Poddar; two *s* one *d. Educ:* Univ. of Calcutta (BSc Hons Physics, MSc Physics; PhD Biophysics); Associateship Dip., Saha Inst. of Nuclear Physics. Progressively, Research Asst, Lecturer, Reader, Associate Prof., Biophysics Div., Saha Inst. of Nuclear Physics, 1953–73; Calcutta University: Pro-Vice-Chancellor (A), 1977–79; Vice-Chancellor, 1979–83. Research experience in Univ. of California, Berkeley, 1958–60, Purdue Univ., 1960–61, California Inst. of Technology, 1970. *Publications:* research papers in jls of internat. repute, contribs to internat. congresses/symposia and to all-India seminars/symposia, in the fields of biophysics, molecular biology and photobiology. *Address:* University College of Science, University of Calcutta, Calcutta 700009, India. *T:* (office) 35–9186; (home) 57–5260; 57–6573.

PODMORE, Ian Laing; Chief Executive, Sheffield City Council, since 1974; *b* 6 Oct. 1933; *s* of Harry Samuel Podmore and Annie Marion (*née* Laing); *m* 1961, Kathleen Margaret (*née* Langton); one *s* one *d. Educ:* Birkenhead School. Admitted Solicitor 1960. Asst Solicitor, Wallasey County Borough, 1960–63; Sen. Asst Solicitor, Southport Co. Borough, 1963–66; Deputy Town Clerk: Southport, 1966–70; Sheffield, 1970–74. *Recreations:* golf, gardening, watching football. *Address:* Town Hall, Sheffield S1 2HH. *T:* Sheffield 734000; 55 Devonshire Road, Sheffield S17 3NU. *Club:* Abbeydale Golf.

POETT, Gen. Sir (Joseph Howard) Nigel, KCB 1959 (CB 1952); DSO and Bar, 1945; idc; psc; *b* 20 Aug. 1907; *s* of late Maj.-General J. H. Poett, CB, CMG, CBE; *m* 1937, Julia, *d* of E. J. Herrick, Hawkes Bay, NZ; two *s* one *d. Educ:* Downside; RMC Sandhurst. 2nd Lieut, DLI, 1927; Operations, NW Frontier, 1930–31; Adjt 2nd Bn DLI, 1934–37; GSO2, 2nd Div., 1940; GSO1, War Office, 1941–42; Comd 11th Bn DLI, 1942–43; Comdr, 5th Parachute Bde, 1943–46; served North-West Europe, 1944–45; Far East, 1945–46; Director of Plans, War Office, 1946–48; idc 1948; Dep.-Commander, British Military Mission, Greece, 1949; Maj.-General, 1951; Chief of Staff, FARELF, 1950–52; GOC 3rd Infantry Division, Middle East Land Forces, 1952–54; Dir of Military Operations, War Office, 1954–56; Commandant, Staff Coll., Camberley, 1957–58; Lt-Gen., 1958; General Officer Commanding-in-Chief, Southern Command, 1958–61; Commander-in-Chief, Far East Land Forces, 1961–63; General, 1962. Colonel, The Durham Light Infantry, 1956–65. Dir, British Productivity Council, 1966–71. Silver Star, USA. *Address:* Swaynes Mead, Great Durnford, Salisbury, Wilts. *Club:* Army and Navy.

PÖHL, Karl Otto; Grosses Verdienstkreuz mit Stern und Schulterband des Verdienstordens der Bundesrepublik Deutschland; Governor, Deutsche Bundesbank and German Governor, International Monetary Fund and Bank for International Settlements, since 1980; *b* 1 Dec. 1929; *m* 1974; two *s* two *d. Educ:* Göttingen Univ. (Econs; Diplom.-Volkswirt). Div. Chief for Econ. Res., IFO-Institut, Munich, 1955–60; econ. journalist,

Bonn, 1961–67; Mem. Exec., Fed. Assoc. of German Bank, Cologne, 1968–69; Div. Chief in Fed. Min. of Econs, Bonn, 1970–71; Dept Chief in Fed. Chancellery (Head, Dept for Econ. and Fiscal Policy), Bonn, 1971–72; Sec. of State in Fed. Min. of Finance, 1972–77; Dep. Governor, Deutsche Bundesbank, 1977–79; Chairman: EEC Monetary Cttee, 1976–77; Deputies of Gp of Ten, 1978–80; Gp of Ten, 1983–. Hon. DHL Georgetown Univ., 1983; Hon. DEconSc Ruhr Univ., 1985; Hon. DPhil Tel Aviv, 1986. *Publications*: miscellaneous. *Address*: Deutsche Bundesbank, Wilhelm-Epstein-strasse 14, 6000 Frankfurt 50, Federal Republic of Germany. *T*: Frankfurt 1581.

POITIER, Sidney, KBE (Hon.) 1974; actor, film and stage; director; *b* Miami, Florida, 20 Feb. 1927; *s* of Reginald Poitier and Evelyn (*née* Outten); *m* 1950, Juanita Hardy (marr. diss.); four *d*; *m* 1975, Joanna Shimkus; two *d*. *Educ*: private tutors; Western Senior High Sch., Nassau; Governor's High Sch., Nassau. Served War of 1941–45 with 1267th Medical Detachment, United States Army. Started acting with American Negro Theatre, 1946. *Plays include*: Anna Lucasta, Broadway, 1948; A Raisin in the Sun, Broadway, 1959; *films include*: Cry, the Beloved Country, 1952; Red Ball Express, 1952; Go, Man, Go, 1954; Blackboard Jungle, 1955; Goodbye, My Lady, 1956; Edge of the City, 1957; Band of Angels, 1957; Something of Value, 1957; The Mark of the Hawk, 1958; The Defiant Ones, 1958 (Silver Bear Award, Berlin Film Festival, and New York Critics Award, 1958); Porgy and Bess, 1959; A Raisin in the Sun, 1960; Paris Blues, 1960; Lilies of the Field, 1963 (award for Best Actor of 1963, Motion Picture Academy of Arts and Sciences); The Bedford Incident, 1965; The Slender Thread, 1966; A Patch of Blue, 1966; Duel at Diablo, 1966; To Sir With Love, 1967; In the Heat of the Night, 1967; Guess Who's Coming to Dinner, 1968; For Love of Ivy, 1968; They Call Me Mister Tibbs, 1971; The Organization, 1971; The Wilby Conspiracy, 1975; director and actor: Buck and the Preacher, 1972; A Warm December, 1973; Uptown Saturday Night, 1975; Let's Do It Again, 1976; A Piece of the Action, 1977; *director*: Stir Crazy, 1981; Hanky Panky, 1982. *Publication*: This Life (autobiography), 1980. *Address*: c/o Verdon Productions Ltd, 9350 Wilshire Boulevard, Beverly Hills, Calif 90212, USA.

POLAK, Cornelia Julia, OBE 1964 (MBE 1956); HM Diplomatic Service, retired; *b* 2 Dec. 1908; *d* of late Solomon Polak and late Georgina Polak (*née* Pozner). Foreign Office, 1925–38; Asst Archivist, British Embassy, Paris, 1938–40; Foreign Office, 1940–47; Vice-Consul, Bergen, 1947–49; Consul, Washington, 1949–51; Foreign Office, 1951–55; Consul, Paris, 1955–57; Consul, Brussels, 1957–60; Foreign Office, 1960–63; Head of Treaty and Nationality Department, Foreign Office, 1963–67; Consul General, Geneva, 1967–69, retired; re-employed at FCO, 1969–70. *Address*: 24 Belsize Court, NW3.

POLAND, Rear-Adm. Edmund Nicholas, CB 1967; CBE 1962; *b* 19 Feb. 1917; 2nd *s* of late Major Raymond A. Poland, RMLI; *m* 1941, Pauline Ruth Margaret Pechell; three *s* one *d* (and one *d* decd). *Educ*: Royal Naval Coll., Dartmouth. Served at sea during Abyssinian and Palestine crises, Spanish Civil War; War of 1939–45: convoy duties, Norwegian waters; Motor Torpedo Boats, Channel and Mediterranean; Torpedo Specialist, 1943; Staff Officer Ops to Naval Force Comdr, Burma; Sqdn T. Officer, HMS Royalist; HMS Hornet, 1946; Flotilla Torpedo and Anti-Submarine Officer of Third Submarine Flotilla, HMS Montclare; Air Warfare Div., Admiralty, 1950; British Naval Staff, Washington, 1953; jssc 1955; Directorate of Tactics and Ship Requirements, Admiralty; comd RN Air Station, Abbotsinch, 1956; Nato Standing Gp, Washington; Director of Under Sea Warfare (Naval), Ministry of Defence, 1962; Chief of Staff to C-in-C Home Fleet, 1965–68; retired. Commander, 1950; Capt., 1956; Rear-Adm., 1965. Vice-Pres., Internat. Prisoners' Aid Assoc., 1978, Chm. (UK), 1979; Vice-Pres., Scottish Assoc. for Care and Resettlement of Offenders, 1979 (Dir, 1975–79). *Recreations*: golf, fishing, gardening. *Address*: Bryant's Cottage, Burgate Cross, near Fordingbridge, Hants.
See also R. D. Poland.

POLAND, Richard Domville, CB 1973; *b* 22 Oct. 1914; *er s* of late Major R. A. Poland, RMLI, and late Mrs F. O. Bayly-Jones; *m* 1948, Rosalind Frances, *y d* of late Surgeon-Captain H. C. Devas; one *s* one *d*. *Educ*: RN Coll., Dartmouth. Traffic Trainee, Imperial Airways, 1932; Traffic Clerk, British Continental Airways and North Eastern Airways, 1934–39. Ops Officer, Air Ministry, Civil Aviation Dept, 1939; Civil Aviation Dept Rep., W Africa, 1942–44; Private Secretary to Minister of Civil Aviation, 1944–48; Principal, 1946; Asst Secretary, 1953; Shipping Attaché, British Embassy, Washington, DC, 1957–60; Under-Secretary: Min. of Transport, 1964–70; DoE, 1970–74. Sec., Internat. Maritime Industry Forum, 1976–78. Chm., Kent Branch, CPRE, 1980. *Address*: 63 Alexandra Road, Kew, Surrey. *T*: 01–948 5039.
See also Rear-Admiral E. N. Poland.

POLANI, Prof. Paul Emanuel, MD, DCH; FRCP; FRCOG; FRS 1973; Hon. FRCPath; Prince Philip Professor of Pædiatric Research in the University of London, 1960–80, now Professor Emeritus; Geneticist, Pædiatric Research Unit, Guy's Hospital Medical School, London, since 1983 (Director, 1960–82); Children's Physician, Geneticist, and Consultant Emeritus, Guy's Hospital; Geneticist, Italian Hospital; Director, SE Thames Regional Genetics Centre, 1976–82; *b* 1 Jan. 1914; first *s* of Enrico Polani and Elsa Zennaro; *m* 1944, Nina Ester Sullam; no *c*. *Educ*: Trieste, Siena and Pisa (Scuola Normale Superiore, Italy). MD (Pisa) 1938; DCH 1945; MRCP (London) 1948; FRCP (London) 1961; FRCOG 1979. National Birthday Trust Fund Fellow in Pædiatric Research, 1948; Assistant to Director, Dept of Child Health, Guy's Hospital Medical School, 1950; Research Physician on Cerebral Palsy and Director, Medical Research Unit, National Spastic Society, 1955; Consultant to WHO (Regional Office for Europe) on Pregnancy Wastage, 1959; Consultant, Nat. Inst. Neurol. Disease and Blindness, Nat. Insts of Health, USA, 1959–61. Chm., Mutagenesis Cttee, UK, 1975–. Vis. Prof. of Human Genetics and Develt, Columbia Univ., 1977–. Hon. FRCPath 1985. Sanremo Internat. Award and Prize for Genetic Res., 1984; Baly Medal, RCP, 1985. *Publications*: chapters in books on human genetics, mental deficiency, psychiatry and pædiatrics; papers on human genetics, cytogenetics, experimental meiosis, congenital malformations and neurological disorders of children. *Recreations*: reading, riding, ski-ing. *Address*: Little Meadow, West Clandon, Surrey GU4 7TL. *T*: Guildford 222436. *Club*: Athenæum.

POLANYI, Prof. John Charles, CC (Canada) 1979 (OC 1974); FRS 1971; FRSC 1966; University Professor, since 1974 and Professor of Chemistry, University of Toronto, since 1962; *b* 23 Jan. 1929; *m* 1958, Anne Ferrar Davidson; one *s* one *d*. *Educ*: Manchester Grammar Sch.; Victoria Univ., Manchester (BSc, PhD, DSc). Research Fellow: Nat. Research Council, Ottawa, 1952–54; Princeton Univ., 1954–56; Univ. of Toronto: Lectr, 1956; Asst Prof., 1957–60; Assoc. Prof, 1960–62. Sloan Foundn Fellow, 1959–63; Guggenheim Meml Fellow, 1970–71, 1979–80; Sherman Fairchild Distinguished Scholar, CIT, 1982. Mem., Scientific Adv. Bd, Max Planck Inst. for Quantum Optics, Garching, Germany, 1982–. Lectures: Centennial, Chem. Soc., 1965; Ohio State Univ., 1969 (and Mack Award); Reilly, Univ. of Notre Dame, 1970; Harkins Meml, Univ. of Chicago, 1971; Purves, McGill Univ., 1971; Killam Meml Schol., 1974, 1975; F. J. Toole, Univ. of New Brunswick, 1974; Philips, Haverford Coll., 1974; Kistiakowsky, Harvard Univ., 1975; Camille and Henry Dreyfus, Kansas, 1975; J. W. T. Spinks, Saskatchewan, 1976; Laird, Western Ontario, 1976; CIL Dist., Simon Fraser Univ., 1977; Gucker, Indiana Univ., 1977; Jacob Bronowski Meml, Toronto Univ., 1978; Hutchison, Rochester Univ., 1979; Priestley, Penn State Univ., 1980; Barré, Univ. of Montreal, 1982; Chute, Dalhousie, and Redman, McMaster, 1983; Wiegand, Toronto Univ., 1984; Condon, Colorado Univ., 1984; Allan, Alberta Univ., 1984. Hon. For. Mem., Amer. Acad. of Arts and Sciences, 1976; For. Associate, Nat. Acad. of Sciences, USA, 1978. Hon. DSc: Waterloo, 1970; Memorial, 1976; McMaster, 1977; Carleton, 1981; Harvard, 1982; Rensselaer, 1984; Brock, 1984; Hon. LLD: Trent, 1977; Dalhousie, 1983; St Francis Xavier, 1984. Marlow Medal, Faraday Soc., 1963; Steacie Prize for Natural Scis, 1965; Chem. Inst. Canada Medal, 1976 (Noranda Award, 1967); Chem. Soc. Award, 1970; Henry Marshall Tory Medal, RSC, 1977; Remsen Award, Amer. Chem. Soc., 1978; (jtly) Wolf Prize in Chemistry, 1982. *Film*: Concept in Reaction Dynamics, 1970. *Publications*: (with F. G. Griffiths) The Dangers of Nuclear War, 1979; papers in scientific jls, articles on science policy and on control of armaments. *Address*: 142 Collier Street, Toronto, Ont M4W 1M3, Canada.

POLE; *see* Carew Pole.

POLE; *see* Chandos-Pole.

POLE, Prof. Jack Richon, PhD; FBA 1985; FRHistS; Rhodes Professor of American History and Institutions, Oxford University, and Fellow of St Catherine's College, since 1979; *b* 14 March 1922; *m* 1952, Marilyn Louise Mitchell; one *s* two *d*. *Educ*: Oxford Univ. (BA 1949); Princeton Univ. (PhD 1953). MA Cantab 1963. FRHistS 1970. Instr in History, Princeton Univ., 1952–53; Asst Lectr/Lectr in Amer. History, UCL, 1953–63; Cambridge University: Reader in Amer. History and Govt, 1963–79; Fellow, Churchill Coll., 1963–79 (Vice-Master, 1975–78); Mem., Council of Senate, 1970–74. Vis. Professor: Berkeley, 1960–61; Ghana, 1966; Chicago, 1969; Peking, 1984. Commonwealth Fund Amer. Studies Fellowship, 1956; Fellow, Center for Advanced Study in Behavioral Sciences, 1969–70; Guest Schol., Wilson Internat. Center, Washington, 1978–79. Jefferson Meml Lectr, Berkeley, 1971; Richard B. Russell Lectr, Ga, 1981. Member: Council, Inst. for Early Amer. History and Culture, 1973–76; Acad. Européenne d'Histoire, 1981. Hon. Fellow, Hist. Soc. of Ghana. *Publications*: Abraham Lincoln and the Working Classes of Britain, 1959; Abraham Lincoln, 1964; Political Representation in England and the Origins of the American Republic, 1966 (also USA); (ed) The Advance of Democracy, USA 1967; The Seventeenth Century: the origins of legislative power, USA 1969; (ed) The Revolution in America: documents of the internal development of America in the revolutionary era, 1971 (also USA); (co-ed) The Meanings of American History, USA 1971; Foundations of American Independence, 1763–1815, 1973 (USA 1972); (Gen. Editor) American Historical Documents (ed, Slavery, Secession and Civil War), 1975; The Decision for American Independence, USA 1975; The Idea of Union, USA 1977; The Pursuit of Equality in American History, USA 1978; Paths to the American Past, 1979 (also USA); The Gift of Government: political responsibility from the English Restoration to American Independence, USA 1983; (co-ed) Colonial British America: essays in the new history of the early modern era, USA 1983; articles in Amer. Hist. Rev., William and Mary Qly, and Jl of Southern Hist. *Recreations*: cricket, painting, drawing. *Address*: 20 Divinity Road, Oxford OX1 4LJ; St Catherine's College, Oxford OX1 3UJ. *Club*: Trojan Wanderers Cricket (Co-founder, 1957).

POLE, Sir Peter Van Notten, 5th Bt, *cr* 1791; FASA; ACIS; accountant; *b* 6 Nov. 1921; *s* of late Arthur Chandos Pole and Marjorie, *d* of late Charles Hargrave, Glen Forrest, W Australia; *S* kinsman, 1948; *m* 1949, Jean Emily, *d* of late Charles Douglas Stone, Borden, WA; one *s* one *d*. *Educ*: Guildford Grammar Sch. *Heir*: *s* Peter John Chandos Pole [*b* 27 April 1952; *m* 1973, Suzanne Norah, BAppSc(MT), *d* of Harold Raymond and Gwendoline Maude Hughes; two *s* one *d*]. *Address*: 9 Yeovil Way, Karrinyup, WA 6018, Australia.

POLGE, Dr Ernest John Christopher, FRS 1983; Officer-in-Charge, Agricultural Research Council Animal Research Station, Institute of Animal Physiology, Cambridge, since 1979; Fellow, Wolfson College, Cambridge, since 1984; *b* 16 Aug. 1926; *s* of late Ernest Thomas Ella Polge and Joan Gillet Polge (*née* Thorne); *m* 1954, Olive Sylvia Kitson; two *s* two *d*. *Educ*: Bootham Sch., York; Reading Univ. (BSc Agric.); PhD London 1955. Dept of Agricl Econs, Bristol Univ., 1947–48; Nat. Inst. for Med. Res., London, 1948–54; ARC Unit of Reproductive Physiology and Biochem., later Animal Res. Station, 1954–. Lalor Foundn Fellow, Worcester Foundn for Exptl Biol., Shrewsbury, Mass and Univ. of Illinois, 1967–68. Consultant: WHO, Geneva, 1965; FAO, Rome, 1983. Member Committee: Soc. for Study of Fertility, 1955–64, 1976–83 (Sec., 1960–63; Chm., 1978–81); Soc. for Low Temp. Biol., 1974–79 (Chm., 1976–79). Chm., Journals of Reproduction and Fertility Ltd, 1982– (Mem., Council of Management and Exec. Cttee, 1972–79). Lectures: Sir John Hammond Meml, Soc. for Study of Fertility, 1974; Blackman, Oxford, 1979; Cameron-Gifford, Newcastle, 1984; E. H. W. Wilmott, Bristol, 1986. Hon. FRASE 1984; Hon. ARCVS 1986. (Jtly) John Scott Award, City of Philadelphia, 1969; Sir John Hammond Meml Prize, British Soc. of Animal Prodn, 1971. *Publications*: papers on reproduction in domestic animals and low temp. biol., in biological jls. *Recreations*: gardening, fishing. *Address*: 38 High Street, Girton, Cambridge CB3 0PU. *T*: Cambridge 276056.

POLKINGHORNE, Rev. John Charlton, FRS 1974; Fellow and Dean of Trinity Hall, Cambridge, since 1986; *b* 16 Oct. 1930; *s* of George Baulkwill Polkinghorne and Dorothy Evelyn Polkinghorne (*née* Charlton); *m* 1955, Ruth Isobel Martin; two *s* one *d*. *Educ*: Elmhurst Grammar Sch.; Perse Sch.; Trinity Coll., Cambridge (MA 1956; PhD 1955; ScD 1974); Westcott House, Cambridge, 1979–81. Deacon, 1981; Priest, 1982. Fellow, Trinity Coll., Cambridge, 1954–86; Commonwealth Fund Fellow, California Institute of Technology, 1955–56; Lecturer in Mathematical Physics, Univ. of Edinburgh, 1956–58; Cambridge University: Lecturer in Applied Mathematics, 1958–65; Reader in Theoretical Physics, 1965–68; Prof. of Mathematical Physics, 1968–79. Hon. Prof. of Theoretical Physics, Univ. of Kent at Canterbury, 1985. Curate: St Andrew's, Chesterton, 1981–82; St Michael's, Bedminster, 1982–84. Vicar of St Cosmus and St Damian in the Blean, 1984–86. Mem. SRC, 1975–79; Chm., Nuclear Phys. Bd, 1978–79. Chm. of Governors, Perse Sch., 1972–81; Governor, SPCK, 1984–. Licensed Reader, Diocese of Ely, 1975. *Publications*: (jointly) The Analytic S-Matrix, 1966; The Particle Play, 1979; Models of High Energy Processes, 1980; The Way the World Is, 1983; The Quantum World, 1984; One World, 1986; many articles on elementary particle physics in learned journals. *Recreation*: gardening. *Address*: Flat 3, 51 Bateman Street, Cambridge. *T*: Cambridge 60743.

POLLARD, Maj.-Gen. Barry; *see* Pollard, Maj.-Gen. C. B.

POLLARD, Bernard; Deputy Secretary and Director General (Technical), Board of Inland Revenue, since 1985; *b* 24 Oct. 1927; *m* 1961, Regina (*née* Stone); one *s* one *d*. *Educ*: Tottenham Grammar Sch.; London Univ. (BSc Econ; Gladstone Meml Prize (Econs), 1949). Called to the Bar, Middle Temple, 1968. Served RAF (Flying Officer), 1949–53. Entered Tax Inspectorate, Inland Revenue, 1953; Principal Inspector of Taxes, 1969; Asst Sec., 1973; Under Sec., 1979; Dir of Counter Avoidance and Evasion Div., 1981–85. *Recreations*: reading biographics, watching cricket and National Hunt racing.

Address: 10 Merrows Close, Northwood, Mddx HA6 2RT. *T:* Northwood 24762. *Club:* Surrey County Cricket.

POLLARD, Maj.-Gen. (Charles) Barry; General Manager, Solent Business Fund, since 1984; *b* 20 April 1927; *s* of Leonard Charles Pollard and Rose Constance (*née* Fletcher); *m* 1954, Mary Heyes; three *d. Educ:* Ardingly Coll.; Selwyn Coll., Cambridge. Commnd, Corps of RE, 1947; served in ME, Korea and UK, 1947–58; Student, Staff Coll., Camberley, 1958; GSO 2 (Trng), HQ Eastern Comd, 1959–61; Liaison Officer, Ecole du Genie, France, 1961–63; OC 5 Field Sqdn, 1963–65; JSSC, 1965; Mil. Asst to DCOS, Allied Forces Central Europe, 1966; GSO 1 MoD, 1967; GSO 1 (DS), Staff Coll., Camberley, 1968; CRE 3 Div., 1969–71; Col GS 3 Div., 1971–72; CCRE 1st British Corps, 1972–74; RCDS, 1975; Chief Engr, BAOR, 1976–79. Col Comdt, RE, 1982–. National Dir, Trident Trust, 1980–84. *Recreations:* sailing, golf. *Address:* Yateley, Coombe Road, Salisbury, Wilts. *Club:* Army and Navy.

POLLARD, Sir (Charles) Herbert, Kt 1962; CBE 1957 (OBE 1946; MBE 1943); retired as City Treasurer, Kingston upon Hull, 1961; *b* 23 Oct. 1898; *s* of Charles Pollard; *m* 1922, Elsie (*d* 1970), *d* of Charles Crain; one *d*; *m* 1971, Hilda M. Levitch. *Educ:* Blackpool. City Treasurer, Kingston upon Hull, 1929–61; formerly held appointments in Finance Depts of Blackpool and Wallasey. Fellow, Inst. of Chartered Accountants; Member Council, Inst. of Municipal Treasurers and Accountants, 1944–61 (President Inst. 1952–53); Financial Adviser to Assoc. of Municipal Corporations, 1951–61; Member several cttees and working parties arranged by government departments on various aspects of education, housing, police and local authority finance; Hon. Manager, Savings Bank, Hull Area, 1943–78. Trustee: C. C. Grundy Trust; Chamberlain Trust for over 25 yrs. Life Vice-Pres., Hanover Housing Assoc.; Mem., Nat. Savings Cttee, 1946–51; Official delegate at International Confs on aspects of local government finance (including Education) in Rome and Geneva, held under auspices of International Union of Local Authorities (prepared British paper for this) and UNESCO. Licentiate, London College of Music. Hon. Treas. and Member Council, General Assembly of Unitarian and Free Christian Churches, 1959–70 (President, 1956–57); Hon. Treas., British and Foreign Unitarian Assoc. Inc., 1964–79; Member, St John Council for Lancs, 1962–72. OStJ 1962. *Publications:* contrib. to: Local Government Finance and to other local government journals. *Recreations:* music, theatre; membership of voluntary service organisations. *Address:* St Peter's Court, St Peter's Grove, York YO3 6AQ. *Clubs:* Yorkshire (York); Rotary (Past Pres., Hull and St Annes-on-Sea).

POLLARD, Sir Herbert; *see* Pollard, Sir C. H.

POLLARD, Prof. Sidney; Professor of Economic History, University of Bielefeld, since 1980; *b* 21 April 1925; *s* of Moses and Leontine Pollak; *m* 1st, 1949, Eileen Andrews; two *s* one *d*; 2nd, 1982, Helen Trippett. *Educ:* London School of Economics. University of Sheffield: Knoop Fellow, 1950–52; Asst Lecturer, 1952–55; Lecturer, 1955–60; Senior Lecturer, 1960–63; Prof. of Economic History, 1963–80. *Publications:* Three Centuries of Sheffield Steel, 1954; A History of Labour in Sheffield 1850–1939, 1959; The Development of the British Economy 1914–1950, 1962, 3rd edn, 1914–1980, 1983; The Genesis of Modern Management, 1965; The Idea of Progress, 1968; (with D. W. Crossley) The Wealth of Britain, 1086–1966, 1968; (ed) The Gold Standard and Employment Policies between the Wars, 1970; (ed, with others) Aspects of Capital Investment in Great Britain, 1750–1850, 1971; (ed) The Trades Unions Commission: the Sheffield outrages, 1971; (ed with J. Salt) Robert Owen, prophet of the poor, 1971; (ed with C. Holmes) Documents of European Economic History, vol. 1, 1968, vols 2 and 3, 1972; The Economic Integration of Europe, 1815–1970, 1974; (ed with C. Holmes) Essays in the Economic and Social History of South Yorkshire, 1977; (with Paul Robertson) The British Shipbuilding Industry 1870–1914, 1979; Peaceful Conquest, 1981; The Wasting of the British Economy, 1982; articles in learned journals in field of economics, economic history and history. *Recreations:* walking, music. *Address:* Loebellstrasse 14, D-4800 Bielefeld 1, Germany. *T:* Bielefeld 178390.

POLLEN, Sir John Michael Hungerford, 7th Bt of Redenham, Hampshire, *cr* 1795; *b* 6 April 1919; *s* of late Lieut-Commander John Francis Hungerford Pollen, RN; *S* kinsman, Sir John Lancelot Hungerford Pollen, 6th Bt, 1959; *m* 1st, 1941, Angela Mary Oriana Russi (marr. diss., 1956); one *s* one *d*; 2nd, 1957, Mrs Diana Jubb. *Educ:* Downside; Merton Coll., Oxford. Served War of 1939–45 (despatches). *Heir: s* Richard John Hungerford Pollen [*b* 3 Nov. 1946; *m* 1971, Christianne, *d* of Sir Godfrey Agnew, *qv*; four *s* two *d*]. *Address:* Manor House, Rodbourne, Malmesbury, Wiltshire; Lochportain, Isle of North Uist, Outer Hebrides.

POLLEN, Peregrine Michael Hungerford; Executive Deputy Chairman, 1975–77, Deputy Chairman, 1977–82, Sotheby Parke Bernet and Co.; *b* 24 Jan. 1931; *s* of late Sir Walter Michael Hungerford Pollen, MC, JP, and of Lady Pollen; *m* 1958, Patricia Helen Barry; one *s* two *d. Educ:* Eton Coll.; Christ Church, Oxford. National Service, 1949–51. ADC to Sir Evelyn Baring, Governor of Kenya, 1955–57; Sotheby's, 1957–82: Dir, 1961; Pres., Sotheby Parke Bernet, New York, 1965–72. *Address:* Norton Hall, Mickleton, Glos. *T:* Mickleton 218. *Clubs:* Brooks's, Beefsteak.

POLLINGTON, Viscount; John Andrew Bruce Savile; *b* 30 Nov. 1959; *s* and *heir* of 8th Earl of Mexborough, *qv*.

POLLOCK, family name of **Viscount Hanworth.**

POLLOCK, Alexander; MP (C) Moray, since 1983 (Moray and Nairn, 1979–83); advocate; *b* 21 July 1944; *s* of Robert Faulds Pollock, OBE, and Margaret Findlay Pollock; *m* 1975, Verena Francesca Gertraud Alice Ursula Critchley; one *s* one *d. Educ:* Rutherglen Academy; Glasgow Academy; Brasenose Coll., Oxford (BA Hons); Edinburgh Univ. (LLB); Perugia Univ. Solicitor, Bonar Mackenzie & Kermack, WS, 1970–73; Advocate, Scottish Bar, 1973–. PPS to Sec. of State for Scotland, 1982–86, to Sec. of State for Defence, 1986–. Mem., Commons Select Cttee on Scottish Affairs, 1979–82, 1986–. Sec., British-Austrian Parly Gp, 1979–. Mem., Queen's Body Guard for Scotland, Royal Co. of Archers, 1984–. *Recreations:* music, golf, cycling. *Address:* Drumdarrach, Forres, Moray, Scotland IV36 0DW. *Clubs:* New (Edinburgh); Rothes FC Social (Rothes); Royal Findhorn Yacht.

POLLOCK, David Linton; *b* 7 July 1906; *yr s* of late Rev. C. A. E. Pollock, formerly President of Corpus Christi College, Cambridge, and of Mrs G. I. Pollock; *m* 1st, 1933, Lilian Diana Turner; one *s*; 2nd, 1950, Margaret Duncan Curtis-Bennett (*née* Mackintosh). *Educ:* Marlborough Coll.; Trinity Coll., Cambridge. Partner in the firm of Freshfields, 1938–51; served with HM Treasury, 1939–40; War of 1939–45, Commander RNVR (despatches). Member of British Government Economic Mission to Argentina, 1946. Member of Council, Royal Yachting Assoc., 1950–65. Former Director: S. Pearson & Son Ltd; National Westminster Bank Ltd; Vickers Ltd; Legal and General Assurance Soc. Ltd; Industrial and Commercial Finance Corp. Ltd. President, Société Civile du Vignoble de Château Latour. Member of Council, Marlborough College, 1950–71. *Recreation:* sailing. *Address:* The Old Rectory, Wiggonholt, near Pulborough, West Sussex RH20 2EL. *T:* Pulborough 2531. *Clubs:* Royal Thames Yacht; Itchenor Sailing (Sussex).

POLLOCK, Ellen Clara; actress and director; President, The Shaw Society; Professor at RADA and Webber Douglas School of Acting; *m* 1st, 1929, Lt-Col L. F. Hancock, OBE, RE (decd); one *s*; 2nd, 1945, James Proudfoot (*d* 1971). *Educ:* St Mary's College, W2; Convent of The Blessed Sacrament, Brighton. First appeared, Everyman, 1920, as page in Romeo and Juliet. Accompanied Lady Forbes-Robertson on her S. African tour, and later visited Australia as Moscovitch's leading lady. West End successes include: Hit the Deck, Hippodrome, 1927; Her First Affaire, Kingsway, and Duke of York's, 1930; The Good Companions, Her Majesty's, 1931; Too True to be Good, New, 1933; Finished Abroad, Savoy, 1934; French Salad, Westminster and Royalty, 1934; The Dominant Sex, Shaftesbury and Aldwych, 1935. Open Air Theatre: Lysistrata; As You Like It. Seasons of Shaw's plays: at Lyric, Hammersmith, 1944, and with late Sir Donald Wolfit at King's, Hammersmith, 1953; three seasons of Grand Guignol plays at The Irving and Granville, Walham Green; Six Characters in Search of an Author, New Mayfair Theatre, 1963; Lady Frederick, Vaudeville and Duke of York's, 1969–70; Ambassador, Her Majesty's, 1971; Pygmalion, Albery, 1974; Tales from the Vienna Woods, Nat. Theatre, 1976; The Dark Lady of the Sonnets, Nat. Theatre, 1977; The Woman I Love, Churchill, 1979; Country Life, Lyric, Hammersmith, 1980; Harlequinade, and Playbill, Nat. Theatre, 1980. Has acted in numerous films and TV, incl. Forsyte Saga, The Pallisers, World's End and The Nightingale Saga. *Productions include:* Summer in December, Comedy Theatre, 1949; Miss Turner's Husband, St Martin's, 1949; The Third Visitor, Duke of York's, 1949; Shavings, St Martin's, 1951; Mrs Warren's Profession, Royal Court, 1956; A Matter of Choice, Arts, 1967. *Recreations:* motoring, antiques and cooking. *Address:* 9 Tedworth Square, SW3. *T:* 01–352 5082.

POLLOCK, Sir George, Kt 1959; QC 1951; *b* 15 March 1901; *s* of William Mackford Pollock; *m* 1st, 1922, Doris Evelyn Main (*d* 1977); one *s* one *d*; 2nd, 1977, Mollie (*née* Pedder), *widow* of J. A. Van Santen. Served Merchant Navy, 1914–18 War. Entered journalism as trainee reporter on Leamington Spa Courier; sub-editor Daily Chronicle, 1922–28; called to Bar, Gray's Inn, 1928; Bencher, 1948. Recorder of Sudbury, 1946–51. Served Army (Special Forces), 1940–44, Egypt, N Africa, Sicily and Italy (Colonel, Gen. Staff); Chief Judicial Officer, Allied Control Commn, Italy, 1944. Retired from Bar, 1954; Dir, British Employers' Confedn, 1954–65; Member: Nat. Jt Adv. Council (to advise Minister of Labour), Jt Consultative Cttee (to advise BEC and TUC), Nat. Production Adv. Council on Industry (to advise Pres., BOT), 1955–61; British Productivity Council, 1955–61. Assisted in planning and orgn of newly constituted CBI; Senior Consultant to CBI on Internat. Labour Affairs, 1965–69. Member: Governing Body, ILO, 1963–69; EFTA Consultative Cttee, 1966–69; Royal Commn on Trade Unions and Employers' Organisations. Mem. Council, Sussex Univ., 1974–77. *Publication:* Life of Mr Justice McCardie, 1934. *Address:* 62 Saffrons Court, Eastbourne, East Sussex.

POLLOCK, Sir George F(rederick), 5th Bt, *cr* 1866; Artist-Photographer since 1963; *b* 13 Aug. 1928; *s* of Sir (Frederick) John Pollock, 4th Bt and Alix l'Estom (*née* Soubiran); *S* father, 1963; *m* 1951, Doreen Mumford, *o d* of N. E. K. Nash, CMG; one *s* two *d. Educ:* Eton; Trinity Coll., Cambridge. BA 1953, MA 1957. 2nd Lieut, 17/21 Lancers, 1948–49. Admitted Solicitor, 1956. Hon. FRPS (Past Pres.); FBIPP; FRSA. Past Chm., London Salon of Photography. *Recreation:* ski-ing. *Heir: s* David Frederick Pollock [*b* 13 April 1959; *m* 1985, Helena, *o d* of L. J. Tompsett]. *Address:* Netherwood, Stones Lane, Westcott, near Dorking, Surrey RH4 3QH. *T:* Dorking 885447. *Clubs:* Lansdowne, Ski Club of Great Britain; DHO (Wengen).

POLLOCK, Sir Giles (Hampden) Montagu-, 5th Bt *cr* 1872; Management Consultant in Marketing, since 1974; Associate of John Stork & Partners Ltd, since 1980; *b* 19 Oct. 1928; *s* of Sir George Seymour Montagu-Pollock, 4th Bt, and of Karen-Sofie, Lady Montagu-Pollock, *d* of Hans Ludwig Dedekam, Oslo; *S* father, 1985; *m* 1963, Caroline Veronica, *d* of Richard F. Russell; one *s* one *d. Educ:* Eton; de Havilland Aeronautical Technical School. de Havilland Enterprise, 1949–56; Bristol Aeroplane Co. Ltd, 1956–59; Bristol Siddeley Engines Ltd, 1959–61; Associate Dir, J. Walter Thompson Co. Ltd, 1961–69; Director: C. Vernon & Sons Ltd, 1969–71; Acumen Marketing Group Ltd, 1971–74; 119 Pall Mall Ltd, 1972–78. *Recreations:* bicycling, water-skiing, walking. *Heir: s* Guy Maximilian Montagu-Pollock, *b* 27 Aug. 1966. *Address:* The White House, 7 Washington Road, SW13 9BG. *T:* 01–748 8491. *Club:* Institute of Directors.

POLLOCK, John Denton; General Secretary, Educational Institute of Scotland, since 1975; a Forestry Commissioner, since 1978; *b* 21 April 1926; *s* of John Pollock and Elizabeth (*née* Crawford); *m* 1961, Joyce Margaret Sharpe; one *s* one *d. Educ:* Ayr Academy; Royal Technical Coll., Glasgow; Glasgow Univ.; Jordanhill Coll. of Education. BSc (Pure Science). FEIS 1971. Teacher, Mauchline Secondary Sch., 1951–59; Head Teacher, Kilmaurs Secondary Sch., 1959–65; Rector, Mainholm Acad., 1965–74. Chm., Scottish Labour Party, 1959 and 1971. Vice-Chm., Scottish TUC, 1980–81, Chm., 1981–82 (Mem., Gen. Council, 1975–). Member: (Annan) Cttee on Future of Broadcasting, 1974–77; Gen. Adv. Council, BBC, 1981–84; Broadcasting Council for Scotland, 1985–; Manpower Services Cttee Scotland, 1977–; Council for Tertiary Educn in Scotland, 1979–83; Exec. Bd, European Trade Union Cttee for Educn, 1980–; Chm., European Cttee, World Conf. of Orgns of Teaching Profession, 1980–. *Address:* 52 Douglas Road, Longniddry, East Lothian, Scotland. *T:* Longniddry 52082.

POLLOCK, Martin Rivers, FRS 1962; Professor of Biology, University of Edinburgh, 1965–76, now Emeritus; *b* 10 Dec. 1914; *s* of Hamilton Rivers Pollock and Eveline Morton Pollock (*née* Bell); *m* 1st, 1941, Jean Ilsley Paradise (marr. diss.); two *s* two *d*; 2nd, 1979, Janet Frances Machen. *Educ:* Winchester Coll., Trinity Coll., Cambridge; University College Hospital, London. BA Cantab, 1936; Senior Scholar, Trinity Coll., Cambridge, 1936; MRCS, LRCP 1939; MB, BCh Cantab 1940. House Appointments at UCH and Brompton Hospital, 1940–41; Bacteriologist, Emergency Public Health Laboratory Service, 1941–45; seconded to work on Infective Hepatitis with MRC Unit, 1943–45; apppointment to scientific staff, Medical Research Council, under Sir Paul Fildes, FRS, 1945–; Head of Division of Bacterial Physiology, Nat. Inst. for Medical Research, Mill Hill (MRC), 1949–65. *Publications:* (ed) Report of Conference on Common Denominators in Art and Science, 1983; articles in British Journal of Experimental Pathology, Biochemical Journal, Journal of General Microbiology, etc. *Recreation:* contemplating, planning and occasionally undertaking various forms of mildly adventurous travel, preferably through deserts, painting. *Address:* Marsh Farm House, Margaret Marsh, Shaftesbury, Dorset SP7 0AZ. *T:* Marnhull 820479.

POLLOCK, Adm. of the Fleet Sir Michael (Patrick), GCB 1971 (KCB 1969; CB 1966); LVO 1952; DSC 1944; Bath King of Arms, 1976–85; *b* 19 Oct. 1916; *s* of late C. A. Pollock and of Mrs G. Pollock; *m* 1st, 1940, Margaret Steacy (*d* 1951), Bermuda; two *s* one *d*; 2nd, 1954, Marjory Helen Reece (*née* Bisset); one step *d. Educ:* RNC Dartmouth. Entered Navy, 1930; specialised in Gunnery, 1941. Served War of 1939–45 in Warspite, Vanessa, Arethusa and Norfolk, N. Atlantic, Mediterranean and Indian Ocean. Captain, Plans Div. of Admiralty and Director of Surface Weapons; comd HMS Vigo and Portsmouth Sqdn, 1958–59; comd HMS Ark Royal, 1963–64; Asst Chief of Naval Staff, 1964–66; Flag Officer Second in Command, Home Fleet, 1966–67; Flag Officer Submarines and Nato Commander Submarines, Eastern Atlantic, 1967–69; Controller of the Navy, 1970–71; Chief of Naval Staff and First Sea Lord, 1971–74; First and Principal Naval Aide-de-Camp to the Queen, 1972–74. Comdr, 1950; Capt., 1955; Rear-Adm., 1964; Vice-Adm., 1968; Adm., 1970. *Recreations:* sailing, tennis, shooting, fishing, travel. *Address:* The Ivy House, Churchstoke, Montgomery, Powys SY15 6DU. *T:* Churchstoke 426.

POLLOCK, Sir William H. M.; *see* Montagu-Pollock.

POLSON, Prof. Cyril John; Professor of Forensic Medicine, University of Leeds, 1947–69, now Emeritus Professor; *b* 1901; *s* of William Polson, MB, CM, and A. D., *d* of Thomas Parker, JP, MInstCE, FRSE; *m* 1932, Mary Watkinson Tordoff (*d* 1961); one *d*; *m* 1963, G. Mary Pullan (BSc, MB, ChB, MFCM, DObst, RCOG). *Educ:* Wrekin Coll.; Birmingham Univ. MB, ChB and MRCS, LRCP, 1924; MRCP 1926; FRCP, 1941; FRCPath, 1964; MD 1929, Birmingham. Called to the Bar, Inner Temple, 1940. Assistant Lecturer, Univ. of Manchester, 1927; Univ. of Leeds: Lecturer in Pathology, 1928; Senior Lecturer in Pathology, and Pathologist to St J. Hospital, Leeds, 1945; Hon. Member, N England Laryngological Society, 1948. Corr. Member la Société de Médecine Légale de France, 1950. Vice-President 2nd International Meeting in Forensic Medicine, NY, 1960; President: British Association in Forensic Medicine, 1962–65; British Acad. of Forensic Sciences, 1974–75; Mem., Leeds and West Riding Medico-Legal Society, 1963 (Pres. 1966); Hon. Mem., Leeds and West Riding Medico-Chirurgical Soc., 1970. A. G. Marshall Lectr, Midland Inst. of Forensic Medicine and Bd of Grad. Studies, Birmingham Univ., 1979. *Publications:* Clinical Toxicology (with M. A. Green and M. R. Lee), 2nd edn, 1969, 3rd edn, 1983; The Scientific Aspects of Forensic Medicine, 1969, Swedish trans., 1973; The Essentials of Forensic Medicine, 3rd edn (with D. J. Gee), 1973, 4th edn (with D. J. Gee and Bernard Knight), 1984; The Disposal of the Dead (with T. K. Marshall), 3rd edn, 1975; papers in scientific journals devoted to pathology and forensic medicine. *Recreations:* gardening, photography. *Address:* 16 Tewit Well Road, Harrogate HG2 8JE. *T:* Harrogate 503434.

POLTIMORE, 7th Baron *cr* 1831; **Mark Coplestone Bampfylde;** Bt 1641; *b* 8 June 1957; *s* of Captain the Hon. Anthony Gerard Hugh Bampfylde (*d* 1969) (*er s* of 6th Baron) and of Brita Yvonne (who *m* 2nd, 1975, Guy Elmes), *o d* of late Baron Rudolph Cederström; *S* grandfather, 1978; *m* 1982, Sally Anne, *d* of Dr Norman Miles; one *s*. *Heir:* *s* Hon. Henry Anthony Warwick Bampfylde, *b* 3 June 1985. *Address:* 55 Elsynge Road, SW18 2HR.

POLUNIN, Nicholas, CBE 1976; MS (Yale); MA, DPhil, DSc (Oxon.); FLS; FRGS; Editor (founding), Environmental Conservation, since 1974; Convener and General Editor, Environmental Monographs and Symposia, since 1979; Secretary-General and Editor, International Conferences on Environmental Future, since 1971; President: The Foundation for Environmental Conservation, since 1975; World Council for the Biosphere, since 1984; *b* Checkendon, Oxon, 26 June 1909; *e s* of late Vladimir and Elizabeth Violet (*née* Hart) Polunin; *m* 1st, 1939, Helen Lovat Fraser (*d* 1973); one *s*; 2nd, 1948, Helen Eugenie Campbell; two *s* one *d*. *Educ:* The Hall, Weybridge; Latymer Upper and privately; Oxford, Yale and Harvard Univs. Open Scholar of Christ Church, Oxford, 1928–32; First Class Hons Nat. Sci. Final Examination, Botany and Ecology; Goldsmiths' Senior Studentship for Research, 1932–33; Botanical tutor in various Oxford Colls, 1932–47; Henry Fellowship at Pierson Coll., Yale Univ., USA, 1933–34 (Sigma Xi); Departmental Demonstrator in Botany 1934–35, and Senior (Research) Scholar of New Coll., Oxford, 1934–36; Dept of Scientific and Industrial Research, Senior Research Award, 1935–38; Rolleston Memorial Prize, 1938; DSIR Special Investigator, 1938; Research Associate, Gray Herbarium, Harvard Univ., USA, 1936–37, and subs. Foreign Research Associate; Fielding Curator and Keeper of the Univ. Herbaria, Oxford, and Univ. Demonstrator and Lectr in Botany, 1939–47; Oxford Univ. Botanical Moderator, 1941–45; Macdonald Prof. of Botany, McGill Univ., Canada, 1947–52 (Visiting Prof., 1946–47); Research Fellow, Harvard Univ., 1950–53; Lectr in Plant Science and Research Associate, Yale Univ., 1953–55; Project Dir, US Air Force, 1953–55, and Consultant to US Army Corps of Engineers; formerly Sen. Research Fell. and Lectr, New Coll., Oxford; Prof. of Plant Ecology and Taxonomy, Head of Dept of Botany, and Dir of Univ. Herbarium, etc., Baghdad, Iraq, Jan. 1956–58 (revolution); Founding Prof. of Botany and Head of Dept, Faculty of Science (which he established as Dean), Univ. of Ife, Nigeria, 1962–66 (revolutions, etc). Leverhulme Res. Award, 1941–43; Arctic Inst. Res. Fellowship, 1946–48; Guggenheim Mem. Fellowship, 1950–52. Haley Lectr, Acadia Univ., NS, 1950; Visiting Lectr and Adviser on Biology, Brandeis Univ., Waltham, Mass, 1953–54; Guest Prof., Univ. of Geneva, 1959–61 and 1975–76. US Order of Polaris; Marie-Victorin Medal for services to Canadian botany; Ramdeo Medal for Environmental Scis, India, 1986; FRHS. Fellow: AAAS, Arctic Inst. NA, American Geographical Soc. Member or Leader, numerous scientific expeditions from 1930, particularly in arctic or sub-arctic regions, including Spitsbergen, Lapland (3 times), Iceland, Greenland, Canadian Eastern Arctic (5 times, including confirmation of Spicer Islands in Foxe Basin north of Hudson Bay and discovery in 1946 of last major islands to be added to world map following their naming in 1949 as Prince Charles Is. and Air Force Is.), Labrador—Ungava (many times), Canadian Western Arctic (including Magnetic Pole), Alaska, summer and winter flights over geographical North Pole; subsequently in Middle East and West Africa; Ford Foundation Award, Scandinavia and USSR, 1966–67. International Botanical Congresses: VII (Stockholm, 1950); VIII (Paris, 1954); X (Edinburgh, 1964); XI (Seattle, 1969, symposium chm., etc); XII (Leningrad, 1975, Conservation Section 1st chm., etc.); XIII (Sydney, 1981); International Congresses of Ecology: I (The Hague, 1974); II (Jerusalem, 1978); IV (Syracuse, NY, 1986). Founding Editor: Biological Conservation, 1967–74; Plant Science Monographs, 1954–78; Associate Ed., Environmental Pollution, 1969–; Chm. Editl Bd, Cambridge Studies in Environmental Policy; Mem., Adv. Bd, The Environmentalist, 1981–, and other jls. Chairman: Internat. Steering Cttee, and Editor of Proceedings, 1st Internat. Conf. on Environmental Future, Finland, 1971, 2nd Conf., Iceland, 1978; Chm. (founding), Foundn for Environmental Conservation, 1973– (subsequently consolidated and placed under Swiss cantonal and federal surveillance). *Publications:* Russian Waters, 1931; The Isle of Auks, 1932; Botany of the Canadian Eastern Arctic, vol. I, Pteridophyta and Spermatophyta, 1940; (ed) vol. II, Thallophyta and Bryophyta, 1947; vol. III, Vegetation and Ecology, 1948; Arctic Unfolding, 1949; Circumpolar Arctic Flora, 1959; Introduction to Plant Geography, 1960 (subseq. Amer. and other edns); Eléments de Géographie botanique, 1967; (ed) The Environmental Future, 1972; Growth Without Ecodisasters?, 1980; Ecosystem Theory and Application, 1986; papers chiefly on arctic and boreal flora, phytogeography, ecology, vegetation, aerobiology, and conservation; editor of International Industry, 1943–46, and of World Crops Books, 1954–76; contrib. Encyclopædia Britannica, Encyclopedia of the Biological Scis, etc., and some 450 other scientific papers, editorials, reviews, etc, to various jls. *Recreations:* travel and scientific exploration, nature conservation, stock-markets. *Address:* 7 Chemin Taverney, 1218 Grand-Saconnex, Geneva, Switzerland. *T:* (022) 982383/84; c/o New College, Oxford. *Clubs:* Reform (life); Harvard (life), Torrey Botanical (New York City); New England Botanical (Boston); Canadian Field Naturalists' (Ottawa).

POLWARTH, 10th Lord, *cr* 1690 (Scot.); **Henry Alexander Hepburne-Scott,** TD; DL; Vice-Lord-Lieutenant, Borders Region (Roxburgh, Ettrick and Lauderdale), since 1975; Member, Royal Company of Archers; a Scots Representative Peer, 1945–63; Chartered Accountant; *b* 17 Nov. 1916; *s* of late Hon. Walter Thomas Hepburne-Scott (*d* 1942); *S* grandfather, 1944; *m* 1st, 1943, Caroline Margaret (marr. diss. 1969; she *d* 1982), 2nd *d* of late Captain R. A. Hay, Marlefield, Roxburghshire, and Helmsley, Yorks; one *s* three *d*; 2nd, 1969, Jean, *d* of late Adm. Sir Angus Cunninghame Graham of Gartmore, KBE, CB, and formerly wife of C. E. Jauncey, QC (now Hon. Lord Jauncey); two step *s* one step *d*. *Educ:* Eton Coll.; King's Coll., Cambridge. Served War of 1939–45, Captain, Lothians and Border Yeomanry. Former Partner, firm of Chiene and Tait, CA, Edinburgh; Governor, Bank of Scotland, 1966–72, Director, 1974–; Chm., General Accident, Fire & Life Assurance Corp., 1968–72; Director: ICI Ltd, 1969–72, 1974–81; Halliburton Co., 1974–; Canadian Pacific Ltd, 1975–86; Sun Life Assurance Co. of Canada, 1975–84. Minister of State, Scottish Office, 1972–74. Chm., later Pres., Scottish Council (Develt and Industry), 1955–72. Member: Franco-British Council, 1981–; H of L Select Cttee on Trade, 1984–85. Chm., Scottish Nat. Orchestra Soc., 1975–79. Chancellor, Aberdeen Univ., 1966–86. Hon. LLD: St Andrews; Aberdeen; Hon. DLitt Heriot-Watt; DUniv Stirling. FRSE; FRSA; Hon. FRIAS. DL Roxburgh, 1962. *Heir:* *s* Master of Polwarth, *qv*. *Address:* Harden, Hawick, Roxburghshire. *T:* Hawick 72069. *Clubs:* Pratt's, Army and Navy; New (Edinburgh).

See also Baron Moran.

POLWARTH, Master of; Hon. Andrew Walter Hepburne-Scott; *b* 30 Nov. 1947; *s* and *heir* of 10th Lord Polwarth, *qv*; *m* 1971, Isabel Anna, *e d* of Maj. J. F. H. Surtees, OBE, MC; two *s* two *d*. *Educ:* Eton; Trinity Hall, Cambridge. *Address:* 72 Cloncurry Street, SW6. *Clubs:* New (Edinburgh); Knickerbocker (New York).

POLYNESIA, Bishop in, since 1975; **Rt. Rev. Jabez Leslie Bryce;** Chairman, Pacific Conference of Churches, since 1976; *b* 25 Jan. 1935. *Educ:* St John's College, Auckland, NZ (LTh); St Andrew's Seminary, Manila, Phillipines (BTh). Deacon 1960, priest 1962, Polynesia; Curate of Suva, 1960–63; Priest-in-charge: Tonga, 1964; St Peter's Chinese Congregation, Manila, 1965–67; Archdeacon of Suva, 1967–69; Deputy Vicar-General, Holy Trinity Cathedral, Suva, 1967–72; Lectr, St John Baptist Theological Coll., Suva, 1967–69; Vicar of Viti Levu W, 1969–75; Archdeacon in Polynesia, 1969–75; Vicar-General of Polynesia, 1972–75. *Recreations:* tennis, golf. *Address:* Bishop's House, PO Box 35, Suva, Fiji Islands. *T:* (office) 24357, (home) 23436.

POMEROY, family name of **Viscount Harberton.**

PONCET, Jean André F.; *see* François-Poncet.

PONSFORD, Brian David; Under Secretary (Director of Waste Disposal), Department of the Environment, since 1985; *b* 23 Dec. 1938; *s* of Herbert E. Ponsford and Kathleen W. C. (*née* Parish); *m* 1966, Erica Neumark; one *s*. *Educ:* City of London Sch.; Corpus Christi Coll., Oxford (1st Cl. Classical Mods 1958, 1st Cl. Lit. Hum. 1960). Teacher, Westminster Sch., 1960–61; Asst Principal, Min. of Housing and Local Govt, 1961–67; Asst Private Sec. to Minister, 1964–66; Private Sec. to Minister of State, 1966–67; Principal, 1967–69; Principal, Cabinet Office, 1969–71, DoE, 1971–73; Asst Sec., DoE, 1973; Counsellor, Office of UK Perm. Representative to European Communities, 1975–78; Under Sec., DoE, 1981–; Dir, Local Govt Finance Policy, 1981–84, Housing, 1984–85. Dir, Medical Systems Gp, Smiths Industries, 1985–. *Recreations:* music, books, films. *Address:* 19 Hermitage Lane, NW2. *T:* 01–435 2368.

PONSONBY, family name of **Earl of Bessborough** and of **Barons de Mauley, Ponsonby of Shulbrede,** and **Sysonby.**

PONSONBY OF SHULBREDE, 3rd Baron *cr* 1930, of Shulbrede; **Thomas Arthur Ponsonby;** Chief Opposition Whip, House of Lords, since 1982; *b* 23 Oct. 1930; *o* surv. *s* of 2nd Baron Ponsonby of Shulbrede, and Hon. Elizabeth Bigham (*d* 1985), *o d* of 2nd Viscount Mersey, PC, CMG, CBE; *S* father, 1976; *m* 1st, 1956, Ursula Mary (marr. diss. 1973), *yr d* of Comdr Thomas Stanley Lane Fox-Pitt, OBE, RN; one *s* two *d* (and one *d* decd); 2nd, 1973, Maureen Estelle Campbell-Tiech, *d* of Alfred William Windsor, Reigate, Surrey. *Educ:* St Ronan's Sch.; Bryanston; Hertford Coll., Oxford. Royal Borough of Kensington and Chelsea (formerly Royal Borough of Kensington): Councillor, 1956–65; Alderman, 1964–74; Leader, Labour Gp, 1968–73. GLC: Alderman, 1970–77; Chm. Covent Garden Cttee, 1973–75; Chm., Central Area Bd (Transport and Planning Cttees), 1973–76; Chm. of Council, 1976–77. An Opposition Whip, 1979–81, Dep. Chief Opposition Whip, 1981–82, House of Lords. Chairman: London Tourist Bd, 1976–80; Greater London Citizens Advice Bureaux Service Ltd, 1977–79; Age Concern Greater London, 1977–78; London Convention Bureau, 1977–85; Bd of Trustees, Community Projects Foundn, 1978–82; Tourism Soc., 1980–83 (Pres., 1984–); Local Govt Trng Bd, 1981–; Galleon Trust, 1981– (Pres., Galleon World Travel Assoc. Ltd, 1977–81); Rona-Naïve Artists Ltd, 1978–83. Contested (Lab) Heston and Isleworth, general election, 1959. Fabian Society: Asst Gen. Sec., 1961–64; Gen. Sec., 1964–76. President: British Handball Assoc., 1981–; Hotel Industry Mkty Gp, 1983–; Fedn of Industrial Develt Authorities, 1983–. Governor, London Sch. of Economics, 1970–. Patron New Mozart Orch., 1978–. *Recreations:* eating, drinking, gardening. *Heir:* *s* Hon. Frederick Matthew Thomas Ponsonby, *b* 27 Oct. 1958. *Address:* 9 Harwood Terrace, SW6 2AF. *T:* 01–736 1699.

PONSONBY, Sir Ashley (Charles Gibbs), 2nd Bt *cr* 1956; MC 1945; Chairman: Colville Estate Ltd; Trans-Oceanic Trust Ltd; Director: J. Henry Schroder, Wagg & Co. Ltd, 1962–80; Rowntree Mackintosh Ltd and other companies; Lord-Lieutenant of Oxfordshire, since 1980; *b* 21 Feb. 1921; *o s* of Col Sir Charles Edward Ponsonby, 1st Bt, TD, and Hon. Winifred (*d* 1984), *d* of 1st Baron Hunsdon; *S* father, 1976; *m* 1950, Lady Martha Butler, *yr d* of 6th Marquess of Ormonde, CVO, MC; four *s*. *Educ:* Eton; Balliol College, Oxford. 2nd Lieut Coldstream Guards, 1941; served war 1942–45 (North Africa and Italy, wounded); Captain 1943; on staff Bermuda Garrison, 1945–46. A Church Commissioner, 1963–80; Mem., Council of Duchy of Lancaster, 1977–. DL Oxon, 1974–80. *Heir:* *e s* Charles Ashley Ponsonby [*b* 10 June 1951; *m* 1983, Mary P., *yr d* of late A. R. Bromley Davenport and of Mrs A. R. Bromley Davenport, Over Peover, Knutsford, Cheshire; two *s*]. *Address:* Woodleys, Woodstock, Oxon. *T:* Woodstock 811422. *Club:* Pratt's.

PONSONBY, Myles Walter, CBE 1966; HM Diplomatic Service, retired; Foreign and Commonwealth Office, 1977–80; *b* 12 Sept. 1924; *s* of late Victor Coope Ponsonby, MC and Gladys Edith Ponsonby (*née* Walter); *m* 1951, Anne Veronica Theresa Maynard, *y d* of Brig. Francis Herbert Maynard, CB, DSO, MC, and of Ethel Maynard (*née* Bates); one *s* two *d*. *Educ:* St Aubyn's, Rottingdean; Eton College. HM Forces (Captain, KRRC), 1942–49. Entered Foreign (subseq. Diplomatic) Service, 1951; served in: Egypt, 1951; Cyprus, 1952–53; Beirut, 1953–56; Djakarta, 1958–61; Nairobi, 1963–64; Hanoi (Consul-Gen.), 1964–65; FO, 1966–69; Rome, 1969–71; FCO, 1972–74; Ambassador to Mongolian People's Republic, 1974–77. *Recreation:* gardening. *Address:* The Old Vicarage, Porton, near Salisbury, Wilts SP4 0LH. *T:* Idmiston 610914. *Club:* Army and Navy.

PONSONBY, Robert Noel, CBE 1985; Controller of Music, BBC, 1972–85; *b* 19 Dec. 1926; *o s* of late Noel Ponsonby, BMus, Organist Christ Church Cathedral, Oxford, and Mary White-Thomson (now Mrs L. H. Jaques, Winchester); *m* 1st, 1957, Una Mary (marr. diss.), *er d* of late W. J. Kenny; 2nd, 1977, Lesley Margaret Black, *o d* of late G. T. Black. *Educ:* Eton; Trinity Coll., Oxford. MA Oxon, Eng. Litt. Commissioned Scots Guards, 1945–47. Organ Scholar, Trinity Coll., Oxford, 1948–50; staff of Glyndebourne Opera, 1951–55; Artistic Director of the Edinburgh International Festival, 1955–60; with Independent Television Authority, 1962–64; Gen. Administrator, Scottish Nat. Orchestra, 1964–72. Director, Commonwealth Arts Festival, Glasgow, 1965. Artistic Adviser to Internat. Arts Guild of Bahamas, 1960–72. Mem., Music Adv. Panel, Arts Council of GB, 1986–. Trustee, Young Concert Artists Trust, 1984–. Governor, Purcell Sch., 1985–. Hon. RAM 1975. FRSA 1979. *Publication:* Short History of Oxford University Opera Club, 1950. *Recreations:* fell-walking, English and Scottish painting, music. *Address:* 11 St Cuthbert's Road, NW2 3QJ. *Clubs:* Oriental; Trinity Society.

PONTECORVO, Guido, FRS 1955; FRSE 1946; FLS 1971; PhD (Edinburgh) 1941; DrAgr (Pisa) 1928; *b* Pisa, Italy, 29 Nov. 1907; *s* of Massimo Pontecorvo and Maria (*née* Maroni); *m* 1939, Leonore Freyenmuth, Frauenfeld, Switzerland; one *d. Educ:* Pisa (Classics). Ispettorato Agrario per la Toscana, Florence, 1931–38; Inst. of Animal Genetics, Univ. of Edinburgh, 1938–40 and 1944–45; Dept of Zoology, Univ. of Glasgow, 1941–44; Dept of Genetics, Univ. of Glasgow, 1945–68 (Prof. 1956–68); Mem. Res. Staff, Imperial Cancer Res. Fund, 1968–75, Hon. Consultant Geneticist, 1975–80. Jesup Lectr, Columbia Univ., 1956; Messenger Lectr, Cornell Univ., 1957; Visiting Prof., Albert Einstein Coll. Med., 1965, 1966; Vis. Lectr, Washington State Univ., 1967; Royal Society, Leverhulme Overseas Vis. Prof., Inst. of Biophysics, Rio de Janeiro, 1969 and Dept of Biology, Pahlavi Univ., 1974; Sloane Foundn Vis. Prof., Vermont, 1971; Visiting Professor: UCL, 1968–75; King's Coll., London, 1970–71; Biology Dept, Tehran Univ., 1975; Prof. Ospite Linceo, Scuola Normale Superiore, Pisa, 1976–81; L. C. Dunn Lectr, NY Blood Center, 1976; Raman Prof., Indian Acad. of Scis, 1982–83; J. Weigle Meml Lectr, CIT, 1984; Gandhi Meml Lectr, Raman Inst., 1983. Pres., Genetical Soc., 1964–66; Vice-Pres., Inst. of Biology, 1969–71. For. Hon. Member: Amer. Acad. Arts and Sciences, 1958; Danish Royal Acad. Sci. and Letters, 1966; Peruvian Soc. of Medical Genetics, 1969; Indian National Science Acad., 1983; Indian Acad. of Scis, 1984; For. Associate, Nat. Acad. of Scis, USA, 1983. Hon. DSc: Leicester, 1968; Camerino, 1974; East Anglia, 1974; Hon. LLD Glasgow, 1978. Hansen Prize, Carlsberg Foundn, 1961; Darwin Medal, Royal Soc., 1978. Campano d'Oro, Pisa, 1979. *Publications:* Ricerche sull' economia montana dell' Appennino Toscano, 1933 (Florence); Trends in Genetic Analysis, 1958. Numerous papers on genetics and high mountain botany. *Recreation:* alpine plants photography. *Address:* Flat 25, Cranfield House, 97 Southampton Row, WC1B 4HH. *T:* 01–636 9441.

PONTEFRACT, Bishop Suffragan of, since 1971; **Rt. Rev. Thomas Richard Hare;** *b* 1922; *m* 1963, Sara, *d* of Lt-Col J. E. Spedding, OBE; one *s* two *d. Educ:* Marlborough; Trinity Coll., Oxford; Westcott House, Cambridge. RAF, 1942–45, Curate of Haltwhistle, 1950–52; Domestic Chaplain to Bishop of Manchester, 1952–59; Canon Residentiary of Carlisle Cathedral, 1959–65; Archdeacon of Westmorland and Furness, 1965–71; Vicar of St George with St Luke, Barrow-in-Furness, 1965–69; Vicar of Winster, 1969–71. *Address:* 306 Barnsley Road, Wakefield WF2 6AX. *T:* Wakefield 256935.

PONTEFRACT, Archdeacon of; *see* Unwin, Ven. K.

PONTI, Signora Carlo; *see* Loren, Sophia.

PONTIFEX, Brig. David More, CBE 1977 (OBE 1965; MBE 1956); General Secretary, Army Cadet Force Association and Secretary, Combined Cadet Force Association, since 1977; *b* 16 Sept. 1922; *s* of Comdr John Weddall Pontifex, RN, and Monica Pontifex; *m* 1968, Kathleen Betsy (*née* Matheson); one *s* four *d. Educ:* Worth Preparatory Sch.; Downside Sch. Commnd The Rifle Brigade, 1942; served War, Italy (despatches); Staff Coll., Camberley, 1951; HQ Parachute Brigade, 1952–54; Kenya, 1954–56; War Office, 1956–58; Armed Forces Staff Coll., USA, 1958–59; Brigade Major, 63 Gurkha Brigade, 1961–62; CO 1st Bn Federal Regular Army, Aden, 1963–64; GSO1 2nd Div., BAOR, 1965–66; Col GS, Staff Coll., Camberley, 1967–69; Divisional Brig., The Light Div., 1969–73; Dep. Dir, Army Staff Duties, MoD, 1973–75; Dep. Comdr and COS, SE District, 1975–77, retired 1977. ADC to the Queen, 1975–77. *Address:* 68 Shortheath Road, Farnham, Surrey. *T:* Farnham 723284. *Club:* Naval and Military.

PONTIN, Sir Frederick William, (Sir Fred Pontin), Kt 1976; Founder: Pontin's Ltd, 1946; Pontinental Ltd, 1963; Chairman and Joint Managing Director of Pontin's Ltd, 1946–79, and Pontinental (HS) Ltd, 1972–79; Deputy Chairman, Kunick Leisure, since 1985 (Chairman, 1983–85); *b* 24 Oct. 1906; *m* Dorothy Beatrice Mortimer; one *d. Educ:* Sir George Monoux Grammar Sch., Walthamstow. Began career on London Stock Exchange, 1920. Catering and welfare work for Admiralty, Orkney Is, 1939–46. Acquired: Industrial Catering Bristol, 1946; Brean Sands Holiday Village, 1946. Chief Barker, Variety Club of GB (Raising £1,000,000 for charity), 1968; Mem. Exec. Bd, Variety Club, 1968–, Pres. 1969–75, formed 15 regional centres of club; Companion Mem., Grand Order of Water Rats; co-opted Mem., Stars Orgn for Spastics. Mem., St John Council; Prescot Band. Life Mem., BRCS (Hon. Vice Pres., Dorset Branch). Underwriting Mem., Lloyd's Insurance. Freeman of Christchurch, Dorset. *Recreations:* racing (owner of Specify, winner of 1971 Grand National, and Cala Mesquida, winner of 1971 Schweppes Gold Trophy); connected with Walthamstow Avenue FC for many years prior to 1939–45 war; interested in all sporting activities. *Address:* Flat 64, 3 Whitehall Court, SW1A 2EL. *T:* 01–839 5251. *Clubs:* Farmers', Eccentric, Saints and Sinners, Institute of Directors.

POOLE, family name of **Baron Poole.**

POOLE, 1st Baron, *cr* 1958, of Aldgate; **Oliver Brian Sanderson Poole,** PC 1963; CBE 1945; TD; Member of Lloyd's; lately Director, S. Pearson & Son Ltd; *b* 11 Aug. 1911; *s* of late Donald Louis Poole of Lloyd's; *m* 1st, 1933, Betty Margaret Gilkison (marr. diss., 1951); one *s* three *d*; 2nd, 1952, Mrs Daphne Heber Percy (marr. diss., 1965); 3rd, 1966, Barbara Ann Taylor. *Educ:* Eton; Christ Church, Oxford. Life Guards, 1932–33; joined Warwickshire Yeomanry, 1934. Service in 1939–45 in Iraq, Syria, North Africa, Sicily and NW Europe (despatches thrice, MBE, OBE, CBE, US Legion of Merit, Order of Orange Nassau). MP (C) Oswestry Division of Salop, 1945–50. Conservative Party Organisation: Jt Hon. Treas., 1952–55; Chairman, 1955–57; Dep.-Chm., 1957–59; Jt Chm., May-Oct. 1963, Vice-Chm., Oct. 1963–Oct. 1964. Governor of Old Vic, 1948–63; a Trustee, Nat. Gallery, 1973–81. Hon. DSc City Univ., 1970. *Heir: s* Hon. David Charles Poole [*b* 6 Jan. 1945; *m* 1st, 1967, Fiona, *d* of John Donald, London SW6; one *s*; 2nd, 1975, Philippa, *d* of Mark Reeve]. *Address:* 24 Campden Hill Gate, Duchess of Bedford Walk, W8. *Clubs:* MCC, Buck's; Royal Yacht Squadron (Cowes).
See also Sir John Lucas-Tooth, Bt.

POOLE, Anthony Cecil James; Head of Administration Department, House of Commons, since 1985; *b* 9 Oct. 1927; *s* of Walter James Poole and Daisy Poole (*née* Voyle); *m* 1951, Amelia Keziah (*née* Pracy); one *d. Educ:* Headlands Grammar School, Swindon. Served RN, 1945–47; Department of Employment, 1947–76; Principal Establishments Officer, Manpower Services Commn, 1976–80; House of Commons, 1980, Head of Establishments Office, 1981. *Recreations:* golf, gardening. *Address:* Orchard End, Guildford Road, Woking, Surrey GU22 7UT.

POOLE, Mrs Avril Anne Barker; Chief Nursing Officer, Department of Health and Social Security, since 1982; *b* 11 April 1934; *d* of Arthur George and Norah Heritage; *m* 1959, John Percy Poole. *Educ:* High Sch., Southampton. SRN 1955, SCM 1957, Health Visitors Cert., 1958. Asst Chief Nursing Officer, City of Westminster, 1967–69; Chief Nursing Officer, London Borough of Merton, 1969–73; Area Nursing Officer, Surrey AHA, 1974–81; Dep. Chief Nursing Officer, DHSS, 1981–82. CBIM 1984. *Address:* Ancaster House, Church Hill, Merstham, Surrey. *T:* Merstham 4332.

POOLE, David Anthony; QC 1984; a Recorder of the Crown Court, since 1983; *b* 8 June 1938; *s* of William Joseph Poole and Lena Thomas; *m* 1974, Pauline Ann O'Flaherty; four *s. Educ:* Ampleforth; Jesus Coll., Oxford (MA); Univ. of Manchester Inst. of Science and Technology (DipTechSc). Called to the Bar, Middle Temple, 1968. Chm., Assoc. of Lawyers for the Defence of the Unborn, 1985–. *Address:* 1 Deans Court, Crown Square, Manchester. *T:* 061–834 4097; 5 Essex Court, Temple, EC4. *Clubs:* London Irish Rugby Football, Vincent's, The Wolfhounds, Northern Lawn Tennis.

POOLE, David James, RP 1969; ARCA; artist; President, Royal Society of Portrait Painters, since 1983; *b* 5 June 1931; *s* of Thomas Herbert Poole and Catherine Poole; *m* 1958, Iris Mary Toomer; three *s. Educ:* Stoneleigh Secondary Sch.; Wimbledon Sch. of Art; Royal Coll. of Art. National Service, RE, 1949–51. Sen. Lectr in Painting and Drawing, Wimbledon Sch. of Art, 1962–77. One-man Exhibns, Zurich and London. Portraits include: The Queen, The Duke of Edinburgh, The Queen Mother, Prince Charles, Princess Anne, Princess Margaret, Earl Mountbatten of Burma and The Duke of Kent; also distinguished members of govt, industry, commerce, medicine, the academic and legal professions. Work in private collections of the Queen and the Duke of Edinburgh, and in Australia, S Africa, Bermuda, France, W Germany and Switzerland. *Recreations:* painting, drawing. *Address:* Peartree Cottage, Silkmore Lane, West Horsley, Surrey KT24 6JQ. *T:* East Horsley 3765.

POOLE, Isobel Anne; Sheriff of the Lothian and Borders, since 1979, at Edinburgh, since 1986; *b* 9 Dec. 1941; *d* of late John Cecil Findlay Poole, DM Oxon, and of Constance Mary (*née* Gilkes), SRN. *Educ:* Oxford High Sch. for Girls; Edinburgh Univ. (LLB). Admitted to Faculty of Advocates, 1964. Formerly Standing Jun. Counsel to Registrar Gen. for Scotland. Mem., Sheriffs' Council, 1980–85. *Recreations:* country, arts, houses, gardens, friends. *Address:* 5 Randolph Place, Edinburgh EH3 7TQ. *T:* 031–225 1931.

POOLE, Rev. Canon Joseph Weston; Canon Emeritus of Coventry Cathedral, since 1977; *b* 25 March 1909; *s* of Rev. S. J. Poole and Mrs Poole (*née* Weston); *m* 1945, Esmé Beatrice Mounsey; three *s* two *d. Educ:* St George's School, Windsor; King's School, Canterbury; Jesus Coll., Cambridge (Organ Schol. and Class. Exhibnr); Westcott House, Cambridge. Curate of St Mary-at-the-Walls, Colchester, 1933; Sub-Warden of Student Movement House, 1935; Minor Canon and Sacrist of Canterbury, 1936; Precentor of Canterbury, 1937; Rector of Merstham, Surrey, 1949; Hon. Canon of Coventry, 1958, Precentor, 1958–77; Canon Residentiary, 1963–77. ChStJ, 1974. FRSCM 1977. *Recreations:* music, literature, typography. *Address:* 132 Charminster Drive, Coventry CU3 5AD.

POOLE HUGHES, Rt. Rev. John Richard Worthington; *b* 8 Aug. 1916; *s* of late Canon W. W. Poole Hughes, Warden of Llandovery College and late Bertha Cecil (*née* Rhys). *Educ:* Uppingham School; Hertford College, Oxford; Wells Theological College. BA (Lit. Hum.) 1939, MA 1945. Royal Artillery, 1939–45. Deacon, 1947; Priest, 1948; Curate, St Michael and All Angels, Aberystwyth, 1947–50; UMCA Missionary, 1950–57; Staff, St Michael's College, Llandaff, 1957–59; Home Secretary, Universities' Mission to Central Africa, 1959–62; Bishop of South-West Tanganyika, 1962–74; Asst Bishop of Llandaff and Asst Curate, Llantwit Major, 1975; Bishop of Llandaff, 1976–85. *Publication:* Asomaye na Afahamu (SPCK), 1959. *Recreation:* writing. *Address:* St Ethelbert's House, Castle Hill, Hereford HR1 2NJ.

POOLEY, Dr Derek; Deputy Director, Atomic Energy Establishment, Winfrith, since 1986; *b* 28 Oct. 1937; *s* of Richard Pike Pooley and Evelyn Pooley; *m* 1961; Jennifer Mary Davey; two *s* one *d. Educ:* Sir James Smith's Sch., Camelford, Cornwall; Birmingham Univ. (BSc 1958; PhD 1961). FInstP 1979; FInstE 1984. A. A. Noyes Res. Fellow, Calif Inst. of Technol., Pasadena, 1961–62; UKAEA, Harwell: Res. Scientist, 1962–68; Leader of Defects Gp, later of Physics Applications Gp, 1968–76; Head of Materials Develt Div., 1976–81; Dir of Non-nuclear Energy Res., 1981–83; Chief Scientist, Dept of Energy, 1983–86. *Publications:* Real Solids and Radiation, 1975; chapters in: Treatise on Materials Science and Technology, 1974; Radiation Damage Processes in Materials, 1975; Shaping Tomorrow, 1981; Energy and Feedstocks in the Chemical Industry, 1983. *Recreations:* photography, gardening, walking, *Address:* 19a Park Homer Drive, Wimborne Minster, Dorset BH21 2SR. *T:* Wimborne 841741.

POOLEY, Frederick Bernard, CBE 1968; PPRIBA; Architect to Greater London Council, 1978–80, Controller of Planning and Transportation, 1974–80, and Superintending Architect of Metropolitan Buildings, 1978–80; *b* 18 April 1916; *s* of George Pooley and Elizabeth Pawley; *m* 1944, Hilda Olive Williams; three *d. Educ:* West Ham Grammar Sch.; RIBA, FRICS, FRTPI, MIStructE, FCIArb. Served war, RE, 1940–45. Deputy Borough Architect and Planning Officer, County Borough of West Ham, 1949–51; Deputy City Architect and Planning Officer, Coventry, 1951–54; County Architect and Planning Officer, Bucks, 1954–74. Major projects include: public and sch. bldg programme; scheme for public acquisition of bldgs of arch. or hist. interest for preservation and resale; new methods for assembling and servicing land; early planning work for new Milton Keynes. RIBA: Mem. Council, 1962–; Treasurer, 1972; Pres., 1973–75. *Publications:* contribs on planning, transport and architecture. *Address:* Long Ridge, Whiteleaf, Aylesbury, Bucks HP17 0LZ. *T:* Princes Risborough 6151. *Club:* Arts.

POOLEY, Peter; Deputy Director General, Agriculture, European Commission, since 1983; *b* 19 June 1936; *er* (twin) *s* of late W. M. Pooley, OBE, Truro, and of Grace Lidbury; *m* 1966, Janet Mary, *er d* of Jack Pearson, Banbury; one *s* one *d. Educ:* Brentwood Sch.; Clare Coll., Cambridge (BA); Royal Tank Regt. Joined MAFF as Asst Principal, 1959; seconded to: Diplomatic Service, 1961–63 (served in Brussels) and 1979–82 (Minister (Agric.), Office of UK Perm. Rep. to EEC, Brussels); CSD, 1977–79; Under-Sec., 1979, Fisheries Sec., 1982, MAFF. *Address:* 53 De Reymaekerlaan, 1980 Tervuren, Belgium; 24 Burghley House, Oakfield, Somerset Road, Wimbledon SW19.
See also R. Pooley.

POOLEY, Robin; Chief Executive, Potato Marketing Board, since 1981; Director: Butchers Co. Estates Ltd, since 1977; Solanex Ltd, since 1981; Member, British Agricultural Council, since 1981; *b* 19 June 1936; *yr* (twin) *s* of late W. Melville Pooley, OBE and of Grace M. Pooley (*née* Lidbury); *m* 1972, Margaret Anne, *yr d* of Jack Pearson, Banbury; one *d. Educ:* Brentwood School. Various posts, Towers & Co. Ltd, 1954–71; Gen. Manager, CWS Gp, 1971–76; Man. Dir, Buxted Poultry Ltd, 1976–81. Renter Assistant, Butchers' Co., 1986. *Recreations:* country pursuits. *Address:* Potato Marketing

Board, 50 Hans Crescent, Knightsbridge, SW1. *T:* 01–589 4874. *Clubs:* Farmers', City Livery.
See also P. Pooley.

POORE, Dennis; *see* Poore, R. D.

POORE, Duncan; *see* Poore, M. E. D.

POORE, Sir Herbert Edward, 6th Bt, *cr* 1795; *b* April 1930; *s* of Sir Edward Poore, 5th Bt, and Amelia Guliemone; *S* father 1938. *Heir: u* Nasionceno Poore [*b* 1900; *m* Juana Borda (*d* 1943); three *s* three *d*]. *Address:* Curuzu Cuatia, Corrientes, Argentine Republic.

POORE, Dr (Martin Edward) Duncan, MA, PhD; FIBiol; Director, Forestry and Land Use Programme (formerly Senior Fellow), International Institute for Environment and Development, and consultant in conservation and land use, since 1983; *b* 25 May 1925; *s* of T. E. D. Poore and Elizabeth McMartin; *m* 1948, Judith Ursula, *d* of Lt-Gen. Sir Treffry Thompson, KCSI, CB, CBE, and late Mary Emily, *d* of Rev. Canon Medd; two *s*. *Educ:* Trinity Coll., Glenalmond; Edinburgh Univ.; Clare Coll., Cambridge. MA, PhD Cantab.; MA Oxon. MICFor. Japanese interpreter, 1943–45. Nature Conservancy, 1953–56; Consultant Ecologist, Hunting Technical Services, 1956–59; Prof. of Botany, Univ. of Malaya, Kuala Lumpur, 1959–65; Dean of Science, Univ. of Malaya, 1964–65; Lectr, Forestry Dept, Oxford, 1965–66; Dir, Nature Conservancy, 1966–73; Scientific Dir, Internat. Union for Conservation of Nature and Natural Resources, Switzerland, 1974–78; Prof. of Forest Science and Dir, Commonwealth Forestry Inst., Oxford Univ., 1980–83; Fellow of St John's Coll., Oxford, 1980–83. Member: Thames Water Authority, 1981–83; Nature Conservancy Council, 1981–84. FRSA; FRGS. *Publications:* papers on ecology and land use in various jls and scientific periodicals. *Recreations:* hill walking, natural history, music, gardening, photography. *Address:* Evenlode, Stonesfield, Oxon. *T:* Stonesfield 246. *Club:* Royal Commonwealth Society.

POORE, Roger Dennistoun; Executive Chairman: Manganese Bronze Holdings plc (Chairman, since 1963; Director, since 1961); Federated Trust Corporation Ltd, since 1967; Chairman, The Scottish & Mercantile Investment plc, since 1971 (Director, since 1965); Member Lloyd's, since 1950; *b* 19 Aug. 1916; *s* of Lt-Col Roger Alvin Poore, DSO, and Lorne Margery, *d* of Major R. J. W. Dennistoun; *m* 1949, Mrs Peta Farley; one *d*. *Educ:* Eton; King's College, Cambridge (MA). Served War, Royal Air Force, 1939–46 (Wing Comdr 1944). Motor racing successes, 1947–55 (British Hill Climb Champion, 1950). *Recreations:* tennis, golf, bridge. *Address:* 33 Phillimore Gardens, W8. *T:* 01–937 1384.

POOT, Anton; Chairman and Managing Director, Philips Electronics & Associated Industries Ltd, since 1984; *b* 23 Nov. 1929; *m* 1983, Jesmond Masters; one *s* one *d* by a former marriage. *Educ:* High School in Holland; studied Electronics and Economics, Johannesburg. NV Philips' Gloeilampenfabrieken, Hilversum, Utrecht, Eindhoven, 1946–51; Philips S Africa, Fedn of Rhodesia and Nyasaland, 1951–63; NV Philips' Gloeilampenfabrieken, Eindhoven, 1963–66; Chairman and Man. Dir, Philips East Africa, 1967–71; Man. Dir, Ada (Halifax) Ltd and Philips Electrical Ltd UK, 1971–76; Div. Man. Dir, NV Philips' Gloeilampenfabrieken, Eindhoven, 1976–78; Chm. and Man. Dir, Philips Appliances Div., 1978–83. Dep. Chm., Netherlands–British Chamber of Commerce. FBIM; FRSA. *Recreations:* golf, sailing, ski-ing. *Address:* (office) Arundel Great Court, 8 Arundel Street, WC2R 3DT. *T:* 01–689 2166. *Clubs:* Buck's; Wimbledon Park Golf.

POPA, Pretor; Order Star of Socialist Republic of Romania; Order of Labour and other medals; Deputy Foreign Trade Minister, Romania, since 1980; *b* 20 April 1922; *m* Ileana Popa. *Educ:* Academy for High Commercial and Industrial Studies, Bucharest. Director, Ministry for Oil Extraction and Processing, 1950–66; Gen. Director, Ministry for Foreign Trade, 1966–70; Deputy Minister, Ministry for Foreign Trade, and Vice-Chairman at Chamber of Commerce, 1970–73; Ambassador of Romania to the UK, 1973–80. *Address:* Ministry for Foreign Trade, 1 University Square, Bucharest, Romania.

POPE, His Holiness the; *see* John Paul II.

POPE, Andrew Lancelot, CMG 1972; CVO 1965; OBE 1959; HM Diplomatic Service, retired; *b* 27 July 1912; *m* 1st, 1938 (marr. diss.); 2nd, 1948, Ilse Migliarina; one *step d*. *Educ:* Harrow School. Served War of 1939–45 (despatches): Lieut, Royal Fusiliers, 1939; POW 1940–45. Served in Mil. Govt and Allied High Commn in Germany, 1945–56; entered Foreign (subseq. Diplomatic) Service, 1959; Counsellor, Bonn, 1962–72. Director: Conf. Bd, NY, 1972–80; Gerling Global General and Reinsurance Co. Ltd. Liveryman, Worshipful Co. of Grocers. Order of Merit (Germany), 1965; Order of Merit (Bavaria), 1970; Order of Merit (Lower Saxony), 1972. *Recreations:* shooting, gardening. *Address:* Goldhill Grove, Lower Bourne, Farnham, Surrey. *T:* Farnham 721662.

POPE, Dudley Bernard Egerton; Naval historian and author; *b* 29 Dec. 1925; *s* of late Sydney Broughton Pope and late Alice Pope (*née* Meehan); *m* 1954, Kathleen Patricia Hall; one *d*. *Educ:* Ashford (Kent). Served War of 1939–45: Midshipman, MN, 1941–43 (wounded and invalided). The Evening News: naval and defence correspondent, 1944–57, Dep. Foreign Editor, 1957–59; resigned to take up full-time authorship, 1959. Counsellor, Navy Record Soc., 1964–68. Cruising trans-Atlantic and Caribbean in own yacht, doing naval historical research, 1965–. Created: "Lt Ramage RN" series of historical novels covering life of naval officer in Nelson's day, 1965; series of novels portraying sea life of Yorke family, 1979. Hon. Mem., Mark Twain Soc., 1976. *Publications: non-fiction:* Flag 4, the Battle of Coastal Forces in the Mediterranean, 1954; The Battle of the River Plate, 1956; 73 North, 1958; England Expects, 1959; At 12 Mr Byng was Shot, 1962; The Black Ship, 1963; Guns, 1965; The Great Gamble, 1972; Harry Morgan's Way, 1977; Life in Nelson's Navy, 1981; *fiction: the Ramage series:* Ramage (Book Society Choice) 1965; Ramage and the Drum Beat (Book Society Alternative Choice), 1967; Ramage and the Freebooters (Book of the Month Club Alt. Choice), 1969; Governor Ramage, RN, 1973; Ramage's Prize, 1974; Ramage and the Guillotine, 1975; Ramage's Diamond, 1976; Ramage's Mutiny, 1977; Ramage and the Rebels, 1978; The Ramage Touch, 1979; Ramage's Signal, 1980; Ramage and the Renegades, 1981; Ramage's Devil, 1982; Ramage's Trial, 1984; Ramage's Challenge, 1985; Ramage at Trafalgar, 1986; *the Yorke series:* Convoy (Book Club Associates' Choice), 1979; Buccaneer, 1981; Admiral, 1982; Decoy, (World Book Club Choice), 1983; Galleon, 1986. *Recreations:* ocean cruising, skin-diving. *Address:* c/o Campbell Thomson & McLaughlin, 31 Newington Green, N16 9PU. *Club:* Royal Temple Yacht.

POPE, Sir Ernle; *see* Pope, Sir J. E.

POPE, Geoffrey George, CB 1986; PhD, FRAeS; Director, Royal Aircraft Establishment, since 1984; *b* 17 April 1934; *s* of Sir George Reginald Pope and of Susie (*née* Hendy); *m* 1961, Rosemary Frances Harnden; two *s*. *Educ:* Epsom Coll.; Imperial Coll., London. MSc (Eng), PhD, CEng, DIC, FCGI. Junior Technical Asst, Hawker Aircraft Ltd, 1952–53; Student, Imperial Coll., 1953–58; Royal Aircraft Establishment: Structures Dept, 1958–73 (Head, Research Div., 1969–73); Aerodynamics Dept, 1973–77 (Head, 1974–77); Gp Head, Aerodynamics, Structures and Materials Depts, 1978–79; Dep. Dir (Weapons), 1979–81; Asst Chief Scientific Advr (Projects), MoD, 1981–82; Dep. Controller and Adviser (Res. and Technol.), MoD, 1982–84. *Publications:* technical papers, mainly on structural mechanics and optimum design of structures, in ARC (R&M series) and various technical jls. *Recreations:* music, photography, walking. *Address:* Royal Aircraft Establishment, Farnborough, Hants GU14 6TD.

POPE, Jeremy James Richard, OBE 1985; Joint Managing Director, Eldridge, Pope & Co. plc, since 1982; *b* 15 July 1943; *s* of Philip William Rolph Pope and Joyce Winifred Harcourt Pope (*née* Slade); *m* 1969, Hon. Jacqueline Best; three *s*. *Educ:* Charterhouse; Trinity Coll., Cambridge. Law tripos, MA. Solicitor. Joined Eldridge, Pope & Co., 1969, Finance and Planning Dir, 1972–82. Chm., Smaller Firms Council, CBI, 1981–83; Member: NEDC, 1981–85; Exec. Cttee, Food and Drinks Fedn, 1986–. Mem., Royal Commn on Environmental Pollution, 1984–. Chm., Winterbourne Hosp. plc, 1981–. Gov., Forres Sch., Swanage, 1984–. *Recreations:* shooting, fishing, gardening, cooking the resultant produce. *Address:* (office) Dorchester Brewery, Dorchester, Dorset DT1 1QT. *T:* Dorchester 64801; (home) Field Cottage, West Compton, Dorchester, Dorset DT2 0EY. *T:* Maiden Newton 20469.

POPE, Air Vice-Marshal John Clifford, CB 1963; CBE 1959; CEng, FIMechE; FRAeS; RAF (retired); *b* 27 April 1912; *s* of George Newcombe-Pope; *m* 1950, Christine Agnes (*d* 1982), *d* of Alfred Hames, Chichester; one *s* two *d*. *Educ:* Tiverton Sch.; RAF Coll., Cranwell. Commnd, 1932; served with No 3 Sqdn, 1933, Nos 27 and 39, on NW Frontier, 1933–36. War of 1939–45; Comd RAF Station, Cleave, 1940–42; served in Egypt and Palestine, 1943–46; Asst Dir Research and Develt, Min. of Supply, 1947–50; Dir of Engineering, RNZAF, 1951–53; Comd RAF Station, Stoke Heath, 1954–57; Sen. Tech. Staff Officer, No 3 Gp Bomber Comd, 1957–59 and Flying Trng Comd, 1960–61; AOC and Comdt, RAF Technical College, 1961–63; Senior Technical Staff Officer, Transport Command, 1963–66. Life Vice-Pres., RAF Boxing Assoc. *Recreation:* scale model steam engineering. *Address:* Dilston, 47 Oxford Road, Stone, near Aylesbury, Bucks. *T:* Aylesbury 748467. *Club:* Royal Air Force.

POPE, Vice-Adm. Sir (John) Ernle, KCB 1976; *b* 22 May 1921; *s* of Comdr R. K. C. Pope, Homme House, Herefordshire. *Educ:* RN Coll., Dartmouth. Royal Navy, 1935. Served throughout War of 1939–45, in Destroyers. CO, HMS Decoy, 1962–64; Dir, Naval Equipment, 1964–66; CO, HMS Eagle, 1966–68; Flag Officer, Western Fleet Flotillas, 1969–71; C of S to C-in-C Western Fleet, 1971–74; Comdr, Allied Naval Forces, S Europe, 1974–76; Rear-Adm. 1969; Vice-Adm. 1972. Pres., Royal Naval Assoc. *Recreations:* sailing, shooting. *Address:* Homme House, Much Marcle, Herefordshire. *Club:* Army and Navy.
See also Rear-Adm. M. D. Kyrle Pope.

POPE, Sir Joseph (Albert), Kt 1980; DSc, PhD (Belfast), WhSc; Chairman, TecQuipment Group, Nottingham (Director, since 1960); *b* 18 October 1914; *s* of Albert Henry and Mary Pope; *m* 1940, Evelyn Alice Gallagher; one *s* two *d*. *Educ:* School of Arts and Crafts, Cambridge; King's College, London. Apprentice, Boulton & Pauls, Norwich, 1930–35. Whitworth Scholarship, 1935. Assistant Lecturer in Engineering, Queen's Univ., Belfast, 1938–44; Assistant Lecturer in Engineering, Univ. of Manchester, 1944–45; Lecturer, then Senior Lecturer, Univ. of Sheffield, 1945–49; Professor of Mechanical Engineering, Nottingham University, 1949–60; Research Dir, Mirrlees Nat. Research Div., Stockport, and Dir, Mirrlees National Ltd 1960–69; Vice-Chancellor, Univ. of Aston in Birmingham, 1969–79. Director: John Brown & Co. Ltd, 1970–82; Midlands Electricity Bd, 1975–80; Royal Worcester Ltd, 1979–83; Chm., W Midlands Econ. Planning Council, 1977–79. Gen. Treasurer, British Assoc., 1975–82; Pres., Whitworth Soc., 1978–79; Chm., Birmingham Civic Soc., 1978–79. Hon. LLD Birmingham, 1979; Hon. DUniv Heriot-Watt, 1979; Hon. DSc: Aston, 1979; Belfast, 1980; Salford, 1980. *Publications:* papers on the impact of metals and metal fatigue published in Proc. of Inst. of Mech. Engineers and Jl of Iron and Steel Inst. *Address:* 3 Mapperley Hall Drive, Nottingham NG3 5EP. *T:* Nottingham 621146.

POPE, Rear-Adm. Michael Donald K.; *see* Kyrle Pope.

POPE, Very Rev. Robert William, OBE 1971; Dean of Gibraltar, 1977–82; *b* 20 May 1916; *s* of late Rev. Jonas George Pope and Marjorie Mary Pope (*née* Coates); *m* 1940, Elizabeth Beatrice Matilda (*née* Bressey); two *s* one *d*. *Educ:* English College, Temuco, Chile; Harvey Grammar Sch., Folkestone; Maidstone Grammar Sch.; St Augustine's Coll., Canterbury; Durham Univ. (LTh). Deacon 1939, priest, 1940, Rochester; Curate: Holy Trinity, Gravesend, 1939–41; St Nicholas, Guildford, 1942–43; Priest in charge, Peaslake, 1943–44; Chaplain, Royal Navy, 1944–71; Vicar of Whitchurch with Tufton and Litchfield, Dio. Winchester, 1971–77. Member of Sion College. Provincial Guardian of European Province, Third Order of Soc. of St Francis, 1985. *Address:* 5 Wreath Green, Tatworth, Chard, Somerset TA20 2SN. *T:* Chard 20987.

POPE-HENNESSY, Sir John (Wyndham), Kt 1971; CBE 1959 (MBE 1944); FBA 1955; FSA; FRSL; Consultative Chairman, Department of European Paintings, Metropolitan Museum, New York, since 1977; Professor of Fine Arts, New York University, since 1977; *b* 13 Dec. 1913; *er s* of late Major-General L. H. R. Pope-Hennessy, CB, DSO, and late Dame Una Pope-Hennessy, DBE. *Educ:* Downside School; Balliol Coll., Oxford (Hon. Fellow). Joined staff of Victoria and Albert Museum, 1938. Served Air Ministry, 1939–45. Victoria and Albert Museum: Keeper, Dept of Architecture and Sculpture, 1954–66; Dir and Sec., 1967–73; Dir, British Museum, 1974–76. Slade Professor of Fine Art, Univ. of Oxford, 1956–57; Clark Professor of Art, Williams College, Mass., USA, 1961–62; Slade Professor of Fine Art, and Fellow of Peterhouse, University of Cambridge, 1964–65. Member: Arts Council, 1968–76; Ancient Monuments Bd for England, 1969–72; Dir, Royal Opera House, 1971–76. Fellow, Amer. Acad. of Arts and Scis, 1978; Corresponding Member: Accademia Senese degli Intronati; Bayerische Akademie der Wissenschaften; Hon. Academician, Accademia del Disegno, Florence; For. Mem., Amer. Philosophical Soc., 1974; Hon. Fellow, Pierpoint Morgan Library, 1975. Serena Medal of British Academy for Italian Studies, 1961; New York University Medal, 1965; Torch of Learning Award, Hebrew Univ., Jerusalem, 1977; Art Dealers Assoc. Award, 1984; Jerusalem Prize of Arts and Letters, 1984. Hon. LLD Aberdeen, 1972; Hon. Dr RCA, 1973. Hon. Citizen, Siena, 1982. Mangia d'Oro, 1982. *Publications:* Giovanni di Paolo, 1937, Sassetta, 1939; Sienese Quattrocento Painting, 1947; A Sienese Codex of the Divine Comedy, 1947; The Drawings of Domenichino at Windsor Castle, 1948; A Lecture on Nicholas Hilliard, 1949; Donatello's Ascension, 1949; The Virgin with the Laughing Child, 1949; edition of the Autobiography of Benvenuto Cellini, 1949; Paolo Uccello, 1950, rev. edn, 1972; Italian Gothic Sculpture in the Victoria and Albert Museum, 1952; Fra Angelico, 1952, rev. edn, 1974; Italian Gothic Sculpture, 1955, rev. edn 1972; Italian Renaissance Sculpture, 1958, rev. edn 1971; Italian High Renaissance and Baroque Sculpture, 1963, rev. edn 1970; Catalogue of Italian Sculpture in the Victoria and Albert Museum, 1964; Renaissance Bronzes in the Kress Collection, 1965; The Portrait in the Renaissance, 1967; Essays on Italian Sculpture, 1968; Catalogue of Sculpture in the Frick Collection, 1970; Raphael (Wrightsman lectures),

1970; (with others) Westminster Abbey, 1972; Luca della Robbia, 1980 (Mitchell Prize, 1981); The Study and Criticism of Italian Sculpture, 1980; Cellini, 1985; Contributor, Apollo, etc. *Recreation:* music. *Address:* 1130 Park Avenue, New York, NY 10128, USA.

POPHAM, Maj.-Gen. Christopher John, CB 1982; Director, British Atlantic Committee, since 1982; *b* 2 April 1927; *s* of late Gordon F. B. Popham and Dorothy A. L. Popham (*née* Yull); *m* 1950, Heather Margaret, *y d* of late Lt-Col and Mrs H. R. W. Dawson; two *s*. *Educ:* Merchant Taylors' School. Commnd Royal Engineers, 1946; served with King George V's Own Bengal Sappers and Miners, RIE and Royal Pakistan Engineers, 1946–48; UK and Germany, 1948–57; Staff Coll., 1958; Cyprus, 1959–62; OC 4 Field Sqdn, 1963–65; JSSC 1965; Mil. Asst to QMG, 1966–68; CO 36 Engineer Regt, 1968–70; CRE 4 Div., 1971–73; Comd 12 Engineer Bde, 1973–75; BGS Intelligence and Security, HQ BAOR and ACOS G-2 HQ Northern Army Group, 1976–79; Asst Chief of Staff (Intell.), SHAPE, 1979–82. Col Comdt, RE, 1982–. FBIM. *Recreations:* music, photography, railways. *Address:* c/o Barclays Bank, High Street, Andover, Hants.

POPJÁK, George Joseph, DSc (London), MD; FRS 1961; FRSC; Professor of Biochemistry at University of California in Los Angeles, 1968–84, now Emeritus; *b* 5 May 1914; *s* of late George and Maria Popják, Szeged, Hungary; *m* 1941, Hasel Marjorie, *d* of Duncan and Mabel Hammond, Beckenham, Kent. *Educ:* Royal Hungarian Francis Joseph University, Szeged. Demonstrator at Department of Morbid Anatomy and Histology, University of Szeged, 1938–39; Br. Council Scholar, Postgraduate Med. School of London, 1939–41; Demonstrator in Pathology, Dept of Pathology, St Thomas's Hosp. Med. School, London, 1941–43; Beit Mem. Fellow for medical research at St Thomas's Hosp. Med. School, London, 1943–47; Member scientific staff of Med. Research Council at Nat. Inst. for Med. Research, 1947–53; Director of Medical Research Council Experimental Radiopathology Research Unit, Hammersmith Hosp., 1953–62; Jt Dir, Chemical Enzymology Lab., Shell Res. Ltd, 1962–68; Assoc. Prof. in Molecular Sciences, Warwick Univ., 1965–68. Foreign member of Belgian Roy. Flemish Acad. of Science, Literature and Fine Arts, 1955; Hon. Member: Amer. Soc. of Biological Chemists, 1968; Alpha-Omega-Alpha, 1970; Mem., Amer. Acad. of Arts and Sciences, 1971. (With Dr J. W. Cornforth, FRS) CIBA Medal of Biochemical Soc., 1965 (first award); Stouffer Prize, 1967; Davy Medal, Royal Soc., 1968; Award in Lipid Chem., Amer. Oil Chem. Soc., 1977; Distinguished Scientific Achievement award, Amer. Heart Assoc., 1978. *Publications:* Chemistry, Biochemistry and Isotopic Tracer Technique (Roy. Inst. of Chemistry monograph), 1955; (jtly) Lipids, Chemistry, Biochemistry and Nutrition, 1986; articles on fat metabolism in Jl Path. Bact., Jl Physiol., Biochemical Jl, etc. *Recreations:* music, modelling and gardening. *Address:* Departments of Medicine and Biological Chemistry, University of California at Los Angeles, Center for the Health Sciences, Los Angeles, Calif 90024, USA.

POPLE, John Anthony, FRS 1961; John Christian Warner University Professor of Natural Sciences (formerly Professor of Chemical Physics), Carnegie-Mellon University, Pittsburgh, USA, since 1964; *b* 31 Oct. 1925; *e s* of Herbert Keith Pople and Mary Frances Jones, Burnham-on-Sea, Som.; *m* 1952, Joy Cynthia Bowers; three *s* one *d*. *Educ:* Bristol Grammar School; Cambridge University, MA, PhD. Mayhew Prize, 1948, Smith Prize, 1950, Cambridge; Fellow, Trinity College, 1951–58, Lecturer in Mathematics, 1954–58, Cambridge; Superintendent of Basic Physics Division, National Physical Laboratory, 1958–64. Ford Visiting Professor, Carnegie Inst. of Technology, Pittsburgh, 1961–62. Fellow: Amer. Physical Soc., 1970; Amer. Acad. of Arts and Scis, 1971; AAAS, 1980. For. Associate, Nat. Acad. of Sci., 1977. Marlow Medal, Faraday Soc., 1958; ACS Pauling Award, 1977; Awards from American Chemical Society: Langmuir, 1970; Harrison Howe, 1971; Gilbert Newton Lewis, 1973; Pittsburgh, 1975. Sen. US Scientist Award, Alexander von Humboldt Foundn, 1981; G. Willard Wheland Award, Univ. of Chicago, 1981; Evans Award, Ohio State Univ., 1982; Oesper Award, Univ. of Cincinnati, 1984. *Publications:* High Resolution nuclear magnetic resonance, 1959; Approximate Molecular Orbital Theory, 1970; scientific papers on molecular physics and theoretical chemistry. *Recreations:* music, travel. *Address:* Carnegie-Mellon University, 4400 Fifth Avenue, Pittsburgh, Pa 15213, USA; 415 W, 100 Bryn Mawr Court, Pittsburgh, Pa 15221, USA.

POPONDETTA, Bishop of; *see* Papua New Guinea, Archbishop of.

POPOV, Viktor Ivanovich; Soviet Ambassador to the Court of St James's, 1980–86; *b* 19 May 1918; *m* Natalia Aleksandrovna Popova; two *s*. *Educ:* Moscow Inst. of History and Philosophy; Higher Diplomatic Sch. of USSR. Entered Min. of Foreign Affairs, 1954; Vietnam, 1960–61; Australia, 1967–68; UK, 1968; Ambassador on special assignments, UN and Unesco, and Rector, Diplomatic Acad. of USSR, 1968–80. Many Soviet and foreign awards. *Publications:* Anglo-Soviet Relations 1927–29; Anglo-Soviet Relations 1929–39; (jtly) History of Diplomacy series III. *Address:* c/o Ministry of Foreign Affairs, 32–34 Smolenskaya Sennaya Ploshchad, Moscow, USSR.

POPPER, Prof. Sir Karl (Raimund), CH 1982; Kt 1965; FRS 1976; FBA 1958; PhD (Vienna), MA (New Zealand), DLit (London); Professor of Logic and Scientific Method in the University of London (London School of Economics and Political Science), 1949–69; Emeritus Professor, 1969; Guest Professor in the Theory of Science, University of Vienna, since 1986; Head of the Ludwig Boltzmann Institute for the Theory of Science, Vienna; Senior Research Fellow, Hoover Institution, Stanford University; *b* Vienna, 28 July 1902; *s* of Dr Simon Siegmund Carl Popper, Barrister, of Vienna, and of Jenny Popper (*née* Schiff); *m* 1930, Josefine Anna Henninger (*d* 1985); no *c*. *Educ:* University of Vienna. Senior Lecturer in Philosophy, Canterbury University College, Christchurch (Univ. of NZ), 1937–45; Reader in Logic and Scientific Method, LSE, Univ. of London, 1945–49. Fellow, Center for Advanced Study in the Behavioral Sciences, Stanford, Calif, 1956–57; Visiting Professor: Harvard (Wm James Lectures in Philosophy), 1950; Univ. of California Berkeley, 1962; Minnesota Center for Phil. of Science, 1962; Indiana Univ., 1963; Inst. for Advanced Studies, Vienna, 1964; Denver Univ., 1966; Vis. Fellow, The Salk Institute for Biological Studies, 1966–67; Kenan Univ. Prof., Emory Univ., 1969; Jacob Ziskind Vis. Prof. in Philosophy and the History of Thought, Brandeis Univ., 1969; William Evans Vis. Prof., Otago, 1973; Vis. Erskine Fellow, Canterbury, NZ, 1973; Lectures: Yale, Princeton, Chicago, Emory Univs, 1950, 1956; Eleanor Rathbone, Bristol, 1956; Annual Philos. to British Acad., 1960; Herbert Spencer, Oxford, 1961 and 1973; Shearman Meml, UCL, 1961; Farnum, Princeton, 1963; Arthur H. Compton Meml, Washington, 1965; Romanes, Oxford, 1972; Broadhead Meml, Canterbury NZ, 1973; First Darwin, Darwin Coll., Cambridge, 1977; Tanner, Ann Arbor, 1978; Frank Nelson Doubleday, Smithsonian Inst., 1979; first Morrell Meml, York, 1981; first Medawar, Royal Soc., 1986. Member: Editorial Bd: Foundations of Physics; British Jl Phil. of Science; Studi Internat. di Filosofia; Jl of Political Theory; Biologie et Logique; Board of Consulting Editors: Theory and Decision; Idea; Advisory Board: Medical Hypotheses; The Monist; Co-Editor: Ratio; Studies in the Foundations Methodology and Philosophy of Science; Methodology and Science; Rechtstheorie; Schriftenreihe Erfahrung und Denken; Library of Exact Philosophy; Ed. Correspond., Dialectica. Chairman, Phil. of Science Group, 1951–53; President: The Aristotelian Soc., 1958–59; British Society for the Phil. of Science, 1959–61; Mem. Council, Assoc. for Symb. Logic, 1951–55. Mem., Académie Internat. de Philosophie des Sciences, 1949; Hon. Mem., RSNZ, 1965; For. Hon. Mem., Amer. Acad. of Arts and Sciences, 1966; Correspondant de l'Institut de France, 1974–80; Associate Mem., Académie Royale de Belgique, 1976; Membre d'Honneur, Académie Internationale d'Histoire des Sciences, 1977; Hon. Mem., Deutsche Akademie für Sprache und Dichtung, 1979; Membre de l'Académie Européenne des Sciences, des Arts et des Lettres (Delegn of GB), 1980; Membre de l'Institut de France, 1980; Socio Straniero dell'Accademia Nazionale dei Lincei, 1981; Ehrenmitglied, Oesterreichische Akademie der Wissenschaften, 1982. Hon. Mem., Harvard Chapter of Phi Beta Kappa, 1964; Hon. Fellow, LSE, 1972; Hon. Mem., Allgemeine Gesellschaft für Philosophie in Deutschland, 1979; Hon. Fellow, Darwin Coll., Cambridge, 1980; Hon. Research Fellow, Dept of History & Philosophy of Science, KCL, 1982; Hon. Mem., Gesellschaft der Ärzte, Vienna, 1986. Hon. Prof. of Econs, Vienna. Ehrenring der Stadt Wien, 1983. Hon. LLD: Chicago, 1962; Denver, 1966; Hon. LittD: Warwick, 1971; Canterbury, NZ, 1973; Cantab, 1980; Hon. DLitt: Salford, 1976; City Univ., 1976; Guelph, Ontario, 1978; Oxon 1982; Hon. Dr.rer.nat, Vienna, 1978; Dr. phil *hc*: Mannheim, 1978; Salzburg, 1979; Hon. Dr.rer.pol, Frankfurt, 1979; Hon. DSc: Gustavus Adolphus Coll., 1981; London, 1986. Prize of the City of Vienna for 'Geisteswissenschaften' (mental and moral sciences) 1965; Sonning Prize for merit in work that has furthered European civilization, Univ. of Copenhagen, 1973; Lippincott Award, Amer. Pol. Sci. Assoc., 1976; Dr Karl Renner Prize, Vienna, 1978; Dr Leopold Lucas Prize, Univ. of Tübingen, 1981; Alexis de Tocqueville Prize, Fondation Tocqueville, 1984. Grand Decoration of Honour in Gold (Austria), 1976; Gold Medal for Disting. Service to Sci., Amer. Mus. of Nat. Hist., NY, 1979; Ehrenzeichen für Wissenschaft und Kunst (Austria), 1980; Order Pour le Mérite (German Fed. Rep.), 1980; Grand Cross with Star, Order of Merit (German Fed. Rep.), 1983; Ring of Honour, City of Vienna, 1983. *Publications:* (trans. into 26 languages): Logik der Forschung, 1934, rev. 2nd edn 1966, rev. 8th edn 1984; The Open Society and Its Enemies, 1945, 5th edn, rev. 1966, 14th impr. 1984; The Poverty of Historicism, 1957, 11th impr. 1984; The Logic of Scientific Discovery, 1959, 12th impr. 1985; On the Sources of Knowledge and of Ignorance, 1961; Conjectures and Refutations, 1963, 9th impr. 1984; Of Clouds and Clocks, 1966; Objective Knowledge, 1972, 7th impr. 1983; Unended Quest: An Intellectual Autobiography, 1976, 7th impr. 1985; (with Sir John Eccles) The Self and Its Brain, 1977, rev. pbk edn (UK), 1984, 3rd impr. rev. edn 1985; Die beiden Grundprobleme der Erkenntnistheorie, 1979; Postscript to The Logic of Scientific Discovery (ed W. W. Bartley), 3 vols, 1982–83 (vol. 1, Realism and the Aim of Science; vol. 2, The Open Universe; vol. 3, Quantum Theory and the Schism in Physics, 1982); (with F. Kreuzer) Offene Gesellschaft—Offene Universum, 1982, 3rd edn 1983; A Pocket Popper (ed David Miller), 1983; Auf der Suche nach einer besseren Welt, 1984; (with Konrad Lorenz) Die Zukunft ist Offen, 1984, 2nd edn 1985; (ed David Miller) Popper Selections, 1985; contribs to: learned jls; anthologies; The Philosophy of Karl Popper, Library of Living Philosophers (ed P. A. Schilpp), 1974. *Recreation:* music. *Address:* c/o London School of Economics, Houghton Street, Aldwych, WC2A 2AE.

POPPLEWELL, Hon. Sir Oliver Bury, Kt 1983; **Hon. Mr Justice Popplewell;** Judge of the High Court of Justice, Queen's Bench Division, since 1983; *b* 15 Aug. 1927; *s* of late Frank and Nina Popplewell; *m* 1954, Catharine Margaret Storey; four *s* (and one *s* decd). *Educ:* Charterhouse (Schol.); Queens' Coll., Cambridge (Class. exhibnr). BA 1950; LLB 1951; MA. CUCC, 1949–51. Called to the Bar, Inner Temple, 1951, Bencher, 1978; QC 1969. Recorder, Burton-on-Trent, 1970–71; Dep. Chm., Oxon QS, 1970–71; a Recorder of the Crown Court, 1972–82. Indep. Mem., Wages Councils, 1962–82, Chm. 1973–82; Mem., Home Office Adv. Bd on Restricted Patients, 1981–82; Vice-Chm., Parole Bd, 1986 (Mem., 1985–); Chm., Inquiry into Crowd Safety and Control at sports grounds, 1985–86; Pres., Employment Appeal Tribunal, 1986– (Mem., 1984–85). MCC: Mem. Cttee, 1971–74, 1976–79, 1980–; Trustee, 1983–. Gov., Sutton's Hosp. in Charterhouse, 1986–. *Recreations:* sailing, cricket, tennis. *Address:* Royal Courts of Justice, Strand, WC2. *Clubs:* MCC; Hawks (Cambridge), Blakeney Sailing.

PORCHER, Michael Somerville, CMG 1962; OBE 1960; Secretary (Operations Division), Royal National Life-Boat Institution, 1964–83; *b* 9 March 1921; *s* of late Geoffrey Lionel Porcher and Marjorie Fownes Porcher (*née* Somerville); *m* 1955, Mary Lorraine Porcher (*née* Tweedy); two *s*. *Educ:* Cheltenham College; St Edmund Hall, Oxford. Military Service, 1941–42. Joined Colonial Admin. Service: Sierra Leone; Cadet, 1942; Asst Dist, Comr, 1945; Dist Comr, 1951; British Guiana: Dep. Colonial Sec., 1952; Governor's Sec. and Clerk Exec. Council, 1953; Dep. Chief Sec., 1956. British Honduras: Colonial Secretary, 1960; Chief Secretary, 1961; retired, 1964. *Recreations:* fishing, shooting, sailing. *Address:* Bladon, Worth Matravers, near Swanage, Dorset.

PORCHESTER, Lord; Henry George Reginald Molyneux Herbert, KCVO 1982; KBE 1976; DL; *b* 19 Jan. 1924; *o s* of 6th Earl of Carnarvon, *qv*; *m* 1956, Jean Margaret, *e d* of Hon. Oliver Wallop, Big Horn, Sheridan Co., Wyoming, USA; two *s* one *d*. Late Lieut RHG; retired pay, 1947. Hon. Col, Hampshire Fortress Regt, RE (TA) 1963–67, retaining rank of Hon. Col. Racing Manager to the Queen, 1969–. Chairman: South East Economic Planning Council, 1971–79; Agricultural Research Council, 1978–82; Game Research Assoc., 1960–67 (Vice-Pres., 1967–); Stallion Adv. Cttee to Betting Levy Bd, 1974–; Standing Conf. on Countryside Sports, 1978–; President: Thoroughbred Breeders' Assoc., 1969–74 (Chm. 1964–66); RASE, 1980–81. Member: Hampshire Agriculture Exec. Cttee, 1955–65; Nature Conservancy, 1963–66; Sports Council, 1965–70 (Chm., Planning Cttee, 1965–70); Forestry Commission, 1967–70; President: Amateur Riders' Assoc., 1969–75; Hampshire County Cricket Club, 1966–68; Mem., Jockey Club, 1964– (Chm., Flat Pattern Cttee, 1967–85). CC Hants, 1954; County Alderman, 1965–74; Vice-Chm. County Council, 1971–74, Chm., New County Council, 1973–77; Vice-Chm., CC Assoc., 1972–74 (Chm. Planning Cttee, 1968–74); Member: Basingstoke Town Develt Jt Cttee, 1960–73; Andover Town Develt Jt Cttee, 1960–65. Verderer of the New Forest, 1961–65. DL Hants 1965. High Steward of Winchester, 1977. Hon. Fellow, Portsmouth Polytech., 1976. Hon. DSc Reading, 1980. *Address:* Milford Lake House, Burghclere, Newbury, Berks RG16 9EL. *T:* Highclere 253387. *Clubs:* White's, Portland.

PORRITT, family name of **Baron Porritt.**

PORRITT, Baron *cr* 1973 (Life Peer), of Wanganui, NZ, and of Hampstead; **Arthur Espie Porritt,** GCMG 1967 (KCMG 1950); GCVO 1970 (KCVO 1957); CBE 1945 (OBE 1943); Bt 1963; Life Vice-President, African Medical and Research Foundation, since 1981 (Chairman, 1973–81); President, Arthritis and Rheumatism Council, since 1979 (Chairman, 1973–79); *b* 10 Aug. 1900; *e s* of late E. E. Porritt, VD, MD, FRCS, Wanganui, New Zealand; *m* 1st, 1926, Mary Frances Wynne, *d* of William Bond; 2nd, 1946, Kathleen Mary, 2nd *d* of late A. S. Peck and Mrs Windley, Spalding, Lincs; two *s* one *d*. *Educ:* Wanganui Collegiate School, NZ; Otago University, NZ; Magdalen College, Oxford (Rhodes Scholar); St Mary's Hospital, London. MA Oxon.; MCh Oxon. Surgeon; St Mary's Hosp.; Hosp. of St John and St Elizabeth; King Edward VII Hosp. for Officers; Royal Masonic Hosp.; Consulting Surgeon: Princess Louise Kensington Hosp. for Children; Paddington Hosps; Royal Chelsea Hosp.; Civil Consulting Surgeon to the Army, 1954–67, Emeritus, 1971; Brigadier, RAMC, 21 Army Group; Surgeon-in-Ordinary to the Duke of York; Surgeon to HM Household; a Surgeon to King George

VI, 1946–52; Sergeant-Surgeon to the Queen, 1952–67; Governor-General of New Zealand, 1967–72. Dir, Sterling Winthrop and Sterling Europa. Chairman: Medical Advisory Cttee, Ministry of Overseas Develt; Medical Services Review Cttee, 1958; Red Cross Comr for NZ in UK; Chapter-Gen., Order of St John; Hunterian Soc., 1934–39 (Past Pres.); President: RCS, 1960–63; BMA, 1960–61 (Gold Medallist, 1964); RSM, 1966–67; Assoc. of Surgeons of Gt Britain and Ireland; Patron, Med. Council on Alcoholism; Pres., Med. Commn on Accident Prevention; Past Master, Soc. of Apothecaries, 1964–66; Vice-Pres., Royal Commonwealth Soc.; Pres., OUAC, 1925–26; holder of 100 yards and 220 yards hurdles records at Oxford and 100 yards Oxford v. Cambridge (9 9/10 seconds); represented Oxford in Athletics, 1923–26; Finalist, Olympic 100 metres (Bronze Medallist), Paris, 1924, Captain NZ Olympic Team, Paris, 1924, Amsterdam, 1928, Manager Berlin, 1936; Mem., Internat. Olympic Cttee, British Olympic Council; Vice-Pres., British Empire and Commonwealth Games Federation. Olympic Order (1st cl.), 1985. FRCS (Eng.); Fellow: Amer. Surgical Assoc.; Amer. Soc. of Clinical Surgery; French Acad. of Surgery; Hon. FRACS; Hon. FRCS (Ed.); Hon. FACS; Hon. FRCS (Glas.); Hon. FRCS (Can.); Hon. FCS (SAf); Hon. FRCS (I); Hon. FRCP; Hon. FRACP; Hon FRCOG; Hon. FRACR; Hon. Fellow, Magdalen College, Oxford, 1961. Hon. LLD: St Andrews; Birmingham; New Zealand; Otago. Hon. MD Bristol; Hon. DSc Oxon. Legion of Merit (USA); KStJ. *Publications:* Athletics (with D. G. A. Lowe), 1929; Essentials of Modern Surgery (with R. M. Handfield-Jones), 1938, 6th edn 1956; various surgical articles in medical jls. *Recreations:* riding, golf, swimming; formerly athletics and Rugby football. *Heir* (to baronetcy only)*: s* Hon. Jonathon Espie Porritt, *qv. Address:* 57 Hamilton Terrace, NW8 9RG. *Club:* Buck's.

PORRITT, Hon. Jonathon (Espie); Director, Friends of The Earth, since 1984; *b* 6 July 1950; *s* and *heir* (to Baronetcy) of Baron Porritt, *qv. Educ:* Eton; Magdalen Coll., Oxford (BA (First Cl.) Modern Languages). ILEA Teacher, 1975–84: Head of English and Drama, Burlington Danes School, W12, 1980–84. Ecology Party: candidate: General Elections, 1979 and 1983; European Elections, 1979 and 1984; Local Elections, 1977, 1978, 1982; Party Council Member, 1978–80, 1982–84; Chairman, 1979–80, 1982–84. *Publication:* Seeing Green - the Politics of Ecology, 1984. *Recreation:* walking. *Address:* 17A Laurier Road, NW5. *T:* 01–485 2452.

PORT ELIZABETH, Bishop of, since 1975; **Rt. Rev. Bruce Read Evans;** *b* 10 Nov. 1929; *s* of Roy Leslie and Lilia Evans; *m* 1955, Joan Vanda Erlangsen; two *s* one *d. Educ:* King Edward Sch., Johannesburg; Univ. of the Witwatersrand, Johannesburg; Oak Hill Theological Coll., London. ACIS 1952; director of companies, 1952–54. Ordained into CofE, Southwark, 1957; Curate, Holy Trinity, Redhill, Surrey, 1957–59; Senior Curate, St Paul's, Portman Square, W1, and Chaplain to West End Business Houses in London, 1959–61; Curate-in-Charge: St Luke's, Diep River, Cape, 1962; Christ Church, Kenilworth, Cape, 1963–69; Rector of St John's, Wynberg, Cape, 1969–75. International speaker. *Recreations:* formerly boxing and hockey; now painting. *Address:* Bishop's House, 75 River Road, Walmer, Port Elizabeth, CP, 6065, South Africa. *T:* 51–4296. *Club:* Port Elizabeth.

PORT MORESBY, Archbishop of, (RC), since 1981; **Most Rev. Sir Peter Kurongku,** KBE 1986; DD; *b* 1932; *s* of Adam Mapa and Eve Kawa. *Educ:* Holy Spirit National Seminary. Ordained priest, 1966; consecrated Bishop, 1978. *Address:* PO Box 1032, Boroko, Papua New Guinea. *T:* (office) 251192, (home) 253126.

PORT OF SPAIN, Archbishop of, since 1968; **Most Rev. Anthony Pantin,** CSSp; *b* 27 Aug. 1929; *s* of Julian and Agnes Pantin, both of Trinidad. *Educ:* Sacred Heart Private Sch., Belmont Boys' Intermediate Sch., St Mary's Coll., Port of Spain; Seminary of Philosophy, Montreal; Holy Ghost Missionary Coll., Dublin. Ordained Dublin, 1955; Guadeloupe, French West Indies, 1956–59; Fatima College, Port of Spain, 1959–64; Superior, St Mary's Coll., Port of Spain, 1965–68. Mem., Vatican Secretariat for Christian Unity, 1971–83. Vice-Pres., Antilles Episcopal Conference, 1984– (Pres., 1979–84). Hon. FCP 1982. *Address:* Archbishop's House, 27 Maraval Road, Port of Spain, Trinidad. *T:* 21103.

PORTAL, family name of **Baroness Portal of Hungerford.**

PORTAL OF HUNGERFORD, Baroness (2nd in line), *cr* 1945; **Rosemary Ann Portal;** *b* 12 May 1923; *d* of 1st Viscount Portal of Hungerford, KG, GCB, OM, DSO, MC, and Joan Margaret, *y d* of Sir Charles Glynne Earle Welby, 5th Bt; *S* to barony of father, 1971. Formerly Section Officer, WAAF. *Heir:* none. *Address:* West Ashling House, Chichester, West Sussex PO18 8DN.

PORTAL, Sir Jonathan (Francis), 6th Bt *cr* 1901; ACA; Financial Controller, City Business Machines Group; *b* 13 Jan. 1953; *s* of Sir Francis Spencer Portal, 5th Bt, and of Jane Mary, *d* of late Albert Henry Williams, OBE; *S* father, 1984; *m* 1982, Louisa Caroline, *er d* of F. J. C. G. Hervey-Bathurst, Somborne Park, near Stockbridge, Hants. *Educ:* Marlborough; Univ. of Edinburgh (BCom). ACA 1977. Mem., Clothworkers' Co. *Heir: b* Philip Francis Portal, *b* 6 July 1957. *Address:* 21 Yeomans Row, SW3 2AL.

PORTARLINGTON, 7th Earl of, *cr* 1785; **George Lionel Yuill Seymour Dawson-Damer;** Baron Dawson 1770; Viscount Carlow 1776; *b* 10 Aug. 1938; *er s* of Air Commodore Viscount Carlow (killed on active service, 1944) and Peggy (who *m* 2nd, 1945, Peter Nugent; she *d* 1963), *yr d* of late Charles Cambie; *S* grandfather, 1959; *m* 1961, Davina, *e d* of Sir Edward Windley, KCMG, KCVO; three *s* one *d. Educ:* Eton. Page of Honour to the Queen, 1953–55. Director: G. S. Yuill & Co. Ltd, Sydney, 1964; Cold Storage Holdings plc, London, 1965 (Dir, Malaysia Bd, Kuala Lumpur); Queensland Trading Holding Co. Ltd, Brisbane, 1967; Australian Stock Breeders Co. Ltd, Brisbane, 1966. *Heir: s* Viscount Carlow, *qv. Recreations:* fishing, ski-ing, books. *Address:* 19 Coolong Road, Vaucluse, NSW 2030, Australia. *T:* Sydney 337–3013. *Club:* Union (Sydney).

PORTEOUS, Christopher, MA; Headmaster of Eltham College, 1959–83; *b* 2 April 1921; *e s* of late Rev. Gilbert Porteous; *m* 1944, Amy Clunis, *d* of Theodore J. Biggs; one *s* three *d. Educ:* Nottingham High Sch. (Foundation Scholar); Emmanuel Coll., Cambridge (Senior Scholar). First Classes, with distinction, in Classical Tripos. Master of Classical Sixth, Mill Hill Sch., 1947–55; Asst Director, HM Civil Service Commission, 1955–59. FRSA. *Recreations:* travel, the countryside. *Address:* Little Thatch, Edwardstone, Suffolk CO6 5PR.

PORTEOUS, James, FEng 1986; FIEE; FInstE; FSS; Chairman, Yorkshire Electricity Board, since 1984; *b* 29 Dec. 1926; *e s* of James and Isabella Porteous; *m* 1960, Sheila Beatrice (*née* Klotz); two *d. Educ:* Jarrow Grammar School; King's College, Durham University. BSc Hons. NESCo Ltd, NE Electricity Bd, NE Div., BEA, 1945–62; Central Electricity Generating Board: Operations Dept, HQ, 1962–66; System Op. Eng., Midlands Region, 1966–70; Dir, Operational Planning, SE Region, 1970–72; NE Region, 1972–75; Dir-Gen., Midlands Region, 1975–84. Member: E Midlands Economic Planning Council, 1976–79; Electricity Council, 1984–; British Railways Bd (Eastern Reg.), 1986–. Dir, Peter Peregrinus Ltd, 1981–. CBIM. *Recreations:* highland life, railways. *Address:* c/o Yorkshire Electricity Board, Scarcroft, Leeds LS14 3HS. *T:* Leeds 892123. *Club:* Caledonian.

PORTEOUS, Rev. Norman Walker, MA Edinburgh et Oxon, BD Edinburgh, DD St Andrews; *b* Haddington, 9 Sept. 1898; *yr s* of late John Dow Porteous, MA, formerly Rector of Knox Memorial Inst, Haddington, and Agnes Paton Walker; *m* 1929, May Hadwen (*d* 1981), *y d* of late John Cook Robertson, Kirkcaldy; three *s* three *d. Educ:* Knox Memorial Institute, Haddington; Universities of Edinburgh, Oxford (Trinity College), Berlin, Tübingen and Münster; New Coll., Edinburgh. MA Edinburgh with 1st Class Honours in Classics; MA Oxon with 1st Class in Literæ Humaniores; BD Edinburgh with distinction in Old Testament; 1st Bursar at Edinburgh University, 1916; C. B. Black Scholar in New Testament Greek, 1920; John Edward Baxter Scholar in Classics, 1923; Ferguson Scholar in Classics, 1923; Senior Cunningham Fellow at New College and Kerr Travelling Scholar, 1927; served in army, 1917–19, commissioned 2nd Lieut, March 1918, served overseas with 13th Royal Scots; Ordained to Ministry of United Free Church of Scotland, 1929; Minister of Crossgates Church, Church of Scotland, 1929–31; Regius Professor of Hebrew and Oriental Languages in the University of St Andrews, 1931–35; Professor of Old Testament Language, Literature and Theology in the University of Edinburgh, 1935–37; Prof. of Hebrew and Semitic Languages, Univ. of Edinburgh, 1937–68; Principal of New Coll., and Dean of Faculty of Divinity, Univ. of Edinburgh, 1964–68; retd, 1968; now Emeritus Professor. Hon. DD St Andrews, 1944; Lectures: Stone, Princeton Theological Seminary, 1953; Montague Burton, Leeds, 1974. President, Soc. for Old Testament Study, 1954. *Publications:* Das Alte Testament Deutsch 23: Das Danielbuch, 1962, 4th edn 1985 (English edition, 1965, 2nd, 1979); Living the Mystery: Collected Essays, 1967; Old Testament and History, 5 lectures in Annual of Swedish Theological Inst., vol. VIII, 1970–71; contributions to: Theologische Aufsätze Karl Barth zum 50 Geburtstag, 1936; Record and Revelation, 1938; The Old Testament and Modern Study, 1951; Peake's Commentary on the Bible, 1962. *Address:* 3 Hermitage Gardens, Edinburgh EH10 6DL. *T:* 031–447 4632.

PORTEOUS, Colonel Patrick Anthony, VC 1942; RA, retired 1970; *b* 1 Jan. 1918; *s* of late Brig.-General C. McL. Porteous, 9th Ghurkas, and late Mrs Porteous, Fleet, Hampshire; *m* 1943, Lois Mary (*d* 1953), *d* of late Maj.-General Sir H. E. Roome, KCIE; one *s* one *d*; *m* 1955, Deirdre, *d* of late Eric King; three *d. Educ:* Wellington Coll.; Royal Military Acad., Woolwich. BEF France, Sept. 1939–May 1940, with 6th AA Regt, RA; Dieppe, Aug. 1942 (VC); No 4 Commando, Dec. 1940–Oct. 1944; BLA June-Sept. 1944; 1st Airborne Div. Dec. 1944–July 1945; 6th Airborne Div., July 1945–March 1946; Staff Coll., Camberley, May-Nov. 1946; 16 Airborne Div. TA, Jan. 1947–Feb. 1948; 33 Airborne Lt Regt, RA, Feb. 1948–April 1949; No 1 Regular Commission Board, 1949; Instructor, RMA, Sandhurst, July 1950–July 1953; GHQ, Far East Land Forces, Singapore, Sept. 1953–July 1955; 1st Singapore Regt, RA, July-Dec. 1955; 14 Field Regt, RA, 1956–58; RAF Staff Coll., Jan. 1958–Dec. 1958; AMS, HQ Southern Comd, 1959–60; Colonel Junior Leaders Regt, RA, 1960–63; Colonel, General Staff War Office, later Ministry of Defence, 1963–66; Comdr Rheindahlen Garrison, 1966–69. *Recreation:* sailing. *Address:* Christmas Cottage, Church Lane, Funtington, W Sussex PO18 9LQ. *T:* Chichester 575315.

PORTER, Alastair Robert Wilson, CBE 1985; Secretary and Registrar, Royal College of Veterinary Surgeons, since 1966; barrister; *b* 28 Sept. 1928; *s* of late James and Olivia Porter (*née* Duncan); *m* 1954, Jennifer Mary Priaulx Forman; two *s* one *d. Educ:* Irvine Royal Academy; Glasgow Academy; Merton Coll., Oxford (MA). Called to Bar, Gray's Inn, 1952. Resident Magistrate, N Rhodesia, 1954; Registrar of High Court of N Rhodesia, 1961; Permanent Secretary: Min. of Justice, N Rhodesia, 1964; Min. of Justice, Govt of Republic of Zambia, Oct. 1964. Mem., Fedn (formerly Liaison Cttee) of Veterinarians of the EEC, 1966–, Sec.-Gen., 1973–79; Chm., EEC's Adv. Cttee on Veterinary Trng, 1986– (Vice-Chm., 1981–86). Wooldridge Meml Lectr, BVA Congress, 1976; MacKellar Meml Lectr, Western Counties Veterinary Assoc., Tavistock, 1978; Centenary Prize Lectr, Central Vet. Soc., 1981; Weipers Lectr, Glasgow Univ., 1985. Hon. Mem., BVA, 1978; Hon. Associate, RCVS, 1979. *Publication:* (jtly) An Anatomy of Veterinary Europe, 1972. *Address:* 4 Savill Road, Lindfield, Haywards Heath, West Sussex RH16 2NX. *T:* Lindfield 2001. *Club:* Caledonian.

PORTER, Alfred Ernest, CSI 1947; CIE 1942; *b* 2 Nov. 1896; *s* of F. L. Porter; *m* 1929, Nancy Florence (decd), *d* of late E. L. Melly; two *s. Educ:* Manchester Grammar Sch.; Corpus Christi Coll., Oxford. Manchester Regt, 1915; Machine Gun Corps, 1916; Indian Civil Service, 1922 48. *Address:* The Old Hall, Chawleigh, Chulmleigh, Devon EX18 7HH. *T:* Chulmleigh 80280.

PORTER, Prof. Arthur, OC 1983; MSc, PhD (Manchester); FIEE; FRSC 1970; Professor of Industrial Engineering, and Chairman of Department, University of Toronto, Toronto, 1961–76, now Emeritus Professor; President, Arthur Porter Associates Ltd, since 1973; Associate, Institute for Environmental Studies, University of Toronto, since 1981; *b* 8 Dec. 1910; *s* of late John William Porter and Mary Anne Harris; *m* 1941, Phyllis Patricia Dixon; one *s. Educ:* The Grammar Sch., Ulverston; University of Manchester. Asst Lecturer, University of Manchester, 1936–37; Commonwealth Fund Fellow, Massachusetts Inst. of Technology, USA, 1937–39; Scientific Officer, Admiralty, 1939–45; Principal Scientific Officer, National Physical Laboratory, 1946; Prof. of Instrument Technology, Royal Military Coll. of Science, 1946–49; Head, Research Division, Ferranti Electric Ltd, Toronto, Canada, 1949–55; Professor of Light Electrical Engineering, Imperial College of Science and Technology, University of London, 1955–58; Dean of the College of Engineering, Saskatchewan Univ., Saskatoon, 1958; Acting Dir, Centre for Culture and Technology, Toronto Univ., 1967–68; Academic Comr, Univ. of W Ontario, 1969–71. Dir and Founding Chm., Scientists and Engineers for Energy and Environment Inc., 1981–84. Chairman: Canadian Environmental Adv. Council, 1972–75; Ontario Royal Commn on Electric Power Planning, 1975–80. *Publications:* An Introduction to Servomechanisms, 1950; Cybernetics Simplified, 1969; Towards a Community University, 1971; articles in Trans. Royal Society, Proc. Royal Society, Phil. Mag., Proc. Inst. Mech. Eng, Proc. IEE, Nature, etc. *Recreations:* landscape architecture, energy conservation. *Address:* Watendlath, Belfountain, Ontario L0N 1B0, Canada. *T:* (519) 927–5732; (winter) Apt 21W Beacon House, 2170 Gulf Shore Boulevard N, Naples, Fla 33940, USA. *T:* (813) 263–2540. *Clubs:* Athenæum; Arts and Letters, Empire (Toronto), Wyndemere (Naples, Florida).

PORTER, Arthur Thomas, MRSL 1979; MA, PhD; Vice-Chancellor, University of Sierra Leone, Freetown, Sierra Leone, 1974–84; *b* 26 Jan. 1924; *m* 1953, Rigmor Sondergaard (*née* Rasmussen); one *s* one *d. Educ:* Fourah Bay Coll. (BA Dunelm); Cambridge Univ. (BA (Hist Tripos), MA); Boston Univ. (PhD). Asst, Dept of Social Anthropology, Edinburgh Univ., UK, 1951–52. Prof. of History and Head of Dept of Hist., also Dir of Inst. of African Studies, Fourah Bay Coll., 1963–64; Principal, University Coll., Nairobi, Univ. of E Africa, 1964–70; UNESCO Field Staff Officer; Educl Planning Adviser, Min. of Educn, Kenya, 1970–74. Mem. Exec. Bd, UNESCO, 1976–80. Africanus Horton Meml Lectr, Edinburgh Univ., 1983; Fulbright Schol.-in-Residence, Bethany Coll., Kansas, 1986–June 1987. Chm., Bd of Dirs, Sierra Leone Nat. Diamond Mining

Co., 1976–85. Hon. LHD Boston 1969; Hon. LLD Royal Univ. of Malta 1969. Phi Beta Kappa 1972. Symonds Medal, ACU, 1985. *Publications:* Creoledom, a Study of the Development of Freetown Society, 1963; contribs to The Times, Africa, African Affairs. *Recreation:* photography. *Address:* 26b Spur Road, Wilberforce, PO Box 1363, Freetown, Sierra Leone, West Africa. *T:* 31736; 81 Fitzjohn Avenue, Barnet, Herts EN5 2HN. *T:* 01–441 1551.

PORTER, Barry; *see* Porter, G. B.

PORTER, Rt. Rev. David Brownfield; *b* 10 May 1906; *s* of Sydney Lawrence Porter and Edith Alice Porter; *m* 1936, Violet Margaret Eliot (*d* 1956); one *s*; *m* 1961, Mrs Pamela Cecil (*née* Lightfoot) (*d* 1974), *widow* of Neil McNeill. *Educ:* Hertford Coll., Oxford. Curate of St Augustine's, Leeds, 1929; Tutor of Wycliffe Hall, Oxford, 1931; Chaplain, 1933; Chaplain of Wadham Coll., Oxford, 1934; Vicar of All Saints', Highfield, Oxford, 1935; Vicar of Darlington, 1943; Rector of St John's, Princes Street, Edinburgh, 1947–61; Dean of Edinburgh, 1954–61; Bishop Suffragan of Aston, 1962–72. Select Preacher, Oxford Univ., 1964. *Recreations:* fishing and painting. *Address:* Silver Leys, Brockhampton, near Cheltenham.

PORTER, Dorothea Noelle Naomi, (Thea Porter); fashion designer, since 1967; *b* 24 Dec. 1927; *d* of Rev. Dr M. S. Seale and Renée Seale; *m* 1953, Robert S. Porter (marr. diss. 1967); one *d*. *Educ:* Lycée français, Damascus; Fernhill Manor; Royal Holloway Coll., London Univ. Embassy wife, Beirut; fashion designer, 1967–, interior and fabric designer. *Recreations:* cooking, travelling, music, painting, collecting antique Islamic fabrics and objets; consulting clairvoyants. *Club:* Colony Room.

PORTER, Eric (Richard); actor; *b* London, 8 April 1928; *s* of Richard John Porter and Phoebe Elizabeth (*née* Spall). *Educ:* LCC and Wimbledon Technical College. First professional appearance with Shakespeare Memorial Theatre Company, Arts, Cambridge, 1945; first appearance on London stage as Dunois' Page in Saint Joan with the travelling repertory company, King's, Hammersmith, 1946; Birmingham Repertory Theatre, 1948–50; under contract to H. M. Tennant, Ltd, 1951–53. *Plays include:* The Silver Box, Lyric, Hammersmith, 1951; The Three Sisters, Aldwych, 1951; Thor, With Angels, Lyric, Hammersmith, 1951; title-role in Noah, Whitehall, 1951; The Same Sky, Lyric, Hammersmith, 1952; Under the Sycamore Tree, Aldwych, 1952; season at Lyric, Hammersmith, directed by John Gielgud, 1953–plays: Richard II, The Way of the World, Venice Preserved; with Bristol Old Vic Company, 1954, and again 1955–56; parts included title roles in King Lear, Uncle Vanya, Volpone; with Old Vic Company, 1954–55: parts included Jacques in As You Like It, title role in Henry IV, Bolingbroke in Richard II, Christopher Sly in The Taming of the Shrew; Romanoff and Juliet, Piccadilly, 1956; A Man of Distinction, Edinburgh Festival and Princes, 1957; Time and Again, British tour with the Lunts, 1957, and New York in The Visit, 1958; The Coast of Coromandel, English tour, 1959; Rosmersholm, Royal Court, 1959, Comedy, 1960. (Evening Standard Drama Award as Best Actor of 1959); under contract to Royal Shakespeare Company, 1960–65; parts: Malvolio in Twelfth Night, Stratford, 1960, Aldwych, 1961; Duke in The Two Gentlemen of Verona, Stratford, 1960; Leontes in The Winter's Tale, Stratford, 1960; Ulysses in Troilus and Cressida, Stratford, 1960; Ferdinand in The Duchess of Malfi, Stratford, 1960, Aldwych, 1961; Lord Chamberlain in Ondine, Aldwych, 1961; Buckingham in Richard III, Stratford, 1961; title role in Becket, Aldwych, 1961, Globe, 1962; title role in Macbeth, Stratford, 1962; Iachimo in Cymbeline, Stratford, 1962; Pope Pius XII in The Representative, Aldwych, 1963. Stratford Season, 1964; Bolingbroke in Richard II; Henry IV in Henry IV Parts I and II; Chorus in Henry V; Richmond in Richard III; Stratford Season, 1965: Barabas in The Jew of Malta; Shylock in The Merchant of Venice; Chorus in Henry V, Aldwych, 1965; Ossip in The Government Inspector, Aldwych, 1966; Stratford Season, 1968; Lear in King Lear; Faustus in Dr Faustus (US tour, 1969); Paul Thomsen in My Little Boy-My Big Girl (also directed), Fortune, 1969; The Protagonist, Brighton, 1971; Peter Pan, Coliseum, 1971; Malvolio, inaugural season, St George's Elizabethan Theatre, 1976. *Films:* The Fall of the Roman Empire, 1964; The Pumpkin Eater, 1964; The Heroes of Telemark, 1965; Kaleidoscope, 1966; The Lost Continent, 1968; Hands of the Ripper, Nicholas and Alexandra, Antony and Cleopatra, 1971; Hitler: the last ten days, 1973; The Day of the Jackal, 1973; The Belstone Fox, 1973; Callan, 1974; Hennessy, 1975; The Thirty-Nine Steps, 1978; Little Lord Fauntleroy, 1980; *television parts include:* Soames Forsyte in The Forsyte Saga, BBC (Best Actor Award, Guild of TV Producers and Directors, 1967); Karenin, in Anna Karenina, BBC, 1977; Alanbrooke in Churchill and the Generals, BBC, 1979; Polonius in Hamlet, BBC, 1980; Dep. Governor Danforth in The Crucible, BBC, 1981; Neville Chamberlain in Winston Churchill: The Wilderness Years, Southern, 1981; Count Bronowsky in The Jewel in the Crown, 1983; Moriarty in Sherlock Holmes, 1984; Fagin in Oliver Twist, 1985. *Recreations:* walking, swimming, sailing. *Address:* c/o London Management, 235 Regent Street, W1A 2JT.

PORTER, Prof. Sir George, Kt 1972; FRS 1960; BSc (Leeds); MA, PhD, ScD, (Cambridge); FRSC; Chancellor of Leicester University, since 1986; President of the Royal Society, since 1985; Fullerian Professor of Chemistry, Royal Institution of Great Britain, since 1966 (Director, 1966–86); Visiting Professor: Department of Chemistry: University College, London, since 1967; Imperial College, London, since 1978; *b* 6 Dec. 1920; *m* 1949, Stella Jean Brooke; two *s*. *Educ:* Thorne Grammar Sch.; Leeds Univ.; Emmanuel Coll., Cambridge. Ackroyd Scholar, Leeds Univ., 1938–41. Served RNVR in Western Approaches and Mediterranean, 1941–45. Cambridge: Demonstrator in Physical Chemistry, 1949–52, Fellow of Emmanuel Coll., 1952–54; Hon. Fellow, 1967; Asst Director of Research in Physical Chemistry, 1952–54. Asst Director of British Rayon Research Assoc., 1954–55. Prof. of Physical Chemistry, 1955–63, Firth Prof. of Chemistry, 1963–66, Univ. of Sheffield; Prof. of Chemistry, Royal Institution, 1963–66. Member: ARC, 1964–66; Open Univ. Council, 1969–75; Science Mus. Adv. Council, 1970–73; Council and Science Bd, SRC, 1976–80; Council, KCL (KQC), 1985–. President: Chemical Soc., 1970–72 (Pres. Faraday Div., 1973–74); Comité Internat. de photobiologie, 1968–72; Nat. Assoc. for Gifted Children, 1975–80; R&D Soc., 1977–80; Assoc. for Science Educn, 1985; BAAS, 1985–86. Counsellor, Inst. for Molecular Sci., Okazaki, Japan, 1980. Hon. Member: NY Acad. of Sciences, 1968; Leopoldina Acad., 1970; Chemical Soc. of Japan, 1982; For. Associate, Nat. Acad. of Sciences, 1974; Corresp. Mem., Göttingen Acad. of Sciences, 1974; Mem. Pontifical Acad. of Sciences, 1974; For. Corresp. Mem., La Real Academia de Ciencias, Madrid, 1978; For. Hon. Mem., Amer. Acad. of Arts and Scis, 1979; For. Mem., Acad. of Sciences, Lisbon, 1983; Hon. Prof. of Phys. Chem., Univ. of Kent at Canterbury, 1966–; Hon. Professor: Chinese Acad. of Scis, 1980; Amer. Philosophical Soc., 1986. Lectures: Tilden, 1958; Remsen Meml, Amer. Chem. Soc., 1962; Liversidge, 1970; Geoffrey Frew, Aust. Acad. of Sci., 1976; Robbins, USA, 1976; Pahlavi, Iran, 1977; Bakerian, 1977, Humphry Davy, 1985, Royal Soc., 1977; Robertson Meml, Nat. Acad. of Sciences, USA, 1978; Romanes, Oxford, 1978; Goodman, London, 1979. Trustee, British Museum, 1972–74. Hon. Fellow: Inst. of Patentees and Inventors, 1970; QMC, 1986; Hon. FRSE, 1983; Hon. Freeman, Livery of Salters' Co., 1981. Hon. Doctorates: Utah, Sheffield, East Anglia, Durham, Leeds, Leicester, Heriot-Watt, City, Manchester, St Andrews, London, Kent, Oxon, Hull, Rio de Janeiro, Instituto Quimica de Sarria, Barcelona, Pennsylvania, Coimbra, Lille, Open, Surrey, Univ. of Phillipines, Bristol, Notre Dame, Reading. Fairchild Dist. Scholar, California Inst. of Technology, 1974; Hitchcock Prof., Univ. of California, Berkeley, 1978. Corday-Morgan Medal, Chem. Soc., 1955; Nobel Prize (Jt) for Chemistry, 1967; Silvanus Thompson Medal, 1969; Royal Society: Davy Medal, 1971; Rumford Medal, 1978; Kalinga Prize, 1977; Faraday Medal, Chem. Soc., 1980; Longstaff Medal, RSC, 1981. *Publications:* Chemistry for the Modern World, 1962; scientific papers in Proc. Royal Society, Trans. Faraday Society, etc. TV Series: Laws of Disorder, 1965–66; Time Machines, 1969–70; Natural History of a Sunbeam, 1976–77. *Recreation:* sailing. *Address:* The Royal Society, 6 Carlton House Terrace, SW1. *Club:* Athenæum.

PORTER, George Barrington, (Barry); MP (C) Wirral South, since 1983 (Bebington and Ellesmere Port, 1979–83); *b* 11 June 1939; *s* of Kenneth William Porter and Vera Porter; *m* 1965, Susan Carolyn James; two *s* three *d*. *Educ:* Birkenhead Sch.; University Coll., Oxford (BA Hons). Admitted solicitor, 1965. Councillor: Birkenhead County Bor. Council, 1967–74; Wirral Bor., 1975–79 (Chm., Housing Cttee, 1976–77, and Educn Cttee, 1977–79). Mem., Select Cttee on Trade and Industry; Sec., All Party Parly Solicitors Gp. *Recreations:* golf, Rugby Union football, watching cricket, real ale. *Address:* House of Commons, SW1A 0AA. *Clubs:* Royal Commonwealth Society, Royal Automobile; Oxton Conservative, Ellesmere Port Conservative; Birkenhead Park Football, Wirral Ladies Golf, Birkenhead Squash Racquets, Oxton Cricket.

PORTER, Prof. Helen Kemp, FRS 1956; DSc; FRSC; Emeritus Professor, University of London; Scientific Adviser to the Secretary, Agricultural Research Council, 1971–72 (Second Secretary, 1969–71); Fellow, Imperial College of Science and Technology, 1966; *b* 10 Nov. 1899; *d* of George Kemp Archbold and Caroline E. B. Archbold (*née* Whitehead); *m* 1937, William George Porter, MD, MRCP (decd); *m* 1962, Arthur St George Huggett, FRS, DSc, MB, BS (*d* 1968). *Educ:* Clifton High School for Girls, Bristol; University of London, Research Assistant, Food Investigation Board, 1922–32; DSc London, 1932. On staff of Research Institute of Plant Physiology, Imperial Coll., 1932–59; Reader in Enzymology, University of London, Imperial College of Science and Technology, 1957–59; Prof. of Plant Physiology, Imperial Coll. of Science and Technology, London Univ., 1959–64; Dir, ARC Unit of Plant Physiology, 1959–64. Hon. ARCS 1964. *Publications:* contributions to Annals of Botany, Biochemical Journal, Journal of Experimental Botany, etc. *Recreation:* needlework. *Address:* 49e Beaumont Street, W1N 1RE. *T:* 01–935 5862.

PORTER, Ivor Forsyth, CMG 1963; OBE 1944; HM Diplomatic Service, retired; *b* 12 Nov. 1913; *s* of Herbert and Evelyn Porter; *m* 1951, Ann, *o d* of late Dr John Speares (marr. diss., 1961); *m* 1961, Katerina, *o c* of A. T. Cholerton; one *s* one *d*. *Educ:* Barrow Grammar Sch.; Leeds Univ. (BA, PhD). Lecturer at Bucharest Univ., 1939–40; Temp. Secretary, at Bucharest Legation, 1940–41; Raiding Forces, 1941–45 (Major). Joined Foreign (subseq. Diplomatic) Service, May 1946, as 2nd Secretary in Sen. Branch; 1st Secretary 1948; transferred to Washington, 1951; Foreign Office, 1953; UK Delegation to NATO Paris as Counsellor and Head of Chancery, 1956; Nicosia, 1959 (Deputy Head UK Mission), Deputy High Commissioner, 1961–62, Cyprus; Permanent Rep. to Council of Europe, Strasbourg, 1962–65 (with personal rank of Minister); Dep. High Commissioner, Eastern India, 1965–66; Ambassador, UK Delegn to Geneva Disarmament Conf., 1968–71 (Minister, 1967–68); Ambassador to Senegal, Guinea, Mali and Mauritania, 1971–73; later Dir, Atlantic Region, Research Dept, FCO, retired. *Publication:* The Think Trap, 1972. *Recreations:* writing, walking. *Address:* 17 Redcliffe Road, SW10. *Clubs:* Travellers', PEN.

PORTER, James Forrest; Director of the Commonwealth Institute, since 1978; *b* Frodsham, Cheshire, 2 Oct. 1928; *s* of Ernest Porter and Mary Violetta Porter; *m* 1952, Dymphna, *d* of Leo Francis Powell, London; two *d*. *Educ:* Salford Grammar Sch.; LSE (BSc Sociol.); Univ. of London Inst. of Educn (MA). Asst Master, St George in the East Sec. Sch., Stepney, 1948–50; Leverhulme Scholar, Univ. of London, 1950–55; Lectr in Sociol. and Educn, Worcester Coll., 1955–60; Head of Educn Dept, Chorley Coll., 1960–62; Dep. Principal, Coventry Coll., 1962–67; Principal, Bulmershe Coll. of Higher Educn, Reading, 1967–78. Director: bi-annual internat. courses on teacher educn, Brit. Council, 1975, 1977, 1979, on Museum Educn, 1982; Adult Literacy Support Services Fund, 1977–81. Consultant: Finland, 1976; Unesco, Paris, 1979–; Commonwealth Fellow, Australia, 1977. Chairman: World Educn Fellowship, 1979–82; Newsconcern Foundn, 1984–; Member: Nat. Cttee of Inquiry into Teacher Educn and Trng (James Cttee), 1971; Educn Cttee, UGC, 1970–78; Educnl Adv. Council, IBA, 1970–80; Nat. Council for Dance Educn, 1978; Exec. Cttee, Internat. Council of Museums, 1981–; Pres., British Comparative Educn Soc., 1983–84. Member: UK Delegn to Unesco, Geneva, 1975 (Vice-Pres., Commn on Changing Role of Teacher); Unesco Missions to Morocco and Senegal, 1982, to Jordan, 1983; UK Nat. Commn for Unesco, 1984–. Governor, Polytechnic of Central London. Mem., Editorial Bd, Higher Education Review, 1974–; Chm., Editorial Bd, Commonwealth Magazine, 1985– (Mem., 1982). FRSA 1978; Hon. FCP 1978; FRGS 1984. *Publications:* (ed) Rural Development and the Changing Countries of the World, 1969; (with N. Goble) The Changing Role of the Teacher, Paris 1977. *Recreations:* writing, river watching. *Address:* Commonwealth Institute, Kensington High Street, W8 6NQ. *T:* 01–603 4535; House by the Water, Bolney Avenue, Shiplake, Oxon. *Club:* Royal Commonwealth Society.

PORTER, Air Vice-Marshal John Alan, OBE 1973; CEng, FRAeS, FIEE; Director-General Aircraft 2, Ministry of Defence Procurement Executive, since 1984; *b* 29 Sept. 1934; *s* of late Alan and Etta Porter; two *s*. *Educ:* Lawrence Sheriff School, Rugby; Bristol Univ. (BSc); Southampton Univ. (Dip Soton). Commissioned in Engineer Branch, RAF, 1953; appts in UK, USA and Cyprus, 1953–79; Royal College of Defence Studies, 1980; Dep. Gen. Manager, NATO MRCA Develt and Production Agency (NAMMA), Munich, 1981–84. *Recreations:* music, horology. *Address:* c/o R3, Cox's and King's Branch, Lloyds Bank, 6 Pall Mall, SW1. *Club:* Royal Air Force.

PORTER, John Andrew, TD; JP; DL; Director, Anglia Building Society (formerly Anglia, Hastings and Thanet Building Society), since 1978 (Chairman, 1978–81); Partner, Porter and Cobb, as Chartered Surveyor, 1940–81; Consultant, Cobbs (formerly Porter, Cobb and Prall), since 1981; *b* 18 May 1916; *s* of late Horace Augustus Porter, DFC, JP, and Vera Marion Porter; *m* 1941, Margaret Isobel Wisnom; two *d*. *Educ:* Radley Coll.; Sidney Sussex Coll., Cambridge (MA). Commissioned RA, TA, 1938; served War, 1939–46, Lt-Col. Dir, Kent County Building Soc., 1947 (Chm., 1965–68); Dir, Hastings and Thanet Building Soc., 1968 (Chm., 1972–78). JP Gravesham PSD, 1952, Chm., Gravesham Div., 1976–83, Dep. Chm., 1983–. Pres., Gravesend Cons. Assoc., 1965–77. General Commissioner of Taxes, 1970–. DL Kent, 1984. *Recreations:* cricket, hockey, golf. *Address:* Leaders, Hodsoll Street, near Wrotham, Kent TN15 7LH. *T:* Fairseat 822260. *Clubs:* Royal Automobile, MCC; Hawks (Cambridge); Kent CC (Pres., 1985–86).

PORTER, Sir John Simon H.; *see* Horsbrugh-Porter.

PORTER, Prof. Rev. Canon Joshua Roy; Professor of Theology, University of Exeter, 1962–86 (Head of Department, 1962–85), now Professor Emeritus; *b* 7 May 1921; *s* of

Joshua Porter and Bessie Evelyn (*née* Earlam). *Educ:* King's Sch., Macclesfield; Merton Coll., Oxford (Exhibnr); S Stephen's House, Oxford. BA: Mod. Hist. (Cl. I), Theology (Cl. I), MA Oxon. Liddon Student, 1942; Deacon 1945, Priest 1946; Curate of S Mary, Portsea, 1945–47; Resident Chaplain to Bp of Chichester, 1947–49; Hon. Chaplain, 1949–50; Examining Chaplain from 1950; Fellow, Chaplain and Lectr, Oriel Coll., Oxford, 1949–62; Tutor, 1950–62; Kennicott Hebrew Fellow, 1955; Sen. Denyer and Johnson Schol., 1958; Select Preacher: Univs of Oxford, 1953–55, Cambridge, 1957, TCD, 1958; Canon and Preb. of Wightring and Theol Lectr in Chichester Cath., 1965–; Vis. Prof., Southeastern Seminary, Wake Forest, N Carolina, 1967; Dean of Arts, Univ. of Exeter, 1968–71; Proctor in Convocation of Canterbury for dio. of Exeter, 1964–75; for Other Univs (Canterbury), 1975–; Examining Chaplain to Bps of Peterborough, 1973–, of Truro, 1973–81, and of London, 1981–. Ethel M. Wood Lectr, Univ. of London 1979; Michael Harrah Wood Lectr, Univ. of the South, Sewanee, Tenn, 1984. Member: Gen. Synod, 1970– (Panel of Chairmen, 1984–); ACCM, 1975–86; Council of Management, Coll. of St Mark and St John, 1980–85; Vice-Pres., Folklore Soc., 1979– (Pres., 1976–79); Pres., Soc. for OT Study, 1983. FAMS. *Publications:* World in the Heart, 1944; Moses and Monarchy, 1963; The Extended Family in the Old Testament, 1967; Proclamation and Presence, 1970, 2nd rev. edn, 1983; The Non-Juring Bishops, 1973; Leviticus, 1976, Japanese edn 1984; Animals in Folklore, 1978; The Crown and the Church, 1978; Folklore and the Old Testament, 1981; contributor to: Promise and Fulfilment, 1963; A Source Book of the Bible for Teachers, 1970; The Journey to the Other World, 1975; Tradition and Interpretation, 1979; A Basic Introduction to the Old Testament, 1980; Divination and Oracles, 1981; Folklore Studies in the Twentieth Century, 1981; The Folklore of Ghosts, 1981; Israel's Prophetic Tradition, 1982; Tracts for Our Times, 1983; The Hero in Tradition and Folklore, 1984; Harper's Bible Dictionary, 1985; Arabia and the Gulf: from traditional society to modern states, 1986; numerous articles in learned jls and dictionaries. *Recreations:* theatre and opera, book-collecting, travel. *Address:* 36 Theberton Street, Barnsbury, N1 0QX. *T:* 01–354 5861. *Club:* Royal Over-Seas League.

PORTER, Sir Leslie, Kt 1983; President, Tesco PLC, since 1985 (Chairman, 1973–85; Deputy Chairman and Managing Director, 1972–73); Chairman, Sports Aid Foundation, since 1985; *b* 10 July 1920; *s* of late Henry Alfred and Jane Porter; *m* 1949, Shirley Cohen; one *s* one *d*. *Educ:* Holloway County Sch. Joined family textile business (J. Porter & Co), 1938. Served War: Techn. Quartermaster Sergt, 1st Bn The Rangers, KRRC, in Egypt, Greece, Crete, Libya, Tunisia, Algeria, Italy, 1939–46. Re-joined J. Porter & Co, 1946; became Managing Dir, 1955. Joined Tesco Stores (Holdings) Ltd: Dir, 1959; Asst Managing Dir, 1964; Dep. Chm., 1970. Member of Lloyd's, 1964– (John Poland syndicate). Pres., Inst. of Grocery Distribution, 1977–80. Vice Pres., Age Concern England. Mem. Court, Cranfield Inst. of Technology, 1977–; Chm., Bd of Governors, Tel Aviv Univ.; Governor, Hong Kong Baptist Coll.; Vice-Pres., Nat. Playing Fields Assoc. Hon. PhD (Business Management), Tel Aviv Univ., 1973. *Recreations:* golf, yachting, bridge. *Clubs:* Royal Automobile, City Livery; Dyrham Park County (Barnet, Herts); Coombe Hill Golf (Kingston Hill, Surrey); Frilford Heath Golf (Abingdon).

PORTER, Marguerite Ann, (Mrs Nicky Henson); Guest Artist, Royal Ballet Co., since 1986 (Senior Principal Dancer, 1976–85); *b* 30 Nov. 1948; *d* of William Albert and Mary Porter; *m* (marr. diss.); *m* 1986, Nicky Henson. *Educ:* Doncaster. Joined Royal Ballet School, 1964; graduated to Royal Ballet Co., 1966; soloist, 1972; Principal, 1976; favourite roles include: Juliet in Romeo and Juliet, Manon, Natalia in A Month in the Country. *Recreation:* friends. *Address:* c/o Jean Diamond, London Management, 235/241 Regent Street, W1.

PORTER, Air Marshal Sir (Melvin) Kenneth (Drowley), KCB 1967 (CB 1959); CBE 1945 (OBE 1942); *b* 19 Nov. 1912; *s* of late Edward Ernest Porter, MBE, DCM and late Helen Porter; *m* 1940, Elena, *d* of F. W. Sinclair; two *s* one *d*. *Educ:* No. 1 School of Technical Training, Halton; RAF Coll., Cranwell. Aircraft apprentice, RAF Halton; cadetship to RAF Coll., Cranwell; commissioned, 1932; Army Co-operation Sqdn, Fleet Air Arm, 1933–36, as PO and FO; specialised on Signals, 1936–37, Flt-Lieut; Sqdn Leader, 1939. Served War of 1939–45 (despatches thrice, OBE, CBE); Chief Signals Officer, Balloon Command, 1939; DCSO and CSO, HQ No. 11 Group, 1940–42; Temp. Wing Comdr, 1941; CSO, HQ 2nd TAF, 1943–45; Temp Gp Captain, 1943; Actg Air Commodore, 1944–45; CSO, HQ Bomber Command, 1945; Air Min. Tech. Plans, 1946–47, Gp Captain, 1946; Member Directing Staff, RAF Staff Coll., Andover, 1947–49; Senior Tech. Staff Officer, HQ No. 205 Group, 1950–52; Comdg Nos 1 and 2 Air Signallers Schools, 1952–54; CSO HQ 2nd ATAF, 1954–55; CSO, HQ Fighter Command, Actg Air Commodore, 1955–58, Air Cdr, 1958; Student Imperial Defence Coll., 1959; Commandant of No 4 School of Technical Training, RAF St Athan, Glamorgan, and Air Officer Wales, 1960–61; Actg Air Vice-Marshal, 1961; Air Vice-Marshal, 1962; Director-General: Ground Training, 1961–63; of Signals (Air), Ministry of Defence, 1964–66; AOC-in-C, Maintenance Command, 1966–70; Hd of RAF Engineer Branch, 1968–70; Actg Air Marshal, 1966; Air Marshal, 1967. Dir of Tech. Educn Projects, UC Cardiff, 1970–74. CEng 1966; FIEE; FRAeS; CBIM; FInstProdE. Officer, Legion of Merit (US), 1945. *Recreation:* reading. *Address:* c/o Lloyds Bank, Redland Branch, 163 Whiteladies Road, Clifton, Bristol BS8 8RW.

PORTER, Hon. Sir Murray (Victor), Kt 1970; Agent-General for Victoria in London, 1970–76; *b* 20 Dec. 1909; *s* of late V. Porter, Pt Pirie, SA; *m* 1932, Edith Alice Johnston, *d* of late C. A. Johnston; two *d*. *Educ:* Brighton (Victoria) Grammar Sch., Australia. Served War, 2nd AIF, 1941–45. MLA (Liberal) Sandringham, Victoria, 1955–70; Govt Whip, 1955–56; Asst Minister, 1956–58; Minister for: Forests, 1958–59; Local Govt, 1959–64; Public Works, 1964–70. *Recreations:* golf, swimming. *Address:* Flat 7, The Point, 405 Beach Road, Beaumaris, Victoria 3193, Australia. *Clubs:* Melbourne Cricket, Royal Melbourne Golf, Royal Automobile Club of Victoria.

PORTER, Peter Neville Frederick, FRSL; freelance writer, poet; *b* Brisbane, 16 Feb. 1929; *s* of William Ronald Porter and Marion Main; *m* 1961, Jannice Henry (*d* 1974); two *d*. *Educ:* Church of England Grammar Sch., Brisbane; Toowoomba Grammar Sch. Worked as journalist in Brisbane before coming to England in 1951; clerk, bookseller and advertising writer, before becoming full-time poet, journalist, reviewer and broadcaster in 1968. Chief work done in poetry and English literature. Hon. DLitt Melbourne, 1985. *Publications:* Once Bitten, Twice Bitten, 1961; Penguin Modern Poets No 2, 1962; Poems, Ancient and Modern, 1964; A Porter Folio, 1969; The Last of England, 1970; Preaching to the Converted, 1972; (trans.) After Martial, 1972; (with Arthur Boyd) Jonah, 1973; (with Arthur Boyd) The Lady and the Unicorn, 1975; Living in a Calm Country, 1975; (jt ed) New Poetry 1, 1975; The Cost of Seriousness, 1978; English Subtitles, 1981; Collected Poems, 1983 (Duff Cooper Prize); Fast Forward, 1984; (with Arthur Boyd) Narcissus, 1985. *Recreations:* buying records and listening to music; travelling in Italy. *Address:* 42 Cleveland Square, W2. *T:* 01–262 4289.

PORTER, Raymond Alfred James; *b* 14 Oct. 1896; *o s* of Philip and Alice Porter; *m* 1922, Nellie (*d* 1979), *er d* of George Edward Loveland; no *c*. *Educ:* Reigate Grammar Sch. Entered Lloyd's, 1912, Under-writing Member, 1934. Served European War, 1914–19, in Queen's Royal (West Surrey) Regt. Member, Cttee of Lloyd's, 1950–53, 1955–58, 1960–63 (Deputy Chairman of Lloyd's, 1961); Member, Cttee, Lloyd's Underwriters' Assoc., 1945–65 (Chairman, 1949–54, 1962); Chairman Joint Hull Cttee, 1958 and 1959. Member: Local Govt Management Cttee, 1964–67; Godstone RDC, 1946–60 and 1962–69 (Chairman, 1952–54); Surrey CC, 1955–58. Silver Medal for Services to Lloyd's, 1978. *Address:* Mashobra, Limpsfield, Oxted, Surrey. *T:* Oxted 2509.

PORTER, Prof. Robert, DM, FRACP, FAA; Howard Florey Professor of Medical Research and Director, John Curtin School of Medical Research, Australian National University, since 1980; *b* 10 Sept. 1932; *s* of William John Porter and late Amy Porter (*née* Tottman); *m* 1961, Anne Dorothy Steell; two *s* two *d*. *Educ:* Univ. of Adelaide (BMedSc, DSc); Univ. of Oxford (MA, BCh, DM). Rhodes Scholarship, South Australia, 1954; Radcliffe Travelling Fellowship in Med. Sci., University Coll., Oxford, 1962; Lectr, Univ. Lab. of Physiology, Oxford, 1960–67; Fellow, St Catherine's Coll., and Medical Tutor, Oxford, 1963–67; Prof. of Physiology and Chm., Dept of Physiology, Monash Univ., 1967–79. *Publications:* Cortico-Spinal Neurones: their role in movement (with C. G. Phillips), 1977; articles on neurophysiology and control of movement by the brain. *Recreations:* outdoor sports. *Address:* 85 Brereton Street, Garran, ACT 2605, Australia. *T:* (home) (062) 810383; (office) (062) 492597.

PORTER, Rt. Rev. Robert George; *see* Murray, Bishop of The.

PORTER, Robert Stanley, CB 1972; OBE 1959; Deputy Secretary (Chief Economist), Overseas Development Administration, Foreign and Commonwealth Office (formerly Ministry of Overseas Development), 1980–84; retired; *b* 17 Sept. 1924; *s* of S. R. Porter; *m* 1st, 1953, Dorothea Naomi (marr. diss. 1967), *d* of Rev. Morris Seale; one *d*; 2nd, 1967, Julia Karen, *d* of Edmund A. Davies. *Educ:* St Clement Danes, Holborn Estate, Grammar Sch.; New Coll., Oxford. Research Economist, US Economic Cooperation Administration Special Mission to the UK, 1949; British Middle East Development Division: Asst Statistical Adviser, Cairo, 1951; Statistical Adviser and Economist, Beirut, 1955; Min. of Overseas Development: Dir, Geographical Div., Economic Planning Staff, 1965; Dep. Dir-Gen. of Economic Planning, 1967; Dir-Gen. of Economic Planning, 1969. Vis. Prof., David Livingstone Inst. for Overseas Develt Studies, 1984–87. *Publications:* articles in Oxford Economic Papers, Kyklos, Review of Income and Wealth. *Recreations:* music, theatre. *Address:* Lower Saunders, Cheriton Fitzpaine, Crediton, Devon EX17 4JA. *T:* Cheriton Fitzpaine 645. *Club:* Athenæum.

PORTER, Rt. Hon. Sir Robert (Wilson), Kt 1971; PC (NI) 1969; QC (NI) 1965; County Court Judge, Northern Ireland, since 1978; *b* 23 Dec. 1923; *s* of late Joseph Wilson Porter and late Letitia Mary (*née* Wasson); *m* 1953, Margaret Adelaide, *y d* of late F. W. Lynas; one *s* one *d* (and one *d* decd). *Educ:* Model Sch. and Foyle Coll., Londonderry; Queen's Univ., Belfast. RAFVR, 1943–46; Royal Artillery (TA), 1950–56. Foundation Schol., Queen's Univ., 1947 and 1948; LLB 1949. Called to Bar of N Ireland, 1950. Lecturer in Contract and Sale of Goods, Queen's Univ., 1950–51; Jun. Crown Counsel, Co. Londonderry, 1960–63, Co. Down, 1964–65; Counsel to Attorney-General for N Ireland, 1963–64 and 1965; Recorder of Londonderry, 1979–81. Vice-Chairman, 1959–61, Chairman, 1961–66, War Pensions Appeal Tribunal for N Ireland. MP (U) Queen's Univ. of Belfast, 1966–69, Lagan Valley, 1969–73, Parlt of N Ireland; Minister of Health and Social Services, N Ireland, 1969; Parly Sec., Min. of Home Affairs, 1969; Minister of Home Affairs, Govt of NI, 1969–70. *Recreations:* gardening, golf. *Address:* Larch Hill, Ballylesson, Belfast, N Ireland BT8 8JX. *Club:* Royal Air Force.

PORTER, Shirley, (Lady Porter); Councillor, Hyde Park Ward, Westminster City Council, since 1974, Leader of the Council since 1983; *b* 29 Nov. 1930; *d* of late Sir John (Edward) Cohen and Lady (Sarah) Cohen; *m* 1949, Sir Leslie Porter, *qv*; one *s* one *d*. *Educ:* Warren Sch., Worthing, Sussex; La Ramée, Lausanne, Switzerland. Founded Designers' Guild, 1970; Sec., Porter Investments, 1970–; Dir, Capital Radio, 1982–. Westminster City Council: Conservative Whip, 1974–77; Chm., Highways and Works Cttee, 1978–82 (Vice-Chm., 1977–78); Mem., Road Safety Cttee, 1974–82; Mem., Co-ordinating Cttee, 1981–82; Chm., Gen. Purposes Cttee, 1982–; Chm., Policy Review Cttee, 1982–. Chairman: (also Founder), WARS Campaign (Westminster Against Reckless Spending), 1981–; Cleaner City Campaign, 1979–81; Vice-Pres., Cleaner London Campaign, 1979–81; Mem. Exec., Keep Britain Tidy Gp, 1977–81. Dep. Chm., London Festival Ballet, 1980–; Vice-Chm., London Union of Youth Clubs, 1978–; Member: Family Service Unit, 1978–; Court, Guild of Cleaners, 1976–. Governor, Tel Aviv Univ., 1982. JP Inner London, 1972–84. *Recreations:* golf, tennis, ballet, cleaning up London, waste-hunting. *Address:* Westminster City Hall, Victoria Street, SW1E 6QP. *T:* 01–828 8070. *Clubs:* Queen's, Racquets; Frilford Heath Golf (Oxford); Coombe Hill Golf, Dyrham Park Golf.

PORTER, Thea; *see* Porter, D. N. N.

PORTER, Walter Stanley, TD 1950; MA (Cantab); Headmaster of Framlingham College, 1955–71; *b* 28 Sept. 1909; *s* of late Walter Porter, Rugby; *m* 1937, Doreen, *o d* of B. Haynes, Rugby; one *d*. *Educ:* Rugby Sch.; Gonville and Caius Coll., Cambridge. Assistant Master and Officer Commanding Training Corps, Trent Coll., 1933–36; Felsted Sch., 1936–43; Radley Coll., 1944–55. FRSA 1968. *Recreations:* travel, amateur dramatics; formerly Rugby football, hockey. *Address:* The Hermitage, 29 Cumberland Street, Woodbridge, Suffolk. *T:* Woodbridge 2340.

PORTERFIELD, Dr James Stuart; Reader in Bacteriology, Sir William Dunn School of Pathology, Oxford University, and Senior Research Fellow, Wadham College, Oxford, since 1977; *b* 17 Jan. 1924; *yr s* of late Dr Samuel Porterfield and Mrs Lilian Porterfield, Widnes, Lancs, and Portstewart, Co. Londonderry, NI; *m* 1950, Betty Mary Burch; one *d* (one *s* decd). *Educ:* Wade Deacon Grammar Sch., Widnes; King's Sch., Chester; Liverpool Univ. MB, ChB 1947, MD 1949. Asst Lectr in Bacteriology, Univ. of Liverpool, 1947–49; Bacteriologist and Virologist, Common Cold Res. Unit, Salisbury, Wilts, 1949–51; Pathologist, RAF Inst. of Pathology and Tropical Med., Halton, Aylesbury, Bucks, 1952–53; seconded to W African Council for Med. Res. Labs, Lagos, Nigeria, 1953–57; Mem. Scientific Staff, Nat. Inst. for Med. Res., Mill Hill, 1949–77; WHO Regional Ref. Centre for Arthropod-borne Viruses, 1961–65; WHO Collaborating Lab., 1965–; Ref. Expert on Arboviruses, Public Health Lab. Service, 1967–76. Chm., Arbovirus Study Gp, Internat. Cttee for Nomenclature of Viruses, 1968–78; Meetings Sec., Soc. for General Microbiology, 1972–77; Vice-Pres., Royal Soc. for Tropical Med. and Hygiene, 1980–81 (Councillor, 1973–76); Secretary and Vice-Pres., Royal Institution, 1973–78. *Publications:* contribs to medical and scientific jls. *Recreations:* fell-walking, gardening. *Address:* Sir William Dunn School of Pathology, South Parks Road, Oxford OX1 3RE.

PORTES, Prof. Richard David, DPhil; Professor of Economics, Birkbeck College, University of London, since 1972; Director, Centre for Economic Policy Research, since 1983; *b* 10 Dec. 1941; *s* of Herbert Portes and Abra Halperin Portes; *m* 1963, Barbara Diana Frank; one *s* one *d*. *Educ:* Yale Univ. (BA 1962 *summa cum laude* maths and philosophy); Balliol and Nuffield Colls, Oxford (Rhodes Schol., Woodrow Wilson

Fellow, Danforth Fellow; MA 1965; DPhil 1969). Official Fellow and Tutor in Econs, Balliol Coll., Oxford, 1965–69; Asst Prof. of Econs and Internat. Affairs, Princeton Univ., 1969–72; Head, Dept of Econs, Birkbeck Coll., 1975–77 and 1980–83. Dir d'Etudes Associé, Centre d'Economie Quantitative et Comparative, Ecole des Hautes Etudes en Sciences Sociales, Paris, 1978–. Hon. Res. Fellow, UCL, 1971–72; Guggenheim Fellow, 1977–78; British Acad. Overseas Vis. Fellow, 1977–78; Res. Associate, Nat. Bureau of Econ. Res., Cambridge, Mass, 1980–; Vis. Prof., Harvard Univ., 1977–78. Vice-Chm., Econs Cttee, SSRC, 1981–84 (Mem. 1980–84). Member: Bd of Dirs, Soc. for Econ. Analysis (Rev. of Econ. Studies), 1967–69, 1972–80 (Sec. 1974–77); RIIA, 1973– (Res. Cttee, 1982–); Council on Foreign Relations, 1978–; Hon. Degrees Cttee, Univ. of London, 1984–; Channel 4 Current Affairs Adv. Gp, 1986–. Fellow, Econometric Soc., 1983–; Mem. Council, Royal Econ. Soc., 1986–. Mem. Adv. Bd, Inst. for Internat. Econ. Studies, Stockholm Univ., 1983–. Co-Chm., Bd of Governors, and Sen. Editor, Economic Policy, 1985–. Member Editorial Board: Applied Economics, 1973–85; Jl of Comparative Economics, 1980–85; Economic Modelling, 1983–; Annales d'Economie et de Statistique, 1984–; Science and Technology Review (Beijing), 1985–. Governor, Birkbeck Coll., 1981–82. *Publications:* (ed) Planning and Market Relations, 1971; The Polish Crisis, 1981; Deficits and Détente, 1983; contribs to many learned jls. *Recreation:* living beyond my means. *Address:* Centre for Economic Policy Research, 6 Duke of York Street, SW1Y 6LA. *T:* 01–930 7182.

PORTILLO, Michael Denzil Xavier; MP (C) Enfield, Southgate, since December 1984; an Assistant Government Whip, since 1986; *b* 26 May 1953; *s* of Luis Gabriel Portillo and Cora Waldegrave Blyth; *m* 1982, Carolyn Claire Eadie. *Educ:* Harrow County Boys' School; Peterhouse, Cambridge (1st cl. Hons MA History). Ocean Transport & Trading Co., 1975–76; Conservative Res. Dept., 1976–79; Special Advr, Sec. of State for Energy, 1979–81; Kerr McGee Oil (UK) Ltd, 1981–83; Special Adviser: to Sec. of State for Trade and Industry, 1983; to Chancellor of the Exchequer, 1983–84. *Address:* House of Commons, SW1A 0AA. *Club:* Carlton.

PORTLAND, 9th Duke of, *cr* 1716; **Victor Frederick William Cavendish-Bentinck,** CMG 1942; Earl of Portland, Viscount Woodstock, Baron Cirencester, 1689; Marquess of Titchfield, 1716; *b* 18 June 1897; *s* of (William George) Frederick Cavendish-Bentinck (*d* 1948) (*ggs* of 3rd Duke) and Ruth Mary St Maur (*d* 1953); granted, 1977, the same title and precedence that would have been due to him if his father had succeeded to the Dukedom of Portland; *S* brother, 1980; *m* 1st, 1924 (marr. diss.); one *d* (one *s* decd); 2nd, 1948, Kathleen Elsie, *yr d* of Arthur Barry, Montreal. *Educ:* Wellington Coll., Berks. Attaché HM Legation, Oslo, 1915; 2nd Lieut, Grenadier Guards, 1918; 3rd Sec., HM Legation, Warsaw, 1919; transferred to Foreign Office, 1922; attended Lausanne Conference, 1922–23; 2nd Sec., HM Embassy, Paris, 1923; HM Legation, The Hague, 1924; transferred to Foreign Office, 1925; attended Locarno Conference, 1925; 1st Sec., HM Embassy, Paris, 1928; HM Legation, Athens, 1932; HM Embassy, Santiago, 1934; transferred to Foreign Office, 1937; Asst Under-Sec. of State, 1944; Chm. Jt Intelligence Cttee of Chiefs of Staff, 1939–45, also Foreign Office Adviser to Directors of Plans, 1942–45; Ambassador to Poland, 1945–47; retired from Diplomatic Service, 1947. Former Chm., Bayer (UK) Ltd. Hon. Life Pres., British Nuclear Forum. (Pres. Council, 1969–84). Grosses Verdienstkreuz (Germany). *Recreations:* travelling and antiques. *Heir* (to earldom only): *kinsman* Henry Noel Bentinck, Count of the Holy Roman Empire [*b* 2 Oct. 1919; *m* 1st, 1940, Pauline Ursula (*d* 1967), *y d* of late Frederick William Mellowes; one *s* two *d*; 2nd, 1974, Jenifer, *d* of late Reginald Hopkins]. *Address:* 21 Carlyle Square, SW3. *T:* 01–352 1258. *Clubs:* Turf, Beefsteak.

PORTMAN, family name of **Viscount Portman.**

PORTMAN, 9th Viscount, *cr* 1873; **Edward Henry Berkeley Portman;** Baron 1873; *b* 22 April 1934; *s* of late Hon. Michael Berkeley Portman (*d* 1959) (*yr s* of 7th Viscount), and June Charles (*d* 1947); *S* uncle, 1967; *m* 1st, 1956, Rosemary Farris (marr. diss., 1965); one *s* one *d*; 2nd, 1966, Penelope Allin; four *s*. *Educ:* Canford; Royal Agricultural College. Farmer. *Recreations:* shooting, fishing, music. *Heir:* *s* Hon. Christopher Edward Berkeley Portman [*b* 30 July 1958; *m* 1983, Caroline Steenson; one *s*]. *Address:* Clock Mill, Clifford, Herefordshire. *T:* Clifford 235. *Club:* White's.

PORTSMOUTH, 10th Earl of, *cr* 1743; **Quentin Gerard Carew Wallop;** Viscount Lymington, Baron Wallop, 1720; Hereditary Bailiff of Burley, New Forest; *b* 25 July 1954; *s* of Oliver Kintzing Wallop (Viscount Lymington) (*d* 1984) and Ruth Violet (*d* 1978), *yr d* of Brig.-Gen. G. C. Sladen, CB, CMG, DSO, MC; *S* grandfather, 1984; *m* 1981, Candia (*née* McWilliam), adopted *d* of Baron Strathcona and Mount Royal, *qv*; one *s* one *d*. *Educ:* Eton. *Heir:* *s* Viscount Lymington, *qv*. *Address:* Farleigh Wallop, Basingstoke, Hants.

PORTSMOUTH, Bishop of, since 1985; **Rt. Rev. Timothy John Bavin;** *b* 17 Sept. 1935; *s* of Edward Sydney Durrance and Marjorie Gwendoline Bavin. *Educ:* Brighton Coll.; Worcester Coll., Oxford (2nd Cl. Theol., MA); Cuddesdon Coll. Curate, St Alban's Cathedral Pretoria, 1961–64; Chaplain, St Alban's Coll., Pretoria, 1965–68; Curate of Uckfield, Sussex, 1969–71; Vicar of Good Shepherd, Brighton, 1971–73; Dean and Rector of Cathedral of St Mary the Virgin, Johannesburg, 1973–74; Bishop of Johannesburg, 1974–84. ChStJ 1975. *Recreations:* music, theatre, walking, gardening. *Address:* Bishopswood, Fareham, Hants PO14 1NT.

PORTSMOUTH, Bishop of, (RC), since 1976; **Rt. Rev. Anthony Joseph Emery;** *b* Burton-on-Trent, 17 May 1918. Ordained 1953. Auxiliary Bishop of Birmingham (Titular Bishop of Tamallula), 1968–76. Chm., Catholic Education Council, 1968–84. *Address:* Bishop's House, Edinburgh Road, Portsmouth PO1 3HG.

PORTSMOUTH, Archdeacon of; *see* Crowder, Ven. N. H.

PORTSMOUTH, Provost of; *see* Stancliffe, Very Rev. D. S.

POSKITT, Prof. Trevor John, DSc, PhD; Professor of Civil Engineering, Queen Mary College, University of London, since 1972; *b* 26 May 1934; *s* of late William Albert Poskitt, Worthing, and Mrs D. M. Poskitt, Lincoln; *m* 1968, Gillian Mary, *d* of L. S. Martin, MBE, Romiley, Cheshire; one *s* one *d*. *Educ:* Corby Technical Sch.; Huddersfield Technical Coll.; Univ. of Leeds; Univ. of Cambridge. HND (Mech. Eng.); BSc Leeds, PhD Cambridge, DSc Manchester; FICE, FIStructE. Apprentice Engineer to Thos. Broadbent & Sons, Huddersfield, 1949–53; Graduate Assistant, English Electric Co. Ltd, 1958–60; Whitworth Fellow, 1960–63; Lectr, 1963–71, Senior Lectr, 1971–72, in Civil Engineering, Univ. of Manchester. *Publications:* numerous on civil engineering topics. *Recreations:* tennis, music. *Address:* Queen Mary College, Mile End Road, E1 4NS. *T:* 01–980 4811.

POSNER, Michael Vivian, CBE 1983; Secretary-General, European Science Foundation, since 1986; *b* 25 Aug. 1931; *s* of Jack Posner; *m* 1953, Rebecca Posner, *qv*; one *s* one *d*. *Educ:* Whitgift Sch.; Balliol Coll., Oxford. Research Officer, Oxford Inst. of Statistics, 1953–57; University of Cambridge: Asst Lecturer, Lecturer, then Reader in Economics, 1958–79; Fellow, Pembroke Coll., 1960–83; Chm., Faculty Bd of Economics, 1974–75. Vis. Prof., Brookings Instn, Washington, 1971–72. Director of Economics, Ministry of Power, 1966–67; Economic Adviser to Treasury, 1967–69; Economic Consultant to Treasury, 1969–71; Consultant to IMF, 1971–72; Energy Adviser, NEDO, 1973–74; Econ. Adviser, Dept of Energy, 1974–75; Dep. Chief Econ. Adviser, HM Treasury, 1975–76. Chm., SSRC, 1979–83; Econ. Dir, NEDO, 1984–86. Member: BRB, 1976–84; Post Office Bd, 1978–79; Member: Adv. Council for Energy Conservation, 1974–82; Standing Commn on Energy and the Environment, 1978–81. Mem. Council, PSI, 1978–83 (Senior Res. Fellow, 1983–84). *Publications:* (co-author) Italian Public Enterprise, 1966; Fuel Policy: a study in applied economics, 1973; (ed) Resource Allocation in the Public Sector, 1977; (ed) Demand Management, 1978; (co-author) Energy Economics, 1981; (ed) Problems of International Money 1972–1985, 1986; books and articles on economics. *Recreation:* country life. *Address:* Rushwood, Jack Straw's Lane, Oxford. *T:* Oxford 63578; European Science Foundation, 1 Quai Lezay-Marnésia, Strasbourg, France. *Club:* United Oxford & Cambridge University.

POSNER, Prof. Rebecca; Professor of the Romance Languages, University of Oxford, since 1978; Fellow, St Hugh's College, Oxford, since 1978; *b* 17 Aug. 1929; *d* of William and Rebecca Reynolds; *m* 1953, Michael Vivian Posner, *qv*; one *s* one *d*. *Educ:* Somerville Coll., Oxford. MA, DPhil (Oxon); PhD (Cantab). Fellow, Girton Coll., Cambridge, 1960–63; Prof. of French Studies, Univ. of Ghana, 1963–65; Reader in Language, Univ. of York, 1965–78. Vis. Prof. of Romance Philology, Columbia Univ., NY, 1971–72; Vis. Senior Fellow, Princeton Univ., 1983. *Publications:* Consonantal Dissimilation in the Romance Languages, 1961; The Romance Languages, 1966; (with J. Orr and I. Iordan) Introduction to Romance Linguistics, 1970; (ed with J. N. Green) Trends in Romance Linguistics and Philology, 4 vols, 1980–82; numerous articles. *Recreations:* walking, gardening, theatre, music. *Address:* St Hugh's College, Oxford OX2 6LE. *T:* Oxford 57341; Rushwood, Jack Straw's Lane, Oxford OX3 0DN. *T:* Oxford 63578.

POSNETT, Sir Richard (Neil), KBE 1980 (OBE 1963); CMG 1976; HM Diplomatic Service, retired; Member, Lord Chancellor's Panel of Independent Inspectors, since 1983; *b* 19 July 1919; *s* of Rev. Charles Walker Posnett, K-i-H, Medak, S India, and Phyllis (*née* Barker); *m* 1st; two *s* one *d*; 2nd, 1959, Shirley Margaret Hudson; two *s* one *d*. *Educ:* Kingswood; St John's Coll., Cambridge. BA 1940, MA 1947. Called to the Bar, Gray's Inn, 1951. HM Colonial Administrative Service in Uganda, 1941; Chm., Uganda Olympic Cttee, 1956; Colonial Office, London, 1958; Judicial Adviser, Buganda, 1960; Perm. Sec. for External Affairs, Uganda, 1962; Perm. Sec. for Trade and Industry, 1963; joined Foreign (subseq. Diplomatic) Service, 1964; FO, 1964; served on UK Mission to UN, NY, 1967–70; briefly HM Comr in Anguilla, 1969; Head of W Indian Dept, FCO, 1970–71; Governor and C-in-C of Belize, 1972–76; Special Mission to Ocean Island, 1977; Dependent Territories Adviser, FCO, 1977–79; British High Comr, Kampala, 1979. UK Comr, British Phosphate Comrs, 1978–81. Governor and C-in-C, Bermuda, 1981–83. First ascent of South Portal Peak on Ruwenzori, 1942. Member: RIIA; Royal Forestry Soc.; Royal African Soc. Pres., Kingswood Assoc., 1980; Chm., Godalming Joigny Friendship Cttee, 1984. Governor: Broadwater Sch., 1984; Kingswood Sch., 1985. KStJ 1972. *Publications:* articles in Uganda Journal, World Today. *Address:* Timbers, Northway, Godalming, Surrey. *Clubs:* Royal Commonwealth Society, Achilles; West Surrey Golf; Mid-Ocean Golf; Privateers Hockey.

POSNETTE, Prof. Adrian Frank, CBE 1976; FRS 1971; VMH 1982; Director, East Malling Research Station, Kent, 1972–79 (Deputy Director, 1969–72, and Head of Plant Pathology Section, 1957–72); *b* 11 Jan. 1914; *e s* of late Frank William Posnette and Edith (*née* Webber), Cheltenham; *m* 1937, Isabelle, *d* of Dr Montgomery La Roche, New York; one *s* two *d*. *Educ:* Cheltenham Grammar Sch.; Christ's Coll., Cambridge. MA, ScD Cantab; PhD London; AICTA Trinidad; FIBiol. Research at Imperial Coll. of Tropical Agriculture, Trinidad, 1936–37; Colonial Agric. Service, Gold Coast, 1937; Head of Botany and Plant Pathology Dept, W African Cacao Research Inst., 1944; research at East Malling Research Stn, 1949–. Vis. Prof. in Plant Sciences, Wye Coll., Univ. of London, 1971–78. *Publications:* Virus Diseases of Apples and Pears, 1963; numerous research papers in Annals of Applied Biology, Jl of Horticultural Science, Nature, Tropical Agriculture. *Recreations:* ornithology, sailing, gardening. *Address:* Walnut Tree, East Sutton, Maidstone, Kent. *T:* Maidstone 843282. *Clubs:* Farmers'; Hawks (Cambridge); Helford River Sailing.

POST, Col Kenneth Graham, CBE 1945; TD; *b* 21 Jan. 1908; *s* of Donnell Post and Hon. Mrs Post; *m* 1st, 1944, Stephanie Bonté Wood (marr. diss., 1963); one *s* two *d*; 2nd, 1963, Diane Allen; two *s*. *Educ:* Winchester; Magdalen, Oxford. London Stock Exchange, 1929–37; 2nd Lieut, RA (TA) 1937; Norway, 1940; War Office, 1941–42; Ministry of Supply, 1943–44; Ministry of Works, 1945–47; Ministry of Housing, 1956–57; Ministry of Defence, 1957–59. Member Corby New Town Development Corporation, 1955–62; Director, Civic Trust, 1957–63. *Address:* 3 Shepherds Walk, Pembury Road, Tunbridge Wells, Kent. *T:* Tunbridge Wells 48560. *Club:* Pratt's.

POSTGATE, Prof. John Raymond, FRS 1977; FIBiol; Director, AFRC Unit of Nitrogen Fixation, since 1980 (Assistant Director, 1963–80), and Professor of Microbiology, University of Sussex, since 1965; *b* 24 June 1922; *s* of Raymond William Postgate and Daisy Postgate (*née* Lansbury); *m* 1948, Mary Stewart; three *d*. *Educ:* Woodstock Sch., Golders Green; Kingsbury County Sch., Mddx; Balliol Coll., Oxford. BA, MA, DPhil, DSc. Research in chemical microbiology: with D. D. Woods on action of sulfonamide drugs, 1946–48, with K. R. Butlin on sulphate-reducing bacteria, 1948–59. Research on bacterial death, 1959–63, incl. Visiting Professor: Univ. of Illinois, 1962–63, working on sulphate-reducing bacteria; Oregon State Univ., 1977–78. President: Inst. of Biology, 1982–84; Soc. for Gen. Microbiology, 1984–87. *Publications:* Microbes and Man (Pelican), 1969, 2nd edn 1986; Biological Nitrogen Fixation, 1972; Nitrogen Fixation, 1978; The Sulphate-Reducing Bacteria, 1979, 2nd edn 1984; The Fundamentals of Nitrogen Fixation, 1982; A Plain Man's Guide to Jazz, 1973; ed, 3 scientific symposia; regular columnist in Jazz Monthly, 1952–72; numerous scientific papers in microbiol/biochem. jls; many jazz record reviews in specialist magazines; articles on jazz. *Recreations:* listening to jazz and attempting to play it. *Address:* 1 Houndean Rise, Lewes, Sussex BN7 1EG. *T:* Lewes 472675.

POSTGATE, Richmond Seymour, MA; FCP; Consultant, education and broadcasting; *b* 31 Dec. 1908; *s* of Prof. J. P. Postgate, FBA and Edith Postgate; *m* 1949, Audrey Winifred Jones; one *s* two *d*. *Educ:* St George's Sch., Harpenden, Herts; Clare Coll., Cambridge. Editorial staff, Manchester Guardian newspaper; teaching in Public and Elementary Schools; County LEA Administration; RAFVR. In BBC: Head of School Broadcasting, etc; Director-General, Nigerian Broadcasting Corporation, 1959–61; Controller, Educnl Broadcasting, BBC, 1965–72. FCP 1973. *Recreation:* walking. *Address:* 3 Stanford Road, Faringdon, Oxon. *T:* Faringdon 20172.

POSWILLO, Prof. David Ernest, FDSRCS, FRACDS, FIBiol, FRCPath; Professor of Oral and Maxillofacial Surgery, United Medical and Dental Schools of Guy's and St Thomas' Hospitals, University of London, since 1983; *b* 1 Jan. 1927; *s* of Ernest and Amelia Poswillo, Gisborne, NZ; *m* 1956, Elizabeth Alison, *d* of Whitworth and Alice

Russell, Nelson, NZ; two *s* two *d. Educ*: Gisborne Boys' High, NZ; Univ. of Otago. BDS 1948, DDS 1962, DSc 1975, Westminster Hosp.; FDSRCS 1952, FRACDS 1966, FIBiol 1974, FRCPath 1981. OC S District Hosp., RNZDC, 1949–51; Hill End Hosp., St Albans, 1952; Dir of Oral Surgery, Christchurch Hosp., NZ, 1953–68; Prof. of Teratology, RCS, 1969–77; Consultant Oral Surgeon, Queen Victoria Hosp., East Grinstead, 1969–77; Prof. of Oral Path. and Oral Surgery, Univ. of Adelaide, and Sen. Oral and Maxillofacial Surgeon, Royal Adelaide and Childrens' Hosps, 1977–79; Prof. of Oral Surgery, and Mem. Council, Royal Dental Hosp., London, 1977–83. Consultant Adviser to Chief MO, DHSS, 1979–86; Mem., Bd of Faculty of Dental Surgery, RCS, 1981–; Medical Defence Union: Vice-Pres. and Council Mem., 1983–; Chm., Dental Cttee, 1983–; Sec. Gen., Internat. Assoc. of Oral and Maxill. Surgeons, 1983–. Trustee, Tobacco Products Research Fund, 1980–; Human Task Force, WHO, 1976–78. Mem. Council of Govs, UMDS of Guy's and St Thomas's Hosps, 1983–. Lectures: Arnott Demonstrator, 1972; Erasmus Wilson, 1973; Hunterian Prof., RCS, 1968, 1976; Darwin-Lincoln, Johns Hopkins, 1975; Waldron, Harvard, 1976; Richardson, Harvard, 1981; Tomes, RCS, 1982; President's, BAOMS, 1985. RNZADC Prize, 1948; Tomes Prize, 1966; Down Medal, 1973; Kay-Kilner Prize, 1975; ASOMS Research Award, 1976; Hunter Medal and Triennial Prize, 1976; 2nd Orthog. Surg. Award, Univ. of Texas, 1982. Hon. MD Zürich, 1983. Hon. FFDRCSI, 1984; Hon. FIMFT, 1985. *Publications*: (with C. L. Berry) Teratology, 1975; (with B. Cohen and D. K. Mason) Oral Surgery and Pathology, 1978; (with B. Cohen and D. K. Mason) Oral Medicine and Diagnosis, 1978; (with D. J. Simpson and D. David) The Craniosynostoses, 1982; (with D. Henderson) Atlas of Orthognathic Surgery, 1984; (jtly) Dental, Oral and Maxillofacial Surgery, 1986; papers on surgery, pathology and teratology in dental medical and sci jls. *Recreations*: art, reading, gardening. *Address*: Ferndale, Oldfield Road, Bickley BR1 2LE *T*: 01–467 1578.

POTTER, Prof. Allen Meyers, PhD; James Bryce Professor of Politics, University of Glasgow, 1970–84, retired; *b* 7 March 1924; *s* of Maurice A. and Irene M. Potter; *m* 1949, Joan Elizabeth Yeo; two *d. Educ*: Wesleyan Univ., Conn (BA 1947, MA 1948); Columbia Univ., NY (PhD 1955). FSS 1967. Instructor, College of William and Mary, 1949–51; Lectr/Sen. Lectr, Univ. of Manchester, 1951–62; Vis. Professor, Univ. of Texas, 1960; Professor: Univ. of Strathclyde, 1963–65; Univ. of Essex, 1965–70; Pro-Vice-Chancellor, Univ. of Essex, 1969–70. Vice-Principal, Univ. of Glasgow, 1979–82. Member, US-UK Educational Commn, 1979–84. Governor, Glasgow Sch. of Art, 1979–82. *Publications*: American Government and Politics, 1955, 2nd edn 1978; Organised Groups in British National Politics, 1961; articles in American and British social science jls. *Recreation*: inventing table games. *Address*: 14 Severn Drive, Malvern, Worcs WR14 2SZ. *T*: Malvern 69315.

POTTER, Arthur Kingscote, CMG 1957; CBE 1946; *b* 7 April 1905; *s* of late Richard Ellis Potter, Ridgewood, Almondsbury, Glos and Harriott Isabel (*née* Kingscote, of Kingscote, Glos); *m* 1950, Hilda, *d* of late W. A. Butterfield, OBE; one *d. Educ*: Charterhouse; New Coll., Oxford (BA). Entered Indian CS, 1928; posted to Burma; in charge of Pegu earthquake relief, 1930–31; District Comr, 1934; Controller of Finance ('reserved' subjects), 1937; Financial Adviser, Army in Burma, 1942 (despatches); Finance Secretary, Government of Burma (in Simla), 1942–43; Financial Adviser (Brigadier), 11th Army Group, 1943, and Allied Land Forces, South-East Asia, 1943–44; Chief Financial Officer (Brig.), Military Administration of Burma, 1944–47; HM Treasury Representative in India, Pakistan and Burma, 1947–50; Asst Secretary, HM Treasury, 1950–56; Counsellor, UK Delegation to NATO, Paris, 1956–65. *Address*: Lower House Barns, Bepton, Midhurst, W Sussex GU29 0JB.

POTTER, Dennis (Christopher George); playwright, author and journalist (freelance since 1964); *b* 17 May 1935; *e s* of Walter and Margaret Potter; *m* 1959, Margaret Morgan; one *s* two *d. Educ*: Bell's Grammar Sch., Coleford, Glos; St Clement Danes Grammar Sch.; New Coll., Oxford. Editor, Isis, 1958; BA (Hons) in PPE Oxon, 1959. BBC TV (current affairs), 1959–61; Daily Herald, feature writer, then TV critic, 1961–64; contested (Lab) East Herts, 1964; Leader writer, The Sun, Sept.-Oct. 1964, then resigned; TV Critic, Sunday Times, 1976–78. First television play, 1965. NFT retrospective, 1980. *Television plays*: Vote Vote Vote for Nigel Barton (also at Bristol Old Vic, 1968; SFTA Award, 1966); Stand Up Nigel Barton; Where the Buffalo Roam; A Beast with Two Backs; Son of Man; Traitor; Paper Roses; Casanova; Follow the Yellow Brick Road; Only Make Believe; Joe's Ark; Schmoedipus; (adapted from novel by Angus Wilson) Late Call, 1975; Brimstone and Treacle, 1976 (not transmitted); Double Dare, 1976; Where Adam Stood, 1976; Pennies from Heaven (sextet), 1978 (BAFTA award, 1978); Blue Remembered Hills, 1979 (BAFTA award, 1980); Blade on the Feather, Rain on the Roof, Cream in my Coffee, 1980 (Prix Italia, 1982); Tender is the Night (sextet, from Scott Fitzgerald), 1985; The Singing Detective (sextet), 1986; *screenplays*: Pennies from Heaven, 1981; Brimstone and Treacle, 1982; Gorky Park, 1983; Dreamchild, 1985; *stage play*: Sufficient Carbohydrate, 1983. *Publications*: The Glittering Coffin, 1960; The Changing Forest, 1962; *plays*: The Nigel Barton Plays (paperback, 1968); Son of Man, 1970; Brimstone and Treacle, 1979; Sufficient Carbohydrate, 1983; Waiting for the Boat (3 plays), 1984; *novels*: Hide and Seek, 1973; Pennies from Heaven, 1982; Ticket to Ride, 1986. *Recreations*: nothing unusual, ie the usual personal pleasures, sought with immoderate fervour. *Address*: Morecambe Lodge, Duxmere, Ross-on-Wye, Herefordshire HR9 5BB. *T*: Ross-on-Wye 63199.

POTTER, Donald Charles, QC 1972; *b* 24 May 1922; *s* of late Charles Potter, Shortlands, Kent. *Educ*: St Dunstan's Coll.; London Sch. of Economics. RAC (Westminster Dragoons), 1942–46 (Lieut); served England, NW Europe (D-day), Germany; mentioned in despatches; Croix de Guerre (France). LLB London 1947; called to Bar, Middle Temple, 1948; Bencher, Lincoln's Inn, 1979. Asst Lectr in Law, LSE, 1947–49; practised at Bar, 1950–. Chm., Revenue Bar Assoc., 1978–. *Publication*: (with H. H. Monroe) Tax Planning with Precedents, 1954. *Recreations*: farming, travel, theatre, reading. *Address*: 27 Old Buildings, Lincoln's Inn, WC2A 3UJ; Bow Cottage, East Portlemouth, Devon TQ8 8PE. *Clubs*: Garrick, Farmers'.

POTTER, Ernest Frank; Director, Finance, since 1979 (Director of Finance and Corporate Planning, 1977–79), Cable & Wireless Ltd; *b* 29 April 1923; *s* of Frank William and Edith Mary Potter; *m* 1945, Madge (*née* Arrowsmith); one *s. Educ*: Dr Challoner's Grammar Sch., Amersham. FCMA, FCIS, MIMC. Commissioned Pilot and Navigator, RAF, 1941–49. Chief Accountant, Bulmer & Lumb Ltd, 1950–58; Director, Management Consulting, Coopers & Lybrand, 1959–71; British Steel Corporation, Cammell Laird Shipbuilders Ltd, 1972–77. Mem., Accounting Standards Cttee, 1985–. *Recreations*: golf, squash. *Address*: Long Meadow, Gorse Hill Road, Virginia Water, Surrey GU25 4AS. *T*: Wentworth 2178. *Clubs*: Royal Air Force, Royal Commonwealth Society; Wentworth (Surrey).

POTTER, Francis Malcolm; His Honour Judge Malcolm Potter; a Circuit Judge, since 1978; *b* 28 July 1932; *s* of Francis Martin Potter and Zilpah Jane Potter; *m* 1970, Bertha Villamil; one *s* one *d. Educ*: Rugby Sch.; Jesus Coll., Oxford. Called to Bar, Lincoln's Inn, 1956. A Recorder of the Crown Court, 1974–78. *Recreation*: painting. *Address*: 5 Fountain Court, Steelhouse Lane, Birmingham B4 6DR.

POTTER, Sir Ian; *see* Potter, Sir W. I.

POTTER, Jeremy; *see* Potter, R. J.

POTTER, Maj.-Gen. Sir John, KBE 1968 (CBE 1963; OBE 1951); CB 1966; Chairman, Traffic Commissioners and Licensing Authority, Western Traffic Area, 1973–83; *b* 18 April 1913; *s* of late Major Benjamin Henry Potter, OBE, MC; *m* 1st, 1943, Vivienne Madge (*d* 1973), *d* of late Captain Henry D'Arcy Medlicott Cooke; one *s* one *d*; 2nd, 1974, Mrs D. Ella Purkis; one step *s* one step *d*. Served War of 1939–45. Major-General, 1962; Colonel Comdt: RAOC, 1965–69; RCT, 1968–73. Director of Supplies and Transport, 1963–65; Transport Officer in Chief (Army), 1965–66; Dir of Movements (Army), MoD, 1966–68; retired. *Address*: Orchard Cottage, The Orchard, Freshford, Bath, Avon.

POTTER, John Herbert, MBE 1974; HM Diplomatic Service, retired; *b* 11 Jan. 1928; *s* of Herbert George and Winifred Eva Potter; *m* 1953, Winifred Susan Florence Hall; one *d. Educ*: elementary education at various state schools. Electrical Engineering jobs, 1942–45; served HM Forces, 1945–48; GPO, 1948–53; Foreign Office, 1953–55; Commercial Attaché, Bangkok, 1955–57; FO, 1957–60; Istanbul, 1960; Ankara, 1960–64; Second Secretary, Information, 1962; Second Sec., Information, Addis Ababa, 1964; Vice-Consul, Information, Johannesburg, 1964–66; DSAO, later FCO, 1966–70; First Sec. (Administration): Brussels, 1970–74; Warsaw, 1974–76; FCO (Inspectorate), 1976–80; Counsellor (Admin.) and Consul-Gen., Moscow, 1980–81; Counsellor (Administration), Bonn, 1981–82. *Recreations*: reading, languages, walking, gardening. *Address*: Newlands, Westcourt Drive, Bexhill-on-Sea, E Sussex TN39 3NA.

POTTER, John McEwen, DM, FRCS; Director of Postgraduate Medical Education and Training, Oxford University, 1972–Oct. 1987; Fellow, Wadham College, Oxford, 1969–Oct. 1987, Emeritus Fellow, 1987 (Professorial Fellow, 1974–87; Sub-Warden, 1978–81); Hon. Consultant Neurosurgeon, Oxford Regional Health Authority and Oxfordshire Health Authority, since 1972; *b* 28 Feb. 1920; *er s* of Alistair Richardson Potter and Mairi Chalmers Potter (*née* Dick); *m* 1943, Kathleen Gerrard; three *s. Educ*: Clifton Coll.; Emmanuel Coll., Cambridge; St Bartholomew's Hosp. BA, MB, BChir Cantab, 1943; MA 1945; FRCS 1951; MA, BM, BCh Oxon, 1963, DM 1964. Active service (Captain, RAMC), Europe, India and Burma, 1944–47. Lectr in Physiol. and Jun. Chief Asst, Surg. Professorial Unit, St Bart's Hosp., 1948–51; Graduate Asst to Nuffield Prof. of Surgery, Oxford, 1951–56; E. G. Fearnsides Scholar, Cambridge, 1954–56; Hunterian Prof., 1955; Cons. Neurosurgeon: Manchester Royal Infirmary, 1956–61; Radcliffe Infirm., Oxford, 1961–72; Vis. Prof., UCLA, 1967; Univ. of Oxford: Clin. Lectr in Neurosurgery, 1962–68, Univ. Lectr, 1968–; Mem., Gen. Bd of Faculties, 1975–83; Hebdomadal Council, 1983–; Fellow, Linacre Coll., 1967–69. Governor, United Oxford Hosps, 1973. Cairns Lectr, Adelaide, 1974. Examr for Final BM, BCh Oxon; Ext. Examr, Med. Sciences Tripos Pt II, Cambridge Univ. FRSM (Pres., Sect. of Neurol., 1975–76); Member: GMC, 1973– (Chm., Registration Cttee, 1979–); Oxfordshire HA, 1982–; Soc. of British Neurol Surgeons (Archivist; formerly Hon. Sec.); Vice-Pres., 4th Internat. Congress of Neurol Surgery. Corres. Member: Amer. Assoc. of Neurol Surgeons; Deutsche Gesellschaft für Neurochirurgie; Sociedad Luso-Espanhola de Neurocirurgia; Hon. Mem., Egyptian Soc. of Neurol Surgeons. *Publications*: The Practical Management of Head Injuries, 1961, 4th edn 1984; contrib. to books and jls on subjects relating mostly to neurology and med. educn. *Recreation*: fishing. *Address*: 47 Park Town, Oxford OX2 6SL. *T*: Oxford 57875; Myredykes, Newcastleton, Roxburghshire TD9 05R. *Club*: Kielder Working Men's.

See also R. J. Potter.

POTTER, Sir (Joseph) Raymond (Lynden), Kt 1978; Chairman, Halifax Building Society, 1974–83; *b* 21 April 1916; *s* of Rev. Henry Lynden and Mabel Boulton Potter; *m* 1939, Daphne Marguerite, *d* of Sir Crawford Douglas-Jones, CMG; three *s* one *d. Educ*: Haileybury Coll.; Clare Coll., Cambridge (MA). War Service, 1939–46, Queen's Own Royal W Kent Regt, England and Middle East; GSO2 Staff Duties, GHQ, MEF; AQMG War Office. Sec., Royal Inst. of Internat. Affairs, 1947–51; joined Halifax Building Soc., 1951; Gen. Man. 1956; Chief Gen. Man., 1960–74; Dir, 1968–83. Mem., Board, Warrington and Runcorn (formerly Warrington) New Town Develt Corp., 1969–. Vice Pres., Building Socs Assoc., 1981– (Mem. Council, 1965–81; Chm., 1975–77). Freeman, City of London, 1981. Life Governor, Haileybury Coll. *Recreation*: hill walking. *Address*: Oakwood, Chilbolton, Stockbridge, Hampshire SO20 6BE. *T*: Chilbolton 523. *Club*: Hawks (Cambridge).

POTTER, Malcolm; *see* Potter, F. M.

POTTER, Mark Howard, QC 1980; a Recorder, since 1986; *b* 27 Aug. 1937; *s* of Prof. Harold Potter, LLD, PhD, and Beatrice Spencer Potter (*née* Crowder); *m* 1962, Undine Amanda Fay Miller; two *s. Educ*: Perse Sch., Cambridge; Gonville and Caius Coll., Cambridge (Schol.; BA (Law Tripos) 1960, MA 1963). National Service, 15 Med. Regt RA, 1955–57 (commnd 1956); Territorial Army, 289 Lt Parachute Regt RHA(TA), 1958–64. Asst Supervisor, Legal Studies, Gonville and Caius, Queens' and Sidney Sussex Colls, 1961–68; called to Bar, Gray's Inn, 1961; in practice, 1962–; Member: Senate of Inns of Court and Bar, 1976–79, 1982–; Supreme Ct Rule Cttee, 1980–84; Council of Legal Educn, 1983–; Lord Chancellor's Civil Justice Review Cttee, 1985–; Chm., Senate Law Reform Cttee, 1984–. *Recreations*: family and sporting. *Address*: Fountain Court, Temple, EC4 9DH. *T*: 01–353 7356. *Club*: Garrick.

POTTER, Rev. Philip Alford; Chaplain to University of West Indies and Lecturer, United Theological College of West Indies, since 1985; *b* 19 Aug. 1921; *s* of Clement Potter and Violet Peters, Roseau, Dominica, Windward Is, WI; *m* 1st, 1956, Ethel Olive Doreen Cousins (*d* 1980), Jamaica; WI; 2nd, 1984, Rev. Barbel von Wartenberg, FRG. *Educ*: Dominica Grammar Sch.; United Theological Coll., Jamaica; London Univ. BD, MTh. Methodist Minister. Overseas Sec., British SCM, 1948–50; Superintendent, Cap Haitien Circuit, Methodist Church, Haiti, 1950–54; Sec., later Dir, Youth Dept, WCC, 1954–60; Sec. for WI and W Africa, Methodist Missionary Society, London, 1961–66; Dir, Commn on World Mission and Evangelism, and Associate Gen. Sec., WCC, 1967–72; Gen. Sec., WCC, 1972–84. Mem., then Chm., Youth Dept Cttee, WCC, 1948–54; Chm., World Student Christian Fedn, 1960–68. Editor: Internat. Review of Mission, 1967–72; Ecumenical Rev., 1972–84. Hon. Doctor of Theology: Hamburg Univ., Germany, 1971; Geneva, 1976; Theol Inst. of Rumanian Orthodox Church, 1977; Humboldt Univ., Berlin (GDR), 1982; Uppsala, 1984; Hon. LLD W Indies, 1974; Hon. DD Birmingham, 1985. Niwano Peace Prize, Japan, 1986. *Publications*: (with Prof. Hendrik Berkhof) Key Words of the Gospel, 1964; The Love of Power or the Power of Love, 1974; Life in all its Fullness, 1981; chapter in Explosives Lateinamerika (ed by T. Tschuy), 1969; essays in various symposia; contrib. various jls, incl. Ecumenical Rev., Internat. Rev. of Mission, Student World. *Recreations*: swimming, hiking, music, geology. *Address*: United Theological College of the West Indies, PO Box 136, Golding Avenue, Kingston 7, Jamaica, WI.

POTTER, Sir Raymond; *see* Potter, Sir J. R. L.

POTTER, Raymond; Deputy Secretary (Head of Legal Administration), Lord Chancellor's Department, since 1986; *b* 26 March 1933; *s* of William Thomas Potter and Elsie May Potter; *m* 1959, Jennifer Mary Quicke; one *s*. *Educ:* Henry Thornton Grammar School. Called to the Bar, Inner Temple, 1971. Central Office, Royal Courts of Justice, 1950; Western Circuit, 1963; Chief Clerk, Bristol Crown Court, 1972; Dep. Circuit Administrator, Western Circuit, 1976; Circuit Administrator, Northern Circuit, 1982–86. *Recreation:* painting. *Address:* Neville House, Page Street, SW1P 4LS. *Club:* Civil Service.

POTTER, (Ronald) Jeremy; Director: LWT (Holdings) plc, since 1979; London Weekend Television Ltd, since 1979; Page and Moy (Holdings) plc, since 1979; *b* 25 April 1922; *s* of Alistair Richardson Potter and Mairi Chalmers (*née* Dick); *m* 1950, Margaret, *d* of Bernard Newman; one *s* one *d*. *Educ:* Clifton Coll.; Queen's Coll., Oxford (Neale Exhibnr, MA). Served War, Intell. Officer, Indian Army. Manager, subseq. Man. Dir, Dep. Chm., New Statesman, 1951–69; Man. Dir, Independent Television Publications Ltd, 1970–79; Chm., Independent Television Books Ltd, 1971–79; Chm., Hutchinson Ltd, 1982–84 (Dir, 1978; Dep. Chm., 1980–82). Pres., Periodical Publishers Assoc., 1978–79; Appeals Chm., Newsvendors' Benevolent Instn, 1979; Chairman: Twickenham Arts Council, 1967–68; Richard III Soc., 1971–. FRSA. Captain, Hampstead Hockey Club, 1954–57. *Publications:* Good King Richard?, 1983; *novels:* Hazard Chase, 1964; Death in Office, 1965; Foul Play, 1967; The Dance of Death, 1968; A Trail of Blood, 1970; Going West, 1972; Disgrace and Favour, 1975; Death in the Forest, 1977; *lectures:* ITV: Critics and Viewers, 1975; Problems in Mass Communication, 1976. *Recreations:* reading, writing, Real tennis. *Address:* The Old Pottery, Larkins Lane, Headington, Oxford OX3 9DW. *Clubs:* Garrick, MCC, Puritans Hockey.

See also J. McE. Potter.

POTTER, Ronald Stanley James; Director of Social Services, Surrey County Council, 1970–81; *b* 29 April 1921; *e s* of late Stanley Potter and Gertrude Mary Keable, Chelmsford; *m* 1954, Ann (Louisa Eleanor) Burnett; one *s* one *d*. *Educ:* King Edward VI Grammar Sch., Chelmsford. MISW. Territorial Army, 1939, War Service, 1939–47; commnd RA, 1942; Captain 1946. Area Welfare Officer, Essex CC, 1953–61; Dep. Co. Welfare Officer, Lindsey CC, 1962; County Welfare Officer: Lindsey CC, 1962–64; Herts CC, 1964–70. Dir, Watford Sheltered Workshop Ltd, 1964–70; Mem. Cttee of Enquiry into Voluntary Workers in Social Services, 1966–69; Dir, Industrial Advisers to Blind Ltd, 1969–74; Vice Pres., SE Regional Assoc. for Deaf, 1984– (Vice-Chm., 1968–76; Chm., 1976–84); Member: Council of Management, RNID, 1968–71, 1976–84; Nat. Jt Council for Workshops for the Blind, 1970–81; Adv. Council, Nat. Corp. for Care of Old People, 1974–77; Local Authorities Adv. Cttee on Conditions of Service of Blind Workers, 1974–81; Exec. Council, RNIB, 1975–81; Nat. Adv. Council on Employment of Disabled People, 1978–81; Dir, Remploy Ltd, 1974–86. *Recreations:* walking, swimming, caravanning, bowls. *Address:* Ridge Cottage, 16 Howard Ridge, Burpham Lane, Guildford, Surrey GU4 7LY. *T:* Guildford 504272.

POTTER, Maj.-Gen. Sir Wilfrid John; *see* Potter, Maj.-Gen. Sir John.

POTTER, Sir (William) Ian, Kt 1962; Stockbroker, Melbourne, Australia; *b* 25 Aug. 1902; *s* of James William Potter and Maria Louisa (*née* McWhinnie); *m* 1975; two *d* of former *m*. *Educ:* University of Sydney. Economist to Federal Treas., 1935–36; Commonwealth Rep. Rural Debt Adjustment Cttee, 1936; founded Ian Potter & Co., 1937; Principal Partner, 1937–67. Served RANVR, 1939–44. Member: Cttee Stock Exchange of Melbourne, 1945–62; Melbourne University Council, 1947–71; Commonwealth Immigration Planning Council, 1956–62; Victorian Arts Centre Building Cttee, 1960–78. President, Australian Elizabethan Theatre Trust, 1964–66 and 1983– (Chairman 1968–83); Vice-Pres., Howard Florey Inst., Melbourne. *Publications:* contrib. articles on financial and economic subjects to learned journals and press. *Recreations:* yachting, tennis, golfing. *Address:* 99 Spring Street, Melbourne, Victoria 3000, Australia. *Clubs:* Melbourne, Australian, Royal Melbourne Golf (Melbourne); The Links (NY).

POTTERTON, Homan, FSA; Director, National Gallery of Ireland, since 1980; *b* 9 May 1946; sixth *s* of late Thomas Edward Potterton and of Eileen Potterton (*née* Tong). *Educ:* Kilkenny Coll.; Trinity Coll., Dublin (BA 1968, MA 1973); Edinburgh Univ. (Dip. Hist. Art 1971). FSA 1981. Cataloguer, National Gall. of Ireland, 1971–73; Asst Keeper, National Gall., London, 1974–80. HRHA 1982. *Publications:* Irish Church Monuments 1570–1880, 1975; A Guide to the National Gallery, 1976, rev. edn 1980 (German, French, Italian and Japanese edns 1977); The National Gallery, London, 1977; Reynolds and Gainsborough: themes and painters in the National Gallery, 1976; Pageant and Panorama: the elegant world of Canaletto, 1978; (jtly) Irish Art and Architecture, 1978; Venetian Seventeenth Century Painting (National Gallery Exhibn Catalogue), 1979; introd. to National Gallery of Ireland Illustrated Summary Catalogue of Paintings, 1981; (jtly) National Gallery of Ireland, 50 Pictures, 1981; Dutch 17th and 18th Century Paintings at the National Gallery of Ireland, 1986; contrib. Burlington Mag., Apollo, Connoisseur, and Country Life. *Recreations:* Pimlico, daydreaming. *Address:* National Gallery of Ireland, Merrion Square West, Dublin 2. *T:* Dublin 767571.

POTTINGER, (William) George; *b* 11 June 1916; *e s* of late Rev. William Pottinger, MA, Orkney, and Janet Woodcock; *m* 1946, Margaret Rutherfurd Clark McGregor; one *s*. *Educ:* George Watson's; High School of Glasgow; Edinburgh Univ.; Heidelberg; Queens' Coll., Cambridge (Major Scholar). Entered Scottish Home Dept, as Assistant Principal, 1939. Served War of 1939–45, RFA; France, N Africa, Italy (despatches), Lieut-Col RA. Principal, 1945; Private Secretary to successive Secretaries of State for Scotland, 1950–52; Asst Secretary, Scottish Home Dept, 1952; Secretary, Royal Commn on Scottish Affairs, 1952–54; Under-Secretary: Scottish Home Dept, 1959–62; Scottish Home and Health Dept, 1962–63; Scottish Development Dept, 1963–64; Scottish Office, 1964–68; Dept of Agriculture and Fisheries for Scotland, 1968–71; Secretary, Dept of Agriculture and Fisheries for Scotland, 1971. *Publications:* The Winning Counter, 1971; Muirfield and the Honourable Company, 1972; St Moritz: an Alpine caprice, 1972; The Court of the Medici, 1977; The Secretaries of State for Scotland 1926–76, 1979; Whisky Sour, 1979; The Afghan Connection, 1983; papers and reviews. *Recreations:* real tennis, golf, fishing. *Address:* West Lodge, Balsham, Cambridge CB1 6EP. *T:* Cambridge 892958. *Club:* Savile.

POTTLE, Frederick Albert, BA Colby, MA, PhD Yale, Hon. LittD Colby, Rutgers, Hon. LHD Northwestern; Hon. LLD Glasgow; Sterling Professor of English, Yale University, 1944–66, now Professor Emeritus; Fellow Emeritus of Davenport College, Yale University; Public Orator, Yale University, 1942 and 1946; *b* Lovell, Maine, 3 Aug. 1897; *y s* of late Fred Leroy Pottle and Annette Wardwell Kemp; *m* 1920, Marion Isabel Starbird, Oxford, Maine; one *s*. *Educ:* Colby Coll. (*Summa cum laude*); Yale (John Addison Porter Prize). Served as private in Evacuation Hospital No 8, AEF, 1918–19; formerly Assistant Professor of English, University of New Hampshire; Editor of the Private Papers of James Boswell (succeeding the late Geoffrey Scott); Hon. member of Johnson Club; Vice-Pres., Johnson Soc., London; Pres., Johnson Soc., Lichfield, 1974; Trustee: General Theological Seminary, 1947–68; Colby Coll., 1932–59, 1966–78, Hon. Life Trustee, 1978; Messenger Lecturer, Cornell Univ., 1941; Member of Joint Commission on Holy Matrimony of the Episcopal Church, 1940–46; Guggenheim Fellow, 1945–46, 1952–53; Chancellor Academy of American Poets, 1951–71; Chairman of Editorial Cttee of Yale Editions of Private Papers of James Boswell, 1949–79; Member Provinciaal Utrechtsch Genootschap van Kunsten en Wetenschappen, 1953–; Member American Academy of Arts and Sciences, 1957–; FIAL, 1958–; Member, American Philosophical Society, 1960. Wilbur Lucius Cross Medal, Yale, 1967; William Clyde DeVane Medal, Yale, 1969; Lewis Prize, Amer. Philosophical Soc., 1975; Dist. Alumnus Award, Colby, 1977. *Publications:* Shelley and Browning, 1923; A New Portrait of James Boswell (with Chauncey B. Tinker), 1927; The Literary Career of James Boswell, 1929; Stretchers, the Story of a Hospital on the Western Front, 1929; The Private Papers of James Boswell: A Catalogue (with Marion S. Pottle), 1931; Vols 7–18 of The Private Papers of James Boswell, 1930–34; Boswell's Journal of a Tour to the Hebrides, from the Original Manuscript (with Charles H. Bennett), 1936, revised edition, 1963; Index to the Private Papers of James Boswell (with Joseph Foladare, John P. Kirby and others), 1937; Boswell and the Girl from Botany Bay, 1937; The Idiom of Poetry, 1941, revised and enlarged edition, 1946; James Boswell, the Earlier Years, 1966; Pride and Negligence, A History of the Boswell Papers, 1982; *editions of Boswell's journals:* Boswell's London Journal (1762–63), 1950; Boswell in Holland (1763–64), 1952; Boswell on the Grand Tour: Germany and Switzerland (1764), 1953; Boswell on the Grand Tour: Italy, Corsica and France, 1765 (with Frank Brady), 1955; Boswell in Search of a Wife, 1766–1769 (with Frank Brady), 1956; Boswell for the Defence, 1769–1774 (with William K. Wimsatt), 1959; Boswell: The Ominous Years, 1774–1776 (with Charles Ryskamp), 1963; Boswell in Extremes, 1776–1778 (with Charles McC. Weis), 1970; Boswell, Laird of Auchinleck, 1778–1782 (with Joseph W. Reed), 1977; Boswell, the Applause of the Jury, 1981; various articles. *Recreation:* gardening. *Address:* Edgehill Road, New Haven, Conn 06511, USA. *Clubs:* Elizabethan (New Haven); Grolier, Ends of the Earth (New York).

POTTS, Archibold; Head of School of Business Administration, Newcastle upon Tyne Polytechnic, since 1980; *b* 27 Jan. 1932; *s* of late Ernest W. Potts and Ellen Potts; *m* 1957, Marguerite Elsie (*née* Elliott) (*d* 1983); one *s* one *d*. *Educ:* Monkwearmouth Central Sch., Sunderland; Ruskin and Oriel Colls, Oxford (Dip. Econ. and Pol. Sci., 1958; BA PPE 2nd cl. hons, 1960); ext. postgrad. student, London Univ. (Postgrad. CertEd 1964) and Durham Univ. (MEd 1969). Nat. Service, RAF, 1950–53. Railway Clerk, 1947–50 and 1953–56. Lecturer: N Oxfordshire Tech. Coll., 1961; York Tech. Coll., 1962–65; Rutherford Coll. of Technology and Newcastle upon Tyne Polytechnic, 1965–80. Tyne and Wear County Council: Councillor, 1979–86; Vice-Chm., Planning Cttee, 1981–86; Vice-Chm., Council, 1983–84; Chm., Council, 1984–85. Mem., N Regl Exec. Cttee, Nat. Housing and Town Planning Council, 1981–86. Contested (Lab) Westmorland, 1979. Director: Tyne and Wear Building Preservation Trust Ltd, 1985–; Town Teacher Ltd, 1986–. *Publications:* Stand True, 1976; Bibliography of Northern Labour History, 1982–; contribs to Dictionary of Labour Biography, vol. 2 1974, vol. 4 1977, vol. 5 1979; articles on economics and economic history. *Recreations:* local history, military modelling. *Address:* 41 Kenton Avenue, Kenton Park, Newcastle upon Tyne NE3 4SE. *T:* Tyneside 2856361. *Club:* Victory Service.

POTTS, Archie; Under-Secretary, and Director of Scientific and Technical Intelligence, Ministry of Defence, 1964–74; *b* 28 Dec. 1914; *s* of late Mr and Mrs A. Potts, Newcastle upon Tyne; *m* 1951, Winifred Joan Bishop, MBE, *d* of late Mr and Mrs Reginald Bishop; two *s*. *Educ:* University of Durham. BSc (Hons) Physics, 1935. Research in Spectroscopy, King's Coll., University of Durham, 1936–39. War of 1939–45: Operational Research in Radar and Allied Fields, Fighter Command, and N Africa and Italy, 1939–45; Hon. Sqdn Leader, RAFVR, 1943–45. Chief Research Officer, Fighter Command, 1946–51; Defence Research Staff, Min. of Defence, 1951–53; Scientific Adviser, Allied Air Forces Central Europe, 1954–56; Asst Scientific Adviser, Air Ministry, 1957; Dep. Director for Atomic Energy, Jt Intell. Bureau, 1957–63. FInstP 1945. *Recreation:* listening to music. *Address:* 3 The Keir, West Side, SW19 4UG. *T:* 01-946 7077. *Club:* Royal Air Force.

POTTS, Hon. Sir Francis Humphrey, Kt 1986; **Hon. Mr Justice Potts;** a Judge of the High Court of Justice, Queen's Bench Division, since 1986; *b* 18 Aug. 1931; *er s* of late Francis William Potts and Elizabeth Hannah Potts (*née* Humphrey), Penshaw, Co. Durham; *m* 1971, Philippa Margaret Campbell, *d* of the late J. C. H. Le B. Croke and of Mrs J. F. G. Downes; two *s* and two step-*s*. *Educ:* Royal Grammar Sch., Newcastle upon Tyne; St Catherine's Society, Oxford. BCL 1954, MA 1957. Barrister-at-Law, Lincoln's Inn, 1955 (Tancred Student, 1953; Cholmeley Scholar, 1954), Bencher, 1979; North Eastern Circuit, 1955; admitted to Hong Kong Bar, 1984. QC 1971; a Recorder, 1972–86. Member: Mental Health Review Tribunal, 1984–86; Criminal Injuries Compensation Bd, 1985–. *Address:* Royal Courts of Justice, Strand, WC2A 2LL.

POTTS, Kenneth Hampson; Chief Executive, Leeds City Council, 1973–79; *b* 29 Sept. 1921; *s* of late James Potts and Martha Ann Potts; *m* 1945, Joan Daphne Wilson; two *s*. *Educ:* Manchester Grammar Sch.; Liverpool Univ. (LLB Hons). Solicitor. Captain, RA, 1942–46. Deputy Town Clerk, Leeds, 1965; Chief Management and Legal Officer, Leeds, 1969. Member: Yorks and Humberside Economic Planning Council, 1974–79; Data Protection Cttee, 1976–79. *Recreations:* Dandie Dinmonts, gardening, theatre, music, reading. *Address:* 8 Burlyn Road, Hunmanby, Filey, N Yorks YO14 0QA. *T:* Scarborough 891100.

POTTS, Peter; JP; General Secretary, General Federation of Trade Unions, since 1977; *b* 29 June 1935; *s* of late John Peter Potts and of Margaret (*née* Combs); *m* 1st, 1956, Mary Longden (*d* 1972); two *s* one *d*; 2nd, 1974, Angela Elouise van Lieshout (*née* Liddelow); one step *s* one step *d*. *Educ:* Chorlton High Sch., Manchester; Ruskin Coll., Oxford; Oxford Univ. (Dip. in Econs and Pol. Science). Served RAF, 1953–55. USDAW, 1951–65; Res. Officer, Union of Tailors and Garment Workers, 1965–74; National Officer, Clerical and Supervisory Staffs, 1974–77. Member: Clothing EDC, 1970–77 (Trade Union Advisor, 1966–70); Jt Textile Cttee, NEDO, 1970–77; Trade Union Unit Trust Investors Cttee, 1977– (Chm., 1984–); Trade Union Res. Unit, 1975–; Trade Union Internat. Res. and Educn Gp, 1979–; Governing Council, Ruskin Coll., 1977– (Mem. Exec. Cttee, 1977–; Vice-Chm., 1984–). JP N Beds, 1983. *Recreations:* tennis, do-it-yourself hobbies, art, listening to jazz. *Address:* 3 Tadmere, Two Mile Ash, Milton Keynes, Bucks.

POTTS, Robin, QC 1982; barrister; *b* 2 July 1944; *s* of William and Elaine Potts; *m*; one *s*; *m* Helen Elizabeth Sharp. *Educ:* Wolstanton Grammar Sch.; Magdalen Coll., Oxford (BA, BCL). Called to the Bar, Gray's Inn, 1968. *Publication:* (contrib.) Gore-Browne on Companies, 43rd edn. *Address:* The Grange, Church Lane, Pinner, Mddx HA5 3AB. *T:* 01-866 9013.

POTTS, Thomas Edmund, ERD 1957; Company Director, retired; *b* 23 March 1908; *s* of late T. E. Potts, Leeds; *m* 1932, Phyllis Margaret, *d* of late J. S. Gebbie, Douglas, Isle of Man; one *s*. *Educ:* Leeds Modern School. Joined The British Oxygen Co. Ltd, 1928. Commissioned RE, Supp. R of O, 1938; served War of 1939–45, Madras Sappers and Miners in India, Eritrea, Western Desert, Tunisia, with 4th and 5th Indian Divs (despatches,

1942 and 1943; Major); CRE 31st Indian Armoured Div., 9th Army (Lt-Col); released from active service and transferred to RARO (resigned Commission, RE, 1950). Rejoined British Oxygen Co. Ltd, London, 1945; Managing Director, African Oxygen Ltd, Johannesburg, 1947; Director, British Oxygen Co. Ltd, 1955; Group Managing Director, The British Oxygen Co. Ltd, 1958–63; UK Atomic Energy Authority: Consultant, 1968–78, a Dir, 1971–78, Radiochemical Centre; Dir, Amersham Corp., Chicago, 1968–78. Pres. South African Instn of Welding, 1951; Vice-Pres., Inst. of Welding, 1963–64. CBIM 1979. *Recreations:* golf, gardening. *Address:* Cleeve, Brayfield Road, Bray-on-Thames, Berks SL6 2BW. *T:* Maidenhead 26887. *Clubs:* Rand (Johannesburg); Temple Golf.

POULTON, Rev. Canon John Frederick; Residentiary Canon, Norwich Cathedral, 1979–86, Canon Emeritus since 1986; *b* 15 June 1925; *m* 1946, Iris Joan Knighton; two *s* two *d*. *Educ:* King's Coll., London (BA Hons); Ridley Hall, Cambridge. Tutor, 1955–60, and Actg Principal, 1960–61, Bishop Tucker Coll., Mukono, Uganda; Dir, Church of Uganda Literature and Radio Centre, 1962–66; Res. Sec., World Assoc. of Christian Communication, 1966–68; Exec. Sec., Archbishops' Council on Evangelism, 1968–78. *Publications:* A Today Sort of Evangelism, 1972; People under Pressure, 1973; Jesus in Focus, 1975; Dear Archbishop, 1976; The Feast of Life, 1982; Fresh Air: a vision for the rural church, 1985; (contrib.) David Watson, a portrait by his friends, 1985; (contrib.) My Call to Preach, 1986. *Address:* 22 St Michael-at-Pleas, Norwich NR3 1EP. *T:* Norwich 618755.

POULTON, Richard Christopher, MA; Head Master, Christ's Hospital, Horsham, since 1987; *b* 21 June 1938; *e s* of Rev. Christopher Poulton and Aileen (*née* Sparrow); *m* 1965, Zara, *o d* of Prof. P. and Mrs J. Crossley-Holland; two *s* one *d*. *Educ:* King's Coll., Taunton; Wesleyan Univ., Middletown, Conn, USA; Pembroke Coll., Cambridge (BA 1961, CertEd 1962, MA 1965). Asst Master: Bedford Sch., 1962–63; Beckenham and Penge Grammar Sch., 1963–66; Bryanston School: Asst Master, 1966–80; Head of History Dept, 1971–76; Housemaster, 1972–80; Headmaster, Wycliffe Coll., 1980–86. JP S Glos, 1985–86. *Publications:* Victoria, Queen of a Changing Land, 1975; Kings and Commoners, 1977; A History of the Modern World, 1980. *Recreations:* writing, hill walking, choral music. *Address:* The Head Master's House, Christ's Hospital, Horsham, W Sussex RH13 7LS. *T:* Horsham 52547.

POUNCEY, Denys Duncan Rivers, MA, MusB Cantab; FRCO; Organist and Master of the Choristers, Wells Cathedral, 1936–70; Conductor of Wells Cathedral Oratorio Chorus and Orchestra, 1946–66; Hon. Diocesan Choirmaster, Bath and Wells Choral Association, 1946–70; *b* 23 Dec. 1906; *s* of late Rev. George Ernest Pouncey and late Madeline Mary Roberts; *m* 1937, Evelyn Cottier. *Educ:* Marlborough College; Queens' College, Cambridge. Asst to Dr Cyril Rootham, Organist and Choirmaster of St John's Coll., Cambridge, 1928–34; Organist and Choirmaster, St Matthew's, Northampton, 1934–36; Founder Conductor of Northampton Bach Choir. *Address:* Waverley Hotel, 10 Tregonwell Road, Minehead, Somerset.
See also P. M. R. Pouncey.

POUNCEY, Philip Michael Rivers, MA; FBA 1975; a Director of Sothebys, 1966–83, now consultant; Hon. Keeper of Italian Drawings, Fitzwilliam Museum, since 1975; *b* 15 Feb. 1910; *s* of Rev. George Ernest Pouncey and Madeline Mary Roberts; *m* 1937, Myril Gros; two *d*. *Educ:* Marlborough; Queens' Coll., Cambridge (MA). Hon. Attaché, Fitzwilliam Museum, 1931–33; Assistant, National Gall., London, 1934–45; Asst Keeper, 1945–54, Dep. Keeper, 1954–66, British Museum; Visiting Professor: Columbia Univ., NY, 1958; Inst. of Fine Arts, New York Univ., 1965. *Publications:* Catalogues of Italian Drawings in the British Museum: (with A. E. Popham) XIV-XV Centuries, 1950; (with J. A. Gere) Raphael and his Circle, 1962; Lotto disegnatore, 1965; (with J. A. Gere) Italian Artists Working in Rome *c* 1550–*c* 1640, 1983; articles in Burlington Magazine, etc. *Recreation:* travel in Italy and France. *Address:* 5 Lower Addison Gardens, W14 8BG.
See also D. D. R. Pouncey.

POUND, Sir John David, 5th Bt *cr* 1905; *b* 1 Nov. 1946; *s* of Sir Derek Allen Pound, 4th Bt; *S* father, 1980; *m* 1st, 1968 (marr. diss.); one *s*; 2nd, 1978, Penelope Ann, *er d* of Grahame Arthur Rayden, Bramhall, Cheshire; one *s*. Liveryman, Leathersellers' Co. *Heir:* *s* Robert John Pound, *b* 12 Feb. 1973.

POUND, Ven. Keith Salisbury; Chaplain-General and Archdeacon to the Prison Service, since 1986; *b* 3 April 1933; *s* of Percy Salisbury Pound and Annie Florence Pound. *Educ:* Roan School, Blackheath; St Catharine's Coll., Cambridge (BA 1954, MA 1958); Cuddesdon Coll., Oxford. Curate, St Peter, St Helier, Dio. Southwark, 1957–61; Training Officer, Hollowford Training and Conference Centre, Sheffield, 1961–64; Warden 1964–67; Rector of Holy Trinity, Southwark, with St Matthew, Newington, 1968–78; RD, Southwark and Newington, 1973–78; Rector of Thamesmead, 1978–86; Sub-Dean of Woolwich, 1984–86; Dean of Greenwich, 1985–86. Hon. Canon of Southwark Cathedral, 1985. *Publication:* Creeds and Controversies, 1976. *Recreations:* theatre, music, books, walking, crosswords. *Address:* Prison Service Chaplaincy, Cleland House, Page Street, SW1P 4LN. *T:* 01–211 8108. *Club:* Civil Service.

POUNDER, Rafton John; Secretary, Northern Ireland Bankers' Association, since 1977; *b* 13 May 1933; *s* of late Cuthbert C. Pounder, Gefion, Ballynahatty, Shaw's Bridge, Belfast; *m* 1959, Valerie Isobel, *d* of late Robert Stewart, MBE, Cherryvalley, Belfast; one *s* one *d*. *Educ:* Charterhouse; Christ's College, Cambridge. Qualified as a Chartered Accountant, 1959. Chm. Cambridge Univ. Cons. and Unionist Assoc., 1954; Ulster rep. on Young Cons. and Unionist Nat. Adv. Cttee, 1960–63; Hon. Mem., Ulster Young Unionist Council, 1963; Member: UK delegn (C) to Assembly of Council of Europe, and to Assembly of WEU, 1965–68; UK Delegn to European Parlt, Strasbourg, 1973–74; Exec. Cttee, Nat. Union of Cons. and Unionist Assocs, 1967–72; Exec. Cttee, Ulster Unionist Council, 1967–73. MP (UU) Belfast S, Oct. 1963–Feb. 1974; Mem., House of Commons Select Cttee on Public Accounts, 1970–73; Vice-Chm., Cons. Parly Party's Technology Cttee, 1970; PPS to Minister for Industry, 1970–71. Mem. CPA Delegn to: Jamaica and Cayman Is, Nov. 1966; Malawi, Sept. 1968. Hon. Secretary: Ulster Unionist Parly Party at Westminster, 1964–67; Cons. Parly Party's Power Cttee, 1969–70. Pres., Ulster Soc. for Prevention of Cruelty to Animals, 1968–74. Dir, Progressive Building Soc., 1968–77. Lay Member, General Synod of the Church of Ireland, 1966–78. *Recreations:* golf, reading, music, sailing. *Address:* Gunpoint, Coastguard Lane, Orlock, Groomsport, Co. Down BT19 2LR.

POUNDS, Maj.-Gen. Edgar George Derek, CB 1975; Chief Executive, British Friesian Cattle Society, since 1976; Executive Committee, National Cattle Breeders' Association, since 1978; *b* 13 Oct. 1922; *s* of Edgar Henry Pounds, MBE, MSM, and Caroline Beatrice Pounds; *m* 1944, Barbara Winifred May Evans; one *s* one *d*. *Educ:* Reading Sch. War of 1939–45: enlisted, RM, 1940 (King's Badge, trng); HMS Kent, 1941–42 (Atlantic); commissioned as Reg. Off., Sept. 1942 (sword for dist., trng); HMS Berwick, 1943–44 (Atlantic and Russia). Co. Comdr, RM, 1945–51: Far East, Palestine, Malta, UK (Sniping Wing), Korea (US Bronze Star, 1950); Captain 1952. Instr, RM Officers' Trng Wing, UK, 1952–54; Adjt, 45 Commando, RM, 1954–57, Malta, Cyprus (despatches), Suez;

RAF Staff Coll., Bracknell, 1958; Staff Captain, Dept of CGRM, London, 1959–60; Major 1960; Amphibious Ops Officer, HMS Bulwark, 1961–62, Kuwait, Aden, E Africa, Borneo; Corps Drafting Off., UK, 1962–64; 40 Commando RM: 2nd in Comd, 1964–65, Borneo, and CO, 1966–67, Borneo and Far East; CO, 43 Commando, RM, 1967–68, UK based; GSO1 Dept CGRM, 1969–70; Col 1970; Naval Staff, MoD, 1970–72; Comdt Commando Trng Centre, RM, 1972–73; Actg Maj.-Gen. 1973; Maj.-Gen., RM, 1974; Comdt Commanding Commando Forces, RM, 1973–76, retired. *Publications:* articles on strategy, amphibious warfare, and tactics in professional jls, and cattle breeding and dairying in farming jls. *Recreations:* hunting, target rifle shooting, boating, reading. *Clubs:* Army and Navy, Farmers'.

POUNDS, Prof. Kenneth Alwyne, CBE 1984; FRS 1980; Professor of Space Physics, and Director, X-ray Astronomy Group, University of Leicester, since 1973; *b* 17 Nov. 1934; *s* of Harry and Dorothy Pounds; *m* 1st, 1961, Margaret Mary (*née* Connell); two *s* one *d*; 2nd, 1983, Joan Mary (*née* Millit); one *s*. *Educ:* Salt Sch., Shipley, Yorkshire; University Coll. London (BSc, PhD). Department of Physics, University of Leicester: Asst Lectr, 1960; Lecturer, 1961; Sen. Lectr, 1969. Member: SERC, 1980–84 (Chm., Astronomy, Space and Radio Bd); Management Bd, British Nat. Space Centre, 1986–. DUniv York, 1984. *Publications:* many, in Monthly Notices, Nature, Astrophysical Jl, etc. *Recreations:* cricket, music. *Address:* 12 Swale Close, Oadby, Leicester LE2 4GF. *T:* Leicester 719370.

POUNTAIN, Sir Eric (John), Kt 1985; DL; Group Chief Executive, since 1979, and Chairman, since 1983, Tarmac PLC; Director (non-executive), Glynwed PLC, since 1983; Deputy Chairman, James Beattie PLC, since 1985 (Director since 1984); Director, Midland Bank, since 1986; *b* 5 Aug. 1933; *s* of Horace Pountain and Elsie Pountain; *m* 1960, Joan Patricia Sutton; one *s* one *d*. *Educ:* Queen Mary Grammar Sch., Walsall. CBIM; FFB, FIHE. Joined F. Maitland Selwyn & Co., auctioneers and estate agents, 1956, joint principal, 1959; founded Midland & General Develts, 1964, acquired by John McLean & Sons Ltd, 1969; Chief Exec., John McLean & Sons, 1969, acquired by Tarmac PLC, 1973; Chief Exec., newly formed Tarmac Housing Div., until 1979. Dir, Tarmac PLC, 1977–. President: Haflinger Soc. of GB; Shropshire Enterprise Trust; Patron, Staffs Agricl Soc. DL Stafford, 1985. *Recreations:* farming, horse breeding. *Address:* Edial House, Edial, Lichfield. *T:* Burntwood 2229.

POUNTNEY, David Willoughby; Director of Productions, English National Opera, since 1982; *b* 10 Sept. 1947; *s* of Dorothy and Willoughby Pountney; *m* 1980, Jane Henderson; one *s* one *d*. *Educ:* St John's College Choir School, Cambridge; Radley College; St John's College, Cambridge (MA). Joined Scottish Opera, 1970; 1st major production Katya Kabanova (Janacek), Wexford Fest., 1972; Dir of Productions, Scottish Opera, 1976–80; individual guest productions for all British Opera companies, also USA, Aust., Italy, Germany, The Netherlands; productions for ENO include: Rusalka (Dvorak); Osud (Janacek); Dr Faust (Busoni). *Publications:* numerous trans. of opera, esp. Czech and Russian repertoire. *Recreations:* croquet, food and wine. *Address:* 142 Hemingford Road, N1 1DE. *T:* 01–609 6931. *Club:* Garrick.

POUT, Harry Wilfrid, CB 1978; OBE 1959; CEng, FIEE; Defence consultant, since 1980; Marconi Underwater Systems Ltd, since 1982; *b* 11 April 1920; British; *m* 1949, Margaret Elizabeth (*née* Nelson); three *d*. *Educ:* East Ham Grammar Sch.; Imperial Coll., London. BSc (Eng); ACGI 1940. RN Scientific Service, 1940; Admty Signal Estab. (later Admty Signal and Radar Estab.), 1940–54; Dept of Operational Research, Admty, 1954–59; idc 1959; Head of Guided Weapon Projects, Admty, 1960–65; Asst Chief Scientific Adviser (Projects), MoD, 1965–69; Dir, Admiralty Surface Weapons Estabt, 1969–72; Dep. Controller, Guided Weapons, 1973, Guided Weapons and Electronics, 1973–75, Air Systems, 1975–79, Aircraft Weapons and Electronics, 1979–80, MoD. FCGI 1972. *Publications:* (jtly) The New Scientists, 1971; classified books; contribs to jls of IEE, RAeS, RUSI, etc. *Recreations:* mountaineering, gardening and do-it-yourself activities, amateur geology. *Address:* Oakmead, Fox Corner, Worplesdon, near Guildford, Surrey. *T:* Worplesdon 232223.

POVER, Alan John; HM Diplomatic Service; Counsellor and Consul-General, Washington, since 1986; *b* 16 Dec. 1933; *s* of John Pover and Anne (*née* Hession); *m* 1964, Doreen Elizabeth Dawson; one *s* two *d*. *Educ:* Salesian College, Thornleigh, Bolton. Served HM Forces, 1953–55; Min. of Pensions and Nat. Insce, 1955–61; Commonwealth Relations Office, 1961; Second Secretary: Lagos, 1962–66; Tel Aviv, 1966–69; Second, later First, Sec., Karachi/Islamabad, 1969–73; First Sec., FCO, 1973–76; Consul, Cape Town, 1976–80; Counsellor, Diplomatic Service Inspector, 1983–86. *Recreations:* cricket, golf, gardening. *Address:* c/o Foreign and Commonwealth Office, SW1; 6 Wetherby Close, Emmer Green, Reading, Berks. *T:* Reading 477037. *Club:* Royal Commonwealth Society.

POWDITCH, Alan (Cecil Robert), MC 1944; JP; District Administrator, NW District, Kensington and Chelsea and Westminster Area Health Authority, 1974–77, retired; *b* 14 April 1912; *s* of Cecil John and Annis Maudie Powditch; *m* 1942, Barbara Leggat; one *s* one *d*. *Educ:* Mercers School. Entered Hospital Service, 1933; Accountant, St Mary's Hospital, W2, 1938. Served War of 1939–45, with 51st Royal Tank Regt, 1941–46. Dep. House Governor, St Mary's Hospital, 1947–50, Sec. to Bd of Governors, 1950–74. Mem. Nat. Staff Cttee (Min. of Health) 1964–72; Chm., Juvenile Panel, Gore Div., 1973–76. Mem. Council, Sue Ryder Foundn, 1977–85; Mem. Magistrates' Courts Cttee, 1979–81. JP Co. Middlesex 1965, supp. List 1982. *Recreations:* golf; interested in gardening when necessary. *Address:* 27 Gateway Close, Northwood, Mddx HA6 2RW.

POWELL; *see* Baden-Powell.

POWELL, Albert Edward, JP; General President of Society of Graphical and Allied Trades, 1973–82, of SOGAT '82 1982–83; *b* 20 May 1927; *s* of Albert and Mary Powell; *m* 1947, Margaret Neville; one *s* two *d*. *Educ:* Holy Family Elementary Sch., Morden. FIWSP. London Organiser, SOGAT, 1957, Organising Secretary, 1967. Has served on various Committees and Boards, including: past Chairman, Croydon College of Art, past Governor, London College of Printing. Chairman, Paper & Paper Products Industry Trng Bd, 1975– (Mem. Central Arbitration Cttee, 1976–); Member: TUC Printing Industries Cttee, 1971–; NEDO Printing Industries Sector Working Party, 1980–; Methods-Time Measurement Assoc., 1966–. Member: Industrial Tribunal, 1983–; Social Security Appeal Tribunal, 1984–; Parole Bd, 1986–. JP: Wimbledon, 1961–75; Southend-on-Sea, 1975–80; Bexley, 1980–. Queen's Silver Jubilee Medal, 1977. *Recreations:* gardening reading (science fiction), music. *Address:* 31 Red House Lane, Bexleyheath, Kent DA6 8JF. *T:* 01–304 7480.

POWELL, Anthony Dymoke; CBE 1956; *b* 21 Dec. 1905; *o s* of late Lt-Col P. L. W. Powell, CBE, DSO; *m* 1934, Lady Violet Pakenham, 3rd *d* of 5th Earl of Longford, KP; two *s*. *Educ:* Eton; Balliol College, Oxford, MA; Hon. Fellow, 1974. Served War of 1939–45, Welch Regt and Intelligence Corps, Major. A Trustee, National Portrait Gallery, 1962–76. Hon. Mem., Amer. Acad. of Arts and Letters, 1977; Hon. Fellow, Mod. Lang. Assoc. of Amer., 1981. Hon. DLitt: Sussex, 1971; Leicester, 1976; Kent, 1976; Oxon,

1980; Bristol, 1982. Hudson Review Bennet Prize, 1984; T. S. Eliot Prize for Creative Lit., Ingersoll Foundn, 1984. Orders of: the White Lion, (Czechoslovakia); the Oaken Crown and Croix de Guerre (Luxembourg); Leopold II (Belgium). *Publications:* Afternoon Men, 1931; Venusberg, 1932; From a View to a Death, 1933; Agents and Patients, 1936; What's become of Waring, 1939; John Aubrey and His Friends, 1948; Selections from John Aubrey, 1949; A Dance to the Music of Time, 12 vol. sequence, 1951–75: A Question of Upbringing, 1951; A Buyer's Market, 1952; The Acceptance World, 1955; At Lady Molly's, 1957 (James Tait Black Memorial Prize); Casanova's Chinese Restaurant, 1960; The Kindly Ones, 1962; The Valley of Bones, 1964; The Soldier's Art, 1966; The Military Philosophers, 1968; Books do Furnish a Room, 1971; Temporary Kings, 1973 (W. H. Smith Prize, 1974); Hearing Secret Harmonies, 1975; O, How The Wheel Becomes It!, 1983; The Fisher King, 1986; *memoirs:* To Keep the Ball Rolling, 4 vols, 1976–82 (abridged one vol. edn 1983): Infants of the Spring, 1976; Messengers of Day, 1978; Faces In My Time, 1980; The Strangers All are Gone, 1982; *plays:* Afternoon Men (adapted by Riccardo Aragno), Arts Theatre Club, 1963; The Garden God, 1971; The Rest I'll Whistle, 1971. *Address:* The Chantry, near Frome, Somerset. *T:* Nunney 314. *Clubs:* Travellers', Pratt's.

POWELL, Sir Arnold Joseph Philip; *see* Powell, Sir Philip.

POWELL, Arthur Barrington, CMG 1967; *b* 24 April 1918; *er s* of late Thomas and Dorothy Powell, Maesteg, Glam; *m* 1945, Jane, *d* of late Gen. Sir George Weir, KCB, CMG, DSO; four *s* one *d. Educ:* Cowbridge; Jesus Coll. Oxford. Indian Civil Service, 1939–47; served in Province of Bihar. Asst Princ., Min. of Fuel and Power, 1947; Princ. Private Sec. to Minister, 1949–51; Asst Sec., 1955; Petroleum Div., 1957–68; Petroleum Attaché, HM Embassy, Washington, 1962–64; Gas Div., 1968–72; Reg. Finance Div., DoI, 1972–76; Exec. Dir, Welsh Develt Agency, 1976–83. *Address:* The Folly, Newchurch West, Chepstow, Gwent. *Clubs:* United Oxford & Cambridge University; Royal Porthcawl Golf.

POWELL, Charles David; Private Secretary to the Prime Minister, since 1984; *b* 6 July 1941; *s* of Air Vice Marshal John Frederick Powell, *qv*; *m* 1964, Carla Bonardi; two *s. Educ:* King's Sch., Canterbury; New Coll., Oxford (BA). Entered Diplomatic Service, 1963; Third Sec., FO, 1963–65; Second Sec., Helsinki, 1965–67; FCO, 1968–71; First Sec. and Private Sec. to HM Ambassador, Washington, 1971–74; First Sec., Bonn, 1974–77; FCO, 1977–80 (Counsellor, 1979; Special Counsellor for Rhodesia, 1979–80); Counsellor, UK Perm. Repn to European Communities, 1980–84. *Recreation:* walking. *Address:* c/o 10 Downing Street, SW1 *Club:* Turf.

POWELL, David; *see* Powell, E. D. B.

POWELL, David; *b* 1914; *s* of Edward Churton Powell and Margaret (*née* Nesfield); *m* 1941, Joan Boileau (Henderson); one *s* four *d. Educ:* Charterhouse. Served 1939–46: Lt, Kent Yeomanry RA; Captain and Major on Staff. Qualified as Chartered Accountant, 1939, admitted, 1943; in practice, 1946–47; joined Booker McConnell Ltd, 1947; Finance Dir, 1952; Dep. Chm. 1957; Man. Dir, 1966; Chm. and Chief Exec., 1967, retired 1971. *Recreations:* stalking, golf, English water-colours, fishing, reading. *Address:* The Cottage, 20 Coldharbour Lane, Hildenborough, Kent TN11 9JT. *T:* Hildenborough 833103.

POWELL, Dewi Watkin, JP; **His Honour Judge Watkin Powell;** a Circuit Judge, since 1972; *b* Aberdare, 29 July 1920; *o s* of W. H. Powell, AMICE and of M. A. Powell, Radyr, Glam; *m* 1951, Alice, *e d* of William and Mary Williams, Nantmor, Caerns; one *d. Educ:* Penarth Grammar Sch.; Jesus Coll., Oxford (MA). Called to Bar, Inner Temple, 1949. Dep. Chm., Merioneth and Cardigan QS, 1966–71; Dep. Recorder of Cardiff, Birkenhead, Merthyr Tydfil and Swansea, 1965–71; Junior, Wales and Chester Circuit, 1968; Liaison Judge for Dyfed; Vice-Pres., South and Mid Glamorgan branch of Magistrates' Assoc. Mem. Exec. Cttee, Plaid Cymru, 1943–55, Chm., Constitutional Cttee, 1967–71; Mem. Council, Hon. Soc. of Cymmrodorion, 1965– (Chm., 1978–84). Member: Court, Univ. of Wales; Court and Council, Univ. Coll. of Wales, Aberystwyth and Univ. Coll. Cardiff (and Vice-Pres., UC Cardiff); Welsh Council of Social Services; Magistrates Courts and Probation and After-Care Cttees for Co. of Dyfed. Hon. Mem., Gorsedd of Bards. JP Dyfed. *Recreations:* gardening, reading, theology, Welsh history and literature. *Address:* Crown Court, Law Courts, Cathays Park, Cardiff.

POWELL, (Elizabeth) Dilys, CBE 1974; FRSL; TV Film Critic of The Sunday Times, since 1976 (Film Critic, 1939–76); Film Critic, Punch, since 1979; *yr d* of late Thomas and Mary Powell; *m* 1st, 1926, Humfry Payne, later Director of the British School of Archæology at Athens (*d* 1936); 2nd, 1943, Leonard Russell (*d* 1974); no *c. Educ:* Bournemouth High School; Somerville College, Oxford. Editorial Staff, Sunday Times, 1928–31 and 1936–41. Lived and travelled extensively in Greece, 1931–36. Member: Bd of Governors of British Film Institute, 1948–52 (Fellow, BFI, 1986); Independent Television Authority, 1954–57; Cinematograph Films Council, 1965–69; President, Classical Association, 1966–67. Hon. Mem., ACTT. Award of Honour, BAFTA, 1984. *Publications:* Descent from Parnassus, 1934; Remember Greece, 1941; The Traveller's Journey is Done, 1943; Coco, 1952; An Affair of the Heart, 1957; The Villa Ariadne, 1973. *Address:* 14 Albion Street, Hyde Park, W2. *T:* 01–723 9807.

POWELL, Rt. Hon. Enoch; *see* Powell, Rt Hon. J. E.

POWELL, (Evan) David (Brynmor); Regional Chairman of Industrial Tribunals (Cardiff), since 1968; *b* 31 July 1927; *s* of David Harold Idris and Mary Powell; *m* 1962, Margaret Gwynne Thomas; one *s* two *d. Educ:* Swansea Grammar Sch.; Winchester Coll.; Trinity Coll., Oxford (MA); King's Coll., London (LLB). Called to the Bar, Gray's Inn, 1953; practised on Wales and Chester Circuit, 1953–68. *Address:* 74 Pencisely Road, Cardiff CF5 1DH. *T:* Cardiff 566216.

POWELL, Francis Turner, MBE 1945; Chairman, Laing & Cruickshank, Stockbrokers, 1978–80; *b* 15 April 1914; *s* of Francis Arthur and Dorothy May Powell; *m* 1940, Joan Audrey Bartlett; one *s* one *d. Educ:* Lancing College. Served War, Queen's Royal Regt (TA), 1939–45 (Major). Joined L. Powell Sons & Co. (Stockbrokers), 1932, Partner, 1939; merged with Laing & Cruickshank, 1976. Mem. Council, Stock Exchange, 1963–78 (Dep. Chm., 1976–78). *Recreations:* golf, gardening. *Address:* Tanglewood, Oak Grange Road, West Clandon, Surrey. *T:* Guildford 222698.

POWELL, Geoffry Charles Hamilton; Founding Partner, Chamberlin, Powell & Bon, since 1952; *b* 7 Nov. 1920; *s* of late Col D. H. Powell and Violet (*née* Timins); *m* 1st, Philippa Cooper; two *d*; 2nd, Dorothy Williams; one *s. Educ:* Wellington College; AA School of Architecture. RIBA; AA Dipl. Asst to Frederick Gibberd, 1944, to Brian O'Rorke, 1946; teaching at Kingston School of Art (School of Architecture), 1949. Work includes: Golden Lane Estate; expansion of Leeds Univ.; schools, houses, commercial buildings; Barbican. Member: Council, Architectural Assoc.; SE Economic Planning Council. *Recreations:* travel, painting. *Address:* Glen Cottage, River Lane, Petersham, Surrey. *T:* 01–940 6286.

POWELL, Harry Allan Rose, (Tim Powell), MBE 1944; TD 1973; Chairman: Massey-Ferguson Holdings Ltd, 1970–80 (Managing Director, 1962–78); Holland and Holland Holdings Ltd, since 1982; *b* 15 Feb. 1912; *er s* of late William Allan Powell and Marjorie (*née* Mitchell); *m* 1936, Elizabeth North Hickley; two *d. Educ:* Winchester; Pembroke Coll., Cambridge (MA). Joined Corn Products Ltd, 1934. Commissioned Hertfordshire Yeomanry, 1938; Staff Coll., 1942; War Office 1942; Joint Planning Staff, 1943; seconded to War Cabinet Secretariat, 1943–44; Head of Secretariat, Supreme Allied Commander, South East Asia, 1944–45 (Col). Mitchells & Butlers Ltd, 1946–49; Gallaher Ltd, 1949–52. Joined Harry Ferguson Ltd, 1952. British Inst. of Management: Fellow, 1963; Vice-Chm., 1970–77. Governor, St Thomas' Hosp., 1971–74. *Recreations:* fishing, lapidary, arguing. *Address:* Ready Token, near Cirencester, Glos. *T:* Bibury 219; 12 Shafto Mews, Cadogan Square, SW1. *T:* 01–235 2707. *Clubs:* Buck's, MCC.

POWELL, Herbert Marcus, FRS 1953; BSc, MA; Professor of Chemical Crystallography, Oxford University, 1964–74, now Emeritus; *s* of William Herbert and Henrietta Powell; *m* 1973, Primrose Jean Dunn. *Educ:* St John's College, Oxford. MA Oxon 1931. Reader in Chemical Crystallography in the University of Oxford, 1944–64; Fellow of Hertford College, Oxford, 1963–74, Emeritus Fellow, 1974. *Address:* 46 Davenant Road, Oxford.

POWELL, John Alfred, MA, DPhil, CEng, FIEE, FRSE; consultant; *b* 4 Nov. 1923; *s* of Algernon Powell and Constance Elsie (*née* Honour); *m* 1949, Zena Beatrice (*née* Steventon); one *s* one *d. Educ:* Bicester County Sch.; The Queen's Coll., Oxford. No 1 Sch. of Technical Trng, RAF Halton, 1940–42. The Queen's Coll., Oxford, 1945–48. DPhil, Clarendon Lab., Oxford, 1948–51; Post-Doctorate Research Fellowship, Nat. Research Council, Ottawa, Canada, 1952–54; Marconi Research Labs, 1954–57; Texas Instruments Ltd: joined, 1957; Gen. Manager, 1959; Man. Dir, 1963; Asst Vice-Pres., TI Inc. (US), 1968; EMI Ltd: Main Bd Dir, Group Tech. Dir, 1971; Dir, Commercial Electronics, 1972; Dep. Man. Dir, 1973; Gp Man. Dir, 1974–78; Vice Chm., 1978–79. Mem., Honeywell Adv. Council, 1978–82. Faraday Lectr, 1978–79. CBIM (FBIM 1974); FRSA 1975; SMIEE (US). Member: Electronic Components Bd, 1968–71; Court of Cranfield Coll. of Technology, 1968–72; Electronics Research Council, 1972–74; Cttee of Inquiry into Engrg Profession, 1977–80; Physical Scis Sub-Cttee, UGC, 1980–85. Hon. Mem., BIR, 1980. *Recreations:* arts, sports, the rural scene. *Address:* Kym House, 21 Buccleuch Road, Branksome Park, Poole, Dorset BH13 6LF.

POWELL, Rt. Hon. (John) Enoch, PC 1960; MBE 1943; MA (Cantab); MP (UU) South Down, since Oct. 1974 (resigned seat Dec. 1985 in protest against Anglo-Irish Agreement; re-elected Jan. 1986); *b* 16 June 1912; *s* of Albert Enoch Powell and Ellen Mary Breese; *m* 1952, Margaret Pamela (*née* Wilson); two *d. Educ:* King Edwards, Birmingham; Trinity College, Cambridge. Craven Scholar, 1931; First Chancellor's Classical Medallist; Porson Prizeman; Browne Medallist, 1932; BA (Cantab); Craven Travelling Student, 1933; Fellow of Trinity College, Cambridge, 1934–38; MA (Cantab) 1937; Professor of Greek in the University of Sydney, NSW, 1937–39; Pte and L/Cpl R Warwickshire Regt, 1939–40; 2nd Lieut General List, 1940; Captain, General Staff, 1940–41; Major, General Staff, 1941; Lieut-Col, GS, 1942; Col, GS, 1944; Brig. 1944; Diploma in Oriental and African Studies. MP (C) Wolverhampton SW, 1950–Feb. 1974; Parly Sec., Ministry of Housing and Local Government, Dec. 1955–Jan. 1957; Financial Secretary to the Treasury, 1957–58; Minister of Health, July 1960–Oct. 1963. *Publications:* The Rendel Harris Papyri, 1936; First Poems, 1937; A Lexicon to Herodotus, 1938; The History of Herodotus, 1939; Casting-off, and other poems, 1939; Herodotus, Book VIII, 1939; Llyfr Blegywryd, 1942; Thucydidis Historia, 1942; Herodotus (translation), 1949; Dancer's End and The Wedding Gift (poems), 1951, repr. 1976; The Social Services; Needs and Means, 1952; (jointly) One Nation, 1950; Change is our Ally, 1954; Biography of a Nation (with Angus Maude), 1955, 2nd edn 1970; Great Parliamentary Occasions, 1960; Saving in a Free Society, 1960; A Nation not Afraid, 1965; Medicine and Politics, 1966, rev. edn 1976; The House of Lords in the Middle Ages (with Keith Wallis), 1968; Freedom and Reality, 1969; Common Market: the case against, 1971; Still to Decide, 1972; Common Market: renegotiate or come out, 1973; No Easy Answers, 1973; Wrestling with the Angel, 1977; Joseph Chamberlain, 1977; A Nation or No Nation (ed R. Ritchie), 1978; numerous political pamphlets. *Address:* 33 South Eaton Place, SW1. *T:* 01–730 0988.

POWELL, Air Vice-Marshal John Frederick, OBE 1956; Warden and Director of Studies, Moor Park College, 1972–77; *b* 12 June 1915; *y s* of Rev. Morgan Powell, Limpley Stoke, Bath; *m* 1939, Geraldine Ysolda, *e d* of late Sir John Fitzgerald Moylan, CB, CBE; four *s. Educ:* Lancing; King's Coll., Cambridge (MA). Joined RAF Educnl Service at No 1 Sch. of Techn Trng, 1937; Junior Lectr, RAF College, 1938–39; RAFVR (Admin. and Special Duties) ops room duties, Coastal Comd, 1939–45 (despatches); RAF Educn Br., 1946; Sen. Instructor in History, RAF Coll., 1946–49; RAF Staff Coll., 1950; Air Min., 1951–53; Sen. Tutor, RAF Coll., 1953–59; Educn Staff, HQ, FEAF, 1959–62; Min. of Def., 1962–64; Comd Educn Off., HQ Bomber Comd, 1964–66; OC, RAF Sch. of Educn, 1966–67; Dir of Educational Services, RAF, 1967–72; Air Commodore, 1967; Air Vice-Marshal, 1968. *Recreations:* choral music, tennis, gardening. *Address:* Old Post Office, Northington, near Alresford, Hants. *T:* Alresford 2221. *Club:* Royal Air Force.

See also C. D. Powell.

POWELL, John Geoffrey; consultant surveyor to Gerald Eve & Co., since 1985; arbitrator; Deputy Chairman, Local Government Boundary Commission for England, since 1984; *b* 13 Jan. 1928; *s* of H. W. J. and W. A. S. Powell; *m* 1954, Anne (*née* Evans); one *s* three *d. Educ:* Shrewsbury. FRICS; FSVA; ACIArb. Lieut, Welsh Guards, 1945–48. Joined Gerald Eve & Co., Chartered Surveyors, 1948, Partner, 1957, Joint Senior Partner, 1973–85. Chm., Property Adv. Gp, DoE (Chm., New Towns Sub-Gp); Member: Skelmersdale New Town Corp., 1978–85; Review Cttee of Govt Valuation Services, 1982; British Rail Property Board, 1985–. Sec.-Gen., European Group of Valuers of Fixed Assets, 1982–; European Rep., Internat. Assets Valuation Standards Cttee, 1984–. Chm., RICS Cttees, 1960–83, incl. Assets Valuation Standards Cttee, 1981–83. External Examr, City Univ. Centre for Studies in Property Valuation and Management, 1983–. *Recreation:* aviation. *Address:* (office) 117 Temple Chambers, Temple Avenue, EC4Y 0HP. *T:* 01–353 9353; (home) 01–876 0792. *Club:* Cavalry and Guards.

POWELL, Jonathan Leslie; Head of Drama Series and Serials, BBC Television, since 1983 (producer, drama serials, 1977–83); *b* 25 April 1947; *s* of James Dawson Powell and Phyllis Nora Sylvester (*née* Doubleday). *Educ:* Sherborne; University of East Anglia. BA Hons (English and American Studies). Script editor and producer of drama, Granada TV, 1970–77. *TV serials include:* Testament of Youth, 1979 (BAFTA award); Tinker Tailor Soldier Spy, 1979; Pride and Prejudice, 1980; Thérèse Raquin, 1980; The Bell, 1982; Smiley's People, 1982 (Peabody Medal, USA); The Old Men at the Zoo, 1983; Bleak House, 1985; Tender is the Night, 1985. Royal Television Soc. Silver Award for outstanding achievement, 1979–80. *Address:* c/o Union House, BBC TV, Shepherd's Bush Green, W12 7RJ. *T:* 01–743 8000.

POWELL, Lewis Franklin, Jr; Associate Justice of US Supreme Court, since Dec. 1971; *b* Suffolk, Va, USA, 19 Sept. 1907; *s* of Lewis Franklin Powell and Mary Lewis (*née*

Gwathmey); *m* 1936, Josephine Pierce Rucker; one *s* three *d*. *Educ:* McGuire's Univ. Sch., Richmond, Va; Washington and Lee Univ., Lexington, Va (BS *magnum cum laude*, LLB); Harvard Law Sch. (LLM). Admitted to practice, Bar of Virginia, 1931; subseq. practised law; partner in firm of Hunton, Williams, Gay, Powell and Gibson, in Richmond, 1938–71. Served War, May 1942–Feb. 1946, USAAF, overseas, to rank Col; subseq. Col. US Reserve. Legion of Merit and Bronze Star (US), also Croix de Guerre with Palms (France). Member: Nat. Commn on Law Enforcement and Admin of Justice, 1965–67; Blue Ribbon Defence Panel, 1969–70. Chairman or Dir of companies. Pres., Virginia State Bd of Educn; Past Chm. and Trustee, Colonial Williamsburg Foundn; Trustee, Washington and Lee Univ., etc. Mem., Amer. Bar Assoc. (Pres. 1964–65); Fellow, Amer. Bar Foundn (Pres. 1969–71); Pres. or Mem. various Bar Assocs and other legal and social instns; Hon. Bencher, Lincoln's Inn. Holds several hon. degrees. Phi Beta Kappa. Is a Democrat. *Publications:* contribs to legal periodicals, etc. *Address:* Supreme Court Building, Washington, DC 20543, USA. *Club:* University (NYC).

POWELL, Prof. Michael James David, FRS 1983; John Humphrey Plummer Professor of Applied Numerical Analysis, University of Cambridge, since 1976; Professorial Fellow of Pembroke College, Cambridge, since 1978; *b* 29 July 1936; *s* of William James David Powell and Beatrice Margaret (*née* Page); *m* 1959, Caroline Mary Henderson; two *d* (one *s* decd). *Educ:* Eastbourne Coll.; Peterhouse, Cambridge (Schol.; BA 1959; ScD 1979). Mathematician at Atomic Energy Research Estabt, Harwell, 1959–76; special merit research appt to banded level, 1969, and to senior level, 1975. George B. Dantzig prize in Mathematical Programming, 1982; Naylor Prize, London Math. Soc., 1983. *Publications:* Approximation Theory and Methods, 1981; papers on numerical mathematics, especially approximation and optimization calculations. *Recreations:* canals, golf, walking. *Address:* 134 Milton Road, Cambridge.

POWELL, Michael Latham, FRGS; film director; *b* Bekesbourne, near Canterbury, Kent, 30 Sept. 1905; *s* of Thomas William Powell and Mabel, *d* of Frederick Corbett, Worcester; *m* 1st, Frances (*d* 1983), *d* of Dr J. J. Reidy, JP, MD; two *s*; 2nd, 1984, Thelma Colbert Schoonmaker, *d* of Bertram Schoonmaker. *Educ:* King's Sch., Canterbury; Dulwich Coll. Hon. DLitt: East Anglia, 1978; Kent, 1984. BFI Special Award (with Emeric Pressburger), 1978; Fellow: BAFTA, 1981; BFI, 1983. Golden Lion of Venice Award, 1982. Joined National Provincial Bank, 1922; Metro-Goldwyn-Mayer film co., 1925, making Mare Nostrum, in the Mediterranean, with Rex Ingram as Dir; various capacities on 2 subseq. Ingram films: Somerset Maugham's The Magician and Robert Hichens' The Garden of Allah; was brought to Elstree, 1928, by the painter and film director, Harry Lachman; worked on 3 Hitchcock silent films, incl. script of Blackmail (later made into talking film). Travelled in Albania; wrote scripts for films of Caste and 77 Park Lane; given chance to direct by Jerry Jackson, 1931; dir Two Crowded Hours and Rynox (both melodramas of 40 mins); went on to make a dozen short features, incl. 4 for Michael Balcon at Shepherd's Bush Studios, incl. The Fire Raisers and The Red Ensign (both orig. stories by Jackson and Powell); wrote and dir The Edge of the World, on Foula, Shetland, 1936 (prod. Joe Rock); given a contract by Alexander Korda, 1938, travelled in Burma, up the Chindwin; met Emeric Pressburger, together wrote and then dir The Spy in Black, and Contraband; co-dir, Thief of Bagdad and The Lion has Wings; prod. and dir 49th Parallel (from orig. story by Pressburger); formed The Archers Company and together with Pressburger wrote, prod. and dir 16 films, incl. Colonel Blimp, I Know Where I'm Going, A Matter of Life and Death, Black Narcissus, The Red Shoes, all for J. Arthur Rank; returned to Korda, 1948, to make 4 films, incl. The Small Back Room and Tales of Hoffman; returned to Rank for The Battle of the River Plate (The Archers' second Royal Perf. film) and Ill Met By Moonlight; also made Rosalinda (film of Fledermaus) at Elstree; The Archers Company then broke up; since then has dir Honeymoon, Peeping Tom, The Queen's Guards, Bluebeard's Castle (Bartók opera); The Sorcerer's Apprentice (ballet film); film (for Children's Film Foundn) from a story and script by Pressburger, The Boy Who Turned Yellow; They're a Weird Mob (Aust.); Age of Consent (Aust.); Return to the Edge of the World, 1978; lectured on film, Dartmouth Coll., New Hampshire, 1980; joined F. Coppola as Sen. Dir in Res., Zoetrope Studios, 1981; supervisor for Pavlova (Anglo-USSR prod.), 1983–85. *In the theatre:* prod. and dir (Hemingway's) The Fifth Column, 1945; (Jan de Hartog's) The Skipper Next to God, 1947; (James Forsyth's) Heloise, 1951; (Raymond Massey's) Hanging Judge, 1955. TV Series (several episodes): Espionage and The Defenders, for Herbert Brodkin. *Publications:* 200,000 Feet on Foula; Graf Spee; A Waiting Game, 1975; (with Emeric Pressburger) The Red Shoes, 1978; A Life in Movies (autobiog.), 1986. *Recreation:* leaning on gates. *Address:* Lee Cottages, Avening, Tetbury, Glos. *Clubs:* Savile, Royal Automobile.

POWELL, Sir Nicholas (Folliott Douglas), 4th Bt *cr* 1897; Company Director; *b* 17 July 1935; *s* of Sir Richard George Douglas Powell, 3rd Bt, MC, and Elizabeth Josephine (*d* 1979), *d* of late Lt-Col O. R. McMullen, CMG; *S* father, 1980; *m* 1960, Daphne Jean, 2nd *d* of G. H. Errington, MC; one *s* one *d*. *Educ:* Gordonstoun. Lieut Welsh Guards, 1953–57. *Heir:* *s* James Richard Douglas Powell, *b* 17 Oct. 1962. *Address:* Petrunella Coffee Estate, Box 58, Chipinga, Zimbabwe.

POWELL, Prof. Percival Hugh, MA, DLitt, Dr Phil.; Professor of German, Indiana University, 1970–83, now Emeritus; *b* 4 Sept. 1912; 3rd *s* of late Thomas Powell and late Marie Sophia Roeser; *m* 1944, Dorothy Mavis Pattison (*née* Donald) (marr. diss. 1964); two *s* one adopted *d*; *m* 1966, Mary Kathleen (*née* Wilson); one *s*. *Educ:* University College, Cardiff (Fellow 1981); Univs of Rostock, Zürich, Bonn. 1st Class Hons German (Wales), 1933; Univ. Teachers' Diploma in Education, 1934; MA (Wales) Dist. 1936; Research Fellow of Univ. of Wales, 1936–38; Modern Languages Master, Towyn School, 1934–36; Dr Phil. (Rostock) 1938; Lektor in English, Univ. of Bonn, 1938–39; Asst Lectr, Univ. Coll., Cardiff, 1939–40; War Service, 1940–46 (Capt. Intelligence Corps); Lecturer in German, Univ. Coll., Leicester, 1946, Head of Department of German, 1954; Prof. of German, Univ. of Leicester, 1958–69. Barclay Acheson Prof. of Internat. Studies at Macalester Coll., Minn., USA, 1965–66. DLitt (Wales) 1962. British Academy award, 1963; Fritz Thyssen Foundation Award, 1964; Leverhulme Trust Award, 1968. *Publications:* Pierre Corneilles Dramen in Deutschen Bearbeitungen, 1939; critical editions of dramas of Andreas Gryphius, 1955–72; critical edn of J. G. Schoch's Comœdia vom Studentenleben, 1976; articles and reviews in English and foreign literary jls. *Recreation:* music. *Address:* c/o Department of Germanic Studies, Ballantine Hall, Indiana University, Bloomington, Indiana 47405, USA.

POWELL, Sir Philip, CH 1984; Kt 1975; OBE 1957; RA 1977 (ARA 1972); FRIBA; Partner of Powell and Moya, Architects, since 1946, and Powell, Moya and Partners, since 1976; *b* 15 March 1921; *yr s* of late Canon A. C. Powell and late Mary Winnifred (*née* Walker), Epsom and Chichester; *m* 1953, Philippa, *d* of Lt-Col C. C. Eccles, Tunbridge Wells; one *s* one *d*. *Educ:* Epsom Coll.; AA Sch. of Architecture (Hons Diploma). *Works include:* Churchill Gdns flats, Westminster, 1948–62 (won in open competition); houses and flats at Gospel Oak, St Pancras, 1954, Vauxhall Park, Lambeth, 1972, Covent Garden, 1983; houses at: Chichester, 1950; Toys Hill, 1954; Oxshott, 1954; Baughurst, Hants, 1954; Skylon for Fest. of Britain, 1951 (won in open competition); British Pavilion, Expo 70, Osaka, Japan, 1970; Mayfield Sch., Putney, 1955; Plumstead Manor Sch., Woolwich, 1970; Dining Rooms at Bath Acad. of Art, Corsham, 1970, and Eton Coll., 1974; extensions, Brasenose Coll., Oxford, 1961, and Corpus Christi Coll., Oxford, 1969; picture gall. and undergrad. rooms, Christ Church, Oxford, 1967; Wolfson Coll., Oxford, 1974; Cripps Building, St John's Coll., Cambridge, 1967; Cripps Court, Queens' Coll., Cambridge, 1976; Chichester Fest. Theatre, 1961; Swimming Baths, Putney, 1967; Hosps at Swindon, Slough, High Wycombe, Wythenshawe, Woolwich, Maidstone; Museum of London, 1976; London and Manchester Assurance HQ, near Exeter, 1978; Sch. for Advanced Urban Studies, Bristol Univ., 1981; NatWest Bank, Shaftesbury Ave, London, 1982; Queen's Building, RHBNC, Egham, 1986; Queen Elizabeth II Conf. Centre, Westminster, 1986. Has won numerous medals and awards for architectural work, inc. Royal Gold Medal for Architecture, RIBA, 1974. Mem. Royal Fine Art Commn, 1969–; Treas. RA, 1985–. *Recreations:* travel, listening to music. *Address:* 16 The Little Boltons, SW10 9LP. *T:* 01–373 8620; 21 Upper Cheyne Row, SW3 5JW. *T:* 01–351 3881.

POWELL, Raymond; MP (Lab) Ogmore, since 1979; *b* 19 June 1928; *s* of Albert and Lucy Powell; *m* 1951, Marion Grace Evans; one *s* one *d*. *Educ:* Pentre Grammar Sch.; National Council of Labour Colls; London School of Economics. British Rail, 1945–50; Shop Manager, 1950–66; Secretary/Agent to Walter Padley, MP, 1967–69, voluntarily, 1969–79; Sen. Administrative Officer, Welsh Water Authority, 1969–79. Welsh Regl Opposition Whip. Chairman: Labour Party Wales, 1977–78; S Wales Euro-Constituency Labour Party, 1979–. Secretary: Welsh PLP, 1984–85; Anglo-Bulgarian All Party Gp, 1984–85; Treas., Anglo-Romanian All Party Gp, 1984–85. *Recreations:* gardening, sport, music. *Address:* 8 Brynteg Gardens, Bridgend, Mid-Glam. *T:* Bridgend 2159. *Club:* Ogmore Constituency Labour Party Social.

POWELL, Sir Richard (Royle), GCB 1967 (KCB 1961; CB 1951); KBE 1954; CMG 1946; Deputy Chairman, Permanent Committee on Invisible Exports, 1968–76; Chairman, Alusuisse (UK) Ltd and subsidiary companies, 1969–84; *b* 30 July 1909; *er s* of Ernest Hartley and Florence Powell; unmarried. *Educ:* Queen Mary's Grammar Sch., Walsall; Sidney Sussex Coll., Cambridge (Hon. Fellow, 1972). Entered Civil Service, 1931 and apptd to Admiralty; Private Sec. to First Lord, 1934–37; Member of British Admiralty Technical Mission, Canada, and of British Merchant Shipbuilding Mission, and later of British Merchant Shipping Mission in USA, 1940–44; Civil Adviser to Commander-in-Chief, British Pacific Fleet, 1944–45; Under-Secretary, Ministry of Defence, 1946–48. Dep. Sec., Admiralty, 1948–50; Dep. Sec., Min. of Defence, 1950–56; Permanent Secretary, Board of Trade, 1960–68 (Min. of Defence, 1956–59). Dir, Philip Hill Investment Trust, 1968–81; Director: Whessoe Ltd, 1968–; Sandoz Gp of Cos, 1972– (Chm.); Clerical, Medical and General Life Assurance Soc., 1972–85; BPB Industries PLC, 1973–83; Ladbroke Gp, 1980–; Bridgewater Paper Co. Ltd, 1984–. Pres., Inst. for Fiscal Studies, 1970–78. *Address:* 56 Montagu Square, W1. *T:* 01–262 0911. *Club:* Athenæum.

POWELL, Robert Lane B.; *see* Bayne-Powell.

POWELL, Robert William; Headmaster of Sherborne, 1950–70; retired; *b* 29 October 1909; *s* of late William Powell and Agnes Emma Powell; *m* 1938, Charity Rosamond Collard; one *s*. *Educ:* Bristol Grammar School; Christ Church, Oxford. Assistant Master, Repton, May-Dec. 1934; Assistant Master, Charterhouse, 1935. Served War of 1939–45, 1940–45. Housemaster of Gownboys, Charterhouse, 1946–50. *Recreations:* fishing, music. *Address:* Manor Farm House, Child Okeford, near Blandford, Dorset. *T:* Child Okeford 860648.

POWELL, Roger, OBE 1976; bookbinder; *b* 17 May 1896; *er s* of late Oswald Byrom Powell and Winifred Marion Powell (*née* Cobb); *m* 1924, Rita Glanville, *y d* of late Frank and Katherine F. Harvey; one *s* twin *d*. *Educ:* Bedales Sch. Served European War, 1914–18: Hampshire Regt, Palestine, 1917; Flt Lt, RAF, Egypt, 1918. Poultry farming, 1921–30; studied bookbinding at LCC Central Sch., 1930–31; joined Douglas Cockerell & Son, bookbinders, 1935; Partner, 1936; opened own bindery at Froxfield, 1947. Member: Art Workers' Guild; Double Crown Club; Red Rose Guild. Has repaired and bound many early manuscripts, incunabula and other early printed books including: for Winchester (both Coll. and Cathedral); for TCD, The Book of Kells, 1953; The Book of Durrow, The Book of Armagh, The Book of Dimma (in accommod. Brit. Mus.), 1954–57; for Lichfield Cath., The St Chad Gospels, 1961–62; for RIA, The Book of Lecan, Lebor na hUidre, Leabhar Breac, The Book of Fermoy, The Cathach of St Columba, 1968–81; for Durham Cathedral, The A. II. 17 Gospels, 1976. Tooled Memorial Bindings, incl: WVS Roll of Honour, Civilian War Dead, 1939–45, in Westminster Abbey. Rolls of Honour: for RMA Sandhurst and Woolwich; Coastal Command, RAF; S Africa, India, Pakistan. Other tooled bindings, in: Brit. Mus., Victoria and Albert Mus.; in Libraries: (Bodleian, Oxford; Pierpont Morgan; Syracuse Univ.; Grolier Club, New York; Newberry, Chicago), and in private collections in Britain, Ireland and USA. Visited, to advise on book-conservation: Iceland, 1965; Florence, 1966; Portugal, 1967. Hon. For. Corresp. Mem., Grolier Club, NY. Hon. MA Dublin, 1961. *Publications:* various contribs to The Library; Scriptorium, Brussels; Ériu, Dublin, 1956–69. *Recreations:* cricket, singing, 'finding out', photography, amateur operatics and dramatics, organic cultivations, bee-keeping, golf. *Address:* The Slade, Froxfield, Petersfield, Hants GU32 1EB. *T:* Hawkley 229.

POWELL, Tim; *see* Powell, H. A. R.

POWELL, Victor George Edward; Senior Partner, Victor G. Powell Associates, Management Consultants, since 1963; Professor of Management, ILO International Centre for Advanced Training, since 1982; Director, Mosscare Housing Association Ltd, since 1974; *b* London, 1 Jan. 1929; *s* of George Richard Powell and Kate Hughes Powell, London; *m* 1956, Patricia Copeland Allen; three *s* one *d*. *Educ:* Beckenham Grammar Sch.; Univs of Durham and Manchester. BA 1st cl. hons Econs 1954, MA Econ. Studies 1957, Dunelm; PhD Manchester 1963. RN Engrg Apprentice, 1944–48. Central Work Study Dept, ICI, London, 1954–56; Chief Work Study Engr, Ind Coope Ltd, 1956–58; Lectr in Industrial Administration, Manchester Univ., 1959, Hon. Lectr 1959–63; Asst Gen. Manager, Louis C. Edwards & Sons Ltd, 1959–63; Chm., Food Production & Processing Ltd, 1971–74. Sen. Advr, 1976, Dir and Chief Advr, 1977–82, ILO. Gen. Sec., 1970–72, Dir, 1972–73, War on Want. MBIM 1957; Mem. Inst. Management Consultants, 1968. *Publications:* Economics of Plant Investment and Replacement Decisions, 1964; Techniques for Improving Distribution Management, 1968; Warehousing, 1976; Improving the Performance of Public Enterprises, 1986; various articles. *Recreations:* music, walking. *Address:* Inglewood, Coppice Lane, Disley, Stockport, Cheshire SK12 2LT. *T:* Disley 2011.

POWELL, William Rhys; MP (C) Corby, since 1983; *s* of Rev. Canon Edward Powell and Anne Powell; *m* 1973, Elizabeth Vaudin; three *d*. *Educ:* Lancing College; Emmanuel College, Cambridge. BA 1970, MA 1973. Called to the Bar, Lincoln's Inn, 1971; Barrister, South Eastern Circuit, 1971–. PPS to Minister for Overseas Develt, 1985–. Jt Sec., Cons. Back Bench For. Affairs Cttee, 1985. Mem. Council, British Atlantic Cttee, 1985–. As Private Mem. piloted Copyright (Computer Software) Amendment Act, 1985. *Address:* House of Commons, SW1. *Club:* Corby Conservative.

POWELL-COTTON, Christopher, CMG 1961; MBE 1951; MC 1945; JP; Uganda CS, retired; *b* 23 Feb. 1918; *s* of Major P. H. G. Powell-Cotton and Mrs H. B. Powell-Cotton (*née* Slater); unmarried. *Educ:* Harrow School; Trinity College, Cambridge. Army Service, 1939–45: commissioned Buffs, 1940; seconded KAR, Oct. 1940; T/Major, 1943. Apptd to Uganda Administration, 1940, and released for Mil. Service. District Commissioner, 1950; Provincial Commissioner, 1955; Minister of Security and External Relations, 1961. Landowner in SE Kent. Dir, Powell-Cotton Museum of Nat. History and Ethnography. *Address:* Quex Park, Birchington, Kent. *T:* Thanet 41836. *Club:* MCC.

POWELL-JONES, John Ernest, CMG 1974; HM Diplomatic Service, retired; Ambassador to Switzerland, 1982–85; *b* 14 April 1925; *s* of late Walter James Powell-Jones and Gladys Margaret (*née* Taylor); *m* 1st, 1949, Ann Murray (marr. diss. 1967); two *s* one *d*; 2nd, 1968, Pamela Sale. *Educ:* Charterhouse; University Coll., Oxford (1st cl. Modern Hist.). Served with Rifle Bde, 1943–46. HM Foreign (now Diplomatic) Service, 1949; 3rd Sec. and Vice-Consul, Bogota, 1950–52; Eastern and later Levant Dept, FO, 1952–55; 2nd, later 1st Sec., Athens, 1955–59; News Dept, FO, 1959–60; 1st Sec., Leopoldville, 1961–62; UN Dept, FO, 1963–67; ndc Canada 1967–68; Counsellor, Political Adviser's Office, Singapore, 1968–69; Counsellor and Consul-General, Athens, 1970–73; Ambassador at Phnom Penh, 1973–75; RCDS 1975; Ambassador to Senegal, Guinea, Mali, Mauritania and Guinea-Bissau, 1976–79, to Cape Verde, 1977–79; Ambassador and Perm. Rep., UN Conf. on Law of the Sea, 1979–82. *Recreations:* gardening, walking. *Address:* Gascons, Gaston Gate, Cranleigh, Surrey. *T:* Cranleigh 274313. *Club:* Travellers'.

POWER, Sir Alastair John Cecil, 4th Bt *cr* 1924, of Newlands Manor; *b* 15 Aug. 1958; *s* of Sir John Patrick McLannahan Power, 3rd Bt and of Melanie, *d* of Hon. Alastair Erskine; *S* father, 1984. *Heir: b* Adam Patrick Cecil Power, *b* 22 March 1963.

POWER, Mrs Brian St Quentin; *see* Stack, (Ann) Prunella.

POWER, Eugene Barnum, Hon. KBE 1977; microphotographer, retired 1970; business executive; *b* Traverse City, Mich, 4 June 1905; *s* of Glenn Warren Power and Annette (*née* Barnum); *m* 1929, Sadye L. Harwick; one *s*. *Educ:* Univ. of Mich (AB 1927, MBA 1930). With Edwards Bros, Inc., Ann Arbor, Mich, 1930–38; engaged in expts with methods and uses of microfilm technique for reprodn of materials for res., 1935; Founder: Univ. Microfilms (merged with Xerox Corp. 1962), 1938; Univ. Microfilms, Ltd London, 1952; Dir, Xerox Corp., 1962–68. Organized: 1st large microfilming proj. for libraries, copying all books printed in England before 1640; Microfilms, Inc., as distbn agency, using microfilm as reprodn medium for scientific and technical materials, 1942–62; Projected Books, Inc. (non-profit corp.), for distbn of reading and entertainment materials in photog. form to physically incapacitated, 1944–70; Eskimo Art, Inc. (non-profit corp.). During War, dir. large-scale copying of important Brit. MSS in public and private archives, also enemy documents. Pres. and Chm., Power Foundn, 1968–; Mem. Bd of Dirs, Domino's Pizza Inc., Ann Arbor, 1978–. Special Rep. Co-ordinator of Inf. and of Library of Congress, London 1942, Office of Strategic Services, 1943–45. President: Internat. Micrographic Congress, 1964–65; Nat. Microfilm Assoc., 1946–54. Chm., Mich Co-ordinating Council for State Higher Educn; Regent, Univ. of Michigan, 1956–66. Chm., Ann Arbor Summer Festival Inc., 1978–85. Member: Council of Nat. Endowment for the Humanities, 1968–74; Amer. Philos. Soc., 1975. Fellow, Nat. Microfilm Assoc., 1963 (Award of Merit, 1956); Fellow of Merit, Internat. Micrographic Congress, 1978; Paul Harris Fellow, Rotary Internat., 1979. Hon. Fellow: Magdalene Coll., Cambridge, 1967; Northwestern Mich Coll., 1967. Hon. LHD: St John's Univ., 1966; Univ. of Michigan, 1971. *Publications:* numerous articles on techniques and uses of microfilm. *Recreations:* swimming, sailing, fishing, hunting, music. *Address:* (home) 989 Forest Road, Barton Hills, Ann Arbor, Mich 48105, USA. *T:* (313) 662–2886; (office) 2929 Plymouth Road, Ann Arbor, Mich 48105. *T:* (313) 769–8424. *Clubs:* American; Rotary (Ann Arbor).

POWER, Michael George; Director, Greenwich Hospital, since 1982; *b* 2 April 1924; *s* of Admiral of the Fleet Sir Arthur Power, GCB, GBE, CVO, and Amy Isabel (*née* Bingham); *m* 1954, Kathleen Maeve (*née* McCaul); one *s* two *d* and two step *d*. *Educ:* Rugby Sch.; Corpus Christi Coll., Cambridge. Served War, Rifle Bde, 1942–46 (Captain); ME Centre of Arab Studies (Jerusalem), 1946–47; Colonial Admin. Service, 1947–63: District Officer: Kenya, 1948–53; Malaya, 1953–57; Kenya, 1957–63; Home Civil Service, 1963–81; Under-Sec., MoD, 1973–81. Mem., Royal Patriotic Fund Corp., 1982. Almoner, Christ's Hosp., 1983–. *Recreations:* sailing, golf, gardening. *Address:* Wancom Way, Puttenham Heath Road, Compton, Guildford. *T:* Guildford 810470.

POWER, Noel Plunkett; Hon. Mr Justice Power; Judge of the High Court, Hong Kong, since 1979; *b* 4 Dec. 1929; *s* of John Joseph Power and Hilda Power; *m* 1965, Irma Maroya; two *s* one *d*. *Educ:* Downlands Coll.; Univ. of Queensland (BA, LLB). Called to the Bar, Supreme Court of Queensland and High Court of Australia, 1955; Magistrate, Hong Kong, 1965–76; Pres., Lands Tribunal, Hong Kong, 1976–79. *Publications:* (ed) Lands Tribunal Law Reports, 1976–79. *Recreations:* travel, cooking, reading, tennis. *Address:* 76 G Peak Road, Hong Kong. *T:* 5–96798. *Clubs:* Hong Kong (Hong Kong); Queensland (Brisbane).

POWERSCOURT, 10th Viscount *cr* 1743; **Mervyn Niall Wingfield;** Baron Wingfield, 1743; Baron Powerscourt (UK), 1885; *b* 3 Sept. 1935; *s* of 9th Viscount Powerscourt and of Sheila Claude, *d* of late Lt-Col Claude Beddington; *S* father, 1973; *m* 1962, Wendy Ann Pauline (marr. diss. 1974), *d* of R. C. G. Slazenger; one *s* one *d*; *m* 1978, Pauline, *d* of W. P. Vann, San Francisco. *Educ:* Stowe; Trinity Coll., Cambridge. Formerly Irish Guards. *Heir: s* Hon. Mervyn Anthony Wingfield, *b* 21 Aug. 1963.
See also Sir H. R. H. Langrishe, Bt.

POWIS, 6th Earl of, *cr* 1804; **Christian Victor Charles Herbert;** Baron Clive (Ire.), 1762; Baron Clive, 1794; Viscount Clive, Baron Herbert, Baron Powis, 1804; *b* 28 May 1904; 2nd *s* of Colonel Edward William Herbert, CB (*d* 1924) (*g s* of 2nd Earl of Powis) and Beatrice Anne (*d* 1928), *d* of Sir Hedworth Williamson, 8th Bt; *S* brother, 1974. *Educ:* Oundle; Trinity Coll., Cambridge (BA); University Coll., London. Barrister, Inner Temple, 1932; Private Secretary to: Governor and C-in-C, British Honduras, 1947–55; Governor of British Guiana, 1955–64. Served War of 1939–45 with RAOC, UK and India; Major, 1943. *Heir: cousin* George William Herbert [*b* 4 June 1925; *m* 1949, Hon. Katharine Odeyne de Grey, *d* of 8th Baron Walsingham, DSO, OBE; four *s* two adopted *d*]. *Address:* Powis Castle, Welshpool, N Wales. *T:* 3360. *Clubs:* Brooks's, MCC.

POWLES, Sir Guy (Richardson), KBE 1961; CMG 1954; ED 1944; first Ombudsman of New Zealand, 1962–75, Chief Ombudsman, 1975–77; *b* 5 April 1905; *s* of late Colonel C. G. Powles, CMG, DSO, New Zealand Staff Corps; *m* 1931, Eileen, *d* of A. J. Nicholls; two *s*. *Educ:* Wellington Coll., NZ; Victoria Univ. (LLB). Barrister, Supreme Court, New Zealand, 1929; served War of 1939–45 with NZ Military Forces, to rank of Colonel; Counsellor, NZ Legation, Washington, DC, USA, 1946–48; High Comr, Western Samoa, 1949–60, for NZ in India, 1960–62, Ceylon, 1960–62, and Ambassador of NZ to Nepal, 1960–62. President, NZ Inst. of Internat. Affairs, 1967–71. NZ Comr, Commn of the Churches on Internat. Affairs, World Council of Churches, 1971–80; Comr, Internat. Commn of Jurists, Geneva, 1975–. Race Relations Conciliator, 1971–73. Patron: Amnesty International (NZ); NZ-India Soc.; Environmental Defence Soc. Hon. LLD Victoria Univ. of Wellington, 1969. *Publications:* articles and speeches on international affairs, administrative law and race relations. *Address:* 34 Wesley Road, Wellington, NZ.

POWLETT; *see* Orde-Powlett.

POWLETT, Rear-Adm. Philip Frederick, CB 1961; DSO 1941 (and Bar 1942); DSC 1941; DL; retired; *b* 13 Nov. 1906; *s* of late Vice-Admiral F. A. Powlett, CBE; *m* 1935, Frances Elizabeth Sykes (*née* Elwell); two *s* one *d*. *Educ:* Osborne and Dartmouth. War of 1939–45 (DSC, DSO and Bar; Polish Cross of Valour, 1942); in command of destroyers and corvettes, Shearwater, Blankney, Cassandra. Deputy Director of Naval Air Organisation and Training, 1950; Senior Officer, Reserve Fleet, Clyde, 1952–53; Captain (F), 6th Frigate Squadron, 1954–55; Director (RN), Joint Anti-Submarine School, and Senior Naval Officer, Northern Ireland, 1956–58; Flag Officer and Admiral Superintendent, Gibraltar, 1959–62; retired, 1962. DL Norfolk, 1974. *Address:* The Mill House, Lyng, Norwich, Norfolk NR9 5QZ. *T:* Norwich 872334.

POWLEY, John Albert; MP (C) Norwich South, since 1983; *b* 3 Aug. 1936; *s* of Albert and Evelyn Powley; *m* 1957, Jill (*née* Palmer); two *s* one *d*. *Educ:* Cambridge Grammar Sch.; Cambridgeshire Coll. of Arts and Technology. Apprenticeship, Pye Ltd, 1952–57; RAF, 1957–59; retail shop selling and servicing radio, television and electrical goods, 1960–. Cambs CC, 1967–77; Cambridge City Council, 1967–79; Leader, Cons. Group, 1973–79; Chm., Housing Cttee, 1972–74, 1976–79; Leader of Council, 1976–79. Contested (C) Harlow, 1979. *Recreations:* golf, cricket, football. *Address:* House of Commons, SW1A 0AA; 32 Sunningdale, Eaton, Norwich NR4 6AN. *Club:* Carlton.

POWNALL, Henry Charles; QC 1979; **His Honour Judge Pownall;** a Circuit Judge, since 1984; *b* 25 Feb. 1927; *er s* of late John Cecil Glossop Pownall, CB, and of Margaret Nina Pownall (*née* Jesson); *m* 1955, Sarah Bettine, *d* of late Major John Deverell; one *s* one *d* (and one *d* decd). *Educ:* Rugby Sch.; Trinity Coll., Cambridge; BA 1950, MA 1963; LLB 1951. Served War, Royal Navy, 1945–48. Called to Bar, Inner Temple, 1954, Bencher, 1976; joined South-Eastern Circuit, 1954. Junior Prosecuting Counsel to the Crown at the Central Criminal Court, 1964–71; a Sen., subseq. 2nd, Prosecuting Counsel, 1971–79; a Recorder of the Crown Court, 1972–84; a Judge, Courts of Appeal of Jersey and Guernsey, 1980–86. Mem. Cttee: Orders and Medals Research Soc., 1961–69, and 1970– (Pres., 1971–75, 1977–81); Nat. Benevolent Instn, 1964–. Hon. Legal Advr, ABA, 1976–. *Publication:* Korean Campaign Medals, 1950–53, 1957. *Recreations:* travel; medals and medal ribbons. *Address:* 57 Ringmer Avenue, SW6 5LP; Knightsbridge Crown Court, 1 Hans Crescent, SW1X 0LQ. *Clubs:* Pratt's; Hurlingham; Ebury Court.
See also J. L. Pownall.

POWNALL, John Harvey; Under Secretary (Head of Electricity Division), Department of Energy, since 1985; *b* 24 Oct. 1933; *s* of Eric Pownall and Gladys M. Pownall (*née* Baily); *m* 1958, Pauline M. Marsden, *o d* of William Denton Marsden; one *s* two *d*. *Educ:* Tonbridge School; Imperial College, London (BSc Eng Met). ARSM, MIMM, CEng. Scientific Officer, Atomic Energy Research Estab., Harwell, 1955–59; Warren Spring Lab., DSIR, 1959–64; Dept of Economic Affairs, 1964–66; Board of Trade/Dept of Trade and Industry, 1966–83; Dir-Gen., Council of Mechanical and Metal Trade Assocs, 1983–85. *Publications:* papers in professional jls. *Address:* 27 The Reddings, Welwyn Garden City, Herts AL8 7LA. *T:* Welwyn Garden 327149. *Club:* Athenæum.

POWNALL, Brig. John Lionel, OBE 1972; Deputy Chairman, Police Complaints Authority, since 1986 (Member, since 1985); *b* 10 May 1929; *yr s* of John Cecil Glossop Pownall, CB and of Margaret Nina Pownall (*née* Jesson); *m* 1962, Sylvia Joan Cameron, *d* of late J. Cameron Conn, WS; two *s*. *Educ:* Rugby School; RMA Sandhurst. Commissioned 16th/5th Lancers, 1949; served Egypt, Cyrenaica, Tripolitania, BAOR, Hong, Kong, Cyprus; psc, jssc; Comd 16th/5th The Queen's Royal Lancers, 1969–71; Adjutant-Gen.'s Secretariat, 1971–72; Officer i/c RAC Manning and Records, 1973–75; Col, GS Near East Land Forces/Land Forces Cyprus, 1975–78; Asst Dir, Defence Policy Staff, MoD, 1978–79; Brig. RAC, UKLF, 1979–82; Brig. GS, MoD, 1982–84; retired 1984. Col, 16th/5th The Queen's Royal Lancers, 1985–. *Recreations:* equitation, ski-ing, gardening, arts. *Address:* c/o Coutts & Co., 440 Strand, WC2R 0QS. *Club:* Cavalry and Guards.
See also H. C. Pownall.

POWNALL, Leslie Leigh, MA, PhD; Chairman, NSW Planning and Environment Commission, 1974–77, retired; *b* 1 Nov. 1921; *y s* of A. de S. Pownall, Wanganui, New Zealand; *m* 1943, Judith, *d* of late Harold Whittaker, Palmerston North. *Educ:* Palmerston North Boys' High Sch.; Victoria University College, University of Canterbury, University of Wisconsin. Asst Master, Christchurch Boys' High Sch., 1941–46; Lecturer in Geography: Christchurch Teachers' Coll., 1946–47; Ardmore Teachers' Coll., 1948–49; Auckland University College, 1949–51; Senior Lecturer in Geography, 1951–60, Prof. of Geography, 1960–61, Vice-Chancellor and Rector, 1961–66, University of Canterbury; Clerk of the University Senate, Univ. of London, 1966–74. Consultant, Inter-University Council for Higher Educn Overseas, London, 1963; Consultant to Chm. of Working Party on Higher Educn in E Africa, 1968–69. Member Meeting, Council on World Tensions on Social and Economic Development (S Asia and Pacific), Kuala Lumpur, Malaysia, 1964; Governor, Internat. Students Trust, London, 1967–74; Member: Central Governing Body, City Parochial Foundation, London, 1967–74 (Mem., Grants Sub-Cttee; Chm., Finance and Gen. Purposes Cttee); UK Commonwealth Scholarship Commn, 1979–80. *Publications:* New Zealand, 1951 (New York); geographic contrib. in academic journals of America, Netherlands and New Zealand. *Recreations:* music, literature. *Clubs:* Canterbury, University (Christchurch, NZ).

POWYS, family name of **Baron Lilford.**

POYNTON, Sir (Arthur) Hilton, GCMG 1964 (KCMG 1949; CMG 1946); *b* 20 April 1905; *y s* of late Arthur Blackburne Poynton, formerly Master of University College, Oxford; *m* 1946, Elisabeth Joan, *d* of late Rev. Edmund Williams; two *s* one *d*. *Educ:* Marlborough Coll.; Brasenose Coll., Oxford (Hon. Fellow 1964). Entered Civil Service, Department of Scientific and Industrial Research, 1927; transferred to Colonial Office, 1929; Private Secretary to Minister of Supply and Minister of Production 1941–43; reverted to Colonial Office, 1943; Permanent Under-Secretary of State, CO, 1959–66. Mem. Governing Body, SPCK, 1967–72. Mem., Ct of Governors, London Sch. Hygiene and Tropical Med., 1965–77; Treas., Soc. Promotion Roman Studies, 1967–76; Dir, Overseas Branch, St John Ambulance, 1968–75. KStJ 1968. *Recreations:* music, travel. *Address:* Craigmillar, 47 Stanhope Road, Croydon CR0 5NS. *T:* 01–688 3729.

POYNTON, (John) Orde, CMG 1961; MD; Consulting Bibliographer, University of Melbourne, 1962–74; Fellow of Graduate House, University of Melbourne, 1971–84; *b* 9 April 1906; *o s* of Frederick John Poynton, MD, FRCP, and Alice Constance, *d* of Sir John William Powlett Campbell-Orde, 3rd Bt, of Kilmory; *m* 1965, Lola, *widow* of Group Captain T. S. Horry, DFC, AFC. *Educ:* Marlborough Coll.; Gonville and Caius

Coll., Cambridge; Charing Cross Hospital (Univ. Schol. 1927–30). MA, MD (Cambridge); MD (Adelaide) 1948; MRCS, LRCP; Horton-Smith prize, University of Cambridge, 1940. Sen. Resident MO, Charing Cross Hosp., 1932–33; Health Officer, Fed. Malay States, 1936–37; Res. Officer Inst. for Med. Research, FMS, 1937–38, Pathologist, 1938–46; Lectr in Pathology, Univ. of Adelaide, 1947–50; Pathologist, Inst. of Med. and Veterinary Science, S Australia, 1948–50, Director, 1950–61. Dir, Commercial Finance Co., 1960–70. Hon. LLD Melbourne, 1977. *Publications:* monographs and papers relating to medicine and bibliography. *Recreation:* bibliognostics. *Address:* 8 Seymour Avenue, Mount Eliza, Victoria 3930, Australia. *Club:* MCC.

POYNTZ, Rt. Rev. Samuel Greenfield; *see* Cork, Cloyne and Ross, Bishop of.

PRACY, Robert, FRCS; Dean of the Institute of Laryngology and Otology, University of London, 1981–84; *b* 19 Sept. 1921; *s* of Douglas Sherrin Pracy and Gwendoline Blanche Power; *m* 1946, Elizabeth Patricia Spicer; one *s* two *d* (and one *s* decd). *Educ:* Berkhamsted Sch.; St Bartholomew's Hosp. Med. Coll. (MB BS 1945); MPhil (Lond.) 1984. LRCP 1944; MRCS, FRCS 1953. Former Captain, RAMC. House Surgeon appts, St Bartholomew's Hosp.; formerly: Registrar, Royal Nat. Throat, Nose and Ear Hosp.; Consultant Surgeon: Liverpool Regional Board, 1954; United Liverpool Hosps, 1959; Alder Hey Childrens' Hosp., 1960; Royal Nat. Throat, Nose and Ear Hosp.; Hosp. for Sick Children, Gt Ormond St; Dir, Dept of Otolaryngology, Liverpool Univ. Mem. Ct of Examnrs, RCS and RCSI. Lectures: Yearsley, 1976; Joshi, 1978; Wilde, 1979; Semon, London Univ., 1980. Pres., British Assoc. of Otolaryngologists; FRSocMed (Pres., Sect. of Laryngology, 1982–83). Hon. FRCSI 1982; Hon. Fellow: Irish Otolaryngol Assoc.; Assoc. of Otolaryngologists of India; Polish Otolaryngological Assoc. *Publications:* (jtly) Short Textbook: Ear, Nose and Throat, 1970, 2nd edn 1974 (trans. Italian, Portuguese, Spanish); (jtly) Ear, Nose and Throat Surgery and Nursing, 1977; contribs to learned jls. *Recreations:* cabinet making, painting, engraving, reading, theatre. *Address:* Wardens Post, Moor Lane, South Newington, near Banbury, Oxon OX15 4JQ. *T:* Banbury 720433.

PRAG, Derek; Member (C) Hertfordshire, European Parliament, since 1979; *b* 6 Aug. 1923; *s* of Abraham J. Prag and Edith Prag; *m* 1948, Dora Weiner; three *s*. *Educ:* Bolton Sch.; Emmanuel Coll., Univ. of Cambridge (MA; Cert. of Competent Knowledge in Russian). Served War, Intelligence Corps, England, Egypt, Italy, Austria, 1942–47. Economic journalist with Reuters News Agency in London, Brussels and Madrid, 1950–55; Information Service of High Authority, European Coal and Steel Community, 1955–59; Head of Division, Jt Information Service of European Communities, 1959–65; Director, London Information Office of European Communities, 1965–73; ran own consultancy company on relations with EEC, 1973–79. Mem., Institutional Cttee, 1979– (Europ. Democratic Gp spokesman, 1982–84); Political spokesman for European Democratic (Cons.) Group, 1984–; Chm., European Parlt All-Party Disablement Gp, 1980–. Associate Mem., RIIA, 1973–. Hon. Dir, EEC Commn, 1974. Silver Medal of European Merit, Luxembourg, 1974. *Publications:* Businessman's Guide to the Common Market, 1973; various reports on Europe's internat. role, and booklets and articles on European integration. *Recreations:* reading, theatre, music, walking, swimming, gardening. *Address:* The Euro-centre, Maynard House, The Common, Hatfield, Herts AL10 0NF. *Clubs:* Carlton, English-Speaking Union, Europe House; St Anne's (Brussels).

PRAGNELL, Anthony William, CBE 1982 (OBE 1960); DFC 1944; Deputy Director-General, Independent Broadcasting Authority (formerly Independent Television Authority), 1961–83; Director, Channel Four Television, since 1983; *b* 15 Feb. 1921; *s* of William Hendley Pragnell and Silvia Pragnell; *m* 1955, Teresa Mary, *d* of Leo and Anne Monaghan, Maidstone; one *s* one *d*. *Educ:* Cardinal Vaughan Sch., London. Asst Examiner, Estate Duty Office, 1939. Joined RAF as aircrew cadet, 1942; Navigator, Bomber Command, one tour of ops with 166 Squadron; second tour with 109 Squadron (Pathfinder Force), 1943–46. Examiner, Estate Duty Office, 1946. LLB London Univ., 1949. Asst Principal, General Post Office, 1950; Asst Secretary, ITA, 1954; Secretary, ITA, 1955. Vis. Fellow, European Inst. for the Media, Univ. of Manchester, 1983. Fellow, Royal Television Soc., 1980. *Publication:* Television in Europe: quality and values in a time of change, 1985. *Recreations:* reading, music. *Address:* Ashley, Grassy Lane, Sevenoaks, Kent. *T:* Sevenoaks 451463. *Club:* Royal Air Force.

PRAIN, Alexander Moncur, CBE 1964; Sheriff: of Perth and Angus at Perth, 1946–71; of Lanarkshire at Airdrie, 1943–46; *b* Longforgan, Perthshire, 19 Feb. 1908; 2nd *s* of A. M. Prain, JP, and Mary Stuart Whytock; *m* 1936, Florence Margaret Robertson; one *s*. *Educ:* Merchiston Castle; Edinburgh Academy; Edinburgh Univ. Called to Scottish Bar, 1932; Army, 1940–43, Major, RAC. *Recreations:* fishing, reading. *Address:* Castellar, Crieff, Perthshire.

PRAIN, Sir Ronald (Lindsay), Kt 1956; OBE 1946; Chief Executive, 1943–68, Chairman, 1950–72, RST international group of companies; Director, Pan-Holding SA, and other companies; *b* Iquiqui, Chile, 3 Sept. 1907; *s* of Arthur Lindsay Prain and Amy Prain (*née* Watson); *m* 1938, Esther Pansy, *d* of late Norman Brownrigg, Haslemere; two *s*. *Educ:* Cheltenham Coll. Controller (Ministry of Supply): Diamond Die and Tool Control, 1940–45; Quartz Crystal Control, 1943–45. First Chairman: Agricultural Research Council of Rhodesia & Nyasaland, 1959–63; Merchant Bank of Central Africa Ltd, 1956–66; Merchant Bank (Zambia) Ltd, 1966–72; Director: Metal Market & Exchange Co. Ltd, 1943–65; San Francisco Mines of Mexico Ltd, 1944–68; Selection Trust Ltd, 1944–78; Internat. Nickel Co. of Canada Ltd, 1951–72; Wankie Colliery Co. Ltd, 1953–63; Minerals Separation Ltd, 1962–78; Foseco Minsep Ltd, 1969–80; Barclays Bank International, 1971–77. Chairman, Council of Commonwealth Mining & Metallurgical Institutions, 1961–74; President, British Overseas Mining Assoc., 1952; President, Inst. of Metals, 1960–61; Hon. Pres., Copper Develt Assoc.; Hon. Member: Inst. of Metals; Amer. Inst. of Min. & Metall. Engrs. Trustee, Inst. for Archaeo-Metallurgical Studies; Pres. Council, Cheltenham College, 1972–80. ANKH Award, Copper Club, New York, 1964; Gold Medal, 1968, and Hon. Fellow, Instn of Mining and Metallurgy; Platinum Medal, Inst. of Metals, 1969. *Publications:* Selected Papers (4 Vols); Copper: the anatomy of an industry, 1975 (Japanese trans. 1976; Spanish trans. 1980); Reflections on an Era, 1981. *Recreations:* cricket, real tennis, travel. *Address:* Waverley, St George's Hill, Weybridge, Surrey KT13 0QJ. *T:* Weybridge 42776. *Clubs:* White's, MCC.

PRAIS, Prof. Sigbert Jon, FBA 1985; Senior Research Fellow, National Institute of Economic and Social Research, London, since 1970; Visiting Professor of Economics, City University, since 1975; *b* 19 Dec. 1928; *s* of Samuel and Bertha Prais; *m* 1971, Vivien Hennessy, LLM, solicitor; one *s* three *d*. *Educ:* King Edward's School, Birmingham; Univ. of Birmingham (MCom); Univ. of Cambridge (PhD, ScD); Univ. of Chicago. Dept of Applied Economics, Cambridge, 1950–57; research officer, NIESR, 1953–59; UN Tech. Assistance Orgn, 1959–60; IMF Washington, 1960–61; Finance Dir, Elbief Co., 1961–70. Mem. Council, Royal Economic Soc., 1979–83. *Publications:* Analysis of Family Budgets (jtly), 1955, 2nd edn 1971; Evolution of Giant Firms in Britain, 1976, 2nd edn 1981; Productivity and Industrial Structure, 1981; articles in economic and statistical jls, esp. on influence of educn on economic progress. *Address:* 83 West Heath Road, NW3. *T:* 01–458 4428; (office) 01–222 7665.

PRANKERD, Thomas Arthur John, FRCP; Professor of Clinical Haematology, 1965–79 and Dean, 1972–77, University College Hospital Medical School; Hon. Consultant Physician: University College Hospital; Whittington Hospital; *b* 11 Sept. 1924; *s* of late H. A. Prankerd, Barrister-at-Law, and J. D. Shorthose; *m* 1950, Margaret Vera Harrison Cripps; two *s* (and one *s* one *d* decd). *Educ:* Charterhouse Sch.; St Bartholomew's Hospital Med. Sch. MD (London) Gold Medal 1949; FRCP 1962. Jnr med. appts, St Bart's and University Coll. Hosp., 1947–60. Major, RAMC, 1948–50. Univ. Travelling Fellow, USA, 1953–54; Consultant Physician, University Coll. Hosp., 1960–65. Goulstonian Lectr, RCP, 1963; Examr, RCP, and various univs. Vis. Prof., Univ. of Perth, WA, 1972. Mem., NE Thames RHA, 1976–79. Mem. Bd of Governors, UCH, 1972–74. *Publications:* The Red Cell, 1961; Haematology in Medical Practice, 1968; articles in med. jls. *Recreations:* fishing, gardening, music. *Address:* Milton Lake, Milton Abbas, Blandford, Dorset DT11 0BJ. *T:* Milton Abbas 880278.

PRASADA, Krishna, CIE 1943; JP; ICS retired; Director-General, Posts and Telegraphs, New Delhi, 1945–53; *b* 4 Aug. 1894; *s* of Pandit Het Ram, CIE; *m* 1911, Bishan Devi (*d* 1950); three *s*. *Educ:* Bareilly; New Coll., Oxford. Joined ICS 1921; Joint Magistrate and subsequently a District Magistrate in UP. Services borrowed by Government of India in 1934, when he was appointed as Postmaster-General. Led Government of India deputations to International Tele-communications Conference, Cairo, 1938, Buenos Aires, 1952, and to International Postal Congress, Paris, 1947. Retired, 1954. Director, Rotary International, 1961–63. *Recreation:* tennis, Oxford Tennis Blue (1921) and played for India in the Davis Cup in 1927 and 1932. Won All India Tennis Championships. *Address:* D/152, East of Kailash, New Delhi 24, 65 India.

PRASHAR, Usha Kumari, (Mrs V. K. Sharma); Director, National Council for Voluntary Organisations, since 1986; *b* 29 June 1948; *d* of Nauhria Lal Prashar and Durga Devi Prashar; *m* 1973, Vijay Kumar Sharma. *Educ:* Duchess of Gloucester Sch., Nairobi; Wakefield Girls' High Sch. (Head Girl, 1966–67); Univ. of Leeds (BA Hons Pol. Studies); Univ. of Glasgow (postgrad. Dip. Social Admin). Race Relations Bd, 1971–75; Asst Dir, Runnymede Trust, 1976–77, Dir, 1977–84; Res. Fellow, PSI, 1984–86. Member: Arts Council of GB, 1979–81; Study Commn on the Family, 1980–83; Social Security Adv. Cttee, 1980–83; Exec. Cttee, Child Poverty Action Gp, 1984–85; GLAA, 1984–; London Food Commn, 1984–. Trustee, Thames Help Trust. *Publications: contributed to:* Britain's Black Population, 1980; The System: a study of Lambeth Borough Council's race relations unit, 1981; Scarman and After, 1984; Sickle Cell Anaemia, Who Cares? a survey of screening, counselling, training and educational facilities in England, 1985; Routes or Road Blocks, a study of consultation arrangements between local authorities and local communities, 1985. *Recreations:* painting, reading, country walks, squash, music. *Address:* National Council for Vountary Organisations, 26 Bedford Square, WC1.

PRATLEY, Alan Sawyer; Director of Administration, Commission of the European Communities, since 1981; *b* 25 Nov. 1933; *s* of Frederick Pratley and Hannah Pratley (*née* Sawyer); *m* 1st, 1960, Dorothea Rohland (marr. diss. 1979); two *d*; 2nd, 1979, Josette Kairis; one *d*. *Educ:* Latymer Upper School; Sidney Sussex Coll., Cambridge. BA Modern Languages (German, Russian). Head, German Dept, Stratford Grammar Sch., West Ham, 1958–60; Asst Dir, Examinations, Civil Service Commn, 1960–68; Home Office, 1968–73; Commission of the European Communities: Head, Individual Rights Div., 1973–79; Dep. Chef de cabinet to Christopher Tugendhat, 1979–80; Adviser to Michael O'Kennedy, 1980–81. *Recreations:* squash, gardening. *Address:* Avenue de l'Abbaye d'Affligem 3, 1300 Wavre, Belgium. *T:* Wavre 22.66.06. *Club:* Travellers'.

PRATLEY, Clive William; Under Secretary, Lord Chancellor's Department, 1976–85; Circuit Administrator: Midland and Oxford Circuit, 1976–82; North-Eastern Circuit, 1982–85; *b* 23 Jan. 1929; *s* of late F. W. Pratley and late Minnie Pratley (*née* Hood); *m* 1962, Eva, *d* of Nils and Kerstin Kellgren, Stockholm; one *s* one *d*. *Educ:* RMA Sandhurst; and after retirement from Army, at Univs of Stockholm, 1961–62, and Hull, 1962–65 (LLB Hons). Commissioned into Royal Tank Regt, 1949; Adjt, 2nd Royal Tank Regt, 1959–61; retired from active list, 1961. Entered Administrative Class of Home Civil Service as Principal, 1966; Lord Chancellor's Department: Sen. Principal, 1971; Asst Sec., 1974. *Recreations:* horses, the countryside, badminton, lawn tennis, gardening, music. *Address:* The Old Chapel, Aldfield, near Ripon, North Yorkshire HG4 3BE. *Clubs:* Army and Navy; Durham County (Durham).

PRATLEY, David Illingworth; Arts consultant; *b* 24 Dec. 1948; *s* of Arthur George Pratley and Olive Constance Illingworth. *Educ:* Westminster Abbey Choir Sch.; Westminster Sch.; Univ. of Bristol (LLB). PRO, Thorndike Theatre, Leatherhead, 1970–71; Gen. Asst, Queen's Univ. Festival, Belfast, 1971–73; Dep. Dir, Merseyside Arts Assoc., 1973–76; Dir, Greater London Arts Assoc., 1976–81; Regl Dir, Arts Council of GB, 1981–86. *Publication:* (co-ed) Culture for All, 1981. *Recreations:* music, theatre, art, countryside, travel. *Address:* 13 St James Street, W6 9RW. *Club:* Athenæum.

PRATT, family name of **Marquess Camden.**

PRATT, Anthony Malcolm G.; *see* Galliers-Pratt.

PRATT, (Arthur) Geoffrey, CBE 1981; Hon. Secretary, Institution of Gas Engineers, since 1982; *b* 19 Aug. 1922; *s* of William Pratt, Willington, Co. Durham; *m* 1946, Ethel Luck; two *s* twin *d*. *Educ:* King James I Grammar Sch., Bishop Auckland. CEng, FIGasE. Joined E Mids Gas Bd, 1951: Chief Engr, 1964; Dir of Engrg, 1967; Dep. Chm., S Eastern Gas Bd, 1970–72; Chm., SE Gas Region, 1972–81; part-time Mem., British Gas Corp., 1981–82. Chm., Metrogas Building Soc., 1977–. Pres., IGasE, 1974–75. *Recreations:* golf, squash, swimming, bridge. *Address:* c/o Institution of Gas Engineers, 17 Grosvenor Crescent, SW1.

PRATT, His Honour Hugh MacDonald; a Circuit Judge (formerly County Court Judge) 1947–72; *b* 15 Sept. 1900; *o c* of late Sir John William Pratt; *m* 1928, Ingeborg, *e d* of late Consul Johannes Sundför, MBE, Haugesund, Norway; one *s*. *Educ:* Hillhead High Sch., Glasgow; Aske's Haberdashers' Sch., London; Balliol Coll., Oxford. Called to Bar, Inner Temple, 1924; practised London and Western Circuit; member General Council of the Bar; President, Hardwicke Society; contested Drake Div. of Plymouth, 1929; Dep. President War Damage (Valuation Appeals) Panel, 1946. Chairman, Devon Quarter Sessions, 1958–64. Hon. LLD Exeter, 1972. *Publications:* English trans. of Professor Axel Möller's International Law (Vol. I, 1931, Vol. II, 1935); trans. of various articles in Norwegian, Danish and Swedish on commercial and international law. *Recreations:* reading, gardening. *Address:* New Pond Farm, New Pond Road, Compton, Surrey GU3 1HY. *T:* Godalming 6049.

PRATT, Very Rev. John Francis, MA; Provost Emeritus, since 1978; *s* of late Rev. J. W. J. Pratt, Churchill, Somerset; *m* 1939, Norah Elizabeth (*d* 1981), *y d* of late F. W. Corfield, Sandford, Somerset; two *d*. *Educ:* Keble Coll., Oxford; Wells Theological Coll. Priest, 1937. CF, 1st KSLI, 1941–46; (despatches, 1943); SCF, Cyprus, 1946. Vicar of: Rastrick,

1946–49; Wendover, 1949–59; Reading S Mary's (with All Saints, S Saviour's, S Mark's and S Matthew's), 1959–61; Vicar of Chilton with Dorton, 1961–70; Archdeacon of Buckingham, 1961–70; Provost of Southwell, 1970–78; Priest-in-charge, Edingley with Halam, 1975–78. RD of Wendover, 1955–59; Chaplain to High Sheriff of Bucks, 1956, 1962; Examining Chaplain to Bishop of Southwell, 1971–78. *Address:* 42 Bickerton Road, Headington, Oxford OX3 7LS. *T:* Oxford 63060.

PRATT, Michael John; QC 1976; a Recorder of the Crown Court, since 1974; *b* 23 May 1933; *o s* of W. Brownlow Pratt; *m* 1960, Elizabeth Jean Hendry; two *s* three *d. Educ:* West House Sch., Edgbaston; Malvern Coll. LLB (Birmingham). Army service, 2nd Lieut, 3rd Carabiniers (Prince of Wales's Dragoon Guards); Staff Captain. Called to the Bar, Middle Temple, 1954, Bencher, 1986. *Recreations:* music, theatre, sport generally. *Address:* 9 Moorland Road, Edgbaston, Birmingham B16 9JP. *T:* 021–454 1071. *Clubs:* Cavalry and Guards; Birmingham Conservative.

PRATT, Prof. Peter Lynn, PhD; FInstP; CEng, FIM; Professor of Crystal Physics, Imperial College of Science and Technology, London University, since 1963; *b* 10 March 1927; *s* of late William Lynn Pratt and Margery Florence Pratt; *m* 1951, Lydia Elizabeth Anne, *y d* of late G. A. Lyon Hatton, Edgbaston; two *s. Educ:* Cheltenham Coll.; Birmingham Univ. (BSc 1948); Pembroke Coll., Cambridge (PhD 1952). FInstP 1967; FIM 1980. Res. Fellow, AERE, 1951–53; Lectr, Univ. of Birmingham, 1953–58; Reader in Physical Metallurgy, Imperial Coll., 1959–63; Dean, Royal Sch. of Mines, and Mem. Governing Body, Imperial Coll., 1977–80; Dir of Continuing Educn, Imperial Coll., 1981–. Vis. Scientist, N Amer. Aviation Centre, 1963; Vis. Prof., Univ. of Stanford, 1964. Consultant at various times to: AERE; Commonwealth Trans-Antarctic Expedn; Commonwealth Develt Corp.; indust. firms and publishing houses. Chm., Adv. Cttee on Trng and Qualification of Patent Agents, 1972–73. Pres., RSM Assoc., 1984–85. Sir George Beilby Gold Medal and Prize, Institute of Metals, 1964. *Publications:* (ed) Fracture, 1969; technical appendix to Longbow (by Robert Hardy), 1976; articles on materials science and engrg in learned jls. *Recreations:* toxophily (esp. the English longbow), sailing, music, motor racing. *Address:* 20 Westfield Road, Beaconsfield, Bucks HP9 1EF. *T:* Beaconsfield 3392.

PRAWER, Prof. Siegbert Salomon, FBA 1981; Taylor Professor of German Language and Literature, University of Oxford, 1969–86, now Professor Emeritus; Fellow of The Queen's College, Oxford, since 1969; *b* 15 Feb. 1925; *s* of Marcus and Eleonora Prawer; *m* 1949, Helga Alice (*née* Schaefer); one *s* two *d* (and one *s* decd). *Educ:* King Henry VIII Sch., Coventry; Jesus Coll. (Schol.) and Christ's Coll., Cambridge. Charles Oldham Shakespeare Scholar, 1945, MA 1950, LittD 1962, Cantab; PhD Birmingham, 1953; MA 1969, DLitt 1969, Oxon. Adelaide Stoll Res. Student, Christ's Coll., Cambridge, 1947–48; Asst Lecturer, Lecturer, Sen. Lecturer, University of Birmingham, 1948–63; Prof. of German, Westfield Coll., London Univ., 1964–69. Visiting Professor: City Coll., NY, 1956–57; University of Chicago, 1963–64; Harvard Univ., 1968; Hamburg Univ., 1969; Univ. of Calif, Irvine, 1975; Otago Univ., 1976; Pittsburgh Univ., 1977; Visiting Fellow: Knox Coll., Dunedin, 1976; Humanities Research Centre, ANU, 1980; Tauber Inst., Brandeis Univ., 1981–82. Hon. Director, London Univ. Inst. of Germanic Studies, 1966–68. Pres., British Comp. Lit. Assoc., 1984–. Hon. Dr. phil. Cologne, 1984. Goethe Medal, 1973; Friedrich Gundolf Prize, 1986. Co-editor: Oxford German Studies, 1971–75; Anglica Germanica, 1973–79. *Publications:* German Lyric Poetry, 1952; Mörike und seine Leser, 1960; Heine's Buch der Lieder: A Critical Study, 1960; Heine: The Tragic Satirist, 1962; The Penguin Book of Lieder, 1964; The Uncanny in Literature (inaug. lect.), 1965; (ed, with R. H. Thomas and L. W. Forster) Essays in German Language, Culture and Society, 1969; (ed) The Romantic Period in Germany, 1970; Heine's Shakespeare, a Study in Contexts (inaug. lect.), 1970; (ed) Seventeen Modern German Poets, 1971; Comparative Literary Studies: an Introduction, 1973; Karl Marx and World Literature, 1976 (Isaac Deutscher Meml Prize, 1977); Caligari's Children: the film as tale of terror, 1980; Heine's Jewish Comedy: a study of his portraits of Jews and Judaism, 1983; A. N. Stencl: poet of Whitechapel (Stencl Meml Lect.), 1984; Coalsmoke and Englishmen (Bithell Meml Lecture), 1984; Frankenstein's Island: England and the English in the writings of Heinrich Heine, 1986; articles on German, English and comparative literature in many specialist periodicals and symposia. *Recreation:* portrait drawing. *Address:* 9 Hawkeswell Gardens, Oxford OX2 7EX
     See also Mrs R. P. Jhabvala.

PRAWER JHABVALA, Mrs Ruth; *see* Jhabvala.

PREBBLE, David Lawrence; Master, Queen's Bench Division, Supreme Court of Justice, since 1981; *b* 21 Aug. 1932; *s* of late George Wilson Prebble and of Margaret Jessie Prebble (*née* Cuthbertson); *m* 1959, Fiona W. Melville; three *d. Educ:* Cranleigh; Christ Church, Oxford. MA. National Service, 1950–52; commissioned in 3rd Carabiniers (Prince of Wales's Dragoon Guards); served TA, 1952–61, City of London Yeomanry (Rough Riders) TA (Captain). Called to the Bar, Middle Temple, 1957; practised at Bar, 1957–81. *Recreations:* reading; operetta; wine and food; hounds and dogs; friends' horses; own wife and family; (not necessarily in foregoing order as to precedence). *Address:* 16 Wool Road, Wimbledon, SW20. *T:* 01–946 1804. *Club:* Royal Wimbledon Golf.

PREBBLE, John Edward Curtis, FRSL; Writer; *b* 23 June 1915; *o s* of late John William Prebble, Petty Officer, RN, and Florence (*née* Wood); *m* 1936, Betty, *d* of late Ernest Golby; two *s* one *d. Educ:* Sutherland Public Sch., Saskatchewan; Latymer Upper Sch., London. Entered journalism, 1934; in ranks with RA, 1940–45; Sergeant-reporter with No 1 British Army Newspaper Unit (Hamburg), 1945–46; reporter, columnist and feature-writer for British newspapers and magazines, 1946–60; novelist, historian, film-writer and author of many plays and dramatised documentaries for radio and TV. *Publications: novels:* Where the Sea Breaks, 1944; The Edge of Darkness, 1948; Age Without Pity, 1950; The Mather Story, 1954; The Brute Streets, 1954; The Buffalo Soldiers, 1959; *short stories:* My Great Aunt Appearing Day, 1958; Spanish Stirrup, 1972; *biography:* (with J. A. Jordan) Mongaso, 1956; *history:* The High Girders, 1956; Culloden, 1961; The Highland Clearances, 1963; Glencoe, 1966; The Darien Disaster, 1968; The Lion in the North, 1971; Mutiny: Highland Regiments in Revolt, 1975; John Prebble's Scotland, 1984. *Recreation:* serendipity. *Address:* Hill View, The Glade, Kingswood, Surrey. *T:* Mogador 832142.

PRELOG, Prof. Dr Vladimir; Professor of Organic Chemistry, Swiss Federal Institute of Technology, 1950–76; *b* 23 July 1906; *m* 1933, Kamila Vitek; one *s. Educ:* Inst. of Technology, Prague. Chemist, Prague, 1929–34; Lecturer and Professor, University of Zagreb, 1935–41. Privatdozent, Swiss Federal Inst. of Technology, Zürich, 1941; Associate Professor, 1947. Mem. Bd, CIBA-GEIGY Ltd, Basel. Vis. Prof. of Chemistry, Univ. of Cambridge, 1974. Mem. Leopoldina, Halle/Saale, 1963; Hon. Member: American Acad. of Arts and Sciences, 1960; Chem. Society, 1960; Nat. Acad. of Sciences, Washington, 1961; Royal Irish Acad., Dublin, 1971; Foreign Member: Royal Society, 1962; Acad. of Sciences, USSR, 1966; Acad. dei Lincei, Roma 1965; Istituto Lombardo, Milano, 1964; Royal Danish Acad. of Sciences, 1971; Amer. Philosophical Soc. Philadelphia, 1976; Acad. Sciences, Paris, 1981; Mem., Papal Acad. of Science, 1986–. Dr *hc* Universities of: Zagreb,

1954; Liverpool, 1963; Paris, 1963; Bruxelles, 1969. Hon. DSc: Cambridge, 1969; Manchester, 1977; Inst. Quimico Sarria, Barcelona, 1978. Davy Medal, Royal Society, 1967; A. W. Hofmann Medal, Gesell. deutscher Chem., 1967; Marcel Benoist Prize, 1965; Roger Adams Award, 1969; (jtly) Nobel Prize for Chemistry, 1975. Order of Rising Sun, Japan; Order of Yugoslav Star. *Publications:* numerous scientific papers, mainly in Helvetica chimica acta. *Address:* (office) Laboratorium für organische Chemie, ETH-Zentrum, Universitätstrasse 16, CH-8092 Zürich, Switzerland; (home) Bellariastr. 33, 8002 Zürich. *T:* CH 01 202 17 81.

PREMADASA, Ranasinghe; Member of Parliament of Sri Lanka, since 1960; Prime Minister of Sri Lanka, since 1978; also Minister of Local Government, Housing and Construction and Leader of the National State Assembly, since 1977; *b* 23 June 1924; *m* 1964, Hema Wickrematunge; one *s* one *d. Educ:* Lorenz Coll.; Colombo; St Joseph's Coll., Colombo. Member, Colombo Municipal Council, 1950; Dep. Mayor of Colombo, 1955. Joined United Nat. Party and contested Ruvanwella, 1956; MHR(Colombo): 3rd Mem., 1960; 2nd Mem., 1965; 1st Mem. 1970; Nat. State Assembly (Colombo): 1st Mem., 1977–. Chief Whip, Opp. Parly Gp, in House of Reps, 1970; Dep. Leader, United Nat. Party, 1976. Has visited, as state guest or member of delegns: UK, USA, Australia, China, USSR, Japan, Singapore, Hong Kong, and several European countries, 1955–. *Publications:* 10 books in Sinhalese language. *Address:* Prime Minister's Office, Colombo, Sri Lanka. *T:* 27447.

PRENDERGAST, (Christopher) Anthony, CBE 1981; Chairman, Dolphin Square Trust Ltd, since 1967; Director General, Location of Industry Bureau Ltd, since 1983; an Underwriting Member of Lloyd's; *b* 4 May 1931; *s* of Maurice Prendergast, AINA, and Winifred Mary Prendergast, Falmouth; *m* 1959, Simone Ruth Laski, OBE 1981, CStJ, JP, DL; one *s. Educ:* Falmouth Grammar School. Westminster City Council: Mem., 1959–; Chairman: Housing Cttee, 1962–65; Health Cttee, 1965–68; Town Planning Cttee, 1972–75, 1976–78; Gen. Purposes Cttee, 1978–80; Management Services, 1981–83; Licensing Sub Cttee, 1983–; Lord Mayor and Dep. High Steward of Westminster, 1968–69; High Sheriff of Greater London, 1980. Additional Mem., GLC (Covent Garden Cttee), 1971–75; Member: London Boroughs Trng Cttee, 1965–68; Docklands Develt Cttee, 1974; AMA Cttee, 1976–; Nat Jt Council (Manual Workers), 1978–82, 1983–; LEB, 1983–; Conf. of Regl and Local Auths of Europe, 1983–. Chairman: Location of Offices Bureau, 1971–79; LACSAB, 1983–; Joint Nat. Cttee for Chief Execs of Local Authorities, 1984–, for Chief Officers of Local Authorities, 1984–; Gen. Purposes Cttee, London Boroughs Assoc., 1986–. Governor, Westminster Sch., 1974–. Master, Pattenmakers' Co., 1983–84. FRSA 1984. *Recreations:* fishing, shooting, photography. *Address:* 52 Warwick Square, SW1V 2AJ. *T:* 01–821 7653. *Clubs:* Carlton, Brooks's, Irish; MCC.

PRENDERGAST, Sir John (Vincent), KBE 1977 (CBE 1960); CMG 1968; GM 1955; CPM 1955; QPM 1963; retired; Deputy Commissioner and Director of Operations, Independent Commission Against Corruption, Hong Kong, 1973–77; *b* 11 Feb. 1912; *y s* of late John and Margaret Prendergast; *m* 1943, Enid Sonia, *yr d* of Percy Speed; one *s* one *d. Educ:* in Ireland; London Univ. (External). Local Government, London, 1930–39. War Service, 1939–46 (Major). Asst District Comr, Palestine Administration, 1946–47; Colonial Police Service, Palestine and Gold Coast, 1947–52; seconded Army, Canal Zone, on special duties, 1952–53; Colonial Police Service, Kenya, 1953–58 (Director of Intelligence and Security, 1955–58); Chief of Intelligence, Cyprus, 1958–60; Director, Special Branch, Hong Kong (retired as Dep. Comr of Police), 1960–66. Director of Intelligence, Aden, 1966–67. *Recreations:* racing, collecting first editions. *Address:* 20 Westbourne Terrace, W2 3UP. *T:* 01–262 9514. *Clubs:* East India; Hong Kong, Royal Hong Kong Jockey (Hong Kong).

PRENDERGAST, (Walter) Kieran; HM Diplomatic Service; Head of South African Department, Foreign and Commonwealth Office, since 1986; *b* 2 July 1942; *s* of Lt-Comdr J. H. Prendergast and Mai Hennessy; *m* 1967, Joan Reynolds; two *s* two *d. Educ:* St Patrick's College, Strathfield, Sydney, NSW; Salesian College, Chertsey; St Edmund Hall, Oxford. Turkish language student Istanbul, 1964; Ankara, 1965; FO (later FCO), 1967; 2nd Sec. Nicosia, 1969; Civil Service Coll., 1972; 1st Sec. FCO, 1972; The Hague, 1973; Asst Private Sec. to Foreign and Commonwealth Sec. (Rt Hon. Anthony Crosland, Rt Hon. Dr David Owen), 1976; UK Mission to UN, NY, 1979 (detached for duty Jan.-March 1980 at Govt House, Salisbury); Counsellor, Tel Aviv, 1982. Rhodesia Medal, 1980; Zimbabwe Independence Medal, 1980. *Recreations:* family, walking, reading, sport, wine. *Address:* c/o Foreign and Commonwealth Office, SW1A 2AH.

PRENTICE, (Hubert Archibald) John, CEng; FInstP; consultant on manufacturing and management strategies to several UK and USA companies; *b* 5 Feb. 1920; *s* of Charles Herbert Prentice and Rose Prentice; *m* 1947, Sylvia Doreen Elias; one *s. Educ:* Woolwich Polytechnic, London; Salford Univ. (BSc, MSc). CEng; MRAeS 1962; FInstP 1967. Min. of Supply, 1939–56; R&D posts, res. estabts and prodn, MoD, 1956–60; Space Dept, RAE, Min. of Aviation, 1960–67; Head, Road User Characteristics Res., 1967–70, and Head, Driver Aids and Abilities Res., 1970–72, MoT; Head, Road User Dynamics Res., DoE, 1972–75; Counsellor (Sci. and Technol.), British Embassy, Tokyo, 1975–80. *Recreations:* walking, climbing. *Address:* 5 Foxhill Crescent, Camberley, Surrey GU15 1PR. *T:* Camberley 66373.

PRENTICE, Rt. Hon. Reginald Ernest; PC; JP; MP (C) Daventry, since 1979 (MP (Lab) East Ham North, May 1957–1974, Newham North East, 1974–Oct. 1977, MP (C) Newham North East, Oct. 1977–1979); *b* 16 July 1923; *s* of Ernest George and Elizabeth Prentice; *m* 1948, Joan Godwin; one *d. Educ:* Whitgift Sch.; London School of Economics. Temporary Civil Servant, 1940–42; RA, 1942–46; commissioned 1943; served in Italy and Austria, 1944–46. Student at LSE, 1946–49. BSc (Econ). Member staff of Transport and General Workers' Union, Asst to Legal Secretary; in charge of Union's Advice and Service Bureau, 1950–57; Minister of State, Department of Education and Science, 1964–66; Minister of Public Building and Works, 1966–67; Minister of Overseas Develt, 1967–69; Opposition Spokesman on Employment, 1972–74; Sec. of State for Educn and Science, 1974–75; Minister for Overseas Develt, 1975–76; Minister of State (Minister for Social Security), DHSS, 1979–81. Alderman, GLC, 1970–71. JP County Borough of Croydon, 1961. *Publications:* (jt) Social Welfare and the Citizen, 1957; Right Turn, 1978. *Recreations:* walking, golf. *Address:* Bridle Cottage, Ballards Farm Road, Croydon CR0 5RL; St Hilda's Cottage, The Green, Creaton, Northants. *Club:* Addington Palace Golf.

PRENTICE, Thomas, MC 1945; Chairman, Harrisons & Crosfield plc, since 1977; *b* 14 Oct. 1919; *s* of Alexander and Jean Young Prentice; *m* 1949, Peggy Ann Lloyd; two *s* two *d. Educ:* McLaren High Sch., Callander, Perthshire. Served Army, 1939–46. Harrisons & Crosfield (Sabah) Sdn. Bhd., Malaysia, 1947–67; Harrisons & Crosfield plc, 1967–. *Recreations:* golf, gardening. *Address:* Harrisons & Crosfield plc, 1/4 Great Tower Street, EC3. *Club:* East India, Devonshire, Sports and Public Schools.

PRENTICE, Hon. Sir William (Thomas), Kt 1977; MBE 1945; Senior Member, Administrative Appeals Tribunal, Australia, since 1981; *b* 1 June 1919; *s* of Claud Stanley and Pauline Prentice; *m* 1946, Mary Elizabeth, *d* of F. B. Dignam; three *s* one *d. Educ:* St

Joseph's College, Hunters Hill; Sydney Univ. (BA, LLB). AIF, Middle East and New Guinea, 2–33 Inf. Bn and Staff Captain 25 Aust. Inf. Bde, Owen Stanleys and Lae Ramu campaigns; Staff Course, Duntroon, 1944; Staff Captain, 7 Aust. Inf. Bde, Bougainville campaign, 1944–45. Resumed law studies, 1946; admitted Bar, NSW, 1947; Judge, Supreme Court, PNG, 1970; Senior Puisne Judge, 1975; Deputy Chief Justice on independence, PNG, 1975, Chief Justice 1978–80. *Recreations:* bush walking, swimming, reading. *Address:* 16 Olympia Road, Naremburn, NSW 2065, Australia. *Clubs:* Tattersall's, NSW Leagues, Cricketers' (Sydney).

PRENTICE, Dame Winifred (Eva), DBE 1977 (OBE 1972); SRN; President, Royal College of Nursing, 1972–76; *b* 2 Dec. 1910; *d* of Percy John Prentice and Anna Eva Prentice. *Educ:* Northgate Sch. for Girls, Ipswich; E Suffolk and Ipswich Hosp. (SRN); W Mddx Hosp. (SCM Pt I); Queen Elizabeth Coll., London Univ. (RNT); Dip. in Nursing, London Univ. Ward Sister: E Suffolk and Ipswich Hosp., 1936–39; Essex County Hosp., 1941–43; Nurse Tutor, King's Lynn Hosp., 1944–46; Principal Tutor, Stracathro Hosp., Brechin, Angus, 1947–61, Matron, 1961–72. *Publications:* articles in Nursing Times and Nursing Mirror. *Recreations:* music, amateur dramatics, gardening. *Address:* Marleish, 4 Duke Street, Brechin, Angus. *T:* Brechin 2606. *Club:* New Cavendish.

PRESCOTT, James Arthur, CBE 1947; DSc; FRS 1951; FAA; retired; Director, Waite Agricultural Research Institute, 1938–55; Professor of Agricultural Chemistry, University of Adelaide, 1924–55, Emeritus Professor since 1956; *b* 7 Oct. 1890; *e s* of Joseph Arthur Prescott, Bolton, Lancs; *m* 1915, Elsie Mason, Accrington, Lancs; one *s*. *Educ:* Ecole Littré, Lille; Accrington Grammar Sch.; Manchester Univ.; Leipzig Univ. Rothamsted Experimental Station; Chief Chemist and Superintendent of Field Experiments, Bahtim Experimental Station, Sultanic Agricultural Society of Egypt, 1916–24; Chief, Division of Soils, Commonwealth Council for Scientific and Industrial Research, 1929–47. Mem. Council and Scientific Adviser, Australian Wine Research Inst., 1954–69. Hon. DAgSc Melbourne, 1956. Hon. Member: Internat. Society of Soil Science, 1964; All-Union (Soviet) Soc. of Soil Science, 1977. (Foundn) FAA 1954. *Publications:* various scientific, chiefly on soils, climatology and principles of crop production. *Address:* 6 Kinross Lodge, 2 Netherby Avenue, Netherby, SA 5062, Australia.

PRESCOTT, Prof. John Herbert Dudley, PhD; FIBiol; Director of Grassland and Animal Production Research, Agricultural and Food Research Council, since 1986; *b* 21 Feb. 1937; *s* of Herbert Prescott and Edith Vera Prescott; *m* 1960, Diana Margaret Mullock; two *s* two *d*. *Educ:* Haileybury; Univ. of Nottingham (BSc (Agric), PhD). FIBiol 1983. Lectr in Animal Prodn, Univ. of Newcastle upon Tyne, 1963–72; Animal Prodn Officer in Argentina, FAO, UN, 1972–74; Head of Animal Prodn Advisory and Develt, E of Scotland Coll. of Agric., 1974–78; Prof. of Animal Prodn, 1978–84, and Head of Animal Div., 1978–84, Sch. of Agric., Univ. of Edinburgh; Dir, Grassland, later Animal and Grassland, Res. Inst., 1984–86. Vis. Prof., Univ. of Reading, 1985–. *Publications:* scientific papers in Animal Prodn and Agricultural Science; technical articles. *Recreations:* farming, walking, wildlife, the countryside. *Address:* Institute of Grassland and Animal Production Research, Hurley, Maidenhead, Berks SL6 5LR. *T:* Littlewick Green 3631.

PRESCOTT, John Leslie; MP (Lab) Hull East, since 1983 (Kingston upon Hull (East), 1970–83); *b* 31 May 1938; *s* of John Herbert Prescott, JP, and Phyllis Prescott; *m* 1961, Pauline Tilston; two *s*. *Educ:* Ellesmere Port Secondary Modern Sch.; WEA; correspondence courses; Ruskin Coll., Oxford (DipEcon/Pol Oxon); Hull Univ. (BSc Econ). Trainee Chef, 1953–55; Steward, Passenger Lines, Merchant Navy, 1955–63; Ruskin Coll., Oxford, 1963–65; Recruitment Officer, General and Municipal Workers Union (temp.), 1965; Hull Univ., 1965–68. Contested (Lab) Southport, 1966; Full-time Official, National Union of Seamen, 1968–70. Member: Select Cttee Nationalized Industries, 1973–79; Council of Europe, 1972–75; European Parlt, 1975–79 (Leader, Labour Party Delegn, 1976–79); PPS to Sec. of State for Trade, 1974–76; opposition spokesman on Transport, 1979–81; opposition front bench spokesman on Regional Affairs and Devolution, 1981–83, on Transport, 1983–84, on Employment, 1984–; Mem., Shadow Cabinet, 1983–. *Publication:* Not Wanted on Voyage, 1966. *Address:* 365 Saltshouse Road, Sutton-on-Hull, North Humberside.

PRESCOTT, Sir Mark, 3rd Bt, *cr* 1938, of Godmanchester; Racehorse Trainer, in Newmarket; *b* 3 March 1948; *s* of late Major W. R. Stanley Prescott (MP for Darwen Div., 1943–51; 2nd *s* of Colonel Sir William Prescott, 1st Bt) and of Gwendolen (who *m* 2nd, 1952, Daniel Orme (*d* 1972)), *o c* of late Leonard Aldridge, CBE; *S* uncle, Sir Richard Stanley Prescott, 2nd Bt, 1965. *Educ:* Harrow. *Address:* Heath House, Moulton Road, Newmarket, Suffolk CB8 8DU. *T:* Newmarket 662117.

PRESCOTT, Brig. Peter George Addington, MC 1944; Secretary, National Rifle Association, since 1980; *b* 22 Sept. 1924; *s* of Col and Mrs John Prescott; *m* 1953, June Marian Louise Wendell; one *s* one *d*. *Educ:* Eton Coll.; Staff Coll. (psc 1957); Royal Coll. of Defence Studies (rcds 1973). Commnd Grenadier Guards, 1943; 2nd Armoured Bn Gren. Gds, 1944–45; comd 2nd Bn Gren. Gds, 1966–69; Comdr 51st Inf. Bde, 1970–72; Dep. Comdr NE Dist, 1974–77; Dep. Dir of Army Trng, 1977–79, retd. Chevalier, Royal Order of the Sword, Sweden, 1954. *Recreations:* sailing, painting, gardening. *Address:* The Bourne, Church Lane, Holybourne, Alton, Hants.

PRESCOTT, Peter John; British Council Representative, France, and Cultural Counsellor, British Embassy, Paris, since 1984; *b* 6 April 1936; *s* of Wentworth James and Ellen Marie Prescott; *m* 1971, Gillian Eileen Lowe. *Educ:* Windsor Grammar School; Pembroke College, Oxford (MA). Joined British Council, 1963; Asst Cultural Attaché, Egypt, 1963–67; London, 1967–70; Sussex Univ., 1970–71; France, 1971–75; London, 1975–79; on secondment to Dept of Education and Science, 1979–81; Australia, 1981–84. *Recreations:* reading, music, walking, swimming. *Address:* British Council, 9 rue de Constantine, 75007 Paris, France. *T:* 45.55.95.95.

PRESCOTT, Westby William P.; *see* Percival-Prescott.

PRESLAND, John David; Executive Vice-Chairman, Port of London Authority, 1978–82; *b* 3 July 1930; *s* of Leslie and Winifred Presland; *m* 1969, Margaret Brewin. *Educ:* St Albans Sch.; London Sch. of Economics. BScEcon. FCA, IPFA, MBCS. Knox Cropper & Co., Chartered Accountants, 1950–58; Pfizer Ltd (various financial posts), 1958–64; Berk Ltd: Chief Accountant, 1964–67; Financial Controller, 1967–68; Dir and Financial Controller, 1968–71; Port of London Authority: Financial Controller, 1971–73; Asst Dir-Gen. (Finance), 1973–76; Exec. Dir (Finance), 1976–78. Freeman of City of London; Freeman of Company of Watermen and Lightermen of River Thames. *Recreations:* history, natural history, music. *Address:* c/o British Ports Association, Commonwealth House, 1–19 New Oxford Street, WC1A 1DZ. *Club:* Oriental.

PRESS, John Bryant, FRSL; author and poet; *b* 11 Jan. 1920; *s* of late Edward Kenneth Press and late Gladys (*née* Cooper); *m* 1947, Janet Crompton; one *s* one *d*. *Educ:* King Edward VI Sch., Norwich; Corpus Christi Coll., Cambridge, 1938–40 and 1945–46. Served War of 1939–45: RA, 1940–45. British Council, 1946–79: Athens, 1946–47; Salonika, 1947–50; Madras, 1950–51; Colombo, 1951–52; Birmingham, 1952–54; Cambridge, 1955–62; London, 1962–65; Paris, 1966–71 (also Asst Cultural Attaché, British Embassy); Regional Dir, Oxford, 1972–78; Literature Advr, London, 1978–79. Mem. Council, RSL, 1961–. Gave George Elliston Poetry Foundation Lectures at Univ. of Cincinnati, 1962; Vis. Prof., Univ. of Paris, 1981–82. *Publications:* The Fire and the Fountain, 1955; Uncertainties, 1956; (ed) Poetic Heritage, 1957; The Chequer'd Shade, 1958 (RSL Heinemann Award); Andrew Marvell, 1958; Guy Fawkes Night, 1959; Herrick, 1961; Rule and Energy, 1963; Louis MacNeice, 1964; (ed) Palgrave's Golden Treasury, Book V, 1964; A Map of Modern English Verse, 1969; The Lengthening Shadows, 1971; John Betjeman, 1974; Spring at St Clair, 1974; Aspects of Paris, (with illus by Gordon Bradshaw), 1975; (with Edward Lowbury and Michael Riviere) Troika, 1977; Poets of World War I, 1983; Poets of World War II, 1984; A Girl with Beehive Hair, 1986. Libretto, new version of Bluebeard's Castle, for Michael Powell's colour television film of Bartok's opera, 1963. *Recreations:* travel (especially in France), theatre, opera, concerts, cinema; architecture and visual arts; watching football and cricket. *Address:* 5 South Parade, Frome BA11 1EJ.

PRESSBURGER, Emeric; Author, Film Producer; *b* 5 Dec. 1902; one *d*. *Educ:* Universities of Prague and Stuttgart. Journalist in Hungary and Germany, author and writer of films in Berlin and Paris; came to England in 1935; formed jointly with Michael Powell, The Archers Film Producing Company, and Vega Productions Ltd, and made the following films: Spy in Black, 1938; 49th Parallel, 1940 (USA Academy Award 1942, under American title, The Original Story of The Invaders); One of our Aircraft is Missing, 1941; Colonel Blimp, 1942; I Know Where I'm Going, 1944; A Matter of Life and Death, 1945; Black Narcissus, 1946; The Red Shoes, 1947; Small Back Room, 1948; Gone to Earth, 1949; The Tales of Hoffmann, 1951; Oh Rosalinda!!, 1955; The Battle of the River Plate, 1956; Ill Met by Moonlight, 1956. Wrote, produced, and directed first film Twice Upon a Time, 1952; wrote and produced Miracle in Soho, 1957; wrote The Boy who Turned Yellow (film). British Film Institute Special Award (with Michael Powell), 1978; Fellow: BAFTA, 1981; BFI, 1983. *Publications:* Killing a Mouse on Sunday (novel), 1961; The Glass Pearls (novel), 1966; (with Michael Powell) The Red Shoes, 1978. *Recreations:* music, travel, and sports. *Address:* Shoemaker's Cottage, Aspall, Stowmarket, Suffolk. *Club:* Savile.

PRESSMAN, Mrs J. J.; *see* Colbert, Claudette.

PRESTON, family name of **Viscount Gormanston.**

PRESTON, Alan; Director of Fisheries Research, Ministry of Agriculture, Fisheries and Food, since 1980; *b* 23 May 1929; *s* of Ivor Gordon Preston and Lottie May Preston (*née* Bentley); *m* 1952, Beatrice Patricia Smith; two *s* two *d*. *Educ:* Newcastle High Sch., Staffs; Univ. of Reading (BSc (Gen.) 1950, BSc Hons Marine Zoology 1951). Nat. Service, RCS, 1953–55; 2nd Lieut 1954. Joined Fisheries Lab., Lowestoft, 1951: Head, Fisheries Radiobiol Lab., 1965–72; Dep. Dir, Fisheries Res., 1972–80; Co-ordinator, Fisheries Res. and Develt for GB, 1983–85. Buckland Foundation Professor, 1981 (Chm., Buckland Foundn Trustees, 1983–); Hon. Prof., Univ. of East Anglia, 1980–. Founder Mem., Soc. for Radiological Protection (Council Mem., 1969–73, 1981–84; Pres., 1982–83); Governor and Council Mem., Marine Biol Assoc. of the UK, 1981–. Delegate, 1981–, Vice-Pres., 1985–, Internat. Council for Exploration of the Sea. FRSA 1983. *Publications:* papers in learned jls. *Recreations:* gardening, haute cuisine, American history. *Address:* The Hall, Oulton, Lowestoft, Suffolk. *T:* Lowestoft 65115. *Club:* Rotary (Lowestoft South).

PRESTON, Frederick Leslie, FRIBA; AADip; formerly Senior Partner in firm of Easton Robertson Preston and Partners, Architects; *b* 27 Nov. 1903; *m* 1927, Rita Lillian (*d* 1982), *d* of late T. H. J. Washbourne; one *d*. *Educ:* Dulwich Coll.; Architectural Association Sch., London. Henry Jarvis Student, 1924; joined firm of Easton & Robertson, 1925, and engaged on: in London: Royal Horticultural Society's New Hall; Royal Bank of Canada; Metropolitan Water Board's Laboratories; in Cambridge: reconstruction of Old Library; Zoological laboratories; School of Anatomy; Gonville and Caius new buildings; in New York: British Pavilion, World's Fair, 1939. Hon. Citizen of City of New York, 1939. Served War of 1939–45, RAF, Wing Comdr, Airfield Construction Branch (despatches). *Principal works:* laboratories for Brewing Industry Research Foundation; laboratories for Coal Research Establishment, NCB, Cheltenham; Bank of England, Bristol; offices for Lloyds Bank, Plymouth; Birmingham; plans for development of Reading University: Faculty of Letters, Library, Windsor Hall, Depts of Physics and Sedimentology, Dept of Mathematics. Applied Physical Science Building, Palmer Building, Whiteknights House, Students Union, Animal Biology and Plant Sciences Buildings; additions to St Patrick's Hall and to Depts of Horticulture and Dairying, Reading Univ.; Buildings for Dulwich Coll.; office building for Salters' Co., London; Laboratories and Aquarium for Marine Biological Association, Plymouth; offices for Friends' Provident & Century Life Office, Dorking; Research Laboratories for Messrs Arthur Guinness Son & Co. (Park Royal) Ltd; University of Keele, Library; Midland Hotel, Manchester, alterations; University of Kent at Canterbury, Chemistry Laboratories, Biology Laboratories, Physics 11; Bank of England Printing Works Extension, Debden; Eagle Star Insurance Head Office, City; Plans for Aquarium, Rangoon Zoological Gardens. Member of RIBA Practice Cttee, 1951–55; Member Council of Architects' Registration Council of the UK, 1954–60. Governor of Westminster Technical College, 1957–67. Hon. DLitt, Reading, 1964. *Recreations:* seeing friends and places of interest, reading. *Address:* Wintershaw, Westcott, Surrey RH4 3NU. *T:* Dorking 885472. *Clubs:* Athenæum, Reform.

PRESTON, Geoffrey Averill; Assistant Counsel to Chairman of Committees, House of Lords, since 1982; *b* 19 May 1924; *s* of George and Winifred Preston; *m* 1953, Catherine Wright. *Educ:* St Marylebone Grammar Sch. Barrister-at-Law. Served, RNVR, 1942–46. Called to Bar, Gray's Inn, 1950. Treasury Solicitor's Dept, 1952–71; Solicitor's Department: Dept of Environment, 1971–74; Dept of Trade, 1974–75; Under-Sec. (Legal), Dept of Trade, 1975–82. *Recreations:* gardening, carpentry, chess. *Address:* Ledsham, Glaziers Lane, Normandy, Surrey. *T:* Guildford 811250.

PRESTON, Jeffrey William; Deputy Secretary, Welsh Office, since 1985; *b* 28 Jan. 1940; *s* of William and Sybil Grace Preston (*née* Lawson). *Educ:* Liverpool Collegiate Sch.; Hertford Coll., Oxford (MA 1966). Asst Principal, Min. of Aviation, 1963; Private Sec. to Permanent Sec., BoT, 1966; Principal: BoT, 1967; HM Treasury, 1970; DTI, 1973; Asst Sec., Dept of Trade, 1975–82; Under Sec. and Regional Dir, Yorks and Humberside Region, DTI, 1982–85. *Recreations:* motoring, opera, swimming. *Address:* Welsh Office, Cathays Park, Cardiff CF1 3NQ. *T:* Cardiff 823579. *Clubs:* United Oxford & Cambridge University; Leeds (Leeds).

PRESTON, Sir Kenneth (Huson), Kt 1959; *b* 19 May 1901; *e s* of late Sir Walter Preston, Tetbury, Glos; *m* 1st, 1922, Beryl Wilmot (decd), *d* of Sir William Wilkinson; one *s* one *d*; 2nd, 1984, Mrs V. E. Dumont. *Educ:* Rugby; Trinity Coll., Oxford. Dir, J. Stone & Co, 1925; Chm. Platt Bros, 1946; Chm. Stone-Platt Industries, 1958–67; Dir, Midland Bank Ltd, 1945–76. Mem. S Area Bd, BR. Mem. British Olympic Yachting team, 1936 and 1952, Captain 1960. *Recreations:* yachting, hunting. *Address:* Court Lodge, Avening, Tetbury, Glos. *T:* Nailsworth 4402. *Clubs:* Royal Yacht Squadron (Vice-Cdre, 1965–71); Thames Yacht (Vice-Cdre, 1953–56).

PRESTON, Leslie; *see* Preston, F. L.

PRESTON, Myles Park; HM Diplomatic Service, retired; *b* 4 April 1927; *s* of Robert and Marie Preston; *m* 1st, 1951, Ann Betten (marr. diss.); one *s* one *d*; 2nd, 1981, Joy Moore (*née* Fisher). *Educ:* Sudley Road Council Sch.; Liverpool Inst. High Sch.; Clare Coll., Cambridge. Instructor Lieut, RN, 1948–51; Asst Principal, Admty, 1951–53; CRO, 1953–54; 2nd Sec., British High Commn, New Delhi, 1954–56; 1st Sec., CRO, 1956–59; 1st Sec., Governor-General's Office and British High Commn, Lagos, 1959–62; CRO, 1962–64; 1st Sec., British High Commn, Kampala, 1964–67; Commonwealth Office and FCO, 1967–69; Counsellor and Consul-Gen., Djakarta, 1969–72; Canadian Nat. Defence Coll., 1972–73; FCO, 1973–77; Dep. Governor, Solomon Islands, 1977–78; Consul-Gen., Vancouver, 1978–79. *Address:* 20 Prince Edwards Road, Lewes, East Sussex BN7 1BE. *T:* Lewes 475809.

PRESTON, Peter John; Editor, The Guardian, since 1975; *b* 23 May 1938; *s* of John Whittle Preston and Kathlyn (*née* Chell); *m* 1962, Jean Mary Burrell; two *s* two *d*. *Educ:* Loughborough Grammar Sch.; St John's Coll., Oxford (MA EngLit). Editorial trainee, Liverpool Daily Post, 1960–63; Guardian: Political Reporter, 1963–64; Education Correspondent, 1965–66; Diary Editor, 1966–68; Features Editor, 1968–72; Production Editor, 1972–75. Hon. DLitt Loughborough, 1982. *Recreations:* football, films; four children. *Address:* The Guardian, 119 Farringdon Road, EC1R 3ER.

PRESTON, Sir Peter (Sansome), KCB 1978 (CB 1973); Permanent Secretary, Overseas Development Administration, Foreign and Commonwealth Office (formerly Ministry of Overseas Development), 1976–82; *b* Nottingham, 18 Jan. 1922; *s* of Charles Guy Preston, Solicitor; *m* 1951, Marjory Harrison; two *s* three *d*. *Educ:* Nottingham High School. War Service, RAF, 1942–46; Board of Trade: Exec. Officer, 1947; Higher Exec. Off., 1950; Asst Principal, 1951; Principal, 1953; Trade Comr, New Delhi, 1959; Asst Sec., 1964; idc 1968; Under-Sec., BoT later DTI, 1969–72; Dep. Sec., Dept of Trade, 1972–76. Mem., BOTB, 1975–76. Dir, Wellcome Internat. Trading Co. Ltd, 1985–; Dep. Chm., CARE Britain, 1985–; Adviser, Land-Rover Leyland Ltd, 1983–; Mem. Council, Overseas Develt Inst. *Address:* 5 Greville Park Avenue, Ashtead, Surrey. *T:* Ashtead 72099.

PRESTON, Prof. Reginald Dawson, FRS 1954; retired; Professor of Plant Biophysics, 1953–73 (now Professor Emeritus), and Head, Astbury Department of Biophysics, 1962–73, University of Leeds; Chairman, School of Biological Sciences, 1970–73; Dean of the Faculty of Science, 1955–58; *b* 21 July 1908; *s* of late Walter C. Preston, builder, and late Eliza Preston; *m* 1935, Sarah J. Pollard (decd); two *d* (one *s* decd); *m* 1963, Dr Eva Frei. *Educ:* Leeds University; Cornell University, USA. BSc (Hons Physics, Class I), 1929; PhD (Botany), 1931; 1851 Exhibition Fellowship, 1932–35; Rockefeller Foundation Fellowship, 1935–36. Lecturer, Botany Dept, Univ. of Leeds, 1936–46; Sen. Lectr, 1946–49; Reader, 1949–53. Vis. Prof. of Botany, Imperial Coll., London, 1976–79. Mem. NY Acad. Sci., 1960. Hon. Mem., Internat. Assoc. of Wood Anatomists, 1981. DSc 1943; CPhys (FInstP 1944); FLS 1958; FIWSc 1960; FIAWS 1973. Anselme Payen Award, Amer. Chem. Soc., 1983; Disting. Service Medal, Leeds Phil. Lit. Soc., 1983. Editor: Proc. Leeds Phil. Soc. Sci. Sec., 1950–74; Advances in Botanical Research, 1968–77; Associate Editor, Jl Exp. Bot., 1950–77. *Publications:* Molecular Architecture of Plant Cell Walls, 1952; Physical Biology of Plant Cell Walls, 1974; about 180 articles in Proc. Roy. Soc., Nature, Ann. Bot., Biochem. Biophys Acta, Jl Exp. Bot., etc. *Recreations:* walking, climbing, music. *Address:* 117 St Anne's Road, Leeds, West Yorks LS6 3NZ. *T:* 785248.

PRESTON of Ardchattan, Robert Modan Thorne C.; *see* Campbell-Preston of Ardchattan.

PRESTON, Sir Ronald (Douglas Hildebrand), 7th Bt *cr* 1815; country landowner and journalist; *b* 9 Oct. 1916; *s* of Sir Thomas Hildebrand Preston, 6th Bt, OBE, and of Ella Henrietta, *d* of F. von Schickendantz; *S* father, 1976; *m* 1st, 1954, Smilya Stefanovic (marr. diss.); 2nd, 1972, Pauleen Jane, *d* of late Paul Lurcott. *Educ:* Westminster School; Trinity Coll., Cambridge (Hons History and Economics, MA); Ecole des Sciences Politiques, Paris. Served War, 1940–46, in Intelligence Corps, reaching rank of Major: Western Desert, Middle East, Italy, Austria, Allied Control Commn, Bulgaria. Reuter's Correspondent, Belgrade, Yugoslavia, 1948–53; The Times Correspondent: Vienna and E Europe, 1953–60; Tokyo and Far East, 1960–63. HM Diplomatic Service, 1963–76; retired, 1976. *Recreations:* shooting, tennis, picture frame making. *Heir: cousin* Philip Charles Henry Hulton Preston, *b* 31 Aug. 1946. *Address:* Beeston Hall, Beeston St Lawrence, Norwich NR12 8YS. *T:* Horning 630771. *Clubs:* Travellers'; Norfolk (Norwich); Tokyo (Tokyo).

PRESTON, Rev. Prof. Ronald Haydn, DD; Professor of Social and Pastoral Theology in the University of Manchester, 1970–80, now Emeritus; *b* 12 March 1913; *o s* of Haydn and Eleanor Jane Preston; *m* 1948, Edith Mary Lindley; one *s* two *d*. *Educ:* London School of Economics, University of London; St Catherine's Coll., Oxford. BSc (Econ.) 1935, Cl. II, Div. I; Industrial Secretary of Student Christian Movement, 1935–38; BA Cl. I Theology, 1940; MA 1944; MA Manchester 1974; BD, DD Oxon 1983. Curate, St John, Park, Sheffield, 1940–43; Study Secretary, Student Christian Movement, 1943–48; Warden of St Anselm Hall, University of Manchester, 1948–63; Lectr in Christian Ethics, Univ. of Manchester, 1948–70; Examining Chaplain: to Bishop of Manchester, 1948–; to Bishop of Sheffield, 1971–80; Canon Residentiary of Manchester Cathedral, 1957–71, Sub-Dean 1970–71, Hon. Canon 1971, Canon Emeritus, 1980. Editor, The Student Movement, 1943–48. *Publications:* (jointly) Christians in Society, 1939; (jointly) The Revelation of St John the Divine, 1949; Technology and Social Justice, 1971; (ed) Industrial Conflicts and their Place in Modern Society, 1974; (ed) Perspectives on Strikes, 1975; (ed) Theology and Change, 1975; Religion and the Persistence of Capitalism, 1979; (ed jtly) The Crisis in British Penology, 1980; (ed) Explorations in Theology, No 9, 1981; Church and Society in the late Twentieth Century, 1983; The Future of Christian Ethics, 1986; reviews, etc in The Guardian, Theology, etc. *Address:* 161 Old Hall Lane, Manchester M14 6HJ. *T:* 061–225 3291.

PRESTON, Simon John; Organist and Master of the Choristers, Westminster Abbey, since 1981; *b* 4 Aug. 1938. *Educ:* Canford Sch.; King's Coll., Cambridge (Dr Mann Organ Student). BA 1961, MusB 1962, MA 1964. ARCM, FRAM. Sub Organist, Westminster Abbey, 1962–67; Acting Organist, St Albans Abbey, 1967–68; Organist and Lecturer in Music, Christ Church, Oxford, 1970–81. Conductor, Oxford Bach Choir, 1971–74. Hon. FRCO; Hon. FRCCO. Edison Award, 1971; Grand Prix du Disque, 1979. *Recreations:* croquet, photography, cooking. *Address:* 8 The Little Cloister, Westminster Abbey, SW1P 3PL. *T:* 01–222 6222.

PRESTON, Timothy William; QC 1982; a Recorder of the Crown Court, since 1979; *b* 3 Nov. 1935; *s* of Charles Frank Preston, LDS, RCS and Frances Mary, *o d* of Captain W. Peters, 5th Lancers; *m* 1965, Barbara Mary Haygarth. *Educ:* Haileybury; Jesus Coll., Oxford (BA 1960). 2/Lieut 16/5 Lancers, 1955; Captain, Staffs Yeomanry, retd. Called to the Bar, Inner Temple, 1964. *Recreations:* hunting, golf. *Address:* 2 Temple Gardens, EC4Y 9AY. *T:* 01–583 6041. *Club:* Cavalry and Guards.

PRESTT, Arthur Miller, QC 1970; **His Honour Judge Prestt;** a Circuit Judge (formerly Judge of County Courts), since 1971; Hon. Recorder of Manchester and Senior Circuit Judge, Manchester, since 1982; *b* 23 April 1925; *s* of Arthur Prestt and Jessie (*née* Miller), Wigan; *m* 1949, Jill Mary, *d* of late Graham Dawbarn, CBE, FRIBA, FRAeS, and of Olive Dawbarn (*née* Topham); one *s* one *d*. *Educ:* Bootham Sch., York; Trinity Hall, Cambridge (MA). Served 13th Bn Parachute Regt, France, Belgium, India, Malaya, Java, 1944–46; Major Legal Staff, Singapore, 1946–47, War Crimes Prosecutor. Called to Bar, Middle Temple, 1949. Mental Health Review Tribunal, 1963–70; Dep. Chm., Cumberland QS, 1966–69, Chm., 1970–71. Has held various appts in Scout Assoc. (Silver Acorn, 1970); Pres., Chorley and Dist Scout Council. Pres., SW Lancs Parachute Regt Assoc. JP Cumberland, 1966. 5 years Medal, Ampleforth Lourdes Hospitalite, 1976. *Recreations:* gardening, golf. *Address:* Glebe House, Eccleston, Chorley, Lancs PR7 6LY. *T:* Eccleston (Lancs) 451397. *Club:* St James's (Manchester).
See also I. Prestt.

PRESTT, Ian, CBE 1986; Director General (formerly Director), Royal Society for the Protection of Birds, since 1975; *b* 26 June 1929; *s* of Arthur Prestt and Jessie Prestt (*née* Miller); *m* 1956, Jennifer Ann Wagstaffe; two *d* (one *s* decd). *Educ:* Bootham School, York; Univ. of Liverpool (BSc, MSc). FIBiol. 2nd Lt, RA, 1947–49. Joined staff of Nature Conservancy, 1956; Asst Regional Officer (SW England), 1956–59; Asst to Dir-Gen. and Ornithological Officer (GB, HQ), 1959–61; Dep. Regional Officer (N England), 1961–63; PSO, Monks Wood Experimental Station, 1963–70; Dep. Dir, Central Unit on Environmental Pollution, Cabinet Office and DoE, 1970–74; Dep. Dir, Nature Conservancy Council, 1974–75. Member: Council and Exec. Cttee, Wildfowl Trust, 1976–; Adv. Cttee on Birds, Nature Conservancy Council, 1981–; Chairman: Exec. Cttee, Internat. Council for Bird Preservation, 1982– (Mem., 1979–); Huntingdon Div., CPRE, 1975–. *Publications:* scientific papers in ecol and ornithol jls. *Recreations:* sketching, architecture, reading. *Address:* Willowdene, London Road, St Ives, Huntingdon, Cambs PE17 4EU. *T:* St Ives 62313. *Club:* Athenæum.
See also A. M. Prestt.

PRESTWOOD, Viscount; John Richard Attlee; *b* 3 Oct. 1956; *s* and *heir* of 2nd Earl Attlee, *qv*.

PRETORIA, Bishop of, since 1982; **Rt. Rev. Richard Austin Kraft;** *b* 3 June 1936; *s* of Arthur Austin Kraft and Mary Roberta Hudson Kraft; *m* 1958, Phyllis Marie Schaffer; three *s* one *d*. *Educ:* Ripon Coll., Ripon, Wisconsin, USA (BA); General Theolog. Seminary, New York (MDiv; Hon. DD 1983). Deacon then priest, 1961; Asst priest, St Alphege's, Scottsville, dio. Natal, 1961–63; Asst priest and Rector, St Chad's Mission, Klip River, 1963–67; Dir of Christian Education, Diocese of Zululand, 1968–76; Rector, All Saints Parish, Melmoth, 1974–76; Dir of Education Dept, Church of Province of S Africa, 1977–79; Dean and Rector, St Alban's Cathedral, Diocese of Pretoria, 1979–82. Canon, Dio. of Zululand, 1971; Canon Emeritus, 1977. *Recreation:* woodwork. *Address:* Bishop's House, 264 Celliers Street, Muckleneuk, Pretoria, 0002, S Africa. *T:* (home) (012) 443163, (office) (012) 266956.

PRETYMAN, Sir Walter (Frederick), KBE 1972; President, Usina Santa Cruz: *b* 17 Oct. 1901; *s* of Rt Hon. E. G. Pretyman and Lady Beatrice Pretyman; *m* 1st, 1929, Margaret Cunningham (*d* 1942); one *d*; 2nd, 1947, Vera de Sa Sotto Maior (*d* 1986); two *s*; 3rd, 1986, Marie Therese de Castro Brandão. *Educ:* Eton; Magdalen Coll., Oxford. From 1923 onwards, industrial and agricultural activities in Brasil. Served War, with RAFVR, 1943–45; despatches, 1946; retd with rank of Sqdn Ldr. *Address:* (*Office*) 90 Rua Mexico, Rio de Janeiro, Brazil. *T:* 232–8179. *Clubs:* Gavea Golf and Country, Jockey (Rio de Janeiro).

PREVIN, André (George); conductor and composer; Music Director: Royal Philharmonic Orchestra, since 1985; Los Angeles Philharmonic Orchestra, since 1986; *b* Berlin, Germany, 6 April 1929; *s* of Jack Previn and Charlotte Epstein; *m* 1970; three *s* (inc. twin *s*), three *d*; *m* 1982, Heather, *d* of Robert Sneddon; one *s*. *Educ:* Berlin and Paris Conservatoires; private study with Pierre Monteux, Castelnuovo-Tedesco. Composer of film scores, 1950–62 (four Academy Awards). Music Dir, Houston Symphony Orchestra, 1967–69; Principal Conductor, London Symphony Orchestra, 1968–79, Conductor Emeritus, 1979; Music Dir, Pittsburgh Symphony Orchestra, 1976–84; Guest Conductor, most major orchestras, US and Europe, Covent Garden Opera, Salzburg Festival, Edinburgh Festival, Osaka Festival; Music Dir, London South Bank Summer Festival, 1972–74. Member: Composers Guild of GB; Amer. Composers League; Dramatists League. Recording artist. Principal compositions: Cello Concerto; Guitar Concerto; Wind Quintet; Serenades for Violin; piano preludes; Piano Concerto, 1984; Symphony for Strings; overtures; Principals, Reflections (for orchestra); Every Good Boy Deserves Favour (text by Tom Stoppard); Six Songs Mezzo-Soprano (text by Philip Larkin). Annual TV series: specials for BBC; PBS (USA). *Publications:* Music Face to Face, 1971; (ed) Orchestra, 1979; André Previn's Guide to Music, 1983; *relevant publications:* André Previn, by Edward Greenfield, 1973; Previn, by H. Ruttencutter, 1985. *Address:* c/o Harrison/Parrott Ltd, 12 Penzance Place, W11 4PA. *Club:* Garrick.

PREVOST, Sir Christopher (Gerald), 6th Bt *cr* 1805; Chairman and Managing Director, Mailtronic Ltd, since 1977; *b* 25 July 1935; *s* of Sir George James Augustine Prevost, 5th Bt and Muriel Emily (*d* 1939), *d* of late Lewis William Oram; *S* father, 1985; *m* 1964, Dolores Nelly, *o d* of Dezo Hoffman; one *s* one *d*. *Educ:* Cranleigh School. Served 60th Regt (formed by Provost family) and Rifle Bde; Kenya Service Medal, 1955. IBM, 1955–61; Pitney-Bowes, 1963–76; founder of Mailtronic Ltd, manufacturers and suppliers of mailroom equipment, 1977. Mem., Business Equipment Trade Assoc., 1983–. *Recreations:* squash; skiing (Member of British Jetski Assoc. and Team sponsor). *Heir: s* Nicholas Marc Prevost, *b* 13 March 1971. *Address:* Highway Cottage, Berry Grove Lane, Watford, Herts WD2 8AE. *Club:* Cloisters Wood (Stanmore, Middx).

PREY, Hermann; baritone; *b* Berlin, 11 July 1929; *s* of Hermann Prey; *m* Barbara Pniok; one *s* two *d*. *Educ:* Humanistisches Gymnasium, Berlin; Staatliche Musikhochschule, Berlin. With State Opera, Wiesbaden, 1952; appearances in Germany, Vienna, (La Scala) Milan, (Metropolitan Opera) New York, Buenos Aires, San Francisco, Covent Garden, etc. Festivals include: Salzburg, Bayreuth, Edinburgh, Vienna, Tokyo, Aix-en-Provence, Perugia, Berlin. *Address:* D-8033 Krailling vor München, Fichtenstrasse 14, Federal Republic of Germany; c/o Lies Askonas, 186 Drury Lane, WC2B 5QD.

PRICA, Srdja; Member: Council of the Federation of Yugoslavia, since 1972; Council for Foreign Affairs of the Presidency of the Republic of Yugoslavia, since 1971; *b* 20 Sept. 1905; *m* 1956, Vukica Tomanović-Prica. *Educ:* University of Zagreb, Yugoslavia. Newspaperman until 1946; Director of Department, Foreign Office, Belgrade, 1947–49; Asst Min., FO, Belgrade, 1949–51; Ambassador of Yugoslavia, Paris, 1951–55; Under-Sec. of State for Foreign Affairs, Belgrade, 1955–60; Ambassador: to Court of St James's, 1960–65; to Italy, 1967–71; to Malta, 1968–72. Grand Officier, Légion d'Honneur (France); Egyptian, Italian, Norwegian, Austrian and Greek Orders. *Address:* c/o Council of the Federation of Yugoslavia, Belgrade, Yugoslavia.

PRICE, (Alan) Anthony; author and journalist; Editor, The Oxford Times, since 1972; *b* 16 Aug. 1928; *s* of Walter Longsdon Price and Kathleen Price (*née* Lawrence); *m* 1953, Yvonne Ann Stone; two *s* one *d*. *Educ:* King's Sch., Canterbury; Merton Coll., Oxford (Exbnr; MA). Oxford & County Newspapers, 1952–. *Publications:* The Labyrinth Makers, 1970 (CWA Silver Dagger); The Alamut Ambush, 1971; Colonel Butler's Wolf, 1972; October Men, 1973; Other Paths to Glory, 1974 (CWA Gold Dagger, 1974; Swedish Acad. of Detection Prize, 1978); Our Man in Camelot, 1975; War Game, 1976; The '44 Vintage, 1978; Tomorrow's Ghost, 1979; The Hour of the Donkey, 1980; Soldier No More, 1981; The Old Vengeful, 1982; Gunner Kelly, 1983; Sion Crossing, 1984; Here Be Monsters, 1985; For the Good of the State, 1986. *Recreation:* military history. *Address:* Wayside Cottage, Horton-cum-Studley, Oxford OX9 1AW. *T:* Stanton St John 326.

PRICE, Arnold Justin, QC 1976; a Recorder of the Crown Court, since 1972; *b* 16 Aug. 1919; *s* of late Sydney Walter Price, LLB, Solicitor, and Sophia Price (*née* Marks); *m* 1948, Ruth Corinne, *d* of Ralph and Dorothy Marks; four *d*. *Educ:* St Christopher's Sch., Liverpool; Kingsmead Sch., Meols; Liverpool Coll.; Liverpool Univ. Bd of Legal Studies. Served War, Royal Engrs, 42nd Inf. Div. TA (invalided), later 2nd Lieut Royal Corps Mil. Police, 42nd Inf. Div. TA. Called to Bar, Middle Temple, 1952; practised Wales and Chester Circuit; Resident Magistrate, Nyasaland, 1955; Magistrate, N Nigeria, 1957; Actg Chief Magistrate and Judge, High Court N Nigeria, 1957–60; returned to practice, Wales and Chester Circuit, 1960; Northern Circuit, 1969. CC Chester, 1963–68. *Publications:* articles on politics, agriculture and legal subjects. *Recreations:* fishing, the countryside, beekeeping. *Address:* Thicket Ford, Thornton Hough, Wirral. *T:* 051–336 4444; Peel House, Harrington Street, Liverpool. *T:* 051–236 5072, 051–227 5661; 2 Pump Court, Temple, EC4. *T:* 01–353 3106. *Club:* Athenæum (Liverpool).

PRICE, (Arthur) Leolin; QC 1968; *b* 11 May 1924; 3rd *s* of late Evan Price and Ceridwen Price (*née* Price), Hawkhurst, Kent; *m* 1963, Hon. Rosalind Helen Penrose Lewis, *er d* of 1st Baron Brecon, PC, and of Mabel, Baroness Brecon, CBE, JP; two *s* two *d*. *Educ:* Judd Sch., Tonbridge; Keble Coll., Oxford (Schol.; MA). War service, 1943–46 with Army: Capt., RA; Adjt, Indian Mountain Artillery Trng Centre and Depot, Ambala, Punjab, 1946. Treas., Oxford Union, 1948; Pres., Oxford Univ. Conserv. Assoc., 1948. Tutor (part-time), Keble Coll., Oxford, 1951–59. Called to Bar, Middle Temple, 1949; Bencher, 1970–; Barrister of Lincoln's Inn, 1959. QC Bahamas, 1969. Member: Editorial Cttee, Modern Law Review, 1954–65; Bar Council Law Reform Cttee, 1969–75; Cttee, Soc. of Cons. Lawyers, 1971–; Cttee of Management, Inst. of Child Health, 1972– (Chm., 1976–). Director: Child Health Res. Investment Trust plc, 1980–; Marine Adventure Sailing Trust plc, 1981–. Governor, Gt Ormond St Hosp. for Sick Children, 1972–; Mem., Falkland Islands Cttee, 1972–. Governor, Christ Coll., Brecon, 1977–. Chancellor, Diocese of Swansea and Brecon, 1982–. *Publications:* articles and notes in legal jls. *Address:* 32 Hampstead Grove, NW3 6SR. *T:* 01–435 9843; 10 Old Square, Lincoln's Inn, WC2A 3SU. *T:* 01–405 0758; Moor Park, Llanbedr, near Crickhowell, Powys NP8 1SS. *T:* Crickhowell 810443. *Club:* Carlton.

See also V. W. C. Price.

PRICE, Barry; *see* Price, W. F. B.

PRICE, (Benjamin) Terence; Secretary-General, Uranium Institute, since 1974; *b* 7 January 1921; *er s* of Benjamin and Nellie Price; *m* 1947, Jean Stella Vidal; one *s* one *d*. *Educ:* Crypt School, Gloucester; Queens' College, Cambridge. Naval electronics res., 1942–46; Atomic Energy Research Establishment, Harwell (Nuclear Physics Division), 1947–59; Head of Reactor Development Division, Atomic Energy Estabt, Winfrith, 1959; Chief Scientific Officer, Ministry of Defence, 1960–63; Assistant Chief Scientific Adviser (Studies), Ministry of Defence, 1963–65; Director, Defence Operational Analysis Establishment, MoD, 1965–68; Chief Scientific Adviser, Min. of Transport, 1968–71; Dir of Planning and Development, Vickers Ltd, 1971–73. Chm., NEDO Mechanical Handling Sector Working Party, 1976–80. *Publication:* Radiation Shielding, 1957. *Recreations:* flying, ski-ing, making music. *Address:* Seers Bough, Wilton Lane, Jordans, Buckinghamshire. *T:* Chalfont St Giles 4589. *Club:* Athenæum.

PRICE, Bernard Albert; County Clerk and Chief Executive, Staffordshire County Council, and Clerk to the Lieutenancy, since 1983; *b* 6 Jan. 1944; *s* of Albert and Doris Price; *m* 1966, Christine Mary, *d* of Roy William Henry Combes; two *s* one *d*. *Educ:* Whitchurch Grammar Sch., Salop; King's Sch., Rochester, Kent; Merton Coll., Oxford (BA 1965, MA 1970). DMS, Wolverhampton Polytechnic, 1972. Articled, later Asst Solicitor, Worcs CC, 1966–70; Asst Solicitor, subseq. Dep. Dir of Admin, Staffs CC, 1970–80; Sen. Dep. Clerk, Staffs CC, 1980–83. *Recreations:* sailing, walking. *Address:* The Cottage, Yeatsall Lane, Abbots Bromley, Rugeley, Staffs WS15 3DY. *T:* Burton on Trent 840269.

PRICE, Rear-Adm. Cecil Ernest, CB 1978; AFC 1953; Deputy Assistant Chief of Staff (Operations), SHAPE, 1976–80, retired; *b* 29 Oct. 1921; *s* of Ernest C. Price and Phyllis M. Price; *m* 1946, Megan Morgan; one *s* one *d*. *Educ:* Bungay Grammar Sch. Joined Royal Navy, 1941; served as Pilot in several aircraft carriers, 1942–46; completed Empire Test Pilot School, and Test Flying, Boscombe Down, 1948–52; CO 813 Sqdn, 1953–54; Comdr 1956; CO Naval Test Sqdn, Boscombe Down, 1956–58; British Navy Staff, Washington, 1959–61; Captain 1966; idc 1970; Director: Naval Air Warfare, 1971–72; Naval Operational Requirements, 1972–73; CO RNAS, Culdrose, 1973–75; Rear-Adm. 1976. *Recreations:* golf, fishing, gardening. *Address:* Low Farm, Mendham, Harleston, Norfolk. *T:* Harleston 852676.

PRICE, Maj.-Gen. Cedric Rhys, CB 1951; CBE 1945 (OBE 1943); Principal Staff Officer to Secretary of State for Commonwealth Relations, 1959–64; ADC to the Queen, 1954–57; *b* 13 June 1905; *o s* of late Colonel Sir Rhys H. Price, KBE, CMG, Highlands, Purley Downs; *m* 1935, Rosamund, *e d* of late Arthur W. Clifford, Dursley, Glos; two *d*. *Educ:* Wellington College; RMA Woolwich; Trinity College, Cambridge. Commissioned Royal Engineers, 1925; served in India, 1932–38; Staff College, 1938–39; Military Assistant Secretary, offices of War Cabinet, 1940–46; Secretary, British Joint Services Mission, Washington, USA, 1946–48; Secretary, Chiefs of Staff Cttee, Ministry of Defence, 1948–50; student, Imperial Defence College, SW1, 1951; Chief of Staff to Chairman of British Joint Services Mission, Washington, 1952–54; Brigadier, General Staff, Eastern Command, 1955–56; Director of Military Intelligence, War Office, 1956–59. *Recreations:* golf, tennis, riding. *Address:* Furze Field Cottage, Hoe Lane, Peaslake, Guildford, Surrey. *T:* Dorking 730586. *Club:* Army and Navy.

PRICE, Charles H., II; American Ambassador to the Court of St James's, since 1983; *b* 1 April 1931; *s* of Charles Harry Price and Virginia (*née* Ogden); *m* 1969, Carol Ann Swanson; two *s* three *d*. *Educ:* University of Missouri. Pres., Linwood Securities, 1960–81; Chairman: Price Candy Co., 1969–81; American Bancorpn, 1973–81; American Bank & Trust Co., 1973–81; American Mortgage Co., 1973–81; Dir, Ameribanc, Inc.; Ambassador to Belgium, 1981–83. Vice-Chm. and Mem. Exec. Cttee, Midwest Res. Inst., 1978–81; Mem. Bd of Dirs, Civic Council, Greater Kansas City, 1979–80. Hon. Dr Westminster Coll., Missouri. *Recreations:* tennis, golf. *Address:* American Embassy, 24 Grosvenor Square, W1A 1AE. *T:* 01–499 9000. *Clubs:* White's, Mark's, Swinley Forest Golf; Metropolitan (Washington); Mill Reef (Antigua).

PRICE, Sir Charles (Keith Napier) Rugge-, 9th Bt *cr* 1804; Supervisor Compensation, City of Edmonton; *b* 7 August, 1936; *s* of Lt-Col Sir Charles James Napier Rugge-Price, 8th Bt, and of Lady (Maeve Marguerite) Rugge-Price (*née* de la Peña); *S* father, 1966; *m* 1965, Jacqueline Mary (*née* Loranger); two *s*. *Educ:* Middleton College, Eire. 5th Regt Royal Horse Artillery, Germany and Wales, 1954–59. Actuarial Dept, William Mercers Ltd, Canada, 1959–60; Alexander and Alexander Services Ltd, Montreal, Canada, 1960–67; with Domtar Ltd, 1968–71; Manager, Tomenson Alexander Ltd, Toronto, 1971–76. *Heir: s* James Keith Peter Rugge-Price, *b* 8 April 1967. *Address:* 23 Lambert Crescent, St Albert, Alberta T8N 1M1, Canada.

PRICE, Christopher; Director, Leeds Polytechnic, since 1986; freelance journalist and broadcaster; *b* 26 Jan. 1932; *s* of Stanley Price; *m* 1956, Annie Grierson Ross; two *s* one *d*. *Educ:* Leeds Grammar School; Queen's College, Oxford. Sec., Oxford Univ. Labour Club, 1953; Chm., Nat. Assoc. of Labour Student Organisations, 1955–56. Sheffield City Councillor, 1962–66; Dep. Chm., Sheffield Educn Cttee, 1963–66. Contested (Lab): Shipley, 1964; Birmingham, Perry Barr, 1970; Lewisham W, 1983. MP (Lab): Perry Barr Division of Birmingham, 1966–70; Lewisham W, Feb. 1974–1983; PPS to Secretary of State for Education and Science, 1966–67 and 1975–76; Chm., H of C Select Cttee on Educn, Science and the Arts, 1980–83. Mem., European Parlt, 1977–78. Dir, London Internat. Festival of Theatre Ltd, 1982–86; Pro-Asst Dir, The Polytechnic of the South Bank, 1983–86. Chm., Council, Nat. Youth Bureau, 1977–80; Mem. Bd, Phoenix House Ltd (Britain's largest gp of drug rehabilitation houses), 1986– (Chm., 1980–86); Member: Council, Inst. for Study of Drug Dependence, 1984–; Delegacy, Univ. of London Goldsmiths' Coll., 1981–86; Court, Polytechnic of Central London, 1982–86; London Centre for Biotechnology Trust, 1984–; Fellow, Inst. for Biotechnol Studies, 1984. Editor, New Education, 1967–68; Educn corresp., New Statesman, 1969–74; Columnist, TES, 1983–85. *Publications:* (contrib.) A Radical Future, 1967; Crisis in the Classroom, 1968; (ed) Your Child and School, 1968; Which Way?, 1969; (contrib.) Life and Death of the Schools Council, 1985; (contrib.) Police, the Constitution and the Community, 1985. *Address:* Leeds Polytechnic, Calverley Street, Leeds LS1 3HE; Flat 1, 6 Montpelier Grove, NW5. *Club:* Athenæum.

PRICE, Maj.-Gen. David; *see* Price, Maj.-Gen. M. D.

PRICE, Sir David (Ernest Campbell), Kt 1980; DL; MP (C) Eastleigh Division of Hampshire, since 1955; *b* 20 Nov. 1924; *o s* of Major Villiers Price; *m* 1960, Rosemary Eugénie Evelyn, *o d* of late Cyril F. Johnston, OBE; one *d*. *Educ:* Eton; Trinity College, Cambridge; Yale University, USA; Rosebery Schol., Eton; Open History Schol., Trinity College, Cambridge. Served with 1st Battalion Scots Guards, CMF; subsequently Staff Captain (Intelligence) HQ, 56 London Div., Trieste, 1942–46. Trin. Coll., Cambridge, BA Hons, MA. Pres. Cambridge Union; Vice-Pres. Fedn of Univ. Conservative and Unionist Assocs, 1946–48; Henry Fellow of Yale Univ., USA, 1948–49. Industrial Consultant. Held various appts in Imperial Chemical Industries Ltd, 1949–62. Parly Sec., Board of Trade, 1962–64; Opposition Front-Bench spokesman on Science and Technology, 1964–70; Parly Sec., Min. of Technology, June-Oct. 1970; Parly Sec., Min. of Aviation Supply, 1970–71; Parly Under-Sec. of State, Aerospace, DTI, 1971–72. Member: Public Accounts Cttee, 1974–75; Select Cttee on Transport, 1979–83; Select Cttee on Social Services, 1983–; Vice-Pres., Parly and Scientific Cttee, 1975–79 and 1982– (Vice-Chm., 1965–70, Chm., 1973–75 and 1979–82). Vice-Chm., Cons. Arts and Heritage Cttee, 1979–81 and 1983–; Chm., Cons. Shipping and Ship-Building Cttee; Pres., Wessex Area Cons. and Unionist Party, 1986. British Representative to Consultative Assembly of the Council of Europe, 1958–61. Dir, Assoc. British Maltsters, 1966–70. Gen. Cons. to IIM (formerly IWM), 1973–; Cons. to Union International Ltd. Vice-Pres., IIM, 1980–. Governor, Middlesex Hospital, 1956–60. DL Hants, 1982. *Recreations:* swimming, arts and heritage, history, ornithology, wine, cooking. *Address:* 16 Laxford House, Cundy Street, SW1. *T:* 01–730 3326; Flat 2, Lepe House, Exbury, Southampton. *Club:* Beefsteak.

PRICE, Eric Hardiman Mockford; Under Secretary, Head of Economics and Statistics Division, Department of Energy, since 1980; Director, Robinson Brothers (Ryders Green) Ltd, since 1985; *b* 14 Nov. 1931; *s* of Frederick Hardiman Price and Florence Nellie Hannah Price (*née* Mockford); *m* 1963, Diana Teresa Mary Stanley Robinson; one *s* three *d*. *Educ:* St Marylebone Grammar Sch.; Christ's Coll., Cambridge. Econs Tripos, 1955; MA 1958. FREconS, 1956; FSS 1958. Army service, 1950–52; HAC, 1952–57. Supply Dept, Esso Petroleum Co. Ltd, 1955–56; Economist: Central Electricity Authority, 1956–57; Electricity Council, 1957–58; British Iron & Steel Fedn, 1958–62; Chief Economist, Port of London Authority, 1962–67; Sen. Econ. Adviser, Min. of Transport, 1966–69; Chief Econ. Adviser, Min. of Transport, 1969–71; Dir of Econs, 1971–75, Under Sec., 1972–76, Dir of Econs and Stats, 1975–76, DoE; Under Sec., Econs and Stats Div., Depts of Industry, Trade and Consumer Protection, 1977–80. Member: Soc. of Business Economists, 1961; Northern Regional Strategy Steering Gp, 1976–77; Soc. of Strategic and Long-range Planning, 1980–; Council, British Inst. of Energy Economics, 1986 (Mem., 1980–; Vice-Chm., 1981–82); Chm., 1982–85). *Publications:* various articles in learned jls on transport economics, energy and energy efficiency, investment, public sector industries, technological innovation in industry and regional planning. *Recreations:* tennis, squash, local history. *Address:* Batchworth Heath Farm, London Road, Rickmansworth, Herts. *Clubs:* Moor Park Golf; Northwood Squash.

PRICE, Sir Francis (Caradoc Rose), 7th Bt *cr* 1815; barrister and solicitor; *b* 9 Sept. 1950; *s* of Sir Rose Francis Price, 6th Bt and of Kathleen June, *d* of late Norman W. Hutchinson, Melbourne; *S* father, 1979; *m* 1975, Marguerite Jean, *d* of Roy S. Trussler, Cobble Hill, BC; three *d*. *Educ:* Eton; Trinity College, Melbourne Univ. (Sen. Student 1971, LLB Hons 1973); Univ. of Alberta (LLM 1975); Canadian Petroleum Law Foundn Fellow, 1974–75. Admitted Province of Alberta 1976, Northwest Territories 1978, Canada. Lectr, 1979– and Course Head, 1983–, Alberta Bar Admission Course. *Publications:* Pipelines in Western Canada, 1975; Mortgage Actions in Alberta, 1985; contribs to Alberta and Melbourne Univ. Law Revs, etc. *Recreations:* cricket, skiing, squash, running, theatre. *Heir: b* Norman William Rose Price, *b* 17 March 1953. *Address:* 9677 95th Avenue, Edmonton, Alberta T6C 2A3, Canada. *Clubs:* Centre, Faculty (Edmonton).

PRICE, Sir Frank (Leslie), Kt 1966; DL; Chairman: Elite Design and Security Ltd, since 1983; Sir Frank Price Associates, since 1984; Swansong Developments Ltd, since 1984; Signet Securities PLC, since 1986; Sir Frank Price Associates SA, since 1986; *b* 26 July 1922; *s* of G. F. Price; marr. diss.; one *s*; married again. *Educ:* St Matthias Church Sch., Birmingham; Vittoria Street Arts Sch. Elected to Birmingham City Council, 1949; Alderman, 1958–74; Lord Mayor, 1964–65. Member: Council, Town and Country Planning Assoc., 1958–74; W Midlands Economic Planning Council, 1965–72; Nat. Water Council, 1975–79; Chm., British Waterways Bd, 1968–84. Founder/Chm., Midlands Art Centre for Young People, 1960–71; Chairman: W Midlands Sports Council, 1965–69; Telford Development Corporation, 1968–71; Dir, National Exhibn

Centre, 1968–74. Member: Minister of Transport's Cttee of Inquiry into Major Ports, 1961; English Tourist Board, 1976–83; Pres., BAIE, 1979–83. Livery Co. of Basketmakers. FSVA; FCIT. FRSA. DL Herefordshire and Worcestershire, 1977–84, and County of West Midlands, 1977. Freeman, City of London. *Publications:* various pamphlets and articles on planning and transport, etc. *Recreations:* painting, cruising. *Club:* Reform.

PRICE, Gareth; Controller, BBC Wales, since 1986; *b* 30 Aug. 1939; *s* of Rowena and Morgan Price; *m* 1962, Mari Griffiths; two *s* one *d*. *Educ:* Aberaeron Grammar School and Ardwyn Grammar School, Aberystwyth; University College of Wales, Aberystwyth (BA Econ). Asst Lectr in Economics, Queen's Univ., Belfast, 1962–64; BBC Wales: Radio Producer, Current Affairs, 1964–66; Television Producer, Features and Documentaries, 1966–74; Dep. Head of Programmes, 1974–81; Head of Programmes, 1981–85. *Publication:* David Lloyd George (with Emyr Price and Bryn Parry), 1981. *Recreations:* all sports and restaurants. *Address:* 98 Pencisely Road, Llandaff, Cardiff, South Glamorgan. *T:* Cardiff 568332. *Club:* Cardiff and County (Cardiff).

PRICE, Geoffrey Alan, IPFA, FBIM; Chief Executive, Hereford and Worcester County Council, since 1983. Formerly County Treasurer, Hants CC; previous appts in: Gloucester CC; Southend-on-Sea; Cheshire CC; West Sussex CC. *Address:* County Hall, Spetchley Road, Worcester WR5 2NP.

PRICE, Rt. Hon. George (Cadle), PC 1982; Prime Minister of Belize, 1981–84 (Premier from 1964 until Independence, 1981); *b* 15 Jan. 1919; *s* of William Cadle Price and Irene Cecilia Escalante de Price. *Educ:* Holy Redeemer Primary Sch., Belize City; St John's Coll., Belize City. Private Sec. to late Robert S. Turton; entered politics, 1944; City Councillor, 1947–65 (Mayor of Belize City several times); founding Mem., People's United Party, 1950; Party Sec., 1950–56; became Leader, 1956; elected to National Assembly, 1954; under 1961 Ministerial System, led People's United Party to 100% victory at polls and became First Minister; under 1964 Self-Govt Constitution, title changed to Premier; has led delegns to Central American and Caribbean countries; spearheaded internationalization of Belize problem at internat. forums; addressed UN's Fourth Cttee, 1975, paving way for overwhelming victory at UN when majority of nations voted in favour of Belize's right to self-determination and territorial integrity.

PRICE, Prof. Harold Louis; Professor of Mathematics for Applied Science, University of Leeds, 1968–82, now Emeritus Professor; *b* 3 Sept. 1917; *s* of Reuben Price and Annie Boltsa; *m* 1941, Gertrude Halpern; two *d*. *Educ:* Manchester Grammar Sch.; Sidney Sussex Coll., Cambridge; Univ. of Leeds. MA Cantab; MSc (distinction), PhD Leeds; FRAeS; FIMA. Mathematician, Rotol Airscrews Ltd, 1939–40; Aerodynamicist, Blackburn Aircraft, 1940–45; Research Mathematician, Sperry Gyroscope Co., 1945–46; Univ. of Leeds: Lectr in Applied Maths, 1946–60; Sen. Lectr, 1960–64; Prof. of Maths, 1964–68; Chm., Sch. of Mathematics, 1970–73. *Publications:* research papers on aircraft dynamics, etc. *Address:* 11 West Park Place, Leeds LS8 2EY. *T:* Leeds 664212.

PRICE, Very Rev. Hilary Martin Connop; Rector and Provost of Chelmsford, 1967–77, now Provost Emeritus; *b* 1912; *s* of late Rev. Connop Lewis Price and late Shirley (*née* Lewis); *m* 1939, Dorothea (*née* Beaty-Pownall); one *s* two *d*. *Educ:* Cheltenham Coll.; Queens' Coll., Cambridge (MA); Ridley Hall, Cambridge. Asst Curate, St Peter's, Hersham, Surrey, 1936–40; Sen. Chaplain, Portsmouth Cathedral, 1940–41; Asst Curate, Holy Trinity, Cambridge, 1941–46; Chaplain, RAFVR, 1943–46; Vicar, St Gabriel's, Bishopwearmouth, 1946–56; Rector and Rural Dean, Newcastle-under-Lyme, 1956–67. Prebendary of Lichfield, 1964–67. Proctor in Convocation: of York for Durham Dio., 1954–56; of Canterbury for Lichfield Dio., 1962–67. Mem., General Synod, 1970–75. *Address:* 98 St James Street, Shaftesbury, Dorset SP7 8HF. *T:* Shaftesbury 2118.

PRICE, Sir (James) Robert, KBE 1976; FAA 1959; Chairman of the Executive, Commonwealth Scientific and Industrial Research Organization, 1970–77; *b* 25 March 1912; *s* of Edgar James Price and Mary Katherine Price (*née* Hughes); *m* 1940, Joyce Ethel (*née* Brooke); one *s* two *d*. *Educ:* St Peter's Coll., Adelaide; Univ. of Adelaide (BSc Hons, MSc, DSc); Univ. of Oxford (DPhil). Head, Chemistry Section, John Innes Horticultural Inst., London, 1937–40; (UK) Min. of Supply, 1941–45; Div. of Industrial Chemistry, Council for Scientific and Industrial Research (CSIR), Australia, from 1945; CSIRO: Officer-in-Charge, Organic Chem. Section, 1960, subseq. Chief of Div. of Organic Chem.; Mem., Executive, 1966. Pres., Royal Aust. Chemical Inst., 1963–64. *Publications:* numerous scientific papers in learned jls. *Recreations:* squash; growing Australian native plants. *Address:* Yangoora, 2 Ocean View Avenue, Red Hill South, Victoria 3937, Australia. *Club:* Melbourne (Melb.).

PRICE, John Alan, QC 1980; a Recorder of the Crown Court, since 1980; a Deputy Circuit Judge, since 1975; *b* 11 Sept. 1938; *s* of Frederick Leslie Price and Gertrude Davilda Alice Price; *m* 1964, Elizabeth Myra (*née* Priest); one *s* one *d*. *Educ:* Stretford Grammar Sch.; Manchester Univ. (LLB Hons 1959). Called to the Bar, Gray's Inn, 1961; in practice on Northern Circuit; Head of 60 King St Chambers, Manchester, 1978–80. *Recreations:* tennis, squash, football, golf. *Address:* 5 Essex Court, Temple, EC4Y 9AH. *Clubs:* Northern Lawn Tennis; Wilmslow Golf; Wilmslow Rugby Union Football.

PRICE, John Lister Willis, CVO 1965; HM Diplomatic Service, retired; *b* 25 July 1915; *s* of Canon John Willis Price, Croughton, Brackley, Northants; *m* 1940, Frances Holland (marr. diss.); one *s* one *d*. *Educ:* Bradfield; New College, Oxford. Military Service, 1940–46 (despatches). Joined Foreign Office News Dept, 1946; apptd First Secretary, Paris, 1950; transf. to FO, 1952; to Sofia, 1956; FO, 1959; Counsellor, Head of British Information Services, Bonn, 1962–66; IDC 1967; seconded as Dir of Information, NATO, 1967–72; retired 1972. Dir, Merseyside Develt Office in London, 1972–79. *Recreations:* ski-ing, hill walking. *Address:* Flat 3, 12 Salisbury Road, Hove, East Sussex BN3 3AD. *Club:* Ski Club of Great Britain.

PRICE, J(ohn) Maurice, QC 1976; *b* 4 May 1922; second *s* of Edward Samuel Price and Hilda M. Price, JP; *m* 1945, Mary, *d* of Dr Horace Gibson, DSO and bar, Perth, WA; two *s*. *Educ:* Grove Park Sch., Wrexham; Trinity Coll., Cambridge (MA). Served in Royal Navy, 1941–46 (Submarines, 1943–46), Lieut RNVR. Called to Bar, Gray's Inn, 1949 (Holt Scholar, Holker Sen. Scholar; Bencher 1981), and to Lincoln's Inn (*ad eundem*), 1980; called to Singapore Bar, 1977. Mem., Senate of Inns of Court and the Bar, 1975–78. *Recreations:* fishing, opera. *Address:* Bowzell Place, Weald, Sevenoaks, Kent TN14 6NF; (chambers) 2 New Square, Lincoln's Inn, WC2A 3RU. *T:* 01–242 6201. *Club:* Flyfishers'.

PRICE, John Playfair; *b* 4 July 1905; *s* of William Arthur Price and Edith Octavia Playfair; *m* 1932, Alice Elizabeth Kendall, Boston, Mass; two *d*. *Educ:* Gresham School; New College, Oxford. Hon. Exhib., New Coll., Oxford; Pres. Oxford Union Society. Diplomatic and Consular posts at Peking, Nanking, Tientsin, Canton, Chinkiang, Harbin (Manchuria), Katmandu (Nepal), Gangtok (Sikkim), Los Angeles, Kansas City, Tunis, Tangier, Lisbon, Santiago (Chile), and Geneva. Additional Judge, China, 1933–37; Foreign Office, 1938; 1st Secretary of Embassy, 1943; Consul-General for Khorasan, Sistan and Persian Baluchistan, 1948; retired from Diplomatic Service, 1950. Civil Service and Foreign Service Selection and Final Selection Boards, 1950; Dir and Chm. of Exec., Central African Rhodes Centenary Exhibition, 1951–52; British Council, 1959–61. *Address:* 3 rue Pasteur, 74200 Thonon, France. *T:* (50) 26.63.96.

PRICE, Air Vice-Marshal John Walter, CBE 1979 (OBE 1973); Administrative Manager, Clyde Petroleum plc, since 1984; *b* Birmingham, 26 Jan. 1930; *s* of late Henry Walter Price and Myrza Price (*née* Griffiths); *m* 1956, Margaret Sinclair McIntyre, Sydney, Aust. *Educ:* Solihull Sch.; RAF Coll., Cranwell. MRAeS 1971, FBIM 1979. Joined RAF, 1948; Adjutant, No 11 (Vampire) Sqn, 1950–52; No 77 (Meteor) Sqn, RAAF, Korea, 1952–53 (mentioned in despatches, 1953); No 98 Sqn (Venoms and Vampires), 1953–54; No 2 (F) Op. Trng Unit (Vampires) and No 75 (F) Sqn (Meteors), RAAF, 1954–56; Cadet Wing Adjutant, RAF Tech. Coll., Henlow, 1956–60; RAF Staff Coll., 1960; Air Ministry (Ops Overseas), 1961–64; Comd No 110 Sqn (Sycamore and Whirlwind), 1964–66; Directing Staff, RAF Staff Coll., 1966–68; PSO to Chief of Air Staff, 1968–70; Comd No 72 (Wessex) Sqn, 1970–72; Air Warfare Course, 1973; Dep. Dir Ops (Offensive Support and Jt Warfare), MoD (Air), 1973–75; sowc 1975–76; Comd RAF Laarbruch, 1976–78; Gp Capt. Ops, HQ Strike Comd, 1979; Dir of Ops (Strike), MoD (Air), 1980–82; ACAS (Ops), 1982–84, retd. Governor, Solihull Sch., 1979–, Chm., 1983–. *Recreations:* golf, cabinet making. *Address:* c/o Royal Bank of Scotland, 21 Broad Street, Hereford. *Club:* Royal Air Force.

PRICE, Leolin; *see* Price, A. L.

PRICE, Leonard Sidney, OBE 1974; HM Diplomatic Service, retired 1981; Hon. Treasurer, St John Ambulance in Somerset, since 1983 (Association Deputy Director, 1982–84); *b* 19 Oct. 1922; *s* of late William Price and late Dorothy Price; *m* 1958, Adrienne Mary (*née* Wilkinson); two *s* one *d*. *Educ:* Central Foundation Sch., EC1. Served War, 1942–45. Foreign Office, 1939–42 and 1945–48; Chungking, later Vice-Consul, 1948; Mexico City, 1950; Rome, 1953; Vice-Consul, later Second Sec., Katmandu, 1954; FO, 1957; Consul, Split, 1960; Consul and First Sec., Copenhagen, 1963; FO, later FCO, 1967; First Sec. i/c, Kuching, 1970; Suva, 1972; Parly Clerk, FCO, 1975; Counsellor (Admin), Canberra, 1977–81. *Recreations:* carpentry, wine making. *Address:* 5 Staplegrove Manor, Taunton, Somerset TA2 6EG. *T:* Taunton 87093. *Club:* Civil Service.

PRICE, Leontyne; Opera Prima Donna (Soprano), United States; *b* 10 Feb. 1927. *Educ:* Public Schools, Laurel, Mississippi; Central State College, Wilberforce, Ohio. Four Saints, 1952; Porgy and Bess, 1952–54. Operatic Debut on TV, 1955, as Tosca; Concerts in America, England, Australia, Europe. Operatic debut as Madame Lidoine in Dialogues of Carmelites, San Francisco, 1957; Covent Garden, Verona Arena, Vienna Staatsoper, 1958; five roles, inc. Leonora in Il Trovatore, Madame Butterfly, Donna Anna in Don Giovanni, Metropolitan, 1960–61; Salzburg debut singing soprano lead in Missa Solemnis, 1959; Aida in Aida, Liu in Turandot, La Scala, 1960; opened season at Metropolitan in 1961 as Minnie in Fanciulla del West; opened new Metropolitan Opera House, 1966, as Cleopatra in world premiere of Samuel Barber's Antony and Cleopatra; debut Teatre Dell'Opera, Rome, in Aida, 1967; debut Paris Opera, in Aida, 1968; debut Teatro Colon, Buenos Aires, as Leonora in Il Trovatore, 1969; opened season at Metropolitan Opera, in Aida, 1969. Numerous recordings. Fellow, Amer. Acad. of Arts and Sciences. Hon. Dr of Music: Howard Univ., Washington, DC, 1962; Central State Coll., Wilberforce, Ohio, 1968; Hon. DHL, Dartmouth Univ., 1962; Hon. Dr of Humanities, Rust Coll., Holly Springs, Miss, 1968; Hon. Dr of Humane Letters, Fordham Univ., New York, 1969. Hon. Mem. Bd of Dirs, Campfire Girls, 1966. Presidential Medal of Freedom, 1966; Spingarn Medal, NAACP, 1965. Order of Merit (Italy), 1966. *Recreations:* cooking, dancing, shopping for clothes, etc, antiques for homes in Rome and New York. *Address:* c/o Columbia Artists Management Inc., 165 W 57th Street, New York, NY 10019, USA.

PRICE, Sir Leslie Victor, Kt 1976; OBE 1971; Chairman, Australian Wheat Board, since 1977 (Member since 1971); *b* Toowoomba, Qld, 30 Oct. 1920; *s* of late H. V. L. Price; *m* Lorna Collins; one *s* two *d*. President: Queensland Graingrowers Assoc., 1966–77; Australian Wheatgrowers Fedn, 1970–72; Mem., Queensland State Wheat Bd, 1968–77. *Recreation:* clay target shooting. *Address:* 80 Studley Park Road, Kew, Victoria 3101, Australia. *Clubs:* Queensland; Melbourne.

PRICE, (Llewelyn) Ralph, CBE 1972; Director, Honeywell, since 1971 (Chairman, 1971–81); Chairman, ML Holdings Ltd, since 1976; *b* 23 Oct. 1912; *s* of late L. D. Price, schoolmaster, and late Lena Elizabeth (*née* Dixon); *m* 1939, Vera Patricia Harrison; one *s* two *d*. *Educ:* Quarry Bank Sch., Liverpool. Chartered Accountant, 1935; Sec. to Honeywell Ltd, 1936; Cost Investigator, Min. of Supply, 1943–46; Dir of Manufacturing (Scotland), Honeywell Ltd, 1947; Financial Dir, Honeywell Europe, 1957; Dir, Computer Div., Honeywell, 1960; Managing Dir, Honeywell Ltd, 1965; Chm., Honeywell UK Adv. Council, 1981–. Pres., British Industrial, Measuring & Control Apparatus Manufrs Assoc., 1971–76. CBIM. *Recreations:* golf, bridge, music. *Address:* Nascot, Pinkneys Drive, Pinkneys Green, Maidenhead, Berks. *T:* Maidenhead 28270. *Clubs:* Royal Automobile; Temple Golf (Maidenhead).

PRICE, Margaret Berenice, CBE 1982; opera singer; *b* Tredeger, Wales, 13 April 1941; *d* of late Thomas Glyn Price and of Lilian Myfanwy Richards. *Educ:* Pontllanfraith Secondary Sch.; Trinity Coll. of Music, London. Debut as Cherubino in Marriage of Figaro, Welsh Nat. Opera Co., 1962; debut, in same rôle, at Royal Opera House, Covent Garden, 1963; has subseq. sung many principal rôles at Glyndebourne, San Francisco Opera Co., Cologne Opera House, Munich State Opera, Hamburg State Opera, Vienna State Opera, Lyric Opera, Chicago, Paris Opera; La Scala, Milan; Metropolitan Opera House, NY. Major rôles include: Countess in Marriage of Figaro; Pamina in The Magic Flute; Fiordiligi in Cosi Fan Tutte; Donna Anna in Don Giovanni; Konstanze in Die Entführung; Amelia in Simone Boccanegra; Agathe in Freischütz; Desdemona in Otello; Elisabetta in Don Carlo; title rôles in Aida, Norma and Ariadne auf Naxos. BBC recitals and concerts, also TV appearances. Has made recordings. Hon. FTCL; Hon. DMus Wales, 1983. Elisabeth Schumann Prize for Lieder; Ricordi Prize for Opera; Silver Medal, Worshipful Co. of Musicians. *Recreations:* cooking, driving, reading, walking, swimming. *Address:* c/o Bayerische Staatsoper München, Max Josef Platz 2, 8000 München 22, W Germany.

PRICE, Maj.-Gen. (Maurice) David, CB 1970; OBE 1956; *b* 13 Feb. 1915; *s* of Edward Allan Price and Edna Marion Price (*née* Turner); *m* 1st, 1938, Ella Lacy (*d* 1971), *d* of late H. L. Day; two *s* two *d*; 2nd, 1972, Mrs Olga Marion Oclee. *Educ:* Marlborough; RMA, Woolwich. 2nd Lt R Signals, 1935; Vice-Quartermaster-Gen., MoD (Army), 1967–70, retired. Col Comdt, Royal Corps of Signals, 1967–74. *Recreation:* fishing. *Address:* The Cross, Chilmark, Salisbury, Wiltshire SP3 5AR. *T:* Teffont 212.

PRICE, Sir Norman (Charles), KCB 1975 (CB 1969); Member, European Court of Auditors, 1977–83; Chairman, Board of Inland Revenue, 1973–76 (Deputy Chairman, 1968–73); *b* 5 Jan. 1915; *s* of Charles William and Ethel Mary Price; *m* 1940, Kathleen Beatrice (*née* Elston); two *d*. *Educ:* Plaistow Grammar School. Entered Civil Service as Executive Officer, Customs and Excise, 1933; Inspector of Taxes, Inland Revenue, 1939; Secretaries' Office, Inland Revenue, 1951; Board of Inland Revenue, 1965. *Recreations:*

music, history. *Address:* 306 Gilbert House, Barbican, EC2Y 8BD. *T:* 01–638 0391; 14 Ravens Croft, St Johns Road, Eastbourne BN20 7HX. *T:* Eastbourne 25941.

PRICE, Norman Stewart, CMG 1959; OBE 1946; *b* 9 Aug. 1907; *s* of late Lt-Col Ivon Henry Price, DSO, LLD, Asst Inspr-Gen., RIC, and May Emily (*née* Kinahan), Greystones, Ireland; *m* 1933, Rosalind Evelyn Noelle (*née* Ormsby) (*d* 1973); two *d. Educ:* Portora Royal School, Enniskillen; Exeter Sch.; Trinity Coll., Dublin; Queens Coll., Oxford. LLB 1929, BA Hons 1930. Cadet, Northern Rhodesia, 1930, District Officer, 1932, Provincial Comr, Northern Rhodesia, 1951–59; retired, 1959. Coronation Medal, 1953. *Recreations:* gardening; Captain Dublin University Harriers and Athletic Club, 1928–29; Half-Blue Oxford University Cross Country, 1929. *Address:* 24 Halcombe, Chard, Somerset TA20 2DS. *T:* Chard 61688.

PRICE, Peter Nicholas; Member (C) London South East, since 1984 (Lancashire West, 1979–84), European Parliament; *b* 19 Feb. 1942; *s* of Rev. Dewi Emlyn Price and Kate Mary Price (*née* Thomas). *Educ:* Worcester Royal Grammar Sch.; Aberdare Boys' Grammar Sch.; Univ. of Southampton (BA (Law)); Coll. of Law, Guildford. Solicitor. Interviewer and current affairs freelance broadcaster, 1962–67; Asst Solicitor, Glamorgan CC, 1967–68; solicitor in private practice, 1966–67 and 1968–85. Contested (C) Gen. Elecs: Aberdare 1964, 1966; Caerphilly 1970; Nat. Vice-Chm., Young Conservatives, 1971–72; Mem., Nat. Union Exec. Cttee, 1969–72 and 1978–79; Vice-Chm., Cons. Pol. Centre Nat. Cttee, 1978–79; Hon. Sec., For. Affairs Forum, 1977–79; Vice-Chm., Cons. Gp for Europe, 1979–81; Mem. Council, Europ. Movement, 1971–81. Vice-Chm., Europ. Parlt Budgetary Control Cttee, 1979–84, and its Rapporteur for series of 4 major reports on Community finances, 1985–86; spokesman for Europ. Democratic Gp: Legal Affairs Cttee, 1984–; Budgets Cttee, 1986–; Mem., ACP/EEC Jt Assembly, 1981–. Fellow, Industry and Parlt Trust, 1981–82; Vice-Pres., UK Cttee, Europ. Year of Small and Med.-sized Enterprises, 1983. Vice-Pres., Llangollen Internat. Eisteddfod, 1981–. *Publications:* misc. pol. pamplets and newspaper articles. *Recreations:* theatre, music, photography. *Address:* 7 Juniper Close, Biggin Hill, Westerham, Kent TN16 3LZ. *T:* Biggin Hill 76161.

PRICE, Rev. Peter Owen, CBE 1983; BA; FPhS; RN retired; Minister of Blantyre Old Parish Church, Glasgow, since 1985; *b* Swansea, 18 April 1930; *e s* of late Idwal Price and Florence Price; *m* 1st, 1957, Margaret Trevan (*d* 1977); three *d*; 2nd, 1982, Marilyn Lorne Campbell (*née* Murray). *Educ:* Wyggeston Sch., Leicester; Didsbury Theol Coll., Bristol. BA Open Univ. Ordained, 1960, Methodist Minister, Birmingham; commnd RN as Chaplain, 1960; served: HMS Collingwood, 1960; RM, 1963–64; Staff of C-in-C Med., 1964–68; RNAS Brawdy, 1968–69; RM, 1970–73; HMS Raleigh, 1973; HMS Drake, 1974–78; BRNC Dartmouth, 1978–80; Principal Chaplain, Church of Scotland and Free Churches (Naval), MoD, 1981–84. Hon. Chaplain to the Queen, 1981–84. *Recreations:* warm water sailing, music. *Address:* The Manse of Blantyre Old, High Blantyre, Glasgow G72 9UA.

PRICE, Peter S.; *see* Stanley Price.

PRICE, Ralph; *see* Price, L. R.

PRICE, Sir Robert; *see* Price, Sir J. R.

PRICE, Air Vice-Marshal Robert George, CB 1983; *b* 18 July 1928; *s* of Charles and Agnes Price, Hale, Cheshire; *m* 1958, Celia Anne Mary Talamo; one *s* four *d. Educ:* Oundle Sch.; RAF Coll., Cranwell. 74 Sqn, 1950; Central Flying Sch., 1952; 60 Sqn, 1956; Guided Weapons Trials Sqn, 1958; Staff Coll., 1960; Bomber Comd, 1961; JSSC 1964; CO 31 Sqn, 1965; PSO to Dep. SACEUR, 1968; CO RAF Linton-on-Ouse, 1970; RCDS 1973; Dep. Dir Operations, 1974; Group Captain Flying Trng, Support Comd, 1978; Dep. Chief of Staff, Support HQ, 2nd Allied Tactical Air Force, 1979; AOA, RAF Germany, 1980; AOA, HQ Strike Comd, 1981–83. *Recreations:* golf, ski-ing, bridge. *Address:* c/o Barclays Bank, Easingwold, Yorkshire. *Club:* Royal Air Force.

PRICE, Sir Robert (John) G.; *see* Green-Price.

PRICE, Brig. Rollo Edward Crwys, CBE 1967; DSO 1961; *b* 6 April 1916; *s* of Eardley Edward Carnac Price, CIE; *m* 1945, Diana Budden; three *d. Educ:* Canford; RMC Sandhurst. Commissioned 2nd Lt in S Wales Borderers, 1936; War Service, Middle East and Italy, 1939–45; Lt-Col and seconded for service with Queen's Own Nigeria Regt, 1959–61; Col 1962; Comdr 160 Inf. Bde, 1964–67; Brig. 1966, Comdr, British Troops, Malta, 1968–69, retired. *Address:* Elsford, Netherton, near Yeovil, Somerset. *T:* Yetminster 872377.

PRICE, Roy Kenneth, CB 1980; Under-Secretary (Legal), in office of HM Treasury Solicitor, 1972–81; *b* 16 May 1916; *s* of Ernest Price and Margaret Chapman Price (*née* Scott); *m* 1948, Martha (*née* Dannhauser); one *s* one *d. Educ:* Eltham Coll. Qualified as Solicitor, 1937. Town Clerk, Borough of Pembroke, and Clerk to Castlemartin Justices, 1939–40. Served War, Army, 1940–46. Officer in Charge, Legal Aid (Welfare), Northern Command, 1946 (Lt-Col). Joined HM Treasury Solicitor, as Legal Asst, 1946; Sen. Legal Asst, 1950; Asst Solicitor, 1962. Pres., Richmond Assoc., Nat. Trust; Mem. Exec. Council, RNIB; Chm., Portcullis Trust. *Recreations:* gardening, theatre, travel. *Address:* 6 Old Palace Lane, Richmond, Surrey. *T:* 01–940 6685. *Club:* Law Society.

PRICE, Terence; *see* Price, B. T.

PRICE, Mrs Vincent; *see* Browne, C. E.

PRICE, Vivian William Cecil; QC 1972; *b* 14 April 1926; 4th *s* of late Evan Price, Hawkhurst, Kent; *m* 1961, Elizabeth Anne, *o c* of late Arthur Rawlins and Georgina (*née* Guinness); three *s* two *d. Educ:* Judd Sch., Tonbridge, Kent; Trinity Coll., Cambridge (BA); Balliol Coll., Oxford (BA). Royal Navy, 1946–49, Instructor Lieut. Called to the Bar: Middle Temple, 1954 (Bencher, 1979); Hong Kong, 1975; Singapore, 1979. Dep. High Court Judge (Chancery Div.), 1975–85; a Recorder of the Crown Court, 1984. Sec., Lord Denning's Cttee on Legal Educn for Students from Africa, 1960; Junior Counsel (Patents) to the Board of Trade, 1967–72; Mem., Patents Procedure Cttee, 1973. Mem., Incorporated Council of Law Reporting for England and Wales, 1980–. *Address:* Redwall Farmhouse, Linton, Kent. *T:* Maidstone 43682; New Court, Temple, EC4. *T:* 01–353 1769. *Club:* Travellers'.

See also A. L. Price.

PRICE, Walter Robert; Executive Director: Latin American and South African Operations, General Motors, since 1984; Overseas Assembly, North American Vehicles, since 1982; Joint Ventures and African Operations, General Motors, since 1981; Managing Director, GM de Venezuela, since 1983; *b* 26 Feb. 1926; *m* 1951, Mary Alice Hubbard; one *s* three *d. Educ:* Wesleyan Univ., Middletown, Conn, USA (BA). Managing Director: General Motors Suisse, Bienne, Switzerland, 1967; General Motors Continental, Antwerp, Belgium, 1970; General Motors South African (Pty) Ltd, Port Elizabeth, S Africa, 1971; Chm. and Man. Dir, Vauxhall Motors Ltd, Luton, 1974–79; Vice Pres., General Motors Corp., 1978–. Vice Pres., SMMT, 1978–79. *Recreations:* tennis, squash, golf. *Address:* General Motors Corporation, General Motors Building, 3044 West Grand Boulevard, Detroit, Mich 48202, USA.

PRICE, Prof. William Charles, FRS 1959; Wheatstone Professor of Physics, University of London, at King's College, 1955–76, now Emeritus; *b* 1 April 1909; *s* of Richard Price and Florence Margaret (*née* Charles); *m* 1939, Nest Myra Davies; one *s* one *d. Educ:* Swansea Grammar Sch.; University of Wales, Swansea (Hon. Fellow, 1985); Johns Hopkins University, Baltimore; Trinity Coll., Cambridge, BSc (Wales) 1930; Commonwealth Fellow, 1932; PhD (Johns Hopkins), 1934; Cambridge: Senior 1851 Exhibitioner, 1935, University Demonstrator, 1937–43, PhD (Cantab) 1937. Prize Fellow, Trinity Coll., 1938; ScD (Cantab) 1949; Meldola Medal of Inst. of Chem., 1938; Senior Spectroscopist, ICI (Billingham Div.), 1943–48; Research Associate, University of Chicago, 1946–47; Reader in Physics, University of London (King's Coll.) 1948. FKC 1970. FRIC 1944; FIP 1950. Co-editor, British Bulletin of Spectroscopy, 1950–. Hon. DSc Wales, 1970. *Publications:* research and review articles on physics and chemistry in scientific journals. *Address:* 38 Cross Way, Orpington, Kent BR5 1PE. *T:* Orpington 28815.

PRICE, (William Frederick) Barry, OBE 1977; HM Diplomatic Service, retired; Consul-General, Amsterdam, 1983–85; *b* 12 Feb. 1925; *s* of William Thomas and Vera Price; *m* 1948, Lorraine Elisabeth Suzanne Hoather; three *s* two *d. Educ:* Worcester Royal Grammar Sch.; St Paul's Training Coll., Cheltenham. Served War: Armed Forces, 1944–47: commissioned Royal Warwicks, 1945; demobilised, 1947. Primary Sch. Teacher, 1948. Joined Bd of Trade, 1950; Asst Trade Comr: in Delhi, 1954; in Nairobi, 1957; Trade Commissioner, Accra, 1963; transferred to HM Diplomatic Service, 1966; 1st Sec., Sofia, 1967; seconded to East European Trade Council, 1971; Consul-Gen., Rotterdam, 1973–77; Consul, Houston, 1978–81; Counsellor (Commercial and Economic), Bangkok, 1981–82; Kuala Lumpur, 1982. *Recreation:* Open University student. *Address:* 46 Finchley Park, N12 9JL. *T:* 01–445 4642. *Club:* Oriental.

PRICE, William George; Consultant, National Union of Licensed Victuallers, since 1979; *b* 15 June 1934; *s* of George and Lillian Price; *m* 1963, Joy Thomas (marr. diss. 1978); two *s. Educ:* Forest of Dene Technical Coll.; Gloucester Technical Coll. Staff Journalist: Three Forest Newspapers, Cinderford, until 1959; Coventry Evening Telegraph, 1959–62; Birmingham Post & Mail, 1962–66. MP (Lab) Rugby, Warks, 1966–79; PPS: to Sec. of State for Educn and Science, 1968–70; to Dep. Leader, Labour Party, 1972–74; Parliamentary Secretary: ODM, March-Oct. 1974; Privy Council Office, 1974–79. Contested (Lab) Rugby, 1979, 1983. *Recreation:* sport. *Address:* 54 Kings Grove, Peckham, SE15 2NB.

PRICE, Winford Hugh Protheroe, OBE 1983; FCA; City Treasurer, Cardiff City Council, 1975–83; *b* 5 Feb. 1926; *s* of Martin Price and Doris Blanche Price. *Educ:* Cardiff High Sch. IPFA 1952; FCA 1954. Served War, RAFVR, 1944–48. City Treasurer's and Controller's Dept, Cardiff, 1942; Dep. City Treasurer, Cardiff, 1973–75. Public Works Loan Comr, 1979–83. Treasurer and Financial Adviser, Council for the Principality, 1975–83; Financial Adviser, Assoc. of Dist Councils Cttee for Wales, 1975–83; Treasurer: The Queen's Silver Jubilee Trust (S Glam), 1976–83; Royal National Eisteddfod of Wales (Cardiff), 1978. Occasional lectr on local govt topics. *Publications:* contrib. to jls. *Recreation:* chess. *Address:* 3 Oakfield Street, Roath, Cardiff CF2 3RD. *T:* Cardiff 494635.

PRICE EVANS, David Alan; *see* Evans.

PRICHARD, Mathew Caradoc Thomas; Chairman: Agatha Christie Ltd, since 1971; Authors' Division, Booker McConnell PLC, since 1985; *b* 21 Sept. 1943; *s* of late Major H. de B. Prichard and of Rosalind Hicks; *m* 1967, Angela Caroline Maples; one *s* two *d. Educ:* Eton College; New College, Oxford. BA (PPE). Penguin Books, 1965–69; Advisory Local Dir, Barclays Bank plc, 1977–. Pres., Welsh Group of Artists, 1974–; Member: Court of Governors and Council, Nat. Museum of Wales, 1975–; Welsh Arts Council, 1980– (Vice-Chm., 1983–86; Chm., 1986–); Arts Council of GB, 1983–. High Sheriff, Glamorgan, 1972–73. *Recreations:* golf, cricket, bridge. *Address:* Pwllywrach, Cowbridge, South Glamorgan CF7 7NJ. *T:* Cowbridge 2256. *Clubs:* Boodle's, MCC; Cardiff and County; Royal & Ancient Golf (St Andrews); Royal Porthcawl Golf.

PRICHARD, Sir Montague (Illtyd), Kt 1972; CBE 1965; MC 1944; Chairman: Belgrave Holdings PLC, since 1985; Scientific Applied Research plc, since 1985; Director: Polysius Ltd, since 1975; United Management Services Ltd, since 1985; *b* 26 Sept. 1915; *s* of late George Montague Prichard; *m* 1942, Kathleen Georgana Hamill; two *s* one *d. Educ:* Felsted Sch., Essex. Served War of 1939–45 (despatches thrice, MC): Royal Engineers: Somaliland, India, Burma, Malaya and Far East, Lt-Col as CRE 20 Indian Division. R. A. Lister & Co. Ltd, 1933–53 (excluding war service), Dir, 1950–53; Perkins Engineering Group Ltd, 1953, Man. Dir, 1958, Chm., 1959–75; Dir, Massey-Ferguson Ltd (Canada), 1961–75; retired from exec. capacities, 1975; Dir, Tozer, Kemsley & Millbourn (Holdings) plc, 1976–85 (Chm., 1982–85). Member: British Productivity Council; BNEC, 1965–72; Founder Chairman: Nat. Marketing Council, 1963; British Industry Roads Campaign. Vice-Pres., SMMT, 1966–70; Pres., Motor Industry Res. Assoc., 1972–74. FInstMSM. *Address:* Willowdale House, Apethorpe, Peterborough PE8 5DP. *T:* Kingscliffe 211. *Club:* East India, Devonshire, Sports and Public Schools.

PRICHARD, Air Vice-Marshal Richard Augustin R.; *see* Riseley-Prichard.

PRICHARD, Air Commodore Richard Julian Paget, CB 1963; CBE 1958; DFC 1942; AFC 1941; *b* 4 Oct. 1915; *o s* of Major W. O. Prichard, 24th Regt; unmarried. *Educ:* Harrow; St Catharine's Coll., Cambridge. Entered RAF, 1937; Air Armament Sch., Eastchurch and Manby, 1937–39; Flying Instructor, South Cerney, 1939–41; No. 21 (LB) Squadron, 1942–43; Staff Coll. (psa), 1943; AEAF, 1943–45; Chief Intelligence Officer, Burma and FEAF, 1946–47; Chief Flying Instructor, RAF Coll., Cranwell, 1947–49; Ministry of Defence, 1949–52; Instructor, RAF Staff Coll., 1953–55; Station Comdr, RAF Tengah, Singapore, 1956–58. IDC, 1959; Director Air Plans, Air Ministry, 1960–63; AOC No 13 Scottish Sector, Fighter Command, 1963–64; AOC Northern Sector of Fighter Command, 1965–66; retired, 1966. US Legion of Merit, 1944. *Recreations:* tennis, fishing. *Address:* c/o Lloyds Bank, 6 Pall Mall, SW1Y 5NH. *Club:* Royal Air Force.

PRICHARD-JONES, Sir John, 2nd Bt, *cr* 1910; barrister; farmer and bloodstock breeder; *b* 20 Jan. 1913; *s* of 1st Bt and Marie, *y d* of late Charles Read, solicitor; *S* father, 1917; *m* 1937, Heather, (from whom he obtained a divorce, 1950), *er d* of late Sir Walter Nugent, 4th Bt; one *s*; *m* 1959, Helen Marie Thérèse, *e d* of J. F. Liddy, dental surgeon, 20 Laurence Street, Drogheda; one *d. Educ:* Eton; Christ Church, Oxford (BA Hons; MA). Called to Bar, Gray's Inn, 1936. Commnd, Queen's Bays, 1939, and served throughout War. *Heir: s* David John Walter Prichard-Jones, BA (Hons) Oxon, *b* 14 March 1943. *Address:* Allenswood House, Lucan, Co. Dublin.

PRICKETT, Air Chief Marshal Sir Thomas (Other), KCB 1965 (CB 1957); DSO 1943, DFC 1942; RAF retired; *b* 31 July 1913; *s* of late E. G. Prickett; *m* 1st, 1942, Elizabeth Gratian, (*d* 1984), *d* of late William Galbally, Laguna Beach, Calif, USA; one *s* one *d*; 2nd, 1985, Shirley Westerman. *Educ:* Stubbington House Sch.; Haileybury Coll. Joined RAF, 1937; commanded RAF Tangmere, 1949–51; Group Captain operations, HQ Middle East Air Force, 1951–54; commanded RAF Jever, 1954–55; attended Imperial Defence Coll., 1956; Chief of Staff Air Task Force, 1956; Director of Policy, Air Ministry, 1957–58; SASO, HQ No 1 Group, 1958–60; ACAS (Ops) Air Ministry, 1960–63; ACAS (Policy and Planning) Air Ministry, 1963–64; AOC-in-C, NEAF, Comdr British Forces Near East, and Administrator, Sovereign Base Area, 1964–66; AOC-in-C, RAF Air Support Command, 1967–68; Air Mem. for Supply and Organisation, MoD, 1968–70. *Recreations:* polo, sailing, golf. *Address:* East House, Petworth, West Sussex. *Club:* Royal Air Force.

PRICKMAN, Air Cdre Thomas Bain, CB 1953; CBE 1945; *b* 1902; *m* 1st, Ethel Serica (*d* 1949), *d* of John Cubbon, Douglas, IOM; 2nd, 1952, Dorothy (who *m* 1946, Group Captain F. C. Read, *d* 1949), *d* of John Charles Clarke. *Educ:* Blundell's Sch. Joined RAF, 1923. Served War of 1939–45, with Fighter Command; RAF Liaison staff in Australia, 1946–48; AOA, Home Command, 1950–54; retired, 1954. *Address:* Tilsmore Cottage, Cross-in-Hand, Heathfield, Sussex TN21 0LS.

PRIDAY, Christopher Bruton; QC 1986; *b* 7 Aug. 1926; *s* of Arthur Kenneth Priday and Rosemary Priday; *m* 1953, Jill Holroyd Sergeant, *o d* of John Holroyd Sergeant and Kathleen Sergeant; two *s*. *Educ:* Radley College; University College, Oxford (MA). Called to the Bar, Gray's Inn, 1951; Hon. *ad eundem* Mem., Middle Temple, 1985. *Publications:* jt editor, publications on law of landlord and tenant. *Recreations:* opera, golf at St Enodoc. *Address:* 29 Tedworth Square, SW3 4DP. *T:* 01–352 4492. *Club:* St Enodoc Golf.

PRIDDLE, Robert John; Under Secretary and Head of Telecommunications and Posts Division, Department of Trade and Industry, since 1985; *b* 9 Sept. 1938; *s* of Albert Leslie Priddle and Alberta Edith Priddle; *m* 1962, Janice Elizabeth Gorham; two *s*. *Educ:* King's Coll. Sch., Wimbledon; Peterhouse, Cambridge (MA). Asst Principal, Min. of Aviation, 1960, Principal 1965; Private Sec. to Minister for Aerospace, 1971–73; Asst Sec., DTI, 1973, and Dept of Energy, 1974; Under Sec., Dept of Energy, 1977–85. *Publication:* Victoriana, 1959 (2nd edn 1963). *Address:* Department of Trade and Industry, 1 Victoria Street, SW1H 0ET.

PRIDEAUX, Sir Humphrey (Povah Treverbian), Kt 1971; OBE 1945; DL; Chairman, Morland & Co., since 1983 (Director, 1981; Vice Chairman, 1982); Director, The London Life Association Ltd, since 1964 (Vice-President, 1965–72; President, 1973–84); Chairman, Lord Wandsworth Foundation, since 1966; *b* 13 Dec. 1915; 3rd *s* of Walter Treverbian Prideaux and Marion Fenn (*née* Arbuthnot); *m* 1939, Cynthia, *er d* of late Lt-Col H. Birch Reynardson, CMG; four *s*. *Educ:* St Aubyns, Rottingdean; Eton; Trinity Coll., Oxford (MA). Commissioned 3rd Carabiniers (Prince of Wales's Dragoon Guards) 1936; DAQMG Guards Armd Div., 1941; Instructor, Staff Coll., 1942; AQMG 21 Army Gp, 1943; AA QMG Guards Armd Div., 1944; Joint Planning Staff, War Office, 1945; Naval Staff Coll., 1948; Commandant School of Administration, 1948; Chiefs of Staff Secretariat, 1950; retired, 1953. Director, NAAFI, 1956–73 (Man. Dir, 1961–65; Chm., 1963–73); Chm., Brooke Bond Liebig Ltd, 1972–80 (Dir, 1968; Dep. Chm., 1969–71); Vice-Chm., W. H. Smith & Son Ltd, 1977–81 (Dir, 1969–77); Dir, Grindleys, 1982–85. DL Hants 1983. *Recreations:* country pursuits. *Address:* Summers Farm, Long Sutton, Basingstoke, Hants RG25 1TQ. *T:* Basingstoke 862295. *Club:* Cavalry and Guards.

See also Sir J. F. Prideaux, W. A. Prideaux.

PRIDEAUX, Sir John (Francis), Kt 1974; OBE 1945; DL; Director: Dow Scandia Holdings, since 1982; Arbuthnot Latham Bank, since 1982; *b* 30 Dec. 1911; 2nd *s* of Walter Treverbian Prideaux and Marion Fenn (*née* Arbuthnot); *m* 1934, Joan, *er d* of late Captain Gordon Hargreaves Brown, MC, and Lady Pigott Brown; two *s* one *d*. *Educ:* St Aubyns, Rottingdean; Eton. Middlesex Yeomanry, 1933; served War of 1939–45, Colonel Q, 2nd Army, 1944. Joined Arbuthnot Latham & Co. Ltd, Merchant Bankers, 1930, Dir, 1936–69, Chm., 1964–69. Mem., London Adv. Bd, Bank of NSW, 1948–74; Director: Westminster Bank Ltd, later National Westminster Bank Ltd, 1955–81 (Chm., 1971–77); Westminster Foreign Bank Ltd, later Internat. Westminster Bank Ltd, 1955–81 (Chm., 1969–77). Chm., Cttee of London Clearing Bankers, 1974–76; Vice-Pres., British Bankers' Assoc., 1972–77. Pres., Inst. of Bankers, 1974–76. Mem., Wilson Cttee to review functioning of financial instns in the City, 1977–80. Dep. Chm., Commonwealth Develt Corp., 1960–70; Chm., Victoria League for Commonwealth Friendship, 1977–81. Mem., Lambeth, Southwark and Lewisham AHA(T), 1974–82 (Commissioner, Aug. 1979–March 1980); Treasurer and Chm., Bd of Governors, St Thomas' Hosp., 1964–74; Chm., Special Trustees, St Thomas' Hosp., 1974–. Prime Warden, Goldsmiths' Company, 1972. DL Surrey 1976. Legion of Merit, USA, 1945. *Address:* Elderslie, Ockley, Surrey. *T:* Dorking 711263. *Clubs:* Brooks's, Overseas Bankers (Pres. 1976–77).

See also Sir H. P. T. Prideaux, W. A. Prideaux.

PRIDEAUX, Walter Arbuthnot, CBE 1973; MC 1945; TD 1948; *b* 4 Jan. 1910; *e s* of Walter Treverbian Prideaux and Marion Fenn (*née* Arbuthnot); *m* 1937, Anne, *d* of Francis Stewart Cokayne; two *s* two *d*. *Educ:* Eton; Trinity Coll., Cambridge. Solicitor, 1934. Assistant Clerk of the Goldsmiths' Company, 1939–53, Clerk 1953–75. Chm., City Parochial Foundn, 1972–80. Kent Yeomanry, 1936–48. *Recreation:* rowed for Cambridge, 1930, 1931. *Address:* 16 Tanbridge Place, Horsham, West Sussex RH12 1RY. *T:* Horsham 58891.

See also Sir H. P. T. Prideaux, Sir J. F. Prideaux.

PRIDHAM, Brian Robert; HM Diplomatic Service, retired; Research Fellow, Centre for Arab Gulf Studies, since 1983, and Lecturer in Arabic, Department of Arabic and Islamic Studies, since 1984, University of Exeter; *b* 22 Feb. 1934; *s* of Reginald Buller Pridham and Emily Pridham (*née* Winser); *m* 1954, Fay Coles; three *s*. *Educ:* Hele's Sch., Exeter. MA Exon, 1984. RWAFF (Nigeria Regt), 1952–54; Foreign Office, 1954–57; MECAS, 1957–59; Bahrain, 1959; Vice-Consul, Muscat, 1959–62; Foreign Office, 1962–64; 2nd Sec., Algiers, 1964–66, 1st Sec., 1966–67; Foreign Office, 1967–70; Head of Chancery: La Paz, 1970–73; Abu Dhabi, 1973–75; Dir of MECAS, Shemlan, Lebanon, 1975–76; Counsellor, Khartoum, 1976–79; Head of Communications Ops Dept, FCO, 1979–81; Centre for Arab Gulf Studies, Exeter Univ., 1981– (Dep. Dir, 1984–85; Dir, 1985–86). *Publications:* (ed) Contemporary Yemen: politics and historical background, 1984; (ed) Economy, Society and Culture in Contemporary Yemen, 1984; (ed) The Arab Gulf and the West, 1985; (ed) Oman: economic, social and strategic developments, 1986. *Recreations:* sailing, old roses. *Address:* c/o Barclays Bank, Exeter.

PRIDHAM, Kenneth Robert Comyn, CMG 1976; HM Diplomatic Service, retired; *b* 28 July 1922; *s* of late Colonel G. R. Pridham, CBE, DSO, and Mignonne, *d* of late Charles Cumming, ICS; *m* 1965, Ann Rosalind, *d* of late E. Gilbert Woodward, Metropolitan Magistrate, and of Mrs Woodward. *Educ:* Winchester; Oriel Coll., Oxford. Lieut, 60th Rifles, 1942–46; served North Africa, Italy, Middle East (despatches). Entered Foreign (subseq. Diplomatic) Service, 1946; served at Berlin, Washington, Belgrade and Khartoum, and at the Foreign Office; Counsellor: Copenhagen, 1968–72; FCO, 1972–74; Asst Under Sec. of State, FCO, 1974–78; Ambassador to Poland, 1978–81. Vis. Res. Fellow, RIIA, 1981–82. *Address:* c/o Lloyds Bank, 16 St James's Street, SW1. *Club:* Travellers'.

PRIEST, Prof. Robert George, MD, FRCPsych; Professor of Psychiatry, University of London and Head of Department of Psychiatry at St Mary's Hospital Medical School, since 1973; Hon. Consultant Psychiatrist, St Mary's Hospital, London, since 1973; *b* 28 Sept. 1933; *er s* of late James Priest and of Phoebe Priest; *m* 1955, Marilyn, *er d* of late Baden Roberts Baker and of Evelyn Baker; two *s*. *Educ:* University Coll., London and University Coll. Hosp. Med. Sch. MB, BS 1956; DPM 1963; MRCPE 1964; MD 1970; MRCPsych 1971 (Foundn Mem.); FRCPE 1974; FRCPsych 1974. Lectr in Psychiatry, Univ. of Edinburgh, 1964–67; Exchange Lectr, Univ. of Chicago, 1966; Consultant, Illinois State Psychiatric Inst., Chicago, 1966; Sen. Lectr, St George's Hosp. Med. Sch., London, 1967–73; Hon. Consultant: St George's Hosp., London, 1967–73; Springfield Hosp., London, 1967–73; Recognised Teacher, Univ. of London, 1968–; Examiner in Psychiatry, NUI, 1975–78, 1980–83. Chairman: Psychiatric Adv. Sub-Cttee, NW Thames RHA, 1976–79 (Vice-Chm., Reg. Manpower Cttee, 1980–83); Psych. Sub-Cttee, Central Cttee for Hosp. Med. Services, 1983–. Member: Council (Chm. Membership Cttee), British Assoc. for Psychopharmacology, 1977–81; World Psychiatric Assoc., 1980– (Mem. Cttee, 1985–); Pres., Soc. for Psychosomatic Res., 1980–81 (Vice-Pres., 1978–80); Chm., Mental Health Gp Cttee, BMA, 1982–85 (Mem. 1978–); Internat. Coll. of Psychosomatic Medicine: Fellow, 1977; Mem. Gov. Body and UK Delegate, 1978–81; Treasurer, 1981–83; Secretary, 1981–85; Vice-Pres., 1985–; Royal Coll. of Psychiatrists: Mem. Council, 1982–; Registrar, 1983–; Chm., Public Policy Cttee, 1983–; Chm., Gen. Psych. Cttee, 1985–. A. E. Bennett Award, Soc. for Biol Psychiatry, USA (jtly), 1965; Doris Odlum Prize (BMA), 1968; Gutheil Von Domarus Award, Assoc. for Advancement of Psychotherapy and Amer. Jl of Psychotherapy, NY, 1970. *Publications:* Insanity: A Study of Major Psychiatric Disorders, 1977; (ed jtly) Sleep Research, 1979; (ed jtly) Benzodiazepines Today and Tomorrow, 1980; (ed) Psychiatry in Medical Practice, 1982; Anxiety and Depression, 1983; (ed) Sleep, 1984; Psychological Disorders in Obstetrics and Gynaecology, 1985; (jtly) 8th edn, Handbook of Psychiatry, 1986; chapters in: Current Themes in Psychiatry, 1978; Mental Illness in Pregnancy and the Puerperium, 1978; Psychiatry in General Practice, 1981; Modern Emergency Department Practice, 1983; The Scientific Basis of Psychiatry, 1983; The Psychosomatic Approach: contemporary practice of wholeperson care, 1986; articles in BMJ, Brit. Jl of Psychiatry, Amer. Jl of Psychotherapy and other learned jls. *Recreations:* squash, tennis, foreign languages, nature study. *Address:* Woodeaves, 29 Old Slade Lane, Richings Park, Iver, Bucks SL0 9DY. *T:* Iver 653178.

PRIESTLAND, Gerald Francis; Religious Affairs Correspondent, BBC, 1977–82; *b* 26 Feb. 1927; *s* of late Frank Priestland and Nelly Priestland (*née* Renny); *m* 1949, Helen Sylvia (*née* Rhodes); two *s* two *d*. *Educ:* Charterhouse; New Coll., Oxford (BA). Subeditor, BBC News, 1949–54; BBC Correspondent: New Delhi, 1954–58; Washington, 1958–61; Beirut, 1961–65; Washington, 1965–70; news presenter on Radio and TV, 1970–76. Hon. Fellow, Manchester Polytechnic, 1978. M Open Univ., 1985. Sandford St Martin Prize for religious broadcasting, 1982. *Television:* Priestland Right and Wrong (series), 1983. *Publications:* America the Changing Nation, 1968; Frying Tonight (the Saga of Fish and Chips), 1971; The Future of Violence, 1976; Yours Faithfully, Vol. 1, 1979; Dilemmas of Journalism, 1979; (with Sylvia Priestland) West of Hayle River, 1980; Yours Faithfully, Vol. 2, 1981; Priestland's Progress, 1981; Reasonable Uncertainty (Swarthmore Lect.), 1982; Who Needs the Church? (William Barclay Lects), 1983; Gerald Priestland at Large, 1983; Priestland Right and Wrong, 1983; The Case Against God, 1984; For All the Saints (Backhouse Lect.), 1985; Something Understood (autobiog.), 1986. *Recreation:* trying to think of a recreation. *Address:* 4 Temple Fortune Lane, NW11 7UD. *T:* 01–455 3297; The Old Sunday School, Carfury, Cornwall. *T:* Penzance 69191.

PRIESTLEY, Prof. Charles Henry Brian, AO 1976; FAA 1954; FRS 1967; Professor of Meteorology, Monash University, Australia, 1978–80; *b* 8 July 1915; *s* of late T. G. Priestley; *m* 1946, Constance, *d* of H. Tweedy; one *s* two *d*. *Educ:* Mill Hill Sch.; St John's Coll., Cambridge. MA 1942, ScD 1953. Served in Meteorological Office, Air Ministry, 1939–46; subseq. with CSIRO, Australia; Chief of Div. of Meteorological Physics, 1946–71; Chm., Environmental Physics Res., 1971–78. David Syme Prize, University of Melbourne, 1956. Member Exec. Cttee, International Assoc. of Meteorology, 1954–60, Vice-Pres., 1967–75; Vice-Pres., Australian Acad. of Science, 1959–60; Mem., Adv. Cttee, World Meteorological Organisation, 1964–68 (Chm., 1967; Internat. Met. Orgn Prize, 1973). FRMetSoc (Hon. Life Fellow, 1978; Buchan Prize, 1950 and Symons Medal, 1967, of Society); FInstP. Hon. Mem., Amer. Met. Soc., 1978 (Rossby Medal, 1975). *Publications:* Turbulent Transfer in the Lower Atmosphere, 1959; about 60 papers in scientific journals. *Recreation:* golf. *Address:* Flat 2, 862 Malvern Road, Armidale, Vic 3143, Australia.

PRIESTLEY, Clive, CB 1983; an HQ Director, since 1983, and Director, Inland Communications, Southern England and Wales, since 1986, British Telecom; *b* 12 July 1935; *s* of late Albert Ernest and Annie May Priestley; *m* 1st, 1961, Barbara Anne (marr. diss. 1984), *d* of George Gerard and Ann Doris Wells; two *d*; 2nd, 1985, Daphne June Challis Loasby, JP, *o d* of late W. Challis and Dorothy Franks. *Educ:* Loughborough Grammar Sch.; Nottingham Univ. BA 1956; MA 1958. Nat. Service, 1958–60. Joined HM Home Civil Service, 1960; Min. of Educn, later DES, 1960–65; Schools Council, 1965–67; Harkness Commonwealth Fund Fellow, Harvard Univ., 1967–68; CSD, 1969–79; Prime Minister's Office, 1979–83 (Chief of Staff to Sir Derek Rayner); Under Sec., 1979–83; MPO, 1982–83; Director: Special Projs, BT, 1983–85; Management Control Systems, 1985. Member: Council, Univ. of Reading, 1984–; Univ. of Cambridge Careers Service Syndicate, 1986–. Governor, Royal Shakespeare Co., 1984–; Mem. Philharmonia Trust, 1985–. *Publications:* financial scrutinies of the Royal Opera House, Covent Garden Ltd, and of the Royal Shakespeare Co., 1984. *Address:* c/o British Telecom, Bond Street, Bristol BS1 3TD. *Club:* Army and Navy.

PRIESTLEY, Mrs J. B.; *see* Hawkes, Jacquetta.

PRIESTLEY, Leslie William, TD 1974; FIB; CBIM; Chief General Manager, TSB England and Wales and Central Trustee Savings Bank, since 1985; *b* 22 Sept. 1933; *s* of Winifred and George Priestley; *m* 1960, Audrey Elizabeth (*née* Humber); one *s* one *d*. *Educ:* Shooters Hill Grammar School. Head of Marketing, Barclaycard, 1966–73; Asst Gen. Manager, Barclays Bank, 1974–77, Local Dir, 1978–79; Sec. Gen., Cttee of London Clearing Bankers, 1979–83; Dir, Bankers' Automated Clearing Services, 1979–83; Man. Dir, Barclays Insurance Services Co., 1983–84; Regional Gen. Manager, Barclays Bank, 1984–85. Dir, London Electricity Board, 1984–. Consultant Editor, Bankers' Magazine, 1972–81. *Publication:* (ed) Bank Lending with Management Accounts, 1981. *Recreations:* reading, gardening. *Address:* TSB, 60 Lombard Street, EC3V 9EA. *T:* 01–623 6000. *Clubs:* Royal Automobile, Wig and Pen.

PRIESTLEY, Prof. Maurice Bertram, MA, PhD; Professor of Statistics, University of Manchester Institute of Science and Technology, since 1970 and Head of Department of Mathematics, 1973–75, 1977–78 and since 1980; *b* 15 March 1933; *s* of Jack and Rose Priestley; *m* 1959, Nancy, *d* of late Ralph and Hilda Nelson; one *s* one *d*. *Educ:* Manchester

Grammar Sch.; Jesus Coll., Cambridge. BA (Wrangler, 1954), MA, DipMathStat (Cambridge); PhD (Manchester). Scientific Officer, RAE, 1955–56; Asst Lectr, Univ. of Manchester, 1957–60, Lectr, 1960–65; Vis. Professor, Princeton and Stanford Univs, USA, 1961–62; Sen. Lectr, UMIST, 1965–70; Dir, Manchester-Sheffield Sch. of Probability and Stats, and Hon. Prof. of Probability and Stats, Sheffield Univ., 1976–79. Mem. Court and Council, UMIST, 1971–74. FIMS; FSS; Mem. Council, Royal Statistical Soc., 1971–75; Mem., ISI. Editor-in-chief, Jl of Time Series Analysis, 1980–. *Publications:* Spectral Analysis and Time Series, Vols I and II, 1981; papers and articles in Jl RSS, Biometrika, Technom., Automatica, Jl of Sound and Vibration. *Recreations:* music, hi-fi and audio, golf. *Address:* Department of Mathematics, University of Manchester Institute of Science and Technology, PO Box 88, Manchester M60 1QD. *T:* 061–236 3311.

PRIESTMAN, John David; Clerk of the Parliamentary Assembly of the Council of Europe, 1971–Dec. 1986; *b* 29 March 1926; *s* of Bernard Priestman and Hermine Bréal; *m* 1951, Nada Valić; two *s* two *d*. *Educ:* private sch. in Paris; Westminster Sch.; Merton Coll. and Christ Church, Oxford (Hon. Mods, Lit. Hum.) Served Coldstream Guards, 1944–47, Temp. Captain. Third, subseq. Second, Sec., Belgrade, 1949–53; Asst Private Sec. to Rt Hon. Anthony Eden, 1953–55; joined Secretariat, Council of Europe, 1955; Head of Sec. Gen's Private Office, 1961; Sec., Cttee of Ministers, 1966; Dep. Clerk of Parly Assembly, 1968–71. *Recreations:* off-piste Alpine ski-ing, music, competition bridge, gastronomic research. *Address:* 6 rue Adolphe Wurtz, 67000 Strasbourg, France. *T:* 88–354049; 13 chemin de la Colle, 06160 Antibes, France. *T:* 93–617724.

PRIGOGINE, Prof. Ilya; Grand-Croix de l'Ordre de Léopold II, Belgium; Professor, Université Libre de Bruxelles, since 1951; Director, Instituts Internationaux de Physique et de Chimie, since 1959; Director, Ilya Prigogine Center of Statistical Mechanics and Thermodynamics, University of Texas at Austin, since 1967; *b* 25 Jan. 1917; *m* 1961, Marina Prokopowicz; two *s*. *Educ:* Univ. of Brussels (Dr en Sciences Physiques, 1941). Prof., Dept of Chemistry, Enrico Fermi Inst. for Nuclear Studies, and Inst. for Study of Metals, Univ. of Chicago, 1961–66; Member: Académie Royale de Belgique, 1958; Royal Soc. of Sciences, Uppsala, Sweden, 1967; German Acad. Naturforscher Leopoldina, GDR, 1970; Acad. Internat. de Philosophie des Sciences, 1973; Acad. Européenne des Scis, des Arts et des Lettres, Paris, 1980 (Vice-Pres., 1980); Accademia Mediterranea delle Scienze, Catania, 1982. Hon. Member: Amer. Acad. of Arts and Sciences, 1960; Chem. Soc., Warsaw, 1971. Fellow, Acad. of Sciences, New York, 1962; Centennial Foreign Fellow, Amer. Chem. Soc., 1976; For. Fellow, Indian Nat. Sci. Acad., 1979; Foreign Associate, Nat. Acad. of Sciences, USA, 1967; Foreign Member: Akad. der Wissenschaften der DDR, Berlin, 1980; USSR Acad. of Scis, 1982; Corresponding Member: Acad. of Romania, 1965; Soc. Royale des Sciences, Liège, 1967; Section of Phys. and Math., Akad. der Wissenschaften, Göttingen, 1970; Akad. der Wissenschaften, Vienna, 1971; Rheinish-Westfählische Akad. der Wissenschaften, Düsseldorf, 1980; Archives de Psychologie, Univ. of Geneva, 1982. Dr *(hc)*: Newcastle upon Tyne, 1966; Poitiers, 1966; Chicago, 1969; Bordeaux, 1972; Uppsala, 1977; Liège, 1978; Aix-Marseille, 1979; Georgetown, 1980; Rio de Janeiro, 1981; Cracow, 1981; Stevens Inst. of Technology, Hoboken, 1981; Tours, France, 1984; Heriot-Watt, 1985. Prizes: Van Laar, Société Chimique de Belgique, 1947; A. Wetrems 1950, and Annual (jtly) 1952, Acad. Royale de Belgique; Francqui, 1955; E. J. Solvay, 1965. Nobel Prize for Chemistry, 1977. Gold Medals: Swante Arrhenius, Royal Acad. of Sciences, Sweden, 1969; Cothenius, German Acad. Naturforscher Leopoldina, 1975; Rumford, Royal Soc., 1976. Bourke Medal, Chem. Soc., 1972; Medal, Assoc. for the Advancement of Sciences, Paris, 1975; Southwest Science Forum Prize, NY Acad. of Science; Karcher Medal, Amer. Crystallographic Assoc., 1978; Descartes Medal, Univ. Descartes, Paris, 1979. Commandeur, l'Ordre du Mérite, France; Commandeur, l'Ordre des Arts et des Lettres, France, 1984. *Publications:* (with R. Defay) Traité de Thermodynamique, conformément aux méthodes de Gibbs et de Donder: Vol. I, Thermodynamique Chimique, 1944 (Eng. trans. 1954); Vol. II, Tension Superficielle et Adsorption, 1951 (Eng. trans. 1965); Etude Thermodynamique des Phénomènes Irreversibles, 1947; Introduction to Thermodynamics of Irreversible Processes, New York 1954 (3rd edn 1967); (with A. Bellemans and V. Mathot) The Molecular Theory of Solutions, Amsterdam 1957; Non. Equilibrium Statistical Mechanics, 1962 (also New York); (with R. Herman) Kinetic Theory of Vehicular Traffic, New York 1971; (with P. Glansdorff) Thermodynamic Theory of Structure, Stability and Fluctuations, London and New York 1971 (also French edn); (with G. Nicolis) Self-Organization in Non Equilibrium Systems, 1977 (also New York); From Being to Becoming: time and complexity in the physical sciences, 1980 (also French, German, Japanese, Russian and Italian edns); (with I. Stengers) La Nouvelle Alliance: les métamorphoses de la science, 1981 (Prix du Haut Comité de la langue française, Paris, 1981) (also English, German, Italian, Yugoslavian, Spanish, Rumanian, Swedish, Dutch, Danish and Portuguese edns). *Recreations:* art, music. *Address:* avenue Fond'Roy 67, 1180 Bruxelles, Belgium. *T:* 02/3742952.

PRIME, Derek Arthur, RDI 1982; FSIAD; Managing Director, J. C. B. Research, since 1973; *b* 16 July 1932; *s* of Thomas Beasley Prime and Lucy Prime; *m* 1963, Pamela Dix; one *s* one *d*. *Educ:* Alleynes Grammar Sch., N Staffs Technical Coll. (HNC Mech. Engrg). MIED 1964; FSIAD 1979; FRSA 1983. Engrg Apprentice, Thomas Bolton & Sons Ltd, 1948–52; Designer, J. C. Bamford Excavators Ltd, 1952–59; J. C. B. Research: Asst Chief Designer, 1959; Chief Designer, 1964; Technical Dir, 1970. Queen's Award for Technical Innovation, 1973; Design Council Awards, 1973, 1975 and 1984; RSA Award for Design Management, 1979. Listed as inventor on 22 patents in field of construction machinery. *Recreations:* gardening, photography, equestrian events as a spectator. *Address:* Bladon House, Lodge Hill, Tutbury, Burton on Trent, Staffs DE13 9HF. *T:* Burton on Trent 813839.

PRIME, Prof. Henry Ashworth, CEng, FIEE; Professor of Electronic and Electrical Engineering, University of Birmingham, 1963–86, now Professor Emeritus; *b* 11 March 1921; *s* of late E. V. Prime and Elsie (*née* Ashworth); *m* 1943, Ella Stewart Reid; one *s* one *d*. *Educ:* N Manchester High Sch.; Manchester Univ. (MSc). CEng, FIEE 1964. Scientific Officer, Admiralty Signal and Radar Estab., 1942–46; Lectr, Univ. of Liverpool, 1946–50; Sen. Lectr, Univ. of Adelaide, 1950–55; Chief Electronic Engr and Manager Control Div., Brush Elec. Engrg Co., 1955–63. Pro-Vice-Chancellor, Univ. of Birmingham, 1978–82. Vis. Professor: Univ. of Teheran, 1971; Univ. of Hanover, 1978; Univ. of Cape Town, 1984. Member: CNAA Elec. Engrg Bd, 1970–74; Naval Educn Adv. Cttee, 1973–79 (Chm., 1978–79). Mem. Council, IEE, 1974–77, 1980–84, 1985–; Chm., Computing and Control Divl Bd, IEE, 1982–83. *Publications:* (contrib.) Telecommunication Satellites, ed Gatland, 1964; Modern Concepts in Control Theory, 1970; papers in scientific jls on electrical discharges, microwave interaction with ionised gases, and control systems. *Recreation:* golf. *Address:* 2 Oakdene Drive, Birmingham B45 8LQ. *T:* 021–445 2545.

PRIMROSE, family name of **Earl of Rosebery.**

PRIMROSE, Sir Alasdair Neil, 4th Bt *cr* 1903, of Redholme, Dumbreck, Govan; Senior Master, St Andrews Scots School, Olivos, Buenos Aires; *b* 11 Dec. 1935; *s* of Sir John Ure Primrose, 3rd Bt and of Enid, *d* of James Evans Sladen, British Columbia; *S* father, 1984;

m 1958, Elaine Noreen, *d* of Edmund Cecil Lowndes, Buenos Aires; two *s* two *d*. *Educ:* St George's College, Buenos Aires. *Heir:* *s* John Ure Primrose [*b* 28 May 1960; *m* 1983, Marion Cecilia, *d* of Hans Otto Altgelt; two *d*]. *Address:* Ada Elflein 3155, 1609 Boulogne, Provincia Buenos Aires, Argentina.

PRIMUS, The; see Brechin, Bishop of.

PRINCE, (Celestino) Anthony; solicitor; Taxing Master of the Supreme Court, since 1983; *b* 20 Aug. 1921; *s* of Charles Prince and Amelia (*née* Daubenspeck); *m* 1950, Margaret (*née* Walker) (rep., 200 metres, GB in Olympic Games, 1948 and England in British Empire Games, 1950); one *s* one *d*. *Educ:* Finchley Grammar Sch. Served War, RN, 1939–45: Western Mediterranean in HMS Antelope; Atlantic, Indian Ocean and Pacific in HMS Arbiter; commnd Sub-Lt, 1944. Articled to Kenneth George Rigden of Beaumont Son & Rigden, Fleet Street, 1939; admitted solicitor, 1947; founded firm of C. Anthony Prince & Co., Ealing, 1952; retd as Sen. Partner, 1981. Mem., No 1 (London), later No 14, Legal Aid Area Cttee, 1966–71. Founder Chm., Ealing Family Housing Assoc., 1963. Hon. Sec., Bucks CCC, 1954–69 (played in Minor Counties Comp., 1946–49); Captain, W Mddx Golf Club, 1970–71. *Recreations:* cricket, golf, sailing (Mem., Australian Sardinia Cup team, 1978; Fastnet Race, 1981). *Address:* 16 Park View Road, Ealing, W5 2JB. *T:* 01–997 8872. *Clubs:* MCC; West Middlesex Golf; Pevero Golf, Costa Smeralda Yacht (Sardinia).

PRINCE, Prof. Frank Templeton, MA (Oxon); *b* Kimberley, South Africa, 13 Sept. 1912; 2nd *s* of late H. Prince and Margaret Templeton (*née* Hetherington); *m* 1943, Pauline Elizabeth, *d* of late H. F. Bush; two *d*. *Educ:* Christian Brothers' Coll., Kimberley, South Africa; Balliol Coll., Oxford. Visiting Fellow, Graduate Coll., Princeton, NJ, 1935–36. Study Groups Department, Chatham House, 1937–40. Served Army, Intelligence Corps, 1940–46. Department of English, 1946–57, Prof. of English, 1957–74, Southampton Univ.; Prof. of English, Univ. of WI, Jamaica, 1975–78. Hurst Vis. Prof., Brandeis Univ., 1978–80; Vis. Prof., Washington Univ., St Louis, 1980–81, Sana'a Univ., N Yemen, 1981–83; Visiting Fellow, All Souls Coll., 1968–69. Clark Lectr, Cambridge, 1972–73. Pres., English Assoc., 1985–86. Hon. DLitt Southampton, 1981; DUniv York, 1982. *Publications:* Poems, 1938; Soldiers Bathing (poems), 1954; The Italian Element in Milton's Verse, 1954; The Doors of Stone (poems), 1963; Memoirs in Oxford (verse), 1970; Drypoints of the Hasidim (verse), 1975; Collected Poems, 1979; Later On (poems), 1983. *Recreations:* music, etc. *Address:* 32 Brookvale Road, Southampton. *T:* Southampton 555457.

PRINCE, Harold Smith; theatrical director/producer; *b* NYC, 30 Jan. 1928; *s* of Milton A. Prince and Blanche (*née* Stern); *m* 1962, Judith Chaplin; two *d*. *Educ:* Univ. of Pennsylvania (AB 1948). Co-Producer: The Pajama Game, 1954–56 (co-prod film, 1957); Damn Yankees, 1955–57 (co-prod film, 1958); New Girl in Town, 1957–58; West Side Story, 1957–59; Fiorello!, 1959–61 (Pulitzer Prize); Tenderloin, 1960–61; A Call on Kuprin, 1961; They Might Be Giants, London 1961; Side By Side By Sondheim, 1977–78. Producer: Take Her She's Mine, 1961–62; A Funny Thing Happened on the Way to the Forum, 1962–64; Fiddler on the Roof, 1964–72; Poor Bitos, 1964; Flora the Red Menace, 1965. Director-Producer: She Loves Me, 1963–64, London 1964; Superman, 1966; Cabaret, 1966–69, London 1968; Zorba, 1968–69; Company, 1970–72, London 1972; A Little Night Music, 1973–74, London 1975 (dir. film, 1977); Pacific Overtures, 1976. Director: A Family Affair, 1962; Baker Street, 1965; Something For Everyone (film), 1970; New Phoenix Rep. prodns of Great God Brown, 1972–73, The Visit, 1973–74, and Love for Love, 1974–75; Some of my Best Friends, 1977; On the Twentieth Century, 1978; Evita, London 1978, USA 1979–80, Australia, Vienna, 1980, Mexico City, 1981; Sweeney Todd, 1979, London 1980; Girl of the Golden West, San Francisco Op., 1979; world première, Willie Stark, Houston Grand Opera, 1981; Merrily We Roll Along (musical) 1981; A Doll's Life (musical), 1982; Madame Butterfly, Chicago Lyric Op., 1982; Turandot, Vienna state Op., 1983; Play Memory, 1984; End of the World, 1984; Diamonds, 1985; The Phantom of the Opera, London, 1986; Directed for NY City Opera: Ashmedai, 1976; Kurt Weill's Silverlake, 1980; Candide, 1982; co-Director-Producer, Follies, 1971–72; co-Producer-Director: Candide, 1974–75; Merrily We Roll Along, 1981; A Doll's Life, 1982; Grind (musical), 1985. Antoinette Perry Awards for: The Pajama Game; Damn Yankees; Fiorello!; A Funny Thing Happened on the Way to the Forum; Fiddler on the Roof; Cabaret; Company; A Little Night Music; Candide; Sweeney Todd; Evita; SWET award: Evita, 1977–78. Member: League of New York Theatres (Pres., 1964–65); Council for National Endowment for the Arts. Hon. DLit, Emerson College, 1971; Hon. Dr of Fine Arts, Univ. of Pennsylvania, 1971. Drama Critics' Circle Awards; Best Musical Award, London Evening Standard, 1955–58, 1972. *Publication:* Contradictions: notes on twenty-six years in the theatre, 1974. *Recreation:* tennis. *Address:* Suite 2410, 1270 Avenue of the Americas, New York, NY 10020, USA. *T:* 212–399–0960.

PRINCE, Maj.-Gen. Hugh Anthony, CBE 1960; retired as Chief, Military Planning Office, SEATO, Bangkok; *b* 11 Aug. 1911; *s* of H. T. Prince, FRCS, LRCP; *m* 1st, 1938, Elizabeth (*d* 1959), *d* of Dr Walter Bapty, Victoria, BC; two *s*; 2nd, 1959, Claude-Andrée, *d* of André Romanet, Château-de-Tholot, Beaujeu, Rhône; one *s*. *Educ:* Eastbourne Coll.; RMC, Sandhurst. Commissioned, 1931; served in 6th Gurkha Rifles until 1947; The King's Regt (Liverpool), 1947. *Recreations:* golf, gardening, antiques. *Address:* 36 Route de la Crau, 13200 Raphèle-les-Arles, France. *T:* (90) 98.46.93.

PRINCE-SMITH, Sir (William) Richard, 4th Bt, *cr* 1911; *b* 27 Dec. 1928; *s* of Sir William Prince-Smith, 3rd Bt, OBE, MC, and Marjorie, Lady Prince-Smith (*d* 1970); *S* father, 1964; *m* 1st, 1955, Margaret Ann Carter; one *s* one *d*; 2nd, 1975, Ann Christina Faulds. *Educ:* Charterhouse; Clare Coll., Cambridge (MA). BA (Agric.) 1951. *Recreations:* music, photography, tennis. *Heir:* *s* James William Prince-Smith, Capt. 13th/18th Royal Hussars (QMO), *b* 2 July 1959. *Address:* 40–735 Paxton Drive, Rancho Mirage, Calif 92270, USA. *T:* (619) 321–1975.

PRING, David Andrew Michael, CB 1980; MC 1943; Clerk of Committees, House of Commons, since 1976; *b* 6 Dec. 1922; *s* of late Captain John Arthur Pring and Gladys Pring; *m* 1962, Susan Brakspear, Henley-on-Thames; one *s* one *d*. *Educ:* King's Sch., Rochester; Magdalene Coll., Cambridge (MA). Served Royal Engineers, N Africa, Sicily, Italy, Austria, 1941–46; attached staff Governor-General, Canada, 1946. A Clerk of the House of Commons, 1948–. *Publications:* various, incl. (with Kenneth Bradshaw) Parliament and Congress, 1972. *Recreation:* living in the country. *Address:* Bushy Platt, Stanford Dingley, Berks RG7 6DY. *T:* Woolhampton 712585. *Club:* Athenæum.

PRINGLE, Air Marshal Sir Charles (Norman Seton), KBE 1973 (CBE 1967); MA, FEng, FRAeS; CBIM; Director, FR Group plc (formerly Flight Refuelling Holdings plc), since 1985; *b* 6 June 1919; *s* of late Seton Pringle, OBE, FRCSI, Dublin; *m* 1946, Margaret, *d* of late B. Sharp, Baildon, Yorkshire; one *s*. *Educ:* Repton; St John's Coll., Cambridge. Commissioned, RAF, 1941; served India and Ceylon, 1942–46. Air Ministry, 1946–48; RAE, Farnborough, 1949–50; attached to USAF, 1950–52; appts in UK, 1952–60; STSO No 3 Group, Bomber Comd, 1960–62, and Air Forces Middle East, 1962–64; Comdt RAF St Athan and Air Officer Wales, 1964–66; MoD, 1967; IDC, 1968. Dir-Gen. of

Engineering (RAF) MoD, 1969–70; Air Officer Engineering, Strike Command, 1970–73; Dir-Gen. Engineering (RAF), 1973; Controller, Engrg and Supply (RAF), 1973–76; Sen. Exec., Rolls Royce Ltd, 1976–78; Dir, Hunting Engineering Ltd, 1976–78; Dir and Chief Exec., SBAC, 1979–84. Pres., RAeS, 1975–76; Vice-Chm., 1976–77, Chm., 1977–78, CEI. Mem. Council, RSA, 1978–83 and 1986–. Chm. Governors, Repton Sch., 1985–. *Recreations:* photography, ornithology, motor sport. *Address:* Appleyards, Fordingbridge, Hants SP6 3BP. *T:* Fordingbridge 52357; K9 Sloane Avenue Mansions, SW3 3JP. *T:* 01–584 3432. *Clubs:* Institute of Directors, Royal Air Force, Buck's.

PRINGLE, Dr Derek Hair, CBE 1980; BSc, PhD, DSc; FRSE; FInstP; Chairman, SEEL Ltd, since 1980; *b* 8 Jan. 1926; *s* of Robert Pringle and Lilias Dalgleish Hair; *m* 1949, Anne Collier Caw; three *s* one *d. Educ:* George Heriot's Sch., Edinburgh; Edinburgh Univ. (BSc 1948, PhD 1954). FInstP 1957; FRSE 1970. Res. Physicist, Ferranti Ltd, Edinburgh, 1948–59; Nuclear Enterprises Ltd: Technical Dir, 1960–76; Man. Dir, 1976–78; Chm., 1978–80; Chm., Bioscot, 1983–; Director: Amersham Internat. Ltd, 1978–; Creative Capital Nominees Ltd, 1982–; Melville Street Investments (Edinburgh) Ltd, 1983–. Member: Nat. Radiol Protection Bd, Harwell, 1969–81; Council for Applied Science in Scotland, 1981–; CNAA, 1982–85. Vice-Pres., RSE, 1985– (Mem. Council, 1982–); Member: Council, Scottish Museums Adv. Bd, 1984–; Bd of Trustees, Nat. Museums of Scotland, 1985–. Mem., Court, Heriot-Watt Univ., 1968–77. Pres., Edinburgh Chamber of Commerce and Manufactures, 1979–81; Chm., Assoc. of Scottish Chambers of Commerce, 1985–; Mem. Council, Assoc. of British Chambers of Commerce, 1986–. Faraday Lectr, 1978–79. Hon. DSc Heriot Watt Univ., 1981. *Publications:* papers on microwave engrg, gas discharge physics and nuclear science in scientific jls. *Recreations:* golf, gardening. *Address:* Earlyvale, Eddleston, Peebles-shire EH45 8QX. *T:* Eddleston 231. *Clubs:* Royal Over-Seas League, English-Speaking Union.
See also R. W. Pringle.

PRINGLE, John Martin Douglas; *b* 1912; *s* of late J. Douglas Pringle, Hawick, Scotland; *m* 1936, Celia, *d* of E. A. Carroll; one *s* two *d. Educ:* Shrewsbury Sch.; Lincoln Coll., Oxford. First Class Literae Humaniores, 1934. Editorial Staff of Manchester Guardian, 1934–39. Served War of 1939–45 with King's Own Scottish Borderers, 1940–44; Assistant Editor, Manchester Guardian, 1944–48; Special Writer on The Times, 1948–52; Editor of The Sydney Morning Herald, 1952–57; Deputy Editor of The Observer, 1958–63; Managing Editor, Canberra Times, 1964–65; Editor, Sydney Morning Herald, 1965–70. *Publications:* China Struggles for Unity, 1938; Australian Accent, 1958; Australian Painting Today, 1963; On Second Thoughts, 1971; Have Pen, Will Travel, 1973; The Last Shenachie, 1976. *Address:* 8/105A Darling Point Road, Darling Point, NSW 2027, Australia.

PRINGLE, Dr Robert William, OBE 1967; BSc, PhD; FRSE; FRSC; President, Nuclear Enterprises Ltd, Edinburgh, since 1976; *b* 2 May 1920; *s* of late Robert Pringle and late Lillias Dalgleish Hair; *m* 1948, Carol Stokes; three *s* one *d. Educ:* George Heriot's Sch., Edinburgh; Edinburgh Univ. (Vans Dunlop Scholar in Natural Philosophy). Lecturer, Natural Philosophy, Edinburgh, 1945; Associate Professor of Physics, Manitoba, 1949; Prof. and Chairman of Physics, Manitoba, 1953–56; Chm. and Man. Dir, Nuclear Enterprises Ltd, 1956–76 (Queen's Award to Industry, 1966, 1979); Dir, N Sea Assets Ltd, 1977–78. Member: Scottish Council, CBI (Cttee), 1966–72; Scottish Univs Industry Liaison Cttee, 1968–75; Bd, Royal Observatory (Edinburgh), 1968–79; Council, SRC, 1972–76; Bd, Astronomy, Space and Radio (SRC), 1970–72; Bd, Nuclear Physics (SRC), 1972–76; Economic Council for Scotland, 1971–75; Bd, Scottish Sch. Business Studies, 1972–83. University of Edinburgh: Mem. Court, 1967–75; Mem., Finance Cttee, 1967–75; Mem. Bd, Centre for Indust. Liaison and Consultancy, 1968–84; Mem., Press Cttee, 1977–78. Trustee: Scottish Hospitals Endowments Res. Trust, 1976–; Scottish Trust for the Physically Disabled, 1977–84. Hon. Adviser, Nat. Museum of Antiquities of Scotland, 1969–. FInstP 1948; Fellow, American Inst. Physics, 1950; FRS(Can) 1955; FRSE 1964; Hon. Fellow, Royal Scottish Soc. Arts, 1972; CPhys 1985. *Publications:* (with James Douglas) 20th Century Scottish Banknotes, Vol. II, 1986; papers on nuclear spectroscopy and nuclear geophysics in UK and US scientific journals. *Recreations:* golf, book-collecting, Rugby (Edinburgh, Edinburgh and Glasgow, Rest of Scotland, 1945–48). *Address:* 27 avenue Princesse Grace, Monaco. *Clubs:* Athenæum; New (Edinburgh); Yacht Club de Monaco, Golf de Monte Carlo.
See also D. H. Pringle.

PRINGLE, Lt-Gen. Sir Steuart (Robert), 10th Bt, *cr* 1683, Stichill, Roxburghshire; KCB 1982; Commandant General Royal Marines 1981–84; Chairman and Chief Executive, Chatham Historic Dockyard Trust, since 1984; *b* 21 July 1928; *s* of Sir Norman H. Pringle, 9th Bt and Lady (Oonagh) Pringle (*née* Curran) (*d* 1975); *S* father, 1961; *m* 1953, Jacqueline Marie Gladwell; two *s* two *d. Educ:* Sherborne. Royal Marines: 2nd Lieut, 1946; 42 Commando, 1950–52; 40 Commando, 1957–59; Chief Instructor, Signal Trng Wing, RM, 1959–61; Bde Signal Officer, 3 Commando Bde, RM, 1961–63; Defence Planning Staff, 1964–67; Chief Signal Officer, RM, 1967–69; 40 Commando, Far East, 1969–71; CO 45 Commando Group, 1971–74; HQ Commando Forces, 1974–76; RCDS, 1977; Maj.-Gen. RM Commando Forces, 1978–79; Chief of Staff to Comdt Gen., RM, 1979–81. Pres., St Loye's Coll. for the Disabled, 1984–; Vice-Pres., Officers Pensions Assoc., 1984–; Mem. Council, Union Jack Club, 1982–85; Vice-Patron, Royal Naval Benevolent Trust, 1984–. CBIM. Liveryman, Plaisterers' Co., 1984. Hon. DSc City, 1982. Hon. Admiral, Texas Navy; Hon. Mem., Co. of Bear Tamers. *Publications:* (contrib) The Price of Peace, 1982; contribs to RUSI Jl, Navy International, etc. *Heir: s* Simon Robert Pringle, *b* 6 Jan. 1959. *Address:* 76 South Croxted Road, Dulwich, SE21. *Clubs:* Army and Navy; Royal Thames Yacht, MCC.

PRIOR, Ven. Christopher, CB 1968; Archdeacon of Portsmouth, 1969–77, Archdeacon Emeritus since 1977; *b* 2 July 1912; *s* of late Ven. W. H. Prior; *m* 1945, Althea Stafford (*née* Coode); two *d. Educ:* King's Coll., Taunton; Keble Coll., Oxford; Cuddesdon Coll. Curate of Hornsea, 1938–41; Chaplain RN from 1941, Chaplain of the Fleet, 1966–69. Served in: HMS Royal Arthur, 1941; HMHS Maine, 1941–43; HMS Scylla, 1943–44; HMS Owl, 1944–46; various ships, 1946–58; Britannia RNC, Dartmouth, 1958–61; HMS Blake, 1961–62; HM Dockyard, Portsmouth, 1963–66; QHC, 1966–69. *Recreation:* walking. *Address:* Ponies End, West Melbury, Shaftesbury, Dorset SP7 0LY. *T:* Shaftesbury 811239.

PRIOR, Rt. Hon. James Michael Leathes, PC 1970; MP (C) Waveney, since 1983 (Lowestoft, Suffolk, 1959–83); Chairman, The General Electric Company plc, since 1984; *b* 11 Oct. 1927; 2nd *s* of late C. B. L. and A. S. M. Prior, Norwich; *m* 1954, Jane Primrose Gifford, 2nd *d* of late Air Vice-Marshal O. G. Lywood, CB, CBE; three *s* one *d. Educ:* Charterhouse; Pembroke College, Cambridge. 1st class degree in Estate Management, 1950; commissioned in Royal Norfolk Regt, 1946; served in India and Germany; farmer and land agent in Norfolk and Suffolk. PPS to Pres. of Bd of Trade, 1963, to Minister of Power, 1963–64, to Mr Edward Heath, Leader of the Opposition, 1965–70; Minister of Agriculture, Fisheries and Food, 1970–72; Lord Pres. of Council and Leader of House of Commons, 1972–74; Opposition front bench spokesman on Employment, 1974–79; Sec. of State for Employment, 1979–81; Sec. of State for NI, 1981–84. A Dep. Chm., Cons. Party, 1972–74 (Vice-Chm., 1965). Director: United Biscuits (Holdings), 1984–; Barclays Bank, 1984–; Barclays International, 1984–; J. Sainsbury, 1984–. *Publication:* A Balance of Power, 1986. *Recreations:* cricket, tennis, golf, gardening. *Address:* Old Hall, Brampton, Beccles, Suffolk. *T:* Brampton 278; 36 Morpeth Mansions, SW1. *T:* 01–834 5543. *Clubs:* MCC; Butterflies Cricket.

PRIOR, Peter James, CBE 1980; DL; Deputy Chairman, Holden Hydroman PLC, since 1984; *b* 1 Sept. 1919; *s* of Percy Prior; *m* 1957, Prinia Mary, *d* of late R. E. Moreau, Berrick Prior, Oxon; two *s. Educ:* Royal Grammar Sch., High Wycombe; London Univ. BSc(Econ). FCA, FIMC, CBIM, FIIM, FRSA. Royal Berks Regt, 1939; Intell. Corps, 1944–46 (Captain) (Croix-de-Guerre 1944). Company Sec., Saunders-Roe (Anglesey) Ltd, 1948; Consultant, Urwick, Orr & Partners, 1951; Financial Dir, International Chemical Co., 1956; Financial Dir, British Aluminium Co., 1961; Man. Dir, H. P. Bulmer Ltd, 1966; Director: H. P. Bulmer Holdings, 1977–84 (Chm., 1977–82); Dir, Trebor, 1982–. Member: English Tourist Bd, 1969–75; Midlands Electricity Bd, 1973–83; Chairman: Inquiry into Potato Processing Industry, 1971; Motorway Service Area Inquiry, 1977–78; Home Office Deptl Inquiry into Prison Discipline, 1984–85. Pres., Incorp. Soc. of British Advertisers' Council, 1980–83; Mem. Council, BIM, 1974–82. Chm. Trustees, Leadership Trust, 1975–79; Member: Council, Regular Forces Employment Assoc., 1981–; Council, Operation Raleigh, 1984–. DL Hereford and Worcester, 1983. Communicator of the Year Award, British Assoc. of Industrial Editors, 1982. *Publications:* Leadership is not a Bowler Hat, 1977; articles on management and leadership. *Recreations:* free-fall parachuting (UK record for longest delayed drop (civilian), 1981), flying (Vice Chm., Hereford Air Sports Centre, 1979–84), motor-cycling, sub-aqua swimming. *Address:* Rathays, Sutton Saint Nicholas, Herefordshire HR1 3AY. *T:* Sutton Saint Nicholas 313. *Clubs:* Army and Navy, Special Forces.

PRIOR, William Johnson, CBE 1979; CEng, FIEE; CBIM; Chairman, Manx Electricity Authority, 1984–85; *b* 28 Jan. 1924; *s* of Ernest Stanley and Lilian Prior; *m* 1945, Mariel (*née* Irving); two *s* one *d. Educ:* Goole and Barnsley Grammar Schs. Barugh, Mexborough, Stuart Street (Manchester) and Stockport Power Stations, 1944–52; Keadby, 1952–56, Supt, 1954–56; Supt, Berkeley, 1957–58; Supt, Hinkley Point Generating Station, 1959–66; CEGB and predecessors: Asst Reg. Dir (Generation), NW Region, 1967–70; Dir (Generation), SW Region, 1970–72; Dir-Gen., SE Region, 1972–76; Mem., Electricity Council, 1976–79; Chm., Yorks Electricity Bd, 1979–84. Member: NCB, 1977–83; Adv. Cttee on Safety of Nuclear Installations, 1980–. *Recreation:* country walking. *Address:* Highfield House, Lime Kiln Lane, Kirk Deighton, Wetherby, W Yorks LS22 4EA. *T:* Wetherby 64434.

PRITCHARD, family name of **Baron Pritchard.**

PRITCHARD, Baron *cr* 1975 (Life Peer), of West Haddon, Northamptonshire; **Derek Wilbraham Pritchard;** Kt 1968; DL; *b* 8 June 1910; *s* of Frank Wheelton Pritchard and Ethel Annie Pritchard (*née* Cheetham); *m* 1941, Denise Arfor Pritchard (*née* Huntbach); two *d. Educ:* Clifton College, Bristol. Took over family business of E. Halliday & Son, Wine Merchants, 1929, Man. Dir, 1930–51. Called up in TA and served War of 1939–45; demob. as Col and joined Bd of E. K. Cole, Ltd, 1946. Joined Ind Coope Ltd, as Man. Dir of Grants of St James's Ltd, 1949, Chm., 1960–69; Chm., Victoria Wine & Co. Ltd, 1959–64. Former Director: Ind Coope Ltd, 1951; Ind Coope Tetley Ansell Ltd on merger of those companies, 1961; Allied Breweries Ltd, 1961–80 (Chm., 1968–70); Allied Breweries Investments Ltd, 1957–80; Guardian Assurance Ltd, 1960–80; Guardian Royal Exchange Assurance Ltd, 1968–80; George Sandeman Sons & Co. Ltd, 1952–80; Carreras Ltd, 1970–72 (Chm.); Dorchester Hotel Ltd, 1976–80 (Chm.); Rothmans of Pall Mall Canada Ltd, 1972–77; Rothmans of Pall Mall (Australia) Ltd, 1972–77; Rothmans of Pall Mall (Malaysia) Berhad, 1972–77; Rothmans of Pall Mall (Singapore) Ltd, 1972–77; Deltec International, 1975–77; London-American Finance Corp., 1976–78. Director: J. & W. Nicholson (Holdings) Ltd, 1952–85; Midland Bank Ltd, 1968–; Samuel Montagu Ltd, 1969–86; Adelaide Associates Ltd, 1970–; Rothmans International Ltd, 1972– (Chm., 1972–75); Rothmans Group Services SA, 1972–; Rothmans of Pall Mall (London) Ltd, 1980–; Rothmans Group Holdings Ltd, 1981–; Carreras Group (Jamaica) Ltd, 1972–; Paterson, Zochonis & Co. Ltd, 1977–; Philips Electronic & Associated Industries Ltd, 1978–; Tiedmann-Goodnow Internat. Capital Corp., 1983– (Chm., 1983); Matterhorn Investment Co. Ltd, 1983– (Chm., 1983); Thoroughbred Holdings Internat. Ltd, 1982– (Chm.); Euro-Canadian Bank Inc., 1984–; International Intelligence Inc., 1984–; Templeton Investments International Inc., 1980–; Templeton Investments International Ltd, 1980–. Chairman: Dorchester Hotel Bd of Trustees, 1980–; Adv. Bd, Rembrandt-Rothmans World Gp, 1980–; Mem., Salomon Bros Adv. Bd, USA, 1980–83; Dep Chm., British National Export Council, 1965–66, Chm. 1966–68; Member: Nat. Inds Appts Bd, 1973–80; Top Salaries Review Body, 1975–78; House of Lords EEC Cttee, 1975–79, EEC Sub-Cttee A, 1975–81; British Overseas Trade Adv. Council, 1976–82; Fund Raising Cttee, RCS, 1976–; Chancellor of the Duchy of Lancaster's Cttee on Business Sponsorship of the Arts, 1980–84; Amer. European Community Assoc., 1981–; President: Inst. of Directors, 1968–74; British Export Houses Assoc., 1976–83; Northants Co. Branch, Royal Agricl Benevolent Instn, 1981–; Patron, Northants British Red Cross Soc., 1982– (Pres., 1975–82); Vice-President: Inst. of Export, 1976– (Pres., 1962–64); Wine and Spirit Assoc. of GB, 1964– (Pres., 1962–64); Northants Youth Club Assoc., 1965–; East of England Agricl Soc., 1974–; Co-Chm., UK-Jamaica Cttee, 1981–; Trustee: Age Action Trust, 1975–84; St Giles Church, Northampton, 1976–; Patron: Northampton and County Chamber of Commerce, 1978–; Three Shires Indept Hosp., 1978–; Abbeyfield Soc. for the Aged, 1979– (Pres., 1970–79); Governor: Clifton Coll., Bristol; Nene Coll., Northampton; Lyford Cay Club, Bahamas; British Foundn for Age Research, 1975–84. DL Northants, 1974. *Recreations:* farming, tennis, golf, swimming, hunting. *Address:* West Haddon Hall, Northampton NN6 7AU. *T:* West Haddon 210.

PRITCHARD, Arthur Alan, CB 1979; JP; management consultant; formerly Deputy Under Secretary of State, Ministry of Defence; *b* 3 March 1922; *s* of Arthur Henry Standfast Pritchard and Sarah Bessie Myra Pritchard (*née* Mundy); *m* 1949, Betty Rona Nevard (*née* Little); two *s* one *d. Educ:* Wanstead High Sch., Essex. Board of Trade, 1939. RAFVR Pilot, 1941–52. Joined Admiralty, 1952; Asst Sec., 1964; Royal College of Defence Studies, 1972; Asst Under-Sec. of State, Naval Personnel and Op. Requirements, MoD, 1972–76; seconded as Dep. Sec., NI Office, 1976–78; Secretary to the Admiralty Bd, 1978–81. JP Ringwood (Totton and New Forest, 1981). *Recreations:* caravanning, walking. *Address:* Courtlands, Manor Farm Road, Fordingbridge, Hants. *Club:* Royal Air Force.

PRITCHARD, Sir Asa Hubert, Kt 1965; Merchant, retired; President, Asa H. Pritchard Ltd, Nassau; *b* 1 Aug. 1891; *s* of William Edward Pritchard, Bahamas; *m* 1915, Maud Pauline Pyfrom (*d* 1978); two *s* two *d. Educ:* Queen's College, Bahamas. MHA, Bahamas, 1925–62; Deputy Speaker, 1942–46; Speaker, 1946–62. Member: Board of Education, 1930–35; Electricity Board, 1940–46; Chm., Bahamas Develt Bd, 1946. *Address:* Breezy Ridge, PO Box 6218 ES, Nassau, Bahamas.

PRITCHARD, Rear-Adm. Gwynedd Idris, CB 1981; *b* 18 June 1924; *s* of Cyril Idris Pritchard and Lily Pritchard; *m* 1975, Mary Thérèsa (*née* Curtin); three *s* (by previous marriage). *Educ:* Wyggeston Sch., Leicester. FBIM, MNI. Joined Royal Navy, 1942; Sub-Lieut 1944; Lieut 1946; Lt-Comdr 1954; Comdr 1959; Captain 1967; Rear-Adm. 1976; Flag Officer Sea Training, 1976–78; Flag Officer Gibraltar, 1979–81; retired list, 1981. Mem., Dorset CC, 1985–. *Recreations:* riding, caravanning. *Address:* Hoofprints, Beach Road, Burton Bradstock, Dorset.

PRITCHARD, Hugh Wentworth, CBE 1969; Member of Council of Law Society, 1947–66; *b* 15 March 1903; *s* of late Sir Harry G. Pritchard; *m* 1934, Barbara Stableforth; two *s.* *Educ:* Charterhouse; Balliol College, Oxford. Admitted a solicitor, 1927, partner in Sharpe Pritchard & Co., 1928–80. Pres. Soc. of Parliamentary Agents, 1952–55; Member: Statute Law Committee, 1954–81; Committee on Administrative Tribunals and Enquiries, 1955; Council on Tribunals, 1958–70. Lay Reader, 1947. Served War of 1939–45, in England, France, Belgium and Germany; joined The Queen's as a private; commissioned in RAOC, attaining rank of Lt-Col. *Recreation:* golf. *Address:* Barton, Great Woodcote Drive, Purley, Surrey CR2 3PL. *T:* 01–660 9029.

PRITCHARD, Sir John (Michael), Kt 1983; CBE 1962; Chief Conductor: Cologne Opera, since 1978; BBC Symphony Orchestra, since 1982 (Chief Guest Conductor, 1979–82); Music Director, Belgian Opera Nationale, since 1981; San Francisco Opera, since 1986; *b* 5 Feb. 1921; *s* of Albert Edward Pritchard and Amy Edith Shaylor. *Educ:* Sir George Monoux School, London; privately. Conductor: Derby String Orchestra, 1943–51; Music Staff, Glyndebourne Opera, 1947, Chorus master, 1949; Conductor, Jacques Orchestra, 1950–52; Asst to Fritz Busch, Vittorio Gui, 1950–51; Conductor Glyndebourne Festivals, 1952–77; Conductor and Musical Director, Royal Liverpool Philharmonic Orchestra, 1957–63; Musical Director, London Philharmonic Orchestra, 1962–66; Principal Conductor, 1967–77, and Musical Director, 1969–77, Glyndebourne Opera; Guest Conductor: Vienna State Opera, 1952–53, 1964–65; Covent Garden Opera, 1952–77; Edinburgh Internat. Festivals, opera and symphony concerts 1951–55, 1960–63, 1979–81; Aix-en-Provence Festival, 1963, 1981; Frankfurt Radio Orchestra, 1953; Cologne Radio Orchestra, 1953; Vienna Symphony Orchestra, 1953–55; Berlin Festival, 1954, 1964; Zürich Radio Orchestra, 1955, 1961; Santa Cecilia Orchestra, Rome, 1958, 1972, 1979; Orchestre Nationale, Brussels, 1958, 1965–67; Cracow Philharmonic Orch., 1961; Basel, Winterthur Orch., 1961, 1969; RIAS Orchestra, Berlin, 1961, 1966; Royal Philharmonic Soc., London, 1959, 1961, 1963, 1964, 1965, 1966, 1970, 1974, 1979–83, 1985; Wexford Festival, 1959, 1961; Oslo Philharmonic Orch., 1960, 1961, 1966, 1975; Pittsburgh Symphony Orch., 1963, 1964, and San Francisco Symphony, 1964; BBC Promenade Concerts, 1960–77, 1979–85; tour of Switzerland, 1962, 1966, 1985; of Australia, 1962; of Germany, 1963, 1966; with BBC Symph. Orch., 1968, 1982; tour of Jugoslavia, 1968; Georges Enesco Festival, Bucharest, 1964; Lausanne Festival, 1964; Berlin Philharmonic, 1964; New York Opera Assoc., 1964; Société Philharmonique, Brussels, 1965, 1967; Helsinki Philharmonic, 1966; Salzburg Festival, 1966; Teatro Colon, Buenos Aires, 1966; RAI Symphony Orch., Turin, 1967; Sjaellands Symphony Orch., Copenhagen, 1967–70; SABC Orchestra, Johannesburg, 1967–70; Scandinavian Tour, Glyndebourne Opera, 1967; Teatro San Carlo, Naples, 1969–70; Danish Radio Symph., 1968; Palermo Sinfonia, 1968; Munich State Opera, 1968–69, 1983; Athens Festival, 1968–70; Leipzig Gewandhaus, 1968–70; Dresden Staatskapelle, 1968–70, 1972; Berlin Radio, 1968–70, 1972; Chicago Lyric Opera, 1969, 1975, 1977, 1978, 1984; Florence Maggio Musicale, 1977, 1978, 1979; Zürich Tonhalle, 1977–78, 1979; London Philharmonic Tours: Far East, 1969; USA, 1971; Hong Kong and China, 1973; New Philharmonia Orch., Osaka, Tokyo, 1970; San Francisco Opera, 1970, 1973–74, 1976, 1977, 1979, 1985; Geneva Opera, 1971, 1974; Metropolitan Opera, NY, 1971, 1973–74, 1977–79, 1983–84; Yomiuri Nippon Orch., Tokyo, 1972; English Chamber Orch. Tour, Latin America, 1972; Australian Opera, Sydney, 1974, 1977; Cologne Opera, 1975, 1976, 1977; Philadelphia Orch., 1975, 1976, 1978; Opera Orch., Monte Carlo, 1976–78, 1984; Houston Grand Opera, 1976, 1978, 1979; Vancouver Symphony, 1978; Paris Opéra, 1979, 1981. Shakespeare Prize, Hamburg, 1975. *Recreations:* good food and wine, theatre. *Address:* c/o Basil Horsfield, Estoril (B), Avenue Princesse Grace 31, Monte Carlo.

PRITCHARD, Kenneth John, CB 1982; Director, Greenwich Hospital, since 1986; *b* 18 March 1926; *s* of William Edward Pritchard and Ethel Mary Pritchard (*née* Cornfield); *m* 1st, 1949, Elizabeth Margaret Bradshaw (*d* 1978); two *d*; 2nd, 1979, Angela Madeleine Palmer; one *s* two *d.* *Educ:* Newport High Sch.; St Catherine's Coll., Oxford (BA 1951). Served Army, 1944–48; Indian Mil. Acad., Dehra Dun, 1945; served with 8th/12th Frontier Force Regt and 2nd Royal W Kent Regt. Asst Principal, Admiralty, 1951; Private Sec. to Sec. of State for Wales, 1964; Asst Sec., Min. of Aviation, 1966; RCDS, 1972; Principal Supply and Transport Officer (Naval), Portsmouth, 1978, Exec. Dir 1980; Dir Gen. of Supplies and Transport (Naval), MoD, 1981–86, retd. FInstPS 1986. *Recreations:* squash, tennis. *Address:* Pickford House, Beckington, Som BA3 6SJ. *T:* Frome 830329.

PRITCHARD, Kenneth William; Secretary of the Law Society of Scotland, since 1976; *b* 14 Nov. 1933; *s* of Dr Kenneth Pritchard, MB, BS, DPH, and Isobel Pritchard, LDS (*née* Broom); *m* 1962, Gretta (*née* Murray); two *s* one *d.* *Educ:* Dundee High Sch.; Fettes Coll.; St Andrews Univ. (BL). National Service, Argyll and Sutherland Highlanders, 1955–57; commnd 2nd Lieut, 1956; TA 1957–62 (Captain). Joined J. & J. Scrimgeour, Solicitors, Dundee, 1957, Sen. Partner, 1970–76. Hon. Sheriff, Dundee, 1978–. Member: Sheriff Court Rules Council, 1973–76; Lord Dunpark's Cttee Considering Reparation upon Criminal Conviction, 1973–77; Secretary, Scottish Council of Law Reporting, 1976. Governor, Moray House Coll. of Educn, 1982–84; Mem., National Trust for Scotland Jubilee Appeal Cttee, 1980–82. Pres., Dundee High Sch. Old Boys Club, 1975–76; Captain of the School's RFC, 1959–62. *Recreation:* golf. *Address:* 36 Ravelston Dykes, Edinburgh EH4 3EB. *T:* 031–332 8584. *Clubs:* New, Bruntsfield Links Golfing Association (Edinburgh); Hon. Company of Edinburgh Golfers (Muirfield).

PRITCHARD, Sir Neil, KCMG 1962 (CMG 1952); HM Diplomatic Service, retired; Ambassador in Bangkok, 1967–70; *b* 14 January 1911; *s* of late Joseph and Lillian Pritchard; *m* 1943, Mary Burroughes, Pretoria, S Africa; one *s.* *Educ.* Liverpool Coll.; Worcester Coll., Oxford. Dominions Office, 1933; Private Secretary to Permanent Under-Sec., 1936–38; Assistant Secretary, Rhodesia-Nyasaland Royal Commission, 1938; Secretary, Office of UK High Commissioner, Pretoria, 1941–45; Principal Secretary, Office of UK Representative, Dublin, 1948–49; Assistant Under-Secretary of State, Commonwealth Relations Office, 1951–54; Dep. UK High Commissioner: Canada, 1954–57; Australia, 1957–60; Actg Dep. Under-Sec. of State, CRO, 1961; British High Comr in Tanganyika, 1961–63; Deputy Under-Secretary of State, Commonwealth Office (formerly CRO), 1963–67. *Recreation:* golf. *Address:* Little Garth, Daglingworth, Cirencester, Glos GL7 7AQ.

PRITCHETT, Sir Victor (Sawdon), Kt 1975; CBE 1968; FRSL; Author and Critic; *b* 16 Dec. 1900; *s* of Sawdon Pritchett and Beatrice Martin; *m* Dorothy, *d* of Richard Samuel Roberts, Welshpool, Montgomeryshire; one *s* one *d.* *Educ:* Alleyn's School. Christian Gauss Lectr, Princeton Univ., 1953; Beckman Prof., Univ. California, Berkeley, 1962; Writer-in-Residence, Smith Coll., Mass, 1966; Vanderbilt Univ., Tenn., 1981; Visiting Professor: Brandeis Univ., Mass; Columbia Univ.; Clark Lectr, 1969. Foreign Member: Amer. Acad. and Inst., 1971; Amer. Acad. Arts and Sciences, 1971. Pres., Internat. PEN, 1974–76; Soc. of Authors, 1977–. Hon. LittD Leeds, 1972; Hon. DLitt: Columbia, 1978; Sussex, 1980; Harvard, 1985. *Publications:* Marching Spain, 1928; Clare Drummer, 1929; The Spanish Virgin, 1930; Shirley Sanz, 1932; Nothing Like Leather, 1935; Dead Man Leading, 1937; You Make Your Own Life, 1938; In My Good Books, 1942; It May Never Happen, 1946; The Living Novel, 1946; Why Do I Write?, 1948; Mr Beluncle, 1951; Books in General, 1953; The Spanish Temper, 1954; Collected Stories, 1956; When My Girl Comes Home, 1961; London Perceived, 1962; The Key to My Heart, 1963; Foreign Faces, 1964; New York Proclaimed, 1965; The Working Novelist, 1965; Dublin: A Portrait, 1967; A Cab at the Door (autobiog.), 1968 (RSL Award); Blind Love, 1969; George Meredith and English Comedy, 1970; Midnight Oil (autobiog.), 1971; Balzac, 1973; The Camberwell Beauty, 1974; The Gentle Barbarian, 1977; Selected Stories, 1978; The Myth Makers, 1979; On the Edge of the Cliff, 1980; The Tale Bearers, 1980; (ed) The Oxford Book of Short Stories, 1981; (with Reynolds Stone) The Turn of the Years, 1982; Collected Stories, 1982; More Collected Stories, 1983; The Other Side of a Frontier, 1984; Man of Letters, 1985. *Address:* 12 Regent's Park Terrace, NW1. *Clubs:* Savile, Beefsteak.

PRITTIE, family name of **Baron Dunalley.**

PROBERT, David Henry, FCIS, FCMA, FCCA; Chairman, W. Canning plc, since 1986; Deputy Chairman, Crown Agents for Oversea Governments and Administrations, since 1985 (Crown Agent since 1981); Crown Agent for Holdings and Realisation Board, since 1981; *b* 11 April 1938; *s* of William David Thomas Probert and Doris Mabel Probert; *m* 1968, Sandra Mary Prince; one *s* one *d.* *Educ:* Bromsgrove High School. Director: BSA Ltd, 1971–73; Mills and Allen International Ltd, 1974–76; W. Canning plc, 1976– (Chief Exec., 1979–86); HB Electronics plc, 1977– (Chm., 1986); British Hallmarking Council, 1983–; Linread Public Limited Company, 1983–; Associated Steel Distributors plc, 1985–; Sandvik Ltd, 1985–. *Recreations:* theatre, music, sport. *Address:* 4 Blakes Field Drive, Barnt Green, Birmingham B45 8JT. *Clubs:* City Livery, Lord's Taverners.

PROBINE, Dr Mervyn Charles, CB 1986; FRSNZ; FInstP; FNZIM; company director and consultant, since 1986; *b* 30 April 1924; *s* of Frederick Charles and Ann Kathleen Probine; *m* 1949, Marjorie Walker; one *s* one *d.* *Educ:* Univ. of Auckland (BSc); Victoria Univ. of Wellington (MSc); Univ. of Leeds (PhD). Physicist, DSIR, 1946–67; Dir, Physics and Engineering Lab., 1967–77; Asst Dir-Gen., DSIR, 1977–79; State Services Commission: Comr, 1979–80; Dep. Chm., 1980–81; Chm., 1981–86, retired. *Publications:* numerous scientific research papers and papers on application of science in industry. *Recreations:* bridge, sailing, angling. *Address:* 24 Bloomfield Terrace, Lower Hutt, New Zealand. *T:* (04) 663492. *Club:* Wellington (Wellington, NZ).

PROBY, Sir Peter, 2nd Bt *cr* 1952; FRICS; Lord-Lieutenant of Cambridgeshire, 1981–85; *b* 4 Dec. 1911; *s* of Sir Richard George Proby, 1st Bt, MC, and Betty Monica (*d* 1967), *d* of A. H. Hallam Murray; *S* father, 1979; *m* 1944, Blanche Harrison, *o d* of Col Henry Harrison Cripps, DSO; one *s* three *d* (and one *s* decd). *Educ:* Eton; Trinity College, Oxford. BA 1934. Served War of 1939–45, Captain, Irish Guards. Bursar of Eton College, 1953–71. *Heir: s* William Henry Proby, MA, FCA [*b* 13 June 1949; *m* 1974, Meredyth Anne Brentnall; three *d.* *Educ:* Eton; Lincoln Coll., Oxford (MA)]. *Address:* Pottle Green, Elton, Peterborough.

PROBYN, Air Commodore Harold Melsome, CB 1944; CBE 1943; DSO 1917; *b* 8 Dec. 1891; *s* of late William Probyn; *m* 1920, Marjory (*d* 1961), *d* of late Francis Evance Savory. Served European War, 1914–17 (despatches, DSO); commanded: 208 (AC) Squadron, Egypt; No 2 (AC), Squadron, Manston; 25 (Fighter) Squadron at Hawkinge; RAF School of Photography, 1932; No 22 Group, RAF, 1932–34; Senior Personnel Staff Officer, Middle East, Cairo, 1934–35; Senior Engineer Staff Officer, Middle East, Cairo, 1935–37; No 12 (Fighter) Group Royal Air Force, Hucknall, Notts, 1937; served War of 1939–45 (despatches); SASO, No 11 Fighter Group, Uxbridge, 1939–40; commanded RAF Station, Cranwell, 1940–44; retired, 1944. *Recreations:* flying, fishing, golf. *Address:* The Cottage, PO Box 61, Nyeri, Kenya. *T:* 2248. *Clubs:* Naval and Military; Nairobi (Kenya).

PROCKTOR, Patrick, RWS 1981; painter since 1962; *b* 12 March 1936; 2nd *s* of Eric Christopher Procktor and Barbara Winifred (*née* Hopkins); *m* 1973, Kirsten Bo (*née* Andersen) (*d* 1984); one *s.* *Educ:* Highgate; Slade Sch. (Diploma). Many one-man exhibns, Redfern Gallery, from 1963. *Publications:* One Window in Venice, 1974; Coleridge's Rime of the Ancient Mariner (new illustrated edn), 1976; A Chinese Journey (aquatint landscapes), 1980; (illustrated) Sailing through China, by Paul Theroux, 1983; Patrick Procktor Prints 1959–85 (catalogue raisonné), 1985; *relevant publication:* Patrick Procktor (monograph by Patrick Kinmonth), 1985. *Recreation:* Russian ballet. *Address:* 26 Manchester Street, W1M 5PG. *T:* 01–486 1763.

PROCTER, Norma; Contralto Singer; *b* Cleethorpes, Lincolnshire, 1928. Studied under Roy Henderson and Alec Redshaw. Made first London appearance at Southwark Cathedral; debut at Covent Garden, in Gluck's Orpheus, 1961. Has sung at major British music and European festivals. Numerous concerts and recitals throughout Europe; frequent broadcasts in Britain, Holland and Germany; has made many recordings. Hon. RAM 1974. *Address:* 194 Clee Road, Grimsby, Lincolnshire.

PROCTER, Sidney, CBE 1986; FCIS, FIB; Adviser to the Governor of the Bank of England, since 1985; Commissioner, Building Societies Commission, since 1986; company director; *b* 10 March 1925; *s* of Robert and Georgina Margaret Procter; *m* 1952, Isabel (*née* Simmons); one *d.* *Educ:* Ormskirk Grammar School. Served RAF, 1943–47. Entered former Williams Deacon's Bank, 1941; Asst General Manager, 1969; Dep. Dir, Williams & Glyn's Bank, 1970; Divl Dir, 1975; Exec. Dir, 1976–85; Asst Chief Executive, 1976; Dep. Chief Executive, 1977; Chief Exec., 1978–82; Dep. Gp Man. Dir, Royal Bank of Scotland Gp, 1979–82; Gp Chief Exec., 1982–85; Vice Chm., 1986; Director: Royal Bank of Scotland, 1978–86 (Vice Chm., 1986); Provincial Insurance Co., 1985–; Provincial Group, 1986–. Chm., Exeter Trust, 1986 (Dir, 1985). *Address:* The Piece House, Bourton-on-the-Water, Glos GL54 2AZ. *T:* Cotswold 20425.

PROCTOR, David Victor; Head of Printed Books and Manuscripts Department, National Maritime Museum, since 1976; *b* 1 March 1930; *s* of Comdr Victor William Lake Proctor, RN and Marjorie Proctor (*née* Weeks); *m* 1st, 1959, Margaret Graham (marr. diss. 1984); three *s*; 2nd, 1984, Marion Clara Calver; one step *s* five step *d.* *Educ:* Dauntsey's Sch.; Clare Coll., Cambridge (MA; DipEd 1955); Imperial Coll., London (DIC). Shipbroking, 1953–54; Teacher: Lycée de Brest, France, 1955–56; Clifton Coll., Bristol, 1956–62; National Maritime Museum: Educn Officer, 1962–72; Sec. and Educn Officer, 1972–74; Hd of Educn and Res. Facilities, 1974–76. Internat. Congress of Maritime Museums: Sec. Gen., 1972–78; Mem. Exec. Council, 1978–81; Vice-Pres., 1981–84; Trustee, 1984–. Chm., Gp for Educnl Services in Museums, 1971–75; Member: Adv. Council, Internat. Council of Museums, 1983–; Exec. Council, Internat. Commn for Maritime Hist., 1985– (Sec. Gen., 1980–85); Trustee, Madeleine Mainstone Trust, 1980–. Fellow, Huguenot Soc. of London, 1986–. *Publications:* Child of War, 1972; contribs to jls on museums, museum educn and hist. of science. *Recreations:* sailing, piano, walking, travel, DIY. *Address:* 6 Vinge Mews, Rochester, Kent ME1 1RA. *T:* Medway 49592. *Clubs:* Royal Cruising; Rochester Cruising.

PROCTOR, Harvey; *see* Proctor, K. H.

PROCTOR, Ian Douglas Ben, RDI 1969; FSIAD 1969; FRSA 1972; Chairman, Ian Proctor Metal Masts Ltd, 1959–76 and 1981–86 (Director, since 1959); freelance industrial designer since 1950; *b* 12 July 1918; *s* of Douglas McIntyre Proctor and Mary Albina Louise Proctor (*née* Tredwen); *m* 1943, Elizabeth Anne Gifford Lywood, *d* of Air Vice-Marshal O. G. Lywood, CB, CBE; three *s* one *d*. *Educ:* Gresham's Sch., Holt; London University. RAFVR (Flying Officer), 1946–47. Man. Dir, Gosport Yacht Co., 1947–48; Joint Editor Yachtsman Magazine, 1948–50; Daily Telegraph Yachting Correspondent, 1950–64. Yachtsman of the Year, 1965; Council of Industrial Design Award, 1967; Design Council Awards, 1977, 1980. *Publications:* Racing Dinghy Handling, 1948; Racing Dinghy Maintenance, 1949; Sailing: Wind and Current, 1950; Boats for Sailing, 1968; Sailing Strategy, 1977. *Recreation:* sailing. *Address:* Ferry House, Duncannon, Stoke Gabriel, near Totnes, Devon. *Clubs:* Nash House; Hayling Island Sailing, Aldenham Sailing.

PROCTOR, Ven. Jesse Heighton, MA (London); Archdeacon of Warwick, 1958–74, now Emeritus; Vicar of Sherbourne, Warwick, 1958–69; *b* 26 May 1908; *s* of Thomas and Sophia Proctor, Melton Mowbray; *m* 1938, Helena Mary Wood, *d* of John Thomas and Jessie Wood, Melton Mowbray; one *s* two *d*. *Educ:* County Grammar Sch. of King Edward VII, Melton Mowbray; Coll. of St Mark and St John, Chelsea, Univ. of London; St Andrew's Theological Training House, Whittlesford. Asst Master, Winterbourne Sch., Croydon, 1929–32; Sen. History Master, Melton Mowbray Gram. Sch., 1932–35; Deacon 1935, Priest 1936; Chap. and Tutor, St Andrew's, Whittlesford, 1935–38; Curate, St Philip's, Leicester, 1938–39; Vicar, Glen Parva and South Wigston, and Chap., Glen Parva Barracks, Leicester, 1939–46; Precentor of Coventry Cath., 1946–58; Hon. Canon of Coventry, 1947; Chaplain, Gulson Hosp., 1953–58; Sen. Examining Chap. to Bishop of Coventry, 1947–65; Canon Theologian of Coventry, 1954–59; Vice-Pres. CMS. Governor: Univ. of Warwick, 1966–68; City of Coventry Coll. of Educn, 1966–70. Barnabas of Coventry Evening Telegraph, 1955–75. *Publication:* contrib. to Neville Gorton (SPCK), 1957. *Recreations:* study of theology and history; the countryside. *Address:* Dilkusha, Bank Crescent, Ledbury, Herefordshire HR8 1AA. *T:* Ledbury 2241.

PROCTOR, (Keith) Harvey; MP (C) Billericay, since 1983 (Basildon, 1979–83); *b* 16 Jan. 1947; *s* of Albert Proctor and Hilda Tegerdine. *Educ:* High School for Boys, Scarborough; Univ. of York. BA History Hons, 1969. Asst Director, Monday Club, 1969–71; Research Officer, Conservative 1970s Parliamentary Gp, 1971–72; Exec. Director, Parliamentary Digest Ltd, 1972–74; British Paper & Board Industry Federation: Asst Sec., 1974–78; Secretary, 1978–79; Consultant, 1979–. Mem., Exec. Council, Monday Club, 1983–. *Publication:* Billericay in Old Picture Postcards. *Recreation:* tennis. *Address:* House of Commons, SW1. *T:* 01–219 4110.

PROCTOR, Sir Roderick (Consett), Kt 1978; MBE 1946; FCA; company director; *b* 28 July 1914; *s* of Frederick William Proctor and Ethel May (*née* Christmas); *m* 1st, 1943, Kathleen Mary (*née* Murphy; *d* 1978); four *s*; 2nd, 1980, Janice Marlene (*née* Pryor). *Educ:* Hale Sch., Perth, WA; Melbourne C of E Grammar Sch., Vic. FCA 1958. Served War, 1939–45. Commenced career as chartered accountant, 1931, as Jun. Clerk with R. Goyne Miller, Perth; joined Clarke & Son, Chartered Accountants, Brisbane, Qld, 1937; Partner, 1950, Sen. Partner, 1966 (firm merged with Aust. national firm, Hungerfords, 1960); retd as Partner, 1976. *Recreations:* surfing, boating. *Address:* Unit 102, The Gardens, Alice Street, Brisbane, Qld 4000, Australia. *Clubs:* Queensland, Brisbane, United Service (Brisbane); Southport Yacht, Runaway Bay Yacht.

PROCTOR-BEAUCHAMP, Sir Christopher Radstock P.; *see* Beauchamp.

PROFUMO, John Dennis, CBE 1975 (OBE (mil.) 1944); 5th Baron of the late United Kingdom of Italy; *b* 30 Jan. 1915; *e s* of late Baron Albert Profumo, KC; *m* 1954, Valerie Hobson, *qv*; one *s*. *Educ:* Harrow; Brasenose College, Oxford. 1st Northamptonshire Yeomanry, 1939 (despatches); Brigadier, Chief of Staff UK Mission in Japan, 1945. MP (C) Kettering Division, Northamptonshire, 1940–45; MP (C) Stratford-on-Avon Division of Warwickshire, 1950–63; Parliamentary Secretary, Ministry of Transport and Civil Aviation, Nov. 1952–Jan. 1957; Parliamentary Under-Secretary of State for the Colonies, 1957–58; Parliamentary Under-Sec. of State, Foreign Affairs, Nov. 1958–Jan. 1959; Minister of State for Foreign Affairs, 1959–60; Secretary of State for War, July 1960–June 1963. Dir, Provident Life Assoc. of London, 1975– (Dep. Chm., 1978–82). Mem., Bd of Visitors, HM Prison, Grendon, 1968–75. Chm., Toynbee Hall, 1982–85, Pres. 1985–. *Recreations:* fishing, gardening, DIY. *Heir:* *s* David Profumo [*b* 30 Oct. 1955; *m* 1980, Helen, *o d* of Alasdair Fraser; two *s*]. *Club:* Boodle's.

See also Baron Balfour of Inchrye.

PROKHOROV, Prof. Alexander Mikhailovich; Hero of Socialist Labour, 1969, 1986; Order of Lenin (five-fold); Physicist; Director, General Physics Institute, Academy of Sciences of the USSR, Moscow, since 1983; Editor-in-Chief, Bolshaya Sovetskaya Encyclopedia Publishing House, since 1970; *b* Atherton, Australia, 11 July 1916; *s* of Mikhail Prokhorov; *m* 1941, Galina Alexeyevna (*née* Shelepina); one *s*. *Educ:* Leningrad State University; Lebedev Inst. of Physics. Corresp. Mem., Academy of Sciences of the USSR (Department of General Physics and Astronomy), 1960–66, Full Mem., 1966–, Mem. Presidial Body, 1970, Academician-Secretary, 1973–. Chm., Nat. Commn of Soviet Physicists. Professor, Moscow University, 1958–. Hon. Professor: Delhi Univ.; Bucharest Univ., 1971; Cluz Univ., 1977; Praha Politechnical Inst., 1980. Member: European Phys. Soc., 1977; European Acad. of Scis, Art and Literature, 1986; Hon. Member: Amer. Acad. of Arts and Sciences, 1972; Acad. of Sciences of Hungary, 1976; Acad. of Sciences, German Democratic Republic, 1977; Acad. of Scis of Czechoslavakia, 1982; Acad. of Scis Leopoldina, 1984. Member, Communist Party of the Soviet Union, 1950–. Awarded Lenin Prize, 1959; Nobel Prize for Physics (jointly with Prof. N. G. Basov and Prof. C. H. Townes), 1964. *Publications:* contributions on non-linear oscillations, radiospectroscopy and quantum radio-physics. *Address:* General Physics Institute, Academy of Sciences of the USSR, Vavilov Street 38, 117942, GSP-1 Moscow, USSR.

PROKHOROVA, Violetta; *see* Elvin, V.

PROKOSCH, Frederic; Writer; *b* 17 May 1908; *s* of Eduard (Professor of Linguistics, Yale University) and Mathilde Prokosch. *Educ:* Yale University (PhD, 1933); King's College, Cambridge. Educated as a child in Wisconsin, Texas, Munich, Austria; travelled extensively all his life; research work in Chaucerian MSS, 1933–38 (PhD Dissertation: The Chaucerian Apocrypha). *Publications:* The Asiatics (novel), 1935; The Assassins (poems), 1936; The Seven Who Fled (novel), 1937; The Carnival (poems), 1938; Night of The Poor (novel), 1939; Death at Sea (poems), 1940; The Skies of Europe (novel), 1942; The Conspirators (novel), 1943; Some Poems of Hölderlin, 1943; Chosen Poems, 1944; Age of Thunder (novel), 1945; The Idols of the Cave (novel), 1946; The Medea of Euripides, 1947; The Sonnets of Louise Labé, 1947; Storm and Echo (novel), 1948; Nine Days to Mukalla (novel), 1953; A Tale for Midnight (novel), 1955; A Ballad of Love (novel), 1960; The Seven Sisters (novel), 1962; The Dark Dancer (novel), 1964; The Wreck of the Cassandra (novel), 1966; The Missolonghi Manuscript (novel), 1968; America, My Wilderness (novel), 1972; Voices (a memoir), 1983. *Recreations:* squash racquets (Champion of France, 1938, 1939, Champion of Sweden, 1944), lawn tennis (Champion of Mallorca). *Address:* Ma Trouvaille, 06 Plan de Grasse, France. *Clubs:* Pitt (Cambridge); Yale (New York); France-Amérique (Paris).

PROOM, Major William Arthur, TD 1953; *b* 18 Dec. 1916; *s* of Arthur Henry Proom and Nesta Proom; *m* 1941, Nellie Lister; one *s* one *d*. *Educ:* Richmond Sch., Yorks; Keighley Technical Coll. Commnd TA, 1/6 Bn Duke of Wellington's Regt, 1938; served War: Iceland, 1940–42; REME/IEME, India and Burma, 1943–46; Major, retd. Mayor of Keighley, 1973; Member: W Yorks Metropolitan CC, 1974–81 (Chm., 1979–80); City of Bradford Metrop. Dist Council, 1975–79. Chm., NE Gas Consumers' Council, 1973–77. *Recreations:* gardening, reading. *Address:* 15 The Hawthorns, Sutton-in-Craven, Keighley, W Yorks BD20 8BP.

PROOPS, Mrs Marjorie, OBE 1969; journalist; *d* of Alfred and Martha Rayle; *m* 1935; one *s*. *Educ:* Dalston Secondary Sch. Daily Mirror, 1939–45; Daily Herald, 1945–54; Daily Mirror, 1954–. Broadcaster, Television, 1960–. Member: Royal Commn on Gambling, 1976–78; Council for One Parent Families. Woman Journalist of the Year, 1969. *Publications:* Pride, Prejudice & Proops, 1975; Dear Marje, 1976. *Address:* 9 Sherwood Close, SW13.

PROPHET, Prof. Arthur Shelley, CBE 1980; DDS; DpBact; FDSRCS; FFDRCSI; Professor of Dental Surgery, University of London, 1956–83, now Emeritus; *b* 11 Jan. 1918; *s* of Eric Prophet and Mabel Wightman; *m* 1942, Vivienne Mary Bell; two *s*. *Educ:* Sedbergh School; University of Manchester. BDS Hons (Preston Prize and Medal), 1940; Diploma in Bacteriology (Manchester), 1948; DDS (Manchester) 1950; FDSRCS 1958; FFDRCS Ireland, 1964. RNVR (Dental Branch), 1941–46; Nuffield Dental Fellow, 1946–48; Lecturer in Dental Bacteriology, University of Manchester, 1948–54; Lecturer in Dental Surgery, QUB, 1954–56; Dir of Dental Studies, 1956–74, Dean of Dental Studies, 1974–77, UCH Dental Sch.; Dean, UCH Medical Sch., 1977–80; Dean, 1980–82, Vice-Dean, 1982–83, Faculty of Clinical Scis, UCL. Lectures: Charles Tomes, RCS, 1977; Wilkinson, Univ. of Manchester, 1978; Elwood, QUB, 1979; Shefford, UCL, 1983. Rep. of University of London on Gen. Dental Council, 1964–84. Elected Mem. Bd, Faculty of Dental Surgery, RCS, 1964–80 (Vice-Dean, 1972–73); Member: Cttee of Management, Inst. of Dental Surgery, 1963–83; Dental Sub-Cttee, UGC, 1968–78; Bd of Governors, UCH, 1957–74; Camden and Islington AHA(T), 1974–82; Bloomsbury HA, 1982–83. WHO Consultant, 1966; Consultant Dental Advr, DHSS, 1977–83. *Publications:* contrib. to medical and dental journals. *Recreation:* golf. *Address:* Little Orchard, Minstead, Lyndhurst, Hants SO43 7FW. *T:* Southampton 814003.

PROPPER, Arthur, CMG 1965; MBE 1945; *b* 3 Aug. 1910; 2nd *s* of late I. Propper; *m* 1941, Erica Mayer; one *d*. *Educ:* Owen's Sch.; Peterhouse, Cambridge (schol.). 1st class, Hist. Tripos, Pt 2. With W. S. Crawford Ltd (Advertising Agents), 1933–38, and the J. Walter Thompson Co. Ltd, 1939; Min. of Economic Warfare, 1940; transf. to Min. of Food, 1946 (subseq. to Min. of Agric., Fisheries and Food); established in Home Civil Service, 1949; Asst Sec., 1952; Mem. UK Delegn at Common Market negotiations, with rank of Under-Sec., 1962–63; seconded to Foreign Office, 1963; Counsellor (Agric.), UK Delegn to the European Communities, Brussels, and HM Embassy, Bonn, 1963–64; Under-Sec., Min. of Agriculture, Fisheries and Food, 1964–70; Common Mkt Advr, Unigate Ltd, 1970–73; Sec., Food Panel, Price Commn, 1973–76. *Recreations:* the theatre, music, buying books, visiting Scotland. *Address:* 3 Hill House, Stanmore Hill, Stanmore, Mddx. *T:* 01–954 1242. *Club:* United Oxford & Cambridge University.

PROSSER, Hon. Lord; William David Prosser; a Senator of the College of Justice in Scotland and Lord of Session, since 1986; *b* 23 Nov. 1934; *yr s* of David G. Prosser, MC, WS, Edinburgh; *m* 1964, Vanessa, *er d* of Sir William O'Brien Lindsay, KBE, Nairobi; two *s* two *d*. *Educ:* Edinburgh Academy; Corpus Christi Coll., Oxford (MA); Edinburgh Univ. (LLB). Advocate, 1962; QC (Scotland) 1974; Standing Junior Counsel in Scotland, Board of Inland Revenue, 1969–74; Advocate-Depute, 1978–79; Vice-Dean, Faculty of Advocates, 1979–83; Dean of Faculty, 1983–86. Mem., Scottish Cttee, Council on Tribunals, 1977–84. *Address:* 7 Randolph Crescent, Edinburgh EH3 7TH. *T:* 031–225 2709; Netherfoodie, Dairsie, Fife. *T:* Balmullo 870438. *Clubs:* New, Scottish Arts (Edinburgh).

PROSSER, (Albert) Russell (Garness), CMG 1967; MBE 1953; Senior Adviser (formerly Adviser), Social Development, Overseas Development Administration, 1967–80; *b* 8 April 1915; *s* of late Thomas Prosser; *m* 1957, Ruth Avalon Moore; one *s* (and one *s* decd). *Educ:* Godlys Sch.; London Sch. of Economics. Principal, Sch. of Social Welfare, Accra, 1947; Dep. Sec., Uganda, 1959; Permanent Secretary, Uganda, 1962; Adviser, Social Development, Kenya, 1963. Alternate UK delegate, UN Social Develt Commn, 1965–72, UK delegate, 1973–80. Associate Mem., Inst. of Develt Studies, Univ. of Sussex; External Examr Rural Develt, Univ. of Reading. Editor, Clare Market Review, 1939–40. FRSA 1974. Golden Medallion, Belgian Govt, 1962 (now known as La Belgique Reconnaissante). *Recreations:* angling, gardening. *Address:* 18b Wray Park Road, Reigate, Surrey. *T:* Reigate 42792.

PROSSER, (Elvet) John; QC 1978; a Recorder of the Crown Court, since 1972; *b* 10 July 1932; *s* of David and Hannah Prosser; *m* 1957, Mary Louise Cowdry; two *d*. *Educ:* Pontypridd Grammar Sch.; King's Coll., London Univ. LLB. Flt Lt, RAF, 1957–59. Called to the Bar, Gray's Inn, 1956; Mem., Senate of Inns of Court and the Bar, 1980–. Leader, Wales and Chester Circuit, 1984–. Part-time Chm. of Industrial Tribunals, 1975–81. An Asst Boundary Comr for Wales, 1977–. *Recreations:* watching cricket and television. *Address:* 78 Marsham Court, Westminster, SW1. *T:* 01–834 9779; Hillcroft, Mill Road, Lisvane, Cardiff CF4 5XJ. *T:* Cardiff 752380. *Clubs:* East India, Devonshire, Sports and Public Schools; Cardiff and County (Cardiff).

PROSSER, Ian Maurice Gray, FCA; Vice Chairman, since 1982, and Group Managing Director, since 1984, Bass PLC; *b* 5 July 1943; *s* of Maurice and Freda Prosser; *m* 1964, Elizabeth Herman; two *d*. *Educ:* King Edward's School, Bath; Watford Grammar School; Birmingham Univ. (BComm). Coopers & Lybrand, 1964–69; Bass Charrington Ltd, later Bass PLC, 1969–; Financial Dir, 1978. Dir, Boots Co., 1984–. Dir, Brewers' Soc., 1983–. *Recreations:* bridge, squash, gardening. *Address:* Bass PLC, 30 Portland Place, W1N 3DF. *T:* 01–637 5499. *Club:* Royal Automobile.

PROSSER, Raymond Frederick, CB 1973; MC 1942; *b* 12 Sept. 1919; *s* of Frederick Charles Prosser and Jane Prosser (*née* Lawless); *m* 1949, Fay Newmarch Holmes; two *s* three *d*. *Educ:* Wimbledon Coll.; The Queen's Coll., Oxford (1938–39 and 1946). Served Royal Artillery (Field), 1939–45 (MC, despatches): service in Egypt, Libya, India and Burma; Temp. Major. Asst Principal, Min. of Civil Aviation, 1947; Sec., Air Transport

Advisory Council, 1952–57; Private Sec. to Minister of Transport and Civil Aviation, 1959, and to Minister of Aviation, 1959–61; Counsellor (Civil Aviation), HM Embassy, Washington, DC, 1965–68; Under-Sec., Marine Div., BoT, later DTI, 1968–72; Deputy Sec., Regional Industrial Organisation and Policy, DTI, later DoI, 1972–77; Principal Estabt and Finance Officer, Depts of Industry, Trade, and Prices and Consumer Protection, 1977–79, retired. Dir, European Investment Bank, 1973–77. Mem. (part-time), CAA, 1980–85. *Address:* Juniper House, Shalford Common, Shalford, Guildford, Surrey. *T:* Guildford 66498.

PROSSER, Russell; *see* Prosser, A. R. G.

PROSSER, Thomas Vivian, CBE 1963; chartered builder, retired; *b* 25 April 1908; *er s* of T. V. Prosser, Liverpool; *m* 1935, Florence Minnie (Billie), 2nd *d* of W. J. Boulton, Highworth, Wilts; one *s* one *d*. *Educ:* Old Swan Technical Institute (now West Derby High School); College of Technology, Liverpool. Pupil of A. E. Cuddy, LRIBA, Architect, 1924. Joined Wm Thornton & Sons Ltd, Contractors of Liverpool, 1925, Man. Dir, 1945–64; Founder, Chm. and Man. Dir, Nat. Building Agency, 1964–67; Chm., T. V. Prosser & Son (Estates) Ltd, 1968–76. Formerly: President, Liverpool Regional Fedn of Building Trades Employers, 1956; Pres., Nat. Fedn of Building Trades Employers, 1959–60. *Recreations:* gardening, reading. *Address:* Priory Cottage, 1 Mill Street, Steventon, near Abingdon, Oxon OX13 6SP. *T:* Abingdon 831219. *Club:* Lyceum.

PROSSER, William David; *see* Prosser, Hon. Lord.

PROTHEROE, Alan Hackford, MBE (mil.) 1980; TD 1981; Assistant Director General, BBC, since 1982; *b* 10 Jan. 1934; *s* of Rev. B. P. Protheroe and R. C. M. Protheroe; *m* 1956, Anne Miller; two *s*. *Educ:* Maesteg Grammar Sch., Glamorgan. FBIM. Nat. Service, 2nd Lieut The Welch Regt, 1954–56; Lt-Col, Royal Regt of Wales (TA), 1979–84; Col, 1984–. Reporter, Glamorgan Gazette, 1951–53; BBC Wales: Reporter, 1957–59; Industrial Correspondent, 1959–64; Editor, News and Current Affairs, 1964–70; BBC TV News: Asst Editor, 1970–72; Dep. Editor, 1972–77; Editor, 1977–80; Asst Dir, BBC News and Current Affairs, 1980–82. During BBC career has made films and radio progs, reported wars, and travelled widely; seconded to Greek Govt to assist in reorganisation of Greek TV, 1973. Mem., Steering Cttee, EBU News Gp, 1977–; Dir, Visnews Ltd, 1982–. Mem. Council, RUSI, 1984–; Founder Mem. and Dep. Chm., Assoc. of British Editors, 1984–. *Publications:* contribs to newspapers and specialist jls on industrial, defence and media affairs. *Recreations:* writing, pistol and rifle shooting. *Address:* c/o Broadcasting House, Portland Place, W1A 1AA. *T:* 01–580 4468.

PROUD, Air Cdre Harold John Granville Ellis, CBE 1946; *b* 23 Aug. 1906; *s* of late Ralph Henry Proud, Glasgow; *m* 1937, Jenefer Angela Margaret, *d* of late Lt-Col J. Bruce, OBE, 19th Lancers; two *d*. HAC (Inf.), 1924–26; commissioned RAF, pilot, 1926; Staff Coll., 1936; served in: Mediterranean (FAA), 1928; India, 1937 and 1942 (Inspector Gen. Indian Air Force, 1942–43; AOA Air HQ, 1943–45); Dir of Ground Def., Air Min., 1945–47; served in Singapore, 1949; AOC 67 (NI) Gp and Senior Air Force Officer N Ire., 1951–54; Provost Marshal and Chief of Air Force Police, 1954; retired 1956; in business, 1957–71; now domiciled in Switzerland; Mem. Council, British Residents Assoc. of Switzerland, 1973–77, Chm., 1974–75. *Address:* Appt 10, Les Libellules, 1837 Chateau d'Oex, Switzerland. *T:* (029) 46223.

PROUD, Sir John (Seymour), Kt 1978; mining engineer; director and chairman of companies; *b* 9 Aug. 1907; *s* of William James Proud and Hannah Seymour; *m* 1964, Laurine, *d* of M. Ferran. *Educ:* Univ. of Sydney (Bachelor of Engrg, Mining and Metallurgy). CEng, FIMM, FIE(Aust), M(Aus)IMM. Chm., Newcastle Wallsend Coal Co., which merged with Peko Mines NL, 1960; Chm., Peko-Wallsend Investments Ltd, then Chm., Peko-Wallsend Ltd; retd from chair, 1978; Dir/Consultant, 1978–82. Chairman: Electrical Equipment Ltd (Group), 1978–82 (Dir, 1943–83); Oil Search Ltd, 1978– (Dir, 1974–); Oil Co. of Australia NL, 1979–83; Dir, CSR Ltd, 1974–79. Fellow of Senate, Univ. of Sydney, 1974–83. Chm. Trustees, Lizard Island Reef Res. Foundn, 1978–; Trustee, Aust. Museum, 1971–77. Hon. DEng Sydney, 1984. *Recreations:* yachting, pastoral activity. *Address:* 9 Finlay Road, Turramurra, NSW 2074, Australia. *Clubs:* Union, Royal Sydney Yacht Squadron, Royal Prince Alfred Yacht, American National (Sydney).

PROUDFOOT, Bruce; *see* Proudfoot, V. B.

PROUDFOOT, Bruce Falconer; Publicity Officer, Ulster Savings Committee, 1963–69; Editor, Northern Whig and Belfast Post, 1943–63; *b* 1903; 2nd *s* of G. A. Proudfoot, Edinburgh; *m* 1928, Cecilia, *er d* of V. T. T. Thompson, Newcastle on Tyne; twin *s*. *Educ:* Edinburgh Education Authority's Primary and Secondary Schools. Served with Edinburgh Evening Dispatch, Galloway Gazette (Newton-Stewart) and Newcastle Daily Chronicle before joining Northern Whig, 1925. *Address:* 10 Ophir Gardens, Belfast BT15 5EP. *T:* 776368.

See also V. B. Proudfoot.

PROUDFOOT, (George) Wilfred; owner, self-service stores; consultant in distribution; owner, Proudfoot School of Hypnosis and Hypnotherapy; *b* 19 December 1921; *m* 1950, Margaret Mary, *d* of Percy Clifford Jackson, Pontefract, Yorks; two *s* one *d*. *Educ:* Crook Council Sch.; Scarborough Coll. Served War of 1939–45, NCO Fitter in RAF, 1940–46. Served Scarborough Town Council, 1950–58 (Chm. Health Cttee, 1952–58). MP (C) Cleveland Division of Yorkshire, Oct. 1959–Sept. 1964; PPS to Minister of State, Board of Trade, Apr.–July 1962, to Minister of Housing and Local Govt and Minister for Welsh Affairs (Rt Hon. Sir Keith Joseph, Bt, MP), 1962–64; MP (C) Brighouse and Spenborough, 1970–Feb. 1974; Minister of State, Dept of Employment, 1970; contested (C) Brighouse and Spenborough, Oct. 1974. Man. Dir, Radio 270, 1965–. Chm., Scarborough Cons. Assoc., 1978–80; Chm., Cleveland European Constituency Cons. Assoc., 1979–. Professional hypnotist; face lifted by Dr John Williams, USA, 1978. Chm., Hypnotist Examiners Council, 1983–. *Publication:* The Two Factor Nation, or How to make the people rich, 1977. *Recreations:* reading, photography, caravanning, travel, walking, skiing, jogging. *Address:* 278 Scalby Road, Scarborough, North Yorkshire. *T:* Scarborough 67027. *Club:* St Stephen's Constitutional.

PROUDFOOT, Prof. (Vincent) Bruce, FSA 1963; FRSE 1979; Professor of Geography, University of St Andrews, since 1974; *b* 24 Sept. 1930; *s* of Bruce Falconer Proudfoot, *qv*; *m* 1961, Edwina Valmai Windram Field; two *s*. *Educ:* Royal Belfast Academical Instn; Queen's Univ., Belfast (BA, PhD). Research Officer, Nuffield Quaternary Research Unit, QUB, 1954–58; Lectr in Geography, QUB, 1958–59, Durham Univ., 1959–67; Tutor, 1960–63, Librarian, 1963–65, Hatfield Coll., Durham; Visiting Fellow, Univ. of Auckland, NZ, and Commonwealth Vis. Fellow, Australia, 1966; Associate Prof., 1967–70, Prof., 1970–74, Univ. of Alberta, Edmonton, Canada; Acting Chm., Dept of Geography, Univ. of Alberta, 1970–71; Co-ordinator, Socio-Economic Opportunity Studies, and Staff Consultant, Alberta Human Resources Research Council, 1971–72. Trustee, Nat. Mus. of Antiquities of Scotland, 1982–85. Chairman: Rural Geog. Study Gp, Inst. of British Geographers, 1980–84; Soc. for Landscape Studies, 1979–83. Vice-President: RSE, 1985– (Mem. Council, 1982–85); Soc. of Antiquaries of Scotland, 1982–85; Pres., Section H (Anthrop. and Archaeol.), BAAS, 1985; Hon. Pres., Scottish Assoc. of Geography Teachers, 1982–84. Lectures: Lister, BAAS, 1964; Annual, Soc. for Landscape Studies, 1983; Estyn Evans, QUB, 1985. Hon. Editor, RSGS, 1979–. *Publications:* The Downpatrick Gold Find, 1955; (with R. G. Ironside *et al*) Frontier Settlement Studies, 1974; (ed) Site, Environment and Economy, 1983; numerous papers in geographical, archaeological and soils jls. *Recreation:* gardening. *Address:* Westgate, Wardlaw Gardens, St Andrews, Scotland KY16 9DW. *T:* St Andrews 73293.

PROUDFOOT, Wilfred; *see* Proudfoot, G. W.

PROUT, Christopher James, DPhil; Member (C) Shropshire and Stafford, European Parliament, since 1979; Chief Whip, European Democratic Group, since 1983; barrister-at-law; *b* 1 Jan. 1942; *s* of late Frank Yabsley Prout, MC and bar, and Doris Lucy Prout (*née* Osborne). *Educ:* Sevenoaks Sch.; Manchester Univ. (BA); The Queen's Coll., Oxford (Scholar; BPhil, DPhil). TA Officer (Major): OU OTC, 1966–74; 16/5 Lancers, 1974–82; 3rd Armoured Div., 1982–. Called to the Bar, The Middle Temple, 1972. English-Speaking Union Fellow, Columbia Univ., NYC, 1963–64; Staff Mem., World Bank Group (UN), Washington DC, 1966–69; Leverhulme Fellow and Lectr in Law, Sussex Univ., 1969–79. Dep. Whip, Europ. Democratic Gp, 1979–82; Chm., Parlt Cttee No 16 (Electoral Law), 1982–84. *Publications:* Market Socialism in Yugoslavia, 1985; (contrib.) International Economic Relations in the 1960s, ed A. Shonfield, 1976; (contrib.) vols 51 and 52, Halsbury's Laws of England, 1986; articles in legal jls. *Recreations:* riding, sailing. *Address:* 2 Queen Anne's Gate, SW1. *T:* 01–222 1729; 2 Paper Buildings, Temple, EC4. *T:* 01–353 5835. *Clubs:* Beefsteak, Royal Ocean Racing.

PROVAN, James Lyal Clark; Member (C) NE Scotland, European Parliament, since 1979; farmer; *b* 19 Dec. 1936; *s* of John Provan and Jean (*née* Clark); *m* 1960, Roweena Adele Lewis; twin *s* one *d*. *Educ:* Ardvreck Sch., Crieff; Oundle Sch., Northants; Royal Agricultural Coll., Cirencester. Member: Tayside Regional Council, 1978–82; Tay River Purification Bd, 1978–82. Member: Agriculture and Fisheries Cttee, European Parlt, 1979– (European Democratic Gp spokesman on agricl and fisheries affairs); Environment, Consumer Affairs and Public Health Cttee, European Parlt, 1979–. Area President, Scottish NFU, 1965 and 1971; Manager, Scottish Farming News, 1966–68; Founder Vice-Chm., East of Scotland Grassland Soc., 1972– (Chm., 1973–75). Treasurer, Perth and E Perthshire Conservative Assoc., 1975–77; Member, Lord Lieutenant's Queen's Jubilee Appeal Cttee, 1977. *Recreations:* country pursuits, sailing, flying, musical appreciation, travel. *Address:* Wallacetown, Bridge of Earn, Perth, Scotland PH2 8QA. *T:* Bridge of Earn 812243. *Clubs:* Farmers', East India, Devonshire, Sports and Public Schools; Royal Perth Golfing Society.

PROWSE, Florence Irene; *see* Calvert, F. I.

PRUDE, Mrs Walter F.; *see* de Mille, Agnes George.

PRYCE, George Terry; Managing Director, since 1978, and Chief Executive, since 1981, Dalgety Ltd; *b* 26 March 1934; *s* of Edwin Pryce and Hilda Florence (*née* Price); *m* 1957, Thurza Elizabeth Tatham; two *s* one *d*. *Educ:* Welshpool Grammar Sch.; National Coll. of Food Technol. MFC, FIFST, CBIM. Dir, various food cos in THF Gp, 1965–70; Asst Man. Dir, Dalgety (UK) Ltd, 1970, Man. Dir, 1971; Dir, Dalgety Ltd, 1972–; Chairman: Dalgety (UK) Ltd, 1978–; Dalgety Spillers Ltd, 1980–; Dir, H. P. Bulmer Holdings. Chm., Bd of Food Studies, Reading Univ.; Mem., AFRC, 1986–. Governor, National Coll. of Food Technol., 1981–. *Recreations:* sport, esp. golf; reading. *Address:* Dalgety Ltd, 19 Hanover Square, W1.

PRYCE, Rt. Rev. James Taylor; a Suffragan Bishop of Toronto (Area Bishop of York-Simcoe), since 1985; *b* 3 May 1936; *s* of James Pryce and Florence Jane (*née* Taylor); *m* 1962, Marie Louise Connor; three *s* (one decd) one *d*. *Educ:* Bishop's Univ., Lennoxville, Quebec (BA, LST). Asst Curate, Church of the Ascension, Don Mills, 1962–65; Incumbent: St Thomas' Church, Brooklin, Ont, 1965–70; St Paul's, Lorne Park, 1970–75; Christ Church, Scarborough, 1975–81; St Leonard's, North Toronto, 1981–85. Hon. DD, Wycliffe Coll., 1986. *Address:* 8 Pinehurst Court, Aurora, Ontario L4G 3Z3, Canada. *T:* 1–416–727–7863.

PRYCE, Maurice Henry Lecorney, FRS 1951; Professor of Physics, University of British Columbia, 1968–78, now Hon. Professor; *b* 24 Jan. 1913; *e s* of William John Pryce and Hortense Lecorney; *m* 1939, Susanne Margarete Born (marr. diss., 1959); one *s* three *d*; *m* 1961, Freda Mary Kinsey. *Educ:* Royal Grammar Sch., Guildford; Trinity Coll., Cambridge. Commonwealth Fund Fellow at Princeton, NJ, USA, 1935–37; Fellow of Trinity Coll., Cambridge, and Faculty Asst Lecturer, University of Cambridge, 1937–39; Reader in Theoretical Physics, University of Liverpool, 1939–45. Engaged on Radar research with Admiralty Signal Establishment, 1941–44, and on Atomic Energy Research with National Research Council of Canada, Montreal, 1944–45. University Lecturer in Mathematics and Fellow of Trinity Coll., Cambridge, 1945–46; Wykeham Professor of Physics, University of Oxford, 1946–54; Henry Overton Wills Professor of Physics, University of Bristol, 1954–64; Prof. of Physics, University of Southern California, 1964–68. Visiting Professor: Princeton Univ., NJ, USA, 1950–51; Duke Univ., NC, USA, 1958; Univ. of Sussex, 1976–77. *Publications:* various on Theoretical Physics, in learned journals. *Recreations:* lawn tennis, badminton. *Address:* Physics Department, University of British Columbia, 2075 Wesbrook Mall, Vancouver V6T 1W5, Canada; 4754 West 6th Avenue, Vancouver, BC V6T 1C5, Canada. *Club:* Athenæum.

PRYCE, Prof. Roy; Director, Federal Trust for Education and Research, since 1983; *b* 4 Oct. 1928; *s* of Thomas and Madeleine Pryce; *m* 1954, Sheila Rose, *d* of Rt Hon. James Griffiths, CH; three *d*. *Educ:* Grammar Sch., Burton-on-Trent; Emmanuel Coll., Cambridge (MA, PhD). MA Oxon. Research Fellow: Emmanuel Coll., Cambridge, 1953–55; St Antony's Coll., Oxford, 1955–57; Head of London Information Office of High Authority of European Coal and Steel Community, 1957–60; Head of London Inf. Office, Jt Inf. Service of European Communities, 1960–64; Rockefeller Foundn Res. Fellow, 1964–65; Dir, Centre for Contemp. European Studies, Univ. of Sussex, 1965–73; Directorate General for Information, Commission of the European Communities: Dir, 1973–78; Sen. Advr for Direct Elections, 1978–79; Chief Advr for Programming, 1979–81. Vis. Professorial Fellow, Centre for Contemporary European Studies, Univ. of Sussex, 1973–81; Vis. Professor: Coll. of Europe, Bruges, 1965–72; Eur. Univ. Inst., Florence, 1981–83; Eur. Inst. for Public Admin, Maastricht, 1983 . *Publications:* The Italian Local Elections 1956, 1957; The Political Future of the European Community, 1962; (with John Pinder) Europe After de Gaulle, 1969, German and Ital. edns 1970; The Politics of the European Community, 1973; contrib. Encyl. Brit., Jl Common Market Studies, etc. *Recreations:* gardening, collecting water colours and prints.

PRYCE-JONES, Alan Payan, TD; book critic, author and journalist; *b* 18 Nov. 1908; *s* of late Colonel Henry Morris Pryce-Jones, CB; *m* 1934, Thérèse (*d* 1953), *d* of late Baron Fould-Springer and of Mrs Frank Wooster, Paris; one *s*; *m* 1968, Mrs Mary Jean Kempner Thorne (*d* 1969), *d* of late Daniel Kempner. *Educ:* Eton; Magdalen Coll., Oxford. Formerly Asst Editor, The London Mercury, 1928–32; subseq. Times Literary Supplement; Editor,

Times Literary Supplement, 1948–59; Book critic: New York Herald Tribune, 1963–66; World Journal Tribune, 1967–68; Newsday, 1969–71; Theatre Critic, Theatre Arts, 1963–. Trustee, National Portrait Gallery, 1950–61; Director, Old Vic Trust, 1950–61; Member Council, Royal College of Music, 1956–61; Program Associate, The Humanities and Arts Program, Ford Foundation, NY, 1961–63. Served War of 1939–45, France, Italy, Austria; Lieut-Colonel, 1945. *Publications:* The Spring Journey, 1931; People in the South, 1932; Beethoven, 1933; 27 Poems, 1935; Private Opinion, 1936; Nelson, an opera, 1954; Vanity Fair, a musical play (with Robin Miller and Julian Slade), 1962. *Recreations:* music, travelling. *Address:* 46 John Street, Newport, RI 02840, USA. *Clubs:* Travellers', Garrick, Beefsteak, Pratt's; Knickerbocker, Century (New York); Artillery (Galveston, Texas).

PRYER, Eric John, CB 1986; Chief Land Registrar, since 1983; *b* 5 Sept. 1929; *s* of late Edward John and Edith Blanche Pryer; *m* 1962, Moyra Helena Cross; one *s* one *d*. *Educ:* Beckenham and Penge County Grammar Sch.; Birkbeck Coll., London Univ. (BA Hons). Associate Mem., RICS, 1986. Called to the Bar, Gray's Inn, 1957. Exec. Officer, Treasury Solicitor's Dept, 1948; Legal Asst, HM Land Registry, 1959; Asst Land Registrar, 1965; Dist Land Registrar, Durham, 1976; Dep. Chief Land Registrar, 1981–83. *Publications:* official pubns; articles in jls. *Recreation:* reading. *Address:* HM Land Registry, Lincoln's Inn Fields, WC2A 3PH. *T:* 01–405 3488.

PRYKE, Sir David Dudley, 3rd Bt *cr* 1926; *b* 16 July 1912; *s* of Sir William Robert Dudley Pryke, 2nd Bt; *S* father 1959; *m* 1945, Doreen Winifred, *er d* of late Ralph Bernard Wilkins; two *d*. *Educ:* St Lawrence Coll., Ramsgate. Liveryman Turners' Company, 1961 (Master, 1985–86). *Heir: b* William Dudley Pryke [*b* 18 Nov. 1914; *m* 1940, Lucy Irene, *d* of late Frank Madgett; one *s* one *d*]. *Address:* Flatholme, Brabant Road, North Fambridge, Chelmsford, Essex. *T:* Maldon 740227.

PRYN, Maj.-Gen. William John, OBE 1973; MB, BS; FRCS, FRCSEd; Director of Army Surgery, and Consulting Surgeon to the Army, 1982–86, retired; *b* 25 Jan. 1928; *s* of late Col Richard Harold Cotter Pryn, FRCS, late RAMC and Una St George Ormsby (*née* Roe); *m* 1st, 1952, Alison Lynette (marr. diss.), 2nd *d* of Captain Norman Arthur Cyril Hardy, RN; two *s* one *d*; 2nd, 1982, June de Medina, *d* of Surg. Comdr Norman Bernard de Medina Greenstreet, RN; one step *s* one step *d*. *Educ:* Malvern Coll.; Guy's Hosp. Med. Sch., London Univ. (MB, BS 1951). MRCS, LRCP 1951; FRCS 1958; FRCSEd 1984. Trooper, 21st SAS Regt (Artists Rifles), TA, 1948–50. House appts, Gen. Hosp., Ramsgate and Royal Berks Hosp., Reading, 1951–52; commnd into RAMC, 1952; Regtl MO to No 9 Training Regt RE, 1952–53; surg. appts in mil. hosps in UK, Cyprus and N Africa, 1953–58; seconded as Surg. Registrar, Royal Postgrad. Med. Sch., Hammersmith Hosp., 1958–59; Officer i/c Surg. Div. and Consultant Surgeon to mil. hosps, Malaya, Singapore, N Borneo and UK, 1959–69; CO BMH Dhekelia, 1969–72; Sen. Consultant Surgeon in mil. hosps, UK and NI, 1972–77; Consulting Surgeon to BAOR, 1977–82; Consultant in Surgery to Royal Hosp., Chelsea, 1982–86; Hon. Consultant to S Dist, Kensington and Chelsea and Westminster AHA (T), 1981. Member: EUROMED Gp on Emergency Medicine, 1980–86; Specialty Bd in Surgery, and Reg. Trng Cttee in Gen. Surgery, Defence Medical Services, 1982–86; Med. Cttee, Defence Scientific Adv. Council, 1982–86; BMA, 1950–; Wessex Surgeons Club, 1976–. Member Council: RAMC, 1982–86; Mil. Surgical Soc., 1982–. Fellow, Assoc. of Surgeons of GB and Ireland, 1960 (Mem., Educn Adv. Cttee, 1982–86). QHS 1981–86. OStJ 1984. Mem., Editorial Bd, Injury, 1982–86. *Publications:* (contrib.) Field Surgery Pocket Book, 1981; original articles in the Lancet and British Jl of Surgery. *Recreations:* fishing, shooting and other country pursuits, golf, tennis, sailing, gardening, joinery, house maintenance.

PRYOR, Arthur John, PhD; Under Secretary, and Regional Director, West Midlands Region, Department of Trade and Industry, since 1985; *b* 7 March 1939; *s* of Quinton Arthur Pryor, FRICS and Elsie Mary (*née* Luscombe); *m* 1964, Marilyn Kay Petley; one *s* one *d*. *Educ:* Harrow County Grammar Sch.; Downing Coll., Cambridge (MA; PhD). Asst Lectr, then Lectr, in Spanish and Portuguese, UC Cardiff, 1963–66; Asst Principal, BoT and ECGD, 1966–69; Principal, DTI, 1970–73; First Sec., British Embassy, Washington, 1973–75; Principal, Dept of Trade, 1975–77; Assistant Secretary: Shipping Policy Div., Dept of Trade, 1977–80; Air Div., DoI, 1980–83; Internat. Trade Policy Div., DTI, 1984–85. *Publications:* contribs to modern lang. jls. *Recreations:* tennis, squash, book collecting. *Address:* 35 Bloomsbury Grove, Kings Heath, Birmingham B14 7NU. *T:* 021–443 2891.

PRYOR, John Pembro, MS; FRCS; Consultant Urological Surgeon to King's College Hospital and St Peter's Hospital, since 1975; Dean, Institute of Urology, London University, 1978–85; *b* 25 Aug. 1937; *s* of William Benjamin Pryor and Kathleen Pryor; *m* 1959, Marion Hopkins; four *s*. *Educ:* Reading Sch.; King's Coll. and King's Coll. Hosp. Med. Sch. (MB, BS). AKC 1961; FRCS 1967; MS London 1971. Training appointments: Doncaster Royal Infirm., 1965–66; Univ. of Calif, San Francisco, 1968–69; King's Coll. Hosp. and St Paul's Hosp., 1971–72. Hunterian Prof., RCS, 1971. Chm. (first), British Andrology Soc., 1979–84. *Publications:* articles on urology and andrology in scientific jls. *Address:* 147 Harley Street, W1N 1DL. *T:* 01–935 4444.

PRYOR, Robert Charles, QC 1983; *b* 10 Dec. 1938; *s* of Charles Selwyn Pryor and Olive Woodall Pryor; *m* 1969, Virginia Sykes; one *s* one *d*. *Educ:* Eton; Trinity Coll., Cambridge (BA). National Service, KRRC, 2nd Lieut 1958. Called to the Bar, Inner Temple, 1963. Director, Sun Life Assurance plc, 1977–. *Recreations:* fishing, shooting. *Address:* Chitterne House, Warminster, Wilts BA12 0LG. *T:* Warminster 50255.

PRYS-DAVIES, family name of **Baron Prys-Davies.**

PRYS-DAVIES, Baron *cr* 1982 (Life Peer), of Llanegryn in the County of Gwynedd; **Gwilym Prys Prys-Davies;** Partner, Morgan Bruce & Nicholas, Solicitors, Cardiff, Pontypridd and Porth, since 1957; *b* 8 Dec. 1923; *s* of William and Mary Matilda Davies; *m* 1951, Llinos Evans; three *d*. *Educ:* Towyn Sch., Towyn, Merioneth; University College of Wales, Aberystwyth. Served RN, 1942–46. Faculty of Law, UCW, Aberystwyth, 1946–52; President of Debates, Union UCW, 1949; President Students' Rep. Council, 1950; LLB 1949; LLM 1952. Admitted Solicitor, 1956. Contested (Lab) Carmarthen, 1966. Special Adviser to Sec. of State for Wales, 1974–78; Chm., Welsh Hosps Bd, 1968–74; Member: Welsh Council, 1967–69; Welsh Adv. Cttee, ITA, 1966–69; Working Party on 4th TV Service in Wales, Home Office and Welsh Office, 1975–; Adv. Gp, Use of Fetuses and Fetal Material for Res., DHSS and Welsh Office, 1972; Econ. and Social Cttee, EEC, 1978–82. OStJ. *Publications:* A Central Welsh Council, 1963; Y Ffermwr a'r Gyfraith, 1967. *Address:* Lluest, 78 Church Road, Tonteg, Pontypridd, Mid Glam. *T:* Newtown Llantwit 2462.

PUGH, Alastair Tarrant, CBE 1986; Executive Vice Chairman/Director of Strategy, Caledonian Aviation Group plc, since 1985; *b* 16 Sept. 1928; *s* of Sqdn Leader Rev. Herbert Cecil Pugh, GC, MA, and Amy Lilian Pugh; *m* 1957, Sylvia Victoria Marlow; two *s* one *d*. *Educ:* Tettenhall Coll., Staffs; De Havilland Aeronautical Tech. Sch. FRAeS; FCIT; FIFF; CBIM. Design Dept, De Havilland Aircraft Co., 1949–52; Sen. Designer, H. M. Hobson, 1952–55; journalist, Flight, 1955–61; Channel Air Bridge, 1961–63; British United Airways, 1963–70: Planning Dir, 1968; British Caledonian Airways: Dir, R&D, 1970; Production Dir, 1973–74; Corporate Planning Dir, 1974–77; Dep. Chief Exec., 1977–78; Man. Dir, 1978–85. Pres., Inst. of Freight Forwarders, 1981–82. *Recreation:* the chain-driven Frazer Nash. *Address:* England's Cottage, Sidlow Bridge, Reigate, Surrey. *T:* Reigate 43456.

PUGH, Charles Edward, (Ted Pugh); Managing Director, National Nuclear Corporation Ltd, since 1984; *b* 17 Sept. 1922; *s* of Gwilym Arthur and Elsie Doris Pugh; *m* 1945, Edna Wilkinson; two *s* and *d*. *Educ:* Bolton and Salford Technical Colleges. CEng, MIMechE, MInstE. Lancashire Electric Power Co., 1941–48; CEGB Project Manager responsible for construction of 6 power stations, 1951–71; Chief Electrical and Control and Instrumentation Engineer, CEGB, Barnwood, 1971–73; Special Services, CEGB, 1973–76; Dir of Projects, CEGB, 1976–82; PWR Project Dir, NNC, 1982–84. Hon. FINucE. *Recreations:* power stations, sculpture, painting, music, gardening and walking. *Address:* Hazelmere, Cranage, Holmes Chapel, Cheshire. *T:* Holmes Chapel 34565.

PUGH, Harold Valentine, CBE 1964; Chairman, Northern Ireland Joint Electricity Authority, 1967–70, retired; *b* 18 Oct. 1899; *s* of Henry John Valentine Pugh and Martha (*née* Bott); *m* 1934, Elizabeth Mary (*née* Harwood); two *s* one *d*. *Educ:* The High Sch., Murree, India; Manchester College of Technology. Trained Metropolitan-Vickers (asst engineer erection, 1925–30). Chief Engineer, Cory Bros, 1930–35; Deputy Superintendent and later Superintendent, Upper Boat Power Station, 1935–43; Generation Engineer, South Wales Power Company, 1943–44; Deputy Chief Engineer, Manchester Corporation Electricity Dept, 1944–48; Controller, British Electricity Authority, South Wales Division, 1948; Controller, British (later Central) Electricity Authority, London Division, 1951; Chairman: Eastern Electricity Board, 1957–63; South-Eastern Electricity Board, 1963–66. Director: Aberdare Holdings, 1966–70. AMCT; FIEE; FIMechE. *Recreations:* gardening, golf. *Address:* Clontaff, Doggetts Wood Lane, Chalfont St Giles, Bucks HP8 4TH. *T:* Little Chalfont 2330.

PUGH, Sir Idwal (Vaughan), KCB 1972 (CB 1967); Chairman, Chartered Trust Ltd, since 1979; Director: Standard Chartered Bank, since 1979; Halifax Building Society, since 1979; *b* 10 Feb. 1918; *s* of late Rhys Pugh and Elizabeth Pugh; *m* 1946, Mair Lewis (*d* 1985); one *s* one *d*. *Educ:* Cowbridge Grammar Sch.; St John's Coll., Oxford (Hon. Fellow, 1979). Army Service, 1940–46. Entered Min. of Civil Aviation, 1946; Alternate UK Rep. at International Civil Aviation Organisation, Montreal, 1950–53; Asst Secretary, 1956; Civil Air Attaché, Washington, 1957–59; Under Secretary, Min. of Transport, 1959; Min. of Housing and Local Govt, 1961; Dep. Sec., Min. of Housing and Local Govt, 1966–69; Permanent Sec., Welsh Office, 1969–71; Second Permanent Sec., DoE, 1971–76. Parly Comr for Administration and Health Service Comr for England, Wales and Scotland, 1976–79. Chm., Develt Corp. of Wales, 1980–83. *Address:* Nant-y-Garreg, Bontddu, Gwynedd. *Club:* Brooks's.

PUGH, John Arthur, OBE 1968; HM Diplomatic Service, retired; British High Commissioner to Seychelles, 1976–80; *b* 17 July 1920; *er s* of late Thomas Pugh and Dorothy Baker Pugh; unmarried. *Educ:* Brecon Grammar Sch.; Bristol Univ. RN, 1941–45. Home CS, 1950–54; Gold Coast Admin. Service, 1955–58; Adviser to Ghana Govt, 1958–60; First Sec., British High Commn, Lagos, 1962–65; First Sec. (Economic), Bangkok, and British Perm. Rep. to Economic Commn for Asia and Far East, 1965–68; British Dep. High Comr, Ibadan, 1971–73; Diplomatic Service Inspector, 1973–76. *Recreations:* Oriental ceramics, anthropology, the sea. *Address:* Pennybrin, Hay on Wye, Hereford HR3 5RS. *T:* Hay on Wye 820695. *Club:* Royal Commonwealth Society.

PUGH, John Stanley; Editor, Liverpool Echo, 1978–82; *b* 9 Dec. 1927; *s* of John Albert and Winifred Lloyd Pugh; *m* 1953, Kathleen Mary; two *s* one *d*. *Educ:* Wallasey Grammar School. Editor, Liverpool Daily Post, 1969–78. *Recreation:* golf. *Address:* 26 Westwood Road, Noctorum, Birkenhead, Merseyside L43 9RQ. *Club:* Royal Liverpool (Hoylake).

PUGH, Lionel Roger Price, CBE 1975; VRD 1953; Deputy Chairman, Bridon plc, since 1977 (Director since 1973); *b* 9 May 1916; *s* of late Henry George Pugh, Cardiff; *m* 1942, Joyce Norma Nash; one *s* one *d*. *Educ:* Clifton. FCA. Supply Officer, RNVR, 1938–60; war service mainly in Mediterranean, 1939–46; retired as Lt Comdr, RNR, 1960. With Deloitte & Co., 1933–47; joined Guest Keen & Bladwins Iron & Steel Co. Ltd, 1947; Dir 1955; Man. Dir 1960; Chm. 1962; Jt Man. Dir, GKN Steel, 1964. Dir, Product Co-ordination, British Steel Corp., 1967; Dep. Commercial Man. Dir, 1969; Man. Dir, Ops and Supplies, 1970; Mem., Corporate Finance and Planning, 1972; Exec. Mem., 1972–77. Dir, Ryan Internat., 1979–85. Pres., Iron and Steel Inst., 1973; Hon. Member: American Iron and Steel Inst. 1973; Metals Soc., 1976; Inst. of Metals, 1985. Mem., Civil Aviation Council for Wales, 1962–66; part-time Mem., S Wales Electricity Bd, 1963–67. DL S Glamorgan (formerly Glamorgan), 1963–78. Gold Cross of Merit (Poland), 1942. *Address:* Brook Cottage, Bournes Green, Oakridge, Glos. *T:* Gloucester 770554. *Clubs:* Naval and Military; Cardiff and County; Royal Porthcawl Golf, Cirencester Golf.

PUGH, Surg. Rear-Adm. Patterson David Gordon, OBE 1968; surgeon and author; *b* 19 Dec. 1920; *o s* of late W. T. Gordon Pugh, MD, FRCS, Carshalton, and Elaine V. A. Pugh (*née* Hobson), Fort Beaufort, S Africa; *m* 1st, 1948, Margaret Sheena Fraser; three *s* one *d*; 2nd, 1967, Eleanor Margery Jones; one *s* one *d*. *Educ:* Lancing Coll.; Jesus Coll., Cambridge; Middlesex Hosp. Med. Sch. MA (Cantab), MB, BChir; FRCS, LRCP. Ho. Surg., North Middlesex Hosp., 1944. RNVR, 1945; served, HMS Glasgow and HMS Jamaica, 1945–47; perm. commn, 1950; served, HMS Narvik, 1952, HMS Warrior, 1956; Consultant in Orthopaedics, RN Hospitals: Malta, 1960; Haslar, 1962; Plymouth, 1968; Sen. MO (Admin.), RN Hosp., Plymouth, 1973; MO i/c, RN Hosp., Malta, 1974–75; Surgeon Rear-Adm. (Naval Hosps), 1975–78. QHS, 1975–78. MO, Home Office Prison Dept, 1978–80. Fellow, British Orthopaedic Assoc.; FRSA; Mem., Soc. of Authors. CStJ 1976. *Publications:* Practical Nursing, 16th edn 1945, to 21st edn 1969; Nelson and his Surgeons, 1968; Staffordshire Portrait Figures and Allied Subjects of the Victorian Era, 1970, enlarged edn 1981; Naval Ceramics, 1971; Heraldic China Mementos of the First World War, 1972; Pugh of Carshalton, 1973. *Recreation:* travel. *Address:* 3 Chilworth Road, Camps Bay, Cape Town 8001, Republic of South Africa. *T:* 021–481122.

PUGH, Peter David S.; *see* Storie-Pugh.

PUGH, Roger Courtenay Beckwith, MD; Pathologist to St Peter's Hospitals and the Institute of Urology, London, 1955–82; *b* 23 July 1917; *y s* of late Dr Robert Pugh, Talgarth, Breconshire, and of late Margaret Louise Pugh (*née* Gough); *m* 1942, Winifred Dorothy, *yr d* of late Alfred Cooper and late Margaret Cooper (*née* Evans); one *s* one *d*. *Educ:* Gresham's Sch., Holt; St Mary's Hospital (University of London). MRCS, LRCP 1940; MB, BS, 1941; MD 1948; MCPath 1964, FRCPath 1967; FRCS 1983. House Surgeon, St Mary's Hospital and Sector Hospitals, 1940–42; War Service in RAF (Mediterranean theatre), 1942–46, Sqdn Leader; Registrar, Department of Pathology, St Mary's Hospital, 1946–48; Asst Pathologist and Lecturer in Pathology, St Mary's Hospital, 1948–51; Asst Morbid Anatomist, The Hospital for Sick Children, Great Ormond Street,

1951–54. Erasmus Wilson Demonstrator, RCS, 1959, 1961; Member: Board of Governors, St Peter's Hospitals, 1961–82; Pathological Society of Great Britain and Ireland; Assoc. of Clin. Pathologists (Marshall Medal, 1982); Internat. Society of Urology; Internat. Acad. of Pathology (former Pres., British Div.); Hon. Member British Assoc. of Urological Surgeons (St Peter's Medal, 1981); FRSocMed (former Pres., Sect. of Urology). *Publications:* (ed) Pathology of the Testis, 1976; various contributions to Pathological, Urological and Paediatric Journals. *Recreations:* gardening, photography. *Address:* 19 Manor Way, Beckenham, Kent. *T:* 01–658 6294.

PUGH, Ted; *see* Pugh, C. E.

PUGH, William David, CBE 1965; FIM; CBIM; FIIM; JP; Deputy Chairman, English Steel Corporation Ltd, 1965–67 (Managing Director, 1955–65); Director of Personnel, British Steel Corporation (Midland Group), 1967–70; *b* 21 Nov. 1904; *s* of late Sir Arthur and Lady Pugh; *m* 1936, Mary Dorothea Barber; one *d. Educ:* Regent Street Polytechnic; Sheffield Univ. Joined Research Dept, Vickers Ltd, Sheffield, 1926, Director, Vickers Ltd, 1962–67; Chairman: The Darlington Forge Ltd, 1957–66; Taylor Bros & Co. Ltd, 1959–66; Director: (and alternate Chairman), Firth Vickers Stainless Steels Ltd, 1948–67; High Speed Steel Alloys Ltd, 1953–68; Industrial Training Council Service, 1960–67; British Iron and Steel Corp. Ltd, 1962–67; Sheffield Boy Scouts Holdings Ltd, 1965–; Sheffield Centre for Environmental Research Ltd. Associate of Metallurgy (Sheffield University; Mappin Medallist). Hon. DMet (Sheffield), 1966. *Recreations:* gardening, golf, reading, voluntary work, drystone-walling. *Address:* Freebirch Cottage, Freebirch, Chesterfield, Derbyshire S42 7DQ. *T:* Baslow 3153. *Club:* Sheffield (Sheffield).

PUGSLEY, Sir Alfred Grenvile, Kt 1956; OBE 1944; DSc; FRS 1952; FEng; Professor of Civil Engineering, University of Bristol, 1944–68, now Emeritus; Pro-Vice-Chancellor, 1961–64; *b* May 1903; *s* of H. W. Pugsley, BA, FLS, London; *m* 1928, Kathleen M. Warner (*d* 1974); no *c. Educ:* Rutlish Sch.; London Univ. Civil Engineering Apprenticeship at Royal Arsenal, Woolwich, 1923–26; Technical Officer, at the Royal Airship Works, Cardington, 1926–31; Member scientific and technical staff at Royal Aircraft Establishment, Farnborough, 1931–45, being Head of Structural and Mechanical Engineering Dept there, 1941–45. Visiting Lecturer on aircraft structures at Imperial Coll., London, 1938–40. Chairman of Aeronautical Research Council, 1952–57; Member: Advisory Council on Scientific Policy, 1956–59; Tribunal of Inquiry on Ronan Point, 1968; Member of various scientific and professional institutions and cttees; President: IStructE, 1957–58; Section G, British Assoc. for Advancement of Science, 1960; a Vice-Pres., ICE, 1971–73. Hon. FRAeS 1963; Hon. FICE 1981. Hon. DSc: Belfast, 1965; Cranfield, 1978; Birmingham, 1982; Hon. DUniv Surrey, 1968. Structural Engineers' Gold Medal, 1968; Civil Engineers' Ewing Gold Medal, 1979. *Publications:* The Theory of Suspension Bridges, 1957 (2nd edn 1968); The Safety of Structures, 1966; (ed and contrib.) The Works of Isambard Kingdom Brunel, 1976; numerous Reports and Memoranda of Aeronautical Research Council; papers in scientific journals and publications of professional engineering bodies; articles and reviews in engineering press. *Address:* 4 Harley Court, Clifton Down, Bristol BS8 3JU. *Club:* Athenæum.

PUGSLEY, Rear-Admiral Anthony Follett, CB 1944; DSO 1943; retired; *b* 7 Dec. 1901; *e s* of late J. Follett Pugsley, Whitefield, Wiveliscombe, Somerset; *m* 1931, Barbara, *d* of late J. Byam Shaw; one *s. Educ:* RN Colleges, Osborne and Dartmouth. Midshipman, 1918; Commander, 1936; Captain, 1942; Rear-Admiral, 1952; retired, 1954. Served European War from May 1918; on Upper Yangtse, 1925–27, and in command HM Ships P.40, Antelope and Westcott, 1933–36; during War of 1939–45, in command HM Ships Javelin, Fearless, Paladin; Captain (D) 14th Flotilla, Jervis (despatches thrice, DSO and bar, Greek War Cross); Assault Gp Comdr, Normandy landing, 1944 (2nd bar to DSO); Naval Force Commander in assault on Walcheren, 1944 (CB); Captain (D) 19th Flotilla (Far East), 1945–46; Directing Staff, Senior Officers War Course, 1947–48; Naval Officer in charge, Londonderry and Director (RN) Joint Anti-Submarine School, 1948–50; in command HMS Warrior, 1951; Flag Officer, Malayan Area, Dec. 1951–Nov. 1953. *Publication:* Destroyer Man, 1957. *Address:* Javelin, Milverton, Taunton, Somerset. *T:* Milverton 400355.

PUGSLEY, David Philip; Chairman of Industrial Tribunals, Birmingham Region, since 1985; *b* 11 Dec. 1944; *s* of Rev. Clement Pugsley and Edith (*née* Schofield); *m* 1966, Judith Mary Mappin; two *d. Educ:* Shebbear College; St Catharine's College, Cambridge (MA). Called to the Bar, Middle Temple, 1968; practised Midland and Oxford Circuit until 1985. *Recreations:* golf, fly fishing, theatre. *Address:* 41 Pilkington Avenue, Sutton Coldfield, West Midlands B72 1LA. *T:* 021–354 1464. *Club:* National Liberal.

PUIG DE LA BELLACASA, José Joaquín; Grand Cross of Isabel la Católica; Incomienda de Numero de Carlos III; Spanish Ambassador to the Court of St James's, since 1983; *b* 5 June 1931; *s* of José Maria Puig de la Bellacasa and Consuelo de Urdampilleta; *m* 1960, Paz de Aznar Ybarra; four *s* two *d. Educ:* Areneros Jesuit Coll., Madrid; Madrid Univ. Barrister-at-law. Entered Diplomatic Service, 1959; Dirección General Politica Exterior, 1961–62; Minister's Cabinet, 1962–69; Counsellor, Spanish Embassy, London, 1971–74; Private Sec. to Prince of Spain, 1974–75, to HM King Juan Carlos, 1975–76; Director-General: Co-op. Tecnica Internacional, 1976; Servicio Exterior, 1977–78; Under-Sec. of State for Foreign Affairs, 1978–80; Ambassador to Holy See, 1980–83. Holds several foreign decorations. *Address:* 24 Belgrave Square, SW1X 8QA; Felipe IV 7, Madrid 14, Spain. *Clubs:* Athenæum, Beefsteak, Hurlingham, White's; Nuevo, Golf de Puerta de Hierro, Club de Campo (Madrid).

PULFORD, Richard Charles; General Director (Administration), South Bank Board, since 1986; *b* 14 July 1944; *s* of late Charles Edgar Pulford and Grace Mary Pulford (*née* Vickors). *Educ:* Royal Grammar Sch., Newcastle upon Tyne; St Catherine's Coll., Oxford (BA Jurisprudence). Voluntary service in the Sudan, 1966–67; Home Civil Service, 1967–79: Department of Education and Science: Asst Principal, 1967–72, Principal, 1972–75; HM Treasury, 1975–77; Asst Secretary, DES, 1977–79; Dep. Sec.-Gen., 1979–85, South Bank Planning Dir, 1985–86, Arts Council of GB. Mem., South Bank Theatre Bd. *Recreations:* the arts, smoking, playing games and watching sports. *Address:* 905 Beatty House, Dolphin Square, SW1. *T:* 01–798 8308.

PULLAN, Prof. Brian Sebastian, PhD; FBA 1985; Professor of Modern History, University of Manchester, since 1973; *b* 10 Dec. 1935; *s* of Horace William Virgo Pullan and Ella Lister Pullan; *m* 1962, Janet Elizabeth Maltby; two *s. Educ:* Epsom Coll.; Trinity Coll., Cambridge (MA, PhD); MA Manchester. Nat. Service, RA, 1954–56. Cambridge University: Res. Fellow, Trinity Coll., 1961–63; Official Fellow, Queens' Coll., 1963–72; Univ. Asst Lectr in History, 1964–67; Lectr, 1967–72; Dean, Faculty of Arts, Manchester Univ., 1982–84. Feoffee of Chetham's Hosp. and Library, Manchester, 1981–. Corresp. Fellow, Ateneo Veneto, 1986. *Publications:* (ed) Sources for the History of Medieval Europe, 1966; (ed) Crisis and Change in the Venetian Economy in the Sixteenth and Seventeenth Centuries, 1968; Rich and Poor in Renaissance Venice, 1971; A History of Early Renaissance Italy, 1973; The Jews of Europe and the Inquisition of Venice, 1983; articles and reviews in learned jls and collections. *Recreations:* dogs, theatre. *Address:* 30 Sandhurst Road, Didsbury, Manchester M20 0LR. *T:* 061–445 3665.

PULLAN, John Marshall, MChir, FRCS; Surgeon, King Edward VII Hospital; Hon. Surgeon, St Thomas' Hospital, London; late of Bolingbroke Hospital, London and Royal Masonic Hospital, London; *b* 1 Aug. 1915; *e s* of late William Greaves Pullan and of Kathleen, *d* of Alfred Marshall, Otley, Yorkshire; *m* 1940, Leila Diana, *d* of H. C. Craven-Veitch, Surgeon; one *s* three *d. Educ:* Shrewsbury; King's Coll., Cambridge; St Thomas' Hospital, London. MA Cantab (1st Cl. Nat. Sc. Tripos) 1937; MB, BChir 1940; FRCS, 1942; MChir 1945. Teacher in Surgery, Univ. of London; Examiner in Surgery, Univs of: London, 1956; Cambridge. Member: Court of Examiners, RCS, 1964; Board of Governors, St Thomas' Hospital. *Publications:* Section on Diseases of the Liver, Gall Bladder and Bile Ducts, in Textbook of British Surgery, ed Sir Henry Souttar, 1956; articles in surgical journals. *Address:* Palings, Warboys Road, Kingston Hill, Surrey KT2 7LS. *T:* 01–546 5310. *Clubs:* White's, Flyfishers', Boodle's.

PULLAR, Hubert Norman, CBE 1964; MA; HM Diplomatic Service, retired; *b* 26 Dec. 1914; *y s* of late William Laurence and Christine Ellen Pullar, formerly of Uplands, Bridge-of-Allan, Stirlingshire; *m* 1943, Helen Alice La Fontaine; one *s* one *d. Educ:* Trin. Coll., Glenalmond; Trin. Coll., Oxford. Entered HM Consular Service, 1938. Served in Turkey, 1938–42; USA, 1943–46; Persia, 1946–48; Morocco, 1949–52; Foreign Office, 1952–54; Finland, 1954–56; Syria, 1956; Iraq, 1957–59; Consul-Gen., Antwerp, 1960–64; HM Consul-General, Jerusalem, 1964–67; Foreign Office, 1967–68; Consul-General, Durban, 1968–71. Order of Ouissam Alouite, Morocco, 1952. CStJ 1966. Coronation Medal, 1953. *Recreations:* golf, motoring, travel. *Address:* Camelot, Ringles Cross, Uckfield, East Sussex. *T:* Uckfield 2159.

PULLÉE, Ernest Edward, CBE 1967; ARCA, ASIA, FSAE, NEAC; painter; Chief Officer, National Council for Diplomas in Art and Design, 1967–74; retired; *b* 19 Feb. 1907; *s* of Ernest and Caroline Elizabeth Pullée; *m* 1933, Margaret Fisher, ARCA, NEAC; one *s. Educ:* St Martin's Sch., Dover; Royal Coll. of Art, London. Principal: Gloucester Coll. of Art, 1934–39; Portsmouth Coll. of Art, 1939–45; Leeds Coll. of Art, 1945–56; Leicester Coll. of Art and Design, 1956–67. Regular exhibitor, RA summer exhibns and at London and provincial galls. Pres., Nat. Soc. for Art Educn, 1945, 1959; Chm., Assoc. of Art Instns, 1959; Mem., Nat. Adv. Coun. for Art Educn, 1959; Mem., Nat. Coun. for Diplomas in Art and Design, 1961. Hon. Fellow: Portsmouth Polytechnic, 1976; Leicester Polytechnic, 1977. Hon. DA (Manchester), 1961. *Publications:* contribs to professional and academic jls. *Recreation:* travel. *Address:* 3 March Square, The Drive, Summersdale, Chichester, W Sussex PO19 4AN. *Club:* Chelsea Arts.

PULLEIN-THOMPSON, Denis; *see* Cannan, D.

PULLEN, William Reginald James, CVO 1975 (MVO 1966); LLB; FCIS; JP; Receiver-General, since 1959, and Chapter Clerk since 1963, Westminster Abbey (Registrar, 1964–84); *b* 17 Feb. 1922; *er s* of late William Pullen and Lillian Pullen (*née* Chinn), Falmouth; *m* 1948, Doreen Angela Hebron; two *d. Educ:* Falmouth Gram. School; King's College, London; private study. Served War of 1939–45; Flt Lt, RAFVR (admin and special duties) SE Asia. Asst to Chief Accountant, Westminster Abbey, 1947; Dep. Registrar, 1951; Sec. Westminster Abbey Appeal, 1953. Westminster City Council, 1962–65. JP Inner London, 1967. Freeman, Worshipful Co. of Wax Chandlers. CStJ 1981 (OStJ 1969). *Publication:* contrib. A House of Kings, 1966. *Recreations:* reading, walking, cooking. *Address:* 4b Dean's Yard, Westminster, SW1. *T:* 01–222 4023. *Clubs:* Royal Air Force, MCC.

PULLEYBLANK, Prof. Edwin George, PhD; FRSC; Professor of Chinese, University of British Columbia, since 1966; *b* Calgary, Alberta, 7 Aug. 1922; *s* of W. G. E. Pulleyblank, Calgary; *m* 1945, Winona Ruth Relyea (decd), Arnprior, Ont; one *s* two *d. Educ:* Central High School, Calgary; University of Alberta; University of London. BA Hons Classics, Univ. of Alberta, 1942; Nat. Research Council of Canada, 1943–46. School of Oriental and African Studies, Univ. of London: Chinese Govt Schol., 1946; Lectr in Classical Chinese, 1948; PhD in Classical Chinese, 1951; Lectr in Far Eastern History, 1952; Professor of Chinese, University of Cambridge, 1953; Head, Dept of Asian Studies, Univ. of British Columbia, 1968–75. Fellow of Downing Coll., Cambridge, 1955–66. *Publications:* The Background of the Rebellion of An Lu-Shan, 1955; Middle Chinese, 1984; articles in Asia Major, Bulletin of School of Oriental and African Studies, etc. *Address:* Department of Asian Studies, University of British Columbia, Vancouver, BC V6T 1W5, Canada.

PULLICINO, Dr Anthony Alfred; *b* 14 March 1917; *s* of late Sir Philip Pullicino; *m* 1944, Edith Baker; three *s* two *d. Educ:* St Aloysius Coll., Malta; Royal Univ. of Malta; Melbourne University. BA 1939, LLD 1943, Malta; LLB Melbourne 1963. Served in Royal Malta Artillery, 1944–45 (Lieut). MLA Malta, 1951–55 (Speaker, 1951–52). Mem. Council, CPA, attending sessions in London 1952, Nairobi 1953. Practised as Solicitor, Melbourne, 1963–65; High Comr for Malta in Canberra, 1965–69; High Comr in London and Ambassador of Malta to USSR, 1970–71. *Recreation:* golf. *Address:* 191/4 Tower Road, Sliema, Malta. *Club:* Casino Maltese (Malta).

PULLING, Martin John Langley, CBE 1958 (OBE 1954); *b* 30 May 1906; *o s* of late Rev. Augustine J. Pulling and Dorothea Fremlin Key; *m* 1939, Yvonne Limborgh, Antwerp, Belgium; no *c. Educ:* Marlborough College; King's College, Cambridge (Scholar). Mech. Scis Tripos, BA 1928; MA 1943. Various posts in radio industry, 1929–34; joined BBC Engrg Div., 1934; retired as Dep. Dir of Engrg, 1967. Was Chm. of Technical Cttee (of European Broadcasting Union) responsible for development of "Eurovision" from its inception in 1952 until 1962. Chairman: The Ferrograph Co., 1968–72; Rendar Instruments Ltd, 1968–72; Dir, Compagnie Générale d'Electricité Internationale (UK) Ltd, 1971–76. FIEE 1967 (MIEE 1945, AMIEE 1935); Chm., Electronics and Communications Section, IEE, 1959–60; Mem. Council, IEE, 1963–66; MITE 1966; Hon. FBKS. *Address:* 6 Cadogan House, 93 Sloane Street, SW1X 9PD. *T:* 01–235 1739. *Clubs:* Hurlingham, MCC, Anglo-Belgian; Phyllis Court (Henley-on-Thames).

PULLINGER, Sir (Francis) Alan, Kt 1977; CBE 1970; DL; Chairman, Haden Carrier Ltd, 1961–79; *b* 22 May 1913; *s* of William Pullinger; *m* 1st, 1946, Felicity Charmian Gotch Hobson (decd); two *s* one *d*; 2nd, 1966, Jacqueline Louise Anne Durin. *Educ:* Marlborough Coll.; Balliol Coll., Oxford (MA). Pres., IHVE, 1972–73. Chm., Hertfordshire Scouts, 1976–. Vice Chm. Council, Benenden Sch., 1980–. Hon. FCIBSE, 1977. DL Herts, 1982. *Recreations:* mountaineering, sailing, beagling. *Address:* Barnhorn, Meadway, Berkhamsted, Herts. *T:* Berkhamsted 3206. *Clubs:* Alpine, Travellers'.

PULLINGER, John Elphick; His Honour Judge Pullinger; a Circuit Judge, since 1982; *b* 27 Aug. 1930; *s* of late Reginald Edward Pullinger and of Elsie Florence Pullinger; *m* 1956, Carette Maureen, *d* of late Flt Lieut and late Mrs E. D. Stephens; one *s* one *d. Educ:* Friern Barnet Grammar Sch.; Quintin Sch.; London Sch. of Econs and Pol. Science (LLB 1955). Called to the Bar, Lincoln's Inn, 1958; Sir Thomas More Bursary, 1958. Legal Sec. to Lord Shrewsbury's Commn of Enquiry into the Infantile Paralysis Fellowship, 1958–59; Dep. Judge Advocate, 1965; AJAG, 1972–82; Judge Advocate to NZ Force SE Asia, 1973–75; served on JAG's staff in Germany, Mediterranean, Near East and Far East.

Member: NSRA, 1977–; NRA, 1979–; Historical Breechloading Smallarms Assoc., 1984–; BFSS; HAC, 1950–. *Publication:* The Position of the British Serviceman under the Army and Air Force Acts 1955, 1975. *Recreations:* shottist, bibliophile. *Address:* 1 Essex Court, Temple, EC4Y 9AR.

PULVERTAFT, Prof. Robert James Valentine, OBE 1944; MD Cantab; FRCP; FRCPath; Emeritus Professor of Clinical Pathology, University of London (Professor, 1950–62); Visiting Professor of Pathology, Makerere University College; Visiting Professor of Pathology, University of Ibadan, W Nigeria; President Association of Clinical Pathologists, 1953; Director of Laboratories, Westminster Hospital, until 1962; Lieutenant-Colonel RAMC, 1943, serving Middle East Forces; subsequently Assistant Director of Pathology, Northern Command and MEF; lately Hon. Consultant in Pathology to the Army at Home; *b* 14 Feb. 1897; *s* of Rev. T. J. Pulvertaft and B. C. Denroche; *m* E. L. M. Costello (*d* 1985); one *s* two *d. Educ:* Westminster School; Trinity College, Cambridge (Classical Scholar); St Thomas' Hosp. Lt 3rd Royal Sussex 1915–19; served with 4th Royal Sussex (Palestine); seconded to RFC as observer (Palestine) and pilot in 205 Squadron RAF (France); Senior Exhibitioner and Scholar, Nat. Science, Trinity College Cantab. 2nd class Part II Tripos Nat. Science (Physiology); Entrance University Scholar St Thomas' Hospital; Asst Bacteriologist, VD Dept St Thomas' Hospital; Pathologist to Units, St Thomas' Hosp., 1923–32; Plimmer Research Fellow in Pathology, 1929–32; EMS Sept.-Nov. 1939; National Institute Medical Research, 1939–40. Examiner in Pathology, Univs of Cambridge, Oxford, London, Trinity College, Dublin, National University of Ireland, Liverpool University; also for the Conjoint Board and Royal Army Medical Coll. Hon. FRSM 1972. *Publications:* Studies on Malignant Disease in Nigeria by Tissue Culture; various papers on bacteriology and pathology, particularly in relation to the study of living cells by cinemicrography. *Address:* 31 Izaak Walton Way, Chesterton, Cambridge.

PULZER, Prof. Peter George Julius, PhD; FRHistS; Gladstone Professor of Government and Public Administration, University of Oxford, since Jan. 1985; Fellow of All Souls College, since 1985; *b* 20 May 1929; *s* of Felix and Margaret Pulzer; *m* 1962, Gillian Mary Marshall; two *s. Educ:* Surbiton County Grammar Sch.; King's Coll., Cambridge (1st Cl. Hons Historical Tripos 1950; PhD 1960); London Univ. (BSc Econ 1954). FRHistS 1971. Lectr in Politics, Magdalen Coll. and Christ Church, Oxford, 1957–62; University Lectr in Politics, Oxford, 1960–84; Official Student and Tutor in Politics, Christ Church 1962–84. Vis. Professor: Univ. of Wisconsin, 1965; Sch. of Advanced Internat. Studies, Johns Hopkins Univ., 1972; Univ. of Calif, LA, 1972. *Publications:* The Rise of Political Anti-Semitism in Germany and Austria, 1964 (German edn 1966); Political Representation and Elections in Britain, 1967, 3rd edn 1975; contrib. to jls, year books and symposia. *Recreations:* opera, walking. *Address:* All Souls College, Oxford OX1 4AL. *T:* Oxford 722251.

PUMPHREY, Sir (John) Laurence, KCMG 1973 (CMG 1963); HM Diplomatic Service, retired; Ambassador to Pakistan (formerly High Commissioner), 1971–76; *b* 22 July 1916; *s* of late Charles Ernest Pumphrey and Iris Mary (*née* Moberly-Bell); *m* 1945, Jean, *e d* of Sir Walter Buchanan Riddell, 12th Bt; four *s* one *d. Educ:* Winchester; New College, Oxford. Served War of 1939–45 in Army. Foreign Service from 1945. Head of Establishment and Organisation Department, Foreign Office, 1955–60; Counsellor, Staff of British Commissioner-General for SE Asia, Singapore, 1960–63; Counsellor, HM Embassy, Belgrade, 1963–65; Deputy High Commissioner, Nairobi, 1965–67; British High Comr, Zambia, 1967–71. Military Cross, 3rd Class (Greece), 1941. *Address:* Caistron, Thropton, Morpeth, Northumberland NE65 7LG.

PUNGAN, Vasile; Minister of Foreign Trade and International Economic Co-operation, Romania, since 1982; *b* 2 Nov. 1926; *m* 1952, Liliana Niță (*d* 1973); one *d. Educ:* Inst. of Econs, Bucharest. Dr in Econ. Scis and Univ. Prof.; Dean of Faculty, Agronomical Inst., Bucharest, 1954; Gen. Dir, Min. of Agric. and Forestry, 1955–58; Counsellor, Romanian Embassy, Washington, 1959–62; Dir and Mem. College, Min. of Foreign Affairs, 1963–66; Ambassador of Socialist Republic of Romania to Court of St James's, 1966–72; Counsellor to Pres. of Romania, 1973–78 and 1979–82; Minister and Sec. of State, State Council, 1979–82. Mem., Central Cttee of Romanian Communist Party, 1972 (Alternate Mem. 1969); Mem., Grand National Assembly, 1975. Holds orders and medals of Socialist Republic of Romania and several foreign countries. *Address:* Ministry of Foreign Trade, Str. Gheorghe Asan 1, Bucharest, Romania.

PURCELL, Denis; *see* Purcell, J. D.

PURCELL, Prof. Edward Mills, PhD; Gerhard Gade University Professor, Harvard University, 1960–80, now Emeritus; *b* 30 Aug. 1912; *s* of Edward A. Purcell and Mary Elizabeth Mills; *m* 1937, Beth C. Busser; two *s. Educ:* Purdue University; Harvard University. PhD Harvard, 1938. Instructor in Physics, Harvard, 1938–40; Radiation Laboratory, Mass. Inst. of Technology, 1940–45; Associate Professor of Physics, Harvard, 1945–49; Professor of Physics, 1949–60. Senior Fellow, Society of Fellows, Harvard, 1950–71. Halley Lectr, Oxford Univ., 1982. Hon. DEng Purdue, 1953; Hon. DSci Washington Univ., St Louis, 1963. (Jointly) Nobel Prize in Physics, 1952; Nat. Medal of Science, 1979. *Publications:* Principles of Microwave Circuits, 1948; Physics for Students of Science and Engineering, 1952; Electricity and Magnetism, 1965; papers in Physical Review, Astrophys. Jl, Biophys. Jl. *Address:* 5 Wright Street, Cambridge, Mass, USA. *T:* 547–9317.

PURCELL, Harry, CBE 1982; Member (C) for Chaddesley Corbett, Hereford and Worcester County Council, since 1974; *b* 2 Dec. 1919; *s* of Charles and Lucy Purcell; *m* 1941, Eunice Mary Price; three *s* one *d. Educ:* Bewdley C of E Sch.; Kidderminster Coll. Joined TA, 1938; served War, 1939–46, Queen's Own Worcester Hussars; Transport Officer, Berlin, 1946–48. Carpet industry, 1949–60; self-employed, 1961. Formerly Mem., Kidderminster Bor. Council; Mayor of Kidderminster, 1967–68. Chairman: West Mercia Police Authority, 1979–82; Police Cttee, National Assoc. of County Councils, 1977–; Chm., National Police Negotiating Bd, 1978–82; Vice-Chm., ACC, 1982–85. *Recreations:* theatre, tennis, public service. *Address:* Meadowsmead, Woodrow, Chaddesley Corbett, near Kidderminster, Worcs. *T:* Chaddesley Corbett 347. *Club:* Carlton.

PURCELL, (John) Denis; Metropolitan Magistrate, Clerkenwell Magistrates' Court, 1963–86; *b* 7 Dec. 1913; *s* of John Poyntz Purcell and Dorothy Branston, Newark; *m* 1951, Pauline Mary, *e d* of Rev. Hiram Craven, Painswick, Glos; two *s. Educ:* Marlborough; Wadham College, Oxford. Called to Bar, Gray's Inn, 1938; SE Circuit; Sussex QS. Served War of 1939–45: commnd from HAC, 1939, to Shropshire Yeo., 1940; ADC to GOC-in-C, Western Command, 1941; Staff Capt., Western Command; GSO3, Italy; DAAG, HQ British Troops, Palestine. Actg Dep. Chm., London QS, 1962. *Recreations:* back-yard gardening, racing. *Address:* 1 Cheltenham Terrace, SW3. *T:* 01–730 2896.

PURCELL, Robert Michael, CMG 1983; HM Diplomatic Service, retired; Adviser and Secretary, East Africa Association, 1984–87; *b* 22 Oct. 1923; *s* of late Lt-Col Walter Purcell and Constance (*née* Fendick); *m* 1965, Julia Evelyn, *o d* of late Brig. Edward Marsh-Kellett; two *d. Educ:* Ampleforth Coll. Commnd 60th Rifles (Greenjackets), 1943–47. Colonial Service, later HMOCS, Uganda, 1949–62: Dist Officer, 1949–60; Dist Comr,

1961–62; retd 1962. 1st Sec., CRO, later FCO, 1964–68; 1st Sec. (Commercial/Economic), Colombo, 1968–69; FCO, 1969–71; 1st Sec. (Aid), Singapore, 1971–73; Head of Chancery, HM Legation to the Holy See, 1973–76; Counsellor and Dep. High Comr, Malta, 1977–80; Ambassador to Somali Democratic Republic, 1980–83. KCSG 1976. *Recreation:* country life. *Address:* Lythe House, Selborne, Hants GU34 3JA. *T:* Selborne 231. *Club:* Naval and Military.

PURCELL, Rev. Canon William Ernest; author and broadcaster; Residentiary Canon of Worcester Cathedral, 1966–76; *b* 25 May 1909; *s* of Will and Gwladys Purcell; *m* 1939, Margaret Clegg; two *s* one *d. Educ:* Keble Coll., Oxford (MA); Univ. of Wales (BA); Queens Coll., Birmingham. Curate: St. John's Church, Keighley, 1938; Dover Parish Church, 1939–43; Vicar: St. Peter's, Maidstone, 1944–47; Sutton Valence, 1947–53; Chaplain, HM Borstal Instn, East Sutton, 1947–53; Religious Broadcasting Organiser, BBC Midlands, 1953–66. *Publications:* These Thy Gods, 1950; Pilgrim's Programme, 1957; Onward Christian Soldier (biog. of S. Baring Gould), 1957; A Plain Man Looks At Himself, 1962; Woodbine Willie (biog. of G. Studdert Kennedy), 1962; This Is My Story, 1963; The Plain Man Looks At The Commandments, 1966; Fisher of Lambeth (biog. of Archbp of Canterbury), 1969; Portrait of Soper (biog. of Lord Soper), 1972; British Police in a Changing Society, 1974; A Time to Die, 1979; Pilgrim's England, 1981; The Christian in Retirement, 1982; Martyrs of Our Time, 1983; Seekers and Finders, 1985. *Address:* 14 Conifer Close, Cumnor Hill, Oxford OX2 9HP. *Club:* National Liberal.

PURCELL, Ven. William Henry Samuel, MA; Archdeacon of Dorking, 1968–82; *b* 22 Jan. 1912; *m* 1941, Kathleen Clough, Leeds; one *s* (and one *s* decd). *Educ:* King Edward VI School, Norwich; Fitzwilliam House, Cambridge (MA). Asst Curate, St Michael's, Headingley, Leeds, 1937; Minor Canon of Ripon Cathedral, 1940; Vicar: St Matthew, Holbeck, Leeds, 1943; St Matthew, Chapel Allerton, Leeds, 1947; St Martin's, Epsom, 1963. Rural Dean of Epsom, 1965. Hon. Canon of Ripon Cathedral, 1962; Hon. Canon of Guildford Cathedral, 1968, Canon Emeritus, 1982. *Recreations:* walking, travel. *Address:* 55 Windfield, Epsom Road, Leatherhead, Surrey KT22 8UQ. *T:* Leatherhead 375708.

PURCHAS, Rt. Hon. Sir Francis (Brooks), Kt 1974; PC 1982; **Rt. Hon. Lord Justice Purchas;** a Lord Justice of Appeal, since 1982; *b* 19 June 1919; *s* of late Captain Francis Purchas, 5th Royal Irish Lancers and late Millicent Purchas (*née* Brooks); *m* 1942, Patricia Mona Kathleen, *d* of Lieut Milburn; two *s. Educ:* Summerfields Sch., Oxford; Marlborough Coll.; Trinity Coll., Cambridge. Served RE, 1940–46: North Africa, 1943 (despatches); Hon. Lt-Col retd (Africa Star, Italy Star, 1939–45 Medal; Defence Medal). Allied Mil. Commission, Vienna. Called to Bar, Inner Temple, 1948, QC 1965, Bencher, 1972; practised at Bar, 1948–74; Leader, SE Circuit, 1972–74; Dep. Chm., E Sussex QS, 1966–71; Recorder of Canterbury, 1969–71 (Hon. Recorder of Canterbury, 1972–74); Recorder of the Crown Court, 1972–74; a Judge of the High Court of Justice, Family Div., 1974–82; Presiding Judge, SE Circuit, 1977–82. Comr, Central Criminal Court, 1970–71. Mem., Bar Council, 1966–68, 1969–71, 1972–74. Mem. of Livery, Worshipful Co. of Broderers, 1962. *Recreations:* shooting, golf, fishing. *Address:* Parkhurst House, near Haslemere, Surrey GU27 3BY. *T:* North Chapel 280; 1 Temple Gardens, Temple, EC4Y 9BB. *T:* 01–353 5124. *Club:* Hawks (Cambridge).

PURDEN, Roma Laurette, (Laurie Purden; Mrs J. K. Kotch), MBE 1973; journalist and writer; Editor-in-Chief, Woman's Journal, since 1978; *b* 30 Sept. 1928; *d* of George Cecil Arnold Purden and Constance Mary Sheppard; *m* 1957, John Keith Kotch (*d* 1979); two *d. Educ:* Harecroft Sch., Tunbridge Wells. Fiction Editor, Home Notes, 1948–51; Asst Editor, Home Notes, 1951–52; Asst Editor, Woman's Own, 1952; Sen. Asst Editor, Girl, 1952–54; Editor of: Housewife, 1954–57; Home, 1957–62; House Beautiful, 1963–65; Good Housekeeping, 1965–73; Editor-in-Chief: Good Housekeeping, and Womancraft, 1973–77; Woman & Home, 1982–83. Dir, Brickfield Publications Ltd, 1978–80. Magazine Editor of the Year, 1979, British Soc. of Magazine Editors; Consumer Magazine of the Year awarded by Periodical Publishers Assoc. to Woman's Journal, 1985. *Address:* 174 Pavilion Road, SW1X 0AW.

PURDON, Maj.-Gen. Corran William Brooke, CBE 1970; MC 1945; CPM 1982; Director, Defence Services Limited; *b* 4 May 1921; *s* of Maj.-Gen. William Brooke Purdon, DSO, OBE, MC, KHS, and Dorothy Myrtle Coates; *m* 1945, Maureen Patricia, *d* of Major J. F. Petrie, Guides Infantry, IA; two *s* one *d. Educ:* Rokeby, Wimbledon; Campbell Coll., Belfast; RMC Sandhurst. MBIM. Commnd into Royal Ulster Rifles, 1939; service with Army Commandos, France and Germany, 1940–45 (wounded; MC); 1st Bn RU Rifles, Palestine, 1945–46; GHQ MELF, 1949–51; psc 1955; Staff, Malayan Emergency, 1956–58; Co. Comdr, 1 RU Rifles, Cyprus Emergency, 1958; CO, 1st Bn RU Rifles, BAOR and Borneo War, 1962–64; GSO1 and Chief Instructor, Sch. of Infantry, Warminster, 1965–67; Comdr, Sultan's Armed Forces, Oman, and Dir of Ops, Dhofar War, 1967–70 (Sultan's Bravery Medal, 1968 and Distinguished Service Medal for Gallantry, 1969, Oman; CBE); Commandant: Sch. of Infantry, Warminster, 1970–72; Small Arms Sch. Corps, 1970–72; GOC, NW Dist, 1972–74; GOC Near East Land Forces, 1974–76, retired. Dep. Comr, Royal Hong Kong Police Force, 1978–81; Comdr, St John Ambulance, Wilts, 1981–84 (Mem. Council, 1981–86); Dir, Falconstar (British Military and Police Training Teams) Ltd, 1983–86. Hon. Colonel: Queen's Univ. Belfast OTC, 1975–78; D (London Irish Rifles) Co., 4th (V) Bn, Royal Irish Rangers, 1986–. Pres., Army Gymnastic Union, 1973–76; Patron, Small Arms Sch. Corps Assoc., 1985–; Governor, Royal Humane Soc., 1985–. KStJ 1983. *Publications:* articles in British Army Review and Infantryman. *Recreations:* physical training, swimming, collecting military pictures and military commemorative plates. *Address:* Old Park House, Devizes, Wilts SN10 5JR. *Clubs:* Army and Navy; Hong Kong.

PURDY, Prof. Richard Little; *b* 21 April 1904; *s* of Leander Crawford Purdy and Louisa Canfield Purdy. *Educ:* Yale Univ. (BA 1925, PhD 1930). Associate Professor and Fellow of Berkeley Coll., Yale Univ., 1928–70, retired. *Publications:* The Larpent MS of The Rivals, 1935; Thomas Hardy, a Bibliographical Study, 1954, 1978; (ed with Prof. Michael Millgate) The Collected Letters of Thomas Hardy: Vols I-V, 1978–84. *Address:* 245 Whitney Avenue, New Haven, Connecticut, USA. *Clubs:* Athenæum, Bibliographical Society; Elizabethan (New Haven, Connecticut).

PURDY, Robert John, CMG 1963; OBE 1954; Bursar, Gresham's School, Holt, 1965–81; retired from HM Overseas Civil Service, 1963; *b* 2 March 1916; 2nd *s* of late Lt-Col T. W. Purdy, Woodgate House, Aylsham, Norfolk; *m* 1957, Elizabeth (*née* Sharp); two *s* one *d. Educ:* Haileybury College; Jesus College, Cambridge (BA). Served 1940–46 with 81 West African Division Reconnaissance Regt, 3rd and 4th Burma Campaigns (despatches, Major). Appointed to Colonial Administrative Service, Northern Nigeria, 1939; promoted Resident, 1956; Senior Resident, Staff Grade, 1957. Resident, Adamawa Province, 1956; Senior Resident, Plateau Province, 1958–61; Senior Resident, Sokoto Province, 1961–63, retd. *Recreations:* shooting, fishing, gardening. *Address:* Spratt's Green House, Aylsham, Norwich NR11 6TX. *T:* Aylsham 732147.

PURNELL, Anthony Guy, QC 1984; a Recorder of the Crown Court, since 1982; *b* 7 Sept. 1944; *s* of Peter A. Medcraft; *m* 1973, Christina Elizabeth, *d* of Comdr T. D.

Handley, RN; one *s* two *d*. *Educ:* Stancliffe Hall; Haileybury; Univ. of Sheffield (LLB Hons). Called to the Bar, Inner Temple, 1967; Member, North Eastern Circuit, 1968. *Recreations:* biblical research, music. *Address:* 11 King's Bench Walk, Temple, EC4Y 7EQ. *T:* 01–353 3337. *Club:* Royal Automobile.

PURNELL, Nicholas Robert; QC 1985; a Recorder, since 1986; *b* 29 Jan. 1944; *s* of late Oliver Cuthbert Purnell and of Pauline Purnell; *m* 1970, Melanie Jill Stanway; four *s*. *Educ:* Oratory Sch.; King's Coll. Cambridge (Open Exhibnr; MA). Called to the Bar, Middle Temple, 1968 (Astbury Schol.); Junior of Central Criminal Court Bar Mess, 1972–75; Member: Bar Council and Senate, 1973–77 and 1982–85. Prosecuting Counsel to Inland Revenue, 1977–79; Jun. Treasury Counsel, 1979–85. Member, Lord Chancellor's and Home Secretary's Working Party on the Training of the Judiciary, 1975–78; Crown Court Rules Cttee, 1982–. *Recreation:* family holidays in Brittany. *Address:* 3 Temple Gardens, Temple, EC4. *T:* 01–353 3533.

PURNELL, Paul Oliver; QC 1982; a Recorder, since 1985; *b* 13 July 1936; *s* of Oliver Cuthbert Purnell and Pauline (*née* Brailli); *m* 1966, Celia Consuelo Ocampo; one *s* two *d*. *Educ:* The Oratory Sch.; Jesus Coll., Oxford (MA). Served 4th/7th Royal Dragoon Guards, 1958–62. Called to the Bar, Inner Temple, 1962. Jun. Treasury Counsel at Central Criminal Court, 1976–82. *Recreations:* windsurfing, tennis. *Address:* 3 Temple Gardens, Temple, EC4Y 9AU. *T:* 01–353 3533.

PURSEGLOVE, John William, CMG 1973; Tropical Crops Specialist, Overseas Development Administration at East Malling Research Station, Kent, 1967–75; *b* 11 Aug. 1912; *s* of late Robert and Kate Purseglove; *m* 1947, Phyllis Agnes Adèle, *d* of late George and Mary Turner, Falkland Is; one *s* one *d*. *Educ:* Lady Manners Sch., Bakewell; Manchester Univ. (BSc Hons Botany); Gonville and Caius Coll, Cambridge; Imperial Coll. of Tropical Agriculture, Trinidad (AICTA). Agricultural and Sen. Agricl Officer, Uganda, 1936–52; Lectr in Tropical Agriculture, Univ. of Cambridge, 1952–54; Dir, Botanic Gardens, Singapore, 1954–57; Prof. of Botany, Imperial Coll. of Tropical Agriculture and Univ. of the West Indies, Trinidad, 1957–67. Pres., Assoc. for Tropical Biology, 1962–65. FLS 1945; FIBiol 1970; Hon. Mem., Trop. Agric. Assoc., 1984. *Publications:* Tobacco in Uganda, 1951; Tropical Crops, Dicotyledons, 2 vols, 1968; Tropical Crops, Monocotyledons, 2 vols, 1972; (with E. G. Brown, C. L. Green and S. R. J. Robbins) Spices, 2 vols, 1981; papers on land use, ethnobotany, etc, in scientific jls and symposia vols. *Recreations:* gardening, natural history. *Address:* Walnut Trees, Sissinghurst, Cranbrook, Kent TN17 2JL. *T:* Cranbrook 712836.

PURSSELL, Anthony John Richard; Member of the Board, Civil Aviation Authority, since 1984; *b* 5 July 1926; *m* 1952, Ann Margaret Batchelor; two *s* one *d*. *Educ:* Oriel Coll., Oxford (BA Hons Chemistry). Managing Director: Arthur Guinness Son & Co. (Park Royal) Ltd, 1968; Arthur Guinness Son & Co. (Dublin) Ltd, 1973; Arthur Guinness & Sons plc, 1975–81; Jt Dep. Chm., 1981–83. Mem. IBA, 1976–81. Regional Dir, Thames Valley and S Midlands Bd, Lloyds Bank plc. *Recreations:* travel, golf, sailing, books. *Address:* Allendale, Bulstrode Way, Gerrards Cross, Bucks SL9 7QT. *Club:* Leander (Henley).

PURVES, Dame Daphne (Helen), DBE 1979; Senior Lecturer in French, Dunedin Teachers College, 1967–73, retired (Lecturer, 1963–66); *b* 8 Nov. 1908; *d* of Irvine Watson Cowie and Helen Jean Cowie; *m* 1939, Herbert Dudley Purves; one *s* two *d*. *Educ:* Otago Girls' High Sch., Dunedin, NZ; Univ. of Otago, Dunedin (MA 1st Cl. Hons English and French). Secondary sch. teacher, 1931–40 and 1957–63. Pres., NZ Fedn of University Women, 1962–64; Internat. Fedn of University Women: Mem., Cultural Relations Cttee, 1965–68, Convener, 1968–71; 3rd Vice-Pres., 1971–74; 1st Vice-Pres., 1974–77; Pres., 1977–80. Chm., National Theme Cttee, The Child in the World, NZ Nat. Commn for Internat. Year of the Child, 1978–80; Mem., Internat. Year of the Child Telethon Trust, 1978–81; Exec. Mem., NZ Cttee for Children (IYC) Inc., 1980–82. Mem., NZ Nat. Commn, Unesco, 1964–68. Vice-Pres. for Women, Global Cooperation Soc. Club, 1980. *Recreations:* reading, croquet, gardening, bridge, travel, public speaking. *Address:* 12 Grendon Court, 36 Drivers Road, Dunedin, New Zealand. *T:* Dunedin 779 105.

PURVES, Elizabeth Mary, (Libby), (Mrs Paul Heiney); writer and broadcaster; *b* 2 Feb. 1950; *d* of late James Grant Purves, CMG; *m* 1980, Paul Heiney; one *s* one *d*. *Educ:* Convent of the Sacred Heart, Tunbridge Wells; St Anne's Coll., Oxford (1st Cl. Hons Eng. Lang. and Lit.). BBC Local Radio (Oxford), 1972–76; Today, Radio 4: Reporter, 1976–79; Presenter, 1979–81; freelance writer, broadcaster; BBC TV Choices, 1982, Midweek (Presenter, 1984–), documentaries; writer for The Times, Punch, Observer, Options, et al; Editor, Tatler, March–Oct. 1983, resigned. *Publications:* (ed) The Happy Unicorns, 1971; (ed) Adventures Under Sail, H. W. Tilman, 1982; Britain At Play, 1982; Sailing Weekend Book, 1985; How Not to be a Perfect Mother, 1986. *Recreations:* sailing, walking, writing, radio. *Address:* Pattles Farm, near Saxmundham, Suffolk IP17 1TL; c/o A. P. Watt Ltd, Bedford Row, WC1. *Club:* Royal Thames Yacht.

PURVES, William, DSO 1951; Chairman and Chief Executive, Hongkong and Shanghai Banking Corporation, since 1986; *b* 27 Dec. 1931; *s* of Andrew and Ida Purves; *m* 1958, Diana Troutbeck Richardson; two *s* two *d*. *Educ:* Kelso High School. AIBScot. National Service, with Commonwealth Div. in Korea (Subaltern; DSO). National Bank of Scotland, 1948–54; Hongkong and Shanghai Banking Corporation: Germany, Hong Kong, Malaysia, Singapore, Sri Lanka, Japan, 1954–70; Chief Accountant, Hong Kong, 1970; Manager, Tokyo, 1974; Sen. Manager Overseas Operations, 1976; Asst General Manager, Overseas Operations, 1978; General Manager, 1979; Executive Director, 1982; Dep. Chm., 1984. *Recreations:* golf, Rugby. *Address:* 19 Middle Gap Road, Hong Kong. *T:* 5–8496134. *Clubs:* New (Edinburgh); Royal Hong Kong Jockey, Royal Hong Kong Golf, Shek-o Country, Hong Kong, Rugby Union (Hong Kong).

PURVIS, Air Vice-Marshal Henry R.; *see* Reed-Purvis.

PURVIS, John Robert; Managing Director, Gilmerton Management Services Ltd, since 1973; *b* 6 July 1938; *s* of Lt-Col R. W. B. Purvis, MC, JP, and Mrs R. W. B. Purvis, JP; *m* 1962, Louise S. Durham; one *s* two *d*. *Educ:* Cargilfield, Barnton, Edinburgh; Trinity Coll., Glenalmond, Perthshire; St Salvator's Coll., Univ. of St Andrews (MA Hons). National Service, Lieut Scots Guards, 1956–58. First National City Bank, New York, 1962–69: London, 1962–63; New York, 1963–65; Milan, 1965–69; Treasurer, Noble Grossart Ltd, Edinburgh, 1969–73. Mem. (C) Mid-Scotland and Fife, European Parlt, 1979–84, contested same seat, 1984; European Democratic Gp spokesman on energy, research and technology, European Parlt, 1982–84. Mem., IBA, 1985– (Chm., Scottish Adv. Cttee, 1985–). *Publication:* (section 'Money') in Power and Manoeuvrability, 1978. *Address:* Gilmerton, Dunino, St Andrews, Fife, Scotland KY16 8NB. *T:* St Andrews 73275. *Clubs:* Cavalry and Guards, Farmers'; New (Edinburgh); Royal and Ancient (St Andrews).

PUSACK, George Williams, MS; Chief Executive, Mobil Oil Australia Ltd, 1980–85, retired; *b* 26 Sept. 1920; *s* of George F. Pusack and Winifred (*née* Williams); *m* 1942, Marian Preston; two *s* one *d*. *Educ:* Univ. of Michigan; Univ. of Pennsylvania. BSE (AeroEng), BSE (Eng.Math), MS (MechEng). Aero Engr, US Navy, 1942–45; Corporal, US Air Force, 1945–46; Mobil Oil Corp.: Tech. Service and Research Manager, USA, 1946–53; Product Engrg Manager, USA, 1953–59; International Supply Manager, USA, 1959–69; Vice-Pres., N Amer. Div., USA, 1969–73; Regional Exec., Mobil Europe, London, 1973–76; Chm. and Chief Exec, Mobil Oil Co. Ltd, 1976–80. Trustee, Victorian State Opera Foundn. Teacher, layreader, vestryman and warden of Episcopal Church. *Recreations:* golf, travel. *Address:* 23 Hickory Nut Lane, Clover, SC 29710, USA. *T:* 803–831–7628. *Clubs:* River Hills Country (Clover, USA); Australian, Royal Melbourne Golf (Melbourne).

PUSEY, Nathan Marsh, PhD; President Emeritus, Harvard University; *b* Council Bluffs, Iowa, 4 April 1907; *s* of John Marsh Pusey and Rosa Pusey (*née* Drake); *m* 1936, Anne Woodward; two *s* one *d*. *Educ:* Harvard University, USA. AB 1928, AM 1932, PhD, 1937. Assistant, Harvard, 1933–34; Sophomore tutor, Lawrence Coll., 1935–38; Asst Prof., history and literature, Scripps Coll., Claremont, Calif., 1938–40; Wesleyan Univ.: Asst Prof., Classics, 1940–43, Assoc. Prof., 1943–44; President: Lawrence Coll., Appleton, Wisconsin, 1944–53; Harvard Univ., 1953–71; Andrew Mellon Foundn, 1971–75. Pres., United Bd for Christian Higher Educn in Asia, 1979–83. Holds many hon. degrees from Universities and colleges in USA and other countries. Officier de la Légion d'Honneur, 1958. *Publications:* The Age of the Scholar, 1963; American Higher Education 1945–1970, 1978. *Address:* 200 East 66th Street, New York, NY 10021, USA.

PUSINELLI, (Frederick) Nigel (Molière), CMG 1966; OBE 1963; MC 1940; HM Overseas Civil Service, retired; *b* 28 April 1919; second *s* of late S. Jacques and T. May Pusinelli, Frettenham, Norfolk and Fowey, Cornwall; *m* 1941, Joan Mary Chaloner, *d* of late Cuthbert B. and Mildred H. Smith, Cromer, Norfolk and Bexhill-on-Sea, Sussex; one *s* one *d*. *Educ:* Aldenham School; Pembroke College, Cambridge (BA Hons in law). Commissioned RA 1939; served BEF, 1940; India/Burma, 1942–45; Major, 1942; Staff College, Quetta, 1945. Administrative officer, Gilbert and Ellice Islands Colony, 1946–57. Transferred to Aden, 1958; Dep. Financial Sec. and frequently Actg Financial Sec. till 1962; Director of Establishments, 1962–68, and Assistant High Commissioner, 1963–68, Aden and Federation of South Arabia. Member E African Currency Board, 1960–62. Salaries Commissioner various territories in West Indies, 1968–70. Chm., Overseas Service Pensioners' Assoc., 1978; Vice-Chm., Chichester Harbour Conservancy, 1985 (and Mem. its Adv. Cttee); Chairman: RYA Southern Region, 1979; Chichester Harbour Fedn of sailing clubs and yachting orgns, 1980. *Publication:* Report on Census of Population of Gilbert and Ellice Islands Colony, 1947. *Recreation:* dinghy racing. *Address:* Routledge Cottage, Westbourne, Emsworth, Hants PO10 8SE. *T:* Emsworth 372915. *Clubs:* Royal Commonwealth Society; Royal Yachting Assoc., Cambridge University Cruising, Emsworth Sailing.

PUTT, S(amuel) Gorley, OBE 1966; MA; Fellow, Christ's College, Cambridge, since 1968 (Senior Tutor, 1968–78; Praelector, 1976–80); Vice-President, English Association, since 1972 (Chairman, Executive Council, 1964–72); *b* 9 June 1913; *o c* of late Poole Putt and late Ellen Blake Gorley, Brixham. *Educ:* Torquay Grammar School; Christ's College, Cambridge; Yale University. 1st Class English Tripos Pts I and II, MA 1937, Cambridge; Commonwealth Fund Fellow, MA 1936, Yale. BBC Talks Dept, 1936–38; Warden and Sec., Appts Cttee, Queen's Univ. of Belfast, 1939–40; RNVR, 1940–46, Lieut-Comdr; Warden and Tutor to Overseas Students and Director International Summer School, Univ. Coll., Exeter, 1946–49; Warden of Harkness House, 1949–68 and Director, Div. of International Fellowships, The Commonwealth Fund, 1966–68. Visiting Professor: Univ. of Massachusetts, 1968; Univ. of the South, Sewanee, 1976; Univ. of Pisa, 1979; Texas Christian Univ., 1985. Member: English-Speaking Union, London Cttee, 1952–57; UK-US Educational Commn: Travel Grants Cttee, 1955–64; Cttee of Management, Inst. of US Studies, London Univ., 1965–69. Contested (L) Torquay, 1945. FRSL 1952. Cavaliere, Order of Merit of Italy, 1980. *Publications:* Men Dressed As Seamen, 1943; View from Atlantis, 1955; (ed) Cousins and Strangers, 1956; Coastline, 1959; Scholars of the Heart, 1962; (ed) Essays and Studies, 1963; A Reader's Guide to Henry James, 1966; The Golden Age of English Drama, 1981; A Preface to Henry James, 1986. *Address:* Christ's College, Cambridge. *T:* Cambridge 334915. *Club:* Athenæum.

PUTTICK, Richard George; Chairman, 1974–85 and Chief Executive, 1978–85, Taylor Woodrow plc, retired; *b* Kingston, Surrey, 16 March 1916; *e s* of late George Frederick Puttick and Dorothea (*née* Bowerman); *m* 1943, Betty Grace Folbigg; two *s*. *Educ:* St Mark's, Teddington. Joined Taylor Woodrow Construction Ltd, 1940 (the Taylor Woodrow Group's largest contracting subsidiary co.); Dir, 1955; Asst Managing Dir, 1968; Dir, Taylor Woodrow Ltd, 1969; Jt Dep. Chm., 1972. Mem. Council, CBI, July 1967–Dec. 1969; Pres., NW Mddx Branch, BIM, 1976–85. FCIOB; CBIM. Liveryman, Worshipful Co. of Joiners and Ceilers; Mem., Co. of Constructors, 1978. *Recreations:* music, reading, gardening, supporting sports. *Address:* Woodlawn, Hanger Hill, Weybridge, Surrey KT13 9XU. *T:* Weybridge 45131.

PUTTNAM, David Terence, CBE 1983; film producer; Chairman and Chief Executive, Columbia Pictures, since 1986; *b* 25 Feb. 1941; *s* of Leonard Arthur Puttnam and Marie Beatrix Puttnam; *m* 1961, Patricia Mary (*née* Jones); one *s* one *d*. *Educ:* Minchenden Grammar Sch., London. Advertising, 1958–66; photography, 1966–68; film prodn, 1968–. Producer of feature films including: That'll Be The Day; Mahler; Swastika; Stardust; Brother can you Spare a Dime; Bugsy Malone (four BAFTA awards, 1976); The Duellists (Jury Prize, Cannes, 1977); Midnight Express (two Acad. Awards, three BAFTA Awards, 1978); Chariots of Fire (four Acad. Awards, three BAFTA Awards incl. Best Film, 1981); Local Hero (two BAFTA Awards, 1984); The Killing Fields (three Acad. Awards, eight BAFTA Awards, 1985); Cal; Defence of the Realm; The Mission (Palme d'Or, Cannes, 1986). Producer of films and series for television. Vis. Industrial Prof., Drama Dept, Bristol Univ., 1986. Director: National Film Finance Corp., 1980–; Anglia Television, 1984–; Governor, National Film Sch. Pres., CPRE, 1985–. Trustee, Tate Gall., 1986–. Michael Balcon Award for outstanding contribn to British Film Industry, BAFTA, 1982. Hon. LLD Bristol, 1983; Hon. DLitt Leicester, 1986. Chevalier, l'Ordre des Arts et des Lettres, France, 1986. *Recreations:* watching cricket, going to the cinema, following the fortunes of Tottenham Hotspur Football Club. *Club:* MCC.

PUXON, (Christine) Margaret, (Mrs Margaret Williams); QC 1982; MD, FRCOG; practising barrister, since 1954; a Recorder, since 1986; *b* 25 July 1915; *d* of Reginald Wood Hale and Clara Lilian Hale; *m* 1955, F. Morris Williams (*d* 1986), MBE; two *s* one *d*. *Educ:* Abbey Sch., Malvern Wells; Birmingham Univ. (MB, ChB; MD Obstetrics 1944). MRCS, LRCP 1942; FRCOG 1976. Gynaecological Registrar, Queen Elizabeth Hosp., Birmingham, and later Consultant Gynaecologist, Essex CC, 1942–49. Called to the Bar, Inner Temple, 1954. A Dep. Circuit Judge, 1970–86. Privy Council Member, Council of Pharmaceutical Soc., 1971–; Member: Genetic Manipulation Adv. Gp, 1979–84; Ethical Cttee, RCGP, 1981–. Liveryman, Worshipful Soc. of Apothecaries, 1982–. *Publications:* The Family and the Law, 1963, 2nd edn 1971; contrib. to Progress in Obstetrics and Gynaecology, 1983; contrib. to In Vitro Fertilisation: Past, Present and Future, 1986; contrib. med. and legal jls, incl. Proc. RSM, Practitioner and Solicitors' Jl.

Recreations: cooking, travel, opera, gardening. *Address:* 5 Pump Court, Temple, EC4Y 7AP. *T:* 01–583 7133; Pearl Chambers, 22 East Parade, Leeds LS1 5BU. *T:* Leeds 452702.

PYATT, Rt. Rev. William Allan, CBE 1985; MA; formerly Bishop of Christchurch, retired; *b* Gisborne, NZ, 4 Nov. 1916; *e s* of A. E. Pyatt; *m* 1942, Mary Lilian Carey; two *s* one *d. Educ:* Gisborne High Sch.; Auckland Univ.; St John's Coll., Auckland; Westcott House, Cambridge. BA 1938 (Senior Schol. in Hist.); MA 1939. Served War of 1939–45: combatant service with 2 NZEF; Major, 2 IC 20 NZ Armd Regt 1945. Ordained, 1946; Curate, Cannock, Staffs, 1946–48; Vicar: Brooklyn, Wellington, NZ, 1948–52; Hawera, 1952–58; St Peter's, Wellington, 1958–62; Dean of Christchurch, 1962–66; Bishop of Christchurch, 1966–83. *Publications:* contribs to NZ Jl of Theology. *Recreations:* Rugby referee; political comment on radio; golf. *Address:* 55a Celia Street, Christchurch 8, New Zealand.

PYBUS, William Michael; Partner, Herbert Oppenheimer, Nathan & Vandyk, Solicitors, since 1953; Chairman: AAH Holdings plc, since 1968; British Fuel Co., since 1968; *b* 7 May 1923; *s* of Sydney James Pybus and Evelyn Mary (*née* Wood); *m* 1959, Elizabeth Janet Whitley; two *s* two *d. Educ:* Bedford Sch.; New College, Oxford (1st cl. hons Jurisprudence). Served War, 1942–46: commissioned 1st King's Dragoon Guards; Lieut attached XIth Hussars in Normandy (wounded); King's Dragoon Guards, Egypt, Palestine, Syria, Lebanon; Prosecutor, Mil. Courts, Palestine, 1946 (Major). Admitted Solicitor (Scott Schol.), 1950. Chairman: Siebe PLC (formerly Siebe Gorman Hldgs), 1980– (Dir, 1972–); Leigh Interests, 1982–; Inter-Continental Fuels Ltd, 1975–; Overseas Coal Developments Ltd, 1979–; Ashdown House School Trust Ltd, 1975–; Vestric Ltd, 1985–; Dep. Chm., R. Mansell Ltd, 1980–85; Director: National Westminster Bank (Outer London Region), 1977–; Cornhill Insurance PLC, 1977–; Bradford & Bingley Building Soc., 1983–; Homeowners Friendly Soc., 1980–. Part-time Member: British Railways (London Midland) Bd, 1974; British Railways (Midlands and West) Bd, 1975–77; Chm., BR Midlands and N Western Bd, 1977–. Dir, Coal Trade Benevolent Assoc., 1969–; Vice-Pres., Coal Industry Soc., 1981– (Pres., 1976–81). Governor, Harpur Trust, 1979–. Master, Pattenmakers' Co., 1972–73. CBIM 1974; FInstM 1974; FRSA 1984. *Recreation:* fishing. *Address:* 20 Copthall Avenue, EC2R 7JH. *T:* 01–628 9611; Beades, Old Malden Lane, Worcester Park, Surrey. *T:* 01–337 1496. *Clubs:* Cavalry and Guards, MCC.

PYE, Prof. John David, FLS; Professor of Zoology, Queen Mary College, University of London, since 1973; *b* 14 May 1932; *s* of Wilfred Frank Pye and Gwenllian Pye (*née* Davies); *m* 1958, Dr Ade Pye (*née* Kuku). *Educ:* Queen Elizabeth's Grammar School for Boys, Mansfield; University Coll. of Wales, Aberystwyth (BSc 1954, Hons 1955); Bedford Coll., London Univ. (PhD 1961). Research Asst, Inst. of Laryngology and Otology, London Univ., 1958–64; Lectr in Zoology, 1964–70, Reader, 1970–73, King's Coll. London; Head of Dept of Zoology and Comparative Physiology, Queen Mary Coll., 1977–82. A founder Dir, QMC Instruments Ltd, 1976–. Linnean Society: Editor, Zoological Jl, 1981–85; Editl Sec. and Mem. Council, 1985–; Mem., IEE Professional Gp Cttee E15, Radar, Sonar, Navigation and Avionics, 1983–86. Member Editorial Boards: Zoolog. Soc., 1972–77, 1978–83, 1985–; Jl of Exper. Biol., 1974–78; Jl of Comp. Physiol. A, 1978–. Associate Mem., Royal Instn, 1979– (delivered Friday discourses 1979, 1983, and televised Christmas Lects for Children, 1985–86). *Publications:* Bats, 1968; (with G. D. Sales) Ultrasonic Communication by Animals, 1974; (ed with R. J. Bench and A. Pye) Sound Reception in Mammals, 1975; articles and research papers. *Recreations:* viticulture and vinification, travelling in warm climates. *Address:* Woodside, 24 St Mary's Avenue, Finchley, N3 1SN. *T:* 01–346 6869; (office) 01–980 4811.

PYE, Prof. Norman; Professor of Geography, University of Leicester, 1954–79, now Emeritus; Pro-Vice-Chancellor, 1963–66; Dean, Faculty of Science, 1957–60; Chairman of Convocation, 1982–85; *b* 2 Nov. 1913; *s* of John Whittaker Pye and Hilda Constance (*née* Platt); *m* 1940, Isabella Jane (*née* Currie); two *s. Educ:* Wigan Grammar School; Manchester University. Manchester University: BA Hons Geography Class I, 1935, Diploma in Education Class I, 1936. Asst Lecturer in Geography, Manchester Univ., 1936–37 and 1938–46; Mem., Cambridge Univ. Spitsbergen Expedn, 1938. Seconded to Hydrographic Dept, Admiralty, for War Service, 1940–46. Lecturer in Geography, 1946–53, Sen. Lecturer, 1953–54, Manchester Univ. Chm., Conf. of Heads of Depts of Geography in British Univs, 1968–70. Vis. Professor: Univ. of Ghana, 1958, 1960; Univ. of BC, 1964, 1983; Univ. of Alberta, Edmonton, 1967, 1968, 1969, 1973, 1974, 1975, 1978; External Examnr: Univ. of E Africa, 1964–67; Univ. of Guyana, 1974–78. Editor, "Geography", 1965–80. Member Corby Development Corp., 1965–80. Governor, Up Holland Grammar Sch., 1953–74; Member: Northants CC Educn Cttee, 1956–74; Court, Nottingham Univ., 1964–79; Standing Conf. on Univ. Entrance, 1966–79; Schools Council, 1967–78. Member: Council, RMetS, 1953–56; Council, Inst. of Brit. Geographers, 1954, 1955; Council, RGS, 1967–70; Council for Urban Studies Centres, 1974–81; Brit. Nat. Cttee for Geography, 1970–75; Heritage Educn Gp, 1976–; Young Enterprise Leics Area Bd, 1983–; Hon. Mem., Geographical Assoc., 1983– (Hon. Vice-Pres., 1979–83). *Publications:* Leicester and its Region (ed and contrib.), 1972; research papers and articles in learned journals. *Recreations:* travel, oenology, music, gardening. *Address:* 127 Spencefield Lane, Evington, Leicester LE5 6GG. *T:* Leicester 415167. *Club:* Geographical.

PYKE, David Alan, CBE 1986; MD, FRCP; Physician-in-charge, Diabetic Department, King's College Hospital, London, 1971–86; *b* 16 May 1921; *s* of Geoffrey and Margaret Pyke; *m* 1948, Janet, *d* of Dr J. Gough Stewart; one *s* two *d. Educ:* Leighton Park Sch., Reading; Cambridge Univ.; University Coll. Hosp. Med. Sch., London. MD Cantab; FRCP. Junior med. appts in London and Oxford, 1945–59. Service in RAMC, 1946–48. Apptd to staff of King's Coll. Hosp., 1959. Hon. Sec.: Assoc. of Physicians of GB and Ire., 1968–73; Royal Soc. of Med., 1972–74. Registrar, Royal Coll. of Physicians of London, 1975–. *Publications:* (jt ed) Clinical Diabetes and its Biochemical Basis, 1968; (ed) Clinics in Endocrinology and Metabolism, Vol. 1, No 3, 1972; (jtly) Diabetes and its Management, 1973, 3rd edn 1978; articles in med. and sci. jls. *Recreations:* golf, opera. *Address:* 17 College Road, SE21 7BG. *T:* 01–693 2313.

PYKE, Sir Louis (Frederick), Kt 1978; ED 1946; FAIB; FAIM; Chairman and Managing Director, Costain (Aust.) Pty Ltd, 1971–77 (Managing Director, 1965–73); Chairman (Victoria), Haden Engineering Pty Ltd; consultant to Meldrum Burrows & Partners, architects; *b* 21 Nov. 1907; *m* 1936, Sierlah, *d* of H. J. Cohen; two *s* one *d. Educ:* Melbourne C of E Grammar Sch. Director: Pyke Simmie, Master Builders, 1947; Union Assce, 1963–74; Costain Investments (Aust.) Pty Ltd, 1977–; Steel Deck Industries Pty Ltd, 1978–; Davis Vindin Pty Ltd, 1978–. Lt-Col, AASC. Mem., United Services Inst., 1936. Member Council: S Melbourne Tech. Sch., 1963–73; Master Builders Assoc., Vic, 1972–. Mem., Melbourne South Rotary, 1962–; Pres., Multiple Sclerosis Soc. of Vic, 1975–82; Dep. Nat. Chm., Business Adv. Bd, Multiple Sclerosis Soc. of Aust., 1979–. Hon. Life Fellow, Aust. Inst. of Bldg. *Recreation:* farming. *Address:* 419 Wattletree Road, East Malvern, Victoria 3145, Australia. *T:* 25 6961. *Clubs:* Naval and Military, Melbourne Cricket, Victoria Racing (Melbourne).

PYKE, Magnus, OBE 1978; PhD, CChem, FRSC, FInst Biol, FIFST, FRSE; *b* 29 Dec. 1908; *s* of Robert Bond Pyke and Clara Hannah Pyke (*née* Lewis); *m* 1937, Dorothea Mina Vaughan (*d* 1986); one *s* one *d. Educ:* St Paul's Sch., London; McGill Univ.;

Montreal; University Coll. London (Fellow, 1984–). BSc, PhD. Scientific Adviser's Div., Min. of Food, London, 1941–45; Nutritional Adviser, Allied Commn for Austria, Vienna, 1945–46; Principal Scientific Officer (Nutrition), Min. of Food, London, 1946–48; Distillers Co. Ltd: Dep. Manager, Yeast Research Outstation, 1949–55; Manager, Glenochil Research Station, 1955–73; Sec. and Chm. of Council, British Assoc. for the Advancement of Science, 1973–77 (Mem. Council, 1968–77; Pres. Section X, 1965). Member: (Vice-Pres.) Soc. for Analytical Chemistry, 1959–61; Council, Royal Inst. of Chemistry, 1953–56, 1962–65; Council, Royal Soc. of Edinburgh, 1961–64; Council, Soc. of Chemical Industry, 1967–69; (Chm.) Scottish Section, Nutrition Soc., 1954–55; (Vice-Pres.) Assoc. for Liberal Education, 1964–81; (Pres.) Inst. of Food Science and Technology of the UK, 1969–71; Participated in Don't Ask Me, 1974–78, Don't Just Sit There, 1979–80, Yorkshire TV. FInstBiol (Mem. Council, Scottish Sect., 1959–62); Hon. Fellow: Australian IFST, 1973; NZ IFST, 1979. DUniv Stirling, 1974; Hon. DSc: Lancaster, 1976; McGill, 1981. Pye Colour TV Award: the most promising newcomer to television, 1975; BBC Multi-Coloured Swap Shop Star Award (Expert of the Year), 1977–78. *Publications:* Manual of Nutrition, 1945; Industrial Nutrition, 1950; Townsman's Food, 1952; Automation, Its Purpose and Future, 1956; Nothing Like Science, 1957; Slaves Unaware, 1959; The Boundaries of Science, 1961; Nutrition, 1962; The Science Myth, 1962; Food Science and Technology, 1964; The Science Century, 1967; Food and Society, 1968; Man and Food, 1970; Synthetic Food, 1970; Technological Eating, 1972; Catering Science and Technology, 1973; Success in Nutrition, 1975; Butterside Up, 1976; There and Back, 1978; Food for all the Family, 1980; Long Life, 1980; Our Future, 1980; (with P. Moore) Everyman's Scientific Facts and Feats, 1981; Six Lives of Pyke, 1981; Curiouser and Curiouser, 1983; Red Rag to a Bull, 1983; (contrib.) Diet and Health in Modern Britain, ed D. J. Oddy and D. S. Miller, 1985; (contrib.) The World's Food Supply, ed J. Asimov, 1985; Dr Magnus Pyke's 101 Inventions, 1986. *Recreation:* Until he was 75 he wrote a page a day and savoured the consequences. *Address:* 3 St Peter's Villas, W6 9BQ. *T:* 01–748 9920. *Club:* Savage.

PYLE, Cyril Alfred; Head Master, South East London School, 1970–80; *s* of Alfred John Pyle and Nellie Blanche Pyle; *m* 1940, Jean Alice Cotten; one *s* one *d. Educ:* Shooters Hill Grammar Sch.; Univ. of London, Goldsmiths' Coll. Dep. Headmaster, Woolwich Polytechnic Secondary Sch., 1940–66; Headmaster, Bow Sch., 1966–70. Pres., London Teachers' Assoc., 1962; Chm., Council for Educnl Advance, 1964–76; Sec., Conference of London Comprehensive School Heads, 1973–79. *Recreations:* Rotary Club, motoring, gardening. *Address:* Barleyfields, Hartlip, Sittingbourne, Kent ME9 7TH. *T:* Newington 842719.

PYM, Rt. Hon. Francis Leslie, PC 1970; MC 1945; DL; MP (C) Cambridgeshire South East, since 1983 (Cambridgeshire, 1961–83); *b* 13 Feb. 1922; *s* of late Leslie Ruthven Pym, MP, and Iris, *d* of Charles Orde; *m* 1949, Valerie Fortune Daglish; two *s* two *d. Educ:* Eton; Magdalene Coll., Cambridge (Hon. Fellow 1979). Served War of 1939–45 (despatches, 1944 and 1945, MC): 9th Lancers, 1942–46; African and Italian campaigns. Contested (C) Rhondda West, 1959. Asst Govt Whip (unpaid), Oct. 1962–64; Opposition Whip, 1964–67; Opposition Dep. Chief Whip, 1967–70; Parly Sec. to the Treasury and Govt Chief Whip, 1970–73; Sec. of State for NI, 1973–74; Opposition spokesman on: agriculture, 1974–76; H of C affairs and devolution, 1976–78; Foreign and Commonwealth affairs, 1978–79; Sec. of State for Defence, 1979–81; Chancellor of the Duchy of Lancaster and Paymaster Gen., and Leader of the House of Commons, 1981; Lord Pres. of the Council and Leader of the House of Commons, 1981–82; Sec. of State for Foreign and Commonwealth Affairs, 1982–83. Pres., Atlantic Treaty Assoc., 1985–. Mem. Herefordshire County Council, 1958–61. DL Cambs, 1973. *Publication:* The Politics of Consent, 1984. *Address:* Everton Park, Sandy, Beds. *Clubs:* Buck's, Cavalry and Guards.

PYMAN, Lancelot Frank Lee, CMG 1961; HM Diplomatic Service, retired; *b* 8 August 1910; *s* of late Dr F. L. Pyman, FRS, and of Mrs I. C. Pyman; *m* 1936, Sarah Woods Gamble (*d* 1981). *Educ:* Dover College; King's College, Cambridge (Exhibitioner). Entered Levant Consular Service, 1933; various posts in Persia, 1933–38; Consul, Cernauti, Roumania, 1939–40; Vice-Consul, Beirut. Lebanon, 1940–41. Served with HM Forces in Levant States, 1941. Asst Oriental Secretary, HM Embassy, Tehran, Dec. 1941–44; Foreign Office, 1944–48; Consul, St Louis, Missouri, Dec. 1948–49; Oriental Counsellor, Tehran, Dec. 1949–Sept. 1952; Counsellor, British Embassy, Rio de Janeiro, 1952–53; Consul-General, Tetuan, 1953–56; Counsellor, British Embassy, Rabat, 1956–57; HM Consul-General: Zagreb, 1957–61; Basra, March–Dec. 1961; Ambassador to the Somali Republic, 1961–63; Consul-General, San Francisco, 1963–66. *Recreations:* listening to music, duplicate bridge. *Address:* Knockroe, Delgany, Co. Wicklow, Ireland.

PYRAH, Prof. Leslie Norman, CBE 1963; retired as Senior Consultant Surgeon, Department of Urology, Leeds General Infirmary (1950–64); Hon. Director, Medical Research Council Unit, Leeds General Infirmary, 1956–64; Professor of Urological Surgery, Leeds University, 1956–64, now Emeritus; *b* 11 April 1899; *s* of Arthur Pyrah; *m* 1934, Mary Christopher Batley; one *s* one *d* (and one *s* decd). *Educ:* University of Leeds; School of Medicine, Leeds. Hon. Asst Surgeon, Leeds Gen. Infirmary, 1934; Hon. Consultant Surgeon, Dewsbury Infirmary, Leeds Public Dispensary, Goole Hosp., and Lecturer in Surgery, Univ. of Leeds, 1934; Hon. Cons. Surgeon, St James' Hosp., Leeds, 1941; Surgeon with charge of Out-patients, Leeds Infirmary, 1944; Weild Lectr, Royal Faculty Physicians and Surgeons, Glasgow, 1955; Ramon Guiteras Lectr, Amer. Urological Assoc., Pittsburgh, USA, 1957; Pres., Section of Urology, Royal Soc. Med., 1958; Litchfield Lectr, Univ. of Oxford, 1959; Hunterian Orator, RCS, 1969. Chm., Specialist Adv. Cttee in Urology, Jt Royal Colls of Surgeons of GB and Ireland, 1968–72. Pres., British Assoc. of Urological Surgeons, 1961, 1962; Pres. Leeds and W Riding Medico-Chirurgical Soc., 1959. Mem. Council (elected), Royal College of Surgeons of England, 1960–68. Hon. Mem. Soc. Belge de Chirurgie, 1958; Corresponding Member: Amer. Assoc. of Genito-Urinary Surgeons, 1962; Amer. Soc. of Pelvic Surgeons, 1962; Australasian Soc. of Urology, 1963. St Peter's Medal (British Assoc. of Urological Surgeons) for outstanding contributions to urology, 1959; Honorary Medal, RCS, 1975. DSc (*hc*) Leeds, 1965; Hon. FRSM, 1978. *Publications:* Renal Calculus, 1979; (contrib.) British Surgical Progress, 1956; numerous contribs to British Journal of Surgery, British Journal of Urology, Proc. Royal Soc. Med., Lancet, BMJ. *Recreations:* tennis, music. *Address:* Fieldhead, Weetwood Lane, Leeds LS16 5NP. *T:* 52777.

PYTCHES, Rt. Rev. George Edward David; Vicar of St Andrew's, Chorleywood, Rickmansworth, since 1977; *b* 9 Jan. 1931; 9th *c* and 6th *s* of late Rev. Thomas Arthur Pytches and late Eirene Mildred Pytches (*née* Welldon); *m* 1958, Mary Trevisick; four *d. Educ:* Old Buckenham Hall, Norfolk; Framlingham Coll., Suffolk; Univ. of Bristol (BA); Trinity Coll., Bristol. MPhil Nottingham, 1984. Deacon 1955, priest 1956; Asst Curate, St Ebbe's, Oxford, 1955–58; Asst Curate, Holy Trinity, Wallington, 1958–59; Missionary Priest in Chol Chol, Chile, 1959–62; in Valparaiso, Chile, 1962–68; Rural Dean, Valparaiso, 1966–70; Asst Bishop of Diocese of Chile, Bolivia and Peru, 1970–72; Vicar General of Diocese, 1971–72; Bishop in Chile, Bolivia and Peru, 1972–77. *Recreations:* collecting semi-precious stones, walking. *Address:* The Vicarage, Quickley Lane, Chorleywood, Rickmansworth, Herts.

Q

QUANT, Mary, (Mrs A. Plunket Greene), OBE 1966; RDI 1969; Director of Mary Quant Group of companies since 1955; *b* 11 Feb. 1934; *d* of Jack and Mildred Quant; *m* 1957, Alexander Plunket Greene; one *s. Educ:* 13 schools; Goldsmiths' College of Art. Fashion Designer. Mem., Design Council, 1971–. Member: British/USA Bicentennial Liaison Cttee, 1973–; Adv. Council, V&A Museum, 1976–78. Exhibition, Mary Quant's London, London Museum, 1973–74. Maison Blanche Rex Award (US), 1964; Sunday Times Internat. Award, 1964; Piavola d'Oro Award (Italy), 1966; Annual Design Medal, Inst. of Industrial Artists and Designers, 1966. FSIA 1967. *Publication:* Quant by Quant, 1966. *Address:* 3 Ives Street, SW3. *T:* 01–584 8781.

QUANTRILL, Prof. Malcolm, RIBA; architect, author and critic; *b* Norwich, Norfolk, 25 May 1931; *s* of Arthur William Quantrill and Alice May Newstead; *m* 1971, Esther Maeve, *d* of James Brignell Dand and Winifred Dand, Chester; two *s* two *d. Educ:* City of Norwich Sch.; Liverpool Univ. (BArch); Univ. of Pennsylvania (MArch); Univ. of Wroclaw (Doc. Ing Arch). RIBA 1961. Fulbright Scholar and Albert Kahn Meml Fellow, Univ. of Pennsylvania, 1954–55; Asst Prof., Louisiana State Univ., 1955–60; Lecturer: Univ. of Wales, Cardiff, 1962–65; UCL, 1965–66; Asst to Dir, Architectural Assoc., 1966–67, Dir, 1967–69; Lectr, Univ. of Liverpool, 1970–73; Dean, Sch. of Environmental Design, Polytechnic of N London, 1973–80; Prof. of Architecture and Urban Design, Univ. of Jordan, Amman-Jordan, 1980–83. Vis. Professor: Univ. of Illinois, Chicago, 1973–75; Carleton Univ., Ottawa, 1978; Gastprofessor, Technische Universität, Wien, 1975–77; Fellow, Graham Foundn for Advanced Studies in the Fine Arts, Chicago, 1984. Sir William Dobell Meml Lectr in Modern Art, Sydney, NSW, 1978. Plays performed: Honeymoon, 1968; Life Class, 1968 (TV); radio plays include: The Fence, 1964; Let's Get This Straight, 1977; Immortal Bite, 1982. *Publications:* The Gotobed Trilogy (novels), 1962–64; Ritual and Response in Architecture, 1974; Monuments of Another Age, 1975; On the Home Front (novel), 1977; The Art of Government and the Government of Art, 1978; Alvar Aalto—a critical study, 1983; Reima Pietilä—architecture, context and modernism, 1985; The Environmental Memory, 1986; articles in RIBA Jl, Arch. Assoc. Qly, Arch. Design, and Art Internat. *Address:* 18 Causton Road, Highgate, N6. *T:* 01–348 1064; School of Architecture, Texas A&M University, College Station, Texas 77843-3137, USA. *Club:* Garrick.

QUANTRILL, William Ernest; HM Diplomatic Service; Counsellor and Head of Chancery, Caracas, since 1984; *b* 4 May 1939; *s* of late Ronald Frederick Quantrill and Norah Elsie Quantrill (*née* Matthews); *m* 1964, Rowena Mary Collins; three *s* one *d. Educ:* Colston's Sch., Bristol; Hatfield Coll., Univ. of Durham (BA Hons French). Entered FO, 1962; served Brussels, Havana, Manila, Lagos, 1964–80; Head of Training Dept, FCO, 1980–81; Dep. Head of Personnel Ops Dept, FCO, 1981–84. *Recreations:* wild life, travel. *Address:* c/o Foreign and Commonwealth Office, SW1A 2AH. *T:* 01–233 3000.

QUARMBY, David Anthony, MA, PhD; FCIT; MIRTE; Director, J. Sainsbury plc, since 1984; *b* 22 July 1941; *s* of Frank Reginald and Dorothy Margaret Quarmby; *m* 1968, Hilmary Hunter; four *d. Educ:* Shrewsbury Sch.; King's Coll., Cambridge (MA), Leeds Univ. (PhD, Dip. Industrial Management). Asst Lectr, then Lectr, Dept of Management Studies, Leeds Univ., 1963; Economic Adviser, Economic Planning Directorate, Min. of Transport, 1966; London Transport Executive: Dir of Operational Research, 1970; Chief Commercial and Planning Officer, 1974; Mem., 1975–84; Man. Dir (Buses), 1978–84; Mem., London Regional Transport, 1984. Vice-Pres., Bus and Coach Council, 1981–84; Mem., Nat. Council, Freight Transport Assoc., 1985–. Member: Southwark Diocesan Synod, 1982–85; London Adv. Bd, Salvation Army, 1982–. *Publications:* Factors Affecting Commuter Travel Behaviour (PhD Thesis, Leeds), 1967; contribs to Jl of Transport Economics and Policy, Regional Studies, Enterprise Management, and to books on transport, economics and operational research. *Recreations:* music, singing. *Address:* 13 Shooters Hill Road, Blackheath, SE3 7AR. *T:* 01–858 7371.

QUARREN EVANS, John Kerry; His Honour Judge Quarren Evans; a Circuit Judge, on South Eastern circuit, since 1980; *b* 4 July 1926; *s* of late Hubert Royston Quarren Evans, MC and of Violet Soule Quarren Evans; *m* 1958, Janet Shaw Lawson; one *s* one *d. Educ:* King Edward VIII Sch., Coventry; Cardiff High Sch.; Trinity Hall, Cambridge, 1948–51 (MA, LLM). 21st Glam. (Cardiff) Bn Home Guard, 1943–44; enlisted, Grenadier Gds, 1944; commnd Royal Welch Fusiliers, 1946, from OTS Bangalore; att. 2nd Bn The Welch Regt, Burma, 1946–47; Captain 1947. Admitted solicitor, 1953; Partner: Lyndon Moore & Co., Newport, 1954–71; T. S. Edwards & Son, Newport, 1971–80; Recorder, Wales and Chester Circuit, 1974–80. *Recreations:* golf, Rugby football, oenology. *Address:* 2 Mount Park Crescent, Ealing, W5 2RN. *Clubs:* Denham Golf, Newport Golf.

QUARTANO, Ralph Nicholas, CEng, MIChemE; Chief Executive, Postel Investment Management Ltd, since 1983; Director: Britoil, since 1982; London American Energy NV, since 1981; Member, Securities and Investments Board, since 1985; *b* 3 Aug. 1927; *s* of late Charles and Vivienne Mary Quartano; *m* 1954, Cornelia Johanna de Gunst; two *d. Educ:* Sherborne Sch.; Pembroke Coll., Cambridge (MA). Bataafsche Petroleum Mij, 1952–58; The Lummus Co, 1958–59; Temple Press, 1959–65; Man. Director: Heywood Temple Industrial Publications, 1965–68; Engineering Chemical and Marine Press, 1968–70; The Post Office, 1971–; Sen. Dir, Central Finance, 1973–74; Chief Exec., Staff Superannuation Fund, 1974–83. Dir, John Lewis Partnership Pensions Trust, 1986–. Member: Engrg Council, 1981–83; City Capital Markets Cttee, 1985–; City Adv. Gp to Dir-Gen., CBI, 1984–. Sloan Fellow of London Business School. Trustee, Monteverdi Trust, 1986–. *Address:* 9 Oakcroft Road, SE13 7ED. *T:* 01 852 1607.

QUASTEL, Juda Hirsch, CC 1970; DSc London; PhD Cantab; ARCS London; FRS 1940; FRSC; Hon. FRSE; Professor of Neurochemistry, University of British Columbia, Canada, 1966–83, now Emeritus; *b* 2 Oct. 1899; *e s* of late Jonas and Flora Quastel, Sheffield, Yorks; *m* 1st, 1931, Henrietta Jungman, MA (*d* 1973); two *s* one *d*; 2nd, 1975, Susan Ricardo. *Educ:* Central Secondary School, Sheffield; Imperial College of Science, London University; Trinity College, Cambridge. Commenced research in biochemistry in Cambridge University, Oct. 1921; awarded Senior Studentship by Royal Commissioners for Exhibition of 1851, 1923; Demonstrator and lecturer in biochemistry, Cambridge Univ. 1923; Fellow of Trinity College, Cambridge, 1924; Meldola Medallist 1927; Beit Memorial Research Fellow, 1928; Director of Research, Cardiff City Mental Hospital, 1929–41; Rockefeller Foundation Fellow, 1936; Director of ARC Unit of Soil Metabolism, 1941–47; Prof. of Biochemistry, McGill Univ., Montreal, 1947–66; Director: McGill-Montreal Gen. Hosp. Research Inst., 1947–65; McGill Unit of Cell Metabolism, 1965–66. Member of Council of Royal Institute of Chemistry, 1944–47; Member: Water Pollution Research Board, 1944–47; Bd of Governors, Hebrew Univ., Jerusalem, 1950; Pres., Montreal Physiological Soc., 1950; Pres. Canadian Biochemical Soc., 1963; Canadian Microbiological Soc. Award, 1965; Flavelle Medal, RSC, 1974; Gairdner Internat. Award for Med. Res., 1974. Member, British, Can. and Amer. scientific societies; Consultant, Montreal General Hosp. Leeuwenhoek Lectr, Royal Society, 1954; Bryan Priestman Lectr, Univ. New Brunswick, 1956; Kearney Foundation Lectr, Univ. Calif, 1958; Seventh Jubilee Lectr, Biochemical Soc. UK, 1974; Royal Society Leverhulme Visiting Professor, in India, 1965–66; Vis. Prof., Nat. Hospital for Nervous Diseases (Neurology Dept), London, 1976–77. Hon. Pres., Internat. Congress of Biochem., 1979. Fellow: NY Academy of Science, 1954; Amer. Assoc. for Advancement of Science, 1964. Hon. Fellow: Japanese Pharmacological Soc., 1963; Canadian Microbiological Soc., 1965; N Pacific Soc. of Neurology and Psychiatry, 1966. Hon. Mem., Biochemical Soc. UK, 1973. Hon. DSc McGill, 1969; Hon. PhD Jerusalem, 1970. *Publications:* since 1923 mainly on subjects of biochemical interest; author and co-editor: Neurochemistry, 1955– (1963); Methods in Medical Research, Vol. 9, 1961; Chemistry of Brain Metabolism, 1962; Metabolic Inhibitors, vol. 1, 1963, vol. 2, 1964, vol. 3, 1972, vol. 4, 1973. *Address:* 4585 Langara Avenue, Vancouver, BC V6R 1C9, Canada.

QUAYLE, Sir Anthony; *see* Quayle, Sir J. A.

QUAYLE, Bronte Clucas, CB 1980; OBE 1969; QC 1978; *b* 24 Oct. 1919; *s* of late Alfred Clucas Quayle and Edith Anne Quayle; *m* 1944, Joan Proctor Strickland; two *s. Educ:* St Peter's Coll., Adelaide; Adelaide Univ. (LLB). AIF, 1940–45. Admitted Barrister and Solicitor, Adelaide, 1948; Office of Parliamentary Counsel, Canberra, 1950–82, First Parly Counsel, 1977–81. Consulting Draftsman, Pakistan Constitution, 1962. Sitara-i-Pakistan 1962. *Recreations:* yachting, motor sport, music, reading. *Address:* 68 Stradbroke Street, Deakin, ACT 2600, Australia. *Clubs:* Canberra Yacht, Canberra Sporting Car, Canberra Wine and Food, University House, ANU (all in Canberra).

QUAYLE, Sir (John) Anthony, Kt 1985; CBE 1952; Actor; *b* 7 September 1913; *s* of Arthur Quayle and Esther Quayle (*née* Overton); *m* 1947, Dorothy Hyson; one *s* two *d. Educ:* Rugby. First appeared on stage, 1931; acted in various London productions between then and 1939, including several appearances at Old Vic; also acted in New York. Served War of 1939–45, Royal Artillery. After 1945 became play-producer as well as actor; produced: Crime and Punishment; The Relapse; Harvey; Who is Sylvia. Director, Shakespeare Memorial Theatre, 1948–56; productions: The Winter's Tale, Troilus and Cressida, Macbeth, Julius Caesar, King Lear (with John Gielgud), Richard II, Henry IV, Part I (with John Kidd), Henry V, Othello and Measure for Measure. *Stratford rôles include:* The Bastard, Petruchio, Claudius, Iago, Hector in Troilus and Cressida; Henry VIII, 1949; Antony and Henry VIII, 1950; Falstaff in Henry IV, Parts I and II, 1951; Coriolanus; Mosca in Volpone, 1952; Othello, Bottom in a Midsummer Night's Dream, Pandarus in Troilus and Cressida, 1954; Falstaff in The Merry Wives of Windsor; Aaron in Titus Andronicus, 1955. Took Shakespeare Memorial Theatre Company to Australia, 1949, 1953. *Other appearances include:* Tamburlaine, NY, 1956; A View from the Bridge, Comedy Theatre, 1956; Titus Andronicus, European tour, 1957; (also dir) The Firstborn, NY, 1958; Long Day's Journey into Night, Edinburgh Festival and London, 1958; Look After Lulu!, Royal Court, 1959; Chin-Chin, Wyndham's, 1960; The Right Honourable Gentleman, Her Majesty's, 1964; Incident at Vichy, Phœnix, 1966; Galileo, NY, 1967; Halfway Up The Tree, NY 1967; Sleuth, St Martin's, 1970, NY, 1970–71; The Idiot, National Theatre, 1970; The Headhunters, Washington, 1974; Old World, RSC, 1976–77; Do You Turn Somersaults, USA, 1977; Heartbreak House, Lord Arthur Saville's Crime, Malvern Festival, 1980; Hobson's Choice, A Coat of Varnish, Haymarket, 1982; (also dir) The Clandestine Marriage, Albery, 1984; After the Ball is Over, Old Vic, 1985. Prospect Theatre at Old Vic: (also co-prod.) The Rivals, 1978; King Lear (as Lear), 1978; (also prod.) The Clandestine Marriage, Albery and UK tour, 1984; (also dir) The Tempest, Brighton, 1985. *Directed:* Lady Windermere's Fan, 1967; Tiger at the Gates, New York, 1968; Harvey, Prince of Wales, 1975; Rip Van Winkle, Washington, 1976; The Old Country, Queen's, 1978; The Rules of the Game, Haymarket, 1982. Founded Compass Theatre, 1983. *Films:* Saraband for Dead Lovers, Hamlet, Oh Rosalinda, Battle of the River Plate, The Wrong Man, Woman in a Dressing Gown, The Man Who Wouldn't Talk, Ice Cold in Alex, Serious Charge, Tarzan's Greatest Adventure, The Challenge, The Guns of Navarone, HMS Defiant, Lawrence of Arabia, The Fall of the Roman Empire, Operation Crossbow, A Study in Terror, Incompreso, MacKenna's Gold, Before Winter Comes, Anne of the Thousand Days, Bequest to the Nation, The Tamarind Seed, Moses the Lawgiver, Great Expectations, 21 Hours in Munich, The Eagle has Landed, The Antagonists, Masada, Dial M for Murder; Last Days of Pompeii. *Publications:* Eight Hours from England, 1945; On Such a Night, 1947. *Club:* Special Forces.

QUAYLE, Prof. John Rodney, PhD; FRS 1978; Vice-Chancellor, University of Bath, since 1983; *b* 18 Nov. 1926; *s* of John Martin Quayle and Mary Doris Quayle (*née*

Thorp); *m* 1951, Yvonne Mabel (*née* Sanderson); one *s* one *d*. *Educ:* Alun Grammar Sch., Mold; University Coll. of North Wales, Bangor (BSc, PhD); Univ. of Cambridge (PhD); MA Oxon. Res. Fellow, Radiation Lab., Univ. of California, 1953–55; Sen. Scientific Officer, Tropical Products Institute, London, 1955–56; Mem. Scientific Staff, MRC Cell Metabolism Res. Unit, Univ. of Oxford, 1956–63; Lectr, Oriel Coll., Oxford, 1957–63; Sen. Lectr in Biochemistry, 1963–65, West Riding Prof. of Microbiol., 1965–83, Sheffield Univ. Vis. Res. Prof. of Gesellschaft für Strahlen und Umweltforschung, Institut für Mikrobiologie, Universität Göttingen, 1973–74; Walker-Ames Vis. Prof., Univ. of Washington, Seattle, 1981. Chm., British Nat. Cttee for Microbiol., 1985–; Member: AFRC, 1982–84; Adv. Council, RMCS, 1983–; Council, Royal Soc., 1982–84; Biol Sciences Cttee, SERC, 1981–84. Trustee, Bath Festival Soc., 1984–. Korrespondierendes Mitglied, Akademie der Wissenschaften, Göttingen, 1976. Ciba Medal, Biochem. Soc., 1978. *Publications:* articles in scientific jls. *Recreations:* hill-walking, gardening, bread-making. *Address:* The Lodge, North Road, Claverton Down, Bath BA2 6HE.

QUEBEC, Archbishop of, (RC), and Primate of Canada, since 1981; **His Eminence Cardinal Louis-Albert Vachon,** CC (Canada) 1969; OQ 1985; FRSC 1974; Officier de l'Ordre de la fidélité française, 1963; *b* 4 Feb. 1912; *s* of Napoléon Vachon and Alexandrine Gilbert. *Educ:* Laval Univ. (PhD Philosophy, 1947); PhD Theology, Angelicum, Rome, 1949. Ordained priest, 1938; Prof. of Philosophy, 1941–47, Prof. of Theology, 1949–55, Laval Univ. Superior, Grand Séminaire de Québec, 1955–59; Superior General, 1960–77; Auxiliary Bishop of Quebec, 1977–81; Cardinal, 1985. Vice-Rector of Laval Univ., 1959–60, Rector, 1960–72. Mem., Royal Canadian Soc. of Arts. Hon. FRCP&S (Canada), 1972. Hon. doctorates: Montreal, McGill and Victoria, 1964; Guelph, 1966; Moncton, 1967; Queen's, Bishop's and Strasbourg, 1968; Notre-Dame (Indiana), 1971; Carleton, 1972; Laval, 1982. Centennial Medal, 1967. *Publications:* Espérance et Présomption, 1958; Vérité et Liberté, 1962; Unité de l'Université, 1962; Apostolat de l'universitaire catholique, 1963; Mémorial, 1963; Communauté universitaire, 1963; Progrès de l'université et consentement populaire, 1964; Responsabilité collective des universitaires, 1964; Les humanités aujourd'hui, 1966; Excellence et loyauté des universitaires, 1969. *Address:* (home) 2 Port-Dauphin, PO Box 459, Quebec G1R 4R6, Canada. *T:* 692–3935; (office) 1073 boulevard St Cyrille ouest, Sillery, Quebec G1S 4R5, Canada. *T:* 688–1211.

QUEBEC, Bishop of, since 1977; **Rt. Rev. Allen Goodings;** *b* Barrow-in-Furness, Lancs, 7 May 1925; *s* of late Thomas Jackson Goodings and Ada Tate; *m* 1959, Joanne Talbot; one *s* one *d*. *Educ:* Sir George Williams Univ. (BA); McGill Univ. (BD); Diocesan Theological Coll., Montreal (LTh; Hon. DD). Studied engineering and worked for Vickers Armstrongs (Britain) and Canadian Vickers (Montreal); studied in Montreal and ordained into Ministry of Anglican Church of Canada, 1959. Chaplain, Canadian Grenadier Guards, Montreal, 1966–69. Dean of Holy Trinity Cathedral, Quebec, 1969–77. Played Rugby Union (capped for Lancashire, 1947/8, including County Championship). *Recreations:* skiing, tennis, squash, cycling. *Address:* 29 Rue des Jardins, Quebec, PQ G1R 4L5, Canada. *T:* 694–9329. *Clubs:* Cercle Universitaire (Quebec); Mess (Royale 22nd Regiment, Quebec); Quebec Garrison (Hon. Mem.).

QUEENSBERRY, 12th Marquess of, *cr* 1682; **David Harrington Angus Douglas;** late Royal Horse Guards; Viscount Drumlanrig and Baron Douglas, 1628; Earl of Queensberry, 1633; Bt (Nova Scotia), 1668; Professor of Ceramics, Royal College of Art, 1959–83; Partner, Queensberry Hunt design group; *b* 19 Dec. 1929; *s* of 11th Marquess of Queensberry and late Cathleen Mann; *S* father, 1954; *m* 1st, 1956, Mrs Ann Radford; two *d*; 2nd, 1969, Alexandra (marr. diss.), *d* of Guy Wyndham Sich; three *s* one *d*. *Educ:* Eton. Mem. Council, Crafts Council; Pres., Design and Industries Assoc., 1976–78. FSIAD. *Heir:* *s* Viscount Drumlanrig, *qv*.

QUEENSLAND, NORTH, Bishop of, since 1971; **Rt. Rev. Hurtle John Lewis;** *b* 2 Jan. 1926; *s* of late Hurtle John Lewis and late Hilda Lewis. *Educ:* Prince Alfred Coll.; London Univ. (BD). ThL of ACT. Royal Australian Navy, 1943–46; Student, St Michael's House, S Aust., 1946–51; Member, SSM, 1951–; Provincial Australia, SSM, 1962–68; Prior, Kobe Priory, Japan, 1969–71. *Recreations:* rowing, horse riding. *Address:* Box 1244, Townsville, Queensland 4810, Australia. *T:* 71–2297.

QUEGUINER, Jean; Légion d'Honneur, 1970; Administrateur Général des Affaires Maritimes, France; maritime consultant, since 1985; Deputy Chairman, Union Chantiers Navals, since 1985; *b* 2 June 1921; *s* of Etienne Quéguiner and Anne Trehin; *m* 1952, Marguerite Gaillard; one *s* one *d*. *Educ:* Lycée Buffon, Collège Stanislas and Faculté de Droit, Paris; Coll. of Administration of Maritime Affairs, St Malo. Docteur en Droit (maritime), Bordeaux. Head of Maritime Dist of Caen, 1953; Dep. Head of Coll. of Admin. of Maritime Affairs, 1955; Head of Safety of Navigation Section, 1963; Vice-Chm. of Maritime Safety Cttee, 1965–68, Dep. Sec.-Gen., 1968–77, IMCO; Chm., Chantiers Navals de l'Esterel, 1981–85. *Publications:* Législation et réglementation maritime, 1955; Le code de la mer, 1965; La croisière cotière, 1967; Le code fluvial à l'usage des plaisanciers, 1970. *Recreation:* sailing. *Address:* 13 rue de l'Horizon, 17480 Le Château d'Oléron, France.

QUENINGTON, Viscount; Michael Henry Hicks Beach; *b* 7 Feb. 1950; *s* and *heir* of 2nd Earl St Aldwyn, *qv*; *m* 1982, Gilda Maria, *o d* of Barão Saavedra, Copacabana, Rio de Janeiro; one *d*. *Educ:* Eton; Christ Church, Oxford. MA. *Address:* Williamstrip Park, Cirencester, Glos; 13 Upper Belgrave Street, SW1; 145 West 58 Street, Apartment 4A, New York, NY 10019, USA. *T:* (212) 664–7626.

QUENNELL, Joan Mary, MBE 1958; *b* 23 Dec. 1923; *o c* of late Walter Quennell, Dangstein, Rogate. *Educ:* Dunhurst and Bedales Schools. War Service, WLA and BRCS. Vice-Chairman, Horsham Division Cons. Assoc., 1949 (Chairman, 1958–61); W Sussex CC, 1951–61. Served on Finance, Local Government, Selection and Education Cttees, etc; also as Governor various schools and colleges; Governor, Crawley Coll., Further Education, 1956–69; Member: Southern Reg. Council for Further Education, 1959–61; Reg. Adv. Council, Technological Education (London and Home Counties), 1959–61. MP (C) Petersfield, 1960–Sept. 1974; PPS to the Minister of Transport, 1962–64; Member: Select Cttee on Public Accounts, 1970–74; Speaker's Panel of Temporary Chairmen of House of Commons, 1970–74; Cttee of Selection, House of Commons, 1970–74; Select Cttee on European Secondary Legislation, 1973–74. Chm., EUW, Hampshire, 1978–80. JP W Sussex, 1959–80. *Recreations:* reading, gardening. *Address:* Dangstein, Rogate, near Petersfield, Hants.

QUENNELL, Peter, CBE 1973; *b* March 1905; *s* of late Marjorie and C. H. B. Quennell. *Educ:* Berkhamsted Grammar Sch.; Balliol Coll., Oxford. Editor, History To-day, 1951–79; edited The Cornhill Magazine, 1944–51. *Publications:* Poems, 1926; Baudelaire and the Symbolists, 1929, 2nd edn 1954; A Superficial Journey through Tokyo and Peking, 1932, 2nd edn 1934; Sympathy, and Other Stories, 1933; Byron, 1934; Byron: the years of fame, 1935, 3rd edn 1967; Victorian Panorama: a survey of life and fashion from contemporary photographs, 1937; Caroline of England, 1939; Byron in Italy, 1941; Four Portraits, 1945, 2nd edn 1965; John Ruskin, 1949; The Singular Preference, 1952; Spring in Sicily, 1952; Hogarth's Progress, 1955; The Sign of the Fish, 1960; Shakespeare: the poet and his background, 1964; Alexander Pope: the education of Genius 1688–1728, 1968; Romantic England, 1970; Casanova in London and other essays, 1971; Samuel Johnson: his friends and enemies, 1972; The Marble Foot (autobiog.), 1976; The Wanton Chase (autobiog.), 1980; Customs and Characters, 1982; *edited:* Aspects of Seventeenth Century Verse, 1933, 2nd edn 1936; The Private Letters of Princess Lieven to Prince Metternich, 1820–1826, 1948; Byron: selected letters and journals, 1949; H. Mayhew, Mayhew's Characters, 1951; Diversions of History, 1954; H. Mayhew, Mayhew's London, 1954; George Borrow, The Bible in Spain, 1959; H. Mayhew, London's Underworld, 1960; G. G. N. Byron, Lord Byron, Byronic Thoughts, 1960; H. de Montherlant, Selected Essays, 1960; W. Hickey, Memoirs, 1960; T. Moore, The Journal of Thomas Moore, 1964; H. Mayhew, Mayhew's Characters, 1967; Marcel Proust, 1871–1922: a centenary volume, 1971; (with H. Johnson) A History of English Literature, 1973; Vladimir Nabokov, his Life, his Work, his World, 1979; A Lonely Business: a self-portrait of James Pope-Hennessy, 1981. *Address:* 26 Cheyne Row, SW3. *Club:* White's.

QUEREJAZU CALVO, Roberto; Cross of the Chaco and Award of Military Merit (Bolivia); Bolivian Ambassador to the Court of St James's 1966–70, and to the Court of The Hague, 1966–70; *b* 24 Nov. 1913; *m* 1944, Dorothy Lewis; one *s* one *d*. *Educ:* Sucre Univ., Bolivia. Director of Minister's Cabinet, Legal Dept, and Political Dept, Bolivian Foreign Service, 1939–42; First Secretary, Embassy in Brazil, 1943; Secretary-General, Bolivian Delegn to UN, 1946; Bolivian Embassy, London: Counsellor, 1947; Chargé d'Affaires, 1948–52; Bolivian Rep.: to UN Conference on Tin, 1951; to Interamerican Conference for De-Nuclearization of Latin America, Mexico, 1964; Bolivian Delegate: XX UN General Assembly, 1965; 2nd Interamerican Conference Extraord., Rio de Janeiro, 1965; Under-Secretary of State for Foreign Affairs, Bolivia, 1966. Holds foreign awards. *Publications:* Masamaclay (history of Chaco War), 1966; Bolivia and the English, 1973; Llallagua (history of a mountain), 1976; Guano, Salitre, Sangre (history of the Pacific War), 1979; Adolfo Costa du Rels (biography of a diplomat and writer), 1981. *Address:* Casilla 4243, Cochabamba, Bolivia.

QUICK, Anthony Oliver Hebert; Headmaster of Bradfield College, 1971–85, retired; *b* 26 May 1924; *er s* of late Canon O. C. Quick, sometime Regius Prof. of Divinity at Oxford, and late Mrs F. W. Quick; *m* 1955, Eva Jean, *er d* of late W. C. Sellar and of Mrs Hope Sellar; three *s* one *d*. *Educ:* Shrewsbury Sch.; Corpus Christi Coll., Oxford; Sch. of Oriental and African Studies, Univ. of London (Govt Schol.). 2nd cl. hons Mod. History, Oxford. Lieut, RNVR, serving mainly on East Indies Stn, 1943–46. Asst Master, Charterhouse, 1949–61; Headmaster, Rendcomb Coll., Cirencester, 1961–71. *Publications:* (jtly) Britain 1714–1851, 1961; Britain 1851–1945, 1967; Twentieth Century Britain, 1968. *Recreations:* walking, gardening, sailing, fishing. *Address:* Corbin, Scorriton, Buckfastleigh, Devon. *Club:* Naval.

QUICK, Norman, CBE 1984; Chairman, H. & J. Quick Group plc, since 1965 (Managing Director, 1965–84); *b* 19 Nov. 1922; *s* of James and Jessie Quick; *m* 1949, Maureen Cynthia Chancellor; four *d*. *Educ:* Arnold Sch., Blackpool. FIMI. H. & J. Quick Ltd to H. & J. Quick Group plc, 1939–; served RNVR, Lieut 1941–46 (despatches Mediterranean, 1943); Non Executive Director, Williams & Glyn's Bank, 1979–85; Royal Bank of Scotland, 1985–; Dir, Piccadilly Radio (formerly Greater Manchester Independent Radio), 1972– (Chm., 1980–). Mem., NW Indust. Council. Pres., Stretford Cons. Assoc., 1974– (formerly Chm.). Mem., Lancs CC, 1954–57. Treasurer, 1975–80, Chm., 1980–83, Univ. of Manchester Council; Member: Wilmslow Prep. Sch. Trust, 1966–; Bd of Governors, Arnold Sch. Ltd, Blackpool, 1980–. Hon. MA Manchester, 1977; Hon. LLD Manchester, 1984. *Recreations:* golf, Rugby. *Address:* Birkin House, Rostherne, Altrincham, Cheshire WA14 3QL. *T:* Bucklow Hill 830 175. *Clubs:* Army and Navy, Royal Automobile; St James's (Manchester).

QUICKE, John Godolphin, CBE 1978; DL; *b* 20 April 1922; *s* of Captain Noel Arthur Godolphin Quicke and Constance May Quicke; *m* 1953, Prudence Tinné Berthon, *d* of Rear-Adm. (E) C. P. E. Berthon; three *s* three *d*. *Educ:* Eton; New Coll., Oxford. Vice-Chm., North Devon Meat, 1982–; Mem., SW Reg. Bd, National Westminster Bank, 1974–. Chairman: Minister of Agriculture's SW Regional Panel, 1972–75; Agricl EDC, NEDC, 1983–; Member: Consultative Bd for R&D in Food and Agric., 1981–84; Severn Barrage Cttee, 1978–80; Countryside Commn, 1981–. Pres., CLA, 1975–77. DL Devon, 1985. Bledisloe Gold Medal for Landowners, RASE, 1985. *Recreations:* reading, music, trees. *Address:* Sherwood, Newton St Cyres, near Exeter, Devon EX5 5BT. *T:* Newton St Cyres 216. *Club:* Boodle's.

QUIGLEY, Johanna Mary, (Mrs D. F. C. Quigley); *see* Foley, J. M.

QUIGLEY, William George Henry, CB 1982; PhD; Permanent Secretary, Department of Finance and Personnel, Northern Ireland, since 1982; *b* 26 Nov. 1929; *s* of William George Cunningham Quigley and Sarah Hanson Martin; *m* 1971, Moyra Alice Munn, LLB. *Educ:* Ballymena Academy; Queen's Univ., Belfast, BA (1st Cl. Hons), 1951; PhD, 1955. Apptd Asst Principal, Northern Ireland Civil Service, 1955; Permanent Secretary: Dept of Manpower Services, NI, 1974–76; Dept of Commerce, NI, 1976–79; Dept of Finance, NI, 1979–82. CBIM. *Publication:* (ed with E. F. D. Roberts) Registrum Iohannis Mey: The Register of John Mey, Archbishop of Armagh, 1443–1456, 1972. *Recreations:* historical research, reading, music.

QUILL, Colonel Raymond Humphrey, CBE 1947; DSO 1947; LVO 1934; Colonel (retired), Royal Marines; *b* 4 May 1897; *s* of late Maj.-General Richard Henry Quill, CB, MD; unmarried. *Educ:* Wellington Coll.; Cheltenham. Joined Royal Marines, 1914. Served European War, 1914–19. Major, RM, 1934; Lieut-Colonel, 1943; Colonel, 1944. Served War of 1939–45. ADC to the King, 1948–50; retired, 1950. Legion of Merit, USA, 1948. Fellow, British Horological Institute, 1954–; Master, Worshipful Co. of Clockmakers, 1967. *Publication:* John Harrison: the man who found Longitude, 1967. *Recreations:* athletics, fishing, horology. *Clubs:* Boodle's, Royal Thames Yacht, Royal Automobile.

QUILLEY, Denis Clifford; actor; *b* 26 Dec. 1927; *s* of Clifford Charles Quilley and Ada Winifred (*née* Stanley); *m* 1949, Stella Chapman; one *s* two *d*. *Educ:* Bancroft's, Woodford, Essex. First appearance, Birmingham Rep. Theatre, 1945; The Lady's not for Burning, Globe, 1949; Old Vic and Young Vic Cos, 1950–51: parts included: Fabian in Twelfth Night (on tour, Italy), Gratiano in Merchant of Venice; Revue, Airs on a Shoe String (exceeded 700 perfs), Royal Court, 1953; first leading rôle in West End as Geoffrey Morris in Wild Thyme, Duke of York's, 1955; subseq. parts incl.: Tom Wilson in Grab Me a Gondola (over 600 perfs), Lyric; Captain Brassbound, and Orlando, Bristol Old Vic; Candide, Saville; Benedick in Much Ado about Nothing, Open Air Th.; Archie Rice in The Entertainer, Nottingham Playhouse; Krogstad in A Doll's House, Brighton; Privates on Parade, Aldwych, 1977, Piccadilly, 1978 (SWET award, 1977); Deathtrap, Garrick, 1978; title rôle in Sweeney Todd, Theatre Royal Drury Lane (SWET award), 1980; Molokov in Chess, Barbican, 1985; Antony, in Antony and Cleopatra, Chichester, 1985; Fatal Attraction, Haymarket, 1985; La Cage aux Folles, Palladium, 1986. Nat. Theatre, 1971–76: Aufidius (Coriolanus); Macbeth; Bolingbroke (Richard II); Caliban

(The Tempest); Lopakin (Cherry Orchard); Jamie (Long Day's Journey into Night); Claudius (Hamlet); Hector (Troilus and Cressida); Bajazeth (Tamburlaine); Morell (Candida), Albery Theatre, 1977. Has played in NY, Melbourne and Sydney. *Films:* Life at the Top, Anne of the Thousand Days, Murder on the Orient Express, The Antagonists, Evil Under the Sun, Privates on Parade, King David. *TV plays and series* incl.: Merchant of Venice; The Father; Henry IV (Pirandello); Murder in the Cathedral; Time Slip; Contrabandits (Aust.); Clayhanger; The Serpent Son; The Crucible; Gladstone, in No 10; Masada; Anno Domini; Murder of a Moderate Man. *Recreations:* playing the piano, flute and cello, walking. *Address:* 22 Willow Road, Hampstead, NW3. *T:* 01–435 5976.

QUILLIAM, Prof. Juan Pete, (Peter), OBE 1986; DSc; FRCP; Professor of Pharmacology, University of London, at St Bartholomew's Hospital Medical College, 1962–83, now Emeritus; Hon. Clinical Assistant, St Bartholomew's Hospital; Chairman of Convocation of the University of London, since 1973; *b* 20 Nov. 1915; *e s* of late Thomas Quilliam, Peel, IoM and Maude (*née* Pavitt); *m* 1st, 1946, Melita Kelly (*d* 1957); one *s* one *d*; 2nd, 1958, Barbara Lucy Marion, *y d* of late Rev. William Kelly, Pelynt, Cornwall. *Educ:* University Coll. Sch.; UCL (exhibnr); UCH Med. Sch. MSc 1938, MB BS 1941; DSc 1969; FRCP 1975. Vice-Pres., London Univ. Athletic Union, 1938; Pres., London Univ. Boat Club, 1939–40 (rowing purple 1938). Sharpey Physiol Schol., UCL, 1939–41; House Phys. and House Surg., UCH, 1941; House Phys., Brompton Hosp. for Diseases of Chest, 1941–42; Asst TB Officer, Chelsea, 1941–42; Exptl Officer, Min. of Supply, 1942–43; served RAFVR Med. Br. (Central Fighter Estabt), 1943–46; Lectr in Pharmacol., KCL, 1945–55; London Univ. Travelling Fellow, 1949–50; Fellow, Johns Hopkins Hosp. Med. Sch., 1949–50; Sen. Lectr and Head of Pharmacol. Dept, 1956, Reader, 1958, St Bartholomew's Hosp. Med. Coll. Gresham Prof. of Physic, 1967–68. London University Convocation: Mem. Standing Cttee, 1966–74; Senator, Medicine, 1968–74; Chm., Trust, 1973–; Mem. Ct and Senate, London Univ. Examiner in Pharmacol. and Clinical Pharmacol. to Univs of London, Edinburgh, Cambridge, Dundee, Liverpool, Manchester and Cardiff, also to Fac. of Anaesthetists and Apothecaries Soc. Mem., 1960–, Dep. Chm., 1975–, Gen. Optical Council; Gen. Sec., British Pharmacol Soc., 1968–71; British Medical Association: Mem. Council, 1971–; Chairman: Med. Academic Staff Cttee, 1978, 1980, 1982; Bd of Sci. and Educn, 1982–; Fellow, 1981. Trustee: City Parochial Foundn, 1977–; Trust for London, 1986–; Trustee and Co-Chm., Help the Hospices Trust, 1984–. Press Editor, British Jl of Pharmacol., 1957–60. *Publications: jointly:* Medical Effects of Nuclear War, 1983; Boxing, 1984; Young People and Alcohol, 1986; Long term environment effects of nuclear war, 1986; Alternative Therapy, 1986; The Torture Report, 1986; papers on visual purple, blood/acqueous humour barrier permability, intra-ocular fluid, DFP and synaptic transmission in heart and muscle, action drugs on the iris, the ocular critical flicker fusion frequency, the auditory flutter fusion frequency, the electro-pharmacology of sedatives, general anaesthetics on autonomic ganglia as a model of brain synapses, GABA-like actions on lobster muscle, effects of staphylococcal α-toxin on intestine, the ultrastructural effects in autonomic ganglia in the presence of chemical substances, World Medicine, University "Cuts" 1983. *Recreations:* work, sailing. *Address:* Senate House, University of London, Malet Street, WC1E 7HU. *T:* 01–636 8000, ext. 3701. *Clubs:* Athenæum; United Hospitals Sailing (Burnham-on-Crouch) (Cdre, 1974–).

QUILTER, Sir Anthony (Raymond Leopold Cuthbert), 4th Bt, *cr* 1897; landowner since 1959; *b* 25 March 1937; *s* of Sir (John) Raymond (Cuthbert) Quilter, 3rd Bt and Margery Marianne (*née* Cooke); *S* father 1959; *m* 1964, Mary Elise, *er d* of late Colonel Brian (Sherlock) Gooch, DSO, TD; one *s* one *d*. *Educ:* Harrow. Is engaged in farming. *Recreations:* shooting, golf. *Heir: s* Guy Raymond Cuthbert Quilter, *b* 13 April 1967. *Address:* Sutton Hall, Sutton, Woodbridge, Suffolk. *T:* Shottisham 411246.

QUILTER, David (Cuthbert) Tudway; Vice Lord-Lieutenant of Somerset, since 1978; Local Director, Barclays Bank, Bristol, 1962–84 (Director, Barclays Bank UK Ltd, 1971–81); Director, Bristol Evening Post, since 1982; *b* 26 March 1921; *o s* of Percy Cuthbert Quilter and Clare Tudway; *m* 1953, Elizabeth Mary, *er d* of Sir John Carew Pole, Bt, *qv*; one *s* two *d*. *Educ:* Eton. Served War of 1939–45, Coldstream Guards, 1940–46. JP London Juvenile Courts, 1959–62. Mayor of Wells, 1974–75; Chm. of Trustees, Wells Cathedral Preservation Trust, 1976–; Treasurer, Bristol Univ., 1976–; Governor, Wells Cathedral Sch., 1968–; Member: Council, Outward Bound Trust, 1959–; Garden Soc., 1973–; Life Trustee, Carnegie UK Trust, 1981–. DL 1970, High Sheriff 1974–75, Somerset. *Publications:* No Dishonourable Name, 1947; A History of Wells Cathedral School, 1985. *Recreations:* gardening, music, tennis, golf, shooting. *Address:* Milton Lodge, Wells, Somerset BA5 3AQ. *T:* Wells 72168. *Club:* Boodle's.

QUIN; *see* Wyndham-Quin, family name of **Earl of Dunraven.**

QUIN, Rt. Rev. George Alderson. *Educ:* Trinity College, Dublin (MA). Deacon, 1937, priest 1938, Down; Curate of St Jude, Ballynafeigh, Belfast, 1937–39; Dean's Vicar of St Anne's Cathedral, Belfast, 1939–41; Holywood, 1941–43; Incumbent of Magheralin, 1943–51; Vicar of Ballymacarrett, 1951–58; Canon of St Anne's Cathedral, Belfast, 1955–56; Archdeacon of Down, 1956–70; Exam. Chaplain to Bishop of Down and Dromore, 1957–70; Rector of Bangor, Dio. Down, 1958–70; Bishop of Down and Dromore, 1970–80. *Address:* c/o The See House, Knockdene Park, S Belfast.

QUIN, Joyce Gwendolen; Member (Lab) Tyne and Wear, European Parliament, since 1984 (South Tyne and Wear, 1979–84); *b* 26 Nov. 1944; *d* of Basil Godfrey Quin and Ida (*née* Ritson). *Educ:* Univ. of Newcastle upon Tyne (BA French, 1st Cl. Hons); Univ. of London (MSc Internat. Relns). Research Asst, Internat. Dept, Labour Party Headquarters, Transport House, 1969–72; Lecturer in French, Univ. of Bath, 1972–76; Resident Tutor, St Mary's Coll., and Lectr in French and Politics, Univ. of Durham, 1977–79. *Publications:* articles on French and European politics in various academic jls. *Recreations:* North-East local history (Newcastle upon Tyne City Guide), music, theatre, walking, cycling. *Address:* European Parliament, Centre européen, Plateau du Kirchberg, Luxembourg. *T:* 43001.

QUINCE, Peter; *see* Thompson, John W. McW.

QUINE, Prof. Willard Van Orman; American author; Professor of Philosophy, 1948, and Edgar Pierce Professor of Philosophy, 1956–78, Harvard University, now Emeritus Professor; *b* Akron, Ohio, 25 June 1908; *s* of Cloyd Robert and Hattie Van Orman Quine; *m* 1st, 1930, Naomi Clayton; two *d*; 2nd, 1948, Marjorie Boynton; one *s* one *d*. *Educ:* Oberlin Coll., Ohio (AB); Harvard Univ. (AM, PhD). Harvard: Sheldon Travelling Fellow, 1932–33 (Vienna, Prague, Warsaw); Jun. Fellow, Society of Fellows, 1933–36 (Sen. Fellow, 1949–78, Chairman, 1957–58); Instructor and Tutor in Philosophy, 1936–41; Assoc. Professor of Philosophy, 1941–48; Chairman, Dept of Philosophy, 1952–53. Visiting Professor, Universidade de São Paulo, Brazil, 1942. Lieut, then Lieut-Commander, USNR, active duty, 1942–46. Consulting editor, Journal of Symbolic Logic, 1936–52; Vice-President, Association for Symbolic Logic, 1938–40; President, 1953–55; Vice-President, Eastern Division, American Philosophical Assoc., 1950, President, 1957; Member: Amer. Philos. Soc., 1957– (Councillor, 1966–68, 1982–); Acad. Internat. de Philosophie de Science, 1960; Institut International de Philosophie, 1983–. FAAAS, 1945– (Councillor, 1950–53); Fellow, Nat. Acad. of Sciences, 1977–. Corres. Member: Instituto Brasileiro de Filosofia, 1963–; Institut de France, 1978–; Corres. Fellow: British Acad., 1959–; Norwegian Acad. of Scis, 1979–; Trustee, Institute for Unity of Science, 1949–56; Syndic, Harvard University Press: 1951–53; 1954–56, 1959–60, 1962–66. George Eastman Visiting Prof., Oxford Univ., 1953–54; Vis. Professor: Univ. of Tokyo, 1959; Rockefeller Univ., 1968; Collège de France, 1969. A. T. Shearman Lecturer, University of London, 1954; Gavin David Young Lectr in Philosophy, Univ. of Adelaide, 1959; John Dewey Lectr, Columbia Univ., 1968; Paul Carus Lectr, Amer. Philos. Assoc., 1971; Hägerström Lectr, Uppsala, 1973; Vis. Lectr, Calcutta, 1983. Member Institute for Advanced Study, Princeton, USA, 1956–57. Fellow: Centre for Advanced Study in the Behavioural Sciences, Palo Alto, California, 1958–59; Centre for Advanced Studies, Wesleyan Univ., Conn, 1965; Sir Henry Saville Fellow, Merton Coll., Oxford, 1973–74. Hon. degrees: MA Oxon, 1953; DLitt Oxon, 1970; LittD: Oberlin, 1955; Akron, 1965; Washington, 1966; Temple, 1970; Cambridge, 1978; Ripon, 1983; LLD: Ohio State, 1957; Harvard, 1979; DèsL Lille, 1965; LHD: Chicago, 1967; Syracuse, 1981; DPh: Uppsala, 1980; Berne, 1982. N. M. Butler Gold Medal, 1970. *Publications:* A System of Logistic, 1934; Mathematical Logic, 1940, rev. edn 1951; Elementary Logic, 1941, rev. edn 1965; O sentido da nova logica, 1944 (São Paulo); Methods of Logic, 1950, rev. edn 1982; From a Logical Point of View, 1953, rev. edn 1961; Word and Object, 1960; Set Theory and its Logic, 1963, revised edn 1969; Ways of Paradox and Other Essays, 1966, rev. edn 1976; Selected Logic Papers, 1966; Ontological Relativity and Other Essays, 1969; Philosophy of Logic, 1970; (with J. S. Ullian) The Web of Belief, 1970; The Roots of Reference, 1974; Theories and Things, 1981; The Time of My Life, 1985; contribs to Journal of Symbolic Logic; Journal of Philosophy; Philosophical Review; Mind; Rivista di Filosofia; Scientific American; NY Review of Books; Library of Living Philosophers. *Recreation:* travel. *Address:* 38 Chestnut Street, Boston, Mass 02108, USA. *T:* 723–6754.

QUINLAN, Maj.-Gen. Henry, CB 1960; *b* 5 Jan. 1906; *s* of Dr Denis Quinlan, LRCP, LRCS (Edinburgh), of Castletownroche, Co. Cork; *m* 1936, Euphemia Nancy, *d* of John Tallents Wynyard Brooke of Shanghai, and Altrincham, Cheshire; two *s* two *d*. *Educ:* Clongowes Wood Coll., Sallins, Co. Kildare. BDS 1926; FFD RCS (I) 1964. Royal Army Dental Corps; Lieut, 1927; Captain, Dec. 1930; Major, 1937; Lieut-Colonel, Dec. 1947; Colonel, 1953; Maj.-General, Oct. 1958; Director Army Dental Service, 1958–63; QHDS 1954–64, retired; Colonel Comdt Royal Army Dental Corps, 1964–71. Officer OStJ 1958. *Address:* White Bridges, Redlands Lane, Crondall, Hants. *T:* Aldershot 850239.

QUINLAN, Sir Michael (Edward), KCB 1985 (CB 1980); Permanent Secretary, Department of Employment, since 1983; *b* 11 Aug. 1930; *s* of late Gerald and Roseanne Quinlan, Hassocks; *m* 1965, Margaret Mary Finlay; two *s* two *d*. *Educ:* Wimbledon Coll.; Merton Coll., Oxford. 1st Cl. Hon. Mods, 1st Cl. LittHum. RAF, 1952–54. Asst Principal, Air Ministry, 1954; Private Sec. to Parly Under-Sec. of State for Air, 1956–58; Principal, Air Min., 1958; Private Sec. to Chief of Air Staff, 1962 65; Asst Sec., MoD, 1968; Defence Counsellor, UK Delegn to NATO, 1970–73; Under-Sec., Cabinet Office, 1974–77; Dep. Under-Sec. of State, MoD, 1977–81; Dep. Sec., HM Treasury, 1981–82. Chm., Civil Service Sports Council, 1985–. Governor, Henley Management Coll., 1983–. CBIM 1983. *Recreations:* squash, watching cricket, listening to music. *Address:* c/o Department of Employment, Caxton House, Tothill Street, SW1. *Club:* Royal Air Force.

QUINN, Brian; Assistant Director since 1982, and Head of Banking Supervision since 1986, Bank of England; *b* 18 Nov. 1936; *s* of Thomas Quinn and Margaret (*née* Cairns); *m* 1961, Mary Bradley; two *s* one *d*. *Educ:* Glasgow Univ. (MA Hons); Manchester Univ. (MA Econs); Cornell Univ. (PhD). Economist, African Dept, IMF, 1964–70, Rep., Sierra Leone, 1966–68; joined Bank of England, 1970; Economic Div., 1970–74; Chief Cashier's Dept, 1974–77; Head of Information Div., 1977–82. *Publications:* (contrib.) Surveys of African Economies, vol. 4, 1971; (contrib.) The New Inflation, 1976; articles in learned jls. *Recreations:* fishing, golf. *Club:* Overseas Bankers'.

QUINN, Brian; *see* Quinn, J. S. B.

QUINN, Prof. David Beers, DLit (QUB), PhD (London), MRIA, FRHistS; Andrew Geddes and John Rankin Professor of Modern History, University of Liverpool, 1957–76; *b* 24 April 1909; *o s* of late David Quinn, Omagh and Belfast, and Albertina Devine, Cork; *m* 1937, Alison Moffat Robertson, MA, *d* of late John Ireland Robertson, Edinburgh; two *s* one *d*. *Educ:* Clara (Offaly) No 2 National Sch.; Royal Belfast Academical Institution; Queen's Univ., Belfast; King's Coll., University of London. University Schol., QUB, 1928–31 (1st Class Hons in Medieval and Modern History, 1931); PhD London, 1934. Asst Lecturer, 1934, and Lecturer, 1937, University College, Southampton; Lecturer in History, QUB, 1939–44; seconded to BBC European Service, 1943; Prof. of History, University College, Swansea, 1944–57; DLit (QUB), 1958. Secretary, Ulster Society for Irish Historical Studies, 1939–44; Member: Council of Hakluyt Society, 1950–54, 1957–60 (Vice-Pres., 1960–82, Pres., 1982–); Council of Royal Historical Society, 1951–55, 1956–60 (Vice-Pres., 1964–68, Hon. Vice-Pres., 1983); Fellow, Folger Shakespeare Lib. (Washington, DC), 1957, 1959, 1963–64; Fellow, John Carter Brown Lib., 1970, 1982; Leverhulme Res. Fellow, 1963; British Council Visiting Scholar, NZ, 1967; Hungary, 1972; Fellow, Huntington Library, 1980; Fellow, Nat. Inst. for the Humanities, 1983; Harrison Vis. Prof., Coll. of William and Mary, Williamsburg, Va, 1969–70; Visiting Professor: St Mary's Coll., St Mary's City, Md, 1976–78, 1980–82, 1984; Michigan Univ., 1979. Hon. FBA 1984. Hon. DLitt: Newfoundland, 1964; New Univ. of Ulster, 1975; NUI, 1981; Hon. DHL St Mary's Coll., 1978; Hon. LLD Univ. of N Carolina, 1980. Hon. Phi Beta Kappa, 1984. *Publications:* The Port Books or Petty Customs Accounts of Southampton for the Reign of Edward IV, 2 vols, 1937–38; The Voyages and Colonising Enterprises of Sir Humphrey Gilbert, 2 vols, 1940; Raleigh and the British Empire, 1947; The Roanoke Voyages, 1584–90, 2 vols, 1955; (with Paul Hulton) The American Drawings of John White, 1577–1590, 1964; (with R. A. Skelton) R. Hakluyt's Principall Navigations (1589), 1965; The Elizabethans and the Irish, 1966; Richard Hakluyt, Editor, 1967; North American Discovery, 1971; (with W. P. Cumming and R. A. Skelton) The Discovery of North America, 1972; (with N. M. Cheshire) The New Found Land of Stephen Parmenius, 1972; (with A. M. Quinn) Virginia Voyages from Hakluyt, 1973; England and the Discovery of America 1481–1620, 1974; The Hakluyt Handbook, 2 vols, 1974; (with W. P. Cumming, S. E. Hillier and G. Williams) The Exploration of North America, 1630–1776, 1974; The Last Voyage of Thomas Cavendish, 1975; North America from First Discovery to Early Settlements, 1977; (with A. M. Quinn and S. Hillier) New American World, 5 vols, 1979; Early Maryland and a Wider World, 1982; (with A. M. Quinn) The First Settlers, 1982; (with A. M. Quinn) English New England Voyages 1602–1608, 1983; (with A. N. Ryan) England's Sea Empire, 1550–1642, 1983; Set Fair for Roanoke, 1985; (ed) John Derricke, The Image of Ireland, 1986; contribs on Irish history and the discovery and settlement of N America in historical journals. *Address:* 9 Knowsley Road, Cressington Park, Liverpool L19 0PF. *T:* 051–427 2041.

QUINN, James Charles Frederick; film producer and exhibitor; Chairman, The Minema, since 1984; *b* 23 Aug. 1919; *y s* of Rev. Chancellor James Quinn and Muriel Alice May (*née* MaGuire); *m* 1942, Hannah, 2nd *d* of Rev. R. M. Gwynn, BD (Sen. Fellow and Vice-Provost, TCD), and Dr Eileen Gwynn; one *s* one *d*. *Educ:* Shrewsbury Sch.;

TCD (Classical Exhibnr); Christ Church, Oxford (MA; Dip. in Econ. and Polit. Sci.). Served War, Irish Guards, Italy, NW Europe; British Army Staff, France, and Town Major, Paris, 1945–46. Courtaulds Ltd, 1949–55. Dir, BFI, 1955–64: National Film Theatre built, London Film Festival inaugurated, and 1st Univ. Lectureship in Film Studies in UK estabd at Slade Sch. of Fine Art, University Coll., London. Council of Europe Fellowship, 1966. Chairman: Internat. Short Film Conf., 1971–78 (Life Pres., 1979); National Panel for Film Festivals, 1974–83. Member: Gen. Adv. Council, BBC, 1960–64; Bd, Gardner Arts Centre, Sussex Univ., 1968–71; British Council Film Television and Video Adv. Cttee, 1983–. Trustee: Imperial War Museum, 1968–78; Grierson Meml Trust, 1975–. Invited to stand by New Ulster Movement as Indep. Unionist Parly candidate, S Down, 1968. Foreign Leader Award, US State Dept, 1962. Films: co-producer, Herostratus, 1966; Producer, Overlord, 1975. Silver Bear Award, Berlin Internat. Film Festival, 1975; Special Award, London Evening News British Film Awards, 1976. Chevalier de l'Ordre des Arts et des Lettres, France, 1979. *Publications:* Outside London, 1965; The Film and Television as an Aspect of European Culture, 1968; contrib. Chambers's Encyclopaedia (cinema), 1956–59. *Recreations:* lawn tennis; formerly Eton Fives. *Address:* Crescent Cottage, 108 Marine Parade, Brighton, E Sussex. *T:* Brighton 607888. *Clubs:* Cavalry and Guards; Vincent's (Oxford).

QUINN, (James Steven) Brian; Managing Director, Visnews, since 1980; *b* 16 June 1936; *s* of James and Elizabeth Quinn; *m* 1962, Blanche Cecilia James; two *s* one *d. Educ:* St Mary's Coll., Crosby; Waterpark Coll., Ireland; University Coll., Dublin (BCL, LLB). Kings Inn, Dublin. Director: Johnson Radley, 1966–68; United Glass Containers, 1968–69; Head of Industrial Activities, Prices and Incomes Board, 1969–71; Dir, M. L. H. Consultants, 1971–79; Corporate Develt Advr, Midland Bank Internat., 1977–80; Chief Industrial Advr, Price Commn, 1977–78. Chairman: BrightStar Communications, 1983–; BAJ Holdings, 1985–; Director: Digital Computer Services, 1985–; Telematique Services, 1985–. British Institute of Management: FBIM 1978; Mem. Council, 1981–; Mem. Finance Cttee, 1981–; Chm., City of London Branch, 1981–83; Vice Pres., 1983–. Trustee, Internat. Inst. of Communications, 1982– (Chm., Exec. Cttee, 1984–); Mem., Exec. Cttee, Inst. of European Trade and Technology, 1983–. Chm., Finance Cttee, Great Japan Exhbn, 1979–82. *Recreations:* golf, reading. *Address:* Craiglea House, Austenwood Lane, Gerrards Cross, Bucks. *Club:* Athenæum.

QUINN, Sheila Margaret Imelda, CBE 1978; FHSM; FRCN; Nursing Adviser, British Red Cross Society, since 1983; *b* 18 Sept. 1920; *d* of late Wilfred Amos Quinn and Ada Mazella (*née* Bottomley). *Educ:* Convent of Holy Child, Blackpool; London Univ. (BScEcon Hons); Royal Lancaster Infirmary (SRN 1947); Birmingham (SCM); Royal Coll. of Nursing, London (RNT). FHSM (FHA 1971); FRCN 1978. Admin. Sister, then Principal Sister Tutor, Prince of Wales' Gen. Hops., London, 1950–61; Internat. Council of Nurses, Geneva: Dir, Social and Econ. Welfare Div., 1961–66; Exec. Dir, 1967–70; Chief Nursing Officer, Southampton Univ. Hosps, 1970–74; Area Nursing Officer, Hampshire AHA (Teaching), 1974–78; Regional Nursing Officer, Wessex RHA, 1978–83. Pres., Standing Cttee of Nurses of EEC, 1983–; Member: Council, Royal Coll. of Nursing, 1971–79 (Chm. Council, 1974–79; Dep. Pres., 1980–82; Pres., 1982–86); Bd of Dirs, Internat. Council of Nurses, 1977–85 (first Vice-Pres., 1981–85); Mem., EEC Adv. Cttee on Trng in Nursing, 1978–. Hon. DSc (Social Sciences) Southampton, 1986. *Publications:* Nursing in The European Community, 1980; Caring for the Carers, 1981; articles, mainly on internat. nursing and EEC, in national and internat. jls. *Recreations:* boating, gardening. *Address:* Far Close, Wickham Lodge, Wickham, Fareham, Hants. *T:* Wickham 832942. *Club:* New Cavendish.

QUINTON, family name of **Baron Quinton.**

QUINTON, Baron *cr* 1982 (Life Peer), of Holywell in the City of Oxford and County of Oxfordshire; **Anthony Meredith Quinton,** FBA 1977; President of Trinity College, Oxford, 1978–Sept. 1987; Chairman of the Board, British Library, since 1985; *b* 25 March 1925; *s* of late Richard Frith Quinton, Surgeon Captain, RN, and late Gwenllyan Letitia Quinton; *m* 1952, Marcelle Wegier; one *s* one *d. Educ:* Stowe Sch.; Christ Church, Oxford (St Cyres Scholar; BA 1st Cl. Hons PPE 1948). Served War, RAF, 1943–46: flying officer and navigator. Fellow: All Souls Coll., Oxford, 1949–55; New Coll., Oxford, 1955–78. Delegate, OUP, 1970–76. Mem., Arts Council, 1979–81; Vice Pres., British Acad., 1985–. Vis. Professor: Swarthmore Coll., Pa, 1960; Stanford Univ., Calif, 1964; New Sch. for Social Res., New York, 1976–77. Lecturer: Dawes Hicks, British Acad., 1971; Gregynog, Univ. of Wales, Aberystwyth, 1973; T. S. Eliot, Univ. of Kent, Canterbury, 1976. Pres., Aristotelian Soc., 1975–76. Governor, Stowe Sch., 1963–84 (Chm. Governors, 1969–75); Fellow, Winchester Coll., 1970–85; Emeritus Fellow, New College, Oxford, 1980. Vice Chm., Bd of Editors, Encyclopaedia Britannica, 1985–. Order of Leopold II, Belgium. *Publications:* Political Philosophy (ed), 1967; The Nature of Things, 1973; Utilitarian Ethics, 1973; (trans.) K. Ajdukiewicz (with H. Skolimowski) Problems and Theories of Philosophy, 1973; The Politics of Imperfection, 1978; Francis Bacon, 1980; Thoughts and Thinkers, 1982. *Recreations:* sedentary pursuits. *Address:* (from Oct. 1987) President's Lodgings, Trinity College, Oxford. *T:* Oxford 242888; 22

St James's Square, SW1. *Clubs:* Garrick, Beefsteak, United Oxford & Cambridge University.

QUINTON, John Grand; Chairman: Barclays Bank UK, since 1985; Barclays Bank PLC, from May 1987 (Deputy Chairman, 1985–87); *b* 21 Dec. 1929; *s* of William Grand Quinton and Norah May (*née* Nunn); *m* 1954, Jean Margaret Chastney; one *s* one *d. Educ:* Norwich Sch.; St John's Coll., Cambridge (MA 1954); FIB 1964. Joined Barclays Bank, 1953: Asst Manager, Piccadilly, 1961; Dep. Principal, Staff Trng Centre, 1963; Manager, King's Cross, 1965; seconded to Min. of Health as Principal, Internat. Div. and UK Deleg., World Health Assembly, 1966; Asst Gen. Manager, 1968; Local Dir, Nottingham, 1969; Reg. Gen. Manager, 1971; Gen. Manager, 1975; Dir and Sen. Gen. Man., 1982–84; Vice-Chm., 1985. Dep. Chm., Mercantile Credit Co. Ltd, 1975–79. Chairman: Chief Exec. Officers, Cttee of London Clearing Bankers, 1982–83; Adv. Council, London Enterprise Agency, 1985–; Member: City Capital Markets Cttee, 1981–; NE Thames RHA, 1974–; Accounting Standards Cttee, 1982–85; Econ. and Financial Policy Cttee, CBI, 1985–. Chm., Motability Finance Ltd, 1978–85; Treasurer, Inst. of Bankers, 1980–; Hon. Treas. and Bd Mem., Business in the Community, 1986–. Governor, Motability, 1985–; Mem. Court of Governors, Royal Shakespeare Theatre, 1986–. *Recreations:* tennis, gardening, music, occasional golf. *Address:* Chenies Place, Chenies, Bucks. *T:* Chorleywood 2579. *Club:* Reform.

QUIRK, Prof. Sir (Charles) Randolph, Kt 1985; CBE 1976; FBA 1975; FIC; President, British Academy, since 1985; Fellow of University College London; *b* 12 July 1920; *s* of late Thomas and Amy Randolph Quirk, Lambfell, Isle of Man. *Educ:* Cronk y Voddy Sch.; Douglas High Sch., IOM; University College London. MA, PhD, DLit London; Fil.Dr Lund and Uppsala; DUP; DU Essex; DUniv Open; DHC Liège; DLitt Reading, Newcastle upon Tyne, Durham, Bath, Salford and Nijmegen; LLD Leicester. Served RAF, 1940–45. Lecturer in English, University College London, 1947–54; Commonwealth Fund Fellow, Yale Univ. and University of Michigan, 1951–52; Reader in English Language and Literature, University of Durham, 1954–58; Professor of English Language in the University of Durham, 1958–60, in the University of London, 1960–68; Quain Prof. of English Language and Literature, University Coll. London, 1968–81; Vice-Chancellor, Univ. of London, 1981–85. Dir, Survey of English Usage, 1959–. Member: Senate, Univ. of London, 1970–75 (Chm., Acad. Council, 1972–75); Ct, Univ. of London, 1972–75; Bd, British Council, 1983–; BBC Archives Cttee, 1975–; RADA Council, 1985–. Pres., Inst. of Linguists, 1982–85; Governor: British Inst. of Recorded Sound, 1975–80; E-SU, 1980–85; Amer. Internat. Coll. of London, 1981–. Chairman: Cttee of Enquiry into Speech Therapy Services, 1969–72; Hornby Educnl Trust, 1979–; Anglo-Spanish Foundn, 1983–85; British Library Adv. Cttee, 1984–. For. Fellow, Royal Belgian Acad. of Scis, 1975. Hon. FCST; Hon. FIL; Hon. Fellow, QMC, 1986. Jubilee Medal, Inst. of Linguists, 1973. *Publications:* The Concessive Relation in Old English Poetry, 1954; Studies in Communication (with A. J. Ayer and others), 1955; An Old English Grammar (with C. L. Wrenn), 1955, revised edn, 1958; Charles Dickens and Appropriate Language, 1959; The Teaching of English (with A. H. Smith), 1959, revised edn, 1964; The Study of the Mother-Tongue, 1961; The Use of English (with Supplements by A. C. Gimson and J. Warburg), 1962, enlarged edn, 1968; Prosodic and Paralinguistic Features in English (with D. Crystal), 1964; A Common Language (with A. H. Marckwardt), 1964; Investigating Linguistic Acceptability (with J. Svartvik), 1966; Essays on the English Language—Mediaeval and Modern, 1968; (with S. Greenbaum) Elicitation Experiments in English, 1970; (with S. Greenbaum, G. Leech, J. Svartvik) A Grammar of Contemporary English, 1972; The English Language and Images of Matter, 1972; (with S. Greenbaum) A University Grammar of English, 1973; The Linguist and the English Language, 1974; (with V. Adams, D. Davy) Old English Literature: a practical introduction, 1975; (with J. Svartvik) A Corpus of English Conversation, 1980; Style and Communication in the English Language, 1982; (with S. Greenbaum, G. Leech, J. Svartvik) A Comprehensive Grammar of the English Language, 1985; (with H. Widdowson) English in the World, 1985; Words at Work: lectures on textual structure, 1986; contrib. to: Proc. 8th Internat. Congress of Linguists, 1958; Language and Society (Festschrift for Arthur M. Jensen), 1961; Proc. 9th International Congress of Linguists, 1962; English Teaching Abroad and the British Universities (ed G. Bullough), 1961; Dictionaries and that Dictionary (ed J. H. Sledd and W. R. Ebbitt), 1962; World Book Encyclopædia Dictionary (ed C. L. Barnhart), 1963; Early English and Norse Studies (Festschrift for A. H. Smith), 1963; (ed Lady Birkenhead) Essays by Divers Hands, 1969; Essays and Studies, 1970; Charles Dickens (ed S. Wall), 1970; A New Companion to Shakespeare Studies, 1971; Linguistics at Large, 1971; The Crown and the Thistle, 1979; The State of the Language, 1980; papers in linguistic and literary journals. *Address:* University College London, Gower Street, WC1E 6BT. *Club:* Athenæum.

QUIRK, John Stanton S.; *see* Shirley-Quirk.

QVIST, Dame Frances; *see* Gardner, Dame Frances.

R

RABBI, The Chief; *see* Jakobovits, Rabbi Sir Immanuel.

RABI, Prof. Isidor Isaac, PhD; University Professor Emeritus, Columbia University, NY; Member: Naval Research Advisory Committee, since 1952; (US Member) Science Committee of United Nations, since 1954; (US Member) Science Committee of NATO, since 1958; General Advisory Committee, Arms Control and Disarmament Agency since 1962; Consultant: to General Advisory Committee, Atomic Energy Commission, since 1956 (Chairman, 1952–56, Member, since 1946); to Department of State, since 1958; etc; *b* Rymanov, Austria, 29 July 1898; *s* of David and Scheindel Rabi; *m* Helen Newmark; two *d. Educ:* Cornell University (BChem 1919); Columbia University (PhD, 1927). Lecturer, Physics, Columbia University, New York, 1929; then various posts, there, 1930–50, when Higgins Professor of Physics until 1964, University Professor, 1964–67. Associate Director, Radiation Laboratory, Massachusetts Institute of Technology, Cambridge, Mass, 1940–45. Mem., National Academy of Sciences; Fellow, American Physics Soc. (Pres., 1950–51). Holds numerous honorary doctorates; awarded medals and prizes, 1939 onwards, including: Nobel prize in physics, 1944; Atoms for Peace Award (jointly), 1967; Franklin Delano Roosevelt Freedom Medal, 1985; Vannevar Bush Award, 1986. *Publications:* My Life and Times as a Physicist, 1960; communications to The Physical Review, 1927–; contrib. to scientific jls on magnetism, quantum mechanics, nuclear physics, and molecular beams. *Recreations:* the theatre, travel, walking. *Address:* 450 Riverside Drive, New York City, NY 10027, USA. *Clubs:* Athenæum (London); Cosmos (Washington); Century Association (New York).

RABIN, Prof. Brian Robert; Professor of Biochemistry and Head of Department of Biochemistry, since 1970, Fellow since 1984, University College, London; *b* 4 Nov. 1927; *s* of Emanuel and Sophia Rabin, both British; *m* 1954; one *s* one *d. Educ:* Latymer Sch., Edmonton; University Coll., London. BSc 1951, MSc 1952, PhD 1956. University College, London: Asst Lectr, 1954–57; Lectr, 1957–63; Reader, 1963–67; Prof. of Enzymology, 1967–70. Rockefeller Fellow, Univ. of California, 1956–57. Founder Dir, London Biotechnology Ltd, 1985–. *Publications:* numerous in Biochem. Jl, European Jl of Biochem., Nature, Proc. Nat. Acad. Sciences US, etc. *Recreations:* travel, listening to music, carpentry. *Address:* 34 Grangewood, Potters Bar, Herts. *T:* Potters Bar 54576. *Club:* Athenæum.

RABINOWITZ, Harry, MBE 1977; freelance conductor and composer; *b* 26 March 1916; *s* of Israel and Eva Rabinowitz; *m* 1944, Lorna Thurlow Anderson; one *s* two *d. Educ:* Athlone High Sch., S Africa; Witwatersrand Univ.; Guildhall Sch. of Music. Conductor, BBC Radio, 1953–60; Musical Dir, BBC TV Light Entertainment, 1960–68; Head of Music, LWT, 1968–77; freelance film, TV, radio and disc activities, 1977–. Conductor: Cats, New London Th., 1981; Song and Dance, Palace Th., 1982; Hollywood Bowl Concerts, 1983 and 1984; Boston "Pops" concerts, 1985 and 1986; concerts with RPO, LSO and London Concert Orch.; *films:* conductor: La Dentellière, 1977; Mon Oncle d'Amérique, 1980; The Time Bandits, 1980; Chariots of Fire, 1981; Heat and Dust, 1982; The Missionary, 1983; Electric Dreams (actor/conductor), 1984; The Bostonians, 1984; Return to Oz, Lady Jane Grey, and Revolution—1776, 1985; F/x, and Manhattan Project, 1986; *television:* composer-conductor: Agatha Christie Hour, 1982; Reilly Ace of Spies, 1983; Glorious Day, 1985; conductor: Dizzy Feet, 1982 (Montreux Fest. First Prize); Nicholas Nickleby, 1982; Top Cs and Tiaras, 1984; Julia Migenes Sings, Theme Dreams, Zastrozzi, and Absent Friends, 1985; TV specials, Dickie Henderson Memorial, Julia McKenzie and Friends, and the Paul Nicholas Show, 1986. *Recreations:* listening to others making music, gathering edible fungi, wine tasting. *Address:* Hope End, Holmbury St Mary, Dorking, Surrey RH5 6PE. *T:* Dorking 730605.

RABORN, Vice-Adm. William Francis, Jr, DSM 1960; President, W. F. Raborn Company Inc., McLean, Virginia, since 1966; Director: Curtiss Wright Corporation; Avemco; E-Sys Inc.; S.A.I. Corporation; Wackenhut Corporation; *b* Decatur, Texas, 8 June 1905; *s* of William Francis, Sr, and Mrs Cornelia V. Raborn (*née* Moore); *m* 1955, Mildred T. Terrill; one *s* one *d. Educ:* US Naval Acad., Annapolis, Md (BS); Naval War Coll., Newport, RI. Ensign, USN, 1928; Naval Aviator, 1934; Sea duty, 1928–40; Aviation Gunnery Sch., 1940–42; Exec. Off., USS Hancock, 1943–45; Chief Staff Comdr Task Force 77, W Pacific, 1945–47; Ops Off. Comdr for Air W Coast, 1947–49; R & D Guided Missiles, 1949–50; Guided Missile Div., Office of Naval Ops, 1952–54; CO, USS Bennington, 1954–55; Asst Chief of Staff to C-in-C, Atlantic Fleet, 1955; Dir, Office of Special Projects, Polaris program, 1955; Dep. Chief, Naval Ops (Develt), 1962; retd from USN, 1963; Vice-Pres., Program management Aerojet Gen. Corp., Azusa, Calif, 1963–65; Director of Central Intelligence, USA, 1965–66; Industrial Consultant, Aerojet Gen. Corp. Silver Star, 1945; Bronze Star Medal, 1951; Commendation Medal, 1954; National Security Medal, 1966. *Address:* (home and business) 1606 Crestwood Lane, McLean, Virginia 22101, USA. *Clubs:* Army-Navy, Metropolitan (Washington, DC); Burning Tree (Bethesda, Md); Fair Oaks Golf and Country (San Antonio, Texas).

RABUKAWAQA, Sir Josua Rasilau, KBE 1977 (CBE 1974; MBE 1968); MVO 1970; Ambassador-at-Large for Fiji and Chief of Protocol, Fiji, 1977–80; *b* 2 Dec. 1917; *s* of Dr Aisea Rasilau and Adi Mereoni Dimaicakau, Bau, Fiji; *m* 1944, Mei Tolanivutu; three *s* two *d. Educ:* Suva Methodist Boys' Sch.; Queen Victoria Sch.; Teachers' Trng Coll., Auckland. Diploma in Public and Social Admin. 1958. Teaching in schools throughout Fiji, 1938–52; Co-operatives Inspector, 1952. Joined Fiji Mil. Forces, 1953; attached Gloucester Regt at Warminster Sch. of Infantry and Support Weapons Wing, Netheravon; comd Mortar Platoon, Malaya, 1954–55. Subseq. Econ. Develt Officer, Fiji, 1957; District Officer, Fiji Admin. Service, 1961; Comr, Central Div., 1968. MLC, Fiji, 1964–66; Delegate, Constitutional Conf., London, 1965; (first) High Comr for Fiji in London, 1970–76. Active worker for Scouts, Red Cross and Methodist Church Choir. Formed Phoenix Choir. Compiled manual of singing in Fijian language, 1956, and guide for Fijian pronunciation for use by Fiji Broadcasting Commn, 1967; Chm., Fijian Adv. Cttee of Fiji Broadcasting Commn, 1965–70; Chm. Bd of Examrs for High Standard Fijian and Interpreters Exams, 1965–70; Mem., Housing Authority; Mem., Educn Adv. Council. *Recreations:* cricket, Rugby football (toured NZ as player/manager for Fiji, 1967). *Address:* 6 Vunivivi Hill, Nausori, Fiji. *Clubs:* Royal Commonwealth Society; Defence, Union (Fiji).

RABY, Sir Victor Harry, KBE 1956; CB 1948; MC; Deputy Under-Secretary of State, Department of the Permanent Under-Secretary of State for Air, 1946–57, retired December 1957; *b* 1897; *s* of Harry Raby, Menheniot, Cornwall; *m* 1921, Dorothy Alys, *d* of Rodney Buzzard, Ditchling, Sussex; one *s. Educ:* Grey College, Bloemfontein, S Africa. Served European War, 1914–19, with London Regt (MC). *Address:* New Way, Forder Lane, Bishopsteignton, Devon.

RACE, (Denys Alan) Reg; Special Research Officer, Association of Cinematograph, Television and Allied Technicians, 1986; *b* 23 June 1947; *s* of Denys and Elsie Race. *Educ:* Sale Grammar School; Univ. of Kent. BA (Politics and Sociology), PhD (Politics). Senior Research Officer, National Union of Public Employees, 1972. MP (Lab) Haringey, Wood Green, 1979–83; Head of Programme Office, GLC, 1983–86. *Publications:* numerous pamphlets and articles in Labour Movement press.

RACE, Ruth Ann; *see* Sanger, Dr R. A.

RACE, Steve, (Stephen Russell Race); broadcaster, musician and author; *b* Lincoln, 1 April 1921; *s* of Russell Tinniswood Race and Robina Race (*née* Hurley); *m* 1st, Marjorie Clair Leng (*d* 1969); one *d*; 2nd, Léonie Rebecca Govier Mather. *Educ:* Lincoln Sch. (now Christ's Hospital Sch.); Royal Academy of Music. FRAM 1978. Served War, RAF, 1941–46; free-lance pianist, arranger and composer, 1946–55; Light Music Adviser to Associated-Rediffusion Ltd, 1955–60; conductor for many TV series incl. Tony Hancock and Peter Sellers Shows. Appearances in radio and TV shows include: My Music, A Good Read, Jazz in Perspective, Any Questions?, Music Now, Music Weekly, Kaleidoscope, Look What they've done to my Song, Jazz Revisited, With Great Pleasure, Desert Island Discs; radio reviews in The Listener, 1975–80; long-playing records and commentary for Nat. Gall., London, Glasgow Art Gall. and Nat. Mus. of Wales, 1977–80. Member: Council, Royal Albert Hall of Arts and Scis, 1976–; Exec. Council, Musicians' Benevolent Fund, 1985–. FRSA 1975. Governor of Tokyo Metropolis Prize for Radio, 1979. Founder Mem., SDP. *Principal compositions:* Nicola (Ivor Novello Award); Faraway Music; The Pied Piper; incidental music for Richard The Third, Cyrano de Bergerac, Twelfth Night (BBC); Cantatas: Song of King David; The Day of the Donkey; Song of Praise; misc. works incl. ITV advertising sound-tracks (Venice Award, 1962; Cannes Award, 1963); film scores include: Calling Paul Temple, Three Roads to Rome, Against The Tide, Land of Three Rivers. *Publications:* Musician at Large: an autobiography, 1979; My Music, 1979; Dear Music Lover, 1981; Steve Race's Music Quiz, 1983; The Illustrated Counties of England, 1984; You Can't be Serious, 1985; The Penguin Masterquiz, 1985. *Recreations:* reading about the past, looking at paintings, the open air. *Address:* Martins End Lane, Great Missenden, Bucks HP16 9HS.

RACZYNSKI, Count Edward, Dr Juris; Chairman, Polish Cultural Foundation, since 1970; Hon. President, The Polish Institute and Sikorski Museum, since 1977 (Chairman, 1966–77); Polish President-in-exile, 1979–86; *b* 19 Dec. 1891; *s* of Count Edouard Raczynski and Countess Rose Potocka; *m* 1st, 1925, Joyous (*d* 1930), *d* of Sir Arthur Basil Markham, 1st Bt, and Lucy, CBE, *d* of Captain A. B. Cunningham, late RA; 2nd, 1932, Cecile (*d* 1962), *d* of Edward Jaroszynski and Wanda Countess Sierakowska; three *d. Educ:* Universities of Krakow and Leipzig; London School of Economics and Political Science. Entered Polish Ministry of Foreign Affairs, 1919; served in Copenhagen, London, and Warsaw; Delegate to Disarmament Conference, Geneva, 1932–34; Polish Minister accredited to the League of Nations, 1932–34; Polish Ambassador to the Court of St James's, 1934–45; Acting Polish Minister for Foreign Affairs, 1941–42; Minister of State in charge of Foreign Affairs, Cabinet of Gen. Sikorski, 1942–43; Chief Polish Rep. on Interim Treasury Cttee for Polish Questions, 1945–47; Hon. Chief Polish Adviser, Ministry of Labour and National Service, 1952–Dec. 1956; Chairman: Polish Research Centre, London, 1940–67. Grand Officier of the Order of Polonia Restituta, Order of White Eagle, Poland, Grand Cross of the Crown of Rumania, etc. *Publications:* In Allied London: Diary 1939–45 (in Polish); In Allied London: (Wartime Diaries), (in English), 1963; Rogalin and its Inhabitants (in Polish), 1963; Pani Róża (in Polish), 1969; Book of Verse (in Polish), 1960; Memoirs of Viridianne Fiszer (translated from French to Polish), 1975; From Narcyz Kulikowski to Winston Churchill (in Polish), 1976. *Recreations:* tennis, golf, skating, ski-ing. *Address:* 8 Lennox Gardens, SW1; 5 Krakowskie Przedmieście, Warsaw, Poland.

RADCLIFFE, Anthony Frank; Keeper of Sculpture, Victoria and Albert Museum, since 1979; *b* Wivenhoe, Essex, 23 Feb. 1933; *s* of Dr Walter Radcliffe and Muriel Laure Radcliffe (*née* Brée); *m* 1960, Enid Clair Cawkwell; two *s. Educ:* Oundle Sch.; Gonville and Caius Coll., Cambridge (MA). Victoria and Albert Museum: joined Dept of Circulation, 1958; transferred to Dept of Architecture and Sculpture, 1960; Res. Asst, Dept of Circulation, 1961–67; Personal Asst to Dir, 1967–74; Asst Keeper, Dept of Architecture and Sculpture, 1974–79. *Publications:* European Bronze Statuettes, 1966; Jean-Baptiste Carpeaux, 1968; (with J. Pope-Hennessy and T. Hodgkinson) The Frick Collection: an illustrated catalogue, III, IV, 1970; (with C. Avery) Giambologna, sculptor to the Medici, 1978; contribs to Burlington Mag., Apollo, Connoisseur, etc. *Address:* 5 Kennylands Road, Sonning Common, Reading RG4 9JR. *T:* Kidmore End 722182.

RADCLIFFE, Francis Charles Joseph; *b* 23 Oct. 1939; *s* of Charles Joseph Basil Nicholas Radcliffe and Norah Radcliffe (*née* Percy); *m* 1968, Nicolette, *e d* of Eugene Randag; one *s* two *d. Educ:* Ampleforth Coll.; Gonville and Caius Coll., Cambridge (MA). Called to the Bar, Gray's Inn, 1962; a Recorder of the Crown Court, 1979. Mem., Assoc. of Lawyers for the Defence of the Unborn. Contested (Christian: stop abortion candidate) York, 1979; founded York Christian Party, 1981. *Recreations:* shooting, beagling, gardening, etc. *Address:* 11 King's Bench Walk, Temple, EC4Y 7EQ.

RADCLIFFE, Hugh John Reginald Joseph, MBE 1944; Chairman, Dun and Bradstreet Ltd, 1974–76; *b* 3 March 1911; 2nd *s* of Sir Everard Radcliffe, 5th Bt; *m* 1937, Marie Therese, *d* of late Maj.-Gen. Sir Cecil Pereira, KCB, CMG; five *s* one *d. Educ:* Downside. Dep. Chm., London Stock Exchange, 1967–70. Kt Comdr St Silvester (Papal), 1965; Kt of St Gregory (Papal), 1984. *Address:* The White House, Stoke, Andover, Hants.
See also Sir S. E. Radcliffe, Bt.

RADCLIFFE, Percy, CBE 1985; farmer; Chairman, Isle of Man Government Executive Council (Manx Cabinet), 1981–85; *b* 14 Nov. 1916; *s* of Arthur and Annie Radcliffe; *m* 1942, Barbara Frances Crowe; two *s* one *d. Educ:* Ramsey Grammar Sch., Isle of Man. Member (Ind.) Isle of Man Govt, 1963, re-elected 1966, 1971, 1976; elected by House of Keys to be Mem. Legislative Council, 1980; Chairman: IoM Local Govt Board, 1966–76; Finance Board, 1976–81; elected by Tynwald (Govt of IoM) first Chm. of Manx Cabinet, 1981. Member: Isle of Man Agricultural Marketing Soc., 1945–75; British Horse Driving Soc., 1979–. Silver Jubilee Medal, 1977. *Address:* Kellaway, Sulby, Isle of Man. *T:* Sulby 7257.

RADCLIFFE, Sir Sebastian Everard, 7th Bt *cr* 1813; *b* 8 June 1972; *s* of Sir Joseph Benedict Everard Henry Radcliffe, 6th Bt, MC and of Marcia Anne Helen, *y d* of Major David Turville Constable Maxwell, Bosworth Hall, Husbands Bosworth, Rugby; *S* father, 1975. *Heir: uncle* Hugh John Reginald Joseph Radcliffe, *qv. Address:* Le Château de Cheseaux, 1033 Cheseaux, Vaud, Switzerland.

RADCLYFFE, Sir Charles Edward M.; *see* Mott-Radclyffe.

RADDA, Prof. George K., MA, DPhil; FRS 1980; British Heart Foundation Professor of Molecular Cardiology, University of Oxford, since 1984; Professorial Fellow, Merton College, Oxford, since 1984; *b* 9 June 1936; *s* of Dr Gyula Radda and Dr Anna Bernolak; *m* 1961, Mary O'Brien; two *s* one *d. Educ:* Pannonhalma, Hungary; Eötvös Univ., Budapest, Hungary; Merton Coll., Oxford (BA Cl. 1, Chem., 1960; DPhil 1962). Res. Associate, Univ. of California, 1962–63; Lectr in Organic Chemistry, St John's Coll., Oxford, 1963–64; Fellow and Tutor in Organic Chem., Merton Coll., Oxford, 1964–84; University Lectr in Biochem., Oxford Univ., 1966–84. Mem., various Editorial Bds of scientific jls including: Editor, Biochemical and Biophysical Research Communications, 1977–; Man. Editor, Biochimica et Biophysica Acta, 1977–. Founder Mem., Oxford Enzyme Gp, 1970–; Pres., Soc. for Magnetic Resonance in Medicine, 1985–86. Hon. FRCR 1985. Hon. DM Bern, 1985. Colworth Medal, Biochem. Soc., 1969; Feldberg Prize, Feldberg Foundn, 1982; British Heart Foundn Prize and Gold Medal for cardiovascular research, 1982; CIBA Medal and Prize, Biochem. Soc., 1983; Gold Medal, Soc. for Magnetic Resonance in Medicine, 1984. *Publications:* articles in books and in jls of biochemistry and medicine. *Recreations:* opera, swimming, jazz. *Address:* Merton College, Oxford. *T:* Oxford 249651.

RADFORD, (Courtenay Arthur) Ralegh, FBA 1956; *b* 7 Nov. 1900; *o s* of late Arthur Lock and Ada M. Radford; unmarried. *Educ:* St George's School, Harpenden; Exeter College, Oxford. BA 1921; MA 1937; Inspector of Ancient Monuments in Wales and Monmouthshire, 1929–34; Director of the British School at Rome, 1936–39; Member of Royal Commission on Ancient Monuments in Wales and Monmouthshire, 1935–46; Member of Royal Commission on Historical Monuments (England), 1953–76; supervised excavations at Tintagel, Ditchley, Castle Dore, the Hurlers, Whithorn, Glastonbury, Birsay and elsewhere; FSA 1928 (Vice-Pres. 1954–58; Gold Medal, 1972); FRHistS 1930; President: Prehistoric Soc., 1954–58; Roy. Archæological Inst., 1960–63; Cambrian Archæological Assoc., 1961; Soc. of Medieval Archæology, 1969–71. Hon. DLitt Glasgow, 1963; Univ. of Wales, 1963; Exeter, 1973; *Publications:* Reports on the Excavations at Tintagel, Ditchley, Whithorn, etc.; various articles on archæological subjects. *Address:* Culmcott, Uffculme, Devon EX15 3AT. *Club:* Athenæum.

RADFORD, Joseph; Public Trustee, 1978–80; *b* 7 April 1918; *s* of Thomas Radford and Elizabeth Ann Radford (*née* Sanders); *m* 1976, Rosemary Ellen Murphy. *Educ:* Herbert Strutt, Belper; Nottingham Univ. Admitted solicitor, 1940. First Cl. Hons, Law Soc. Intermediate, 1937; Dist., Law Soc. Final, 1940. Served War, 1940–47, RA; 41st (5th North Staffordshire) RA; 1st Maritime Regt, RA; Staff, MELF (Major). Joined Public Trustee Office, 1949; Chief Admin. Officer, 1973–75; Asst Public Trustee, 1975–78. Mem., Law Soc., 1945– (Hon. Auditor, 1963–65). Freeman, City of London, 1983. Silver Jubilee Medal, 1977. *Address:* 80 Cunningham Park, Harrow, Mddx HA1 4QJ.

RADFORD, Ralegh; *see* Radford, C. A. R.

RADFORD, Robert Edwin, CB 1979; Assistant Director General, St John Ambulance Association, 1981–84; Deputy Secretary and Principal Finance Officer, Department of Health and Social Security, 1977–81; *b* 1 April 1921; *s* of late Richard James Radford and late May Eleanor Radford (*née* Briant); *m* 1945, Eleanor Margaret, *d* of late John Idwal Jones; one *s* one *d. Educ:* Royal Grammar Sch., Guildford. Board of Educn, 1938. Served War, Lieut, RNVR, 1940–46. Colonial Office: Asst Principal, 1947; Private Sec. to Permanent Under-Sec. of State for the Colonies, 1950–51; Principal, 1951; First Sec., UK Commn, Singapore, 1961–63; Asst Sec., Dept of Techn. Co-op., 1963; transferred to ODM, 1964; Counsellor, British Embassy, Washington, and UK Alternate Exec. Dir, IBRD, 1965–67; Under Secretary: FCO (ODA), 1973; DHSS, 1974–76. Mem., SW Surrey HA, 1982–. *Recreations:* walking, reading. *Address:* Highfield, Nether Mount, Guildford, Surrey GU2 5LL. *T:* Guildford 61822.

RADFORD, Sir Ronald (Walter), KCB 1976 (CB 1971); MBE 1947; Hon. Secretary-General, Customs Co-operation Council, since 1983 (Secretary-General, 1978–83); *b* 28 Feb. 1916; *er s* of late George Leonard Radford and Ethel Mary Radford; *m* 1949, Jean Alison Dunlop Strange; one *s* one *d. Educ:* Southend-on-Sea High Sch.; St John's Coll., Cambridge (Schol., Wrangler, MA). Joined ICS, 1939; Dist Magistrate and Collector, Shahabad, Bihar, 1945; on leave, prep. to retirement from ICS, 1947; Admin. Class, Home CS, and posted to HM Customs and Excise, 1947; Asst Sec., 1953; Comr, 1965; Dep. Chm., 1970; Chm., 1973–77. Mem. Management Cttee, RNLI, 1977– (Vice-Chm., 1986–). *Address:* 4 Thomas Close, Brentwood, Essex CM15 8BS. *T:* Brentwood 211567. *Clubs:* Reform, Civil Service, City Livery; MCC.

RADICE, Edward Albert, CBE 1946; *b* 2 Jan. 1907; *s* of C. A. Radice, ICS and Alice Effie (*née* Murray), DSc (Econ); *m* 1936, Joan Keeling; one *s* one *d. Educ:* Winchester Coll.; Magdalen Coll., Oxford (1st in Maths Mods; 1st in Lit. Hum.; DPhil). Commonwealth Fund Fellow, Columbia Univ., New York, 1933–35; Assistant Professor of Economics, Wesleyan University, Middletown, Conn., 1937–39; League of Nations Secretariat, 1939; Ministry of Economic Warfare, 1940–44; HM Foreign Service, 1945–53; Min. of Defence, 1953–70 (Dir of Economic Intelligence, 1966–70); Senior Research Fellow, St Antony's Coll., Oxford, 1970–73. *Publications:* (jt) An American Experiment, 1936; Fundamental Issues in the United States, 1936; Savings in Great Britain, 1922–35, 1939; (contrib.) Communist Power in Europe 1944–1949, 1977; (jtly, also co-ed) The Economic History of Eastern Europe 1919–1975, Vols I and II, 1986; papers in Econometrica, Oxford Economic Papers, Economic History Review. *Address:* 2 Talbot Road, Oxford. *T:* Oxford 515573.
See also I. de L. Radice.

RADICE, Fulke Rosavo, CBE 1959; MA; late Vice-Director International Bureau of Universal Postal Union (1946–58); *b* Naples, 8 Feb. 1888; British subject; *s* of Albert Hampden Radice, Thistleborough, NI and Adelaide Anna Teresa (*née* Visetti); *m* 1917, Katharine Stella Mary Speck (*d* 1974) *d* of late Canon J. H. Speck and Mrs Speck (*née* Dalrymple); two *s* (and one *s* killed fighting in French Maquis, 1944). *Educ:* Bedford School (Scholar); Brasenose Coll., Oxford (open scholarship in History; 2nd Cl. Hons Mods (classical), 1909; 1st Cl. Mod. History, 1911). Home Civil Service, 1911; Secretary's Office, Gen. Post Office, 1911–46. Head of Brit. Secretariat of Universal Postal Union Congress, 1929, Head of Congress Secretariat at UPU Congresses, 1947, 1952, 1957. Served European War, 1914–18, in France, Salonica, Egypt, Italy; War of 1939–45 in Home Guard. *Publications:* The Radice Family, 1979; Rootlings, 1982; articles in Nineteenth Century and After, and in History. *Recreations:* rifle shooting (Oxford half blue, Oxford long range; English XX, 1909, 1910; King's Prize at Bisley, gold and silver medals, 1910; record score); Rugby football; ski-ing; freemasonry; historical studies. *Address:* 32 Jersey Avenue, Cheltenham, Glos GL52 2SZ; c/o Coutts & Co., 440 Strand, WC2.

RADICE, Giles Heneage; MP (Lab) Durham North, since 1983 (Chester-le-Street, March 1973–1983); *b* 4 Oct. 1936. *Educ:* Magdalen Coll., Oxford. Head of Research Dept, General and Municipal Workers' Union (GMWU), 1966–73. Front Bench Spokesman on foreign affairs, 1981, on employment, 1981–83, on education, 1983–. Member: Council, Policy Studies Inst., 1978–83; Exec., Fabian Soc. *Publications:* Democratic Socialism, 1965; (ed jointly) More Power to People, 1968; (co-author) Will Thorne, 1974; The Industrial Democrats, 1978. *Recreations:* reading, tennis. *Address:* 58A Dartmouth Park Road, NW5.

RADICE, Italo de Lisle, CB 1969; Appointed Member, Royal Patriotic Fund Corporation, since 1969; *b* 2 March 1911; *s* of Charles Albert Radice, ICS, and Alice Effie (*née* Murray); *m* 1935, Betty Dawson (*d* 1985); three *s* (and one *d* decd). *Educ:* Blundell's School; Magdalen College, Oxford (demy). Admitted Solicitor, 1938; Public Trustee Office, 1939; Military Government East and North Africa, Italy, and Germany, 1941–46; Treasury, 1946, Under-Secretary, 1961–68; Sec. and Comptroller General, Nat. Debt Office, 1969–76. Dir, Central Trustee Savings Bank Ltd, 1976–80. Comr for Income Tax, City of London, 1972–86. Cavaliere Ufficiale dell'Ordine al Merito (Italy), 1981. *Address:* 2 Fitzroy Road, NW1 8TX. *T:* 01–586 4856; Old Post Office, Berrick Salome, Oxford. *T:* Stadhampton 891100.
See also E. A. Radice.

RADJI, Parviz Camran; diplomat; Ambassador of Iran to the Court of St James's, 1976–79; *b* 1936; *m* 1986, Golgoun Goli Partovi. *Educ:* Trinity Hall, Cambridge (MA Econs). National Iranian Oil Co., 1959–62; Private Sec. to Minister of Foreign Affairs, 1962–65; Private Sec. to Prime Minister, subseq. Personal Asst, 1965–72; Special Adviser to Prime Minister, 1972–76. *Publication:* In the Service of the Peacock Throne: the diaries of the Shah's last Ambassador to London, 1983. *Address:* 20 Holland Park Road, W14.

RADLEY-SMITH, Eric John, MS; FRCS; Surgeon: Royal Free Hospital, London; Brentford Hospital; Epsom Hospital; Neurosurgeon, Royal National Throat, Nose and Ear Hospital. *Educ:* Paston; King's College, London; King's College Hospital. MB, BS (Hons, Distinction in Medicine, Surgery, Forensic Medicine and Hygiene), 1933; MS, London, 1936; LRCP, 1933; FRCS 1935 (MRCS 1933). Served War of 1939–45, Wing Comdr i/c Surgical Div. RAFVR. Formerly: Surgical Registrar, King's Coll. Hosp.; House Surgeon, National Hosp. for Nervous Diseases, Queen Square. Examnr in Surgery, Univs of London and West Indies. Mem. Court, RCS. Mem. Assoc. of British Neurosurgeons; Fellow, Assoc. of Surgeons of Great Britain. *Publications:* papers in medical journals. *Recreations:* football and farming.

RADNOR, 8th Earl of, *cr* 1765; **Jacob Pleydell-Bouverie;** Bt 1713–14; Viscount Folkestone, Baron Longford, 1747; Baron Pleydell-Bouverie, 1765; *b* 10 Nov. 1927; *e s* of 7th Earl of Radnor, KG, KCVO, and Helen Olivia, *d* of late Charles R. W. Adeane, CB; *S* father, 1968; *m* 1st, 1953, Anne (marr. diss. 1962), *d* of Donald Seth-Smith, Njoro, Kenya and Whitsbury Cross, near Fordingbridge, Hants; two *s*; 2nd, 1963, Margaret Robin (marr. diss. 1985), *d* of late Robin Fleming, Catter House, Drymen; four *d*; *m* 1986, Mrs A. C. Pettit. *Educ:* Harrow; Trinity Coll., Cambridge (BA Agriculture). *Heir: s* Viscount Folkestone, *qv. Address:* Longford Castle, Salisbury, Wilts. *T:* Salisbury 29732.

RADO, Prof. Richard, FRS 1978; Professor of Pure Mathematics, University of Reading, 1954–71, Emeritus since 1971; Canadian Commonwealth Fellow, University of Waterloo, Ontario, 1971–72; *b* 28 April 1906; 2nd *s* of Leopold Rado, Berlin; *m* 1933, Luise, *e d* of Hermann Zadek, Berlin; one *s. Educ:* University of Berlin (DPhil); University of Göttingen; University of Cambridge (PhD). Lecturer, Sheffield Univ., 1936–47; Reader, King's College, Univ. of London, 1947–54. Vis. Prof., Calgary, Alberta, 1973. London Mathematical Society: Mem. of Council, 1948–57; Hon. Sec., 1953–54; Vice-President, 1954–56. Chm., British Combinatorial Cttee, 1977–83. Richard Rado Lecture instituted at British Combinatorial Conf., 1985. FIMA. Dr rer. nat. *hc* Freie Univ., Berlin, 1981; Hon. DMath Univ. of Waterloo, Canada, 1986. Sen. Berwick Prize, London Mathematical Soc., 1972. *Publications:* (with P. Erdös, A. Hajnal and A. Máté) Combinatorial Set Theory: partition relations for cardinals, 1984; articles in various journals on topics in pure mathematics; Mem. Editorial Bds of *Aequationes mathematicae*, Discrete Mathematics, Jl Combinatorial Theory, Combinatorica, Graphs and Combinatorics (Asian Jl); *relevant publication:* Festschrift: Studies in Pure Mathematics, ed Prof. L. Mirsky, 1971. *Recreations:* music, reading, walking. *Address:* 14 Glebe Road, Reading RG2 7AG. *T:* 871281.

RADZINOWICZ, Sir Leon, Kt 1970; MA, LLD; FBA 1973; Fellow of Trinity College, Cambridge, since 1948; Wolfson Professor of Criminology, University of Cambridge, 1959–73, and Director of the Institute of Criminology, 1960–72; Associate Fellow, Silliman College, Yale, since 1966; Adjunct Professor of Law and Criminology, Columbia Law School, since 1966; *b* Poland, 15 Aug. 1906; *m* 1st, 1933, Irene Szereszewski (marr. diss., 1955); 2nd, 1958, Mary Ann (marr. diss. 1979), *d* of Gen. Nevins, Gettysburg, Pa, USA; one *s* one *d*; 3rd, 1979, Isolde Klarmann, *d* of late Prof. Emil and Elfriede Doernenburg, and widow of Prof. Adolph Klarmann, Philadelphia; naturalised British subject, 1947. *Educ:* Warsaw, Paris, Geneva and Rome. University of Paris, 1924–25;

Licencié en Droit, Univ. of Geneva, 1927; Doctor of Law, Rome, 1928; LLD Cambridge, 1951. Lectr, Univ. of Geneva, 1928–31; Doctor of Law, Cracow, 1929; Reported on working of penal system in Belgium, 1930; Lectr, Free Univ. of Warsaw, 1932, and Asst Prof., 1936. Came to England on behalf of Polish Ministry of Justice to report on working of English penal system, 1938; Asst Dir of Research, Univ. of Cambridge, 1946–49; Dir, Dept of Criminal Science, Univ. of Cambridge, 1949–59; Walter E. Meyer Research Prof. of Law, Yale Law Sch., 1962–63; Distinguished Prof. of Criminal Justice, John Jay Coll. of Criminal Justice, City of NY Univ., 1978–79; Vis. Prof. and Carpentier Lectr, Columbia Law Sch.; Dist. Prof. of Criminology, Rutgers Univ., 1970; Dist. Prof., Minnesota Law Sch., 1977; Visiting Professor: Virginia Law School, 1968–; Univ. of Pennsylvania, 1970–73; (also Consultant) Inst. of Criminology, UCT, 1972; Benjamin Cardozo Law Sch., Yeshiva Univ., 1979; Lionel Cohen Lectr, Univ. of Jerusalem, 1969; Visitor, Princeton Inst. for Advanced Study, 1975; Overseer, Pennsylvania Law Sch. and Associate Trustee, Pennsylvania Univ., 1978–82. Mem., Conseil de Direction de l'Assoc. Intern. de Droit Pénal, Paris, 1947–; Vice-Pres. Internat. Soc. of Social Defence, 1956–; Head of Social Defence Section, UN, New York, 1947–48. Member: Roy. Commn on Capital Punishment, 1949–53; Advisory Council on the Treatment of Offenders, Home Office, 1950–63; Adv. Council on the Penal System, Home Office, 1966–74; Jt Chm., Second UN Congress on Crime, 1955; Chief Rapporteur, 4th UN Congress on Crime, Kyoto, 1970; Chm. Sub-Cttee on Maximum Security in Prisons, 1967–68; Mem. Advisory Coun. on the Penal System, 1966–; first Pres., Brit. Acad. of Forensic Sciences, 1960–61, Vice-Pres., 1961–; First Chm. Council of Europe Sci. Cttee, Problems of Crime, 1963–70; Mem. Royal Commn on Penal System in Eng. and Wales, 1964–66; Consultant: Ford Foundn and Bar Assoc., NYC, on teaching and res. in criminol., 1964–65; President's Nat. Commn on Violence, Washington, 1968–69; Min. of Justice, NSW, and Nat. Inst. of Criminology, Canberra, 1973; Hon. Vice-Chm., Fifth UN Congress on Crime, Geneva, 1975. For. Hon. Mem., Amer. Acad. of Arts and Sciences, 1973; Hon. For. Mem., Aust. Acad. Forensic Scis, 1973; Hon. Mem., Amer. Law Inst., 1981; Hon. Fellow, Imperial Police Coll., 1968. Hon. LLD Leicester, 1965. James Barr Ames Prize and Medal, Faculty of Harvard Law School, 1950; Bruce Smith Sr award, Amer. Acad. Criminal Justice Sciences, 1976; Sellin-Glueck Award, Amer. Assoc. of Criminology, 1976. Coronation Medal, 1953. Chevalier de l'Ordre de Léopold, Belgium, 1930. *Publications:* Sir James Fitzjames Stephen (Selden Soc. Lect.), 1957; In Search of Criminology, 1961 (Italian edn 1965; French edn 1965; Spanish edn 1971); The Need for Criminology, 1965; Ideology and Crime (Carpentier Lectures), 1966, (Italian edn 1968); The Dangerous Offender (Frank Newsam Memorial Lecture), 1968; History of English Criminal Law, Vol. I, 1948 (under auspices of Pilgrim Trust), Vols II and III, 1956, Vol. IV, 1968 (under auspices of Rockefeller Foundation), Vol. V (with R. Hood), 1986 (under auspices of Home Office and MacArthur Foundn); (ed with Prof. M. E. Wolfgang) Crime and Justice, 3 vols, 1971, 2nd edn 1977; (with Joan King) The Growth of Crime, 1977 (trans. Italian, 1981); (with R. Hood) Criminology and the Administration of Criminal Justice: a Bibliography (Joseph L. Andrews Award, Amer. Assoc. of Law Libraries 1977), 1976; (ed) English Studies in Criminal Science, now Cambridge Studies in Criminology, 50 vols; numerous articles in English and foreign periodicals. *Address:* Trinity College, Cambridge. *Club:* Athenæum.

RAE, Allan Alexander Sinclair, CBE 1973; Chairman, CIBA-GEIGY PLC, since 1972; *b* 26 Nov. 1925; *s* of John Rae and Rachel Margaret Sinclair; *m* 1st, 1955, Sheila Grace (*née* Saunders) (*d* 1985); two *s* one *d*; 2nd, 1986, Gertrud (*née* Dollinger). *Educ:* Ayr Acad.; Glasgow Univ. LLB. Admitted Solicitor, 1948. Served Army, RA then JAG's Dept (Staff Captain), 1944–47. Partner, 1950, Sen. Partner, 1959, Crawford Bayley & Co., Bombay (Solicitors); Dir and Hd of Legal and Patents Dept, CIBA Ltd, Basle, 1964, Mem. Management Cttee, 1969; Mem. Exec. Cttee, CIBA-GEIGY Ltd, Basle and Chm., CIBA-GEIGY Gp of Cos in UK, 1972; Chairman: Clayton Aniline Co. Ltd, 1965–; CIBA-GEIGY Chemicals, 1965–; Ilford Ltd, 1972–; GRETAG CX Ltd, 1984–; Director: British Brown Boveri Ltd, 1973–; Turner & Newall PLC, 1979–; Brown Boveri Kent (Hldgs) Ltd, 1980–; Mettler Instruments Ltd, 1985–; AP Bank Ltd, 1986–. Member of Council: Chemical Industries Assoc., 1976– (Pres., 1986–); CBI, 1980–; British Swiss Chamber of Commerce, 1965– (Pres., 1969–72). *Recreations:* sailing, golf, ski-ing. *Address:* (office) 30 Buckingham Gate, SW1E 6LH. *T:* 01–828 5676. *Clubs:* Buck's; Royal Thames Yacht, Sunningdale Golf Club.

RAE, Charles Robert Angus; *b* 20 Feb. 1922; *s* of Charles E. L. Rae and Gladys M. Horsfall; *m* 1948, Philippa Neild; one *s* two *d*. *Educ:* Eton Coll.; Trinity Coll., Cambridge; London Sch. of Slavonic Studies. BA (Hons History) Cantab, 1945, MA 1948. War service in N Russia, RNVR, 1943–45. Foreign Office, 1947, service in Rome, 1950–54, Mexico City, 1957–59, Moscow, 1959–60; Private Sec. to Parly Under-Sec., 1954–57; seconded to Dept of Technical Co-operation on its formation, 1961; transf. to ODM as Asst Sec., 1964; Under Sec., 1975–79. Mem., Bd of Exec. Dirs, Inter-American Development Bank, 1979–82. Chm., Chelsham and Farleigh Parish Council, 1974–79. *Recreations:* walking, gardening. *Address:* The Limes, Shabbington, near Aylesbury, Bucks. *T:* Long Crendon 201139.

RAE, Henry Edward Grant, JP; Lord Provost, City of Aberdeen, since 1984; Lord Lieutenant, City of Aberdeen, since 1984; *b* 17 Aug. 1925; *s* of late James and Rachel Rae; *m* 1955, Margaret Raffan Burns; one *d*. *Educ:* Queen's Cross School, Aberdeen; Ruthrieston School, Aberdeen. Chairman: Aberdeen Dist Cttee, TGWU, 1969–82; Grampian and Northern Isles Dist Cttee, 1982–85. Councillor, Aberdeen City Council, 1974– (Convener, Libraries Cttee, 1977–80, Manpower Cttee, 1980–84). JP Aberdeen 1984 (Chm., Justices' Cttee). *Address:* 76 Whitehouse Street, Aberdeen AB1 1QH. *T:* Aberdeen 640425; (office) Town House, Aberdeen AB9 1LP. *T:* Aberdeen 642121.

RAE, John Malcolm, MA, PhD; Director: Laura Ashley Foundation, since 1986; The Observer Ltd, since 1986; *b* 20 March 1931; *s* of late Dr L. John Rae, radiologist, London Hospital, and Blodwen Rae; *m* 1955, Daphné Ray Simpson, *d* of John Phimester Simpson; two *s* four *d*. *Educ:* Bishop's Stortford Coll.; Sidney Sussex Coll., Cambridge. MA Cantab 1958; PhD 1965. 2nd Lieut Royal Fusiliers, 1950–51. Asst Master, Harrow School, 1955–66; Dept of War Studies, King's Coll., London, 1962–65; Headmaster: Taunton School, 1966–70; Westminster School, 1970–86. Chairman: HMC, 1977; Council for Educn in World Citizenship, 1983–. Member: NERC, 1986–; Council, Nat. Cttee for Electoral Reform; Council, King's Coll. London, 1981–84. Trustee, Imperial War Mus., 1980–85. JP Middlesex, 1961–66. Hon. FCP 1982. *Publications:* The Custard Boys, 1960 (filmed 1979); (jtly, film) Reach for Glory (UN Award); Conscience and Politics, 1970; The Golden Crucifix, 1974; The Treasure of Westminster Abbey, 1975; Christmas is Coming, 1976; Return to the Winter Palace, 1978; The Third Twin: a ghost story, 1980; The Public School Revolution: Britain's independent schools, 1964–1979, 1981; Letters to Parents, 1987; articles in The Times, Encounter; columnist in Times Ed. Supp. *Recreations:* writing, swimming, children, cinema. *Address:* 101 Millbank Court, 24 John Islip Street, Westminster, SW1P 4LG. *T:* 01–828 1595; Laura Ashley Foundation, 31 Old Burlington Street, W1X 1LB. *T:* 01–437 9367. *Clubs:* Royal Automobile; Hawks (Cambridge).

RAE, Robert Wright; Civil Service, retired; Clerk to the General Commissioners of Income Tax, Blackheath Division, since 1977 (Clerk, Bromley Division, 1977–85); *b* 27 March 1914; *s* of Walter Rae and Rachel Scott; *m* 1st, 1945, Joan McKenzie (*d* 1966); two *s*; 2nd, 1977, Marjorie Ann Collyer. *Educ:* George Heriot's Sch., Edinburgh; Edinburgh Univ. MA 1st cl. hons. Asst Inspector of Taxes, 1936; Dep. Chief Inspector of Taxes, 1973–75; Dir Personnel, Inland Revenue, 1975–77. *Recreations:* gardening, walking. *Address:* Oak Lodge, Blackbrook Lane, Bickley, Bromley BR1 2LP. *T:* 01–467 2377.

RAE, Air Vice-Marshal Ronald Arthur R.; *see* Ramsay Rae.

RAE, Hon. Sir Wallace (Alexander Ramsay), Kt 1976; Agent-General for Queensland, in London, 1974–80; Hon. Chairman, Brisbane Forest Park Advisory Board, since 1981, grazier, Ramsay Park, Blackall, Queensland; *b* 31 March 1914; *s* of George Ramsay Rae and Alice Ramsay Rae. *Educ:* Sydney, Australia. Served War: RAAF Coastal Command, 1939; Pilot, Flt Lt, UK, then OC Test Flight, Amberley, Qld. Mem., Legislative Assembly (Nat. Party of Australia) for Gregory, Qld, 1957–74; Minister for: Local Govt and Electricity, 1969–74; Lands and Forestry, Qld, 1974. Founder Pres., Pony Club Assoc. of Queensland. *Recreations:* bowls, golf. *Address:* 6 Ondine Street, Mermaid Waters, Gold Coast, Qld 4218, Australia. *Clubs:* Queensland, Tattersall's (Brisbane); Longreach (Longreach).

See also Air Vice-Marshal R. A. Ramsay Rae.

RAE SMITH, David Douglas, CBE 1976; MC 1946; MA; FCA; Senior Partner, Deloitte Haskins & Sells, Chartered Accountants, 1973–82 (Partner, 1954); *b* 15 Nov. 1919; *s* of Sir Alan Rae Smith, KBE, and Lady (Mabel Grace) Rae Smith; *m* 1947, Margaret Alison Watson, *d* of James Watson; three *s* one *d*. *Educ:* Radley Coll.; Christ Church, Oxford (MA). FCA 1959. Served War, RA, 1939–46: ME, N Africa and NW Europe; Captain; MC and mentioned in despatches. Chartered accountant, 1950. Hon. Treasurer, RIIA, 1961–81. Director: Thomas Tilling Ltd, 1982–83; Sandoz Products Ltd, 1983–; Dep. Chm., Bankers Trustee Co., 1984–. Member: Licensed Dealers Tribunal, 1974–; Council, Radley Coll., 1966– (Chm., 1976–). *Recreations:* horse racing, golf, travel. *Address:* Oakdale, Crockham Hill, Edenbridge, Kent. *T:* Edenbridge 866220. *Club:* Gresham.

RAEBURN, David Antony; Headmaster of Whitgift School, Croydon, since 1970; *b* 22 May 1927; *e s* of late Walter Augustus Leopold Raeburn, QC; *m* 1961, Mary Faith, *d* of Arthur Hubbard, Salisbury, Rhodesia; two *s* one *d*. *Educ:* Charterhouse; Christ Church, Oxford (Schol., MA). 1st cl. hons Hon. Mods, 2nd in Greats. Nat. Service, 1949–51: Temp. Captain, RAEC. Asst Master: Bristol Grammar Sch., 1951–54; Bradfield Coll., 1955–58 (prod. Greek Play, 1955 and 1958); Senior Classics Master, Alleyn's Sch., Dulwich, 1958–62; Headmaster, Beckenham and Penge Grammar Sch., 1963–70 (school's name changed to Langley Park School for Boys, Beckenham in 1969). Schoolteacher Fellow-Commoner, Jesus Coll., Cambridge, 1980. Chm. Classics Cttee, Schs Council, 1974–80; Pres., Jt Assoc. of Classical Teachers, 1983–85. FRSA 1969. *Publications:* articles on Greek play production. *Recreation:* play production (produced Cambridge Greek Play, 1980, 1983). *Address:* Haling House, 38 Haling Park Road, South Croydon CR2 6NE. *T:* 01–688 8114.

RAEBURN, Maj.-Gen. Sir Digby; *see* Raeburn, Maj.-Gen. Sir W. D. M.

RAEBURN, Prof. John Ross, CBE 1972; BSc (Agric.), PhD, MS; FRSE; FIBiol; Strathcona-Fordyce Professor of Agriculture, Aberdeen University, 1959–78; Principal, North of Scotland College of Agriculture, 1963–78; *b* 20 Nov. 1912; *s* of late Charles Raeburn and Margaret (*née* Ross); *m* 1941, Mary, *o d* of Alfred and Kathrine Roberts; one *s* three *d*. *Educ:* Manchester Grammar School; Edinburgh and Cornell Universities. Professor of Agricultural Economics, Nanking University, 1936–37; Research Officer, Oxford University, 1938–39; Ministry of Food Divisional statistician, 1939–41, Head Agricultural Plans Branch, 1941–46; Senior research officer, Oxford University, 1946–49; Reader in Agricultural Economics, London University, 1949–59. Visiting Professor: Cornell, 1950; Wuhan, 1983. Consultant to UN. Member: Agricultural Mission to Yugoslavia, 1951; Mission of Enquiry into Rubber Industry, Malaya, 1954; Colonial Economic Research Committee, 1949–61; Scottish Agricultural Improvement Council, 1960–71; Scottish Agricultural Develt Council, 1971–76; Verdon-Smith Committee, 1962–64; Council, Scottish Agricultural Colls, 1974–78. Hon. MA Oxford, 1946. FRSE 1961; FIBiol 1968. Vice-President, International Association of Agricultural Economists, 1964–70 (Hon. Life Mem., 1976–); President, Agric. Econ. Society, 1966–67 (Hon. Life Mem., 1981–). *Publications:* Preliminary economic survey of the Northern Territories of the Gold Coast, 1950; (jtly) Problems in the mechanisation of native agriculture in tropical African Territories, 1950; Agriculture: foundations, principles and development, 1984; research bulletins and contributions to agricultural economic journals. *Recreations:* gardening, travel. *Address:* 30 Morningfield Road, Aberdeen AB2 4AQ.

RAEBURN, Michael Edward Norman; (4th Bt, *cr* 1923, but does not use the title); *b* 12 Nov. 1954; *s* of Sir Edward Alfred Raeburn, 3rd Bt, and of Joan, *d* of Frederick Hill; *S* father, 1977; *m* 1979, Penelope Henrietta Theodora, *d* of Alfred Louis Penn; one *s* one *d*. *Heir: s* Christopher Edward Alfred Raeburn, *b* 4 Dec. 1981. *Address:* 1 Spring Cottages, Fletching Street, Mayfield, E Sussex TN20 6TN

RAEBURN, Maj.-Gen. Sir (William) Digby (Manifold), KCVO 1979; CB 1966; DSO 1945; MBE 1941; Major and Resident Governor, HM Tower of London, and Keeper of the Jewel House, 1971–79; *b* 6 Aug. 1915; *s* of late Sir Ernest Manifold Raeburn, KBE, and Lady Raeburn; *m* 1960, Adeline Margaret (*née* Pryor). *Educ:* Winchester; Magdalene College, Cambridge (MA). Commnd into Scots Guards, 1936; comd 2nd Bn Scots Guards, 1953; Lieut-Col Comdg Scots Guards, 1958; Comdr, 1st Guards Bde Group, 1959; Comdr, 51st Infty Bde Group, 1960; Director of Combat Development (Army), 1963–65; Chief of Staff to C-in-C, Allied Forces, N Europe, 1965–68; Chief Instructor (Army), Imperial Defence College, 1968–70. Freeman of City of London, 1972. *Recreations:* ski-ing, shooting, sailing. *Address:* c/o Lloyds Bank, 6 Pall Mall, SW1. *Clubs:* Pratt's, Cavalry and Guards; Royal Yacht Squadron.

RAFAEL, Gideon; Ambassador of Israel, retired 1978; *b* Berlin, 5 March 1913; *s* of Max Rafael; *m* 1940, Nurit Weissberg; one *s* one *d*. *Educ:* Berlin Univ. Went to Israel, 1934; Member, kibbutz, 1934–43; Jewish Agency Polit. Dept, 1943; in charge of prep. of Jewish case for JA Polit. Dept, Nuremberg War Crimes Trial, 1945–46; Member: JA Commn to Anglo-American Commn of Enquiry, 1946, and of JA Mission to UN Special Commn for Palestine, 1947; Israel Perm. Deleg. to UN, 1951–52; Alt. Rep. to UN, 1953; Rep. at UN Gen. Assemblies, 1947–66; Counsellor in charge of ME and UN Affairs, Min. for Foreign Affairs, 1953–57. Ambassador to Belgium and Luxembourg, 1957–60, and to the European Economic Community, 1959. Head, Israel Delegn to 2nd Geneva Conf. on Maritime Law, 1960; Dep. Dir-Gen., Min. of Foreign Affairs, 1960–65; Perm. Rep. to UN and Internat. Organizations in Geneva, Sept. 1965–April 1966; Special Ambassador and Adviser to Foreign Minister, 1966–67; Perm. Rep. to UN, 1967; Dir-Gen., Min. for Foreign Affairs, 1967–71; Head, Israel Delegn to UNCTAD III, 1972; Sen. Polit. Adviser, Foreign Ministry, 1972–73; Ambassador to the Court of St James's, 1973–77, and non-resident Ambassador to Ireland, 1975–77; Sen. Advr to Foreign Minister, 1977–78.

Publications: Destination Peace: three decades of Israeli foreign policy, 1981; articles on foreign affairs in Israel and internat. periodicals. *Address:* Ministry for Foreign Affairs, Jerusalem, Israel.

RAFF, Prof. Martin Charles, FRS 1985; Professor of Biology, University College London, since 1979; *b* 15 Jan. 1938; *s* of David and Reba Raff; *m* Carol Winters; two *s* one *d*. *Educ:* McGill Univ. (BSc; MD; CM). House Officer, Royal Victoria Hosp., Montreal, 1963–65; Resident in Neurology, Massachusetts General Hosp., 1965–68; Postdoctoral Fellow, Nat. Inst. for Med. Res., 1968–71; Co-director, MRC Neuroimmunology Programme, 1971–. *Publications:* (jtly) T and B Lymphocytes, 1973; (jtly) Molecular Biology of the Cell, 1983. *Address:* 67 Upper Park Road, NW3 2UL. *T:* 01–722 5610.

RAFFAN, Keith William Twort; MP (C) Delyn, since 1983; *b* 21 June 1949; *s* of A. W. Raffan, TD, MB, ChB, FFARCS. *Educ:* Robert Gordon's Coll., Aberdeen; Trinity Coll., Glenalmond; Corpus Christi Coll., Cambridge. BA 1971, MA 1977. Parly Correspondent, Daily Express, 1981–83. Candidate's Parly Aide, Cynon Valley and Brecon and Radnor by-elections. Mem., Select Cttee on Welsh Affairs, 1983–. Introduced Controlled Drugs (Penalties) Act (Private Member's Bill, 1985). Vice-Chm., Cons. Party Orgn Cttee; Pres., Wales Cons. Trade Unionists; Vice-Pres., Wales Young Conservatives. Nat. Chm., PEST, 1970–74; Vice-President: Clwyd Pre-School Playgroups Assoc.; Delyn and Deeside Multiple Sclerosis Soc. Contested (C) Dulwich, Feb. 1974, and East Aberdeenshire, Oct. 1974. Mem. NUJ. *Address:* House of Commons, SW1A 0AA. *T:* 01–219 3000. *Clubs:* Carlton; Flint Conservative; Prestatyn Conservative; Mold Conservative.

RAFFERTY, Hon. Joseph Anstice, BA; FAIM, FID; Agent General for Victoria in London, 1979–83; investor and primary producer, Australia, since 1983; *s* of late Col Rupert A. Rafferty, DSO, and Rose Sarah Anne Rafferty; *m* 1st, 1940, Miriam K. (decd), *d* of late Frank Richards, Devonport, Tas; two *s*; 2nd, 1973, Lyn, *d* of Grace Jones, Brisbane, Qld. *Educ:* Christ Coll., Univ. of Tas (BA); Univ. of Melbourne. FAIM 1954; FID 1960. Commonwealth Public Service, 1934–45; Personnel Manager, Australian National Airways, 1945–53; Personnel Management and Indust. Relations Consultant, 1953–70 (own practice; co. dir). MP (Lib) for: Caulfield, Vic, 1955–58; Ormond, Vic, 1958–67; Glenhuntly, Vic, 1967–79; Chm. Cttees and Dep. Speaker, Victorian Legislative Assembly, 1961–65; Parly Sec. for Cabinet, 1965–70; Minister for Labour and Industry, 1970–76; Asst Minister for Educn, 1970–72; Minister for Consumer Affairs, 1972–76; Minister for Fed. Affairs, 1974–76; Minister for Transport, 1976–78; Chief Sec., 1978–79; Leader, Aust. Delegn to ILO Conf., Geneva, 1974. Pres., Melbourne Jun. Chamber of Commerce, 1950; Treasurer, Nat. Assoc. of Jun. Chambers of Commerce of Australia, 1951; Councillor: Melbourne Chamber of Commerce, 1950–76; Victorian Employers' Fedn, 1952–65. Dep. Leader, Aust. Delegn, 5th World Congress, Jun. Chamber of Commerce, Manila, 1950; Aust. Delegate, 6th World Congress, Jun. Chamber of Industry, Montreal, 1951; Delegate, 17th Triennial Congress, British Empire Chambers of Commerce, London, 1951. Mem. Council, La Trobe Univ., Vic, 1964–70; Trustee, Caulfield Racecourse Reserve, 1965–. *Recreations:* golf, swimming, walking, travel. *Address:* 8 Matlock Court, Caulfield North, Vic 3161, Australia. *Clubs:* Royal Wimbledon Golf; Athenæum, Metropolitan Golf, MCC (Melbourne).

RAFFO, Carlos; Ambassador of Peru to the Court of St James's, since 1986; *b* 23 Aug. 1927; *s* of Carlos Raffo and Maria Julia Dasso de Raffo; *m* 1953, Araceli Quintana de Raffo; one *s* two *d*. *Educ:* Univ. Nacional Mayor de San Marcos; Univ. Católica, Peru (Law and Humanities). Dir, Banco Industrial, 1960–66; Founder, Inst. Peruano de Admin. de Empresas, 1963; Pres., Bd of Dirs, Volvo del Perú SA and Volvo Distrib. SA, 1969–; President: Conductores Eléctricos Pirelli SA, 1984–; Alfa Laval SA, 1984–; Dir, Vice-Pres. and Pres., numerous companies. Grand Cross, Peruvian Orders: El Sol del Perú, 1986; Commander, Al Mérito por Serviciós Distinguidos, 1980; Officer, Al Mérito Agrícola, 1969; Comdr, Swedish Order of Vassa, 1974. *Recreation:* golf. *Address:* 34 Porchester Terrace, W2. *T:* 01–262 5113. *Clubs:* Travellers'; Sunningdale Golf; Nacional (Lima); Lima Golf.

RAFTERY, Peter Albert, CVO 1984 (MVO 1979); MBE 1972; HM Diplomatic Service; High Commissioner to Botswana, since 1986; *b* 8 June 1929; *s* of John Raftery and Mary (*née* Glynn); *m* 1st, 1949, Margaret Frances Hulse (decd); four *d*; 2nd, 1975, Fenella Jones. *Educ:* St Ignatius Coll., London. Nat. Service, 1947–49. India Office, 1946; CRO, 1949; New Delhi, 1950; Peshawar, 1956; Cape Town, 1959; Kuala Lumpur, 1963; Nairobi, 1964; Asst Political Agent, Bahrain, 1968; First Sec., FCO, 1973; Head of Chancery, Gabarone, 1976; Asst Head, E Africa Dept, FCO, 1980; Counsellor and Consul Gen., Amman, 1982–85. *Recreations:* tennis, squash. *Address:* c/o Foreign and Commonwealth Office, SW1A 2AH.

RAGG, Rt. Rev. Theodore David Butler, DD; *b* 23 Nov. 1919; *s* of late Rt Rev. Harry Richard Ragg and Winifred Mary Ragg (*née* Groves); *m* 1945, Dorothy Mary Lee; one *s* two *d*. *Educ:* Univ. of Manitoba; Trinity Coll., Univ. of Toronto (BA, LTh); General Synod (BD). Deacon, 1949; priest, 1950; Asst Curate, St Michael and All Angels, Toronto, 1949; Rector: Nokomis, 1951; Wolseley, 1953; St Clement's N Vancouver, 1955; St Luke's, Victoria, 1957; Bishop Cronyn Memorial, London, 1962; St George's, Owen Sound, 1967. Examining Chaplain to Bishop of Huron, 1964–67; Archdeacon of Saugeen, 1967; elected Suffragan Bishop of Huron, 1973; Bishop of Huron, 1974–84, retired. Hon. DD: Huron Coll., London, Ont., 1975; Trinity Coll., Toronto, Ont., 1975. *Recreations:* woodworking, golf. *Address:* 1771 McRae Avenue, Victoria, BC V8P 1J2, Canada.

RAGLAN, 5th Baron, *cr* 1852; **FitzRoy John Somerset;** JP; DL; Chairman, Cwmbran New Town Development Corporation, 1970–83; *b* 8 Nov. 1927; *er s* of 4th Baron and Hon. Julia Hamilton, CStJ (*d* 1971), *d* of 11th Baron Belhaven and Stenton, CIE; *S* father, 1964; *m* 1973, Alice Baily (marr. diss. 1981), *yr d* of Peter Baily, Great Whittington, Northumberland. *Educ:* Westminster; Magdalen College, Oxford; Royal Agricultural College, Cirencester. Captain, Welsh Guards, RARO. Crown Estate Comr, 1970–74. Chm., Agriculture and Consumer Affairs sub-cttee, House of Lords Select Cttee on the European Community, 1975–77. Pres., UK Housing Trust, 1983–. Pres., Pre Retirement Assoc., 1970–77, Vice-Pres. 1977–. Chairman: The Courtyard Arts Trust, 1974–; Bath Preservation Trust, 1975–77; The Bath Soc., 1977–; President: Gwent Foundn Concert Soc.; Usk Civic Soc.; Usk Farmers Club; Bath Centre of Nat. Trust; S Wales Reg., RSMHCA, 1971–; Mem., Distinguished Members Panel, National Secular Soc.; Patron, The Raglan Baroque Players. JP 1958, DL 1971, Gwent (formerly Monmouthshire). Farms 600 acres at Usk. *Recreation:* being mechanic to a Bugatti. *Heir:* *b* Hon. Geoffrey Somerset [*b* 29 Aug. 1932; *m* 1956, Caroline Rachel, *d* of Col E. R. Hill, *qv*; one *s* two *d*]. *Address:* Cefntilla, Usk, Gwent. *T:* Usk 2050. *Clubs:* Beefsteak, Bugatti Owners, Vintage Sports Car; Usk Farmers'.

RAHIMTOOLA, Habib Ibrahim, BA, LLB, FRPS (Gt Br.); Chairman: Pakistan Red Cross, 1970–73; Pakistan Government Shipping Rates Advisory Board, 1959–71; Diplomatist, Pakistan; *b* 10 March 1912; *s* of late Sir Ibrahim Rahimtoola, GBE, KCSI, CIE, and Lady Kulsum Rahimtoola (*née* Mitha); *m* Zubeida, *d* of Sir Sultan Chinoy; two *s* one *d*. *Educ:* St Xavier's School and College and Govt Law Coll., Bombay. High Commissioner for Pakistan in London, 1947–52; Ambassador for Pakistan to France, 1952–53; Governor of Sind Province, 1953–54, of Punjab Province, June-Nov. 1954; Minister for Commerce, Central Govt, Nov. 1954–Aug. 1955; Minister for Commerce and Industries, 1955–56. President: Fed. of Muslim Chambers of Commerce and Industry, New Delhi, 1947–48; Bombay Provincial Muslim Chamber of Commerce, 1944–47; Bombay Provincial Muslim League Parly Board for Local Bodies, 1945–47; Young Men's Muslim Association, 1946–47; Bombay Muslim Students' Union, 1946–47–48. Director, Rotary Club, 1944–46; Chairman Membership Committee, 1945–46, Classification Cttee, 1944–45; Member: Govt of India Food Delegation to UK and USA, 1946; Govt of India Policy Cttee on Shipping; Govt of Bombay Housing Panel; Civil Aviation Conference, Govt of India, 1947; Cttee on Trade Policy, Govt of India, 1947; Indian Delegation to Internat. Trade and Employment Conference, Geneva, 1947; alternate Leader Indian Delegation Special Cereals Conference, Paris, 1947; Delegate or Leader of Pakistan Delegations: Inter-Allied Reparations Agency, Brussels, 1947–48–49–50–51; FAO, Geneva, 1947; Dollar Talks, London, 1947; Internat. Trade and Employment Conf., Geneva, 1947; Freedom of Information Conf., Geneva, 1948; Safety of Life at Sea (1948), and Sterling Balance (1948, 1949, 1950, 1951) Confs, London; Prime Ministers' Conferences, London, 1948, 1949, 1951; Foreign Ministers' Conference, Ceylon, 1950; ILO, 1950; Commonwealth Finance Ministers' Conf., 1948–52; SE Asia Conf. on Colombo Plan, 1950; Commonwealth Talks on Japanese Peace Treaty, London, 1950; General Agreement on Tariffs and Trade Conf., 1950–52; Supply Ministers' Conf., London, 1951; UNESCO, Paris, 1953; Afro-Asian Conf., Bandung, 1955; Leader Pakistan Trade Delegation to Brit. E Africa, 1956; Leader, Flood Control Conf., New Delhi, 1956; Chm. Karachi Development Authority, 1958–60; Chm. Water Co-ordination Council, 1958–60. Chm., or Dir, numerous companies. Internat. Counsellor, Lions Internat.; Chairman: Karachi Race Club Ltd, 1958–70 (Pres., 1970–71); Pak-Japan Cultural Assoc., 1959–. District Governor 305W, Lions International, 1964–67. FRSA; FRPS. Melvin Jones Award, USA; several photography awards. Order of Sacred Treasure, Japan. *Recreations:* photography, horse racing, golf, tennis. *Address:* Bandenawaz Ltd, Standard Insurance House, I. I. Chundrigar Road, PO Box 4792, Karachi 2, Pakistan. *T:* 221267; Kulib, KDA 1, Habib I. Rahimtoola Road, Karachi 8. *T:* 432125. *Clubs:* MCC; Sind, Boat, Gymkhana (Karachi); Willingdon (Bombay).

RAHMAN PUTRA, Tunku (Prince) Abdul; *see* Abdul Rahman Putra.

RAHTZ, Prof. Philip Arthur; Professor of Archaeology, University of York, 1979–86; *b* 11 March 1921; *s* of Frederick John Rahtz and Ethel May Rahtz; *m* 1st, 1940, Wendy Hewgill Smith (*d* 1977); three *s* two *d*; 2nd, 1979, Lorna Rosemary Jane Watts. *Educ:* Bristol Grammar Sch. MA Bristol 1964. FSA. Served RAF, 1941–46. Articled to accountant, 1937–41; photographer (Studio Rahtz), 1946–49; schoolteacher, 1950–53; archaeological consultant, 1953–63; Univ. of Birmingham: Lectr, 1963–75; Sen. Lectr, later Reader, 1975–79. *Publications:* Rescue Archaeology, 1973; Chew Valley Lake Excavations, 1978; Saxon and Medieval Palaces at Cheddar, 1979; Invitation to Archaeology, 1985; contrib. nat. and regional jls in England, W Africa and Poland. *Recreations:* swimming, sunbathing, music, travel. *Address:* Old School, Harome, Helmsley, North Yorkshire. *T:* Helmsley 70862.

RAIKES, Vice-Adm. Sir Iwan (Geoffrey), KCB 1976; CBE 1967; DSC 1943; DL; Flag Officer Submarines, and Commander Submarines, Eastern Atlantic Area, 1974–76; retired 1977; *b* 21 April 1921; *s* of late Adm. Sir Robert Henry Taunton Raikes, KCB, CVO, DSO, and Lady (Ida Guinevere) Raikes; *m* 1947, Cecilia Primrose Hunt; one *s* one *d*. *Educ:* RNC Dartmouth. Entered Royal Navy, 1935; specialised in Submarines, 1941; comd HM Submarines: H43, 1943; Varne, 1944; Virtue, 1946; Talent, 1948–49; Aeneas, 1952; comd HM Ships: Loch Insh, 1961; Kent, 1968; Exec. Officer, HMS Newcastle, 1955–57; Dep. Dir, Undersurface Warfare, 1962–64; Dir, Plans & Operations, Staff of C-in-C Far East, 1965–66; JSSC, 1957; IDC, 1967. Rear-Adm., 1970; Naval Sec., 1970–72; Vice-Adm., 1973; Flag Officer, First Flotilla, 1973–74. Mem., Governing Body, Church in Wales, 1979–. DL Powys, 1983. *Recreations:* shooting, fishing, sailing, skiing, tennis, gardening. *Address:* Aberyscir Court, Brecon, Powys. *Club:* Naval and Military.

RAILTON, Brig. Dame Mary, DBE 1956 (CBE 1953); *b* 28 May 1906; *d* of late James and Margery Railton. *Educ:* privately. Joined FANY, 1938; commissioned in ATS, 1940; WRAC 1949; Director WRAC, 1954–57; Deputy Controller Commandant, 1961–67. *Address:* 1 Frogmore Cottages, Great Bedwyn, Marlborough, Wilts.

RAILTON, Dame Ruth, DBE 1966 (OBE 1954); Founder and Musical Director of the National Youth Orchestra and National Junior Music School, 1947–65; *b* 14 Dec. 1915; *m* 1962, Cecil Harmsworth King, *qv*. *Educ:* St Mary's School, Wantage; Royal Academy of Music, London. Director of Music or Choral work for many schools and societies, 1937–49; Adjudicator, Fedn of Music Festivals, 1946–74; Pres., Ulster Coll. of Music, 1960–; Governor, Royal Ballet School, 1966–74. Founder and Pres., Irish Children's Theatre, 1978–; Vice-Pres., Cork Internat. Fest., 1975–85; Mem., Bd of Dirs, Nat. Concert Hall, Dublin, 1981–86; Advr, Nat. Children's Orchestra, 1985–. Hon. Professor: Chopin Conservatoire, Warsaw, 1960; Conservatoire of Azores, 1972. FRAM 1956; FRCM 1965; Hon. RMCM 1959; Hon. FTCL 1969. Hon. LLD Aberdeen Univ., 1960. Harriet Cohen Medal for Bach, 1955. *Recreations:* interested in everything. *Address:* The Pavilion, Greenfield Park, Dublin 4. *T:* Dublin 695870.

RAINBOW, (James) Conrad (Douglas), CBE 1979; Chairman, Sovereign Country House Ltd, since 1979; *b* 25 Sept. 1926; *s* of Jack Conrad Rainbow and Winifred Edna (*née* Mears); *m* 1974, Kathleen Margaret (*née* Holmes); one *s* one *d*. *Educ:* William Ellis Sch., Highgate; Selwyn Coll., Cambridge (MA). Asst Master, St Paul's Sch., London, 1951–60; HM Inspector of Schools, 1960–69; Dep. Chief Educn Officer, Lancashire, 1969–74, Chief Educn Officer, 1974–79. Vis. Prof., Univ. of Wisconsin, 1979. Education Consultant: ICI, 1980–85; Shell Petroleum Co. Ltd, 1980–; Advr to H of C Select Cttee on Educn, 1980–82. Mem., Exec. Cttee, Council of British Internat. Schs in the European Community. Mem., Inst. of Dirs. Chm. of Governors, Northcliffe Sch., Hants. *Publications:* various articles in educnl jls. *Recreations:* rowing (now as an observer), music, reading. *Address:* Freefolk House, Laverstoke, Whitchurch, Hants. *Clubs:* Royal Commonwealth Society; Leander.

RAINE, Craig Anthony; poet; Poetry Editor, Faber & Faber, since 1981; *b* 3 Dec. 1944; *s* of Norman Edward Raine and Olive Marie Raine; *m* 1972, Ann Pasternak Slater; one *d* two *s*. *Educ:* Barnard Castle Sch.; Exeter Coll., Oxford (BA Hons in English; BPhil). College Lecturer, Oxford University: Exeter Coll., 1971–72; Lincoln Coll., 1974–75; Exeter Coll., 1975–76; Christ Church, 1976–79. Books Editor, New Review, 1977–78; Editor, Quarto, 1979–80; Poetry Editor, New Statesman, 1981. Cholmondeley Poetry Award, 1983. *Publications:* The Onion, Memory, 1978, 4th edn 1983; A Martian Sends a Postcard Home, 1979, 5th edn 1983; A Free Translation, 1981, 2nd edn 1981; Rich, 1984, 2nd edn 1984; The Electrification of the Soviet Union, 1986. *Recreation:* publishing. *Address:* c/o Faber & Faber, 3 Queen Square, WC1N 3AU.

RAINE, (Harcourt) Neale, CBE 1986; Chairman, Business and Technician Education Council, since 1983 (of Technician Education Council, 1976–83); *b* 5 May 1923; *s* of late Harold Raine and Gertrude Maude Healey; *m* 1947, Eileen Daphne, *d* of A. A. Hooper; one *s*. *Educ:* Dulwich and London. MSc (Eng) London; CEng, FIProdE, MICE, FIMC. Various appts as professional civil engr, 1947–52; Industrial Management Consultant with Production Engrg Ltd, 1953–59; Jt Man. Dir, Mycalex & TIM Ltd, 1959–63; Chief Exec., Car Div., Wilmot Breedon Ltd, 1963; Management Consultancy in assoc. with Production Engrg Ltd, 1964–65; Dep. Man. Dir, 1965, later Chm. and Man. Dir, Brico Engrg Ltd (Associated Engrg Gp); Chm., Coventry Radiator & Presswork Co. Ltd (Associated Engrg Gp), 1968–70; Man. Dir, Alfred Herbert Ltd, 1970–75. Dir, Associated Engineering Ltd and Man.-Dir of Gen. Div., 1968–70; Dir, Stothert & Pitt Ltd, 1978–86. Pres., Coventry and District Engrg Employers' Assoc., 1975–77. Governor, Lanchester Polytechnic, Coventry and Rugby, 1970–80. *Address:* Penn Lea, The Avenue, Charlton Kings, Cheltenham, Glos GL53 9BJ. *T:* Cheltenham 26185.

RAINE, Kathleen Jessie, (Mrs Madge), FRSL; poet; *b* 1908; *o d* of late George Raine, schoolmaster, and Jessie Raine; *m* Charles Madge (marr. diss.); one *s* one *d*. *Educ:* Girton College, Cambridge. Hon. DLitt: Leicester, 1974; Durham, 1979. *Publications:* Stone and Flower, 1943; Living in Time, 1946; The Pythoness, 1949; The Year One, 1952; Collected Poems, 1956; The Hollow Hill (poems), 1965; Defending Ancient Springs (criticism), 1967; Blake and Tradition (Andrew Mellon Lectures, Washington, 1962), Princeton 1968, London 1969 (abridged version, Blake and Antiquity, Princeton 1978, London 1979); (with George Mills Harper) Selected Writings of Thomas Taylor the Platonist, Princeton and London, 1969; William Blake, 1970; The Lost Country (verse), 1971 (W. H. Smith & Son Award, 1972); On a Deserted Shore (verse), 1973; Yeats, the Tarot and The Golden Dawn (criticism), 1973; Faces of Day and Night, 1973; Farewell Happy Fields (autobiog.), 1973 (French trans. as Adieu prairies heureuses, 1978; Prix du meilleur livre étranger); Death in Life and Life in Death (criticism), 1974; The Land Unknown (autobiog.), 1975 (French trans. as Le royaume inconnu, 1978), The Oval Portrait (verse), 1977; The Lion's Mouth (autobiography), 1977; David Jones and the Actually Loved and Known (criticism), 1978; From Blake to a Vision (criticism), 1979; The Oracle in the Heart, (verse), 1979; Blake and the New Age (criticism), 1979; Collected Poems, 1981; The Human Face of God, 1982; The Inner Journey of the Poet and other papers (criticism), 1982; L'Imagination Créatrice de William Blake; French trans. of verse: Isis errante, 1978; Sur un rivage désert, 1978; Le Premier Jour, 1980; Spanish trans.: En una desierta orilla, 1980; Co-Editor, Temenos, a bi-annual Review devoted to the Arts of the Imagination, 1981– (6th issue 1985); contributions to literary journals. *Address:* 47 Paultons Square, SW3. *Club:* University Women's.

RAINE, Neale; *see* Raine, H. N.

RAINER, Luise; actress and painter; *b* Vienna, 12 Jan.; *d* of Heinz Rainer; *m* 1937, Clifford Odets, (*d* 1963) (from whom she obtained a divorce, 1940); *m* 1945, Robert, *s* of late John Knittel; one *d*. *Educ:* Austria, France, Switzerland and Italy. Started stage career at age of sixteen under Max Reinhardt in Vienna; later was discovered by Metro-Goldwyn-Mayer talent scout in Vienna; came to Hollywood; starred in: Escapade, The Great Ziegfeld, The Good Earth, Emperor's Candlesticks, Big City, Toy Wife (Frou Frou), The Great Waltz, Dramatic School; received Motion Picture Academy of Arts and Sciences Award for the best feminine performance in 1936 and 1937. One-man exhibn of paintings at Patrick Seale Gallery, SW1, 1978. US Tour in recitation of Tennyson's Enoch Arden with music by Richard Strauss, 1981–82, 1983. George Eastman Award, George Eastman Inst., Rochester, NY, 1982. Grand Cross 1st class, Order of Merit (Federal Republic of Germany), 1985. *Recreation:* mountain climbing. *Address:* Casa Isola, Vico Morcote, Lake Lugano, CH 6911, Switzerland. *T:* (091) 692201.

RAINEY, Dr Reginald Charles, OBE 1979; FRS 1975; Consultant, tropical pest management; *b* 18 June 1913; *s* of Charles Albert Rainey and Ethel May Rainey; *m* 1943, Margaret Tasman; three *s* (one *d* decd). *Educ:* Purbrook Park County High Sch., Hants; Imperial Coll. of Science and Technology (ARCS); London Sch. of Hygiene and Trop. Med. DSc London; FIBiol. Res. biologist, Empire Cotton Growing Corp., Transvaal, 1938–40 and 1946–49; Meteorological Officer, S African Air Force, S and E Africa and ME, 1940–46; Sen. Entomologist, Desert Locust Survey, E Africa High Commn (res. and develt work on use of meteorology and aircraft in forecasting and control of desert locust invasions), 1949–58; SPSO, Centre for Overseas Pest Research, ODM (formerly Anti-Locust Research Centre), 1958–78; i/c FAO Desert Locust Inf. Service (desert locust forecasting, with co-operation and support of countries concerned, in Africa and Asia), 1960–67; res. and develt work on use of meteorology and aircraft in forecasting and control of other insect pests, with co-operation and support of E African Agric. and Forestry Res. Org., Sudan Gezira Bd, Canadian Forestry Service, Agricl Aviation Res. Unit (Ciba-Geigy Ltd), Cranfield Coll. of Aeronautics, Univ. of New Brunswick, FAO, Acad. Sinica, 1967–. Pres., Royal Entomological Soc., 1979–81. Fitzroy Prize, Royal Meteorological Soc., 1971. *Publications:* Meteorology and the Migration of Desert Locusts, 1963; (ed) Insect Flight, 1975; (ed with D. L. Gunn) Migrant Pests, 1979; papers in sci. jls. *Recreations:* as above. *Address:* Elmslea, Old Risborough Road, Stoke Mandeville, Bucks. *T:* Stoke Mandeville 2493.

RAINGER, Peter, CBE 1978; FRS 1982; FEng; Deputy Director of Engineering, British Broadcasting Corporation, 1978–84, retired; *b* 17 May 1924; *s* of Cyril and Ethel Rainger; *m* 1st, 1953, Josephine Campbell (decd); two *s*; 2nd, 1972, Barbara Gibson. *Educ:* Northampton Engrg Coll.; London Univ. (BSc(Eng)). CEng, FIEE; FEng 1979. British Broadcasting Corporation: Head of Designs Dept, 1968–71; Head of Research Dept, 1971–76; Asst Dir of Engrg, 1976–78. Chairman: Professional Gp E14, IEE, 1973–76; various working parties, EBU, 1971–84. Fellow, Royal Television Soc., 1969. Geoffrey Parr Award, Royal TV Soc., 1964; J. J. Thompson Premium, IEE, 1966; TV Acad. Award, Nat. Acad. of Arts and Scis, 1968; David Sarnoff Gold Medal, SMPTE, 1972. *Publications:* Satellite Broadcasting, 1985; technical papers in IEE, Royal TV Soc. and SMPTE jls. *Recreations:* sailing, model engineering. *Address:* Applehurst, West End Avenue, Pinner, Mddx. *T:* 01–868 5166.

RAINS, Prof. Anthony John Harding, CBE 1986; MS, FRCS; Hon. Librarian, since 1984, and Hunterian Trustee, since 1982, Royal College of Surgeons of England; *b* 5 Nov. 1920; *s* of late Dr Robert Harding Rains and Mrs Florence Harding Rains; *m* 1943, Mary Adelaide Lillywhite; three *d*. *Educ:* Christ's Hospital School, Horsham; St Mary's Hospital, London. MB, BS London, MS London 1952; MRCS; LRCP 1943; FRCS 1948. Ho. Surg. and Ho. Phys. St Mary's, 1943. RAF, 1944–47. Ex-Service Registrar to Mr Handfield-Jones and Lord Porritt, 1947–48; Res. Surgical Officer, Bedford County Hosp., 1948–50; Lectr in Surgery, Univ. of Birmingham, 1950–54, Sen. Lectr, 1955–59; Prof. of Surgery, Charing Cross Hosp. Medical Sch., Univ. of London, and Hon. Consultant Surgeon, Charing Cross Hosp., 1959–81; Asst Dir, BPMF, Univ. of London, and Postgraduate Dean, SW Thames RHA, 1981–85. Hon. Consulting Surgeon, United Birmingham Hospitals, 1954–59; Hon. Consultant Surgeon to the Army, 1972–82. Royal College of Surgeons of England: Mem. Court of Examiners, 1968–74; Mem. Council, 1972–84; Dean, Inst. of Basic Med. Scis, 1976–82; Vice-President, 1983–84. Chm., Med. Commn on Accident Prevention, 1974–83. Pres., Nat. Assoc. of Theatre Nurses, 1979–81. Sir Arthur Keith medal, RCS. Editor: Annals of RCS; Jl of RSocMed, 1985–. *Publications:* (ed with Dr P. B. Kunkler) The Treatment of Cancer in Clinical Practice, 1959; Gallstones: Causes and Treatment, 1964; (ed) Bailey and Love's Short Practice of Surgery, rev. edn 1984; Edward Jenner and Vaccination, 1975; Emergency and Acute Care, 1976; Lister and Antisepsis, 1977; 1,001 Multiple Choice Questions and Answers in Surgery, 1978; articles on the surgery of the gall bladder, on the formation of gall stones, inguinal hernia and arterial disease. *Recreations:* rough work, country garden, painting. *Address:* Church Orchard, Far End Lane, Sheepscombe, near Stroud, Glos GL6 7RQ. *T:* Painswick 813338.

RAINSFORD, Surg. Rear-Adm. (retd) Seymour Grome, CB 1955; FRCPath 1964; ARC Research Fellow, Bone and Joint Research Unit, London Hospital Medical College, since 1975; Hon. Consultant in Coagulation Disorders, Wessex Regional Hospital Board, since 1975; *b* 24 April 1900; *s* of Frederick Edward Rainsford, MD, Palmerstown Hse, Co. Dublin; *m* 1st, 1929, Violet Helen (*née* Thomas) (decd); 2nd, 1972, Caroline Mary Herschel, *d* of late Sir Denis Hill, FRCP, FRCPsych; twin *s*. *Educ:* St Columba's College, Co. Dublin; Trinity College, Dublin. MD 1932; ScD 1939; DPH 1937; FRCPath 1964; FRCP 1977. Joined RN as Surg. Lieut, 1922. North Persian Forces Memorial Medal, for research on Mediterranean Fever, 1933; Gilbert Blane Gold Medal for research on Typhoid Fever, 1938; Chadwick Gold Medal and Prize for research on typhoid vaccine and on blood transfusion in the Royal Navy, 1939. Surgeon Rear-Adm. 1952; Deputy Medical Director-General of the Royal Navy, 1952–55. Chevalier de la Légion d'Honneur, 1948; CStJ 1955. *Publications:* papers on typhoid fever and other tropical diseases, haematology, blood transfusion, blood clotting disorders and physiological problems concerned in diving and submarine escape, in Jl Hygiene, Lancet, BMJ, British Jl of Haematology, Jl Clin. Pathology, Thrombosis et Diathesis and Journal RN Med. Serv. *Recreations:* shooting, golf. *Address:* The Ashes, 25 Colletts Close, Corfe Castle, Wareham, Dorset BH20 5HG. *Club:* Army and Navy.

RAINWATER, Prof. (Leo) James; Professor of Physics, Columbia University, New York, since 1952; *b* 9 Dec. 1917; *s* of Leo Jasper Rainwater and Edna Eliza (*née* Teague); *m* 1942, Emma Louise Smith; three *s*. *Educ:* California Inst. of Technol.; Columbia Univ., NY (BS, MA, PhD). Asst in Physics, 1939–42, Instr 1946–47, Asst Prof. 1947–49, Assoc. Prof., 1949–52, Columbia Univ.; Scientist, OSRD and Manhattan Project, 1942–46; Dir, Nevis Cyclotron Lab., 1951–53 and 1956–61; scientific research contracts with US naval research, Atomic Energy Commn and Nat. Science Foundn, 1947–. Fellow: Amer. Phys. Soc.; AAAS; IEEE; NY Acad. of Science; Optical Soc. of Amer.; Mem., Nat Acad. of Sciences. Hon. Mem., Royal Swedish Acad., 1982. Ernest Orlando Lawrence Physics Award, US Atomic Energy Commn, 1963; (jtly) Nobel Prize for Physics, 1975. *Recreations:* classical music, environmental problems, astronomy. *Publications:* numerous articles in Phys. Review, 1946–, and other professional jls. *Address:* Physics Department, Columbia University, New York, NY 10027, USA. *T:* 212–280–3345; (home) 342 Mt Hope Boulevard, Hastings-on-Hudson, NY 10706, USA. *T:* 914–GR8–1368.

RAIS, Tan Sri Abdul J.; *see* Jamil Rais.

RAISMAN, John Michael, CBE 1983; Chairman, 1979–85 and Chief Executive, 1978–85, Shell UK Ltd; *b* 12 Feb. 1929; *er s* of Sir Jeremy Raisman, GCMG, GCIE, KCSI, and Renee Mary Raisman; *m* 1953, Evelyn Anne, *d* of Brig. J. I. Muirhead, CIE, MC; one *s* three *d*. *Educ:* Dragon Sch., Oxford; Rugby Sch.; The Queen's Coll., Oxford (Jodrell Schol., BA Lit Hum). CBIM 1980. Joined Royal Dutch/Shell Group, 1953; served in Brazil, 1954–60; General Manager, Shell Panama, 1961–62; Asst to Exploration and Production Coordinator, The Hague, 1963–65; Gen. Man., Shell Co. of Turkey, 1966–69; President, Shell Sekiyu K. K. Japan, 1970–73; Head, European Supply and Marketing, 1974–77; Man. Dir, Shell UK Oil, 1977–78; Regional Coordinator, UK and Eire, Shell Internat. Pet. Co. Ltd, 1978–85; Dep. Chm., Shell UK Ltd, 1978–79. Director: Vickers PLC, 1981–; Glaxo Hldgs PLC, 1982–; Lloyds Bank Plc, 1985–; Lloyds Merchant Bank Hldgs Ltd, 1985–; Govt Dir, British Telecom, 1984–. Chairman: Adv. Council, London Enterprise Agency, 1979–85; UK Oil Industry Emergency Cttee, 1980–85; Council of Industry for Management Educn, 1981–85; Investment Bd, Electra-Candover Partners, 1985–. Member: Council, CBI, 1979– (Chm., CBI Europe Cttee, 1980–; Mem., President's Cttee, 1980–); Council, Inst. of Petroleum, 1979–81; Council, Inst. for Fiscal Studies, 1982–; Governing Council, Business in the Community, 1982–85; Council, UK Centre for Econ. and Environmental Develt, 1985–; Royal Commn on Environmental Pollution, 1986–; Chm., Electronics Industry EDC, 1986–. Chm., RA Appeal Cttee, 1983–; Trustee, RA, 1983–; Governor, National Inst. of Econ. and Social Res. DUniv Stirling, 1983; Hon. LLD: Aberdeen, 1985; Manchester, 1986. *Recreations:* golf, skiing, listening to music. *Address:* Netheravon House, Netheravon Road South, W4 2PY. *Clubs:* Brooks's; Royal Mid-Surrey; Sunningdale Golf.

RAISON, Dr John Charles Anthony, MA, MD; MFCM; Specialist in Community Medicine, Wessex Regional Health Authority, since 1982; *b* 13 May 1926; *s* of late Cyril A. Raison, FRCS, Edgbaston, Birmingham, and of Ceres Raison; *m* 1st, 1951 (marr. diss. 1982); one *s* two *d*; 2nd, 1983, Ann Alexander, *d* of Captain and Mrs J. H. R. Faulkner, Southampton; three step *d*. *Educ:* Malvern Coll.; Trinity Hall, Cambridge; Birmingham Univ. Consultant Clinical Physiologist in Cardiac Surgery, Birmingham Reg. Hosp. Bd, 1962; Hon. Associate Consultant Clinical Physiologist, United Birmingham Hosps, 1963; Sen. Physiologist, Dir of Clinical Res. and Chief Planner, Heart Research Inst., Presbyterian-Pacific Medical Center, San Francisco, 1966; Chief Scientific Officer and Sen. Princ. Medical Officer, Scientific Services, DHSS, 1974–78; Dep. Dir, Nat. Radiological Protection Bd, 1978–81. Vis. Consultant, Civic Hosps, Lisbon (Gulbenkian Foundn), 1962; Arris and Gale Lectr, Royal College of Surgeons, 1965. Councillor, Southam RDC, 1955–59. FRSM. *Publications:* chapters in books, and papers in medical jls on open-heart surgery, extracorporeal circulation, intensive care, scientific services in health care, and computers in medicine. *Recreations:* tennis, squash, gardening, theatre, sailing, beach life at Mudeford. *Address:* 141 Kingsway, Chandlers Ford, Hants SO5 1BX. *T:* Chandlers Ford 3627.

RAISON, Rt. Hon. Timothy (Hugh Francis), PC 1982; MP (C) Aylesbury since 1970; *b* 3 Nov. 1929; *s* of Maxwell and late Celia Raison; *m* 1956, Veldes Julia Charrington; one *s* three *d*. *Educ:* Dragon Sch., Oxford; Eton (King's Schol.); Christ Church, Oxford (Open History Schol.). Editorial Staff: Picture Post, 1953–56; New Scientist, 1956–61; Editor: Crossbow, 1958–60; New Society, 1962–68. Member: Youth Service Develt Council, 1960–63; Central Adv. Council for Educn, 1963–66; Adv. Cttee on Drug Dependence, 1966–70; Home Office Adv, Council on Penal System, 1970–74; (co-opted) Inner London Educn Authority Educn Cttee, 1967–70; Richmond upon Thames Council, 1967–71. PPS to Sec. of State for N Ireland, 1972–73; Parly Under-Sec. of State, DES, 1973–74; Opposition spokesman on the Environment, 1975–76; Minister of State, Home Office, 1979–83; Minister of State, FCO, and Minister for Overseas Develt, 1983–86. Sen. Fellow, Centre for Studies in Soc. Policy, 1974–77; Mem. Council, PSI, 1978–79; Consultant, Selection Trust, 1977–79. Nansen Medal (for share in originating World Refugee Year), 1960. *Publications:* Why Conservative?, 1964; (ed) Youth in New Society,

1966; (ed) Founding Fathers of Social Science, 1969; Power and Parliament, 1979; various political pamphlets. *Recreation:* golf. *Address:* 66 Riverview Gardens, SW13. *T:* 01–748 4724. *Clubs:* Beefsteak, MCC.

RAITZ, Vladimir Gavrilovich; Chairman, Hickie Borman Grant & Co. Ltd, and associated travel companies; Director, Medallion Holidays, since 1976; *b* 23 May 1922; *s* of Dr Gavril Raitz and Cecilia Raitz; *m* 1954, Helen Antonia (*née* Corkrey); three *d. Educ:* Mill Hill Sch.; London University. BSc(Econ.), Econ. History, 1942. British United Press, 1942–43; Reuters, 1943–48; Chm., Horizon Holidays, 1949–74. Member: NEDC for Hotels and Catering Industry, 1968–74; Cinematograph Films Council, 1969–74; Ct of Governors, LSE, 1971–. Cavaliere Ufficiale, Order of Merit (Italy), 1971. *Recreations:* reading, ski-ing. *Address:* 32 Dudley Court, Upper Berkeley Street, W1. *T:* 01–262 2592. *Club:* Reform.

RAJ, Prof. Kakkadan Nandanath; Hon. Emeritus Fellow, Centre for Development Studies, Trivandrum, Kerala State, since 1983 (Fellow, 1973–84); *b* 13 May 1924; *s* of K. N. Gopalan and Karthiayani Gopalan; *m* 1957, Dr Sarasamma Narayanan; two *s. Educ:* Madras Christian Coll., Tambaram (BA (Hons), MA, in Economics); London Sch. of Economics (PhD (Econ); Hon. Fellow, 1982). Asst Editor, Associated Newspapers of Ceylon, Nov. 1947–July 1948; Research Officer, Dept of Research, Reserve Bank of India, Aug. 1948–Feb. 1950; Asst Chief, Economic Div., Planning Commn, Govt of India, 1950–53; Prof. of Economics, Delhi Sch. of Economics, Univ. of Delhi, 1953–73 (Vice-Chancellor, Univ. of Delhi, 1969–70; Nat. Fellow in Economics, 1971–73). Mem., Economic Adv. Council to Prime Minister of India, 1983–. Visiting Prof., Johns Hopkins Univ., Jan.-June, 1958; Vis. Fellow, Nuffield Coll., Oxford, Jan.-June, 1960; Corresp. Fellow, British Academy, 1972. Hon. Fellow, Amer. Economic Assoc. *Publications:* The Monetary Policy of the Reserve Bank of India, 1948; Employment Aspects of Planning in Underdeveloped Economies, 1956; Some Economic Aspects of the Bhakra-Nangal Project, 1960; Indian Economic Growth-Performance and Prospects, 1964; India, Pakistan and China-Economic Growth and Outlook, 1966; Investment in Livestock in Agrarian Economies, 1969; also articles in Economic Weekly, Economic and Political Weekly, Indian Economic Review, Oxford Economic Papers. *Address:* "Nandavan", Kumarapuram, Trivandrum 695011, Kerala State, India. *T:* (home) 73309, (office) 8881–8884, 8412.

RAJAH, Hon. Arumugam Ponnu; Hon. Mr Justice Rajah; a Judge of the Supreme Court, Singapore, since 1976; *b* Negri Sembilan, Malaysia, 23 July 1911; *m* Vijaya Lakshmi; one *s* one *d. Educ:* St Paul's Inst., Seremban; Raffles Instn and Raffles Coll., Singapore; Lincoln Coll., Oxford Univ. (BA). Barrister-at-law, Lincoln's Inn. City Councillor, Singapore: nominated, 1947–49; elected, 1949–57; MLA for Farrer Park, Singapore, 1959–66, Chm., Public Accounts Cttee, 1959–63, Speaker, 1964–66; first High Comr for Singapore to UK, 1966–71; High Comr to Australia, 1971–73; practised law, Tan Rajah & Cheah, Singapore, 1973–76. Mem. Bd of Trustees, Singapore Improvement Trust, 1949–57; Mem., Raffles Coll. Council and Univ. of Malaya Council, 1955–63; Chm., Inst. of SE Asian Studies, 1975–84; Pro-Chancellor, Nat. Univ. of Singapore, 1975–. Hon. Dr Laws Nat. Univ. of Singapore, 1984. *Address:* Supreme Court, Singapore; 7–D Balmoral Road, Singapore 10.

RALLI, Sir Godfrey (Victor), 3rd Bt, *cr* 1912; TD; *b* 9 Sept. 1915; *s* of Sir Strati Ralli, 2nd Bt, MC; *S* father 1964; *m* 1st, 1937, Nora Margaret Forman (marriage dissolved, 1947); one *s* two *d*; 2nd, 1949, Jean, *er d* of late Keith Barlow. *Educ:* Eton. Joined Ralli Bros Ltd, 1936. Served War of 1939–45 (despatches), Captain, Berkshire Yeomanry RA. Director and Vice-Chairman, Ralli Bros Ltd, 1946–62; Chm., Greater London Fund for the Blind, 1962–82. *Recreations:* fishing, golf. *Heir:* *s* David Charles Ralli [*b* 5 April 1946; *m* 1975, Jacqueline Cecilia, *d* of David Smith; one *s* one *d*]. *Address:* Great Walton, Eastry, Sandwich, Kent CT13 0DN. *T:* Sandwich 611355. *Clubs:* White's, Naval and Military.

RALPHS, Enid Mary, (Lady Ralphs), CBE 1984; JP; DL; Chairman of the Council, Magistrates' Association, 1981–84; *b* 20 Jan. 1915; *d* of Percy William Cowlin and Annie Louise Cowlin (*née* Willoughby); *m* 1938, Sir (Frederick) Lincoln Ralphs Kt 1973 (*d* 1978); one *s* two *d. Educ:* Camborne Grammar Sch.; University Coll., Exeter (BA); DipEd Cambridge. Pres., Guild of Undergrads, Exeter, 1936–37; Vice-Pres., NUS, 1937–38. Teacher, Penzance Grammar Sch., 1937–38; Staff Tutor, Oxford Univ. Tutorial Classes Cttee, 1942–44; pt-time Sen. Lectr, Keswick Hall Coll. of Educn, 1948–80. Member: Working Party on Children and Young Persons Act 1969, 1977–78; Steering Cttee on Community Alternatives for Young Offenders, NACRO, 1979–82; Consultative Cttee on Educn in Norwich Prison, 1982–. Member: Religious Adv. Council, BBC Midland Reg., 1963–66; Guide Council for GB, 1965–68. Pres., Norwich and Dist Br., UNA, 1973–. Governor: Norwich Sch.; Culford Sch.; Wymondham Coll. Trustee, Norfolk Children's Projects, 1982–. JP Norwich 1958; Chairman: Norwich Juvenile Panel, 1964–79; Norwich Bench, 1977–85; former Mem., Licensing Cttee; Mem., Domestic Panel, 1981–85; Chm., Norfolk Br., Magistrates' Assoc.; Dep. Chm., Norfolk Magistrates' Courts Cttee, 1978–85 (Chm., Trng Sub-Cttee); Mem., Central Council, Magistrates' Courts Cttees, 1974–81. DL Norfolk 1981. *Publications:* contribs to various jls. *Recreations:* gardening, travel. *Address:* Jesselton, 218 Unthank Road, Norwich NR2 2AH. *T:* Norwich 53382. *Club:* Royal Over-Seas League.

RAM CHANDRA, CIE 1933; MBE 1919; MA (Punjab); MA (Cantab); a Trustee of The Tribune (English daily newspaper in Chandigarh), 1949–76, President of Board of Trustees, 1967–76; *b* 1 March 1889; *m* 1917; one *s* one *d. Educ:* Government College, Lahore (Fuller Exhibitioner); Panjab Univ. (MA English 1907; MA 1st class, Mathematics, 1908); Trinity College, Cambridge (Senior Scholar, Mathematical Tripos and Wrangler, b star, 1913); Govt of India Bd of Examrs Cert. of High Proficiency in Persian, 1915; Degree of Honour in Urdu, 1921. Assistant Professor of Mathematics, Government College, Lahore, 1908–10; joined ICS, 1913; served in Punjab as Assistant Commissioner in various districts; Colonisation Officer, 1915; Under-Secretary, 1919–21; Settlement Officer, 1921–25; Director of Land Records, 1924; Deputy Commissioner, 1925; Secretary to Punjab Government, Transferred Department, 1926–27; Home Secretary to Punjab Government, 1928; Deputy Secretary to Govt of India, Department of Education, Health, and Lands, 1928; Joint Secretary, 1932; Secretary, 1935; Member Council of State, 1935; Member, Punjab Legislative Council, 1936; Finance Secretary to Punjab Govt, 1936–37; Commissioner, 1938–39; Sec. to Punjab Govt, Medical and Local Govt Depts, 1939–41; Chief Controller of Imports, India, 1941–44; Leader of Indian Delegation to Egypt for Cotton Conference, 1943; Secretary to Government of India, Commerce Dept, 1944–45; Secretary to Govt of India, Defence Dept, 1945–46; Financial Comr, Punjab, 1946–48; Chairman, Punjab (India) Public Service Commission, 1948–53; Mem., Punjab Legislative Council (elected by Graduates' Constituency), 1954–60; Fellow of Panjab Univ., Chandigarh, 1947–68, Syndic, 1949–64; Syndic and Fellow, Punjabi Univ., Patiala, 1962–72. Chief Comr, Scouts and Guides, Punjab, 1955–68. *Recreation:* gardening. *Address:* Forest Hill, Simla 2, India. *T:* 2129.

RAMACHANDRAN, Prof. Gopalasamudram Narayana, FRS 1977; Indian National Science Academy Albert Einstein National Professor, since 1984; *b* 8 Oct. 1922; *s* of G. R. Narayana Iyer and Lakshmi Ammal; *m* 1945, Rajalakshmi Sankaran; two *s* one *d. Educ:* Maharaja's Coll., Ernakulam, Cochin; Indian Inst. of Science; Univ. of Madras (MA, MSc, DSc); Univ. of Cambridge (PhD). Lectr in Physics, Indian Inst. of Science, 1946–47, Asst Prof., 1949–52; 1851 Exhibn Scholar, Univ. of Cambridge, 1947–49; Prof., Univ. of Madras, 1952–70 (Dean, Faculty of Science, 1964–67); Prof. of Biophysics, 1970–78, Inst. Prof. of Mathematical Philosophy, 1978–81, Hon. Fellow, 1984, Indian Inst. of Science; Dist. Scientist, Centre for Cellular and Molecular Biology, Hyderabad, 1981–83. Dir, Univ. Grants Commn Centre of Advanced Study in Biophysics, 1962–70; part-time Prof. of Physics, Univ. of Chicago, 1967–78. Member: Physical Res. Cttee, 1959–; Nat. Cttee for Biophysics, 1961–; Bd of Sci. and Ind. Res., India, 1962–65; Council, Internat. Union of Pure and Applied Biophysics, 1969–72; Commn on Macromolecular Biophysics, 1969; Chm., Nat. Cttee for Crystallography, 1963–70; Senior Vis. Prof., Univ. of Michigan, 1965–66; Jawaharlal Nehru Fellow, 1968–70; Fogarty Internat. Schol., NIH, 1977–78. Fellow, Indian Acad. of Sciences, 1950 (Mem. Council, 1953–70; Sec., 1956–58; Vice-Pres., 1962–64); Fellow, Nat. Inst. of Sciences, 1963; FRSA 1971. Hon. Mem., Amer. Soc. of Biological Chem., 1965; Hon. Foreign Mem., Amer. Acad. of Arts and Scis; Founder Mem., Indian Acad. of Yoga, 1980; Mem., Third World Acad., Rome, 1982. Hon. DSc: Roorkee, 1979; Indian Inst. Technology, Madras, 1985. Bhatnagar Meml Prize, 1961; Watumull Prize, 1964; John Arthur Wilson Award, 1967; Ramanujan Medal, 1971; Maghnad Saha Medal, 1971; J. C. Bose Gold Medal and Prize of Bose Inst., 1975; Fogarty Medal, 1978; Distinguished Alumni Award, Indian Inst. of Sci., 1978; C. V. Raman Award, 1982; Birla Award for Medical Science, 1984. Editor: Current Science, 1950–58; Jl Indian Inst. of Sci., 1973–77; Member Editorial Board: Jl Molecular Biol., 1959–66; Biochimica et Biophysica Acta, 1965–72; Indian Jl Pure and Applied Physics, 1963–; Internat. Jl Peptide and Protein Res., 1969–; Indian Jl Biochem. and Biophys., 1970–; Connective Tissue Research 1972–; Biopolymers, 1973–; Jl Biomolecular Structure and Dynamics, 1984–. *Publications:* Crystal Optics, in Handbuch der Physik, vol. 25; Molecular Structure of Collagen, in Internat. Review of Connective Tissue Research, vol. 1; Conformation of Polypeptides and Proteins, in Advances in Protein Chemistry, vol. 23; Conformation Polypeptide Chains, in Annual Reviews in Biochemistry, vol. 39; Fourier Methods in Crystallography, 1970; (ed) Advanced Methods of Crystallography; (ed) Aspects of Protein Structure; (ed) Treatise on Collagen, 2 vols, 1967; (ed) Conformation of Biopolymers, vols 1 and 2, 1967; (ed) Crystallography and Crystal Perfection; (ed) Biochemistry of Collagen. *Recreations:* Indian and Western music; detective fiction. *Address:* Mathematical Philosophy Group, Indian Institute of Science, Bangalore 560 012, India. *T:* 364411 ext. 461; Gita, 5, 10–A Main Road, Malleswaram West, Bangalore 560055. *T:* 360362.

RAMADHANI, Most Rev. John Acland; *see* Tanzania, Archbishop of.

RAMAGE, Captain Cecil Beresford, MC; *b* 17 Jan. 1895; *o s* of John Walker Ramage, Edinburgh; *m* 1921, Cathleen Nesbitt, CBE (*d* 1982); one *s* one *d. Educ:* Edinburgh Academy; Pembroke College, Oxford (open Classical Scholar); President Oxford Union Society. Commissioned in the Royal Scots, 1914; served Gallipoli, Egypt, Palestine, until 1919 (despatches, Order of the Nile). Contested Newcastle upon Tyne, General Election, 1922; MP (L) Newcastle upon Tyne (West Division), 1923–24; contested Southport, 1929. Barrister-at-Law, Middle Temple, 1921; subseq. Oxford Circuit. *Recreation:* golf. *Address:* Flat 2, 11 Dean Park Road, Bournemouth, Dorset.

RAMAGE, (James) Granville (William), CMG 1975; HM Diplomatic Service, retired; *b* 19 Nov. 1919; *s.* of late Rev. George Granville Ramage and Helen Marion (*née* Middlemass); *m* 1947, Eileen Mary Smith; one *s* two *d. Educ:* Glasgow Acad.; Glasgow University. Served in HM Forces, 1940–46 (despatches). Entered HM Foreign Service, 1947; seconded for service at Bombay, 1947–49; transf. to Foreign Office, 1950; First Sec. and Consul at Manila, 1952–56; South-East Asia Dept, FO, 1956–58; Consul at Atlanta, Ga, 1958–62; Gen. Dept, FO, 1962–63; Consul-General, Tangier, 1963–67; High Comr in The Gambia, 1968–71; Ambassador, People's Democratic Republic of Yemen, 1972–75; Consul General at Boston, Massachusetts, 1975–77. *Recreations:* music, golf. *Address:* 4 Merton Hall Road, Wimbledon, SW19 3PP. *T:* 01–542 5492.

RAMBAHADUR LIMBU, Captain, VC 1966; MVO 1984; HM the Queen's Gurkha Orderly Officer, 1983–85; employed in Sultanate of Negara Brunei Darussalam, since 1985; *b* Nov. 1939; *s* of late Tekbir Limbu; *m* 1st, 1960, Tikamaya Limbuni (*d* 1966); two *s*; 2nd, 1967, Purnimaya Limbuni; three *s.* Army Cert. of Educn 1st cl. Enlisted 10th Princess Mary's Own Gurkha Rifles, 1957; served on ops in Borneo (VC); promoted Sergeant, 1971; WOII, 1976; commissioned, 1977. Hon. Captain (GCO), 1985. *Publication:* My Life Story, 1978. *Recreations:* football, volley-ball, badminton, basketball. *Address:* Gurkha Reserve Unit, Sungei Akar Camp, Post Box No 420, Negara Brunei Darussalam; Ward No 13 Damak, Nagar Panchayat, PO Box Damak, District Jhapa, Mechi Zone, East Nepal. *Clubs:* VC and GC Association, Royal Society of St George (England).

RAMELSON, Baruch, (Bert); Member, Editorial Board, World Marxist Review, published in Prague, and Editor of the English edition, since 1977; *b* 22 March 1910; *s* of Jacob and Liuba Mendelson; *m* 1st, 1939, Marion Jessop (*d* 1967); 2nd, 1970, Joan Dorothy Smith; one step *s* two step *d. Educ:* Univ. of Alberta. 1st cl. hons LLB. Barrister and Solicitor, Edmonton, Alta, 1934–35; Internat. Bde, Mackenzie-Pappinard Bn, Spanish Civil War, 1937–39; Adjt, Canadian Bn of Internat. Bde; Tank Driver, Royal Tank Corps, 1941; captured, Tobruk, 1941; escaped Prison Camp, Italy, 1943; OCTU, Catterick, 1944–45, commnd RA 1945; served in India, 1945–46 (Actg Staff Captain Legal). Communist Party of GB: full-time Sec., Leeds, 1946–53; Sec., Yorks, 1953–65; Mem. Nat. Exec., 1953–78; Mem. Polit. Cttee, 1954–78; National Industrial Organiser, 1965–77. *Publications:* The Case for an Alternative Policy, 1977; various pamphlets and booklets; contrib. Communist (Moscow), Marxism Today, World Marxist Review. *Recreations:* travel, reading. *Address:* 160A Conisborough Crescent, Catford, SE6 2SF. *T:* 01–698 0738.

RAMIN, Mme Manfred; *see* Cotrubas, I.

RAMM, Rev. Canon (Norwyn) MacDonald; Vicar of St Michael at North Gate with St Martin and All Saints, Oxford, since 1961 (Curate, 1957–61); City Rector, Oxford; Chaplain to the Queen, since 1985; *b* 8 June 1924; *s* of Rev. Ezra Edward and Dorothy Mary Ramm; *m* 1962, Ruth Ellen, *d* of Robert James Kirton, *qv*; two *s* one *d. Educ:* Berkhamsted School; St Peter's Theological College, Jamaica; Lincoln College, Oxford. Jamaica appointments: Curate, St James, 1951–53, deacon 1951, priest, 1952; Master, Cornwall College; Rector, Stony Hill with Mount James, 1953–57; Master, Wolmers Girls' School; Chaplain to Approved Sch., Stony Hill; Priest in charge, St Martin and All Saints, Oxford, 1961–71; Hon. Canon, Christ Church Cathedral, Oxford, 1985–. Chaplain to: HM Prison, Oxford, 1975–; British Fire Services Assoc., 1980–; The Sea Cadets, RAF Assoc., RTR, Para Regtl Assoc., Desert Forces (all Oxford branches), Oxford City Police Assoc. Pres., Isis Dist Scout Assoc., 1984–; Chm. Council, Headington Sch., 1984–; Founder, Samaritans of Oxford, 1963. *Recreations:* ski-ing, gardening, collecting Graces. *Address:* 24 St Michael's Street, Oxford OX1 2EB. *T:* Oxford 242444. *Clubs:* Clarendon, Frewen (Oxford), Oxford Rotary.

RAMPHAL, Sir Shridath Surendranath, OE 1983; AC 1982; Kt 1970; CMG 1966; QC (Guyana) 1965, SC 1966; Secretary-General of the Commonwealth, since 1975; *b* 1928; *m. Educ:* King's Coll., London (LLM 1952). FKC 1975; Fellow, London Sch. of Econs, 1979. Called to the Bar, Gray's Inn, 1951 (Hon. Bencher 1981). Colonial Legal Probationer, 1951; Arden and Atkin Prize, 1952; John Simon Guggenheim Fellow, Harvard Law Sch., 1962. Crown Counsel, British Guiana, 1952–54; Asst to Attorney-Gen., 1954–56; Legal Draftsman, 1956–58; First Legal Draftsman, West Indies, 1958–59; Solicitor-Gen., British Guiana, 1959–61; Asst Attorney-Gen., West Indies, 1961–62, Attorney-Gen., Guyana, 1965–73; Minister of State for External Affairs, Guyana, 1967–72; Foreign Minister and Attorney General, Guyana, 1972–73; Minister, Foreign Affairs and Justice, 1973–75; Mem., National Assembly, Guyana, 1965–75. Member: Hon. Adv. Cttee, Center for Internat. Studies, NY Univ., 1966–; Internat. Commn of Jurists, 1970–; Bd, Vienna Inst. of Develt, 1973–; Internat. Hon. Cttee, Dag Hammarskjold Foundn, 1977–; Independent (Brandt) Commn on International Development Issues, 1977–; Ind. (Palme) Commn on Disarmament and Security Issues, 1980–; Ind. Commn on Internat. Humanitarian Issues, 1983–; World Commn on Environment and Develt, 1984–; Council, Television Trust for the Environment, 1984–; Internat. Bd, United World Colls, 1984–; Bd of Governors, World Maritime Univ., Oslo, 1984–. Chairman: Selection Cttee, Third World Prize, 1979–; UN Cttee on Develt Planning, 1984–87; Vice-Chm., Centre for Research on New Internat. Econ. Order, Oxford, 1977–. FRSA 1981; Hon. Fellow, Magdalen Coll., Oxford, 1982; Hon. LLD: Panjab, 1975; Southampton, 1976; St Francis Xavier, NS, 1978; Univ. of WI, 1978; Aberdeen, 1979; Cape Coast, Ghana, 1980; London, 1981; Benin, Nigeria, 1982; Hull, 1983; Yale, 1985; Cambridge, 1985; DUniv: Surrey, 1979; Essex, 1980; Hon. DHL: Simmons Coll., Boston, 1982; Duke Univ., 1985; Hon. DCL: Oxon, 1982; E Anglia, 1983; Hon. DLitt, Bradford, 1985. *Publications:* One World to Share: selected speeches of the Commonwealth Secretary-General 1975–79, 1979; Nkrumah and the Eighties: Kwame Nkrumah Memorial Lectures, 1980; Sovereignty and Solidarity: Callander Memorial Lectures, 1981; Some in Light and Some in Darkness: the long shadow of slavery (Wilberforce Lecture), 1983; The Message not the Messenger (STC Communication Lecture), 1985; contrib. various political, legal and other jls incl. International and Comparative Law Qly, Caribbean Qly, Public Law, Guyana Jl, Round Table, Foreign Policy, Third World Qly, RSA Jl Internat. Affairs. *Address:* Commonwealth Secretariat, Marlborough House, Pall Mall, SW1Y 5HX. *Clubs:* Athenæum, Royal Automobile, Travellers'.

RAMPTON, Sir Jack (Leslie), KCB 1973 (CB 1969); Director, London Atlantic Investment Trust, since 1981; *b* 10 July 1920; *s* of late Leonard Wilfrid Rampton and of Sylvia (*née* Davies); *m* 1950, Eileen Joan (*née* Hart); one *s* one *d. Educ:* Tonbridge Sch.; Trinity Coll., Oxford. MA. Treasury, 1941; Asst Priv. Sec. to successive Chancellors of the Exchequer, 1942–43; Priv. Sec. to Financial Sec., 1945–46; Economic and Financial Adv. to Comr-Gen. for SE Asia and to British High Comr, Malaya, 1959–61; Under-Secretary, HM Treasury, 1964–68; Dep. Sec., Min. of Technology (formerly Min. of Power), 1968–70; Dep. Sec., DTI, 1970–72; Second Permanent Sec. and Sec. (Industrial Develt), DTI, 1972–74; Perm. Under-Sec. of State, Dept of Energy, 1974–80. Dep. Chm., Sheerness Steel Co., 1985– (Dir, 1982–); Special Adviser: North Sea Sun Oil Co., 1982–; Sun Exploration and Development Co. Inc., 1982–; Magnet Gp, WA, 1981–84; Director: ENO Co., 1982–; Flextech plc, 1985–. Member: Council, Victoria League, 1981– (Dep. Chm. 1985–); Honeywell UK Adv. Council, 1981–; Oxford Energy Policy Club, 1978–; Council, Cook Soc., 1984– (Chm., 1986–87); British Library of Tape Recordings Adv. Council, 1977–; Council, Britain-Australia Soc., 1986– (Hon. Sec., 1986–). CBIM; CIGasE; FInstPet 1982. Hon. DSc Aston, 1979. *Recreations:* gardening, games, photography, travel; Oxford Squash V (Capt.) 1939–40; Authentic, 1940. *Address:* 17 The Ridgeway, Tonbridge, Kent. *T:* Tonbridge 352117. *Clubs:* Pilgrims, Britain Australia Society; Vincent's (Oxford).

RAMSAY, family name of **Earl of Dalhousie.**

RAMSAY, Lord; James Hubert Ramsay; Executive Director, Enskilda Securities, Skandinaviska Enskilda Ltd, since 1982; *b* 17 Jan. 1948; *er s* and *heir* of 16th Earl of Dalhousie, *qv*; *m* 1973, Marilyn, *yr d* of Major David Butter, *qv*; one *s* two *d. Educ:* Ampleforth. 2nd Bn Coldstream Guards, commnd 1968–71, RARO 1971. Dir, Hambros Bank Ltd, 1981–82. *Heir: s* Hon. Simon David Ramsay, *b* 18 April 1981. *Address:* Dalhousie Lodge, Edzell, Angus; 3 Vicarage Gardens, W8. *Clubs:* White's, Pratt's, Turf.

RAMSAY, Sir Alexander William Burnett, 7th Bt, *cr* 1806, of Balmain (also *heir-pres* to Btcy of Burnett, *cr* 1626 (Nova Scotia), of Leys, Kincardineshire, which became dormant, 1959, on death of Sir Alexander Edwin Burnett of Leys, and was not claimed by Sir Alexander Burnett Ramsay, 6th Bt, of Balmain); *b* 4 Aug. 1938; *s* of Sir Alexander Burnett Ramsay, 6th Bt and Isabel Ellice, *e d* of late William Whitney, Woodstock, New South Wales; *S* father, 1965; *m* 1963, Neryl Eileen, *d* of J. C. Smith Thornton, Trangie, NSW; three *s. Heir: s* Alexander David Ramsay, *b* 20 Aug. 1966. *Address:* Bulbah, Warren, NSW 2824, Australia.

RAMSAY, Allan John Heppel Ramsay; HM Diplomatic Service; Counsellor and Head of West Indian and Atlantic Department, Foreign and Commonwealth Office, since 1985; *b* 19 Oct. 1937; *s* of Norman Ramsay Ramsay and Faith Evelyn Sorel-Cameron; *m* 1966, Pauline Therese Lescher; two *s* one *d. Educ:* Bedford Sch.; RMA Sandhurst; Durham Univ. Served Army, 1957–70: Somerset Light Infantry, 1957–65; DLI, 1965–70. Entered FCO, 1970. *Address:* c/o Foreign and Commonwealth Office, SW1A 2AH. *Clubs:* Brooks's, Hurlingham.

RAMSAY, Arthur; *see* Ramsay, James A.

RAMSAY, Maj.-Gen. Charles Alexander, OBE 1979; General Officer Commanding Eastern District, since 1984; *b* 12 Oct. 1936; *s* of Adm. Sir Bertram Home Ramsay, KCB, KBE, MVO, Allied Naval C-in-C, Invasion of Europe, 1944 (killed on active service, 1945), and Helen Margaret (*née* Menzies); *m* 1967, Hon. Mary Margaret Hastings MacAndrew, *d* of 1st Baron MacAndrew, PC, TD; two *s* two *d. Educ:* Eton; Sandhurst. Commissioned Royal Scots Greys, 1956; served Germany, Middle East, Canada, N Ireland; commanded Royal Scots Dragoon Guards, 1977–79; Colonel General Staff, MoD, 1979–80; Comdr 12th Armoured Bde, BAOR, 1980–82; Dep. Dir of Mil. Ops, MoD, 1983–84. Member, Queen's Body Guard for Scotland, Royal Company of Archers. *Recreations:* field sports, equitation, travel. *Address:* Bughtrig, Coldstream, Berwickshire. *T:* Leitholm 221; Chesthill, Glenlyon, Perthshire. *T:* Glenlyon 224. *Clubs:* Boodle's, Cavalry and Guards, Farmers'; New (Edinburgh).

RAMSAY, Donald Allan, ScD; FRS 1978, FRSC 1966; Principal Research Officer, National Research Council of Canada, since 1968; *b* 11 July 1922; *s* of Norman Ramsay and Thirza Elizabeth Beckley; *m* 1946, Nancy Brayshaw; four *d. Educ:* Latymer Upper Sch.; St Catharine's Coll., Cambridge. BA 1943, MA 1947, PhD 1947, ScD 1976 (all Cantab). Research Scientist (Div. of Chemistry, 1947, Div. of Physics, 1949, Herzberg Inst. of Astrophysics, 1975), Nat. Research Council of Canada. Fellow, Amer. Phys. Soc., 1964; FCIC, 1970; Vice-Pres., Acad. of Science, 1975–76; Hon. Treas., RSC, 1976–79, Centennial Medal, RSC, 1982. Dr *hc* Reims, 1969; Fil.Hed. Stockholm, 1982. Queen Elizabeth II Silver Jubilee Medal, 1977. *Publications:* numerous articles on molecular spectroscopy and molecular structure, espec. free radicals. *Recreations:* sailing, fishing, organ playing. *Address:* 1578 Drake Avenue, Ottawa, Ontario K1G 0L8, Canada. *T:* 613–733–8899. *Club:* Leander (Henley).

RAMSAY, Henry Thomas, CBE 1960; Director, Safety in Mines Research Establishment, Ministry of Technology (formerly Ministry of Power), Sheffield, 1954–70, retired; *b* 7 Dec. 1907; *s* of Henry Thomas and Florence Emily Ramsay, Gravesend, Kent; *m* 1953, Dora Gwenllian Burgoyne Davies (*d* 1979); one *s* one *d*; *m* 1983, Vivian Ducatel Prague, Bay St Louis, Miss. *Educ:* Gravesend Junior Techn. Sch.; thereafter by evening study. On scientific staff, Research Labs, GEC, 1928–48; RAE, 1948–54. Chartered engineer; FInstP; FIMinE; Pres., Midland Inst. Mining Engrs, 1970–71. *Publications:* contrib. to: Trans of Instn of Electrical Engrs; Jl of Inst. of Mining Engrs; other technical jls. *Recreations:* gardening, horses.

RAMSAY, J(ames) Arthur, MBE 1945; FRS 1955; Fellow of Queens' College, Cambridge, 1934–76, now Hon. Fellow; Professor of Comparative Physiology, University of Cambridge, 1969–76, now Emeritus Professor (Reader, 1959); *b* 6 Sept. 1909; *s* of late David Ramsay and Isabella Rae Ramsay (*née* Garvie); *m* 1939, Helen Amelie, *d* of late Oscar Dickson, Stockholm; one *s* one *d. Educ:* Fettes College; Gonville and Caius College, Cambridge. University Demonstrator and Fellow of Queens', 1934. Major RA Coast and Anti-Aircraft Defence Experimental Establishment, 1939–45. Joint Editor, Journal of Experimental Biology, 1952–74. *Publications:* Physiological Approach to the Lower Animals, 1952; The Experimental Basis of Modern Biology, 1965; A Guide to Thermodynamics, 1972; papers in Jl of Experimental Biology. *Recreations:* mountaineering, ski-ing. *Address:* The Boxer's Croft, Achbuie 3, Abriachan, Inverness-shire. *T:* Dochgarroch 269.

RAMSAY, Prof. John Graham, FRS 1973; Professor of Geology, Eidgenössische Technische Hochschule and University of Zürich, since 1977; *b* 17 June 1931; *s* of Robert William Ramsay and Kathleen May Ramsay; *m* 1st, 1952, Sylvia Hiorns (marr. diss. 1957); 2nd, 1960, Christine Marden; three *d* (and one *d* decd). *Educ:* Edmonton County Grammar Sch.; Imperial Coll., London. DSc, PhD, DIC, BSc, ARCS, FGS. Musician, Corps of Royal Engineers, 1955–57; academic staff Imperial Coll., London, 1957–73: Prof. of Geology, 1966–73; Prof. of Earth Sciences, Leeds Univ., 1973–76. Vice-Pres., Société Géologique de France, 1973. For. Associate, US Nat. Acad. of Scis, 1985. Dr *hc* Rennes, 1978. *Publications:* Folding and Fracturing of Rocks, 1967; The Techniques of Modern Structural Geology, 1983. *Recreations:* chamber music, mountaineering, ski-ing. *Address:* Eidgenössische Technische Hochschule Zürich, ETH Zentrum, CH 8092 Zürich, Switzerland.

RAMSAY, Norman James Gemmill; Sheriff of South Strathclyde, Dumfries and Galloway at Kirkcudbright, Stranraer and Dumfries (formerly Dumfries and Galloway, Western Division), 1971–85, now Hon. Sheriff; *b* 26 Aug. 1916; *s* of late James Ramsay and late Mrs Christina Emma Ramsay; *m* 1952, Rachael Mary Berkeley Cox, *d* of late Sir Herbert Charles Fahie Cox; two *s. Educ:* Merchiston Castle Sch.; Edinburgh Univ. (MA, LLB). Writer to the Signet, 1939; Advocate, Scotland, 1956. War Service, RN, 1940–46; Lt (S), RNVR. Colonial Legal Service, Northern Rhodesia: Administrator-General, 1947; Resident Magistrate, 1956; Sen. Resident Magistrate, 1958; Puisne Judge of High Court, Northern Rhodesia, later Zambia, 1964–68. Mem., Victoria Falls Trust, 1950–58. *Address:* Mill of Borgue, Kirkcudbright DG6 4SY.

RAMSAY, Patrick George Alexander; Controller, BBC Scotland, 1979–83; *b* 14 April 1926; *yr s* of late Rt Rev. Ronald Erskine Ramsay, sometime Bishop of Malmesbury, and Winifred Constance Ramsay (*née* Partridge); *m* 1948, Hope Seymour Dorothy, *y d* of late Rt Rev. Algernon Markham, sometime Bishop of Grantham, and Winifred Edith Markham (*née* Barne); two *s. Educ:* Marlborough Coll.; Jesus Coll., Cambridge (MA). Served War, Royal Navy (Fleet Air Arm), 1944–46. Joined BBC as Report Writer, Eastern European Desk, Monitoring Service, 1949; Liaison Officer, US Foreign Broadcasts Information Service, Cyprus, 1951–52; Asst, Appts Dept, 1953–56; Sen. Admin. Asst, External Broadcasting, 1956–58; Admin. Officer News and Head of News Administration, 1958–64; Planning Manager, Television Programme Planning, 1964–66; Asst Controller: Programme Services, 1966–69; Programme Planning, 1969–72; Controller, Programme Services, 1972–79. General Managerial Advr, Oman Broadcasting Service, 1984–85. A Dir, Windsor Festival Soc., 1973–76. Councillor and Alderman, Royal Borough of New Windsor, 1962–67; Chm., Windsor and Eton Soc., 1971–76. FRSA. *Recreations:* fellwalking, gardening, foreign travel, history, looking in junk shops, thwarting bureaucrats. *Address:* Englefield Green House, Surrey. *Clubs:* Naval, National Liberal; New (Edinburgh).

RAMSAY, Richard Alexander McGregor; Director, Hill Samuel & Co. Ltd, since 1984; *b* 27 Dec. 1949; *s* of Alexander John McGregor Ramsay and Beatrice Kent De Lanauze; *m* 1975, Elizabeth Catherine Margaret Blackwood; one *s* one *d. Educ:* Dalhousie Sch.; Trinity Coll., Glenalmond; Aberdeen Univ. (MA Hons in Politics and Sociology). ACA 1975; FCA. Price Waterhouse & Co., 1972–75; Grindlay Brandts, 1976–78; Hill Samuel & Co. Ltd, 1979–; on secondment as Dir, Industrial Develt Unit, DTI, 1984–86. *Recreations:* squash, hill walking, ski-ing, computing, classic cars. *Address:* 23 Pinfold Road, SW16 2SL. *T:* 01–769 2703.

RAMSAY, Thomas Anderson; *b* 9 Feb. 1920; *s* of David Mitchell Ramsay and Ruth Bramfitt Ramsay; *m* 1949, Margaret Lilian Leggat Donald; one *s* two *d. Educ:* Glasgow Univ. BSc, MB, ChB. FRCSGlas; FFCM; FRSH; FRCP. Surg. Lieut, RNVR, 1945–47. Various posts in general and clinical hospital practice (mainly paediatric and orthopaedic surg.), 1943–56; Asst, later Dep. Sen. Admin. Med. Officer, NI Hospitals Authority, 1957–58; Dep. Sen., later Sen. Admin. Med. Officer, NE Metropolitan Reg. Hospital Bd, 1958–72; Post-Grad. Dean and Prof. of Post-Grad. Med., Univ. of Aberdeen, 1972–76; Dir of Post-Grad. Med. Educn, NE Region (Scotland), 1972–76; Med. Officer, W Midlands RHA, 1976–79; Prof. of Post Graduate Med. Educn, Univ. of Warwick, 1980–83; Dir, Post Graduate Med. Educn, Coventry AHA, Warwicks Post Graduate Med. Centre, 1980–85. Vis. Prof. of Health Services Admin, London Sch. of Hygiene and Tropical Medicine, 1971–72; Vis. Prof., Health Services Admin., Univ. of Aston, 1979–. Mem. Bd, Faculty of Community Medicine, 1972–. Governor, London Hosp., 1965–72. *Publications:* several papers in learned jls regarding post-graduate medical educn and community medicine. *Recreations:* travel, photography. *Address:* 1 Vallum Close, Carlisle, Cumbria. *T:* Carlisle 33870.

RAMSAY, Sir Thomas (Meek), Kt 1972; CMG 1965; Chairman: The Kiwi International Company Ltd, Melbourne, 1967–80; joined The Kiwi Polish Co. Pty Ltd, Melbourne, 1926, Managing Director, 1956–72 (Joint Managing Director, 1945); *b* Essendon, Victoria, 24 Nov. 1907; *s* of late William Ramsay, Scotland; *m* 1941, Catherine Anne, *d* of John William Richardson, Adelaide, SA; four *s* one *d. Educ:* Malvern Grammar; Scotch Coll.; Melbourne Univ. (BSc). CMF, 1940–41 (Lieut); Asst Controller, Min. of Munitions, 1941–45. Chairman: Norwich Union Life Insurance Soc. (Aust. Bd), 1968–79; Collie (Aust.) Ltd Group, 1977–79; Industrial Design Council of Australia, 1969–76;

ANZAC Fellowship Selection Cttee, 1971–78; Director: Australian Consolidated Industries Ltd Group, 1965–79; Alex Harvey Industries Group, NZ. President: Associated Chambers of Manufrs of Australia, 1962–63; Victorian Chamber of Manufrs, 1962–64; Mem., Selection Cttee (Industrial) Sir Winston Churchill Fellowships. FRHistS of Queensland, 1964; FRHistS of Victoria, 1965; FAIM; FSAScot. Hon. Sen. Fellow, Mus. of Victoria. *Recreations:* gardening, Australian historical research. *Address:* 23 Airlie Street, South Yarra, Victoria 3141, Australia. *T:* 26 1751. *Clubs:* Athenæum, Australian, Melbourne (Melbourne).

RAMSAY-FAIRFAX-LUCY, Sir Edmund J. W. H. C.; *see* Fairfax-Lucy.

RAMSAY RAE, Air Vice-Marshal Ronald Arthur, CB 1960; OBE 1947; *b* 9 Oct. 1910; *s* of late George Ramsay Rae, Lindfield, NSW, and Alice Ramsay Rae (*née* Haselden); *m* 1939, Rosemary Gough Howell, *d* of late Charles Gough Howell, KC, Attorney General, Singapore; one *s* one *d*. *Educ:* Sydney, New South Wales, Australia. Served Australian Citizen Force and then as Cadet, RAAF, at Point Cook, 1930–31; transf. to RAF, 1932; flying duties in UK and Middle East with Nos 33 and 142 Sqdns until 1936; Advanced Armament Course; Armament officer in Far East, 1938–42; then Comdr RAF Tengah, Singapore; POW, 1943–45; Gp Captain in comd Central Gunnery Sch., Leconfield, Yorks, 1946; despatches, 1946. RAF Staff Coll., Andover, 1948; Dep. Dir Organisation (Estabt), Middle East; in comd RAF North Luffenham and then RAF Oakington (206 Advanced Flying Sch.); Commandant, Aircraft and Armament Exptl Estabt, Boscombe Down, 1955–57; Dep. Air Sec., Air Min., 1957–59; AOC No 224 Group, RAF, 1959–62, retd. NPFA, 1963–71. AFRAeS 1956. *Recreations:* cricket, golf, tennis, winter sports (Cresta Run and ski-ing; Pres., St Moritz Tobogganing Club, 1978–84). *Address:* Commonwealth Bank of Australia, 71 Aldwych, WC2; Little Wakestone, Bedham, Fittleworth, W Sussex. *Club:* Royal Air Force.
See also Hon. Sir Wallace A. R. Rae.

RAMSBOTHAM, family name of **Viscount Soulbury.**

RAMSBOTHAM, Maj.-Gen. David John, CBE 1980 (OBE 1974); Commander, 3rd Armoured Division, 1984–87; United Kingdom Land Forces, Salisbury, from April 1987; *b* 6 Nov. 1934; *s* of Rt Rev. J. A. Ramsbotham, *qv*; *m* 1958, Susan Caroline (*née* Dickinson); two *s*. *Educ:* Haileybury Coll.; Corpus Christi Coll., Cambridge (BA 1957, MA 1973). Nat. Service, 1952–54; Rifle Bde, UK and BAOR, 1958–62; seconded to KAR, 1962–63; Staff Coll., 1964; Rifle Bde, Far East, 1965; Staff, 7 Armoured Bde, 1966–68; 3 and 2 Green Jackets (BAOR), 1968–71; MA to CGS (Lt-Col), 1971–73; CO, 2 RGJ, 1974–76; Staff, 4 Armd Div., BAOR, 1976–78; Comd, 39 Infantry Bde, 1978–80; RCDS, 1981; Dir of Public Relns (Army), 1982–84. *Recreations:* sailing, shooting, gardening. *Address:* Morteyn, Piddlehinton, Dorset. *T:* Piddletrenthide 378. *Club:* MCC.

RAMSBOTHAM, Rt. Rev. John Alexander; *b* 25 Feb. 1906; *s* of late Rev. Alexander Ramsbotham and of late Margaret Emily Ramsbotham; *m* 1933, Eirian Morgan Owen; three *s* two *d*. *Educ:* Haileybury College; Corpus Christi College, Cambridge; Wells Theological College. Travelling Secretary, 1929–30, Missionary Secretary, 1930–33, Student Christian Movement; Chaplain, 1933–34. Vice-Principal, 1934–36, Wells Theol. Coll.; Priest-Vicar Wells Cathedral, 1933–36; Warden, College of the Ascension, Selly Oak, 1936–40; Rector of Ordsall, Notts, 1941–42; Vicar of St George's, Jesmond, Newcastle on Tyne, 1942–50; Bishop Suffragan of Jarrow, 1950–58, also Archdeacon of Auckland and Canon of Durham; Bishop of Wakefield, 1958–67; Asst Bishop, Dio. Newcastle, 1968–76. *Publication:* Belief in Christ and the Christian Community, 1949. *Recreation:* music. *Address:* West Lindeth Home, Silverdale, Lancs LA5 0TA.
See also Brig. D. J. Ramsbotham.

RAMSBOTHAM, Hon. Sir Peter (Edward), GCMG 1978 (KCMG 1972; CMG 1964); GCVO 1976; HM Diplomatic Service, retired; Director: Lloyds Bank, since 1981; Lloyds Bank UK Management, since 1983; Regional Director, Southern Regional Board, Lloyds Bank, since 1981 (Chairman 1983); Director, Commercial Union Assurance Co., since 1981; *b* 8 Oct. 1919; *yr s* of 1st Viscount Soulbury, PC, GCMG, GCVO, OBE, MC; *b* and *heir pres.* to 2nd Viscount Soulbury, *qv*; *m* 1st, 1941, Frances Blomfield (*d* 1982); two *s* one *d*; 2nd, 1985, Dr Zaida Hall, *widow* of Ruthven Hall. *Educ:* Eton College; Magdalen College, Oxford. HM Forces, 1943–46 (despatches; Croix de Guerre, 1945). Control Office for Germany and Austria from 1947; Regional Political Officer in Hamburg; entered Foreign Service, Oct. 1948; Political Division of Allied Control Commission, Berlin, Nov. 1948; transferred to Foreign Office, 1950; 1st Secretary, 1950; Head of Chancery, UK Delegation, New York, 1953; Foreign Office, 1957; Counsellor, 1961, Head of Western Organisations and Planning Dept; Head of Chancery, British Embassy, Paris, 1963–67; Foreign Office, 1967–69 (Sabbatical year, Inst. of Strategic Studies, 1968); High Comr, Nicosia, 1969–71; Ambassador to Iran, 1971–74; Ambassador to the United States, 1974–77; Governor and C-in-C of Bermuda, 1977–80. Dir, Lloyds Bank Internat., 1981–83. Trustee, Leonard Cheshire Foundn, 1981–; Chm., Ryder-Cheshire Mission for the Relief of Suffering, 1982–; Governor, King's Sch., Canterbury, 1981–. Hon. LLD: Akron Univ., 1975; Coll. of William and Mary, 1975; Maryland Univ., 1976; Yale Univ., 1977. KStJ 1976. *Recreations:* gardening, fishing. *Address:* East Lane, Ovington, near Alresford, Hants SO24 0RA. *T:* Alresford 2515. *Clubs:* Garrick; Metropolitan (Washington).

RAMSBURY, Area Bishop of; Rt. Rev. John Robert Geoffrey Neale, AKC; appointed Bishop Suffragan of Ramsbury, 1974; Hon. Canon of Salisbury Cathedral since 1974; *b* 21 Sept. 1926; *s* of late Geoffrey Brockman Neale and Stella Beatrice (*née* Wild). *Educ:* Felsted Sch.; King's Coll., London Univ. Served War of 1939–45: Lieut RA; Army, 1944–48. Business, G. B. Neale & Co Ltd, EC2, 1948–51. King's Coll. London, 1951–55 (Jelf Prize, 1954). Deacon, 1955, priest, 1956; Curate, St Peter, St Helier, Dio. Southwark, 1955–58. Chaplain, Ardingly Coll., Sx, 1958–63; Recruitment Sec., CACTM (ACCM), 1963–67; Archbishops' Rep. for ordination candidates, 1967–68; Canon Missioner, Dio. Guildford, Hon. Canon of Guildford Cath. and Rector of Hascombe, Surrey, 1968–74; Archdeacon of Wilts, 1974–80. *Publication:* Ember Prayer (SPCK), 1965. *Recreation:* horticulture. *Address:* Bishop's House, High Street, Urchfont, Devizes SN10 4QH. *T:* Chirton 373. *Club:* Royal Commonwealth Society.

RAMSDEN, Sir Caryl (Oliver Imbert), 8th Bt *cr* 1689, of Byram, Yorks; CMG 1965; CVO 1966; *b* 4 April 1915; *s* of Lt-Col Josslyn Vere Ramsden, CMG, DSO (*d* 1952) (*g g s* of 4th Bt) and Olive Clotilde Bouhier (*d* 1977), *d* of Frederic William Imbert-Terry; *S* kinsman, Sir Geoffrey William Pennington-Ramsden, 7th Bt, 1986; *m* 1945, Anne, *d* of late Sir Charles Wickham, KCMG, KBE, DSO; one *s*. *Educ:* Eton; New Coll., Oxford. Served in Royal Regiment of Artillery, 1937–49; Assistant Military Attaché, Bucharest, 1947–49. Entered HM Foreign Service, 1949, retired 1967; Private Secretary to Prime Minister, 1957; Consul-General, Hanover, 1957–59; Counsellor, Rio de Janeiro, 1959; acted as Chargé d'Affaires, 1960; Counsellor, Brussels 1962. Pro-Principal (Admin), University College at Buckingham, 1975–79. Commander of the Star of Ethiopia, 1954; Commander, Order of Leopold, 1966. *Heir: s* John Charles Josslyn Ramsden [*b* 19 Aug. 1950; *m* 1985, Jane Jennifer Bevan]. *Address:* The Old Brewery, Helperby, York YO6 2NS. *Club:* Cavalry and Guards.

RAMSDEN, Sir Geoffrey Charles Frescheville, Kt 1948; CIE 1942; *b* 21 April 1893; *s* of Colonel H. F. S. Ramsden, CBE, and Hon. Edwyna Fiennes, *d* of 17th Lord Saye and Sele, DL, JP, CC; *m* 1930, Margaret Lovell (*d* 1976), *d* of late Rev. J. Robinson; no *c*. *Educ:* Haileybury College; Sidney Sussex Coll., Cambridge (MA). Served in the Army, 1914–19; Capt. 1st Bn Royal Sussex Regt, NW Frontier (India) 1915–19; joined ICS 1920; Secretary Indian Tariff Board, 1923–25; Deputy Commissioner of Jubbulpore, 1926 and 1931–34, and of various other Districts; Commissioner, Jubbulpore Div., 1936 and 1941–44, and Chhatisgarh Div., 1937–40; Development Adviser to Governor, 1945; Financial Comr CP and Berar, 1941–45 and 1946–47; retd, 1948. *Recreations:* travel, photography, tennis and fishing. *Address:* Longdown Nursing Home, Hindhead Road, Hindhead, Surrey. *Club:* Royal Over-Seas League.

RAMSDEN, Prof. Herbert, MA, Dr en Filosofía y Letras; Professor of Spanish Language and Literature, University of Manchester, 1961–82, now Emeritus; *b* 20 April 1927; *s* of Herbert and Ann Ramsden; *m* 1953, Joyce Robina Hall, SRN, ONC, CMB; three *s* (incl. twin *s*) twin *d*. *Educ:* Sale Grammar Sch.; Univs of Manchester, Strasbourg, Madrid and Sorbonne. National Service, Inf. and Intell. Corps, 1949–51 (commnd). Travel, study and research abroad (Kemsley Travelling Fellow, etc), 1951–54; Univ. of Manchester: Asst Lectr in Spanish, 1954–57; Lectr in Spanish, 1957–61; Chm. of MA Cttee, 1964–65; Pres., Philological Club, 1966–68. *Publications:* An Essential Course in Modern Spanish, 1959; Weak-Pronoun Position in the Early Romance Languages, 1963; (ed with critical study) Azorín, La ruta de Don Quijote, 1966; Angel Ganivet's Idearium español: A Critical Study, 1967; The Spanish Generation of 1898, 1974; The 1898 Movement in Spain, 1974; (ed with critical study) Lorca, Bodas de sangre, 1980; Pío Baroja: La busca, 1982; Pío Baroja: La busca 1903 to La busca 1904, 1982; (ed with critical study) Lorca, La casa de Bernarda Alba, 1983; articles in Bulletin of Hispanic Studies, Modern Language Review, Modern Languages, etc. *Recreations:* family, hill-walking, foreign travel. *Address:* 7 Burford Avenue, Bramhall, Stockport, Cheshire. *T:* 061–439 4306.

RAMSDEN, Rt. Hon. James Edward, PC 1963; Director: Prudential Assurance Co. Ltd, since 1972 (Deputy Chairman, 1976–82); Prudential Corporation Ltd, since 1979 (Deputy Chairman, 1979–82); *b* 1 Nov. 1923; *s* of late Capt. Edward Ramsden, MC, and Geraldine Ramsden, OBE, Breckamore Hall, Ripon; *m* 1949, Juliet Barbara Anna, *y d* of late Col Sir Charles Ponsonby, 1st Bt, TD, and Hon. Lady Ponsonby, *d* of 1st Baron Hunsdon; three *s* two *d*. *Educ:* Eton; Trinity College, Oxford (MA). Commnd KRRC, 1942; served North-West Europe with Rifle Brigade, 1944–45. MP (C) Harrogate, WR Yorks, March 1954–Feb. 1974; PPS to Home Secretary, Nov. 1959–Oct. 1960; Under-Sec. and Financial Sec., War Office, Oct. 1960–Oct. 1963; Sec. of State for War, 1963–64; Minister of Defence for the Army, April-Oct. 1964. Director: UK Board, Colonial Mutual Life Assurance Society, 1966–72; Standard Telephones and Cables, 1971–81. Chm., London Clinic, 1984– (Dir, 1973–). Mem., Historic Buildings Council for England, 1971–72. *Address:* Old Sleningford Hall, Ripon, North Yorks. *T:* Ripon 85229. *Club:* Pratt's.

RAMSDEN, (John) Michael; Editor-in-Chief, Flight International, since 1981; *b* 2 Oct. 1928; *s* of John Leonard Ramsden and Edith Alexandra Ramsden; *m* 1953, Angela Mary Mortimer; one *s* one *d*. *Educ:* Bedford Sch.; de Havilland Aeronautical Tech. Sch. CEng, FRAeS, FSLAET. With de Havilland Aircraft Co. Ltd, 1946–55; Flight, 1955–: Air Transport Editor, 1961–64; Editor, 1964–81. Chm., Press and Broadcasting Side, Defence Press and Broadcasting Cttee, 1983–. Dir, de Havilland Aircraft Mus., 1970–. Queen's Silver Jubilee Medal, 1977. *Publications:* The Safe Airline, 1976, 2nd edn 1978; Caring for the Mature Jet, 1981. *Recreations:* light-aircraft flying, water-colour painting. *Club:* London School of Flying (Elstree).

RAMSDEN, Michael; *see* Ramsden, J. M.

RAMSDEN, Sally, OBE 1981; Director, North East Broadcasting Co. Ltd (Metro Radio), 1973–81; *d* of John Parkin and Hannah Bentley; *m* 1948, Allan Ramsden. *Educ:* Ryhope Grammar Sch.; Neville's Cross Coll., Durham (Teaching Diploma). Teacher, 1930–47; Headmistress, 1947–69; Asst. Group Officer (part time), Nat. Fire Service, 1941–45; Hon. Organiser, Citizens' Advice Bureau, 1971–73; Pres., UK Fedn of Business and Professional Women, 1972–75; Member: Women's Nat. Commn, 1972–75; Women's Internat. Year Cttee, 1974–75; VAT Tribunals, 1973–84; Royal Commn on Legal Services, 1976–79; Durham Posts and Telecom Adv. Cttee, 1980–. *Recreations:* fly fishing, gardening, reading. *Address:* 1 Westcott Drive, Durham Moor, Durham City DH1 5AG. *T:* Durham 42989.

RAMSEY OF CANTERBURY, Baron *cr* 1974 (Life Peer), of Canterbury; **Rt. Rev. and Rt. Hon. Arthur Michael Ramsey,** PC 1956; Royal Victorian Chain, 1974; MA, BD; Hon. Fellow: Magdalene College, Cambridge, since 1952; Merton College, Oxford, since 1974; Keble College, Oxford, since 1975; St Cross College, Oxford, since 1981; Selwyn College, Cambridge, since 1983; *b* 14 Nov. 1904; *s* of late Arthur Stanley Ramsey, Fellow and sometime President of Magdalene Coll., Cambridge; *m* 1942, Joan, *d* of Lieut-Colonel F. A. C. Hamilton. *Educ:* Repton; Magdalene Coll., Cambridge (Scholar); Cuddesdon. 2nd Class, Classical Tripos, 1925; 1st Class, Theological Tripos, 1927; President of Cambridge Union, 1926; ordained, 1928; curate of Liverpool Parish Church, 1928–30; subwarden of Lincoln Theological Coll., 1930–36; Lecturer of Boston Parish Church, 1936–38; Vicar of S Benedict, Cambridge, 1939–40; Canon of Durham Cathedral and Professor of Divinity in Univ. of Durham, 1940–50, Emeritus Prof., 1977, Hon. Fellow, St Chad's Coll., 1980; Regius Professor of Divinity, Univ. of Cambridge, and Fellow of Magdalene Coll., 1950–52; Canon and Prebendary in Lincoln Cathedral, 1951–52; Bishop of Durham, 1952–56; Archbishop of York, 1956–61; Archbishop of Canterbury, 1961–74. Examining Chaplain to Bishop of Chester, 1932–39, to Bishop of Durham, 1940–50, and to Bishop of Lincoln, 1951–52; Select Preacher, Cambridge 1934, 1940, 1948, 1959, 1964, Oxford, 1945–46; Hulsean Preacher, Cambridge, 1969–70. Hon. Master of the Bench, Inner Temple, 1962. A President of World Council of Churches, 1961–68. Trustee, British Museum, 1963–69. Hon. FBA 1983. Hon. degrees include: Hon. DD: Durham, 1951; Leeds, Edinburgh, Cambridge, Hull, 1957; Manchester, 1961; London, 1962; Hon. DCL: Oxford, 1960; Kent, 1966; Hon. DLitt Keele, 1967, and a number from universities overseas. *Publications:* The Gospel and the Catholic Church, 1936; The Resurrection of Christ, 1945; The Glory of God and the Transfiguration of Christ, 1949; F. D. Maurice and the Conflicts of Modern Theology, 1951; Durham Essays and Addresses, 1956; From Gore to Temple, 1960; Introducing the Christian Faith, 1961; Canterbury Essays and Addresses, 1964; Sacred and Secular, 1965; God, Christ and the World, 1969; (with Cardinal Suenens) The Future of the Christian Church, 1971; The Christian Priest Today, 1972; Canterbury Pilgrim, 1974; Holy Spirit, 1977; Jesus and the Living Past, 1980; Be Still and Know, 1982. *Recreation:* walking. *Address:* North Wing Flat, Bishopthorpe, York YO2 1QE.

RAMSEY, Sir Alfred (Ernest), Kt 1967; Director: Sadler & Sons, since 1974; Gola Sports, since 1975; *b* Dagenham, 1920; *m* 1951, Victoria Phyllis Answorth, *d* of William Welch. *Educ:* Becontree Heath School. Started playing for Southampton and was an International with them; transferred to Tottenham Hotspur, 1949; with Spurs (right back), 1949–51; they won the 2nd and 1st Division titles in successive seasons. Manager of Ipswich Town Football Club, which rose from 3rd Division to Championship of the League, 1955–63; Manager, FA World Cup Team, 1963–74. Played 31 times for England. Dir, Birmingham City, 1976–77, Consultant, 1977–78. *Address:* 41 Valley Road, Ipswich, Suffolk.

RAMSEY, Rt. Rev. Kenneth Venner; an Assistant Bishop, Diocese of Manchester, since 1975; *b* 26 Jan. 1909; *s* of James Ernest and Laura Rebecca Ramsey, Southsea, Hants; unmarried. *Educ:* Portsmouth Grammar Sch.; University Coll., Oxford; Manchester Univ. Curate of St Matthew, Stretford, 1933–35; Vice-Prin., Egerton Hall, Manchester, and Lectr in Christian Ethics, Manchester Univ., 1935–38; Vice-Prin., Bishop Wilson Coll., Isle of Man, 1938–39; Prin., Egerton Hall, Manchester, 1939–41; Vicar of St Paul, Peel, Little Hulton, Lancs, 1941–48, Rector of Emmanuel Church, Didsbury, Manchester, 1948–55; Hon. Canon, Manchester Cathedral, 1950–53; Proctor in Convocation and mem. Church Assembly, 1950–55; Rural Dean of Heaton, 1950–53; Bishop Suffragan of Hulme, 1953–75. *Address:* 41 Bradwell Drive, Heald Green, Cheadle, Cheshire SK8 3BX. *T:* 061–437 8612.

RAMSEY, Leonard Gerald Gwynne; Editor of The Connoisseur, 1951–72; *b* 17 March 1913; *s* of late L. B. Ramsey, London Stock Exchange; *m* 1941, Dorothy Elizabeth, *y d* of late W. J. McMillan, Belfast; one *s* one *d. Educ:* Radley College. Commissioned Oxfordshire and Buckinghamshire Light Infantry (T), 1938; invalided out of Army, 1944; on General Staff, War Office, 1941–44, and other staff appointments. Public Relations Officer, The National Trust, 1946–49; Press Officer at Board of Trade and Colonial Office, 1950–51. Member of several Committees associated with ecclesiastical art and charitable matters. FSA 1949. *Publications:* (ed) The Connoisseur Encyclopædia of Antiques, 5 vols, 1954–60; (ed. with Ralph Edwards) The Connoisseur Period Guides, 6 vols, 1956–59; Montague Dawson, marine artist, a biography, 1967; (ed with Helen Comstock) The Connoisseur's Guide to Antique Furniture, 1969. *Recreations:* historic buildings, works of art, gardening. *Address:* 28 Morley Avenue, Woodbridge, Suffolk IP12 4AZ. *Club:* Light Infantry.

RAMSEY, Prof. Norman Foster; Higgins Professor of Physics, Harvard University, since 1947; Senior Fellow, Harvard Society of Fellows, since 1971; *b* 27 Aug. 1915; *s* of Brig.-Gen. and Mrs Norman F. Ramsey; *m* 1940, Elinor Stedman Jameson (*d* 1983); four *d*; *m* 1985, Ellie A. Welch. *Educ:* Columbia Univ.; Cambridge Univ. (England). Carnegie Fellow, Carnegie Instn of Washington, 1939–40; Assoc., Univ. of Ill, 1940–42; Asst Prof., Columbia Univ., 1942–45; Research Assoc., MIT Radiation Laboratory, 1940–43; Cons. to Nat. Defense Research Cttee, 1940–45; Expert Consultant to Sec. of War, 1942–45; Grp Leader and Assoc. Div. Head, Los Alamos Lab. of Atomic Energy Project, 1943–45; Chief Scientist of Atomic Energy Lab. at Tinian, 1945; Assoc. Prof., Columbia Univ., 1945–47; Head of Physics Dept, Brookhaven Nat. Lab., 1946–47; Assoc. Prof., Harvard Univ., 1947–50; John Simon Guggenheim Fell., Oxford Univ., 1953–54; George Eastman Vis. Prof., Oxford Univ., 1973–74; Luce Prof. of Cosmology, Mt Holyoke, 1982–83; Prof., Univ. of Virginia, 1983–84. Dir Harvard Nuclear Lab., 1948–50, 1952; Chm., Harvard Nuclear Physics Cttee, 1948–60; Science Adviser, NATO, 1958–59; Fell. Amer. Phys. Soc. and Amer. Acad. of Arts and Sciences; Nat. Acad. of Sciences; Amer. Philos. Soc.; Sigma Xi; Phi Beta Kappa; Amer. Assoc. for Advancement of Science, 1940– (Chm., Phys. Sect., 1976). Bd of Directors, Varian Associates, 1964–66; Bd of Trustees: Associated Univs; Brookhaven Nat. Lab., 1952–55; Carnegie Endowment for Internat. Peace; Univ. Research Assoc. (Pres., 1966–81, Pres. Emeritus 1981–); Rockefeller Univ., 1976–; Air Force Sci. Adv. Bd, 1948–54; Dept of Defense Panel on Atomic Energy, 1953–59; Bd of Editors of Review of Modern Physics, 1953–56; Chm. Exec. Cttee for Camb. Electron Accelerator, 1956–63; Coun. Amer. Phys. Soc., 1956–60 (Vice-Pres., 1977; Pres., 1978); Chm., Bd of Governors, Amer. Inst. of Physics, 1980–. Gen. Adv. Cttee, Atomic Energy Commn, 1960–72. Chm., High Energy Accelerator Panel of President's Sci. Adv. Cttee and AEC, 1963. Pres., Phi Beta Kappa, 1985 (Vice-Pres., 1982). Presidential Certificate of Merit, 1947; E. O. Lawrence Award, 1960; Davisson-Germer Prize, 1974; Award for Excellence, Columbia Univ. Graduate Alumni, 1980; Medal of Honor, IEEE, 1984; Rabi Prize, Frega Control Symposium, IEEE, 1985; Monie Ferst Prize, Sigma Xi, 1985; Compton Award, Amer. Inst. of Physics, 1985; Rumford Premium, Amer. Acad. of Arts and Scis, 1985. Hon. MA Harvard, 1947; Hon. ScD Cambridge, 1953; Hon. DSc: Case Western Reserve, 1968; Middlebury Coll., 1969; Oxford, 1973; Rockefeller Univ., 1986. *Publications:* Experimental Nuclear Physics, 1952; Nuclear Moments, 1953; Molecular Beams, 1956; Quick Calculus, 1965; and numerous articles in Physical Review and other scientific jls. *Recreations:* tennis, ski-ing, walking, sailing, etc. *Address:* 21 Monmouth Court, Brookline, Mass 02146, USA. *T:* 617–277–2313.

RAMSEY, Waldo Emerson W.; see Waldron-Ramsey.

RANCE, Gerald Francis, OBE 1985 (MBE 1968); HM Diplomatic Service; High Commissioner to Tonga, since 1984; *b* 20 Feb. 1927; *s* of Cecil Henry and Jane Carmel Rance; *m* 1949, Dorothy (*née* Keegan); one *d. Educ:* Brompton Oratory. HM Forces (RCMP), 1945–48; joined Foreign Service, 1948; Foreign Office, 1948–51; served Belgrade, Rome, Bucharest, Istanbul, Munich, Kabul, New York and Dallas; Inspectorate, FCO, 1973–77; Head of Chancery, Mbabane, 1977–79; First Sec. (Comm.), Nicosia, 1980–83. *Recreations:* golf, tennis, reading. *Address:* c/o Foreign and Commonwealth Office, SW1A 2AH. *Clubs:* Royal Commonwealth Society; Chislehurst Golf.

RANCHHODLAL, Sir Chinubhai Madhowlal, 2nd Bt, *cr* 1913; *b* 18 April 1906; *s* of 1st Bt and Sulochana, *d* of Chunilal Khushalrai; *S* father, 1916; *m* 1924, Tanumati, *d* of late Jhaverilal Bulakhiram Mehta of Ahmedabad; three *s*. Father was only member of Hindu community to receive a baronetcy. *Heir: s* Udayan [*b* 25 July 1929; *m* 1953, Muneera Khodadad Fozdar; one *s* three *d.* Arjuna Award, 1972]. *Address:* Shantikunj, PO Shahibaug, Ahmedabad, India. *T:* 26953. *Club:* Willingdon (Bombay).

RANDALL, Col Charles Richard, OBE 1969; TD 1947; Vice Lord-Lieutenant for the County of Bedfordshire, since 1978; *b* 21 Jan. 1920; *s* of Charles Randall and Elizabeth Brierley; *m* 1945, Peggy Dennis; one *s* one *d. Educ:* Bedford Sch. Served War, 1939–45: commissioned Bedfordshire Yeomanry, 1939. Chm., Randalls Group Ltd, 1965–81. Chm., Bedfordshire County TA&VR, 1978–; Dep. Hon. Col, The Royal Anglian Regt (Bedfordshire), TAVR, 1979–84. Hon. rank of Col, 1984. High Sheriff, Bedfordshire, 1974–75. *Recreations:* shooting, fishing, gardening. *Address:* The Rookery, Aspley Guise, Milton Keynes MK17 8HP. *T:* Milton Keynes 582188. *Clubs:* Naval and Military, MCC.

RANDALL, Rev. Edmund Laurence, AM 1980; Warden, St Barnabas' Theological College, 1964–85; Hon. Canon of Adelaide, 1979–86; *b* 2 June 1920; *s* of Robert Leonard Randall and Grace Annie Randall (*née* Young); unmarried. *Educ:* Dulwich College; Corpus Christi College, Cambridge. BA 1941. MA 1947. Served War, 1940–45, with Royal Artillery (AA). Corpus Christi Coll., 1938–40 and 1945–47. Wells Theological College, 1947–49. Deacon, 1949; Priest, 1950. Assistant Curate at St Luke's, Bournemouth, 1949–52; Fellow of Selwyn College, Cambridge, 1952–57; Chaplain, 1953–57; Residentiary Canon of Ely and Principal of Ely Theological Coll., 1957–59; Chaplain, St Francis Theological Coll., Brisbane, 1960–64. *Recreations:* travel, motoring. *Address:* 44

Mackay Street, Wangaratta, Vic 3677, Australia. *T:* 057 219007. *Club:* Naval, Military and Air Force, South Australia.

RANDALL, Stuart; MP (Lab) Kingston upon Hull West, since 1983; *b* 22 June 1938; *m* 1963, Gillian Michael; three *d. Educ:* University Coll., Cardiff (BSc Elect. Engrg). English Electric Computers and Radio Corp. of America, USA, 1963–66; Marconi Automation, 1966–68; Inter-Bank Res. Orgn, 1968–71; BSC, 1971–76; BL, 1976–80; Nexos Office Systems, 1980–81; Plessey Communications Systems, 1981–83. PPS to Shadow Chancellor of the Exchequer, 1984–85, to Front Bench Spokesman on Agricl, Food and Fisheries Affairs, 1985–. *Recreation:* sailing. *Address:* House of Commons, SW1A 0AA. *T:* 01–219 3000.

RANDALL, William Edward, CBE 1978; DFC 1944; AFC 1945; Chairman, Chubb & Son Ltd, 1981–84 (Managing Director, 1971–81, Deputy Chairman, 1976–81); *b* 15 Dec. 1920; *s* of William George Randall and Jane Longdon (*née* Pannell); *m* 1st, 1943, Joan Dorothea Way; two *s* one *d*; 2nd, 1975, Iris Joyce Roads. *Educ:* Tollington Sch., London. FRSA. Served RAF, Flt Lieut, 1941–46. Commercial Union Assce Co., 1946–50; Chubb & Sons Lock and Safe Co., 1950, Man. Dir, 1965; Dir, Chubb & Son Ltd, 1965; Dir, Metal Closures Gp, 1976–86. Member: Home Office Standing Cttee on Crime Prevention, 1967–85; Exec. Cttee, British Digestive Foundn, 1982–86; Chairman: Council, British Security Industry Assoc., 1981–85; Airport Export Gp, NEDO, 1983. *Recreations:* reading, gardening. *Address:* Villa Oleander, Lote 5, Vale de Milho, 8400 Lagoa, Portugal.

RANDELL, Peter Neil; Secretary, Administration and Personnel, British Technology Group (National Research Development Corporation and National Enterprise Board), since 1981; *b* 18 Nov. 1933; *s* of Donald Randell and Dorothy (*née* Anthonisz); *m* 1962, Anne Loraine Mudie; one *s* one *d. Educ:* Bradfield Coll.; Wye Coll., Univ. of London (BSc (Agric) Hons). FCIS. Farming and other employments, Rhodesia, 1955–61; Asst to Sec., British Insulated Callenders Cables Ltd, 1962–65; Asst Sec., NRDC, 1965–73, Sec. 1973–81, Board Member 1980–81. *Recreations:* the outdoors, reading. *Address:* Wood Dene, Golf Club Road, Hook Heath, Woking, Surrey. *T:* Woking 63824.

RANDLE, Prof. Sir Philip (John), Kt 1985; MD, FRCP; FRS 1983; Professor of Clinical Biochemistry, University of Oxford, since 1975; Fellow of Hertford College, Oxford, since 1975; *b* 16 July 1926; *s* of Alfred John and Nora Anne Randle; *m* 1952, Elizabeth Ann Harrison; three *d* (one *s* decd). *Educ:* King Edward VI Grammar Sch., Nuneaton; Sidney Sussex Coll., Cambridge (MA, PhD, MD); UCH, London. Med. and Surg. Officer, UCH, 1951; Res. Fellow in Biochem., Cambridge, 1952–55; Univ. Lectr, Biochem., Cambridge, 1955–64; Fellow of Trinity Hall and Dir of Med. Studies, 1957–64; Prof. of Biochem., Univ. of Bristol, 1964–75. Member: Board of Governors, United Cambridge Hospitals, 1960–64; Clinical Endocrinology Cttee, MRC, 1957–64; Chm., Grants Cttee, MRC, 1975–77; Pres., European Assoc. for Study of Diabetes, 1977–80; Chm., Research Cttee, British Diabetic Assoc., 1971–78. DHSS: Mem. Cttee on Med. Aspects Food Policy, 1981–; Chm., COMA Panel on Diet and Cardiovascular Disease, 1981–84; Consultant Adviser in Biochemistry to CMO, 1981–. Member: General Medical Council, 1967–75; Gen. Dental Council, 1971–75; Res. Cttee, British Heart Foundn, 1982–85. Lectures: Banting, British Diabetic Assoc., 1965; Minkowski, European Assoc. for Study of Diabetes, 1966; Copp, La Jolla, 1972; Humphry Davy Rolleston, RCP, 1983; Ciba Medal and Lectr, Biochem. Soc., 1984. Corresp. Mem. of many foreign medical and scientific bodies. *Publications:* numerous contribs to books and med. sci. jls on diabetes mellitus, control of metabolism and related topics. *Recreations:* travel, swimming, bricklaying. *Address:* John Radcliffe Hospital, Headington, Oxford OX3 9DU; 11 Fitzherbert Close, Iffley, Oxford OX4 4EN.

RANDOLPH, Denys, BSc; CEng, MRAeS, FIProdE, FInstD, CBIM; Chairman: Woodrush Investments Ltd, since 1980; Haddon Rocking Horses, since 1981; Poitires Eyots Ltd, since 1972; *b* 6 Feb. 1926; *s* of late Harry Beckham Randolph and Margaret Isabel Randolph; *m* 1951, Marjorie Hales; two *d. Educ:* St Paul's School: Queen's Univ., Belfast (BSc). Served Royal Engineers, 1944–48 (Captain). Queen's Univ., Belfast, 1948–52; post-grad. apprenticeship, Short Bros & Harland, 1952–55; Wilkinson Sword Ltd: Prod. Engr/Prod. Dir, Graviner Div., 1955–66; Man. Dir, Hand Tools Div., 1966–69; Chm., Graviner Div., 1969–79; Chm., 1972–79; Pres., 1980–85; Wilkinson Match Ltd: Dir, 1974–80; Chm., 1976–79. Institute of Directors: Chm., 1976–79; Vice-Pres., 1979–; Mem., Policy Cttee. Past Master, Worshipful Co. of Scientific Instrument Makers, 1977; Master, Cutlers' Co., 1985–86. Mem. Council, Brunel Univ.; Governor, Henley Admin. Staff Coll. FRSA (Manufactures and Commerce). *Publication:* From Rapiers to Razor Blades—The Development of the Light Metals Industry (paper, RSA). *Recreations:* yachting, golf, viticulture. *Address:* The Cottages, Rush Court, Wallingford OX10 8LJ. *T:* Wallingford 36586. *Clubs:* Army and Navy, Royal Automobile, City Livery, Little Ship.

RANDOLPH, John Hugh Edward; His Honour Judge Randolph; a Circuit Judge, since 1972; *b* 14 Oct. 1913; *s* of late Charles Edward Randolph and Phyllis Randolph; *m* 1959, Anna Marjorie (*née* Thomson). *Educ:* Bradford Grammar Sch.; Leeds University. RAF, 1940–46. Called to Bar, Middle Temple, 1946; practised on NE Circuit until 1965; Stipendiary Magistrate of Leeds, 1965–71. Deputy Chairman: E Riding QS, 1958–63; W Riding QS, 1963–71. *Recreation:* golf. *Address:* Crown Court, Leeds. *Club:* Leeds (Leeds).

RANDOLPH, Michael Richard Spencer; Editor since 1957, Director since 1967, British Reader's Digest; Deputy Executive Editor, Reader's Digest International Editions, since 1978; *b* 2 Jan. 1925; *s* of late Leslie Richard Randolph and late Gladys (*née* Keen); *m* 1952, Jenefer Scawen Blunt; two *s* two *d. Educ:* Merchant Taylors' Sch.; New Rochelle High Sch., NY, USA; Queen's Coll., Oxford. Served RNVR, Intell. Staff Eastern Fleet, 1944–46, Sub-Lieut. Editorial staff, Amalgamated Press, 1948–52; Odham's Press, 1952–56; Reader's Digest, 1956–; Press Mem., Press Council, 1975–. Chm., Reader's Digest Pension Trustees Ltd, 1975–; Chm., Soc. of Magazine Editors, 1973; Mem. Council, British Atlantic Cttee, 1970–. Chm., Weald of Kent Preservation Soc., 1981–. Churchwarden, St Michael the Archangel, Smarden, 1978–. *Recreation:* grandparenthood. *Address:* The Cloth Hall, Smarden, Kent TN27 8QB. *Club:* Savile.

RANDOLPH, Ven. Thomas Berkeley; Archdeacon of Hereford, 1959–70, Archdeacon Emeritus, since 1970; Canon Residentiary of Hereford Cathedral, 1961–70; *b* 15 March 1904; *s* of Felton George Randolph, Barrister-at-law, and Emily Margaret Randolph, Chichester, Sx; *m* 1935, Margaret, *d* of Rev. H. C. R. F. Jenner, Vennwood, Hereford and Wenvoe, Glam; two *s* one *d. Educ:* Christ's Hospital; Queen's College, Oxford (Scholar). BA (2nd Class Theology) 1927; MA 1932; Cuddesdon Coll., 1927; Curate of St Mary's, Portsea, 1928–33; Chaplain (Eccles. Est.) St Paul's Cathedral, Calcutta, 1934–37; Vicar of Eastleigh, 1938–46; Vicar of St Mary the Virgin with All Saints, St Saviour's, St Mark's and St Matthew's, Reading, 1946–59. Proctor in Convocation for the Diocese of Oxford, 1950–55; Hon. Canon of Christ Church, Oxford, 1957–59; Vicar of Wellington, Hereford, 1959–61. *Address:* 14 Heatherwood, Midhurst, West Sussex. *T:* Midhurst 2765.

RANELAGH, John O'B.; see O'Beirne Ranelagh.

RANFURLY, 6th Earl of, *cr* 1831; **Thomas Daniel Knox,** KCMG 1955; Baron Welles, 1781; Viscount Northland, 1791; Baron Ranfurly (UK) 1826; Chairman, Inchcape Insurance Holdings Ltd, 1966–83; Director: Inchcape & Co. Ltd, 1966–83; a Member of Lloyd's, since 1947; *b* 29 May 1913; *s* of late Viscount Northland (killed in action, 1915) and Hilda, *d* of late Sir Daniel Cooper, 2nd Bt; *S* grandfather 1933; *m* 1939, Hermione, *e d* of late G. R. P. Llewellyn, Baglan Hall, Monmouth Road, Abergavenny, Mon; one *d*. *Educ:* Eton; Trinity Coll., Cambridge. ADC to Gov.-Gen. of Australia, 1936–38; served European War of 1939–45 (prisoner). Governor and C-in-C, Bahamas, 1953–56. Colonial Mutual Life Assurance Soc. Ltd (London Bd), 1966–82. Chairman London Scout Council, 1957–65; Chief Scout's Commissioner, Greater London, 1965–79. President, Shaftesbury Homes and "Arethusa" Training Ship, 1959–83; Chairman: Madame Tussauds Ltd, 1971–80; Bd of Governors, London Clinic, 1973–84; Ranfurly Library Service Ltd. Steward, Jockey Club, 1973–75. *Heir: kinsman* Gerald Françoys Needham Knox [*b* 4 Jan. 1929; *m* 1955, Rosemary, *o d* of late Air Vice-Marshal Felton Vesey Holt, CMG, DSO; two *s* two *d*]. *Address:* Great Pednor, Chesham, Bucks. *T:* Gt Missenden 2155. *Clubs:* White's; Jockey (Newmarket).

RANG, Prof. Humphrey Peter, DPhil; FRS 1980; Director, Sandoz Institute for Medical Research, University College London, since 1983; *b* 13 June 1936; *s* of Charles Rang and Sybil Rang; *m* 1960, Elizabeth Harvey Clapham; one *s* three *d*. *Educ:* University Coll. Sch.; University Coll. London (MSc 1960); UCH Med. Sch. (MB, BS 1961); Balliol Coll., Oxford (DPhil 1965). J. H. Burn Res. Fellow, Dept of Pharmacol., Oxford, 1961–65; Vis. Res. Associate, Albert Einstein Coll. of Medicine, NY, 1966–67; Univ. Lectr in Pharmacol., Oxford, 1966–72; Fellow and Tutor in Physiol., Lincoln Coll., Oxford, 1967–72; Prof. of Pharmacology: Univ. of Southampton, 1972–74; St George's Hosp. Med. Sch., London, 1974–79; Prof. of Pharmacol., 1979–83, Fellow and Vis. Prof., 1983–, UCL. *Publication:* Drug Receptors, 1973. *Recreations:* sailing, music. *Address:* 1 Belvedere Drive, SW19 7BX. *T:* 01–947 7603.

RANGER, Sir Douglas, Kt 1978; FRCS; Otolaryngologist, The Middlesex Hospital, 1950–82; Dean, The Middlesex Hospital Medical School, 1974–83; Hon. Civil Consultant in Otolaryngology, RAF, since 1983; *b* 5 Oct. 1916; *s* of William and Hatton Thomasina Ranger; *m* 1943, Betty, *d* of Captain Sydney Harold Draper and Elsie Draper; two *s*. *Educ:* Church of England Grammar Sch., Brisbane; The Middlesex Hosp. Med. Sch. MB BS 1941, FRCS 1943. Surgical Registrar, The Mddx Hosp., 1942–44. Served War, Temp. Maj. RAMC and Surgical Specialist, 1945–48 (SEAC and MELF). Otolaryngologist, Mount Vernon Hosp., 1958–74; Hon. Sec., Brit. Assoc. of Otolaryngologists, 1965–71. RCS: Mem. Court of Examiners, 1966–72; Mem. Council, 1967–72; Pres., Assoc. of Head and Neck Oncologists of GB, 1974–77. Civil Consultant in Otolaryngology, RAF, 1965–83. Dir, Ferens Inst. of Otolaryngology, 1965–83; Cons. Adviser in Otolaryngology, DHSS, 1971–82. *Publications:* The Middlesex Hospital Medical School, Centenary to Sesquicentenary, 1985; papers and lectures on otolaryngological subjects, esp. with ref. to malignant disease. *Address:* The Tile House, The Street, Chipperfield, King's Langley, Herts WD4 9BH. *T:* King's Langley 68910; 44 Wimpole Street, W1M 7DG. *T:* 01–935 3332.

RANK, Sir Benjamin (Keith), Kt 1972; CMG 1955; MS, FRCS; FRACS; FACS; Consulting Plastic Surgeon, Royal Melbourne Hospital, Repatriation Department, Victoria Eye and Ear Hospital, Queen Victoria Hospital, etc, and in Tasmania; *b* 14 Jan. 1911; *s* of Wreghitt Rank and Bessie Rank (*née* Smith); *m* 1938, Barbara Lyle Facy; one *s* three *d*. *Educ:* Scotch College, Melbourne; Ormond College, University of Melbourne. MB, BS Melbourne, 1934; Resident Medical Officer, Royal Melbourne Hospital, 1935–36; MS (Melb.), 1937; MRCS, LRCP 1938; Resident Surgical Officer, London County Council, 1938–39 (St James' Hospital, Balham); FRCS 1938; Assistant Plastic Surgeon (EMS) at Hill End (Bart's), 1939–40; AAMC, 1940–45; Officer i/c AIF Plastic Surgery Unit in Egypt, and later at Heidelberg Military Hospital, Victoria, Australia (Lt-Col); Hon. Plastic Surgeon, Royal Melbourne Hosp., 1946–66. Carnegie Fellow, 1947. Member: Dental Board of Victoria 1949–73, Joske Orator 1974; BMA State Council, 1950–60; Chm. Exec. Cttee, RACS (Pres., 1966–68); Chm., Cttee of Management, Victorian Plastic Surgery Unit (Preston Hosp.), 1966–; Member: Bd of Management, Royal Melbourne Hosp., 1976–82 (Vice-Pres., 1979–82); Motor Accident Bd, Victoria, 1972–82. Chm., Consult. Council on Casualty Services, Victoria Health Council; Pres., St John's Ambulance Council, Victoria, 1983– (Chm. 1978–83). Sir Arthur Sims Commonwealth Travelling Prof., RCS, 1958; Moynihan Lectr, 1972; Vis. Prof., Harvard Med. Sch., 1976. Syme Orator, RACS, 1976; Stawell Orator, 1977. 87th Mem., James IV Assoc. of Surgeons; Pres., British Assoc. of Plastic Surgeons, 1965. Pres., 5th Internat. Congress of Plastic Surgery, Melbourne, 1971. FRACS 1943; Hon. FACST 1952; Hon. FRCS Canada; Hon. FRCSE 1973; Hon. FACS. Hon. DSc Punjabi Univ., 1970; Hon. Member: Société Française de Chirurgie Plastique; Indian Association of Surgeons. CStJ 1982. *Publications:* (jointly) Surgery of Repair as applied to Hand Injuries, 1953. Papers in British, American and Australian Surgical Jls. *Recreations:* golf, gardening. *Address:* 12 Jerula Avenue, Mount Eliza, Victoria 3930, Australia. *Clubs:* Melbourne (Melbourne); Peninsula Golf (Vice-Pres.).

RANK, Joseph McArthur; President, Ranks Hovis McDougall Ltd, since 1981; *b* 24 April 1918; *s* of late Rowland Rank and of Margaret McArthur; *m* 1946, Hon. Moira (who *m* 1940, Peter Anthony Stanley Woodwark, killed in action, 1943; one *d*), *d* of 3rd Baron Southborough; one *s* one *d*. *Educ:* Loretto. Joined Mark Mayhew Ltd, 1936. Served RAF, 1940–46. Personal Pilot to Air C-in-C, SEAC, 1945; Jt Man. Dir, Joseph Rank Ltd, 1955–65; Dep. Chm. and Chief Exec., Ranks Hovis McDougall Ltd, 1965–69, Chm., 1969–81. Pres., Nat. Assoc. of British and Irish Millers, 1957–58, Centenary Pres., 1978. Chm., Millers Mutual Assoc., 1969–; Chm. Council, British Nutrition Foundation, 1968–69; Dir, Royal Alexandra and Albert Sch., 1952–, Chm., Governing Body, 1975–84; Friend of the Royal Coll. of Physicians, 1967–; Council, Royal Warrant Holders Assoc., 1968–71. Mem., Shrievalty Assoc., 1974. First High Sheriff of East Sussex, 1974. Hon. FRCP, 1978. *Recreations:* boating, travelling. *Address:* Landhurst, Hartfield, East Sussex. *T:* Hartfield 293. *Clubs:* Royal Air Force; Sussex.

RANKEILLOUR, 4th Baron *cr* 1932, of Buxted; **Peter St Thomas More Henry Hope;** *b* 29 May 1935; *s* of 3rd Baron Rankeillour and Mary Sibyl, *d* of late Col Wilfrid Ricardo, DSO; *S* father, 1967; unmarried. *Educ:* Ampleforth College; privately. *Recreations:* hunting, shooting, boating; agricultural machinery inventor. *Heir: cousin* Michael Richard Hope [*b* 21 Oct. 1940; *m* 1964, Elizabeth Rosemary, *e d* of Col F. H. Fuller; one *s* two *d*]. *Address:* Achaderry House, Roy Bridge, West Inverness-shire. *T:* Spean Bridge 206.

RANKIN, Andrew, QC 1968; a Recorder of the Crown Court, since 1972; *b* 3 Aug. 1924; *s* of William Locke Rankin and Mary Ann McArdle, Edinburgh; *m* 1st, 1944, Winifred (marr. diss. 1963), *d* of Frank McAdam, Edinburgh; two *s* two *d* (and one *s* decd); 2nd, 1964, Veronica, *d* of George Aloysius Martin, Liverpool. *Educ:* Royal High Sch., Edinburgh; Univ. of Edinburgh; Downing Coll., Cambridge. Served War of 1939–45: Sub-Lt, RNVR, 1943. BL (Edin.) 1946; BA, 1st cl. hons Law Tripos (Cantab), 1948. Royal Commonwealth Soc. Medal, 1942; Cecil Peace Prize, 1946; Lord Justice Holker Exhibn, Gray's Inn, 1947–50; Lord Justice Holker Schol., Gray's Inn, 1950–53; Univ. Blue, Edin., 1943 and 1946 and Camb., 1948. Lectr in Law, Univ. of Liverpool, 1948–52. Called to Bar, Gray's Inn, 1950. *Publications:* (ed, 4th edn) Levie's Law of Bankruptcy in Scotland, 1950; various articles in UK and foreign legal jls. *Recreations:* swimming, travel by sea, racing (both codes), watching soccer (especially Liverpool FC). *Address:* Chelwood, Pine Walks, Prenton, Cheshire. *T:* 051–608 2987; 69 Cliffords Inn, EC4. *T:* 01–405 2932; 2 Serjeants Inn, Temple, EC4. *T:* 01–353 7825.

RANKIN, Sir Hugh (Charles Rhys), 3rd Bt, *cr* 1898; FSAScot 1948; Member, Standing Council of the Baronetage, since 1979; Representative to District Council Perth CC (Eastern District), 1949, Perth CC 1950; Councillor for Boro' of Rattray and Blairgowrie, 1949; joined RASC as 2nd Lieut, May 1940, at age of 41 years; Captain 1940–45, India; sheep farming and is a judge of sheep at prominent shows; formerly Senior Vice-President of the Western Islamic Association; a former Vice-President of Scottish National Liberal Association; has lived during the reigns of six sovereigns; *b* 8 Aug. 1899; *er s* of Sir Reginald Rankin, 2nd Bt, and Hon. Nest Rice (*d* 1943), 2nd *d* of 6th Baron Dynevor; changed his names by Scotch law in July 1946 to above; *S* father, 1931; *m* 1932, Helen Margaret (*d* 1945), *e d* of Sir Charles Stewart, KBE, 1st Public Trustee, and *widow* of Capt. Colin Campbell, Scots Guards; *m* 1946, Robina Kelly, FSA (Scot.), SRN, Cordon Bleu (Edin.), Crieff, Perthshire. *Educ:* Harrow. Served in 1st Royal Dragoon Guards in Sinn Feinn Campaign, 1920–22 (oldest surviving mem.); ex-Pres. Clun Forest Sheep Breeders Assoc., 1928, and their representative to National Sheep Breeders Association that year; whole-time 'piece-work' shearer, in W Australia, covering area between Bunbury and Broome, 1929–31; in 1938 was a representative on committee of British sheep breeders in London appointed to petition Government *re* sheep industry. Runner-up All Britain Sheep Judging Competition (6,000 entrants), 1962. A writer on agricultural stock; expert on Highland problems; was Brit. Rep., 1937, to 1st all European Muslim Congress at Geneva; a practising Non-Theistic Theravada Buddhist since 1944, and performed Holy Buddhist Pilgrimage, Nov. 1944, the 2nd Britisher to do so; Vice-Pres. World's Buddhist Assoc., 1945. Joined Labour Party 1939 and holds extreme political views; has been a Dominion Home Ruler for Scotland, member Scottish National Party; joined Scottish Communist Party, 1945, resigned 1980; Welsh Republican Nationalist and Welsh speaker; now left-side Labour; also zealous SNP who desires an independent Red Republic of all Scotland, exc. Orkneys and Shetlands. Has made archaeological discoveries in Dumfries, 1977–. Mem. Roy. Inst. and Roy. Soc. of Arts; is Hereditary Piper of the Clan Maclaine. News of the World Kt of the Road (for courtesy in motor driving). Broadsword Champion of British Army (Cavalry), 1921. *Publications:* articles in agricultural publications, etc. *Recreations:* golf (holds an amateur record amongst golfers of Gt Britain in having played on 382 separate courses of UK and Eire), shooting, coarse fishing, hunting, motoring, cycling on mountain tracks to tops of British mountains (Pres. Rough Stuff Cycling Assoc., 1956); study of ancient track ways; bowls, tennis, archæology (wife and himself are only persons who have crawled under dwarf fir forest for last ½ mile of most northerly known section of any Roman road in Europe, terminating opposite end of Kirriemuir Golf Course), study of domestic animals, speaking on politics, especially *re* Scottish Home Rule and Highland problems. *Heir: nephew* Ian Niall Rankin [*b* 19 Dec. 1932; *s* of Arthur Niall Talbot Rankin and of Lady Jean Rankin, *qv*; *m* 1st, 1959, Alexandra, *o d* of Adm. Sir Laurence Durlacher, KCB, OBE, DSC; one *s* one *d*; 2nd, 1980, Mrs June Norman, *d* of late Captain Thomas Marsham-Townshend; one *d*]. *Address:* The Cottage, Kindallachan, Pitlochry, Perthshire PH9 0NW. *T:* Ballinluig 258. *Clubs:* Royal and Ancient Golf (St Andrews), Burns (Dumfries).

RANKIN, James Deans, CBE 1983; PhD; Chief Inspector, Cruelty to Animals Act (1876), Home Office, 1976–83; *b* 17 Jan. 1918; *s* of late Andrew Christian Fleming Rankin and Catherine Sutherland (*née* Russell); *m* 1950, Hilary Jacqueline Bradshaw; two *d*. *Educ:* Hamilton Acad.; Glasgow Veterinary Coll. (MRCVS); Reading Univ. (PhD Microbiology). FIBiol. Gen. practice, 1941; Res. Officer, Min. of Agriculture and Fisheries, 1942; Principal Res. Officer, ARC, 1952; Inspector, Home Office, 1969. *Publications:* scientific contribs in standard works and in med. and veterinary jls. *Recreations:* golf, DIY. *Club:* Farmers'.

RANKIN, Lady Jean (Margaret), DCVO 1969 (CVO 1957); Woman of the Bedchamber to Queen Elizabeth The Queen Mother, 1947–81, Extra Woman of the Bedchamber, since 1982; *b* 15 Aug. 1905; *d* of 12th Earl of Stair; *m* 1931, Niall Rankin (*d* 1965), *s* of Sir Reginald Rankin, 2nd Bt; two *s*. Governor: Thomas Coram Foundation; Magdalen Hosp. Trust. *Address:* House of Treshnish, Dervaig, Isle of Mull. *T:* Dervaig 249; 3 Catherine Wheel Yard, SW1. *T:* 01–493 9072.

See also Sir Hugh C. R. Rankin, Bt.

RANKIN, Prof. Robert Alexander, MA, PhD, ScD; FRSE, FRSAMD, Dean of Faculties, since 1986, Professor Emeritus, since 1982, Glasgow University (Professor of Mathematics, 1954–82; Clerk of the Senate, 1971–78); *b* 27 Oct. 1915; *s* of late Rev. Prof. Oliver Shaw Rankin, DD, and late Olivia Theresa Shaw; *m* 1942, Mary Ferrier Llewellyn, *d* of late W. M. Llewellyn and late K. F. Llewellyn, JP; one *s* three *d*. *Educ:* Fettes; Clare Coll., Cambridge. Wrangler, 1936; Fellow of Clare College, 1939–51; Vis. Fellow, Clare Hall, 1971. Ministry of Supply (work on rockets), 1940–45; Faculty Asst Lecturer, Cambridge Univ., 1945–48; Univ. Lecturer, Cambridge, 1948–51; Asst Tutor, Clare Coll., 1947–51; Praelector, Clare Coll., 1949–51; Mason Professor of Pure Mathematics at Birmingham University, 1951–54. Mathematical Sec. and Editor of Proceedings of Cambridge Philosophical Soc., 1947–51; Hon. Pres. Glasgow Gaelic Soc., 1957–; Pres. Edinburgh Mathematical Soc., 1957–58, 1978–79; Mem., Special Cttee, Advisory Coun. on Educn in Scotland, 1959–61; Vis. Prof., Indiana Univ., 1963–64; Vice-Pres. Roy. Soc. of Edinburgh, 1960–63; Vice-Pres., Scottish Gaelic Texts Soc., 1967–; Founder Mem., and Chm., Scottish Mathematical Council, 1967–73; Chm., Clyde Estuary Amenity Council, 1969–82. Keith Prize, RSE, 1961–63. *Publications:* Matematicheskaya Teorija Dvizhenija Neupravljaemykh Raket, 1951; An Introduction to Mathematical Analysis, 1963; The Modular Group and its Subgroups, 1969; Modular Forms and Functions, 1977; (ed) Modular Forms, 1985; papers on the Theory of Numbers, Theory of Functions, Rocket Ballistics and Gaelic Subjects in various journals. *Recreations:* hill-walking, Gaelic studies, organ music. *Address:* 98 Kelvin Court, Glasgow G12 0AH. *T:* 041–339 2641.

RANKINE, Jean Morag; Deputy Director of the British Museum, since 1983; *b* 5 Sept. 1941; *d* of Alan Rankine and Margaret Mary Sloan Rankine (*née* Reid). *Educ:* Central Newcastle High Sch.; University College London (BA, MPhil); Univ. of Copenhagen. Grad. Assistant, Durham Univ. Library, 1966–67; British Museum: Res. Assistant, Dept of Printed Books, 1967–73; Asst Keeper, Director's Office, 1973–78; Dep. Keeper, Public Services, 1978–83. *Recreations:* sculling, ski-ing, fell-walking, opera, motorcycling. *Address:* British Museum, WC1B 3DG. *Clubs:* Thames Rowing; Clydesdale Amateur Rowing (Glasgow).

RANKINE, Sir John (Dalzell), KCMG 1954 (CMG 1947); KCVO 1956; *b* 8 June 1907; *o s* of late Sir Richard Rankine, KCMG; *m* 1939, Janet Grace (*d* 1976), *d* of Major R. L. Austin, Clifton, Bristol; one *d*. *Educ:* Christ's College, Christchurch, New Zealand; Exeter College, Oxford. BA 1930; entered Colonial Administration Service as Cadet,

Uganda, 1931; Asst Sec. East African Governor's Conference, 1939; First Asst Sec., 1942; Asst Colonial Sec., Fiji, 1942; Colonial Sec., Barbados, 1945; Chief Secretary, Kenya, 1947–51; Chairman, Development and Reconstruction Authority. British Resident, Zanzibar, 1952–54; administered Govts of Barbados and Kenya on various occasions; Governor, Western Region, Nigeria, 1954–60. KStJ 1958. Brilliant Star of Zanzibar (1st Class), 1954. *Recreations:* tennis, squash, golf. *Address:* 12A Crittles Court, Townsland Road, Wadhurst, East Sussex TN5 6BY. *T:* Wadhurst 3642. *Clubs:* Athenæum, MCC, Queen's.

RANKING, Robert Duncan; His Honour Judge Ranking; a Circuit Judge (formerly County Court Judge), since 1968; Judge of the Mayors and City of London Court, since 1980; *b* 24 Oct. 1915; *yr s* of Dr R. M. Ranking, Tunbridge Wells, Kent; *m* 1949, Evelyn Mary Tagart (*née* Walker); one *d. Educ:* Cheltenham Coll.; Pembroke Coll., Cambridge (MA). Called to Bar, 1939. Served in Queen's Own Royal W Kent Regt, 1939–46. Dep. Chm. E Sussex QS, 1962–71; Dep. Chm., Agricultural Land Tribunal (S Eastern Area), 1963. *Address:* Little Oakfield, Camden Hill, Tunbridge Wells, Kent. *T:* 27551.

RANNIE, Prof. Ian; FRCPath 1964; FIBiol 1964; Professor of Pathology (Dental School), University of Newcastle upon Tyne, 1960–81, Professor Emeritus 1981; *b* 29 Oct. 1915; *o s* of James Rannie, MA, and Nicholas Denniston McMeekan; *m* 1943, Flora Welch; two *s. Educ:* Ayr Academy; Glasgow University. BSc (Glas), 1935; MB, ChB (Glas), 1938; BSc Hons Pathology and Bacteriology (Glas), 1939; Hutcheson Research Schol. (Pathology), 1940. Assistant to Professor of Bacteriology, Glasgow, 1940–42; Lecturer in Pathology, 1942–60, King's College, Univ. of Durham. Consultant Pathologist, United Newcastle upon Tyne Hospitals, 1948–81, Hon. Consultant 1981–. Pres., International Soc. of Geographical Pathology, 1969–72; Vice-President: Assoc. of Clinical Pathologists, 1978–80; Internat. Union of Angiology. Hon. Mem., Hungarian Arteriosclerosis Res. Soc. *Publications:* papers on various subjects in medical journals. *Recreation:* golf. *Address:* 5 Osborne Villas, Newcastle upon Tyne NE2 1JU. *T:* Tyneside 2813163. *Clubs:* East India, Royal Over-Seas League.

RANT, James William, QC 1980; **His Honour Judge Rant;** a Circuit Judge, since 1984; *b* 16 April 1936; *s* of Harry George Rant, FZS and Barbara Rant; *m* 1963, Helen Rant (*née* Adnams), BA; two *s* two *d. Educ:* Stowe Sch.; Selwyn Coll., Cambridge (MA, LLM). Called to the Bar, Gray's Inn, 1961; pupillage with late James N. Dunlop, 1962–63; a Dep. Circuit Judge, 1975–79; a Recorder, 1979–84. Freeman, City of London, 1986. *Recreations:* cookery, music, family life. *Address:* 6 Barnstaple Road, Thorpe Bay, Essex.

RANTZEN, Esther Louise, (Mrs Desmond Wilcox); Television Producer/Presenter, since 1968; *b* 22 June 1940; *d* of Harry and Katherine Rantzen; *m* 1977, Desmond Wilcox, *qv*; one *s* two *d. Educ:* North London Collegiate Sch.; Somerville Coll., Oxford (MA). Studio manager making dramatic sound effects, BBC Radio, 1963; BBC TV: Researcher, 1965; Dir, 1967; Reporter, Braden's Week, 1968–72; Producer/Presenter, That's Life, 1973–, scriptwriter, 1976–; Producer, documentary series, The Big Time, 1976; Presenter, Drugwatch, Childwatch, and Producer/Presenter, The Lost Babies and other progs on social issues; reporter/producer, various documentaries, religious and current affairs TV progs. Mem., Nat. Consumer Council. Chm., Childline; Pres., Meet-a-Mum Assoc.; a Vice-President: ASBAH; Health Visitors' Assoc.; Spastics Soc.; Patron: Addenbrookes Kidney Patients Assoc.; Contact-a-Family (families of disabled children); DEMAND (furniture for the disabled); Downs Children's Assoc.; Trustee, Ben Hardwick Meml Fund. Personality of 1974, RTS award; BBC TV Personality of 1975, Variety Club of GB; European Soc. for Organ Transplant Award, 1985. *Publications:* (with Desmond Wilcox): Kill the Chocolate Biscuit, 1981; Baby Love, 1985; (with Shaun Woodward) Ben: the story of Ben Hardwick, 1985. *Recreations:* family life, the countryside, appearing in pantomime. *Address:* BBC TV, Lime Grove Studios, Lime Grove, W12. *T:* 01–743 8000; Noel Gay Artists, 24 Denmark Street, WC2. *T:* 01–836 3941.

RAO, Calyampudi Radhakrishna, FRS 1967; University Professor, University of Pittsburgh, since 1979; Director, Research and Training School, Indian Statistical Institute 1964–76, and Secretary, 1972–76; *b* 10 Sept. 1920; *s* of C. D. Naidu and A. Laksmikantamma; *m* 1948, C. Bhargavi Rao; one *s* one *d. Educ:* Andhra Univ. (MA, 1st Class Maths); Calcutta Univ. (MA, 1st Class Statistics; Gold Medal); PhD, ScD, Cambridge (Hon. Fellow, King's Coll., Cambridge, 1975). Indian Statistical Institute: Superintending Statistician, 1943–49; Professor and Head of Division of Theoretical Research and Training, 1949–64; Jawaharlal Nehru Professor, 1976–84. Co-editor, Sankhya, Indian Jl of Statistics, 1964–72, Editor, 1972–. Member, Internat. Statistical Inst., 1951 (Mem. Statistical Educn Cttee, 1958–; Treasurer, 1962–65; Pres.-elect, 1975–77, Pres., 1977–79, Hon. Mem. 1982); Chm., Indian Nat. Cttee for Statistics, 1962–; President: Biometric Soc., 1973–75; Indian Econometric Soc., 1971–76; Forum for Interdisciplinary Mathematics, 1982–. Fellow: Indian Nat. Sci. Acad., 1953 (Vice-Pres., 1973, 1974); Inst. of Math. Statistics, USA, 1958 (Pres., 1976–77); Amer. Statistical Assoc., 1972; Econometric Soc., 1972; Indian Acad. of Sciences, 1974; Founder Fellow, Third World Science Acad., 1983. Hon. Fellow: Royal Stat. Soc., 1969; Amer. Acad. of Arts and Sciences, 1975; Biometric Soc., 1986. Shanti Swarup Bhatnagar Memorial Award, 1963; Guy Medal in Silver, Royal Stat. Soc., 1965; Padma Bhushan, 1968; Meghnad Saha Medal, 1969; J. C. Bose Gold Medal, 1979. Hon. DSc: Andhra; Leningrad; Athens; Osmania; Ohio State; Philippines; Tampere; Hon. DLitt Delhi. Hon. Prof., Univ. of San Marcos, Lima. *Publications:* (with Mahalanobis and Majumdar) Anthropometric Survey of the United Provinces, 1941, a statistical study, 1949; Advanced Statistical Methods in Biometric Research, 1952; (with Mukherjee and Trevor) The Ancient Inhabitants of Jebal Moya, 1955; (with Majumdar) Bengal Anthropometric Survey, 1945, a statistical study, 1959; Linear Statistical Inference and its Applications, 1965; (with A. Matthai and S. K. Mitra) Formulae and Tables for Statistical Work, 1966; Computers and the Future of Human Society, 1968; (with S. K. Mitra) The Generalised Inverse of Matrices and its Applications, 1971; (with A. M. Kagan and Yu. V. Linnik) Characterization Problems of Mathematical Statistics, 1973. *Address:* Department of Mathematics and Statistics, University of Pittsburgh, Pittsburgh, Pa 15260, USA.

RAO, Prof. Chintamani Nagesa Ramachandra, Padma Shri, 1974; Padma Vibhushan, 1985; FRS 1982; CChem, FRSC; Director, since 1984, Professor of Chemical Sciences, since 1976, Indian Institute of Science, Bangalore, India; *b* 30 June 1934; *s* of H. Nagesa Rao; *m* 1960, Indumati; one *s* one *d. Educ:* Univ. of Mysore (DSc); Univ. of Purdue, USA (PhD). Research Chemist, Univ. of California, Berkeley, 1958–59; Lectr, Indian Inst. of Science, 1959–63; Prof., Indian Inst. of Technology, Kanpur, 1963–76, Head of Chemistry Dept, 1964–68, Dean of Research, 1969–72; Jawaharlal Nehru Fellow, 1973–75; Commonwealth Vis. Prof., Univ. of Oxford and Fellow, St Catherine's Coll., 1974–75; Jawaharlal Nehru Vis. Prof., Univ. of Cambridge, and Professorial Fellow, Kings' Coll., Cambridge, 1983–84. Chm., Solid State and Structural Chemistry Unit and Materials Res. Laboratory, Indian Inst. of Science, Bangalore, 1976–; President: INSA, 1986–; IUPAC, 1985–. Member: First Nat. Cttee of Science and Technology, Govt of India, 1971–74; Science Adv. Cttee to Union Cabinet of India, 1981–86; Chm., Science Adv. Council to Prime Minister, 1986–. Hon. DSc: Purdue, 1982; Bordeaux, 1983; Tirupati 1984; Roorkee 1985; Fellow, Indian Acad. of Scis; Foreign Member: Slovenian Acad. of Scis; Serbian Acad. of Scis; Amer. Acad. of Arts and Scis; Founder Mem., Third World Acad. Sci.; many awards and medals, incl.: Marlow Medal of Faraday Soc. (London), 1967; Royal Soc. of Chemistry (London) Medal, 1981; Centennial For. Fellowship of Amer. Chemical Soc., 1976. *Publications:* Ultraviolet and Visible Spectroscopy, 1960, 3rd edn 1975; Chemical Applications of Infrared Spectroscopy, 1964; Spectroscopy in Inorganic Chemistry, 1970; Modern Aspects of Solid State Chemistry, 1970; University General Chemistry, 1973; Solid State Chemistry, 1974; Phase Transitions in Solids, 1978; Preparation and Characterization of Materials, 1981; The Metallic and the Non-metallic States of Matter, 1985; New Directions in Solid State Chemistry, 1986; 400 research papers. *Recreations:* gourmet cooking, gardening. *Address:* Solid State and Structural Chemistry Unit, Indian Institute of Science, Bangalore-560012, India. *T:* 361690.

RAO, P. V. Narasimha; Member, Lok Sabha; Minister of Human Resources Development, India, since 1985 and Minister of Health and Family Welfare, since 1986; *b* Karimnagar, Andhra Pradesh, 28 June 1921; widower; three *s* five *d. Educ:* Osmania Univ., Hyderabad; Bombay Univ.; Nagpur Univ. (BSc, LLB). Career as leader, writer, poet, agriculturalist, advocate and administrator. Member, Andhra Pradesh Legislative Assembly, 1957–77; Minister in Andhra Pradesh Govt, 1962–71; Chief Minister of the State, 1971–73. Chm., Telugu Academy, Andhra Pradesh, 1968–74; Vice-Pres., Dakshin Bharat Hindi Prachar Sabha, Madras, 1972–; Gen. Sec., All India Congress Cttee, 1975–76. Elected to Lok Sabha (from Hanamkonda, Andhra Pradesh) 1972, 1977 and 1980, (from Ramtek) 1984; Minister: for External Affairs, 1980–84; for Home Affairs, 1984; of Defence, 1985. Chairman: Public Accounts Cttee, 1978–79; Bharatiya Vidya Bhavan's Andhra Centre. Has lectured on political matters in univs in USA and Federal Republic of Germany, and has visited many countries. *Publications:* many, including Sahasra Phan (Hindi trans.). *Recreations:* music, cinema, theatre. *Address:* Ministry of Human Resources Development, New Delhi, India; Vangara Post, Karimnagar District, Andhra Pradesh, India.

RAPER, Vice-Adm. Sir (Robert) George, KCB 1971 (CB 1968); FEng; Director-General, Ships, 1968–May 1974; Chief Naval Engineer Officer, 1968–74; *b* 27 Aug. 1915; *s* of Major Robert George Raper and Ida Jean (*née* MacAdam Smith); *m* 1940, Frances Joan St John (*née* Phillips); one *s* two *d. Educ:* RNC Dartmouth; RN Engineering College, Keyham; Advanced Engineering Course RNC Greenwich. Sen. Engineer, HMS Edinburgh, 1940 until ship was sunk, 1942 (despatches); Turbine Research Section, Admiralty, 1942–45; Engineer Officer, HMS Broadsword, Battleaxe, Crossbow, 1945–47; Comdr, 1947; Engineer-in-Chief's Dept, Admiralty, 1948–51; Engr Officer, HMS Birmingham, 1952–54; lent to RCN, 1954; Technical Sec. to Engineer-in-Chief of the Fleet, 1955–57; Capt. 1957; IDC 1958; in command HMS Caledonia, 1959–61; Dep. Dir of Marine Engineering, Admiralty, 1961–63; CSO (T) to Flag Officer Sea Training, 1963–65; Dir, Marine Engineering, MoD (Navy Dept), 1966–67. FEng 1976; FRINA; FIMechE; FIMarE (Pres. 1972); FRSA. *Address:* Hollytree Farm, Moorlinch, near Bridgwater, Somerset. *T:* Ashcott 210510.

RAPHAEL, Adam Eliot Geoffrey; Political Editor, The Observer, since 1981; *b* 22 April 1938; *s* of Geoffrey George Raphael and Nancy Raphael (*née* Rose); *m* 1970, Caroline Rayner Ellis; one *s* one *d. Educ:* Arnold House, Charterhouse; Oriel Coll., Oxford (BA Hons History). 2nd Lieut Royal Artillery, 1956–58. Copy Boy, Washington Post, USA, 1961; Swindon Evening Advertiser, 1962–63; Film Critic, Bath Evening Chronicle, 1963–64; The Guardian: Reporter, 1965; Motoring Correspondent, 1967–68; Foreign Correspondent, Washington and S Africa, 1969–73; Consumer Affairs Columnist, 1974–76; Political Correspondent, The Observer, 1976–81. Awards include: Granada Investigative Journalist of the Year, 1973; British Press Awards, Journalist of the Year, 1973. *Recreations:* tennis, ski-ing. *Address:* 50 Addison Avenue, W11 4QP. *T:* 01–603 9133. *Clubs:* Hurlingham, Royal Automobile, Ski Club of Great Britain.

RAPHAEL, Chaim, CBE 1965 (OBE 1951); *b* Middlesbrough, 14 July 1908; *s* of Rev. David Rabinovitch and Rachel Rabinovitch (name Hebraised by deed poll 1936); *m* 1934, Diana Rose (marr. diss. 1964); one *s* one *d. Educ:* Portsmouth Grammar Sch.; University Coll., Oxford. PPE 1930. James Mew Post-Grad. Schol. in Hebrew, 1931. Kennicott Fellowship, 1933–36. Cowley Lectr in Post-Biblical Hebrew, 1932–39. Liaison Officer for Internment Camps: UK 1940; Canada 1941. Adviser, British Information Services, NY, 1942–45; Dir (Economics), 1945–57; Dep. Head of Information Div., HM Treasury, 1957–59; Head of Information Division: HM Treasury, 1959–68; Civil Service Dept, 1968–69. Research Fellow, Univ. of Sussex, 1969–75. *Publications:* Memoirs of a Special Case, 1962; The Walls of Jerusalem, 1968; A Feast of History, 1972; A Coat of Many Colours, 1979; The Springs of Jewish Life, 1982 (jtly, Wingate Prize, 1983); The Road from Babylon, 1985; A Jewish Book of Common Prayer, 1986; *novels:* (under pseudonym Jocelyn Davey): The Undoubted Deed, 1956; The Naked Villany, 1958; A Touch of Stagefright, 1960; A Killing in Hats, 1964; A Treasury Alarm, 1976; Murder in Paradise, 1982. *Recreation:* America. *Address:* 27 Langdale Road, Hove, East Sussex BN3 4HQ. *T:* Brighton 770563. *Club:* Reform.

RAPHAEL, Prof. David Daiches, DPhil, MA; Emeritus Professor of Philosophy, University of London, since 1983; *b* 25 Jan. 1916; 2nd *s* of late Jacob Raphael and Sarah Warshawsky, Liverpool; *m* 1942, Sylvia, er *d* of late Rabbi Dr Salis Daiches and Flora Levin, Edinburgh; two *d. Educ:* Liverpool Collegiate School; University College, Oxford (scholar). 1st Class, Classical Moderations, 1936; Hall-Houghton Junior Septuagint Prizeman, 1937; 1st Class, Literae Humaniores, 1938; Robinson Senior Scholar of Oriel College, Oxford, 1938–40; Passmore Edwards Scholar, 1939. Served in Army, 1940–41. Temporary Assistant Principal, Ministry of Labour and National Service, 1941–44; temp. Principal, 1944–46. Professor of Philosophy, University of Otago, Dunedin, NZ, 1946–49; Lecturer in Moral Philosophy, Univ. of Glasgow, 1949–51; Senior Lecturer, 1951–60; Edward Caird Prof. of Political and Social Philosophy, Univ. of Glasgow, 1960–70; Prof. of Philosophy, Univ. of Reading, 1970–73; Prof. of Philosophy, Imperial Coll., Univ. of London, 1973–83 (Acad. Dir of Associated Studies, 1973–80; Head of Dept of Humanities, 1980–83). Visiting Professor of Philosophy, Hamilton Coll., Clinton, NY (under Chauncey S. Truax Foundation), and Univ. of Southern California, 1959; Mahlon Powell Lectr, Indiana Univ., 1959; Vis. Fellow, All Souls Coll., Oxford, 1967–68; John Hinkley Vis. Prof. of Political Sci., Johns Hopkins Univ., 1984. Independent Member: Cttee on Teaching Profession in Scotland (Wheatley Cttee), 1961–63; Scottish Agricultural Wages Board, 1962–84; Agricultural Wages Bd for England and Wales, 1972–78. Mem. Academic Adv. Cttee, Heriot-Watt Univ., Edinburgh, 1964–71; Mem. Cttee on Distribution of Teachers in Scotland (Roberts Cttee), 1965–66; Independent Member Police Advisory Board for Scotland, 1965–70; Member Social Sciences Adv. Cttee, UK Nat. Commission, UNESCO, 1966–74; Vice-Pres., Internat. Assoc. Philosophy of Law and Social Philosophy, 1971–; Pres., Aristotelian Soc., 1974–75. Academic Mem., Bd of Governors, Hebrew Univ. of Jerusalem, 1969–81, Hon. Governor 1981–. *Publications:* The Moral Sense, 1947; Edition of Richard Price's Review of Morals, 1948; Moral Judgement, 1955; The Paradox of Tragedy, 1960; Political Theory and the Rights of Man, 1967; British Moralists 1650–1800, 1969; Problems of Political Philosophy, 1970; (ed jtly) Adam Smith's Theory of Moral Sentiments, 1976; Hobbes: Morals and Politics, 1977; (ed jtly) Adam Smith's Lectures on Jurisprudence, 1978; (ed jtly) Adam Smith's

Essays on Philosophical Subjects, 1980; Justice and Liberty, 1980; Moral Philosophy, 1981; (trans. jtly with Sylvia Raphael) Richard Price as Moral Philosopher and Political Theorist, by Henri Laboucheix, 1982; Adam Smith, 1985; articles in jls of philosophy and of political studies. *Address:* Imperial College of Science and Technology, SW7 2AZ.

RAPHAEL, Frederic Michael; author; *b* 14 Aug. 1931; *s* of late Cedric Michael Raphael and of Irene Rose (*née* Mauser); *m* 1955, Sylvia Betty Glatt; two *s* one *d*. *Educ:* Charterhouse; St John's Coll., Cambridge (MA (Hons)). FRSL 1964. *Publications: novels:* Obbligato, 1956; The Earlsdon Way, 1958; The Limits of Love, 1960; A Wild Surmise, 1961; The Graduate Wife, 1962; The Trouble with England, 1962; Lindmann, 1963; Orchestra and Beginners, 1967; Like Men Betrayed, 1970; Who Were You With Last Night?, 1971; April, June and November, 1972; Richard's Things, 1973; California Time, 1975; The Glittering Prizes, 1976; Heaven and Earth, 1985; *short stories:* Sleeps Six, 1979; Oxbridge Blues, 1980 (also pubd as scripts of TV plays, 1984); Think of England, 1986; *biography:* Somerset Maugham and his World, 1977; Byron, 1982; *essays:* Bookmarks (ed), 1975; Cracks in the Ice, 1979; *screenplays:* Nothing but the Best, 1964; Darling, 1965 (Academy Award); Two For The Road, 1967; Far From the Madding Crowd, 1967; A Severed Head, 1972; Daisy Miller, 1974; The Glittering Prizes, 1976 (sequence of TV plays) (Writer of the Year 1976, Royal TV Soc.); Rogue Male, 1976; (and directed) Something's Wrong (TV), 1978; School Play (TV), 1979; The Best of Friends (TV), 1979; Richard's Things, 1981; *play:* From The Greek, Arts, Cambridge, 1979; *translations:* (with Kenneth McLeish): Poems of Catullus, 1976; The Oresteia, 1978 (televised as The Serpent Son, BBC, 1979). *Recreation:* tennis. *Address:* The Wick, Langham, Colchester, Essex CO4 5PE. *Clubs:* Savile, Queen's.

RAPHAEL, Prof. Ralph Alexander, CBE 1982; PhD, DSc (London), ARCS, DIC; FRS 1962, FRSE, FRSC; Fellow of Christ's College, Professor of Organic Chemistry, and Head of Department of Organic and Inorganic Chemistry, Cambridge University, since June 1972; *b* 1 Jan. 1921; *s* of Jack Raphael; *m* 1944, Prudence Marguerite Anne, *d* of Col P. J. Gaffikin, MC, MD; one *s* one *d*. *Educ:* Wesley College, Dublin; Tottenham County School; Imperial College of Science and Technology. Chemist, May & Baker Ltd, 1943–46. ICI Research Fellow, Univ. of London, 1946–49; Lecturer in Organic Chemistry, Univ. of Glasgow, 1949–54; Professor of Organic Chemistry, Queen's University, Belfast, 1954–57; Regius Prof. of Chemistry, Glasgow Univ., 1957–72. Tilden Lectr, Chem. Soc., 1960, Corday-Morgan Vis. Lectr, 1963; Roy. Soc. Vis. Prof., 1967; Pedler Lectr, Chem. Soc., 1973; Pacific Coast Lectr, West Coast Univs tour from LA to Vancouver, 1979; Lady Davis Vis. Prof., Hebrew Univ. of Jerusalem, 1980; Sandin Lectr, Univ. of Alberta, 1985; Andrews Lectr, Univ. of NSW, 1985. Vice-Pres. Chemical Soc., 1967–70; Mem., Academic Adv. Bd, Warwick Univ. Hon. DUniv Stirling, 1982; Hon. DSc East Anglia, 1986. Meldola Medallist, RIC, 1948; Chem. Soc. Ciba-Geigy Award for Synthetic Chemistry, 1975; Davy Medal, Royal Soc., 1981. *Publications:* Chemistry of Carbon Compounds, Vol. IIA, 1953; Acetylenic Compounds in Organic Synthesis, 1955; papers in Journal of Chemical Society. *Recreations:* music, bridge. *Address:* University Chemical Laboratory, Lensfield Road, Cambridge CB2 1EW. *T:* Cambridge 66499; 4 Ivy Field, High Street, Barton, Cambs. *Club:* Athenæum.

RAPHAEL, Ven. Timothy John; Archdeacon of Middlesex, since 1983; *b* 26 Sept. 1929; *s* of Hector and Alix Raphael; *m* 1957, Anne Elizabeth Shepherd; one *s* two *d*. *Educ:* Christ's College, Christchurch, NZ; Leeds Univ. (BA). Asst Curate, St Stephen, Westminster, 1955–60; Vicar of St Mary, Welling, Kent, 1960–63; Vicar of St Michael, Christchurch, NZ, 1963–65; Dean of Dunedin, 1965–73; Vicar, St John's Wood, London, 1973–83. *Recreations:* contemporary poetry, theatre, beach-combing. *Address:* 12 St Ann's Villas, W11 4RS. *T:* 01–603 0856.

RAPHOE, Bishop of, (RC), since 1982; **Most Rev. Séamus Hegarty;** *b* 26 Jan. 1940; *s* of James Hegarty and Mary O'Donnell. *Educ:* Kilcar National School; St Eunan's Coll., Letterkenny; St Patrick's Coll., Maynooth; University Coll., Dublin. Priest, 1966; post-grad. studies, University Coll., Dublin, 1966–67; Dean of Studies 1967–71, President 1971–82, Holy Cross College, Falcarragh. *Publication:* contribs to works on school administration and student assessment. *Recreations:* bridge, fishing. *Address:* Ard Adhamhnain, Letterkenny, Co. Donegal, Ireland. *T:* Letterkenny 21208.

RASCH, Sir Richard Guy Carne, 3rd Bt, *cr* 1903; a Member of HM Body Guard, Honourable Corps of Gentlemen-at-Arms, since 1968; *b* 10 Oct. 1918; *s* of Brigadier G. E. C. Rasch, CVO, DSO (*d* 1955); *S* uncle, 1963; *m* 1st, 1947, Anne Mary, *d* of late Major J. H. Dent-Brocklehurst; one *s* one *d*; 2nd, 1961, Fiona Mary, *d* of Robert Douglas Shaw. *Educ:* Eton; RMC, Sandhurst. Major, late Grenadier Guards. Served War of 1939–45; retired, 1951. *Recreations:* shooting, fishing. *Heir:* *s* Simon Anthony Carne Rasch [*b* 26 Feb. 1948. *Educ:* Eton; Royal Agric. Coll., Cirencester]. *Address:* 30 Ovington Square, SW3. *T:* 01–589 9973; The Manor House, Lower Woodford, near Salisbury, Wilts. *Clubs:* White's, Pratt's, Cavalry and Guards.

RASH, Mrs D. E. A.; *see* Wallace, Doreen.

RASHLEIGH, Sir Richard (Harry), 6th Bt *cr* 1831; Management Accountant, United Biscuits PLC, since 1985; *b* 8 July 1958; *s* of Sir Harry Evelyn Battie Rashleigh, 5th Bt and of Honora Elizabeth, *d* of George Stuart Sneyd; *S* father, 1984. *Educ:* Allhallows School, Dorset. Management Accountant with Arthur Guinness Son & Co., 1980–82; Dexion-Comino International Ltd, 1982–84. *Recreation:* sailing. *Heir:* *uncle* Peter Rashleigh [*b* 21 Sept. 1924; *m* 1949, Lola Evan, NSW; three *d*]. *Address:* Stowford Grange, Lewdown, near Okehampton, Devon. *T:* Lewdown 237. *Club:* Naval.

RASHLEIGH BELCHER, John; *see* Belcher, J. R.

RASMINSKY, Louis, CC (Canada), 1968; CBE 1946; Governor, Bank of Canada, 1961–73; *b* 1 Feb. 1908; *s* of David and Etta Rasminsky; *m* 1930, Lyla Rotenberg; one *s* one *d*. *Educ:* University of Toronto; London School of Economics. Financial Section, League of Nations, 1930–39; Chairman, Foreign Exchange Control Board, Canada, 1940–51; Deputy Governor, Bank of Canada, 1956–61. Executive Director: IMF, 1946–62; International Bank, 1950–62; Alternate Governor for Canada, IMF, 1969–73. Chm., Bd of Governors, Internat. Develt Res. Centre, 1973–78. Hon. Fellow, LSE, 1960. Hon. LLD: Univ. of Toronto, 1953; Yeshiva Univ., 1965; Queen's Univ., 1967; Bishop's Univ., 1968; McMaster Univ., 1969; Trent Univ., 1972; Concordia Univ., 1975; Univ. of Western Ontario, 1978; Univ. of British Columbia, 1979; Hon. DHL Hebrew Union Coll., 1963. Outstanding Achievement Award of Public Service of Canada, 1968; Vanier Medal, Inst. of Public Admin, 1974. *Recreations:* golf, fishing. *Address:* 20 Driveway, Apt 1006, Ottawa, Ont K2P 1C8, Canada. *T:* 613–594–0150. *Clubs:* Rideau, Cercle Universitaire d'Ottawa (Ottawa); Five Lakes (Wakefield, PQ).

RASMUSSEN, Prof. Steen Eiler; architect; Professor of Architecture, Royal Academy of Fine Arts, Copenhagen, 1938–68; *b* Copenhagen, 9 Feb. 1898; *s* of General Eiler Rasmussen; *m* 1934, Karen Margrete Schrøder (*d* 1985); two *d*. *Educ:* Metropolitanskolen; Royal Academy of Fine Arts, Copenhagen. Three first prizes in town planning competitions, 1919. Mem. Danish Roy. Acad. of Fine Arts, 1922; Lecturer at Architectural Sch. of the Academy, 1924; Architect to Municipal Town Planning Office, Copenhagen, 1932–38. Pres. Copenhagen Regional Planning Cttee, 1945–58. Visiting Professor in USA: Massachusetts Inst. of Technology, 1953, Yale, 1954, Philadelphia, 1958, Berkeley, 1959. Lethaby Professor, Roy. College of Art, London, 1958. Designed: Tingbjerg Housing Estate, Copenhagen, 1953–; Schools, Town Hall. Hon. Corr. Member: RIBA London, Bavarian Acad. of Fine Arts, 1958; American Institute of Architects, 1962; Hon. Royal Designer for Industry, London, 1947; Hon. Dr: Technische Hochschule Munich; Univ. of Lund. *Publications:* London, the Unique City, 1937; Towns and Buildings, 1951; Experiencing Architecture, 1959. *Recreation:* to doze in a chair thinking of future books. *Address:* Dreyersvej 9, 2960 Rungsted Kyst, Denmark. *T:* 0286 3510.

RASUL, Syed Alay; Hon. Chairman, Federation of Bangladesh Associations, UK and Europe, since 1974; consultant, Ethnic Advice and Information, since 1983; *b* 1 Feb. 1931; *s* of late Syed Ahmed Rasul and Khodeja Rasul; *m* 1956, Kamrunnessa Rasul; three *s* one *d* (and one *d* decd). *Educ:* Univ. of Aligarh, India (BA 1950); Univ. of Dacca, Bangladesh (MA 1953); Univ. of Manchester (Dipls: Adult Educn and Community Development 1963, Social Admin. 1964; Pres., Pakistan Students Soc., 1963–64); High Wycombe Coll. of Technology. NEBSS Cert., 1974; UN and Govt of Pakistan Cert. of Merit in Community Develt, 1956. Manpower Survey Officer, Pakistan Govt, 1955; E Pakistan Government: Social Welfare Organiser, 1956–60; Divl Welfare Organiser, 1960–62; Exec. Sec., Pakistan Welfare and Inf. Centre, Manchester, 1964–67; Sen. Community Relations Officer, Sheffield, 1967–82. Gen. Sec., E Pakistan Conf. of Social Work, 1956–57; Hon. Sec. Gen., Standing Conf. of Asian Organisations, UK, 1970–82; EC Mem., UK Immigrants Advisory Service, 1977– (Hon. Vice-Chm. 1975); Convenor, EEC Migrant Workers Forum, 1975–; founder Mem., Bangladesh Immigration and Adv. Service, 1978–; Chm., Campaign for Increases in Pensions Paid Abroad, 1980–81. Member: BBC Adv. Council for Asian Unit, 1965–70; Electricity Consumer Council, 1977–; presenter and broadcaster, Asian programme, Radio Sheffield, 1966–76. Governor, Waltheaf Comp. Sch., Sheffield, 1978–; Gen. Sec., Aligarh Muslim Univ. Old Boys' Assoc., UK, 1983– (Pres., 1981–83). *Publications:* 6 special brochures; weekly column on immigration and race relations in Janomot. *Recreations:* billiards, music; visiting places and meeting people. *Address:* 47 Blenheim Gardens, Wembley, Mddx HA9 7NP. *T:* 01–904 6007.

RATCLIFF, Antony Robin Napier; Deputy Chairman and Chief Executive, Eagle Star Insurance, since 1985; *b* 26 Sept. 1925; *m* 1956, Helga Belohlawek, Vienna; one *s*. FIA 1953; ASA. Nat. Correspondent for England, Internat. Actuarial Assoc., 1965–70; Mem. Council, Assoc. of British Insurers (formerly British Insurance Assoc.), 1969–. Pres., Inst. of Actuaries, 1980–82; Vice-Pres., London Insce Inst., 1964–. Vice-Pres., Assoc. internat. pour l'Etude de l'Economie de l'Assurance, 1986–. Corresponding Member: Deutsche Gesellschaft für Versicherungsmathematik; Verein zur Förderung der Versicherungswirtschaft. FRSA. Hon. Treasurer, German Christ Church, London. Messenger and Brown Prize-Winner, Inst. of Actuaries, 1963. *Publications:* (jtly) Lessons from Central Forecasting, 1965; (jtly) Strategic Planning for Financial Institutions, 1974; (jtly) A House in Town, 1984; contribs to Jl of Inst. of Actuaries, Trans of Internat. Congress of Actuaries, Jl London Insce Inst., Jl Chartered Insce Inst., Blätter der Deutschen Gesellschaft für Versicherungsmathematik. *Address:* 1 Threadneedle Street, EC2R 8BE. *T:* 01–588 1212. *Clubs:* Actuaries, Roehampton, Anglo-Austrian Society.

RATCLIFFE, Frederick William, MA, PhD; JP; University Librarian, University of Cambridge, since 1980; Fellow, Corpus Christi College, Cambridge, since 1980; *b* 28 May 1927; *y s* of late Sydney and Dora Ratcliffe, Leek, Staffs; *m* 1952, Joyce Brierley; two *s* one *d*. *Educ:* Leek High Sch., Staffs; Manchester Univ. (MA, PhD); MA Cantab. Served in N Staffs Regt, 1945–48. Manchester University: Graduate Res. Scholarship, 1951; Res. Studentship in Arts, 1952; Asst Cataloguer and Cataloguer, 1954–62; Sub-Librarian, Glasgow Univ., 1962–63; Dep. Librarian, Univ. of Newcastle upon Tyne, 1963–65; University Librarian, 1965–80, Dir, John Rylands University Library, 1972–80, Manchester University. Trustee, St Deiniol's Library, Hawarden, 1975–. Hon. Lectr in Historical Bibliography, Manchester Univ., 1970–80; External Prof., Dept of Library and Inf. Studies, Loughborough Univ., 1981–86; Fellow, Chapter of Woodard Schools (Eastern Div.), 1981–. JP Stockport, 1972–80, Cambridge, 1981. *Publications:* Preservation Policies and Conservation in British Libraries, 1984; many articles in learned journals. *Recreations:* book collecting, hand printing, cricket. *Address:* 84 Church Lane, Girton, Cambs. *T:* Cambridge 277512; Light Alders Farm, Light Alders Lane, Disley, Cheshire SK12 2LW. *T:* Disley 2234.

RATCLIFFE, John Ashworth, CB 1965; CBE 1959 (OBE 1947); FRS 1951; FEng; MA; Director of Radio and Space Research Station, Slough, Oct. 1960–Feb. 1966; *b* 12 Dec. 1902; *s* of H. H. Ratcliffe, Rawtenstall, Lancs; *m* 1930, Nora Disley; two *d*. *Educ:* Giggleswick School; Sidney Sussex College, Cambridge. Taught Physics at Cambridge and Research in Radio Wave Propagation, 1924–60 (War Service with Telecommunications Res. Est., Malvern); Reader in Physics, Cambridge University, 1947–60; Fellow of Sidney Sussex College, 1927–60, Hon. Fellow 1962. President: Physical Society, 1959–60; Section A, British Association, 1964; Chairman, Electronics Board, IEE, 1962–63; Vice-Pres., IEE, 1963–66, Pres., 1966. Hon. Pres., URSI; Foreign Fellow, Indian Nat. Sci. Acad. FEng 1976; FIEEE. Hon. FInstP; Hon. FIEE; Hon. DSc Kent, 1979. Faraday Medal (IEE), 1966; Royal Medal (Roy. Soc.), 1966; Guthrie Medal (Inst. Physics), 1971; Gold Medal (RAS), 1976. *Publications:* numerous papers in scientific journals on Radio Wave Propagation. *Address:* 193 Huntingdon Road, Cambridge CB3 0DL.

RATFORD, David John Edward, CMG 1984; CVO 1979; HM Diplomatic Service; Assistant Under-Secretary of State (Europe), Foreign and Commonwealth Office, since 1986; *b* 22 April 1934; *s* of George Ratford and Lilian (*née* Jones); *m* 1960, Ulla Monica, *d* of Oskar and Gurli Jerneck, Stockholm; two *d*. *Educ:* Whitgift Middle Sch.; Selwyn Coll., Cambridge (1st Cl. Hons Mod. and Med. Langs). National Service (Intell. Corps), 1953–55. Exchequer and Audit Dept, 1952; FO, 1955; 3rd Sec., Prague, 1959–61; 2nd Sec., Mogadishu, 1961–63; 2nd, later 1st Sec., FO, 1963–68; 1st Sec. (Commercial), Moscow, 1968–71; FCO, 1971–74; Counsellor (Agric. and Econ.), Paris, 1974–78; Counsellor, Copenhagen, 1978–82; Minister, Moscow, 1983–85. Comdr, Order of the Dannebrog, Denmark, 1979. *Recreations:* music, squash, tennis. *Address:* c/o Foreign and Commonwealth Office, SW1; Käringön, Bohuslän, Sweden. *Club:* Travellers'.

RATHBONE, John Francis Warre, CBE 1966; TD 1950; Secretary of National Trust for Places of Historic Interest or Natural Beauty, 1949–68; President, London Centre of the National Trust, since 1968; *b* 18 July 1909; *e s* of Francis Warre Rathbone and Edith Bertha Hampshire, Allerton Beeches, Liverpool. *Educ:* Marlborough; New College, Oxford. Solicitor, 1934. Served War of 1939–45; AA Comd and staff (Col 1945). Dir Ministry of Justice Control Branch, CCG (British Element), 1946–49. Member Bd of Governors, UCH, 1968–74. Mem. Management Cttee, Mutual Households Assoc. Ltd; Hon. Treas., Friends of UCH; Mem. Council, Over Forty Assoc. *Recreations:* music, travel. *Address:* 15 Furlong Road, N7 8LS. *T:* 01–607 4854. *Club:* Travellers'.

RATHBONE, John Rankin, (Tim Rathbone); MP (C) Lewes since Feb. 1974; *b* 17 March 1933; *s* of J. R. Rathbone, MP (killed in action 1940) and Lady Wright (*see*

Beatrice Wright); *m* 1st, 1960, Margarita Sanchez y Sanchez (marr. diss. 1981); two *s* one *d*; 2nd, 1982, Mrs Susan Jenkin Stopford Sackville. *Educ:* Eton; Christ Church, Oxford; Harvard Business School. 2nd Lieut KRRC, 1951–53. Robert Benson Lonsdale & Co., Merchant Bankers, 1956–58; Trainee to Vice-Pres., Ogilvy & Mather Inc., NY, 1958–66; Chief Publicity and Public Relations Officer, Conservative Central Office, 1966–68; Director: Charles Barker Group, 1968–; Ayer Barker Ltd, 1971– (Man. Dir 1971–73; Dep. Chm., 1973–79); Charles Barker City, 1981–; Charles Barker Manchester (formerly Charles Barker Cross Courtenay), 1983– (Chm., 1983–). PPS to Minister of Health, 1979–82, to Minister for Trade (Consumer Affairs), 1982–83, to Minister for the Arts, 1985. Founder Member: All Party Parly Drugs Misuse Gp, 1984; Conservatives for Fundamental Change in South Africa, 1986, Council Member. Nat. Cttee for Electoral Reform; RSA (FRSA 1979). *Recreation:* family. *Address:* 30 Farringdon Street, EC4A 4EA. *T:* 01–634 1098. *Clubs:* Brooks's, Pratt's; Sussex; Society of Sussex Downsmen.

RATHBONE, Very Rev. Norman Stanley; Dean of Hereford, 1969–82, now Dean Emeritus; *b* 8 Sept. 1914; *er s* of Stanley George and Helen Rathbone; *m* 1952, Christine Olive Gooderson; three *s* two *d*. *Educ:* Lawrence Sheriff Sch., Rugby; Christ's Coll., Cambridge; Westcott House, Cambridge. BA 1936, MA 1939. St Mary Magdalen's, Coventry: Curate, 1938; Vicar, 1945; Canon Theologian, Coventry Cathedral, 1954; Canon Residentiary and Chancellor, Lincoln Cathedral, 1959. *Address:* The Daren, Newton St Margarets, Herefordshire. *T:* Michaelchurch 623.

RATHBONE, Philip Richardson; Secretary, Royal Town Planning Institute, 1960–75; *b* 21 May 1913; *s* of Herbert R. Rathbone, sometime Lord Mayor of Liverpool, and Winifred Richardson Evans, Wimbledon; *m* 1940, Angela, *d* of Captain A. B. de Beer, Liverpool; one *s* two *d*. *Educ:* Clifton Coll., Bristol; University Coll., Oxford. BA Hons Mod. History 1934. Sec., Housing Centre, London, 1935–39. Army, King's Regt, Liverpool; Personnel Selection, WO, 1939–45 (Major). Principal, Min. of Town and Country Planning, 1945–53; Sec., Royal Instn of Chartered Surveyors (Scotland), 1953–60. Hon. MRTPI, 1975. *Publications:* Paradise Merton: The Story of Nelson and the Hamiltons at Merton Place, 1973; The Angel and the Flame: the two marriages of Sir William Hamilton, 1978; A Wheelchair for all Seasons, 1981. *Recreations:* writing, Lady Hamilton. *Address:* 19 Raymond Road, SW19 4AD. *T:* 01–946 2478.

RATHBONE, Tim; *see* Rathbone, J. R.

RATHCAVAN, 2nd Baron *cr* 1953, of The Braid, Co. Antrim; **Phelim Robert Hugh O'Neill;** Bt 1929; PC (N Ireland) 1969; Major, late RA; *b* 2 Nov. 1909; *s* of 1st Baron Rathcavan, PC and Sylvia (*d* 1972), *d* of Walter A. Sandeman; *S* father, 1982; *m* 1st, 1934, Clare Désirée (from whom he obtained a divorce, 1944), *d* of late Detmar Blow; one *s* one *d*; 2nd, 1953, Mrs B. D. Edwards-Moss, *d* of late Major Hon. Richard Coke; three *d* (and one *d* decd). *Educ:* Eton. MP (UU) for North Antrim (UK Parliament), 1952–59; MP (U) North Antrim, Parliament of N Ireland, 1959–72; Minister, N Ireland: Education, 1969; Agriculture, 1969–71. *Heir:* *s* Hon. Hugh Detmar Torrens O'Neill [*b* 14 June 1939; *m* 1983, Mrs Sylvie Chittenden, *d* of Georges Wichard, Provence; one *s*]. *Address:* The Lodge, Killala, Co. Mayo, Ireland. *T:* Ballina 32252.

RATHCREEDAN, 2nd Baron, *cr* 1916; **Charles Patrick Norton,** TD; *b* 26 Nov. 1905; *er s* of 1st Baron and Marguerite Cecil (*d* 1955), *d* of Sir Charles Huntington, 1st Bart, MP; *S* father, 1930; *m* 1946, Ann Pauline, *er d* of late Surgeon Capt. William Bastian, RN; two *s* one *d*. *Educ:* Wellington Coll.; Lincoln Coll., Oxford, MA. Called to Bar, Inner Temple, 1931; admitted Solicitor, 1936; Major 4th Battalion Oxford and Buckinghamshire Light Inf., TA; served France, 1940; prisoner of war, 1940–45. Master, Founders' Co., 1970. *Recreation:* gardening. *Heir:* *s* Hon. Christopher John Norton [*b* 3 June 1949; *m* 1978, Lavinia, *d* of A. G. R. Ormiston, Coln Orchard, Arlington, Bibury, Glos; one *d*]. *Address:* Church Field, Fawley, Henley-on-Thames, Oxon. *T:* Henley 574160.

RATHDONNELL, 5th Baron, *cr* 1868; **Thomas Benjamin McClintock Bunbury;** *b* 17 Sept. 1938; *o s* of William, 4th Baron Rathdonnell and Pamela, *e d* of late John Malcolm Drew; *S* father 1959; *m* 1965, Jessica Harriet, *d* of George Gilbert Butler, Scatorish, Bennettsbridge, Co. Kilkenny; three *s* one *d*. *Educ:* Charterhouse; Royal Naval College, Dartmouth. Lieutenant RN. *Heir:* *s* Hon. William Leopold McClintock Bunbury, *b* 6 July 1966. *Address:* Lisnavagh, Rathvilly, County Carlow, Ireland. *T:* Carlow 66104.

RATTEE, Donald Keith, QC 1977; Attorney General of the Duchy of Lancaster, since 1986; *b* 9 March 1937; *s* of Charles Ronald and Dorothy Rattee; *m* 1964, Diana Mary Howl; four *d*. *Educ:* Clacton County High School; Trinity Hall, Cambridge (MA, LLB). Called to Bar, Lincoln's Inn, 1962, Bencher, 1985; Second Junior Counsel to the Inland Revenue (Chancery), 1972–77. Mem., Gen. Council of the Bar, 1970–74. *Recreations:* tennis, golf, music, gardening. *Address:* 29 Shirley Avenue, Cheam, Surrey. *T:* 01–642 3062; 7 New Square, Lincoln's Inn, WC2. *T:* 01–405 1266. *Clubs:* Sutton Tennis and Squash (Sutton, Surrey); Banstead Downs Golf Club (Banstead).

RATTLE, Simon; Principal Conductor, City of Birmingham Symphony Orchestra since Sept. 1980; Principal Guest Conductor, Los Angeles Philharmonic, since 1981; *b* Liverpool, 1955; *m* 1980, Elise Ross, American soprano; one *s*. Won Bournemouth John Player Internat. Conducting Comp., when aged 19. Has conducted: Bournemouth Sinfonietta; Philharmonia; Northern Sinfonia; London Philharmonic; London Sinfonietta; Boston Symphony; Chicago Symphony; Cleveland; Concertgebouw; Stockholm Philharmonic; Toronto Symphony, etc. Festival Hall début, 1976. Royal Albert Hall (Proms. etc.), 1976–; Asst Conductor, BBC Scottish Symphony Orch. (début Glasgow 1976), 1977–80; Associate Conductor, Royal Liverpool Philharmonic Soc., 1977–80; Glyndebourne début, 1977; Principal Conductor, London Choral Soc., 1979–83; Artistic Dir, South Bank Summer Music, 1981–83; Principal Guest Conductor, Rotterdam Philharmonic, 1981–84. Exclusive contract with EMI Records. *Address:* c/o Harold Holt Ltd, 31 Sinclair Road, W14 0NS. *T:* 01–603 4600.

RAU, Santha Rama; free-lance writer since 1945; English teacher at Sarah Lawrence College, Bronxville, NY, since 1971; *b* Madras, India, 24 Jan. 1923; *d* of late Sir Benegal Rama Rau, CIE; *m* 1st, 1952, Faubion Bowers (marr. diss. 1966); one *s*; 2nd, Gurdon W. Wattles. *Educ:* St Paul's Girls' School, London, England; Wellesley College, Mass., USA. Feature writer for the Office of War Information, New York, USA, during vacations from college, 1942–45. Hon. doctorate: Bates College, USA, 1961; Russell Sage College, 1965; Phi Beta Kappa, Wellesley College, 1960. *Publications:* Home to India, 1945; East of Home, 1950; This is India, 1953; Remember the House, 1955; View to the South-East, 1957; My Russian Journey, 1959; A Passage to India (dramatization), 1962; Gifts of Passage, 1962; The Adventuress, 1971; Cooking of India, 1971 (2 vols); A Princess Remembers (with Maharani Gayatri Devi of Jaipur), 1976; An Inheritance (with Dhanvanthi Rama Rau), 1977. Many articles and short stories in New Yorker, Art News, Horizon, Saturday Evening Post, Reader's Digest, etc. *Address:* RR Box 200, Leedsville Road, Amenia, NY 12501, USA.

RAVEN, John Armstrong, CBE 1982; Consultant, World Bank, since 1983; Chairman, Aleph Systems Ltd, since 1983; *b* 23 April 1920; *s* of late John Colbeck Raven; *m* 1st,

1945, Megan Humphreys (*d* 1963); one *s* one *d*; 2nd, 1965, Joy Nesbitt (*d* 1983); one step *d*. *Educ:* High Sch., Cardiff; Downing Coll., Cambridge (MA). Called to Bar, Gray's Inn, 1955. Dir, British Coal Exporters' Fedn, 1947–68; Section Head, Nat. Economic Develt Office, 1968–70; Dir of Bd, 1970–72, Chief Exec., 1974–83, SITPRO. Dir-Gen., Assoc. of British Chambers of Commerce, 1972–74. *Recreation:* wondering. *Address:* 203 Avenue de Messidor, 1180 Brussels, Belgium. *T:* 343 6194. *Club:* United Oxford & Cambridge University.

RAVEN, Rear-Adm. John Stanley, CB 1964; BSc, FIEE; *b* 5 Oct. 1910; *s* of Frederick William Raven; *m* 1935, Nancy, *d* of William Harold Murdoch; three *s*. *Educ:* Huddersfield College; Leeds University (BSc). Temp. RNVR Commission, 1939; transferred to RN, 1946; retired, 1965. *Recreation:* painting. *Address:* East Garth, School Lane, Collingham, Yorks.

RAVEN, Dame Kathleen, (Dame Kathleen Annie Ingram), DBE 1968; FRCN 1986; SRN 1936; SCM 1938; Chief Nursing Officer in the Department of Health and Social Security (formerly Ministry of Health), 1958–72; *b* 9 Nov. 1910; *o d* of late Fredric William Raven and late Annie Williams Mason; *m* 1959, Prof. John Thornton Ingram, MD, FRCP (*d* 1972). *Educ:* Ulverston Grammar School; privately; St Bartholomew's Hosp., London; City of London Maternity Hospital. St Bartholomew's Hospital: Night Superintendent, Ward Sister, Administrative Sister, Assistant Matron, 1936–49; Matron, Gen. Infirmary, Leeds, 1949–57; Dep. Chief Nursing Officer, Min. of Health, 1957–58. Mem. Gen. Nursing Council for England and Wales, 1950–57; Mem. Council and Chm. Yorkshire Br., Roy. Coll. of Nursing, 1950–57; Mem. Central Area Advisory Bd for Secondary Education, Leeds, 1953–57; Area Nursing Officer, Order of St John, 1953–57; Mem. Exec. Cttee Assoc. of Hospital Matrons for England and Wales, 1955–57; Mem. Advisory Cttee for Sister Tutor's Diploma, Univ. of Hull, 1955–57; Internal Examr for Diploma of Nursing, Univ. of Leeds, 1950–57; Member: Area Nurse Trg Cttee, 1951–57; Area Cttee Nat. Hosp. Service Reserve, 1950–57; Central Health Services Council, 1957–58; Council and Nursing Advisory Bd, British Red Cross Soc., 1958–72; Cttee of St John Ambulance Assoc., 1958–72; National Florence Nightingale Memorial Cttee of Great Britain and Northern Ireland, 1958–72; WHO Expert Advisory Panel on Nursing, 1961–79; WHO Fellow, 1960; a Vice-Pres., Royal Coll. of Nursing, 1972–. Civil Service Comr, 1972–80. Chief Nursing Adviser, Allied Med. Gp, 1974–. Nursing missions to Saudi Arabia and Egypt, 1972–. Freedom, City of London, 1986. Hon. Freewoman, Worshipful Co. of Barbers, 1981. FRSA 1970. Officer (Sister) Order of St John, 1963. *Recreations:* painting, reading, travel. *Address:* Jesmond, Burcott, Wing, Leighton Buzzard, Bedfordshire. *T:* Aylesbury 688244; 29 Harley Street, W1. *T:* 01–580 3765. *Club:* Royal Commonwealth Society.
See also R. W. Raven.

RAVEN, Ronald William, OBE (mil.) 1946; TD; FRCS 1931; Consulting Surgeon, Westminster Hospital and Royal Marsden Hospital, since 1969; Surgeon, French Hospital, London, since 1936; Cons. Surgeon (General Surgeon) Eversfield Chest Hospital since 1937; Cons. Surgeon, Royal Star and Garter Home for Disabled Sailors, Soldiers and Airmen since 1948; *b* 28 July 1904; *e s* of late Fredric William Raven and Annie Williams Mason, Coniston. *Educ:* Ulverston Grammar School; St Bartholomew's Hospital Medical College, Univ. of London. St Bart's Hosp.: gained various prizes and Brackenbury surgical schol.; resident surgical appts, 1928–29; Demonstrator in Pathology, St Bart's Hosp., 1929–31; Registrar Statistics Nat. Radium Commn, 1931–34; jun. surgical appts, 1931–35; Asst Surg. Gordon Hosp., 1935; Asst Surg. Roy. Cancer Hosp., 1939–46, Surg. 1946–62; Jt Lectr in Surgery, Westminster Med. Sch., Univ. of London, 1951–69; Surgeon, Westminster (Gordon) Hosp., 1947–69; Sen. Surgeon, Royal Marsden Hosp. and Inst. of Cancer Research, Royal Cancer Hosp., 1962–69. Lectr, RIPH&H, 1965–85. Member: DHSS Standing Sub-Cttee on Cancer; DHSS Adv. Cttee on Cancer Registration; Chairman: Jt Nat. Cancer Survey Cttee; Cancer Rehabilitation and Continuing Care Cttee, UICC, 1983–. Fellow Assoc. of Surg. of GB; Mem., Internat. Soc. of Surgery; FRSM (PP, Section of Proctology, PP, Section of Oncology); Mem. Council, 1968–76, Mem. Court of Patrons, 1976–, RCS; Founder Pres., British Assoc. of Surgical Oncology (1973–77); Past (Founder) Pres., Assoc. of Head and Neck Oncologists of GB; Mem., European Soc. Surgical Oncology. Chm. Council, 1961–, and Chm Exec. Cttee, 1948–61, Marie Curie Meml Foundn; Vice-Pres. and Chm., Council of Epsom Coll., 1954–; late Chm., Conjoint Cttee; late Mem. Bd of Governors Royal Marsden Hosp.; formerly Mem. Council of Queen's Institute of District Nursing; Mem. (late Chm.), Cttee of Management Med. Insurance Agency; Formerly Mem. Council, Imperial Cancer Res. Fund; Founder Pres., World Fedn for Cancer Care, 1982–; Vice-Pres., Malta Meml District Nursing Assoc., 1982–. Surg. EMS, 1939; joined RAMC, 1941, and served in N Africa, Italy and Malta (despatches); o/c Surg. Div. (Lt-Col); and o/c Gen. Hosp. (Col), 1946; Lt-Col RAMC (TA); o/c Surg. Div. Gen. Hosp., 1947–53; Col RAMC (TA); o/c No 57 (Middlesex) General Hospital (TA), 1953–59; Colonel TARO, 1959–62; Hon. Colonel RAMC. OStJ 1946. Hon. Professor National Univ. of Colombia, 1949; Hon. MD Cartagena, 1949; Corresponding Foreign Member: Soc. of Head and Neck Surgeons of USA; Roman Surg. Soc.; Soc. Surg. of Bogotà; Société de Chirurgie de Lyon; Acad. of Athens, 1983; Member: Nat. Acad. Med. of Colombia; NY Acad. of Sciences; Soc. of Surgeons of Colombia; Italian Soc. Thoracic Surg.; Czechoslovak Soc. of J. E. Purkyne; Hon. Mem., Indian Assoc. of Oncology, 1983; Diploma de Socio Honorario, Soc. de Cancerologia de El Salvador, 1983. Diploma de Honor al Merito, Liga Nacional de El Salvador, 1983. Lectures: Arris and Gale, 1933; Erasmus Wilson, 1935, 1946, 1947; Malcolm Morris Meml, 1954; Blair Bell Meml, 1960; Elizabeth Matthai Endowment, Madras Univ., 1965; First W. Emory Burnett Honor, Temple Univ., USA, 1966; Edith A. Ward Meml, 1966; Gerald Townsley Meml, 1974; Bradshaw, RCS, 1975; Ernest Miles Meml, 1980; Honor, Amer. Soc. of Surg. Oncology, 1981; Honor, 1st Congress, Eur. Soc. of Surg. Oncology, Athens, 1982; Honor-Centenary, George N. Papanicolaou, Athens, 1983; First Kitty Cookson Meml, Royal Free Hosp., 1985. Hunterian Prof., RCS, 1948; Vis. Prof. of Surgery: Ein-Shams University, Cairo, 1961; Cancer Inst., Madras, 1965; Maadi Hosp., Cairo, 1974. Surgical missions to: Colombia, 1949; Saudi Arabia, 1961, 1962, 1975, 1976; United Arab Emirates, 1975, 1985. Consulting Editor, Clinical Oncology, 1979–82. Mem. Court, 1973–, Master, 1980–81, Worshipful Co. of Barbers; Mem., Livery Consultative Cttee, 1981–86. Freeman, City of London, 1956. Chevalier de la Légion d'Honneur, 1952. *Publications:* Treatment of Shock, 1942 (trans. Russian); Surgical Care, 1942, 2nd edn 1952; Cancer in General Practice (jointly), 1952; Surgical Instruments and Appliances (jointly), 1952; War Wounds and Injuries (jt editor and contrib.). 1940; chapters on Shock and Malignant Disease in Encyclopædia British Medical Practice, 1952, 1955, 1962–69, and Medical Progress, 1970–71; Handbook on Cancer for Nurses and Health Visitors, 1953; Cancer and Allied Diseases, 1955; contrib. chapters in Operative Surgery (Rob and Rodney Smith), 1956–57; Editor and contrib. Cancer (7 vols), 1957–60; Cancer of the Pharynx, Larynx and Oesophagus and its Surgical Treatment, 1958; (ed) Cancer Progress, 1960 and 1963; (ed jtly) The Prevention of Cancer, 1967; (ed) Modern Trends in Oncology 1, part 1, Research Progress, part 2, Clinical Progress, 1973; (ed and contrib.) The Dying Patient, 1975 (trans. Japanese and Dutch); (ed and contrib.) Principles of Surgical Oncology, 1977; (ed and contrib.) Foundations of Medicine, 1978; Rehabilitation and Continuing Care in Cancer, 1986;

(jtly) Cancer Care—an international survey; papers on surgical subjects, especially relating to Cancer in British and foreign journals. *Recreations:* philately (medallist Internat. Stamp Exhibn, London, 1950), music, ceramics and pictures, travel. *Address:* 29 Harley Street, W1N 1DA. *T:* 01–580 3765; Manor Lodge, Wingrave, Aylesbury, Bucks. *T:* Aylesbury 681287; Meadow View, Coniston, Cumbria. *Clubs:* MCC, Pilgrims.

See also Dame Kathleen Raven.

RAVEN, Simon (Arthur Noël); author, critic and dramatist since 1957; *b* 28 Dec. 1927; *s* of Arthur Godart Raven and Esther Kate Raven (*née* Christmas); *m* 1951, Susan Mandeville Kilner (marriage dissolved); one *s.* *Educ:* Charterhouse; King's Coll., Cambridge (MA). Research, 1951–52; regular commn, King's Shropshire Light Inf., 1953–57 (Capt.): served in Kenya; resigned, 1957. Member, Horatian Society. *Publications: novels:* The Feathers of Death, 1959; Brother Cain, 1959; Doctors Wear Scarlet, 1960; Close of Play, 1962; The Roses of Picardie, 1980; An Inch of Fortune, 1980; September Castle, 1983. The Alms for Oblivion sequence: The Rich Pay Late, 1964; Friends in Low Places, 1965; The Sabre Squadron, 1966; Fielding Gray, 1967; The Judas Boy, 1968; Places Where They Sing, 1970; Sound the Retreat, 1971; Come like Shadows, 1972; Bring Forth the Body, 1974; The Survivors, 1976; The First-born of Egypt sequence: Morning Star, 1984; The Face of the Waters, 1985; Before the Cock Crow, 1986; *short stories:* The Fortunes of Fingel, 1976; *memoirs:* Shadows on the Grass, 1982; *general:* The English Gentleman, 1961; Boys Will be Boys, 1963; Royal Foundation and Other Plays, 1965; contribs to Observer, Spectator, Punch, etc. *Plays and dramatisations for broadcasting:* BBC TV: Royal Foundation, 1961; The Scapegoat, 1964; Sir Jocelyn, 1965; Huxley's Point Counter-Point, 1968; Trollope's The Way We Live Now, 1969; The Pallisers, a serial in 26 episodes based on the six Palliser novels of Anthony Trollope, 1974; Iris Murdoch's An Unofficial Rose, 1975; Sexton Blake, 1978; ABC TV: The Gaming Book, 1965; Thames TV: Edward and Mrs Simpson, a serial based on Edward VIII by Frances Donaldson, 1978; Love in a Cold Climate, a dramatisation of Nancy Mitford's Pursuit of Love and Love in a Cold Climate, 1980; BBC Radio: Triad, a trilogy loosely based on Thucydides' History of the Peloponnesian War, 1965–68. *Recreations:* cricket, travel, reading, the turf. *Address:* c/o Curtis Brown Ltd, 162–168 Regent Street, W1R 5TB. *Clubs:* Brooks's, Reform; MCC, Butterflies Cricket, Trogs' Cricket.

RAVENSCROFT, John Robert Parker, (John Peel); broadcaster/journalist, since 1961; *b* 30 Aug. 1939; *s* of Robert Leslie and Joan Mary Ravenscroft; *m* 1974, Sheila Mary Gilhooly; two *s* two *d.* *Educ:* Woodlands Sch., Deganwy, N Wales; Shrewsbury. National Service, Royal Artillery (B2 Radar Operator), 1957–59. Mill operative, Rochdale, 1959–60; office boy, Dallas, Texas, 1960–65; part-time disc-jockey, 1961–; computer programmer, 1965; Pirate Radio, London, 1967; BBC Radio 1, 1967–. *Recreations:* cycling, staring out of the window. *Address:* c/o BBC Radio 1, W1A 4WW. *T:* 01–580 4468. *Clubs:* Liverpool Supporters; Eddie Grundy Fan (Sutton).

RAVENSDALE, 3rd Baron *cr* 1911; **Nicholas Mosley,** MC 1944; Bt 1781; *b* 25 June 1923; *e s* of Sir Oswald Mosley, 6th Bt (*d* 1980) and Lady Cynthia (*d* 1933), *d* of 1st Marquess Curzon of Kedleston; *S* to barony of aunt, who was also Baroness Ravensdale of Kedleston (Life Peer), 1966, and to baronetcy of father, 1980; *m* 1st, 1947, Rosemary Laura Salmond (marr. diss. 1974); three *s* one *d;* 2nd, 1974, Mrs Verity Bailey; one *s.* *Educ:* Eton; Balliol College, Oxford. Served in the Rifle Brigade, Captain, 1942–46. *Publications:* (as Nicholas Mosley): Spaces of the Dark, 1951; The Rainbearers, 1955; Corruption, 1957; African Switchback, 1958; The Life of Raymond Raynes, 1961; Meeting Place, 1962; Accident, 1964; Experience and Religion, 1964; Assassins, 1966; Impossible Object, 1968; Natalie Natalia, 1971; The Assassination of Trotsky, 1972; Julian Grenfell: His Life and the Times of his Death, 1888–1915, 1976; Catastrophe Practice, 1979; Imago Bird, 1980; Serpent, 1981; The Rules of the Game: Sir Oswald and Lady Cynthia Mosley 1896–1933, 1982; Beyond the Pale: Sir Oswald Mosley 1933–80, 1983; Judith, 1986. *Heir:* *s* Hon. Shaun Nicholas Mosley [*b* 5 August 1949; *m* 1978, Theresa Clifford; one *s*]. *Address:* Church Row Studios, 21a Heath Street, NW3. *T:* 01–435 8222.

RAVENSDALE, Thomas Corney, CMG 1951; retired; *b* 17 Feb. 1905; *s* of late Henry Ravensdale and late Lilian (*née* Corney); *m* (marriage dissolved); two *s;* *m* 1965, Mme Antoine Watteau (*née* Ricard). *Educ:* Royal Masonic Sch., Bushey, Herts; St Catharine's Coll., Cambridge. Acting Vice-Consul, Smyrna, 1928; 3rd Secretary, British Embassy, Ankara, 1929–34; 2nd Asst Oriental Sec., The Residency, Cairo, 1934–37; Vice-Consul, Bagdad, 1937–42; 1st Asst Oriental Sec., Brit. Embassy, Cairo, 1942–47; Oriental Counsellor, Cairo, 1948–51; Political Adviser, British Residency, Benghazi, 1951; Couns., Brit. Embassy in Libya, 1952–55; Ambassador to Dominican Republic, 1955–58; Insp. Foreign Service Establishments, 1958–60; Ambassador to the Republics of Dahomey, Niger, Upper Volta and the Ivory Coast, 1960–63. *Recreation:* gardening. *Address:* The Cottage, 13 rue de Penthièvre, Petit Andely, 27700 Les Andelys, France. *T:* (32) 54–16–38. *Club:* Athenæum.

RAVENSWORTH, 8th Baron *cr* 1821; **Arthur Waller Liddell,** Bt 1642; JP; *b* 25 July 1924; *s* of late Hon. Cyril Arthur Liddell (2nd *s* of 5th Baron) and Dorothy L., *d* of William Brown, Slinfold, Sussex; *S* cousin 1950; *m* 1950, Wendy, *d* of J. S. Bell, Cookham, Berks; one *s* one *d.* *Educ:* Harrow. Radio Engineer, BBC, 1944–50. JP Northumberland, 1959. *Heir:* *s* Hon. Thomas Arthur Hamish Liddell [*b* 27 Oct. 1954; *m* 1983, Linda, *d* of H. Thompson]. *Address:* Eslington Park, Whittingham, Alnwick, Northumberland. *T:* Whittingham 239.

RAW, Rupert George, CMG 1979; UK Director, European Investment Bank, 1973–81; *b* 5 April 1912; *s* of late Captain Rupert George Raw, DSO, and late Winifred Melville (*née* Francis), later Lady Stuart-Menteth; *m* 1936, Joan Persica, *d* of Sir Alban Young, 9th Bt, KCMG, MVO; one *s* two *d.* *Educ:* Eton; Oxford (BA Hons History). Supplementary Reserve Scots Guards, Lt-Col; parachuted Yugoslavia. CCG, 1946–48; joined OEEC; Finance Director, 1952–55; Bank of England, 1955; Adviser to Governor, 1962–72, retired; Director of Banque Belge, 1973, resigned, 1977; Dep. Chm., Italian Internat. Bank, 1973–76, Chm. 1976–79, retired 1980. *Recreations:* tennis, skiing. *Address:* 23 Warwick Square, SW1.

RAWBONE, Rear-Adm. Alfred Raymond, CB 1976; AFC 1951; *b* 19 April 1923; *s* of A. Rawbone and Mrs E. D. Rawbone (*née* Wall); *m* 1943, Iris Alicia (*née* Willshaw); one *s* one *d.* *Educ:* Saltley Grammar Sch., Birmingham. Joined RN, 1942; 809 Sqdn War Service, 1943; CO 736 Sqdn, 1953; CO 897 Sqdn, 1955; CO Loch Killisport, 1959–60; Comdr (Air) Lossiemouth and HMS Ark Royal, 1961–63; Chief Staff Officer to Flag Officer Naval Air Comd, 1965–67; CO HMS Dido, 1968–69; CO RNAS Yeovilton, 1970–72; CO HMS Kent, 1972–73; Dep. ACOS (Operations), SHAPE, 1974–76. Comdr 1958; Captain 1964; Rear-Adm. 1974. Director: Vincents of Yeovil, 1983–; Vindata, 1984–; Vincents (Bridgewater) Ltd, 1984–. *Address:* Halstock Leigh, Halstock, near Yeovil, Somerset.

RAWCLIFFE, Rt. Rev. Derek Alec; *see* Glasgow and Galloway, Bishop of.

RAWES, Francis Roderick, MBE 1944; MA; *b* 28 Jan. 1916; *e s* of late Prescott Rawes and Susanna May Dockery; *m* 1940, Dorothy Joyce, *d* of E. M. Hundley, Oswestry; two *s* one *d.* *Educ:* Charterhouse; St Edmund Hall, Oxford. Served in Intelligence Corps, 1940–46; GSO3(I) 13 Corps; GSO1 (I) HQ 15 Army Group and MI14 WO. Asst Master at Westminster School, 1938–40 and 1946–64; Housemaster, 1947–64; Headmaster, St Edmund's School, Canterbury, 1964–78. Chm. Governing Body, Westonbirt Sch., 1983– (Governor, 1979–). *Address:* Peyton House, Chipping Campden, Glos.

RAWLEY, Alan David, QC 1977; a Recorder of the Crown Court, since 1972; *b* 28 Sept. 1934; *er s* of late Cecil David Rawley and of Theresa Rawley (*née* Pack); *m* 1964, Ione Jane Ellis; two *s* one *d.* *Educ:* Wimbledon Coll.; Brasenose Coll., Oxford. Nat. Service, 1956–58; commnd Royal Tank Regt. Called to the Bar, Middle Temple, 1958; Bencher, 1985. Dep. Chairman, Cornwall Quarter Sessions, 1971. *Address:* Lamb Building, Temple, EC4. *T:* 01–353 6381. *Clubs:* Garrick, Pilgrims, MCC; Hampshire (Winchester).

RAWLINGS, Margaret; actress; *b* Osaka, Japan, 5 June 1906; *d* of Rev. G. W. Rawlings and Lilian Boddington; *m* 1st, 1927, Gabriel Toyne, actor (marr. diss. 1938); no *c;* 2nd, 1942, Robert Barlow (knighted 1943; *d* 1976); one *d.* *Educ:* Oxford High School for Girls; Lady Margaret Hall, Oxford. Left Oxford after one year, and joined the Macdona Players Bernard Shaw Repertory Company on tour, 1927; played Jennifer in the Doctor's Dilemma and many other parts; toured Canada with Maurice Colbourne, 1929; First London engagement Bianca Capello in The Venetian at Little Theatre in 1931, followed by New York; played Elizabeth Barrett Browning, in The Barretts of Wimpole Street in Australia and New Zealand; Oscar Wilde's Salome at Gate Theatre; Liza Kingdom, The Old Folks at Home, Queen's; Mary Fitton in This Side Idolatry, Lyric; Jean in The Greeks had a word for it, Liza Doolittle in Pygmalion and Ann in Man and Superman, Cambridge Theatre, 1935; Katie O'Shea in Parnell, Ethel Barrymore Theatre, New York 1935, later at New, London; Lady Macbeth for OUDS 1936; Mary and Lily in Black Limelight, St James's and Duke of York's, 1937–38; Helen in Trojan Women, Karen Selby in The Flashing Stream, Lyric, 1938–39, and in New York; Revival of Liza in Pygmalion, Haymarket, 1939; You of all People, Apollo, 1939; A House in the Square, St Martin's, 1940; Mrs Dearth in Dear Brutus, 1941–42; Gwendolen Fairfax in the Importance of Being Earnest, Royal Command Perf., Haymarket, 1946; Titania in Purcell's Fairy Queen, Covent Garden, 1946; Vittoria Corombona in Webster's The White Devil, Duchess, 1947; Marceline in Jean-Jacques Bernard's The Unquiet Spirit, Arts, 1949; Germaine in A Woman in Love, tour and Embassy, 1949; The Purple Fig Tree, Piccadilly, 1950; Lady Macbeth, Arts, 1950; Spring at Marino, Arts, 1951; Zabina in Tamburlaine, Old Vic, 1951–52; Lysistrata in The Apple Cart, Haymarket, 1953; Countess in The Dark is Light Enough, Salisbury and Windsor Repertory, 1955; Paulina and Mistress Ford, Old Vic, 1955–56; Title Rôle in Racine's Phèdre, Theatre in the Round, London and tour, 1957–58; Sappho in Sappho, Lyceum, Edinburgh, 1961; Ask Me No More, Windsor, 1962; Title role in Racine's Phèdre, Cambridge Arts, 1963; Ella Rentheim in John Gabriel Borkman, Duchess, 1963; Jocasta in Œdipus, Playhouse (Nottingham), 1964; Gertrude in Hamlet, Ludlow Festival, 1965; Madame Torpe in Torpe's Hotel, Yvonne Arnaud Theatre, Guildford, 1965; Mrs Bridgenorth, in Getting Married, Strand, 1967; Carlotta, in A Song at Twilight, Windsor, 1968; Cats Play, Greenwich, 1973; Mixed Economy, King's Head Islington, 1977; Lord Arthur Saville's Crime, Malvern Fest. and tour, 1980; Uncle Vanya, Haymarket, 1982. One-woman performance, Empress Eugénie, May Fair, London, transf. to Vaudeville, UK tour and Dublin Fest., 1979; repeated at King's Lynn Fest., Riverside Theatre, London, New Univ. of Ulster, 1980; Cologne, Horsham, MacRobert Arts Centre, Stirling, Pitlochry Fest., New Univ. of Ulster, 1981; Spoleto Fest., Charleston, SC, 1983. *Films:* Roman Holiday; Beautiful Stranger; No Road Back; Hands of the Ripper. *Television:* Criss Cross Quiz; Somerset Maugham Hour; Sunday Break; Compact; Maigret; Planemakers; solo performance, Black Limelight, Armchair Theatre, 1969; Wives and Daughters, 1971; Folio, 1983. Innumerable broadcasts, incl. We Beg to Differ, Brains Trust, Desert Island Discs (an early castaway); poetry recitals; recordings of: Keats, Gerard Manley Hopkins, Alice in Wonderland; (Marlowe Soc.) King Lear, Pericles; New English Bible Gospels. *Publication:* (trans.) Racine's Phèdre, 1961, (US, 1962). *Recreation:* poetry. *Address:* Rocketer, Rocky Lane, Wendover, Bucks. *T:* Wendover 622234. *Club:* Arts Theatre.

RAWLINS, Colin Guy Champion, OBE 1965; DFC 1941; Director of Zoos and Chief Executive Officer, Zoological Society of London, 1966–84; *b* 5 June 1919; *s* of R. S. C. Rawlins and Yvonne Blanche Andrews; *m* 1946, Rosemary Jensen; two *s* one *d.* *Educ:* Prince of Wales Sch., Nairobi; Charterhouse; Queen's Coll., Oxford (BA). Served with RAF, 1939–46: Bomber Comd, NW Europe; POW, 1941–45; Sqdn-Leader. HM Overseas Civil Service, 1946–66: Administrative Officer, Northern Rhodesia (later Zambia); appointments at Headquarters and in field; Provincial Commissioner, Resident Secretary. Mem., Pearce Commn on Rhodesian Opinion, 1972. Past Pres., Internat. Union of Dirs of Zool. Gardens. FCIS 1967. *Recreations:* aviation, travel, gardening. *Address:* Birchgrove, Earl Howe Road, Holmer Green, Bucks.

RAWLINS, Surg. Vice-Adm. Sir John (Stuart Pepys), KBE 1978 (OBE 1960; MBE 1956); *b* 12 May 1922; *s* of Col S. W. H. Rawlins, CB, CMG, DSO and Dorothy Pepys Cockerell; *m* 1944, Diana Colbeck; one *s* three *d.* *Educ:* Wellington Coll.; University Coll., Oxford; St Bartholomew's Hospital. BM, BCh 1945; MA, FRCP, FFCM, FRAeS. Surg. Lieut RNVR, HMS Triumph, 1947; Surg. Lieut RN, RAF Inst. Aviation Med., 1951; RN Physiol Lab., 1957; Surg. Comdr RAF Inst., Aviation Med., 1961; HMS Ark Royal, 1964; US Navy Medical Research Inst., 1967; Surg. Captain 1969; Surg. Cdre, Dir of Health and Research (Naval), 1973; Surg. Rear-Adm. 1975; Dean of Naval Medicine and MO i/c, Inst. of Naval Medicine, 1975–77; Actg Surg. Vice-Adm. 1977; Medical Dir-Gen. (Navy), 1977–80. QHP 1975. Chairman: Deep Ocean Technology Inc., 1983–; Deep Ocean Engineering Inc., 1983–; Medical Express Ltd, 1984–; Dir, Diving Unlimited International Ltd, 1980–. Pres., Soc. for Underwater Technology, 1980–84; Vice-Pres., Underseas Med. Soc.; Founder-Mem. European Underseas Biomed. Soc.; Fellow Aerospace Med. Soc.; FRAeS 1973; FRSM. Hon. Fellow, Lancaster Univ., 1986. Erroll-Eldridge Prize 1967; Sec. of US Navy's Commendation 1971; Gilbert Blane Medal 1971; Tuttle Meml Award 1973; Chadwick Medal and Prize 1975; Armstrong Lectr (Aerospace Med. Soc.), 1980; Man of the Year, British Council for Rehabilitation of the Disabled, 1964. *Publications:* papers in fields of aviation and diving medicine. *Recreations:* diving, fishing, stalking, riding. *Address:* Wey House, Standford Lane, Headley, Bordon, Hants GU35 8RH. *T:* Bordon 2830. *Clubs:* Army and Navy; Vincent's (Oxford).

RAWLINSON, family name of **Baron Rawlinson of Ewell.**

RAWLINSON OF EWELL, Baron *cr* 1978 (Life Peer), of Ewell in the County of Surrey; **Peter Anthony Grayson Rawlinson,** PC 1964; Kt 1962; QC 1959; QC (NI) 1972; *b* 26 June 1919; *o surv. s* of late Lt-Col A. R. Rawlinson, OBE, and of Ailsa, *e d* of Sir Henry Mulleneux Grayson, Bt, KBE; *m* 1st, 1940, Haidee Kavanagh; three *d;* 2nd, 1954, Elaine Dominguez, Newport, Rhode Island, USA; two *s* one *d.* *Educ:* Downside; Christ's Coll., Cambridge (Exhibitioner 1938, Hon. Fellow 1980). Officer Cadet Sandhurst, 1939; served in Irish Guards, 1940–46; N Africa, 1943 (despatches); demobilized with rank of

Major, 1946. Called to Bar, Inner Temple, 1946, Bencher, 1962, Reader, 1983, Treas., 1984; Recorder of Salisbury, 1961–62; called to Bar, Northern Ireland, 1972. Recorder of Kingston upon Thames, 1975–85; Leader, Western Circuit, 1975–82. Contested (C) Hackney South, 1951; MP(C) Surrey, Epsom, 1955–74, Epsom and Ewell, 1974–78. Solicitor-General, July 1962–Oct. 1964; Opposition Spokesman: for Law, 1964–65, 1968–70; for Broadcasting, 1965; Attorney-General, 1970–74; Attorney-General for NI, 1972–74. Chm., Parly Legal Cttee, 1967–70. Member of Council, Justice, 1960–62, 1964; Trustee of Amnesty, 1960–62; Member, Bar Council, 1966–68; Mem. Senate, Inns of Court, 1968, Vice-Chm., 1974; Vice-Chm., Bar, 1974–75; Chairman of the Bar and Senate, 1975–76; Pres., Senate of Inns of Court and Bar, 1986–. Chm., Enquiry into Constitution of the Senate, 1985–86. Steward, RAC, 1985. Director: Pioneer Concrete Services Ltd, Sydney (Chm., UK subsidiary); Mercantile & General Reinsurance Co. PLC; Daily Telegraph plc; OCI plc; STC plc; Mem., London Adv. Cttee, Hongkong and Shanghai Banking Corp. Hon. Fellow, Amer. Coll. of Trial Lawyers, 1973; Hon. Mem., Amer. Bar Assoc., 1976. SMO Malta. *Publications:* War Poems and Poetry today, 1943; Public Duty and Personal Faith—the example of Thomas More, 1978; articles and essays in law jls. *Recreations:* the theatre and painting. *Address:* 9 Priory Walk, SW10 9SP. *T:* 01–370 1656. *Clubs:* White's, Pratt's, MCC.

RAWLINSON, Sir Anthony Henry John, 5th Bt *cr* 1891; fashion photographer; *b* 1 May 1936; *s* of Sir Alfred Frederick Rawlinson, 4th Bt and of Bessie Ford Taylor, *d* of Frank Raymond Emmatt, Harrogate; *S* father, 1969; *m* 1st, 1960, Penelope Byng Noel (marr. diss. 1967), 2nd *d* of Rear-Adm. G. J. B. Noel, RN; one *s* one *d*; 2nd, 1967, Pauline Strickland (marr. diss. 1976), *d* of J. H. Hardy, Sydney; one *s*; 3rd, 1977, Helen Leone, *d* of T. M. Kennedy, Scotland; one *s*. *Educ:* Millfield School. Coldstream Guards, 1954–56. *Heir: s* Alexander Noel Rawlinson, *b* 15 July 1964. *Address:* Heath Farm, Guist, near Dereham, Norfolk. *Club:* Clermont.

RAWLINSON, Charles Frederick Melville; Joint Chairman, Morgan Grenfell & Co. Ltd, since 1985; Director, Morgan Grenfell Group plc, since 1985; *b* 18 March 1934; *s* of Rowland Henry Rawlinson and Olivia Melville Rawlinson; *m* 1962, Jill Rosalind Wesley; three *d*. *Educ:* Canford Sch.; Jesus Coll., Cambridge (MA). FCA, FCT. With A. E. Limehouse & Co., Chartered Accts, 1955–58; Peat Marwick Mitchell & Co., 1958–62; Morgan Grenfell & Co. Ltd, Bankers, 1962–, Dir, 1970–; seconded as Man. Dir, Investment Bank of Ireland Ltd, Dublin, 1966–68; Director: Associated Paper Industries plc, 1972– (Chm., 1979–); Willis Faber plc, 1981–. Joint Hon. Treas., Nat. Assoc. of Boys' Clubs, 1983–. Chm., Peache Trustees, 1980–. *Recreations:* music, sailing, shooting, walking in the hills. *Address:* (office) 23 Great Winchester Street, EC2P 2AX. *Clubs:* Brooks's, City of London; Leander (Henley-on-Thames); Royal Harwich Yacht.

RAWLINSON, Dennis George Fielding, OBE 1978; Member Board, National Bus Management Ltd, since 1974; Company Director, since 1964; *b* 3 Sept. 1919; *s* of George and Mary Jane Rawlinson; *m* 1943, Lilian Mary; one *s* one *d*. *Educ:* Grocers' Co.'s Sch. Army, 1939–46. Various progressive positions in omnibus industry. *Recreations:* theatre, music, golf and various lesser sports. *Address:* 62 Cleveland Avenue, Darlington, Co. Durham DL3 7HG. *T:* Darlington 461254. *Club:* Army and Navy.

RAWNSLEY, Prof. Kenneth, CBE 1984; FRCP, FRCPsych, DPM; Professor and Head of Department of Psychological Medicine, University of Wales College of Medicine (formerly Welsh National School of Medicine), 1964–85, now Emeritus; *b* 1926; *m* Dr Elinor Kapp; one *s* one *d* (two *s* one *d* by previous marr.). *Educ:* Burnley Grammar Sch.; Univ. of Manchester Med. Sch. MB ChB Manchester 1948; MRCP 1951; DPM Manchester 1954; FRCP 1967; FRCPsych 1971. Member, Scientific Staff of Medical Research Council, 1954–64; Registrar, Bethlem Royal and Maudsley Hosps; Pres., Royal College of Psychiatrists, 1981–84 (Dean, 1972–77); Former Vice-Provost, Welsh Nat. Sch. of Medicine, 1979–80. former Hon. Consultant Psychiatrist, S Glam. AHA(T); Chairman: Welsh Scheme for Develt of Health and Social Res.; Management Cttee, Nat. Counselling Service for Sick Doctors. MRSM. Postgrad. Organiser and Clinical Tutor in Psychiatry, S Glam. *Publications:* contribs to Brit. Jl Psych., Postgrad. Med. Jl, Jl Psychosom. Res., etc. *Address:* 46 Cathedral Road, Cardiff. *T:* 397850. *Club:* Athenæum.

RAWSON, Christopher Selwyn Priestley; an Underwriting Member of Lloyd's; *b* 25 March 1928; *e s* of late Comdr Selwyn Gerald Caygill Rawson, OBE, RN (retd) and late Dr Doris Rawson, MB, ChB (*née* Brown); *m* 1959, Rosemary Ann Focke; two *d*. *Educ:* The Elms Sch., Colwall, near Malvern, Worcs; The Nautical College, Pangbourne, Berks. Navigating Apprentice, Merchant Service, T. & J. Brocklebank Ltd, 1945–48. Sheriff of the City of London, 1961–62; Member of Court of Common Council (Ward of Bread Street), 1963–72; Alderman, City of London, (Ward of Lime Street), 1972–83; one of HM Lieutenants of City of London, 1980–83. Chairman: Governors, The Elms Sch., Colwall, near Malvern, Worcs, 1965–84; Port and City of London Health Cttee, 1967–70; Billingsgate and Leadenhall Mkt Cttee, 1972–75. Silver Medal for Woollen and Worsted Raw Materials, City and Guilds of London Institute, 1951; Livery of Clothworkers Company, 1952, Mem. Court of Assistants, 1977; Freeman, Company of Watermen and Lightermen, 1966, Mem. Ct of Assts, 1974, Master, 1982–84. President: Lime St Ward Club, 1973–83 (Hon. Patron, 1983); Sowerby St Peter's Cricket Club, 1975–. Hon. Mem., London Metal Exchange, 1979. ATI 1953; AIMarE 1962. CStJ 1985. Commander: National Order of Senegal, 1961; Order of the Ivory Coast, 1962; Star of Africa, Liberia, 1962. *Recreations:* shooting, sailing. *Address:* 56 Ovington Street, SW3. *T:* 01–589 3136; College Hill Chambers, 23 College Hill, EC4R 2RT. *T:* 01–236 1471. *Clubs:* Royal London Yacht, City Livery.

RAWSON, Prof. Kenneth John, MSc; FEng; RCNC; Professor and Head of Department of Design and Technology, since 1983, Dean of Education and Design, since 1984, Brunel University; *b* 27 Oct. 1926; *s* of late Arthur William Rawson and Beatrice Anne Rawson; *m* 1950, Rhona Florence Gill; two *s* one *d*. *Educ:* Northern Grammar Sch., Portsmouth; HM Dockyard Technical Coll., Portsmouth; RN Colls, Keyham and Greenwich. RCNC; FEng 1984; FRINA; FSIAD. WhSch. At sea, 1950–51; Naval Construction Res. Estabt, Dunfermline, 1951–53; Ship Design, Admiralty, 1953–57; Lloyd's Register of Shipping, 1957–59; Ship and Weapons Design, MoD, Bath, 1959–69; Naval Staff, London, 1969–72; Prof. of Naval Architecture, University Coll., Univ. of London, 1972–77; Ministry of Defence, Bath: Head of Forward Design, Ship Dept, 1977–79; Dep. Dir, Ship Design and Chief Naval Architect (Under Sec.), 1979–83. FRSA. *Publications:* Photoelasticity and the Engineer, 1953; (with E. C. Tupper) Basic Ship Theory, 1968, 3rd edn 1983, contrib. numerous technical publications. *Recreations:* cabinet making, wine making, gardening, walking. *Address:* Moorlands, The Street, Chilcompton, Bath BA3 4HB. *T:* Stratton-on-the-Fosse 232793.

RAWSTHORNE, Rt. Rev. John; Titular Bishop of Rotdon and an Auxiliary Bishop of Liverpool, (RC), since 1981; President, St Joseph's College, since 1982; *b* Crosby, Merseyside, 12 Nov. 1936. Priest, 1962. Administrator, St Mary's, Highfield, 1982. *Address:* St Joseph's College, Upholland, Lancs WN8 0PZ.

RAY, Hon. Ajit Nath; Chief Justice of India, Supreme Court of India, 1973–77; *b* Calcutta, 29 Jan. 1912; *s* of Sati Nath Ray and Kali Kumari Debi; *m* 1944, Himani Mukherjee; one *s*. *Educ:* Presidency Coll., Calcutta; Calcutta Univ. (Hindu Coll. Foundn Schol., MA); Oriel College, Oxford (MA; Hon. Fellow, 1975). Called to Bar, Gray's Inn, 1939; practised at Calcutta High Court, 1940–57; Judge, Calcutta High Court, 1957–69; Judge, Supreme Court of India, 1969–73. Pres., Governing Body, Presidency Coll., Calcutta, 1959–70; Vice-President: Asiatic Soc., 1963–65 (Hon. Treas. 1960–63); Internat. Law Assoc., 1977– (Pres., 1974–76; Pres., Indian Br., 1973–77); Indian Law Inst., New Delhi, 1973–77; Ramakrishna Mission Inst. of Culture, 1981–; Mem., Internat. Court of Arbitration, 1976–; Pres., Soc. for Welfare of Blind, Narendrapur, 1959–80; Member: Karma Samiti (Exec. Council), 1963–67 and 1969–72, and Samsad (Court), 1967–71, Visva-Bharati Univ., Santiniketan. *Address:* 15 Panditia Place, Calcutta 700029, India. *T:* Calcutta 475213. *Club:* Calcutta (Calcutta).

RAY, Cyril; *b* 16 March 1908; *e s* of Albert Benson Ray (who changed the family name from Rotenberg, 1913), and Rita Ray; *m* 1953, Elizabeth Mary, JP, *o d* of late Rev. H. C. Brocklehurst; one *s*. *Educ:* elementary sch., Bury, Lancs; Manchester Gr. Sch. (Foundation schol.); Jesus Coll., Oxford (open schol.). Manchester Guardian and BBC war correspondent: 5th Destroyer Flotilla, 1940 (Hon. Mem. HMS Kelly Reunion); N African landings, 1942; 8th Army, Italy (despatches); US 82nd Airborne Div. (US Army citation, Nijmegen), and 3rd Army, 1944–45. UNESCO missions, Italy, Greece, East, Central and S Africa, 1945–50. Sunday Times, 1949–56 (Moscow Correspondent, 1950–52); Editor, The Compleat Imbiber, 1956–71 (Wine and Food Soc.'s first André Simon Prize, 1964); Asst Editor, The Spectator, 1958–62; Wine Correspondent: The Director, 1958–76; The Observer, 1959–73; Punch, 1978–84; Wine Steward to the Punch Table, 1984–; Chief Consltnt, The Good Food Guide, 1968–74; Founder and past President, Circle of Wine Writers. Trustee, Albany, 1967– (Chm. Trustees, 1981–86). Much occasional broadcasting, 1940–62 (The Critics, 1958–62), Southern TV, 1958–59. Hon. Life Mem., NUJ. Glenfiddich Wine and Food Writer of the Year, 1979; Special Glenfiddich Award, 1985. Freeman, City of London; Liveryman, Fan-Makers Co. Mem. Labour Party. Commendatore, Italian Order of Merit, 1981 (Cavaliere 1972); Chevalier, French Order of Merit, 1985 (Mérite Agricole, 1974). *Publications:* (ed) Scenes and Characters from Surtees, 1948; From Algiers to Austria: The History of 78 Division, 1952; The Pageant of London, 1958; Merry England, 1960; Regiment of the Line: The Story of the Lancashire Fusiliers, 1963; (ed) The Gourmet's Companion, 1963; (ed) Morton Shand's Book of French Wines, 1964; (ed) Best Murder Stories, 1965; The Wines of Italy, 1966 (Bologna Trophy, 1967); In a Glass Lightly, 1967; Lafite: The Story of Château Lafite-Rothschild, 1968, rev. edn 1985; Bollinger: the story of a champagne, 1971, rev. edn 1982; Cognac, 1973, rev. edn 1985; Mouton: the story of Mouton-Rothschild, 1974; (with Elizabeth Ray) Wine with Food, 1975; The Wines of France, 1976; The Wines of Germany, 1977; The Complete Book of Spirits and Liqueurs, 1978; The Saint Michael Guide to Wine, 1978; (with C. Mozley) Ruffino: the story of a Chianti, 1979, Lickerish Limericks, with Filthy Pictures by Charles Mozley, 1979; Ray on Wine (Glenfiddich Wine Book of the Year), 1979; The New Book of Italian Wines, 1982; (ed) Vintage Tales, 1984; Robert Mondavi of the Napa Valley, 1984; (ed) The New Compleat Imbiber, 1986. *Recreation:* riding. *Address:* Albany, Piccadilly, W1. *T:* 01–734 0270. *Clubs:* Athenæum, Brooks's, MCC, Special Forces; Puffin's (Edinburgh) (Hon. Life Mem.); Kildare Street and University (Dublin).

RAY, Edward Ernest; Senior Partner, Spicer and Pegler, Chartered Accountants, since 1984 (Partner, 1957); *b* 6 Nov. 1924; *s* of Walter James Ray and Cecilia May Ray; *m* 1949, Margaret Elizabeth, *d* of George Bull; two *s*. *Educ:* Holloway Co. Sch.; London Univ. (External) (BCom). Served RN, 1943–46. Qualified, Inst. of Chartered Accountants: Mem., 1950; FCA 1955; Council Mem., 1973; Vice Pres., 1980; Dep. Pres., 1981; Pres., 1982, 1983. Chm., London Chartered Accountants, 1972–73. Director: HM Hldgs plc, 1984–; Securities and Investment Bd Ltd, 1985–; Member: City Capital Markets Cttee, 1984–; Marketing of Investments Bd Organising Cttee, 1985–. *Publications:* Partnership Taxation, 1972, 2nd edn 1978; (jtly) VAT for Accountants and Businessmen, 1972; contrib. accountancy magazines. *Recreations:* walking, birdwatching, golf. *Address:* 1 Brooklands Court, Bush Hill, N21 2BZ. *T:* 01–360 0028. *Club:* City of London.

RAY, Gordon Norton; President of the John Simon Guggenheim Memorial Foundation, since 1963; *b* New York City, 8 Sept. 1915; *s* of Jesse Gordon and Jessie Norton Ray; unmarried. *Educ:* University of Indiana (AM); Harvard Univ. (AM, PhD). Instructor in English, Harvard, 1940–42; Guggenheim Fellow, 1941–42, 1946, 1956–57. Lt, US Navy, serving aboard aircraft carriers Belleau Wood and Boxer, Pacific, 1942–46; Professor of English, 1946–60, Head of Dept, 1950–57, Vice-President and Provost, 1957–60, University of Illinois. Associate Secretary General, Guggenheim Foundn, 1960–61; Sec.-Gen., 1961–63. Rockefeller Fellow, 1948–49; Member US Educational Commn in UK, which established Fulbright program, 1948–49. Lowell Lectures, Boston, 1950; Walls Lectures, Pierpont Morgan Lib., 1982; Berg Professor, New York Univ. 1952–53; Professor of English, 1962–80, now Emeritus Professor; Lyell Reader in Bibliography, Oxford Univ., 1984–85. Advisor in literature, Houghton Mifflin Co., 1953–71. Member Commission on Trends in Education, Mod. Lang. Assoc., 1953–59, Trustee 1966–; Mem. Council, Smithsonian Instn, 1968–, Chm. 1970–; Dir and Treasurer, Amer. Council of Learned Socs, 1973–. Advisory Bd, Guggenheim Foundation, 1959–60, Trustee, 1963–; Trustee: Pierpont Morgan Library, 1970–; Rosenbach Foundn, 1972–81; New York Public Library, 1975–84 (Hon. Trustee, 1984–); Columbia Univ. Press, 1977–82; Winterthur Museum, 1977–; American Trust for the British Library, 1979–. Dir, Yaddo, 1979–. Hon. LittD: Monmouth Coll., 1959; Syracuse, 1961; Duke, 1965; Illinois, 1968; Northwestern, 1974; Maryland, 1982; Hon. LLD: New York, 1961; Tulane, 1963; California, 1968; Columbia, 1969; Southern California, 1974; Pennsylvania, 1978; Hon. LHD, Indiana, 1964. FRSL 1948. Fellow, Amer. Acad. of Arts and Sciences, 1962; Mem., Amer. Philosophical Soc., 1977. Joseph Henry Medal, Smithsonian Instn, 1980. *Publications:* Letters and Private Papers of Thackeray, 4 vols, 1945–46; The Buried Life, 1952; Thackeray: The Uses of Adversity, 1955; Henry James and H. G. Wells, 1958; Thackeray: The Age of Wisdom, 1958; H. G. Wells and Rebecca West, 1974; The Illustrator and the Book in England from 1790 to 1914, 1976; The Art of the French Illustrated Book 1700–1914, 2 vols, 1982, etc; contrib. to magazines and learned jls. *Recreations:* book-collecting, travel. *Address:* (business) 90 Park Avenue, New York, NY 10016; (home) 25 Sutton Place South, New York, NY 10022, USA. *Clubs:* Athenæum, Roxburghe (London); Harvard, Grolier (President, 1965–69), Century (New York).

RAY, Philip Bicknell, CMG 1969; Ministry of Defence 1946–76, retired; *b* 10 July 1917; *s* of late Basil Ray and Clare (*née* Everett); *m* 1946, Bridget Mary Robertson (decd); two *s* one *d*. *Educ:* Felsted Sch.; Selwyn Coll., Cambridge (MA). Indian Police, 1939–46. *Address:* The Cottage, Little Shoddesden, Andover, Hants.

RAY, Robin; freelance broadcaster and entertainer; *s* of Ted Ray and Sybil (*née* Olden); *m* 1960, Susan Stranks; one *s*. *Educ:* Highgate Sch. West End Stage debut, The Changeling, 1960. Chief Technical Instructor, RADA, 1961–65; Associate Dir, Meadowbrook Theatre, Detroit, USA, 1965–66. As writer/broadcaster, over 750 progs for radio and television, mainly music and arts for BBC, including: Music Now; The Lively Arts; Robin Ray's Picture Gallery; Face the Music; A Touch of Genius; current series, Film

Buff of the Year, 1984–. Reviewer of classical records for Capital Radio, 1977–84. Script for Café Puccini, Wyndham's Th., 1986. *Publications:* Time For Lovers (anthology), 1975; Robin Ray's Music Quiz, 1978; Favourite Hymns and Carols, 1982; Words on Music, 1984. *Recreations:* music, cinema, property hunting. *Address:* 8 Waterloo Place, Pall Mall, SW1Y 4AW.

RAY, Satyajit; Padma Shree, 1957; Padma Bhushan, 1964; Padma Bibhushan, 1976; Indian film producer and film director since 1953; *b* 2 May 1921; *s* of late Sukumar and Suprabha Ray (*née* Das); *m* 1949, Bijoya (*née* Das); one *s. Educ:* Ballygunge Govt School; Presidency College, Calcutta. Joined British advertising firm, D. J. Keymer & Co., as visualiser, 1943; Art Director, 1950. In 1952, started first feature film, Pather Panchali, finished in 1955 (Cannes Special Award, 1956, San Francisco, best film, 1957). Left advertising for whole-time film-making, 1956. Other films: Aparajito, 1957 (Venice Grand Prix, 1957, San Francisco, best direction); Jalsaghar, 1958; Devi, 1959; Apur Sansar, 1959 (Selznick Award and Sutherland Trophy 1960); Teen Kanya (Two Daughters), 1961; Kanchanjangha, 1962; Mahanagar, 1963; Charulata, 1964; The Coward and The Holy Man (Kapurush-O-Mahapurush), 1965; The Hero (Nayak), 1965; Goopy Gyne and Bagha Byne, 1969; Days and Nights in the Forest, 1970; Pratidwandi (The Adversary), 1970; Company Limited, 1971; Distant Thunder, 1973 (Golden Bear, Berlin Film Festival, 1973); The Golden Fortress, 1974; The Middleman, 1975; The Chess Players, 1977; The Elephant God, 1979; The Kingdom of Diamonds, 1980; Pikoo, Deliverance, 1981; Ghare Baire (The Home and the World), 1984. Founded first Film Society in Calcutta, 1947. Composes background music for own films. Fellow, BFI, 1983. Hon. DLitt Oxon, 1978. *Publications:* Our Films, Their Films, 1976; film articles in Sight and Sound, Sequence; (Editor, 1961–) children's magazine Sandesh, with contributions of stories, poems. *Recreations:* listening to Indian and Western classical music, and reading science-fiction. *Address:* Flat 8, 1–1 Bishop Lefroy Road, Calcutta 20, India. *T:* 44–8747.

RAYLEIGH, 5th Baron *cr* 1821; **John Arthur Strutt;** *b* 12 April 1908; *e s* of 4th Baron Rayleigh, FRS, and late Mary Hilda, 2nd *d* of 4th Earl of Leitrim; *S* father 1947; *m* 1934, Ursula Mary (*d* 1982), *o d* of Lieut-Colonel R. H. R. Brocklebank, DSO and Charlotte Carissima, *o d* of General Sir Bindon Blood, GCB, GCVO. *Educ:* Eton; Trinity College, Cambridge. *Heir: nephew* John Gerald Strutt, *b* 4 June 1960. *Address:* Terling Place, Chelmsford, Essex. *T:* Terling 235; 01–453 3235.

RAYMER, Michael Robert, OBE 1951; Assistant Secretary, Royal Hospital, Chelsea, 1975–82; *b* 22 July 1917; surv. *s* of late Rev. W. H. Raymer, MA; *m* 1948, Joyce Marion Scott; two *s* one *d. Educ:* Marlborough College (Foundation Scholar); Jesus College, Cambridge (Rustat Schol.). BA (Hons) 1939. Administrative Officer, Nigeria, 1940–49 and 1952–55. Served in Royal W African Frontier Force, 1940–43. Colonial Sec. to Govt of the Falkland Islands, 1949–52; Prin. Estab. Officer, N Nigeria, 1954; Controller of Organisation and Establishments, to Government of Fiji, 1955–62; retired, 1962; Principal, MoD, 1962–75. *Recreation:* gardening. *Address:* The Stable House, Manor Farm, Apethorpe, Northants PE8 5DG.

RAYMOND, Sir Stanley (Edward), Kt 1967; FCIT; FBIM; *b* 10 Aug. 1913; *s* of late Frederick George and Lilian Grace Raymond; *m* 1st, 1938, Enid (*d* 1979), *d* of Capt. S. A. Buley, Polruan-by-Fowey; one *s*; 2nd, 1982, Mrs Constance Clarke. *Educ:* Orphanage; Grammar Sch., Hampton, Mx. Entered Civil Service, 1930. Asst Sec., Soc. of Civil Servants, 1939–45. War service in Royal Artillery, 1942–45; Lieutenant-Colonel on demobilisation. London Passenger Transport Board, 1946; British Road Services, 1947; BTC, 1955; Director of Establishment and Staff, 1956; Chief Commercial Manager, Scottish Region, British Railways, 1957 and Asst Gen. Manager, 1959; Traffic Adviser, BTC, 1961; Chm. Western Railway Board, and General Manager, Western Region, British Railways, 1962–63; Member, 1963, a Vice-Chm., 1964–65, and Chm., 1965–67, British Railways Bd. Chairman: Horserace Betting Levy Bd, 1972–74; Gaming Bd for GB, 1968–77. *Recreations:* walking, travelling the world. *Address:* 41 Veric, 16/18 Eaton Gardens, Hove, Sussex BN3 3UB.

RAYMOND, William Francis, CBE 1978; FRSC; Agricultural Science Consultant; *b* 25 Feb. 1922; *m* 1949, Amy Elizabeth Kelk; three *s* one *d. Educ:* Bristol Grammar Sch.; The Queen's Coll., Oxford (MA). Research Officer, MRC, 1943–45; Head of Animal Science Div. and later Asst Dir, Grassland Research Inst., Hurley, 1945–72; Dep. Chief Scientist, 1972–81, Chief Scientist (Agriculture and Horticulture), 1981–82, MAFF. Mem., ARC, 1981–82. Sec., 8th Internat. Grassland Congress, 1960; President: Brit. Grassland Soc., 1974–75; Brit. Soc. Animal Production, 1981–82. Vis. Prof. in Agriculture, Wye Coll., 1978–83. Chm., Stapledon Meml Trust, 1983–. Consultant, World Bank, 1986. *Publications:* (with Shepperson and Waltham) Forage Conservation and Feeding, 1972, 4th edn (with Redman and Waltham), 1986; EEC Agricultural Research Framework Programme, 1983; Research in Support of Agricultural Policies in Europe, FAO Regional Conf., Reykjavik, 1984; over 160 papers in scientific jls. *Recreation:* gardening. *Address:* Periwinkle Cottage, Christmas Common, Watlington OX9 5HR. *T:* Watlington 2942. *Club:* Farmers'.

RAYNE, family name of **Baron Rayne.**

RAYNE, Baron *cr* 1976 (Life Peer), of Prince's Meadow in Greater London; **Max Rayne,** Kt 1969; Chairman, London Merchant Securities plc, since 1960; *b* 8 Feb. 1918; *er s* of Phillip and Deborah Rayne; *m* 1st, 1941, Margaret Marco (marr. diss., 1960); one *s* two *d*; 2nd, 1965, Lady Jane Antonia Frances Vane-Tempest-Stewart, *er d* of 8th Marquess of Londonderry; two *s* two *d. Educ:* Central Foundation Sch. and University Coll., London. Served RAF 1940–45. Chm., Westpool Investment Trust plc, 1980–; Dep. Chm., First Leisure Corp. plc, 1984–; Dir, other companies. Governor: Royal Ballet Sch., 1966–79; Yehudi Menuhin Sch., 1966–; Malvern Coll., 1966–; Centre for Environmental Studies, 1967–73; Special Trustee, St Thomas' Hosp., 1974– (Governor, 1962–74); Member: Gen. Council, King Edward VII's Hosp. Fund for London, 1966–; Council, St Thomas's Hospital Medical School, 1965–82; Council of Governors, United Med. Schs of Guy's and St Thomas's Hosps, 1982–; Internat. Council, Salk Inst., 1982–. Hon. Vice-Pres., Jewish Welfare Bd, 1966–; Chairman: London Festival Ballet Trust, 1967–75; Nat. Theatre Board, 1971–; Founder Patron, The Rayne Foundation, 1962–. Hon. Fellow: Darwin Coll., Cambridge, 1966; UCL, 1966; LSE 1974; King's Coll. Hosp. Med. Sch., 1980; UC, Oxford, 1982. Hon. FRCPsych, 1977. KCL, 1983. Hon. LLD London, 1968. Chevalier Légion d'Honneur, 1973. *Address:* 33 Robert Adam Street, W1M 5AH. *T:* 01–935 3555.

RAYNE, Edward, CVO 1977; Chairman and Managing Director of H. & M. Rayne Ltd, since 1951; Executive Chairman, Harvey Nichols, since 1979; *b* 19 Aug. 1922; *s* of Joseph Edward Rayne and Meta Elizabeth Reddish (American); *m* 1952, Phyllis Cort; two *s. Educ:* Harrow. Pres., 1961–72, Exec. Chm., 1972–86, Rayne-Delman Shoes Inc.; Dir, Debenhams Ltd, 1975–86; Pres., Debenhams Inc., 1976–86; Chairman Fashion Multiple Div., Debenhams Ltd, 1978–86; Harvey Nichols Ltd, 1978–; Lotus Ltd, 1978–86. Member: Export Council for Europe, 1962–71; European Trade Cttee, 1972–84; Bd of Governors, Genesco Inc., 1967–73; Franco British Council, 1980–. Chairman: Incorp. Soc. of London Fashion Designers, 1960–; British Fashion Council, 1985–; Pres., Royal

Warrant Holders' Assoc., 1964, Hon. Treas. 1974–; President: British Footwear Manufacturers' Fedn, 1965; British Boot and Shoe Instn, 1972–79; Clothing and Footwear Inst., 1979–80. Master, Worshipful Co. of Pattenmakers, 1981. FRSA 1971. Harper's Bazaar Trophy, 1963. Chevalier, l'Ordre Nat. du Mérite, France, 1984. *Recreations:* golf and bridge (Mem., winning British team, European Bridge Championship, 1948, 1949). *Address:* 15 Grosvenor Square, W1. *T:* 01–493 2871. *Clubs:* Portland, White's, Brooks's; Travellers' (Paris).

RAYNER, family name of **Baron Rayner.**

RAYNER, Baron *cr* 1983 (Life Peer), of Crowborough in the County of East Sussex; **Derek George Rayner;** Kt 1973; Chairman, since 1984, Chief Executive, since 1983, Joint Managing Director, since 1973, Marks and Spencer plc; *b* 30 March 1926; *o s* of George William Rayner and Hilda Jane (*née* Rant); unmarried. *Educ:* City Coll., Norwich; Selwyn Coll., Cambridge (Hon. Fellow 1983). Fellow, Inst. Purchasing and Supply, 1970. Nat. Service, commnd RAF Regt, 1946–48. Joined Marks & Spencer, 1953; Dir, 1967. Special Adviser to HM Govt, 1970; Chief Exec., Procurement Executive, MoD, 1971–72. Mem., UK Permanent Security Commn, 1977–80. Dep. Chm., Civil Service Pay Bd, 1978–80. Member: Design Council, 1973–75; Council RCA, 1973–76. Adviser to Prime Minister on improving efficiency and eliminating waste in Government, 1979–83. Chm., Coronary Artery Disease Res. Assoc., 1985–. *Recreations:* music, food, travel. *Address:* Michael House, Baker Street, W1A 1DN.

RAYNER, Bryan Roy; Deputy Secretary, Department of Health and Social Security, since 1984; *b* 29 Jan. 1932; *s* of Harold and Florence Rayner; *m* 1957, Eleanora Whittaker; one *d. Educ:* Stationers' Company's School, N8. Clerical Officer, Customs and Excise, 1948; Asst Private Sec. to Minister of Health, 1960–62; Principal, 1965, Asst Sec., 1970, Under Sec., 1975, DHSS. *Recreations:* listening to music, gardening. *Address:* 8 West Common Drive, Haywards Heath, W Sussex RH16 2AP.

RAYNER, Claire Berenice; writer and broadcaster; *b* 22 Jan. 1931; *m* 1957, Desmond Rayner; two *s* one *d. Educ:* City of London Sch. for Girls; Royal Northern Hosp. Sch. of Nursing, London (Gold Medal; SRN 1954); Guy's Hosp. (midwifery). Formerly: Nurse, Royal Free Hosp.; Sister, Paediatric Dept, Whittington Hosp. Woman's Own: Med. Correspondent, as Ruth Martin, 1966–75, as Claire Rayner, 1975–. Advice column: The Sun, 1973–80; The Sunday Mirror, 1980–. Radio and television broadcasts include: family advice, Pebble Mill at One, BBC, 1972–74; (co-presenter) Kitchen Garden, ITV, 1974–77; Contact, BBC Radio, Wales, 1974–77; Claire Rayner's Casebook (series), BBC, 1980, 1983, 1984; TV-am Advice Spot, 1985–. FRSM. Freeman, City of London, 1981. *Publications:* Mothers and Midwives, 1962; What Happens in Hospital, 1963; The Calendar of Childhood, 1964; Your Baby, 1965; Careers with Children, 1966; Essentials of Out-Patient Nursing, 1967; For Children, 1967; Shall I be a Nurse, 1967; 101 Facts an Expectant Mother should know, 1967; 101 Key Facts of Practical Baby Care, 1967; Housework - The Easy Way, 1967; Home Nursing and Family Health, 1967; A Parent's Guide to Sex Education, 1968; People in Love, 1968 (subseq. publd as About Sex, 1972); Protecting Your Baby, 1971; Woman's Medical Dictionary, 1971; When to Call the Doctor - What to Do Whilst Waiting, 1972; The Shy Person's Book, 1973; Childcare Made Simple, 1973; Where Do I Come From?, 1975; (ed and contrib.) Atlas of the Body and Mind, 1976; (with Keith Fordyce) Kitchen Garden, 1976; (with Keith Fordyce) More Kitchen Garden, 1977; Family Feelings, 1977; Claire Rayner answers your 100 Questions on Pregnancy, 1977; (with Keith Fordyce) Claire and Keith's Kitchen Garden, 1978; The Body Book, 1978; Related to Sex, 1979; (with Keith Fordyce) Greenhouse Gardening, 1979; Everything your Doctor would Tell You if He Had the Time, 1980; Claire Rayner's Lifeguide, 1980; Baby and Young Child Care, 1981; Growing Pains, 1984; Claire Rayner's Marriage Guide, 1984; The Getting Better Book, 1985; Woman, 1986; When I Grow Up, 1986; *fiction:* Shilling a Pound Pears, 1964; The House on the Fen, 1967; Starch of Aprons, 1967 (subseq. publd as The Hive, 1968); Lady Mislaid, 1968; Death on the Table, 1969; The Meddlers, 1970; A Time to Heal, 1972; The Burning Summer, 1972; Sisters, 1978; Reprise, 1980; The Running Years, 1981; Family Chorus, 1984; The Virus Man, 1985; Lunching at Laura's, 1986; The Performers: Book 1, Gower Street, 1973; Book 2, The Haymarket, 1974; Book 3, Paddington Green, 1975; Book 4, Soho Square, 1976; Book 5, Bedford Row, 1977; Book 6, Long Acre, 1978; Book 7, Charing Cross, 1979; Book 8, The Strand, 1980; Book 9, Chelsea Reach, 1982; Book 10, Shaftesbury Avenue, 1983; Book 11, Piccadilly, 1985; Book 12, Seven Dials, 1986; *as Sheila Brandon: fiction:* The Final Year, 1962; Cottage Hospital, 1963; Children's Ward, 1964; The Lonely One, 1965; The Doctors of Downlands, 1968; The Private Wing, 1971; Nurse in the Sun, 1972; *as Ann Lynton:* Mothercraft, 1967; contrib. Lancet, Med. World, Nursing Times, Nursing Mirror, and national newspapers and magazines, incl. Design. *Recreations:* talking, cooking, party-giving, theatre-going. *Address:* Holly Wood House, Roxborough Avenue, Harrow-on-the-Hill, Mddx HA1 3BU. *T:* 01–864 9898.

RAYNER, David Edward; General Manager, British Rail, Eastern Region, since 1986; *b* 26 Jan. 1940; *s* of Marjory and Gilbert Rayner; *m* 1966, Enid Cutty; two *d. Educ:* St Peter's School, York; Durham University (BSc Hons). Joined British Railways, 1963; Passenger Marketing Manager, BR Board, 1982; Dep. Gen. Manager, BR, London Midland Region, 1984–86. *Recreation:* collector. *Address:* Bilbrough, York YO2 3NT. *T:* Tadcaster 835538.

RAYNER, Edward John; Controller, Europe and North Asia Division, British Council, since 1986; *b* 27 Feb. 1936; *s* of Edward Harold Rayner and Edith Rayner; *m* 1960, Valerie Anne Billon; one *s* one *d. Educ:* Slough Grammar Sch.; London Univ. (BSc Econs). British Council: Asst Regional Rep., Lahore, Pakistan, 1959–62; Asst Rep., Lagos, Nigeria, 1962–65; Inspector, Complements Unit, 1965–67; Head, Overseas Careers, Personnel Dept, 1967–70; Dep. Rep., Pakistan, 1970–71; Regional Dir, Sao Paulo, Brazil, 1972–75; Controller, Estabts Div., 1975–78; Secretary, 1978–82; Rep., Brazil, 1983–86. *Recreations:* golf, tennis, theatre, music. *Address:* c/o British Council, 10 Spring Gardens, SW1A 2BN.

RAYNER, Most Rev. Keith; see Adelaide, Archbishop of.

RAYNER, Neville, JP, FRSA; Underwriting Member of Lloyd's, since 1963; General Commissioner of Income Tax, since 1965; property consultant, since 1936; *b* 1914; *m* 1941, Elsie Mary (*née* Lindley); two *s. Educ:* Emanuel Sch., SW11. Commd RAFVR(T), 1941–45. Mem., Court of Common Council, City of London, 1960–81; Sheriff of London, 1971–72. Former Mem., LCC and Wandsworth Borough Council. Director, Bedford Building Soc. Parish Clerk, Priory Church of St Bartholomew-the-Great, Smithfield; Mem., Honourable Artillery Co.; Liveryman: Painter Stainers Co.; Basketmakers Co. (Prime Warden 1980–81); Glovers' Co. (Master, 1982–83); Playing Card Makers Co.; Mem. Ct of Assts, Worshipful Co. of Parish Clerks. JP, Inner London, 1959; Dep. Chm., Greater London (SW) Valuation Appeals Court, 1950–56; Pres., Greater London Council Br., Royal British Legion, 1962– (Gold Badge, 1979); Vice-Pres., Nat. Union of Ratepayers. FRVA, FSVA, FCIArb, FInstD, F Land Inst. Past Pres., Farringdon Ward Club. Member: Magistrates Assoc.; British Olympic Assoc.; Magic

Circle; Council, Gardeners' Royal Benevolent Soc.; Royal Soc. St George (Vice-Pres., City of London Br.); Luxembourg Soc.; Netherlands Soc.; Sheriff's Soc.; Court, Nene Coll., Northampton; Chm., Rayner Court and Red Oaks Sheltered Housing, Henfield. OStJ. Order of Sacred Treasure (Japan), 1972; Star of Afghanistan, 1972; Comdr, Order of Orange-Nassau (Holland), 1972; Couronne de Chêne (Luxembourg), 1972; Comendador de la Orden del Merito Civil (Spain), 1975. *Recreations:* magic, travel, carpentry. *Address:* Old Selsfield, Turners Hill, West Sussex RH10 4PS. *T:* Copthorne 715203; 1 Montpelier Mews, SW7 1HB. *T:* 01-589 3939. *Clubs:* Guildhall, United Wards (Past Pres.), City Livery, Pilgrims, Press, Anglo-Spanish, Wig and Pen, Belfry, St Stephen's Constitutional.

RAYNHAM, Viscount; Charles George Townshend; *b* 26 Sept. 1945; *s* and *heir* of 7th Marquess Townshend, *qv*; *m* 1975, Hermione (*d* 1985), *d* of Lt-Cdr R. M. D. Ponsonby and Mrs Dorothy Ponsonby; one *s* one *d.* *Educ:* Eton; Royal Agricultural College, Cirencester. Chm. and Dir, AIMS Ltd, 1977–; Dir, Veroncroft Properties Ltd, 1978–. Mem. Council, RASE, 1982–. Chm., Local Radio Assoc., 1981–84. *Heir:* *s* Hon. Thomas Charles Townshend, *b* 2 Nov. 1977. *Address:* Pattesley House, Fakenham, Norfolk. *T:* Fakenham 2133. *Clubs:* White's, Farmers'.

RAYNSFORD, Nick; *see* Raynsford, W. R. N.

RAYNSFORD, Wyvill Richard Nicolls, (Nick); MP (Lab) Fulham, since April 1986; *b* 28 Jan. 1945; *s* of Wyvill Raynsford and Patricia Raynsford (*née* Dunn); *m* 1968, Anne Raynsford (*née* Jelley); three *d.* *Educ:* Repton Sch.; Sidney Sussex Coll., Cambridge (MA); Chelsea Sch. of Art (DipAD). Market research, A. C. Nielsen Co. Ltd, 1966–68; Gen. Sec., Soc. for Co-operative Dwellings, 1972–73; SHAC: Emergency Officer, 1973–74; Research Officer, 1974–76; Dir, 1976–86. Councillor (Lab) London Borough of Hammersmith & Fulham, 1971–75 (Chm., Leisure and Recreation Cttee, 1972–74). *Publication:* A Guide to Housing Benefit, 1982, 7th edn 1986. *Recreations:* running, walking, sleeping. *Address:* 31 Cranbury Road, Fulham, SW6 2NS. *T:* 01–731 0675.

RAZ, Prof. Joseph; Professor of the Philosophy of Law, Oxford, since 1985, and Fellow of Balliol College, Oxford; *b* 21 March 1939. *Educ:* Hebrew University, Jerusalem (MJur 1963); University Coll., Oxford (DPhil 1967). Lectr, Hebrew Univ., Jerusalem, 1967–70; Research Fellow, Nuffield Coll., Oxford, 1970–72; Tutorial Fellow, Balliol Coll., Oxford, 1972–85. *Publications:* The Concept of a Legal System, 1970, 2nd edn 1980; Practical Reason and Norms, 1975; The Authority of Law, 1979; The Morality of Freedom, 1986. *Address:* Balliol College, Oxford OX12 3BJ. *T:* Oxford 244574.

RAZZALL, Leonard Humphrey; a Master of the Supreme Court (Taxing), 1954–81; *b* 13 Nov. 1912; *s* of Horace Razzall and Sarah Thompson, Scarborough; *m* 1936, Muriel (*d* 1968), *yr d* of late Pearson Knowles; two *s.* *Educ:* Scarborough High Sch. Admitted solicitor, 1935; founded firm Humphrey Razzall & Co., 1938. Served in Royal Marines, 1941–46, Staff Captain; Staff Coll., Camberley (jsc). Contested (L) Scarborough and Whitby Division, 1945. Sometime Examr in High Court practice and procedure for solicitors final examination. *Publications:* A Man of Law's Tale, 1982; Law, Love and Laughter, 1984. *Recreations:* travel, cricket, book-collecting and book-selling. *Address:* 69 Westfields Avenue, SW13. *T:* 01–878 5670; (shop) 01–878 7859. *Clubs:* National Liberal, English-Speaking Union.

REA, family name of **Baron Rea.**

REA, 3rd Baron *cr* 1937, of Eskdale; **John Nicolas Rea,** MD; Bt 1935; General Medical Practitioner in James Wigg Group Practice, Kentish Town Health Centre, NW5, since 1968; *b* 6 June 1928; *s* of Hon. James Russell Rea (*d* 1954) (2nd *s* of 1st Baron) and Betty Marion (*d* 1965), *d* of Arthur Bevan, MD; *S* uncle, 1981; *m* 1951, Elizabeth Anne, *d* of late William Hensman Robinson; four *s.* *Educ:* Dartington Hall School; Belmont Hill School, Mass, USA; Dauntsey's School; Christ's Coll., Cambridge Univ.; UCH Medical School. MA, MD (Cantab); MRCGP; DPH, DCH. Research Fellow in Paediatrics, Lagos, Nigeria, 1962–65; Lecturer in Social Medicine, St Thomas's Hosp. Medical School, 1966–68. Exec. Chm., Nat. Coordinating Cttee on Prevention of Coronary Heart Disease, 1985–. FRSocMed (Pres., Section of Gen. Practice, 1985–86). *Publications:* Interactions of Infection and Nutrition (MD Thesis, Cambridge Univ.), 1969; (jtly) Learning Teaching—an evaluation of a course for GP Teachers, 1980; articles on epidemiology and medical education in various journals. *Recreations:* music (bassoon), fishing, sailing, winter sports, walking. *Heir:* *s* Hon. Matthew James Rea, *b* 28 March 1956. *Address:* 11 Anson Road, N7 0RB. *T:* 01–607 0546.

REA, James Taylor, CMG 1958; HM Overseas Civil Service, retired; *b* 19 Oct. 1907; *s* of Rev. Martin Rea, Presbyterian Minister, and Mary Rea (*née* Fisher); *m* 1934, Catharine, *d* of Dr W. H. Bleakney, Whitman College, Walla Walla, Washington, USA; one *s* one *d.* *Educ:* Royal School, Dungannon; Queen's University, Belfast (BA); St John's College, Cambridge (MA). HM Colonial Administrative Service (now known as HM Overseas Civil Service) serving throughout in Malaya and Singapore, 1931–58; Principal offices held: Asst Sec., Chinese Affairs, Fedn of Malaya, 1948; Dep. Comr for Labour, Fedn of Malaya, 1949; Dep. Malayan Establishment Officer, 1950; Dep. Pres., 1952–55, Pres., 1955–58, City Council, Singapore. Retired, 1958. Chairman: Hotel Grants Adv. Cttee, NI, 1963–75; NI Training Exec., 1972–75; Down District Cttee, Eastern Health and Social Services Bd, 1974–78; Mem., NI Housing Trust, 1959–71, Vice Chm., 1970–71. Indep. Mem.: Catering Wages Council, N Ireland, 1965–82; Retail Bespoke Tailoring Wages Council, 1965–82; Laundry Wages Council, 1965–82; Shirtmaking Wages Council, 1965–82. Nominated Member General Dental Council, under Dentist Act, 1957, 1961–79. Mem. Downpatrick HMC, 1966–73, Chm., 1971–73. *Address:* Craigduff, Downpatrick, N Ireland. *T:* Seaforde 258.

REA, Dr John Rowland, FBA 1981; Lecturer in Documentary Papyrology, University of Oxford, since 1965; Senior Research Fellow, Balliol College, Oxford, since 1969; *b* 28 Oct. 1933; *s* of Thomas Arthur Rea and Elsie Rea (*née* Ward); *m* 1959, Mary Ogden. *Educ:* Methodist Coll., Belfast; Queen's Univ., Belfast (BA); University Coll. London (PhD). Asst Keeper, Public Record Office, 1957–61; Res. Lectr, Christ Church, Oxford, 1961–65. *Publications:* The Oxyrhynchus Papyri, Vol. XL, 1972, Vol. XLVI, 1978, Vol. LI, 1983, also contribs to Vols XXVII, XXXI, XXXIII, XXXIV, XXXVI, XLI, XLIII, XLIX, L; (with P. J. Sijpesteijn) Corpus Papyrorum Raineri V, 1976; articles in classical jls. *Address:* Balliol College, Oxford.

REA, Rupert Lascelles P.; *see* Pennant-Rea.

READ, Prof. Alan Ernest Alfred, MD, FRCP; Professor of Medicine and Director of Medical Professorial Unit, since 1969, University of Bristol; *b* 15 Nov. 1926; *s* of Ernest Read and Annie Lydia; *m* 1952, Enid Malein; one *s* two *d.* *Educ:* Wembley County Sch.; St Mary's Hosp. Med. Sch., London. House Phys., St Mary's Hosp., 1950; Med. Registrar, Royal Masonic Hosp., 1951; Mil. Service Med. Specialist, Trieste, 1952–54; Registrar and Sen. Registrar, Central Mddx and Hammersmith Hosps, 1954–60; Lectr in Medicine and Cons. Phys., University of Bristol, 1961, Reader in Medicine, 1966, Dean of Faculty of Medicine, 1983–85; Associate Prof. of Medicine, Univ. of Rochester, USA, 1967. *Publications:* Clinical Apprentice (jtly), 1948, 5th edn 1978; (jtly) Basic Gastroenterology, 1965, 3rd edn 1980; (jtly) Modern Medicine, 1975, 3rd edn 1984. *Recreations:* boating, fishing. *Address:* Riverbank, 77 Nore Road, Portishead, Bristol BS20 9JZ.

READ, Rt. Rev. Allan Alexander; *see* Ontario, Bishop of.

READ, Gen. Sir Antony; *see* Read, Gen. Sir J. A. J.

READ, Charles; *see* Read, Cyril N.

READ, Air Marshal Sir Charles (Frederick), KBE 1976 (CBE 1964); CB 1972; DFC 1942; AFC 1958; Chief of the Air Staff, RAAF, 1972–75, retired; *b* Sydney, NSW, 9 Oct. 1918; *s* of J. F. Read, Bristol, England; *m* 1946, Betty E., *d* of A. V. Bradshaw; three *s.* *Educ:* Sydney Grammar Sch. Former posts include: OC, RAAF Base, Point Cook, Vic., 1965–68; OC, RAAF, Richmond, NSW, 1968–70; Dep. Chief of Air Staff, 1969–72. *Recreation:* yachting. *Address:* 2007 Pittwater Road, Bayview, NSW 2104, Australia. *T:* 997–1686.

READ, Cyril Norman, (Charles), CBE 1983; Director of Information Technology, Post Office, since 1983; *b* 5 Feb. 1925; *s* of Ernest Archibald Read and Rosa Read; *m* 1950, Patricia Edna May King; one *s* two *d.* *Educ:* Chatham House Grammar Sch., Ramsgate; London Sch. of Econs and Pol. Science (BSc Econ 1951). Served War, Royal Corps of Signals, 1943–47. ITT Gp, 1951–56; Philips Electrical Industries, 1956–64; Scicon, 1964–67; Logica, 1967–68; Dir, IBRO, 1968–83. Chairman: Prime Minister's IT Adv. Panel, 1981–; Confedn of Information Communication Industries, 1984–; Member: Computers System and Electronics Requirements Bd, Dept of Industry, 1973–78; Lindop Cttee on Data Protection, 1977–78; Alvey Cttee on 5th Generation Computing Res., 1983. *Publications:* articles in jls and conf. papers on information technology and on payment systems and banking. *Recreations:* walking, classical music and opera, art, crafts, DIY.

READ, Rev. David Haxton Carswell, MA, DD; Minister of Madison Avenue Presbyterian Church, New York City, USA, since 1956; regular broadcaster on: National Radio Pulpit; Thinking It Over; *b* Cupar, Fife, 2 Jan. 1910; *s* of John Alexander Read and Catherine Haxton Carswell; *m* 1936, Dorothy Florence Patricia Gilbert; one *s.* *Educ:* Daniel Stewart's College, Edinburgh. Edinburgh Univ.; Univs of Montpellier, Strasbourg, Paris, and Marburg; New Coll., Edinburgh. MA Edin. (first class Hons in Lit.) 1932; BD (dist. in Dogmatics) 1936. Ordained Minister of the Church of Scotland, 1936; Minister of Coldstream West Church, 1936–39. CF, 1939–45 (despatches; POW, 1940–45, Germany). Minister of Greenbank Parish, Edinburgh, 1939–49; first Chaplain, Univ. of Edinburgh, 1949–55; Chaplain to the Queen in Scotland, 1952–55. Pres., Japan Internat. Christian Univ. Foundn. Guest Lectr and Preacher in USA, Scotland, Canada, Australia. Hon. DD: Edinburgh, 1956; Yale, 1959; Lafayette Coll., 1965; Hope Coll., 1969; Knox Coll., Canada, 1979; Hon. LHD: Hobart Coll., 1972; Trinity Univ., 1972; Hon. LittD Coll. of Wooster, 1966; Hon. DHL: Japan Internat. Christian Univ., 1979; Rockford Coll., 1982. *Publications:* The Spirit of Life, 1939; The Church to Come (trans. from German), 1939; Prisoners' Quest, Lectures on Christian doctrine in a POW Camp, 1944; The Communication of The Gospel, Warrack Lectures, 1952; The Christian Faith, 1955 (NY 1956); I am Persuaded, 1961 (NY 1962); Sons of Anak, 1964 (NY); God's Mobile Family, 1966 (NY); Whose God is Dead?, 1966 (Cin); Holy Common Sense, 1966 (Tenn); The Pattern of Christ, 1967 (NY); The Presence of Christ, 1968 (NJ); Christian Ethics, 1968 (NY 1969); Virginia Woolfe Meets Charlie Brown, 1968 (Mich); Giants Cut Down To Size, 1970; Religion Without Wrappings, 1970; Overheard, 1971; Curious Christians, 1972; Sent from God, 1974; Good News in the Letters of Paul, 1975; Go and make Disciples, 1978; Unfinished Easter, 1978; The Faith is Still There, 1980; *autobiography:* This Grace Given, 1984; Grace Thus Far, 1986; articles and sermons in Atlantic Monthly, Scottish Jl of Theology, Expository Times, etc. *Recreations:* languages; drama; travel, especially in France. *Address:* 1165 Fifth Avenue, New York, NY 10029, USA. *Clubs:* Pilgrims of the US, The Century (New York).

READ, Prof. Frank Henry, FRS 1984; Professor of Physics, Victoria University of Manchester, since 1975; *b* 6 Oct. 1934; *s* of late Frank Charles Read and of Florence Louise Read; *m* 1961, Anne Stuart (*née* Wallace); two *s* two *d.* *Educ:* Haberdashers' Aske's Hampstead Sch. (Foundn Scholar, 1946); Royal Coll. of Science, Univ. of London (Royal Scholar, 1952; ARCS 1955; BSc 1955). PhD 1959, DSc 1975, Victoria Univ. of Manchester. FInstP 1968; MIEE 1982; CEng. Univ. of Manchester: Lectr, 1959; Sen. Lectr, 1969; Reader, 1974. Vis. Scientist: Univ. of Paris, 1974; Univ. of Colorado, 1974–75; Inst. for Atomic and Molecular Physics, Amsterdam, 1979–80. Vice Pres., Inst. of Physics, 1985–. Hon. Editor, Jl of Physics B, Atomic and Molecular Physics, 1980–84. *Publications:* (with E. Harting) Electrostatic Lenses, 1976; Electromagnetic Radiation, 1980; papers in physics jls. *Recreations:* dry-stone walling, farming, shooting. *Address:* Hardingland Farm, Macclesfield Forest, Cheshire SK11 0ND. *T:* Macclesfield 25759.

READ, Gen. Sir (John) Antony (Jervis), GCB 1972 (KCB 1967; CB 1965); CBE 1959 (OBE 1957); DSO 1945; MC 1941; Governor of Royal Hospital, Chelsea, 1975–81; *b* 10 Sept. 1913; *e s* of late John Dale Read, Heathfield, Sussex; *m* 1947, Sheila, *e d* of late F. G. C. Morris, London, NW8; three *d.* *Educ:* Winchester; Sandhurst. Commissioned Oxford and Bucks Lt Inf., 1934; seconded to Gold Coast Regt, RWAFF, 1936; comd 81 (WA) Div. Reconnaissance Regt, 1943; comd 1 Gambia Regt, 1944; war service Kenya, Abyssinia, Somaliland, Burma; DAMS, War Office, 1947–49; Company Comd RMA Sandhurst, 1949–52; AA&QMG 11 Armd Div., 1953–54; comd 1 Oxford and Bucks Lt Inf., 1955–57; comd 3 Inf. Bde Gp, 1957–59; Comdt School of Infantry, 1959–62; GOC Northumbrian Area and 50 (Northumbrian) Division (TA), 1962–64; Vice-Quarter-Master-General, Min. of Defence, 1964–66; GOC-in-C, Western Comd, 1966–69; Quartermaster-General, 1969–72; Comdt, Royal Coll. of Defence Studies, 1973. ADC (Gen.) to the Queen, 1971–73. Colonel Commandant: Army Catering Corps, 1966–76; The Light Division, 1968–73; Small Arms School Corps, 1969–74; Hon. Col, Oxfordshire Royal Green Jackets Bn ACF, 1983. President: TA Rifle Assoc.; Ex-Services Fellowship Centres, 1975–; ACF Assoc., 1982– (Chm., 1973–82). Treas., Lord Kitchener Nat. Meml Fund, 1980. Governor: Royal Sch. for Daughters of Officers of the Army, 1966–83 (Chm., 1975–81); St Edward's Sch., Oxford, 1972–; Special Comr, Duke of York's Royal Mil. Sch., 1974. FBIM 1972. *Address:* Brackles, Little Chesterton, near Bicester, Oxon. *T:* Bicester 252189. *Club:* Army and Navy.

READ, Sir John (Emms), Kt 1976; FCA 1947; Chairman: TSB Group plc, since 1986; Trustee Savings Banks Central Board, since 1980; Director, TSB England and Wales plc, since 1986; Deputy Chairman, Thames Television Ltd, since 1981 (Director, since 1973); *b* 29 March 1918; *s* of late William Emms Read and of Daysie Elizabeth (*née* Cooper); *m* 1942, Dorothy Millicent Berry; two *s.* *Educ:* Brighton, Hove and Sussex Grammar Sch. Served Royal Navy, 1939–46 (rank of Comdr (S) RNVR); Admiral's Secretary: to Asst Chief of Naval Staff, Admty, 1942–45; to Brit. Admty Technical Mission, Ottawa, Canada, 1945–46. Ford Motor Co. Ltd, 1946–64 (Admin. Staff Coll., Henley, 1952), Dir of Sales, 1961–64; Dir, Electric and Musical Industries Ltd, 1965–; EMI Group: Jt Man. Dir, 1967; Chief Exec., 1969–79; Dep. Chm., 1973–74; Chm., 1974–79; Thorn EMI: Dep. Chm., 1979–81, Dir, 1981–. Director: Capitol Industries-EMI Inc., 1970–83; Group

Five Holdings Ltd, 1984–; Dunlop Holdings Ltd, 1971–84; Wonder World plc, 1985–; Chairman: CBI Finance & GP Cttee, 1978–84; TSB Holdings Ltd, 1980–86; Central TSB Ltd, 1983–86; TSB England and Wales Ltd, 1983–86; UDT, 1981–85. Chm., EDC for Electronics Industry, 1977–80. Member: (part time), PO Bd, 1975–77; Engineering Industries Council, 1975–80; BOTB, 1976–79; Armed Forces Pay Review Body, 1976–83; Nat. Electronics Council, 1977–80; Groupe des Présidents des Grandes Enterprises Européennes, 1977–80. Vice-Pres., Inst. of Bankers, 1982–. Member: RN Film Corp., 1975–83; Brighton Festival Soc. Council of Management, 1977–82; CBI Council, 1977– (Mem., Presidents' Cttee, 1977–84); White Ensign Assoc. Council of Management, 1979–; Governing Body and Finance and Gen. Purposes Cttee, Brit. Post-Grad. Med. Fedn, London Univ., 1982–; Governing Council, Business in the Community, 1985–; Council, British Heart Foundn, 1986–; Chm., Inst. of Neurology Council of Management, 1980–; Trustee: Westminster Abbey Trust, 1978–85; Brain Res. Trust, 1982– (Chm., 1986–); Charities Aid Foundn, 1985–; Dir and Trustee, Brighton Fest. Trust, 1977–; Trustee, LSO Trust, 1985–; President: Sussex Assoc. of Boys' Clubs, 1982–; Cheshire Homes, Seven Rivers, Essex, 1979–85; Governor, Admin. Staff Coll., Henley, 1974–. CBIM (FBIM 1974); CompIERE 1974; FRSA 1974; FIB 1982. *Recreations:* music, arts, sports. *Address:* Muster House, 12 Muster Green, Haywards Heath, W Sussex RH16 4AG; (office) 25 Milk Street, EC2V 8LU. *T:* 01–606 7070. *Club:* MCC.

READ, Lt-Gen. Sir John (Hugh Sherlock), KCB 1972; OBE 1944; retired; Adviser, West Africa Committee, since 1975; *b* 6 Sept. 1917; *s* of late Group Captain John Victor Read, Blunham, Bedfordshire, and Chacewater, Cornwall, and Elizabeth Hannah (*née* Link); *m* 1942, Mary Monica Wulfhilde Curtis (*d* 1985), *d* of late Henry Curtis, Spofforth, Yorks, and Harrogate; two *s* one *d*. *Educ:* Bedford School; RMA Woolwich; Magdalene Coll., Cambridge. BA (Cantab.) 1939. MA (Cantab.) 1944. Commissioned 2nd Lt RE, 1937. Served UK, France, Belgium, Egypt, Palestine, Greece, Austria at regimental duty and on staff, 1939–45, and UK, Austria, Germany, Hong Kong, 1945–57; GSO1, Singapore Base Dist, 1957; CO, Training Regt, RE, 1959; IDC, 1962; Min. of Defence (War Office), 1963; Comdr, Training Bde, RE, 1963; Asst Comdt, RMA, 1966–68; Director of Military Operations, MoD, 1968–70; ACDS (Policy), MoD, 1970–71; Dir, Internat. Mil. Staff, HQ, NATO, Brussels, 1971–75. Col Comdt, Corps of Royal Engineers, 1972–77. *Recreations:* fishing, shooting, gardening. *Address:* Bathealton Court, Bathealton, Taunton, Som TA4 2AJ. *T:* Wivelscombe 24134. *Club:* Oriental.

READ, John Leslie, FCA; Chairman, LEP Group plc, since 1982; *b* 21 March 1935; *s* of Robert and Florence Read; *m* 1958, Eugenie Ida (*née* Knight); one *s* one *d*. *Educ:* Sir William Turner's School. Partner, Price Waterhouse & Co., 1966–75; Finance Dir, then Jt Chief Exec., Unigate plc, 1975–80; Director: Metal Box plc, 1979–; Equity Law Life Assurance Soc. plc, 1980–; Border and Southern Stockholders Investment Trust plc, 1985–. Chm., Audit Commn for Local Authorities in England and Wales, 1983–86. *Recreations:* music, sport, reading, photography. *Address:* LEP Group, Sunlight Wharf, Upper Thames Street, EC4P 4AD. *T:* 01–236 5050. *Club:* Royal Automobile.

READ, Leonard Ernest, (Nipper), QPM 1976; National Security Adviser to the Museums and Galleries Commission, 1978–86; *b* 31 March 1925; *m* 1st, 1951, Marion Alexandra Millar (marr. diss. 1979); one *d*; 2nd, 1980, Patricia Margaret Allen. *Educ:* elementary schools. Worked at Players Tobacco factory, Nottingham, 1939–43; Petty Officer, RN, 1943–46; joined Metropolitan Police, 1947; served in all ranks of CID; Det. Chief Supt on Murder Squad, 1967; Asst Chief Constable, Notts Combined Constabulary, 1970; National Co-ordinator of Regional Crime Squads for England and Wales, 1972–76. Mem. Council, British Boxing Bd of Control, 1976–. Freeman, City of London, 1983. *Recreations:* cine photography, collecting club ties. *Address:* 23 North Barn, Broxbourne, Herts EN10 6RR.

READ, Lionel Frank, QC 1973; a Recorder of the Crown Court, since 1974; a General Commissioner of Income Tax, Gray's Inn Division, since 1986; *b* 7 Sept. 1929; *s* of late F. W. C. Read and Lilian (*née* Chatwin); *m* 1956, Shirley Greenhalgh; two *s* one *d*. *Educ:* Oundle Sch.; St John's Coll., Cambridge (MA Hons). Mons OCS Stick of Honour; commnd 4 RHA, 1949. Called to Bar, Gray's Inn, 1954; Bencher, 1981; Mem., Senate of the Inns of Court and the Bar, 1974–77. Vice-Chm., Local Government and Planning Bar Assoc., 1986. *Recreations:* golf, gardening. *Address:* Cedarwood, Church Road, Ham Common, Surrey. *T:* 01–940 5247. *Club:* Garrick.

READ, Prof. Margaret (Helen), CBE 1949; MA (Cantab), PhD (London); *b* 5 Aug. 1889; *d* of Mabyn Read, MD, Worcester, and Isabel Margaret Lawford. *Educ:* Roedean School, Brighton; Newnham College, Cambridge. Social work in India, 1919–24; lecturing on international affairs in Gt Britain and USA, 1924–30; LSE, student of anthropology and occasional lecturer, 1930–34; Research Fellow, Internat. African Inst. and field work in N Rhodesia and Nyasaland, 1934–39; Asst Lecturer, LSE, 1937–40; Univ. of London Inst. of Educ., Prof. and Head of Dept of Educ. in Tropical Areas, 1940–55; Prof. of Educ., Univ. Coll., Ibadan, Nigeria, 1955–56; occasional Consultant to WHO, 1956–62; Consultant to Milbank Memorial Fund, New York, 1964, 1965, 1966, 1967, 1968, 1969. Vis. Prof., Cornell Univ., 1951–52, Northwestern Univ., 1955, Michigan State Univ., 1960, Yale Univ. Medical School, 1965, 1966, 1967, 1968. *Publications:* Indian Peasant Uprooted, 1931; Africans and their Schools, 1953; Education and Social Change in Tropical Areas, 1955; The Ngoni of Nyasaland, 1956; Children of their Fathers, 1959; Culture, Health and Disease, 1966; articles in Africa, Bantu Studies, Journal of Applied Anthropology, Annals of the American Academy, etc. *Recreations:* gardening, music. *Address:* 9 Paradise Walk, Chelsea, SW3. *T:* 01–352 0528.

READ, Piers Paul, FRSL; author; *b* 7 March 1941; 3rd *s* of Sir Herbert Read, DSO, MC and Margaret Read, Stonegrave, York; *m* 1967, Emily Albertine, *o d* of Evelyn Basil Boothby, *qv*; two *s* two *d*. *Educ:* Ampleforth Coll.; St John's Coll., Cambridge (MA). Artist-in-residence, Ford Foundn, Berlin, 1963–64; Sub-Editor, Times Literary Supplement, 1965; Harkness Fellow, Commonwealth Fund, NY, 1967–68. Member: Council, Inst. of Contemporary Arts, 1971–75; Cttee of Management, Soc. of Authors, 1973–76; Literature Panel, Arts Council, 1975–77. Adjunct Prof. of Writing, Columbia Univ., NY, 1980. TV plays: Coincidence, 1968; The House on Highbury Hill, 1972; The Childhood Friend, 1974; radio play: The Family Firm, 1970. *Publications: novels:* Game in Heaven with Tussy Marx, 1966; The Junkers, 1968 (Sir Geoffrey Faber Meml Prize); Monk Dawson, 1969 (Hawthornden Prize and Somerset Maugham Award); The Professor's Daughter, 1971; The Upstart, 1973; Polonaise, 1976; A Married Man, 1979 (televised 1983); The Villa Golitsyn, 1981; The Free Frenchman, 1986; *non-fiction:* Alive, 1974; The Train Robbers, 1978. *Address:* 50 Portland Road, W11 4LG.

READ, Simon Holcombe Jervis, CBE 1977; MC 1944; HM Diplomatic Service, retired 1977; Secretary, Game Farmers' Association, since 1977; Chairman, UK Committee of Federation of Field Sports Associations of EEC, since 1983; *b* 7 Feb. 1922; *s* of John Dale Read and Evelyn Constance Read (*née* Bowen); *m* 1st, 1946, Bridget Elizabeth Dawson (marr. diss. 1959); two *s* one *d*; 2nd, 1960, Coelestine von der Marwitz. *Educ:* Winchester Coll. Served War: Private soldier, Essex Regt, 1940; commissioned 10th Baluch Regt, 1941; SOE and Detachment 101 (US Army), 1942, in Burma; service in Burma, Malaya, Thailand, Cambodia, Indo-China, China. Joined FCO, 1946; 3rd/2nd Sec., Singapore, Thailand, 1946–50; 1st Secretary: Hongkong, 1952–54; Iran, 1954–59; Berlin, 1959–64; UK, 1964–77. *Publication:* provisional check list of Birds of Iran (Teheran Univ.), 1958. *Recreations:* ornithology, shooting, gardening. *Address:* The Cottage, Little Chart, near Ashford, Kent. *T:* Pluckley 610. *Club:* Special Forces.

READE, Brian Anthony; HM Diplomatic Service; Counsellor, Foreign and Commonwealth Office, since 1986; *b* 5 Feb. 1940; *s* of Stanley Robert Reade and Emily Doris (*née* Lee); *m* 1964, Averille van Eugen; one *s* one *d*. *Educ:* King Henry VIII Sch., Coventry; Univ. of Leeds (BA Hons 1963). Interlang Ltd, 1963–64; Lectr, City of Westminster Coll., 1964–65; 2nd Sec., FCO, 1965–69; 2nd Sec., Bangkok, 1970–71, 1st Sec., 1971–74; FCO, 1974–77; Consul (Econ.), Consulate-General, Düsseldorf, 1977–81; FCO, 1981–82; 1st Sec., Bangkok, 1982–84; Counsellor (ESCAP), Bangkok, 1984–86. *Recreations:* watching sport, conversation, reading. *Address:* c/o Foreign and Commonwealth Office, SW1. *Clubs:* East India; Coventry Rugby Football; Royal Bangkok Sports (Thailand).

READE, Sir Clyde Nixon, 12th Bt *cr* 1661; *b* 1906; *s* of Sir George Reade, 10th Bt; *S* brother, Sir John Reade, 11th Bt, 1958; *m* 1930, Trilby (*d* 1958), *d* of Charles McCarthy. Is a Royal Arch Mason. *Address:* Box 242, Mason, Michigan 48854, USA.

READER, Dame Audrey Tattie Hinchcliff, DBE 1978 (OBE 1966); voluntary worker in several community organizations and in politics; *b* 9 Dec. 1903; *d* of William Henry Nicholls and Mabel Tattie Brimacombe Nicholls (*née* Mallett); *m* 1928, Reginald John Reader; one *d*. *Educ:* Macedon Primary Sch., Victoria; Malvern Coll., Melbourne. Housewife. Member: Victoria League for Commonwealth Friendship, Melbourne; Royal Soc. of St George. Patron, Victorian Br., Freedom Coalition.*Recreations:* reading, writing, gardening. *Address:* 68 Millewa Avenue, Chadstone, Victoria 3148, Australia. *T:* 5688716.

READER HARRIS, Dame (Muriel) Diana, DBE 1972; Headmistress, Sherborne School for Girls, Dorset, 1950–75; *b* Hong Kong, 11 Oct. 1912; *er d* of late Montgomery Reader Harris. *Educ:* Sherborne School for Girls; University of London (external student). BA 1st Class Honours (English), 1934. Asst Mistress, Sherborne School for Girls, 1934, and House Mistress, 1938. Organised Public Schools and Clubs Camps for Girls, 1937–39; in charge of group evacuated from Sherborne to Canada, 1940; joined staff of National Association of Girls' Clubs, 1943; Chm. Christian Consultative Cttee Nat. Assoc. of Mixed Clubs and Girls' Clubs, 1952–68, Vice-Pres., 1968; Chm. Outward Bound Girls' Courses, 1954–59; Mem. Council, Outward Bound Trust, 1956–64. Member: Women's Consultative Cttee, Min. of Labour, 1958–77; Women's Nat. Commn, 1976–78. Member: Dorset Educn Cttee, 1952–70; Exec. Cttee, Assoc. of Headmistresses, 1953–58, 1960 (Pres., 1964–66); Pres., Assoc. of Headmistresses of Boarding Schs, 1960–62; Member: Cttee on Agricl Colls, Min. of Agric., 1961–64; Schs Council, 1966–75. Member: Archbishop's Council on Evangelism, 1966–68; Panel on Broadcasting, Synod of C of E, 1975–86; Bd, Christian Aid, 1976–83 (Chm., 1978–83); Exec. Cttee and Assembly, BCC, 1977–83. Pres., CMS, 1969–82 (Mem., 1953–82, Chm., 1960–63, Exec. Cttee). King George's Jubilee Trust: Mem., Standing Res. and Adv. Cttee, 1949; Mem., Admin. Council, 1955–67; Member: Council, 1951–62, Exec. and Council, 1976–79, Nat. Youth Orch. of GB; ITA, 1956–60; Council, Westminster Abbey Choir Sch., 1976–; Court, Royal Foundn of St Katharine, 1979– (Chm., 1981–). Patron, Jt Educational Trust, 1986– (Chm., 1982–84, Trustee, 1975–86); President: Sch. Mistresses and Governesses Benevolent Instn, 1980–; Time and Talents Assoc., 1981–; British and For. Sch. Soc., 1982–; Churches' Commn on Overseas Students, 1984–. Governor: Godolphin Sch., Salisbury, 1975–; St Michael's Sch., Limpsfield, 1975–83 (Chm., 1977–83). FRSA 1964 (Mem. Council, RSA, 1975–; Chm., 1979–81; Vice-Pres., 1981–); Mem., The Pilgrims, 1979–. Hon. FCP 1975. *Address:* 35 The Close, Salisbury, Wilts SP1 2EL. *T:* Salisbury 26889.

READHEAD, James (Templeman), 3rd Bt, *cr* 1922 (but discontinued style of Sir and the use of his title, 1965); Lieutenant late King's Own Yorkshire Light Infantry, TA; *b* 12 Feb. 1910; *s* of late Stanley Readhead, Stanhope House, Westoe, South Shields, and late Hilda Maud, *d* of Thomas John Templeman, Weymouth, Dorset; *S* uncle, 1940; *m* 1946, Hilda Rosemary, *o d* of George Henry Hudson, The Manor, Hatfield, nr Doncaster, Yorks; one *d*. *Educ:* Repton School. Electrical Engineer, retired. *Recreations:* various.

READING, 4th Marquess of, *cr* 1926; **Simon Charles Henry Rufus Isaacs;** Baron 1914; Viscount 1916; Earl 1917; Viscount Erleigh 1917; *b* 18 May 1942; *e s* of 3rd Marquess of Reading, MBE, MC, and of Margot Irene, *yr d* of late Percy Duke, OBE; *S* father, 1980; *m* 1979, Melinda Victoria, *yr d* of Richard Dewar, Shoelands House, Seale, Surrey; one *s* two *d*. *Educ:* Eton. Short service commission, 1st Queen's Dragoon Guards, 1961–64. Member of Stock Exchange, 1970–74. Marketing Director of several companies. *Heir:* *s* Viscount Erleigh, *qv*. *Address:* Jayne's Court, Bisley, Gloucs. *Clubs:* Cavalry and Guards, MCC.

READING, Area Bishop of; Rt. Rev. Ronald Graham Gregory Foley; appointed Bishop Suffragan of Reading, 1982, Area Bishop, 1985; *b* 13 June 1923; *s* of Theodore Gregory Foley and Cessan Florence Page; *m* 1944, Florence Redman; two *s* two *d*. *Educ:* King Edward's Grammar Sch., Aston, Birmingham; Wakefield Grammar Sch.; King's Coll., London; St John's Coll., Durham BA Hons Theol., LTh. Curate, South Shore, Blackpool, 1950; Vicar, S Luke, Blackburn, 1954; Dir of Educn, Dio. of Durham, and Rector of Brancepeth, 1960; Chaplain, Aycliffe Approved Sch., 1962; Vicar of Leeds, 1971–82; Chaplain to the Queen, 1977–82. Hon. Canon: Durham Cathedral, 1965–71; Ripon Cath., 1971–82. Dir, Yorks Electricity Bd, 1976–82. Chm. of Trustees, Dorothy Kerin Trust, Burrswood, 1983–. *Publication:* (jtly) Religion in Approved Schools, 1969. *Recreations:* journalism, reading detective stories, watching other people mow lawns. *Address:* Greenbanks, Old Bath Road, Sonning-on-Thames, Reading RG4 0SY. *T:* Reading 692187. *Club:* Royal Commonwealth Society.

READWIN, Edgar Seeley, CBE 1971; retired; *b* 7 Nov. 1915; *s* of Ernest Readwin, Master Mariner and Edith Elizabeth Readwin; *m* 1940, Lesley Margaret (*née* Barker); two *s* one *d*. *Educ:* Bracondale Sch., Norwich. FCA. Articled Clerk, Harman & Gowen, Norwich, 1932–37; Asst Auditor, Bengal & North Western Railway, 1938–40; commnd service 14th Punjab Regt, 1941–45, PoW Far East, Singapore, Siam-Burma Railway, 1942–45; Indian Railway Accounts Service, 1945–49. Booker Group of Companies in Guyana: Asst to Accounts Controller, 1950; Finance Dir, 1951–56; Dep. Chm., 1956–62; Chm., 1962–71. Dir, West Indies Sugar Assoc., 1962–71; Finance Dir, Indonesia Sugar Study, 1971–72; Chm., Minvielle & Chastenet Ltd, St Lucia, 1973–76. Hon. Treas., Guyana Lawn Tennis Assoc., 1951–67, Pres., 1968–70, Hon. Life Vice-Pres., 1971–. *Recreations:* lawn tennis, golf, gardening, chess, bridge. *Address:* Lane End Farmhouse, Ancton Lane, Middleton-on-Sea, Sussex. *T:* Middleton-on-Sea 2131. *Clubs:* Veterans' Lawn Tennis of Great Britain; Bognor Tennis; Littlehampton Golf.

REAGAN, Ronald; President of the United States of America, since 1981; *b* Tampico, Ill, 6 Feb. 1911; *m* 1st, 1940, Jane Wyman (marr. diss. 1948); one *s* one *d*; 2nd, 1952, Nancy Davis; one *s* one *d*. *Educ:* public schools in Tampico, Monmouth, Galesburg, and Dixon,

Ill; Eureka Coll., Ill (AB). Sports Announcer, WHO, Des Moines, 1932–37; actor, films and television, 1937–66; Host and Program Superviser, Gen. Electric Theater (TV), 1954–62; Host, Death Valley Days (TV), 1962–65. Pres., Screen Actors' Guild, 1947–52, 1959–60; Chm., Motion Picture Industry Council, 1949. Served with USAAF, 1942–45. Governor, State of California, 1967–74; Chairman, State Governors' Assoc., 1969. Republican Candidate for nomination for the Presidency, 1976. Operates horsebreeding and cattle ranch. *Publications:* Where's the Rest of Me? (autobiog.), 1965 (repr. 1981 as My Early Life); Abortion and the Conscience of the Nation, 1984. *Address:* The White House, 1600 Pennsylvania Avenue NW, Washington, DC 20500, USA.

REARDON, Rev. Canon Martin Alan; Secretary, Board for Mission and Unity, General Synod of the Church of England, since 1978; *b* 3 Oct. 1932; *s* of Ernest William Reardon, CBE and Gertrude Mary; *m* 1964, Ruth Maxim Slade; one *s* one *d*. *Educ:* Cumnor House Sch.; St Edward's Sch., Oxford; Selwyn Coll., Cambridge (MA); Cuddesdon Coll., Oxford; Univ. of Geneva; Univ. of Louvain. Asst Curate, Rugby Parish Church, 1958–61; Sec., Sheffield Council of Churches, 1962–71; Sub-Warden, Lincoln Theol Coll., 1971–78. *Publications:* Christian Unity in Sheffield, 1967; (with Kenneth Greet) Social Questions, 1964; What on Earth is the Church For?, 1985; contribs to One in Christ, Theology, Clergy Review, etc. *Recreations:* walking, sketching. *Address:* Board for Mission and Unity, Church House, Dean's Yard, SW1P 3NZ. *T:* 01-222 9011.

REARDON-SMITH, Sir William; *see* Smith.

REASON, Dr Richard Edmund, OBE 1967; FRS 1971; Consultant, Rank Taylor-Hobson. *Address:* 5 Manor Road, Great Bowden, Leicestershire LE16 7HE. *T:* Market Harborough 63219.

REAY, 14th Lord, *cr* 1628, of Reay, Caithness; **Hugh William Mackay;** Bt of Nova Scotia, 1627; Baron Mackay of Ophemert and Zennewijnen, Holland; Chief of Clan Mackay; Delegate to the Council of Europe and to WEU, since 1979; *b* 19 July 1937; *s* of 13th Lord Reay and Charlotte Mary Younger; *S* father, 1963; *m* 1st, 1964, Hon. Annabel Thérèse Fraser (marr. diss. 1978; she *m* 1985, Henry Neville Lindley Keswick, *qv*), *y d* of 17th Baron Lovat, *qv*; two *s* one *d*; 2nd, 1980, Hon. Victoria Isabella Warrender, *d* of Baron Bruntisfield, *qv*; two *d*. *Educ:* Eton; Christ Church. Mem., European Parlt, 1973–79 (Vice-Chm., Cons. Gp). *Heir: s* The Master of Reay, *qv*. *Address:* House of Lords, SW1; Kasteel Ophemert, Ophemert, (Gld) Holland.

REAY, Master of; Aeneas Simon Mackay, *b* 20 March 1965; *s* and *heir* of 14th Lord Reay, *qv*. *Educ:* Westminster School; Brown Univ., USA. *Recreations:* most sports, especially football, cricket and shooting.

REAY, Lt-Gen. Sir Alan; *see* Reay, Lt-Gen. Sir H. A. J.

REAY, Basil; *see* Reay, S. B.

REAY, David William, CEng, FIERE; CPhys, FInstP; Managing Director, Tyne Tees Television Ltd, since 1984; *b* 28 May 1940; *s* of Stanley Reay and Madge Reay (*née* Hall); *m* 1964, Constance Susan Gibney; two *d*. *Educ:* Monkwearmouth Grammar School, Sunderland; Newcastle upon Tyne Polytechnic. Independent Television Authority, 1960–62; Alpha Television (ATV and ABC) Services Ltd, 1962–64; Tyne Tees Television Ltd, 1964–72; HTV Ltd: Engineering Manager, 1972–75; Chief Engineer, 1975–79; Dir of Engineering, 1979–84. FBIM; FRTS 1984. *Recreations:* walking, reading, music, watching soccer (particularly Sunderland AFC). *Address:* Warreners House, Northgate, Morpeth, Northumberland. *Club:* Savile.

REAY, Lt-Gen. Sir (Hubert) Alan (John), KBE 1981; FRCP, FRCP(Edin); Director General, Army Medical Services, 1981–85; *b* 19 March 1925; *s* of Rev. John Reay; *m* 1960, Ferelith Haslewood Deane; two *s* two *d* (and one *s* decd). *Educ:* Lancing College; Edinburgh Univ. MB, DTMQ&H, DCH. Field Medical Services, Malaya, 1949–52 (despatches); Exchange Physician, Brooke Hosp., San Antonio, Texas, 1957; Command Paediatrician: Far East, 1962; BAOR, 1965; Adviser in Paediatrics, MoD (Army), 1968; Hon. Out-patient Consultant, Great Ormond Street Hosp., 1975–79, 1985–; QHP 1976–85; Postgraduate Dean and Comdt, Royal Army Med. Coll., 1977–79; DMS, HQ BAOR, 1979–81. Hon. Col, 217 (London) General Hosp. RAMC (Volunteers) TA, 1986–. Chief Hon. Steward, Westminster Abbey, 1985–. Pres., Paediatric Section, RSocMed, 1984–85. Inaugural Lectr, Soc. of Armed Forces Med. Consultants, Univ. of Health Scis, Bethesda, 1984. CStJ 1981 (OStJ 1979). *Publications:* paediatric articles in med. jls. *Address:* 63 Madrid Road, Barnes, SW13 9PQ.

REAY, Dr John Sinclair Shewan; Director, Warren Spring Laboratory, Department of Trade and Industry, since 1985; *b* Aberdeen, 8 June 1932; *s* of late George Reay, CBE and Tina (*née* Shewan); *m* 1958, Rhoda Donald Robertson; two *s* one *d*. *Educ:* Robert Gordon's College, Aberdeen; Univ. of Aberdeen; Imperial College, London (Beit Fellow). BSc, PhD, DIC. CChem, FRSC. Joined Scottish Agricultural Industries, 1958; Warren Spring Lab., Min of Technology, 1968; Head of Air Pollution Div., DoI, 1972–77; Head, Policy and Perspectives Unit, DTI, 1977–79; Head of Branch, Research Technology Div., DoI, 1979–81; Dep. Dir, Warren Spring Lab., 1981–85. *Publications:* papers on surface chemistry and air pollution. *Recreations:* playing violin, listening to music. *Address:* 13 Grange Hill, Welwyn, Herts Al6 9RH. *T:* Welwyn 5587.

REAY, (Stanley) Basil, OBE 1957; Secretary, Lawn Tennis Association, 1948–73; *b* 2 Feb. 1909; *s* of Robert and Maud Reay (*née* Cox), Stockton on Tees; *m* 1935, Beatrice Levene; one *s* one *d*. *Educ:* Queen Elizabeth Grammar School, Hexham; St John's College. Schoolmaster in England, 1929–32; Min. of Education, Egypt, 1932–39. Chairman Inter-Services Language Training Cttee, 1945–47. Served RAF, 1939–47, chiefly in ME (Wing Comdr, 1944). Wing Comdr, RAFVR. Sec. Gen., Internat. Lawn Tennis Fedn and Davis Cup Competition, 1973–76 (Hon. Sec., 1948–73; Hon. Life Counsellor, 1976–). Chm., British Schs LTA, 1980–84. Commandeur, Ordre de Merite Sportif (France), 1960; Gold Medal of Jerusalem (Israel); sports decorations from Yugoslavia, Brazil and others. *Recreations:* travel and sports. *Address:* Molende, Molember Road, East Molesey, Surrey. *Clubs:* Royal Automobile, Queen's; All England (Wimbledon); International Lawn Tennis Clubs of Great Britain, USA, France, Italy and several other countries.

REBBECK, Dr Denis, CBE 1952; JP, DL; MA, MSc, PhD, BLitt; FEng, FICE, FIMechE, FRINA, FIMarE, FCIT; *b* 22 Jan. 1914; *er s* of late Sir Frederick Ernest Rebbeck, KBE; *m* 1938, Rosamond Annette Kathleen, *e d* of late Henry Jameson, Bangor, Co. Down; four *s*. *Educ:* Campbell Coll., Belfast; Pembroke Coll., Cambridge. BA (Hons) Mech. Sciences Tripos, 1935; MA (Cantab) 1939; MA (Dublin) 1945; BLitt (Dublin) 1946; MSc (Belfast) 1946; PhD (Belfast) 1950; Part-time Post-grad. Research. Harland & Wolff, Ltd: Director, 1946–70; Dep. Man. Director, 1953; Man. Dir, 1962–70; Chm., 1965–66. Chm., 1972–84, Dir, 1950–84, Iron Trades Employers' Insurance Association Ltd and Iron Trades Mutual Insurance Co. Ltd (Vice-Chm., 1969–72); Director: Nat. Shipbuilders Security Ltd, 1952–58; Colvilles Ltd, 1963–67; Brown Brothers & Co. Ltd, 1967–68; Shipbuilding Corporation Ltd, 1963–73; National Commercial Bank of Scotland Ltd, 1965–69; Royal Bank of Scotland Ltd, 1969–84; Belships Co. Ltd, 1970–76 (Chm., 1972–76); John Kelly Ltd, 1968–79 (Dep. Chm., 1968; Chm., 1969–79); Howdens Ltd, 1977–79; Norman Canning Ltd, 1977–79; Nationwide Building Soc., 1980–; General Underwriting Agencies Ltd, 1984– (Chm. 1984–); Nordic Business Forum for Northern Britain Ltd, 1980–84. Special Consultant, Swan Hunter Group Ltd, 1970–79; Consultant, Ellerman Travel, 1979–84. Belfast Harbour Commissioner, 1962–85. Member Research Council, and Chairman, Design Main Committee, British Ship Research Association, 1965–73; Pres., Shipbuilding Employers' Fedn, 1962–63; Past Chm. Warship Gp., Shipbuilding Conf.; NI Economic Council, 1965–70; Lloyd's Register of Shipping General Cttee, 1962–85 and Technical Cttee, 1964–76; Management Board: Engineering Employers Fedn, 1963–75; Shipbuilders & Repairers Nat. Assoc., 1966–71; Council, RINA, 1964–72; Council for Scientific R&D in NI, 1948–59; Member Inst. of Engineers and Shipbuilders in Scotland; Past Chm. and Trustee, Belfast Savings Bank; Cambridge Univ. Engineers' Assoc.; Science Masters' Assoc. (Pres. NI Branch, 1954–55); NI Grammar Schools Careers Assoc. (Pres., 1964–65); Life Mem. Brit. Assoc. for the Advancement of Science; National Playing Fields Assoc. (NI Exec. Cttee), 1952–77; Chairman: Adv. Cttee on Marine Pilotage, 1977–79; Pilotage Commn, 1979–83; Member: Drummond Technical Investigation Cttee, 1955–56; Lord Coleraine's Committee to enquire into Youth Employment Services in NI, 1957–58; Sir John Lockwood's Cttee on Univ. and Higher Techn. Educn in Northern Ireland, 1963–64; Queen's Univ., Better Equipment Fund Exec. Cttee, 1951–82; Hon. Life Mem., Irish Port Authorities Assoc., 1985; Vice-Pres. of Belfast Savings Council; Visitor, Linen Industry Research Assoc., DSIR, 1954–57; President: Belfast Assoc. of Engineers, 1947–48; NI Society of Incorporated Secretaries, 1955–70; Glencraig Curative Schools, NI, 1953–70; World Ship Soc., 1978–81 (Vice Pres., 1956); Past Mem. Council IMechE; IMarE; Chm. NI Assoc., ICE, 1952–53; FEng 1979. Member: Smeatonian Soc. of Civil Engrs; Incorp. of Hammermen of Glasgow. Liveryman, Worshipful Company of Shipwrights, 1952– (Prime Warden, 1980–81). Hon. Mem., BUPA, 1984. Vice-Pres., Queen's Univ. Guild, 1951–65; Board Governors Campbell Coll., Belfast, 1952–60 (Vice-Chm. 1957–60); Member of Court, New Univ. of Ulster. Mem., T&AFA for Belfast, 1947–65; Dep.-Chm. NI Festival of Britain, 1948–51; papers read before British Association, ICE, etc; Akroyd Stuart Award, IMarE, 1943. JP County Borough of Belfast, 1949; DL County of the City of Belfast, 1960. *Recreation:* sailing. *Address:* The White House, Craigavad, Holywood, County Down, N Ireland BT18 0HE. *T:* Holywood 2294. *Clubs:* Royal Yacht Squadron, Royal Automobile, City Livery, Den Norske; Cambridge Union; Shippingklubben (Oslo); Royal Norwegian Yacht; Royal North of Ireland Yacht (Cultra, Co. Down).

RECKITT, Lt-Col Basil Norman, TD 1946; Director, Reckitt and Colman Ltd, retired 1972 (Chairman, 1966–70); *b* 12 Aug. 1905; *s* of Frank Norman Reckitt, Architect, and Beatrice Margaret Hewett; *m* 1st, 1928, Virginia Carre-Smith (*d* 1961); three *d*; 2nd, 1966, Mary Holmes (*née* Peirce), *widow* of Paul Holmes, Malham Tarn, near Settle. *Educ:* Uppingham; King's Coll., Cambridge (MA). Joined Reckitt & Sons Ltd, 1927; Dir, Reckitt & Colman Ltd, 1938. 2nd Lieut, 62nd HAA Regt (TA), 1939; Bde Major, 39th AA Brigade, 1940; CO 141 HAA (M) Regt, 1942; Military Government, Germany, 1944–45. Chm. Council, 1971–80, and Pro-Chancellor, 1971–, Hull Univ. Sheriff of Hull, 1970–71. Chm., Friends of Abbot Hall Art Gall. and Museums, Kendal, 1982–; Vice-Chm., YMCA Nat. Centre, Lakeside, Windermere, 1982–. Hon. LLD, Hull University, 1967. *Publications:* History of Reckitt & Sons Ltd, 1951; Charles I and Hull, 1952; The Lindley Affair, 1972. *Recreations:* riding and walking. *Address:* Haverbrack, Milnthorpe, Cumbria LA7 7AH. *T:* Milnthorpe 3142.

REDDAWAY, (Arthur Frederick) John, CMG 1959; OBE 1957; Deputy Commissioner-General, United Nations Relief and Works Agency, 1960–68; *b* 12 April 1916; *s* of Arthur Joseph Reddaway, Chartered Accountant, and Thirza May King; *m* 1945, Anthoula, *d* of Dr Christodoulos Papaioannou, Nicosia; two *s*. *Educ:* County High School, Ilford; University of Reading. Colonial Administrative Service, Cyprus, 1938; Imperial Defence College, 1954; Administrative Sec., Cyprus, 1957–60. Dir-Gen., Arab-British Centre, London, 1970–80. *Address:* 19 Woodsyre, Sydenham Hill, SE26. *Club:* Royal Commonwealth Society.

REDDAWAY, Brian; *see* Reddaway, W. B.

REDDAWAY, (George Frank) Norman, CBE 1965 (MBE 1946); HM Diplomatic Service, retired; *b* 2 May 1918; *s* of late William Fiddian Reddaway and late Kate Waterland Reddaway (*née* Sills); *m* 1944, Jean Brett, OBE; two *s* three *d*. *Educ:* Oundle School; King's College, Cambridge. Scholar Modern Langs, 1935; 1st Class Hons Mod. Langs Tripos Parts 1 and 2, 1937 and 1939. Served in Army, 1939–46; psc Camberley, 1944. Foreign Office, 1946; Private Sec. to Parly Under Sec. of State, 1947–49; Rome, 1949; Ottawa, 1952; Foreign Office, 1955; Imperial Defence College, 1960; Counsellor, Beirut, 1961; Counsellor, Office of the Political Adviser to the C-in-C, Far East, Singapore, 1965–66; Counsellor (Commercial), Khartoum, 1967–69; Asst Under-Sec. of State, FCO, 1970–74; Ambassador to Poland, 1974–78. Chm., English International, 1978–; Dir, Catalytic International, 1978–; Trustee, Thomson Foundn, 1978–. Commander, Order of Merit, Polish People's Republic, 1985. *Recreations:* gardening, family history. *Address:* 51 Carlton Hill, NW8. *T:* 01-624 9238. *Clubs:* Athenæum, United Oxford & Cambridge University, Royal Commonwealth Society.

REDDAWAY, John; *see* Reddaway, A. F. J.

REDDAWAY, Norman; *see* Reddaway, G. F. N.

REDDAWAY, Prof. (William) Brian, CBE 1971; FBA 1967; Professor of Political Economy, University of Cambridge, 1969–80; Fellow of Clare College, Cambridge, since 1938; *b* 8 Jan. 1913; *s* of late William Fiddian Reddaway and late Kate Waterland Reddaway (*née* Sills); *m* 1938, Barbara Augusta Bennett; three *s* one *d*. *Educ:* Oundle Sch.; King's Coll., Cambridge; Maj. schol. natural science; 1st cl. Maths tripos, part I, 1st cl. 1st div. Economics tripos, part II; Adam Smith Prize; MA. Assistant, Bank of England, 1934–35; Research Fellow in Economics, University of Melbourne, 1936–37; Statistics Division, Board of Trade (final rank Chief Statistician), 1940–47; University Lectr in Economics, 1939–55, Reader in Applied Economics, 1957–65, Dir of Dept of Applied Economics, 1955–69, Univ. of Cambridge. Economic Adviser to OEEC, 1951–52; Visiting Economist, Center for International Studies, New Delhi, 1959–60; Vis. Lectr, Economic Develt Inst. (Washington), 1966–67; Consultant, Harvard Develt Adv. Service (in Ghana), 1967; Vis. Prof., Bangladesh Inst. of Develt Studies, 1974–75. Economic Consultant to CBI, 1972–83. Regional Adviser, Economic Commn for Western Asia, 1979–80; Consultant to World Bank on Nigerian economy, 1983–85. Member: Royal Commn on the Press, 1961–62; NBPI, 1967–71; Chm., Inquiry into Consulting Engineering Firms' Costs and Earnings, 1971–72. Editor, Economic Jl, 1971–76. *Publications:* Russian Financial System, 1935; Economics of a Declining Population, 1939; (with C. F. Carter, Richard Stone) Measurement of Production Movements, 1948; The Development of the Indian Economy, 1962; Effects of UK Direct Investment Overseas, Interim Report, 1967, Final Report, 1968; Effects of the Selective Employment Tax, First Report, 1970, Final Report, 1973; (with G. C. Fiegehen) Companies, Incentives and Senior

Managers, 1981; articles in numerous economic journals. *Recreations:* skating, squash, walking. *Address:* 4 Adams Road, Cambridge. *T:* 350041.

REDDINGTON, Clifford Michael; Chief Executive, Liverpool City Council, since 1986; *b* 14 Sept. 1932; *s* of Thomas Reddington and Gertrude (*née* Kenny); *m* 1968 Ursula Moor. *Educ:* St Michael's Coll., Leeds; St Edward's Coll., Liverpool; Liverpool Univ. BCom 1953; IPFA 1958; MBCS 1964. Served RAF, 1958–60. City Treasury, Liverpool, 1953–58 and 1960–86; Dep. City Treasurer, 1974, City Treasurer, 1982–86. *Recreations:* fell-walking, choral singing, cooking. *Address:* Entwood, Westwood Road, Noctorum, Birkenhead L43 9RQ.

REDDISH, Prof. Vincent Cartledge, OBE 1974; Professor Emeritus, Edinburgh University, 1980; industrial and scientific consultant, with business interests in the Scottish Tourist industry, since 1980; *b* 28 April 1926; *s* of William H. M. Reddish and Evelyn Reddish; *m* 1951, Elizabeth Waltho; two *s*. *Educ:* Wigan Techn. Coll.; London Univ. BSc Hons, PhD, DSc. Lectr in Astronomy, Edinburgh Univ., 1954; Lectr in Radio Astronomy, Manchester Univ., 1959; Royal Observatory, Edinburgh: Principal Scientific Officer, 1962; Sen. Principal Sci. Off., 1966; Dep. Chief Sci. Off., 1974; Regius Prof. of Astronomy, Edinburgh Univ., Dir, Royal Observatory, Edinburgh, and Astronomer Royal for Scotland, 1975–80. Governor, Rannoch Sch., 1981–. *Publications:* Evolution of the Galaxies, 1967; The Physics of Stellar Interiors, 1974; Stellar Formation, 1978; numerous sci. papers in Monthly Notices RAS, Nature and other jls. *Recreations:* hill walking, sailing, ornithology, do-it-yourself. *Address:* Croiscrag, Rannoch Station, Perthshire PH17 2QG. *T:* Bridge of Gaur 255.

REDDY, (Neelam) Sanjiva; farmer and lemon grower; President of India, 1977–82; *b* 13 May 1913; *m* Nagaratnamma; one *s* three *d*. *Educ:* Adyar Arts Coll., Anantapur. Andhra Provincial Congress: Sec., Congress Cttee, 1936–46; Pres., 1951–; Leader, Congress Legislature Party, 1953–; Mem. and Sec., Madras Legislative Assembly, 1946; Mem., Indian Constituent Assembly, 1947; Minister for Prohibition, Housing and Forests, Madras Govt, 1949–51; Mem., Rajya Sabha, 1952–53; Andhra Pradesh: Mem., Legislative Assembly, 1953–64; Dep. Chief Minister, 1953–56; Chief Minister, 1956–57 and 1962–64; Pres., All-India Congress Party, 1960–62; Member: Rajya Sabha, 1964–67; Lok Sabha, 1967–71, and 1977; Minister: of Steel and Mines, 1964–65; of Transport, Aviation, Shipping and Tourism, 1966–67; Speaker of Lok Sabha, 1967–69, 1977. *Address:* Illure, Anantapur, Andhra Pradesh, India.

REDESDALE, 5th Baron, *cr* 1902; **Clement Napier Bertram Mitford;** Vice President, Corporate Communications Europe, Africa and Middle East, Chase Manhattan Bank NA; *b* 28 Oct. 1932; *o s* of late Hon. E. R. B. O. Freeman-Mitford, 5th *s* of 1st Baron; *S* uncle, 1963; *m* 1958, Sarah Georgina Cranston Todd; one *s* five *d* (and one *d* decd). *Educ:* Eton. MCAM. Joined Colin Turner (London) Ltd, 1953; joined Erwin Wasey (Advertising), 1955, Associate Director, 1960–64. Pres., Guild of Cleaners and Launderers, 1968–70. Chm., Nat. Council of Royal Soc. of St George, 1970–75, Pres., 1975–79. Governor, Yehudi Menuhin Sch., 1973–. *Heir: s* Hon. Rupert Bertram Mitford, *b* 18 July 1967. *Address:* 2 St Mark's Square, NW1 7TP. *T:* 01–722 1965. *Club:* Lansdowne.

REDFEARN, Sir Herbert, Kt 1973; JP; DL; wire and wire goods manufacturer; Chairman, John Brown (Brighouse) Ltd, since 1949; *b* 26 Sept. 1915; *s* of Harry Reginald and Annie Elizabeth Redfearn; *m* 1942, Doris Vickerman, *y d* of Joseph Vickerman and Sarah Elizabeth Vickerman; one *s* one *d*. *Educ:* local council and technical schs. Brighouse: Borough Council, 1943–74; Alderman of Borough, 1953–74; Mayor, 1967. Chm., Brighouse and Spenborough Conservative Constituency Assoc., 1961–66, Pres., 1966–83; Treas., Yorks Provincial Area Council of Conservative and Unionist Assoc., 1966–70, Chm., 1971–76. Member: Conservative Party Bd of Finance, 1966–70; Nat. Union Exec. Cttee, 1966–83; Superannuation Fund Management Cttee, 1972–79 (Trustee 1979–); Vice Chm., Nat. Union of Cons. and Unionist Assocs, 1976–77, Chm. 1978; Pres., Calder Valley Cons. Assoc., 1983. JP W Yorks, 1956; DL W Yorks, 1977. *Recreations:* freemasonry, gardening. *Address:* Ash Lea, Woodhouse Lane, Brighouse, West Yorkshire. *Club:* Carlton.

REDFERN, Philip, CB 1983; Deputy Director, Office of Population Censuses and Surveys, 1970–82; *b* 14 Dec. 1922; *m* 1951, Gwendoline Mary Phillips; three *d*. *Educ:* Bemrose Sch., Derby; St John's Coll., Cambridge. Wrangler, Mathematical Tripos, Cambridge, 1942. Asst Statistician, Central Statistical Office, 1947; Chief Statistician, Min. of Education, 1960; Dir of Statistics and Jt Head of Planning Branch, Dept of Educn and Science, 1967.

REDFORD, Donald Kirkman, CBE 1980; DL; Chairman, The Manchester Ship Canal Company, since 1972 (Managing Director, 1970–80); *b* 18 Feb. 1919; *er s* of T. J. and S. A. Redford; *m* 1942, Mabel (*née* Wilkinson), Humberstone, Lincs; one *s* one *d*. *Educ:* Culford Sch.; King's Coll., Univ. of London (LLB). Served, 1937–39, and War until 1945, in RAFVR (retd as Wing Comdr). Practice at the Bar until end of 1946, when joined The Manchester Ship Canal Company, with which Company has since remained. Chairman, Nat. Assoc. of Port Employers, 1972–74; Dep. Chm., British Ports Assoc., 1973–74, Chm. 1974–78. Member: Cttee of Management, RNLI, 1977– (Chm., Search and Research Cttee, 1984–); Court and Council, Manchester Univ., 1977– (Dep. Treas., 1980–82, Treas., 1982–83, Chm. of Council, 1983–). CBIM, FRSA. DL Lancs 1983. *Recreations:* reading, history, sailing, golf. *Address:* North Cotes, 8 Harrod Drive, Birkdale, Southport. *T:* Southport 67406; The Manchester Ship Canal Co., Dock Office, Trafford Road, Manchester M5 2XB. *T:* 061–872 2411. *Clubs:* Oriental; St James's (Manchester).

REDGRAVE, Lynn; actress; *b* 8 March 1943; *d* of late Sir Michael Redgrave, CBE, and of Rachel Kempson, *qv*; *m* 1967, John Clark; one *s* two *d*. *Educ:* Queensgate Sch.; Central Sch. of Speech and Drama. Nat. Theatre of GB, 1963–66 (Tulip Tree, Mother Courage, Andorra, Hay Fever, etc); Black Comedy, Broadway 1967; The Two of Us, Slag, Zoo Zoo Widdershins Zoo, Born Yesterday, London 1968–71; A Better Place, Dublin 1972; My Fat Friend, Knock Knock, Mrs Warren's Profession, Broadway 1973–76; The Two of Us, California Suite, Hellzapoppin, US tours 1976–77; Saint Joan, Chicago and NY 1977; Twelfth Night, Amer. Shakespeare Festival, Conn, 1978; Les dames du jeudi, LA, 1981; Sister Mary Ignatius Explains It All For You, LA, 1983; The King and I, N American Tour, 1983. *Films include:* Tom Jones, Girl with Green Eyes, Georgy Girl (NY Film Critics, Golden Globe and IFIDA awards, Academy nomination Best Actress), Deadly Affair, Smashing Time, Virgin Soldiers, Last of the Mobile Hotshots, Every Little Crook and Nanny, National Health, Happy Hooker, Everything You Always Wanted to Know about Sex, The Big Bus, Sunday Lovers. *USA television includes:* Co-host of nationally televised talk-show, Not For Women Only, appearances in documentaries, plays, The Muppets, Centennial, Beggarman Thief, The Seduction of Miss Leona, Rehearsal for Murder, and series: Housecalls (CBS); Teachers Only (NBC). *Recreations:* cooking, gardening, horse riding. *Address:* PO Box 1207, Topanga, Calif 90290, USA. *T:* (213) 455–1334.

REDGRAVE, Rachel, (Lady Redgrave); *see* Kempson, R.

REDGRAVE, Maj.-Gen. Sir Roy Michael Frederick, KBE 1979; MC 1945; FRGS; Director, Onsky Ltd (Hong Kong), since 1985; *b* 16 Sept. 1925; *s* of late Robin Roy Redgrave and Michelene Jean Capsa; *m* 1953, Caroline Margaret Valerie, *d* of Major Arthur Wellesley; two *s*. *Educ:* Sherborne Sch. Served War of 1939–45: enlisted Trooper, Royal Horse Guards, 1943; Lieut, 1st Household Cavalry Regt, NW Europe, 1944–45. GSO III Intell., HQ Rhine Army, 1950; Canadian Army Staff Coll., 1955; GSO II Ops HQ, London Dist, 1956; Recce, Sqn Ldr, Cyprus, 1959 (despatches); Mil. Assistant to Dep. SACEUR, Paris, 1960–62; JSSC 1962; Comd Household Cavalry Regt (Mounted), 1963–64; Comd Royal Horse Guards (The Blues), 1965–67; AAG PS12, MoD, 1967–68; Chief of Staff, HQ 2nd Div., 1968–70; Comdr, Royal Armoured Corps, 3rd Div., 1970–72; Nat. Defence Coll., Canada, 1973; Comdt Royal Armoured Corps Centre, 1974–75; British Comdt, Berlin, 1975–78; Comdr, British Forces, Hong Kong, and Maj.-Gen. Brigade of Gurkhas, 1978–80. Hon. Col 31st (GL) Signal Regt (V). Dir Gen., Winston Churchill Meml Trust, 1980–82. Member: Council Charing Cross and Westminster Med. Sch.; Hammersmith SHA, 1981–85; Council, Victoria League for Commonwealth Friendship. Chairman: Hammersmith and Fulham HA, 1981–85; Lambrook Appeal, 1984–85. Special Trustee, Charing Cross and West London Hosps. *Recreations:* walking, archaeology, philately. *Address:* c/o Lloyds Bank, Wareham, Dorset BH20 4LX. *Club:* Cavalry and Guards.

REDGRAVE, Vanessa, CBE 1967; Actress since 1957; *b* 30 Jan. 1937; *d* of late Sir Michael Redgrave, CBE, and of Rachel Kempson, *qv*; *m* 1962, Tony Richardson, *qv* (marr. diss., 1967); two *d*. *Educ:* Queensgate School; Central School of Speech and Drama. Frinton Summer Repertory, 1957; Touch of the Sun, Saville, 1958; Midsummer Night's Dream, Stratford, 1959; Look on Tempests, 1960; The Tiger and the Horse, 1960; Lady from the Sea, 1960; Royal Shakespeare Theatre Company: As You Like It, 1961, Taming of the Shrew, 1961, Cymbeline, 1962; The Seagull, 1964; The Prime of Miss Jean Brodie, Wyndham's, 1966; Daniel Deronda, 1969; Cato Street, 1971; The Threepenny Opera, Prince of Wales, 1972; Twelfth Night, Shaw Theatre, 1972; Antony and Cleopatra, Bankside Globe, 1973; Design for Living, Phoenix, 1973; Macbeth, LA, 1974; Lady from the Sea, NY, 1976, Roundhouse, 1979; The Aspern Papers, Haymarket, 1984; The Seagull, Queen's, 1985; Chekhov's Women, Lyric, 1985; The Taming of the Shrew and Antony and Cleopatra, Haymarket, 1986. *Films:* Morgan-A Suitable Case for Treatment, 1966 (Cannes Fest. Award, Best Actress 1966); The Sailor from Gibraltar, 1967; Blow-Up, 1967; Camelot, 1967; Red White and Zero, 1967; Charge of the Light Brigade, 1968; Isadora, 1968; A Quiet Place in the Country, 1968; The Seagull, 1969; Drop-Out, 1970; La Vacanza, 1970; The Trojan Women, 1971; The Devils, 1971; Mary, Queen of Scots, 1972; Murder on the Orient Express, 1974; Out of Season, 1975; Seven Per Cent Solution, 1975; Julia, 1976 (Academy Award, 1977; Golden Globe Award); Agatha, 1978; Yanks, 1978; Bear Island, 1978; Playing for Time, 1980; My Body, My Child, 1981; Wagner, 1983; The Bostonians, 1984; Wetherby, 1985; Steaming, 1985. Has appeared on TV. *Publication:* Pussies and Tigers (anthology of writings of school children), 1963.

REDGROVE, Peter William, FRSL; poet; Resident Author, Falmouth School of Art, 1966–83; *b* 2 Jan. 1932; *s* of Gordon James Redgrove and late Nancy Lena Cestrilli-Bell; *m* Penelope Shuttle, *qv*; one *d*; (two *s* one *d* by former marr.). *Educ:* Taunton Sch.; Queens' Coll., Cambridge. Scientific journalist and copywriter, 1954–61; Visiting Poet, Buffalo Univ., NY, 1961–62; Gregory Fellow in Poetry, Leeds Univ., 1962–65; study with John Layard, 1968–69. O'Connor Prof. of Literature, Colgate Univ., NY, 1974–75; Leverhulme Emeritus Fellow, 1985–87. George Rylands' Verse-speaking Prize, 1954; Fulbright Award, 1961; Poetry Book Society Choices, 1961, 1966, 1979, 1981; Arts Council Awards, 1969, 1970, 1973, 1975, 1977, 1982; Guardian Fiction Prize, 1973; Prudence Farmer Poetry Award, 1977; Cholmondeley Award, 1985. FRSL 1982. *Publications: poetry:* The Collector, 1960; The Nature of Cold Weather, 1961; At the White Monument, 1963; The Force, 1966; Penguin Modern Poets 11, 1968; Work in Progress, 1969; Dr Faust's Sea-Spiral Spirit, 1972; Three Pieces for Voices, 1972; The Hermaphrodite Album (with Penelope Shuttle), 1973; Sons of My Skin: Selected Poems, 1975; From Every Chink of the Ark, 1977; Ten Poems, 1977; The Weddings at Nether Powers, 1979; The Apple-Broadcast, 1981; The Working of Water, 1984; The Man Named East, 1985; The Mudlark Poems and Grand Buveur, 1986; In the Hall of the Saurians, 1987; New Selected Poems, 1987; *novels:* In the Country of the Skin, 1973; The Terrors of Dr Treviles (with Penelope Shuttle), 1974; The Glass Cottage, 1976; The Sleep of the Great Hypnotist, 1979; The God of Glass, 1979; The Beekeepers, 1980; The Facilitators, 1982; *plays:* Miss Carstairs Dressed for Blooding (play-book containing several dramatic pieces), 1976; (for radio): In the Country of the Skin, 1973; The Holy Sinner, 1975; Dance the Putrefact, 1975; The God of Glass, 1977 (Imperial Tobacco Award 1978); Martyr of the Hives, 1980 (Giles Cooper Award 1981); Florent and the Tuxedo Millions, 1982 (Prix Italia); The Sin-Doctor, 1983; Dracula in White, 1984; The Scientists of the Strange, 1984; Time for the Cat-Scene, 1985; Trelamia, 1986; (for television): The Sermon, 1963; Jack Be Nimble, 1980; *psychology:* The Wise Wound (with Penelope Shuttle), 1978, rev. edn 1986. *Recreations:* work, photography, judo (1st Kyu Judo: Otani and Brit. Judo Assoc.), yoga. *Address:* c/o David Higham Associates, 5–8 Lower John Street, Golden Square, W1R 4HA.

REDHEAD, Brian; Presenter, Today programme, BBC Radio, since 1975; *b* 28 Dec. 1929; *s* of Leonard Redhead and Janet Fairley; *m* 1954, Jean, (Jenni), Salmon; two *s* one *d* (and one *s* decd). *Educ:* Royal Grammar Sch., Newcastle upon Tyne; Downing Coll., Cambridge. Northern Editor, The Guardian, 1965–69; Editor, Manchester Evening News, 1969–75. Dir, World Wide Pictures, 1980–. *Address:* 171 Shakespeare Tower, Barbican, EC2Y 8DR. *T:* 01–638 5111. *Club:* Savage.

REDMAN, Maj.-Gen. Denis Arthur Kay, CB 1963; OBE 1942; retired; Colonel Commandant, REME, 1963–68; Director, Electrical and Mechanical Engineering, War Office, 1960–63; *b* 8 April 1910; *s* of late Brig. A. S. Redman, CB; *m* 1943, Penelope, *d* of A. S. Kay; one *s* one *d*. *Educ:* Wellington Coll.; London Univ. BSc (Eng) 1st class Hons (London); FCGI, MIMechE, AMIEE. Commissioned in RAOC, 1934; served in Middle East, 1936–43; transferred to REME, 1942; Temp. Brig., 1944; DDME 1st Corps, 1951; Comdt REME Training Centre 1957–59. Graduate of Staff Coll., Joint Services Staff Coll. and Imperial Defence Coll. *Recreations:* normal. *Club:* Army and Navy.

REDMAN, Maurice; Chairman, Scottish Region, British Gas Corporation, 1974–82 (Deputy Chairman, 1970–74); *b* 30 Aug. 1922; *s* of Herbert Redman and Olive (*née* Dyson); *m* 1960, Dorothy (*née* Appleton); two *d*. *Educ:* Hulme Grammar Sch., Oldham; Manchester Univ. BSc(Tech), 1st cl. Hons. Joined staff of Co. Borough of Oldham Gas Dept, 1943; Asst, later Dep. Production Engr, North Western Gas Bd, 1951; Chief Develt Engr, NW Gas Bd, 1957; Chief Engr, Southern Gas Bd, 1966; Dir of Engrg, Southern Gas Bd, 1970. Mem., Internat. Gas Union Cttee on Manufactured Gases, 1961–82. *Publications:* papers to Instn of Gas Engrs, Inst. of Fuel, various overseas conferences, etc. *Recreations:* gardening, music, photography. *Address:* Avington, 3 Cramond Regis, Edinburgh EH4 6LW. *T:* 031–336 6178. *Club:* New (Edinburgh).

REDMAN, Sydney, CB 1961; *b* 12 Feb. 1914; *s* of John Barritt Redman and Ann Meech; *m* 1939, Barbara Mary Grey; one *s* two *d*. *Educ*. Manchester Gram. Sch.; Corpus Christi

Coll., Oxford. Asst Principal, WO, 1936; Principal Private Sec. to Secretary of State for War, 1942–44; Asst Under-Sec. of State: War Office, 1957–63; Ministry of Defence, 1963–64; Dep. Under-Sec. of State, MoD, 1964–73. Dir-Gen., Timber Trade Fedn, 1973–82. *Address:* Littlehurst, Birch Avenue, Haywards Heath, West Sussex. *T:* Haywards Heath 413738.

REDMAYNE, Clive; aeronautical engineering consultant; *b* 27 July 1927; *s* of late Procter Hubert Redmayne and Emma (*née* Torkington) *m* 1952, Vera Muriel, *d* of late Wilfred Toplis and Elsie Maud Toplis; one *s* one *d*. *Educ:* Stockport Sch. BSc (Hons Maths) London External. CEng, MIMechE; FRAeS. Fairey Aviation Co.: apprentice, 1944–48; Stress Office, 1948–50; English Electric Co., Warton: Stress Office, 1950–51; A. V. Roe & Co., Chadderton: Stress Office, 1951–55; A. V. Roe & Co., Weapons Research Div., Woodford: Head of Structural Analysis, 1955–62; Structures Dept, RAE, 1962–67; Asst Director, Project Time and Cost Analysis, Min. of Technology, 1967–70; Sen. Officers' War Course, RNC, Greenwich, 1970; Asst Dir, MRCA, MoD(PE), 1970–74; Division Leader, Systems Engrg, NATO MRCA Management Agency (NAMMA), Munich, 1974–76; Chief Supt, A&AEE, Boscombe Down, 1976–78; Dir, Harrier Projects, MoD(PE), 1978–80; Director General, Future Projects, MoD(PE), 1980–81; Dir Gen. Aircraft 3, Procurement Exec., MoD, 1981–84. *Recreations:* reading, chess, ski-ing, squash, sailing, caravanning. *Address:* Pennycot, 47 Old Bisley Road, Frimley, Camberley, Surrey GU16 5RE. *T:* Camberley 21610. *Clubs:* Civil Service, Caravan.

REDMAYNE, Hon. Sir Nicholas (John), 2nd Bt *cr* 1964; Director, Kleinwort, Grieveson and Co., stockbrokers; *b* 1 Feb. 1938; *s* of Baron Redmayne, DSO, PC (Life Peer) and Anne (*d* 1982), *d* of John Griffiths; *S* to baronetcy of father, 1983; *m* 1st, 1963, Ann Saunders (marr. diss. 1976; she *d* 1985); one *s* one *d*; 2nd, 1978, Christine Diane Wood Hewitt (*née* Fazakerley); two step *s*. *Educ:* Radley College; RMA Sandhurst. Grenadier Guards, 1957–62. *Recreations:* shooting, skiing. *Heir:* *s* Giles Martin Redmayne, *b* 1 Dec. 1968. *Address:* Walcote Lodge, Walcote, Lutterworth, Leics.

REDMOND, Sir James, Kt 1979; FEng, FIEE; Director of Engineering, BBC, 1968–78; *b* 8 Nov. 1918; *s* of Patrick and Marion Redmond; *m* 1942, Joan Morris; one *s* one *d*. *Educ:* Graeme High Sch., Falkirk. Radio Officer, Merchant Navy, 1935–37 and 1939–45; BBC Television, Alexandra Palace, 1937–39; BBC: Installation Engr, 1949; Supt Engr Television Recording, 1960; Sen. Supt Engr TV, 1963; Asst Dir of Engrg, 1967. Pres., Soc. of Electronic and Radio Technicians, 1970–75; Pres., IEE, 1978–79. Mem. Bd, Services Sound and Vision Corporation, 1983–. Member: Council, Brunel Univ., 1980–; Council, Open Univ., 1981–. *Recreation:* golf. *Address:* 43 Cholmeley Crescent, Highgate, N6. *T:* 01-340 1611. *Club:* Athenæum.

REDMOND, Martin; MP (Lab) Don Valley, since 1983; *b* 15 Aug. 1937. *Educ:* Woodlands RC Sch.; Sheffield Univ. Mem., Doncaster Borough Council, 1975–; Chm. of Labour Gp and Leader of Council, 1982–. Vice-Chm., Doncaster AHA. Mem., NUM. *Address:* House of Commons, SW1A 0AA.

REDMOND, Robert Spencer, TD 1953; Director and Chief Executive, National Federation of Clay Industries, 1976–84; *b* 10 Sept. 1919; *m* 1949, Marjorie Helen Heyes; one *s*. *Educ:* Liverpool Coll. Served War, Army, 1939–46: commissioned The Liverpool Scottish, 1938; transferred, RASC, 1941; Middle East, Junior Staff Sch., 1943; DAQMG, HQ Special Ops (Mediterranean), 1943–45; released, rank of Major, 1946. Conservative Agent, 1947–56 (Wigan, 1947–49, Knutsford, 1949–56). Managing Dir, Heyes & Co. Ltd, Wigan, 1956–66; Ashley Associates Ltd: Commercial Manager, 1966–69; Managing Dir, 1969–70; Dir, 1970–72. Dir, Manchester Chamber of Commerce, 1969–74. MP (C) Bolton West, 1970–Sept. 1974; Vice-Chm., Cons. Parly Employment Cttee, 1972–74 (Sec., 1971–72). Pres., Alderley Edge British Legion, 1968–76; Chm. (and Founder), NW Export Club, 1958–60. *Address:* 194 Grove Park, Knutsford, Cheshire WA16 8QE. *T:* Knutsford 2657. *Club:* Army and Navy.

REDPATH, John Thomas, CB 1969; MBE 1944; FRIBA; architect in private practice, since 1977; *b* 24 Jan. 1915; *m* 1st, 1939, Kate (*née* Francis) (*d* 1949); one *d*; 2nd, 1949, Claesina (*née* van der Vlerk); three *s* one *d*. *Educ:* Price's Sch.; Southern Coll. of Art. Served with RE, 1940–47. Asst Architect: Kent CC, 1936–38; Oxford City Coun., 1938–40; Princ. Asst Architect, Herts, CC, 1948–55; Dep. County Architect, Somerset CC, 1955–59; Chief Architect (Abroad), War Office, 1959–63; MPBW later DoE: Dir of Development, 1963–67; Dir Gen. of Research and Development, 1967–71; Dir Gen. of Develt, 1971–72; Dep. Ch. Exec., Property Services Agency, 1972–75; Man. Dir, Millbank Technical Services Educn Ltd, 1975–77. *Publications:* various articles in architectural jls. *Recreation:* golf. *Address:* Pines Edge, Sandy Lane, Cobham, Surrey. *Club:* Arts.

REDSHAW, Sir Leonard, Kt 1972; FEng 1976; FRINA; industrial consultant; Member, Safety Committee, Pacific Nuclear Transport Ltd (BNFL), since 1978; *b* 15 April 1911; *s* of late Joseph Stanley Redshaw, Naval Architect; *m* 1939, Joan Mary, *d* of Wm White, London; one *s* one *d*. *Educ:* Barrow Grammar Sch.; Univ. of Liverpool. 1st cl. Hons degree in naval architecture; 1851 Exhibn Royal Comr's post grad. Schol., Master's degree. Joined the Management Staff of Vickers-Armstrongs, 1936; Asst to Shipbuilding Manager, 1950; Special Dir, 1953; when Vickers-Armstrongs (Shipbuilders) Ltd was formed he was apptd Shipbuilding Gen. Man. of Yards at Barrow-in-Furness and Newcastle, 1955; Dir, Vickers-Armstrongs (Shipbuilders) Ltd, 1956, Deputy Managing Director, 1961; Builders' Chief Polaris Exec., 1963; Man. Dir, Vickers Ltd Shipbuilding Group, 1964; Special Dir, Vickers Ltd, 1965; Dir, 1967, Asst Man. Dir, 1967–76; Chairman: Vickers Ltd Shipbuilding Group, 1967–76; Vickers Oceanics Ltd, 1972–78; Vickers Offshore Engineering Group, 1975–78; Slingsby Sailplanes, 1969–77; Brown Brothers & Co. Ltd, 1973–77; Director: Rolls Royce & Associates, Ltd, 1966–77; Shipbuilding Corp. Ltd, 1970–77; Brown Bros & Co. Ltd, 1970–77; Cockatoo Docks & Eng. Co. Pty Ltd, 1972–76; Fillite (Runcorn) Ltd, 1971–85; Silica Fillers Ltd, 1971–85. Jt Chm., Technical Cttee, Lloyd's Register of Shipping, 1972–81; Mem., Lloyd's Gen. Cttee, 1972–81. Mem., Nat. Defence Industries Council, 1971–76; Chairman: Assoc. W European Shipbuilders, 1972–73; Warshipbuilders Cttee; President: Shipbuilders and Repairers Nat. Assoc., 1971–72; Inst. of Welding, 1963–65 (Mem. Council); Welding Institute, 1977–79. Hon. FWeldI. John Smeaton Medal, CEI, 1977; William Froude Medal, RINA, 1977. *Publications:* British Shipbuilding-Welding, 1947; Application of Welding to Ship Construction, 1962. *Recreations:* gliding, fishing, farming. *Address:* Netherclose, Ireleth, Askam-in-Furness, Cumbria LA16 7EZ. *T:* Dalton-in-Furness 62529.

REDSHAW, Emeritus Prof. Seymour Cunningham, DSc (Wales), PhD (London), FICE, FIStructE, FRAeS; Beale Professor and Head of Civil Engineering Department, University of Birmingham, 1950–69; Dean of Faculty of Science, 1955–57; Member of Aeronautical Research Council, 1955; a Governor of Coll. of Aeronautics, 1951–69; *b* 20 March 1906; *s* of Walter James Redshaw and Edith Marion Cunningham; *m* 1935, Mary Elizabeth Jarrold; three *s*. *Educ:* Blundell's School; University of Wales. Technical Assistant, Bristol Aeroplane Co. Ltd, 1927–31; Asst Designer General Aircraft Ltd, 1931–32; Member of Staff: Imperial College, London, 1933–35; Building Research Station, 1936–40; Boulton Paul Aircraft Ltd, 1940–50: Chief Engineer, 1945; Director, 1949. Mem. Adv. Cttee on Building Research, 1965–67; Mem. Council, Univ. of Aston, 1966–67; Chm., Acad. Adv. Cttee, and Mem. Council, Univ. of Bath, 1966. Hon. DSc: Bath, 1966; Cranfield, 1976. *Publications:* numerous papers in scientific and engineering journals. *Address:* 22 Newport Street, Brewood, Staffs. *T:* Brewood 850274.

REDWOOD, John Alan, DPhil; Investment Manager and Director, N. M. Rothschild & Sons, since 1977; Joint Deputy Chairman, since 1986, and Director, Norcros PLC; *b* 15 June 1951; *s* of William Charles Redwood and Amy Emma Redwood (*née* Champion); *m* 1974, Gail Felicity Chippington; one *s* one *d*. *Educ:* Kent Coll., Canterbury; Magdalen and St Antony's Colls, Oxford. MA, DPhil Oxon. Fellow, All Souls Coll., 1972. Investment Adviser, Robert Fleming & Co., 1973–77. Adviser, Treasury and Civil Service Select Cttee, 1981; Head of PM's Policy Unit, 1984–85. Councillor, Oxfordshire CC, 1973–77. Prosp. Party Cand. (C) Wokingham, 1985–. Governor of various schools, 1974–83. *Publications:* Reason, Ridicule and Religion, 1976; Public Enterprise in Crisis, 1980; (with John Hatch) Value for Money Audits, 1981; (with John Hatch) Controlling Public Industries, 1982; Going for Broke, 1984; Equity for Everyman, 1986. *Recreations:* water sports, village cricket. *Address:* 506 Queens Quay, Upper Thames Street, EC4V 3EH. *T:* 01-248 6777.

REDWOOD, Sir Peter (Boverton), 3rd Bt *cr* 1911; Colonel, late King's Own Scottish Borderers; *b* 1 Dec. 1937; *o s* of Sir Thomas Boverton Redwood, 2nd Bt, TD, and of Ruth Mary Redwood (*née* Creighton, now Blair); *S* father, 1974; *m* 1964, Gilian, *o d* of John Lee Waddington Wood, Limuru, Kenya; three *d*. *Educ:* Gordonstoun. National Service, 1956–58, 2nd Lieut, Seaforth Highlanders; regular commn, KOSB, 1959; served in UK (despatches 1972), BAOR, Netherlands, ME, Africa and Far East; Staff Coll., Camberley, 1970; Nat. Defence Coll., Latimer, 1978–79. Mem., Queen's Body Guard for Scotland (Royal Co. of Archers). Liveryman, Goldsmiths' Co. *Heir:* *half-b* Robert Boverton Redwood [*b* 24 June 1953; *m* 1978, Mary Elizabeth Wright; one *s* one *d*]. *Address:* c/o National Westminster Bank, Thames House, Millbank, SW1. *Club:* Army and Navy.

REECE, Dr Charles Hugh; Research and Technology Director, Imperial Chemical Industries, since 1979; *b* 2 Jan. 1927; *s* of Charles Hugh Reece and Helen Youlle; *m* 1951, Betty Linford; two *d*. *Educ:* Pocklington Sch., E Riding; Huddersfield Coll.; Leeds Univ. (PhD, BSc Hons). FRSC. ICI: joined Dyestuffs Div., 1949; Head of Medicinal Process Develt Dept, Dyestuffs Div., 1959; Manager, Works R&D Dept, 1965; Jt Research Manager, Mond Div., 1967; Dir, R&D, Mond Div., 1969; Dep. Chm., Mond Div., 1972; Chm., Plant Protection Div., 1975. Dir, Finnish Chemicals, 1971–75; Chm., Teijin Agricultural Chemicals, 1975–78; Non-Exec. Dir, APV Holdings, 1984–. Chm., Univ. of Surrey Robens Inst. of Indust. and Envtl Health and Safety Cttee, 1985; Member: Adv. Council for Applied R&D, 1983–; Adv. Cttee on Industry, Cttee of Vice-Chancellors and Principals, 1983–; Council, RSC, 1985–; Council, SERC, 1985–; Council, Royal Instn of GB, 1985–; SCI; Parly and Sci. Cttee, 1979– (Vice-Chm., 1986–). Hon. DSc St Andrews, 1986. *Publications:* reports and papers in learned jls. *Recreations:* Sailing, gardening. *Address:* ICI plc, Imperial Chemical House, Millbank, SW1P 3JF. *T:* 01-834 4444.

REECE, Courtenay Walton; Puisne Judge, Hong Kong, 1952–61, retired; *b* 4 Dec. 1899; 3rd *s* of H. Walter Reece, KC (Barbados); *m* 1927, Rosa U. E. Parker (*d* 1956); two *d*. *Educ:* Harrison College and Codrington College, Barbados; Jesus College, Oxford (BA). Called to Bar, Middle Temple, 1925; Police Magistrate, Barbados, 1926; Registrar, Barbados, 1931; Magistrate, Nigeria, 1938; Crown Counsel, Nigeria, 1939; Senior Crown Counsel, Nigeria, 1946; Puisne Judge, Nigeria, 1949. *Recreations:* motor-boating, swimming, carpentry, fishing. *Address:* 108 Macdonnell Road, 7th Floor, Hong Kong. *T:* 5-231705.

REECE, (Edward Vans) Paynter; His Honour Judge Paynter Reece; a Circuit Judge, since 1982; *b* 17 May 1936; *s* of Clifford Mansel Reece and Catherine Barbara Reece (*née* Hathorn); *m* 1967, Rosamund Mary Reece (*née* Roberts); three *s* one *d*. *Educ:* Blundell's Sch.; Magdalene Coll., Cambridge (MA). Called to the Bar, Inner Temple, 1960; a Recorder of the Crown Court, 1980–82. *Recreation:* fishing. *Address:* 2 Harcourt Buildings, Temple, EC4Y 9DB.

REECE, Paynter; *see* Reece, E. V. P.

REED, Adrian Harbottle, CMG 1981; HM Diplomatic Service, retired; Consul-General, Munich, 1973–80; *b* 5 Jan. 1921; *s* of Harbottle Reed, MBE, FRIBA, and Winifred Reed (*née* Rowland); *m* 1st, 1947, Doris Davidson Duthie (marr. diss. 1975); one *s* one *d*; 2nd, 1975, Maria-Louise, *d* of Dr and Mrs A. J. Boekelman, Zeist, Netherlands. *Educ:* Hele's Sch., Exeter; Emmanuel Coll., Cambridge. Royal Artillery, 1941–47. India Office, 1947; Commonwealth Relations Office, 1947; served in UK High Commission: Pakistan, 1948–50; Fedn of Rhodesia and Nyasaland, 1953–56; British Embassy, Dublin, 1960–62; Commonwealth Office, 1962–68; Counsellor (Commercial), and Consul-Gen., Helsinki, 1968–70; Economic Counsellor, Pretoria, 1971–73. Bavarian Order of Merit, 1980. *Recreations:* maritime history, the English countryside. *Address:* Old Bridge House, Uffculme, Cullompton, Devon. *T:* Craddock 40595.

REED, Air Cdre April Anne, RRC 1981; Director of RAF Nursing Services, 1984–85, retired; *b* 25 Jan. 1930; *d* of Captain Basil Duck Reed, RN, and Nancy Mignon Ethel Reed. *Educ:* Channing Sch., Highgate. SRN, SCM. SRN training, Middlesex Hosp., 1948–52; midwifery training, Royal Maternity Hosp., Belfast, 1953; joined Royal Air Force, 1954; Dep. Matron, 1970; Sen. Matron, 1976; Principal Matron, 1981; Matron in Chief (Director), 1984. *Recreations:* sailing, ornithology, antiques, gardening, interest in oriental carpets. *Address:* 3 Edieham Cottages, Angle Lane, Shepreth, Royston, Herts SG8 6QJ. *T:* Royston 61329. *Club:* Royal Air Force.

REED, David; Director of Communications, Hewlett-Packard, since 1975; *b* 24 April 1945; *s* of Wilfred Reed and Elsie Swindon; *m* 1973, Susan Garrett, MA Oxon, MScEcon. *Educ:* West Hartlepool Grammar Sch. Journalist: Northern Echo, 1963–64; Imperial Chemical Industries, 1964–65; Public Relations Officer: NE Development Council, 1966–68; Vickers Ltd, 1968–70. MP (Lab) Sedgefield, Co. Durham, 1970–Feb. 1974. *Publications:* many articles in national newspapers and other jls, on regional and consumer affairs. *Recreations:* many and varied. *Address:* 34 St Andrews Road, Henley-on-Thames, Oxon RG9 1JB. *T:* Henley 3777.

REED, Edward John; Clerk to the Clothworkers' Company of the City of London, 1963–78; *b* 2 Sept. 1913; *o c* of late Edward Reed; *m* 1939, Rita Isabel Venus Cheston-Porter; one *s* one *d*. *Educ:* St Paul's School. Admitted Solicitor, 1938. Territorial Service with HAC; commnd 1940; served BEF and BAOR with 63 (WR) Medium Regt RA; Capt. 1942. Clerk to Governors of Mary Datchelor Girls' Sch., 1963–78. Vice Pres., Metropolitan Soc. for the Blind, 1979– (Chm., 1965–79); Chm., Indigent Blind Visiting Society, 1965–79; Vice-Pres., N London District, St John Ambulance, 1969–81. Chm., City Side, Joint Grand Gresham Cttee, 1984. Member: Court of Common Council, City of London, for Tower Ward, 1978–86; Lloyds, 1979–. Clothworkers' Co.: Liveryman, 1964; Sen. Warden, 1981; Mem., Ct of Assistants, 1982–. Governor: Christ's Hosp., 1981–; City of London Freemen's Sch., 1982–. Hon. MA Leeds, 1979. CStJ 1968.

Chevalier, Order of Leopold with Palm, and Croix de Guerre with Palm, Belgium, 1944. *Recreations:* sailing, photography. *Address:* 54 Hillcrest Gardens, Hinchley Wood, Esher, Surrey KT10 0BX. *T:* 01–398 3984. *Club:* City Livery.

REED, Henry; poet, radio-dramatist, translator; *b* 22 Feb. 1914; *s* of late Henry Reed and late Mary Ann Ball; unmarried. *Educ:* King Edward VI Sch., Aston, Birmingham; Birmingham Univ. (BA 1st cl. Hons Lang. and Lit., 1934; Charles Grant Robertson Scholar, 1934; MA 1936). From then on, verse and journalism. Taught for a year before call-up in 1941; served (or rather *studied*) in Army, 1941–42; transf. to Naval Intelligence, FO, 1942–45; released VJ day, 1945; recalled to Army, 1945; did not go, 1945; matter silently dropped, 1945. During war continued to write and publish verse and book-reviews; began occasional broadcasting; began writing radio-plays, 1946 (Premio della Radio Italiana, 1953), and doing much translation from Italian and French. Academic appts at Univ. of Washington, Seattle: Vis. Prof. of Poetry, winter quarter 1964; Asst Prof. of English, 1965–66; Vis. Prof. of Poetry, winter quarter 1967. Pye gold award (Soc. of Authors), 1979. *Publications:* A Map of Verona (poems), 1946, enl. edn NY 1948; Moby Dick (radio-version in prose and verse of Melville's novel), 1947; The Novel since 1939 (British Council booklet), 1947; The Lessons of the War (poems), 1970; Hilda Tablet and others, 1971; The Streets of Pompeii and other plays for radio, 1971. Numerous published translations include: Paride Rombi: Perdu and his Father (novel), 1954; Ugo Betti: Three Plays (with foreword), 1956, NY 1958; Ugo Betti: Crime on Goat Island, 1961 (staged NY 1960); Dino Buzzati: Larger than Life (novel), 1962; Balzac: Père Goriot, NY 1962; Balzac: Eugénie Grandet, NY 1964; Natalia Ginzburg: The Advertisement (play), 1969 (Nat. Theatre 1969). *Address:* c/o Messrs Jonathan Cape Ltd, 32 Bedford Square, WC1. *Club:* Savile.

REED, Jane Barbara; Managing Editor, Today, since 1986; 2nd *d* of William and late Gwendoline Reed, Letchworth, Herts. *Educ:* Royal Masonic Sch.; sundry further educational establishments. Worked on numerous magazines; returned to Woman's Own, 1965; Editor, 1970–79; Publisher, IPC Women's Monthly Group, 1979–81; Editor-in-Chief, Woman magazine, 1981–82; IPC Magazines: Asst Man. Dir, Specialist Educn and Leisure Gp, 1983; Man. Dir, Holborn Publishing Gp, 1983–85; News (UK) Ltd, 1985–. Chairman: Editorial Cttee, Fédération International de la Presse Périodique, 1979–85; Publicity Cttee, Birthright, 1979–. *Publications:* Girl About Town, 1964; (jtly) Kitchen Sink—or Swim?, 1982. *Address:* Allen House, 70 Vauxhall Bridge Road, SW1.

REED, Laurance Douglas; *b* 4 Dec. 1937; *s* of Douglas Austin Reed and late Mary Ellen Reed (*née* Philpott). *Educ:* Gresham's Sch., Holt; University Coll., Oxford (MA). Nat. Service, RN, 1956–58; worked and studied on Continent (Brussels, Bruges, Leyden, Luxembourg, Strasbourg, Paris, Rome, Bologna, Geneva), 1963–66; Public Sector Research Unit, 1967–69. MP (C) Bolton East, 1970–Feb. 1974; PPS to Chancellor of Duchy of Lancaster, 1973–74. Jt Sec., Parly and Scientific Cttee, 1971–74; Member: Soc. for Underwater Technology; Select Cttee on Science and Technology, 1971–74. *Publications:* Europe in a Shrinking World, 1967; An Ocean of Waste, 1972; Political Consequences of North Sea Oil, 1973. *Recreations:* gardening, painting. *Address:* Water-Flag House, Isle of Soay, Inverness-shire. *T:* Soay 4. *Club:* Carlton.

REED, Leslie Edwin, PhD; CEng, MIMechE, FInstE; Chief Industrial Air Pollution Inspector, Health and Safety Executive, 1981–85; *b* 6 Feb. 1925; *s* of Edwin George and Maud Gladys Reed; *m* 1947, Ruby; two *s*. *Educ:* Sir George Monoux Grammar Sch., Walthamstow; University Coll. London (BScEng, MScEng, PhD). Engineering Officer, RNVR, 1945–47; Fuel Research Station, 1950–58; Warren Spring Laboratory, 1958–70; Central Unit on Environmental Pollution, DoE, 1970–79; Head, Air and Noise Div., DoE, 1979–81. *Address:* 20 Deards Wood, Knebworth, Herts SG3 6PG. *T:* Stevenage 813272.

REED, Sir Nigel (Vernon), Kt 1970; CBE 1967 (MBE (mil.) 1945); TD 1950; Chief Justice of the Northern States of Nigeria, 1968–75; *b* 31 Oct. 1913; *s* of Vernon Herbert Reed, formerly MP and MLC New Zealand, and of Eila Mabel Reed; *m* 1945, Ellen Elizabeth Langstaff; one *s* two *d*. *Educ:* Wanganui Collegiate School, NZ; Victoria University College, NZ; Jesus College, Cambridge. LLB (NZ) and LLB (Cantab). Called to the Bar, Lincoln's Inn, 1939. Military Service, 1939–45, Lt-Col 1944. Appointed to Colonial Legal Service, 1946; Magistrate, Nigeria, 1946; Chief Magistrate, Nigeria, 1951; Chief Registrar, High Court of the Northern Region of Nigeria, 1955; Judge, High Court of the Northern Region of Nigeria, 1956; Sen. Puisne Judge, High Court of Northern Nigeria, 1964. *Address:* Old Farm Cottage, Corton, Warminster, Wilts.

REED, Oliver; *see* Reed, R. O.

REED, Philip Dunham; Corporation Director; *b* Milwaukee, Wisconsin, 16 Nov. 1899; *s* of William Dennis Reed and Virginia Brandreth Dunham; *m* 1921, Mabel Mayhew Smith (*d* 1984); one *s* one *d*. *Educ:* University of Wisconsin (BS in Electrical Engineering); Fordham Univ. (LLB). Hon. LLD, Union Coll. and Brooklyn Poly. Inst., Hon. DEng Rensslaer Poly. Inst.; Hon. Dr of Commercial Science, New York Univ. 1950; Hon. Dr of Laws, Univ. of Wisconsin, 1950. Swarthmore Coll., 1954. With General Electric Co. (Law Dept), 1926–; Asst to Pres. and Dir, 1937–39; Chm. of Bd, 1940; resigned Chairmanship Dec. 1942 to continue war work in England; re-elected Chm. of Bd, 1945–58; Chm., Finance Cttee, General Electric Co., NY, 1945–59, Director Emeritus, 1968–. Chm. of Board: of Internat. General Electric Company, 1945 until merger with parent co., 1952; Federal Reserve Bank of NY, 1960–65. Director: American Express Co.; American Express Internat. Banking Corp., 1958–72; US Financial, 1970–72; Otis Elevator Company, 1958–72; Kraftco Corp., 1958–70; Scott Paper Co., 1958–66; Metropolitan Life Insurance Co., 1940–73; Tiffany & Co., 1956–81; Bigelow-Sanford Inc., 1959–74; Bankers Trust Co., 1939–58 and 1966–72; Cowles Communications Inc., 1972–83; Cowles Broadcasting Inc., 1983–85; Metropolitan Opera Assoc. Inc., 1945–53; Mem. Business Advisory Council for Dept of Commerce, 1940– (Vice-Chm. 1951–52); US Adv. Commn on Information, 1948–61; Member: Executive Commn, Payroll Savings Adv. Cttee for US Treasury Dept, 1946–56; Dir, Council on Foreign Relations, 1946–69; Trustee: Carnegie Endowment for Internat. Peace, 1945–53; Cttee for Economic Development (and Member Research and Policy Cttee); Member of the Visiting Cttee, Graduate School of Business Admin., Harvard Univ., 1940–60; Director, Ford Foundation Fund for Advancement of Education, 1951–53; Consultant to US Deleg., San Francisco Conf. on World Organization; Chm. US Associates (now US Council), Internat. Chamber of Commerce, 1945–Jan. 1948; mem. Exec. Cttee, US Council, ICC; Hon. Pres. Internat. Chamber of Commerce (Pres., 1949–51); Chm. US Side of Anglo-American Productivity Council, 1948–52; Vice-Chm. Eisenhower Exchange Fellowships, 1953–74; Chm. Finance Cttee, 1955–56. Mem. President's Cttee on Information Activities Abroad, 1960; Mem. Cttee on the Univ. and World Affairs (Ford Foundn), 1960; Trustee of Kress Foundn, 1960–65. Entered War work, 1941, with Office of Production Management, Washington, and its successor the War Production Board (Chief of Bureau of Industry Branches responsible for organising and converting peacetime industries to war production). Went to London, July 1942, as Deputy Chief of Economic Mission headed by W. Averell Harriman; Chief of Mission for Economic Affairs, London, with rank of Minister, Oct. 1943–31 Dec. 1944. Special Ambassador to Mexico, 1958. President's Certificate of Merit Award, 1947; Comdr Légion d'Honneur (France), 1951 (Officer, 1947). *Address:* 375 Park Avenue, New York, NY 10022, USA; (home) Rye, NY. *Clubs:* University, The Links (NY City); Apawamis (Rye, NY); Blind Brook (Purchase, NY); Bohemian (San Francisco); Mill Reef (Antigua, WI).

REED, (Robert) Oliver; actor; *b* 13 Feb. 1938; *s* of Peter and Marcia Reed; one *s* one *d*; *m* 1985, Josephine Burge. *Educ:* Ewel Castle. Films include: Oliver, 1967; Women In Love, 1969; The Devils, 1971; Three Musketeers, 1974; Tommy, 1975; The Prince and the Pauper, 1977; Lion of the Desert, Condorman, 1981; Venom, The Sting II, 1982; Second Chance, 1983; Castaway, 1986. *Publication:* Reed All About Me, 1979. *Recreations:* rugby, racing. *Address:* c/o 314 High Street, Dorking, Surrey. *T:* Dorking 888058.

REED, Stanley William; Director, British Film Institute, 1964–72, Consultant on Regional Development, 1972–76; *b* 21 Jan. 1911; *s* of Sidney James Reed and Ellen Maria Patient; *m* 1937, Alicia Mary Chapman; three *d*. *Educ:* Stratford Grammar Sch.; Coll. of St Mark and St John, Chelsea. Teacher in E London schools, 1931–39. In charge of school evacuation parties, 1939–45. Teacher and Visual Aids Officer, West Ham Education Cttee, 1939–50. British Film Institute: Educn Officer, 1952–56; Sec., 1956–64. *Publications:* The Cinema, 1952; How Films are Made, 1955; A Guide to Good Viewing, 1961. Neighbourhood 15 (film, also Dir). *Recreations:* opera and exploring London's suburbs. *Address:* 54 Felstead Road, Wanstead, E11. *T:* 01–989 6021.

REED, Most Rev. Thomas Thornton, CBE 1980; MA, DLitt, ThD; *b* Eastwood, South Australia, 9 Sept. 1902; *s* of Alfred Ernest Reed, Avoca, Vic; *m* 1932, Audrey Airlie, *d* of Major Harry Lort Spencer Balfour-Ogilvy, MBE, DCM, Tannadice, Renmark, South Australia; two *d* (and one *d* decd). *Educ:* Collegiate Sch. of St Peter, Adelaide; Trinity College, University of Melbourne (Hon. Schol., BA, MA); St Barnabas' Theol. Coll., Adelaide. ThL, ATC, 1st cl. hons. Fred Johns Schol. for Biography, Univ. of Adelaide, 1950. Deacon, 1926; Priest, 1927; Curate, St Augustine's, Unley, 1926–28; Priest in Charge, Berri Mission, 1928–29; Resident Tutor, St Mark's Coll., Univ. of Adelaide, and Area Padre, Toc H, 1929–31; Asst Chaplain, Melbourne Grammar Sch., 1932–36; Rector, St Michael's, Henley Beach, 1936–44; Rector, St Theodore's, Rose Park, 1944–54; Chaplain, Australian Mil. Forces, 1939–57; Chaplain, AIF with HQ, New Guinea Force, 1944–45; Asst Tutor, St Barnabas' Coll., 1940–46; Senior Chaplain, RAAChD, HQ, C Command, South Australia, 1953–56; Editor, Adelaide Church Guardian, 1940–44; Rural Dean, Western Suburbs, 1944; Priest Comr, Adelaide Dio. Centenary, 1947; Canon of Adelaide, 1947–49; Archdeacon of Adelaide, 1949–53; Dean of Adelaide, 1953–57; Bishop of Adelaide, 1957–73; Archbishop of Adelaide, and Metropolitan of S Australia, 1973–75. Pres., Toc H, S Aust., 1960; Pres., St Mark's Coll., Univ. of Adelaide, 1961–74, Hon. Fellow, 1973. Hon. ThD, Australian Coll. of Theology, 1955; DLitt, Univ. of Adelaide, 1954. Chaplain and Sub Prelate of Venerable Order of St John of Jerusalem, 1965. *Publications:* Henry Kendall: A Critical Appreciation, 1960; Sonnets and Songs, 1962; (ed) The Poetical Works of Henry Kendall, 1966; A History of the Cathedral Church of St Peter, Adelaide, 1969; Historic Churches of Australia, 1978. *Recreations:* golf, research on Australian literature, heraldry, and genealogy. *Address:* 44 Jeffcott Street, North Adelaide, SA 5006, Australia. *T:* 2674841; PO Box 130, North Adelaide, SA 5006, Australia. *Clubs:* Adelaide, Naval, Military and Air Force, Royal Adelaide Golf (Adelaide).

REED-PURVIS, Air Vice-Marshal Henry, CB 1982; OBE 1972; Sales Director, British Aerospace Dynamics Group, Stevenage Division, since 1986; *b* 1 July 1928; *s* of late Henry Reed and of Nancy Reed-Purvis; *m* 1951, Isabel Price; three *d*. *Educ:* King James I School, Durham; Durham Univ. BSc Hons 1950. Entered RAF, 1950; various Op. Sqdns, 1951–58; Instr, Jt Nuclear Biological and Chemical Sch., 1958–60; RMCS Shrivenham (Nuclear Sci. and Tech.), 1961; MoD Staff, 1962–64; OC No 63 Sqdn, RAF Regt, Malaya, 1964–66; Exchange Duties, USAF, 1966–69; USAF War Coll., 1969–70; OC No 5 Wing RAF Regt, 1970–72; Gp Capt. Regt, HQ Strike Comd, 1972–74, HQ RAF Germany, 1974–76; ADC to the Queen, 1974–76; Dir, RAF Regt, 1976–79; Comdt Gen. RAF Regt and Dir Gen. of Security (RAF) 1979–83. Dep. Dir Sales, BAe Dynamics Gp, Stevenage Div., 1983–86. *Recreations:* golf, bridge and music. *Address:* Westbury House, Ashwell, Herts SG7 5PH. *T:* Ashwell 2075. *Club:* Royal Air Force.

REEDY, Norris John, (Jack); Regional Officer (Midlands), Independent Broadcasting Authority, since 1983; editorial consultant; *b* 1934; *s* of John Reedy; *m* 1964, Sheila Campbell McGregor; one *d*. *Educ:* Chorlton High Sch., Manchester; Univ. of Sheffield. Sheffield Telegraph, 1956; Sunday Times, 1961; Lancashire Evening Telegraph, 1962; Guardian, 1964; Birmingham Post: Features Editor, 1964; Sen. Asst Editor, 1968; Dep. Editor, 1973; Editor, 1974–82. Mem. Cttee, RTS Midland Centre, 1984–; Dir, Birmingham Press Club Ltd, 1984–; Council Mem., Rotary Club of Birmingham, 1985–. Guild of British Newspaper Editors: Chm., W Midlands Region, 1979–80, Sec. and Councillor, 1980–82; Nat. Vice-Pres., 1981–82. *Recreations:* astronomy, natural history, painting, photography. *Address:* The Old Manor, Rowington, near Warwick. *T:* Lapworth 3129.

REEKIE, Henry Enfield; Headmaster of Felsted School, 1951–68; *b* Hayfield, Derbyshire, 17 Oct. 1907; *s* of John Albert Reekie and Edith Dowson; *m* 1936, Pauline Rosalind, *d* of Eric W. Seeman; one *s* three *d*. *Educ:* Oundle; Clare College, Cambridge. Asst Master, Felsted School, 1929, Housemaster, 1933, Senior Science Master, 1945; Headmaster, St Bees School, 1946. *Recreations:* ski-ing, gardening, travel. *Address:* Tarn House, Mark Cross, Crowborough, East Sussex. *T:* Mayfield 873100. *Club:* East India, Devonshire, Sports and Public Schools.

REES, Anthony John David; Head Master, Blundell's School, Tiverton, Devon, since 1980; *b* 20 July 1943; *s* of Richard Frederick and Betty Rees; *m* 1967, Carol Stubbens; one *s* one *d* (and one *d* decd). *Educ:* Newcastle Royal Grammar Sch.; Clare Coll., Cambridge (Exhibr; BA 2nd Cl. Hons Geog.); PGCE 1966. Head of Economics, Harrow Sch., 1966–80. Established Notting Dale Urban Study Centre, 1972; Vis. Tutor, London Inst. of Education, 1973–. Member Executive Committee: Queen's Silver Jubilee Appeal, 1976–82; and Admin. Council, Royal Jubilee Trusts, 1978–82; Chm., Prince's Trust for Devon, 1981–83; Member: CoSIRA Cttee for Devon, 1981–83; Council, Drake Fellowship, 1981–; Cttee, HMC, 1986; Founder Dir, Mid Devon Enterprise Agency, 1984–; Mem. Bd, Youth Business Initiatives, 1984–; Prince of Wales Community Venture, 1985–; Trustee, Life Educn Centres, 1986–. *Publications:* articles on economics and community service in many jls incl. Economics, Youth in Society, etc. *Recreations:* hill walking, family and friends. *Address:* Blundell's School, Tiverton, Devon. *T:* Tiverton 252543.

REES, Arthur Morgan, CBE 1974 (OBE 1963); QPM 1970; DL; Chairman, St John's Staffordshire, since 1974; *b* 20 Nov. 1912; *s* of Thomas and Jane Rees, The Limes, Llangadog; *m* 1943, Dorothy Webb; one *d*. *Educ:* Llandovery Coll.; St Catharine's Coll., Cambridge. BA 1935, MA 1939. Metropolitan Police, 1935–41; RAF (Pilot), 1941–46 (Subst. Sqdn Ldr; Actg Wing Comdr); Metropolitan Police, 1946–57; Chief Constable: Denbighshire, 1957–64; Staffordshire, 1964–77. Consultant Director: for Wales, Britannia

Building Soc., 1983–; Inter-Globe Security Services Ltd, 1986–. Chm. (Founder), EPIC, ExPolice in Industry and Commerce, 1978–. Life Mem., Midlands Sports Adv. Cttee, 1981; Chm., Queen's Silver Jubilee Appeal (Sport), 1976–; Mem., King George's Jubilee Trust Council, 1973–. Chm., British Karate Fedn, 1982–; Pres., Welsh Karate Fedn. Chm., Staffs St John Ambulance Brigade, 1970. Trustee and Board of Governors, Llandovery College. Founder Pres., Eccleshall Rugby Football Club, 1980–. DL Staffs, 1967. KStJ 1977 (CStJ 1969). *Recreations:* former Rugby International for Wales (14 caps), Cambridge Rugby Blue, 1933 and 1934; Chairman: Crawshays Welsh Rugby XV, 1960–; Welsh Schs Hockey Internat., 1970–. *Address:* The Old Vicarage, Ellenhall, Stafford. *T:* Eccleshall 850789. *Clubs:* Royal Air Force, Hawks (Cambridge) (Vice-Chm. 1985).

REES, Brian, MA Cantab; Headmaster, Rugby School, 1981–84; *b* 20 Aug. 1929; *s* of late Frederick T. Rees; *m* 1959, Julia (*d* 1978), *d* of Sir Robert Birley, KCMG; two *s* three *d*. *Educ:* Bede Grammar Sch., Sunderland; Trinity Coll., Cambridge (Scholar). 1st cl. Historical Tripos, Part I, 1951; Part II, 1952. Eton College: Asst Master, 1952–65; Housemaster, 1963–65; Headmaster: Merchant Taylors' Sch., 1965–73; Charterhouse, 1973–81. Pres., Conference for Independent Further Education, 1973–82; Chm., ISIS, 1982–84. Patron, UC of Buckingham, 1973–; Chm., Tormead Sch. Council. Liveryman, Merchant Taylors' Co., 1981. *Publication:* A Musical Peacemaker: biography of Sir Edward German, 1986. *Recreations:* music, painting. *Address:* 52 Spring Lane, Flore, Northants NN7 4LS. *T:* Weedon 40045. *Club:* Beefsteak.

REES, Prof. Brinley Roderick, MA Oxon; PhD, Hon. LLD Wales; Principal, Saint David's University College, Lampeter, 1975–80; *b* 27 Dec. 1919; *s* of John David Rees and Mary Ann (*née* Roderick); *m* 1951, Zena Muriel Stella Mayall; two *s*. *Educ:* Christ Coll., Brecon; Merton Coll., Oxford (Postmaster). 1st Cl., Class. Hons Mods and Hon. Mention, Craven and Ireland Schols, 1946. Welch Regt, 1940–45. Asst Classics Master, Christ Coll., Brecon, 1947; Cardiff High Sch., 1947–48; Asst Lectr in Classics, University Coll. of Wales Aberystwyth, 1948–49; Lectr 1949–56; Sen. Lectr in Greek, Univ. of Manchester, 1956–58; UC Cardiff: Prof. of Greek, 1958–70; Dean of Faculty of Arts, 1963–65; Dean of Students, 1967–68; Hon. Lectr, 1980–; Prof. Emeritus, 1981; University of Birmingham: Prof. of Greek, 1970–75; Dean of Faculty of Arts, 1973–75; Hon. Life Mem. of Court, 1983. Welsh Supernumerary Fellow, Jesus Coll., Oxford, 1975–76; Leverhulme Emeritus Fellow, 1984–86. Hon. Secretary, Classical Association, 1963–69, Vice-Pres., 1969–78, 1979–, Pres., 1978–79. Hon. LLD Wales, 1981. *Publications:* The Merton Papyri, Vol. II (with H. I. Bell and J. W. B. Barns), 1959; The Use of Greek, 1961; Papyri from Hermopolis and other Byzantine Documents, 1964; (with M. E. Jervis) Lampas: a new approach to Greek, 1970; Classics: an outline for intending students, 1970; Aristotle's Theory and Milton's Practice, 1972; Strength in What Remains, 1980; articles and reviews in various classical and other jls. *Address:* 4 Cranmer Court, Ely Road, Llandaff, Cardiff CF5 2JD. *T:* Cardiff 566037.

REES, Prof. Charles Wayne, DSc; FRS 1974; FRSC; Hofmann Professor of Organic Chemistry, Imperial College, London, since 1978; *b* 15 Oct. 1927; *s* of Percival Charles Rees and Daisy Alice Beck; *m* 1953, Patricia Mary Francis; three *s*. *Educ:* Farnham Grammar Sch.; University Coll., Southampton (BSc, PhD). Lectr in Organic Chem.: Birkbeck Coll., Univ. of London, 1955–57; King's Coll., Univ. of London, 1957–63, Reader, 1963–65; Prof. of Organic Chem., Univ. of Leicester, 1965–69; Prof. of Organic Chem., 1969–77, Heath Harrison Prof. of Organic Chem., 1977–78, Univ. of Liverpool. Visiting Prof., Univ. of Würzburg, 1968; Royal Society of Chemistry (formerly Chemical Society): Tilden Lectr, 1973–74; Award in Heterocyclic Chem., 1980; Pres., Perkin Div., 1981–83; Pedler Lectr, 1984–85. Pres., Chemistry Sect., BAAS, 1984. *Publications:* Organic Reaction Mechanism (8 annual vols), 1965–72; Carbenes, Nitrenes, Arynes, 1969; (ed jtly) Comprehensive Heterocyclic Chemistry (8 vols), 1984; about 300 research papers and reviews, mostly in jls of Chemical Soc. *Recreations:* music, wine. *Address:* Department of Chemistry, Imperial College of Science and Technology, South Kensington, SW7 2AY. *T:* 01-589 5111.

REES, Sir (Charles William) Stanley, Kt 1962; TD 1949; DL; Judge of High Court of Justice, Family Division (formerly Probate, Divorce and Admiralty Division), 1962–77; *b* 30 Nov. 1907; *s* of Dr David Charles Rees, MRCS, LRCP, and Myrtle May (*née* Dolley); *m* 1934, Jean Isabel Munro Wheildon (*d* 1985); one *s*. *Educ:* St Andrew's College, Grahamstown, S Africa; University College, Oxford. BA, BCL (Oxon). Called to the Bar, 1931; Bencher, Inner Temple, 1962. 2nd Lt 99th Regt AA RA (London Welsh), 1939; JAG's office in Home Commands, 1940–43; Lt-Col in charge JAG's Branch, HQ Palestine Command, 1944–45; released from military service as Hon. Lt-Col, 1945. QC 1957; Recorder of Croydon, 1961–62; Commissioner of Assize, Stafford, Dec. 1961; Dep. Chm., 1959–64, Chm., 1964–71, E Sussex QS. DL E Sussex (formerly Sussex), 1968. Chm., Statutory Cttee, Pharmaceutical Soc. of GB, 1980–81. Governor, Brighton College, 1954–83 (Pres., 1973–83; Vice Patron, 1983). *Recreations:* walking, gardening. *Address:* Lark Rise, Lyoth Lane, Lindfield, Sussex RH16 2QA. *Clubs:* United Oxford & Cambridge University, Sussex.
See also Harland Rees.

REES, Prof. David, FRS 1968; Emeritus Professor of Pure Mathematics, University of Exeter (Professor, 1958–83); *b* 29 May 1918; *s* of David and Florence Gertrude Rees; *m* 1952, Joan Sybil Cushen; four *d*. *Educ:* King Henry VIII Grammar School, Abergavenny; Sidney Sussex College, Cambridge. Manchester University: Assistant Lecturer, 1945–46, Lecturer, 1946–49; Cambridge University: Lecturer, 1949–58; Fellow of Downing College, Cambridge, 1950–58, Hon. Fellow, 1970–. Mem. Council, Royal Soc., 1979–81. *Publications:* papers on Algebraic topics in British and foreign mathematical journals. *Recreations:* reading and listening to music. *Address:* 6 Hillcrest Park, Exeter EX4 4SH. *T:* Exeter 59398.

REES, Dr David Allan, BSc, PhD, DSc; FRS 1981; FRSC, FIBiol; Director, National Institute for Medical Research, Mill Hill, since 1982; *b* 28 April 1936; *s* of James Allan Rees and Elsie Bolam; *m* 1959, Myfanwy Margaret Parry Owen; two *s* one *d*. *Educ:* Hawarden Grammar Sch., Clwyd; University Coll. of N Wales, Bangor, Gwynedd (BSc 1956; PhD 1959). DSc Edinburgh, 1970. DSIR Res. Fellow, University Coll., Bangor, 1959, and Univ. of Edinburgh, 1960; Asst Lectr in Chem., 1961, Lectr, 1962–70, Univ. of Edinburgh; Section Manager, 1970–72, Principal Scientist, 1972–82, and Sci. Policy Exec., 1978–82, Unilever Res., Colworth Lab.; Chm., Science Policy Gp for Unilever Res., 1979–82. Associate Dir (pt-time), MRC Unit for Cell Biophysics, KCL, 1980–82. Vis. Professorial Fellow, University Coll., Cardiff, 1972–77. Philips Lecture, Royal Soc., 1984. Member: MRC, 1984–; Council, Royal Soc., 1985–. Hon. FRCP 1986. Colworth Medal, Biochemical Soc., 1970; Carbohydrate Award, Chemical Soc., 1970. *Publications:* various, on carbohydrate chem. and biochem. and cell biology. *Recreations:* the countryside, reading, listening to music.

REES, Dame Dorothy (Mary), DBE 1975 (CBE 1964); Member, Central Training Council, 1964–67; *b* 1898; widow. *Educ:* Elementary and Secondary Schools. Formerly: school teacher; Member of Barry Borough Council. Alderman of Glamorgan CC; former Mem. Nat. Advisory Committee for National Insurance; Member: Joint Education Committee for Wales (Chm., Technical Educn Sub-Cttee); Welsh Teaching Hospitals Board. Liaison Officer, Ministry of Food, during War of 1939–45. MP (Lab) Barry Division of Glamorganshire, 1950–51; formerly Parliamentary Private Secretary to the Minister of National Insurance. *Address:* Mor-Hafren, 341 Barry Road, Barry, S Glam.

REES, Dr (Florence) Gwendolen, FRS 1971; FIBiol; a Professor of Zoology, University of Wales, at University College of Wales, Aberystwyth, 1971–73, now Emeritus; *b* 3 July 1906; *yr d* of late E. and E. A. Rees; unmarried. *Educ:* Girls' Grammar Sch., Aberdare; UCW Cardiff. BSc 1927; PhD 1930; DSc 1942. FIBiol 1971. UCW, Aberystwyth: Lectr in Zoology, 1930–46; Sen. Lectr, 1946–66; Reader, 1966–71. Vis. Scientist, Univ. of Ghana, 1961. Research grants from Royal Soc., SRC, Shell Grants Cttee, Nat. Research Council, USA. Hon. Member: Amer. Soc. of Parasitologists, 1975; British Soc. for Parasitology, 1976. *Publications:* numerous papers on parasitology (helminthology) in scientific jls. *Recreations:* riding, amateur dramatics, the arts. *Address:* Grey Mist, North Road, Aberystwyth, Dyfed. *T:* Aberystwyth 612389.

REES, Prof. Garnet; Professor of French, 1957–79, now Emeritus Professor, University of Hull; Pro-Vice-Chancellor, 1972–74; *b* 15 March 1912; *o s* of William Garnet and Mabel Rees; *m* 1941, Dilys, *o d* of Robert and Ellen Hughes; two *d*. *Educ:* Pontardawe Grammar School; University College of Wales, Aberystwyth; University of Paris. BA (Wales), 1934; MA (Wales), 1937; Docteur de l'Université de Paris, 1940; Fellow of Univ. of Wales, 1937–39; Asst Lecturer in French, Univ. Coll., Aberystwyth, 1939–40. Served War of 1939–45, in Roy. Regt of Artillery (Captain, Instructor in Gunnery), 1940–45. Lecturer in French, Univ. of Southampton, 1945–46; Sen. Lecturer in French, Univ. Coll., Swansea, 1946–57. Hon. DLitt Hull, 1979. Officier des Palmes Académiques (France), 1961. Chevalier de la Légion d'Honneur, 1967. *Publications:* Remy de Gourmont, 1940; Guillaume Apollinaire, Alcools, 1975; Baudelaire, Sartre and Camus: lectures and commentaries, 1976; articles on modern French literature and bibliography in learned journals. *Recreations:* gardening and motoring. *Address:* 45 Exeter Gardens, Stamford, Lincs PE9 2RN. *T:* Stamford 63672.

REES, Gwendolen; *see* Rees, F. G.

REES, Harland, MA, MCh, FRCS; Hon. Consultant Urological Surgeon, King's College Hospital; Hon. Consultant Surgeon and Urological Surgeon, Royal Free Hospital; *b* 21 Sept. 1909; *yr s* of Dr David Charles Rees, MRCS, LRCP, and Myrtle May (*née* Dolley); *m* 1950, Helen Marie Tarver; two *s* (one *d* decd). *Educ:* St Andrew's Coll., Grahamstown, S Africa; University Coll., Oxford; Charing Cross Hospital. Rhodes Scholar, Oxford University. Served RAMC, 1942–46; OC Surgical Div. 53, Indian General Hospital. Adviser in Surgery, Siam (Thailand). Examiner in Surgery, University of Cambridge, 1963–73. Chm., S Beds DC, 1986. *Publications:* articles and chapters in various books and journals, 1952–63. *Recreations:* walking, cultivation of trees; Rugby football, Oxford *v* Cambridge, 1932–33. *Address:* Kensworth Gorse, Kensworth, near Dunstable, Beds LU6 3RF. *T:* Whipsnade 872411. *Club:* Vincent's (Oxford).
See also Hon. Sir C. W. S. Rees.

REES, Haydn; *see* Rees, T. M. H.

REES, Prof. Hubert, DFC 1945; PhD, DSc; FRS 1976; Professor of Agricultural Botany, University College of Wales, Aberystwyth, since 1968; *b* 2 Oct. 1923; *s* of Owen Rees and Tugela Rees, Llangennech, Carmarthenshire; *m* 1946, Mavis Hill; two *s* two *d*. *Educ:* Llandovery and Llanelli Grammar Schs; University Coll. of Wales, Aberystwyth (BSc). PhD, DSc Birmingham. Served RAF, 1942–46. Student, Aberystwyth, 1946–50; Lectr in Cytology, Univ. of Birmingham, 1950–58; Sen. Lectr in Agric. Botany, University Coll. of Wales, Aberystwyth, 1958, Reader 1966. *Publications:* Chromosome Genetics, 1977; B Chromosomes, 1982; articles on genetic control of chromosomes and on evolutionary changes in chromosome organisation. *Recreation:* fishing. *Address:* Irfon, Llanbadarn Road, Aberystwyth, Dyfed. *T:* Aberystwyth 3668.

REES, Hugh; *see* Rees, J. E. H.

REES, Hugh Francis E.; *see* Ellis-Rees.

REES, (John Edward) Hugh; Chartered Surveyor; *b* 8 Jan. 1928; *s* of David Emlyn Rees, Swansea; *m* 1961, Gillian Dian Milo-Jones (decd); two *s*. MP (C) Swansea, West Division, Oct. 1959–64; Assistant Government Whip, 1962–64. UK Rep., Econ. and Soc. Cttee, EEC, 1972–78. Dir, Abbey National Building Soc., 1976–; Chm., Abbey Housing Association Ltd., 1980–. Mem., Welsh Develt Agency, 1980–86. Trustee, Ffynone House Sch. Trust, 1977–85. Governor, Nat. Mus. of Wales. FRICS, FRVA. *Address:* Sherwood, 35 Caswell Road, Newton, Mumbles, Swansea, W Glamorgan.

REES, Very Rev. John Ivor; Dean of Bangor, since 1976; Vicar of Cathedral Parish of Bangor, since 1979; *b* 19 Feb. 1926; *o s* of David Morgan Rees and Cecilia Perrott Rees; *m* 1954, Beverley Richards; three *s*. *Educ:* Llanelli Gram. Sch.; University Coll. of Wales (BA 1950); Westcott House, Cambridge. Served RN, Coastal Forces and British Pacific Fleet, 1943–47. Deacon 1952, priest 1953, Dio. St David's; Curate: Fishguard, 1952–55; Llangathen, 1955–57; Priest-in-Charge, Uzmaston, 1957–59; Vicar: Slebech and Uzmaston, 1959–65; Llangollen, 1965–74; Rural Dean of Llangollen, 1970–74; Rector of Wrexham, 1974–76; Canon of St Asaph, 1975–76; Chaplain, Order of St John for County of Clwyd, 1974–76, County of Gwynedd, 1976–. SBStJ 1975, OStJ 1981. *Publication:* Monograph—The Parish of Llangollen and its Churches, 1971. *Recreations:* music and good light reading. *Address:* The Deanery, Bangor, Gwynedd LL57 1LH. *T:* Bangor 351693.

REES, John Samuel; Editor, Western Mail, since 1981; *b* 23 Oct. 1931; *s* of John Richard Rees and Mary Jane Rees; *m* 1957, Ruth Jewell; one *s* one *d*. *Educ:* Cyfarthfa Castle Grammar Sch., Merthyr Tydfil. Nat. Service, Welch Regt and RAEC, 1950–52. Reporter, 1948–50, Sports Editor, 1952–54, Merthyr Express; The Star, Sheffield: Reporter, 1954–56; Sub Editor, 1956–58; Dep. Chief Sub Editor, 1958–59; Dep. Sports Editor, 1959–61; Asst Editor, 1961–66; Dep. Editor, Evening Echo, Hemel Hempstead, 1966–69; Editor: Evening Mail, Slough and Hounslow, 1969–72; The Journal, Newcastle upon Tyne, 1972–76; Evening Post-Echo, Hemel Hempstead, 1976–79, Asst Man. Dir, Evening Post-Echo Ltd, 1979–81. *Recreations:* marquetry, watching cricket and rugby, walking, gardening. *Address:* Timbertops, St Andrew's Road, Dinas Powys, S Glam CF6 4HB. *T:* Cardiff 513254.

REES, Rt. Rev. Leslie Lloyd; *b* 14 April 1919; *s* of Rees Thomas and Elizabeth Rees; *m* 1944, Rosamond Smith; two *s*. *Educ:* Pontardawe Grammar Sch.; Kelham Theological College. Asst Curate, St Saviour, Roath, 1942; Asst Chaplain, HM Prison, Cardiff, 1942; Chaplain, HM Prison; Durham, 1945; Dartmoor, 1948; Vicar of Princetown, 1948; Chaplain, HM Prison, Winchester, 1955; Chaplain General of Prisons, Home Office Prison Dept, 1962–80; Bishop Suffragan of Shrewsbury, 1980–86. Chaplain to the Queen, 1971–80. Hon. Canon of Canterbury, 1966–80, of Lichfield, 1980–. Freeman, City of London. ChStJ. *Recreations:* music, brass bands. *Address:* Kingfisher Lodge, Arle Gardens, Alresford, Hants.

REES, Linford; *see* Rees, W. L. L.

REES, Llewellyn; *see* Rees, (Walter) L.

REES, Prof. Martin John, FRS 1979; Plumian Professor of Astronomy and Experimental Philosophy, Cambridge University, since 1973; Director, Institute of Astronomy, Cambridge, 1977–82 and since 1987; Fellow of King's College, since 1973 (and 1969–72); Regents Fellow of Smithsonian Institution, Washington, since 1984; *b* 23 June 1942; *s* of Reginald J. and Joan Rees; *m* 1986, Dr Caroline Humphrey, *d* of late Prof. C. H. Waddington. *Educ:* Shrewsbury Sch.; Trinity Coll., Cambridge. MA, PhD (Cantab). Fellow, Jesus Coll., Cambridge, 1967–69; Research Associate, California Inst. of Technology, 1967–68 and 1971; Mem., Inst. for Advanced Study, Princeton, 1969–70; Visiting Prof., Harvard Univ., 1972; Prof., Univ. of Sussex, 1972–73; Vis. Prof., Inst. for Advanced Studies, Princeton, 1982. Chm., Science Adv. Cttee, ESA, 1976–78; Mem. Council, Royal Soc., 1983–85. Lectures: H.P.Robertson Meml, US Nat. Acad. Sci, 1975; George Darwin, Royal Astron. Soc., 1976; Halley, Oxford, 1978; Milne, Oxford, 1980; Loeb, Harvard, 1980; Bakerian, Royal Soc., 1982; Danz, Univ. of Washington, 1984. For. Hon. Mem., Amer. Acad. of Arts and Sciences, 1975; Foreign Associate, Nat. Acad. of Sciences, USA, 1982. Heinemann Prize, Amer. Inst. Physics, 1984; Bappu Award, Indian Nat. Science Acad., 1986. *Publications:* mainly articles and reviews in scientific jls. *Address:* c/o King's College, Cambridge. *T:* Cambridge 350411; (office) Cambridge 337548.

REES, Rt. Hon. Merlyn, PC 1974; MP (Lab) Morley and Leeds South, since 1983 (South Leeds, June 1963–83); *b* Cilfynydd, South Wales, 18 Dec. 1920; *s* of late L. D. and E. M. Rees; *m* 1949, Colleen Faith (*née* Cleveley); three *s*. *Educ:* Elementary Schools, S Wales and Wembley, Middx; Harrow Weald Grammar School; Goldsmiths' Coll., Univ. of London; London School of Economics; London Univ. Institute of Education. Nottingham Univ. Air Sqdn; Served RAF, 1941–46; demobilised as Sqdn Ldr. Teacher in Economics and History, Harrow Weald Grammar School, 1949–60. Organised Festival of Labour, 1960–62. Lecturer in Economics, Luton Coll. of Technology, 1962–63; contested (Lab) Harrow East, Gen. Elections 1955 and 1959 and by-election, 1959; PPS to Chancellor of the Exchequer, 1964; Parly Under-Sec. of State, MoD (Army), 1965–66; MoD (RAF), 1966–68; Home Office, 1968–70; Mem., Shadow Cabinet, 1972–74; Opposition spokesman on NI affairs, 1972–74; Sec. of State for NI, 1974–76; Home Sec., 1976–79; Shadow Home Sec., 1979–80; Opposition spokesman on Energy, 1980–83; Opposition Coordinator of Industry, Energy, Employment and Trade. Member: Cttee to examine operation of Section 2 of Official Secrets Act, 1971; Falkland Is Inquiry Cttee, 1982. Vice-Pres., British American Parly Assoc. *Publications:* The Public Sector in the Mixed Economy, 1973; Northern Ireland: a personal perspective, 1985. *Recreation:* reading. *Address:* House of Commons, SW1. *Club:* Reform.

REES, Meuric; *see* Rees, R. E. M.

REES, Rev. Michael; *see* Rees, Rev. R.M.

REES, Owen; Under Secretary, Welsh Office, since 1977, and Head of Economic and Regional Policy Group, since 1985; *b* 26 Dec. 1934; *s* of late John Trevor and Esther Rees, Trimsaran, Dyfed; *m* 1958, Elizabeth Gosby; one *s* two *d*. *Educ:* Llanelli Grammar Sch.; Univ. of Manchester. BA(Econ). Bank of London and South America, 1957; regional development work in Cardiff, Birmingham and London, BoT, 1959–69; Cabinet Office, 1969–71; Welsh Office, 1971–; Asst Sec. (European Div.), 1972; Sec. for Welsh Educn, 1977–78; Dir, Industry Dept, 1980–85. *Address:* 4 Llandennis Green, Cyncoed, Cardiff CF2 6JX. *T:* Cardiff 759712.

REES, Peter Magnall; a Senior Clerk, House of Lords, 1981–84; *b* 17 March 1921; *s* of late Edward Saunders Rees and of Gertrude Rees (*née* Magnall); *m* 1949, Moya Mildred Carroll. *Educ:* Manchester Grammar Sch.; Jesus Coll., Oxford. Served War, RA, 1941–46 (SE Asia, 1942–45). HM Overseas Service, Nigeria, 1948; Dep. Govt Statistician, Kenya, 1956; Dir of Economics and Statistics, Kenya, 1961; HM Treasury, 1964; Chief Statistician, 1966; Under-Sec., DTI later Dept of Industry, 1973–81. Consultant, OECD, 1981. *Publications:* articles in statistical jls. *Recreations:* choral singing, music, studying architecture. *Address:* The Old Orchard, Sandford Orcas, Sherborne, Dorset DT9 4RP. *T:* Corton Denham 244. *Club:* Royal Commonwealth Society.

REES, Rt. Hon. Peter Wynford Innes, PC 1983; QC 1969; MP (C) Dover, 1970–74 and since 1983 (Dover and Deal, 1974–83); *b* 9 Dec. 1926; *s* of late Maj.-Gen. T. W. Rees, Indian Army, Goytre Hall, Abergavenny; *m* 1969, Mrs Anthea Wendell, *d* of late Major H. J. M. Hyslop, Argyll and Sutherland Highlanders. *Educ:* Stowe; Christ Church, Oxford. Served Scots Guards, 1945–48. Called to the Bar, 1953, Bencher, Inner Temple, 1976; Oxford Circuit. Contested (C): Abertillery, 1964 and 1965; Liverpool, West Derby, 1966. PPS to Solicitor General, 1972; Minister of State, HM Treasury, 1979–81; Minister for Trade, 1981–83; Chief Sec. to HM Treasury, 1983–85. *Address:* 39 Headfort Place, SW1; Goytre Hall, Abergavenny, Gwent; 5 Church Street, St Clement's, Sandwich, Kent. *Club:* Boodle's.

REES, Philip; a Recorder of the Crown Court, since 1983; *b* 1 Dec. 1941; *s* of John Trevor Rees and Olwen Muriel Rees; *m* 1969, Catherine Good; one *s* one *d*. *Educ:* Monmouth Sch.; Bristol Univ. (LLB Hons). Called to the Bar, Middle Temple, 1965. *Recreations:* music, sport. *Address:* 34 Park Place, Cardiff CF1 3BA. *T:* Cardiff 382731. *Club:* Cardiff and Counties (Cardiff).

REES, Prof. Ray; Professor of Economics, University College, Cardiff, since 1978; *b* 19 Sept. 1943; *s* of Gwyn Rees and Violet May (*née* Powell); *m* 1976, Denise Sylvia (*née* Stinson); two *s*. *Educ:* Dyffryn Grammar Sch., Port Talbot; London School of Economics and Political Science (MScEcon). Lectr 1966–76, Reader 1976–78, Queen Mary Coll., Univ. of London; Economic Advr, HM Treasury (on secondment), 1968–72. Member (part-time), Monopolies and Mergers Commn, 1985–. *Publications:* A Dictionary of Economics, 1968, 3rd edn 1984; Public Enterprise Economics, 1975, 2nd edn 1984; Microeconomics, 1981; articles in Economic Jl, Amer. Econ. Rev., Jl of Public Econs, Economica, and others. *Recreations:* playing the guitar, losing chess games, learning German. *Address:* Lane Farm, Catbrook, Chepstow, Gwent NP6 6NA. *T:* Trelleck 860797.

REES, (Richard Ellis) Meuric, CBE 1982; JP; FRAgS; Member: Countryside Commission, since 1981 (Chairman, Committee for Wales); Agriculture Training Board, since 1974 (Chairman, Committee for Wales); Vice Chairman, Hill Farming Advisory Committee (Chairman, Committee for Wales); *b* Pantydwr, Radnorshire, 1924; *m*; three *d*. President: YFC in Wales, 1961; Merioneth Agricl Soc., 1972; Royal Welsh Agricl Show, 1978; former Chm., Welsh Council of NFU; Mem., CLA. Governor: Welsh Agricl Coll., Aberystwyth; Coleg Meirionnydd, Dolgellau. Mem., Tywyn UDC, 1967–73. Chm., N Wales Police Authority, 1982–84. JP Tywyn, 1957 (Chm. of Bench, 1974–); High Sheriff of Gwynedd, 1982–83. FRAgS 1973. *Address:* Escuan Hall, Tywyn, Gwynedd.

REES, Dr Richard John William, CMG 1979; FRCP, FRCPath; Grant holder, Division of Communicable Diseases, Clinical Research Centre, Harrow; Head, Laboratory for Leprosy and Mycobacterial Research, and WHO Collaborating Centre for Reference and Research on *M. leprae*, National Institute for Medical Research, London, 1969–82; *b* 11 Aug. 1917; *s* of William and Gertrude Rees; *m* 1942, Kathleen Harris; three *d*. *Educ:* East Sheen County Sch., London; Guy's Hosp., London (BSc 1939; MB, BS 1942). MRCS, LRCP 1941, FRCP 1983; MRCPath 1963, FRCPath 1964. Served War, 1942–46: Captain, RAMC Army Blood Transfusion Service, N Africa and Italy campaigns. House Surg. and Phys., Southern Hosp., Kent, 1941–42; Asst Clin. Pathologist, Guy's Hosp., 1946–49; Mem. of Scientific Staff, NIMR, 1949–69. Sec., MRC Leprosy Cttee, 1959–; Consultant, US Japanese Co-op. Scientific Prog. on Leprosy, 1969–73. Chairman: LEPRA Med. Adv. Bd, 1963– (Mem. Exec. Cttee, 1964–); Acid Fast Club, 1960; Pres., Section of Comparative Medicine, RSM, 1975. Member: Trop. Medicine Res. Bd, 1968–72; Council, Internat. Leprosy Assoc., 1963–; 3rd WHO Expert Cttee on Leprosy, 1965; WHO IMMLEP Steering Cttee, 1974–; WHO THELEP Steering Cttee, 1977–82. Almoth Wright Lectr, 1971; Erasmus Wilson Demonstration, RCS, 1973; 1st Clayton Meml Lectr, 1974; BMA Film, Silver Award, Leprosy, 1974. Mem. Editorial Boards: Leprosy Review; Internat. Jl of Leprosy; Excerpta Medica Leprosy. Hon. Mem., RSM Comparative Medicine Section, 1982. Manson Medal, 1980. *Publications:* scientific papers on basic and applied studies in animals and man relevant to pathogenesis, immunology and chemotherapy of leprosy and tuberculosis. *Address:* Highfield, Highwood Hill, Mill Hill, NW7 4EU. *T:* 01–959 2021; Division of Communicable Diseases, Clinical Research Centre, Harrow, Mddx HA1 3OJ. *T:* 01–864 5311 ex. 2697.

REES, Rev. (Richard) Michael; Chief Secretary, Church Army, since 1984; *b* 31 July 1935; *s* of Richard and Margaret Rees; *m* 1958, Yoma Patricia; one *s* one *d*. *Educ:* Brighton College; St Peter's College, Oxford (MA Theol); Tyndale Hall, Bristol. Curate: Crowborough, 1959–62; Christ Church, Clifton, Bristol, 1962–64; Vicar: Christ Church, Clevedon, 1964–72; Holy Trinity, Cambridge, 1972–84; Proctor, General Synod for Ely Diocese, 1975–85. Editor, Missionary Mandate, 1955–68. *Recreations:* photography, filling waste paper baskets. *Address:* Church Army, Independents Road, Blackheath, SE3 9LG. *T:* 01–318 1226.

REES, Sir Stanley; *see* Rees, Sir C. W. S.

REES, (Thomas Morgan) Haydn, CBE 1975; JP; DL; Chairman, Welsh Water Authority, 1977–82; Member: National Water Council, 1977–82; Water Space Amenity Commission, 1977–82; *b* 22 May 1915; *y s* of late Thomas Rees and Mary Rees, Gorseinon, Swansea; *m* 1941, Marion, *y d* of A. B. Beer, Mumbles, Swansea; one *d*. *Educ:* Swansea Business Coll. Served War, 1939–45. Admitted solicitor, 1946; Sen. Asst Solicitor, Caernarvonshire CC, 1947; Flints County Council, 1948–65: Dep. Clerk, Dep. Clerk of the Peace, Police Authority, Magistrates Courts Cttee, and of Probation Cttee; 1966–74: Chief Exec.; Clerk of Peace (until office abolished, 1971); Clerk, Flints Police Authority (until merger with N Wales Police Authority, 1967); Clerk of Probation, Magistrates Courts, and of Justices Adv. Cttees; Clerk to Lieutenancy; Chief Exec., Clwyd CC, and Clerk, Magistrates Courts Cttee, 1974–77; Clerk to Lieutenancy and of Justices Adv. Cttee, Clwyd, 1974–77. Clerk, N Wales Police Authority, 1967–77; Secretary: Welsh Counties Cttee, 1968–77; (Corresp.) Rep. Body (Ombudsman) Cttee for Wales, 1974–77; Mem., Severn Barrage Cttee, 1978–81. Asst Comr, Royal Commn on Constitution, 1969–73. Chm., New Jobs Team, Shotton Steelworks, 1977–82; part-time Mem. Bd, BSC (Industry) Ltd, 1979–83. Chm., N Wales Arts Assoc., 1981–. Member: Lord Chancellor's Circuit Cttee for Wales and Chester Circuit, 1972–77; Welsh Council, 1968–79; Welsh Arts Council, 1968–77 (Mem. Regional Cttee 1981–); Gorsedd, Royal National Eisteddfod for Wales; Prince of Wales Cttee, 1976–79. Clerk, 1974–77, Mem., 1983–, Theatr Clwyd Governors. Chairman: Govt Quality of Life Experiment in Clwyd, 1974–76; Deeside Enterprise Trust Ltd, 1982–. DL Flints 1969, Clwyd 1974; JP Mold, 1977 (Dep. Chm., 1978–84; Chm., 1985). *Recreations:* the arts, golf. *Address:* Cefn Bryn, Gwernaffield Road, Mold, Clwyd CH7 1RQ. *T:* Mold 2421. *Club:* Mold Golf.

REES, (Walter) Llewellyn, MA; Actor and Theatre Administrator; Hon. Life Member: British Actors' Equity Association, 1981 (General Secretary, 1940–46); Theatrical Management Association, 1985; Honorary President of International Theatre Institute since 1951; *b* 18 June 1901; *s* of Walter Francis Rees and Mary Gwendoline Naden; *m* 1961, Madeleine Newbury; one *s* one *d*. *Educ:* King Edward's School, Birmingham; Keble College, Oxford. Private Tutor, 1923–26; studied at RADA, 1926–28; Actor, 1928–40; Jt Secretary: London Theatre Council, 1940–46, Prov. Theatre Council, 1942–46; Sec. of Fed. of Theatre Unions, 1944–46; Governor of the Old Vic, 1945–47; Drama Director, Arts Council of Great Britain, 1947–49; Administrator of the Old Vic, 1949–51; Administrator of Arts Theatre, 1951–52; General Administrator, Donald Wolfit's Company, 1952–58; Chairman Executive Committee of International Theatre Institute, 1948–51; Hon. Counsellor to Council of Repertory Theatres, 1951–77. Returned to West End Stage, 1956, as Bishop of Buenos Aires in The Strong are Lonely, Theatre Royal, Haymarket; Olmeda in The Master of Santiago, Lyric Theatre, Hammersmith, 1957; Polonius in Hamlet, Bristol Old Vic, 1958; Dean of College in My Friend Judas, Arts Theatre, 1959; Mr Brandy in Settled out of Court, Strand Theatre, 1960–61; Justice Worthy in Lock Up Your Daughters, Mermaid Theatre and Her Majesty's, 1962–63; Sir Henry James in the Right Honourable Gentleman, Her Majesty's, 1964–65; Father Ambrose in The Servants and the Snow, Greenwich, 1970; Duncan in Macbeth, Greenwich, 1971; Mr Justice Millhouse in Whose Life Is It Anyway?, Savoy, 1978–79. Many film and television appearances. *Recreation:* travel. *Address:* 6 Byfeld Gardens, Barnes, SW13 9HP.

REES, William Howard Guest; Chief Veterinary Officer, State Veterinary Service, since 1980; *b* 21 May 1928; *s* of Walter Guest Rees and Margaret Elizabeth Rees; *m* 1952, Charlotte Mollie (*née* Collins); three *s* one *d*. *Educ:* Llanelli Grammar Sch.; Royal Veterinary Coll., London (BSc). MRCVS; DVSM. Private practice, Deal, Kent, 1952–53; joined MAFF as Veterinary Officer, 1953; stationed Stafford, 1953–66; Divl Vet. Officer, Vet. Service HQ, Tolworth, 1966–69; Divl Vet. Officer, Berks, 1969–71; Dep. Regional Vet. Officer, SE Reg., 1971–73; Regional Vet. Officer, Tolworth, 1973–76, Asst Chief Vet. Officer, 1976–80. Mem. AFRC (formerly ARC), 1980–. *Recreations:* Rugby and cricket follower, golf. *Address:* Taliesin, Paddocks Way, Ashtead, Surrey KT21 2QY. *T:* Ashtead 76522.

REES, William Hurst; Member of Lands Tribunal, since 1973; *b* 12 April 1917; *s* of Richard and Florence A. Rees; *m* 1941, Elizabeth Mary Wight; two *s* one *d*. *Educ:* College of Estate Management, Univ. of London (BSc Est. Man.). FRICS. Served War, RA and RE (SO2), 1940–46; Liaison Officer, Belgian Army Engrs. Head of Valuation Dept, Coll. of Estate Management, 1948–51. Principal in Private Practice as Chartered Surveyor: City of London, Richard Ellis & Son, 1951–61; East Grinstead, Sx, Turner, Rudge & Turner, 1961–73. Gov., Coll. of Estate Management, 1965–72; Mem. Council, RICS, 1967–70; Chm. Bd of Studies in Estate Management, Univ. of London, 1970–74; Chm., Surveying Bd, CNAA, 1976–77; Hon. Mem., Rating Surveyors Assoc. Pres., BSc (Estate Management) Club, 1961–62; Chm., Exams Bd, Incorporated Soc. of Valuers and

Auctioneers, 1984–. *Publications:* Modern Methods of Valuation, 1943, (jointly) 6th edn 1971; (ed) Valuations: Principles into Practice, 1980, 2nd edn 1984. *Recreation:* music, mainly opera. *Address:* Brendon, Carlton Road, South Godstone, Godstone, Surrey RH9 8LD. *T:* South Godstone 892109.

REES, (William) Linford (Llewelyn), CBE 1978; FRCP; FRCPsych; Emeritus Professor of Psychiatry, University of London, 1980; Consulting Physician, St Bartholomew's Hospital, since 1981; Lecturer in Psychological Medicine, St Bartholomew's Medical College, since 1958; Recognised Clinical Teacher in Mental Diseases, Institute of Psychiatry, University of London, since 1956; Chairman: University of London Teachers of Psychiatry Committee; Armed Services Consultant Advisory Board in Psychiatry, since 1979; *b* 24 Oct. 1914; *e s* of late Edward Parry Rees and Mary Rees, Llanelly, Carmathenshire; *m* 1940, Catherine, *y d* of late David Thomas, and of Angharad Thomas, Alltwen, Glam; two *s* two *d. Educ:* Llanelly Grammar School; University Coll., Cardiff; Welsh Nat. Sch. of Medicine; The Maudsley Hosp.; Univ. of London. BSc 1935; MB, BCh 1938; DPM 1940; DSc London, 1978; MRCP 1942; MD 1943; FRCP 1950; FRCPsych 1971 (Pres., 1975–78); Hon. FRCPsych 1978. David Hepburn Medal and Alfred Hughes Medal in Anatomy, 1935; John Maclean Medal and Prize in Obstetrics and Gynaecology, 1937, etc. Specialist, EMS, 1942; Dep. Med. Supt, Mill Hill Emergency Hosp., 1945; Asst Physician and Postgrad. Teacher in Clinical Psychiatry, The Maudsley Hosp., 1946; Dep. Physician Supt, Whitchurch Hosp., 1947; Regional Psychiatrist for Wales and Mon, 1948; Consultant Physician, The Bethlem Royal Hosp. and The Maudsley Hosp., 1954–66; Med. Dir, Charter Clinic, London, 1980–; Chief Psychiatrist and Exec. Med. Dir, Charter Medical, 1984–. Consultant Advisor in Psychiatry to RAF; WHO Consultant to Sri Lanka, 1973; Hon. Consultant, Royal Sch. for Deaf Children. Lectures to Univs and Learned Socs in Europe, USA, Asia, Australia and S America. Examiner: Diploma Psychological Medicine, RCP, 1964–69; MRCP, RCP, RCPE and RCPGlas, 1969–; MB and DPM, Univ. of Leeds, 1969–. President: Soc. for Psychosomatic Research, 1957–58; Royal Coll. of Psychiatrists, 1975–78 (Vice-Pres., 1972–75; Chm., E Anglian Region); Section of Psychiatry, RSM, 1971–72 (Vice-Pres., 1968; Hon. Mem., 1982); BMA, 1978– (Fellow, 1981); Vice-Pres., Stress Foundn, 1984–; Chm., Medico-Pharmaceutical Forum, 1982 (Vice-Chm., 1981). Treasurer, World Psychiatric Assoc., 1966– (Hon. Mem., 1982). Member: Clinical Psychiatry Cttee, MRC, 1959–; Council, Royal Medico-Psychological Assoc. (Chm., Research and Clinical Section, 1957–63); Soc. for Study of Human Biology; Asthma Research Council; Cttee on Safety of Medicines (also Toxicity and Clinical Trials Sub-Cttee), 1971–; Psychological Medicine Group, BMA, 1967–; Bd of Advanced Med. Studies, Univ. of London, 1966–69; Higher Degrees Cttee, Univ. of London; Acad. Council Standing Sub-Cttee in Medicine, Univ. of London; Cttee of Management, Inst. of Psychiatry, Maudsley Hosp., 1968–; Council and Exec. Cttee, St Bartholomew's Hosp. Med. Coll., 1972–; Jt Policy Cttee, QMC, St Bartholomew's Hosp. and London Hosp., 1973–; Cttee on Review of Medicines (Chm., Psychotropic Drugs Sub-Cttee); Central Health Services Council; Standing Medical Adv. Cttee; Jt Consultants Cttee; Conference of Presidents of Royal Colls; GMC, 1980–84 (Mem., Educn Cttee, Preliminary Health Cttee and Prof. Conduct Cttee). Founder Mem., Internat. Coll. of Neuro-psychopharmacology. Hon. Mem. Learned Socs in USA, Sweden, Venezuela, East Germany, Spain and Greece. FRSM; Fellow: Eugenics Soc.; and Vice-Pres., Internat. Coll. of Psychosomatic Medicine, 1973; University Coll., Cardiff, 1980 (Governor, 1984–); Distinguished Fellow, Amer. Psychiatric Assoc., 1968; Hon. Fellow: Amer. Soc. of Physician Analysts; Amer. Coll. Psychiatrists; Hon. Member: Biological Psychiatry Assoc., USA; Hong Kong Psychiatric Soc., 1982. Chm. Bd of Trustees, Stress Syndrome Foundn, 1981– (Chm., Scientific Adv. Council). Governor: The Bethlem Royal Hosp. and The Maudsley Hosp.; Med. Coll. of St Bartholomew's Hosp., 1980–. Pres., Golden Jubilee Appeal, Welsh Nat. Sch. of Med., 1980; Patron of Extend, 1976. Co-Editor, Jl of Psychosomatic Research. Liveryman: Barber Surgeons; Apothecaries. Hon. LLD Wales, 1981. Bard of Welsh Gorsedd. *Publications:* (with Eysenck and Himmelweit) Dimensions of Personality, 1947; Short Textbook of Psychiatry, 1967. Chapters in: Modern Treatment in General Practice, 1947; Recent Progress in Psychiatry, 1950; Schizophrenia: Somatic Aspects, 1957; Psychoendocrinology, 1958; Recent Progress in Psychosomatic Research, 1960; Stress and Psychiatric Disorders, 1960. Papers in: Nature, BMJ, Jl of Mental Sci., Jl of Psychosomatic Research, Eugenics Review, etc. Contribs to Med. Annual, 1958–68. *Recreations:* swimming, photography, amusing grandchildren. *Address:* Penbryn, 62 Oakwood Avenue, Purley, Surrey. *Club:* Athenæum.

REES-DAVIES, William Rupert, QC 1973; Barrister-at-law; *b* 19 Nov. 1916; *o s* of late Sir William Rees-Davies, KC, DL, JP, formerly Chief Justice of Hong Kong and Liberal MP for Pembroke and of late Lady Rees-Davies; *m* 1st, 1959, Jane (marr. diss. 1981), *d* of Mr and Mrs Henry Mander; two *d*; 2nd, 1982, Sharlie Kingsley. *Educ:* Eton; Trinity Coll., Cambridge; Eton Soc., Eton XI, 1934–35; Eton Victor Ludorum; Cambridge Cricket XI, 1938; Honours in History and Law. Called to Bar, Inner Temple, 1939. Commissioned HM Welsh Guards, 1939; served War of 1939–45 (discharged disabled with loss of arm, 1943). Contested (C) South Nottingham in 1950 and 1951. MP (C) Isle of Thanet, March 1953–1974, Thanet W, 1974–83; Cons. Leader, Select Cttee on Health and the Social Services, 1980–83; Chm., Cons. Cttee on Tourism. *Recreations:* racing, collecting pictures and antiques. *Address:* 5 Lord North Street, SW1. *Clubs:* Turf, Guards' Polo, MCC; Hawks, University Pitt (Cambridge).

REES-JONES, Geoffrey Rippon, MA Oxon; Principal, King William's College, Isle of Man, 1958–79; *b* 8 July 1914; *er s* of W. Rees-Jones, BA, Ipswich; *m* 1950, Unity Margaret McConnell (*d* 1982), *d* of Major P. M. Sanders, Hampstead; one *s* one *d. Educ:* Ipswich School (scholar); University College, Oxford (open scholar). Assistant Master, Eastbourne College, 1936–38, Marlborough College, 1938–54 (Housemaster, C2, 1946–54); Headmaster, Bembridge School, 1954–58. Served War mainly in Commandos, 1940–45; Commandant, Commando Mountain Warfare School, 1943; Staff College, Camberley, 1944 (sc); Brigade Major, 4 Commando Bde, 1944–45 (despatches). *Recreations:* sailing, cricket, golf, fives; Oxford Rugby 'blue', 1933–35, Wales XV, 1934–36. *Address:* Red Lion Cottage, Braaid, Isle of Man. *T:* Castletown 851360.

REES-MOGG, Sir William, Kt 1981; Chairman and Proprietor, Pickering & Chatto Ltd, since 1981; Director, General Electric Co., since 1981; Chairman, Sidgwick & Jackson, since 1985; Chairman, Arts Council of Great Britain, since 1982; Member, International Committee, Pontifical Council for Culture, since 1983; *b* 14 July 1928; *s* of late Edmund Fletcher Rees-Mogg and late Beatrice Rees-Mogg (*née* Warren), Temple Cloud, Somerset; *m* 1962, Gillian Shakespeare Morris, *d* of T. R. Morris; two *s* three *d. Educ:* Charterhouse; Balliol Coll., Oxford (Brackenbury Scholar). President, Oxford Union, 1951. Financial Times, 1952–60, Chief Leader Writer, 1955–60; Asst Editor, 1957–60; Sunday Times, City Editor, 1960–61; Political and Economic Editor, 1961–63; Deputy Editor, 1964–67; Editor, The Times, 1967–81; Mem., Exec. Bd, Times Newspapers Ltd, 1968–81; Director: The Times Ltd, 1968–81; Times Newspapers Ltd, 1978–81. Vice-Chm., Bd of Governors, BBC, 1981–86. Contested (C) Chester-le-Street, Co. Durham, By-election 1956; General Election, 1959. Treasurer, Institute of Journalists, 1960–63, 1966–68, Pres., 1963–64; Vice-Chm. Cons. Party's Nat. Advisory Cttee on Political Education, 1961–63. Pres., English Assoc., 1983–84. Vis. Fellow, Nuffield Coll.,

Oxford, 1968–72. High Sheriff, Somerset, 1978. Hon. LLD Bath, 1977. *Publications:* The Reigning Error: the crisis of world inflation, 1974; An Humbler Heaven, 1977; How to Buy Rare Books, 1985. *Recreation:* collecting. *Address:* 3 Smith Square, SW1; The Old Rectory, Hinton Blewitt, near Bristol, Avon. *Club:* Garrick.

REES-WILLIAMS, family name of **Baron Ogmore.**

REESE, Prof. Colin Bernard, PhD; ScD; FRS 1981; Daniell Professor of Chemistry, King's College, University of London, since 1973; *b* 29 July 1930; *s* of Joseph and Emily Reese; *m* 1968, Susanne Bird; one *s* one *d. Educ:* Dartington Hall Sch.; Clare Coll., Cambridge (BA 1953, PhD 1956, MA 1957, ScD 1972). 1851 Sen. Student, 1956–58; Research Fellow: Clare Coll., Cambridge, 1956–59; Harvard Univ., 1957–58; Official Fellow and Dir of Studies in Chem., Clare Coll., 1959–73; Cambridge University: Univ. Demonstrator in Chem., 1959–63; Asst Dir of Res., 1963–64; Univ. Lectr in Chem., 1964–73. Pacific Coast Lectr, USA and Canada, 1986. *Publications:* scientific papers, mainly in chemical jls. *Address:* Department of Chemistry, King's College, London, Strand, WC2R 2LS. *T:* 01-836 5454.

REESE, Surg. Rear-Adm. John Mansel, CB 1962; OBE 1953; *b* 3 July 1906; *s* of late Dr D. W. Reese, and late Mrs A. M. Reese; *m* 1946, Beryl (*née* Dunn) (*d* 1973); two *d* (and one *s* decd). *Educ:* Epsom Coll.; St Mary's Hosp. Med. Sch., London University. MRCS, LRCP 1930; DPH 1934. Entered Royal Navy, Jan. 1931; Naval Medical Officer of Health, Orkney and Shetland Comd, 1942–44; Naval MOH, Ceylon, 1944–46; Admiralty, 1947–53; Medical Officer-in-Charge RN Hospital, Plymouth, 1960–63; QHP 1960–63. Surgeon Comdr, 1943; Surgeon Captain, 1954; Surgeon Rear-Adm., 1960; retd 1963. FRSTM&H. Sir Gilbert Blane Gold Medal, 1939. Member Gray's Inn, 1953. CStJ 1961. *Address:* 4 Meldon Court, East Budleigh Road, Budleigh Salterton, Devon.

REESE, (John) Terence; bridge expert, author and journalist; *b* 28 Aug. 1913; *s* of John and Anne Reese; *m* 1970, Alwyn Sherrington. *Educ:* Bilton Grange; Bradfield Coll. (top scholar); New Coll., Oxford (top class. scholar). Worked at Harrods, 1935–36; left to follow career as bridge expert and journalist. Became bridge correspondent of the Evening News, 1948, the Observer, 1950, the Lady, 1954, and the Standard, 1981. Winner of numerous British, European and World Championships. *Publications:* The Elements of Contract, 1938; Reese on Play, 1948; The Expert Game, 1958; Play Bridge with Reese, 1960; Story of an Accusation, 1966; Precision Bidding and Precision Play, 1972; Play These Hands With Me, 1976; Bridge at the Top (autobiog.), 1977; *with Albert Dormer:* The Acol System Today, 1961; The Play of the Cards, 1967; Bridge for Tournament Players, 1969; The Complete Book of Bridge, 1973; and many others. *Recreations:* golf, backgammon. *Address:* 18a Woods Mews, Park Lane, W1. *T:* 01-629 5553.

REEVE, Anthony, CMG 1986; HM Diplomatic Service; Assistant Under Secretary of State (Africa), Foreign and Commonwealth Office, since 1986; *b* 20 Oct. 1938; *s* of Sidney Reeve and Dorothy (*née* Mitchell); *m* 1964, Pamela Margaret Angus; one *s* two *d. Educ:* Queen Elizabeth Grammar Sch., Wakefield; Marling Sch., Stroud; Merton Coll., Oxford (MA). Lever Brothers & Associates, 1962–65; joined HM Diplomatic Service, 1965; Middle East Centre for Arab Studies, 1966–68; Asst Political Agent, Abu Dhabi, 1968–70; First Secretary, FCO, 1970–73; First Sec., later Counsellor, Washington, 1973–78; Head of Arms Control and Disarmament Dept, FCO, 1979–81; Counsellor, Cairo, 1981–84; Head of Southern Africa Dept, FCO, 1984–86. *Recreations:* writing, music. *Address:* c/o Foreign and Commonwealth Office, SW1; 44 Priory Road, Kew, Richmond, Surrey TW9 3DH. *T:* 01-940 1093. *Clubs:* United Oxford & Cambridge University; Leander (Henley-on-Thames).

REEVE, Hon. Sir (Charles) Trevor, Kt 1973; **Hon. Mr Justice Reeve;** a Judge of the High Court of Justice, Family Division, since 1973; *b* 4 July 1915; *o s* of William George Reeve and Elsie (*née* Bowring), Wokingham; *m* 1941, Marjorie, *d* of Charles Evelyn Browne, Eccles, Lancs. *Educ:* Winchester College; Trinity College, Oxford. Commissioned 10th Royal Hussars (PWO) 1940; served BEF, CMF (Major) 1940–44 (despatches); Staff College, Camberley, 1945. Called to Bar, Inner Temple, 1946, Bencher, 1965; Mem., Bar Council, 1950–54. QC 1965; County Court Judge, 1968; Circuit Judge, 1972. Mem., Appeals Tribunal for E Africa in respect of Commonwealth Immigration Act, 1968. *Recreations:* golf, dancing. *Address:* 95 Abingdon Road, Kensington, W8 6QU. *T:* 01-937 7530. *Clubs:* Garrick; Royal North Devon Golf (Westward Ho!); Sunningdale Golf.

REEVE, James Ernest, CMG 1982; HM Diplomatic Service, retired; Secretariat, International Primary Aluminium Institute, London, since 1985; *b* 8 June 1926; *s* of Ernest and Anthea Reeve; *m* 1947, Lillian Irene Watkins; one *s* one *d. Educ:* Bishops Stortford Coll. Vice-Consul, Ahwaz and Khorramshahr, Iran, 1949–51; UN General Assembly, Paris, 1951; Asst Private Sec. to Rt Hon. Selwyn Lloyd, Foreign Office, 1951–53; 2nd Secretary: Brit. Embassy, Washington, 1953–57; Brit. Embassy, Bangkok, 1957–59; FO, 1959–61; HM Consul, Frankfurt, 1961–65; 1st Secretary: Brit. Embassy in Libya, 1965–69; Brit. Embassy, Budapest, 1970–72; Chargé d'Affaires, Budapest, 1972; Counsellor (Commercial), East Berlin, 1973–75; Consul-Gen., Zurich and Principality of Liechtenstein, 1975–80; HM Minister and Consul-Gen., Milan, 1980–83. Dir, Sprester Investments Ltd, 1986–. *Recreations:* theatre, tennis, skiing, travel. *Address:* 20 Glenmore House, Richmond Hill, Surrey. *Club:* Royal Automobile.

REEVE, Mrs Marjorie Frances Wentworth, CBE 1944; TD 1950; JP; *d* of late Charles Fry, Bedford; *m* 1st, Lieutenant-Commander J. K. Laughton, Royal Navy (*d* 1925); one *s*; 2nd, Major-General C. M. Wagstaff, CB, CMG, CIE, DSO (*d* 1934); 3rd, 1950, Major-General J. T. Wentworth Reeve, CB, CBE, DSO (*d* 1983). Joined ATS, 1938; served with BEF, and in Middle East and BAOR; late Controller ATS. Was i/c Public Welfare Section of Control Commission for Germany (BE); Principal in Board of Trade (Overseas) till 1950; Swedish Red Cross Medal in Silver, 1950; County Director, BRCS, 1953–57; Dep. Pres. Suffolk BRCS, 1957, Hon. Vice-Pres., 1977. Badge of Honour (2nd Class) BRCS, 1970. JP (W Suffolk), 1954. *Address:* 7 Clare Park, Crondall, near Farnham, Surrey GU10 5DT. *T:* Aldershot 850681.

REEVE, Prof. Michael David, FBA 1984; Kennedy Professor of Latin, and Fellow of Pembroke College, University of Cambridge, since 1984; *b* 11 Jan. 1943; *s* of Arthur Reeve and Edith Mary Barrett; *m* 1970, Elizabeth Klingaman; two *s* one *d. Educ:* King Edward's Sch., Birmingham; Balliol Coll., Oxford (MA). Harmsworth Senior Scholar, Merton Coll., Oxford, 1964–65; Woodhouse Research Fellow, St John's Coll., Oxford, 1965–66; Tutorial Fellow, Exeter Coll., Oxford, 1966–84, now Emeritus Fellow. Visiting Professor: Univ. of Hamburg, 1976; McMaster Univ., 1979; Univ. of Toronto, 1982–83. Editor, Classical Quarterly, 1981–86. *Publications:* Longus, Daphnis and Chloe, 1982; contribs to Texts and Transmission, ed L. D. Reynolds, 1983; articles in European and transatlantic jls. *Recreations:* chess, music, gardening, mountain walking. *Address:* Pembroke College, Cambridge CB2 1RF.

REEVE, Robin Martin, MA; Head Master, King's College School, Wimbledon, since 1980; *b* 22 Nov. 1934; *s* of Percy Martin Reeve and Cicely Nora Parker; *m* 1959, Brianne Ruth Hall; one *s* two *d. Educ:* Hampton Sch.; Gonville and Caius Coll., Cambridge (Foundation Schol.; BA cl. 1 Hist. Tripos, 1957; MA). Asst Master, King's Coll. Sch.,

Wimbledon, 1958–62; Head of History Dept, 1962–80, and Dir of Studies, 1975–80, Lancing Coll. Chm., Governors, Rosemead Sch., Littlehampton, 1983–. *Publication*: The Industrial Revolution 1750–1850, 1971. *Recreations*: English history and architecture, gardening. *Address*: 20 Burghley Road, SW19 5BH. *T*: 01–947 3190; The Old Rectory, Coombes, Lancing, W Sussex BN15 0RS. *Club*: East India, Devonshire, Sports and Public Schools.

REEVE, Suzanne Elizabeth; Secretary, Economic and Social Research Council, since 1985; *b* 12 Aug. 1942; *d* of Charles Clifford Reeder and Elizabeth Joan Armstrong Reeder; *m* 1967, Jonathan Reeve; one *s* (marr. diss. 1980); one *s*. *Educ*: Badminton Sch., Bristol; Univ. of Sussex (BA Hons History); Univ. of Cambridge (Dip. Criminology). Home Office Res. Unit, 1966–67; Personal Assistant to Sec. of State for Social Services, DHSS, 1968–70; Principal, DHSS, 1970–73; Central Policy Review Staff, 1973–74; Asst Sec., DHSS, 1979–85. *Recreations*: family life, cooking, gardening, reading, films. *Address*: 8 College Gardens, Dulwich, SE21 7BE.

REEVE, Hon. Sir Trevor; *see* Reeve, Hon. Sir C. T.

REEVES, Christopher Reginald; Deputy Chairman and Group Chief Executive, Morgan Grenfell Group PLC; Joint Chairman, Morgan Grenfell & Co. Ltd; *b* 14 Jan. 1936; *s* of Reginald and Dora Reeves; *m* 1965, Stella, *d* of Patrick and Maria Whinney; three *s*. *Educ*: Malvern College. National Service, Rifle Bde, 1955–57. Bank of England, 1958–63; Hill Samuel & Co. Ltd, 1963–67; joined Morgan Grenfell & Co. Ltd, 1968; Dir, 1970. Director: London Board, Westpac Banking Corp. (formerly Commercial Bank of Australia Ltd) 1972– (Chm., 1976–82, Dep. Chm., 1982–); Midland and International Banks Ltd, 1976–83; BICC, 1982–; Andrew Weir & Co., 1982–; Allianz Internat. Insurance Co. Ltd, 1983–; Oman Internat. Bank, 1984–. Member: Adv. Panel, City University Business Sch., 1972–81 (Chm., 1979–81); Council, City Univ. Business Sch., 1986–; Council, Inst. for Fiscal Studies, 1982–; Governor: Stowe Sch., 1976–81; Dulwich College Prep. Sch., 1977–; Mermaid Theatre Trust, 1981–85. *Recreations*: sailing, shooting, ski-ing. *Address*: c/o 23 Great Winchester Street, EC2P 2AX. *T*: 01–588 4545. *Clubs*: Boodle's; Royal Southern Yacht (Southampton).

REEVES, Marjorie Ethel, MA (Oxon), PhD (London), DLitt (Oxon); FRHistS; FBA 1974; Vice-Principal, St Anne's College, Oxford, 1951–62, 1964–67; *b* 17 July 1905; *d* of Robert J. W. Reeves and Edith Saffery Whitaker. *Educ*: The High School for Girls, Trowbridge, Wilts; St Hugh's Coll., Oxford; Westfield Coll., London. Asst Mistress, Roan School, Greenwich, 1927–29; Research Fellow, Westfield Coll., London, 1929–31; Lecturer, St Gabriel's Trng Coll., London, 1931–38; Tutor, later Fellow of St Anne's College, 1938–72, Hon. Fellow, 1973. Member: Central Advisory Council, Min. of Educn, 1947–61; Academic Planning Bd, Univ. of Kent; Academic Advisory Cttee, University of Surrey; formerly Member: Educn Council, ITA; British Council of Churches; School Broadcasting Council. Corresp. Fellow, Medieval Acad. of America, 1979. *Publications*: Growing Up in a Modern Society, 1946; (ed, with L. Tondelli, B. Hirsch-Reich) Il Libro delle Figure dell'Abate Gioachino da Fiore, 1953; Three Questions in Higher Education (Hazen Foundation, USA), 1955; Moral Education in a Changing Society (ed W. Niblett), 1963; ed, Eighteen Plus: Unity and Diversity in Higher Education, 1965; The Influence of Prophecy in the later Middle Ages: a study in Joachimism, 1969; Higher Education: demand and response (ed W. R. Niblett), 1969; (with B. Hirsch-Reich) The Figurae of Joachim of Fiore, 1972; Joachim of Fiore and the Prophetic Future, 1976; Sheep Bell and Ploughshare, 1978; Why History, 1980; (with W. Gould) Joachim of Fiore and the Myth of the Eternal Evangel, 1986; Then and There Series: The Medieval Town, 1954, The Medieval Village, 1954, Elizabethan Court, 1956, The Medieval Monastery, 1957, The Norman Conquest, 1958, Alfred and the Danes, 1959; The Medieval Castle, 1960, Elizabethan Citizen, 1961; A Medieval King Governs, 1971; Explorers of the Elizabethan Age, 1977; Elizabethan Country House, 1984; contributions on history in Speculum, Medieval and Renaissance Studies, Traditio, Sophia, Recherches de Théologie, etc, and on education in Times Educational Supplement, New Era, etc. *Recreations*: music, gardening, bird-watching. *Address*: 38 Norham Road, Oxford. *T*: Oxford 57039. *Club*: University Women's.

REEVES, Prof. Nigel Barrie Reginald, DPhil; FIL; Professor of German, since 1975, Head of Department of Linguistic and International Studies, since 1979, and Dean of the Faculty of Human Studies, since 1986, University of Surrey; *b* 9 Nov. 1939; *s* of Reginald Arthur Reeves and Marjorie Joyce Reeves; *m* 1982, Minou (*née* Samimi); one *s* one *d*. *Educ*: Merchant Taylors' Sch.; Worcester Coll., Oxford (MA); St John's Coll., Oxford (DPhil 1970). FIL 1981. Lectr in English, Univ. of Lund, Sweden, 1964–66; Lectr in German, Univ. of Reading, 1968–74; Alexander von Humboldt Fellow, Univ. of Tübingen, 1974–75. Guest Prof. of German, Royal Holloway Coll., London Univ., 1976; Vis. Prof., European Business Sch., 1981–; Sen. Alexander von Humboldt Fellow, Univ. of Hamburg, 1986. Chairman: Council, Inst. of Linguists, 1985–; Nat. Congress on Langs in Educn; Pres., Nat. Assoc. of Language Advisers, 1986–. FRSA 1986. *Publications*: Merkantil-Tekniska Stilar, 2 Vols, 1965–66; Heinrich Heine: poetry and politics, 1974; (with K. Dewhurst) Friedrich Schiller: medicine, psychology and literature, 1978; (with D. Liston) Business Studies, Languages and Overseas Trade, 1985; over 30 articles in learned jls on language, language educn and literature. *Recreations*: gardening, walking. *Address*: Department of Linguistic and International Studies, University of Surrey, Guildford GU2 5XH. *T*: Guildford 509174.

REEVES, Most Rev. Sir Paul Alfred, GCMG 1985; GCVO 1986; Kt 1985; Governor-General of New Zealand since 1985; *b* 6 Dec. 1932; 2nd *s* of D'Arcy Lionel and Hilda Mary Reeves; *m* 1959, Beverley Gwendolen Watkins; three *d*. *Educ*: Wellington Coll., New Zealand; Victoria Univ. of Wellington (MA); St John's Theol. Coll., Auckland (LTh); St Peter's Coll., Univ. of Oxford (MA; Hon. Fellow, 1980). Deacon, 1958; Priest, 1960; Curate: Tokoroa, NZ, 1958–59; St Mary the Virgin, Oxford, 1959–61; Kirkley St Peter, Lowestoft, 1961–63; Vicar, St Paul, Okato, NZ, 1964–66; Lectr in Church History, St John's Coll., Auckland, NZ, 1966–69; Dir of Christian Educn, Dio. Auckland, 1969–71; Bishop of Waiapu, 1971–79; Bishop of Auckland, 1979–85; Primate and Archbishop of New Zealand, 1980–85. Chm., Environmental Council, 1974–76. KStJ 1986. Hon. DCL Oxford. *Recreations*: jogging, sailing, swimming. *Address*: Government House, Wellington, New Zealand.

REEVES, Philip Thomas Langford, RSA 1976 (ARSA 1971); artist in etching and other mediums; Senior Lecturer, Glasgow School of Art, since 1973; *b* 7 July 1931; *s* of Herbert Reeves and Lilian; *m* 1964, Christine MacLaren; one *d*. *Educ*: Naunton Park Sch., Cheltenham. Student, Cheltenham Sch. of Art, 1947–49. Army service, 4th/7th Royal Dragoon Guards, Middle East, 1949–51. RCA, 1951–54 (ARCA 1st Cl.); Lectr, Glasgow Sch. of Art, 1954–73. Associate, Royal Soc. of Painter Etchers, 1954, Fellow 1964; RSW 1962; RGI 1981. Works in permanent collections: Arts Council; V&A; Gall. of Modern Art, Edinburgh; Glasgow Art Gall.; Glasgow Univ. Print Collection; Hunterian Art Gall., Glasgow; Manchester City Art Gall.; Royal Scottish Acad.; Aberdeen Art Gall.; Paisley Art Gall.; Inverness Art Gall.; Milngavie Art Gall.; Dept of the Environment; Dundee Art Gall.; Scottish Develt Agency; Stirling and Strathclyde Univs; Contemporary

Art Soc. *Recreation*: walking. *Address*: 13 Hamilton Drive, Glasgow G12 8DN. *Club*: Traverse (Edinburgh).

REEVES, William Desmond; Assistant Under Secretary of State (Systems), Office of Management and Budget, Ministry of Defence, since 1985; *b* 26 May 1937; *s* of Thomas Norman and Anne Reeves; *m* 1967, Aase Birte Christensen; two *d*. *Educ*: Darwen Grammar Sch.; King's Coll., Cambridge (BA Hist.). National service, RAEC, 1959–61. Joined Admiralty as Asst Principal, 1961; MoD, 1964; Asst Sec., 1973; seconded to Pay Board, 1973–74; Asst Under Sec. of State, Air, MoD (PE), 1982–84, Resources and Progs, MoD, 1984. *Address*: 2 Downs Bridge Road, Beckenham, Kent BR3 2HX. *T*: 01–650 5943.

REFFELL, Vice-Adm. Sir Derek (Roy), KCB 1984; Controller of the Navy, since 1984; *b* 6 Oct. 1928; *s* of late Edward (Roy) and Murielle Reffell; *m* 1956, Janne Gronow Davis; one *s* one *d*. *Educ*: Culford Sch., Suffolk; Royal Naval Coll., Dartmouth. FNI. Various ships at Home, Mediterranean, West Indies and Far East, 1946–63; qualified Navigating Officer, 1954; Comdr 1963; Comd HMS Sirius, 1966–67; Comdr BRNC Dartmouth, 1968–69; Captain 1970; Chief Staff Officer Plans Far East, 1970–71; Naval Staff, 1971–74; Comd HMS Hermes, 1974–76; Director Naval Warfare, 1976–78; Commodore Amphibious Warfare, 1978–79; Asst Chief of Naval Staff (Policy), 1979–82; Flag Officer Third Flotilla and Comdr Anti-Submarine Group Two, March 1982–Aug. 1983; Flag Officer, Naval Air Comd, 1983–84. CBIM. Assistant, Coachmakers Company, 1976–. *Recreation*: wine-making. *T*: Hindhead 5184; 01–834 3159. *Club*: Army and Navy.

REFSHAUGE, Maj.-Gen. Sir William (Dudley), AC 1980; Kt 1966; CBE 1959 (OBE 1944); ED 1965; Secretary-General, World Medical Association, 1973–76; Hon. Consultant to Australian Foundation on Alcoholism and Drugs of Dependence, since 1979; *b* 3 April 1913; *s* of late F. C. Refshauge, Melbourne; *m* 1942, Helen Elizabeth, *d* of late R. E. Allwright, Tasmania; four *s* one *d*. *Educ*: Hampton High Sch.; Scotch Coll., Melbourne; Melbourne University. MB, BS (Melbourne) 1938; FRCOG 1961; FRACS 1962; FRACP 1963; Hon. FRSH 1967; FACMA 1967; FRACOG 1978. Served with AIF, 1939–46; Lt-Col, RAAMC (despatches four times). Medical Supt, Royal Women's Hosp., Melbourne, 1948–51; Col, and Dep. DGAMS, Aust., 1951–55; Maj.-Gen. and DGAMS, Aust., 1955–60; QHP, 1955–64. Commonwealth Dir-Gen. of Health, Australia, 1960–73. Chairman: Council, Aust. Coll. of Nursing, 1958–60 (Chm. Educn Cttee, 1951–58); Nat. Health and MRC, 1960–73; Nat. Fitness Council, 1960–; Nat. Tuberculosis Adv. Council, 1960–; Prog. and Budget Cttee, 15th World Health Assembly, 1962; Admin., Fin. and Legal Cttee 19th World Health Assembly (Pres., 24th Assembly, 1971); Exec. Bd, WHO, 1969–70 (Mem., 1967–70). Member: Council, Aust. Red Cross Soc., 1954–60; Mem. Nat. Blood Transfusion Cttee, ARCS 1955–60; Nat. Trustee, Returned Services League Aust., 1961–73, 1976–; Mem. Bd of Management, Canberra Grammar Sch., 1963–68; Mem. Bd of Trustees, Walter and Eliza Hall Inst. of Med. Res., Melbourne, 1977– (Chm., Ethics Cttee, 1983–); Chm., Governing Bd, Menzies Sch. of Health Research, Darwin. Chm., ACT Cttee, Mem., Nat. Cttee and Mem. Nat. Exec., Sir Robert Menzies Foundn, 1979–. Hon. Life Mem., Australian Dental Assoc., 1966. Patron: Australian Sports Medicine Assoc., 1971–; ACT Br., Aust. Sports Medicine Fedn, 1980–; Totally and Permanently Incapacitated Assoc., ACT, 1982–; 2/2 Field Regtl Assoc., 1984–. Leader, Commemorative Tour of Europe for 60th anniversary, RSL. Nat. Pres., 1st Pan Pacific Conf. on alcohol and drugs, 1980. *Publications*: contribs to Australian Med. Jl, NZ Med. Jl, etc. *Recreations*: bowls, rug-making, gardening. *Address*: 26 Birdwood Street, Hughes, Canberra, ACT 2605, Australia. *Clubs*: Royal Society of Medicine (London); Naval and Military, Cricket (Melbourne); Commonwealth (Canberra); Bowling (Canberra); Royal Automobile (Victoria).

REGAN, Charles Maurice; Clerk to the Trustees, Hampstead Wells and Campden Trust, since 1985; Under-Secretary, Department of Health and Social Security, 1972–79 and 1981–85; *b* 31 Oct. 1925; *m* 1961, Susan (*née* Littmann) (*d* 1972); one *s* one *d*. *Educ*: Taunton Sch.; London Sch. of Economics and Political Science (BSc(Econ)). Academic research, 1950–52. Asst Principal, Min. of National Insurance, 1952; Principal Private Sec. to Minister of Pensions and National Insurance, 1962–64; Asst Sec., 1964; Treasury/Civil Service Dept, 1967–70; Under-Sec., DES, 1979–81. *Recreations*: walking, travel. *Address*: 35 Crediton Hill, NW6 1HS. *T*: 01–794 6404.

REGAN, Donald Thomas; Chief of Staff at the White House, since 1985; *b* 21 Dec. 1918; *s* of late William F. Regan and Kathleen A. Regan; *m* 1942, Ann Gordon Buchanan; two *s* two *d*. *Educ*: Cambridge Latin Sch.; Harvard Univ. (BA). Served War, US Marine Corps, 1940–46; retd as Lt Col, Marine Corps Reserve. Merrill Lynch, Pierce, Fenner & Smith Inc., 1946–81: Vice Pres., 1959–64; Exec. Vice Pres., 1964–68; Pres., 1968–71; Chm. of Bd, 1971–80; Chm. of Bd, Merrill Lynch & Co., Inc., 1973–81; Sec. of the Treasury, US Treasury Dept, 1981–85. Hon. LLD: Hahnemann Med. Coll. and Hosp., 1968; Tri-State Coll., 1969; Univ. of Penn., 1972; Hon. Dr of Commercial Science, Pace Univ., 1973. Fortune magazine's Hall of Fame for business leadership, 1981. *Publication*: A View from the Street, 1972. *Recreations*: golf, reading. *Address*: The White House, Capitol Hill, Washington DC, USA. *Clubs*: Metropolitan, Army-Navy (Washington, DC); Burning Tree (Bethesda, Md).

REGAN, Hon. Gerald Augustine, PC (Can.) 1980; QC (Can.) 1970; President, Hawthorne Developments, since 1984; lawyer; *b* Windsor, NS, 13 Feb. 1929; *s* of Walter E. Regan and Rose M. Greene; *m* 1956, A. Carole, *d* of John H. Harrison; three *s* three *d*. *Educ*: Windsor Academy; St Mary's and Dalhousie Univs, Canada; Dalhousie Law Sch. (LLB). Called to Bar of Nova Scotia, 1954. Liberal candidate in Provincial gen. elecs, 1956 and 1960, and in Fed. gen. elec., 1962. MP for Halifax, NS, House of Commons of Canada, 1963–65; Leader, Liberal Party of Nova Scotia, 1965–80; MLA for Halifax-Needham, Provincial gen. elec., 1967, re-elected, 1970–74 and 1978; Premier of Nova Scotia, 1970–78, Leader of the Opposition 1978–80; Minister of Labour, Govt of Canada, 1980–81, Minister responsible for Fitness and Amateur Sport 1980–82; Secretary of State for Canada, 1981–82; Minister for International Trade, 1982–84; Minister of Energy, Mines and Resources, June–Sept. 1984. Mem., NS Barristers Soc.; Chm. Exec. Cttee, Commonwealth Parly Assoc., 1973–76; Mem., Canadian Delegn, UN, 1965. Director: Nabisco Brands Inc.; Sceptre Resources; Roman Corp.; Provigo Inc. Governor, Olympic Trust of Canada. *Recreations*: tennis, ski-ing. *Address*: PO Box 828 Station B, Ottawa, Ontario K1P 5P9, Canada; (home) 2332 Georgina Drive, Ottawa, K2B 7M4, Canada. *Club*: Halifax (Halifax, NS).

REGINA, Archbishop of, (RC), since 1973; **Most Rev. Charles A. Halpin;** *b* 30 Aug. 1930; *s* of John S. Halpin and Marie Anne Gervais. *Educ*: St Boniface Coll. (BA); St Boniface Seminary (BTh); Gregorian Univ., Rome (JCL). Priest, 1956; Vice-Chancellor of Archdiocese of Winnipeg and Secretary to Archbishop, 1960; Officialis of Archdiocesan Matrimonial Tribunal, 1962; Chaplain to the Holy Father with title of Monsignor, 1969; ordained Bishop, Nov. 1973; installed as Archbishop of Regina, Dec. 1973. *Address*: 3225 13th Avenue, Regina, Saskatchewan S4T 1P5, Canada. *T*: (306) 352–1651.

REHNQUIST, William H.; Chief Justice of the United States, since 1986; *b* 1 Oct. 1924; *s* of William Benjamin and Margery Peck Rehnquist; *m* 1953, Natalie Cornell; one *s* two *d*. *Educ:* Stanford and Harvard Univs. BA, MA 1948, LLB 1952, Stanford; MA Harvard 1949. Law Clerk for Mr Justice Robert H. Jackson, 1952–53; Partner, Phoenix, Ariz: Evans, Kitchell & Jenckes, 1953–55; Ragan & Rehnquist, 1956–57; Cunningham, Carson & Messenger, 1957–60; Powers & Rehnquist, 1960–69; Asst Attorney-Gen., Office of Legal Counsel, Dept of Justice, 1969–72; Associate Justice, Supreme Court, 1972–86. Phi Beta Kappa; Order of the Coif. *Publications:* contrib. US News and World Report, Jl of Amer. Bar Assoc., Arizona Law Review. *Recreations:* swimming, tennis, reading, hiking. *Address:* Supreme Court of the United States, Washington, DC 20543, USA. *Club:* National Lawyers (Washington, DC).

REICH, Peter Gordon, FRIN; Assistant Chief Scientist (G), Royal Air Force, since 1984; *b* 16 Sept. 1926; *s* of Douglas Gordon Reich and Josephine Grace Reich; *m* 1948, Kathleen, *d* of Alan and Florence Lessiter, Banstead; three *d*. *Educ:* Sutton Grammar Sch.; London Univ. (BSc). FRIN 1967 (Bronze Medal, 1967). Served RN, 1944–47. Entered Civil Service as Scientific Officer, 1952; Armament Res. Estab., 1952–54; Opl Res. Br., Min. of Transport and Civil Aviation, 1955–60; RAE, 1960–68; Asst Dir of Electronics Res. and Develt (2), Min. of Technol., 1968–70; Asst Dir of Res. (Avionics, Space and Air Traffic), Min. of Aviation Supply, 1971–73; Supt, Def. Opl Analysis Estab., MoD, 1973–76; Mem., Reliability and Costing Study Gp, MoD, 1976–79; Counsellor (Defence Res.), Canberra, and Head of British Defence Res. and Supply Staffs, Australia, 1979–83. *Publications:* papers in Jl of Inst. of Nav., and Jl of Opl Res. Soc. *Recreations:* racquet games, walking, aural pleasures. *Address:* MoD Main Building, Whitehall.

REICHSTEIN, Prof. Tadeus, Dr ing chem; Ordentlicher Professor, Head of Department of Organic Chemistry, University of Basel, 1946–60, now Emeritus; *b* Wloclawek, Poland, 20 July 1897; *s* of Isidor Reichstein and Gustava Brockmann; *m* 1927, Henriette Louise Quarles van Ufford; two *d*. *Educ:* Oberrealschule and Eidgenössische Technische Hochschule, Department of Chemistry, Zürich. Assistant, ETH, Zürich, 1922–34; professor of organic chemistry, ETH, Zürich, 1934; head of department of pharmacy, University of Basel, 1938. Dr *hc* Sorbonne, Paris, 1947, Basel 1951, Geneva, 1967, ETH, Zürich, 1967, Abidjan 1967, London 1968, Leeds 1970. Marcel Benoît Prize, 1948; (jointly) Nobel Prize for Medicine, 1950; Cameron Prize, 1951; Copley Medal, Royal Soc., 1968; Dale Medal, Soc. for Endocrinology, 1975. Foreign Member: Royal Society, 1952; Linnean Society, 1974. Hon. Member: British Pteridological Soc., 1967; Amer. Fern Soc., 1974; Deutsche Botanische Gesellschaft, 1976; Schweizerische Botanische Gesellschaft, 1977. *Publications:* numerous papers. *Recreations:* botany (ferns), devoted gardener, mountain-climber. *Address:* Institut für Organische Chemie der Universität, St Johanns-Ring 19, CH 4056 Basel, Switzerland. *T:* (061) 576060.

REID, Sir Alexander (James), 3rd Bt *cr* 1897; JP; DL; *b* 6 Dec. 1932; *s* of Sir Edward James Reid, 2nd Bt, KBE, and of Tatiana, *d* of Col Alexander Fenoult, formerly of Russian Imperial Guard; *S* father, 1972; *m* 1955, Michaela Ann, *d* of late Olaf Kier, CBE; one *s* three *d*. *Educ:* Eton; Magdalene Coll., Cambridge. Nat. Certificate Agriculture (NCA). 2nd Lieut, 1st Bn Gordon Highlanders, 1951; served Malaya; Captain, 3rd Bn Gordon Highlanders (TA), retired 1964. Director: Ellon Castle Estates Co. Ltd, 1965–; Cristina Securities Ltd, 1970–; Kingston Agricultural Services Ltd, 1977–; Cytozyme (UK) Ltd, 1985–. Governor, Heath Mount Prep. Sch., Hertford, 1970, Chm., 1976. JP Cambridgeshire and Isle of Ely, 1971, DL 1973. *Recreation:* shooting. *Heir:* *s* Charles Edward James Reid, *b* 24 June 1956. *Address:* Kingston Wood Manor, Arrington, Royston, Herts SG8 0AP. *T:* Caxton 231. *Clubs:* Farmers', Caledonian.

REID, Andrew Milton; Deputy Chairman, Imperial Group, since 1986; *b* 21 July 1929; *s* of late Rev. A. R. R. Reid, DD and of Lilias Symington Tindal; *m* 1953, Norma Mackenzie Davidson; two *s*. *Educ:* Glasgow Academy; Jesus Coll., Oxford. Imperial Tobacco Management Pupil, 1952; Asst Managing Director, John Player & Sons, 1975; Director Imperial Group Ltd, 1978; Chm., Imperial Tobacco Ltd, 1979–86. Director: Trade Indemnity plc, 1982–; Renold PLC, 1983–; Mem. S and W Adv. Bd, Legal and General Assurance Soc. Ltd. Member, Tobacco Adv. Council, 1977–. Mem. Court and Council, Bristol Univ., 1986. Chm. Governors, Colston's Sch., 1986. *Recreations:* sailing, golf, fishing. *Address:* Parsonage Farm, Publow, Pensford, near Bristol BS18 4JD. *Club:* Clifton (Bristol).

REID, Archibald Cameron, CMG 1963; CVO 1970; retired 1971; *b* 7 Aug. 1915; *s* of William Reid; *m* 1941, Joan Raymond Charlton; two *s* two *d*. *Educ:* Fettes; Queen's College, Cambridge. Apptd Admin. Officer, Class II, in Colony of Fiji, 1938; Admin. Officer, Class I, 1954; British Agent and Consul, Tonga, 1957–59; Sec. for Fijian Affairs, 1959–65; British Comr and Consul, Tonga, 1965–70; Dep. High Comr, Tonga, 1970–71. Engaged in Pacific History research. *Publications:* sundry articles. *Recreations:* walking, painting, golf. *Address:* 37 Kevin Avenue, Avalon Beach, NSW 2107, Australia. *T:* 918 6402.

REID, Beryl, OBE 1986; actress; *b* 17 June 1920. *Educ:* Lady Barne House Sch.; Withington High Sch.; Levenshulme High Sch., Manchester. First stage appearance, Bridlington, 1936; on London stage, 1951; appeared in variety, numerous sketches, revues and pantomimes, 1951–64. *Plays:* The Killing of Sister George, Duke of York's, 1965, NY, 1966 (Tony Award for Best Actress); Blithe Spirit, Globe, 1970; Entertaining Mr Sloane, Royal Court, Duke of York's, 1975; National Theatre: Spring Awakening, Romeo and Juliet, 1974; Il Campiello, Counting the Ways, 1976; The Way of the World, RSC, Aldwych, 1978; Born in the Gardens, Bristol Old Vic, 1979, Globe (SWET Award), 1980; The School for Scandal, Haymarket, and Duke of York's, 1983; A Little Bit on the Side, Yvonne Arnaud, Guildford, 1983; Gigi, Lyric, 1985. *Films include:* The Belles of St Trinians, Star, The Killing of Sister George, Entertaining Mr Sloane, No Sex Please—We're British!, Joseph Andrews, Carry On Emmanuelle, Yellowbeard, The Doctor and the Devils. Frequent television and radio performances, including her own series on several occasions; Best TV actress award, BAFTA, 1983 (for Smiley's People). *Publications:* So Much Love (autobiog.), 1984; (with Eric Braun) The Cats Whiskers, 1986. *Recreations:* gardening, cooking. *Address:* c/o Eric Braun Enterprises, 36 Michelham Gardens, Strawberry Hill, Twickenham TW1 4SB. *T:* 01-892 6795.

REID, Dougal Gordon, CMG 1983; HM Diplomatic Service, retired; Director of Studies, Overseas Services Unit, Royal Institute of Public Administration, since 1985; *b* Hong Kong, 31 Dec. 1925; *e s* of late Douglas Reid and Catherine Jean (*née* Lowson), Forfar; *m* 1950, Georgina Elizabeth Johnston; one *s* (and one *s* decd). *Educ:* Sedbergh Sch.; Trinity Hall, Cambridge; LSE. Served in Royal Marines, 1944–46. Cadet, Colonial Admin. Service (later HMOCS), Sierra Leone, 1949; District Comr 1956; retd as Perm. Sec., Min. of Natural Resources, 1962. Arthur Guinness Son & Co. Ltd, 1962–63. Entered CRO, 1963; 1st Sec., Accra, 1964–65; Commonwealth Office, 1966; Accra, 1966–68 (concurrently Lomé, 1967–68); Seoul, 1968–71; FCO, 1971–74; Counsellor (Commercial) and Consul-General, Kinshasa (and concurrently at Brazzaville, Bujumbura and Kigali), 1974–77; Counsellor, New Delhi, 1977–78; Counsellor (Economic and Commercial), Singapore, 1979–80; Ambassador to Liberia, 1980–85. Member: Internat. Cttee, Leonard Cheshire Foundn, 1985–; VSO, 1984–. *Recreations:* golf, music, watching sport. *Clubs:* Travellers', Royal Commonwealth Society, MCC; Sadan Pubin (Seoul).

REID, Francis Alexander; QC (NI) 1956; Social Security Commissioner, 1970–85; retired; *b* 2 March 1915; *s* of Frank Reid and Annie Stevenson; *m* 1940, Barbara Colville Welsh; one *d*. *Educ:* Trinity Public Elementary Sch., Bangor, Co. Down; Bangor Grammar Sch.; The Queen's Univ., Belfast (BA). Called to Bar of N Ireland, 1939; Bencher of Inn of Court, NI, 1965; admitted Advocate and Solicitor, FMS, 1939. War service in FMS Volunteer Force, 1939–45. Sen. Crown Prosecutor, successively, Armagh, Londonderry, Antrim and Belfast, 1954–67. Member, National Arbitration Tribunal (NI), 1947–56; Chm., War Pensions Appeal Tribunal (NI), 1956–61; President of Industrial Tribunals, 1970. Chm., Bar Council, NI, 1967–69. *Recreation:* reading. *Address:* Flat D, Newfaan Isle House, 65 Abbotsford Road, Galashiels TD1 3HN. *T:* Galashiels 4635. *Club:* New (Edinburgh).

REID, George Newlands; Director of Public Affairs, League of Red Cross and Red Crescent Societies in Geneva, since 1984; *b* 4 June 1939; *s* of late George Reid, company director, and of Margaret Forsyth; *m* 1968, Daphne Ann MacColl; two *d*. *Educ:* Tullibody Sch.; Dollar Academy; Univ. of St Andrews (MA Hons). Pres., Students' Representative Council. Features Writer, Scottish Daily Express, 1962; Reporter, Scottish Television, 1964; Producer, Granada Television, 1965; Head of News and Current Affairs (Scottish Television), 1968; freelance broadcaster and journalist, 1972–84; presenter, political and documentary progs, BBC. MP (SNP) Stirlingshire E and Clackmannan, Feb. 1974–1979; Member, Select Committee on: Assistance to Private Members, 1975–76; Direct Elections to European Assembly, 1976–77; Mem., British Parly Delegn to Council of Europe and WEU, 1977–79. Dir, Scottish Council Res. Inst., 1974–77. League rep. to UN, 1986–. *Address:* 23 Avenue du Bouchet, Petit Saconnex, Geneva, Switzerland. *T:* 34.67.05.

REID, Hon. Sir George Oswald, Kt 1972; QC (Vic) 1971; Attorney-General, Victoria, Australia, 1967–73; Barrister and Solicitor; *b* Hawthorn, Vic, 22 July 1903; *s* of late George Watson Reid and Lillias Margaret Reid (*née* Easton); *m* 1st, 1930, Beatrix Waring McCay, LLM (*d* 1972), *d* of Lt-Gen. Hon. Sir James McCay; one *d*; 2nd, 1973, Dorothy, *d* of late C. W. F. Ruttledge. *Educ:* Camberwell Grammar Sch. and Scotch Coll., Melbourne; Melbourne Univ. (LLB). Admitted to practice as Barrister and Solicitor, Supreme Ct of Vic., 1926. Has practised as Solicitor in Melbourne, 1929–. Served War, RAAF, 1940–46, Wing Comdr. MLA (Liberal) for Box Hill, 1947–52, and 1955–73. Government of Victoria: Minister without Portfolio, 1955–56; Minister of Labour and Industry and Electrical Undertakings, 1956–65; Minister: for Fuel and Power, 1965–67; of Immigration, 1967–70; Chief Secretary, March 9–Apr. 27, 1971. *Recreations:* bowls, golf, reading. *Address:* Nilja, Alexander Road, Warrandyte, Vic 3113, Australia. *Clubs:* Melbourne, Savage, Melbourne Cricket (Melbourne); Royal Automobile (Victoria).

REID, Air Vice-Marshal Sir (George) Ranald Macfarlane, KCB 1945 (CB 1941); DSO 1919; MC and bar; Extra Gentleman Usher to the Queen, 1959; Gentleman Usher to the Queen, 1952 (formerly to King George VI, 1952); *b* 25 Oct. 1893; *s* of late George Macfarlane Reid and Gertrude Macquisten, Prestwick; *m* 1934, Leslie Livermore Washburne, *d* of late Hamilton Wright, Washington, DC, USA, and *g d* of Senator William Washburne; one *s* one *d*. *Educ:* Routenburn; Malvern Coll. Regular Officer, 1914–46 in: 4th (SR) Argyll and Sutherland Highlanders; 2nd Black Watch; RFC and RAF. Served European War, 1914–18 (wounded, despatches, MC and Bar, DSO); Egypt, 1919–21; Sudan, 1927–29; RAF Staff Coll., 1930; Imperial Defence Coll., 1932; Air Attaché, British Embassy, Washington, 1933–35; AOC Halton, 1936–38; Air Officer Commanding British Forces, Aden, 1938–41; Air Officer Administration Flying Training Command; AOC 54 Group; AOC West Africa, 1944–45; retired from Royal Air Force, 1946. *Address:* c/o R3 Section, Lloyds Bank, 6 Pall Mall, SW1Y 5NH. *Clubs:* Royal Air Force; Weld (Perth, Western Australia).

REID, Very Rev. George Thomson Henderson, MC 1945; Chaplain to the Queen in Scotland, 1969–80, Extra Chaplain since 1980; *b* 31 March 1910; *s* of Rev. David Reid, DD; *m* 1938, Anne Guilland Watt, *d* of late Principal Very Rev. Hugh Watt, DD, Edinburgh; three *s* one *d*. *Educ:* George Watson's Boys' Coll.; Univ. of Edinburgh. MA 1932, BD 1935, Edinburgh. Served as Chaplain to 3rd Bn Scots Guards, 1940–45, Sen. Chaplain to 15th (S) Div., 1945. Minister at: Port Seton, E Lothian, 1935–38; Juniper Green, Edinburgh, 1938–49; Claremont Church, Glasgow, 1949–55; West Church of St Andrew, Aberdeen, 1955–75. Moderator of the General Assembly of the Church of Scotland, 1973–74. Hon. DD Aberdeen, 1969. *Recreations:* golf, bird-watching, painting. *Address:* 33 Westgarth Avenue, Colinton, Edinburgh.
See also Prof. J. K. S. Reid.

REID, Prof. Gordon Stanley, AC 1986; Governor of Western Australia, since 1984; Professor Emeritus, University of Western Australia; *b* 22 Sept. 1923; *s* of Emily Matilda Reid (*née* Hewitt) and Stanley Archibald James Reid; *m* 1945, Ruth Amelia Fish; two *s* two *d*. Educ: Univ. of Melbourne (BCom 1953); London Sch. of Economics (PhD 1957; Hon. Fellow, 1984); FASSA; Fellow, Royal Aust. Inst. of Public Admin. Flying Officer, RAAF, Europe, RAF Sqdns Nos 83 and 106, 1942–46. Serjeant-at-Arms, House of Representatives, Canberra, 1955–58; Senior Lectr, then Reader, in Politics, Univ. of Adelaide, 1958–66; Prof. of Politics, Univ. of Western Australia, 1966–71, 1974–78, 1983–84 (Dep. Vice-Chancellor, 1978–83); Prof. of Political Science, ANU, 1971–74. *Publications:* The Politics of Financial Control, 1966; (with C. J. Lloyd), Out of the Wilderness: the return of Labour, 1974; (with M. Oliver) The Premiers of Western Australia, 1983. *Recreation:* tennis. *Address:* Government House, Perth, WA 6000, Australia. *T:* 325 3222; 69 Tyrell Street, Nedlands, WA 6009, Australia. *Clubs:* University House (Canberra); Western Australian Cricket.

REID, Graham Livingstone; Chief Economic Adviser and Head of Economic and Social Division, Department of Employment, since 1984; *b* 30 June 1937; *s* of late William L. Reid and of Louise M. Reid; *m* 1973, Eileen M. Loudfoot (marr. diss. 1983). *Educ:* Univ. of St Andrews (MA); Queen's Univ., Kingston, Canada (MA). Dept of Social and Economic Res., Univ. of Glasgow: Asst Lectr in Applied Economics, 1960, Lectr 1963, Sen. Lectr 1968, Reader 1971; Sen. Econ. Adviser and Head of Econs and Statistics Unit, Scottish Office, 1973–75; Dir, Manpower Intelligence and Planning Div., MSC, 1975–84. Vis. Associate Prof., Mich State Univ., 1967; Vis. Res. Fellow, Queen's Univ., Canada, 1969. *Publications:* Fringe Benefits, Labour Costs and Social Security (ed with D. J. Robertson), 1965; (with K. J. Allen) Nationalised Industries, 1970 (3rd edn 1975); (with L. C. Hunter and D. Boddy) Labour Problems of Technological Change, 1970; (with K. J. Allen and D. J. Harris) The Nationalised Fuel Industries, 1973; contrib. to Econ. Jl, Brit. Jl of Indust. Relations, Scot. Jl of Polit. Econ., Indust & Lab. Relns Rev. *Recreations:* golf, music. *Address:* 16c Abercorn Place, NW8 9XP. *Club:* Royal Commonwealth Society.

REID, (Harold) Martin (Smith), CMG 1978; HM Diplomatic Service; High Commissioner to Jamaica, and Ambassador (non-resident) to Haiti, since 1984; *b* 27 Aug. 1928; *s* of late Marcus Reid and late Winifred Mary Reid (*née* Stephens); *m* 1956, Jane Elizabeth Harwood; one *s* three *d*. *Educ:* Merchant Taylors' Sch.; Brasenose Coll., Oxford (Open Scholar). RN, 1947–49. Entered HM Foreign Service, 1953; served in: FO,

1953–54; Paris, 1954–57; Rangoon, 1958–61; FO, 1961–65; Georgetown, 1965–68; Bucharest, 1968–70; Dep. High Comr, Malaŵi, 1970–73; Private Sec. to successive Secs of State for NI, 1973–74; Head of Central and Southern Africa Dept, FCO, 1974–78; Minister, British Embassy, Pretoria/Cape Town, 1979–82; Resident Chm. (Dip. Service) CS Selection Bd, 1983–84. *Recreations:* painting and drawing; chess. *Address:* c/o Foreign and Commonwealth Office, SW1.

See also M. H. M. Reid.

REID, Sir Hugh, 3rd Bt *cr* 1922; farmer; *b* 27 Nov. 1933; *s* of Sir Douglas Neilson Reid, 2nd Bt, and of Margaret Brighton Young, *d* of Robert Young Maxtone, MBE, JP; *S* father, 1971. *Educ:* Loretto. Royal Air Force, 1952–56; RAFVR, 1956–78 (Flying Officer, Training Branch, 1965–78). *Recreations:* skiing, travel. *Heir:* none. *Address:* Caheronaun Park, Loughrea, Co. Galway.

REID, Ian George; Director, Centre for European Agricultural Studies, Wye College, University of London, 1974–86; *b* 12 May 1921; 2nd *s* of James John Reid and Margaret Jane Reid; *m* 1946, Peggy Eileen Bridgman. *Educ:* Merchant Taylors' Sch.; London Sch. of Econs (BScEcon); Christ's Coll., Cambridge (Dip. Agric.). Lectr, Reading Univ., 1945–53; Lectr, 1953–63, and Sen. Lectr, 1963–86, Wye Coll. Pres., Agricultural Econs Soc., 1981–82. *Recreations:* enjoying music, gardening, art. *Address:* 20 Bridge Street, Wye, Ashford, Kent TN25 5EA. *T:* Wye (Kent) 812388. *Clubs:* Athenæum, Farmers'.

REID, Col Ivo; *see* Reid, Col P. F. I.

REID, James, OBE (mil.) 1968; VRD 1967; Director, Investments and Loans, Commission of European Communities, 1973–76; *b* 23 Nov. 1921; *s* of William Reid, MBE, and Dora Louisa Reid (*née* Smith); *m* 1949, Margaret James; two *d. Educ:* City of London Sch.; Emmanuel Coll., Cambridge (MA). Served War, RN: RNVR (Sub. Lieut), 1942–45. Served RNVR and RNR (Comdr), 1953–72. Entered Northern Ireland Civil Service, 1948 (Asst Principal); Min. of Finance, 1948–61 and 1963–73; Min. of Commerce, 1961–63; Principal, 1953; Asst Sec., 1963; Sen. Asst Sec., 1971; Dep. Sec., 1972. *Recreations:* reading, music. *Address:* 6 Avenue Guillaume, Luxembourg–1650. *Club:* United Oxford & Cambridge University.

REID, James Robert; QC 1980; a Recorder, since 1985; *b* 23 Jan. 1943; *s* of late Judge J. A. Reid, MC and of Jean Ethel Reid; *m* 1974, Anne Prudence Wakefield; two *s* one *d. Educ:* Marlborough Coll.; New Coll., Oxford (MA). Called to the Bar, Lincoln's Inn, 1965. *Recreations:* fencing, cricket. *Address:* 9 Old Square, Lincoln's Inn, WC2.

REID, John, CB 1967; Chief Veterinary Officer, Ministry of Agriculture, Fisheries and Food, 1965–70; *b* 14 May 1906; *s* of late John and Jessie Jamieson Reid, Callander, Perthshire; *m* 1933, Molly Russell; one *d. Educ:* McLaren High Sch., Callander; Royal (Dick) Veterinary Coll., Edinburgh. FRCVS 1971; DVSM 1931. Asst Veterinary Officer, Midlothian County Council, 1931; Asst Veterinary Officer, Cumberland County Council, 1932; Ministry of Agriculture and Fisheries: Divisional Veterinary Officer, 1938; Superintending Veterinary Officer, 1952; Ministry of Agriculture, Fisheries and Food: Regional Veterinary Officer, 1958; Deputy Chief Veterinary Officer, 1960; Director of Veterinary Field Services, 1963. Mem. ARC, 1965–70. Vice-Chm., FAO European Commn for Control of Foot-and-Mouth Disease, 1967–70; Member: Cttee of Inquiry into Veterinary Profession, 1971–75; Scientific Authority for Animals, DoE, 1976–77. *Recreations:* gardening, bird watching. *Address:* Owl's Green Cottage, Dennington, Woodbridge, Suffolk IP13 8BY. *T:* Badingham 205. *Club:* Farmers'.

REID, John Boyd, AO 1980; LLB; FAIM; Chairman, James Hardie Industries, since 1973; *b* 27 Dec. 1929; *s* of Sir John Thyne Reid, CMG; *m* 1954, Patricia, *d* of late D. J. Ferrier; two *d. Educ:* Scotch College; Melbourne Univ. Chm., Comsteel Vickers Ltd, 1983–86; Vice-Chm., Qantas Airways, 1981–86 (Dir, 1977–86); Director: Broken Hill Pty Co., 1972–; Barclays Internat. Australia, 1982–85. Chm., Australian Bicentennial Authy, 1979–85; Member: Admin. Review Cttee, 1975–76; Indep. Inquiry into Commonwealth Serum Labs, 1978; Australia Japan Business Co-operation Cttee, 1978–; Patron, Australia Indonesia Business Co-operation Cttee, 1979– (Pres., 1973–79); Mem., Internat. Adv. Bd, Swiss Banking Corp., 1986–; Chm., Review of Commonwealth Admin, 1981–82. Internat. Counsellor, Conference Bd USA, Stanford Res. Inst., USA.Chm. Council, Pymble Ladies Coll., 1975–82 (Mem., 1965–75); Governor, Ian Clunies Ross Meml Foundn, 1975–; Member, Nat. Councils: Scout Assoc. of Aust.; Aust. Opera; Mem. Sydney Adv. Cttee, Salvation Army, 1985–. Melbourne Univ. Graduate Sch. of Business Admin Award, 1983; John Storey Medal, AIM, 1985. *Address:* c/o James Hardie Industries Ltd, GPO Box 3935, Sydney, NSW 2001, Australia. *Clubs:* Caledonian; Australian (Sydney); Commonwealth (Canberra); Royal Sydney Yacht Squadron.

REID, Sir John (James Andrew), KCMG 1985; CB 1975; TD 1958; MD, FRCP, FRCPE; Consultant Adviser on International Health, Department of Health and Social Security, since 1986; Hon. Consultant in Community Medicine to the Army, since 1971; *b* 21 Jan. 1925; *s* of Alexander Scott Reid and Mary Cullen Reid (*née* Andrew); *m* 1949, Marjorie Reid (*née* Crumpton), MB, ChB; one *s* four *d. Educ:* Bell-Baxter Sch.; Univ. of St Andrews. BSc 1944; MB, ChB 1947; DPH 1952; MD 1961; Hon. DSc 1979; FRCP (Edin.) 1970; FRCP 1971; FFCM 1972; FRCP (Glas) 1980. Lt-Col RAMC (TA). Hospital, Army (Nat. Service) and junior Public Health posts, 1947–55; Lectr in Public Health and Social Medicine, Univ. of St Andrews, 1955–59; Dep. County MOH, Northamptonshire, 1959–62; County MOH, Northamptonshire, 1962–67; County MOH, Buckinghamshire, 1967–72; Dep. Chief MO, DHSS, 1972–77, Chief MO, SHHD, 1977–85. Member: GMC (Crown Nominee), 1973–81, 1985; Council for Post-grad. Med. Educn, 1973–77; Scottish Council for Post-grad. Med. Educn, 1977–85; Scottish Health Service Planning Council, 1977–85; Exec. Bd, WHO, 1973–75, 1976–79, 1980–83, 1984– (Vice Chm., 1977–78; Chm., 1978–79; consultant); MRC, 1977–85; EC Adv. Cttee on Med. Training, 1976–85. WHO Fellow, 1962; Mem., Standing Med. Adv. Cttee, DHSS, 1966–72; Chm., Jt Sub-Cttee on Health and Welfare Services for People with Epilepsy (Report, People with Epilepsy, 1969); Chm., Jt Working Party for Health Services in Milton Keynes, 1968–74; Dep. Co-Chm., UK/USSR Cttee on Health Care, 1975–77; Jt Chm., Scottish/Finnish Health Agreement, 1978–85; Mem., Working Party on Medical Administrators (Report, 1972); Public Health Lab. Service Bd, 1974–77; Hospital Management Committees: St Crispins, 1959–69; Northampton, 1962–67; St Johns, 1967–72. Vis. Prof. in Health Services Admin, London Sch. of Hygiene and Tropical Medicine, 1973–78 (Governor and Mem. Bd of Management, 1977–); Vis. Lectr and Examr, univs in UK and abroad; Governor, United Oxford Hosps, 1962–66. Hon. LLD Dundee, 1985. *Publications:* papers on public and international health, community medicine, diabetes, epilepsy, etc, in BMJ, Lancet, etc. *Address:* The Manor House, Manor Road, Oving, Aylesbury, Bucks HP22 4HW.

REID, Rev. Prof. John Kelman Sutherland, CBE 1970; TD 1961; Professor of Christian Dogmatics, 1961–70, of Systematic Theology 1970–76, University of Aberdeen; *b* 31 March 1910; *y s* of late Reverend Dr David Reid, Calcutta and Leith, and of late Mrs G. T. Reid (*née* Stuart); *m* 1950, Margaret Winifrid Brookes. *Educ:* George Watson's Boys' College, Edinburgh; Universities of Edinburgh (MA and BD), Heidelberg, Marburg, Basel, and Strasbourg. MA 1st Cl. Hons Philosophy, 1933. Prof. of Philosophy in Scottish Church Coll., Univ. of Calcutta, 1935–37; BD (dist. in Theol.), 1938, and Cunningham Fellow. Ordained into Church of Scotland and inducted into Parish of Craigmillar Park, Edinburgh, 1939. CF, chiefly with Parachute Regt, 1942–46. Jt Ed. Scot. Jl Theol. since inception, 1947; Hon. Sec. Jt Cttee on New Translation of the Bible, 1949–82; Prof. of Theology and Head of Department of Theology, University of Leeds, 1952–61. Hon. DD (Edinburgh), 1957. *Publications:* The Authority of Scripture, 1957; Our Life in Christ, 1963; Christian Apologetics, 1969. Translation of: Oscar Cullmann's The Earliest Christian Confessions, 1949; Baptism in the New Testament, 1952; Calvin's Theological Treatises, ed and trans. 1954; Jean Bosc's The Kingly Office of the Lord Jesus Christ, 1959; Calvin's Concerning the Eternal Pre-destination of God, ed and trans., 1961, repr. 1982. *Address:* 1 Camus Park, Fairmilehead, Edinburgh EH10 6RY. *Club:* Mortonhall Golf (Edinburgh).

See also Very Rev. G. T. H. Reid.

REID, Prof. John Low, DM; Regius Professor of Materia Medica, University of Glasgow, since 1978; *b* 1 Oct. 1943; *s* of Dr James Reid and Irene M. Dale; *m* 1964, Randa Pharaon; one *s* one *d. Educ:* Fettes Coll., Edinburgh; Magdalen Coll., Oxford. MA; DM; FRCP. House Officer, Radcliffe Infirmary, Oxford, and Brompton Hosp., 1967–70; Res. Fellow, RPMS, 1970–73; Vis. Fellow, Nat. Inst. of Mental Health, USA, 1973–74; Royal Postgraduate Medical School: Sen. Lectr in Clin. Pharmacol., and Consultant Physician, 1975–77; Reader in Clin. Pharmacol., 1977–78. *Publications:* Central Action of Drugs in Regulation of Blood Pressure, 1975; Lecture Notes in Clinical Pharmacology, 1982; Handbook of Hypertension, 1983; papers on cardiovascular and neurological diseases in clinical and pharmacological journals. *Recreations:* books, gardening, jogging. *Address:* Department of Materia Medica, Stobhill General Hospital, Glasgow G21 3UW. *T:* 041–558 0111.

REID, Rt. Rev. John Robert; Bishop of South Sydney since 1983 (Assistant Bishop, Diocese of Sydney, since 1972); *b* 15 July 1928; *s* of John and Edna Reid; *m* 1955, Alison Gertrude Dunn; two *s* four *d. Educ:* Melbourne Univ. (BA); Moore Coll., Sydney (ThL). Deacon 1955, Priest 1955; Curate, Manly, 1955–56; Rector, Christ Church, Gladesville, NSW, 1956–69; Archdeacon of Cumberland, NSW, 1969–72. *Recreation:* walking. *Address:* 33 Fairfax Road, Bellevue Hill, NSW 2023, Australia. *T:* 327–3320.

REID, John (Robson); architect and consultant designer; Partner, John and Sylvia Reid, since 1951; Pageantmaster to the Lord Mayors of London, since 1972; *b* 1 Dec. 1925; *s* of late Thomas Robson Reid and Olive Reid; *m* 1948, Sylvia Reid (*née* Payne), Dip. Arch., RIBA, FSIAD; one *s* twin *d. Educ:* Wellingborough Grammar Sch.; Sch. of Architecture, The Polytechnic, WI (Dip. in Architecture with dist.). RIBA, FSIAD, FCIBS. Capt., Green Howards, 1944–47; Mem. HAC, 1980. *Architectural work includes:* hotels, showrooms, museums, houses and pubs: Civic Suite, Wandsworth Town Hall; Savile Room, Merton Coll., Oxford; Great Room, Grosvenor House; Dunhill Res. Lab., Inst. of Dermatology; Westminster Theatre; Lawson House, ICI, Runcorn; Heatherside Shopping Centre; Savoy Grill; Exec. Suite, British Telecoms HQ; Barbican Exhibition Halls, Corporation of City of London; *industrial design work includes:* furniture, lighting fittings, road and rail transport, carpets, textiles, civic regalia; lighting consultant for Coventry Cathedral; some-time design consultant to Thorn, Rotaflex, Stag, CMC, BR, N General Transport, PO; UNIDO consultant on industrial design in India, Pakistan, Egypt and Turkey, 1977–79; British Council tour, India, 1985. *Exhibitions:* 350th Anniversary Celebration, Jamestown, Virginia, USA, 1957; various exhibns for BR, Cardiff Corp., City of London, etc. Leader, British delegn of design educn in Soviet Union, Anglo-Soviet Cultural Exchange Treaty, 1967. Dean of Art and Design, Middx Polytechnic, 1975–78; some-time mem. of adv. cttees, Central Sch. of Art and Design, Leeds Coll. of Art and Design, Newcastle-upon-Tyne Sch. of Art and Design, Carleton Univ., Ottawa; Governor, Hornsey Coll. of Art. Lectured in Canada, Czechoslovakia, Eire, Hungary, Japan, Poland, USA, USSR. PSIAD, 1965–66; Pres., Internat. Council of Socs of Ind. Design, 1969–71; Vice-Pres., Illuminating Engrg Soc., 1969–71. RIBA Mem., Bd of Nat. Inspection Council for Electrical Installation Contracting (Chm., 1972–73). Liveryman and Mem. Court of Assts, Worshipful Co. of Furniture Makers. Four CoID Awards; Silver Medals of 12th and 13th Milan Internat. Triennales. *Publications:* International Code of Professional Conduct, 1969; A Guide to Conditions of Contract for Industrial Design, 1971; Industrial Design in India, Pakistan, Egypt and Turkey, 1978; various articles in professional jls. *Recreations:* music, dinghy-sailing, gardening. *Address:* Arnoside House, The Green, Old Southgate, N14 7EG. *T:* 01–882 1083. *Clubs:* City Livery, Wig and Pen.

REID, Leslie, CBE 1978; HM Diplomatic Service, retired; Director General, The Association of British Mining Equipment Companies, 1980–83; *b* 24 May 1919; *s* of late Frederick Sharples and Mary Reid; *m* 1942, Norah Moorcroft; three *d. Educ:* King George V Sch., Southport, Lancs. Served War of 1939–45, W Europe and SEAC, Major, XX The Lancashire Fusiliers. Board of Trade, 1947–49; Asst Trade Commissioner: Salisbury, Rhodesia, 1949–55; Edmonton, Alberta, 1955–56; Trade Comr, Vancouver, 1956–60; Principal, BoT, 1960–62; Trade Comr and Economic Adviser, British High Commn, Cyprus, 1962–64; BoT, 1964–66; 1st Sec., FCO, 1966–68; Sen. Commercial Sec., British High Commn, Jamaica, and 1st Sec., British Embassy, Port-au-Prince, Haiti, 1968–70; Commercial and Economic Counsellor, Ghana, 1970–73; Consul Gen., Cleveland, Ohio, 1973–79. *Recreations:* golf, reading. *Address:* Abbotswood, Guildford, Surrey GU1 1UY.

REID, Prof. Lynne McArthur; S. Burt Wolbach Professor of Pathology, Harvard Medical School, since 1976; Chairman, Department of Pathology, Children's Hospital Medical Center, Boston, since 1976; *b* Melbourne, 12 Nov. 1923; *er d* of Robert Muir Reid and Violet Annie Reid (*née* McArthur). *Educ:* Wimbledon Girls' Sch. (GPDST); Janet Clarke Hall, Trinity Coll., Melbourne Univ.; Royal Melbourne Hosp. MB, BS Melb. 1946; MRACP 1950; MRCP 1951; FRACP, MRCPath (Foundn Mem.) 1964; FRCPath 1966; FRCP 1969; MD Melb. 1969. House Staff, Royal Melb. Hosp., 1946–49; Res. Fellow, Nat. Health and MRC, Royal Melb. Hosp. and Eliza Hall, 1949–51; Res. Asst, Inst. Diseases of Chest, 1951–55; Sen. Lectr founding Res. Dept of Path., Inst. Diseases of Chest, 1955; Reader in Exper. Path., London Univ., 1964; Prof. of Exper. Path., Inst. of Diseases of Chest (later Cardiothoracic Inst.), 1967–76; Hon. Lectr, UC Med. Sch., 1971–76; Hon. Consultant in Exper. Path., Brompton Hosp., 1963–76; Dean, Cardiothoracic Inst. (British Postgrad. Med. Fedn), 1973–76. 1st Hastings Vis. Prof. in Path., Univ. of California, 1965; Holme Lectr, UC Med. Sch., 1969; Walker-Ames Prof., Univ. of Washington, 1971; Neuhauser Lectr, 1976; Fleischner Lectr, 1976; Waring Prof., Stanford and Denver, 1977; Amberson Lectr, Amer. Thoracic Soc., 1978. Mem. Fleischner Soc., 1971 (Pres., 1977); 1st Hon. Fellow, Canadian Thoracic Soc., 1973; Chm., Cystic Fibrosis Res. Trust, 1974 (Mem. Med. Adv. Cttee 1964); Royal Soc. Medicine (Sect. Pathology): Vice-Pres. 1974; Standing Liaison Cttee on Sci. Aspects of Smoking and Health, 1971; Commn of European Cttees (Industrial Safety and Medicine), 1972; Mem. Bd of Governors, Nat. Heart and Chest Hosps, 1974; Manager, Royal Instn of Gt Britain, 1973 (Vice-Pres. 1974); Mem. Gov. Body, British Postgrad. Med. Fedn, 1974. *Publications:* The Pathology of Emphysema, 1967; numerous papers in sci jls. *Recreations:* music, travel, reading. *Address:* 75 Montrose Court, Princes Gate, SW7; Children's

Hospital Medical Center, Harvard Medical School, 300 Longwood Avenue, Boston, Mass 02115, USA. *Clubs:* University Women's; Harvard (Boston).

REID, Malcolm Herbert Marcus; Chief Executive, Life Assurance and Unit Trust Regulatory Organisation, since 1986; *b* 2 March 1927; *s* of late Marcus Reid and Winifred Stephens; *m* 1st, 1956, Eleanor (*d* 1974), *d* of late H. G. Evans, MC; four *s*; 2nd, 1975, Daphne, *e d* of Sir John Griffin, *qv*. *Educ:* Merchant Taylors' Sch.; St John's Coll., Oxford. Served in Navy, 1945–48 and in RNVR, 1949–53. Entered Board of Trade, 1951; Private Secretary to Permanent Secretary, 1954–57; Trade Comr in Ottawa, 1957–60; Board of Trade, 1960–63; Private Secretary to successive Prime Ministers, 1963–66; Commercial Counsellor, Madrid, 1967–71; Asst Sec., DTI, 1972–74; Under Sec., Dept of Industry, 1974–78, of Trade, 1978–83, DTI, 1983–84; Registrar, Registry of Life Assurance Commn, 1984. *Recreation:* National Hunt racing. *Address:* 71 Thurleigh Road, SW12 8TZ. *T:* 01–675 1172; Collins Cottage, Duton Hill, Essex. *T:* Great Easton 462. *Club:* United Oxford & Cambridge University.
See also H. M. S. Reid.

REID, Martin; *see* Reid, H. M. S.

REID, Sir Norman (Robert), Kt 1970; DA (Edinburgh); FMA; FIIC; Director, the Tate Gallery, 1964–79; *b* 27 December 1915; *o s* of Edward Daniel Reid and Blanche, *d* of Richard Drouet; *m* 1941, Jean Lindsay Bertram; one *s* one *d*. *Educ:* Wilson's Grammar School; Edinburgh Coll. of Art; Edinburgh Univ. Served War of 1939–46, Major, Argyll and Sutherland Highlanders. Joined staff of Tate Gallery, 1946; Deputy Director, 1954; Keeper, 1959. Fellow, International Institute for Conservation (IIC) (Secretary General, 1963–65; Vice-Chm., 1966); British Rep. Internat. Committee on Museums and Galleries of Modern Art, 1963–79; President, Penwith Society of Arts; Member: Council, Friends of the Tate Gall., 1958–79 (Founder Mem.); Arts Council Art Panel, 1964–74; Inst. of Contemporary Arts Adv. Panel, 1965–; Contemporary Art Soc. Cttee, 1965–72, 1973–77; "Paintings in Hospitals" Adv. Cttee, 1965–69; British Council Fine Arts Cttee, 1965–77 (Chm. 1968–75); Culture Adv. Cttee of UK Nat. Commn for Unesco, 1966–70; Univ. of London, Bd of Studies in History of Art, 1968; Cttee, The Rome Centre, 1969–77 (Pres. 1975–77); Adv. Council, Paul Mellon Centre, 1971–78; Council of Management, Inst. of Contemp. Prints, 1972–78; Council, RCA, 1974–77. Mem. Bd, Burlington Magazine, 1971–75. Trustee, Graham and Kathleen Sutherland Foundn, 1980–85. Hon. LittD East Anglia, 1970. Officer of the Mexican Order of the Aztec Eagle. *Address:* 50 Brabourne Rise, Park Langley, Beckenham, Kent.

REID, Patrick Robert, MBE 1940; MC 1943; Managing Director, Kem Estates Ltd; *b* 13 Nov. 1910; *s* of John Reid, CIE, ICS, and Alice Mabel Daniell; *m* 1943, Jane Cabot (marr. diss. 1966); three *s* two *d*; *m* 1977, Mrs Mary Stewart Cunliffe-Lister (*d* 1978); *m* 1982, Mrs Nicandra Hood. *Educ:* Clongowes Wood College, Co. Kildare; Wimbledon College; King's College, London University. BSc (London) 1932; AMICE, 1936; Pupilage, Sir Alex Gibb & Partners, 1934–37. Served War of 1939–45, BEF, France, Capt. RASC 2nd Div., Ammunition Officer, 1939–40; POW Germany, 1940–42; Asst Mil. Attaché, Berne, 1943–46; First Sec. (Commercial), British Embassy, Ankara, 1946–49; Chief Administrator, OEEC, Paris, 1949–52. Prospective Parly Candidate (C) Dartford and Erith, 1953–55. Director, Richard Costain (Projects) Ltd, 1959–62; Dir, Richard Costain (Middle East) Ltd, 1959–62. W. S. Atkins & Partners, Consulting Engineers, 1962–63. *Publications:* The Colditz Story, 1953; The Latter Days, 1955 (omnibus edn of the two, as Colditz, 1962, televised as The Colditz Story, BBC, 1973–74); (with Sir Olaf Caroe and Sir Thomas Rapp) From Nile to Indus, 1960; Winged Diplomat, 1962; Economic Survey Northern Nigeria, 1962; My Favourite Escape Stories, 1975; Prisoner of War, 1983; Colditz: the full story, 1984. *Recreations:* ski-ing, yachting, gardening. *Address:* Picket House, Avening, Glos. *Club:* Lansdowne.

REID, Col (Percy Fergus) Ivo, OBE 1953; DL; *b* 2 Nov. 1911; *er s* of Col Percy Lester Reid, CBE, DL, JP; *m* 1940, Mary Armida, *d* of Col James Douglas Macindoe, MC; two *s* one *d*. *Educ:* Stowe; Pembroke Coll., Oxford. Joined Irish Guards, 1933; Egypt, 1936–38; served in 2nd World War, Guards Armd Div., Europe (Despatches); Staff Coll., 1945; Comdt, Guards Depot, 1950–53; Lt Col 1951; comd Irish Guards and Regt District, 1955–59; Col 1955; retd 1959. Mem., HM Bodyguard of Hon. Corps of Gentlemen at Arms, 1961–81; Harbinger, 1979–81. Northamptonshire: High Sheriff 1967; DL 1969. *Recreations:* hunting, shooting. *Address:* The Glebe House, Marston St Lawrence, Banbury, Oxon OX17 2DA. *T:* Banbury 710300. *Club:* White's.

REID, Maj.-Gen. Peter Daer, CB 1981; Defence Adviser to GKN plc, 1983; Military Adviser to Howden Airdynamics, 1982; Associate Member, Burdeshaw Associates Ltd (USA), 1982; *b* 5 Aug. 1925; *s* of Col S. D. Reid and Dorothy Hungerford (*née* Jackson) *m* 1958, Catherine Fleetwood (*née* Boodle); two *s* two *d*. *Educ:* Cheltenham College; Wadham Coll., Oxford. Commissioned into Coldstream Guards, 1945; transferred Royal Dragoons, 1947; served: Germany, Egypt, Malaya, Gibraltar, Morocco; Staff Coll., 1959; Comdg Officer, The Royal Dragoons, 1965–68; student, Royal College of Defence Studies, 1973; Commander RAC, 3rd Div., 1974–76; Dir, RAC, 1976–78; Chief Exec., Main Battle Tank 80 Proj., 1979–80; Dir, Armoured Warfare Studies, 1981. *Recreations:* sailing, skiing, fishing, bird watching. *Address:* The Border House, Cholderton, near Salisbury, Wilts. *Clubs:* Army and Navy; Royal Western Yacht; Kandahar Ski.

REID, Philip; *see under* Ingrams, R. R.

REID, Air Vice-Marshal Sir Ranald; *see* Reid, Sir G. R. M.

REID, Sir Robert (Basil), Kt 1985; CBE 1980; FCIT; Chairman, British Railways Board, since 1983; *b* 7 Feb. 1921; *s* of Sir Robert Niel Reid, KCSI, KCIE, ICS and Lady (A.H.) Reid (*née* Disney); *m* 1951, Isobel Jean McLachlan (*d* 1976); one *s* one *d*. *Educ:* Malvern Coll.; Brasenose Coll., Oxford (MA; Hon. Fellow, 1985). Commnd Royal Tank Regt, 1941, Captain 1945. Traffic Apprentice, LNER, 1947; Goods Agent, York, 1958; Asst Dist Goods Manager, Glasgow, 1960, Dist Passenger Man., 1961, Divl Commercial Man., 1963; Planning Man., Scottish Region, 1967; Divl Man., Doncaster, 1968; Dep. Gen. Man., Eastern Region, York, 1972; Gen. Manager, Southern Reg., BR, 1974–76; British Railways Board: Exec. Mem. for Marketing, 1977–80; Chief Exec. (Railways), 1980–83; a Vice-Chm., 1983. Dir, British Transport Hotels Ltd, 1977–83; Chm., Freightliner Co. Ltd, 1978–80. Pres., CIT, 1982–83. FInstM; CBIM. CStJ 1985. *Recreations:* golf, sailing, fishing, shooting. *Address:* Rail House, Euston Square, PO Box 100, NW1 2DZ. *T:* 01–262 3232. *Club:* Naval and Military.

REID, Robert Paul; Chairman and Chief Executive, Shell UK, since 1985; *b* 1 May 1934; *m* 1958, Joan Mary; three *s*. *Educ:* St Andrews Univ. (BA Pol. Econ. and Mod. Hist.). Joined Shell, 1956; Sarawak Oilfields and Brunei, 1956–59; Nigeria 1959–67 (Head of Personnel); Africa and S Asia Regional Orgn, 1967–68; PA and Planning Adviser to Chairman, Shell & BP Services, Kenya, 1968–70; Man. Dir, Nigeria, 1970–74; Man. Dir, Thailand, 1974–78; Vice-Pres., Internat. Aviation and Products Trading, 1978–80; Exec. Dir, Downstream Oil, Shell Co. of Australia, 1980–83; Co-Ordinator for Supply and Marketing, London, 1983; Dir, Shell International Petroleum Co., 1984–. *Recreations:* golf, sailing. *Address:* 24 Ashley Gardens, Ambrosden Avenue, SW1P 1QD. *Clubs:* MCC; Royal and Ancient Golf; Royal Melbourne (Melbourne); Frilford Heath Golf.

REID, Whitelaw; President and Director, Reid Enterprises; *b* 26 July 1913; *s* of late Ogden Reid and Mrs Ogden Reid; *m* 1st, 1948, Joan Brandon (marr. diss., 1959); two *s*; 2nd, 1959, Elizabeth Ann Brooks; one *s* one *d*. *Educ:* Lincoln Sch., NYC; St Paul's Sch., Concord, New Hampshire; Yale Univ. (BA). New York Herald Tribune: in various departments, 1938–40; foreign correspondent, England, 1940; Assistant to Editor, 1946; Editor (and Pres., 1953–55), 1947–55; Chm. of Bd, 1955–58; Director, 1946–65; Pres., Herald Tribune Fresh Air Fund, 1946–62, Dir 1962–. Served War of 1939–45, 1st Lieut naval aviator, USNR. Formerly Director: Farfield Foundn; Freedom House; Golden's Bridge Hounds Inc., 1970–83; Dir, Yale Westchester Alumni Assoc. Chm., NY State Cttee on Public Employee Security Procedures, 1956–57. Ambassador to inauguration of President Ponce, Ecuador, 1956. Member: Nat. Commn for Unesco, 1955–60; President's Citizen Advisers on the Mutual Security Program, 1956–57; Yale Alumni Board (Vice-Chm., 1962–64), Yale Univ. Council (Chm., Publications Cttee, 1965–70); Council on Foreign Relations; Nat. Inst. of Social Sciences. District Comr, Purchase Pony Club, 1964–70; Pres., New York State Horse Council (formerly Empire State Horsemen's Assoc.), 1975–80. Fellow, Pierson Coll., Yale, 1949–. *Address:* (home and office) Reid Enterprises, Ophir Farm North, 73 West Patent Road, Bedford Hills, New York 10507, USA. *Clubs:* Century, Overseas Press, Silurians, Pilgrims, Amateur Ski (New York); Metropolitan (Washington); St Regis Yacht.

REID, Flight Lt William, VC 1943; agricultural consultant; Agriculture Adviser, The MacRobert Trust, Douneside, Tarland, Aberdeenshire, since 1950; *b* 21 Dec. 1921; *s* of late William Reid, Baillieston, Glasgow; *m* 1952, Violet Gallagher, 11 Dryburgh Gdns, Glasgow, NW1; one *s* one *d*. *Educ:* Coatbridge Secondary Sch.; Glasgow Univ.; West of Scotland Coll. of Agriculture. Student of Metallurgy, Sept. 1940; BSc (Agric.), 1949; Post-Graduate World Travelling Scholarship for 6 months, to study Agric. and Installations in India, Australia, NZ, USA and Canada, 1949–50. Joined RAF 1941; trained in Lancaster, Calif, USA. Won VC during a trip to Düsseldorf, 3 Nov. 1943, when member of 61 Squadron; pilot RAFVR, 617 Squadron (prisoner); demobilised, 1946; recalled to RAF for 3 months, Dec. 1951. Joined RAFVR, commissioned Jan. 1949, 103 Reserve Centre, Perth. Nat. Cattle and Sheep Advr, Spillers Ltd, 1959–81. *Recreations:* golf, shooting, fishing, etc. *Address:* Cranford, Ferntower Place, Crieff, Perthshire. *T:* Crieff 2462. *Club:* Royal Air Force.

REID, William, FSA; FMA; Director, National Army Museum, since 1970; *b* Glasgow, 8 Nov. 1926; *o s* of Colin Colquhoun Reid and Mary Evelyn Bingham; *m* 1958, Nina Frances Brigden. *Educ:* Glasgow and Oxford. Commnd RAF Regt, 1946–48. Joined staff of Armouries, Tower of London, 1956. Organising Sec., 3rd Internat. Congress of Museums of Arms and Military History, London, Glasgow and Edinburgh, 1963; Sec.-Gen., Internat. Assoc. of Museums of Arms and Military History, 1969–81, Pres., 1981–; Member: British Nat. Cttee, ICOM, 1973–; Council, Chelsea Soc., 1979–85; Founding Council, Army Records Soc., 1983–. FSA 1965 (Mem. Council, 1975–76); FMA 1974. Trustee: The Tank Museum, 1970–; RAEC Museum, 1985–. Hon. Member: Amer. Soc. of Arms Collectors, 1975; Indian Army Assoc., 1981. *Publications:* The Lore of Arms, 1976 (Military Book Society choice) (also trans. French, German, Danish, Italian and Swedish); contribs to British and foreign jls. *Recreations:* the study of armour and arms, music, ornithology. *Address:* 66 Ennerdale Road, Richmond, Surrey. *T:* 01–940 0904. *Club:* Athenæum.

REID, Very Rev. William Gordon; Provost of St Andrew's Cathedral, Inverness, since 1984; *b* 28 Jan. 1943; *s* of William Albert Reid and Elizabeth Jean Inglis. *Educ:* Galashiels Academy; Edinburgh Univ. (MA); Keble Coll., Oxford (MA); Cuddesdon College. Deacon 1967, priest 1968; Curate, St Salvador's, Edinburgh, 1967–69; Chaplain and Tutor, Salisbury Theological Coll., 1969–72; Rector, St Michael and All Saints, Edinburgh, 1972–84. Councillor, Lothian Regional Council, 1974–84; Chm., Lothian and Borders Police Bd, 1982–84. *Recreations:* travel and languages, Church and politics. *Address:* St Andrew's House, 15 Ardross Street, Inverness IV3 5NS. *T:* Inverness 233535. *Club:* New (Edinburgh).

REID, William Kennedy, CB 1981; Secretary, Scottish Home and Health Department, since 1984; *b* 15 Feb. 1931; 3rd *s* of late James and Elspet Reid; *m* 1959, Ann, *d* of Rev. Donald Campbell; two *s* one *d*. *Educ:* Robert Gordon's Coll.; George Watson's Coll.; Univ. of Edinburgh; Trinity Coll., Cambridge. MA 1st cl. Classics Edinburgh and Cantab. Ferguson scholar 1952; Craven scholar 1956. Nat. service, 1952–54. Min. of Educn, 1956; Asst Private Sec. to Minister, 1958–60; Cabinet Office, 1964; Private Sec. to Sec. of Cabinet, 1965–67; Asst Sec., DES, 1967; Sec., Council for Scientific Policy, 1967–72; Under Sec., 1974–78, Accountant-General, 1976–78, DES; Dep. Sec. (Central Services), Scottish Office, 1978–84. *Address:* 11 Inverleith Terrace, Edinburgh EH3 5NS. *T:* 031–556 1089. *Club:* New (Edinburgh).

REID, William Macpherson; Sheriff of Tayside, Central and Fife, since 1983; *b* 6 April 1938; *s* of William Andrew Reid and Mabel McLeod; *m* 1971, Vivien Anne Eddy; three *d*. *Educ:* Elgin Academy; Aberdeen Univ.; Edinburgh Univ. MA; LLB. Admitted Advocate, 1963; Sheriff of: Lothian and Borders, 1978; Glasgow and Strathkelvin, 1978–83. *Address:* Sheriffs' Chambers, Sheriff Court House, Mar Street, Alloa FK10 1HR.

REID BANKS, Lynne; *see* Banks.

REIDHAVEN, Viscount, (Master of Seafield); James Andrew Ogilvie-Grant; *b* 30 Nov. 1963; *s* and *heir* of Earl of Seafield, *qv*.

REIDY, Joseph Patrick Irwin, FRCS; Consulting Plastic Surgeon, retired: Westminster Hospital, 1948–72; Stoke Mandeville Hospital, Bucks, 1951–72 (Director, Plastic Surgery, 1957–72); Oldchurch Hospital, Romford, 1946–72; Consulting Plastic Surgeon (Hon.), St Paul's Hospital, WC, 1959–72; *b* 30 October 1907; 2nd *s* of late Dr Jerome J. Reidy, JP, MD, Co. Limerick and London and of Alderman Mrs F. W. Reidy, JP (*née* Dawson), Castle Dawson, Co. Derry; *m* 1943, Anne (*d* 1970), *e d* of late T. Johnson, and of late Mrs T. Johnson, County Durham; three *d*; *m* 1972, Freda M. Clout (*née* Lowe), Gosfield Hall, Essex. *Educ:* Stonyhurst College, Lancs; St John's Coll., Cambridge; London Hospital. MA (Nat. Sci. Trip.) (Cantab); MD, BCh (Cantab); FRCS. Casualty Officer and Ho. Phys., Poplar Hosp., 1932; Ho. Surg. and Casualty Officer, London Hosp., 1933; Ho. Surg., Leicester Roy. Inf., 1934; General Practitioner, 1934–37. Surgeon H. Div., Metropolitan Police, 1934–37. Hon. Dem. of Anatomy, Med. Sch., Middx Hosp., 1938; Civilian Surg., RAF Hosp., Halton, Bucks, 1939; Res. Surg. Officer; EMS, Albert Dock Hosp., 1939–40; EMS, St Andrew's Hosp., Billericay, 1940–42; Chief Asst, Plastic Surgery, St Thomas' Hosp., 1943–48. Cons. Plastic Surgeon, Essex Co. Hosp., Colchester, 1943–46; Senior Grade Surgeon, Plastic Surg. Unit, Min. of Pensions: Stoke Mandeville Hosp., Bucks, 1942–51; Queen Mary's Hosp., Roehampton, 1942–51. Consulting Plastic Surgeon: Middlesex CC, 1944–48; Nelson Hosp., Kingston, 1948–50; Metropolitan ENT Hosp., 1948–50; West Middlesex Hosp.; Lord Mayor Treloar Hosp., Alton, 1953–56. Hon. Chief MO, Amateur Boxing Association, 1948; Hon. Secretary and Treas.

United Hospitals Rugby Football Club, 1957–62. Liveryman Soc. of Apothecaries; Freeman of City of London; FRSocMed; FMedSoc Lond.; Fellow Hunterian Soc.; Pres., Chiltern Medical Soc., 1958–60; Pres., Brit. Assoc. of Plastic Surgeons, 1962. Member: BMA; British Assoc. of Surgeons; Brit. Acad. of Forensic Sciences; Colchester Med. Soc. Hunterian Prof., RCS, 1957, 1968; Lecturer, London Univ., 1952; Purkinje Medal, Czechoslovak Acad. of Sciences, 1965. *Publications*: contrib. since 1944 to: Proc. Roy. Soc. Med., Medical Press, West London Medico-Chirurgical Journal, British Journal of Plastic Surgery, BMJ, Medical History 2nd World War, Monograph Plastic Surgery and Physiotherapy, Annals RCS, etc. *Recreations*: gardening, reading. *Address*: Priory Cottage, Earls Colne, Essex CO6 2PG. *T*: Earls Colne 2271.

REIGATE, Baron *cr* 1970 (Life Peer), of Outwood, Surrey; **John Kenyon Vaughan-Morgan;** Bt 1960; PC 1961; *b* 2 Feb. 1905; *yr s* of late Sir Kenyon Vaughan-Morgan, DL, OBE, MP and late Lady Vaughan-Morgan; *m* 1940, Emily, *d* of late Mr and Mrs W. Redmond Cross, New York City; two *d*. *Educ*: Eton; Christ Church, Oxford. Mem. Chelsea Borough Council, 1928; Member of London County Council for Chelsea, 1946–52; Chm. East Fulham Conservative and Unionist Assoc., 1935–38 (Pres. 1945); MP (C) Reigate Div. of Surrey, 1950–70. Parly Sec., Min. of Health, 1957; Minister of State, BoT, 1957–59. Dir, Morgan Crucible Co. Ltd, now retired. Chm. Bd of Govs, Westminster Hosp., 1963–74 (Mem., 1960). Pres., Royal Philanthropic Sch., Redhill. Dep. Chm., South Westminster Justices, now retired. Mem., Court of Assistants, Merchant Taylors Co. (Master 1970). Hon. Freeman, Borough of Reigate, 1971. Served War of 1939–45; Welsh Guards, 1940; GSO2, War Office; GSO1, HQ 21 Army Group (despatches). *Address*: 36 Eaton Square, SW1. *T*: 01–235 6506. *Clubs*: Brooks's, Beefsteak, Hurlingham.

REIGATE, Archdeacon of; *see* Jacob, Ven. B. V.

REIHER, Frederick Bernard Carl, CMG 1982; Director, Harrisons & Crosfield (PNG) Ltd, since 1982; Chairman, Harcos Trading, since 1982; Manager, Protocol and Overseas Service Hospitality (POSH); *b* 7 Feb. 1945; *s* of William and Ruth Reiher; *m* 1974, Helen Perpetua; one *s* two *d*. *Educ*: Holy Spirit National Seminary; Univ. of Papua New Guinea (BD). Private Sec. to Minister for Finance, PNG, 1973–76. Joined Diplomatic Service, 1976; established Diplomatic Mission for PNG in London, 1977; High Comr for PNG in London, 1978–80; Sec. to Prime Minister of PNG, and accredited Ambassador to FRG, Belgium, EEC, Israel, and Turkey, 1980–82. *Address*: PO Box 7500, Boroko, Papua New Guinea. *Clubs*: Royal Commonwealth Society, Travellers' (Hon.); Aviat Social & Sporting, South Pacific Motor Sports, PNG Pistol.

REILLY, family name of **Baron Reilly.**

REILLY, Baron *cr* 1978 (Life Peer), of Brompton in the Royal Borough of Kensington and Chelsea; **Paul Reilly;** Kt 1967; Director: Conran Design Group; The Building Trades Exhibition Ltd; Director, Design Council (formerly Council of Industrial Design), 1960–77; *b* 29 May 1912; *s* of late Prof. Sir Charles Reilly, formerly Head of Liverpool Sch. of Architecture; *m* 1st, 1939, Pamela Wentworth Foster; one *d*; 2nd, 1952, Annette Stockwell, *d* of Brig-Gen. C. I. Stockwell, CB, CMG, DSO. *Educ*: Winchester; Hertford College, Oxford; London School of Economics. Salesman and Sales Manager, Venesta Ltd, 1934–36; Leader Page Editor and Features Editor, News Chronicle, 1936–40. RAC, 1940; RNVR 1941–45. Editorial Staff, Modern Plastics, New York, 1946; Co-Editor, British Plastics Encylopædia, 1947; Chief Information Officer, Council of Industrial Design, 1948; Deputy Director, 1954. Member: Council, Royal Society of Arts, 1959–62, 1963–70; Council, BTA, 1960–70; Council, RCA, 1963–81; BBC General Advisory Council, 1964–70; BNEC, 1966–70; British Railways Bd Design Panel, 1966–, Environment Panel, 1977–84; GLC Historic Buildings Cttee, 1967–82; Post Office Stamp Adv. Cttee, 1967–, Design Adv. Cttee, 1970–84; British Telecom Design Cttee, 1981–83; British Council Fine Arts Adv. Cttee, 1970–80; Conseil Supérieur de la Création Esthétique Industrielle (France), 1971–73; Adv. Council of Science Policy Foundn, 1971–; British Crafts Centre Bd, 1972–77; Nat. Theatre Design Adv. Cttee, 1974–; Royal Fine Art Commn, 1976–81; Crafts Advisory Cttee, 1977–81 (Chief Exec., 1971–77). Chairman: Trustees, Building Conservation Trust, 1977–82; Conran Foundn, 1981–86. President: Soc. of Designer-Craftsmen, 1976–84; Assoc. of Art Institutions, 1977–80; World Crafts Council, 1978–80; Vice-President: ICSID, 1963–67; Modular Soc., 1968–77; London Soc., 1977–; ICA, 1979–; Rye Conservation Soc., 1980–. Governor: Hammersmith Coll. of Art and Building, 1948–67; Central Sch. of Art and Design, 1953–74; Camberwell Sch. of Art and Design, 1967–77; City of Birmingham Polytechnic, 1970–77. Mem., Ct of Governors, LSE, 1975–80. Hon. FSIA, 1959; Hon. FRIBA, 1965; Sen. Fellow, RCA, 1972; Hon. Assoc. Manchester Coll. of Art, 1963; Hon. Member, Art Workers Guild, 1961; Ornamo, Finland, 1981; Hon. Corresponding Mem., Svenskaslöjdforeningen, 1956; Hon. Comr, Japan Design Foundn, 1983. Hon. Liveryman, Furniture Makers' Co., 1980. Hon. DSc: Loughborough, 1977; Aston, 1981; Cranfield, 1983; Hon. Dr RCA, 1978. Comdr, Royal Order of Vasa (Sweden), 1961. Bicentenary Medal, RSA, 1963. *Publication*: An Introduction to Regency Architecture (Art and Technics), 1948. *Recreation*: looking at buildings. *Address*: 3 Alexander Place, SW7 2SG. *T*: 01–589 4031. *Club*: Arts.

REILLY, Brian Thomas; Chairman, Panasonic UK Ltd (formerly National Panasonic (UK) Ltd), since 1979; *b* 9 Dec. 1924; *s* of Thomas Joseph and Eugene Reilly; *m* 1952, Jean Cynthia Gilbey; one *s* four *d*. *Educ*: Mount St Mary's Coll., Spinkhill, near Sheffield. Captain, KRRC, 1943–47. Various pursuits, 1947–51; Dist Sales Man., Thomas Hedley & Co. Ltd (now Proctor & Gamble Ltd), 1951–60; Sales Dir, Man. Dir and Dep. Chm., Radio & Allied Industries Ltd (wholly owned subsid. of GEC Co. Ltd), 1960–79; Associate Dir, GEC Co. Ltd, 1976–79. *Address*: (office) 300–306 Bath Road, Slough, Berks SL1 6JB. *T*: Slough 34522; Nutfield, 25 The Fair Mile, Henley-on-Thames, Oxon. *Clubs*: Annabel's, St James's.

REILLY, Sir (D'Arcy) Patrick, GCMG 1968 (KCMG 1957; CMG 1949); OBE 1942; Chairman, Banque Nationale de Paris Ltd (formerly British and French Bank), 1969–80; *b* 17 March 1909; *s* of late Sir D'Arcy Reilly, Indian Civil Service; *m* 1938, Rachel Mary (*d* 1984), *d* of late Brigadier-General Sir Percy Sykes, KCIE, CB, CMG; two *d*. *Educ*: Winchester; New Coll., Oxford. (1st class Hon. Mods, 1930, Lit Hum 1932), Hon. Fellow 1972. Laming Travelling Fellow, Queen's College, 1932; Fellow of All Souls College, 1932–39, 1969–; Diplomatic Service, 1933; Third Secretary, Tehran, 1935–38; Ministry of Economic Warfare, 1939–42; First Secretary, Algiers, 1943; Paris, 1944; Athens, 1945. Counsellor, HM Foreign Service, 1947; Counsellor at Athens, 1947–48; Imperial Defence College, 1949; Assistant Under-Secretary of State, Foreign Office, 1950–53; Minister in Paris, 1953–56; Dep. Under-Sec. of State, Foreign Office, Oct. 1956; Ambassador to the USSR, 1957–60; Dep. Under-Sec. of State, Foreign Office, 1960–64; Official Head of UK Delegation to UN Conference on Trade and Development, 1964; Ambassador to France, 1965–68. Pres., 1972–75, Vice-Pres., 1975–, London Chamber of Commerce and Industry. Chairman: London Chamber of Commerce Standing Cttee for Common Market countries, 1969–72; Overseas Policy Cttee, Assoc. of British Chambers of Commerce, 1970–72; London Univ. Management Cttee, British Inst. in Paris, 1970–79; Council, Bedford Coll., London Univ., 1970–75. Hon. DLitt Bath, 1982. Comdr Légion d'Honneur, 1979. *Address*: Hampden Cottage, Ramsden, Oxford OX7 3AU. *T*: Ramsden 348. *Club*: Athenæum.

REILLY, Lt-Gen. Jeremy Calcott, DSO 1973; Commander Training and Arms Directors, since 1986; *b* 7 April 1934; *s* of late Lt-Col J. F. C. Reilly and of E. N. Reilly (*née* Moreton); *m* 1960, Julia Elizabeth (*née* Forrester); two *d* (and one *d* decd). *Educ*: Uppingham; RMA Sandhurst. Commissioned Royal Warwickshire Regt, 1954; served Egypt, Cyprus (Despatches), Ireland, Hong Kong, Germany, Borneo, BJSM Washington DC; psc 1965; Brigade Major, BAOR, 1967–69; Chief Instructor, RMA, 1969–71; CO 2nd Bn Royal Regt of Fusiliers, 1971–73 (DSO); Instructor, Staff Coll., 1974–75; Col GS (Army Deployment), MoD, 1975–77; PSO to Field Marshal Lord Carver and attached FCO (Rhodesia), 1977–79; Comdr 6 Field Force and UK Mobile Force, 1979–81; Comdr 4th Armoured Div., BAOR, 1981–83; Dir Battle Develt, MoD, 1983–84; ACDS (Concepts), MoD, 1985–86. Dep. Col, RRF (Warwickshire), 1981–; Col, RRF, 1986–. *Publications*: minor articles in various jls. *Address*: RHQ RRF, HM Tower of London, EC3N 4AB.

REILLY, Noel Marcus Prowse, CMG 1958; *b* 31 Dec. 1902; *s* of late Frederick Reilly and late Ellen Prowse; *m* 1st, 1927, Dolores Albra Pratten (marr. diss., 1963); one *s* one *d*; 2nd, 1963, Dorothy Alma Rainsford. *Educ*: University Coll. Sch.; Gonville and Caius College, Cambridge (MA 1928); London Univ. (BSc Econ., 1st Cl. Hons 1946, PhD 1972). Schoolmaster, Boston, Massachusetts, USA, 1924; business in New Zealand, 1926, England, 1928; Secretary, Area Cttee for National Fitness for Oxon, Bucks, and Berks, 1938; Press Censor, Ministry of Information, 1939; Principal, HM Treasury, 1946; Economic Counsellor, Persian Gulf, 1953–59; Financial Counsellor and Dep. Head, UK Treasury Delegation, British Embassy, Washington, 1960–65; Alternate Exec. Dir for the UK, IBRD, and Affiliates, 1962–65. *Publication*: The Key to Prosperity, 1931. *Recreations*: ski-ing, windsurfing, whitewater kayaking. *Address*: North Sandwich, New Hampshire 03259, USA. *T*: 603–284–7730.

REILLY, Sir Patrick; *see* Reilly, Sir D. P.

REINDORP, Rt. Rev. George Edmund, DD; an Assistant Bishop, Diocese of London, since 1982; *b* 19 Dec. 1911; *s* of Rev. Hector William Reindorp and Dora Lucy (*née* George), Goodmayes, Essex; *m* 1943, Alix Violet Edington, MB, ChB, *d* of Alexander Edington, MD, and Helen Edington, Durban, Natal; three *s* one *d* (and one *d* decd). *Educ*: Felsted Sch.; Trinity Coll., Cambridge; Westcott House, Cambridge. MA Cantab, 1939. Deacon, 1937; Priest, 1938; Curate, S Mary Abbots, Kensington, 1937–39; Chaplain RNVR, 1938–46; Vicar St Stephen with St John, Westminster, 1946–57. Commissary for Bishop of Natal, 1948–61; Provost of Southwark and Rector of St Saviour with All Hallows, Southwark, 1957–61; Bishop of Guildford, 1961–73; Bishop of Salisbury, 1973–81. Mem., House of Lords, 1970. With BBC Radio Religious Dept, arranging and performing Daily Service and arranging and producing Morning Service and other programmes, 1982–83. Chaplain, RCGP, 1965. Hon. DD Lambeth, 1961; DUniv Surrey, 1971. *Publications*: What about You?, 1956; No Common Task, 1957; Putting it Over: ten points for preachers, 1961; Over to You, 1964; Preaching Through the Christian Year, 1973. *Recreations*: ski-ing, radio and television; avoiding committees. *Address*: 17 Vincent Square, Westminster, SW1P 2NA. *Clubs*: Ski Club of Great Britain, Kandahar.

See also Sir Humphrey Mynors, Bt.

REINERS, William Joseph; Director of Research Policy, Departments of the Environment and Transport, 1977–78, retired 1978; *b* 19 May 1923; *s* of late William and Hannah Reiners; *m* 1952, Catharine Anne Palmer; three *s* one *d*. *Educ*: Liverpool Collegiate Sch.; Liverpool Univ. RAE Farnborough, 1944–46; Min. of Works, 1946–50; Head, Building Operations and Economics Div., Building Research Station, 1950–63; Dir of Research and Information, MPBW, 1963–71; Dir of Research Requirements, DoE, 1971–77. *Publications*: various on building operations and economics. *Address*: Valais, Berks Hill, Chorleywood, Herts. *T*: Chorleywood 3293.

REINHARDT, Max; Joint Chairman, Chatto, Virago, Bodley Head and Jonathan Cape Ltd, since 1973; Chairman, Bodley Head Group of Publishers, since 1981; Chairman, Max Reinhardt Ltd and Reinhardt Books Ltd, since 1948; *b* 30 Nov. 1915; *s* of Ernest Reinhardt and Frieda Reinhardt (*née* Darr); *m* 1st, 1947, Margaret Leighton, CBE (marr. diss. 1955; she *d* 1976); 2nd, 1957, Joan, *d* of Carlisle and Dorothy MacDonald, New York City; two *d*. *Educ*: English High Sch. for Boys, Istanbul; Ecole des Hautes Etudes Commerciales, Paris; London School of Economics. Acquired HFL (Publishers) Ltd, 1947; founded Max Reinhardt Ltd, 1948, which bought: The Bodley Head Ltd, 1956 (Man. Dir, 1957–81); Putnam & Co., 1963. Dir, Compass Theatre Ltd, 1983–. Mem. Council: Publishers' Assoc., 1963–69; Royal Academy of Dramatic Art, 1965–. *Recreations*: tennis, swimming, bridge. *Address*: 16 Pelham Crescent, SW7 2NR. *T*: 01–589 5527. *Clubs*: Beefsteak, Garrick, Savile, Royal Automobile.

REISS, Sir John (Anthony Ewart), Kt 1967; BEM 1941; Chairman of Associated Portland Cement Manufacturers Ltd (now Blue Circle Industries), 1957–74; *b* 8 April 1909; *m* 1st, 1938, Marie Ambrosine Phillpotts; one *s* one *d*; 2nd, 1951, Elizabeth Booth-Jones (*née* MacEwan); two *d*. *Educ*: Eton. Cotton, Banking, Insurance, 1928–34. Joined Associated Portland Cement Manufacturers, 1934; Dir, 1946. Chm., Foundn for Business Responsibilities; Pres., Aims of Industry, 1978– (Hon. Treasurer, 1967–78); Vice-Chm., CRC. *Recreations*: shooting, cricket. *Address*: Barrow House, Barrow, Oakham, Leics. *Club*: Buck's.

REISS, John Henry, OBE 1972; British Ambassador to Liberia, 1973–78, retired; *b* 26 March 1918; *s* of late Rev. Leopold Reiss and Dora Lillian (*née* Twisden-Bedford); *m* 1943, Dora Lily (*née* York); one *s* two *d*. *Educ*: Bradfield Coll.; St Thomas' Hosp. Served War, Army, 1939–42. Kenya Govt, 1945–59; Dir of Information, 1954–59; Commonwealth Office, 1959; Dir of Information Services: Johannesburg, 1961–63; Wellington, New Zealand, 1963–65. Foreign and Commonwealth Office, 1966–69; Dep. British Govt Representative, Antigua/St Kitts, 1969–73. *Recreations*: bridge, computing. *Address*: 1 Manor Crescent, Tytherington, Macclesfield, Cheshire.

REISZ, Karel; film director; *b* 21 July 1926; *s* of Joseph Reisz and Frederika; *m* 1963, Betsy Blair; three *s*. *Educ*: Leighton Park Sch., Reading; Emmanuel Coll., Cambridge (BA). Formerly: co-ed with Lindsay Anderson, film magazine, Sequence; worked for BFI; first Programme Dir, National Film Theatre. Co-directed, with Tony Richardson, Momma Don't Allow, 1956; produced: Every Day Except Christmas, 1957; This Sporting Life, 1960; directed: We Are the Lambeth Boys, 1958; Saturday Night and Sunday Morning, 1959; Night Must Fall, 1963; Morgan, a Suitable Case for Treatment, 1965; Isadora, 1967; The Gambler, 1975; Dog Soldiers, 1978; The French Lieutenant's Woman, 1981; Sweet Dreams, 1986. *Publication*: The Technique of Film Editing (also ed), 1953. *Address*: c/o Film Contracts, 2 Lower James Street, Golden Square, W1.

REITH, Barony of (*cr* 1940); title disclaimed by 2nd Baron; *see under* Reith, Christopher John.

REITH, Christopher John; farmer; *b* 27 May 1928; *s* of 1st Baron Reith, KT, PC, GCVO, GBE, CB, TD, of Stonehaven, and Muriel Katharine, *y d* of late John Lynch Odhams; *S* father, 1971, as 2nd Baron Reith, but disclaimed his peerage for life, 1972; *m* 1969, Penelope Margaret Ann, *er d* of late H. R. Morris; one *s* one *d*. *Educ:* Eton; Worcester College, Oxford (MA Agriculture). Served in Royal Navy, 1946–48; farming thereafter. *Recreations:* fishing, gardening, forestry. *Heir (to disclaimed peerage):* *s* Hon. James Harry John Reith, *b* 2 June 1971. *Address:* Whitebank Farm, Methven, Perthshire. *T:* Methven 333.

REITH, Douglas, QC (Scotland) 1957; a Social Security (formerly National Insurance) Commissioner, since 1960; *b* 29 June 1919; *s* of William Reith and Jessie McAllan; *m* 1949, Elizabeth Archer Stewart; one *s* one *d*. *Educ:* Aberdeen Grammar School; Aberdeen University (MA, LLB). Became Member of Faculty of Advocates in Scotland, 1946. Served in Royal Signals, 1939–46. Standing Junior Counsel in Scotland to Customs and Excise, 1949–51; Advocate-Depute, Crown Office, Scotland, 1953–57; Pres., Pensions Appeal Tribunal (Scotland), 1958–64; Chm., Nat. Health Service Tribunal (Scotland), 1963–65. *Address:* 11 Heriot Row, Edinburgh EH3 6HP. *T:* 031–556 6966. *Club:* New (Edinburgh).

REITH, Martin; HM Diplomatic Service; High Commissioner in Swaziland, since 1983; *b* 6 Dec. 1935; *s* of late James Reith and of Christian (*née* Innes); *m* 1964, Ann Purves; four *s*. *Educ:* Royal High Sch. of Edinburgh. Served: India (Calcutta), 1957–59; Uganda, 1962–66; Scottish Office, Edinburgh, 1966–68; Australia (Canberra), 1969–72; Asst Head of Central and Southern Africa Dept, FCO, 1974–77; Commercial Sec., Beirut, 1977–78; UN Dept, FCO, 1979; Counsellor, NATO Def. Coll., Rome, 1980; Dep. High Comr, Malta, 1980–83. *Recreations:* hill-walking, bridge, watching the Scottish literary scene. *Address:* c/o Foreign and Commonwealth Office, SW1A 2AH.

RELLIE, Alastair James Carl Euan; HM Diplomatic Service; Counsellor, Foreign and Commonwealth Office, since 1979; *b* 5 April 1935; *s* of William and Lucy Rellie; *m* 1961, Annalisa (*née* Modin); one *s* two *d*. *Educ:* Michaelhouse, SA; Harvard Univ., USA (BA). Rifle Bde, 1958–60. Second Sec., FCO, 1963–64; Vice-Consul, Geneva, 1964–67; First Secretary: FCO, 1967–68; (Commercial), Cairo, 1968–70; Kinshasa, 1970–72; FCO, 1972–74; (and later Counsellor), UK Mission to UN, New York, 1974–79. *Recreations:* travel, talk, newspapers. *Address:* 50 Smith Street, SW3 4EP. *T:* 01–352 5734. *Clubs:* Brooks's, Greenjackets.

RELLY, Gavin Walter Hamilton; Chairman: Anglo American Corporation of South Africa Ltd, since 1983 (Deputy Chairman, 1977–82); AECI Ltd, since 1983; *b* 6 Feb. 1926; *s* of Cullis Hamilton Relly and Helen Relly; *m* 1951, Jane Margaret Glenton; one *s* two *d*. *Educ:* Diocesan Coll., Cape Town; Trinity Coll., Oxford (MA). Joined Anglo American Corp., 1949 (Sec. to H. F. Oppenheimer and then to Sir Ernest Oppenheimer); Manager, Chm.'s Office, 1958; elected to Bd of Corp., 1965; Exec. Dir, 1966; Chm., Exec. Cttee, 1978; Mem. Bd, Anglo American Industrial Corp., 1973– (Chm., 1973–83). Mem. Bd, Charter Consolidated Ltd, 1971–; Dir, Minerals & Resources Corp. Ltd, 1974–. Member: South Africa Foundn, 1975– (Pres., 1981–82); Bd of Governors, Urban Foundn, 1985. *Recreations:* fishing, golf. *Address:* PO Box 61587, Marshalltown, 2107, South Africa. *T:* 638–3234. *Clubs:* Rand, Country (Johannesburg).

RELPH, Michael Leighton George; film producer, director, designer, writer; *s* of late George Relph and Deborah Relph (later Harker); *m* 1st, 1939, Doris Gosden (marr. diss.); one *s*; 2nd, 1950, Maria Barry; one *d*. *Educ:* Bembridge Sch. Stage designer, 1940–50: West-end prodns include: Indoor Fireworks; The Doctor's Dilemma; Up and Doing; Watch on the Rhine; The Man Who Came to Dinner; Frieda; Saloon Bar; Old Acquaintance; Quiet Week-end; Heartbreak House; Relative Values; A Month in the Country; The Last of Summer; Love in Idleness; The White Carnation; The Petrified Forest; The Banbury Nose; They Came to a City. Began film career as apprentice, then Asst Art Dir, Gaumont British Studios; Art Dir, Warner Brothers Studios; Art Dir, Ealing Studios, 1942–45: prodns include: The Bells Go Down; Dead of Night; Champagne Charley; Nicholas Nickleby; Saraband for Dead Lovers (nominated Hollywood Oscar); Associate Producer to Michael Balcon, 1945; subseq. Producer with Basil Dearden as Dir until Dearden's death, 1972: prodns include: The Captive Heart; Kind Hearts and Coronets; The Blue Lamp (Best British Film Award, Brit. Film Acad.); Frieda; Saraband for Dead Lovers; I Believe in You (co-author); The Ship that Died of Shame; The Rainbow Jacket; The Square Ring; The Gentle Gunman; Cage of Gold; Pool of London. Director: Davy, 1957; Rockets Galore, 1958; Producer: Violent Playground; Sapphire (Best British Film Award, Brit. Film Acad.); All Night Long; The Smallest Show on Earth. Founder Dir, Allied Film Makers: produced: League of Gentlemen; Victim; Man in the Moon (co-author); Life for Ruth; The Mind Benders; Woman of Straw; Masquerade (co-author); The Assassination Bureau (also author and designer); The Man Who Haunted Himself (co-author); in charge of production, Boyd's Company, 1978–82: Scum (exec. producer), 1979; An Unsuitable Job for a Woman (co-producer), 1982; Treasure Houses of Britain (TV; exec. producer), 1985; Heavenly Pursuits, 1986. Chm., Film Prodn Assoc. of GB, 1971–76; Mem., Cinematograph Films Council, 1971–76; Governor, BFI, 1972–79 (Chm., Prodn Bd, 1972–79). *Recreations:* reading, theatre going, painting. *Address:* The Lodge, Primrose Hill Studios, Fitzroy Road, NW1 8JP. *T:* 01–586 0249.

See also S. G. M. Relph.

RELPH, Simon George Michael; Chief Executive, British Screen Finance Ltd, since 1985; *b* 13 April 1940; *s* of Michael Leighton George Relph, *qv*; *m* 1963, Amanda, *d* of Anthony Grinling, MC; one *s* one *d*. *Educ:* Bryanston School; King's College, Cambridge (MA Mech. Scis). Asst Dir, Feature Films, 1961–73; Production Administrator, Nat. Theatre, 1974–78; *films* include: Production Executive: Yanks, 1978; Reds, 1980; Producer/Co-Producer: The Return of the Soldier, 1981; Privates on Parade, 1982; Ploughman's Lunch, 1983; Secret Places, 1984; Wetherby, 1985; Comrades, 1986. *Recreations:* gardening, photography, golf. *Address:* 338 Liverpool Road, N7 8PZ.

RELTON, Stanley; HM Diplomatic Service, retired; Counsellor (Administration), British Embassy, Brussels, 1978–83; *b* 19 May 1923; *m* 1953, José Shakespeare; four *d*. Army, 1942–47. Joined HM Diplomatic Service, 1948: Haifa, 1949; Seoul, 1950; Tokyo, 1951; FCO, 1952–53; Vice-Consul, Stuttgart, 1954–57; Bremen, 1957–59; Consul, Rotterdam, 1959–61; Budapest, 1961–64; Second Sec., Buenos Aires, 1964–68; First Sec., Algiers, 1968–71; FCO, 1971–75; First Sec., Blantyre, Malawi, 1975–78. *Recreations:* music, chess. *Address:* 20A Waldegrave Park, Twickenham, Mddx.

REMEDIOS, Alberto Telisforo, CBE 1981; opera and concert singer; *b* 27 Feb. 1935; *s* of Albert and Ida Remedios; *m* 1965, Judith Annette Hosken; two *s* one *d*. *Educ:* studied with Edwin Francis, Liverpool. Début with Sadler's Wells Opera, 1956; sings regularly: English Nat. Opera; Royal Opera House, Covent Garden; Welsh Nat. Opera; Metropolitan NY, San Francisco, San Diego, Seattle, Australia, NZ, S Africa, Frankfurt, Bonn, France, Spain; sang Peter Grimes, Teatro Colon, Buenos Aires, 1979; also with major English orchestras. Recordings include Wagner's Ring; Tippett: A Midsummer Marriage. Queen's Prize, RCM, 1958; 1st prize, Union of Bulgarian Composers, 1963. *Recreations:* soccer, motoring, record collecting. *Address:* c/o Kaye Artists Management Ltd, Kingsmead House, 250 King's Road, SW3; 27 The Ridgeway, N14 6NX. *T:* 01–882 0599.

REMEZ, Aharon; sculptor; *b* 8 May 1919; *m* 1952, Rita (*née* Levy); one *s* three *d*. *Educ:* Herzliah Grammar Sch., Tel Aviv. Volunteered for service with RAF, and served as fighter pilot in Gt Brit. and in European theatre of war; after end of war with British Occupation forces in Germany. Mem., kibbutz Kfar Blum, 1947–. Dir Planning and of Ops and subseq. Chief of Staff, and C-in-C Israel Air Force (rank Brig.-Gen.), 1948–51; Head of Min. of Defence Purchasing Mission, USA, 1951–53; Aviation Adviser to Minister of Def., 1953–54; Mem. Bd of Dirs, Solel Boneh Ltd, and Exec. Dir, Koor Industries Ltd, 1954–59; MP (Israel Lab Party) for Mapai, 1956–57; Admin. Dir, Weizmann Inst. of Science, Rehovot, 1959–60. Dir, Internat. Co-op. Dept, Min. for Foreign Affairs, Jerusalem, 1960; Adviser on Internat. Co-operation to Min. for Foreign Affairs, also Consultant to OECD, 1964–65; Ambassador of Israel to the Court of St James's, 1965–70. Dir Gen., Israel Ports Authority, 1970–77. Chairman: Nat. Council for Civil Aviation, 1960–65; Bd of Dirs, Airports Authority, 1977–81. *Recreations:* handicrafts, sculpture. *Address:* San Martin Street, Cottage 11, Jerusalem 93341, Israel.

REMNANT, family name of **Baron Remnant.**

REMNANT, 3rd Baron *cr* 1928, of Wenhaston; **James Wogan Remnant,** Bt 1917; CVO 1979; FCA; Chairman, Touche, Remnant & Co., since 1981 (Managing Director, 1970–80); *b* 23 October 1930; *s* of 2nd Baron and of Dowager Lady Remnant; *S* father, 1967; *m* 1953, Serena Jane Loehnis, *o d* of Sir Clive Loehnis, *qv*; three *s* one *d*. *Educ:* Eton. Partner, Touche Ross & Co., 1958–70; Chairman: TR Energy, 1980–; TR City of London Trust, 1981–; TR Pacific Basin Investment Trust, 1983–; London Bd, Bank of Scotland, 1979– (Dir, 1979–). Deputy Chairman: Union Discount Co. of London, 1970–86 (Dir, 1968–); Ultramar, 1981–; Dir, Australia and New Zealand Banking Group, 1968–81, and other cos. Chm., Assoc. of Investment Trust Cos, 1977–79. A Church Comr, 1976–84. Chm., Royal Jubilee Trusts, 1980– (Hon. Treasurer, 1972–80); Pres., Nat. Council of YMCAs, 1983–. FCA 1955. *Heir:* *s* Hon. Philip John Remnant [*b* 20 December 1954; *m* 1977, Caroline Elizabeth Clare, *yr d* of late Godfrey H. R. Cavendish; one *s* two *d*]. *Address:* Bear Ash, Hare Hatch, Reading RG10 9XR.

RENALS, Sir Stanley, 4th Bt, *cr* 1895; formerly in the Merchant Navy; *b* 20 May 1923; 2nd *s* of Sir James Herbert Renals, 2nd Bt; *S* brother, Sir Herbert Renals, 3rd Bt, 1961; *m* 1957, Maria Dolores Rodriguez Pinto, *d* of late José Rodriguez Ruiz; one *s*. *Educ:* City of London Freemen's School. *Heir:* *s* Stanley Michael Renals, BSc, CEng, MIMechE, MIProdE [*b* 14 January 1958; *m* 1982, Jacqueline Riley; one *s*]. *Address:* 47 Baden Road, Brighton, East Sussex BN2 4DP.

RENAUD, Madeleine, (Mme Jean-Louis Barrault); Officier de la Légion d'Honneur; actress; formed Madeleine Renaud-Jean-Louis Barrault Company, 1946, Co-director and player leading parts; *b* Paris, 21 Feb. 1903; *d* of Prof. Jean Renaud; *m*; one *s*; *m* 1940, Jean-Louis Barrault, *qv*. *Educ:* Lycée Racine; Conservatoire de Paris (Ier Prix de Comédie). Pensionnaire, Comédie Française, 1921–46. Jt Founder, Madeleine Renaud-Jean-Louis Barrault Company, 1947. Has appeared in classical and modern plays, and in films. Mem., Conseil d'administration, ORTF, 1967–68. Grand Officier de l'ordre national du Mérite; Commandeur des Arts et Lettres. *Publications:* novels, short stories, plays. *Address:* 18 Avenue du Président Wilson, 75116 Paris, France.

RENDALL, Archibald, OBE 1967; HM Diplomatic Service, retired; Consul General, Lille, France, 1977–81; *b* 10 Aug. 1921; *s* of late James Henry Rendall; *m* 1951, Sheila Catherine (*née* Martin); one *d*. *Educ:* Broughton Sch., Edinburgh. Inland Revenue Dept, 1938; served in RN, 1941–46; joined Foreign (subseq. Diplomatic) Service, 1948; Vice-Consul, Monrovia, 1948–49; Vice-Consul and 2nd Sec., Baghdad, 1950–54; FO, 1954–57; 1st Sec. (Commercial), Beirut, 1957–60; Consul (Commercial), New York, 1960–65; 1st Sec. (Commercial), Bucharest, 1965–68; FCO, 1969–72; Consul-Gen., St Louis, 1972–77. *Address:* 37 Albany Villas, Hove, Sussex BN3 2RT. *T:* Brighton 772968.

RENDALL, Peter Godfrey; Headmaster, Bembridge School, Isle of Wight, 1959–74; *b* 25 April 1909; *s* of Godfrey A. H. Rendall and Mary Whitshaw Rendall (*née* Wilson); *m* 1944, Ann McKnight Kauffer; two *s* one *d*. *Educ:* Rugby School; Corpus Christi College, Oxford. Assistant Master: Felsted School, Essex, 1931–34; Upper Canada College, Toronto, 1934–35; Felsted School, Essex, 1935–43. Served War of 1939–45, RAF, 1943–46, Flight-Lieut. Second Master, St Bees School, Cumberland, 1946–48; Headmaster Achimota School, Gold Coast, 1949–54; Assistant Master, Lancing College, 1954–59. Clerk to Burford Town Council, 1977–85. Coronation Medal, 1953. *Recreations:* reading, gardening, carpentry, painting. *Address:* Chippings, The Hill, Burford, Oxon. *Clubs:* Royal Commonwealth Society; Oxford Union Society.

RENDELL, Ruth Barbara; crime novelist, since 1964; *b* 17 Feb. 1930; *d* of Arthur Grasemann and Ebba Kruse; *m* 1950, Donald Rendell; marr. diss. 1975; remarried Donald Rendell, 1977; one *s*. *Educ:* Loughton County High School. Arts Council National Book Award for Genre Fiction, 1981. *Publications:* From Doon with Death, 1964; To Fear a Painted Devil, 1965; Vanity Dies Hard, 1966; A New Lease of Death, 1967; Wolf to the Slaughter, 1967; The Secret House of Death, 1968; The Best Man to Die, 1969; A Guilty Thing Surprised, 1970; One Across Two Down, 1971; No More Dying Then, 1971; Murder Being Once Done, 1972; Some Lie and Some Die, 1973; The Face of Trespass, 1974; Shake Hands for Ever, 1975; A Demon in my View, 1976; The Fallen Curtain, 1976; A Judgement in Stone, 1977; A Sleeping Life, 1978; Make Death Love Me, 1979; Means of Evil, 1979; The Lake of Darkness, 1980; Put on by Cunning, 1981; Master of the Moor, 1982; The Fever Tree, 1982; The Speaker of Mandarin, 1983; The Killing Doll, 1984; The Tree of Hands, 1984; An Unkindness of Ravens, 1985; The New Girl Friend, 1985; Live Flesh, 1986; (as Barbara Vine) A Dark-Adapted Eye, 1986. *Recreations:* reading, walking, opera. *Address:* Nussteads, Polstead, Suffolk. *Clubs:* Groucho, Detection.

RENDELL, Sir William, Kt 1967; General Manager, Commonwealth Development Corporation, 1953–73, retired; *b* 25 Jan. 1908; *s* of William Reginald Rendell and Hon. Janet Marion Rendell; *m* 1950, Annie Henriette Maria (*née* Thorsen). *Educ:* Winchester; Trinity Coll., Cambridge. FCA. Partner, Whinney Murray & Co., 1947–52. Mem., PLA, 1967–78. *Recreations:* shooting, fishing, gardening. *Address:* 10 Montpelier Place, SW7. *T:* 01–584 8232.

RENDLE, Michael Russel; Managing Director, British Petroleum Co. plc, 1981–86; Deputy Chairman: Imperial Continental Gas Association, since 1986; British-Borneo Petroleum Syndicate plc, since 1986; Director, Willis Faber plc, since 1985; *b* 20 Feb. 1931; *s* of late H. C. R. Rendle and of Valerie Patricia (*née* Gleeson); *m* 1957, Heather, *d* of J. W. J. Rinkel; two *s* two *d*. *Educ:* Marlborough; New College, Oxford. MA. Joined Anglo-Iranian Oil Co. (now BP), 1954; Man. Dir, BP Trinidad, 1967–70; Man. Dir, BP Australia, 1974–78; Dir, BP Trading Ltd, 1978–81; Chairman: BP Chemicals Int., 1981–83; BP Coal, 1983–86; BP Nutrition, 1981–86; Dir, Petrofina SA, 1986–; Mem., London Adv. Bd, Westpac Banking Corp. (formerly Commercial Bank of Australia), 1978–. Mem. BOTB, 1982–; Chm., European Trade Cttee, 1982–86. Chm. Social Affairs Cttee, UNICE, 1984–; Mem. Internat. Council and UK Adv. Bd, INSEAD, 1984–86.

Recreations: golf, music, outdoor sports, gardening. *Address:* c/o Imperial Continental Gas Association, 14 Moorfields Highwalk, EC2Y 9BS. *T:* 01–628 3272. *Clubs:* Vincent's (Oxford); Australian, Royal Melbourne Golf (Melbourne).

RENDLE, Peter Critchfield; Under-Secretary (Principal Finance Officer), Scottish Office, 1978–80, retired; *b* Truro, 31 July 1919; *s* of late Martyn and Florence Rendle; *m* 1944, Helen Barbara Moyes; three *s*. *Educ:* Queen Elizabeth's Sch., Hartlebury. Clerical Officer, Min. of Transport, 1936–49. Served War, Royal Navy, 1940–46 (Lieut RNVR). Min. of Town and Country Planning, 1949; Dept of Health for Scotland, 1950–59 (Sec., Guest Cttee on Bldg Legislation in Scotland) and other Scottish Depts; Under Sec., Housing, Scottish Development Dept, 1973–78. Member: Legal Aid Central Cttee for Scotland, 1980–; Scottish Is Councils Cttee of Inquiry, 1982–84. *Publication:* Rayner Report, Scrutiny of HM Inspectors of Schools in Scotland, 1981. *Recreations:* hockey, taking photographs. *Address:* St Clair, 159 Granton Road, Edinburgh EH5 3NL. *T:* 031–552 3396. *Club:* Scottish Arts (Edinburgh).

RENDLESHAM, 8th Baron, *cr* 1806; **Charles Anthony Hugh Thellusson;** Royal Corps of Signals; *b* 15 March 1915; *s* of Lt-Col Hon. Hugh Edmund Thellusson, DSO (3rd *s* of 5th Baron); *S* uncle, 1943; *m* 1st, 1940, Margaret Elizabeth (marr. diss. 1947; she *m* 1962, Patrick P. C. Barthropp), *d* of Lt-Col Robin Rome, Monk's Hall, Glemsford; one *d*; 2nd, 1947, Clare, *d* of Lt-Col D. H. G. McCririck; one *s* three *d*. *Educ:* Eton. *Heir:* *s* Hon. Charles William Brooke Thellusson [*b* 10 Jan. 1954; *m* 1983, Susan Fielding]. *Address:* 498 King's Road, SW10 0LE.

See also Sir William Goring, Bt.

RENÉ, (France) Albert; barrister-at-law; President of the Republic of Seychelles since 1977 (elected, since 1979); Minister of Administration, Finance and Industries, Transport, Planning and External Relations, since 1984; *b* Mahé, Seychelles, 16 Nov. 1935; *s* of Price René and Louisa Morgan; *m* 1st, 1956, Karen Handlay; one *d*; 2nd, 1975, Geva Adam; one *s*. *Educ:* St Louis Coll., Seychelles; St Moritz, Switzerland; St Mary's Coll., Southampton, England; King's Coll., Univ. of London; Council of Legal Educn, 1956; LSE, 1961. Called to Bar, 1957. Leader, Founder, 1964, Sec.-Gen., 1984–, Seychelles People's United Party (first effective political party and liberation movement in Seychelles); MP, 1965; Mem. in Governing Council, 1967; Mem., Legal Assembly, 1970 and 1974; Minister of Works and Land Development, 1975, Prime Minister, 1976–77. Founder, Leader and Pres., Seychelles People's Progressive Front, 1978. Advocates positive non-alignment, the development of a Seychellois-socialist society and the promotion of the Indian Ocean as a zone of peace. Order of the Golden Ark (1st cl.), 1982. *Address:* President's Office, State House, Republic of Seychelles.

RENFREW, Prof. (Andrew) Colin; FBA 1980; Disney Professor of Archaeology, University of Cambridge, since 1981; Master of Jesus College, Cambridge, since 1986; *b* 25 July 1937; *s* of late Archibald Renfrew and Helena Douglas Renfrew (*née* Savage); *m* 1965, Jane Margaret, *d* of Ven. Walter F. Ewbank, *qv*; two *s* one *d*. *Educ:* St Albans Sch.; St John's Coll., Cambridge (Exhibr); British Sch. of Archaeology, Athens. Pt I Nat. Scis Tripos 1960; BA 1st cl. hons Archaeol. and Anthrop. Tripos 1962; MA 1964; PhD 1965; ScD 1976. Pres., Cambridge Union Soc., 1961; Sir Joseph Larmor Award 1961. Nat. Service, Flying Officer (Signals), RAF, 1956–58. Res. Fellow, St John's Coll., Cambridge, 1965, Professorial Fellow, 1981–86; Bulgarian Govt Schol., 1966; Univ. of Sheffield: Lectr in Prehistory and Archaeol., 1965–70; Sen. Lectr, 1970–72; Reader, 1972; Prof. of Archaeology, Southampton Univ., 1972–81. Vis. Lectr, Univ. of Calif at Los Angeles, 1967. Contested (C) Sheffield Brightside, 1968; Vice-Chm., Sheffield Brightside Conserv. Assoc., 1968–72. Member: Ancient Monuments Bd for England, 1974–84; Royal Commn on Historical Monuments (England), 1977–87; Historic Buildings and Monuments Commn for England, 1984–86; Ancient Monuments Adv. Cttee, 1984–; UK Nat. Commn for UNESCO, 1984–86 (Mem. Culture Adv. Cttee, 1984–86); Trustee, Antiquity Trust, 1974–; Chm., Hants Archaeol Cttee, 1974–81; a Vice-Pres., RAI, 1982–85. Chm., Governors, The Leys, 1984–. Lectures: Dalrymple in Archaeol., Univ. of Glasgow, 1975; George Grant MacCurdy, Harvard, 1977; Patten, Indiana Univ., 1982; Harvey, New Mexico Univ., 1982. Excavations: Saliagos near Antiparos, 1964–65; Sitagroi, Macedonia, 1968–70; Phylakopi in Melos, 1974–76; Quanterness, Orkney, 1972–74; Maes Howe, 1973–74; Ring of Brodgar, 1974; Liddle Farm, 1973–74. Rivers Meml Medal, RAI, 1979. FSA 1968; FSAScot 1970. *Publications:* (with J. D. Evans) Excavations at Saliagos near Antiparos, 1968; The Emergence of Civilisation, 1972; (ed) The Explanation of Culture Change, 1973; Before Civilisation, 1973; (ed) British Prehistory, a New Outline, 1974; Investigations in Orkney, 1979; (ed) Transformations: Mathematical Approaches to Culture Change, 1979; Problems in European Prehistory, 1979; (with J. M. Wagstaff) An Island Polity, 1982; (ed) Theory and Explanation in Archaeology, 1982; Approaches to Social Archaeology, 1984; The Prehistory of Orkney, 1985; The Archaeology of Cult, 1985; articles in archaeol jls. *Recreations:* modern art, numismatics, travel. *Address:* Master's Lodge, Jesus College, Cambridge CB5 8BL. *T:* Cambridge 353310; Department of Archaeology, Downing Street, Cambridge CB2 3DZ. *T:* Cambridge 333520. *Clubs:* Athenæum, United Oxford & Cambridge University.

RENFREW, Rt. Rev. Charles McDonald; Titular Bishop of Abula and Auxiliary to the Archbishop of Glasgow, (RC), since 1977; Vicar General of Archdiocese of Glasgow, since 1974; *b* 21 June 1929; *s* of Alexander Renfrew and Mary (*née* Dougherty). *Educ:* St Aloysius College, Glasgow; Scots College, Rome. PhL, STL (Gregorian). Ordained Rome, 1953; Assistant at Immaculate Conception, Glasgow, 1953–56; Professor and Procurator, Blairs Coll., Aberdeen, 1956–61; First Rector and founder of St Vincent's Coll., Langbank, 1961–74. Sound and television broadcasts for BBC and STV. Comdr, Order of Merit (Republic of Italy), 1982. *Publications:* St Vincent's Prayer Book, 1971; pamphlets and articles in newspapers and magazines. *Recreation:* music, especially grand and light opera. *Address:* St Joseph's, 38 Mansionhouse Road, Glasgow G41 3DN. *T:* 041–649 2228.

RENFREW, Prof. Colin; *see* Renfrew, Prof. A. C.

RENFREW, Glen McGarvie; Managing Director and Chief Executive, Reuters Ltd, since 1981; *b* 15 Sept. 1928; *s* of Robert Renfrew and Jane Grey Watson; *m* 1954, Daphne Ann Hailey; one *s* two *d* (and one *d* decd). *Educ:* Sydney Univ., NSW, Australia (BA). Joined Reuters, London, 1952; reporting and/or management assignments in Asia, Africa and Europe, 1956–64; London management posts in computer and economic information services, 1964–70; Manager, Reuters N America, 1971–80. *Recreation:* sailing. *Address:* c/o Reuters, 85 Fleet Street, EC4. *T:* 01–250 1122. *Clubs:* Manhasset Bay Yacht (Long Island, NY), National Press (Washington).

RENFREY, Rt. Rev. Lionel Edward William; Dean of Adelaide, since 1966; Assistant Bishop of Adelaide, since 1969; Rector of Mallala and Two Wells, since 1981; *b* Adelaide, SA, 26 March 1916; *s* of late Alfred Cyril Marinus Renfrey and Catherine Elizabeth Rose Frerichs (*née* Dickson); *m* 1948, Joan Anne, *d* of Donal Smith, Cooke's Plains, SA; one *s* five *d*. *Educ:* Unley High School; St Mark's Coll., Univ. of Adelaide; St Barnabas' Theological Coll., Adelaide. BA (First Cl. Hons English), ThL (ACT) (Second Cl. Hons). Deacon 1940, priest 1941, Dio. Adelaide; Curate, St Cuthbert's, Prospect, 1940–43; Mission Chaplain, Mid Yorke Peninsula, 1943–44; Warden, Brotherhood of St John Baptist, 1944–47; Priest-in-charge: Berri-Barmera, 1948–50; Kensington Gardens, 1950–57; Rector, St James', Mile End, 1957–63; Rural Dean, Western Suburbs, 1962–63; Organising Chaplain, Bishop's Home Mission Soc., 1963–66; Editor, Adelaide Church Guardian, 1961–66; Archdeacon of Adelaide, 1965–66; Examining Chaplain to Bishop of Adelaide, 1965–; Administrator (*sede vacante*), Diocese of Adelaide, 1974–75. OStJ 1981 (SBStJ 1969). *Publications:* Father Wise: a Memoir, 1951; Short History of St Barnabas' Theological College, 1965; What Mean Ye By This Service?, 1978; (ed) Catholic Prayers, 1980; (ed) SS Peter and Paul Prayer Book, 1982. *Recreations:* reading, golf, motoring. *Address:* Church Office, 44 Currie Street, Adelaide, SA 5000, Australia. *Clubs:* Adelaide, Royal Adelaide Golf (Adelaide).

RENNELL, 3rd Baron *cr* 1933, of Rodd, Herefordshire; **John Adrian Tremayne Rodd;** *b* 28 June 1935; *s* of Hon. Gustaf Guthrie Rennell Rodd (*d* 1974) (*yr s* of 1st Baron) and Yvonne Mary Rodd (*d* 1982), *d* of late Sir Charles Murray Marling, GCMG, CB; *S* uncle, 1978; *m* 1977, Phyllis, *d* of T. D. Neill; one *s* one *d*. *Educ:* Downside; RNC, Dartmouth. Served Royal Navy, 1952–62. With Morgan Grenfell & Co. Ltd, 1963–66; free-lance journalist, 1966–67; Marks of Distinction Ltd, 1968–79; Dir, Tremayne Ltd, 1980–. *Recreations:* Scotland Rugby XV, 1958–65; golf, Real tennis. *Heir:* *s* Hon. James Roderick David Tremayne Rodd, *b* 9 March 1978. *Clubs:* White's, Queen's; Sunningdale (Ascot).

RENNIE, Alexander Allan, CBE 1980; QPM 1971; Chief Constable, West Mercia Constabulary, 1975–81, retired; *b* 13 June 1917; *s* of Charles Rennie and Susan Parsons Rennie; *m* 1941, Lucy Brunt; one *s* one *d*. *Educ:* Ellon Acad., Aberdeenshire. Armed Services, 1941–45: commnd 30 Corps Royal Northumberland Fusiliers; active service in Europe (mentioned in despatches, 1945). Joined Durham County Constab., 1937; Chief Supt, 1963; Dep. Chief Constable, Shropshire, 1963–67; Dir, Sen. Comd Course, Police Coll., Bramshill, 1967–69; Asst Chief Constable, West Mercia, 1969–72, Dep. Chief Constable, 1973–75. OStJ 1975. *Recreations:* golf, hill walking. *Address:* 14 Minter Avenue, St Andrews Gardens, Droitwich, Worcs WR9 8RP.

RENNIE, Sir Alfred (Baillie), Kt 1960; formerly a Federal Justice of the West Indies Federation (1958–62); *b* 18 March 1896; *s* of James Malcolm and Mary Jane Rennie; *m* 1925, Patricia Margaret O'Gorman; one *s* two *d*. *Educ:* Wolmer's School, Kingston, Jamaica; King's College, London. Lieut, British West Indies Regt, 1916–19. Called to the Bar, 1922; practised in Jamaica and Bermuda, 1922–29; Clerk of the Courts, Jamaica, 1929–33; Resident Magistrate, 1933–34; Crown Solicitor, 1934–49; Judge of Supreme Court of Jamaica, 1949–58. *Recreation:* shooting. *Address:* 65 Friary Park, Ballabeg, Isle of Man.

RENNIE, Archibald Louden, CB 1980; Secretary, Scottish Home and Health Department, 1977–84, retired; *b* 4 June 1924; *s* of John and Isabella Rennie; *m* 1950, Kathleen Harkess; four *s*. *Educ:* Madras Coll.; St Andrews University. Experimental Officer, Mine Design Dept, Admty, 1944–47; Dept of Health for Scotland, 1947–62; Private Sec. to Sec. of State for Scotland, 1962–63; Asst Sec., Scottish Home and Health Dept, 1963–69; Registrar Gen. for Scotland, 1969–73; Under-Sec., Scottish Office, 1973–77. Gen. Council Assessor, St Andrews Univ. Court, 1984–85; Chancellor's Assessor, 1985–; Vice-Chm., Adv. Cttee on Distinction Awards for Consultants, 1985–. *Recreations:* Scottish literature, sailing, gardening. *Address:* Baldinnie, Park Place, Elie, Fife KY9 1DH. *T:* Elie 330741. *Club:* Scottish Arts (Edinburgh).

RENNIE, Compton Alexander, CMG 1969; Nuclear Energy Consultant since 1968; *b* 12 Dec. 1915; *s* of George Malcolm Rennie, Southampton; *m* 1941, Marjorie Dorothy Pearson; no *c*. *Educ:* Sutton Valence Sch., Kent; Sidney Sussex Coll., Cambridge. Radar Officer, TRE, Malvern, 1940–45. Atomic Energy Research Estabt, Harwell, 1945–59: Overseas Liaison Officer, 1955; Dep. Head, Reactor Div., 1957; Head, High Temperature Reactor Div., 1958; Atomic Energy Estabt, Winfrith, Dorset, and Chief Exec. of OECD High Temperature Reactor Project (Dragon Project), 1959–68; Dir, Nuclear Power and Reactors Div., Internat. Atomic Energy Agency, Vienna, 1970–72. Ford Foundn Atoms for Peace Award, 1969. *Recreation:* gardening. *Address:* 43 East Street, Wareham, Dorset BH20 4NW. *T:* Wareham 2671.

RENNIE, James Douglas Milne, CB 1986; Parliamentary Counsel, since 1976; *b* 2 Nov. 1931; *s* of Douglas Frederick Milne Rennie and Margaret Wilson Fleming Rennie (*née* Keanie); *m* 1962, Patricia Margaret Calhoun Watson; one *s* one *d*. *Educ:* Charterhouse; New Coll., Oxford (Schol.). 1st cl. Hon. Mods 1953; 2nd cl. Lit. Hum. 1955; 2nd cl. Jurisprudence 1957; MA. Called to Bar, Lincoln's Inn, 1958 (Cholmeley Schol.). Asst Lectr, UCW Aberystwyth, 1957; practised at Chancery Bar, 1958–65; Asst Parly Counsel, HM Treasury, 1965; Sen. Asst Parly Counsel, 1972; Dep. Parly Counsel, 1973–75. *Recreations:* opera, travel. *Address:* 8 Wellesley Road, W4 4BL. *T:* 01–994 6627.

RENNIE, John Chalmers; Town Clerk of Aberdeen, 1946–68; retired; *b* 16 April 1907; *s* of late John Chalmers Rennie, Pharmacist, Wishaw; *m* 1937, Georgina Stoddart, *d* of late Henry Bell, Engineer and Ironfounder, Wishaw; one *s*. *Educ:* University of Glasgow (BL). Town Clerk Depute, Motherwell and Wishaw, 1929–43; Town Clerk Depute, Aberdeen, 1943–46. *Recreation:* do-it-yourself. *Address:* 34 Morningfield Road, Aberdeen AB2 4AQ. *T:* Aberdeen 316904.

RENNIE, Sir John Shaw, GCMG 1968 (KCMG 1962; CMG 1958); OBE 1955; Commissioner-General, United Nations Relief and Works Agency for Palestine Refugees, 1971–77 (Deputy Commissioner-General, 1968–71); *b* 12 Jan. 1917; *s* of late John Shaw Rennie, Saskatoon, Sask, Canada; *m* 1946, Mary Winifred Macalpine Robertson; one *s*. *Educ:* Hillhead High School; Glasgow University; Balliol College, Oxford. Cadet, Tanganyika, 1940; Asst District Officer, 1942; District Officer, 1949; Deputy Colonial Secretary, Mauritius, 1951; British Resident Comr, New Hebrides, 1955–62; Governor and C-in-C of Mauritius, 1962–March 1968, Governor-General, March-Aug. 1968. Hon. LLD Glasgow, 1972. *Address:* 26 College Cross, N1 1PR; via Roma 33, 06050 Collazzone (PG), Italy. *Club:* Royal Commonwealth Society.

RENOWDEN, Very Rev. Charles Raymond; Dean of St Asaph since 1971; *b* 27 Oct. 1923; *s* of Rev. Canon Charles Renowden; *m* 1951, Ruth Cecil Mary Collis; one *s* two *d*. *Educ:* Llandysil Grammar Sch.; St David's Univ. Coll., Lampeter; Selwyn Coll., Cambridge. BA (Hons Philosophy, cl. I), Lampeter; BA, MA (Hons Theology, cl. I), Cambridge. Served War, Army, Intelligence Corps, in India and Japan, 1944–47. Cambridge Ordination Course; Deacon, 1951, Priest, 1952, Wales. Asst Curate, Hubberston, Milford Haven, 1951–55. St David's Univ. Coll., Lampeter: Lectr in Philosophy and Theology, 1955–57; Head of Dept of Philosophy, 1957–69; Sen. Lectr in Philosophy and Theology, 1969–71. *Publications:* (monograph) The Idea of Unity, 1965; New Patterns of Ministry, 1973; The Rôle of a Cathedral Today and Tomorrow, 1974; contributor to: Theology, The Modern Churchman, Church Quarterly Review, Trivium, Province. *Recreations:* music, gardening, ornithology. *Address:* The Deanery, St Asaph, Clwyd. *T:* St Asaph 583597.

RENOWDEN, Ven. Glyndwr Rhys; QHC 1980; Chaplain in Chief, Royal Air Force, since 1983; *b* 13 Aug. 1929; *s* of Charles and Mary Elizabeth Renowden; *m* 1956, Mary

Kinsey-Jones; one *d*. *Educ:* Llanelli Grammar Sch.; St David's Coll., Lampeter (BA, LTh). Curate: St Mary's, Tenby, 1952–55; St Mary's, Chepstow, 1955–58; Chaplain, RAF, 1958–; Asst Chaplain in Chief, 1975–83. *Recreations:* Rugby football, bridge. *Address:* Ministry of Defence (Air), Adastral House, Theobald's Road, WC1X 8RU. *Club:* Royal Air Force.

RENSHAW, Sir (Charles) Maurice (Bine), 3rd Bt *cr* 1903; *b* 7 Oct. 1912; *s* of Sir (Charles) Stephen (Bine) Renshaw, 2nd Bt and of Edith Mary, *d* of Rear-Adm. Sir Edward Chichester, 9th Bt, CB, CMG; *S* father, 1976; *m* 1942, Isabel Bassett (marr. diss. 1947), *d* of late Rev. John L. T. Popkin; one *s* one *d* (and one *s* decd); *m* 2nd, Winifred May, *d* of H. F. Gliddon, Ashwater, Devon, and formerly wife of James H. T. Sheldon; three *s* three *d*. *Educ:* Eton. Served as Flying Officer, RAF (invalided). *Heir:* *s* John David Renshaw [*b* 9 Oct. 1945; *m* 1970, Jennifer, *d* of Group Captain F. Murray, RAF; one *s* two *d*]. *Address:* Tam-na-Marghaidh, Balquhidder, Perthshire; Linwood, Instow, N Devon.

RENSHAW, Hon. John Brophy, AC 1979; Agent-General for New South Wales in London, 1980–83; *b* 8 Aug. 1909; *s* of late J. I. Renshaw; *m* 1st, 1943 (she *d* 1964); one *s*; 2nd, 1966, Mrs M. McKay. *Educ:* Ryde Sch. Mem., Coonabarabran Shire Council, 1937–40 (Pres., 1939–40); MLA, Castlereagh, NSW, 1941–80; Assistant Minister: for Lands, 1950; for Local Govt, 1952; Minister: for Public Works, 1952, and for Local Govt, 1953–56; for Local Govt and Highways, 1956–59; Treasurer, 1959–65; Dep. Premier and Minister for Industrial Develt and Decentralisation, 1962–64; Premier of NSW, 1964–65; Leader of the Opposition, 1965–68 (resigned); Treasurer, 1976–80.

RENTON, family name of **Baron Renton.**

RENTON, Baron *cr* 1979 (Life Peer), of Huntingdon in the County of Cambridgeshire; **David Lockhart-Mure Renton,** KBE 1964; TD; PC 1962; QC 1954; MA; BCL; DL; a Deputy Speaker of the House of Lords, since 1982; *b* 12 Aug. 1908; *s* of late Dr Maurice Waugh Renton, The Bridge House, Dartford, Kent, and Eszma Olivia, *d* of late Allen Walter Borman, Alexandria; *m* 1947, Claire Cicely Duncan (*d* 1986); three *d*. *Educ:* Stubbington; Oundle; University College, Oxford. BA (Hons Jurisprudence), 1930; BCL, 1931; MA. Called to Bar, Lincoln's Inn, 1933; South-Eastern Circuit; elected to General Council of the Bar, 1939; Bencher, Lincoln's Inn, 1962, Treasurer, 1979. Commnd RE (TA), 1938; transferred to RA 1940; served throughout War of 1939–45; Capt. 1941; Major, 1943; served in Egypt and Libya, 1942–45. MP (Nat L) 1945–50, (Nat L and C) 1950–68, (C) 1968–79, Huntingdonshire; Parly Sec., Min. of Fuel and Power, 1955–57, Ministry of Power, 1957–58; Joint Parly Under-Sec. of State, Home Office, 1958–61; Minister of State, Home Office, 1961–62; Chm., Select Cttee for Revision of Standing Orders, House of Commons, 1963 and 1970; Dep. Chm., Select Cttee on H of C Procedure, 1976–78; Mem., Cttee of Privileges, 1973–79. Recorder of Rochester, 1963–68, of Guildford, 1968–71; Vice-Chm., Council of Legal Educn, 1968–70, 1971–73. Member: Senate of Inns of Court, 1967–69, 1970–71, 1975–79; Commn on the Constitution, 1971–73; Chm., Cttee on Preparation of Legislation, 1973–75. Pres., Statute Law Soc., 1980–. Pres., Royal Soc. for Mentally Handicapped Children, 1982– (Hon. Treas., 1976–78; Chm., 1978–82). President: Conservation Soc., 1970–71; Nat. Council for Civil Def., 1980–. Patron: Nat. Law Library, 1979–; Huntingdonshire Conservative Assoc., 1979–; Ravenswood Foundn, 1979–; Gtr London Assoc. for the Disabled, 1986–; DEMAND (Design and Manufacture for Disablement), 1986–. DL Huntingdonshire, 1962, Huntingdon and Peterborough, 1964, Cambs, 1974. Coronation and Jubilee Medals. *Recreations:* outdoor sports and games, gardening. *Address:* Moat House, Abbots Ripton, Huntingdon, Cambs PE17 2PE. *T:* Abbots Ripton 227; 22 Old Buildings, Lincoln's Inn, WC2. *T:* 01-242 8986. *Clubs:* Carlton, Pratt's.

RENTON, Gordon Pearson; Assistant Under-Secretary of State, Department of Trade and Industry, 1983–84; *b* 12 Dec. 1928; *s* of Herbert Renton and Annie (*née* Pearson); *m* 1st, 1952, Joan Mary Lucas (marr. diss. 1971); two *s*; 2nd, 1978, Sylvia Jones. *Educ:* King Edward VII Sch., Sheffield; Lincoln Coll., Oxford (Scholar, BA Lit. Hum.). Served Royal Signals, 1951–53. Teacher, W Riding, 1953–54; Asst Principal, Home Office, 1954; Asst Private Sec. to Home Sec. and Lord Privy Seal, 1959–60; Principal, 1960; Asst Sec., 1967; Asst Under-Sec. of State, 1978. Mem., Parole Bd, 1985–. *Recreations:* music, gardening, sailing. *Address:* Ship Cottage, Pwll Du, Bishopston, Swansea SA3 2AU. *T:* Bishopston 3796. *Club:* Reform.

RENTON, Air Cdre Helen Ferguson, CB 1982; Director, Women's Royal Air Force, 1980–86; *b* 13 March 1931; *d* of late John Paul Renton and Sarah Graham Renton (*née* Cook). *Educ:* Stirling High Sch.; Glasgow Univ. (MA). Joined WRAF, 1954; commnd, 1955; served in UK, 1955–60; Cyprus, 1960–62; HQ Staff, Germany, 1967; MoD Staff, 1968–71; NEAF, 1971–72; Training Comd, 1973–76; MoD Staff, 1976–78. Hon. LLD Glasgow, 1981. *Publications:* (jtly) Service Women, 1977. *Recreations:* needlework, travel, reading. *Club:* Royal Air Force.

RENTON, Ronald Timothy; MP (C) Mid-Sussex since Feb. 1974; Minister of State, Foreign and Commonwealth Office, since 1985; *b* 28 May 1932; *yr s* of R. K. D. Renton, CBE, and Mrs Renton, MBE; *m* 1960, Alice Fergusson of Kilkerran, Ayrshire; two *s* three *d*. *Educ:* Eton Coll. (King's Schol.); Magdalen Coll., Oxford (Roberts Gawen Schol.). First cl. degree in History, MA Oxon. Joined C. Tennant Sons & Co. Ltd, London, 1954; with Tennants' subsidiaries in Canada, 1957–62; Dir, C. Tennant Sons & Co. Ltd and Managing Dir of Tennant Trading Ltd, 1964–73; Director: Silvermines Ltd, 1967–84; Australia & New Zealand Banking Group, 1967–76; J. H. Vavasseur & Co. Ltd, 1971–74. Mem., BBC Gen. Adv. Council, 1982–84. Contested (C) Sheffield Park Div., 1970; PPS to Rt Hon. John Biffen, MP, 1979–81, to Rt Hon. Geoffrey Howe, MP, 1983–84; Parly Under Sec. of State, FCO, 1984–85. Mem., Select Cttee on Nationalised Industries, 1974–79; Vice-Chm., Cons. Parly Trade Cttee, 1974–79; Chm., Cons. Foreign and Commonwealth Council, 1982–; Vice-Pres., 1978–80, Pres., 1980–84, Cons. Trade Unionists; Fellow, Industry and Parlt Trust, 1977–79. Mem. Council, Roedean Sch., 1982–. Trustee, Mental Health Foundn, 1985–. *Recreations:* gardening, tennis, growing trees. *Address:* Mount Harry House, Offham, Lewes, E Sussex. *T:* Lewes 474456. *Club:* Garrick.

RENWICK, family name of **Baron Renwick.**

RENWICK, 2nd Baron *cr* 1964, of Coombe; **Harry Andrew Renwick;** Bt 1927; *b* 10 Oct. 1935; *s* of 1st Baron Renwick, KBE, and of Mrs John Ormiston, Miserden House, Stroud, *er d* of late Major Harold Parkes, Alveston, Stratford-on-Avon; *S* father, 1973; *m* 1965, Susan Jane, *d* of late Captain Kenneth S. B. Lucking and of Mrs Moir P. Stormonth-Darling, Lednathie, Glen Prosen, Angus; two *s*. *Educ:* Eton. Grenadier Guards (National Service), 1955–56. Partner, W. Greenwell & Co., 1964–80. Dir, General Technology Systems Ltd, 1975–. Vice-Pres., British Dyslexia Assoc., 1982– (Chm., 1977–82); Chm., Dyslexia Educnl Trust, 1986–. *Heir:* *s* Hon. Robert James Renwick, *b* 19 Aug. 1966. *Address:* House of Lords, SW1A 0PW. *Clubs:* White's, Turf.

RENWICK, Prof. James Harrison, DSc, FRCP, FRCPath; Professor of Human Genetics and Teratology, University of London, since 1979; *b* 4 Feb. 1926; *s* of late Raymond Renwick and of Edith Helen Renwick; *m* 1st, 1959, Helena Verheyden (marr. diss. 1979); one *s* one *d*; 2nd, 1981, Kathleen Salafia; two *s*. *Educ:* Sedbergh School; Univ. of St Andrews; MB ChB (commend), 1948; University Coll. London; PhD 1956, DSc 1970; FRCP 1972, MFCM 1972; FRCPath 1982. Captain RAMC, Korean war; research on genetical effects of atomic bomb, Hiroshima, 1951–53. Univ. of Glasgow, 1959, Prof. of Human Genetics, 1967–68; London Sch. of Hygiene and Tropical Medicine, 1968, Head of Preventive Teratology Unit, 1977–. Hon. Treasurer, Genetical Soc., 1960–65, Hon. Auditor, 1965–72. FRSocMed. Freeman, Co. of Stationers and Newspaper Makers. *Publications:* numerous scientific articles on mapping of genes on human chromosomes and on prevention of human congenital malformations. *Recreations:* walking, music. *Address:* 402 Seddon House, Barbican, EC2. *T:* (home) 01-638 3332; (office) 01-637 2839.

RENWICK, Sir Richard Eustace, 4th Bt *cr* 1921; *b* 13 Jan. 1938; *er s* of Sir Eustace Deuchar Renwick, 3rd Bt, and of Diana Mary, *e d* of Colonel Bernard Cruddas, DSO; *S* father, 1973; *m* 1966, Caroline Anne, *er d* of Major Rupert Milburn; three *s*. *Educ:* Eton. *Heir:* *s* Charles Richard Renwick, *b* 10 April 1967. *Address:* Whalton House, Whalton, Morpeth, Northumberland. *T:* Whalton 383. *Club:* Northern Counties (Newcastle).

RENWICK, Robin William, CMG 1980; HM Diplomatic Service; Assistant Under-Secretary of State, Foreign and Commonwealth Office, since 1984; *b* 13 Dec. 1937; *s* of Richard Renwick, Edinburgh, and the late Clarice Henderson; *m* 1965, Anne Colette Giudicelli; one *s* one *d*. *Educ:* St Paul's Sch.; Jesus Coll., Cambridge (1st Cl. Hons History Tripos; Newling Prize); Univ. of Paris (Sorbonne). Army, 1956–58. Entered Foreign Service, 1963; Dakar, 1963–64; FO, 1964–66; New Delhi, 1966–69; Private Sec. to Minister of State, FCO, 1970–72; First Sec., Paris, 1972–76; Counsellor, Cabinet Office, 1976–78; Head, Rhodesia Dept, FCO, 1978–80; Political Adviser to Governor of Rhodesia, 1980; Vis. Fellow, Center for Internat. Affairs, Harvard, 1980–81; Head of Chancery, Washington, 1981–84. *Publication:* Economic Sanctions, 1981. *Recreation:* tennis. *Address:* c/o Foreign and Commonwealth Office, SW1. *Clubs:* Hurlingham, Travellers'.

REPORTER, Sir Shapoor (Ardeshirji), KBE 1973 (OBE 1969); Consultant on Economic and Political Matters concerning Iran, since 1962; *b* 26 Feb. 1921; *s* of Ardeshirji Reporter and Shirin Reporter; *m* 1952, Assia Alexandra; one *s* one *d*. *Educ:* Zoroastrian Public Sch., Teheran; matriculated in Bombay (specially designed course in Political Science under Cambridge Univ. Tutors, UK). PRO, British Legation, Teheran, 1941–43; in charge of Persian Unit of All India Radio, New Delhi, 1943–45; Teaching English, Imperial Staff Coll., Teheran, 1945–48; Political Adviser, US Embassy, Teheran, 1948–54; Free-lance Correspondent, 1954–62; Economic Consultant to major British interests in Iran, 1962–73. *Publications:* English-Persian Phrases, 1945 (Delhi); Dictionary of English-Persian Idioms, 1956 (Teheran); Dictionary of Persian-English Idioms, 1972 (Teheran Univ.). *Recreations:* tennis, walking, travelling.

REPTON, Bishop Suffragan of, since 1986; **Rt. Rev. Francis Henry Arthur Richmond,** MA; *b* 6 Jan. 1936; *s* of Frank and Lena Richmond; *m* 1966, Caroline Mary Berent; two *s* one *d*. *Educ:* Portora Royal School, Enniskillen; Trinity Coll., Dublin (MA); Univ. of Strasbourg (BTh); Linacre Coll., Oxford (MLitt); Wycliffe Hall, Oxford. Deacon, 1963; Priest, 1964; Asst Curate, Woodlands, Doncaster, 1963–66; Sir Henry Stephenson Research Fellow, Sheffield Univ. and Chaplain, Sheffield Cathedral, 1966–69; Vicar, St George's, Sheffield, 1969–77; Warden, Lincoln Theolog. Coll., and Canon and Prebendary of Lincoln Cathedral, 1977–86. Anglican Chaplain to Sheffield Univ. and Mem. Sheffield Chaplaincy for Higher Education, 1974–77. Examng Chaplain to Bishop of Lincoln; Proctor in Convocation for Lincoln, 1980. Select Preacher, Univ. of Oxford, 1985. *Recreations:* listening to classical music, reading, theatre, walking, gardening. *Address:* Repton House, Lea, Matlock, Derbys DE4 5JP. *T:* Dethick 644.

RESNAIS, Alain; French film director; *b* Vannes, 3 June 1922; *s* of Pierre Resnais and Jeanne (*née* Gachet); *m* 1969, Florence Mairaux. *Educ:* Collège St François-Xavier, Vannes; Institut des hautes études cinématographiques. Assistant to Nicole Védrée for film Paris 1900, 1947–48; has directed his own films (many of which have won prizes), since 1948. Short films, 1948–59, include: Van Gogh, 1948; Guernica (jtly with Robert Hessens), 1950, Les statues meurent aussi (jtly with Chris Marker), 1952, Nuit et brouillard, 1955. Full length films include: Hiroshima mon amour, 1959; L'année dernière à Marienbad, 1961; Muriel, 1963; La guerre est finie, 1966; Je t'aime, je t'aime, 1968; Stavisky, 1974; Providence, 1977; Mon Oncle d'Amérique, 1980; La vie est un roman, 1983; L'amour à Mort, 1984. *Address:* Artmedia, 10 Avenue George V, 75008 Paris, France.

RESO, Sidney Joseph; Executive Vice President, Exxon Co. International, since 1986; *b* 12 Feb. 1934; *s* of late James A. Reso and of J. Agnes Reso; *m* 1955, Patricia M. Armond; two *s* three *d*. *Educ:* Louisiana State Univ. (BS Petroleum Engrg). Joined Humble Oil & Refining Co., Houston, Texas (now Exxon Co., USA), as engineer, 1957; USA and Australia: engrg assignments, 1961–66; managerial assignments, 1967–71; Dir, Esso Australia Ltd, Sydney, 1972; managerial assignments, USA, 1973–74; Vice-Pres., Esso Europe Inc. and Managing Dir, Esso Petroleum Co., 1975–78; Vice-Pres., Exxon Corp., 1978–80; Exxon Co. USA: Vice-Pres., 1980–81; Sen. Vice-Pres., 1981–85; Exec. Vice-Pres., 1985–86. *Recreations:* golf, tennis, photography, reading. *Address:* 200 Park Avenue, Florham Park, NJ 07932–1002, USA. *Club:* River Oaks Country.

RESTIEAUX, Rt. Rev. Cyril Edward; *b* 25 Feb. 1910; *s* of Joseph and Edith Restieaux. *Educ:* English Coll., Rome; Gregorian University. Ordained, 1932; Curate at Nottingham, 1933; Parish Priest at Matlock, 1936; Hon. Canon of Nottingham, 1948; Vicar-General of Nottingham, 1951; Provost and Domestic Prelate to HH Pope Pius XII, 1955; Bishop of Plymouth, 1955–86. *Address:* Stoodley Knowle, Anstey's Cove Road, Torquay TQ1 2JB.

RESTREPO-LONDOÑO, Andrés; Order of Boyacá, Colombia; Colombian Ambassador to the Court of St James's, 1981–82; former Chairman, Proban SA (Banana Exporting Company); President, Industrias e Inversiones Samper SA (Cement Company), since 1985; *b* 20 Jan. 1942; *m* 1968, Ghislaine Ibiza; one *s* three *d*. *Educ:* Universidad de Antioquia; Université de Paris (postgraduate courses, 1966). Professor and Head of Economic Dept., Univ. de Antioquia, 1967–68; Gen. Man., La Primavera chain of stores, 1969–76; Finance Man., Empresas Públicas de Medellin, 1976–79; Gen. Man., Carbones de Colombia (Colombian Coal Bd), 1979–80; Minister for Economic Develt, May 1980–March 1981. Order Sol of Peru; Order Cruzeiro do Sul, Brazil. *Publications:* Carbones Térmicos en Colombia, Bases para una Política Contractual, 1981; several articles in El Colombiano, daily newspaper of Medellin, Colombia. *Recreations:* fishing, tennis. *Address:* Calle 136A No 57B-17, Bogotá, DE, Colombia. *Clubs:* Bogotá Sports, Lagartos (Bogotá).

RETTIE, (James) Philip, TD 1962; Chairman, Sea Fish Industry Authority, since 1981; *b* 7 Dec. 1926; *s* of James Rettie and Rachel Buist; *m* 1st, 1955, Helen Grant; two *s* one *d*; 2nd, 1980, Mrs Diana Harvey (*née* Ballantyne). *Educ:* Trinity College, Glenalmond. Royal Engineers, 1945–48; RE (TA), 1949–65. Wm Low & Co. plc, 1948–; (Chm., 1980–85); farmer, 1964–. Mem., TSB Scotland Area Bd, 1983–. Trustee, Scottish Civic Trust, 1983–. Hon. Colonel: 117 (Highland) Field Support Squadron, RE, TAVR, 1982–; 277 Airfield

Damage Repair Sqdn, RE(T), 1984–. *Recreations:* shooting, gardening, hill-walking. *Address:* Wester Ballindean, Inchture, Perthshire PH14 9QS. *T:* Inchture 86337. *Club:* Caledonian.

REUTER, Prof. Gerd Edzard Harry, MA Cantab; Professor of Mathematics, Imperial College of Science and Technology, London, 1965–83, now Emeritus; *b* 21 Nov. 1921; *s* of Ernst Rudolf Johannes Reuter and Gertrud Charlotte Reuter (*née* Scholz); *m* 1945, Eileen Grace Legard; one *s* three *d*. *Educ:* The Leys School and Trinity College, Cambridge. Mem. of Dept of Mathematics, Univ. of Manchester, 1946–58; Professor of Pure Mathematics, Univ. of Durham, 1959–65. *Publications:* Elementary Differential Equations and Operators, 1958; articles in various mathematical and scientific jls. *Address:* 47 Madingley Road, Cambridge CB3 0EL.

REVANS, Sir John, Kt 1977; CBE 1967 (MBE 1943); retired; *b* 7 June 1911; *s* of Thomas William Revans, MINA and Ethel Amelia Revans; *m* 1936, Eileen Parkhurst Mitchell; two *d*. *Educ:* Middlesex Hosp. Med. Sch. (Broderip Schol. in Med., Surgery and Path.; Forensic Medicine Prize, 1935); Royal Army Med. Coll. (Montefiore Prize in Surgery, 1936). London Univ. DCH 1946; FRCP 1969. Served War of 1939–45 (despatches 1941): Col Indian Med. Service, 1936–47, retd. Sen. Admin. MO, Wessex RHB, 1959–73; Regional MO, Wessex RHA, 1973–76. Adviser on hosps and health services to Royal Commn on Health, Newfoundland and Labrador, 1965–66; Member: Med. Cons. Cttee, Nuffield Provincial Hosps Trust, 1961–76; Standing Nursing Adv. Cttee, Central Health Services Council; Cttee on Gen. Practice of CHSC; Cttee on Senior Nursing Staff Structure in Hosp. Service; Cttee on Rehabilitation; Cttee on Hosp. Complaints; Central Midwives Bd, 1963–67. Vis. Prof. of Health Service Admin, Univ. of London, 1969. Mem. Council, Univ. of Southampton, 1978. Hon. LLD Southampton, 1970. Hon. FRCGP 1974. OStJ 1946. *Recreation:* sailing (RYA/DTI Yachtmaster (Offshore)). *Address:* The Triangle, Durley, Southampton SO3 2AJ. *T:* Durley 348. *Club:* Little Ship.

See also Prof. R. W. Revans.

REVANS, Prof. Reginald William, PhD; MIMinE; Founder, Action Learning Trust, 1977; Professorial Fellow in Action Learning, University of Manchester, since 1986; *b* 14 May 1907; *s* of Thomas William Revans, Principal Ship Surveyor, Board of Trade; *m* 1st, 1932, Annida Aquist, Gothenburg (marriage dissolved, 1947); three *d*; 2nd, 1955, Norah Mary Merritt, Chelmsford; one *s*. *Educ:* Battersea Grammar School; University Coll., London; Emmanuel Coll., Cambridge. BSc London, PhD Cantab. Commonwealth Fund Fellow, Univ. of Michigan, 1930–32; Research Fellow, Emmanuel Coll., Cambridge, 1932–35; Dep. Chief Education Officer, Essex CC, 1935–45; Dir of Education, Mining Assoc. of Gt Britain, 1945–47 and NCB, 1947–50; Research on management of coalmines, 1950–55; Prof., Industrial Admin., Univ. of Manchester, 1955–65; Res. Fellow, Guy's Hosp. Med. Sch., 1965–68; External Prof., Management Studies, Leeds Univ., 1976–78. Dist. Vis. Scholar, Southern Methodist Univ., USA, 1972. Pres., Internat. Management Centre from Buckingham, 1983–. Hon. DSc Bath, 1969. Chevalier, Order of Leopold, Belgium, 1971. *Publications:* Report on Education for Mining Industry, 1945; Education of the Young Worker, 1949; Standards for Morale, 1964; Science and the Manager, 1965; The Theory and Practice of Management, 1965; Developing Effective Managers, 1971; (ed) Hospitals, Communication, Choice and Change, 1972; Workers' Attitudes and Motivation (OECD Report), 1972; Childhood and Maturity, 1973; Action Learning in Hospitals, 1976; The ABC of Action Learning, 1978; Action Learning, 1979; The Origins and Growth of Action Learning, 1982; various in professional magazines upon application of analytical methods to understanding of industrial morale. *Recreations:* British Olympic Team, 1928; holder of Cambridge undergraduate long jump record, 1929–62. *Address:* 8 Higher Downs, Altrincham, Cheshire. *Club:* National Liberal.

See also Sir John Revans.

REVELSTOKE, 4th Baron *cr* 1885; **Rupert Baring;** *b* 8 Feb. 1911; *o s* of 3rd Baron and Maude (*d* 1922), *d* of late Pierre Lorillard; *S* father, 1934; *m* 1934, Flora (who obtained a divorce 1944), 2nd *d* of 1st Baron Hesketh; two *s*. *Educ:* Eton. 2nd Lt Royal Armoured Corps (TA). *Heir:* *s* Hon. John Baring, *b* 2 Dec. 1934. *Address:* Lambay Island, Rush, Co. Dublin, Ireland.

REVERDIN, Prof. Olivier, DrLitt; Professor of Greek, University of Geneva, 1958–83 (Hon. Professor, since 1983); Member, Consultative Assembly of Council of Europe, 1963–74 (President, 1969–72); Deputy (Liberal) for Geneva, Swiss National Council, 1955–71, Council of States (Senate), 1971–79; *b* 15 July 1913; *m* 1936, Renée Chaponnière; two *s* one *d*. *Educ:* Geneva, Paris and Athens. LicLitt 1935; DrLitt Geneva, 1945. Foreign Mem., French Sch. of Archaeology, Athens, 1936–38; Attaché Swiss Legation, Service of Foreign Interests, Rome, 1941–43; Privatdocent of Greek, Univ. of Geneva, 1945–57; Parly Redactor, 1945–54; Chief Editor 1954–59, Manager 1954–67, Pres., 1972–79, Journal de Genève. Mem. 1963–80, Pres. 1968–80, Swiss National Research Council; Mem., Swiss Science Council, 1958–80; Président: Fondation Hardt pour l'étude de l'antiquité classique, Geneva, 1959–; Fondation Archives Jean Piaget, 1973–; Vice-Pres., European Science Foundn, 1974–77, Mem. Exec. Council, 1977–80; Chm., Collections Baur, Geneva, 1984–. *Publications:* La religion de la cité platonicienne, 1945; La guerre du Sonderbund, 1947; La Crète, berceau de la civilisation occidentale, 1960; Connaissance de la Suisse, 1966. *Address:* 8 rue des Granges, 1204 Geneva, Switzerland. *T:* 022–21–51–91.

REVIE, Donald, OBE; formerly professional footballer, then football manager, now retired; *b* 10 July 1927; *m* 1949, Elsie May Leonard Duncan; one *s* one *d*. *Educ:* Archibald Secondary Modern Sch., Middlesbrough, Yorks. Professional footballer with Leicester, Hull, Manchester City, Sunderland, and Leeds United, 1945–61; Player-Manager, then Manager, Leeds United Football Club, 1961–74; Manager of England Team, FA, 1974–77; National Team Coach, UAE FA, 1977–80; Manager: Al Nasr Football Club, 1980; National Football Club, Cairo, 1984. *Publication:* Soccer's Happy Wanderer, 1955. *Recreations:* golf, reading.

REX, Prof. John Arderne; Research Professor on Ethnic Relations, since 1984 and Associate Director, Centre for Research in Ethnic Relations, since 1974, University of Warwick; *b* 5 March 1925; *s* of Frederick Edward George Rex and Winifred Natalie Rex; *m* 1st, 1949, Pamela Margaret Rutherford (marr. diss. 1963); two *d*; 2nd, 1965, Margaret Ellen Biggs; two *s*. *Educ:* Grey Institute High Sch. and Rhodes University Coll., S Africa. BA (S Africa), PhD (Leeds). Served War, Royal Navy (Able Seaman), 1943–45. Graduated, 1948; Lecturer: Univ. of Leeds, 1949–62; Birmingham, 1962–64; Prof. of Social Theory and Institutions, Durham, 1964–70; Prof. of Sociology, Univ. of Warwick, 1970–79; Dir, SSRC Research Unit on Ethnic Relations, Univ. of Aston in Birmingham, 1979–84. Vis. Prof., Univ. of Toronto, 1974–75. *Publications:* Key Problems of Sociological Theory, 1961; (with Robert Moore) Race Community and Conflict, 1967, 2nd edn 1973; Race Relations in Sociological Theory, 1970; Discovering Sociology, 1973; Race, Colonialism and the City, 1974; (ed) Approaches to Sociology, 1974; Sociology and the Demystification of the Modern World, 1974; (with Sally Tomlinson) Colonial Immigrants in a British City, 1979; Social Conflict, 1980; (ed) Apartheid and Social Research, 1981; Race and Ethnicity, 1986. *Recreations:* politics, race relations work. *Address:* Centre for Research in Ethnic Relations, University of Warwick, Coventry CV4 7AL.

REX, Hon. Sir Robert (Richmond), KBE 1984 (OBE 1973); CMG 1978; Prime Minister of Niue, since 1974; Representative of Alofi South on the Niue Island Council, since 1952; *b* 25 Jan. 1909; *s* of Leslie Lucas Richmond Rex and Monomono Paea; *m* 1941, Tuagatagaloa Patricia Vatolo; two *s* two *d*. *Educ:* Tufukia Technical Sch., Niue. Engrg Apprentice, Rakiraki Sugar-mills, Fiji Islands, 1926; Employee, NZ Steamship Union Co., 1927; farmer, Niue, 1930; Businessman (retailing), R. R. Rex & Sons Ltd, 1952. Clerk and Official Interpreter (Jack-of-all-trades), Niue Govt, 1934; Mem. Exec. Cttee, Niue Island Assembly, 1960; Leader of Govt Business, 1966; is known as the longest-serving statesman in the Pacific. Mem., Commonwealth Parly Assoc. *Recreations:* cricket, Rugby, fishing, planting, billiards. *Address:* Alofi South, Niue Island, New Zealand. *T:* 275. *Club:* Niue Sports.

REYES, Narciso G., Bintang Mahaputera, 1964; Order of Diplomatic Service Merit, 1972; President, Philippine Council for Foreign Relations, 1986–87; *b* Manila, 6 Feb. 1914; *m*. *Educ:* Univ. of Sto Tomas (AB). Mem., English Faculty, Univ. of Sto Tomas, 1935–36; Assoc. Ed., Philippines Commonweal, 1935–41; Nat. Language Faculty, Ateneo de Manila, 1939–41; Assoc. Ed., Manila Post, 1945–47; Assoc. News Ed., Evening News, Manila, 1947–48; Man. Ed., Philippine Newspaper Guild Organ, 1947–48; various advisory and UN posts, 1948–; Dir, Philippine Information Agency, 1954–55; Minister-Counsellor, Bangkok, 1956; Public Relations Dir, SEATO, 1956–58; Minister, later Amb., Burma, 1958–62; Ambassador to: Indonesia, 1962–67; London, Stockholm, Oslo, Copenhagen, 1967–70; Permanent Rep. to UN, 1970–77; Philippine Ambassador to People's Republic of China, 1977–80; Sec. Gen., ASEAN, 1980–82. Mem. various delegns and missions, incl. sessions of UN; Philippine Rep. to UN Commn for Social Devt, 1967–72 (Vice-Chm., 1967; Chm., 1968); Special UN Rep. on Social Develt, 1968; Rep. to UN Human Rights Commn, 1970–72; Chairman: UNICEF Exec. Bd, 1972–74; UN Gen. Assembly Finance and Economic Cttee, 1971; Pres., UNDP Governing Council; Vice-Pres., UN Environment Governing Council. Outstanding Alumnus, Univ. of Sto Tomas, 1969. Dr of Laws (*hc*), Philippine Women's Univ., 1977. *Publications:* essays, poems and short stories. *Address:* 8 Lipa Road, Philamlife Homes, Quezon City, Manila, Philippine.

REYNOLD, Frederic, QC 1982; *b* 7 Jan. 1936; *s* of Henry and late Regina Reynold. *Educ:* Battersea Grammar School; Magdalen College, Oxford. BA Hons Jurisprudence. Called to the Bar, Gray's Inn, 1960; commenced practice, 1963. *Publication:* The Judge as Lawmaker, 1967. *Recreations:* music, the arts, association croquet, dining out among friends. *Address:* 5 Hillcrest, 51 Ladbroke Grove, W11. *T:* 01–229 3848. *Club:* Sussex County Croquet.

REYNOLDS, Alan (Munro); painter, maker of reliefs, and printmaker; *b* 27 April 1926; *m* 1957, Vona Darby. *Educ:* Woolwich Polytechnic Art School; Royal College of Art (Scholarship and Medal). One man exhibitions: Redfern Gall., 1952, 1953, 1954, 1956, 1960, 1962, 1964, 1966, 1970, 1972, 1974; Durlacher Gall., New York, 1954, 1959; Leicester Galleries, 1958; Aldeburgh, Suffolk, 1965; Arnolfini Gall., Bristol, 1971 (graphics); Annely Juda Fine Art, 1978; Juda Rowan Gall., 1982, 1986; Thomas Agnew, Albemarle Street Gall., 1982. Work in exhibitions: Carnegie (Pittsburgh) Internat., USA, 1952, 1955, 1958, 1961; Internat. Exhibn, Rome, (awarded one of the three equal prizes), subsequently Musée d'Art Moderne, Paris, and Brussels; British Council Exhibn, Oslo and Copenhagen, 1956; Redfern Gall., 1971; Spectrum, Arts Council of GB, 1971; British Painting 1952–77, Royal Academy, 1977; Galerie Loyse Oppenheim, Nyon, Switzerland, 1977; Galerie Renée Ziegler, Zürich, 1981; group exhibitions: Scottish Nat. Gall. of Modern Art, Edinburgh, 1984; Annely Juda Fine Art and Juda Rowan Gall., London, 1985; Galeries Renée Ziegler, Zürich, 1985–86. Works acquired by: Tate Gall.; V&A; National Galleries of: S Aust.; Felton Bequest, Vic., Aust.; NZ; Canada; City Art Galleries of: Birmingham; Bristol; Manchester; Wakefield; Mus. of Modern Art, NY; Contemporary Art Soc.; British Council; Arts Council of GB; Rothschild Foundn; The Graves Art Gall., Sheffield; Nottingham Castle Mus.; Fitzwilliam Mus., Cambridge; Mus. of Modern Art, São Paulo, Brazil; Leeds Art Gall.; Toledo Art Gall., Ohio, USA; Barnes Foundn, USA; Oriel Coll., Oxford; Warwick Univ.; Mus. and Art Galls, Brighton and Plymouth; Texas Univ., Austin, USA; Berlin Nat. Gall.; McCrory Corp., NY. CoID Award, 1965; Arts Council of GB Purchase Award, 1967. *Relevant Publication:* The Painter, Alan Reynolds, by J. P. Hodin, 1962. *Address:* Briar Cottage, High Street, Cranbrook, Kent.

REYNOLDS, (Arthur) Graham, OBE 1984; Keeper of the Department of Prints and Drawings, 1961–74 (of Engraving, Illustration and Design, 1959–61), and of Paintings, Victoria and Albert Museum, 1959–74; *b* Highgate, 10 Jan. 1914; *o s* of late Arthur T. Reynolds and Eva Mullins; *m* 1943, Daphne, *d* of late Thomas Dent, Huddersfield. *Educ:* Highgate School; Queens' College, Cambridge. Joined staff of Victoria and Albert Museum, 1937. Seconded to Ministry of Home Security, 1939–45. Member: Adv. Council, Paul Mellon Centre for Studies in British Art, 1977–84; Reviewing Cttee on the Export of Works of Art, 1984–. Trustee, William Morris Gallery, Walthamstow, 1972–75; Chm., Gainsborough's House Soc., Sudbury, 1977–79. Leverhulme Emeritus Fellowship, 1980–81. *Publications:* Twentieth Century Drawings, 1946; Nicholas Hilliard and Isaac Oliver, 1947, 2nd edn, 1971; Van Gogh, 1947; Nineteenth Century Drawings, 1949; Thomas Bewick, 1949; An Introduction to English Water-Colour Painting, 1950; Gastronomic Pleasures, 1950; Elizabethan and Jacobean Costume, 1951; English Portrait Miniatures, 1952; Painters of the Victorian Scene, 1953; Catalogue of the Constable Collection, Victoria and Albert Museum, 1960, rev. edn, 1973; Constable, the Natural Painter, 1965; Victorian Painting, 1966; Turner, 1969; A Concise History of Water Colour Painting, 1972; Catalogue of Portrait Miniatures, Wallace Collection, 1980; Constable's England, 1983; The Later Paintings and Drawings of John Constable, 2 vols, 1984 (Mitchell Prize); Editor of series English Masters of Black and White; contribs to Burlington Magazine, Apollo, etc. *Address:* The Old Manse, Bradfield St George, Bury St Edmunds, Suffolk IP30 0AZ. *T:* Sicklesmere 610. *Club:* Athenæum.

REYNOLDS, Barbara, MA Cantab; BA (Hons), PhD London; author, lexicographer; Reader in Italian Studies, University of Nottingham, 1966–78; *b* 13 June 1914; *d* of late Alfred Charles Reynolds; *m* 1st, 1939, Prof. Lewis Thorpe (*d* 1977); one *s* one *d*; 2nd, 1982, Kenneth Imeson, *qv*. *Educ:* St Paul's Girls' Sch.; UCL. Asst Lectr in Italian, LSE 1937–40. Chief Exec. and Gen. Editor, The Cambridge Italian Dictionary, 1948–81; Man. Editor, Seven, an Anglo-American Literary Review, 1980–. Mem. Coun. Senate, Cambridge Univ., 1961–62. University Lecturer in Italian Literature and Language, Cambridge, 1945–62 (Faculty Assistant Lecturer, 1940–45); Warden of Willoughby Hall, Univ. of Nottingham, 1963–69. Vis. Professor: Univ. of Calif., Berkeley, 1974–75; Wheaton Coll., Illinois, 1977–78, 1982; Trinity Coll., Dublin, 1980, 1981; Hope Coll., Mich., 1982. Hon. Reader in Italian, Univ. of Warwick, 1975–80. Hon. DLitt: Wheaton Coll., Illinois, 1979; Hope Coll., Mich., 1982. Silver Medal for Services to Italian culture (Italian Govt), 1964; Edmund Gardner Prize, 1964; Silver Medal for services to Anglo-Veneto cultural relations, Prov. Admin of Vicenza, 1971; Cavaliere Ufficiale al Merito della Repubblica Italiana, 1978. *Publications:* (with K. T. Butler) Tredici Novelle Moderne, 1947; The Linguistic Writings of Alessandro Manzoni: a Textual and Chronological Reconstruction, 1950; rev. edn with introd., Dante and the Early Astronomers, by M. A. Orr, 1956; The Cambridge Italian Dictionary, Vol. I, Italian-English, 1962, Vol. II, English-Italian, 1981; (with Dorothy L. Sayers) Paradise: a translation into English triple rhyme, from the Italian of Dante Alighieri, 1962; (with Lewis Thorpe) Guido Farina, Painter of Verona, 1967; La Vita Nuova (Poems of Youth); trans. of Dante's Vita Nuova, 1969; Concise Cambridge Italian Dictionary, 1975; Orlando Furioso, trans. into rhymed octaves of Ariosto's epic, Vol. I, 1975 (Internat. Literary Prize, Monselice, Italy, 1976) Vol. II, 1977; (ed) Cambridge-Signorelli Dizionario Italiano-Inglese, Inglese-Italiano, 1986; numerous articles on Italian literature in learned jls. *Address:* 220 Milton Road, Cambridge CB4 1LQ. *T:* Cambridge 357894. *Clubs:* University Women's, Authors'.

See also A. C. Thorpe.

REYNOLDS, Sir David James, 3rd Bt, *cr* 1923; Member of Lloyd's Insurance; *b* 26 Jan. 1924; *er s* of Sir John Francis Roskell Reynolds, 2nd Bt, MBE, JP and Milicent (*d* 1931), *d* of late Major James Orr-Ewing and late Lady Margaret Orr-Ewing; *S* father 1956; *m* 1966, Charlotte Baumgartner; one *s* two *d. Educ:* Downside. Active service in Army, 1942–47, Italy, etc; on demobilisation, Captain 15/19 Hussars. *Recreation:* sport. *Heir: s* James Francis Reynolds, *b* 10 July 1971. *Address:* Blanche Pierre House, St Lawrence, Jersey, CI.

REYNOLDS, Eric Vincent, TD 1948; MA; Headmaster of Stowe, 1949–58, retired; *b* 30 April 1904; *o s* of late Arthur John and Lily Reynolds; unmarried. *Educ:* Haileybury College; St John's College, Cambridge. Modern and Mediæval languages Tripos, Parts 1 and 2; Lector in English at University of Leipzig, 1926–27; MA 1930. Assistant Master: Rugby School, 1927–31; Upper Canada College, Toronto, 1931–32; Rugby School, 1932–49 (Housemaster, 1944–49). CO, Rugby School JTC, 1938–44. *Recreations:* ski-ing and mountaineering. *Address:* 48 Lemsford Road, St Albans, Herts AL1 3PR. *T:* 53599.

REYNOLDS, Eva Mary Barbara; *see* Reynolds, Barbara.

REYNOLDS, Frank Arrowsmith, OBE 1974; LLB; HM Diplomatic Service, retired; *b* 30 March 1916; *s* of late Sydney Edward Clyde Reynolds and Bessie (*née* Foster); *m* 1938, Joan Marion Lockyer; one *s* two *d. Educ:* Addey and Stanhope Sch.; London University. Army, 1941–46 (Lieut, RE). District Officer, Tanganyika, 1950; Commonwealth Relations Office, 1962–63; First Secretary, Bombay, 1964–67; CO, later FCO, 1967–69; Consul-Gen., Seville, 1969–71; Head of Chancery, Maseru, 1971–75. *Publication:* Guide to Super-8 Photography, 1981. *Recreations:* music, sailing, photography. *Address:* 26 Nelson Street, Brightlingsea, Essex CO7 0DZ. *Clubs:* Royal Bombay Yacht; Colne Yacht.

REYNOLDS, Graham; *see* Reynolds, A. G.

REYNOLDS, Guy Edwin K.; *see* King-Reynolds.

REYNOLDS, Maj.-Gen. Jack Raymond, CB 1971; OBE 1945; ERD 1948; DL; President, British Equestrian Federation, since 1985 (Director-General, 1975–85); *b* 10 June 1916; *s* of Walter Reynolds and Evelyn Marion (*née* Burrows); *m* 1940, Joan Howe Taylor; one *s* one *d. Educ:* Haberdashers' Aske's. Student Apprentice, AEC Ltd, 1934. Commissioned RASC (SR), 1936. Served War of 1939–45, France, Middle East and Italy (despatches). CRASC 7th Armoured Div., 1955–57; GSO 1 War Office, 1958–60; Col GS; UK Delegn to NATO Standing Group, Washington, DC, 1960–62; DDST, Southern Command, 1962–64; Commandant, RASC Training Centre, 1964–65; Imperial Defence College, 1966; Dep. Quarter-Master-General, BAOR, 1967–68; Dir of Movements (Army), MoD, 1968–71, retired. Col Comdt, Royal Corps of Transport, 1972–78. Dir-Gen., BHS, 1971–75. FCIT. DL Northants, 1984. *Recreation:* fishing. *Address:* Old Mill House, Hellidon, near Daventry, Northants. *Club:* Army and Navy.

REYNOLDS, James; Judge of the High Court, Eastern Region of Nigeria, 1956–63; *b* Belfast, May, 1908; *yr s* of late James Reynolds and late Agnes Forde (*née* Cully); *m* 1946, Alexandra Mary Erskine Strain; two *s* two *d. Educ:* Belfast Roy. Acad.; Queen's Univ., Belfast. Called to Bar of N Ire., 1931; practised at N Ire Bar, 1931–40. Colonial Legal Service as Crown Counsel in Hong Kong, 1940. Prisoner-of-war in Japanese hands, 1941–45. Returned to Hong Kong, 1946; apptd District Judge, 1953. Chairman: Local Tribunal under Nat. Insce Acts, 1964; Industrial Tribunal, 1969–81. *Address:* 10 Church Road, Helen's Bay, Co. Down, Northern Ireland.

REYNOLDS, John Arthur, JP; Member (Lab), since 1973, and Opposition Leader, since 1983, Cardiff City Council (Leader of Council, 1982–83); Principal Lecturer, South Glamorgan Institute of Higher Education, since 1981; *b* 28 Oct. 1925; *s* of William Thomas and Elsie Mary Reynolds; *m* 1955, Dorothy Grace Leigh; one *s* one *d. Educ:* London Univ. (BSc Econ); Trinity Coll., Carmarthen (CertEd Univ. of Wales). Teacher, 1954–64; Technical Coll. Lectr, 1965–. Member: Regional Cttee, S and W Wales, CRS Ltd, 1962–; Nat. Council for Training Journalists, 1974–85; Local Govt Training Bd, 1979–. Cardiff City Council: Chairman: Policy (Finance) Cttee, 1973–76, 1979–82; Policy Cttee, 1982–83. JP Cardiff, 1977. *Recreations:* reading, TV, theatre, music. *Address:* 46 Richmond Road, Cardiff CF2 3AT. *T:* Cardiff 482183. *Club:* Victory Services.

REYNOLDS, Joyce Maire, FBA 1982; Fellow of Newnham College, 1951–84, now Hon. Fellow, and Reader in Roman Historical Epigraphy, 1983–84, University of Cambridge; *b* 18 Dec. 1918; *d* of late William Howe Reynolds and Nellie Farmer Reynolds. *Educ:* Walthamstow County High Sch. for Girls; St Paul's Girls' Sch., Hammersmith; Somerville Coll., Oxford. Temp. Civil Servant, BoT, 1941–46; Rome Scholar, British Sch. at Rome, 1946–48; Lectr in Ancient History, King's Coll., Newcastle upon Tyne, 1948–51; Cambridge University: Asst Lectr in Classics, 1952–57; Univ. Lectr 1957–83; Dir of Studies in Classics, 1951–79 and Lectr in Classics, 1951–84, Newnham Coll. Woolley Travelling Fellow, Somerville Coll., Oxford, 1961; Mem., Inst. for Advanced Study, Princeton, USA, 1984–85. President: Soc. for Libyan Studies, 1981–86; Soc. for the Promotion of Roman Studies, 1986–. Corresp. Mem., German Archaeol Inst., 1971–. Hon. DLitt Newcastle upon Tyne, 1984. *Publications:* (with J. B. Ward Perkins) The Inscriptions of Roman Tripolitania, 1952; Aphrodisias and Rome, 1982; articles on Roman history and epigraphy in jls, 1951–. *Recreation:* walking. *Address:* Newnham College, Cambridge CB3 9DF. *T:* Cambridge 335700.

REYNOLDS, Dr Martin Richard Finch; Specialist in Community Medicine, Hull Health Authority, since 1986; *b* 26 July 1943; 2nd *s* of Gerald Finch Reynolds and Frances Bertha (*née* Locke); *m* 1965, Shelagh (*née* Gray); two *d. Educ:* Newton Abbot Grammar Sch.; Univ. of Bristol. MB ChB, DPH; FFCM. House posts in medicine, surgery, infectious diseases and paediatrics, 1966–67; Dep. Med. Officer, Glos CC, 1967–70; Sen. Dep. Med. Officer, Bristol City and Asst Sen. Med. Officer, SW Regional Hosp. Bd, 1970–74; Dist Community Physician, Southmead Dist of Avon AHA (Teaching) and Med. Officer for Environmental Health, Northavon Dist Council, 1974–79; Area Med. Officer, Wilts AHA, 1979–80; Regional MO/Chief Med. Advr, South Western RHA, 1980–86. *Publications:* contrib. various articles in professional jls on subjects in community medicine. *Address:* Knights Garth, Callas, Bishop Burton, Beverley, N Humberside HU17 8QL. *T:* Leconfield 50276.

REYNOLDS, Michael Emanuel, CBE 1977; *b* 22 April 1931; *s* of Isaac Mark and Henrietta Rosenberg; *m* 1964, Susan Geraldine Yates; two *d. Educ:* Haberdashers' Aske's (HSC). Marks & Spencer Ltd, 1951–61; Food Controller, British Home Stores Ltd, 1961–64; Spar (UK) Ltd, 1964–77: Trading Controller, 1964–67; Chm. and Managing Dir, 1967–77; BV Intergroup Trading (IGT), 1974–77: Founder Mem., Bd of Admin.; Dir, 1974–75; Chm. and Dir, 1975–77; Founder/Owner, Susan Reynolds Books Ltd, 1977–84. FRSA. *Recreations:* tennis, squash, bridge. *Address:* 3 Melbourne Terrace, Moore Park Road, SW6 2JU. *T:* 01–731 6750.

REYNOLDS, Maj.-Gen. Michael Frank, CB 1983; *b* 3 June 1930; *s* of Frank Reynolds and Gwendolyn Reynolds (*née* Griffiths); *m* 1955, Anne Bernice (*née* Truman); three *d Educ:* Cranleigh Sch.; RMA, Sandhurst. Commnd Queen's Royal Regt, 1950; served Germany, Korea, Cyprus, Canada, Persian Gulf, Netherlands; *psc* 1960; GSO 1 Ops, HQ AFCENT, 1970–71; comd 2 Queen's, BAOR and Ulster, 1971–73; GSO 1 Ops, N Ireland, 1973–74; comd 12 Mech Bde BAOR, 1974–76; RCDS, 1977; Dep. Adjt Gen., BAOR, 1978–80; Comdr, Allied Command Europe Mobile Force (Land), 1980–83; Asst Dir, IMS, HQ NATO, 1983–86. Col Comdt, Queen's Division, 1984. *Recreations:* military history, architecture, gardening.

REYNOLDS, Sir Peter (William John), Kt 1985; CBE 1975; Chairman, Ranks Hovis McDougall plc, since 1981; *b* 10 Sept. 1929; *s* of Harry and Gladys Victoria Reynolds; *m* 1955, Barbara Anne, *d* of Vincent Kenneth Johnson, OBE; two *s. Educ:* Haileybury Coll., Herts. National Service, 2nd Lieut, RA, 1948–50. Unilever Ltd, 1950–70: Trainee; Managing Dir, then Chm., Walls (Meat & Handy Foods) Ltd. Asst Gp Managing Dir, Ranks Hovis McDougall Ltd, 1971, Gp Man. Dir, 1972–81. Mem., Consultative Bd for Resources Develt in Agriculture, 1982–84; Dir, Industrial Develt Bd for NI, 1982–; Chm., Resources Cttee, Food and Drink Fedn (formerly Food and Drink Industries Council), 1983–. *Recreations:* gardening, beagling. *Address:* The White House, Beamond End, Amersham, Bucks. *T:* High Wycombe 713248. *Clubs:* Naval and Military, Farmers'.

REYNOLDS, Prof. Philip Alan, CBE 1986; DL; Vice-Chancellor, University of Lancaster, 1980–85; *b* 15 May 1920; *s* of Harry Reynolds and Ethel (*née* Scott); *m* 1946, Mollie Patricia (*née* Horton); two *s* one *d. Educ:* Worthing High Sch.; Queen's Coll., Oxford (BA 1940, 1st Cl. Mod. Hist.; MA 1950). Served War, 1940–46: HAA and Staff, UK, ME and Greece; Major 1945. Asst Lectr, then Lectr in Internat. History, LSE, 1946–50; Woodrow Wilson Prof. of Internat. Politics, UCW Aberystwyth, 1950–64 (Vice-Principal, 1961–63); Prof. of Politics and Pro-Vice-Chancellor, Univ. of Lancaster, 1964–80. Vis. Professor: in Internat. Relations, Toronto, 1953; in Commonwealth History and Instns, Indian Sch. of Internat. Studies, New Delhi, 1958; Anspach Fellow, Univ. of Pa, 1971; Vis. Res. Fellow, ANU Canberra, 1977. Vice-Chm., Cttee of Vice-Chancellors and Principals, 1984–85; Chm., Brit. Internat. Studies Assoc., 1976, Hon. Pres., 1981–84; Mem. Council, RIIA, 1975–80. DL Lancs, 1982. Hon. DLitt Lancaster, 1985. *Publications:* War in the Twentieth Century, 1951; Die Britische Aussenpolitik zwischen den beiden Weltkriegen, 1952 (rev. edn, 1954, as British Foreign Policy in the Inter-War Years); An Introduction to International Relations, 1971, rev. edn 1980 (Japanese edn 1977, Spanish edn 1978); (with E. J. Hughes) The Historian as Diplomat: Charles Kingsley Webster and the United Nations 1939–46, 1976; contrib. New Cambridge Mod. Hist., History, Slavonic Rev., Pol. Qly, Pol. Studies, Internat. Jl, Internat. Studies, Brit. Jl of Internat. Studies, Educn Policy Bulletin, Higher Educn, Univs Qly. *Recreations:* music, bridge, eating and drinking. *Address:* Lattice Cottage, The Green, Borwick, Carnforth, Lancs. *T:* Carnforth 732518.

REYNOLDS, Seymour John Romer, MA, MB, BChir (Cambridge) 1936; MRCS, LRCP, 1935; DMRE 1938; Physician to Radiological Department, Charing Cross Hospital, 1945–76; Consultant Radiologist: Kingston Hospital Group, 1948–73; New Victoria Hospital, Kingston-upon-Thames; *b* 26 April 1911; *s* of late Russell J. Reynolds, CBE, FRCP; *m* 1939, Margaret Stuart McCombie; one *s. Educ:* Westminster School; Trinity Coll., Cambridge; Charing Cross Hosp. Med. School. Formerly: House Surgeon, House Physician and Clin. Asst at Charing Cross Hosp.; Univ. Demonstrator in Anatomy, Cambridge Univ., 1937; Radiologist: Victoria Hosp., Kingston-upon-Thames, 1939; Prince of Wales Gen. Hosp., Tottenham, 1939; Highlands Hosp.; Hackney Hosp.; Epsom Hosp. 1943; Queen Mary's Hosp., Roehampton, 1946. Dean of Charing Cross Hosp. Med. Sch., 1962–76. Mem. Bd of Governors, Charing Cross Hosp., 1962–74; Mem., Ealing, Hammersmith and Hounslow AHA, 1974–76. *Recreations:* gardening, visiting art galleries. *Address:* Camelot, Renfrew Road, Kingston Hill, Surrey. *T:* 01–942 3808.

REYNOLDS, William Oliver, OBE 1973 (MBE 1944); *b* 2 Nov. 1915; General Manager, Eastern Region, British Rail, 1973–76; *s* of Edgar Ernest Reynolds and Elizabeth Wilson Biesterfield; *m* 1944, Eleanor Gill; two *s. Educ:* Royal Grammar Sch., Newcastle upon Tyne. LNER Traffic apprentice, 1936. Served War, with Royal Engineers, 1940–46: despatches, 1942 and 1944; Lt-Col, 1944. Lt-Col, Engineer and Railway Staff Corps, RE (T&AVR IV), 1971–. Divisional Manager, London Midland, BR, 1960; Asst Gen. Manager, Scottish Region, 1964; Chief Operating Manager, BR Bd, 1968; Exec. Dir, BR Bd, 1969. Mem., Adv. Council, Science Mus. 1975–84; Chm., Friends of Nat. Railway Mus. 1984–. FCIT. *Recreations:* fishing, golf, gardening. *Address:* Oak House, Follifoot, Harrogate, N Yorks. *Club:* Oriental.

REYNOLDS, William Vaughan; Principal, St Marylebone Literary Institute, 1965–70, retired; *b* 10 May 1908; *yr s* of late William Reynolds, MBE, editor of The Midland Daily Telegraph; *m* 1932, Gertrude Mabel, *yr d* of late Arthur Charles Flint; four *s. Educ:* King Henry VIII School, Coventry; St Edmund Hall, Oxford. First class in Final Hons School of Eng. Lang. and Lit., 1930; BLitt, 1931; MA 1934; Senior Exhibitioner, St Edmund Hall, 1930–31. Assistant Lecturer in English Literature, University of Sheffield, 1931–34; Lecturer, 1934–41. Deputy Regional Officer, Ministry of Information (NE Region), 1941–45; Sec., East and West Ridings Industrial Publicity Cttee, 1943–45. Joined staff of The Birmingham Post as Leader-writer and Editorial Asst, 1945; served in London office, 1949; Editor, 1950–64, retired. Mem. British Cttee, Internat. Press Inst., 1952–64; Pres., Rotary Club of Birmingham, 1962–63; Mem., Church Information Adv. Cttee, 1966–72. *Publications:* Selections from Johnson, 1935; articles contributed to The Review of English Studies and to Notes and Queries; literary and dramatic reviews in various periodicals and newspapers. Has broadcast frequently in Gt Britain and US. *Recreations:* motoring, cats, theatre going, and reading. *Address:* 36 Laurel Avenue, Moreton Park, Bideford, North Devon.

REYNTIENS, Nicholas Patrick, OBE 1976; Head of Fine Art, Central School of Art and Design, London, since 1976; *b* 11 Dec. 1925; *s* of Nicholas Serge Reyntiens, OBE, and Janet MacRae; *m* 1953, Anne Bruce; two *s* two *d. Educ:* Ampleforth; Edinburgh Coll. of Art (DA). Served Scots Guards, 1943–47. St Marylebone Sch. of Art, 1947–50; Edinburgh Coll. of Art, 1950–51. Founder, Reyntiens Trust, 1970. Mem., Architectural Adv. Cttee, Westminster Abbey. Numerous commns for stained glass, 1950–. *Publication:* Technique of Stained Glass, 1967, 2nd edn 1977. *Address:* Ilford Bridges Farm, Close Stocklinch, Ilminster, Som. *T:* Ilminster 2241.

RHEA, Alexander Dodson, III; *b* 10 May 1919; *s* of Alexander D. Rhea, Jr and Annie Rhea; *m* 1945, Suzanne Menocal; one *s*. *Educ:* Princeton Univ. BA Econs and Social Instns. Active service as Lt-Comdr USNR, 1941–45. Vice-Pres., Govt Employees Ins. Corp., Washington, DC, 1946–48; Treas. and Man. Dir, General Motors de Venezuela, Caracas, 1949–55; Vice-Pres., General Motors Overseas Corp., 1960–68; Regional Gp Dir, NY, 1960–66, Staff Man., 1966–67, General Motors Overseas Operations; Chm. and Man. Dir, General Motors-Holden's, Melbourne, 1968–70; Chm. and Man. Dir., Vauxhall Motors Ltd, 1970–74; Chm., General Motors Corp. European Adv. Council, 1974–77; Exec. Vice-Pres. and Dir, General Motors Overseas Corp., 1974–77. *Recreations:* reading, golf. *Address:* 580 Park Avenue, New York, NY 10021, USA. *Clubs:* Knickerbocker, Princeton, Colony (New York); Fort Worth, River Crest Country (Fort Worth, Texas); Melbourne (Melbourne); Greenbrier Golf and Tennis (White Sulphur Springs, West Virginia).

RHIND, Prof. David William; Professor of Geography, since 1982 and Co-ordinator for Information Technology, since 1985, Birkbeck College, London University; *b* 29 Nov. 1943; *s* of late William Rhind and of Christina Rhind; *m* 1966, Christine Young; one *s* two *d*. *Educ:* Berwick Grammar School; Bristol Univ. (BSc); Edinburgh Univ. (PhD). Research Fellow, Royal College of Art, 1969–73; Lectr then Reader, Univ. of Durham, 1973–81; Birkbeck College: Dean, Faculty of Economics, 1984–86; Governor, 1986–. Visiting Fellow: Internat. Trng Centre, Netherlands, 1975; ANU, 1979. Vice-Pres., Internat. Cartographic Assoc., 1984–; Member: Council, RGS, 1984–; Govt Cttee on Enquiry into handling of geographic inf., 1985–; Advisor, H of L Select Cttee on Sci. and Tech., 1983–84; Chm., Royal Soc. Digital Cartography Sub-Cttee, 1983–. *Publications:* Land Use, 1980; The Census User's Handbook, 1983; (jtly) Atlas of EEC Affairs, 1984; numerous papers on map-making and computerised databases. *Recreation:* enjoying good company. *Address:* Birkbeck College, 7–15 Gresse Street, W1P 1PA. *T:* 01–631 6474. *Club:* Athenæum.

RHODES, family name of **Baron Rhodes.**

RHODES, Baron *cr* 1964, of Saddleworth (Life Peer); **Hervey Rhodes,** KG 1972; PC 1969; DFC and Bar; DL; *b* 12 August 1895; *s* of John Eastwood and Eliza Ann Rhodes; *m* 1925, Ann Bradbury (*d* 1983); two *d*. *Educ:* Greenfield, St Mary's Elementary Sch.; Huddersfield Technical College; evening classes. Woollen worker pre-1914; joined King's Own Royal Lancs, 1914, commissioned, seconded to Flying Corps (wounded, DFC and Bar). Discharged from Hospital, 1921. Commenced business as woollen manufacturer. Served on Local Authority. Chairman of Urban District Council, 1944–45. Chairman, Saddleworth War Charities. Commanded 36th West Riding Bn Home Guard. MP (Lab) Ashton-under-Lyne, 1945–64; PPS, Min. of Pensions, 1948–51; Parliamentary Secretary, Board of Trade, 1950–51, 1964–67. Led all-party Parly delegns to China, 1978, 1979, 1981 and 1983. President: SELCARE, 1971–; North West Arts, 1972–; Saddleworth Fest. of the Arts, 1957–. Lord Lieutenant of Lancashire, 1968–71; DL Lancs, 1971. Freedom of Borough of Ashton-under-Lyne, 1965, and of Saddleworth, Yorks, 1966. KStJ 1968. Fellow, Huddersfield Polytechnic, 1976; Hon. Mem., RNCM, 1982. Hon. DTech Bradford, 1966; Hon LLD Manchester, 1971. *Address:* Cribbstones, Delph, Oldham, Lancs OL3 5BZ. *T:* Saddleworth 4500.

RHODES, Rev. Canon Cecil; Canon Residentiary of St Edmundsbury Cathedral, 1964–80; retired 1980; Founder and Editor, Church News, since 1946; *b* Preston, Lancs, 5 Oct. 1910; *s* of James Rhodes; *m* 1940, Gladys, *d* of H. B. Farlie; one *s* two *d*. *Educ:* Preston Gram. Sch.; St Peter's Hall, Oxford; Wycliffe Hall, Oxford (MA). Deacon, 1936; Priest, 1937. Curate, St Stephen, Selly Hill, Birmingham, 1936–38; Asst Editor and Youth Sec., The Pathfinder, 1938–40; Jt Editor, Light and Life Publications, 1941–44; Diocesan Chaplain-in-charge, St Mary, Pype Hayes, Birmingham, 1940–44; Vicar: St Luke, Tunbridge Wells, 1944–49; St Augustine, Edgbaston, Birmingham, 1949–64; Birmingham Diocesan Adviser for Stewardship, 1960–64; Hon. Canon of Birmingham, 1961–64. Diocesan Dir of Lay Training, Diocese of St Edmundsbury and Ipswich, 1968–74; Chm., Diocesan Information Cttee, 1968–76. Jt Editor, The Pilgrim, C of E youth magazine, 1949–50; regular contributor to The Birmingham Post, 1950–64; East Anglian Daily Times, 1970–78. *Recreations:* writing, books, travel. *Address:* College Gate House, Bury St Edmunds, Suffolk. *T:* Bury St Edmunds 3530.

RHODES, George Harold Lancashire, TD 1946; Regional Chairman of Industrial Tribunals (Manchester), since 1985; *b* 29 Feb. 1916; *er s* of Judge Harold and Ena Rhodes of Bowdon, Cheshire. *Educ:* Shrewsbury School; The Queen's College, Oxford (MA 1941). Commissioned 52nd Field Regt RA TA, 1938; war service, BEF, 1940, Middle East, 1942, Italy, 1943–46 (Major). Called to the Bar, Gray's Inn, 1947; practised on N Circuit; the Junior, 1948; Office of Judge Advocate General (Army and RAF), 1953; Asst Judge Advocate General, 1967; Chm., Industrial Tribunals (Manchester), 1974, Dep. Regional Chm., 1975. *Recreations:* walking, golf. *Address:* 8 Newington Court, The Firs, Bowdon, Cheshire WA14 2UA. *T:* 061–928 1200. *Clubs:* Bowdon Warlocks; Hong Kong (Hong Kong).

RHODES, Sir John (Christopher Douglas), 4th Bt, *cr* 1919; *b* 24 May 1946; *s* of Sir Christopher Rhodes, 3rd Bt, and of Mary Florence, *d* of late Dr Douglas Wardleworth; *S* father, 1964. *Heir:* *b* Michael Philip James Rhodes [*b* 3 April 1948; *m* 1973, Susan, *d* of Patrick Roney-Dougal; one *d*].

RHODES, John Ivor McKinnon, CMG 1971; *b* 6 March 1914; *s* of late Joseph Thomas Rhodes and late Hilda (*née* McKinnon); *m* 1939, Eden Annetta (*née* Clark); one *s* one *d*. *Educ:* Leeds Modern School. Exec. Officer, WO, 1933; Financial Adviser's Office, HQ British Forces in Palestine, 1938; Major 1940; Asst Comd Sec., Southern Comd, 1944; Financial Adviser, London District, 1946; Principal 1947, Asst Sec. 1959, HM Treasury; Minister, UK Mission to UN, 1966–74. Member: UN Pension Board, 1966–71; UN Cttee on Contributions, 1966–71, 1975–77; Chm., UN Adv. Cttee on Admin. and Budgetary Questions, 1971–74; Senior Adviser (Asst Sec.-Gen.) to Administrator, UNDP, 1979–80. *Recreations:* gardening, playing the electronic organ. *Address:* Quintins, Watersfield, Sussex. *T:* Bury 634.

RHODES, Marion, RE 1953 (ARE 1941); etcher, painter in water colour and oils; *b* Huddersfield, Yorks, 1907; *d* of Samuel Rhodes and Mary Jane Mallinson. *Educ:* Greenhead High School, Huddersfield; Huddersfield Art School; Leeds College of Art; The Central School of Arts and Crafts, London. Art Teachers' Certificate (Univ. of Oxford), 1930; teaching posts, 1930–67; pt-time lecturer in Art at Berridge House Training Coll., 1947–55. SGA 1936, Hon. Life Mem., 1969; FRSA 1944; Member, Manchester Acad. of Fine Art, 1955–81; Paris Salon: Honourable Mention, 1952; Bronze Medal, 1956; Silver Medal 1961; Gold Medal, 1967. Exhibited from 1934 at: Royal Academy, Royal Scottish Academy, Mall Gall., The Paris Salon, Walker Art Gall., Towner Art Gall., Atkinson Art Gall., Southport, Brighton, Bradford, Leeds, Manchester and other provincial Art Galls, also USA and S Africa. Etching of Jordans' Hostel and drawing of The Meeting House purchased by Contemporary Art Soc. and presented to British Museum; other works in the Print Room, BM, and Print Room, V&A; work also purchased by Bradford Corp. Art Gall., Brighouse Art Gall., Huddersfield Art Gall., Stoke-on-Trent Educn Cttee's Loan Scheme, and South London (Camberwell) Library Committee; works reproduced. Fellow, Ancient Monuments Soc.; Associate, Artistes Français, 1971–79; Hon. Mem., Tommasso Campanella Acad., Rome (Silver Medal, 1970). Cert. of Merit, Dictionary of Internat. Biography, 1972. Mem., Accademia delle Arti e de Lavoro (Parma), 1979–82; Academic of Italy with Gold Medal, 1979. *Publication:* illustrations for Robert Harding's Snettisham, 1982. *Recreations:* gardening and geology. *Address:* 2 Goodwyn Avenue, Mill Hill, NW7 3RG. *T:* 01–959 2280. *Club:* English-Speaking Union.

RHODES, Sir Peregrine (Alexander), KCMG 1984 (CMG 1976); HM Diplomatic Service, retired; Director-General, British Property Federation, since 1986; *b* 14 May 1925; *s* of Cyril Edmunds Rhodes and Elizabeth Jocelyn Rhodes; *m* 1st, 1951, Jane Marion Hassell (marr. diss.); two *s* one *d*; 2nd, 1969, Margaret Rosemary Page. *Educ:* Winchester Coll.; New Coll., Oxford. Served with Coldstream Guards, 1944–47. Joined FO, 1950; 2nd Sec., Rangoon, 1953–56; Private Sec. to Minister of State, 1956–59; 1st Sec., Vienna, 1959–62; 1st Sec., Helsinki, 1962–65; FCO, 1965–68, Counsellor 1967; Inst. for Study of Internat. Organisation, Sussex Univ., 1968–69; Counsellor: Rome, 1970–73; E Berlin, 1973–75; on secondment as Under Sec., Cabinet Office, 1975–78; High Comr, Cyprus, 1979–82; Ambassador, Greece, 1982–85. Chm., Anglo-Hellenic League, 1986–. *Recreations:* photography, reading. *Address:* Pond House, Thorpe Morieux, Bury St Edmunds, Suffolk. *Club:* Travellers'.

RHODES, Philip, FRCS, FRCOG, FRACMA; Regional Postgraduate Dean of Medical Studies, and Professor of Postgraduate Medical Education, Southampton University, since 1980; *b* 2 May 1922; *s* of Sydney Rhodes, Dore, Sheffield; *m* 1946, Mary Elizabeth Worley, Barrowden, Rutland; three *s* two *d*. *Educ:* King Edward VII Sch., Sheffield; Clare Coll., Cambridge; St Thomas's Hospital Medical School. BA(Cantab) 1943, MB, BChir(Cantab) 1946; FRCS 1953; MRCOG 1956; FRCOG 1964; FRACMA 1976. Major RAMC, 1948–50. Medical appointments held in St Thomas' Hosp., Folkestone, Harrogate, Chelsea Hosp. for Women, Queen Charlotte's Hosp., 1946–58; Consultant Obstetric Physician, St Thomas' Hosp., 1958–63; Prof. of Obstetrics and Gynæcol., St Thomas's Hosp. Med. Sch., Univ. of London, 1964–74, Dean, 1968–74; Dean, Faculty of Medicine, Univ. of Adelaide, 1975–77; Postgrad. Dean and Dir, Regional Postgrad. Inst. for Med. and Dentistry, Newcastle Univ., 1977–80. Member: SW Metropolitan Regional Hosp. Board, 1967–74; SE Thames Reg. Health Authority, 1974; GMC, 1979– (Educn Cttee, 1984–). Mem. Steering Cttee of DHSS on management of NHS, 1971–72. Mem., Adv. Cttee, Nat. Inst. of Medical Hist., Australia, 1976. Chm., Educn Cttee, King Edward's Hosp. Fund for London, 1981–; Member: UGC Working Party on Continuing Educn, 1983; Council for Postgrad. Med. Educn in England and Wales, 1984–. Governor: Dulwich Coll., 1966–74; St Thomas' Hosp., 1969–74; Pembroke Sch., Adelaide, 1976–77. *Publications:* Fluid Balance in Obstetrics, 1960; Introduction to Gynæcology and Obstetrics, 1967; Reproductive Physiology for Medical Students, 1969; Woman: A Biological Study, 1969; The Value of Medicine, 1976; Dr John Leake's Hospital, 1978; Letters to a Young Doctor, 1983; An Outline History of Medicine, 1985; Associate Editor, The Oxford Companion to Medicine, 1986; articles in Jl of Obstetrics and Gynæcology of the British Empire, Lancet, Brit. Med. Jl, Med. Jl of Australia. *Recreations:* reading, gardening, photography. *Address:* Postgraduate Department, Southampton General Hospital, Southampton SO9 4XY.

RHODES, Reginald Paul; CBIM; Chairman, Southern Gas Region, 1975–83; *b* 10 April 1918; *s* of Edwin Rhodes and Dorothy Lena Molyneux; *m* 1940, Margaret Frances Fish; two *s* three *d*. *Educ:* Merchant Taylors Sch., Northwood. Joined Gas Light & Coke Co., 1937; North Thames Gas, 1948 (Dep. Chm., 1972). Chairman: Southampton Industrial Therapy Organisation, 1980–; Solent Productivity Assoc., 1983–; Solent Business Fund, 1983–; Member: Wessex RHA, 1984–; Wessex Rehabilitation Assoc., 1981–; Shaw Trust, 1984–. Member, Co. of Pikemen, Honourable Artillery Company. FIGasE. *Recreations:* music, gardening. *Address:* Tidebrook Lodge, Royden Lane, Boldre, near Lymington, Hants SO41 8PE. *T:* Lymington 22399.

RHODES, Robert Elliott; First Prosecuting Counsel to Inland Revenue at Central Criminal Court and Inner London Crown Courts, since 1981; *b* 2 Aug. 1945; *s* of late Gilbert G. Rhodes, FCA and of Elly, who *m* 2nd, Leopold Brook, *qv*; *m* 1971, Georgina Caroline, *d* of J. G. Clarfelt, *qv*; two *s* one *d*. *Educ:* St Paul's School; Pembroke Coll., Oxford. MA. Called to the Bar, Inner Temple, 1968. Second Prosecuting Counsel to Inland Revenue at Central Criminal Court and Inner London Crown Courts, 1979. *Recreations:* opera, reading, cricket, fishing. *Address:* 114 Loudoun Road, NW8. *T:* 01–722 0818. *Club:* MCC.

RHODES, Stephen, OBE 1969; solicitor; Secretary, Association of District Councils, 1973–81; *b* 19 Jan. 1918; *s* of late Edward Hugh Rhodes, CBE, and Helen Edith Laurie Patricia Rhodes; *m* 1958, Jane, *d* of late Norman S. Bradley, Sydney, Aust.; one *s* two *d*. *Educ:* St Paul's Sch.; Law Society's Sch. of Law. LLB (London). Articled to Sir Cecil Oakes, CBE, Clerk of East Suffolk CC; admitted solicitor, 1941. Served RAF, 1939–46: commnd 1941; Sqdn-Ldr, 1944 (despatches). Asst Solicitor, East Suffolk CC, 1946–47; Sen. Asst Solicitor, Norfolk CC, 1947–49; Asst Sec., County Councils Assoc., 1949–59; Secretary, Rural District Councils Assoc., 1959–73; Jt Sec., Internat. Union of Local Authorities, 1975–81. Mem., Health Educn Council, 1968–74; Jt Sec., Standing Adv. Cttee on Local Authorities and the Theatre, 1975–81; Sec., Local Authorities Management Services and Computer Cttee, 1980–81. Vice-Chm., London Region, Royal Soc. for Mentally Handicapped Children and Adults, 1978–85. *Recreation:* wine making. *Address:* 14 Hale Avenue, New Milton, Hants BH25 6JA. *T:* New Milton 611225. *Clubs:* National Liberal, English-Speaking Union.

RHODES, Zandra Lindsey, RDI, DesRCA, FSIAD; Managing Director, Zandra Rhodes (UK) Ltd and Zandra Rhodes (Shops) Ltd, since 1975; *b* 19 Sept. 1940; *d* of Albert James Rhodes and Beatrice Ellen (*née* Twigg). *Educ:* Medway Technical Sch. for Girls, Chatham; Medway Coll. of Art; Royal Coll. of Art (DesRCA 1964). RDI 1977, FSIAD 1982. With Alexander MacIntyre, set up print factory and studio, 1965; sold designs (and converted them on to cloth) to Foale and Tuffin and Roger Nelson; formed partnership with Sylvia Ayton and began producing dresses using her own prints, 1966; opened Fulham Road Clothes Shop, designing dresses as well as prints, first in partnership, 1967–68, then (Fulham Road shop closed) alone, producing first clothes range in which she revolutionised use of prints in clothes by cutting round patterns to make shapes never before used; took collection to USA, 1969; sold to Fortnum and Mason, London, through Anne Knight, 1969, then to Piero de Monzi, 1971; began building up name and business in USA (known for her annual spectacular Fantasy Shows); also started designing in jersey and revolutionised its treatment with lettuce edges and seams on the outside; with Anne Knight and Ronnie Stirling founded Zandra Rhodes (UK) Ltd and Zandra Rhodes (Shops) Ltd, 1975–86; opening first shop in London, 1975; others opened in Bloomingdales NY, Marshall Field, Chicago, and Harrods, London, 1976; new factory premises opened in

Hammersmith, London, 1984. Licensees: Wamsutta, USA, 1976 (sheets and pillowcases); CVP Designs, 1977 (patterns for the interior); Regal Rugs, USA, 1977 (rugs); Baar and Beard Inc., USA, 1978 (scarves); Sari Fabrics, 1979 (kitchen accessories); Wagner Furs, 1979 (furs); Sabrina Coats, 1979 (coats); Jack Mulqueen, USA, 1980 (printed silk dresses and blouses); Green and Makofsky, USA, 1980 (coats); Senko, Japan, 1980 (rugs and bathroom accessories); Suffola, USA, 1980 (sheets and bed accessories); Falmers, 1981 (jeans and T-shirts); Seibu, Japan, 1981 (blouses); Courtaulds, 1981 (knitted silk lingerie); Zandra Rhodes Sportswear, 1982; Lyle & Scott, 1982 (cashmere knitwear); Zandra Rhodes 'Designs on Legs' Jambetex, 1984 (hosiery); Universal Leather, 1984 (handbags); Japan Feather Bedding Co., Japan, 1984 (bedlinen, cushions and bedroom accessories); Zandra Rhodes Shoes for Pentland Industries, 1984, Monitor Designs, 1985 (bedlinen). Launched: Zandra Rhodes Ready-to-Wear, Australia, 1979; Zandra Rhodes II Ready-to-Wear, UK, 1984. One-man exhibitions: Oriel, Cardiff (Welsh Arts Council), 1978; Texas Gall., Houston, 1981; Otis Parsons, Los Angeles, 1981; La Jolla Museum of Contemporary Art, San Diego, 1982; ADITI Creative Power, Barbican Centre, 1982; Sch. of Art Inst., Chicago, 1982; Parsons Sch. of Design, NY, 1982; Art Museum of Santa Cruz Co., Calif, 1983; retrospective exhibition of 'Works of Art' with textiles, Museum of Art, El Paso, Texas, 1984. Work represented in major costume collections: UK: V & A; City Mus. and Art Gall., Stoke-on-Trent; Bath Mus.; Royal Pavilion Brighton Mus.; Platt Fields Costume Mus., Manchester; City Art Gall., Leeds; overseas: Metropolitan Mus., NY; Chicago Historical Soc.; Smithsonian Instn; Royal Ontario Mus.; Mus. of Applied Arts and Scis, Sydney; Nat. Mus. of Victoria, Melbourne; La Jolla Mus. of Contemp. Art. Opening speaker, Famous Women of Fashion, Smithsonian Inst., Washington, 1978. DFA Internat. Fine Arts Coll., Miami, Florida. Emmy Award for Best Costume Designs in Romeo and Juliet on Ice, CBS TV, 1984; citations and commendations from USA estabs. *Publication:* The Art of Zandra Rhodes, 1984, US edn 1985; *relevant publications:* in English Vogue, 1978 and 1982; Architectural Digest, 1978; The Connoisseur, 1981; comment and illus. in numerous books and articles since 1971. *Recreations:* travelling, drawing. *Address:* (factory) 87 Richford Street, Hammersmith, W6 7HJ. *T:* (business) 01–749 9561.

RHODES JAMES, Robert Vidal; MP (C) Cambridge, since Dec. 1976; Chairman, Buchan and Enright, Publishers, since 1982; Chairman, History of Parliament Trust, since 1983; *b* 10 April 1933; *y s* of late Lieut-Col W. R. James, OBE, MC; *m* 1956, Angela Margaret Robertson, *er d* of late R. M. Robertson; four *d*. *Educ:* private schs in India; Sedbergh Sch.; Worcester Coll., Oxford. Asst Clerk, House of Commons, 1955–61; Senior Clerk, 1961–64. Fellow of All Souls Coll., Oxford, 1965–68, 1979–; Dir, Inst. for Study of Internat. Organisation, Univ. of Sussex, 1968–73; Principal Officer, Exec. Office of Sec.-Gen. of UN, 1973–76. Kratter Prof. of European History, Stanford Univ., Calif., 1968. Consultant to UN Conf. on Human Environment, 1971–72; UK Mem., UN Sub-Commn on Prevention of Discrimination and Protection of Minorities, 1972–73. PPS, FCO, 1979–82. Conservative Party Liaison Officer for Higher Educn, 1979–85. FRSL 1964; NATO Fellow, 1965; FRHistS 1973; Professorial Fellow, Univ. of Sussex, 1973. Hon. Dr of Letters, Westminster Coll., Fulton, Missouri. *Publications:* Lord Randolph Churchill, 1959; An Introduction to the House of Commons, 1961 (John Llewelyn Rhys Memorial Prize); Rosebery, 1963 (Royal Society Lit. Award); Gallipoli, 1965; Standardization and Production of Military Equipment in NATO, 1967; Churchill: a study in failure, 1900–39, 1970; Ambitions and Realities: British politics 1964–70, 1972; Victor Cazalet: a portrait, 1976; The British Revolution 1880–1939, vol. I, 1976, vol. II, 1977, 1 Vol. edn, 1978; Albert, Prince Consort, 1983; Anthony Eden, 1986; (ed) Chips: The Diaries of Sir Henry Channon, 1967; (ed) Memoirs of a Conservative: J. C. C. Davidson's Memoirs and Papers, 1969; (ed) The Czechoslovak Crisis 1968, 1969; (ed) The Complete Speeches of Sir Winston Churchill, 1897–1963, 1974; contrib. to: Suez Ten Years After, 1967; Essays From Divers Hands, 1967; Churchill: four faces and the man, 1969; International Administration, 1971; The Prime Ministers, vol. II, 1975. *Address:* The Stone House, Great Gransden, near Sandy, Beds. *T:* Great Gransden 7025. *Clubs:* Travellers', Pratt's; Century (New York).

RHYMES, Rev. Canon Douglas Alfred; Canon Residentiary and Librarian, Southwark Cathedral, 1962–69, Hon. Canon, 1969, Canon Emeritus since 1984, Lecturer in Ethics, Chichester Theological College; *b* 26 March 1914; *s* of Peter Alfred and Jessie Rhymes; unmarried. *Educ:* King Edward VI School, Birmingham; Birmingham Univ.; Ripon Hall Theological College, Oxford. BA (2nd Cl. Hons 1st Div.) Philosophy 1939. Asst Curate, Dovercourt, Essex, 1940–43; Chaplain to the Forces, 1943–46; Asst Curate, Romford, Essex (in charge of St George's, Romford and St Thomas', Noak Hill), 1946–49; Priest-in-charge, Ascension, Chelmsford, 1949–50; Sacrist, Southwark Cathedral, 1950–54; Vicar, All Saints, New Eltham, SE9, 1954–62; Director of Lay Training, Diocese of Southwark, 1962–68; Vicar of St Giles, Camberwell, 1968–76; Parish Priest of Woldingham, 1976–84. Proctor in Convocation and Mem. of Gen. Synod, 1975–85. *Publications:* (jtly) Crisis Booklets, Christianity and Communism, 1952; (jtly) Layman's Church, 1963; No New Morality, 1964; Prayer in the Secular City, 1967; Through Prayer to Reality, 1974; (jtly) Dropping the Bomb, 1985. *Recreations:* theatre, conversation, country walks. *Address:* Chillington Cottage, 7 Dukes Road, Fontwell, W Sussex BH18 0SP. *T:* Eastergate 3268.

RHYS, family name of **Baron Dynevor.**

RHYS, Keidrych; poet and writer; proprietor, Druid Books, Antiquarian and Out-of-print Booksellers, Heath Street, Hampstead; editor (founder) of magazine Wales, 1937–60; *b* Bethlehem, Llandilo, 26 Dec. 1915; *m* 1st, 1939, Lynette Roberts, poet and novelist, of Buenos Aires; one *s* one *d*; 2nd, 1956, Eva Smith; one *s*. *Educ:* Bethlehem; Llangadog; Llandovery Grammar Sch., etc. Literary and other journalism, London, etc, 1935. Served in Army (London Welsh AA) (1939–45 medals); with Ministry of Information, London, 1943–44; War Correspondent Europe, 1944–45. Public Relations Consultant, various charities and organisations, 1950–54; Welsh columnist and correspondent, The People, 1954–60; London Editor, Poetry London-New York, 1956–60. Arts Council Award in Literature, 1969–70. Vice-President International Musical Festival and Eisteddfod; Executive Committee (writers' group); Chairman Friends of Wales Soc.; Vice-Pres. Carmarthen Arts Club; Carmarthenshire County Drama Cttee and Rural Community Council. *Publications:* The Van Pool and other poems, 1941; Poems from the Forces, 1942; More Poems from the Forces, 1943; Modern Welsh Poetry, 1945; Angry Prayers, 1952; Poems; Contributor to: Wales, Times Lit. Supp., New Statesman, anthologies, and to European and American jls. *Recreations:* Welsh National affairs, lecturing, theatre. *Address:* 40 Heath Street, NW3 6TE. *T:* 01–794 2970.

RHYS WILLIAMS, Sir Brandon (Meredith), 2nd Bt, *cr* 1918; MP (C) Kensington, since 1974 (Kensington South, March 1968–1974); *b* 14 Nov. 1927; *s* of Sir Rhys Rhys Williams, 1st Bt, DSO, QC, and Lady (Juliet) Rhys Williams, DBE (*d* 1964); *S* father, 1955; *m* 1961, Caroline Susan, *e d* of L. A. Foster, Greatham Manor, Pulborough, Sussex; one *s* two *d*. *Educ:* Eton. Served in Welsh Guards, 1946–48 (Lt). Contested (C) Pontypridd Div., 1959, and Ebbw Vale Div., 1960 and 1964. Consultant, Management Selection Ltd, 1963–71; formerly with ICI Ltd. Asst Dir, Spastics Soc., 1962–63. Mem. (ED) European Parlt, 1973–84 (elected Mem. for London SE, 1979–84); Vice-Chm., European Parlt Economic and Monetary Affairs Cttee, 1973–79. *Publications:* The New Social Contract, 1967; More Power to the Shareholder?, 1969; Redistributing Income in a Free Society, 1969. *Heir:* *s* Arthur Gareth Ludovic Emrys Rhys Williams, *b* 9 Nov. 1961. *Address:* 32 Rawlings Street, SW3. *T:* 01–584 0636; Gadairwen, Groes Faen, near Pontyclun, Mid-Glamorgan. *Clubs:* White's, Pratt's; Cardiff and County (Cardiff).

RIABOUCHINSKA, Tatiana, (Mme Lichine); Ballerina of Russian Ballet; owns and operates the Lichine Ballet Academy, Beverly Hills; *b* 23 May 1916; *d* of Michael P. Riabouchinsky, Moscow (Banker), and Tatiana Riabouchinska (*d* 1935), Dancer of Moscow Imperial School of Dance; *m* 1942, David Lichine (*d* 1972); one *d*. *Educ:* Cour Fénelon, Paris. Trained first by her mother; then by Volinine (dancer of the Moscow Imperial Grand Theatre); then by Mathilde Kchesinska. First appeared as child dancer with Balieff's Chauve Souris in London, 1931; joined new Russian Ballet (de-Basil), 1932, and danced with them in nearly all countries of Western Europe, Australia and N and S America. Contribution to books on dancing by: Andre Levinson, Arnold L. Haskell, Irving Deakin, Rayner Heppenstall, Kay Ambrose, Prince Peter Lieven, Cyril W. Beaumont, Cyril Brahms, Adrian Stokes, A. V. Coton, Ninette de Valois, etc. *Address:* 965 Oakmont Drive, Los Angeles, Calif 90049, USA.

RIBBANS, Prof. Geoffrey Wilfrid, MA; Kenan University Professor of Hispanic Studies, Brown University, USA, since 1978; *b* 15 April 1927; *o s* of late Wilfrid Henry Ribbans and Rose Matilda Burton; *m* 1956, Magdalena Cumming (*née* Willmann), Cologne; one *s* two *d*. *Educ:* Sir George Monoux Grammar Sch., Walthamstow; King's Coll., Univ. of London. BA Hons Spanish 1st cl., 1948; MA 1953. Asst Lectr, Queen's Univ., Belfast, 1951–52; Asst, St Salvator's Coll., Univ. of St Andrews, 1952–53; Univ. of Sheffield: Asst Lectr, 1953–55; Lectr, 1955–61; Sen. Lectr, 1961–63; Gilmour Prof. of Spanish, Univ. of Liverpool, 1963–78; First Director, Centre for Latin-American Studies, 1966–70; Dean, Faculty of Arts, 1977–78; Chm., Dept of Hispanic and Italian Studies, Brown Univ., USA, 1981–84. Andrew Mellon Vis. Prof., Univ. of Pittsburgh, 1970–71; Leverhulme Res. Fellow, 1975. Norman Maccoll Lectr, Univ. of Cambridge, 1985. Vice-Pres., Internat. Assoc. of Hispanists, 1974–80 (Pres., Local Organising Cttee, 8th Congress, Brown Univ., 1983); Pres., Anglo-Catalan Soc., 1976–78; Dir, Liverpool Playhouse, 1974–78. Editor, Bulletin of Hispanic Studies, 1964–78. Hon. Fellow, Inst. of Linguists, 1972. Corresp. Member: Real Academia de Buenas Letras, Barcelona, 1978; Hispanic Soc. of Amer., 1981. MA *ad eund.* Brown Univ., 1979. *Publications:* Catalunya i València vistes pels viatgers anglesos del segle XVIIIè, 1955; Niebla y Soledad: aspectos de Unamuno y Machado, 1971; ed, Soledades, Galerias, otros poemas, by Antonio Machado, 1975, 2nd edn 1984; Antonio Machado (1875–1939): poetry and integrity, 1975; B. Pérez Galdós: Fortunata y Jacinta, a critical guide, 1977; numerous articles on Spanish and Catalan literature in specialised publications. *Recreations:* travel, fine art. *Address:* c/o Department of Hispanic and Italian Studies, Box E, Brown University, Providence, Rhode Island 02912, USA.

RICE; *see* Spring Rice, family name of Baron Monteagle of Brandon.

RICE, Dennis George, PhD; Social Security (formerly National Insurance) Commissioner, since 1979; *b* 27 Nov. 1927; *s* of George Henry Rice and Ethel Emily Rice; *m* 1959, Jean Beryl Wakefield; one *s*. *Educ:* City of London Sch.; King's Coll., Cambridge (Scholar and Prizeman; 1st Cl. Classical Tripos Pt I, Law Tripos Pt II; BA 1950, LLB 1951, MA 1955); London Sch. of Econs (PhD 1956). Called to the Bar, Lincoln's Inn, 1952. Served RAF, 1946–48. Entered J. Thorn and Sons Ltd, 1952; Dir, 1955; Man. Dir, 1956; Chm. and Man. Dir, 1958–69; in practice at Chancery Bar, 1970–79. Member: Cttee of Timber Bldg Manufrs Assoc., 1967–69; Cttee of Joinery and Woodwork Employers Fedn, 1968–69. *Publications:* Rockingham Ornamental Porcelain, 1965; Illustrated Guide to Rockingham Pottery and Porcelain, 1971; Derby Porcelain: the golden years, 1750–1770, 1983; articles on company law in legal jls and on Rockingham porcelain in art magazines. *Recreations:* history of English porcelain, gardening. *Address:* c/o Office of the Social Security Commissioners, 6 Grosvenor Gardens, Victoria, SW1W 0DH. *Club:* Reform.

RICE, Maj.-Gen. Desmond Hind Garrett, CVO 1985; CBE 1976 (OBE 1970); Secretary, Central Chancery of the Orders of Knighthood, since 1980; *b* 1 Dec. 1924; *s* of Arthur Garrett Rice and Alice Constance (*née* Henman); *m* 1954, Denise Ann (*née* Ravenscroft); one *d*. *Educ:* Marlborough College. Commissioned into The Queen's Bays, 1944; psc 1954; 1st The Queen's Dragoon Guards, 1958; jssc 1963; First Comdg Officer, The Royal Yeomanry, 1967–69; Col GS 4 Div., 1970–73; BGS (MO) MoD, 1973–75; rcds 1976; Director of Manning (Army), 1977–78; Vice Adjutant General, 1978–79; Col, 1st The Queen's Dragoon Guards, 1980–86. *Recreations:* field sports, skiing, gardening. *Address:* Fairway, Malacca Farm, West Clandon, Surrey. *T:* Guildford 222677. *Club:* Cavalry and Guards.

RICE, Gordon Kenneth; His Honour Judge Rice; a Circuit Judge, since 1980; *b* 16 April 1927; *m* 1967. *Educ:* Brasenose Coll., Oxford (MA). Called to the Bar, Middle Temple, 1957. *Address:* 83 Beach Avenue, Leigh-on-Sea, Essex.

RICE, Peter Anthony Morrish; stage designer; *b* 13 Sept. 1928; *s* of Cecil Morrish Rice and Ethel (*née* Blacklaw); *m* 1954, Patricia Albeck; one *s*. *Educ:* St Dunstan's Coll., Surrey; Royal Coll. of Art (ARCA 1951). Designed first professional prodn, Sex and the Seraphim, Watergate Theatre, London, 1951, followed by The Seraglio, Sadler's Wells Opera, 1952, and Arlecchino, Glyndebourne, 1954; subsequently has designed over 100 plays, operas and ballets, including: *plays:* Time Remembered, 1954; The Winter's Tale, and Much Ado About Nothing, Old Vic, 1956; Living for Pleasure, 1956; A Day in the Life of . . ., 1958; The Lord Chamberlain Regrets, and Toad of Toad Hall, 1961; The Farmer's Wife, The Italian Straw Hat, and Heartbreak House, Chichester, 1966; Flint, and Arms and the Man, 1970; Happy Birthday, 1977; Private Lives, Greenwich and West End, 1980; Present Laughter, Greenwich and West End, 1981; Cavell, and Goodbye Mr Chips, Chichester, 1982; The Sleeping Prince, Chichester and West End, 1983; Forty Years On, Chichester and West End, 1984; *operas:* Count Ory, Sadler's Wells, 1962; Arabella, Royal Opera, 1964, Paris Opera, 1981, Chicago, 1984, and Covent Garden, 1986; The Thieving Magpie, and The Violins of St Jacques, Sadler's Wells, 1967; La Bohème, Scottish Opera, 1970; The Magic Flute, Ottawa, 1974; Tosca, Scottish Opera, 1980; The Secret Marriage, Buxton Fest., 1981; The Count of Luxembourg, Sadler's Wells, 1982; Death in Venice, Antwerp, and Die Fledermaus, St Louis, USA, 1983; *ballets:* Romeo and Juliet, Royal Danish Ballet, 1955, and London Festival Ballet, 1985; Sinfonietta, Royal Ballet, 1966; The Four Seasons, Royal Ballet, 1974. Theatre interiors: Vaudeville Theatre, London; Grand Theatre, Blackpool; His Majesty's Theatre, Aberdeen. *Publications:* The Clothes Children Wore, 1973; Farming, 1974; Narrow Boats, 1976. *Recreation:* ancient films. *Address:* 4 Western Terrace, W6 9TX. *T:* 01–748 3990. *Club:* Garrick.

RICE, Peter D.; *see* Davis-Rice.

RICE, Timothy Miles Bindon; writer and broadcaster; *b* 10 Nov. 1944; *s* of Hugh Gordon Rice and Joan Odette Rice; *m* 1974, Jane Artereta McIntosh; one *s* one *d*. *Educ:* Lancing Coll. EMI Records, 1966–68; Norrie Paramor Org., 1968–69. Lyrics for musicals (with music by Andrew Lloyd Webber): Joseph and the Amazing Technicolor Dreamcoat, 1968 (rev. 1973); Jesus Christ Superstar, 1970; Evita, 1976 (rev. 1978); Cricket, 1986; (with music by Stephen Oliver) Blondel, 1983; (with music by Benny Andersson and Björn Ulvaeus) Chess, 1984 (rev. 1986). Lyrics for songs, 1975–, with other composers, incl. Marvin Hamlisch, Elton John, Rick Wakeman, Vangelis, Paul McCartney, Mike Batt, Francis Lai and John Barry. Awards include gold and platinum records in over 20 countries, 2 Tony Awards and 2 Grammy Awards. Founder and Director: GRRR Books, 1978–; Pavilion Books, 1981–. Presenter, TV series incl. Musical Triangles, Friday Night Saturday Morning, Tim Rice. Film début as actor in insultingly small rôle, The Survivor, 1980. Chairman: Stars Organization for Spastics, 1983–85; Shaftesbury Avenue Centenary Cttee, 1984–86. *Publications:* Heartaches Cricketers' Almanack, yearly, 1975–; (ed) Lord's Taverners Sticky Wicket Book, 1979; (with Andrew Lloyd Webber): Evita, 1978; Joseph and the Amazing Technicolour Dreamcoat, 1982; (jtly) Guinness Books of British Hit Singles and Albums and associated pubns, 1977–, vol. 12, 1986. *Recreations:* cricket, history of popular music. *Address:* 196 Shaftesbury Avenue, WC2. *T:* 01–240 5617. *Clubs:* MCC, Royal Automobile, Dramatists'; Fonograf (Budapest).

RICE-OXLEY, James Keith, CBE 1981; Chairman, Merchant Navy Training Board, since 1981; *b* 15 Aug. 1920; *o s* of late Montague Keith Rice-Oxley and Margery Hyacinth Rice-Oxley (*née* Burrell), Kensington; *m* 1949, Barbara, *yr d* of late Frederick Parsons, Gerrards Cross; two *d. Educ:* Marlborough Coll.; Trinity Coll., Oxford. MA(Law). Served War of 1939–45: Wiltshire Regt, Royal West Kents (wounded El Alamein); GSO III, HQ 3 Corps; GSO II, HQ Land Forces, Greece (despatches). Joined Shipping Fedn, 1947, Dir, 1965–75; Dir, Internat. Shipping Fedn, 1970–80; Dir, Gen. Council of British Shipping, 1975–80. Chm., Nat. Sea Training Trust, 1965–80; Mem. Nat. Maritime Bd, 1965–80; Mem., Merchant Navy Welfare Bd, 1965–80; Internat. Shipowners' Chm. and British Shipowners' Rep. on Jt Maritime Commn of ILO, 1970–80; Chm., Shipowners' Gp at Internat. Labour (Maritime) Confs, 1969, 1970, 1975, 1976; a Vice-Pres., IMCO/ILO Maritime Conf., 1978. Chm., Maritime Studies Cttee, BTEC, 1980–; Mem. Industrial Tribunals (England and Wales), 1981–; General Comr of Income Tax, 1986–. Chm., Shaftesbury Civic Soc., 1982–85; Member: Council and Exec. Cttee, Dr Barnardo's, 1981–; Council, King George's Fund for Sailors, 1965–82; UK Mem., Bd of Governors, World Maritime Univ., Malmö, 1983–. *Recreations:* squash, ceramics. *Address:* Ox House, Bimport, Shaftesbury SP7 8AX. *T:* Shaftesbury 2741.

RICH, Jacob Morris, MA, LLB; Hon. Consultant, South African Jewish Board of Deputies (Secretary 1939–74); *b* Longton, Stoke-on-Trent, 4 March 1897; *m* 1940, Sylvia Linken; two *d. Educ:* Hanley High School; Fitzwilliam Hall, Cambridge. Served in Palestine with Jewish Battalions of the Royal Fusiliers during European War; Secretary to the Board of Deputies of British Jews, 1926–31; Secretary of the Joint Foreign Committee of the Board of Deputies of British Jews and the Anglo-Jewish Association, 1930–31; Hon. Secretary Jewish Historical Society of England, 1924–31; Editor, The Jewish Chronicle, 1931–36. *Address:* 17 Campbell Road, Parktown West, Johannesburg, S Africa.

RICH, John Rowland, CMG 1978; HM Diplomatic Service; Ambassador to Switzerland, since 1985; *b* 29 June 1928; *s* of late Rowland William Rich, Winchester, and of Phyllis Mary, *e d* of Charles Linstead Chambers, Southgate; *m* 1956, Rosemary Ann, *yr d* of late Bertram Evan Williams, Ferndown, Dorset; two *s* one *d. Educ:* Sedbergh; Clare Coll., Cambridge (Foundn Exhibnr 1948). BA 1949, MA 1954. HM Forces, 1949–51; FO, 1951–53; 3rd, later 2nd Sec., Addis Ababa, 1953–56; 2nd, later 1st Sec., Stockholm, 1956–59; FO, 1959–63; 1st Sec. (Economic) and Head of Chancery, Bahrain (Political Residency), 1963–66; FCO, 1966–69; Counsellor and Head of Chancery, Prague, 1969–72; Diplomatic Service Inspector, 1972–74; Commercial Counsellor, Bonn, 1974–78; Consul-Gen., Montreal, 1978–80; Ambassador to Czechoslovakia, 1980–84. *Recreations:* walking, wild orchids, steam locomotives. *Address:* c/o Foreign and Commonwealth Office, SW1A 2AH. *Club:* Travellers'.

RICH, Michael Samuel, QC 1980; a Recorder, since 1986; *b* 18 Aug. 1933; *s* of late Sidney Frank Rich, OBE and of Erna Babette; *m* 1963, Janice Sarita Benedictus; three *s* one *d. Educ:* Dulwich Coll.; Wadham Coll., Oxford (MA, 1st Class Hons PPE). Called to the Bar, Middle Temple, 1958, Bencher, 1985. Medal of Merit, Boy Scouts Assoc., 1970. *Publication:* (jtly) Hill's Law of Town and Country Planning, 5th edn, 1968. *Recreations:* "prog-nosed" activities. *Address:* 2 Paper Buildings, Temple, EC4. *T:* 01–353 5835; 18 Dulwich Village, SE21. *T:* 01–693 1957.

RICH, Nigel Mervyn Sutherland, FCA; Director, Jardine Matheson & Co., since 1984; Director since 1983, Chief Operating Officer since 1986, Hongkong Land Co.; *b* 30 Oct. 1945; *s* of Charles Albert Rich and Mina Mackintosh Rich; *m* 1970, Cynthia Elizabeth (*née* Davies); two *s* two *d. Educ:* Sedbergh Sch.; New Coll., Oxford (MA). Deloitte, Plender Griffiths, London, 1967–71; Deloitte, Haskins & Sells, New York, 1971–73; Jardine Matheson & Co., Hong Kong, 1974–; served in varying positions in Hong Kong, Johannesburg (Rennies Consolidated Holdings) and Manila (Jardine Davies Inc.); seconded to Hongkong Land Co. as Finance Dir, 1983. Liveryman, Tobacco Pipemakers and Tobacco Blenders Co.; Freeman, City of London, 1970. *Recreations:* tennis, golf, windsurfing. *Address:* 16 Shek O, Hong Kong. *T:* 5–8094477. *Clubs:* Hurlingham, Army and Navy; Shek O, Ladies Recreation, Tennis, American (Hong Kong).

RICHARD, Cliff, OBE 1980; singer, actor; *b* 14 Oct. 1940; *s* of Rodger Webb and Dorothy Webb. *Educ:* Riversmead Sch., Cheshunt. Awarded 11 Gold Discs for records: Living Doll, 1959; The Young Ones, 1962; Bachelor Boy, 1962; Lucky Lips, 1963; Congratulations, 1968; Power to all Our Friends, 1973; Devil Woman, 1976; We Don't Talk Anymore, 1979; Wired for Sound, 1981; Daddy's Home, 1981; Living Doll, 1986; also 30 Silver Discs and 1 Platinum Disc (Daddy's Home, 1981). Films: Serious Charge, 1959; Expresso Bongo, 1960; The Young Ones, 1962; Summer Holiday, 1963; Wonderful Life, 1964; Finders Keepers, 1966; Two a Penny, 1968; His Land, 1970; Take Me High, 1973. Own TV series, ATV and BBC. Stage: rep. and variety seasons; Time, Dominion, 1986. Top Box Office Star of GB, 1962–63 and 1963–64. *Publications:* Questions, 1970; The Way I See It, 1972; The Way I See It Now, 1975; Which One's Cliff, 1977; Happy Christmas from Cliff, 1980; You, Me and Jesus, 1983; Mine to Share, 1984; Jesus, Me and You, 1985. *Recreations:* swimming, tennis. *Address:* c/o Peter Gormley, PO Box 46C, Esher, Surrey KT10 9AF. *T:* Esher 67752.

RICHARD, Ivor Seward; QC 1971; *b* 30 May 1932; *s* of Seward Thomas Richard, mining and electrical engineer, and Isabella Irene Richard; *m;* two *s* one *d. Educ:* St Michael's Sch., Bryn, Llanelly; Cheltenham Coll.; Pembroke Coll., Oxford (Wightwick Scholar; Hon Fellow, 1981). BA Oxon (Jurisprudence) 1953; MA 1970; called to Bar, Inner Temple, 1955, Bencher, 1985. Practised in chambers, London, 1955–74. UK Perm. Representative to UN, 1974–79; Mem., Commn of EEC, 1981–84; Chm., Rhodesia Conf., Geneva, 1976. Parly Candidate, S Kensington, 1959; MP (Lab) Barons Court, 1964–Feb. 1974. Delegate: Assembly, Council of Europe, 1965–68; Western European Union, 1965–68; Vice-Chm., Legal Cttee, Council of Europe, 1966–67; PPS, Sec. of State for Defence, 1966–69; Parly Under-Sec. (Army), Min. of Defence, 1969–70; Opposition Spokesman, Broadcasting, Posts and Telecommunications, 1970–71; Dep. Spokesman,

Foreign Affairs, 1971–74. Chm., World Trade Centre Wales Ltd (Cardiff), 1985–; Dir, Job Creation Ltd, 1985–. Member: Fabian Society; Society of Labour Lawyers; Inst. of Strategic Studies; Royal Inst. of Internat. Affairs. *Publications:* (jt) Europe or the Open Sea, 1971; We, the British, 1983 (USA); articles in various political jls. *Recreations:* playing piano, watching football matches, talking. *Address:* 169 Temple Chambers, Temple Avenue, EC4Y 0DT.

RICHARDS, family name of **Baron Milverton.**

RICHARDS, Alun; *see* Richards, R. A.

RICHARDS, Archibald Banks, CA; retired; *b* 29 March 1911; *s* of late Charles Richards and Margaret Pollock Richards; *m* 1941, Edith Janet Sinclair; one *s* one *d. Educ:* Daniel Stewart's Coll., Edinburgh. Partner, A. T. Niven & Co., Chartered Accountants, Edinburgh, 1939–69, Touche Ross & Co., Chartered Accountants, 1964–78. Inst. of Chartered Accountants of Scotland: Mem., 1934; Mem. Council, 1968–73; Vice Pres., 1974–76; Pres., 1976–77. *Address:* 7 Midmar Gardens, Edinburgh EH10 6DY. *T:* 031–447 1942. *Club:* New (Edinburgh).

RICHARDS, Arthur Cyril, FIA; Chairman, Blackwood Hodge plc, since 1983 (Director, since 1978); *b* 7 April 1921; *s* of Ernest Arthur Richards and Kate Richards (*née* Cooper); *m* 1st, 1944, Joyce Bertha Brooke (marr. diss. 1974); two *s* two *d;* 2nd, 1975, Els Stoyle (*née* van der Stoel); two step *s* one step *d. Educ:* Tollington Sch., London. FIA 1949; FSVA 1962. Insurance, 1937–41. Served RAF, 1941–46. Insurance, consulting actuary, steel manufacture, investment banking, internat. property develt, 1946–64; Advr, Samuel Montagu & Co. Ltd, 1965–67; Gp Finance Dir, Bovis Ltd, 1967–71; United Dominions Trust Ltd: Gp Finance Dir, 1971–76; Gp Man. Dir, 1976–80; Chief Exec., 1981–83. Chm., Federated Land, 1982; Director: MSL Gp Internat., 1970–81; TSB Trust Co., 1981–; Combined Lease Finance PLC, 1985–. *Recreations:* sailing, windsurfing, reading. *Address:* Caboose, Tilt Meadow, Cobham, Surrey. *Club:* Overseas Bankers'.

RICHARDS, Bertrand; *see* Richards, E. B. B.

RICHARDS, Sir Brooks; *see* Richards, Sir F. B.

RICHARDS, Charles Anthony Langdon, CMG 1958; *b* 18 April 1911; *s* of T. L. Richards, Bristol, Musician; *m* 1937, Mary Edith Warren-Codrington; two *s. Educ:* Clifton Coll.; Brasenose Coll., Oxford. Appointed Colonial CS, Uganda, 1934; Major, 7th King's African Rifles, 1939–41: duties in Mauritius, 1941–46; District Officer, Uganda, 1946–50; Commissioner for Social Development, Tanganyika, 1950–53; Commissioner for Community Development, Uganda, 1953–54; Resident, Buganda, Oct. 1954–60; Minister of Local Government, Uganda, 1960–61. *Recreation:* gardening. *Address:* The Wall House, Oak Drive, Highworth, Wilts SN6 7BP.

RICHARDS, Rev. Canon Daniel; Residentiary Canon of Llandaff Cathedral since 1949; Priest-in-charge of Merthyr Mawr and Ewenny, 1968–77; *b* 13 February 1892; *s* of John and Elizabeth Richards; *m* 1919, Hilda Roberts; one *s* (and one *s* killed 1944). *Educ:* St David's College, Lampeter, Cards. LD 1915, Mathews Scholar, 1928–29, BA and BD 1929; Curate of St Mary's Church, Court Henry, Carms, 1915–18; Curate of St Mary's Church, Burry Port, Carms, 1918–24; Rector of Llangeitho, Cards, 1924–31; Vicar of: Llangynwyd with Maesteg, 1931–66; Grouped Parish of Troedyrhiw Garth, Maesteg, 1950–60; Precentor of Llandaff Cathedral, 1961–67; SPCK Hon. Group Secretary for Dioceses of St David's, Swansea and Brecon, Llandaff and Monmouth, 1966–. Fellow of Philosophical Society of England, 1942. MTh 1980, PhD 1984, Geneva Theol Coll.; STh Lambeth Diploma of Student in Theology, 1981. *Publications:* Honest to Self (autobiog.), 1971; History of the Lampeter Society, 1972, revd edn 1982; Honest Memories (autobiog.), 1985. *Address:* Llandre, 26 Brynteg Avenue, Bridgend, Mid Glamorgan. *T:* Bridgend 5117.

RICHARDS, David Gordon, FCA; Deputy Chairman, Monopolies and Mergers Commission, since 1983; *b* 25 Aug. 1928; *s* of late Gordon Charles Richards and Vera Amy (*née* Barrow); *m* 1960, Stephanie, *er d* of late E. Gilbert Woodward, Metropolitan Magistrate and of Mrs Woodward; one *s* two *d. Educ:* Highgate Sch. FCA 1961. Articled to Harmood Banner & Co., 1945; served, 8th Royal Tank Regt, 1947–49; Partner: Harmood Banner & Co., 1955–74; Deloitte Haskins & Sells, 1974–84. Admitted Associate Mem. Inst. of Chartered Accountants in England and Wales, 1951 (Council, 1970; Vice-Pres., 1977–78; Dep. Pres., 1978–79; Centenary Pres., 1979–80; Mem., Gen. Purposes and Finance Cttee, 1977–83; Chm., Internat. Affairs Cttee, 1980–83); Member: Cttee of London Soc. of Chartered Accountants, 1966–70, 1981–82 (Chm., 1969–70); Cttees of Investigation under Agricultural Marketing Act (1958), 1972–; Council for Securities Industry, 1979–80; Panel on Take Overs and Mergers, 1979–80; Review Body on Doctors' and Dentists' Remuneration, 1984–; Chm., Cons. Cttee of Accountancy Bodies, 1979–80; UK and Ireland rep. on Council, Internat. Fedn of Accountants, 1981–83. Governor, Highgate Sch., 1982– (Chm. 1983–); Trustee, The Bob Champion Cancer Trust, 1983–; Trustee and Chm. Exec. Cttee, Fairbridge Youth Employment Soc.; Hon. Treasurer, Royal Acad. of Music Appeal Fund, 1985–. Master, Worshipful Co. of Chartered Accountants in England and Wales, 1986–87. *Publications:* numerous contribs to professional press and lectures on professional topics given internationally. *Recreations:* golf, lawn tennis, sailing, shooting, silviculture, music. *Address:* Eastleach House, Eastleach, Glos GL7 3NW. *T:* Southrop 416.

RICHARDS, Denis Edward, CMG 1981; HM Diplomatic Service, retired; Ambassador to the United Republic of Cameroon and the Republic of Equatorial Guinea, 1979–81; *b* 25 May 1923; *m* 1947, Nancy Beryl Brown; two *d. Educ:* Wilson's Grammar Sch., London; St Peter's Coll., Oxford. Lieut RNVR, 1941–46; Colonial Service (HMOCS), 1948–60: District Admin. and Min. of Finance, Ghana (Gold Coast); HM Diplomatic Service, 1960–81: CRO, 1960; Karachi, 1961–63; FO (News Dept), 1964–68; Brussels (NATO), 1969; Brussels (UK Negotiating Delegn), 1970–72; Counsellor, Kinshasa, 1972–74; Consul-Gen., Philadelphia, 1974–79. *Recreations:* music, amateur dramatics. *Address:* Tresco House, Spencer Road, Birchington, Kent CT7 9EY. *T:* Thanet 45637.

RICHARDS, Denis George; author; *b* 10 Sept. 1910; *s* of late George Richards and Frances Amelia Gosland; *m* 1940, Barbara, *d* of J. H. Smethurst, Heaton, Bolton; four *d. Educ:* Owen's Sch.; Trinity Hall, Cambridge (Scholar). BA 1931 (1st Cl. in both Parts of Historical Tripos); MA 1935; Asst Master, Manchester Grammar School, 1931–39; Senior History and English Master, Bradfield Coll., 1939–41; Narrator in Air Ministry Historical Branch, writing confidential studies on various aspects of the air war, 1942–43; Sen. Narrator, 1943–47; Hon. Sqdn Ldr RAFVR, 1943–47; engaged in writing, under Air Min. auspices, an official History of the Royal Air Force in the Second World War, 1947–49; was established in Admin. Civil Service, Principal, Department of Permanent Under Secretary of State for Air, 1949–50; Principal, Morley College, 1950–65; Longman Fellow in Univ. of Sussex, 1965–68. Chm., Women's League of Health and Beauty; Vice-Pres., Purcell Sch. for Young Musicians, 1984–. *Publications:* An Illustrated History of Modern Europe, 1938; Modern Europe (1919–39 section for revised edn of work by Sydney Herbert), 1940; (with J. W. Hunt) An Illustrated History of Modern Britain,

1950; (with late Hilary St G. Saunders) Royal Air Force 1939–45–an officially commissioned history in 3 volumes, 1953–54 (awarded C. P. Robertson Memorial Trophy, 1954); (with J. Evan Cruikshank) The Modern Age, 1955; Britain under the Tudors and Stuarts, 1958; Offspring of the Vic: a History of Morley College, 1958; (with Anthony Quick) Britain 1714–1851, 1961; (with J. A. Bolton) Britain and the Ancient World, 1963; (with Anthony Quick) Britain, 1851–1945, 1967; (with Anthony Quick) Twentieth Century Britain, 1968; (with A. W. Ellis) Medieval Britain, 1973; Portal of Hungerford, 1978. *Recreations:* music, pictures, golf, travel in the more civilized parts of Europe, the lighter tasks in the garden. *Address:* 16 Broadlands Road, N6 4AN. *T:* 01–340 5259. *Clubs:* Arts, Garrick, PEN.

See also W. P. Shovelton.

RICHARDS, (Edmund) Bertrand (Bamford); His Honour Judge Bertrand Richards; a Circuit Judge since 1972; *b* 14 Feb. 1913; *s* of Rev. Edmund Milo Richards, Llewesog Hall, Denbigh; *m* 2nd, 1966, Jane, *widow* of Edward Stephen Porter. *Educ:* Lancing Coll.; Corpus Christi Coll., Oxford. Served War, RA, 1940–46. Called to Bar, Inner Temple, 1941. Dep. Chm., Denbighshire QS, 1964–71. Hon. Recorder of Ipswich, 1975. *Address:* Melton Hall, near Woodbridge, Suffolk.

RICHARDS, Hon. Sir Edward (Trenton), Kt 1970; CBE 1967; Premier of Bermuda, 1972–75 (Leader, 1971; Deputy Leader, 1968–71); MP 1948–76; *b* 4 Oct. 1908; 2nd *s* of late George A. Richards and Millicent Richards, British Guiana; *m* 1940, Madree Elizabeth Williams; one *s* two *d. Educ:* Collegiate Sch.; Queen's Coll., Guyana; Middle Temple. Secondary School-teacher, 1930–43; called to Bar, 1946. Elected to House of Assembly, Bermuda, 1948; served numerous Select Cttees of Parliament; served on Commns; Member, Exec. Council (now Cabinet), 1963–75; Mem. of Govt responsible for Immigration, Labour and Soc. Security, 1968–71. Served on many Govt Boards; Chairman: Public Transportation Board; Transport Control Board. Bermuda Representative: CPA Confs, Lagos, 1962, Kuala Lumpur, 1971; Guyana's Independence Celebrations, 1966, Bahamas Independence Celebrations, 1973; Mem., Constitution Conf., 1966; Leader Bermuda Delegn, ILO Confs Geneva, 1969–71. Magistrate, 1958. Chm., Berkeley Educational Soc., 1956–72. Hon. Life Vice-Pres., Bermuda Football Assoc. Hon. LLD, Wilberforce, USA, 1960. *Recreations:* music, reading, walking. *Address:* Wilton, Keith Hall Road, Warwick East, Bermuda. *T:* 2–3645. *Clubs:* Somerset Cricket, Warwick Workman's, Blue Waters Anglers (Bermuda); Royal Hamilton Amateur Dinghy.

RICHARDS, Prof. Elfyn John, OBE 1958; FEng; FRAeS; FIMechE; Research Professor, Southampton University, and Acoustical Consultant, 1975–84, now Emeritus. *b* Barry, Glamorgan, South Wales, 28 Dec. 1914; *s* of Edward James Richards, Barry, schoolmaster, and of Catherine Richards; *m* 1941, Eluned Gwenddydd Jones (*d* 1978), Aberporth, Cardigan; three *d. Educ:* Barry County School; Univ. Coll. of Wales, Aberystwyth (BSc); St John's Coll., Cambridge (MA). DSc (Wales), 1959. Research Asst, Bristol Aeroplane Company, 1938–39; Scientific Officer, National Physical Laboratory, Teddington, 1939–45, and Secretary, various Aeronautical Research Council sub-cttees; Chief Aerodynamicist and Asst Chief-Designer, Vickers Armstrong, Ltd, Weybridge, 1945–50; Prof. of Aeronautical Engineering, 1950–64, and Founder Dir, Inst. of Sound and Vibration Research, 1963–67, Univ. of Southampton, also Aeronautical Engineering Consultant; Vice-Chancellor, Loughborough Univ., 1967–75. Res. Prof., Florida Atlantic Univ., 1983. Member: SRC, 1970–74; Noise Adv. Council; Noise Research Council, ARC, 1968–71; Construction Research and Adv. Council, 1968–71; Inland Transport and Develt Council, 1968–71; Gen. Adv. Council of BBC (Chm. Midlands Adv. Council, 1968–71); Cttee of Scientific Advisory Council; Wilson Cttee on Problems of Noise; Planning and Transport Res. Adv. Council, 1971–. Chm., Univs Council for Adult Educn; President: British Acoustical Soc., 1968–70; Soc. of Environmental Engrs, 1971–73. Mem. Leics CC. Hon. LLD Wales, 1973; Hon. DSc: Southampton, 1973; Heriot-Watt, 1983; Hon. DTech Loughborough, 1975. Hon. FIOA 1978; Hon. Fellow Acoustical Soc. of America, 1980. Taylor Gold Medal, RAeS, 1949; James Watt Medal, ICE, 1963; Silver Medal, RSA, 1971. *Publications:* books and research papers (250) in acoustics, aviation, education. *Recreations:* swimming, walking. *Address:* 53 The Harrage, Romsey, Hants.

RICHARDS, Sir (Francis) Brooks, KCMG 1976 (CMG 1963); DSC and Bar, 1943; *b* 18 July 1918; *s* of Francis Bartlett Richards; *m* 1941, Hazel Myfanwy, *d* of Lt-Col Stanley Price Williams, CIE; one *s* one *d. Educ:* Stowe School; Magdalene College, Cambridge. Served with RN, 1939–44 (Lieut-Comdr RNVR). HM Embassy: Paris, 1944–48; Athens, 1952–54; First Sec. and Head of Chancery, Political Residency, Persian Gulf, 1954–57; Assistant Private Secretary to Foreign Secretary, 1958–59; Counsellor (Information), HM Embassy, Paris, 1959–64; Head of Information Policy Dept, 1964–65, and of Jt Inf. Policy and Guidance Dept, FO/CRO, 1964–65; seconded to Cabinet Office, 1965–69; HM Minister, Bonn, 1969–71; HM Ambassador, Saigon, 1972–74; HM Ambassador, Greece, 1974–78; Dep. Sec., Cabinet Office, 1978–80; NI Office, 1980–81. Chairman: CSM European Consultants Ltd, 1983–; CSM Parliamentary Consultants Ltd, 1984–; Dir, Ramsden International Trade Finance Ltd, 1985–. Chm., Cttee of Management, British Inst. in Paris; Member: IISS; RIIA. Chevalier, Légion d'Honneur and Croix de Guerre (France), 1944. *Recreations:* sailing, gardening, travelling. *Address:* The Ranger's House, Farnham, Surrey. *Clubs:* Travellers', Special Forces (Pres.); Royal Ocean Racing.

See also F. N. Richards.

RICHARDS, Francis Neville; HM Diplomatic Service; Economic and Commercial Counsellor, New Delhi, since 1985; *s* of Sir Francis Brooks Richards, *qv*; *m* 1971, Gillian Bruce Nevill, *d* of late I. S. Nevill, MC and of Dr L. M. B. Dawson; one *s* one *d. Educ:* Eton; King's Coll., Cambridge (MA). Royal Green Jackets, 1967 (invalided, 1969). FCO, 1969; Moscow, 1971; UK Delegn to MBFR negotiations, Vienna, 1973; FCO, 1976–85 (Asst Private Sec. to Sec. of State, 1981–82). *Recreations:* walking, looking at buildings and pictures. *Address:* c/o Foreign and Commonwealth Office, SW1. *Club:* Travellers'.

RICHARDS, Sir Gordon, Kt 1953; Racing Manager, since 1970 (Jockey, retired 1954, then Trainer, 1955–70); *b* 5 May 1904; *s* of Nathan Richards; *m* Marjery (*d* 1982); two *s.* Started life as a clerk; went as a stable apprentice to Mr Martin G. Hartigan, 1919; has headed the list of winning jockeys, 1925, 1927–29, 1931–33, 1938–40, 1942; 259 winners in 1933, breaking Fred Archer's record; passed Archer's record total of 2,749 winners, 26 April 1943; passed own record with 269 winners, 1947; rode 4000th winner 4 May 1950; broke world record with 4,500 winners 17 July 1952; final total, 4,870. Won the 1953 Derby on Pinza. Hon. Member, Jockey Club, 1970. *Publication:* My Story, 1955. *Recreations:* shooting, watching football. *Address:* Duff House, Kintbury, Berks.

RICHARDS, Very Rev. Gwynfryn; Dean of Bangor, 1962–71; Archdeacon of Bangor, 1957–62; Rector of Llandudno, 1956–62; *b* 10 Sept. 1902; *er s* of Joshua and Elizabeth Ann Richards, Nantyffyllon, Glam; *m* 1935, Margery Phyllis Evans; one *s* one *d. Educ:* Universities of Wales, Oxford and Boston. Scholar, Univ. Coll., Cardiff, 1918–21; BSc (Wales), 1921; Jesus Coll., Oxford, 1921–23; Certificate, School of Geography, Oxford, 1922; BA 1st Cl. Hons School of Natural Science, 1923; MA 1928. In industry (USA), 1923–25. Boston Univ. Sch. of Theology, 1926–28; STB First Cl., 1928; Scholar and Travelling Fellow, 1928–29; Oxford, 1928–29; St Michael's Coll., Llandaff, 1929–30; deacon, 1930; priest, 1931. Curate of: Llanrhos, 1930–34; Aberystwyth, St Michael, 1934–38; Rector of Llanllyfni, 1938–49; Vicar of Conway with Gyffin, 1949–56. Canon of Bangor Cathedral, 1943–62, Treas., 1943–57; Examining Chaplain to Bp of Bangor, 1944–71; Rural Dean of Arllechwedd, 1953–57. Pantyfedwen Lectr, Univ. Coll., Aberystwyth, 1967. *Publications:* Ffurfiau Ordeinio Holl Eglwysi Cymru, 1943; Yr Hen Fam, 1952; Ein Hymraniadau Annedwydd, 1963; Gwir a Diogel Obaith, 1972; Ar Lawer Trywydd, 1973; A Fynn Esgyn, Mynn Ysgol, 1980; contrib. to Journal of the Historical Society of the Church in Wales, Nat. Library of Wales Jl, Trans of Caernarvonshire Hist. Soc. *Recreations:* gardening, photography, local history. *Address:* Llain Werdd, Llandegfan, Menai Bridge, Gwynedd LL59 5LY. *T:* Menai Bridge 713429.

RICHARDS, James Alan, OBE 1979; Agent-General for Western Australia in London, 1975–78, retired; *b* 8 Oct. 1913; *s* of James Percival Richards and Alice Pearl Richards (*née* Bullock) Adelaide; *m* 1939, Mabel Joyce, *d* of R. H. Cooper, Riverton, S Austr.; three *s* one *d. Educ:* Unley High Sch.; Coll. of Business Admin, Univ. of Hawaii. Served War of 1939–45, 2nd AIF. Ampol Petroleum Ltd, 1946–75: Sales Man., South Australia, 1952–53; State Man., Western Australia, 1954–75. *Recreation:* bowls. *Address:* 4 Nuytsia Avenue, Sorrento, WA 6020, Australia.

RICHARDS, Sir James (Maude), Kt 1972; CBE 1959; FSA 1980; architectural writer, critic and historian; Editor, Architectural Review, 1937–71; Editor, Architects' Journal, 1947–49 (editorial board, 1949–61); Architectural Correspondent, The Times, 1947–71; *b* 13 Aug. 1907; 2nd *s* of late Louis Saurin Richards and Lucy Denes (*née* Clarence); *m* 1st, 1936, Margaret (marr. diss., 1948), *d* of late David Angus; (one *s* decd) one *d*; 2nd, 1954, Kathleen Margaret (Kit), *widow* of late Morland Lewis and 2nd *d* of late Henry Bryan Godfrey-Faussett-Osborne, Queendown Warren, Sittingbourne, Kent; one *s* decd. *Educ:* Gresham's School, Holt; AA School of Architecture. ARIBA, AADipl 1930. Studied and practised architecture in Canada and USA, 1930–31, London and Dublin, 1931–33; Asst Editor, The Architects' Jl, 1933; The Architectural Review, 1935; Editor, Publications Div., 1942, Director of Publications, Middle East, Cairo, 1943–46, MOI; Gen. Editor, The Architectural Press, 1946. Hoffman Wood Prof. of Architecture, Leeds Univ., 1957–59. Editor, European Heritage, 1973–75. Member: exec. cttee Modern Architectural Research Gp, 1946–54; AA Council, 1948–51, 1958–61, 1973–74; Advisory Council, Inst. of Contemporary Arts, 1947–68; Architecture Council, Festival of Britain, 1949–51; British Cttee, Internat. Union of Architects, 1950–66; Royal Fine Art Commn, 1951–66; Fine Art Cttee, Brit. Council, 1954–78; Council of Industrial Design, 1955–61; Min. of Transport (Worboys) Cttee on traffic signs, 1962–63; World Soc. of Ekistics, 1965–; Council, Victorian Soc., 1965–; National Trust, 1977–83; Vice-Pres. Nat. Council on Inland Transport, 1963–; Exec. Cttee, Venice in Peril Fund, 1969–; Chm., Arts Council inquiry into provision for the arts in Ireland, 1974–76; British Cttee, Icomos, 1975–. Broadcaster, television and sound (regular member, BBC Critics panel, 1948–68). FRSA 1970; Hon. AILA, 1955; Hon. FAIA, 1985. Chevalier (First Class), 1960, Comdr, 1985, Order of White Rose of Finland; Gold Medal, Mexican Institute of Architects, 1963; Bicentenary Medal, RSA, 1971. *Publications:* Miniature History of the English House, 1938; (with late Eric Ravilious) High Street, 1938; Introduction to Modern Architecture, 1940, new edn 1970 (trans. seven langs); (with John Summerson) The Bombed Buildings of Britain, 1942; Edward Bawden, 1946; The Castles on the Ground, 1946, new enl. edn 1973; The Functional Tradition in Early Industrial Buildings, 1958; (ed) New Building in the Commonwealth, 1961; An Architectural Journey in Japan, 1963; Guide to Finnish Architecture, 1966; A Critic's View, 1970; (ed, with Nikolaus Pevsner) The Anti-Rationalists, 1972; Planning and Redevelopment in London's Entertainment Area, 1973 (Arts Council report); The Professions: Architecture, 1974; (ed) Who's Who in Architecture: from 1400 to the present day, 1977; 800 Years of Finnish Architecture, 1978; Memoirs of an Unjust Fella (autobio.), 1980; The National Trust Book of English Architecture, 1981; Goa, 1982; The National Trust Book of Bridges, 1984. *Recreations:* travel and topography. *Address:* 29 Fawcett Street, SW10. *T:* 01–352 9874. *Clubs:* Athenæum, Beefsteak.

RICHARDS, Ven. John; Archdeacon of Exeter and Canon Residentiary of Exeter Cathedral, since 1981; *b* 4 Oct. 1933; *s* of William and Ethel Mary Richards; *m* 1958, Ruth Haynes; two *s* three *d. Educ:* Reading School; Wyggeston Grammar School, Leicester; Sidney Sussex Coll., Cambridge (MA); Ely Theological Coll. Asst Curate, St Thomas, Exeter, 1959–64; Rector of Holsworthy with Hollacombe and Cookbury, 1964–74; RD of Holsworthy, 1970–74; Rector of Heavitree with St Paul's, Exeter, 1974–81; RD of Exeter, 1978–81. Chm. of House of Clergy, Exeter Diocesan Synod, 1979–82; Mem. Gen. Synod, 1985–. *Recreations:* gardening, fishing, walking. *Address:* 12 The Close, Exeter. *T:* Exeter 75745.

RICHARDS, John Arthur; Under-Secretary, Department of Education and Science, 1973–77; *b* 23 June 1918; *s* of late Alderman A. J. Richards and Mrs Annie Richards, Dulwich; *m* 1946, Sheelagh, *d* of late Patrick McWalter and Katherine McWalter, Balla, Co. Mayo; two *s* one *d. Educ:* Brockley Sch.; King's Coll., London. BA, AKC, Dip. in Educn. Hon. Sec., King's Coll. Union Soc., 1939. Served War: Captain RA; Directorate of Personnel Selection, War Office, 1945–46. Temp. Third Sec., Foreign Office, 1946; Staff, Hackney Downs Grammar Sch., 1948; Ministry of Education: Asst Principal and Principal, 1949 (Jt Sec., Secondary Schs Examinations Council, 1956–57); Asst Sec. (also Dept of Educn and Science), 1963–73. *Publications:* occasional verse and contribs to journals. *Recreations:* journalism, writing verse. *Address:* 14 Blacksmiths Hill, Sanderstead, Surrey CR2 9AY. *T:* 01–657 1275.

RICHARDS, Lt-Gen. Sir John (Charles Chisholm), KCB 1980; HM Marshal of the Diplomatic Corps, since 1982; *b* 21 Feb. 1927; *s* of Charles C. Richards and Alice Milner; *m* 1953, Audrey Hidson; two *s* one *d. Educ:* Worksop Coll., Notts. Joined Royal Marines, 1945; 45 Commando, Malaya, 1950–52; HMS Birmingham, 1955–56; Canadian Army Staff Coll., 1959–61; 43 Commando, 1962–63; Naval staff, 1963–64; Instructor, Staff Coll., Camberley, 1965–67; 45 Commando: Aden, 1967; CO, 1968–69; GSO1 Plymouth Gp, 1969; CO 42 Commando, 1970–72; Chief of Staff, Brit. Def. Staff, Washington DC, UN Deleg., and Mem. Mil. Staff Cttee, 1972–74; Comdr 3rd Commando Bde, 1975–76; Comdt Gen., Royal Marines, 1977–81. Col Comdt, RM, 1987–. CBIM 1980. Freeman, City of London, 1982. *Recreations:* golf, gardening. *Address:* St James's Palace, SW1. *Club:* Army and Navy.

RICHARDS, John Deacon, CBE 1978; ARSA 1974; RIBA; PPRIAS; architect; Senior Consultant, Robert Matthew, Johnson-Marshall and Partners (Partner, 1964–86); *b* 7 May 1931; *s* of late William John Richards and Ethel Richards; *m* 1958, Margaret Brown, RIBA, ARIAS; one *s* three *d. Educ:* Geelong Grammar Sch., Vic.; Cranleigh Sch.; Architect. Assoc. Sch. of Arch., London (Dipl. 1954). RIBA 1955; FRIAS 1968 (PRIAS, 1983–85). RE, 1955–57. Buildings include: Stirling Univ., 1965–; Royal Commonwealth Pool, Edinburgh, 1970; airport terminals, Edinburgh and Aberdeen, 1977. Member: Royal Fine Art Commn for Scotland, 1975–; Bd, Housing Corp., 1982– (Chm., Scottish Cttee, 1982–). Mem., Agrément Bd, 1980–83. Trrustee, Nat. Galleries of Scotland, 1986–.

Hon. DUniv Stirling, 1976. Gold Medallist, RSA, 1972. *Recreation*: country life. *Address*: Lady's Field, Whitekirk, Dunbar, East Lothian EH42 1XS. *T*: Whitekirk 206. *Clubs*: Athenæum; Scottish Arts (Edinburgh).

RICHARDS, Rt. Rev. John Richards, DD (Lambeth); President, St David's University College, Lampeter, 1971–77; *b* 3 March 1901; *s* of Thomas and Elizabeth Richards, Llanbadarn, Fawr, Aberystwyth; *m* 1929, Katherine Mary (*d* 1980), *d* of W. E. and M. Hodgkinson, Inglewood, St Michael's, Tenterden; one *s* one *d*. *Educ*: Ardwyn School, Aberystwyth; Univ. College of Wales; St Michael's College Llandaff. BA 1922 (2nd Cl. Hons Mod. Langs); MA 1955; DD 1956. Deacon, 1924; priest, 1925; Curate of Pembrey w Burry Post, 1924–27; CMS missionary in Iran, 1927–45, at Shiraz, 1927–36, at Yezd, 1938–42, at Isfahan, 1942–45; Archdeacon in Iran, 1937–45. Mem. of Near East Christian Council, 1932–38; Hon. CF, Paiforce, 1942–45; Vicar of Skewen, 1945–52, Vicar of St Catherine, Pontypridd, 1952–54; Canon of St Andrew in Llandaff Cathedral, 1949–54; Dean of Bangor, 1955–56; Vicar of St James', Bangor, and Canon of Bangor Cathedral, 1954–55; Bishop of St David's, 1956–March 1971. Pantyfedwen Lectr, UC Swansea, 1972. Mem. of Governing Body of the Church in Wales, 1948–71. Chaplain and Sub-Prelate, Order of St John, 1961. Hon. LLD Wales, 1971. *Publications*: The Religion of the Baha'is, 1932; The Open Road in Persia, 1932; Baha'ism, 1965; Under His Banner, 1973; Jesus: Son of God and Son of Man, 1974. *Address*: Lluest Wen, Llanbadarn Road, Aberystwyth SY23 1EY.

RICHARDS, Michael; Director, Samuel Montagu & Co. Ltd, 1960–85; *b* 4 Oct. 1915; *s* of Frank Richards and Jenny Charlotte (*née* Levinsen); *m* 1942, Lucy Helen Quirey; three *d*. *Educ*: Roundhay High Sch., Leeds; Leeds Univ. (LLB). Solicitor, 1936. Partner, Ashurst, Morris Crisp & Co., Solicitors, City of London, 1936–54; Chm. and Man. Dir, Hart, Son & Co. Ltd, Merchant Bankers, 1954–60. Chm., Wood Hall Trust Ltd, 1950–82. *Recreations*: work, farming, collecting works of art. *Address*: Wood Hall, Shenley, Radlett, Herts. *T*: Radlett 6624.

RICHARDS, Michael Anthony, CBiol; FIBiol 1985; Chief Inspector, Cruelty to Animals Act (1876), Home Office, since 1982; *b* 12 Oct. 1926; *s* of Edward Albert Richards and Clara Muriel (*née* Webb); *m* 1956, Sylvia Rosemary, *d* of Geoffrey Charles Pain, JP; two *d*. *Educ*: St Albans Coll., St George's Coll., and J. M. Estrada Coll., all in Buenos Aires; Royal Vet. Coll., London Univ. MRCVS 1953. Served Army, Intell. Corps, 1945–47. In general practice, 1953; Lectr in Vet. Medicine, Univ. of London, 1963–67; Lectr in Vet. Pathology, Univ. of Edinburgh, 1967–69; Home Office, 1969–. *Publications*: scientific contribs to standard works and med. and vet. jls. *Recreation*: philately. *Address*: Home Office, 50 Queen Anne's Gate, SW1H 9AT. *T*: 01-213 6269. *Club*: Civil Service.

RICHARDS, Prof. Peter; Dean and Professor of Medicine, St Mary's Hospital Medical School, University of London, since 1979; *b* 25 May 1936; *s* of William and Barbara Richards; *m* 1959, Anne Marie Larsen (marr. diss. 1986); one *s* three *d*. *Educ*: Monkton Combe Sch.; Emmanuel Coll., Cambridge (BA 1957; MB BChir 1960; MA 1961; MD 1971); St George's Hosp. Medical Sch.; Royal Postgraduate Medical Sch. PhD London, 1966. FRCP. Consultant Physician, St Peter's Hosp., Chertsey and Hon. Sen. Lectr in Medicine, St Mary's Hosp. Med. Sch., 1970–73; Sen. Lectr in Medicine, St George's Hosp. Med. Sch., 1973–79. *Publications*: The Medieval Leper, 1977; (ed jtly) Clinical Medicine and Therapeutics, Vol. I, 1977, Vol. II, 1979; Understanding Water, Electrolyte and Acid/Base Metabolism, 1983; Learning Medicine, 1983, 2nd edn 1985; scientific papers esp. concerning kidney disease and criteria for selection of medical students in Lancet, BMJ, etc. *Recreations*: walking, listening to music, Finland, social history. *Address*: St Mary's Hospital Medical School, Paddington, W2 1PG. *Club*: Garrick.

RICHARDS, Sir Rex (Edward), Kt 1977; DSc Oxon 1970; FRS 1959; FRSC; Director, The Leverhulme Trust, since 1985; Chancellor, Exeter University, since 1982; *b* 28 Oct. 1922; *s* of H. W. and E. N. Richards; *m* 1948, Eva Edith Vago; two *d*. *Educ*: Colyton Grammar School, Devon; St John's College, Oxford. Senior Demy, Magdalen College, Oxford, 1946; MA; DPhil; Fellow, Lincoln College, Oxford, 1947–64, Hon. Fellow, 1968; Research Fellow, Harvard University, 1955; Dr Lee's Prof. of Chemistry, Oxford, 1964–70; Fellow, Exeter College, 1964–69; Warden, Merton Coll., Oxford, 1969–84, Hon. Fellow, 1984; Vice-Chancellor, Oxford Univ., 1977–81; Hon. Fellow, St John's Coll., Oxford, 1968; Associate Fellow, Morse Coll., Yale, 1974–79. Director: IBM-UK Ltd, 1978–83; Oxford Instruments Group, 1982–. Chm., BPMF, 1986–; Member: Chemical Society Council, 1957; Faraday Society Council, 1963; Royal Soc. Council, 1973–75; Scientific Adv. Cttee, Nat. Gall., 1978–; ABRC, 1980–83; ACARD, 1984–; Comr, Royal Comm for the Exhibition of 1851, 1984–; Trustee: CIBA Foundn, 1978–; Nat. Heritage Memorial Fund, 1980–84; Tate Gall., 1982–; Nat. Gall., 1982–. Tilden Lectr, 1962. Corday-Morgan Medal of Chemical Soc., 1954; Davy Medal, Royal Soc., 1976; Award in Theoretical Chemistry and Spectroscopy, Chem. Soc., 1977; Educn in Partnership with Industry or Commerce Award, DTI, 1982; Medal of Honour, Rheinische Friedrich-Wilhelms Univ., Bonn, 1983; Royal Medal, Royal Soc., 1986. FRIC 1970. Hon. DSc: East Anglia, 1971; Exeter, 1975; Leicester, 1978; Salford, 1979; Edinburgh, 1981; Leeds, 1984; Hon. LLD Dundee, 1977. *Publications*: various contributions to scientific journals. *Recreation*: 20th century painting and sculpture. *Address*: 13 Woodstock Close, Oxford OX2 8DB. *T*: Oxford 513621; 214 The Colonnades, Porchester Square, W2 6AS. *T*: 01-402 2955.

RICHARDS, (Richard) Alun; Welsh Secretary in charge of Welsh Office Agriculture Department, 1978–81; *b* 2 Jan. 1920; *s* of Sylvanus and Gwladys Richards, Llanbrynmair, Powys; *m* 1944, Ann Elonwy Mary (Nansi) Price, Morriston, Swansea; two *s*. *Educ*: Machynlleth County Sch.; Liverpool Univ. (BVSc, MRCVS, 1942). Veterinary Officer with State Vet. Service, Caernarfon and Glamorgan, 1943–57; Divl Vet. Officer, HQ Tolworth and in Warwick, 1957–65; Dep. Reg. Vet. Officer (Wales), 1965–67; seconded to NZ Govt to advise on control of Foot and Mouth disease, 1967–68; Reg. Vet. Officer, HQ Tolworth, 1968–71; Asst Chief Vet. Officer, 1971–77; Asst Sec., Welsh Dept, MAFF, 1977–78; Under-Sec., 1978. *Publications*: contrib. to vet. jls. *Recreations*: gardening, fishing, shooting. *Address*: Isfryn, Llandre, Aberystwyth, Dyfed. *T*: Aberystwyth 828246.

RICHARDS, Rt. Rev. Ronald Edwin, MA, ThD (*jure dig*); *b* Ballarat, Vic., 25 Oct. 1908; *s* of Edward and Margaret Elizabeth Richards, Ballarat; *m* 1937, Nancy, *d* of W. E. Lloyd Green; one *d*. *Educ*: Ballarat High Sch.; Trinity Coll., Melbourne Univ. BA 2nd Cl. Hons Phil., 1932, MA 1937; Asst Master, Ballarat C of E Gram. Sch., 1926, Malvern C of E Gram. Sch., 1927–28; deacon, 1932; priest, 1933; Curate of Rokewood, 1932–33, Priest-in-charge, 1934; Priest-in-charge, Lismore, 1934–41 and 1945–46; Chaplain AIF, 1941–45; Vicar of Warrnambool, 1946–50; Archdeacon of Ballarat, and Examining Chapl. to Bp of Ballarat, 1950–57; Vicar-Gen., 1952–57; Bishop of Bendigo, 1957–74. *Address*: Madron, 119 Dare Street, Ocean Grove, Victoria 3226, Australia. *Clubs*: Royal Automobile of Victoria (Melbourne); Barwon Heads Golf.

RICHARDSON, family name of **Barons Richardson** and **Richardson of Duntisbourne.**

RICHARDSON, Baron *cr* 1979 (Life Peer), of Lee in the County of Devon; **John Samuel Richardson,** 1st Bt, *cr* 1963; Kt 1960; LVO 1943; MD, FRCP; retired; President, General Medical Council, 1973–80; Hon. Consulting Physician: St Thomas' Hospital; King Edward VII's Hospital for Officers; Consultant Emeritus to the Army; Consulting Physician: Metropolitan Police, 1957–80; London Transport Board, since 1964; *b* 16 June 1910; *s* of Major John Watson Richardson, solicitor, and Elizabeth Blakeney, *d* of Sir Samuel Roberts, 1st Bt, both of Sheffield; *m* 1933, Sybil Angela Stephanie, *d* of A. Ronald Trist, Stanmore; two *d*. *Educ*: Charterhouse; Trinity Coll., Cambridge (Hon. Fellow, 1979). MB BChir 1936, MD 1940; MRCP 1937, FRCP 1948; FRCPE 1975. Major, RAMC (temp.), 1939; Lt-Col, RAMC (temp.), 1942. 1st asst, Med. Professorial Unit, St Thomas's Hosp., 1946; Physician to St Thomas's Hosp., 1947–75. Examiner to Univs of Cambridge, London, Manchester, NUI, RCP London and Edinburgh Conjoint Bd. President: Internat. Soc. of Internal Medicine, 1966–70 (Hon. Pres. 1970); Royal Soc. of Medicine, 1969–71 (Hon. Librarian, 1957–63; Pres., Med. Educn Sect., 1967–68); BMA, 1970–71; 2nd Congress, Assoc. Européene de Médicine Interne d'Ensemble, Bad-Godesberg, 1973 (Hon. Mem. 1974); Assoc. for the Study of Med. Educn, 1978–80 (Vice-Pres., 1974–78, Hon. Mem., 1980); Vice-President: Med. Soc. of London, 1961–63 (Hon. Fellow, 1981); Royal Coll. of Nursing, 1972–; Chairman: Jt Consultants Cttee, 1967–72; Council for Postgrad. Med. Educn in England and Wales, 1972–80; Medico-Pharmaceutical Forum, 1973–76; Armed Forces Med. Adv. Bd, MoD, 1975–80. Mem., Bd of Governors, St Thomas's Hosp., 1953–59, 1964–74. Mem. Ct, Soc. of Apothecaries, 1960–85 (Master, 1971–72). Lectures: Lettsomian, Med. Soc. of London, 1963; Scott Heron, Royal Victoria Hosp., Belfast, 1969; Maudsley, RCPsych, 1971; Wilkinson Meml, Inst. of Dental Surgeons, London Univ., 1976; Harveian Oration, RCP, 1978; Orator, Med. Soc. of London, 1981. Hon. Fellow: Swedish Soc. Med. Scis, 1970; RSocMed 1973; Heberden Soc., 1973; Osler Club of London, 1973; Hon. Mem., Assoc. of Clinical Tutors of GB, 1980; Hon. FPS, 1974; Hon. FRCPI 1975; Hon. FFCM 1977; Hon. FRCPsych 1979; Hon. FRCS 1980; Hon. FRCPSG 1980; Hon. FRCPE 1981. Hon. Bencher, Gray's Inn, 1974. Hon. DSc: NUI, 1975; Hull, 1981; Hon. DCL Newcastle, 1980; Hon. LLD: Nottingham, 1981, Liverpool, 1983. CStJ 1970. Baron de Lancey Law Prize, RSM, 1978; Gold Medal, BMA, 1982; Guthrie Medal, RAMC, 1982. Editor-in-Chief, British Encylopaedia of Medical Practice, 1970–74. *Publications*: The Practice of Medicine, 2nd edn 1960; Connective Tissue Disorders, 1963; Anticoagulant Prophylaxis and Treatment (jointly), 1965. *Heir* to baronetcy: none. *Address*: Windcutter, Lee, near Ilfracombe, North Devon EX34 8LW. *T*: Ilfracombe 63198.

RICHARDSON OF DUNTISBOURNE, Baron *cr* 1983 (Life Peer), of Duntisbourne in the County of Gloucestershire; **Gordon William Humphreys Richardson,** KG 1983; MBE 1944; TD 1979; PC 1976; DL; Chairman, Morgan Stanley International, since 1986; Governor, Bank of England, 1973–83, Member, Court of the Bank of England, 1967–83; *b* 25 Nov. 1915; *er s* of John Robert and Nellie Richardson; *m* 1941, Margaret Alison, *er d* of Canon H. R. L. Sheppard; one *s* one *d*. *Educ*: Nottingham High School; Gonville and Caius College, Cambridge (BA, LLB). Commnd S Notts Hussars Yeomanry, 1939; Staff Coll., Camberley, 1941; served until 1946. Called to Bar, Gray's Inn, 1946 (Hon. Bencher, 1973); Mem. Bar Council, 1951–55; ceased practice at Bar, Aug. 1955. Industrial and Commercial Finance Corp. Ltd, 1955–57; Director: J. Henry Schroder & Co., 1957; Lloyds Bank Ltd, 1960–67 (Vice-Chm., 1962–66); Legal and General Assurance Soc., Ltd, 1956–70 (Vice-Chm. 1959–70); Director: Rolls Royce (1971) Ltd, 1971–73; ICI Ltd, 1972–73; Chairman: J. Henry Schroder Wagg & Co. Ltd, 1962–72; Schroders Ltd, 1966–73; Schroders Inc. (NY), 1968–73. Chm., Industrial Develt Adv. Bd, 1972–73. Mem. Company Law Amendment Committee (Jenkins Committee), 1959–62; Chm. Cttee on Turnover Taxation, 1963. Chm., RIIA, 1984–. Member: Court of London University, 1962–65; NEDC, 1971–73, 1980–83; Trustee, National Gallery, 1971–73, Chm., Pilgrim Trust, 1984. One of HM Lieutenants, City of London, 1974–; High Steward of Westminster, 1985–; DL Glos, 1983. Deputy High Steward, Univ. of Cambridge, 1982; Hon. Fellow: Gonville and Caius Coll., 1977; Wolfson Coll., Cambridge, 1977. Hon. LLD Cambridge, 1979; Hon. DSc: City Univ., 1976; Aston, 1979; Hon. DCL East Anglia, 1984. Benjamin Franklin Medal, RSA, 1984. *Address*: c/o Morgan Stanley International Inc., Commercial Union Building, 1 Undershaft, Leadenhall Street, EC3P 3HB. *Clubs*: Athenæum, Brooks's.

See also Sir John Riddell, Bt.

RICHARDSON, Alexander Stewart, CBE 1943; BSc; *b* 17 May 1897; *e s* of late Alexander Stewart Richardson and Susan Hamilton Horsburgh; *m* 1931, Kathleen Margaret, *o d* of late Angus McColl, Inverness; one *s* one *d*. *Educ*: Edinburgh University. Military Service, 1916–19; Agricultural Officer, Tanganyika Territory, 1924; Senior Agricultural Officer, 1930; Deputy Director of Agriculture, Uganda, 1937; Director of Agriculture, Nyasaland, 1940–44; MLC 1940; Chairman Supply Board and Controller of Essential Supplies and Prices, 1941 and 1942; Controller of Production and Food, 1943. Member of Executive and Legislative Councils; Officer in general charge of Supplies, Prices and Distribution of Commodities; Uganda Govt Rep. on East African Production and Supply Council; Leader of East African Cotton deleg. to New Delhi, India, 1946; retired, 1947; Director of Agriculture, Uganda, 1944–47. *Recreations*: golf, shooting, fishing. *Address*: 24 Drummond Road, Inverness IV2 4NF. *T*: Inverness 233497.

RICHARDSON, Anthony; *see* Richardson, H. A.

RICHARDSON, Sir Anthony (Lewis), 3rd Bt *cr* 1924; *b* 5 Aug. 1950; *s* of Sir Leslie Lewis Richardson, 2nd Bt, and of Joy Patricia, Lady Richardson, *d* of P. J. Rillstone, Johannesburg; *S* father, 1985; *m* 1985, Honor Gillian Dauney. *Educ*: Diocesan College, Cape Town, S Africa. Stockbroker with L. Messel & Co., London, 1973–75; Insurance Broker with C. T. Bowring, London and Johannesburg, 1975–76; Stockbroker with Fergusson Bros, Hall, Stewart & Co., Johannesburg and Cape Town, 1976–78; Stockbroker with W. Greenwell & Co., London, 1979–81; with Rowe & Pitman, London, 1981. *Recreations*: various sports, photography. *Heir*: *b* Charles John Richardson, *b* 8 Dec. 1955. *Address*: c/o Potter Partners, 325 Collins Street, Melbourne, Victoria 3000, Australia. *Clubs*: Boodle's, Hurlingham.

RICHARDSON, Gen. Sir Charles (Leslie), GCB 1967 (KCB 1962; CB 1957); CBE 1945; DSO 1943; Member of the Army Board (Quartermaster General to the Forces, then Master-General of the Ordnance), 1965–71; *s* of late Lieutenant-Colonel C. W. Richardson, RA, and Mrs Richardson; *m* 1947, Audrey Styles (*née* Jorgensen); one *s* one *d* and one step *d*. *Educ*: Wellington College; Royal Military Acad., Woolwich (King's Medal); Cambridge Univ. (BA). Commissioned Royal Engineers, 1928; Exhibitioner, Clare College, Cambridge, 1930, 1st Cl. Hons Mech Sciences Tripos. Served France and Belgium, 1939–40; GSO1 Plans HQ, Eighth Army, 1942; BGS Eighth Army, 1943; Deputy Chief of Staff Fifth US Army, 1943; BGS Plans, 21st Army Group, 1944; Brigade Commander, 1953–54; Commandant, Royal Military College of Science, 1955–58; General Officer Commanding Singapore District, 1958–60; Director of Combat Development, War Office, 1960–61; Director-General of Military Training, 1961–63; General Officer Commanding-in-Chief, Northern Command, 1963–65; ADC (General) to the Queen, 1967–70; Chief Royal Engr, 1972–77. Col Comdt, RAOC, 1967–71.

Consultant, International Computers Ltd, 1971–76. Treasurer, Kitchener Nat. Meml Fund, 1971–81; Chm., Gordon Boy's Sch., 1977–. Legion of Merit (US), 1944. *Publication:* Flashback: a soldier's story, 1985. *Address:* The Stables, Betchworth, Surrey RH3 7AA. *Club:* Army and Navy.

See also J. B. W. McDonnell.

RICHARDSON, Brigadier (Retd) Charles Walter Philipps, DSO and Bar 1945; *b* 8 Jan. 1905; *s* of W. J. Richardson and E. C. Philipps; *m* 1st, 1932, Joan Kathleen Constance Lang (from whom he obtained a divorce, 1946); one *s*; 2nd, 1946, Hon. Mrs Averil Diana Going; one *s*. *Educ:* RNC Osborne and Dartmouth; RMC Sandhurst. 2nd Lieut KOSB, 1924; served in Egypt, China and India; Bde Maj. 52nd (Lowland) Div., 1942; Comdr 6th Bn KOSB 15th (Scottish) Div., 1944–46; Colonel 1946; Comdt, Tactical Wing, School of Infantry, Warminster, 1947–48; GSO(1) Singapore District, 1948–49 (despatches, Malaya, 1948); Deputy Comdt Malay Regt, 1949; Dir Amphibious Warfare Trg, 1951; Comdr 158 Inf. Bde (TA), 1952; Brig. 1952; Dep. Comdr Lowland District, 1955–57. Retired 1957. Order of Leopold and Belgian Croix de Guerre, 1945; King Haakon Victory Medal, 1945. *Recreations:* shooting, fishing. *Address:* Quintans, Steventon, Hants. *T:* Dummer 473.

RICHARDSON, David; Director, London Office, International Labour Organisation, since 1982; *b* 24 April 1928; *s* of Harold George Richardson and Madeleine Raphaële Richardson (*née* Lebret); *m* 1951, Frances Joan Pring; three *s* one *d*. *Educ:* Wimbledon Coll.; King's Coll., London (BA Hons). RAF, 1949. Unilever, 1951. Inland Revenue, 1953; Min. of Labour, 1956; Sec., Construction Industry Training Bd, 1964; Chm., Central Youth Employment Exec., 1969; Royal Coll. of Defence Studies, 1971; Under Sec., Dept of Employment, 1972; Dir, Safety and Gen. Gp, Health and Safety Exec., 1975; Dir and Sec., ACAS, 1977. *Recreations:* music, walking, landscape gardening. *Address:* 183 Banstead Road, Carshalton, Surrey. *T:* 01–642 1052. *Club:* Royal Air Force.

RICHARDSON, Air Marshal Sir (David) William, KBE 1986; Chief Engineer, Royal Air Force, since 1986; *b* 10 Feb. 1932; *s* of Herbert Cyril Richardson and Emily Lydia Richardson; *m* 1954, Mary Winifred Parker; two *s* one *d*. *Educ:* Southend Grammar Sch.; Birmingham Univ. (BSc Maths); Cranfield Inst. of Technology (MSc Eng). CEng, FIMechE, MRAeS. Joined RAF from Univ. Air Sqdn, 1953 and completed flying and technical trng; served in Fighter Comd before attending Staff Coll. 1964; Staff: HQ Middle East, 1965–67; HQ RAF Germany, 1969–71; CO, RAF Colerne, 1971–74; RCDS, 1974; AO Engrg and Supply, HQ NEAF, 1975; Dir, Engrg and Supply Policy, 1976–78; AO Engrg and Supply, HQ RAF Germany, 1978–81; AOC Maintenance Gp, RAF Support Comd, 1981–83; AO Engrg, RAF Strike Comd, 1983–86. *Publications:* contrib. RUSI Jl. *Recreation:* sailing. *Address:* c/o Lloyds Bank, Hull HU1 1XW. *Club:* Royal Air Force.

RICHARDSON, Sir Earl; see Richardson, Sir L. E. G.

RICHARDSON, Sir Egerton (Rudolf), OJ 1975; Kt 1968; CMG 1959; Permanent Representative of Jamaica to the United Nations, New York, since 1981; *b* 15 Aug. 1912; *s* of James Neil Richardson and Doris Adel (*née* Burton); *m*; one *s* one *d*. *Educ:* Calabar High School, Kingston, Jamaica; Oxford University. Entered Civil Service, 1933; Secretary Land Policy Co-ordinating Committee, 1943–53; Permanent Sec., Min. of Agric. and Lands, 1953–54; Under-Sec. Finance, 1954–56; on secondment, CO, London, 1953–54; Financial Secretary, Jamaica, 1956–62; Ambassador and Permanent Representative at UN, 1962–67; to USA, 1967–72; to Mexico, 1967–75; Permanent Sec., Min. of the Public Service, 1973–75. *Recreations:* swimming, golf, astronomy. *Address:* 215 E 68th Street, New York, NY 10021, USA.

RICHARDSON, Elliot Lee; Partner, Milbank, Tweed, Hadley & McCloy, Washington DC, since 1980; *b* 20 July 1920; *s* of Dr Edward P. and Clara Lee Richardson; *m* 1952, Anne F. Hazard; two *s* one *d*. *Educ:* Harvard Coll.; Harvard Law Sch. BA 1941, LLB 1947, *cum laude*. Served with US Army, 1942–45 (Lieut): litter-bearer platoon ldr, 4th Inf. Div., Normandy Landing (Bronze Star, Purple Heart). Law clerk, 1947–49; Assoc., Ropes, Gray, Best, Coolidge and Rugg, lawyers, Boston, 1949–53 and 1955–56; Asst to Senator Saltonstall, Washington, 1953 and 1954; Asst Sec. for Legislation of Dept of Health, Educn and Welfare, 1957–59 (Actg Sec., April-July 1958); US Attorney for Massachusetts, 1959–61; Special Asst to Attorney General of US, 1961; Partner, Ropes & Gray, 1961–62 and 1963–64; Lieut Governor of Mass, 1964; Attorney General of Mass, 1966; Under Sec. of State, 1969–70; Sec. of Health, Educn and Welfare, 1970–73; Sec. of Defense, Jan.-May 1973; Attorney General of US, May-Oct. 1973, resigned; Ambassador to UK, 1975–76; Sec. of Commerce, 1976–77; Ambassador-at-large and Special Rep. of the US Pres. to the Law of the Sea Conf., 1977–80. Fellow, Woodrow Wilson Internat. Center for Scholars, 1973–74. Holds numerous hon. degrees. *Publications:* The Creative Balance, 1976; numerous articles on law, social services and govt policy. *Address:* 1100 Crest Lane, McLean, Va 22101, USA.

RICHARDSON, Sir Eric; see Richardson, Sir J. E.

RICHARDSON, Maj.-Gen. Frank McLean, CB 1960; DSO 1941; OBE 1945; MD; Director Medical Services, BAOR, 1956–61; *b* 3 March 1904; *s* of late Col Hugh Richardson, DSO, and of Elizabeth Richardson; *m* 1944, Sylvia Innes, *d* of Col S. A. Innes, DSO; two *s* one *d*. *Educ:* Glenalmond; Edinburgh Univ. MB, ChB 1926. MD 1938. Joined RAMC, 1927; Captain 1930; Major 1936; Lt-Col 1945; Col 1949; Brig. 1956; Maj.-Gen. 1957. Honorary Surgeon to the Queen, 1957–61. Hon. Col 51 (H) Div. Dist RAMC, TA, 1963–67. Vice-Pres., Piobaireachd Soc. *Publications:* Napoleon: Bisexual Emperor, 1972; Napoleon's Death: An Inquest, 1974; Fighting Spirit: psychological factors in war, 1978; The Public and the Bomb, 1981; Mars without Venus: a study of some homosexual Generals, 1981. *Address:* c/o Royal Bank of Scotland, Kirkland House, SW1; 4B Barnton Avenue West, Edinburgh EH4 6DE.

RICHARDSON, George Barclay, CBE 1978; Fellow of St John's College, Oxford, since 1951; Secretary to the Delegates and Chief Executive of the Oxford University Press, since 1974; *b* 19 Sept. 1924; *s* of George and Christina Richardson; *m* 1957, Isabel Alison Chalk; two *s*. *Educ:* Aberdeen Central Secondary Sch. and other schs in Scotland; Aberdeen Univ.; Corpus Christi Coll., Oxford. BSc Physics and Maths, 1944 (Aberdeen); MA (Oxon) PPE 1949. Admty Scientific Res. Dept, 1944; Lieut, RNVR, 1945. Intell. Officer, HQ Intell. Div. BAOR, 1946–47; Third Sec., HM Foreign Service, 1949; Student, Nuffield Coll., Oxford, 1950; University Reader in Economics, 1969–73. Economic Advr, UKAEA, 1968–74. Member: Economic Develt Cttee for Electrical Engineering Industry, 1964–73; Monopolies Commn, 1969–74; Royal Commn on Environmental Pollution, 1973–74. Deleg., Oxford Univ. Press, 1971–74; Council, Publishers Assoc., 1981–. *Publications:* Information and Investment, 1960; Economic Theory, 1964; articles in academic jls. *Address:* Ridgeway, The Hill, Burford, Oxon. *Club:* United Oxford & Cambridge University.

RICHARDSON, George Taylor; President, James Richardson & Sons, Limited, Winnipeg, Canada, since 1966 (Vice-President 1954); Chairman, Richardson Greenshields of Canada Ltd; *b* 22 Sept. 1924; *s* of late James Armstrong Richardson and Muriel (*née* Sprague); *m* 1948, Tannis Maree Thorlakson; two *s* one *d*. *Educ:* Grosvenor Sch. and Ravenscourt Sch. Winnipeg; Univ. of Manitoba (BComm). Joined family firm of James Richardson & Sons Ltd, 1946. Chm. and Dir, Pioneer Grain Co. Ltd and of other cos owned by James Richardson & Sons Ltd; Director: Inco Ltd; United Canadian Shares Ltd; Canada Packers Inc. Member: Chicago Bd of Trade; Chicago Mercantile Exchange; Bd of Trade, Kansas City; Winnipeg Commodity Exchange. Hon. Dir, Canada's Aviation Hall of Fame. Hon. LLD Manitoba. *Recreations:* hunting, helicopter flying. *Address:* (business) James Richardson & Sons, Limited, Richardson Building, One Lombard Place, Winnipeg, Manitoba R3B 0Y1, Canada. *T:* 934–5811. *Clubs:* Manitoba, St Charles (Winnipeg); Vancouver (Vancouver); Toronto (Toronto).

RICHARDSON, Graham Edmund; Rector, Dollar Academy, Clackmannanshire, 1962–75; *b* 16 July 1913; *s* of H. W. Richardson, BSc, MIEE, AMIMechE, Studland, Dorset; *m* 1939, Eileen Cynthia, *d* of Lewis Beesly, FRCSE, Brightwalton, Newbury, Berks; one *s* one *d*. *Educ:* Tonbridge School; Strasbourg University; Queen's College, Oxford. Asst Master, Fettes College, Edinburgh, 1935–55; Housemaster, 1946–55; Headmaster, Melville College, Edinburgh, 1955–62. Mem., Scottish Adv. Cttee, IBA, 1968–73. *Recreations:* sailing, fishing, natural history. *Address:* Sunnyholme, Studland, Dorset.

RICHARDSON, (Henry) Anthony; a Recorder of the Crown Court, since 1978; barrister; *b* 28 Dec. 1925; *er s* of late Thomas Ewan Richardson and Jessie (*née* Preston), Batley, W Yorks; *m* 1954, Georgina (*née* Lawford), *d* of Rosamond Bedford and step *d* of Gp Captain G. R. Bedford, MB, ChB, RAF retd. *Educ:* Giggleswick Sch.; Leeds Univ. (LLB 1950, LLM 1956). Called to the Bar, Lincoln's Inn, 1951; North-Eastern Circuit; Dep. Circuit Judge, 1972–78. Chm., a Police Disciplinary Appeal Tribunal, 1983. *Publications:* articles in legal periodical. *Recreations:* walking, swimming, listening to music. *Address:* (home) Grey Thatch, Wetherby Road, Scarcroft, Leeds LS14 3BB. *T:* Leeds 892555; (chambers) 38 Park Square, Leeds LS1 2PA. *T:* Leeds 439422.

RICHARDSON, Horace Vincent, OBE 1968; HM Diplomatic Service, retired; *b* 28 Oct. 1913; *s* of late Arthur John Alfred Richardson and late Mrs Margaret Helena Jane Richardson (*née* Hooson); *m* 1942, Margery Tebbutt; two *s* one *d* (and one *d* decd). *Educ:* Abergele Grammar Sch.; King's Coll., London (LLB). Served with Army, 1940–45. LCC, 1931–35; Supreme Court of Judicature, 1935–47; FO, 1947–48; British Vice-Consul, Shanghai, 1948–50; Washington, 1950–53; 2nd Sec., Rome, 1953–56; FO, 1956–61; Consul, Philadelphia, 1961–63; FO, 1963–66; Consul, Cairo, 1966–68; 1st Sec., Washington, 1968–70; Head of Nationality and Treaty Dept, FCO, 1970–73. Rep. HM Govt at 9th and 10th Sessions of Hague Conf. of Private Internat. Law. *Recreations:* golf, gardening, tennis. *Address:* 34 Friern Barnet Lane, N11. *T:* 01–368 1983. *Clubs:* MCC, Civil Service; Turf (Cairo); Highgate Golf.

RICHARDSON, Hugh Edward, CIE 1947; OBE 1944; *b* 22 Dec. 1905; *s* of Hugh Richardson, DSO, MD, and Elizabeth (*née* McLean); *m* 1951, Huldah (*née* Walker), *widow* of Maj.-Gen. T. G. Rennie, Black Watch, killed in action 1945. *Educ:* Trinity College, Glenalmond; Keble College, Oxford (Hon. Fellow, 1981). Entered Indian Civil Service, 1930; SDO, Tamluk, Midnapore Dist, Bengal, 1932–34; entered Foreign and Political Service of Govt of India, 1934; APA Loralai, Baluchistan, 1934–35; British Trade Agent, Gyantse, and O-in-C British Mission, Lhasa, 1936–40; service in NWFP, 1940–42; 1st Sec. Indian Agency-General in China, Chungking, 1942–43; Dep. Sec. to Govt of India, EA Dept, 1944–45; British Trade Agent, Gyantse, and O-in-C, British Mission, Lhasa, 1946–47; Indian Trade Agent, Gyantse and Officer-in-charge, Indian Mission, Lhasa, 1947–50. Retd from ICS, 1950. Hon. FBA 1986. Hon. DLitt St Andrews, 1985. *Publications:* Tibet and its History, 1962; (with D. L. Snellgrove) A Cultural History of Tibet, 1968; A Corpus of Early Tibetan Inscriptions, 1985. *Recreation:* golf. *Address:* c/o Grindlay's Bank, 13 St James's Square, SW1. *Club:* Royal and Ancient Golf (St Andrews).

RICHARDSON, Ian; actor; *b* 7 April 1934; *s* of John Richardson and Margaret Drummond; *m* 1961, Maroussia Frank; two *s*. *Educ:* Tynecastle; Edinburgh; Univ. of Glasgow. Studied for stage at Coll. of Dramatic Art, Glasgow (James Bridie Gold Medal, 1957). FRSAMD 1971. Joined Birmingham Repertory Theatre Co. 1958 (leading parts incl. Hamlet); joined Shakespeare Meml Theatre Co. (later RSC), 1960; rôles, Stratford and Aldwych, 1960–: Arragon in Merchant of Venice; Sir Andrew Aguecheek, 1960; Malatesti in Duchess of Malfi, 1960; Oberon in A Midsummer Night's Dream, 1961; Tranio in Taming of the Shrew, 1961; the Doctor in The Representative, 1963; Edmund in King Lear, 1964; Antipholus of Ephesus in Comedy of Errors, 1964; Herald and Marat in Marat/Sade, 1964, 1965; Ithamore, The Jew of Malta, 1964; Ford, Merry Wives of Windsor, 1964, 1966, 1969; Antipholus of Syracuse in Comedy of Errors, 1965; Chorus, Henry V, 1965; Vindice, The Revengers Tragedy, 1965, 1969; Coriolanus, 1966; Bertram, All's Well That Ends Well, 1966; Malcolm, Macbeth, 1966; Cassius, Julius Caesar, 1968; Pericles, 1969; Angelo, Measure for Measure, 1970; Buckingham, Richard III, 1970; Proteus, Two Gentlemen of Verona, 1970; Prospero, The Tempest, 1970; Richard II/Bolingbroke, Richard II, 1973; Berowne, Love's Labour's Lost, 1973; Iachimo, Cymbeline, 1974; Shalimov, Summer Folk, 1974; Ford, Merry Wives of Windsor, 1975; Richard III, 1975; tours with RSC: Europe and USSR, NY, 1964; NY, 1965; USSR, 1966; Japan, 1970; NY, 1974, 1975; Tom Wrench in musical Trelawny, Sadler's Wells, 1971–72; Professor Higgins, My Fair Lady, Broadway, 1976 (Drama Desk Award, 1976); Jack Tanner, in Man and Superman, and Doctor in The Millionairess, Shaw Festival Theatre, Niagara, Ont; The Government Inspector, Old Vic, 1979; Romeo and Juliet, Old Vic, 1979; Lolita, Broadway, 1981. *Films:* Captain Fitzroy in The Darwin Adventure, 1971; Priest in Man of la Mancha, 1972; Montgomery in Ike—the War Years, 1978; Charlie Muffin, 1979; The Sign of Four, 1982; Hound of the Baskervilles, 1982; Brazil, 1984. *Television:* plays: Danton's Death, 1978; Churchill and the Generals, 1979; A Cotswold Death, Passing Through, 1981; Russian Night, Kisch-Kisch, Beauty and the Beast, Salad Days, 1982; Slimming Down, 1984; Star Quality, 1985; films: Monsignor Quixote, 1985; serials: Eyeless in Gaza, 1971; Tinker, Tailor, Soldier, Spy, 1979; Private Schulz, 1981; The Woman in White, 1982; The Master of Ballantrae, 1984; Six Centuries of Verse, 1984; Mistral's Daughter; Blunt; series: Ramsay Macdonald, in Number 10, 1982; Nehru, in Mountbatten—the last Viceroy, 1986. RTS Award, 1982. *Publication:* Preface to Cymbeline (Folio Soc.), 1976. *Recreations:* music, exploring churches and castles. *Address:* c/o London Management, Regent House, 235–241 Regent Street, W1. *T:* 01–493 1610. *Club:* Garrick.

RICHARDSON, Rt. Hon. Sir Ivor (Lloyd Morgan), Kt 1986; PC 1978; SJD; **Rt. Hon. Mr Justice Richardson;** Judge, Court of Appeal of New Zealand, since 1977; *b* 24 May 1930; *s* of W. T. Richardson; *m* 1955, Jane, *d* of I. J. Krchma; three *d*. *Educ:* Canterbury Univ. (LLB); Univ. of Mich (LLM, SJD). Partner, Macalister Bros, Invercargill, 1957–63; Crown Counsel, Crown Law Office, Wellington, 1963–66; Prof. of Law, Victoria Univ. of Wellington, 1967–73 (Dean of Law Faculty, 1968–71; Pro-Chancellor, 1979–84; Chancellor, 1984–86); Partner, Watts & Patterson, Wellington, 1973–77. Chm., Cttees of Inquiry into Inflation Accounting, 1975–76, into Solicitors Nominee Cos, 1983. Chm., Council of Legal Educn, 1983–. *Publications:* books and articles on legal subjects. *Address:* 29 Duthie Street, Wellington 5, New Zealand. *T:* 769–310. *Club:* Wellington (Wellington, NZ).

RICHARDSON, Hon. James Armstrong, PC (Can.); *b* Winnipeg, Manitoba, 28 March 1922; *s* of James Armstrong Richardson and Muriel Sprague; *m* 1949, Shirley Anne, *d* of John Rooper, Shamley Green, Surrey, England; two *s* three *d*. *Educ:* St John's-Ravenscourt, Winnipeg; Queen's Univ., Kingston, Ont. (BA). Pilot with No 10 BR Sqdn, before entering family firm of James Richardson & Sons, Ltd, Winnipeg, Oct. 1945; he was Chm. and Chief Exec. Officer of this company, but resigned to enter public life, 1968. MP (L), June 1968 (re-elected Oct. 1972, July 1974); Minister, Canadian Federal Cabinet, July 1968; Minister of Supply and Services, May 1969; Minister of Nat. Defence, 1972–76; resigned from Federal Cabinet over constitutional language issue, Oct. 1976; crossed floor of House to sit as an Independent MP, 27 June 1978. Chm., Westmead Ltd; Pres., Jarco Ltd; Director: James Richardson & Sons Ltd; Lombard Place Ltd. Director: Max Bell Foundn; Canada's America's Cup Challenge; Hon. Pres., Commonwealth Games Assoc. of Canada, Inc. *Address:* 5209 Roblin Boulevard, Winnipeg, Manitoba R3R 0G8, Canada.
See also G. T. Richardson.

RICHARDSON, Joanna, MA Oxon; FRSL; author; *o d* of late Frederick Richardson and late Charlotte Elsa (*née* Benjamin). *Educ:* The Downs School, Seaford; St Anne's College, Oxford. Mem. Council, Royal Soc. of Literature, 1961–86. Contributor, BBC. *Publications:* Fanny Brawne: a biography, 1952; Rachel, 1956; Théophile Gautier: his Life and Times, 1958; Sarah Bernhardt, 1959; Edward FitzGerald, 1960; The Disastrous Marriage: a Study of George IV and Caroline of Brunswick, 1960; (ed) FitzGerald: Selected Works, 1962; The Pre-Eminent Victorian: a study of Tennyson, 1962; The Everlasting Spell: a study of Keats and his Friends, 1963; (ed) Essays by Divers Hands (trans. Royal Soc. Lit.), 1963; introd. to Victor Hugo: Choses Vues (The Oxford Lib. of French Classics), 1964; Edward Lear, 1965; George IV: a Portrait, 1966; Creevey and Greville, 1967; Princess Mathilde, 1969; Verlaine, 1971; Enid Starkie, 1973; (ed and trans.) Verlaine, Poems, 1974; Stendhal: a critical biography, 1974; (ed and trans.) Baudelaire, Poems, 1975; Victor Hugo, 1976; Zola, 1978; Keats and his Circle: an album of portraits, 1980; (trans.) Gautier, Mademoiselle de Maupin, 1981; The Life and Letters of John Keats, 1981; Letters from Lambeth: the correspondence of the Reynolds family with John Freeman Milward Dovaston 1808–1815, 1981; Paris under Siege, 1982; Colette, 1983; Judith Gautier, 1986; The Brownings, 1986; contribs to The Times, The Times Literary Supplement, Sunday Times, Spectator, New Statesman, New York Times Book Review, The Washington Post, French Studies, French Studies Bulletin, Modern Language Review, Keats-Shelley Memorial Bulletin, etc. *Recreations:* antique-collecting, sketching. *Address:* 55 Flask Walk, NW3. *T:* 01–435 5156.

RICHARDSON, John David Benbow, MC 1942, and Bar 1943; President, Northern Rent Assessment Panel, since 1979 (Vice-President, 1968–79); *b* 6 April 1919; *s* of His Honour Judge Thomas Richardson, OBE, and Winifred Ernestine (*née* Templer); *m* 1946, Kathleen Mildred (*née* Price-Turner); four *s*. *Educ:* Harrow; Clare Coll., Cambridge. Called to Bar, Middle Temple, 1947. Served War of 1939–45, as Captain in King's Dragoon Guards (wounded; MC and Bar). ADC to Governor of South Australia (Lt-Gen. Sir Willoughby Norrie, later Lord Norrie), 1946–47. Dep. Chm., Durham County Quarter Sessions, 1964–71, and Recorder, 1972–73. Mem., Police Complaints Bd, 1977–82. *Recreations:* fishing, gardening, golf. *Address:* The Old Rectory, Whitfield, Hexham, Northumberland NE47 8JH. *T:* Whitfield 228. *Clubs:* MCC; York County Stand; Northern Counties (Newcastle upon Tyne).

RICHARDSON, Sir (John) Eric, Kt 1967; CBE 1962; PhD, DSc, BEng, CEng, FIEE, MIMechE, FBHI, FBOA, FPS; FRSA; Director, The Polytechnic of Central London, 1969–70; *b* 30 June 1905; *e surv. s* of late William and Mary Elizabeth Richardson, Birkenhead; *m* 1941, Alice May, *d* of H. M. Wilson, Hull; one *s* two *d* (and one *d* decd). *Educ:* Birkenhead Higher Elementary Sch.; Liverpool Univ. BEng 1st Cl. Hons, 1931, PhD 1933, Liverpool. Chief Lectr in Electrical Engineering, 1933–37, Head of Engineering Dept, 1937–41, Hull Municipal Technical Coll.; Principal: Oldham Municipal Technical Coll., 1942–44; Royal Technical Coll., Salford, 1944–47; Northampton Polytechnic, London, EC1, 1947–56; Dir Nat. Coll. of Horology and Instrument Technology, 1947–56; Dir of Educn, Regent Street Polytechnic, W1, 1957–69. Hon. Sec., Assoc. of Technical Insts, 1957–67, Chm., 1967–68; Pres. Assoc. of Principals of Technical Instns, 1961–62; Dep. Chm., Council for Overseas Colls of Arts, Science and Technology, 1949–62; Member: Council for Tech. Educn and Trng in Overseas Countries, 1962–73 (Chm. Technical Educn Cttee, 1971–73); and Vice-Chm. Council and Cttees, London and Home Counties Regional Adv. Council for Technol Educn, 1972–; Chm., Adv. Cttee on Educn for Management, 1961–66; Member: Governing Council of Nigerian Coll. of Art, Science and Technology, 1953–61; Council, Univ. Coll., Nairobi, 1961–70; Provisional Council, Univ. of East Africa, 1961–63; Governing Body, College of Aeronautics, Cranfield, 1956–59; Council of British Horological Institute, 1951–; Gen. Optical Council, 1959–78 (Chm., 1975–78); Assoc. of Optical Practitioners (Vice-Pres., 1983–84; Pres., 1984–); Science and Technol Cttee of CNAA, 1965–71; Electrical Engrg Bd of CNAA (Chm.); Industrial Trg Bd for Electricity Supply Industry, 1965–71; Univ. and Polytechnic Grants Cttee, Hong Kong, 1972–77; Council, RSA, 1968–78 (Chm. Exams Cttee, 1969–78, Hon. Treasurer, 1974–78); Council and Exec. Cttee, Leprosy Mission, 1970–84 (Chm., 1974–84; Vice-Pres., 1984–); Council and Exec. Cttee, City and Guilds of London Inst., 1969–80 (Chm. Policy and Overseas Cttees; Vice-Chm. Technical Educn Cttee; Jt Hon. Sec., 1970–80; Vice-Pres., 1979–82; Hon. FCGI 1981); Chm., Ealing Civic Soc., 1972–76. Chairman: Africa Evangelical Fellowship (SAGM), 1950–70; Nat. Young Life Campaign, 1949–64; Council, Inter-Varsity Fellowship of Evangelical Unions, 1966–69; President: Crusaders Union, 1972–; Governors of London Bible Coll., 1968– (Chm., 1970–77; Pres., 1978–); Chm., Governors, Clarendon Sch., Abergele, 1971–75. *Publications:* paper in IEE Jl (Instn Prize); various papers on higher technological education in UK and Nigeria. *Recreations:* gardening, photography. *Address:* 73 Delamere Road, Ealing, W5 3JP. *T:* 01–567 1588.

RICHARDSON, John Eric, MS; FRCS; Member, Medical Appeal Tribunal, since 1980; Surgeon: The London Hospital, 1949–81; The Royal Masonic Hospital, 1960–81; King Edward VII's Hospital for Officers, 1960–81; Prince of Wales Hospital, Tottenham, N15, 1958–65; former Consultant Surgeon to the Navy; *b* Loughborough, 24 February 1916; *s* of late C. G. Richardson, MD, FRCS; *m* 1943, Elisabeth Jean, *d* of late Rev. John Webster; one *s* one *d*. *Educ:* Clifton College; London Hospital. MB, BS London (Hons and Distinction, Pathology), 1939; MRCS, LRCP 1939. Andrew Clarke Prize, London Hosp., 1939. Resident Appointments, London Hospital and Poplar Hospital, 1939–41; Surgeon Lieut RNVR, HMS Prince of Wales (Surgical Specialist), 1941–46; Surgical Registrar, London Hosp., 1946–47; Rockefeller Travelling Fellow, 1947–48; Research Fellow in Surgery, Harvard Univ., 1947–48; Fellow in Clinical Surgery, Massachusetts Gen. Hosp., Boston, Mass, 1947–48. Surgeon, St Andrews Hosp., Dollis Hill, 1965–73. Hunterian Prof., RCS, 1953; Lettsomian Lectr, Med. Soc. of London, 1973. Pres., Med. Soc. of London, 1974–75. Examr in Surgery to Soc. of Apothecaries, London, 1959–67 and Univ. of London, 1962–63, 1965–66. Mem., Bd of Governors, London Hosp., 1964–73. *Publications:* contrib. to Lancet, BMJ and Brit. Jl of Surgery on gastro-enterology and endocrine disease. *Address:* Allen's Barn, Swinbrook, Oxon OX8 4EA. *T:* Burford 2456.

RICHARDSON, Ven. John Farquhar, MA; Archdeacon of Derby, 1952–73, now Emeritus; Chaplain to The Queen, 1952–76; First Residentiary Canon of Derby Cathedral 1954–73; *b* 23 April 1905; 2nd *s* of late William Henry Richardson and Gertrude Richardson (*née* Walker); *m* 1936, Elizabeth Mary, *d* of Henry Roy Dean; one *s* two *d*. *Educ:* Winchester; Trinity Hall, Cambridge; Westcott House, Cambridge. Curate of Holy Trinity, Cambridge, 1929–32; Chaplain of Repton School, 1932–35; Curate of St Martin-in-the-Fields, 1935–36; Vicar of Christ Church, Hampstead, 1936–41; Rector of Bishopwearmouth, 1941–52; Rural Dean of Wearmouth, 1947–52. Proctor in Convocation, 1950–52; Hon. Canon of Durham, 1951–52. Vice Chm., Trent Coll., 1972–82; Vice Provost, Midlands Div., Woodard Schs, 1971–80. *Recreation:* golf. *Address:* 474 Kedleston Road, Derby DE3 2NE. *T:* Derby 559135. *Clubs:* Royal Automobile; Jesters; Hawks (Cambridge).

RICHARDSON, John Flint; Chairman of Tyne and Wear County Council, 1976–77; *b* 5 May 1906; *s* of Robert Flint Richardson and Jane Lavinia; *m* 1932, Alexandra Graham; two *s*. *Educ:* Cone Street, South Shields. Councillor, 1938, Alderman, 1954, Mayor, 1960–61, South Shields; Freeman, South Shields, 1973. *Recreations:* serving people, reading.

RICHARDSON, John Francis; Director and Chief Executive, National & Provincial Building Society, 1985–86; *b* 16 June 1934; *s* of Francis and Stella Richardson; *m* 1960, Jacqueline Mary Crosby; two *d*. *Educ:* Wadham College, Oxford (PPE). FCBSI. Burnley Building Society, 1959–82; Chief General Manager, 1980–82; Dep. Chief Executive, National & Provincial Building Society, 1983–85. Pres., CBSI, 1985. *Recreations:* golf, gardening, military history. *Address:* Beckfield, Weeton, Leeds LS17 0AY. *T:* Harrogate 74388. *Club:* Pannal Golf.

RICHARDSON, Josephine, (Jo Richardson); MP (Lab) Barking, since Feb. 1974. Opposition spokesperson on women's rights, 1983–. Mem., Labour Party NEC, 1979–; a Vice President, Campaign for Nuclear Disarmament; Chairperson, Tribune Group, 1978–79 (Secretary, 1948–78; formerly Keep Left Group, then Bevan Group); Member: ASTMS; APEX. *Recreations:* politics, cooking. *Address:* House of Commons, SW1A 0AA. *T:* 01–219 5028.

RICHARDSON, Kenneth Albert; QC 1985; a Recorder of the Crown Court, since 1980; First Senior Prosecuting Counsel to the Crown at the Central Criminal Court, 1981–85; *b* 28 July 1926; *s* of Albert Robert Richardson and Ida Elizabeth Richardson (*née* Williams); *m* 1956, Dr Eileen Mary O'Cleary, Galway; two *s* one *d* (and one *s* decd). *Educ:* Ruthin Sch.; Merton Coll., Oxford. MA (in English and Jurisprudence). Called to the Bar, Middle Temple, 1952 (Harmsworth Scholar; Bencher, 1975). Commissioned RWF, 1945 (attached 8th Punjab Regt). Junior Prosecuting Counsel to the Crown, 1967–73; Senior Prosecuting Counsel to the Crown, 1973–81. Mem., Bar Council, 1972; Senate of the Inns and Bar, 1974–80. *Recreations:* skiing, golf, sailing, music. *Address:* Queen Elizabeth Building, Temple, EC4. *Clubs:* Blackheath FC; Vincent's (Oxford).

RICHARDSON, Sir (Lionel) Earl (George), Kt 1986; JP; Chairman, Masport Ltd, Auckland, New Zealand, since 1984; *b* 24 Nov. 1921; *s* of Lionel Harcourt Richardson and Doris Evelyn Richardson; *m* 1st, 1942, June Cecil Stretton (*d* 1984); two *d*; 2nd, 1985, Alison Valerie Langford. *Educ:* Seddon Memorial Coll.; Auckland Univ. ACA; FNZIM. Served War: NZ Army (Lieut), 1939–43; RNZN (Sub Lieut), on loan to RN, 1943–46. Dep. Man. Dir, 1946–73, Cons. and Co. Dir, 1973–, Holeproof (NZ) Ltd; Director: Bendon Industries Ltd; MacJays Ltd; Garman Holdings Ltd; First City Finance Ltd. President: Textile and Garment Fedn, 1973–76 (Life Mem.); NZ Manufrs' Fedn, 1982–85; Foundn Pres., Papatoetoe RSA; Life Mem., Papatoetoe and Dist RSA; Chm., Auckland Maritime Foundn; Founder, Half Moon Bay Marina, 1968. *Recreations:* golf, yachting. *Address:* 5 Shore Road, Reumera, Auckland, New Zealand. *T:* 505701. *Club:* Royal New Zealand Yacht Squadron (Auckland).

RICHARDSON, Group Captain Michael Oborne, RAF, retired; *b* Holmfirth, Yorks, 13 May 1908; *s* of Rev. Canon G. L. Richardson, MA, BD, and Edith Maria (*née* Ellison); *m* 1st, 1935, Nellie Marguerita (*d* 1974), *d* of Walter Ross Somervell, Elizavetgrad, Russia; one *s* one *d*; 2nd, 1979, Gwendolyn Oenone Jane Bevan, *e d* of William Stuart Rashleigh, JP, Menabilly and Stoketon, Cornwall. *Educ:* Lancing Coll.; Keble Coll., Oxford; Guy's Hospital. BA 1929; MRCS, LRCP 1938; DPH 1955; MA Oxon 1963; DPhysMed 1964. Oxford House, Bethnal Green, 1930. Commissioned RAF, 1939; served at Kenley; War Service included HQ Fighter Comd (Unit), S Africa, Western Desert, Malta, Sicily, Italy (despatches). Post-war service in Germany and Aden and comdt various hosps and Medical Rehabilitation Units; Commandant, Royal Star and Garter Home for Disabled Sailors, Soldiers and Airmen, 1967–73. OStJ 1965. *Recreation:* the countryside. *Address:* Tremethek, Penscott Lane, Tregorrick, St Austell, Cornwall. *T:* St Austell 63768. *Clubs:* Royal Air Force; Webbe.

RICHARDSON, Prof. Peter Damian, FRS 1986; Professor of Engineering and Physiology, Brown University, USA, since 1984; *b* West Wickham, Kent, 22 Aug. 1935; *s* of Reginald William Merrells Richardson and Marie Stuart Naomi (*née* Ouseley; now M. S. N. Moss). *Educ:* Imperial College, Univ. of London (BSc (Eng) 1955; PhD 1958; DSc (Eng) 1974; ACGI 1955; DIC 1958; DSc 1983); MA Brown Univ. 1965. Demonstrator, Imperial Coll., 1955–58; Brown University: Vis. Lectr, 1958–59; Research Associate, 1959–60; Asst Prof. of Engrg, 1960–65; Associate Prof. of Engrg, 1965–68; Prof. of Engrg, 1968–84; Vice-Chair, University Faculty, 1986–. Sen. Vis. Fellow, Univ. of London, 1967; Prof. d'échange, Univ. of Paris, 1968; leave at Orta Doğu Teknik Univ., Ankara, 1969. FASME 1983. Humboldt-Preis, A. von Humboldt Sen. Scientist Award, 1976. *Publications:* numerous articles in learned jls. *Recreations:* photography, travel, country life. *Address:* Box D, Brown University, Providence, Rhode Island 02912, USA. *T:* 010–1–401–863–2687.

RICHARDSON, Robert Augustus; HM Chief Inspector of Schools, Department of Education and Science, 1968–72; *b* 2 Aug. 1912; *s* of late Ferdinand Augustus Richardson and Muriel Emma Richardson; *m* 1936, Elizabeth Gertrude Williamson; one *d*. *Educ:* Royal College of Art. Schoolmaster, 1934; Headmaster, Sidcup School of Art, 1937. Served in Royal Navy, 1941–46. Principal: Folkestone Sch. of Art, 1946; Maidstone Coll. of Art, 1948. Dept of Education and Science: HM Inspector of Schools, 1958; HM Staff Inspector, 1966. ARCA 1934. *Recreations:* theatre, music. *Address:* Amber Cottage, Sigglesthorne, Hull, North Humberside. *T:* Hornsea 4596.

RICHARDSON, Rev. Canon Robert Douglas, DD, MLitt, MA; *b* 26 February 1893; *er s* of late Frederick Richardson; *m* 1929, Professor Linetta P. de Castelvecchio (*d* 1975). *Educ:* Hertford College and Ripon Hall, Oxford. Served European War, 1914–18, in RN; Curate of Stourport-on-Severn; Succentor of Birmingham Cathedral; Vicar of Four Oaks and Vicar of Harborne; Select Preacher, Cambridge University; Lectr, Univ. of Oxford; sometime External Lectr in Biblical Studies to Univ. of Birmingham; Examining Chaplain to Bishop of Birmingham, 1932–53; Canon Emeritus of Birmingham Cathedral;

Principal of Ripon Hall, Oxford, 1948–52; Rector of Boyton with Sherrington, 1952–67. *Publications:* The Conflict of Ideals in the Church of England, 1923; The Gospel of Modernism, 1933; Sectional Editor of Webster's Dictionary (1934 edn); A Revised Order of Holy Communion, 1936; Christian Belief and Practice, 1940; The Psalms as Christian Prayers and Praises, 1960; article on Luke and the Eucharistic Tradition, in Studia Evangelica, 1957, in The Gospels Reconsidered, 1960; Studies in the Origins of the Liturgy (publ. with Lietzmann's Studies in the History of the Liturgy in Mass and Lord's Supper), 1979; Christianity for To-day, 1986; contrib. to various theological jls. *Address:* Corton Parva, Warminster, Wilts. *T:* Warminster 50286.

RICHARDSON, Lt-Gen. Sir Robert (Francis), KCB 1982; CVO 1978; CBE 1975 (OBE 1971; MBE 1965); Administrator, MacRobert Trusts; General Officer Commanding Northern Ireland, 1982–85; *b* 2 March 1929; *s* of late Robert Buchan Richardson and Anne (*née* Smith); *m* 1956, Maureen Anne Robinson (*d* 1986); three *s* one *d*. *Educ:* George Heriot's Sch., Edinburgh; RMA Sandhurst. Commnd into The Royal Scots, 1949; served in BAOR, Korea, and Middle East with 1st Bn The Royal Scots until 1960; Defence Services Staff Coll., India, 1960–61; psc 1961; GSO II MO4, MoD, 1961–64; jssc 1964; Brigade Major Aden Bde, 1967 (Despatches); GSO II ACDS (Ops), MoD, 1968–69; CO 1st Bn The Royal Scots, 1969–71; Col Gen. Staff, Staff Coll. Camberley, 1971–74; Comdr 39 Infantry Bde, Northern Ireland, 1974–75; Deputy Adjutant General, HQ BAOR, 1975–78; GOC Berlin (British Sector), 1978–80; Vice Adjutant Gen. and Dir of Army Manning, 1980–82. Col, The Royal Scots (The Royal Regt), 1980–. *Recreations:* golf and other outdoor sports, gardening. *Address:* c/o Lloyds Bank, Cox's and King's Branch, 6 Pall Mall, SW1. *Clubs:* Caledonian; Royal Scots (Edinburgh), Hon. Co. of Edinburgh Golfers (Muirfield).

RICHARDSON, Ronald Frederick, CBE 1973 (MBE 1945); Deputy Chairman, Electricity Council, 1972–76; *b* 1913; *s* of Albert F. Richardson and Elizabeth Jane (*née* Sayer); *m* 1946, Anne Elizabeth McArdle; two *s*. *Educ:* Coopers' Company's School; Northampton Engineering Inst.; Polytechnic Inst.; Administrative Staff College. Served War of 1939–45: Major, Field Park Company RE, 1942–46. Callenders Cables, 1929–36; Central London Electricity, 1936–39, 1946–48; London Electricity Board, 1948–52; British Electricity Authority, 1952–57; South Western Electricity Board, 1957–63; Chm., North Western Electricity Board, 1964–71. Chm., Nat. Inspection Council for Electrical Installation Contracting, 1969–70; Dep. Chm., NW Regional Council, CBI, 1971; Member: North West Economic Planning Council, 1965–70; Adv. Council on Energy Conservation, 1974–76; (part-time): NCB, 1975–77; Electricity Council, 1976; Price Commn, 1977–79. Member: Court of Manchester Univ., 1969–71; Council, 1970–71, Court, 1970–, Salford Univ., 1970–74; Governor, William Temple Coll., 1971–74. *Recreations:* music, the open air. *Address:* 12 Ryecotes Mead, Dulwich Common, SE21 7EP.

RICHARDSON, Dr Sam Scruton, AO 1980; CBE 1965 (OBE 1960); Foundation Principal, Canberra College of Advanced Education, 1969–84, Emeritus Fellow, since 1984; *b* 31 Dec. 1919; *s* of Samuel and Gladys Richardson; *m* 1949, Sylvia May McNeil; two *s* one *d*. *Educ:* Magnus Sch., Newark-on-Trent; Trinity Coll., Oxford (State Scholarship, 1937; BA PPE, 1940; MA 1946); Sch. of Oriental and African Studies, Univ. of London. Called to the Bar, Lincoln's Inn, 1958. Served War, 1940–46: commnd Royal Marines; Commando Bdes, Europe and Far East (despatches); demob., Temp. Major, 1946. Dist Comr, Sudan Polit. Service, 1946–53 (served in Kordofan and Darfur Provinces); Resident, Dar Masalit, 1954; HMOCS, Nigeria, 1954–67: Dist Comr, Bornu Prov., 1954–58; Comr for Native Courts in Attorney Gen.'s Chambers, N Nigeria, 1958–60; Dir, Inst. of Admin, Zaria, 1960–67; Dep. Vice-Chancellor, Ahmadu Bello Univ., Nigeria, 1962–67; Prof. of Public Admin, Mauritius, 1967–68; occasional Lectr in Islamic Law, ANU, 1971–. Consultant: Aust. Law Reform Commn, 1980–; Museum of Australia, 1985–. Chm., Aust. Conf. of Principals, 1979–80; Pres., Internat. Assoc. of Schs and Insts of Admin, 1982–; Member: Academic Adv. Council, RAN Coll., Jervis Bay, 1978–84; Adv. Council, Aust. Jt Services Staff Coll., 1977–84; Inst. of Admin, Papua New Guinea, 1970–84; Council, ANU, 1981–84; Immigration Adv. Council, 1971–74; National Standing Control Cttee on Drugs of Dependence, 1974–84; Bd of Management, Aust. Inst. of Sport, 1980–84. Nat. Pres., Australia Britain Soc., 1980–84; Vice-Pres., Britain Australia Soc., 1984–. Hon. Fellow, Portsmouth Polytech., 1984. Hon. LLD Ahmadu Bello, 1967. *Publications:* Notes on the Penal Code of N Nigeria, 1959, 3rd edn 1967; (with T. H. Williams) The Criminal Procedure Code of N Nigeria, 1963; (with E. A. Keay) The Native and Customary Courts of Nigeria, 1965; Parity of Esteem—the Canberra College of Advanced Education 1968–78, 1979; regular book revs in Canberra Times, 1970–; articles on public admin, customary law and higher educn in learned jls. *Recreations:* travel, reading, community service. *Address:* The Malt House, Wylye, Wilts BA12 0QP. *T:* Wylye 348. *Clubs:* United Oxford & Cambridge University; University House (ANU, Canberra).

RICHARDSON, Sir Simon Alaisdair S.; *see* Stewart-Richardson.

RICHARDSON, Maj.-Gen. Thomas Anthony, (Tony), CB 1976; MBE 1960; Deputy Chairman, Tree Council, since 1984; Secretary, British Christmas Tree Growers Association, since 1980; *b* 9 Aug. 1922; *s* of late Maj.-Gen. T. W. Richardson, Eaton Cottage, Unthank Road, Norwich, and late Mrs J. H. Boothby, Camberley; *m* 1945, Katharine Joanna Ruxton Roberts, Woodland Place, Bath; one *s* one *d*. *Educ:* Wellington Coll., Berks. Technical Staff Course, psc, Fixed Wing Pilot, Rotary Wing Pilot, Parachutist. War of 1939–45: enlisted, Feb. 1941; commissioned, RA, March 1942; Essex Yeomanry (France and Germany), 1942–45; Air Observation Post, 1945–46. Tech. Staff/G Staff, 1949–52, 1954–55, 1959–60, 1963–64; Regt duty, 1942–45, 1952–54, 1957–58, 1961–62. Instr, Mil. Coll. Science, 1955–56; CO, 7th Para, RHA, 1965–67; CRA, 2 Div., 1967–69; Dir, Operational Requirements (Army), 1969–71; Dir, Army Aviation, 1971–74; Defence and Military Advr, India, 1974–77. Col Comdt, RA, 1978–83. Sec., Timber Growers England and Wales Ltd, 1980–84 (Asst Sec., 1978–80). *Recreations:* sailing, skiing, fishing, shooting. *Address:* 12 Lauriston Road, Wimbledon, SW19 4TQ. *Club:* Army and Navy.

RICHARDSON, Thomas Legh; HM Diplomatic Service; Head of Economic Relations Department, Foreign and Commonwealth Office, since 1986; *b* 6 Feb. 1941; *s* of Arthur Legh Turnour Richardson and Penelope Margaret Richardson; *m* 1979, Alexandra Frazier Wasiqullah (*née* Ratcliff). *Educ:* Westminster Sch.; Christ Church, Oxford. MA (Hist.). Joined Foreign Office, 1962; seconded to Univ. of Ghana, 1962–63; FO, 1963–65; Third Sec., Dar-Es-Salaam, 1965–66; Vice-Consul (Commercial), Milan, 1967–70; seconded to N. M. Rothschild & Sons, 1970; FCO, 1971–74; First Sec., UK Mission to UN, 1974–78; FCO, 1978–80; seconded to Central Policy Review Staff, Cabinet Office, 1980–81; Head of Chancery, Rome, 1982–86. *Recreations:* reading, walking, travel, music. *Address:* c/o Foreign and Commonwealth Office, SW1. *Club:* United Oxford & Cambridge University.

RICHARDSON, Maj.-Gen. Tony; *see* Richardson, Maj.-Gen. Thomas A.

RICHARDSON, Tony; Director, Woodfall Film Productions Ltd, since 1958; *b* 5 June 1928; *s* of Clarence Albert and Elsie Evans Richardson; *m* 1962, Vanessa Redgrave, *qv* (marr. diss., 1967); two *d*. *Educ:* Wadham College, Oxford. Associate Artistic Dir, English Stage Co., Royal Court Theatre, 1956–64. *Plays directed or produced:* Look Back in Anger, 1956; The Chairs, 1957; Pericles and Othello (Stratford), 1958; The Entertainer, 1958; A Taste of Honey, NY, 1961; Luther, 1961; Semi-Detached, 1962; Arturo Ui, 1963; Natural Affection, 1963; The Milk Train Doesn't Stop Here Any More, 1963; The Seagull, 1964; St Joan of the Stockyards, 1964; Hamlet, 1968; The Threepenny Opera, Prince of Wales, 1972; I Claudius, Queen's, 1972; Antony and Cleopatra, Bankside Globe, 1973; Lady from the Sea, New York, 1977; As You Like It, Los Angeles, 1979. *Films directed or produced:* Look Back in Anger, 1958; The Entertainer, 1959; Saturday Night and Sunday Morning (prod), 1960; Taste of Honey, 1961; The Loneliness of the Long Distance Runner (prod and dir.), 1962; Tom Jones (dir.), 1962; Girl with Green Eyes (prod), 1964; The Loved One (dir.), 1965; Mademoiselle (dir.), 1965; The Sailor from Gibraltar (dir.), 1965; Red and Blue (dir.) 1966; The Charge of the Light Brigade (dir.), 1968; Laughter in the Dark (dir.), 1969; Hamlet (dir.), 1969; Ned Kelly (dir.), 1969; A Delicate Balance, 1972; Dead Cert, 1974; Joseph Andrews, 1977; A Death in Canaan, 1978; The Border, 1981; The Hotel New Hampshire, 1983. *Recreations:* travel, tennis, birds, directing plays and films. *Address:* 1478 North King's Road, Los Angeles, Calif 90069, USA.

RICHARDSON, Air Marshal Sir William; *see* Richardson, Air Marshal Sir D. W.

RICHARDSON, William, CBE 1981; DL; CEng; FRINA; Chairman: Vickers Shipbuilding and Engineering Ltd, 1976–83 (Managing Director, 1969–76); Vosper Thornycroft (UK) Ltd, 1978–83; Barclay Curle Ltd, 1978–83; Brook Marine Ltd, 1981–83; Member Board, British Shipbuilders (from incorporation), 1977–83, Deputy Chairman 1981–83; Director, Vickers Cockatoo Dockyard Pty Ltd, Australia, 1977–84; *b* 15 Aug. 1916; *s* of Edwin Richardson, marine engr, and Hannah (*née* Remington); *m* 1941, Beatrice Marjorie Iliffe; one *s* one *d*. *Educ:* Ocean Road Boys' Sch., Walney Is, Barrow-in-Furness; Jun. Techn. and Techn. Colls, Barrow-in-Furness (part-time). HNC (Dist.) Naval Architecture; HNC (1st Cl.) Mech. Engrg. CBIM 1981 (FBIM 1977); FInstD 1977–83. Vickers Ltd, Barrow-in-Furness: Shipbldg Apprentice, 1933–38; Techn. Dept, 1938–39; Admiralty Directorate of Aircraft Maintenance and Repair, UK and Far East, 1939–46; Vickers Ltd Barrow Shipyard: Techn. Depts, 1946–51; Asst Shipyard Manager, 1951–60; Dockside Outfitting Man., 1960–61; Dep. Shipyard Man., 1961–63; Shipyard Man., 1963–64; Dir and Gen. Man., 1964–66; Dir and Gen. Man., Vickers Ltd Naval Shipyard, Newcastle upon Tyne, 1966–68; Dep. Man. Dir, Swan Hunter & Tyne Shipbldrs Ltd, 1968–69. Director: Slingsby Sailplanes, 1969–70 (co. then incorp. into Vickers Ltd); Vickers Oceanics, 1972–77; Chm., Clark & Standfield (subsid. of Vickers Gp), 1976–83; Dir, Vosper Shiprepairers, 1978–82. Dir of Trustees, 1976–, Mem. Res. Council and Office Bearer, 1976–78, BSRA; Mem. Exec. Council, 1969–77, Chm. Management Bd, 1976–78, SRNA; Pres. Brit. Productivity Assoc., Barrow and Dist, 1969–72; Shipbldg Ind. Rep., DIQAP, 1972–82; Mem., Shipbuilding Industry Trng Bd, 1979–82; Mem., NE Coast IES, 1967–. FRINA 1970 (ARINA 1950, MRINA 1955). Liveryman, Shipwrights' Co., 1978. DL Cumbria, 1982. Queen's Silver Jubilee Medal, 1977. *Publications:* papers on various aspects of UK shipbldg industry; contribs to techn. jls. *Recreations:* sailing, small-bore shooting, golf, fishing. *Address:* Hobroyd, Pennybridge, Ulverston, Cumbria LA12 7TD. *T:* Greenodd 86 226. *Clubs:* Grange-over-Sands Golf, National Small-Bore Rifle Association.

RICHARDSON, William Eric, CEng, FIEE, FBIM; Chairman, South Wales Electricity Board, 1968–77; Member, Electricity Council, 1968–77; retired 1977; *b* 21 May 1915; *o s* of William Pryor and Elizabeth Jane Richardson, Hove, Sussex; *m* (she *d* 1975); one *s*; *m* 1976, Barbara Mary Leech. *Educ:* Royal Masonic Sch., Bushey. Engineer with Brighton Corp., 1934–37; Southampton Corp., 1937–39; Norwich Corp., 1939–46; Distribution Engr with Newport (Mon) Corp., 1946–48; Area Engr with S Wales Electricity Bd, 1948–57; Area Manager, 1957–65; Chief Commercial Engr, 1965–67; Dep. Chm., 1967–68. *Recreations:* sailing, golf, gardening. *Address:* Beaumont, 92 Allt-yr-yn Avenue, Newport, Gwent. *T:* Newport (Gwent) 64388.

RICHARDSON-BUNBURY, Sir (Richard David) Michael, *see* Bunbury.

RICHES, Sir Derek (Martin Hurry), KCMG 1963 (CMG 1958); Ambassador to Lebanon, 1963–67, retired; *b* 26 July 1912; *s* of late Claud Riches and Flora Martin; *m* 1942 Helen Barkley Hayes, Poughkeepsie, NY, USA; one *d*. *Educ:* University College School; University College, London. Appointed Probationer Vice-Consul, Beirut, Dec. 1934. Subsequently promoted and held various appts, Ethiopia and Cairo; Foreign Office, 1944; promoted one of HM Consuls serving in FO, 1945. Kabul, 1948 (in charge, 1948 and 1949); Consul at Jedda, 1951 (Chargé d'Affaires, 1952); Officer Grade 6, Branch A, Foreign Service and apptd Trade Comr, Khartoum, 1953. Attached to Imperial Defence College, 1955; returned to Foreign Office, 1955; Counsellor in the Foreign Office, Head of Eastern Department, 1955; British Ambassador in Libya, 1959–61; British Ambassador to the Congo, 1961–63. *Address:* 48 The Avenue, Kew Gardens, Surrey.

RICHES, Sir Eric (William), Kt 1958; MC; MS (London), FRCS; Emeritus Surgeon and Urologist to Middlesex Hospital; Hon. Consultant Urologist to Hospital of St John and St Elizabeth; formerly Consulting Urologist to the Army and to Ministry of Pensions Spinal Injury Centre; lately Urologist, St Andrew's Hospital, Dollis Hill; lately Urologist, Royal Masonic Hospital; Hon. Curator, Historical Surgical Instruments Collection, Royal College of Surgeons, 1962; *b* Alford, Lincolnshire, 29 July 1897; *s* of William Riches; *m* 1st, 1927, Annie M. S. (*d* 1952), *d* of late Dr A. T. Brand, Driffield, E Yorks; two *d*; 2nd, 1954, Susan Elizabeth Ann, *d* of late Lt-Col L. H. Kitton, MBE, MC; one *d*. *Educ:* Christ's Hospital; Middlesex Hospital. Served European War, 10th Lincoln and 11th Suffolk Regt, Capt. and Adjutant (MC); Senior Broderip Scholar and Lyell Gold Medallist, Middlesex Hospital, 1925. Past Vice-President, Royal College of Surgeons, Member of Court of Examiners, 1940–46; Hunterian Professor 1938 and 1942, Jacksonian Prizeman, 1942; Bradshaw Lecturer, 1962; Gordon-Taylor Lecturer, 1967. Hon. Fellow Royal Society of Medicine, 1966, lately Hon. Librarian, ex-President Clinical Section, Section of Urology, and Section of Surgery. Past-President Medical Society of London; Lettsomian Lecturer, 1958, Orator, 1970; Senior Fellow Association of Surgeons of Great Britain and Ireland; Past President Hunterian Society, Orator, 1967; Vice-President, Internat. Soc. of Urology (Pres. XIII Congress, 1964); Hon. Fellow and Past Pres. of British Assoc. of Urological Surgeons; St Peters medallist, 1964; Member Association Française d'Urologie; Honorary Member: Urological Society of Australasia; Canadian Urological Assoc.; Swedish Urological Soc.; American Urological Assoc.; American Assoc. of Genito-Urinary Surgeons; Ramon Guitéras Lectr, 1963; Hon. Associate Mem. French Academy of Surgery, 1961; Emeritus Mem. Internat. Soc. of Surgery; Past Treas. British Journal of Surgery; Past Chm., Ed. Cttee, British Jl of Urology; Mem. of Biological and Medical Cttee, Royal Commission on Population. Visiting Professor, Urol.; University of Texas and State University of New York, 1965; Visiting Professor and Balfour Lecturer, University of Toronto, 1966. Treasurer, Christ's Hospital, and Chm., Council of Almoners, 1970–76. *Publications:* Modern Trends in Urology, Series 1, 1953, Series 2, 1960, Series 3, 1969; Tumours of the Kidney and Ureter, 1964; various articles on Surgery and Urology in Scientific journals; contributor to Text Book of Urology, British Surgical Practice, and to Encyclopædia of Urology. *Recreations:* golf, music, photography. *Address:* 23 Eresby House, Rutland Gate, SW7 1BG. *T:* 01–589 7129.

See also Rev. Canon J. F. Hester.

RICHES, General Sir Ian (Hurry), KCB 1960 (CB 1959); DSO 1945; *b* 27 Sept. 1908; *s* of C. W. H. Riches; *m* 1936, Winifred Eleanor Layton; two *s*. *Educ:* Univ. Coll. Sch., London. Joined Royal Marines, 1927; Major, 1946; Lt-Colonel, 1949; Colonel, 1953; Maj.-Gen., 1957; Lt-Gen., 1959; General, 1961. Maj.-Gen., RM, Portsmouth Group, 1957–59; Commandant-General, Royal Marines, 1959–62; Regional Dir of Civil Defence, 1964–68; Representative Col Comdt, 1967–68. *Address:* 34 Cheriton Road, Winchester, Hants.

RICHES, Rt. Rev. Kenneth, DD, STD; Assistant Bishop of Louisiana, USA, 1976–77; *b* 20 Sept. 1908; *s* of Capt. A. G. Riches; *m* 1942, Kathleen Mary Dixon, JP 1964; two *s* one *d*. *Educ:* Royal Gram. Sch., Colchester; Corpus Christi Coll., Cambridge. Curate of St Mary's, Portsea, 1932–35; St John's, East Dulwich, 1935–36; Chaplain and Librarian, Sidney Sussex Coll., Cambridge, 1936–42; Examining Chaplain to Bishops of Bradford and Wakefield, 1936; Editorial Sec., Cambridgeshire Syllabus, 1935; Editor, Cambridge Review, 1941–42; Rector of Bredfield with Boulge, Suffolk, and Dir of Service Ordination Candidates, 1942–45; Principal of Cuddesdon Theological Coll., Oxford, and Vicar of Cuddesdon, 1945–52; Hon. Canon of Portsmouth Cathedral, 1950–52; Bishop Suffragan of Dorchester, Archdeacon of Oxford and Canon of Christ Church, 1952–56; Bishop of Lincoln, 1956–74. Select Preacher: University of Cambridge, 1941, 1948, 1961, and 1963; University of Oxford, 1954–55. Mem. Archbishops' Commission on Training for the Ministry, 1942; Sec. of Theol. Commn on the Church of Faith and Order Movement. Visiting Lecturer the General Theological Seminary, New York, 1956 and 1962. Hon. Fellow: Sidney Sussex Coll., Cambridge, 1958; Lincoln Coll., Oxford, 1975; Corpus Christi Coll., Cambridge, 1975. Chm., Central Advisory Council for the Ministry, 1959–65. *Recreations:* gardening, antiques, and country life. *Address:* Little Dingle, Dunwich, Saxmundham, Suffolk. *T:* Westleton 316.

RICHINGS, Lewis David George; *b* 22 April 1920; *s* of Lewis Vincent Richings and Jessie Helen (*née* Clements); *m* 1944, Margaret Alice Hume; three *d*. *Educ:* Battersea Grammar Sch.; Devonport High Sch.; Darlington Grammar Sch.; London Sch. of Econs and Polit. Science (part-time). Served War, Army, 1939–46: commnd 2 Lieut Inf., 1940; attached 8 DLI, 1940–41; seconded 11 KAR, 1941–45; Actg Major, 1945; various postings, UK, 1945–46. MAFF, 1937–58; attached MoD, 1958; Gen. Administrator, AWRE, 1958–65; Health and Safety Br., UKAEA, 1965–70; Sec., Nat. Radiol Protection Bd, 1970–79, Dep. Dir, 1978–80. Mem., Radiol Protection and Public Health Cttee, Nuclear Energy Agency, OECD, 1966–80 (Chm., 1972–74). FRSA. *Publications:* articles in press and jls on admin and technical matters relating to common land, rural electrification, earthquakes, and radiol protection. *Recreation:* boats. *Address:* 2873 Nepean Highway, Blairgowrie, Vic 3942, Australia; 28 Endymion Road, N4 1EE.

RICHLER, Mordecai; author; *b* 27 Jan. 1931; *s* of late Moses Isaac Richler and Lily Rosenberg; *m* 1960, Florence Wood; three *s* two *d*. *Educ:* Sir George Williams Univ., Montreal (left without degree). Writer-in-residence, Sir George Williams Univ., 1968–69; Vis. Prof., English Dept, Carleton Univ., Ottawa, 1972–74. Edit. Bd, Book-of-the-Month Club, NY. Canada Council Senior Arts Fellowship, 1960; Guggenheim Fellowship, Creative Writing, 1961; Governor-General's Award for Literature, 1969 and 1972; Paris Review Humour Prize, 1969. *Publications: novels:* The Acrobats, 1954; A Choice of Enemies, 1955; Son of a Smaller Hero, 1957; The Apprenticeship of Duddy Kravitz, 1959, repr. 1972 (filmed, Golden Bear Award, Berlin Film Fest., 1974; Writers Guild of America Annual Award, 1974; Academy Award nomination, 1974); The Incomparable Atuk, 1963; Cocksure, 1968; St Urbain's Horseman, 1971; Joshua Then and Now, 1980 (filmed, 1985); *essays:* Hunting Tigers Under Glass, 1969; Shovelling Trouble, 1973; Home Sweet Home, 1984; *autobiography:* The Street, 1972; *children's book:* Jacob Two-Two Meets the Hooded Fang, 1975; *anthology:* (ed) The Best of Modern Humour, 1983; contrib. Encounter, Commentary, New York Review of Books, etc. *Recreations:* poker, snooker. *Address:* Apt 80C, 1321 Sherbrooke Street W, Montreal, Quebec H3G 1J4, Canada. *T:* 514–288–2008.

RICHMAN, Stella; Chairman, White Elephant Club Ltd, since 1960; *b* 9 Nov. 1922; *d* of Jacob Richman and Leoni Richman; *m* 1st, Alec Clunes; 2nd, 1953, Victor Brusa (*d* 1965); one *s* one *d*. *Educ:* Clapton County Secondary Sch. for Girls. Started TV career at ATV, running Script Dept 1960; created and produced Love Story, 1963; joined Rediffusion, 1964; Exec. Head of Series (prod The Informer); Exec. Prod., award-winning Man of Our Times, Half Hour Story and Blackmail; prod first 6 plays, Company of Five, for newly formed London Weekend Television, 1968; Man. Dir, London Weekend Internat., 1969, and Controller of Programmes, London Weekend Television, 1970–71 (first woman to sit on bd of a television co.); in partnership with David Frost formed Stella Richman Productions, 1972–78: resp. for Miss Nightingale, Jennie, Clayhanger, Bill Brand, Just William. FRTS 1982. *Publications:* The White Elephant Cook Books, 1973, 1979. *Recreations:* travel, wine, herb growing, reading biographies. *Address:* 28 Curzon Street, W1Y 8EA. *Club:* White Elephant (owner).

RICHMOND, 9th Duke of, *cr* 1675, **AND GORDON,** 4th Duke of, *cr* 1876; **Frederick Charles Gordon-Lennox;** Earl of March, Baron Settrington, Duke of Lennox, Earl of Darnley, Baron Methuen, 1675; Earl of Kinrara, 1876; Duke d'Aubigny (France), 1683–84; Hereditary Constable of Inverness Castle; Flight Lieut, RAFVR; *b* 5 Feb. 1904; *o* surv. *s* of 8th Duke and Hilda, DBE, *d* of late Henry Arthur Brassey, Preston Hall, Kent; *S* father, 1935; *m* 1927, Elizabeth Grace, *y d* of late Rev. T. W. Hudson; two *s*. *Educ:* Eton; Christ Church, Oxford. *Heir:* *s* Earl of March, *qv*. *Address:* Carne's Seat, Goodwood, Chichester, W Sussex; 29 Hyde Park Street, W2.

See also Sir Alastair Coats, Bt, Lord N. C. Gordon Lennox, C. G. Vyner.

RICHMOND, Archdeacon of; *see* McDermid, Ven. N. G. L. R.

RICHMOND, Sir Alan (James), Kt 1969; engineering consultant, expert witness and arbitrator; *b* 12 Oct. 1919. Trained and employed Engineering Industry, 1938–45; London Univ., BSc(Eng) 1945, PhD 1954; Lecturer, Battersea Polytechnic, 1946–55; Head of Engineering Dept, Welsh Coll. of Advanced Technology, 1955–58; Principal, Lanchester College of Technology, Coventry, 1959–69; Director, Lanchester Polytechnic, 1970–71; Principal, Strode Coll., Street, 1972–81; Associate Tutor, Further Education Staff Coll., Blagdon, Bristol, 1982–85. FIMechE; FCIArb. Hon. DSc CNAA, 1972. *Publications:* (with W. J. Peck) Applied Thermodynamics Problems for Engineers, 1950; Problems in Heat Engines, 1957; various lectures, reviews and articles. *Recreations:* gardening, reading. *Address:* Juglans, 9 Springfield Drive, Wedmore, Som. *T:* Wedmore 712829. *Club:* Royal Commonwealth Society.

RICHMOND, Rear-Adm. Andrew John; Assistant Chief of Defence Staff (Logistics), since 1985 and Chief Naval Supply and Secretariat Officer, since 1986; *b* 5 Nov. 1931; *s* of Albert George Richmond and Emily Margaret (*née* Denbee); *m* 1957, Jane Annette (*née* Ley); one *s* two *d*. *Educ:* King's School, Bruton; Nautical College, Pangbourne. Joined RN 1950; staff of C-in-C East Indies, 1953; flying training, 1955; Cyprus 847 Sqdn, 1956; HMS Victorious 824 Sqdn, 1958; staff of FO Arabian Sea, 1960; BRNC Dartmouth, 1963; Sec., FO Carriers and Amphibious Ships, 1968; Supply School, HMS Pembroke, 1970; Fleet Supply Officer, 1974; Asst Dir Naval Manpower, 1976; Sec., C-in-C Naval Home Comd, 1977; Captain, HMS Cochrane, 1979; Dir, Naval Logistic Planning, 1982. *Recreations:* home, gardening, golf. *Address:* c/o Royal Bank of Scotland, South Street, Chichester, West Sussex. *Clubs:* Royal Commonwealth Society; Goodwood Golf.

RICHMOND, Rt. Hon. Sir Clifford (Parris), PC 1973; KBE 1977; Kt 1972; Judge of the Court of Appeal of New Zealand, 1972–81, President, 1976–81; *b* 23 June 1914; *s* of Howard Parris Richmond, QC, and Elsie Wilhelmina (*née* MacTavish); *m* 1938, Valerie Jean Hamilton; two *s* one *d*. *Educ:* Wanganui Collegiate Sch.; Victoria and Auckland Univs. LLM (1st cl. Hons). Served War of 1939–45: 4 Field Regt 2NZEF, North Africa and Italy, 1942–45 (despatches, 1944). Partner, legal firm, Buddle Richmond & Co., Auckland, 1946–60. Judge of the Supreme Court of New Zealand, 1960–71. *Recreations:* golf, fishing. *Address:* 21 McFarlane Street, Mount Victoria, Wellington, New Zealand. *T:* 846–974. *Club:* Wellington (NZ).

RICHMOND, Rt. Rev. Francis Henry Arthur; *see* Repton, Bishop Suffragan of.

RICHMOND, Prof. John, MD, FRCP, FRCPE; Professor of Medicine, since 1973, Chairman, Academic Division of Medicine, 1978–85, Honorary Director of Cancer Research, since 1983, and Dean of Medicine and Dentistry, since 1985, University of Sheffield; *b* 30 May 1926; *er s* of late Hugh Richmond and Janet Hyslop Brown; *m* 1951, Jenny Nicol, 2nd *d* of T. Nicol; two *s* one *d*. *Educ:* Doncaster Grammar Sch.; Univ. of Edinburgh. MB, ChB 1948 (with Distinction in Medicine); MD 1963. FRCPE 1963, FRCP 1970. House Officer, in Edinburgh hosps and Northants, 1948–49, 1952–54; RAMC, Military Mission to Ethiopia, Captain 1st Bn King's African Rifles, N Rhodesia, 1949–50; Rural Gen. Practice, Galloway, Scotland, 1950–52; Res. Fellow, Meml Sloan Kettering Cancer Center, New York, 1958–59; Sen. Lectr, later Reader in Medicine, Univ. of Edinburgh, 1963–73. Censor, 1981–82, Sen. Vice-Pres. and Sen. Censor, 1984–85, RCP; Chm., MRCP (UK) Part 2 Examining Bd. Mem., Sheffield HA, 1982–84. High Constables of Edinburgh, 1961–70. *Publications:* Mem. Editorial Bd and contribs, A Companion to Medical Studies, ed R. Passmore and J. S. Robson, vols I-III; contribs: Davidson's Principles and Practice of Medicine, ed J. G. Macleod; Abdominal Operations, ed Rodney Maingot; (jtly) The Spleen, 1973; papers in med. jls mainly on haematology and oncology. *Recreations:* gardening, photography. *Address:* Stumper Lea, 42 Stumperlowe Hall Road, Sheffield S10 3QS. *T:* Sheffield 301395.

RICHMOND, Sir John (Christopher Blake), KCMG 1963 (CMG 1959); retired; *b* 7 September 1909; *s* of E. T. Richmond, FRIBA, and M. M. Richmond (*née* Lubbock); *m* 1939, D. M. L. Galbraith; two *s* three *d*. *Educ:* Lancing College; Hertford College, Oxford; University College, London. Various archaeological expeditions, 1931–36; HM Office of Works, 1937–39; served War, Middle East, 1939–46; Dept of Antiquities, Palestine Govt, 1946–47; HM Diplomatic Service, Baghdad, 1947; Foreign Office, 1951; Counsellor, British Embassy, Amman, 1953–55; HM Consul-General, Houston, Texas, 1955–58; Foreign Office, 1958–59; Counsellor, British Property Commission, Cairo, 1959; HM Ambassador to Kuwait, 1961–63 (Political Agent, Kuwait, 1959–61); Supernumerary Fellow of St Antony's College, Oxford, 1963–64; Ambassador to Sudan, 1965–66; Lectr, Modern Near East History, Sch. of Oriental Studies, Univ. of Durham, 1966–74. *Publication:* Egypt 1798–1952, 1977. *Address:* 21 The Avenue, Durham City DH1 4ED.

RICHMOND, Sir John (Frederick), 2nd Bt, *cr* 1929; *b* 12 Aug. 1924; *s* of Sir Frederick Henry Richmond, 1st Bt (formerly Chm. Debenham's Ltd and Harvey Nichols & Co. Ltd), and Dorothy Agnes (*d* 1982), *d* of Frances Joseph Sheppard; *S* father 1953; *m* 1965, Mrs Anne Moreen Bentley; one *d*. *Educ:* Eton; Jesus Coll., Cambridge. Lt 10th Roy. Hussars; seconded Provost Br., 1944–47. *Address:* Shimpling Park Farm, Bury St Edmunds, Suffolk. *Club:* MCC.

RICHMOND, Sir Mark (Henry), Kt 1986; PhD, ScD; FRCPath; FRS 1980; Vice-Chancellor, and Professor of Molecular Microbiology, Victoria University of Manchester, since 1981; *b* 1 Feb. 1931; *s* of Harold Sylvester Richmond and Dorothy Plaistowe Richmond; *m* 1958, Shirley Jean Townrow; one *s* two *d*. *Educ:* Epsom College; Clare Coll., Cambridge. BA, PhD, ScD. Scientific Staff, MRC, 1958–65; Reader in Molecular Biology, Univ. of Edinburgh, 1965–68; Prof. of Bacteriology, Univ. of Bristol, 1968–81. Member: Bd, PHLS, 1976–85; Fulbright Commn, 1980–84; SERC, 1981–85; Chm., British Nat. Cttee for Microbiol., 1980–85; Member: Genetic Manipulation Adv. Gp 1976–84; Adv. Cttee on Genetic Manipulation, 1984–85. Member: IBM Academic Adv. Bd, 1984–; Knox Fellowship Cttee, 1984–; CIBA-Geigy Fellowship Trust, 1984–; Jarrett Cttee for University Efficiency, 1985. *Publications:* several in microbiology and biochemistry jls. *Recreation:* hill-walking. *Address:* Victoria University of Manchester, Oxford Road, Manchester M13 9PL. *Club:* Athenæum.

RICHNELL, Donovan Thomas, CBE 1973; Director General, British Library Reference Division, 1974–79; *b* 3 Aug. 1911; *o s* of Thomas Hodgson Richnell and Constance Margaret Richnell (*née* Allen); *m* 1957, Renée Norma Hilton; one *s* one *d*. *Educ:* St Paul's School; Corpus Christi Coll., Cambridge; University Coll., London (Fellow 1975). BA, FLA. Sub-Librarian, Royal Soc. Med., 1946–49; Dep. Librarian, London Univ. Library, 1949–60; Librarian, Univ. of Reading, 1960–67; Dir, and Goldsmiths' Librarian, Univ. of London Library, 1967–74. Library Association: Mem. Council, 1962–; President 1970; Hon. Fellow 1979; Chm. of Council, Aslib, 1968–70. Member: Library Adv. Council for England, 1966–71, 1974–77; British Library Organising Cttee, 1971–73; Adv. Cttee for Scientific and Technical Information, 1970–74; British Library Bd, 1974–79; Chm., Standing Conf. of Nat. and Univ. Libraries, 1973–75. Hon. DLitt Loughborough, 1977. *Address:* 2 Queen Anne's Gardens, Bedford Park, W4.

RICHTER, Prof. Burton; Paul Pigott Professor in the Physical Sciences, Stanford University, USA, since 1980 (Professor of Physics, since 1967), and Director, Stanford Linear Accelerator Center, since 1984 (Technical Director, 1982–84); *b* 22 March 1931; *s* of Abraham Richter and Fannie Pollack; *m* 1960, Laurose Becker; one *s* one *d*. *Educ:* Massachusetts Inst. of Technology. BS 1952, PhD (Physics) 1956. Stanford University: Research Associate, Physics, High Energy Physics Lab., 1956–60; Asst Prof., 1960–63; Associate Prof., 1963–67; full Prof., 1967. E. O. Lawrence Award, 1975; Nobel Prize for Physics (jointly), 1976. *Publications:* over 180 articles in various scientific journals. *Address:* Stanford Linear Accelerator Center, PO Box 4349, Stanford University, Stanford, California 94305, USA.

RICHTER, Sviatoslav; Hero of Socialist Labour, 1975; pianist; *b* Zhitomir, Ukraine, 20 March 1915; *m* Nina Dorliak. *Educ:* Moscow State Conservatoire. Gave first piano recital at age of nineteen and began to give concerts on a wide scale in 1942. Appeared at the Royal Albert Hall and the Royal Festival Hall, London, 1961; Royal Festival Hall, 1963, 1966, 1977, 1979. Was recently awarded Lenin Prize, and also holds the title of "Peoples'

Artist of the USSR"; Order of Lenin, 1965. *Recreations:* walking, ski-ing and painting. *Address:* c/o Victor Hochhauser Ltd, 4 Holland Park Avenue, W11.

RICKARD, Prof. Peter, DPhil, PhD, LittD; Drapers Professor of French, University of Cambridge, 1980–82, Emeritus since 1983; Fellow of Emmanuel College, Cambridge, 1953, Professorial Fellow, 1980, Life Fellow, since 1983; *b* 20 Sept. 1922; *yr s* of Norman Ernest Rickard and Elizabeth Jane (*née* Hosking); unmarried. *Educ:* Redruth County Grammar Sch., Cornwall; Exeter Coll., Oxford (Pt I Hons Mod. Langs (French and German), Cl. I, 1942; Final Hons Cl. I, 1948; MA 1948). DPhil Oxon 1952; PhD Cantab 1952; LittD Cambridge 1982. Served War, 1st Bn Seaforth Highlanders and Intell. Corps, India, 1942–46. Heath Harrison Travelling Scholar (French), 1948; Amelia Jackson Sen. Scholar, Exeter Coll., Oxford, 1948–49; Lectr in Mod. Langs, Trinity Coll., Oxford, 1949–52; Univ. of Cambridge: Asst Lectr in French, 1952–57, Lectr, 1957–74; Reader in French Lang., 1974–80; Mem., St John's Coll., 1952–; Tutor, Emmanuel Coll., 1954–65. *Publications:* Britain in Medieval French Literature, 1956; La langue française au XVIe siècle, 1968; (ed with T. G. S. Combe) The French Language: studies presented to Lewis Charles Harmer, 1970; (ed and trans.) Fernando Pessoa, Selected Poems, 1971; A History of the French Language, 1974; Chrestomathie de la langue française au XVe siècle, 1976; (ed with T. G. S. Combe) L. C. Harmer, Uncertainties in French Grammar, 1979; The Embarrassments of Irregularity, 1981; articles in Romania, Trans Phil Soc., Neuphilologische Mitteilungen, Cahiers de Lexicologie, and Zeitschrift für Romanische Philologie. *Recreations:* travel, photography, music. *Address:* Emmanuel College, Cambridge CB2 3AP. *T:* Cambridge 334223; Upper Rosevine, Portscatho, Cornwall. *T:* Portscatho 582.

RICKETS, Brig. Reginald Anthony Scott, (Tony); Managing Director, Irvine Development Corporation, since 1981; Vice-President, 1985, and President, 1986, Ayrshire Chamber of Industries (Director, since 1981); *b* 13 Dec. 1929; *s* of Captain R. H. Rickets and Mrs V. C. Rickets (*née* Morgan) *m* 1952, Elizabeth Ann Serjeant; one *s* one *d*. *Educ:* St George's Coll., Weybridge; RMA Sandhurst. 2nd Lieut, RE, 1949; served with airborne, armoured and field engrs in UK, Cyrenaica, Egypt, Malaya, Borneo, Hong Kong and BAOR; special employment military forces Malaya, 1955–59; Staff Coll., Camberley, 1962; BM Engr Gp, BAOR, 1963–66; OC 67 Gurkha Indep. Field Sqn, 1966–68; DS Staff Coll., 1968–70; Comdt Gurkha Engrs/CRE Hong Kong, 1970–73; COS British Sector, Berlin, 1973–77; Col GS RSME, 1977–78; Chief Engr UKLF, 1978–81. *Recreation:* sailing (DTI Ocean skipper and RYA coach/examiner). *Address:* Irvine Development Corporation, Perceton House, Irvine, Ayrshire, Scotland. *Clubs:* Naval and Military; Royal Engineer Yacht (Commodore, 1979–81; Rear Commodore, 1984–).

RICKETT, Sir Denis Hubert Fletcher, KCMG 1956 (CMG 1947); CB 1951; Director: Schroder International, 1974–79; De La Rue Co., 1974–77; Adviser, J. Henry Schroder Wagg & Co., 1974–79; *b* 27 July 1907; *s* of late Hubert Cecil Rickett, OBE, JP; *m* 1946, Ruth Pauline (MB, BS, MRCS, LRCP), *d* of late William Anderson Armstrong, JP; two *s* one *d*. *Educ:* Rugby School; Balliol College, Oxford (Schol. 1925; Jen Ryns Exhibnr 1929; 1st cl. Hons Mods 1927; 1st cl. Lit.Hum. 1929). Fellow of All Souls College, Oxford, 1929–49. Joined staff of Economic Advisory Council, 1931; Offices of War Cabinet, 1939; Principal Private Secretary to Right Honourable Oliver Lyttelton, when Minister of Production, 1943–45; Personal Assistant (for work on Atomic Energy) to Rt Hon. Sir John Anderson, when Chancellor of the Exchequer, 1945; transferred to Treasury, 1947; Principal Private Secretary to the Rt Hon. C. R. Attlee, when Prime Minister, 1950–51; Economic Minister, British Embassy, Washington, and Head of UK Treasury and Supply Delegation, 1951–54; Third Secretary, HM Treasury, 1955–60, Second Secretary, 1960–68. Vice-Pres., World Bank, 1968–74. *Recreations:* music, travel. *Address:* 9 The Close, Salisbury, Wilts. *Clubs:* Athenæum, Brooks's.

RICKETT, Dr Raymond Mildmay Wilson, CBE 1984; BSc, PhD, CChem, FRSC; Director, Middlesex Polytechnic, since 1972; *b* 17 March 1927; *s* of Mildmay Louis Rickett and Winifred Georgina Rickett; *m* 1958, Naomi Nishida; one *s* two *d*. *Educ:* Faversham Grammar Sch.; Medway Coll. of Technology (BSc London); Illinois Inst. of Technology (PhD). Royal Navy, 1946–48; Medway Coll. of Technology, 1953–55; Illinois Inst. of Technology, 1955–59; Plymouth Coll. of Technology, 1959; Lectr, Liverpool Coll. of Technology, 1960–62; Senr Lectr/Principal Lectr, West Ham Coll. of Technology, 1962–64; Head of Dept, Wolverhampton Coll. of Technology, 1965–66; Vice-Principal, Sir John Cass Coll., 1967–69; Vice-Provost, City of London Polytechnic, 1969–72. Chm., Cttee of Dirs of Polytechnics, 1980–82 and 1986–; Chm., UK Nat. Commn for UNESCO Educn Adv. Cttee; Member: Higher Educn Review Group for NI; IUPC; Cttee for Internat. Cooperation in Higher Educn; Working Group, Management of Higher Educn (Oakes Cttee); Educnl Credit Transfer Steering Cttee, DES; Council for Industry and Higher Educn; CNAA Adv. Bd for Credit Accumulation Scheme; NAB Bd for PSHE; Hong Kong 2nd Polytechnic Sub-Cttee; Open University Council; SE Regional Adv. Council for Tech. Educn; Governor, Yehudi Menuhin Live Music Now Scheme; Pres., N London English-Speaking Union. *Publications:* Experiments in Physical Chemistry (jtly), 1962, new edn 1968; 2 chapters in The Use of the Chemical Literature, 1962, new edn 1969; articles on Polytechnics in the national press and contribs to learned jls. *Recreations:* cricket, theatre-going, opera. *Address:* Principal's Lodge, Trent Park, Cockfosters Road, Barnet, Herts EN4 0PS. *T:* 01–449 9012.

RICKETTS, Maj.-Gen. Abdy Henry Gough, CBE 1952; DSO 1945; DL; *b* 8 Dec. 1905; *s* of Lt-Col P. E. Ricketts, DSO, MVO, and L. C. Ricketts (*née* Morant); *m* 1932, Joan Warre, *d* of E. T. Close, Camberley; one *s* one *d*. *Educ:* Winchester. Sandhurst, 1924; Durham LI, 1925; Shanghai Defence Force, 1927; NW Frontier, India (medal and clasp), 1930; Burma "Chindit" campaign, 1944–45; Gen. Service Medal and clasp, Malaya, 1950; comd British Brigade, Korea, 1952; Comdr (temp. Maj.-Gen.), Cyprus District, 1955–56. Col, Durham LI, 1965–68; Dep. Col, The Light Infantry (Durham), 1968–70. DL Somerset, 1968. Officer, Legion of Merit (USA), 1953. *Address:* The Old Rectory, Pylle, Shepton Mallet, Som. *T:* Ditcheat 248. *Club:* Army and Navy.

RICKETTS, (Anne) Theresa, (Lady Ricketts), CBE 1983; Chairman, National Association of Citizens' Advice Bureaux, 1979–84; *b* 12 April 1919; *d* of late Rt Hon. Sir (Richard) Stafford Cripps, CH, FRS, QC, and Dame Isobel Cripps, GBE; *m* 1945, Sir Robert Ricketts, Bt, *qv*; two *s* two *d*. *Educ:* Oxford University. Second Officer, WRNS, War of 1939–45. Joined Citizens' Advice Bureaux Service, 1962. Member: Electricity Consumers' Council, 1977–; Council, Direct Mail Services Standards Board, 1983–. *Recreations:* gardening, field botany. *Address:* Forwood House, Minchinhampton, Stroud, Glos GL6 9AB. *T:* Brimscombe 882160. *Club:* Royal Commonwealth Society.

See also Sir J. S. Cripps.

RICKETTS, Michael Rodney, MA; Headmaster, Sutton Valence School, 1967–80; *b* 29 Sept. 1923; *er s* of late Rt Rev. C. M. Ricketts, Bishop of Dunwich, and Dorothy Ricketts; *m* 1958, Judith Anne Caroline Corry; two *s* two *d*. *Educ:* Sherborne; Trinity Coll., Oxford. Served War of 1939–45: in 8th Army with 60th Rifles, 1942–47. Trinity Coll., Oxford, 1947–50; Asst Master and Housemaster, Bradfield Coll., 1950–67. *Recreations:* cricket, shooting, country activities. *Address:* Church Farm, Saxlingham, Holt, Norfolk. *T:* Binham 307. *Clubs:* East India, Devonshire, Sports and Public Schools, MCC.

RICKETTS, Sir Robert (Cornwallis Gerald St Leger), 7th Bt, *cr* 1828; retired Solicitor; *b* 8 Nov. 1917; *s* of Sir Claude Albert Frederick Ricketts, 6th Bt, and Lilian Helen Gwendoline (*d* 1955), *o d* of Arthur M. Hill, late 5th Fusiliers; *S* father 1937; *m* 1945, Anne Theresa Cripps (*see* A. T. Ricketts); two *s* two *d*. *Educ:* Haileybury; Magdalene College, Cambridge (2nd Cl. Hons in History and Law, BA 1939, MA 1943). Served War of 1939–45 (Captain, Devon Regiment); Personal Assistant to Chief of Staff, Gibraltar, 1942–45; ADC to Lieutenant-Governor of Jersey, 1945–46. Formerly Partner in Wellington and Clifford. FRSA. Hon. Citizen, Mobile, USA, 1970. *Heir:* *s* Robert Tristram Ricketts [*b* 17 April 1946; *m* 1969, Ann, *yr d* of late E. W. C. Lewis, CB; one *s* one *d*]. *Address:* Forwood House, Minchinhampton, Stroud, Glos GL6 9AB. *TA* and *T:* Brimscombe 882160.

See also G. F. P. Mason.

RICKETTS, Theresa; *see* Ricketts, A. T.

RICKFORD, Jonathan Braithwaite Keevil; Solicitor, Department of Trade and Industry, since 1985; *b* 7 Dec. 1944; *s* of R.B.K. Rickford, *qv*; *m* 1968, Dora R. Sargant; one *s* two *d*. *Educ:* Sherborne School; Magdalen College, Oxford (BA (Jurisp.); BCL). Barrister at Law. Teaching Associate, Univ. of California Sch. of Law, 1968–69; Lectr in Law, LSE, 1969–72; Legal Asst, Dept of Trade, 1972–73; Senior Legal Assistant: Dept of Prices and Consumer Protection, 1974–76; Law Officers' Dept, Attorney General's Chambers, 1976–79; Dept of Trade and Industry (formerly Dept of Trade): Asst Solicitor (Company Law), 1979–82; Under Sec. (Legal), 1982–85. *Publications:* articles in learned jls. *Recreation:* sailing. *Address:* 42 Half Moon Lane, SE24. *T:* 01–693 3998. *Club:* Royal Dart Yacht.

RICKFORD, Richard Braithwaite Keevil, MD (London), BS, FRCS, FRCOG; Consulting Physician, Obstetric Department, St Thomas' Hospital, London, 1979–85 (Physician, 1946–79); Consulting Surgeon, Chelsea Hospital for Women, 1979–85 (Surgeon, 1950–79); Gynæcologist, Oxted Hospitals, 1952–82; formerly Dean, Institute of Obstetrics and Gynaecology; *b* 1 June 1914; *e s* of late L. T. R. Rickford; *m* 1939, Dorothy, *d* of late Thomas Lathan; three *s* (and one *s* decd). *Educ:* Weymouth College; University of London. Various surgical, obstetric and gynæcological appointments at Norfolk and Norwich Hospital and St Thomas' Hospital. Examiner to: Universities of London, Cambridge and Glasgow; Royal Coll. of Obstetricians and Gynæcologists; Conjoint Board; Central Midwives Board. *Publications:* contributions to medical journals. *Recreations:* gardening, sailing. *Address:* Kingswear Lodge, Kingswear, Devon TQ6 0BS. *T:* Kingswear 361. *Club:* Royal Dart Yacht (Kingswear, Devon).

See also J. B. K. Rickford.

RICKS, Prof. Christopher Bruce, FBA 1975; Professor of English, Boston University, since 1986; *b* 18 Sept. 1933; *s* of James Bruce Ricks and Gabrielle Roszak; *m* 1st, 1956, Kirsten Jensen (marr. diss.); two *s* two *d*; 2nd, 1977, Judith Aronson; one *s* two *d*. *Educ:* King Alfred's Sch., Wantage; Balliol Coll., Oxford. 2nd Lieut, Green Howards, 1952. BA 1956, BLitt 1958, MA 1960, Oxon. Andrew Bradley Jun. Res. Fellow, Balliol Coll., Oxford, 1957; Fellow of Worcester Coll., Oxford, 1958–68; Prof. of English, Bristol Univ., 1968–75; University of Cambridge: Prof. of English, 1975–82; King Edward VII Prof. of English Lit., 1982–86; Fellow, Christ's Coll., 1975–86. Visiting Professor: Berkeley and Stanford, 1965; Smith Coll., 1967; Harvard, 1971; Wesleyan, 1974; Brandeis, 1977, 1981, 1984. A Vice-Pres., Tennyson Soc. Co-editor, Essays in Criticism. George Orwell Meml Prize, 1979; Beefeater Club Prize for Literature, 1980. *Publications:* Milton's Grand Style, 1963; (ed) The Poems of Tennyson, 1969, rev. edn 1987; Tennyson, 1972; Keats and Embarrassment, 1974; (ed with Leonard Michaels) The State of the Language, 1980; The Force of Poetry, 1984. *Address:* 39 Martin Street, Cambridge, Mass 02138, USA; Lasborough Cottage, Lasborough Park, near Tetbury, Glos. *T:* Leighterton 252.

RICKS, David Trulock, OBE 1981; British Council Representative, Italy, since 1985; *b* 28 June 1936; *s* of Percival Trulock Ricks and Annetta Helen (*née* Hood); *m* 1960, Nicole Estelle Aimée Chupeau; two *s*. *Educ:* Kilburn Grammar Sch.; Royal Acad. of Music; Merton Coll., Oxford (MA); Univ. of London Inst. of Educn; Univ. of Lille (LèsL). Teaching in Britain, 1960–67; joined British Council, 1967: Rabat, 1967–70; Univ. of Essex, 1970–71; Jaipur, 1971–74, New Delhi, 1974; Dar Es Salaam, 1974–76; Tehran, 1976 80; London, 1980 85. *Recreations:* music, ski ing. *Address:* c/o The British Council, 10 Spring Gardens, SW1A 2BN. *T:* 01–930 8466.

RICKS, Sir John (Plowman), Kt 1964; Solicitor to the Post Office, 1953–72; *b* 3 April 1910; *s* of late James Young Ricks; *m* 1st, 1936, May Celia (*d* 1975), *d* of late Robert William Chubb; three *s*; 2nd, 1976, Mrs Doreen Ilsley. *Educ:* Christ's Hosp.; Jesus Coll., Oxford. Admitted Solicitor, 1935; entered Post Office Solicitor's Department, 1935; Assistant Solicitor, Post Office, 1951. *Address:* 8 Sunset View, Barnet, Herts. *T:* 01–449 6114.

RICKUS, Gwenneth Margaret, CBE 1981; Director of Education, London Borough of Brent, 1971–84; *b* 1925; *d* of Leonard William Ernest and Florence Rickus. *Educ:* Latymer Sch., Edmonton; King's Coll., Univ. of London. BA, PGCE. Teaching, 1948–53; Asst Sec., AAM, 1953–61; Education Administration: Mddx CC, 1961–65; London Borough of Brent, 1965–84. Co-opted Mem. Educn Cttee, Hampshire CC, 1985–. Comr for Racial Equality, 1977–80. *Recreations:* walking, reading, crafts, gardening, music, politics.

RIDD, John William Gregory; HM Diplomatic Service; Foreign and Commonwealth Office, since 1978; *b* 4 June 1931; *s* of William John and Lilian Gregory Cooke; adoptive *s* of Philip and Elizabeth Anne Ridd; *m* 1956, Mary Elizabeth Choat; three *s* one *d*. *Educ:* Lewis' Sch., Pengam; Wallington County Grammar Sch.; St Edmund Hall, Oxford (BA Hons 1954). National Service, 1949–51 (Army). Foreign Office, 1954; Buenos Aires, 1957–61; First Sec., Cairo, 1963–66, Prague, 1968–70, Brasilia, 1974–77; First Sec., later Counsellor, FCO, 1978–. *Recreations:* books, distance running, allotment gardening, travel, music, singing. *Address:* c/o Foreign and Commonwealth Office, SW1.

RIDDELL, Sir John (Charles Buchanan), 13th Bt, *cr* 1628; CA; Private Secretary to TRH the Prince and Princess of Wales, since 1985; *b* 3 Jan. 1934; *o s* of Sir Walter Buchanan Riddell, 12th Bt, and Hon. Rachel Beatrice Lyttelton (*d* 1965), *y d* of 8th Viscount Cobham; *S* father 1934; *m* 1969, Hon. Sarah, *o d* of Baron Richardson of Duntisbourne, *qv*; three *s*. *Educ:* Eton; Christ Church, Oxford. 2nd Lieut Rifle Bde, 1952–54. With IBRD, Washington DC, 1969–71; with Credit Suisse First Boston Ltd, 1972–85 (Dir, 1975–85); Director: First Boston (Europe) Ltd, 1975–78; UK Provident Instn, 1975–85; Northern Rock Bldg Soc., 1981–85. Dep Chm., IBA, 1981–85. Contested (C): Durham NW, Feb. 1974; Sunderland S, Oct. 1974. Mem., Bloomsbury DHA, 1982–85; Trustee, Buttle Trust, 1981–. *Heir:* *s* Walter John Buchanan Riddell, *b* 10 June 1974. *Address:* Hepple, Morpeth, Northumberland. *TA:* Hepple; 49 Campden Hill Square, W8. *Clubs:* Garrick; Northern Counties (Newcastle upon Tyne).

See also Sir J. L. Pumphrey.

RIDDELL-WEBSTER, John Alexander, MC 1943; farmer; Member, Tayside Regional Council, since 1986; *b* 17 July 1921; *s* of Gen. Sir Thomas Riddell-Webster, GCB, DSO; *m* 1960, Ruth, *d* of late S. P. L. A. Lithgow; two *s* one *d*. *Educ:* Harrow; Pembroke Coll., Cambridge. Seaforth Highlanders (Major), 1940–46. Joined Anglo-Iranian Oil Co., 1946; served in Iran, Iraq, Bahrain, Aden; Vice-Pres. Marketing, BP Canada, 1959; Dir, Shell-Mex and BP, 1965, Man. Dir, Marketing, 1971–75; Dir, BP Oil Ltd, 1975–82 (Dep. Man. Dir, 1976–80); Dir, Public Affairs, Scotland, BP, 1979–81. Mem. Cttee, AA, 1980–; Mem. Exec. Cttee, Scottish Council (Develt and Industry), 1981–84; Member of Council: Advertising Assoc., 1974–80; Inc. Soc. of British Advertisers, 1968–80; for Vehicle Servicing and Repair, 1972–80 (Chm., 1975); Royal Warrant Holders' Assoc. (Vice-Pres., 1979; Pres., 1980); British Road Fedn, 1971–80; Chm., Transport Action Scotland, 1982–; Pres., Oil Industries Club, 1977–78. CBIM. *Recreations:* shooting, fishing, gardening. *Address:* Lintrose, Coupar Angus, Perthshire. *T:* Coupar Angus 27472. *Clubs:* New (Edinburgh); Royal Perth Golfing Society.

RIDDELSDELL, Dame Mildred, DCB 1972; CBE 1958; Second Permanent Secretary, Department of Health and Social Security, 1971–73; (Deputy Secretary, 1966–71); *b* 1 Dec. 1913; 2nd *d* of Rev. H. J. Riddelsdell. *Educ:* St Mary's Hall, Brighton; Bedford Coll., London. Entered Min. of Labour, 1936; Asst Sec., Min. of National Insurance, 1945; Under Secretary, 1950; On loan to United Nations, 1953–56; Secretary, National Incomes Commission, 1962–65; Ministry of Pensions and National Insurance, 1965, Social Security, 1966. Chm., CS Retirement Fellowship, 1974–77. *Recreation:* gardening. *Address:* 26A New Yatt Road, Witney, Oxon.

RIDDLE, Hugh Joseph, (Huseph), RP 1960; Artist; Portrait Painter; *b* 24 May 1912; *s* of late Hugh Howard Riddle and late Christine Simons Brown; *m* 1936, Joan Claudia Johnson; one *s* two *d*. *Educ:* Harrow; Magdalen, Oxford; Slade School of Art; Byam Shaw School of Art and others. *Recreations:* sailing, ski-ing, swimming, tennis, golf. *Address:* 18 Boulevard Verdi, Domaine du château de Tournon, Montauroux 83710, France.

RIDDOCH, John Haddow, CMG 1963; Under-Secretary, Board of Trade, 1966–69, retired; *b* 4 Feb. 1909; *s* of Joseph Riddoch, Gourock, Renfrewshire; *m* 1st, 1938, Isobel W. Russell (*d* 1972); one *s* two *d*; 2nd, 1975, Margaret C. McKimmie. *Educ:* Greenock Acad.; Glasgow Univ. Entered Inland Revenue Dept (Inspectorate of Taxes), 1932; Asst Principal in Air Ministry (Dept of Civil Aviation), 1939; Principal, 1942; Asst Sec., Min. of Civil Aviation, 1945; Under-Sec., Min. of Transport and Civil Aviation, 1957, Min. of Aviation, 1959; United Kingdom Representative on the Council of the ICAO, 1957–62 (First Vice-Pres. of Council, 1961–62); Under-Sec., Min. of Aviation, 1962–66. *Recreations:* music, bowls, gardening. *Address:* 10 The Fairway, New Barnet, Herts EN5 1HN.

RIDEALGH, Mrs Mabel; General Secretary of Women's Co-operative Guild, 1953–63; Member, Women's Advisory Committee, British Standards Institute, 1953–63; *b* 11 Aug. 1898; *d* of M. A. Jewitt, Wallsend-on-Tyne, Northumberland; *m* 1919, Leonard, *s* of W. R. Ridealgh, Sunderland, Durham; one *s* one *d*. National Pres. Women's Co-op. Guild, 1941–42; Hon. Regional Organiser Bd of Trade (Make-do and Mend), 1942–44; MP (Lab) Ilford North, 1945–50. *Address:* 2 Eastwood Road, Goodmayes, Ilford, Essex. *T:* 01–599 8960.

RIDEOUT, Prof. Roger William; Professor of Labour Law, University College, London, since 1973; *b* 9 Jan. 1935; *s* of Sidney and Hilda Rideout; *m* 1st, 1959, Marjorie Roberts (marr. diss. 1976); one *d*; 2nd, 1977, Gillian Margaret Lynch. *Educ:* Bedford School; University Coll., London (LLB, PhD). Called to the Bar, Gray's Inn, 1964. National Service, 1958–60; 2nd Lt RAEC, Educn Officer, 1st Bn Coldstream Guards. Lecturer: Univ. of Sheffield, 1960–63; Univ. of Bristol, 1963–64. University Coll., London: Sen. Lectr, 1964–65; Reader, 1965–73; Dean of Faculty of Laws, 1975–77. Dep. Chairman: Central Arbitration Cttee; Industrial Tribunals. Vice-Pres., Industrial Law Society; Industrial Arbitrator. Mem., Zool Soc. of London. Jt Editor, Current Legal Problems, 1975–. *Publications:* The Right to Membership of a Trade Union, 1962; The Practice and Procedure of the NIRC, 1973; Trade Unions and the Law, 1973; Principles of Labour Law, 1972, 4th edn 1983. *Address:* 255 Chipstead Way, Woodmansterne, Surrey. *T:* Downland 52033. *Club:* MCC.

RIDGE, Anthony Hubert; Director-General, International Bureau, Universal Postal Union, Bern, 1973–74 (Deputy Director-General, 1964–73); *b* 5 Oct. 1913; *s* of Timothy Leopold Ridge and Magdalen (*née* Hernig); *m* 1938, Marjory Joan Sage; three *s* one *d*. *Educ:* Christ's Hospital; Jesus College, Cambridge. Entered GPO, 1937; seconded to Min. Home Security, 1940; GPO Personnel Dept, 1944; PPS to Postmaster General, 1947; Dep. Dir, London Postal Region, 1949; Asst Sec., Overseas Mails, 1951, Personnel, 1954, Overseas Mails, 1956; Director of Clerical Mechanization and Buildings, and Member of Post Office Board, GPO, 1960–63. Mem., Postling Parish Council, 1979–. Governor, Christ's Hosp. *Recreations:* music, languages, transport, gardening. *Address:* Staple, Postling, Hythe, Kent CT21 4HA. *T:* Lyminge 862315. *Clubs:* Christ's Hospital, United Oxford & Cambridge University, Cambridge Society.

RIDGERS, John Nalton Sharpe; Deputy Chairman and Treasurer, Lloyd's Register of Shipping, 1973–78; Director: Smit International (UK) Ltd, 1974–84; *b* 10 June 1910; 4th *c* and *o s* of Sharpe Ridgers; *m* 1936, Barbara Mary, *o d* of Robert Cobb; five *d*. *Educ:* Wellington College. Entered Lloyd's, 1928; underwriting member, 1932. Member Cttee Lloyd's Underwriters' Association, 1951–61, 1964–69, Chm. 1961; Member Joint Hull Cttee, 1957–69, Dep. Chm., 1968, Chm., 1969. Mem. Cttee of Lloyd's, 1957–60, 1962–65, Dep. Chm., 1962, Chm., 1963. Director: London Trust Co. Ltd, 1963–80; Arbuthnot Insurance Services Ltd, 1974–80; Danae Investment Trust Ltd, 1975–80. *Recreations:* snooker, carpentry. *Address:* Little Watlynge, 4 Chestnut Lane, Sevenoaks, Kent TN13 3AR.

RIDGWAY, Gen. Matthew Bunker, DSC (with Oak Leaf Cluster); DSM (with 3rd Oak Leaf Cluster); Silver Star (with Oak Leaf Cluster); Legion of Merit; Bronze Star Medal V (with Oak Leaf Cluster); Purple Heart; Hon. KCB 1955 (Hon. CB 1945); Chairman of The Mellon Institute of Industrial Research 1955–60, retired; *b* 3 March 1895; *s* of Thomas Ridgway and Ruth Starbuck Bunker; *m* 1917; two *d*; *m* 1930; one *d*; *m* 1947, Mary Anthony; (one *s* decd). *Educ:* United States Military Academy, 1913–17. Inf. School (Company Officers' Course), 1924–25; Mem. Am. Electoral Commn, Nicaragua, 1927–28; Mem. Commn on Bolivian-Paraguayan boundary dispute, 1929; Inf. School (Advanced Course), 1929–30; Liaison Officer to Govt in Philippine Is, Tech. Adviser to Gov.-Gen., 1932–33; Comd and Gen. Staff School, 1933–35; Asst Chief of Staff, 6th Corps Area, 1935–36; Dep. Chief of Staff, Second Army, 1936; Army War College, 1936–37; Assistant Chief of Staff, Fourth Army, 1937–39; accompanied Gen. Marshall on special mission to Brazil, 1939; War Plans Div., War Department Gen. Staff, 1939–42; Asst Div. Comdr, 82nd Inf. Div., 1942; Comdr 1942; Comdg Gen. 82nd Airborne Div., Sicily, Italy, Normandy, 1942–44; Comdr 18th Airborne Corps, Belgium, France, Germany, 1944–45; Comdr Luzon Area Command, 1945; Comdr Medit. Theater, and Dep. Supreme Allied Comdr, Medit., 1945–46; Senior US Army Member Military Staff Cttee, UN, 1946–48; Chm. Inter-Am. Defense Bd, 1946–48; C-in-C Caribbean Command, 1948–49; Dep. Army Chief of Staff for Admin., 1949–50 (and Chm. Inter-Am. Defense Bd, 1950); Comdg Gen. Eighth Army in Korea, 1950–51; Comdr UN Comd in Far East, C-in-C of Far East Comd and Supreme Comdr for Allied Powers in Japan, 1951–52; Supreme Allied Comdr, Europe, 1952–53; Chief of Staff, United States Army, 1953–55, retired. Holds many American and foreign decorations. *Address:* 918 W Waldheim Road, Fox Chapel, Pittsburgh, Pa 15215, USA.

RIDING, Laura, (Mrs Schuyler B. Jackson); *b* New York City, 16 Jan. 1901; American mother and naturalised (Austrian-born) father (Nathaniel S. Reichenthal); *m* 1941, Schuyler B. Jackson (*d* 1968) (American writer; poetry-editor of Time, 1938–43). *Educ:* American public schools; Cornell University. First published poems in American poetry magazines; member of group of Southern poets, The Fugitives; went to England in 1926, remaining abroad until 1939; engaging in writing and allied activities, seeking a single terminology of truth to supersede our confused terminological diversity (*eg*, as Editor of Epilogue, a critical miscellany); was co-operator of Seizin Press, first author of A Survey of Modernist Poetry (Robert Graves, collaborator), 1927; devoted herself to helping other poets with their work. Has since renounced poetry as humanly inadequate and concentrated on direct linguistic handling of truth-problem, studying ways to intensify people's consciousness of word-meanings; working long with husband on a book in which the principles of language and the principles of definition are brought into relation, to be entitled Rational Meaning: A New Foundation for the Definition of Words (publishing arrangements pending). Mark Rothko Appreciation Award, 1971; Guggenheim Fellowship award, 1973; Nat. Endowment for the Arts Fellowship Award (for writing of her memoirs, now in progress), 1979. *Publications include:* (as Laura Riding, until 1941, thereafter as Laura (Riding) Jackson) individual books of poems (10), from 1926; Contemporaries and Snobs, 1928; Anarchism Is Not Enough, 1928; Experts are Puzzled, 1930; Progress of Stories, 1935, new edn with additional stories, and new prefatory and supplementary material, 1982; A Trojan Ending, 1937, new edn 1984 (Spanish trans., 1986); The World and Ourselves, 1938; Collected Poems, 1938, new edn with new preface and extensive appendix 1980; Lives of Wives, 1939, new edn 1986; The Telling (a personal evangel-complete magazine publication, Chelsea, USA), 1967, enl. edn in book form, UK 1972, USA 1973; Selected Poems: in five sets, 1970, USA 1973; Writings of 50 Years—Author's Miscellany, entire biannual issue, Chelsea (USA), autumn 1976; Description of Life, 1980; Some Communications of Broad Reference, 1983; contribs to magazines. *Address:* Box 35, Wabasso, Florida 32970, USA.

RIDLER, Anne (Barbara); author; *b* 30 July 1912; *o d* of late H. C. Bradby, housemaster of Rugby School, and Violet Milford; *m* 1938, Vivian Ridler, *qv*; two *s* two *d*. *Educ:* Downe House School; King's College, London; and in Florence and Rome. *Publications: poems:* Poems, 1939; A Dream Observed, 1941; The Nine Bright Shiners, 1943; The Golden Bird, 1951; A Matter of Life and Death, 1959; Selected Poems (New York), 1961; Some Time After, 1972; (contrib.) Ten Oxford Poets, 1978; *plays:* Cain, 1943; The Shadow Factory, 1946; Henry Bly and other plays, 1950; The Trial of Thomas Cranmer, 1956; Who is my Neighbour?, 1963; The Jesse Tree (libretto), 1972; The King of the Golden River (libretto), 1975; The Lambton Worm (libretto), 1978; *translations:* Italian opera libretti: Rosinda, 1973; Orfeo, 1975; Eritrea, 1975; Return of Ulysses, 1978; Orontea, 1979; Agrippina, 1981; Calisto, 1984; Così fan Tutte, 1986; *biography:* Olive Willis and Downe House, 1967; Editor: Shakespeare Criticism, 1919–35; A Little Book of Modern Verse, 1941; Best Ghost Stories, 1945; Supplement to Faber Book of Modern Verse, 1951; The Image of the City and other essays by Charles Williams, 1958; Shakespeare Criticism 1935–60, 1963; Poems of James Thomson, 1963; Thomas Traherne, 1966; (with Christopher Bradby) Best Stories of Church and Clergy, 1966; Selected Poems of George Darley, 1979; Poems of William Austin, 1983. *Recreations:* music; the theatre; the cinema. *Address:* 14 Stanley Road, Oxford.

RIDLER, Vivian Hughes, CBE 1971; MA Oxon 1958 (by decree; Corpus Christi College); Printer to the University of Oxford, 1958–78; *b* 2 Oct. 1913; *s* of Bertram Hughes Ridler and Elizabeth Emmeline (*née* Best); *m* 1938, Anne Barbara Bradby (*see* A. B. Ridler); two *s* two *d*. *Educ:* Bristol Gram. Sch. Appren. E. S. & A. Robinson, Ltd, 1931–36. Works Manager University Press, Oxford, 1948; Assistant Printer, 1949–58. Pres., British Federation of Master Printers, 1968–69. Professorial Fellow, St Edmund Hall, 1966, Emeritus Fellow, 1978. *Recreations:* printing, theatre, cinema, cinematography. *Address:* 14 Stanley Road, Oxford. *T:* Oxford 247595.

RIDLEY, family name of **Viscount Ridley.**

RIDLEY, 4th Viscount, *cr* 1900; **Matthew White Ridley,** TD 1960; DL; Baron Wensleydale, *cr* 1900; Bt 1756; Lord-Lieutenant and Custos Rotulorum of Northumberland, since Jan. 1984; *b* 29 July 1925; *e s* of 3rd Viscount Ridley; *S* father, 1964; *m* 1953, Lady Anne Lumley, 3rd *d* of 11th Earl of Scarbrough, KG, PC, GCSI, GCIE, GCVO; one *s* three *d*. *Educ:* Eton; Balliol College, Oxford. ARICS 1951. Coldstream Guards (NW Europe), 1943–46, Captain, 1946; Bt-Col Northumberland Hussars (TA); Hon. Colonel: Northumberland Hussars Sqdn, Queen's Own Yeomanry, 1979–86; Queen's Own Yeomanry RAC TA, 1984–86; Northumbrian Univs OTC, 1986–; Col Comdt, Yeomanry RAC TA, 1982–86. Director: Northern Rock Building Society; Tyne Tees Television; Barclays Bank (NE) Ltd; Municipal Mutual Insurance. Pres., British Deer Soc., 1970–73. Mem., Layfield Cttee of Enquiry into Local Govt Finance, 1974–. Chm., N of England TA Assoc., 1980–84; Pres., TA & VRA Council, 1984–. Chm., Newcastle Univ. Develt. Trust, 1981–84; Hon. Fellow, Newcastle upon Tyne Polytechnic, 1980; Hon. FRHS 1986. JP 1957, CC 1958, CA 1963, DL 1968, Northumberland; Chm., Northumberland CC, 1967–74, Chm., new Northumberland CC, 1974–79; Pres., ACC, 1979–84. KStJ 1984. Order of Merit, West Germany, 1974. *Heir: s* Hon. Matthew White Ridley, *b* 7 Feb. 1958. *Address:* Blagdon, Seaton Burn, Newcastle upon Tyne NE13 6DD. *T:* Stannington 236. *Clubs:* Turf, Pratt's; Northern Counties (Newcastle upon Tyne).

See also Rt Hon. Nicholas Ridley.

RIDLEY, Sir Adam (Nicholas), Kt 1985; Director, Hambros PLC, and Executive Director, Hambros Bank, since 1985; *b* 14 May 1942; *s* of Jasper Maurice Alexander Ridley and Helen Cressida Ridley (*née* Bonham Carter); *m* 1981, Margaret Anne Passmore. *Educ:* Eton Coll.; Balliol Coll., Oxford (1st cl. hons PPE 1965); Univ. of California, Berkeley. Foreign Office, 1965, seconded to DEA, 1965–68; Harkness Fellow, Univ. of California, Berkeley, 1968–69; HM Treasury, 1970–71, seconded to CPRS, 1971–74; Economic Advr to shadow cabinet and Asst Dir, Cons. Res. Dept, 1974–79; Special Advr to Chancellor of the Exchequer, 1979–84, to Chancellor of the Duchy of Lancaster, 1985. *Publications:* articles on regional policy, public spending, international economics. *Recreations:* music, painting, travel. *Address:* c/o Hambros Bank, 41 Bishpsgate, EC2P 2AA. *Clubs:* Zanzibar, Garrick.

RIDLEY, Dame Betty; *see* Ridley, Dame M. B.

RIDLEY, Edward Alexander Keane, CB 1963; Principal Assistant Solicitor, Treasury Solicitor's Department, 1956–69, retired; *b* 16 April 1904; *s* of late Major Edward Keane Ridley, Dudswell House, near Berkhamsted, Herts, and late Ethel Janet Ridley, *d* of

Alexander Forbes Tweedie; unmarried. *Educ:* Wellington College; Keble College, Oxford. Admitted Solicitor, 1928. Entered Treasury Solicitor's Department, 1934. Hon. RCM 1977. *Publications:* Wind Instruments of European Art Music, 1975; Catalogue of Wind Instruments in the Museum of the Royal College of Music, 1982. *Recreation:* music. *Address:* c/o Coutts & Co., 440 Strand, WC2.

RIDLEY, Prof. Frederick Fernand, OBE 1978; PhD; Professor of Political Theory and Institutions, University of Liverpool, since 1965; *b* 11 Aug. 1928; *s* of late J. and of G. A. Ridley; *m* 1967, Paula Frances Cooper Ridley, *qv*; two *s* one *d*. *Educ:* The Hall, Hampstead; Highgate Sch.; LSE (BScEcon, PhD); Univs of Paris and Berlin. Lectr, Univ. of Liverpool, 1958–65. Vis. Professor: Graduate Sch. of Public Affairs, Univ. of Pittsburgh, 1968; Coll. of Europe, Bruges, 1975–83. Manpower Services Commission, Merseyside: Chm., Job Creation Prog., 1975–77; Vice-Chm., Special Progs Bd, then Area Manpower Bd, 1978–. Member: Jt Univ. Council for Social and Public Admin, 1964– (Chm., 1972–74); Exec., Polit. Studies Assoc., 1967–75; Council, Hansard Soc., 1970–; Polit. Science Cttee, SSRC, 1972–76; Europ. Cttee, Internat. Inst. of Admin. Sciences, Brussels, 1973–; Public and Social Admin Bd, CNAA, 1975–82; Social Studies Res. Cttee, CNAA, 1980–83 (Chm.); Res. Adv. Gp, Arts Council, 1979–82; Exec., Merseyside Arts (RAA), 1979–84; Adv. Council, Granada Foundn, 1984–; Trustee, Friends of Merseyside Museums and Galleries, 1977–. Hon. Pres., Politics Assoc., 1976–81. Editor: Political Studies, 1969–75; Parliamentary Affairs, 1975–. *Publications:* Public Administration in France, 1964; (ed) Specialists and Generalists, 1968; Revolutionary Syndicalism in France, 1970; The Study of Government, 1975; (ed) Studies in Politics, 1975; (ed) Government and Administration in W Europe, 1979; (ed) Policies and Politics in W Europe, 1984. *Address:* Riversdale House, Grassendale Park, Liverpool L19 0LR. *T:* 051–427 1630.

RIDLEY, Gordon, OBE 1980; MA; FICE, FIHT; Director of Planning and Transportation, Greater London Council, 1978–80; *b* 1 Nov. 1921; *s* of Timothy Ridley and Lallah Sarah Ridley; *m* 1952, Doreen May Browning; one *s* one *d*. *Educ:* Selwyn Coll., Cambridge (MA). FICE 1965; FIMunE 1964; FInstHE 1966. Served War, Admiralty Signals Estab., 1941–46. Engrg appts, various local authorities, 1946–55; Bridges Br., MoT, 1955–58; AEA, 1958–63; LCC, 1963–65; engrg appts, GLC, 1965–78. *Publications:* papers on engrg topics presented to learned instns. *Recreations:* words, walking, photography. *Address:* 26 Greenacres, Preston Park Avenue, Brighton BN1 6HR. *T:* Brighton 559951.

RIDLEY, Jasper Godwin; author; *b* 25 May 1920; *s* of Geoffrey Ridley and Ursula (*née* King); *m* 1949, Vera, *d* of Emil Pollak; two *s* one *d*. *Educ:* Felcourt Sch.; Sorbonne, Paris; Magdalen Coll., Oxford. Certif. of Honour, Bar Finals. Called to Bar, Inner Temple, 1945. St Pancras Borough Council, 1945–49. Pres., Hardwicke Soc., 1954–55. Contested (Lab): Winchester, 1955; Westbury, 1959. Vice-Pres., English Centre of Internat. PEN. Middle Warden, Carpenters' Co. Has written many radio scripts on historical subjects. FRSL 1963. *Publications:* Nicholas Ridley, 1957; The Law of Carriage of Goods, 1957; Thomas Cranmer, 1962; John Knox, 1968; Lord Palmerston, 1970 (James Tait Black Meml Prize, 1970); Mary Tudor, 1973; Garibaldi, 1974; The Roundheads, 1976; Napoleon III and Eugénie, 1979; History of England, 1981; The Statesman and the Fanatic: Thomas Wolsey and Thomas More, 1982; Henry VIII, 1984. *Recreations:* walking, tennis, chess. *Address:* 6 Oakdale Road, Tunbridge Wells, Kent. *T:* Tunbridge Wells 22460.

RIDLEY, Michael Kershaw; Clerk of the Council, Duchy of Lancaster, since 1981; *b* 7 Dec. 1937; *s* of George K. and Mary Ridley; *m* 1968, Diana Loraine McLernon; two *s*. *Educ:* Stowe; Magdalene College, Cambridge. MA. FRICS. Grosvenor Estate, Canada and USA, 1965–69, London, 1969–72; Property Manager, British & Commonwealth Shipping Co., 1972–81. A Gen. Comr of Income Tax, 1984–. Mem., Adv. Panel, Greenwich Hosp., 1978–. *Recreation:* golf. *Address:* Duchy Office, Lancaster Place, Strand, WC2. *Club:* Royal Mid-Surrey Golf.

RIDLEY, Dame (Mildred) Betty, DBE 1975; MA (Lambeth) 1958; Third Church Estates Commissioner, 1972–81; a Church Commissioner, 1959–81; *b* 10 Sept. 1909; *d* of late Rt Rev. Henry Mosley, sometime Bishop of Southwell; *m* 1929, Rev. Michael Ridley (*d* 1953), Rector of Finchley; three *s* one *d*. *Educ:* North London Collegiate School; Cheltenham Ladies' College. Member: General Synod of Church of England, 1970–81, and its Standing Cttee, 1971–81; Central Board of Finance, 1955–79; Mem., Faculty Jurisdiction Commn, 1980–83; Vice-Pres. British Council of Churches, 1954–56. Governor, King Alfred's Coll., Winchester, 1985–. FRSA 1981. *Recreations:* walking, gardening. *Address:* Little Dickers, Hannington, Basingstoke, Hants RG26 5TZ. *T:* Kingsclere 298191. *Club:* Reform.

RIDLEY, Rt. Hon. Nicholas, PC 1983; MP (C) Cirencester and Tewkesbury Division of Gloucestershire since 1959; Secretary of State for the Environment, since 1986; *b* 17 Feb. 1929; *yr s* of 3rd Viscount Ridley, CBE, TD; *m* 1st, 1950, Hon. Clayre Campbell (marr. diss. 1974), 2nd *d* of 4th Baron Stratheden and Campbell, CBE; three *d*; 2nd, 1979, Judy Kendall. *Educ:* Eton; Balliol College, Oxford. Civil Engineering Contractor, Brims & Co. Ltd, Newcastle upon Tyne, 1950–59, Director, 1954–70; Director: Heenan Group Ltd, 1961–68; Ausonia Finance, 1973–79; Marshall Andrew Ltd, 1975–79. Contested (C) Blyth, Gen. Election, 1955; PPS to Minister of Education, 1962–64; Delegate to Council of Europe and WEU, 1962–66; Parly Sec., Min. of Technology, June-Oct. 1970; Parly Under-Sec. of State, DTI, 1970; Minister of State, FCO, 1979–81; Financial Sec. to HM Treasury, 1981–83; Sec. of State for Transport, 1983–86. Mem., Royal Commn on Historical Manuscripts, 1967–79. *Recreations:* painting, architecture, gardening, fishing. *Address:* Old Rectory, Naunton, Cheltenham, Glos. *T:* Guiting Power 252; 50 Warwick Square, SW1.

RIDLEY, Nicholas Harold Lloyd, MD, FRCS; FRS 1986; Hon. Consultant Surgeon, Moorfields Eye Hospital, 1971 (Surgeon, 1938–71); Hon. Consultant Surgeon, Ophthalmic Department, St Thomas' Hospital, 1971 (Ophthalmic Surgeon, 1946–71); *b* 10 July 1906; *s* of late N. C. Ridley, MB (London), FRCS, Royal Navy retired, Leicester; *m* 1941, Elisabeth Jane, *d* of late H. B. Wetherill, CIE; two *s* one *d*. *Educ:* Charterhouse; Pembroke Coll., Cambridge; St Thomas' Hospital, London. MB 1931, MD 1946, Cambridge; FRCS 1932. Originator in 1949 of intraocular implants. Late Hon. Ophthalmic Surgeon, Royal Buckinghamshire Hospital. Temp. Major, RAMC. Hon. Cons. in Ophthalmology to Min. of Defence (Army), 1964–71; Life Pres., Internat. Intraocular Implants Club, 1972; late Vice-Pres., Ophthalmological Soc. of UK; Mem. Advisory Panel, WHO, 1966–71; Hon. Mem., Oxford Ophthalmological Congress. Hon. Fellow International College of Surgeons, Chicago, 1952; Hon. FRSM 1986; Hon. Member: Peruvian Ophthalmic Society, 1957; Ophthalmological Society of Australia, 1963; Irish Ophthalmological Society; Ophthalmological Soc. of UK, 1984; Amer. Intraocular Implants Soc., 1974; European Intra-Ocular Implantlens Council, 1983. Galen Medal, Apothecaries' Soc., 1986. *Publications:* Monograph on Ocular Onchocerciasis; numerous contrib. in textbooks and medical journals on intraocular implant surgery and other subjects. *Recreation:* fly-fishing. *Address:* Keeper's Cottage, Stapleford, Salisbury, Wilts SP3 4LT. *T:* Salisbury 790209. *Club:* Flyfishers'.

RIDLEY, Paula Frances Cooper, JP; MA; Member, Independent Broadcasting Authority, since 1982; Director, Community Initiatives Research Trust, 1983–; *b* 27 Sept. 1944; *d* of Ondrej Clyne and Ellen (*née* Cooper); *m* 1967, Frederick Fernand Ridley, *qv*; two *s* one *d*. *Educ:* Greenhead High Sch., Huddersfield; Kendal High Sch., Westmorland; Univ. of Liverpool. BA, MA; Lady Pres., Guild of Undergraduates. Standing Cttee of Convocation, Univ. of Liverpool, 1966–74 (Clerk of Convocation, 1972–74); Mem., Univ. Court, 1972–. Lectr in Politics and Public Admin., Liverpool Polytechnic, 1966–71; Proj. Coordinator, Regeneration Projects Ltd, 1981–84; Dir, New Enterprise Workshops (Toxteth) Ltd, 1984–; Consultant BAT Industries Small Businesses Ltd, 1983–; Associate, Centre for Employment Initiatives, 1984–. Member: Governing Body, Stocktonwood County Primary Sch., 1970–81 (Chm., 1976–79); Liverpool Heritage Bureau, 1971–; Management Cttee, Liverpool Victoria Settlement, 1971–86 (Vice-Chm., 1977–86); IBA Adv. Cttee for Radio in Liverpool, 1975–78; Barnardo's Intermediate Treatment Adv. Gp in Liverpool, 1980–; Council, Liverpool and Huyton Colls, 1979– (Life Governor); Cttee of Friends of Merseyside Maritime Mus., 1980–82; Merseyside Enterprise Forum, 1986–; Merseyside Civic Society: Hon. Sec., 1971–82; Vice-Chm., 1982–86; Chm., 1986–; Dir, Liverpool City Develt Trust, 1982–86. JP Liverpool, 1977; Juvenile Panel, 1979–; Jt Cttee, Juv. Panel and Educn and Social Services Cttees, Liverpool City Council, 1981–. *Address:* Riversdale House, Grassendale Park, Liverpool L19 0LR. *T:* 051–427 1630.

RIDLEY, Philip Waller, CB 1978; CBE 1969; Director: Avon Rubber Co., since 1980; consultant to other companies; *b* 25 March 1921; *s* of Basil White Ridley and Frida (*née* Gutknecht); *m* 1942, Foye Robins; two *s* one *d*. *Educ:* Lewes County Grammar Sch.; Trinity Coll., Cambridge. Intelligence Corps, 1941–47 (Major); German Section, FO, 1948–51; Min. of Supply, 1951–55; BoT, 1955–56 and 1960–66; Atomic Energy Office, 1956–60; Counsellor (Commercial), British Embassy, Washington, 1966–70; Under-Sec., 1971–75, Dep. Sec., 1975–80, Dept of Industry. *Recreations:* music, gardening, skiing, sailing. *Address:* Old Chimneys, Plumpton Green, Lewes, East Sussex. *T:* Plumpton 890342.

RIDLEY, Sir Sidney, Kt 1953; Emeritus Fellow, St John's College, Oxford, 1969 (Fellow, 1962); Indian Civil Service, retired; *b* 26 March 1902; *s* of John William and Elizabeth Janet Ridley; *m* 1929, Dorothy Hoole; three *d*. *Educ:* Lancaster Royal Grammar Sch.; Sidney Sussex Coll., Cambridge. MA Cantab, MA Oxon. Joined ICS, 1926; Finance Secretary, Govt of Sind, 1936; Secretary to the Agent-General for India in South Africa, 1936–40; Chief Secretary, Govt of Sind, 1944; Commissioner: Northern Division, Ahmedabad, 1946; Central Div., Poona, 1947; Revenue Commissioner in Sind and Secretary to Government, 1947–54. Representative of W Africa Cttee in Ghana, Sierra Leone and the Gambia, 1957–60; Domestic Bursar, St John's Coll., Oxford, 1960–68. *Recreation:* golf. *Address:* Lambrook Cottage, Waytown, Bridport, Dorset. *T:* Netherbury 337.

RIDLEY, Tony Melville, CBE 1986; PhD; CEng, FICE; FCIT; Chairman and Managing Director, London Underground Ltd, since 1985; Board Member, London Regional Transport (formerly London Transport Executive), since 1980; *b* 10 Nov. 1933; *s* of late John Edward and of Olive Ridley; *m* 1959, Jane (*née* Dickinson); two *s* one *d*. *Educ:* Durham Sch.; King's Coll. Newcastle, Univ. of Durham (BSc); Northwestern Univ., Ill (MS); Univ. of California, Berkeley (PhD). Nuclear Power Group, 1957–62; Univ. of California, 1962–65; Chief Research Officer, Highways and Transportation, GLC, 1965–69; Director General, Tyne and Wear Passenger Transport Exec., 1969–75; Man. Dir, Hong Kong Mass Transit Rly Corp., 1975–80; Man. Dir (Rlys), LTE, then LRT, 1980–85. Dir, Halcrow Fox and Associates, 1980–; Chm., London Transport Internat., 1982–. Visiting Professor: Imperial Coll., London, 1981–; Univ. of Newcastle upon Tyne, 1985–. Pres., Light Rail Transit Assoc., 1974–. Freeman, City of London, 1982. FHKIE, MITE. *Publications:* articles in transport, engrg and other jls. *Recreations:* theatre, music, international affairs, rejuvenation of Britain. *Address:* 77 Church Road, Richmond, Surrey TW10 6LX. *T:* 01–948 3898. *Clubs:* Hong Kong, Jockey (Hong Kong).

RIDLEY, Rear-Adm. William Terence Colborne, CB 1968; OBE 1954; Admiral Superintendent/Port Admiral, Rosyth, 1966–72; Chairman, Ex-Services Mental Welfare Society, 1973–83; *b* 9 March 1915; *s* of late Capt. W. H. W. Ridley, RN and late Vera Constance (*née* Walker); *m* 1938, Barbara Allen; one *s*. *Educ:* Emsworth House; RNC, Dartmouth (Robert Roxburgh Prize); RNEC, Keyham. HMS Exeter, 1936; HMS Valiant, 1939; HMS Firedrake, 1940 (despatches twice); E-in-C Dept Admty, 1941; HMS Indefatigable, 1944; Admty Fuel Experimental Stn, 1947; Seaslug Project Officer, RAE Farnborough, 1950; HMS Ark Royal, 1956; E-in-C Dept Admty, Dreadnought Project Team, 1958; CO, RNEC, 1962; Staff of C-in-C Portsmouth, 1964. Lt-Comdr 1944; Comdr 1947; Capt. 1957; Rear-Adm. 1966. *Recreations:* gardening, do-it-yourself. *Address:* 12 New King Street, Bath, Avon. *T:* Bath 318371.

RIDSDALE, Sir Julian (Errington), Kt 1981; CBE 1977; MP (C) Harwich Division of Essex, since Feb. 1954; *b* 8 June 1915; *m* 1942, Victoire Evelyn Patricia Bennett; one *d*. *Educ:* Tonbridge; Sandhurst. 2nd Lieutenant, Royal Norfolk Regiment, 1935; attached British Embassy, Tokyo, 1938–39; served War of 1939–45: Royal Norfolk Regt, Royal Scots, and Somerset Light Infantry; Asst Mil. Attaché, Japan, 1940; GSO3, Far Eastern Sect., War Office, 1941; GSO2, Joint Staff Mission, Washington, 1944–45; retired from Army with rank of Major, 1946. Contested SW Islington (C), LCC, 1949, N Paddington (C), Gen. Elec., 1951. PPS to Parly Under-Sec. of State for Colonies, 1957–58; PPS to Minister of State for Foreign Affairs, 1958–60; Parly Under-Sec. of State: for Air and Vice-President of the Air Council, 1962–64; for Defence for the Royal Air Force, Ministry of Defence, April-Oct. 1964. Chairman: British Japanese Parly Group, 1964–; Parly Gp for Engrg Develt, 1985–; Vice-Chm., UN Parly Assoc., 1966–82; Mem., Select Cttee of Public Accounts, 1970–74. Leader, Parly Delegns to Japan, 1973, 1975, and annually 1977–82. Member: Trilateral Commn, EEC, USA and Japan, 1973–; North Atlantic Assembly, 1979– (Vice-Pres., Political Cttee, 1983–). Dep. Chm., Internat. Triangle, USA, Japan and Europe, 1981–85. Chm., Japan Soc., London, 1976–79. Master, Skinners' Co., 1970–71. Order of the Sacred Treasure, Japan. *Recreations:* tennis, chess, gardening, travelling, and sailing. *Address:* 12 The Boltons, SW10. *T:* 01–373 6159; Fiddan, St Osyth, Essex. *T:* St Osyth 367. *Clubs:* Carlton, MCC, Hurlingham; Frinton Tennis.

RIE, Lucie, CBE 1981 (OBE 1968); studio potter since 1927; *b* 16 March 1902; *d* of Prof. Dr Benjamin and Gisela Gomperz. *Educ:* Vienna Gymnasium (matriculate); Kunstgewerbe Schule. Pottery workshop: Vienna, 1927; London, 1939. Work included in V&A Museum, Fitzwilliam Museum, Cambridge Museum, Boymans-van Beuningen Museum, Stedelijk Museum, Museum of Modern Art, NY, Aust. Nat. Gall., Canberra, and other public collections in England and abroad. Exhibitions include: Arts Council retrospective, 1967; (with Hans Coper) Boymans-van Beuningen Museum, 1967; Expo '70, Osaka, 1970; (with Hans Coper) Museum of Art and Crafts, Hamburg, 1972; Hetjens Museum, Düsseldorf, 1978; retrospective, Sainsbury Centre and V&A Mus, 1981–82. Gold medals: Internat. Exhibn, Brussels, 1935; Triennale, Milan, 1936, 1954; Internat. Exhib., Munich, 1964. Hon. Doctor, Royal College of Art, 1969.

RIFKIND, Rt. Hon. Malcolm (Leslie), PC 1986; QC (Scot.) 1985; MP (C) Edinburgh, Pentlands, since Feb. 1974; Secretary of State for Scotland, since 1986; *b* 21 June 1946; *yr s* of E. Rifkind, Edinburgh; *m* 1970, Edith Amalia Rifkind (*née* Steinberg); one *s* one *d*. *Educ:* George Watson's Coll.; Edinburgh Univ. LLB, MSc. Lectured at Univ. of Rhodesia, 1967–68. Called to Scottish Bar, 1970. Contested (C) Edinburgh, Central, 1970. Opposition front-bench spokesman on Scottish Affairs, 1975–76; Parly Under Sec. of State, Scottish Office, 1979–82, FCO, 1982–83; Minister of State, FCO, 1983–86. Chm., Scottish Cons. Devolution Cttee, 1976; Jt Sec., Cons. Foreign and Commonwealth Affairs Cttee, 1978; Member: Select Cttee on Europ. Secondary Legislation, 1975–76; Select Cttee on Overseas Develt, 1978–79. Hon. Pres., Scottish Young Conservatives, 1975–76. *Address:* House of Commons, SW1. *Club:* New (Edinburgh).

RIGBY, Bryan; Managing Director, UK Operations, BASF Group, since 1984; *b* 9 Jan. 1933; *s* of William George Rigby and Lily Rigby; *m* 1978, Marian Rosamund; one *s* one *d* of a former marriage, and one step *s* one step *d*. *Educ:* Wigan Grammar Sch.; King's Coll., London (BSc Special Chemistry, Dip. Chem. Engrg). UKAEA Industrial Gp, Capenhurst, 1955–60; Beecham Gp, London and Amsterdam, 1960–64; Laporte Industries (Holdings) Ltd, 1964–78; Dep. Dir-Gen., CBI, 1978–83. *Recreations:* music, squash, golf, gardening. *Address:* Cluny, 61 Penn Road, Beaconsfield, Bucks HP9 2LW. *T:* Beaconsfield 3206. *Club:* Reform.

RIGBY, Herbert Cecil, DFC 1943, and Bar 1944; **His Honour Judge Rigby;** a Circuit Judge since 1980; Senior Partner, H. P. & H. C. Rigby, Solicitors, Sandbach, Cheshire; *b* 2 April 1917; *s* of Captain Herbert Parrot Rigby, TD; *m* 1st, 1939, Ethel Muriel Horton; two *d*; 2nd, 1949, Florence Rita Scotts; one *s*. *Educ:* Sandbach Sch.; Ellesmere Coll.; Liverpool Univ. (Law Faculty). Articled R. S. Rigby, Winsford. Commissioned, 7th Cheshire Regt, 1937. Served War: Expeditionary Force, France, 1939; evacuated, Dunkirk, 1940; transfer to RAF, 1941; Wings, 11 Gp, Hornchurch (Spitfires), 1942; Landing, N Africa, 1942; commanded 222 Sqdn, Invasion of France, 1944–45 (Bt Militaire de Pilote D'Avion, 1945); demobilised, 1946. Commanded 610 City of Chester Auxiliary Sqdn, 1947–49. Law Final, and admitted solicitor, 1947; partner, H. P. & H. C. Rigby, Sandbach, Cheshire, 1947–; a Recorder of the Crown Court, Wales and Chester Circuit, 1972–80. Member: Cheshire Brine Compensation Bd, 1952–74 (Chm., 1969–74); Cheshire CC, 1955–69; Runcorn Develt Corp., 1964–80 (Dep. Chm., 1974–80). *Recreations:* fishing, golf, boating, gardening. *Address:* Shelbourre, New Platt Lane, Cranage, *via* Crewe, Cheshire.

RIGBY, Lt-Col Sir (Hugh) John (Macbeth), 2nd Bt, *cr* 1929; ERD and 2 clasps; Director, Executors of James Mills Ltd, retired 1977; *b* 1 Sept. 1914; *s* of Sir Hugh Mallinson Rigby, 1st Bt, and Flora (*d* 1970), *d* of Norman Macbeth; *S* father, 1944; *m* 1946, Mary Patricia Erskine Leacock; four *s*. *Educ:* Rugby; Magdalene Coll., Cambridge. Lt-Col RCT, retd, 1967. *Heir: s* Anthony John Rigby [*b* 3 Oct. 1946; *m* 1978, Mary, *e d* of R. G. Oliver, Park Moor Cottage, Pott Shrigley, Macclesfield; three *s*]. *Address:* 5 Park Street, Macclesfield, Cheshire SK11 6SR. *T:* Macclesfield 613959; Casa das Palmeiras, Armação de Pêra, 8365 Alcantarilha, Algarve, Portugal. *T:* 82–32548.

RIGBY, Sir Ivo (Charles Clayton), Kt 1964; a Metropolitan Stipendiary Magistrate, 1976–83; a Recorder of the Crown Court, 1975–83, retired; *b* 2 June 1911; *s* of late James Philip Clayton Rigby and late Elisabeth Mary Corbett; *m* 1st, 1938, Agnes Bothway; 2nd, Kathleen Nancy, *d* of late Dr W. E. Jones, CMG; no *c*. *Educ:* Magdalen College School, Oxford. Called to the Bar (Inner Temple), 1932; Magistrate, Gambia, 1935–38; Chief Magistrate, Crown Counsel, and President of a District Court, Palestine, 1938–48; Assistant Judge, Nyasaland, 1948–54; President of Sessions Court, Malaya, 1954–55; Puisne Judge, Malaya, 1956–61; Senior Puisne Judge, Hong Kong, 1961–70; Chief Justice of Hong Kong and of Brunei, 1970–73; Pres., Court of Appeal, Brunei, 1973–79. *Publications:* The Law Reports of Nyasaland, 1934–1952. *Recreations:* cricket and bridge. *Address:* 1 Dalmeny House, Thurloe Place, SW7 2RY. *T:* 01–589 0267. *Clubs:* Naval and Military, Hurlingham, East India, Devonshire, Sports and Public Schools, MCC.

RIGBY, Sir John; *see* Rigby, Sir H. J. M.

RIGBY, Norman Leslie; company chairman, retired; *b* 27 June 1920; *s* of Leslie Rigby and Elsie Lester Wright; *m* 1950, Mary Josephine Calderhead; two *d* (one *s* decd). *Educ:* Cowley Sch., St Helens. Served War, RAF, 1939–45, Intell. Officer to Free French Air Force. Management Trainee, Simon Engineering Group, 1946–48; Marketing Exec., Procter & Gamble Ltd, 1948–55; Marketing Dir, Macleans Ltd (Beecham Group), 1955–59; Nabisco Ltd: Marketing Dir 1959; Man. Dir 1960; Vice-Chm. 1962; Chm. 1964; Industrial Adviser, 1968–70, Co-ordinator of Industrial Advisers, HM Govt, 1969–70; Dir, Spillers Ltd, 1970–80 (Divl Man. Dir, 1977–80); Chm., Allan H. Williams Ltd and associated cos, 1981–82. CBIM. *Recreations:* gardening, golf. *Address:* 38 West Common Way, Harpenden, Herts. *T:* Harpenden 5448.

RIGBY, Reginald Francis, TD 1950 and Clasp 1952; a Recorder of the Crown Court, 1977–83; Consultant with Rigby, Rowley Cooper & Co., Solicitors, Newcastle-under-Lyme; *b* Rudyard, Staffs, 22 June 1919; *s* of Reginald Rigby, FRIBA, FRICS, and Beatrice May Rigby, *d* of John Frederick Green, Woodbridge, Suffolk; *m* 1949, Joan Edwina, *d* of Samuel E. M. Simpson, Newcastle-under-Lyme, and of Dorothy C. Simpson; one *s* (and one *s* decd). *Educ:* Manchester Grammar Sch.; Victoria Univ., Manchester. Solicitor, 1947, Hons; John Peacock and George Hadfield Prizeman, Law Society Art Prize, 1962. Served War: commissioned 2nd Lieut 41 Bn, Royal Tank Corps, TA, 1939; served AFV Sch.; volunteered for maritime service: Captain in RASC motor boat companies in home coastal waters, India, Burma, Malaya and its Archipelago; demob. 1946; Major, QORR, The Staffordshire Yeomanry. Mem., Market Drayton RDC, 1966–71; Chm., Woore Parish Council, 1971–79; Hon. Sec., North Staffs Forces Help Soc., 1964–84; Mem., Staffs War Pensions Cttee; Member: 1745 Assoc. and Mil. Hist. Soc., 1960–84; Pres., Uttoxeter Flyfishing Club, 1975–77; Trustee, Birdsgrove Flyfishing Club, Ashbourne. Life Mem., Clan Morrison Soc. Member, Military and Hospitaller Order of St Lazarus of Jerusalem. *Recreation:* fishing. *Address:* The Rookery, Woore, Salop CW3 9RG. *T:* Pipe Gate 414. *Club:* Army and Navy.

RIGG, Diana; actress; Director, United British Artists, since 1982; *b* Doncaster, Yorks, 20 July 1938; *d* of Louis Rigg and Beryl Helliwell; *m* 1982, Archibald Stirling; one *d*. *Educ:* Fulneck Girls' Sch., Pudsey. Trained for the stage at Royal Academy of Dramatic Art. First appearance on stage in RADA prod. in York Festival, at Theatre Royal, York, summer, 1957 (Natella Abashwili in The Caucasian Chalk Circle); after appearing in repertory in Chesterfield and in York she joined the Royal Shakespeare Company, Stratford-upon-Avon, 1959; first appearance in London, Aldwych Theatre, 1961 (2nd Ondine, Violanta and Princess Berthe in Ondine); at same theatre, in repertory (The Devils, Becket, The Taming of the Shrew), 1961; (Madame de Tourvel, The Art of Seduction), 1962; Royal Shakespeare, Stratford-upon-Avon, Apr. 1962 (Helena in A Midsummer Night's Dream, Bianca in The Taming of the Shrew, Lady Macduff in Macbeth, Adriana in The Comedy of Errors, Cordelia in King Lear); subseq. appeared in the last production at the Aldwych, Dec. 1962, followed by Adriana in The Comedy of Errors and Monica Stettler in The Physicists, 1963. Toured the provinces, spring, 1963, in A Midsummer Night's Dream;

subseq. appeared at the Royal Shakespeare, Stratford, and at the Aldwych, in Comedy of Errors, Dec. 1963; again played Cordelia in King Lear, 1964, prior to touring with both plays for the British Council, in Europe, the USSR, and the US; during this tour she first appeared in New York (State Theatre), 1964, in same plays; Viola in Twelfth Night, Stratford, June 1966; Heloise in Abelard and Heloise, Wyndham's, 1970, also at the Atkinson, New York, 1971; joined The National Theatre, 1972: in Jumpers, 'Tis Pity She's a Whore and Lady Macbeth in Macbeth, 1972; The Misanthrope, 1973, Washington and NY, 1975; Phaedra Britannica, 1975 (Plays and Players Award for Best Actress); The Guardsman, 1978; Pygmalion, Albery, 1974; Night and Day, Phoenix, 1978 (Plays and Players award, 1979); Colette, USA, 1982; Heartbreak House, Haymarket, 1983; Little Eyolf, Lyric, Hammersmith, 1985; Antony and Cleopatra, Chichester, 1985; *films include:* A Midsummer Night's Dream, Assassination Bureau, On Her Majesty's Secret Service, Julius Caesar, The Hospital, Theatre of Blood, A Little Night Music, The Great Muppet Caper, Evil Under the Sun (Film Actress of the Year Award, Variety Club, 1983); *TV appearances include:* Sentimental Agent, The Comedy of Errors, The Avengers, Married Alive, Diana (US series), In This House of Brede (US), Three Piece Suite, The Serpent Son, Hedda Gabler, The Marquise, Little Eyolf, King Lear, Witness of the Prosecution, Bleak House, and others. *Publication:* No Turn Unstoned, 1982. *Recreations:* reading and trying to get organized. *Address:* c/o London Management, 235 Regent Street, W1A 2JT.

RIGNEY, Howard Ernest; HM Diplomatic Service, retired; Consul-General, Lyons, 1977–82; *b* 22 June 1922; *o s* of late Wilbert Ernest and Minnie Rigney; *m* 1950, Margaret Grayling Benn; one *s*. *Educ:* Univs of Western Ontario, Toronto and Paris. BA Western Ont. 1945, MA Toronto 1947. Lectr, Univ. of British Columbia, 1946–48; grad. studies, Paris Univ., 1948–50; COI, 1953–56; CRO, 1956; Regional Information Officer, Dacca, 1957–60, Montreal, 1960–63; CRO, 1963–65; FO/CO, 1965–67; Consul (Information), Chicago, 1967–69; Dep. Consul-Gen., Chicago, 1969–71; Head of Chancery and Consul, Rangoon, 1971–73; Head of Migration and Visa Dept, FCO, 1973–77. Hon DLitt, Winston Churchill Coll., Ill, 1971. *Recreations:* opera, book-collecting, gardening, golf. *Address:* c/o Lloyds Bank, 6 Pall Mall, SW1. *Clubs:* Cercle de l'Union (Lyon), Golf Club de Lyon.

RILEY, Bridget Louise, CBE 1972; Artist; *b* 24 April 1931; *d* of John Riley and late Louise (*née* Gladstone). *Educ:* Cheltenham Ladies' College; Goldsmiths' School of Art; Royal College of Art. ARCA 1955. AICA critics Prize, 1963; Stuyvesant Bursary, 1964; Ohara Mus. Prize, Tokyo, 1972; Gold Medal, Grafik Biennale, Norway, 1980. Mem., RSA. One-man shows: London, 1962, 1963, 1969, 1971 (retrospective, at Hayward Gall.), 1976, 1981, 1983; New York, Los Angeles, 1965; New York, 1967, 1975, 1978; Hanover, 1970; Turin, Düsseldorf, Berne, Prague, 1971; Basle, 1975; Sydney, 1976; Tokyo, 1977, 1983; touring retrospective, USA, Aust. and Japan, 1978–80. Exhibited in group shows: England, France, Israel, America, Germany, Italy. Represented Britain: Paris Biennale, 1965; Venice Biennale, 1968 (awarded Chief internat. painting prize). Public collections include: Tate Gallery, Victoria and Albert Museum, Arts Council, British Council, Museum of Modern Art, New York', Australian Nat. Gallery, Canberra, Museum of Modern Art, Pasadena, Ferens Art Gallery, Hull, Allbright Knox, Buffalo, USA, Museum of Contemporary Art, Chicago, Ulster Museum, Ireland, Stedelijk Museum, Berne Kunsthalle. Designed Colour Moves, for Ballet Rambert, 1983. Trustee, Nat. Gallery, 1981–. Hon. DLit: Manchester, 1976; Ulster, 1986.

RILEY, Major John Roland Christopher; Chairman, Channel Television, since 1982; *b* 4 July 1925; *s* of Christopher John Molesworth Riley and Bridget Maisie Hanbury; *m* 1956, Penelope Ann Harrison (*d* 1978); two *d*. *Educ:* Winchester College. Commissioned Coldstream Guards, 1943; served NW Europe, Palestine, Malaya; Instructor, Army Staff Coll., 1960–62; retired 1962; Elected Deputy, States of Jersey, 1963, Senator, 1975; retired from Govt, 1981. Director: Air UK, 1963–; Jersey Gas Co., 1970–; Chase Bank & Trust Co. (CI), 1975–; Fuel Supplies CI, 1976–; Servisair Jersey, 1976–; Arbuthnot Latham Securities CI, 1980–; Securicor Jersey, 1982–; Arbuthnot Latham Trustees CI Ltd, 1984–. Seigneur de la Trinité. *Recreations:* horse riding (Master Jersey Drag Hunt), yachting. *Address:* Trinity Manor, Jersey, Channel Islands. *T:* Jersey 61026. *Clubs:* Cavalry and Guards, Royal Yacht Squadron.

RILEY, Sir Ralph, Kt 1984; DSc; FRS 1967; Deputy Chairman, 1983–85, Secretary, 1978–85, Agricultural and Food Research Council; *b* 23 Oct. 1924; *y c* of Ralph and Clara Riley; *m* 1949, Joan Elizabeth Norrington; two *d*. *Educ:* Audenshaw Gram. Sch.; Univ. of Sheffield. Infantry Soldier, 1943–47; Univ. of Sheffield, 1947–52; Research worker, Plant Breeding Inst., Cambridge, 1952–78; Head of Cytogenetics Dept, 1954–72; Dir, 1971–78. National Research Council/Nuffield Foundn Lectr at Canadian Univs, 1966; Special Prof. of Botany, Univ. of Nottingham, 1970–78. Fellow of Wolfson Coll., Cambridge, 1967–. Lectures: Sir Henry Tizard Meml, 1973; Holden, Univ. of Nottingham, 1975; Woodhull, Royal Instn, 1976; Bewley, Glasshouse Crops Res. Inst., 1980; Bernal, Birkbeck Coll., 1983. Pres., Genetical Soc., 1973–75; Sec., Internat. Genetics Fedn, 1973–78; Pres., Sect. K, BAAS, 1979. For. Fellow, INSA, 1976; For. Correspondent, Acad. d'Agriculture de France, 1981; For. Associate, Nat. Acad. Scis, USA, 1982. Hon. FRASE, 1980. Hon. DSc: Edinburgh, 1976; Hull, 1982; Cranfield, 1985; Hon. LLD Sheffield, 1984. William Bate Hardy Prize, Cambridge Phil. Soc., 1969; Royal Medal, Royal Soc., 1981; Wolf Foundn Prize in Agriculture, 1986. *Publications:* scientific papers and articles on genetics of chromosome behaviour, plant cytogenetics and evolution and breeding of crop plants especially wheat. *Address:* 2 High Street, Little Shelford, Cambridge CB2 5ES. *T:* Cambridge 843845. *Club:* Athenæum.

RIMBAULT, Brig. Geoffrey Acworth, CBE 1954; DSO 1945; MC 1936; DL; Director, Army Sport Control Board, 1961–73; *b* 17 April 1908; *s* of late Arthur Henry Rimbault, London; *m* 1933, Joan, *d* of late Thomas Hallet-Fry, Beckenham, Kent; one *s*. *Educ:* Dulwich College. 2nd Lieut, The Loyal Regt (N Lancs), 1930; served: India, Waziristan, 1931–36; Palestine, 1937; Staff Coll., Camberley; N Africa, Anzio, Italy and Palestine, 1939–46; Chief Instructor, RMA Sandhurst, 1950–51; Chief of Staff, E Africa, 1952–54; comd 131 Inf. Bde, 1955–57; comd Aldershot Garrison, 1958–61. Colonel, The Loyal Regt, 1959–70. Life Vice-Pres., Surrey CCC (Pres., 1982–83). Liveryman, Mercers' Co., 1961, Master, 1970–71. DL Surrey, 1971. *Recreations:* cricket, tennis, golf, shooting. *Address:* 10 Clarke Place, Elmbridge, Cranleigh, Surrey. *T:* Cranleigh 271207. *Clubs:* Army and Navy, MCC.

RIMINGTON, Claude, FRS 1954, MA, PhD Cantab, DSc London; Emeritus Professor of Chemical Pathology, University of London; Head of Department of Chemical Pathology, University College Hospital Medical School, 1945–67; *b* 17 Nov. 1902; *s* of George Garthwaite Rimington, Newcastle upon Tyne; *m* 1929, Soffi, *d* of Clemet Andersen, Askerøy, Lyngør, Norway; one *d*. *Educ:* Emmanuel College, Cambridge. Benn W. Levy Research Scholar, Univ. of Cambridge, 1926–28; Biochemist, Wool Industries Research Association, Leeds, 1928–30; Empire Marketing Board Senior Research Fellow, then Scientific Research Officer, Division of Veterinary Services, Govt of Union of South Africa, at Onderstepoort Veterinary Research Laboratory, Pretoria, 1931–37; Biochemist, National Institute for Medical Research, Medical Research Council, London, 1937–45. Hon. FRCP Edinburgh, 1967; Hon. Mem. Brit. Assoc. of Dermatology, 1967. Graham

Gold Medal, Univ. of London, 1967. *Publications:* (with A. Goldberg), Diseases of Porphyrin Metabolism, 1962; numerous biochemical and scientific papers. *Recreations:* sailing, languages, Scandinavian literature. *Address:* Askerøy, Per Vestre Sandøy 4915, Norway.

RIMINGTON, John David; Director-General, Health and Safety Executive, since 1984; *b* 27 June 1935; *s* of John William Rimington and Mabel Dorrington; *m* 1963; two *d. Educ:* Nottingham High Sch.; Jesus Coll., Cambridge (Cl. I Hons History, MA). Nat. Service Commn, RA, 1954–56. Joined BoT, 1959; seconded HM Treasury (work on decimal currency), 1961; Principal, Tariff Div., BoT, 1963; 1st Sec. (Economic), New Delhi, 1965; Mergers Div., DTI, 1969; Dept of Employment, 1970; Asst Sec. 1972 (Employment Policy and Manpower); Counsellor, Social and Regional Policy, UK perm. representation to EEC, Brussels, 1974; MSC, 1977–81; Under Sec. 1978; Dir, Safety Policy Div., HSE, 1981–83; Dep. Sec., 1984. *Publications:* contrib. to RIPA Jl, New Asia Review. *Recreations:* walking, gardening, watching cricket.

RIMMER, Prof. Frederick William, CBE 1980; MA (Cantab), BMus (Dunelm); FRCO; FRSAMD; Gardiner Professor of Music, University of Glasgow, 1966–80, now Emeritus Professor; Director of Scottish Music Archive, 1968–80; *b* 21 Feb. 1914; 2nd *s* of William Rimmer and Amy Graham McMillan, Liverpool; *m* 1941, Joan Doreen, *d* of Major Alexander Hume Graham and Beatrice Cecilia Myles; two *s* one *d. Educ:* Quarry Bank High Sch., Liverpool. FRCO (Harding Prize), 1934; BMus (Dunelm), 1939. Served War: 11th Bn, The Lancashire Fusiliers, Middle East, 1941–45 (Maj. 1944). Selwyn Coll., Cambridge (Organ Scholar), 1946–48; Sen. Lectr in Music, Homerton Coll., Cambridge, 1948–51; Cramb Lectr in Music, Univ. of Glasgow, 1951–56; Sen. Lectr, 1956–66, and Organist to the Univ., 1954–66. Henrietta Harvey Vis. Prof., Memorial Univ. of Newfoundland, 1977. A Dir of Scottish Opera, 1966–80; Chm., BBC's Scottish Music Adv. Cttee, 1972–77; Mem., Music Adv. Cttee, British Council, 1973–82, Scottish Adv. Cttee, 1979–82. Hon. Fellow, Selwyn Coll., Cambridge, 1982. Special Award for services to contemp. music in Scotland, Composers' Guild of GB, 1975. *Publications:* contrib. to: A History of Scottish Music, 1973; Companion to Scottish Culture, 1981; articles on 20th century music, in: Tempo; Music Review; Organists' Review; compositions for solo organ: Five Preludes on Scottish Psalm Tunes, Pastorale and Toccata, Invenzione e Passacaglia Capricciosa, Ostinato Mesto, Fugato Giocoso; anthems for choir and organ: Sing we merrily; Christus natus est alleluia; O Lord, we beseech thee; O Blessed God in Trinity; Five carols of the Nativity; for solo soprano and organ: Of a Rose; Born is the Babe. *Recreations:* reading and gardening. *Address:* Manor Farmhouse, 6 Mill Way, Grantchester, Cambridge CB3 9NB. *T:* Cambridge 840716.

RINFRET, Hon. Gabriel-Edouard, OC 1983; PC (Canada) 1949; Chief Justice of Québec, 1977–80, retired; Counsel, Pepin, Le Tourneau and Associates, since 1981; *b* St-Jérôme, PQ, 12 May 1905; *s* of Rt Hon. Thibaudeau Rinfret, Chief Justice of Canada, and Georgine, *d* of S. J. B. Rolland; *m* 1929; two *s*; *m* 1982. *Educ:* Collège Notre-Dame, Côte des Neiges, PQ; Petit Séminaire, Montréal; Collège Ste-Marie (BA with distinction); McGill Univ., Montréal (LLM with distinction); pupil of Hon. J. L. Perron. Admitted to practice, 1928; joined law office of Campbell, McMaster, Couture, Kerry and Bruneau; partner, Campbell, Weldon, MacFarlane and Rinfret, 1945. KC 1943. Sec. or Legal Adviser to various provincial govt commns of enquiry, 1934–45. Pres., Jeunesse Libérale de Montréal, 1934; Co-founder and 1st Pres., Assoc. de la Jeunesse Libérale de la Province de Québec, 1934–35; MP (L) Outremont, 1945–49, Outremont-St Jean 1949–52, House of Commons of Canada; Postmaster General in St Laurent Cabinet. A Judge of the Court of Appeal of Québec, 1952–80. Pres. or Director: Concerts Symphoniques de Montréal; Inst. Internat. de Musique; Grands Ballets Canadiens; Dominion Drama Festival (organised Montréal Festival, 1961; Pres., W Québec Region, and Mem., Nat. Exec. Cttee, 1962–68; Canadian Drama Award, 1969); Vice Pres., Conservatoire Lassalle, 1967–. Hon. LLD, Univ. of British Columbia, 1979. *Publications:* Répertoire du théâtre canadien d'expression française, vol. 1, 1975, vol. 2, 1976, vol. 3, 1977, vol. 4, 1978. *Recreations:* cabinet-work, Canadian paintings; formerly baseball, lacrosse, tennis, hockey, ski-ing. *Address:* 121 Melbourne Avenue, Town of Mount Royal, Québec, H3P 1G3, Canada.

RING, Prof. James, CBE 1983; Emeritus Professor of Physics, Imperial College of Science and Technology, since 1984; Deputy Chairman, Cable Authority, since 1984; *b* 22 Aug. 1927; *s* of James and Florence Ring; *m* 1949, Patricia, *d* of Major H. J. Smith, MBE; two *s. Educ:* Univ. of Manchester (BSc, PhD). FInstP, FRAS. Reader in Spectrometry, Univ. of Manchester, 1957; Prof. of Applied Physics, Hull Univ., 1962; Prof. of Physics, 1962, and Associate Hd of Physics Dept, 1979, Imperial Coll. of Sci. and Technol. Chm., Queensgate Instruments, 1979–; Director: Infrared Engrg, 1970–; IC Optical Systems, 1970–. Member: IBA, 1974–81; Inquiry into Cable Expansion and Broadcasting Policy, 1982. *Publications:* numerous papers and articles in learned jls. *Recreations:* stargazing, dinghy sailing. *Address:* 8 Riverview Gardens, Barnes, SW13.

RING, Sir Lindsay (Roberts), GBE 1975; JP; Chairman, Ring & Brymer (Birchs) Ltd; Lord Mayor of London for 1975–76; *b* 1 May 1914; *y s* of George Arthur Ring and Helen Rhoda Mason Ring (*née* Stedman); *m* 1940, Hazel Doris, *d* of A. Trevor Nichols, CBE; two *s* one *d. Educ:* Dulwich Coll.; Mecklenburg, Germany. Served 1939–45, Europe and Middle East, Major RASC. Underwriting Member of Lloyd's, 1964. Fellow, Hotel and Catering Inst.; Chm., Hotel and Catering Trades Benevolent Assoc., 1962–71; Member: Bd of Verge of Royal Palaces, 1977–84; Gaming Bd for GB, 1977–83; NI Develt Agency, 1977–81. Chm., City of London (Arizona) Corp., 1981–84. Chancellor, City Univ., 1975–76. Governor, Farringtons Sch. Freeman, City of London, 1935; Member, Court of Assistants: Armourers' and Brasiers' Co. (Master 1972); Chartered Secretaries' and Administrators' Co. Common Councilman, City of London (Ward of Bishopsgate), 1964–68; Alderman (Ward of Vintry), 1968–84; Sheriff, City of London, 1967–68; Governor, Hon. Irish Soc., 1980–84. HM Lieut for City of London; JP Inner London, 1964. Hon. Col, 151 (Greater London) Regt, RCT(V). Hon. Burgess, Borough of Coleraine, NI. KStJ 1976. FCIS 1976. Hon. DSc City Univ., 1976; Hon. DLitt Ulster, 1976. Comdr, Legion of Honour, 1976; Order of Rio Branca (Brazil), 1976. *Address:* Chalvedune, Wilderness Road, Chislehurst, Kent, BR7 5EY. *T:* 01–467 3199. *Club:* City Livery.

RINGADOO, Hon. Sir Veerasamy, GCMG 1986; Kt 1975; Officier de l'Ordre National Malgache 1969; Governor-General and Commander-in-Chief of Mauritius, since 1986; *b* 1920; *s* of Nagaya Ringadoo; *m* 1954, Lydie Vadamootoo; one *s* one *d. Educ:* Port Louis Grammar Sch.; LSE Eng. (LLB); Hon. Fellow, 1976. Called to Bar, 1949; Municipal Councillor, 1956; MLC for Moka-Flacq, 1951–67; Minister: Labour and Social Scurity, 1959–64; Education, 1964–67; Agriculture and Natural Resources, 1967–68; Finance, 1968–82; attended London Constitutional Conf., 1965; first MLA (Lab) for Quartier Militaire and Moka, 1967, re-elected 1976. Governor, IMF; Chm., Bd of Governors, African Development Bank and African Development Fund, 1977–78. Hon. Fellow, LSE, 1976. Hon LLD Mauritius, 1975; Hon. DLit Andhra, 1978. *Address:* Government House, Port Louis, Mauritius.

RINGROSE, Prof. John Robert, FRS 1977; FRSE; Professor of Pure Mathematics, since 1964, and a Pro-Vice-Chancellor, since 1983, University of Newcastle upon Tyne; *b* 21 Dec. 1932; *s* of Albert Frederick Ringrose and Elsie Lilian Ringrose (*née* Roberts); *m* 1956, Jean Margaret Bates; three *s. Educ:* Buckhurst Hill County High School, Chigwell, Essex; St John's Coll., Cambridge (MA, PhD). Lecturer in Mathematics: King's Coll., Newcastle upon Tyne, 1957–61; Univ. of Cambridge (also Fellow of St John's Coll.), 1961–63; Sen. Lectr in Mathematics, Univ. of Newcastle upon Tyne, 1963–64. *Publications:* Compact Non-self-adjoint Operators, 1971; (with R. V. Kadison) Fundamentals of the Theory of Operator Algebras, 1983; mathematical papers in various research jls. *Address:* School of Mathematics, The University, Newcastle upon Tyne NE1 7RU. *T:* Newcastle upon Tyne 328511.

RINGWOOD, Prof. Alfred Edward, FAA 1966; FRS 1972; Professor of Geochemistry, Australian National University, since 1967; *b* 19 April 1930; *s* of Alfred Edward Ringwood and Wilhelmena Grace Bruce Ringwood (*née* Robertson); *m* 1960, Gun Ivor Karlsson, Halsingborg, Sweden; one *s* one *d. Educ:* Hawthorn Central Sch., Melbourne; Geelong Grammar Sch.; Melbourne Univ. BSc 1950, MSc 1953, PhD 1956, Melbourne. Research Fellow, Geochemistry, Harvard Univ., 1957–58; Australian National University: Sen. Res. Fellow, 1959; Sen. Fellow, 1960; Personal Prof., 1963; Dir, Res. Sch. of Earth Scis, 1978–84. William Smith Lectr, Geol Soc. of London, 1973; Vernadsky Lectr, USSR Acad. of Scis, 1975; Centenary Lectr and Medallist, Chem. Soc., London, 1977; Matthew Flinders Lecture, Australian Acad. of Sci., 1978; Hallimond Lectr, Mineralogical Soc. of GB, 1983; Bakerian Lect., Royal Soc., 1983. Commonwealth and Foreign Mem., Geol Soc., London, 1967; Fellow, Amer. Geophysical Union, 1969; Vice-Pres., Australian Acad. of Science, 1971. For. Associate, Nat. Acad. of Scis of Amer., 1975; Hon. Mem., All-Union Mineralog. Soc., USSR, 1976. Mineralogical Soc. of America Award, 1967; Britannica Australia Award for Science, 1969; Rosentiel Award, AAAS, 1971; Werner Medaille, German Mineralogical Soc., 1972; Bowie Medal, American Geophysical Union, 1974; Day Medal, Geological Soc. of America, 1974; Mueller Medal, Aust. and NZ Assoc. for Advancement of Sci., 1975; Holmes Medal, European Union of Geosciences, 1985. *Publications:* Composition and Petrology of the Earth's Mantle, 1975; Safe Disposal of High Level Nuclear Reactor Wastes: a new strategy, 1978; Origin of Earth and Moon, 1979; numerous papers in learned jls dealing with nature of earth's interior, phase transformations under high pressures, origin and evolution of earth, moon, planets and meteorites, and safe immobilization of high level nuclear reactor wastes. *Recreations:* music, travel. *Address:* 3 Vancouver Street, Red Hill, Canberra, ACT 2603, Australia. *T:* Canberra 062–953635.

RINK, Margaret Joan; *see* Suttill, Dr. M. J.

RIPA DI MEANA, Carlo; Member for Italy, Commission of the European Communities, since 1985; *b* 15 Aug. 1929; *m* 1982, Marina Punturieri. Editor, Il Lavoro (Ital. Gen. Conf. of Labour weekly newspaper), and Editor, foreign dept, Unita (Ital. Communist Party daily paper), 1950–53; rep. of Italy on UIE, Prague, 1953–56; founded jointly Nuova Generazione, 1956; left Ital. Communist Party, 1957; founded jointly Passato e Presente, 1957 (chief editor); joined Italian Socialist Party (PSI), 1958; worked in publishing until 1966; Councillor for Lombardy (PSI), 1970–74 (Chm., Constitutional Cttee); leader, PSI Group, regional council; head, international relations PSI, 1979–80; Mem., European Parlt, 1979–84. Pres., Inst. for Internat. Economic Cooperation and Develt Problems, 1983; Sec.-Gen., Club Turati, Milan, 1967–76; Mem. Board, Scala Theatre, Milan, 1970–74; Mem. Council, Venice Biennale 1974–82 (Chm., 1974–79); founder Mem., Crocodile Club; Pres., Fernando Santi Inst.; Pres., Unitary Fedn, Italian Press abroad; Vice-Chm., Internat. Cttee for Solidarity with Afghan People. *Publications:* Un viaggio in Viet-Nam (A Voyage to Vietnam), 1956; A tribute to Raymond Roussel and his Impressions of Africa, 1965; Il governo audiovisio (Audiovisual Government), 1973. *Recreations:* horse riding, sailing. *Address:* 200 Rue de la Loi, 1049 Brussels, Belgium.

RIPLEY, Dillon; *see* Ripley, S. D.

RIPLEY, Sir Hugh, 4th Bt, *cr* 1880; former Director, John Walker & Sons Ltd, Scotch Whisky Distillers, retired 1981; *b* 26 May 1916; *s* of Sir Henry William Alfred Ripley, 3rd Bt, and Dorothy (*d* 1964), *e d* of late Robert William Daker Harley; *S* father 1956; *m* 1st, 1946, Dorothy Mary Dunlop Bruce-Jones (marr. diss. 1971); one *s* one *d*; 2nd, 1972, Susan, *d* of W. Parker, Leics; one *d. Educ:* Eton. Served in Africa and Italy with 1st Bn KSLI (despatches twice, American Silver Star); retired regular Major. *Recreations:* golf, fishing, shooting. *Heir: s* William Hugh Ripley, *b* 13 April 1950. *Address:* 20 Abingdon Villas, W8; The Oak, Bedstone, Bucknell, Salop. *Club:* Boodle's.

RIPLEY, (Sidney) Dillon, II, Hon. KBE 1979; PhD; Secretary, Smithsonian Institution, 1964–84, now Secretary Emeritus; *b* 20 Sept. 1913; *s* of Louis Arthur Ripley and Constance Baillie (*née* Rose); *m* 1949, Mary Moncrieffe Livingston; three *d. Educ:* St Paul's Sch., Concord, NH; Yale Univ. (BA 1936); Harvard Univ. (PhD 1943). Staff, Acad. of Natural Sciences, Philadelphia, 1936–39; Volunteer Asst, Amer. Museum of Natural History, New York, 1939–40; Teaching Asst, Harvard Univ., 1941–42; Asst Curator of Birds, Smithsonian Instn, 1942; OSS, 1942–45; Lectr, Curator, Associate Prof. of Zool. and Prof. of Biol., Yale Univ., 1946–64; Dir, Peabody Museum of Nat. Hist., 1959–64. Dir, Riggs Nat. Corp., Washington, 1984. Chm. (US), E-SU, 1984. Pres., 1958–82, Pres. Emeritus, 1982–, ICBP. Benjamin Franklin Fellow, RSA, 1968. Mem., Amer. Acad. of Arts and Scis, 1984; Hon. Mem., Amer. Inst. of Architects, 1975–. Hon. MA Yale Univ., 1961; Hon DHL: Marlboro Coll., 1965; Williams Coll., 1972; Johns Hopkins, 1984; Washington Coll., 1986; Hon. DSc: George Washington Univ., 1966; Catholic Univ., 1968; Univ. of Md, 1970; Cambridge Univ., 1974; Brown Univ., 1975; Trinity Coll., 1977; Hon. LLD: Dickinson Coll., 1967; Hofstra Univ., 1968; Yale Univ., 1975; Gallaudet Coll., 1981; Harvard, 1984; Hon. DE Stevens Inst. of Technol., 1977. Order of White Elephant, Thailand, 1949; Order of the Sacred Treasure, 2nd Cl., Japan, 1982; Officer: l'Ordre des Arts et des Lettres, France, 1975; Order of Leopold, Belgium, 1981; Commander: Order of Golden Ark, Netherlands, 1976; Order of Merit, State Council of Polish People's Republic, 1979; Order of Orange-Nassau, Netherlands, 1982; Officier, Légion d'Honneur, France, 1985; Comdr's Cross, Order of the Dannebrog, Denmark, 1976; Caballero Gran Cruz, Orden del Merito Civil, Spain, 1976; Order of James Smithson, Smithsonian Instn, 1984; Padma Bhushan, India, 1986. Freedom Medal, Thailand, 1949; President's Medal of Freedom, USA, 1985; Gold Medal: New York Zool Soc., 1966; Royal Zool Soc. of Antwerp, 1970; Thomas Jefferson Award, Amer. Soc. of Interior Designers, 1974; Medal for Distinguished Achievement, Holland Soc. of New York, 1977; F. K. Hutchinson Medal, Garden Club of America, 1979; Medal of Honor, National Soc. of Daughters of Amer. Revolution, 1981; Delacour Medal, ICBP, 1982; Henry Shaw Medal, St Louis Botanical Garden, 1982; Gold Medal, Acad. of Soc. Sci., New York, 1982; Addison Emery Verrill Medal, Peabody Mus., Yale Univ., 1984; Olympia Prize, Onassis Foundn, 1984; Medal of Distinction, Barnard Coll., 1985. *Publications:* The Trail of the Money Bird, 1942; Search for the Spiny Babbler, 1952, re-issued as A Naturalist's Adventure in Nepal, 1978; A Paddling of Ducks, 1957; A Synopsis of the Birds of India and Pakistan, 1961, rev. edn 1982; (with Lynette L. Scribner) Ornithological Books in the Yale University Library, 1961; (co-ed) The Land and Wildlife of Tropical Asia, 1964, rev. edns 1971 and 1974; (with H. G. Deignan and R. A. Paynter, Jr) Check-list of Birds of the World, Vol. X (continuation of work of James L.

Peters), 1964; The Sacred Grove, 1969; The Paradox of the Human Condition, 1975; Rails of the World, 1977; (with Sálim Ali) Handbook of the Birds of India and Pakistan: Vol. I, 1968, rev. edn 1978; Vol. II, 1969, rev. edn 1979; Vol. III, 1969, rev. edn 1981; Vol. IV, 1970, rev. edn 1984; Vol. V, 1972; Vol. VI, 1971; Vol. VII, 1972; Vol. VIII, 1973; Vol. IX, 1973; Vol. X, 1974; (with Sálim Ali) A Pictorial Guide to Birds of the Indian Subcontinent, 1983. *Recreation*: watching ducks. *Address*: 2324 Massachusetts Avenue, NW, Washington, DC 20008, USA. *T*: (202) 232–3131; Duck Pond Road, Litchfield, Conn 06759, USA. *T*: (203) 567–8208. *Clubs*: Pilgrims of the US, Knickerbocker, Century Association, Yale (New York); Cosmos, Society of Cincinnati, Alibi, Metropolitan, Army–Navy (Washington, DC); Himalayan (New Delhi).

RIPLEY, Sydney William Leonard; Member, Greater London Council (Kingston-upon-Thames Borough), 1964–86; *b* 17 July 1909; *o s* of late Leonard Ripley; *m* 1st, 1934, Doris Emily (from whom he obtained a divorce, 1966), *d* of late William Gray; one *s* two *d*; 2nd, 1972, Mrs Pida Polkinghorne, *d* of Capt. Peter Russell. *Educ*: King's School, Canterbury; London. Served War of 1939–45, with RAF, Flight-Lieut (despatches). Contested (C) Ipswich, 1950, Watford, 1951; Chairman Malden and Coombe Conservative Assoc., 1938–49, Pres., 1950–; Vice-Pres., Kingston Division, 1955–79, Pres., 1979–. Formerly Chairman Leonard Ripley and Co. Ltd and other printing and outdoor advertising companies, resigned 1973; Dir, Mills and Allen Ltd, 1970–73 (Consultant, 1975–). Member, Malden and Coombe Borough Council, 1938–48, formerly Chm. Finance Cttee; DL Surrey 1960; DL Greater London, 1966–84; JP 1959–69, CC 1946, CA 1955, Surrey (Chairman, Finance Cttee, 1962–64); Vice-Chm. Surrey CC, 1956–59; Chm. General Purposes Cttee, 1952–59; Chm. Surrey County Council, 1959–62; Mem., Surrey Jt Standing Cttee, 1959–65; County Council rep. on Metrop. Water Bd, 1956–65; County Councils Assoc., 1958–65; Surrey T&AFA, 1959–65; Governor Westminster Hosp., 1963–65; Jt Dep. Leader, Cons. Opposition, GLC, 1964–66; GLC rep. on Surrey T&AFA, 1965–68; London Tourist Board, 1965–68; Thames Water Authority, 1975–86; Chm., Open Spaces and Recreation Cttee, GLC, 1977–81. Chm., SW Regional Hosp. Bd, 1963–65. Freeman, City of London. *Recreations*: golf, swimming, tennis. *Address*: 41 Green Street, W1. *Clubs*: Brooks's, Carlton.

RIPON, Bishop of, since 1977; **Rt. Rev. David Nigel de Lorentz Young;** *b* 2 Sept. 1931; *s* of late Brig. K. de L. Young, CIE, MC; *m* 1962, Rachel Melverley Lewis (*d* 1966); one *s* one *d*; *m* 1967, Jane Havill Collison; three *s*. *Educ*: Wellington Coll.; Balliol Coll., Oxford (MA). Director, Dept of Buddhist Studies, Theological Coll. of Lanka, 1964; Lecturer in Comparative Religion, Manchester Univ., 1967; Vicar of Burwell, Cambridge, 1970–75; Archdeacon of Huntingdon, 1975–77; Vicar of Great with Little and Steeple Gidding, 1975–77; Rector of Hemingford Abbots, 1977; Hon. Canon of Ely Cathedral, 1975–77. Mem., Doctrine Commn, 1978–81; Chairman: Partnership for World Mission, 1978–86; Governing Body, SPCK, 1979–; Anglican Interfaith Consultants, 1981–; Scargill Council, 1984–. *Publications*: contribs to Religious Studies. *Recreations*: tennis, sailing. *Address*: Bishop Mount, Ripon, N Yorks HG4 5DP. *Club*: Royal Commonwealth Society.

RIPON, Dean of; *see* Campling, Very Rev. C. R.

RIPPENGAL, Derek, CB 1982; QC 1980; Counsel to Chairman of Committees, House of Lords, since 1977; *b* 8 Sept. 1928; *s* of William Thomas Rippengal and Margaret Mary Rippengal (*née* Parry); *m* 1963, Elizabeth Melrose (*d* 1973); one *s* one *d*. *Educ*: Hampton Grammar Sch.; St Catharine's Coll., Cambridge (MA). Called to Bar, Middle Temple, 1953 (Harmsworth schol.). Entered Treasury Solicitor's Office, 1958, after Chancery Bar and univ. posts; Sen. Legal Asst, 1961; Asst Treasury Solicitor, 1967; Principal Asst Treasury Solicitor, 1971; Solicitor to DTI, 1972–73; Dep. Parly Counsel, 1973–74, Parly Counsel, 1974–76, Law Commn. *Recreations*: music, fishing. *Address*: Wychwood, Bell Lane, Little Chalfont, Amersham, Bucks HP6 6PF. *Club*: Athenæum.

RIPPON, Rt. Hon. (Aubrey) Geoffrey (Frederick), PC 1962; QC 1964; MP (C) Hexham, since 1966; *b* 28 May 1924; *o s* of late A. E. S. Rippon; *m* 1946, Ann Leyland, OBE 1984, *d* of Donald Yorke, MC, Prenton, Birkenhead, Cheshire; one *s* three *d*. *Educ*: King's College, Taunton; Brasenose College, Oxford (Hulme Open Exhibitioner; MA), Hon. Fellow, 1972. Secretary and Librarian of the Oxford Union, 1942; Pres. Oxford University Conservative Assoc., 1942; Chm., Federation of University Conservative Associations, 1943. Called to the Bar, Middle Temple, 1948 (Robert Garraway Rice Pupillage Prizeman), Bencher, 1979. Member Surbiton Borough Council, 1945–54; Alderman, 1949–54; Mayor, 1951–52; Member: LCC (Chelsea), 1952–61 (Leader of Conserv. Party on LCC, 1957–59); Court, Univ. of London, 1958–; Chairman: British Section of the Council of European Municipalities; British Sect., European League for Economic Co-operation; President: London Mayors' Assoc., 1968–71; Surrey Mayors' Assoc., 1974–76; Admiral of the Manx Herring Fleet, 1971–74. Chm. Conservative National Advisory Committee on Local Government, 1957–59, Pres., 1972–74; Vice-Pres., Council of Europe's Local Government Conference, 1957 and 1958; Contested (C) Shoreditch and Finsbury, General Elections, 1950 and 1951; MP (C) Norwich South, 1955–64. PPS, Min. of Housing and Local Govt, 1956–57, Min. of Defence, 1957–59; Parly Sec., Min. of Aviation, 1959–61; Jt Parly Sec., Min. of Housing and Local Govt, Oct. 1961–July 1962; Minister of Public Building and Works, 1962–64 (Cabinet, 1963–64); Chief Opposition Spokesman on housing, local govt and land, 1966–68, on defence, 1968–70; Minister of Technology (incorporating Mins of Industry, Fuel and Power, Aviation and Supply), 1970; Chancellor of the Duchy of Lancaster, 1970–72 (resp. for negotiating Britain's entry into the EEC); Sec. of State for the Environment (incorporating Mins of Trans., Housing, Land, Local Govt, Public Bldg and Works), 1972–74; Chief Opposition Spokesman on Foreign and Commonwealth Affairs, 1974–75. Chm., Parly Foreign and Commonwealth Affairs Cttee, 1979–81; Leader: Cons. Party Delegn to Council of Europe and WEU, 1967–70; Cons. Gp, European Parlt, 1977–79; Chm., Council of Ministers, EFTA, 1970–72. Chairman: Dun and Bradstreet Ltd, 1976–; Britannia Arrow Hldgs, 1977–; Brassey's Defence Publishers, 1977–; Singer & Friedlander Hldgs, 1984–; Robert Fraser and Partners, 1985–; formerly: Chm., Holland, Hannen & Cubitts; Dep. Chm., Drake & Gorham; Director: Fairey Co. Ltd; Bristol Aeroplane Co.; Hotung Estates. FCIArb; Hon. Mem., Rating and Valuation Assoc. Knight Grand Cross, Royal Order of North Star (Sweden); Grand Cross, Order of Merit (Liechtenstein). *Publications*: (Co-author) Forward from Victory, 1943; The Rent Act, 1957; various pamphlets and articles on foreign affairs, local government and legal subjects. *Recreations*: watching cricket, travel. *Address*: Mantle Hill, Hesleyside, Hexham, Northumberland; 22 Chipstead Street, SW6; 2 Paper Buildings, Temple, EC4. *T*: 01–353 5835. *Clubs*: Whites, Pratt's, MCC; Northern Counties, Northern Conservative and Unionist (Newcastle upon Tyne).

RISELEY-PRICHARD, Air Vice-Marshal Richard Augustin; Principal Medical Officer, Royal Air Force Support Command, 1980–85, retired; *b* 19 Feb. 1925; *s* of late Dr J. A. Prichard and Elizabeth (*née* Riseley); *m* 1953, Alannah *d* of late Air Cdre C. W. Busk, CB, MC, AFC; four *d*. *Educ*: Beaudesert Park; Radley Coll.; Trinity Coll., Oxford (MA, BM, BCh); St Bartholomew's Hosp., London. FFCM. Commnd RAF Med. Br., 1951; pilot trng, 1951–52; served at RAF Coll., Cranwell, 1953–56; Dep. Principal Med.

Officer (Flying), HQ Transport Comd and HQ RAF Germany, 1956–63; RAF Staff Coll., 1964; SMO, British Forces, Aden, 1967; Dep. Principal Med. Officer, HQ Strike Comd, 1970–73; Commanding Officer: RAF Hosp. Wegberg, Germany, 1973–76; Princess Alexandra Hosp., Wroughton, 1977–80. QHS 1980–85. Governor, Dauntsey's Sch., 1982– (Vice-Chm., 1985–). CStJ. *Recreations*: tennis, squash, bridge, gardening. *Address*: The Little House, Allington, Devizes, Wilts SN10 3NN. *T*: Cannings 662. *Clubs*: Royal Air Force; All England Lawn Tennis.

RISHBETH, John, OBE 1985; ScD; FRS 1974; Reader in Plant Pathology, University of Cambridge, 1973–84, now Emeritus; Fellow of Corpus Christi College, Cambridge, since 1964; *b* 10 July 1918; *e s* of late Prof. Oswald Henry Theodore Rishbeth and Kathleen (*née* Haddon), Cambridge; *m* 1946, Barbara Sadler; one *s* one *d*. *Educ*: St Lawrence Coll., Ramsgate; Christ's Coll., Cambridge. MA, PhD, ScD (Cantab). Frank Smart Prize, 1940, and Studentship, 1944, 1946, in Botany. Chemist, Royal Ordnance Factories, 1940–43; Bacteriologist, Scientific Adviser's Div., Min. of Food, 1943–45; Demonstrator in Botany, Univ. of Cambridge, 1947–49; Plant Pathologist, West Indian Banana Research Scheme, 1950–52; Lectr in Botany, Univ. of Cambridge, 1953–73. Visiting Prof. in Forest Pathology, N Carolina State Univ., 1967. Hon. Dr.agro Royal Veterinary and Agricl Univ., Copenhagen, 1976. *Publications*: papers on: root diseases, especially of trees, caused by fungi; biological control. *Recreations*: hill walking, tennis. *Address*: 36 Wingate Way, Cambridge CB2 2HD. *T*: Cambridge 841298. *Club*: Hawks (Cambridge).

RISK, Douglas James; Sheriff of Grampian, Highland and Islands, at Aberdeen, since 1979; *b* 23 Jan. 1941; *s* of James Risk and Isobel Katherine Taylor Risk (*née* Dow); *m* 1967, Jennifer Hood Davidson; three *s* one *d*. *Educ*: Glasgow Academy; Gonville and Caius Coll., Cambridge (BA 1963, MA 1967); Glasgow Univ. (LLB 1965). Admitted to Faculty of Advocates, 1966; Standing Junior Counsel, Scottish Education Dept, 1975; Sheriff of Lothian and Borders at Edinburgh, 1977–79. Hon. Lectr, Faculty of Law, Univ. of Aberdeen, 1981–. *Address*: Sheriff's Chambers, Sheriff Court House, Exchequer Row, Aberdeen AB9 1AP. *T*: Aberdeen 572780. *Club*: Royal Northern and University (Aberdeen).

RISK, Sir Thomas (Neilson), Kt 1984; Governor of the Bank of Scotland, since 1981 (Director, 1971; Deputy Governor, 1977–81); *b* 13 Sept. 1922; *s* of late Ralph Risk, CBE, MC, and Margaret Nelson Robertson; *m* 1949, Suzanne Eiloart; four *s*. *Educ*: Kelvinside Academy; Glasgow Univ. Flight Lieut, RAF, 1941–46; RAFVR, 1946–53. Partner, Maclay Murray & Spens, Solicitors, 1950–81; Director: Standard Life Assurance Co., 1965– (Chm., 1969–77); British Linen Bank, 1968– (Governor, 1977–86); Howden Group, 1971–; Merchants Trust, 1973–; MSA (Britain) Ltd, 1958–; Shell UK Ltd, 1982–; Barclays Bank, 1983–85. Member: Scottish Industrial Develt Bd, 1972–75; Scottish Econ. Council, 1983–. Trustee, Hamilton Bequest. *Address*: 10 Belford Place, Edinburgh EH4 3DH. *T*: 031–332 9425. *Clubs*: Royal Air Force; New (Edinburgh); Royal and Ancient (St Andrews); Prestwick Golf.

RISK, William Symington, CA; Chairman, Fleming & Ferguson Ltd, since 1980; *b* 15 Sept. 1909; *er s* of late William Risk and Agnes Hetherington Symington, Glasgow; *m* 1937, Isobel Brown McLay; one *s* one *d*. *Educ*: Glasgow Academy; Glasgow Univ.; Edinburgh Univ. (BCom). FCMA 1944, JDipMA 1969. Served War, with Admiralty, on torpedo production at RN Torpedo Factory, at Greenock and elsewhere, 1940–45. Partner, Robson, Morrow & Co., 1945–53; Managing Director: H. W. Nevill Ltd (Nevill's Bread), 1953; Aerated Bread Co. Ltd, 1956; Chm., The London Multiple Bakers' Alliance, 1958–59; Regional Dir for Southern England, British Bakeries Ltd, 1960; Industrial Consultant, Hambros Bank Ltd, 1963; Chm., Martin-Black Ltd, 1976–79. Inst. of Chartered Accountants of Scotland: Mem. Exam. Bd, 1951–55; Mem. Council, 1963–68; Pres., 1974–75; Jt Dip. in Management Accounting Services, and First Chm. of Bd, 1966; Inst. of Cost and Management Accountants: Mem. Council, 1952–70; Pres. of Inst., 1960–61; Gold Medal of Inst., for services to the Inst. and the profession, 1965. Mem. Bd of Governors, Queen Charlotte's Hosp., 1970–80. *Publications*: technical papers on Accountancy and Management subjects; papers to internat. Congress of Accountants (London, 1952, Paris, 1967). *Recreation*: reading. *Address*: Craigowrie, Strathspey Drive, Grantown on Spey, Morayshire PH26 3EY. *T*: Grantown on Spey 3001. *Club*: Caledonian.

RISNESS, Eric John, CBE 1982; FIEE; Managing Director, Admiralty Research Establishment, Portland, since 1984; *b* 27 July 1927; *s* of Kristen Riisnaes and Ethel Agnes (*née* Weeks); *m* 1952, Colleen Edwina Armstrong; two *s* two *d*. *Educ*: Stratford Grammar School, London; Corpus Christi College, Cambridge (MA, PhD). RN Scientific Service, Admiralty Research Lab., 1954; Naval Staff Coll., 1959; Admiralty Underwater Weapons Estabt, 1961; RCDS 1970; Ministry of Defence: Defence Science, 1974; Underwater Research, 1975; Sting Ray Torpedo Project, 1977; Underwater Weapons Projects, 1979; Admiralty Surface Weapons Estabt, 1980; Dir of Naval Analysis, 1982; Dir-Gen., Surface Weapons Projects, 1983. *Recreations*: music, genealogy, golf. *Address*: 8 Orchard Road, Shalford, Guildford, Surrey GU4 8ER. *T*: Guildford 34581.

RISSON, Maj.-Gen. Sir Robert Joseph Henry, Kt 1970; CB 1958; CBE 1945 (OBE 1942); DSO 1942; ED 1948; Chairman Melbourne and Metropolitan Tramways Board, 1949–70; Chairman, National Fitness Council of Victoria, 1961–71; *b* 20 April 1901; *s* of late Robert Risson; *m* 1934, Gwendolyn, *d* of late C. A. Spurgin; no *c*. *Educ*: Gatton High Sch.; Univ. of Queensland. BE (Civil); FICE; FIEAust; FAIM. Served AIF, War of 1939–45: GOC 3 Div. (Australian), 1953–56; Citizen Military Forces Member Australian Military Board, 1957–58. Chief Commissioner, Boy Scouts, Victoria, 1958–63; Pres., Instn Engineers, Australia, 1962–63. OStJ 1966. *Address*: 39 Somers Street, Burwood, Victoria 3125, Australia. *Clubs*: Australian (Melbourne); Naval and Military (Melbourne); United Service (Brisbane).

RIST, Prof. John Michael, FRSC; Professor of Classics and Philosophy, University of Toronto, since 1983; *b* 6 July 1936; *s* of Robert Ward Rist and Phoebe May (*née* Mansfield) *m* 1960, Anna Thérèse (*née* Vogler); two *s* two *d*. *Educ*: Trinity Coll., Cambridge (BA 1959, MA 1963). FRSC 1976. Univ. of Toronto: firstly Lectr, finally Prof. of Classics, 1959–80; Chm., Grad. Dept of Classics, 1971–75; Regius Prof. of Classics, Aberdeen Univ., 1980–83. *Publications*: Eros and Psyche, Canada 1964; Plotinus: the road to reality, 1967; Stoic Philosophy, 1969; Epicurus: an introduction, 1972; (ed) The Stoics, USA 1978; On the Independence of Matthew and Mark, 1978; Human Value, 1982; contrib. classical and phil jls. *Recreations*: travel, swimming, hill-walking. *Address*: University of Toronto, Toronto, Ontario M5S 1A1, Canada.

RITBLAT, John Henry, FSVA; Chairman and Managing Director, The British Land Co. Plc, since 1970; *b* 3 Oct. 1935; *m* 1960, Isabel Paja (*d* 1979); two *s* one *d*. *Educ*: Dulwich Coll.; London Univ.; College of Estate Management. Articles with West End firm of Surveyors and Valuers, 1952–58. Founder Partner, Conrad Ritblat & Co., Consultant Surveyors and Valuers, 1958; Man. Dir, Union Property Holdings (London) Ltd, 1969. Comr, Crown Estate Paving Commn, 1969–. Hon. Surveyor, King George's Fund for Sailors, 1979. FRGS 1982. *Recreations*: antiquarian books and libraries, old buildings and the countryside, squash, golf, skiing. *Address*: 10 Cornwall Terrace, Regent's Park, NW1

4QP. *T:* 01–486 4466. *Clubs:* Naval and Military, Royal Automobile, MCC, The Pilgrims.

RITCHESON, Prof. Charles Ray; Lovell University Professor, University Librarian, Dean and Vice Provost, University of Southern California, since 1984; *b* 26 Feb. 1925; *s* of Charles Frederick and Jewell Vaughn Ritcheson; *m* 1st, 1953, Shirley Spackman (marr. diss. 1964); two *s*; 2nd, 1965, Alice Luethi; four *s. Educ:* Univs of Harvard, Zürich, Oklahoma and Oxford. DPhil (Oxon). FRHistS. Prof. and Chm. of History, Kenyon Coll., 1953–65; Chm. and Dir, Graduate Studies, Southern Methodist Univ., 1965–70; Lovell Prof. of History, Univ. of Southern Calif., 1971–74; Cultural Attaché, US Embassy, 1974–77; Lovell Distinguished Prof. of History, Univ. of Southern Calif., 1977–84. Chm., British Inst. of the US, 1979–81. Vice-Pres., Board of Dirs, Amer. Friends of Covent Garden; Member: National Council for the Humanities, 1983–; Adv. Council, Ditchley Foundn, 1977–; Adv. Council, UC, Buckingham, 1977–. Hon. DLitt Leicester, 1976. *Publications:* British Politics and the American Revolution, 1954; Aftermath of Revolution: British policy toward the United States 1783–1795, 1969 (paperback, 1971); The American Revolution: the Anglo-American relation, 1969; (with E. Wright) A Tug of Loyalties, 1971. *Recreations:* horseback riding, swimming, opera. *Address:* 10433 Wilshire Boulevard, Los Angeles, Calif 90024, USA. *T:* (213)475–4357. *Clubs:* Beefsteak, Brooks's, Garrick; Regency (Los Angeles).

RITCHIE, family name of **Baron Ritchie of Dundee.**

RITCHIE OF DUNDEE, 5th Baron *cr* 1905; **Harold Malcolm Ritchie;** English and Drama Teacher, Bedgebury School, Kent, retired 1984; *b* 29 Aug. 1919; 4th *s* of 2nd Baron Ritchie of Dundee and Sarah Ruth (*d* 1950), *d* of J. L. Jennings, MP; *S* brother, 1978; *m* 1948, Anne, *d* of late Col C. G. Johnstone, MC; one *s* one *d. Educ:* Stowe School; Trinity College, Oxford. MA 1940. Served in Middle East, Italy and Greece, Captain KRRC, 1940–46. Assistant Headmaster, Brickwall House School, Northiam, Sussex, 1952–65; Headmaster, 1965–72. *Recreations:* gardening, drama, music. *Heir: s* Hon. Charles Rupert Rendall Ritchie [*b* 15 March 1958; *m* 1984, Tara Van Tuyl Koch]. *Address:* House of Lords, SW1.

RITCHIE, Albert Edgar, CC 1975; Canadian Diplomat, retired Nov. 1981; *b* 20 Dec. 1916; *m;* two *s* two *d. Educ:* Mount Allison Univ., New Brunswick (BA 1938); Queen's College, Oxford (Rhodes Scholar, 1940; BA). Officer, Econ. Affairs Dept, UN, and Secretariat of Gen. Agreement on Tariffs and Trade, 1946–48; Counsellor, Office of Canadian High Comr, London, UK, 1948–52; Deputy Under-Secretary of State for External Affairs, Canada, 1964–66; Canadian Ambassador to USA, 1966–70; Under-Sec. of State for External Affairs, Canada, 1970–74; Special Advisor to Privy Council Office, Canada, 1974–76; Canadian Ambassador to Republic of Ireland, 1976–81. Hon. LLD: Mount Allison Univ., 1966; St Thomas Univ., 1968; Carleton Univ., 1985. *Address:* 336 Frost Avenue, Ottawa, Ont K1H 5J2, Canada. *Club:* Rideau (Ottawa).

RITCHIE, Alexander James Otway; Chairman: Grindlays Bank plc, since 1984; ANZ Holdings (UK) Ltd, since 1985; Union Discount Co. of London plc, since 1970; *b* 5 May 1928; *s* of Charles Henry Ritchie and Marjorie Alice Ritchie (*née* Stewart); *m* 1953, Joanna Willink Fletcher; two *s* one *d. Educ:* Stowe; St John's Coll., Cambridge (MA). Joined Glyn, Mills and Co., 1951 (Dir, 1964); Exec. Dir, Williams & Glyn's Bank, 1970; resigned Williams & Glyn's Bank, 1977, for present post; Dep. Chm., Grindlays Bank plc, 1977–83, Ch. Exec. 1980–83; Dep. Chm., Grindlays Holdings, 1978–83. Mem., London Cttee, Ottoman Bank, 1966–; Mem., Export Guarantees Adv. Council, 1977–82 (Dep. Chm., 1980–81). *Recreation:* inland waterways. *Address:* Thornfield House, Vine Road, SW13 0NE. *T:* 01-876 4450. *Club:* Boodle's.

RITCHIE, Anthony Elliot, CBE 1978; MA, BSc, MD; FRSE; Secretary and Treasurer, Carnegie Trust for the Universities of Scotland, 1969–86; *b* 30 March 1915; *s* of late Prof. James Ritchie; *m* 1941, Elizabeth Lambie Knox, MB, ChB, *y d* of John Knox, Dunfermline; one *s* three *d. Educ:* Edinburgh Academy; Aberdeen and Edinburgh Universities. MA (Aber), 1933; BSc 1936, with Hunter Memorial Prize. MB, ChB (Edin.) 1940. Carnegie Research Scholar, Physiology Dept, Edin. Univ., 1940–41; Asst Lectr 1941; Lectr 1942. Ellis Prize in Physiology, 1941; Gunning Victoria Jubilee Prize, 1943; MD (Edin.) with Gold Medal Thesis, 1945; senior lecturer grade, 1946. Lecturer in Electrotherapy, Edin. Royal Infirmary, 1943–48, 1972–; Chandos Prof. of Physiology, Univ. of St Andrews, 1948–69; Dean, Faculty of Science, 1961–66. Hon. Physiologist Gogarburn Nerve Injuries Hospital, 1941–46; Honeyman Gillespie Lecturer, 1944; Hon. Consultant in Electrotherapy, Scot. E Regional Hospital Board, 1950–69; Fellow Royal Soc. of Edinburgh, 1951 (Council RSE 1957–60, 1979–80; Secretary to Ordinary Meetings, 1960–65, Vice-President, 1965–66 and 1976–79; General Secretary, 1966–76); Scientific Adviser, Civil Defence, 1961–80; Adv. Cttee on Med. Research, Scotland, 1961–, Vice-Chm., 1967–69; Chairman: Scottish Cttee on Science Educn, 1970–78; Blood Transfusion Adv. Gp, 1970–80; Scottish Universities Entrance Bd, 1963–69; St Leonard's Sch., St Andrews, 1968–69; Mem., Council for Applied Science in Scotland, 1978–; Mem., British Library Bd, 1973–80; Trustee, Nat. Library of Scotland. Mem., Cttee of Inquiry into Teachers' Pay. Examiner, Chartered Soc. of Physiotherapy, Pharmaceutical Soc. of Great Britain, and RCSE. RAMC (TA) commission, 1942–44. Hon. FCSP, 1970; Hon. FRCPE 1986. Hon. DSc St Andrews, 1972; Hon. LLD Strathclyde, 1985. Bicentary Medal, RSE, 1983. *Publications:* (with J. Lenman) Clinical Electromyography, 1976, 3rd edn 1983; medical and scientific papers on nerve injury diagnosis and medical electronics. *Recreations:* reading, mountaineering, motor cars. *Address:* 12 Ravelston Park, Edinburgh EH4 3DX. *T:* 031–332 6560. *Clubs:* Caledonian; New (Edinburgh).

RITCHIE, Charles Stewart Almon, CC 1972; FRSL 1982; *b* 23 Sept. 1906; *s* of William Bruce Almon Ritchie, KC and Lilian Constance Harriette Ritchie (*née* Stewart), both of Halifax, Nova Scotia; *m* 1948, Sylvia Catherine Beatrice Smellie; no *c. Educ:* University of King's College; Ecole Libre des Sciences Politiques, Paris. BA, MA Oxford 1929, MA Harvard, 1930. Joined Dept of External Affairs, 3rd Sec. Ottawa, 1934; 3rd Sec., Washington, 1936; 2nd Sec., London, 1939; 1st Sec., London, 1943; 1st Sec., Ottawa, 1945; Counsellor, Paris, 1947; Asst Under-Secretary of State for External Affairs, Ottawa, 1950, Deputy Under-Secretary of State for External Affairs, 1952; Ambassador to Federal Republic of Germany, Bonn, and Head of Military Mission, Berlin, 1954; Permanent Rep. to UN, New York 1958; Ambassador of Canada to the United States, 1962; Ambassador and Permanent Representative of Canada to the North Atlantic Council, 1966–67; Canadian High Comr in London, 1967–71; Special Adviser to Privy Council, Canada, 1971–73. Hon. DCL: Univ. of King's College, Halifax, NS; McGill Univ., Montreal. Hon. Fellow, Pembroke College, Oxford. *Publications:* 4 vols of diaries: The Siren Years: undiplomatic diaries 1937–1945, 1974; An Appetite for Life: the education of a young diplomat, 1978; Diplomatic Passport, 1981; Storm Signals, 1983. *Address:* Apt 10, 216 Metcalfe Street, Ottawa, Canada. *Clubs:* Brooks's, Beefsteak; Rideau (Ottawa).

RITCHIE, Douglas Malcolm; Managing Director, Chief Executive Officer and European Regional Director, British Alcan Aluminium, since 1986; *b* Parry Sound, Ont., 8 Jan. 1941; *s* of Ian David Ritchie and Helen Mary Ritchie (*née* Jamieson); *m* 1965, Cydney Ann Brown; three *s. Educ:* McGill University (BSc 1962, MBA 1966). Alcan Group Cos,

1966–73; Vice-Pres. Gen. Manager, 1973–75, Exec. Vice-Pres., 1975–78, Alcan Can. Products; Corp. Vice-Pres., Aluminium Co. Can., 1978–80; Exec. Vice-Pres., 1980–82, Pres., 1982–86, Alcan Smelters & Chems; Dir Exec. Vice-Pres., Alcan Aluminium, Cleveland, 1985–86. *Address:* 48A Upper Brook Street, W1.

RITCHIE, Rear-Adm. George Stephen, CB 1967; DSC 1942; writer; retired hydrographer; *b* 30 Oct. 1914; *s* of Sir (John) Douglas Ritchie, MC and late Margaret Stephen, OBE 1946, JP, Officer of the Order of Orange-Nassau, *d* of James Allan, Methlick, Aberdeenshire; *m* 1942, Mrs Disa Elizabeth Smith (*née* Beveridge); three *s* one *d. Educ:* RNC, Dartmouth. Joined RN Surveying Service, 1936; attached Eighth Army, 1942–43; served in HM Survey Ship Scott for invasion of Europe, 1944; comd HMS Challenger on scientific voyage round world, 1950–51; comd HM New Zealand Survey Ship Lachlan and NZ Surveying Service, 1953–56; comd HM Surveying Ship Dalrymple, Persian Gulf, 1959; comd HM Surveying Ship Vidal, West Indies and Western Europe, 1963–65; ADC to the Queen, 1965; Hydrographer of the Navy, 1966–71; Vis. Research Fellow, Southampton Univ., 1971–72; Pres., Directing Cttee, Internat. Hydrographic Bureau, Monaco, 1972–82; Founder Pres., Hydrographic Soc., 1972–73. Founder's Medal, RGS, 1972; Prix Manley-Bendall, Académie de Marine, Paris, 1977; Gold Medal, Royal Inst. of Navigation, 1978. *Publications:* Challenger, 1957; The Admiralty Chart, 1967; papers on navigation and oceanography in various jls, including Developments in British Hydrography since days of Captain Cook (RSA Silver Medal, 1970). *Recreations:* Trinidad Carnival, boules, hunting. *Address:* Seaview, Collieston, Ellon, Aberdeenshire AB4 9RS. *Clubs:* Reform; Collieston Boules (Pres.); Monte Carlo (Emeritus Mem.), Bouliste Monegasque.

RITCHIE, Harry Parker, CMG 1966; Fiscal Adviser to Government of Falkland Islands, since 1978; *b* 3 June 1919; *s* of W. S. Ritchie; *m* 1949, Mary Grace, *née* Foster; two *s. Educ:* Royal Belfast Academical Institution; Queen's University, Belfast. Served War of 1939–45 (Captain). Administrative Cadet, Bechuanaland Protectorate, 1946; Swaziland, 1948; District Officer, 1953; seconded to Office of High Commissioner, as Assistant Secretary, 1954; Deputy Financial Secretary, Fiji, 1957, Financial Secretary, 1962–67, Minister of Finance, 1967–70; Secretary for Finance, Papua New Guinea, 1971–74. Financial and Econ. Consultant to Papua New Guinea Govt, 1974–75; Consultant on Civil Service Salaries to Govt of Tonga (report pubd 1976), to Govt of Seychelles (report pubd 1977), to Govt of Falkland Islands (reports pubd 1977, 1981); to Govt of St Helena (report pubd 1980). *Recreations:* gardening, reading. *Address:* 6 Mill Rise, Mill Lane, Bourton, Dorset.

RITCHIE, Horace David; Emeritus Professor of Surgery, University of London, and former Director of the Surgical Unit at The London Hospital; *b* 24 Sept. 1920; marr. diss.; three *s. Educ:* Universities of Glasgow, Cambridge and Edinburgh. Dean, London Hosp. Med. Coll. and Dental Sch., 1982–83. *Publications:* contribs to various scientific journals.

RITCHIE, Sir James Edward Thomson, 2nd Bt, *cr* 1918 (2nd creation); TD 1943 (2 clasps); FRSA; Chairman M. W. Hardy & Co. Ltd, 1948–78; Director, Wm Ritchie & Son (Textiles) Ltd; Member Court of Assistants, Merchant Taylors' Co. (Master, 1963–64); *b* 16 June 1902; *s* of 1st Baronet and Ada Bevan, *d* of late Edward ap Rees Bryant; *S* father, 1937; *m* 1st, 1928, Esme Phyllis (*d* 1939), *o d* of late J. M. Oldham, Ormidale, Ascot; 2nd, 1936, Rosemary, *yr d* of late Col. Henry Streatfeild, DSO, TD; two *d. Educ:* Rugby; The Queen's Coll., Oxford. Joined Inns of Court Regt, 1936; commissioned, 1938; served 1939–45 (CMF 1944–45), various staff and regimental appts; Lt-Col 1945; re-commissioned, 1949, to command 44 (Home Counties) Div. Provost Co. RCMP (TA); retired 1953. Co-opted Mem. Kent TA&AFA (Mem. General Purposes Cttee), 1953–68. Chm., Chatwood-Milner (formerly Milners Safe Co. Ltd), 1937–70; Director: Caledonian Insurance Co. (London Bd), 1951–67; Guardian Assurance Co. Ltd (Local London Bd, 1967–71). Pres., Royal British Legion, Ashford (Kent) Br., 1952–75; Patron, Ashford and Dist Caledonian Society; Chm. Finance and General Purposes Cttee and joint Hon. Treas., London School of Hygiene and Tropical Medicine, Univ. of London, 1951–61; co-opted Mem. Bd of Management and Finance and Gen. Purposes Cttee, 1964–67. *Heir:* none. *Address:* 3 Farquhar Street, Bengeo, Hertford SG14 3BN.

RITCHIE, (James) Martin; Chairman: British Enkalon Ltd, 1975–83; Haymills Holdings Ltd, 1977–83; Director, Sun Alliance and London Insurance Ltd; *b* 29 May 1917; *s* of late Sir James Ritchie, CBE and Lady Ritchie (*née* Gemmell); *m* 1939, Noreen Mary Louise Johnston; three *s. Educ:* Strathallan Sch., Perthshire. Joined Andrew Ritchie & Son Ltd, Glasgow, corrugated fibre container manufrs, 1934; Dir, 1938. TA Officer, 1938; served War of 1939–45: HAA Regt; Capt. 1941; psc 1943; DAA&QMG, MEF, Middle East, 1944–45 (Maj.). Rejoined Andrew Ritchie & Son Ltd, then part of Eburite Organisation; Man. Dir, 1950; Gen. Man., Bowater-Eburite Ltd, on merger with Bowater Organisation, 1956; Bowater Paper Corp. Ltd: Dir, 1959; Man. Dir, 1964; Dep. Chm. and Man. Dir, 1967; Chm. 1969–72. FBIM 1971; FRSA 1971. *Recreations:* golf, fishing. *Address:* The Court House, Fulmer, Bucks. *T:* Fulmer 2585. *Clubs:* Caledonian; Denham Golf.

RITCHIE, James Walter, MC; Master of Foxhounds; a Managing Director, Inchcape & Co. Ltd, 1976–84, retired; *b* 12 Jan. 1920; *m* 1951, Penelope June (*née* Forbes); two *s* two *d. Educ:* Ampleforth Coll.; Clare Coll., Cambridge. Gordon Highlanders. *Recreations:* hunting, fishing, golf. *Address:* Lockeridge Down, Lockeridge, near Marlborough, Wilts. *T:* Lockeridge 244. *Clubs:* City of London, Oriental.

RITCHIE, John, MBE 1944; Senior Master of the Supreme Court of Judicature (Queen's Bench Division), and Queen's Remembrancer, 1980–82 (Master, 1960); *b* 7 Feb. 1913; *e s* of W. Tod Ritchie, JP, Rector of Hutchesons' Grammar School, Glasgow; *m* 1936, Nora Gwendolen Margaret, *yr d* of Sir Frederic G. Kenyon, GBE, KCB, FBA; one *s* two *d. Educ:* Glasgow Academy; Magdalen College, Oxford. BA 1935; MA 1948. Called to the Bar, Middle Temple, 1935; practised in London and on South-Eastern Circuit, 1935–60; Recorder of King's Lynn, 1956–58. Served War of 1939–45 (MBE, Belgian Croix de Guerre, despatches twice): BEF 1940; BLA 1944–45; private, Royal Fusiliers, 1939; commissioned Queen's Own Cameron Highlanders, 1940; Major, 1942. Belgian Croix de Guerre, 1944. *Recreations:* painting, rose-growing, wine-tasting. *Address:* 4 Millwood Rise, Overton-on-Dee, near Wrexham, Clwyd LL13 0EL. *T:* Overton-on-Dee 485.

RITCHIE, Dr John Hindle, MBE 1985; RIBA; Chief Executive, Merseyside Development Corporation, since 1985; *b* 4 June 1937; *s* of Charles A. Ritchie; *m* 1963, Anne Leyland; two *d. Educ:* Royal Grammar School, Newcastle upon Tyne; Univ. of Liverpool (BArch Hons); Univ. of Sheffield (PhD Building Science). Science Research Council, 1963–66; Liverpool City Council, 1966–69; Rowntree Housing Trust, Univ. of Liverpool, 1969–72; Cheshire County Council, 1972–74; Merseyside CC, 1974–80; Dir of Develt, Merseyside Develt Corp., 1980–85. Chm., Merseyside Educn Training Enterprise Ltd, 1986–; Mem., Merseyside Tourism Bd, 1986–. FBIM. *Publications:* scientific and planning papers on urban environment and obsolescence. *Address:* c/o Merseyside Development Corporation, Royal Liver Building, Pierhead, Liverpool L3 1JH. *T:* 051–236 6090.

RITCHIE, Prof. J(oseph) Murdoch, PhD, DSc; FRS 1976; Eugene Higgins Professor of Pharmacology, Yale University, since 1968; *b* 10 June 1925; *s* of Alexander Farquharson Ritchie and Agnes Jane (*née* Bremner); *m* 1951, Brenda Rachel (*née* Bigland); one *s* one *d*. *Educ:* Aberdeen Central Secondary Sch.; Aberdeen Univ. (BSc Maths); UCL (BSc Physiol., PhD, DSc; Fellow 1978). MInstP. Res. in Radar, Telecommunications Res. Estabt, Malvern, 1944–46; University Coll. London: Hon. Res. Asst, Biophysics Res. Unit, 1946–49; Lectr in Physiol., 1949–51; Mem. staff, Nat. Inst. for Med. Res., Mill Hill, 1951–55; Asst Prof. of Pharmacology, 1956–57, Associate Prof., 1958–63 and Prof., 1963–68, Albert Einstein Coll. of Medicine, NY; Overseas Fellow, Churchill Coll., Cambridge, 1964–65; Chm., Dept of Pharmacol., 1968–74, Dir, Div. of Biol Scis, 1975–78, Yale Univ. Hon. MA Yale, 1968. *Publications:* papers on nerve and muscle physiol. and biophysics in Jl of Physiol. *Recreations:* skiing, chess. *Address:* 47 Deepwood Drive, Hamden, Conn 06517, USA. *T:* (home) (203) 777–0420; (office) (203) 785–4567. *Club:* Yale (NYC).

RITCHIE, Kenneth Gordon, CMG 1968; HM Diplomatic Service, retired; *b* 19 Aug. 1921; *s* of Walter Ritchie, Arbroath; *m* 1951, Esme Stronsa Nash. *Educ:* Arbroath High Sch.; St Andrews Univ. (MA). Joined FO, 1944; Embassy, Ankara, 1944–47; Foreign Office, 1947–49; Khorramshahr, 1949–50; Tehran, 1950–52; Djakarta, 1952–55; Foreign Office, 1955–57; Peking, 1957–62; Santiago, 1962–64; Elisabethville, 1965–66; Dep. High Commissioner, Lusaka, 1966–67; High Commissioner, Guyana, 1967–70; Head of Perm. Under-Sec.'s Dept, FCO, 1970–73; High Comr, Malaŵi, 1973–77. *Recreations:* cinephotography, model railways. *Address:* Dalforbie, North Esk Road, Edzell, Angus.

RITCHIE, Margaret Claire; Headmistress of Queen Mary School, Lytham, since 1981; *b* 18 Sept. 1937; *d* of Roderick M. Ritchie, Edinburgh. *Educ:* Leeds Girls' High Sch.; Univ. of Leeds (BSc). Postgraduate Certificate in Education, Univ. of London. Asst Mistress, St Leonards Sch., St Andrews, 1960–64; Head of Science Dept, Wycombe Abbey Sch., High Wycombe, 1964–71; Headmistress, Queenswood Sch., 1972–81. *Address:* Queen Mary School, Clifton Drive South, Lytham St Annes, Lancs FY8 1DS.

RITCHIE, Martin; *see* Ritchie, J. M.

RITCHIE, Robert Blackwood; grazier running family sheep and cattle properties, Western Victoria, since 1958; Director, Agricultural Investments Australia Ltd, since 1968 (Chairman, 1968–85); *b* 6 April 1937; *s* of Alan Blackwood Ritchie and Margaret Louise (*née* Whitcomb); *m* 1965, Eda Natalie Sandford Beggs; two *s* one *d*. *Educ:* Geelong Grammar Sch.; Corpus Christi Coll., Cambridge (MA; Rowing Blue, 1958). Exec. Mem., Graziers Assoc. of Vic, 1968–72; Mem., National Rural Adv. Council, 1974–75. Dir-Gen., Min. for Economic Develt, Vic, 1981–83. Geelong Grammar School: Mem. Council, 1966–78 (Chm., 1973–78); Chief Exec., 1979–80 (during period between Head Masters). *Recreation:* sailing. *Address:* Blackwood, Penshurst, Vic 3289, Australia. *T:* (055) 765432. *Clubs:* Melbourne (Melbourne, Australia); Royal Yacht of Victoria (Australia).

RITCHIE, Shirley Anne, (Mrs R. H. C. Anwyl), QC 1979; a Recorder of the Crown Court, since 1981; *b* 10 Dec. 1940; *d* of James Ritchie and Helen Sutherland Ritchie; *m* 1969, Robin Hamilton Corson Anwyl; two *s*. *Educ:* St Mary's Diocesan Sch. for Girls, Pretoria; Rhodes Univ., S Africa (BA, LLB). Called to the South African Bar, 1963; called to the Bar, Inner Temple, 1966, Bencher, 1985. Member: Senate of Inns of Court and Bar, 1978–81; Criminal Injuries Compensation Bd, 1980–; Mental Health Review Tribunal, 1983–. Dep. Chm., Barristers' Benevolent Assoc., 1980–. *Recreations:* theatre, sailing. *Address:* 4 Paper Buildings, Temple, EC4Y 7EX. *T:* 01–353 3420.

RITTNER, Luke Philip Hardwick; Secretary General, the Arts Council of Great Britain, since 1983; *b* 24 May 1947; *s* of late George Stephen Hardwick Rittner and of Joane (*née* Thunder); *m* 1974, Corinna Frances Edholm; one *d*. *Educ:* Blackfriars School, Laxton; City of Bath Technical Coll.; Dartington Coll. of Arts; London Acad. of Music and Dramatic Art. Asst Administrator, Bath Festival, 1968–71, Jt Administrator, 1971–74, Administrative Director, 1974–76; Dir, Assoc. for Business Sponsorship of the Arts, 1976–83. Member: Adv. Council, V&A Museum, 1980–83; Music Panel, British Council, 1979–83. Trustee: Bath Preservation Trust, 1968–73; Theatre Royal, Bath, 1979–82; Foundn Trustee, Holburne Museum, Bath, 1981–; Governor, Urchfont Manor, Wiltshire Adult Educn Centre, 1982–83. *Recreations:* the arts, people, travel. *Address:* c/o Arts Council of Great Britain, 105 Piccadilly, W1V 0AU.

RIVERDALE, 2nd Baron, *cr* 1935; **Robert Arthur Balfour,** Bt 1929; DL; President, Balfour Darwins Ltd, 1969–75 (Chairman, 1961–69); *b* Sheffield, 1 Sept. 1901; *er s* of 1st Baron Riverdale, GBE; *S* father, 1957; *m* 1st, 1926, Nancy Marguerite (*d* 1928), *d* of late Rear-Adm. Mark Rundle, DSO; one *s*; 2nd, 1933, Christian Mary, *er d* of late Major Rowland Hill; one *s* one *d*. *Educ:* Aysgarth; Oundle. MRINA. Served with RNVR, 1940–45, attaining rank of Lt-Comdr. Joined Arthur Balfour & Co. Ltd, 1918; Dir, 1924; Man. Dir, 1949; Chm. and Man. Dir, 1957–61; Exec. Chm., 1961–69. Director: National Provincial Bank, Main Central Bd, 1964–69 (Local Bd, 1949–69); National Westminster Bank, E Region, 1969–71; Light Trades House Ltd, 1956–65; Yorkshire Television, 1967–73. The Association of British Chambers of Commerce: Mem. Exec. Council, 1950–; Vice-Pres., 1952–54; Dep. Pres., 1954–57; Pres., 1957–58; Chm., Overseas Cttee, 1953–57. President: Nat. Fedn of Engineers' Tool Manufacturers, 1951–57 (Hon. Vice-Pres., 1957–; Representative on Gauge and Tool Adv. Council, 1946–64); Sheffield Chamber of Commerce, 1950 (Jt Hon. Sec., 1957–); Milling Cutter and Reamer Trade Assoc., 1936–54 (Vice-Pres., 1954–57); Twist Drill Traders' Assoc., 1946–55; Chm., British Council, Aust. Assoc. of British Manufacturers, 1954–57 (Vice-Chm., 1957–65; Hon. Mem., 1965–); Member: Management and Tech. Cttee, High Speed Steel Assoc., 1947–65; British Nat. Cttee of Internat. Chamber of Commerce Adv. Cttee, 1957–58; Nat. Production Adv. Cttee, 1957–58; Consultative Cttee for Industry, 1957–58; Standing Cttee, Crucible and High Speed Steel Conf., 1951–64; Western Hemisphere Exports Council (formerly Dollar Exports Council), 1957–61; Governor, Sheffield Savings Bank, 1948–58 (Patron, 1958–); Master Cutler, 1946; Trustee, Sheffield Town Trust, 1958–; Town Collector, Sheffield, 1974–; Guardian of Standard of Wrought Plate within City of Sheffield, 1948–; Belgian Consul for Sheffield area, 1945–. JP, City of Sheffield, 1950–66 (Pres., S Yorks Br. Magistrates' Assoc., 1971–); DL, S Yorks (formerly WR Yorks and City and County of York), 1959–. Pres., Derwent Fly Fishing Club. Is a Churchman and a Conservative. Chevalier of Order of the Crown, Belgium, 1956; La Médaille Civique de première classe; Officier de l'Ordre de Leopold II, 1971. *Recreations:* yachting, yacht designing, shooting, stalking, fishing. *Heir:* *s* Hon. Mark Robin Balfour, *qv*. *Address:* Ropes, Grindleford, via Sheffield S30 1HX. *T:* Hope Valley 30408. *Clubs:* Royal Cruising; Sheffield (Sheffield).

RIVERINA, Bishop of, since 1971; **Rt. Rev. Barry Russell Hunter;** *b* Brisbane, Queensland, 15 Aug. 1927; *s* of late John Hunter; *m* 1961, Dorothy Nancy, *d* of B. P. Sanders, Brisbane; three *d*. *Educ:* Toowoomba Grammar Sch.; St Francis' Theological Coll., Brisbane; Univ. of Queensland (BA, ThL). Assistant Curate, St Matthew's, Sherwood, 1953–56; Member, Bush Brotherhood of St Paul, Cunnamulla, Queensland, 1956–61; Rector, St Cecilia's, Chinchilla, 1961–66; Rector, St Gabriel's, Biloela, 1966–71; Archdeacon of the East, Diocese of Rockhampton, 1969–71. *Recreation:* music. *Address:* Bishop's Lodge, 127 Audley Street, Narrandera, NSW 2700, Australia. *T:* Narrandera (069) 59 1177. *Club:* Griffith Aero (Griffith).

RIVERS, Georgia; *see* Clark, Marjorie.

RIVERS, Mrs Rosalind V.; *see* Pitt-Rivers.

RIVET, Prof. Albert Lionel Frederick, FBA 1981; Professor of Roman Provincial Studies, University of Keele, 1974–81, now Emeritus; *b* 30 Nov. 1915; *s* of Albert Robert Rivet, MBE and Rose Mary Rivet (*née* Bulow); *m* 1947, Audrey Catherine Webb; one *s* one *d*. *Educ:* Felsted Sch. (schol.); Oriel Coll., Oxford. BA 1938, MA 1946. FSA 1953; FSAScot 1959. Schoolmaster, 1938–39; ARP, 1939–40; mil. service, mainly in E Africa, 1940–46 (Major, Royal Signals); bookseller, 1946–51; Asst Archaeology Officer, Ordnance Survey, 1951–64; Keele University: Lectr in Classics, 1964–67; Reader in Romano-British Studies, 1967–74. Member: Royal Commn on Historical Monuments (England), 1979–85; Exec. Cttee, British Sch. at Rome, 1974–83. Pres., Soc. for Promotion of Roman Studies, 1977–80. Corresp. Mem., German Archaeol Inst., 1960–. Editor, Procs of Soc. of Antiquaries of Scotland, 1961–64. *Publications:* Town and Country in Roman Britain, 1958, 2nd edn 1964; (ed) The Iron Age in Northern Britain, 1966; (ed) The Roman Villa in Britain, 1969; (with C. C. Smith) The Place-Names of Roman Britain, 1979; contribs to books, atlases, encyclopaedias and learned journals. *Recreation:* conversation. *Address:* 7 Springpool, The University, Keele, Staffs ST5 5BN.

RIVETT, Dr Geoffrey Christopher; Senior Principal Medical Officer, Department of Health and Social Security, since 1985; *b* 11 Aug. 1932; *s* of Frank Andrew James Rivett and Catherine Mary Rivett; *m* 1976, Elizabeth Barbara Hartman; two *s* by previous marr. *Educ:* Manchester Grammar Sch.; Brasenose Coll., Oxford (MA 1st Cl. Hons Animal Physiol.); University Coll. Hosp. (BM, BCh); MRCGP, DObst RCOG. House Officer, Radcliffe Inf., Oxford, 1957; House Phys., London Chest Hosp., 1958; RAMC, 1958–60; GP, Milton Keynes, 1960–72; DHSS, 1972–. Mem., Soc. of Apothecaries, 1981–; ARPS 1971. *Publication:* The Development of the London Hospital System 1823–1982, 1986. *Recreations:* photography, house conversion. *Address:* 4 Courtside, N8 8EW. *T:* 01–348 3242; Shilling Orchard, Shilling Street, Lavenham, Suffolk CO10 9RH. *T:* Lavenham 247808. *Clubs:* Wig and Pen, Royal Society of Medicine.

RIVETT-CARNAC, Rev. Canon Sir (Thomas) Nicholas, 8th Bt *cr* 1836; Priest-in-charge, St Mark's, Kennington Oval, SE11, since 1972; Hon. Canon of Southwark Cathedral, since 1980; *b* 3 June 1927; *s* of Vice-Admiral James William Rivett-Carnac, CB, CBE, DSC (2nd *s* of 6th Bt) (*d* 1970), and of Isla Nesta Rivett-Carnac (*d* 1974), *d* of Harry Officer Blackwood; *S* uncle, 1972; *m* 1977, Susan Marigold MacTier Copeland, *d* of late Harold and Adeline Copeland. *Educ:* Marlborough College. Scots Guards, 1945–55. Probation Service, 1957–59. Ordained, 1963; Curate: Holy Trinity, Rotherhithe, 1963–68; Holy Trinity, Brompton, 1968–72; Rural Dean of Lambeth, 1978–82. *Heir:* *b* Miles James Rivett-Carnac, Commander, RN [*b* 7 Feb. 1933; *m* 1958, April Sally, *d* of late Major Arthur Andrew Sidney Villar; two *s* one *d*]. *Address:* St Mark's Vicarage, Kennington Oval, SE11. *T:* 01–735 4609.

RIVETT-DRAKE, Brig. Dame Jean (Elizabeth), DBE 1964 (MBE 1947); JP; DL; Member, Hove Borough Council, 1966–84; Mayor of Hove, 1977–78; Lay Member, Press Council, 1973–78; Director, Women's Royal Army Corps, 1961–64, retd; *b* 13 July 1909; *d* of Comdr Bertram Gregory Drake and of late Dora Rivett-Drake. Served War of 1939–45 (despatches, 1946). Hon. ADC to the Queen, 1961–64. Mem., East Sussex CC, 1973–77 (Mem. Educn and Social Services Cttees, AHA). JP 1966; DL E Sussex, 1984. *Address:* 9 Kestrel Close, Hove, East Sussex BN3 6NS. *T:* Brighton 505839; c/o Barclays Bank, 92 Church Road, Hove, East Sussex. *Club:* English-Speaking Union.

RIVLIN, Geoffrey, QC 1979; a Recorder of the Crown Court, since 1978; *b* 28 Nov. 1940; *s* of late M. Allenby Rivlin and late May Rivlin; *m* 1974, Maureen Smith, violinist; two *d*. *Educ:* Bootham Sch.; Leeds Univ. (LLB). Called to the Bar, Middle Temple, 1963 (Colombos Prize, Internat. Law). NE Circuit Junior 1967. Mem., Senate of Inns of Court and the Bar, 1976–79. *Address:* 4 Paper Buildings, Temple, EC4Y 7EX; 2 Park Square, Leeds LS1 2NE.

RIX, Bernard Anthony, QC 1981; *b* 8 Dec. 1944; *s* of Otto Rix and Sadie Silverberg; *m* 1983, Hon. Karen Debra, *er d* of Baron Young of Graffham, *qv*. *Educ:* St Paul's School, London; New College, Oxford (BA: Lit.Hum. 1966, Jur. 1968); Harvard Law School (Kennedy Scholar 1968; LLM 1969). Called to Bar, Inner Temple, 1970. Member: Senate, Inns of Court and Bar, 1981–83; Bar Council, 1981–83. *Recreations:* music, opera, Italy, fencing. *Address:* 3 Essex Court, Temple, EC4. *T:* 01–583 9294.

RIX, Sir Brian (Norman Roger), Kt 1986; CBE 1977; actor-manager, 1948–77; Secretary-General, Mencap (Royal Society for Mentally Handicapped Children and Adults), since 1980; *b* 27 Jan. 1924; *s* of late Herbert and Fanny Rix; *m* 1949, Elspet Jeans Macgregor-Gray; two *s* two *d*. *Educ:* Bootham Sch., York. Stage career: joined Donald Wolfit, 1942; first West End appearance, Sebastian in Twelfth Night, St James's, 1943; White Rose Players, Harrogate, 1943–44. Served War of 1939–45, RAF and Bevin Boy. Became actor-manager, 1948; ran repertory cos at Ilkley, Bridlington and Margate, 1948–50; toured Reluctant Heroes and brought to Whitehall Theatre, 1950–54; Dry Rot, 1954–58; Simple Spymen, 1958–61; One For the Pot, 1961–64; Chase Me Comrade, 1964–66; went to Garrick Theatre, 1967, with repertoire of farce: Stand By Your Bedouin; Uproar in the House; Let Sleeping Wives Lie; after 6 months went over to latter, only, which ran till 1969; then followed: She's Done It Again, 1969–70; Don't Just Lie There, Say Something!, 1971–73 (filmed 1973); New Theatre, Cardiff, Robinson Crusoe, 1973; Cambridge Theatre, A Bit Between The Teeth, 1974; Fringe Benefits, Whitehall Theatre, 1976. Entered films, 1951: subsequently made eleven, including Reluctant Heroes, 1951, Dry Rot, 1956. BBC TV contract to present farces on TV, 1956–72; first ITV series Men of Affairs, 1973; A Roof Over My Head, BBC TV series, 1977. Presenter, Let's Go ..., BBC TV series (first ever for mentally handicapped), 1978–83; Disc Jockey (for first time) BBC Radio 2 series, 1978–80. Dir and Theatre Controller, Cooney-Marsh Group, 1977–80; Trustee, Theatre of Comedy, 1983–; Chm., Arts Council Drama Panel, 1986–. Chm., Indep. Develt Council for People with Mental Handicap, 1981–86; Governor, Mencap City Foundation, 1984–. Hon. MA: Hull, 1981; Open, 1983; DUniv Essex, 1984; Hon. LLD Manchester, 1986. Hon. Fellow, Humberside Coll. of Higher Educn, 1984. *Publication:* My Farce from My Elbow: an autobiography, 1975. *Recreations:* cricket, amateur radio (G2DQU; Hon. Vice-Pres., Radio Soc. of GB, 1979). *Address:* 3 St Mary's Grove, Barnes Common, SW13 0JA. *T:* 01–785 9626. *Clubs:* Lord's Taverners (Pres. 1970), MCC; Yorkshire County Cricket.

RIX, Sir John, Kt 1977; MBE 1955; DL; FEng 1979; Chairman, Seahorse International Ltd, since 1986; Director: Vosper PLC, since 1958 (Chairman, 1978–85); Charismarine Ltd, since 1976; Southampton Cable Ltd, since 1986; Chilworth Centre Ltd, since 1986; *b* 1917; *s* of Reginald Arthur Rix; *m* 1953, Sylvia Gene Howe; two *s* one *d*. *Educ:* Southampton Univ. FRINA; FIMarE. Chm. and Chief Exec., Vosper Thornycroft (UK) Ltd, 1970–78; Chairman: Vosper Shiprepairers Ltd, 1977–78; David Brown Vosper (Offshore) Ltd, 1978–85; Vosper Hovermarine Ltd, 1980–85; David Brown Gear

Industries Ltd, 1980–85; Mainwork Ltd, 1980–85; Dir, Vosper Private Ltd, 1966–77 and 1978–85. DL Hants 1985. *Recreations:* sailing, tennis, golf, walking. *Address:* Lower Baybridge House, Owslebury, Winchester, Hants. *T:* Owslebury 306. *Club:* Royal Thames Yacht.

RIX, Timothy John; Chief Executive, since 1976, and Chairman since 1984, Longman Group Ltd; *b* 4 Jan. 1934; *s* of late Howard Terrell Rix and Marguerite Selman Rix; *m* 1st, 1960, Wendy Elizabeth Wright (marr. diss. 1967); one *d*; 2nd, 1967, Gillian Diana Mary Greenwood; one *s* one *d*. *Educ:* Radley Coll.; Clare Coll., Cambridge (BA); Yale Univ., USA. Sub-Lieut, RNVR, 1952–54. Mellon Fellow, Yale, 1957–58; joined Longmans, Green & Co. Ltd, 1958; Overseas Educnl Publisher, 1958–61; Publishing Manager, Far East and SE Asia, 1961–63; Head of English Language Teaching Publishing, 1964–68; Divl Man. Dir, 1968–72; Jt Man. Dir, 1972–76; Director: Pearson Longman Ltd, 1979–83; Goldcrest Television, 1981–83; Yale Univ. Press, London, 1984–. Publishers Association: Chm., Trng Cttee, 1974–78; Chm., Book Develt Council, 1979–81; Vice-Pres., 1980–81 and 1983–84; Pres., 1981–83. Member: Exec. Cttee, NBL, 1979– (Dep. Chm., 1984–86; Chm., 1986–); Publishers Adv. Panel, British Council, 1978–; Arts Council Literature Panel, 1983–86; British Library Adv. Council, 1982–86; British Library Bd, 1986–. CBIM 1981; FRSA 1986. *Publications:* articles on publishing in trade jls. *Recreations:* reading, landscape, wine. *Address:* 24 Birchington Road, N8 8HP. *T:* 01–348 4143. *Club:* Garrick.

RIZK, Waheeb, CBE 1984 (OBE 1977); MA, PhD, FEng, FIMechE; Consulting Engineer, and Deputy President, British Standards Institution (Chairman of Board, 1982–85); *b* 11 Nov. 1921; *s* of Dr and Mrs I. Rizk; *m* 1952, Vivien Moyle, MA (Cantab); one *s* one *d* (and one *d* decd). *Educ:* Emmanuel College, Cambridge. MA, PhD. Joined English Electric Co., 1954, Chief Engineer, Gas Turbine Div., 1957, Gen. Manager, new div., combining gas turbines and industrial steam turbines, 1967; after merger with GEC became Man. Dir, GEC Gas Turbines Ltd, 1971; Chairman: GEC-Ruston Gas Turbines Ltd, 1983–86; GEC Diesels Ltd, 1983–86. Member Council: IMechE, 1978– (Pres., 1984–85); Fellowship of Engrg, 1982–85. Pres., Internat Council on Combustion Engines (CIMAC), 1973–77. Mem. Council, Cranfield Inst. of Technology; Mem. Court, Brunel Univ. Liveryman and Mem. Ct of Assistants, Worshipful Co. of Engineers. Gold Medal, CIMAC, 1983. *Publications:* technical papers to IMechE and Amer. Soc. of Mech. Engineers. *Recreations:* intelligent tinkering with any mechanism, photography, old motor cycles. *Address:* 231 Hillmorton Road, Rugby CV22 5BD. *T:* Rugby 65093. *Club:* Athenæum.

RIZZELLO, Michael Gaspard, OBE 1977; sculptor and coin designer; *b* 2 April 1926; *s* of Arthur Rizzello and Maria Rizzello (*née* D'Angelo); *m* 1950, Sheila Semple Maguire; one *d*. *Educ:* Oratory Central Boys Sch., SW3; Royal College of Art. Military Service, 1944–48; served in India and Far East; commissioned 1945. Major Travelling Scholarship (Sculpture) and Drawing Prize, RCA, 1950. ARCA 1950; ARBS 1955, FRBS 1961, PRBS 1976–86; FSIAD 1978. Pres., Soc. of Portrait Sculptors, 1968. Prix de Rome (Sculpture), 1951. Sir Otto Beit Medal for Sculpture, 1961. Sculptor: National Memorial to David Lloyd George, Cardiff; Official Medals for Investiture of HRH Prince of Wales, 1969; 900th Anniversary of Westminster Abbey, 1965; Churchill Centenary Trust, 1974; Sir Thomas Beecham bust, Royal Opera House, 1979, and Royal Festival Hall, 1986. Designer and Sculptor of coinages for over 90 countries. *Recreation:* people. *Address:* Melrose Studio, 7 Melrose Road, SW18 1ND. *T:* 01–870 8561.

ROACH, Prof. Gary Francis, FRSE; Professor of Mathematics, University of Strathclyde, since 1979; *b* 8 Oct. 1933; *s* of John Francis Roach and Bertha Mary Ann Roach (*née* Walters); *m* 1960, Isabella Grace Willins Nicol. *Educ:* University Coll. of S Wales and Monmouthshire (BSc); Univ. of London (MSc); Univ. of Manchester (PhD). FRAS, FIMA. RAF (Educn Branch), Flying Officer, 1955–58; Research Mathematician, BP, 1958–61; Lectr, UMIST, 1961–66; Vis. Prof., Univ. of British Columbia, 1966–67; University of Strathclyde: Lectr, 1967; Sen Lectr, 1970; Reader, 1971; Prof., 1979; Dean, Faculty of Science, 1982–. Mem., Edinburgh Mathematical Soc. (Past Pres.). *Publications:* Green's Functions, 1970, 2nd edn 1982; articles in learned jls. *Recreations:* mountaineering, photography, philately, gardening, music. *Address:* 11 Menzies Avenue, Fintry, Glasgow G63 0YE. *T:* Fintry 335.

ROADS, Dr Christopher Herbert; Director, National Sound Archive, since 1983; consultant in museums and audio visual archives; *b* 3 Jan. 1934; *s* of late Herbert Clifford Roads and of Vera Iris Roads; *m* 1976, Charlotte Alicia Dorothy Mary Lothian; one *d*. *Educ:* Cambridge and County Sch.; Trinity Hall, Cambridge (MA; PhD 1961). Adviser to WO on Disposal of Amnesty Arms, 1961–62; Imperial War Museum: Keeper of Dept of Records, 1962–70; Dep. Dir-Gen. at Main Building, Southwark, 1964–79, at Duxford, Cambridge, 1976–79, HMS Belfast, Pool of London, 1978–79. Dir, Museums & Archives Develt Associates Ltd, 1977–85. UNESCO consultant designing major audio visual archives or museums in Philippines, Panama, Bolivia, Kuwait, Jordan and Saudi Arabia, 1976–. Founder and Dir, Cambridge Coral/Starfish Res. Gp, 1968–; Dir, Nat. Discography Ltd, 1986–; Chm., Coral Conservation Trust, 1972–; President: Archives Commn, Internat. Films and TV Council, 1970–; Historical Breechloading Small Arms Assoc., 1973–; Vice President: World Expeditionary Assoc., 1971–; Duxford Aviation Soc., 1974–; English Eight Club, 1980–. Member Council: Scientific Exploration Soc., 1971–82; Cambridge Univ. Rifle Assoc., 1955–; Hon. Sec., Cambridge Univ. Long Range Rifle Club, 1979–. Trustee: HMS Belfast Trust, 1970–78; Historic Cable Ship John W. Mackay, 1986–. Adjt, English VIII, 1964–. Churchill Fellowship, 1970; Vis. Fellow, Centre of Internat. Studies, Univ. of Cambridge, 1983–84. FRGS. Order of Independence, 2nd cl. (Jordan), 1977. *Publications:* The British Soldier's Firearm, 1850–1864, 1964; (jtly) New Studies on the Crown of Thorns Starfish, 1970; The Story of the Gun, 1978. *Recreations:* rifle shooting, marine and submarine exploration, wind surfing, motorcycling, cine and still photography. *Address:* The White House, 90 High Street, Melbourn, near Royston, Herts SG8 6AL. *T:* Royston 60866. *Clubs:* United Oxford & Cambridge University; Hawks (Cambridge).

ROADS, Peter George, MD; FFCM; Regional Medical Officer, South West Thames Regional Health Authority, 1973–82, retired; *b* 14 Nov. 1917; *s* of Frank George Roads and Mary Dee Hill (*née* Bury); *m* 1949, Evelyn Clara (*née* Daniel); one *s* one *d*. *Educ:* Bedford Sch.; Univ. of London (St Mary's Hosp. Med. Sch.), Hon. Society of Inner Temple. MD (London); FFCM, Royal Colls of Physicians. Served War, in China, 1944–46. MRC, Pneumoconiosis Unit, 1949–50; Dep. MOH, etc, City and Co. of Bristol, 1956–59; MOH, Principal Sch. Med. Officer and Port Med. Officer for City and Port of Portsmouth, 1959–73; Med. Referee to Portchester Crematorium, 1959–73. Mem., Central Midwives Bd, 1964–76; Adviser on Health Services, Assoc. of Municipal Corporations, 1966–74. FRSocMed; Fellow, Soc. of Community Medicine. *Publications:* Care of Elderly in Portsmouth, 1970; Medical Importance of Open Air Recreation (Proc. 1st Internat. Congress on Leisure and Touring), 1966. *Recreations:* open air, walking, forestry, riding, ski-ing, history, touring. *Address:* Pasture Cottage, School Lane, Dinton, near Aylesbury, Bucks HP17 8UG. *T:* Aylesbury 748504.

ROARK, Helen Wills; *b* California, 1905; *d* of Dr Clarence A. Wills (surgeon) and Catherine A. Wills; *m* 1st, 1929, Frederick Schander Moody (marr. diss. 1937); 2nd, 1939, Aidan Roark. *Educ:* Anna Head School, Berkeley, California; University of California; Phi Beta Kappa (Scholarship Society). *Publications:* three books on tennis; Mystery Book, 1939; articles in various magazines and periodicals. *Recreations:* American Lawn Tennis Championship, 1923–24–25–27–28–29 and 1931; English Lawn Tennis Championship, 1927–28–29–30–32–33–35–38; French, 1927–28–29–30; has held exhibitions of drawing and paintings at Cooling Galleries, London, 1929 (drawings); Grand Central Art Galleries, New York, 1930 (drawings), 1936 (flower paintings in oil); Berheim-Jenne Galleries, Paris, 1932 (etchings). *Clubs:* All England Lawn Tennis; Colony, West Side Lawn Tennis (New York); Burlingame Country (California).

ROB, Prof. Charles Granville, MC 1943; Professor of Surgery, Uniformed Services University of the Health Sciences, Bethesda, Maryland, since 1983; *b* 4 May 1913; *s* of Joseph William Rob, OBE, MD; *m* 1941, Mary Dorothy Elaine Beazley; two *s* two *d*. *Educ:* Oundle School; Cambridge Univ.; St Thomas's Hospital. FRCS 1939; MChir Cantab, 1941. Lt-Col RAMC Surgeon, St Thomas' Hospital, 1948; Professor of Surgery, London University, 1950–60; Professor and Chm. Dept of Surgery, Univ. of Rochester, NY, 1960–78; Prof. of Surg., E Carolina Univ., 1978–83. Formerly Surgeon and Director of the Surgical Professorial Unit, St Mary's Hospital; Consultant Vascular Surgeon to the Army. *Publications:* (ed, with Rodney Smith) Operative Surgery (8 vols), 1956–57, (14 vols), 1968–69; various surgical. *Recreations:* mountaineering, ski-ing. *Address:* Uniformed Services University of the Health Services, Bethesda, Md 20814, USA. *Club:* Alpine.

ROBARTS, (Anthony) Julian; Managing Director, Coutts & Co., since 1986; *b* 6 May 1937; *s* of late Lt-Col Anthony V. C. Robarts, DL and of Grizel Mary Robarts (Grant); *m* 1961, Edwina Beryl Hobson; two *s* one *d*. *Educ:* Eton College. National Service, 11th Hussars (PAO), 1955–57; joined Coutts & Co., 1958, Dir, 1963, Dep. Man. Dir, 1976–86; Director: Coutts Finance Co., 1967–; F. Bolton Group, 1970–; International Fund for Institutions Inc., USA, 1983–; Regional Dir, Nat. Westminster Bank, 1971–. Hon. Treasurer, Union Jack Club. *Recreations:* shooting, gardening, opera. *Address:* c/o Coutts & Co., 440 Strand, WC2R 0QS. *T:* 01–379 6262. *Club:* MCC.

ROBARTS, Basil; Director, 1964–85, and Chief General Manager, 1963–75, Norwich Union Insurance Group; *b* 13 Jan. 1915; *s* of late Henry Ernest Robarts and Beatrice Katie (*née* Stevens); *m* 1941, Sheila Margaret Cooper Thwaites; one *s* one *d*. *Educ:* Gresham's Sch., Holt. Served Army, 1939–45 (Lt-Col, RA). Joined Norwich Union Life Insce Soc., 1934; Gen. Man. and Actuary, 1953. Institute of Actuaries: Fellow (FIA), 1939; Treas., 1965–67; Gen. Commissioner of Income Tax, 1958–; Chm., British Insce Assoc., 1969–71. Trustee, Charities Official Investment Fund, 1977–85. *Recreation:* music. *Address:* 466B Unthank Road, Norwich. *T:* Norwich 51135. *Club:* Naval and Military.

ROBARTS, David John; Director of Robert Fleming & Co. Ltd, 1944–76; Director of other companies; Chairman, Committee of London Clearing Bankers and President, British Bankers' Association, 1956–60 and 1968–70; *b* 1906; *e s* of Capt. Gerald Robarts; *m* 1951, Pauline Mary, *d* of Colonel Francis Follett, and *widow* of Clive Stoddart; three *s* one *d*. *Educ:* Eton; Magdalen College, Oxford. Dir, National Westminster Bank Ltd, to 1976 (Chm., 1969–71; Chm., National Provincial Bank Ltd, 1954–68). Church Commissioner, 1957–65. High Sheriff of Buckinghamshire, 1963. *Address:* 7 Smith Square, Westminster, SW1. *T:* 01–222 2428; Lillingstone House, Buckingham. *T:* Lillingstone Dayrell 202. *Club:* Pratt's.

ROBARTS, Eric Kirkby; *b* 20 Jan. 1908; *s* of Charles Martin Robarts and Flora Robarts (*née* Kirkby); *m* 1930, Iris Lucy Swan; five *d*. *Educ:* Bishops Stortford Coll.; Herts Inst. of Agriculture. Ran family business, C. M. Robarts & Son, until Aug. 1942. Joined Express Dairy Co. Ltd, 1942: Dir, 1947–73; Man. Dir, 1960–73; Dep. Chm., 1966; Chm., 1967–73. FRSA; FBIM. *Recreations:* hunting, shooting. *Address:* Frithcote, Watford Road, Northwood, Middx. *T:* Northwood 22533. *Club:* Farmers'.

ROBARTS, Julian; *see* Robarts, A. J.

ROBATHAN, Rev. Canon Frederick Norman, OBE 1945; MA; Hon. CF (1st Cl.); Canon Emeritus of Ely Cathedral, since 1960; *b* 4 Jan. 1896; *s* of Reverend Thomas Frederick and Edith Jane Robathan, St Andrew's College, Gorakpur, India; *m* 1st, 1922, Renée Wells (*d* 1972) (JP 1947–53); one *s* (and one *s* decd); 2nd, 1972, Ruth Elizabeth Emma Corfe (*d* 1984), 3rd *d* of late Canon E. C. Corfe and Mrs Emma Corfe. *Educ:* King's School, Chester; Dean Close Sch., Cheltenham; St Edmund Hall, Oxford (MA); Wycliffe Hall, Oxford. Served as Commissioned Officer, European War, 1914–19 (campaign medals), France, 1915–16. Ordained, 1921; Curate, Quarry Bank, Staffs, 1921; Priest Vicar, Truro Cathedral, 1923–25; Priest Vicar, Lincoln Cathedral, 1925–28; Chaplain HM Prison, Lincoln, 1926–28; Minor Canon and Sacrist and Junior Cardinal, St Paul's Cathedral, 1928–34; Chaplain Guy's Hosp., 1932–33; Minor Canon, Westminster Abbey, 1934–37, and Chaplain, Westminster Hospital; Rector of Hackney, 1937–45, and Chaplain East London Hospital, CF, RARO, 1923. War of 1939–45 (campaign medals); BEF 1940; Evacuation, Dunkirk, 1940; Sen. Chaplain 43 Div., 1941; Army Technical Sch., Arborfield, 1941; Sen. Chaplain Royal Garrison Church, Aldershot, 1942; Dep. Asst Chaplain-Gen. 12th Corps, 1943; Asst Chaplain-Gen. 21 Army Grp., 1944; Normandy Landings, 1944 (despatches). Vicar of Brighton, Sussex and Canon and Prebendary of Waltham in Chichester Cathedral, 1945–53; Canon Residentiary and Treasurer, Ely Cathedral, 1953–59; Vicar of Cardington, Bedford, 1959. Sen. Chaplain Army Cadet Force, Cambs, 1954–59. Councillor, Bedford RDC, 1960. Chaplain to High Sheriff of Beds., 1962; Rector of Charleton with Buckland tout Saints, Kingsbridge, S Devon, 1962–66. Hon. Priest Vicar, Truro Cathedral, 1967. Coronation Medal, 1937. *Recreations:* rowing, hockey, cricket, antiquaries. *Address:* Myrtle Court, Mevagissey, Cornwall. *T:* Mevagissey 842233.

ROBB, Prof. James Christie; Professor of Physical Chemistry, 1957–84, and Head of Department of Chemistry, 1981–84, University of Birmingham; *b* 23 April 1924; *s* of James M. Robb, Rocklands, The House of Daviot, Inverurie, Aberdeenshire; *m* 1951, Joyce Irene Morley; three *d*. *Educ:* Daviot School; Inverurie Academy; Aberdeen University (BSc Hons, 1945, PhD 1948); DSc Birmingham, 1954. DSIR Senior Research Award, Aberdeen, 1948–50. ICI Fellow, Birmingham Univ., 1950–51; on Birmingham Univ. staff, 1951–84. A Guardian of Birmingham Assay Office, 1980–. Mem. Council, Birmingham Civic Soc., 1981–. Pres., Birmingham Rotary Club, 1982–83. *Publications:* scientific contrib. to Proc. Royal Soc., Trans. Faraday Soc., etc. *Recreations:* motoring, photography, computing. *Address:* 42 School Road, Moseley, Birmingham B13 9SN. *T:* 021–449 2610.

ROBBE-GRILLET, Alain, literary consultant, writer and cinéaste; Editions de Minuit, Paris, since 1955; *b* 18 Aug. 1922; *s* of Gaston Robbe-Grillet and Yvonne Canu; *m* 1957, Catherine Rstakian. *Educ:* Lycée Buffon, Paris; Lycée St Louis, Paris; Institut National Agronomique, Paris. Engineer: Institut National de la Statistique, 1945–49; Institut des Fruits et Agrumes Coloniaux, 1949–51. *Films:* L'Immortelle, 1963; Trans-Europ-Express, 1967; L'Homme qui ment, 1968; L'Eden et après, 1970; Glissements progressifs du plaisir,

1974; Le jeu avec le feu, 1975; La belle captive, 1983. *Publications:* Les Gommes, 1953 (The Erasers, 1966); Le Voyeur, 1955 (The Voyeur, 1959); La Jalousie, 1957 (Jealousy, 1960); Dans le labyrinthe, 1959 (In the Labyrinth, 1967); L'Année dernière à Marienbad, 1961 (Last Year in Marienbad, 1962); Instantanés, 1962 (Snapshots, and, Towards a New Novel, 1965); L'Immortelle, 1963 (The Immortal One, 1971); Pour un nouveau roman, 1964; La Maison de rendezvous, 1965; Projet pour une révolution à New York, 1970 (Project for a Revolution in New York, 1972); Glissements progressifs du plaisir, 1974; Topologie d'une cité fantôme, 1976 (Topology of a Phantom City, 1978); La Belle captive, 1976; Souvenirs du Triangle d'or, 1978; Un Régicide, 1978; Djinn, 1981; Le Miroir qui revient, 1985. *Address:* 18 Boulevard Maillot, 92200 Neuilly-sur-Seine, France. *T:* (1) 47 22 31 22.

ROBBINS, Edgar Carmichael, CBE 1957; Legal Adviser to The British Broadcasting Corporation, 1959–74; *b* 22 March 1911; *s* of John Haldeman Robbins; *m* 1936, Alice Eugenia, *d* of Rev. Herbert Norman Nash; two *s* two *d. Educ:* Westminster Sch.; London Univ. (LLB). Admitted a solicitor, 1933. Employed by The British Broadcasting Corporation, 1934–74, Solicitor to the BBC 1945–59. Clerk, City of London Solicitors' Company, 1976–84. *Publications:* William Paston, Justice, 1932; The Cursed Norfolk Justice, 1936. *Address:* 9 Pensioners' Court, The Charterhouse, EC1. *T:* 01–250 0555. *Club:* Athenæum.

ROBBINS, Prof. Frederick C., MD; Bronze Star (US Army), 1945; President, Institute of Medicine, National Academy of Sciences, Washington, DC, since 1980; University Professor, Case Western Reserve University, since 1980 (Professor of Pediatrics, School of Medicine, 1952–80, Dean, 1966–80, now Emeritus); *b* 25 Aug. 1916; *s* of William J. Robbins and Christine Chapman Robbins; *m* 1948, Alice Havemeyer Northrop; two *d. Educ:* University of Missouri (AB); University of Missouri Medical School (BS); Harvard Medical School (MD). US Army, 1942–46; rank on discharge, Major. Various posts in the Children's Hospital, Boston, from 1940, finishing as Chief Resident in Medicine, 1948; Sen. Fellow in Virus Diseases, National Research Council, 1948–50; Research Fellow in Pediatrics, Harvard Med. Sch., 1948–50; Instr in Ped., 1950–51, Associate in Ped., 1951–52, at Harvard Medical School; Dir, Department of Pediatrics, Cleveland Metropolitan General Hospital, 1952–66. Associate, Research Div. of Infectious Diseases, the Children's Medical Center, Boston, 1950–52; Research Fellow in Ped., the Boston Lying-in Hospital, Boston, Mass, 1950–52; Asst to Children's Medical Service, Mass Gen. Hosp., Boston, 1950–52. Visiting Scientist, Donner Lab., Univ. of California, 1963–64. President: Soc. for Pediatric Research, 1961–62; Amer. Pediatric Soc., 1973–74. Member: Nat. Acad. of Sciences, 1972 (Co-Chm., Forum on Human Experimentation, 1974); Amer. Philosophical Soc., 1972; Adv. Cttee, Office of Technol. Assessment for Congress, 1973; Adv. Cttee on Med. Research, Pan American Health Organization, WHO, 1981–. First Mead Johnson Award, 1953; Nobel Prize in Physiology and Medicine, 1954; Award for Distinguished Achievement (Modern Medicine), 1963; Med. Mutual Honor Award for 1969. Hon. Dr of Science: John Carroll University, 1955; Missouri, 1958; North Carolina, 1979; Tufts, 1983; Med. Coll. of Ohio, 1983; Albert Einstein Coll. of Medicine, 1984; Med. Coll. of Wisconsin, 1984; Hon. Dr of Laws, New Mexico, 1968; Hon. Dr Med. Sci., Med. Coll. of Pa, 1984. *Publications:* numerous in various jls, primarily on subject of viruses and infectious diseases. *Recreations:* music, tennis, sailing. *Address:* 7021 Oak Forest Lane, Bethesda, Maryland 20817, USA; (office) 2101 Constitution Avenue, NW, Washington, DC 20418, USA. *T:* 202/334–3300.

ROBBINS, Harold; writer; *m* Grace; one *d. Educ:* New York. Formerly sugar exporter, film publicist, film impresario, etc. *Publications:* The Dream Merchants, 1949; 79 Park Avenue, 1955; A Stone for Danny Fisher, 1955; Never Leave Me, 1956; Never Love a Stranger, 1958; Stiletto, 1960; The Carpetbaggers, 1961; Where Love Has Gone, 1964; The Adventurers, 1966; The Inheritors, 1969; The Betsy, 1971 (filmed 1978); The Pirate, 1974; The Lonely Lady, 1976; Dreams Die First, 1977; Memories of Another Day, 1979; Goodbye, Janette, 1981; Spellbinder, 1982; Descent from Xanadu, 1984. *Address:* c/o New English Library, 47 Bedford Square, WC1B 3DP.

ROBBINS, Jerome; Choreographer and Director; Co-Ballet Master in Chief, New York City Ballet, since 1983 (Ballet Master, 1969–83; Associate Artistic Director, 1949–59); Founder Director, Ballets: USA, 1958–61; *b* New York, 11 Oct. 1918; *s* of Harry and Lena Robbins. *Educ:* Woodrow Wilson High School, Weehawken, NJ; New York University. Studied ballet with Antony Tudor and Eugene Loring, and Modern, Spanish and oriental dance. First stage experience with Sandor-Sorel Dance Center, New York, 1937; dancer in chorus of American musicals, 1938–40; Ballet Theatre, 1940–44 (soloist 1941), London season, 1946; formed own company, Ballets: USA, 1958. Member: NY State Council on the Arts/Dance Panel, 1973–77; Nat. Council on the Arts, 1974–80. City of Paris Award, 1971; Handel Medallion, NYC, 1976; Kennedy Center Honoree, 1981, and many other awards. Hon. Degrees from Ohio Univ., 1974, City Univ. of NY, 1980. Chevalier, Order of Arts and Letters (France), 1964. *Ballets include:* (for Ballet Theater) Fancy Free, 1944; (for Concert Varieties) Interplay, 1945; (for New York City Ballet) Age of Anxiety, 1950; The Cage, 1951; Afternoon of a Faun, 1953; Fanfare, 1953; The Concert, 1956; (for American Ballet Theater) Les Noces, 1965; Dances at a Gathering, 1969; In the Night, 1970; The Goldberg Variations, 1971; Watermill, 1972; Requiem Canticles, 1972; An Evening's Waltzes, 1973; Dybbuk (later The Dybbuk Variations, then renamed Suite of Dances), 1974; Concerto in G (later in G Major), 1975; Ma Mère l'Oye (later Mother Goose), 1975; Chansons Madécasses, 1975; The Four Seasons, 1979; Opus 19, The Dreamer, 1979; Rondo, 1981; Piano Pieces, 1981; The Gershwin Concerto, 1982; Four Chamber Works, 1982; Glass Pieces, 1983; I'm Old Fashioned, 1983; Antique Epigraphs, 1984; (with Twyla Tharp) Brahms/Handel, 1984; Eight Lines, 1985; In Memory Of, 1985; Quiet City, 1986; Picollo Balleto, 1986; (for Ballets: USA) NY Export: Opus Jazz, 1958; Moves, 1959; (for Star Spangled Gala) Other Dances, 1976. *Musicals include:* On the Town, 1945; Billion Dollar Baby, 1946 (Donaldson award); High Button Shoes, 1947 (Donaldson and Tony awards); Miss Liberty, 1949; Call Me Madam, 1950; The King and I, 1951 (Donaldson award); Two's Company, 1952 (Donaldson award); Peter Pan, 1954; Bells Are Ringing, 1956; West Side Story, 1957 (Tony, Evening Standard, Laurel and two Academy awards); Gypsy, 1959; Fiddler on the Roof, 1964 (two Tony awards and Drama Critics' award). Has directed and choreographed films, drama and TV (inc. Peter Pan with Mary Martin, 1955 (Emmy award)). Hon. Mem., AAIL, 1985. Hon. Dr Fine Arts, NY Univ., 1985. *Address:* c/o New York City Ballet, New York State Theater, Lincoln Center, New York, NY 10023, USA.

ROBBINS, John Dennis, OBE 1945; TD 1950; FCA; *b* 28 July 1915; *s* of Duncan Ross Robbins and Harriette Winifred Robbins (*née* Goodyear); *m* 1942, Joan Mary Mason; one *s* two *d. Educ:* Aldenham School. Commnd Mddx Regt (DCO), 2nd Lieut 1939, Captain 1940, Major 1941, Lt-Col 1944; served N Africa, Italy, Palestine (OBE, despatches twice); retd as Lt-Col 1946. Partner, Kay Keeping & Co., Chartered Accountants, 1946–49; joined British Metal Corp. Ltd, 1950; Dir and Gen. Man., 1952; a Man. Dir, 1963. Amalgamated Metal Corp. Ltd: Dir 1965; Chief Exec. 1971; Exec. Dep. Chm., 1972, Chm., 1975–77; Dir, Smith & Nephew Associated Cos, 1958–85. Mem., Worshipful Co. of Chartered Accountants. Freeman, City of London. *Recreations:* gardening, shooting,

fly-fishing. *Address:* Orpen's Hill House, Birch, Colchester, Essex CO2 0LY. *T:* Colchester 330797. *Club:* Gresham.

ROBBINS, Prof. Keith Gilbert; Professor of Modern History, Glasgow University, since 1980; *b* 9 April 1940; *s* of Gilbert Henry John and Edith Mary Robbins; *m* 1963, Janet Carey Thomson; three *s* one *d. Educ:* Bristol Grammar Sch.; Magdalen and St Antony's Colls, Oxford. MA, DPhil (Oxon); DLitt (Glas.). University of York: Asst Lectr in History, 1963; Lectr in Hist., 1964; Prof. of History, 1971–79, Dean of Faculty of Arts, 1977–79, UCNW, Bangor. Vis. Prof., British Columbia Univ., 1983; Lectures: Enid Muir, Newcastle Univ., 1981; A. H. Dodd, UCNW, Bangor, 1984; Raleigh, British Acad., 1984; Ford, Oxford Univ., 1986–87. Editor, History, 1977–; Editorial Bd, Jl of Ecclesiastical History, 1978–. *Publications:* Munich 1938, 1968; Sir Edward Grey, 1971; The Abolition of War: The British Peace Movement 1914–1919, 1976; John Bright, 1979; The Eclipse of a Great Power: Modern Britain 1870–1975, 1983; The First World War, 1984; articles in Historical Jl, Internat. Affairs, Jl of Contemporary Hist., Jl of Ecclesiastical Hist., Jl of Commonwealth and Imperial Hist., etc. *Recreations:* music, gardening, walking. *Address:* Department of Modern History, The University, Glasgow G12 8QQ. *T:* 041–339 8855.

ROBBINS, Michael; see Robbins, R. M.

ROBBINS, Dr Raymond Frank; Director, Plymouth Polytechnic, since 1974; *b* 15 Feb. 1928; *s* of Harold and Elsie Robbins; *m* 1955, Eirian Meredith Edwards; two *d. Educ:* Grove Park Grammar Sch., Wrexham; UCW Aberystwyth. PhD 1954; FRIC 1962. Research Chemist, Monsanto Chemicals Ltd, 1954–55; Research Fellow, Univ. of Exeter, 1955–56; Lectr, Nottingham Coll. of Technology, 1956–59; Sen. Lectr, Hatfield Coll. of Technology, 1960–61; Head of Dept of Chem. Sciences, Hatfield Polytechnic, 1961–70; Dep. Dir, Plymouth Polytechnic, 1970–74. *Publications:* papers on organic chemistry in chem. jls, various reviews and articles in sci. and educnl press. *Recreations:* hill walking, sailing. *Address:* Lent Hill Cottage, Ashburton, Devon TQ13 7NW. *T:* (office) Plymouth 21312.

ROBBINS, (Richard) Michael, CBE 1976; *b* 7 Sept. 1915; *er s* of late Alfred Gordon Robbins and Josephine, *d* of R. L. Capell, Northampton; *m* 1939, Rose Margaret Elspeth, *er d* of late Sir Robert Reid Bannatyne, CB, Lindfield, Sussex; one *s* two *d. Educ:* Westminster Sch. (King's Schol.); Christ Church, Oxford (Westminster Schol.; MA); Univ. of Vienna. Joined London Passenger Transport Board, 1939. War service, RE (Transportation), 1939–46: Persia and Iraq, 1941–43; GHQ, MEF, 1943–44; Major, AML (Greece), 1944–45. Rejoined London Transport, 1946; Sec. to Chm., 1947–50; Sec., London Transp. Exec., 1950–55; Sec. and Chief Public Relations Off., 1955–60; Chief Commercial and Pub. Rel. Off., 1960–65; Mem., London Transport Exec., 1965–80 (Man. Dir, Rlys, 1971–78). Chm., Transport Adv. Cttee, Transport and Road Res. Lab., 1977–81. Pres., Inst. of Transport, 1975–76 (Mem. Council, 1957–60 and 1962–64; Chm., Metrop. Sect., 1962–63; Chm., Educn and Trg Cttee, 1969–72; Vice-Pres., 1972–75); Pres., Omnibus Soc., 1965; Chairman: Middx Victoria County History Council, 1963–76; Middx Local History Council, 1958–65; Internat. Metrop. Rlys Cttee, Internat. Union of Public Transport, 1976–81; Victorian Soc., 1978–81; President: London and Middx Archæol. Soc., 1965–71 (Mem. Council, 1951–56 and 1960–65); Greater London Industrial Archæol. Soc., 1969–; Rly Students Assoc., 1967–68; St Marylebone Soc., 1971–74; Mem., Ancient Monuments Adv. Cttee, English Heritage, 1986–. Dunhill lectr on industrial design, Australia, 1974. FSA 1957; Treasurer, Soc. of Antiquaries, 1971– (Mem. Council, 1965–67, 1970–71); Chm., Museum of London, 1979– (Governor, 1968–); Trustee: London Museum, 1970–75; Greater Manchester Museum of Science and Industry, 1982–. *Publications:* The North London Railway, 1937; 190 in Persia, 1951; The Isle of Wight Railways, 1953; Middlesex, 1953; (ed) Middlesex Parish Churches, 1955; The Railway Age, 1962; (with T. C. Barker) History of London Transport, vol. 1, 1963, vol. 2, 1974; George and Robert Stephenson, 1966, rev. edn 1981; Points and Signals, 1967; A Public Transport Century, 1985; Joint Editor, Journal of Transport History, 1953–65; contribs to transport and historical jls. *Recreations:* exploring cities and suburbs; travelling abroad and in branch railway trains; concert-going. *Address:* 7 Courthope Villas, Wimbledon, SW19 4EH. *T:* 01–946 7308.

ROBENS, family name of **Baron Robens of Woldingham.**

ROBENS OF WOLDINGHAM, Baron *cr* 1961, of Woldingham (Life Peer); **Alfred Robens,** PC 1951; Chairman: Snamprogetti, since 1980; Alfred Robens Associates, since 1984; a Director: Times Newspapers Holdings Ltd, 1980–83 (Times Newspapers Ltd, 1967–80); British Fuel Co., since 1967; AAH, since 1971; AMI (Europe) Ltd, since 1981; Chairman, Engineering Industries Council, since 1976; *b* 18 Dec. 1910; *s* of George and Edith Robens; *m* 1937, Eva, *d* of Fred and late Elizabeth Powell. *Educ:* Manchester Secondary Sch. Official of Union of Distributive and Allied Workers, 1935–45; Manchester City Councillor, 1942–45. MP (Lab) Wansbeck Div. of Northumberland, 1945–50, and for Blyth, 1950–60. Parliamentary Private Secretary to Minister of Transport, 1945–47; Parliamentary Secretary, Ministry of Fuel and Power, 1947–51; Minister of Labour and National Service, April-Oct. 1951. Chairman: National Coal Bd, 1961–71; Vickers Ltd, 1971–79; St Regis Internat., 1976–81; MLH Consultants, 1971–81; Johnson Matthey PLC, 1971–83 (Hon. Pres., 1983–); St Regis Newspapers, Bolton, 1975–80 (Dir, 1976); a Director: Bank of England, 1966–81; St Regis Paper Co. (NY), 1976–80; Trust House Forte Ltd, 1971–86. Chairman: Foundation on Automation and Employment, 1962; Engrg Industries Council, 1976–80; Member: NEDC, 1962–71; Royal Commn on Trade Unions and Employers' Assocs, 1965–68. President: Advertising Assoc., 1963–68; Incorporated Soc. of British Advertisers, 1973–76; Chairman: Jt Steering Cttee for Malta, 1967; Jt Econ. Mission to Malta, 1967. Member: Council of Manchester Business School, 1964–79 (Dep. Chm., 1964–70; Chm., 1970–79); Court of Governors, LSE, 1965; Chancellor, Univ. of Surrey, 1966–77. Governor, Queen Elizabeth Training Coll. for the Disabled, 1951–80; Chairman: Bd of Govs, Guy's Hosp., 1965–74; Guy's Hosp. Medical and Dental Sch., 1974–82; Cttee on Safety and Health of people at their place of work, 1970–72; Fellow, Manchester Coll. of Science and Technology, 1965–; Hon. FRCR, 1975. Hon. DCL: Univ. of Newcastle upon Tyne, 1964; Manchester Univ., 1974; Hon. LLD: Leicester, 1966; London, 1971. Hon. MInstM, 1968; Hon. FIOB, 1974. Mackintosh Medal, Advertising Assoc., 1970; Albert Medal, RSA, 1977. *Publications:* Engineering and Economic Progress, 1965; Industry and Government, 1970; Human Engineering, 1970; Ten Year Stint, 1972; sundry articles to magazines, journals and newspapers. *Recreation:* gardening. *Club:* Reform.

ROBERGE, Guy, QC (Can.); Counsel, Clarkson, Tétrault, Barristers and Solicitors, since 1982; *b* 26 Jan. 1915; *s* of P. A. Roberge and Irène Duchesneau; *m* 1957, Marie Raymond; one *s* one *d. Educ:* Laval Univ., Quebec. Called to Bar, 1937; Mem., Quebec Legislative Assembly, 1944–48; Mem., Restrictive Trade Practices Commn of Canada, 1955–57; Chm. and Chief Exec. Officer, Nat. Film Bd of Canada, 1957–66; Agent-General for Govt of PQ in UK, 1966–71; Vice-Pres. (Law), Canadian Transport Commn, 1971–81. Hon. DCL: Bishop's Univ., 1967; Hon. doctorat d'université, Laval Univ., 1975. *Address:*

555 Wilbrod, Ottawa, Ontario K1N 5R4, Canada. *Clubs:* Quebec Garrison (Quebec City); Rideau (Ottawa).

ROBERTHALL, family name of **Baron Roberthall.**

ROBERTHALL, Baron *cr* 1969 (Life Peer), of Silverspur, Queensland, and Trenance, Cornwall; **Robert Lowe Roberthall,** KCMG 1954; CB 1950; MA; Principal Hertford College, Oxford, 1964–67, Hon. Fellow since 1969; Member of Economic Planning Board, 1947–61; *b* New South Wales, 6 March 1901; *s* of late Edgar Hall and Rose Helen, *d* of A. K. Cullen; changed surname to Roberthall by deed poll, 1969; *m* 1932, Laura Margaret (marr. diss. 1968), *d* of G. E. Linfoot; two *d*; *m* 1968, Perilla Thyme, *d* of late Sir Richard Southwell, FRS. *Educ:* Ipswich, Qld; Univ. of Queensland; Magdalen College, Oxford. BEng, Queensland, 1922; Rhodes Scholar, 1923–26 (First in Modern Greats, 1926); Lecturer in Economics, Trinity College, 1926–47; Fellow, 1927–50; Hon. Fellow, 1958; Junior Dean, 1927; Dean, 1933–38; Bursar, 1938–39; Proproctor, 1933; Ministry of Supply, 1939–46; British Raw Materials Mission, Washington, 1942–44; Adviser, Board of Trade, 1946–47; Director Economic Section, Cabinet Office, 1947–53; Economic Adviser to HM Government, 1953–61; Advisory Dir, Unilever, 1961–71; advr to Tube Investments, 1961–76. Fellow of Nuffield College, 1938–47, Visiting Fellow, 1961–64. Mem. of Economic and Employment Commn UN, 1946–49; Chm., OEEC Gp of Economic Experts, 1955–61; UK Mem., Commonwealth Economic Cttee, 1961–67; Mem., (Franks) Commn of Inquiry into Oxford Univ., 1964–66; Chm. Exec. Cttee, NIESR, 1962–70; Chm. Select Cttee on Commodity Prices, 1976–77. Royal Economic Society: Hon. Sec., 1948–58; Pres., 1958–60; Vice-Pres., 1960–86; Pres., Soc. of Business Economists, 1968–73, Hon. Fellow, 1973. Rede Lecturer, Cambridge University, 1962. Hon. DSc, University of Queensland. Joined SDP, 1981. *Publications:* Earning and Spending, 1934; The Economic System in a Socialist State, 1936; various articles, etc on economics. *Recreations:* walking, gardening. *Address:* Quarry, Trenance, Newquay, Cornwall. *T:* St Mawgan 860456.

ROBERTS, family name of **Baron Clwyd.**

ROBERTS, Prof. Adam; *see* Roberts, E. A.

ROBERTS, Albert, JP; DL; *b* 14 May 1908; *s* of Albert Roberts and Annie Roberts (*née* Ward); *m* 1932, Alice Ashton; one *s* one *d. Educ:* Woodlesford School; Normanton and Whitwood Technical College, Yorks. Sec., Woodlesford Br., Yorks Miners Assoc., 1935–41; Safety Board, Mines Inspector, 1941–51. Mem., Rothwell UDC, 1937–52. MP (Lab) Normanton, 1951–83; Exec. Mem., British Group, Inter-Parly Union, 1955–83 (Chm., 1968–70). Exec. Mem., Yorkshire Area Heart Foundn; Vice-Pres., Yorkshire Soc. JP 1946, DL 1967, W Yorks. Order of Isabela la Católica (Spain), 1967; Diplomatic Order of Merit, Korean Republic, 1979. *Recreations:* cricket, bowls. *Address:* Cordoba, 14 Aberford Road, Oulton-Woodlesford, near Leeds. *T:* Leeds 822303.

ROBERTS, Dr Albert, MSc, PhD; MIMinE, MIMM, AMInstCE, FGS, CEng; Head of Department of Mining Engineering, University of Nevada, 1969–75, retired 1975; *b* 25 April 1911; British; *m* 1938, May Taberner; two *s* one *d. Educ:* Wigan Mining and Techn. College. Mining Engr, Wigan Coal Corp., 1931–35, 1938–40; Ashanti Goldfields Corp., 1935–38; Lectr: Sunderland Techn. Coll., 1940–45; Nottingham Univ., 1945–55; Sheffield Univ., 1955; Dir, Postgraduate Sch. of Mining, Sheffield Univ., 1956–69. Ed., Internat. Jl of Rock Mechanics and Mining Sciences, 1964–68. *Publications:* Geological Structures, 1946; Underground Lighting, 1959; Mine Ventilation, 1959; Mineral Processing, 1965; Geotechnology, 1977; Applied Geotechnology, 1981. *Recreations:* gardening, photography, music, fishing.

ROBERTS, Allan; MP (Lab) Bootle, since 1979; *b* 28 Oct. 1943; *s* of Ernest and Anne Roberts. *Educ:* Droylesden, Little Moss Boys' County Sec. Sch.; Didsbury Coll. of Education (Teachers' Cert.); Manchester Univ. Extra-Mural Dept (CQSW). School teacher, 1967–70; at Manchester Univ., 1970–72; Social Worker and Sen. Social Worker, 1972–74; Training Officer, City of Salford Social Services Dept, 1974–76; Principal Officer (Child Care) with Salford Social Services Dept, 1976–79. Chm., Parly Labour Party Environment Gp; Mem. Environment Select Cttee. Mem., CND. *Publications:* contribs to Tribune; regular columnist, Labour Herald. *Recreations:* reading, films, eating, drinking, theatre. *Address:* House of Commons, SW1A 0AA. *Clubs:* Bootle Labour; Litherland Trades & Labour; Seaforth Socialist.

ROBERTS, Alwyn; Vice Principal, since 1985, and Director of Extra Mural Studies, since 1979, University College of North Wales, Bangor; *b* 26 Aug. 1933; *s* of late Rev. Howell Roberts and Buddug Roberts; *m* 1960, Mair Rowlands Williams; one *s. Educ:* Penygroes Grammar Sch.; Univ. of Wales, Aberystwyth and Bangor (BA, LLB); Univ. of Cambridge (MA). Tutor, Westminster Coll., Cambridge, 1959; Principal, Pachhunga Meml Govt Coll., Aijal, Assam, India, 1960–67; Lectr in Social Admin, University Coll., Swansea, 1967–70; Lectr, subseq. Sen. Lectr, Dept of Social Theory and Instns, UCNW, Bangor, 1970–79. BBC National Governor for Wales, 1979–86; Chm., Broadcasting Council for Wales, 1979–86 (Mem., 1974–78); Member: Welsh Fourth TV Channel Auth., 1979–86; Gwynedd CC, 1973–81 (Chm., Social Services Cttee, 1977–81); Gwynedd AHA, 1973–80; Royal Commn on Legal Services, 1976–79; Council, Royal National Eisteddfod of Wales, 1979–; Bd, CWMN 1 Theatr Cymru, 1982–. *Address:* Gwynfryn, Holyhead Road, Bangor, Gwynedd LL57 2EE. *T:* Bangor 364052.

ROBERTS, Angus Thomas; Director of Litigation and Prosecution, Post Office Solicitor's Office (formerly Principal Assistant Solicitor to General Post Office), 1965–74; *b* 28 March 1913; *s* of late Edward Roberts and late Margaret (*née* Murray); *m* 1940, Frances Monica, *d* of late Frederick and late Agnes Bertha Cane; two *s. Educ:* Felsted School. Admitted Solicitor, 1936. Entered Post Office Solicitor's Dept, 1939. Served in Royal Navy, 1941–46 (Lieut, RNVR). Asst Solicitor to GPO, 1951. *Recreations:* golf, fishing, gardening. *Address:* 1 The Mulberries, The Inner Silk Mill, Malmesbury, Wilts. *T:* Malmesbury 4981.

ROBERTS, Ann Clwyd; *see* Clwyd, Ann.

ROBERTS, (Anthony) John; Managing Director, Counter Services, and Board Member, The Post Office, since 1985; *b* 26 Aug. 1944; *s* of Douglas and Margaret Roberts; *m* 1970, Diana June (*née* Lamdin); two *s. Educ:* Hampton Sch.; Exeter Univ. (BA Hons). CBIM. Open Entrant, Administrative Class Civil Service, The Post Office, 1967; PA to Dep. Chairman and Chief Executive, 1969–71; Principal, Long Range Planning, 1971–74; Controller Personnel and Finance, North Western Postal Board, 1974–76; Principal Private Sec. to Chairman, 1976–77; Director, Chairman's Office, 1977–80; Secretary Designate, 1980–81, Sec., 1981–82; Dir, Counter Services, 1981–85. Freeman, City of London, 1983. *Recreations:* squash, golf, gardening, music. *Address:* The Post Office, Counters Business Headquarters, Streets House, 20–21 Lawrence Lane, EC2V 8HQ. *T:* 01–432 3452. *Clubs:* Oxshott Squash Rackets, Betchworth Park Golf.

ROBERTS, Arthur Loten, OBE 1971; Emeritus Professor, formerly Livesey Professor of Coal Gas and Fuel Industries, 1947–71, and Chairman of the Houldsworth School of

Applied Science, 1956–70, University of Leeds; Pro-Vice-Chancellor, 1967–69; *b* 1 April 1906; *s* of Arthur James Roberts, Hull, and Alice Maude Loten, Hornsea, E Yorks; *m* 1941, Katherine Mary Hargrove; one *s* one *d. Educ:* Christ's Hospital; Univ. of Leeds. BSc 1928, PhD 1930, Assistant Lecturer, Lecturer, Senior Lecturer, Leeds Univ. Part-time mem. North-Eastern Area Gas Board, 1950–71; Mem. Gas Corp. Res. Cttee (formerly Gas Council Research Cttee), 1951–79; Hon. Sec. Advisory Research Cttee of Gas Council and University, 1947–71; Chm., former Joint Refractories Cttee of British Ceramic Research Assoc. and the Gas Corporation; Pres. British Ceramic Society, 1957–58; Member of Technology Sub-Cttee, UGC, 1960–69. FRIC, FInstF, Hon. Fellow Inst. Ceram., Hon. FInstGasE, Hon. FIChemE. *Publications:* numerous contributions to chemical, ceramic and fuel jls. *Recreations:* painting, pianoforte, garden. *Address:* Hillside, 6 King's Road, Bramhope, Leeds, W Yorks. *T:* Leeds 674977.

ROBERTS, Barbara Haig; *see* MacGibbon, B. H.

ROBERTS, Prof. Benjamin Charles, MA Oxon; Professor of Industrial Relations, London School of Economics, University of London, 1962–84, now Emeritus; *b* 1 Aug. 1917; *s* of Walter Whitfield Roberts and Mabel Frances Roberts; *m* 1945, Veronica Lilian, *d* of George Frederick and Vera Lilian Vine-Lott; two *s. Educ:* LSE; New Coll., Oxford. Research Student, Nuffield Coll., Oxford, 1948–49; Part-time Lectr, Ruskin Coll., Oxford, 1948–49; London Sch. of Economics: Lectr in Trade Union Studies, 1949–56; Reader in Industrial Relations, 1956–62; Mem. Ct of Govs, 1964–69, 1979–83. Vis. Prof: Princeton Univ., 1958; MIT 1959; Univ. of Calif., Berkeley, 1965. Assoc., Internat. Inst. of Labour Studies, Geneva, 1966; Member: Council, Inst. Manpower Studies; British-N American Cttee; Nat. Reference Tribunal of Coal Mining Industry, 1970–; Council, ACAS, 1979–. Editor, British Jl of Industrial Relations, 1963–. Pres., British Univs Industrial Relations Assoc., 1965–68; Pres., Internat. Industrial Relations Assoc., 1967–73. Consultant to EEC, 1976–79. Chm., Economists' Bookshop, 1979–. *Publications:* Trade Unions in the New Era, 1947; Trade Union Government and Administration in Great Britain, 1956; National Wages Policy in War and Peace, 1958; The Trades Union Congress, 1868–1921, 1958; Trade Unions in a Free Society, 1959; (ed) Industrial Relations: Contemporary Problems and Perspectives, 1962; Labour in the Tropical Territories of the Commonwealth, 1964; (ed) Manpower Planning and Employment Trends 1966; (with L. Greyfié de Bellecombe) Collective Bargaining in African Countries, 1967; (ed) Industrial Relations: Contemporary Issues, 1968; (with John Lovell) A Short History of the TUC, 1968; (with R. O. Clarke and D. J. Fatchet) Workers' Participation in Management in Britain, 1972; (with R. Loveridge and J. Gennard) Reluctant Militants: a study of industrial technicians, 1972; (with H. Okomoto and G. Lodge) Collective Bargaining and Employee Participation in Western Europe, North America and Japan, 1979; also Evidence to Royal Commn on Trade Unions, 1966, and Report to ILO on Labour and Automation: Manpower Adjustment Programmes in the United Kingdom, 1967; Industrial Relations in Europe: the imperatives of change, 1985. *Address:* 28 Temple Fortune Lane, NW11. *T:* 01–458 1421. *Club:* Reform.

ROBERTS, Bertie; Director, Department of the Environment (Property Services Agency), 1971–79; *b* 4 June 1919; *y s* of late Thomas and Louisa Roberts, Blaengarw, S Wales; *m* 1st, 1946, Dr Peggy Clark; one *s*; 2nd, 1962, Catherine Matthew. *Educ:* Garw Grammar School. Entered Civil Service (HM Office of Works), 1936; HM Forces, 1942–46, Captain RAOC; leader of study on feasibility of using computers in Min. of Public Bldg and Works, 1958; formed and directed operational computer orgn, 1962; Comptroller of Accounts, 1963; Dir of Computer Services, 1967; Head of Organisation and Methods, 1969; Dir of Estate Management Overseas, Dept of the Environment (with FCO), 1971; Reg. Dir, DoE (Maj.-Gen.), British Forces Germany, 1976–79. Mem., Community Health Council and Ethical Cttee (Hastings Health Dist), 1982–. *Recreations:* travel, music. *Address:* Fairmount, 41 Hollington Park Road, St Leonards on Sea, E Sussex. *T:* Hastings 714177. *Clubs:* Civil Service; Rotary of St Leonard's-on-Sea.

ROBERTS, Brian Richard; Editor, The Sunday Telegraph, 1966–76 (Managing Editor, 1961–66); *b* 16 Sept. 1906; *e s* of late Robert Lewis Roberts, CBE; *m* 1935, Elisabeth Franziska Dora, *er d* of late Dr Leo Zuntz, Berlin; one adopted *s. Educ:* Merchant Taylors' Sch.; St John's Coll., Oxford (MA); Hon. Fellow 1975. Editorial staff, Oxford Mail, 1930–33; Daily Mail, 1933–38 (Night Editor, 1936–38); Joined The Daily Telegraph, 1939 (Night Editor, 1944–57, Chief Asst Editor 1957–60). Pres., Inst. of Journalists, 1954–55; Pres., Guild of Agricultural Journalists, 1976; Mem. Governing Body, Northern Polytechnic, London, 1946–71 (Chm. 1956–71); Polytechnic of North London: Chm., Formation Cttee, 1970–71; Mem. Ct of Governors, 1971–79, Chm., 1971–74; Hon. Fellow 1981; Chm. of Council, Assoc. of Colls for Further and Higher Educn (formerly Assoc. of Technical Instns), 1964–65, Hon. Treasurer, 1967–77. Gold Medal, Inst. of Journalists, 1971; special award, National Press Awards, 1974; Silver Jubilee Medal, 1977. *Recreation:* agriculture. *Address:* Old Foxhunt Manor, Waldron, near Heathfield, Sussex TN21 0RU. *T:* Horam Road 2618.

See also C. H. Roberts, Rev. R. L. Roberts.

ROBERTS, Brian Stanley; HM Diplomatic Service; Counsellor, Stockholm, since 1983; *b* 1 Feb. 1936; *s* of Stanley Victor Roberts and Flora May (*née* McInnes); *m* 1st, 1961, Phyllis Hazel Barber (marr. diss. 1976); two *s*; 2nd, 1985, Jane Catharine Chisholm. Educ: Liverpool Collegiate Sch., Christ's Coll., Cambridge (MA); Courtauld Institute, London (MA). Served Royal Navy, 1955–57. Staff, Edinburgh Univ., 1960–62; Lecturer in Art History, Goldsmiths' Coll., London, 1962–69; entered FCO, 1970: First Secretary, Capetown/Pretoria, 1972; FCO, 1974; attached to Hong Kong Govt, 1977; FCO, 1980. *Recreations:* walking, looking at pictures. *Address:* c/o Foreign and Commonwealth Office, SW1; c/o British Embassy, Stockholm, Sweden. *Clubs:* United Oxford & Cambridge University, Lansdowne.

ROBERTS, Sir Bryan Clieve, KCMG 1973 (CMG 1964); QC; JP; a Metropolitan Stipendiary Magistrate, since 1982; Chairman, Commonwealth Magistrates' Association, since 1979; *b* 22 March 1923; *s* of late Herbert Roberts, MA, and Doris Evelyn Clieve; *m* 1st, 1958, Pamela Dorothy Campbell (marr. diss. 1975); 2nd, 1976, Brigitte Patricia Reilly-Morrison (marr. diss. 1981); 3rd, 1985, Mrs Barbara Forter. *Educ:* Whitgift School; Magdalen Coll., Oxford (BA Hons). Served War of 1939–45: commissioned in RA and RHA, 1941–46; active service in Normandy, Belgium, Holland and Germany, 1944–45. Called to Bar, Gray's Inn, 1950; in chambers in Temple, 1950–51; Treasury Solicitor's Dept, 1951–53. Crown Counsel, N Rhodesia, 1953–60; Dir of Public Prosecutions, N Rhodesia, 1960–61; QC (Fedn of Rhodesia and Nyasaland) 1961; Nyasaland: Solicitor-General, 1961–64; Minister of Justice, 1962–63; Mem., Legislative Council, 1961–63; Attorney-Gen. of Malawi, 1964–72; Perm. Sec. to Office of the President, Sec. to the Cabinet, and Head of Malawi Civil Service, 1965–72; Chairman: Malawi Army Council; Nat. Security and Intell. Council; Nat. Develt and Planning Council, 1966–72. Lord Chancellor's Office, 1973–82 (Under Sec., 1977–82). JP Inner London, 1975 (Dep. Chm., South Westminster Bench, 1977–82). Officer of the Order of Menelik II of Ethiopia, 1965; Comdr, Nat. Order of Republic of Malagasy, 1969. *Address:* 3 Caroline Place, W2; Stonebarrow Lodge, Charmouth, Dorset. *Club:* Royal Commonwealth Society.

ROBERTS, Dr Brynley Francis, FSA; Librarian, National Library of Wales, since 1985; *b* 3 Feb. 1931; *s* of Robert F. Roberts and Laura Jane Roberts (*née* Williams); *m* 1957, Rhiannon Campbell; twin *s*. *Educ:* Grammar School, Aberdare; University College of Wales, Aberystwyth (BA Hons Welsh, MA, PhD). Fellow, Univ. of Wales, 1956–57; Lectr, Sen. Lectr, Reader, Dept of Welsh, University Coll. of Wales, Aberystwyth, 1957–78; Prof. of Welsh Language and Literature, University Coll. Swansea, 1978–85. Sir John Rhys Fellow, Jesus Coll., Oxford, 1973–74. Chairman: United Theological Coll., Aberystwyth, 1977–; Gwasg Pantycelyn, Caernarfon, 1977–. *Publications:* Gwasanaeth Meir, 1961; Brut y Brenhinedd, 1971, 2nd edn 1984; Cyfranc Lludd a Llefelys, 1975; Brut Tysilio, 1980; Edward Lhuyd: the making of a scientist, 1980; articles in learned jls. *Recreations:* walking, music. *Address:* Hengwrt, Llanbadarn Road, Aberystwyth. *T:* Aberystwyth 3577.

ROBERTS, Rear-Adm. Cedric Kenelm, CB 1970; DSO 1952; *b* 19 April 1918; *s* of F. A. Roberts; *m* 1940, Audrey, *d* of T. M. Elias; four *s*. *Educ:* King Edward's Sch., Birmingham. Joined RN as Naval Airman 2nd Cl., 1940; commnd Temp. Sub-Lt (A), RNVR, 1940; sunk in HMS Manchester, 1942, Malta Convoy; interned in Sahara; released, Nov. 1942; Personal Pilot to Vice-Adm. Sir Arthur Lyster, 1943; HMS Trumpeter, Russian Convoys, 1944; perm. commn as Lt RN, HMS Vindex, Pacific, 1945; CO 813 Sqdn, 1948; Naval Staff Coll., 1949; CO 767 Sqdn, 1950–51; CO 825 Sqdn, 1951–52: served Korean War; shot down, rescued by US Forces; lent to RAN as Dep. Dir, Air Warfare, 1953–55; CO, RNAS Eglinton, 1958–59; Chief Staff Officer: FONFT, 1959–61; FOAC, 1961–62; Capt., HMS Osprey, 1962–64; Capt., RNAS Culdrose, 1964–65; Chief Staff Officer (Ops), Far East Fleet, 1966–67; Flag Officer, Naval Flying Training, 1968–71; retired 1971; farmed in Somerset, 1971–79; emigrated to Australia, 1979. Comdr 1952; Capt. 1958; Rear-Adm. 1968. *Recreations:* sitting in the sun, drinking plonk, and watching the sheilas go by. *Address:* 11 Collins Street, Merimbula, NSW 2548, Australia. *T:* Merimbula 51754.

ROBERTS, Charles Stuart, CMG 1975; HM Diplomatic Service, retired; High Commissioner in Barbados, 1973–78; *b* 24 May 1918; *s* of late Charles William Roberts and of Dorothy Roberts; *m* 1946, Margaret Ethel Jones; one *s* two *d*. *Educ:* Merchant Taylors' School. Entered Colonial Office, 1936. Naval Service (Lieut RNVR), 1940–46. Economic and Financial Adviser, Leeward Is, 1955–57; transferred to HM Diplomatic Service (Counsellor), 1966; British Govt Representative, W Indies Associated States, 1967–70; Head of Caribbean Dept, FCO, 1970–73. *Recreations:* chess, crosswords. *Address:* 10 Montacute Road, Tunbridge Wells, Kent TN2 5QR. *T:* Tunbridge Wells 25553. *Clubs:* MCC; Royal Commonwealth Society (West Indian).

ROBERTS, Christopher William, CB 1986; Deputy Secretary, Department of Trade and Industry, and Chief Executive, British Overseas Trade Board, since 1983; *b* 4 Nov. 1937; *s* of Frank Roberts and Evelyn Dorothy Roberts. *Educ:* Rugby Sch.; Magdalen Coll., Oxford (MA). Lectr in Classics, Pembroke Coll., Oxford, 1959–60; Asst Principal, BoT, 1960; Second Sec. (Commercial), British High Commn, New Delhi, 1962–64; Asst Private Sec. to Pres. of BoT, 1964–65; Principal, 1965; Cabinet Office, 1966–68; Private Sec. to Prime Minister, 1970–73; Asst Sec., 1972; Dept of Trade, 1973–77; Under Secretary: Dept of Prices and Consumer Protection, 1977–79; Dept of Trade, 1979–82. *Recreations:* travel, cricket, opera. *Address:* 11 Sprimont Place, SW3 3HT. *T:* 01–581 1860. *Clubs:* United Oxford & Cambridge University, MCC.

ROBERTS, Colin Henderson, CBE 1973; Secretary to Delegates of Oxford University Press, 1954–74; Fellow of St John's College, Oxford, 1934–76, Hon. Fellow, 1976; *b* 8 June 1909; *s* of late Robert Lewis Roberts, CBE; *m* 1947, Alison Muriel, *d* of Reginald Haynes and Phyllis Irene Barrow; one *d*. *Educ:* Merchant Taylors' School; St John's College, Oxford (MA). 1st Cl., Hon. Class. Mods, 1929; 1st Cl., Lit. Hum. 1931; Sen. Schol., St John's Coll., 1931–34; Craven Univ. Fellow, 1932–34. Studied Berlin Univ., 1932; Univ. of Michigan, Near East Research (Egypt), 1932–34; Dept of Foreign Office, 1939–45. Lecturer in Classics, St John's College, Oxford, 1939–53; tutor, 1946–53; University Lecturer in Papyrology, 1937–48; Reader, 1948–53. Delegate of Oxford Univ. Press, 1946–53; FBA 1947–80; Visiting Mem. of Inst. for Advanced Study, Princeton, NJ, 1951–52; Sandars Reader in Bibliography, University of Cambridge, 1960–61. Schweich Lectr, British Acad., 1977. Hon. DLitt Oxon, 1975. *Publications:* An Unpublished Fragment of the Fourth Gospel, 1935; Catalogue of the Greek Papyri in the Rylands Library, Manchester, Vol. III, 1938, Vol. IV (with E. G. Turner), 1952; part editor of the Oxyrhynchus Papyri, Parts XVIII-XX, 1941–52 and XXII, 1954; The Antinoopolis Papyri, 1950; The Merton Papyri (with H. I. Bell), 1948; The Codex, 1955; The Greek Bookhand, 1955; Manuscript, Society and Belief in Early Christian Egypt, 1979; (with T. C. Skeat) The Birth of the Codex, 1983. *Recreation:* gardening. *Address:* Hursey House, Broadwindsor, near Beaminster, Dorset. *T:* Broadwindsor 68281.

See also B. R. Roberts, Rev. R. L. Roberts.

ROBERTS, Cyril Alfred, CBE 1947 (MBE 1944); DL; *b* 4 June 1908; *s* of late A. W. Roberts; *m* 1932, Christine Annabel Kitson, *d* of late Hon. E. C. Kitson, Leeds; three *s* one *d*. *Educ:* Eton; Trinity Coll., Oxford. Called to the Bar, 1932, and practised until 1939. Served War of 1939–45, HM Forces, 1939–46; France, 1940; Western Desert, 1941–42; Instructor, Staff Coll., Haifa, 1943; War Office, Army Council Secretariat, 1943–45; Brigadier AG Co-ordination, 1945–46. Asst Sec., NCB, 1946–47, Under-Sec. 1947–51, Sec., 1951–59; Member of the Board, 1960–67. Dir, later Dep. Chm., Woodall-Duckham Gp Ltd, 1968–73. Chm., Inst. of Cardiology, 1967–72; Mem. Bd of Governors, Brompton Hosp., Chm. House Cttee, Nat. Heart Hosp., 1973–76. Adviser to Minister of Defence on Resettlement from the Forces, 1968–70; Mem., Armed Forces Pay Review Bd, 1971–79. Mem. Bd of Dirs, Coronary Artery Disease Res. Assoc. (Chm., 1979–81); Chm., League of Friends, Nat. Heart Hosp., 1984–86. Chm., Chichester District Council, 1981–83. DL West Sussex, 1982. *Address:* Bury Gate House, Pulborough, West Sussex. *T:* Bury 440.

ROBERTS, Sir David (Arthur), KBE 1983; CMG 1975; CVO 1979; HM Diplomatic Service, retired; Chairman, Herefordshire District Health Authority; *b* 8 Aug. 1924; *s* of late Rev. T. A. and Mrs Roberts; *m* 1st, 1951, Nicole Marie Fay (*d* 1965); two *d*; 2nd, 1968, Hazel Faith Arnot. *Educ:* Hereford Cathedral Sch.; Jesus Coll., Oxford (Scholar; BA). Served Royal Armoured Corps, 1943–46. HM Foreign Service, Dec. 1947. Served: Baghdad, 1948–49; Tokyo, 1949–51; FO, 1951–53; Alexandria, 1953–55; Khartoum, 1955–58; FO, 1958–60; Dakar, 1960–61 (Chargé d'Affairs at Bamako and at Lomé during same period); FO, 1962–63; Damascus, 1963–66; Political Agent in the Trucial States, Dubai, 1966–68; Head of Accommodation Dept, FCO, 1968–71; High Comr in Barbados, 1971–73; Ambassador to Syria, 1973–76; High Comr in Sierra Leone, 1976–77; Ambassador to: the United Arab Emirates, 1977–81; Lebanon, 1981–83. Dir-Gen., Middle East Assoc., 1983–85; Chm., British Lebanese Assoc., 1984–. Hon. Fellow, Faculty of Middle East and Islamic Studies, Durham Univ., 1985. *Publications:* The Ba'Ath and the Creation of Modern Syria, 1986; lectures and contribs to symposia, etc. *Club:* Reform.

ROBERTS, David Ewart; His Honour Judge David Roberts; a Circuit Judge, since 1982; *b* 18 Feb. 1921; *s* of John Hobson Roberts and Dorothy Roberts. *Educ:* Abingdon Sch.; St John's Coll., Cambridge. MA, LLB. Served War, 1941–46; commnd RA (Field); service in Middle East, North Africa, Italy, Yugoslavia and Germany. Called to Bar, Middle Temple, 1948. Asst Recorder, Coventry QS, 1966–71; a Recorder of the Crown Court, 1978–82. *Recreations:* golf, skiing, photography. *Address:* 4 Greville Drive, Birmingham B15 2UU. *T:* 021–440 3231.

ROBERTS, David Francis; Minister (Agriculture), UK Representation to the European Communities, Brussels, since 1985; *b* 28 Aug. 1941; *s* of Arthur Roberts and Mary Roberts; *m* 1974, Astrid Suhr Henriksen; two *s* one *d*. *Educ:* Priory Grammar School, Shrewsbury; Worcester College, Oxford (MA). Joined MAFF, 1964; seconded to FCO as First Sec. (Agric.), Copenhagen, 1971–74; Principal Private Sec. to Minister of Agriculture, 1975–76; seconded to HM Treasury as Head of Agric. Div., 1979–80; Under Sec., seconded to FCO, 1985. *Recreations:* sailing, squash. *Address:* c/o Foreign and Commonwealth Office, SW1.

ROBERTS, (David) Gwilym (Morris), FEng; Senior Partner and Chairman, John Taylor & Sons, since 1981; *b* 24 July 1925; *er s* of late Edward and Edith Roberts of Crosby; *m* 1st, 1960, Rosemary Elizabeth Emily (*d* 1973), *d* of late J. E. Giles of Tavistock; one *s* one *d*; 2nd, 1978, Wendy Ann, *d* of late Dr J. K. Moore of Beckenham and Alfriston. *Educ:* Merchant Taylors' School, Crosby; Sidney Sussex College, Cambridge (Minor Scholar, MA). FICE, FIMechE. Engineering Officer, RNVR, 1945–47; Lieut Comdr RNR, retired 1961. Asst Engineer, 1947–55, then Partner, 1956–, John Taylor & Sons; principally development of water and wastewater projects, UK towns and regions, and Abu Dhabi, Bahrain, Egypt, Iraq, Kuwait, Mauritius, Qatar, Saudi Arabia and Thailand. President: IPHE, 1968–69 (IPHE Silver Medal 1974); ICE, 1986–87 (Vice-Pres., 1983–86; Overseas Premium, 1978; Halcrow Premium, 1985; George Stephenson Medal, 1986); Member: UK Cttee, IAWPRC, 1967–83; Exec. Cttee, Taylor Binnie & Partners, 1976–; Bd of Control, AMBRIC (American British Consultants), 1978–; (Construction Industry) Group of Eight, 1983–85; Council, Brighton Polytechnic, 1983–. Freeman, City of London, 1977; Liveryman, Engineers' Co., 1985; Mem., Constructors' Co. (formerly Co. of Builders), 1976–. *Publications:* (co-author) Civil Engineering Procedure, 3rd edn, 1979; papers to Royal Soc., Arab League, ICE, IPHE. *Recreations:* tennis, walking, local history, engineering archaeology in Middle East. *Address:* (office) Artillery House, Artillery Row, SW1P 1RY. *T:* 01–222 7050; North America Farm, Hundred Acre Lane, Westmeston, Hassocks, Sussex BN6 8SH. *T:* Plumpton 890324. *Clubs:* St Stephen's Constitutional, United Oxford & Cambridge University, MCC.

ROBERTS, Rt. Rev. (David) John; Abbot of Downside, since 1974; *b* 31 March 1919; *s* of Albert Edward and Elizabeth Minnith Roberts. *Educ:* Downside School; Trinity Coll., Cambridge (MA). Royal Sussex Regt, Oct. 1939–Nov. 1945 (POW Germany, May 1940–April 1945). Entered monastery, Feb. 1946; ordained, 1951. House Master, Downside School, 1953–62; Novice Master, 1962–66; Prior 1966–74. *Address:* Downside Abbey, Stratton-on-the-Fosse, Bath BA3 4RH.

ROBERTS, Maj.-Gen. David Michael, MD; FRCP, FRCPE; QHP; Director of Army Medicine and Consulting Physician to the Army, since 1984; *b* 9 Sept. 1931; *s* of James Henry and Agnes Louise Roberts; *m* 1964, Angela Louise Squire; one *s* two *d*. *Educ:* Emanuel Sch., London; Royal Free Hospital School of Medicine (MB, BS). Qualified in medicine, 1954; commissioned RAMC, 1955; service in field units, BAOR, 1955–59; Hon. Registrar in Medicine, Radcliffe Infirmary, Oxford, 1960; various medical specialty appts in military hosps in UK, BAOR and Hong Kong, 1960–75; graded consultant physician, 1968; Joint Professor of Military Medicine, RAMC and RCP, London, 1975–81; Command Cons. Physician, BAOR, 1981–84. Consulting Physician, Royal Hosp., Chelsea, 1984–. Lectr in Tropical Medicine, Mddx Hosp. Medical Sch., 1976–81; Examiner in Tropical Medicine for RCP, 1981–. Mem., British Soc. of Gastroenterology, 1973–. QHP 1984. *Publications:* many articles on gastroenterological subjects. *Recreations:* mixing concrete, building things. *Address:* Elmgrove, Normandy, Surrey GU3 2AS. *T:* Worplesdon 234943.

ROBERTS, Dr Denis; *see* Roberts, Dr E. F. D.

ROBERTS, Denis Edwin, CBE 1974 (MBE 1945); Managing Director, Posts, 1970–80; *b* 6 Jan. 1917; *s* of late Edwin and Alice G. Roberts; *m* 1940, Edith (*née* Whitehead); two *s*. *Educ:* Holgate Grammar Sch., Barnsley. Served War of 1939–45, Royal Signals, France, N Africa, Italy and Austria. Entered Post Office, Barnsley, 1933; various appts, 1933–71; Dir Postal Ops, 1971–75; Sen. Dir, Postal Services, 1975–77. Chm., British Philatelic Trust, 1981–85. *Address:* 302 Gilbert House, Barbican, EC2Y 8BD. *T:* 01–638 0881. *Clubs:* City of London, City Livery.

ROBERTS, Hon. Sir Denys (Tudor Emil), KBE 1975 (CBE 1970; OBE 1960); SPMB; **Hon. Mr Justice Roberts;** Chief Justice of Hong Kong and Negara Brunei Darussalam, since 1979; *b* 19 Jan. 1923; *s* of William David and Dorothy Elizabeth Roberts; *m* 1st, 1949, Brenda Marsh (marr. diss. 1973); one *s* one *d*; 2nd, 1985, Anna Fiona Dollar Alexander; one *s*. *Educ:* Aldenham; Wadham Coll., Oxford, 1942 and 1946–49 (MA 1948, BCL 1949; Hon. Fellow, 1984); served with Royal Artillery, 1943–46, France, Belgium, Holland, Germany, India (Captain). English Bar, 1950–53; Crown Counsel, Nyasaland, 1953–59; QC Gibraltar 1960; QC Hong Kong 1964; Attorney-General, Gibraltar, 1960–62; Solicitor-General, Hong Kong, 1962–66; Attorney-General, Hong Kong, 1966–73; Chief Secretary, Hong Kong, 1973–78. Hon. Bencher, Lincoln's Inn, 1978. SPMB (Negara Brunei Darussalam), 1984. *Publications:* Smuggler's Circuit, 1954; Beds and Roses, 1956; The Elwood Wager, 1958; The Bones of the Wajingas, 1960; How to Dispense with Lawyers, 1964. *Recreations:* cricket, walking, writing. *Address:* The Supreme Court, Hong Kong; High Point, 35 Beaucroft Lane, Colehill, Wimborne, Dorset. *Clubs:* MCC; Hong Kong (Hong Kong).

ROBERTS, Derek Harry, CBE 1983; FRS 1980, FEng, FInstP; Joint Deputy Managing Director (Technical), General Electric Company plc, since 1985 (Technical Director, 1983–85); *b* 28 March 1932; *s* of Harry and Alice Roberts; *m* 1958, Winifred (*née* Short); one *s* one *d*. *Educ:* Manchester Central High Sch.; Manchester Univ. (BSc). MIEE. Joined Plessey Co.'s Caswell Res. Lab., 1953; Gen. Man., Plessey Semiconductors, 1967; Dir, Allen Clark Res. Centre, 1969; Man. Dir, Plessey Microelectronics Div., 1973. Hon. DSc: Bath, 1982; Loughborough, 1984; DUniv Open, 1984. *Publications:* about 20 pubns in scientific and technical jls. *Recreations:* reading, gardening. *Address:* The Old Rectory, Maids Moreton, Buckingham. *T:* Buckingham 813470.

ROBERTS, Prof. (Edward) Adam; Montague Burton Professor of International Relations, Oxford, since 1986; *b* 29 Aug. 1940; *s* of Michael Roberts and Janet Roberts (*see* Janet Adam Smith); *m* 1966, Frances P. Dunn; one *s* one *d*. *Educ:* Westminster School; Magdalen College, Oxford (BA 1962, MA 1981). Asst Editor, Peace News Ltd, 1962–65; Noel Buxton Student in Internat. Relations, LSE, 1965–68; Lectr in Internat. Relations, LSE, 1968–81; Alastair Buchan Reader in Internat. Relations, Oxford, and Professorial Fellow, St Antony's Coll., Oxford, 1981–86. Mem., Council, RIIA, 1985–. *Publications:* (ed) The Strategy of Civilian Defence, 1967; (jtly) Czechoslovakia 1968, 1969; Nations in Arms, 1976, 2nd edn, 1986; (ed jtly) Documents on the Laws of War, 1982. *Recreations:*

rock climbing, mountaineering, running. *Address:* Balliol College, Oxford OX1 3BJ. *T:* Oxford 249601. *Club:* Alpine.

ROBERTS, Rev. Canon Edward Eric, JP; Canon Emeritus of Southwell, since 1980; Secretary, Nottingham Council of Churches, since 1980; *b* 29 April 1911; *o s* of late Edward Thomas Roberts and Mrs Charlotte Roberts, Liverpool; *m* 1938, Sybil Mary (*née* Curren); two *d. Educ:* Univ. of Liverpool; St Augustine's Coll., Canterbury. Youth Officer: City of Oxford LEA, 1938–43; Wallasey CB, LEA, 1943–44; Training Officer, Church of England Youth Council, 1944–52; Southwell Diocesan Director: of Further Educn, 1952–61; of Educn, 1961–68. Canon, 1964; Canon Residentiary, Vice-Provost of Southwell Cathedral and Personal Chaplain to Bishop of Southwell, 1969–79; Ecumenical Officer, Diocese of Southwell, 1973–79. JP, City of Nottingham, 1958–. *Recreation:* photography. *Address:* 24 Manor Close, Southwell, Nottinghamshire NG25 0AP. *T:* Southwell 813246.

ROBERTS, Sir (Edward Fergus) Sidney, Kt 1978; CBE 1972; former Federal President, Australian Country Party; grazier and manager of companies; *b* 19 April 1901; *s* of late E. J. Roberts. *Educ:* Scots Coll., Sydney. Gen. Manager, Ungra, Brisbane, 1957–70; owner, Boolaroo Downs, Clermont, Qld, 1928–63. United Graziers' Assoc., Qld: Mem. Council, 1948–76; Vice-Pres., 1950–52. Aust. Road Fedn: Mem., 1954–63; Nat. Pres., 1962–63. Mem. Bd, Queensland Country Life Newspaper, 1969–77; Pres., Aust. Country Party, Qld, 1967; Chm., Federal Council, ACP, 1969–74. Knighthood awarded for distinguished service to Primary Industry, Australia. *Address:* 53 Eldernell Avenue, Hamilton, Queensland 4007, Australia. *Club:* Queensland (Brisbane).

ROBERTS, Dr (Edward Frederick) Denis, FRSE 1980; Librarian, National Library of Scotland, since 1970; *b* 16 June 1927; *s* of Herbert Roberts and Jane Spottiswoode Roberts (*née* Wilkinson); *m* 1954, Irene Mary Beatrice (*née* Richardson); one *s* one *d. Educ:* Royal Belfast Academical Institution; Queen's University of Belfast. BA (1st cl. Hons Modern History) 1951; PhD 1955. Research Assistant, Dept of History, Queen's Univ. of Belfast, 1951–55; National Library of Scotland: Asst Keeper, Dept of Manuscripts, 1955–66; Secretary of the Library, 1966–67; Librarian, Trinity College Dublin, 1967–70; Hon. Prof., Univ. of Edinburgh, 1975. Hon. FLA 1983. *Publication:* (with W. G. H. Quigley) Registrum Iohannis Mey: The Register of John Mey, Archbishop of Armagh, 1443–1456, 1972. *Address:* 6 Oswald Court, Edinburgh EH9 2HY. *T:* 031–667 9473. *Club:* New (Edinburgh).

ROBERTS, Rt. Rev. Edward James Keymer; *b* 18 April 1908; *s* of Rev. Arthur Henry Roberts; *m* 1st, 1941, Dorothy Frances (*d* 1982), *d* of Canon Edwin David Bowser, Deal; three *s* one *d*; 2nd, 1984, Diana, *widow* of Dr Christopher Grey. *Educ:* Marlborough; Corpus Christi Coll., Cambridge; Cuddesdon Theological Coll. BA 2nd class Theological Tripos, 1930; MA 1935; DD (*hc*) Cambridge, 1965. FRSCM 1977. Deacon, 1931; priest, 1932; Curate of All Saints, Margaret Street, 1931–35; Vice-Principal Cuddesdon Coll., 1935–39; Examining Chaplain to Bishop of Portsmouth and Commissary, Johannesburg, 1936–39; Vicar of St Matthew, Southsea, 1940–45; Curate-in-charge of St Bartholomew, Southsea, 1941–45; Examining Chaplain to Bishop of Portsmouth, 1942–56; Proctor in Convocation, Portsmouth, 1944–49; Commissary, Northern Rhodesia, 1946–51; Hon. Canon of Portsmouth, 1947–49; Archdeacon of Isle of Wight, Vicar of Brading, Rector of Yaverland, 1949–52; Archdeacon of Portsmouth, 1952–56; Suffragan Bishop of Malmesbury, 1956–62; Examining Chaplain to Bishop of Bristol, 1959–62; Suffragan Bishop of Kensington, 1962–64; Bishop of Ely, 1964–77. Episcopal Commissary, Portsmouth, 1984–85. Hon. Fellow, Corpus Christi Coll., Cambridge, 1964–. Select Preacher, University of Cambridge, 1966, 1978. *Recreation:* shoe cleaning. *Address:* The House on the Marsh, Quay Lane, Brading, IoW. *T:* Isle of Wight 407434.

See also Hon. P. J. S. Roberts.

ROBERTS, Eirlys Rhiwen Cadwaladr, CBE 1977 (OBE 1971); Deputy Director, Consumers' Association (Which?), 1973–77 (Head of Research and Editorial Division, 1958–73); *b* 3 Jan. 1911; *d* of Dr Ellis James Roberts and Jane Tennant Macaulay; *m* 1941, John Cullen (marr. diss.); no *c. Educ:* Clapham High School; Girton College, Cambridge. BA (Hons) Classics. Sub-editor in Amalgamated Press; Military, then Political Intelligence, 1943–44 and 1944–45; Public Relations in UNRRA, Albanian Mission, 1945–47; Information Division of the Treasury, 1947–57. Chief Exec., Bureau of European Consumer Orgns, 1973–78. Mem., Royal Commn on the Press, 1974–77. Chm., European Res. into Consumer Affairs, 1978–; Mem., Economic and Social Cttee of EEC, 1973–82 (Chm., Environment and Consumer Protection section, 1978–82). *Publication:* Consumers, 1966. *Recreations:* walking, ice-skating, reading detective novels. *Address:* 8 Lloyd Square, WC1. *T:* 01–837 2492.

ROBERTS, Emrys, CBE 1976 (MBE 1946); *b* 22 Sept. 1910; *s* of late Owen Owens Roberts and of Mary Grace Williams, both of Caernarfon; *m* 1948, Anna Elisabeth Tudor; one *d* (one *s* decd). *Educ:* Caernarfon; Aberystwyth; Gonville and Caius Coll., Cambridge; Geneva. MA (Cantab); LLB (Wales); 1st Class, Parts I and II, Law Tripos, Cambridge, 1933; 1st Class Hons, University of Wales, 1931, S. T. Evans Prize; Solicitor, 1936, 1st Class Hons, Clements Inn Prize. Squadron Leader RAF, 1941–45. Barrister, Gray's Inn, 1944. MP (L) for Merioneth, 1945–51; Member of Parliamentary Delegations to Yugoslavia, Germany, Rumania, and Sweden; Representative at Council of Europe, 1950 and 1951. Director: Tootal Broadhurst Lee Co. Ltd, English Sewing Ltd, English Calico Ltd and Tootal Ltd, 1958–75; Cambrian & General Securities Ltd, 1974–81. Chairman: Mid-Wales Develt Corp., 1968–77; Develt Bd for Rural Wales, 1977–81; Mem., Welsh Develt Agency, 1977–81; Dir, Develt Corp. of Wales, 1978–81. Mem. Court and Council, Univ. Coll. of Wales, Aberystwyth, 1972–85; Chm. of Council, Nat. Eisteddfod of Wales, 1964–67, and Hon. Counsel, 1957–74; Vice-Pres. Hon. Soc. of Cymmrodorion. *Publication:* (jointly) The Law of Restrictive Trade Practices and Monopolies. *Address:* 24 Glyn Garth Court, Menai Bridge, Anglesey, Gwynedd LL59 5PB. *T:* Menai Bridge 713665; 8 Kent House, 62–66 Holland Park Avenue, W11 3RA.

ROBERTS, Rt. Rev. Eric Matthias; *b* 18 Feb. 1914; *s* of Richard and Jane Roberts; *m* 1944, Nancy Jane Roberts (*née* Davies); two *s. Educ:* Friars Sch., Bangor; University Coll., Bangor; St Edmund Hall, Oxon (MA); St Michael's Coll., Llandaff. Curate, Penmaenmawr, 1938–40; Sub-Warden, St Michael's Coll., Llandaff, 1940–47; Vicar: Port Talbot, 1947–56; Roath, 1956–65; Archdeacon of Margam, 1965–71; Bishop of St David's, 1971–81. ChStJ 1973. *Address:* 2 Tudor Close, Westbourne Road, Penarth, South Glamorgan.

ROBERTS, Ernest Alfred Cecil; MP (Lab) Hackney North and Stoke Newington, since 1979; *b* 20 April 1912; *s* of Alfred and Florence Roberts; *m* 1953, Joyce Longley; one *s* two *d. Educ:* St Chad's Boys' Elementary Sch., Shrewsbury. Engineer, 1925–57; Assistant General Secretary, AUEW, 1957–77. Chairman: PLP Health and Social Security Cttee; Lab. Party Parly Assoc. Tom Mann Gold Medal for services to trade unionism, 1943. *Publication:* Workers' Control, 1973. *Recreations:* work and politics, reading. *Address:* House of Commons, Westminster, SW1A 0AA.

ROBERTS, Sir Frank (Kenyon), GCMG 1963 (KCMG 1953; CMG 1946); GCVO 1965; Director: Hoechst (UK); Mercedes-Benz (UK); Amalgamated Metal Corporation PLC; German Securities Investment Trust; Vice-President: European Atlantic Group, since 1983 (Chairman, 1970–73; President, 1973–83); Atlantic Treaty Association, since 1973 (President, 1969–73); British Atlantic Committee, since 1982 (President, 1968–81); *b* Buenos Aires, 27 Oct. 1907; *s* of Henry George Roberts, Preston, and Gertrude Kenyon, Blackburn; *m* 1937, Celeste Leila Beatrix, *d* of late Sir Said Shoucair Pasha, Cairo, Financial Adviser to Sudan Government; no *c. Educ:* Bedales; Rugby; Trinity College, Cambridge (Scholar). Entered Foreign Office, 1930; served HM Embassy, Paris, 1932–35 and at HM Embassy, Cairo, 1935–37; Foreign Office, 1937–45; Chargé d'Affaires to Czechoslovak Govt, 1943; British Minister in Moscow, 1945–47; Principal Private Secretary to Secretary of State for Foreign Affairs, 1947–49; Deputy High Commr (UK) in India, 1949–51; Deputy-Under Secretary of State, Foreign Office, 1951–54; HM Ambassador to Yugoslavia, 1954–57; United Kingdom Permanent Representative on the North Atlantic Council, 1957–60; Ambassador: to the USSR, 1960–62; to the Federal Republic of Germany, 1963–68. Vice-Pres., German Chamber of Commerce in UK, 1974– (Pres., 1971–74); Dep. Chm., British Nat. Cttee, Internat. Chamber of Commerce, 1978–81. Mem., FCO Review Cttee on Overseas Representation, 1968–69. Pres., Anglo-German Assoc.; Vice-Pres., GB-USSR Assoc. Grand Cross, German Order of Merit, 1965. *Address:* 25 Kensington Court Gardens, W8 5QF. *Clubs:* Brooks's, Royal Automobile.

ROBERTS, Prof. Gareth Gwyn, FRS 1984; Chief Scientist, since 1985, Director of Research, since 1986, Thorn EMI; Professor of Applied Physics, Department of Engineering Science and Fellow, Brasenose College, Oxford University, since 1985; *b* 16 May 1940; *s* of Edwin and Meri Roberts; *m* 1962, Charlotte Standen; two *s* one *d. Educ:* UCNW, Bangor (BSc, PhD, DSc). Lectr in Physics, Univ. of Wales, 1963–66; Res. Physicist, Xerox Corp., USA, 1966–68; Sen. Lectr, Reader, and Professor of Physics, NUU, 1968–76; Prof. of Applied Physics and Head, Dept of Applied Physics and Electronics, Univ. of Durham, 1976–85. *Publications:* Insulating Films on Semiconductors, 1979; Langmuir-Blodgett Films, 1982; many publications and patents on physics of semiconductor devices and molecular electronics. *Recreations:* soccer, duplicate bridge, classical music. *Address:* Galleons Lap, Templewood Lane, Farnham Common, Bucks. *T:* Farnham Common 4430.

ROBERTS, Prof. Geoffrey Frank Ingleson, CBE 1978; FEng 1978; Chairman, British Pipe Coaters Ltd, since 1978; British Gas Professor of Gas Engineering, University of Salford, since 1983; *b* 9 May 1926; *s* of late Arthur and Laura Roberts; *m* 1949, Veronica, *d* of late Captain J. Busby, Hartlepool; two *d. Educ:* Cathedral Sch., and High Sch. for Boys, Hereford; Leeds Univ. (BSc hons). FIChemE; FInstE. Pupil engr, Gas Light & Coke Co., and North Thames Gas Bd, 1947–50; North Thames Gas Board: Asst Engr, 1950–59; Stn Engr, Slough, 1959–61; Dept. Stn Engr, Southall Stn, 1961–66; Group Engr, Slough Group, 1966–68; Dep. Dir (Ops) Gas Council, 1968–71; Mem. for Production and Supply, Gas Council, later British Gas Corp., 1972–78; Mem. for External Affairs, British Gas Corp., 1979–81, retired. President: IGasE, 1980–81 (Hon. FIGasE); Inst. of Energy, 1983–84. Liveryman: Basketmakers' Co., 1981; Engineers' Co., 1984. *Recreations:* gardening, reading. *Address:* Ranmoor, St Nicholas Road, Middleton, Ilkley, West Yorks LS29 0AN. *T:* Ilkley 608915. *Club:* Royal Automobile.

ROBERTS, Air Cdre Sir Geoffrey Newland, Kt 1973; CBE 1946; AFC 1942; FRAeS; Company Director, retired; *b* Inglewood, Taranaki, New Zealand, 8 Dec. 1906; *s* of Charles Oxford Roberts, England, and Hilda Marion Newland, New Zealand; *m* 1934, Phyllis Hamilton Bird; one *s* one *d. Educ:* New Plymouth Boys' High Sch., New Plymouth, Taranaki, NZ. In commerce, NZ, 1924–28; RAF, England/India, 1928–34; commerce, UK, 1935–36; commerce, NZ, 1936–39. Served War: RNZAF, NZ and Pacific (final rank Air Cdre), 1939–46. Air New Zealand, General Manager, 1946–58; Dir, 1958–65; Chm., 1965–75. Chairman: Lion Breweries Ltd Mimiwhangata Farm Park Trust Board, 1975–86; Kaipara Edible Oils Refinery Ltd, 1978–82; Director: MFL Mutual Fund Ltd, 1971–86; Saudi NZ Capital Corp., 1980–84. Patron: Soc. of Licensed Aircraft Engrs and Technologists, 1964–86; Internat. Fedn of Airworthiness, 1976–84. US Legion of Merit, 1944. *Relevant publication:* To Fly a Desk, by Noel Holmes, 1982. *Address:* Puketiro, No 2: RD, Wellsford, North Auckland, New Zealand. *T:* Wellsford 7219. *Clubs:* Northern, Auckland (Auckland, NZ); Rotary (Wellsford, NZ).

ROBERTS, Brig. Sir Geoffrey P. H.; *see* Hardy-Roberts.

ROBERTS, Maj.-Gen. (George) Philip (Bradley), CB 1945; DSO 1942; MC 1941; late RTR; *b* 5 Nov. 1906; *m* 1st, 1936, Désirée (*d* 1979), *d* of Major A. B. Godfray, Jersey; two *s* two *d*; 2nd, 1980, Annie Cornelia, *d* of Lt-Col F. E. W. Toussieng, Kt of Dannebrog, and *widow* of Brig. J. K. Greenwood, OBE. *Educ:* Marlborough; RMC, Sandhurst. 2nd Lieut Royal Tank Corps, 1926; served War of 1939–45 (MC, DSO and two Bars, CB, despatches thrice); Officier Légion d'Honneur; Croix de Guerre avec palmes. Adjt 6 RTR 1939; DAQMG 7th Armed Div., Bde Maj. 4th Armed Bde, GSO II 7th Armed Div., AQMG 30 Corps, CO 3 RTR 1939–41; Comd 22nd Armed Bde, Comd 26th Armed Bde, Comd 30th Armed Bde, 1941–43; Commander 11th Armoured Div., 1943–46; Comdr 7th Armoured Div., 1947–48; Dir, Royal Armoured Corps, War Office, 1948–49; retired pay, 1949. Hon. Col Kent and County of London Yeomanry Squadron, The Royal Yeomanry Regt, T&AVR, 1963–70. JP County of Kent, 1960–70. *Address:* Greenbank, West Street, Mayfield, E Sussex; c/o Royal Bank of Scotland, Kirkland House, Whitehall, SW1. *Club:* Army and Navy.

See also Sir R. M. H. Vickers.

ROBERTS, Sir Gilbert (Howland Rookehurst), 7th Bt *cr* 1809; *b* 31 May 1934; *s* of Sir Thomas Langdon Howland Roberts, 6th Bt, CBE, and of Evelyn Margaret, *o d* of late H. Fielding-Hall; *S* father, 1979; *m* 1958, Ines, *o d* of late A. Labunski; one *s* one *d. Educ:* Rugby; Gonville and Caius Coll., Cambridge (BA 1957). CEng, MIMechE. *Heir: s* Howland Langdon Roberts, *b* 19 Aug. 1961. *Address:* 3340 Cliff Drive, Santa Barbara, Calif 93109, USA.

ROBERTS, Gillian Frances; Academic Registrar, University of London, since 1983; *b* 3 Nov. 1944; *d* of late Frank Murray and of Mabel Murray; *m* 1969, Andrew Clive Roberts. *Educ:* Sydenham High Sch.; Southampton Univ. (BA Hist., 1966). Academic Dept, London Univ., 1967–83. *Address:* Senate House, University of London, Malet Street, WC1E 7HU. *T:* 01–636 8000.

ROBERTS, Sir Gordon (James), Kt 1984; CBE 1975; JP; DL; Chairman, Oxford Regional Health Authority, since 1978; Member, Commission for the New Towns, since 1978 (Deputy Chairman, 1978–82); *b* 30 Jan. 1921; *s* of Archie and Lily Roberts; *m* 1944, Barbara Leach; one *s* one *d. Educ:* Deanshanger Sch., Northants. Chairman: Northants AHA, 1973–78; Supervisory Bd, NHS Management Adv. Service, 1982–85; NHS Computer Policy Cttee, 1981–85; RHA Chairmen, 1982–84; Member: Oxford Reg. Hosp. Bd, 1968–74; St Crispin Hosp. Management Cttee, 1965–74; Northants Exec. Council, NHS, 1954–74; E Midlands Econ. Planning Council, 1975–79; Bd, Northampton Develt Corp., 1976–85 (Dep. Chm., 1985). Contested (Lab) S Northants, 1970. Mem., Towcester RDC, 1953–56; Mem., Northants CC, 1954–77 (Leader, 1973–77). JP

Northants, 1952; Chm., Towcester Bench, 1977–83. DL Northants, 1984. FRSA 1985. *Publication:* (with Dr O. F. Brown) Passenham—the history of a forest village, 1975. *Recreations:* music, reading, walking, local history. *Address:* 114 Ridgmont, Deanshanger, Milton Keynes, Bucks MK19 6JG. *T:* Milton Keynes 562605.

ROBERTS, Gwilym; *see* Roberts, D. G. M.

ROBERTS, Gwilym Edffrwd; *b* 7 Aug. 1928; *s* of William and Jane Ann Roberts; *m* 1954, Mair Griffiths; no *c. Educ:* Brynrefail Gram. Sch.; UCW (Bangor). Industrial Management, 1952–57; Lecturer (Polytechnic and University), 1957–66, 1970–74. MP (Lab): South Bedfordshire, 1966–70; Cannock, Feb. 1974–1983; PPS, DoI, 1976–79. Contested (Lab): Conway, 1964; Ormskirk, 1969; S Beds, 1970; Cannock and Burntwood, 1983. Industrial Consultant, Economic Forecasting, Market and Operational Research, 1957–. Institute of Statisticians: Vice-Pres., 1978–; Hon. Officer, 1983–84; Editor, Newsletter, 1967–78. *Recreations:* cricket, table tennis, journalism. *Address:* 60 Swasedale Road, Luton, Beds. *T:* Luton 573893; 8 Main Road, Brereton, Rugeley, Staffs. *T:* Rugeley 3601.

ROBERTS, (Herbert) John, CMG 1965; a Director, Rural Development Corporation of Zambia, since 1980; *b* 22 Nov. 1919; *m* 1946, Margaret Pollard; three *s* one *d. Educ:* Holy Trinity, Weymouth; Milton, Bulawayo. Served War of 1939–45; Somaliland, Ethiopia, Burma. Elected MLC, 1954; Leader of Northern Rhodesia United Federal Party, 1959–63; Founder of National Progress Party, 1963; MP Zambia, Nat. Progress Party 1964–66, Ind. 1967–69; Min. of Labour and Mines, 1959–61; Leader of Opposition (NR), 1961–64; Leader of Opposition (Zambia), 1964–65; disbanded Nat. Progress Party, 1966. *Address:* Chanyanya Ranch, PO Box 32037, Lusaka, Zambia.

ROBERTS, Hugh Eifion Pritchard, QC 1971; **His Honour Judge Eifion Roberts;** a Circuit Judge, since 1977; *b* 22 Nov. 1927; *er s* of late Rev. and Mrs E. P. Roberts, Anglesey; *m* 1958, Buddug Williams; one *s* two *d. Educ:* Beaumaris Grammar Sch.; University Coll. of Wales, Aberystwyth (LLB); Exeter Coll., Oxford (BCL). Called to Bar, Gray's Inn, 1953; practised as a Junior Counsel on Wales and Chester Circuit, Sept. 1953–April 1971. Dep. Chairman: Anglesey QS, 1966–71; Denbighshire QS, 1970–71; a Recorder of the Crown Court, 1972–77. Formerly Asst Parly Boundary Comr for Wales; Mem. for Wales of the Crawford Cttee on Broadcasting Coverage. *Recreation:* gardening. *Address:* Maes-y-Rhedyn, Gresford Road, Llay, Wrexham, Clwyd. *T:* Gresford 2292.

ROBERTS, Hugh Martin P.; *see* Plowden Roberts.

ROBERTS, Ian White; HM Diplomatic Service, retired; Hon. Research Fellow, School of Slavonic and East European Studies, University of London, 1985; *b* 29 March 1927; *s* of George Dodd Roberts and Jessie Dickson Roberts (*née* White); *m* 1956, Pamela Johnston; one *d. Educ:* Royal Masonic Sch., Bushey, Herts; Gonville and Caius Coll., Cambridge (MA 1st Cl. Hons Mod. Langs). Served Royal Air Force (Pilot Officer), 1948–50; postgrad. student, Cambridge (Scarborough Award), 1950. Joined Foreign Office, 1951–: Klagenfurt, 1952; Munich, 1954; Berlin, 1955; FCO, 1957–61; Second (later First) Secretary, Budapest, 1961–63; FCO, 1963; Bujumbura, 1965; FCO, 1965–66; Buenos Aires, 1966; FCO, 1969–74; Oslo, 1974–76; FCO, 1976–84; Counsellor, 1976. *Recreations:* music, reading, philately (Mem., Royal Philatelic Soc.). *Address:* c/o Lloyds Bank, 1 Butler Place, SW1H 0PR. *Club:* Travellers'.

ROBERTS, (Ieuan) Wyn (Pritchard); MP (C) Conwy, since 1983 (Conway, 1970–83); Parliamentary Under Secretary of State, Wales, since 1979; *b* 10 July 1930; *s* of late Rev. E. P. Roberts and Margaret Ann; *m* 1956, Enid Grace Williams; three *s. Educ:* Harrow; University Coll., Oxford. Sub-editor, Liverpool Daily Post, 1952–54; News Asst, BBC, 1954–57; TWW Ltd: News, Special Events and Welsh Language Programmes Producer, 1957–59; Production Controller, 1959–60; Exec. Producer, 1960–68; Welsh Controller, 1964–68; Programme Exec., Harlech TV, 1969. PPS to Sec. of State for Wales, 1970–74; Opposition Front-Bench Spokesman on Welsh Affairs, 1974–75, 1976–79. Vice-Pres., Assoc. of District Councils, 1975–79. Mem. of Gorsedd, Royal National Eisteddfod of Wales, 1966. Member, Court of Governors: Nat. Library of Wales; Nat. Museum of Wales; University Coll. of Wales, Aberystwyth, 1970–. *Recreation:* gardening. *Address:* Tan y Gwalia, Conway, Gwynedd. *T:* Tyn y Groes 371. *Clubs:* Savile; Cardiff and County (Cardiff).

ROBERTS, Hon. Jane; *see* Roberts, Hon. P. J. S.

ROBERTS, Dame Jean, DBE 1962; JP; DL; *m* 1922, Cameron Roberts (decd), Headmaster of Albert Senior Secondary Sch., Springburn; one *d. Educ:* Albert Sch.; Whitehill Sch. Taught at Bishopstreet School and later in a special school for handicapped children. Representative of Kingston Ward in Corp. of City of Glasgow from Nov. 1929–May 1966; DL 1964, JP 1934, Glasgow; Sen. Magistrate; held the following posts as first woman to do so: Convener of Electrical Cttee; Dep. Chm. of Corporation; Leader of the Labour Group; City Treasurer; Lord Provost of the City of Glasgow and Lord Lieut of the county of the City of Glasgow, 1960–63. Chm., Cumbernauld Develt Corp., 1965–72. Chm., Scottish National Orchestra Society, 1970–75; Member: Scottish Arts Council, 1963; Arts Council of Gt Britain, 1965–68. Since 1930: apptd by Secretary of State for Scotland to serve on many Advisory Cttees dealing with Local Govt, Social and Economic matters in Scotland. Hon. LLD Glasgow, 1977. Order of St Olav, 1962. *Recreations:* music and public service. *Address:* 35 Beechwood Drive, Glasgow G11 7ET. *T:* 041–334 1930.

ROBERTS, Jeremy Michael Graham; QC 1982; Barrister; a Recorder of the Crown Court, since 1981; *b* 26 April 1941; *s* of late Lt-Col J. M. H. Roberts and E. D. Roberts; *m* 1964, Sally Priscilla Johnson. *Educ:* Winchester; Brasenose Coll., Oxford. BA. Called to the Bar, Inner Temple, 1965. *Recreations:* racing, reading, theatre, opera. *Address:* 2 Dr Johnson's Buildings, Temple, EC4Y 7AY. *T:* 01–353 5371.

ROBERTS, Dame Joan (Howard), DBE 1978; President, Yooralla Society of Victoria, 1977–78; *b* 27 June 1907; *d* of Charles A. Norris and Rose M. A. Norris; *m* 1937, Allan Edwin Tainsh Roberts; two *s* one *d. Educ:* Presbyterian Ladies' Coll., Melbourne, Australia; Univ. of Melb. (MSc). Res. Biochemist, Dept of Pathology, Univ. of Melb., 1930–34; Biochemist, Prince Henry's Hosp., Melb., 1935–37. Yooralla Hosp. Sch. for Crippled Children: Mem. Cttee, 1948–68; Pres., 1968–77. Member: Council, Presbyterian Ladies' Coll., Melb., 1948–80; Council of Management, Arthritis Foundn of Victoria (formerly Rheumatism and Arthritis Assoc. of Victoria), 1979–. *Recreations:* travel, reading, classical music. *Address:* 2 Prowse Avenue, Balwyn, Vic 3103, Australia. *T:* 836–1258. *Club:* Lyceum (Melbourne).

ROBERTS, John; *see* Roberts, A. J.

ROBERTS, Rt. Rev. John; *see* Roberts, Rt Rev. D. J.

ROBERTS, John; *see* Roberts, H. J.

ROBERTS, John Alexander Fraser, CBE 1965; FRS 1963; MA Cantab; MD, DSc (Edinburgh); FRCP; FRCPsych; *b* 8 Sept. 1899; *er s* of late Robert Henry Roberts, Foxhall, Denbigh, and late Elizabeth Mary; *m* 1st, 1941, Doris, *y d* of late Herbert and Kate Hare; two *d*; 2nd, 1975, Margaret, *d* of late Sydney and Dorothy Ralph. *Educ:* Denbigh Gram. Sch.; privately; Gonville and Caius Coll., Cambridge; Univs of Edinburgh, Wales and Bristol. 2nd Lieut Royal Welch Fusliliers, 1918–19; War of 1939–45: Surgeon-Comdr RNVR and Cons. in Med. Statistics, RN, 1942–46. Research Asst, Inst. of Animal Genetics, Univ. of Edinburgh, 1922–28; Biologist, Wool Industries Research Assoc., 1928–31; Macaulay Research Fellow, Univ. of Edinburgh, 1931–33; Dir, Burden Mental Research Dept, Stoke Park Colony, Bristol, 1933–57; Lectr in Med. Genetics, London School of Hygiene and Trop. Med., 1946–57; Consultant in Medical Genetics, Royal Eastern Counties Hosp., Colchester, 1946–80; Dir, Clinical Genetics Research Unit (MRC), Inst. of Child Health, Univ. of London, and Hon. Consultant in Med. Genetics, The Hospital for Sick Children, Gt Ormond St, 1957–64; Geneticist, Paediatric Res. Unit, Guy's Hosp. Med. Sch. and Hon. Clinical Geneticist, Guy's Hosp., 1964–81. President: Royal Anthropological Inst. of Gt Britain and Ire., 1957–59; Biometric Society (British Region), 1960–62; Section of Epidemiology and Preventive Medicine, RSM, 1960–62, Lectures: Charles West, RCP, 1961; Leonard Parsons, Univ. of Birmingham, 1963; Donald Paterson, Univ. of British Columbia (and Vis. Prof.), 1967; Lumleian, RCP, 1971. Ballantyne Prize, RCPE 1976. *Publications:* An Introduction to Medical Genetics, 1940, 7th edn 1978; papers in medical, biological and genetical journals. *Recreation:* country walks. *Address:* 10 Aspley Road, Wandsworth, SW18 2DB. *T:* 01–874 4826. *Club:* Athenæum.

ROBERTS, John Arthur, CEng, FIEE; Under-Secretary, Department of Energy, 1974–77; *b* 21 Dec. 1917; *s* of late John Richard and Emily Roberts; *m* 1st, 1944, Winifred Wilks Scott (*d* 1976); two *s* one *d*; 2nd, 1977, Rosetta Mabel Price. *Educ:* Liverpool Institute; Liverpool Univ. (BEng). Apprentice, Metropolitan-Vickers Electrical Co Ltd, 1939. Served War, Royal Signals, 1940–46, Major. Sen. Lectr, Applied Science, RMA, Sandhurst, 1947–49; SSO and PSO, RAE, Farnborough, 1949–59; Head, Control and Computers Section, Applications Br., Central Electricity Generating Bd, 1959–62; Project Ldr, Automatic Control, CEGB, 1962–67; DCSO, Min. of Tech. and DTI, 1967–72; Under-Sec., DTI, 1972–74. *Address:* Gorse Hill Lane, Virginia Water, Surrey. *T:* Wentworth 2457.

ROBERTS, John Charles Quentin; Director, Great Britain-USSR Association, since 1974; *b* 4 April 1933; *s* of Hubert and Emilie Roberts; *m* 1st, 1959, Dinah Webster-Williams (marr. diss.); one *s* one *d*; 2nd, 1982, Elizabeth Roberts (Pres., Cooper Estates Inc., LA, Calif.), *y d* of late W. H. Gough-Cooper, Farningham, Kent. *Educ:* King's Coll., Taunton (scholar); Merton Coll., Oxford (MA). MIL 1972. Royal Air Force CSC Interpreter, 1953; Shell International Petroleum Co. Ltd, 1956; Shell Co. of E Africa Ltd: Representative, Zanzibar and S Tanganyika, 1957, Kenya Highlands, 1958; PA to Man. Dir, Shell Austria AG Vienna, 1960; Pressed Steel Co. Ltd, Oxford, 1961; Asst Master, Marlborough Coll., 1963. Chm., Organising Cttee for British Week in Siberia, 1978. Mem. Council, SSEES, Univ. of London, 1981–; Vice Pres., Assoc. of Teachers of Russian, 1984–. Governor, Cobham Hall, 1984–. *Recreations:* family, the arts, walking and combing the dogs, collecting. *Address:* 52 Paultons Square, SW3. *T:* 01–352 3882. *Club:* Athenæum.

ROBERTS, John Eric, DSc (Leeds); CPhys; FInstP; Emeritus Professor of Physics, University of London, 1969; Physicist to Middlesex Hospital, W1, 1946–70; Consultant Adviser in Physics, Department of Health and Social Security, 1960–71; *b* Leeds, 1907; *e s* of late James J. Roberts, Normanton, Yorks; *m* Sarah, *o d* of late Thomas Raybould, Normanton, Yorks; two *d. Educ:* Normanton Grammar School; University of Leeds (Brown Scholar; Univ. Res. Schol., 1930; BSc (Physics Hons) 1928; PhD 1930; DSc 1944). FInstP 1938; CPhys 1985. Research Assistant in Physics, University of Leeds, 1930; Assistant Physicist, Royal Cancer Hospital, 1932; Senior Asst Physicist, Middlesex Hosp., 1937; Joel Prof. of Physics Applied to Medicine, Univ. of London, 1946–69; Regional Adviser, ME, Internat. Atomic Energy Agency, 1963–64. Pres., British Inst. of Radiology, 1951–52; Pres. Hospital Physicists Assoc., 1950–51; Editor, Physics in Medicine and Biology, 1956–60; Editor, British Jl of Radiology, 1964–67. Hon. Member: Royal Coll. of Radiologists; Inst. of Physical Scis in Med. *Publications:* Nuclear War and Peace, 1956; scientific papers in various journals. *Address:* Windrush, Malthouse Lane, Ludham, Great Yarmouth, Norfolk NR29 5QL. *T:* St Benets 459.

ROBERTS, Air Vice-Marshal John Frederick, CB 1967; CBE 1960 (OBE 1954); *b* 24 Feb. 1913; *y s* of late W. J. Roberts, Pontardawe; *m* 1st, 1942, Mary Winifred (*d* 1968), *d* of late J. E. Newns; one *s*; 2nd, 1976, Mrs P. J. Hull, *d* of A. Stiles. *Educ:* Pontardawe Gram. Sch., Glam. Chartered Accountant, 1936. Joined RAF, 1938; service in Middle East, 1942–45; Mem. Directing Staff, RAF Staff Coll., Bracknell, 1954–56; SASO, RAF Record Office, 1958–60; Dep. Comptroller, Allied Forces Central Europe, 1960–62; Stn Comdr RAF Uxbridge, 1963; Dir of Personal Services I, Min. of Def. (Air), 1964–65; Dir-Gen. of Ground Training (RAF), 1966–68; retd, 1968. With Deloitte & Co., Chartered Accountants, Swansea, 1969–78. *Recreations:* cricket, golf, cabinet-making. *Address:* Cefneithrym, 1 Lon Cadog, Sketty, Swansea SA2 0TS. *T:* Swansea 203763. *Clubs:* Royal Air Force, MCC; Pontardawe Golf (Pres., 1978–).

ROBERTS, John Herbert; Director, Technical Division 2, Inland Revenue, since 1985; *b* 18 Aug. 1933; *s* of late John Emanuel Roberts and Hilda Mary Roberts; *m* 1965, Patricia Iris; one *s* three *d. Educ:* Canton High Sch.; London School of Economics (BScEcon Hons). Entered Civil Service by Open Competition as Inspector of Taxes, 1954; National Service, commnd RASC, 1955–57; returned to Inland Revenue, 1957; Principal Inspector, 1974; Sen. Principal Inspector, 1979; Under Secretary, 1981; Director of Operations, 1981–85. *Recreations:* music, walking, Welsh Springers. *Address:* Somerset House, WC2R 1LB. *T:* 01–438 7649.

ROBERTS, Dr John Laing; Regional Prevention Manager, North Western Regional Health Authority, since 1985; *b* 26 Dec. 1939; *s* of Charles F. Roberts and May Roberts; *m* 1st, 1963, Meriel F. Dawes (marr. diss. 1980); three *d*; 2nd, 1981, Judith Mary Hare. *Educ:* Latymer Upper School; Univ. of Birmingham. PhD, BSocSc. FHA. NHS Nat. Administrative Trainee, 1962–63; Senior Administrative Asst, United Birmingham Hosps, 1964–66; Sen. Res. Associate, Dept of Social Medicine, Univ. of Birmingham, 1966–69; Dep. Dir, Res. Div., Health Education Council, 1969–74; Operational Services Gen. Administrator, S Glamorgan AHA (T), 1974–77; Regional Gen. Administrator, W Midlands RHA, 1977–82; Regional Administrator, N Western RHA, 1983–85. *Publications:* papers on health education, health service administration, economics and health; PhD thesis, Studies of Information Systems for Health Service Resource Planning and Control. *Recreations:* village cricket, hill walking. *Address:* 20 Crabtree Avenue, Disley, Stockport, Cheshire SK12 2DD. *T:* 061–236 7594.

ROBERTS, John Lewis; Assistant Under-Secretary of State (Equipment Collaboration), Ministry of Defence, since 1985; *b* 21 April 1928; *s* of Thomas Hubert and Meudwen Roberts; *m* 1952, Maureen Jocelyn (*née* Moriarty); two *s. Educ:* Pontardawe Grammar

Sch.; Trinity Hall, Cambridge. BA (Hons) History. Joined Min. of Civil Aviation, 1950; Private Sec. to the Parly Sec., 1953; Principal: in Railways, then in Sea Transport; branches of MoT and Civil Aviation, 1954–59; Civil Air Attaché, Bonn Embassy, 1959–62; Defence Supply Counsellor, Paris Embassy, 1966–69; Ministry of Defence: Asst Sec., Internat. Policy Div., 1971–74; Assistant Under-Secretary of State: Air MoD PE, 1974–76; Sales, 1976–77; Personnel, (Air), 1977–80; Supply and Organisation, (Air), 1980–82; Internat. and Industrial Policy, PE, 1982–85. *Recreations:* angling, sailing. *Address:* 23 Mount Ararat Road, Richmond, Surrey TW10 6PQ. *T:* 01–940 1035. *Club:* Fly Fishers'.

ROBERTS, Dr John Morris; Warden, Merton College, Oxford, since 1984; *b* 14 April 1928; *s* of late Edward Henry Roberts and late Dorothy Julia Roberts, Bath, Som.; *m* 1964, Judith Cecilia Mary, *e d* of late Rev. James Armitage and Monica Armitage; one *s* two *d*. *Educ:* Taunton Sch.; Keble Coll., Oxford (Schol.; Hon. Fellow, 1981). National Service, 1949–50; Prize Fellow, Magdalen Coll., Oxford, 1951–53; Commonwealth Fund Fellow, Princeton and Yale, 1953–54; Merton College, Oxford: Fellow and Tutor, 1953–79 (Hon. Fellow, 1980–84); acting Warden, 1969–70, 1977–79; Sen. Proctor, Oxford Univ., 1967–68; Vice-Chancellor and Prof., Southampton Univ., 1979–85. Mem., Inst. for Advanced Study, Princeton, 1960–61; Vis. Prof., Univ. of S Carolina, 1961; Sec. of Harmsworth Trust, 1962–68; Member: Council, European Univ. Inst., 1980–; US/UK Educn Commn, 1981–. Mem., Gen. Cttee, Royal Literary Fund, 1975–. Trustee, Nat. Portrait Gall., 1984–. Editor, English Historical Review, 1967–77. Pres. Council, Taunton Sch., 1978–. Presenter, TV series, The Triumph of the West, 1985. *Publications:* French Revolution Documents, 1966; Europe 1880–1945, 1967; The Mythology of the Secret Societies, 1972; The Paris Commune from the Right, 1973; Revolution and Improvement: the Western World 1775–1847, 1976; History of the World, 1976; The French Revolution, 1978; The Triumph of the West, 1985; (Gen. Editor) Purnell's History of the 20th Century; articles and reviews in learned jls. *Recreation:* music. *Address:* Merton College, Oxford OX1 4JD. *Club:* United Oxford & Cambridge University.

ROBERTS, Rear-Adm. John Oliver, CB 1976; MNI; Managing Director, Demak Ltd, International Consultants, since 1983; *b* 4 April 1924; *er s* of J. V. and M. C. Roberts; *m* 1st, 1950, Lady Hermione Mary Morton Stuart (marr. diss. 1960; she *d* 1969); one *d*; 2nd, 1963, Honor Marigold Gordon Gray; one *s* one *d*. *Educ:* RN Coll., Dartmouth. Served War: Midshipman, HM Ships Renown and Tartar, 1941–43; Sub-Lt, HMS Serapis, 1943–44; Lieut, 1945; Pilot Trg, 1944–46. HMS Triumph, 1947–49; RNAS, Lossiemouth, 1949–51; Flag-Lt to FOGT, 1952; Lt-Comdr, 1953; HMAS Vengeance and Sydney, 1953–54; RNVR, Southern Air Div., 1954–56; CO, No 803 Sqdn, HMS Eagle, 1957–58; Comdr, 1958; RNAS, Brawdy, 1958–60; CO, HMS St Bride's Bay, 1960–61; Naval Staff, 1962–64; Captain, 1964; CSO, Flag Officer Aircraft Carriers, 1964–66; CO, HMS Galatea, 1966–68; Naval Staff, 1968–70; CO, HMS Ark Royal, 1971–72; Rear-Adm., 1972; Flag Officer Sea Training, 1972–74; COS to C-in-C Fleet, 1974–76; Flag Officer, Naval Air Command, 1976–78. Non-exec. Dir, Aeronautical & General Instruments Ltd, 1981–82 (Head of Marketing and Sales, Defence Systems Div., 1980–81); Dir Gen., British Printing Industries Fedn, 1981–82. FRSA. *Recreations:* Rugby football, cricket, athletics, sailing, skiing. *Club:* East India, Devonshire, Sports and Public Schools.

ROBERTS, Prof. Lewis Edward John, CBE 1978; FRS 1982; Wolfson Professor of Environmental Risk Assessment, University of East Anglia, since 1986; *b* 31 Jan. 1922; *s* of William Edward Roberts and Lilian Lewis Roberts; *m* 1947, Eleanor Mary Luscombe; one *s*. *Educ:* Swansea Grammar Sch.; Jesus Coll., Oxford (MA, DPhil). Clarendon Laboratory, Oxford, 1944; Scientific Officer, Chalk River Res. Estabt, Ont, Canada, 1946–47; AERE, Harwell, 1947, Principal Scientific Officer, 1952; Commonwealth Fund Fellow, Univ. of Calif, Berkeley, 1954–55; Dep. Head, Chemistry Div., 1966, Asst Dir, 1967, Dir, 1975–86, AERE. Mem., UKAEA, 1979–86. Pres., British Nuclear Energy Soc., 1985–. R. M. Jones Lectr, QUB, 1981. Governor, Abingdon Sch., 1978–86. *Publications:* Nuclear Power and Public Responsibility, 1984; papers in qly revs and in scientific journals and IAEA pubns. *Recreations:* reading, gardening. *Address:* School of Environmental Sciences, University of East Anglia, Norwich NR4 7TJ. *Club:* United Oxford & Cambridge University.

ROBERTS, Prof. Michael, FBA 1960; Director, Institute for Social and Economic Research, Rhodes University, 1974–76; Professor of Modern History, The Queen's University, Belfast, 1954–73; Dean of the Faculty of Arts, 1957–60; *b* 21 May 1908; *s* of Arthur Roberts and Hannah Elizabeth Landless; *m* 1941, Ann McKinnon Morton; one *d*. *Educ:* Brighton Coll.; Worcester Coll., Oxford. Gladstone Meml Prizeman, 1931; A. M. P. Read Scholar (Oxford), 1932. Procter Vis. Fell., Princeton Univ., USA, 1931–32; Lectr, Merton Coll., Oxford, 1932–34; Asst Lectr, Univ. of Liverpool, 1934–35; DPhil, Oxford, 1935; Prof. of Modern History, Rhodes Univ., S Africa, 1935–53. Lieut, SA Int. Corps, 1942–44. British Council Representative, Stockholm, 1944–46. Public Orator, Rhodes Univ., 1951–53; Hugh Le May Vis. Fellow, Rhodes Univ., 1960–61; Lectures: A. L. Smith, Balliol Coll., Oxford, 1962; Enid Muir Meml, Univ. of Newcastle upon Tyne, 1965; Creighton in History, Univ. of London, 1965; Stenton, Univ. of Reading, 1969; James Ford special, Oxford Univ., 1973; Wiles, QUB, 1977. Hon. Fellow, Worcester Coll., Oxford, 1966; Vis. Fellow, All Souls Coll., Oxford, 1968–69; Leverhulme Faculty Fellow in European Studies, 1973; Vis. Fellow, Pomona Coll., Claremont, Calif, 1978. Vis. Fellow, Trevelyan Coll., Univ. of Durham, 1981. MRIA 1968. For. Member: Roy. Swedish Acad. of Letters, History and Antiquities; Royal Swedish Academy of Science; Hon. Mem. Samfundet för utgivande av handskrifter rörande Skandinaviens historia. FRHistS; Fil dr (*hc*) (Stockholm), 1960; DLit (*hc*) QUB, 1977. Kungens medalj i Serafimerband (Sweden), 1981. Chevalier, Order of North Star (Sweden), 1954. *Publications:* The Whig Party, 1807–1812, 1939; (with A. E. G. Trollip) The South African Opposition, 1939–1945, 1947; Gustavus Adolphus: A History of Sweden, 1611–1632, Vol. I, 1953, Vol. II, 1958; Essays in Swedish History, 1967; The Early Vasas: A History of Sweden 1523–1611, 1968; Sweden as a Great Power 1611–1697, 1968; Sverige och Europa, 1969; Gustav Vasa, 1970; Gustavus Adolphus and the Rise of Sweden, 1973; (ed) Sweden's Age of Greatness, 1973; Macartney in Russia, 1974; The Swedish Imperial Experience 1560–1718, 1979; British Diplomacy and Swedish Politics, 1758–1773, 1980; Sverige som Stormakt, 1980; The Age of Liberty: Sweden 1719–1772, 1986; trans. from Swedish of works by Nils Ahnlund, F. G. Bengtsson, Gunnar Wennerberg (Gluntarne), Birger Sjöberg (Fridas bok), Carl Michael Bellman (Epistles and Songs, I-III), Anna Maria Lenngren; articles in New Cambridge Mod. Hist., EHR, History, Historical Jl, Past and Present, Scandia, Karolinska Förbundets Årsbok, South African Archives Yearbook, etc. *Recreation:* music. *Address:* 38 Somerset Street, Grahamstown, CP, South Africa. *T:* Grahamstown 24855.

ROBERTS, Norman Stafford, MA, DPA; Headmaster, Taunton School, 1970–Aug. 1987; *b* 15 Feb. 1926; *s* of late Walter S. Roberts, LLM and Florence E. Roberts (*née* Phythian), Calderstones, Liverpool; *m* 1965, Beatrice, *o d* of late George and Winifred Best, Donaghadee, Co. Down; one *s* two *d*. *Educ:* Quarry Bank High Sch., Liverpool; Hertford Coll., Oxford (Open Exhibnr, History). Served in RA, Egypt and Palestine, 1945–47 (Lieut). 2nd cl. hons PPE 1950; DipEd Oxford 1951; DPA London 1951. Asst Master, Berkhamsted Junior Sch., 1951–55; House Master, Sixth Form Master, Berkhamsted Sch., 1955–59; Walter Hines Page Scholar to USA, 1959, 1980; Senior History Master, CO CCF (Hon. Major 1965), Monkton Combe Sch., 1959–65, Housemaster 1962–65; Schoolmaster Student, Merton Coll., Oxford, 1964; Headmaster, Sexey's Sch., Bruton, 1965–70. *Recreations:* foreign travel, bridge, hockey, tennis. *Address:* (until Aug. 1987) Headmaster's House, Private Road, Staplegrove, Taunton, Somerset. *T:* Taunton 72588; (from July 1987) 23 Mount Street, Taunton, Somerset. *T:* Taunton 81623. *Club:* East India, Devonshire, Sports and Public Schools.

ROBERTS, Prof. Paul Harry, PhD, ScD; FRS 1979; FRAS; Professor of Mathematics, University of California at Los Angeles, since 1986; *b* 13 Sept. 1929; *s* of Percy Harry Roberts and Ethel Frances (*née* Mann); *m* 1959, Joyce Atkinson *Educ:* Ardwyn Grammar Sch., Aberystwyth; University Coll. of Wales, Aberystwyth; Gonville and Caius Coll., Cambridge (George Green Student; BA, MA, PhD, ScD). FRAS 1955. Res. Associate, Univ. of Chicago, 1954–55; Scientific Officer, AWRE, 1955–56; ICI Fellow in Physics, 1956–59, Lectr in Phys, 1959–61, Univ. of Newcastle upon Tyne; Associate Prof. of Astronomy, Univ. of Chicago, 1961–63; Prof. of Applied Maths, Univ. of Newcastle upon Tyne, 1963–85. Editor, Geophysical and Astrophysical Fluid Dynamics, 1976–. *Publications:* An Introduction to Magnetohydrodynamics, 1967; contrib. to Geophys. and Astrophys. Fluid Dyn., Jl Low Temp. Phys., Astrophys. Jl, Jl Fluid Mech., and Jl Phys. Soc. *Recreations:* playing bassoon, chess. *Address:* 2642 Cordelia Street, Los Angeles, Calif 90049, USA. *T:* 213–471–5491; Department of Mathematics or Institute of Geophysics and Planetary Physics UCLA, Los Angeles, Calif 90024, USA. *T:* 213–825–7764; 213–206–2707.

ROBERTS, Percy Charles; Chairman and Chief Executive, Mirror Group Newspapers Ltd, 1977–80; *b* 30 July 1920; *s* of late Herbert Bramwell Roberts and Alice (*née* Lang); *m* 1st 1946, Constance Teresa Violet Butler (marr. diss. 1977); two *s*; 2nd, 1978, Pauline Moore. *Educ:* Brighton Hove and Sussex Grammar Sch. Reporter, Sussex Daily News, 1936–39. Served War of 1939–45: Sussex Yeomanry, in France and ME (Captain). Sub-Editor, Egyptian Mail, Cairo, 1946; Reporter, Mid-East Mail, Palestine, 1947; Sub-Editor: Sussex Daily News, 1948; Liverpool Daily Post, 1949; Editor, Nigerian Citizen, 1949–51; Editorial Adviser, Gen. Manager, Managing Dir, Nigerian Daily Times, 1951–60; Managing Dir, Mirror Gp Newspapers in Caribbean, 1960–62; Gen. Manager, Mirror Newspapers in Manchester, 1962–66; Dir, 1964–80, Managing Dir, 1966–80, Daily Mirror Newspapers Ltd; Vice-Chm., West of England Newspapers Ltd, 1965–69; Managing Dir, IPC Newspapers Ltd, 1968–75; Dir, Scottish Daily Record & Sunday Mail Ltd, 1969–74; Chm., Overseas Newspapers Ltd, 1969–75; Dep. Chm. and Chief Exec., Mirror Gp Newspapers Ltd, 1975 77. Dir, Reed Publishing Holdings Ltd, 1975–80; Mem., Reed Internat. UK Cttee, 1975–80. Mem., CBI Employment Policy Cttee, 1975–78. Mem. Council, CPU, 1979–83. CBIM. *Address:* Merrick House, Weston-under-Penyard, near Ross-on-Wye, Herefordshire HR9 7PG. *Clubs:* MCC, Royal Automobile; Ross Rotary.

ROBERTS, Maj.-Gen. Philip; *see* Roberts, Maj.-Gen. G. P. B.

ROBERTS, Philip Bedlington; a Recorder of the Crown Court, since 1982; Regional Chairman of Industrial Tribunals (Bristol), since 1984; *b* 15 Dec. 1921; *s* of late R. J. S. Roberts, solicitor and A. M. Roberts; *m* 1944, Olive Margaret, *d* of E. R. Payne, Mugswell, Chipstead, Surrey; one *s* one *d*. *Educ:* Dawson Court, Kensington; St Matthew's Sch., Bayswater. RAFVR, 1940–46. Admitted solicitor, 1949; in private practice with Scholfield Roberts & Hill, 1950–75; Chm. of Industrial Tribunals, 1975– (part-time, 1966–75). Chairman: Nat. Insce Tribunals, 1959–75; Compensation Appeals Tribunal, 1962. Solicitor, Somerset British Legion, 1960–75. *Publications:* contribs to professional jls. *Recreation:* gardening. *Address:* Charlynch House, Spaxton, Bridgwater, Somerset TA5 1BY. *T:* Spaxton 356. *Club:* Royal Air Force.

ROBERTS, Hon. (Priscilla) Jane (Stephanie), (Hon. Mrs Roberts), MVO 1985; Curator of the Print Room, Royal Library, Windsor Castle, since 1975; *b* 4 Sept. 1949; *d* of Baron Aldington, *qv*; *m* 1975, Hugh Ashley Roberts, *s* of Rt Rev. Edward James Keymer Roberts, *qv*; two *d*. *Educ:* Cranborne Chase School; Westfield College, Univ. of London (BA Hons); Courtauld Inst., Univ. of London (MA). *Publications:* Holbein, 1979; Leonardo: Codex Hammer, 1981; Master Drawings in the Royal Collection, 1985; articles in Burlington Magazine, Report of Soc. of Friends of St George's. *Recreations:* singing, sewing. *Address:* Salisbury Tower, Windsor Castle, Berks. *T:* Windsor 855581.

ROBERTS, Ven. Raymond Harcourt, CB 1984; General Secretary, Jerusalem and Middle East Church Association, since 1986; Licensed, Diocese of Guildford, since 1986; *b* 14 April 1931; *s* of Thomas Roberts and Carrie Maud Roberts. *Educ:* St Edmund Hall, Oxford (MA English); St Michael's Theol Coll., Llandaff. Deacon 1956, priest 1957, dio. of Monmouth (Curate of Bassaleg); Chaplain RNVR, 1958, RN, 1959; Destroyers and Frigates, Far East, 1959; HMS Pembroke, 1962; Dartmouth Trng Sqdn, 1963; RM Commando Course, 1965; 45 Commando, S. Arabia, 1965; RN Engrg Coll., 1967; HMS Bulwark, 1968; BRNC Dartmouth, 1970; HMS Ark Royal, 1974; Commando Trng Centre, RM, 1975; HMS Drake and HM Naval Base, Plymouth, 1979; Chaplain of the Fleet and Archdeacon for RN, 1980–84; Archdeacon Emeritus, 1985–. QHC, 1980–84. Hon. Canon, Cathedral of Holy Trinity, Gibraltar, 1980–84. *Address:* 13 Oast House Crescent, Upper Hale, Farnham, Surrey GU9 0NP. *T:* Farnham 722014. *Club:* Royal Commonwealth Society.

ROBERTS, Richard (David Hallam); freelance academic and wordsmith, yachtmaster, bookbinder's mate, trainee househusband, gardener, woodman, antiquarian cyclist; *b* 27 July 1931; *s* of Arthur Hallam Roberts, Barrister-at-law, sometime Attorney-General, Zanzibar, and Ruvé Constance Jessie Roberts; *m* 1960, Wendy Ewen Mount; three *s*. *Educ:* King's Sch., Canterbury; Jesus Coll., Cambridge. Commissioned into RA 6th Field Regt, 1952. Asst Master, King's Sch., Canterbury, 1956; Housemaster, 1957; Head of Modern Language Dept, 1961; Senior Housemaster, 1965; Headmaster: Wycliffe Coll., Stonehouse, 1967–80; King Edward's Sch., Witley, 1980–85. *Address:* Smithy Cottage, Orford, Suffolk IP12 2NW. *Club:* Orford Sailing.

ROBERTS, Rear-Adm. Richard Douglas, CB 1971; CEng; FIMechE; Rear-Admiral Engineering on staff Flag Officer Naval Air Command, 1969–72; *b* 7 Nov. 1916; *s* of Rear-Adm. E. W. Roberts and Mrs R. E. Roberts (*née* Cox); *m* 1943, Mary Norma Wright; one *s* one *d*. *Educ:* RNC Dartmouth; RNEC Keyham. Frobisher, 1934; RNEC Keyham, 1935–38 (qual. Marine Eng); HM Ships: Kent, 1938–40; Exeter, 1941; Bermuda, 1942; Mauritius, 1943–45; RNEC Manadon, 1945 (qual. Aero Eng); RNAY Donibristle, 1946 (AMIMechE); RNAS Worthy Down, 1947; RNAS Yeovilton, 1948–49; Staff of Rear-Adm. Reserve Aircraft, 1949–50; Comdr, 1950; RN Staff Coll., 1951; RNAY Fleetlands, 1952–53 (Production Man.); HMS Newfoundland, 1954–56 (Engr Officer); Engr-in-Chief's Dept, Bath, 1956–60; Captain 1960; RNAY Belfast, 1961–62 (Supt); idc, 1963 (MIMechE); Dir, Fleet Maintenance, 1964–66; Dir, Naval Officer Appts (E), 1966–68; Rear-Adm. 1969. FBIM 1982. *Recreations:* sailing (RNSA,

1936), fishing; light railways; Vice Pres., Axe Vale Conservation Soc. *Club*: Army and Navy.

ROBERTS, Richard Frederick Anthony, CBE 1985; High Commissioner for the Commonwealth of the Bahamas in London, 1977–84; *b* 12 May 1932; *s* of Enoch Pedro Roberts and Gladys Raine Roberts (*née* Archer); *m* 1960, Melvern Hollis Bain; on *s* two *d. Educ*: St John's College. Personnel Officer, Bahamas Airways, 1963–67; Exec. Dir and Partner, Venn, Livingstone, Roberts (Public Relns), 1967–68; Personnel Dir, New Providence Develt Co. Ltd (Land Develt), March-Oct. 1968; MP Centreville, 1968–77; Parly Sec.: Min. of Finance, 1969–72; Min. of Agric., 1971–72; Minister of Agric. and Fisheries, Oct. 1972–Feb. 1973; Minister of Home Affairs, March-Dec. 1973; Minister of Agric., Fisheries and Local Govt, 1974–77. Pres., Airline Workers Union; Sec. Gen., Amalgamated Building Constructional Engrg Trade Union; Asst Gen. Sec., Bahamas Fedn of Labour; Pres. and Gen. Sec., Bahamas TUC. Progressive Liberal Party: Asst Gen. Sec.; first Vice-Chm.; Mem., Nat. Gen. Council. Mem., Adv. Cttee to Labour Bd; Chm., Maritime Bd; Mem., Broadcasting and TV Commn; Vice-Chm., Bahamas Agricl Corp. Sec., Methodist Preachers' Cttee. Asst Scout Master; Lt, Boys Brigade. Mem. Internat. Cultural Exchange. *Recreations*: fishing, reading, sports, religion. *Address*: Carmichael Road, PO Box 565, Nassau, Bahamas. *Clubs*: Royal Automobile, Hurlingham.

ROBERTS, Robert Evan, CBE 1976; National General Secretary, National Council of YMCAs, 1965–75; *b* 16 July 1912; *s* of late Robert Thomas Roberts, Llanilar, Denbighshire; *m* 1939, Rhoda, *d* of late William Driver, Burnley, Lancs; one *s* one *d. Educ*: Cilcain, Flintshire; Liverpool. YMCA: Asst Sec.: Central YMCA Liverpool, 1933; Hornsey (N London), 1935; Asst Div. Sec., Lancs/Cheshire, 1937; Div. Sec., NW Div., 1939; Dep. Dir, YMCA Welfare Services, NW Europe, 1944–46 (despatches); Mem. 21st Army Gp, Council of Voluntary Welfare Work, 1944–46. Nat. Sec., Ireland, 1946; Sec., Personnel Dept, Nat. Council of YMCAs, London, 1948; Nat. Sec., Nat. Council of YMCAs, Wales, 1956–65; Hon. Sec/Treasurer, Assoc. of Secs of YMCAs of Gt Brit. and Ireland, 1963–65; Dep. Chm., Welsh Standing Conf. of Nat. Vol. Youth Orgs. 1963–65. Past Member: Welsh Nat. Council of Social Service; Welsh Jt Educn Cttee; Nat. Inst. of Adult Educn. Member: Nat. Council of Social Service, 1965–75; Brit. Council of Churches (and its Exec.), 1965–74; Council of Voluntary Welfare Work, 1965–75; World Council of YMCAs (and its Finance Cttee), 1965–75; Vice-Pres., Welsh Nat. Council of YMCAs, 1975; Chm., Job Creation Programme, Barrow and S Lakeland, 1976–80; Exec. Member: SE Cumbria Community Health Council, 1977–82; S Lakeland Voluntary Action, 1978–85; S Cumbria Community Health Council, 1982–; S Cumbria DHA Ethics of Research Cttee, 1983–; Community Health Council Observer, Cumbria FPC, 1984–. Trustee: Framlington Trust, 1973–. Age Concern: Mem., 1976–82, Vice Chm., 1981–82, Exec. Cttee, Cumbria; Chm., S Lakeland, 1977–82; Exec. Mem. and Trustee, Kendal and Ulveston. Dist Judge, Cumbria Best Kept Village, 1977–85; Warden, Lakeland Horticultural Soc. Gardens, 1977–. Fellow, Royal Commonwealth Soc., 1974. Silver Jubilee Medal, 1977. *Recreations*: fell-walking, gardening. *Address*: 5 Priory Crescent, Kents Bank, Grange over Sands, Cumbria LA11 7BL. *T*: Grange over Sands 2161.

ROBERTS, Rev. Roger Lewis, CVO 1973; MA Oxon; Chaplain, the Queen's Chapel of the Savoy, and Chaplain of the Royal Victorian Order, 1961–73; Chaplain to the Queen, 1969–81; *b* 3 Aug. 1911; 3rd *s* of late Robert Lewis Roberts, CBE; *m* 1935, Katie Agnes Mary Perryman; one *s. Educ*: Highgate School; Exeter College, Oxford. 1st Class Hon. Mods, 1931; 1st Class Lit. Hum., 1933; Charles Oldham Prize, 1933; BA 1933; MA 1938; Sixth Form Master, The Liverpool Institute, 1933–34; Sixth Form Master, Rugby School, 1934–40; enlisted RRA, 1940; Army Educational Corps, 1941–43 (Major). Headmaster, Blundell's Sch., 1943–47; Deacon, Exeter, 1946; Priest, St Albans, 1948; Assistant Priest, Cathedral and Abbey Church of St Alban, 1948–49. Vicar of Sharnbrook, Bedfordshire, 1949–54. Vicar of the Guild Church of All Hallows, London Wall, 1954–58, of St Botolph without Aldersgate, 1958–61. Warden, The Church of England Men's Society, 1957–61 (Gen. Sec. 1954–57, Vice-Pres. 1962–). Member of editorial staff, The Church Times, 1950–76 (Editor, 1960–68). Chaplain: Instn of Electrical Engineers, 1961–73; Worshipful Co. of Glaziers, 1967–77. *Address*: Thorn Farm Cottage, Chagford, Devon. *T*: Chagford 2493. *Club*: United Oxford & Cambridge University.

See also B. R. Roberts and C. H. Roberts.

ROBERTS, Roy Ernest James, CBE 1986; FEng, FIMechE, FIProdE; AMIBF; Managing Director, GKN Group, since 1980; Deputy Chairman and Chairman elect, Simon Engineering plc, since 1986; Deputy Chairman, Dowty Group PLC, since 1986; *b* 14 Dec. 1928; *s* of Douglas Henry Roberts and Elsie Florence (*née* Rice); *m* 1950, Winson Madge Smith; two *s. Educ*: Farnham Grammar Sch.; Royal Aircraft Estabt, Farnborough (student apprentice). Management trainee, Guest, Keen and Nettlefolds, 1951–55; Asst to Directors, C. & B. Smith Ltd, 1956–57, Works Director, 1958–66, Dir and Gen. Manager, 1966–70 (C. & B. Smith was acquired by GKN, 1966); Managing Director: GKN Cwmbran Ltd, 1970–72; GKN Engineering Ltd, 1972–74; Chairman, GKN Engineering Ltd and GKN Building Supplies & Services Ltd, 1974–77; Member, main board of GKN, 1975; Group Director, GKN, with special responsibilities for engrg and construction services activities, also for interests in India, Pakistan, S Africa and the Middle East, 1977–79. Mem. (pt-time), UKAEA, 1981–. Instn of Mechanical Engineers: Vice Pres., 1986–; Chm. Bd, Manufg Industries Div., 1983–86; Mem. Council, 1983–; Instn of Production Engineers: Vice Pres., 1983–; Mem., Exec. Policy Bd, 1983–; Mem. Exec. Cttee, SMMT, 1983–. Member: Council, Cranfield Inst. of Technol., 1983–; Management Bd and Council, 1984–; Policy Cttee, 1985–, Engrg Employers' Fedn; Engineering Council, 1986–. CBIM 1979; FInstD 1980; FRSA 1980. *Recreations*: field sports, walking, music. *Address*: GKN plc, Group Headquarters-Corporate Centre, 7 Cleveland Row, SW1A 1DB. *T*: 01–930 2424. *Telex*: 24911. *Club*: Royal Automobile.

ROBERTS, Sir Samuel, 4th Bt *cr* 1919, of Ecclesall and Queen's Tower, City of Sheffield; Director, Chartfield Holdings Ltd, since 1984; *b* 16 April 1948; *s* of Sir Peter Geoffrey Roberts, 3rd Bt, and of Judith Randell, *d* of late Randell G. Hempson; *S* father, 1985; *m* 1977, Georgina Ann, *yr d* of David Cory; three *d. Educ*: Harrow School; Sheffield Univ. (LLB); Manchester Business School. Called to the Bar, Inner Temple, 1972. Director: Wombwell Management Co. Ltd, 1974–84; Curzon Steels Ltd, 1978–84; Sterling Silverware Ltd, 1978–84; Wellman plc, 1981–84; Old Master Drawings Ltd, 1984–. *Address*: Cockley Cley Hall, Swaffham, Norfolk. *T*: Swaffham 21308.

ROBERTS, Dame Shelagh (Marjorie), DBE 1981; former Industrial Relations Consultant; Member (C) London South West, European Parliament, since Sept. 1979; *b* 13 Oct. 1924; *d* of Glyn and Cecelia Roberts, Ystalyfera. *Educ*: St Wyburn Sch., Birkdale, Lancs. Member: Kensington Borough Council, 1953–71; GLC, 1970–81; Bd of Basildon Development Corp., 1971–75; Occupational Pensions Bd, 1973–79; Race Relations Bd, 1973–77; Panel of Industrial Tribunals, 1973–79; PLA, 1976–79; Chm., National Women's Advisory Cttee of Conservative Party, 1972–75; Chm., Nat. Union of Conservative Party, 1976–77. Leader, Planning and Communications Policy Cttee, GLC, 1977–79. Co-Chm., Jt Cttee Against Racialism, 1978–80. *Publications*: (co-author) Fair Share for the Fair Sex, 1969; More Help for the Cities, 1974. *Recreation*: enjoying the sun

and fresh air. *Address*: 23 Dovehouse Street, Chelsea, SW3 6JY. *T*: 01–352 3711. *Clubs*: Hurlingham, St Stephen's Constitutional.

ROBERTS, Sir Sidney; see Roberts, Sir E. F. S.

ROBERTS, Sir Stephen (James Leake), Kt 1981; Chairman, Milk Marketing Board, since 1977; *b* 13 April 1915; *s* of Frank Roberts and Annie Leake; *m* 1940, Muriel Hobbins; two *s* two *d. Educ*: Wellington Grammar Sch. Farmer; founded Wrekin Farmers Ltd, 1960 (Chm., 1960–77); Shropshire delegate to NFU Council, 1962–70; Member: MMB for W Midland Region, 1966– (Vice-Chm., 1975–77); Food from Britain Council, 1983–. *Recreation*: football (now spectator). *Address*: Littleworth, Little Wenlock, Wellington, Telford, Shropshire TF6 5AX. *T*: Telford 504569. *Club*: Farmers'.

ROBERTS, Stephen Pritchard; baritone; professional singer, since 1972; *b* 8 Feb. 1949; *s* of Edward Henry Roberts and Violet Pritchard. *Educ*: Royal College of Music (schol.). ARCM 1969; GRSM 1971. Professional Lay-Cleric, Westminster Cathedral Choir, 1972–76; now sings regularly in London, UK and Europe, with all major orchs and choral socs; has also sung in USA, Canada, Israel, Hong Kong, Singapore and S America. *Opera* rôles include: Count, in Marriage of Figaro; Falke, in Die Fledermaus; Ubalde, in Armide; Ramiro, in Ravel's L'Heure Espagnole; Aeneas, in Dido and Aeneas; Don Quixote, in Master Peter's Puppet Show; Mittenhofer, in Elegy for Young Lovers; *television* appearances include: Britten's War Requiem; Weill's Seven Deadly Sins; Delius' Sea Drift; Handel's Jeptha; Handel's Judas Maccabaeus; Penderecki's St Luke Passion, 1983 Proms; Walton's Belshazar's Feast, 1984 Proms; *recordings* include: Tippett's King Priam; Birtwistle's Punch and Judy; Gluck's Armide; Orff's Carmina Burana; Vaughan Williams' Five Mystical Songs; Fauré's Requiem; and works by J. S. Bach, C. P. E. Bach and Duruflé. *Address*: 144 Gleneagle Road, SW16 6BA. *T*: 01–769 1512.

ROBERTS, Thomas Arnold, OBE 1962; TD 1947; FRICS; Chartered Surveyor; former Senior Partner, Richard Ellis, Chartered Surveyors, London, EC3; *b* 5 Nov. 1911; *s* of Sidney Herbert Roberts, Liverpool; *m* Kathleen Audrey Robertshaw. *Educ*: Bedford Sch. Joined Westminster Dragoons, 1932; transf. to Royal Signals, 1938. Served War, in N Africa and Italy, 1942–44. Partnership in Richard Ellis & Son, Chartered Surveyors, 1946. Surrey TA Assoc., 1950–72 (Chm., 1956–60); Hon. Col: 381 Lt Regt (TA), 1957–61; Surrey Yeomanry, 1961–68. Property Adviser to Electricity Council, 1957–73. A Church Commissioner, 1973–81. A Governor of Cranleigh Sch., 1960–73 (Chm., 1965–72). DL Surrey, 1958–75. *Recreations*: vintage and sporting motor vehicles, travel. *Address*: Purslow Hall, Clunbury, Craven Arms, Shropshire. *Clubs*: Athenæum, Naval and Military.

ROBERTS, Thomas Somerville, JP; FCIT; Chairman, Milford Haven Conservancy Board, 1976–82; *b* Ruabon, N Wales, 10 Dec. 1911; *s* of Joseph Richard Roberts, Rhosllanerchrugog and Lily Agnes (*née* Caldwell); *m* 1st, 1938, Ruth Moira Teasdale; two *s*; 2nd, 1950, Margaret Peggy Anderson, Sunderland. *Educ*: Roath Park Elem. Sch., Cardiff; Cardiff High Sch.; Balliol Coll., Oxford (Domus Exhibnr). Traffic Apprentice, LNER, 1933; Docks Manager, Middlesbrough and Hartlepool, 1949; Chief Docks Manager: Hull, 1959; S Wales, 1962; Port Dir, S Wales Ports, 1970–75. Chm., S Wales Port Employers, 1962–75; Member: Nat. Jt Council for Port Transport Industry, 1962–75; Nat. Dock Labour Bd, 1970–75; Race Relations Bd, 1968–76. Dir, Develt Corp. for Wales, 1965–80, Vice-Pres. 1979–83; Dep. Chm., Welsh Develt Agency, 1976–80. Member: Council, University Coll., Cardiff; Court, Univ. of Wales; Pwyllgor Tywysog Cymru (Prince of Wales' Cttee), 1977–81; Exec. Cttee, Welsh Environment Foundn, 1977–. Hon. Fellow and Life Governor, University Coll., Cardiff; Life Governor, UWIST. JP City of Cardiff, 1966. *Recreation*: TV. *Address*: Marcross Lodge, 9 Ely Road, Llandaff, Cardiff CF5 2JE. *T*: Cardiff 561153.

ROBERTS, Wilfrid Hubert Wace, JP; *b* 28 Aug. 1900; *s* of Charles and Lady Cecilia Roberts, Boothby, Brampton, Cumberland; *m* 1928, Anne Constance Jennings; three *d. Educ*: Gresham School; Balliol College, Oxford. MP (L) North Cumberland, 1935–50; joined Labour Party, July 1956. *Address*: Boothby Manor House, Brampton, Cumbria.

ROBERTS, Sir William (James Denby), 3rd Bt *cr* 1909; *b* 10 Aug. 1936; *s* of Sir James Denby Roberts, 2nd Bt, OBE, and of Irene Charlotte D'Orsey, *yr d* of late William Dunn, MB, CM; *S* father, 1973. *Educ*: Rugby; Royal Agricultural Coll., Cirencester. MRAC, ARICS. Farms at Strathallan Castle, and Combwell Priory, Flimwell, Wadhurst, Sussex. Founder, 1969, and owner 1969–81, Strathallan Aircraft Collection. *Recreations*: swimming and flying. *Heir*: *b* Andrew Denby Roberts, *b* 21 May 1938. *Address*: Strathallan Castle, Auchterarder, Perthshire. *T*: Auchterarder 2131.

ROBERTS, Wyn; see Roberts, I. W. P.

ROBERTS-JONES, Ivor, CBE 1975; RA 1973 (ARA 1969); sculptor; Teacher of sculpture, Goldsmiths' College School of Art, 1946–68; *b* 2 Nov. 1913; *s* of William and Florence Robert-Jones; *m* 1940, Monica Florence Booth; one *d* (one *s* decd). *Educ*: Oswestry Grammar Sch.; Worksop Coll.; Goldsmiths' Coll. Art Sch.; Royal Academy Schs. Served in RA, 1939–46; active service in Arakan, Burma. One-man Exhibitions of Sculpture: Beaux Arts Gall., 1957; Oriel, Welsh Arts Council Gall., Cardiff 1978; Eisteddfod, 1983. Works purchased by: Tate Gall.; National Portrait Gall.; Arts Council of Gt Brit.; Welsh Arts Council; Beaverbrook Foundation, New Brunswick; Nat. Mus. of Wales. Public commissions: Winston Churchill, Parliament Square; Augustus John Memorial, Fordingbridge; Saint Francis, Lady Chapel, Ardleigh, Essex; Apsley Cherry Garrard, Wheathampstead; Winston Churchill, Oslo, 1975; Winston Churchill, New Orleans, 1977; Earl Attlee, Members' Lobby, House of Commons, 1979; Janus Rider (equestrian group), Harlech Castle, 1982, etc. Exhibited at: The John Moore, Leicester Galls, Royal Academy, Arts Council travelling exhibitions, Jubilee Exhibn of Modern British Sculpture, Battersea Park, 1977, etc. Work is in many private collections. Best known portraits include: Paul Claudel, Somerset Maugham, Yehudi Menuhin, The Duke of Edinburgh, Geraint Evans, Speaker George Thomas. Hon. LLD Wales, 1983. *Publications*: poetry published in Welsh Review, Poets of the Forties, etc. Sculpture illustr. in British Art since 1900 by John Rothenstein; British Sculptors, 1947; Architectural Review, etc. *Address*: The Bridles, Hall Lane, Shimpling, near Diss, Norfolk IP21 4UH. *T*: Diss 740204.

ROBERTS-WEST, Lt-Col George Arthur Alston-; see West.

ROBERTSON, family name of **Baron Robertson of Oakridge.**

ROBERTSON, Hon. Lord; Ian Macdonald Robertson, TD 1946; a Senator of the College of Justice in Scotland (with judicial title of Lord Robertson) since 1966; *b* 30 Oct. 1912; *s* of late James Robertson and Margaret Eva Wilson, Broughty Ferry, Angus, and Edinburgh; *m* 1938, Anna Love Glen, *d* of late Judge James Fulton Glen, Tampa, Florida, USA; one *s* two *d. Educ*: Merchiston Castle School; Balliol College, Oxford; Edinburgh University. BA Oxford (Mod. Greats), 1934; LLB Edinburgh 1937; Vans Dunlop Schol. in Law, Edinburgh 1937. Member Faculty of Advocates, 1939; Advocate-Depute, 1949–51; QC (Scot.), 1954; Sheriff of Ayr and Bute, 1961–66; Sheriff of Perth and

Angus, 1966. Chairman: Medical Appeals Tribunal, 1957–63; Scottish Jt Council for Teachers' Salaries, 1965–81; Scottish Valuation Adv. Council, 1977–86; Member Court of Session Rules Council; UK Rep., Central Council, Internat. Union of Judges, 1974–. Formerly, External Examiner in law subjects, Aberdeen, Glasgow, Edinburgh and St Andrews Universities; Member Committee on Conflicts of Jurisdiction affecting Children, 1958; Governor of Merchiston Castle School, 1954, Chm., 1970; Assessor on Court of Edinburgh Univ., 1967–81. Chairman: Edinburgh Centre of Rural Economy, 1967–85; Edinburgh Centre for Tropical Veterinary Medicine. Served War of 1939–45, 8th Bn The Royal Scots (The Royal Regt); commd 1939; SO (Capt.), 44th Lowland Brigade (15th Scottish Division), Normandy and NW Europe (despatches). *Publication:* From Normandy to the Baltic, 1945. *Recreation:* golf. *Address:* 13 Moray Place, Edinburgh EH3 6DT. *T:* 031–225 6637. *Clubs:* New, Honourable Company of Edinburgh Golfers (Captain 1970–72).

ROBERTSON OF OAKRIDGE, 2nd Baron *cr* 1961; **William Ronald Robertson;** Bt 1919; Member of the London Stock Exchange, since 1973; *b* 8 Dec. 1930; *s* of General Lord Robertson of Oakridge, GCB, GBE, KCMG, KCVO, DSO, MC, and Edith (*d* 1982), *d* of late J. B. Macindoe; *S* father, 1974; *m* 1972, Celia Jane, *d* of William R. Elworthy; one *s*. *Educ:* Hilton Coll., Natal; Charterhouse; Staff Coll., Camberley (psc). Served The Royal Scots Greys, 1949–69. Mem. Salters' Co (Master, 1985–86). *Heir: s* Hon. William Brian Elworthy Robertson, *b* 15 Nov. 1975. *Club:* Anglo-German Association.

ROBERTSON, Alan, OBE 1965; FRS 1964; FRSE 1966; BA; DSc; Deputy Chief Scientific Officer, ARC Unit of Animal Genetics, Edinburgh, 1966–85; *b* 21 Feb. 1920; *s* of late John Mouat Robertson and Annie Grace; *m* 1947, Margaret Sidney, *y d* of late Maurice Bernheim; two *s* one *d*. *Educ:* Liverpool Institute; Gonville and Caius College, Cambridge. Operational Research Section, Coastal Command, RAF, 1943–46. ARC Unit of Animal Genetics, Edinburgh, 1947–85. Hon. Prof., Edinburgh Univ., 1967. For. Assoc., Nat. Acad. of Sci., USA, 1979. Hon. Dr rer nat Univ. of Hohenheim, 1968; Hon. DAgrSc: Norway, 1984; Agricl Univ., Denmark, 1986. Gold Medal, Royal Agric. Soc., 1958. *Publications:* papers in scientific jls. *Recreations:* gardening, tennis. *Address:* 47 Braid Road, Edinburgh EH10 6AW. *T:* 031–447 4239. *Club:* Farmers'.

ROBERTSON, Prof. Sir Alexander, Kt 1970; CBE 1963; Professor of Tropical Animal Health, University of Edinburgh, 1971–78, now Emeritus Professor; Director: Veterinary Field Station, 1968–78; Centre for Tropical Veterinary Medicine, Edinburgh University, 1971–78; *b* 3 Feb. 1908; *m* 1936, Janet McKinlay; two *d*. *Educ:* Stonehaven Mackie Acad.; Aberdeen University; and Royal (Dick) Veterinary College, Edinburgh. MA Aberdeen, 1929; BSc Aberdeen, 1930; PhD Edinburgh, 1940; MRCVS, 1934. Demonstrator in Anatomy, Royal (Dick) Veterinary College, Edinburgh, 1934; Vet. Inspector, Min. of Agriculture, 1935–37; Sen. Lectr in Physiology, 1938–44, Prof. of Vet. Hygiene, 1944–53, William Dick Prof. of Animal Health, 1953–71, Director, 1957–63, Royal (Dick) School of Veterinary Studies, Univ. of Edinburgh; Dean of Faculty of Vet. Medicine, Univ. of Edinburgh, 1964–70. Exec. Officer for Scotland, Farm Livestock Emergency Service, 1942–47. FRSE, 1945; FRIC, 1946; FRSH, 1950; FRZSScot, 1952; Mem. Departmental Cttee on Foot and Mouth Disease, 1952–54; Pres. Brit. Vet. Assoc., 1954–55; Vice-Pres. Roy. Zoological Soc. of Scotland, 1959– (and Hon. Fellow); Mem. Governing Body, Animal Virus Research Inst., Pirbright, 1954–62; Member: Council Royal Coll. of Veterinary Surgeons, 1957–78 (Treasurer, 1964–67; Vice-Pres., 1967–68, 1969–70; Pres., 1968–69); Artificial Insemination Adv. Cttee for Scotland, 1958–65; ARC Tech. Adv. Cttee on Nutrient Requirements, 1959–78; Departmental Cttee of Inquiry into Fowl Pest, 1960–61; Governing Body Rowett Research Institute, 1962–77; ARC Adv. Cttee on Meat Research, 1968–73; Trustee, Internat. Laboratory for Res. in Animal Diseases, 1973–82 (Chm., 1980–81); Chairman: Sci. Adv. Panel, Pig Industry Develt Authority, 1962–68; Research Adv. Cttee, Meat and Livestock Commn, 1969–73; Vet. Adv. Panel, British Council, 1971–78; Member: FAO/WHO Expert Panel on Veterinary Educn, 1962–78; East African Natural Resources Research Council, 1963–78; Cttee of Inquiry into Veterinary Profession, 1971–75; Council, RSE, 1963–65, Vice-Pres., 1969–72; Inter Univ. Council, 1973–75. Editor, Jl of Tropical Animal Health and Production. Hon. FRCVS, 1970. Hon. Mem., World Veterinary Assoc., 1975. Hon. LLD Aberdeen, 1971; Hon. DVSc Melbourne, 1973. *Publications:* (ed) International Encyclopædia of Veterinary Medicine; numerous articles in veterinary and other scientific journals. *Recreations:* gardening, motoring, hill climbing. *Address:* 205 Mayfield Road, Edinburgh EH9 3BD. *T:* 031–667 1242. *Club:* New (Edinburgh).

ROBERTSON, Anne Elisabeth; *see* Mueller, A. E.

ROBERTSON, Prof. Anne Strachan, DLitt; FRSE; FSA, FSAScot; Titular Professor of Roman Archaeology, Glasgow University, 1974–75, retired; *d* of John Anderson Robertson and Margaret Purden. *Educ:* Hillhead High Sch.; Glasgow High Sch. for Girls; Glasgow Univ. (MA, DLitt); London Univ. (MA). FRSE 1975; FMA 1958; FRNS 1937; FSA 1958; FSAScot 1941. Glasgow University: Dalrymple Lectr in Archaeol., 1939; Under-Keeper, Hunterian Museum and Curator, Hunter Coin Cabinet, 1952; Reader in Roman Archaeol., Keeper of Cultural Collections and of Hunter Coin Cabinet, Hunterian Museum, 1964; Keeper of Roman Collections and of Hunter Coin Cabinet, 1974. Silver Medal, RNS, 1964; Silver Huntington Medal, Amer. Numismatic Soc., 1970. *Publications:* An Antonine Fort: Golden Hill, Duntocher, 1957; The Antonine Wall, 1960 (new edn 1979); Sylloge of Anglo-Saxon Coins in the Hunter Coin Cabinet, 1961; Catalogue of Roman Imperial Coins in the Hunter Coin Cabinet: Vol. 1, 1962; Vol. 2, 1971; Vol. 3, 1977; Vol. 4, 1978; Vol. 5, 1982; The Roman Fort at Castledykes, 1964; Birrens (Blatobulgium), 1975; contrib. to Britannia, Numismatic Chron., Proc. Soc. of Antiquaries of Scotland. *Recreations:* reading, writing, photography, walking, gardening. *Address:* 31 Upper Glenburn Road, Bearsden, Glasgow G61 4BN. *T:* 041–942 1136.

ROBERTSON, Bryan Charles Francis, OBE 1961; author, broadcasting and television, etc; regular contributor to The Spectator; *b* 1 April 1925; *yr s* of A. F. Robertson and Ellen Dorothy Black; unmarried. *Educ:* Battersea Grammar School. Worked and studied in France and Germany, 1947–48; Director: Heffer Gallery, Cambridge, 1949–51; Whitechapel Art Gallery, London, 1952–68. Mem. Arts Council Art Panel, 1958–61, 1980–84; Mem. Contemporary Art Soc. Cttee, 1958–73. US Embassy Grant to visit United States, 1956; Lectr on art, Royal Ballet School, 1958; Ford Foundn Grant for research for writing, 1961; British Council Lecture Tour, SE Asia and Australian State Galleries, 1960. Dir, State Univ. of NY Museum, 1970–75. Since 1953 has organized major exhibitions at Whitechapel, including Turner, Hepworth, Moore, Stubbs, John Martin, Rowlandson and Gillray, Bellotto, Mondrian, de Staël, Nolan, Davie, Smith, Malevich, Pollock, Richards, Australian Painting, Rothko, Tobey, Vaughan, Guston, Poliakof, Caro, Medley, etc. *Publications:* Jackson Pollock, a monograph, 1960; Sidney Nolan, a monograph, 1961; (jtly) Private View, 1965; (with H. Tatlock Miller) Loudon Sainthill, 1973; Edward Burra, 1978; contribs (art criticism) to London Magazine, Art News (US), Spectator, Harpers & Queen, Twentieth Century, Listener, Cambridge Review, Museums Jl, etc. *Address:* 73 Barnsbury Street, N1 1EJ. *Club:* Athenæum.

ROBERTSON, Prof. Charles Martin; FBA 1967; Lincoln Professor of Classical Archæology and Art, University of Oxford, 1961–78; *b* 11 Sept. 1911; *s* of late Professor Donald Struan Robertson, FBA, FSA, and Petica Coursolles Jones; *m* 1942, Theodosia Cecil Spring Rice (*d* 1984); four *s* two *d*. *Educ:* Leys School, Cambridge; Trinity College, Cambridge. BA Cambridge, 1934, MA 1947; student at British School of Archæology, Athens, 1934–36; Asst Keeper, Dept of Greek and Roman Antiquities, British Museum, 1936–48 (released for service, War of 1939–45, 1940–46); Yates Professor of Classical Art and Archæology in the Univ. of London (Univ. Coll.), 1948–61. Corresp. Mem., German Archæological Inst., 1953; Ordinary Mem., 1953; Chm., Man. Cttee, British School at Athens, 1958–68. Mem., Inst. for Advanced Study, Princeton, 1968–69. Guest Schol., J. Paul Getty Museum, Malibu, 1980. Hon. Fellow: Lincoln Coll., Oxford, 1980; UCL, 1980. For. Hon. Mem., Archaeological Inst. of America, 1985. Hon. DLit QUB, 1978. *Publications:* Why Study Greek Art? (Inaugural Lecture), 1949; Greek Painting, 1959; The Visual Arts of the Greeks (in The Greeks), 1962; Between Archæology and Art History (Inaugural Lecture), 1963; Crooked Connections (poems), 1970; indexes and editorial work in late Sir John Beazley's Paralipomena, 1971; For Rachel (poems), 1972; A History of Greek Art, 1975; (with Alison Frantz) The Parthenon Frieze, 1975; A Hot Bath at Bedtime (poems), 1977; The Sleeping Beauty's Prince (poem), 1977; (with John Boardman) Corpus Vasorum Antiquorum, Castle Ashby, 1978; A Shorter History of Greek Art, 1981; The Attic Black-figure and Red-figure Pottery, in Karageorghis, Excavations at Kition IV, 1981; (contrib.) Greek Religion and Society (ed P. E. Easterling and J. V. Muir), 1985; articles, notes and reviews since 1935, in British and foreign periodicals. *Address:* 7a Parker Street, Cambridge CB1 1JL. *T:* Cambridge 311913.

ROBERTSON, Charles Robert Suttie; Member, Management Committee of The Distillers Company plc, 1970–82, retired; chartered accountant; *b* 23 Nov. 1920; *s* of late David Young McLellan Robertson and Doris May Beaumont; *m* 1949, Shona MacGregor Riddel (*d* 1985), *d* of late Robert Riddel, MC, and Phyllis Mary Stewart; one *s*. *Educ:* Dollar Academy. Joined DCL group, 1949; appointed: Managing Director, Scottish Malt Distillers, 1960; Sec., DCL, 1966, Finance Director, 1967. *Recreation:* hill walking. *Address:* The Arch, Edzell, Angus DD9 7TF. *T:* Edzell 484.

ROBERTSON, Sheriff Daphne Jean Black, WS; Sheriff of Glasgow and Strathkelvin, since 1979; *b* 31 March 1937; *d* of Rev. Robert Black Kincaid and Ann Parker Collins; *m* 1965, Donald Buchanan Robertson, *qv*. *Educ:* Hillhead High Sch.; Greenock Acad.; Edinburgh Univ. (MA); Glasgow Univ. (LLB). Admitted solicitor, 1961; WS 1977. *Address:* Sheriff Court House, Glasgow G5 9DA. *Club:* New (Edinburgh).

ROBERTSON, David Lars Manwaring; JP; Director, Kleinwort, Benson, Lonsdale plc; *b* 29 Jan. 1917; *m* 1939, Pamela Lauderdale Meares; three *s*. *Educ:* Rugby; University Coll., Oxford. Served Welsh Guards, 1940–45. Man. Dir, Charterhouse Finance Corp. Ltd, 1945–55; joined Kleinwort, Sons & Co. Ltd, 1955; Dir, Kleinwort, Benson Ltd, 1955–81; Chairman: MK Electric Group plc, 1975 ; Provident Mutual Life Assurance Assoc., 1973–; Provident Mutual Managed Pensions Funds Ltd, 1974–; Director: Berry Bros and Rudd; The Rouse Co., Columbia, Maryland. JP Crowborough, 1971. *Recreations:* skiing, golf, fishing, shooting. *Address:* Kleinwort, Benson, Lonsdale plc, 20 Fenchurch Street, EC3P 3DB. *Clubs:* Boodle's, MCC.

ROBERTSON, Donald Buchanan, QC (Scot.) 1973; *b* 29 March 1932; *s* of Donald Robertson, yachtbuilder, Sandbank, Argyll, and Jean Dunsmore Buchanan; *m* 1st, 1955, Louise Charlotte, *d* of Dr J. Linthorst-Homan; one *s* one *d*; 2nd, 1965, Daphne Jean Black Kincaid (*see* D. J. B. Robertson). *Educ:* Dunoon Grammar Sch.; Glasgow Univ. (LLB). Admitted Solicitor, 1954; Royal Air Force (National Service), 1954–56. Passed Advocate, 1960; Standing Junior to Registrar of Restrictive Practices, 1970–73. Member: Sheriff Court Rules Council, 1972–76; Royal Commn on Legal Services in Scotland, 1976–80; Legal Aid Central Cttee, 1982–85; Criminal Injuries Compensation Bd, 1986; Chm., VAT Tribunal, 1978–85. Hon. Sheriff, Lothian and Peebles, 1982–. FSA (Scot.) 1982. *Recreations:* shooting, numismatics, riding. *Address:* 11 Grosvenor Crescent, Edinburgh EH12 5ED. *T:* 031–337 5544; Cranshaws Castle, By Duns, Berwickshire. *T:* Longformacus 268. *Clubs:* New (Edinburgh); RNVR (Glasgow).

ROBERTSON, Douglas William, CMG 1947; DSO 1918; MC 1918; *b* 30 Nov. 1898; 2nd surv. *s* of late Rev. J. A. Robertson, MA; *m* 1924, Mary Eagland (*d* 1968), *y d* of late W. E. Longbottom, Adelaide; no *c*. *Educ:* George Watson's College, Edinburgh. 2nd Lt KRRC, 1917; France, 1918 (wounded, MC, DSO, despatches); Administrative Service, Uganda, 1921–50; Resident of Buganda, 1945; Secretary for African Affairs, Uganda, 1947–50, retired, 1950. *Address:* 3a Ravelston Park, Edinburgh EH4 3DX. *Club:* East India, Devonshire, Sports and Public Schools.

ROBERTSON, Eric Desmond, OBE 1964; Controller, English Services, BBC External Services, and Deputy Managing Director, External Broadcasting, 1973–74; *b* 5 Oct. 1914; *s* of late Major Frank George Watt Robertson, Indian Army, and Amy Robertson (*née* Davidson); *m* 1943, Aileen Margaret Broadhead; two *s*. *Educ:* Aberdeen Grammar Sch.; Univ. of Aberdeen. BSc (Forestry) 1934, BSc 1936, Hunter Meml Prize, 1936. Scientific Adviser, Guthrie & Co. Ltd, Malaya, 1938–39; Malayan Forest Service, Asst Conservator, 1939–40. War of 1939–45: Malaya Command, on special duty, 1940–41. Producer, Malaya Broadcasting Corp., 1941–42; Special Officer, Far Eastern Broadcasting, All India Radio, 1942–45; Malay Editor, BBC, 1945–46; Far Eastern Service Organiser, BBC, 1946–49; Asst Head of Far Eastern Service, BBC, 1949–52; Head of Far Eastern Service, BBC, 1952–58; Head of Asian Services, BBC, 1958–64; Asst Controller, Overseas Services, BBC, 1964–70; Controller, Overseas Services, BBC, 1970–73. *Publication:* The Japanese File, 1979. *Address:* B2 Albany, Piccadilly, W1. *T:* 01–734 3355. *Club:* Naval and Military.

ROBERTSON, Francis Calder F.; *see* Ford Robertson.

ROBERTSON, George Islay Macneill; MP (Lab) Hamilton, since 1978; *b* 12 April 1946; *s* of George Phillip Robertson and Marion I. Robertson; *m* 1970, Sandra Wallace; two *s* one *d*. *Educ:* Dunoon Grammar Sch.; Univ. of Dundee (MA Hons 1968). Res. Asst, Tayside Study, 1968–69; Scottish Res. Officer, G&MWU, 1969–70, Scottish Organiser, 1970–78. PPS to Sec. of State for Social Services, 1979; opposition spokesman on Scottish Affairs, 1979–80, on Defence, 1980–81, on Foreign and Commonwealth Affairs, 1981–; principal spokesman on European Affairs, 1984–. Chm., Scottish Council of Labour Party, 1977–78; Mem., Scottish Exec. of Lab. Party, 1973–79; Sec., Manifesto Gp of PLP, 1979–84. Vice Chm. Bd, British Council, 1985–; Member: Bd, Scottish Develt Agency, 1975–78; Bd, Scottish Tourist Bd, 1974–76; Council, National Trust for Scotland, 1976–82 and 1983–85; Police Adv. Bd for Scotland, 1974–78; Council, British Atlantic Cttee, 1981–; Council, Operation Raleigh, 1982–; Governing Body, GB/E Europe Centre, 1983–; Council, RIIA, 1984–. Chm., Seatbelt Survivors Club, 1981–. *Publications:* articles in Contemp. Review, Financial Times and other pubns; contrib. management jls and trade press. *Recreations:* photography, golf. *Address:* House of Commons, SW1A 0AA. *T:* 01–219 3000; 3 Argyle Park, Dunblane, Central Scotland.

ROBERTSON, (Harold) Rocke, CC (Canada) 1969; MD, CM, FRCS(C), FRCSE, FACS, FRSC; Principal and Vice-Chancellor of McGill University, 1962–70; *b* 4 Aug. 1912; *s* of Harold Bruce Robertson and Helen McGregor Rogers; *m* 1937, Beatrice

Roslyn Arnold; three s one d. *Educ*: St Michael's Sch., Victoria, BC; Ecole Nouvelle, Switzerland; Brentwood College, Victoria, BC; McGill University. Montreal Gen. Hospital: rotating, 1936; pathology, 1937–38; Clin. Asst in Surg., Roy. Infirmary, Edinburgh, 1938–39; Demonstr in Anat., Middx Hosp. Med. Sch., 1939; Jun. Asst in Surg., Montreal Gen. Hosp., 1939–40; RCAMC, 1940–45; Chief of Surgery: Shaughnessy Hosp., DVA, Vancouver, 1945–59 (Prof. of Surg., Univ. of BC, 1950–59); Vancouver Gen. Hosp., 1950–59; Montreal Gen. Hosp., 1959–62 (Prof. of Surg., McGill University, 1959–62). Member: Nat. Research Coun., 1964; Science Council of Canada, 1976–82. Hon. DCL, Bishop's Univ., 1963; Hon. LLD: Manitoba, 1964; Toronto, 1964; Victoria, 1964; Glasgow, 1965; Michigan, 1967; Dartmouth, 1967; Sir George Williams, 1970; McGill, 1970; Hon. DSc: Brit. Columbia, 1964; Memorial, 1968; Jefferson Med. Coll., 1969; Dr de l'Univ., Montreal, 1965. FRSA 1963. *Publications*: article on wounds, Encyclopædia Britannica; numerous contribs to scientific journals and text books. *Recreations*: tennis, fishing, gardening, golf. *Address*: RR2, Mountain, Ontario K0E 1S0, Canada. *T*: 613–989–2967.

ROBERTSON of Brackla, Maj.-Gen. Ian Argyll, CB 1968; MBE 1947; MA; DL; Vice-Lord-Lieutenant, Highland Region (Nairn), since 1980; Representative in Scotland of Messrs Spink & Son, 1969–76; Chairman, Royal British Legion, Scotland, 1974–77 (Vice-Chairman, 1971–74); b 17 July 1913; 2nd s of John Argyll Robertson and Sarah Lilian Pitt Healing; m 1939, Marjorie Violet Isobel Duncan; two d. *Educ*: Winchester Coll.; Trinity Coll., Oxford. Commnd Seaforth Highlanders, 1934; Brigade Major: 152 Highland Bde, 1943; 231 Infantry Bde, 1944; GSO2, Staff College, Camberley, 1944–45; AAG, 15 Indian Corps, 1945–46; GSO1, 51 Highland Div., 1952–54; Comdg 1st Bn Seaforth Highlanders, 1954–57; Comdg Support Weapons Wing, 1957–59; Comdg 127 (East Lancs) Inf. Bde, TA, 1959–61; Nat. Defence College, Delhi, 1962–63; Comdg School of Infantry, 1963–64; Commanding 51st Highland Division, 1964–66; Director of Army Equipment Policy, Ministry of Defence, 1966–68; retd. Mem. Council, Nat. Trust for Scotland, 1972–75. DL Nairn 1973. *Recreations*: various in a minor way. *Address*: Brackla House, Nairn. *T*: Cawdor 220. *Clubs*: Army and Navy, MCC; Vincent's (Oxford).

ROBERTSON, Rear-Adm. Ian George William, CB 1974; DSC 1944; b 21 Oct. 1922; s of late W. H. Robertson, MC, and Mrs A. M. Robertson; m 1947, Barbara Irène Holdsworth; one s one d. *Educ*: Radley College. Joined RNVR, 1941; qual. Pilot; Sub-Lt 1943; air strike ops against enemy shipping and attacks against German battleship Tirpitz, 1944 (DSC); Lieut, RN, 1945; flying and instructional appts, 1944–53; Comdr (Air): RNAS Culdrose, 1956; HMS Albion, 1958; in comd: HMS Keppel, 1960; HMS Mohawk, 1963; RNAS Culdrose, 1965; HMS Eagle, 1970; Admiral Comdg Reserves, 1972–74; retd 1974. Comdr 1954; Captain 1963; Rear-Adm. 1972; idc 1968. Dir-Gen., Navy League, 1975–76; Scoutreach Resources Organiser, Scout Assoc., 1976–79. *Recreations*: golf, sailing, fishing. *Address*: Moons Oast, Barcombe Road, Piltdown, Sussex TN22 3XG. *T*: Newick 2279. *Clubs*: Naval; Rye Golf, Piltdown Golf.

ROBERTSON, Ian Macbeth, CB 1976; LVO 1956; JP; Secretary of Commissions for Scotland, 1978–83; b 1 Feb. 1918; s of late Sheriff-Substitute J. A. T. Robertson; m 1947, Anne Stewart Marshall. *Educ*: Melville College; Edinburgh University. Served War of 1939–45 in Middle East and Italy; Royal Artillery and London Scottish, Captain. Entered Dept of Health for Scotland, 1946. Private Secretary to Minister of State, Scottish Office, 1951–52 and to Secretary of State for Scotland, 1952–55. Asst Secretary, Dept of Health for Scotland, 1955; Assistant Under-Secretary of State, Scottish Office, 1963–64; Under-Secretary: Scottish Development Department, 1964–65; Scottish Educn Dept, 1966–78. Mem., Williams Cttee on Nat. Museums and Galls in Scotland, 1979–81. Chm. of Governors, Edinburgh Coll. of Art, 1981–. JP Edinburgh 1978. *Address*: Napier House, 8 Colinton Road, Edinburgh EH10 5DS. *T*: 031–447 4636. *Club*: New (Edinburgh).

ROBERTSON, Ian Macdonald; see Robertson, Hon. Lord.

ROBERTSON, James, CBE 1969; MA; FRCM; Hon. FTCL; Hon. GSM; Hon. RAM; b 17 June 1912; s of Ainslie John Robertson and Phyllis Mary Roughton; m 1st, 1949, Rachel June Fraser (d 1979); one s (and one s decd); 2nd, 1980, Oswalda Viktoria Pattrick. *Educ*: Winchester College; Trinity College, Cambridge; Conservatorium, Leipzig; Royal College of Music, London. On musical staff, Glyndebourne Opera, 1937–39; Conductor, Carl Rosa Opera, Co., 1938–39; Conductor, Canadian Broadcasting Corp., 1939–40; Air Ministry, 1940–42; RAFVR (Intelligence), 1942–46. Director, Sadler's Wells Opera Company, 1946–54; Conductor of National Orchestra of New Zealand Broadcasting Service, Sept. 1954–Nov. 1957. Conductor, Touring Opera, 1958; Adviser on Opera, Théâtre de la Monnaie, Brussels, 1960–61; Artistic and Musical Director, New Zealand Opera Co., 1962–63; Dir, London Opera Centre, 1964–77, Consultant, 1977–78; Musical Dir, Nat. Opera of NZ, 1979–81. *Recreation*: languages. *Address*: Ty Helyg, Llwynmawr, Pontfadog, Llangollen, Clwyd LL20 7BG. *T*: Glynceiriog 480.

ROBERTSON, Maj.-Gen. James Alexander Rowland, CB 1958; CBE 1956 (OBE 1949; MBE 1942); DSO 1944 (Bar 1945); DL; b 23 March 1910; s of Colonel James Currie Robertson, CIE, CMG, CBE, IMS, and Catherine Rowland Jones; m 1st, 1949, Ann Madeline Tosswill (d 1949); 2nd, Joan Wills (née Abercromby), widow of R. L. Wills, CBE, MC. *Educ*: Aysgarth School; Epsom College, RMC, Sandhurst. Commissioned 2 Lieutenant IA, 1930, attached 1st KOYLI; posted 6th Gurkha Rifles, 1931; Instructor Sch. of Physical Training, 1936–37; Staff Coll., Quetta, July-Dec. 1941; Bde Major 1 (Maymyo) Bde, Jan.-June, 1942; Bde Major, 106 I Inf. Bde, 1942–44; Comdr 1/7 Gurkha Rifles, 1944–45; Comdr 48 Ind. Inf. Bde, 1945–47; GSO 1, Instr Staff Coll., Quetta, June-Nov., 1947; Comdr 1/6th Gurkha Rifles, 1947–48; GSO 1 Gurkha Planning Staff, March-June, 1948; GSO 1 Malaya comd, June-Nov. 1948; BGS 1948–49. GSO 1, War Office, 1950–52; Col GS, 1 Corps, Germany, 1952–54; Comdr 51 Indep. Bde, 1955–57; Commander 17 Gurkha Division Overseas Commonwealth Land Forces, and Maj.-Gen. Brigade of Gurkhas, 1958–61; GOC Land Forces, Middle East Command, 1961–63; Gurkha Liaison Officer, War Office, 1963–64, retd. Personnel Dir, NAAFI, 1964–69. Colonel, 6th Queen Elizabeth's Own Gurkha Rifles, 1961–69; Chm., 1968–80, Pres. 1980–, Gurkha Brigade Assoc. DL Greater London, 1977. *Recreations*: fishing, sculpture, an outdoor life.

ROBERTSON, Sir James (Anderson), Kt 1968; CBE 1963 (OBE 1949; MBE 1942); QPM 1961; b Glasgow, 8 April 1906; s of James Robertson, East Haugh, Pitlochry, Perthshire and later of Glasgow, and Mary Rankin Anderson, Glasgow; m 1942, Janet Lorraine Gilfillan Macfarlane, Largs, Ayrshire; two s one d. *Educ*: Provanside Sch., Glasgow and Glasgow Univ. BL 1936. Chief Constable of Glasgow, 1960–71. Chairman: Scotland Cttee; Nat. Children's Home; Glasgow Standing Conf. of Voluntary Youth Organisations; Hon. President: Glasgow Bn Boys' Brigade. OStJ 1964. *Recreations*: golf and gardening. *Address*: 3 Kirklee Road, Glasgow G12 0RL. *T*: 041–339 4400.

ROBERTSON, James Geddes, CMG 1961; formerly Under-Secretary, Department of the Environment, and Chairman, Northern Economic Planning Board, 1965–71, retired 1971; b 29 Nov. 1910; s of late Captain A. M. Robertson, Portsoy, Banffshire; m 1939, Marion Mitchell Black; one s one d. *Educ*: Fordyce Academy, Banffshire; George Watson's

College, Edinburgh; Edinburgh University. Kitchener Schol., 1928–32, MA 1st cl. Hons History (Edinburgh), 1932. Entered Ministry of Labour as Third Class Officer, 1933; Principal, 1943; on exchange to Commonwealth Dept of Labour and Nat. Service, Australia, 1947–49; Asst Sec., Min of Labour, 1956; Member of Government Delegations to Governing Body and Conference of ILO, 1956–60, and Social Cttee, Council of Europe, 1953–61; Safety and Health Dept, 1961–63; Training Department, Ministry of Labour, 1963–65. Member: Industrial Tribunals Panel, 1971–73; Northern Rent Scrutiny Bd, 1973–74; Rent Assessment Panel for Scotland, 1975–81. Served War of 1939–45, RAF 1942–45. *Address*: 12a Abbotsford Crescent, Edinburgh EH10 5DY. *T*: 031–447 4675.

ROBERTSON, Maj.-Gen. James Howden, CB 1974; Director, Army Dental Service, 1970–74; b 16 Oct. 1915; s of John and Marion Robertson, Glasgow and Creetown; m 1942, Muriel Edna, d of Alfred Jefferies, Elgin; two s one d. *Educ*: White Hill Sch., Glasgow; Glasgow Dental Hospital. LDS, RFPS(G) 1939; FDS, RCSE 1957. Lieut, Army Dental Corps, 1939; Captain 1940; Major 1943; Lt-Col 1954; Col 1962; Brig. 1967; Maj.-Gen. 1970. Served in UK and Norway, 1939–44, Europe, 1944–50; Senior Specialist in Dental Surgery, 1957; Middle East, 1958–61; Consultant, CMH Aldershot, 1962–67; Consulting Dental Surgeon to the Army, 1967–70. Col Comdt, RADC, 1975–80. QHDS, 1967–74. Pres., Oral Surgery Club of GB, 1975–76. OStJ 1969. *Publications*: various articles in medical and dental jls on oral and maxillo-facial surgery. *Recreations*: wildfowling, fishing, gardening. *Address*: Struan, Hethfelton Hollow, East Stoke, Dorset. *T*: Bindon Abbey 462272.

ROBERTSON, Rev. Canon James Smith, OBE 1984; Canon Emeritus, Zambia, 1965; Secretary, United Society for the Propagation of the Gospel, 1973–83; a Chaplain to the Queen, since 1980; Vice-President, British Council of Churches, 1984–March 1987; b 4 Sept. 1917; s of Stuart Robertson and Elizabeth Mann Smith, Forfar; m 1950, Margaret Isabel Mina Mounsey; one d. *Educ*: Glasgow Univ.; Edinburgh Theol Coll.; London Univ. MA Glasgow 1938; PCE London 1953. Curate, St Salvador's, Edinburgh, 1940–45; Mission Priest, UMCA, N Rhodesia, 1945–50; St Mark's Coll., Mapanza, 1950–55; Chalimbana Trng Coll., Lusaka, 1955–65, Principal 1958–65; Head, Educn Dept, Bede Coll., Durham, 1965–68; Sec., Church Colls of Educn, Gen. Synod Bd of Educn, 1968–73. Chm., Conf. for World Mission, BCC, 1977–81. *Publications*: contributed to: Education in South Africa, 1970; The Training of Teachers, 1972; Values and Moral Development in Higher Education, 1974; Grow or Die, 1981; A Dictionary of Religious Education, 1984. *Recreations*: music, electronics, philosophy. *Address*: 13 Onslow Mansions, Onslow Avenue, Richmond, Surrey TW10 6QD. *T*: 01–940 8574.

ROBERTSON, Jean, CBE 1986; RRC 1981; Matron-in-Chief, Queen Alexandra's Royal Naval Nursing Service, 1983–86; Director of Defence Nursing Services, Ministry of Defence, and Director of Royal Naval Nursing Services, 1985–86; b 21 Sept. 1928; d of late Alexander Robertson and of Jean Robertson (née McCartney). *Educ*: Mary Erskine's School for Girls, Edinburgh. Registered Sick Children's Nurse, 1948, General Nurse, 1951; Ward Sister, Edinburgh Sick Children's Hospital, 1953; QARNNS 1955; QHNS, 1983–86. SSStJ 1981. *Recreations*: gardening, reading. *Address*: 14 The Haven, Alverstoke, Hants PO12 2BD. *T*: Gosport 82301. *Club*: Soroptimists' International.

ROBERTSON, John; b 3 Feb. 1913; s of William Robertson; m 1st, 1939 (marr. diss. 1977); two s three d; 2nd, 1977, June Robertson (d 1978); 3rd, 1979, Mrs Sheena Lynch. *Educ*: elementary and secondary schools. Formerly District Secretary and Assistant Divisional Organizer of the Amalgamated Engineering Union, West of Scotland. Mem., Lanarkshire County Council, Motherwell and Wishaw Town Council, 1946–52. Member of Labour Party, 1943–; contested (Lab) Scotstoun Division of Glasgow, General Election, Oct. 1951; MP Paisley, (Lab) Apr. 1961–76, (SLP) 1976–79. Among the founders of the Scottish Labour Party, Jan. 1976. *Recreations*: politics, painting, bowling and Trade Union. *Address*: 28 Davidson Place, Ayr. *T*: Ayr 261849.

ROBERTSON, Maj.-Gen. John Carnegie; Director of Army Legal Services, Ministry of Defence, 1973–76; b 24 Nov. 1917; s of late Sir William C. F. Robertson, KCMG and Dora (née Whelan); m 1961, Teresa Mary Louise, d of Cecil T. Porter. *Educ*: Cheltenham Coll.; RMC, Sandhurst. Served War of 1939–45: Officer in Gloucestershire Regt (PoW, Germany, 1940). Called to the Bar, Gray's Inn, 1949. Joined Judge Advocate's Dept, 1948; served subseq. in Middle East, BAOR, East Africa and the Far East. Dep. Dir, Army Legal Services, HQ, BAOR, 1971–73. Steward, Nat. Greyhound Racing Club, 1984. *Address*: Berry House, Nuffield, Henley-on-Thames, Oxon. *T*: Nettlebed 641740. *Clubs*: Naval and Military; Huntercombe Golf, St Enodoc Golf, Senior Golfers' Soc.

ROBERTSON, John David H.; see Home Robertson.

ROBERTSON, Rear Adm. John Keith, CB 1983; FIEE, FBIM; consultant; b 16 July 1926; s of G. M. and J. L. Robertson; m 1951, Kathleen (née Bayntun); one s three d. *Educ*: RNC Dartmouth; Clare Coll., Cambridge (BA 1949). FIEE 1981; FBIM 1980. RNC Dartmouth, 1940–43; served, 1943–83 (Clare Coll., Cambridge, 1946–49): HM Ships Queen Elizabeth, Zest, Gabbard, Aisne and Decoy; Staff, RNC Dartmouth; Grad. Recruiting; Weapon Engr Officer, HMS Centaur; Comdr, RNEC Manadon; RCDS; Captain Technical Intell. (Navy), 1974–76; Captain Fleet Maintenance, Portsmouth, 1976–78; Dir, Naval Recruiting, 1978–79; Dir, Management and Support of Intelligence, MoD, 1980–82; ACDS (Intelligence), 1982–83. *Recreations*: hockey, tennis, golf, wood carving. *Address*: Alpina, Kingsdown, Corsham, Wilts SN14 9BJ. *Clubs*: Pilgrims; Corkscrew (Bath).

ROBERTSON, John Monteath, CBE 1962; FRS 1945; FRSC, FInstP, FRSE; MA, PhD, DSc (Glasgow); Gardiner Professor of Chemistry, University of Glasgow, 1942–70, now Professor Emeritus; Director of Laboratories, 1955–70; b 24 July 1900; s of William Robertson and Jane Monteath, of Nether Fordun, Auchterarder; m 1930, Stella Kennard Nairn, MA; two s one d. *Educ*: Perth Academy; Glasgow University. Commonwealth Fellow, USA, 1928; Member staff of Davy Faraday Laboratory of Royal Institution, 1930; Senior Lecturer in Physical Chemistry, University of Sheffield, 1939; Scientific Adviser (Chemical) to Bomber Command, 1941; Hon. Scientific Adviser to RAF, 1942. George Fisher Baker Lecturer, Cornell Univ., USA, 1951; Visiting Prof., Univ. of California, Berkeley, USA, 1958. Member, University Grants Committee, 1960–65; President, Chemical Society, 1962–64. Corresp. Member Turin Academy of Sciences, 1962. Hon. LLD Aberdeen, 1963; Hon. DSc Strathclyde, 1970. Davy Medal, Royal Soc., 1960; Longstaff Medal, Chemical Soc., 1966; Paracelsus Medal, Swiss Chem. Soc., 1971; Gregori Aminoff Medal, Royal Swedish Acad., 1983. *Publications*: Organic Crystals and Molecules, 1953; papers and articles on chemical, physical, and X-ray diffraction subjects in Proc. Royal Soc., Jl of Chem. Soc., etc. *Address*: 11a Eriskay Road, Inverness IV2 3LX. *T*: Inverness 225561. *Club*: Athenæum.

ROBERTSON, John Windeler; Deputy Chairman, Barclays de Zoete Wedd (BZW), since 1986; b 9 May 1934; s of John Bruce Robertson and Evelyn Windeler Robertson; m 1959, Jennifer-Ann Gourdou (marr. diss.); one s one d. *Educ*: Winchester Coll. National Service, RNVR, 1953–55. Joined Wedd Jefferson & Co. (Members of Stock Exchange),

1955; Partner, 1961; Sen. Partner, Wedd Durlacher Mordaunt, 1979–86. Dep. Chm., Stock Exchange, 1976–79 (Mem. Council, 1966–). Mem., City Capital Markets' Cttee, 1981–. *Recreations:* golf, deer stalking, motor boating. *Address:* Flat 9, 4 Tedworth Square, SW3 4DY. *T:* 01-351 7918. *Club:* City of London.

ROBERTSON, Julia Ann; *see* Burdus, J. A.

ROBERTSON, Lewis, CBE 1969; FRSE; industrialist and administrator; Chairman: F. H. Lloyd Holdings plc, since 1982; Triplex plc, since 1983; National Girobank Scotland, since 1984; Thomas Borthwick & Sons plc, since 1985; Director, Scottish and Newcastle Breweries plc, since 1975; *b* 28 Nov. 1922; *s* of John Farquharson Robertson and Margaret Arthur; *m* 1950, Elspeth Badenoch; three *s* one *d*. *Educ:* Trinity Coll., Glenalmond. Accountancy training; RAF Intelligence. Chm., 1968–70, and Man. Dir, 1965–70, Scott & Robertson Ltd; Chief Executive, 1971–76, and Dep. Chm., 1973–76, Grampian Holdings Ltd; Mem, 1975–76, Dep. Chm. and Chief Exec., Scottish Develt Agency, 1976–81. Chm. Eastern Regional Hosp. Bd (Scotland), 1960–70; Trustee (Exec. Cttee), Carnegie Trust for Univs of Scotland, 1963–; Member: Provincial Synod, Episcopal Church of Scotland, 1963–83 (Chm. Policy Cttee, 1974–76); (Sainsbury) Cttee of Enquiry, Pharmaceutical Industry, 1965–67; Court (Finance Convener), Univ. of Dundee, 1967–70; Monopolies and Mergers Commn, 1969–76; Arts Council of GB (and Chm., Scottish Arts Council), 1970–71; Scottish Economic Council, 1977–83; Scottish Postal Bd, 1984–; British Council, 1978– (Chm., Scottish Adv. Cttee); Council, Scottish Business School, 1978–82; Restrictive Practices Court, 1983–; Edinburgh Univ. Press Cttee, 1985–; Bd, Friends of Royal Scottish Acad., 1986–; Chm., Bd for Scotland, BIM, 1981–83. Mem., Adv. Bd, critical edn of Waverley novels, 1984–. Trustee, Foundn for Study of Christianity and Society, 1980–. FRSE 1978; FRSA 1981; CBIM 1976. Hon. LLD Dundee, 1971. *Recreations:* work, foreign travel, computer use, music, reading, things Italian. *Address:* 32 Saxe Coburg Place, Edinburgh EH3 5BP. *T:* 031-332 5221. *Clubs:* Athenæum; New (Edinburgh).

ROBERTSON, Commandant Dame Nancy (Margaret), DBE 1957 (CBE 1953; OBE 1946); retired as Director of Women's Royal Naval Service (Dec. 1954–April 1958); *b* 1 March 1909; *er d* of Rev. William Cowper Robertson and Jessie Katharine (*née* McGregor). *Educ:* Esdaile School, Edinburgh; Paris. Secretarial work, London and Paris, 1928–39; WRNS, 1939. *Recreations:* needlework, gardening. *Address:* 14 Osborne Way, Wigginton, Tring, Herts. *T:* Tring 2560.

ROBERTSON, Prof. Noel Farnie, CBE 1978; BSc Edinburgh; MA Cantab; PhD Edinburgh; FRSE; Professor of Agriculture and Rural Economy, University of Edinburgh, and Principal, East of Scotland College of Agriculture, 1969–83; Chairman of Governors, Scottish Crop Research Institute, since 1983 (Governor since 1973); *b* 24 Dec. 1923; *o s* of late James Robertson and Catherine Landles Robertson (*née* Brown); *m* 1948, Doreen Colina Gardner; two *s* two *d*. *Educ:* Trinity Academy, Edinburgh; University of Edinburgh; Trinity College, Cambridge. Plant Pathologist, West African Cacao Research Institute, 1946–48; Lecturer in Botany, University of Cambridge, 1948–59; Prof. of Botany, Univ. of Hull, 1959–69. Pres., British Mycol Soc., 1965; Trustee, Royal Botanic Garden, Edinburgh, 1986–. *Address:* Woodend, Juniper Bank, Walkerburn, Peeblesshire. *Club:* Farmers'.

ROBERTSON, Patrick Allan Pearson, CMG 1956; *b* 11 Aug. 1913; *s* of A. N. McI. Robertson; *m* 1st, 1939, Penelope Margaret Gaskell (*d* 1966); one *s* two *d*; 2nd, 1975, Lady Stewart-Richardson. *Educ:* Sedbergh School; King's College, Cambridge. Cadet, Tanganyika, 1936; Asst Dist Officer, 1938; Clerk of Exec. and Legislative Councils, 1945–46; Dist Officer, 1948; Principal Asst Sec., 1949; Financial Sec., Aden, 1951; Asst Sec., Colonial Office, 1956–57; Chief Sec., Zanzibar, 1958; Civil Sec., Zanzibar, 1961–64; Deputy British Resident, Zanzibar, 1963–64; retired, 1964. Associate Member, Commonwealth Parliamentary Association. Freeman, City of London. *Recreations:* golf, tennis, fishing. *Address:* Lynedale, Longcross, Chertsey, Surrey. *T:* Ottershaw 2329. *Club:* Royal Commonwealth Society.

See also Sir Simon Stewart-Richardson, Bt.

ROBERTSON, (Richard) Ross, RSA, FRBS; DA; sculptor; *b* Aberdeen, 10 Sept. 1914; *s* of Rev. R. R. Robertson; *m* Kathleen May Matts; two *d*. *Educ:* Glasgow School of Art; Gray's School of Art, Aberdeen (DA). Lectr, Gray's Sch. of Art, 1946–79. FRBS 1963 (ARBS 1951); RSA 1977 (ARSA 1969). *Recreation:* study of art. *Address:* Creaguir, Woodlands Road, Rosemount, Blairgowrie, Perthshire.

ROBERTSON, Robert, CBE 1967; JP; Member, Strathclyde Regional Council, 1974–86; *b* 15 Aug. 1909; *s* of late Rev. William Robertson, MA; *m* 1938, Jean, *d* of late James Moffatt, MA, Invermay, Broomhill, Glasgow; one *s* one *d*. *Educ:* Forres Academy; Royal Technical Coll., Glasgow. Civil Engr, retd 1969. Mem., Eastwood Dist Council, 1952–58; Chm., Renfrewshire Educn Cttee, 1962–73; Convener, Renfrewshire County Council, 1973–75 (Mem., 1958); Mem., Convention of Scottish Local Authorities, 1975–86. Chm., Sec. of State's Cttee on Supply and Trng of Teachers for Further Educn, 1962–78; Chm., Nat. Cttee for Inservice Trng of Teachers, 1965–78. Mem. Scottish Council for: Research in Educn, 1962–80; Commercial Admin. and Professional Educn, 1960–69; Development of Industry, 1973–75. Chm., Sch. of Further Educn for training of teachers in Scotland, 1969–83. Governor: Jordanhill Coll. of Educn, 1966–83; Watt Memorial and Reid Kerr Colls, 1966–75, 1977–86. Member: Scottish Nat. School Camps Assoc., 1975–80; Scottish Assoc. of Young Farmers' Clubs, 1975–83; Glasgow Educnl Trust, 1978–86; Hutchison Educnl Trust, 1978–86; Council, Glasgow Coll. of Bldg and Printing, 1978–86. Fellow, Educnl Inst. of Scotland (FEIS), at Stirling Univ., 1970; Hon. Warden, Co. of Renfrew, Ont., Canada, 1970. JP Renfrewshire, 1958. *Publications:* Robertson Report on: The Training of Teachers in Further Education (HMSO), 1965. *Recreations:* fishing, painting. *Address:* 24 Broadwood Park, Alloway, Ayrshire. *T:* Alloway 43820; Castlehill, Maybole, Ayrshire. *T:* Dunure 337. *Clubs:* RNVR (Scotland); SV Carrick, Clarkston Rugby (Glasgow).

ROBERTSON, Robert Henry; Permanent Representative of Australia to the Office of the United Nations in Geneva, since 1984; *b* 23 Dec. 1929; *s* of James Rowland Robertson and Hester Mary (*née* Kay); *m*; 2nd, 1958, Jill Bryant Uther (marr. diss. 1982); two *s* one *d*; 3rd, 1986, Isabelle Costa de Beauvegard, *d* of Comte and Comtesse Reré Costa de Beauvegard. *Educ:* Geelong Church of England Grammar Sch.; Trinity Coll., Univ. of Melbourne (LLB). Third Secretary, Australian High Commn, Karachi, 1954–56; Second Sec., Mission to UN, New York, 1958–61; First Sec., later Counsellor, Washington, 1964–67; Ambassador to Jugoslavia, Romania and Bulgaria, 1971–73; Asst Sec., Personnel Br., Dept of Foreign Affairs, Canberra, 1974–75; First Asst Sec., Western Div., 1975–76, Management and Foreign Service Div., 1976–77; Ambassador to Italy, 1977–81; Dep. High Comr in London, 1981–84. *Address:* c/o Australian Permanent Mission to Office of UN, 56–58 Rue de Moillebeau, Petit Saconnex, 1211 Geneva 19, Switzerland. *T:* 346200. *Club:* Commonwealth (Canberra).

ROBERTSON, Ronald Foote, CBE 1980; MD, FRCP, FRCPE, FRCPGlas; Physician to the Queen in Scotland, 1977–85; *b* 27 Dec. 1920; *s* of Thomas Robertson and Mary Foote; *m* 1949, Dorothy Tweedy Wilkinson; two *d* (and one *d* decd). *Educ:* Perth Acad.; Univ. of Edinburgh. MB, ChB (Hons) 1945; MD (High Commendation) 1953; FRCPEdin. 1952; FRCP London 1969; FRCPGlas 1978. Consultant Physician: Leith Hosp., 1959–74; Deaconess Hosp., 1958–83; Royal Infirmary of Edinburgh, 1975–. Sec., RCPEdin., 1958–63; Vice-Pres., 1973–76; Pres., 1976–79. Principal MO, Scottish Life Assce Co., 1968–86. Mem., Assoc. of Phys. of Gt Britain and Ireland; Pres., BMA, 1983–84. Has served on numerous NHS cttees; Mem. GMC, 1979–. Hon. Fellow, Coll. of Physicians and Surgeons, Pakistan, 1977; Hon. FACP 1978; Hon. FRCPI 1978; Hon. FRACP 1979. *Publications:* several articles in scientific jls. *Recreations:* gardening, curling, fishing. *Address:* 15 Wester Coates Terrace, Edinburgh EH12 5LR. *T:* 031–337 6377. *Clubs:* New, University Staff (Edinburgh).

ROBERTSON, Ross; *see* Robertson, R. R.

ROBERTSON, Prof. Sir Rutherford (Ness), AC 1980; Kt 1972; CMG 1968; DSc; PhD; FRS 1961; FAA; Emeritus Professor; Hon. Visitor, School of Biological Sciences, University of Sydney, since 1979; *b* 29 Sept. 1913; *o c* of Rev. J. Robertson, MA, and Josephine Robertson; *m* 1937, Mary Helen Bruce Rogerson; one *s*. *Educ:* St Andrew's Coll., NZ; Univ. of Sydney; St John's Coll., Cambridge (Hon. Fellow 1973). DSc Sydney 1961; FAA 1954. Sydney Univ. Science Res. Schol., 1934–35, Linnean Macleay Fell., 1935–36. Exhibn of 1851 Res. Schol., 1936–39; Res. at Botany Sch., Cambridge, in plant physiology, 1936–39, PhD 1939; Asst Lectr, later Lectr, Botany Sch., Univ. of Sydney, 1939–46; Sen. Res. Offr, later Chief Res. Offr, Div. of Food Preservation, CSIRO, 1946–59 (res. in plant physiol. and biochem.); Sydney University: jointly in charge of Plant Physiol. Unit, 1952–59, Hon. Res. Associate, 1954–59; Visiting Prof., Univ. of Calif, Los Angeles, 1958–59; Kerney Foundn Lectr, Univ. of Calif, Berkeley, 1959; Mem. Exec., CSIRO 1959–62; Prof. of Botany, Univ. of Adelaide, 1962–69, now Emeritus; Dir, Res. Sch. of Biol Scis, ANU, 1973–78, now Emeritus Professor (Master, University House, 1969–72); Pro-Chancellor, ANU, 1984–. Chm., Aust. Res. Grants Cttee, 1965–69; Dep. Chm., Aust. Sci. and Tech. Council, 1977–81. Pres. Linnean Soc. of NSW, 1949; Hon. Sec. Austr. Nat. Res. Council, 1951–55; President: Australian Academy of Science, 1970–74 (Sec. Biological Sciences, 1957–58); Aust. and NZ Assoc. for the Advancement of Science, 1964–66; XIII Internat. Botanical Congress, Sydney, 1981; Corresp. Mem., Amer. Soc. of Plant Physiologists, 1953; For. Associate, US Nat. Acad. of Scis, 1962; Hon. Mem., Royal Soc. of NZ, 1971; Hon. FRSE 1983; For. Mem., Amer. Philosophical Soc., 1971; For. Hon. Mem., Amer. Acad. of Arts and Scis, 1973. Hon. DSc: Tasmania, 1965; Monash, 1970; ANU, 1979; Hon ScD Cambridge, 1969. Clarke Meml Medal, Royal Soc. of NSW, 1955; Farrer Meml Medal, 1963; ANZAAS Medal, 1968; Mueller Medal, 1970; Burnet Medal, 1975. *Publications:* (with G. E. Briggs, FRS, and A. B. Hope) Electrolytes and Plant Cells, 1961; Protons, Electrons, Phosphorylation and Active Transport, 1968; The Lively Membranes, 1983; various scientific papers on plant physiology and biochemistry. *Recreations:* reading, water colours. *Address:* School of Biological Sciences, A12, University of Sydney, NSW 2006, Australia. *Club:* Union (Sydney).

ROBERTSON, Toby, (Sholto David Maurice Robertson), OBE 1978; Director, theatre, opera and television; Director, Theatr Clwyd, Mold, since 1985; *b* 29 Nov. 1928; *s* of David Lambert Robertson and Felicity Douglas (*née* Tomlin); *m* 1963, Teresa Jane McCulloch (marr. diss. 1981); two *s* two *d*. *Educ:* Stowe; Trinity Coll., Cambridge (BA 1952, MA 1981). Formerly an actor. Dir. first prof. prodn, The Iceman Cometh, New Shakespeare, Liverpool, 1958. Dir. plays, London, Pitlochry and Richmond, Yorks, and for RSC, 1959–63. Director of over 40 prodns for Prospect Theatre Co., incl.: 1964: The Soldier's Fortune; You Never Can Tell; The Confederacy; The Importance of Being Earnest; 1965: The Square; Howard's End; The Man of Mode; 1966: Macbeth; The Tempest; The Gamecock; 1967: A Murder of No Importance; A Room with a View (Edinburgh Fest.; co-Dir for London season, 1975); 1968: Twelfth Night (also 1973, 1978); No Man's Land; The Beggar's Opera (also Edinburgh and London; for Phoenix Opera, 1972); The Servant of Two Masters (London); 1969: Edward II (also Edinburgh and London); 1970: Much Ado About Nothing (also Edinburgh); Boswell's Life of Johnson (also Edinburgh); Venice Preserved; 1971: King Lear (also 1978), and Love's Labour's Lost (Edinburgh, Australian tour, London); Alice in Wonderland (Ashcroft, Croydon); 1972: Richard III; Ivanov (also 1978); 1973: The Grand Tour (also 1978, 1979); Twelfth Night, Pericles, and The Royal Hunt of the Sun (internat. festivals, Moscow, Leningrad and Hong Kong); 1974: The Pilgrim's Progress (also Edinburgh and Round House, 1975); A Month in the Country (Chichester Fest.; London season, 1975); 1977: Hamlet (also 1979), War Music, and Antony and Cleopatra (Edinburgh, ME Fest., London); Smith of Smiths (also 1978, 1979); Buster (Edinburgh); 1978: The Lunatic, The Lover and The Poet (also 1979); 1979: Romeo and Juliet; The Government Inspector; The Padlock; Hamlet, Elsinore, 1979 and 1st visit by British co., China, 1980, Old Vic Co.; 1980: Next Time I'll Sing to You, Greenwich; Beggar's Opera, Lyric, Hammersmith; Pericles, NY (OBIE Award for outstanding direction, 1981); 1981: Measure for Measure, People's Arts Theatre, Peking; The Revenger's Tragedy, NY (Villager Award for outstanding treatment of classical text, 1982); Night and Day (opening prodn), 1982 and The Taming of the Shrew, 1983, Huntingdon Theatre Co., Boston; 1983: The Tempest (opening prodn), New Cleveland Playhouse; Love's Labour's Lost, Shakespeare Workshop, also Circle Rep., NYC, 1984; 1984: York Cycle of Mystery Plays, York Fest.; 1985: Midsummer Night's Dream, Open Air Th., Regent's Park; 1986: Medea, Theatr Clwyd and Young Vic; (jt Dir) Antony and Cleopatra, The Taming of the Shrew, Haymarket; Coriolanus, festivals in Spain. *Opera:* for Scottish Opera, incl.: A Midsummer Night's Dream, 1972; Hermiston, 1975; Marriage of Figaro, 1977; for Opera Co. of Philadelphia: Elisir d'Amore (with Pavarotti and winner of Pavarotti competition), Dido and Aeneas, Oedipus Rex, 1982; Faust, 1984; Wiesbaden: A Midsummer Night's Dream, 1984; NY City Opera: Barber of Seville, 1984; Wexford Opera: The Kiss, 1984. Asst Dir, Lord of the Flies (film), 1961. Dir of more than 25 television prodns, incl.: The Beggar's Opera; Richard II; Edward II. Member: Bd, Cambridge Theatre Co., 1970–74; Bd, Prospect Productions Ltd, 1964– (Artistic Dir, Prospect Theatre Co., 1964–79); Director: Old Vic Theatre, 1977–80, Old Vic Co., 1979–80; Acting Co., Kennedy Centre, Washington, 1983; Associate Dir, Circle Rep., New York, 1983–84. Drama Advr, Argo Records, 1979–; Prof. of Theatre, Brooklyn Coll., City Univ. NY, 1981–82. Lectures: Wilson Meml, Cambridge Univ., 1974; Hamlet, Athens Univ., 1978; Rikstheatre, Stockholm, 1980. *Recreations:* painting, sailing, Bunburying. *Address:* 210 Brixton Road, SW9. *Clubs:* Garrick, Bunbury.

ROBERTSON, Vernon Colin, OBE 1977; self employed consultant, specialising in environmental issues in developing countries; Board Member, Commonwealth Development Corporation, since 1982; *b* 19 July 1922; *s* of Colin John Trevelyan Robertson and Agnes Muriel Robertson (*née* Dolphin). *Educ:* Imperial Service College, Windsor; Univ. of Edinburgh (BSc Agr subs. Forestry); Univ. of Cambridge (Dip Agr 1950; MA). Joined Home Guard, 1940; enlisted RA, 1941, commissioned 1942; served 12th HAC Regt RHA, N Africa, Italy, Austria, 1942–45 (despatches 1945); with 1st Regt RHA, Italy, 1945–46 (Adjutant). Staff, Sch. of Agric., Cambridge, 1950; joined Hunting Aerosurveys Ltd, 1953, as ecologist heading new natural resources survey dept; developed this into overseas land and water resource consultancy, renamed Hunting Technical

Services Ltd (Managing Director, 1959–77; after retirement continuing as Director and Consultant), development planning in Africa, Asia and Latin America. Director: Hunting Surveys and Consultants Ltd, 1962–77; Groundwater Development Consultants (International) Ltd, 1975–85; Vice-Chm. and acting Chm., Environmental Planning Commn, Internat. Union for Conservation of Nature, 1972–78; Chm., Trop. Agric. Assoc. (UK), 1981–85. *Publications:* articles in learned jls. *Recreations:* natural history, esp. plants and birds, gardening, painting, photography, music, sailing. *Address:* The Saltings, Manor Road, Great Holland, Frinton-on-Sea, Essex CO13 0JT. *T:* Frinton-on-Sea 4585. *Clubs:* Honourable Artillery Company, Farmers'.

ROBERTSON, Prof. William Bruce, MD, FRCPath; Professor of Histopathology, St George's Hospital Medical School, 1968–84, now Emeritus; Director of Studies, Royal College of Pathologists, since 1984; *b* 17 Jan. 1923; *s* of late William Bruce Robertson and Jessie Robertson (*née* McLean); *m* 1948, Mary Patricia Burrows two *d*. *Educ:* The Academy, Forfar; Univ. of St Andrews. BSc 1944, MB ChB 1947, MD 1959; MRCPath 1963, FRCPath 1969. Junior appts, Cumberland Infirm., Carlisle, 1947–48; RAMC, E Africa, 1948–50; Registrar Pathology, Cumberland Infirm., 1950–53; Demonstr Pathology, Royal Victoria Infirm., Newcastle upon Tyne, 1953–56; Sen. Lectr Pathology, Univ. of the West Indies, Jamaica, 1956–64; Reader in Morbid Anatomy, St George's Hosp. Med. Sch., Univ. of London, 1964–68. Visiting Professor: Louisiana State Univ., New Orleans, USA, 1961–62; Katholieke Universiteit te Leuven, Belgium, 1972–73. *Publications:* scientific papers and book chapters in various med. jls and publns. *Address:* 3 Cambisgate, Church Road, Wimbledon, SW19 5AL. *T:* 01–947 6731.

ROBERTSON, Air Cdre William Duncan, CBE 1968; Royal Air Force, retired; Senior Air Staff Officer, HQ 38 Group, Royal Air Force, 1975–77; *b* 24 June 1922; *s* of William and Helen Robertson, Aberdeen; *m* 1st, 1952, Doreen Mary (*d* 1963), *d* of late Comdr G. A. C. Sharp, DSC, RN (retd); one *s* one *d*; 2nd, 1968, Ute, *d* of late Dr R. Koenig, Wesel, West Germany; one *d*. *Educ:* Robert Gordon's Coll., Aberdeen. Sqdn Comdr, No 207 Sqdn, 1959–61. Gp Dir, RAF Staff Coll., 1962–65; Station Comdr, RAF Wildenrath, 1965–67; Dep. Dir, Administrative Plans, 1967; Dir of Ops (Plans), 1968; Dir of Ops Air Defence and Overseas, 1969–71; RCDS, 1971–72; SASO RAF Germany, 1972–74; SASO 46 Group, 1975. *Recreations:* golf, tennis. *Address:* Parkhouse Farm, Leigh, Surrey. *Club:* Royal Air Force.

ROBERTSON, William Walter Samuel, CBE 1957 (OBE 1950); *b* 3 July 1906; *s* of W. H. A. and A. M. Robertson (*née* Lane); *m* 1935, Kathleen Elizabeth Chawner East; one *s* two *d*. *Educ:* Bedford School; King's College, London. BSc (Eng.) First Class Hons, 1926. Apprenticeship to W. H. A. Robertson & Co. Ltd (Director, 1929) and to Torrington Mfg Co., USA, 1926–28. Regional Controller and Chm. of North Midland Regional Bd for Production, 1943–45; Chairman, Eastern Regional Bd for Industry, 1949–64 (Vice-Chm., 1945–49); Member Advisory Committee, Revolving Fund for Industry, 1955–58. MIMechE, 1943. High Sheriff of Bedfordshire, 1963. Governor, St Felix School, Southwold. *Recreations:* rowing, golf. *Address:* The Dale, Pavenham, Beds. *T:* Oakley 2895. *Clubs:* Caledonian; Leander (Henley-on-Thames).

ROBEY, Douglas John Brett, CMG 1960; HM Diplomatic Service, retired; *b* 7 Aug. 1914; *s* of late E. J. B. and Margaret Robey; *m* 1943, Elizabeth, *d* of late Col David D. Barrett, US Army; two *s* one *d*. *Educ:* Cranleigh School; St John's College, Oxford; Ecole des Sciences Politiques, Paris. BA (History); Editor of The Cherwell. Joined HM Foreign Service, 1937. Served in China, USA, Paris, Berlin, Baghdad; Consul-Gen., Chicago, 1966–69; Ambassador and Permanent UK Representative, Council of Europe, Strasbourg, 1969–74. *Publication:* The Innovator, 1945. *Recreations:* reading, writing, and the Niebelung Ring. *Address:* Allan Down House, Rotherfield, East Sussex TN6 3RT. *T:* Rotherfield 2329. *Club:* Cercle Européen de Strasbourg (Hon. Life Pres.).

ROBIN, Dr Gordon de Quetteville; Director, Scott Polar Research Institute, University of Cambridge, 1958–82; Fellow since 1964 and Vice-Master, 1974–78, Darwin College, Cambridge; *b* Melbourne, 17 Jan. 1921; *s* of Reginald James Robin and Emily Mabel Robin; *m* 1953, Jean Margaret Fortt, Bath; two *d*. *Educ:* Wesley Coll., Melbourne; Melbourne Univ. ScD Cantab, MSc Melbourne, PhD Birmingham; FInstP. War service, RANVR: anti-submarine, 1942–44; submarine, RN, 1944–45 (Lieut). Physics Dept, Birmingham Univ.: research student, lectr, ICI Research Fellow, 1945–56; Sen. Fellow, Geophysics Dept, ANU, 1957–58. Meteorologist and Officer i/c Signy Is, South Orkneys, with Falkland Is Dependencies Survey, 1947–48; Physicist and Sen. British Mem. of Norwegian-British-Swedish Antarctic Expedn, 1949–52 (made first effective measurements of Antarctic ice thickness); further researches in Antarctic in 1959, 1967, 1969, 1974, and in Arctic, 1964, 1966, 1973; Sec., 1958–70, Pres., 1970–74, and Hon. Mem., Scientific Cttee on Antarctic Research of Internat. Council of Scientific Unions. Hon. DPhil Stockholm, 1978. Kongens Fortjensmedalje, Norway, 1952; Back Grant, RGS, 1953; Bruce Medal, RSE, 1953; Polar Medal, 1956; Patrons Medal, RGS, 1974; Seligman Crystal, Internat. Glaciological Soc., 1986. *Publications:* scientific reports of Norwegian-British-Swedish Antarctic Expedition (Glaciology III, 1958; Upper Winds, 1972); (ed) Annals of the IGY, Vol. 41, Glaciology, 1967; (ed and contrib.) The Climatic Record in Polar Ice Sheets, 1983; papers and articles on polar glaciology in scientific jls. *Recreations:* travel, walking. *Address:* 10 Melbourne Place, Cambridge CB1 1EQ. *T:* Cambridge 358463.

ROBIN, Ian (Gibson), FRCS; *b* 22 May 1909; *s* of Dr Arthur Robin, Edinburgh, and Elizabeth Parker; *m* 1939, Shelagh Marian (*d* 1978), *d* of late Colonel C. M. Croft; one *s* two *d*. *Educ:* Merchiston Castle School; Clare College, Cambridge. MA, MB, BCh Cantab 1933; LRCP 1933; FRCS 1935. Guy's Hosp.; late House Phys.; Sen. Science Schol., 1930; Treasurer's Gold Medals in Clinical Surgery and Medicine, 1933; Arthur Durham Travelling Schol., 1933; Charles Oldham Prize in Ophthalmology, 1933; Registrar and Chief Clin. Asst, ENT Dept, 1935–36; late Consulting ENT Surgeon: Royal Chest Hosp., 1939–44; Royal Northern Hosp., 1937–74; St Mary's Hosp., Paddington, 1948–74; Princess Louise (Kensington) Hosp. for Children, 1948–69; Paddington Green Children's Hosp., 1969–74; Surgeon EMS, Sector III London Area, 1939–45. Late Vice-Chm., Royal Nat. Institute for the Deaf. Member Hunterian Soc.; Council of Nat. Deaf Children's Soc.; Past Pres., Brit. Assoc. of Otolaryngologists, 1971–72; Past Pres., Laryng. Section, RSM, 1967–68; Vice-Pres., Otolog. Section, RSM, 1967–68, 1969; late Examiner for DLO of RCS of England. Lectures: Yearsley, 1968; Jobson Horne, 1969. Mem., Royal Water-Colour Soc. *Publications:* (jt) Diseases of Ear, Nose and Throat (Synopsis Series), 1957; papers in various med. treatises, jls, etc. *Recreations:* golf, gardening, sketching; formerly athletics and Rugby. *Address:* Stowe House, 3 North End, Hampstead, NW3. *T:* 01–458 2292; 86 Harley Street, W1. *T:* 01–580 3625. *Clubs:* Hawks (Cambridge); Achilles (Great Britain); Hampstead Golf.

ROBINS, Daniel Gerard; QC 1986; *b* 12 March 1942; *o s* of W. A. and H. M. Robins; *m* 1968, Elizabeth Mary Gerran, *e d* of Baron Lloyd of Kilgerran, *qv*; three *d*. *Educ:* City of London School; London School of Economics (BSc, LLB). FRAI. Called to the Bar, Lincoln's Inn, 1966; Hardwicke Scholar 1963, Mansfield Scholar 1966. Trustee: Education Trust Ltd; Brantwood (John Ruskin) Trust. *Recreations:* ornithology, squash, golf. *Address:* 2 Harcourt Buildings, Temple, EC4. *T:* 01–353 8415. *Clubs:* Savile; Royal Wimbledon Golf; Royal Naval (Portsmouth).

ROBINS, Group Captain Leonard Edward, CBE (mil.) 1979; AE 1958 (and 2 clasps); DL; on Lord Mayor of London's personal staff, since 1986; Representative DL, Borough of Wandsworth, since 1979; Inspector, Royal Auxiliary Air Force, 1973–83; *b* 2 Nov 1921; *yr s* of late Joseph Robins, Bandmaster RM, and late Louisa Josephine (*née* Kent); *m* 1949, Jean Ethelwynne (Headteacher) (*d* 1985), *d* of late Roy and Bessie Searle, Ryde, IoW. *Educ:* Singlegate, Mitcham, Surrey; City Day Continuation School, EC. Entered Civil Service, GPO, 1936; War service RAF, UK, SEAC, Ceylon, India, 1941–46; resumed with GPO, 1946; Min. of Health, 1948; Min. of Housing and Local Govt, 1962; DoE, 1970–80, retired. Airman, No 3700 (Co. of London) Radar Reporting Unit RAuxAF, 1950; Commissioned 1953, radar branch; transf. to No 1 (Co. of Hertford) Maritime HQ Unit RAuxAF, intelligence duties, 1960; OC No 1 Maritime Headquarters Unit, RAuxAF, 1969–73; Gp Capt., Inspector RAuxAF, 1973. ADC to the Queen, 1974–83. Selected Air Force Mem., Greater London TAVRA, 1973–83 and City of London TAVRA, 1980–84. Lord Mayor of London's personal staff, 1977–78, 1980–81 and 1982–83. Pres., Wandsworth Victim Support, 1980–. Trustee, Royal Foundn of Greycoat Hosp., 1983–. Freeman, City of London, 1976. Coronation Medal, 1953; Jubilee Medal, 1978. Officer of Merit with Swords, SMO Malta, 1986. DL Greater London, 1978–. FBIM. *Recreations:* naval, military and aviation history; book hunting; kipping. *Address:* 16 Summit Way, Upper Norwood, SE19 2PU. *T:* 01–653 3173; Higher Bosigran Cottage, Pendeen, Penzance, Cornwall TR20 8YX. *Club:* Royal Air Force.

ROBINS, Malcolm Owen, CBE 1978; Learned Societies Officer, Royal Society/British Academy, 1979–81; a Director, Science Research Council, 1972–78; *b* 25 Feb. 1918; *s* of late Owen Wilfred Robins and Amelia Ada (*née* Wheelwright); *m* 1944, Frances Mary, *d* of late William and Frances Hand; one *s* one *d*. *Educ:* King Edward's Sch., Stourbridge; The Queen's Coll., Oxford (Open Scholar in Science). MA (Oxon) 1943. On scientific staff of Royal Aircraft Establishment, 1940–57; a Div. Supt in Guided Weapons Dept, RAE, 1955–57; Asst Dir, Guided Weapons, Min. of Supply, London, 1957–58; UK Project Manager for jt UK/USA Space Research programme, and hon. Research Associate, University Coll. London, 1958–62; a Dep. Chief Scientific Officer and Head of Space Research Management Unit, Office of Minister for Science (later Dept of Educn and Science), 1962–65; Head of Astronomy, Space and Radio Div., SRC, 1965–68; a Research Planning post in Min. of Technology (later Dept of Trade and Industry), 1968–72. Vis. Prof., University Coll., London, 1974–77. FInstP 1945; FRAS 1974. *Publications:* (with Sir Harrie Massey) History of British Space Science, 1986; papers on space research in scientific jls. *Recreation:* gardening. *Address:* Wychbury, Gorse Lane, Farnham, Surrey GU10 4SD. *T:* Farnham 723186.

ROBINS, Ralph Harry; Managing Director, Rolls-Royce plc, since 1984; *b* 16 June 1932; *s* of Leonard Haddon and Maud Lillian Robins; *m* 1962, Patricia Maureen Grimes; two *d*. *Educ:* Imperial Coll., Univ. of London (BSc, ACGI). CEng, MIMechE. Development Engr, Rolls-Royce, Derby, 1955–66; Exec. Vice-Pres., Rolls-Royce Inc., 1971; Man. Dir, RR Industrial & Marine Div., 1973; Commercial Dir, RR Ltd, 1978; Chm., International Aero Engines AG, 1983–84. Chm., Defence Industries Council, 1986–; Pres., Soc. of British Aerospace Companies, 1986–87. *Recreations:* tennis, golf, music. *Address:* Rolls-Royce plc, 65 Buckingham Gate, SW1E 6AT.

ROBINS, Prof. Robert Henry, FBA 1986; Professor of General Linguistics, 1966–86, now Emeritus, and Dean, Faculty of Arts, 1984–86, University of London; Head of Department of Phonetics and Linguistics, School of Oriental and African Studies, University of London, 1970–85; *b* 1 July 1921; *s* of John Norman Robins, medical practitioner, and Muriel Winifred (*née* Porter); *m* 1953, Sheila Marie Fynn (*d* 1983). *Educ:* Tonbridge Sch.; New Coll., Oxford, 1940–41 and 1945–48, MA 1948; DLit London 1968. Served war, RAF Intelligence, 1942–45. Lectr in Linguistics, Sch. of Oriental and African Studies, London, 1948–55; Reader in General Linguistics, Univ. of London, 1955–65. Mem. Senate, Univ. of London, 1980–85. Research Fellow, Univ. of California, 1951; Vis. Professor: Washington, 1963; Hawaii, 1968; Minnesota, 1971; Florida, 1975; Salzburg, 1977, 1979. Hon. Sec., Philological Soc., 1961–; President: Societas Linguistica Europea, 1974; CIPL, 1977–87 (British Rep., 1970–77). Hon. Mem., Linguistic Soc. of Amer., 1981–. *Publications:* Ancient and Mediaeval Grammatical Theory in Europe, 1951; The Yurok Language, 1958; General Linguistics: an introductory survey, 1964; A Short History of Linguistics, 1967; Diversions of Bloomsbury, 1970; Ideen- und Problemgeschichte der Sprachwissenschaft, 1973; System and Structure in Sundanese, 1983; articles in Language, TPS, BSOAS, Lingua, Foundations of Language, Man, etc. *Recreations:* gardening, travel. *Address:* 65 Dome Hill, Caterham, Surrey CR3 6EF. *T:* Caterham 43778. *Clubs:* Athenæum; Royal Commonwealth Society.

ROBINS, William Edward Charles; Metropolitan Stipendiary Magistrate since 1971; solicitor; *b* 13 March 1924; *s* of late E. T. and late L. R. Robins; *m* 1946, Jean Elizabeth, *yr d* of Bruce and Flora Forsyth, Carlyle, Saskatchewan, Canada; one *s* one *d*. *Educ:* St Alban's Sch. Served War: commissioned as Navigator, RAF, 1943–47. Admitted as a Solicitor, 1948; joined Metropolitan Magistrates' Courts' service, 1950; Dep. Chief Clerk, 1951–60; Chief Clerk, 1960–67; Sen. Chief Clerk, Thames Petty Sessional Div., 1968–71. Sec., London Magistrates' Clerks' Assoc., 1953–60 (Chm. 1965–71). Member, Home Office working parties, on: Magistrates' Courts' Rules; Legal Aid; Motor Vehicle Licences; Fines and Maintenance Orders Enforcement, 1968–71; Member: Lord Chancellor's Sub-Cttee on Magistrates' Courts' Rules, 1969–70; Adv. Council on Misuse of Drugs, 1973–. Fellow Commoner, Corpus Christi Coll., Cambridge, Michaelmas 1975. *Recreations:* touring off the beaten track, music, theatre. *Address:* Bow Street Magistrates' Court, WC2.

ROBINSON, family name of **Baron Martonmere.**

ROBINSON, Sir Albert (Edward Phineas), Kt 1962; Director, Anglo American Corporation of SA Ltd, since 1965; *b* 30 December 1915; *s* of late Charles Phineas Robinson (formerly MP Durban, S Africa) and of late Mabel V. Robinson; *m* 1st, 1944, Mary Judith Bertish (*d* 1973); four *d*; 2nd, 1975, Mrs M. L. Royston-Piggot (*née* Barrett). *Educ:* Durban High School; Universities of Stellenbosch, London, Cambridge (Trinity Coll.) and Leiden; MA (Cantab). Pres., Footlights Club, Cambridge, 1937. Barrister, Lincoln's Inn. Served War of 1939–45, in Imperial Light Horse, Western Desert, N Africa, 1940–43. Member Johannesburg City Council, 1945–48 (Leader United Party in Council, 1946–47); MP (United Party), S African Parlt, 1947–53; became permanent resident in Rhodesia, 1953. Dep. Chm., General Mining and Finance Corp. Ltd, 1963–71; Chairman: Johannesburg Consolidated Investment Co., 1971–80; Rustenburg Platinum Mines, 1971–80; Australian Anglo American Ltd, 1980–85; Director: Anglo American Corp., Zimbabwe Ltd, 1964–86; Founders Bldg Soc., 1954–86; Rand Mines Ltd, 1965–71; Johannesburg Consolidated Investment Co., 1965–85; Standard Bank Investment Corp., 1972–86; Director, in Zimbabwe and South Africa, of various Mining, Financial and Industrial Companies. Chm. Central African Airways Corp., 1957–61. Member, Monckton Commission, 1960; High Commissioner in the UK for the Federation of Rhodesia and Nyasaland, 1961–63. Chancellor, Univ. of Bophuthatswana, 1981–.

Recreations: people, music and conversation. *Address:* 36 Smits Road, Dunkeld, Johannesburg, South Africa. *Clubs:* Carlton (London); City (Capetown).

ROBINSON, Alwyn Arnold; Managing Director, Daily Mail, since 1975; *b* 15 Nov. 1929. Director: Associated Newspapers Holdings; Associated Newspapers Group Ltd; Harmsworth Publishing Ltd; Mail on Sunday Ltd. Mem., Press Council (Jt Vice-Chm., 1982–83). *Address:* The Daily Mail, EC4. *T:* 01-353 6000.

ROBINSON, Arthur Alexander; Director of Computing, University of Wales Institute of Science and Technology, since 1976; *b* 5 Aug. 1924; *o s* of Arthur Robinson and Elizabeth (*née* Thompson); *m* 1956, Sylvia Joyce Wagstaff; two *s* one *d. Educ:* Epsom Coll.; Clare Coll., Cambridge (MA); Univ. of Manchester (PhD). English Electric Co. Ltd, 1944; Ferranti Ltd, 1950; Dir and Gen. Man., Univ. of London Atlas Computing Service, 1962; Dir, Univ. of London Computer Centre, 1968; Dir, National Computing Centre Ltd, 1969–74. *Publications:* papers in Proc. IEE. *Recreation:* gardening. *Address:* 6 Portland Close, Penarth, S Glamorgan.

ROBINSON, (Arthur) Geoffrey, CBE 1978; Chairman, Medway Ports Authority, since 1978; *b* 22 Aug. 1917; *s* of Arthur Robinson and Frances M. Robinson; *m* 1st, 1943, Patricia MacAllister (*d* 1971); three *s* one *d*; 2nd, 1973, Hon. Mrs Treves, *d* of Rt Hon. Lord Salmon, *qv*; three step *s* one step *d. Educ:* Lincoln Sch.; Jesus Coll., Cambridge (MA); Sch. of Oriental and African Studies, London Univ. Served War, RA, 1939–46. Solicitor, 1948; Treasury Solicitor's Dept, 1954–62; PLA, 1962–66; Man. Dir, Tees and Hartlepool Port Authority, 1966–77; Chm., English Indust. Estates Corp., 1977–83. Member: National Dock Labour Bd, 1972–77; National Ports Council, 1980–81; Chm., British Ports Assoc., 1983–85. *Publications:* Hedingham Harvest, 1977; various articles. *Recreation:* music. *Address:* Salts End, Goss Hall Lane, Ash, Kent CT3 2AN. *T:* Ash 812366; 38 Paxton Road, W4 2QX. *T:* 01-994 1848. *Club:* United Oxford & Cambridge University.
See also P. H. Robinson.

ROBINSON, Arthur Napoleon Raymond; barrister; Chairman, Tobago House of Assembly, since 1980; Chairman, Democratic Action Congress, Trinidad and Tobago, since 1971; *b* 16 Dec. 1926; *s* of late James Alexander Andrew Robinson, Headmaster, and Emily Isabella Robinson; *m* 1961, Patricia Rawlins; one *s* one *d. Educ:* Bishop's High Sch., Tobago; St John's Coll., Oxford. LLB (London); MA (PPE) Oxon. Called to Bar, Inner Temple; in practice, 1956–61, 1970–. Treas., People's Nat. Movt (governing Party) 1956; Mem. Federal Parlt, 1958; MHR for Tobago East, 1961–71 and 1976–80; Minister of Finance, 1961–66; Dep. Political Leader of Party, 1966; Actg Prime Minister (during his absence), April and Aug. 1967; Minister of External Affairs, Trinidad and Tobago, 1967–68. Member: Legal Commn on US Leased Areas under 1941 Agreement, 1959; Industrial Develt Corp., 1960; Council, Univ. of West Indies, 1960–62. Consultant, Foundn for establishment of an Internat. Criminal Court, 1972–75, Exec. Dir, 1976–77. Mem., UN Expert Gp on Crime and the Abuse of Power, 1979. Dist. Internat. Criminal Law Award, Internat. Criminal Court Foundn, 1977. *Publications:* The New Frontier and the New Africa, 1961; Fiscal Reform in Trinidad and Tobago, 1966; The Path of Progress, 1967; The Teacher and Nationalism, 1967; The Mechanics of Independence, 1971; Caribbean May, 1986; articles and addresses. *Address:* 21 Ellerslie Park, Maraval, Trinidad; Robinson Street, Scarborough, Tobago.

ROBINSON, Sir Austin; *see* Robinson, Sir E. A. G.

ROBINSON, Basil William, FBA 1981; retired; *b* 20 June 1912; *o c* of William Robinson and Rebecca Frances Mabel, *d* of Rev. George Gilbanks; *m* 1st, 1945, Ailsa Mary Stewart (*d* 1954); 2nd, 1958, Oriel Hermione Steel; one *s* one *d. Educ:* Winchester (Exhibitioner); CCC Oxford. BA 1935; MA, BLitt, 1938. Asst Keeper, Victoria and Albert Museum, 1939. Min. of Home Security, 1939–40. Served as Captain, 2nd Punjab Regt, India, Burma, Malaya, 1943–46. Deputy Keeper, V&A Museum, 1954, Keeper, Dept of Metalwork, 1966–72, Keeper Emeritus, 1972–76. Pres., Royal Asiatic Soc., 1970–73; Vice-Pres., Arms and Armour Soc., 1953; Hon. Pres., Tō-ken Soc. of Great Britain, 1967. FSA 1974. *Publications:* A Primer of Japanese Sword-blades, 1955; Persian Miniatures, 1957; Japanese Landscape Prints of the 19th Century, 1957; A Descriptive Catalogue of the Persian Paintings in the Bodleian Library, 1958; Kuniyoshi, 1961; The Arts of the Japanese Sword, 1961, 2nd edn, 1971; Persian Drawings, 1965; part-author, vols 2 and 3, Catalogue of Persian MSS and Miniatures in the Chester Beatty Library, 3 vols, 1958–62; Persian Miniature Painting, 1967; Persian Paintings in the India Office Library, 1976; (ed. and jt author) Islamic painting in the Keir Collection, 1976; Japanese Sword-fittings in the Baur Collection, 1980; Persian Paintings in the John Rylands Library, 1980; Kuniyoshi: the Warrior Prints, 1982 (Uchiyama Meml Proze, Japan Ukiyoe Soc.); Persian Painting and the National Epic (Hertz Lecture, British Acad.), 1983; numerous booklets, articles and reviews on Persian and Japanese art. *Recreations:* catch singing (founder and Chairman, Aldrich Catch Club); cats. *Address:* 41 Redcliffe Gardens, SW10 9JH. *T:* 01-352 1290. *Club:* Hurlingham.

ROBINSON, Air Vice-Marshal Bruce, CB 1968; CBE 1953; Air Officer Commanding No 24 Gp, RAF, 1965–67; retired, 1967; *b* 19 Jan. 1912; *s* of late Dr G. Burton Robinson, Cannington, Somerset; *m* 1940, Elizabeth Ann Compton, *d* of Air Commodore D. F. Lucking; one *s* one *d. Educ:* King's School, Bruton. Commissioned in SR of O, The Somerset Light Infty, 1931–33; Commissioned in RAF, 1933; No 16 (Army Co-op. Sqdn), 1934–37; Specialist Engineer course, 1937–39. Served War of 1939–45: Technical duties in Fighter and Bomber Commands, UK Senior Technical Staff Officer, Rhodesian Air Training Group, 1946–48; on loan to Indian Air Force (Director of Technical Services), 1951–53; Commandant, No 1 Radio School, RAF Locking, 1953–55; Sen. RAF Officer at Wright Patterson Air Force Base, Dayton, Ohio, 1958–60; Commandant No 1 Sch. of Technical Training, RAF Halton, Bucks, 1961–63. Director of RAF Aircraft Development, Min. of Aviation, 1963–65. *Recreations:* golf, sailing, painting, writing. *Address:* Bent Hollow, Bromeswell, Woodbridge, Suffolk. *T:* Eyke 460295.

ROBINSON, Rt. Rev. Christopher James Gossage, MA; *b* 10 June 1903; *s* of late Canon Albert Gossage Robinson; unmarried. *Educ:* Marlborough, Christ's Coll., Cambridge. Lecturer at St Stephen's Coll., Delhi, 1926–29; Deacon, 1929; Priest, 1930; Curate St Mary's, Portsea, 1929–31; Asst Priest, St James, Delhi, 1931–32; Vicar of St James, and Chaplain of Delhi, 1932–42; Vicar of St Thomas, New Delhi, 1942–45; Hon. Canon of Lahore Cathedral, 1944–47; Bishop of Lucknow, 1947–62; Bishop of Bombay, 1962–70. Member, Brotherhood of the Ascended Christ (formerly Cambridge Brotherhood of the Ascension), Delhi, since 1931. *Address:* Brotherhood House, 7 Court Lane, Delhi 110–054, India. *Club:* Royal Commonwealth Society.
See also Sir E. A. G. Robinson.

ROBINSON, Christopher John, LVO 1986; Organist and Master of the Choristers, St George's Chapel, Windsor Castle, since 1974; *b* 20 April 1936; *s* of late Prebendary John Robinson, Malvern, Worcs; *m* 1962, Shirley Ann, *d* of H. F. Churchman, Sawston, Cambs; one *s* one *d. Educ:* St Michael's Coll., Tenbury; Rugby; Christ Church, Oxford. MA, BMus; FRCO, Hon. RAM. Assistant Organist of Christ Church, Oxford, 1955–58; Assistant Organist of New College, Oxford, 1957–58; Music Master at Oundle School, 1959–62; Assistant Organist of Worcester Cathedral, 1962–63; Organist and Master of Choristers, Worcester Cathedral, 1963–74. Conductor: City of Birmingham Choir, 1963–; Oxford Bach Choir, 1977–; Leith Hill Musical Festival, 1977–80. Pres., RCO, 1982–84. *Recreations:* watching cricket, motoring. *Address:* 23 The Cloisters, Windsor Castle, Berks.

ROBINSON, Mrs Clare; *see* Panter-Downes, M. P.

ROBINSON, Clifton Eugene Bancroft, CBE 1985 (OBE 1973); JP; a Deputy-Chairman, Commission for Racial Equality, 1977–85; *b* 5 Oct. 1926; *s* of Theodore Emanuel and Lafrance Robinson; *m* (marr. diss.); one *s* three *d*, *m* 1977, Margaret Ann Ennever. *Educ:* Kingston Technical Coll., Jamaica; Birmingham Univ.; Leicester Univ.; Lancaster Coll. of Educn. BA, DipEd. Served War, RAF, 1944–49. Teacher: Mellor Sch., Leicester, 1951–61; i/c Special Educn Unit, St Peter's Sch., Leicester, 1961–64; Dep. Headteacher, Charnwood Sch., Leicester, 1964–68; Headteacher: St Peter's Sch., Leicester, 1968–70; Uplands Sch., Leicester, 1970–77. JP Leicester, 1974. *Recreations:* music (mainly classical), walking; when there is time, gardening. *Address:* 80 Numa Court, Justin Close, Brentford, Middlesex TW8 8QF.

ROBINSON, Sir David, Kt 1985; *b* Cambridge, 1904; *s* of Herbert Robinson; *m. Educ:* Cambridgeshire High School for Boys. Started in business, 1930; Robinson Rentals, Bedford, 1954–68. Former race-horse owner; won 997 races, 1960–75. Founder, Robinson Trust; Robinson Coll., Cambridge, opened 1981.

ROBINSON, (David) Duncan; Director, Yale Center for British Art, New Haven, Connecticut, Chief Executive, Paul Mellon Centre for Studies in British Art, London, and Adjunct Professor of the History of Art, Yale University, since 1981; *b* 27 June 1943; *s* of Tom and Ann Robinson; *m* 1967, Elizabeth Anne Sutton; one *s* one *d. Educ:* King Edward VI Sch., Macclesfield; Clare Coll., Cambridge (MA); Yale Univ. (Mellon Fellow, 1965–67; MA). Asst Keeper of Paintings and Drawings, 1970–76, Keeper, 1976–81, Fitzwilliam Museum, Cambridge; Fellow and Coll. Lectr, Clare Coll., Cambridge, 1975–81. Mem. Cttee of Management, and Chm., Exhibns Cttee, Kettle's Yard, Cambridge Univ., 1970–81. Member: Art Panel, Eastern Arts Assoc., 1973–81 (Chm., 1979–81); Arts Council of GB, 1981 (Mem., 1978–81, Vice-Chm., 1981, Art Panel); Assoc. of Art Mus. Dirs (USA), 1982–; Bd of Managers, Lewis Walpole Library, Farmington Ct, USA, 1982–; Council of Management, The William Blake Trust, 1983–; Vis. Cttee, Dept of Paintings Conservation, Metropolitan Museum of Art, NY, 1984–; Walpole Soc., 1983– (Mem. Council, 1985–). Organised Arts Council exhibitions: Stanley Spencer, 1975; William Nicholson, 1980. *Publications:* Companion Volume to the Kelmscott Chaucer, 1975, re-issued as Morris, Burne-Jones and the Kelmscott Chaucer, 1982; Stanley Spencer, 1979; (with Stephen Wildman) Morris & Company in Cambridge, 1980; Town, Country, Shore & Sea: English Watercolours from van Dyck to Paul Nash, 1982; catalogues; articles and reviews in Apollo, Burlington Magazine, etc. *Address:* 142 Huntington Street, New Haven, Conn 06511, USA. *T:* (203) 787 7199. *Clubs:* Athenæum; Yale (NY); Mory's (New Haven).

ROBINSON, David Julien; Film Critic, The Times, since 1974; *b* 6 Aug. 1930; *s* of Edward Robinson and Dorothy Evelyn (*née* Overton). *Educ:* Lincoln Sch.; King's Coll., Cambridge (BA Hons). Associate Editor, Sight and Sound, and Editor, Monthly Film Bulletin, 1956–58; Programme Dir, NFT, 1959; Film Critic, Financial Times, 1959–74; Editor, Contrast, 1962–63. *Publications:* Hollywood in the Twenties, 1969; Buster Keaton, 1969; The Great Funnies, 1972; World Cinema, 1973, 2nd edn 1980 (US edn The History of World Cinema, 1974, 1980); Chaplin: the mirror of opinion, 1983; Chaplin: his life and art, 1985; (ed and trans.) Luis Buñuel (J. F. Aranda); (ed and trans.) Cinema in Revolution (anthology). *Recreations:* collecting optical toys, model theatres. *Address:* 96–100 New Cavendish Street, W1M 7FA. *T:* 01-580 4959; 4 Sion Hill Place, Bath. *T:* Bath 338578.

ROBINSON, Derek, CBE 1979; Fellow of Magdalen College, Oxford, since 1969; Senior Research Officer, Oxford Institute of Economics and Statistics; *b* 9 Feb. 1932; *s* of Benjamin and Mary Robinson; *m* 1956, Jean Evelyn (*née* Lynch); one *s* one *d. Educ:* Barnsley Holgate Grammar Sch.; Ruskin Coll., Oxford; Lincoln Coll., Oxford. MA (Oxon), DipEcPolSci (Oxon). Civil Service, 1948–55. Sheffield Univ., 1959–60; Senior Research Officer, Oxford Inst. of Economics and Statistics, 1961–. Economic Adviser, Nat. Bd for Prices and Incomes, 1965–67; Sen. Economic Adviser, Dept of Employment and Productivity, 1968–70; Dep. Chm., Pay Bd, 1973–74; Chm., SSRC, 1975–78. Mem., British Library Bd, 1979–82. Visiting Professor: Cornell Univ., 1983; Univ. of Hawaii, 1983. Chairman: Oxfordshire Dist Manpower Cttee, 1980–83 (Oxf. and S Bucks, 1975–79); Cttee of Inquiry into the remuneration of members of local authorities, 1977; Chilterns Area Bd, Manpower Services Commn Special Programmes, 1978–79. Inter-regional Adviser on Wage Policy, ILO, 1986–. *Publications:* Non-Wage Incomes and Prices Policy, 1966; Wage Drift, Fringe Benefits and Manpower Distribution, 1968; Workers' Negotiated Savings Plans for Capital Formation, 1970; (ed) Local Labour Markets and Wage Structures, 1970; Prices and Incomes Policy: the Austrian Experience (with H. Suppanz), 1972; Incomes Policy and Capital Sharing in Europe, 1973; (with J. Vincens) Research into Labour Market Behaviour, 1974; (with K. Mayhew *et al*) Pay Policies for the Future, 1983; Introduction to Economics, 1986; Monetarism and the Labour Market, 1986; contributor to Bulletin of Oxford Univ. Inst. of Economics and Statistics; Industrial Relations Jl, etc. *Address:* 56 Lonsdale Road, Oxford. *T:* Oxford 52276. *Club:* Reform.

ROBINSON, Derek Anthony, DPhil; Keeper, Department of Museum Services, Science Museum, London, since 1978; *b* 21 April 1942; *s* of late Charles Frederick Robinson and of Mary Margaret Robinson; *m* 1965, Susan Gibson; two *s. Educ:* Hymers Coll., Hull; The Queen's Coll., Oxford (BA 1963; MA, DPhil 1967). Post-doctoral Res. Fellow, Dept of Chemistry, Univ. of Reading, 1967–69; Mem. scientific staff, Molecular Pharmacology Unit of MRC, Cambridge, 1969–72; Sen. Asst in Res., Dept of Haematol Medicine, Cambridge Univ. Med. Sch., 1972–74; Science Museum: Asst Keeper I, Dept of Chem., 1974–77; Dep. Keeper (formerly Asst Keeper I), Wellcome Mus. of History of Medicine, and Sec. of Adv. Council, 1977–78. Mem., CGLI, 1984. *Publications:* (contrib.) 2nd edn Acridines, ed R. M. Acheson, 1973; (contrib.) Vol. VI, The History of Technology, ed T. I. Williams, 1978; papers on heterocyclic chemistry, molecular pharmacol., and leukaemia chemotherapy, in Jl Chem. Soc., Brit. Jl Pharmacol., and Biochem. Trans. *Recreations:* cricket, mini rugby, travel, walking, eating Indian and Chinese food. *Address:* 3 Broadwater Avenue, Letchworth, Herts SG6 3HE. *T:* Letchworth 686961, (office) 01-589 3456.

ROBINSON, Most Rev. Donald William Bradley; *see* Sydney, Archbishop of.

ROBINSON, Sir Dove-Myer, Kt 1970; JP; MRSH; Mayor of Auckland, New Zealand, 1959–65 and 1968–80; *b* Sheffield, 15 June 1901; 6th *c* of Moss Robinson and Ida Robinson (*née* Brown); of Jewish race; *m* 1st, Bettine Williams; 2nd, Thelma Ruth Thompson; one *s* five *d. Educ:* primary schools in Sheffield, Manchester, London and Devonport (Auckland, NZ). Mem., Auckland City Council, 1952–59; Chm., Auckland Metropolitan Drainage Bd, 1953–55; Chm., Auckland Airport Cttee, 1959–61; Mem.,

Auckland Univ. Council, 1952–80; Chm., Auckland Regional Authority, 1963–65, Mem., 1963–80 (Chm. Rapid Transit Cttee, 1968–74); Sen. Vice-Pres., NZ Municipal Assoc., 1959–65 and 1968–80; President: Auckland Rugby League, 1964–; Auckland Festival Soc., 1959–65 and 1968–80. Fellow, NZ Inst. of Management, 1948, Hon. Fellow, 1974; Patron, NZ Pure Water Assoc., 1954–; Hon. Mem., Inst. Water Pollution Control. CStJ 1979. *Publications:* Utilization of Town and Country Wastes, Garbage and Sewage, 1946; Soil, Food and Health, 1947; Passenger Transport in Auckland, 1969; numerous leaflets and pubns on Pollution, Conservation, Fluoridation, Nutrition, Local and Regional Govt, Town Planning, Rapid Transit, etc. *Recreations:* golf, fishing, boating, photography, motoring, local government. *Address:* 12a Aldred Road, Remuera, Auckland 5, New Zealand. *T:* 503–693. *Clubs:* Remuera Golf, Rugby League (Auckland).

ROBINSON, Duncan; *see* Robinson, David D.

ROBINSON, Prof. Sir (Edward) Austin (Gossage), Kt 1975; CMG 1947; OBE 1944; FBA 1955; Emeritus Professor of Economics, Cambridge University since 1966 (Professor, 1950–65); Fellow of Sidney Sussex College, Cambridge, since 1931; Secretary of Royal Economic Society, 1945–70; *b* 20 Nov. 1897; *s* of late Rev. Canon Albert Gossage Robinson; *m* 1926, Joan (*d* 1983), *d* of late Major-General Sir Frederick Maurice, KCMG, CB; two *d. Educ:* Marlborough College (Scholar); Christ's College, Cambridge (Scholar). BA 1921; MA 1923; RNAS and RAF (Pilot), 1917–19; Fellow of Corpus Christi Coll., Cambridge, 1923–26; Tutor to HH The Maharaja of Gwalior, 1926–28; University Lecturer, Cambridge, 1929–49; Asst Editor of Economic Journal, 1934–44, Joint Editor, 1944–70; Member of Economic Section, War Cabinet Office, 1939–42; Economic Adviser and Head of Programmes Division, Ministry of Production, 1942–45; Member of British Reparations Mission, Moscow and Berlin, 1945; Economic Adviser to Board of Trade, 1946; returned to Cambridge, Sept. 1946. Mem. of Economic Planning Staff, 1947–48; Treasurer of International Economic Association, 1950–59, President 1959–62; Mem. Council, DSIR, 1954–59; Dir of Economics, Min. of Power, 1967–68. Chairman: Council Nat. Inst. of Economic and Social Research, 1949–62; European Energy Advisory Commn, OEEC, 1957–60; Exec. Cttee, Overseas Develt Inst. *Publications:* The Structure of Competitive Industry, 1931; Monopoly, 1941; Economic Consequences of the Size of Nations, 1960; Economic Development of Africa South of the Sahara, 1964; Problems in Economic Development, 1965; The Economics of Education (with J. E. Vaizey), 1966; Backward Areas in Advanced Countries, 1969; Economic Development in South Asia, 1970; (ed jtly) The Economic Development of Bangladesh within a Socialist Framework, 1974; (ed jtly) Employment Policy in a Developing Country; contributor to: Modern Industry and the African, 1933; Lord Hailey's African Survey, 1938; articles in Economic Journal, etc. *Address:* Sidney Sussex College, Cambridge. *T:* Cambridge 357548. *Club:* Reform.
See also Rt. Rev. C. J. G. Robinson.

ROBINSON, Eric Embleton; Director, Lancashire Polytechnic (formerly Preston Polytechnic), since 1982; *b* 12 March 1927; *s* of Cyril Robinson and Florence Mary Embleton. *Educ:* local authority schools, Nelson and Colne, Lancs; London Univ. (MSc). Teaching, Prescot Grammar Sch., 1948, Acton Tech. Coll., 1949–56, Brunel Coll., 1956–62, Enfield Coll., 1962–70; Dep. Dir, NE London Polytechnic, 1970–73; Principal, Bradford Coll., 1973–82. Pres., Assoc. of Teachers in Tech. Instns, 1962; Exec. Mem., Nat. Union of Teachers, 1961–67; Member: Burnham Cttees, 1961–67; Nat. Council for Training and Supply of Teachers, 1964–66; Minister's Working Party on Polytechnics, 1965–66; Equal Opportunities Commn, 1976–81; CNAA, 1976–82; UNESCO Nat. Commn, 1975–78. *Publications:* The New Polytechnics, 1968; numerous articles and papers. *Address:* Lancashire Polytechnic, Preston PR1 2TQ. *T:* Preston 22141. *Club:* Savile.

ROBINSON, Forbes; Principal Artist (Bass), Royal Opera House, Covent Garden, 1954–83; *b* Macclesfield, 21 May 1926; *s* of Wilfred and Gertrude Robinson; *m* 1952, Marion Stubbs; two *d. Educ:* King's Sch., Macclesfield. St Paul's Coll., Cheltenham (teacher's trg), 1943–45. Capt. in RAEC, 1946–48. Loughborough Coll. (Hons Dipl., Phys. Educn), 1949–50; La Scuola di Canto (Scala, Milan), 1952–53. Promenade Debut, 1957. Guest artist with Dublin, Handel, Sadler's Wells, Opera North, London Savoyards, Scottish and Welsh National Opera Cos. Has sung at Festivals at Aldeburgh, Barcelona, Edinburgh, Holland, Leeds, Lucerne, Ottawa, Portugal and Schwetzingen. Has also sung in Argentina, Belgium, Canada, Denmark, France, Germany, Luxembourg, Sweden, USA, South Korea, Japan and South Africa. First British singer to sing Don Giovanni at Royal Opera House, Covent Garden, for 100 years. Hon. DLitt Loughborough, 1979. Awarded Opera Medal for 1963, for creating King Priam (Tippett). Several recordings, inc. 4 solo albums and 2 TV videos. *Recreations:* walking, talking, gardening, croquet, jazz. *Address:* 225 Princes Gardens, W3. *T:* 01–992 5498. *Club:* Savage.

ROBINSON, Frank Arnold, CBE 1980; DSc, CChem, FRSC; Director of Twyford Laboratories Ltd & Twyford Pharmaceutical Services Ltd, retired; *b* 3 Dec. 1907; *s* of Frank Robinson and Edith Robinson (*née* Jagger); *m* 1st, 1930, Margaret Olive Jones; two *s*; 2nd, 1958, Beth Clarence Smith. *Educ:* Elland Grammar Sch.; Univ. of Manchester (James Gaskill Scholar; Hon. Fellow, UMIST, 1981); BSc Tech (Hons) 1929, MSc Tech 1930, DSc 1958; Univ. of London LLB (Hons.) 1940. Laboratory of Govt Chemist, 1930–33; Research Chemist, Glaxo Laboratories Ltd, Greenford, 1933–45; Manager, Distillers Co. Research Labs, Epsom, 1945–48; Dir of Research, Allen & Hanburys Ltd, Ware, 1948–60. FRIC 1940 (now FRSC). Hon. Professorial Fellow, University Coll., Cardiff, 1967–72; Hon. DSc: Bath, 1968; Salford, 1972. Chm., Biochemical Soc., 1946, and Treas., 1952–62; Pres., Section I (Biomedical) of BAAS, 1972–73; Mem., British National Cttee for Biochemistry, 1973–78; President: Royal Inst. Chem., 1972–74 (Vice-Pres., 1961–63, 1970–72); Chemical Soc., 1975–76; 12th Congress of Assoc. Internat. d'Expertise Chimique, Cambridge, 1972; Mem., UNESCO Cttee on status of scientific researchers, 1974; Chairman: Council, Science and Technology Insts Ltd, 1975–76; Council for Environmental Science and Engineering, 1975–81; Vice-Pres., Parly and Scientific Cttee, 1978–81. Assessor, Sci. Board, SRC, 1978–81. First medal awarded by Royal Soc. of Chem. for service to the Soc., 1983. *Publications:* Principles and Practice of Chromatography, 1941; The Vitamin B Complex, 1951; Antibiotics, 1951; Vitamin Co-Factors of Enzyme Systems, 1966; Chemists and the Law, 1967; research papers and reviews in scientific jls. *Recreations:* gardening, archæology. *Address:* 40 Handside Court, Handside Lane, Welwyn Garden City, Herts. *T:* Welwyn Garden 324751.

ROBINSON, Geoffrey; *see* Robinson, A. G.

ROBINSON, Geoffrey; MP (Lab) Coventry North-West, since March 1976; *b* 25 May 1938; *s* of Robert Norman Robinson and Dorothy Jane Robinson (*née* Skelly); *m* 1967, Marie Elena Giorgio; one *s* one *d. Educ:* Emanuel School; Cambridge and Yale Univs. Labour Party Research Assistant, 1965–68; Senior Executive, Industrial Reorganisation Corporation, 1968–70; Financial Controller, British Leyland, 1971–72; Managing Director, Leyland Innocenti, Milan, 1972–73; Chief Exec., Jaguar Cars, Coventry, 1973–75; Chief Exec. (unpaid), Meriden Motor Cycle Workers' Co-op, 1978–80 (Dir, 1980–82). Opposition spokesman on science, 1982–83, on regional affairs and industry, 1983–. Dir, W Midlands Enterprise Bd, 1980–84. *Recreations:* reading, squash. *Address:* House of Commons, SW1A 0AA. *T:* 01–219 3000.

ROBINSON, Harold George Robert, OBE 1961; FRAeS; CEng, MIEE; Director-General Research (General), Ministry of Defence (Procurement Executive), and Assistant Chief Scientific Adviser (Research), Ministry of Defence, 1981–84, retired; Senior Consultant, General Technology Systems Ltd, Brentford, since 1984; *b* 2 April 1924; *s* of Harold Arthur Robinson and Winifred Margaret (*née* Ballard); *m* 1955, Sonja (*née* Lapthorn); two *s. Educ:* Portsmouth Northern Grammar Sch.; Imperial Coll., London Univ.; California Inst. of Technology. WhSch 1944; BSc 1948; FCGI 1970. Joined RAE as Scientific Officer, 1948; Head of Satellite Launcher Div., Space Dept, RAE, 1961; Head of Avionics Dept, RAE, 1965–69; Head of Research Planning Div., Min. of Technology, 1969–71; Dir Gen., Aerospace Assessment and Res., DTI, 1971–74; Under-Sec., Space and Air Res., DoI, 1974–76; a Dep. Dir, RAE, 1976–81. Pres., Astronautics Commn, FAI, 1969–70 (Paul Tissandier Diploma, 1971); FRAeS 1981 (Bronze Medal, 1961). Pres., Whitworth Soc., 1982–83. *Publications:* various scientific and technical papers, contribs to books, primarily on rocket and space research. *Recreations:* painting, photography. *Address:* 39 Crosby Hill Drive, Camberley, Surrey. *T:* Camberley 23771.

ROBINSON, John Armstrong, CMG 1969; HM Diplomatic Service, retired; Ambassador to Israel, 1980–81; *b* 18 Dec. 1925; *m* 1952, Marianne Berger; one *s* one *d.* HM Forces, 1944–46; Foreign Office, 1949–50; Second Secretary, Delhi, 1950–52; Foreign Office, 1952–53; Helsinki, 1953–56; Second later First Secretary, Paris, 1956–58; Foreign Office, 1958–61; First Secretary in UK Delegation to European Communities, Brussels, 1962–67; Counsellor, Foreign Office, 1967; Head of European Economic Integration Dept, FCO, 1968–70; appointed Member of team of nine officials for negotiations on British entry into the Common Market, Brussels, 1970–71; Asst Under-Sec. of State, FCO, 1971–73; Ambassador to Algeria, 1974–77; Minister, Washington, 1977–80. *Address:* La Sirgarié, St Martin Laguépie, 81170 Cordes, Tarn, France.

ROBINSON, Sir John Beverley, 7th Bt, *cr* 1854; *b* 3 Oct. 1913; *s* of Sir John Beverley Robinson, 6th Bt, and Constance Marie (*d* 1977), *d* of Robert W. Pentecost; *S* father 1954. *Heir: kinsman* Christopher Philipse Robinson [*b* 10 Nov. 1938; *m* 1962, Barbara Judith, *d* of Richard Duncan; two *s* (and one *s* decd)].

ROBINSON, John Foster, CBE 1968; TD; DL; Honorary President, DRG plc, since 1974; *b* 2 Feb. 1909; *s* of late Sir Foster Gotch Robinson; *m* 1st, 1935, Margaret Eve Hannah Paterson (*d* 1977); two *s* two *d*; 2nd, 1979, Mrs Joan De Moraville. *Educ:* Harrow; Christ Church, Oxford. Dir, E. S. & A. Robinson Ltd, 1943, Jt Man. Dir 1948; Chm., E. S. & A. Robinson (Holdings) Ltd, 1961; Dep. Chm., The Dickinson Robinson Group Ltd, 1966, Chm., 1968–74. DL Glos 1972; High Sheriff, Avon, 1975. *Recreations:* shooting, fishing, golf. *Address:* Honor Farm, Failand Lane, Portbury, Bristol BS20 9SR. *T:* Pill 2108. *Clubs:* Houghton; Clifton, Bristol, Constitutional (Bristol).
See also M. N. F. Robinson.

ROBINSON, Sir John (James Michael Laud), 11th Bt *cr* 1660; DL; *b* 19 Jan. 1943; *s* of Michael Frederick Laud Robinson (*d* 1971) and Elizabeth (*née* Bridge); *S* grandfather, 1975; *m* 1968, Gayle Elizabeth (*née* Keyes); two *s* one *d. Educ:* Eton; Trinity Coll., Dublin (MA, Economics and Political Science). Chartered Financial Analyst. Chm., Celebrity Fabrics Ltd, 1982–. Pres., Northants Br., British Red Cross, 1982–; Chm., St Andrews Hosp., Northampton, 1984–. Chm., BBC Northants Radio Adv. Council, 1985–. DL Northants, 1984. *Heir: s* Mark Christopher Michael Villiers Robinson, *b* 23 April 1972. *Address:* Cranford Hall, Cranford, Kettering, Northants.

ROBINSON, Rev. Canon Joseph, MTh, FKC; Master of the Temple since 1980; *b* 23 Feb. 1927; *er s* of Thomas and Maggie Robinson; *m* 1953, Anne Antrobus; two *s* two *d. Educ:* Upholland Grammar Sch., Lancs; King's Coll., London. BD (1st cl. Hons); AKC (1st cl.) 1951; MTh 1958; FKC 1973. Deacon, 1952; Priest, 1953; Curate, All Hallows, Tottenham, 1952–55; Minor Canon of St Paul's Cathedral, 1956–68; Sacrist, 1958–68; Lectr in Hebrew and Old Testament Studies, King's Coll., London, 1959–68; Canon Residentiary, Canterbury Cathedral, 1968–80, now Canon Emeritus; Librarian, 1968–73; Treasurer, 1972–80; Exam. Chaplain to Archbishop of Canterbury, 1968–80. Golden Lectr, 1963; St Antholin Lectr, 1964–67. Chaplain, Worshipful Co. of Cutlers, 1963–; Sub Chaplain, Order of St John of Jerusalem, 1965–. *Publications:* The Cambridge Bible Commentary on 1 Kings, 1972, 2 Kings, 1976; articles in: Church Quarterly Review, Expository Times, Church Times; many reviews in various jls. *Recreations:* reading, gardening. *Address:* The Master's House, The Temple, EC4. *T:* 01–353 8559. *Club:* Athenæum.

ROBINSON, Kathleen Marian, (Mrs Vincent F. Sherry; Kathleen M. Sherry); FRCS, FRCOG, MD; Hon. Obstetrician, and Hon. Gynæcologist, Royal Free Hospital; Hon. Obstetrician, Queen Charlotte's Hospital; *b* 25 May 1911; *d* of late James Robinson and Ruth Robinson (*née* Edmeston); *m* 1946, Vincent Francis Sherry; one *s* one *d* (and one *d* decd). *Educ:* Penrhos College, Colwyn Bay; Royal Free Hospital School of Medicine, London University. MB, BS, 1936; MRCS, LRCP 1936; MD London 1940; FRCS 1940; MRCOG 1941; FRCOG 1953. House Surgeon: Royal Free Hospital; Samaritan Hospital, Royal Marsden Hospital, Queen Charlotte's Hospital. Resident Obstetrician, Queen Charlotte's Hospital. Recognised Teacher of the London University. FRSM; FRHS. *Publications:* contributor to Queen Charlotte's Text Book of Obstetrics, also to Practical Motherhood and Parentcraft. *Recreations:* gardening, cooking, travel. *Address:* 17 Herondale Avenue, SW18 3JN. *T:* 01–874 8588.

ROBINSON, Keith; *see* Robinson, L. K.

ROBINSON, Rt. Hon. Sir Kenneth, Kt 1983; PC 1964; Hon. DLitt; FCIT; Chairman, Arts Council of Great Britain, 1977–82; *b* Warrington, Lancs, 19 March 1911; *s* of late Clarence Robinson, MRCS, LRCP; *m* 1941, Helen Elizabeth Edwards; one *d. Educ:* Oundle Sch. Insurance Broker at Lloyd's, 1927–40. Served War of 1939–45, RN 1941–46; Ord. Seaman, 1941; commissioned, 1942; Lieut-Comdr RNVR, 1944; served Home Fleet, Mediterranean, Far East and Pacific. Company Secretary, 1946–69. MP (Lab) St Pancras N, 1949–70; Asst Whip (unpaid), 1950–51, an Opposition Whip, 1951–54; Minister of Health, 1964–68; Minister for Planning and Land, Min. of Housing and Local Govt, 1968–69. Dir, Social Policy, 1970–72, Man. Dir (Personnel and Social Policy Div.), 1972–74, British Steel Corp.; Chm., LTE, 1975–78. Chairman: English National Opera, 1972–77; Young Concert Artists Trust, 1983–; Carnegie Council Arts and Disabled People, 1985–; Jt Treas., RSA, 1983–. Trustee, Imperial War Mus., 1978–84. Hon. FRCGP; Hon. DLitt Liverpool, 1980. *Publications:* Wilkie Collins, a Biography, 1951; Policy for Mental Health, 1958; Patterns of Care, 1961; Look at Parliament, 1962. *Recreations:* looking at paintings, reading, listening to music. *Address:* 12 Grove Terrace, NW5.

ROBINSON, Kenneth Dean, MA Oxon; Administrator, Advertising Code, British Herbal Medicine Association, since 1978 (General Secretary, 1979–86); *b* 9 March 1909; *s* of late Rev. Arthur Edward and late Mary Edith Robinson; *m* 1936, Marjorie Belle Carter, Bradford, Yorks; two *s* two *d. Educ:* Bradford Grammar Sch.; Corpus Christi

Coll., Oxford (Scholar). Classical Honour Mods Class I, Litt Hum. Class II. Sixth Form Classical Master, St Edmund's, Canterbury, 1932–34; Head of Classical Dept, Wellington College, Berks, 1934–41; Intelligence Corps, 1941–45; Asst to Director of Education, Shire Hall, Reading, Berks, 1945–46; Headmaster: Birkenhead Sch., Cheshire, 1946–63 (Hon. Pres., Old Birkonian Soc., 1986–); Bradford Grammar Sch., 1963–74. Classics panel Secondary Sch. Examinations Council, 1948–50; Pres. Liverpool Br., Class. Assoc., 1958; Council, IAHM, 1949–53; HMC Cttee, 1956–60; Chm. NW Div., HMC, 1958–59; Chm. Direct Grant Cttee, HMC, 1958–59, Mem., 1967–70; Chm., NE Div., HMC, 1971–72; Chm. Op. Res. Sect. Div. XII, IAHM, 1952–60; Chm. Div. XII, IAHM, 1961–62; Mem. Council, 1962–63, Chm., 1975–79, Hon. Pres., 1979, Leeds/Bradford Branch, Nat. Assoc. for Gifted Children. Governor, Giggleswick Sch., 1974–84. *Publications:* (with R. L. Chambers) Septimus: a First Latin Reader, 1936; The Latin Way, 1947. *Recreations:* gardening, chess, painting, canals, country. *Address:* Lane House, Cowling, near Keighley, West Yorks BD22 0LX. *T:* Crosshills 34487.

ROBINSON, Kenneth Ernest, CBE 1971; MA, FRHistS; *b* 9 March 1914; *o s* of late Ernest and Isabel Robinson, Plumstead, Kent; *m* 1938, Stephanie, *o d* of late William Wilson, Westminster; one *s* one *d*. *Educ:* Monoux Grammar School, Walthamstow; Hertford College, Oxford (Scholar, 1st Cl. PPE; 1st Cl. Mod. Hist.; Beit Senior Schol. in Colonial History); London School of Economics. Colonial Office, 1936; Asst Sec. 1946; resigned 1948. Fellow of Nuffield Coll. (Hon. Fellow, 1984) and Reader in Commonwealth Govt, Oxford, 1948–57; Dir, Inst. of Commonwealth Studies and Prof. of Commonwealth Affairs, Univ. of London, 1957–65 (Hon. Life Mem., 1980–); Vice-Chancellor, Univ. of Hong Kong, 1965–72; Hallsworth Res. Fellow, Univ. of Manchester, 1972–74; Dir, Commonwealth Studies Resources Survey, Univ. of London, 1974–76. Leverhulme Res. Fellow, 1952–53; Vis. Lectr, Sch. of Advanced Internat. Studies, Johns Hopkins Univ., 1954; Carnegie Travel Grant, East, Central and S Africa, 1960; Reid Lectr, Acadia Univ., 1963; Vis. Prof., Duke Univ., NC, 1963; Callander Lectr, Aberdeen, 1979. Editor, Jl of Commonwealth Political Studies, 1961–65; Special Commonwealth Award, ODM, 1965. Member: (part-time) Directing Staff, Civil Service Selection Bd, 1951–56, Assessor Panel, 1973–77; Colonial Economic Res. Cttee, 1949–62; Colonial SSRC, 1958–62; Inter-Univ. Council for Higher Educn Overseas, 1973–79; Mem. Council: Overseas Develt Inst. 1960–65; RIIA, 1962–65; Internat. African Inst., 1960–65; African Studies Assoc., UK, 1963–65, 1978–81; ACU, 1967–68; Hong Kong Management Assoc., 1965–72; Chinese Univ. of Hong Kong, 1965–72; Univ. of Cape Coast, 1972–74; Royal Commonwealth Soc., 1974– (Vice Pres., 1984–); Royal African Soc., 1983–; Life Mem. Ct, Univ. of Hong Kong, 1972. Governor, LSE, 1959–65. Corresp. Mem., Académie des Sciences d'Outre-Mer, Paris. Hon. LLD Chinese Univ. of Hong Kong, 1969; Hon. DLitt, Univ. of Hong Kong, 1972; DUniv Open, 1978. JP Hong Kong, 1967–72. *Publications:* (with W. J. M. Mackenzie) Five Elections in Africa, 1960; (with A. F. Madden) Essays in Imperial Government presented to Margery Perham, 1963; The Dilemmas of Trusteeship, 1965; (with W. B. Hamilton & C. D. Goodwin) A Decade of the Commonwealth 1955–64 (USA), 1966. Contrib. to Africa Today (USA), 1955; Africa in the Modern World (USA), 1955; University Cooperation and Asian Development (USA), 1967; L'Europe du XIXe et du XXe Siècle, Vol. 7 (Italy), 1968; Experts in Africa, 1980; papers in learned jls. *Address:* The Old Rectory, Church Westcote, Oxon. *T:* Shipton under Wychwood 830586. *Clubs:* Royal Commonwealth Society, United Oxford & Cambridge University, Lansdowne; Hong Kong.

ROBINSON, Lee Fisher; Chief Executive and Deputy Chairman, Turriff Construction Corporation Ltd, since 1970; Chairman, Biotechna Ltd, since 1982; Consultant, International Management Consultants, since 1972; Director and Vice-President, RTL SA, since 1977; Director and Chief Executive, RTR SA, since 1977; Director and Chairman, Ingeco Laing Ltd (UK), since 1977; *b* 17 July 1923; *m* 1st, 1944, Zelda Isobel Fisher; three *d*; 2nd, 1976, June Edna Hopkins. *Educ:* Howard Sch.; Cardiff Tech. College. CEng; MICE; ACIArb. Royal Engrs, Sappers and Miners, IE, 1942–45. Turriff Const. Corp. Ltd, HBM (BCC), 1963; Man. Dir, Power Gas Corp. Ltd, 1964; Director: Davy-Ashmore Ltd, 1970; Combustion Systems (NRDC), 1972– (Chm., 1978); Redwood Internat. (UK) Ltd, 1972; Altech SA, 1976–; Protech SA, 1976–; Altech of Canada, 1976–; Danks Gowerton, 1976–; Hewlee Ltd, 1976–; BCS Ltd, 1976–; Charterhouse Strategic Development Ltd, 1976–80 (Gp Indust. Adviser, Charterhouse Gp); Altech (Canada) Ltd, 1976–; Ingeco Laing SA, 1977–; RTR (Oil Sands) Alberta, 1977–; RTR Canada Ltd, 1977–; SPO Minerals Co. Ltd, 1980–81; Thalassa (North Sea) Ltd, 1980–; Marcent Natural Resources Ltd (Man. Dir), 1980–; WGI Engineering Ltd, 1980–; Hydromet Mineral Co., 1983–. Chm., Warren Spring Adv. Bd, 1969–72; Mem. Adv. Council for Technology, 1968–69. *Publications:* Cost and Financing of Fertiliser Projects in India, 1967; various articles. *Recreations:* badminton, sailing. *Address:* Flat 3, Athenaeum Hall, Vale-of-Health, NW3 1AP. *Clubs:* East India, Devonshire, Sports and Public Schools, Wig and Pen.

ROBINSON, (Leonard) Keith, CBE 1981; DL; management consultant, since 1985; County Chief Executive, Hampshire County Council, 1973–85; Clerk of Lieutenancy, 1973–85; *b* 2 July 1920; *s* of Cuthbert Lawrence Robinson and Hilda Robinson; *m* 1948, Susan May Tomkinson; two *s* two *d*. *Educ:* Queen Elizabeth's Grammar Sch., Blackburn; Victoria Univ. of Manchester (LLB). Solicitor. RAFVR, 1940–46 (Navigator, Sqdn-Ldr). Asst Solicitor, City and County of Bristol, 1948–55; Dep. Town Clerk, Birkenhead Co. Borough Council, 1955–66; Town Clerk, Stoke-on-Trent City Council, 1966–73. Association of County Councils: Mem., Officers Adv. Gp, 1974–83 (Chm., 1977–82); Adviser, Policy Cttee, 1975–82; Adviser, Local Govt Finance Cttee, 1976–85; Chm., Assoc. of County Chief Execs, 1975–77. Member: W Mids Econ. Planning Council, 1967–73; Keele Univ. Council, 1968–73; Central Cttee for Reclamation of Derelict Land, 1971–74; Quality Assce Council, BSI, 1973–77; Job Creation Programme Action Cttee for London and SE, 1976–77; District Manpower Cttee, 1980–83; Adv. Council for Energy Conservation, 1982–84; Local Authorities' Mutual Investment Trust, 1982–83; Hillier Arboretum Management Cttee, 1985– (Sec., 1977–85); Southern Arts, 1985–; Exec. Cttee, Hampshire Develt Assoc., 1985–; Vice-Chm., Nuffield Theatre Bd, 1985–. Trustee, and Mem. Council of Management, New Theatre Royal (Portsmouth) Ltd, 1976–; Mem. Exec. Cttee, Hampshire Gardens Trust, 1985–; Dir, Salisbury Playhouse, 1979–. DL Hants, 1985. *Publications:* contrib. local govt and legal jls. *Recreations:* fly-fishing, theatre, photography, gardening. *Address:* Bransbury Mill Cottage, Bransbury, Barton Stacey, Winchester, Hants SO21 3QJ. *Clubs:* National Liberal, MCC.

ROBINSON, Lloyd; *see* Robinson, T. L.

ROBINSON, Group Captain Marcus, CB 1956; AFC 1941 and Bar 1944; AE 1942; DL; Chairman, Robinson, Dunn & Co. Ltd and subsidiary companies, 1966–77, retired; *b* 27 May 1912; *s* of Wilson and Eileen Robinson; *m* 1st, 1941, Mrs Mary Playfair (marr. diss. 1951); 2nd, 1953, Mrs Joan E. G. O. Weatherlake (*née* Carter); one *s* one *d*. *Educ:* Rossall. Commissioned AAF, 602 Sqdn, 1934; Squadron Ldr, 1940, commanding 616 Squadron; Wing Comdr, 1942; Group Capt., 1945; re-formed 602 Squadron, 1946; Member Air Advisory Council, Air Ministry, 1952–56; Chairman Glasgow TA and AFA, 1953–56; Chairman Glasgow Rating Valuation Appeals Cttee, 1963–74 (Dep. Chm., 1958–63). A Vice-Pres., Earl Haig Fund, Scotland, 1978– (Chm., 1974–78). DL Glasgow, 1953. Silver Jubilee Medal, 1977. *Recreations:* ski-ing, sailing. *Address:* Rockfort, Helensburgh, Dunbartonshire G84 7BA. *Clubs:* Western (Glasgow); Royal Northern and Clyde Yacht (Rhu).

ROBINSON, Mark Noel Foster; MP (C) Newport West, since 1983; Parliamentary Under Secretary of State, Welsh Office, since 1985; *b* 26 Dec. 1946; *s* of John Foster Robinson, *qv*; *m* 1982, Vivien Radclyffe (*née* Pilkington); one *s* one *d*. *Educ:* Harrow School; Christ Church, Oxford. MA Hons Modern History. Called to the Bar, Middle Temple, 1975. Research Assistant to Patrick Cormack, 1970–71; Special Asst to US Congressman Hon. F. Bradford Morse, 1971–72; Special Asst to Chief of UN Emergency Operation in Bangladesh, 1972–73; Second Officer, Exec. Office, UN Secretary-General, 1974–77; Asst Dir, Commonwealth Secretariat, 1977–83. Mem., Foreign Affairs Select Cttee, 1983–84; PPS to Sec. of State for Wales, 1984–85. Hon. Sec., UN Parly Gp, 1983–85. *Recreations:* include the countryside and fishing. *Address:* House of Commons, SW1. *Club:* Travellers'.

ROBINSON, Air Vice-Marshal Michael Maurice Jeffries, CB 1982; Secretary (Welfare) to the RAF Benevolent Fund, since 1982; *b* 11 Feb. 1927; *s* of Dr Maurice Robinson and Muriel (*née* Jeffries); *m* 1952, Drusilla Dallas Bush; one *s* two *d*. *Educ:* King's Sch., Bruton; Queen's Coll., Oxford; RAF Coll., Cranwell. psa 1961, jssc 1965. Commnd, 1948; 45 Sqdn, Malaya, 1948–51; CFS, 1953–55; OC 100 Sqdn, 1962–64; Comd, RAF Lossiemouth, 1972–74; Asst Comdt, RAF Coll., Cranwell, 1974–77; SASO No 1 Gp, 1977–79; Dir Gen. of Organisation (RAF), 1979–82, retd. Wing Comdr 1961, Gp Captain 1970, Air Cdre 1976, Air Vice-Marshal 1980. Governor, King's Sch., Bruton, 1980–. *Recreations:* golf, gardening, going to the opera. *Address:* Lloyds Bank (Cox's and King's Branch), 6 Pall Mall, SW1Y 5NH. *Club:* Royal Air Force.

ROBINSON, Sir Niall B. L.; *see* Lynch-Robinson.

ROBINSON, Oliver John; Editor, Good Housekeeping, 1947–65, Editor-in-Chief, 1965–67; *b* 7 April 1908; *s* of late W. Heath and Josephine Constance Robinson; *m* 1933, Evelyn Anne Laidler. *Educ:* Cranleigh Sch. Art Editor, Good Housekeeping, 1930; Art Editor, Nash's, 1933. Temporary commission, Queen's Royal Regt, 1941; Camouflage Development and Training Centre, 1942; Staff Officer, War Office, 1944. *Address:* 92 Charlbert Court, Eamont Street, NW8 7DA. *T:* 01–722 0723. *Club:* Savage.

ROBINSON, Oswald Horsley, CMG 1983; OBE 1977; HM Diplomatic Service, retired; *b* 24 Aug. 1926; *s* of Sir Edward Stanley Gotch Robinson, CBE, FSA, FBA, and Pamela, *d* of Sir Victor Horsley, CB, FRS; *m* 1954, Helena Faith, *d* of Dr F. R. Seymour; two *s* one *d*. *Educ:* Bedales Sch.; King's Coll., Cambridge. Served RE, 1943–48. Joined FO, 1951; served: Rangoon and Maymyo, 1954; FO, 1958; Mexico and Guatemala, 1961; Quito and Bogotá, 1963; FO (later FCO), 1965; Georgetown, Guyana, 1973; Bangkok, 1976; FCO, 1979–84. *Recreation:* sailing. *Clubs:* Royal Cruising; West Mersea Yacht.

ROBINSON, Peter; Director, Tootal Ltd, since 1973; *b* 18 Jan. 1922; *s* of Harold Robinson and Jane Elizabeth Robinson; *m* Lesley Anne, step-*d* of Major J. M. May, TD; two *s* two *d*. *Educ:* Prince Henry's Sch., Otley; Leeds Coll. of Technology (Diploma in Printing). Mem., Inst. of Printing; CBIM. Management Trainee, 1940–41; flying duties, RAFVR, 1942–46; Leeds Coll. of Technol., 1946–49; Asst Manager, Robinson & Sons Ltd, Chesterfield, 1949–53; Works Dir and Man. Dir, Taylowe Ltd, 1953–62; Director: Hazell Sun, 1964; British Printing Corp., 1966–81, Man. Dir 1969–75; Chm. and Chief Exec., BPC Ltd (formerly British Printing Corp.), 1976–81. Formerly Council Mem., PIRA. *Recreations:* military history, cricket, golf. *Address:* 20 Links Road, Flackwell Heath, High Wycombe, Bucks.

ROBINSON, Peter Damian, CB 1983; Adviser on the Hong Kong Judiciary, since 1986; *b* 11 July 1926; *s* of late John Robinson and Jill Clegg (*née* Easten); *m* 1st, 1956, Mary Katinka Bonner (*d* 1978), Peterborough; two *d*; 2nd, 1985, Mrs Sheila Suzanne Gibbins (*née* Guille). *Educ:* Corby Sch., Sunderland; Lincoln Coll., Oxford. MA. Royal Marine Commandos, 1944–46. Called to Bar, Middle Temple, 1951; practised common law, 1952–59; Clerk of Assize, NE Circuit, 1959–70; Administrator, NE Circuit, 1970–74; Circuit Administrator, SE Circuit, 1974–80; Dep. Sec., 1980–86, and Dep. Clerk of the Crown in Chancery, 1982–86, Lord Chancellor's Dept. Member, Home Office Departmental Cttee on Legal Aid in Criminal Proceedings (the Widgery Cttee), 1964–66; Chm., Interdeptl Cttee on Conciliation, 1982–83. *Recreations:* reading, the countryside. *Address:* c/o Hayes Dixon, 146 Strand, WC2R 1JH. *Club:* Athenæum.

ROBINSON, Peter David; MP (DemU) Belfast East, since 1979 (resigned seat Dec. 1985 in protest against Anglo-Irish Agreement; re-elected Jan. 1986); *b* 29 Dec. 1948; *s* of David McCrea Robinson and Sheliah Robinson; *m* 1970, Iris Collins; two *s* one *d*. *Educ:* Annadale Grammar School; Castlereagh Further Education College. Gen. Secretary, Ulster Democratic Unionist Party, 1975–79, Dep. Leader, 1980–. Mem. (DemU) Belfast E, NI Assembly, 1982–86; Member, Castlereagh Borough Council, 1977; Deputy Mayor, 1978; Mayor of Castlereagh, 1986. *Publications:* (jtly) Ulster—the facts, 1982; booklets: The North Answers Back, 1970; Capital Punishment for Capital Crime, 1978; Self Inflicted, 1981; Ulster in Peril, 1981; Savagery and Suffering, 1981. *Address:* 51 Gransha Road, Dundonald, Northern Ireland.

ROBINSON, Philip Henry; Chairman, Sunbury Investment Co. Ltd, since 1985; *b* 4 Jan. 1926; *s* of Arthur Robinson and Frances M. Robinson; *m* 1st, 1959, Helen Wharton (marr. diss. 1979); one *s* one *d*; 2nd, 1985, Mrs A. L. D. Baring; two step *s*. *Educ:* Lincoln Sch.; Jesus Coll., Cambridge (Exhibr, MA); Sch. of Oriental and African Studies, London Univ.; NY Univ. Graduate Sch. of Business Admin. Member, Gray's Inn. Royal Navy, 1944–47; N. M. Rothschild & Sons, 1950–54; Actg Sec., British Newfoundland Corp., Montreal, 1954–56; Asst Vice-Pres., J. Henry Schroder Banking Corp., NY, 1956–61; J. Henry Schroder Wagg & Co. Ltd, 1961; Director: J. Henry Schroder Wagg & Co. Ltd, 1966–85; Siemens Ltd, 1967–86; Schroders & Chartered Ltd Hong Kong, 1971–85; Standard Chartered PLC, 1986–; Exec. Vice-Pres., Schroder International Ltd, 1977–85 (Dir, 1973–85); Chm., Schroder Leasing Ltd, 1979–85. Managing Trustee, Municipal Mutual Insurance Ltd, 1977–. Mem., Nat. Coal Board, 1973–77. Hon. Treasurer, Nat. Council for One Parent Families, 1977–79. *Publications:* contrib. Investor's Chronicle. *Recreations:* music, walking. *Address:* Stone Hall, Great Mongeham, Deal, Kent; Saint-Maximin, 30700 Uzès, France. *Club:* Brooks's.
See also A. G. Robinson.

ROBINSON, Robert Henry; writer and broadcaster; *b* 17 Dec. 1927; *o s* of Ernest Redfern Robinson and Johanna Hogan; *m* 1958, Josephine Mary Richard; one *s* two *d*. *Educ:* Raynes Park Grammar Sch.; Exeter Coll., Oxford (MA). Editor of Isis, 1950. TV columnist, Sunday Chronicle, 1952; film and theatre columnist, Sunday Graphic, and radio critic, Sunday Times, 1956; editor Atticus, Sunday Times, 1960; weekly column, Private View, Sunday Times, 1962; film critic, Sunday Telegraph, 1965. Writer and/or presenter of TV programmes: Picture Parade, 1959; Points of View, 1961; Divided We Stand, 1964; The Look of the Week, 1966; Reason to Believe?, The Fifties, 1969; Chm., Call My Bluff, Ask The Family, 1967; The Book Programme, Vital Statistics, 1974;

Word for Word, 1978; The Book Game, 1983 and 1985; films for TV: Robinson's Travels - the Pioneer Trail West, 1977; From Shepherd's Bush to Simla, 1979; B. Traven: a mystery solved, 1978; Robinson Cruising, 1981; The Auden Landscape, 1982; Robinson Country, 1983, 1986; presenter of: BBC radio current affairs programme Today, 1971–74; Chm., Brain of Britain, 1973–; Chm., Stop the Week, 1974–. Pres., Johnson Soc. of Lichfield, 1982. Radio Personality of the Year: Radio Industries Club, 1973; Variety Club of GB, 1980. *Publications:* (ed) Poetry from Oxford, 1951; Landscape with Dead Dons, 1956; Inside Robert Robinson (essays), 1965; (contrib.) To Nevill Coghill from Friends, 1966; The Conspiracy, 1968; The Dog Chairman, 1982; (ed) The Everyman Book of Light Verse, 1984; In Trust—Houses and Heritage, 1986; Robinson Country, 1987; contrib. The Times, Punch, Listener, etc. *Address:* 16 Cheyne Row, SW3; Laurel Cottage, Buckland St Mary, Somerset. *Clubs:* Garrick, Savile.

ROBINSON, Prof. Roger James, FRCP; Professor of Paediatrics, United Medical and Dental Schools of Guy's and St Thomas's Hospitals (formerly Guy's Hospital Medical School), University of London, since 1975; *b* 17 May 1932; *s* of Albert Edward and Leonora Sarah Robinson; *m* 1962, Jane Hippisley Packham; two *s* one *d.* *Educ:* Poole Grammar Sch.; Balliol Coll., Oxford (Brackenbury schol.; MA, DPhil, BM, BCh). Lectr of Christ Church, Oxford, 1953; appts at Radcliffe Infirmary, Oxford, National Hosp., Queen Square, and Hammersmith Hosp., 1960–66; Visiting Fellow, Harvard, 1967; Sen. Lectr, Inst. of Child Health, Hammersmith Hosp., 1967; Cons. Paediatrician, Guy's Hosp., 1971. *Publications:* Brain and Early Behaviour: development in the fetus and infant, 1969; (jtly) Medical Care of Newborn Babies, 1972; papers on paediatrics and child neurology. *Address:* 60 Madeley Road, Ealing, W5 2LU.

ROBINSON, Prof. Ronald Edward, CBE 1970; DFC 1944; Beit Professor of the History of the British Commonwealth, and Fellow of Balliol College, Oxford University, since 1971; Director, University of Oxford Development Records Project, since 1978; *b* 3 Sept. 1920; *e s* of William Edward and Ada Theresa Robinson, Clapham; *m* 1948, Alice Josephine Denny; two *s* two *d.* *Educ:* Battersea Grammar Sch.; St John's Coll., Cambridge. Major Scholar in History, St John's Coll., 1939; BA 1946, PhD 1949, Cantab. F/Lt, 58 Bomber Sqn, RAF, 1942–45. Research Officer, African Studies Branch, Colonial Office, 1947–49; Lectr in History, 1953–66, Smuts Reader in History of the British Commonwealth, 1966–71, Univ. of Cambridge; Tutor 1961–66, Fellow 1949–71, St John's Coll., Cambridge; Chm., Faculty Bd of Modern Hist., Oxford, 1974–76, Vice-Chm., 1979–. Inst. for Advanced Studies, Princeton, 1959–60. Mem., Bridges Cttee on Trng in Public Administration, 1961–62; Chm., Cambridge Confs on Problems of Developing Countries, 1961–70. UK observer, Zimbabwe election, 1980. *Publications:* Africa and the Victorians, 1961; Developing the Third World, 1971; articles in Cambridge History of the British Empire, Vol. III, 1959, and The New Cambridge Modern History, Vol. XI, 1963; reports on Problems of Developing Countries, 1963–71; articles and reviews in learned jls. *Recreation:* room cricket. *Address:* Balliol College, Oxford. *Clubs:* Royal Commonwealth Society; Hawks (Cambridge); Gridiron (Oxford).

ROBINSON, Stanley Scott, MBE 1944; TD 1950; Sheriff of Grampian, Highland and Islands (formerly Inverness (including Western Isles), Ross, Cromarty, Moray and Nairn), 1973–83; retired; *b* 27 March 1913; *s* of late William Scott Robinson, Engineer, and of Christina Douglas Robinson; *m* 1937, Helen Annan Hardie; three *s.* *Educ:* Boroughmuir Sch., Edinburgh; Edinburgh Univ. Admitted as solicitor, 1935; Solicitor in the Supreme Courts. Commissioned in TA, 1935. Served War: France and Belgium, 1939–40, Captain RA; France, Holland and Germany, 1944–45 (despatches twice); Major, RA, 1943; Lt-Col, 1948. Solicitor in gen. practice in Montrose, Angus, 1935–72 (except during war service). Hon. Sheriff: of Perth and Angus, 1970–72; of Inverness, 1984. Mem. Council of Law Society of Scotland, 1963–72 (Vice-Pres., 1971–72); Dean, Soc. of Solicitors of Angus, 1970–72. *Publications:* contribs to Stair Memorial Encyclopaedia and Jl of Law Society of Scotland. *Recreations:* golf, bowling, military history. *Address:* Flat 3, Drumallin House, Drummond Road, Inverness. *T:* Inverness 233488. *Club:* Highland (Inverness).

ROBINSON, Stephen Joseph, OBE 1971; FRS 1976; FEng, FIEE; on secondment as Deputy Director, Royal Signals and Radar Establishment, Ministry of Defence, since 1985; *b* 6 Aug. 1931; *s* of Joseph Allan Robinson and Ethel (*née* Bunting); *m* 1957, Monica Mabs Scott; one *s* one *d.* *Educ:* Sebright Sch., Wolverley; Jesus Coll., Cambridge (MA Natural Sciences). RAF, 1950–51. Mullard Res. Labs, 1954–72; MEL Div., Philips Industries (formerly MEL Equipment Co. Ltd), 1972–79; Product Dir, 1973–79; Man. Dir, Pye TVT Ltd, 1980–84. Mem. Council, Royal Soc., 1982–. *Recreations:* sailing, skiing. *Address:* 140 The Street, Kirtling, near Newmarket, Suffolk. *T:* Newmarket 730104.

ROBINSON, Thomas Lloyd, TD; Honorary Vice-President, The Dickinson Robinson Group Ltd, since 1978 (Chairman, 1974–77, Deputy Chairman, 1968); *b* 21 Dec. 1912; *s* of late Thomas Rosser Robinson and Rebe Francis-Watkins; *m* 1939, Pamela Rosemary Foster; one *s* two *d.* *Educ:* Wycliffe Coll. Served War, 1939–45: Royal Warwickshire Regt, 61 Div., and SHAEF; Staff Coll., Camberley. Director, E. S. & A. Robinson Ltd, 1952; Jt Managing Dir, 1958; Dep. Chm., E. S. & A. Robinson (Holdings) Ltd, 1963; Director: Bristol Waterworks Co., 1978–84; Van Leer Groep Stichting, Holland, 1977–81; Legal & General Assurance Society (now Legal & General Group plc), 1970–83 (Vice-Chm., 1978–83); Chm., Legal & General South and Western Advisory Bd, 1972–84. Chm., Council of Governors, Wycliffe Coll., 1970–83; Mem. Council, Univ. of Bristol, 1977–83, Pro-Chancellor, 1983–. Master, Soc. of Merchant Venturers, Bristol, 1977–78. High Sheriff, Avon, 1979–80; Pres., Glos CCC, 1980–83. Hon. LLD Bristol, 1985. *Recreations:* music, antiques, golf. *Address:* Lechlade, 23 Druid Stoke Avenue, Stoke Bishop, Bristol BS9 1DB. *T:* Bristol 681957. *Clubs:* Army & Navy, MCC; Royal and Ancient (St Andrews); Clifton (Bristol).

ROBINSON, Victor, CEng, FIChemE; non-executive Director, Davy International Projects (concerned with major multi-discipline overseas projects); *b* 31 July 1925; *s* of Arthur Worsley Robinson and Nellie (*née* Halliwell); *m* 1948, Sadie Monica (*née* Grut); one *s* five *d.* *Educ:* Manchester Grammar Sch.; Cambridge Univ. (MA); Admin. Staff Coll., Henley. CEng, FIChemE 1960. Simon Carves Ltd: R&D Proj. Engrg, 1945; Technical Dir, 1961; Dir, 1964; Man. Dir Overseas Ops and Dir, Sim-Chem Ltd and subsid. cos, 1966; Man. Dir, Turriff Taylor Ltd, 1974–76; Industrial Adviser, Dept of Trade (on secondment from Davy Corp. Ltd), 1978–81. *Recreation:* fell and alpine walking. *Address:* 1A The Crest, Surbiton, Surrey KT5 8JZ. *T:* 01–399 1753.

ROBINSON, Vivian; QC 1986; a Recorder, since 1986; *b* 29 July 1944; *s* of William and Ann Robinson; *m* 1975, Louise Marriner; one *s* two *d.* *Educ:* Queen Elizabeth Grammar School, Wakefield; The Leys School, Cambridge; Sidney Sussex College, Cambridge (BA). Called to the Bar, Inner Temple, 1967. *Address:* Queen Elizabeth Building, Temple, EC4Y 9BS.

ROBINSON, Sir Wilfred (Henry Frederick), 3rd Bt, *cr* 1908; Finance Officer, Society of Genealogists, since 1980; Staff, Diocesan College School, Rondebosch, South Africa, 1950–77, Vice-Principal, 1969–77; *b* 24 Dec. 1917; *s* of Wilfred Henry Robinson (*d* 1922) (3rd *s* of 1st Bt), and Eileen (*d* 1963), *d* of Frederick St Leger, Claremont, SA; *S* uncle, Sir Joseph Benjamin Robinson, 2nd Bt, 1954; *m* 1946, Margaret Alison Kathleen, *d* of late Frank Mellish, MC, Bergendal, Gansbaai, Cape Province, SA; one *s* two *d.* *Educ:* Diocesan Coll., Rondebosch; St John's Coll., Cambridge, MA 1944. Served War of 1939–45, Devonshire Regt and Parachute Regt, Major. *Heir:* *s* Peter Frank Robinson, *b* 23 June 1949. *Address:* 8 Charlotte Road, Barnes, SW13.

ROBINSON, Ven. William David; Archdeacon of Blackburn, since 1986; Vicar of Balderstone, since 1986; *b* 15 March 1931; *s* of William and Margaret Robinson; *m* 1955, Carol Averil Roma Hamm; one *s* one *d.* *Educ:* Queen Elizabeth's Grammar School, Blackburn; Durham Univ. (MA, DipTh). Curate: Standish, 1958–61; Lancaster Priory (i/c St George), 1961–63; Vicar, St James, Blackburn, 1963–73; Diocesan Stewardship Adviser, Blackburn, and Priest-in-charge, St James, Shireshead, 1973–86; Hon. Canon, Blackburn Cathedral, 1975–86. *Recreation:* fell walking. *Address:* Balderstone Vicarage, Blackburn, Lancs BB2 7LL. *T:* Mellor 2232.

ROBINSON, William Good; Deputy Secretary, Department of the Civil Service, Northern Ireland, 1978–80, retired; *b* 20 May 1919; *s* of William Robinson and Elizabeth Ann (*née* Good); *m* 1947, Wilhelmina Vaughan; two *d.* *Educ:* Clones High Sch.; Queen's Univ. of Belfast (BScEcon, BA). Served War, RAF, 1941–46 (Flt Lieut, Navigator). Entered NI Civil Service, 1938; Min. of Labour and National Insurance, NI, 1946–63; Principal, Min. of Home Affairs, NI, 1963; Asst Sec., 1967; Sen. Asst Sec., NI Office, 1973. *Recreations:* do-it-yourself, reading history. *Address:* Stormochree, 47 Castlehill Road, Belfast BT4 3GN. *T:* Belfast 63646.

ROBINSON, Rt. Rev. William James; *b* 8 Sept. 1916; *s* of Thomas Albert Robinson and Harriet Mills; *m* 1946, Isobel Morton; one *s* three *d.* *Educ:* Bishop's Univ., Lennoxville, PQ. BA in Theology; DCL (*hc*) 1973. Deacon, 1939; Priest, 1940; Asst Curate in Trenton, 1939–41; Rector of: Tweed and Madoc, 1941–46, Tweed and N Addington, 1946–47; Napanee, 1948–53; St Thomas' Church, Belleville, 1953–55; St John's Church, Ottawa, 1955–62; Church of Ascension, Hamilton, 1962–67; St George's Church, Guelph, 1967–70. Canon of Christ Church Cathedral, Hamilton, 1964–68; Archdeacon of Trafalgar (Niagara Diocese), 1968–70; Bishop of Ottawa, 1970–81; retired. *Recreations:* woodworking and gardening. *Address:* 168 Inverness Crescent, Kingston, Ontario, K7M 6N7. *T:* (613) 549–7599.

ROBINSON, William Rhys Brunel; Under Secretary, Overseas Division, Department of Employment, since 1980; *b* 12 July 1930; *s* of late William Robinson and Elizabeth Myfanwy Robinson (*née* Owen). *Educ:* Chepstow Secondary Grammar Sch.; St Catherine' Soc., Oxford (MA,BLitt). Entered Min. of Labour, 1954; Asst Private Sec. to Minister, 1958–59; Principal, Min. of Labour, 1959; Asst Sec., 1966; London Sch. of Economics, 1972–73 (MSc Industrial Relations, 1973); Asst Sec., Trng Services Agency, 1973–75; Dep. Chief Exec., Employment Service Agency, 1975–77; Under-Sec. and Dir of Establishments, Dept of Employment, 1977–80. Chm., Governing Body, ILO, 1986. FSA 1978. *Publications:* articles in historical jls. *Recreation:* historical research. *Address:* 7 Shere Avenue, Cheam, Surrey SM2 7JU. *T:* 01–393 3019.

ROBLES, Marisa, (Mrs Christopher Hyde-Smith); harpist; Professor of Harp: Madrid Conservatoire, since 1958; Royal College of Music, since 1971; *b* 4 May 1937; *d* of Cristobal Robles and Maria Bonilla; *m* 1968, Christopher Hyde-Smith; two *s* one *d.* *Educ:* Madrid National Sch.; Madrid Conservatoire. Recitals in Europe, Africa and America; soloist with major internat. orchestras. Hon. Royal Madrid Conservatoire 1958; Hon. RCM 1973. *Recreations:* theatre, indoor plants, family life in general. *Address:* 38 Luttrell Avenue, Putney, SW15 6PE. *T:* 01–788 3753. *Club:* Anglo-Spanish.

ROBOROUGH, 2nd Baron, *cr* 1938, of Maristow; **Massey Henry Edgcumbe Lopes;** Bt, *cr* 1805; JP; Brevet Major Reserve of Officers Royal Scots Greys; Lord-Lieutenant and Custos Rotulorum of Devon, 1958–78; *b* 4 Oct. 1903; *o s* of 1st Baron and Lady Albertha Louisa Florence Edgcumbe (*d* 1941), *d* of 4th Earl of Mount Edgcumbe; *S* father 1938; *m* 1936, Helen, *o d* of late Colonel E. A. F. Dawson, Launde Abbey, Leicestershire; two *s* (and one *d* decd). *Educ:* Eton Coll.; Christ Church, Oxford (BA). Served in Royal Scots Greys, 1925–38; served again 1939–45 (twice wounded). ADC to Earl of Clarendon, when Governor of Union of South Africa, 1936–37. CA Devon, 1956–74; DL 1946; Vice-Lieutenant of Devon, 1951; Member of Duchy of Cornwall Council, 1958–68; High Steward of Barnstaple. Chairman: Dartmoor National Park, 1965–74; SW Devon Div. Educn Cttee, 1954–74; Devon Outward Bound, 1960–75; President: SW Reg., YMCA, 1958–67; Devon British Legion, 1958–68; Devon Conservation Forum, 1972–78; President, Devon, 1958–78: Magistrates Cttee; Council of St John; CPRE; Trust for Nature Conservation; Boy Scouts Assoc.; Football Assoc.; Assoc. of Youth Clubs. Governor: Exeter Univ.; Seale-Hayne, Kelly, Plymouth and Exeter Colls. Hon. Col, Devon Army Cadet Force, 1967–78. Hon. LLD Exeter, 1969. KStJ. *Heir:* *s* Hon. Henry Massey Lopes [*b* 2 Feb. 1940; *m* 1968, Robyn, *e d* of John Bromwich, Melbourne, Aust.; two *s* two *d*]. *Address:* Bickham Barton, Roborough, Plymouth, Devon. *T:* Yelverton 2478. *Club:* Cavalry and Guards.

ROBSON, family name of **Baroness Robson of Kiddington.**

ROBSON OF KIDDINGTON, Baroness *cr* 1974 (Life Peer), of Kiddington; **Inga-Stina Robson,** JP; Chairman, South-West Thames Regional Health Authority, 1974–82; *b* 20 Aug. 1919; *d* of Erik R. Arvidsson and Lilly A. Arvidsson (*née* Danielson); *m* 1940, Sir Lawrence W. Robson (*d* 1982); one *s* two *d.* *Educ:* Stockholm, Sweden. Swedish Foreign Office, 1939–40; Min. of Information, 1942–43. Contested (L) Eye Div., 1955 and 1959, Gloucester City, 1964 and 1966. President: Women's Liberal Fedn, 1968–69 and 1969–70; Liberal Party Org., 1970–71; Chm., Liberal Party Environment Panel, 1971–77. Chairman: Bd of Governors, Queen Charlotte's and Chelsea Hosps, 1970–84; Midwife Teachers Training Coll.; Nat. Assoc. of Leagues of Hosp. Friends, 1985–; Member: Cttee of Management, Inst. of Obst. and Gynaecology; Bd of Governors, University Coll. Hosp., 1966–74; Council, Surrey Univ., 1974. Chm., Anglo-Swedish Soc., 1983–. JP Oxfordshire, 1955. *Recreations:* sailing, skiing. *Address:* Kiddington Hall, Woodstock, Oxon.

ROBSON, Brian Ewart, CB 1985; Deputy Under-Secretary of State (Personnel and Logistics), Ministry of Defence, 1984–86; *b* 25 July 1926; 2nd *s* of late Walter Ewart Robson; *m* 1962, Cynthia Margaret, *o d* of late William James Scott, Recife, Brazil; two *d.* *Educ:* Steyning Grammar Sch.; Varndean Sch., Brighton; The Queen's Coll., Oxford (BA Modern History). Royal Sussex Regt and Kumaon Regt, Indian Army, 1944–47. Air Min., 1950; Asst Private Sec. to Sec. of State for Air, 1953–55; Principal, 1955; Asst Sec., 1965; Imperial Defence Coll., 1970; Ecole Nationale d'Administration, Paris, 1975; Asst Under-Sec. of State, MoD, 1976–82; Dep. Under-Sec. of State (Army), 1982–84. Mem., Central Finance Bd of C of E, 1985–. Comr, Royal Hosp., 1982–85; Member Council: Soc. for Army Historical Res., 1977–; Army Records Soc., 1984–; Nat. Army Museum, 1982; Trustee, Imperial War Museum, 1984–86. *Publications:* Swords of the British Army, 1975; The Road to Kabul: the Second Afghan War 1878–1880, 1986; numerous articles on weapons and military history. *Recreations:* military history, cricket, travel. *Address:* 17 Woodlands, Hove, East Sussex BN3 6TJ. *T:* Brighton 505803. *Club:* Naval and Military.

ROBSON, David Ernest Henry, QC 1980; a Recorder of the Crown Court (NE Circuit), since 1979; *b* 1 March 1940; *s* of late Joseph Robson and of Caroline Robson. *Educ:* Robert Richardson Grammar Sch., Ryhope; Christ Church, Oxford (MA). Called to the Bar, Inner Temple, 1965; NE Circuit, 1965–. Profumo Prize, Inner Temple, 1963. *Recreations:* acting, Italy. *Address:* Whitton Grange, Whitton, Rothbury, Northumberland NE65 7RL. *T:* Rothbury 20929. *Club:* County (Durham).

ROBSON, Prof. Elizabeth Browel; Galton Professor of Human Genetics and Head of Department of Genetics and Biometry, University College London, since 1978; *b* 10 Nov. 1928; *d* of Thomas Robson and Isabella (*née* Stoker); *m* 1955, George Macbeth, *qv* (marr. diss. 1975). *Educ:* Bishop Auckland Girls' Grammar Sch., King's Coll., Newcastle upon Tyne. BSc Dunelm; PhD London. Rockefeller Fellowship, Columbia Univ., New York City, 1954–55; external scientific staff of MRC (London Hosp. Med. Coll. and King's Coll. London), 1955–62; Member and later Asst Director, MRC Human Biochemical Genetics Unit, University Coll. London, 1962–78. Member, Board of Trustees, Royal Botanic Gardens, Kew, 1984–. Jt Editor, Annals of Human Genetics, 1978–. *Publications:* papers on biochemical human genetics and gene mapping in scientific jls. *Address:* 44 Sheen Road, Richmond, Surrey TW9 1AW.

ROBSON, Frank Elms; Partner, Trollope and Winckworth, Solicitors, Oxford and Westminster, since 1962; Registrar: Diocese of Oxford, since 1970; Province of Canterbury, since 1982; *b* 14 Dec. 1931; *s* of Joseph A. Robson and Barbara Robson; *m* 1958, Helen (*née* Jackson) four *s* one *d*. *Educ:* King Edward VI Grammar Sch., Morpeth; Selwyn Coll., Cambridge (MA). Admitted solicitor, 1954. *Recreations:* fell-walking, clocks, following Oxford United. *Address:* 2 Simms Close, Stanton St John, Oxford OX9 1HB. *T:* Stanton St John 393.

ROBSON, Vice-Adm. Sir Geoffrey; *see* Robson, Vice-Adm. Sir W. G. A.

ROBSON, Prof. Sir (James) Gordon, Kt 1982; CBE 1977; MB, ChB; FRCS; FFARCS; Professor of Anaesthetics, University of London, Royal Postgraduate Medical School and Hon. Consultant, Hammersmith Hospital, 1964–86, retired; Master, Hunterian Institute, Royal College of Surgeons, since 1982; Chairman, Advisory Committee on Distinction Awards, since 1984; *b* Stirling, Scot., 18 March 1921; *o s* of late James Cyril Robson and Freda Elizabeth Howard; *m* 1st, 1945, Dr Martha Graham Kennedy (*d* 1975); one *s*; 2nd, 1984, Jennifer Kilpatrick. *Educ:* High Sch. of Stirling; Univ. of Glasgow. FRCS 1977. RAMC, 1945–48 (Captain). Sen. Registrar in Anaesthesia, Western Inf., Glasgow, 1948–52; First Asst, Dept of Anaesthetics, Univ. of Durham, 1952–54; Cons. Anaesth., Royal Inf., Edinburgh, 1954–56; Wellcome Res. Prof. of Anaesth., McGill Univ., Montreal, 1956–64. Consultant Advr in Anaesthetics to DHSS, 1975–84; Hon. Consultant in Anaesthetics to the Army, 1983–. Mem. Bd of Faculty of Anaesthetists, RCS, 1968–85 (Dean of Faculty, 1973–76); Mem. Council, RCS, 1973–81 (a Vice-Pres., 1977–79); Chm., Jt Cttee on Higher Trng of Anaesthetists, 1973–76; Member: AHA, Ealing, Hammersmith and Hounslow, 1974–77 (NW Met. RHB, 1971–74); Chief Scientists' Res. Cttee and Panel on Med. Res., DHSS, 1973–77; Neurosciences Bd, MRC, 1974–77; Clin. Res. Bd, MRC (Chm. Grants Cttee II), 1969–71; Mem. Council, RPMS (Vice-Chm. Academic Bd, 1973–76; Chm. 1976–80); Mem., Rock Carling Fellowship Panel, 1976–78; Vice-Chm., Jt Consultants' Cttee, 1974–79. Special Trustee, Hammersmith Hosp., 1974–77; Chm., Cttee of Management, Inst. of Basic Med. Scis, 1982–85; Hon. Sec., Conf. of Med. Royal Colls and Their Faculties, UK, 1976–82; Examiner, Primary FFARCS, 1967–73; Member: Editorial Bd (and Cons. Editor), British Jl of Anaesthesia, 1965–85; Edit. Bd, Psychopharmacology; Council, Assoc. of Anaesths of GB and Ire., 1973–84; Physiol. Soc., 1966–; Cttee of AA, 1979–; Council, RCS, 1982–; Hon. Mem., Assoc. of Univ. Anaesths (USA), 1963–; President: Scottish Soc. of Anaesthetists, 1985–86; RSocMed, 1986–. Sir Arthur Sims Commonwealth Trav. Prof., 1968; Visiting Prof. to many med. centres, USA and Canada; Lectures: Wesley Bourne, McGill Univ., 1965; First Gillies Meml, Dundee, 1978; 2nd Gilmartin, Faculty of Anaesthetists, RCSI, 1986. Joseph Clover Medal and Dudley Buxton Prize, Fac. of Anaesths, RCS, 1972; John Snow Medal, Assoc. of Anaesthetists of GB and Ireland, 1986. Hon. FFARACS 1968; Hon. FFARCSI 1980; Hon. FDSRCS, 1979. Hon. DSc McGill, 1984. *Publications:* on neurophysiol., anaesthesia, pain and central nervous system mechanisms of respiration, in learned jls. *Recreations:* practice of anaesthesia; golf, wet fly fishing. *Clubs:* Council of Royal College of Surgeons; Denham Golf.

ROBSON, James Jeavons, CBE 1972; FICE; MIStructE; FIArb; Secretary for the Environment, Hong Kong, 1973–76; Member of Legislative Council, Hong Kong, 1969–76; in private practice, since 1976; *b* 4 July 1918; *m* 1945, Avis Metcalfe; one *s*. *Educ:* Constantine Coll., Middlesbrough. MICE 1948, FICE 1958; MIStructE 1946; FIArb 1969. War Service, RM, 1942–46 (Captain). Engrg Trng, Messrs Dorman Long & Co. and ICI, 1936–41; joined Colonial Engrg Service and posted to PWD, Hong Kong, 1946; Dir of Public Works, 1969. Mem. Council, ICE, 1967; Telford Premium (for paper, Overall Planning in Hong Kong), ICE, 1971. *Publications:* articles on civil engineering in Jl ICE. *Recreations:* golf, racing, gardening. *Address:* Labéjan, 32300 Mirande, France. *Clubs:* Oriental; Hong Kong, Royal Hong Kong Jockey, Royal Hong Kong Golf.

ROBSON, Prof. James Scott, MD; FRCP, FRCPE; Professor of Medicine, University of Edinburgh, 1977–86, now Emeritus; Consultant Physician, and Physician in charge, Medical Renal Unit, Royal Infirmary, Edinburgh, 1959–86; *b* 19 May 1921; *s* of William Scott Robson, FSA and Elizabeth Hannah Watt; *m* 1948, Mary Kynoch MacDonald, MB ChB, FRCP, *d* of late Alexander MacDonald, Perth; two *s*. *Educ:* Edinburgh Univ. (Mouat Schol.). MB ChB (Hons) 1945, MD 1946; FRCPE 1960, FRCP 1977. Captain, RAMC, India, Palestine and Egypt, 1945–48. Rockefeller Student, NY Univ., 1942–44; Rockefeller Res. Fellow, Harvard Univ., 1949–50. Edinburgh University: Sen. Lectr in Therapeutics, 1959; Reader, 1961; Reader in Medicine, 1968. Hon. Associate Prof., Harvard Univ., 1962; Merck Sharp & Dohme Vis. Prof., Australia, 1968. External examnr in medicine to several univs in UK and overseas. Mem., Biomed. Res. Cttee, SHHD, 1979–84; Chm., Sub-cttee in Medicine, Nat. Med. Consultative Cttee, 1983–85. Pres., Renal Assoc., London, 1977–80. Hon. Mem., Australasian Soc. of Nephrology. Sometime Mem. Editl Bd, and Dep. Chm., Clinical Science, 1969–73, and other med. jls. *Publications:* (ed with R. Passmore) Companion to Medical Studies, vol. 1, 1968, 3rd edn 1985; vol. 2, 1970, 2nd edn 1980; vol. 3, 1974; contribs on renal physiology and disease to med. books, symposia and jls. *Recreations:* gardening, theatre, reading, writing. *Address:* 1 Grant Avenue, Edinburgh EH13 0DS. *T:* 031–441 3508. *Club:* University Staff (Edinburgh).

ROBSON, John Adam, CMG 1983; HM Diplomatic Service; Ambassador to Colombia, since 1982; *b* 16 April 1930; *yr s* of Air Vice-Marshal Adam Henry Robson, CB, OBE, MC; *m* 1958, Maureen Molly, *er d* of E. H. S. Bullen; three *d*. *Educ:* Charterhouse; Gonville and Caius Coll., Cambridge (Major Scholar). BA 1952, MA 1955, PhD 1958. Fellow, Gonville and Caius Coll., 1954–58; Asst Lectr, University Coll. London, 1958–60. HM Foreign Service (later Diplomatic Service), 1961; Second Sec., British Embassy, Bonn, 1962–64; Second, later First, Secretary, Lima, 1964–66; First Sec., British High Commn, Madras, 1966–69; Asst Head, Latin American Dept, FCO, 1969–73; Head of Chancery, Lusaka, 1973–74; RCDS, 1975; Counsellor, Oslo, 1976–78; Head of E African Dept, FCO, and Comr for British Indian Ocean Territory, 1979–82. *Publications:* Wyclif and the Oxford Schools, 1961; articles in historical jls. *Recreation:* gardening. *Address:* c/o Foreign and Commonwealth Office, Whitehall, SW1.

ROBSON, Lawrence Fendick; Member, Electricity Council, 1972–76; *b* 23 Jan. 1916; *s* of (William) Bertram Robson and Annie (*née* Fendick); *m* 1945, Lorna Winifred Jagger, Shafton, Yorks; two *s* one *d*. *Educ:* Rotherham Grammar Sch.; Clare Coll., Cambridge (BA). FIEE. North Eastern Electric Supply Co. Ltd, 1937; Royal Corps of Signals, 1939–45; various positions with NE and London Electricity Bds, 1948–65; Commercial Adviser, Electricity Council, 1965–72. *Recreations:* music, open air. *Address:* Millers Hill, Priestman's Lane, Thornton Dale, N Yorks.

ROBSON, Nigel John; London Adviser to Bank of Tokyo Group, since 1984; Deputy Chairman, London Committee, Ottoman Bank, since 1983 (Member, since 1949); Chairman: Royal Trust Company of Canada, since 1984; TSB England & Wales, since 1986; Alexander Howden & Beck Ltd, since 1986; Director: TSB Group, since 1985; Royal Trustco Ltd, Toronto, since 1985; *b* 25 Dec. 1926; *s* of late Col the Hon. Harold Burge Robson, TD, DL, JP, Pinewood Hill, Wormley, Surrey, and late Iris Robson (*née* Abel Smith); *m* 1957, Anne Gladstone, *yr d* of late Stephen Deinol Gladstone and late Clair Gladstone; three *s*. *Educ:* Eton. Grenadier Guards, 1945–48. Joined Arbuthnot Latham & Co. Ltd, Merchant Bankers, 1949, a Director, 1953, Chm., 1969–75; Dir, Arbuthnot Latham Holdings Ltd, 1968–81; Dir, Grindlays Bank plc, 1969–83, Dep. Chm., 1975–76, Chm. 1977–83; Director: British Sugar plc, 1982–86; Central Trustee Savings Bank, 1984–86. Mem., Bd of Banking Supervision, 1986–. Chm., F&GP, British Heart Foundn, 1985– (Hon. Treas., 1986–); Treas., Automobile Assoc., 1986–. Gov., King Edward's Sch., Witley, 1975–. *Recreations:* tennis, walking, music. *Address:* Pinewood Hill, Wormley, Godalming, Surrey GU8 5UD. *Clubs:* Brooks's, City of London, MCC.
See also W. M. Robson.

ROBSON, Air Cdre Robert Michael, OBE 1971; Director of Public Relations, Royal Air Force, since 1984; *b* 22 April 1935; *s* of Dr John Alexander and Edith Robson; *m* 1959, Brenda Margaret (*née* Croysdill); one *s* two *d*. *Educ:* Sherborne; RMA Sandhurst. Commissioned 1955; RAF Regt, 1958; Navigator Training, 1959; Strike Squadrons, 1965; Sqdn Comdr, RAF Coll., 1968; Defence Adviser to British High Comr, Sri Lanka, 1972; Nat. Defence Coll., 1973; CO 27 Sqdn, 1974–75; MoD staff duties, 1978; CO RAF Gatow, 1978–80; RCDS 1981; Dir of Initial Officer Training, RAF Coll., 1982–84; ADC to the Queen, 1979–80. *Recreations:* sheep farming, photography. *Address:* Long Row Cottage, North Rauceby, Sleaford, Lincs. *T:* South Rauceby 631. *Club:* Royal Air Force.

ROBSON, Robert William; Manager, England Association Football Team and National Coach, since 1982; *b* 18 Feb. 1933; *s* of Philip and Lilian Robson; *m* 1955, Elsie Mary Gray; three *s*. *Educ:* Langley Park Primary Sch.; Waterhouses Secondary Mod. Sch., Co. Durham. Professional footballer: Fulham FC, 1950–56 and 1962–67; West Bromwich Albion FC, 1956–62; twenty appearances for England; Manager: Vancouver FC, 1967–68; Fulham FC, 1968–69; Ipswich Town FC, 1969–82. *Publications:* Time on the Grass (autobiog.), 1982; (with Bob Harris) So Near and Yet So Far, 1986. *Recreations:* golf, squash, reading, gardening. *Address:* The Football Association, 16 Lancaster Gate, W2. *T:* 01–262 4542.

ROBSON, Sir Thomas (Buston), Kt 1954; MBE 1919; FCA; Partner in Price Waterhouse & Co., Chartered Accountants, 1934–66; Chairman, Renold Ltd, 1967–72; *b* Newcastle upon Tyne, 4 Jan. 1896; *s* of late Thomas Robson, Langholm, Dumfriesshire, and Newcastle upon Tyne; *m* 1936, Roberta Cecilia Helen (*d* 1980), *d* of late Rev. Archibald Fleming, DD, St Columba's Church of Scotland, Pont St, SW1; two *d*. *Educ:* Rutherford College, Newcastle upon Tyne; Armstrong Collge, University of Durham. BA Hons, Modern History, 1920; MA 1923. Served European War, 1914–18, with British Salonika Force in Macedonia; Captain RGA; MBE, despatches 1919; articled with Sisson & Allden, Chartered Accountants, Newcastle upon Tyne, 1920; W. B. Peat gold medal in final examination of Inst. Chartered Accountants in England and Wales, 1922; joined staff of Price Waterhouse & Co., London, 1923; ACA, 1923, FCA, 1939; Mem. Council of Inst., 1941–66 (Vice-Pres. 1951–52; Pres., 1952–53); rep. Inst. at overseas mtgs of accountants; FCA (Ont.). Member: Committee on Amendment of Census of Production Act, Bd of Trade, 1945; Central Valuation Bd for Coal Industry, 1947; Accountancy Advisory Cttee on Companies Act, Bd of Trade, 1948–68 (Chm. 1955–68); Cttee of Inquiry into London Transport Exec., Min. of Transport and Civil Aviation, 1953; Chm. Cttees of Inquiry into Coal Distribution Costs, Min. of Fuel and Power, 1956 and Min. of Commerce, N Ireland, 1956; Mem. Advisory Cttee on Replacement of the "Queen" ships, Min. of Transport and Civil Aviation, 1959; Chm. Economic Development Cttee for Paper and Board Industry under National Economic Development Council, 1964–67. Vice-Pres. Union Européenne des Experts Comptables, Economiques et Financiers, 1963–64; Mem. Transport Tribunal, 1963–69. *Publications:* Garnsey's Holding Companies and their Published Accounts, 3rd edn, 1936; The Construction of Consolidated Accounts, 1936; Consolidated and other Group Accounts, 1st edn, 1946, 4th edn, 1969; numerous papers and addresses on professional subjects. *Recreations:* walking and reading; for many years an active worker in Boy Scout movement (Vice-Pres., Gr London Central Scout Council). *Address:* 3 Gonville House, Manor Fields, SW15 3NH. *T:* 01–789 0597.

ROBSON, Thomas Snowdon, CBE 1986 (OBE 1970; MBE 1964); CEng, FIEE; FRTS; FBKSTS; Director of Engineering, Independent Broadcasting Authority, 1978–86; *b* 6 Aug. 1922; *s* of Thomas Henry Robson and Annie Jessie (*née* Snowdon); *m* 1951, Ruth Bramley; one *s* one *d*. *Educ:* Portsmouth Grammar Sch. BBC, 1941–42; RAF Techn. Br., 1942–46; EMI Research Labs, 1947–57; ITA: Engr in Charge, Black Hill, 1957–58; Sen. Engr, Planning and Construction, 1958–67; Head of Station Design and Construction, 1967–69; Asst Dir of Engrg, 1969–73; IBA, Dep. Dir of Engrg, 1973–77. Eduard Rhein Prize, Eduard Rhein Foundn, Berlin, 1984. *Recreations:* golf, home computing. *Address:* 3 Sleepers Hill Gardens, Winchester, Hants SO22 4NT. *T:* Winchester 68540.

ROBSON, Vice-Adm. Sir (William) Geoffrey (Arthur), KBE 1956; CB 1953; DSO 1940 (Bar 1941); DSC 1941; Lieutenant-Governor and Commander-in-Chief of Guernsey, 1958–64; *b* 10 March 1902; *s* of Major John Robson; *m* 1st, 1925, Sylvia Margaret Forrester (*d* 1968); one *s*; 2nd, 1969, Elizabeth Kathleen, *widow* of Lt-Col V. H. Holt. *Educ:* RN Colleges, Osborne and Dartmouth. Midshipman, HMS Malaya, 1918; served in Destroyers, 1922–37. Commanded Rowena, 1934; Wren, 1935–36; RN Staff Course, 1937; RAF Staff Course, 1938. Served War of 1939–45 (despatches thrice, DSO and Bar, DSC): Comd HMS Kandahar, 1939–41; Combined Operations, 1942–43; Commanded the 26th Destroyer Flotilla, 1944, in HMS Hardy; Captain of Coastal Forces (Nore), 1945; HMS Superb in command, 1945–47; Comd HMS Ganges, 1948–50; President of Admiralty Interview Board, 1950–51; Flag Officer (Flotillas), Home Fleet, 1951–53; Flag Officer, Scotland, 1952–56; Commander-in-Chief, South Atlantic, 1956–58; retd, 1958. Commander of the Order of St Olav (Norway). *Recreations:*

shooting, fishing. *Address:* Amat, Ardgay, Ross-shire; Le Paradou, Forest, Guernsey. *Club:* Army and Navy.

ROBSON, William Michael; Deputy Chairman: The Standard Bank Ltd, 1965–83 (Director, 1960–83); The Chartered Bank, 1974–83; Standard and Chartered Banking Group Ltd, 1974–83 (Director, 1970–83); Member of Lloyd's, since 1937; *b* 31 Dec. 1912; *e s* of late Col the Hon. Harold Burge Robson, TD, DL, JP, Pinewood Hill, Witley, Surrey and late Ysolt Robson (*née* Leroy-Lewis); *m* 1st, 1939, Audrey Isobel Wales (*d* 1964), *d* of late Maj. William Dick, Low Gosforth Hall, Northumberland; two *s* one *d*; 2nd, 1965, Frances Mary Wyville, *d* of late James Anderson Ramage Dawson, Balado House, Kinross, and widow of Andrew Alexander Nigel Buchanan (he *d* 1960). *Educ:* Eton; New College, Oxford. Served War of 1939–45: with Grenadier Guards (Maj. 1944), England and Europe BAOR. A Vice-Chm., Victoria League for Commonwealth Friendship, 1962–65. Director: Booker McConnell Ltd, 1955–78 (Chm., Booker Pensions, 1957–78); United Rum Merchants Ltd, 1965–78; British South Africa Co., 1961–66 (Vice-Chm., Jt East & Central African Bd, 1956–63); Antony Gibbs & Sons (Insurance) Ltd, 1946–48, 1973–76; Antony Gibbs (Insurance Holdings), 1976–80; Antony Gibbs, Sage Ltd, 1976–80; Anton Underwriting Agencies Ltd, 1977–82; Chm., Standard Bank Finance & Develt Corp. Ltd, 1966–73; Mem., BNEC, Africa, 1965–71 (Dep. Chm., 1970–71). High Sheriff of Kent, 1970. Liveryman, Vintners Co., 1953. Mem. Council of The Shrievalty Assoc., 1971–76. *Address:* 28 Smith Terrace, Chelsea, SW3. *T:* 01–352 2177; Hales Place, Tenterden, Kent. *T:* Tenterden 2932. *Club:* Brooks's.
See also N. J. Robson.

ROBSON, Prof. William Wallace; Masson Professor of English Literature, University of Edinburgh, since 1972; *b* 20 June 1923; *o s* of late W. Robson, LLB, barrister, and Kathleen Ryan; *m* 1962, Anne-Varna Moses, MA; two *s. Educ:* Leeds Modern School; New College, Oxford (R. C. Sherriff Scholar; BA 1944, MA 1948). Asst Lectr, King's College London, 1944–46; Lectr, Lincoln College, Oxford, 1946–48, Fellow, 1948–70; Prof. of English, Univ. of Sussex, 1970–72. Visiting Lecturer: Univ. of S California, 1953; Univ. of Adelaide, 1956; Vis. Prof., Univ. of Delaware, 1963–64; Elizabeth Drew Prof., Smith Coll., USA, 1969–70; Vis. Fellow: All Souls Coll., Oxford, 1982; New Coll., Oxford, 1985. *Publications:* Critical Essays, 1966; The Signs Among Us, 1968; Modern English Literature, 1970, 5th edn 1984; The Definition of Literature, 1982; A Prologue to English Literature, 1986. *Address:* Department of English Literature, The University, Edinburgh EH8 9YL. *T:* 031–667 1011.

ROCH, Hon. Sir John (Ormond), Kt 1985; **Hon. Mr Justice Roch;** a Judge of the High Court of Justice, Queen's Bench Division, since 1985; Presiding Judge, Wales and Chester Circuit, since 1986; *b* 19 April 1934; *s* of Frederick Ormond Roch and Vera Elizabeth (*née* Chamberlain); *m* 1967, Anne Elizabeth Greany; three *d. Educ:* Wrekin Coll.; Clare Coll., Cambridge (BA, LLB). Called to Bar, Gray's Inn, 1961, Bencher, 1985; QC 1976; a Recorder, 1975–85. *Recreations:* sailing, music. *Address:* c/o Royal Courts of Justice, Strand, WC2. *Club:* Dale Yacht.

ROCH, Muriel Elizabeth Sutcliffe, BA; Headmistress, School of S Mary and S Anne, Abbots Bromley, Staffs, 1953–77; *b* 7 Sept. 1916; *d* of late Rev. Sydney John Roch, MA Cantab, Pembroke and Manchester. *Educ:* Manchester High Sch.; Bedford Coll., London; Hughes Hall, Cambridge. Teaching appointments at: Devonport High School, 1939–41; Lady Manners, Bakewell, 1941–44; Howells School, Denbigh, 1944–47; Talbot Heath, Bournemouth, 1947–53. *Recreations:* music, travel. *Address:* Northdown Cottage, Lamphey, Dyfed. *T:* Lamphey 2577.

ROCHDALE, 1st Viscount *cr* 1960; **2nd Baron** 1913; **John Durival Kemp,** OBE 1945; TD; DL; *b* 5 June 1906; *s* of 1st Baron and Lady Beatrice Egerton, 3rd *d* of 3rd Earl of Ellesmere; *S* father, 1945; *m* 1931, Elinor Dorothea Pease (CBE 1964; JP); one *s* (one *d* decd). *Educ:* Eton; Trin. Coll., Cambridge. Hons degree Nat. Science Tripos. Served War of 1939–45 (despatches); attached USA forces in Pacific with rank of Col, 1944; Temp. Brig., 1945. Hon. Col 251 (Westmorland and Cumberland Yeomanry) Field Regiment, RA, TA, late 851 (W&CY) Field Bty, RA, 1959–67. Joined Kelsall & Kemp Ltd, 1928, Chm., 1952–71; Director: Consett Iron Co. Ltd, 1957–67; Williams Deacon's Bank Ltd, 1960–70; Nat. and Commercial Banking Gp Ltd, 1971–77; Deputy Chairman: West Riding Worsted & Woollen Mills, 1969–72; Williams & Glyn's Bank Ltd, 1973–77 (Director, 1970–); Chm., Harland & Wolff, 1971–75. President: National Union of Manufacturers, 1953–56; NW Industrial Develt Assoc., 1974–84; Member: Dollar Exports Council, 1953–61; Central Transport Consultative Cttee for GB, 1953–57; Western Hemisphere Exports Council, 1961–64; Chairman: Cotton Board, 1957–62; Docks and Harbours Committee of Inquiry, 1961; National Ports Council, 1963–67; Cttee of Inquiry into Shipping, 1967–70. A Governor of the BBC, 1954–59. Pres., British Legion, NW Area, 1955–61. Companion, Textile Inst. 1959; MInstT 1964. Upper Bailiff, Weavers' Co., 1949–50, 1956–57. DL Cumberland, 1948–84. *Heir: s* Hon. St John Durival Kemp [*b* 15 Jan. 1938; *m* 1st, 1960, Serena Jane Clark-Hall (marr. diss. 1974); two *s* two *d*; 2nd, 1976, Elizabeth Anderton]. *Address:* Lingholm, Keswick, Cumbria. *T:* Keswick 72003. *Club:* Lansdowne.
See also Sir J. K. Barlow, Bt, Duke of Sutherland.

ROCHDALE, Archdeacon of; *see* Bonser, Ven. D.

ROCHE, family name of **Baron Fermoy.**

ROCHE, Sir David (O'Grady), 5th Bt *cr* 1838 of Carass, Limerick; FCA; Chairman: Roche & Co. Ltd (licensed dealers in securities); Carass Property Ltd; *b* 21 Sept. 1947; *s* of Sir Standish O'Grady Roche, 4th Bt, DSO, and of Evelyn Laura, *d* of Major William Andon; *S* father, 1977; *m* 1971, Hon. (Helen) Alexandra Briscoe Frewen, *d* of 3rd Viscount Selby; one *s* one *d* (and one *s* decd). *Educ:* Wellington Coll., Berks; Trinity Coll., Dublin. *Heir: s* David Alexander O'Grady Roche, *b* 28 Jan. 1976. *Address:* Bridge House, Starbotton, Skipton, N Yorks BD23 5HY; 36 Coniger Road, SW6. *T:* 01–736 0382. *Clubs:* Buck's; Kildare Street and University (Dublin); Royal Yacht Squadron.

ROCHE, Frederick Lloyd, CBE 1985; Deputy Chairman and Managing Director, Conran Roche, since 1981; *b* 11 March 1931; *s* of John Francis Roche and Margaret Roche. *Educ:* Regent Street Polytechnic. DipArch, ARIBA. Architect (Schools), City of Coventry, 1958–62; Principal Develt Architect, Midlands Housing Consortium, 1962–64; Chief Architect and Planning Officer, Runcorn Develt Corp., 1964–70; Gen. Manager, Milton Keynes Develt Corp., 1970–80. Mem., Environmental Bd, 1976–79; Vice-Pres., RIBA, 1983. *Publications:* numerous technical articles. *Address:* Conran Roche, Norfolk House, 435 Silbury Boulevard, Central Milton Keynes MK9 3HB. *T:* Milton Keynes 663330.

ROCHE, Hon. Thomas Gabriel, QC 1955; Recorder of the City of Worcester, 1959–71; *b* 1909; *yr s* of late Baron Roche, PC. *Educ:* Rugby; Wadham Coll., Oxford. Called to the Bar, Inner Temple, 1932. Served War of 1939–45 (Lt-Col 1944, despatches). Church Commissioner, 1961–65; Member, Monopolies Commission, 1966–69. *Address:* Chadlington, Oxford. *Club:* United Oxford & Cambridge University.

ROCHESTER, 2nd Baron, of the 4th creation, *cr* 1931, of Rochester in the County of Kent; **Foster Charles Lowry Lamb,** DL; *b* 7 June 1916; *s* of 1st Baron Rochester, CMG, and Rosa Dorothea (*née* Hurst); *S* father 1955; *m* 1942, Mary Carlisle, *yr d* of T. B. Wheeler, CBE; two *s* one *d* (and one *d* decd). *Educ:* Mill Hill; Jesus College, Cambridge. MA. Served War of 1939–45: Captain 23rd Hussars; France, 1944. Joined ICI Ltd, 1946: Labour Manager, Alkali Div., 1955–63; Personnel Manager, Mond Div., 1964–72. Pro-Chancellor, Univ. of Keele, 1976–86. Chairman: Cheshire Scout Assoc., 1974–81; Governors of Chester Coll., 1974–83. DL Cheshire, 1979. DUniv Keele, 1986. *Heir: s* Hon. David Charles Lamb [*b* 8 Sept. 1944; *m* 1969, Jacqueline Stamp; two *s. Educ:* Shrewsbury Sch.; Univ. of Sussex]. *Address:* The Hollies, Hartford, Cheshire CW8 1PG. *T:* Northwich 74733. *Clubs:* Reform, MCC.
See also Hon. K. H. L. Lamb.

ROCHESTER, Bishop of, since 1961; **Rt. Rev. Richard David Say,** DD (Lambeth) 1961; High Almoner to HM the Queen, since 1970; *b* 4 Oct. 1914; *s* of Commander Richard Say, OBE, RNVR, and Kathleen Mary (*née* Wildy); *m* 1943, Irene Frances (OBE 1980, JP 1960), *e d* of Seaburne and Frances Rayner, Exeter; one *s* two *d* (and one *s* decd). *Educ:* University Coll. Sch.; Christ's College, Cambridge (MA); Ridley Hall, Cambridge. Ordained deacon, 1939; priest, 1940. Curate of Croydon Parish Church, 1939–43; Curate of St Martin-in-the-Fields, London, 1943–50; Asst Sec. Church of England Youth Council, 1942–44; Gen. Sec., 1944–47; Gen. Sec. British Council of Churches, 1947–55; Church of England delegate to World Council of Churches, 1948, 1954 and 1961. Select Preacher, University of Cambridge, 1954 and University of Oxford, 1963; Rector of Bishop's Hatfield, 1955–61; Hon. Canon of St Albans, 1957–61. Domestic Chaplain to Marquess of Salisbury and Chaplain of Welfield Hospital, 1955–61; Hon. Chaplain of The Pilgrims, 1968–. Entered House of Lords, 1969. Chaplain and Sub-Prelate, Order of St John, 1961. Mem., Court of Ecclesiastical Causes Reserved, 1984–. Dep. Pro-Chancellor, 1977–83, Pro-Chancellor, 1983–, Kent Univ.; Governor, University Coll. Sch., 1980. Freeman of City of London, 1953. Hon. Mem., Smeatonian Soc., 1977. *Recreations:* walking, travel. *Address:* Bishopscourt, Rochester ME1 1TS. *T:* Medway 42721. *Club:* United Oxford & Cambridge University.

ROCHESTER, Dean of; *see* Arnold, Very Rev. J. R.

ROCHESTER, Archdeacon of; *see* Turnbull, Ven. A. M. A.

ROCHESTER, Prof. George Dixon, FRS 1958; FInstP; Professor of Physics, University of Durham, 1955–73, now Professor Emeritus; *b* 4 Feb. 1908; *s* of Thomas and Ellen Rochester; *m* 1938, Idaline, *o d* of Rev. J. B. Bayliffe; one *s* one *d. Educ:* Wallsend Secondary Sch. and Technical Inst.; Universities of Durham, Stockholm and California. BSc, MSc, PhD (Dunelm). Earl Grey Memorial Scholar, Armstrong College, Durham University, 1926–29; Earl Grey Fellow, at Stockholm Univ., 1934–35; Commonwealth Fund Fellow at California Univ., 1935–37; Manchester University: Asst Lectr, 1937–46; Lectr, 1946–49; Sen. Lectr, 1949–53; Reader, 1953–55. Scientific Adviser in Civil Defence for NW Region, 1952–55. (Jt) C. V. Boys Prizeman of the Physical Society of London, 1956; Symons Memorial Lecturer of the Royal Meteorological Soc., 1962. Member: Council CNAA, 1964–74; Council, British Assoc. for Advancement of Science, 1971–72; Council, Royal Soc., 1972–74; Chm., NE Branch, Inst. of Physics, 1972–74. Second Pro-Vice-Chancellor, Univ. of Durham, 1967–69, Pro-Vice-Chancellor, 1969–70. Hon. DSc: Newcastle upon Tyne, 1973; CNAA, 1975; Hon. Fellow, Newcastle upon Tyne Polytechnic, 1977. Methodist. *Publications:* (with J. G. Wilson) Cloud Chamber Photographs of the Cosmic Radiation, 1952; scientific papers on cosmic rays and spectroscopy. *Recreations:* gardening, history of science. *Address:* 18 Dryburn Road, Durham DH1 5AJ. *T:* Durham 64796.

ROCHETA, Dr Manuel Farrajota; Military Order of Christ of Portugal; Ambassador for Portugal in Madrid, 1968–74, retired; *b* 6 Aug. 1906; *s* of Manuel and Rosa Rocheta; *m* 1933, Maria Luiza Belmarco Rocheta; one *d. Educ:* Lisbon University. Entered Diplomatic Service, 1931; Assistant Consul Hamburg, 1934; Consul Copenhagen, 1935–39; First Sec. and Chargé d'Affaires *ai*, Bucarest, 1943–45; First Sec. and Chargé d'Affaires *ai*, Dublin, 1945; First Secretary, Washington, 1946, Counsellor, 1947, Minister-Counsellor, 1950 (Chargé d'Affaires, 1 Nov. 1946–31 March 1947 and 11 Feb. 1950–6 June 1950); Asst Dir-Gen. of Political Dept, Foreign Affairs Ministry, Lisbon, 1951; Minister-Plen. and Dir-Gen. of Political Dept, Foreign Ministry, Lisbon, 1954; Minister in Bonn, 1956, Ambassador, 1956–58; Ambassador: to Rio de Janeiro, 1958–61; to the Court of St James's, 1961–68. Doctor in Law, Univ. of Bahia, Brazil. Knight Grand Cross of Royal Victorian Order, Gt Brit. (Hon. GCVO) 1955, and holds Grand Cross of several foreign orders. *Recreations:* walking and swimming. *Address:* c/o Ministry of Foreign Affairs, Lisbon, Portugal.

ROCKE, John Roy Mansfield; Vice-Chairman, J. Bibby & Sons, 1975–82, retired; *b* 13 April 1918; *s* of late Frederick Gilbert Rocke and late Mary Susan Rocke; *m* 1948, Pauline Diane Berry; no *c. Educ:* Charterhouse; Trinity Coll., Cambridge (BA). War Service, Grenadier Guards, 1940–46 (Maj.). Orme & Eykyn (Stockbrokers), 1946–50; Booker McConnell Ltd, 1950–70, Dir, 1954, Vice-Chm., 1962–70. Mem., BNEC, and Chm., BNEC (Caribbean), 1965–68; Chm., Nat. Econ. Development Cttee for the Food Manufacturing Industry, 1967–71. *Address:* 22 Bruton Street, W1. *T:* 01–629 3393; Pendomer Manor, Pendomer, near Yeovil, Somerset. *Club:* Boodle's.

ROCKEFELLER, David; banker; *b* New York City, 12 June 1915; *s* of John Davison Rockefeller, Jr and Abby Greene (Aldrich) Rockefeller; *m* 1940, Margaret, *d* of Francis Sims McGrath, Mount Kisco, NY; two *s* four *d. Educ:* Lincoln School of Columbia University's Teachers College; Harvard Univ. (BS); London School of Economics; Univ. of Chicago (PhD). Sec. to Mayor Fiorello H. LaGuardia, 1940–41; Asst Regional Dir, US Office of Defense Health and Welfare Services, 1941. Served in US Army, N Africa and France, 1942–45 (Captain). Joined Chase National Bank, NYC, 1946; Asst Manager, Foreign Dept, 1946–47; Asst Cashier, 1947–48; Second Vice-Pres., 1948–49; Vice-Pres., 1949–51; Senior Vice-Pres., 1951–55; Exec. Vice-Pres., Chase Manhattan Bank (formed by merging Chase Nat. Bank and Bank of Manhattan Co.), 1955–57; Dir, 1955–81; Vice-Chm., 1957–61; Pres. and Chm., Exec. Cttee, 1961–69; Chm. of Bd, 1969–81 and Chief Exec. Officer, 1969–80; Chairman: Chase Internat. Investment Corp., 1961–81; Chase Internat. Adv. Cttee, 1980–. Chm., Rockefeller Brothers Fund Inc., 1981– (Vice-Chm., 1968–80); Trustee: Univ. of Chicago, 1947–62 (Life Trustee, 1966); Carnegie Endowment for Internat. Peace, 1947–60; Council of the Americas (Chm., 1965–70); Sleepy Hollow Restorations, 1981–; Chairman: Americas Soc.; Council on Foreign Relations; NY Chamber of Commerce and Industry; NYC Partnership, 1979–; US Business Cttee on Jamaica, 1980–; N American Chm., Trilateral Commn; Mem. Exec. Cttee, Museum of Modern Art (Chm. 1962–72); Chairman: The Rockefeller Group Inc.; Exec. Cttee, Rockefeller Univ., 1950–75; Director: Downtown-Lower Manhattan Assoc., Inc. (Chm. 1958–75); Internat. Exec. Service Corps (Chm., 1964–68); NY Clearing House, 1971–78; Center for Inter-Amer. Relations (Chm. 1966–70); Overseas Develt Council; US-USSR Trade and Econ. Council, Inc.; Member: Harvard Coll. Bd of Overseers, 1954–60, 1962–68; Urban Develt Corp., NY State, Business Adv. Council,

1968–72; US Adv. Cttee on Reform of Internat. Monetary System, 1973–; Sen. Adv. Gp, Bilderberg Meetings; US Exec. Cttee, Dartmouth Conf.; American Friends of LSE; US Hon. Fellows, LSE; Municipal Union Financial Leaders; Bd, Inst. of International Economics, 1985–. Hon. Mem., Commn on White House Fellows, 1964–65; Founding Mem., Business Cttee for the Arts. Director: Morningside Heights, 1947–70 (Pres., 1947–57, Chm., 1957–65); Internat. House, NY, 1940–63; Equitable Life Assce Soc. of US, 1960–65; B. F. Goodrich Co., 1956–64. Hon. Chm., Japan Soc. World Brotherhood Award, Jewish Theol Seminary, 1953; Gold Medal, Nat. Inst. Social Sciences, 1967; Medal of Honor for city planning, Amer. Inst. Architects, 1968; C. Walter Nichols Award, NY Univ., 1970; Reg. Planning Assoc. Award, 1971. Hon. LLD: Columbia Univ., 1954; Bowdoin Coll., 1958; Jewish Theol Seminary, 1958; Williams Coll., 1966; Wagner Coll., 1967; Harvard, 1969; Pace Coll., 1970; St John's Univ., 1971; Middlebury, 1974; Univ. of Liberia, 1979; Rockefeller Univ., 1980; Hon. DEng Colorado Sch. of Mines, 1974. Holds civic awards. Officer, Legion of Honour, France, 1955; Order of Merit of the Republic, Italy; Order of the Southern Cross, Brazil; Order of the White Elephant and Order of the Crown, Thailand; Order of the Cedar, Lebanon; Order of the Sun, Peru; Order of Humane African Redemption, Liberia; Order of the Crown, Belgium; National Order of Ivory Coast. *Publications:* Unused Resources and Economic Waste, 1940; Creative Management in Banking, 1964. *Recreation:* sailing. *Address:* 30 Rockefeller Plaza, New York, NY 10112, USA. *Clubs:* Century, Harvard, River, Knickerbocker, Links, University, Recess (New York); New York Yacht.

See also L. S. Rockefeller.

ROCKEFELLER, James Stillman; President and Director, Indian Spring Land Co.; Vice-President and Director, Indian Rock Corp.; Director, Cranston (RI) Print Works Co.; *b* New York, 8 June 1902; *s* of William Goodsell Rockefeller and Elsie (*née* Stillman); *m* 1925, Nancy Carnegie; two *s* two *d*. *Educ:* Yale University (BA). With Brown Bros & Co., NYC, 1924–30; joined National City Bank of New York (later First Nat. City Bank; now Citibank, NA), 1930; Asst Cashier, 1931; Asst Vice-Pres. 1933; Vice-Pres., 1940–48; Sen. Vice-Pres., 1948–52; Exec. Vice-Pres., 1952; Pres. and Director, 1952–59; Chairman, 1959–67. Rep. Greenwich (Conn.) Town Meeting, 1933–42. Served as Lieutenant-Colonel in US Army, 1942–46. Member Board of Overseers, Memorial Hospital for Cancer and Allied Diseases, NY; Trustee of Estate of William Rockefeller; Trustee American Museum of National History. Hon. Dir, NCR Corp. *Address:* Room 2900, 399 Park Avenue, New York, NY 10043, USA. *Clubs:* Links, Down Town Assoc., Union League, University (New York); Metropolitan (Washington, DC); Field (Greenwich, Conn).

ROCKEFELLER, Laurance Spelman, OBE (Hon.) 1971; conservationist and business executive; Director, Rockefeller Center Inc., 1936–78 (Chairman, 1953–56, 1958–66); *b* New York, 26 May 1910; *s* of John Davison Rockefeller, Jr, FRS and Abby Greene Aldrich; *m* 1934, Mary French; one *s* three *d*. *Educ:* Lincoln School of Teachers College; Princeton University (BA). War service, Lt-Comdr, USNR, 1942–45. Chairman: Citizens' Adv. Cttee on Environmental Quality, 1969–73 (Mem., 1973–79); Meml Sloan-Kettering Cancer Center, 1960–82 (Hon. Chm., 1982–); NY Zool Soc., 1970–75 (Hon. Chm., 1975–); Caneel Bay Inc.; Amer. Conservation Assoc.; Rockresorts Inc.; Woodstock Resort Corp.; Grand Teton Lodge Co.; Director: Eastern Air Lines, 1938–60, 1977–81, Adv. Dir, 1981–; Readers' Digest Assoc., 1973–; President: Jackson Hole Preserve, Inc.; Palisades Interstate Park Commn, 1970–77 (Chm. Emeritus, 1978–); Adv. Trustee, Rockefeller Bros Fund, 1982–85 (Chm., 1958–80; Vice-Chm., 1980–82); Charter Trustee, Princeton Univ.; Trustee: Alfred P. Sloan Foundn, 1950–82; Greenacre Foundn; Nat. Geog. Soc.; Sleepy Hollow Restorations, 1975– (Chm., 1981–85); Life Mem., Mass Inst. of Technology; Dir, Community Blood Council of Gtr NY; Mem., Nat. Cancer Adv. Bd, 1977–79; Chairman: Outdoor Recreation Resources Review Commn, 1958–65; Hudson River Valley Commn, 1956–66; 1965 White House Conf. on Nat. Beauty; Delegate UN Conf. on Human Environment, 1972. Holds numerous awards, medals and hon. degrees. Comdr, Royal Order of the Lion, Belgium, 1950; US Medal of Freedom, 1969. *Address:* Room 5600, 30 Rockefeller Plaza, New York, NY 10112, USA. *Clubs:* Boone and Crockett, River, Princeton, Downtown Association, Brook, New York Yacht, Links, Knickerbocker (New York City); Cosmos, Metropolitan (Washington, DC).

See also David Rockefeller.

ROCKHAMPTON, Bishop of, since 1981; **Rt. Rev. George Arthur Hearn;** *b* 17 Nov. 1935; *s* of Albert Frederick and Edith Maxham Hearn; *m* 1957, Adele Taylor; two *s* one *d*. *Educ:* Northcote High School; University High School; Latrobe Univ., Melbourne. BA, ThL 1965, DipRE, ThSchol Aust. Coll. of Theology; MACE. Deacon 1964, priest 1965, Diocese of Gippsland; Curate of Traralgon, 1964–66; Vicar of Omeo, 1966–69; Rector of Wonthaggi, 1969–73; Rector of Kyabram, dio. Bendigo, 1973–77; Field Officer, Dept of Christian Education, Diocese of Melbourne, 1977–79; Dir, Gen. Bd of Religious Education, 1978–81. *Recreations:* gardening, reading, golf and music. *Address:* PO Box 116, Rockhampton, Queensland 4700, Australia. *T:* (079) 27 3188.

ROCKLEY, 3rd Baron *cr* 1934; **James Hugh Cecil;** Director: Kleinwort Benson Ltd, since 1970; Equity and Law Life Assurance Society Ltd, since 1980; *b* 5 April 1934; *s* of 2nd Baron Rockley, and Anne Margaret (*d* 1980), *d* of late Adm. Hon. Sir Herbert Meade-Featherstonhaugh, GCVO, CB, DSO; *S* father, 1976; *m* 1958, Lady Sarah Primrose Beatrix, *e d* of 7th Earl Cadogan, *qv*; one *s* two *d*. *Educ:* Eton; New Coll., Oxford. Wood Gundy & Co. Ltd, 1957–62; Kleinwort Benson Ltd, 1963–. Trustee, Nat. Portrait Gall., 1981–. *Heir:* *s* Hon. Anthony Robert Cecil, *b* 29 July 1961. *Address:* Lytchett Heath, Poole, Dorset. *T:* Lytchett Minister 622228.

ROCKSAVAGE, Earl of; David George Philip Cholmondeley; *b* 27 June 1960; *s* and *heir* of 6th Marquess of Cholmondeley, *qv*.

RODD, family name of **Baron Rennell.**

RODDAN, Gilbert McMicking, CMG 1957; Deputy Agricultural Adviser, Department of Technical Co-operation, 1961 (to Secretary of State for Colonies, 1956); retired 1965; *b* 13 May 1906; *m* 1934, Olive Mary Wetherill; two *d*. *Educ:* Dumfries Academy; Glasgow and Oxford Universities; Imperial College of Tropical Agriculture, Trinidad. Colonial Service, 1930–56. *Address:* Wayland, Edinburgh Road, Peebles. *Club:* Royal Commonwealth Society.

RODDICK, (George) Winston; QC 1986; *b* Caernarfon, 2 Oct. 1940; *s* of William and Aelwen Roddick; *m* 1966, Cennin Parry; one *s* one *d*. *Educ:* University Coll. London (LLB, LLM). Called to the Bar, Gray's Inn, 1968. Chairman: Welsh Liberal Party, 1982–84; Alliance in Wales, 1985–87. Chm., Lloyd George Soc., 1985–87. *Recreations:* reading The Times on holidays, walking the countryside. *Address:* 17 Llandennis Avenue, Cyncoed, Cardiff CF2 6JD. *T:* Cardiff 759376. *Clubs:* Cardiff and County (Cardiff); Caernarfon Sailing.

RODDIE, Prof. Ian Campbell, TD 1967; FRCPI; Dunville Professor of Physiology, since 1964, and Pro-Vice-Chancellor, since 1983, Queen's University, Belfast; *b* 1 Dec. 1928; *s* of Rev. J. R. Wesley Roddie and Mary Hill Wilson; *m* 1958, Elizabeth Ann Gillon Honeyman (decd); one *s* three *d*. *Educ:* Methodist Coll., Belfast; Queen's Univ., Belfast. Malcolm Exhibnr, 1951, McQuitty Schol., 1953; BSc (1st cl. Hons Physiol.), MB BCh, BAO, MD (with gold medal), DSc; MRCPI; MRIA. Major RAMC (T&AVR); OC Med. Sub-unit, QUB OTC, retd 1968. Resident MO, Royal Victoria Hosp., Belfast, 1953–54; Queen's University, Belfast: Lectr in Physiology, 1954–60; Sen. Lectr, 1961–62; Reader, 1962–64; Dep. Dean, 1975–76, Dean, 1976–81, Faculty of Medicine. Consultant Physiologist: NI Hosps Authority, 1962–72; Eastern Health Bd, NI, 1972–. Harkness Commonwealth Fund Fellow, Washington Univ., 1960–61; Vis. Prof., Univ. of NSW, 1983–; Res. Fellow, Japan Soc. for Promotion of Science, Matsumoto, Japan, 1984. External Examiner: Univs of Aberdeen, Baghdad, Benghazi, Birmingham, Bristol, Glasgow, Ireland, Jos, Leeds, London, Sheffield, Southampton; RCS, RCSE, RCPGlas, RCSI. Chief Reg. Sci. Advr for Home Defence, NI, 1977–; Member: Home Defence Sci. Adv. Conf., 1977–; Eastern Area Health and Social Services Bd, NI, 1976–81; Physiol Systems Bd, MRC, 1974–76; Med. Adv. Cttee, Cttee of Vice-Chancellors and Principals, 1976–81; GMC, 1979–81; GDC, 1979–81. President: Royal Acad. of Medicine in Ireland, 1985–; Biol Scis Sect., Royal Acad. of Medicine in Ireland, 1964–66; Ulster Biomed. Engrg Soc., 1979–; Chm. Cttee, Physiol Soc., 1985– (Mem. Cttee, 1966–69). Arris and Gale Lectr, RCS, 1962. Conway Bronze Medal, Royal Acad. of Medicine in Ireland, 1977. *Publications:* Physiology for Practitioners, 1971, 2nd edn 1975; Multiple Choice Questions in Human Physiology, 1971, 2nd edn 1977; The Physiology of Disease, 1975; papers on physiology and pharmacology of vascular, sudorific and lymphatic systems. *Recreations:* gardening, carpentry. *Address:* Seapark, Marino, Holywood, Co. Down BT18 0LH. *T:* Holywood 3212. *Club:* Royal Commonwealth Society.

RODEN, 9th Earl of, *cr* 1771; **Robert William Jocelyn;** Baron Newport, 1743; Viscount Jocelyn, 1755; a baronet of England, 1665; Captain Royal Navy; retired; *b* 4 Dec. 1909; *S* father 1956; *m* 1937, Clodagh, *d* of late Edward Kennedy, Bishopscourt, Co. Kildare; three *s*. Retired 1960. *Address:* 75 Bryansford Village, Newcastle, Co. Down BT33 0PT. *T:* Newcastle 23469.

RODERICK, Caerwyn Eifion; Councillor, South Glamorgan County Council, since 1980; *b* 15 July 1927; *m* 1952, Eirlys Mary Lewis; one *s* two *d*. *Educ:* Maes-y-Dderwen County Sch., Ystradgynlais; University Coll. of North Wales, Bangor. Asst Master, Caterham Sch., Surrey, 1949–52; Sen. Master, Chartesey Sch., LCC, 1952–54; Sen. Maths Master, Boys' Grammar Sch., Brecon, 1954–57; Method Study Engineer, NCB, 1957–60; Sen. Maths Master, Hartridge High Sch., Newport, Mon, 1960–69; Lecturer, Coll. of Educn, Cardiff, 1969–70. MP (Lab) Brecon and Radnor, 1970–79; PPS to Rt Hon. Michael Foot. Mem. Council: UC, Cardiff; UMIST; formerly Mem. Council, RCVS. *Address:* 29 Charlotte Square, Rhiwbina, Cardiff. *T:* Cardiff 68269.

RODERICK, Rev. Charles Edward Morys; Chaplain to the Queen, 1962–80; Rector of Longparish and Hurstbourne Priors, 1971–80; *b* 18 June 1910; *s* of Edward Thomas and Marion Petronella Roderick; *m* 1940, Betty Margaret Arrowsmith; two *s*. *Educ:* Christ's College, Brecon; Trinity College, Oxford (MA). Schoolmaster, 1932–38; training for ordination, 1938–39; ordained, 1939; Curate, St Luke's Parish Church of Chelsea, 1939–46; Chaplain to the Forces, 1940–45; Rector of Denham, Bucks, 1946–53. Vicar of St Michael's, Chester Square, London, 1953–71. HCF. *Address:* 135 Little Ann, Abbotts Ann, Andover, Hants.

RODGER, Alan Ferguson; QC(Scot) 1985; Home Advocate Depute, since 1986; *b* 18 Sept. 1944; *er s* of Prof. Thomas Ferguson Rodger and Jean Margaret Smith Chalmers. *Educ:* Kelvinside Acad., Glasgow; Glasgow Univ. (MA, LLB); New Coll., Oxford (MA (by decree), DPhil). Dyke Jun. Res. Fellow, Balliol Coll., Oxford, 1969–70; Fellow, New Coll., Oxford, 1970–72; Mem., Faculty of Advocates, 1974; Clerk of Faculty, 1976–79; Advocate Depute, 1985. Member: Mental Welfare Commn for Scotland, 1981–84; UK Delegn to CCBE, 1984. *Publications:* Owners and Neighbours in Roman Law, 1972; articles mainly on Roman Law. *Recreation:* walking. *Address:* 72 Northumberland Street, Edinburgh EH3 6JG. *T:* 031–556 4754; Earlsknowe, Grange Road, Earlsferry, Fife KY9 1AL. *Club:* Athenæum.

RODGER, Allan George, OBE 1944; Under-Secretary, Scottish Education Department, 1959–63, retired; *b* Kirkcaldy, 7 Jan. 1902; *s* of Allan Rodger, Schoolmaster, and Annie Venters; *m* 1930, Barbara Melville Simpson; one *s* one *d*. *Educ:* Pathhead Primary School, Kirkcaldy; Kirkcaldy High School; Edinburgh University (MA (Hons) Maths, BSc, MEd, Dip Geog). Teacher, Viewforth School, Kirkcaldy, 1926–29; Lecturer, Moray House Training Coll. and Univ. Dept of Educ. (Edinburgh), 1929–35; HM Inspector of Schools, 1935–45, with special duties in regard to geography, special schools, and training colleges (seconded to special administrative duties in Education Dept, 1939–45); Asst Secretary, Scottish Educ. Dept, 1945–59. Served on Educational Commission for Govts of Uganda and Kenya, 1961. Chairman of various Govt Cttees on Scottish Educ. matters. *Publications:* contrib. to Jl of Educational Psychology and other educational journals. *Recreations:* reading, music. *Address:* 9 Viewpark, Milngavie, Glasgow. *T:* 041–956 6114.

RODGER, Rt. Rev. Patrick Campbell; *b* 28 Nov. 1920; *s* of Patrick Wylie and Edith Ann Rodger; *m* 1952, Margaret Menzies Menzies, MBE; one *s* (and one *s* decd). *Educ:* Cargilfield; Rugby; Christ Church, Oxford; Theological College, Westcott House, Cambridge; Deacon, 1949; Priest, 1950. Asst Curate, St John's Church, Edinburgh, 1949–51, and Chaplain to Anglican Students in Edinburgh, 1951–54. Study Secretary, SCM of Gt Brit. and Ire., 1955–58; Rector, St Fillan's, Kilmacolm, with St Mary's Bridge of Weir, 1958–61; Exec. Sec. for Faith and Order, World Council of Churches, 1961–66; Vice-Provost, St Mary's Cathedral, Edinburgh, 1966–67; Provost, 1967–70; Bishop of Manchester, 1970–78; Bishop of Oxford, 1978–86. Chm., Churches' Unity Commn, 1974–78; Pres., Conf. of European Churches, 1974–86. *Publication:* The Fourth World Conference on Faith and Order, Montreal (ed), 1964. *Recreations:* music and walking. *Address:* 12 Warrender Park Terrace, Edinburgh EH9 1EG. *T:* 031–229 5075.

RODGER, Sir William (Glendinning), Kt 1978; OBE 1957; FCA (NZ), FCIS; JP; chartered accountant; *b* Glasgow, 5 June 1912; *s* of William Rodger, Eaglesham; *m* 1937, Dulcie Elizabeth, *d* of Frank Bray, Auckland, NZ; one *s* one *d*. *Educ:* Univ. of Auckland; Victoria Univ. of Wellington. BCom. FCA (NZ) 1935; FCIS 1936; FCAI 1937; FIANZ 1946; FNZIM 1947. Commercial appts, 1927–41; with public accountancy firm, 1945–54. Victoria Univ. of Wellington: Mem. Professorial Bd, 1951–61; Dean, Faculty of Commerce, 1953–54, 1957, and 1959–60; Sen. Lectr in Accountancy, Univ. of Auckland, 1967–77. Vis. Prof. of Business Admin (Fulbright Award), Univ. of Calif at LA, 1957–58; Vis. Prof. of Commerce, Sch. of Business, Queen's Univ., Ont, 1962–63; Vis. Lectr in Farm Management Accounting, Wye Coll., Univ. of London, 1965–66; Agricl Economist, Min. of Agriculture, 1965–66; Vis. Fellow: Centre for Continuing Educn, Univ. of Auckland, 1978–; Mitchell Coll. of Advanced Educn, Bathurst, NSW, 1978–79. Founder Mem., NZ Admin. Staff Coll., 1950–65 (Course Dir, 1953–59). Dir, Civic Trust, Auckland, 1978. President: NZ Inst. of Cost Accountants, 1955 (Maxwell Award, 1956); NZ Inst. of Management, 1957. Member: NZ Govt Co. Law Cttee, 1951–55; Jamaican Govt Sugar Industry Commn, 1966–67; Nat. Res. Cttee, NZ Soc. of Accts, 1951–66; Nat. Exec., NZ Statistical Assoc., 1952–54; NZ Div., Chartered Inst. of

Secs, 1945–66 (Nat. Pres., 1958; Wellington Pres., 1960); Wellington Br., Econ. Soc. of Aust. and NZ, 1946–52. Hon. Member: NZ Inst. of Valuers, 1952; NZ Libraries Assoc., 1978; NZ Council Mem., Royal Commonwealth Soc., 1979–; founded Auckland Exec. Management Club 1968 (Pres., 1969–72). Pres., NZ Br. of Heraldry Soc., 1980–. Hon. Treas., Boy Scout Assoc., 1937–58. JP Auckland, 1946. Editor: The New Zealand Accountants Journal, 1945–47; Contemporary Commercial Practice, 1946; Management Review, 1948–53; Farm Accounting Research Reports, 1961 and 1966. *Publications:* Balance Sheet Significance, Preparation and Interpretation, 1949; (jtly) Auditing, 1950 (3rd edn 1962); Valuation of Unquoted Shares in New Zealand, 1953; Interpretation of Financial Data and Company Reports, 1955 (2nd edn 1960); Bibliography of Accountancy, 1955; (rev. edn) Yorston's Advanced Accounting, 3 vols, 1956; Private Companies in NZ, 1956; NZ Company Secretary, 1956, 2nd edn 1960; An Introduction to Accounting Theory, 1957; Company Accounts in NZ, 1962; A Study Guide to Auditing, 1963; Estate Planning, 1964; An Introduction to Cost and Management Accounting, 1965; The Management Audit, 1966; Business Administration in Pharmacy, 1969; Management in the Modern Medical Practice, 1975; Introduction to Genealogy and Heraldry in New Zealand, 1980; The Arms of the New Zealand Society of Accountants, 1980; The Heraldry of the Anglican Church in New Zealand, 1982; Case Studies on Heraldry in New Zealand, 1983; reports; contrib. prof. jls. *Address:* 61 Speight Road, St Heliers Bay, Auckland, New Zealand. *T:* 555 947.

RODGERS, (Andrew) Piers (Wingate); Secretary, Royal Academy of Arts, London, since 1982; *b* 24 Oct. 1944; second *s* of Sir John Rodgers, Bt, *qv*; *m* 1979, Marie Agathe Houette; two *s*. *Educ:* Eton Coll.; Merton Coll., Oxford (BA 1st Cl. Honour Mods, Prox. acc. Hertford and De Paravicini Prizes). J. Henry Schroder Wagg & Co. Ltd, London, 1967–73: Personal Asst to Chairman, 1971–73; Director, International Council on Monuments and Sites (ICOMOS), Paris, 1973–79; Consultant, UNESCO, Paris, 1979–80; Member, Technical Review Team, Aga Khan Award for Architecture, 1980, 1983; Secretary, UK Committee of ICOMOS, 1981. FRSA 1973. *Publications:* articles on protection of cultural heritage. *Recreations:* music, Islamic art. *Address:* 18 Hertford Street, W1. *T:* 01–409 3110. *Clubs:* Brooks's, Pratt's, MCC.

RODGERS, Mrs Barbara Noel, OBE 1975; *b* 1912; *d* of F. S. Stancliffe, Wilmslow, Cheshire; *m* 1950, Brian Rodgers; no *c*. *Educ:* Wycombe Abbey Sch.; (Exhibitioner) Somerville Coll., Oxford (MA). Social work and travel, 1935–39; Jt appt with Manch. and Salford Council of Social Service and Manchester Univ. (practical work Tutor and special Lectr), 1939–45; Lectr 1945, Sen. Lectr, 1955, and Reader, 1965–73, Manchester Univ.; Teaching Fellowship in Grad. Sch. of Social Work, Toronto Univ., 1948–49; Sen. Res. Fellow, Centre for Studies in Social Policy, 1973–75. Member: various wages councils and Industrial Tribunal Panel, 1950–85; National Assistance Bd, 1965; Supplementary Benefits Commn, 1966–76. Served and serving on numerous voluntary welfare organisations. *Publications:* (co-author) Till We Build Again, 1948; (with Julia Dixon) Portrait of Social Work, 1960; A Follow Up Study of Manchester Social Administration Students, 1940–60, 1963; Careers of Social Studies Graduates, 1964; (co-author) Comparative Social Administration, 1968; (with June Stevenson) A New Portrait of Social Work, 1973; chapter on Comparative Studies in Social Administration, in Foundations of Social Administration (ed H. Heisler), 1977; The Study of Social Policy: a comparative approach, 1979; numerous articles in learned jls mainly on social security and social services in America, France and Canada. *Recreations:* walking, bird watching, travel. *Address:* 19 High Street, Great Budworth, Cheshire CW9 6HF. *T:* Comberbach 892068.

RODGERS, George; Circulation and Promotion Manager, Labour Weekly; *b* 7 Nov. 1925; *s* of George and Lettitia Georgina Rodgers; *m* 1952, Joan, *d* of James Patrick and Elizabeth Graham; one *s* two *d*. *Educ:* St Margaret's and Holy Trinity, Liverpool; St Michael's, Sylvester, Rupert Road and Longview, Huyton. Co-operative Soc., Whiston, Lancs, 1939–43. Served War, RN, 1943–46 (War Medals, France, Germany Star). White's, Engrs, Widnes, 1946–50; with Civil Engineers: Eave's, Blackpool, 1950–53; Costain, Liverpool, 1953–54; Brit. Insulated Callender Cables, 1954–74. MP (Lab) Chorley, Feb. 1974–1979; Chm., NW Region Lab MPs, 1975–79. Sales Organiser, Labour Weekly, 1980. Contested (Lab) Pendle, 1983. Mem., Huyton UDC, 1964–74 (Chm., Educn Cttee, 1969–73; Chm., Local Authority, 1973–74); Mem. Liverpool Regional Hosp. Bd, 1967–74. *Publication:* (with Ivor Clemitson) A Life to Live: beyond full employment, 1981. *Recreations:* cycling, political history, amateur boxing (spectator). *Address:* 32 Willoughby Road, Huyton, Liverpool L14 6XB. *T:* 051–489 1913, (office) 01–703 0833. *Club:* Labour (Huyton).

RODGERS, Gerald Fleming; HM Diplomatic Service, retired; *b* 22 Sept. 1917; *s* of Thomas Fleming Rodgers and Mary Elizabeth (*née* Gillespie); *m* 1965, Helen Lucy, *y d* of late Dr Wall, Coleshill; two *s*. *Educ:* Rugby; Queens' Coll., Cambridge. Served War of 1939–45, Army, 1939–46. Foreign (subseq. Diplomatic) Service, 1947; served at: Jedda, 1947–49; British Middle East Office, Cairo and Fayid, 1949–53; FO, 1953–59; Peking, 1959–61; UK Delegation to OECD, 1961–64; Djakarta, 1964–65; Counsellor, Paris, 1965–67. *Address:* Laurelcroft, North Street, Kilsby, Rugby, Warwickshire CV23 8XU. *T:* Crick 822314.

RODGERS, Prof. Harold William, OBE 1943; FRCS 1933; Professor of Surgery, Queen's University of Belfast, 1947–73; Professor Emeritus, 1973; *b* 1 Dec. 1907; *s* of Major R. T. Rodgers; *m* 1938, Margaret Boycott; one *s* three *d*. *Educ:* King's College School; St Bartholomew's Hospital. St Bartholomew's Hospital: House Surgeon, Demonstrator in Anatomy, Chief Asst, Casualty Surgeon, Senior Asst Surgeon. Served War of 1939–45, RAMC, North Africa, Italy, France; Hon. Lt-Col. Prof. of Surgery and Head of Div. of Hosp. Care, Univ. of Ife, Nigeria, 1974–77, retd. Nuffield Medical Visitor to African Territories; WHO Vis. Prof. to India; Vice-Pres. Intervarsity Fellowship; FRC Soc.; Past President: Section of Surgery, RSM; British Society of Gastro-enterology; Christian Medical Fellowship; British Surgical Research Soc.; YMCA (Belfast); Past Chairman, Ct of Examiners of RCS; Pres., Hibernian CMS. District Surgeon, St John's Ambulance Brigade. Mem., RIIA, 1947–. Hon. Fellow, Polish Soc. of Surgeons, 1972. Hon. MD QUB, 1981. OStJ 1968. *Publications:* Gastroscopy, 1937; general articles in surgical and medical journals. *Recreations:* painting, travel, gardening, poetry. *Address:* 47 Fordington Road, N6.

RODGERS, Sir John (Charles), 1st Bt, *cr* 1964; DL; *b* 5 Oct. 1906; *o s* of Charles and Maud Mary Rodgers; *m* Betsy, JP, East Sussex, *y d* of Francis W. Aikin-Sneath, JP, and of Louisa, *d* of Col W. Langworthy Baker; two *s*. *Educ:* St Peter's, York; Ecole des Roches, France; Keble College, Oxford (scholar). MA. Sub-Warden, Mary Ward Settlement, 1929; Lectr and Administrative Asst, Univ. of Hull, 1930; FO, 1938–39 and 1944–45; Special Mission to Portugal, December 1945; Dir, Commercial Relations Div., MOI, 1939–41; Dir, Post-War Export Trade Develt, Dept of Overseas Trade, 1941–42; Head Industrial Inf. Div., Min. of Production, 1942–44; Foundation Gov. of Administrative Staff Coll.; Exec. Council Member, Foundation for Management Education, 1959–; BBC General Advisory Council, 1946–52; Hon. Secretary Smuts Memorial Committee, 1953; Chm. Cttee on Litter in Royal Parks, 1954; Exec. Cttee of British Council, 1957–58; Governor, British Film Institute, 1958; Member Tucker Cttee on Proceedings before Examining Justices, 1957; Leader, Parliamentary Panel, and on Exec. and Coun., Inst. of Dirs, 1955–58; Vice-Chm. Exec. Cttee Political and Economic Planning (PEP), 1962–68; Mem. Exec., London Library, 1963–71. MP (C) Sevenoaks, Kent, 1950–79 (where Winston Churchill was one of his constituents); PPS to Rt Hon. Viscount Eccles (at Ministries of Works, Education and Board of Trade), 1951–57; Parliamentary Sec., Bd of Trade, and Minister for regional development and employment, 1958–60. UK Delegate and Leader of the Conservatives to Parly Assembly, Council of Europe, and Vice-Pres., WEU, 1969–79; Chm., Independent Gp, Council of Europe, 1974–79; Chm., Political Affairs Cttee, 1976–79; Vice-Pres., European League for Econ. Co-operation, 1970–79; Hon. Treasurer, Europe-Atlantic Gp, 1975–; Mem., UK Cttee, European Cultural Foundn, 1982–. President: Centre Européen de Documentation et Information, 1963–66; Friends of Free China, 1969–. Dep. Chm., J. Walter Thompson Co. Ltd, 1931–70; Chairman: Cocoa Merchants Ltd, 1959–81; British Market Research Bureau Ltd, 1933–54; New English Library, 1961–70; Radio Luxembourg London, 1979–83 (Hon. Pres., 1983–); dir of Comweld Ltd and other cos. Mem. Council, Nat. Trust, 1978–83; Vice-Chm., Heritage of London Trust, 1980–. Mem. Court: City Univ., 1969–; Brunel Univ., 1981–84. President: Inst. of Practitioners in Advertising, 1967–69; Soc. for Individual Freedom, 1970–73; Inst. of Statisticians, 1971–77; Master, Worshipful Company of Masons, 1968–69; Freeman of the City of London. DL Kent 1973. CBIM; FSS; FIS; FRSA. Knight Grand Cross, Order of Civil Merit (Spain), 1965; Grand Cross of Liechtenstein, 1970; Comdr, Order of Dom Infante Henrique (Portugal), 1972; Grand Officier, Order of Leopold II (Belgium), 1978; Order of Brilliant Star (China), 1979; Kt Comdr, 1st cl., Royal Order of North Star, Sweden, 1980; Comdr, 1st cl., Order of Lion of Finland, 1980; Medal of Merit, Council of Europe, 1980; Grand Officer, Order of Merit of Grand Duchy of Luxembourg, 1983. *Publications:* Mary Ward Settlement: a history, 1930; The Old Public Schools of England, 1938; The English Woodland, 1941; (jtly) Industry looks at the New Order, 1941; English Rivers, 1948; (jtly) One Nation, 1950; York, 1951; (ed) Thomas Gray, 1953; (jtly) Change is our Ally, 1954; (jtly) Capitalism—Strength and Stress, 1958; One Nation at Work, 1976; and other pamphlets. *Recreations:* travel, theatre. *Heir:* *s* John Fairlie Tobias Rodgers, *b* 2 July 1940. *Address:* 72 Berkeley House, Hay Hill, W1. *T:* 01–629 5220; The Dower House, Groombridge, Kent. *T:* Groombridge 213. *Clubs:* Brooks's, Pratt's, Beefsteak, Royal Thames Yacht.

See also A. P. W. Rodgers.

RODGERS, Piers; *see* Rodgers, A. P. W.

RODGERS, Rt. Hon. William Thomas, PC 1975; Vice-President, Social Democratic Party, since 1982; *b* 28 Oct. 1928; *s* of William Arthur and Gertrude Helen Rodgers; *m* 1955, Silvia, *d* of Hirsch Szulman; three *d*. *Educ:* Sudley Road Council Sch.; Quarry Bank High School, Liverpool; Magdalen College, Oxford. General Secretary, Fabian Society, 1953–60. Contested: (Lab) Bristol West, March 1957; (SDP) Stockton N, 1983. MP (Lab 1962–81, SDP 1981–83) Stockton-on-Tees, 1962–74, Teesside, Stockton, 1974–83; Parly Under-Sec. of State: Dept of Econ. Affairs, 1964–67, Foreign Office, 1967–68; Leader, UK delegn to Council of Europe and Assembly of WEU, 1967–68; Minister of State: BoT, 1968–69; Treasury, 1969–70; MoD, 1974–76; Sec. of State for Transport, 1976–79. Chm., Expenditure Cttee on Trade and Industry, 1971–74. Borough Councillor, St Marylebone, 1958–62. *Publications:* Hugh Gaitskell, 1906–1963 (ed), 1964; (jt) The People into Parliament, 1966; The Politics of Change, 1982; pamphlets, etc. *Address:* 48 Patshull Road, NW5 2LD. *T:* 01–485 9997.

RODNEY, family name of **Baron Rodney.**

RODNEY, 9th Baron *cr* 1782; **John Francis Rodney;** Bt 1764; Director, Sulby Vacuumatic Division of Portals Holdings Ltd (formerly Marketing Director); *b* 28 June 1920; *s* of 8th Lord Rodney and Lady Marjorie Lowther (*d* 1968), *d* of 6th Earl of Lonsdale; *S* father, 1973; *m* 1952, Régine, *d* of late Chevalier Pangaert d'Opdorp, Belgium, and the late Baronne Pangaert d'Opdorp; one *s* one *d*. *Educ:* Stowe Sch., Buckingham; McGill Univ., Montreal. Served War of 1939–45 with Commandos, Burma, 1943–45 (despatches). Alternate Delegate to Council of Europe and WEU; Chm., Standing Cttee on Drug Abuse; Past Chm. and Council Mem., British Fedn of Printing Machinery and Supplies. *Recreations:* sailing, shooting, gardening, travelling round the world (not all recreation). *Heir:* *s* Hon. George Brydges Rodney, *b* 3 Jan. 1953. *Address:* 38 Pembroke Road, W8. *T:* 01–602 4391. *Clubs:* White's; Royal Yacht Squadron; Royal Southampton Yacht.

RODRIGUES, Sir Alberto, Kt 1966; CBE 1964 (OBE 1960; MBE (mil.) 1948); ED; General Medical Practitioner, Hong Kong; Senior Unofficial Member Executive Council 1964–74; Pro-Chancellor and Chairman of Executive Council, University of Hong Kong; *b* 5 November 1911; *s* of late Luiz Gonzaga Rodrigues and late Giovanina Remedios; *m* 1940, Cynthia Maria da Silva; one *s* two *d*. *Educ:* St Joseph's College and University of Hong Kong. MBBS Univ. of Hong Kong, 1934; Post graduate work, London and Lisbon, 1935–36; Medical Practitioner, 1937–40; also Medical Officer in Hong Kong Defence Force. POW, 1940–45. Medical Practitioner, 1945–50; Post graduate work, New York, 1951–52; Resident, Winnipeg Maternity Hosp. (Canada), 1952–53; General Medical Practitioner, 1953–. Member: Urban Council (Hong Kong), 1940–41; 1947–50; Legislative Council, 1953–60; Executive Council, 1960–74. Med. Superintendent, St Paul's Hospital, 1953–. Director: Jardine Securities, 1969–; Lap Heng Co. Ltd, 1970–; Hill & Shanghai Hotels Ltd, 1969–; Peak Tramways Co. Ltd, 1971–; Li & Fung Ltd, 1973; Hill Antenna and Engineering Co. Ltd, 1972–; Computer Data (Hill) Ltd, 1973–; Hill Commercial Broadcasting Co. Ltd, 1974–; Hong Kong and Shanghai Banking Corporation, 1974–. Officer, Ordem de Cristo (Portugal), 1949; Chevalier, Légion d'Honneur (France), 1962; Knight Grand Cross, Order of St Sylvester (Vatican), 1966. *Recreations:* cricket, hockey, tennis, swimming, badminton. *Address:* St Paul's Hospital Annexe, Causeway Bay, Hong Kong. *T:* 760017. *Clubs:* Hong Kong, Royal Hong Kong Jockey, Hong Kong Country, Lusitano, Recreio (all Hong Kong).

RODWELL, Daniel Alfred Hunter; QC 1982; **His Honour Judge Rodwell;** a Circuit Judge, since 1986; *b* 3 Jan. 1936; *s* of late Brig. R. M. Rodwell, AFC, and Nellie Barbara Rodwell (*née* D'Costa); *m* 1967, Veronica Ann Cecil; two *s* one *d*. *Educ:* Munro Coll., Jamaica; Worcester Coll., Oxford, 1956–59 (BA Law). National service, 1954–56; 2/Lieut 1st West Yorks, PWO, 1955; TA, 1956–67: Captain and Adjt 3 PWO, 1964–67. Called to Bar, Inner Temple, 1960. A Deputy Circuit Judge, 1977; a Recorder, 1980–86. *Recreations:* hunting, gardening, sailing. *Address:* Roddimore House, Winslow Road, Great Horwood, Milton Keynes MK17 0NY. *T:* Winslow (Aylesbury) 2536.

ROE, Marion Audrey; MP (C) Broxbourne, since 1983; *b* 15 July 1936; *d* of William Keyte and Grace Mary (*née* Bocking); *m* 1958, James Kenneth Roe; one *s* two *d*. *Educ:* Bromley High Sch. (GPDST); Croydon High Sch. (GPDST); English Sch. of Languages, Vevey. Member: London Adv. Cttee, IBA, 1978–81; Gatwick Airport Consultative Cttee, 1979–81; SE Thames RHA, 1980–83. Member (C): Bromley Borough Council, 1975–78; for Ilford N, GLC, 1977– (Cons. Dep. Chief Whip, 1978–82). Contested (C) Barking, 1979. Parly Private Secretary to: Parly Under-Secs of State for Transport, 1985;

Minister of State for Transport, 1986. Mem., Agriculture Select Cttee, 1984–85; Secretary: Cons. Backbench Horticulture Cttee, 1983–85; Cons. Backbench Party Orgn Cttee, 1985. Vice-Pres., Women's Nat. Cancer Control Campaign, 1985–; Patron, UK Nat. Cttee for UN Develt Fund for Women, 1985–. *Recreations:* ballet, opera. *Address:* House of Commons, SW1A 0AA. *Club:* Carlton (Associate Member).

ROE, Dame Raigh (Edith), DBE 1980 (CBE 1975); JP; Director, Airlines of Western Australia, since 1981; World President, Associated Country Women of the World, 1977–80; *b* 12 Dec. 1922; *d* of Alwyn and Laura Kurts; *m* 1941, James Arthur Roe; three *s. Educ:* Perth Girls' Sch., Australia. Country Women's Association: State Pres., 1967–70; National Pres., 1969–71. World Ambassador, WA Council, 1978–; Hon. Ambassador, State of Louisiana, USA, 1979–. Comr, ABC, 1978–83; Nat. Dir (Aust.), Queen Elizabeth II Silver Jubilee Trust for Young Australians, 1978–. JP Western Australia, 1966. Australian of the Year, 1977; Brooch of Merit, Deutscher Landfrauenverband, Fed. Republic of Germany, 1980. *Address:* 76 Regency Drive, Crestwood, Thornlie, WA 6108, Australia. *T:* 4598765.

ROE, Air Chief Marshal Sir Rex (David), GCB 1981 (KCB 1977; CB 1974); AFC; retired 1981; *b* 1925; *m* 1948, Helen Sophie (*née* Nairn) (*d* 1981); one *s* two *d. Educ:* City of London Sch.; London University. Joined RAF 1943; trained in Canada; served with Metropolitan Fighter Sector, No 11 Group, 203 Sqn, 1950–51; Sch. of Maritime Reconnaissance, 1951–53; Central Flying School and Flying Training Units, 1953–55; Commanded RNZAF Central Flying School, 1956–58; RAF Staff College, 1959; Commanded No 204 Sqn, 1960–62; College of Air Warfare, 1962–64; SASO No 18 (Maritime) Gp, 1964–67; Stn Comdr RAF Syerston, 1967–69; Director of Flying Trng, 1969–71; RCDS, 1971; Deputy Controller Aircraft (C), MoD (Procurement Executive), 1972–74; SASO HQ Near East Air Force, 1972–76; AOC-in-C Training Comd, 1976–77; AOC-in-C, Support Command, 1977–78; Air Mem. for Supply and Organisation, 1978–81. *Recreations:* reading, Rugby football. *Address:* c/o Lloyds Bank, 6 Pall Mall, SW1. *Club:* Royal Air Force.

ROE, Rt. Rev. William Gordon; *see* Huntingdon, Bishop Suffragan of.

ROEBUCK, Roy Delville; Barrister-at-law; *b* Manchester, 25 Sept. 1929; *m* 1957, Dr Mary Ogilvy Adams; one *s. Educ:* various newspapers. Called to the Bar, Gray's Inn, 1974. Served RAF, 1948–50 (National Service). Journalist, Stockport Advertiser, Northern Daily Telegraph, Yorkshire Evening News, Manchester Evening Chronicle, News Chronicle, Daily Express, Daily Mirror and Daily Herald, 1950–66; freelance, 1966–. MP (Lab) Harrow East, 1966–70. Contested (Lab): Altrincham and Sale, 1964 and Feb. 1965; Leek, Feb. 1974. Mem., Bd of Governors, Moorfields Eye Hospital, 1984–. *Recreations:* ski-ing, music, reading Hansard. *Address:* 12 Brooksby Street, N1 1HA. *T:* 01–607 7057; 5 Pump Court, Temple, EC4Y 7AP. *T:* 01–353 2532. *Club:* Royal Automobile.

ROEG, Nicolas Jack; film director; *b* 15 Aug. 1928; *s* of Jack Roeg and Gertrude Silk; *m* 1957, Susan (marr. diss.), *d* of Major F. W. Stephen, MC; four *s*; *m* Theresa Russell; two *s. Educ:* Mercers Sch. Original story of Prize of Arms; Cinematographer: The Caretaker; Masque of the Red Death; Nothing But the Best; Petulia; A Funny Thing Happened on the Way to the Forum; Fahrenheit 451; Far From the Madding Crowd, etc; 2nd Unit Director and Cinematographer: Judith; Lawrence of Arabia; Co-Dir, Performance; Director: Walkabout; Don't Look Now; The Man who Fell to Earth; Bad Timing; Eureka, 1983; Insignificance, 1985; Castaway, 1986. *Address:* Flat E, 2 Oxford and Cambridge Mansions, Old Marylebone Road, NW1. *T:* 01–262 8612.

ROFF, Derek Michael, OBE 1972; HM Diplomatic Service; Counsellor, Foreign and Commonwealth Office, since 1981; *b* 1 Aug. 1932; *m* 1957, Diana Susette Barrow; three *s. Educ:* Royal Grammar Sch., Guildford; St Edmund Hall, Oxford (BA). National Service with The Cameronians (Scottish Rifles) and King's African Rifles, 1952–54. ICI Ltd, 1958–67; entered Foreign Office, 1967; Consul (Economic), Frankfurt, 1968; First Sec., UK Delegn to the European Communities, Brussels, 1970; Consul (Economic), Düsseldorf, 1973; First Sec., FCO, 1977. *Recreations:* Dutch painting, sheep, countryside, music. *Address:* c/o Foreign and Commonwealth Office, SW1A 2AH. *Club:* Royal Commonwealth Society.

ROFFEY, Harry Norman, CMG 1971; Assistant Secretary, Department of Health and Social Security, 1954–72, retired; *b* 2 March 1911; *s* of Henry Roffey and Ella Leggatt; *m* 1964, Florence Dickie; no *c. Educ:* Brighton Grammar Sch.; St Catharine's Coll., Cambridge (BA Hons, MA); Inst. of Education, London Univ. (Teacher's Dip.). Teaching (languages), 1935–40. Air Ministry and Foreign Office, 1940–45 (left as Wing Comdr); Min. of Health (Principal), 1946–54; Dept of Health and Social Security, 1954–72 (as Asst Sec. i/c Internat. Affairs, on the Health side). *Recreations:* travel, music, etc. *Address:* 2 Sunnyside Place, Wimbledon, SW19 4SJ. *T:* 01–946 4991.

ROGAN, Very Rev. John; Canon Residentiary, Bristol Cathedral, since 1983; Bishop's Adviser in Social Responsibility; *b* 20 May 1928; *s* of William and Jane Rogan; *m* 1953, Dorothy Margaret Williams; one *s* one *d. Educ:* Manchester Central High School; St John's Coll., Univ. of Durham. BA 1949, MA 1951; DipTheol with distinction, 1954; BPhil 1981. Education Officer, RAF, 1949–52. Asst Curate, St Michael and All Angels, Ashton-under-Lyne, 1954–57; Chaplain, Sheffield Industrial Mission, 1957–61; Secretary, Church of England Industrial Cttee, 1961–66; Asst Secretary, Board for Social Responsibility, 1962–66; Vicar of Leigh, Lancs, 1966–78; Sec., Diocesan Bd for Social Responsibility, 1967–74, Chm. 1974–78; Rural Dean of Leigh, 1971–78; Hon. Canon of Manchester, 1975–78; Provost, St Paul's Cathedral, Dundee, 1978–83. *Publication:* (ed jtly) Principles of Church Reform: Thomas Arnold, 1962. *Recreations:* Roman history, walking, music. *Address:* 5 Elmgrove Road, Bristol BS6 6AH. *T:* Bristol 422168.

ROGAN, Rev. William Henry; an Extra Chaplain to the Queen, since 1978 (Chaplain to the Queen, 1966–78); *b* 1908; *s* of late Rev. John Rogan and Christian Ann McGhie; *m* 1940, Norah Violet Henderson, Helensburgh; one *s* two *d. Educ:* Royal High Sch. of Edinburgh; Univ. of Edinburgh. MA 1928; BD 1931. Asst, St Cuthbert's Parish Church, Edinburgh, 1930–32; Minister: Whithorn Parish, 1932; St Bride's Parish, Helensburgh, 1936–50; Paisley Abbey, 1950–69; Humbie, East Lothian, 1969–74. Supt, Church of Scotland Huts and Canteens in Orkney and Shetland, 1941–42; Army Chaplain, 1943–46. Select Preacher: Glasgow Univ., 1960–65; Aberdeen Univ., 1959–66; St Andrews Univ., 1959; Convener, Church of Scotland Youth Cttee, 1965–70. Founder and formerly Chm., Soc. of Friends of Paisley Abbey. Pres., Scottish Church Soc., 1977–78. Hon. DD Edinburgh, 1963. *Recreation:* angling. *Address:* Westwood, Edinburgh Road, Lauder, Berwickshire TD2 6PA. *T:* Lauder 415.

ROGERS, Rt. Rev. Alan Francis Bright, MA; an Hon. Assistant Bishop, Diocese of London (Kensington Area), since 1985; Hon. Assistant Curate, St Mary's, Twickenham, since 1985; *b* 12 Sept. 1907; *s* of Thomas and Alice Rogers, London, W9; *m* 1st, 1932, Millicent Boarder (*d* 1984); two *s*; 2nd, 1985, Barbara Gower. *Educ:* Westminster City Sch.; King's Coll., London; Leeds Univ.; Bishop's Coll., Cheshunt. Curate of St Stephen's, Shepherds Bush, 1930–32; Holy Trinity, Twickenham, 1932–34; Civil Chaplain, Mauritius, 1934–49; Archdeacon of Mauritius, 1946–49; Commissary to Bishop of Mauritius, 1949–59; Vicar of Twickenham, 1949–54; Proctor in Convocation, 1951–59; Vicar of Hampstead, 1954–59; Rural Dean of Hampstead, 1955–59; Bishop of Mauritius, 1959–66; Suffragan Bishop of Fulham, 1966–70; Suffragan Bishop of Edmonton, 1970–75; Priest-in-Charge: Wappenham, 1977–80; Abthorpe with Slapton, 1977–83. An Hon. Asst Bishop of Peterborough, 1975–84. Chm., Archbishops' Bd of Examiners, USPG, 1972–83. MA Lambeth 1959. *Recreations:* walking, light music. *Address:* 20 River Way, Twickenham, Middx TW2 5JP. *T:* 01–894 2031. *Club:* Royal Over-Seas League.

ROGERS, Allan Ralph, FGS; MP (Lab) Rhondda, since 1983; *b* 24 Oct. 1932; *s* of John Henry Rogers and Madeleine Rogers (*née* Smith); *m* 1955, Ceridwen James; one *s* three *d. Educ:* University College of Swansea (BSc Hons Geology). Geologist, UK, Canada, USA, Australia, 1956–63; Teacher, 1963–65; Tutor-organiser, WEA, 1965–70, District Sec., 1970–79. European Parliament: Mem. (Lab) SE Wales, 1979–84; Vice-Pres., 1979–82. *Recreations:* all sports, jazz bands. *Address:* 70 Cemetery Road, Porth, Rhondda, Mid-Glamorgan. *Clubs:* Workmen's (Ystrad Mynach); Workmen's (Treorchy); Penallta Colliery Rugby Football (Hengoed).

ROGERS, General Bernard William; General, United States Army; Supreme Allied Commander, Europe, since 1979; *b* 16 July 1921; *s* of late Mr and Mrs W. H. Rogers; *m* 1944, Ann Ellen Jones; one *s* two *d. Educ:* Kansas State Coll.; US Mil. Acad. (BS); Oxford Univ. (Rhodes Scholar; BA, MA); US Army Comd Staff Coll., Fort Leavenworth, Kansas; US Army War Coll., Carlisle Barracks, Pa. CO 3rd Bn, 9th Inf. Regt, 2nd Inf. Div., Korea, 1952–53; Bn Comdr 1st Bn, 23rd Inf., 2nd Inf. Div., Fort Lewis, Washington, 1955–56; Comdr, 1st Battle Gp, 19th Inf., Div. COS, 24th Inf. Div., Augsburg, Germany, 1960–61; Exec. Officer to Chm., Jt Chiefs of Staff, Washington, DC, 1962–66; Asst Div. Comdr, 1st Inf. Div., Republic of Vietnam, 1966–67; Comdt of Cadets, US Mil. Acad., 1967–69; Comdg Gen., 5th Inf. Div., Fort Carson, Colo, 1969–70; Chief of Legislative Liaison, Office of Sec. to the Army, Washington, DC, 1971–72; Dep. Chief of Staff for Personnel, Dept of the Army, Washington, DC, 1972–74; Comdg Gen., US Army Forces Comd, Fort McPherson, Ga, 1974–76; Chief of Staff, US Army, Washington, DC, 1976–79. Mem., Council on Foreign Relations, 1983–. Hon. Fellow, University Coll., Oxford, 1979. Hon. LLD: Akron, 1978; Boston, 1981; Hon. DCL Oxon, 1983. *Publications:* Cedar Falls-Junction City: a Turning Point, 1974; contribs to: Foreign Affairs, RUSI, 1982; Strategic Review, NATO's Sixteen Nations, 1983; Europa Archiv, Defense, NATO Review, 1984; Europäische Wehrkunde, Rivista Militaire, 1985; The Adelphi Papers, 1986. *Recreations:* golf, reading. *Address:* Supreme Allied Commander, Europe, Supreme Headquarters Allied Powers Europe, 7010 SHAPE, Belgium. *T:* 065–444113.

ROGERS, Surgeon Rear-Adm. (D) Brian Frederick, CB 1980; Director of Naval Dental Services, 1977–80; *b* 27 Feb. 1923; *s* of Frederick Reginald Rogers, MIMechE, MIMarE, and Rosa Jane Rogers; *m* 1946, Mavis Elizabeth (*née* Scott); one *s* two *d. Educ:* Rock Ferry High Sch.; Liverpool Univ. (LDS 1945). House Surgeon, Liverpool Dental Hosp., 1945; joined RNVR, 1946; transf. to RN, 1954; served HMS Ocean, 1954–56 and HMS Eagle, 1964–66; Fleet Dental Surg. on staff of C-in-C Fleet, 1974–77; Comd Dental Surg. to C-in-C Naval Home Comd, 1977. QHDS 1977. *Recreations:* European touring, photography, DIY. *Address:* 22 Trerieve, Downderry, Torpoint, Cornwall PL11 3LY. *T:* Downderry 526; Montana roja, Lanzarote, Canary Islands.

ROGERS, Prof. C(laude) Ambrose, FRS 1959; Astor Professor of Mathematics, University College, London, 1958–86, now Emeritus; *b* 1 Nov. 1920; *s* of late Sir Leonard Rogers, KCSI, CIE, FRS; *m* 1952, Mrs J. M. Gordon, *widow* of W. G. Gordon, and *d* of F. W. G. North; two *d. Educ:* Berkhamsted School; University Coll., London; Birkbeck Coll., London. BSc, PhD, DSc (London, 1941, 1949, 1952). Experimental officer, Ministry of Supply, 1940–45; lecturer and reader, University College, London, 1946–54; Prof. of Pure Mathematics, Univ. of Birmingham, 1954–58. Mem. Council, Royal Soc., 1966–68 and 1983–84; Pres., London Mathematical Soc., 1970–72; Chm., Jt Mathematical Council, 1982–84. *Publications:* Packing and Covering, 1964; Hausdorff Measures, 1970; articles in various mathematical journals. *Recreation:* string figures. *Address:* Department of Statistical Science, University College, WC1E 6BT; 8 Grey Close, NW11 6QG. *T:* 01–455 8027.

ROGERS, Ven. David Arthur; Archdeacon of Craven, 1977–86; *b* 12 March 1921; *s* of Rev. Canon Thomas Godfrey Rogers and Doris Mary Cleaver Rogers (*née* Steele); *m* 1951, Joan Malkin; one *s* three *d. Educ:* Saint Edward's School, Oxford (scholar); Christ's College, Cambridge (exhibitioner). BA 1947, MA 1952. War service with Green Howards and RAC, 1940–45; Christ's Coll. and Ridley Hall, Cambridge, 1945–49; Asst Curate, St George's, Stockport, 1949–53; Rector, St Peter's, Levenshulme, Manchester, 1953–59; Vicar of Sedbergh, Cautley and Garsdale, 1959–79; Rural Dean of Sedbergh and then of Ewecross, 1959–77; Hon. Canon of Bradford Cathedral, 1967. *Address:* Borrens, Leck, via Carnforth, Lancs.

ROGERS, David Bryan, CB 1984; Deputy Secretary and Director General, Board of Inland Revenue, since 1981; *b* 8 Sept. 1929; *s* of Frank Rogers and Louisa Rogers; *m* 1955, Marjory Geraldine Gilmour Horribine; one *s* two *d. Educ:* Grove Park, Wrexham; University Coll., London (BA Classics). Inspector of Taxes, 1953; Principal Inspector, 1968; Sen. Principal Inspector, 1976; Under Sec. and Dir of Operations, Bd of Inland Revenue, 1978–81. Mem. Council, UCL, 1983–. *Recreations:* piano, organ, singing, reading. *Address:* 2 Abbotswood Close, Guildford, Surrey. *T:* Guildford 69135.

ROGERS, Rev. Edward; General Secretary, Methodist Division of Social Responsibility (formerly Christian Citizenship Department), 1950–75; *b* 4 Jan. 1909; *s* of Capt. E. E. Rogers, Fleetwood; *m* 1st, 1937, Edith May, *o d* of A. L. Sutton, Plaistow; 2nd, 1979, Lucy Eveline Howlett. *Educ:* Baines's Poulton-Le-Fylde Grammar School; Manchester University; Hartley Methodist Coll. Kitchener Scholar, Shuttleworth Scholar, Hulme Hall, Manchester. MA (Econ. and Pol.) 1931, BD, 1933, Manchester Univ. Methodist Circuit Minister: East London Mission, Bakewell, Birmingham (Sutton Park), Southport, 1933–50. Lectures: Fernley, 1951; Ainslie, 1952; Beckly, 1957; Peake 1971. Editorial Dir, Methodist Newspaper Co., 1949–; Organising Dir, Methodist Relief Fund, 1953–75; Chairman, Inter-Church Aid and Refugee Service, British Council of Churches, 1960–64; Pres., Methodist Conf., 1960; Moderator, Free Church Federal Council, 1968 (Chm., Exec., 1974–80); Vice-Pres., British Council of Churches, 1971–74. Chairman: Standing Commn on Migration, 1964–70; Churches Cttee on Gambling Legislation, 1967–73; Exec. Council, UK Immigrants Adv. Service, 1970–; Community and Race Relations Unit, 1971–75; Avec Board, 1977–; Select Committee on Cruelty to Animals, 1963. *Publications:* First Easter, 1948; A Commentary on Communism, 1951; Programme for Peace, 1954; God's Business, 1957; That They Might Have Life, 1958; The Christian Approach to the Communist, 1959; Church Government, 1964; Living Standards, 1964; Law, Morality and Gospel, 1969; Search for Security, 1973; Plundered Planet, 1973; Money, 1976; Thinking About Human Rights, 1978. *Recreations:* travel, indiscriminate reading. *Address:* 49 Fernhurst Road, Croydon, Surrey CR0 7OJ. *T:* 01–656 1729.

ROGERS, Eric William Evan, DSc(Eng); FRAeS; aeronautical research consultant; Deputy Director (A), Royal Aircraft Establishment, Farnborough, Hants, 1978–85; *b* 12 April 1925; *o s* of late W. P. Rogers, Southgate, N London; *m* 1950, Dorothy Joyce Loveless; two *s* one *d*. *Educ:* Southgate County Grammar Sch.; Imperial Coll., London. FCGI, DIC. Aerodynamics Div., NPL, 1945–70 (Head of Hypersonic Research, 1961); Aerodynamics Dept, RAE, 1970 (Head, 1973). *Publications:* various papers on aerodynamics and on industrial aerodynamics, in ARC (R and M series), RAeS jls and elsewhere. *Recreations:* music, philately. *Address:* 64 Thetford Road, New Malden, Surrey. *T:* 01–942 7452.

ROGERS, Frank J.; Chairman, EMAP plc (formerly East Midland Allied Press), since 1973 (Director, since 1971); Deputy Chairman: Argyll Investments Ltd, since 1982; Daily Telegraph plc, since 1986 (Director, since 1985); *b* 24 Feb. 1920; *s* of Percy Rogers, Stoke-on-Trent; *m* 1949; two *d*. *Educ:* Wolstanton Grammar School. Journalist, 1937–49; Military Service, 1940–46; Gen. Man., Nigerian Daily Times, 1949–52; Manager, Argus, Melbourne, 1952–55; Man. Dir, Overseas Newspapers, 1958–60; Dir, Daily Mirror, 1960–65; Man. Dir, IPC, 1965–70. Chm., Nat. Newspaper Steering Gp, 1970–72; Dir, Newspaper Publishers Assoc., 1971–73. Adviser on Corporate Affairs, The Plessey Co. Ltd, 1973–81. Chm., British Exec. Cttee, Internat. Press Inst., 1978–. Mem. Council and Chm., Exec. Cttee, Industrial Soc., 1976–79; Chm. Council, Industry and Parliament Trust, 1979–81; Mem. Council, Advertising Standards Authority, 1985–. *Recreations:* motoring, golf. *Address:* Greensleeves, Loudwater Drive, Rickmansworth, Herts. *T:* Rickmansworth 775358. *Club:* Reform.

ROGERS, George Theodore; retired; Under-Secretary, Department of Trade, 1974–79; *b* 26 Feb. 1919; *s* of George James and late Margaret Lilian Rogers; *m* 1944, Mary Katherine Stedman; three *s* two *d*. *Educ:* Portsmouth Grammar Sch.; Keble Coll., Oxford (Open Schol. in Classics). Served War, Indian Infy, Burma, 1939–45. Resumed univ. educn (PPE), 1945–48; NATO Defence Coll., 1953–54. Min. of Supply/Min. of Aviation, 1948–65; Univ. Grants Cttee, 1965–68; Min. of Technology, 1968–70; DTI, 1970–74; Under-Sec., 1973. *Recreations:* gardening, travel, aviation. *Address:* 39 Sandy Lane, Cheam, Surrey SM2 7PQ. *T:* 01–642 6428.

ROGERS, Henry Augustus, OBE 1976 (MBE 1967); HM Diplomatic Service, retired; *b* 11 Dec. 1918; *s* of Henry Augustus Rogers and Evelyn Mary Rogers (*née* Casey); *m* 1947, Margaret May Stainsby; three *s*. *Educ:* The Fox Sch.; West Kensington Central Sch., London, W. With Solicitors, Wedlake Letts & Birds, Temple, prior to war. Joined RNVR, 1938; served war, 1939–45. Joined Foreign Office, 1945; Buenos Aires, 1946; Havana, 1953; Vice-Consul, Guatemala City, 1954; Vice-Consul, Los Angeles, 1958; Second Sec., Belgrade, 1961; FO, 1963; Second Sec., Kaduna, 1965; First Sec., Head of Chancery and Consul, Tegucigalpa, 1967; FCO, 1971; Consul, Luanda, Angola, 1973; Consul-Gen., Brisbane, 1976–77; FCO, 1978. *Recreations:* reading, classical literature and modern history, art (the Impressionists), music. *Address:* 7 Fitzgerald Close, Silverdale Road, Eastbourne, East Sussex BN20 7EP. *T:* Eastbourne 30915.

ROGERS, Prof. Howard John, FRCP; Professor of Clinical Pharmacology, United Medical and Dental Schools, and Physician, Guy's Hospital, since 1984; *b* 18 June 1943; *er s* of George Howard Rogers and Vivienne Rogers; *m* 1968, Moira O'Boyle; three *d*. *Educ:* Chislehurst and Sidcup Grammar School; Downing College, Cambridge (Open Major Scholar 1962; MA, MB, BChir); Guy's Hosp. Med. Sch. (Open Scholar 1965, Governors' Research Scholar 1969; PhD). Registrar, Guy's Hosp., 1973; MRC Research Fellow, Johns Hopkins Med. Sch., USA, 1974; Lectr, Sen. Lectr, Reader in Clinical Pharmacology, Guy's Hosp. Med. Sch., 1975–84. *Publications:* jointly: An Introduction to Mechanisms in Pharmacology and Therapeutics, 1976; Aids to Pharmacology, 1980, 2nd edn 1986; Aids to Clinical Pharmacology, 1984; Psychiatry: common drug treatments, 1984; A Textbook of Clinical Pharmacology, 1981, 2nd edn 1986; papers on clinical pharmacology and oncology. *Recreations:* music, reading, Ireland. *Address:* 5 Grovebury Close, Erith, Kent DA8 3DJ. *T:* Dartford 341976.

ROGERS, Hugh Charles Innes, MA, FIMechE; Director, Avon Rubber Co., 1968–79 (Chairman, 1968–78); Vice-Chairman, Bristol and West Building Society, 1972–82; *b* 2 November 1904; *s* of late Hugh Innes Rogers, OBE, MIEE; *m* 1930, Iris Monica Seymour; one *s* three *d*. *Educ:* Marlborough; Clare College, Cambridge. Brecknell Munro & Rogers, 1926–31 (Chairman and Jt Man. Dir, 1931–41); SW Reg. Controller, Min. of Supply, 1941; SW Reg. Controller, Min. of Production and Chm. of Regional Bd, 1942–44; Dep. Controller (Production) in Admiralty, 1944–46. Imperial Tobacco Co. Ltd, Bristol: Chief Engr, 1948; Dir, 1949–67; a Dep. Chm., 1964–67; Dir, British American Tobacco Co., 1964–67. Member Bristol University Council, 1938, Chm., 1968–72. Chairman: SW Regional Housing Bd, 1952–53; SW Regional Council, FBI, 1954. High Sheriff of Avon, 1974. Hon. LLD Bristol, 1971; Hon. DSc Bath, 1971. *Recreations:* sailing, shooting, tennis, farming. *Address:* Beach House, Bitton, near Bristol BS15 6NP. *T:* Bitton 3127.

ROGERS, John Michael Thomas; QC 1979; barrister-at-law; a Recorder of the Crown Court, since 1976; *b* 13 May 1938; *s* of Harold Stuart Rogers and Sarah Joan Thomas; *m* 1971, Jennifer Ruth Platt (marr. diss. 1984); one *d*. *Educ:* Rydal Sch.; Birkenhead Sch.; Fitzwilliam House, Cambridge (MA, LLB). Schoolmaster, 1962–64; called to Bar, Gray's Inn, 1963. *Recreations:* farming, gardening. *Address:* c/o J. Case, off Mordda Road, Oswestry, Shropshire. *T:* Oswestry 653726; 2 Dr Johnson's Building, Temple, EC4. *T:* 01–353 5371. *Clubs:* Reform; Pragmatists (Wirral); Ruthin Rugby Football; Bristol Channel Yacht.

ROGERS, Air Chief Marshal Sir John (Robson), KCB 1982; CBE 1971; FRAeS; Director, First Security Group plc, since 1986; Controller Aircraft, Ministry of Defence Procurement Executive, 1983–86, retired; *b* 11 Jan. 1928; *s* of B. R. Rogers; *m* 1955, Gytha Elspeth Campbell; two *s* two *d*. *Educ:* Brentwood Sch.; No 1 Radio Sch., Cranwell; Royal Air Force Coll., Cranwell. OC 56(F) Sqdn, 1960–61; Gp Captain, 1967; OC RAF Coningsby, 1967–69; Air Commodore, 1971; Dir of Operational Requirements (RAF), 1971–73; Dep. Comdt, RAF Coll., 1973–75; RCDS, 1976; Air Vice-Marshal, 1977; Dir-Gen. of Organisation, RAF, 1977–79; AOC Training Units, RAF Support Comd, 1979–81; Air Mem. for Supply and Organisation, MoD, 1981–83. CBIM 1983; FRAeS 1983. *Recreation:* motor racing. *Address:* c/o Lloyds Bank, 27 High Street, Colchester, Essex. *Club:* Royal Air Force.

ROGERS, John Willis; QC 1975; a Recorder of the Crown Court, since 1974; *b* 7 Nov. 1929; *s* of late Reginald John Rogers and late Joan Daisy Alexandra Rogers (*née* Willis); *m* 1952, Sheila Elizabeth Cann; one *s* one *d*. *Educ:* Sevenoaks Sch.; Fitzwilliam House, Cambridge (MA). Called to Bar, Lincoln's Inn, 1955 (Cholmeley Schol.); Bencher, 1984. 1st Prosecuting Counsel to Inland Revenue, SE Circuit, 1969–75. Hon. Recorder, City of Canterbury, 1985. *Recreations:* cricket, gardening, change ringing. *Address:* 3 Serjeant's Inn, Temple, EC4Y 1BQ. *T:* 01–353 5537. *Clubs:* Garrick, MCC, Band of Brothers.

ROGERS, Malcolm Austin, DPhil; FSA; Deputy Director since 1983, and Keeper since 1985, National Portrait Gallery (Deputy Keeper, 1983–85); *b* 3 Oct. 1948; *s* of late James Eric Rogers and Frances Anne (*née* Elsey). *Educ:* Oakham School; Magdalen College, Oxford (Open Exhbr); Christ Church, Oxford (Senior Scholar). MA 1973; DPhil 1976. Assistant Keeper, National Portrait Gallery, 1974. *Publications:* Dictionary of British Portraiture, 4 vols (ed jtly), 1979–81; Museums and Galleries of London, 1983; William Dobson, 1983; John and John Baptist Closterman: a catalogue of their works, 1983; articles and reviews in Burlington Magazine, Apollo, Connoisseur, TLS. *Recreations:* food and wine, opera, travel. *Address:* 14 Talfourd Road, SE15 5NY. *T:* 01–701 4007; Tudor Barn, Wardley, Uppingham, Rutland, Leics LE15 8AZ. *T:* Belton 311. *Club:* Beefsteak.

ROGERS, Martin Hartley Guy; HM Diplomatic Service, retired; *b* 11 June 1925; *s* of late Rev. Canon T. Guy Rogers and Marguerite Inez Rogers; *m* 1959, Jean Beresford Chinn; one *s* three *d*. *Educ:* Marlborough Coll.; Jesus Coll., Cambridge. CRO, 1949; 2nd Sec., Karachi, 1951–53; CRO, 1953–56 and 1958–60; seconded to Govt of Fedn of Nigeria, 1956–57; ndc 1960–61; 1st Sec., Ottawa, 1961–62; Adviser to Jamaican Min. of External Affairs, 1963; CRO, later Commonwealth Office, 1963–68; Dep. High Comr, Bombay, 1968–71, Kaduna, 1972–75; High Comr, The Gambia, 1975–79; on loan to CS Selection Bd, 1979–85. *Recreations:* golf, bridge. *Address:* Croftside, Harrow Road East, Dorking, Surrey. *T:* Dorking 883789.

ROGERS, Martin John Wyndham; Chief Master, King Edward's School, Birmingham, Headmaster of the Schools of King Edward VIth in Birmingham, since 1982; *b* 9 April 1931; *s* of late John Frederick Rogers and Grace Mary Rogers; *m* 1957, Jane Cook; two *s* one *d*. *Educ:* Oundle Sch.; Heidelberg Univ.; Trinity Hall, Cambridge (MA). Henry Wiggin & Co., 1953–55; Westminster School: Asst Master, 1955–60; Sen. Chemistry Master, 1960–64; Housemaster, 1964–66; Under Master and Master of the Queen's Scholars, 1967–71; Headmaster of Malvern Coll., 1971–82. Seconded as Nuffield Research Fellow (O-level Chemistry Project), 1962–64; Salter's Company Fellow, Dept of Chemical Engrg and Chemical Technology, Imperial Coll., London, 1969. Chairman: Curriculum Cttees of HMC, GSA and IAPS, 1979–86; HMC, 1987. Mem., Council, Birmingham Univ., 1985–. *Publications:* John Dalton and the Atomic Theory, 1965; Chemistry and Energy, 1968; (Editor) Foreground Chemistry Series, 1968; Gas Syringe Experiments, 1970; (co-author) Chemistry: facts, patterns and principles, 1972. *Address:* Vince House, King Edward's School, Birmingham B15 2UA. *T:* 021–472 0652. *Club:* East India, Devonshire, Sports and Public Schools.

ROGERS, Maurice Arthur Thorold; Secretary, Royal Institution, 1968–73; Joint Head, Head Office Research and Development Department, ICI, 1962–72; *b* 8 June 1911; *s* of A. G. L. Rogers; *g s* of Prof. J. E. Thorold Rogers; *m* 1947, Margaret Joan (*née* Craven) one *s* two *d*. *Educ:* Dragon Sch.; Westminster Sch.; University Coll., London. 1st Class hons BSc (Chem.) UCL 1932, PhD (Chem.) 1934. Chemist, ICI Dyestuffs Div., 1934–45; Head of Academic Relations Dept, 1946–58; Head of Head Office Research Dept, ICI, 1958–62. *Publications:* numerous papers in: Jl of Chem. Soc.; Nature; etc. *Recreations:* climbing, gardening, china restoration, conservation of countryside. *Address:* Mount Skippet, Ramsden, Oxford OX7 3AP. *T:* Ramsden 253.

ROGERS, Murray Rowland Fletcher; Member, Courts of Appeal for the Seychelles, St Helena, The Falkland Islands Colony and Dependencies, and the British Antarctic Territory, 1965–75; *b* 13 Sept. 1899; *s* of Geoffrey Pearson and Adeline Maud Rogers; *m* 1924, Dorothy Lilian Bardsley (*d* 1950); one *s* (one *d* decd). *Educ:* St Edward's School; RMC, Sandhurst; 2nd Lieut 8th Hussars, 1918–21; Liverpool Univ. (BA 1924). Schoolmaster until 1929; called to Bar, Gray's Inn, 1929; Northern Circuit until 1937; Magistrate, Nigeria, 1937–42; Chief Magistrate, Palestine, 1942–47; District Judge, Malaya, 1947–49; President Sessions Court, Malaya, 1949–52; Judge of Supreme Court, Sarawak, N Borneo and Brunei, 1952–63, retd. *Publication:* Law Reports of the Seychelles Court of Appeal, vol 1, 1965–76, 1976. *Address:* Flat 10, 2 Mountview Road, N4. *Clubs:* Athenæum; Artists' (Liverpool).

ROGERS, Nigel David; free-lance singer, conductor and teacher; Professor of Singing, Royal College of Music, since 1978; *b* 21 March 1935; *m* 1961, Frederica Bement Lord (marr. diss. 1974); one *d*. *Educ:* Wellington Grammar Sch.; King's Coll., Cambridge (MA). Studied in Italy and Germany. Professional singer, 1961–; began singing career in Munich with group Studio der frühen Musik. Is a leading specialist in field of Baroque music, of which he has made about 70 recordings; gives concerts, recitals, lectures and master classes in many parts of world; most acclaimed role in opera as Monteverdi's Orfeo. Formed vocal ensemble Chiaroscuro, to perform vast repertory of Italian Baroque music, 1979. Has lectured and taught at Schola Cantorum Basiliensis, Basle. Hon. RCM 1981. *Publications:* articles on early Baroque performance practice in various periodicals in different countries. *Recreations:* good food and wine, country pursuits, travel, especially Italy. *Address:* Chestnut Cottage, East End, East Woodhay, near Newbury, Berks. *T:* Highclere 253319.

ROGERS, Maj.-Gen. Norman Charles, FRCS 1949; Civilian Consultant Surgeon: BMH Iserlohn, 1983–86; BMH Munster, 1986; *b* 14 Oct. 1916; *s* of Wing Comdr Charles William Rogers, RAF, and Edith Minnie Rogers (*née* Weaver); *m* 1954, Pamela Marion (*née* Rose); two *s* one *d*. *Educ:* Imperial Service Coll.; St Bartholomew's Hosp. MB, BS London; MRCS, LRCP 1939. Emergency Commn, Lieut RAMC, Oct. 1939; 131 Field Amb. RAMC, Dunkirk (despatches); RMO, 4th Royal Tank Regt, N Africa, 1941–42; Italy, 1942–43 (POW); RMO 1st Black Watch, NW Europe, 1944–45 (wounded, despatches twice). Ho. Surg., St Bartholomew's Hosp., 1946–47; Registrar (Surgical) Appts, Norwich, 1948–52; Sen. Registrar Appts, Birmingham, 1952–56; granted permanent commn, RAMC, 1956; surgical appts in mil. hospitals: Chester, Dhekelia (Cyprus), Catterick, Iserlohn (BAOR), 1956–67; Command Consultant Surgeon, BAOR, 1967–69; Dir, Army Surgery, 1969–73; QHS, 1969–73; Clin. Supt, 1975–80, and Consultant, 1973–81, Accident and Emergency Dept, Guy's Hosp. *Publications:* contribs on surgical subjects. *Address:* 29 Ponsonby Terrace, SW1.

ROGERS, Mrs P. E.; *see* Box, B. E.

ROGERS, Paul; actor; *b* Plympton, Devon, 22 March 1917; *s* of Edwin and Dulcie Myrtle Rogers; *m* 1st, 1939, Jocelyn Wynne (marr. diss. 1955); two *s*; 2nd, 1955, Rosalind Boxall; two *d*. *Educ:* Newton Abbot Grammar School, Devon. Michael Chekhov Theatre Studio, 1936–38. First appearance on stage as Charles Dickens in Bird's Eye of Valour, Scala, 1938; Stratford-upon-Avon Shakespeare Memorial Theatre, 1939; Concert Party and Colchester Rep. Co. until 1940. Served Royal Navy, 1940–46. Colchester Rep. Co. and Arts Council Tour and London Season, Tess of the D'Urbervilles, 1946–47; Bristol Old Vic, 1947–49; London Old Vic (incl. tour S Africa and Southern Rhodesia), 1949–53; also at Edinburgh, London and in USA, 1954–57; London, 1958; tour to Moscow, Leningrad and Warsaw, 1960. Roles with Old Vic include numerous Shakespearean leads. Other parts include: Sir Claude Mulhammer in The Confidential Clerk, Edinburgh Festival and Lyric, London, 1953; Lord Claverton in The Elder Statesman, Edinburgh Fest. and Cambridge Theatre, London, 1958; Mr Fox in Mr Fox of Venice, Piccadilly, 1959; Johnny Condell in One More River, Duke of York's and Westminster, 1959; Nickles in JB, Phœnix, 1961; Reginald Kinsale in Photo Finish, Saville, 1962; The Seagull, Queen's, 1964; Season of Goodwill, Queen's, 1964; The Homecoming, Aldwych, 1965; Timon of Athens, Stratford-upon-Avon, 1965; The Government Inspector, Aldwych,

1966; Henry IV, Stratford-upon-Avon, 1966; Max in The Homecoming, New York, 1967 (Tony Award and Whitbread Anglo-American Award); Plaza Suite, Lyric, 1969; The Happy Apple, Apollo, 1970; Sleuth, St Martin's, 1970, NY, 1971 and 1974; Othello, Nat. Theatre Co., Old Vic, 1974; Heartbreak House, Nat. Theatre, 1975; The Marrying of Ann Leete, Aldwych, 1975; The Return of A. J. Raffles, Aldwych, 1975; The Zykovs, Aldwych, 1976; Volpone, The Madras House, Nat. Theatre, 1977; Eclipse, Royal Court, 1978; You Never Can Tell, Lyric, Hammersmith, 1979; The Dresser, New York, 1981, 1982; The Importance of Being Earnest, A Kind of Alaska, Nat. Theatre, 1982; The Apple Cart, Theatre Royal, Haymarket, 1986. Appears in films and television. *Publication*: a Preface to Folio Soc. edition of Shakespeare's Love's Labour's Lost, 1959. *Recreations*: gardening, carpentry, books. *Address*: 9 Hillside Gardens, Highgate, N6 5SU. *T*: 01–340 2656. *Club*: Naval.

ROGERS, Rev. Percival Hallewell, MBE 1945; Priest-in-Charge of Sandford-on-Thames since 1985; *b* 13 Sept. 1912; *m* 1940, Annie Mary Stuart, 2nd *d* of Lt-Col James Morwood; two *s* one *d*. *Educ*: Brentwood School; St Edmund Hall, Oxford. BA Class II, Hons English, Oxford, 1935; Diploma in Education, 1936; MA 1946. Two terms of teaching, Westminster School; Master in charge of English, Haileybury, 1936; served War, 1940–45 (despatches twice, MBE): RA, Major; DAA QMG; Bishop's College, Cheshunt, 1946; ordained, 1947; Asst Chaplain and English Master, Haileybury, 1947; Chaplain and English Master, 1949; Headmaster, Portora Royal Sch., Enniskillen, 1954–73; student, Internat. Acad. for Continuous Educn, Cheltenham, 1973–74; Chaplain, Gresham's Sch., Holt, 1974–75; Dean, Internat. Acad. for Continuous Educn, 1975–76; Asst Priest, Trinity Episcopal Church, New Orleans, 1976–80; Dir of Ordinands, Warden of Lay Readers, Dio. of Clogher, 1982–84. *Publications*: The Needs of the Whole Man, Systematics, 1971; Editor and contrib. to A Guide to Divinity Teaching (SPCK), 1962. *Address*: 7 Eyot Place, Iffley Fields, Oxford OX4 1SA. *T*: Oxford 244976. *Club*: East India, Devonshire, Sports and Public Schools.

ROGERS, Peter Brian; Director of Finance, Independent Broadcasting Authority, since 1982; Director, Channel Four Television Company Ltd, since 1982; *b* 8 April 1941; *s* of late William Patrick Rogers and Margaret Elizabeth Rogers; *m* 1966, Jean Mary Bailey; one *s* two *d*. *Educ*: De La Salle Grammar Sch., Liverpool; Manchester Univ. (1st Cl. Hons BAEcon; Cobden Prize); London Sch. of Econs and Pol. Science, London Univ. (MSc Econs). Tax Officer, Inland Revenue, 1959–67; Res. Associate, Manchester Univ., 1967–68; Econ. Adviser, HM Treasury, 1968–73; Sen. Econ. Adviser, Central Policy Review Staff, Cabinet Office, 1973–74; Dir of Econ. Planning, Tyne and Wear CC (on secondment from Central Govt), 1974–76; Sen. Econ. Adviser, DoE, 1976–79; Dep. Chief Exec., Housing Corp., 1979–82. *Recreations*: woodwork, photography. *Address*: Riverhead Cottage, Kilmeston Road, Cheriton, Alresford, Hants SO24 0NJ. *T*: Bramdean 790.

ROGERS, Sir Philip, GCB 1975 (KCB 1970; CB 1965); CMG 1952; Chairman, Universities Superannuation Scheme, 1977–84; Director: Glaxo Ltd, 1978–84; Greater London Regional Board, Lloyds Bank, 1980–85; *b* 19 Aug. 1914; *s* of William Edward and Sarah Jane Rogers; *m* 1940, Heather Mavis Gordon; one *s* one *d*. *Educ*: William Hulme's Grammar School, Manchester; Emmanuel Coll., Cambridge. Apptd to administrative class of Home Civil Service, as an Asst Principal in Colonial Office, 1936; seconded to be Private Secretary to Governor of Jamaica, Jan.-Dec. 1939; Asst Secretary, Colonial Office, 1946–53; Assistant Under-Secretary of State, Colonial Office, 1953–61; Under-Secretary, Department of Technical Co-operation, 1961–64; Dep. Sec. of Cabinet, 1964–67; Third Secretary, Treasury, 1967–68; Dep. Secretary, 1968–69, Second Permanent Secretary, 1969–70, Civil Service Dept; Permanent Secretary, DHSS, 1970–75. Chm., Bd of Management, London Sch. of Hygiene and Trop. Medicine, 1977–82; Member: SHA, Hammersmith Hosp., 1982–85; Court, London Univ., 1978–85; Council, Reading Univ., 1978– (Pres., 1980–). Outward Bound Trust: Mem. Council, 1976–82; Chm., 1976–80; Vice-Pres., 1982–. *Recreation*: gardening. *Address*: 96 King's Road, Henley-on-Thames, Oxon RG9 2DQ. *T*: Henley-on-Thames 575228. *Club*: Phyllis Court (Henley-on-Thames).

ROGERS, Sir Philip (James), Kt 1961; CBE 1952; Chairman, Tobacco Research Council, 1963–71; *b* 1908; *s* of late James Henry Rogers; *m* 1939, Brenda Mary Sharp, CBE, *d* of late Ernest Thompson Sharp. *Educ*: Blundell's Sch. Served War (RWAFF and Intell. Corps), 1940–44. MLC, Nigeria, 1947–51; MLC, Kenya, 1957–62; Elected Representative, Kenya, East African Legislative Assembly, 1962 and 1963. President: Nigerian Chamber of Commerce, 1948 and 1950 (Vice-Pres. 1947 and 1949); Nairobi Chamber of Commerce, 1957 (Vice-Pres. 1956); AAA of Nigeria, 1951; Dir, Nigerian Elec. Corp., 1951; Governor, Nigeria Coll. of Technology, 1951; Member: Nigerian Exec. Cttee, Rd Transport Bd, 1948–51; Central Council Red Cross Soc. of W Africa, 1950–51; Trades Adv. Cttee, Nigeria, 1950 and 1951–; Wages Adv. Bd, Kenya, 1955–61; EA Industrial Council, 1954–63; EA Air Licensing Appeals Trib., 1958–60; EA Air Adv. Council, 1956–60; Kenya Road Authority, 1957–61; Provl Council, Univ. of E Africa, 1961–63; Gov. Council, Roy. Tech. Coll. of E Africa, 1957–58 (Chm. 1958/59/60). Chairman: East African Tobacco Co. Ltd, 1951–63; Rift Valley Cigarette Co. Ltd, 1956–63; EA Rd Fedn, 1954–56; Kenya Cttee on Study and Trg in USA, 1958–63; Bd of Govs, Coll. of Social Studies, 1960–63; Nairobi Special Loans Cttee, 1960–63; African Teachers' Service Bd, 1956–63; Council, Royal College (now University Coll., Nairobi), 1961–63; Fedn of Sussex Amenity Socs, 1968–; Trustee, Outward Bound Trust of Kenya, 1959–63; Rep. of Assoc. Chambers of Commerce & Indust. of Eastern Africa; Mem. of Industrial Tribunals, England and Wales, 1966–80. Governor, Plumpton Agric. Coll., 1967–76. Member: E Sussex Educn Cttee, 1969–75; Finance Cttee, UCL, 1972–79; Indep. Schools Careers Orgn, 1972–79; Chairman: Fedn of Sussex Amenity Socs, 1968–80; Age Concern, East Sussex, 1974–80. *Address*: Church Close, Newick, East Sussex BN8 4JZ. *T*: Newick 2210.

ROGERS, Richard George, RA 1984 (ARA 1978); MArch; RIBA; Chairman: Richard Rogers and Partners, Rogers PA Technical and Science Centre; Piano and Rogers, France; *b* 23 July 1933; *m*; three *s*; *m* 1973, Ruth Elias; two *s*. *Educ*: Architectural Assoc. (graduate, Dip.); Yale Univ. (Fulbright, Edward D. Stone, and Yale Scholar; MArch). Winner of internat. competition from 680 entries for Centre Pompidou (1 million sq. ft in Paris for Min. of Culture), 1977; winner of Lloyd's internat. competition for 600,000 sq. ft Headquarters in City of London, 1978. Projects include: Electronics factory for Reliance Controls Ltd, Swindon, 1967; PA Technology Centre, Phases 1, 2 and 3, near Cambridge, 1970–84; B & B Factory, Como, Italy, 1972; Music res. centre for Pierre Boulez and Min. of Cultural Affairs, Paris, 1977; Cummins/Fleetguard factory, Quimper, France, 1980; Inmos semi-conductor manufg facility, Newport, 1982; HQ Wellcome Pharmaceuticals, Esher, 1984; PA Science Lab., Princeton, 1984; Urban Conservation, Florence, 1984; Royal Docks Strategy Planning, London, 1984–; Roundhouse Centre for Performing Arts, London, 1984–; Thames Wharf Offices, indust. units and housing, 1984/85–; Citibank Trading Floor and Offices, Billingsgate, London, 1985–. Visiting Lecturer/Professor: UCLA, Princeton, Harvard, Berkeley, Cornell, McGill, Hong Kong, Aachen, Cambridge; Saarinen Prof., Yale, 1985. Member: Council, RIBA; UN Architects Cttee; Chm. Trustees, Tate Gallery, 1984– (Trustee, 1981–). Adjudicator: Mem. and Chm., AA External Examining Bd, 1979–84; RIBA Awards, 1977, 1978; Dunlop Design Award 1981, 1983; R. S. Reynolds Meml Award, 1982; Tele Defense Comp., Paris, 1982–83; Urban Design Comp., Center for Innovative Tech., Virginia, and Progressive Arch. Design Award, USA, 1985. Hon. Fellow: Royal Acad. of the Hague; Amer. Inst. of Architects; IBM Fellow. Prizes include: Architectural Design Awards, 1964, 1965, 1968; Financial Times Indust. Arch. Award for Most Outstanding Indust. Bldg, 1967 (Reliance Controls, Swindon), 1976 (Patscentre), and 1983 (Inmos); RIBA Res. Award, 1970; British Steel Structural Design Award, 1975, 1982; RIBA Commendation, 1976; Auguste Perret Prize, Internat. Union of Architects, 1978; Premier Europeo Umberto Biancamano, 1979; Eurostructpress Award, 1983; Royal Gold Medal, RIBA, 1985. Subject of BBC documentary, Building for Change, 1980. *Publications*: By Their Own Design, 1980; contribs to Architectural Design, Global Arch., Progressive Arch., Arch. Review, and Arch. and Urbanism. *Address*: Thames Wharf, Rainville Road, W6 9HA. *T*: 01–385 1235.

ROGERS, Thomas Edward, CMG 1960; MBE 1945; HM Diplomatic Service, retired; *b* 28 Dec. 1912; *s* of T. E. Rogers and Lucy Jane Browne; *m* 1950, Eileen Mary, *d* of R. J. Speechley; no *c*. *Educ*: Bedford Sch.; Emmanuel Coll., Cambridge (Exhibnr); School of Oriental Studies, London. Selected for Indian Civil Service, 1936, and for Indian Political Service, 1941. Served in Bengal, 1937–41; in Persia and Persian Gulf, 1941–45; Political Agent, Quetta, 1947; Dep. Sec. (Cabinet Secretariat), Pakistan Govt, 1947–48. Entered Foreign Service, 1948: FO, 1948–50; Bogotá, 1950–53; jssc, 1953–54; Coun. (Comm.), Madrid, 1954–58; Coun. (Econ.), Belgrade, 1958–62; Minister (Econ.), Buenos Aires, 1963–65; Dep. UK High Comr, Canada, 1966–70, Actg High Comr, 1967–68; Ambassador to Colombia, 1970–73. Chm., Anglo-Colombian Soc., 1981–. Grand Cross of St Carlos, Colombia, 1974. *Recreation*: travel. *Address*: Chintens, Firway, Grayshott, Hants. *Club*: United Oxford & Cambridge University.

ROGERS, Thomas Gordon Parry; Chairman, Institute of Directors, since 1985; Chairman: Plessey Pension Trust, since 1980; Percom Ltd, since 1984; Education Technology Ltd; Director: Hobsons Ltd; Butler Cox & Partners Ltd; Norman Broadbent International Ltd; *b* 7 Aug. 1924; *s* of late Victor Francis Rogers and Ella (*née* May); *m* 1st, 1947, Pamela Mary (*née* Greene) (marr. diss. 1973); one *s* seven *d*; 2nd, 1973, Patricia Juliet (*née* Curtis); one *s* one *d*. *Educ*: West Hartlepool Grammar Sch.; St Edmund Hall, Oxford. MA; CIPM, CBIM; FRSA; FInstD. Procter & Gamble Ltd, 1948–54; Mars Ltd, 1954–56; Hardy Spicer Ltd, 1956–61 (Dir, 1957–61); IBM United Kingdom Ltd, 1961–74; Plessey Co. plc, 1974–86 (Dir, 1976–86); Director: IBM UK Holdings, 1964–74; Management Selection Ltd, 1970–78; MSL Gp Internat., 1970–78; ICL, 1977–79. Chairman: Salisbury HA; Adv. Cttee on Charitable Fund Raising, NCSS, 1970–76; Inst. of Manpower Studies; BTEC; Pres., Inst. of Personnel Management, 1975–77; Member: Council of Careers Research Adv. Centre, 1968–; Council, Industrial Participation Assoc., 1972–86; CBI/BIM Panel on Management Educn, 1968–78; CBI Employment Policy Cttee, 1980–86; Oxford Univ. Appts Cttee, 1972–; Employment Appeal Tribunal, 1978–; Standing Commn on Pay Comparability, 1980–81; Management Bd, EEF, 1980–86; E European Trade Council, 1982–85; Econ. League, 1982–86; Nat. Steering Gp, Technical and Vocational Educn Initiative, MSC, 1983–86; IT Skill Shortages Cttee, DTI, 1984; IT Skills Agency, 1985–; CBI Educn Foundn, 1985–; Review Team, Children and Young Persons Benefits, DHSS, 1984–85. *Publications*: The Recruitment and Training of Graduates, 1970; contribs to: The Director's Handbook, Management and the Working Environment, and various newspapers and jls. *Recreations*: birdwatching, golf, tennis. *Address*: St Edward's Chantry, Bimport, Shaftesbury, Dorset. *T*: Shaftesbury 2789; 32 Romulus Court, Brentford Dock, Mddx. *T*: 01–568 6060. *Clubs*: Savile, Royal Automobile; Royal Wimbledon Golf, Sherborne Golf.

ROGERS, William Pierce; Partner, law firm of Rogers & Wells, since 1973 (of Royall, Koegel, Rogers and Wells, 1961–69); *b* 23 June 1913; *s* of Harrison A. and Myra Beswick Rogers; *m* 1937, Adele Langston; three *s* one *d*. *Educ*: Canton High School, Canton, New York; Colgate University; Cornell Law School. Law firm of Cadwalader, Wickersham and Taft, NY City, 1937; an Asst District Attorney in NY County, 1938; US Navy, 1942–46; Dist Attorney's Office in New York, 1946; Chief Counsel, Senate Investigating Cttee, 1947; Counsel, Senate Permanent Investigating Cttee, 1949; law firm of Dwight, Royall, Harris, Koegel and Caskey, offices in New York and Washington, 1950; Dep. Attorney-General, 1953; Attorney-General of the US, 1957–61; Secretary of State, USA, 1969–73. Holds several hon. degrees in Law, from Univs and Colls in the USA, 1956–60. Mem. Bar Assocs in the USA. US Representative: to 20th Session of UN General Assembly, 1965; on UN Ad Hoc Cttee on SW Africa, 1967; Mem., President's Commn on Law Enforcement and Administration of Justice, 1965–67. *Recreations*: golf, tennis, swimming. *Address*: Rogers & Wells, 200 Park Avenue, New York, NY 10166, USA. *Clubs*: Metropolitan (Washington); Burning Tree (Bethesda); Racquet and Tennis, The Sky (NYC); Chevy Chase (Chevy Chase).

ROGERSON, Rt. Rev. Barry; *see* Bristol, Bishop of.

ROGERSON, John; Part-time Inspector, Department of the Environment, 1973–75; *b* 9 March 1917; *s* of late Walter John Lancashire Rogerson and Anne Marion Rogerson; *m* 1972, Audrey, *d* of late Adrian and Dorothy Maitland-Heriot. *Educ*: Tonbridge Sch.; St John's Coll., Oxford (BA). Served War, 2nd Lieut, later Captain, Royal Norfolk Regt, 1940–46. Principal: Min. of Town and Country Planning, 1947–49; HM Treasury, 1949–51; Min. of Housing and Local Govt (later Dept of the Environment), 1951–73; Asst Sec., 1955; Under-Sec., 1963; retd 1973. *Recreations*: botany, archaeology, mycophagy. *Address*: 95 Ridgmount Gardens, WC1E 7AZ. *T*: 01–636 0433.

ROGG, Lionel; organist and composer; Professor of Organ and Improvisation, Geneva Conservatoire de Musique, since 1961; *b* 1936; *m* Claudine Effront; three *s*. *Educ*: Conservatoire de Musique, Geneva (1st prize for piano and organ). Concerts or organ recitals on the five continents. Records include works by Alain, Buxtehude (complete organ works; Deutscher Schallplatten Preis, 1980), Couperin and Martin; also complete works of J. S. Bach (Grand Prix du Disque, 1970, for The Art of the Fugue). *Compositions*: Acclamations, 1964; Chorale Preludes, 1971; Partita, 1975; Variations on Psalm 91, 1983; Cantata "Geburt der Venus", 1984; Introduction, Ricerare and Toccata, 1985. *Publication*: Eléments de Contrepoint, 1969. *Address*: Conservatoire de Musique, Place Neuve, Geneva, Switzerland; 38A rte de Troinex, CH 1234 Vessy-Genève, Switzerland.

ROIJEN, Jan Herman Van; Grand Cross, Order of Orange Nassau; Commander, Order of the Netherlands Lion; Netherlands Ambassador to the United Kingdom, 1964–70; Netherlands Ambassador to the Icelandic Republic, 1964–70; Netherlands Permanent Representative to Council of Western European Union, 1964–70; *b* Istanbul, 10 April 1905; *s* of Jan Herman van Roijen (sometime Netherlands Min. to USA), and (American-born) Albertina Winthrop van Roijen; *m* 1934, Anne Snouck Hurgronje; two *s* two *d*. *Educ*: Univ. of Utrecht. Doctor in Law, 1929. Joined Foreign Service, 1930; Attaché to Neths Legn, Washington, 1930–32; Min. of For. Affairs, 1933–36; Sec. to Neths Legn, Tokyo, 1936–39; Chief of Polit. Div. of Min. of For. Affairs, 1939. Jailed during German occupation; escaped to London, 1944. Minister without Portfolio, 1945; Minister of For. Affairs, March-July 1946; Asst Deleg. and Deleg. to UN Conf. and Assemblies, 1945–48; Ambassador to Canada, 1947–50. Leader, Neths Delegn to bring about Netherlands-Indonesian Round Table Conf., Batavia, 1949; Dep. Leader, Neths Delegn at Round Table Conf., The Hague, 1949. Ambassador to the United States, 1950–64. Leader, Neths Delegn in negotiations with Indonesia about W New Guinea, Middleburg (Va.) and New York, 1962. Holds several hon. doctorates in Laws, of Univs and Colls in USA; Gr. Cross, Order of Oak Crown, Luxembourg; Gr. Cross, Order of Falcon, Iceland; Comdr, Order of British Empire (CBE); Comdr, Order of Holy Treasure, Japan. *Recreations*: reading, theatre, golf. *Address*: Stoephoutflat, Stoeplaan 11, Wassenaar, Netherlands. *Club*: De Haagsche (The Hague).

ROITH, Oscar, FEng, FIMechE; Chief Engineer and Scientist, Department of Trade and Industry, since 1982; *b* London, 14 May 1927; *s* of late Leon Roith and Leah Roith; *m* 1950, Irene Bullock; one *d*. *Educ*: Gonville and Caius Coll., Cambridge (minor schol.; Mech. Scis Tripos; MA). FIMechE 1967; FEng 1983. CBIM. FRSA. Research Dept, Courtaulds, 1948; Distillers Co. Ltd: Central Engrg Dept, 1952; Engrg Manager, Hull Works, 1962; Works Manager, 1968, Works Gen. Manager, 1969, BP Chemicals, Hull; General Manager: Engrg and Technical, BP Chemicals, 1974; Engrg Dept, BP Trading, 1977; Chief Exec. (Engrg), BP Internat., 1981. Mem., Yorks and Humberside Economic Planning Council, 1972–74. Chm., Mech. and Electrical Engrg Requirements Bd, 1981–82; Member: Mech. Engrg and Machine Tools Requirements Bd, 1977–81; ACORD, 1982–; ACARD, 1982–; Process Plant EDC, NEDO, 1979–82; SERC, 1982–; NERC, 1982–. Dep. Pres., IMechE, 1985– (Mem. Council, 1981–; Mem., Process Engrg Gp Cttee, 1962–68). *Recreations*: cricket, gardening, walking. *Address*: (office) 1 Victoria Street, SW1H 0ET.

ROITT, Prof. Ivan Maurice, FRS 1983; Professor, since 1968 and Head of Department of Immunology, since 1968 and of Rheumatology Research, since 1984, Middlesex Hospital Medical School; *b* 30 Sept. 1927; *e s* of Harry Roitt; *m* 1953, Margaret Auralie Louise, *d* of F. Haigh; three *d*. *Educ*: King Edward's Sch., Birmingham; Balliol Coll., Oxford (exhibnr; BSc 1950; MA 1953; DPhil 1953; DSc 1968). FRCPath 1973. Res. Fellow, 1953, Reader in Immunopathol., 1965–68, Middlesex Hosp. Med. Sch. Chm., WHO Cttee on Immunolog. Control of Fertility, 1976–79; Mem., Biol. Sub-Cttee, UGC. Mem., Harrow Borough Council, 1963–65; Chm., Harrow Central Lib. Assoc., 1965–67. Florey Meml Lectr, Adelaide Univ., 1982. Hon. MRCP (London). (Jtly) Van Meter Prize, Amer. Thyroid Assoc., 1957; Gairdner Foundn Award, Toronto, 1964. *Publications*: Essential Immunology, 1971, 5th edn 1984; (jtly) Immunology of Oral Diseases, 1979; (jtly) Immunology, 1985; contribs to Lancet, etc. *Address*: Department of Immunology, Middlesex Hospital Medical School, Arthur Stanley House, 40–50 Tottenham Street, W1.

ROKISON, Kenneth Stuart; QC 1976; *b* 13 April 1937; *s* of Frank Edward and Kitty Winifred Rokison; *m* 1973, Rosalind Julia (*née* Mitchell); one *s* two *d*. *Educ*: Whitgift School, Croydon; Magdalene College, Cambridge (BA 1960). Called to the Bar, Gray's Inn, 1961, Bencher, 1985. *Recreation*: acting. *Address*: Ashcroft Farm, Gadbrook, Betchworth, Surrey. *T*: Dawes Green 244.

ROLAND, Nicholas; *see* Walmsley, Arnold Robert.

ROLF, Percy Henry; a Recorder of the Crown Court, since 1978; Consultant, Robinson Jarvis & Rolf, Solicitors, Isle of Wight, since 1986 (Partner 1948; Senior Partner, 1964); *b* 25 Dec. 1915; *s* of Percy Algernon Rolf and Lydia Kate (*née* Arnold); *m* 1939, Cecilia Florence Cooper; one *s* one *d*. *Educ*: Sandown Grammar Sch.; London Univ. (LLB). Solicitor. Served War, RAF, 1940–46: Wing Comdr; Sen. Air Traffic Control Officer, Transport Comd, 1945–46. *Recreations*: golf, gardening. *Address*: Ashlake Water, Fishbourne, Isle of Wight. *T*: Isle of Wight 882513.

ROLFE, Rear-Adm. Henry Cuthbert Norris, CB 1959; *b* 1908; *s* of Benedict Hugh Rolfe, MA Oxon; *m* 1931, Mary Monica Fox; one *s* two *d*. *Educ*: Pangbourne Nautical College. Joined Royal Navy, 1925. Served War of 1939–45: HMS Hermes, 1939; South-East Asia, 1944; Staff of Director of Air Warfare, Admiralty, 1947; commanded HMS Veryan Bay, 1948; service with Royal Canadian Navy, 1949; commanded: HMS Vengeance, 1952; RN Air Station, Culdrose, 1952; HMS Centaur, 1954–56; RN Air Station, Ford, 1956–57; Asst Chief of Naval Staff (Warfare) 1957–60; Regional Director, Northern Region, Commonwealth Graves Commission, 1961–64, retd. Naval ADC to the Queen, 1957; Rear-Admiral, 1957. Liveryman, Worshipful Company of Coachmakers and Coach Harnessmakers, 1962. *Address*: 43 Nuns Road, Winchester, Hants.

ROLFE, Hume B.; *see* Boggis-Rolfe.

ROLL, family name of Baron Roll of Ipsden.

ROLL OF IPSDEN, Baron *cr* 1977 (Life Peer), of Ipsden in the County of Oxfordshire; **Eric Roll,** KCMG 1962 (CMG 1949); CB 1956; Director of the Bank of England, 1968–77; Chancellor, University of Southampton, 1974–84; Joint Chairman, S. G. Warburg & Co. Ltd, since 1983 (Chairman, 1974–83; Deputy Chairman, 1967–74); President: Mercury Securities Ltd, since 1985 (Chairman, 1974–84); Mercury International Group, since 1985; *b* 1 Dec. 1907; *yr s* of Mathias and Fany Roll; *m* 1934, Winifred, *o d* of Elliott and Sophia Taylor; two *d*. *Educ*: on the Continent; Univ. of Birmingham. BCom 1928; PhD 1930; Gladstone Memorial Prize, 1928; Univ. Research Scholarship, 1929. Prof. of Economics and Commerce, Univ. Coll. of Hull, 1935–46 (leave of absence 1939–46). Special Rockefeller Foundation Fellow, USA, 1939–41. Member, later Dep. Head, British Food Mission to N America, 1941–46; UK Dep. Member and UK Exec. Officer, Combined Food Board, Washington, until 1946; Asst Sec., Ministry of Food, 1946–47; Under-Secretary, HM Treasury (Central Economic Planning Staff), 1948; Minister, UK Delegation to OEEC, 1949. Deputy Head, United Kingdom Delegation to North Atlantic Treaty Organization, Paris, 1952; Under Secretary Ministry of Agriculture, Fisheries and Food, 1953–57; Executive Dir, International Sugar Council, 1957–59; Chm., United Nations Sugar Conf., 1958; Deputy Secretary, Ministry of Agriculture, Fisheries and Food, 1959–61; Deputy Leader, UK Delegation for negotiations with the European Economic Community, 1961–63; Economic Minister and Head of UK Treasury Delegation, Washington, 1963–64, also Exec. Dir for the UK International Monetary Fund and International Bank for Reconstruction and Development; Permanent Under-Sec. of State, Dept of Economic Affairs, 1964–66. Chm., subseq. Hon. Chm., Book Development Council, 1967–. Independent Mem., NEDC, 1971–80. Director: Times Newspapers Ltd, 1967–80; Times Newspapers Holdings Ltd, 1980–83; also other Directorships. Hon. DSc Hull, 1967; Hon. DSocSci Birmingham, 1967; Hon. LLD Southampton, 1974. Grosses Goldene Ehrenzeichen mit Stern (Austria), 1979; Comdr 1st Cl., Order of the Dannebrog (Denmark), 1981; Officier, Légion d' Honneur, 1984. *Publications*: An Early Experiment in Industrial Organization, 1930; Spotlight on Germany, 1933; About Money, 1934; Elements of Economic Theory, 1935; Organized Labour (collaborated), 1938; The British Commonwealth at War (collaborated), 1943; A History of Economic Thought, 1954,

new edn, 1973; The Combined Food Board, 1957; The World After Keynes, 1968; The Uses and Abuses of Economics, 1978; (ed) The Mixed Economy, 1982; Crowded Hours (autobiog.), 1985; articles in Economic Jl, Economica, American Economic Review, etc. *Recreation*: reading. *Address*: D2 Albany, Piccadilly, W1. *Clubs*: Brooks's, Groucho.

ROLL, Rev. Sir James (William Cecil), 4th Bt, *cr* 1921; Vicar of St John's, Becontree, 1958–83, retired; *b* 1 June 1912; *s* of Sir Cecil Ernest Roll, 3rd Bt, and Mildred Kate (*d* 1926), *d* of William Wells, Snaresbrook; *S* father, 1938; unmarried. *Educ*: Chigwell School, Essex; Pembroke College, Oxford; Chichester Theological College. Deacon, 1937. Curate East Ham Parish Church, 1944–58. *Heir*: none. *Address*: 82 Leighcliff Road, Leigh on Sea, Essex. *T*: Southend on Sea 76177.

ROLLAND, Lawrence Anderson Lyon, PRIBA; PPRIAS; Senior Partner: L. A. Rolland & Partners, since 1959; Robert Hurd and Partners, since 1965; President of Royal Institute of British Architects, 1985–July 1987; *b* 6 Nov. 1937; *s* of Lawrence Anderson Rolland and Winifred Anne Lyon; *m* 1960, Mairi Melville; two *s* two *d*. *Educ*: George Watson Boys' College, Edinburgh; Duncan of Jordanstone College of Art. Diploma of Art (Architecture) 1959; ARIBA 1960; FRIAS 1965 (Pres., RIAS, 1979–81). Founder Mem., Scottish Construction Industry Group, 1979–81; Mem., Bldg EDC, NEDC. Architect for: Queen's Hall, Edinburgh; restoration and renovation of Bryce Bank of Scotland Head Office; much housing in Fife's royal burghs. A Trustee, Church of Scotland. *Recreations*: music, fishing, food, wine, cars. *Address*: Rossend Castle, Burntisland, Fife KY3 0DF. *T*: Burntisland 873535. *Clubs*: Reform; Scottish Arts (Edinburgh).

ROLLO, family name of **Lord Rollo.**

ROLLO, 13th Lord *cr* 1651; **Eric John Stapylton Rollo;** Baron Dunning, 1869; JP; *b* 3 Dec. 1915; *s* of 12th Lord and Helen Maud (*d* 1928), *o c* of Frederick Chetwynd Stapylton of Hatton Hill, Windlesham, Surrey; *S* father, 1947; *m* 1938, Suzanne Hatton; two *s* one *d*. *Educ*: Eton. Served War of 1939–45, Grenadier Guards, retiring with rank of Captain. JP Perthshire, 1962. *Heir*: *s* Master of Rollo, *qv*. *Address*: Pitcairns, Dunning, Perthshire. *T*: Dunning 202.

ROLLO, Master of; Hon. David Eric Howard Rollo; *b* 31 March 1943; *s* and *heir* of 13th Lord Rollo, *qv*; *m* 1971, Felicity Anne Christian, *o d* of Lt-Comdr J. B. Lamb; three *s*. *Educ*: Eton. Late Captain Grenadier Guards. *Address*: 20 Draycott Avenue, SW3. *Clubs*: Cavalry and Guards, Turf.

ROLO, Cyril Felix, CMG 1975; OBE 1959; HM Diplomatic Service, retired; *b* 13 Feb. 1918; *s* of late I. J. Rolo and Linda (*née* Suares); *m* 1948, Marie Luise Christine (*née* Baeurle); one *s*. *Educ*: Charterhouse; Oriel Coll., Oxford (MA). Served with Armed Forces, 1940–46 (Major): Oxf. and Bucks LI, later on Gen. Staff; Western Desert, E Africa, Italy, Austria. Joined HM Foreign (subseq. Diplomatic) Service, 1946: Allied Commn for Austria, 1947–48; 2nd Sec., Rome, 1948–50; Political Adviser's Office, Berlin, 1950–52; FO, 1952–57; 1st Sec., Vienna, 1957–62; FO (subseq. FCO), 1962–76; Counsellor, 1971. *Recreations*: travel, golf, reading. *Address*: 32 Roxburghe Mansions, Kensington Court, W8 5BH. *T*: 01–937 4696. *Clubs*: Travellers'; Sunningdale Golf.

ROLPH, C. H., (Cecil Rolph Hewitt); *b* London, 23 Aug. 1901; *s* of Frederick Thompson Hewitt and Edith Mary Speed; *m* 1st, 1926, Audrey Mary Buttery (marr. diss., 1946; she *d* 1982); one *d*; 2nd, 1947, Jenifer Wayne (*d* 1982), author and scriptwriter; one *s* two *d*. *Educ*: State schools. City of London Police, 1921–46 (Chief Inspector); editorial staff, New Statesman, 1947–70; editor, The Author, 1956–60; Dir, New Statesman, 1965–80. Mem. Council, Soc. of Authors. *Publications*: A Licensing Handbook, 1947; Crime and Punishment, 1950; Towards My Neighbour, 1950; On Gambling, 1951; Personal Identity, 1956; (ed) The Human Sum, 1957; Mental Disorder, 1958; Commonsense About Crime and Punishment, 1961; The Trial of Lady Chatterley, 1961; (with Arthur Koestler) Hanged by the Neck, 1961; All Those in Favour? (The ETU Trial), 1962; The Police and The Public, 1962; Law and the Common Man, 1967; Books in the Dock, 1969; Kingsley, 1973; Believe What You Like, 1973; Living Twice (autobiog.), 1974; Mr Prone, 1977; The Queen's Pardon, 1978; London Particulars (autobiog.), 1980; The Police (child's history), 1980; As I Was Saying, 1985; Further Particulars (autobiog.), 1987; contributor to The Encyclopædia Britannica, Chambers's Encyclopædia, Punch, The Week-End Book, The New Law Journal, The Times Literary Supplement, The Author, The Nation (NY), daily and weekly press. *Recreations*: music, reading, and the contemplation of work. *Address*: Rushett Edge, Bramley, Surrey GU5 0LH. *T*: Guildford 893227.

ROMAIN, Roderick Jessel Anidjar; Metropolitan Stipendiary Magistrate, 1972–83; *b* 2 Dec. 1916; *s* of late Artom A. Romain and Winifred (*née* Rodrigues); *m* 1947, Miriam, *d* of late Semtob Sequerra; one *s* one *d*. *Educ*: Malvern Coll.; Sidney Sussex Coll., Cambridge. Called to the Bar, Middle Temple, 1939. Commissioned from HAC to 27th Field Regt, RA, 1940. Served War of 1939–45: France and Belgium, also N Africa and Italy, JAG Staff, 1943–45; JA at Neuengamme War Crimes Trial. Admitted a Solicitor, 1949, in practice as Partner, in Freke Palmer, Romain & Gassman, until 1972; recalled to Bar, 1973; a Dep. Circuit Judge, 1975–78. *Recreations*: golf, gardening. *Address*: 43 Lyndale Avenue, NW2 2QB. *T*: 01–435 5913. *Clubs*: Garrick; Hampstead Golf.

ROMANES, Professor George John, CBE 1971; PhD; Professor of Anatomy, 1954–84, and Dean of Faculty of Medicine, 1979–83, Edinburgh University; Professor of Anatomy, Royal Scottish Academy, since 1983; *b* 2 Dec. 1916; *s* of George Romanes, BSc, AMICE, and Isabella Elizabeth Burn Smith; *m* 1945, Muriel Grace Adam, Edinburgh; four *d*. *Educ*: Edinburgh Academy; Christ's College, Cambridge (BA, PhD); Edinburgh University (MB, ChB). Marmaduke Sheild Scholar in Human Anatomy, 1938–40; Demonstrator in Anatomy, Cambridge, 1939; Beit Memorial Fellow for Medical Research, Cambridge, 1944–46; Lectr in Neuroanatomy, Edinburgh, 1946; Prof. of Anatomy, Edinburgh, 1954. Commonwealth Fund Fell., Columbia Univ., NY, 1949–50. Chm., Bd of Management, Edinburgh Royal Infirmary, 1959–74. Mem. Anatomical Soc. of Gt Brit. and Ireland; Mem. Amer. Assoc. of Anatomists; Assoc. Mem. Amer. Neurological Assoc. FRSE 1955; FRCSE 1958. Hon. DSc Glasgow, 1983. *Publications*: (ed) Cunningham's Textbook and Manuals of Anatomy; various papers on the anatomy and development of the nervous system in Jl of Anatomy and Jl of Comparative Neurology. *Recreations*: angling and curling. *Address*: 9 Campbell Park Drive, Edinburgh EH13 0HS. *T*: 031–441 2826.

ROMER, Mark Lemon Robert; a Metropolitan Stipendiary Magistrate since 1972; *b* 12 July 1927; *s* of late Rt Hon. Sir Charles Romer, OBE, and Hon. Lady Romer; *m* 1953, Philippa Maynard Tomson; one *s* two *d*. *Educ*: Bryanston; Trinity Hall, Cambridge (MA, LLM). Called to Bar, Lincoln's Inn, 1952; practised privately until 1958 when joined Govt Legal Service. *Recreations*: bird-watching, reading, music. *Address*: The Old Vicarage, Braughing, Ware, Herts. *T*: Ware 821434.

ROMNEY, 7th Earl of, *cr* 1801; **Michael Henry Marsham;** Bt 1663; Baron of Romney, 1716; Viscount Marsham, 1801; *b* 22 Nov. 1910; *s* of Lt-Col the Hon. Reginald Hastings Marsham, OBE (*d* 1922) (2nd *s* of 4th Earl) and Dora Hermione (*d* 1923), *d* of late Charles North; *S* cousin, 1975; *m* 1939, Frances Aileen, *o d* of late Lt-Col James Russell Landale,

IA. *Educ:* Sherborne. Served War of 1939–45, Major RA. *Heir: cousin* Julian Charles Marsham [*b* 28 March 1948; *m* 1975, Catriona Ann, *d* of Lt-Col Robert Christie Stewart, *qv*; two *s* one *d*]. *Address:* Wensum Farm, West Rudham, King's Lynn, Norfolk. *T:* East Rudham 249.

ROMSEY, Lord; Norton Louis Philip Knatchbull; *b* 8 Oct. 1947; *s* and *heir* of Baron Brabourne, *qv* and of Countess Mountbatten of Burma, *qv*; *m* 1979, Penelope Meredith Eastwood; one *s* two *d*. *Educ:* Dragon School, Oxford; Gordonstoun; University of Kent (BA Politics). *Heir: s* Hon. Nicholas Louis Charles Norton Knatchbull, *b* 15 May 1981. *Address:* Broadlands, Romsey, Hants SO51 9ZD. *T:* Romsey 517888.

RONALD, Edith, (Mrs Edmund Ronald); *see* Templeton, Mrs Edith.

RONALDSHAY, Earl of; Lawrence Mark Dundas; *b* 28 Dec. 1937; *e s* of 3rd Marquess of Zetland, *qv*; *m* 1964, Susan, 2nd *d* of Guy Chamberlin, Oatlands, Wrington Hill, Wrington, Bristol, and late Mrs Chamberlin; two *s* two *d*. *Educ:* Harrow School; Christ's College, Cambridge. Late 2nd Lieut, Grenadier Guards. *Heir: s* Lord Dundas, *qv*. *Address:* Copt Hewick Hall, Ripon, N Yorks HG4 5DE. *T:* Ripon 3946. *Clubs:* All England Lawn Tennis and Croquet, Jockey.

RONAY, Egon; Founder of the Egon Ronay hotel and restaurant guides (taken over by the Automobile Association, 1985); *m* 1967, Barbara Greenslade; one *s* (two *d* of previous marr.). *Educ:* School of Piarist Order, Budapest; Univ. of Budapest (LLD); Academy of Commerce, Budapest. Dip. Restaurateurs' Guild, Budapest; FHCIMA. After univ. degree, trained in kitchens of family catering concern; continued training abroad, finishing at Dorchester Hotel, London; progressed to management within family concern of 5 restaurants, of which eventually he took charge; emigrated from Hungary, 1946; Gen. Manager, Princes Restaurant, Piccadilly, then Society Restaurant, Jermyn Street, followed by 96 Restaurant, Piccadilly; opened own restaurant, The Marquee, SW1, 1952–55; started eating-out and general food, wine and tourism weekly column in Daily Telegraph and later Sunday Telegraph, 1954–60, also eating-out guide, 1957; weekly dining out column in Evening News, 1968–74. Mem. l'Académie des Gastronomes, France, 1979; Pres., British Acad. of Gastronomes, 1983; Vice Pres., Internat. Acad. of Gastronomy, 1985. *Publications:* Egon Ronay's Lucas Guide to Hotels and Restaurants, annually, 1956–85; Egon Ronay's Lucas Just A Bite, annually, 1979–85; Egon Ronay's Guinness Pub Guide, annually, 1980–85; Egon Ronay's Guide to 500 Good Restaurants in Europe's main cities, annually, 1983–85; various other tourist guides to Britain, to ski resorts in Europe, to Scandinavian hotels and restaurants and to eating places in Greece. *Address:* Alliance House, 12 Caxton Street, SW1H 0QS. *T:* 01–828 6032.

RONSON, Gerald Maurice; Chairman and Chief Executive, Heron Corporation PLC and Heron International PLC; *b* 26 May 1939; *s* of Henry and Sarah Ronson; *m* 1967, Gail; four *d*. Chief Executive, 1976–, Chairman, 1979–, Heron Corp. PLC; Chm. and Chief Exec., Heron International PLC, 1983–. *Recreations:* yachting, shooting. *Address:* Heron House, 19 Marylebone Road, NW1 5JP. *T:* 01–486 4477. *Club:* Royal Southern Yacht (Southampton).

ROOK, Dr John Allan Fynes, CBE 1985; FRSE, FRSC, FIBiol; Second Secretary, Agricultural and Food Research Council (formerly Agricultural Research Council), London, 1981–86; Visiting Professor in Animal Nutrition, Wye College, University of London, 1981–86; *b* 1 May 1926; *s* of Edward Fynes Rook and Annie Rook; *m* 1952, Marion Horsburgh Millar; two *s* one *d*. *Educ:* Scarborough Boys' High Sch.; University College of Wales, Aberystwyth. BSc, DSc (Wales); PhD (Glasgow). National Institute for Research in Dairying, Shinfield, Berks, 1954–65; Prof. of Agricultural Chemistry, Univ. of Leeds, 1965–70; Dir, Hannah Res. Inst., Ayr, and Hannah Prof. of Animal Nutrition, Univ. of Glasgow, 1971–80. *Publications:* (ed jtly) Nutritional Physiology of Farm Animals, 1983; numerous articles in British Jl of Nutrition, Jl of Dairy Research, etc. *Recreations:* gardening, golf; shutting doors and switching off lights after other members of the family. *Address:* Corbiestow, Mill Lane, Rathmell, near Settle, North Yorks BD24 0LA. *Club:* Farmers'.

ROOKE, Daphne Marie; author; *b* 6 March 1914; *d* of Robert Pizzey and Marie Knevitt; *m* 1937, Irvin Rooke; one *d*. *Educ:* Durban, S Africa. *Publications:* A Grove of Fever Trees, 1950; Mittee, 1951; Ratoons, 1953; The South African Twins, 1953; The Australian Twins, 1954; Wizards' Country; The New Zealand Twins, 1957; Beti, 1959; A Lover for Estelle, 1961; The Greyling, 1962; Diamond Jo, 1965; Boy on the Mountain, 1969; Double Ex!, 1970; Margaretha de la Porte, 1974; A Horse of his Own, 1976. *Recreation:* bushwalking. *Address:* 34 Bent Street, Fingal Bay, NSW 2315, Australia.

ROOKE, Sir Denis (Eric), Kt 1977; CBE 1970; BSc (Eng.); FRS 1978; FEng 1977; Chairman, British Gas Corporation (formerly The Gas Council), since 1976 (Deputy Chairman, 1972–76); *b* 2 April 1924; *yr s* of F. G. Rooke; *m* 1949, Elizabeth Brenda, *d* of D. D. Evans, Ystradgynlais, Brecon; one *d*. *Educ:* Westminster City Sch.; Addey and Stanhope Sch.; University Coll., London (Fellow, 1972). Served with REME, UK and India, 1944–49 (Major). Joined staff of S Eastern Gas Bd as Asst Mechanical Engr in coal-tar by-products works, 1949; Dep. Man. of works, 1954; seconded to N Thames Gas Bd, 1957, for work in UK and USA on liquefied natural gas; mem. technical team which sailed in Methane Pioneer on first voyage bringing liquefied natural gas to UK, 1959; S Eastern Gas Bd's Development Engr, 1959; Development Engr, Gas Council, 1960; Mem. for Production and Supplies, 1966–71. Chm., CNAA, 1978–83; Member: Adv. Council for R&D, 1972–77; Adv. Council for Energy Conservation, 1974–77; Offshore Energy Technology Bd, 1975–78; BNOC, 1976–82; NEDC, 1976–80; Energy Commn, 1977–79. President: IGasE, 1975; Assoc. for Science Educn, 1981; Fellowship of Engineering, 1986–. Trustee, Science Museum, 1984–. Hon. DSc: Salford, 1978; Leeds, 1980; City, 1985; Durham, 1986. *Publications:* papers to Instn of Gas Engrs, World Power Conf., World Petroleum Conf., etc. *Recreations:* photography, listening to music. *Address:* 23 Hardy Road, Blackheath, SE3. *Clubs:* Athenæum, English-Speaking Union.

ROOKE, Giles Hugh, TD 1963; QC 1979; **His Honour Judge Rooke;** a Circuit Judge, since 1981; *b* 28 Oct. 1930; *s* of late Charles Eustace Rooke, CMG, and Irene Phyllis Rooke; *m* 1968, Anne Bernadette Seymour, *d* of His Honour John Perrett, *qv*; three *s* one *d*. *Educ:* Stowe; Exeter Coll., Oxford (MA). Kent Yeomanry, 1951–61, Kent and County of London Yeomanry, 1961–65 (TA), Major. Called to Bar, Lincoln's Inn, 1957; practised SE Circuit, 1957–81; a Recorder of the Crown Court, 1975–81. Hon. Recorder of Margate, 1980–. *Address:* St Stephen's Cottage, Bridge, Canterbury CT4 5AH. *T:* Canterbury 830298.

ROOKE, James Smith, CMG 1961; OBE 1949; Grand Decoration of Honour in Gold, of the Austrian Republic, 1981; Chief Executive, British Overseas Trade Board, 1972–75; HM Diplomatic Service, retired; now lecturer, Diplomatic Academy, Vienna; *b* 6 July 1916; *s* of Joseph Nelson Rooke and Adeline Mounser (*née* Woodgate); *m* 1938, Maria Theresa Rebrec, Vienna; one *s* two *d*. *Educ:* Workington Grammar Sch.; University College, London; Vienna Univ. Apptd to Dept of Overseas Trade, 1938. Military service, 1940–45, KRRC and AEC. Second Secretary (Commercial), British Embassy, Bogotá, 1946; UK Delegation to ITO Conf., Havana, 1947; Dep. UK Commercial Rep., Frankfurt, 1948; First Secretary (Commercial), British Embassy, Rome, 1951; Consul (Commercial), Milan, 1954; Deputy Consul-General (Commercial), New York, 1955–59; HM Counsellor (Commercial) British Embassy, Berne, 1959–63, Rome, 1963–66; Minister (Commercial), British High Commn, Canberra, 1966–68; Minister (Economic), British Embassy, Paris, 1968–72. *Recreations:* climbing, tennis, ski-ing. *Address:* Kreuzwiesengasse 4, 1170 Vienna, Austria. *Club:* East India, Devonshire, Sports and Public Schools.

ROOKE, Brig. Vera Margaret, CB 1984; CBE 1980; RRC 1973; Matron-in-Chief (Army) and Director of Army Nursing Services, 1981–84; *b* 21 Dec. 1924; *d* of late William James Rooke and Lily Amelia Rooke (*née* Cole). *Educ:* Girls' County Sch., Hove, Sussex. Addenbrooke's Hosp., Cambridge (SRN); Royal Alexandra Children's Hosp., Brighton (RSCN); St Helier Hosp., Carshalton (Midwifery). Joined Queen Alexandra's Royal Army Nursing Corps, 1951; appointments include: service in military hospitals, UK, Egypt, Malta, Singapore; Staff Officer in Work Study; Liaison Officer, QARANC, MoD, 1973–74; Assistant Director of Army Nursing Services and Matron: Military Hosp., Hong Kong, 1975; Royal Herbert Hosp. and Queen Elizabeth Military Hosp., Woolwich, 1976–78; Dep. Dir, Army Nursing Services, HQ UKLF, 1979–80. QHNS, 1981–84. Lt-Col 1972, Col 1975, Brig. 1981. *Recreations:* gardening, walking, cookery, opera. *Address:* c/o Lloyds Bank, 208 Portland Road, Hove, Sussex.

ROOKER, Jeffrey William, CEng; MP (Lab) Birmingham, Perry Barr, since Feb. 1974; *b* 5 June 1941; *m* 1972, Angela. *Educ:* Handsworth Tech. Sch.; Handsworth Tech. Coll.; Warwick Univ. (MA); Aston Univ. (BScEng). CEng, FIProdE, Grad. IMechE; MBIM. Apprentice toolmaker, King's Heath Engrg Co. Ltd, Birmingham, 1957–63; student apprentice, BLMC, 1963–64; Asst to Works Manager, Geo. Salter & Co., West Bromwich, 1964–65, Assembly Manager, 1965–67; Prodn Manager, Rola Celestion Ltd, Thames Ditton and Ipswich, 1967–70; Industrial Relations and Safety Officer, Metro-Cammell, Birmingham, 1971; Lectr, Lanchester Polytechnic, Coventry, 1972–74. Opposition spokesman on social services, 1979–80, on social security, 1980–83, on treasury and economic affairs, 1983–84, on housing, 1984–. Mem. Council, Instn of Prodn Engrs, 1975–81. *Recreation:* full-time MP. *Address:* House of Commons, SW1. *T:* (home) 021–350 6186.

ROOLEY, Anthony; lutenist; Artistic Director, The Consort of Musicke, since 1969; *b* 10 June 1944; *s* of Madge and Henry Rooley; *m* 1967, Carla Morris; three *d*. *Educ:* Royal Acad, of Music. LRAM (Performers). Recitals in Europe, USA, Middle East, Japan, S America, New Zealand; radio and TV in UK and Europe; numerous recordings, British and German. *Publication:* Penguin Book of Early Music. 1982. *Recreations:* food, wine, gardening, philosophy. *Address:* 54A Leamington Road Villas, W11.

ROOME, Maj. Gen. Oliver McCrea, CBE 1973; DL; *b* 9 March 1921; *s* of late Maj. Gen. Sir Horace Roome, KCIE, CB, CBE, MC, DL, late Royal Engineers; *m* 1947, Isobel Anstis, *d* of Rev. A. B. Jordan; two *s* one *d*. *Educ:* Wellington Coll. Commissioned in Royal Engineers, 1940. Served War: UK, Western Desert, Sicily, Italy, 1939–45. Various appts, UK, Far and Middle East, Berlin, 1946–68; IDC, 1969; Director of Army Recruiting, 1970–73; Chief, Jt Services Liaison Organisation, Bonn, 1973–76; retired. Col Comdt, RE, 1979–84. County Comr, Scouts, Isle of Wight, 1977–85. DL Isle of Wight, 1981; High Sheriff of the Isle of Wight, 1983–84. *Recreations:* sailing, maritime and military history. *Address:* Lloyds Bank, 6 Pall Mall, SW1. *Clubs:* Army and Navy, Royal Ocean Racing, Royal Cruising; Royal Yacht Squadron.

ROONEY, Denis Michael Hall, CBE 1977; FEng, FIMechE, FIEE; CBIM; industrial consultant; Consultant, Goddard, Kay, Rogers, since 1983; Chairman, Laserfix Ltd, since 1984; *b* 9 Aug. 1919; *s* of late Frederick and Ivy Rooney; *m* 1st, 1942, Ruby Teresa (*née* Lamb) (*d* 1984); three *s* three *d*; 2nd, 1986, Muriel Franklin; one step *d*. *Educ:* Stonyhurst Coll.; Downing Coll., Cambridge (MA). Served War, Royal Navy, 1941–46. Various appts with BICC Ltd, 1946–69; Balfour Beatty Ltd: Dep. Managing Dir, 1969–72; Man. Dir, 1973–77; Chm., 1975–80; BICC Ltd: Exec. Dir, 1973–80; Exec. Vice-Chm., 1978–80; Chm., BICC Internat., 1978–80; Dep. Chm., Metal Manufactures Ltd, Australia, 1978–80; Chm., Nat. Nuclear Corp., 1980–81. Chm., SE Asia Trade Adv. Gp, BOTB, 1975–79; Member: British Overseas Trade Adv. Council, 1976–80; Overseas Projects Bd, BOTB, 1976–79; BOTB, 1979–80; Council: Export Gp for Construction Industries, 1964–80; Christian Assoc. of Business Execs, 1979–. Liveryman, Worshipful Company of Turners of London. *Publication:* contrib. (Brazilian Rlwy Electrification) IEE Jl. *Recreation:* golf. *Address:* 36 Edwardes Square, W8. *T:* 01–603 9971. *Clubs:* Institute of Directors; Tandridge Golf (Oxted).

ROOT, Rev. Canon Howard Eugene; Director of the Anglican Centre, Rome, since 1981; St Augustine Canon of Canterbury Cathedral, since 1980; Counsellor on Vatican Affairs to Archbishop of Canterbury, since 1981; Guest Professor, Pontifical Gregorian University, Rome, since 1984; *b* 13 April 1926; *s* of Dr Howard Root and Flora Hoskins; *m* 1952, Celia, *e d* of Col R. T. Holland, CBE, DSO, MC; two *s* two *d*. *Educ:* Univ. of Southern California; St Catherine's Coll. and Magdalen Coll., Oxford; Ripon Hall, Oxford. BA S Calif 1945; BA Oxon 1951; MA Oxon 1970; MA Cantab 1953. Teaching Fellow, 1945–47; Instructor, American Univ., Cairo, 1947–49; Sen. Demy, Magdalen Coll., Oxford, and Liddon Student, 1952–53. Deacon, 1953; Priest, 1954. Curate of Trumpington, 1953; Asst Lectr in Divinity, Cambridge, 1953–57; Lectr, 1957–65; Fellow, Emmanuel Coll., Cambridge, 1954–65, Chaplain, 1954–56, Dean, 1956–65; Prof. of Theology, Univ. of Southampton, 1966–81. Wilde Lectr, Oxford Univ., 1957–60; Senior Denyer and Johnson Scholar, Oxford, 1963–64; Bampton Lectr, Univ. of Oxford, 1972; Pope Adrian VI Chair, Univ. of Louvain, 1979; Exam. Chaplain to Bishops of Ripon, 1959–76, Southwark, 1964–81, Bristol, 1965–81, Winchester, 1971–81, and Wakefield, 1977–81; Commissary to Bishop in Jerusalem, 1976–. Official Anglican Observer at Second Vatican Council, 1963–65; Consultant, Lambeth Conf., 1968. Chm., Archbishops' Commn on Marriage, 1968–71; Member: Academic Council, Ecumenical Inst., Jerusalem, 1966–81; Anglican-RC Preparatory Commn, 1967–68; Archbishops' Commn on Christian Doctrine, 1967–74; Anglican-Roman Catholic Internat. Commn, 1969–81. Hon. Chaplain, Winchester Cathedral, 1966–67; Canon Theologian of Winchester, 1967–80. Mem., BBC Central Religious Adv. Cttee, 1971–75. Jt Editor, Jl of Theol Studies, 1969–74. *Recreations:* music, silence. *Address:* Anglican Centre, Palazzo Doria, via del Corso 303, Rome, Italy; c/o Barclays Bank, Old Bank, High Street, Oxford. *Club:* Brooks's.

ROOTES, family name of **Baron Rootes.**

ROOTES, 2nd Baron *cr* 1959; **William Geoffrey Rootes;** Chairman, 1967–73, Chrysler United Kingdom (lately Rootes Motors Ltd); *b* 14 June 1917; *er s* of 1st Baron Rootes, GBE; *S* father, 1964; *m* 1946, Marian, *widow* of Wing Comdr J. H. Slater, AFC, and *d* of late Lt-Col H. R. Hayter, DSO; one *s* one *d*. *Educ:* Harrow; Christ Church, Oxford. Served War of 1939–45 in RASC (France, E Africa, Western Desert, Libya, Tunisia and Italy), demobilised, Actg Major, 1946. Rejoined Rootes Group, 1946: Man. Dir, 1962–67; Dep. Chm., 1965–67; Chm. 1967–70. Director: Rank Hovis McDougall, 1973–84; Joseph Lucas Industries Ltd, 1973–85. President: SMMT, 1960–61 (Hon. Officer, 1958–62,

Chm. Exec. Cttee, 1972–73); Motor & Cycle Trades Benevolent Fund, 1968–70; Motor Ind. Research Assoc., 1970–71; Inst. of Motor Industry, 1973–75. Member: Nat. Adv. Council, Motor Manufrg Industry, 1964–71; Nat. Economic Development Cttee, Motor Manufacturing Industry, 1968–73; BNEC (Chm., American Cttee, 1969–71); Council, CBI, 1967–74, Europe Cttee CBI, 1972–76; Council, Inst. of Dirs, 1953–78; Council, Warwick Univ., 1968–74 (Chm., Careers Adv. Bd). Vice-President: Game Conservancy, 1979– (Chm., 1975–79); British Field Sports Soc., 1978–; Mem. Council and Trustee, WWF UK. County Pres., St John Ambulance, Berks; CStJ 1983. FRSA; FBIM; FIMI; FIPE. *Recreations:* shooting, fishing. *Heir:* s Hon. Nicholas Geoffrey Rootes [*b* 12 July 1951; *m* 1976, Dorothy Anne Burn-Forti, *d* of Cyril Wood]. *Address:* North Standen House, Hungerford, Berks RG17 0QZ. *Clubs:* Buck's, Flyfishers'.

ROOTHAM, Jasper St John, MA; *b* 21 Nov. 1910; *s* of Dr Cyril Bradley and Rosamond Margaret Rootham; *m* 1944, Joan McClelland; one *s* one *d*. *Educ:* Tonbridge Sch. (Judd Schol.); St John's Coll., Cambridge (Maj. Schol.). 1st cl. Class. Tripos Pts I and II. Entered Civil Service, 1933; Min. of Agric., 1933–34; CO, 1934–36; Treasury, 1936–38; Pte Sec. to Prime Minister, 1938–39; Treasury, 1939–40; resigned to join Army, 1940; served Middle East, Balkans, Germany (despatches); demobilized, 1946 (Col); entered Bank of England as Actg Asst Adviser, 1946; Adviser to Governor, 1957; Chief of Overseas Dept, 1962; Asst to Governor, 1964; retd, 1967. Man. Dir, Lazard Bros & Co. Ltd, 1967–75; Dir, Agricultural Mortgage Corp., 1967–77 (Dep. Chm., 1973–77); Director: British Sugar Corp., 1968–80; Stanley Miller Holdings, Newcastle, 1977–84. *Publications:* Miss Fire, 1946; Demi-Paradise, 1960; Verses 1928–72, 1972; The Celestial City and Other Poems, 1975; Reflections from a Crag, 1978; Selected Poems, 1980; Stand Fixed in Steadfast Gaze, 1981; Affirmation, 1982; Lament for a dead Sculptor and other poems, 1985. *Recreations:* music, country life. *Address:* 30 West Street, Wimborne Minster, Dorset BH21 1JS. *T:* Wimborne 888121. *Club:* United Oxford & Cambridge University.

ROOTS, Paul John; Director of Industrial Relations, Ford Motor Co. Ltd, 1981–86, retired; *b* 16 Oct. 1929; *s* of John Earl and Helen Roots; *m* 1951, Anna Theresa Pateman; two *s* two *d*. *Educ:* Dormers Wells Sch.; London Sch. of Economics. Cert. in Personnel Admin. CIPM; CBIM. RN, 1947–54: service in Korean War. Personnel Officer, Brush Gp, 1955; Labour Officer, UKAEA, 1956, Labour Manager, 1959; Ford Motor Co. Ltd: Personnel Manager, Halewood, 1962; Forward Planning Manager, 1966; Labour Relations Manager, 1969; Dir of Employee Relations, 1974. Vice-Pres., IPM, 1981–83. Chairman: CBI Health and Safety Policy Cttee, 1984–; CBI Health and Safety Consultative Cttee, 1984–; Member: Council of Management, CBI Educn Foundn, 1981–; CBI Working Party on the Employment of Disabled People, 1981–; CBI Employment Policy Cttee, 1983–; CBI Council, 1984–; Engrg Industry Training Bd, 1985–. *Publications:* (jtly) Communication in Practice, 1981; (jtly) Personnel Management: planning for performance, 1986; articles in personnel management jls. *Recreations:* riding, theatre, music. *Address:* Hillcot House, Bitterley, Ludlow, Shropshire.

ROPER; *see* Trevor-Roper.

ROPER, Hon. Sir Clinton Marcus, Kt 1985; Judge of the Court of Appeal, Fiji, and of the High Court, Cook Islands, since 1985; Judge of the High Court of New Zealand, 1968–85; *b* Christchurch, 19 June 1921; *s* of Wilfred Marcus Roper; *m* 1947, Joan Elsa Turnbull; one *s* one *d*. *Educ:* Christchurch West High Sch.; Canterbury Univ.; Victoria Univ. of Wellington. LLB. Served War of 1939–45, Pacific, Italy and Japan (Lieut). Crown Solicitor, Christchurch, 1961–68. Chm., Prisons Parole Bd, 1970–85. Tongan Privy Council, 1986–. *Address:* 6 Amherst Place, Christchurch, New Zealand.

ROPER, John Charles Abercromby, CMG 1969; MC; HM Diplomatic Service, retired; *b* 8 June 1915; *s* of late Charles Roper, MD, and of Mrs Roper; *m* 1st, 1945, Valerie Armstrong-MacDonnell (marr. diss.); two *d*; 2nd, 1960, Kathryn (*d* 1984), *d* of late Edgar Bibas, New York; 3rd, 1986, Phoebe, *d* of late R. B. Foster, London and New York. *Educ:* Harrow; Universities of Cambridge and Princeton (Commonwealth Fellow). Served 1939–46, Scots Guards and Special Forces, Major (MC). HM Diplomatic Service, 1946; Athens, 1947–51; Foreign Office, 1951–54; Washington, 1954–59. Seconded to Min. of Defence and apptd Dep. Commandant (Civil) of NATO Defence College, Paris, 1960–62; Asst Sec., Cabinet Office, 1962–64; Counsellor, UK Delegn to OECD, 1964–70; Ambassador to Luxembourg, 1970–75. *Address:* 58048 Paganico, Provincia di Grosseto, Italy; Island of Hydra, Greece. *Club:* Special Forces.

ROPER, John (Francis Hodgess); Research Fellow, since 1984, and Editor, since 1983, International Affairs, Royal Institute of International Affairs; *b* 10 Sept. 1935; *e s* of Rev. Frederick Mabor Hodgess Roper and Ellen Frances (*née* Brockway); *m* 1959, Valerie Hope, *er d* of late Rt Hon. L. John Edwards, PC, OBE, MP, and late Mrs D. M. Edwards; one *d*. *Educ:* William Hulme's Grammar Sch., Manchester; Reading Sch.; Magdalen Coll., Oxford; Univ. of Chicago. Nat. Service, commnd RNVR, 1954–56; studied PPE, Oxford, 1956–59 (Pres. UN Student Assoc., 1957; organised Univ. referendum on Nuclear Disarmament); Harkness Fellow, Commonwealth Fund, 1959–61; Research Fellow in Economic Statistics, Univ. of Manchester, 1961; Asst Lectr in Econs, 1962–64, Lectr 1964–70, Faculty Tutor 1968–70. Contested: (Lab) High Peak (Derbs), 1964; (SDP) Worsley, 1983. MP (Lab and Co-op 1970–81, SDP 1981–83) Farnworth, 1970–83; PPS to Minister of State, DoI, 1978–79; opposition front bench spokesman on defence, 1979–81; Social Democrat Chief Whip, 1981–83. Vice-Chairman: Anglo-German Parly Gp, 1974–83; Anglo-Benelux Parly Gp, 1979–83; Chm., British-Atlantic Gp of Young Politicians, 1974–75. Council of Europe: Consultant, 1965–66; Mem., Consultative Assembly, 1973–80; Chm., Cttee on Culture and Educn, 1979–80; Mem., WEU, 1973–80; Chm., Cttee on Defence Questions and Armaments, WEU, 1977–80. Hon. Treasurer, Fabian Soc., 1976–81; Chm., Labour Cttee for Europe, 1976–80; Vice-Chm., GB East Europe Centre, 1974–. Research Adviser (part-time), DEA in NW, 1967–69. Director: Co-op. Wholesale Soc., 1969–74; Co-op Insurance Soc., 1973–74. Pres., Gen. Council, UNA, 1972–78; Mem. Council, Inst. for Fiscal Studies, 1975–; Mem. Gen. Adv. Council, IBA, 1974–79. Vice-Pres., Manchester Statistical Soc., 1971–. Trustee, Hist. of Parlt Trust, 1974–84. *Publications:* (with Lloyd Harrison) Towards Regional Co-operatives, 1967; The Teaching of Economics at University Level, 1970; The Future of British Defence Policy, 1985; articles and reviews in Co-operative jls and Manchester School. *Recreations:* reading, travel. *Address:* 137 Hampstead Way, NW11 7JN. *T:* 01-458 5106.

ROPER, Robert Burnell, CB 1978; Chief Land Registrar, 1975–83 (Deputy Chief Land Registrar, 1973–75); *b* 23 Nov. 1921; *s* of late Allen George and Winifred Roper; *m* 1948, Mary Brookes; two *s*. *Educ:* King's College Sch., Wimbledon; King's Coll., London. LLB (Hons) 1941. Called to Bar, Gray's Inn, 1948. Served War, RAF, 1942–46. Miners' Welfare Commn, 1946–48; Nat. Coal Bd, 1948–49; Treasury Solicitor's Dept, 1949–50; HM Land Registry, 1950–83. *Publications:* (Ruoff and Roper) The Law and Practice of Registered Conveyancing, 3rd edn 1972, to 5th edn 1987; Consulting Editor on Land Registration matters for Encyclopaedia of Forms and Precedents (4th edn). *Recreations:* gardening, watching sport. *Address:* 11 Dukes Road, Lindfield, Haywards Heath, West Sussex RH16 2JH.

ROPER-CURZON, family name of **Baron Teynham.**

ROPNER, David; *see* Ropner, W. G. D.

ROPNER, Sir John (Bruce Woollacott), 2nd Bt *cr* 1952; Director, Ropner PLC; *b* 16 April 1937; *s* of Sir Leonard Ropner, 1st Bt, MC, TD, and of Esmé, *y d* of late Bruce Robertson; *S* father, 1977; *m* 1st, 1961, Anne Melicent (marr. diss. 1970), *d* of late Sir Ralph Delmé-Radcliffe; two *d*; 2nd, 1970, Auriol, *d* of Captain Graham Lawrie Mackeson-Sandbach, Caerllo, Llangernyw; one *s* two *d*. *Educ:* Eton; St Paul's School, USA. *Heir:* *s* Henry John William Ropner, *b* 24 Oct. 1981. *Address:* Thorp Perrow, Bedale, Yorks.

ROPNER, John Raymond; Consultant, Ropner PLC, and other companies; *b* 8 May 1903; *s* of William Ropner; *m* 1928, Joan Redhead; two *s* one *d*. *Educ:* Harrow; Clare College, Cambridge (BAEcon 1925). Durham Heavy Bde, RA (TA), 1922–28; joined Sir R. Ropner & Co. Ltd, 1925; Ministry of War Transport, North Western Europe, 1944–45. High Sheriff of Durham, 1958. Member, Shipping Advisory Panel, 1962. Order of Oranje-Nassau, 1947. *Recreations:* gardening, fishing; formerly golf (Cambridge blue, 1925). *Address:* The Limes, Dalton, Richmond, N Yorkshire. *T:* Teesdale 21447.

ROPNER, Sir Robert Douglas, 4th Bt, *cr* 1904; *b* 1 Dec. 1921; *o s* of Sir (E. H. O.) Robert Ropner, 3rd Bt; *S* father, 1962; *m* 1943, Patricia Kathleen, *d* of W. E. Scofield, W. Malling, Kent; one *s* one *d*. *Educ:* Harrow. Formerly Captain, RA. *Heir:* *s* Robert Clinton Ropner, *b* 6 Feb. 1949.

ROPNER, (William Guy) David, FICS; Director, Ropner PLC, since 1953 (Chairman, 1973–85); *b* 3 April 1924; *s* of late Sir William Guy Ropner and Lady (Margarita) Ropner; *m* 1st, 1955, Mildred Malise Hare Armitage (marr. diss. 1978); three *s* one *d*; 2nd, 1985, Hon. Mrs Charlotte M. Taddei. *Educ:* Harrow. FICS 1953. Served War, 1942–47: 2nd Lieut RA, Essex Yeomanry; Captain 3rd Regt, RHA. Joined Sir R. Ropner and Co. Ltd, 1947; dir of various Ropner PLC gp cos, 1953–. Member: Baltic Exchange, 1949–; Lloyd's, 1952–; Gen. Cttee, Lloyd's Register of Shipping, 1961–; Pres., Gen. Council of British Shipping, 1979–80; Chairman: Deep Sea Tramp Section, Chamber of Shipping, 1970–72; Lights Adv. Cttee, GCBS, 1978–; Merchant Navy Welfare Bd, 1980–; Cleveland & Durham Industrial Council, 1980–; Dir, British Shipowners Assoc., 1954–. Director: Croft Autodrome Ltd, 1979–; Guidehouse Expansion Management, 1984–. *Recreations:* country and garden pursuits. *Address:* 1 Sunningdale Gardens, Stratford Road, W8 6PX. *T:* 01-937 3862. *Clubs:* Boodle's, City of London; St Moritz Tobogganing.

RORKE, Prof. John, CBE 1979; PhD, FRSE, FIMechE; Professor of Mechanical Engineering, since 1980, and Vice-Principal, since 1984, Heriot-Watt University; *b* 2 Sept. 1923; *s* of John and Janet Rorke; *m* 1948, Jane Craig Buchanan; two *d*. *Educ:* Dumbarton Acad.; Univ. of Strathclyde (BSc, PhD). Lectr, Strathclyde Univ., 1946–51; Asst to Engrg Dir, Alexander Stephen & Sons Ltd, 1951–56; Technical Manager, subseq. Gen. Man., and Engrg Dir, Wm Denny & Bros Ltd, 1956–63; Tech. Dir, subseq. Sales Dir, Man. Dir, and Chm., Brown Bros & Co. Ltd (subsid. of Vickers Ltd), 1963–78; Man. Dir, Vickers Offshore Engrg Gp, 1978; Dir of Planning, Vickers Ltd, 1979–80. Pres., Instn of Engineers and Shipbuilders in Scotland, 1985–. *Recreations:* golf, bridge. *Address:* 3 Barnton Park Grove, Edinburgh EH3 6HG. *T:* 031-336 3044. *Club:* Bruntsfield Links Golfing Society (Edinburgh).

ROSCOE, Air Cdre Peter Henry, CB 1967; FCA; *b* 1912. Dept of Air Member for Personnel, 1963–67; Dir of Personnel (Ground) Min. of Defence (RAF), 1966; retired 1967. *Address:* Fairhaven, Tan-y-Bryn Road, Holyhead, Gwynedd LL65 1AR.

ROSCOE, Sir Robert Bell, KBE 1981; FASA, ABIA, ABINZ; Director, Chase-NBA Group Ltd (Australia and New Zealand), 1969–80; Chairman: Melbourne Underground Rail Loop Authority, 1971–81; First Federation Discount Co. Ltd, 1975–84; *b* 7 August 1906; *s* of T. B. Roscoe; *m* 1931, Daphne, *d* of G. Maxwell; one *d*. *Educ:* Central Tech. Coll., Brisbane. Liquidator, Qld Nat. Bank Ltd, 1949; State Manager, Qld, 1951–54; Nat. Bank of Australasia: State Manager, Victoria, 1954–60; Chief Inspector, 1960–65; Sen. Chief Inspector, 1965–66; Asst Chief Manager, 1966–69. Director: Hoechst Australia Ltd, 1970–; All States Commercial Bills Ltd; Oceania Capital Corp. Ltd. *Address:* 833 Burwood Road, Hawthorn East, Victoria 3123, Australia. *Club:* Australian (Melbourne).

ROSE, Sir Alec (Richard), Kt 1968; *b* 13 July 1908; *s* of Ambrose Rose; *m* 1st, 1931, Barbara Kathleen (*née* Baldwin); two *s* two *d*; 2nd, 1960, Dorothy Mabel (*née* Walker). *Educ:* Simon Langton Boys School, Canterbury. Farming in Canada, 1928–30; Haulage Contractor, 1930–39; served RNVR, 1939–45; Market Gardener, 1945–57; Fruit Merchant, 1957–71. Member: Fruiterers Co.; Worshipful Co. of Basketmakers; Worshipful Co. of Shipwrights. Hon. Life Governor, RNLI, 1975–. Freedom of Portsmouth, 1968. Blue Water Medal, Cruising Club of America, 1969; Seamanship Medal, Royal Cruising Club. *Publication:* My Lively Lady, 1968. *Recreation:* sailing (inc. circumnavigation of world, 1968). *Address:* Woodlands Cottage, Eastleigh Road, Havant, Hants. *T:* Havant 477124. *Clubs:* City Livery; Portsmouth County, Royal Naval and Royal Albert Yacht (Portsmouth); Royal Yacht Squadron, Royal Naval Sailing Assoc., Eastney Cruising Assoc., Ocean Cruising (Admiral).

ROSE, Andrew; *see* Rose, W. A.

ROSE, (Arthur) James; HM Chief Inspector for Primary Education, Department of Education and Science, since 1986; *m* 1960, Pauline; one *d*. *Educ:* Kesteven College; Leicester University. Formerly Headteacher of Shaftesbury Junior School and Shenton Primary School, Leicester. *Address:* Department of Education and Science, Elizabeth House, York Road, SE1 7PH. *T:* 01-934 9000.

ROSE, Captain Arthur Martin Thomas, MC 1944; solicitor; a Recorder of the Crown Court, since 1979; *b* 22 Nov. 1918; *s* of Stanley Arthur Rose and Hilda Mary Martin Rose (*née* Hayward); *m* 1952, Patricia Cameron (*d* 1978); two *s*. *Educ:* Perse Sch.; Uppingham; Trinity Hall, Cambridge (MA, LLM). Served War: commnd Royal Artillery, 1941–46 (MC, twice wounded). Partner in firm of Few & Kester, solicitors, 1949–82, Senior Partner, 1981–82. *Recreations:* sport, freemasonry. *Address:* 10 Marlborough Court, Grange Road, Cambridge CB3 9BQ. *T:* Cambridge 312726. *Clubs:* Camden Cricket; Gog Magog Golf.

ROSE, Barry, MBE 1981; editor and publisher; Chairman, own group of companies, since 1970; *b* 17 July 1923; *s* of late William George Rose and Beatrice Mary (*née* Castle); *m* 1963, Dorothy Jean Colthrup, *d* of Lt-Col W.R. Bowden; one *d*. Editor: Justice of the Peace and Local Government Review, 1944–72; Justice of the Peace, 1972–74; Local Government Review, 1972–76; law and local govt oriented periodicals. Member: Chichester RDC, 1951–61; West Sussex CC, 1952–73 (Leader, Cons. Group, 1967–72; Alderman, 1972); Pagham Parish Council, 1952–62; Bognor Regis UDC, 1964–68; Hon. Editor, Rural District Review, 1959–63; Mem., RDCA, 1960–63, CCA 1968–72; Chm., SE Area Cons. Local Govt Adv. Cttee, 1969–73; Pres., Assoc. of Councillors, 1975– (Treasurer, 1960–69; Chm., Exec. Cttee, 1969–75); posts in Cons. Party, 1945–74, incl. Constituency Chm., Chichester, 1961–69; Pres., Chichester Div., Young Conservatives,

1959–69. Liveryman, Stationers' Co., 1974. FRSA 1960. Hon. Life Mem., Justices' Clerks' Soc., 1985. *Publications:* Change of Fortune (play), 1950; Funny Business (play), 1951; England Looks at Maud, 1970; A Councillor's Work, 1971. *Recreations:* entertaining and being entertained. *Address:* Courtney Lodge, Sylvan Way, Bognor Regis, West Sussex. *T:* Bognor Regis 829902. *Clubs:* Garrick, MCC, Press, United Oxford & Cambridge University; West Sussex County (Chichester).

ROSE, Barry Michael, FRSCM; Master of the Choirs, King's School, Canterbury, since 1985; *b* 24 May 1934; *s* of Stanley George Rose and Gladys Mildred Rose; *m* 1965, Elizabeth Mary Ware; one *s* two *d*. *Educ:* Sir George Monoux Grammar Sch., Walthamstow; Royal Acad. of Music (ARAM). FRSCM 1973. First Organist and Master of the Choristers, new Guildford Cathedral, 1960–74; Sub-Organist, St Paul's Cath., 1974–77; Master of the Choir, 1977–84. Music Adviser to Head of Religious Broadcasting, BBC, 1970–. *Recreation:* running a record company (Guild Records, founded 1967). *Address:* Mill Cottage, Milner Lane, Sturry, Canterbury, Kent CT2 0AE.

ROSE, Bernard William George, OBE 1980; MusB Cantab 1938, MA Oxon, Cantab 1944, DMus Oxon 1955, FRCO; Fellow, Organist, Informator Choristarum, Magdalen College, Oxford, 1957–81, Vice-President, 1973 and 1974, Emeritus Fellow since 1981; University Lecturer in Music, 1950–81; Choragus in the University, 1958–63; *b* Little Hallingbury, Herts, 9 May 1916; *s* of William and Jessie Rose; *m* 1939, Molly Daphne, JP, DL, 5th *d* of D. G. Marshall, MBE, Cambridge; three *s*. *Educ:* Salisbury Cathedral Sch.; Royal Coll. of Music; St Catharine's Coll., Cambridge. Organ Scholar, St Catharine's, Cambridge, 1935–39; Stewart of Rannoch Scholar in Sacred Music, Cambridge, 1935–39; Organist, and Conductor of the Eaglesfield Musical Soc., The Queen's Coll., Oxford, 1939–57, Fellow, 1949. Served with 4th Co. of London Yeomanry (Sharpshooters), 1941–44, Adjutant 1942 (PoW 1943–44). Conductor, Oxford Orchestral Soc., 1971–74. Mem. Council, Royal Coll. of Organists (Pres. 1974–76). *Publications:* contrib. Proc. Roy. Mus. Assoc., 1955; various church music compositions and edns of church music; edns of Anthems of Thomas Tomkins; (ed) Early English Church Music, Vols 5, 9, 14 and 27; Hallische Händel Ausgabe, 'Susanna'; reviews in Music and Letters, articles in Musical Times. *Recreation:* DIY. *Address:* Bampton House, Bampton, Oxford OX8 2LX. *T:* Bampton Castle 850135.

ROSE, Brian; HM Diplomatic Service; Commercial and Economic Counsellor, Helsinki, since 1985; *b* 26 Jan. 1930; *s* of Edwin and Emily Rose; *m* 1952, Audrey Barnes; one *d*. *Educ:* Canford Sch., Dorset. MIL 1983. Intelligence Corps, 1948–50. Min. of Food, 1950–54; CRO, 1954; Peshawar, 1955–56; Ottawa, 1958–61; Kingston, Jamaica, 1962–65; Rome, 1966; Zagreb, 1966–68; Zomba, Malawi, 1968–71; FCO, 1971–74; Düsseldorf, 1974–77; E Berlin, 1977–78; Zürich, 1978–82; Consul-Gen., Stuttgart, 1982–85. *Recreations:* tennis, squash. *Address:* c/o Foreign and Commonwealth Office, SW1A 2AH. *Club:* Travellers'.

ROSE, Major Charles Frederick, MBE 1968; CEng, MICE, MCIT; Chief Inspecting Officer of Railways, Department of Transport, since 1982; *b* 9 July 1926; *s* of Charles James Rose and Ida Marguerite Chollet; *m* 1956, Huguette Primerose Lecoultre; one *s* one *d*. *Educ:* Xaverian Coll., Brighton; Royal School of Military Engineering, 1951–52 and 1957–59. Student engineer, Southern Railway Co., 1942–46; commnd RE, 1947; service with mil. railways, Palestine and Egypt, 1947–51; with a Field Sqdn in Germany, 1952–53; Engr SO, Korea, 1953–54; Instructor: Mons Officer Cadet Sch., 1954–57; Transportation Centre, Longmoor, 1959–62; OC a Field Sqdn, Germany, 1962–64; Instr, Royal Sch. of Mil. Engrg, 1964–66; Engr, RE road construction project, Thailand, 1966–68; Inspecting Officer of Railways, MoT, 1968–82. *Recreations:* cycling, walking, music, reading. *Address:* Hollybank, Shadyhanger, Godalming, Surrey GU7 2HR. *T:* Godalming 6429.

ROSE, Christine Brooke; *see* Brooke-Rose.

ROSE, Hon. Sir Christopher (Dudley Roger), Kt 1985; **Hon. Mr Justice Rose;** a Judge of the High Court, Queen's Bench Division, since 1985; Presiding Judge, Northern Circuit, since 1987; *b* 10 Feb. 1937; *s* of Roger Rose and late Hilda Rose, Morecambe; *m* 1964, Judith, *d* of late George and Charlotte Brand, Didsbury; one *s* one *d*. *Educ:* Morecambe Grammar Sch.; Repton; Leeds Univ.; Wadham Coll., Oxford. LLB and Hughes Prize, Leeds, 1957; 1st cl. hons BCL 1959, Eldon Scholar 1959, Oxon. Lectr in Law, Wadham Coll., Oxford, 1959–60; called to Bar, Middle Temple, 1960 (Bencher, 1983); Bigelow Teaching Fellow, Law Sch., Univ. of Chicago, 1960–61; Harmsworth Scholar, 1961; joined Northern Circuit, 1961; QC 1974; a Recorder, 1978–85. Mem., Senate of Inns of Court and Bar, 1983–. *Recreations:* playing the piano, listening to music, golf, travel. *Address:* Royal Courts of Justice, Strand, WC2A 2LL. *Clubs:* Big Four (Manchester); Wilmslow Golf.

ROSE, Clifford; *see* Rose, F.C.

ROSE, Sir Clive (Martin), GCMG 1981 (KCMG 1976; CMG 1967); HM Diplomatic Service, retired; Director: Control Risks (GS) Ltd, since 1985; Control Risks Information Services Ltd, since 1986; *b* 15 Sept. 1921; *s* of late Rt Rev. Alfred Carey Wollaston Rose; *m* 1946, Elisabeth Mackenzie, *d* of late Rev. Cyril Lewis, Gilston; two *s* three *d*. *Educ:* Marlborough College; Christ Church, Oxford. Rifle Bde, 1941–46 (Maj.; despatches): served in Europe, 1944–45; India, 1945; Iraq, 1945–46. Commonwealth Relations Office, 1948; Office of Deputy High Comr, Madras, 1948–49; Foreign Office, 1950–53; UK High Commn, Germany, 1953–54; British Embassy, Bonn, 1955; FO, 1956–59; 1st Sec. and HM Consul, Montevideo, 1959–62; FO, 1962–65; Commercial Counsellor, Paris, 1965–67; Imp. Defence Coll., 1968; Counsellor, British Embassy, Washington, 1969–71; Asst Under-Sec. of State, FCO, 1971–73; Head, British Delegn to Negotiations on Mutual Reduction of Forces and Armaments and Associated Measures in Central Europe, 1973–76; Dep. Secretary, Cabinet Office, 1976–79; UK Permanent Rep. on North Atlantic Council, 1979–82. Member: Adv. Council, Control Risks Ltd, 1983–86; RCDS Adv. Bd, 1985–; Chairman: Council, RUSI, 1983–86; Internat. Commn on Violence in the Basque Country, 1985–86. Chm., Suffolk Preservation Soc., 1985–. FRSA 1982. *Publications:* Campaigns Against Western Defence: NATO's adversaries and critics, 1985, 2nd edn 1986; various articles on NATO and arms control. *Recreation:* gardening. *Address:* Chimney House, Lavenham, Suffolk CO10 9QT. *Club:* Army and Navy.

ROSE, David Edward; Senior Commissioning Editor (Fiction), Channel Four Television, since 1981; *b* 22 Nov. 1924; *s* of Alvan Edward Rose and Gladys Frances Rose; *m* 1st, 1952, Valerie Edwards (*d* 1966); three *s* three *d*; 2nd, 1966, Sarah Reid; one *d*, and one step *s* one step *d* adopted. *Educ:* Kingswood Sch., Bath; Guildhall Sch. of Music and Drama. Repertory Theatre, 1952; Ballets Jooss, and Sadler's Wells Theatre Ballet, 1954; BBC Television, 1954–81 (in production and direction; Head of Television Training, 1969; Head of Regional Television Drama, 1971–81). Mem., BAFTA. Prix Italia TV Award (for film Medico), 1959; BAFTA Producer and Director's Award, (for Z Cars (prod original series)), 1963; BFI Award (for Film on Four and work of new writers and directors), 1985. *Address:* 1 Ufton Grove, N1 4HG. *T:* 01–249 4410.

ROSE, Donald Henry Gair, LVO 1982; HM Diplomatic Service, retired; Consul-General, Jedda, 1983–86; *b* 24 Sept. 1926; *m* 1950, Sheila Munro; three *s*. HM Forces, 1944–48; Scottish Office, 1948–66; Commonwealth Office, 1966; Nairobi, 1967; Tripoli, 1971; First Sec., Cairo, 1974–77; FCO, 1977–79; High Comr, Kiribati, 1979–83.

ROSE, Eliot Joseph Benn, (Jim Rose), CBE 1979; Chairman, Penguin Books, 1973–80; Director, Pearson Longman, 1974–81; *b* 7 June 1909; *s* of late Colonel E. A. Rose, CBE, and Dula, *e d* of Eliot Lewis, JP; *m* 1946, Susan Pamela Gibson; one *s* one *d*. *Educ:* Rugby; New College, Oxford. Served War of 1939–45, RAF, Wing-Comdr. Literary Editor, The Observer, 1948–51; Director: International Press Institute, Zürich, 1951–62; Survey of Race Relations in Britain, 1963–69; Editorial Dir, Westminster Press Ltd, 1970–74. Chm., Inter-Action Trust, 1968–84; Co-founder and Chm., Runnymede Trust; Mem., Cttee of Inquiry into educn of children from ethnic minority groups, 1979–81; Special Consultant to Unicef, 1981. Sidney Ball Meml Lectr, Oxford, 1970. Legion of Merit (US). *Publication:* Colour and Citizenship, 1969. *Address:* 37 Pembroke Square, W8. *T:* 01–937 3772. *Club:* Garrick.

ROSE, Francis Leslie, CBE 1978 (OBE 1949); PhD, DSc; FRS 1957; FRSC; Consultant, Imperial Chemical Industries Ltd, since 1974; *b* 27 June 1909; *s* of late Frederick William and Elizabeth Ann Rose, Lincoln; *m* 1935, Ailsa Buckley; one *s*. *Educ:* City Sch., Lincoln; Univ. Coll. of Nottingham. BSc (Hons Chemistry) London, 1930; PhD London 1934; DSc Nottingham 1950. Research Chemist, ICI Ltd, 1932; Res. Manager, Pharmaceutical Div., ICI, 1954–71, Res. Fellow, 1971–74. Hon. Reader in Organic Chem., UMIST, 1959–72, Hon Fellow, 1972. Mem., later Consultant, Home Office Forensic Science Cttee, 1965–78. Former Mem., Court of Governors, Manchester University and Court of Governors, Univ. of Manchester Inst. of Science and Technology. Hon. Fellow, Manchester Polytechnic. Hon. DSc Loughborough, 1982. Gold Medal, Soc. of Apothecaries, 1948; Tilden Lecture and Medal, Chem. Soc., 1951; Medal, Soc. of Chem. Industry, 1975; Leverhulme Medal, Royal Soc., 1975. *Publications:* numerous scientific papers on chemotherapeutic themes, mainly in Jl of Chem. Soc., Brit. Jl of Pharmacol., Biochem. Jl, etc. *Recreations:* music, in particular the organ; sailing. *Address:* 27 Green Hall Mews, Parkway, Wilmslow, Cheshire SK9 1LP. *T:* Wilmslow 530499; ICI Ltd, Alderley Park, Macclesfield, Cheshire. *Club:* Athenæum.

ROSE, Dr Frank Clifford, FRCP; Physician in Charge, Department of Neurology, Charing Cross Hospital, since 1965; Director, Academic Unit of Neuroscience, Charing Cross and Westminster Medical School, since 1985; Principal Medical Officer, Allied Dunbar Assurance Co. (formerly Hambro Life Assurance Co.), since 1970; *b* 29 Aug. 1926; *s* of James and Clare Rose; *m* 1963, Angela Juliet Halsted; three *s*. *Educ:* King's Coll., London; Westminster Hosp. Med. Sch.; Univ. of California, San Francisco; Hôpital de la Salpêtrière, Paris. MB BS London; DCH; MRCS; FRCP 1971 (LRCP 1949, MRCP 1954). Medical Registrar, Westminster Hosp., 1955; Resident MO, National Hosp., Queen Square, 1957; Sen. Registrar, Dept of Neurology, St George's Hosp., 1960; Consultant Neurologist: Medical Ophthalmology Unit, St Thomas' Hosp., 1963–85; Moor House Sch. for Speech Disorders, 1965–70. Chm., European Stroke Prevention Study, 1981–; President: Med. Soc. London, 1983–84 (Treas., 1984–); Assurance Med. Soc., 1983–85. Medical Patron, Motor Neurone Disease Assoc.; Trustee, Migraine Trust. Examr in Clinical Pharmacology and Therapeutics, Univ. of London. Lettsomian Lectr, Med. Soc. London, 1979; Guest Lectr, Scandinavian Migraine Soc., 1983. Harold Wolff Award, 1981 and 1984, and Distinguished Clinician Award, 1986, Amer. Assoc. for the Study of Headache. *Publications:* Hypoglycaemia, 1965, 2nd edn, 1981; Basic Neurology of Speech, 1970, 3rd edn 1983; Physiological Aspects of Clinical Neurology, 1976; Medical Ophthalmology, 1976; Motor Neurone Disease, 1977; Clinical Neuroimmunology, 1978; Paediatric Neurology, 1979; Optic Neuritis and its Differential Diagnosis, 1979; Progress in Stroke Research 1, 1979; Progress in Neurological Research, 1979; Migraine: the facts, 1979; Clinical Neuroepidemiology, 1980; Animal Models of Neurological Disorders, 1980; Research Progress in Parkinson's Disease, 1981; Metabolic Disorders of the Nervous System, 1981; Progress in Migraine Research 1, 1981; Stroke: The Facts, 1981; Historical Aspects of the Neurosciences, 1982; Cerebral Hypoxia in the Pathogenesis of Migraine, 1982; Advances in Stroke Therapy, 1982; Advances in Migraine Research and Therapy, 1982; Research Progress in Epilepsy, 1982; Immunology of Nervous System Infections, 1983; The Eye in General Disease, 1983; Progress in Stroke Research 2, 1983; Research Progress in Motor Neurone Disease, 1984; Progress in Migraine Research 2, 1984; Progress in Aphasiology, 1985; Modern Approaches to the Dementias (2 vols), 1985; Neuro-oncology, 1985; Migraine: clinical and research advances, 1985; Handbook of Clinical Neurology: headache, 1986; papers in neurological and gen. med. jls. *Recreations:* travel, reading. *Address:* Department of Neurology, Charing Cross Hospital, Fulham Palace Road, W6 8RF. *T:* 01–741 7833. *Clubs:* Savile, Royal Society of Medicine.

ROSE, Gerald Gershon, PhD; CChem, FRSC; Director, Thornton Research Centre, Shell Research Ltd, 1975–80; *b* 4 May 1921; *m* 1945, Olive Sylvia; one *s* two *d*. *Educ:* Hendon County Grammar Sch.; Imperial Coll. of Science and Technology (BSc, ARCS, DIC, PhD). Joined Shell Group, 1944; served in refineries, Stanlow, Trinidad, Singapore and South Africa; General Manager, Shell/BP South Africa Petroleum Refineries, 1963; Manufacturing and Supply Director, Shell/BP Service Co., 1968; Manager, Teesport Refinery, 1971. *Recreations:* golf, tennis, gardening. *Address:* The Tithe Barn, Great Barrow, Chester, Cheshire CH3 7HW. *T:* Tarvin 40623.

ROSE, Prof. Harold Bertram; Group Economic Adviser, Barclays Bank, since 1975; Professor of Finance, London Graduate School of Business Studies, since 1965 (Esmée Fairbairn Chair until 1975, then part-time); *b* 9 Aug. 1923; *s* of late Isaac Rose and Rose Rose (*née* Barnett); *m* 1st, 1949, Valerie Frances Anne Chubb (marr. diss. 1974); three *s* one *d*; 2nd, 1974, Diana Mary Campbell Scarlett; one *s* one *d*. *Educ:* Davenant Foundn Sch.; LSE (BCom). Served with RA in Britain, India and Burma, 1942–45 (Captain). Head of Econ. Intell. Dept, Prudential Assce Co., Ltd, 1948–58; Sen. Lectr, then Reader, in Business Finance, LSE, 1958–65; Member: Council, Consumers' Assoc., 1958–63; Central Adv. Council on Primary Educn (Plowden Cttee), 1963–65; Business Studies Cttee, SSRC, 1967–68, and Univ. Grants Cttee, 1968–69; Reserve Pension Bd, 1973–75; HM Treasury Inquiry into Value of Pensions, 1980; Special Adviser to: H of C Treasury and Civil Service Cttee, 1980–81; DoI, 1980–81. Dir, Abbey National Building Soc., 1975–83. Mem., Retail Prices Adv. Cttee, 1985–86. *Publications:* The Economic Background to Investment, 1959; Disclosure in Company Accounts, 1963; Management Education in the 1970's, 1970; various papers in econ. and financial jls. *Address:* 33 Dartmouth Park Avenue, NW5. *T:* 01–485 7315.

ROSE, Jack, CMG 1963; MBE 1954; DFC 1942; *b* 18 Jan. 1917; *s* of late Charles Thomas Rose; *m* 1st, 1940, Margaret Valerie (*d* 1966), 2nd *d* of late Alec Stuart Budd; two *s*; 2nd, 1967, Beryl Elizabeth, 4th *d* of late A. S. Budd. *Educ:* Shooters Hill School; London University. Served RAF, 1938–46 (Wing Commander); served in fighter, fighter/bomber and rocket firing sqdns; France, 1940 and 1944; Battle of Britain; Burma, 1944–45. Joined Colonial Administrative Service, N Rhodesia, 1947; Private Secretary to Governor of Northern Rhodesia, 1950–53; seconded to Colonial Office, 1954–56; Administrative posts, Northern Rhodesia, 1956–60; Administrator, Cayman Islands (seconded), 1960–63; Assistant to Governor, British Guiana, 1963–64 (Actg Governor and Dep. Governor for periods). Member: Professional and Technical 'A' Whitley Council for Health Services, 1965–75 (Chm., 1973–75); Gen. Whitley Council for Health Services, 1973–75. Secretary: Chartered Soc. of Physiotherapy, 1965–75; Salmon and Trout Assoc., 1975–79 (Vice-Pres., 1980–). *Recreations:* gardening, walking. *Address:* The Little House, The Hill, Burford, Oxon OX8 4QZ. *T:* Burford 2553.

ROSE, James; *see* Rose, A. J.

ROSE, Jeffrey David; Chairman of the Royal Automobile Club, since 1981 (Deputy Chairman, 1979–81); *b* 2 July 1931; *s* of late Samuel and Daisy Rose; *m* 1958, Joyce (*née* Clompus); one *s* two *d*. *Educ:* Southend High Sch.; London Sch. of Econs and Pol. Science. Chm., RAC Motoring Services, 1980–; Dir, Young & Co.'s Brewery PLC, 1976–. Vice Chm., British Road Fedn, 1982–; Vice Pres., Fédn Internationale de l'Automobile, 1983–85 (Mem. Cttee, 1980–); Mem., Management Cttee, Alliance Internationale de Tourisme, 1982–. Liveryman, Worshipful Co. of Coachmakers and Coach Harness Makers, 1981. *Recreations:* skiing, walking, dining, music. *Address:* 5 Wadham Gardens, NW3. *Clubs:* Royal Automobile, MCC.

ROSE, Jim; *see* Rose, E. J. B.

ROSE, Sir Julian (Day), 4th Bt *cr* 1909, of Hardwick House, and 5th Bt *cr* 1872, of Montreal; *b* 3 March 1947; 3rd and *o* surv. *s* of Sir Charles Henry Rose, 3rd Bt and of Phoebe, *d* of 2nd Baron Phillimore (*d* 1947); *S* father, 1966, and cousin, Sir Francis Cyril Rose, 4th Bt, 1979; *m* 1976, Elizabeth Goode Johnson, Columbus, Ohio, USA; one *d*. *Educ:* Stanbridge School. Actor/asst dir, Players' Theatre of New England, 1973–79; Co-founder, Inst. for Creative Develt, Antwerp, 1978–83. Co-ordinator, Organic Farming practice, Hardwick Estate, 1984–. Member: Council, Soil Assoc., 1984–; Agricl Panel, Intermediate Technology Develt Gp, 1984–. *Address:* Hardwick House, Whitchurch-on-Thames, Oxfordshire RG8 7RB.

ROSE, Kenneth Vivian, FRSL; writer; *b* 15 Nov. 1924; *s* of Dr J. Rose, MB, ChB. *Educ:* Repton Sch.; New Coll., Oxford (scholar; MA). Served Welsh Guards, 1943–46; attached Phantom, 1945. Asst master, Eton Coll., 1948; Editorial Staff, Daily Telegraph, 1952–60; founder and writer of Albany column, Sunday Telegraph, 1961–. *Publications:* Superior Person: a portrait of Curzon and his circle in late Victorian England, 1969; The Later Cecils, 1975; William Harvey: a monograph, 1978; King George V, 1983 (Wolfson Award for History, 1983; Whitbread Award for Biography, 1983; Yorkshire Post Biography of the Year Award, 1984); Kings, Queens and Courtiers: intimate portraits of the Royal House of Windsor, 1985; contribs to Dictionary of National Biography. *Address:* 38 Brunswick Gardens, W8 4AL. *T:* 01–221 4783. *Clubs:* Beefsteak, Pratt's.

ROSE, Paul (Bernard); Barrister-at-Law; *b* 26 Dec. 1935; *s* of Arthur and Norah Rose; *m* 1957, Eve Marie-Thérèse; two *s* one *d*. *Educ:* Bury Gram. Sch.; Manchester Univ.; Gray's Inn. LLB (Hons) Manch., 1956; Barrister-at-Law, 1957. Legal and Secretarial Dept, Co-op. Union Ltd, 1957–60; Lectureship, Dept of Liberal Studies, Royal Coll. of Advanced Technology, Salford, 1961–63; Barrister-at-Law, practising on SE circuit; Asst Recorder (formerly Dep. Circuit Judge). MP (Lab) Manchester, Blackley, 1964–79; PPS to Minister of Transport, 1967–68; Opposition Front Bench Spokesman, Dept of Employment, 1970–72. Chairman: Parly Labour Home Office Group, 1968–70; Parly Labour Employment Group, 1974–79; Campaign for Democracy in Ulster, 1965–73. Delegate to Council of Europe and WEU, 1968–69; Vice-Chm., Labour Cttee for Europe, 1977–79. Mem., Commn on Electoral Reform, 1975–. Founder Mem., SDP (Brent Area Sec., 1981–82). Chm., NW Regional Sports Council, 1966–68. AIL. *Publications:* Handbook to Industrial and Provident Societies Act, 1960; Guide to Weights and Measures Act 1963, 1965; The Manchester Martyrs, 1970; Backbencher's Dilemma, 1981; The Moonies' Unmasked, 1981; (jt) A History of the Fenian Movement in Britain, 1982; contrib. to many periodicals on political and legal topics. *Recreations:* sport, theatre, languages, travel. *Address:* 10 King's Bench Walk, Temple, EC4Y 7EB.

ROSE, Prof. Richard; Director and Professor of Public Policy, Centre for the Study of Public Policy, Strathclyde University, since 1976; *b* 9 April 1933; *o s* of Charles Imse and late Mary Conely Rose, St Louis, Mo, USA; *m* 1956, Rosemary J., *o d* of late James Kenny, Whitstable, Kent; two *s* one *d*. *Educ:* Clayton High Sch., Mo; Johns Hopkins Univ., BA (Double distinction, Phi Beta Kappa) comparative drama, 1953; London Sch. of Economics, 1953–54; Oxford University, 1957–60, DPhil (Lincoln and Nuffield Colls). Political public relations, Mississippi Valley, 1954–55; Reporter, St Louis Post-Dispatch, 1955–57; Lecturer in Govt, Univ. of Manchester, 1961–66; Prof. of Politics, Strathclyde Univ., 1966–82. Consultant Psephologist, The Times, Independent Television, Daily Telegraph, STV, UTV, 1964–. American SSRC Fellow, Stanford Univ., 1967; Vis. Lectr in Political Sociology, Cambridge Univ., 1967; Dir, ISSC European Summer Sch., 1973. Sec., Cttee on Political Sociology, Internat. Sociological Assoc., 1970–85; Founding Mem., European Consortium for Political Res., 1970; Member: US/UK Fulbright Commn, 1971–75; Eisenhower Fellowship Programme, 1971. Guggenheim Foundn Fellow, 1974; Visiting Scholar: Woodrow Wilson Internat. Centre, Washington DC, 1974; Brookings Inst., Washington DC, 1976; Fiscal Affairs Dept, IMF, Washington, 1984; Vis. Prof., European Univ. Inst., Florence, 1977, 1978; Vis. Schol., Amer. Enterprise Inst., Washington, 1980; Visitor, Japan Foundn, 1984. Consultant Chm., NI Constitutional Convention, 1976; Home Office Working Party on Electoral Register, 1975–77. BBC Radio 3: Man of Action, 1974. Co-Founder, British Politics Gp, 1974–; Convenor, Work Gp on UK Politics, Political Studies Assoc., 1976–; Mem. Council, Internat. Political Science Assoc., 1976–82; Keynote Speaker, Aust. Inst. of Political Science, Canberra, 1978; Technical Consultant, OECD; Dir, ESRC (formerly SSRC) Res. Programme, Growth of Govt, 1982–86. Editor, Jl of Public Policy, 1985– (Chm., 1981–85). Foreign Mem., Finnish Acad. of Science and Letters, 1985. *Publications:* The British General Election of 1959 (with D. E. Butler), 1960; Must Labour Lose? (with Mark Abrams), 1960; Politics in England, 1964, 4th edn 1985; (ed) Studies in British Politics, 1966, 3rd edn 1976; Influencing Voters, 1967; (ed) Policy Making in Britain, 1969; People in Politics, 1970; (ed, with M. Dogan) European Politics, 1971; Governing Without Consensus: an Irish perspective, 1971; (with T. Mackie) International Almanack of Electoral History, 1974, 2nd edn, 1982; (ed) Electoral Behaviour: a comparative handbook, 1974; (ed) Lessons from America, 1974; The Problem of Party Government, 1974; (ed) The Management of Urban Change in Britain and Germany, 1974; Northern Ireland: a time of choice, 1976; Managing Presidential Objectives, 1976; (ed) The Dynamics of Public Policy, 1976; (ed, with D. Kavanagh) New Trends in British Politics, 1977; (ed with J. Wiatr) Comparing Public Policies, 1977; What is Governing?: Purpose and Policy in Washington, 1978; (ed, with G. Hermet and A. Rouquié) Elections without Choice, 1978; (with B. G. Peters) Can Government Go Bankrupt?, 1978; (ed with W. B. Gwyn) Britain: progress and decline, 1980; Do Parties Make a Difference?, 1980, 2nd edn 1984; (ed) Challenge to Governance, 1980; (ed) Electoral Participation, 1980; (ed with E. Suleiman) Presidents and Prime Ministers, 1980; Understanding the United Kingdom, 1982; (with I. McAllister) United Kingdom Facts, 1982; (ed with P. Madgwick) The Territorial Dimension in United Kingdom Politics, 1982; (ed with E. Page) Fiscal Stress in Cities, 1982; Understanding Big Government, 1984; (with I. McAllister) The Nationwide Competition for Votes, 1984; Public Employment in Western Nations, 1985; (with I. McAllister) Voters Begin to Choose, 1986; (with D. Van Mechelen) Patterns of Parliamentary Legislation, 1986; (ed with R. Shiratori) The Welfare State East and West, 1986; Ministers and Ministries, 1987; contribs to academic journals in Europe and America; trans. into many foreign languages; broadcasts on British, Irish and American politics and public policy. *Recreations:* architecture (historical, Britain; modern, America), music, writing. *Address:* Centre for the Study of Public Policy, Livingstone Tower, Glasgow G1 1XH. *T:* 041–552 4400; Bennochy, 1 East Abercromby Street, Helensburgh, Dunbartonshire G84 7SP. *T:* Helensburgh 2164. *Clubs:* Reform; Cosmos (Washington DC).

ROSE, (Thomas) Stuart, CBE 1974; FSIAD; Design Adviser, The Post Office, 1968–76; *b* 2 Oct. 1911; *s* of Thomas and Nellie Rose; *m* 1940, Dorothea Winifred, *d* of F. G. Ebsworth, Petrograd; two *d*. *Educ:* Choral Scholar, Magdalen College Sch., Oxford; Central Sch. of Arts and Crafts. Designer, Crawfords Advertising, 1934–39; free-lance graphics designer and typographer, 1946–68; Typographer, Cement and Concrete Assoc., 1946–51; Print Consultant, Fedn of British Industries, 1947–68; Art Editor, Design Magazine, 1947–53; Typographic Adviser to Postmaster General, 1962–68; Associate, Design Research Unit, industrial design partnership, 1964–68. Member: Industrial Design Cttee, FBI, 1948–65 (Chm. 1965–68); CoID Stamp Adv. Cttee, 1960–62; Post Office Stamp Adv. Cttee, 1968–76. Mem., Soc. of Industrial Artists and Designers, 1936, Pres. 1965. Governor, Central Sch. of Art and Design, 1965–74 (Vice-Chm., 1971–74). FRSA 1970. Phillips Gold Medal for Stamp Design, 1974. *Publication:* Royal Mail Stamps, 1980. *Recreations:* drawing, music, the country. *Address:* 25 Balcombe Street, NW1 6HE. *T:* 01–262 8242; Walpole House, Coggeshall, Essex CO6 1SH. *T:* Coggeshall 62409. *Club:* Arts (Chairman 1982–85).

ROSE, (Wilfred) Andrew; agriculturist, diplomat, industrialist, banker; Hon. chartered surveyor (Estate Management); Chairman and Managing Director, Photo-Scan International of South America Ltd; Chairman: Trinidad and Tobago Oil Co. Ltd; Eagle Enterprises, Trinidad; President and Chairman, Trinidad Co-operative Bank Ltd; Deputy Chairman, National Energy Corporation of Trinidad and Tobago; Director: Interstate Investment (Management) Ltd; Guyana and Trinidad Mutual Fire Insurance Co. Ltd; *b* 4 Oct. 1916; *s* of James Emmanuel Rose and Eleanora Rose; *m* 1944, Pamphylia Marcano; one *s*. *Educ:* Tranquility Boys' Intermediate Sch.; Queen's Royal Coll.; Imperial Coll. of Tropical Agriculture, Trinidad (DipAgr); Coll. of Estate Management, London; London University. FRICS. Agric. Technologist, Food Control Dept, during War of 1939–45. Subseq. Cane Farmers' Superintendent; Estate Manager; Housing Manager, Planning and Housing Commission, Trinidad and Tobago. Editor, Jl of Agricl Soc. of Trinidad and Tobago. Dir, Assoc. of Professional Agrologists of Trinidad and Tobago; Pres., Professional Valuation and Land Economy Surveyors of Trinidad and Tobago; Member: Roy. Soc. of Health; Agricl Soc. of Trinidad and Tobago (Life); W India Cttee (Life); West Indies National Party; People's National Movement (several cttees). Chm., Commn of Enquiry on Road Passenger Transport. Elected Member for St Ann's, Trinidad, Federal Elections of the West Indies, 1958. Minister of Communications and Works, Federal Govt, West Indies, 1958–62 (twice acted as Dep. Prime Minister); High Commissioner for Trinidad and Tobago: in Canada, 1962–64; in UK, 1964–69, Ambassador to EEC, 1965–69, and Ambassador to UN Agencies, Europe, and Permanent Representative to GATT, 1965–68; Ambassador to Brazil, 1969–72; led West Indies delegn to various confs; Rep. of Govt, frequently abroad. Chm., Commonwealth Rhodesia Sanctions Cttee, 1968–69; Vice-Chm., UNCTAD II, New Delhi, 1968; Member: Commonwealth Telecommunications Bd, 1964–68; Commonwealth Telecommunications Council, 1968. Chm., Nat. Museum Task Force. Freeman, City of London, 1967. *Publications:* articles on agriculture in the Trinidad Press, 1942–45. *Recreations:* agriculture, horse-riding, golf. *Address:* PO Box 1041, Port of Spain, Trinidad, WI. *Clubs:* Royal Commonwealth Society; Union (Trinidad).

ROSEBERY, 7th Earl of, *cr* 1703; **Neil Archibald Primrose,** DL; Bt 1651; Viscount of Rosebery, Baron Primrose and Dalmeny, 1700; Viscount of Inverkeithing, Baron Dalmeny and Primrose, 1703; Baron Rosebery (UK), 1828; Earl of Midlothian, Viscount Mentmore, Baron Epsom, 1911; *b* 11 Feb. 1929; *o* surv. *s* of 6th Earl of Rosebery, KT, PC, DSO, MC, and of Eva Isabel Marian (Eva Countess of Rosebery, DBE), *d* of 2nd Baron Aberdare; *S* father, 1974; *m* 1955, Alison Mary Deirdre, *d* of late Ronald William Reid, MS, FRCS; one *s* four *d*. *Educ:* Stowe; New Coll., Oxford. DL Midlothian, 1960. *Heir:* *s* Lord Dalmeny, *qv*. *Address:* Dalmeny House, South Queensferry, West Lothian.

ROSEHILL, Lord; David John MacRae Carnegie; estate manager/owner; *b* 3 Nov. 1954; *s* and *heir* of 13th Earl of Northesk, *qv*; *m* 1979, Jacqueline Reid, *d* of Mrs Elizabeth Reid, Sarasota, Florida, USA; one *s* one *d*. *Educ:* West Hill Park, Titchfield; Eton; Brooke House, Market Harborough; UCL. *Heir:* *s* Hon. Alexander Robert MacRae Carnegie, *b* 16 Nov. 1980. *Address:* Fair Oak, Rogate, Petersfield, Hants GU31 5HR. *T:* Rogate 508.

ROSEN, Charles; pianist; Professor of Music, State University of New York at Stony Brook; *b* New York, 5 May 1927; *s* of Irvin Rosen and Anita Gerber. *Educ:* studied piano with Mr and Mrs Moriz Rosenthal; Princeton Univ. (PhD). Début, NY, 1951. His many recordings include: first complete recording of Debussy Etudes, 1951; late keyboard works of Bach, 1969; last six Beethoven Sonatas, 1970; Beethoven's Five Piano Concerti; Diabelli Variations; also works by Liszt, Elliott Carter, Boulez, etc. Eliot Norton Prof. of Poetry, Harvard Univ., 1980. Hon. MusD Trinity Coll., Dublin, 1976; Hon. DMus Durham, 1980. *Publications:* The Classical Style, 1971; Schoenberg, 1976; Sonata Forms, 1980; (with H. Zerner) Romanticism and Realism: the mythology of nineteenth century art, 1984. *Recreations:* music, books. *Address:* c/o Basil Douglas Ltd, 8 St George's Terrace, NW1 8XJ. *T:* 01–722 7142.

ROSEN, Rabbi Jeremy, MA; Minister, Western Synagogue, London, since 1985; *b* 11 Sept. 1942; *s* of Rabbi Kopul Rosen and Bella Rosen; *m* 1971, Vera Giuditta Zippel; two *s* two *d*. *Educ:* Carmel Coll.; Pembroke Coll., Cambridge (MA); Mir Academy, Jerusalem. Minister, Bulawayo Hebrew Congregation, Rhodesia, 1966; Minister, Giffnock Hebrew Congregation, Scotland, 1968–71; Headmaster, 1971–85, Principal, 1983–85, Carmel Coll. *Address:* Western Synagogue, Crawford Place W1H 5HD.

ROSENBLUM, Prof. Robert; Professor of Fine Arts, New York University, USA, since 1966; *b* 24 July 1927; *m* 1977, Jane Kaplowitz; one *s* one *d*. *Educ:* Queens Coll., Flushing, NY (BA); Yale Univ. (MA); New York Univ. (PhD); Oxford Univ. (MA). Prof. of Art and Archaeology, Princeton Univ., USA, 1956–66; Slade Prof. of Fine Art, Oxford Univ., 1971–72. Fellow, Amer. Acad. of Arts and Scis, 1984. Frank Jewett Mather Award for Art Criticism, 1981. *Publications:* Cubism and Twentieth-Century Art, 1960; Transformations in Late Eighteenth Century Art, 1967; Jean-Auguste-Dominique Ingres, 1967; Frank Stella, 1971; Modern Painting and the Northern Romantic Tradition: Friedrich to Rothko, 1975; French Painting, 1774–1830 (exhibn catalogue), 1975; Andy Warhol: Portraits of the Seventies, 1979; (with H. W. Janson) Nineteenth Century Art,

1984; articles in learned jls: Art Bulletin; Burlington Magazine; Jl of the Warburg and Courtauld Institutes; La Revue de l'Art, etc. *Address:* Department of Fine Arts, New York University, New York, NY 10003, USA. *T:* (212)–598–3471.

ROSENBROCK, Prof. Howard Harry, DSc, FEng; FRS 1976; FIEE, FIChemE; FInstMC; Professor of Control Engineering, since 1966, Vice-Principal, 1977–79, University of Manchester Institute of Science and Technology, (UMIST); Science Research Council Senior Fellow, 1979–83; *b* 16 Dec. 1920; *s* of Henry Frederick Rosenbrock and Harriett Emily (*née* Gleed); *m* 1950, Cathryn June (*née* Press); one *s* two *d*. *Educ:* Slough Grammar Sch.; University Coll. London. BSc, PhD; Fellow 1978. Served War, RAFVR, 1941 46. GEC, 1947 48; Electrical Research Assoc., 1949–51; John Brown & Co., 1951–54; Constructors John Brown Ltd, 1954–62 (latterly Research Manager); ADR, Cambridge Univ., 1962–66. Mem. Council, IEE, 1966–70, Vice-Pres., 1977–78; Pres., Inst. of Measurement and Control, 1972–73; Member: Computer Bd, 1972–76; SRC Engineering Bd, 1976–78; SERC/ESRC Jt Cttee, 1981–85. *Publications:* (with C. Storey) Computational Techniques for Chemical Engineers, 1966; (with C. Storey) Mathematics of Dynamical Systems, 1970; State-space and Multivariable Theory, 1970; Computer-aided Control System Design, 1974; contribs Proc. IEE, Trans IChemE, Proc. IEEE, Automatica, Internat. Jl Control, etc. *Recreations:* microscopy, photography, 17th and 18th Century literature. *Address:* Linden, Walford Road, Ross-on-Wye, Herefordshire HR9 5PQ. *T:* Ross-on-Wye 65372.

ROSENFELD, Alfred John, CB 1981; Deputy Chairman, Shoreham Port Authority, since 1984 (Member, since 1983); Deputy Secretary, 1979–82, and Principal Finance Officer, 1976–82, Department of Transport; *b* 27 Feb. 1922; *s* of late Ernest Rosenfeld and late Annie Jeanette Rosenfeld (*née* Samson); *m* 1955, Mary Elisabeth (*née* Prudence); two *s* one *d*. *Educ:* Leyton County High Sch. Entered Public Trustee Office, 1938. Served War, Fleet Air Arm, 1942–46. Min. of Civil Aviation, 1947 (later, Min. of Transport, and Dept of Environment); Private Sec. to Jt Parliamentary Sec., 1958–59; Asst Sec., 1967; Under-Sec., 1972. Hon. Treas., PHAB. *Recreations:* chess, bridge, gardening. *Address:* 33 Elmfield Road, Chingford, E4 7HT. *T:* 01–529 8160.

ROSENTHAL, Erwin Isak Jacob, LittD, DrPhil, MA; Reader in Oriental Studies, University of Cambridge, 1959–71, now Emeritus Reader; Fellow of Pembroke College, 1962–71, now Emeritus Fellow; *b* 18 Sept. 1904; *y s* of Moses and Amalie Rosenthal; *m* 1933, Elizabeth Charlotte Marx; one *s* one *d*. *Educ:* Heilbronn; Universities of Heidelberg, Munich, Berlin. Goldsmid Lectr in Hebrew, Lectr in North-Semitic Epigraphy, Head of Dept of Hebrew, University Coll., Univ. of London, 1933–36; Special Lectr, Semitic Langs and Lits, Univ. of Manchester, 1936–44, Nat. Service: RASC, 1944–45; attached FO, 1945; German Sect., FO, 1946–48. Lectr, Central Advisory Coun. for Educn, HM Forces, 1940–44; Tutor, Adult Educn, Univ. Tutorial Class, WEA, London, 1946–48 (Part-time); Univ. Lectr in Hebrew, Cambridge, 1948–59. Vis. Professor: Columbia Univ., 1967–68; El Colegio de Mexico, 1968; Leverhulme Emeritus Fellow, 1974, 1975. Pres., British Assoc. for Jewish Studies, 1977. Corresp. Fellow, Amer. Acad. for Jewish Res., 1984; Corresp. Mem., Rhenish-Westphalian Acad. of the Sciences, 1986. *Publications:* Ibn Khalduns Gedanken über den Staat, 1932; Law and Religion (Vol. 3 Judaism and Christianity), 1938 (ed and contrib.); Saadya Studies, 1943 (ed and contrib.); Averroes' Commentary on Plato's Republic, 1956, 1966, 1969 (ed and trans.); Political Thought in Medieval Islam, 1958, 1962, 1968, 1985 (Spanish trans., 1967; Japanese trans., 1970); Griechisches Erbe in der jüdischen Religionsphilosophie des Mittelalters, 1960; Judaism and Islam, 1961; Islam in the Modern National State, 1965; (ed) Judaism section, in Religion in the Middle East, 1969; Studia Semitica (I: Jewish Themes; II: Islamic Themes), 1971; articles in learned jls; Festschriften. *Recreations:* music, walking, travelling. *Address:* 199 Chesterton Road, Cambridge CB4 1AH; Pembroke College, Cambridge. *T:* Cambridge 357648.
See also T. G. Rosenthal.

ROSENTHAL, Harold David, OBE 1983; Editor of Opera, 1953–86, now Editor Emeritus; Lecturer and Broadcaster since 1950; *b* 30 Sept. 1917; *s* of Israel Victor Rosenthal and Leah Samuels; *m* 1944, Lillah Phyllis Weiner; one *s* one *d*. *Educ:* City of London School; University College, London (BA); Inst. of Education, London. Asst Editor, Opera, 1950–53; Archivist, Royal Opera House, Covent Garden, 1950–56. Member: Arts Council Patrons of Music Fund Cttee, 1960–70; Council, Friends of Covent Garden, 1962–; Chairman, Music Section, Critics' Circle of Gt Britain, 1965–67. Cavaliere Ufficiale, Order of Merit of the Republic (Italy), 1977. *Publications:* Sopranos of Today, 1956; Two Centuries of Opera at Covent Garden, 1958; A Concise Oxford Dictionary of Opera (with John Warrack), 1964, paperback edn, 1972, rev. and enl. edn, 1979; Great Singers of Today, 1966; Mapleson Memoires (ed and annotated), 1966; The Opera Bedside Book, 1965; Opera at Covent Garden, 1967; Covent Garden, 1976; (ed) Loewenberg's Annals of Opera 1597–1940, 3rd edn, 1979; My Mad World of Opera, 1982; Annals of Opera 1940–80, 1986. *Recreations:* travel, food; collecting playbills, prints, programmes, etc. *Address:* 6 Woodland Rise, N10 3UH. *T:* 01–883 4415.

ROSENTHAL, Jack Morris; writer; *b* 8 Sept. 1931; *s* of Samuel and Leah Rosenthal; *m* 1973, Maureen Lipman, *qv*; one *s* one *d*. *Educ:* Colne Grammar School; Sheffield Univ. (BA Eng. Lit. and Lang). *Television:* writer of over 250 productions, incl. That Was the Week That Was, 1963; 150 episodes of Coronation Street, 1961–69; The Evacuees, 1975; Bar Mitzvah Boy, 1976; Ready When You Are, Mr McGill, 1976; Spend Spend Spend, 1977; The Knowledge, 1979; P'tang Yang Kipperbang, 1982; Mrs Capper's Birthday, 1985; London's Burning, 1986; Fools on the Hill, 1986; Day to Remember, 1986; *stage:* five plays, incl. Smash!, 1981; *films:* six feature films including: Lucky Star, 1980; Yentl, 1983 (co-written with Barbra Streisand); The Chain, 1985. BAFTA Writer's Award, 1976; RTS Writer's Award, 1976. *Publications:* (contrib.) The Television Dramatist, 1973; (anthology) First Love, 1984; numerous TV plays. *Recreations:* work, frying fish, polishing almost anything tarnished, playing the violin in enforced privacy, remembering how Manchester United used to play, collecting models of rhinoceri and tortoisi. *Address:* c/o Margaret Ramsay Ltd, 14A Goodwin's Court, St Martin's Lane, WC2N 4LL. *T:* 01–240 0691. *Club:* Dramatists'.

ROSENTHAL, Maureen Diane, (Mrs J. M. Rosenthal); *see* Lipman, M. D.

ROSENTHAL, Norman Leon; Exhibitions Secretary, Royal Academy of Arts, since 1977; *b* 8 Nov. 1944; *s* of Paul Rosenthal and Kate Zucker. *Educ:* Westminster City Grammar School; University of Leicester. BA Hons History. Librarian, Thomas Agnew & Sons, 1966–68; Exhibitions Officer, Brighton Museum and Art Gallery, 1970–71; Exhibition Organiser, ICA, 1974–76; jointly responsible for contemporary art exhbns including: Art into Society, ICA, 1974; A New Spirit in Painting, RA, 1981; Zeitgeist, West Berlin, 1982; German Art of the Twentieth Century, Royal Acad., London and Staatsgalerie, Stuttgart, 1985–86. TV and radio broadcasts on contemporary art. *Recreations:* music, especially opera. *Address:* The Royal Academy of Arts, Burlington House, W1. *T:* 01–734 9052.

ROSENTHAL, Thomas Gabriel; publisher, critic and broadcaster; Joint Chairman and Joint Managing Director, André Deutsch Ltd, since 1984; Chairman, Frew McKenzie

(Antiquarian Booksellers), since 1985; *b* 16 July 1935; *o s* of Erwin I. J. Rosenthal, *qv*; *m* Ann Judith Warnford-Davis; two *s*. *Educ:* Perse Sch., Cambridge; Pembroke Coll., Cambridge (Exhibnr, MA). Served RA, 1954–56, 2nd Lieut; subseq. Lieut Cambridgeshire Regt (TA). Joined Thames and Hudson Ltd, 1959; Man. Dir, Thames & Hudson Internat., 1966; joined Martin Secker & Warburg Ltd as Man. Dir, 1971; Dir, Heinemann Gp of Publishers, 1972–84; Man. Dir, William Heinemann International Ltd, 1979–84; Chairman: World's Work Ltd, 1979–84; Heinemann Zsolnay Ltd, 1979–84; William Heinemann Ltd, 1980–84; Martin Secker & Warburg Ltd, 1980–84; Kaye & Ward Ltd, 1980–84; William Heinemann, Australia and SA, 1981–82; Pres., Heinemann Inc., 1981–84. Art Critic of The Listener, 1963–66. Chm., Soc. of Young Publishers, 1961–62; Member: Cambridge Univ. Appts Bd, 1967–71; Exec. Cttee, NBL, 1971–74; Cttee of Management, Amateur Dramatic Club, Cambridge (also Trustee); Council, RCA, 1982–; Trustee, Phoenix Trust. *Publications:* Monograph on Jack B. Yeats, 1964; (with Alan Bowness) Monograph on Ivon Hitchens, 1973; (with Ursula Hoff) Monograph on Arthur Boyd, 1986; A Reader's Guide to European Art History, 1962; A Reader's Guide to Modern American Fiction, 1963; introdns to paperback edns of Theodore Dreiser's The Financier, The Titan and Jennie Gerhardt; articles in The Times, Guardian, TLS, London Magazine, Encounter, New Statesman, Jl of Brit. Assoc. for Amer. Studies, Studio Internat., DNB, Bookseller, Nature, etc. *Recreations:* opera, bibliomania, looking at pictures, reading other publishers' books. *Address:* c/o André Deutsch Ltd, 105 Great Russell Street, WC1B 3LJ. *T:* 01–580 2746. *Clubs:* Garrick, MCC.

ROSEVEARE, Robert William, CBE 1977; retired; Board Member, Community Industry Ltd, since 1983; Secretary, 1967–83, and Managing Director, Policy Co-ordination, 1973–83, British Steel Corporation; *b* Mandalay, Burma, 23 Aug. 1924; *s* of late William Leonard Roseveare, MC and of Marjory C. Roseveare; *m* 1954, Patricia Elizabeth, *d* of Guy L. Thompson, FRCS, Scarborough; one *s* three *d*. *Educ:* Gresham's Sch., Holt; St John's Coll., Cambridge (MA). Served in Fleet Air Arm, 1943–46. Home Civil Service, Admin. Class, 1949. Asst Private Sec. to Minister of Fuel and Power, 1952–54; seconded to Cabinet Office, 1958–60; British Embassy, Washington, 1960–62; Asst Sec., Ministry of Power, 1964. Special Asst to Chm. of Organising Cttee for British Steel Corporation (Lord Melchett), 1966; seconded to British Steel Corporation on its formation, 1967; Dir, Admin. Services, 1969; Man. Dir, Corporate Administration, 1971. *Recreations:* hill-walking, bird-watching, singing. *Address:* Littlecroft, Bank Crescent, Ledbury, Herefordshire. *T:* Ledbury 2913.

ROSIER, Air Chief Marshal Sir Frederick (Ernest), GCB 1972 (KCB 1966; CB 1961); CBE 1955 (OBE 1943); DSO 1942; RAF, retired; *b* 13 Oct. 1915; *s* of E. G. Rosier; *m* 1939, Hettie Denise Blackwell; three *s* one *d*. *Educ:* Grove Park School, Wrexham. Commissioned RAF, 1935; 43 (F) Sqdn, 1936–39. Served War of 1939–45 in France, UK, Western Desert and Europe. OC Horsham St Faith, 1947; exchange duties with USAF, 1948–50; Instructor at Jt Services Staff College, 1950–52; Gp Capt. Operations at Central Fighter Establishment, 1952–54; Gp Capt. Plans at Fighter Command, 1955–56; ADC to the Queen, 1956–58; idc 1957; Director of Joint Plans, Air Ministry, 1958; Chm. Joint Planning Staff, 1959–61; AOC Air Forces Middle East, 1961–63; Senior Air Staff Officer, HQ Transport Command, 1964–66; Air Officer C-in-C, RAF, Fighter Command, 1966–68; UK Mem., Permanent Military Deputies Group, Central Treaty Organisation, Ankara, 1968–70; Dep. C-in-C, Allied Forces Central Europe, 1970–73. Air ADC to the Queen, 1972–73. Mil. Advr and Dir, British Aircraft Corp. (Preston) Ltd, 1973–77; Director i/c BAC Ltd, Saudi Arabia, 1977–80. Commander: Order of Orange Nassau, 1947; Order of Polonia Restituta. *Address:* Ty Haul, Sun Bank, Llangollen, N Wales. *T:* Llangollen 861068; Flat 286, Latymer Court, Hammersmith, W6. *T:* 01–741 0765. *Club:* Royal Air Force.

ROSIER, Rt. Rev. Stanley Bruce; *see* Willochra, Bishop of.

ROSKELL, Prof. John Smith, MA, DPhil; FBA 1968; Professor of Medieval History, University of Manchester, 1962–79, now Professor Emeritus; *b* Norden, Rochdale, 2 July 1913; *s* of John Edmund and Lucy A. Roskell; *m* 1942, Evelyn Liddle; one *s* one *d*. *Educ:* Rochdale Municipal Secondary School; Accrington Grammar Sch.; University of Manchester; Balliol College, Oxford. Asst Lecturer in History, Manchester University, 1938; Lecturer, 1945; Senior Lecturer, 1950–52; Professor of Medieval History, University of Nottingham, 1952–62. President: Lancashire Parish Register Soc., 1962–84; Chetham Soc., 1972–84. Royal Navy, 1940–45; Lieut RNVR, 1942–45. *Publications:* The Knights of the Shire of the County Palatine of Lancaster (1377–1460), Chetham Society, 1937; The Commons in the Parliament of 1422, 1954; The Commons and their Speakers in English Parliaments, 1376–1523, 1965; (ed with F. Taylor) Gesta Henrici Quinti, 1975; Parliament and Politics in Late Medieval England, (3 vols), 1981–83; The Impeachment of Michael de la Pole, Earl of Suffolk, in 1386, 1984. *Recreation:* cricket. *Address:* 42 Barcheston Road, Cheadle, Cheshire. *T:* 061–428 4630.

ROSKILL, family name of **Baron Roskill.**

ROSKILL, Baron *cr* 1980 (Life Peer), of Newtown in the County of Hampshire; **Eustace Wentworth Roskill;** Kt 1962; PC 1971; DL; a Lord of Appeal in Ordinary 1980–86; *b* 6 Feb. 1911; *y s* of late John Roskill, KC and of late Sybil Mary Wentworth, *d* of Ashton Wentworth Dilke, MP; *m* 1947, Elisabeth Wallace Jackson, 3rd *d* of late Thomas Frame Jackson, Buenos Aires; one *s* two *d*. *Educ:* Winchester College (exhibnr; Fellow, 1981–86); Exeter Coll., Oxford (exhibnr). 1st Cl. hons, Hon. Sch. of Mod. Hist. Oxford, BA 1932; MA 1936; Harmsworth Law Schol. Middle Temple, 1932; called to Bar, Middle Temple, 1933, Bencher 1961, Reader 1978, Dep. Treasurer 1979, Treasurer 1980; Hon. Bencher of The Inner Temple, 1980. Worked at Ministries of Shipping and War Transport, 1939–45. QC 1953. Dep. Chm. Hants QS, 1951–60, Chm. 1960–71; Comr of Assize (Birmingham), 1961; Judge of the High Court of Justice, Queen's Bench Division, 1962–71; a Lord Justice of Appeal, 1971–80. Vice-Chm., Parole Bd, 1967–69; Chm., Commn on Third London Airport, 1968–70. Pres., Senate of Four Inns of Court, 1972–74; Hon. Mem., 1974; Life Mem., Canadian Bar Assoc., 1974. Chairman: Average Adjusters Assoc., 1977–78; London Internat. Arbitration Trust, 1981–; Fraud Trials Cttee, 1983–85. Hon. Fellow, Exeter College, Oxford, 1963. Hampshire: JP 1950; DL 1972. *Recreations:* music, swimming, gardening. *Address:* Heatherfield, Newtown, Newbury, Berks RG15 9DB. *T:* Newbury 40606; New Court, Temple, EC4. *T:* 01–353 8870; House of Lords, SW1. *Club:* Reform.
See also Sir Patrick Dean, Sir A. W. Roskill, O. W. Roskill.

ROSKILL, Sir Ashton (Wentworth), Kt 1967; QC 1949; MA Oxon; Chairman, Monopolies and Mergers Commission (formerly Monopolies Commission), 1965–75 (Part-time Member, 1960–65); *b* 1 Jan. 1902; *e s* of late John Roskill, KC, and Sybil Mary Wentworth, *d* of late Ashton Dilke, MP; *m* 1st, 1932, Violet Willoughby (*d* 1964), *d* of late Charles W. Waddington, CIE, MVO; one *s* one *d*; 2nd, 1965, Phyllis Sydney, *y d* of late Sydney Burney, CBE. *Educ:* Winchester; Exeter Coll., Oxford (Schol.). 1st class hons Modern History, 1923; Barrister-at-Law, Inner Temple, 1925; Certificate of Honour, Council of Legal Education, 1925. Attached War Office, Intelligence Staff, 1940–45. Bencher, Inner Temple, 1958, Treasurer, 1980; Hon. Bencher, Middle Temple, 1980.

Chm., Barristers Benevolent Assoc., 1968–79. *Address:* Heath Cottage, Newtown, Newbury, Berks. *T:* Newbury 40328. *Club:* Reform.
See also Baron Roskill, O. W. Roskill.

ROSKILL, Oliver Wentworth, CChem, FRSC, CEng, FIChemE, CIMechE, SFInstE, CBIM, FIMC; Senior Partner, O. W. Roskill Industrial Consultants, 1930–74; Chairman: O. W. Roskill & Co (Reports) Ltd, 1957–74; Roskill Information Services Ltd, 1971–74; *b* 28 April 1906; *s* of John Roskill, KC, and Sibyl Mary Wentworth, *d* of Ashton Wentworth Dilke, MP. *Educ:* Oundle Sch.; Lincoln Coll., Oxford (scholar). MA, BSc (Oxon) (1st Cl. Hons). Captain, Oxford Univ. Rugby Fives Club, 1927. Imperial Chemical Industries Ltd, 1928–30. Min. of Economic Warfare, Dep. Head, Enemy Countries Intell., 1939–41. Mem. Exec. Cttee of Political and Economic Planning (now Policy Studies Inst.), 1931, Vice-Pres., 1975; Founder Mem. Council, British Inst. of Management, 1947–53 (Chm. Inf. and Research Cttee); Mem. British Nat. Export Council, Caribbean Cttee, 1965–69; Mem. Council, Inst. of Management Consultants, 1963–74 (Pres., 1970–71). Consultant on industrial development projects to Govts of Iran, Pakistan, Malta, Fed. Govt of Rhodesia, and others. *Publications:* Founder and part author of 'Who Owns Whom' series of directories; part author of Fifty Years of Political and Economic Planning; author of monographs on economics of metals and minerals (incl. tungsten, titanium, chromium, fluorspar); contributor to many jls of learned societies (incl. Inst. Fuel, RIBA, Town Planning Inst.). *Recreations:* mountain walking, playing chamber music, choral singing, real tennis, gardening. *Address:* The Priory, Beech Hill, Reading, Berks. *T:* Reading 883146. *Clubs:* Brooks's; Woodmen of Arden; Hampton Court Tennis, Holyport Tennis, Hatfield Tennis.
See also Baron Roskill, Sir A. W. Roskill.

ROSLING, Peter Edward, LVO 1972; HM Diplomatic Service; High Commissioner, Lesotho, since 1984; *b* 17 June 1929; *s* of Peregrine Starr and Jessie Rosling; *m* 1950, Kathleen Nuell; three *s*. *Educ:* grammar school. Served Royal Navy, 1948–50. HM Diplomatic Service, 1946–; Belgrade, Innsbruck, Cape Town, Rome (NATO Defence College), FCO; Consul-Gen., Zagreb, 1980–83. *Recreations:* walking, fishing, painting, bridge. *Address:* c/o Foreign and Commonwealth Office, SW1A 2AH. *Club:* Royal Commonwealth Society.

ROSOMAN, Leonard Henry, OBE 1981; RA 1969 (ARA 1960); FSA; Tutor, Royal College of Art, since 1957; *b* 27 Oct. 1913; *s* of Henry Rosoman; *m* 1963, Jocelyn (marr. diss. 1969), *d* of Bertie Rickards, Melbourne, Australia. *Educ:* Deacons Sch., Peterborough; Durham Univ. Teacher of Drawing and Painting, Reimann Sch. of Art, London, 1938–39; Official War Artist to Admiralty, 1943–45; Teacher: Camberwell Sch. of Art, London, 1947–48; (Mural Painting) Edinburgh Coll. of Art, 1948–56; Chelsea School of Art, 1956–57; Tutor, Royal Coll. of Art, 1957–. One Man Shows: St George's Gallery, London, 1946 and 1949; Roland, Browse and Delbanco Gallery, London, 1954, 1957, 1959, 1965 and 1969; Fine Art Soc., 1974, 1978, 1983. Works bought by: HM Govt, Arts Council, British Council, York Art Gall., Contemporary Art Soc., Adelaide Art Gallery, V&A Museum. Executed large mural paintings for: Festival of Britain, 1951; British Pavilion, Brussels World Fair, 1958; Harewood House, 1959. FSIA; Hon. ARCA; HRSW. *Recreation:* travelling as much as possible. *Address:* 7 Pembroke Studios, Pembroke Gardens, W8. *T:* 01–603 3638.

ROSPIGLIOSI, family name of **Earl of Newburgh.**

ROSS, family name of **Baron Ross of Marnock.**

ROSS, Rt. Hon. Lord; Rt. Hon. Lord Justice-Clerk; Donald MacArthur Ross, PC 1985; a Senator of the College of Justice, Scotland, and Lord of Session, since 1977; Lord Justice-Clerk, since 1985; *b* 29 March 1927; *s* of late John Ross, solicitor, Dundee; *m* 1958, Dorothy Margaret, *d* of late William Annand, Kirriemuir; two *d*. *Educ:* Dundee High School; Edinburgh University. MA (Edinburgh) 1947; LLB with distinction (Edinburgh) 1951. National Service with The Black Watch (RHR), 2nd Lt, 1947–49. Territorial Service, 1949–58, Captain. Advocate, 1952; QC (Scotland) 1964; Vice-Dean, Faculty of Advocates of Scotland, 1967–73; Dean, 1973–76; Sheriff Principal of Ayr and Bute, 1972–73. Dep. Chm., Boundary Commn for Scotland, 1977–85. Member: Scottish Cttee of Council on Tribunals, 1970–76; Cttee on Privacy, 1970. Mem. Court, Heriot-Watt Univ., 1978– (Chm., 1984–). *Recreation:* gardening. *Address:* 33 Lauder Road, Edinburgh EH9 2JG. *T:* 031–667 5731. *Club:* New (Edinburgh).

ROSS OF MARNOCK, Baron *cr* 1979 (Life Peer), of Kilmarnock in the District of Kilmarnock and Loudoun; **William Ross;** PC 1964; MBE (mil.) 1945; MA; Lord High Commissioner, General Assembly of Church of Scotland, 1978–80; *b* 7 April 1911; *s* of W. Ross, Ayr; *m* 1948, Elizabeth Jane Elma Aitkenhead, Ayr; two *d*. *Educ:* Ayr Academy; Glasgow University. MA 1932; Schoolmaster. Served War of 1939–45, HLI, R Signals, Major; India, SACSEA. Contested Ayr Burgh, General Election, 1945; MP (Lab) Kilmarnock, Ayr and Bute, 1946–79; Secretary of State for Scotland, 1964–70, 1974–76; Opposition spokesman on Scottish Affairs, 1970–74; Mem., Labour Parly Cttee, 1970–79. Hon. Pres., Scottish Football Assoc., 1978. FEIS 1971. Hon. LLD: St Andrews, 1967; Strathclyde, 1969; Glasgow, 1978. *Recreation:* golf. *Address:* 10 Chapelpark Road, Ayr. *T:* Ayr 65673.

ROSS, Alan, CBE 1982; author, publisher and journalist; Editor of London Magazine; Managing Director, London Magazine Editions (Publishers), since 1965; *b* Calcutta, 6 May 1922; *o s* of John Brackenridge Ross, CBE and Clare, *d* of Captain Patrick Fitzpatrick, Indian Army; *m* 1949, Jennifer, *d* of Sir Geoffrey Fry, 1st and last Bt, KCB, CVO; one *s*. *Educ:* Haileybury; St John's College, Oxford. RN 1942–47; general service, Arctic and North Seas, 1942–44; Asst Staff Officer, Intelligence, 16th Destroyer Flotilla, 1944; on staff of Flag Officer, Western Germany, 1945, and Interpreter to British Naval Commander-in-Chief, Germany, 1946. British Council, 1947–50; on staff of The Observer 1950–71. Toured Australia as correspondent, with MCC, 1954–55, 1962–63; toured South Africa, 1956–57, 1964–65; toured West Indies, 1960, 1968. Atlantic Award for Literature (Rockefeller Foundation), 1946. FRSL 1971. *Publications:* The Derelict Day, 1947; Time Was Away, 1948; The Forties, 1950; The Gulf of Pleasure, 1951; The Bandit on the Billiard Table, 1954 (revised edition South to Sardinia, 1960); Something of the Sea, 1954; Australia 55, 1956, 2nd edn, 1985; Abroad (ed), 1957; Cape Summer and the Australians in England, 1957, 2nd edn, 1986; To Whom It May Concern, 1958; The Onion Man, 1959; Through the Caribbean, 1960; The Cricketer's Companion (ed), 1960; Danger on Glass Island, 1960; African Negatives, 1962; Australia 63, 1963; West Indies at Lord's, 1963, 2nd edn 1986; North from Sicily, 1965; Poems 1942–67, 1968; Tropical Ice, 1972; The Taj Express, 1973; (ed) London Magazine Stories 1–11, 1964–80; (ed) Living in London, 1974; Open Sea, 1975; (ed) Selected Poems of Lawrence Durrell, 1977; Death Valley and Other Poems, 1980; (ed) The Turf, 1982; Colours of War, 1983; Ranji, 1983; (ed) Living out of London, 1984; Blindfold Games, 1986; (ed) London Magazine 1961–85, 1986; The Emissary, 1986; several trans and introductions; contrib. to various jls in England and America. *Recreations:* travel, sport (played cricket and squash for Oxford University and Royal Navy), racing. *Address:* 4 Elm Park Lane, SW3. *Clubs:* Garrick, MCC; Vincent's (Oxford).

ROSS, Sir Alexander, Kt 1971; Chairman: United Dominions Trust Ltd, 1963–74 (Director, 1955; Vice-Chairman, 1962); Australia and New Zealand Banking Group Ltd, 1970–75; Deputy Chairman: Eagle Star Insurance Co. Ltd, 1963–82; Eagle Star Holdings Ltd, retired 1982; *b* 2 Sept. 1907; *s* of William Alexander Ross and Kathleen Ross; *m* 1st, 1933, Nora Bethia Burgess (*d* 1974); two *s* two *d*; 2nd, 1975, Cynthia Alice Barton. *Educ:* Mount Albert Grammar Sch.; Auckland University (Dip. Banking). Joined Nat. Bank of NZ, 1927, and Reserve Bank of NZ on its establishment in 1934; Dep. Gov., 1948–55. Director: Whitbread Investment Trust Ltd, 1972–83; Drayton Far Eastern Trust Ltd (formerly British Aust. Investment Trust Ltd), 1975–82; Power Components Ltd, 1976–82. Rep. NZ on numerous occasions overseas, including Commonwealth Finance Ministers' Conf. in Australia, 1954. Rep. NZ in rowing, at Empire Games, 1930; Manager, NZ team to Commonwealth Games, Vancouver, 1954; NZ rowing selector for Olympic and Commonwealth Games, NZ; Chairman: Commonwealth Games Fedn, 1968–82 (Vice Chm., 1966–68); Cttee for British Exports to NZ, 1965–67; East European Trade Council, 1967–69; British Aust. Soc., 1970–75; Vice-Pres., British Export Houses Assoc., 1968–71; Dir, NRDC, 1966–74; Mem., BNEC, 1967–69. Member: New Zealand Soc. (Past Pres.); Council, Dominion Students' Hall Trust; Governor, Royal Caledonian Schs, 1964–69; Trustee, Aust. Musical Soc. Foundn; a past Governor, E-SU. Pres., Fellowship of British Motor Industry, 1971–73. Dep. Chm., Central Council, Royal Over-Seas League, 1979–82, Life Vice Pres., 1982. Chm. Ct of Advisers, St Paul's Cathedral, 1981–82. Qld Pres., St John's Ambulance; Life Vice-Pres., Commonwealth Games Fedn. Freeman, City of London. Hon. Mem., NUR. *Recreations:* walking, writing. *Address:* 20 Compass Way, Tweed Heads West, NSW 2485, Australia. *T:* (075) 36 7430.

ROSS, Alfred William, OBE 1955; MA, MIEE; Technical and Operational Research Consultant, 1974–84, retired; Deputy Chief Scientist (Navy), Ministry of Defence, 1972–74; *b* 13 Sept. 1914; *m* 1946, Margaret Elizabeth Wilson; three *d*. *Educ:* King Edward VI School, Stourbridge; Christ's Coll., Cambridge. Joined HM Signal Sch., Portsmouth, 1936. Worked on Radar during War at Admiralty Signal and Radar Establishment. Defence Research Policy Staff, Ministry of Defence, 1946–47; Chief Superintendent, Army Operational Research Group, 1951–56. Director, Naval Physical Research, MoD, 1956–68; Chief of Naval Research, MoD, 1968–72. *Publications:* scientific papers on radar, electronics and operational research. *Recreation:* golf. *Address:* 336 Fir Tree Road, Epsom Downs, Surrey KT17 3NW. *T:* Burgh Heath 56774. *Club:* Walton Heath Golf.

ROSS, Rev. Dr Andrew Christian; Senior Lecturer in Ecclesiastical History, University of Edinburgh, since 1966; Principal of New College and Dean of the Faculty of Divinity, 1978–84; *b* 10 May 1931; *s* of George Adams Ross and Christian Glen Walton; *m* 1953, Isabella Joyce Elder; four *s* (one *d* decd). *Educ:* Dalkeith High Sch.; Univ. of Edinburgh (MA, BD, PhD); Union Theol Seminary, New York (STM). Served Royal Air Force, Pilot Officer, then FO, 1952–54. Ordained Minister of Church of Scotland, 1958; Minister, Church of Central Africa Presbyterian (Malâwi), 1958–65; Chm., Lands Tribunal of Nyasaland, then Malâwi Govt, 1963–65; Vice-Chm., Nat. Tenders Bd of Nyasaland, then Malâwi, 1963–65. Sen. Studentship in African History, Univ. of Edinburgh, 1965–66; Mem. Court of Univ. of Edinburgh, 1971–73, Chm. Student Affairs Cttee of the Court, 1977–83. Kerr Lectr, Glasgow Univ., 1984; Vis. Prof., Univ. of Witwatersrand, 1984; Coll. Lectr, Assembly's Coll., Belfast, 1985. *Publications:* chapter in: The Zambesian Past, 1965; Religion in Africa, 1965; Witchcraft and Healing, 1969; David Livingstone and Africa, 1973; Malâwi, Past and Present, 1974; introd. and ed for micro film-prodn: Life and Work in Central Africa 1885–1914, 1969; The Records of the UMCA 1859–1914, 1971; John Philip: missions, race and politics in South Africa, 1986; contribs to Union Qly Rev., New Left Rev., Scottish Historical Rev. *Recreation:* playing and watching soccer. *Address:* 27 Colinton Road, Edinburgh EH10 5DR. *T:* 031–447 5987. *Club:* University of Edinburgh Staff.

ROSS, Sir Archibald (David Manisty), KCMG 1961 (CMG 1953); HM Diplomatic Service, retired; *b* 12 Oct. 1911; *s* of late J. A. Ross, Indian Civil Service, and Dorothea, *e d* of late G. Eldon Manisty, Indian Civil Service; *m* 1939, Mary Melville, *d* of Melville Macfadyen; one *s* one *d* (and one *s* decd). *Educ:* Winchester; New College, Oxford (MA). 1st Class Hon. Mods 1932, Lit. Hum. 1934; Gaisford Greek Verse Prize, 1932; Laming Travelling Fellow, Queen's College, 1934–35. Diplomatic Service, 1936; Berlin, 1939, Stockholm, 1939–44; Foreign Office, 1944–47, Tehran, 1947–50; Counsellor, Foreign Office, 1950–53; HM Minister, Rome, 1953–56; Assistant Under Secretary of State for Foreign Affairs, 1956–60; Ambassador to Portugal, 1961–66; Ambassador to Sweden, 1966–71. Chairman: Alfa-Laval Co., 1972–82; Saab (GB), 1972–82; Scania (GB), 1972–82; Ericsson Information Systems, 1981–86. Mem. Council, RASE, 1980–85. Grand Cross, Order of the North Star, Sweden, 1981. *Address:* 17 Ennismore Gardens, SW7. *Clubs:* Travellers'; Leander.

ROSS, (Claud) Richard, CB 1973; British financial executive and economist; Vice-President, and Vice-Chairman Board of Directors, European Investment Bank, since 1978; *b* 24 March 1924; *o s* of late Claud Frederick Ross and Frances Muriel Ross, Steyning, Sussex; *m* 1954, Leslie Beatrice, *d* of Oliver Arnell and late Dr H. M. Arnell, Kitale, Kenya; two *d*. *Educ:* Ardingly Coll.; Hertford Coll., Oxford (Open Schol., Mod. Hist.). 1st cl. PPE, 1950; MA. Fellow of Hertford Coll., 1951–63; Lectr in Economics, Oxford Univ., 1951–52 and 1955–63; Economic Advr to HM Treasury, 1952–55; Junior Proctor, Oxford Univ., 1958–59; Bursar, Hertford Coll., 1959–63; Prof. of Economics and Dean, School of Social Studies, Univ. of East Anglia, 1963–68 (Pro-Vice-Chancellor, 1964–68); Special Consultant, OECD, Paris, 1968–71; Dep. Sec., Central Policy Review Staff, Cabinet Office, 1971–78. Adviser, Bankers' Mission to India and Pakistan, 1960. Represented HM Treasury on OECD Working Party on Policies for Economic Growth, 1961–68. Leader, British Economic Mission to Tanzania, 1965; Member: East Anglia Regional Economic Planning Council, 1966–69 (Dep. Chm., 1967–69); Jt Mission for Malta, 1967. *Publications:* Financial and Physical Problems of Development in the Gold Coast (with D. Seers), 1952; articles on economics. *Address:* European Investment Bank, 100 boulevard Konrad Adenauer, L-2950 Luxembourg. *T:* 43 79–1; 2a Oliver's Wharf, 64 Wapping High Street, E1.

ROSS, Donald MacArthur; *see* Ross, Hon. Lord.

ROSS, Donald Nixon, FRCS; Consultant Cardiac Surgeon, National Heart Hospital, since 1963; *b* 4 Oct. 1922; *m* 1956, Dorothy Curtis; one *d*. *Educ:* Boys' High Sch., Kimberley, S Africa; Univ. of Capetown (BSc, MB, ChB 1st Cl. Hons, 1946). FRCS 1949; FACC 1973; FACS 1976. Sen. Registrar in Thoracic Surgery, Bristol, 1952; Guy's Hospital: Res. Fellow, 1953; Sen. Thoracic Registrar, 1954; Cons. Thoracic Surg., 1958; Cons. Surg., National Heart Hosp., 1963, Sen. Surg., 1967; Dir, Dept of Surgery, Inst. of Cardiology, 1970. Hon. FRCSI 1984. Hon. DSc CNAA, 1982. Clement Price Thomas Award, RCS, 1983. Order of Cedar of Lebanon, 1975; Order of Merit (1st cl.), West Germany, 1981. *Publications:* A Surgeon's Guide to Cardiac Diagnosis, 1962; (jtly) Medical and Surgical Cardiology, 1968; (jtly) Biological Tissue in Heart Valve Replacement, 1972; contrib. BMJ, Lancet, Proc. RSM, Annals Royal Coll. Surg., Amer. Jl Cardiol. *Recreations:*

horseriding, gardening. *Address:* 69 Gloucester Crescent, NW1. *T:* 01–935 8805. *Clubs:* Garrick; Kimberley (SA).

ROSS, Duncan Alexander, CEng, FIEE; Chairman, Southern Electricity Board, since 1984; Member, Electricity Council, since 1981; *b* 25 Sept. 1928; *s* of William Duncan Ross and Mary Ross; *m* 1958, Mary Buchanan Clarke Parsons; one *s* one *d. Educ:* Dingwall Academy; Glasgow Univ. (BSc Elec. Engrg). CBIM. Various engineering posts, South of Scotland Electricity Board, 1952–57; engineering, commercial and management posts, Midlands Electricity Board, 1957–72; Area Manager, South Staffs Area, 1972–75, Chief Engineer, 1975–77; Dep. Chm., 1977–81, Chm., 1981–84, South Wales Electricity Bd. *Recreations:* golf, squash. *Address:* Holly House, Canon Hill Way, Bray, Maidenhead, Berks SL6 2EX. *T:* Maidenhead 782753.

ROSS, Ernest; MP (Lab) Dundee West, since 1979; *b* Dundee, July 1942; *m*; two *s* one *d. Educ:* St John's Jun. Secondary Sch. Quality Control Engineer, Timex Ltd. Mem., AUEW (TASS). *Address:* House of Commons, SW1.

ROSS, Rear-Adm. George Campbell, CB 1952; CBE 1945; FRGS; CEng, MIMechE; MRAeS; retired; *b* 9 Aug. 1900; *s* of late Sir Archibald Ross, KBE; *m* 1st, 1929, Alice Behrens; 2nd, 1950, Lucia Boer (marr. diss. 1969); two *d*; 3rd, 1975, Manolita Harris. *Educ:* Royal Naval Colleges, Osborne and Dartmouth. Served European War, 1914–18, Grand Fleet (HM Ships Warspite, P59, Vendetta). Engineering Courses at RN College, Greenwich, and RNE College, Keyham, 1919–21; HMS Hawkins, Flagship China Station, 1921–24; RNE Coll., Lecturer in Marine Engineering, 1924–27; HMS Effingham, Flagship East Indies Station, 1927–29; HM Dockyard, Chatham, 1929–31; HMS Rodney, Atlantic Fleet, 1931–33 (incl. Invergordon Mutiny); Comdr 1933; Asst Naval Attaché, Embassy, Tokyo, 1933–36; Liaison Officer to Japanese Flagship Asigara, Coronation Review, 1937; introduced the Oerlikon 20mm gun to the Royal Navy, 1937 (adopted in 1939 largely owing to Lord Mountbatten and the First Sea Lord, Sir Roger Backhouse); HMS Manchester, E Indies Station, 1937–39; Engineer-in-Chief's Dept, Admiralty, 1939–41; Engineer Officer, HMS Nelson, and Staff Engineer Officer to Flag Officer, Force "H", Malta Convoy, N Africa and Sicily, 1941–Aug. 1943; Capt. 1943; HMS St Angelo, Malta, as Staff Engineer Officer (D), on staff of Captain (D), Force "H", Aug. 1943–Dec. 1943 (first officer to go aboard flagship of Italian Fleet after its surrender); Aircraft Maintenance and Repair Dept, Admiralty, 1943–47; ADC to the King, 1948–49; Chief of Staff to Rear-Admiral Reserve Aircraft, 1948–49; Rear-Adm. (E) 1949; Director of Aircraft Maintenance and Repair, Admiralty, 1949–53; retd, Oct. 1953. Joined Hawker Siddeley group, Nov. 1953, and retd Sept. 1965. Consultant to Grieveson Grant, Stockbrokers (1965–79), and other cos. Chairman, Combined Services Winter Sports Assoc., 1951–67. Freeman, City of London, 1955. *Recreations:* fishing, travel, painting, writing. *Address:* 11 Redcliffe Close, Old Brompton Road, SW5. *T:* 01–373 0609. *Club:* Hurlingham.

ROSS, James; QC 1966; **His Honour Judge Ross;** a Senior Circuit Judge, since 1985 (a Circuit Judge (formerly a Judge of County Courts), since 1971); *b* 22 March 1913; *s* of John Stuart Ross, FRCSE; *m* 1939, Clare Margaret, *d* of Alderman Robert Cort-Cox, Stratford-on-Avon; one *d. Educ:* Glenalmond; Exeter Coll., Oxford. BA Oxon 1934. Admitted Solicitor, 1938; called to Bar, Gray's Inn, 1945. Legal Member, Mental Health Review Tribunal, Birmingham Region, 1962; Deputy Chairman, Agricultural Land Tribunal, East Midland Area, 1963; Dep. Chm. QS, Parts of Lindsey, 1968–71; Recorder of Coventry, 1968–71; Mem., Parole Bd, 1974–76. Hon. Recorder, City of Birmingham, 1985. *Address:* 2 Dr Johnson's Buildings, Temple, EC4. *T:* 01–353 5371. *Clubs:* Bar Yacht, Royal Yachting Association.

ROSS, James Alexander, MBE (mil.) 1944; MD, FRCSEd, FRCSGlas; Professor of Anatomy, King Saud University, Riyadh, 1983–84, retired; *b* 25 June 1911; *s* of James McMath Ross and Bessie Hopper Flint; *m* 1940, Catherine Elizabeth, *d* of Clark Booth Curtis; one *s* three *d. Educ:* Merchiston Castle Sch.; Edinburgh Univ. MB ChB Ed 1934, MD Ed 1947; FRCSEd 1938, FRCSGlas 1965. Served War: RAMC, 1939–45: France, ME, Europe; then Lt-Col RAMC, RARO, 1953–55. Surgeon, Leith Hosp., 1946–61, and Royal Infirmary, Edinburgh, 1947–61; Surgeon, Eastern Gen. Hosp., 1961–76 and Edenhall Hosp., 1970–76. Hon. Sec., Royal Coll. of Surgeons of Edinburgh, 1960–68; Vice-Pres., 1971–73; Pres., RCSEd, 1973–76; Pres., Edinburgh Harveian Soc., 1977–78; Vice-Pres., Internat. Fedn of Surgical Colls, 1975–81. Hon. Cons. Surgeon to Army in Scotland, 1970–76. Lectures: McCombe, RCSE, 1977; Mason Brown Meml, RCSE, 1978; Hutchinson, Edinburgh Univ., 1979; Mitchiner Meml, RAMC, 1979; Douglas Guthrie Hist. of Medicine, RCSE, 1983. Hon. FRCSI, 1976; Hon. FRACS, 1977; Hon. FDSRCSE, 1983; Hon. Fellow: Pakistan Coll., P and S, 1976; Sri Lanka Coll. of Surgeons, 1976; Hong Kong Surgical Soc., 1976. Guthrie Medallist, RAMC, 1976; Farquharson Award (teaching of anatomy and surgery), RCSE, 1986. *Publications:* Memoirs of an Army Surgeon, 1948; (jtly) Manual of Surgical Anatomy, 1964; (jtly) Behaviour of the Human Ureter, in Health and Disease, 1972; The Edinburgh School of Surgery after Lister, 1978. *Recreations:* walking, swimming, watching cricket. *Address:* 5 Newbattle Terrace, Edinburgh EH10 4RU. *T:* 031–447 2292.

ROSS, Sir (James) Keith, 2nd Bt *cr* 1960; RD 1967; MS, FRCS; Consultant Cardiac Surgeon: Wessex Region, since 1972; King Edward VII Hospital, Midhurst, since 1979; *b* 9 May 1927; *s* of Sir James Paterson Ross, 1st Bt, KCVO, FRCS, and Marjorie Burton Townsend (*d* 1978); *S* father, 1980; *m* 1956, Jacqueline Annella Clarke; one *s* three *d. Educ:* St Paul's School; Middlesex Hospital. MB BS 1950; MS 1965; FRCS 1956. House Surgeon, Registrar, Sen. Registrar, Middlesex Hosp., 1950–67. Surgn Lieut, RNVR, 1952–54; Surg. Lt Comdr, RNR, retd 1972. Heller Fellowship, San Francisco, 1959; Registrar, Brompton Hosp., 1958, 1960. Consultant Thoracic Surgeon, Harefield Hosp., 1964–67; Consultant Surgeon, Nat. Heart Hosp., 1967–72. Hunterian Prof., RCS, 1961. *Publications:* on cardiac surgery in appropriate medical jls. *Recreations:* fly fishing, sailing, painting. *Heir: s* Andrew Charles Paterson Ross, *b* 18 June 1966. *Address:* Moonhills Gate, Exbury Road, Beaulieu, Brokenhurst, Hants SO42 7YS. *T:* Beaulieu 612104. *Clubs:* MCC; Royal Southampton Yacht, Royal Lymington Yacht.

ROSS, Leonard Q.; *see* Rosten, L. C.

ROSS, Sir Lewis (Nathan), Kt 1984; CMG 1974; FCA; Chartered Accountant (Fellow) in Public Practice, since 1932; company director, New Zealand; *b* 7 March 1911; *e s* of Robert and Raie Ross; *m* 1937, Ella Myrtle Burns, Melbourne, Australia; two *s* one *d. Educ:* Auckland Grammar Sch.; Univ. of Auckland. Commenced practice as CA, founding firm now known as Ross, Melville, Bridgman & Co, 1932; withdrew from partnership in 1965 to practise as consultant. Pres., Associated Chambers of Commerce of NZ, 1955–56; Chm., Govt Cttee: on PAYE taxation, 1964; to review all aspects of Central Govt Taxation in NZ, 1966–67. Chm., Aotea Centre Trust Bd, Auckland, 1984–; Pres., NZ Soc. of Accountants, 1972–73. Director: Bank of NZ (Chm.), 1966–; Bradbury Wilkinson (NZ) Ltd; Sanford Ltd; James Hardie Impey Ltd; Revertex Ind. Ltd; Bank of Western Samoa (Chm.). Hon. LLD Auckland, 1983. *Publications:* Taxation—Principles, Purpose and Incidence, 1964 (rev. edn 1973); Finance for Business, 1964; Accounting Problems that arise from Business Combinations, 1973; articles in Accountants' Jl and other business pubns. *Recreations:* bowls, contract bridge. *Address:* (private) 11 Rewiti Street, Orakei, Auckland, New Zealand. *T:* 547–449; (business) PO Box 881, Auckland, New Zealand. *T:* 798–665. *Club:* Northern (Auckland).

ROSS, Malcolm Keir; Headmaster of Crown Woods School, London, 1957–71; *b* 8 June 1910; *m* 1937, Isabel Munkley (*d* 1983); two *d. Educ:* Grangefield Grammar Sch., Stockton-on-Tees; Keble Coll., Oxford. Schoolmaster: Gordonstoun, 1933–34; Haverfordwest Grammar Sch., 1934–36; Bromley Grammar Sch., 1936–40; war service with RAF, 1940–45; Warden of Village Coll., Sawston, Cambs, 1945–57. Mem., Cttee of Enquiry into conditions of service life for young servicemen, 1969. Governor, Rachel McMillan Coll. of Education. Book reviewer for The Times Educational Supplement. FRSA. *Recreations:* gardening, reading. *Address:* 45 Winn Road, SE12 9EX.

ROSS, Rear-Adm. Maurice James, CB 1962; DSC 1940; retired; *b* 31 Oct. 1908; *s* of Basil James Ross and Avis Mary (*née* Wilkinson); *m* 1946, Helen Matheson McCall; one *d. Educ:* Charterhouse. Entered Royal Navy, 1927; specialised in gunnery, 1935; Comdr, 1943; Captain, 1951; Rear-Adm., 1960. Master, Gardeners' Company, 1983. *Publication:* Ross in the Antarctic 1839–1843, 1982. *Address:* The School House, Chippenham, Ely, Cambs CB7 5PP. *Club:* Army and Navy.

ROSS, Mrs Nicholas; *see* Phillpotts, M. Adelaide Eden.

ROSS, Norman Stilliard; Assistant Under-Secretary of State, Fire Department, Home Office, 1976–79; *b* 10 April 1919; *s* of late James Ross and Mary Jane Elizabeth Ross; *m* 1946, Sarah Cahill; one *s* two *d. Educ:* Solihull Sch., Warwickshire; Birmingham Univ. (BA). Served in local govt, City of Birmingham, 1935–39. War service, Army, RAMC and RAOC, in France, Belgium, Kenya, Ceylon, Burma and India, 1939–46 (despatches, France and Belgium, 1940). Asst Principal, Min. of Fuel and Power, 1949; Home Office, 1950; Asst Private Sec. to Sec. of State, 1950–52; Principal, 1952; Asst Sec., 1963; Asst Under-Sec. of State, 1976. *Recreations:* walking, music, reading. *Address:* 27 Detillens Lane, Limpsfield, Oxted, Surrey RH8 0DH. *T:* Oxted 2579.

ROSS, Richard; Professor of Film and Television, Royal College of Art, since 1980; *b* 22 Dec. 1935; *s* of Lawrence Sebley Ross and Muriel Ross; *m* 1957, Phyllis Ellen Hamilton; one *s* one *d. Educ:* Westland High School, Hokitika, NZ; Canterbury University College, NZ. Exchange Telegraph, 1958–60; Visnews Ltd, 1960–65; BBC TV News, 1965–80. Consultant: Univ. Sains, Penang, Malaysia, 1984–; Calouste Gulbenkian Foundn, Lisbon, 1983–. Chm., Educn Cttee, British Film Year, 1985–86. Fellow in Fine Arts, Trent Polytechnic, 1970–72. Fellow, RCA, 1981. *Recreations:* walking in London, eating in France, talking and drinking anywhere. *Address:* Royal College of Art, Kensington Gore, SW7 2EU; 51 Hanbury Street, E1.

ROSS, Richard; *see* Ross, C. R.

ROSS, Robert, MA, FLS; Keeper of Botany, British Museum (Natural History), 1966–77; *b* 14 Aug. 1912; *e s* of Robert Ross, Pinner, Middx; *m* 1939, Margaret Helen Steadman; one *s* three *d. Educ:* St Paul's Sch.; St John's Coll., Cambridge. Asst Keeper, British Museum (Natural History), 1936; Principal Scientific Officer, 1950; Deputy Keeper, 1962. Royal Microscopical Society: Hon. Librarian, 1947–51; Hon. Editor, 1953–71; Vice-Pres., 1959–60. Administrator of Finances, Internat. Assoc. of Plant Taxonomy, 1964–69; Sec., Gen. Cttee for Plant Nomenclature, 1964–69, Chm., 1969–81. President: British Phycological Soc., 1969–71; Quekett Microscopical Club, 1974–76. *Publications:* various papers in scientific jls on botanical subjects. *Recreations:* morris dancing (Bagman, Morris Ring of England, 1946–50); walking; gardening. *Address:* The Garden House, Evesbatch, Bishop's Frome, Worcester. *T:* Bosbury 366.

ROSS, Comdr Ronald Douglas, OBE 1984; RN; *b* 30 July 1920; *o s* of Captain James Ross, FRGS, Scottish Horse of Chengtu, Szechwan Province, China; *m* 1952, Elizabeth Mary, *er d* of Canon S. J. S. Groves; one *d. Educ:* Cargilfield; Sedbergh; RN Staff Coll. Joined Accountant Br. of RN and went to sea, 1937; war service in HM Ships Exeter, Devonshire and Tartar. Called to Bar, Middle Temple, 1950; called to the Bar, Supreme Court of Hong Kong, 1963; officiated frequently as Judge Advocate; Admiralty Prize Medal for Naval History, 1957; retired list, 1967. Clerk, Vintners' Co., 1969–84. Mem., Wine Standards Bd, 1973–84. Chevalier du Sacavin d'Anjou, 1974; Citizen and Vintner, 1975. *Publications:* contribs to The Times, Scotsman, New York Times, Investors' Chronicle, Brassey's Naval Annual, etc. *Recreation:* scripophily. *Address:* c/o National Westminster Bank, 1 Princes Street, EC2.

ROSS, Stephen Sherlock, FRICS; MP (L) Isle of Wight, since Feb. 1974; *b* 6 July 1926; *s* of Reginald Sherlock Ross and Florence Beryl (*née* Weston); *m* 1949, Brenda Marie Hughes; two *s* two *d. Educ:* Bedford Sch. Served War of 1939–45, RN, 1944–48. Articled Nock & Joseland, Kidderminster, 1948–51; Assistant: Heywood & Sons, Stone, Staffs, 1951–53; Sir Francis Pittis & Son, Newport, IoW, 1953–57 (Partner, 1958–73). County Councillor, IoW CC, 1967–74 and 1981–85 (Chm. Policy and Resources Cttee, 1973–74 and 1981–83). *Recreations:* cricket; antique porcelain collector. *Address:* 47 Quay Street, Newport, Isle of Wight PO30 5BA. *T:* Newport 522215. *Club:* National Liberal.

ROSS, Timothy David M.; *see* Melville-Ross.

ROSS, Victor; Chairman, Reader's Digest Association Ltd, 1978–84; *b* 1 Oct. 1919; *s* of Valentin and Eva Rosenfeld; *m* 1st, 1944, Romola Wallace; two *s*; 2nd, 1970, Hildegard Paiser. *Educ:* schs in Austria, Germany and France; London Sch. of Economics. Served in Army, 1942–45. Journalist and writer, 1945–55; joined Reader's Digest, 1955; Man. Dir and Chief Exec., 1972–81. Pres., Assoc. of Mail Order Publishers, 1979–80, 1983–84; Mem., Data Protection Tribunal, 1985–. *Publications:* A Stranger in my Midst, 1948; Tightrope, 1952; Basic British, 1956. *Recreations:* collecting 20th century dedication copies, fishing. *Address:* c/o 25 Berkeley Square, W1X 6AB. *T:* 01–629 8144.

ROSS, William; MP (UU) Londonderry East, since 1983 (Londonderry, Feb. 1974–1983), resigned seat Dec. 1985 in protest against Anglo-Irish Agreement; re-elected Jan. 1986; *b* 4 Feb. 1936; *m* 1974, Christine; three *s* one *d. Recreations:* fishing, shooting. *Address:* Hillquarter, Turmeel, Dungiven, Northern Ireland. *T:* Dungiven 41428. *Club:* Northern Counties (Londonderry).

ROSS, William Mackie, TD 1969; DL; MD; FRCS; FRCR; Consultant Radiotherapist, Northern Regional Health Authority, since 1953; Lecturer in Radiotherapy, University of Newcastle upon Tyne, since 1973; *b* 14 Dec. 1922; *s* of Harry Caithness Ross and Catherine Ross; *m* 1948, Mary Burt; one *s* two *d. Educ:* Durham and Newcastle. MB, BS 1945, MD 1953; FRCS 1956, FRCR 1960. Trainee in Radiotherapy, 1945–53; National Service, 1951–53; RAMC TA, 1953–72; Col, CO 201 Gen. Hosp., 1967–72, Hon. Col, 1977–82. President: Section of Radiology, RSM, 1978; British Inst. of Radiology, 1979; North of England Surgical Soc., 1983; Royal Coll. of Radiologists, 1983–86. DL Northumberland, 1971–74, Tyne and Wear, 1974. *Publications:* articles on cancer, its causation and treatment. *Address:* 62 Archery Rise, Durham City DH1 4LA. *T:* Durham 69256.

ROSS-MUNRO, Colin William Gordon, QC 1972; *b* 12 Feb. 1928; *s* of late William Ross-Munro and of Adela Chirgwin; *m* 1958, Janice Jill Pedrana; one step *d*. *Educ:* Lycée Français de Londres; Harrow Sch.; King's Coll., Cambridge. Served in Scots Guards and in Army Education Corps. Called to the Bar, Middle Temple, 1951 (Master of the Bench, 1983). *Recreations:* tennis and travel. *Address:* (home) 7 Onslow Gardens, SW7; 2 Hare Court, Temple EC4Y 7BH.

ROSS RUSSELL, Graham; stockbroker; Senior Partner, Laurence Prust & Co. Ltd (Partner, since 1967); *b* 3 Jan. 1933; *s* of Robert Ross Russell and Elizabeth Ross Russell (*née* Hendry); *m* 1963, Jean Margaret Symington; three *s* one *d*. *Educ:* Loretto; Trinity Hall, Cambridge (BA); Harvard Business School (MBA; Frank Knox Fellow, 1958–60). Sub Lieut, RNVR, 1951–53 (Mediterranean Fleet). Merchant banking: Morgan Grenfell & Co. and Baring Brothers, 1956–58; Philip Hill Higginson Erlanger, 1960–63; Stockbroker, Laurence Prust & Co., 1963–; Dep.Chm., Stock Exchange Council, 1984– (Mem. Council, 1973–). Chm., Braham Miller Group, 1981–84; non-exec. Director: Fordath, 1971–84; EMAP, 1971–; Norton and Wright Group, 1980–82; Automation & Technical Services (Holdings), 1981–84; Barlow Rand International, 1984–. Comr, Public Works Loan Bd, 1980–. *Publications:* occasional articles in esoteric financial and fiscal jls. *Recreations:* tennis, reading. *Address:* 30 Ladbroke Square, W11 3NB. *T:* 01–727 5017. *Clubs:* Hawks (Cambridge); Woodpeckers (Oxford and Cambridge).

ROSSE, 7th Earl of, *cr* 1806; **William Brendan Parsons;** Bt 1677; Baron Oxmantown 1792; Member, Advisory Council on Development Co-operation, Government of Ireland, since 1984; *b* 21 Oct. 1936; *s* of 6th Earl of Rosse, KBE, and of Anne, *o d* of Lt-Col Leonard Messel, OBE; *S* father, 1979; *m* 1966, Alison Margaret, *er d* of Major J. D. Cooke-Hurle, Startforth Hall, Barnard Castle, Co. Durham; two *s* one *d*. *Educ:* Eton; Grenoble Univ.; Christ Church, Oxford. BA 1961, MA 1964. 2nd Lieut, Irish Guards, 1955–57. UN Official 1963–80, appointed successively to Accra, Cotonou, New York, Teheran, Dacca and Algiers, in posts ranging from Area Officer to Dep. Resident Rep., with specific responsibility for directing the first teams of UN volunteers (in Iran) and co-ordinating disaster relief (in Bangladesh). Mem. Council: Agency for Personal Service Overseas; Food and Agriculture Res. Mission. Dir, Historic Irish Tourist Houses and Gardens Assoc.; Trustee, Edward de Bono Foundn; Patron, Halley's Comet Soc. FRAS. *Heir: s* Lord Oxmantown, *qv*. *Address:* (home) Birr Castle, Co. Offaly, Ireland. *T:* 353.509.20023.

See also Earl of Snowdon.

ROSSER, Sir Melvyn (Wynne), Kt 1974; DL; Chairman, HTV Group, since 1986; non-executive Director, Buckley Brewery Plc, since 1986; *b* 11 Nov. 1926; *s* of late David John and of Anita Rosser; *m* 1957, Margaret; one *s* two *d*. *Educ:* Glanmor Sch., Swansea; Bishop Gore Grammar Sch., Swansea. Chartered Accountant, qual. 1949; joined staff Deloitte & Co. (later Deloitte, Haskins & Sells), Swansea, 1950, Partner 1961; practised in Swansea, 1961–68, in Cardiff, 1968–80, in London, 1980–85, retired. Director: Develt Corp. for Wales, 1965–80; Nat. Bus Co., 1969–72; Wales and Marches Telecom. Bd, 1970–80; Welsh Regional Council, CBI, 1970–80; BSC, 1972–80; pt-time Mem., British Coal (formerly NCB), 1983–; Chm., Manpower Services Cttee for Wales, 1980–. Member: Welsh Econ. Council, 1965–68; Welsh Council, 1968–80 (Chm., 1971–80); Royal Commn on Standards of Conduct in Public Life, 1974; Prime Minister's Adv. Cttee on Outside Business Appts, 1976–83. Pres., UCW, Aberystwyth, 1986– (Vice-Pres., 1977–86). Mem. Gorsedd of Bards, Royal Nat. Eisteddfod of Wales. DL West Glamorgan, 1986. *Recreations:* music, gardening. *Address:* Corlan, 53 Birchgrove Road, Lonlas, Swansea SA7 9JR. *T:* Swansea 812286. *Clubs:* Reform, Royal Automobile; Cardiff and County (Cardiff).

ROSSI, Sir Hugh (Alexis Louis), Kt 1983; MP (C) Hornsey and Wood Green, since 1983 (Hornsey, 1966–83); *b* 21 June 1927; *m* 1955, Philomena Elizabeth Jennings; one *s* four *d*. *Educ:* Finchley Catholic Gram. Sch.; King's Coll., Univ. of London (LLB; FKC 1986). Solicitor with Hons, 1950; consultant in London practice. Member: Hornsey Borough Coun., 1956–65; Haringey Council, 1965–68; Middlesex CC, 1961–65. Govt Whip, Oct. 1970–April 1972; Europe Whip, Oct. 1971–1973; a Lord Comr, HM Treasury, 1972–74; Parly Under-Sec. of State, DoE, 1974; opposition spokesman on housing and land, 1974–79; Minister of State: NI Office, 1979–81; for Social Security and the Disabled, DHSS, 1981–83. Chm., Select Cttee on the Environment, 1983–. Dep. Leader, UK Delegn to Council of Europe and WEU, 1972–73 (Mem., 1970–73). Knight of Holy Sepulchre, 1966; KCSG 1985. *Publications:* Guide to the Rent Act, 1974; Guide to Community Land Act, 1975; Guide to Rent (Agriculture) Act, 1976. *Address:* House of Commons, SW1.

ROSSITER, Rt. Rev. (Anthony) Francis, OSB; Abbot of Ealing, since 1967; Abbot President of the English Benedictine Congregation since 1985 (Second Assistant, 1976–85); *b* 26 April 1931; *s* of Leslie and Winifred Rossiter. *Educ:* St Benedict's, Ealing; Sant Anselmo, Rome (LCL). Priest, 1955; Second Master, St Benedict's School, 1960–67; Vicar for Religious, Archdiocese of Westminster, 1969–; Pres., Conf. of Major Religious Superiors of England and Wales, 1970–74. *Address:* Ealing Abbey, W5 2DY. *T:* 01–998 2158.

ROSSITER, Hon. Sir John Frederick, KBE 1978; Agent-General for Victoria, in London, 1976–79; *b* 17 Dec. 1913; *s* of James and Sarah Rossiter; *m* 1st, 1939, Joan Durrant Stewart (*d* 1979); one *s* two *d*; 2nd, 1981, Heather Steer. *Educ:* Melbourne Univ. (BA 1937). Senior Lecturer in English, Royal Melbourne Inst. of Technology, 1946–55; MLA (Lib.), Brighton, Vic., 1955; Minister of Labour and Industry; Minister of Health; Chief Secretary, 1964–76. *Recreation:* golf. *Address:* 14 Pretoria Avenue, Balmoral, Sydney, NSW 2088, Australia. *Clubs:* Wig and Pen, United Oxford & Cambridge University, Les Ambassadeurs; Naval and Military (Melbourne), Melbourne CC; Elenora Golf, Sydney CC; Hon. Company of Edinburgh Golfers (Muirfield).

ROSSLYN, 7th Earl of, *cr* 1801; **Peter St Clair-Erskine;** Bt 1666; Baron Loughborough, 1795; *b* 31 March 1958; *s* of 6th Earl of Rosslyn, and of Athenais de Mortemart, *o d* of late Duc de Vivonne; *S* father, 1977; *m* 1982, Helen, *e d* of Mr and Mrs C. R. Watters, Christ's Hospital, Sussex; one *s*. *Educ:* Eton; Bristol Univ. Metropolitan Police, 1980–. Trustee, Dunimarle Museum. *Recreations:* opera, church music, piano. *Heir: s* Lord Loughborough, *qv*. *Address:* 30 Trigon Road, SW8. *Club:* White's.

ROSSMORE, 7th Baron, *cr* 1796; **William Warner Westenra;** *b* 14 Feb. 1931; *o s* of 6th Baron and Dolores Cecil (*d* 1981), *d* of late Lieut-Col James Alban Wilson, DSO, West Burton, Yorks; *S* father, 1958; *m* 1982, Valerie Marion, *d* of Brian Tobin; one *s*. *Educ:* Eton; Trinity Coll., Cambridge (BA). 2nd Lieut, Somerset LI. Co-founder, Coolemine Therapeutic Community, Dublin. *Recreations:* drawing, painting. *Heir: s* Hon. Benedict William Westenra, *b* 6 March 1983. *Address:* Rossmore Park, Co. Monaghan, Eire. *T:* Monaghan 81947.

ROST, Peter Lewis; MP (C) Erewash, since 1983 (Derbyshire South-East, 1970–83); *b* 19 Sept. 1930; *s* of Frederick Rosenstiel and Elisabeth Merz; *m* 1961, Hilary Mayo; two *s* two *d*. *Educ:* various primary schs; Aylesbury Grammar Sch. National Service, RAF, 1948–50; Birmingham Univ. (BA Hons Geog.), 1950–53. Investment Analyst and Financial Journalist with Investors Chronicle, 1953–58; firstly Investment Advisor, 1958, and then, 1962, Mem. London Stock Exchange, resigned 1977. Secretary: Cons. Parly Trade and Industry Cttee, 1972–73; Cons. Parly Energy Cttee, 1974–77; Select Cttee on Energy, 1979. Treasurer, Anglo-German Parly Gp, 1974–. FRGS (Mem. Council, 1980–83). Grand Cross, Order of Merit, Germany, 1979. *Recreations:* tennis, ski-ing, gardening, antique map collecting. *Address:* Norcott Court, Berkhamsted, Herts. *T:* Berkhamsted 6123.

ROSTAL, Professor Max, CBE 1977; Professor at the Guildhall School of Music, London, 1944–58; Professor of the Master-Class, State Academy of Music, Cologne, since 1957; Professor of the Master-Class, Conservatoire, Berne, Switzerland, since 1958; *b* 7 Aug. 1905; *m*; two *d*; *m* 1980, Maria Busato. *Educ:* State Acad., Vienna (Prof. Rosé); State Academy, Berlin (Prof. Flesch). Concert artist since age of 6; gave concerts in all parts of the world; at age of 23 Assistant to Prof. Flesch; Professor at State Academy of Music, Berlin, 1928–33. Lived in London, 1934–58; now residing in Switzerland. Has made various recordings for HMV, Decca, Argo, Concert Hall Soc., and Deutsche Grammophon Companies. FGSM 1945. Hon. RAM 1981. Silver Medal, State Acad. of Music, Cologne, 1965; Music Award, City of Berne, Switzerland, 1972. Bundesverdienstkreuz 1st Class, 1968, Grand Cross of Merit, 1981, German Federal Govt; Commendatore della Repubblica Italiana, 1984. *Publications:* Thoughts on the interpretation of Beethoven's Violin Sonatas, 1981; many compositions, transcriptions, arrangements, editions. *Recreations:* motoring, photography, reading. *Address:* Frikartweg 4, CH-3006 Berne, Switzerland. *T:* (0)31–431101; CH-3084, Gunten, Lake of Thun, Switzerland. *T:* (0)33–511867.

ROSTEN, Leo C., (pseudonym: **Leonard Q. Ross);** author and social scientist; *b* 11 April 1908; *s* of Samuel C. and Ida F. Rosten; *m* 1st, 1935, Priscilla Ann Mead (decd); one *s* two *d*; 2nd, 1960, Gertrude Zimmerman. *Educ:* University of Chicago (PhD); London School of Economics (Hon. Fellow, 1975). Research Assistant, Political Science Dept, Univ. of Chicago, 1933–35; Fellow, Social Science Research Council, 1934–36; Grants from Rockefeller Foundation and Carnegie Corporation, 1938–40. Dir, Motion Picture Research Project, 1939–41. Spec. Consultant, Nat. Defense Advisory Commn, Washington, 1939; Chief, Motion Picture Div., Office of Facts and Figures, Washington, 1941–42; Dep. Dir, Office of War Information, Washington, 1942–45; Special Consultant, Sec. of War, Washington, 1945; special mission to France, Germany, England, 1945. Faculty Associate, Columbia Univ., 1953–; Lectr in Political Science, Yale Univ., 1955, New School for Social Research, NY, 1959. Ford Vis. Prof. in Pol. Sci., Univ. of California (Berkeley), USA, 1960–61. Wrote film screenplays: Sleep, My Love; The Velvet Touch; Walk East on Beacon; The Dark Corner, etc. Member: Amer. Acad. of Political and Social Science; Amer. Assoc. for Advancement of Science; Nat. Acad. of Lit. and the Arts; Authors League of America; Authors Guild of America; Educnl Policies Cttee of Nat. Educnl Assoc. Phi Beta Kappa, 1929; Freedom Foundation's Award, 1955; George Polk Meml Award, 1955; Distinguished Alumnus Award, Univ. of Chicago, 1970. Hon. DHL: Univ. of Rochester, 1973; Hebrew Union Theol Coll., 1980. *Publications:* The Education of H*y*m*a*n K*a*p*l*a*n, 1937; The Washington Correspondents, 1937; The Strangest Places, 1939; Hollywood: The Movie Colony, The Movie Makers, 1941; The Dark Corner, 1945; (ed) Guide To The Religions of America, 1957; The Return of H*y*m*a*n K*a*p*l*a*n, 1959; Captain Newman, MD, 1961; The Story Behind the Painting, 1961; The Many Worlds of Leo Rosten; The Leo Rosten Bedside Book, 1965; A Most Private Intrigue, 1967; The Joys of Yiddish, 1968; A Trumpet for Reason, 1970; People I have Loved, Known or Admired, 1970; Rome Wasn't Burned in a Day, 1971; Leo Rosten's Treasury of Jewish Quotations, 1973; Dear "Herm", 1974; (ed) The Look Book, 1975; The 3.10 to Anywhere, 1976; O Kaplan! My Kaplan!, 1976; The Power of Positive Nonsense, 1977; Passions and Prejudices, 1978; (ed) Infinite Riches: Gems from a Lifetime of Reading, 1979; Silky!, 1979; King Silky!, 1980; Hooray for Yiddish!, 1983; Leo Rosten's Giant Book of Laughter, 1985; contrib. learned journals. *Recreations:* photography, travel. *Address:* 36 Sutton Place South, NY 10022, USA. *Clubs:* Savile, Reform, Garrick (London); Cosmos (Washington); Chaos (New York).

ROSTOW, Prof. Eugene Victor; Sterling Professor of Law, Yale University, 1938–84, now Emeritus; Distinguished Visiting Research Professor of Law and Diplomacy, National Defense University, Washington, since 1984; *b* 25 Aug. 1913; *s* of Victor A. and Lillian H. Rostow; *m* 1933, Edna B. Greenberg; two *s* one *d*. *Educ:* Yale Coll.; King's Coll., Cambridge (LLD 1962); Yale Law Sch. Practised law, New York, 1937–38; Yale Law Faculty, 1938–; Prof. of Law, 1944–84; Dean of Law Sch., 1955–65. Asst to Asst Sec. of State Acheson, 1942–44; Asst to Exec. Sec., Econ. Commn for Europe, UN, Geneva, 1949–50; Under-Sec. of State for Political Affairs, 1966–69. Dir, Arms Control and Disarmament Agency, 1981–83. Pres., Atlantic Treaty Assoc., 1973–76. Pitt Prof., Cambridge, 1959–60; Eastman Prof., Oxford, 1970–71. Dir, American Jewish Cttee, 1972–74; Chm. Exec. Cttee, Cttee on the Present Danger (Washington), 1976–81. Hon. LLD Boston, 1976. Chevalier, Legion of Honour (France), 1960; Grand Cross, Order of the Crown (Belgium), 1969. *Publications:* A National Policy for the Oil Industry, 1948; Planning for Freedom, 1959; The Sovereign Prerogative, 1962; Law, Power and the Pursuit of Peace, 1968; (ed) Is Law Dead?, 1971; Peace in the Balance, 1972; The Ideal in Law, 1978; contribs to legal and economic jls. *Address:* 208 St Ronan Street, New Haven, Conn 06511, USA. *T:* 203–776–3906; Peru, Vermont 05152, USA. *T:* 802–824–6627; National Defense University, Ft L. J. McNair, Washington, DC 20319–6000, USA. *Clubs:* Century (New York); Elizabethan, Lawn (New Haven); Cosmos (Washington).

See also W. W. Rostow.

ROSTOW, Walt Whitman; Professor of Economics and of History, University of Texas at Austin, Texas, since 1969; *b* 7 Oct. 1916; 2nd *s* of Victor and Lillian Rostow; *m* 1947, Elspeth, *o d* of Milton J. and Harriet Vaughan Davies; one *s* one *d*. *Educ:* Yale (BA 1936; PhD 1940); Oxford (Rhodes Scholar). Social Science Research Council Fellow, 1939–40; Instructor, Columbia Univ., 1940–41; Office Strategic Services, 1941–45 (Army of the United States, 1943–45, Major; Legion of Merit; Hon. OBE); Assistant Chief Division German-Austrian Economic Affairs, Department of State, 1945–46; Harmsworth Professor American History, Oxford, 1946–47; Special Assistant to Executive Secretary, Economic Commission for Europe, 1947–49; Pitt Professor of American History, Cambridge, 1949–50; Professor of Economic History, Massachusetts Institute of Technology, 1950–61. Deputy Special Assistant to the President (USA) for National Security Affairs, Jan. 1961–Dec. 1961; Counselor and Chairman, Policy Planning Council, Department of State, 1961–66; US Mem., Inter-Amer. Cttee on Alliance for Progress, 1964–66; Special Assistant to the President, The White House, 1966–69. Member: Royal Economic Society, England; American Academy of Arts and Sciences, 1957; Amer. Philos. Soc.; Massachusetts Historical Soc. Hon. LLD: Carnegie Inst. of Tech., Pittsburgh, 1962; Univ. Miami, 1965; Univ. Notre Dame, 1966; Middlebury Coll., 1967; Jacksonville Univ., 1974. Presidential Medal of Freedom, with distinction, 1969. *Publications:* The American Diplomatic Revolution, 1947; Essays on the British Economy of the Nineteenth Century, 1948; The Process of Economic Growth, 1952; (with A. D. Gayer and A. J. Schwartz) The Growth and Fluctuation of the British Economy,

1790–1850, 1953, new edn 1975; (with A. Levin and others) The Dynamics of Soviet Society, 1953; (with others) The Prospects for Communist China, 1954; (with R. W. Hatch) An American Policy in Asia, 1955; (with M. F. Millikan) A Proposal: Key to An Effective Foreign Policy, 1957; The Stages of Economic Growth, 1960, 2nd edn 1971; The United States in the World Arena, 1960; The Economics of Take-off into Sustained Growth (ed), 1963; View from the Seventh Floor, 1964; A Design for Asian Development, 1965; Politics and the Stages of Growth, 1971; The Diffusion of Power, 1972; How It All Began: origins of the modern economy, 1975; The World Economy: history and prospect, 1978; Getting from Here to There, 1978; Why the Poor Get Richer and the Rich Slow Down, 1980; Pre-Invasion Bombing Strategy: General Eisenhower's Decision of March 25, 1944, 1981; The Division of Europe after World War II: 1946, 1981; British Trade Fluctuations 1868–1896: a chronicle and a commentary, 1981; Europe after Stalin: Eisenhower's Three Decisions of March 11, 1953, 1982; Open Skies: Eisenhower's proposal of July 21, 1955, 1982; The Barbaric Counter-Revolution, 1983; Eisenhower, Kennedy and Foreign Aid, 1985; The United States and the Regional Organization of Asia and the Pacific 1965–85, 1985; various articles contributed to: The Economist, Economic Journal, Economic History Review, Journal of Econ. History, American Econ. Review, etc. *Address:* 1 Wild Wind Point, Austin, Texas 78746, USA. *Clubs:* Elizabethan (New Haven, Conn, USA); Cosmos (Washington, DC).

See also E. V. Rostow.

ROSTRON, Sir Frank, Kt 1967; MBE 1954; FIEE; Director, Ferranti Ltd, Hollinwood, Lancs, 1958–68; *b* 11 Sept. 1900; *s* of late Samuel Ernest and Martha Rostron, Oldham; *m* 1929, Helen Jodrell Owen (*d* 1984); one *s* one *d*. *Educ:* Oldham High Sch.; Manchester Coll. of Tech. Ferranti Ltd, 1917–68. Served War of 1939–45: Electrical Engineer Officer, RAF; released with rank of Squadron Leader. President, Manchester Chamber of Commerce, 1956 and 1957. Director: National and Vulcan Boiler and General Insurance Co. Ltd, 1961–70; Aron Meters Ltd, 1961–68; McKechnie Brothers Ltd, 1966–71. Chairman: Cotton Board, 1963–67 (Independent Member, 1959); Cotton and Allied Textiles Industry Training Board, 1966–67; Textile Council, 1967–68. *Address:* 344 Varsity Close, NW, Calgary, Alberta T3B 2Z1, Canada.

ROSTROPOVICH, Mstislav; 'cellist; Music Director and Conductor, National Symphony Orchestra, Washington, since 1977; *b* 1927; *m* Galina Vishnevskaya, *qv*; two *d*. *Educ:* State Conservatoire, Moscow. Has played in many concerts in Russia and abroad from 1942; first performance of Shostakovich's 'cello concerto (dedicated to him), Edinburgh Festival, 1960. Series of concerts with London Symphony Orchestra under Gennadi Rozhdestvensky, Festival Hall, 1965 (Gold Medal); first perf. Britten's third cello suite, Aldeburgh, 1974. An Artistic Dir, Aldeburgh Festival, 1977–. Mem. Union of Soviet Composers, 1950–78. Lenin Prize, 1964. Holds 23 honorary degrees including Hon. MusD: St Andrews, 1968; Cambridge, 1975; Harvard, 1976; Yale, 1976; Oxon, 1980. Officier de la Légion d'Honneur (France), 1981. *Address:* c/o National Symphony Orchestra, J. F. Kennedy Center for the Performing Arts, Washington, DC 20566, USA.

ROTBLAT, Prof. Joseph, CBE 1965; MA, DSc (Warsaw); PhD (Liverpool); DSc (London); FInstP; Professor of Physics in the University of London, at St Bartholomew's Hospital Medical College, 1950–76, now Emeritus; Physicist to St Bartholomew's Hospital, 1950–76; *b* 4 Nov. 1908; *e s* of late Z. Rotblat, Warsaw. *Educ:* University of Warsaw, Poland. Research Fellow of Radiological Laboratory of Scientific Society of Warsaw, 1933–39; Asst Director of Atomic Physics Institute of Free Univ. of Poland, 1937–39; Oliver Lodge Fellow of Univ. of Liverpool, 1939–40; Lecturer and afterwards Senior Lecturer in Dept of Physics, Liverpool Univ., 1940–49; Director of Research in nuclear physics at Liverpool Univ., 1945–49; work on atomic energy at Liverpool Univ. and Los Alamos, New Mexico. Treasurer, St Bartholomew's Hosp. Med. Coll., 1974–76; Vice-Dean, Faculty of Sci., London Univ., 1974–76. Mem., Advy. Cttee on Med. Res., WHO, 1972–75; Mem., WHO Management Gp, 1984–. Ed., Physics in Medicine and Biol., 1960–72. Sec.-Gen., Pugwash Confs on Science and World Affairs, 1957–73; Chm., British Pugwash, 1978–. Pres., Hosp. Physicists' Assoc, 1969–70; Pres., British Inst. of Radiology, 1971–72. Mem. Governing Body of Stockholm Internat. Peace Res. Inst., 1966–71. Pres., Internat. Youth Sci. Fortnight, 1972–74. Vis. Prof. of Internat. Relations, Univ. of Edinburgh, 1975–76. Member, Polish Academy of Sciences, 1966; Hon. For. Mem., Amer. Acad. of Arts and Sciences, 1972. Hon. Fellow, UMIST, 1985. Hon. DSc Bradford, 1973. Bertrand Russell Soc. Award, 1983. *Publications:* Progress in Nuclear Physics, 1950; (with Chadwick) Radio-activity and Radioactive Substances, 1953; Atomic Energy, a Survey, 1954; Atoms and the Universe, 1956; Science and World Affairs, 1962; Aspects of Medical Physics, 1966; Pugwash, the First Ten Years, 1967; Scientists in the Quest for Peace, 1972; Nuclear Reactors: to breed or not to breed, 1977; Nuclear Energy and Nuclear Weapon Proliferation, 1979; Nuclear Radiation in Warfare, 1981; Scientists, The Arms Race and Disarmament, 1982; The Arms Race at a Time of Decision, 1984; Nuclear Strategy and World Security, 1985; World Peace and the Developing Countries, 1986; Strategic Defence and the Future of the Arms Race, 1986; papers on nuclear physics and radiation biology in Proceedings of Royal Society, Radiation Research, Nature, etc. *Recreations:* recorded music, travel. *Address:* 8 Asmara Road, West Hampstead, NW2 3ST. *T:* 01–435 1471. *Club:* Athenæum.

ROTH, Andrew; Political Correspondent, New Statesman, since 1984; Director, Parliamentary Profiles, since 1955; *b* NY, 23 April 1919; *s* of Emil and Bertha Roth; *m* 1949, Mathilda Anna Friederich (marr. diss. 1984); one *s* one *d*. *Educ:* City Coll. of NY (BSS); Columbia Univ. (MA); Harvard Univ. Reader, City Coll., 1939; Res. Associate, Inst. of Pacific Relations, 1940; US Naval Intell., 1941–45 (Lieut, SG); Editorial Writer, The Nation, 1945–46; Foreign Corresp., Toronto Star Weekly, 1946–50; London Corresp., France Observateur, Sekai, Singapore Standard, 1950–60; Political Corresp., Manchester Evening News, 1972–84. *Publications:* Japan Strikes South, 1941; French Interests and Policies in the Far East, 1942; Dilemma in Japan, 1945 (UK 1946); The Business Background of MPs, 1959, 7th edn 1980; The MPs' Chart, 1967, 5th edn 1979; Enoch Powell: Tory Tribune, 1970; Can Parliament Decide . . ., 1971; Heath and the Heathmen, 1972; Lord on the Board, 1972; The Prime Ministers, Vol. II (Heath chapter), 1975; Sir Harold Wilson: Yorkshire Walter Mitty, 1977; Parliamentary Profiles, Vols I–IV, 1984–85. *Recreations:* tennis, sketching, jazz-dancing. *Address:* 34 Somali Road, NW2 3RL. *T:* 01–435 6673; 2 Queen Anne's Gate Buildings, Dartmouth Street, SW1H 9BP. *T:* 01–222 5884/9.

ROTH, Prof. Klaus Friedrich, FRS 1960; Professor of Pure Mathematics (Theory of Numbers) at Imperial College of Science and Technology, since 1966; *b* 29 Oct. 1925; *s* of late Dr Franz Roth and Mathilde Roth (*née* Liebrecht); *m* 1955, Melek Khairy, BSc, PhD. *Educ:* St Paul's Sch.; Peterhouse, Cambridge; Univ. College, London (Fellow, 1979). BA (Cambridge, 1945); MSc, PhD (London, 1948, 1950). Asst Master, Gordonstoun School, 1945–46. Member of Dept of Mathematics, University College, London, 1948–66; title of Professor in the University of London conferred 1961. Visiting Lecturer, 1956–57, Vis. Prof., 1965–66, at Mass Inst. of Techn., USA. Foreign Hon. Mem., Amer. Acad. of Arts and Scis, 1966. Fields Medal awarded at International Congress of Mathematicians, 1958; De Morgan Medal, London Math. Soc., 1983. *Publications:* papers in various mathematical jls. *Recreations:* chess, cinema, ballroom dancing. *Address:* Department of Mathematics, Imperial College, Queen's Gate, SW7 5HH; 24 Burnsall Street, SW3 3ST. *T:* 01–352 1363.

ROTH, Prof. Sir Martin, Kt 1972; MD; FRCP; FRCPsych; DPM; Professor of Psychiatry, University of Cambridge, since March 1977; Fellow, Trinity College, Cambridge, since 1977; *b* 6 Nov. 1917; *s* of late Samuel Simon and Regina Roth; *m* 1945, Constance Heller; three *d*. *Educ:* University of London, St Mary's Hospital. FRCP 1958. MA Cantab; MD Cantab 1984. Formerly: Senior Registrar, Maida Vale, and Maudsley Hosps; Physician, Crichton Royal Hosp., Dumfries; Director of Clinical Research, Graylingwell Hosp.; Prof. of Psychological Medicine, Univ. of Newcastle upon Tyne, 1956–77. Visiting Assistant Professor, in the Department of Psychiatry, McGill University, Montreal, 1954; Consultant, WHO Expert Cttee on Mental Health Problems of Ageing and the Aged, 1958; Member: Med. Cons. Cttee, Nuffield Provincial Hosp. Trust, 1962; Central Health Services Council, Standing Med. Adv. Cttee, Standing Mental Health Adv. Cttee, DHSS, 1966–75; Scientific Adv. Cttee, CIBA Foundn, 1970–; Syndic of Cambridge Univ. Press, 1980–. Mayne Vis. Prof., Univ. of Queensland, 1968; Albert Sterne Vis. Prof., Univ. of Indiana, 1976; first Andrew Woods Vis. Prof., Univ. of Iowa, 1976. Adolf Meyer Lectr, Amer. Psychiatric Assoc., 1971; Linacre Lectr, St John's Coll., Cambridge, 1984. Pres., Section of Psychiatry, RSM, 1968–69; Member: MRC, 1964–68; Clinical Research Board, MRC, 1964–70; Hon. Dir, MRC Group for study of relationship between functional and organic mental disorders, 1962–67. FRCPsych (Foundn Fellow; Pres., 1971–75; Hon. Fellow, 1975); Distinguished Fellow, Amer. Psychiatric Assoc., 1972; Hon. FRCPSGlas. Corresp. Mem., Deutsche Gesellschaft für Psychiatrie und Nervenheilkunde; Hon. Mem., Société Royale de Médecine Mentale de Belgique. Hon. Fellow: Amer. Coll. Neuropsychopharmacology; Australian and New Zealand College of Psychiatry; Canadian Psychiatric Assoc., 1972. Hon. ScD TCD, 1977. Burlingame Prize, Royal Medico Psychol Assoc., 1951; First Prize, Anna Monika Foundn, 1977; Paul Hoch Prize, Amer. Psychopathological Assoc., 1979; Gold Florin, City of Florence, 1979; Gold Medal, Soc. of Biological Psychiatry, 1980; Kesten Prize, Univ. of Southern Calif, 1983; Sandoz Prize, Internat. Assoc. of Gerontology, 1985. Co-Editor, British Jl of Psychiatry, 1967; Editor, Psychiatric Developments, 1983–. *Publications:* (with Mayer-Gross and Slater) Clinical Psychiatry, 1954, (with Slater) rev. 3rd edn 1977; Studies in the Classification of Affective Disorders, 1977; papers on psychiatric aspects of ageing, depressive illness, anxiety states, in various psychiatric and medical journals. *Recreations:* music, literature, conversation, travel. *Address:* Department of Psychiatry, New Addenbrooke's Hospital, University of Cambridge, Hills Road, Cambridge CB2 2QQ. *Club:* Athenæum.

ROTHENSTEIN, Sir John (Knewstub Maurice), Kt 1952; CBE 1948; KCStG 1977; PhD (London 1931); Hon. LLD (New Brunswick 1961; St Andrews 1964); writer; Director of the Tate Gallery, 1938–64; Hon. Fellow: Worcester College, Oxford, 1963; University College London, 1976; Member: Architectural and Art Advisory Committee, Westminster Cathedral, since 1979 (of Advisory Committee on Decoration, 1953–79); Council, Friends of the Tate Gallery, since 1958; President: Friends of the Bradford City Art Gallery and Museums, since 1973; Friends of the Stanley Spencer Gallery, Cookham, since 1981; *b* London, 11 July 1901; *er s* of Sir William Rothenstein and Alice Mary, *e c* of Walter John Knewstub, of Chelsea; *m* 1929, Elizabeth Kennard Whittington, 2nd *d* of Charles Judson Smith, of Lexington, Kentucky; one *d*. *Educ:* Bedales School; Worcester College, Oxford (MA); University College, London (PhD). Assistant Professor: of Art History in the University of Kentucky, 1927–28; Department of Fine Arts, University of Pittsburgh, 1928–29; Director: City Art Gallery, Leeds, 1932–34; City Art Galleries and Ruskin Museum, Sheffield, 1933–38; Member: Executive Committee, Contemporary Art Society, 1938–65; British Council, 1938–64; Art Panel, Arts Council of Great Britain, 1943–56. Rector, University of St Andrews, 1964–67. Visiting Professor: Dept of Fine Arts, Fordham Univ., USA, 1967–68; of History of Art, Agnes Scott Coll., Ga, USA, 1969–70; Distinguished Prof., City Univ. of NY, at Brooklyn Coll., 1971, 1972; Regents' Lectr, Univ. of Calif at Irvine, 1973. Pres., Friends of the Stanley Spencer Gall., 1980–. Editor, The Masters, 1965–67; Hon. Editor, Museums Jl, 1959–61. Knight Commander, Mexican Order of the Aztec Eagle, 1953. *Publications:* The Portrait Drawings of William Rothenstein, 1889–1925, 1926; Eric Gill, 1927; The Artists of the 1890's, 1928; Morning Sorrow: a novel, 1930; British Artists and the War, 1931; Nineteenth Century Painting, 1932; An Introduction to English Painting, 1933; The Life and Death of Conder, 1938; Augustus John (Phaidon British Artists), 1944; Edward Burra (Penguin Modern Painters), 1945; Manet, 1945; Modern Foreign Pictures in the Tate Gallery, 1949; Turner, 1949; London's River, 1951 (with Father Vincent Turner, SJ); Modern English Painters, vol. I, Sickert to Smith, 1952, vol. II, Lewis to Moore, 1956, vol. III, Wood to Hockney, 1973, new enl. edn, as Modern English Painters: Sickert to Hockney, 1984; The Tate Gallery, 1958 (new edn 1962); Turner, 1960; British Art since 1900: an Anthology, 1962; Sickert, 1961; Paul Nash, 1961; Augustus John, 1962; Matthew Smith, 1962; Turner (with Martin Butlin), 1963; Francis Bacon (with Ronald Alley), 1964; Edward Burra, 1973; Victor Hammer: artist and craftsman, 1978; (ed) Sixteen Letters from Oscar Wilde, 1930; (ed) Stanley Spencer the Man: Correspondence and Reminiscences, 1979; John Nash, 1984; *autobiography:* Summer's Lease (I), 1965; Brave Day, Hideous Night (II), 1966; Time's Thievish Progress (III), 1970; contribs to DNB. *Television:* Churchill the Painter, COI, 1968; Collection and Recollection, BBC, 1968. *Address:* Beauforest House, Newington, Dorchester-on-Thames, Oxon OX9 8AG. *Clubs:* Athenæum (Hon. Mem.), Chelsea Arts (Hon. Mem.).

See also Baron Dynevor.

ROTHENSTEIN, Michael, RA 1983 (ARA 1977); Hon. RE; Painter and print-maker; *b* 1908; *yr s* of late Sir William Rothenstein; *m* 1936, Betty Desmond Fitz-Gerald (marr. diss., 1957); one *s* one *d*; *m* 1958, Diana, 2nd *d* of late Comdr H. C. Arnold-Forster, CMG. Retrospective exhibitions: Kunstnernes Hus, Oslo, 1969; Bradford Art Gallery, 1972; ICA, 1974. Works acquired by: Museum of Modern Art and Brooklyn Museum, New York; Tate Gallery; British Museum; Victoria and Albert Museum; Library of Congress, Washington; British Council; Arts Council; museums of: Sydney; Victoria; Dallas; Boston; Cincinnati; Lugano; etc. Exhibited: Cincinnati Biennial, 1954, 1960; Ljubljana Biennial of Graphic Art, 1957, 1961, 1963; Albertina, Vienna (Prints), 1963; Internat. Triennale, Grechen, 1961, 1964, 1967; 8th Internat. Exhibition, Lugano; 4th Internat. Print Exhibn, Tokyo, 1966; Internat. Print Biennale, Cracow, 1970–78; retrospective exhibn, Norway, 1980. Trust House Award, 1963; Gold Medal, first internat. Engraving Biennale, Buenos Aires; Prix d'Achat, Cracow Internat. Print Biennale, 1974; Grand Prix, Norwegian Internat. Print Biennale, 1976. *Publications:* Frontiers of Printmaking, 1966; Relief Printing, 1970; Suns and Moons, 1972; Seven Colours (with Edward Lucie Smith), 1975; Song of Songs (folio), 1979. *Address:* Columbia House, Stisted, Braintree, Essex. *T:* Braintree 25444.

ROTHERHAM, Air Vice-Marshal John Kevitt, CB 1962; CBE 1960; Director-General (Engineering), RAF, 1967–69; retired; *b* 28 Dec. 1910; *s* of Colonel Ewan Rotherham; *m* 1st, 1936, Joan Catherine Penrose (*d* 1940); one *d*; 2nd, 1941, Margot Susan Hayter. *Educ:* Uppingham; Exeter College, Oxford. Joined RAF with Univ. perm.

commn, 1933; 17 (F) Sqdn, 1934; 605 (B) Sqdn, 1936; School of Aeronautical Engineering, Henlow, 1936; post-grad. course, Imperial Coll., 1938; 43 (M) Group, 1939; Kidbrooke, 1940; MAP 1941; 41 (M) Group, 1942; HQ Flying Training Comd, 1946; exchange posting with USAF, 1947; Air Ministry, 1948; Joint Services Staff Coll., 1951; No 205 Group, Middle East, 1952; Air Ministry, 1954; seconded to Pakistan Air Force, 1957; Senior Technical Staff Officer, Transport Command, RAF, 1960–63; AOC No 24 (Training) Group, Technical Training Command, RAF, 1963–65; Senior Tech. Staff Officer, Bomber Command, 1965–67. AFRAeS 1949, FRAeS 1967. *Recreations:* sailing, fishing. *Address:* South Meadow, Shore Road, Old Bosham, Chichester, Sussex PO18 8QL. *T:* Bosham 573346. *Clubs:* Royal Air Force; Bosham Sailing.
See also R. J. S. McDowall.

ROTHERHAM, Leonard, CBE 1970; DSc; FRS 1963; FEng, FIEE, SFInstE, FIM, FInstP; Hon. Professor, Bath University, since 1985 (Vice-Chancellor, 1969–76); *b* 31 Aug. 1913; *m* 1937, Nora Mary Thompson; one *s* two *d.* *Educ:* Strutt School, Belper; University College, London. Physicist, Brown Firth Research Laboratories, 1935–46; Head of Metallurgy Dept, RAE Farnborough, 1946–50; Dir, R&D, UKAEA, Industrial Group, Risley, 1950–58. Mem. for Research, Central Electricity Generating Bd, 1958–69; Head of Research, Electricity Supply Industry and Electricity Council, 1965–69. Chm., Adv. Cttee for Scientific and Technical Information, 1970–74. Member: Defence Scientific Adv. Council, 1967–77 (Chm., 1974–77); Central Adv. Council for Science and Technology, 1968–70; Adv. Council for Energy Conservation, 1974–79; Adv. Council for Applied R&D, 1976–81. Governor, Imperial Coll., 1977–. Hon. LLD Bristol, 1972; Hon. DSc Bath, 1976. Fellow UCL, 1959; Hon. Fellow, Inst. of Welding, 1965; Hon. Life Mem., American Society of Mechanical Engineers, 1963; President, Instn of Metallurgists, 1964; Inst. of Metals, 1965; Member of Council, Royal Society, 1965–66. Founder Fellow, Fellowship of Engineering, 1976 (Mem. Exec. Council, 1978–80). *Publications:* Creep of Metals, 1951; Research and Innovation, 1984; various scientific and technical papers; also lectures: Hatfield Memorial, 1961; Coal Science, 1961; Calvin Rice (of Amer. Soc. of Mech. Engrs), 1963; 2nd Metallurgical Engineering, Inst. of Metals, 1963. *Address:* Westhanger, Horningsham, Warminster, Wilts. *Club:* Athenæum.

ROTHERMERE, 3rd Viscount *cr* 1919, of Hemsted; **Vere Harold Esmond Harmsworth;** Bt 1910; Baron 1914; Chairman: Associated Newspapers Group Ltd, since 1971; Daily Mail and General Trust Ltd, since 1978; Evening Standrd Co. Ltd, since 1985; *b* 27 Aug. 1925; *s* of 2nd Viscount Rothermere and of Margaret Hunam, *d* of late William Redhead; *S* father, 1978; *m* 1957, Mrs Patricia Evelyn Beverley Brooks, *d* of John William Matthews, FIAS; one *s* two *d* (and one step *d*). *Educ:* Eton; Kent Sch., Conn, USA. With Anglo Canadian Paper Mills, Quebec, 1948–50; Associated Newspapers Ltd, 1951–; launched: New Daily Mail, 1971; Mail on Sunday, 1982. Trustee, Reuters; Director, Consolidated Bathurst (Canada). Pres., Commonwealth Press Union, 1983– (Chm., UK Section, 1976); Trustee, Vis-News; Pres., London Press Club, 1976–81; Patron, London Sch. of Journalism, 1980–. FRSA, FBIM. Commander: Order of Merit (Italy); Order of Lion (Finland). *Recreations:* painting, sailing, reading. *Heir:* *s* Hon. Harold Jonathan Esmond Vere Harmsworth, *b* 3 Dec. 1967. *Address:* New Carmelite House, Carmelite Street, EC4. *Clubs:* Boodle's, Beefsteak; Royal Yacht Squadron; Brook (New York City); Travellers' (Paris).
See also Lord Ogilvy.

ROTHERWICK, 2nd Baron *cr* 1939; **Herbert Robin Cayzer;** Bt 1924; *b* 5 Dec. 1912; *s* of 1st Baron Rotherwick; *S* father 1958; *m* 1952, Sarah-Jane (*d* 1978), *o d* of Sir Michael Nial Slade, 6th Bt; three *s* one *d.* *Educ:* Eton; Christ Church, Oxford (BA). Supplementary Reserve Royal Scots Greys, 1938; served War of 1939–45 with them in Middle East. Deputy Chairman British & Commonwealth Shipping Co. Ltd, and Director of other and associated companies. *Heir:* *s* Hon. (Herbert) Robin Cayzer, Lt Life Guards (T&AVR) [*b* 12 March 1954; *m* 1982, Sara, *o d* of R. J. McAlpine, Swettenham Hall, Cheshire; one *d*]. *Address:* Cornbury Park, Charlbury, Oxfordshire. *T:* Charlbury 311; 44 Chelsea Square, SW3. *Club:* White's.

ROTHES, 21st Earl of, *cr* before 1457; **Ian Lionel Malcolm Leslie;** Lord Leslie 1445; Baron Ballenbreich 1457; *b* 10 May 1932; *o s* of 20th Earl of Rothes and of Beryl, *o d* of J. Lionel Dugdale; *S* father, 1975; *m* 1955, Marigold, *o d* of Sir David M. Evans Bevan, 1st Bt; two *s.* *Educ:* Eton. Sub-Lt RNVR, 1953. *Heir:* *s* Lord Leslie, *qv.* *Address:* Tanglewood, West Tytherley, Salisbury, Wilts.

ROTHMAN, Sydney; Chairman of Rothmans Tobacco (Holdings) Ltd, 1953–79 (Chairman and Managing Director, Rothmans Ltd, 1929–53); *b* 2 December 1897; *s* of Louis and Jane Rothman; *m* 1929, Jeannette Tropp; one *s* one *d.* *Educ:* Highgate School. Joined L. Rothman & Company, 1919, Partner, 1923, Rothmans Ltd. Ministry of Supply, 1941–45. *Recreation:* golf. *Address:* Barclays Bank, Box 8, St Helier, Jersey.

ROTHNIE, Sir Alan (Keir), KCVO 1980; CMG 1967; HM Diplomatic Service, retired; Director, Overseas Technical Service International Ltd, since 1980; *b* 2 May 1920; *s* of late John and Dora Rothnie, Aberdeen; *m* 1953, Anne Cadogan Harris, *d* of Euan Cadogan Harris, *qv*; two *s* one *d.* *Educ:* Montrose Acad.; St Andrews University. Served RNVR, 1939–45. Entered Diplomatic Service, Nov. 1945; Foreign Office, 1945–46; 3rd Sec., HM Legation, Vienna, 1946–48; 2nd Sec., HM Embassy, Bangkok, 1949–50; FO 1951–53; 1st Sec. HM Embassy, Madrid, 1953–55; Asst Political Agent, Kuwait, 1956–58; FO, 1958–60; Middle East Centre for Arab Studies, Shemlan, 1960–62 (Chargé d'Affaires, HM Embassy, Kuwait, 1961); Commercial Counsellor: HM Embassy, Baghdad, 1963–64; HM Embassy, Moscow, 1965–68; Consul-Gen., Chicago, 1969–72; Ambassador to Saudi Arabia, 1972–76, to Switzerland, 1976–80. Mem. Panel of Conciliators, Internat. Centre for Settlement of Investment Disputes, 1980–. Hon. LLD St Andrews, 1981. *Recreations:* shooting, ski-ing. *Address:* Little Job's Cross, Rolvenden Layne, Kent TN17 4PP. *T:* Cranbrook 241350. *Clubs:* White's, MCC.

ROTHSCHILD, family name of **Baron Rothschild.**

ROTHSCHILD, 3rd Baron, *cr* 1885; **Nathaniel Mayer Victor Rothschild;** Bt 1847; GBE 1975; GM 1944; PhD; ScD; FRS 1953; Chairman, Rothschilds Continuation, since 1976; Director, N. M. Rothschild & Sons (Chairman, 1975–76); Chairman: Biotechnology Investments Ltd, since 1981; Rothschilds Continuation Holdings AG, since 1982; *b* 31 Oct. 1910; *s* of late Hon. (Nathaniel) Charles Rothschild, 2nd *s* of 1st Baron Rothschild; *S* uncle, 1937; *m* 1st, 1933, Barbara (marr. diss. 1945), *o d* of late Sir John Hutchinson, KC; one *s* two *d*; 2nd, 1946, Teresa, MBE, MA, JP, *d* of late R. J. G. Mayor, CB; one *s* two *d* (and one *s* decd). *Educ:* Harrow, Trinity Coll., Cambridge. Prize-Fellow of Trinity Coll., Cambridge, 1935–39, Hon. Fellow, 1961. War of 1939–45: Military Intelligence (despatches, American Legion of Merit, American Bronze Star). Director, BOAC, 1946–58; Chm., Agricultural Res. Council, 1948–58; Assistant Dir of Research, Dept of Zoology, Cambridge, 1950–70; Vice-Chm., Shell Research Ltd, 1961–63, Chm., 1963–70; Chm., Shell Research NV, 1967–70; Director: Shell Internationale Research Mij, 1965–70; Shell Chemicals UK Ltd, 1963–70; Shell International Gas, 1969–70; Research Co-ordinator, Royal Dutch Shell Group, 1965–70; Dir Gen. and First Perm. Under-Sec., Central Policy Review Staff, Cabinet Office, 1971–74. Chairman: Royal Commn on Gambling, 1976–78; Enquiry into SSRC, 1982; Member: BBC General Advisory Council, 1952–56; Council for Scientific Policy, 1965–67; Central Adv. Council for Science and Technology, 1969. 4th Royal Soc. Technol. Lect., 1970; Trueman Wood Lect., RSA, 1972; Dimbleby Lecture, 1978. FSS 1984; Hon. Fellow: Bellairs Research Inst. of McGill Univ., Barbados, 1960; Weizmann Inst. of Science, Rehovoth, 1962; Wolfson Coll., Cambridge, 1966; Inst. of Biol., 1971; Imperial Coll., 1975; RSE, 1986. Hon. DSc: Newcastle, 1964; Manchester, 1966; Technion, Haifa, 1968; City Univ., 1972; Bath, 1978; Hon. PhD: Tel Aviv, 1971; Hebrew Univ., Jerusalem, 1975; Bar-Ilan, Israel, 1980; Hon. LLD London, 1977; DUniv York, 1980. KStJ 1948. Melchett Medal, 1971; RSA Medal, 1972. *Publications:* The History of Tom Jones, a Changeling, 1951; The Rothschild Library, 1954, new edn, 1969; Fertilization, 1956; A Classification of Living Animals, 1961, 1965; A Framework for Government Research and Development, 1971; The Rothschild Family Tree, 1973, new edn 1981; Meditations of a Broomstick, 1977; N. M. Rothschild, 1977; 'You Have It, Madam', 1980; The Shadow of a Great Man, 1982; Random Variables, 1984; (with N. Logothetis) Probability Distributions, 1986; scientific papers. *Heir:* *s* Hon. (Nathaniel Charles) Jacob Rothschild, *qv.* *Club:* Pratt's.

ROTHSCHILD, Edmund Leopold de, TD; Director, N. M. Rothschild & Sons, since 1975 (Partner since 1946, Senior Partner, 1960–70, Chairman, 1970–75); Chairman: Straflo Ltd, since 1975; A. U. R. Hydropower Ltd, since 1980; *b* 2 Jan. 1916; *s* of late Lionel Nathan de Rothschild and Marie Louise Beer; *m* 1st, 1948, Elizabeth Edith Lentner (*d* 1980); two *s* two *d*; 2nd, 1982, Anne, JP, *widow* of J. Malcolm Harrison. *Educ:* Harrow Sch.; Trinity Coll., Cambridge. Major, RA (TA). Served France, North Africa and Italy, 1939–46 (wounded). Dep. Chairman: Brit. Newfoundland Corp. Ltd, 1963–69; Churchill Falls (Labrador) Corp. Ltd, 1966–69. Mem., Asia Cttee, BNEC, 1970–71, Chm., 1971. Trustee, Queen's Nursing Inst.; Mem. Council, Royal Nat. Pension Fund for Nurses; Pres., Assoc. of Jewish Ex-Servicemen and Women; Vice-Pres., Council of Christians and Jews. Governor, Tech. Univ. of Nova Scotia. Hon. LLD Memorial Univ. of Newfoundland, 1961; Hon. DSc Salford, 1983. Order of the Sacred Treasure, 1st Class (Japan), 1973. *Publication:* Window on the World, 1949. *Recreations:* gardening, fishing, shooting, cine-photography, hunting butterflies. *Address:* New Court, St Swithin's Lane, EC4P 4DU. *T:* 01–280 5000. *Clubs:* White's, Portland; Mount Royal (Montreal).
See also L. D. de Rothschild.

ROTHSCHILD, Evelyn de; Chairman, N. M. Rothschild & Sons Ltd; *b* 29 Aug. 1931; *s* of late Anthony Gustav de Rothschild; *m* 1973, Victoria Schott; two *s* one *d.* *Educ:* Harrow; Trinity Coll., Cambridge. Chairman: Economist Newspaper, 1972–; United Racecourses Ltd, 1977–. Chm., Accepting Houses Cttee, 1985–. *Recreations:* art, racing.

ROTHSCHILD, Baron Guy (Edouard Alphonse Paul) de; Officier de la Légion d'Honneur, 1959; Director: Centro Asegurador SA, Madrid; Rothschild Inc., New York; *b* 21 May 1909; *s* of late Baron Edouard de Rothschild and late Baronne de Rothschild (*née* Germaine Halphen); *m* 1st, 1937, Baronne Alix Schey de Koromla (marriage dissolved, 1956; she *d* 1982); one *s*; 2nd, 1957, Baronne Marie-Hélène de Zuylen de Nyevelt (who *m* 1st, Comte François de Nicolay); one *s* and one step *s.* *Educ:* Lycées Condorcet et Louis le Grand, Facultés de Droit et des Lettres (Licencié en Droit). Served War of 1939–45 (Croix de Guerre). Chevalier du Mérite Agricole, 1948. Associé de MM de Rothschild Frères, 1936–67; President: Compagnie du Chemin de Fer du Nord, 1949–68; Banque Rothschild, 1968–78; Société Imétal, 1975–79. Mem., Société d'Encouragement. *Publication:* The Whims of Fortune (autobiog.), 1985. *Recreation:* haras et écurie de courses, golf. *Address:* 131 East 66 Street, New York, NY 10021, USA. *Clubs:* Nouveau Cercle, Automobile Club de France, Cercle Interallié.

ROTHSCHILD, Hon. Jacob; *see* Rothschild, Hon. N. C. J.

ROTHSCHILD, Leopold David de, CBE 1985; Director, N. M. Rothschild & Sons Ltd, since 1970 (Partner, 1956–70); *b* 12 May 1927; *yr s* of Lionel de Rothschild and Marie Louise Beer. *Educ:* Bishops Coll. Sch., Canada; Harrow; Trinity Coll., Cambridge. Director of Bank of England, 1970–83. Chairman: Anglo Venezuelan Soc., 1975–78; English Chamber Orchestra and Music Soc. Ltd, 1963; Bach Choir, 1976; Vice Pres., Develt Fund, RCM, 1984– (Chm., Centenary Appeal, 1982–84). FRCM 1977. Order of Francisco de Miranda, 1st cl. (Venezuela), 1978. *Recreations:* music, sailing. *Address:* New Court, St Swithin's Lane, EC4. *T:* 01–280 5000. *Clubs:* Brooks's; Royal Yacht Squadron.
See also E. L. de Rothschild.

ROTHSCHILD, Hon. Miriam Louisa, (Hon. Mrs Miriam Lane), CBE 1982; FRS 1985; *b* 5 Aug. 1908; *e d* of Hon. N. C. Rothschild and Rozsika de Wertheimstein; *m* 1943, Capt. George Lane, MC (marriage dissolved, 1957); one *s* three *d* (and one *s* one *d* decd). *Educ:* home. Member: Zoological and Entomological Research Coun.; Marine Biological Assoc.; Royal Entomological Soc.; Systematics Assoc.; Soc. for Promotion of Nature Reserves, etc.; Ed., Novitates Zoologica, 1938–41; Mem., Publications Cttee, Zoological Soc.; Foreign Office, 1940–42; Trustee, British Museum of Natural History, 1967–75. Mem., Amer. Acad. of Arts and Scis. Vis. Prof. in Biology, Royal Free Hosp. Romanes Lectr, Oxford, 1985. Hon. Fellow, St Hugh's Coll., Oxford. Hon. DSc: Oxford; Gothenburg, 1983; Hull, 1984; Northwestern Univ., 1986. Defence Medal (1940–45). *Publications:* Catalogue Rothschild Collection of Fleas (British Museum): vol. I 1953, vol. II 1956, vol. III 1962, vol. IV 1966, vol. V 1971, vol. VI 1983; (with Theresa Clay) Fleas, Flukes and Cuckoos, 1952; (with Clive Farrell) The Butterfly Gardener, 1983; Dear Lord Rothschild (biog.), 1983; (with Prof. Schlein and Prof. Ito) Atlas of Insect Tissue, 1985; Animals & Man, 1986; 300 contribs to scientific jls. *Recreation:* watching butterflies. *Address:* Ashton, Peterborough. *Clubs:* Queen's, Entomological.
See also Baron Rothschild.

ROTHSCHILD, Hon. (Nathaniel Charles) Jacob; Chairman: J. Rothschild Holdings plc; Five Arrows Ltd; *b* 29 April 1936; *e s* and *heir* of 3rd Baron Rothschild, *qv*; *m* 1961, Serena Mary, *er d* of late Sir Philip Gordon Dunn, 2nd Bt; one *s* three *d.* *Educ:* Eton; Christ Church, Oxford. BA 1st cl. hons History. Chm., Rothschild Investment Trust Ltd, later RIT Ltd, 1971–82, RIT and Northern, 1982–84. Chm., Bd of Trustees, National Gallery, 1985–. Mem. Council, RCA, 1986–. Comdr. Order of Henry the Navigator, 1985. *Address:* 15 St James's Place, SW1A 1NW. *T:* 01–493 8111.

ROTHSCHILD, Baron Robert, KCMG (Hon.) 1963; Grand Officier de l'Ordre de Leopold (Belgium); Belgian Ambassador to the Court of St James's, 1973–76; *b* 16 Dec. 1911; *s* of Bernard Rothschild and Marianne von Rynveld; one *d.* *Educ:* Univ. of Brussels (DrRerPol). Entered Belgian Foreign Office: Brussels, 1937; Lisbon, 1942; Chungking, China, 1944; Shanghai, 1946, Washington, USA, 1950; Paris, NATO, 1952; Brussels, 1954; Ambassador to Yugoslavia, 1958; Head of Mission, Katanga, Congo, 1960; Brussels, 1960; Ambassador to: Switzerland, 1964; France, 1966. *Publication:* La Chute de Chiang Kai-Shek, 1973 (Paris). *Recreations:* gardening, travel. *Address:* 43 Ranelagh Grove, SW1; 51 Avenue du Général de Gaulle, Bruxelles, Belgium.

ROTHSTEIN, Saul; Solicitor to the Post Office, 1976–81; *b* 4 July 1920; *s* of late Simon Rothstein and late Zelda Rothstein; *m* 1949, Judith Noemi (*née* Katz); two *d.* *Educ:*

Church Institute Sch., Bolton; Manchester Univ (LLB). Admitted solicitor, 1947. War service, RAF, 1941–46 (Flt-Lt). Entered Solicitor's Dept, General Post Office, 1949, Asst Solicitor, 1963; Director, Advisory Dept, Solicitor's Office, Post Office, 1972–76. *Recreations:* chamber music, walking, travel. *Address:* 9 Templars Crescent, Finchley, N3 3QR. *T:* 01–346 3701.

ROTHWELL, Margaret Irene; HM Diplomatic Service; Counsellor, Consul-General and Head of Chancery, Jakarta, since 1984; *b* 25 Aug. 1938; *d* of Harry Rothwell and Martha (*née* Goedecke). *Educ:* Southampton Grammar School for Girls; Lady Margaret Hall, Oxford (BA LitHum). Foreign Office, 1961; Third, later Second Secretary, UK Delegn to Council of Europe, Strasbourg, 1964, FO, 1966; Second Sec. (Private Sec. to Special Representative in Africa), Nairobi, 1967; Second, later First Sec., Washington, 1968; FCO, 1972; First Sec. and Head of Chancery, Helsinki, 1976; FCO, 1980; Counsellor and Hd of Trng Dept, FCO, 1981–83. *Recreations:* gardening, cooking, tennis. *Address:* c/o Foreign and Commonwealth Office, SW1A 2AH.

ROTHWELL, Sheila Gwendoline; Director, Centre for Employment Policy Studies, Henley Administrative Staff College, since 1979; *b* 22 Aug. 1935; *d* of Reginald Herbert Paine and Joyce Margaret Paine; *m* 1958, Miles Rothwell (marr. diss. 1968); one *s* one *d*. *Educ:* Wyggeston Sch., Leicester; Westfield Coll., Univ. of London (BA Hons History, 1956); LSE (MScEcon Indust. Relations, 1972). Teaching and res., London, Trinidad and Barbados, 1958–68; Res. Officer/Lectr, Indust. Relations Dept, LSE, 1969–75; Asst Sec. (Negotiations), National Union of Bank Employees, 1975–76; Asst Chief Exec., Equal Opportunities Commn, 1976–78. Res. Sec. to House of Lords Select Cttee on Anti-Discrimination Bill, 1972–73. Mem., Williams Cttee on Obscenity and Film Censorship, 1978–79. Dir, British Consortium for Innovation, 1981–. ACAS Ind. Expert on Equal Pay, 1984–. *Publications:* Labour Turnover, 1980; contrib. Internat. Labour Rev., and Brit. Jl of Indust. Relations. *Recreations:* cinema, theatre, walking, dressmaking, cycling. *Address:* 4 The Gardens, Fingest, Henley, Oxon RG9 6QF.

ROUGIER, Maj.-Gen. Charles Jeremy, CB 1986; FICE; Engineer-in-Chief (Army), since 1985; *b* 23 Feb. 1933; *s* of late Lt-Col and Mrs C. L. Rougier; *m* 1964, Judith Cawood Ellis; three *s* one *d*. *Educ:* Marlborough Coll.; Pembroke Coll., Cambridge (MA). FICE 1986. Aden, 1960; Instructor, RMA Sandhurst, 1961–62; psc 1963; MA to MGO, 1964–66; comd 11 Engineer Sqn, Commonwealth Bde, 1966–68; jssc 1968; Company Comd, RMA Sandhurst, 1969–70; Directing Staff, Staff Coll., Camberley, 1970–72; CO 21 Engineer Regt, BAOR, 1972–74; Staff of Chief of Defence Staff, 1974–77; Commandant, Royal Sch. of Military Engineering, 1977–79; RCDS 1980; COS, Headquarters Northern Ireland, 1981; Asst Chief of General Staff (Trng), 1982–83. Dir of Army Training, 1983–84; Chm., Review of Officer Training and Educn Study, 1985. *Recreations:* squash, hill walking, DIY, gardening. *Address:* c/o Lloyds Bank Plc, 174 Fleet Road, Fleet, Hants. *Club:* Army and Navy.

ROUGIER, Hon. Sir Richard George, Kt 1986; **Hon. Mr Justice Rougier;** Judge of the High Court of Justice, Queen's Bench Division, since 1986; *b* 12 Feb. 1932; *s* of late George Ronald Rougier, CBE, QC, and Georgette Heyer, novelist; *m* 1962, Susanna Allen Flint (*née* Whitworth); one *s*. *Educ:* Marlborough Coll.; Pembroke Coll., Cambridge (Exhibr, BA). Called to Bar, Inner Temple, 1956, Bencher 1979. QC 1972; a Recorder, 1973–86. *Recreations:* fishing, golf, bridge. *Address:* Royal Courts of Justice, WC2A 2LL. *Clubs:* Portland, Garrick; Rye Golf.

ROUND, Prof. Nicholas Grenville; Stevenson Professor of Hispanic Studies, in the University of Glasgow, since 1972; *b* 6 June 1938; *s* of Isaac Eric Round and Laura Christabel (*née* Poole); *m* 1966, Ann Le Vin; one *d*. *Educ:* Boyton CP Sch., Cornwall; Launceston Coll.; Pembroke Coll., Oxford. BA (1st cl. Hons, Spanish and French) 1959; MA 1963; DPhil 1967. Lecturer in Spanish, Queen's Univ. of Belfast, 1962–71, Reader, 1971–72; Warden, Alanbrooke Hall, QUB, 1970–72. *Publications:* Unamuno: Abel Sánchez: a critical guide, 1974; The Greatest Man Uncrowned: a study of the fall of Alvaro de Luna, 1986; trans., Tirso de Molina, Damned for Despair, 1986; contribs to: Mod. Lang. Review, Bulletin Hispanic Studies, Proc. Royal Irish Academy, etc. *Recreations:* reading, music, all aspects of Cornwall. *Address:* Department of Hispanic Studies, The University, Glasgow G12 8QQ. *T:* 041–339 8855. *Club:* (Hon. Life Mem.) Students' Union (Belfast).

ROUNTREE, Peter Charles Robert; His Honour Judge Rountree; a Circuit Judge, since 1986; *b* 28 April 1936; *s* of Francis Robert George Rountree and Mary Felicity Patricia Rountree (*née* Wilson); *m* 1968, Nicola Mary (*née* Norman-Butler); one *s* one step *d*. *Educ:* Uppingham School; St John's College, Cambridge (MA). Called to the Bar, Inner Temple, 1961; a Recorder, April–July 1986. *Recreations:* sailing, golf, tennis. *Address:* 16 Clarendon Road, W11. *T:* 01–727 7795. *Clubs:* Royal Automobile, Royal Yacht Squadron, Royal London Yacht; New Zealand Golf.

ROUS, family name of **Earl of Stradbroke.**

ROUS, Brig. Hon. William Edward, OBE 1981 (MBE 1974); Director of Public Relations (Army), since 1985; *b* 22 Feb. 1939; *s* of 5th Earl of Stradbroke, and late Pamela Catherine Mabell (who *m* 1970, Robert Hugh Pardoe), *d* of Captain Hon. Edward James Kay-Shuttleworth; *m* 1970, Judith Rosemary Persse; two *s*. *Educ:* Harrow; Royal Military Academy. Commissioned Coldstream Guards, 1959; Comd 2nd Bn Coldstream Guards, 1979–81, Comd 1st Inf. Brigade, 1983–84. *Address:* Regimental Headquarters, Coldstream Guards, Wellington Barracks, Birdcage Walk, SW1.

ROUSE, Sir Anthony (Gerald Roderick), KCMG 1969 (CMG 1961); OBE 1945; HM Diplomatic Service, retired; *b* 9 April 1911; *s* of late Lt-Col Maxwell Rouse and of Mrs Rouse, Eastbourne; *m* 1935, Beatrice Catherine Ellis. *Educ:* Harrow; Heidelberg Univ. Joined HAC 1935; RA (T) 1938; 2 Lt 1940; transf. to Intelligence Corps; served MEF and CMF on staff of 3rd Corps (commendation); Lt-Col 1944. Entered Foreign Service, 1946; First Secretary (Information), Athens, 1946; Foreign Office, 1949. British Embassy, Moscow, 1952–54; Counsellor, 1955; Office of UK High Commissioner, Canberra, 1955–57; HM Inspector of Foreign Service Establishments, 1957–59; Counsellor (Information) British Embassy, Bonn, 1959–62; British Deputy Commandant, Berlin, 1962–64; HM Minister, British Embassy, Rome, 1964–66; Consul-General, New York, 1966–71. *Address:* St Ritas, Paradise Drive, Eastbourne, E Sussex.

ROUSE, E(dward) Clive, MBE 1946; Medieval Archæologist; Specialist in Mural and Panel Paintings; Lecturer; *b* 15 October 1901; *s* of late Edward Foxwell Rouse (Stroud, Gloucestershire and Acton, Middlesex) and late Frances Sarah Rouse (*née* Sams). *Educ:* Gresham's School; St Martin's School of Art. On leaving school studied art and medieval antiquities, 1920–21; FSA London, 1937 (Mem. of Council, 1943–44); FRSA 1968. President: Royal Archæological Institute, 1969–72 (Vice-Pres., 1965); Bucks Archaeological Soc., 1969–79. Liveryman, Fishmongers' Company, 1962. Served War of 1939–45, RAFVR (Intelligence); Flight-Lt, 1941–45; MBE for special services at Central Interpretation Unit, Medmenham. Hon. MA Oxon, 1969; Hon. DLitt Sussex, 1983. *Publications:* The Old Towns of England, 1936 (twice reprinted); Discovering Wall Paintings, 1968 (reprinted); (jointly) Guide to Buckinghamshire, 1935; contributor to: The Beauty of Britain, 1935; Collins' Guide to English Parish Churches, 1958. Papers in Archæologia, Antiquaries' Journal, Archæological Journal, and publications of many County Archæological Societies. *Recreation:* travel. *Address:* Oakfield, North Park, Gerrards Cross, Bucks. *T:* Gerrards Cross 882595.

ROUSSEL, (Philip) Lyon, OBE 1974; FRGS; FRSA; retired; *b* 17 Oct. 1923; *s* of late Paul Marie Roussel and Beatrice (*née* Cuthbert; later Lady Murray); *m* 1959, Elisabeth Mary, *d* of Kenneth and Kathleen Bennett; one *s* one *d*. *Educ:* Hurstpierpoint Coll.; St Edmund Hall, Oxford (MA, Cert. Public and Social Admin); Chelsea Sch. of Art. Served Indian Army in Parachute Regt, 1942–46 (Major). Sudan Political Service, 1950–55; Principal, War Office, 1955–56, Associated Newspapers, 1956–57; British Council, 1960–83: India, 1960–67 (Regional Rep., Western and Central India, 1964–67); Dir, Scholarships, 1967–71; Rep. and Cultural Attaché, British Embassy, Belgium and Luxembourg, 1971–76; Europalia-Great Britain Festival Cttee, 1973; Cultural Attaché (Counsellor), British Embassy, Washington, 1976–79; Controller, Arts Div., 1979–83. Sponsorship Consultant, National Theatre, 1983–84. Member: Fest. of India Cttee, 1981–82; British Adv. Cttee, Britain Salutes New York, 1981–83; Bd, The Hanover Band, 1984–. *Recreations:* painting, the arts in general, tennis and a barn in France. *Address:* 4 Holland Park, W11 3TG. *Clubs:* Athenæum; Oxford Union.

ROUSSOS, Stavros G.; Secretary General, Ministry of Foreign Affairs, Greece, 1980–82, retired; *b* 1918; *m*; two *s* one *d*. *Educ:* Univ. of Lyons (LèsL); Univ. of Paris (LèsL, LèsScPol, LLD). Entered Greek Diplomatic Service as Attaché, Min. of Foreign Affairs, 1946; Mem., Greek Delegn to Gen. Assembly of UN, 1948 and 1954–55; Sec. to Permanent Mission of Greece to UN in New York, 1950; Consul, Alexandria, 1955; i/c Greek Consulate General, Cairo, 1956; Counsellor, 1959; Min. of Foreign Affairs, 1959–61; Mem., Perm. Delegn of Greece to EEC, Brussels, 1962; Perm. Rep. to EEC, 1969; Dir-Gen., Econ. and Commercial Affairs, Min. of Foreign Affairs, 1972; Ambassador of Greece to UK, 1974–79; Alternate Sec. Gen., Min. of Foreign Affairs, 1979–80. Grand Comdr, Order of Phoenix; Commander: Order of Belgian Crown; Order of Merit of Egypt. *Publication:* The Status of Dodecanese Islands in International Law, 1940 (Paris). *Address:* 5 Loukianou Street, Athens, Greece.

ROUTH, Donald Thomas; Under Secretary, Department of the Environment, since 1978; *b* 22 May 1936; *s* of Thomas and Flora Routh; *m* 1961, Janet Hilda Allum. *Educ:* Leeds Modern Sch. Entered WO, Northern Comd, York, as Exec. Officer, 1954; Nat. Service, RN, 1954–56; Higher Exec. Officer, Comd Secretariat, Kenya, 1961–64; Asst Principal, Min. of Housing and Local Govt, 1964–66; Asst Private Sec. to Minister, 1966–67; Principal, 1967; on loan to Civil Service Selection Bd, 1971; Asst Sec., DoE, 1972; Under Sec., 1978; Regional Dir, West Midlands, 1978–81; Hd of Construction Industries Directorate, 1981–85; Dir of Senior Staff Management, 1985–. *Address:* 2 Marsham Street, SW1.

ROUTLEDGE, Alan, CBE 1979; *b* 12 May 1919; *s* of George and Rose Routledge, Wallasey, Cheshire; *m* 1949, Irene Hendry, Falkirk, Stirlingshire; one *s* (and one *s* decd). *Educ:* Liscard High Sch., Wallasey. Served Army, Cheshire (Earl of Chester's) Yeomanry, 1939–46. Control Commn for Germany, 1946–51; Diplomatic Wireless Service of FO (now Foreign and Commonwealth Office), 1951–79: Head, Cypher and Signals Branch, 1962; Head, Commns Planning Staff, 1973; Head, Commns Ops Dept, 1979; retired FCO, 1979. *Recreations:* English history, cricket, golf. *Address:* 15 Ilford Court, Elmbridge, Cranleigh, Surrey GU6 8TJ. *T:* Cranleigh 276669. *Clubs:* Civil Service; Old Liscardians.

ROUTLEDGE, Rev. Canon (Kenneth) Graham; Canon Residentiary and Treasurer of St Paul's Cathedral, since 1982; Chancellor, Diocese of Ely since 1973, of Peterborough since 1976, and of Lichfield since 1976; *b* 21 Sept. 1927; *s* of Edgar Routledge and late Catherine (*née* Perry); *m* 1960, Muriel, *d* of late Robert Shallcross. *Educ:* Birkenhead Sch.; Liverpool Univ. (LLB 1st Cl. Hons 1951); Fitzwilliam Coll., Cambridge (BA 1965 Theol Tripos Pt II, MA 1969); Westcott House, Cambridge. Deacon, 1966; priest, 1967. Called to the Bar, Middle Temple, 1952 (Blackstone Entrance Scholar, Harmsworth Law Scholar, Campbell Foster Prize). HM Forces, RE and RAEC, 1945–48. Practice at Chancery Bar, Liverpool, and on Northern Circuit, 1952–63; Tutor and Lectr in Law, Liverpool Univ., 1952–63; Curate, St George's, Stockport, 1966–69; Lectr in Law, Manchester Univ., 1966–69; Corpus Christi Coll., Cambridge: Dean of Chapel, 1969–77; Lectr and Dir of Studies in Law, 1972–77; Fellow, 1969–83; Canon Residentiary and Treasurer of Peterborough Cathedral, 1977–82. Mem., Birkenhead Bor. Council, 1960–63. Contested Birkenhead (Conservative), Gen. Election, 1959. Life Governor and Mem. Council, Haileybury and Imperial Service Coll., 1976–; Mem. Council, Westwood House Sch., Peterborough, 1979–; Fellow, Woodard Schools, 1979–. *Recreations:* Rugby, cricket, golf, bird watching, reading. *Address:* 3 Amen Court, EC4M 7BU. *T:* 01–236 4532. *Clubs:* Royal Commonwealth Society, MCC.

ROUX, Michel André; Director and Chef de Cuisine, since 1967; *b* 19 April 1941; *s* of late Henry Roux and of Germaine Triger; *m* 1984, Robyn (Margaret Joyce); one *s* two *d* by previous marr. *Educ:* Ecole Primaire, Saint Mande; Brevet de Maîtrise (Pâtisserie). Apprenticeship, Pâtisserie Loyal, Paris, 1955–57; Commis Pâtissier-Cuisinier, British Embassy, Paris, 1957–59; Commis de Cuisine with Miss Cécile de Rothschild, Paris, 1959–60; Military service, 1960–62, at Versailles and Colomb Bechar, Sahara; Chef with Miss Cécile de Rothschild, 1962–67; came to England, 1967; restaurants opened: Le Gavroche, 1967; Le Poulbot, 1969; Le Gamin, 1971; Waterside Inn, 1972; Gavvers, 1981. Mem., UK Br., Académie Culinaire de France. Numerous French and British prizes and awards, including: Médaille d'Or, Cuisiniers Français, 1972; Restaurateur of the Year, Caterer & Hotelkeeper, 1985; Personnalité de l'Année, Gastronomie dans le Monde, Paris, 1985. *Publications:* New Classic Cuisine, 1983 (French edn, 1985); The Roux Brothers on Patisserie, 1986. *Recreations:* shooting, walking, skiing. *Address:* The Waterside Inn, Ferry Road, Bray, Berks SL6 2AT. *T:* Maidenhead 20691; Rye Peck, Ferry Road (end of), Bray, Berks. *Club:* The Benedicts.

ROW, Hon. Sir John Alfred, Kt 1974; Sugar Cane Farmer since 1926; retd as Minister for Primary Industries, Queensland, Australia, 1963–72; *b* Hamleigh, Ingham, Qld, Aust., 1 Jan. 1905; *s* of Charles Edward and Emily Harriet Row; *m* 1st, 1929, Gladys M. (decd), *d* of late H. E. Hollins; one *d*; 2nd, 1966, Irene, *d* of late F. C. Gough. *Educ:* Toowoomba Grammar Sch., Qld; Trebonne State Sch., Qld. Mem. for Hinchinbrook, Qld Legislative Assembly, 1960–72. Mem. Victoria Mill Suppliers Cttee and Herbert River Cane Growers Exec., 1932–60. Rep. Local Cane Prices Bd, 1948–60; Dir, Co-op Cane Growers Store, 1955–60; Councillor, Hinchinbrook Shire, and Rep. on Townsville Regional Electricity Bd, 1952–63; Life Mem.: Aust. Sugar Producers' Assoc.; Herbert River Pastoral and Agricultural Assoc. *Recreations:* bowls (past Pres. and Trustee of Ingham Bowls Club), gardening. *Address:* 10 Gort Street, Ingham, Queensland 4850, Australia. *T:* Ingham 761671.

ROW, Commander Sir Philip (John), KCVO 1969 (CVO 1965; MVO 1958); OBE 1944; RN Retired; an Extra Equerry to the Queen since 1969; Deputy Treasurer to the Queen, 1958–68. *Address:* Clare Lodge, Ewshot, Farnham, Surrey.

ROWALLAN, 3rd Baron *cr* 1911; **Arthur Cameron Corbett;** *b* 17 Dec. 1919; *s* of 2nd Baron Rowallan, KT, KBE, MC, TD, and Gwyn Mervyn (*d* 1971), *d* of J. B. Grimond, St Andrews; *S* father, 1977; *m* 1st, 1945, Eleanor Mary (marr. diss. 1962), *o d* of late Captain George Boyle, The Royal Scots Fusiliers; one *s* three *d*; 2nd, 1963, April Ashley (marr. annulled, 1970). *Educ:* Eton; Balliol College, Oxford. Served War of 1939–45. Croix de Guerre (France), 1944. *Heir:* *s* Hon. John Polson Cameron Corbett [*b* 8 March 1947; *m* 1st, 1970, Susan Jane Dianne Green (marr. diss. 1983); one *s* one *d*; 2nd, 1984, Sandrew Filomena, *d* of William Bryson; one *s*]. *Address:* c/o Hon. John Corbett, Rowallan, Kilmarnock, Ayrshire KA3 2LP.

ROWAN, Carl Thomas; Syndicated columnist, correspondent, Chicago Sun-Times; radio and TV commentator, Post-Newsweek Broadcasting; Roving Editor, Reader's Digest; *b* 11 August 1925; *s* of Thomas D. and Johnnie B. Rowan; *m* 1950, Vivien Murphy; two *s* one *d*. *Educ:* Tennessee State University; Washburn University; Oberlin Coll.; University of Minnesota. Mem. Staff of Minneapolis Tribune, 1948–61; Dept of State, 1961–63; US Ambassador to Finland, 1963–64; Director, United States Information Agency, Washington, DC, 1964–65. Hon. DLitt: Simpson Coll., 1957; Hamline Univ., 1958; Oberlin Coll., 1962; Dr of Humane Letters: Washburn Univ., 1964; Talladega Coll., 1965; St Olaf Coll., 1966; Knoxville Coll., 1966; Rhode Island Coll., 1970; Maine Univ., 1971; American Univ., 1980; Dr of Laws: Howard Univ., 1964; Alfred Univ., 1964; Temple Univ., 1964; Atlanta Univ., 1965; Allegheny Coll., 1966; Colby Coll., 1968; Clark Univ., 1971; Notre Dame, 1973; Dr of Public Admin., Morgan State Coll., 1964; Dr of Letters: Wooster Coll., 1968; Miami Univ., 1982; Drexel Inst. of Technology; Dr of Science Georgetown Med. Sch., 1982. *Publications:* South of Freedom, 1953; The Pitiful and the Proud, 1956; Go South to Sorrow, 1957; Wait Till Next Year, 1960; Between Us Blacks, 1974. *Recreations:* tennis, golf and bowling, singing and dancing. *Address:* 3116 Fessenden Street North-West, Washington, DC 20008, USA. *Clubs:* Federal City, Indian Spring, (Washington, DC).

ROWAN-LEGG, Allan Aubrey; Vice President, Western Region, Edcom Ltd, Canada, since 1976; Director, Horticulture Centre of the Pacific, since 1983; *b* 19 May 1912; *m* 1944, Daphne M. Ker; three *d*. Dir, Vice-Pres. and Gen. Sales Man., Interlake Fuel Oil Ltd, and Interlake Steel Products, 1955–57; Pres. and Dir, Superior Propane Ltd, Northern Propane Gas Co., 1957–63; Dir, Vice-Pres. and Gen. Man., Garlock of Canada Ltd, and Yale Rubber Mfg Co. of Canada Ltd, 1963–64; Regional Dir for Ont., Canadian Corp. for 1967 World Exhibn, 1964–67; Agent General for Ontario in UK, 1967–72; Man. Dir, Canada Permanent Mortgage Corp. and Canada Permanent Trust Co., 1973–75. Chm. and Pres., Art Gallery of Greater Victoria, BC, 1980, then ex officio, 1980–83. Dir and Vice-Pres., Craigdarrock Castle Soc. Liveryman, Painter Stainers Co., 1969–. Freeman of City of London, 1969. Canada Centennial Medal. *Recreations:* golfing, swimming. *Address:* 1790 Glastonbury Road, Victoria, British Columbia V8P 2H3, Canada. *Clubs:* Royal Lymington Yacht (Hants); Union, Victoria Golf, Rotary (Victoria, BC; Hon. Director and Hon. Mem.); Harbourside Rotary (Hon. Director and Hon. Mem.).

ROWE, Andrew; MP (C) Mid Kent, since 1983; *b* 11 Sept. 1935; *s* of John Douglas Rowe and Mary Katharine Storr; *m* 1st, 1960, Alison Boyd (marr. diss.); one *s*; 2nd, 1983, Sheila L. Finkle; two step *d*. *Educ:* Eton Coll.; Merton Coll., Oxford (MA). Sub Lt RNVR, 1954–56. Schoolmaster, 1959–62; Principal, Scottish Office, 1962–67; Lectr, Edinburgh Univ., 1967–74; Consultant to Voluntary Services Unit, Home Office, 1974; Dir, Community Affairs, Cons. Central Office, 1975–79; self-employed consultant and journalist, 1979–83. *Publications:* Democracy Renewed, 1975; pamphlets and articles incl. Somewhere to Start. *Recreations:* photography, reading, theatre. *Address:* Tudor Milgate, Milgate Park, Ashford Road, Thurnham, Maidstone ME14 4NN. *T:* Maidstone 63809.

ROWE, Eric George, CMG 1955; *b* 30 June 1904; *s* of late Ernest Kruse Rowe; *m* 1st, 1931, Gladys Ethel (*d* 1985), *d* of late Charles Horace Rogers, ARCA; 2nd, 1985, Margaret Alison, *d* of late Arthur John Howe. *Educ:* Chatham House School, Ramsgate; St Edmund Hall Oxford. Assistant Master, Queen Mary's Grammar School, Walsall, 1926–27. Entered Colonial Service, Tanganyika; Administrative Officer (Cadet), 1928; Asst District Officer, 1930; District Officer, 1940; Provincial Commissioner, 1948; Senior Provincial Commissioner, 1952; Minister for Local Government and Administration, Tanganyika, 1958; Supervisor, Overseas Services Courses, Oxford, 1959–69. *Publication:* paper in Ibis. *Recreation:* ornithology. *Address:* Merlin Cottage, 3 Snuggs Lane, East Hanney, near Wantage, Oxon OX12 0HU. *T:* West Hanney 229. *Club:* Royal Commonwealth Society.

ROWE, Helen, (Mrs Brian Rowe); *see* Cresswell, H.

ROWE, Sir Henry (Peter), KCB 1978 (CB 1971); QC 1978; First Parliamentary Counsel, 1977–81; *b* 18 Aug. 1916; 3rd *s* of late Dr Richard Röhr and Olga Röhr, Vienna; *m* 1947, Patricia, *yr d* of R. W. King, London; two *s* one *d*. *Educ:* Vienna; Gonville and Caius Coll., Cambridge. War service, Pioneer Corps, RAC, Military Govt, British Troops, Berlin, 1941–46. Called to Bar, Gray's Inn, 1947. Joined Parliamentary Counsel Office, 1947; Jt Second Parly Counsel, 1973–76. Commonwealth Fund Travelling Fellowship in US, 1955; with Law Commn, 1966–68. *Recreations:* music, reading, walking. *Address:* 19 Paxton Gardens, Woking, Surrey. *T:* Byfleet 43816.

ROWE, Jeremy, CBE 1980; Deputy Chairman, Abbey National Building Society, since 1979; Chairman: Peterborough Development Corporation, since 1981; Family Assurance Society, since 1986; *b* 31 Oct. 1928; *s* of Charles William Dell Rowe and Alison (*née* Barford); *m* 1957, Susan Mary (*née* Johnstone); four *d*. *Educ:* Wellesley House Sch.; Uppingham Sch.; Trinity Coll., Cambridge (MA (Hons) Hist.). English-Speaking Union Scholarship to USA, 1952. Joined London Brick Co. Ltd as trainee, 1952: Personal Asst to Chm., 1954; Dir and Sales Manager, 1963–67; Man. Dir, 1967–70; Dep. Chm. and Man. Dir, 1970–79; Man. Dir, 1979–82 and Chm., 1979–84; Director: West End Bd, Sun Alliance Insce Co. Ltd, 1978–; John Maunders Group plc, 1984–; Telephone Rentals plc, 1984–. *Recreations:* tennis, shooting, reading, music. *Address:* 23 Devonshire Place, W1. *T:* 01–935 4902; Woodside, Peasmarsh, near Rye, Sussex. *Clubs:* Buck's; All England Lawn Tennis.

ROWE, John Jermyn, QC 1982; Barrister; a Recorder of the Crown Court, since 1978; *b* 23 March 1936; *er s* of John Rowe and late Olga Brookes Rowe; *m* 1966, Susan, *d* of Wing Comdr Walter Dring, DSO, DFC (killed in action, 1945) and of Sheila Mary Patricia (who *m* 2nd, His Honour B. H. Gerrard, *qv*); two *d*. *Educ:* Manchester Grammar School; Brasenose Coll., Oxford (MA). 2nd Lieut RA, 1954–56. Called to the Bar, Middle Temple, 1960 (Harmsworth Schol.; Blackstone Schol.; Bencher, 1985); practice on Northern Circuit; Prosecuting Counsel to the Inland Revenue, Northern Circuit, 1980–82; called to Irish Bar, Kings Inns, 1986. Member: Gen. Council of the Bar, 1970–74; Bar Representative, Senate of the Inns of Court and the Bar, 1978–81; Mem., Rawlinson Cttee on Constitution of Senate, 1985–86. *Address:* The Cottage, 77 Stamford Road, Bowdon, Altrincham, Cheshire WA14 2JJ; 2 Pump Court, Temple, EC4. *Clubs:* United Oxford & Cambridge University; Tennis and Racquet (Manchester); County (Carlisle).

ROWE, Norbert Edward, CBE 1944; FEng 1976; Hon. FRAeS, 1962; FIMechE; Vice-President, Engineering De Havilland Aircraft of Canada, 1962–66, retired, 1966; *b* 18 June 1898; *s* of Harold Arthur and Jane Rowe, Plymouth, Devon; *m* 1929, Cecilia Brown; two *s* two *d*. *Educ:* City and Guilds (Engineering) Coll. Whitworth Exhibition, 1921; BSc Eng. London, 1st Cl. Hons, 1923; Associate of City and Guilds Institute, 1923; DIC 1924; Hon. FRAeS (FRAeS 1944); Air Ministry; Royal Aircraft Establishment, 1924, Junior Technical Officer, 1925; Testing Establishment, Technical Officer, 1926; Senior Technical Officer, 1937; Testing Establishment, Chief Technical Officer, 1937; Headquarters, Asst Director, 1938; Ministry of Aircraft Production Headquarters, Deputy Director, Research and Develt of Aircraft, 1940; Director of Technical Development, Ministry of Aircraft Production, 1941–45; Director-General of Technical Development, 1945–46; Controller of Research and Special Developments, British European Airways Corporation (on resignation from Civil Service), 1946–51; Technical Director Blackburn and General Aircraft Ltd, E Yorks, 1952–61; Joint Managing Director of the Blackburn Aircraft Company, 1960–61; Director, Hawker Siddeley Aviation, 1961–62. Member: Air Registration Bd, 1968; ARC, 1969–72. Fellow Inst. Aeronautical Sciences of Amer., 1953; FCGI 1954. Pres. Royal Aeronautical Society, 1955–56, Hon. Fellow 1962. President: Helicopter Assoc. of GB, 1959–60; Whitworth Soc., 1974–75. Hon. Fellow, Canadian Aeronautics and Space Inst. (formerly Canadian Aerospace Inst.), 1965. *Address:* 22 Westfields Road, Mirfield, West Yorks WF14 9PW.

ROWE, Norman Francis; one of the Special Commissioners of Income Tax, 1950–73; Commissioner of Income Tax, St Marylebone Division, 1974–83, retired; *b* 18 May 1908; *o s* of late Frank Rowe and Eva Eveline (*née* Metcalfe), Watford; *m* 1941, Suzanne Marian (marr. diss., 1964), *o d* of D. S. Richardson; one *s*; *m* 1965, Vittoria, *yr d* of P. Cav. Tondi; one *s*. *Educ:* Sherborne. Chartered Accountant, 1931–37, retired; re-admitted, 1977; FCA. Called to Bar, Lincoln's Inn, 1940; Mem. of Western Circuit. Served War of 1939–45 (despatches); RAF, 1940–45, serving in UK, Middle East, India, Burma and Ceylon; demobilised with rank of Squadron Leader. Freeman, City of London; Liveryman, Worshipful Co. of Glaziers and Painters of Glass. *Publications:* author of Schedule C and Profits Tax sections of Simon's Income Tax, 1st edn. *Recreations:* fishing, yachting. *Address:* Darley House, Darley Road, Eastbourne, East Sussex BN20 7UH. *T:* Eastbourne 30878; Via Leonardo da Vinci 286, 55049 Viareggio, Italy. *T:* Viareggio 30248. *Clubs:* Naval and Military, Bar Yacht, Little Ship; Island Cruising.

ROWE, Norman Lester, CBE 1976; FRCS, FDSRCS; retired; Honorary Consultant in Oral and Maxillofacial Surgery to: Westminster Hospital; Plastic & Oral Surgery Centre, Queen Mary's Hospital, Roehampton; Institute of Dental Surgery, WC1; Emeritus Consultant to the Royal Navy and Retired Consultant to the Army; Recognised Teacher in Oral Surgery, University of London; *b* 15 Dec. 1915; *s* of late A. W. Rowe, OBE and of L. L. Rowe; *m* 1938 Cynthia Mary Freeman; one *s* one *d*. *Educ:* Malvern College; Guy's Hospital; LRCP, LMSSA (London), HDDRCS (Edin.). Gen. Practice, 1937–41; Captain RADC, 1941–46. Formerly Senior Registrar, Plastic and Jaw Injuries Unit, Hill End Hosp., St Albans, 1947, and consultant in Oral Surgery, Plastic and Oral Surgery Centre, Rooksdown House, Park Prewett, Basingstoke, 1948–59; formerly Mem., Army Med. Adv. Bd; Mem. Bd of Faculty of Dental Surgery, RCS, 1956–74; Vice-Dean, 1967; Colyer Gold Medal, 1981. Lectures: Webb-Johnson, RCS, 1969; Richardson Meml, Boston, 1975; President's, BAOS, 1975; William Guy Meml, RCSE, 1981; Wood Meml, RN Portsmouth, 1981; President's, Amer. Soc. Aesth. & Plastic Surg., LA, 1983; Ruscoe Clarke Meml, Inst. Accident Surgery, Birmingham, 1983; Waldron Meml, Amer. Soc. Maxillofacial Surgs, LA, 1986. Formerly Examr, RCS, RCSE, RCPGlas and RCSI. Foundn Fellow, Brit. Assoc. of Oral and Maxillofacial Surgeons (formerly Brit. Assoc. of Oral Surgeons), Hon. Sec., 1962–68, Pres., 1969–70, Hon. Fellow, 1981 (Down's Surgical Prize Medal, 1976); Foundn Mem., European Assoc. for Maxillofacial Surgery, Pres., 1974–76, Vice-Pres., 1977–82; Hon. Fellow Internat. Assoc. of Oral and Maxillofacial Surgeons (Sec. Gen., 1968–71); Member: BMA; BDA (Tomes Medal, 1985); Fedn Dent. Internat.; Oral Surgery Club (GB); Hon. Member: Academia Nacional de Medicina de Buenos Aires, Argentina; Academie de Chirurgie Dentaire, Paris; Egyptian Dental Assoc.; Soc. of Amer. Oral Surgeons in Europe; Asociacion Mexicana de Cirugia Bucal; Amer. Soc. Maxillofacial Surgs; Canadian Assoc. of Oral and Maxillofacial Surgs; Inst. of Accident Surgery; N Californian Soc. of Oral and Maxillofacial Surgs; Emeritus Fellow, Colegio Brasileiro de Cirurgia e Traumatologia Buco-Maxilo-Facial (Le Fort Prize Medal, 1970); Hon. Fellow: Sociedad Venezolana de Cirurgia Bucal; Finnish Soc. of Oral Surgeons; Australian and New Zealand Soc. of Oral Surgeons; Assoc. Française des Chirurgiens Maxillofaciaux; Soc. Royale Belge de Stomatol. et de Chirurgie Maxillofaciale; Deutsche Gesellschaft für Mund-Kiefer und Gesichtschirugie; Soc. of Maxillofacial and Oral Surgeons of S Africa; Polish Stomatological Soc.; Israel Soc. of Oral and Maxillofacial Surgery; Hon. FDSRCPS(Glas.); Hon. FFDRCS (Irel.); Hon. FRCSE; Hon. FDSRCS(Edin.); Hon. FIMFT. *Publications:* (jtly) Fractures of the Facial Skeleton, 1955, 2nd edn, 1968; (jtly) chapters in Plastic Surgery in Infancy and Childhood, 2nd edn, 1979; chapter in Maxillofacial Trauma, 1984; (jtly) Maxillofacial Injuries, 1985; various articles in British and foreign medical and dental jls. *Address:* Brackendale, Holly Bank Road, Hook Heath, Woking, Surrey GU22 0JP. *T:* Woking 60008. *Club:* Royal Naval Medical.

ROWE, Owen John Tressider, MA; Headmaster of Epsom College, 1970–82; *b* 30 July 1922; *e s* of late Harold Ridges Rowe and Emma E. Rowe (*née* Matthews) Lymington, Hampshire; *m* 1946, Marcelle Ljufliny Hyde-Johnson (*d* 1986); one *s* one *d*. *Educ:* King Edward VI School, Southampton; Exeter College, Oxford (Scholar, MA); 1st Cl. Hons in Classical Hon. Mods, 1942. Served War of 1939–45, Lieut in Roy. Hampshire Regt, 1942–45. 1st Cl. Hons in Lit Hum, Dec. 1947; Assistant Master: Royal Grammar School, Lancaster, 1948–50; Charterhouse, 1950–60 (Head of Classical Dept); Officer Comdg Charterhouse CCF, 1954–60; Headmaster of Giggleswick School, 1961–70. *Address:* 8 Pine Hill, Epsom.

ROWE, Prof. Peter Noël, DSc (Eng); FEng, FIChemE; Ramsay Memorial Professor of Chemical Engineering, and Head of Department, University College London, 1965–85, now Professor Emeritus; *b* 25 Dec. 1919; *e s* of Charles Henry Rowe and Kate Winifred (*née* Storry); *m* 1952, Pauline Garmirian; two *s*. *Educ:* Preston Grammar Sch.; Manchester Coll. of Technology; Imperial Coll., London. Princ. Scientific Officer, AERE, Harwell, 1958–65. Crabtree Orator, 1980. Non-exec. Dir, Bentham Fine Chemicals, 1985–. Pres., IChemE, 1981–82; Hon. Sec., Fellowship of Engrg, 1982–85. FCGI 1983. Hon. DSc Brussels, 1978. *Publications:* scientific articles in Trans IChemE, Chem. Eng. Science, etc. *Address:* Pamber Green, Upper Basildon, Reading, Berks RG8 8PG. *T:* Upper Basildon 671382. *Club:* Athenæum.

ROWE, Peter Whitmill, MA; Schoolteacher at Kent College, Canterbury, since 1983; *b* 12 Feb. 1928; British; *s* of Gerald Whitmill Rowe, chartered accountant, one-time General Manager of Morris Commercials Co. Ltd; *m* 1952, Bridget Ann Moyle; two *s* one *d*. *Educ:* Bishop's Stortford College; St John's College, Cambridge. BA 1950; MA (Hons) 1956. VI Form History Master, Brentwood School, Essex, 1951–54; Senior History Master, Repton School, Derbys, 1954–57; Headmaster: Bishop's Stortford Coll., Herts, 1957–70; Cranbrook Sch., Kent, 1970–81; teacher, Williston-Northampton Sch., Mass.,

USA, 1981–83. JP Bishop's Stortford, 1968–70, Cranbrook, 1971–81. *Recreations:* literature, music, cricket, golf. *Address:* Farm Corner, Angley Park, Cranbrook, Kent.

ROWE, Richard Brian; Registrar of the High Court (Family Division), since 1979; *b* 28 April 1933; *s* of Charles Albert Rowe and Mabel Florence Rowe; *m* 1959, Shirley Ann Symons; two *d. Educ:* Greenford County Grammar Sch.; King's Coll., London Univ. (LLB). National Service, RAF, 1952–54. High Court (Probate, Divorce and Admiralty Div.), 1954–66; Land Commn, 1966–69; Lord Chancellor's Office, 1969–75; Sec., High Court (Family Div.), 1975–79. *Publications:* (ed) 10th edn, Rayden on Divorce, 1967; (ed) 25th and 26th edns, Tristram and Coote's Probate Practice, 1978 and 1983. *Recreations:* most sports. *Address:* High Court (Family Division), Somerset House, Strand, WC2R 1LP.

ROWE, Robert Stewart, CBE 1969; Director, Leeds City Art Gallery and Temple Newsam House, 1958–83 (and also of Lotherton Hall, 1968–83); *b* 31 Dec. 1920; *s* of late James Stewart Rowe and late Mrs A. G. Gillespie; *m* 1953, Barbara Elizabeth Hamilton Baynes; one *s* two *d. Educ:* privately; Downing Coll., Cambridge; Richmond Sch. of Art. Asst Keeper of Art, Birmingham Museum and Art Gallery, 1950–56; Dep. Dir, Manchester City Art Galls, 1956–58. Pres., Museums Assoc., 1973–74; Member: Arts Council of GB, 1981–86; Fine Arts Adv. Cttee, British Council, 1972–84; Dir, Henry Moore Study Centre Trust, 1983–. Liveryman, Worshipful Co. of Goldsmiths. Hon. LittD Leeds, 1983. *Publications:* Adam Silver, 1965; articles in Burlington Magazine, Museums Jl, etc. *Recreations:* gardening, reading. *Address:* Grove Lodge, Shadwell, Leeds LS17 8LB. *T:* Leeds 656365.

ROWE, Dr Roy Ernest, CBE 1977; FEng 1979; Director General, Cement and Concrete Association, since 1977; *b* 26 Jan. 1929; *s* of Ernest Walter Rowe and Louisa Rowe; *m* 1954, Lillian Anderson; one *d. Educ:* Taunton's Sch., Southampton; Pembroke Coll., Cambridge (MA, ScD). FICE, FIStructE, FIHE. Cement and Concrete Association: Research Engineer, 1952–57; Head, Design Research Dept, 1958–65; Dir, R&D, 1966–77. Pres., IStructE, 1983–84. Hon. Mem., Amer. Concrete Inst., 1978; For. Associate, Nat. Acad. of Engineering, USA, 1980. Hon. DEng Leeds, 1984. *Publications:* Concrete Bridge Design, 1962, 3rd impr. 1972; numerous papers in technical and professional jls. *Recreations:* fell walking, listening to music (and mutilating it on the piano). *Address:* Cornerway, 2 Sutton Avenue, Slough SL3 7AW. *T:* Slough 23645.

ROWE-HAM, Sir David (Kenneth), GBE 1986; JP; chartered accountant, since 1962; Lord Mayor of London, 1986–87; Consultant, Touche Ross & Co., since 1984; Director of public and private companies; Chairman, Asset Trust plc, since 1982; *b* 19 Dec. 1935; *o s* of Kenneth Henry and Muriel Phyllis Rowe-Ham; *m* Sandra Celia (*née* Nicholls), *widow* of Ian Glover; three *s. Educ:* Dragon School; Charterhouse. FCA; Mem., Soc. of Investment Analysts. Commnd 3rd King's Own Hussars. Mem., Stock Exchange, 1964–84; Sen. Partner, Smith Keen Cutler, 1972–82. Dir, The Nineteen Twenty Eight Investment Trust, 1984–; Regional Dir (London West), Lloyds Bank, 1985–; Director: W. Canning plc, 1981–86 (Consultant 1986–); Savoy Theatre Ltd, 1986–; Mem. Adv. Panel, Guinness Mahon Fund Managers Ltd. Alderman, City of London, Ward of Bridge and Bridge Without, 1976–; Sheriff, City of London, 1984–85. Court Member: City Univ.; Worshipful Co. of Chartered Accountants in England and Wales (Master, 1985–86); Worshipful Co. of Wheelwrights; Hon. Mem., Worshipful Co. of Launderers; Mem. Ct, HAC; Member: Guild of Freemen; VSO Appeal Council; Youth Business Initiative Bd. Chm., Birmingham Municipal Bank, 1970–72; Mem., Birmingham CC, 1965–72. Chm., Political Council, Junior Carlton Club, 1977; Dep. Chm., Political Cttee, Carlton Club, 1977–79. Member: United Wards Club; Royal Soc. of St George. Governor, Christ's Hospital. JP City of London, 1976. Hon. DLitt City Univ., 1986. KStJ 1986. Commandeur de l'Ordre Mérite, France, 1984; Commander, Order of the Lion, Malaŵi, 1985; Order of the Aztec Eagle (Cl. II), Mexico, 1985. *Recreations:* theatre, shooting. *Clubs:* Carlton, City Livery, Guildhall.

ROWELL, Sir John (Joseph), Kt 1980; CBE 1974; Chairman, Legal Aid Commission of Queensland, since 1978; Senior Partner, Neil O'Sullivan & Rowell, Solicitors, Brisbane, since 1968; *b* 15 Feb. 1916; *s* of Joseph Alfred Rowell and Mary Lilian Rowell (*née* Hooper), both born in England; *m* 1947, Mary Kathleen (*née* de Silva); three *s* two *d. Educ:* Brisbane Grammar School; Univ. of Queensland (BA). Served AIF, 1940–46; Captain 2/10 Fd Regt (Efficiency Medal, 1946). Admitted Solicitor, 1939; Notary Public, 1959. Pres., Queensland Law Soc. Inc., 1964–66 (Mem. Council, 1956–67); Treas., Law Council of Aust., 1961–63 (Mem. Exec., 1960–67); Mem. Bd, Faculty of Law, Univ. of Queensland, 1959–78; Chm., Legal Assistance Cttee of Queensland, 1966–79; Mem., Commonwealth Legal Aid Commn, 1980–85. Chairman: Concrete Constructions (Qld) Pty Ltd; Qld Bulk Handling Pty Ltd; Gas Corp. of Qld Ltd; Dir of Principal Bd, Boral Ltd and Boral Resources Ltd; Local Dir, City Mutual Life Assurance Soc. Ltd (Qld Chm., 1986); Director: Boral Gas Ltd; Trans City Mutual Management Ltd, 1986–. Former Hon. Consul of Qld for Federal Repub. of Germany; Dean, Consular Corps of Qld, 1978–80. Officer's Cross, Federal Republic of Germany, 1st class, 1979; Comdr's Cross, Order of Merit, FRG, 1986. *Recreations:* golf, fishing, reading. *Address:* Edgecliffe, 48 Walcott Street, St Lucia, Brisbane, Qld 4067, Australia. *T:* 370–9070. *Clubs:* Union, Australian (Sydney); Brisbane, United Service, Tattersall's (Brisbane); Indooroopilly Golf, Southport Golf.

ROWLAND, David; *see* Rowland, J. D.

ROWLAND, David Powys; Stipendiary Magistrate, Mid Glamorgan (formerly Merthyr Tydfil), since 1961; *b* 7 Aug. 1917; *s* of late Henry Rowland, CBE, Weston-super-Mare; *m* 1st, 1946, Joan (*d* 1958), *d* of late Group Capt. J. McCrae, MBE, Weston-super-Mare; one *s* one *d*; 2nd, 1961, Jenny (marr. diss. 1977), *d* of late Percival Lance, Swanage, and *widow* of Michael A. Forester-Bennett, Alverstoke; one *s* one *d* (and one step-*d*); 3rd, 1980, Diana, *d* of late W. H. Smith, Cannock, and *widow* of Lt-Col W. D. H. McCardie, S Staffs Regt (two step-*d*). *Educ:* Cheltenham Coll.; Oriel Coll., Oxford (BA). Lieut, Royal Welch Fusiliers, 1940–46. Called to Bar, Middle Temple, 1947. Deputy Chairman: Glamorgan QS, 1961–71; Breconshire QS, 1964–71. Mem. Nat. Adv. Council on Training of Magistrates, 1964–73. *Recreations:* fly-fishing, gardening, golf. *Address:* Trosglwyd, Dyffryn Crawnon, Llangynidr, Crickhowell, Powys. *T:* Bwlch 730635.

ROWLAND, Deborah Molly; Her Honour Judge Rowland; a Circuit Judge (formerly a County Court Judge) since 1971; *d* of Samuel and Hilda Rowland. *Educ:* Slade Sch. of Art; Bartlett Sch. of Architecture; Courtauld Inst of Fine Art. Diploma in Fine Art and Architecture. Called to the Bar, Lincoln's Inn, June 1950. *Publication:* Guide to Security of Tenure for Business and Professional Tenants, 1956. *Recreations:* music (Founder, Bar Musical Soc.), painting, sculpture. *Address:* Lincoln's Inn, WC2.

ROWLAND, Herbert Grimley; *b* 10 Feb. 1905; *s* of Frank Rowland, MRCS, LRCP, and Josephine Mary (*née* Quirke); *m* 1938, Margaret Jane Elizabeth, *yr d* of Robert Crawford Higginson and Mary Higginson; one *d. Educ:* Nautical Coll., Pangbourne; Peterhouse, Cambridge. Called to Bar, 1928; admitted Solicitor, 1933; private practice, Solicitor, 1933–40; joined Office of Solicitor of Inland Revenue, 1940; Princ. Asst Solicitor of Inland Revenue, 1961–65; Acting Solicitor of Inland Revenue, 1961; Special Commissioner of Income Tax, 1965–70. Chm., S Middlesex Rent Tribunal, 1972–76. *Recreation:* golf. *Address:* 10 Hillcrest, Durlston Road, Swanage, Dorset. *T:* Swanage 423256. *Clubs:* Bramley Golf (Surrey); Isle of Purbeck (Swanage).

ROWLAND, Air Marshal Sir James (Anthony), KBE 1977; DFC 1944; AFC 1953; BE; CEng, FRAeS, FIE(Aust); Governor of New South Wales, since 1981; *b* 1 Nov. 1922; *s* of Louis Claude Rowland and Elsie Jean Rowland; *m* 1955, Faye Alison (*née* Doughton); one *d. Educ:* Cranbrook Sch., Sydney; St Paul's Coll., Univ. of Sydney (BE Aero). CEng, FRAeS 1969; FIE (Aust) 1978. Served War, Pilot, RAAF and RAF Bomber Comd, 1942–45. Sydney Univ., 1940–41 and 1946–47; Empire Test Pilots' Sch., Farnborough, 1949; Chief Test Pilot, RAAF R&D Unit, 1951–54; Staff Coll., 1956; Staff and unit posts, incl. OC R&D, 1957–60; RAAF Mirage Mission, Paris, 1961–64; CO No 1 Aircraft Depot, 1966; Sen. Engr SO, Ops Comd, 1968–69; RCDS, 1971; Dir Gen., Aircraft Engrg, RAAF, 1972; Air Mem. for Technical Services, 1973; Chief of Air Staff, RAAF, 1975–79. Mem., Admin. Appeals Tribunal, 1979–80; Consultant, OFEMA Australia, 1980. Hon. DEng Sydney, 1983. KStJ 1981. *Publications:* contribs to professional jls. *Recreations:* surfing, reading, golf. *Address:* Government House, Sydney, NSW 2000, Australia. *T:* 233 2233. *Club:* United Services (Brisbane).

ROWLAND, (John) David; Chairman, Stewart Wrightson Holdings plc, since 1981; *b* 10 Aug. 1933; *s* of Cyril Arthur Rowland and Eileen Mary Rowland; *m* 1957, Giulia Powell; one *s* one *d. Educ:* St Paul's School; Trinity College, Cambridge (MA Natural Sciences). Joined Matthews Wrightson and Co., 1956, Dir, 1965; Dir, Matthews Wrightson Holdings, 1972; Dep. Chm., Stewart Wrightson Holdings, 1978–81. Chm., Westminster Insurance Agencies, 1981–; Dir, Royal London Mutual Insurance Soc., 1985–. Dir, Project Full-employ, 1973–. Vice-Pres., British Insurance Brokers Assoc., 1980–; Member of Council: Industrial Soc., 1983–; British Crafts Centre, 1985–. Governor, Coll. of Insurance, 1983–85; Chm., 1985–, Mem. Council, 1980–, Templeton Coll. (Oxford Centre for Management Studies). *Recreations:* golf, running slowly. *Address:* 6 Mountfort Crescent, N1 1JW. *T:* 01–609 2041. *Clubs:* MCC; Royal and Ancient Golf (St Andrews), Royal Worlington and Newmarket Golf, Sunningdale Golf.

ROWLAND, Robert Todd, QC 1969; **His Honour Judge Rowland;** County Court Judge of Northern Ireland, since 1974; President, Lands Tribunal for Northern Ireland, since 1983; *b* 12 Jan. 1922; *yr s* of late Lt-Col Charles Rowland and Jean Rowland; *m* 1952, Kathleen, *er d* of late H. J. Busby, Lambourn, Berks; two *s. Educ:* Crossley and Porter Sch., Halifax, Yorks; Ballyclare High Sch.; Queen's Univ. of Belfast (LLB 1948). Called to Bar of N Ireland, 1949; Mem., Bar Council, 1967–72. Served 2nd Punjab Regt, IA, in India, Assam, Burma, Thailand, Malaya, 1942–46. Counsel to Attorney-Gen. for N Ireland, 1966–69; Sen. Crown Prosecutor for Co. Tyrone, 1969–72; Vice-Pres., VAT Tribunal for N Ireland, 1972–74. Served on County Court Rules Cttee, 1965–72 and 1975–; Chairman: War Pensions Appeal Tribunal, 1962–72; Commn of Inquiry into Housing Contracts, 1978; Member: Bd of Governors, Strathearn Sch., 1969–; Legal Adv. Cttee, Gen. Synod of Church of Ireland, 1975–. Chancellor, dioceses of Armagh, and Down and Dromore, 1978–. *Recreations:* fly-fishing, golf. *Address:* 36 Knocklofty Park, Belfast, N Ireland BT4 3NB.

ROWLANDS, Edward; MP (Lab) Merthyr Tydfil and Rhymney, since 1983 (Merthyr Tydfil, April 1972–1983); *b* 23 Jan. 1940; *e s* of W. S. Rowlands; *m* 1968, Janice Williams, Kidwelly, Carmarthenshire; two *s* one *d. Educ:* Rhondda Grammar Sch.; Wirral Grammar Sch.; King's Coll., London. BA Hons History (London) 1962. Research Asst, History of Parliament Trust, 1963–65; Lectr in Modern History and Govt, Welsh Coll. of Adv. Technology, 1965–. MP (Lab) Cardiff North, 1966–70; Parliamentary Under-Secretary of State: Welsh Office, 1969–70, 1974–75; FCO, 1975–76; Minister of State, FCO, 1976–79. Member: Governing Body and Exec. Cttee, Commonwealth Inst., 1980–; Academic Council, Wilton Park, 1983–. A Booker Prize Judge, 1984. *Recreation:* music. *Address:* House of Commons, SW1; 5 Park Crescent, Thomastown, Merthyr Tydfil, Mid Glamorgan. *T:* Merthyr 4912.

ROWLANDS, John Kendall, FSA; Keeper, Department of Prints and Drawings, British Museum, since 1981; *b* 18 Sept. 1931; *s* of Arthur and Margaret Rowlands; *m* 1st, 1957, Else A. H. Bachmann (marr. diss. 1981); one *s* two *d*; 2nd, 1982, Lorna Jane Lowe; one *d. Educ:* Chester Cathedral Choir Sch.; King's Sch., Chester; Gonville and Caius Coll., Cambridge. MA Cantab 1959; MA Oxon; FSA 1976. Asst Keeper, Dept of Art, City Mus. and Art Gall., Birmingham, 1956–60; Editor, Clarendon Press, Oxford, 1960–65; Asst Keeper, 1965–74, Dep. Keeper, 1974–81, Dept of Prints and Drawings, British Museum. *Publications:* David Cox Centenary Exhibition Catalogue, 1959; Graphic Work of Albrecht Dürer, 1971; Bosch, 1975; Rubens: drawings and sketches . . ., 1977; Urs Graf, 1977; Hercules Segers, 1979; Bosch, the Garden of Earthly Delights, 1979; German Drawings from a Private Collection, 1984; The Paintings of Hans Holbein the Younger, 1985; contribs to specialist journals. *Recreation:* playing the piano and organ. *Address:* 21 St Paul's Place, N1 2QF. *Club:* Beefsteak.

ROWLANDS, (John) Martin, CBE 1980; Secretary for Civil Service, Hong Kong Government, 1978–85; *b* 20 July 1925; *s* of late John Walter Rowlands and of Mary Ace Maitland (*née* Roberts); *m* 1956, Christiane Germaine Madeleine Lacheny; two *d. Educ:* Charterhouse; Selwyn Coll., Cambridge (MA). Military service, 1943–47 (Captain, 3rd Royal Indian Artillery Field Regt, HQ XV Indian Corps, HQ ALFSEA). HMOCS, Hong Kong Admin. Service, 1952–85: Dep. Dir of Urban Services, 1966–68; Principal Asst Colonial Sec., 1968–71; Dep. Sec. for Home Affairs, 1971–74; Dir of Immigration, 1974–78; Mem., Hong Kong Legislative Council, 1978–84. *Recreations:* travel, railways, bird-watching. *Address:* Flat 3, 15 Collingham Road, SW5 0NU. *Clubs:* Hong Kong, Royal Hong Kong Jockey.

ROWLANDS, Air Marshal Sir John (Samuel), GC 1943; KBE 1971 (OBE 1954); Consultant, Civil Aviation Administration, since 1981; *b* 23 Sept. 1915; *s* of late Samuel and Sarah Rowlands; *m* 1942, Constance Wight; two *d. Educ:* Hawarden School; University of Wales (BSc Hons). Joined RAFVR, 1939; permanent commission in RAF, 1945. British Defence Staff, Washington, 1961–63; Imperial Defence College, 1964; Royal Air Force College, Cranwell, 1965–68; First Director General of Training, RAF, 1968–70; AOC-in-C, RAF Maintenance comd, 1970–73; Asst Principal, Sheffield Polytechnic, 1974–80. *Recreations:* photography, tennis, motoring. *Address:* 45 Lyndhurst Road, Sheffield S11 9BJ. *Club:* Royal Air Force.

ROWLANDS, Maldwyn Jones, OBE 1979; FLA, FRGS, FLS; Head of Library Services (designation Museum Librarian, until 1974), British Museum (Natural History), 1965–81, retired; *b* 7 March 1918; *s* of Thomas and Elizabeth Rowlands; *m* 1941, Sybil Elizabeth Price; two *s* one *d. Educ:* Newtown Grammar Sch., Montgomeryshire; University Coll. London. Served in Army, 1940–46: commnd 1941 (Lieut), HQ 21 Army Gp (Staff Captain), 1944–46 (C-in-C's Cert. 1945). Asst Librarian, Science Museum Library, 1946–54; Deputy Librarian: British Museum (Natural History), 1954–63; Patent Office, 1963–65. *Recreations:* old books and bindings, Welsh history and folk-lore. *Address:* Cannon Cottage, Cannongate Close, Hythe, Kent CT21 5PZ.

ROWLANDS, Martin; *see* Rowlands, J. M.

ROWLANDS, Martyn Omar, FSIAD, FPRI; Chairman, Martyn Rowlands Design Consultants Ltd, since 1960; *b* 27 July 1923; *s* of Edward and Mildred Rowlands; *m* 1st, 1951, Ann Patricia (*d* 1974); two *s* one *d*; 2nd, 1978, Mary Winifred. *Educ:* Eltham Coll.; Central Sch. of Art and Design. FSIAD 1960; FPRI 1973. Served War, RAF, 1940–45: India and Burma. Central Sch. of Art and Design, 1946–49; Head of Indust. Design, Ekco Plastics, 1954–59; started own design consultancy, 1959. Past Pres., SIAD. *Recreation:* photography. *Address:* Winchelsea House, Epping, Essex CM16 4DD. *T:* Epping 72887. *Club:* Arts.

ROWLEY, Sir Charles (Robert), 7th Bt *cr* 1836; *b* 15 March 1926; *s* of Sir William Joshua Rowley, 6th Bt and Beatrice Gwendoline, *d* of Rev. Augustus George Kirby; *S* father, 1971; *m* 1952, Astrid, *d* of Sir Arthur Massey, CBE; one *s* one *d*. *Educ:* Wellington. *Heir: s* Richard Charles Rowley, *b* 14 Aug. 1959. *Address:* 21 Tedworth Square, SW3; Naseby Hall, Northamptonshire.

ROWLEY, Frederick Allan, CMG 1978; OBE 1959; MC 1945; Major (retd); HM Diplomatic Service, retired; *b* 27 July 1922; *m* 1951, Anne Crawley; one *s* three *d*. *Educ:* Haig Sch., Aldershot. Served War of 1939–45: Ranks, 8th Worcs Regt (TA), 1939–40; Emergency Commnd Officer, 5th Bn, 10th Baluch Regt (KGVO), Jacob's Rifles, Indian Army, Burma Campaign (MC), June 1941–Nov. 1948. At partition of India, granted regular commn (back-dated, 1942) in Worcestershire Regt, but retd (wounded), sub. Major. Joined HM Diplomatic Service, Nov. 1948: served (with brief periods in FO) in: Egypt; Ethiopia; Turkey; Burma; Singapore; Australia; Malaysia; FCO 1971–72; Under-Sec., N Ireland Office (on secondment), 1972–73; Counsellor, FCO, 1973–79. Joint Services Staff College (jssc), 1959. *Recreations:* cricket, golf. *Address:* Boxalland, Kirdford, West Sussex. *T:* Kirdford 337. *Club:* MCC.

ROWLEY, Geoffrey William; Town Clerk, City of London, since 1982; *b* 9 Sept. 1926; *s* of George Frederick Rowley and Ellen Mary Rowley; *m* 1950, Violet Gertrude Templeman; one *s* one *d*. *Educ:* Owens School. FIPM 1974. Served War, Royal Marines, 1944–47. Corporation of the City of London, 1947–: Head, Personnel Sect., 1965–74; Dep. Town Clerk, 1974–82. Order of White Rose, Finland, 1969; Order of Orange Nassau, Holland, 1982; Légion d'Honneur, France, 1985. *Recreations:* sport: cricket and badminton as a player, soccer as a spectator. *Address:* 3 Wensley Avenue, Woodford Green, Essex. *T:* 01–504 6270.

ROWLEY, John Charles, CMG 1977; Director, Crown Agents Board of Management, 1980–84, retired; *b* 29 Sept. 1919; *s* of John Ernest Rowley and Edith Muriel (*née* Aldridge); *m* 1st, 1945, Pamela Hilda Godfrey (marr. diss. 1971); two *d*; 2nd, 1972, Anne Patricia Dening; one *s*. *Educ:* Ilford; King's College, London (LLB 1948, Upper Second Cl. Hons). Inland Revenue, 1938–40. RAF, 1940–46, pilot, Flight-Lieut; Iceland, 1944 (despatches). Inland Revenue, 1946–64; Min. of Overseas Development, 1964–79, Head, Middle East Develt Div., Beirut, Lebanon and Amman, Jordan, 1971–79; Crown Agents Regional Controller for Middle East, 1979–80. *Recreations:* choral singing, sailing. *Address:* 43 Half Moon Lane, SE24 9JX.

ROWLEY, John Vincent d'Alessio; General Manager, Bracknell New Town Development Corporation, 1955–73; *b* 12 Sept. 1907; 2nd *s* of late Ven. Hugh Rowley, Archdeacon of Kingwilliamstown, S Africa; *m* 1st, 1936, Violet Maud (*d* 1969), *d* of S. H. Day, Grahamstown, S Africa; one *s*; 2nd, 1972, Kathleen Mary Hawkesworth (*née* Pullom). *Educ:* St Andrews Coll., Grahamstown; Trinity Coll., Oxford (Rhodes Schol.). BA 1929; Oxford Univ. Rugby XV, 1929. Entered Sudan Political Service, 1930; Asst District Comr and District Comr, 1930–49; seconded Sudan Defence Force, 1940–42; Dep. Gov., Kordofan Province, 1950–52; Asst Financial Sec., 1952–53; Governor, Darfur Province, 1953–55. Chm., South Hill Park Arts Centre Trust, 1979–. *Recreations:* music, gardening, golf. *Address:* The Spring, Stanford Dingley, near Bradfield, Berks. *T:* Bradfield 744270. *Club:* United Oxford & Cambridge University.

ROWLEY, Sir Joshua Francis, 7th Bt, *cr* 1786; JP; Lord-Lieutenant of Suffolk, since 1978; *b* 31 Dec. 1920; *o s* of 6th Bt and Margery Frances Bacon (*d* 1977); *S* father, 1962; *m* 1959, Hon. Celia Ella Vere Monckton, 2nd *d* of 8th Viscount Galway; one *d*. *Educ:* Eton; Trinity College, Cambridge. Grenadier Guards, 1940–46. Deputy Secretary, National Trust, 1952–55. Chairman: W Suffolk CC, 1971–74; Suffolk CC, 1976–78; DL 1968, High Sheriff 1971, Vice Lord-Lieutenant, 1973–78, JP 1978, Suffolk. *Address:* Holbecks, Hadleigh, Ipswich, Suffolk IP7 5PF. *T:* Hadleigh 823211. *Clubs:* Boodle's, Pratt's, MCC.

ROWLEY, Peter, MC 1944; Chairman, Leonard Cheshire Foundation, since 1982; *b* 12 July 1918; *s* of late Roland and Catherine Isabel Rowley; *m* 1940, Ethnea Louis Florence Mary Howard Kyan; four *d*. *Educ:* Wembley County Sch.; University Coll., Oxford (MA). Served War of 1939–45: Queen's Westminster Rifles, 1938–39; 14th Bn Sherwood Foresters, 1940–46; Adjt, Middle East, N Africa; Company Comdr, Italy; Bde Major 13 Bde, 1944–45; GSOII 8 Corps, 1945–46. Admitted Solicitor, Titmuss Sainer & Webb, 1950; Sen. Partner, 1981–83, retd. Member, Law Society Land Law Cttee, 1970–. Liveryman, Distillers Co., 1975. *Address:* 38 Devonshire Place Mews, W1N 1FJ. *T:* 01–935 1003. *Club:* Royal Automobile.

ROWLEY-CONWY, family name of **Baron Langford.**

ROWLEY HILL, Sir George Alfred; *see* Hill.

ROWLING, Rt. Hon. Sir Wallace (Edward), KCMG 1983; PC 1974; Ambassador of New Zealand to the United States, since 1985; *b* Motueka, 15 Nov. 1927; *s* of A. Rowling; *m* 1951, Glen Elna, *d* of Captain J. M. Reeves; two *s* one *d*. *Educ:* Nelson Coll. MA. Fulbright Schol., 1955–56. Formerly Asst Dir of Educn, NZ Army. MP (Lab) for Buller (later for Tasman), NZ, 1967–84; Minister of Finance, 1972–74; Prime Minister of NZ, 1974–75; Leader of Opposition, 1975–83. Governor for New Zealand, IMF. Rep. NZ at annual meeting of ADB, Kuala Lumpur,1974. Pres., Asia Pacific Socialist Orgn, 1977–. Col Comdt, NZ Army Educn Corps, 1977–82. *Recreation:* golf. *Address:* 37 Observatory Circle, Washington, 20008, DC, USA; 15 Waverley Street, Richmond, New Zealand.

ROWLINSON, Prof. John Shipley, BSc, MA, DPhil Oxon; FRS 1970; FRSC; FEng 1976; FIChemE; Dr Lee's Professor of Physical Chemistry, Oxford University, since 1974; Fellow of Exeter College, since 1974; *b* 12 May 1926; *er s* of late Frank Rowlinson and Winifred Jones; *m* 1952, Nancy Gaskell; one *s* one *d*. *Educ:* Rossall School (Scholar); Trinity College, Oxford (Millard Scholar). Research Associate, Univ. of Wisconsin, USA, 1950–51; ICI Research Fellow, Lecturer, and Senior Lecturer in Chemistry, University of Manchester, 1951–60; Prof. of Chemical Technology, London Univ. (Imperial Coll.), 1961–73. Lectures: Liversidge, Chem. Soc., 1978; von Hofmann, Gesell. Deutscher Chem., 1980; Faraday, 1983, Lennard-Jones, 1985, RSC; Guggenheim, Reading Univ., 1986. Pres., Faraday Div., Chem. Soc., 1979–81; Hon. Treas., Faraday Society, 1968–71; Vice-Pres., Royal Instn of GB, 1974–76; Member, Sale Borough Council, 1956–59. Meldola Medal, Roy. Inst. of Chemistry, 1954; Marlow Medal, Faraday Soc., 1957.

Publications: Liquids and Liquid Mixtures, 1959, (jtly) 3rd edn, 1982; The Perfect Gas, 1963; Physics of Simple Liquids (joint editor), 1968; (trans. jtly) The Metric System, 1969; (jtly) Thermodynamics for Chemical Engineers, 1975; (jtly) Molecular Theory of Capillarity, 1982; papers in scientific journals. *Recreation:* climbing. *Address:* 12 Pullens Field, Headington, Oxford OX3 0BU. *T:* Oxford 67507; Physical Chemistry Laboratory, South Parks Road, Oxford OX1 3QZ. *T:* Oxford 53322. *Club:* Alpine.

ROWNTREE, Sir Norman Andrew Forster, Kt 1970; CEng; FICE; Consultant to Allott and Lomax, Consulting Engineers, since 1979; *b* 11 March 1912; *s* of Arthur Thomas Rowntree, London, and Ethel, *d* of Andrew Forster; *m* 1939, Betty, *d* of William Arthur Thomas; two *s* one *d*. *Educ:* Tottenham County Sch.; London Univ. (BSc(Eng)). Consulting Engineer, 1953–64; Mem. and Dir, Water Resources Bd, 1964–73; Prof. of Civil Engineering, UMIST, 1975–79; Member: Adv. Council for Applied R&D, 1976–80; Meteorological Office Cttee, 1979–80; Commn for Commonwealth Scholarship, 1979–80; Scientific Council, Centre de Formation Internationale à la Gestion des Ressources en Eau (France), 1977–80, Hon. Vice-Pres., 1980–; Expert Adv. Cttee, State of New Jersey Water Supply Master Plan, 1976–80. Pres., Inst. of Water Engineers, 1962–63. Vice-Pres., ICE, 1972–75, Pres. 1975–76. Vis. Prof., KCL, 1972–75; Lectures: CEI Graham Clark, 1972; IMechE Hawksley, 1976. Hon. DSc City Univ, 1974. Gold Medal, Soc. Chem. Ind., 1977. *Address:* 97 Quarry Lane, Kelsall, Tarporley, Cheshire CW6 0NJ. *T:* Kelsall 51195.

ROWNTREE CLIFFORD, Rev. Paul; *see* Clifford.

ROWSE, Alfred Leslie, MA, DLitt; FBA; Emeritus Fellow of All Souls College, Oxford; *b* St Austell, Cornwall, 4 Dec. 1903. *Educ:* Elementary and Grammar Schools, St Austell; Christ Church Oxford (Douglas Jerrold Scholar in English Literature). Sen. Res. Associate, Huntington Library, Calif, 1962–69. Fellow of the Royal Society of Literature; President of the English Association, 1952; Raleigh Lecturer, British Academy, 1957; Trevelyan Lecturer, Cambridge, 1958; Beatty Memorial Lecturer, McGill University, 1963. Pres., Shakespeare Club, Stratford-upon-Avon, 1970–71. Benson Medal, RSL, 1982. *Publications:* Politics and the Younger Generation, 1931; Mr Keynes and the Labour Movement, 1936; Sir Richard Grenville of the Revenge, 1937; Tudor Cornwall, 1941; Poems of a Decade, 1931–41; A Cornish Childhood, 1942; The Spirit of English History, 1943; Poems Chiefly Cornish, 1944; The English Spirit: Essays in History and Literature, 1944, rev. edn 1966; West Country Stories, 1945; The Use of History, 1946; Poems of Deliverance, 1946; The End of an Epoch, 1947; The England of Elizabeth, 1950; The English Past, 1951 (rev. edn, as Times, Persons, Places, 1965); Translation and completion of Lucien Romier's History of France, 1953; The Expansion of Elizabethan England, 1955; The Early Churchills, 1956; The Later Churchills, 1958; Poems Partly American, 1958; The Elizabethans and America, 1959; St Austell: Church, Town, Parish, 1960; All Souls and Appeasement, 1961; Ralegh and the Throckmortons, 1962; William Shakespeare: A Biography, 1963; Christopher Marlowe: A Biography, 1964; A Cornishman at Oxford, 1965; Shakespeare's Southampton: Patron of Virginia, 1965; Bosworth Field and the Wars of the Roses, 1966; Poems of Cornwall and America, 1967; Cornish Stories, 1967; A Cornish Anthology, 1968; The Cornish in America, 1969; The Elizabethan Renaissance: the Life of the Society, 1971; The Elizabethan Renaissance: The Cultural Achievement, 1972; Strange Encounter (poems), 1972; The Tower of London in the History of the Nation, 1972; Westminster Abbey in the History of the Nation, 1972; Shakespeare's Sonnets: a modern edition, 1973, 2nd edn with introduction and prose versions, 1984; Simon Forman: Sex and Society in Shakespeare's Age, 1974; Windsor Castle in the History of the Nation, 1974; (with John Betjeman) Victorian and Edwardian Cornwall, 1974; Oxford in the History of the Nation, 1975; Discoveries and Reviews, 1975; Jonathan Swift: Major Prophet, 1975; A Cornishman Abroad, 1976; Brown Buck: a Californian fantasy, 1976; Matthew Arnold: Poet and Prophet, 1976; Shakespeare the Elizabethan, 1977; Homosexuals in History: Ambivalence in society, literature and the arts, 1977; Heritage of Britain, 1977; Milton the Puritan: Portrait of a mind, 1977; The Road to Oxford: poems, 1978; (ed) The Poems of Shakespeare's Dark Lady, 1978; The Byrons and Trevanions, 1978; The Annotated Shakespeare, 3 vols (introds to vols and plays), 1978; A Man of the Thirties, 1979; Portraits and Views, 1979; Story of Britain, 1979; (ed) A Man of Singular Virtue: Roper's Life of Sir Thomas More, 1980; Memories of Men and Women, 1980; Shakespeare's Globe, 1980; A Life: Collected Poems, 1981; Eminent Elizabethans, 1983; Shakespeare's Characters: a complete guide, 1984; Night at the Carn, and Other Stories, 1984; Prefaces to Shakespeare's Plays, 1984; Shakespeare's Self-Portrait: Passages chosen from his work, with notes, 1984; Glimpses of the Great, 1985; Reflections on the Puritan Revolution, 1986; The Little Land of Cornwall, 1986; Stories from Trenarren, 1986; A Quartet of Cornish Cats, 1986; (ed) The Contemporary Shakespeare. *Address:* Trenarren House, St Austell, Cornwall. *Club:* Athenæum.

ROWSELL, Edmund Lionel P.; *see* Penning-Rowsell.

ROWSON, Lionel Edward Aston, OBE 1955; MA Cantab 1977; FRS 1973; FRCVS; Director, Cambridge and District Cattle Breeders (AI Centre), 1942–84 (part-time, 1979–84); Officer in Charge, Agricultural Research Council Animal Research Station, Cambridge, 1976–79; Fellow of Wolfson College, Cambridge, since 1973; *b* 28 May 1914; *s* of L. F. Rowson, LDS, and M. A. Rowson (*née* Aston); *m* 1942, Audrey Kathleen Foster; two *s* two *d*. *Educ:* King Edward VIth Sch., Stafford; Royal Veterinary Coll., London. MRCVS, FRCVS 1972; FRVC 1975. Engaged in general practice, 1939–42. Dep. Dir, ARC Unit of Reproductive Physiology and Biochemistry, 1955–76. Life Hon. Pres., Internat. Embryo Transfer Soc.; Mem., Acad. Royale de Médecine de Belgique, 1977. Hon. MA Cantab, 1977. Thomas Baxter Prize, 1956; Wooldridge Meml Lecture and Medal, 1974; Dalrymple-Champneys Cup and Medal, 1975; Bledisloe Veterinary Medal, 1978. *Publication:* (jointly) Reproduction in Domestic Animals (ed H. H. Cole and P. T. Cupps). *Recreations:* shooting, cricket, thoroughbred breeding. *Address:* The Grove, Water Lane, Histon, Cambridge. *T:* Histon 2534.

ROXBEE COX, family name of **Baron Kings Norton.**

ROXBURGH, Air Vice-Marshal Henry Lindsay, CBE 1966; FRCP, FRCPE; Commandant, RAF Institute of Aviation Medicine, 1969–73; retired; *b* 5 Dec. 1909; *s* of John Roxburgh, Galston, Ayrshire and Cape Town, and Edith Mary Roxburgh (*née* Smithers), Kenilworth, Cape; *m* 1944, Hermione Babington (*née* Collard); one *s* two *d*. *Educ:* George Watson's College, Edinburgh; Edinburgh University. BSc 1932; PhD 1934; MB, ChB 1940; FRCPE 1966; FRCP 1972. Medical Branch, Royal Air Force, 1941–73. Service mainly at RAF Inst. of Aviation Med.: research undertaken in various aspects of aviation physiology and related subjects; apptd Prof. in Aviation Medicine, 1966. Chairman, Aero-Space Medical Panel of Advisory Gp of Aero-Space Research and Development, Paris, 1965–67. Mem., Internat. Acad. of Aviation and Space Medicine. QHS 1971–73. FRAeS 1965. *Publications:* papers in field of aviation medicine. *Recreation:* gardening. *Address:* 11 Auderville, Alderney, CI. *Club:* Royal Air Force.

ROXBURGH, Rt. Rev. James William; *see* Barking, Area Bishop of.

ROXBURGH, Vice-Adm. Sir John (Charles Young), KCB 1972 (CB 1969); CBE 1967; DSO 1943; DSC 1942 (Bar, 1945); *b* 29 June 1919; *s* of Sir (Thomas) James (Young) Roxburgh, CIE; *m* 1942, Philippa, 3rd *d* of late Major C. M. Hewlett, MC; one *s* one *d*. *Educ*: RNC, Dartmouth. Naval Cadet, 1933; Midshipman, 1937; Sub-Lt 1939; Lt 1941; Lt-Comdr 1949; Comdr 1952; Capt. 1958; Rear-Adm. 1967; Vice-Adm. 1970. Served in various ships, 1937–39; joined Submarine Br., 1940; served in ops off Norway, in Bay of Biscay and Mediterranean, 1940–42; comd HM Submarines H43, United and Tapir, 1942–45 in ops in Mediterranean and off Norway; HMS Vanguard, 1948–50; comd HM Submarine Turpin, 1951–53; HMS Triumph, 1955; HMS Ark Royal, 1955–56; comd HMS Contest, 1956–58; Brit. Jt Services Mission, Wash., 1958–60; comd 3rd Submarine Sqdn and HMS Adamant, 1960–61; idc 1962; Dep. Dir of Defence Plans (Navy), MoD, 1963–65; comd HMS Eagle, 1965–67; Flag Officer: Sea Training, 1967–69; Plymouth, 1969; Submarines, and NATO Comdr Submarines, E Atlantic, 1969–72, retired 1972. Chm., Grovebell Group Ltd, 1972–75. Mem. Management Cttee, The Freedom Assoc., 1978–85. Pres., Royal Naval Benevolent Trust, 1978–84. Co. Councillor, Surrey, 1977–81. *Recreations*: golf, sailing, walking, music. *Address*: Oakdene, Wood Road, Hindhead, Surrey. *T*: Hindhead 5600. *Club*: Army and Navy.

ROXBURGHE, 10th Duke of, *cr* 1707; **Guy David Innes-Ker;** Baron Roxburghe 1600; Earl of Roxburghe, Baron Ker of Cessford and Cavertoun, 1616; Bt (NS) 1625; Viscount Broxmouth, Earl of Kelso, Marquis of Bowmont and Cessford, 1707; Earl Innes (UK), 1837; *b* 18 Nov. 1954; *s* of 9th Duke of Roxburghe, and Margaret Elisabeth (*d* 1983) (who *m* 1976, Jocelyn Olaf Hambro, *qv*), *d* of late Frederick Bradshaw McConnel; *S* father, 1974; *m* 1977, Lady Jane Meriel Grosvenor, *yr d* of 5th Duke of Westminster, TD; two *s* one *d*. *Educ*: Eton; RMA Sandhurst (Sword of Honour, June 1974); Magdalene Coll., Cambridge. BA (Land Economy) 1980. Commnd into Royal Horse Guards/1st Dragoons, 1974; RARO 1977. Mem., Fishmongers' Co.; Freeman of City of London, 1983. *Recreations*: shooting, fishing, cricket, racing, ski-ing. *Heir*: *s* Marquis of Bowmont, *qv*. *Address*: Floors Castle, Kelso. *T*: Kelso 24288. *Clubs*: Turf, White's.

ROXBY, John Henry M.; *see* Maude-Roxby.

ROY, Andrew Donald; economist; *b* 28 June 1920; *er s* of late Donald Whatley Roy, FRCS, FRCOG, and late Beatrice Anne Roy (*née* Barstow); *m* 1947, Katherine Juliet Grove-White; one *s* two *d*. *Educ*: Malvern Coll.; Sidney Sussex Coll., Cambridge. Maths Trip. Pt I 1939 and Econ. Trip. Pt II 1948, Class I hons. 1939–45: served Royal Artillery, in UK, India and Burma (8 Medium Regt; Adjt, 1942–44). Cambridge Univ.: Asst Lecturer, 1949–51; Lecturer, 1951–64; Jun. Proctor, 1956–57; Sidney Sussex Coll.: Fellow, 1951–64; Tutor, 1953–56; Sen. Tutor, 1956–62; Financial Bursar, 1959–61. HM Treasury: Economic Consultant, 1962; Sen. Economic Adviser, 1964; Under-Sec. (Economics), 1969–72; Under-Sec., DTI, 1972–74, MoD, 1974–76; Chief Economic Adviser, DHSS, 1976–80. Consultant, NIESR, 1981–83. Governor, Malvern Coll., 1960–. *Publications*: British Economic Statistics (with C. F. Carter), 1954; articles in economic and statistical jls. *Address*: 15 Rusholme Road, Putney, SW15 3JX. *T*: 01–789 3180. *Club*: United Oxford & Cambridge University.

ROY, Prof. Arthur Douglas, FRCS, FRCSE, FRCSGlas, FRCSI; FACS; Chief of Surgical Services, Ministry of Health, Sultanate of Oman, since 1985; Professor Emeritus, Queen's University of Belfast, 1985; *b* 10 April 1925; *s* of Arthur Roy and Edith Mary (*née* Brown); *m* 1st, 1954, Monica Cecilia Mary Bowley; three *d*; 2nd, 1973, Patricia Irene McColl. *Educ*: Paisley Grammar Sch.; Univ. of Glasgow (MB, ChB, Commendation). RAMC, 1948–50; Surgical Registrar posts in Glasgow and Inverness, 1950–54; Sen. Surgical Registrar, Aylesbury and Oxford, 1954–57; Cons. Surgeon and Hon. Lectr, Western Infirmary, Glasgow, 1957–68; Foundn Prof. of Surgery, Univ. of Nairobi, 1968–72; Prof. of Surgery, QUB, 1973–85. Mem. Council, RCSE, 1979–85. *Publications*: Lecture Notes in Surgery: tropical supplement, 1975; various papers on gastro-enterology, endocrine surgery, tropical medicine, etc. *Recreations*: sailing, squash, gardening. *Address*: Department of Surgery, Knoula Hospital, Box 9090, Mina Al-Fahal, Sultanate of Oman. *T*: 602617. *Club*: Royal Commonwealth Society.

ROY, Ian; Assistant Under-Secretary of State, Home Office, 1963–72; *b* 2 Aug. 1912; *o s* of late John Roy and Annie Froude Marshall; *m* 1939, Betty Louise Blissett; one *s* two *d*. *Educ*: Manchester Grammar School; Peterhouse, Cambridge. Assistant Inspector of Taxes, 1935; Assistant Principal, Home Office, 1936; Private Secretary to Permanent Under-Secretary of State, 1938; to Parliamentary Under-Secretary of State, 1939–40; Asst Secretary, 1947. *Address*: Flat 47, Cholmeley Lodge, Cholmeley Park, Highgate, N6. *T*: 01–340 3143.

ROYCE, David Nowill; Director-General, Institute of Export, 1980–85; *b* 10 Sept. 1920; *s* of late Bernard Royce and Ida Christine (*née* Nowill); *m* 1942, Esther Sylvia Yule; two *s* one *d*. *Educ*: Reading School; Vienna University. Served HM Forces, 1940–46. Major, Intelligence Corps, 1946; Asst Principal, Foreign Office, German Section, 1948; Foreign Service, 1949; First Secretary: Athens, 1953; Saigon, 1955; Foreign Office, 1957; Head of Chancery, Caracas, 1960; Counsellor (Commercial), Bonn, 1963; Counsellor (Commercial) and Consul-Gen., Helsinki, 1967–68; Commercial Inspector, FCO, 1969–71; Dir for Co-ordination of Export Services, DTI, 1971–73; Under-Secretary: Overseas Finance and Planning Div., Dept of Trade, 1973–75; CRE 3 and Export Develt Divs, Dept of Trade, 1975–77; Export Develt Div., Dept of Trade, 1977–80. Hon. Fellow, Inst. of Export, 1985. *Recreation*: gardening. *Address*: 5 Sprimont Place, SW3. *T*: 01–589 9148. *Club*: Travellers'.

ROYDEN, Sir Christopher (John), 5th Bt *cr* 1905; Director, Spencer Thornton & Co., since 1974; *b* 26 Feb. 1937; *s* of Sir John Ledward Royden, 4th Bt, and of Dolores Catherine, *d* of late Cecil J. G. Coward; *S* father, 1976; *m* 1961, Diana Bridget, *d* of Lt-Col J. H. Goodhart, MC; two *s* one *d*. *Educ*: Winchester Coll.; Christ Church, Oxford (MA). Duncan Fox & Co. Ltd, 1960–71; Spencer Thornton & Co., 1971–. *Recreations*: fishing, shooting, gardening. *Heir*: *s* John Michael Joseph Royden, *b* 17 March 1965. *Address*: Flat 2, 8 Nevern Square, SW5. *Club*: Cavalry and Guards.

ROYDS, Rev. John Caress, MA Cantab; with Church Missionary Society, since 1985; *b* 1920; 3rd *s* of Rev. Edward Thomas Hubert Royds, BA. *Educ*: Monkton Combe School, Bath; Queens' College, Cambridge. II 1 hons History, 1947. Military service with British and Indian Armies, 1940–46. Assistant master, Bryanston School, Dorset, 1947–61, Housemaster, 1951–61; Headmaster: General Wingate School, Addis Ababa, 1961 65; Uppingham Sch., 1965–75. Deacon, 1974; Priest, 1975; Dir of Educn for Peterborough diocese, 1976–81; Vicar of St James's, Northampton, 1981–85. *Address*: PO Box 245, Peshawar, Pakistan.

ROYLE, family name of **Baron Fanshawe of Richmond.**

ROYLE, Prof. Joseph Kenneth; Professor and Head of Department of Mechanical Engineering, University of Sheffield, 1966–84; *b* 3 April 1924; *s* of J. Royle, Accrington, Lancs; *m* 1955, P. R. Wallwork; one *s* two *d*. *Educ*: Manchester University. Royal Aircraft Estabt, 1944–48; Manchester Univ., 1949–61; Vis. Assoc. Prof., MIT, 1961–62; Sen. Lectr, Univ. of Manchester Inst. of Science and Technology, 1962–64; Dept of Mech. Engrg, Univ. of Sheffield, 1964–84, retd. *Publications*: contribs to Proc. IMechE, etc. *Recreations*: gardening, music. *Address*: Anselm, Over Lane, Baslow, Derbyshire. *T*: Baslow 3149.

ROYLE, Mrs Julian A. C.; *see* Harwood, Elizabeth Jean.

ROYLE, Timothy Lancelot Fanshawe, FInstM; Chairman: Control Risks Group, since 1975; Berry Palmer & Lyle, since 1984; *b* 24 April 1931; *s* of Sir Lancelot Carrington Royle, KBE, and Barbara Rachel Royle; *m* 1959, Margaret Jill Stedeford; two *s* one *d*. *Educ*: Harrow; Mons Mil. Acad. FInstM 1977; FBIBA. Commnd 15th/19th King's Royal Hussars, 1949, Inns of Court Regt, TA, 1951–63. Joined Hogg Robinson Gp, 1951; Man. Dir, 1980–81. Dep. Chm., Marine Reinsurance Brokers, 1976–. Member: Church Assembly of C of E, 1960–70; Gen. Synod of C of E, 1985–; Church Comr, 1966–83. Chairman: Lindley Educn Trust, 1970–; Christian Weekly Newspapers, 1979–. *Recreations*: country pursuits, ski-ing. *Address*: National Westminster Bank, 11 Leadenhall Street, EC3. *Clubs*: Cavalry and Guards, MCC; St Moritz Tobogganing (St Moritz).
See also Baron Fanshawe of Richmond.

ROZARIO, Most Rev. Michael; *see* Dhaka, Archbishop of, (RC).

ROZHDESTVENSKY, Gennadi Nikolaevich; Founder, Artistic Director and Chief Conductor, State Symphony Orchestra of Ministry of Culture, USSR (New Symphony Orchestra), since 1983; Professor of Conducting, Moscow State Conservatoire, since 1965; *b* 4 May 1931; *m* Victoria Postnikova, concert pianist. Studied piano at Moscow Conservatoire; started conducting at 18. Conductor Bolshoi Theatre, 1956–60 (Assistant Conductor, 1951); Chief Conductor, USSR Radio and Television Symphony Orchestra, 1960–74; Principal Conductor, Bolshoi Theatre, 1965–70; Chief Conductor: Stockholm Philharmonic Orchestra, 1974–77; BBC Symphony Orchestra, 1978–81; Moscow Chamber Opera, 1974–83; Vienna Symphony Orchestra, 1981–83. Guest conductor, Europe, Israel, America, Far East, Australia. Lenin Prize, 1970; People's Artist, USSR, 1972; Order of Red Banner of Labour, 1981. *Recreation*: music. *Address*: c/o Victor Hochhauser, 4 Oak Hill Way, NW3. *Club*: Athenæum.

RUBBIA, Prof. Carlo; physicist; Scientist, European Organization for Nuclear Research, Geneva (CERN), since 1961; Professor of Physics, Harvard University, since 1971; *b* 31 March 1934; *s* of Silvio and Bice Rubbia; *m* Marisa; one *s* one *d*. *Educ*: Scuola Normale Superiore, Pisa; Univ. of Pisa. Research Fellow, Columbia Univ., 1958–59; Lectr, Univ. of Rome, 1960–61; CERN, 1960–; scientist, Fermi Nat. Accelerator Lab., USA, 1969–73. Mem., Papal Acad. of Science, 1986–. Nobel Prize for Physics (jtly), 1984. *Publications*: papers on nuclear physics: weak force quanta (W –, W + and Z particles, intermediate vector bosons); proton-antiproton collision; sixth quark. *Address*: EP Division, CERN, 1211 Geneva 23, Switzerland.

RUBENS, Bernice Ruth; writer and director of documentary films, since 1957; *b* 26 July 1928; *m* 1947, Rudi Nassauer; two *d*. *Educ*: University of Wales, Cardiff (BA, Hons English; Fellow 1982). Followed teaching profession, 1950–55. American Blue Ribbon award for documentary film, Stress, 1968. *Publications*: Set on Edge, 1960; Madame Sousatzka, 1962; Mate in Three, 1965; The Elected Member, 1969 (Booker Prize, 1970); Sunday Best, 1971; Go Tell the Lemming, 1973; I Sent a Letter to my Love, 1975; The Ponsonby Post, 1977; A Five Year Sentence, 1978; Spring Sonata, 1979; Birds of Passage, 1981; Brothers, 1983; Mr Wakefield's Crusade, 1985; Our Father, 1987. *Recreation*: plays piano and 'cello. *Address*: 89 Greencroft Gardens, NW6 3LJ. *T*: 01–328 1415.

RUBIN, Kenneth Warnell; His Honour Judge Rubin; a Circuit Judge since 1972; *b* 8 March 1920; *s* of late Albert Reginald Rubin and late Mary Eales Rubin; *m* 1948, Jeanne Marie Louise de Wilde; one *s* two *d*. *Educ*: King's College Sch., Wimbledon; King's Coll., London (LLB). Served HM Forces, 1939–45. Called to Bar, Gray's Inn, 1948. *Address*: Tyrrellswood, Shere Road, West Horsley, Surrey. *T*: East Horsley 2848.

RUBINS, Jack, FIPA; Chairman and Chief Executive, DFS Dorland Advertising, since 1976; *b* 4 Aug. 1931; *m* 1962, Ruth Davids; three *s*. *Educ*: Northern Polytechnic (Architecture). *Recreation*: philately. *Address*: DFS Dorland, 121 Westbourne Terrace, W2 6JR.

RUBINSTEIN, Hilary Harold; Chairman and Managing Director, A. P. Watt Ltd (Literary Agents), since 1983; *b* 24 April 1926; *s* of H. F. and Lina Rubinstein; *m* 1955, Helge Kitzinger; three *s* one *d*. *Educ*: Cheltenham Coll.; Merton Coll., Oxford (MA). Editorial Dir, Victor Gollancz Ltd, 1952–63; Special Features Editor, The Observer, 1963–64; Dep. Editor, The Observer Magazine, 1964–65. Partner, 1965–, later Director, A. P. Watt Ltd. Mem. Council, ICA, 1976–. Founder-editor, The Good Hotel Guide (published in USA as Europe's Wonderful Little Hotels and Inns), 1978–. *Publications*: The Complete Insomniac, 1974; Hotels and Inns, an Oxford anthology, 1984. *Recreations*: hotel-watching, reading in bed. *Address*: 61 Clarendon Road, W11 4BR. *T*: 01–727 9550. *Club*: Garrick.
See also M. B. Rubinstein.

RUBINSTEIN, Michael Bernard; Consultant, Rubinstein Callingham, Solicitors, since 1986 (Senior Partner, 1976–86); *b* 6 Nov. 1920; *s* of late H. F. Rubinstein and Lina (*née* Lowy); *m* 1955, Joy Douthwaite; two *s* two *d*. *Educ*: St Paul's Sch. Admitted solicitor, 1948. Served War, RE (TA), 1939, and RA; Captain 1945. Sen. Partner, Rubinstein, Nash & Co., later Rubinstein Callingham, 1969–86. Mem., Lord Chancellor's Cttee on Defamation, 1971–74. Trustee: SPNM, 1967– (Chm., 1986–); Aereopagitica Educnl Trust, 1979–. Occasional TV and radio broadcasting. *Publications*: (ed and contrib.) Wicked, Wicked Libels, 1972; Rembrandt and Angels (monograph), 1982; (with Rowland Parker) The Cart-Ruts on Malta and Gozo (monograph), 1984; Music to my Ear, 1985; contrib. legal jls. *Recreations*: experiencing right hemisphere mentation, ruminating, practising. *Address*: 2 Raymond Buildings, Gray's Inn, WC1R 5BZ. *T*: 01–242 8404. *Club*: Garrick.
See also H. H. Rubinstein.

RUBINSTEIN, Prof. Nicolai, FBA 1971; FRHistS; Professor of History, Westfield College, London University, 1965–78, now Emeritus; *b* 13 July 1911; *s* of Bernhard and Irene Rubinstein; *m* 1954, Ruth Kidder Olitsky. *Educ*: Univs of Berlin and Florence. LittD Florence. Lectr, UC Southampton, 1942–45; Lectr, 1945–62, Reader, 1962–65, Westfield Coll., Univ. of London. Corresp. Mem., Accad. Toscana La Colombaria, 1976; Hon. Fellow: Warburg Inst., 1985; Westfield Coll., 1986. Serena Medal, British Acad., 1974; Premio Internazionale galileo galilei, 1985. *Publications*: The Government of Florence under the Medici 1434–94, 1966; (ed) Florentine Studies: politics and society in Renaissance Florence, 1968; Gen. Editor, Letters of Lorenzo de'Medici and ed vol. 3, 1977, and vol. 4, 1981; articles in Jl of Warburg and Courtauld Insts, Italian Studies, Archivio Storico Italiano, Rinascimento, etc. *Address*: 16 Gardnor Mansions, Church Row, NW3. *T*: 01–435 6995.

RUBNER, Ben; General Secretary, Furniture, Timber and Allied Trades Union, since 1976; *b* 30 Sept. 1921; *s* of Charles and Lily Rubner; *m* 1952, Amelia Sonia Bagnari; one *s* one *d. Educ:* Mansford Street Central Sch., Bethnal Green, E2. Apprentice cabinet maker, 1935; Mem. Cttee, Trade Union Br., 1937. Served war in armed forces, Royal Corps of Signals: N Africa, Italy, Sicily, 1941–46. Shop Steward, Sec., Chm. and Convenor, London Furniture Workers Shop Stewards Council, 1947–52; NUFTO: London Dist Cttee, 1954; Gen. Exec. Council, 1958; London Dist Organiser, 1959. Nat. Trade Organiser, 1963; Asst Gen. Sec., FTAT, 1973–76. British TUC: London Delegate, 1955–58; full-time Officer Deleg., 1974–77. Mem., Central Arbitration Cttee, ACAS, 1977. *Recreations:* music (opera, light and grand), chess, table tennis, swimming. *Address:* 6 Oak Avenue, Bricket Wood, St Albans, Herts AL2 3LG. *Club:* Cambridge and Bethnal Green Old Boys.

RUBYTHON, Eric Gerald, CBE 1978; Member of Aerospace Board, British Aerospace, 1977–83, retired (Deputy Chief Executive of Aircraft Group, 1977–82); *b* 11 Feb. 1921; *s* of Reginald Rubython and Bessie Rubython; *m* 1943, Joan Ellen Mills. Joined Hawker Aircraft Ltd, 1948; Co. Sec., 1953; Exec. Dir, 1959; Dir and Gen. Man., 1960; Divl Dir and Gen. Man., Hawker Blackburn Div., 1963; Hawker Siddeley Aviation: Commercial Dir, 1965; Dir and Gen. Manager, 1970; Chm. and Man. Dir, 1977. *Recreations:* golf, gardening. *Address:* 1230 San Julian Drive, Lake San Marcos, Calif 92069, USA.

RUCK, Peter Frederick C.; *see* Carter-Ruck.

RUCK KEENE, John Robert, CBE 1977 (MBE 1946); TD 1950; Secretary General, Royal Society of Chemistry, 1980–81; *b* 2 Jan. 1917; *s* of late Major Robert Francis Ruck Keene, OBE, and Dorothy Mary (*née* Chester); *m* 1951, Beryl M Manistre; two *s. Educ:* Eton; Trinity Coll., Cambridge (BA 1938, MA 1955). Commissioned TA, Oxford and Bucks LI, 1939; served UK and NW Europe, 1939–45 (Major 1944, MBE 1946). First appointment with Chemical Society, 1946; General Secretary, 1947–80, when the Royal Society of Chemistry was formed by unification under Royal Charter of The Chemical Society and The Royal Institute of Chemistry, 1 June 1980. Hon. FRSC, 1982. *Address:* Chenies Cottage, 8 Copperkins Grove, Amersham, Bucks HP6 5QD. *T:* Amersham 7123.

RUCKER, Sir Arthur Nevil, KCMG 1942; CB 1941; CBE 1937; Chairman of Stevenage New Town Corporation, 1962–66 (Vice-Chairman, 1956–62); *b* 20 June 1895; *o s* of late Sir Arthur Rucker, FRS, and Lady Rucker of Everington House, nr Newbury; *m* 1922, Elsie Marion Broadbent; two *s* two *d. Educ:* Marlborough; Trinity College, Cambridge. Served European War (12th Suffolk Regiment, Lieutenant), 1915–18; entered Civil Service as Assistant Principal, 1920; Private Secretary to successive Ministers of Health, 1928–36; Director of Establishments and Public Relations, Ministry of Health, 1937–39; Principal Private Secretary to Prime Minister, 1939–40; seconded for special duties, 1941, returned to Ministry of Health as Deputy Secretary, 1943; Deputy Director-General, IRO, 1948. Deputy Agent-General of the UN Korean Reconstruction Agency, 1951; Member Commonwealth War Graves Commission, 1956–69. Hon. LLD Wales, 1965. Korean Order of Diplomatic Merit, Heung-in Medal, 1974. *Address:* Manor Farm House, Yattendon, Berks. *T:* Hermitage 201205. *Club:* Athenæum.

RUDD-JONES, Derek, CBE 1981; PhD; Director, Glasshouse Crops Research Institute, Littlehampton, Sussex, 1971–86; *b* 13 April 1924; 2nd *s* of late Walter Henry Jones and late Doris Mary, *er d* of H. Rudd Dawes; *m* 1948, Joan, 2nd *d* of late Edward Newhouse, Hong Kong, and Malvern, Worcs; two *s* one *d. Educ:* Whitgift; Repton; Emmanuel Coll., Cambridge. BA, MA, PhD (Cantab); FIBiol; FIHort. Agricultural Research Council, postgrad. student, Botany Sch., Univ. of Cambridge, 1945–48; Plant Pathologist, E African Agric. and Forestry Research Org., Kenya, 1949–52; Nat. Research Council, Postdoctoral Fellow, Univ. of Saskatchewan, Saskatoon, Canada, 1952–53. ICI Ltd, Akers Research Laboratory, The Frythe, Welwyn, Herts, 1953–56; Jealott's Hill Research Station, Bracknell, Berks, 1956–59; Scientific Adviser to Sec., Agricl Research Council, 1959–71; Foundn Chm., 1968–72, Managing Editor, 1986–, British Crop Protection Council (Mem., 1968–86); Pres., Section K, BAAS, 1981–82; Mem., Scientific Cttee, RHS, 1985–; formerly Mem., Adv. Cttee on Pesticides and Other Toxic Chemicals. Vis. Fellow, Univ. of Southampton, 1975–. *Publications:* papers in scientific journals. *Recreations:* gardening, riding, fly-fishing. *Address:* Bignor Park Cottage, near Pulborough, West Sussex RH20 1HQ. *Club:* Farmers'.

RUDDEN, Prof. Bernard (Anthony), LLD; Professor of Comparative Law, University of Oxford, since 1979; Fellow of Brasenose College, Oxford, since 1979; *b* 21 Aug. 1933; *s* of John and Kathleen Rudden; *m* 1957, Nancy Campbell Painter; three *s* one *d. Educ:* City of Norwich Sch.; St John's Coll., Cambridge. LLD Cantab; MA Oxon; PhD Wales. Solicitor. Fellow and Tutor, Oriel Coll., Oxford, 1965–79. *Publications:* Soviet Insurance Law, 1966; The New River, 1985; co-author or editor of: The Law of Mortgages, 1967; Source-Book on French Law, 1973, 2nd edn 1978; Basic Community Laws, 1980, 2nd edn 1986; The Law of Property, 1982; contrib. periodical pubns. *Address:* Brasenose College, Oxford. *T:* Oxford 248641. *Club:* United Oxford & Cambridge University.

RUDDEN, James; Advisory Head Teacher on Secondary Reorganisation, ILEA, 1976–78, retired; President: National Association of Head Teachers, 1971; London Head Teachers Association, 1969; Metropolitan Catholic Teachers Association, 1964; *b* 11 Dec. 1911; *s* of Bernard and Mary Rudden; *m* 1937, Eileen Finlay; one *s* four *d. Educ:* Carlisle Grammar Sch.; St Mary's Coll., Twickenham. BSc (Special, Geo.) (London Univ.); Teacher's Cert. (London Univ.). Asst Teacher, Carlisle, 1933–47; served War, RAF Educn Officer, 1940–45. First Head: St Cuthbert's Sec. Mod. Sch., Cleator, 1948–52; St Thomas More Sec. Mod. Sch., Tottenham, 1952–59; Bishop Thomas Grant Comprehensive Sch., Streatham, 1959–75. External Examnr for BEd, Avery Hill Coll. Chairman: London Comprehensive Head Teachers Conf., 1974–75; Southwark Diocesan Schs Commn; Governing Body of Schs Council; Adv. Council for Supply and Trng of Teachers. KSG 1969. *Publications:* numerous articles on educnl topics in educational and national press. *Recreation:* indulgence in retirement pursuits. *Address:* 5 The Gorse, Rissington Road, Bourton-on-the-Water, Glos. *T:* Cotswold 21052.

RUDDOCK, Joan Mary; Organiser, Reading Citizens Advice Bureau, since 1979; *b* 28 Dec. 1943; *d* of Ken and Eileen Anthony; *m* 1963, Dr Keith Ruddock. *Educ:* Pontypool Grammar Sch. for Girls; Imperial Coll., Univ. of London (BSc; ARCS). Worked for Shelter, national campaign for the homeless, 1968–73; Dir, Oxford Housing Aid Centre, 1973–77; Special Programmes Officer with unemployed young people, MSC, 1977–79; Chairperson, CND, 1981–85, a Vice Chairperson, 1985–. Active in politics and pressure groups, and mem. of anti-racist concerns, throughout working life. Frank Cousins' Peace Award, TGWU, 1984. *Publications:* co-author of pubns on housing; (contrib.) The CND Story, 1983. *Recreations:* music, travel, gardening. *Address:* c/o Campaign for Nuclear Disarmament, 22–24 Underwood Street, N1 7JQ.

RUDÉ, Prof. George Frederick Elliot; Professor of History, Concordia University, Montreal, since 1970; *b* 8 Feb. 1910; *s* of Jens Essendrop Rude, Norway, and Amy Geraldine Elliot Rude, England; *m* 1940, Doreen, *d* of J. W. De la Hoyde, Dublin; no *c. Educ:* Shrewsbury Sch.; Trinity Coll., Cambridge. Dr of Letters (Adelaide), 1967. Taught at: Stowe Sch., Bucks, 1931–35; St Paul's Sch., London, 1936–49; Sir Walter St John's Sch., London, 1950–54; Holloway Sch., London, 1954–59; Univ. of Adelaide: Sen. Lectr in History, 1960–63; Prof. of History, 1964–67; Prof. of History, Flinders Univ., SA, 1968–70; Leverhulme Vis. Prof., Univ. of Tokyo, Sept.-Nov. 1967; Vis. Prof., Univ. of Stirling, 1968; Vis. Prof. Fellow, Univ. of Sussex, 1979–82; Vis. Prof., Coll. of William and Mary, Williamsburg, USA, 1980–81. Mem., Australian Research Grants Cttee, 1969. Alexander Prize, Roy. Hist. Soc., 1955. FRHistSoc. 1957; Fellow, Australian Acad. of Humanities, 1963. *Publications:* The Crowd in the French Revolution, 1959; Wilkes and Liberty, 1962; Revolutionary Europe 1783–1815, 1964; The Crowd in History, 1964; (ed) The Eighteenth Century 1715–1815, 1965; (ed) Robespierre, 1967; (with E. J. Hobsbawm) Captain Swing, 1969; Paris and London in the 18th Century, 1970; Hanoverian London 1714–1808, 1971; Debate on Europe 1815–1850, 1972; Europe in the Eighteenth Century, 1972; Robespierre, 1975; Protest and Punishment, 1978; Ideology and Popular Protest, 1980; Criminal and Victim: crime and society in early 19th century England, 1985; contribs to Eng. Hist. Review, Eng. Econ. Hist. Review, Revue Historique, Past and Present, etc. *Recreations:* swimming, reading, public speaking. *Address:* Concordia University, Sir George Williams Campus, Montreal, PQ, Canada; 24 Cadborough Cliff, Rye, Sussex TN31 7EB.

RUDKIN, (James) David; playwright; *b* 29 June 1936; *s* of David Jonathan Rudkin and Anne Alice Martin; *m* 1967, Alexandra Margaret Thompson; two *s* two *d. Educ:* King Edward's Sch., Birmingham; St Catherine's Coll., Oxford (MA). *Publications:* plays: Afore Night Come, 1963; (trans.) Moses and Aaron, 1965; The Grace of Todd (orig. opera libretto), 1969; Cries from Casement as his Bones are Brought to Dublin, 1974; Penda's Fen (film), 1975; Burglars (for children), 1976; Ashes, 1978; (trans.) Hippolytus, 1980; The Sons of Light, 1981; The Triumph of Death, 1981; (trans.) Peer Gynt, 1983; The Saxon Shore, 1986; articles, reviews etc. for Encounter, Drama, Tempo. *Recreations:* piano, geology, anthropology, languages, swimming, bridge. *Address:* c/o Margaret Ramsay Ltd, 14a Goodwin's Court, WC2. *T:* 01-240 0691.

RUDKIN, Walter Charles, CBE 1981; Director of Economic Intelligence, 1973–81, of Economic and Logistic Intelligence, 1982, Ministry of Defence; retired; *b* 22 Sept. 1922; *e s* of Walter and Bertha Rudkin; *m* 1950, Hilda Mary Hope; two *s. Educ:* Carre's Grammar Sch., Sleaford; UC Hull. BSc (Econ) London. Served with RAF, 1942–46. Lectr, Dept of Econs and Econ. History, Univ. of Witwatersrand, 1948–52. Entered Min. of Defence, 1954; various appts, incl. Hong Kong, 1956–59; Junior Directing Staff, Imperial Defence Coll., 1962–64; Cabinet Office, 1968–71. *Recreation:* fishing. *Address:* 85 Kingsway, Petts Wood, Orpington, Kent BR5 1PW. *T:* Orpington 22603. *Club:* Royal Commonwealth Society.

RUDLAND, Margaret Florence; Headmistress, Godolphin and Latymer School, since 1986; *b* 15 June 1945; *d* of Ernest George and Florence Hilda Rutland. *Educ:* Sweyne School, Rayleigh; Bedford College, Univ. of London (BSc); Inst. of Education (PGCE). Asst Mathematics Mistress, Godolphin and Latymer Sch., 1967–70; VSO, Ilorin, Nigeria, 1970–71; Asst Maths Mistress, Clapham County Sch., 1971–72; Asst Maths Mistress and Head of Dept, St Paul's Girls' Sch., 1972–83; Deputy Headmistress, Norwich High Sch., GPDST, 1983–85. *Address:* The Godolphin and Latymer School, Iffley Road, Hammersmith, W6 0PG. *T:* 01-741 1936.

RUDMAN, Michael Edward; theatre director and producer; Associate Director, National Theatre, since 1979; *b* Tyler, Texas, 14 Feb. 1939; *s* of M. B. Rudman and Josephine Davis; *m* 1963, Veronica Anne Bennett (marr. diss. 1981); two *d*; *m* 1983, Felicity Kendal, *qv. Educ:* St Mark's Sch., Texas; Oberlin Coll. (BA *cum laude* Govt); St Edmund Hall, Oxford (MA). Pres., OUDS, 1963–64. Asst Dir and Associate Producer, Nottingham Playhouse and Newcastle Playhouse, 1964–68; Asst Dir, RSC, 1968; Artistic Director: Traverse Theatre Club, 1970–73; Hampstead Theatre, 1973–78 (Theatre won Evening Standard Award for Special Achievement, 1978); Dir, Lyttelton Theatre (National), 1979–81. *Plays directed* include: Nottingham Playhouse: Changing Gear, Measure for Measure, A Man for All Seasons, 1965; Julius Caesar, She Stoops to Conquer, Who's Afraid of Virginia Woolf, Death of a Salesman, 1966; Long Day's Journey into Night, 1967; Lily in Little India, 1968; RSC Theatregoround: The Fox and the Fly, 1968; Traverse Theatre: Curtains (transf. Open Space, 1971), Straight Up (transf. Piccadilly, 1971), A Game called Arthur (transf. Theatre Upstairs, 1971), Stand for my Father, (with Mike Wearing) A Triple Bill of David Halliwell plays, 1970; The Looneys, Pantagleize, 1971; Carravagio Buddy, Tell Charlie Thanks for the Truss, The Relapse, 1972; Hampstead Theatre: Ride across Lake Constance, A Nightingale in Bloomsbury Square, 1973; The Black and White Minstrels, The Show-off, The Connection, The Looneys, 1974; Alphabetical Order (transf. May Fair), 1975; Clouds, 1977; Cakewalk, Beyond a Joke, Gloo-Joo (transf. Criterion), 1978; National Theatre: For Services Rendered (televised, 1980), Death of a Salesman, 1979; Thee and Me, The Browning Version and Harlequinade, Measure for Measure, 1980; The Second Mrs Tanqueray, 1981; Brighton Beach Memoirs, The Magistrate, 1986; West End: Donkeys Years, Globe, 1976; Clouds, Duke of York's, 1978; Taking Steps, Lyric, 1980; Camelot, 1982; The Winslow Boy, 1983; The Dragon's Tail, Apollo, 1985; New York: The Changing Room, 1973; Hamlet, 1976; Death of a Salesman, 1984; *plays produced or co-produced* include: Traverse Theatre: As Time Goes By, Do It, Lay By, 1971; Flowers, 1972; Hampstead Theatre: Dusa, Fish, Stas and Vi, 1976 (also May Fair, 1977); Abigail's Party, The Elephant Man, 1977; Bodies, 1978; Translations (also National), 1981; National Theatre: Watch on the Rhine, On the Razzle, 1981. Mem., Bd of Directors, Hampstead Theatre, 1979–. *Recreation:* golf. *Address:* c/o Peter Murphy Esq., Curtis Brown Group, 162–168 Regent Street, W1R 5TA. *T:* 01-437 9700. *Clubs:* Royal Automobile; Dyrham Park Country, Cumberland Lawn Tennis, Royal Mid-Surrey Golf.

RUDOE, Wulf, CB 1975; *b* 9 March 1916; *m* 1942, Ellen Trilling; one *s* one *d. Educ:* Central Foundation School; Peterhouse, Cambridge (Open Schol. and Research Schol.). Mathematics Tripos Pt III, 1938, Distinction. Royal Aircraft Establishment, 1939. Operational Research, RAF, 1939–45. Operational Research in Building Industry, Min. of Works, 1946–48, Principal Scientific Officer 1948; Board of Trade, Statistician 1948, Chief Statistician 1952; Dir of Statistics and Research, DHSS (formerly Min. of Health), 1966–76; Asst Sec., Price Commn, 1976–79; Adviser to Govt of Ghana, 1980–81. Fellow Inst. of Statisticians; Mem. Council, 1962–78, Hon. Treasurer, 1965–74, Vice-Pres., 1974–75 and 1976–77, Roy. Statistical Soc. *Recreations:* walking, travel, languages. *Address:* 72 North End Road, NW11 7SY. *T:* 01-455 2890.

RUE, Dr (Elsie) Rosemary, CBE 1977; Regional General Manager, since 1984, and Regional Medical Officer, since 1973, Oxford Regional Health Authority; *b* 14 June 1928; *d* of Harry and Daisy Laurence; divorced; two *s. Educ:* Sydenham High Sch.; Univ. of London; Oxford Univ. Med. School. MB, BS, FRCP, DCH, FRCPsych, PFCM, FRCGP. Gen. Practitioner, 1952–58; Public Health Service, 1958–65; Hospital Service, 1965–73; SAMO, Oxford RHB, 1971. Past-Pres., Medical Women's Fedn. Hon. Fellow, Green Coll., Oxford, 1985. *Publications:* papers on gen. practice, women in medicine, ward design, community hosps, health services, individuals requiring security. *Address:* 2 Stanton St John, Oxford. *T:* Oxford 64861.

RUEGGER, Paul J.; Swiss diplomat and jurist; *b* 14 August 1897; *s* of Prof. J. Ruegger; *m* 1st, 1932, Countess Isabella Salazar y Munatones (*d* 1969); 2nd, 1971, Marquise Isabella

Francesca Fossi. *Educ:* College Lucerne; Univs of Lausanne, Munich, and Zürich (Doctor of Law). Attaché at Swiss Foreign Office and Sec. Swiss Advisory Cttee for League of Nations and post-war problems, 1918; Secretary of the Swiss Delegation to the League of Nations, 1920–25 (technical adviser, 1923–25); Sec. Swiss Delegation to Internat. Econ. Conf. of Genoa, 1922; Asst Prof. of Internat. Law, Univ. of Geneva, 1922–24; Legal Adviser to Swiss Delegation Conference for control of trade of arms, etc., 1925; Deputy Registrar Permanent Court of International Justice, 1926–28; Counsellor Swiss Legation in Rome, 1929–31; Head of Political Office Foreign Affairs Dept in Berne, 1931–33; 1st Counsellor of the Swiss Legation in Paris, 1933–36; Swiss Minister in Rome, 1936–42; Swiss Minister to Great Britain, 1944–48. Head of the Swiss Delegation for establishment of a Convention between Switzerland and UN on diplomatic privileges and immunities of UNO establishments in Switzerland; member of Swiss Deleg. to last League of Nations Assembly, Geneva, 1946; President Internat. Committee of Red Cross, 1948–55, Chm. 1968–; Chm. ILO Committee on Forced Labour, 1956–60. Prof. of Human Rights, Univ. of Strasbourg, 1964. Member of: Perm. Court of Arbitration, 1948–; Curatorium of Acad. of Internat. Law, at The Hague (Hon. Mem., 1985–); Inst. of Internat. Law, 1967–69 (1st Vice-Pres., 1967–69; Hon. Mem., 1979); Commissions of Conciliation: between Switzerland and USA; between Switzerland and Spain; between France and the Netherlands; between Sweden and Denmark (Chm.); UN Nansen Medal Award Cttee, UN High Commn for Refugees, 1958–78. Ambassador, 1957; Chm. Swiss Deleg. to UN Conf. on Law of the Sea, Geneva, 1958 and 1960, and to UN Confs on Diplomatic Relations and Immunities, Vienna, 1961; on Consular Relations and Immunities, Vienna, 1963; on Law of Treaties, Vienna, 1968 and 1969; Chm. Cttee of UN Atomic Energy Agency, Vienna, on Civil Liability and Internat. Responsibility for Nuclear Hazards, 1959–62; Chm. ILO Arbitral Commn, Ghana-Portugal, 1961–62; Pres., prep. UN Conf, 1964, and of conf. of plenipotentiaries, New York, on transit trade of land-locked countries, 1965; Chm., Study Gp on Labour and Trade Union Situation in Spain, 1968–69. Hon. Pres., Acad. Mondiale pour la Paix, Nice, 1978. Gold Medal, Red Cross Internat. Cttee, and other Red Cross awards; Grand Cross of Merit, SMO Malta, 1949. *Publications:* The Nationality of Corporations in International Law, 1918; Terms of Civil Law in International Law, 1920; The Responsibility of States for Crimes committed on their Territory, 1923; The Practice of International Conciliation Committees, 1929; Foreign Administration as Institutional Function of Intercourse between States, 1934; The Economic Foundations of International Law, 1931; Switzerland's Economy and the British Empire, 1946; The Juridical Aspects of the Organisation of the International Red Cross, 1953; Swiss Neutrality and European Integration, 1953; Notes of the International Responsibility of States for Nuclear Hazards, in Mélanges Séféréades, 1961; Introduction to Max Huber's Denkwürdigkeiten, and book on Max Huber, 1974; Le Rôle Actuel et Futur des Commissions Internationales d'Enquête, 1980, etc. *Address:* Villa il Pino, 267 Via Bolognese, Florence, Italy; Palazzo Fossi, 16 Via de'Benci, Florence, Italy. *Club:* Circolo dell' Unione (Florence).

See also Baron Armstrong.

RUETE, Dr jur. Hans Hellmuth; Ambassador of the Federal Republic of Germany at the Court of St James's, 1977–79; *b* 21 Dec. 1914; *s* of Prof. Dr med. Alfred E. Ruete and Margarita (*née* Bohnstedt); *m* 1948, Ruth (*née* Arfsten); one *s* two *d. Educ:* Univs of Kiel, Lausanne, Marburg, Tokyo (Political Science and Law). Doctor's Degree in Law. Judge at Ministry of Justice in Hesse, 1949–50; then at Federal Min. of Justice; Federal Foreign Office, 1952–80; Tokyo, 1952–56; Bonn, 1956–60 (Head of Russian Desk); Center for International Affairs, Harvard Univ., 1960–61; Consul-Gen., Calcutta, 1961–64; Dept for Eastern Affairs, Bonn, 1964–70; Ambassador: Paris, 1970–72; Warsaw, 1972–77. *Publication:* Der Einfluss des abendländischen Rechts auf die Rechtsentwicklung in China und Japan, 1940. *Recreations:* music, literature, theatre. *Address:* Petersbergstrasse 64, 5300 Bonn-Bad Godesberg, Federal Republic of Germany.

RUFF, William Willis, CBE 1973; DL; Clerk of the Surrey County Council, 1952–74; *b* 22 Sept. 1914; *s* of late William Ruff, Whitby, Yorks; *m* 1939, Agnes, *d* of late Howard Nankivell; two *s. Educ:* Durham School. Served War of 1939–45: Royal Signals, North Africa and India, 1940–45; Capt., 1942; Maj., 1943. Asst Solicitor: Scarborough Corp., 1937; Heston and Isleworth Corp., 1938; Surrey County Council: Asst Solicitor, 1939; Senior Asst Solicitor, 1947; Asst Clerk, 1948; Deputy Clerk, 1951. Chm., Soc. of Clerks of Peace and of Clerks of County Councils, 1969–72. Mem., Parly Boundary Commn for England, 1974–83. DL Surrey, 1964. *Recreations:* music, watching cricket. *Address:* 3 Brympton Close, Ridgeway Road, Dorking, Surrey. *T:* Dorking 882406.

RUFFLE, Mary, (Mrs Thomas Ruffle); *see* Dilnot, Mary.

RUGAMBWA, HE Cardinal Laurean; *see* Dar-es-Salaam, Archbishop of, (RC).

RUGBY, 2nd Baron, *cr* 1947, of Rugby; **Alan Loader Maffey;** farmer and inventor; *b* 16 April 1913; *s* of 1st Baron Rugby, GCMG, KCB, KCVO, CSI, CIE, and Dorothy Gladys, OBE 1919 (*d* 1973), *d* of late Charles Lang Huggins, JP, Hadlow Grange, Buxted; *S* father, 1969; *m* 1947, Margaret, *d* of late Harold Bindley; three *s* two *d* (and one *s* decd). *Educ:* Stowe. Served War of 1939–45, RAF. Inventor, Foldgate Herd Handler (RASE Silver Award, 1974). Mem. Court of Assistants, Saddlers' Co. (Master, 1978–79). *Heir: s* Hon. Robert Charles Maffey [*b* 4 May 1951; *m* 1974, Anne Penelope, *yr d* of late David Hale; two *s*]. *Address:* Grove Farm, Frankton, near Rugby, Warwicks.

RUGGE-PRICE, Sir Charles Keith Napier; *see* Price.

RUGGLES-BRISE, Captain Guy Edward, TD, DL; Associate, Brewin, Dolphin & Co., Stockbrokers; *b* 15 June 1914; *s* of late Col Sir Edward Archibald Ruggles-Brise, 1st Bt, MC, TD, DL, JP, MP, and Agatha, *e d* of J. H. Gurney, DL, JP, Keswick Hall, Norfolk; *b* and *heir pres.* of Sir John Ruggles-Brise, Bt, *qv; m* 1940, Elizabeth, *o d* of James Knox, Smithstone House, Kilwinning, Ayrshire; three *s. Educ:* Eton. Captain 104th (Essex Yeo.) Field Bde RHA (TA), No 7 Commando. Served War of 1939–45 (PoW). Pres., Pony Riding for the Disabled Trust, Chigwell, Essex, 1984–86. DL 1967, High Sheriff 1967, Essex. *Recreations:* field sports. *Address:* Housham Tye, Harlow, Essex. *T:* Bishops Stortford 731236; Ledgowan Lodge, Achnasheen, Ross-shire. *T:* Achnasheen 245; (business) 5 Giltspur Street, EC1. *Clubs:* Cavalry and Guards, City of London.

RUGGLES-BRISE, Col Sir John Archibald, 2nd Bt, *cr* 1935; CB 1958; OBE (mil.) 1945; TD; JP; Lord-Lieutenant of Essex, 1958–78; Pro-Chancellor, University of Essex, 1964–79; *b* 13 June 1908; *er s* of Colonel Sir Edward Archibald Ruggles-Brise, 1st Bt, MC, TD, DL, JP, MP, and Agatha (*d* 1937), *e d* of J. H. Gurney, DL, JP, of Keswick Hall, Norfolk; *S* father, 1942. *Educ:* Eton. Served AA Comd, 1939–45 (comd 1st 450 Mixed HAA Regt, and 2nd AA Demonstration and User Trials Regt); formed and comd 599 HAA Regt, 1947. Member of Lloyd's. Pres., CLA, 1957–59 (helped promote Game Fair); Church Comr, 1959–64; Chm., Council of the Baronetage, 1958–63. Patron, Essex Agricl Soc., 1970–78. DL 1945, JP 1946, Vice-Lieutenant, 1947, Co. Essex. Hon. Freeman of Chelmsford. Governor of Felsted and Chigwell Schools, 1950–75. DUniv Essex, 1980. KStJ. *Recreation:* shooting. *Heir: b* Capt. Guy Edward Ruggles-Brise, *qv. Address:* Spains Hall, Finchingfield, Essex. *T:* Great Dunmow 810266. *Club:* Carlton.

RUHFUS, Dr Jürgen; Officer's Cross, Order of Merit, Federal Republic of Germany, 1983; Hon. KBE, 1978; State Secretary, Federal Foreign Office, Federal Republic of Germany, since 1984; *b* 4 Aug. 1930; three *d. Educ:* Universities of Munich, Münster and Denver, USA. Joined Federal Foreign Office, Bonn, 1955; Consulate General: Geneva, 1956–57; Dakar, 1958–59; Embassy, Athens, 1960–63; Dep. Spokesman of Federal Foreign Office, 1964, Official Spokesman, 1966; Ambassador to Kenya, 1970–73; Asst Under-Secretary, Federal Foreign Office, 1973–76; Adviser on Foreign Policy and Defence Affairs to Federal Chancellor Helmut Schmidt, 1976–80; Ambassador to UK, 1980–83; Head of Political Directorate-General (dealing with Third World and other overseas countries), Federal Foreign Office, Dec. 1983–June 1984. *Recreations:* golf, tennis, skiing, shooting. *Address:* Federal Foreign Office, Adenauerallee 99–103, 5300 Bonn-1, Federal Republic of Germany.

RUIZ SOLER, Antonio, (Antonio); Cross of the Order of Isabella the Catholic, 1951; Comdr Order of Civil Merit, 1964; Spanish dancer; Director, Ballet Nacional Español; *b* Seville, 4 November 1921. Studied at the Realito Dance Academy. First stage appearance at the age of eight; subsequently toured North and South America Southern and Western Europe, and Scandinavia. First stage appearance in Great Britain, Edinburgh Festival, 1950; London début, Cambridge Theatre, 1951. Golden Medal, Fine Arts, 1952. Formed Ballet Company, 1953; début in Generalife Theatre, Granada, presenting his Ballet in Europe, S and N America. Has also appeared in many festivals in Spain. Appearances with Ballet in London: Stoll, 1954; Palace, 1956; Coliseum, 1958; Royalty, 1960; Drury Lane, 1963; Coliseum, 1975. Gala perf. in Washington to President Kennedy, Ed Sullivan Show in New York, appearances Europe, 1963. Festivals of Spain, 1964–65; Madrid Season, 1965; N Amer. tour, 1965; Ed Sullivan Show, 1965. Appears on TV. Gold Medal, Swedish Acad. of Dancing, 1963; Medal of Min. of Information and Tourism, Madrid, 1963; Golden Medal, Spanish Inst., NY, 1979. *Address:* Coslada 7, Madrid, Spain.

RULE, Brian Francis; Director General of Information Technology Systems, Ministry of Defence, since 1985; *s* of Sydney John and Josephine Rule, Pen-y-ffordd, near Chester; *m* 1963, Kay M., *d* of late Dr and Mrs N. A. Dyce-Sharp. *Educ:* Daniel Owen Sch., Mold; Loughborough Univ. of Technology (MSc). Engineer, de Havilland Aircraft Co., 1955–59; Res. Assistant, Loughborough Univ., 1963–65; Lectr, Univ. of Glasgow, 1965–67; University of Aberdeen: Lectr, 1967–70; Sen. Lectr, 1970–72; Dir of Computing, 1972–78; Dir, Honeywell Information Systems Ltd, 1978–79; Dir of Scientific Services, NERC, 1979–85. *Publications:* various papers in scientific jls. *Recreation:* antiquarian horology. *Address:* Ministry of Defence, Northumberland House, Northumberland Avenue, WC2N 5BP. *T:* 01–218 4828. *Club:* Royal Commonwealth Society.

RULE, Margaret Helen, (Mrs A. W. Rule), CBE 1983; FSA; Research Director, Mary Rose Trust, since 1983; *b* 27 Sept. 1928; *d* of Ernest Victor and Mabel Martin; *m* 1949, Arthur Walter Rule; one *s. Educ:* Univ. of London. FSA 1967. Dir of Excavations, Chichester Civic Soc., 1961–79; Hon. Curator, Fishbourne Roman Palace and Museum, 1968–79; Archaeol Dir, Mary Rose Trust, 1979–82. Hon. Fellow, Portsmouth Polytechnic, 1982. Hon. DLitt Liverpool, 1984. Reginald Mitchell Medal, Stoke-on-Trent Assoc. of Engrs, 1983. *Publications:* Chichester Excavations 1, 1967; The Mary Rose, 1982; many papers in jls in Britain and USA. *Recreations:* anything in or on the water. *Address:* Mill House, Westbourne, West Sussex PO10 8TG.

RUMBLE, Captain John Bertram, RN (retired); Director General, Royal Over-Seas League, since 1979; *b* 30 Oct. 1928; *s* of late Major Rumble and of Mrs Rumble; *m* 1953, Jennifer, *d* of late Col. R. H. Wilson, MC, CIE, and Ella Wilson; one *s* three *d. Educ:* Hordle House Sch.; Sherborne Sch. FBIM 1980, FIIM 1980. Special Entry Cadet into Royal Navy, 1946; ADC (Lieut) to Governor of Malta, 1952–53; specialised in Communications, 1954; HMS Maidstone, 1955–56; Staff, BRNC Dartmouth, 1956–57; Exchange Service with RCN, 1957–59; Signal Officer, HMS Ark Royal, 1959–61; Comdr 1962; RN sc 1963; CO HMS Torquay, 1964–65; Staff Communications Officer to C-in-C EASTLANT, 1966–67; Exec. Officer, HMS Hermes, 1967–69; Captain 1970; Staff Dir, Gen. Weapons, 1970–71; CO HMS Fearless, 1974–75; Asst Chief of Staff Communications (as Cdre), C-in-C SOUTH, 1976–77; MoD (Intelligence), 1977–79. Younger Brother, Trinity House, 1977; Member: Council, Mayfair, Piccadilly and St James's Assoc., 1979– (Dep. Chm., 1980–); Jt Commonwealth Societies Council, 1980–. *Recreations:* shooting, sailing, fishing, gold leaf gilding. *Address:* 88 Wroughton Road, SW11. *T:* 01–223 9413; 2 Salterns View, Keyhaven, Hants. *T:* Lymington 43462. *Clubs:* Farmers', Royal Navy of 1765 and 1785; Keyhaven Yacht.

RUMBLE, Peter William, CB 1984; Chief Executive, Historic Buildings and Monuments Commission, since 1983; *b* 28 April 1929; *s* of Arthur Victor Rumble and Dorothy Emily (*née* Sadler); *m* 1953, Joyce Audrey Stephenson; one *s* one *d. Educ:* Harwich County High Sch.; Oriel Coll., Oxford (MA). Entered Civil Service, 1952; HM Inspector of Taxes, 1952; Principal, Min. of Housing and Local Govt, 1963; Asst Sec., 1972, Under Sec., 1977, DoE. *Recreation:* music. *Address:* 11 Hillside Road, Cheam, Surrey SM2 6ET. *T:* 01–643 1752. *Club:* Athenæum.

RUMBOLD, Sir Algernon; *see* Rumbold, Sir H. A. F.

RUMBOLD, Mrs Angela Claire Rosemary, CBE 1981; MP (C) Mitcham and Morden (formerly Merton, Mitcham and Morden), since June 1982; Minister of State, Department of Education and Science, since 1986; *b* 11 Aug. 1932; *d* of Harry Jones, *qv; m* 1958, John Marix Rumbold; two *s* one *d. Educ:* Notting Hill and Ealing High Sch.; King's Coll., London. Founder Member, National Assoc. for the Welfare of Children in Hospital, and National Chairman, 1974–76. Royal Borough of Kingston upon Thames: Councillor, 1974–83; Dep. Leader, 1976; Chairman: Education Cttee, 1978–79; Policy and Resources Cttee, 1979–82. Chairman: Educn Cttee, Assoc. of Metropolitan Authorities, 1979–80; Council, Local Educn Authorities, 1979–80. Mem., Social Services Select Cttee, 1982–83; PPS to Financial Sec. to the Treasury, 1983, to Sec. of State for Transport, 1983–85; Parly Under Sec. of State, DoE, 1985–86. Member, Doctors and Dentists Review Body, 1979–82. Governor: Coombe Lodge Further Education Staff College, 1980–82; Nat. Foundn for Educational Research, 1979–82. *Recreations:* swimming, theatre, reading. *Address:* 18 Park Road, Surbiton, Surrey KT5 8QD.

RUMBOLD, Sir Henry (John Sebastian), 11th Bt *cr* 1779; Partner, Stephenson Harwood, since 1982; *b* 24 Dec. 1947; *s* of Sir Horace Anthony Claude Rumbold, 10th Bt, KCMG, KCVO, CB, and Felicity Ann Rumbold (*née* Bailey); *S* father, 1983; *m* 1978, Frances Ann (*née* Hawkes, formerly wife of Julian Berry). *Educ:* Eton College; College of William and Mary, Virginia, USA (BA). Articled Stileman, Neate and Topping, 1975–77; admitted solicitor, 1977; asst solicitor, Stileman, Neate and Topping, 1977–79; Partner, 1979–81; joined Stephenson Harwood, 1981. *Recreations:* riding, shooting, reading. *Heir: cousin* Sir (Horace) Algernon (Fraser) Rumbold, *qv. Address:* 19 Hollywood Road, SW10 9HT. *T:* 01–352 9148; Hatch House, Tisbury, Wilts. *T:* Tisbury 870622.

RUMBOLD, Sir (Horace) Algernon (Fraser), KCMG 1960 (CMG 1953); CIE 1947; *b* 27 Feb. 1906; *s* of late Colonel William Edwin Rumbold, CMG; *m* 1946, Margaret

Adél, *d* of late Arthur Joseph Hughes, OBE; two *d*. *Educ:* Wellington College; Christ Church, Oxford. Assistant Principal, India Office, 1929; Private Sec. to Parliamentary Under-Secretaries of State for India, 1930–33, and to Permanent Under-Secretary of State, 1933–34; Principal, 1934; Asst Sec., 1943; transferred to Commonwealth Relations Office, 1947; Deputy High Commissioner in the Union of South Africa, 1949–53; Asst Under Sec. of State, 1954–58; Dep. Under Sec. of State, 1958–66; retired, 1966. Chm. Cttee on Inter-Territorial Questions in Central Africa, 1963; Advr, Welsh Office, 1967. Dep. Chm., Air Transport Licensing Bd, 1971–72. Mem. Governing Body, SOAS, 1965–80, Hon. Fellow, 1981. Pres., Tibet Soc. of the UK, 1977–. *Publication:* Watershed in India 1914–1922, 1979. *Address:* Shortwoods, West Clandon, Surrey. *T:* Guildford 222757. *Club:* Travellers'.

RUMBOLD, Sir Jack (Seddon), Kt 1984; QC (Zanzibar) 1963; President of the Industrial Tribunals, England and Wales, 1979–84, retired; *b* 5 March 1920; *s* of William Alexander Rumbold and Jean Lindsay Rumbold (*née* Mackay), Christchurch, NZ; *m* 1st, 1949, Helen Suzanne, *d* of Col J. B. Davis, Wanganui, NZ; two *d*; 2nd, 1970, Veronica Ellie Hurt (*née* Whigham). *Educ:* St Andrew's Coll., NZ; Canterbury Univ., NZ (LLB 1940); Brasenose Coll., Oxford (Rhodes Schol.; BCL 1948). Served Royal Navy, Lieut RNZNVR, 1941–45 (despatches). Called to Bar, Inner Temple, 1948; Crown Counsel, Kenya, 1957, Sen. Crown Counsel, 1959; Attorney General, Zanzibar, 1963; Legal Adviser, Kenya Govt, 1964–66; Academic Director, British Campus of Stanford Univ., USA, 1966–72; Chairman of Industrial Tribunals (part-time), 1968; (full-time) 1972; Regional Chairman (London South), 1977. FRSA 1985. *Recreations:* books, music; formerly cricket (Oxford Blue). *Address:* Il Vallone Alto, Sarteano, Siena, Italy; c/o 4 Wandsworth Bridge Road, SW6. *Clubs:* Garrick, MCC.

RUNACRES, Eric Arthur; *b* 22 Aug. 1916; *s* of Arthur Selwyn Runacres and Mildred May Dye; *m* 1950, Penelope Jane Elizabeth Luxmoore; one *s* one *d*. *Educ:* Dulwich College; Merton College, Oxford. 1st cl. hons Lit. Hum. 1939. Commissioned Royal Engineers, Oct. 1939; served UK, Malta, Middle East, India, 1939–46 (Major). J. & P. Coats Ltd, 1946–48. Entered HM Foreign Service, 1948; First Secretary, 1951–53. British Productivity Council, 1954–71 (Deputy Director, 1959–71, and Secretary, 1962–71); Vice-Chm., OECD, Cttee on National Productivity Centres, 1960–66; Exec. Director, Commonwealth Agricultural Bureaux, 1973–77; Consultant, Industrial Facts & Forecasting Ltd, 1978–81. *Recreations:* European thought and literature; gardening. *Address:* Gables, Radbones Hill, Over Norton, Oxon OX7 5RA. *T:* Chipping Norton 3264.

RUNCIE, Most Rev. and Rt. Hon. Robert Alexander Kennedy; *see* Canterbury, Archbishop of.

RUNCIMAN, family name of **Viscount Runciman of Doxford.**

RUNCIMAN OF DOXFORD, 2nd Viscount, *cr* 1937; **Walter Leslie Runciman,** OBE 1946; AFC; AE; DL; Bt 1906; Baron Runciman, 1933, of Shoreston; Director, Walter Runciman Plc, and other cos; *b* 26 Aug. 1900; *er s* of 1st Viscount Runciman of Doxford, PC, and Hilda (*d* 1956), MP (L) St Ives, 1928–29, *d* of J. C. Stevenson; *S* father 1949; *m* 2nd, 1932, Katherine Schuyler, *y d* of late Wm R. Garrison, New York; one *s*. *Educ:* Eton (King's Scholar); Trinity College, Cambridge (Scholar). Director, 1932, Dep. Chm., (1962–71, Lloyds Bank Ltd. Chm., North of England Shipowners Association, 1931–32 and 1970–71; Chairman of Council, Armstrong College, University of Durham, 1935–37; Director-General of British Overseas Airways Corporation, 1940–43; Air Commodore and Air Attaché, Tehran, 1943–46. Pres. Chamber of Shipping of the UK, and Chm. General Council of British Shipping, 1952; Mem. Air Transport Advisory Council, 1946–54, Vice-Chm., 1951–54; President, RINA, 1951–61; Mem. Shipping Advisory Panel, 1962. Chairman: Cttee on Horticultural Marketing, 1955–56; Trustees, Nat. Maritime Museum, 1962–72; Adv. Cttee on Historic Wreck Sites, 1973–; British Hallmarking Council, 1974–82. Cdre, RYS, 1968–74. Pres., Iran Soc., 1979–. Hon. Elder Brother of Trinity House. Hon. Mem., Hon. Co. of Master Mariners. DL Northumberland, 1961. Hon. DCL, Durham. *Recreations:* sailing, shooting. *Heir: s* Hon. Walter Garrison Runciman, *qv*. *Address:* 46 Abbey Lodge, Park Road, NW8; Doxford, Chathill, Northumberland. *Clubs:* Brooks's; Royal Yacht Squadron.

See also Hon. Sir Steven Runciman.

RUNCIMAN, Hon. Garry; *see* Runciman, Hon. W. G.

RUNCIMAN, Hon. Sir Steven, (Hon. Sir James Cochran Stevenson Runciman), CH 1984; Kt 1958; FBA 1957; FSA 1964; MA; *b* 7 July 1903; 2nd *s* of 1st Viscount Runciman of Doxford, PC. *Educ:* Eton (King's Schol.); Trinity College, Cambridge (Schol.). Fellow of Trinity College, Cambridge, 1927–38 (Hon. Fellow 1965); Lecturer at the University of Cambridge, 1932–38; Press Attaché, British Legation, Sofia, 1940; British Embassy, Cairo, 1941; Professor of Byzantine Art and History in Univ. of Istanbul, 1942–45; Rep. Brit. Council in Greece, 1945–47. Lectures: Waynflete, Magdalen Coll., Oxford, 1953–54; Gifford, St Andrews, 1960–62; Birkbeck, Trinity Coll., Cambridge, 1966; Wiles, Queen's Univ., Belfast, 1968; Robb, Auckland, 1970; Regents', Los Angeles, California, 1971; Weir, Cincinnati, 1973. Alexander White Prof., Chicago, 1963. Mem. Advisory Council, Victoria and Albert Museum, 1957; Pres., British Inst. of Archæology at Ankara, 1960–75; Chairman: Anglo-Hellenic League, 1951–67; Nat. Trust for Greece, 1977–84; Councillor Emeritus, Nat. Trust for Scotland, 1985–; Trustee: British Museum, 1960–67; Scottish Nat. Museum of Antiquities, 1972–77; Hon. Vice-Pres., RHistS, 1967–; Vice-Pres., London Library, 1974; Chm., Friends of Scottish Ballet, 1984–. For. Mem., American Philosophical Soc.; Corresp. Mem. Real Academia de Historia, Madrid. Hon. MRIA 1979. Hon. LittD Cambridge, 1955; Hon. LLD Glasgow, 1955; Hon. DLitt: Durham, 1956; St Andrews, 1969; Oxon, 1971; Birmingham, 1973; Hon. LitD London, 1966; Hon. DPhil Salonika, 1951; Hon. DD Wabash, USA, 1962; Hon. DHL Chicago, 1963; Hon. DHum Ball State Univ., 1973; Hon. DLitt New York Univ., 1984. Wolfson Literary Award, 1982. Knight Commander, Order of the Phœnix (Greece), 1961. *Publications:* The Emperor Romanus Lecapenus, 1929; The First Bulgarian Empire, 1930; Byzantine Civilization, 1933; The Medieval Manichee, 1947; A History of the Crusades, Vol. I, 1951 (illustrated edn, as The First Crusade, 1980), Vol. II, 1952, Vol. III, 1954; The Eastern Schism, 1955; The Sicilian Vespers, 1958; The White Rajahs, 1960; The Fall of Constantinople, 1453, 1965; The Great Church in Captivity, 1968; The Last Byzantine Renaissance, 1970; The Orthodox Churches and the Secular State, 1972; Byzantine Style and Civilisation, 1975; The Byzantine Theocracy, 1977; Mistra, 1980; contributions to various historical journals. *Address:* Elshieshields, Lockerbie, Dumfriesshire DG11 1LY. *Club:* Athenæum.

RUNCIMAN, Hon. Walter Garrison, (Hon. Garry), FBA 1975; Chairman, Walter Runciman plc and subsidiary companies, since 1976; Fellow, Trinity College, Cambridge, since 1971; *b* 10 Nov. 1934; *o s* and *heir* of 2nd Viscount Runciman of Doxford, *qv*; *m* 1963, Ruth, *o d* of late Joseph Hellmann and late Dr Ellen Hellmann, Johannesburg; one *s* two *d*. *Educ:* Eton (Oppidan Schol.); Trinity Coll., Cambridge (Schol.; Fellow, 1959–63, 1971–). National Service, 1953–55 (2/Lt, Grenadier Guards); Harkness Fellow, 1958–60; joined Walter Runciman & Co. Ltd, 1964; part-time Reader in Sociology, Univ. of Sussex, 1967–69; Vis. Prof., Harvard Univ., 1970; Vis. Fellow, Nuffield Coll., Oxford, 1979–. Lectures: Radcliffe-Brown, British Acad., 1986; Spencer, Oxford Univ., 1986. Treas., Child Poverty Action Gp, 1972–; Member: SSRC, 1974–79; Securities and Investments Board, 1986–. Pres., Gen. Council of British Shipping, 1986–87 (Vice-Pres., 1985–86). Hon. Foreign Mem., Amer. Acad. of Arts and Sciences, 1986. *Publications:* Plato's Later Epistemology, 1962; Social Science and Political Theory, 1963, 2nd edn 1969; Relative Deprivation and Social Justice, 1966, 2nd edn 1972; Sociology in its Place, and other essays, 1970; A Critique of Max Weber's Philosophy of Social Science, 1972; A Treatise on Social Theory: vol. I, 1983; articles in academic jls. *Address:* 36 Carlton Hill, NW8 0JY. *Club:* Brooks's.

RUNCORN, Prof. (Stanley) Keith, FRS 1965; Professor of Physics and Head of the School of Physics, University of Newcastle upon Tyne, since 1963, and in the University of Durham (King's College), 1956–63; *b* 19 November 1922; *s* of W. H. Runcorn, Southport, Lancs; unmarried. *Educ:* King George V Sch., Southport; Gonville and Caius Coll., Cambridge. ScD 1963. Radar Research and Devel. Establishment (Min. of Supply), 1943–46; Asst Lecturer, 1946–48, and Lecturer, 1948–49, in Physics, Univ. of Manchester; Asst Dir of Research in Geophysics, Cambridge Univ., 1950–55; Research Geophysicist, Univ. of California at Los Angeles, 1952 and 1953; Fellow of Gonville and Caius Coll., Cambridge, 1948–55; Visiting Scientist, Dominion Observatory, Ottawa, 1955; Vis. Prof. of Geophysics: Cal. Inst. of Tech., 1957; Univ. of Miami, 1966; Pa State Univ., 1967; Florida State Univ., 1968; UCLA, 1975; J. Ellerton Becker Senior Visiting Fellow, Australian Academy of Science, 1963; Res. Associate, Mus. of N Arizona, 1957–72; Rutherford Memorial Lectr (Kenya, Tanzania and Uganda), 1970; Halley Lectr, Oxford Univ., 1972–73; Hitchcock Foundn Prof., Univ. of California, Berkeley, 1981. Mem., NERC, 1965–69. Pres., Section A (Phys. and Maths), British Assoc., 1980–81. Mem., Royal Netherlands Acad. of Arts and Sciences, 1970; For. Mem., Indian Nat. Acad. of Science, 1980; Mem., Pontifical Acad. of Sciences, 1981; Mem., Royal Norwegian Acad. of Sci. and Letters, 1985. Napier Shaw Prize, Royal Met. Soc., 1959; Charles Chree Medal and Prize, Inst. of Physics, 1969; Vetlesen Prize, 1971; John Adams Fleming Medal, Amer. Geophysical Union, 1983; Gold Medal, Royal Astronomical Soc., 1984. Hon. DSc: Utrecht, 1969; Ghent, 1971; Paris, 1979; Bergen, 1980. *Publications:* scientific papers. *Recreations:* usual. *Address:* University of Newcastle upon Tyne, Newcastle upon Tyne NE1 7RU. *Club:* Athenæum.

RUNDALL, Sir Francis (Brian Anthony), GCMG 1968 (KCMG 1956; CMG 1951); OBE 1944; Ambassador to Japan, 1963–67; *b* 11 Sept. 1908; *s* of late Lieutenant-Colonel Charles Frank Rundall, CMG, DSO; *m* 1935, Mary, *d* of late Frank Syrett, MD; one *s* one *d*. *Educ:* Marlborough College; Peterhouse, Cambridge. Entered General Consular Service, 1930; served in Antwerp, Colon, Panama, Boston, Barcelona, Piraeus; Consul, New York, 1944; transferred Foreign Office, 1946; HM Inspector of Foreign Service Establishments, 1949–53. Chief Administrative Officer, UK High Commission in Germany during 1953; Consul-General in New York, 1953–57; Ambassador to Israel, 1957–59; Deputy Under-Secretary of State, Foreign Office, 1959–63. *Address:* Lime Tree Cottage, Church Oakley, Basingstoke, Hants. *T:* Basingstoke 780217. *Club:* Travellers'.

RUNDLE, Christopher John Spencer, OBE 1983; HM Diplomatic Service; First Secretary, Foreign and Commonwealth Office, since 1985; *b* 17 Aug. 1938; *s* of Percy William and Ruth Rundle (*née* Spencer); *m* 1970, Qamar Said; one *d*. *Educ:* Cranbrook Sch.; St John's Coll., Cambridge (MA). Served HM Forces, 1957–59. Central Asian Res. Centre, 1962–63; joined Diplomatic Service, 1963; Tehran, 1967–68; Oriental Sec., Kabul, 1968–70; FCO, 1970–75; seconded to Cabinet Office, 1975–77; First Secretary: FCO, 1977–81; Tehran, 1981–84. *Recreations:* sports, television, foreign films and literature. *Address:* c/o Foreign and Commonwealth Office, SW1A 2AH.

RUNDLE, David John, OBE 1986; Director, British Institute of Florence, since 1981; *b* 21 July 1938; *s* of Richard Norman Rundle and Ivy Evelyn Rundle (*née* Cole); *m* 1963, Charlotte Fallenius (marr. diss. 1979); two *s*. *Educ:* Tavistock Sch., Devon; Jesus Coll., Cambridge (BA, MA); Univ. of Leeds (DipEd, MTEFL 1965). Lektor for British Centre, Sweden, 1961–63; Tutor, English Language Centre, Hove, 1963–64; joined British Council career service, 1965; seconded to Zambian Min. of Educn, Lusaka, 1965–67; Education Officer, Amman, Jordan, 1967–70; Director of Studies, Milan, 1970–75; Regional Director: E Midlands, 1975–79; Munich, 1979–81; on leave of absence, 1981–. Senatore Accademico dell' Accademia Internazionale Medicea, Florence, 1984–. *Publications:* An English Medium Course for Zambia, 1967; articles on cultural diplomacy and teaching of English. *Recreations:* theatre, window-boxing, travel. *Address:* Via Santo Spirito 15, Florence, Italy. *T:* (055) 291978. *Club:* Circolo dell' Unione (Florence).

RUNDLE, John Louis, AM 1981; JP; Agent-General for South Australia, 1980–85; *b* 11 Jan. 1930; *s* of late J. A. Rundle; *m* Elizabeth Phillipa, *d* of John P. Little, Melbourne; one *s* one *d*. *Educ:* Rostrevor Coll. Formerly Senior Partner, J. C. Rundle & Co., and Rundle, Parsons & Partners; Former Chairman: J. C. Rundle Holdings Pty Ltd; Seacliff Investments Pty Ltd; Thevenard Hotel Pty Ltd; former Director: Commonwealth Accommodation & Catering Service Ltd; Mallen & Co. Ltd; Commercial & Domestic Finance Ltd. Former Member: Nat. Employers Ind. Council (Dep. Chm., 1979–80); Confed. of Aust. Industry (Mem. Bd, 1978–80); State Develt Council, SA; Ind. Relations Adv. Council, SA; Adv. Curriculum Bd, SA; Council, Royal AA of SA. Pres., Junior Chambers, Adelaide, 1957, SA, 1958, Australia, 1959; Vice-Pres., JCI, 1960, 1963, Exec. Vice-Pres., 1964, World Pres., 1965, Pres. Senate, 1966; Councillor, Adelaide Chamber of Commerce, 1956–57, 1961–72, Vice-Pres., 1968–70, Dep. Pres., 1970–72; Vice-Pres., Chamber of Commerce & Industry, SA, 1973–75, Dep. Pres., 1975–77, Pres. 1977–79 (Chm., Commerce Div., 1973, 1974; Chm., Ind. Matters Cttee); Exec. Mem., Aust. Chamber of Commerce, 1980. Councillor: Red Cross Soc., SA Div., 1957–63 (Chm., Junior Red Cross, 1961–62); Burnside City Council, 1962–64; President: Assoc. of Indep. Schools of SA, 1972–75; Nat. Council of Indep. Schools, 1975–77; Chm., Bd of Governors, Rostrevor Coll., 1967–77. Freeman, City of London, 1981. JP SA, 1956. *Address:* Waggoners, Tower Road, Hindhead, Surrey GU26 6ST. *T:* Hindhead 5217. *Clubs:* East India, Royal Automobile; Stock Exchange (Pres., 1979–80), Naval Military and Air Force, Tattersall's (Adelaide); Royal Automobile (Melbourne); Clipper (USA).

RUOFF, Theodore Burton Fox, CB 1970; CBE 1962; Chief Land Registrar, 1963–75; *b* 12 April 1910; *s* of late Percy Ruoff and late Edith Crane; *m* 1947, Marjorie Alice, *er d* of late George Mawson, Worthing; no *c*. *Educ:* Clarence School, Weston-super-Mare; King Edward VI School, Bury St Edmunds. Admitted as a solicitor, 1933; 2nd class Hons; Hertfordshire Law Society prizeman; Nuffield Fellowship in Australia and New Zealand, 1951–52; Senior Land Registrar of HM Land Registry, 1958. Founder Mem., 1974, and first Hon. Mem., 1982, Soc. for Computers and Law (Mem. Council, 1974–80); Consultant, Oyez Computers Ltd, 1975–85; Consultant, Law Society's Wkg Party on Law Office Management and Technology (formerly Special Cttee on Computer Services), 1985– (Mem., 1976–85); Special Adviser on Conveyancing to Royal Commn on Legal Services, 1976–79. Editor, Computers and Law, 1978–82. *Publications:* An Englishman Looks at the Torrens System, 1957; Concise Land Registration Practice, 1959, 3rd edn (with C. West), 1982; Rentcharges in Registered Conveyancing, 1961; Land Registration

Forms, 1962, 3rd edn (with C. West), 1983; Curtis and Ruoff's The Law and Practice of Registered Conveyancing (2nd edn, 1965); (with R. B. Roper) Ruoff and Roper's Registered Conveyancing, 1972, 4th edn 1979; Searching without Tears: The Land Charges Computer, 1974; The Solicitor and the Silicon Chip, 1981; (Gen. Ed.) Fourmat Legal Directory, 1981; The Solicitor and the Automated Office, 1984; regular contribs to Australian Law Jl, Victoria Law Inst. Jl, Law Soc.'s Gazette, Solicitors' Jl. *Recreations:* sketching, indifferent golf, gardening. *Address:* Flat One, 83 South Hill Park, Hampstead, NW3 2SS. *T:* 01–435 8014. *Clubs:* Travellers', MCC.

RUPERT'S LAND, Bishop of, since 1983; **Rt. Rev. Walter Heath Jones;** *b* 25 Dec. 1928; *s* of Harry Heath Jones and Anne Grace Evelyn Jones (*née* Stoddart); *m* 1951, L. Marilyn Jones (*née* Lunney); one *s* three *d*. *Educ:* Univ. of Manitoba (BA); St John's College (LTh); Nashotah House (STM). Received into Episcopal Church of USA, 1958; Rector, St Mary's Church, Mitchell, S Dak, 1958–62; Vice-Pres. of Chapter, 1962–67; Dean of Calvary Cathedral, Sioux Falls, S Dak, 1968–70; Bishop of South Dakota, Sioux Falls, 1970–83. Hon. DD: St John's Coll., 1970; Nashotah House. Hon. Citizen of St Boniface, 1966; Bush Fellow, 1978. *Address:* 935 Nesbitt Bay, Winnipeg, Manitoba R3T 1W6, Canada. *T:* (204) 453–6248.

RUPP, Rev. Prof. (Ernest) Gordon, MA, DD; FBA 1970; Dixie Professor of Ecclesiastical History, University of Cambridge, 1968–77, now Emeritus Professor; Fellow of Emmanuel College, Cambridge, 1968–77, Hon. Fellow 1983; Principal, Wesley House, Cambridge, 1967–74; *b* 7 Jan. 1910; *m* 1938, Marjorie Hibbard; one *s*. *Educ:* Owen's School, EC; King's College, London (BA); Wesley House, Cambridge (MA, BD 1946, DD Cantab 1955); Universities of Strasbourg and Basel. Methodist Minister, Chislehurst, Kent, 1938–46; Wesley House, Cambridge, 1946–47; Richmond College, Surrey, 1947–52; Birkbeck Lectr, Trinity Coll., Cambridge, 1947; Lecturer in Divinity, Cambridge Univ., 1952–56; Prof. of Ecclesiastical History, Univ. of Manchester, 1956–67. President of the Methodist Conference, 1968–69; Mem., Central Cttee of World Council of Churches, 1969. Hon. Fellow: Fitzwilliam College, 1969; King's Coll., London, 1969. Hon. DD: Aberdeen; Manchester, 1979; Hon. Dr Théol, Paris. *Publications:* Studies in the English Protestant Tradition, 1947; Luther's Progress to the Diet of Worms, 1951; The Righteousness of God (Luther studies), 1953; Some Makers of English Religion, 1957; The Old Reformation and the New, 1967; Patterns of Reformation, 1969; Just Men, 1977; Thomas More, 1978; Religion in England 1688–1791, 1986. *Address:* 42 Malcolm Place, King Street, Cambridge.

RUSBRIDGE, Brian John, CBE 1984; Secretary, Local Authorities' Conditions of Service Advisory Board, since 1973; Secretary: to all Local Authority National Councils; Burnham Committees for Teachers; Police Negotiating Board; Fire Brigades; Probation Service; Whitley Councils for New Towns Staffs and for Industrial Estates Corporations; Adviser to the States of Jersey and Guernsey; *b* 10 Sept. 1922; *s* of late Arthur John and Leonora Rusbridge, Appleton, Berks; *m* 1951, Joyce, *d* of late Joseph Young Elliott, Darlington; two *s*. *Educ:* Willowfield Sch., Eastbourne; Univ. of Oxford Dept of Social and Admin. Studies (Dip. Social Admin.). Served War of 1939–45, Lieut RNVR. Personnel Manager, Imperial Chemical Industries (Teesside), 1949; British Railways Board: Dir of Industrial Relations, 1963; Divisional Manager, London, 1970. Companion, Inst. of Personnel Management; Mem., Chartered Inst. of Transport. *Recreations:* walking, gardening. *Address:* 19 Beauchamp Road, East Molesey, Surrey KT8 0PA. *T:* 01–979 4952.

RUSBY, Vice-Adm. Sir Cameron, KCB 1979; LVO 1965; Chief Executive, Scottish Society for Prevention of Cruelty to Animals, since 1983; *b* 20 Feb. 1926; *s* of Captain Victor Evelyn Rusby, CBE, RN (Rtd), and Mrs Irene Margaret Rusby; *m* 1948, Marion Elizabeth Bell; two *d*. *Educ:* RNC, Dartmouth. Midshipman 1943; specialised in communications, 1950; CO HMS Ulster, 1958–59; Exec. Officer, HM Yacht Britannia, 1962–65; Dep. Dir, Naval Signals, 1965–68; CO HMS Tartar, 1968–69; Dep. ACOS (Plans and Policy), staff of Allied C-in-C Southern Europe, 1969–72; Sen. Naval Off., WI, 1972–74; Rear-Adm. 1974; ACDS (Ops), 1974–77; Vice-Adm. 1977; Flag Officer Scotland and N Ireland, 1977–79; Dep. Supreme Allied Comdr, Atlantic, 1980–82. *Recreations:* sailing, skiing, equitation. *Address:* c/o Bank of Scotland, 70 High Street, Peebles EH45 8AQ. *Club:* New (Edinburgh).

RUSBY, Norman Lloyd, MA, DM Oxon, FRCP; Consulting Physician: London Hospital since 1970 (Physician, 1946–70); London Chest Hospital since 1970 (Physician, 1936–70); King Edward VII Hospital, Midhurst; Benenden Chest Hospital (Civil Service); Civil Consultant in Diseases of the Chest to the Royal Navy; *b* 26 October 1905; *s* of Dr Edward L. M. Rusby, Streatham and Katharine Helen Rusby (*née* Wright); *m* 1941 Elizabeth, *e d* of F. A. Broadhead, FRIBA, Nottingham; three *s*. *Educ:* Lancing College; St John's College, Oxford; St Thomas's Hospital. BA (Hons) Oxon, 1928, MA 1931; DM 1941; BM, BCh 1931. Res. appts, St Thomas' Hosp.; Res. MO and Registrar, London Chest Hosp., 1934–36; Medical Registrar and Tutor, British Postgraduate Medical School, Hammersmith, 1937–39. Member Standing Advisory Committee on Tuberculosis to Min. of Health, 1940–44; Editor of Tubercle, 1938–44; Physician, EMS, 1939; RAMC Med. specialist, 21 Army Gp, 1944–45; Officer i/c Med. Div., ME Chest Unit, 1945–46; Local Brigadier, Consulting Physician Middle East Land Forces, 1946. Nuffield visitor to East Africa, 1950, 1953. Lecturer for British Council: Poland, 1959; Malta, 1966; Nepal, India and Afghanistan, 1973. Examiner in Medicine: Univ. of London, 1951–56; Univ. of Cambridge, 1957–60; Univ. of W Indies, 1967; RCP, 1962–68. Councillor, RCP, 1964–66; Mitchell Lecturer, RCP, 1967. Member: Attendance Allowance Bd and Med. Appeal Tribunal, 1970–77; Council, Chest, Heart and Stroke Assoc. (Vice-Chm., 1957–77); Council, British Heart Foundn; Council, Metropolitan Hosp. Sunday Fund; Assoc. of Physicians of Gt Britain and Ireland; Hon. Mem., Brit. Thoracic Soc. Mem., Board of Governors: Hospitals for Diseases of the Chest, 1962–67; London Hospital, 1967–70. *Publications:* (jtly) Recent Advances in Respiratory Tuberculosis, 4th and 5th edns, (ed jtly) 6th edn 1968; contributions to various journals, chiefly on diseases of the chest. *Address:* 21 Windmill Hill, Hampstead, NW3. *T:* 01–794 6889. *Clubs:* United Oxford & Cambridge University, MCC.

RUSH, His Honour (Edward Antisell) Michael (Stanistreet); a Circuit Judge, 1980–83; *b* 27 March 1933; *s* of Edward Antisell Evans Rush and Karen (*née* Kröyer Copenhagen). *Educ:* St John's Sch., Leatherhead; Queen's Univ., Belfast; Inns of Court Sch. of Law. Pres., Inns of Court Students' Union, 1958; called to the Bar, Lincoln's Inn, 1958 (Sir Thomas More Scholar). Commissioned, Grenadier Guards, 1958–61. Oxford Circuit, 1961–71 (Junior, 1966); Midland and Oxford Circuit, 1972–80. A Recorder of the Crown Court, 1978–80. Mem., Council on Tribunals, 1986–. *Address:* 2 Harcourt Buildings, Temple, EC4Y 9DB.

RUSH, Most Rev. Francis Roberts; *see* Brisbane, Archbishop of, (RC).

RUSH, Michael; *see* Rush, E. A. M. S.

RUSHBROOKE, Prof. G(eorge) Stanley, MA, PhD; FRS 1982; FRSE; Professor of Theoretical Physics, University of Newcastle upon Tyne, 1951–80; Head of Department of Theoretical Physics, 1965–80; Deputy Head, School of Physics, 1972–80; *b* 19 January 1915; *s* of George Henry Rushbrooke and Frances Isobel Rushbrooke (*née* Wright), Willenhall, Staffs; *m* 1949, Thelma Barbara Cox (*d* 1977). *Educ:* Wolverhampton Grammar School; St John's College, Cambridge. Schol. St John's Coll., Camb., 1933–37; Research Asst, Bristol Univ., 1938–39; Senior DSIR award and Carnegie Teaching Fellowship, 1939–44, UC Dundee, Univ. of St Andrews; Lectr in Mathematical Chemistry, The Univ., Leeds, 1944–48; Sen. Lectr in Theoretical Physics, Oxford, Univ. and Lecturer in Mathematics, University Coll., Oxford, 1948–51. Leverhulme Emeritus Fellow, 1981. Visiting Prof., Dept of Chemistry, Univ. of Oregon, USA, 1962–63; Vis. Prof. of Physics and Chemistry, Rice Univ., Houston, 1967. *Publications:* Introduction to Statistical Mechanics, 1949; research papers in scientific journals. *Recreations:* hillwalking, birdwatching. *Address:* 46 Belle Vue Avenue, Newcastle upon Tyne NE3 1AH.

RUSHDIE, (Ahmed) Salman, FRSL; writer; *b* 19 June 1947; *s* of Anis Ahmed Rushdie and Negin Rushdie (*née* Butt); *m* 1976, Clarissa Luard; one *s*. *Educ:* Cathedral Sch., Bombay; Rugby Sch.; King's Coll., Cambridge (MA (Hons) History). Member: Internat. PEN, 1981–; ICA Council, 1985–; BFI Production Bd, 1986–. FRSL 1983. Arts Council Literature Bursary Award. *Publications:* Grimus, 1975; Midnight's Children, 1981 (Booker McConnell Prize for Fiction; James Tait Black Meml Book Prize; E-SU Literary Award); Shame, 1983 (Prix du Meilleur Livre Etranger, 1984); contribs to: Firebird 1: Writing Today, ed T. J. Binding, 1982; London Review of Books: Anthology One, 1982; many journals. *Recreations:* cinema, reading, chess. *Address:* c/o Jonathan Cape Ltd, 32 Bedford Square, WC1.

RUSHFORD, Antony Redfern, CMG 1963; barrister; consultant on constitutional, international and commonwealth law; associate consultant (Barbados), Sir Fred Phillips, CVO; President and Managing Director, Investors Discount Brokerage Inc. (Nevada) (licensed dealers in securities), since 1986; a director of Studies, Royal Institute of Public Administration (Overseas Services Unit) (also associate consultant on statute law), since 1982; *b* 9 Feb.; *m* 1975, June Jeffrey, *d* of late C. R. Morrish, DSC, KPM, and *widow* of Roy Eustace Wells; one step *s* one step *d*. *Educ:* Taunton Sch.; Trinity Coll., Cambridge (BA 1948; LLM (LLB 1948); MA 1951). FRSA. RAFVR, 1942 (active service, 1943–47, reserve, 1947–59); Sqdn Ldr, 1946. Solicitor, 1944–57 (distinction in Law Soc. final exams, 1942); Barrister, Inner Temple. Asst Solicitor, E. W. Marshall Harvey & Dalton, 1948; Director and Secretary: Rushford Investment Co., 1949–73; Phoenix Antiquities & Fine Arts (formerly Stanrush) Ltd, 1949–77. Home Civil Service, Colonial Office, 1949–68; joined HM Diplomatic Service, 1968; CO, later FCO, retd as Dep. Legal Advr (Asst Under-Sec. of State), 1982. Crown Counsel, Uganda, 1954–63; Principal Legal Adviser, British Indian Ocean Territory, 1983; Attorney-Gen., Anguilla, and St Helena, 1983; Legal Adviser for Commonwealth Sec.-Gen. to Governor-Gen. of Grenada, Mem. Interim Govt, Attorney-Gen., and JP, Grenada, 1983; consultancies: FCO (special duties), 1982; Commonwealth Sec.-Gen., St Kitts and Nevis independence, 1982–83, St Lucia treaties, 1983–85; E Caribbean courts, 1983; maritime legislation for Jamaica, Internat. Maritime Orgn, 1983 and 1985; constitutional advr, Govt of St Kitts and Nevis, and Govt of St Lucia, 1982–. Has drafted many constitutions for UK dependencies and Commonwealth countries attaining independence; presented paper on constitutional develt to meeting of Law Officers from Smaller Commonwealth Jurisdictions, IoM, 1983. UK deleg. or advr at many constitutional confs and discussions; CO Rep., Inst. of Advanced Legal Studies; participant, Symposium on Federalism, Chicago, 1962; Advr, Commonwealth Law Ministers Conf., 1973. Lectr, Overseas Legal Officers Course, 1964; Special Examnr, London Univ., 1963. Mem. Editl Bd, Inst. of Internat. Law and Econ. Develt, Washington, 1977–82. Foundn Mem. Exec. Council, Royal Commonwealth Soc. for the Blind, 1969–81, 1983– (Hon. Legal Adviser, 1984–); Hon. Sec., Services Race Club, Hong Kong, 1946–47. Member: Glyndebourne Fest. Soc., 1950–; Inst. of Advanced Motoring, 1959–73; Commonwealth Lawyers Assoc.; Commonwealth Assoc. of Legislative Counsel, 1984–; Commonwealth Magistrates Assoc., 1986–; Associate Mem., CPA (UK Br.), 1986–. Governor, Taunton Sch., 1948–. OStJ 1978 (Hon. Legal Counsellor, 1978–; Mem., Chapter-Gen., 1983–). *Recreations:* writing poetry, prose, casting astrological horoscopes, painting in gouache and acrylic colours, studying psychology, cat-loving, uxoriousness. *Address:* The Penthouse, 63 Pont Street, Knightsbridge, SW1X 0BD. *T:* 01–589 6448; (office) 19–23 Ludgate Hill, EC4M 7AE. *T:* 01–489 0211; 01–236 1106; (chambers) 12 King's Bench Walk, Temple, EC4Y 7EL. *T:* 01–353 5692/6; Royal Institute of Public Administration, Regent's College, Inner Circle, Regent's Park, NW1 4NS. *T:* 01–486 0141. *Club:* Royal Commonwealth Society.

RUSHTON, William George; actor, author, cartoonist and broadcaster; *b* 18 Aug. 1937; *s* of John and Veronica Rushton; *m* 1968, Arlene Dorgan; three *s*. *Educ:* Shrewsbury Sch. Founder/Editor, Private Eye, 1961. Stage début in The Bed-sitting Room, by Spike Milligan, Marlowe Theatre, Canterbury, 1961; Gulliver's Travels, Mermaid, 1971, 1979; Pass the Butler, by Eric Idle, Globe, 1982; *films:* Nothing but the Best, 1963; Those Magnificent Men in their Flying Machines, 1964, and several others; *television* includes: That Was the Week that Was, 1962; Up Sunday, 1975–78; Celebrity Squares, 1979–80; numerous Jackanory progs; *radio* includes: I'm Sorry I Haven't a Clue, 1976–; much other broadcasting in UK and Australia. *Publications:* written and illustrated: William Rushton's Dirty Book, 1964; How to Play Football: the art of dirty play, 1968; The Day of the Grocer, 1971; The Geranium of Flüt, 1975; Superpig, 1976; Pigsticking: a joy for life, 1977; The Reluctant Euro, 1980; The Filth Amendment, 1981; W. G. Grace's Last Case, 1984; Willie Rushton's Great Moments of History, 1985; The Alternative Gardener: a compost of quips for the green-fingered, 1986; illustrations for many others. *Recreations:* losing weight, gaining weight, parking. *Address:* Wallgrave Road, SW5. *Clubs:* Tatty Bogle's, Lord's Taverners, Surrey CCC.

RUSHWORTH, Dr (Frank) Derek; Headmaster, Holland Park School, London, 1971–85; *b* 15 Sept. 1920; *s* of late Frank and Elizabeth Rushworth, Huddersfield; *m* 1941, Hamidah Begum, *d* of late Justice S. Akhlaque Hussain, Lahore, and Edith (*née* Bayliss), Oxford; three *d*. *Educ:* Huddersfield Coll.; St Edmund Hall, Oxford (Schol.; BA 1942, MA 1946); Doctorate of Univ. of Paris (Lettres), 1947. Served 6th Rajputana Rifles, Indian Army, 1942–45 (Major); began teaching, 1947; Head of Modern Languages: Tottenham Grammar Sch., 1953; Holland Park Sch., 1958; Head of Shoreditch Sch., London, 1965. Chairman: Associated Examining Board, French Committee, 1964–74; Schools Council, 16+ Examination Feasibility Study (French), 1971–75; Pres., London Head Teachers' Assoc., 1985. *Publications:* Our French Neighbours, 1963, 2nd edn 1966; French text-books and language-laboratory books; articles in French Studies, Modern Languages, also educnl jls. *Recreation:* photography. *Address:* 25c Lambolle Road, NW3 4HS. *T:* 01–794 3691.

RUSK, Dean, KBE (Hon.) 1976; Professor of International Law, University of Georgia School of Law, Athens, Georgia, since 1971; *b* 9 February 1909; *s* of Robert Hugh Rusk and Frances Elizabeth Clotfelter; *m* 1937, Virginia Foisie; two *s* one *d*. *Educ:* Davidson College, North Carolina; St John's College, Oxford. Assoc. Prof. of Government and Dean of Faculty, Mills Coll., 1934–40; US Army, 1940–46; Special Asst to Secretary of War, 1946; US Dept of State, 1947–51; Asst Sec. of State for UN Affairs, 1949; Dep.

Under Sec. of State, 1949–50; Asst Sec. of State for Far Eastern Affairs, 1950–51; Sec. of State, 1961–69; President, The Rockefeller Foundation, 1952–61, Distinguished Fellow, 1969–. Hon. Fellow, St John's Coll., Oxford, 1955. Hon. LLD: Mills Coll., Calif, 1948; Davidson Coll., 1950; Univ. of Calif, 1961; Emory Univ., Georgia, 1961; Princeton Univ., NJ, 1961; Louisiana State Univ. 1962; Amherst Coll., 1962; Columbia Univ. 1963; Harvard Univ., 1963; Rhode Island Univ., 1963; Valparaiso Univ., 1964; Williams Coll., 1964; Univ. of N Carolina, 1964; George Washington Univ., 1965; Oberlin Coll., 1965; Maryville Coll., 1965; Denver Univ., 1966; Erskine Coll., 1967. Hon. DCL Oxford, 1962; Hon. LHD: Westminster Coll., 1962; Hebrew Union Coll., 1963; Hardin-Simmons Univ., 1967. Cecil Peace Prize, 1933. Legion of Merit (Oak Leaf Cluster). *Address:* 1 Lafayette Square, 620 Hill Street, Athens, Ga 30606, USA.

RUSSELL; *see* Hamilton-Russell.

RUSSELL, family name of **Duke of Bedford, Earl Russell, Baron Ampthill, Baron de Clifford** and **Baron Russell of Liverpool.**

RUSSELL, 4th Earl *cr* 1861; **John Conrad Russell;** Viscount Amberley, 1861; *b* 16 Nov. 1921; *er s* of 3rd Earl Russell, OM, FRS, and Dora Winifred, MBE (*d* 1986), *d* of late Sir Frederick Black, KCB; *S* father, 1970; *m* 1946, Susan Doniphan (marr. diss. 1954), *d* of late Vachel Lindsay; one *d* (and one *d* decd). *Educ:* Beacon Hill Sch., 1927–34; Dartington Hall Sch.,1934–39; University of California, Los Angeles, 1939–41; Harvard University, 1941–43. Served War of 1939–45, in RNVR, 1943–46; Temp. Admin. Asst, FAO of the United Nations, Washington, DC, 1946–47; temp. Admin. Asst, HM Treasury, 1947–49. Took his seat in the House of Lords, 12 May 1976. *Heir:* half-brother Hon. Conrad Sebastian Robert Russell, *qv. Address:* Carn Voel, Porthcurno, near Penzance, Cornwall.

RUSSELL OF LIVERPOOL, 3rd Baron *cr* 1919; **Simon Gordon Jared Russell;** *b* 30 Aug. 1952; *s* of Captain Hon. Langley Gordon Haslingden Russell, MC (*d* 1975) (*o s* of 2nd Baron), and of Kiloran Margaret, *d* of late Hon. Sir Arthur Jared Palmer Howard, KBE, CVO; *S* grandfather, 1981; *m* 1984, Dr Gilda Albano, *y d* of late Signor F. Albano and of Signora Maria Caputo-Albano; one *s. Educ:* Charterhouse; Trinity Coll., Cambridge; INSEAD, Fontainebleau, France. *Heir: s* Hon. Edward Charles Stanley Russell, *b* 2 Sept. 1985. *Address:* Ash Farm, Stourpaine, Blandford, Dorset.

RUSSELL, Alan; *b* 5 Dec. 1910; *s* of late Hon. Cyril Russell; *m* 1st, 1937, Grace Evelyn Moore (decd); one *d*; 2nd, 1944, Jean Patricia, *widow* of Wing Comdr J. R. Cridland, AAF, and *d* of late Stafford Croom Johnson, JP; one step *s* one *s. Educ:* Beaumont. Joined Helbert Wagg & Co. Ltd, 1929. Served War of 1939–45, in Army, London Scottish, Lt-Col, attached US Army, Europe, 1941–45. Director: Helbert Wagg & Co. Ltd, 1946–62; District Bank Ltd, 1948–70; Alexanders Discount Co. Ltd, 1948–79; IBM United Kingdom Ltd, 1956–79; Legal & General Assurance Society Ltd, 1958–76; J. Henry Schroder & Co. Ltd, 1960–62; United Molasses Co. Ltd, 1962–66; J. Henry Schroder Wagg & Co. Ltd, 1962–70; Turner & Newall Ltd, 1962–75; Schroders Ltd, 1963–70; Yorkshire Bank Ltd, 1965–79; National Westminster Bank Ltd, 1968–79. *Address:* 23 Park Lane, Aldeburgh, Suffolk.

RUSSELL, Alan Keith; Fellow and Bursar of Lincoln College, Oxford; *b* 22 Oct. 1932; *s* of Keith Russell and Gertrude Ann Russell; *m* 1959, Philippa Margaret Stoneham; two *s* one *d. Educ:* Ardingly Coll.; Lincoln and Nuffield Colls, Oxford. BA; MA Econ and Pol Sci; DPhil. Colonial Office, ODM, FCO, 1959–69, 1972–75; CS Coll., 1969–71; Dir, Inter University Council for Higher Educn Overseas, 1980–81; EEC, 1976–79 and 1981–86. *Publications:* ed, The Economic and Social History of Mauritius, 1962; Liberal Landslide: the General Election of 1906, 1973; contrib. Edwardian Radicalism, 1974; articles on commodity trade and on development; misc. poems. *Recreations:* West African history, travel, town planning, services for the mentally handicapped. *Address:* 8 Dale Close, Oxford.

RUSSELL, Albert Muir Galloway, QC (Scot.) 1965; Sheriff of Grampian, Highland and Islands (formerly Aberdeen, Kincardine and Banff) at Aberdeen and Stonehaven, since 1971; *b* 26 Oct. 1925; *s* of Hon. Lord Russell; *m* 1954, Margaret Winifred, *o d* of T. McW Millar, FRCS(E), Edinburgh; two *s* two *d. Educ:* Edinburgh Academy; Wellington College; Brasenose College, Oxford. BA (Hons) Oxon, 1949; LLB (Edin.), 1951. Lieut, Scots Guards, 1944–47. Member of Faculty of Advocates, 1951–. *Recreation:* golf. *Address:* Easter Ord House, Skene, Aberdeenshire. *T:* Aberdeen 740228. *Club:* Royal Northern (Aberdeen).

RUSSELL, Alexander William; Commissioner, HM Customs and Excise, since 1985; *b* 16 Oct. 1938; *s* of William and Elizabeth W. B. Russell (*née* Russell); *m* 1962, Elspeth Rae (*née* Robertson). *Educ:* Royal High Sch., Edinburgh; Edinburgh Univ. (MA Hons); Manitoba Univ. (MA). Assistant Principal, Scottish Development Dept, 1961–64; Private Sec. to Parliamentary Under Secretary of State, Scottish Office, 1964–65; Principal, Regional Development Div. and Scottish Development Dept, 1965–72; Principal Private Sec. to Secretary of State for Scotland, 1972–73; Asst Secretary: Scottish Development Dept, 1973–76; Civil Service Dept, 1976–79; Under-Secretary: Management and Personnel Office (formerly CSD), 1979–82; Hd of Treasury MPO Financial Management Unit, 1982–85. *Address:* c/o Drummonds Branch, Royal Bank of Scotland, Trafalgar Square, SW1.

RUSSELL, Anna; International Concert Comedienne; *b* 27 Dec. 1911; *d* of Col C. Russell-Brown, CB, DSO, RE, and Beatrice M. Tandy; single. *Educ:* St Felix School, Southwold; Royal College of Music, London. Folk singer, BBC, 1935–40; Canadian Broadcasting Corp. programmes, 1942–46; Radio interviewer, CBC, 1945–46; Debut, Town Hall, New York, as concert comedienne, 1948; Broadway show, Anna Russell and her Little Show, 1953; Towns of USA, Canada, Great Britain, Australia, New Zealand, the Orient and South Africa, 1948–60. Television, Radio Summer Theatre, USA; recordings, Columbia Masterworks. Resident in Australia, 1968–75. Mayfair Theatre, London, 1976. *Publications:* The Power of Being a Positive Stinker (NY); The Anna Russell Song Book; I'm Not Making This Up, You Know (autobiog.). *Recreation:* gardening. *Address:* 70 Anna Russell Way, Unionville, Ontario L3R 3X3, Canada. *Club:* Zouta International (USA, Toronto Branch, Internat. Mem.).

RUSSELL, Rev. Canon Anthony John, DPhil; Director, Arthur Rank Centre (National Agricultural Centre), since 1983; Chaplain to the Queen, since 1983; *b* 25 Jan. 1943; *s* of Michael John William and Beryl Margaret Russell; *m* 1967, Sheila Alexandra, *d* of Alexander Scott and Elizabeth Carlisle Ronald; two *s* two *d. Educ:* Uppingham Sch.; Univ. of Durham (BA); Trinity Coll., Oxford (DPhil); Cuddesdon Coll., Oxford. Deacon 1970, Priest 1971; Curate, Hilborough Group of Parishes, 1970–73; Rector, Preston on Stour, Atherstone on Stour and Whitchurch, 1973–; Chaplain, Arthur Rank Centre (Nat. Agr. Centre), 1973–82; Canon Theologian, Coventry Cathedral, 1977–. Mem., Gen. Synod, 1980–. Chaplain, Royal Agr. Soc., 1982–; Council Mem., 1983–; Hon. Chaplain, RABI, 1983–. *Publications:* Groups and Teams in the Countryside (ed), 1975; The Village in Myth and Reality, 1980; The Clerical Profession, 1980; The Country Parish, 1986. *Address:* The Rectory, Whitchurch, Stratford-upon-Avon, Warwicks. *T:* Alderminster

225; The Arthur Rank Centre, National Agricultural Centre, Kenilworth, Warwicks. *T:* Coventry 555100.

RUSSELL, Sir Archibald (Edward), Kt 1972; CBE 1954; FRS 1970; FEng 1976; Joint Chairman, Concorde Executive Committee of Directors, 1965–69; Vice-Chairman, BAC-Sud Aviation Concorde Committee, 1969–70, retired; *b* 30 May 1904; *m*; one *s* one *d. Educ:* Fairfield Secondary Sch.; Bristol Univ. Joined Bristol Aeroplane Co. Ltd, 1926; Chief Technician, 1931; Technical Designer, 1938; Chief Engineer, 1944; Dir, 1951; Tech. Dir, 1960–66; Chm., British Aircraft Corporation, Filton Div., 1967–69 (Man. Dir, 1966–67). Wright Bros Memorial Lecture, Washington, 1949; 42nd Wilbur Wright Memorial Lecture, London, 1954; RAeS British Gold Medal, 1951; David Guggenheim Medal, 1971; Hon. DSc Bristol, 1951. FIAeS; Hon. FRAeS 1967. *Publications:* papers in R&M Series of Aeronautical Research Cttee and RAeS Journal. *Address:* Glendower House, Clifton Down, Bristol BS8 3BP. *T:* Bristol 739208.

RUSSELL, Rev. Arthur Colin, CMG 1957; ED; MA; *b* 1906; *e s* of late Arthur W. Russell, OBE, WS; *m* 1939, Elma (*d* 1967), *d* of late Douglas Strachan, Hon. RSA; three *d. Educ:* Harrow; Brasenose College, Oxford. Barrister-at-law, Inner Temple. Cadet, Gold Coast (now Ghana), 1929; Asst Dist Comr, 1930; Dist Comr, 1940; Judicial Adviser, 1947; Senior, 1951; Regional Officer, 1952; Permanent Sec., Min. of Education and Social Welfare, 1953; Governor's Secretary, 1954; Chief Regional Officer, Ashanti, 1955–57, retd. Trained for the Ministry, 1957–59; Ordained (Church of Scotland), 1959; Parish Minister, Aberlemno, 1959–76; retd. District Councillor, Angus District, 1977–84. *Publication:* Stained Glass Windows of Douglas Strachan, 1972. *Address:* Balgavies Lodge, by Forfar, Angus DD8 2TH. *T:* Letham (Angus) 571.

RUSSELL, Audrey; *see* Russell, M. A.

RUSSELL, Barbara Winifred, MA; Headmistress, Berkhamsted School for Girls, 1950–July 1971; *b* 5 Jan. 1910; *er d* of Lionel Wilfred and Elizabeth Martin Russell. *Educ:* St Oran's School, Edinburgh; Edinburgh University; Oxford University, Dept of Education. History Mistress, Brighton and Hove High School, 1932–38; Senior History Mistress, Roedean School, 1938–49. *Recreations:* reading, gardening, travel. *Address:* 1 Beech Road, Thame, Oxon. *T:* Thame 2738. *Club:* East India, Devonshire, Sports and Public Schools.

RUSSELL, Brian Fitzgerald, MD, FRCP; Consulting Physician, formerly Physician, Department of Dermatology, The London Hospital (1951–69); Consulting Physician, formerly Physician, St John's Hospital for Diseases of the Skin (1947–69); formerly Civilian Consultant in Dermatology to the Royal Navy (1955–69); past Dean, Institute of Dermatology; *b* 1 Sept. 1904; *s* of Dr John Hutchinson Russell and Helen Margaret (*née* Collingwood); *m* 1932, Phyllis Daisy Woodward; three *s* one *d. Educ:* Merchant Taylors' School. MD (London) 1929; FRCP 1951; DPH (Eng.) 1943. Medical First Asst, London Hosp., 1930–32; general medical practice, 1933–45; Dermatologist, Prince of Wales's Hosp., Tottenham, 1946–51; Asst Physician, Dept of Dermatology St Bartholomew's Hosp., 1946–51. President: St John's Hosp. Dermatological Soc., 1958–60; Dermatological Sect., RSM, 1968–69 (Hon. Mem., 1977); Corr. Mem.: American Dermatological Soc.; Danish Dermatological Soc. *Publications:* St John's Hospital for Diseases of the Skin, 1863–1963, 1963; (with Eric Wittkower) Emotional Factors in Skin Diseases, 1953; Section on Dermatology in Price's Medicine (ed by Bodley Scott), 1973. *Recreation:* rustication. *Address:* 24 St John's Close, Saffron Walden, Essex CB11 4AR.

RUSSELL, Cecil Anthony Francis; Director of Intelligence, Greater London Council, 1970–76; *b* 7 June 1921; *s* of late Comdr S. F. Russell, OBE, RN retd and late Mrs M. E. Russell (*née* Sneyd-Kynnersley); *m* 1950, Editha May (*née* Birch); no *c. Educ:* Winchester Coll.; University Coll., Oxford (1940–41, 1945–47). Civil Service, 1949–70: Road Research Lab., 1949–50; Air Min., 1950–62; Dep. Statistical Adviser, Home Office, 1962–67; Head of Census Div., General Register Office, 1967–70. FSS. *Recreation:* ocean sailing. *Address:* Pagan Hill, Whiteleaf, Princes Risborough, Bucks. *T:* Princes Risborough 3655. *Clubs:* Cruising Association; Ocean Cruising, Royal Lymington Yacht.

RUSSELL, Sir Charles Ian, 3rd Bt, *cr* 1916; Consultant (formerly Partner), Charles Russell & Co., Hale Court, Lincoln's Inn, WC2; Captain, RHA (despatches); *b* 13 March 1918; *s* of Captain Sir Alec Charles Russell, 2nd Bt, and Monica (who *m* 2nd, 1942, Brig. John Victor Faviell, CBE, MC; she *d* 1978), *d* of Hon. Sir Charles Russell, 1st Bt; *S* father, 1938; *m* 1947, Rosemary, *er d* of late Sir John Prestige; one *s* one *d. Educ:* Beaumont College; University College, Oxford. Admitted Solicitor, 1947. *Recreation:* golf. *Heir: s* Charles Dominic Russell [*b* 28 May 1956; *m* 1986, Sarah Jane Murray Chandor, *o d* of Anthony Chandor, Haslemere, Surrey]. *Address:* Hidden House, Sandwich, Kent. *Clubs:* Garrick, Army and Navy; Royal St George's.

RUSSELL, Prof. Hon. Conrad Sebastian Robert; Astor Professor of British History, University College London, since 1984; *b* 15 April 1937; *s* of 3rd Earl Russell, OM, FRS and Patricia Helen, *d* of H. E. Spence; half-*b* and heir-pres. to 4th Earl Russell, *qv; m* 1962, Elizabeth Franklyn Sanders; two *s. Educ:* Merton College, Oxford (BA 1958, MA 1962); MA Yale 1979. FRHistS 1971. Lectr in History, Bedford College, London, 1960–74, Reader, 1974–79; Prof. of History, Yale Univ., 1979–84. *Publications:* The Crisis of Parliaments: English History 1509–1660, 1971; (ed) The Origins of the English Civil War, 1973; Parliaments and English Politics 1621–1629, 1979; articles in jls. *Recreations:* politics, swimming, uxoriousness, cricket. *Address:* Department of History, University College London, Gower Street, WC1E 6BT.

RUSSELL, Sir David Sturrock W.; *see* West-Russell.

RUSSELL, Rev. David Syme, CBE 1982; MA, DD, DLitt; President, Baptist Union of Great Britain and Ireland, 1983–84 (General Secretary, 1967–82); *b* 21 Nov. 1916; second *s* of Peter Russell and Janet Marshall Syme; *m* 1943, Marion Hamilton Campbell; one *s* one *d. Educ:* Scottish Baptist Coll., Glasgow; Trinity Coll., Glasgow; Glasgow Univ. (MA, BD, DLitt, Hon. DD); Regent's Park Coll., Oxford Univ. (MA, MLitt). Minister of Baptist Churches: Berwick, 1939–41; Oxford, 1943–45; Acton, 1945–53. Principal of Rawdon Coll., Leeds, and lectr in Old Testament languages and literature, 1953–64; Joint Principal of the Northern Baptist College, Manchester, 1964–67. Moderator, Free Church Federal Council, 1974–75. Pres., European Baptist Fedn, 1979–81. Mem., Central Cttee, WCC, 1968–83; Vice-Pres., BCC, 1981–84. *Publications:* Between the Testaments, 1960; Two Refugees (Ezekiel and Second Isaiah), 1962; The Method and Message of Jewish Apocalyptic, 1964; The Jews from Alexander to Herod, 1976; Apocalyptic: Ancient and Modern, 1978; Daniel (The Daily Study Bible), 1981; In Journeyings Often, 1982; From Early Judaism to Early Church, 1986; contrib. to Encyc. Britannica, 1963. *Recreation:* woodwork. *Address:* 40 Northumbria Drive, Henleaze, Bristol BS9 4HP. *T:* Bristol 621410.

RUSSELL, Prof. Donald Andrew Frank Moore, FBA 1971; Fellow, St John's College, Oxford since 1948; Professor of Classical Literature, Oxford, since 1985; *b* 13 Oct. 1920; *s* of Samuel Charles Russell (schoolmaster) and Laura Moore; *m* 1967, Joycelyne Gledhill Dickinson. *Educ:* King's College Sch., Wimbledon; Balliol Coll., Oxford (MA 1946).

DLitt 1985. Served War: Army (R Signals and Intelligence Corps), 1941–45. Craven Scholar, 1946; Lectr, Christ Church, Oxford, 1947; St John's College, Oxford: Tutor, 1948–84; Dean, 1957–64; Tutor for Admissions, 1968–72; Reader in Class. Lit., Oxford Univ., 1978–85. Paddison Vis. Prof., Univ. of N Carolina at Chapel Hill, 1985. Co-editor, Classical Quarterly, 1965–70. *Publications:* Commentary on Longinus, On the Sublime, 1964; Ancient Literary Criticism (with M. Winterbottom), 1972; Plutarch, 1972; (with N. G. Wilson) Menander Rhetor, 1981; Criticism in Antiquity, 1981; Greek Declamation, 1984; articles and reviews in classical periodicals. *Address:* 47 Woodstock Road, Oxford. *T:* Oxford 56135.

RUSSELL, Rev. Prof. Edward Augustine; Principal, Union Theological College, Belfast, since 1981; Professor of New Testament (originally at Presbyterian College, Belfast), since 1961; *b* 29 Nov. 1916; *s* of William Russell and Annie (*née* Sudway); *m* 1st, 1948, Emily Frances Stevenson (*d* 1978); two *s* one *d*; 2nd, 1979, Joan Evelyn Rufli (*née* Craig). *Educ:* Royal Belfast Academical Instn; London Univ. (BA, BD, MTh); Magee UC, 1942–43; Presbyterian Coll., Belfast, 1943–44, 1945–46; New Coll., Edinburgh, 1944–45. Research at Göttingen Univ. Ordained to Ministry of Presbyterian Church in Ireland, 1948; Minister: Donacloney, 1948–53; Mountpottinger Churches, 1953–61. External Examiner, Glasgow Univ., 1968, 1972–73; extra-mural Lectr, QUB, 1972–. Vis. Prof., Southwestern Univ., Memphis, 1980. Member of various clerical associations. Editor, Irish Biblical Studies, 1979–. Hon. DD Presbyterian Theol Faculty of Ireland, 1966. *Publications:* contribs to Studia Evangelica VI, Berlin 1973; Ministry and the Church, 1977; Studia Biblica vol. II, Sheffield 1980; Studia Evangelica VII, Berlin 1982. *Recreations:* music, golf, painting, languages, bird-watching. *Address:* 14 Cadogan Park, Belfast BT9 6HG.

RUSSELL, Edward Walter, CMG 1960; MA Cantab, PhD Cantab; Professor of Soil Science, Reading University, 1964–70, now Professor Emeritus; *b* Wye, Kent, 27 Oct. 1904; *e s* of late Sir (Edward) John Russell, OBE, FRS; *m* 1933, Margaret, *y d* of late Sir Hugh Calthrop Webster; one *s* two *d*. *Educ:* Oundle; Gonville and Caius College, Cambridge. Soil Physicist, Rothamsted Experimental Station, Harpenden, 1930–48; Reader in Soil Science, Oxford Univ., 1948–55; Director, East African Agriculture and Forestry Research Organisation, 1955–64. Member: Scientific Council for Africa, 1956–63; Agricultural Research Council of Central Africa, 1959–64. FInstP; FIBiol; FIAgrE. Hon. Member: British Soc. of Soil Science (Pres., 1968–70); Internat. Soc. of Soil Science. For. Corr. Mem., French Acad. of Agriculture, 1969. Hon. Councillor, Consejo Superior de Investigations Cientificas, Madrid, 1970. Hon DSc Univ. of East Africa, 1970. *Publications:* 8th, 9th and 10th Editions of Soil Conditions and Plant Growth; contrib. on physics and chemistry of soils to agricultural and soil science journals. *Address:* 31 Brooklyn Drive, Emmer Green, Reading, Berks RG4 8SR. *T:* Reading 472934.

RUSSELL, Edwin John Cumming, FRBS 1978; sculptor; *b* 4 May 1939; *s* of Edwin Russell and Mary Elizabeth Russell; *m* 1964, Lorne McKean (sculptor; commnd by the Queen for her personal silver wedding gift to Prince Philip—Prince Philip riding polo pony); two *d*. *Educ:* Brighton Coll. of Art and Crafts; Royal Academy Schs (CertRAS). *Works:* Crucifix, pulpit, St Paul's Cathedral, 1964; St Catherine, Little Cloister, Westminster Abbey, 1966; St Michael, Chapel of St Michael and St George, St Paul's Cath., 1970; Suffragette Memorial, Westminster, 1970; Silver Jubilee Sundial, Nat. Maritime Mus., 1979; Bishop, Wells Cathedral, 1980. Royal Academy Gold Medal for Sculpture, 1960. *Recreation:* philosophy. *Address:* Lethendry, Polecat Valley, Hindhead, Surrey GU26 6BE. *T:* Hindhead 5655.

RUSSELL, Sir Evelyn (Charles Sackville), Kt 1982; Chief Metropolitan Stipendiary Magistrate, 1978–82; *b* 2 Dec. 1912; *s* of late Henry Frederick Russell and late Kathleen Isabel, *d* of Richard Morphy; *m* 1939, Joan, *er d* of Harold Edward Jocelyn Camps; one *d*. *Educ:* Douai School; Château de Mesnières, Seine Maritime, France. Hon. Artillery Co., 1938. Served War of 1939–45, Royal Artillery, in UK, N Africa, Italy and Greece. Called to the Bar, Gray's Inn, 1945 (Hon. Bencher 1980); Metropolitan Stipendiary Magistrate, 1961. KCHS 1980 (KHS 1964). *Address:* The Gate House, Coopersale, Epping, Essex. *T:* Epping 72568.

RUSSELL, Francis Mark; Chairman: B. Elliott plc, since 1975 (Chief Executive, 1972–83); Goldfields Industrial Corporation, Johannesburg, since 1975; *b* 26 July 1927; *s* of W. Sidney and Beatrice M. Russell; *m* 1950, Joan Patricia Ryan; two *s* three *d*. *Educ:* Ratcliffe Coll., Leicester; Clare Coll., Cambridge (MA). CBIM. Palestine Police, 1946–48; Director: S. Russell & Sons Ltd, 1959; B. Elliott & Co. Ltd, 1967; Chief Executive, Goldfields Industrial Corporation, 1969; Dep. Chm., B. Elliott & Co. Ltd, 1971; Dir, Johnson & Firth Brown plc, 1982–. *Recreations:* golf, gardening. *Address:* Welders Wood, Welders Lane, Chalfont St Peter, Bucks SL9 8TT. *T:* Chalfont St Giles 4559. *Clubs:* Boodle's; Denham Golf.

RUSSELL, George, CBE 1985; Group Chief Executive, Marley Plc, since 1986; *b* 25 Oct. 1935; *s* of William H. Russell and Frances A. Russell; *m* 1959, Dorothy Brown; three *d*. *Educ:* Gateshead Grammar Sch.; Durham Univ. (BA Hons). Vice President and General Manager: Welland Chemical Co. of Canada Ltd, 1968; St Clair Chemical Co. Ltd, 1968; Man. Dir, Alcan UK Ltd, 1976; Asst Man. Dir, 1977–81, Man. Dir, 1981–82, Alcan Aluminium (UK) Ltd; Man. Dir and Chief Exec., British Alcan Aluminium, 1982–86; Chairman: Luxfer Holdings Ltd, 1976; Alcan UK Ltd, 1978; Director: Alcan Aluminiumwerke GmbH, Frankfurt, 1982–; Northern Rock Bldg Soc., 1985–. Visiting Professor, Univ. of Newcastle upon Tyne, 1978. Member: Board, Northern Sinfonia Orchestra, 1977–80; Northern Industrial Development Board, 1977–80; Washington Development Corporation, 1978–80; IBA, 1979–; Board, Civil Service Pay Research Unit, 1980–81; Megaw Inquiry into Civil Service Pay, 1981–; Widdicombe Cttee of Inquiry into Conduct of Local Authority Business, 1985. Trustee, Beamish Develt Trust, 1985–. Hon. DEng Univ of Newcastle upon Tyne, 1985. *Recreations:* tennis, badminton, bird watching. *Address:* 46 Downshire Hill, NW3 1NX. *T:* 01–435 7742.

RUSSELL, Sir George Michael, 7th Bt, *cr* 1812; *b* 30 Sept. 1908; *s* of Sir Arthur Edward Ian Montagu Russell, 6th Bt, MBE and late Aileen Kerr, *y d* of Admiral Mark Robert Pechell; *S* father, 1964; *m* 1936, Joy Frances Bedford, *d* of late W. Mitchell, Irwin, Western Australia; two *d*. *Educ:* Radley, Berkshire, England. *Heir:* *half-b* Arthur Mervyn Russell, *b* 7 Feb. 1923.

See also Baron Broughshane.

RUSSELL, Gerald Francis Morris, MD, FRCP, FRCPE, FRCPsych, DPM; Professor of Psychiatry, Institute of Psychiatry, University of London, and Physician, Bethlem Royal and Maudsley Hospital, since 1979; *b* Grammont, Belgium, 12 Jan. 1928; 2nd *s* of late Maj. Daniel George Russell, MC, and late Berthe Marie Russell (*née* De Boe); *m* 1950, Margaret Taylor, MB, ChB; three *s*. *Educ:* Collège St Jean Berchmans, Brussels; George Watson's Coll., Edinburgh (Dux); Univ. of Edinburgh (Mouat Schol. in Practice of Physic). MD (with commendation), 1957. RAMC Regimental Med. Off., Queen's Bays, 1951–53; Neurological Registrar, Northern Gen. Hosp., Edin., 1954–56; MRC Clinical Res. Fellow, 1956–58; Inst. of Psychiatry, Maudsley Hospital: 1st Asst, 1959–60; Senior Lectr, 1961–70; Dean, 1966–70, Bethlem Royal and Maudsley Hospital: Physician, 1961–70; Mem. Bd of Governors, 1966–70; Prof. of Psychiatry, Royal Free Hosp. Sch. of Medicine, 1971–79. Chm., Educn Cttee, Royal Medico-Psychological Assoc., 1970 (Mem. Council, 1966–71); Sec. of Sect. of Psychiatry, Roy. Soc. Med., 1966–68; Member Editorial Boards: British Jl of Psychiatry, 1966–71; Psychological Medicine, 1970–; Jl Neurology, Neurosurgery and Psychiatry, 1971–75; Medical Education, 1975–. Mem. European Soc. for Clinical Investigation, 1968–72. Corr. Fellow, Amer. Psychiatric Assoc., 1967; Mem., 1942 Club, 1978–. *Publications:* contrib. to Psychiatrie der Gegenwart, vol. 3, 1975; Textbook of Medicine (ed J. B. Wyngaarden and L. H. Smith), 1979; (ed jtly with L. Hersov and contrib.) Handbook of Psychiatry, vol. 4, The Neuroses and Personality Disorders, 1984; (contrib. and ed with G. I. Szmukler, P. D. Slade, P. Harris and D. Benton) Anorexia Nervosa and Bulimic Disorders: current perspectives, 1985; articles in med. jls on psychiatry, disorders of eating, education and neurology. *Recreations:* roses, language, photography. *Address:* The Institute of Psychiatry, De Crespigny Park, SE5.

RUSSELL, Graham R.; *see* Ross Russell.

RUSSELL, James Francis Buchanan, QC (NI) 1968; **His Honour Judge Russell;** County Court Judge of Northern Ireland, since 1978; *b* 7 July 1924; *e s* of John Buchanan Russell and Margaret Bellingham Russell; *m* 1946, Irene McKee; two *s* one *d* (and one *d* decd). *Educ:* King's Sch., Worcester; St Andrews Univ.; Queen's Univ., Belfast (LLB). Served Royal Air Force, 1941–47. Called to Bar, NI, 1952; Crown Prosecutor: Co. Fermanagh, 1970; Co. Tyrone, 1974; Co. Londonderry, 1976. Bencher, Inn of Court, N Ireland, 1972–78, Treasurer, 1977. Member, Standing Advisory Commn on Human Rights, 1974–78; Chairman, Pensions Appeal Tribunal, N Ireland, 1970–82. *Recreations:* golf, gardening. *Address:* 5 Grey Point, Helen's Bay, Co. Down, Northern Ireland. *T:* Helen's Bay 852249. *Clubs:* Royal Air Force; Royal Belfast Golf, Ulster (Belfast).

RUSSELL, Prof. James Knox, MD; ChB; FRCOG; Emeritus Professor of Obstetrics and Gynæcology, University of Newcastle upon Tyne, since 1982; Dean of Postgraduate Medicine, 1968–77; Consultant Obstetrician, Princess Mary Maternity Hospital, Newcastle upon Tyne, 1956–82, now Hon. Consultant; Consultant Gynæcologist, Royal Victoria Infirmary, Newcastle upon Tyne, 1956–82, now Hon. Consultant; *b* 5 Sept. 1919; *s* of James Russell, Aberdeen; *m* 1944, Cecillia V. Urquhart, MD, DCH, *o d* of Patrick Urquhart, MA; three *d*. *Educ:* Aberdeen Grammar School; University of Aberdeen. MB, ChB 1942, MD 1954, Aberdeen; MRCOG 1949; FRCOG 1958. Served War, 1943–46, as MO in RAF, UK and Western Europe. First Assistant to Prof. of Obstetrics and Gynæcology, Univ. of Durham, 1950; Senior Lecturer in Obstetrics and Gynæcology, Univ. of Durham, 1956; Prof., first at Durham, then at Newcastle upon Tyne, 1958–82. Hon. Obstetrician, MRC Unit on Reproduction and Growth; Examiner in Obstetrics and Gynæcology, Univs of London, Birmingham, Manchester, Belfast, Aberdeen, Liverpool, RCOG, CMB, Tripoli and Kuala Lumpur; Presiding Examiner, CMB, Newcastle upon Tyne; Consultant in human reproduction, WHO. Commonwealth Fund Fellow 1962. Visiting Professor: New York, 1974; South Africa, 1978; Kuala Lumpur, 1980, 1982; Graham Waite Meml Lectr, Amer. Coll. of Obstetricians and Gynaecologists, Dallas, 1982. *Publications:* Teenage Pregnancy: Medical, Social and Educational Aspects, 1982; various papers, editorials and articles on obstetrical and gynæcological subjects and medical education to learned journals, newspapers and magazines. *Recreations:* writing, gardening, curing and smoking bacon, eels, salmon, etc. *Address:* Newlands, Tranwell Woods, Morpeth, Northumberland NE61 6AG. *T:* Morpeth 55666. *Club:* Royal Over-Seas League.

RUSSELL, John, CBE 1975; Art critic, since 1974, Chief Art Critic, since 1982, The New York Times; *b* 1919; *o s* of Isaac James Russell and Harriet Elizabeth Atkins; *m* 1st, 1946, Alexandrine Apponyi (marr. diss., 1950); one *d*; 2nd, 1956, Vera Poliakoff (marr. diss., 1971); 3rd, 1975, Rosamond Bernier. *Educ:* St Paul's Sch.; Magdalen Coll., Oxford (MA). Hon. Attaché, Tate Gall., 1940–41; MOI, 1941–43; Naval Intell. Div., Admty, 1943–46. Regular contributor, The Sunday Times, 1945–, art critic, 1949–74. Mem. art panel, Arts Council, 1958–68. Organised Arts Council exhibns: Modigliani, 1964, Rouault, 1966 and Balthus, 1968 (all at Tate Gallery); Pop Art (with Suzi Gablik), 1969 (at the Hayward Gallery); organised Vuillard exhibn (Toronto, Chicago, San Francisco), 1971. Frank Jewett Mather Award (College Art Assoc.), 1979; Mitchell Prize for Art Criticism, 1984. Grand Medal of Honour (Austria), 1972; Officier de l'Ordre des Arts et des Lettres, 1975. Order of Merit, Fed. Repub. of Germany, 1982. TV scripts for arts programmes. *Publications:* books include: Shakespeare's Country, 1942; British Portrait Painters, 1945; Switzerland, 1950; Logan Pearsall Smith, 1950; Erich Kleiber, 1956; Paris, 1960, new and enlarged edn, 1983; Seurat, 1965; Private View (with Bryan Robertson and Lord Snowdon), 1965; Max Ernst, 1967; Henry Moore, 1968; Ben Nicholson, 1969; Pop Art Redefined (with Suzi Gablik), 1969; The World of Matisse, 1970; Francis Bacon, 1971; Edouard Vuillard, 1971; The Meanings of Modern Art, 1981. *Recreations:* reading, writing, Raimund (1790–1836). *Address:* c/o The New York Times, 229 West 43rd Street, New York, NY 10036, USA. *Clubs:* Century, Knickerbocker (New York).

RUSSELL, John Harry; Chairman and Chief Executive, Duport plc, since 1981; *b* 21 Feb. 1926; *s* of Joseph Harry Russell and Nellie Annie Russell; *m* 1951, Iris Mary Cooke; one *s* one *d*. *Educ:* Halesowen Grammar Sch. FCA; FBIM. War Service, RN. Joseph Lucas Ltd, 1948–52; Vono Ltd (Duport Gp Co.), 1952–59; Standard Motors Ltd, 1959–61; rejoined Duport Gp, 1961: Man. Dir, Duport Foundries Ltd, 1964; Dir, Duport Parent Bd, 1966; Chm., Burman & Sons Ltd (formerly part of Duport), 1968–72; Chief Exec., Duport Engrg Div., 1972–73; Dep. Gp Man. Dir, 1973–75; Gp Man. Dir, 1975–80, Dep. Chm., 1976–81, Duport Ltd. Non-exec. Dir, Birmingham Local Bd, Barclays Bank Ltd, 1976–. Liveryman, Worshipful Co. of Glaziers and Freeman and Citizen of London, 1976. *Recreations:* reading, music, antiques. *Address:* 442 Bromsgrove Road, Hunnington, Halesowen, West Midlands B62 0JL.

RUSSELL, John Lawson; Commissioner for Local Administration in Scotland, 1978–82; *b* 29 May 1917; *er s* of late George William Russell and Joan Tait Russell; *m* 1946, Rachel Essington Howgate; three *s*. *Educ:* Central School and Anderson Inst., Lerwick; Edinburgh Univ. (BL). Enrolled Solicitor. Served Royal Scots, Royal Artillery, Gordon Highlanders and 30 Commando, 1939–46 (despatches). Assistant Secretary, Assoc. of County Councils in Scotland, 1946–49; Depute County Clerk: West Lothian, 1950–57; Caithness, 1957–58; County Clerk: Caithness, 1958–67; Aberdeen, 1967–75; Chief Executive, Grampian Region, 1974–77. Member, Countryside Commission for Scotland, 1978–82. *Recreations:* sailing, hill-walking, camping, photography. *Address:* 2A Montgomery Court, 110 Hepburn Gardens, St Andrews, Fife KY16 9LT. *T:* St Andrews 75727.

RUSSELL, Ken; film director since 1958; *b* 3 July 1927. Merchant Navy, 1945; RAF, 1946–49. Ny Norsk Ballet, 1950; Garrick Players, 1951; free-lance photographer, 1951–57; Film Director, BBC, 1958–66; free-lance film director, 1966; *Films for TV:* Elgar; Bartok; Debussy; Henri Rousseau; Isadora Duncan; Delius; Richard Strauss; Clouds of Glory; The Planets; Vaughan Williams; *films:* French Dressing, 1964; The Billion Dollar Brain, 1967; Women in Love, 1969; The Music Lovers, 1970; The Devils, 1971; The Boy Friend, 1971; Savage Messiah, 1972; Mahler, 1973; Tommy, 1974; Lisztomania,

1975; Valentino, 1977; Altered States, 1981; Crimes of Passion, 1984; Gothic, 1986; *opera:* The Rake's Progress, Florence, 1982; Madam Butterfly, Spoleto, 1983; La Bohème, Macerata, 1984; Faust, Vienna, 1985. Screen Writers Guild Award for TV films Elgar, Debussy, Isadora and Dante's Inferno. *Recreation:* music, fell walking.

RUSSELL, Mrs Leonard; *see* Powell, (E.) Dilys.

RUSSELL, Hon. Leopold Oliver, CBE 1970 (OBE 1944); TD; Chairman, Cement Makers' Federation, since 1979; *b* 26 Jan. 1907; 4th *s* of 2nd Baron Ampthill, GCSI, GCIE; *m* 1935, Rosemary Wintour (marr. diss., 1954); no *c. Educ:* Eton. Weekly newspaper publishing company, 1925–38; served War of 1939–45, 5th Battalion Beds and Herts Regiment TA; Gen. Staff appts HQ 18th Div., Eastern Command, South-Eastern Command, GHQ Home Forces, HQ 21st Army Group, and CCG; released with rank of Brigadier; Asst Sec. to Board of Trade, 1946–47; Dir, British Institute of Management, 1947–56. Dir-Gen., Cement and Concrete Assoc., 1958–77, Chm. 1976–80. Chm., E Anglian RHA, 1973–78; Member: Bd of Governors, Nat. Hosps for Nervous Diseases, 1963–76; E Anglian Regional Hosp. Bd, 1972–73. *Address:* 17 Onslow Square, SW7. *T:* 01-589 0891; The Old Rectory, Kettlebaston, Ipswich, Suffolk. *T:* Bildeston 740314. *Clubs:* Brooks's, Buck's, Beefsteak, Pratt's.

RUSSELL, Sir Mark; *see* Russell, Sir R. M.

RUSSELL, Martin Guthrie, CBE 1970; Children's Division, Home Office, later Department of Health and Social Security, 1964–74; *b* 7 May 1914; *s* of William James Russell and Bessie Gertrude Meades; *m* 1951, Moira May Eynon, *d* of Capt. Richard Threlfell; one *d. Educ:* Alleyn's School; Sidney Sussex Coll., Cambridge (MA). Asst Principal, Home Office, 1937; Asst Private Sec. to Lord Privy Seal, 1942; Principal, Home Office, 1942; seconded to Treasury, 1949–51 and 1952–54; Asst Sec. 1950; Estabt Officer, 1954, Dep. Chm., 1960–64, Prison Commn. In charge of Interdepartmental Social Work Gp, 1969–70. *Recreations:* gardening, enjoying retirement. *Address:* 23 Sutton Lane, Banstead, Surrey SM7 3QX. *T:* Burgh Heath 54397. *Club:* United Oxford & Cambridge University.

RUSSELL, (Muriel) Audrey, MVO 1976; broadcaster, radio and television; *o d* of late John Strangman Russell and Muriel Russell (*née* Metcalfe), Co Dublin; unmarried. *Educ:* privately, in England, and France. Trained Central School of Speech and Drama. First stage appearance in London in Victoria Regina, Lyric, 1937. National Fire Service, 1939–42; joined war-time staff, BBC, 1942; accredited BBC war correspondent overseas, 1944–45; news reporter, BBC 1946–51. Commentaries on State occasions have included: Funeral of King George VI at Windsor; the Coronation of Queen Elizabeth II in Westminster Abbey; Royal weddings: Princess Elizabeth; Princess Margaret; Princess Alexandra; Duke of Kent; Princess Anne; Prince Charles, Prince of Wales (for CBC); Funeral of Sir Winston Churchill in St Paul's; Royal Silver Wedding, 1972; Silver Jubilee, 1977; opening of Humber Bridge, 1981. BBC Commentator, 1953–: on Commonwealth Tours of the Queen and Duke of Edinburgh to Bermuda, NZ, Australia, Uganda, Malta, Canada, Nigeria, India, Pakistan, Ghana, Sierra Leone, Tanganyika; visits of Queen Elizabeth the Queen Mother to Central and E Africa; State Visits include: Oslo, 1955; Stockholm, 1956; Lisbon, Paris, Copenhagen, USA, 1957; Amsterdam, 1958; Nepal, Iran, Italy, 1961; W Germany, 1965; Austria, 1969; France, 1972. Royal Maundy Distribution broadcasts, 1952–78; numerous TV appearances in connection with history, art, and Royal occasions. FRSA. Freeman of City of London, 1967. *Publication:* A Certain Voice (autobiog.), 1984. *Recreations:* painting in oils, and visiting art galleries. *Address:* 5 Godstow Road, Upper Wolvercote, Oxford OX2 8AJ.

RUSSELL, Hon. Sir Patrick; *see* Russell, Hon. Sir T. P.

RUSSELL, Prof. Peter Edward Lionel Russell, DLitt; FBA 1977; (surname formerly Wheeler); King Alfonso XIII Professor of Spanish Studies, Oxford, 1953–81; *b* 24 Oct. 1913; *er s* of Hugh Bernard Wheeler and late Rita Muriel (*née* Russell), Christchurch, NZ. *Educ:* Cheltenham College; Queen's College, Oxford. DLitt 1981. Lecturer of St John's College, 1937–53 and Queen's College, 1938–45. Enlisted, 1940; commissioned (Intelligence Corps) Dec. 1940; Temp. Lt-Col, 1945; specially employed in Caribbean, W Africa and SE Asia, 1942–46. Fellow of Queen's College, 1946–53, and Univ. Lectr in Spanish Studies, 1946–53; Fellow of Exeter Coll., 1953–81, Emeritus Fellow, 1981; Norman Maccoll Lectr, Cambridge, 1969; Taylorian Special Lectr, Oxford, 1983; Visiting Professor: Univ. of Virginia, 1982; Univ. of Texas, 1983, 1987; Johns Hopkins Univ., 1986. Member: Portuguese Academy of History, 1956; Real Academia de Buenas Letras, Barcelona, 1972; UGC Cttee on Latin-American Studies in British Univs, 1962–64. FRHistS. *Publications:* As Fontes de Fernão Lopes, 1941 (Coimbra); The English Intervention in Spain and Portugal in the Time of Edward III and Richard II, 1955; Prince Henry the Navigator, 1960; (with D. M. Rogers) Hispanic Manuscripts and Books in the Bodleian and Oxford College Libraries, 1962; (ed) Spain: a Companion to Spanish Studies, 1973, Spanish edn, 1982; Temas de la Celestina y otros estudios (del Cid al Quijote), 1978; Prince Henry the Navigator: the rise and fall of a culture hero, 1984; Traducción y traductores en la Península Ibérica 1400–1550, 1985; Cervantes, 1985; articles and reviews in Modern Language Review, Medium Aevum, Bulletin of Hispanic Studies, etc. *Recreations:* photography and travel. *Address:* 23 Belsyre Court, Woodstock Road, Oxford OX2 6HU. *T:* Oxford 56086. *Club:* United Oxford & Cambridge University.

RUSSELL, Most Rev. Philip Welsford Richmond; *b* 21 Oct. 1919; *s* of Leslie Richmond Russell and Clarice Louisa Russell (*née* Welsford); *m* 1945, Violet Eirene, *d* of Ven. Dr. O. J. Hogarth, sometime Archdeacon of the Cape; one *s* three *d. Educ:* Durban High Sch.; Rhodes Univ. College (Univ. of South Africa), BA 1948; LTh 1950. Served War of 1939–45; MBE 1943. Deacon, 1950; Priest, 1951; Curate, St Peter's, Maritzburg, 1950–54; Vicar: Greytown, 1954–57; Ladysmith, 1957–61; Kloof, 1961–66; Archdeacon of Pinetown, 1961–66; Bishop Suffragan of Capetown, 1966–70; Bishop of Port Elizabeth, 1970–74; Bishop of Natal, 1974–81; Archbishop of Cape Town and Metropolitan of Southern Africa, 1981–86. *Recreations:* caravanning, fishing. *Address:* 400 Currie Road, Durban, Natal, South Africa.

RUSSELL, Robert Christopher Hamlyn, CBE 1981; formerly Director, Hydraulics Research Station, Department of the Environment (formerly Ministry of Technology), 1965–81; *b* Singapore, 1921; *s* of late Philip Charles and Hilda Gertrude Russell; *m* 1950, Cynthia Mary Roberts; one *s* two *d. Educ:* Stowe; King's Coll., Cambridge. Asst Engineer: BTH Co., Rugby, 1944; Dunlop Rubber Co., 1946; Sen. Scientific Officer, later PSO, then SPSO, in Hydraulics Research Station, 1949–65. Visiting Prof., Univ. of Strathclyde, 1967. *Publications:* Waves and Tides, 1951; papers on civil engineering hydraulics. *Address:* 29 St Mary's Street, Wallingford, Oxfordshire. *T:* Wallingford 37323.

RUSSELL, Sir (Robert) Mark, KCMG 1985 (CMG 1977); HM Diplomatic Service; Deputy Under-Secretary of State (Chief Clerk), Foreign and Commonwealth Office, since 1986; *b* 3 Sept. 1929; *s* of Sir Robert E. Russell, CSI, CIE; *m* 1954, Virginia Mary Rogers; two *s* two *d. Educ:* Trinity Coll., Glenalmond; Exeter Coll., Oxford (MA). Hon. Mods cl. 2, Lit. Hum. cl. 1. Royal Artillery, 1952–54; FO, 1954–56; 3rd, later 2nd Sec., HM Legation, Budapest, 1956–58; 2nd Sec., Berne, 1958–61; FO, 1961–65; 1st Sec., 1962; 1st Sec. and Head of Chancery, Kabul, 1965–67; 1st Sec., DSAO, 1967–69; Counsellor, 1969; Dep. Head of Personnel (Ops) Dept, FCO, 1969–70; Commercial Counsellor, Bucharest, 1970–73; Counsellor, Washington, 1974–78, and Head of Chancery, 1977–78; Asst Under Sec. of State, FCO and Dep. Chief Clerk and Chief Inspector, HM Diplomatic Service, 1978–82; Ambassador to Turkey, 1983–86. *Recreations:* travel, music. *Address:* c/o Foreign and Commonwealth Office, SW1. *Clubs:* Royal Commonwealth Society; New (Edinburgh).

RUSSELL, Prof. Roger Wolcott; Vice Chancellor, and Professor of Psychobiology, Flinders University of South Australia, 1972–79, now Emeritus Professor (engaged in research, since 1979); Visiting Professor of Pharmacology, School of Medicine, University of California at Los Angeles, 1976–77 and since 1980; *b* 30 Aug. 1914; *s* of Leonard Walker and Sadie Stanhope Russell, Worcester, Mass, USA; *m* 1945, Kathleen Sherman Fortescue; one *s* one *d. Educ:* Worcester (Mass, USA) Public Schools; Clark Univ. (Livermore Schol., Clark Fellow in Psychology); BA 1935, MA 1936; Peabody Coll. (Payne Schol.); University of Virginia (Du Pont Research Fellow); PhD 1939; DSc Univ. of London, 1954. Instructor in Psychology: Univ. of Nebraska, 1939–41, Michigan State Coll., 1941; Research Psychologist, USAF Sch. of Aviation Medicine, 1941–42; Officer USAF, 1942–46; Asst Prof. in Psychol., Univ. of Pittsburgh, 1946–47; Assoc. Prof. of Psychol., Univ. of Pittsburgh and Res. Fellow in Neurophysiol., Western Psychiatric Inst., 1947–49; Fulbright Advanced Research Schol. and Director, Animal Research Lab., Institute of Psychiatry, Univ. of London, 1949–50; Prof. of Psychology and Head of Dept of Psychol., University Coll., London 1950–57 (on leave of absence, 1956–57); Dean of Advanced Studies, Indiana Univ., 1966–67 (Prof. and Chm. Dept of Psychology, 1959–66); Vice Chancellor, Academic Affairs, and Prof. of Psycho-Biology and of Clinical Pharmacology and Therapeutics, Univ. of Calif., Irvine, 1967–72. Member: Australian Vice-Chancellors' Cttee, 1972–79; Bd of Dirs, Australian-American Educnl Foundn, 1972–79; Commonwealth Educnl R&D Cttee, 1974–79. Visiting Professor: Dept of Psychology, Univ. of Reading, 1977; Dept of Psychology, Univ. of Stockholm, 1977. Executive Sec. of the American Psychological Assoc., 1956–59, Board of Directors, 1963–65, Pres. Div. 1, 1968–69; Mem., USPHS Adv. Cttee in Psychopharmacology, 1957–63, 1967–70, 1981–85; Member: Nat. Research Coun. (USA), 1958–61, 1963–65, 1967–71; Army Sci. Adv. Panel (USA), 1958–66; Sec.-Gen. Internat. Union of Psychological Science, 1960–66 (Vice-Pres., 1966–69; Pres., 1969–72; Mem. Exec. Cttee, 1972–80); Aust.-Amer. Educn Foundn Vis. Prof., Dept of Psychol., Univ. of Sydney, 1965–66; Vis. Erskine Fellow, Univ. of Canterbury, NZ, 1966. Member, Scientific and Professional Socs in Europe, USA, Australia. FACE 1972; FASSA 1973. Hon. DSc: Newcastle, NSW, 1978; Flinders, 1979. Bronze Star Medal (USA), 1945. Army Commendation Medal (USA), 1946. *Publications:* (ed) Frontiers in Psychology, 1964; (ed) Frontiers in physiological Psychology, 1966; (ed) Matthew Flinders: The Ifs of History, 1979; research papers on neurochemical bases of behaviour, experimental psychopathology, physiological, child and social psychology, psychopharmacology. *Recreations:* writing, farming. *Address:* The Flinders University of South Australia, Bedford Park, SA 5042, Australia. *T:* Adelaide 275–3911; Kindra, Box 55, Aldinga, SA 5173, Australia. *T:* Adelaide (085) 56–5011.

RUSSELL, Rudolf Rosenfeld; a Recorder of the Crown Court, since 1980; *b* 5 Feb. 1925; *s* of Robert and Johanna Rosenfeld; *m* 1952, Eva Maria Jaray; one *s. Educ:* Bryanston Sch.; Worcester Coll., Oxford (MA). Service in RAF, 1943–46. Called to the Bar, Middle Temple, 1950. *Recreations:* walking, music, skiing. *Address:* Devereux Chambers, Devereux Court, Temple, WC2. *T:* 01–353 7534.

RUSSELL, Spencer Thomas, FCA; FCIS; FNZIM; Governor, Reserve Bank of New Zealand, since 1984; *b* 5 Oct. 1923; *s* of Thomas Spencer Russell and Ann Jane Russell; *m* 1953, Ainsley Russell (*née* Coull); three *s. Educ:* Wanganui Collegiate School. Served War, NZ Division, 1942–45. Joined National Bank of New Zealand, 1946; International Manager, 1956; Asst Gen. Man., 1960; Chief London Man., 1973; Chief Exec. and Dir, 1976. *Publications:* numerous articles in professional jls. *Recreations:* golf, gardening. *Address:* 83 Hatton Street, Wellington 5, New Zealand. *T:* 04764 069. *Clubs:* Wellington, Wellesley (Wellington); Wellington Golf.

RUSSELL, Terence Francis; Sheriff of North Strathclyde at Kilmarnock, since 1983; *b* 12 April 1931; *s* of Robert Russell and Catherine Cusker Russell; *m* 1965, Mary Ann Kennedy; two *d. Educ:* Glasgow Univ. (BL). Qualified as Solicitor, 1955; practised in Glasgow, 1955–58 and 1963–81; Solicitor in High Court, Bombay, 1958–63. Sheriff of N Strathclyde, and of Grampian, Highland and Islands, 1981–83. *Recreations:* gardening, painting. *Address:* 1 Sutherland Avenue, Pollokshields, Glasgow G41 4JJ. *T:* 041–427 1745.

RUSSELL, Thomas, CMG 1980; CBE 1970 (OBE 1963); HM Overseas Civil Service, retired; Representative of the Cayman Islands in UK, since 1982; *b* 27 May 1920; *s* of Thomas Russell, OBE, MC and Margaret Thomson Russell; *m* 1951, Andrée Irma Désfossés; one *s. Educ:* Hawick High Sch.; St Andrews Univ.; Peterhouse, Cambridge. MA St Andrews; Dip. Anthrop. Cantab. War Service, Cameronians (Scottish Rifles), 1941; 5th Bn (Scottish), Parachute Regt, 1943: served in N Africa and Italy; POW, 1944; Captain 1945; OC Parachute Trng Company, 1946. Cambridge Univ., 1946–47. Colonial Admin. Service, 1948; District Comr, British Solomon Is Protectorate, 1948; Asst Sec., Western Pacific High Commn, Fiji, 1951; District Comr, British Solomon Is Protectorate, 1954–56; seconded Colonial Office, 1956–57; Admin. Officer Class A, 1956; Dep. Financial Sec., 1962; Financial Sec., 1965; Chief Sec. to W Pacific High Commn, 1970–74; Governor of the Cayman Islands, 1974–81. FRAI. *Publications:* monographs in Oceania, Jl of Polynesian Society. *Recreations:* anthropology, archæology. *Address:* 6 Eldon Drive, Frensham Road, The Bourne, Farnham, Surrey. *Clubs:* Royal Commonwealth Society, Caledonian.

RUSSELL, Hon. Sir (Thomas) Patrick, Kt 1980; **Hon. Mr Justice Russell;** Judge of the High Court of Justice (Queen's Bench Division), since 1980; *b* 30 July 1926; *s* of late Sidney Arthur Russell and Elsie Russell; *m* 1951, Doreen (Janie) Ireland; two *d. Educ:* Urmston Grammar Sch.; Manchester Univ. (LLB). Served in Intelligence Corps and RASC, 1945–48. Called to Bar, Middle Temple, 1949; Bencher, 1978; QC 1971; Leader, Northern Circuit, 1978–80; Mem. Senate, Inns of Court and Bar, 1978–80. Prosecuting Counsel to the Post Office (Northern Circuit), 1961–70; Asst Recorder of Bolton, 1963–70; Recorder of Barrow-in-Furness, 1970–71; a Recorder of the Crown Court, 1972–80; Presiding Judge, Northern Circuit, 1983–87. Mem., Lord Justice James Cttee on Distribution of Criminal Business, 1973–76. Pres., Manchester and Dist Medico-Legal Soc., 1978–79; Vice-Pres., Lancs CCC, 1980. *Recreation:* cricket. *Address:* Royal Courts of Justice, WC2.

RUSSELL, William Martin, (Willy); author since 1971; *b* 23 Aug. 1947; *s* of William and Margery Russell; *m* 1969, Ann Seagroatt; one *s* two *d. Educ:* St Katherine's Coll. of Educn, Liverpool (Cert. of Educn). Ladies' Hairdresser, 1963–69; Teacher, 1973–74; Fellow of Creative Writing, Manchester Polytechnic, 1977–78. Founder Mem., and Dir, Quintet Films; Hon. Dir, Liverpool Playhouse. *Theatre:* Blind Scouse (3 short plays),

1971–72; When the Reds (adaptation), 1972; John, Paul, George, Ringo and Bert (musical), 1974; Breezeblock Park, 1975; One for the Road, 1976; Stags and Hens, 1978; Educating Rita, 1979; Blood Brothers (musical), 1983; Our Day Out (musical), 1983; *television plays*: King of the Castle, 1972; Death of a Young Young Man, 1972; Break In (for schools), 1974; Our Day Out, 1976; Lies (for schools), 1977; Daughters of Albion, 1978; Boy with Transistor Radio (for schools), 1979; One Summer (series), 1980; *radio play*: I Read the News Today (for schools), 1976; *screenplays*: Band on the Run, 1979 (not released); Educating Rita, 1981. Hon. MA Open Univ., 1983. *Publications*: Breezeblock Park, 1978; One for the Road, 1980; Educating Rita, 1981; Stags and Hens, 1984; Blood Brothers, 1984 (also pubd as short non-musical version for schools, 1984); several other plays included in general collections of plays; songs and poetry. *Recreations*: playing the guitar, composing songs, gardening, cooking. *Address*: c/o Margaret Ramsay Ltd, 14A Goodwin's Court, St Martin's Lane, WC2. *T*: 01–240 0691. *Club*: Woolton Village (Liverpool).

RUSSELL, William Robert; Vice-President, Australian British Trade Association, since 1980 (Chairman, 1967–72 and 1975–77; Deputy Chairman, 1972–74 and 1977–80); *b* 6 Aug. 1913; *s* of William Andrew Russell and Mary Margaret Russell; *m* 1940, Muriel Faith Rolfe; one *s* one *d*. *Educ*: Wakefield Road Central, East Ham. Served War of 1939–45: Mine-Sweeping and Anti-Submarine vessels; Commissioned, 1942; appointed to command, 1943. Joined Shaw Savill & Albion Co. Ltd, 1929; Director, 1958–; Manager, 1959; Gen. Manager, 1961; Dep. Chm., 1966; Chm. and Man. Dir, 1968–73. Chm., London Bd, Bank of NZ, 1981–84 (Dir, 1968–84). Chairman: Council of European and Japanese Nat. Shipowners Assocs, 1969–71 and 1973–75; Aust. and NZ Adv. Cttee to BOTB, 1975–77 (Dep. Chm., 1977–79); NZ/UK Chamber of Commerce and Industry, 1979–84. Mem., Tandridge Dist Council, 1978–82. Mem., Inst. of Directors. *Recreations*: gardening, golf. *Address*: Westland, Uvedale Road, Limpsfield, Oxted, Surrey. *T*: Oxted 3080. *Club*: Naval.

RUSSELL-DAVIS, John Darelan, FRICS; chartered surveyor, retired; *b* 23 Dec. 1912; *s* of Edward David Darelan Davis, FRCS, and Alice Mildred (*née* Russell); *m* 1st, 1938, Barbarina Elizabeth Graham Arnould (*d* 1985); one *s* one *d*; 2nd, 1986, Gaynor, *widow* of Lt-Col A. V. Brooke-Webb, RA. *Educ*: Stowe Sch.; Germany; Coll. of Estate Management, London. FRICS 1934. Served War, HAC, 1939; commnd RA, 1940; Captain 1942; mentioned in despatches, 1945. Partner, C. P. Whiteley & Son, Chartered Surveyors, 1938; Sen. Partner, Whiteley, Ferris & Puckridge, and Kemsley, Whiteley & Ferris, City of London, 1948–72. Mem., Lands Tribunal, 1972–77. Royal Instn of Chartered Surveyors: formerly Mem. Council (twice); Chm., City branch, 1959; Hon. Treasurer, Benevolent Fund. Mem., East Grinstead UDC, 1957–60 (Vice-Chm., 1960). Formerly: Mem. Council, Wycombe Abbey Sch.; Trustee, Cordwainer and Bread Street Foundn; Mem. Court, Turners Co. (Renter-Warden, 1975). *Recreations*: gardening, motoring, Somerset and Dorset countryside. *Address*: 171 Goose Hill, Bower Hinton, Martoch, Somerset TA12 6LJ. *T*: Martoch 822307. *Clubs*: Army and Navy; Somerset CCC.

See also D. R. Davis.

RUSSELL-SMITH, Dame Enid (Mary Russell), DBE 1953; MA; Principal of St Aidan's College, Durham University, 1963–70; Hon. part-time Lecturer in Politics since 1964; *b* 3 March 1903; *d* of late Arthur Russell-Smith, of Hartfield, Sussex. *Educ*: St Felix Sch., Southwold, Suffolk; Newnham Coll., Cambridge. Modern Languages Tripos (French and German). Entered Civil Service as Assistant Principal in Ministry of Health, 1925. Deputy Secretary, Ministry of Health, 1956–63. Co-opted Mem., Teesside (later Cleveland) Educn Cttee, 1968–75; Chairman: Sunderland Church Commn., 1971; Durham County Conservation Trust, 1973–75; St Paul's Jarrow Develt Trust, 1975–80. Associate Fellow, Newnham College, 1956–72, Hon. Fellow, 1974. DCL Durham, 1985. *Publication*: Modern Bureaucracy: the Home Civil Service, 1974. *Address*: 3 Pimlico, Durham DH1 4QW. *Club*: University Women's.

RUSSELL VICK, Arnold Oughtred; His Honour Judge Russell Vick; *see* Vick.

RUSSO, Sir Peter (George), Kt 1964; CBE 1953 (OBE 1939); JP; Barrister-at-Law; Minister of Housing and Economic Development, Gibraltar Council, 1964–68; *b* 1899; *s* of George Russo; *m* 1926, Margot, *d* of late John A. Imossi, Gibraltar; one *d*. Mem. various Govt bodies and cttees; Dir of several local cos; Trustee, John Mackintosh Foundation; past Chm. City Council, former Mem. Exec. Council, Gibraltar. JP Gibraltar, 1947–. *Address*: 2 Red Sands Road, Gibraltar. *T*: Gibraltar 5622. *Club*: Royal Gibraltar Yacht (past Cdre).

RUSTON, Rev. Canon (Cuthbert) Mark; Vicar, Holy Sepulchre with All Saints (The Round Church), Cambridge, 1955–April 1987; Chaplain to The Queen, 1980–86; *b* 23 Aug. 1916; *s* of Samuel Montague Ruston and Florence Mary Ruston, MBE. *Educ*: Tonbridge Sch.; Jesus Coll., Cambridge (Lady Kaye Schol. 1937; BA 1939, MA 1940); Ridley Hall, Cambridge. Curate, St John's, Woking, 1940–42; Chaplain: Cheltenham Coll., 1942–51; Jesus Coll., Cambridge, 1951–53; Emmanuel Coll., Cambridge, 1953–54. *Recreation*: inland waters cruising. *Address*: (until April 1987) 37 Jesus Lane, Cambridge CB5 8BW. *T*: Cambridge 357931. *Club*: Royal Commonwealth Society.

RUTHERFORD, Andrew; Warden of Goldsmiths' College, University of London, since 1984; *b* Helmsdale, Sutherland, 23 July 1929; *s* of Thomas Armstrong Rutherford and Christian P. Rutherford (*née* Russell); *m* 1953, Nancy Milroy Browning, MA, *d* of Dr Arthur Browning and Dr Jean G. Browning (*née* Thomson); two *s* one *d*. *Educ*: Helmsdale Sch.; George Watson's Boys' Coll.; Univ. of Edinburgh; Merton Coll., Oxford. MA Edinburgh Univ., First Cl. Hons Eng. Lang. and Lit., James Elliott Prize, and Vans Dunlop Schol., 1951; Carnegie Schol., 1953; BLitt Oxford, 1959. Seaforth Hldrs, 1952–53, serving with Somaliland Scouts; 11th Bn Seaforth Hldrs (TA), 1953–58. Asst Lectr in English, Univ. of Edinburgh, 1955; Lectr, 1956–64; Vis. Assoc. Prof., Univ. of Rochester (NY), 1963; University of Aberdeen: Sen. Lectr, 1964; Second Prof. of English, 1965–68; Regius (Chalmers) Prof. of Eng. Lit., 1968–84; Mem. Court, 1978–84; Dean, Faculty of Arts and Soc. Scis, 1979–82; Sen. Vice-Principal, 1982–84. Lectures: Byron Foundn, Nottingham Univ., 1964; Chatterton, British Acad., 1965; Stevenson, Edinburgh Univ., 1967; Byron Soc., 1973. Chm., English Bd, CNAA, 1966–73; Pres., Internat. Assoc. of Univ. Profs of English, 1977–80. Mem., BBC Gen. Adv. Council, 1979–84. British Council lecture tours in: India, Greece, Italy, Colombia, Austria, Luxembourg, Malta, Belgium. *Publications*: Byron: A Critical Study, 1961; (ed) Kipling's Mind and Art, 1964; (ed) Byron: The Critical Heritage, 1970; (ed) 20th Century Interpretations of A Passage to India, 1970; (ed) Kipling, A Sahibs' War and other stories, 1971; (ed) Kipling, Friendly Brook and other stories, 1971; The Literature of War, 1979; (ed) Early Verse by Rudyard Kipling, 1986; articles in learned journals. *Recreation*: shooting. *Address*: University of London Goldsmiths' College, New Cross, SE14 6NW. *Clubs*: Athenæum, Royal Commonwealth Society.

RUTHERFORD, Derek Thomas Jones, FCA; Commissioner for Administration and Finance, Forestry Commission, since 1984; *b* 9 April 1930; *s* of late Sydney Watson Rutherford and Elsie Rutherford; *m* 1956, Kathleen Robinson; one *s* four *d*. *Educ*: Doncaster Grammar School. Practising accountant and auditor, 1955–59; Company Sec./Accountant, P. Platt & Sons, 1959–61; Retail Accountant, MacFisheries, 1961–63; Factory Management Accountant, then Company Systems Manager, T. Wall & Son (Ice Cream), 1963–70; Dir of Finance, Alfa-Laval Co., 1970–74; Group Financial Dir, Oxley Printing Group, 1974; HMSO: Chief Accountant, Publications Group, 1975–76; Dir, Management Accounting Project, 1976–77; Dir of Finance and Planning Div., 1977–83; Principal Estabt and Finance Officer, 1983–84. *Recreations*: reading, gardening, home computing. *Address*: 83 Caiyside, Swanston, Edinburgh EH10 7HN. *T*: 031–445 1171. *Club*: Royal Commonwealth Society.

RUTHERFORD, (Gordon) Malcolm; Assistant Editor and Political Columnist, Financial Times, since 1977; *b* 21 Aug. 1939; *s* of Gordon Brown Rutherford and Bertha Brown Rutherford; *m* 1st, 1965, Susan Tyler (marr. diss. 1969); one *d*; 2nd, 1970, Elizabeth Maitland Pelen; three *d*. *Educ*: Newcastle Royal Grammar Sch.; Balliol Coll., Oxford. Arts Editor 1962, Foreign Editor 1964, The Spectator; founded the Newsletter, Latin America, 1965; Financial Times: Diplomatic Correspondent, 1967–69; Chief German Correspondent, 1969–74; Defence Specialist, 1974–77. Founding Mem., Media Law Group, 1983. *Publication*: Can We Save the Common Market?, 1981, 2nd edn 1983. *Recreations*: travel, reading, music, theatre, ballet, tennis. *Address*: 89 Bedford Gardens, W8. *T*: 01–229 2063. *Club*: Travellers'.

RUTHERFORD, Herman Graham, CBE 1966; QPM 1957; DL; Chief Constable of Surrey, 1956–68; retired, 1968; *b* 3 April 1908; *m* 1940, Dorothy Weaver; three *s* one *d*. *Educ*: Grammar School, Consett, County Durham. Metropolitan Police, 1929–45; Chief Constable: of Oxfordshire, 1945–54; of Lincolnshire, 1954–56. Barrister, Gray's Inn, 1941. Served Army, Allied Military Government, 1943–45, Lt-Colonel. DL Surrey, 1968. *Recreation*: sailing. *Address*: Hankley Farm, Elstead, Surrey. *T*: Elstead 702200.

RUTHERFORD, Malcolm; *see* Rutherford, G. M.

RUTHERFORD, Thomas, CBE 1982; Chairman, North Eastern Electricity Board, since 1977; *b* 4 June 1924; *s* of Thomas and Catherine Rutherford; *m* 1950, Joyce Foreman; one *s* one *d*. *Educ*: Tynemouth High Sch.; King's Coll., Durham Univ. BSc(Hons); CEng, FIEE. Engrg Trainee, subseq. Research Engr, A Reyrolle & Co. Ltd, Hebburn-on-Tyne, 1943–49; North Eastern Electricity Bd: various engrg and commercial appts, 1949–61; Personal Asst to Chm., 1961–63; Area Commercial Engr, then Area Engr, Tees Area, 1964–69; Dep. Commercial Man., 1969–70; Commercial Man., 1970–72; Chief Engr, 1972–73; Dep. Chm., 1973–75; Chm., SE Electricity Board, 1975–77. *Address*: 76 Beach Road, Tynemouth, Northumberland NE30 2QW. *T*: Tyneside 2571775.

RUTHVEN; *see* Hore-Ruthven, family name of Earl of Gowrie.

RUTHVEN OF CANBERRA, Viscount; Patrick Leo Brer Hore-Ruthven; *b* 4 Feb. 1964; *s* and *heir* of 2nd Earl of Gowrie, *qv*.

RUTLAND, 10th Duke of, *cr* 1703; **Charles John Robert Manners,** CBE 1962; Marquess of Granby, 1703; Earl of Rutland, 1525; Baron Manners of Haddon, 1679; Baron Roos of Belvoir, 1896; Captain Grenadier Guards; *b* 28 May 1919; *e s* of 9th Duke and Kathleen, 3rd *d* of late F. J. Tennant; *S* father, 1940; *m* 1946, Anne Bairstow Cumming (marr. diss. 1956), *e d* of late Major Cumming Bell, Binham Lodge, Edgerton, Huddersfield; one *d*; *m* 1958, Frances Helen, *d* of Charles Sweeny and of Margaret, Duchess of Argyll; two *s* one *d* (and one *s* decd). *Educ*: Eton; Trinity Coll., Cambridge. Owns 18,000 acres; minerals in Leicestershire and Derbyshire; picture gallery at Belvoir Castle. Chairman: E Midlands Economic Planning Council, 1971–74; Leicestershire County Council, 1974–77. *Heir*: *s* Marquis of Granby, *qv*. *Address*: Belvoir Castle, Grantham; Haddon Hall, Derby.

See also Marquess of Anglesey, Sir R. G. M. Throckmorton, Bt, Earl of Wemyss.

RUTT, Rt. Rev. Cecil Richard; *see* Leicester, Bishop of.

RUTTER, Prof. Arthur John; Emeritus Professor and Senior Research Fellow, Imperial College, University of London (Professor of Botany, 1967–79 and Head of Department of Botany and Plant Technology, 1971–79); *b* 22 Nov. 1917; *s* of late W. Arthur Rutter, CBE, FRIBA and Amy, *d* of William Dyche, BA, Cardiff; *m* 1944, Betsy Rosier Stone (*d* 1978); two *s* one *d*. *Educ*: Royal Grammar Sch., Guildford; Imperial Coll. of Science and Technology. ARCS, BSc, PhD, FIBiol. Mem., ARC team for selection of oil-seed crops and develt selective herbicides, 1940–45; Asst Lectr, Imperial Coll., 1945, Lectr 1946; Reader in Ecology, Univ. of London, 1956. Vis. Prof., Univ. of the Panjab, Pakistan, 1960–61. *Publications*: papers, mainly in Annals of Botany, Jl of Ecology, Jl of Applied Ecology on water relations of plants, forest hydrology and effects of atmospheric pollution on trees. *Recreations*: gardening, walking. *Address*: Fairseat, Bagshot Road, Knaphill, Woking, Surrey. *T*: Brookwood 3347.

RUTTER, Sir Frank (William Eden), KBE 1986 (CBE 1981); Chairman, Auckland Hospital Board, New Zealand, since 1974; *b* 5 June 1918; *s* of Edgar and Nellie Rutter; *m* 1947, Mary Elizabeth Milton; six *d*. *Educ*: Welsh National Sch. of Medicine, Cardiff; Westminster Hosp. Med. Sch., London. MRCGP, MRCS, LRCP; DipObst. Chm., Health Cttee, Cardiff RDC, 1960–62; Mem., Auckland Hosp. Bd, 1971–. Pres., Hosp. Bds Assoc., NZ, 1976–80 and 1982–84; Chairman, National Advisory Committee: Cancer Treatment Services, 1978–; Organ Imaging Services, 1982–; Life-Mem., NZ National Multiple Sclerosis Soc. OStJ 1980. Silver Jubilee Medal, 1977. *Recreations*: private flying, squash, breeding Airedale terriers and Welsh terriers. *Address*: 10 Staffa Street, Parnell, Auckland, New Zealand. *T*: (09) 773070/(09) 2781202. *Clubs*: Northern, Auckland Aero (Auckland).

See also J. C. Rutter.

RUTTER, John Cleverdon; His Honour Judge Rutter; a Circuit Judge, since 1972; *b* 18 Sept. 1919; 2nd *s* of late Edgar John Rutter; *m* 1951, Jill, *d* of Maxwell Duncan McIntosh; one *s* one *d*. *Educ*: Cardiff High Sch.; Univ. Coll., of SW of England, Exeter (Open Schol.); Keble Coll., Oxford. MA Oxon; LLB London. Royal Artillery, 1939–46; commnd 1941; served overseas. Called to the Bar, Lincoln's Inn, 1948; practised Wales and Chester Circuit, 1948–66, Stipendiary Magistrate for City of Cardiff, 1966–71. A Legal Member, Mental Health Review Tribunal for Wales Region, 1960–66. An Assistant Recorder of: Cardiff, 1962–66; Merthyr Tydfil, 1962–66; Swansea, 1965–66; Dep. Chm., Glamorgan QS, 1969–71. *Recreations*: golf, reading. *Address*: Law Courts, Cardiff. *T*: Cardiff 45931.

RUTTER, Prof. Michael Llewellyn, CBE 1985; MD; FRCP, FRCPsych; Professor of Child Psychiatry, University of London Institute of Psychiatry, since 1973; *b* 15 Aug. 1933; *s* of Llewellyn Charles Rutter and Winifred Olive Rutter; *m* 1958, Marjorie Heys; one *s* two *d*. *Educ*: Moorestown Friends' Sch., USA; Wolverhampton Grammar Sch.; Bootham Sch., York; Birmingham Univ. Med. Sch. (MB ChB 1955, MD Hons 1963). MRCS 1955; LRCP 1955, MRCP 1958, FRCP 1972; FRCPsych 1971. Training in paediatrics, neurology and internal medicine, 1955–58; Maudsley Hosp., 1958–61; Nuffield Med. Travelling Fellow, Albert Einstein Coll. of Medicine, NY, 1961–62; Mem., Sci. Staff, MRC Social Psych. Res. Unit, 1962–65; Institute of Psychiatry: Sen.

Lectr, then Reader, 1966–73; Prof., 1973–; Hon. Dir, MRC Child Psych. Unit, 1984–. Fellow, Center for Advanced Study in Behavioral Scis, Stanford, Calif, 1979–80. Lectures: Goulstonian, RCP, 1973; Salmon, NY Acad. of Medicine, 1979; Adolf Meyer, Amer. Psych. Assoc., 1985; Maudsley, RCPsych, 1986. Hon. FBPsS 1978; Hon. Fellow, Amer. Acad. of Pediatrics, 1981. Hon. DSSc Univ. of Leiden, 1985. Numerous awards, UK and USA. *Publications*: Children of Sick Parents, 1966; (jtly) A Neuropsychiatric Study in Childhood, 1970; (ed jtly) Education, Health and Behaviour, 1970; (ed) Infantile Autism, 1971; Maternal Deprivation Reassessed, 1972, 2nd edn 1981; (ed jtly) The Child with Delayed Speech, 1972; Helping Troubled Children, 1975; (jtly) Cycles of Disadvantage, 1976; (ed jtly) Child Psychiatry, 1977, 2nd edn as Child and Adolescent Psychiatry, 1985; (ed jtly) Autism, 1978; Changing Youth in a Changing Society, 1979; (jtly) Fifteen Thousand Hours: secondary schools and their effects on children, 1979; (ed) Scientific Foundations of Developmental Psychiatry, 1981; A Measure of Our Values: goals and dilemmas in the upbringing of children, 1983; (jtly) Lead Versus Health, 1983; (jtly) Juvenile Delinquency, 1983; (ed) Developmental Neuropsychiatry, 1983; (ed jtly) Stress, Coping and Development, 1983; (ed jtly) Depression and Young People, 1986. *Recreations*: fell walking, tennis, wine tasting, theatre. *Address*: 190 Court Lane, Dulwich, SE21 7ED. *Club*: Royal Society of Medicine.

RUTTER, Air Vice-Marshal (Retd) Norman Colpoy Simpson, CB 1965; CBE 1945; idc; jssc; psa; Sen. Tech. Staff Officer, Bomber Command, 1961–65; *b* 1909; *s* of Rufus John Rutter; *m* 1936, Irene Sophia (*d* 1983), *d* of late Colonel A. M. Lloyd; one *s* one *d*. Air Cdre, 1957; Air Officer Commanding and Commandant of the Royal Air Force Technical College, Henlow, 1959–61. CEng, FIMechE; FRAeS. *Address*: 37 Meadow Road, Pinner, Mddx.

RUTTER, Trevor John, OBE 1976; British Council Representative in Germany, since 1986; *b* 26 Jan. 1934; *s* of late Alfred and Agnes Rutter; *m* 1959, Josephine Henson; one *s*. *Educ*: Monmouth Sch.; Brasenose Coll., Oxford (BA). National Service, Army, 1955–57. British Council, Indonesia, W Germany (Munich), London, 1959–66; First Secretary, Foreign Office, 1967; British Council, 1968–: Representative: Singapore, 1968–71; Thailand, 1971–75; Deputy Head, Home Division, 1975–76; Head: Far East Dept, 1977; Educnl Contracts Dept, 1978–79; Home Div., 1980; Asst Dir Gen., 1981–85. *Address*: c/o British Council, 10 Spring Gardens, SW1; West House, West Street, Wivenhoe, Essex CO7 9DE. *T*: Wivenhoe 2562.

RUTTLE, His Honour Henry Samuel; a Circuit Judge (formerly Judge of County Courts), 1959–81; *b* 10 Nov. 1906; *yr s* of late Michael Ruttle, Portlaw, Co. Waterford, Ireland; *m* 1st, 1943, Joyce Mayo Moriarty (*d* 1968), *yr d* of late J. O. M. Moriarty, Plymouth; one *s* two *d*; 2nd, 1978, Mary Kathleen Scott, *d* of late F. T. Scott, Wimbledon. *Educ*: Wesley College, Dublin and Trinity College, Dublin. BA (Moderatorship in Legal and Political Science) and LLB, 1929; LLD 1933; MA 1950. Called to the Bar, Gray's Inn, 1933; practised in Common Law: London and Western Circuit. Served War of 1939–45: RAFVR, 1940–45; Squadron Leader. Deputy Judge Advocate Judge Advocate General's Office. Resumed practice at Bar, 1945. Member of Church Assembly, 1948–55; Mem., General Council of the Bar, 1957–59; Deputy Chairman Agricultural Land Tribunal (SW Area), 1958–59. JP, Co. Surrey, 1961. Mem., County Court Rules Cttee, 1969–81 (Chm., 1978–81). Jt Editor, The County Court Practice, 1973–81. *Recreations*: Rugby football (Leinster Inter-Provincial, 1927; Captain London Irish RFC, 1935–36; Middlesex County); fly-fishing. *Address*: West Lodge, West Side, Wimbledon Common, SW19.

RYAN, Alan James, FBA 1986; Fellow of New College, since 1969, Reader in Politics, since 1978, University of Oxford; *b* 9 May 1940; *s* of James William Ryan and Ivy Ryan; *m* 1971, Kathleen Alyson Lane; one *d*. *Educ*: Christ's Hospital; Balliol Coll., Oxford. Lectr in Politics, Univ. of Keele, 1963–66, Univ. of Essex, 1966–69. Visiting Professor in Politics: City University of New York, 1967–68; Univs of Texas, 1972, California, 1977, the Witwatersrand, 1978; Vis. Fellow, ANU, 1974, 1979; de Carle Lectr, Univ. of Otago, 1983. Official Mem., CNAA, 1975–80. Delegate, Oxford Univ. Press, 1983–. *Publications*: The Philosophy of John Stuart Mill, 1970, 2nd edn 1987; The Philosophy of the Social Sciences, 1970; J. S. Mill, 1975; Property and Political Theory, 1984. *Recreations*: dinghy sailing, long train journeys. *Address*: Savile House, Mansfield Road, Oxford OX1 3TE. *T*: Oxford 241677.

RYAN, Arthur James, CBE 1953; Regional Director, London Postal Region, 1949–60, retired; *b* 10 Oct. 1900; *e s* of late Stephen James Ryan, Little Common, Bexhill on Sea, Sx; *m* 1926, Marjorie, *y d* of late George James Dee; two *d*. *Educ*: City of London College and privately. Clerk, Headquarters, GPO London, 1918; Asst Surveyor, GPO, Class II, 1926, Class I, 1935; served in N Wales, Eastern Counties, South Western District; Chief Superintendent, then Assistant Controller, 1936, Controller (Mails and Transport), 1941, London Postal Region; Assistant Secretary, Min. of Fuel and Power (on loan), 1941; Dep. Regional Director, London Postal Region, 1944; Member of Post Office Board, 1950. Freeman, City of London. *Recreations*: golf, gardening. *Address*: Lindon House, 2 Pound Avenue, Old Stevenage, Herts SG1 3JA. *T*: Stevenage 318513.

RYAN, (Christopher) Nigel (John), CBE 1977; independent television producer; *b* 12 Dec. 1929; *s* of late Brig. C. E. Ryan, MC, RA; *m* 1984, Mrs Susan Crewe. *Educ*: Ampleforth Coll.; Queen's Coll., Oxford (MA). Joined Reuters, London, 1954; Foreign Corresp., 1957–60; joined Independent Television News, 1961, Editor, 1968–71, Editor and Chief Executive, 1971–77; Vice-Pres., NBC News, America, 1977–80; Dir. of Progs, Thames Television, 1980–82. Dir, TV-am News, 1985–. Silver Medal, Royal Television Soc., 1970; Desmond Davis Award, 1972. *Publications*: A Hitch or Two in Afghanistan, 1983; trans. novels from French by Georges Simenon and others. *Address*: 13 St Marks Place, W11. *T*: 01–727 0766. *Club*: Beefsteak.

RYAN, Maj.-Gen. Denis Edgar; Director of Army Education, since 1984; *b* 18 June 1928; *s* of Reginald Arthur Ryan and Amelia (*née* Smith); *m* 1955, Jean Mary Bentley; one *s* one *d*. *Educ*: Sir William Borlase School, Marlow; King's College, London (LLB). Commissioned RAEC, 1950; served BAOR, 1950–54; Instr, RMA Sandhurst, 1954–56; Adjt, Army Sch. of Educn, 1957–59; Staff Coll., 1960; served in Cyprus, Kenya and UK, 1961–67; CAES, HQ 4 Div., BAOR, 1968–70; Cabinet Office, 1970–72; TDA, Staff Coll., 1972–75; Col GS MoD, 1976–78; Chief Education Officer: HQ SE Dist, 1978–79; HQ BAOR, 1979–82; Comd, Education, UK, 1982–84. *Recreations*: cricket, tennis, rugby, music, theatre. *Address*: c/o Royal Bank of Scotland, Kirkland House, Whitehall, SW1. *Club*: Army and Navy.

RYAN, Sir Derek Gerald, 3rd Bt, *cr* 1919; *b* 9 July 1922; *s* of Sir Gerald Ellis Ryan, 2nd Bt, and Hylda Winifryde Herapath; *S* father 1947; *m* 1st, 1947, Penelope Anne Hawkings (marr. diss. 1971); one *s* three *d*; 2nd, 1972, Katja, *d* of Ernst Best. *Educ*: Harrow. Served War of 1939–45. Lieut Grenadier Guards, 1941–45. *Heir*: *s* Derek Gerald Ryan, Junior, *b* 25 March 1954. *Address*: 6228 Eltville, Nikolausstrasse 11, W Germany. *T*: 06123–5333.

RYAN, Gerard Charles, QC 1981; a Recorder of the Crown Court, since 1986; *b* 16 Dec. 1931; *er s* of Frederick Charles Ryan, Hove, and Louie Violet Ryan (*née* Ball); *m* 1960, Sheila Morag Clark Cameron, *qv*; two *s*. *Educ*: Clayesmore Sch.; Brighton Coll.;

Pembroke Coll., Cambridge. MA. Served RA, 1955–57 (Lieut). Called to the Bar, Middle Temple, 1955 (Exhibnr); Harmsworth Scholar, 1956. *Publication*: (with A. O. B. Harris) Outline of the Law of Common Land, 1967. *Recreations*: gardening, natural history, walking. *Address*: 13 Westmoreland Place, SW1; 2 Harcourt Buildings, Temple, EC4. *T*: 01–353 8415.

RYAN, (James) Stewart; Principal Assistant Solicitor, Department of the Environment, 1975–78; *b* 9 Sept 1913; *o s* of late Philip F. Ryan and Bridget Ryan; *m* 1939, Rachel Alleyn; two *s* four *d*. *Educ*: Beaumont Coll.; Balliol Coll., Oxford (BA). Called to Bar, Inner Temple, 1939. Served in Army, 1939–46 (Major). Joined Govt Legal Service, 1946; Asst Solicitor, Min. of Housing and Local Govt, 1957, later DoE. *Address*: 28 Manor Road, Henley-on-Thames RG9 1LU. *T*: Henley-on-Thames 573345. *Club*: Leander (Henley).
   See also S. K. O'Malley.

RYAN, John; Management consultant and lecturer; *b* 30 April 1940; *m* 1964, Eunice Ann Edmonds; two *s*. *Educ*: Lanark Grammar School; Glasgow University. Member, National Association of Labour Student Organisations, 1958–62; formerly Youth Organiser, Lanark City Labour Party; Member, Executive Committee, North Paddington Labour Party, 1964–66. Contested (Lab) Buckinghamshire South, 1964; MP (Lab) Uxbridge, 1966–70. Member, Fabian Society, 1961; Dir, Tribune Publications Ltd, 1969–. Mem., Inst. of Marketing; Associate Member: Market Res. Soc.; BIM. *Recreations*: golf, walking.

RYAN, Rt. Rev. Joseph Francis, DD, JCD; *b* Dundas, Ontario, 1 March 1897; *s* of Wm Ryan and Ellen Manion. *Educ*: St Mary's Sch., Hamilton; St Jerome's Coll., Kitchener; St Augustine's Seminary, Toronto; Appolinaris Univ., Rome, Italy. Ordained 1921; Asst Priest, St Mary's Cathedral, Hamilton, 1921–25; Rector, 1925; First Rector of new Cathedral of Christ the King, Hamilton, 1933; Administrator of diocese after serving several years as Chancellor; Bishop of Hamilton, 1937–73. *Address*: St Joseph's Motherhouse, PO Box 155, Hamilton, Ontario L8N 3A2, Canada.

RYAN, Nigel; *see* Ryan, C. N. J.

RYAN, Sheila Morag Clark, (Mrs G. C. Ryan); *see* Cameron, S. M. C.

RYAN, Stewart; *see* Ryan, J. S.

RYAN, Thomas; County Councillor, South Yorkshire, 1973–86 (Chairman, 1977–78); *b* 26 Sept. 1911; *s* of John Ryan and Bridget (*née* Griffin); *m* 19 Phoebe (*née* Taylor); two *s*. *Educ*: Netherfield Lane Council Sch.; WEA (adult educn); Sheffield Univ. (2 days per week part-time). Coal miner, Aldwarke Main Colliery, at age of 14; life-long NUM Mem.; NUM Sec., Aldwarke Main Colliery, 1955–62, when Colliery closed; transf. to Denaby Main Colliery, 1962; NUM Pres., 1962; resigned, then elected NUM Sec., 1963–68, when Colliery closed and merged with Cadeby Colliery; underground worker, Cadeby, 1968–71; NUM Sec., Cadeby, 1971–73; elected Sec. again but took redundancy, 1973; retd. Councillor, Rawmarsh UDC, 1960–74 (Chm., 1969); County Councillor, W Riding, 1972–73. Silver Jubilee Medal, 1977. *Recreation*: country walks. *Address*: 24 Hawke Close, Manor Farm Estate, Rawmarsh, Rotherham, S Yorks. *T*: Rawmarsh 2581. *Clubs*: Rawmarsh Trades, Rawmarsh Labour.

RYBCZYNSKI, Tadeusz Mieczyslaw, FIB; Economic Adviser, Lazard Brothers & Co Ltd, and Director, Lazard Securities Ltd, since 1969; *b* 21 May 1923; *s* of Karol Rybczynski and Helena (*née* Sawicka); *m* 1951, Helena Perucka; one *d*. *Educ*: primary and secondary schs, Lwow, Poland; LSE, Univ. of London (BCom, MScEcon). FIB 1966. Lloyds Bank, 1949–53; Lazard Brothers & Co. Ltd, 1954–. Vis. Professor: Univ. of Surrey, 1968–74; City Univ., 1974–. Chm., Soc. of Business Economists, 1962–75. Member: Monopolies and Mergers Commn, 1978–81; Council of Management and Exec. Cttee, NIESR, 1968– (also Governor); Council, REconS, 1969–74 (Treasurer, 1976–); Governing Body, Trade Policy Res. Centre, 1968–; Cttee, Foreign Affairs Club, 1968–; Adv. Bd in Banking and Finance, Univ. of Aston Management Centre, 1973–82; Sci. Cttee, Centre for Monetary and Banking Studies, Univ. of Geneva, 1973–; Court, Brunel Univ., 1976–. Harms Award, Inst. for Economic Research, Univ. of Kiel, 1983. *Publications*: (contrib.) Comparative Banking, ed H. W. Auburn, 1960 (3rd edn 1969); (contrib.) Long Range Planning, Paris and New York, 1967; (ed jtly and contrib.) The Economist in Business, 1967; (contrib.) Readings in International Economics, ed R. E. Caves and H. Johnson, 1968; (ed and contrib.) Value Added Tax–the UK position and the European experience, 1969; (contrib.) Money in Britain 1959–69, ed R. Croome and H. Johnson, 1970; (contrib.) Problems of Investment, ed Sir Robert Shone, 1971; (contrib.) Users of Economics, ed G. D. N. Worswick, 1972; (ed) A New Era in Competition, 1973; (ed and contrib.) The Economics of the Oil Crisis, 1976; (contrib.) Financial Management Handbook, 1977; (contrib.) The International Monetary System 1971–80, 1983; (contrib.) International Lending in a Fragile World Economy, 1983; articles in serious jls, and in academic and bank revs. *Recreations*: opera, ballet, history, international affairs, travel. *Address*: 2 Windyridge Close, Parkside Avenue, SW19 5HB. *T*: 01–946 7363. *Club*: Reform.

RYBURN, Rev. Hubert James, CMG 1959; MA (Oxon and NZ), BD (Union); *b* 19 April 1897; *s* of Very Rev. Robert Middelton Ryburn and Anna Jane Steadman; *m* 1st, 1931, Jocelyn Maud Dunlop (*d* 1980), *d* of Prof. F. W. Dunlop; two *s* two *d*; 2nd, 1981, Isabella Paterson May. *Educ*: Otago University; Oxford University; Union Theological Seminary, NY. Rhodes Scholar, 1921–24. Ordained a minister of the Presbyterian Church of New Zealand, 1926; Minister: Bay of Islands, 1926–29; St Andrews', Dunedin, 1929–41; Master of Knox College, Dunedin, 1941–63. Member: Council of Otago University, 1946–71, Pro-Chancellor, 1954–55, Chancellor, 1955–70; Senate of Univ. of NZ, 1948–61. Hon. LLD (Otago). *Publication*: Te Hemara, James Hamlin, 1980. *Recreation*: fishing. *Address*: 15 Cornwall Street, Dunedin, New Zealand. *T*: 42–032.

RYCROFT, Charlotte Susanna, (Mrs W. N. Wenban-Smith); HM Diplomatic Service; Counsellor (Economic and Commercial), Ottawa, since 1985; *b* 14 June 1941; *d* of late Col David Hugh Rycroft, OBE and Cicely Phoebe Susanna Rycroft (*née* Otter-Barry); *m* 1976, William Nigel Wenban-Smith, *qv*; two *s*, and two step *s* two step *d*. *Educ*: Malvern Girls' Coll.; Girton Coll., Cambridge (BA 1964). Joined FCO, 1964; Havana, 1965; Second Sec., Sofia, 1968–71; First Sec., FCO, 1971–76; Mem., UK Representation to EC, Brussels, 1976–80; FCO, 1980–81; Counsellor, 1981; Advr, CPRS, Cabinet Office, 1981–83; RCDS, 1984. *Recreations*: hillwalking, reading, ski touring, tennis. *Address*: c/o Foreign and Commonwealth Office, King Charles Street, SW1.

RYCROFT, Sir Richard Newton, 7th Bt, *cr* 1784; *b* 23 Jan. 1918; *yr s* of Sir Nelson Edward Oliver Rycroft, 6th Bt, and Ethel Sylvia (*d* 1952), *d* of late Robert Nurton, Odcombe, Yeovil; *S* father 1958; *m* 1947, Ann, *d* of late Hugh Bellingham-Smith, Alfriston, Sussex, and Mrs Harvey Robarts; two *d*. *Educ*: Winchester; Christ Church, Oxford (BA). Served War of 1939–45: Bedfordshire and Hertfordshire Regt, on special service work in Balkans (Major, despatches); Knight's Cross of Royal Order of Phœnix with Swords (Greece). *Heir*: *cousin* Richard John Rycroft, *b* 15 June 1946. *Address*: Winalls

Wood House, Stuckton, Fordingbridge, Hampshire. *T*: Fordingbridge 2263.
See also Viscount FitzHarris.

RYDBECK, Olof; Royal Order of the Star of the North, Sweden; Commissioner-General, United Nations Relief and Works Agency, 1979–85; *b* Djursholm, 15 April 1913; *s* of Oscar Rydbeck and Signe Olson; *m* 1940, Monica Schnell; one *s* one *d*. *Educ*: Univ. of Uppsala, Sweden (BA 1934, LLB 1939). Attaché, Min. for Foreign Affairs, 1939; Berlin, 1940; Ankara, 1941; Stockholm, 1942; Second Sec., 1943; Washington, 1945–50 (First Sec., 1946); Bonn, 1950; Head of Press Sect., Min. for For. Affairs, 1952; Dir Gen., Swedish Broadcasting Corp., 1955–70; Perm. Rep. to UN, 1970–76; Rep. of Sweden to Security Council, 1975–76; Special Rep. of Sec Gen on Western Sahara, 1976; Ambassador of Sweden to the UK, 1977–79. Chairman: Adv. Cttee on Outer Space Communications, UNESCO, 1966–70; Working Gp on Direct Broadcast Satellites, UN Cttee on Peaceful Uses of Outer Space, 1969–75; Cttee of Trustees, UN Trust Fund for S Africa, 1970–75; Prep. Cttee, World Food Conf., 1974; Second Cttee, 30th Gen. Assembly, 1975. Chairman: Assoc. of Royal Swedish Nat. Defence Coll., 1957–70; Internat. Broadcasting Inst., Rome, 1967–70; Hon. Pres., EBU, 1964– (Pres., 1961–64). Member: Central Cttee, Swedish Red Cross; Nat. Swedish Preparedness Commn for Psychol. Defence, 1954–70 (Vice Chm., 1962–70); Royal Swed. Acad. of Music, 1962–. Member Boards: Swed. Inst., 1953–55; Amer.-Swed. News Exchange, 1953–55; Swed. Tourist Traffic Assoc., 1953–55; Stockholm Philharmonic Soc., 1955–62; Swed. Central News Agency, 1967–70; Swed. Inst. of Internat. Affairs, 1967–. Order of: White Rose, Finland; Falcon, Iceland; Dannebrog, Denmark; Verdienstkreutz, Fed. Republic of Germany. *Recreations*: music, equitation. *Address*: Boerhaavegasse 7, 1030 Vienna, Austria.

RYDEN, Kenneth, MC and Bar 1945; DL; *b* 15 Feb. 1917; *s* of Walter and Elizabeth Ryden; *m* 1950, Catherine Kershaw (*née* Wilkinson); two *s*. *Educ*: Queen Elizabeth's Grammar School, Blackburn. FRICS; FRVA. Served War of 1939–45 (MC and Bar, despatches 1945): RE, attached Royal Bombay Sappers and Miners, India, Assam and Burma, 1940–46, retd (Captain). Articled pupil and prof. trng, 1936–39; Min. of Works: Estate Surveyor, 1946–47; attached UK High Commns, India and Pakistan, 1947–50; Sen. Estate Surveyor, Scotland, 1950–59. Founder and Sen. Partner, Kenneth Ryden & Partners (Chartered Surveyors) Edinburgh, Glasgow and London, 1959–74, retd, Consultant 1974–80. Chm., Scottish Br. Chartered Auctioneers and Estate Agents' Institute, 1960–61; Member: Edinburgh Valuation Appeal Cttee, 1965–75, 1981–; Scottish Solicitors' Discipline Tribunal, 1985–. Mem. Bd, Housing Corp., 1972–76. Master, Co. of Merchants of City of Edinburgh, 1976–78; Liveryman, Chartered Surveyors' Co. DL City of Edinburgh, 1978. FRCPE 1985. *Recreations*: fishing, golf, Scottish art. *Address*: 19 Belgrave Crescent, Edinburgh EH4 3AJ. *T*: 031–332 5893. *Club*: New (Edinburgh).

RYDER, family name of **Earl of Harrowby** and of **Baron Ryder of Eaton Hastings.**

RYDER OF EATON HASTINGS, Baron *cr* 1975 (Life Peer), of Eaton Hastings, Oxfordshire; **Sydney Thomas Franklin, (Don), Ryder,** Kt 1972; Industrial Adviser to the Government, since 1974; Chairman, National Enterprise Board, 1975–77; *b* 16 Sept. 1916; *s* of John Ryder; *m* 1950; one *s* one *d*. *Educ*: Ealing. Editor, Stock Exchange Gazette, 1950–60; Jt Man. Dir, 1960–61, Sole Man. Dir, 1961–63, Kelly Iliffe Holdings, and Associated Iliffe Press Ltd; Dir, Internat. Publishing Corp., 1963–70; Man. Dir, Reed Paper Gp, 1963–68; Chm. and Chief Executive, Reed International Ltd, 1968–75; Dir, MEPC Ltd, 1972–75. Member: British Gas Corp., 1973–78; Reserve Pension Bd, 1973–; Council and Bd of Fellows, BIM, 1970–; Court and Council, Cranfield Inst. of Technology, 1970–74; Council, UK S Africa Trade Assoc., 1974–; Nat. Materials Handling Centre (Pres., 1970–77); Council, Industrial Soc., 1971–; NEDC, 1976–77. Vice-Pres., RoSPA, 1973–. *Recreations*: sailing, chess. *Address*: House of Lords, SW1.

RYDER OF WARSAW, Baroness *cr* 1979 (Life Peer), of Warsaw in Poland and of Cavendish in the County of Suffolk; **(Sue Ryder),** CMG 1976; OBE 1957; Founder and Social Worker, Sue Ryder Foundation for the Sick and Disabled of all Age Groups; *b* 3 July 1923; *d* of late Charles and Elizabeth Ryder; *m* 1959, Geoffrey Leonard Cheshire, *qv*; one *s* one *d*. *Educ*: Benenden Sch., Kent. Served War of 1939–45 with FANY and with Special Ops Executive. Co-Founder, Mission for the Relief of Suffering; Trustee, Cheshire Foundn. Hon. LLD: Liverpool, 1973; Exeter, 1980; London, 1981; Leeds, 1984; Hon. DLitt Reading, 1982. Holds Officer's Cross of Order of Polonia Restituta, Poland, 1965; Medal of Yugoslav Flag with Gold Wreath and Diploma, 1971; Golden Order of Merit, Polish People's Republic, 1976; Order of Smile (Poland), 1980. *Publications*: Remembrance (annual leaflet of the Sue Ryder Foundation); And the Morrow is Theirs (autobiog.), 1975; Child of My Love (autobiog.), 1986. *Address*: Sue Ryder Home, Cavendish, Suffolk CO10 8AY.

RYDER, Edward Alexander; HM Chief Inspector of Nuclear Installations, Health and Safety Executive, since 1985; *b* 9 Nov. 1931; *s* of Alexander Harry and Gwendoline Gladys Ryder; *m* 1956, Janet; one *s* one *d*. *Educ*: Cheltenham Grammar School; Bristol University (BSc). CPhys; FInstP. Flying Officer, RAF, 1953–55; Engineer, GEC Applied Electronics Labs, 1955–57; Control Engineer, Hawker Siddeley Nuclear Power Co., 1957–61; Sen. Engineer, CEGB, 1961–71; Principal Inspector, then Superintending Inspector, HM Nuclear Installations Inspectorate, 1971–80; Head of Hazardous Installations Policy Branch, 1980–85, Head of Nuclear Installations Policy Branch, 1985, HSE. Sec., Adv. Cttee on Major Hazards, 1980–85. *Recreations*: golf—or is it nature study; small-hill walking. *Address*: 24 Linchfield Road, Datchet, Slough, Berks SL3 9LZ. *T*: Slough 41599.

RYDER, Eric Charles, MA, LLB; Barrister; Professor of English Law in the University of London (University College) 1960–82, now Professor Emeritus; *b* 28 July 1915; *er s* of late Charles Henry Ryder, solicitor, Hanley, Staffs, and of Ellen Miller; *m* 1941, Nancy Winifred Roberts. *Educ*: Hanley High School; Gonville and Caius College, Cambridge (scholar). BA (Law Tripos Parts I and II, 1st Cl.), 1936; LLB (1st Cl.) 1937; MA 1940; Tapp Law Scholar, Gonville and Caius College, 1937; called to Bar, Gray's Inn, 1937; practice at Chancery Bar. Ministry of Food, 1941–44; Lecturer in Law, King's College, Newcastle upon Tyne, 1944; Dean of Faculty of Law, Univ. of Durham, 1947–60; Professor of Law, Univ. of Durham (King's College), 1953–60. Practised as conveyancing counsel, Newcastle upon Tyne, 1944–53. *Publications*: Hawkins and Ryder on the Construction of Wills, 1965; contrib. to legal periodicals. *Address*: 19 Langton Avenue, Whetstone, N20. *T*: 01–445 1588.

RYDER, Peter Hugh Dudley, MBE 1944; Managing Director, Thomas Tilling Ltd, 1957–68; *b* 28 April 1913; *s* of Hon. Archibald Dudley Ryder and Eleanor Frederica Fisher-Rowe; *m* 1940, Sarah Susannah Bowes-Lyon; two *s* one *d*. *Educ*: Oundle School. Provincial Newspapers Ltd, Hull and Leeds, 1930–33; Illustrated Newspapers Ltd, 1933–39; seconded from TA to Political Intell. Dept of FO, 1939–45 (Lt-Col 1944); Jt Man. Dir, Contact Publications Ltd, 1945; Man. Dir, Daimler Hire Ltd, 1950; Commercial Dir, James A. Jobling & Co. Ltd, Sunderland, 1953; Chairman: James A. Jobling & Co. Ltd, 1957–62 and 1967–68; Heinemann Gp of Publishers Ltd, 1961–68; Director: District Bank Ltd, 1961–69; Cornhill Insce Co. Ltd, 1965–68. Mem. Council, BIM,

1966–69 (Mem. Bd of Fellows, 1968–69); Mem. Bd of Govs, Ashridge Management Coll., 1968. *Address*: Ardmore, 21 Riverbank Road, Ramsey, Isle of Man.

RYDER, Richard Andrew, OBE 1981; MP (C) Mid Norfolk, since 1983; an Assistant Government Whip, since 1986; *b* 4 Feb. 1949; *s* of Richard Stephen Ryder, JP, DL, and Margaret MacKenzie; *m* 1981, Caroline, *o d* of Sir David Stephens, *qv*; one *d*. *Educ*: Radley; Magdalene Coll., Cambridge. BA Hons History, 1971. Manager, Private Office of Leader of the Opposition, 1975–79; Political Sec. to Prime Minister, 1979–81. Parliamentary Private Secretary: to Financial Sec. to the Treasury, 1984; to Sec. of State for Foreign and Commonwealth Affairs, 1984–. Contested (C) Gateshead East, Feb. and Oct. 1974. Partner, M. Ryder and Sons.

RYDER, Richard Hood Jack Dudley; campaigner; *b* 3 July 1940; *s* of late Major D. C. D. Ryder; *m* 1974, Audrey Jane Smith; one *s* one *d*. *Educ*: Sherborne Sch.; Cambridge Univ. (MA); Edinburgh Univ. (DCP); Columbia Univ., NY (Fellow). ABPsS; FZS. Sen. Clinical Psychologist, Warneford Hosp., Oxford, 1967–84; Principal Clin. Psychologist, St James Hosp., Portsmouth, 1983–84. Chm., Oxford Div. of Clin. Psych., 1981–83; Member: Oxford Regional Adolescent Service, 1971–84; DHSS Health Adv. Service, 1977–78. Royal Society for Prevention of Cruelty to Animals: Council Mem., 1972–; Chm., 1977–79; Chm. Political Cttee, 1979–80; Chm., Animal Experimentation Adv. Cttee, 1983–85; Mem., Gen. Election Coordinating Cttee on Animal Protection, 1978; Prog. Organiser, IFAW, 1984–; UK Delegate, Eurogroup, 1980. Chm., Liberal Animal Welfare Gp, 1981–; Member: Liberal Party Council, 1983–; Liberal Party Policy Panels on defence, health, home affairs, eur. affairs, environment, 1981–; contested (L) Buckingham, 1983; Prospective Parly Cand. (L) Teignbridge, 1983–. Broadcaster and writer on psychological, political and animal protection subjects. *Publications*: Speciesism, 1970; Victims of Science, 1975, 2nd edn 1984; (ed) Animal Rights—a Symposium, 1979. *Recreations*: history, opera, croquet. *Address*: c/o Liberal Office, 7 Market Street, Newton Abbot, Devon TQ12 2RJ. *Clubs*: National Liberal, Royal Over-Seas League.

RYDILL, Prof. Louis Joseph, OBE 1962; FEng 1982; RCNC; Consultant in Naval Ship Design, 1986; Professor of Naval Architecture, University College London, 1981–85, now Emeritus Professor; *b* 16 Aug. 1922; *s* of Louis and Queenie Rydill; *m* 1949, Eva (*née* Newman); two *d*. *Educ*: HM Dockyard Sch., Devonport; RNEC Keyham; RNC Greenwich; Royal Corps of Naval Constructors. FRINA (Gold Medallist). Asst Constructor, 1946–52; Constructor, 1952–62, incl. Asst Prof. of Naval Architecture, RNC Greenwich, 1953–57; Chief Constructor, 1962–72, incl. Prof. of Naval Architecture, RNC Greenwich and UCL, 1967–72; Asst Dir Submarines, Constructive, 1972–74; Dep. Dir Submarines (Polaris), 1974–76; Dir of Ship Design and Engrg (formerly Warship Design), MoD, 1976–81. Hon. Res. Fellow, UCL, 1974; Vis. Prof., US Naval Acad., Annapolis, Md, 1985–86. Silver Jubilee Medal, 1977. *Recreations*: literature, theatre, jazz and other music. *Address*: The Lodge, Entry Hill Drive, Bath, Avon. *T*: Bath 27888.

RYDON, Prof. (Henry) Norman, DSc, PhD (London), DPhil (Oxon), FRSC; Professor of Chemistry, University of Exeter, 1957–77, now Emeritus; Deputy Vice-Chancellor, 1973–75; Public Orator, 1976–77; *b* 24 March 1912; *o s* of late Henry William Rydon and Elizabeth Mary Anne (*née* Salmon); *m* 1st, 1937, Eleanor Alice Tattersall (*d* 1968); one *d*; 2nd, 1968, Lovis Elna Hibbard (*née* Davies) (*d* 1983); 3rd, 1985, Clare Warfield Hill (*née* Kenner). *Educ*: Central Foundation Sch., London; Imperial Coll., London. BSc (London), 1931; PhD (London), 1933; DSc (London), 1938; DPhil (Oxon), 1939. Demonstrator in Organic Chemistry, Imperial College, London, 1933–37; Demonstrator in Chemistry, Birkbeck College, London, 1933–37; 1851 Exhibition Senior Student, Oxford University, 1937–40; Chemical Defence Experimental Station, Porton, 1940–45; Member Scientific Staff, Medical Research Council, Lister Institute, 1945–47; Reader in Organic Chemistry, Birkbeck Coll., London, 1947–49; Asst Prof. and Reader in Organic Chemistry, Imperial Coll., London, 1949–52; Professor of Chemistry and Director of the Chemical Laboratories, Manchester College of Science and Technology, 1952–57. Member Council: Chem. Society, 1947–50, 1951–52, 1954–57, 1964–67; Roy. Inst. of Chemistry, 1955–58, 1959–62, 1963–66, 1971–73; Soc. of Chemical Industry, 1961–63; Regional Scientific Adviser for Civil Defence, Home Office, 1951–52, 1955–57. Member: Chemical Defence Adv. Bd, MoD, 1955–66; Scientific Adv. Council, MoD, 1960–63. Hon. DSc Exeter, 1981. Meldola Medal, Roy. Inst. of Chemistry, 1939; Harrison Memorial Prize, Chem. Soc., 1941. *Publications*: papers in Jl of Chem. Soc. and other scientific jls, 1933–. *Recreations*: travel, gardening and motoring. *Address*: Stadmans, Dunsford, Exeter EX6 7DD. *T*: Christow 52532; Hunting Hills, 5401 Ijamsville Road, Ijamsville, Md 21754, USA. *T*: (301) 662–2058.

RYKWERT, Prof. Joseph, MA (Cantab), DrRCA; Reader in Architecture, University of Cambridge, since 1985; *b* 5 April 1926; *s* of Szymon Rykwert and Elizabeth Melup; *m* 1st, 1960 (marr. diss. 1967); 2nd, 1972, Anne-Marie Sandersley; one *s* one *d*. *Educ*: Charterhouse; Bartlett Sch. of Architecture; Architectural Assoc. Lectr, Hochschule für Gestaltung, Ulm, 1958; Librarian and Tutor, Royal Coll. of Art, 1961–67; Prof. of Art, Univ. of Essex, 1967–80; Lectr on Arch., Univ. of Cambridge, 1980–85. Fellow, Inst. for Arch. and Urban Studies, NY, 1969–71; Sen. Fellow, Council of Humanities, Princeton Univ., 1971; Visiting Professor: Institut d'Urbanisme, Univ. of Paris, 1974–76; Princeton Univ., 1977; Andrew Mellon Vis. Prof., Cooper Union, NY, 1977; Slade Prof. of Fine Art, Cambridge Univ., 1979–80; Vis. Fellow, Darwin Coll., Cambridge, 1979–80; Sen. Fellow, Center for the Advanced Studies in the Visual Arts. Nat. Gall. of Art, Washington; Visiting Professor: Univ. of Louvain, 1981–84; Univ. of Pennsylvania, 1982–; George Lurcy Vis. Prof., Columbia, 1986. Mem., Comité Internat. des Critiques d'Architecture. Mem. Commn, Venice Biennale, 1974–78. Consultant, Min. of Urban Develt and Ecology, Republic of Mexico, 1986–. Chevalier des Arts et des Lettres, 1984. Co-editor: Lotus, 1974–; RES (Anthropology and Aesthetics), 1981–. *Publications*: The Golden House, 1947; (ed) The Ten Books of Architecture, by L. B. Alberti, 1955; The Idea of a Town, 1963, 2nd edn 1976; Church Building, 1966; On Adam's House in Paradise, 1972, 2nd edn 1982; (ed) Parole nel Vuoto, by A. Loos, 1972; The First Moderns, 1980; The Necessity of Artifice, 1981; (with Anne Rykwert) The Brothers Adam, 1985; contrib. Arch. Rev., Burlington Mag., Lotus. *Recreations*: rare. *Address*: Faculty of Architecture and History of Art, University of Cambridge, 1 Scroope Terrace, Cambridge CB2 1PX. *T*: Cambridge 69501. *Club*: Savile.

RYLAND, Sir (Albert) William (Cecil), Kt 1973; CB 1965; Chairman, Post Office Corporation, 1971–77; *b* 10 Nov. 1913; *s* of late A. E. Ryland, OBE; *m* 1946, Sybil, *d* of late H. C. Wookey; one *s* one *d*. *Educ*: Gosforth County Grammar School. Joined GPO, 1932; Assistant Traffic Superintendent, GPO, 1934; Asst Surveyor, GPO, 1938. Served War of 1939–45 in Royal Engineers (Postal Section), Middle East and Central Mediterranean, Col. Principal, GPO, 1949; Principal Private Secretary to PMG, 1954; Asst Secretary, GPO, 1955; Director of Establishments and Organisation, GPO, 1958; Director of Inland Telecommunications, GPO, 1961–65; Dep. Director-General, 1965–67; Man. Dir, Telecommunications, GPO, 1967–69; PO Corporation: Jt Dep. Chm. and Chief Exec., 1969–70; Acting Chm., 1970–71. Adviser: to Republic of Ireland Posts and Telegraphs Review Gp, 1978–79; to Deloitte, Haskins and Sells, 1981–. Mem., Standing Cttee on Pay Comparability, 1979–80. CompIEE; FBIM; Hon. CGIA. *Address*: 13 Mill

View Gardens, Croydon CR0 5HW. *T*: 01–656 4224. *Clubs*: Reform, City Livery, MCC.

RYLAND, Charles Mortimer Tollemache S.; *see* Smith-Ryland.

RYLAND, Judge John, CIE 1946; RIN (retired); Judge for British Columbia, 1969; retired; *b* 31 March 1900; *s* of late W. J. Ryland, Surbiton; *m* 1938, Lucy Lenore, *d* of J. W. Bryden, Victoria, BC; two *s. Educ*: King's College School; HMS Conway. *Address*: Royston, BC V0R 2V0, Canada.

RYLAND, Timothy Richard Godfrey Fetherstonhaugh; a Recorder of the Crown Court, since 1983; *b* 13 June 1938; *s* of late Richard Desmond Fetherstonhaugh Ryland and of Frances Katharine Vernon Ryland. *Educ*: St Andrew's Coll.; TCD. BA (Moderatorship), LLB. Called to Bar, Gray's Inn, 1961. Dep. Circuit Judge, 1978. *Recreations*: opera, wine. *Address*: Lamb Building, Temple, EC4Y 7AS. *T*: 01–353 0774. *Club*: Kildare Street and University (Dublin).

RYLAND, Sir William; *see* Ryland, Sir A. W. C.

RYLANDS, George Humphrey Wolferstan, CBE 1961; MA; Fellow of King's College, Cambridge; Sometime Dean, Bursar, College Lecturer, and Director of Studies; University Lecturer in English Literature (retd); *b* 23 October 1902; *s* of Thomas Kirkland Rylands. *Educ*: Eton (King's Scholar); King's Coll., Cambridge (Scholar). Chm. of Directors and Trustees of the Arts Theatre, Cambridge, 1946–82; Governor of the Old Vic, 1945–78; Chm. of Apollo Soc., 1946–72. Member: Cheltenham Coll. Council, 1946–76; Council of RADA. Directed Hamlet with Sir John Gielgud, 1945; LP Recordings of the Shakespeare canon and the English Poets, for the British Council. Hon. LittD Cambridge, 1976. *Publications*: Words and Poetry, 1928; Shakespeare the Poet (in a Companion to Shakespeare Studies), 1934; Poems, 1931; The Ages of Man, a Shakespeare Anthology, 1939; Shakespeare's Poetic Energy (British Academy Lecture, 1951); Quoth the Raven "Nevermore": an anthology, 1984. *Address*: King's College, Cambridge CB2 1ST. *T*: Cambridge 350411. *Club*: Athenæum.

RYLE, Kenneth Sherriff, CBE 1964; MC 1945; Secretary to the Church Commissioners for England, 1969–75; *b* 13 April 1912; *s* of Herbert Ryle, CVO, OBE; *m* 1941, Jean Margaret Watt; one *s* one *d. Educ*: Cheltenham Coll. Chartered Accountant, 1936; Queen Anne's Bounty, 1936–48. Served in RA, 1940–45: India, Persia, Middle East, Sicily, Italy, Germany; Captain 1944. Church Commissioners, 1948– (Dep. Sec., 1964–69). *Recreation*: golf. *Address*: 47 Albyfield, Bickley, Kent. *T*: 01–467 6319. *Club*: Chislehurst Golf.

RYLE, Michael Thomas; Clerk of the Journals, House of Commons, since 1985; *b* 30 July 1927; *s* of Peter Johnston Ryle and Rebecca Katie (*née* Boxall); *m* 1952, Bridget Moyes; one *s* two *d. Educ*: Newcastle upon Tyne Royal Grammar Sch.; Merton Coll., Oxford (1st Cl. Hons PPE, 1951; MA). Served RA, 1946–48 and TA, 1950–57. Entered Clerk's Dept, House of Commons, 1951; served in various offices; Clerk of Overseas Office, 1979–83; Principal Clerk, Table Office, 1983–84; attached Nova Scotia Legislature, 1976. Member: Study of Parlt Gp, 1964– (Founding Mem.; Chm., 1975–78; Pres., 1986–); Council, Hansard Soc., 1974–; Council, RIPA, 1982–; Lambeth HMC, 1960–64; Governor, St Thomas' Hosp., 1964–74. *Publications*: (ed with S. Walkland) The Commons in the Seventies, 1977, 2nd edn, as the Commons Today, 1981; (contrib.) The House of Commons in the Twentieth Century, 1979; contrib. to books on parly practice and procedure; articles in Pol Qly, Parly Affairs, The Table, etc. *Recreations*: cricket, golf, bridge, watching birds, caravanning. *Address*: Hillfield, 24 Vicarage Road, East Sheen, SW14 8RU. *T*: 01–876 1582.

RYMAN, John; MP (Lab) Blyth Valley, since 1983 (Blyth, Oct. 1974–1983); *b* 7 Nov. 1930. *Educ*: Leighton Park; Pembroke College, Oxford. Inns of Court Regt (TA), 1948–51. Called to the Bar, Middle Temple, 1957. Harmsworth Law Scholar. Mem. Council, Assoc. of the Clergy, 1976–. *Recreation*: Horses. *Address*: House of Commons, SW1A 0AA; Lowstead, Wark, Hexham, Northumberland.

RYMER-JONES, Brig. John Murray, CBE 1950 (OBE 1941); MC 1917, and Bar 1918; QPM 1959; retired as Assistant Commissioner Metropolitan Police (1950–59); Secretary, Drinking Fountain Association, 1959–76; Committee Member, Royal Humane Society, 1957–77; *b* 12 July 1897; *s* of late John and Lilian Rymer-Jones; *m* 1930, Gertrude Alice Wobey; one *s* two *d. Educ*: Felsted School; RMA, Woolwich. Commissioned RFA 1916; served European War: France and Flanders, 1916–18; Army of Rhine, 1919. Ireland, 1920–21 with KORR (Lancaster); Plebiscite, Upper Silesia, 1921; HQ British Army in Egypt, 1921–25; HQ Shanghai Defence Force, 1927–28; Company Commander and Instructor, RMA, Woolwich, 1929–33; retired as Captain, RA. Joined Metropolitan Police as Chief Inspector, 1934; Superintendent, 1935; Chief Constable, 1936; Inspector-General and Brigadier commanding Palestine Police, 1943–46. Commander Metropolitan Police, 1946–50. Area Comr, St John Ambulance, North Kent, 1963–66. Commander of St John of Jerusalem, 1952; Chevalier, Légion d'Honneur, 1950; *Recreations*: talking and music. *Address*: Lion House Lodge, High Halden, Kent. *T*: High Halden 538. *Club*: Army and Navy.

RYMILL, Hon. Sir Arthur (Campbell), Kt 1954; MLC, South Australia, 1956–75; Chairman, Advertiser Newspapers Ltd, 1980–83; Director, The Bank of Adelaide, 1953–80 (Chairman, 1953–79); Member of Principal Board, Australian Mutual Provident Society, 1964–80; formerly Director of public companies in South Australia; *b* 8 Dec. 1907; *s* of late Arthur Graham Rymill, North Adelaide; *m* 1934, Margaret Earle, *d* of Roland Cudmore; two *d. Educ*: Queen's Sch. and St Peter's Coll., Adelaide; Univ. of Adelaide. Barrister and Solicitor, 1930. Mem. Adelaide City Council, 1933–38, 1946–64; Lord Mayor of Adelaide, 1950–54. Pres., S Australian Liberal and Country League, 1953–55; First Pres., Nat. Trust of S Australia; Vice-Pres., Aust. Elizabethan Theatre Trust, 1954–63; Mem., Found. Bd of Govs, Adelaide Festival of Arts; Vice-Pres., Adelaide Children's Hosp, 1957–84. Won Australasian Unlimited Speedboat Championship, 1933; rep. S Austr. in Australasian Polo Championships, 1938 and 1951. Served War of 1939–45, 2nd AIF: enlisted Private, 2/7th Field Regt, later commissioned. *Recreations*: farming, violin playing, golf. *Address*: 39 Jeffcott Street, North Adelaide, SA 5006, Australia. *T*: 267 2477. *Clubs*: Adelaide (Adelaide); Melbourne (Melbourne); Royal Adelaide Golf, Royal SA Yacht Squadron.

RYRIE, Sir William (Sinclair), KCB 1982 (CB 1979); Executive Vice-President, International Finance Corporation at World Bank, since 1984; *b* 10 Nov. 1928; *s* of Rev. Dr Frank Ryrie and Mabel Moncrieff Ryrie (*née* Watt); *m* 1st, 1953, Dorrit Klein (marr. diss. 1969); two *s* one *d*; 2nd, 1969, Christine Gray Thomson; one *s. Educ*: Mount Hermon Sch., Darjeeling; Heriot's Sch., Edinburgh; Edinburgh Univ. MA 1st cl. hons History, 1951. Nat. Service, 1951–53: Lieut, Intell. Corps, Malaya, 1952–53 (despatches). Colonial Office, 1953; seconded to Uganda, 1956–58; Principal 1958; transf. to Treasury, 1963; Asst Sec., internat. monetary affairs, 1966–69; Principal Private Sec. to Chancellor of Exchequer, 1969–71; Under-Sec., Public Sector Gp, HM Treasury, 1971–75; Econ. Minister and Head of UK Treasury and Supply Delegn, Washington, and UK Exec. Dir, IMF and IBRD, 1975–79; 2nd Perm. Sec. (Domestic Economy Sector), HM Treasury, 1980–82; Permanent Sec., ODA, FCO, 1982–84. *Recreations*: photography, walking, music. *Address*: 1818 H Street, Washington, DC 20433, USA. *Club*: Reform.

S

SAATCHI, Charles; Director, Saatchi & Saatchi Co., since 1970; *b* 9 June 1943; *m* 1973, Doris Lockhart. *Educ:* Christ's Coll., Finchley. Associate Director, Collett Dickenson Pearce, 1966–68; Director, Cramer Saatchi, 1968–70. *Address:* 80 Charlotte Street, W1.

SAATCHI, Maurice; Chairman, Saatchi & Saatchi Co. plc, since 1984; *b* 21 June 1946; *s* of Daisy and Nathan Saatchi; *m* 1984, Josephine Hart; one *s* one step *s*. *Educ:* London School of Economics and Political Science (1st class BSc Econ). Co-Founder of Saatchi & Saatchi Co., 1970. *Recreations:* gardens, plays. *Address:* (office) 80 Charlotte Street, W1A 1AQ. *T:* 01–636 5060.

SABATINI, Lawrence John; retired; Assistant Under Secretary of State, Ministry of Defence, 1972–79; *b* 5 Dec. 1919; *s* of Frederick Laurence Sabatini and Elsie May Sabatini (*née* Friggens); *m* 1947, Patricia Dyson; one *s* one *d*. *Educ:* Watford Grammar School. Joined HM Office of Works, 1938. Army service, 1940–46: commnd in RTR, 1943: service in NW Europe with 5 RTR. Asst Principal, Min. of Works, 1947; Asst Private Sec. to Minister of Works, 1948–49; Principal, 1949; Principal Private Sec. to Ministers of Defence, 1958–60; Asst Sec., MoD, 1960; Defence Counsellor, UK Delegn to NATO, on secondment to Diplomatic Service, 1963–67. *Recreations:* gardening, photography, music. *Address:* 44a Batchworth Lane, Northwood, Mddx HA6 3DT. *T:* Northwood 23249. *Club:* MCC.

SABBEN-CLARE, Ernest E., MA Oxon, BA London; Information Officer to University of Oxford, 1970–77; *b* 11 Aug. 1910; *s* of late Mr and Mrs J. W. Sabben-Clare; *m* 1938, Rosamond Dorothy Mary Scott; two *s* one *d*. *Educ:* Winchester Coll. (schol.); New College, Oxford (schol.). 1st cl. Mod. Hist., Oxford, 1932. Asst Master, Winchester Coll., 1932–34; Asst Dist Officer, Tanganyika, 1935–40; seconded Colonial Office, 1940–47; Lt, 10th Essex Bn Home Guard; Colonial Attaché, British Embassy, Washington, and Comr, Caribbean Commn, 1947–49; Nigerian Govt, 1950–55; Permanent Sec., Min. of Commerce, 1953–55; 1st cl. French, London Univ. (external), 1954; Asst Master, Marlborough Coll., 1955–60, Under-Master from 1957; Headmaster, Bishop Wordsworth's School, Salisbury, 1960–63; Headmaster, Leeds Grammar Sch., 1963–70. Chairman of Governors: Bramcote Sch., Scarborough, 1970–80; Badminton Sch., 1981–85. Editor, Wilts Archaeological and Natural History Magazine, 1956–62. *Publication:* (ed jtly) Health in Tropical Africa during the Colonial Period, 1980. *Recreations:* walking, gardening. *Address:* 4 Denham Close, Abbey Hill Road, Winchester SO23 7BL. *Club:* Athenæum.

See also J.P. Sabben-Clare.

SABBEN-CLARE, James Paley; Headmaster, Winchester College, since 1985; *b* 9 Sept. 1941; *s* of Ernest Sabben-Clare, *qv*; *m* 1969, Geraldine Mary Borton, LLB; one *s* one *d*. *Educ:* Winchester College (Scholar); New College, Oxford (Scholar; 1st Class Classical Hon. Mods and Greats, 1964; MA). Asst Master, Marlborough College, 1964–68; Vis. Fellow, All Souls College, Oxford, 1967–68; Winchester College, 1968–; Head of Classics Dept, 1969–79; Second Master, 1979–85. *Publications:* Caesar and Roman Politics, 1971, 2nd edn 1981; Fables from Aesop, 1976; The Culture of Athens, 1978, 2nd edn 1980; Winchester College, 1981; contribs to jls of Jt Assoc. of Classical Teachers. *Recreations:* fives, Italian opera, mountains. *Address:* Headmaster's House, Winchester College, Winchester, Hants. *T:* Winchester 54328.

SABIN, Professor Albert (Bruce); Emeritus Professor, Medical University of South Carolina, 1982; Consultant to World Health Organization, since 1969; Senior Expert Consultant, Fogarty International Center, National Institutes of Health, Bethesda, Md, since 1984; *b* 26 Aug. 1906; *s* of Jacob Sabin and Tillie Krugman; *m* 1935, Sylvia Tregillus (*d* 1966); two *d*; *m* 1967, Jane Blach Warner (marr. diss. 1971); *m* 1972, Heloisa Dunshee de Abranches. *Educ:* New York Univ. (MD). Ho. Phys., Bellevue Hosp., NY, 1932–33; Nat. Research Council Fellow, Lister Inst., London, 1934; Rockefeller Inst. for Med. Research, NY, 1935–39; Associate Prof. of Research Pediatrics, Univ. of Cincinnati, 1939–43; active duty, US Army, 1943–46 (Legion of Merit, 1945); Prof. of Research Pediatrics, Univ. of Cincinnati Coll. of Medicine and The Children's Hosp. Research Foundn, 1946–60, Distinguished Service Prof., 1960–71, Emeritus, 1971–; Distinguished Res. Prof. of Biomedicine, Med. Univ. of SC, Charleston, 1974–82. Pres., Weizmann Inst. of Science, Israel, 1970–72. Fogarty Scholar, NIH, 1973. Mem. Nat. Acad. of Sciences of the USA; Fellow, Amer. Acad. of Arts and Sciences; Mem. and Hon. Mem. of various Amer. and foreign societies; Hon. Member: Royal Acad. of Med. of Belgium; British Paediatric Association. Holds hon. degrees; awards include: Feltrinelli Prize ($40,000) of Accad. Naz. dei Lincei, Rome, 1964; Lasker ($10,000) Prize for Clinical Medicine Research, 1965. Gold Medal, Royal Soc. of Health, 1969; National Medal of Science (USA), 1970; Statesman in Medicine Award (USA), 1973; US Medal of Freedom, 1986; US Medal of Liberty, 1986. Hon. FRSH London. *Publications:* numerous papers on pneumococcus infection, poliomyelitis, encephalitis, virus diseases of nervous system, toxoplasmosis, sandfly fever, dengue, other topics relating to various infectious diseases and virus-cancer relationships. *Recreations:* reading, music, home. *Address:* Sutton Towers, Apt 1001, 3101 New Mexico Avenue NW, Washington, DC 20016, USA.

SABIN, Howard Westcott; Legal Adviser to Associated Newspapers Group Ltd, 1972–84; *b* 19 Oct. 1916; *s* of late John Howard Sabin and Octavia Roads (*née* Scruby); *m* 1st, 1942, Joan Eunice Noble (marr. diss. 1959); two *s* one *d*; 2nd, 1959, Janet Eileen Baillie. *Educ:* Shrewsbury; St John's Coll., Cambridge; MA (Hons in History and Law). Lieut, RNVR, 1939–46 (despatches 1944). Called to the Bar, Middle Temple, 1946. Dep. Chm., Bedfordshire QS, 1968–72; Assistant Recorder, Portsmouth, 1966, Bournemouth, 1967. Counsel for Post Office (Midland Circuit), 1964. *Recreations:* golf, swimming, music. *Address:* 40 Wynnstay Gardens, W8 6UT. *T:* 01–937 9247. *Club:* Hadley Wood Golf.

SABIN, Paul Robert; Chief Executive, Kent County Council, since 1986; *b* 29 March 1943; *s* of Robert Reginald and Dorothy Maude Sabin; *m* 1965, Vivien Furnival; one *s* two *d*. *Educ:* Oldbury Grammar Sch. DMS Aston Univ.; IPFA 1966; FBIM (MBIM 1967). West Bromwich CBC, 1961–69; Redditch Develt Corp., 1969–81, Chief Finance Officer, 1975–81; City of Birmingham, 1981–86: City Treas., 1982–86; Dep. Chief Exec., 1984–86. *Recreations:* antique maps and books, music. *Address:* County Hall, Maidstone ME14 1XQ. *T:* Maidstone 671411.

SABINE, Neville Warde, CMG 1960; CBE 1957; *b* 6 April 1910; *s* of late John William Sabine; *m* 1954, Zoë Margherita Bargna; two *d*. *Educ:* Manchester Grammar School; Brasenose College, Oxford. BA Hons. (Oxon) 1934. Colonial Service (Colonial Audit Dept) 1934; served Gold Coast, Malaya, Uganda, Leeward Islands, and N Borneo. Served War of 1939–45: Gold Coast Regt, 1939–40; Singapore RA (V), 1940–42; British Military Administration, Malaya, 1945–46. Auditor-General, Ghana, 1954–64; Secretary, Central Bd of Finance of Church of England, 1964–75. Sec., Soc. of Sussex Downsmen, 1976–84. *Recreations:* bridge and tennis. *Address:* 11 Windlesham Road, Brighton BN1 3AG. *T:* Brighton 732157.

SABINE, Peter Aubrey, DSc, FRSE, FRSA, FIMM, FGS; Deputy Director (Chief Scientific Officer, Chief Geologist), British Geological Survey (formerly Institute of Geological Sciences), 1977–84; *b* 29 Dec. 1924; *s* of Bernard Robert and Edith Lucy Sabine; *m* 1946, Peggy Willis Lambert, MSc, FBCS, FRSA, FSS; one *s*. *Educ:* Brockley County Sch.; Chelsea Polytechnic; Royal Coll. of Science, London. BSc, ARCS (1st Cl. Geol.; Watts medal) 1945; PhD 1951, DSc 1970 (London). Apptd Geological Survey of Gt Britain as Geologist, 1945; Geological Museum, 1946–50; in charge Petrographical Dept, Geol Survey and Museum, 1950, Chief Petrographer, 1959; Asst Dir, S England and Wales, 1970; Chief Geochemist, 1977; Dep. Dir, 1977–84. Sec., Geol Soc. of London, 1959–66, Vice-Pres., 1966–67, 1982–84 (Lyell Fund, 1955); International Union of Geological Sciences: Mem. Commn on Systematics of Igneous Rocks, 1969–; Mem. Commn on Systematics in Petrology, 1980– (Chm., 1984–); Chief UK Deleg., 1980–84; Mem. Council, 1980–; Member Council: Geologists' Assoc., 1966–70; Mineralogical Soc., 1950–53; Instn of Mining and Metallurgy, 1976–80; Mineral Industry Res. Orgn, 1983–86; Member: DTI Chem. and Mineral Research Requirements Bd, 1973–82; Minerals, Metals Extraction and Reclamation Cttee, 1981–84; EEC Cttees on minerals and geochemistry; Cttee of Dirs of W European Geolog. Surveys, 1978–84; Chm., Sub-Cttee on geochem. and cosmochem. of British Nat. Cttee for Geology, 1977–86. Visitor, Royal Instn, 1979–82. FMSA. *Publications:* Chemical Analysis of Igneous Rocks (with E. M. Guppy), 1956; (with D. S. Sutherland) Petrography of British Igneous Rocks, 1982; numerous scientific contribs in Mem. Geol. Surv., Qly Jl Geol. Soc., Mineral. Mag., Phil. Trans Roy. Soc., etc. *Recreations:* gardening, geneaology. *Address:* 19 Beaufort Road, Ealing, W5 3EB. *T:* 01–997 2360. *Clubs:* Athenæum; Geological Society's.

SABITI, Most Rev. Erica; *b* 1903; *m* 1934, Geraldine Kamuhigi; four *s* three *d*. *Educ:* Mbarara High Sch.; King's Coll., Budo; Makerere Coll. Teacher, 1920–25 and 1929–30; training in education, 1925–29; training for Ministry, 1931–32; ordained, 1933; Bishop of Ruwenzori, 1960–72; Bishop of Kampala, 1972–74; Archbishop of Uganda, Rwanda, Burundi and Boga Zaire, 1966–74. *Address:* PO Box 134, Mbarara, Uganda.

SACHS, Michael Alexander Geddes; His Honour Judge Sachs; a Circuit Judge, since 1984; *b* 8 April 1932; *s* of Dr Joseph Sachs, MB, ChB, DPH, and Mrs Ruby Mary Sachs; *m* 1957, Patricia Mary (*née* Conroy); two *s* two *d* (and one *s* decd). *Educ:* Sedbergh; Manchester Univ. (LLB 1954). Admitted solicitor, 1957. Partner in Slater, Heelis & Co., Solicitors, Manchester, 1962–84. A Recorder, 1980–84. Pres., Manchester Law Soc., 1978–79; Chm., Greater Manchester Legal Services Cttee, 1977–81; Member: No 7 (NW) Area, Legal Aid Cttee, 1966–80 (Chm., 1975–76); Council, Law Soc., 1979–84 (Chm., Standing Cttee on Criminal Law, 1982–84); Court, Univ. of Manchester, 1977–84. KSS 1980. *Address:* c/o Circuit Administrator, Aldine House, New Bailey Street, Salford M3 5EU.

SACKVILLE, family name of **Earl De la Warr.**

SACKVILLE, 6th Baron, *cr* 1876; **Lionel Bertrand Sackville-West;** *b* 30 May 1913; *s* of late Hon. Bertrand George Sackville-West, *y b* of 4th Baron and Eva Adela Mabel Inigo (*d* 1936), *d* of late Maj.-Gen. Inigo Richmond Jones, CB, CVO; *S* cousin, 1965; *m* 1st, 1953, Jacobine Napier (*d* 1971), *widow* of Captain John Hichens, RA, and *d* of J. R. Menzies-Wilson; five *d*; 2nd, 1974, Arlie, Lady de Guingand (marr. diss. 1983); 3rd, 1983, Jean, *widow* of Sir Edward Imbert-Terry, 3rd Bt. *Educ:* Winchester; Magdalen Coll., Oxford. Formerly Capt. Coldstream Gds; served War, 1939–42 (POW). Member of Lloyd's, 1949. *Heir: b* Hugh Rosslyn Inigo Sackville-West, MC [*b* 1 Feb. 1919; *m* 1957, Bridget Eleanor, *d* of Capt. Robert Lionel Brooke Cunliffe, *qv*; two *s* three *d*]. *Address:* Knole, Sevenoaks, Kent.

See also Sir M. E. S. Imbert-Terry, Bt.

SACKVILLE, Hon. Thomas Geoffrey, (Tom); MP (C) Bolton West, since 1983; *b* 26 Oct. 1950; 2nd *s* of 10th Earl De La Warr, *qv*; *m* 1979, Catherine Theresa, *d* of Brig. James Windsor Lewis; one *s*. *Educ:* St Aubyn's, Rottingdean, Sussex; Eton Coll.; Lincoln Coll., Oxford (BA). Deltec Banking Corp., New York, 1971–74; Grindlays Bank Ltd, London, 1974–77; Internat. Bullion and Metal Brokers (London) Ltd, 1978–83. Sec., All Party Cttee on Drug Misuse, 1984–; PPS to Minister of State at the Treasury, 1985. *Recreations:* music, fishing. *Address:* House of Commons, SW1A 0AA. *T:* 01–219 3000. *Club:* Horwich Golf.

SACKVILLE-WEST, family name of **Baron Sackville.**

SACKWOOD, Dr Mark; Regional Medical Officer, Northern Regional Health Authority, 1973–86, retired; *b* London, 18 Jan. 1926; *s* of Philip and Frances Sackwood; *m* 1953, Anne Harper Wilson; one *s* two *d*. *Educ:* King's Coll., London; Westminster Hosp. Med. School. MB, BS, FFCM, LRCP, MRCS, DPH, DRCOG. Various hosp. appts, South of England, 1949–58; mil. service, Far East, 1951–53; subseq. admin. med. appts, Middlesbrough and Newcastle upon Tyne, incl. Dep. Sen. Admin. MO with Newcastle RHB, 1968–73. *Recreations:* walking, reading, music. *Address:* 11 The Chesters, Beaumont Park, Whitley Bay, Tyne and Wear. *T:* Tyneside 2527401.

SADIE, Stanley (John), CBE 1982; writer on music; Music Critic for The Times, 1964–81, thereafter freelance; Editor: The Musical Times, since 1967; The New Grove Dictionary of Music and Musicians, since 1970; Master Musicians series, since 1976; Musical Consultant, Man and Music, Granada TV, since 1984; *b* 30 Oct. 1930; *s* of David Sadie and Deborah (*née* Simons); *m* 1st, 1953, Adèle Bloom (*d* 1978); two *s* one *d*; 2nd, 1978, Julie Anne Vertrees; one *s* one *d*. *Educ:* St Paul's Sch.; Gonville and Caius Coll., Cambridge Univ. (MA, PhD, MusB). Prof., Trinity Coll. of Music, London, 1957–65. Writer and broadcaster on musical subjects, *circa* 1955–; Editor of many edns of 18th-century music, *circa* 1955–. Vice-Pres., Royal Musical Assoc., 1985–; Member: Internat. Musicological Soc., 1955; Critics' Circle, 1963; American Musicological Soc., 1970. Hon. RAM 1981; Hon. DLitt Leicester, 1981. FRSA 1982. *Publications:* Handel, 1962; Mozart, 1966; Beethoven, 1967; Handel, 1968; (with Arthur Jacobs) Pan Book of Opera/The Opera Guide, 1964, new edns 1969, 1984; Handel Concertos, 1973, new edn 1987; (ed) The New Grove Dictionary of Music and Musicians, 1980; Mozart (The New Grove Biographies), 1982; (ed) New Grove Dictionary of Musical Instruments, 1984; (with Alison Latham) The Cambridge Music Guide, 1985; Mozart Symphonies, 1986; (ed with H. Wiley Hitchcock) The New Grove Dictionary of American Music, 1986; contrib.: The Musical Times, Gramophone, Opera, Music and Letters, Musical Quarterly, Proc. Roy. Musical Assoc. *Recreations:* watching cricket, drinking (mainly wine and coffee), bridge, reading. *Address:* 12 Lyndhurst Road, NW3 5NL. *T:* 01–435 2482.

SADLER, Joan; Principal, Cheltenham Ladies' College, 1979–Sept. 1987; *b* 1 July 1927; *d* of Thomas Harold Sadler and Florence May Sadler. *Educ:* Cambridgeshire High Sch.; Univ. of Bristol (BA Hons (History); DipEd). Downe House, Cold Ash, Newbury, Berks: Asst History teacher, 1950–56; Head of History Dept, 1956–58; Heriots Wood School, Stanmore, Mddx: Head of History Dept, 1958–68; Sen. Mistress, 1966–68; Headmistress, Howell's School, Denbigh, 1968–79. Chm., Boarding Schools' Assoc., 1983–85; Board Member: Central Bureau for Educnl Visits and Exchanges; Common Entrance Examination for Girls' Schools. MInstD 1986. Hon. Freewoman: City of London; Drapers' Co., 1979. FRSA. *Recreations:* music, theatre, reading. *Address:* The Ladies' College, Cheltenham, Glos; Locke's Cottage, Candle Green, Cheltenham, Glos.

SADLER, John Stephen, CBE 1982; Finance Director, since 1971, and Deputy Chairman, since 1984, John Lewis Partnership; *b* 6 May 1930; *s* of Bernard and Phyllis Sadler; *m* 1952, Ella (*née* McCleery); three *s*. *Educ:* Reading Sch.; Corpus Christi Coll., Oxford (MA). Board of Trade, 1952–54; Treasury, 1954–56; Board of Trade, 1956–60; British Trade Commissioner, Lagos, Nigeria, 1960–64; Board of Trade, 1964–66. John Lewis Partnership Ltd, 1966–. Mem., Monopolies and Mergers Commn, 1973–85. Trustee, British Telecommunications Staff Superannuation Scheme, 1983–. *Recreations:* golf, boating. *Address:* 41 Weymouth Mews, W1. *T:* 01–580 6751. *Club:* Reading Golf.

SAGAN, Françoise, pen-name of Françoise Quoirez; authoress; *b* France, 21 June 1935; *y c* of Paul Quoirez; *m* 1958, Guy Schoeller (marr. diss. 1960); *m* 1962, Robert James Westhoff; one *s*. *Educ:* convent and private school. Published first novel at age of 18. Has written some songs and collaborated in scheme for ballet Le Rendez-vous Manqué, produced Paris and London, 1958. *Publications:* (all trans. into Eng., usually French title): Bonjour Tristesse, 1954; Un Certain Sourire, 1956 (filmed, 1958); Dans un mois, dans un an, 1957 (Eng. trans. Those Without Shadows, 1958); Aimez-vous Brahms . . . . 1959 (Eng. trans. 1960); Château en Suède (play), 1960; Les Violons, parfois . . . (play), 1961; La Robe Mauve de Valentine (play), 1963; Bonheur, impair et passe (play), 1964; Toxique . . . (tr. 1965); La Chamade, 1965 (tr. 1966) (film, 1970); Le Cheval Evanoui (play), 1966; L'Echarde, 1966; Le Garde du cœur, 1968 (tr., The Heart-Keeper, 1968); Un peu de soleil dans l'eau froide, 1969 (tr., Sunlight and Cold Water, 1971); Un piano dans l'herbe (play), 1970; Des bleus à l'âme, 1972 (tr., Scars on the Soul, 1974); Zaphorie (play), 1973; Lost Profile, 1976; Silken Eyes (short stories), 1977; The Unmade Bed, 1978; Le Chien Couchant, 1980; La femme fardée, 1981 (tr., The Painted Lady, 1982); The Still Storm, 1984; Incidental Music (short stories), 1985; Avec mon meilleur souvenir (tr. With Fondest Regards), 1986. *Address:* c/o Editions Flammarion, 26 rue Racine, 75006 Paris, France.

SAGE, Lorna; journalist and critic; Senior Lecturer in English Literature, since 1975, Dean of the School of English and American Studies, since 1985, University of East Anglia; *b* 13 Jan. 1943; *d* of Eric and Valma Stockton; *m* 1st, 1959, Victor Sage; one *d*; 2nd, 1979, Rupert Hodson. *Educ:* Univ. of Durham (BA 1st Cl. Hons 1964); Univ. of Birmingham (MA 1966). Asst Lectr in English Literature, Univ. of East Anglia, 1965, Lectr 1968. Florence B. Tucker Vis. Prof., Wellesley Coll., Mass, USA, 1981. *Publications:* (ed) Peacock, Satirical Novels, 1976; Doris Lessing, 1983; reviews in Observer, TLS, etc. *Address:* School of English and American Studies, University of East Anglia, Norwich NR4 7TJ. *T:* Norwich 56161.

SAGITTARIUS; *see* Katzin, Olga.

SAINER, Leonard; *b* 12 Oct. 1909; *s* of late Archer and Sarah Sainer. Director and Life President (formerly Chairman): Sears plc; British Shoe Corporation plc; Lewis's Investment Trust Ltd; Selfridges Ltd; Mappin & Webb Ltd; Garrard Ltd; Sears Industries Inc. (USA); Butler Footwear Hldgs Inc. (USA); Dir, First National Finance Corp. PLC. Consultant, Titmuss, Sainer & Webb, Solicitors. *Address:* (business) 40 Duke Street, W1; (home) 26 Chester Terrace, Regent's Park, NW1.

SAINSBURY, family name of **Baron Sainsbury.**

SAINSBURY, Baron, *cr* 1962, of Drury Lane (Life Peer); **Alan John Sainsbury;** Joint President of J. Sainsbury plc, since 1967 (Chairman, 1956–67); *b* 13 Aug. 1902; *er s* of John Benjamin and Mabel Miriam Sainsbury; *m* 1st, 1925, Doreen Davan Adams (marr. diss. 1939; she *d* 1985); three *s*; 2nd, 1944, Anne Elizabeth Lewy; one *d*. *Educ:* Haileybury. Joined Grocery and Provision Firm of J. Sainsbury, Ltd (founded by his grandparents), 1921. Served on many war-time consultative committees of Ministry of Food; Member Williams' Committee on Milk Distribution, 1947–48; Member: Food Research Advisory Cttee, 1960–70 (Chm., 1965–70); NEDC Cttee for the Distributive Trades, 1964–68; Exec. Cttee, PEP, 1970–76; House of Lords Select Cttee on the European Communities, 1978–81; Chm., Cttee of Inquiry into Relationship of Pharmaceutical Industry with National Health Service, 1965–67. President: Multiple Shops' Fedn, 1963–65; The Grocers' Inst., 1963–66; Internat. Assoc. of Chain Stores, 1965–68; The Royal Inst. of Public Health and Hygiene, 1965–70; Pestalozzi Children's Village Trust, 1963–; Distributive Trades Educn and Trng Council, 1975–83; a Vice-President, Assoc. of Agriculture, 1965–73; Royal Society for the Encouragement of Arts, Manufactures and Commerce, 1962–66; Mem., Court of Univ. of Essex, 1966–76; Governor, City Literary Inst., 1967–69; Chairman of Trustees: Overseas Students Adv. Bureau; Uganda Asian Relief Trust, 1972–74; Vice-President: World Development Movement; Internat. Voluntary Service, 1977–81; Parly Gp for World Govt, 1982–. Liberal candidate, Sudbury Div. of Suffolk, Gen. Elections of 1929, 1931 and 1935. Joined Labour Party, 1945, SDP, 1981. Hon. Fellow, Inst. of Food Sci, and Technology. *Address:* J. Sainsbury plc, Stamford House, Stamford Street, SE1 9LL.

See also Sir J. D. Sainsbury, Hon. T. A. D. Sainsbury.

SAINSBURY, Anya, (Lady Sainsbury); *see* Linden, Anya.

SAINSBURY, David John; Finance Director, J. Sainsbury plc, since 1973; *b* 24 Oct. 1940; *s* of Sir Robert Sainsbury, *qv*; *m* 1973, Susan Carole Reid; three *d*. *Educ:* King's Coll., Cambridge (BA); Columbia Univ., NY (MBA). Joined J. Sainsbury, 1963. Mem., Cttee of Review of the Post Office (Carter Cttee), 1975–77. Trustee, Social Democratic Party, 1982–; Mem. Governing Body, London Business Sch., 1985–. *Publication:* Government and Industry: a new partnership, 1981.

SAINSBURY, Edward Hardwicke; TD 1945; Consultant Partner, Dawson, Hart & Co., Uckfield, since 1983; District Notary Public, Uckfield, since 1965; *b* 17 Sept. 1912; *e s* of Henry Morgan Sainsbury, and *g s* of James C. Hardwicke, a pioneer of technical and other education in S Wales; *m* 1946, Ann, 2nd *d* of late Kenneth Ellis, Tunbridge Wells; one *s* one *d*. *Educ:* Cardiff High School; University of S Wales and Monmouth. Solicitor in private practice, 1935; commissioned (TA) 1936; Prosecuting Solicitor, Cardiff, 1938, Sen. Pros. Solicitor, 1939. Served War of 1939–45; Adjutant, 77th HAA Regt, 1940; comd 240 HAA Battery Gibraltar, 1944; demobilised Nov. 1945. Hong Kong: Asst Crown Solicitor, 1946; commissioner for revision of the laws of Hong Kong, 1947; magistrate, 1948; registrar, High Court, 1949; sen. magistrate, Kowloon, 1951; Barrister, Inner Temple, 1951; Land Officer and sen. crown counsel, Hong Kong, 1952; legal draftsman, Nigeria, 1953; Principal Legal Draftsman, Fed. of Nigeria, 1958. President, Commonwealth Parliamentary Assoc., Southern Cameroons, 1959–63. Judge, High Court of Lagos, 1960–63, and of Southern Cameroons, 1961–63; Speaker, House of Assembly, 1958–63, Chm., Public Service Commn, 1961–63, Southern Cameroons. *Publication:* (jointly) Revised Laws of Hong Kong, 1948. *Recreations:* squash (a memory), golf. *Address:* Little Gassons, Fairwarp, Uckfield, East Sussex. *T:* Nutley 2100.

SAINSBURY, Sir John (Davan), Kt 1980; Chairman, J. Sainsbury plc, since 1969 (Vice-Chairman, 1967–69; Director, since 1958); *b* 2 Nov. 1927; *e s* of Baron Sainsbury, *qv*; *m* 1963, Anya Linden, *qv*; two *s* one *d*. *Educ:* Stowe School; Worcester College, Oxford (Hon. Fellow 1982). Director: Royal Opera House, Covent Gdn, 1969–85; The Economist, 1972–80; Royal Opera House Trust, 1974–84. Member: Council, Retail Consortium, 1975–79; Nat. Cttee for Electoral Reform, 1976–85; President's Cttee, CBI, 1982–84. Vice Pres., Contemporary Art Soc., 1984–; Chm., Friends of Covent Garden, 1969–81 (Mem. Council, 1969–); Jt Hon. Treas., European Movement, 1972–75 (a Pres., 1975–); Governor, Royal Ballet Sch., 1965–76; Associate, V & A, 1976–85; Trustee: Nat. Gall., 1976–83; Westminster Abbey Trust, 1977–83; Tate Gall., 1982–83; Rhodes Trust, 1984–. Fellow, Inst. of Grocery Distribution, 1973–. Hon. Bencher, Inner Temple, 1985. Hon. DScEcon London, 1985. *Address:* c/o Stamford House, Stamford Street, SE1 9LL. *T:* 01–921 6000. *Club:* Garrick.

See also Hon. T. A. D. Sainsbury.

SAINSBURY, Richard Eric, CBE 1964; *b* 15 Sept. 1909; 2nd *s* of E. A. Sainsbury and F. W. Sainsbury (*née* Hill), Trowbridge, Wilts; *m* 1936, Margaret (*née* Horne); one *s*. *Educ:* Lewisham School, Weston-super-Mare; Bristol University. Grad. in Engineering, 1932; time-study with J. Lucas, 1934; subseq. with various firms; Ministry of Aircraft Production, 1940, Deputy Director, 1943; Joint Services Staff College, 1947; Director Instrument and Radio Production, Ministry of Supply, 1950; Imperial Defence College, 1959; Director, Guided Weapons Production, 1960; Dir-Gen., Electronics and Weapons Prodn, Min. of Aviation, 1961–67, Min. of Technology, 1967–70, Min. of Aviation Supply, 1970–71; Dir Gen., Telecommunications, MoD, 1971–72. Dir, Aeromaritime Ltd, Hounslow, 1973–75. Coronation Medal, 1953. *Recreations:* walking, reading. *Address:* c/o Lloyds Bank, Summertown Road, Oxford.

SAINSBURY, Sir Robert, Kt 1967 (for services to the arts); Joint President, J. Sainsbury plc; *b* 24 Oct. 1906; *s* of late John Benjamin Sainsbury and late Mable Miriam (*née* Van den Bergh); *m* 1937, Lisa Ingeborg (*née* Van den Bergh; second cousin); one *s* two *d* (and one *d* decd). *Educ:* Haileybury Coll.; Pembroke Coll., Cambridge (MA; Hon. Fellow, 1983). ACA, 1930, FCA, 1935. Joined J. Sainsbury Ltd, 1930; Dir, 1934; Jt Gen. Man., 1938; Dep. Chm., 1956; Chm. 1967; Jt Pres., 1969. Formerly Mem. Art Panel of Arts Council; Member: Mngt Cttee, Courtauld Inst. of Art, Univ. of London, 1979–82; Vis. Cttee to Primitive Art Dept, Metropolitan Mus of Art, New York, until 1986; Pres., British Assoc. of Friends of Museums, 1985–. Trustee, Tate Gall., 1959–73 (Vice-Chm. 1967, Chm., 1969). Hon. Treasurer, Inst. of Med. Social Workers, 1948–71; Governor, St Thomas' Hospital, 1939–68. Hon. FRIBA 1986. Hon. Dr RCA, 1976; Hon. LittD East Anglia, 1977.

See also D. J. Sainsbury.

SAINSBURY, Hon. Timothy Alan Davan; MP (C) Hove, since Nov. 1973; a Government Whip, since 1983; *b* 11 June 1932; *y s* of Baron Sainsbury, *qv*; *m* 1961, Susan Mary Mitchell; two *s* two *d*. *Educ:* Eton; Worcester Coll., Oxford (MA; Hon. Fellow 1982). Dir, J. Sainsbury, 1962–83. Chm., Council for the Unit for Retail Planning Information Ltd, 1974–79. PPS to Sec. of State for the Environment, 1979–83, to Sec. of State for Defence, 1983. Mem. Council, RSA, 1981–83. *Address:* House of Commons, SW1A 0AA.

See also Sir J. D. Sainsbury.

SAINT, Sir (Sidney) John, Kt 1950; CMG 1946; OBE 1942; BSc, PhD (London); MSc (Reading); CChem; FRSC; Director, Sugar Technological Laboratory, Barbados, 1949–63, retd; *b* 16 Sept. 1897; *m* 1923, Constance Elizabeth Hole; two *s* one *d*. *Educ:* Beaminster Grammar School; Reading University. Served with RFC and RAF, 1916–19; Salter's Research Fellow, 1920–22; Lecturer in Agricultural Chemistry, Leeds University, 1922–27; Chemist, Department of Agriculture, Barbados, 1927–37; Director of Agriculture Barbados, 1937–49; Chm., BWI Sugar Cane Breeding Station, 1937–49; Competent Authority and Controller of Supplies, Barbados, 1939–46; Pres., Barbados Technologists Assoc., 1939–42, 1950–63; Gen. Chm., Internat. Soc. of Sugar Cane Technologists, 1950–53; Chairman: Barbados Public Service Commn, 1952–57; Barbados Development Bd, 1956–59; Interim Federal Public Service Commn, 1956–59. Pres. Museum and Hist. Soc., 1946–59. MEC, 1947–61; PC (Barbados), 1961–63. Hon. Freeman, City of Bridgetown, Barbados, 1963. *Publications:* numerous papers on soils, manuring of tropical crops and sugar technology. *Address:* Selwyn, St George's Lane, Hurstpierpoint, Sussex. *T:* Hurstpierpoint 832335.

SAINT, Dr Stafford Eric, CVO 1956; Medical Practitioner, 1931–70; *b* 13 April 1904; *s* of late Sir Wakelin Saint; *m* 1931, Isabel Mary Fulford; two *s* one *d*. *Educ:* King's School, Ely; The London Hospital. MRCS Eng., LRCP Lond., 1926. *Address:* 28 The Uplands, Gerrard's Cross, Bucks SL9 7JG.

ST ALBANS, 13th Duke of, *cr* 1684; **Charles Frederic Aubrey de Vere Beauclerk,** OBE 1945; Earl of Burford and Baron of Heddington, 1676; Baron Vere, 1750; Hereditary Grand Falconer of England; Hereditary Registrar, Court of Chancery; Chairman, Amalgamated Developers Group; *b* 16 Aug. 1915; *s* of Aubrey Topham Beauclerk and Gwendolen, *d* of late Sir Frederic Hughes; *S* kinsman, 1964; *m* 1st, Nathalie Chatham (who obtained a divorce, 1947; she *d* 1985), *d* of late P. F. Walker; one *s*; 2nd, 1947, Suzanne Marie Adele, *d* of late Emile William Fesq, Mas Mistral, Vence, AM, France; three *s* one *d*. *Educ:* Eton; Magdalene Coll., Cambridge (MA). Served War of 1939–45 in Infantry, Military Intelligence and Psychological Warfare; Col, Intelligence Corps. Controller Inf. Services, Allied Commn for Austria, 1946–50. Central Office of Information: Chief Books Editor, 1951–58; Chief Films Production Officer, 1958–60; Dir, Films Div., 1960–64. Pres., Fedn of Industrial Develt Assocs; Vice-Pres., Ancient Monuments Soc.; Governor General, Royal Stuart Soc.; Pres., Shakespearian Authorship Soc. *Heir: s* Earl of Burford, *qv*. *Address:* 207 Park Palace, Monte Carlo, Monaco. *Club:* Brooks's.

ST ALBANS, Bishop of, since 1980; **Rt. Rev. John Bernard Taylor;** *b* 6 May 1929; *s* of George Ernest and Gwendoline Irene Taylor; *m* 1956, Linda Courtenay Barnes; one *s* two *d*. *Educ:* Watford Grammar Sch.; Christ's Coll., Cambridge; Jesus Coll., Cambridge. MA Cantab. Vicar of Henham and Elsenham, Essex, 1959–64; Vice-Principal, Oak Hill Theological Coll., 1964–72; Vicar of All Saints', Woodford Wells, 1972–75; Archdeacon of West Ham, 1975–80. Examining Chaplain to Bishop of Chelmsford, 1962–80. Chm., Gen. Synod's Cttee for Communications, 1986–. Member: Churches' Council for Covenanting, 1978–82; Liturgical Commn, 1981–. Chairman Council: Haileybury Coll., 1980–85; Wycliffe Hall, Oxford, 1985–. President: Hildenborough Evangelistic Trust, 1985–; Garden Tomb Assoc., Jerusalem, 1986–. Took his seat in House of Lords, 1985. *Publications:* A Christian's Guide to the Old Testament, 1966; Evangelism among Children and Young People, 1967; Tyndale Commentary on Ezekiel, 1969; Preaching through the Prophets, 1983. *Address:* Abbey Gate House, St Albans, Herts AL3 4HD. *T:* St Albans 53305.

ST ALBANS, Dean of; *see* Moore, Very Rev. P. C.

ST ALBANS, Archdeacon of; *see* Norfolk, Ven. E. M.

ST ALDWYN, 2nd Earl, *cr* 1915, of Coln St Aldwyns; **Michael John Hicks Beach,** GBE 1980 (KBE 1964); TD 1949; PC 1959; JP; Bt 1619; Viscount St Aldwyn, 1906; Viscount Quenington, 1915; Vice Lord-Lieutenant, Gloucestershire, since 1981; *b* 9 Oct. 1912; *s* of Visc. Quenington, Roy. Glos. Hussars Yeo. (*d* 1916; *o s* of 1st Earl) and Marjorie (*d* 1916), *d* of late H. Dent Brocklehurst, Sudeley Castle, Gloucs; *S* grandfather, 1916 (his father having been killed in action a week previously); *m* 1948, Diana Mary Christian, DStJ (she *m* 1st, 1939, Major Richard Patrick Pilkington Smyly, MC; marriage annulled, 1942), *o d* of late Henry C. G. and Mrs Mills; three *s*. *Educ:* Eton; Christ Church, Oxford. Major Royal Glos Hussars Yeomanry, 1942. Parliamentary Secretary, Ministry of Agriculture and Fisheries, 1954–58; Captain of the Honorable Corps of Gentlemen-at-Arms and Govt Chief Whip, House of Lords, 1958–64 and 1970–74; Opposition Chief Whip, House of Lords, 1964–70 and 1974–78. DL 1950, JP 1952, Glos. GCStJ 1978; Chancellor, Order of St John, 1978– (Vice-Chancellor, 1969–78). *Heir: s* Viscount Quenington, *qv*. *Address:* Williamstrip Park, Cirencester, Gloucestershire. *T:* Coln St Aldwyns 226; 13 Upper Belgrave Street, SW1. *T:* 01-235 8464. *Clubs:* Carlton, Pratt's, Beefsteak; Royal Yacht Squadron.
See also Sir Richard Keane, Bt.

ST ANDREWS, Earl of; George Philip Nicholas Windsor; *b* 26 June 1962; *s* of HRH the Duke of Kent and HRH the Duchess of Kent. *Educ:* Eton (King's Scholar); Downing College, Cambridge.
See under Royal Family.

ST ANDREWS AND EDINBURGH, Archbishop of, (RC), since 1985; **Most Rev. Keith Michael Patrick O'Brien;** *b* Ballycastle, Co. Antrim, 17 March 1938; *s* of Mark Joseph O'Brien and Alice Mary (*née* Moriarty). *Educ:* schools in Ballycastle, Dumbarton and Edinburgh, Edinburgh Univ. (BSc 1959, DipEd 1966); St Andrew's Coll., Drygrange; Moray House Coll. of Education, Edinburgh. Ordained Priest, 1965; pastoral appointments: Holy Cross, Edinburgh, 1965–66; St Bride's, Cowdenbeath, 1966–71 (while Chaplain and teacher of Maths and Science, St Columba's High Sch., Cowdenbeath and Dunfermline); St Patrick's, Kilsyth, 1972–75; St Mary's, Bathgate, 1975–78. Spiritual Director, St Andrew's Coll., Drygrange, 1978–80; Rector of St Mary's Coll., Blair, Aberdeen, 1980–85. *Address:* St Bennet's, 42 Greenhill Gardens, Edinburgh EH10 4BJ. *T:* 031-447 3337.

ST ANDREWS AND EDINBURGH, Bishop Auxiliary of, (RC); *see* Monaghan, Rt Rev. James.

ST ANDREWS, DUNKELD AND DUNBLANE, Bishop of, since 1969; **Rt. Rev. Michael Geoffrey Hare Duke;** *b* 28 Nov. 1925; *s* of late A. R. A. Hare Duke, Civil Engineer; *m* 1949, Grace Lydia Frances McKean Dodd; one *s* three *d*. *Educ:* Bradfield Coll.; Trinity Coll., Oxford. BA 1949, MA 1951. Sub-Lt, RNVR, 1944–46. Deacon, 1952; Priest, 1953; Curate, St John's Wood Church, 1952–56; Vicar, St Mark's, Bury, 1956–62; Pastoral Dir, Clin. Theol. Assoc., 1962–64; Vicar, St Paul's, Daybrook, and Pastoral Consultant to Clin. Theol. Assoc., 1964–69; OCF, E Midland Dist HQ, 1968–69. Chm., Scottish Assoc. for Mental Health, 1978–85. Mem. Editorial Bd, Contact Magazine, 1962–79. *Publications:* (jtly) The Caring Church, 1963; (jtly) First Aid in Counselling, 1968; Understanding the Adolescent, 1969; The Break of Glory, 1970; Freud, 1972; Good News, 1976; Stories, Signs and Sacraments in the Emerging Church, 1982. Contributor to: Expository Times, Blackfriars, New Christian, Church Quarterly Review, Church Times, Contact. *Address:* Bishop's House, Fairmount Road, Perth PH2 7AP. *T:* Perth 21580.

ST ANDREWS, DUNKELD AND DUNBLANE, Dean of; *see* Shone, Very Rev. J. T.

ST ASAPH, Bishop of, since 1982; **Rt. Rev. Alwyn Rice Jones;** *b* 25 March 1934; *s* of John Griffith and Annie Jones, Capel Curig, Caernarvonshire; *m* 1968, Meriel Anne Thomas; one *d*. *Educ:* Llanrwst Grammar School, Denbighshire; St David's Coll., Lampeter (BA Hons Welsh 1955); Fitzwilliam House, Cambridge (BA 1957 Theology Tripos, MA 1961); St Michael's Coll., Llandaff. Deacon 1958, priest 1959, Bangor Cathedral; Asst Curate, Llanfairisgaer, 1958–62; Secretary for SCM in N Wales Colleges and SCM in schools, 1962–65; Director of Education, Diocese of Bangor, 1965–75; Chaplain, St Winifred's School, Llanfairfechan, 1965–67; Diocesan Warden of Ordinands, 1970–75; Vicar of Porthmadog, dio. Bangor, 1975–79; Exam. Chaplain to Archbishop of Wales, 1970–79; Hon. Canon, Bangor Cathedral, 1974–78, Preb. of Llanfair, 1978–79; Dean of Brecon Cathedral, 1979–82. Mem., IBA Panel of Religious Advisers and Welsh Cttee, IBA, 1972–76; Asst Tutor in Religious Education, UCNW, Bangor, 1973–76. *Recreations:* music and walking. *Address:* Esgobty, St Asaph, Clwyd LL17 0TW. *T:* St Asaph 583503.

ST ASAPH, Dean of; *see* Renowden, Very Rev. C. R.

ST AUBYN, family name of **Baron St Levan.**

ST AUBYN, Sir (John) Arscott M.; *see* Molesworth-St Aubyn.

ST BONIFACE, Archbishop of, (RC), since 1974; **Most Rev. Antoine Hacault,** STD; *b* Bruxelles, Manitoba, 17 Jan. 1926. *Educ:* Sainte-Marie Elem. Sch., Bruxelles; St Boniface Coll. (BA 1947); St Boniface Major Seminary; Angelicum Univ., Rome (STD 1954). Priest, 1951; Prof. of Theology, St Boniface Major Seminary, 1954–64; Auxiliary Bishop of St Boniface and Titular Bishop of Media, 1964; also Rector, St Boniface College, 1967–69; Bishop Coadjutor of St Boniface, 1972. Member: Vatican Secretariat for Non-Believers, 1973–83; Vatican Secretariat for promoting Christian Unity, 1976–; Pastoral Team, Canadian Catholic Conf. of Bishops, 1971–75 and 1983–87; Admin. Bd, St Boniface Gen. Hosp., 1984–; Gen. Bd of Canadian Council of Churches, 1986–. President: Canadian Episcopal Commn for Ecumenism, 1974–; Inter-Church Cttee, 1982–85. *Address:* Archbishop's Residence, 151 avenue de la Cathédrale, St Boniface, Manitoba R2H 0H6, Canada.

SAINT BRIDES, Baron *cr* 1977 (Life Peer), of Hasguard, Dyfed; **John Morrice Cairns James,** PC 1968; GCMG 1975 (KCMG 1962; CMG 1957); CVO 1961; MBE 1944; *b* 30 April 1916; *s* of late Lewis Cairns James and Catherine, *d* of John Maitland Marshall; *m* 1st, 1948, Elizabeth Margaret Roper Piesse (*d* 1966); one *s* two *d*; 2nd, 1968, Mme Geneviève Sarasin. *Educ:* Bradfield; Balliol Coll., Oxford. Dominions Office, 1939; served Royal Navy and Royal Marines, 1940–45; released as Lieut-Col. Asst Sec., Office of UK High Comr in S Africa, 1946–47; Head of Defence Dept, Commonwealth Relations Office, 1949–51, and of Establishment Dept, 1951–52; Dep. High Comr for the UK, Lahore, 1952–53; attended Imperial Defence Coll., 1954; Dep. High Comr for UK in Pakistan, 1955–56; Asst Under-Sec. of State, Commonwealth Relations Office, 1957. Dep. High Comr for UK in India, 1958–61; British High Comr in Pakistan, 1961–66; Dep. Under Sec. of State, CO, 1966–68; Permanent Under-Sec. of State, CO, March-Oct. 1968; British High Commissioner: in India, 1968–71; in Australia, 1971–76. King of Arms, Most Distinguished Order of St Michael and St George, 1975–86. Fellow, Center for Internat. Affairs, Harvard Univ., 1979–80; Distinguished Diplomat-in-Residence, For. Policy Res. Inst., Philadelphia, 1982–81 (took part, as mem. FPRI team, with the Lady Saint Brides, in talks at Zvinigorod with Soviet Inst. for the USA and Canada, Dec. 1981, at Valley Forge, Pa, Nov. 1982 and in Moscow, July 1984); Vis. Scholar, Univ. of Texas at Austin, 1982–83; Dist. Vis. Prof. of Internat. Studies, Rhodes Coll., at Memphis, 1983–84; Mem., Center for Internat. Security and Arms Control, Stanford Univ., 1984–87. Visited Beijing with delegn from Stanford Univ. for talks wih Chinese scholars on security in Asia and the Pacific, 1985. Lectured for E-SU, Council on World Affairs and Council for For. Relns in numerous US cities, 1979–86. *Publications:* articles on internat. affairs in learned US jls incl. Internat. Security, and Orbis. *Recreation:* meeting new and intelligent people. *Address:* Cap Saint-Pierre, 83990 Saint Tropez, France. *T:* 94-97-14-75. *Clubs:* Oriental; Harvard (NY).

ST CLAIR, family name of **Lord Sinclair.**

ST CLAIR, Malcolm Archibald James, farmer; *b* 16 Feb. 1927; *o s* of late Maj.-Gen. George James Paul St Clair, CB, CBE, DSO and late Charlotte Theresa Orme Little; *m* 1955, Mary-Jean Rosalie Alice, *o d* of Wing-Comdr Caryl Liddell Hargreaves, Broadwood House, Sunningdale; two *s* one *d*. *Educ:* Eton. Served with Royal Scots Greys, 1944–48. Formerly Hon. Sec. to Sir Winston Churchill. Contested (C) Bristol South-East, 1959; MP (C) Bristol South-East, 1961–63. Lt Col Comdg, Royal Gloucestershire Hussars (TA), 1967–69. High Sheriff Glos, 1972. *Club:* White's.

ST CLAIR-ERSKINE, family name of **Earl of Rosslyn.**

ST CLAIR-FORD, Capt. Sir Aubrey, 6th Bt, *cr* 1793; DSO 1942; RN, retired; *b* 29 Feb. 1904; *e s* of late Anson and Elsie St Clair-Ford; *S* cousin 1948; *m* 1945, Anne, *o d* of Harold Christopherson, Penerley Lodge, Beaulieu, Hants; one *s* one *d*. *Educ:* Stubbington House; RNC, Osborne and Dartmouth. Served War of 1939–45 (despatches, DSO and bar); Korean War of 1950–53 (despatches, Officer, Legion of Merit, US). *Heir: s* James Anson St Clair-Ford [*b* 16 March 1952; *m* 1977, Jennifer Margaret (marr. diss. 1984), *yr d* of Cdre Robin Grindle]. *Address:* Corner House, Sandle Copse, Fordingbridge, Hants. *Club:* Army and Navy.
See also Maj.-Gen. Sir Peter St Clair-Ford.

ST CLAIR-FORD, Maj.-Gen. Sir Peter, KBE 1961 (CBE 1953); CB 1954; DSO 1943 and Bar 1944; idc; psc; General Secretary of the Officers' Association, 1963–66; *b* 25 Nov. 1905; *s* of late Anson St Clair-Ford and Elsie (*née* Adams); unmarried. *Educ:* Dover College; Royal Military College, Sandhurst. Commissioned into KOYLI, 1925; Somaliland Camel Corps, 1932–39; France, 1939; Staff College, Camberley, 1940 (psc); various Staff appts, UK, 1940–43; Comd 1 Bn KOYLI, 1943–44, Italy and Palestine; Comd 3 Inf. Bde, 1944–46, Italy and Palestine; Comd 129 Inf. Bde (TA), 1947–48; BGS Southern Command (UK), 1948–49; Imperial Defence College (idc), 1950; BGS, FARELF, 1951–52; Training Adviser to Pakistan Army, 1952–54; Commander 1 Federal Division, Malaya, 1954–57; Deputy Chief of Staff, Headquarters Allied Land Forces Central Europe, 1958–60; retd, 1960. *Recreations:* golf, racing. *Address:* Cotswold Lodge, Littlestone, New Romney, Kent. *T:* New Romney 62368. *Club:* East India.
See also Capt. Sir Aubrey St Clair-Ford, Bt.

ST CYRES, Viscount; John Stafford Northcote; *b* 15 Feb. 1957; *s* and *heir* of 4th Earl of Iddesleigh, *qv*; *m* 1983, Fiona Caroline Elizabeth, *d* of P. Wakefield, Barcelona, and Mrs M. Hattrell, Burnham, Bucks; one *s*. *Educ:* Downside Sch.; RAC Cirencester. *Heir: s* Hon. Thomas Stafford Northcote, *b* 5 Aug. 1985. *Address:* Hayne Barton, Newton St Cyres, Devon.

ST DAVIDS, 2nd Viscount, *cr* 1918; **Jestyn Reginald Austen Plantagenet Philipps;** Baron Strange of Knokin, 1299; Baron Hungerford, 1426; Baron de Moleyns, 1445; Bt 1621; Baron St Davids, 1908; Founder and Patron, Pirate Club, Floating Youth Club for Boys and Girls; *b* 19 Feb. 1917; *s* of 1st Viscount and Elizabeth Frances (Baroness Strange of Knokin, Baroness Hungerford and Baroness de Moleyns), *d* of late Hon. Paulyn F. C. Rawdon-Hastings, of The Manor House, Ashby-de-la-Zouch; *S* father, 1938, and to baronies of mother, 1974; *m* 1938, Doreen Guinness (marr. diss., 1954; she *d* 1956), *o d* of Captain Arthur Jowett, Toorak, Australia; one *s* four *d*; *m* 1954, Elisabeth Joyce, *e d* of Dr E. A. Woolf, Hove, Sussex (marr. diss., 1959); *m* 1959, Evelyn Marjorie, *d* of late Dr J. E. G. Harris, Bray, Berks. *Educ:* Eton; Trinity Coll., Cambridge. *Heir: s* Hon. Colwyn Jestyn

John Philipps [*b* 30 Jan. 1939; *m* 1965, Augusta Victoria Correa Larrain, *d* of late Don Estantislao Correa Ugarte; two *s*]. *Address:* 15 St Mark's Crescent, Regent's Park, NW1.

ST DAVIDS, Bishop of, since 1982; **Rt. Rev. George Noakes;** *b* 13 Sept. 1924; *s* of David John and Elizabeth Mary Noakes; *m* 1957, Jane Margaretta Davies. *Educ:* Tregaron Secondary School; University Coll. of Wales, Aberystwyth (BA); Wycliffe Hall, Oxford. Curate of Lampeter, 1950–56; Vicar: Eglwyswrw, 1956–59; Tregaron, 1959–67; Dewi Sant, Cardiff, 1967–76; Rector of Aberystwyth, 1976–79; Canon of St Davids Cathedral, 1977–79; Archdeacon of Cardigan, 1979–82; Vicar of Llanychaearn, 1980–82. *Recreations:* cricket and angling. *Address:* Llys Esgob, Abergwili, Carmarthen, Dyfed SA31 2JG. *T:* Carmarthen 236597.

ST DAVIDS, Dean of; *see* MacWilliam, Very Rev. A.G.

ST EDMUNDSBURY, Provost of; *see* Furnell, Very Rev. R.

ST EDMUNDSBURY AND IPSWICH, Bishop of, since 1986; **Rt. Rev. John Dennis;** *b* 19 June 1931; *s* of Hubert Ronald and Evelyn Dennis; *m* 1956, Dorothy Mary (*née* Hinnels); two *s*. *Educ:* Rutlish School, Merton; St Catharine's Coll., Cambridge (BA 1954; MA 1959); Cuddesdon Coll., Oxford (1954–56). RAF, 1950–51. Curate, St Bartholomew's, Armley, Leeds, 1956–60; Curate of Kettering, 1960–62; Vicar of the Isle of Dogs, 1962–71; Vicar of John Keble, Mill Hill, 1971–79; Area Dean of West Barnet, 1973–79; Prebendary of St Paul's Cathedral, 1977–79; Bishop Suffragan of Knaresborough, 1979–86; Diocesan Dir of Ordinands, Dio. Ripon, 1980–86. Episcopal Guardian of Anglican Focolarini, 1981–. *Recreations:* walking, gardening, wood working. *Address:* Bishop's House, 4 Park Road, Ipswich IP1 3ST. *T:* Ipswich 52829.

ST GEORGE, Sir Denis Howard, 8th Bt *cr* 1766; priest in Holy Orders; *b* 6 Sept. 1902; *s* of Sir Theophilus John St George, 6th Bt, and Florence Emma, *d* of John Vanderplank, Natal; *S* brother, 1983. *Educ:* St Charles Coll., Pietermaritzburg; Rand Univ. (BSc Eng). *Publication:* Failure and Vindication: The Unedited Journal of Bishop Allard, OMI, indexed and fully annotated, 1981. *Heir: b* George Bligh St George [*b* 23 Sept. 1908; *m* 1935, Mary Somerville, *d* of John Francis Fearly Sutcliffe; two *s* three *d*]. *Address:* Emmanuel Cathedral, Cathedral Road, Durban, Natal, 4001, South Africa.

ST GERMANS, 9th Earl of, *cr* 1815; **Nicholas Richard Michael Eliot;** Baron Eliot, 1784; Major, Duke of Cornwall's Light Infantry; *b* 26 Jan. 1914; *er s* of 8th Earl of St Germans, KCVO, OBE, and of Helen Agnes Post (*d* 1962) (*d* of Lady Barrymore and late Arthur Post, New York, USA); *S* father 1960; *m* 1st, 1939, Helen Mary (marr. diss., 1947; she *d* 1951), *d* of late Lt-Col Charles Walter Villiers, CBE, DSO, and late Lady Kathleen Villiers; one *s* one *d*; 2nd, 1948, Mrs Margaret Eleanor Eyston (marr. diss., 1959), *o d* of late Lt-Col William Francis George Wyndham, MVO; 3rd, 1965, Mrs Mary Bridget Lotinga, *d* of late Sir Shenton Thomas and of Lady Thomas, SW7. *Educ:* Eton. Joined Duke of Cornwall's Light Infantry, 1937. Served War of 1939–45: attached Royal Armoured Corps. *Heir: s* Lord Eliot, *qv*. *Address:* Les Arcs, Chemin du Signal, 1807, Blonay, Vaud, Switzerland.
See also Earl of Shelburne.

ST GERMANS, Bishop Suffragan of, since 1985; **Rt. Rev. John Richard Allan Llewellin;** *b* 30 Sept. 1938; *s* of John Clarence Llewellin and Margaret Gwenllian Llewellin; *m* 1965; Jennifer Sally (*née* House); one *s* two *d*. *Educ:* Clifton College, Bristol; Westcott House and Fitzwilliam Coll., Cambridge (MA). Solicitor, 1960. Ordained deacon, 1964; priest, 1965; Curate at Radlett, Herts, 1964–68; Curate at Johannesburg Cathedral, 1968–71; Vicar of Waltham Cross, 1971–79; Rector of Harpenden, 1979–85. *Recreations:* sailing; DIY. *Address:* 32 Falmouth Road, Truro TR1 2HX. *T:* Truro 73190.

ST HELENA, Bishop of, since 1985; **Rt. Rev. James Nathaniel Johnson;** *b* 28 April 1932; *s* of William and Lydia Florence Johnson; *m* 1953, Evelyn Joyce Clifford; one *s* one *d*. *Educ:* Primary and Secondary Selective School, St Helena; Church Army College; Wells Theolog. Coll. Deacon 1964, priest 1965; Curate of St Peter's, Lawrence Weston, dio. Bristol, 1964–66; Priest-in-charge of St Paul's Cathedral, St Helena, 1966–69, Vicar 1969–71; Domestic Chaplain to Bishop of St Helena, 1967–71; USPG Area Sec. for Dioceses of Exeter and Truro, 1972–74; Rector of Combe Martin dio. Exeter, 1974–80; Hon. Canon of St Helena, 1975–85; Vicar of St Augustine, Thorpe Bay, dio. Chelmsford, 1980–85. *Recreations:* music and gardening. *Address:* Bishopsholme, Island of St Helena, South Atlantic Ocean. *T:* (039) St Helena 471. *Clubs:* Royal Commonwealth Society; Exiles (Ascension Island).

ST HELENS, 2nd Baron *cr* 1964; **Richard Francis Hughes-Young;** *b* 4 Nov. 1945; *s* of 1st Baron St Helens, MC, and Elizabeth Agnes (*d* 1956), *y d* of late Captain Richard Blakiston-Houston; *S* father, 1980; *m* 1983, Mrs E. R. Talbot-Smith; one *s*. *Educ:* Nautical College, Pangbourne. *Heir: s* Henry Thomas Hughes-Young, *b* 7 March 1986. *Address:* Marchfield House, Binfield, Berks.

ST JOHN, family name of **Baron St John of Bletso,** and of **Viscount Bolingbroke.**

ST JOHN OF BLETSO, 21st Baron *cr* 1558; **Anthony Tudor St John;** Bt 1660; oil analyst/stockbroker with County Securities, London, since 1986; solicitor in Cape Town; *b* 16 May 1957; *s* of 20th Baron St John of Bletso, TD, and of Katharine, *d* of late A. G. von Berg; *S* father, 1978. *Educ:* Diocesan College, Rondebosch, Cape; Univ. of Cape Town (BSocSc 1977, BA (Law) 1978); Univ. of S Africa (BProc 1982); London Univ. (LLM 1983). Cross-bencher in House of Lords, specific interests in current affairs in S Africa and energy affairs. *Publication:* articles: Quality of Life: Survey on the Squatter Community in the Cape, 1977. *Recreations:* golf, tennis, surfing and skiing; bridge. *Heir: cousin* Edmund Oliver St John, WS [*b* 13 Oct. 1927; *m* 1959, Elizabeth Frances, *o d* of Lt-Col H. R. Nicholl; one *s* two *d*]. *Address:* 46 Reporton Road, SW6. *T:* 01–381 0887. *Clubs:* Royal Cape Golf, Western Province Sports.

ST JOHN, Oliver Beauchamp, CEng, FRAeS; Chief Scientist, Civil Aviation Authority, 1978–82; *b* 22 Jan. 1922; 2nd *s* of late Harold and Ella Margaret St John; *m* 1945, Eileen (*née* Morris); three *s*. *Educ:* Monkton Combe Sch.; Queens Coll., Cambridge (MA); London Univ. (External) (BSc). Metropolitan Vickers, Manchester, 1939; Royal Aircraft Estabt, Farnborough, from 1946, on automatic control of fixed-wing aircraft and helicopters; Supt, Blind Landing Experimental Unit, RAE, Bedford, 1966; Director of Technical Research & Development, CAA, 1969–78. Queen's Commendation for Valuable Services in the Air, 1956. *Publication:* A Gallimaufry of Goffering: a history of early ironing implements, 1982. *Recreations:* mountaineering, skiing, early music, instrument making. *Address:* The Old Stables, Manor Farm Barns, East Hagbourne OX11 9ND. *T:* Didcot 818437. *Club:* Alpine.

ST JOHN, Maj.-Gen. Roger Ellis Tudor, CB 1965; MC 1944; *b* Hexham on Tyne, 4 Oct. 1911; *s* of late Major B. T. St John, Craigveigh, Aboyne, Aberdeenshire; *m* 1943, Rosemary Jean Douglas Vickers, Englefield Green, Surrey; one *s* three *d*. *Educ:* Wellington College; RMC Sandhurst. Joined Fifth Fusiliers, 1931; served War of 1939–45 (despatches, MC), in Hong Kong, UK and NW Europe; Bde Major 11 Armoured Div., 1944–45; GSO 2 Instructor Camberley Staff Coll., 1945–46; AA and QMG 1st Division, Tripoli, 1948–50; comd 1st Bn Royal Northumberland Fusiliers, 1953–55 (despatches), Mau Mau Rebellion; AMS Mil. Secretary's Branch, War Office, 1955–57; Comdr 11 Inf. Bde Group, BAOR, 1957–60; Asst Comdt, Camberley Staff Coll., 1960–62; Comdr, British Army Staff, Military Member, British Defence Staffs, and Military Attaché, Washington, 1963–65; President, Regular Army Commissions Board, 1965–67; retired, 1967. Colonel, Royal Northumberland Fusiliers, 1965–68. Personnel Adminr, Urwick, Orr and Partners Ltd, Management Consultants, 1967–73. *Address:* Harelaw, Gorse Hill Road, Virginia Water, Surrey GU25 4AS.

ST JOHN PARKER, Michael, MA (Cantab); Headmaster, Abingdon School, Oxfordshire, since 1975; *b* 21 July 1941; *s* of Rev. Canon J. W. Parker; *m* 1965, Annette Monica Ugle; two *s* two *d*. *Educ:* Stamford Sch.; King's Coll., Cambridge. Asst Master: Sevenoaks Sch., 1962–63; King's Sch., Canterbury, 1963–69; Winchester Coll., 1969–75; Head of History Dept, Winchester Coll., 1970–75. Member: Council, Hansard Soc., 1972–; Marsh Cttee on Politics and Industry, 1978–79. Chm., Midland Div., HMC, 1984. Governor: St Helen's Sch., 1975–83; Christ Church Cathedral Sch.; Cokethorpe Sch. *Publications:* The British Revolution—Social and Economic History 1750–1970, 1972; various pamphlets and articles. *Recreations:* old buildings, music, books. *Address:* Lacies Court, Abingdon, Oxfordshire. *T:* Abingdon 20163. *Clubs:* East India, Devonshire, Sports and Public Schools; Leander.

ST JOHN-STEVAS, Rt. Hon. Norman Antony Francis, PC 1979; FRSL 1966; MP (C) Chelmsford, since Oct. 1964; Chancellor of the Duchy of Lancaster, Leader of the House of Commons, and Minister for the Arts, 1979–81; Chairman, Royal Fine Art Commission, since 1985; author, barrister and journalist; *b* London, 18 May 1929; *o s* of late Stephen S. Stevas, civil engineer and company director, and late Kitty St John O'Connor; unmarried. *Educ:* Ratcliffe; Fitzwilliam, Cambridge; Christ Church, Oxford; Yale. Scholar, Clothworkers Exhibnr, 1946, 1947; BA (Cambridge) (1st cl. hons in law), 1950, MA 1954; President, Cambridge Union, 1950; Whitlock Prize, 1950; MA 1952, BCL 1954 (Oxon); Sec. Oxford Union, 1952. Contested (C) Dagenham, Gen. Election, 1951; Barrister, Middle Temple, 1952; Blackstone and Harmsworth schol., 1952; Blackstone Prize, 1953. Lecturer, Southampton University, 1952–53, King's Coll., London, 1953–56, tutored in jurisprudence, Christ Church, 1953–55, and Merton, 1955–57, Oxford. Founder member, Inst. of Higher European Studies, Bolzano, 1955; PhD (Lond.) 1957; Yorke Prize, Cambridge Univ., 1957; Fellow Yale Law School, 1957; Fulbright Award, 1957; Fund for the Republic Fellow, 1958; Dr of Sc. of Law (Yale), 1960; Lecture tours of USA, 1958–68. Regents' Prof., Univ. of California at Santa Barbara, 1969, Regents' Lectr 1984. Legal Adviser to Sir Alan Herbert's Cttee on book censorship, 1954–59; joined The Economist, 1959, to edit collected works of Walter Bagehot and became legal, ecclesiastical and political correspondent. Deleg., Council of Europe and WEU, 1967–71; Parly Under-Sec. of State, DES, 1972–73; Min. of State for the Arts, DES, 1973–74; Sec., Cons. Parly Home Affairs Cttee, 1969–72; Vice-Chm., Cons. Parly N Ireland Cttee, 1972–; Mem. Executive, Cons. Parly 1922 Cttee, 1971–72 and 1974; Vice Chm., Cons. Group for Europe, 1972–75; Mem. Shadow Cabinet, 1974–79, and Opposition Spokesman on Educn, 1975–78, Science and the Arts, 1975–79; Shadow Leader of the House, 1978–79; Member: Cons. Nat. Adv. Cttee on Policy, 1971; Fulbright Commission, 1961; Parly Select Cttee: on Race Relations and Immigration, 1970–72; on Civil List, 1971–83; on Foreign Affairs, 1983–. Head, British delegn to Helsinki Cultural Forum, Budapest, 1985. Chm., New Bearings for the Re-Establishment, 1970–. Hon. Sec., Fedn of Cons. Students, 1971–73, Hon. Vice-Pres. 1973. Chm., Booker McConnell Prize, 1985. Mem. Council: RADA, 1983–; Nat. Soc. for Dance, 1983–; Nat. Youth Theatre, 1983– (Patron, 1984–); RCA, 1985–; Patron, Medieval Players, 1984–; Trustee: Royal Philharmonic Orch., 1985–; Royal Soc. of Painters in Watercolours, 1984; Decorative Arts Soc., 1984–. Editor The Dublin (Wiseman) Review, 1961. Vice Pres., Les Amis de Napoléon III, 1974; Mem., Académie du Second Empire, 1975. Presidential Fellow, Aspern Inst., 1980; Hon. Fellow, St Edmund's House, Cambridge, 1985. DD (*hc*) Univ. of Susquehanna, Pa, 1983; DLitt (*hc*) Schiller Univ., 1985. Silver Jubilee Medal, 1977. SBStJ. Commendatore, Order of Merit (Italian Republic), 1965. GCKLJ 1976 (KSLJ 1963). *Publications:* Obscenity and the Law, 1956; Walter Bagehot, 1959; Life, Death and the Law, 1961; The Right to Life, 1963; Law and Morals, 1964; The Literary Works of Walter Bagehot, vols I, II, 1966, The Historical Works, vols III, IV, 1968, The Political Works, vols V, VI, VII, and VIII, 1974, The Economic Works, vols IX, X and XI, 1978, Letters and Miscellany, vols XII, XIII, XIV and XV, 1986; The Agonising Choice, 1971; Pope John Paul II, his travels and mission, 1982; The Two Cities, 1984; contrib. to: Critical Quarterly, Modern Law Review, Criminal Law Review, Law and Contemporary Problems, Twentieth Century, Times Lit. Supp., Dublin Review. *Recreations:* reading, talking, listening (to music), travelling, walking, appearing on television, sleeping. *Address:* 34 Montpelier Square, SW1. *T:* 01–589 3001; The Old Rectory, Preston Capes, Daventry, Northants. *Clubs:* White's, Garrick, Pratt's, Arts (Hon. Mem., 1980), Grillions, The Other.

ST JOHN WILSON, Colin Alexander; *see* Wilson.

ST JOHN'S (Newfoundland), Archbishop of, (RC), since 1979; **Most Rev. Alphonsus Liguori Penney;** *b* 17 Sept. 1924; *s* of Alphonsus Penney and Catherine Penney (*née* Mullaly). *Educ:* St Bonaventure's Coll., St John's, Newfoundland; University Seminary, Ottawa (LPh, LTh). Assistant Priest: St Joseph's Parish, St John's, 1950–56; St Patrick's Parish, St John's, 1956; Parish Priest: Marystown, Placentia Bay, Newfoundland, 1957; Basilica Parish, St John's, 1969. Prelate of Honour, 1971. Bishop of Grand Falls, Newfoundland, 1972. Hon. LLD, Memorial Univ. of Newfoundland, 1980. Confederation Medal, 1967. *Recreations:* walking, golf. *Address:* Basilica Residence, PO Box 37, St John's, Newfoundland A1C 5H5, Canada. *T:* 709–726–3660.

ST JOHNSTON, Colin David; Deputy Managing Director, Ocean Transport and Trading Ltd, since 1986 (Director, since 1974); *b* 6 Sept. 1934; *s* of Hal and Sheilagh St Johnston; *m* 1958, Valerie Paget; three *s* one *d*. *Educ:* Shrewsbury Sch.; Lincoln Coll., Oxford. Booker McConnell Ltd, 1958–70; Ocean Transport and Trading Ltd, 1970–; non-Executive Director, FMC plc, 1981–83. Mem. Council: Royal Commonwealth Society for the Blind, 1967–; Industrial Soc., 1981–; Trustee, Frances Mary Buss Foundn, 1981–; Governor, Camden Sch., 1974–. *Recreations:* music, squash. *Address:* 30 Fitzroy Road, NW1 8TY. *T:* 01–722 5932. *Club:* MCC.

ST JOHNSTON, Kerry; Chairman and Chief Executive, Overseas Containers Ltd, since 1982; *b* 30 July 1931; *s* of George Eric St Johnston and Viola Rhona Moriarty; *m* 1st, 1960, Judith Ann Nichols; two *s* one *d*; 2nd, 1980, Charlotte Ann Taylor. *Educ:* Summer Fields, Oxford; Eton Coll.; Worcester Coll., Oxford (MA Jurisprudence). Joined Ocean Steamship Co. Ltd, 1955, Man. Dir 1963; Overseas Containers Ltd: Founder Dir, 1965; Commerical Dir, 1966; Jt Man. Dir, 1969; Dep. Chm., 1973; Pres. and Chief Exec. Officer, Private Investment Co. for Asia (PICA), SA, Singapore, 1977–82. Dir, Lloyds Bank Internat. Ltd, 1983–85. *Recreations:* fishing, shooting, racing. *Address:* Flat 5, 53 Drayton Gardens, SW10 9RX. *T:* 01–373 3947. *Club:* Boodle's.

ST JOSEPH, Prof. John Kenneth Sinclair, CBE 1979 (OBE 1964); FBA 1978; Professor of Aerial Photographic Studies, University of Cambridge, and Professorial Fellow of

Selwyn College, 1973–80, Professor Emeritus since 1980; *b* 1912; *s* of late John D. St Joseph and of Irma Robertson (*née* Marris); *m* 1945, Daphne Margaret, *d* of late H. March, Worcester; two *s* two *d*. *Educ:* Bromsgrove Sch.; Selwyn Coll., Cambridge (Scholar). BA 1934, PhD 1937, MA 1938, LittD 1976. Harkness Scholar, 1934; Goldsmiths' Company Senior Student, 1935–37; DSIR Sen. Research Award, 1936–37; Fellow, Selwyn Coll., Cambridge, 1939–, Lectr in Natural Sciences and Dean, 1939–62; Tutor, 1945–62; Librarian, 1946–62; Vice Master, 1974–80; Univ. Demonstrator in Geology, 1937–45; Operational Research, Min. of Aircraft Production, 1942–45; Univ. Lectr in Geology, 1945–48; Leverhulme Research Fellow, 1948–49; Curator in Aerial Photography at Cambridge, 1948–62; Dir in Aerial Photography, 1962–80. Has undertaken aerial reconnaissance and photography, in aid of research, over the United Kingdom, Ireland, Denmark, the Netherlands and Northern France. Governor, Stratton Sch., Biggleswade, 1952–64; Hon. Corresp. Mem., German Archæological Inst., 1964–; Member: Council for British Archaeology, 1944–; Ancient Monuments Bd (England), 1969–84; Royal Commn on Historical Monuments (England), 1972–81; Vice-Pres., Soc. for Promotion of Roman Studies, 1975–; Hon. Vice-Pres., Royal Archaeological Inst., 1982–. Lectures: Chatwin Meml, Birmingham, 1969; David Murray, Glasgow Univ., 1973; Kroon, Amsterdam Univ., 1981. Cuthbert Peek Award, RGS, 1976; President's Award, Inst. of Incorporated Photographers, 1977. FGS 1937; FSAScot 1940; FSA 1944; Hon. ScD Trinity Coll., Dublin; Hon. LLD Dundee, 1971; Dr *hc* in Maths and Science, Amsterdam, 1982. *Publications:* The Pentameracea of the Oslo Region, 1939; chapters in The Roman Occupation of SW Scotland (ed S. N. Miller), 1945; Monastic Sites from the Air (with M. C. Knowles), 1952; Medieval England, an aerial survey (with M. W. Beresford), 1958, 2nd rev. edn, 1979; (ed) The Uses of Air Photography, 1966, 2nd rev. edn 1977; The Early Development of Irish Society (with E. R. Norman), 1970; Roman Britain from the Air (with S. S. Frere), 1983; chapters in Inchtuthil: the Roman legionary fortress (ed S. S. Frere), 1985; papers in learned jls on fossil Silurian Brachiopoda, and on aerial photography and archæology, especially of Roman Britain. *Recreations:* gardening, lumbering. *Address:* Selwyn College, Cambridge CB3 9DQ. *T:* Cambridge 335846; Histon Manor, Cambridge CB4 4JJ. *T:* Histon 2383.

SAINT LAURENT, Yves (Henri Donat Mathieu); Officier de la Légion d'Honneur; couturier; *b* 1 Aug. 1936; *s* of Charles Mathieu and Lucienne-Andrée Saint Laurent. *Educ:* Lycée d'Oran. Designer for Christian Dior, 1954–60; Dir, Société Yves Saint Laurent, 1962–. Costume designer for several plays, ballets and films. *Publication:* La Vilaine Lulu, 1967. *Address:* (office) 5 avenue Marceau, 75016 Paris; (home) 55 rue de Babylone, 75007 Paris, France.

ST LEGER, family name of **Viscount Doneraile.**

ST LEONARDS, 4th Baron *cr* 1852; **John Gerard Sugden;** *b* 3 Feb. 1950; *s* of Arthur Herbert Sugden (*g g s* of 1st Baron) (*d* 1958) and of Julia Sheila, *d* of late Philip Wyatt; *S* kinsman, 1972. *Heir: uncle* Dr Edward Charles Sugden, *b* 24 July 1902.

ST LEVAN, 4th Baron *cr* 1887; **John Francis Arthur St Aubyn,** DSC 1942; DL; Bt 1866; landowner and company director; *b* 23 Feb. 1919; *s* of 3rd Baron St Levan, and of Hon. Clementina Gwendolen Catharine Nicolson, *o d* of 1st Baron Carnock; *S* father, 1978; *m* 1970, Susan Maria Marcia, *d* of late Maj.-Gen. Sir John Kennedy, GCMG, KCVO, KBE, CB. *Educ:* Eton Coll.; Trinity Coll., Cambridge (BA). Admitted a Solicitor, 1948. High Sheriff of Cornwall, 1974; DL Cornwall, 1977. Pres., Cornwall Br., CPRE, 1975. FRSA 1974. *Publication:* Illustrated History of St Michael's Mount, 1974. *Recreation:* sailing. *Heir: b* Hon. (Oliver) Piers St Aubyn, MC [*b* 12 July 1920; *m* 1948, Mary, *e d* of late Bailey Southwell; two *s* one *d*]. *Address:* St Michael's Mount, Marazion, Cornwall. *Clubs:* Brooks's; Royal Yacht Squadron.

ST OSWALD, 5th Baron *cr* 1885; **Derek Edward Anthony Winn;** *b* 9 July 1919; *s* of 3rd Baron St Oswald and Eve Carew (*d* 1976), *d* of Charles Greene; *S* brother, 1984; *m* 1954, Charlotte Denise Eileen, *d* of Wilfred Haig Loyd; one *s* one *d*. *Educ:* Stowe. Joined 60th Rifles, KRRC, as 2nd Lieut, 1938; Parachute Regt, 1942; served N Africa (wounded). Malayan Police, 1948–51. Film Producer, 1953–67. Farm owner, Nostell Priory. *Publication:* I Served Caesar, 1972. *Recreation:* shooting. *Heir: s* Hon. Charles Rowland Andrew Winn [*b* 22 July 1959; *m* 1985, Louise Alexandra, *yr d* of Stewart Scott; one *s*]. *Address:* Nostell Priory, Wakefield, Yorks. *T:* Wakefield 862394. *Clubs:* White's, Lansdowne.

ST PAUL'S, Dean of; *see* Webster, Very Rev. A. B.

ST VINCENT, 7th Viscount (*cr* 1801); **Ronald George James Jervis;** *b* 3 May 1905; *o* surv. *s* of 6th Viscount and Marion Annie (*d* 1911), *d* of James Brown, JP, Orchard, Carluke, Scotland; *S* father, 1940; *m* 1945, Phillida, *o d* of Lt-Col R. H. Logan, Taunton; two *s* one *d*. *Educ:* Sherborne. JP Somerset, 1950–55. *Heir: s* Hon. Edward Robert James Jervis [*b* 12 May 1951; *m* 1977, Victoria Margaret, *o d* of Wilton J. Oldham, St Peter, Jersey; one *d*]. *Address:* Les Charrieres, St Ouen, Jersey, CI.

ST VINCENT FERRERI, Marquis of; *see* San Vincenzo Ferreri.

SAINTONGE, Rolland A. A. C. de; *see* Chaput de Saintonge.

SAINTY, Sir John Christopher, KCB 1986; Clerk of the Parliaments, since 1983; *b* 31 Dec. 1934; *s* of late Christopher Lawrence Sainty and Nancy Lee Sainty (*née* Miller); *m* 1965, (Elizabeth) Frances Sherlock; three *s*. *Educ:* Winchester Coll.; New Coll., Oxford (MA). FSA; FRHistS. Clerk, Parlt Office, House of Lords, 1959; seconded as Private Sec. to Leader of House and Chief Whip, House of Lords, 1963; Clerk of Journals, House of Lords, 1965; Res. Asst and Editor, Inst. of Historical Research, 1970; Reading Clerk, House of Lords, 1974. *Publications:* Treasury Officials 1660–1870, 1972; Officials of the Secretaries of State 1660–1782, 1973; Officials of the Boards of Trade 1660–1870, 1974; Admiralty Officials 1660–1870, 1975; Home Office Officials, 1782–1870, 1975; Colonial Office Officials 1794–1870, 1976; (with D. Dewar) Divisions in the House of Lords: an analytical list 1685–1857, 1976; Officers of the Exchequer, 1983; articles in Eng. Hist. Rev., Bull. Inst. Hist. Research. *Address:* 22 Kelso Place, W8 5QG. *T:* 01–937 9460.

SAKHAROV, Dr Andrei Dimitrievich; Member, Academy of Sciences of USSR, since 1953; *b* 21 May 1921; *m* 2nd, 1971, Elena Bonner; one *s* one *d*. *Educ:* Moscow State Univ. Joined P. N. Lebedev Physics Inst. as physicist, 1945; worked with Dr Igor Tamm on nuclear fusion. Member: Amer. Acad. of Arts and Sciences, 1969–; Nat. Acad. of Sciences, 1972–; Foreign Associate, Acad. des Sciences, 1981–. Eleanor Roosevelt Peace Award, 1973; Cino del Duca Prize, 1974; Reinhold Niebuhr Prize, Chicago Univ., 1974; Nobel Peace Prize, 1975; Fritt Ord Prize, 1980. *Publications:* Progress, Peaceful Co-existence and Intellectual Freedom, 1968; Sakharov Speaks, 1974; My Country and the World, 1975; Alarm and Hope, 1979; scientific works, etc. *Address:* Academy of Sciences of USSR, Leninsky prospekt 14, Moscow, USSR; Flat 3, 214 Gagarin prospekt, Sherpinki 2, Gorky, USSR.

SAKZEWSKI, Sir Albert, Kt 1973; FCA, FASA; chartered accountant; Founder, Sir Albert Sakzewski Foundation; Chairman: Avanis Pty Ltd; Blend Investments Pty Ltd; Commercial Finance Pty Ltd; Queensland Securities Pty Ltd; Southern Cross Products Pty Ltd; *b* Lowood, Qld, 12 Nov. 1905; *s* of O. T. Sakzewski, Lowood and Brisbane; *m* 1935, Winifred May (*d* 1972), *d* of W. P. Reade; two *s*. *Educ:* Ipswich High Sch., Qld. Founder and Sen. Partner, A. Sakzewski & Co./Court & Co., Chartered Accountants, 1929–76. Chairman: Qld Bd of Advice, Custom Credit Corp. Ltd, 1964–78; Rover Mowers (Aust) Pty Ltd, 1966–77; Dir, Oswald-Sealy (Australia) Group, 1940–82. Chm. and Govt Nominee, Totalisator Admin Bd of Qld, 1962–81. Dir, Nat. Heart Foundn (Queensland Div.), 1960–76 (Chm., Building Appeal, 1978). Past Pres., Australian Amateur Billiards Council; Member: Aust./Britain Soc.; Nat. Trust of Qld; Aust. Ballet Foundn; Qld Art Gall. Foundn. *Recreations:* horse racing and breeding (administrator (Tattersall's) 1935–, owner 1941–); billiards (Australian Amateur Billiards Champion, 1932, with a then Australian Record break of 206; Qld Amateur Billiards Champion 6 times), snooker (Qld Amateur Snooker Champion 8 times). *Address:* (home) Ilya Lodge, 1 Rossiter Parade, Hamilton, Qld 4007, Australia; (office) National Bank House, 255 Adelaide Street, Brisbane, Qld 4000, Australia; GPO Box 11, Brisbane, 4001. *Clubs:* Royal Commonwealth Society; Brisbane, Tattersall's (Trustee; Life Mem.) (Brisbane); Tattersall's (Sydney); Queensland Turf, Tattersall's Racing (Life Mem.), Brisbane Amateur Turf (Life Mem.), Gold Coast Turf, Rockhampton Jockey (Life Mem.); Royal Queensland Golf, Southport Golf.

SALAM, Professor Abdus, Sitara-i-Pakistan, 1959; Order of Nishan-i-Imtiaz, Pakistan, 1979; PhD; FRS 1959; Professor of Theoretical Physics at the Imperial College of Science and Technology in the University of London since 1957; Director, International Centre for Theoretical Physics, Trieste, since 1964; *b* 29 Jan. 1926. *Educ:* Govt Coll., Lahore, Pakistan (MA); St John's Coll., Camb. (BA, PhD). Fellow, St John's Coll., Cambridge, 1951–56 (Hon. Fellow, 1972); Professor of Mathematics, Government College, Lahore, 1951–54; Lecturer in Mathematics, University of Cambridge, 1954–56. Sci. Advr to Pres. of Pakistan, 1961–74. Has made contributions to the theory of elementary particles. Mem., UN Adv. Cttee on Science and Technology, 1964–75 (Chm., 1971–72); Vice-Pres., IUPAP, 1972–78. Founding Mem. and Pres., Third World Acad. of Scis, 1983; Fellow, Royal Swedish Acad. of Sciences, 1970; For. Mem., USSR Acad. of Scis, 1971. Hon. DSc: Panjab University, Lahore, Pakistan, 1957; Edinburgh, 1971; Hon. ScD Cambridge, 1985. Hopkins Prize, Cambridge Philosophical Soc., 1957; Adams Prize, Cambridge Univ., 1958; Maxwell Medal and Prize, IPPS, 1961; Hughes Medal, Royal Society, 1964; Atoms for Peace Award, 1968; Oppenheimer Prize and Medal, 1971; Guthrie Medal and Prize, IPPS, 1976; Matteuci Medal, Accad. Naz. di XL, Rome, 1978; John Torrence Tate Medal, Amer. Inst. of Physics, 1978; Royal Medal, Royal Society, 1978; (jtly) Nobel Prize for Physics, 1979; Einstein Medal, UNESCO, Paris, 1979; Josef Stefan Medal, Josef Stefan Inst., Ljubljana, 1980; Gold Medal for outstanding contrib. to physics, Czechoslovak Acad. of Scis, Prague, 1981; Peace Medal, Charles Univ., Prague, 1981; Lomonosov Gold Medal, USSR Acad. of Scis, 1983. *Address:* Imperial College of Science and Technology, Prince Consort Road, SW7; International Centre for Theoretical Physics, PO Box 586, 34100 Trieste, Italy.

SALAMAN, Myer Head, MD; Research Pathologist, Royal College of Surgeons, 1968–74; *b* 2 August 1902; *e s* of Redcliffe N. Salaman, MD, FRS and Nina Salaman; *m* 1926, Esther Polianowsky; one *s* three *d*. *Educ:* Clifton College; Bedales School; Trinity College, Cambridge; London Hospital Medical College. Natural Science Tripos Pts I and II, Cambridge, 1921–25; London Hosp.: Clinical training, 1927–30; House Appts, 1931–32; Research on Viruses, 1932–34, and Lister Inst. (Junior Beit Mem. Fellow) 1935–38; Cancer Research, St Bartholomew's Hosp., 1939; Asst Pathologist, Emergency Public Health Service, 1940–42; Cancer and Virus Research, Strangeways Lab., 1942–43; Temp. Major, RAMC, 1943–46. Engaged in Cancer Research at the London Hospital, 1946–48; Dir, Dept of Cancer Research, London Hosp. Med. Sch., 1948–67; engaged in Cancer Research at RCS, 1968–74. MA 1926, MD 1936 Cantab; MRCS, LRCP, 1930; Dipl. Bact. London, 1936. FRSocMed. *Publications:* papers on virus diseases, and on cancer, in Jour. Pathology and Bacteriology, Proc. Roy. Soc. (B), Brit. Jl Cancer, etc. *Recreation:* walking. *Address:* 23 Bisham Gardens, Highgate, N6. *T:* 01–340 1019. *Club:* Athenæum.
See also Prof. H. B. Barlow.

SALAS, Rafael Montinola; Executive Director (with rank of Under-Secretary-General), United Nations Fund for Population Activities, since 1971 (Sen. Consultant to Administrator of UNDP, 1969; Director UNFPA, 1969); Secretary-General, 1984 International Conference on Population; *b* Bago, Negros Occidental, Philippines, 7 Aug. 1928; *s* of Ernesto Salas and Isabel Montinola; *m* 1967, Carmelita J. Rodriguez; two *s*. *Educ:* Coll. of Liberal Arts, Univ. of the Philippines (Associate in Arts (AA) with high honours, 1950; AB *magna cum laude*, 1953); Coll. of Law, Univ. of the Philippines (LLB *cum laude* 1953); Littauer Center of Public Admin. (MPA), Harvard Univ., 1955. Mem., Philippine Bar, 1953. Professorial Lectr in: Polit. Sci. and Economics, Univ. of the Philippines, 1955–59; Economics, Grad. Sch., Far Eastern Univ., 1960–61; Law, Univ. of the Philippines, 1963–66 (Asst. Vice-Pres., 1962–63, Mem., Board of Regents, 1966–69, of the Univ.). Philippine positions: Nat. Economic Council: Exec. Officer (with Cabinet rank), 1960–61; Exec. Dir (with Cabinet rank), 1961; Actg Chm., 1966, 1968. Gen. Manager, the Manila Chronicle, 1963–65; Asst to the President, Meralco Securities Corp., 1963–65. Action Officer, Nat. Rice and Corn Sufficiency Programme, 1967–69 (of vital importance to "Green Revolution"); Nat. Projects Overall Co-ordinator and Action Officer, 1966–69; Exec. Sec. of Republic of the Philippines, 1966–69 (office 2nd to President in executive powers). Holds numerous hon. degrees. Holds foreign orders. *Publications:* People: an international choice, 1976; International Population Assistance: the first decade, 1979; Reflections on Population, 1984, expanded edn, 1985; More Than the Grains: participatory management in the Philippine Rice Sufficiency Program 1967–1969, 1985; Fifty-Six Stones: a collection of poems, 1985. *Recreation:* reading. *Address:* United Nations, New York 10017, USA.

SALE, Geoffrey Stead; Director of Studies, RMA, Sandhurst, Camberley, 1967–71; *b* 6 Aug. 1907; *s* of Frederic W. R. Sale, Solicitor, Carlisle, and Ivy I. Davidson; *m* 1938, Olivia Jean Bell-Scott (*d* 1950), Edinburgh; one *s* three *d*. *Educ:* Berkhamsted School; Lincoln College, Oxford (MA). Diploma in Education; Assistant Master and Housemaster, Fettes College, Edinburgh, 1931–46; Headmaster, King's School, Bruton, 1946–57; Headmaster, Rossall School, 1957–67. Captain TA (General List). Member, House of Laity, Church Assembly, 1960–70. FRSA 1953. *Publications:* Four Hundred Years a School (History of King's School), 1950; History of Casterton School 1823–1983, 1983. *Recreations:* walking, photography, writing. *Address:* 1 Penny's Lane, Wilton, Salisbury, SP2 0BE. *T:* Salisbury 743432.

SALE, Richard; Headmaster of Brentwood School, 1966–81; *b* 4 Oct. 1919; *e s* of late Richard and Rachel Sale; *m* 1943, Elizabeth Thérèse Bauer; four *s* one *d*. *Educ:* Repton Sch. (Schol.); Oriel Coll., Oxford. Commissioned, KSLI, 1940; served War of 1939–45: Canada and Normandy; demobilised, rank of Major, 1946. Asst Master, Repton Sch., 1946–61; Housemaster of The Priory, 1953–61; Headmaster, Oswestry School, Shropshire, 1962–66. Pres., Arthur Dunn Cup; Life Vice-Pres., Essex Co. Football Assoc. President: Old Brentwoods Soc., 1980; Old Reptonian Soc., 1982. FRSA 1969. *Recreations:*

cricket (Oxford Blue; Warwickshire, 1939, 1946, 1947; Derbyshire, 1949–54), golf, fives (Oxford Blue), and other games. *Address:* Whitegates, Homefield Paddock, Beccles, Suffolk. *T:* Beccles 714486. *Clubs:* MCC; Vincent's (Oxford).

SALES, William Henry, BSc (Econ.) Hons. London; Chairman, Yorkshire (late NE) Division of the National Coal Board, 1957–67, retired (Member, National Coal Board, 1953–57); *b* 26 April 1903. *Educ:* pit; Fircroft; London School of Economics. Miners' Welfare Scholarship. Varied career; pit; boys' clubs; WEA Lecturer; schoolmaster. Dep. Labour Director, East Midlands Division, NCB, 1947–51; Deputy Chairman, North-Western Division, 1951–53. Chm. Church of England Industrial Council, 1967–71. Hon. Fellow, LSE, 1960. *Publications:* various papers in Economic and Sociological Journals. *Address:* Handley Cross, Cantley, Doncaster, S Yorks.

SALFORD, Bishop of, (RC), since 1984; **Rt. Rev. Patrick A. Kelly;** *b* 23 Nov. 1938; *s* of John Joseph Kelly and Mary Ann Kelly (*née* Altham). *Educ:* St Mary's Primary School, Morecambe; Preston Catholic Coll.; English College and Gregorian Univ., Rome (STL, PhL). Curate, Lancaster Cathedral, 1964–66; Lectr in Theology, 1966–79 and Rector, 1979–84, St Mary's Coll., Oscott. *Address:* Wardley Hall, Worsley, Manchester M28 5ND.

SALFORD, Auxiliary Bishop of, (RC); *see* Burke, Rt Rev. Geoffrey.

SALINGER, Jerome David; American author; *b* New York City, 1919; *m*; one *s* one *d*. *Educ:* Manhattan public schools; Military Academy, Paris. Served with 4th Infantry Division, US Army, 1942–46 (Staff Sergeant). Travelled in Europe, 1937–38. Started writing at age of 15; first story published, 1940. *Publications:* The Catcher in the Rye, 1951; For Esme-with Love and Squalor, 1953; Franny and Zooey, 1962; Raise High the Roof Beam, Carpenters and Seymour: an Introduction, 1963. *Address:* c/o Harold Ober Associates, 40 East 49th Street, New York, NY 10017, USA.

SALINGER, Pierre (Emil George); Politician, Journalist; Paris Bureau Chief, since 1979, and Chief Foreign Correspondent, ABC News, since 1983, American Broadcasting Company; *b* San Francisco, 14 June 1925; *s* of Herbert and Jehanne Salinger; *m* 1st; one *s* one *d*; 2nd, 1957, Nancy Brook Joy (marr. diss., 1965); 3rd, 1965, Nicole Gillmann, Paris, France; one *s*. *Educ:* Lowell High School, San Francisco; State Coll., San Francisco; Univ. of San Francisco. Served War, 1942–45, with US Navy. With San Francisco Chronicle, 1942–55; Guest Lectr, Mills Coll., Calif, 1950–55; Press Officer, Democratic Presidential Campaign (Calif), 1952; West Coast Editor, Contributing Editor, Collier's Magazine, 1955–56; Investigator, Senate Labor Rackets Cttee, 1957–59; Press Sec. to President Kennedy (when Senator), 1959–61, and to President of the United States, 1961–64; appointed to serve as a US Senator, 4 Aug. 1964–2 Jan. 1965; Roving Editor, L'Express, Paris, 1973–78. Vice Pres.: Continental Airlines, Continental Air Services, 1965–68. Trustee, Robert F. Kennedy Meml Foundn; Chm., Bd of Trustees, American Coll. in Paris. Mem., Legion of Honour, 1978; US Navy and Marine Corps Medal, 1946. *Publications:* articles on county jail conditions in California, 1953; A Tribute to John F. Kennedy, Encyclopedia Britannica, 1964; With Kennedy, 1966; A Tribute to Robert F. Kennedy, 1968; For the Eyes of the President Only, 1971; Je suis un Americain, 1975; La France et le Nouveau Monde, 1976; America Held Hostage—the secret negotiations, 1981; (with Leonard Gross) The Dossier, 1984; (with Robert Cameron) Above Paris, 1985. *Address:* 248 rue de Rivoli, 75001 Paris, France.

SALISBURY, 6th Marquess of, *cr* 1789; **Robert Edward Peter Cecil;** DL; Baron Cecil, 1603; Viscount Cranborne, 1604; Earl of Salisbury, 1605; Captain Grenadier Guards; High Steward of Hertford since 1972; *b* 24 Oct. 1916; *s* of 5th Marquess of Salisbury, KG, PC, FRS, and Elizabeth Vere (*d* 1982), *e d* of late Lord Richard Cavendish, PC, CB, CMG; *S* father, 1972; *m* 1945, Marjorie Olein (Mollie), *d* of late Captain Hon. Valentine Wyndham-Quin, RN; four *s* one *d* (and one *s* decd). MP (C) Bournemouth West, 1950–54. Pres., Monday Club, 1974–81. DL Dorset, 1974. *Heir: s* Viscount Cranborne, *qv*. *Address:* Manor House, Cranborne, Dorset; Hatfield House, Hatfield, Herts.
See also Dowager Duchess of Devonshire.

SALISBURY, Bishop of, since 1982; **Rt. Rev. John Austin Baker;** *b* 11 Jan. 1928; *s* of George Austin Baker and Grace Edna Baker; *m* 1974, Gillian Mary Leach. *Educ:* Marlborough; Oriel Coll., Oxford (MA, MLitt). Asst Curate, All Saints', Cuddesdon, and Lectr in Old Testament, Cuddesdon Theol Coll., 1954–57; Priest 1955; Asst Curate, St Anselm's, Hatch End, and Asst Lectr in NT Greek, King's Coll., London, 1957–59; Official Fellow, Chaplain and Lectr in Divinity, Corpus Christi Coll., Oxford, 1959–73, Emeritus Fellow, 1977; Lectr in Theology, Brasenose and Lincoln Colls, Oxford, 1959–73; Hebrew Lectr, Exeter Coll., Oxford, 1969–73; Canon of Westminster, 1973–82; Treas., 1974–78; Sub-Dean and Lector Theologiae, 1978–82; Rector of St Margaret's, Westminster, and Speaker's Chaplain, 1978–82. Governor of Pusey House, Oxford, 1970–78; Exam. Chaplain to Bp of Oxford, 1960–78, to Bp of Southwark, 1973–78. Governor: Westminster Sch., 1974–81; Ripon Coll., Cuddesdon, 1974–80; Westminster City Sch., 1978–81; Dorset Inst. of Higher Educn, 1982–86; Bishop Wordsworth's Sch., 1982–; Sherborne Sch., 1982–; Salisbury & Wells Theological Coll., 1982–; Pres. of Council, Marlborough Coll., 1982–; Trustee, Harold Buxton Trust, 1973–79. Dorrance Vis. Prof., Trinity Coll., Hartford, Conn, USA, 1967; Vis. Prof., King's Coll., London, 1974–77; Hulsean Preacher, Univ. of Cambridge, 1979; Select Preacher, Univ. of Oxford, 1983. Chairman: Defence Theol Working Party, C of E Bd for Social Responsibility, 1980–82; C of E Doctrine Commn, 1985– (Mem. 1967–76, 1977–81, 1984–); Member: Faith and Order Advisory Gp, C of E Bd for Mission and Unity, 1976–81; Council of Christians and Jews, 1979–; Cttee for Theological Education, 1982–85; Standing Cttee, WCC Faith and Order Commn, 1983–. Chaplain, Playing Card Makers' Co., 1977. *Publications:* The Foolishness of God, 1970; Travels in Oudamovia, 1976; The Living Splendour of Westminster Abbey, 1977; The Whole Family of God, 1981; contrib. to: Man: Fallen and Free (ed Kemp), 1969; Thinking about the Eucharist (ed Ramsey), 1972; Church Membership and Intercommunion (ed Kent and Murray), 1973; What about the New Testament? (ed Hooker and Hickling), 1975; Man and Nature (ed Montefiore), 1975; Studia Biblica I, 1978; Religious Studies and Public Examinations (ed Hulmes and Watson), 1980; Believing in the Church, 1981; Hospice: the living Idea (ed Saunders, Summers and Teller), 1981; Darwin: a Commemoration (ed R. J. Berry), 1982; Unholy Warfare (ed D. Martin and P. Mullen), 1983; Lessons before Midnight (ed J. White), 1984; Dropping the Bomb (ed J. Gladwin), 1985; Theology and Racism, I (ed K. Leech), 1985; Peace Together (ed C. Barrett), 1986; Workers for the Kingdom (ed J. Fuller), 1986; Faith and Renewal (ed T. F. Best), 1986; *translations:* W. Eichrodt, Theology of the Old Testament, vol. 1 1961, vol. 2 1967; T. Bovet, That They May Have Life, 1964; J. Daniélou, Theology of Jewish Christianity, 1964; H. von Campenhausen, Ecclesiastical Authority and Spiritual Power, 1969; H. von Campenhausen, The Formation of the Christian Bible, 1972; J. Daniélou, Gospel Message and Hellenistic Culture, 1973; (with David Smith) J. Daniélou, The Origins of Latin Christianity, 1977. *Recreations:* music, walking. *Address:* South Canonry, 71 The Close, Salisbury, Wilts SP1 2ER.

SALISBURY, Dean of; *see* Dickinson, Very Rev. H. G.

SALISBURY, Harrison Evans; *b* 14 Nov. 1908; *s* of Percy Pritchard Salisbury and Georgiana Evans Salisbury; *m* 1st, 1933, Mary Hollis (marr. diss.); two *s*; 2nd, 1964, Charlotte Young Rand. *Educ:* Univ. of Minnesota (AB). United Press, 1930: London Manager, 1943; Foreign Editor, 1945. New York Times: Moscow Corresp., 1949–54; National Editor, 1962; Asst Man. Editor, 1964–69; Associate Editor and Editor Opposite-Editorial Page, 1970–73. Pres., Amer. Acad. and Inst. of Arts and Letters, 1975–77; Mem., Amer. Acad. of Arts and Letters. Pres., Authors' League, 1980–85. Amer. Philosophical Soc. Pulitzer Prize, International Correspondence, 1955. Holds hon. doctorates. *Publications:* Russia on the Way, 1946; American in Russia, 1955; The Shook-up Generation, 1958; To Moscow-And Beyond, 1960; Moscow Journal, 1961; The Northern Palmyra Affair, 1962; A New Russia?, 1962; Russia, 1965; Orbit of China, 1967; Behind the Lines-Hanoi 1967; The Soviet Union-The 50 Years, 1967; The 900 Days, the Siege of Leningrad, 1969; The Coming War Between Russia and China, 1969; The Many Americas Shall Be One, 1971; The Eloquence of Protest: voices of the seventies, 1972; To Peking-and Beyond, 1973; The Gates of Hell, 1975; Black Night, White Snow: Russia's Revolutions 1905–1917, 1978; Russia in Revolution 1900–1930, 1978; The Unknown War, 1978; Without Fear or Favor: The New York Times and *its* times, 1980; A Journey for Our Times, 1983; China: 100 Years of Revolution, 1983; The Long March: the untold story, 1985. *Address:* Box 70, Taconic, Conn, USA. *Clubs:* Century Association (New York); National Press (Washington, DC).

SALISBURY, John; *see* Caute, J. D.

SALK, Jonas Edward, BS, MD; Founding Director, since 1975, and Distinguished Professor in International Health Sciences, since 1984, Salk Institute for Biological Studies (Director, 1963–75; Fellow, 1963–84); Adjunct Professor of Health Sciences in Departments of Psychiatry, Community Medicine, and Medicine, University of California at San Diego, since 1970; *b* New York, 28 Oct. 1914; *s* of Daniel B. Salk; *m* 1st, 1939, Donna Lindsay (marr. diss. 1968); three *s*; 2nd, 1970, Françoise Gilot. *Educ:* NY University College of Medicine; Coll. of New York City (BS). Fellow, NY Univ. Coll. of Medicine, 1935–40; Mount Sinai Hosp., NYC, 1940–42; Nat. Research Council Fellow, Sch. of Public Health, Univ. of Michigan, 1942–43, Research Fellow in Epidemiology, 1943–44, Research Assoc., 1944–46, Asst Professor, 1946–47; Assoc. Prof. of Bacteriology, 1947–49, and Director of Virus Research Laboratory, 1947–63, School of Medicine, Univ. of Pittsburgh; Research Prof., 1949–54. Consultant in epidemic diseases to: Sec. of War, 1944–47, Sec. of Army, 1947–54; Commonwealth Professor of Experimental Medicine, 1957–62 (Professor of Preventive Med., Sch. of Med., Univ. of Pittsburgh, USA, and Chairman of the Department, 1954–57). Vis. Prof.-at-Large, Pittsburgh, 1963. Specialist in polio research; developed antipoliomyelitis vaccine, 1955. Emeritus Member: Amer. Epidemiological Soc.; Amer. Soc. of Clinical Investigation; Assoc. of Amer. Physicians; Soc. for Exptl Biol. and Medicine; Sen Mem., Inst. of Medicine, Nat. Acad. of Scis; mem. of other socs. Fellow: Amer. Public Health Assoc.; AAAS; Amer. Acad. of Arts and Scis; Hon. Fellow: Amer. Acad. of Pediatrics; Royal Soc. of Health. US Medal of Freedom, 1977. *Publications:* Man Unfolding, 1972; The Survival of the Wisest, 1973; (with Jonathan Salk) World Population and Human Values: a new reality, 1981; Anatomy of Reality: merging of intuition and reason, 1983. *Address:* The Salk Institute, PO Box 85800, San Diego, Calif 92138, USA.

SALMON, family name of **Baron Salmon.**

SALMON, Baron *cr* 1972 (Life Peer), of Sandwich, Kent; **Cyril Barnet Salmon,** PC 1964; Kt 1957; a Lord of Appeal in Ordinary, 1972–80; *b* 28 Dec. 1903; *s* of late Montagu Salmon; *m* 1st, 1929, Rencie (*d* 1942), *d* of late Sidney Gorton Vanderfelt, OBE; one *s* one *d*; 2nd, 1946, Jean, Lady Morris, *d* of late Lt-Col D. Maitland-Makgill-Crichton. *Educ:* Mill Hill; Pembroke College, Cambridge. BA 1925. Called to Bar, Middle Temple, 1925 (Bencher, 1953; Treasurer, 1972); QC 1945; Recorder of Gravesend, 1947–57; Judge of High Court of Justice, Queen's Bench Division, 1957–64; a Lord Justice of Appeal, 1964–72. Chairman: Royal Commission on the Working of the Tribunals of Inquiry (Evidence) Act, 1921, 1966; Royal Commission on Standards of Conduct in Public Life, 1974–76. Commissioned Royal Artillery, 1940. 8th Army HQ Staff, 1943–44. JP (Kent), 1949. Commissioner of Assize, Wales and Chester Circuit, 1955. Captain of the Royal St George's, Sandwich, 1972–73. Commissary of Cambridge Univ., 1979–. Governor of Mill Hill School. Hon. Fellow, Pembroke College, Cambridge. Hon. DCL Kent, 1978; Hon. LLD Cambridge, 1982. *Recreations:* golf, fishing. *Address:* Manwood House, Sandwich, Kent. *T:* Sandwich 612244. *Clubs:* Athenæum, Brooks's.
See also A. G. Robinson.

SALMON, Brian Lawson, CBE 1972; Chairman, J. Lyons & Co. Ltd, 1972–77 (Director, 1961–77, Joint Managing Director, 1967–69, Deputy Chairman, 1969–71); *b* 30 June 1917; *s* of Julius Salmon; *m* 1946, Annette Wilson Mackay; two *s* one *d*. *Educ:* Grenham Hse; Malvern Coll. Chm., Cttee on Sen. Nursing Staff Structure, 1963–66. Vice-Chm., Bd of Governors, Westminster Hosp. Gp, 1963–74; Chairman: Camden and Islington AHA, 1974–77; Supply Bd Working Gp, DHSS, 1977–78. *Recreations:* theatre, ballet, food and wine. *Address:* 34 Kingston House North, Princes Gate, SW7 1LN.
See also N. L. Salmon.

SALMON, Air Vice-Marshal Sir Cyril John Roderic; *see* Salmon, Air Vice-Marshal Sir Roderic.

SALMON, Geoffrey Isidore Hamilton, CBE 1954; President, J. Lyons & Co. Ltd, 1972–77 (Chairman, 1968–72); *b* 14 Jan. 1908; *s* of Harry Salmon and Lena (*née* Gluckstein); *m* 1936, Peggy Rica (*née* Jacobs); two *s* one *d*. *Educ:* Malvern Coll.; Jesus Coll., Cambridge (BA). Hon. Catering Adviser to the Army, 1959–71. *Address:* 10 Stavordale Lodge, Melbury Road, W14 8LW. *T:* 01–602 3425.

SALMON, Dame Nancy (Marion); *see* Snagge, Dame Nancy.

SALMON, Neil Lawson; consultant; *b* 17 Feb. 1921; *s* of Julius and Mimi Salmon; *m* 1944, Yvonne Hélène Isaacs; one *s* one *d*. *Educ:* Malvern Coll., Malvern; Institut Minerva, Zürich. Trainee, J. Lyons & Co. Ltd, 1938–41. Served War (Army), 1941–46. Gen. Manager, J. Lyons & Co., 1947; Chm., Glacier Foods Ltd, 1962; Dir, J. Lyons & Co., 1965; Jt Managing Dir, 1967; Gp Managing Dir, 1969; Dep. Chm. and Man. Dir, 1972; Chm., 1977–78; Dep. Chm., 1978–81. Dir, Allied Breweries (now Allied-Lyons), 1978–81. Member: Restrictive Practices Court, 1971–; Monopolies and Mergers Commn, 1980–. CBIM. *Recreations:* opera, ballet, theatre, wine. *Address:* c/o Eldon House, 1 Dorset Street, W1H 3FB. *T:* 01–581 4501. *Club:* Savile.

SALMON, Thomas David; Assistant to Speaker's Counsel, House of Commons, 1980–86; *b* 1 Nov. 1916; *s* of late Rev. Thomas Salmon and Isabel Salmon (*née* Littleton), North Stoneham, Hants; *m* 1950, Morris Patricia Reyner Turner, Ilford, Essex; one *s* two *d*. *Educ:* Winchester Coll.; Christ Church, Oxford (MA). Served War of 1939–45: Captain 133 Field Regt RA (despatches). Temp. Asst Principal, Cabinet Office, 1946. Admitted Solicitor, 1949; entered Treasury Solicitor's Dept, 1951; transf. to Bd of Trade, 1966; Under-Sec. (Legal), Solicitors' Dept, Depts of Industry and Trade, 1973–80, retired.

Recreations: walking, study of history and languages, gardening. *Address:* Tenures, 23 Sole Farm Road, Great Bookham, Surrey KT23 3DW. *T:* Bookham 52837.

SALMON, Very Rev. Thomas Noel Desmond Cornwall; Dean of Christ Church, Dublin, since 1967; *b* Dublin, 5 Feb. 1913; *s* of Francis Allen Cornwall Salmon, BDS, and Emma Sophia, *d* of Dr Hamilton Jolly, Clonroche, Co. Wexford; unmarried. *Educ:* privately; Trinity College, Dublin; BA 1935, MA, BD. Deacon 1937; Priest 1938. Curate Assistant: Bangor, Co. Down, 1937–40; St James' Belfast, 1940–42; Larne, Co. Antrim, 1942–44; Clerical Vicar, Christ Church Cathedral, 1944–45; Curate Assistant, Rathfarnham, Dublin, 1945–50; Incumbent: Tullow, Carrickmines, 1950–62; St Ann, Dublin, 1962–67. Asst Lectr in Divinity School, TCD, 1945–63; Examining Chaplain to Archbishop of Dublin, 1949–. *Recreations:* in younger days Rugby football (Monkstown FC Dublin) and swimming; now walking, gardening and reading. *Address:* 13 Merlyn Park, Ballsbridge, Dublin 4. *T:* 694780.

SALMON, Col William Alexander, OBE 1956; Assistant Ecclesiastical Secretary to Lord Chancellor, 1964–77, and to Prime Minister, 1964–77, retired; *b* 16 Nov. 1910; *o s* of late Lt-Colonel W. H. B. Salmon, late IA; *m* 1939, Jean Barbara Macmillan (*d* 1982), *o d* of late J. V. Macmillan, DD, OBE (Bishop of Guildford, 1934–49); one *s* two *d*. *Educ:* Haileybury College; RMC, Sandhurst. Commissioned 2nd Lt HLI 1930; ADC to Governor of Sind, 1936–38. Served during War of 1939–45: France, 1939; Middle East, Italy, Greece, Bde Major, 1942; GSO2 HQ Aegean Force, 1943; CO, 2nd Bn Beds and Herts Regt, 1945–46. CO, 2nd Bn Royal Irish Fusiliers, 1946–47; GSO1 (Trng), HQ Scottish Command, 1947–49; Chief of Staff to Lt-Gen. Glubb Pasha, HQ Arab Legion, 1950–53; CO 1st Bn HLI, 1953–55; Col, GS (O and T Div.) SHAPE, 1957–59; AQMG (QAE2), The War Office, 1959–62; AAG (AG14), The War Office, 1962–63; retd 1963. Life Governor, Haileybury and Imperial Service Coll., 1965–. Hashemite Order of El Istiqlal (2nd Cl.), 1953. *Publication:* Churches and Royal Patronage, 1983. *Recreations:* shooting, fishing, gardening. *Address:* Great Maytham Hall, Rolvenden, Kent TN17 4NE. *Club:* Army and Navy.

SALOMON, Sir Walter (Hans), Kt 1982; President, Rea Brothers Plc, Merchant Bank, since 1984 (Chairman, 1950–84); Director, Canal-Randolph Corporation; *b* 16 April 1906; *s* of Henry Salomon and Rena (*née* Oppenheimer); *m* 1935; one *s* one *d*. *Educ:* Oberreal, Eppendorf, Hamburg; Hamburg Univ. FIB 1964. Member of Lloyd's, 1958; Member of Baltic Exchange, 1957; Life President, Young Enterprise (Founder, 1963); Vice-Pres., Cambridge Settlement; Freeman, City of London; Master, Pattenmakers' Co., 1977–78; Member: Luso-Brazilian Council; Anglo-Portuguese Soc.; Hudson Institute, 1976; 1001 Club (World Wildlife), 1973. Has lectured widely on economic and financial matters. Comdr, Southern Cross of Brazil, 1971. Officer's Cross (1 Cl.) of the Order of Merit of the Federal Republic of Germany, 1979. *Publications:* One Man's View, 1973; Fair Warning, 1983; numerous newspaper articles. *Recreations:* yachting, ski-ing, art, bridge, snooker. *Address:* Castlemaine House, 21–22 St James's Place, SW1A 1NH. *T:* 01–493 1273. *Clubs:* Reform, City Livery, Canning House 1001, Royal Automobile, Hurlingham; Wentworth Golf; Norddeutscher Regatta-Verein Hamburg; Poole Harbour and Royal Torbay Yacht.

SALOP, Archdeacon of; *see* Jeffery, Ven. R. M. C.

SALT, Sir Anthony (Houlton), 6th Bt *cr* 1869; Director, Williams de Broe Hill Chaplin & Co. (Stockbrokers), 1968–85 (Chairman, 1981–84); *b* 15 Sept. 1931; *s* of Sir John Salt, 4th Bt, and Stella Houlton Jackson (*d* 1974); *S* brother, 1978; *m* 1957, Prudence Meath Baker; four *d*. *Educ:* Stowe. Member of the Stock Exchange, 1957; Partner, Hill Chaplin & Co. (Stockbrokers), 1957. *Heir: b* Patrick MacDonnell Salt [*b* 25 Sept. 1932; *m* 1976, Ann Elizabeth Mary, *d* of late Dr T. K. MacLachlan]. *Address:* Dellow House, Ugley Green, Bishop's Stortford, Herts. *T:* Bishop's Stortford 813141. *Club:* City of London.

SALT, George, FRS 1956; ScD; Fellow of King's College, Cambridge, since 1933; Reader in Animal Ecology, University of Cambridge, 1965–71, now Emeritus; *b* Loughborough, 12 Dec. 1903; *s* of late Walter Salt and Mary Cecilia (*née* Hulme); *m* 1939, Joyce Laing, Newnham Coll. and Stockton-on-Tees; two *s*. *Educ:* Crescent Heights Collegiate Inst., Calgary; Univ. of Alberta (BSc); Harvard Univ. (SM, SD); Univ. of Cambridge (PhD, ScD). National Research Fellow, Harvard Univ., 1927–28; Entomologist, Imperial Inst. Entom, 1929–31; Royal Soc. Moseley Research Student, 1932–33; Univ. Lectr in Zoology, Cambridge, 1937–65; Fellow of King's Coll., Cambridge, 1933–, Dean, 1939–45, Tutor for Advanced Students, 1945–51. Visiting Prof. Univ. of California, Berkeley, 1966. On biological expedns in NW Canada and Rocky Mts, Cuba, Republic of Colombia, E Africa, Pakistan. *Publications:* The Cellular Defence Reactions of Insects, 1970; papers in scientific jls on insect parasitism and ecology. *Recreations:* mountaineering, gardening, calligraphy and palaeography. *Address:* King's College, Cambridge; 21 Barton Road, Cambridge. *T:* Cambridge 355450.

SALT, Sir (Thomas) Michael (John), 4th Bt, *cr* 1899; *b* 7 Nov. 1946; *s* of Lt-Col Sir Thomas Henry Salt, 3rd Bt, and Meriel Sophia Wilmot, *d* of late Capt. Berkeley C. W. Williams and Hon. Mrs Williams, Herringston, Dorchester; *S* father 1965; *m* 1971, Caroline, *er d* of Henry Hildyard; two *d*. *Educ:* Eton. *Heir: b* Anthony William David Salt [*b* 5 Feb. 1950; *m* 1978, Olivia Anne, *yr d* of Martin Morgan Hudson; two *s*]. *Recreations:* cricket, shooting. *Address:* Shillingstone House, Shillingstone, Dorset. *Club:* Boodle's.

SALTER, Harry Charles, CMG 1983; DFC 1945; Consultant Adviser on European Community Affairs; *b* 29 July 1918; *er s* of late Harry Arnold Salter and Irene Beatrice Salter; *m* 1st, 1946, Anne Hooper (marr. diss. 1980); one *d*; 2nd, 1983, Mrs Janet Watford. *Educ:* St Albans Sch. Entered Ministry of Health, 1936. Served War, Royal Artillery, 1939–46 (despatches, DFC). Asst Sec., Min. of Health, 1963; Under-Sec., DHSS, 1971–73; Dir, Financing of Community Budget, EEC, 1973–82, retd. *Recreations:* golf, bridge, walking, cooking. *Address:* 47 Avenue Chapelle aux Champs, 1200 Brussels, Belgium. *T:* 770 36 71.

SALTER, Vice-Admiral Jocelyn Stuart Cambridge, CB 1954; DSO 1942 (Bar 1951); OBE 1942; *b* 24 Nov. 1901; *s* of late Henry Stuart Salter, of Messrs Lee, Bolton & Lee (Solicitors); *m* 1935, Joan (*d* 1971), *d* of late Rev. C. E. C. de Coetlogon, of the Indian Ecclesiastical Establishment; one *s* one *d*. *Educ:* Royal Naval Colleges, Osborne and Dartmouth. Joined Royal Navy, 1915; Midshipman, 1917; served European War in HMS Ramillies, Grand Fleet, 1917–19; Lieut 1923; Comdr 1937; Comd HMS Foresight in Force H, and in Home Fleet, 1941–42; Capt. 1942. Comd 16th Dest. Flotilla, 1944–45; Comd RN Air Station, Sembawang, Singapore, 1945–47; Comd HMS Jamaica, 1950–51 (served with UN Fleet in Korean waters); served on staff of SHAPE, 1951; ADC, 1951; Rear-Admiral, 1952; Vice-Admiral, 1954; Flag Officer, Malta, and Admiral Superintendent HM Dockyard, Malta, 1952–54; Admiral Superintendent HM Dockyard, Portsmouth, 1954–57; retired, 1957. Mem., Court of Assistants, Haberdashers' Company, Warden, 1958, 1963, 1968, Master, 1970. Norwegian Haakon VII Liberty Cross, 1946; United States Bronze Star medal, 1950. *Address:* Folly House, Hambledon, Hampshire. *T:* Hambledon 732.

SALTHOUSE, Edward Charles, PhD; CEng, FIEE; Master of University College, since 1979, Pro-Vice-Chancellor, since 1985, and First Chairman, School of Applied Science and Engineering, since 1985, Durham University; *b* 27 Dec. 1935; *s* of Edward Salthouse, MBE, and Mrs Salthouse (*née* Boyd); *m* 1961, Denise Kathleen Margot Reid; two *s*. *Educ:* Campbell Coll., Belfast; Queen's University of Belfast (BSc, PhD). Lecturer in Electrical Engrg, Univ. of Bristol, 1962–67; University of Durham: Reader in Elec. Engrg Science, 1967–79; Chairman, Board of Studies in Engrg Science, 1976–79; Dean, Faculty of Science, 1982–85. *Publications:* papers on electrical insulation in Proc. IEE and other appropriate jls. *Recreations:* travel by train, photography. *Address:* The Master's House, The Castle, Durham DH1 3RL. *T:* Durham 65481; Shieldaig, Hume, Kelso.

SALTHOUSE, Leonard; Assistant Under Secretary of State, Ministry of Defence, since 1977; *b* 15 April 1927; *s* of late Edward Keith Salthouse and Dorothy Annie (*née* Clark); *m* 1950, Kathleen May (*née* Spittle); one *s* one *d*. *Educ:* Queen Elizabeth Grammar Sch., Atherstone, Warwickshire; University Coll. London (BScEcon). Home Civil Service: Asst Principal, Min. of Fuel and Power, 1950–55; Principal, Air Min., then Min. of Defence, 1955–66; Asst Sec., 1966–77. *Recreations:* gardening, music. *Address:* Quilon, Hillcrest Waye, Gerrards Cross, Bucks SL9 8QF. *T:* Gerrards Cross 883677.

SALTON, Prof. Milton Robert James, FRS 1979; Professor and Chairman of Microbiology, New York University School of Medicine, since 1964; *b* 29 April 1921; *s* of Robert Alexander Salton and Stella Salton; *m* 1951, Joy Marriott; two *s*. *Educ:* Univ. of Sydney (BSc Agr. 1945); Univ. of Cambridge (PhD 1951, ScD 1967). Beit Meml Res. Fellow, Univ. of Cambridge, 1950–52; Merck Internat. Fellow, Univ. of California, Berkeley, 1952–53; Reader, Univ. of Manchester, 1956–61; Prof. of Microbiology, Univ. of NSW, Australia, 1962–64. Docteur en Médecine, *Dhc*, Université de Liège, 1967. *Publications:* Microbial Cell Walls, 1960; The Bacterial Cell Wall, 1964; Immunochemistry of Enzymes and their Antibodies, 1978; β-Lactam Antibiotics, 1981. *Address:* Department of Microbiology, New York University School of Medicine, 550 First Avenue, New York, NY 10016, USA. *Club:* United Oxford & Cambridge University.

SALTOUN, Lady (20th in line) *cr* 1445, of Abernethy; **Flora Marjory Fraser;** Chief of Clan Fraser; *b* 18 Oct. 1930; *d* of 19th Lord Saltoun, MC, and Dorothy (*d* 1985), *e d* of Sir Charles Welby, 5th Bt; *S* father, 1979; *m* 1956, Captain Alexander Ramsay of Mar, Grenadier Guards retd, *o s* of late Adm. Hon. Sir Alexander Ramsay, GCVO, KCB, DSO, and The Lady Patricia Ramsay, CI, VA, CD; three *d*. *Heiress: d* Hon. Katharine Ingrid Mary Isabel Fraser [*b* 11 Oct. 1957; *m* 1980, Captain Mark Malise Nicolson, Irish Guards; one *d*]. *Address:* Cairnbulg Castle, Fraserburgh, Aberdeenshire AB4 5TN.

SALTZMAN, Charles Eskridge, OBE (Hon.) 1943; DSM 1945 (US); Legion of Merit (US) 1943; Partner, Goldman, Sachs & Co. (investment banking), 1956, Limited Partner since 1973; *b* 19 Sept. 1903; *s* of Maj.-Gen. Charles McKinley Saltzman and Mary Saltzman (*née* Eskridge); *m* 1st, 1931, Gertrude Lamont (marr. diss.); one *s*; 2nd, 1947, Cynthia Southall Myrick (marr. diss.); two *d* (one *s* decd); 3rd, 1978, Clotilde McCormick (*née* Knapp). *Educ:* Cornell Univ.; US Mil. Acad.; Magdalen College, Oxford University. BS (US Mil. Acad.); BA, MA (Rhodes Scholar) (Oxford Univ.). Served as 2nd Lt, Corps of Engrs, US Army, 1925–30; commissioned 1st Lieut, NY National Guard, 1930; Lieutenant-Colonel 1940; on active duty in US Army, 1940–46, serving overseas, 1942–46; Brigadier-General 1945; relieved from active duty, 1946; Maj.-Gen. AUS (Retd). With NY Telephone Co., 1930–35; with NY Stock Exchange, 1935–49 (Asst to Exec. Vice-Pres., later Sec. and Vice-Pres.). Asst Sec. of State, 1947–49; Partner Henry Sears & Co., 1949–56; Under-Sec. of State for Admin., 1954–55. Former Dir, Continental Can Co. and A. H. Robins Co., Inc. President: English-Speaking Union of the US, 1961–66 (now Hon. Director); Assoc. of Graduates, US Mil. Academy, 1974–78 (Emeritus Trustee); Mem. Pilgrims of the United States. Hon. Mem., Soc. of the Cincinnati. Member, Director, or Trustee of many boards, societies and religious, philanthropic and educational institutions. Hon. Dr Mil. Sci. Mil. Coll. of S Carolina, 1984. Holds foreign decorations. *Address:* (home) 30 E 62nd Street, New York, NY 10021, USA. *T:* (212) 759–5655; (office) 85 Broad Street, New York, NY 10004. *T:* (212) 902–1000. *Clubs:* Century Association, Union, University (New York); Metropolitan (Washington).

SALUSBURY-TRELAWNY, Sir J. B.; *see* Trelawny.

SAMARAKOON, Hon. Neville Dunbar Mirahawatte; Chief Justice, Democratic Socialist Republic of Sri Lanka, 1977–84; *b* 22 Oct. 1919; *s* of Alfred Charles Warnabarana Wickremasinghe Samarakoon and Rajapaksa Wasala Mudiyanselage Chandrawati Mirahawatte Kumarihamy; *m* 1949, Mary Patricia Mulholland; one *s* two *d*. *Educ:* Trinity Coll., Kandy; University Coll., Colombo; Law Coll., Colombo. Enrolled as Advocate, 1945; Crown Counsel, Attorney-General's Dept, 1948–51; reverted to Private Bar, 1951; QC 1968. Member: Bar Council, 1964–77; Disciplinary Bd for Lawyers 1971–74, 1976, 1977. Chairman: Judicial Service Commn, 1978–; Council of Legal Educn. *Address:* 129 Wijerama Mawatha, Colombo 7, Sri Lanka. *T:* Colombo 595364.

SAMARANCH, Juan Antonio; President, International Olympic Committee, since 1980 (Member, since 1966); *b* 17 July 1920; *s* of Francisco Samaranch and Juana Torello; *m* 1955, Maria Teresa Salisachs Rowe; one *s* one *d*. *Educ:* Instituto Superior Estudios de Empresas, Barcelona; German College; Higher Inst. of Business Studies, Barcelona. Industrialist, Bank Consultant; Pres., Barcelona Diputacion, 1975; Ambassador to USSR and to People's Republic of Mongolia, 1977–80. Mem., Spanish Olympic Cttee, 1954 (Pres., 1967–70); Nat. Deleg. for Physical Educn and Sport. Holds numerous decorations. *Publications:* Deporte 2000, 1967; Olympic Message, 1980. *Recreation:* philately. *Address:* Avenida Pau Casals, 24 Barcelona-08021, Spain. *T:* 209–07–22; International Olympic Committee, Château de Vidy, 1007 Lausanne, Switzerland. *T:* 253271.

SAMBROOK, Gordon Hartley, CBE 1986; Member, Board, since 1978, and Chairman and Group Executive, General Steels Group, since 1980, British Steel Corporation; *b* 9 Jan. 1930; *m* 1956, Patricia Joan Mary Havard; one *s*. *Educ:* Sheffield Univ. (BA(Hons), DipEd). Graduate Apprentice, Utd Steel, 1954; United Steel Cos, 1954–68; British Steel Corporation: General Manager, Rotherham, 1972; Dir, Tinplate Gp, 1973–75; Man. Dir, Personnel, 1975–77; Man. Dir, Commercial, 1977–80. Director: Allied Steel & Wire Ltd, 1981–; United Merchant Bar PLC, 1985–; United Engineering Ltd, 1986–; Tuscaloosa Steel Inc., 1985–. Chairman: Iron Trades Employers' Insce Assoc., 1984–; Iron Trades Mutual Insce Co., 1984–.

SAMBROOK, Prof. Joseph Frank, PhD; FRS 1985; Professor and Chairman, Department of Biochemistry, University of Texas Health Science Center, Dallas, since 1985; *b* 1 March 1939; *s* of Thomas and Ethel Gertrude (*née* Lightfoot); *m* 1960, Thelma McGrady (marr. diss. 1984); two *s* one *d*; *m* 1986, Mary-Jane Gething. *Educ:* Liverpool Univ. (BSc 1962); Australian Nat. Univ. (PhD 1965). Res. Fellow, John Curtin Sch. of Med. Res., ANU, 1965–66; Postdoctoral Fellow, MRC Lab. of Molecular Biol., 1966–67; Jun. Fellow, Salk Inst. for Biol Studies, 1967–69; Sen. Staff Investigator, 1969–77, Asst Dir, 1977–85, Cold Spring Harbor Lab. Editor-in-chief, Molecular Biology Medicine, 1984–. *Publications:*

contribs to learned jls. *Recreation:* music. *Address:* 4320 Irvin Simmons Drive, Dallas, Texas 75229, USA. *T:* (214) 688–3723.

SAMMAN, Peter Derrick, MD, FRCP; Physician to Dermatological Department, Westminster Hospital, 1951–79, and St John's Hospital for Diseases of the Skin, 1959–79; Consultant Dermatologist, Orpington and Sevenoaks Hospitals, 1951–77; Dean, Institute of Dermatology, 1965–70; *b* 20 March 1914; *y s* of Herbert Frederick Samman and Emily Elizabeth Savage; *m* 1953, Judith Mary Kelly; three *d. Educ:* King William's Coll., IOM; Emmanual Coll., Cambridge; King's Coll. Hosp., London. BA (Nat. Scis. Tripos), 1936; MB, BChir Cantab 1939; MRCP 1946; MA, MD Cantab 1948; FRCP 1963. House Surg., King's Coll. Hosp., 1939; Sqdn Ldr, RAFVR, 1940–45; House Phys. and Registrar, King's Coll. Hosp., 1946; Sen. Dermatological Registrar and Tutor in Dermatology, United Bristol Hosps, 1947–48; Sen. Registrar, St John's Hosp. for Diseases of the Skin, 1949–50. FRSocMed; Mem. Brit. Assoc. of Dermatology; Hon. Mem., Dermatological Soc. of S Africa. *Publications:* The Nails in Disease, 1965, 4th edn 1986; chapters in Textbook of Dermatology (ed Rook, Wilkinson and Ebling), 1968; (jtly) Tutorials in Postgraduate Medicine: Dermatology, 1977; various articles in med. jls. *Recreation:* gardening. *Address:* 18 Sutherland Avenue, Orpington, Kent. *T:* Orpington 20839.

SAMPLES, Reginald McCartney, CMG 1971; DSO 1942; OBE 1963; HM Diplomatic Service, retired; *b* 11 Aug. 1918; *o s* of late William and Jessie Samples; *m* 1947, Elsie Roberts Hide; two *s* one step *d. Educ:* Rhyl Grammar Sch.; Liverpool Univ. (BCom). Served, 1940–46; RNVR (Air Branch); torpedo action with 825 Sqn against German ships Scharnhorst, Gneisenau and Prinz Eugen in English Channel (wounded, DSO); Lieut (A). Central Office of Information (Economic Editor, Overseas Newspapers), 1947–48. CRO (Brit. Inf. Services, India), 1948; Economic Information Officer, Bombay, 1948–52; Editor-in-Chief, BIS, New Delhi, 1952; Dep.-Dir, BIS, New Delhi, 1952–56; Dir, BIS, Pakistan (Karachi), 1956–59; Dir, BIS, Canada (Ottawa), 1959–65, OBE; Counsellor (Information) to Brit. High Comr, India, and Dir, BIS, India (New Delhi), 1965–68; Asst Under-Sec. of State, Commonwealth Office, 1968; Head of British Govt Office, and Sen. British Trade Comr, Toronto, 1969; Consul-Gen., Toronto, 1974–78. Asst Dir, Royal Ontario Museum, 1978–83. *Recreations:* tennis, watching ballet. *Address:* Apartment 1105, 44 Jackes Avenue, Toronto, Ontario M4T 1E5, Canada. *Clubs:* Naval; York, Queens (Toronto).

SAMPSON, Anthony (Terrell Seward); writer and journalist; *b* 3 Aug. 1926; *s* of Michael Sampson and Phyllis, *d* of Sir Albert Seward, FRS; *m* 1965, Sally, *d* of Dr P. G. Bentlif, Jersey, and of Mrs G. Denison-Smith, Islip, Oxon; one *s* one *d. Educ:* Westminster School; Christ Church, Oxford. Served with Royal Navy, 1944–47; Sub-Lieut, RNVR, 1946. Editor of Drum Magazine, Johannesburg, 1951–55; Editorial staff of The Observer, 1955–66; Associate Prof., Univ. of Vincennes, Paris, 1968–70; Chief American Corresp., The Observer, 1973–74. Contributing Editor, Newsweek, 1977–; Editorial Conslt, The Brandt Commn, 1978–79; Editor, The Sampson Letter, 1984–86. *Publications:* Drum, a Venture into the New Africa, 1956; The Treason Cage, 1958; Commonsense about Africa, 1960; (with S. Pienaar) South Africa: two views of Separate Development 1960; Anatomy of Britain, 1962; Anatomy of Britain Today, 1965; Macmillan: a study in ambiguity, 1967; The New Europeans, 1968; The New Anatomy of Britain, 1971; The Sovereign State: the secret history of ITT, 1973; The Seven Sisters, 1975 (Prix International de la Presse, Nice, 1976); The Arms Bazaar, 1977; The Money Lenders, 1981; The Changing Anatomy of Britain, 1982; Empires of the Sky, 1984; (with Sally Sampson) The Oxford Book of Ages, 1985. *Recreations:* vertical gardening, opera. *Address:* 27 Ladbroke Grove, W11. *T:* 01–727 4188, 01–221 5738; Quarry Garden, Wardour, Wilts. *T:* Tisbury 870407. *Clubs:* Beefsteak, Groucho.

SAMPSON, Colin, QPM 1978; Chief Constable of West Yorkshire, since 1983; *b* 26 May 1929; *s* of James and Nellie Sampson; *m* 1953, Kathleen Stones; two *s. Educ:* Stanley Sch., Wakefield. Joined Police Force, 1949; served mainly in the CID (incl. training of detectives), at Dewsbury, Skipton, Doncaster, Goole, Wakefield, Huddersfield, Rotherham, Barnsley; Comdt, Home Office Detective Trng Sch., Wakefield, 1971–72; Asst Chief Constable, West Yorks, 1973; Dep. Chief Constable, Notts, 1976. *Recreations:* choral music, walking, gardening. *Address:* Kidroyd House, Shepley, near Huddersfield.

SAMSOVA, Galina; producer; a Principal Dancer, Sadler's Wells Royal Ballet, since 1980; Teacher with the company in the Royal Ballet and Royal Ballet School; *b* Stalingrad, 1937; *d* of a Byelorussian; *m* 1st, Alexander Ursulia; 2nd, André Prokovsky. *Educ:* the Ballet Sch., Kiev (pupil of N. Verekundova). Joined Kiev Ballet, 1956 and became a soloist; Canadian Ballet, 1961; created chief rôle in Cendrillon, Paris 1963 (Gold Medal for best danseuse of Paris Festival). Ballerina, Festival Ballet, 1964–73; headed the group of André Prokovsky, The New London Ballet, (disbanded in 1977, revived for 3 new productions, The Theatre Royal, York, 1979); has danced principal rôles in Sleeping Beauty, Nutcracker, Giselle, Swan Lake, Anna Karenina, and other classical ballets; danced in Europe, Far East and USA. Produced: Sequence from Paquita, Sadler's Wells, 1980; (with Peter Wright) Swan Lake, Sadler's Wells, 1983; Giselle, London City Ballet, 1986. *Address:* Royal Ballet School, 155 Talgarth Road, W14.

SAMUEL, family name of **Viscounts Bearsted** and **Samuel** and **Baron Samuel of Wych Cross.**

SAMUEL, 3rd Viscount *cr* 1937, of Mount Carmel and of Toxteth, Liverpool; **David Herbert Samuel;** Sherman Professor of Physical Chemistry, since 1967, and Director, Center for Neurosciences and Behavioral Research, since 1978, Weizmann Institute, Rehovot, Israel; *b* 8 July 1922; *s* of 2nd Viscount Samuel, CMG, and Hadassah (*d* 1986), *d* of Judah Goor (Grasovsky); *S* father, 1978; *m* 1st, 1950, Esther Berelowitz (marr. diss. 1957); one *d*; 2nd, 1960, Rinna Dafni (*née* Grossman) (marr. diss. 1978); one *d*; 3rd, 1980, Veronika Engelhardt Grimm. *Educ:* Balliol Coll., Oxford (MA 1948); Hebrew Univ. (PhD 1953). Served War of 1939–45 (despatches); Captain RA, in India, Burma and Sumatra. Member of Isotope Dept, 1949–86, of Dept of Neurobiology, 1986–, Weizmann Inst. of Sci., Rehovot, Israel; Head, Chemistry Gp, Science Teaching Dept, 1967–83; Dean, Faculty of Chemistry, 1971–73; Chm., Bd of Studies in Chemistry, Feinberg Grad. Sch., 1968–74. Post-doctoral Fellow, Chem. Dept, UCL, 1956; Res. Fellow, Chem. Dept, Harvard Univ., 1957–58; Res. Fellow, Lab. of Chemical Biodynamics (Lawrence Radiation Lab.), Univ. of California, Berkeley, 1965–66; Visiting Professor: Sch. of Molecular Scis, Univ. of Warwick, 1967; MRC Neuroimmunology Unit, Zoology Dept, UCL, 1974–75; Pharmacol. Dept, Yale Sch. of Medicine, 1983–84; McLaughlin Prof., Sch. of Medicine, McMaster Univ., 1984. Member: Adv. Bd, Bat-Sheva de Rothschild Foundn for Advancement of Science in Israel, 1970–83; Bd, US-Israel Educnl (Fulbright) Foundn, 1969–74 (Chm., 1974–75); Bd, Israel Center for Scientific and Technol Information, 1970–74; Scientific Adv. Cttee and Bd of Trustees of Israel Center for Psychobiol., 1973–; Acad. Adv. Cttee, Everyman's (Open) Univ., 1976–83; Bd of Govs, Bezalel Acad. of Arts and Design, 1977–; Council, Israel Chemical Soc., 1977–83; Internat. Brain Res. Org. (IBRO), 1977–; Israel Exec. Cttee, America-Israel Cultural Foundn, 1978–; Bd of Governors, Tel Aviv Museum, 1980–; Cttee on Teaching of Chemistry, IUPAC, 1981–; Anglo-Israel Assoc., 1985–; British Israel Arts Foundn, 1986–. *Publications:* more than 200 papers, reviews and parts of collective volumes on isotopes, physical chemistry, reaction mechanisms, neurochemistry, psychopharmacology, animal behavior and science teaching; on editl bds of: Alzheimer Disease and Related Disorders; Brain Behaviour and Immunity; Jl of Labelled Compounds and Radiopharmaceuticals. *Heir: b* Hon. Dan Judah Samuel [*b* 25 March 1925; *m* 1st, 1957, Nonni (Esther) (marr. diss. 1977), *d* of late Max Gordon, Johannesburg; one *s* two *d*; 2nd, 1981, Heather, *d* of Angus and Elsa Cumming, Haywards Heath; one *s* one *d*]. *Address:* Weizmann Institute of Science, Rehovot, Israel. *T:* 08–483117.

SAMUEL OF WYCH CROSS, Baron *cr* 1972 (Life Peer), of Wych Cross, Sussex; **Harold Samuel,** Kt 1963; FRICS; Hon. Fellow: Magdalene College, Cambridge, 1961; University College, London, 1968; Chairman, Land Securities PLC; President, The Central London Housing Trust for the Aged; *b* London, 23 April 1912; *s* of late Vivian and Ada Samuel; *m* 1936, Edna Nedas; two *d* (and one *d* decd). *Educ:* Mill Hill School; College of Estate Management. Dir, Railway Sites Ltd (British Rail), 1962–65. Member: Covent Garden Market Authority, 1961–74; Special (Rebuilding) Cttee, RICS, 1962–76; Land Commn, 1967–70; Reserve Pension Bd, 1974; Crown Estate Comrs Regent St Cttee. Member: Court of The City Univ.; Court of Univ. of Sussex; Court of Univ. Coll. of Swansea; Court of Patrons, RCS; a Vice-Pres., British Heart Foundation; Trustee, Mill Hill Sch. *Recreations:* swimming, horticulture. *Address:* 75 Avenue Road, Regent's Park, NW8 6JD; Wych Cross Place, Forest Row, East Sussex RH18 5JJ. *Club:* East India, Devonshire, Sports and Public Schools.

SAMUEL, Adrian Christopher Ian, CMG 1959; CVO 1963; *b* 20 Aug. 1915; *s* of late George Christopher Samuel and Alma Richards; *m* 1942, Sheila, *er d* of late J. C. Barrett, Killiney, Co. Dublin; three *s* one *d. Educ:* Rugby Sch.; St John's Coll., Oxford. Entered HM Consular Service, 1938; served at Beirut, Tunis and Trieste. Served War, 1940–44, in Royal Air Force. Returned to HM Foreign Service and served at HM Embassies in Ankara, Cairo and Damascus; First Secretary, 1947; Counsellor, 1956; Principal Private Secretary to the Secretary of State for Foreign Affairs, Oct. 1959–63; Minister at HM Embassy, Madrid, 1963–65; resigned 1965. Director: British Chemical Engrg Contractors Assoc., 1966–69; British Agrochemicals Assoc., 1972–78; Dir-Gen., Groupement Internat. des Assocs Nats de Fabricants de Pesticides (GIFAP), 1978–79. *Publication:* An Astonishing Fellow: a life of Sir Robert Wilson, KMT, MP, 1986. *Recreations:* golf, shooting and reading. *Address:* The Laundry House, Handcross, near Haywards Heath, West Sussex RH17 6HQ. *T:* Handcross 400717. *Club:* Garrick.

SAMUEL, Sir John (Michael Glen), 5th Bt, *cr* 1898; Chairman, Whisper Electric Car A/S, Denmark, since 1984; *b* 25 Jan. 1944; *o s* of Sir John Oliver Cecil Samuel, 4th Bt, and of Charlotte Mary, *d* of late R. H. Hoyt, Calgary, Canada; *S* father, 1962; *m* 1st, 1966, Antoinette Sandra, *d* of late Captain Antony Hewitt, RE, 2nd SAS Regt, and of Mrs K. A. H. Casson, Frith Farm, Wolverton, Hants; two *s*; 2nd, 1982, Mrs Elizabeth Ann Molinari, *y d* of Major R. G. Curry, Bournemouth, Dorset. *Educ:* Radley; London Univ. Director: Enfield Automotive, 1967–70; Advanced Vehicle Systems Ltd, 1971–78; Chm., Electric Auto Corp. (USA), 1978–83. *Recreations:* motor racing, water ski-ing. *Heir: s* Anthony John Fulton Samuel, *b* 13 Oct. 1972.

SAMUEL, Hon. Peter Montefiore, MC 1942; TD 1951; Banker; Director, Hill, Samuel Group, since 1965 (Deputy Chairman, after merger with Philip Hill, Higginson & Co., 1965–82); Chairman: Dylon International Ltd, since 1958; Hill Samuel & Co. (Ireland) Ltd, 1964–84; *b* 9 Dec. 1911; second *s* of 2nd Viscount Bearsted and Dorothea, *e d* of late E. Montefiore Micholls; *b* and *heir-pres.* to 3rd Viscount Bearsted, *qv*; *m* 1st, 1939, Deirdre du Barry (marr. diss. 1942); 2nd, 1946, Hon. Elizabeth Adelaide Pearce Serocold (*d* 1983), *d* of late Baron Cohen, PC; two *s* one *d*; 3rd, 1984, Nina Alice Hilary, *widow* of Michael Pocock, CBE. *Educ:* Eton; New College, Oxford (BA). Served Warwickshire Yeo, Middle East and Italy, 1939–45. Director: M. Samuel & Co. Ltd, 1935 (Dep. Chm. 1948); Shell Transport & Trading Co. Ltd, 1938–82; Samuel Properties Ltd, 1961–86 (Chm., 1982–86); Mayborn Products Ltd (Chm.), 1946–; Trades Union Unit Trust Managers Ltd, 1961–82; General Consolidated Investment Trust Ltd, 1975–83. President, Norwood Home for Jewish Children, 1962–79; Hon. Treas., Nat. Assoc. for Gifted Children, 1968–81; Chm. Council, Royal Free Hospital of Medicine, 1973–82 (Mem., 1948–). *Recreations:* golf, fishing, shooting. *Address:* 9 Campden Hill Court, W8 7HX; Farley Hall, Farley Hill, near Reading, Berkshire RG7 1UL. *T:* Eversley 733242. *Club:* White's.

SAMUEL, Richard Christopher, CMG 1983; CVO 1983; HM Diplomatic Service; Under-Secretary for Asia and the Oceans, Overseas Development Administration, Foreign and Commonwealth Office, since 1986; *b* Edinburgh, 8 Aug. 1933. *Educ:* Durham Sch.; St John's Coll., Cambridge (BA). Royal Navy, 1952–54. FO, 1957–58; Warsaw, 1958–59; Rome, 1960–63; FO, 1963; Private Sec. to Parly Under-Sec. of State, 1965–68; Hong Kong, 1968–69; 1st Sec. and Head of Chancery: Singapore, 1969–71; Peking, 1971–73; Counsellor, Washington, 1973–76; Head of Far Eastern Dept, FCO, 1976–79; Counsellor (Commercial), Moscow, 1980–82; Minister and Dep. High Comr, New Delhi, 1982–85. *Recreations:* music, science fiction. *Address:* 41 Northumberland Place, W2 5AS. *T:* 01–229 8357.

SAMUELS; *see* Turner-Samuels.

SAMUELS, John Edward Anthony; QC 1981; a Recorder, since 1985; Joint Chairman, Inner London Education Authority Disciplinary Tribunals, since 1977; Alternate Chairman, Burnham Cttee, since 1981; *b* 15 Aug. 1940; *s* of late Albert Edward Samuels, solicitor, Reigate, Surrey; *m* 1967, Maxine (*née* Robertson), JP; two *s. Educ:* Charterhouse; Perugia; Queens' Coll., Cambridge (MA). Second Lieut, Queen's Royal Regt (TA), 1959; Lieut, Queen's Royal Surrey Regt (TA), 1961–67; RARO 1967. Chairman, Cambridge Univ. United Nations Assoc., 1962. Mansfield Schol., Lincoln's Inn, 1963; called to Bar, 1964; South Eastern Circuit; Mem., Senate of the Inns of Court and the Bar, 1983–; Mem., Council of Legal Educn, 1983–. Co-opted Mem., ILEA Education Cttee, 1964–67. Governor, Brixton College of Further Education, 1964–67. Member: Richmond, Twickenham and Roehampton HA, 1982–85; Kingston and Richmond Family Practitioner Cttee, 1982–86. Trustee, Richmond Parish Lands Charity, 1986–. *Publications:* contributor to Halsbury's Laws of England, 4th edn. *Recreation:* serendipity. *Address:* 3 Hare Court, Temple, EC4Y 7BJ. *T:* 01–583 4555; Spring House, Sheen Road, Richmond, Surrey. *Club:* Athenæum.

SAMUELS, Prof. Michael Louis; Professor of English Language, University of Glasgow, since 1959; *b* 1920; *s* of late Harry Samuels, OBE, MA, barrister-at-law, and Céline Samuels (*née* Aronowitz), London; *m* 1950, Hilary, *d* of late Julius and Ruth Samuel, Glasgow; one *d. Educ:* St Paul's School; Balliol College, Oxford. Domus Exhibitioner in Classics, Balliol College, Oxford, 1938–40 and 1945–47; MA 1947 (First Class Hons English Lang. and Lit.). Worked for Air Ministry (Maintenance Command), 1940–45. Research Fellow, University of Birmingham, 1947–48; Assistant in English Language, University of Edinburgh, 1948–49; Lecturer in English Language, Univ. of Edinburgh, 1949–59. *Publications:* Linguistic Evolution, 1972; articles and reviews in Trans Philological Soc., Medium Aevum, Review of English Studies, Archivum Linguisticum,

English Studies, English and Germanic Studies. *Address:* 4 Queen's Gate, Dowanhill, Glasgow G12 9DN. *T:* 041–334 4999.

SAMUELSON, Sir (Bernard) Michael (Francis), 5th Bt *cr* 1884; *b* 17 Jan. 1917; *s* of Sir Francis Henry Bernard Samuelson, 4th Bt, and Margaret Kendall (*d* 1980), *d* of H. Kendall Barnes; *S* father, 1981; *m* 1952, Janet Amy, *yr d* of Lt-Comdr L. G. Elkington, RN retd, Chelsea; two *s* two *d. Educ:* Eton. Served War of 1939–45 with RA and Leicestershire Regt (despatches). *Heir: s* James Francis Samuelson, *b* 20 Dec. 1956. *Address:* Hollingwood, Stunts Green, Herstmonceux, East Sussex.

SAMUELSON, Prof. Paul A.; Institute Professor, Massachusetts Institute of Technology, 1966–85, now Emeritus; *b* Gary, Indiana, 15 May 1915; *m* 1938, Marion Crawford (*d* 1978); four *s* two *d*; *m* 1981, Risha Claypool. *Educ:* Univs of Chicago (BS) and Harvard (MA, PhD). SSRC Predoctoral Fellow, 1935–37; Soc. of Fellows, Harvard, 1937–40; Guggenheim Fellow, 1948–49; Ford Faculty Research Fellow, 1958–59; Hoyt Vis. Fellow, Calhoun Coll., Yale, 1962; Carnegie Foundn Reflective Year, 1965–66. MIT: Asst Prof. of Econs, 1940; Assoc. Prof. of Econs, 1944; Staff Mem., Radiation Lab., 1944–45; Prof. of Econs, 1947; Prof. of Internat. Economic Relations (part-time), Fletcher Sch. of Law and Diplomacy, 1945. Consultant: to Nat. Resources Planning Bd, 1941–43; to Rand Corp., 1948–75; to US Treasury, 1945–52, 1961–; to Johnson Task Force on Sustained Prosperity, 1964; to Council of Econ. Advisers, 1960–; to Federal Reserve Bd, 1965–; to Congressional Budget Office, 1974–. Economic Adviser to Senator, Candidate and President-elect John F. Kennedy, informal adviser to President Kennedy. Member: War Prodn Bd and Office of War Mobilization and Reconstruction, 1945; Bureau of the Budget, 1952; Adv. Bd of Nat Commn on Money and Credit, 1958–60; Research Adv. Panel to President's Nat. Goals Commn, 1959–60; Research Adv. Bd Cttee for Econ. Develt, 1960; Nat. Task Force on Econ. Educn, 1960–61; Sen. Advr, Brookings Panel on Econ. Activity. Contrib. Editor and Columnist, Newsweek, 1966–81. Lectures: Stamp Meml, London, 1961; Wicksell, Stockholm, 1962; Franklin, Detroit, 1962; Gerhard Colm Meml, NYC, 1971; Davidson, Univ. of New Hampshire, 1971; 12th John von Neumann, Univ. of Wisconsin, 1971; J. Willard Gibbs, Amer. Mathematical Soc., 1974; 1st Sulzbacher, Columbia Law Sch., 1974; John Diebold, Harvard Univ., 1976; Alice Bourneauf, Boston Coll., 1981; Horowitz, Jerusalem and Tel Aviv, 1984; Marschak Meml, UCLA, 1984. Corresp. Fellow, British Acad., 1960; Fellow: Amer. Philosoph. Soc.; Econometric Soc. (Mem. Council; Vice-Pres. 1950; Pres. 1951); AAAS, 1985; Member: Amer. Acad. Arts and Sciences; Amer. Econ. Assoc. (Pres. 1961; Hon. Fellow, 1965); Phi Beta Kappa; Commn on Social Sciences (NSF), 1967–; Internat. Econ. Assoc. (Pres. 1965–68; Hon. Pres. 1968–); Nat. Acad. of Sciences, 1970–; Omicron Delta Epsilon, Bd of Trustees (Internat. Honor Soc. in Econ.). Hon. Fellow: LSE; Peruvian Sch. of Economics, 1980. David A. Wells Prize, Harvard, 1941; John Bates Clark Medal, Amer. Econ. Assoc., 1947; Medal of Honor, Univ. of Evansville, 1970; Nobel Prize in Econ. Science, 1970; Albert Einstein Commemorative Award, 1971; Alumni Medal, Chicago Univ., 1983. Hon. LLD: Chicago, 1961; Oberlin, 1961; Boston Coll., 1964; Indiana, 1966; Michigan, 1967; Claremont Grad. Sch., 1970; New Hampshire, 1971; Keio, Tokyo, 1971; Harvard, 1972; Gustavas Adolphus Coll., 1974; Univ. of Southern Calif, 1975; Univ. of Rochester, 1976; Univ. of Pennsylvania, 1976; Emmanuel Coll., 1977; Widener, 1982; Hon. DLitt: Ripon Coll., 1962; Northern Michigan Univ., 1973; Hon DSc: E Anglia, 1966; Massachusetts, 1972; Rhode Is., 1972; Hon. LHD: Seton Hall, 1971; Williams Coll., 1971; Stonehill Coll., 1978; *Dhc*: Université Catholique de Louvain, Belgium, 1976; Catholic Univ. at Riva Aguero Inst., Lima, 1980; City Univ. of London, 1980; DUniv, New Univ. of Lisbon, Portugal, 1985. *Publications:* Foundations of Economic Analysis, 1947, enlarged edn, 1982; Economics, 1948, 12th edn (ed with W. D. Nordhaus), 1985 (trans. 24 langs); (jtly) Linear Programming and Economic Analysis, 1958 (trans. French, Japanese); Readings in Economics, 1955; The Collected Scientific Papers of Paul A. Samuelson (ed J. E. Stiglitz), vols I and II, 1966, vol. III (ed R. C. Merton), 1972, vol. IV (ed H. Nagatani and K. Crowley), 1977; co-author, other books in field, papers in various jls, etc. *Recreation:* tennis. *Address:* Department of Economics, Massachusetts Institute of Technology E52–383, Cambridge, Mass 02139, USA. *T:* 617–253–3368. *Club:* Belmont Hill (Mass).

SAMUELSON, Sydney Wylie, CBE 1978; Chairman and Chief Executive, Samuelson Group plc; *b* 7 Dec. 1925; 2nd *s* of G. B. and Marjorie Samuelson; *m* 1949, Doris (*née* Magen); three *s. Educ:* Irene Avenue Council Sch., Lancing, Sussex. Served RAF, 1943–47. From age 14, career devoted to various aspects of British film industry: cinema projectionist, 1939–42; Asst Film Editor, 1943; Asst Film Cameraman, Cameraman and Dir of Documentary Films, 1947–59; founded company to service film and TV prodn organisations, supplying cameras and other technical equipment, with purchase of first camera, 1954; continued filming as technician on locations throughout world until 1959, when activities concentrated on expanding his company. Permanent Trustee and currently Chm. Bd of Management, BAFTA (Vice-Chm. Film, 1971–73, Chm. of Council, 1973–76); Member: Exec. Cttee, Cinema and Television Veterans (Pres., 1980–81); Exec. Cttee, Cinema and TV Benevolent Fund (Trustee, 1982–; Pres., 1983–86); Brit. Soc. of Cinematographers (Governor, 1969–79; 1st Vice-Pres., 1976–77; award for Outstanding Contribution to Film Industry, 1967); Associate Mem., Amer. Soc. of Cinematographers. Hon. Technical Adviser, Royal Naval Film Corp.; Hon. Fellow, Brit. Kinematograph Sound and TV Soc., 1970. Guild of Film Production Executives Award of Merit, 1986. Pres., UK Friends of Akim (Israel Assoc. for Mentally Handicapped); Vice Pres., Muscular Dystrophy Assoc. of GB. Michael Balcon Award, BAFTA, 1985. *Recreations:* collecting recorded film music, vintage motoring, veteran jogging (finished 13,006th London Marathon 1982). *Address:* 303–315 Cricklewood Broadway, NW2 6PQ.

SAMUELSSON, Prof. Bengt Ingemar; Professor of Medical and Physiological Chemistry, since 1972, and Rector, since 1983, Karolinska Institutet, Stockholm; *b* Halmstad, Sweden, 21 May 1934; *s* of Anders and Stina Samuelsson; *m* 1958, Inga Karin Bergstein; one *s* two *d. Educ:* Karolinska Institutet (DMedSci 1960, MD 1961). Res. Fellow, Harvard Univ., 1961–62; Asst Prof. of Med. Chemistry, Karolinska Inst, 1961–66; Prof., Royal Vet. Coll., Stockholm, 1967–72; Chm., Dept of Chemistry, 1973–83, Dean of Med. Faculty, 1978–83, Karolinska Inst, Stockholm. Vis. Prof., Harvard, 1976; T. Y. Shen Vis. Prof. in Med. Chem., MIT, 1977. Lectures: MacArthur, Univ. of Edinburgh, 1975; Shirley Johnson Meml, Philadelphia, 1977; Sixth Annual Marrs McLean, Houston, 1978; Rockwood Meml, Univ. of Iowa, 1978; Smith Kline and French, Vanderbilt Univ. Sch. of Medicine, 1979; Harvey, NY, 1979; Smith Kline and French Res., Philadelphia, 1979; Fifth McNeil-Ortho Chem., Philadelphia, 1980; Lane Medical, Stanford Univ., 1981; Shell, Univ. of Calif, 1981; Romanes, Univ. of Edinburgh, 1981; Eighth Annual Sci. in Med., Univ. of Washington, 1981; Fedn of European Chem. Socs, Helsinki, 1981; Arthur C. Corcoran Meml, Cleveland, Ohio, 1981; Carl V. Moore Meml, Washington Univ., 1982; Kober, Assoc. of Amer. Physicians, 1982; first Bayer, Yale Univ., 1983; Lorenzini Foundn, Milan, 1983; Brown-Razor, Rice Univ., Houston, 1984; Solomon A. Berson Meml, Mount Sinai Sch. of Medicine, NY, 1984; Immunology Council Annual, Johns Hopkins Univ., 1984; Dist. Lectr in Med. Scis, Mayo Foundn, 1980. Member: Royal Swedish Acad. of Scis, 1981–; Mediterranean Acad., Catania, 1982–; Swedish Govt Res. Adv. Bd, 1985–; Hon. Prof., Bethune Univ. of Med. Scis, China, 1986; Hon. Member: Amer. Soc. of Biological Chemists, 1976; Assoc. of American Physicians, 1982; Swedish Med. Assoc., 1982; Italian Pharmacological Soc., 1985; For. Associate, US Nat. Acad. of Scis, 1984; For. Hon. Mem., Amer. Acad. of Arts and Scis, 1982–. Nobel Prize in Physiology or Medicine (jtly), 1982; numerous awards, prizes and hon. degrees. *Publications:* papers on biochemistry of prostaglandins, thromboxanes and leukotrienes. *Address:* Department of Physiological Chemistry, Karolinska Institutet, S-104 01 Stockholm, Sweden. *T:* 08/34 05 60.

SAMWORTH, David Chetwode, CBE 1985; DL; Chairman, Samworth Brothers Ltd (formerly Gorran Foods Ltd), since 1984 (Director since 1981); *b* 25 June 1935; *s* of Frank and Phyllis Samworth; *m* 1969, Rosemary Grace Cadell; one *s* three *d. Educ:* Uppingham Sch. Chm., Pork Farms Ltd, 1968–81; Director: Northern Foods Ltd, 1978–81; Imperial Gp, 1983–85. Chm., Meat and Livestock Commn, 1980–84. Member: Leicester No 3 HMC, 1970–74; Trent RHA, 1974–78, 1980–84. DL Leics, 1984. *Recreations:* tennis, hunting. *Address:* Markham House, Thorpe Satchville, Melton Mowbray, Leics. *T:* Melton Mowbray 840510.

SAN VINCENZO FERRERI, 8th Marquis of, **Alfio Testaferrata Ghâxaq** (Marquis Testaferrata); *b* 1911; *s* of Daniel Testaferrata Bonici Ghâxaq and Agnese (*d* 1941), *d* of Baroncino Nicola Galea di San Marciano; *S* father, 1945. *Educ:* Stonyhurst College, Blackburn; University Coll., Oxford. Sometime Member: Cttee of Privileges of Maltese Nobility; Royal Numismatic Society; Société suisse de Numismatique. Hereditary Knight of the Holy Roman Empire; Patrician of Rome, Messina, and Citta di Castello. *Address:* 29 Villegaignon Street, Mdina, Malta, GC. *T:* Rabat 674139. *Club:* Casino Maltese (Valletta).

SANCTUARY, Gerald Philip; Secretary, National Union of Journalists Provident Fund, since 1984; *b* 22 Nov. 1930; *s* of late John Cyril Tabor Sanctuary, MD and of Maisie Toppin Sanctuary (*née* Brooks); *m* 1956, Rosemary Patricia L'Estrange, Dublin; three *s* two *d. Educ:* Bryanston Sch.; Law Soc.'s Sch. of Law. National Service Pilot, 1953–55; Asst Solicitor, Kingston, 1955–56; Partner in Hasties, Solicitors, Lincoln's Inn Fields, 1957–62; Field Sec., Nat. Marriage Guidance Council, 1963–65, Nat. Secretary 1965–69; Exec. Dir, Sex Information and Educn Council of US, 1969–71; Sec., Professional and Public Relations, The Law Soc., 1971–78; Exec. Dir, Internat. Bar Assoc., 1978–79; Legal Adviser and Regional and Local Affairs Dir, Mencap, 1979–84. Hon. Treas., GAPAN. Editor, Law Soc. series: It's Your Law, 1973–79. Regular broadcaster on radio. *Publications:* Marriage Under Stress, 1968; Divorce - and After, 1970, 2nd edn 1976; Before You See a Solicitor, 1973, 2nd edn 1983; After I'm Gone—what will happen to my Handicapped Child?, 1984; contrib., Moral Implications of Marriage Counseling, 1971; Vie Affective et Sexuelle, 1972; Loss Prevention Manual, 1978; The English Legal Heritage, 1979; booklets: Fishpool Street—St Albans, 1984; Tudor St Albans; St Albans and the Wars of the Roses, 1985. *Recreation:* amateur drama. *Address:* 6 Mercer's Row, St Albans, Herts. *T:* St Albans 42666.

SANDARS, Nancy Katharine, FBA 1984; FSA; archaeologist; *b* 29 June 1914; *d* of Edward Carew Sandars and Gertrude Annie Sandars (*née* Phipps). *Educ:* at home; Wychwood School, Oxford; Inst. of Archaeology, Univ. of London (Diploma 1949); St Hugh's College, Oxford (BLitt 1957). Archaeological research and travel in Europe, 1949–69; British School at Athens, 1954–55; Elizabeth Wordsworth Studentship, St Hugh's College, Oxford, 1958–61; travelled in Middle East, 1957, 1958, 1962, 1966; conferences, lectures (Prague, Sofia, McGill Univ.); excavations in British Isles and Greece. *Publications:* Bronze Age Cultures in France, 1957; The Epic of Gilgamesh, an English version, 1960; Prehistoric Art in Europe, 1967, rev. edn 1985; Poems of Heaven and Hell from Ancient Mesopotamia, 1971; The Sea-Peoples: warriors of the ancient Mediterranean, 1978. *Recreations:* walking, translating, looking at pictures. *Address:* The Manor House, Little Tew, Oxford. *Club:* University Women's.

SANDARS, Prof. Patrick George Henry; Professor of Experimental Physics, Oxford University, since 1978; *b* 29 March 1935; *s* of P. R. and A. C. Sandars; *m* 1959, P. B. Hall; two *s. Educ:* Wellington Coll.; Balliol Coll., Oxford (MA, DPhil). Weir Junior Research Fellow, University Coll., and ICI Research Fellow, Clarendon Laboratory, Oxford, 1960–63; Tutorial Fellow, Balliol Coll., and Univ. Lectr, Oxford Univ., 1964–72; Reader in Physics, Oxford Univ., 1972–77. Junior Proctor, Oxford Univ., 1971–72. *Address:* 3 Hawkswell Gardens, Oxford. *T:* Oxford 58535.

SANDBACH, Prof. Francis Henry, FBA 1968; Fellow of Trinity College, Cambridge, since 1927; *b* 23 Feb. 1903; *s* of late Prof. F. E. and Ethel Sandbach; *m* 1932, Mary Warburton Mathews; one *s* one *d* (and one *s* decd). *Educ:* King Edward's Sch., Birmingham; Trinity Coll., Cambridge. Browne Schol., 1922; Craven Schol., 1923; Chancellor's Medallist, 1925; Charles Oldham Class. Schol., 1925. Asst Lectr, Manchester Univ., 1926–28; Lectr in Classics, Univ. of Cambridge, 1929–67; Brereton Reader in Classics, 1951–67; Prof. of Classics, 1967–70. Junior Proctor, 1940–41; Trinity Coll.: Lecturer in Classics, 1929–63; Tutor, 1945–52; Sen. Tutor, 1952–56. For. Mem., Kungl. Vetenskaps- och Vitterhets- Samhället i Göteborg. *Publications:* (some jointly): Plutarch's Moralia, vol. ix, 1961, vol. xi, 1965, vol. xv, 1969; Plutarchus Moralia, vol. vii, 1967; Menandri Reliquiae Selectae, 1972; Menander: a commentary, 1973; The Stoics, 1975; The Comic Theatre of Greece and Rome, 1977; Aristotle and the Stoics, 1985; articles in class. jls. *Address:* 2 Hedgerley Close, Cambridge CB3 0EW. *T:* 353152.

SANDBANK, Charles Peter, FEng; Deputy Director of Engineering, BBC, since 1985 (Assistant Director of Engineering, 1984–85); *b* 14 Aug. 1931; *s* of Gustav and Clare Sandbank; *m* 1955, Audrey Celia (*née* Schonfield); one *s* two *d. Educ:* Bromley Grammar Sch.; London Univ. (BSc, DIC). FEng 1983; FIEE, FInstP. Prodn Engr, 1953–55, Develt Engr, 1955–60, Brimar Valve Co.; Develt Section Head, STC Transistor Div., 1960–64; Head of Electron Devices Lab., 1964–68, Manager, Communication Systems Div., 1968–78, Standard Telecommunication Laboratories; Head of BBC Research Dept, 1978–84. Mem. Council: IEE, 1978–81 (Chm., Electronics Divisional Bd, 1979–80); Royal TV Soc., 1983–86; Chairman: EBU New Systems and Services Cttee, 1984–; EBU High Definition TV Cttee, 1981–84. Ext. Examr, London Univ., 1982–. FRTS; FRSA. *Publications:* Optical Fibre Communication Systems, 1980; papers and patents (about 100) on semiconductor devices, integrated circuits, solid-state bulk effects, compound semiconductors, micro-waves, electron-phonon interactions, navigational aids, electro-optics and broadcasting technology. *Recreations:* boatbuilding, sailing, film-making, music, garden-watching. *Address:* Grailands, Beech Road, Reigate, Surrey RH2 9NA. *T:* (office) 01–580 4468.

SANDBERG, Sir Michael (Graham Ruddock), Kt 1986; CBE 1982 (OBE 1977); JP; Chairman: The Hongkong and Shanghai Banking Corporation, since 1977; The British Bank of the Middle East, since 1980; *b* 31 May 1927; *s* of Gerald Arthur Clifford Sandberg and Ethel Marion Sandberg; *m* 1954, Carmel Mary Roseleen Donnelly; two *s* two *d. Educ:* St Edward's Sch., Oxford. 6th Lancers (Indian Army) and First King's Dragoon Guards, 1945. Joined The Hongkong and Shanghai Banking Corp., 1949. Mem. Exec. Council, Hong Kong, 1978–. JP (Hong Kong), 1972–; Steward, Royal Hong Kong Jockey Club, 1972–, Chm., 1981–; Treasurer, Univ. of Hong Kong, 1977. FIB 1977

(Vice Pres. 1984–); FRSA 1983. Hon. LLD: Hong Kong, 1984; Pepperdine, 1986. *Recreations:* horse racing, bridge, cricket, horology. *Address:* c/o The Hongkong and Shanghai Banking Corporation, 1 Queen's Road Central, Hong Kong. *T:* 5–8221111. *Clubs:* Cavalry and Guards, Carlton, Portland, MCC, Surrey CCC.

SANDELSON, Neville Devonshire; Barrister-at-Law; political and business consultant; Deputy Chairman, Westminster and Overseas Trade Services Ltd, since 1985; *b* Leeds, 27 Nov. 1923; *s* of late David I. Sandelson, OBE, and Dora Sandelson, (*née* Lightman); *m* 1959, Nana Karlinski, Neuilly sur Seine, France; one *s* two *d. Educ:* Westminster School; Trinity College, Cambridge; MA. Called to Bar, Inner Temple, 1946; for some years director of local newspaper and book publishing cos and producer of TV documentary programmes until resuming practice at Bar, 1964. Dep. Circuit Judge and Asst Recorder, 1977–85. Mem. London County Council, 1952–58; junior Whip of majority group. Travelled extensively in USA, Middle East, Europe. Contested (Lab): Ashford (Kent) 1950, 1951 and 1955; Beckenham (by-election) 1957; Rushcliffe 1959; Heston & Isleworth 1966; SW Leicester (by-election) 1967; Chichester 1970; (SDP) Hayes and Harlington, 1983. MP (Lab 1971–81, SDP 1981–83) Hayes and Harlington, June 1971–83; Founder Mem., SDP; Parly spokesman on NI, 1981–82, and on the arts, 1982–83; Vice-Chm., All-Party Productivity Gp; Sec., All-Party Theatre Gp; Jt Sec., British-Greek Parly Gp; Sec., British Gibraltar Parly Gp; Vice-Chm., Afghanistan Parly Support Cttee. Promoted, as a Private Mem's Bill, the Matrimonial Proceedings (Polygamous Marriages) Act, 1972. Mem., SDP Nat. Organisation Sub-Cttee; Jt Hon. Sec., Assoc. for a Social Democratic Europe; Member: Council, Nat. Cttee for Electoral Reform; Cttee, SDP Campaign for Electoral Reform; Nat. Council of European Movement, 1985–; Exec. Cttee, Wider Share Ownership Council; founder Mem., Manifesto Gp (Treas., 1975–80). Sponsor, UK Cttee for Defence of the Unjustly Prosecuted. Member: GMWU; Social Democratic Lawyers Assoc. Mem. Ct, Brunel Univ., 1975–81. *Address:* 1 Hare Court, Temple, EC4. *T:* 01–353 0691; Woodside, Horse Gate Ride, Ascot, Berks. *T:* Ascot 22721. *Club:* Reform.

SANDERS, Christopher Cavania, RA 1961 (ARA 1953); RP 1968; ARCA 1928; artist-painter; *b* near Wakefield, 25 Dec. 1905; *s* of Alfred B. Sanders; *m* 1931, Barbara L. Stubbs (ARCA 1928) (*d* 1967), *d* of Francis F. Stubbs, Isleworth and Felpham; two *s* two *d. Educ:* Ossett Grammar Sch.; Wakefield Sch. of Art; Leeds Coll. of Art; Royal Coll. of Art. Gold Medallist, Paris Salon, 1955. *Address:* 2 Tudor Gardens, Slough, Berks SL1 6HJ.

SANDERS, Cyril Woods, CB 1959; Lord of the Manor of Kavenham-Stoke-Wereham and Wretton in Norfolk; *b* 21 Feb. 1912; *er s* of Cyril Sturgis Sanders and Dorothy (*née* Woods); *m* 1944, Kate Emily Boyes, *qv*; one *s* three *d. Educ:* St Paul's Sch.; Queen's Coll., Oxford. BA Oxon 1934, Lit. Hum. Joined General Post Office as Assistant Principal, 1934; transferred to Board of Trade, 1935; retired from Dept of Trade and Industry (formerly Bd of Trade) as Under-Secretary, 1972. *Recreations:* walking, sailing, painting. *Address:* 41 Smith Street, Chelsea, SW3. *T:* 01–352 8053; Giles Point, Winchelsea, Sussex. *T:* Winchelsea 431; Canower, Cashel, Connemara, Eire. *Clubs:* Ski Club of Gt Britain; Island Cruising (Devon).

SANDERS, Donald Neil, CB 1983; Deputy Governor and Deputy Chairman of Board, Reserve Bank of Australia, since 1975; *b* Sydney, 21 June 1927; *s* of L. G. Sanders; *m* 1952, Betty Elaine, *d* of W. B. Constance; four *s* one *d. Educ:* Wollongong High Sch.; Univ. of Sydney (BEc). Commonwealth Bank of Australia, 1943–60; Australian Treasury, 1956; Bank of England, 1960; Reserve Bank of Australia, 1960–: Supt, Credit Policy Div., Banking Dept, 1964–66; Dep. Manager: Banking Dept, 1966–67; Res. Dept, 1967–70; Aust. Embassy, Washington DC, 1968; Chief Manager: Securities Markets Dept, 1970–72; Banking and Finance Dept, 1972–74; Adviser and Chief Manager, Banking and Finance Dept, 1974–75. *Address:* Reserve Bank of Australia, 65 Martin Place, GPO Box 3947, Sydney, NSW 2001, Australia.

SANDERS, Prof. Ed Parish; Dean Ireland's Professor of Exegesis of Holy Scripture, Oxford, since 1984; *b* 18 April 1937; *s* of Mildred Sanders (*née* Parish) and Eula Thomas Sanders; *m* 1963, Becky Jill Hall (marr. diss. 1978); one *d. Educ:* Texas Wesleyan College (BA); Southern Methodist Univ. (BD); Union Theological Seminary, NY (ThD). Asst Prof. of Religious Studies, McMaster Univ., 1966–70, Associate Prof., 1970–74, Prof., 1974–. Visiting Professor: Jewish Theol. Seminary, 1980; Chair of Judeo-Christian Studies, Tulane Univ., 1980; Walter G. Mason Dist. Vis. Prof., Coll. of William and Mary in Virginia, 1981; Vis. Fellow Commoner, Trinity Coll., Cambridge, 1982. Donnellan Lectr, TCD, 1982. *Publications:* The Tendencies of the Synoptic Tradition, 1969; Paul and Palestinian Judaism, 1977, 2nd edn 1981; (ed) Jewish and Christian Self-Definition, vol. I, The Shaping of Christianity in the Second and Third Centuries, 1980, vol. II, Aspects of Judaism in the Graeco-Roman Period, 1981, vol. III, Self-Definition in the Graeco-Roman World, 1982; Paul, The Law and the Jewish People, 1983; Jesus and Judaism, 1985, 2nd edn 1986; articles in NT Studies, Jl of Biblical Literature, Harvard Theol. Review, Jewish Quarterly Review. *Address:* The Queen's College, Oxford OX1 4AW. *T:* Oxford 57265.

SANDERS, John Derek; Organist and Master of the Choristers, Gloucester Cathedral, since 1967; *b* 26 Nov. 1933; *s* of Alderman J. T. Sanders, JP, CA and Mrs E. M. Sanders (*née* Trivett); *m* 1967, Janet Ann Dawson; one *s* one *d. Educ:* Felsted Sch., Essex; Royal Coll. of Music; Gonville and Caius Coll., Cambridge. ARCM 1952; FRCO 1955; MusB 1956; MA 1958. Dir of Music, King's Sch., Gloucester, and Asst Organist, Gloucester Cathedral, 1958–63; Organist and Master of the Choristers, Chester Cathedral, 1964–67. Dir of Music, Cheltenham Ladies' Coll., 1968–. Conductor: Gloucestershire Symphony Orchestra, 1967–; Gloucester Choral Soc., 1967–. Conductor of Three Choirs Festival, 1968, 1971, 1974, 1977, 1980, 1983, 1986. *Publications:* Festival Te Deum, 1962; Soliloquy for Organ, 1977; Toccata for Organ, 1979; Te Deum Laudamus, 1985; Jubilate Deo, 1986. *Recreations:* gastronomy, travelling. *Address:* 7 Miller's Green, Gloucester GL1 2BN. *T:* 24764.

SANDERS, John Leslie Yorath; HM Diplomatic Service, retired; furniture conservator and restorer; *b* 5 May 1929; *s* of late Reginald Yorath Sanders and Gladys Elizabeth Sanders (*née* Blything); *m* 1953, Brigit Mary Lucine Altounyan; one *s* two *d. Educ:* Dulwich Coll. Prep. Sch.; Cranleigh School. Higher Dip. in Furniture Prodn and Design, London Coll. of Furniture, 1982. Nat. Service in HM Forces (RA), 1948–50; entered HM Foreign Service, 1950; FO, 1950–52; MECAS, Lebanon, 1953; Damascus, 1954–55; Bahrain, 1955–56; Vice-Consul, Basra, 1956–60; Oriental Sec., Rabat, 1960–63; FO, 1964–67; 1st Sec., Beirut, 1968–70; 1st Sec. and Head of Chancery, Mexico City, 1970–73; Counsellor, Khartoum, 1973–75; Counsellor, Beirut, 1975–76; Dir of Res., FCO, 1976–78; Ambassador to Panama, 1978–80. *Recreations:* sailing, music. *Address:* Town Yeat, High Nibthwaite, Ulverston, Cumbria.

SANDERS, Sir John Reynolds M.; *see* Mayhew-Sanders, Sir J. R.

SANDERS, Kate Emily Tyrrell, (Mrs C. W. Sanders); *see* Boyes, K. E. T.

SANDERS, Peter Basil; Director, Commission for Racial Equality, since 1977; *b* 9 June 1938; *s* of Basil Alfred Horace Sanders and Ellen May Sanders (*née* Cockrell); *m* 1961, Janet Valerie (*née* Child) (marr. diss. 1984); two *s* one *d. Educ:* Queen Elizabeth's Grammar Sch., Barnet; Wadham Coll., Oxford (MA, DPhil). Administrative Officer, Basutoland, 1961–66; Research in Oxford for DPhil, 1966–70; Officer, Min. of Defence, 1971–73; Race Relations Bd: Principal Conciliation Officer, 1973–74; Dep. Chief Officer, 1974–77. *Publications:* Lithoko: Sotho Praise-Poems (ed jtly and trans. with an Introd. and Notes), 1974; Moshoeshoe, Chief of the Sotho, 1975. *Address:* 5 Bentfield End Causeway, Stansted Mountfitchet, Essex. *T:* Bishop's Stortford 815096.

SANDERS, Sir Robert (Tait), KBE 1980; CMG 1974; HMOCS; Secretary to the Cabinet, Government of Fiji, 1970–79; Treaties Adviser, Government of Fiji, since 1985; *b* 2 Feb. 1925; *s* of late A. S. W. Sanders and Charlotte McCulloch; *m* 1951, Barbara, *d* of G. Sutcliffe; three *s. Educ:* Canmore Public Sch., Dunfermline; Dunfermline High Sch.; Fettes Coll., Edinburgh; Cambridge Univ. (Major Open Classical Schol., Pembroke Coll., 1943; John Stewart of Rannoch Schol. in Latin and Greek, 1947; 1st cl. Hons, Pts I and II of Classical Tripos); London Sch. of Economics. Served War, 1943–46: Lieut, 1st Bn the Royal Scots, India and Malaya. Sir Arthur Thomson Travelling Schol., 1948; Sir William Browne Medal for Latin Epigram, 1948; MA (Cantab) 1951. Joined HM Overseas Civil Service, Fiji, as Dist Officer, 1950; Sec. to Govt of Tonga, 1956–58; Sec., Coconut Commn of Enquiry, 1963; MLC, Fiji, 1963–64; Sec. for Natural Resources, 1965–67; Actg Sec. Fijian Affairs, and Actg Chm. Native Lands and Fisheries Commn, 1967; MEC, Fiji, 1967; Sec. to Chief Minister and to Council of Ministers, 1967; apptd Sec. to Cabinet, 1970, also Sec. for Foreign Affairs, 1970–74, Sec. for Home Affairs, 1972–74 and Sec. for Information, 1975–76. Fiji Independence Medal, 1970. *Publications:* Interlude in Fiji, 1963; articles in Corona, jl of HMOCS. *Recreations:* golf, music, hill-walking. *Address:* Greystones Lodge, Broich Terrace, Crieff. *Clubs:* Royal Scots (Edinburgh); Nausori Golf (Fiji).

SANDERS, Roger Benedict; Metropolitan Stipendiary Magistrate, since 1980; a Recorder of the Crown Court, since 1986; *b* 1 Oct. 1940; *s* of Maurice and Lilian Sanders; *m* 1969, Susan, *er d* of Simon and Phyllis Brenner; two *s* (one *d* decd). *Educ:* Highgate School. Co-founder, Inner Temple Debating Soc., 1961, Chm. 1962. Called to the Bar, Inner Temple, 1965; South Eastern Circuit. A Chm., Inner London Juvenile Courts, 1980–; Chm., Legal Cttee, Inner London Juvenile Panel, 1983–86; First Chm., No 1 (London S) Regional Duty Solicitor Cttee, 1984–85. Chairman, Walker School Assoc. (Southgate), 1976, 1977; Schools' Debating Assoc. Judge, 1976, 1978, 1981; Mem., Haringey Schools Liaison Group, 1979. *Recreations:* model railways, music, gardening. *Address:* Old Street Magistrates' Court, EC1V 9LJ. *T:* 01–488 5221. *Club:* Players' Theatre.

SANDERS, Ronald; High Commissioner for Antigua and Barbuda to the Court of St James's, since 1984; Ambassador to UNESCO and European Community, since 1983; Ambassador Extraordinary and Plenipotentiary to Federal Republic of Germany, since 1986; *b* 26 Jan. 1948; *m* 1975, Susan Indrani (*née* Ramphal). *Educ:* Sacred Heart RC Sch., Guyana; Westminster Sch., London; Boston Univ., USA. Gen. Man., Guyana Broadcasting Service, 1973–76; Communication Cons. to Pres., Caribbean Develt Bank, Barbados, 1977; UNDP and CFTC Cons. to Govt of Antigua, 1977–81; Advr to For. Minister of Antigua and Barbuda, 1981–82; Dep. Perm. Rep. to UN, 1982–83. Member: Inter-Govtl Council, Internat. Prog. for Develt of Communications, UNESCO, 1983–; Exec. Bd, UNESCO, 1985–; Chm., Gp of Caribbean Ambassadors, UNESCO, 1983–85. *Publications:* Broadcasting in Guyana, 1977; several contribs to internat. jls on communication, Antarctica, also political commentaries. *Recreations:* reading, cinema. *Address:* c/o Antigua and Barbuda High Commission, 15 Thayer Street, W1. *T:* 01–486 7073. *Clubs:* Hurlingham, Royal Automobile.

SANDERS, William George, RCNC, CEng, FRINA; Head of Royal Corps of Naval Constructors; Director General, Submarines, Ministry of Defence (PE), since 1985; *b* 22 Jan. 1936; *s* of George and Alice Irene Sanders; *m* 1956, Marina Charlotte Burford; two *s* one *d. Educ:* Public Secondary Sch., Plymouth; Devonport Dockyard Tech. Coll.; RN Coll., Greenwich. Asst Constructor, Ship Dept, Admiralty, 1961–68; FNCO Western Fleet, 1968–70; Constructor, Ship Dept, MoD (Navy), 1970–77; Principal Naval Overseer, Scotland, 1977–79; Marconi Space and Defence Systems, 1979–82; Project Manager, Type 23, 1982–83; DG Future Material Projects (Naval), MoD (PE), 1983–85. *Recreations:* golf, painting, gardening. *Address:* The Old Barn, London Road West, Bath, Avon. *T:* Bath 317006.

SANDERSON, family name of **Baron Sanderson of Bowden.**

SANDERSON OF AYOT, 2nd Baron *cr* 1960, title disclaimed by the heir, Dr Alan Lindsay Sanderson, 1971.

SANDERSON OF BOWDEN, Baron *cr* 1985 (Life Peer), of Melrose in the District of Ettrick and Lauderdale; **Charles Russell Sanderson,** Kt 1981; Partner, Chas. P. Sanderson, Wool and Yarn Merchants, Melrose, since 1958; Chairman: Edinburgh Financial Trust (formerly Yorkshire & Lancashire Investment Trust), since 1983; Shires Investment Trust, since 1984; company director; *b* 30 April 1933; *s* of Charles Plummer Sanderson and Martha Evelyn Gardiner; *m* 1958, Frances Elizabeth Macaulay; two *s* two *d. Educ:* St Mary's Sch., Melrose; Trinity Coll., Glenalmond; Scottish Coll. of Textiles, Galashiels; Bradford Coll. (now Bradford Univ.). Commnd Royal Signals, 1952; served: 51 (Highland) Inf. Div. Signal Regt TA, 1953–56, KOSB TA, 1956–58. Dir, Clydesdale Bank, 1986–. Chairman, Roxburgh, Selkirk and Peebles Cons. and Unionist Assoc., 1970–73; Scottish Cons. Unionist Association: Chm. Central and Southern Area, 1974–75; Vice-Pres. 1975–77; Pres. 1977–79; Vice-Chm. Nat. Union of Cons Assocs, 1979–81 (Mem. Exec. Cttee, 1975–); Chm. Exec. Cttee, Nat. Union of Cons. Assocs, 1981–86; Member: Cons. Party Policy Cttee, 1979–86; Standing Adv. Cttee of Parly Candidates, 1979–86 (Vice-Chm. with responsibility for Europe, 1980–81). Deacon, Galashiels Manufrs Corp., 1976; Chm., Eildon Housing Assoc., 1978–82. Member of Committee: Scottish Council of Indep. Schs., 1984–; GBA, 1984–. Governor: St Mary's Sch., Melrose, 1977–; Scottish Coll. of Textiles, 1980–; Mem. Council, Trinity Coll., Glenalmond, 1982–. Comr, Gen. Assembly of Ch. of Scotland, 1972. *Recreations:* golf, amateur operatics (Past Pres., Producer and Mem. Melrose Amateur Operatic Soc.). *Address:* Becketts Field, Bowden, Melrose, Roxburgh TD6 0ST. *T:* St Boswell's 22736. *Clubs:* Caledonian; Hon. Co. of Edinburgh Golfers (Muirfield).

SANDERSON, Sir Bryan; *see* Sanderson, Sir F. P. B.

SANDERSON, Charles Denis; HM Diplomatic Service, retired; Domestic Bursar and Fellow of St Peter's College, Oxford, since 1985; *b* 18 Dec. 1934; *s* of Norman and Elsie Sanderson; *m* 1960, Mary Joyce Gillow; one *s* two *d. Educ:* Bishopshalt Sch., Hillingdon, Mddx; Pembroke Coll., Oxford (MA). National Service, 1953–55; Oxford, 1955–58; British Petroleum Co. Ltd, 1958–64; Second, later First Secretary, Commonwealth Relations Office, 1964–67; First Sec., Kingston, and concurrently, Haiti, 1967–70; Acting Consul, Port au Prince, 1969; First Sec., Head of Chancery and Consul, Panama, 1970–73; First Sec., FCO, 1973–75; Consul (Commercial), British Trade Development Office, New York, 1975–77; Dep. Consul General and Director Industrial Development, New York,

1977–79; Counsellor, Caracas, 1979–84; Hd, W Indian and Atlantic Dept, FCO, 1984–85. *Address:* Gilletts Farm, Asthall Leigh, Oxford OX8 5PX. *T:* Asthall Leigh 455. *Clubs:* Royal Commonwealth Society, United Oxford & Cambridge University.

SANDERSON, Sir (Frank Philip) Bryan, 2nd Bt, *cr* 1920; Lt-Comdr RNVR; *b* 18 Feb. 1910; *s* of Sir Frank Bernard Sanderson, 1st Bt, and Amy Edith (*d* 1949), *d* of David Wing, Scarborough; *S* father 1965; *m* 1933, Annette Irene Caroline (*d* 1967), *d* of late Col Korab Laskowski, Warsaw, (*g d* of General Count de Castellaz); two *s* one *d*. *Educ:* Stowe; Pembroke College, Oxford. Served War of 1939–45 with Fleet Air Arm. A Member of Lloyd's. Dir, Humber Fertilisers (formerly Humber Fishing and Fish Manure Co.), Hull (Chm., 1965–80). *Recreation:* shooting. *Heir: s* Frank Linton Sanderson [*b* 21 Nov. 1933; *m* 1961, Margaret Ann, *o d* of John C. Maxwell; two *s* three *d*]. *Address:* Lychgate Cottage, Scaynes Hill, Haywards Heath, West Sussex RH17 7NH. *Club:* Carlton.

SANDERSON, George Rutherford, CBE 1978; *b* 23 Nov. 1919; *er s* of late George Sanderson and Edith Mary Sanderson, Blyth, Northumberland; *m* 1947, Jean Cecilia, *d* of late James C. McDougall, Chesterfield, Derbyshire; two *s*. *Educ:* Blyth Grammar Sch.; Univ. of London (BA 1st Cl. Hons French and Italian). War Service, 1940–46: RA, Malta and Egypt (Major). British Council, 1949–79: Actg Dir, Anglo Argentine Cultural Inst., La Plata, Argentina, 1949; Dir, Tucuman, Argentina, 1950–52; Asst Rep., Santiago, Chile, 1952–58; Dep. Area Officer, Oxford, 1958–62; Reg. Dir, and Dir Anglo Argentine Cultural Assoc., Rosario, Argentina, 1962–66; Asst Rep., Buenos Aires, 1966–69; Reg. Dir, and Dir Anglo Brazilian Cultural Soc., São Paulo, Brazil, 1969–72; Dir, Drama and Music Dept, and Dep. Controller, Arts Div., 1973; Educnl Attaché, British Embassy, Washington, 1973–76; Rep., British Council, Spain, and Cultural Attaché, British Embassy, Madrid, 1976–79; Administering Officer, The Kennedy Scholarships and Knox Fellowships, ACU, 1979–82. *Recreations:* art, reading. *Address:* Leafield House, Holton, Oxford OX9 1PZ. *T:* Wheatley 2526. *Club:* Athenæum.

SANDERSON, Air Vice-Marshal Keith Fred, CB 1986; Air Officer Administration, Headquarters Strike Command, since 1983; *b* 25 Nov. 1932; *s* of late Arnold and Emily Sanderson; *m* 1957, Margaret Ward; two *d*. *Educ:* Hutton Grammar Sch., Lancs. RAF Navigator, 1950–74; Staff of CDS, 1974–75; Comd RAF Leconfield, 1976; RCDS, 1977; AOA RAF Germany, 1978–80; AOC Personnel Management Centre and Dir of Personnel (Air), 1980–83. *Recreations:* walking, golf. *Club:* Royal Air Force.

SANDERSON, Very Rev. Peter Oliver; Provost of St Paul's Cathedral, Dundee, since 1984; *b* 26 Jan. 1929; *s* of Harold and Doris Sanderson; *m* 1956, Doreen Gibson; one *s* one *d* (and one *s* decd). *Educ:* St Chad's College, Durham Univ. (BA, DipTh). Asst Curate, Houghton-le-Spring, Durham Diocese, 1954–59; Rector, Linstead and St Thomas Ye Vale, Jamaica, 1959–63; Chaplain, RAF, 1963–67; Vicar, Winksley-cum-Grantley and Aldfield-with-Studley, Ripon, 1967–74; Vicar, St Aidan, Leeds, 1974–84. *Recreations:* gardening, music, reading. *Address:* St Paul's Cathedral Rectory, 4 Richmond Terrace, Dundee DD2 1BQ. *T:* Dundee 68548.

SANDERSON, Very Rev. Roy; *see* Sanderson, Very Rev. W. R.

SANDERSON, Rt. Rev. Wilfrid Guy; *b* 17 Aug. 1905; *s* of late Wilfrid E. Sanderson; *m* 1934, Cecily Julia Mary Garratt (*d* 1982); one *s* two *d*. *Educ:* Malvern College; Merton College, Oxford (MA). Ordained, 1931; Curate at S Farnborough, Hants, till 1934; Priest-in-charge of St Aidan's, Aldershot, 1934–37; Vicar of All Saints, Woodham, Surrey, 1937–46; Vicar of All Saints, Alton, Hants, 1946–54; Rector of Silverton, Devon, 1954–59; Archdeacon of Barnstaple, 1958–62; Rector of Shirwell, 1959–62; Suffragan Bishop of Plymouth, 1962–72. *Address:* Huish House, Huish Episcopi, Langport, Somerset TA10 9OP. *T:* Langport 252544.

SANDERSON, Very Rev. (William) Roy; Parish Minister at Stenton and Whittingehame, 1963–73; Extra Chaplain to the Queen in Scotland, since 1977 (Chaplain, 1965–77); *b* 23 Sept. 1907; *er s* of late Arthur Watson Sanderson, Leith, and late Ethel Catherine Watson, Dundee; *m* 1941, Annie Muriel Easton, Glasgow; three *s* two *d*. *Educ:* Cargilfield Sch.; Fettes Coll.; Oriel Coll., Oxford; Edinburgh University. BA 1929, MA 1933, Oxon. Ordained, 1933. Asst Minister, St Giles' Cath., Edin., 1932–34; Minister: at St Andrew's, Lochgelly, 1935–39; at the Barony of Glasgow, 1939–63. Moderator: Glasgow Presbytery, 1958; Haddington and Dunbar Presbytery, 1972–74; Convener of Assembly Cttees: on Religious Instruction of Youth, 1950–55; on Deaconesses, 1956–61; Panel of Doctrine, 1960–65; on Gen. Administration, 1967–72. Convener of Business Cttee and Leader of General Assembly of the Church of Scotland, 1965–66, 1968–72. Moderator of Gen. Assembly of the Church of Scotland, May 1967–May 1968. Chm., BBC Scottish Religious Advisory Committee, 1961–71; Member Central Religious Advisory Cttee of BBC and ITA, 1961–71. Governor, Fettes Coll., Edinburgh, 1967–76. Hon. DD Glasgow, 1959. *Publication:* Responsibility (Moderatorial address), 1967. *Recreations:* cooking, reading. *Address:* 1a York Road, North Berwick, East Lothian. *T:* North Berwick 2780.

SANDFORD, 2nd Baron, *cr* 1945, of Banbury; **Rev. John Cyril Edmondson**, DSC 1942; Conservative Peer in House of Lords, since 1959; a Church Commissioner, since 1982; Chairman, Redundant Churches Committee; Director, Ecclesiastical Insurance Office, since 1977; Chairman, Standing Conference of London and South East Regional Planning Authorities, since 1981; *b* 22 Dec. 1920; *e s* of 1st Baron Sandford; *S* father, 1959; *m* 1947, Catharine Mary Hunt; two *s* two *d*. *Educ:* Eton Coll.; Royal Naval Coll., Dartmouth; Westcott House, Cambridge. Served War of 1939–45: Mediterranean Fleet, 1940–41; Home Fleet, 1942; Normandy Landings, 1944 (wounded); Mediterranean Fleet, HMS Saumarez, 1946 (wounded). Staff of RN Coll., Dartmouth, 1947–49; HMS Vengeance, 1950; HMS Cleopatra, 1951–52; Staff Commander-in-Chief Far East, 1953–55; Commander of Home Fleet Flagship, HMS Tyne, 1956; retired 1956. Ordained in Church of England, 1958; Parish of St Nicholas, Harpenden, 1958–63; Exec. Chaplain to Bishop of St Albans, 1965–68. Opposition Whip, House of Lords, 1966–70; Parly Sec., Min. of Housing and Local Govt, June-Oct. 1970; Parliamentary Under-Secretary of State: DoE, 1970–73; DES, 1973–74. Chm., Cttee to review the condition and future of National Parks in England and Wales, 1971. Chairman: Hertfordshire Council of Social Service, 1969–70; Church Army, 1969–70; Community Task Force, 1975–82; Mem., Adv. Council on Penal Reform, 1968–70. President: Anglo-Swiss Soc., 1974–84; Council for Environmental Educn, 1974–84; Assoc. of District Councils, 1980–86; Offa's Dyke Assoc., 1980–84; Countrywide Holidays Assoc., 1982–86; Vice-Pres., YHA, 1979–. Hon Fellow, Inst. of Landscape Architects. *Heir: s* Hon. James John Mowbray Edmondson [*b* 1 July 1949; *m* 1973, Ellen Sarah, *d* of Jack Shapiro, Toronto; one *d*]. *Address:* 6 Smith Square, Westminster, SW1. *T:* 01–222 5715. *Club:* Ski Club of Gt Britain.

SANDFORD, Arthur; Clerk of the County Council and Chief Executive, Nottinghamshire County Council, since 1978; *b* 12 May 1941; *s* of Arthur and Lilian Sandford; *m* 1963, Kathleen Entwistle; two *d*. *Educ:* Queen Elizabeth's Grammar Sch., Blackburn; University Coll., London (LLB Hons (Upper 2nd Class)). Preston County Borough Council: Articled Clerk to Town Clerk, 1962–65; Asst Solicitor, 1965–66; Sen. Asst Solicitor, 1966–68; Asst Solicitor, Hants CC, 1969–70; Nottinghamshire County

Council: Second Asst Clerk, 1970–72; First Asst Clerk, 1972–74; Dep. Dir of Admin, 1973–75; Dir of Admin, 1975–77; Dep. Clerk and County Sec., 1977–78. *Recreations:* half-marathon running, gardening. *Address:* Fairford House, 66 Loughborough Road, Bunny, Nottingham. *T:* Nottingham 212440. *Club:* Royal Over-Seas League.

SANDFORD, Prof. Cedric Thomas; Professor of Political Economy, University of Bath, since 1965, and Director of Bath University Centre for Fiscal Studies, 1974–86; *b* 21 Nov. 1924; *s* of Thomas Sandford and Louisa (*née* Hodge); *m* 1945, Evelyn Belch (*d* 1982); one *s* one *d*; *m* 1984, Christina Privett. *Educ:* Manchester Univ. (BAEcon 1948, MAEcon 1949); London Univ. (BA History (external) 1955). Undergraduate, Manchester Univ., 1942–43 and 1946–48; RAF, 1943–46 (Pilot). Graduate Research Schol., Univ. of Manchester, 1948–49; Lectr, Burnley Municipal Coll., 1949–60; Sen. Lectr, subseq. Head of General and Social Studies Dept, Bristol Coll. of Science and Technology, 1960–65; Head of Sch. of Humanities and Social Sciences, Univ. of Bath, 1965–68, 1971–74, 1977–79. Visiting Prof., Univ. of Delaware, USA, 1969; Vis. Fellow, ANU, 1981, 1985. Mem., Meade Cttee on Reform of Direct Tax System, 1975–78; Consultant: Fiscal Div., OECD, 1976–79, 1985–87; Irish Commn on Taxation, 1982–85; World Bank, 1986. *Publications:* Taxing Inheritance and Capital Gains (Hobart Paper 32, IEA), 1965, 2nd edn 1967; Economics of Public Finance, 1969, 3rd edn 1984; Realistic Tax Reform, 1971; Taxing Personal Wealth, 1971; (sen. editor and jt author) Case Studies in Economics (3 vols), 1971, 2nd edn 1977; National Economic Planning, 1972, 2nd edn 1976; Hidden Costs of Taxation, 1973; (jtly) An Accessions Tax, 1973; (jtly) An Annual Wealth Tax, 1975; Social Economics, 1977; (jtly) Grants or Loans?, 1980; (jtly) The Costs and Benefits of VAT, 1981; The Economic Framework, 1982; (jtly) Tax Policy-Making in the United Kingdom, 1983; (jtly) The Irish Wealth Tax: a study in economics and politics, 1985; numerous articles in wide range of learned jls. *Recreations:* fishing, gardening, violin-playing. *Address:* Old Coach House, Fersfield, Perrymead, Bath BA2 5AR. *T:* Bath 832683.

SANDFORD, Herbert Henry, OBE 1963; DFM 1942; Member for Chelsea, ILEA, since 1986; Chief Whip, minority party; opposition spokesman: Staff Committee; General Purposes Committee; *b* 19 Nov. 1916; *s* of Herbert Charles Sandford and Grace Ellen (*née* Onley); *m* 1st, 1938, Irene Lucy (*née* Porter) (marr. diss. 1944); 2nd, 1948, Jessie Irene (*née* Gray). *Educ:* Minchendon Secondary Sch., Southgate. Served War, Pathfinder Sqdns, RAF, 1939–45. Elected to St Marylebone Metrop. Bor. Council, 1953; Chm., Works Cttee. City of Westminster: Councillor, Lords Ward, 1964–68; Alderman, 1968–78; Dep. Leader of Council, 1975–76; Chairman: Traffic Cttee, 1964–67; Highways and Traffic Cttee, 1967–68; Highways Cttee, 1971–72 (Vice-Chm., 1969–71); Highways and Works Cttee, 1972–75; special sub-cttee of Highways and Town Planning Cttees on redevelt of Piccadilly Circus, 1972–76; Member: Policy Cttee, 1972–74; Town Planning Cttee, 1971–76; Road Safety Cttee, 1972–74; Road Safety Adv. Cttee, 1974–76; Co-ord. Cttee, 1974–75; Housing Management Cttee, 1975–77; London Transport Passenger Cttee, 1974–76. Greater London Council: Mem. for St Marylebone, 1976–86; Dep. Chm., 1985–86; Chm., Central Area Planning Cttee, 1977–81; Member: Public Services Safety Cttee, 1977–81; Covent Garden Cttee, 1977–81; Thames Water Regional Land Drainage Cttee, 1978–82; Leading Opposition Mem., Technical Services Cttee, 1983–86; Dep. Spokesman, Finance Cttee, 1983–86. Opposition Spokesman, Staff and Gen. Cttee, ILEA, 1982–86. Dir, Grove End Housing Assoc., Ltd, 1976–. Chairman: St Marylebone Sea Cadet Corps, 1953; St Marylebone Boy Scouts Assoc., 1958–64. Treasurer, Wiltons Music Hall Trust, 1982–. Governor, St John's Hosp. for Skin Diseases, 1973–76. *Recreations:* golf, bridge, Yoga. *Address:* 5 Elmfield House, Carlton Hill, NW8 9XB. *T:* 01–624 9694. *Clubs:* Royal Air Force, Pathfinder.

SANDFORD, Jeremy; writer, journalist, musician, performer; *s* of late Christopher Sandford, owner/director of the Golden Cockerel Press, and of Lettice Sandford, wood engraver, craft worker; *m* 1956, Nell Dunn; three *s*. *Educ:* Eton; Oxford. Dir, The Cyrenians; Exec., Gypsy Council; Sponsor: Shelter; The Simon Community. Editor, Romano Drom (gypsy newspaper). Screen Writers' Guild of Gt Britain Award, 1967, 1971; Prix Italia prize for TV drama, 1968; Critics Award for TV drama, 1971. *Publications:* Synthetic Fun, 1967; Cathy Come Home, 1967; Whelks and Chromium, 1968; Edna the Inebriate Woman, 1971; Down and Out in Britain, 1971; In Search of the Magic Mushrooms, 1972; Gypsies, 1973; Tomorrow's People, 1974; Prostitutes, 1975; Smiling David, 1975; Virgin of the Clearways, 1977. *Recreations:* painting, music, travel, mountain exploration, riding, wandering, windsurfing, wondering, festivals, getting to know British people. *Address:* c/o 7 Earls Court Square, SW5. *Club:* Chelsea Arts.

SANDFORD, Kenneth Leslie, CMG 1974; barrister; *b* 14 Aug. 1915; *s* of Albert Edgar Sandford and Barbara Ivy (*née* Hill); *m* 1946, Airini Ethel Scott Sergel; one *s* one *d* (and one *d* decd). *Educ:* King's Coll., Auckland, NZ; Auckland University Coll. LLB 1938. Served War: 34 Bn (NZ), rank of Captain, 1940–45. Barrister and Solicitor, 1939–72; Crown Solicitor (Hamilton), 1950–72; Chm., Accident Compensation Commn (NZ), 1972–80. *Publications:* Dead Reckoning, 1955; Dead Secret, 1957; Mark of the Lion, 1962. *Recreation:* cricket (Pres. NZ Cricket Council, 1971–73). *Address:* 144 Lucerne Road, Remuera, Auckland, New Zealand.

SANDFORD, Rear-Adm. Sefton Ronald, CB 1976; *b* 23 July 1925; *s* of Col H. R. Sandford and Mrs Faye Sandford (*née* Renouf); *m* 1st, 1950, Mary Ann Prins (*d* 1972); one *s*; 2nd, 1972, Jennifer Rachel Newell; two *d*. *Educ:* St Aubyns, Rottingdean, 1934–38; Royal Naval Coll., Dartmouth, 1939–42. Served War: went to sea, July 1942; commanded HMMTB 2017, Lieut, 1946–47; ADC to Comdr British Forces, Hong Kong (Lt-Gen. Sir Terence Airey), 1952–53; commanded HMS Teazer (rank Comdr), 1958; Staff of Imperial Defence Coll., 1963–65; comd HMS Protector, Captain, 1965–67; Naval Attaché, Moscow, 1968–70; comd HMS Devonshire, 1971–73; ADC to the Queen, 1974; Flag Officer, Gibraltar, 1974–76. A Younger Brother of Trinity House, 1968. *Recreations:* cricket, sailing, fishing. *Address:* Dolphins, Rue de St Jean, St Lawrence, Jersey, Channel Islands. *T:* Jersey 62200. *Clubs:* Marylebone Cricket (MCC); Royal Yacht Squadron (Cowes).

SANDFORD SMITH, Richard Henry, FCIS; Chairman, Eastern Gas Region (formerly Eastern Gas Board), 1970–73; *b* 29 March 1909; *s* of late Dr H. Sandford Smith; *m* 1936, Dorothy Hewitt, *y d* of late Rev. J. F. Hewitt; one *s*. *Educ:* Haileybury Coll. London Stock Exchange, 1926. Qualified as Chartered Secretary and awarded Sir Ernest Clarke Prize, 1932. Joined Gas Light & Coke Co., 1932; Sec., SE Gas Corp. Ltd, 1939–49; Sec., SE Gas Bd, 1949–56 (Dep. Chm., 1956–69). *Recreations:* theatre, golf, gardening. *Address:* 60 The Marlowes, St John's Wood Park, NW8. *Club:* Savile.

SANDHURST, 5th Baron, *cr* 1871; **(John Edward) Terence Mansfield**, DFC 1944; Managing Director, Leslie Rankin Ltd, Jersey; *b* 4 Sept. 1920; *er s* of 4th Baron Sandhurst, OBE, and Morley Victoria (*née* Upcher; *d* 1961); *S* father 1964; *m* 1947, Janet Mary, *er d* of late John Edward Lloyd, NY, USA; one *s* one *d*. *Educ:* Harrow. Served RAFVR, 1939–46: Bomber Command (as Navigator and Bombing Leader): 149 Sqdn, 1941; 419 (RCAF) Sqdn, 1942; 12 Sqdn, 1943–45. 1946–55: Metropolitan Special Constabulary 'C'

Div., Sergeant, 1949–52; long service medal, 1955. Hon. ADC to Lieutenant-Governor of Jersey, 1969–74. *Recreation:* golf. *Heir: s* Hon. Guy Rhys John Mansfield [*b* 3 March 1949; *m* 1976, Philippa St Clair, *er d* of Digby Verdon-Roe, 06 Le Cannet; one *s*; one *d*. *Educ:* Harrow; Oriel Coll., Oxford (MA). Called to Bar, Middle Temple, 1972]. *Address:* Les Sapins, St Mary, Jersey, CI. *Clubs:* Royal Air Force; MCC, Pathfinder; United (Jersey).

See also Earl of Macclesfield.

SANDILANDS, family name of **Baron Torphichen.**

SANDILANDS, Sir Francis (Edwin Prescott), Kt 1976; CBE 1967; Director, 1965–83 and Chairman, 1972–83, Commercial Union Assurance Co. Ltd; *b* 11 December 1913; *s* of late Lieut-Col Prescott Sandilands, DSO, RM, and late Gladys Baird Murton; *m* 1939, Susan Gillian Jackson; two *s*. *Educ:* Eton; Corpus Christi College, Cambridge (Hon. Fellow, 1975). MA 1938. Served War of 1939–45, Royal Scots Fusiliers and General Staff, UK and NW Europe (Lt-Col; despatches). Joined Ocean Accident and Guarantee Corporation Ltd, 1935, Manager, 1955; General Manager, then Chief General Manager, 1958–72, Vice-Chm., 1968–72, Commercial Union Assurance Co. Ltd; Chairman: Royal Trust Company of Canada, 1974–84; Director: Kleinwort, Benson, Lonsdale Ltd, 1979–86; Plessey Co. Ltd; Lewis & Peat Hldgs. Trustee: British Museum, 1977–85; Royal Opera House, 1974– (Chm. Trustees, 1980–84; Dir, 1975–85); Mem., Royal Fine Art Commn, 1980–85. Chairman: London Salvage Corps, 1962–63; British Insurance Assoc., 1965–67; Pres., Insurance Inst. of London, 1969–70. Chm., Govt Cttee of Enquiry on Inflation and Company Accounts, 1974–75; Cttee on Invisible Exports, 1975–83; Member: BOTB, 1976–83; Adv. Cttee, Queen's Award to Industry, 1976–83. Treas., UCL, 1973–81 (Hon. Fellow, 1981). Commandeur de l'Ordre de la Couronne (Belgium), 1974. *Address:* 53 Cadogan Square, SW1. *T:* 01–235 6384.

SANDLE, Prof. Michael Leonard, ARA 1982; DFA; sculptor; Professor at the Akademie der Bildenden Künste, Karlsruhe, West Germany, since 1980; *b* 18 May 1936; *s* of Charles Edward Sandle and Dorothy Gwendoline Gladys (*née* Vernon); *m* 1971, Cynthia Dora Koppel (marriage annulled 1974). *Educ:* Douglas High Sch., IOM; Douglas Sch. of Art and Technol.; Slade Sch. of Fine Art (DFA 1959). Studied painting and printmaking, Slade Sch. of Fine Art, 1956–59; changed to sculpture, 1962; various teaching posts in Britain, 1961–70, including Lectr, Coventry Coll. of Art, 1964–68; resident in Canada, 1970–73; Vis. Prof., Univ. of Calgary, Alberta, 1970–71; Vis. Associate Prof., Univ. of Victoria, BC, 1972–73; Lectr in Sculpture, Fachhochschule für Gestaltung, Pforzheim, W Germany, 1973–77, Prof., 1977–80. Has participated in exhibns in GB and internationally, 1957–, including: V Biennale, Paris, 1966; Documenta IV, Kassel, W Germany, 1968 and Documenta VI, 1977. Work in public collections, including: Arts Council of GB; Australian Nat. Gall., Canberra; Met. Mus., NY; Sztüki Mus., Lodz; Nat. Gall., Warsaw; Wilhelm Lehmbruck Mus., Duisburg, W Germany. Nobutaka Shikanai Special Prize, Utsukushi-Ga-Hara Open-Air Mus., Tokyo. *Address:* Schloss Scheibenhardt, 7500 Karlsruhe, West Germany. *T:* Karlsruhe 868633.

SANDLER, Prof. Merton, MD, FRCP, FRCPath, FRCPsych; Professor of Chemical Pathology, Institute of Obstetrics and Gynaecology, University of London, since 1973; Consultant Chemical Pathologist, Queen Charlotte's Maternity Hospital, since 1958; *b* 28 March 1926; *s* of Frank Sandler and late Edith (*née* Stein), Salford, Lancs; *m* 1961, Lorna Rosemary, *d* of late Ian Michael and of Sally Grenby, Colindale, London; two *s* two *d*. *Educ:* Manchester Grammar Sch.; Manchester Univ. (MB ChB 1949; MD 1962). FRCPath 1970 (MRCPath 1963); FRCP 1974 (MRCP 1955); FRCPsych 1986. Jun. Specialist in Pathology, RAMC (Captain), 1951–53. Research Fellow in Clin. Path., Brompton Hosp., 1953–54; Lectr in Chem. Path., Royal Free Hosp. Sch. of Med., 1955–58. Visiting Professor: Univ. of New Mexico, 1983; Chicago Med. Sch., 1984. Recognized Teacher in Chem. Path., 1960–; extensive examining experience for various Brit. and for. univs and Royal Colls; Mem. Standing Adv. Cttee, Bd of Studies in Path., Univ. of London, 1972–76 (also Mem. Chem. Path. Sub-Cttee, 1973–); Chm., Academic Bd, 1972–73, Bd of Management, 1975–, Inst. of Obst. and Gyn.; Governor: Brit. Postgrad. Med. Fedn, 1976–78; Queen Charlotte's Hosp. for Women, 1978–84; Council Mem. and Meetings Sec., Assoc. of Clin. Pathologists, 1959–70; Mem. Council, Collegium Internat. Neuro-Psychopharmacologicum, 1982–. Various offices in: RSM, incl. Pres. Section of Med. Exper. Med. and Therapeutics, 1979–80; Brit. Assoc. for Psychopharm., incl. Pres., 1980–; British Assoc. for Postnatal Illness (Pres., 1980–); office in many other learned socs and grant-giving bodies, incl. Med. Adv. Councils of Migraine Trust, 1975–80 (Chm., Scientific Adv. Cttee, 1985–), Schizophrenia Assoc. of GB, 1975–78, Parkinson's Disease Soc., 1981–; Chm. and Sec., Biol Council Symposium on Drug Action, 1979; Sec., Mem. Bd of Management and Chm. Awards Subcttee, Biological Council, 1983–; Mem. Exec. Cttee, Marcé Soc., 1983–86, and organiser or Brit. rep. on org. cttees of many nat. and internat. meetings incl. Internat. Chm., 6th Internat. Catecholamine Congress, 1987. For. Corresp. Mem., Amer. Coll. of Neuropsychopharm., 1975; Hon. Member: Indian Acad. of Neuroscis, 1982; Hungarian Pharmacological Soc., 1985. Jt Editor: British Jl of Pharmacology, 1974–80; Clinical Science, 1975–77; Jl of Neural Transmission, 1979–82; Jt Editor-in-Chief, Jl of Psychiatric Research, 1982–, and present or past Mem. Editorial Bds of 17 other sci. jls; eponymous lectures to various learned socs incl. 1st Cumings Meml, 1976, James E. Beall II Meml, 1980, Biol Council Lecture and Medal, 1984; provision of Nat. Monoamine Ref. Laboratory Service, 1976–. Anna Monika Internat. Prize (jtly), for Res. on Biol Aspects of Depression, 1973; Gold Medal, Brit. Migraine Assoc., 1974. *Publications:* Mental Illness in Pregnancy and the Puerperium, 1978; The Psychopharmacology of Aggression, 1979; Enzyme Inhibitors as Drugs, 1980; Amniotic Fluid and its Clinical Significance, 1980; The Psychopharmacology of Alcohol, 1980; The Psychopathology of Anticonvulsants, 1981; (jointly): The Adrenal Cortex, 1961; The Thyroid Gland, 1967; Advances in Pharmacology, 1968; Monoamine Oxidases, 1972; Serotonin—New Vistas, 1974; Sexual Behaviour: Pharmacology and Biochemistry, 1975; Trace Amines and the Brain, 1976; Phenolsulphotransferase in Mental Health Research, 1981; Tetra-hydroisoquinolines and β-Carbolines, 1982; Progress towards a Male Contraceptive, 1982; Neurobiology of the Trace Amines, 1984; Psychopharmacology and Food, 1985; Neurotransmitter Interactions, 1986; Design of Enzyme Inhibitors as Drugs, 1987; numerous research pubns on aspects of biologically-active monoamine metabolism. *Recreations:* reading, listening to music, lying in the sun. *Address:* 27 St Peter's Road, Twickenham, Mddx TW1 1QY. *T:* 01–892 8433. *Club:* Athenæum.

SANDON, Viscount; Dudley Danvers Granville Coutts Ryder, TD; a Deputy Chairman, National Westminster Bank Plc, since 1971 (Director since 1968); Chairman: International Westminster Bank Plc, since 1977; National Westminster Investment Bank, since 1986; Dowty Group PLC, since 1986 (Director, since 1986); Deputy Chairman, Coutts & Co., since 1970 (Managing Director, 1949); Chairman: Bentley Engineering Co., since 1983; National Biological Standards Board, since 1973; *b* 20 Dec. 1922; *er s* of 6th Earl of Harrowby, *qv*; *m* 1949, Jeannette Rosalthé, *yr d* of late Captain Peter Johnston-Saint; one *s* one *d*. *Educ:* Eton. Lt-Col RA. OC 254 (City of London) Field Regt, RA (TA), 1962–64. Served War of 1939–45: 59 Inf. Div., 5 Para. Bde, in NW Europe (wounded); India and Java (political offr), 56 Armoured Div., 1941–45. Director: Dinorwic Slate Quarries Co., 1951–69; United Kingdom Provident Institution, 1955–86 (Dep. Chm., 1956–64); National Provincial Bank, 1964–69; Olympia Group, 1968–73 (Chm., 1971–73); Sheepbridge Engrg Ltd, 1977–79; Saudi Internat. Bank, 1980–82; Chairman: Powell Duffryn Gp, 1981–86 (Dir, 1976–86); National Westminster Unit Trust Managers, 1979–83; Orion Bank Ltd, 1979–81; Director: Orion Pacific Ltd, 1980–81; Orion Pension Trustee Co. Ltd, 1980–81. Mem. Kensington Borough Council, 1950–65 (Chm., Gen. Purposes Cttee, 1957–59), Kensington and Chelsea BC, 1965–71 (Chm., Finance Cttee, 1968–71); Mem. Exec. Cttee, London area Cons. Assoc., 1949–50; Hon. Treasurer, S Kensington Cons. Assoc., 1953–56; Pres., Wolverhampton SW Cons. Assoc., 1959–68. Hon. Treasurer: Family Welfare Assoc., 1951–65; Central Council for the Care of Cripples, 1953–60. General Commissioner for Income Tax, 1954–71; Member: Lord Chancellor's Adv. Investment Cttees, for Court of Protection, 1965–77, for Public Trustee, 1974–77; Inst. Internat. d'Etudes Bancaires, 1977–; Trilateral Commn, 1980–. Manager, Fulham and Kensington Hosp. Group, 1953–56; Member: Cttee of Management, Inst. of Psychiatry, 1953–73 (Chm. 1965–73); Board of Governors, Bethlem Royal and Maudsley (Postgraduate Teaching) Hosps, 1955–73 (Chm. 1965–73); Dep. Chm., London Postgraduate Cttee, Teaching Hosps Assoc., 1968–69; Trustee, Psychiatry Research Trust, 1982–; Mem. Bd of Govs, Univ. of Keele, 1956–68. Pres., Staffordshire Soc., 1957–59 (Hon. Treas., 1947–51). Mem., Ct of Assts, Goldsmiths Co., 1972–77. Governor, Atlantic Inst. for Internat. Affairs. MRIIA; CBIM; Hon. FRCPsych 1983. *Heir: s* Hon. Dudley Adrian Conroy Ryder [*b* 18 March 1951; *m* 1977, Sarah Nicola Hobhouse Payne, *d* of Captain Anthony Payne; three *s*]. *Address:* 5 Tregunter Road, SW10 9LS. *T:* 01–373 9276; Sandon Hall, Stafford. *T:* Sandon 338; Burnt Norton, Chipping Campden, Glos. *T:* Evesham 840358.

SANDREY, John Gordon, FRCS; Consultant Surgeon, St Peter's Hospital for Stone; Consultant Urologist to the Royal Navy, etc; *b* 20 May 1903; *m* 1932, Eulie Barbara Johnston; one *d*. *Educ:* Sydney, Australia; MB, ChM Sydney, 1926; MRCS, LRCP, 1929; FRCS 1930. Temporary Surgeon-Captain RNVR, 1940–46. Mem. de la Soc. Internat. d'Urol.; FRSocMed. Formerly Surgical Registrar, Royal Prince Alfred Hospital, Sydney, and Resident Surgical Officer, St Mark's and St Peter's Hospital. *Publications:* contributions to medical journals from 1943. *Address:* 134 Walton Street, SW3.

SANDWICH, 10th Earl of, *cr* 1660; Viscount Hinchingbrooke and Baron Montagu of St Neots, 1660 [disclaimed his Peerages for life, 24 July 1964]; *see under* Montagu, A. V. E. P.

SANDYS, *see* Duncan-Sandys.

SANDYS, 7th Baron, *cr* 1802; **Richard Michael Oliver Hill;** DL; Captain of the Yeomen of the Guard (Deputy Government Chief Whip, House of Lords), 1979–82; Landowner; *b* 21 July 1931; *o s* of late Lt-Col the Lord Sandys and of Lady Sandys; *S* father, 1961; *m* 1961, Patricia Simpson Hall, *d* of late Captain Lionel Hall, MC. *Educ:* Royal Naval College, Dartmouth. Lieutenant in The Royal Scots Greys, 1950–55. A Lord in Waiting, 1974; an Opposition Whip, H of L, 1974–79. FRGS. DL Worcestershire, 1968. *Heir: cousin,* Marcus Tufton Hill, *b* 13 March 1931. *Address:* Ombersley Court, Droitwich, Worcestershire WR9 0HH. *T:* Worcester 620220. *Club:* Cavalry and Guards.

SANDYS, Julian George Winston; QC 1983; *b* 19 Sept. 1936; *s* of Baron Duncan-Sandys, *qv*; *m* 1970, Elisabeth Jane, *o d* of late John Besley Martin, CBE; three *s* one *d*. *Educ:* Eton; Salem; Trinity Coll., Melbourne. 2nd Lt, 4th Hussars, 1955; Captain, QRIH (AER), 1964. Called to the Bar, Inner Temple, 1959. Member: Midland Circuit, 1960–76; Western Circuit, 1982–; Gray's Inn, 1970–. Contested (C) Ashfield, Notts, 1959. *Recreations:* flying, computers. *Address:* 2 Serjeants Inn, Temple, EC4. *T:* 01–353 7825; *Telex:* 262303 EQLINC G. *Clubs:* Pratt's, Tiger.

SANER, Robert Morton; *see* Morton-Saner.

SANGER, Frederick, OM 1986; CH 1981; CBE 1963; PhD; FRS 1954; on staff of Medical Research Council, 1951–83; *b* 13 Aug. 1918; *s* of Frederick Sanger, MD, and Cicely Sanger; *m* 1940, M. Joan Howe; two *s* one *d*. *Educ:* Bryanston; St John's College, Cambridge. BA 1939; PhD 1943. From 1940, research in Biochemistry at Cambridge University; Beit Memorial Fellowship for Medical Research, 1944–51; at MRC Lab. of Molecular Biol., Cambridge, 1961–83; Fellowship at King's College, Cambridge, 1954. (Hon. Fellow 1983). For. Hon. Mem., Amer. Acad. of Arts and Sciences, 1958; Hon. Mem. Amer. Society of Biological Chemists, 1961; Foreign Assoc., Nat. Acad. of Sciences, 1967. Hon. DSc: Leicester, 1968; Oxon, 1970; Strasbourg, 1970; Cambridge, 1983. Corday-Morgan Medal and Prize, Chem. Soc., 1951; Nobel Prize for Chemistry, 1958, (jointly) 1980; Alfred Benzon Prize, 1966; Royal Medal, Royal Soc., 1969; Sir Frederick Gowland Hopkins Meml Medal, 1971; Gairdner Foundation Annual Award, 1971, 1979; William Bate Hardy Prize, Cambridge Philosophical Soc., 1976; Hanbury Meml Medal, 1976; Copley Medal, Royal Soc., 1977; Horwitz Prize, Albert Lasker Award, 1979; Biochem. Analysis Prize, German Soc. Clin. Chem., 1980; Gold Medal, RSM, 1983. *Publications:* papers on Chemistry of Insulin and Nucleic Acid Structure in Biochemical and other journals. *Address:* Far Leys, Fen Lane, Swaffham Bulbeck, Cambridge CB5 0NJ.

SANGER, Dr Ruth Ann, (Mrs R. R. Race), FRS 1972; Director, Medical Research Council Blood Group Unit, 1973–83 (Member of Scientific Staff, 1946–83); *b* 6 June 1918; *yr d* of late Rev. Hubert Sanger and late Katharine M. R. Sanger (*née* Cameron), Urunga, NSW; *m* 1956, Robert Russell Race, CBE, FRS (*d* 1984); no *c*. *Educ:* Abbotsleigh, Sydney; Sydney and London Univs. BSc Sydney 1939, PhD London 1948. Scientific Staff of Red Cross Blood Transfusion Service, Sydney, 1940–46. Hon. Member: Sociedad de Hematologia del Instituto Mexicano del Seguro Social; Deutsche Gesellschaft für Bluttransfusion; Toronto Antibody Club; Norwegian Soc. of Immunohaematology; Internat. Soc. of Blood Transfusion. (Jtly with R. R. Race) Landsteiner Meml Award, USA, 1957, Philip Levine Award, USA, 1970, and Gairdner Foundn Award, Canada, 1972; Oliver Meml Award for Blood Transfusion, British Red Cross, 1973. *Publications:* (with R. R. Race) Blood Groups in Man, 1950, 6th edn, 1975; many papers in genetical and med. jls. *Address:* 22 Vicarage Road, East Sheen, SW14 8RU. *T:* 01–876 1508.

SANGSTER, John Laing; Chairman: Exco International, since 1984; London Forfaiting Co. Ltd, since 1984; *b* 21 Nov. 1922; *s* of Albert James Laing Sangster and Ottilie Elizabeth Ritzdorff; *m* 1952, Mary Louise Fitz-Alan Stuart; two *s*. *Educ:* Emanuel Sch., London; Emmanuel Coll., Cambridge (MA). Joined Bank of England, 1949; Adviser, Foreign Exchange, 1965; Deputy Chief Cashier, 1975; Chief Adviser, 1979; Asst Dir, Foreign Exchange Div., 1980–82. *Recreations:* touring, walking, bird watching. *Address:* c/o Astley & Pearce, 80 Cannon Street, EC4N 6LJ. *Clubs:* Overseas Bankers'; Thames Rowing; Leander (Henley on Thames).

SANGSTER, Robert Edmund; Chairman: Vernons Organisation, since 1980; Apollo Leisure Group, since 1984; *b* 23 May 1936; *o c* of Mr Vernon Sangster and Mrs Sangster. *Educ:* Repton Coll. Dir, Newmarket Thoroughbred Breeders plc, 1985–. Owner of: The Minstrel (won Derby, 1977); Alleged (won Prix de l'Arc de Triomphe, 1977, 1978); Detroit (won Prix de l'Arc de Triomphe, 1980); Beldale Ball (won Melbourne Cup,

1980); Our Paddy Boy (won Australian Jockey Club Cup, 1981); Golden Fleece (won Derby, 1982); Assert (won Irish Sweeps Derby, 1982); Lomond (won 2,000 Guineas, 1983); Caerleon (won French Derby, 1983); El Gran Señor (won 2,000 Guineas, Irish Sweeps Derby, 1984); Sadler's Wells (won Irish 2,000 Guineas, 1984); Gildoran (won Ascot Gold Cup, 1984, 1985, Goodwood Cup, 1984); Committed (won Prix de l'Abbaye de Longchamp, Champion European Sprinter, Royal Heroine Champion Grass Mare, USA, 1984); Marooned (won Sydney Cup, 1986). Leading winning race-horse owner, 1977, 1978, 1982, 1983 and 1984 seasons. *Recreation:* golf. *Address:* The Nunnery, Douglas, Isle of Man. *T:* Douglas 23351. *Club:* Jockey.

SANKEY, John Anthony, CMG 1983; HM Diplomatic Service; Ambassador and UK Permanent Representative to United Nations Office, Geneva, and to General Agreement on Tariffs and Trade (GATT), since 1985; *b* 8 June 1930; *m* 1958, Gwendoline Putman; two *s* two *d*. *Educ:* Cardinal Vaughan Sch., Kensington; Peterhouse, Cambridge (Robert Slade Schol.; Classical Tripos Parts 1 and 2, Class 1; MA). 1st (Singapore) Regt, RA (2nd Lieut), 1952. Colonial Office, 1953; UK Mission to United Nations, 1961; Foreign Office, 1964; Dep. High Comr, Guyana, 1968; Counsellor, Singapore, 1971; NATO Defence Coll., Rome, 1973; Dep. High Comr, Malta, 1973–75; Counsellor, The Hague, 1975–79. Govr, British Sch. in the Netherlands, 1975–79; Head of Central African Dept and Special Counsellor for African Affairs, FCO, 1979–82; High Comr, Tanzania, 1982–85. *Address:* c/o Foreign and Commonwealth Office, SW1. *Club:* Athenæum.

SANSBURY, Rt. Rev. (Cyril) Kenneth, MA Cantab; Hon. DD (Trinity College, Wycliffe College, Toronto); *b* 21 Jan. 1905; *s* of late Cyril J. Sansbury; *m* 1931, Ada Ethelreda Mary, *d* of late Captain P. B. Wamsley; one *s* two *d*. *Educ:* St Paul's School; Peterhouse, Cambridge; Westcott House, Cambridge. 2nd cl. Classical Tripos, 1926; 1st cl. Theological Tripos, Pt I 1927 and Pt II 1928. Curate of St Peter's, Dulwich Common, 1928–31 and Wimbledon, 1931–32; SPG Missionary, Numazu, Japan, 1932–34; Prof. at Central Theological Coll. and British Chaplain at St Andrew's, Tokyo, 1934–41; Chaplain to HM Embassy, Tokyo, 1938–41; Chaplain, RCAF, 1941–45; Warden, Lincoln Theological Coll., 1945–52; Canon and Prebendary of Asgarby in Lincoln Cathedral, 1948–53; Warden, St Augustine's College, Canterbury (Central College of the Anglican Communion), 1952–61; Hon. Canon, Canterbury Cathedral, 1953–61; Bishop of Singapore and Malaya, 1961–66; Asst Bishop, dio. London, 1966–73; Gen. Sec., British Council of Churches, 1966–73; Priest-in-Charge of St Mary in the Marsh, Norwich, 1973–83. *Publications:* Truth, Unity and Concord, 1967; Combating Racism, 1975. *Address:* 67C The Close, Norwich NR1 4DD. *Club:* Royal Over-Seas League.

SANTA CRUZ, Marqués de, *cr* 1569; **José Fernandez Villaverde y Roca de Togores;** Marqués de Pozo Rubio; Grandee of Spain; Grand Cross of Carlos III; Grand Cross of Isabel la Católica; Grand Cross of Merito Naval; Knight of Calatrava; Spanish Ambassador to Court of St James's, 1958–72; Permanent Counsellor of State, since 1972; *b* 4 April 1902; *s* of Raimundo F. Villaverde, Marqués de Pozo Rubio and Angela, Marquesa de Pozo Rubio, Grandee of Spain; *m* 1942, Casilda de Silva y Fernandez de Henestrosa, Marquesa de Santa Cruz, Duquesa de San Carlos; three *s* one *d*. *Educ:* privately in Madrid; University of Madrid; New College, Oxford. Entered Diplomatic Service, 1921; Attaché: London, 1921, Rome, 1923; Secretary Legation: Vienna, 1927, Stockholm, 1933, London, 1934; Minister-Counsellor Embassy, London, 1944; Minister: Copenhagen, 1948, The Hague, 1950. Chm. Spanish Delegn, 7th Session The Hague Conf. on Private Internat. Law, 1951; Ambassador to Cairo, 1953; Under Secretary of State for Foreign Affairs, 1955. Representative of Spain on Exec. Council of Latin Union, 1955; Spanish Deleg. to 11th and 12th Gen. Assembly of UN, 1956 and 1957; Chm. of Spanish Delegn to XLVI Conf. of Inter-Parly Union, 1957. Hon. Fellow, New College, Oxford 1959. Holds several foreign decorations. *Recreations:* riding, shooting, golf. *Heir: s* Alvaro Villaverde, Marqués del Viso; *b* 3 Nov. 1943. *Address:* San Bernardino 14, Madrid 8, Spain. *Clubs:* Beefsteak, White's; Nuevo (Madrid).

SANTA CRUZ, Victor (Rafael Andrés), GCVO (Hon.) 1965; Ambassador of Chile to the Court of St James's, 1959–70; *b* 7 May 1913; *s* of Don Gregorio Santa Cruz and Doña Matilde Serrano; *m* 1937, Doña Adriana Sutil Alcalde; two *s* two *d*. *Educ:* Stonyhurst; Instituto Nacional, Chile. Law degree, Chile, 1937; Prof. of Civil Law, in Chile, 1941; elected MP, Chilean Parliament, 1945. *Recreation:* golf. *Address:* Zapallar, V Region, Chile. *Club:* Beefsteak.

SANTER, Rt. Rev. Mark; *see* Kensington, Area Bishop of.

SAOUMA, Edouard; Director-General of the Food and Agriculture Organization of the United Nations, Rome, since 1976; agricultural engineer and international official; *b* Beirut, Lebanon, 6 Nov. 1926; *m* Inés Forero; one *s* two *d*. *Educ:* St Joseph's University Sch. of Engineering, Beirut; École Nat. Supérieure d'Agronomie, Montpellier, France. Director: Tel Amara Agric. Sch., 1952–53; Nat. Centre for Farm Mechanization, 1954–55; Sec. Gen., Nat. Fedn of Lebanese Agronomists, 1955; Dir-Gen., Nat. Inst. for Agric. Research, 1957–62; Mem. Gov. Bd, Nat. Grains Office, 1960–62; Minister of Agric., Fisheries and Forestry, 1970. Food and Agric. Organization of UN: Dep. Regional Rep. for Asia and Far East, 1962–65; Dir, Land and Water Develt Div., 1965–75; Dir-Gen., 1976. Hon. Prof. of Agronomy, Agricl Univ. of Beijing, China. Said Akl Prize, Lebanon; Chevalier du Mérite Agricole, France; Grand Cross: Order of the Cedar, Lebanon; Ordre National du Tchad; Ordre Nat. du Ghana; Ordre National de Haute Volta; Mérito Agrícola of Spain; Kt Comdr, Order of Merit, Greece; Order of Agricl Merit, Colombia; Gran Oficial, Orden de Vasco Nuñez de Balboa, Panamá; Orden al Mérito Agrícola, Peru; Order of Merit, Egypt; Order of Merit, Mauritania; Grand Officier: Ordre de la République, Tunisia; Ordre National, Madagascar. Dr (*hc*): Universidad Nacional Agrarià, Peru; Agric. Univ. La Molina, Peru; Univ. of Seoul, Republic of Korea; Univ. of Uruguay; Univ. of Jakarta, Indonesia; Univ. of Warsaw; Univ. of Los Baños, Philippines; Punjab Agricultural Univ.; Faisalabad Agricultural Univ., Pakistan; Gödöllö Univ., Hungary; Univ. Nacional Autonoma, Nicaragua; Univ. of Florence, Italy; Univ. of Gembloux, Belgium; Univ. of Prague, Czechoslovakia. Accademico Corrispondente, Accademià Nazionale di Agricultura, Italy. *Publications:* technical publications on agriculture. *Address:* Food and Agriculture Organization of the United Nations, Via delle Terme di Caracalla, Rome 00100, Italy. *T:* 5797.

SAPPER, Alan Louis Geoffrey; General Secretary, Association of Cinematograph, Television and Allied Technicians, since 1969; *b* 18 March 1931; *y s* of late Max and Kate Sapper; *m* 1959, Helen Rubens; one *s* one *d*. *Educ:* Upper Latymer Sch.; Univ. of London. Botanist, Royal Botanic Gardens, Kew, 1948–58; Asst Gen. Sec., 1958–64, Dep. Gen. Sec., 1967–69, Assoc. of Cinematograph, Television and Allied Technicians; Gen. Sec., Writers' Guild of Great Britain, 1964–67. Mem. General Council, Trades Union Congress, 1970–84 (Chm., 1982). President: Confedn of Entertainment Unions, 1970–; Internat. Fedn of Audio-Visual Workers, 1974–; Sec., Fedn of Film Unions, 1968–; Treas., Fedn of Broadcasting Unions, 1968–; Member: British Copyright Council, 1964–; British Screen Adv. Council, 1985–. Governor: BFI, 1974–; Nat. Film School, 1980–; Hammersmith Hosp., 1965–72; Ealing Coll. of Higher Educn, 1976–78. Chm., League for Democracy in Greece, 1970–. *Publications:* articles, short stories; stage plays, On Licence, Kith and Kin; TV play, The Return, 1961. *Recreations:* taxonomic botany, hill walking, politics and human nature. *Address:* 19 Lavington Road, West Ealing, W13 9NN. *T:* 01–567 4900.

See also L. J. Sapper.

SAPPER, Laurence Joseph; legal author and broadcaster; part-time Chairman, Social Security Appeal Tribunals, since 1984; General Secretary, Association of University Teachers, 1969–83; *b* 15 Sept. 1922; *s* of late Max and Kate Sapper; *m* 1951, Rita Jeski; one *d*. *Educ:* Univ. of London (External Student). LLB. Called to Bar, Lincoln's Inn, 1950. Churchill Fellow, 1966. Min. of Agric. and Fisheries, 1939–41 and 1946–51; Educn Instructor, RAF, 1941–46; Private Sec. to Minister of Agriculture, 1948–50; Asst Sec., Instn of Professional Civil Servants, 1951–56; Dep. Gen. Sec., Post Office Engrg Union, 1956–69. Mem. Council, Brunel Univ., 1964–; Mem., NW Met. Regional Hosp. Board, 1965–71. *Publications:* Your Job and the Law, 1969; (with G. Socrates) SI Units and Metrication, 1969; papers, articles, broadcasts. *Recreations:* astronomy, writing, law reform. *Address:* 35 Waldeck Road, W13 8LY. *T:* 01–997 1251.

See also A. L. G. Sapper.

SARAGAT, Giuseppe; President of the Italian Republic, 1964–71; a Life Senator; President, Social Democratic Party, 1975–76, and since 1976; *b* 19 Sept. 1898; *s* of Giovanni Saragat and Ernestina Stratta; *m* 1922, Giuseppina Bollani (*d* 1961); one *s* one *d*. *Educ:* University of Economic and Commercial Science, Turin. Served European War, 1915–18 (Lieut); joined Italian Socialist Party, 1924; Member, Exec. Office, Italian Socialist Party, 1925; left Italy for Vienna, Paris and south of France during fascist period, 1926–43; imprisoned by Nazi occupation authorities in Rome, escaped, 1943; Minister without portfolio, 1944; Italian Ambassador in Paris, 1945–46; Pres., Constituent Assembly, 1946; founded Italian Workers Socialist Party (later called Social Democratic Party), 1947; Deputy Prime Minister, 1947–48; Member of Parliament, 1948–64; Deputy Prime Minister and Minister of Merchant Marine, 1948; Deputy Prime Minister, 1954–57; Chm., Standing Cttee for Foreign Affairs, Chamber of Deputies, 1963; Minister of Foreign Affairs, 1963–64. Secretary, Social Democratic Party, 1949–54, 1957–64, and in 1976. *Publications:* L'umanesimo marxista, 1944; Socialismo e libertà, 1944; Per la difesa delle classi lavoratrici, 1951; Il problema della pace, 1951; L'unità socialista, 1956; Per una politica di centrosinistra, 1960; Quaranta anni di lotta per la democrazia, 1965. *Address:* c/o Partito Socialista Democratico, Via Santa Maria in Via 12, 00187 Rome, Italy.

SARAJČIĆ, Ivo; elected Member, Council of the Republic, Croatia, since 1983; President, Board for Foreign Policy and International Relations, National Assembly of Croatia, 1978–82, retired; *b* 10 March 1915; *s* of Ivan and Elizabeth Sarajčić; *m* 1944, Marija Godlar; three *s*. *Educ:* Univ. of Philosophy, Zagreb. Participated in War of Liberation from (beginning) 1941 (Partizan Remembrance Medal); held various prominent political positions. Subsequently: Secretary, Presidium of Nat. Assembly of Croatia; Editor-in-Chief of Borba; Asst Minister of Educn; Dir of Information Office of Yugoslav Govt; MEC, Croatia; also Mem. Central Cttee of League of Communists of Croatia, Mem. Federal Assembly, Mem. Council for Foreign Affairs and Internat. Relations. Yugoslav Diplomatic Service, 1959; Ambassador to Austria, 1960–63; Asst Sec. of State for Foreign Affairs, 1963–66; Ambassador to London, 1966–70; Dir, Inst. for Developing Countries, Zagreb, 1970–78.

SAREI, Alexis Holyweek, CBE 1981; PhD; Papua New Guinea Permanent Representative to the United Nations, and Ambassador to the United States of America, since 1983; *b* 25 March 1934; *s* of late Joseph Nambong and Joanna Mota; *m* 1972, Claire Dionne; three *s* three *d* (all adopted). *Educ:* PNG Primary to Tertiary, 1949–66; Rome Univ., 1968–71 (PhD Canon Law). RC Priest, 1966–72; Secretary to Chief Minister, PNG, 1972–73; District Comr, 1973–75; Advisor to Bougainville people, 1975–76; Premier of North Solomons Provincial Govt, 1976–80; High Comr in UK, 1980–83. PNG Independence Medal 1977; CBE for work in Provincial Govt, pioneering work in the system in PNG. Successor to his uncle, Gregory Moah, as Chief of Clan, Petisuun. *Publication:* The Practice of Marriage Among the Solos, Buka Island, 1974. *Recreations:* music, sketching, golf, swimming, sports. *Address:* Permanent Mission of Papua New Guinea, 100 E 42nd Street, Room 1005, New York, NY 10017, USA; Papua New Guinea Embassy, 1140 19th Street NW, 6th Floor, Washington, DC 20036, USA.

SARELL, Captain Richard Iwan Alexander, DSO 1939; RN retd; *b* 22 Feb. 1909; *s* of late Philip Charles Sarell; *m* 1961, Mrs Ann Morgan (*née* Keenlyside). *Educ:* Royal Naval Coll., Dartmouth. Entered RNC Dartmouth, 1922; Comdr 1943; Capt. 1948; specialised in Gunnery, 1934; DSO for action against enemy submarines while in command of HMS Broke, 1939; despatches, 1943. Naval Attaché, Moscow and Helsinki, 1949–51; student Imperial Defence Coll., 1952; Defence Research Policy Staff, 1954; retd 1957. *Recreation:* fishing. *Address:* 43 Rivermead Court, Ranelagh Gardens, SW6 3RX.

SARELL, Sir Roderick (Francis Gisbert), KCMG 1968 (CMG 1958); KCVO 1971; HM Diplomatic Service, retired; *b* 23 Jan. 1913; *y s* of late Philip Charles Sarell, HM Consular Service and of Ethel Ida Rebecca, *d* of late John Dewar Campbell; *m* 1946, Pamela Muriel, *d* of late Vivian Francis Crowther-Smith; three *s*. *Educ:* Ashdown House, Sussex; Radley; Magdalen College, Oxford. HM Consular Service, 1936; Vice-Consul, Persia, 1937; Italian East Africa, 1939; Iraq, 1940; 2nd Secretary, Addis Ababa, 1942; 1st Secretary, HM Foreign Service, 1946; Rome, Bucharest, 1946; Foreign Office, 1949; Acting Counsellor, 1952; Counsellor and Consul-General, Rangoon, 1953; Consul-General, Algiers, 1956–59; Head of Southern Dept, Foreign Office, 1959–61, General Dept, 1961–63; Ambassador: to Libya, 1964–69; to Turkey, 1969–73. Coronation medal, 1953. *Recreations:* swimming, building, walking. *Address:* The Litten, Hampstead Norreys, Newbury, Berks RG16 0TD. *T:* Hermitage 201274. *Clubs:* Oriental, Royal Over-Seas League; Leander.

SARGAN, Prof. John Denis, FBA 1981; Emeritus Professor, London School of Economics and Political Science, since 1984 (Tooke Professor of Economic Science and Statistics, 1982–84; Professor of Econometrics, 1964–84); *b* 23 Aug. 1924; *s* of H. and G. A. Sargan; *m* 1953, Phyllis Mary Millard; two *s* one *d*. *Educ:* Doncaster Grammar Sch.; St John's Coll., Cambridge. Asst. Lectr, Lectr and Reader, Leeds Univ., 1948–63; Reader, LSE, 1963–64. *Address:* 49 Dukes Avenue, Theydon Bois, Essex.

SARGANT, Sir (Henry) Edmund, Kt 1969; President of the Law Society, 1968–69; Partner in Radcliffes and Co., 1930–71, and Senior Partner for twenty years; *b* 24 May 1906; *s* of Rt Hon. Sir Charles Henry Sargant, Lord Justice of Appeal, and Amelia Julia Sargant, RRC; *m* 1st, 1930, Mary Kathleen Lemmey (*d* 1979); one *s*; 2nd, 1981, Evelyn Noel (*née* Arnold-Wallinger). *Educ:* Rugby School; Trinity College, Cambridge (MA). 3rd Cl. Hons Solicitors' final examination; admitted 1930. Served War of 1939–45 in RAF, Provost and Security Branch; (W Africa; Middle East; Acting Wing Comdr). Member, Council, Law Society, 1951–75; Chm., Disciplinary Cttee of Architects Registration Council, 1964, 1965, 1966. Master, Worshipful Co. of Merchant Taylors, 1954. *Address:* 902 Keyes House, Dolphin Square, SW1V 3LX. *Club:* United Oxford & Cambridge University.

See also Rt Hon. Lord Justice Nourse.

SARGANT, Naomi Ellen; *see* McIntosh, N. E. S.

SARGANT, Thomas, OBE 1966; JP; Founder Secretary, Justice (British Section of International Commission of Jurists), 1957–82; *b* 17 Aug. 1905; *s* of Norman Thomas Carr Sargant and Alice Rose Walters; *m* 1st, 1929, Marie Hlouskova; two *d*; 2nd, 1942, Dorothy Lattimer; one *s*. *Educ:* Highgate School. Founder Mem., Nat. Cttee of Common Wealth, 1941–45. Pioneered campaign for Parliamentary Commissioner. Mem. Council, NACRO, 1966–81. Chm. of Governors, Sydenham Sch., 1956–60. Hon. LLM, QUB, 1977. *Publications:* These Things Shall Be, 1941, 2nd edn 1942; (jtly) More Rough Justice, 1985; articles in legal jls. *Recreations:* playing the piano, travel, helping prisoners. *Address:* 88 Priory Gardens, N6. *T:* 01–348 7530.

See also Prof. A. N. Allott, Prof. N. E. S. McIntosh, W. W. Sargant.

SARGANT, William Walters, MA, MB Cantab, FRCP, Hon. FRCPsych, DPM; Hon. Consulting Psychiatrist, St Thomas' Hospital; Physician in charge of Department of Psychological Medicine, St Thomas' Hospital, London, 1948–72; *b* 1907; *s* of Norman T. C. Sargant, Highgate; *m* 1940, Margaret Heriot Glen. *Educ:* Leys School; St John's College, Cambridge. Geraldine Harmsworth Schol., St Mary's Hosp., 1928; Asst to Medical Professorial Unit, St Mary's Hosp., 1932–34; MO and Phys., Maudsley Hosp., 1935–49; Rockefeller Travelling Fellowship and Research Fellow, Harvard Medical Sch., USA, 1938–39; Asst Clinical Dir Sutton Emergency Hosp., 1939–47; Visiting Prof. of Neuropsychiatry, Duke Univ. Med. Sch., USA, 1947–48; Registrar Royal Medico-Psychological Assoc., 1951–71; Actg Dean, Royal Coll. of Psychiatrists, 1971; Pres., Section of Psychiatry, Royal Society of Medicine, 1956–57; Examiner in Psychological Medicine, Conjoint Board of England, 1960–63; Associate Secretary, World Psychiatric Assoc., 1961–66 (Hon. Mem., 1972). Hon. Mem., Canadian, and Hon. Corres. Mem., Indian and Portuguese Psychiatric Assocs. Lectures: Ernest Parsons Memorial, Amer. Soc. of Biological Psychiatry, 1964; Herman Goldham Internat., New York Coll. of Med., 1964; Watson Smith, RCP, 1966; Maudsley, RMPA, 1968; Belisle Memorial, Michigan, 1968. Taylor Manor Hosp. Award, 1971; Starkey Meml Prize, Royal Soc. of Health, 1973. *Publications:* Physical Methods of Treatment in Psychiatry, 1944, 5th edn, 1972; Battle for the Mind, 1957; The Unquiet Mind, 1967; The Mind Possessed, 1973; Various papers on psychiatric topics, in medical jls. *Recreation:* (formerly) Barbarians RFC, St Mary's Hosp. RFC (Capt.) and Middlesex Co. RFC. *Address:* 19 Hamilton Terrace, NW8. *Club:* Savage.

See also Thomas Sargant.

SARGEANT, Frank Charles Douglas, CMG 1972; HM Diplomatic Service, retired 1977; *b* 7 Nov. 1917; *s* of late John Sargeant and Anna Sargeant; *m* 1946, Joan Adene Bickerton; one *s* one *d*. *Educ:* Lincoln; St Catharine's Coll., Cambridge. MA Cantab, Natural Sciences. Cadbury Bros. Ltd, 1939. Served War: Army, 1939–46; Lt-Col, Royal Signals. Imperial Chemical Industries Ltd, 1947–48. HM Diplomatic Service: Curacao, 1948; The Hague, 1951; Kuwait, 1954; Foreign Office, 1957 (First Sec. 1958); First Sec., Head of Chancery and Consul, Mogadishu, 1959; First Sec. (Commercial) Stockholm, 1962–66; First Sec., Head of Chancery, Colombo, and Consul for the Maldive Islands, 1967; Counsellor, 1968; Consul-General, Lubumbashi, 1968–70; Dep. High Comr, Dacca, 1970–71; Sen. Officers' War Course, RN Coll., Greenwich, 1971–72; Consul Gen., Lyons, 1972–77 (Doyen of the Consular Corps). *Recreations:* shooting, fishing. *Address:* c/o Lloyds Bank, Jersey, Channel Islands.

SARGEANT, Rt. Rev. Frank Pilkington; *see* Stockport, Bishop Suffragan of.

SARGEAUNT, Henry Anthony, CB 1961; OBE 1949; Scientific Consultant, United Nations, New York, 1968–69; *b* 11 June 1907; *o s* of Lt-Col Henry Sargeaunt and Norah Ierne Carden; *m* 1939, Winifred Doris Parkinson; two *s* one *d*. *Educ:* Clifton Coll.; University Coll., Reading (London Univ.); Cambridge Univ. Rhodes Research Grant, 1939–42; served with HM Forces, 1944–46: France, 1944; Staff Capt. with 21 Army Group, 1944; Supt Operational Research Group (ORG) (W&E), Min. of Supply, 1946; Supt, Army ORG, 1947–50; Dep. Scientific Adviser, 1950–52, Scientific Adviser, to Army Council, 1952–55; Asst Scientific Adviser to Supreme Allied Commander in Europe, Sept. 1955–57; Dep. Science Adviser, NATO, 1958–59; re-apptd Scientific Adviser to Army Council, 1959; Dep. Chief Scientist (B), War Office, 1960–62; Chief Scientific Adviser, Home Office, 1962–67. *Recreations:* yachting, horse-racing, bird-watching. *Address:* 4 Arnewood Court, Sway, Lymington, Hants.

SARGENT, Rev. Canon Alexander, MA; Archdeacon of Canterbury, 1942–68, and Canon Residentiary of Canterbury Cathedral, 1939–68; Hon. Canon, 1968, Canon Emeritus, 1974; *b* 9 May 1895; *s* of Frederick George Sargent and Florence Crundall. *Educ:* King's School, Canterbury; St Edmund Hall, Oxford; Cuddesdon Theological Coll. Deacon, 1919; Priest, 1920; Curate of St Margarets-at-Cliffe, 1919; of All Saints, Maidstone, 1921; Chaplain of Cuddesdon Theological College, 1923; Sub-Warden of St Paul's College, Grahamstown, 1927; Resident Chaplain to the Archbishop of Canterbury, 1929–39; Archdeacon of Maidstone, 1939–42; Commissary to the Bishop of Grahamstown, 1931; Six Preacher in Canterbury Cathedral, 1933; Select Preacher, Univ. of Oxford, 1949–51. *Address:* Starr's House, The Precincts, Canterbury, Kent. *T:* Canterbury 65960.

SARGENT, Dick; *see* Sargent, J. R.

SARGENT, John Richard, (Dick); *b* 22 March 1925; *s* of John Philip Sargent and Ruth (*née* Taunton) *m* 1st, 1949, Anne Elizabeth Haigh (marr. diss. 1980); one *s* two *d*; 2nd, 1980, Hester Mary Campbell. *Educ:* Dragon Sch., Oxford; Rugby Sch.; Christ Church, Oxford (MA). Fellow and Lectr in Econs, Worcester Coll., Oxford, 1951–62; Econ. Consultant, HM Treasury and DEA, 1963–65; Prof. of Econs, Univ. of Warwick, 1965–73 (Pro-Vice-Chancellor, 1971–72), Hon. Prof., 1974–81. Vis. Prof. of Econs, LSE, 1981–82; Gp Economic Adviser, Midland Bank Ltd, 1974–84; Houblon-Norman Res. Fellow, Bank of England, 1984–85. Member: Doctors and Dentists Rev. Body, 1972–75; Armed Forces Pay Rev. Body, 1972–86; Channel Tunnel Adv. Gp, 1974–75; SSRC, 1980–85; Pharmacists Review Panel, 1986–. Editor, Midland Bank Rev., 1974–84. *Publications:* British Transport Policy, 1958; (ed with R. C. O. Matthews) Contemporary Problems of Economic Policy, 1983; articles in various economic jls, and in vols of conf. papers etc. *Recreation:* work. *Address:* Trentham House, Fulbrook, Burford, Oxon OX8 4BL. *T:* Burford 3525. *Club:* Reform.

SARGENT, Prof. Roger William Herbert, FEng 1976; Courtaulds Professor of Chemical Engineering, Imperial College, since 1966; *b* 14 Oct. 1926; *s* of Herbert Alfred Sargent and May Elizabeth (*née* Gill); *m* 1951, Shirley Jane Levesque (*née* Spooner); two *s*. *Educ:* Bedford Sch.; Imperial Coll., London. BSc, ACGI, PhD, DScEng, DIC; FIChemE, FIMA. Design Engineer, Société l'Air Liquide, Paris, 1951–58; Imperial College: Sen. Lectr, 1958–62; Prof. of Chem. Engrg, 1962–66; Dean, City and Guilds Coll., 1973–76; Head of Dept of Chem. Engrg and Chem. Technology, 1975–. Member: Engrg and Technol. Adv. Cttee, British Council, 1976– (Chm., 1984–); Technol. Subcttee, UGC, 1984–. Pres., Instn of Chem. Engrs, 1973–74. Fellow, Fellowship of Engineering, 1976; Hon. FCGI 1977. *Publications:* (contrib.) Numerical Methods for Constrained Optimization, 1974; contribs to: Trans Instn Chem. Engrs, Computers and Chemical Engrg, Jl of Optimization Theory and Applications, Mathematical Programming, Internat. Jl of Control, etc. *Address:* Mulberry Cottage, 291A Sheen Road, Richmond, Surrey TW10 5AW. *T:* 01–876 9623.

SARGENT, Prof. Wallace Leslie William, FRS 1981; Ira S. Bowen Professor of Astronomy, California Institute of Technology, since 1981; *b* 15 Feb. 1935; *s* of Leslie William Sargent and Eleanor (*née* Dennis); *m* 1964, Anneila Isabel Cassells, PhD; two *d*. *Educ:* Scunthorpe Tech. High Sch. (first pupil to go to univ., 1953); Manchester Univ. (BSc Hons, MSc, PhD). Research Fellow in Astronomy, California Inst. of Tech., 1959–62; Sen. Research Fellow, Royal Greenwich Observatory, 1962–64; Asst Prof. of Physics, Univ. of California, San Diego, 1964–66; Asst Prof. of Astronomy, Calif Inst. Tech., 1966–68, Associate Prof., 1968–71, Professor, 1971–81; Executive Officer for Astronomy, 1975–81. Fellow, American Acad. of Arts and Sciences, 1977. Warner Prize, American Astronomical Soc., 1968. *Publications:* many papers in learned jls. *Recreations:* reading, gardening, oriental carpets, watching professional sports. *Address:* Astronomy Dept 105–24, California Institute of Technology, Pasadena, Calif 91125, USA. *T:* 818–356–4055; 400 South Berkeley Avenue, Pasadena, Calif 91107, USA. *T:* 818–795–6345. *Club:* Athenæum (Pasadena).

SARGESON, Prof. Alan McLeod, FRS 1983; Professor of Inorganic Chemistry, Australian National University, since 1978; *b* 13 Oct. 1930; *s* of late H. L. Sargeson; *m* 1959, Marietta, *d* of F. Anders; two *s* two *d*. *Educ:* Maitland Boys' High Sch.; Sydney Univ. (BSc, PhD, DipEd). FRACI; FAA. Lectr, Chem. Dept, Univ. of Adelaide, 1956–57; Res. Fellow, John Curtin Sch. of Med. Research, ANU, 1958, Fellow 1960; Sen. Fellow, then Professorial Fellow, 1969–78, Res. Sch. of Chemistry, ANU. *Address:* Research School of Chemistry, Australian National University, GPO Box 4, Canberra, ACT 2601, Australia.

SARGINSON, Edward William; retired from Civil Service, 1976; with Confederation of British Industry until 1982; *b* 22 May 1919; *s* of Frederick William and Edith Sarginson; *m* 1944, Olive Pescod; one *s* one *d*. *Educ:* Barrow-in-Furness Grammar School. Entered Civil Service, War Office, 1936; served Infantry, 1939–46; Principal, Min. of Supply, 1955; Asst Sec., Min. of Aviation, 1965; Asst Under Sec. of State, MoD(PE), 1972–76. *Recreation:* hill walking. *Address:* 41 Kendall Avenue South, Sanderstead, Surrey. *T:* 01–660 4476.

SARGISON, Phillip Harold, MBE 1946; Director-General of Royal Ordnance Factories (Finance and Procurement), Ministry of Defence, 1977–80; *b* 4 Feb. 1920; *s* of Ernest and Ethel Sargison; *m* 1945, Doreen (*née* Rowley); one *s* one *d*. *Educ:* De La Salle Coll., Salford. Apptd to War Office, 1938. Served War of 1939–45, HM Forces, 1940–47 (attained rank of Major). Various War Office appts in UK and British Army of the Rhine, 1947–64; Dep. Dir, Civil Service Pay Research Unit, 1964–67; Ministry of Defence: Dir of Accounts, 1967–73; Dep. Dir Gen. of Defence Accounts, 1974–76. *Recreations:* music, literature. *Address:* 2 Reynard Close, Bickley, Kent BR1 2AB. *T:* 01–467 1477. *Club:* East India.

SARILA, HH Maharaja Mahipal Singh, ju Deo, Maharaja of, CSI 1939; *b* 11 Sept. 1898; *m* 1919, *d* of Landlord of Basela, UP; five *s* three *d*. *Educ:* Daly Coll., Indore. Invested with Ruling Powers, 1919; State Delegate to the First and Second Indian Round Table Conferences, London 1931 and 1932. Late Secretary, General Council and Working Committee, Daly College, Indore. 2nd *s* succeeded, 1942, as HH Maharajadhiraja of Charkhari, UP. *Recreations:* is a keen sportsman and good tennis player and has won tournaments. *Heir:* *s* Raja Bahadur Narendra Singh ju deo, [Indian Ambassador to Switzerland. *Educ:* Mayo Coll., Ajmer, India; Magdalene Coll., Cambridge]. *Address:* Mahipal Niwas Palace, Sarila State, Bundel Khand, UP, India. *TA:* Maharaja Sarila State, India. *Clubs:* National Liberal; Delhi Gymkhana (New Delhi).

SAROOP, Narindar, CBE 1982; Adviser, Development, Clarkson Puckle Group, since 1976; *b* 14 Aug. 1929; *e s* of Chaudhri Ram Saroop, Ismaila, Rohtak, India and late Shyam Devi; *m* 1st, 1952, Ravi Gill (marr. diss. 1967), *o* surv. *c* of the Sardar and Sardarni of Premgarh, India; two *d* (one *s* decd); 2nd 1969, Stephanie Denise, *yr d* of Alexander and Cynthia Amie Cronopulo, Zakynthos, Greece. *Educ:* Aitchison Coll. for Punjab Chiefs, Lahore; Indian Military Acad., Dehra Dun. Served as regular officer, 2nd Royal Lancers (Gardner's Horse) and Queen Victoria's Own The Poona Horse; retired, 1954. Management Trainee, Yule Catto, 1954; senior executive and Dir of subsidiaries of various multinationals, to 1976; Hon. Administrator, Oxfam Relief Project, 1964; Director: Devi Grays Insurance Ltd, 1981–84; Capital Plant International Ltd, 1982–. Mem., BBC Adv. Council on Asian Programmes, 1977–81. Pres., Indian Welfare Soc., 1983–. Member Council: Freedom Assoc., 1978–; Internat. Social Services, 1981–; Inst. of Directors, 1983–; Founder Mem., Tory Asians for Representation Gp, 1984–85; Mem. Adv. Council, Efficiency in Local Govt, 1984. Contested (C) Greenwich, 1979 (first Asian Tory Parliamentary candidate this century); Founder and 1st Chm., UK Anglo Asian Cons. Soc., 1976–79, 1985–. Councillor, Kensington and Chelsea, 1974–82; initiated Borough Community Relations Cttee (Chm., 1975–77, 1980–82); Chm., Working Party on Employment, 1978; Founder and Chm., Durbar Club, 1981–. *Publications:* In Defence of Freedom (jtly), 1978; A Squire of Hindoostan, 1983. *Recreations:* keeping fools, boredom and socialism at bay. *Address:* 25 de Vere Gardens, W8. *Clubs:* Buck's, Cavalry and Guards, Pratt's; Puffin's (Edinburgh); Imperial Delhi Gymkhana; Royal Bombay Yacht, Royal Calcutta Golf.

SARRAUTE, Nathalie; writer; *b* Ivanowo, Russia, 18 July 1900; *d* of Ilya Tcherniak and Pauline Chatounowski; *m* 1925, Raymond Sarraute; three *d*. *Educ:* Sorbonne; Ecole de Droit de Paris; Oxford. *Publications:* Tropismes, 1939 (trans. Tropisms, 1964); Portrait d'un inconnu, 1948 (Portrait of a Man Unknown, 1959); Martereau, 1953 (trans. 1964); L'Ere du soupçon, 1956 (The Age of Suspicion, 1964); Le Planétarium, 1959 (The Planetarium, 1962); Les Fruits d'or, 1963 (The Golden Fruits, 1965) (Prix international de Littérature, 1964); Entre la vie et la mort, 1968 (Between Life and Death, 1969); Vous les entendez?, 1972 (Do You Hear Them?, 1973); "disent les imbéciles", 1976 ("fools say", 1977); L'usage de la parole, 1980 (The Use of Speech, 1983); Enfance, 1983 (Childhood, 1984); *plays:* Le Silence, Le Mensonge, 1967 (Silence and The Lie, 1969); Isma, 1970 (Izzum, 1975); C'est beau, 1973 (It is Beautiful, 1978); Elle est là, 1978 (It is There, 1980); Collected Plays, 1981; Pour un oui ou pour un non, 1982; *essay:* Paul Valéry et l'enfant d'éléphant, 1986. *Address:* 12 avenue Pierre I de Serbie, 75116 Paris, France. *T:* 720.58.28.

SARUM, Archdeacon of; *see* Hopkinson, Ven. B. J.

SASKATOON, Bishop of, since 1981; **Rt. Rev. Roland Arthur Wood;** *b* 1 Jan. 1933; *s* of Cyril Arthur Wood and Evelyn Mae Wood (*née* Cave); *m* 1959, Elizabeth Nora (*née* Deacon); one *s* two *d*. *Educ:* Bishop's Univ., Lennoxville, Quebec (BA 1956, LST 1958). Deacon, May 1958, priest, Dec. 1958; Asst Curate, St Matthew's, Winnipeg, 1958–60; Rector, Christ Church, Selkirk, 1960–64; Assistant Priest, St John's Cathedral, Saskatoon,

1964–67; Rector, Holy Trinity Church, Yorkton, 1967–71; Dean, St John's Cathedral, Saskatoon, 1971–81. Hon. DD, Coll. of Emmanuel and St Chad, Saskatoon, 1979. *Recreation:* model railroading. *Address:* 1104 Elliott Street, Saskatoon, Saskatchewan S7N 0V3, Canada. *T:* 306–653–0890.

SATCHELL, Edward William John, CEng, FIEE, FIERE, RCNC; Director of Engineering (Ships), 1973–76; *b* 23 Sept. 1916; *s* of Horsey John Robert Satchell and Ethel Satchell (*née* Chandler); *m* 1941, Stella Grace Cook; one *d*. *Educ:* Esplanade House Sch., Southsea; Royal Dockyard Sch., Portsmouth; RNC, Greenwich. Electrical Apprentice, Portsmouth Dockyard, 1932; Probationary Asst Electrical Engr, 1936; Asst Electrical Engr, 1939; Electrical Engr, 1943; Suptg Electrical Engr, 1955. Served with British Naval Mission in USA, 1951–53. Warship Electrical Supt, Scotland, 1958–61; Dep. Admty Repair Manager, Malta, 1961–64; Dep. Elec. Engrg Manager, Devonport, 1964–66; Asst Dir of Electrical Engineering, 1966; Dep. Dir of Elec. Engrg, 1970; Head of RN Engrng Service, 1973–75; Dep. Head, RCNC (L), 1975–76; retired 1976. *Recreations:* reading, gardening, bird watching. *Address:* 6 Badminton Gardens, Bath BA1 2XS. *T:* Bath 26974.

SATOW, Rear-Adm. Derek Graham, CB 1977; Chairman, Bath and Wells Diocesan Board of Finance, since 1981; *b* 13 June 1923; *y s* of late Graham F. H. Satow, OBE, and of Evelyn M. Satow (*née* Moore); *m* 1944, Patricia E. A. Penaligon; two *d*. *Educ:* Oakley Hall Sch.; Haileybury Coll.; Royal Naval Engineering Coll. CEng, FIMechE, FIMarE. HMS Ceylon, 1945–46; RNC, Greenwich, 1946–48; HMS Duke of York, 1948–49; RAE Farnborough, 1949–51; HMS Newcastle, 1951–53 (despatches, 1953); Naval Ordnance and Weapons Dept, Admiralty, 1953–59; Dir of Engineering, RNEC, 1959–62; HMS Tiger, 1962–64; Asst and Dep. Dir of Marine Engineering, MoD, 1964–67; IDC, 1968; Captain, RNEC, 1969–71; Dir, Naval Officer Appointments (Eng), MoD, 1971–73; Chief Staff Officer, Technical, later Engineering, to C-in-C Fleet, 1974–76; Dep. Dir-Gen., Ships, MoD, 1976–79; Chief Naval Engr Officer, 1977–79. Comdr, 1955; Captain, 1964; Rear-Adm., 1973.

SATTERTHWAITE, Rt. Rev. John Richard; *see* Gibraltar in Europe, Bishop of.

SATTERTHWAITE, Lt-Col Richard George, LVO 1985; OBE 1961; Director and General Secretary, National Playing Fields Association, 1972–85; *b* 8 April 1920; *s* of R. E. Satterthwaite and A. M. Elers; *m* 1949, Rosemary Ann, *d* of Gen. Sir Frank Messervy, KCSI, KBE, CB, DSO; three *s* (one *d* decd). *Educ:* Rugby Sch.; RMC Sandhurst. 2nd Lieut, 19th King George V's Own Lancers, 1939; served India, Burma, Malaya; transf. to 17th/21st Lancers, 1949; comd 17th/21st Lancers, 1959–61; retd 1962. National Playing Fields Assoc., 1969 (Dir, 1972–85). *Recreations:* cricket, golf. *Club:* MCC. *Address:* Meadow Cottage, East Harting, Petersfield, Hants GU31 5LX. *T:* Harting 516.

SAUGMAN, Per Gotfred; Knight of the Order of Dannebrog; Chairman since 1972, and Managing Director since 1954, Blackwell Scientific Publications Ltd, Oxford; *b* 26 June 1925; *s* of Emanuel A. G. Saugman and Esther (*née* Lehmann); *m* 1950, Patricia (*née* Fulford); two *s* one *d* (and one *s* decd). *Educ:* Gentofte Grammar Sch.; Commercial Coll., Copenhagen. Bookselling and publishing training in Denmark, Switzerland and England, 1941–49; Sales Manager, Blackwell Scientific Publications Ltd, 1952; Director, University Bookshops (Oxford) Ltd, 1963; Mem. Board, B. H. Blackwell Ltd, 1964; Chairman: William George's Sons Ltd, Bristol, 1965; Blackwell North America, Inc., 1975; Ejnar Munksgaard Publishers Ltd, Copenhagen, 1967; Kooyker Boekhandel Leiden, 1973. Member Council: International Publishers' Assoc., 1976–79; Publishers' Assoc. of GB and Ireland, 1977–82; President, Internat. Group of Scientific, Technical and Medical Publishers, 1977–79. Chairman, Oxford Round Table, 1953–55; Hon. Mem., British Ecological Soc., 1960–; Governor: Oxford Polytechnic, 1972–; Dragon Sch., Oxford, 1975–. Fellow, St Cross Coll., Oxford, 1978; Hon. MA Oxford, 1978; Hon. Fellow, Green Coll., Oxford, 1981. Knight of Order of Icelandic Falcon, 1984. *Recreations:* reading, art—English watercolours, golf. *Address:* Sunningwood House, Lincombe Lane, Boars Hill, Oxford OX1 5DZ. *T:* Oxford 735503. *Clubs:* Athenæum, Royal Automobile; Frilford Golf (Oxford).

SAUL, Prof. Samuel Berrick, PhD; Vice Chancellor, University of York, since 1979; *b* 20 Oct. 1924; *s* of Ernest Saul and Maud Eaton; *m* 1953, Sheila Stenton; one *s* one *d*. *Educ:* West Bromwich Grammar Sch.; Birmingham Univ. (BCom 1949, PhD 1953). National Service, 1944–47 (Lieut Sherwood Foresters). Lectr in Econ. History, Liverpool Univ., 1951–63; Edinburgh University: Prof. of Econ. History, 1963–78; Dean, Faculty of Social Sciences, 1970–75; Vice Principal, 1975–77; Actg Principal, 1978. Rockefeller Fellow, Univ. of Calif (Berkeley), and Columbia Univ., 1959; Ford Fellow, Stanford Univ., 1969–70. Vis. Prof., Harvard Univ., 1973. Chm., Central Council for Educn and Trng in Social Work, 1986–. Hon. LLD York, Toronto, 1981; Hon. Dr *hc* Edinburgh, 1986. *Publications:* Studies in British Overseas Trade 1870–1914, 1960; The Myth of the Great Depression, 1969; Technological Change: the US and Britain in the 19th Century, 1970; (with A. S. Milward) The Economic Development of Continental Europe 1780–1870, 1973; (with A. S. Milward) The Development of the Economies of Continental Europe 1850–1914, 1977. *Recreations:* fell walking, brass rubbing, music. *Address:* Vice Chancellor's House, Spring Lane, Heslington, York YO1 5DZ. *T:* York 413601.

SAULL, Rear-Adm. Keith Michael, CB 1982; Chairman, New Zealand Ports Authority, since 1984; *b* 24 Aug. 1927; *s* of Harold Vincent Saull and Margaret Saull; *m* 1952, Linfield Mabel (*née* Barnsdale); two *s* one *d*. *Educ:* Altrincham Grammar Sch.; HMS Conway. Royal Navy, 1945–50; transferred to Royal New Zealand Navy, 1951; commanded HMNZ Ships: Kaniere, Taranaki, Canterbury, 1956–71; Naval Attaché, Washington DC, 1972–75; RCDS 1976; Commodore, Auckland, 1978; Chief of Naval Staff, RNZN, 1980–83. *Recreations:* golf, fishing, sailing. *Address:* 17 Arawa Avenue, Devonport, Auckland, New Zealand. *T:* 452–344.

SAULTER, Paul Reginald; Chief Executive, Association of Exhibition Organisers, since 1985; *b* 27 Aug. 1935; *s* of Alfred Walter Saulter and Mabel Elizabeth Oliver. *Educ:* Truro Sch.; University Coll., Oxford. MA. Admin. Asst, Nat. Council of Social Service, 1960–63; Sen. Asst and Principal, CEGB, 1963–65; Dep. Head, Overseas Div., BEAMA, 1965–69; Dir, Internat. Affairs, ABCC, 1969–73; Sec.-Gen., British Chamber of Commerce in France, 1973–81; Chief Exec., Manchester Chamber of Commerce and Industry, 1981–85. Secretary: For. Trade Working Gp, ORGALIME, 1967–69; Council of British Chambers of Commerce in Continental Europe, 1977–80. *Recreations:* walking, music, theatre. *Address:* 9 Totteridge Avenue, High Wycombe, Bucks HP13 6XG. *T:* High Wycombe 30430. *Club:* St James's (Manchester).

SAUMAREZ, family name of **Baron de Saumarez.**

SAUNDERS, Albert Edward, CMG 1975; OBE 1970; HM Diplomatic Service, retired; Ambassador to the United Republic of Cameroon and the Republic of Equatorial Guinea, 1975–79; *b* 5 June 1919; *s* of late Albert Edward and Marie Marguerite Saunders; *m* 1945, Dorothea Charlotte Mary Whittle (*d* 1985); one *s* one *d*. *Educ:* yes. Westminster Bank Ltd, 1937. Royal Navy, 1942–45: last appt, Asst Chief Port Security Officer, Middle East. Apptd to British Embassy, Cairo, 1938 and 1945; Asst Information Officer, Tripoli, 1949; Asst Admin. Officer, Athens, 1951; Middle East Centre for Arabic Studies, 1952; Third Sec., Office of UK Trade Comr, Khartoum, 1953; Third Sec. (Information), Beirut, 1954; POMEF, Cyprus, 1956; FO, 1957; Second Sec. (Oriental), Baghdad, 1958; FO, 1959; Vice-Consul, Casablanca, 1963; Second Sec. (Oriental), Rabat, 1963; Consul, Jerusalem, 1964; First Sec., FO, 1967; Chancery, Baghdad, 1968; Head of Chancery and Consul, Rabat, 1969; Counsellor and Consul General in charge British Embassy, Dubai, 1972; Chargé d'Affaires, Abu Dhabi, 1972 and 1973; RN War Coll., Greenwich, 1974, sowc, 1975. *Recreation:* iconoclasm (20th Century). *Address:* c/o National Westminster Bank, 30 Wellington Street, Aldershot, Hants GU11 1EB.

SAUNDERS, Andrew Downing; Chief Inspector of Ancient Monuments and Historic Buildings, Historic Buildings and Monuments Commission (formerly Department of the Environment), since 1973; *b* 22 Sept. 1931; *s* of Lionel Edward Saunders; *m* 1961, Hilary Jean (*née* Aikman) (marr. diss. 1980); two *s* one *d*; *m* 1985, Gillian Ruth Hutchinson. *Educ:* Magdalen Coll. Sch., Oxford; Magdalen Coll., Oxford (MA). FSA, FRHistS. Joined Ancient Monuments Inspectorate, 1954; Inspector of Ancient Monuments for England, 1964. Vice-President: Cornwall Archaeol Soc.; Hendon and Dist Archaeol Soc.; Member: Adv. Cttee on Historic Wrecks; UK Cttee, Internat. Council for Monuments and Sites; Cttee for Aerial Photography, Cambridge Univ.; Cttee of Fortress Study Gp; Council for British Archaeology; Nautical Archaeology Cttee. *Publications:* ed jtly and contrib., Ancient Monuments and their Interpretation, 1977; excavation reports on various Roman and Medieval sites and monuments, papers on castles and artillery fortification in various archæological and historical jls; guidebooks to ancient monuments. *Recreations:* opera, sailing, Staffordshire Bull Terriers. *Address:* 12 Ashburnham Grove, Greenwich, SE10 8UH. *T:* 01–691 7192. *Club:* Athenæum.

SAUNDERS, Basil; Director, Traverse-Healy & Regester Ltd, since 1984; *b* 12 Aug. 1925; *s* of late Comdr J. E. Saunders, RN and Marjorie Saunders; *m* 1957, Betty Smith; two *s* four *d*. *Educ:* Merchant Taylors'; Wadham Coll., Oxford (MA). FIPR. Sub-Lt, RNVR, 1944–46. Assistant d'Anglais, Collège de Tarascon, 1950–51; Writer, General Electric Co. (USA), 1952–53; PRO, BIM, 1954–57; Public Relations Exec., Pritchard, Wood and Partners, 1957–63; Head of Public Relations Services, Wellcome Foundn Ltd, 1963–78; Dir-Gen., Aslib, 1978–80; Public Relations Officer, Arts Council, 1981. Consultant, Traverse-Healy Ltd, 1981–84. *Publications:* Crackle of Thorns (verse), 1968; short stories in magazines and on radio; backpagers in Manchester Guardian; reviews, articles, etc. *Recreation:* throwing things away. *Address:* 18 Dartmouth Park Avenue, NW5 1JN. *T:* 01–485 4672. *Club:* Savile.

SAUNDERS, Christopher John, MA; Headmaster, Eastbourne College, since 1981; *b* 7 May 1940; *s* of R. H. Saunders and G. S. Saunders (*née* Harris); *m* 1973, Cynthia Elizabeth Stiles; one *s* one *d*. *Educ:* Lancing Coll.; Fitzwilliam Coll., Cambridge (MA); CertEd Wadham Coll., Oxford. Assistant Master, Bradfield College, 1964–80 (Housemaster, 1972–80). Mem. Council, FA. *Recreations:* soccer (Oxford Blue 1963), cricket (Oxford Blue 1964), theatre, people. *Address:* Headmaster's House, Eastbourne College, Eastbourne, East Sussex BN21 4JX. *Clubs:* MCC, Free Foresters; Hawks (Cambridge).

SAUNDERS, Christopher Thomas, CMG 1953; Visiting Fellow, Sussex European Research Centre and Science Policy Research Unit, University of Sussex, since 1973; *b* 5 Nov. 1907; *s* of Thomas Beckenn Avening Saunders, clergyman, and Mary Theodora Slater; *m* 1947, Cornelia Jacomijntje Gielstra; one *s*. *Educ:* Craig School, Windermere; St Edward's School; Christ Church, Oxford. BA 1929; MA 1932; University of Liverpool: Social Survey of Merseyside, 1930–33; University of Manchester: Economic Research Dept, 1933–35; Joint Committee of Cotton Trade Organisations, Manchester, 1935–40; Cotton Control, 1940–44; Combined Production and Resources Board, Washington, 1944–45; Min. of Labour, 1945–47; Central Statistical Office, 1947–57; Dir, Nat. Inst. of Econ. and Social Research, 1957–64; Economist, UN Econ. Commn for Europe, 1965–72. *Publications:* Red Oxford (with M. P. Ashley), 1929; Social Survey of Merseyside (collaborated in), 1934; Seasonal Variations in Employment, 1936; From Free Trade to Integration?, 1975; Winners and Losers, 1977; Engineering in Britain, West Germany and France, 1978; (with D. Marsden) Pay Inequalities in the European Community, 1981; (ed) The Political Economy of New and Old Industrial Countries, 1981; (ed jtly) Europe's Industries, 1983; (ed) 7 volumes in East-West European Economic Interaction Workshop Papers, 1977–86; articles in Economic Jl, Jl of Royal Statistical Soc., The Manchester School. *Recreations:* walking and other forms of travel; painting. *Address:* 73 Wick Hall, Furze Hill, Hove BN3 1NG. *Club:* Reform.

SAUNDERS, Dame Cicely (Mary Strode), DBE 1980 (OBE 1967); FRCP, FRCS; Chairman, St Christopher's Hospice, since 1985 (Medical Director, 1967–85); *b* 22 June 1918; *d* of Gordon Saunders and Mary Christian Knight; *m* 1980, Prof. Marian Bohusz-Szyszko, *s* of Antoni Bohusz-Szyszko, Wilno, Poland. *Educ:* Roedean Sch.; St Anne's Coll., Oxford; St Thomas's Hosp. Med. Sch.; Nightingale Sch. of Nursing. SRN 1944; MB, BS, 1957; MA 1960 (BA (war degree) 1945). FRCP 1974 (MRCP 1968); FRCN 1981; FRCS 1986. Founded St Christopher's Hospice, 1967 (St Christopher's has been a Registered Charity since 1961 and was opened as a Hospice in 1967). Mem., MRC, 1976–79; Dep. Chm., Attendance Allowance Bd, 1979–85. Hon. Consultant, St Thomas' Hosp., 1985. AIMSW 1947; Hon. Fellow: Sheffield City Polytechnic, 1983; Newnham Coll., Cambridge, 1986. Hon. DSc: Yale, 1969; London, 1983; Dr of Medicine, Lambeth, 1977; Hon. MD Belfast, 1984; DUniv Open, 1978; Hon. LLD: Columbia, NY, 1979; Leicester, 1983; DHL Jewish Theological Seminary of America, 1982; DU Essex, 1983; Hon. DCL: Canterbury, 1984; Cambridge, 1986; Oxford, 1986. Gold Medal, Soc. of Apothecaries of London, 1979. Templeton Foundation Prize, 1981. *Publications:* Care of the Dying, 1960, 2nd edn 1977; (ed) The Management of Terminal Disease, 1978, 2nd edn 1984; (ed jtly) Hospice: the living idea, 1981; Living with Dying, 1983; various papers on terminal care. *Recreations:* music, bird watching, Polish art. *Address:* St Christopher's Hospice, 51–59 Lawrie Park Road, Sydenham, SE26 6DZ. *T:* 01–778 9252.

SAUNDERS, David Martin St George; HM Diplomatic Service; Counsellor, Foreign and Commonwealth Office, since 1983; *b* 23 July 1930; *s* of late Hilary St George Saunders and Helen (*née* Foley); *m* 1960, Patricia, *d* of James Methold, CBE; one *s* one *d*. *Educ:* Marlborough Coll.; RMA Sandhurst; Staff Coll., Quetta, Pakistan. Commnd Welsh Guards, 1950; Staff Captain Egypt, 1954–56; Asst Adjt, RMA Sandhurst, 1956–58; Adjt 1st Bn Welsh Guards, 1958–60; GSO III War Office, 1960–62; sc 1962–63; Company Comdr 1st Bn Welsh Guards, 1964; GSO II British Defence Liaison Staff, Canberra, 1965–67; Guards Depot, Pirbright, 1967–68; joined Foreign Service, 1968; Consul (Economic), Johannesburg, 1970–73; First Secretary: FCO, 1973–74; Dakar, 1974–76; FCO, 1976–77; Pretoria, 1977–79; The Hague, 1979–83. *Recreations:* military history, tennis, skiing, shooting, cinema, wines of Burgundy. *Address:* c/o Foreign and Commonwealth Office, SW1A 2AH.

SAUNDERS, David William; Parliamentary Counsel, since 1980; *b* 4 Nov. 1936; *s* of William Ernest Saunders and Lilian Grace (*née* Ward); *m* 1963, Margaret Susan Rose Bartholomew. *Educ:* Hornchurch Grammar Sch.; Worcester Coll., Oxford (MA).

Admitted solicitor, 1964. Joined Office of Parly Counsel, 1970; Dep. Parly Counsel, 1978–80. *Recreations:* golf, bridge. *Address:* 104A Belgrave Road, SW1V 2BJ. *T:* 01–834 4403. *Club:* United Oxford & Cambridge University.

SAUNDERS, Prof. Derek William, CBE 1986; Professor of Polymer Physics and Engineering, Cranfield Institute of Technology, since 1967; Director, Science and Engineering Research Council/Department of Industry Teaching Company Scheme, since 1981; *b* 4 Dec. 1925; *s* of Alfred and Elizabeth Hannah Saunders; *m* 1949, Mahalah Harrison; three *s* two *d. Educ:* Morley Grammar Sch.; Imperial Coll., Univ. of London. PhD, ARCS, FInstP, FPRI, FIM, CEng. Building Res. Stn, Garston, 1945–47; British Rubber Producers Res. Assoc., 1947–51; Royal Instn, 1951–54; British Rayon Res. Assoc., 1954–60; Cranfield Inst. of Technology: Sen. Lectr 1960, subseq. Reader; Head of Materials Dept, 1969–81; Pro-Vice-Chancellor, 1973–76. Chm. Council, Plastics Inst., 1973–75; Chm. Council, 1975–76, Pres., 1983–85, Plastics and Rubber Inst. Mem. Harpur Trust (Bedford Charity), 1968–. *Publications:* chapters in several books on polymeric materials; sci. papers in various learned jls. *Address:* 64 De Parys Avenue, Bedford. *T:* Bedford 53869.

SAUNDERS, Ernest Walter, MA; FInstM; Chairman, since 1986, and Chief Executive, since 1981, Guinness PLC (formerly Arthur Guinness & Sons plc); Chairman: Arthur Guinness Son & Co. (Great Britain), since 1982; Guinness Brewing Worldwide, since 1982; *b* 21 Oct. 1935; *m* 1963, Carole Ann Stephings; two *s* one *d. Educ:* Emmanuel Coll., Cambridge (MA). Man. Dir, Beecham Products Internat., and Dir, Beecham Products, 1966–73; Chm., European Div., Great Universal Stores, 1973–77; Pres., Nestlé Nutrition SA, and Mem. Worldwide Management Cttee, Nestlé SA, Vevey, Switzerland, 1977–81; Chm., Beechnut Corp., USA, 1977–81; Dir, Brewers' Soc., 1983–. Dir, Queens Park Rangers Football & Athletic Club, 1983–. *Recreations:* skiing, tennis, football. *Address:* c/o Guinness PLC, 39 Portman Square, W1H 9HB. *T:* 01–486 0288. *Club:* Carlton.

SAUNDERS, Air Chief Marshal Sir Hugh (William Lumsden), GCB 1953 (KCB 1950; CB 1943); KBE 1945 (CBE 1941); MC, DFC; MM; *b* 1894; *s* of Frederick William Saunders, Transvaal; *m* 1923, Phyllis Margaret (*d* 1980), *d* of Major P. W. Mabbett, Bidborough, Kent; one *s* (and one *s* decd). *Educ:* Marist Brothers' School, Johannesburg. Served European War, 1914–19, with Witwatersrand Rifles and South African Horse; transf. RFC 1917; Group Capt. 1939; Air Commodore, 1941; temp. Air Vice-Marshal, 1942; Air Marshal, 1947; Air Chief Marshal, 1950; Chief of Air Staff, New Zealand, 1939–41; AOC, No. 11 Group, Fighter Command, 1942–44; Director-General of Postings, Air Ministry, 1944–45; Air Marshal Commanding RAF Burma, 1945–46; AOC-in-C, Bomber Command, 1947; Air Council Member for Personnel, 1947–49; Inspector-General of the RAF, 1949–50; Commander-in-Chief Air Forces Western Europe, Jan.-April 1951. Air Deputy to Supreme Allied Commander Europe, 1951–53; Special Air Adviser to Royal Danish Air Force, 1954–56; Chief Co-ordinator of Anglo-American hospitality activities in UK, 1956–59. A Vice-Chm., Nat. Savings Cttee, 1956–70. Order of Polonia Restituta, 2nd Class (Poland); Commander Order of Merit (US); Officier Légion d'Honneur (France); Grand Cross of Dannebrog (Denmark). *Address:* c/o Barclays Bank PLC, 68 Knightsbridge, SW1X 7LW. *Club:* Royal Air Force.

SAUNDERS, James; playwright; *b* Islington, 8 Jan. 1925; *s* of Walter Percival Saunders and Dorcas Geraldine (*née* Warren); *m* 1951, Audrey Cross; *s* two *d. Educ:* Wembley County Sch.; Southampton Univ. *Plays:* Moonshine, 1955; Alas, Poor Fred, The Ark, 1959; Committal, Barnstable, Return to a City, 1960; A Slight Accident, 1961; Double Double, 1962; Next Time I'll Sing to You, The Pedagogue, Who Was Hilary Maconochie?, 1963; A Scent of Flowers, Neighbours, 1964; Triangle, Opus, 1965; A Man's Best Friend, The Borage Pigeon Affair, 1969; After Liverpool, 1970; Games, Savoury Meringue, 1971; Hans Kohlhaas, 1972; Bye Bye Blues, 1973; The Island, 1975; Bodies, 1977; Birdsong, 1979; Fall, 1981; Emperor Waltz, 1983; Scandella, 1985; *stage adaptations:* The Italian Girl, 1968; The Travails of Sancho Panza, 1969; A Journey to London, 1973; Player Piano, 1978; Random Moments in a May Garden, 1980; The Girl in Melanie Klein, 1980; *television:* Watch Me I'm a Bird, 1964; Bloomers, 1979 (series); television adaptations of works by D. H. Lawrence, Henry James, H. E. Bates and R. F. Delderfield; *screenplays:* Sailor's Return; The Captain's Doll. Arts Council of GB Drama Bursary, 1960; Evening Standard Drama Award, 1963; Writers' Guild TV Adaptation Award, 1966; Arts Council Major Bursary, 1984; BBC Radio Play Award, 1986. *Address:* c/o Margaret Ramsay Ltd, 14a Goodwin's Court, St Martin's Lane, WC2.

SAUNDERS, Sir John (Anthony Holt), Kt 1972; CBE 1970; DSO 1945; MC 1944; formerly Chairman and Chief Manager, Hongkong and Shanghai Banking Corporation, 1962–72; *b* 29 July 1917; *m* 1942, Enid Mary Durant Cassidy; two *d. Educ:* Bromsgrove Sch. Joined The Hongkong and Shanghai Banking Corp., 1937. War Service, 1940–45; OCTU Sandhurst (Belt of Honour); N Africa, Sicily and Italy. Lived in Hong Kong 1950–72; MEC Hong Kong Govt, 1966–72. Chm. of Stewards, Royal Hong Kong Jockey Club, 1967–72. Hon. DSocSc (Hong Kong) 1969. Comdr, Order of Prince Henry the Navigator (Portugal), 1966.

SAUNDERS, Maj.-Gen. Kenneth, CB 1979; OBE 1970; Paymaster in Chief and Inspector of Army Pay Services, 1975–79, retired; *b* 1 Jan. 1920; *m* 1953, Ann Lawrence Addison; one *s. Educ:* Lancastrian Sch., Shrewsbury. Enlisted King's Shropshire LI, 1939; commnd Royal Welch Fus., 1940; served in France, Belgium, Holland and Germany (despatches 1945); various staff appts, NW Europe and Far East, 1945–52; transf. to RAPC, 1952; Staff Paymaster: WO 1962–63; HQ Div./Malaya, 1965–67; MoD, 1967–70; Chief Paymaster: MoD, 1970–71; 1 British Corps, 1971–72; Dep. Paymaster in Chief, 1972–75; Maj.-Gen. 1975; Col Comdt, RAPC, 1979–84. *Recreations:* fishing, travel. *Address:* 31 Prestonville Court, Dyke Road, Brighton BN1 3UG. *T:* Brighton 28866.

SAUNDERS, Kenneth Herbert; Chief Architect, Commission for the New Towns, 1976–82, retired; *b* 5 April 1915; *s* of William James Saunders and Anne Elizabeth Baker; *m* 1940, Kathleen Bettye Fortune (*d* 1981); one *s* one *d. Educ:* elementary sch., Worthing; Sch. of Art, Worthing; Brighton Coll. of Art. ARIBA 1940. Served War: RA Iraq and Persia; OCTU Bengal Sappers and Miners, India and Burma; Major RE ALFSEA, SORE II, 1940 (mentioned in despatches). Articled pupil, 1933; Dept of Architecture, Bor. of Worthing, 1936; City Architect's Dept, Portsmouth, 1937–39, 1946–49; Crawley Develt Corporation: Architect, 1949; Sen. Architect, 1952; Asst Chief Architect, 1958; Commission for New Towns: Asst Chief Architect, 1962; Exec. Architect, 1965; Manager (Crawley), 1978–80. *Recreations:* architecture, buildings. *Address:* Longthorpe, 22 Goffs Park Road, Crawley, West Sussex. *T:* Crawley 21334.

SAUNDERS, Michael Lawrence; Legal Secretary, Law Officers' Department, since 1986; *b* 13 April 1944; *s* of Samuel Reuben Saunders and Doris Saunders; *m* 1970, Anna Stobo; one *s* one *d. Educ:* Clifton College; Birmingham University (LLB Hons); Jesus College, Cambridge (LLB Hons). Called to the Bar, Gray's Inn, 1971. Third Sec., Hague Conf. on Private Internat. Law (Permt Bureau), 1966–68; Second Sec., 1968–72; Senior Legal Assistant: DTI, 1972–73; Treasury Solicitor's Dept (Energy Branch), 1973–76; Law Officers' Dept, 1976–79; Asst Treasury Solicitor (Cabinet Office European Secretariat Asst Legal Adviser), 1979–83; Asst Legal Sec., Law Officers' Dept, 1983–86. *Publications:* contribs to jls on internat. law. *Address:* c/o Law Officers' Department, Royal Courts of Justice, Strand, WC2.

SAUNDERS, Sir Owen (Alfred), Kt 1965; MA, DSc; FRS 1958; FEng; Hon. FIMechE; FInstP; FInstF; FRAeS; Hon. FCGI; Life Member of ASME; Emeritus Professor of Mechanical Engineering, University of London, Imperial College (Professor, 1946; Head of Department, 1946–65; Pro-Rector, 1964–67, Acting Rector, 1966–67); Vice-Chancellor, University of London, 1967–69; *b* 24 September 1904; *s* of Alfred George Saunders and Margaret Ellen Jones; *m* 1st, 1935, Marion Isabel McKechney (*d* 1981); one *s* two *d*; 2nd, 1981, Mrs Daphne Holmes. *Educ:* Emanuel School; Birkbeck College, London; Trinity College, Cambridge (Senior Scholar). Scientific Officer, Dept of Scientific and Industrial Research, 1926; Lecturer in Applied Mathematical Physics, Imperial College, 1932; Clothworkers' Reader in Applied Thermodynamics, Univ. of London, 1937; on loan to Directorate of Turbine Engines, MAP, 1942–45. Dean, City and Guilds Coll., 1955–64. Past Pres., IMechE; Mem., ITA, 1964–69; President: British Flame Research Cttee; Section G, British Assoc., 1959. Founder Fellow, Fellowship of Engineering, 1976. Honorary Member: Yugoslav Acad., 1959–; Japan Soc. of Mechanical Engrs, 1960–; ASME, 1961–; For. Assoc., Nat. Acad. of Engrg, USA, 1979. Hon. Fellow, RHC, 1983 (Chm. Council, 1971–85). Hon. DSc Strathclyde, 1964. Melchett medallist, Inst. of Fuel, 1962; Max Jakob Award, ASME, 1966. Hon. Mem., Mark Twain Soc., 1976. *Publications:* The Calculation of Heat Transmission, 1932; An Introduction to Heat Transfer, 1950; various scientific and technical papers in Proceedings of Royal Society, Phil. Mag., Physical Society, Engineering, and the Institutions. *Recreation:* music. *Address:* Oakbank, Sea Lane, Middleton, Sussex. *T:* Middleton 2966. *Club:* Athenæum.

SAUNDERS, Sir Peter, Kt 1982; Chairman and Managing Director: Peter Saunders Ltd; Volcano Productions Ltd; Peter Saunders Group Ltd; Director: Hampdale Ltd; West End Theatre Managers Ltd; Dominfast Investments Ltd; Duke of York's Theatre Ltd; Theatre Investment Fund Ltd (Vice-Chairman); Theatre Investment Finance Ltd; *b* 23 Nov. 1911; *s* of Ernest and Aletta Saunders; *m* 1st, 1959, Ann Stewart (*d* 1976); no *c*; 2nd, 1979, Catherine Baylis (*née* Imperiali dei Principi di Francavilla) (Katie Boyle); no *c. Educ:* Oundle Sch.; Lausanne. Film cameraman, film director, journalist and press agent; served War of 1939–45 (Captain); started in theatrical production, 1947; has presented over 100 plays incl. The Mousetrap, which has run since 1953 (world's longest ever run, Dec. 1971); other West End productions include: Fly Away Peter; The Perfect Woman; Breach of Marriage; My Mother Said; The Hollow; Witness for the Prosecution; The Manor of Northstead; Spider's Web; The Water Gipsies; The Bride and the Bachelor; Subway in the Sky; Verdict; The Trial of Mary Dugan; The Unexpected Guest; A Day in the Life Of; And Suddenly it's Spring; Go Back For Murder; You Prove It; Fit To Print; Rule of Three; Alfie; The Reluctant Peer; Hostile Witness; Every Other Evening; Return Ticket; Arsenic and Old Lace; Justice Is A Woman; As You Like It; Oh Clarence!; On A Foggy Day; The Jockey Club Stakes; Move Over Mrs Markham; Lover; Cockie; Double Edge; A Murder is Announced; The Family Reunion; Cards On The Table; in 1971 acquired Volcano Productions Ltd., whose productions include No Sex Please, We're British; The Mating Game; Lloyd George Knew My Father; At The End Of The Day; Touch Of Spring; Betzi; operated repertory at Royal Artillery Theatre, Woolwich, 1951, and at Prince of Wales Theatre, Cardiff, 1956; in 1958, took over a long lease of the Ambassadors Theatre; bought the Duchess Theatre, 1961, and sold it in 1968; acquired a long lease of the St Martin's Theatre, 1968; bought the Vaudeville Theatre, 1969, and sold it in 1983; bought the Duke of York's Theatre, 1976 and sold it in 1979 to Capital Radio on condition that it remained a live theatre in perpetuity; has produced more than 1500 programmes for Radio Luxembourg; an original Dir, Yorkshire Television; Mem. consortium awarded London Gen. Radio Station by IBA, which became Capital Radio, 1973. Vice-President: Actors' Benevolent Fund, 1972–; Royal General Theatrical Fund Assoc., 1985–; Mem. Exec. Council, SWET, 1954– (Pres. 1961–62 and 1967–69); Mem. Council, Theatrical Managers' Assoc., 1958–64; Pres., Stage Golfing Soc., 1963; Pres., Stage Cricket Club, 1956–65. Governor, Christ's Hosp. Silver Heart award, Variety Club of GB, 1955. *Publications:* The Mousetrap Man (autobiog.), 1972; Scales of Justice (play), 1978. *Recreations:* cricket, chess, bridge, photography, music of George Gershwin, telephoning. *Address:* Vaudeville Theatre Offices, 10 Maiden Lane, WC2E 7NA. *T:* 01–240 3177. *Clubs:* Garrick, MCC.

SAUNDERS, Raymond; Secretary, British Museum (Natural History), since 1976; *b* 24 July 1933; *s* of late Herbert Charles Saunders and Doris May (*née* Kirkham-Jones); *m* 1959, Shirley Marion (*née* Stringer); two *s. Educ:* Poole Grammar Sch. WO, 1950; Air Min., 1956; Min. of Land and Natural Resources, 1966; Land Commn, 1967; Treasury, 1968; CSD, 1969. *Recreations:* reading biographies, gardening, sport (now mainly as spectator). *Address:* c/o British Museum (Natural History), Cromwell Road, SW7.

SAUNDERS, Prof. Wilfred Leonard, CBE 1982; FLA; Director, University of Sheffield Postgraduate School of Librarianship and Information Science, 1963–82, now Professor Emeritus; *b* 18 April 1920; *s* of Leonard and Annie Saunders; *m* 1946, Joan Mary Rider, *er d* of late Major W. E. Rider; two *s. Educ:* King Edward's Grammar Sch. for Boys, Camp Hill, Birmingham; Fitzwilliam House, Univ. of Cambridge (MA). FLA 1952. Served War: France, 1940; N Africa, 1942–43; Italy, 1943–46; Captain Royal Signals. Library Asst, Birmingham Reference Library, 1936–39; Dep. Lib., Inst. of Bankers, 1948–49; Lib., Univ. of Birmingham Inst. of Educn, 1949–56; Dep. Lib., Univ. of Sheffield, 1956–63; 12 months' secondment to UNESCO as Expert in Educnl Documentation, Uganda, 1962; Univ. of Sheffield: Prof. of Librarianship and Inf. Science, 1968; Dean, Faculty of Educnl Studies, 1974–77. Visiting Professor: Pittsburgh Univ. Grad. Sch. of Library and Inf. Sciences, 1968; UCLA, 1985; Commonwealth Vis. Fellow, Australia, 1969; (1st) Elsie O. and Philip Sang Internat. Lectr, Rosary Grad. Sch. of Library Science, USA, 1974. UK Rep., Internat. Fedn for Documentation/Training of Documentalists Cttee, 1966–70; Hon. Consultant, E Africa Sch. of Librarianship, Makerere Univ., 1967–73; overseas consultancy and adv. missions. Mem. Council, Library Assoc., 1979–83 (Pres. 1980); Member: Council, ASLIB, 1965–71, 1972–78; British Council, 1970– (Mem., Libraries Adv. Panel, 1970–, Chm. 1975–81); Bd of Librarianship, CNAA, 1966–79; Library Adv. Council (England), 1970–73; Adv. Cttee, British Library Ref. Div., 1975–80; *ad hoc* Cttee on Educn and Trng (Gen. Inf. Prog.), UNESCO, 1978–85; Adv. Cttee, British Library R&D Dept, 1980–; British Library Adv. Council, 1981–84; Adv. Council on Public Records, 1986–; Chairman: Jt Consultative Cttee of Library Assoc., Aslib, SCONUL, Soc. of Archivists and IInfSc, 1980–81; Library and Information Services Council (formerly Library Adv. Council for Eng.), 1981–84. Hon. FIInfSc 1977; Hon. FCP 1983. *Publications:* (ed) The Provision and Use of Library and Documentation Services, 1966; (ed) Librarianship in Britain Today, 1967; (with H. Schur and Lisbeth J. Pargeter) Education and Training for Scientific and Technological Library and Information Work, 1968; (ed) University and Research Library Studies, 1968; (with W. J. Hutchins and Lisbeth J. Pargeter) The Language Barrier: a study in depth of the place of foreign language materials in the research activity of an academic community, 1971; (ed) British Librarianship Today, 1977; Guidelines for Curriculum Development in Information Studies, 1978; jl articles and res. reports. *Recreations:* gardening, walking, listening to music, book collecting. *Address:* 15 Princess Drive, Sawston, Cambridge CB2 4DL. *Club:* Royal Commonwealth Society.

SAUNDERS-JACOBS, Brig. John Conrad, CBE 1945; DSO 1944; Indian Army, retired; *b* 12 Nov. 1900; *s* of George Saunders-Jacobs; *m* 1930, Sylvia (*d* 1985), *e d* of Col H. Drury Shaw, DSO; one *d. Educ:* University College, London; RMC, Sandhurst. Joined Royal Garhwal Rifles in India, 1921; Co. comd, RMC, Sandhurst, 1937–38; Bt Major, 1938; War of 1939–45: GSO1, NWF, India, 1941–42; bn, bde and actg div. comdr, Middle East, Italy and Greece, 1942–46. Staff Coll., Quetta, 1934–35; Imperial Defence Coll., London, 1946; Asst Comdt, Staff Coll., Quetta, 1947; GHQ India, Dir of Mil. Operations, Delhi, 1947; retired Indian Army, 1948. FO UK delegate to UN Special Cttee on the Balkans, 1948; Official mil. historian, Cabinet Office, 1949–50; export agent, London, 1950–53; RO II, War Office, 1954; landscape gardener, 1955–57; govt service in Mins of Defence, Aviation and Technology, 1958–71. *Address:* 10 Winsley Road, Cotham, Bristol.

SAUNDERS WATSON, Comdr (Leslie) Michael (Macdonald), RN (retired); DL; President, Historic Houses Association, since 1982 (Deputy President, 1978–82); *b* 9 Oct. 1934; *s* of Captain L. S. Saunders, DSO, RN (retd), and Elizabeth Saunders (*née* Culme-Seymour); *m* 1958, Georgina Elizabeth Laetitia, *d* of Adm. Sir William Davis, *qv*; two *s* one *d. Educ:* Eton; BRNC, Dartmouth. Joined Royal Navy, 1951; specialised in Communications (Jackson Everett Prize); Comdr 1969; retired, 1971, on succession to Rockingham Castle Estate. Chairman: Historic Houses Assoc. Tax and Parliamentary Cttee, 1975–82; Northamptonshire Assoc. Youth Clubs, 1977–; Heritage Educn Year, 1977; Corby Community Adv. Gp, 1979–86; Ironstone Royalty Owners Assoc., 1979–; Northamptonshire Enterprise Agency, 1986–; Vice-Chm., Northamptonshire Small Industries Cttee, 1974–79; Mem., British Heritage Cttee, 1978–; Country Landowners' Association: Member: Taxation Cttee, 1975–; Exec. Cttee, 1977–82; Legal and Land Use Cttee, 1983–; Chm., Northamptonshire Branch, 1981–84. Director: Lamport Hall Preservation Trust, 1978–; English Sinfonia, 1980. Trustee, Royal Botanic Gdns, Kew, 1983–. Chm., Governors Lodge Park Comprehensive Sch., 1977–82; Trustee, Oakham Sch., 1975–77. FRSA 1986. High Sheriff, 1978–79, DL 1979–, Northamptonshire. *Recreations:* sailing, music, gardening. *Address:* Rockingham Castle, Market Harborough, Leicestershire LE16 8TH. *T:* Rockingham 770240/770326. *Club:* Brooks's.

SAUVAGNARGUES, Jean Victor; Commander, Légion d'Honneur, Croix de Guerre avec palme (1939–45); Hon. GCMG 1976; Commander of the National Order of Merit; French Ambassador; former Foreign Minister; *b* Paris, 2 April 1915; *s* of Edmond Sauvagnargues and Alice Caplan; *m* 1948, Lise Marie L'Evesque; two *s* two *d. Educ:* Higher Normal Sch.; Dip., Political Science Sch.; Univ. (German) (Agrégé). Attaché, Embassy, Bucharest, 1941. Served War with Free French Forces, 1943 (Army, June 1944–May 1945). Cabinet of: the High Commn, Beirut, 1943; M Massigli, 1944; Gen. de Gaulle, 1945–46; Specialist on German questions, Quai d'Orsay, 1947–55; Cabinet of M Pinay, 1955. In negotiations about the Saar, Jan.-June 1956; Ambassador to Ethiopia, 1956–60; Director, African and Middle-Eastern Affairs, Min. of Foreign Affairs, 1960–62; Ambassador to: Tunisia, 1962–70; the Federal Republic of Germany, Bonn, 1970–74; Minister for Foreign Affairs, France, 1974–76; Ambassadeur de France, 1976; Ambassador to UK, 1977–81. *Address:* 8 rue Lalo, 75116 Paris, France.

SAUVÉ, Rt. Hon. Jeanne, CC 1984; CMM 1984; CD 1984; PC (Can.) 1972; Governor-General and Commander-in-Chief of Canada, since 1984; *b* 26 April 1922; *d* of Charles Albert Benoit and Mrs Anna Vaillant; *m* 1948, Hon. Maurice Sauvé; one *s. Educ:* Notre-Dame du Rosaire Convent, Ottawa; Ottawa Univ.; Paris Univ. Journalist; Founder, Youth Movements Fedn, 1947; Asst to Dir of Youth Section, UNESCO, Paris, 1951; Union des Artistes, Montreal: Mem., Admin. Council, 1961–72; Deleg. to Film and TV Writers Congress, Moscow, 1968; Vice-Pres., 1968–70; Sec. Gen., Fédération des Auteurs et des Artistes du Canada, 1966–72. MP (L) for Montreal Laval- les-Rapides (formerly Montreal-Ahuntsic), 1972–84; Minister of State for Science and Technol., 1972–74; Minister of the Environment, 1974–75; Minister of Communications, 1975–79; Advisor to Sec. of State for External Affairs for relations with the French-speaking world, 1978; Speaker of the House of Commons, 1980–84. Pres., Canadian Inst. of Public Affairs, 1964 (Vice-Pres., 1962–64); Founding Mem., Inst. of Political Res., 1972; Member: Centennial Commn, 1967; Admin. Council, YMCA, 1969–72. Hon. DSc New Brunswick, 1974; Hon. LLD Calgary, 1982; Hon. DHL Mount St Vincent. *Recreations:* cultivating flowers and plants, reading, tennis. *Address:* Rideau Hall, Ottawa, Ont K1A 0A1, Canada.

SAUZIER, Sir (André) Guy, Kt 1973; CBE 1959; ED; retired General Overseas Representative of Mauritius Chamber of Agriculture, 1959–79; Minister Plenipotentiary, Mauritius Mission to EEC, 1972–79; *b* 20 Oct. 1910; *s* of J. Adrien Sauzier, Mauritius; *m* 1936, Thérèse, *d* of Henri Mallac; six *s* two *d. Educ:* Royal Coll., Mauritius. Served War of 1939–45; late Major, Mauritius TF. A nominated Member of the Legislative Council, Mauritius, 1949–57; Member, Mauritius Political Delegn to the UK, 1955; Minister of Works and Communications, 1957–59. Represented Mauritius at the Coronation, 1953. *Address:* c/o Grosvenor Gardens House, 35–37 Grosvenor Gardens, SW1. *Club:* Royal Gaulois (Brussels).

SAVA, George; (George Alexis Milkomanovich Milkomane); Author and Consulting Surgeon; *b* 15 Oct. 1903; *s* of Col Ivan Alexandrovitch and Countess Maria Ignatiev; *nephew* of Prince Alexander Milkomanovich Milkomane; *m* 1939, Jannette Hollingdale; two *s* two *d. Educ:* Public Schools in Bulgaria and Russia. Entered Russian Imperial Naval Academy in 1913; after the Revolution studied in various medical schools, Univ. of Paris, Florence, Rome, Munich, Berlin and Bonn; domiciled in this country since 1932; further medical education at Manchester, Glasgow and Edinburgh; naturalised British subject in 1938; Research scholarships in medicine and surgery, University of Rome, Libero Docente (Professorship) of Univ. of Rome, 1954. Grand Chev. of the Crown of Bulgaria; Commendatore dell' Ordine al Merito Della Repubblica Italiana, 1961. *Publications: autobiog. medical:* The Healing Knife, 1937; Beauty from the Surgeon's Knife, 1938; A Surgeon's Destiny, 1939; Donkey's Serenade, 1940; Twice the Clock Round, 1941; A Ring at the Door, 1941; Surgeon's Symphony, 1944; They come by Appointment, 1946; The Knife Heals Again, 1948; The Way of a Surgeon, 1949; Strange Cases, 1950; A Doctor's Odyssey, 1951; Patients' Progress, 1952; A Surgeon Remembers, 1953; Surgeon Under Capricorn, 1954; The Lure of Surgery, 1955; A Surgeon at Large, 1957; Surgery and Crime, 1957; All this and Surgery too, 1958; Surgery Holds the Door, 1960; A Surgeon in Rome, 1961; A Surgeon in California, 1962; Appointments in Rome, 1963; A Surgeon in New Zealand, 1964; A Surgeon in Cyprus, 1965; A Surgeon in Australia, 1966; Sex, Surgery, People, 1967; The Gates of Heaven are Narrow, 1968; Bitter-Sweet Surgery, 1969; One Russian's Story, 1970; A Stranger in Harley Street, 1970; A Surgeon and his Knife, 1978; Living with your Psoriasis (essays), 1978; *political and historical books:* Rasputin Speaks, 1941; Valley of Forgotten People, 1942; The Chetniks, 1943; School for War, 1943; They Stayed in London, 1943; Russia Triumphant, 1944; A Tale of Ten Cities, 1944; War Without Guns, 1944; Caught by Revolution, 1952; *novels:* Land Fit for Heroes, 1945; Link of Two Hearts, 1945; Gissy, 1946; Call it Life, 1946; Boy in Samarkand, 1950; Flight from the Palace, 1953; Pursuit in the Desert, 1955; The Emperor Story, 1959; Punishment Deferred, 1966; Man Without Label, 1967; Alias Dr Holtzman, 1968; City of Cain, 1969; The Imperfect Surgeon, 1969; Nothing Sacred, 1970; Of Guilt Possessed, 1970; A Skeleton for My Mate, 1971; The Beloved Nemesis, 1971; On the Wings of Angels, 1972; The Sins of Andrea, 1972; Tell Your Grief Softly, 1972; Cocaine for Breakfast, 1973; Return from the Valley, 1973; Sheilah of Buckleigh Manor, 1974; Every Sweet Hath Its Sour, 1974; The Way of the Healing Knife, 1976; Mary Mary Quite Contrary, 1977; Crusader's Clinic, 1977; Pretty Polly, 1977; No Man is Perfect, 1978; A Stranger in his Skull, 1979; Secret Surgeon, 1979; Crimson Eclipse, 1980; Innocence on Trial, 1981; The Price of Prejudice, 1982; The Killer Microbes, 1982; Betrayal in Style, 1983; Double Identity, 1984; A Smile Through Tears, 1985; Bill of Indictment, 1986; also wrote numerous novels as George Borodin. *Recreations:* tennis, golf, riding, aviation. *Address:* c/o A. P. Watt Ltd, 26/28 Bedford Row, WC1R 4HL.

SAVAGE, Albert Walter, CMG 1954; Director-General (retired), Colonial Civil Aviation Service; *b* 12 June 1898; *s* of William Albert Savage, Wheathampstead, Herts; *m* 1923, Lilian Marie Gertrude Storch; one *s* one *d. Educ:* Northern Polytechnic, Northampton Institute and Sheffield University. Apprentice, Grahame White Flying School, 1914–16. Served European War, 1914–18, RFC, 1916 to end of war. Aeronautical Inspection Directorate, Air Ministry, UK 1921–34, India, 1934–36; seconded to Egyptian Govt as Chief Technical Inspector, Civil Aviation Dept, Cairo, 1936–46; Colonial Civil Aviation Service, 1946–; Director of Civil Aviation, W Africa, 1946–49; Director-General of Civil Aviation, Malaya/Borneo territories, 1949–54; Civil Aviation Adviser, Government of Jordan, 1954–55; Director of Civil Aviation, Leeward and Windward Islands, 1956–60. Director of Civil Aviation, Sierra Leone, 1961–62. *Recreations:* golf, tennis and squash. *Address:* 50 Eridge Road, Eastbourne. *T:* Eastbourne 648174.

SAVAGE, Anthony, CB 1980; Chief Executive, Intervention Board for Agricultural Produce, 1972–80; *b* 23 Aug. 1920; *s* of late Edmund Savage and Dorothy Mary (*née* Gray); *m* 1945, Heather Mary (*née* Templeman); one *s* three *d. Educ:* Johnston Sch., Durham. Entered Min. of Agriculture, 1937. War Service, Royal Artillery, 1939–46: Middle East, Italy and NW Europe, 1940–46; commnd 1943; despatches 1945. Asst Principal, MAFF, 1947; Principal, 1951; Cabinet Office, 1951–53; Asst Sec., 1961; Regional Controller, E Midland Region, 1964–69; Head of Land Drainage Div., 1969–71; Under-Sec., 1972. *Address:* 112 Powys Lane, Palmers Green, N13 4HR. *T:* 01–886 0839.

SAVAGE, Sir Ernest (Walter), Kt 1979; FCA; company director; *b* 24 Aug. 1912; *s* of Walter Edwin Savage and Constance Mary Sutton; *m* 1938, Dorothy Winifred Nicholls; one *s* one *d. Educ:* Brisbane Grammar School; Scots Coll., Warwick, Qld. In public practice as chartered accountant, 1940–76; retd as Sen. Partner of Coopers & Lybrand, Queensland. Chairman, Bank of Queensland, 1960–84; board member of several other public companies and statutory bodies. Institute of Chartered Accountants in Australia: Mem. Queensland State Council, 1951–74 (Chm. three years); Nat. Council, 1961–73; Aust. Pres., 1968–70; elected Life Member, 1978. Hon. Consul for Norway at Brisbane, 1950–76. Member: Bd of Governors, Cromwell Univ. Coll., 1950–77 (Chm. 1958–67); Faculty of Commerce and Economics, Univ. of Queensland, 1960–67; Bd of Advanced Education, 1978–82 (Finance Cttee, 1974–83). Knight 1st class, Order of St Olav (Norway), 1966. *Recreation:* brick and concrete work. *Address:* 12 Mount Ommaney Drive, Jindalee, Brisbane, Queensland 4074, Australia. *T:* 07–376.1086. *Clubs:* Queensland, Brisbane (Brisbane).

SAVAGE, Rt. Rev. Gordon David, MA; *b* 14 April 1915; *s* of Augustus Johnson Savage and Louisa Hannah Atkinson; *m* 1st, Eva Louise, *y d* of H. J. Jessen, Copenhagen; one *s* two *d*; 2nd, Ammanda Lovejoy; one *s. Educ:* Reading Sch.; Tyndale Hall, Bristol; St Catherine's, Oxford. MA Oxon, 1949. Was a Librarian before ordination, 1932–37; deacon, 1940, priest, 1941; Chaplain, Lecturer and Tutor, Tyndale Hall, Bristol, 1940–44; General Secretary Church Society, London, 1945–52; Curate-in-Charge of the City Church, Oxford, 1948–52; Proctor in Convocation, 1951–61; Vicar of Marston, Oxford, 1952–57; Archdeacon of Buckingham and Vicar of Whitchurch, Bucks, 1957–61; Suffragan Bishop of Buckingham, 1960–64; Bishop of Southwell, 1964–70. *Address:* 11 Ranelagh Street, White Cross, Hereford HR4 0DT.

SAVARESE, Signora Fernando; *see* Elvin, Violetta.

SAVERNAKE, Viscount; Thomas James Brudenell-Bruce; *b* 11 Feb. 1982; *s* and *heir* of Earl of Cardigan, *qv*.

SAVILE, family name of **Earl of Mexborough.**

SAVILE, 3rd Baron, *cr* 1888; **George Halifax Lumley-Savile;** DL; JP; *b* 24 Jan. 1919; *s* of 2nd Baron and Esme Grace Virginia (*d* 1958), *d* of J. Wolton; *S* father, 1931. *Educ:* Eton. Served in 1939–45 War in Duke of Wellington's Regiment, and attached Lincolnshire Regiment during the Burma Campaigns. DL W Yorks, 1954. Is Patron of two livings. Owns about 18,000 acres. JP Borough of Dewsbury, 1955. CStJ 1982. *Recreations:* music and shooting. *Heir: b* Hon. Henry Leoline Thornhill Lumley-Savile [*b* 2 Oct. 1923; *m* 1st, 1946, Presiley June (marr. diss. 1951), *o d* of Major G. H. E. Inchbald, Halebourne House, Chobham, Surrey; one *s*; 2nd, 1961, Caroline Jeffie (*d* 1970), *o d* of Peter Clive, California, USA, and Elizabeth Clive, 58 Queens' Gate, SW7; 3rd, 1972, Margaret, *widow* of Peter Bruce; three *s* (triplets). Served War of 1939–45, in Grenadier Guards, Italy (wounded)]. *Address:* Gryce Hall, Shelley, Huddersfield. *T:* Huddersfield 602774; Walshaw, Hebden Bridge, Yorks. *T:* Hebden Bridge 842275. *Clubs:* Brooks's, Sloane.

SAVILE, Jimmy, OBE 1971; TV and radio personality; *b* 31 Oct. 1926. *Educ:* St Anne's, Leeds. Presenter: Radio 1 weekly show; television: Jim'll Fix It, making dreams come true, No 1 in the ratings every year; Mind How You Go, road safety show; Top of the Pops. Man of many parts but best known as a voluntary helper at Leeds Infirmary, Broadmoor Hospital, and Stoke Mandeville where he raised ten million pounds to rebuild the National Spinal Injuries Centre. Hon. LLD Leeds, 1986. Hon. KCSG (Holy See), 1982; Bronze and Gold medals, SMO, St John of Jerusalem. *Publications:* As It Happens (autobiog.), 1975; Love is an Uphill Thing (autobiog.), 1975; God'll Fix It, 1978. *Recreations:* running, cycling, wrestling. *Address:* c/o General Infirmary, Leeds LS1 3EX. *T:* Leeds 432 799. *Club:* Athenæum.

SAVILL, David Malcolm, QC 1969; **His Honour Judge Savill;** a Circuit Judge, since 1984; *b* 18 Sept. 1930; *s* of late Lionel and of Lisbeth Savill; *m* 1955, Mary Arnott (*née* Eadie), JP, *d* of late Lady Hinchcliffe and step *d* of late Hon. Sir (George) Raymond Hinchcliffe; one *s* two *d. Educ:* Marlborough Coll.; Clare Coll., Cambridge. 2nd Lieut Grenadier Guards, 1949–50. BA (Hons) Cambridge, 1953. Called to the Bar, Middle Temple, 1954 (Bencher, 1977); Mem., Senate of Inns of Court and the Bar, 1976, 1980–83. A Recorder, 1972–84; Chancellor, diocese of Bradford, 1976–; Leader, NE Circuit, 1980–83. Chm., Adv. Cttee on Conscientious Objectors, 1978–. *Recreations:* cricket, golf, gardening. *Address:* 11 King's Bench Walk, Temple, EC4. *T:* 01–353 3337. *Club:* MCC.

SAVILL, Colonel Kenneth Edward, CVO 1976; DSO 1945; DL; Member, HM Bodyguard of Hon. Corps of Gentlemen at Arms, 1955–76 (Lieutenant, 1973–76; Standard Bearer, 1972–73); *b* 8 August 1906; *o s* of Walter Savill, Chilton Manor, Alresford and May, *d* of Major Charles Marriott; *m* 1935, Jacqueline (*d* 1980), *o d* of Brig. John Salusbury Hughes, MC; two *d* (and one *d* decd). *Educ*: Winchester College; RMC Sandhurst. Commissioned, 12th Royal Lancers, 1926; 1st King's Dragoon Guards, 1936; The Queen's Bays, 1947. Served War of 1939–45, France, 1939–40; N Africa and Italy, 1943–45; Col 1950; retd 1953. High Sheriff of Hampshire, 1961; DL Hampshire, 1965. Col, 1st The Queen's Dragoon Guards, 1964–68. *Address*: Chilton Manor, Alresford, Hants. *T*: Preston Candover 246. *Club*: Cavalry and Guards.

SAVILLE, Prof. John; Emeritus Professor of Economic and Social History, University of Hull; *b* 2 April 1916; *o s* of Orestes Stamatopoulos, Volos, Greece, and Edith Vessey (name changed by deed poll to that of step-father, 1937); *m* 1943, Constance Betty Saunders; three *s* one *d*. *Educ*: Royal Liberty Sch.; London Sch. of Economics. 1st Cl. Hons BSc (Econ) 1937. Served War, RA, 1940–46; Chief Scientific Adviser's Div., Min. of Works, 1946–47; Univ. of Hull, 1947–82, Prof. of Economic and Social History, 1972–82. Leverhulme Emeritus Fellow, 1984–86. Mem., British Communist Party, 1934–56; Chm., Oral Hist. Soc., 1976–; Vice-Chm., and then Chm., Soc. for Study of Labour Hist., 1974–82; Mem. Exec. Cttee and Founder-Mem., Council for Academic Freedom and Democracy, 1971–81, Chm. 1982–; Chm., Economic and Social Hist. Cttee, SSRC, 1977–79. Trustee, Michael Lipman Trust, 1977–. *Publications*: Ernest Jones, Chartist, 1952; Rural Depopulation in England and Wales 1851–1951, 1957; numerous articles; Co-Editor: (with E. P. Thompson) Reasoner and New Reasoner, 1956–59; (with Asa Briggs) Essays in Labour History, 1960, 1971, 1977; (with Ralph Miliband) Socialist Register (annual, 1964–); (with Joyce M. Bellamy) Dictionary of Labour Biography, 1972–. *Recreations*: working for socialism, looking at churches. *Address*: 152 Westbourne Avenue, Hull HU5 3HZ. *T*: Hull 43425.

SAVILLE, Hon. Sir Mark (Oliver), Kt 1985; **Hon. Mr Justice Saville;** a Judge of the High Court of Justice, Queen's Bench Division, since 1985; *b* 20 March 1936; *s* of Kenneth Vivian Saville and Olivia Sarah Frances Gray; *m* 1961, Jill Gray; two *s*. *Educ*: St Paul's Primary Sch., Hastings; Rye Grammar Sch.; Brasenose Coll., Oxford (BA, BCL). Nat. Service, 2nd Lieut Royal Sussex Regt, 1954–56; Oxford Univ., 1956–60 (Vinerian Schol. 1960); called to Bar, Middle Temple, 1962 (Bencher, 1983); QC 1975. *Recreation*: sailing. *Address*: Royal Courts of Justice, Strand, WC2A 2LL.

SAVORY, Hubert Newman, MA, DPhil Oxon, FSA; Keeper of Archæology, National Museum of Wales, Cardiff, 1956–76; *b* 7 Aug. 1911; *s* of William Charles Newman Savory and Alice Amelia (*née* Minns); *m* 1949, Priscilla Valerie Thirkell; four *s* two *d*. *Educ*: Magdalen College Sch., Oxford; St Edmund Hall, Oxford Univ. BA Oxon 1934 (Lit. Hum. 1st Cl.); DPhil Oxon 1937; Randall MacIver Student in Iberian Archæology, 1936–38. Assistant, 1938, Asst Keeper, 1939, Dept of Archæology, National Museum of Wales. Chm., Royal Commn on Ancient Monuments (Wales), 1979–83 (Mem., 1970–83); Mem., Ancient Monuments Board for Wales, 1957–84; Pres., Cambrian Archæological Assoc., 1975–76; Chm., Glamorgan Gwent Archæological Trust, 1975–84. Conducted excavations of various Welsh cromlechs, round barrows, hill-forts, etc. Served War of 1939–45, in Army, 1940–45. *Publications*: Spain and Portugal: The Prehistory of the Iberian Peninsula, 1968; Guide Catalogues of the Early Iron Age Collections, 1976, and the Bronze Age Collections, 1980, National Museum of Wales; (ed) Glamorgan County History, vol. II, 1984; contrib. to Proc. of Prehistoric Soc.; Archæologia Cambrensis, etc. *Recreations*: walking, gardening. *Address*: 31 Lady Mary Road, Cardiff. *T*: Cardiff 753106.

SAVORY, Sir Reginald (Charles Frank), Kt 1972; CBE 1965; Chairman of Directors, Savory Holdings Ltd, Building Contractors, since 1933; *b* 27 May 1908; *s* of Frank and Margaret Savory, Auckland, NZ; *m* 1935, Fai-Ola, *o c* of Ernest Vaile, Auckland; two *d*. *Educ*: Auckland Grammar Sch. Past Chm., Bd of Governors, Council of Auckland Technical Institutes; Member: Auckland Harbour Bd (Chm., 1961–71); Auckland City Council, 1953–62, Drainage Bd, 1956–62, and Chamber of Commerce, 1961–71. Pres., NZ Harbours Assoc., 1963–67; Past Pres., NZ Technical Assoc.; Life Mem. (Past Pres.) NZ Builders' Fedn; FIOB (Gt Britain) 1959. *Recreations*: boating, fishing, golf, bowls; watching Rugby football. *Address*: Northbridge Residential Home, Akoranga Drive, Northcote, Auckland, New Zealand. *T*: 492–942. *Clubs*: Auckland (Auckland); NZ Royal Yacht Squadron; Newmarket Rotary.

SAVOURS, Dale Norman C.; see Campbell-Savours.

SAWBRIDGE, Henry Raywood, CBE 1960; retired from HM Foreign Service, 1964; Deputy Director, Centre of Japanese Studies, University of Sheffield, 1964–66; *b* 1 Nov. 1907; 2nd *s* of Rev. John Edward Bridgman Sawbridge; *m* 1947, Lilian, *d* of late William Herbert Wood; one *s* one *d*. *Educ*: Eton; Trinity Coll., Oxford. Entered HM Consular Service, 1931, and served in Japan, Korea and at FO; served with Australian Forces, 1943; HM Consul-General, Yokohama, 1949; Chargé d'Affaires, Korea, 1950; HM Consul-General, Geneva, 1953; Counsellor at Foreign Office, 1960. Coronation Medal, 1953. *Recreations*: shooting, fishing. *Address*: The Moorings, Kingsgate, Kent. *Club*: Travellers'.

SAWERS, David Richard Hall; writer and consultant; *b* 23 April 1931; *s* of late Edward and of Madeline Sawers; unmarried. *Educ*: Westminster Sch.; Christ Church, Oxford (MA). Research Asst to Prof. J. Jewkes, Oxford Univ., 1954–58; Journalist, The Economist, 1959–64; Vis. Fellow, Princeton Univ., 1964–65; Econ. Adviser, Min. of Aviation and of Technology, 1966–68; Sen. Econ. Adviser, Min. of Technology, Aviation Supply, and DTI, 1968–72; Under-Sec., Depts of Industry, Trade and Prices and Consumer Protection, 1972–76; Under-Sec., Depts of Environment and Transport, 1976–83; Principal Res. Fellow, Technical Change Centre, 1984–86. *Publications*: (with John Jewkes and Richard Stillerman) The Sources of Invention, 1958; (with Ronald Miller) The Technical Development of Modern Aviation, 1968. *Recreations*: listening to music, looking at pictures, gardening. *Address*: 10 Seaview Avenue, Angmering-on-Sea, Littlehampton BN16 1PP. *T*: Littlehampton 785571.

SAWERS, Maj.-Gen. James Maxwell, CB 1974; MBE 1953; Managing Director, Services Kinema Corporation, 1975–81; *b* 14 May 1920; *s* of late Lt-Col James Sawers, Woking, Surrey; *m* 1945, Grace, *d* of Joseph William Walker, Tynemouth; two *s* one *d*. *Educ*: Rugby; RMA Woolwich. 2nd Lieut, Royal Signals, 1939. Served War of 1939–45 in W Africa and Burma. Lt-Col, 1960; Brig., 1966; BGS, MoD, 1966–68; Comd Corps Royal Signals, 1st British Corps, 1968–69; attended IDC, 1970; Signal Officer in Chief, 1971–74. Col Comdt, Royal Signals, 1974–79; Hon. Col, 71 (Yeomanry) Signal Regt, 1977–83. psc, jssc, idc. CBIM. Managing Trustee: Soldiers' Widows Fund; Single Soldiers' Dependants Fund. *Recreations*: sailing, skiing, gardening, golf, photography. *Address*: Monk's Lantern, Fairfield Close, Lymington, Hants SO4 9NP. *T*: Lymington 73392. *Clubs*: Army and Navy; Royal Lymington Yacht.

SAWKO, Prof. Felicjan, DSc; Professor of Civil Engineering, Liverpool University, since 1967; *b* 17 May 1937; *s* of Czeslaw Sawko and Franciszka (*née* Nawrot); *m* 1960,

Genowefa Stefania (*née* Bak); four *s* one *d*. *Educ*: Leeds Univ. (BSc Civil Engrg, 1958; MSc 1960; DSc 1973). Engr, Rendel Palmer & Tritton, London, 1959–62; Lectr, Leeds Univ., 1962–67, Reader 1967. Henry Adams Award, IStructE, 1980. *Publications*: (ed) Developments in Prestressed Concrete, Vols 1 and 2, 1968; (with Cope and Tickell) Numerical Methods for Civil Engineers, 1981; some 70 papers on computer methods and structural masonry. *Recreations*: travel, bridge, numismatics. *Address*: 9 Harthill Road, Liverpool L18 6HU. *T*: 051–724 2726.

SAWYER, John Stanley, MA; FRS 1962; Director of Research, Meteorological Office, 1965–76; *b* 19 June 1916; *s* of late Arthur Stanley Sawyer and Emily Florence Sawyer (*née* Frost); *m* 1951, Betty Vera Beeching (*née* Tooke), widow; one *d*. *Educ*: Latymer Upper Sch., Hammersmith; Jesus Coll., Cambridge. Entered Meteorological Office, 1937. Mem., NERC, 1975–81. Pres., Commn for Atmospheric Sciences, World Meteorological Organisation, 1968–73 (IMO Prize, 1973); Pres., Royal Meteorological Soc., 1963–65 (Hugh Robert Mill Medal 1956, Buchan Prize 1962, Symons Medal 1971). *Publications*: Ways of the Weather, 1958; scientific papers largely in Quart. Jl Roy. Met. Soc. *Address*: Ivy Corner, Corfe, Taunton, Somerset. *T*: Blagdon Hill 612.

SAXON, David Stephen, PhD; Chairman of the Corporation, Massachusetts Institute of Technology, since 1983; *b* 8 Feb. 1920; *s* of Ivan Saxon and Rebecca Moss; *m* 1940, Shirley Goodman; six *d*. *Educ*: Massachusetts Institute of Technology (BS 1941; PhD 1944). Massachusetts Institute of Technology: Res. physicist, Radiation Lab., 1943–46; Philips Labs, 1946–47. Univ. of California at Los Angeles: Mem. of Faculty, 1947–75; Prof. of Physics, 1958–75; Chm. of Dept, 1963–66; Dean of Physical Sciences, 1966–68; Vice-Chancellor, 1968–75; Provost, Univ. of California, 1974–75, Pres., 1975–83. Guggenheim Fellow, 1956–57 and 1961–62; Fulbright grant, 1961–62. Vis. Prof., Univ. of Paris, Orsay, France, 1961–62; Vis. scientist, Centre d'Etudes Nucléaires, France, 1968–69; Vis. Research Fellow, Merton Coll., Oxford, 1981; consultant to research organisations, 1948–. Special research into theoretical physics: nuclear physics, quantum mechanics, electromagnetic theory and scattering theory. Dir, Eastman Kodak Co., 1983–. Fellow: Amer. Phys. Soc.; Amer. Acad. of Arts and Scis; Member: Amer. Assoc. Physics Teachers; Amer. Inst. Physics; Amer. Assoc. for the Advancement of Science; Technical Adv. Council for Ford Motor Co., 1979–; Corp. of MIT, 1977–; Dir, Houghton Mifflin Co., 1984–. Recipient of several honorary degrees. Member: Phi Beta Kappa; Sigma Pi Sigma; Sigma Xi. Royal Order of the Northern Star (Nordstjärnan), 1979. *Publications*: Elementary Quantum Mechanics, 1968; The Nuclear Independent Particle Model (with A. E. S. Green and T. Sawada), 1968; Discontinuities in Wave Guides (with Julian Schwinger), 1968; Physics for the Liberal Arts Student (with William B. Fretter), 1971. *Address*: Chairman's Office, Massachusetts Institute of Technology, Cambridge, Mass 02139, USA.

SAY, Rt. Rev. Richard David; see Rochester, Bishop of.

SAYCE, Roy Beavan, FRICS; MRAC; Director, Rural Planning Services, Didcot, since 1980; *b* 19 July 1920; *s* of Roger Sayce, BScAgric, NDA, and Lilian Irene Sayce; *m* 1949, Barbara Sarah (*née* Leverton); two *s*. *Educ*: Culford Royal Agricultural Coll. (MRAC; Silver Medal 1948). FRICS 1949. Univ. of London, 1938–40. Served War, Intell., RAFVR, 1940–46. Agricultural Land Service: Asst Land Comr, Chelmsford, 1949–50; Sen. Asst Land Comr, Norwich, 1950–63; Divl Land Comr, Oxford, 1963–71; Reg. Surveyor, Land Service, Agric. Develt and Adv. Service, Bristol, 1971–76; Chief Surveyor, Land Service, Agric. Develt and Adv. Service, MAFF, 1977–80. Royal Instn of Chartered Surveyors: Mem., Gen. and Divl Councils, 1970–80; Divl Pres., Land Agency and Agriculture Div., 1973–74. Chm., Farm Buildings Information Centre, 1980–85. Governor, Royal Agric. Coll., Cirencester, 1975–. FRSA 1975; Hon. Mem., CAAV, 1978. *Publications*: Farm Buildings, 1966; (contrib.) Walmsley's Rural Estate Management, 1969; contrib. professional jls. *Recreations*: golf, non-professional writing. *Address*: 13 Haywards Close, Wantage, Oxon OX12 7AT. *T*: Wantage 4836. *Clubs*: Farmers', Civil Service.

SAYE AND SELE, 21st Baron *cr* 1447 and 1603; **Nathaniel Thomas Allen Fiennes;** DL; Regional Director, South Midlands Region, Lloyds Bank, since 1983; *b* 22 September 1920; *s* of Ivo Murray Twisleton-Wykeham-Fiennes, 20th Baron Saye and Sele, OBE, MC, and Hersey Cecilia Hester, *d* of late Captain Sir Thomas Dacres Butler, KCVO; *S* father, 1968; *m* 1958, Mariette Helena, *d* of Maj.-Gen. Sir Guy Salisbury-Jones, GCVO, CMG, CBE, MC; three *s* one *d* (and one *s* decd). *Educ*: Eton; New College, Oxford. Served with Rifle Brigade, 1941–49 (despatches twice). Chartered Surveyor. Partner in firm of Laws and Fiennes. DL Oxfordshire, 1979. Fellow, Winchester Coll., 1967–83. *Heir*: *s* Hon. Richard Ingel Fiennes, *b* 19 August 1959. *Address*: Broughton Castle, Banbury, Oxon. *T*: Banbury 62624.
See also Very Rev. Hon. O. W. Fiennes.

SAYEED, Dr (Abul Fatah) Akram, OBE 1976; FRSM; General Medical Practitioner in Leicester, since 1963; President, Standing Conference of Asian Organizations in UK, since 1977; Vice-Chairman, Overseas Doctors' Association in UK, since 1984 (Vice-President, 1979–84); *b* Bangladesh, 23 Nov. 1935; *s* of late Mokhles Ahmed, school teacher; registered British; *m* 1959, Hosne-ara Ali, *d* of M. S. Ali; two *s* one *d*. *Educ*: St Joseph's Sch., Khulna; Dacca Univ. MB, BS 1958. Editor, Dacca Med. Coll. Jl and Magazines, 1957–58; Lit. Sec., Students Union. Went to USA, 1960; resident in Britain from 1961. Mem. Staff, Leicester Royal Infirmary; Member: Leics Local Medical Cttee, 1977–; Leics Family Practitioner Cttee, 1982–. Member: DHSS Working Party on Asian Health Gp, 1979; Home Office Statutory Adv. Council on Community and Race Relations, 1983–; Health Care Planning Team, Leics HA, 1984; Unit Management Team, Leics Central Unit, 1986. Sec., Inst. of Transcultural Health Care, 1985. Co-founder, Nat. Fedn of Pakistani Assocs in GB, 1963; Adviser, NCCI, 1965–68; Founder Member: Leicester Council for Community Relations, 1965; British-Bangladesh Soc.; Member: Community Relations Commn, 1968–77; E Midlands Adv. Cttee, CRE, 1978–; Stop Rickets Campaign (Chm., Leicester Campaign); Central Exec. Council, Bangladesh Med. Assoc. in UK; Chm., Standing Conf. of Asian Orgns in UK, 1973–77 (Vice-Chm., 1970–73); Life Mem., Pakistan Soc.; Pres., Pakistan Assoc., Leics, 1965–71. Mem., BBC Asian Programme Adv. Cttee, 1972–77. Special interest in problems of Asians; initiated study of problems of second generation Asians (CRE report Between Two Cultures); Gen. Sec., Overseas Doctors Assoc., 1975–77 (Founder Chm., 1975, Sponsor Chm., 1975; Fellow); attended First World Conf. on Muslim Educn, Mecca, 1977; has done much work with disaster funds, etc. *Publications*: (ed jtly) Asian Who's Who, 1975–76, 2nd edn 1978; contribs on socio-med. aspects of Asians in Britain to various jls. *Recreations*: gardening, reading, stamp collecting. *Address*: Ramna, 2 Mickleton Drive, Leicester LE5 6GD. *T*: Leicester 416703. *Club*: National Liberal (non-political member).

SAYEED, Jonathan; MP (C) Bristol East, since 1983; *b* 20 March 1948; *m* 1980, Nicola Anne Parkes Power; one *s*. *Educ*: Woolverstone Hall; Britannia Royal Naval Coll., Dartmouth; Royal Naval Engrg Coll., Manadon. *Recreations*: riding, squash, classical music, architecture. *Address*: House of Commons, SW1A 0AA. *T*: 01–219 6389.

SAYER, Guy Mowbray, CBE 1978; JP; Director: World Shipping and Investment Co. Ltd, Hong Kong, since 1977; World Finance International Ltd, Bermuda, since 1977; World Maritime Ltd, Bermuda, since 1977; *b* 18 June 1924; *yr s* of late Geoffrey Robley and Winifred Lily Sayer; *m* 1951, Marie Anne Sophie, *o d* of late Henri-Marie and Elisabeth Mertens; one *s* two *d*. *Educ:* Mill Mead Prep. Sch.; Shrewsbury School. FIB 1971. Royal Navy, 1942–46. Joined Hongkong & Shanghai Banking Corp., 1946; service in London, China, Japan, Malaysia, Burma and Hong Kong; Gen. Man. 1969; Exec. Dir 1970; Dep. Chm. 1971; Chm., 1972–77 (now Mem., London Adv. Cttee, 1979–). Chairman: Hongkong Bank of Calif., San Francisco, 1972–77; Mercantile Bank Ltd, 1973–77; Director: Internat. Commercial Bank Ltd, London, 1969–77; Mercantile Credits Ltd, Sydney, 1971–77. Treas., Hong Kong Univ., 1972–77. Member: Exchange Fund Adv. Cttee, Hong Kong, 1971–77; London Adv. Cttee, British Bank of the Middle East, 1980–. MLC, 1973–74, MEC, 1974–77, Hong Kong. JP Hong Kong, 1971. Governor, Suttons Hosp. in Charterhouse. Hon. LLD Hong Kong, 1978. *Recreations:* golf, walking. *Address:* 5 Pembroke Gardens, W8. *T:* 01–602 4578. *Clubs:* Oriental, MCC; Royal Wimbledon Golf; West Sussex Golf; Hong Kong, Shek O Country (Hong Kong).

SAYER, John Raymond Keer, MA; FBIM; Principal, Banbury School, 1973–84; Visiting Fellow, University of London Institute of Education, since 1985; *b* 8 Aug. 1931; *s* of Arthur and Hilda Sayer; *m* 1955, Ilserose (*née* Heyd); one *s* one *d*. *Educ:* Maidstone Grammar Sch.; Brasenose Coll., Oxford (Open Scholar; MA). FBIM 1979. Taught languages, 1955–63; Dep. Head, Nailsea Sch., Somerset, 1963–67; Headmaster, Minehead Sch., Somerset, 1967–73. Chairman: Reform of Assessment at Sixteen-Plus, 1972–75; PUBANSCO publishing gp, 1975–; Chm., External Relations Cttee, Headmasters' Assoc., 1974–77; Secondary Heads Association: Mem. Exec., 1978–86; Press and Publications Officer, 1978–79, 1982–84; Pres., 1979–80. Chm., Jt Council of Heads, 1981; Member: Exec., UCCA, 1975–84; Schools Panel, CBI, 1975–82; Heads Panel, TUC, 1975–80; National Adv. Council on Educn for Industry and Commerce, 1974–77; Adv. Cttee on Supply and Educn of Teachers, 1982–85. Trustee and Member of Executive: Education 2000, 1983–; Schools Curriculum Award, 1986–. *Publications:* (ed) The School as a Centre of Enquiry, 1975; (ed) Staffing our Secondary Schools, 1980; (ed) Teacher Training and Special Educational Needs, 1985; What Future for Secondary Schools?, 1985; Meeting Special Needs in Secondary Schools, 1987; frequent contribs on educnl topics to learned jls and symposia. *Recreation:* postal history. *Address:* 8 Northmoor Road, Oxford OX2 6UP. *T:* Oxford 56932.

SAYERS, Prof. Bruce McArthur, PhD, DScEng; CEng, FIEE; Professor of Computing Applied to Medicine and Head of the Department of Computing, since 1984, Imperial College of Science and Technology; Dean of City and Guilds College, since 1984; *b* 6 Feb. 1928; *s* of John William McArthur Sayers and Mabel Florence Sayers (*née* Howe); *m* 1951, R Woolls Humphery. *Educ:* Melbourne Boys' High School; Univ. of Melbourne (MSc); Imperial Coll., Univ. of London (PhD, DIC, DScEng). Biophysicist, Baker Med. Research Inst. and Clinical Research Unit, Alfred Hosp., Melbourne, 1949–54; Imperial College, London: Research Asst, 1955–56; Philips Elec. Ltd Research Fellow, 1957; Lectr, 1958; Senior Lectr, 1963; Reader, 1965; Prof. of Electrical Engrg Applied to Medicine, 1968–84; Head of Dept of Electrical Engrg, 1979–84. Pres., Section of Measurement in Medicine, Royal Soc. of Medicine, 1971–72; Hon. Consultant, Royal Throat, Nose and Ear Hosp., 1974–; UK rep., Bio-engineering Working Group, EEC Cttee for Med. Res., 1976–80; Temp. Adviser, WHO, 1970–76, 1981–. Consultant: Data Laboratories, 1968–80; Data Beta, 1981–; Advent Eurofund, 1981–; Shinan Investment Services SA, Switzerland, 1984–; Advent Capital Ltd, 1985–; Neuroscience Ltd, 1985–; Transatlantic Capital (Biosciences) Fund, 1985–; Director: Imperial Software Technology Ltd, 1984–; Imperial Information Technology Ltd, 1986–. Former Visiting Prof., Univs of Melbourne, Rio de Janeiro, McGill, Toronto. Travelling Lectr: Nuffield Foundn-Nat. Research Council, Canada, 1971; Inst. of Electron. and Radio Engrs, Australia, 1976. FCGI 1983. Hon. Foreign Mem., Medico-Chirurgical Soc. of Bologna, 1965; Hon. Member, Eta Kappa Nu (USA), 1980. Freeman of the City of London, 1986; Liveryman, Scientific Instrument Makers' Co., 1986. *Publications:* papers, mainly on biomedical signals and control systems, epidemiology, cardiology and audiology. *Recreations:* writing poetry (badly), comic verse (better); painting in oils (with occasional success); music. *Address:* Department of Computing, Imperial College, SW7 2AZ. *T:* 01–589 5111; 40 Queen's Gate, SW7 5HR. *T:* 01–581 3690; Lots Cottage, Compton Abbas, Dorset.

SAYERS, Eric Colin, CBE 1981; FCA; Chairman, Duport Ltd, 1973–81; *b* 20 Sept. 1916; *s* of Alfred William and Emily Clara Sayers; *m* 1940, Winifred Bristow; two *d*. *Educ:* Acton County Grammar School. JDipMA, CBIM. Joined Duport Ltd, 1956; Director, 1962; Managing Director, 1966–75. Director: Ductile Steels PLC, 1973–82; International Timber Corp. PLC, 1977–83; Durapipe Internat. Ltd, 1979–81. Part-time Member, Midlands Electricity Board, 1973–81; Member: Council of CBI, 1975–81 (Chm. Energy Policy Cttee, 1975–81); Government's Advisory Council on Energy Conservation, 1977–79; Energy Commn, 1977–79; Birmingham Cttee of Inst. of Directors, 1974–84. Pres., Birmingham and W Midlands Soc. of Chartered Accountants, 1971–72; Inst. of Chartered Accountants in England and Wales: Council Member, 1966–83; Vice-Pres., 1976; Dep. Pres., 1977; Pres., 1978. Chm., Solihull County Scouts Council, 1983–. Treas., Univ. of Aston in Birmingham, 1976–. Hon. DSc Aston, 1985. *Recreations:* golf, fishing, winemaking. *Address:* 73 Silhill Hall Road, Solihull, West Midlands B91 1JT. *T:* 021–705 3973. *Club:* Lansdowne.

SAYERS, Prof. James, MSc, PhD Cantab; Professor of Electron Physics, University of Birmingham, 1946–72; *b* 2 Sept. 1912; *s* of late J. Sayers; *m* 1943, Diana Ailsa Joan Montgomery; two *s* one *d*. *Educ:* Ballymena Academy; University of Belfast; St John's College, Cambridge. Fellow of St John's College, Cambridge, 1941–46. Research for Admiralty in Univ. of Birmingham, 1939–43, on micro-wave radar; Member of British Group of Atomic Scientists transferred to work on the US Manhattan Project, 1943–45. Award by the Royal Commission on Awards to Inventors, 1949. British delegate to Internat. Scientific Radio Union, Zürich, 1950. Life Fellow, Franklin Inst. of State of Pennsylvania. John Price Wetherill Medallist, for discovery in Physical Science, 1958. *Publications:* papers in Proc. Royal Soc., Proc. Phys. Soc., and in the reports of various Internat. Scientific Conferences, on Upper Atmosphere Physics and the Physics of Ionized Gases. *Recreations:* gardening, photography. *Address:* Edgewood Gables, The Holloway, Alvechurch, Worcestershire. *T:* Redditch 64414.

SAYERS, (Matthew Herbert) Patrick, OBE 1945; MD; FRCPath; Major-General, Army Medical Services (retired); formerly Consulting Pathologist, Employment Medical Advisory Service, Department of Employment and Health and Safety Executive, 1967–75; Hon. Physician to HM The Queen, 1965–67; Director of Army Pathology and Consulting Pathologist to the Army, 1964–67; *b* 17 Jan. 1908; *s* of late Herbert John Ireland Sayers, Musician, and late Julia Alice Sayers (*née* Tabb); *m* 1935, Moira, *d* of Robert Dougall; two *s* one *d*. *Educ:* Whitgift School; St Thomas's Hospital, London. MRCS, LRCP 1932; MB, BS London 1933; MD London 1961; FCPath 1964. Commissioned Lieutenant RAMC, 1935; served India and Far East, 1936–46: Asst Dir of Pathology, HQ 14th Army, 1943–44; Dep. Dir of Pathology, Allied Land Forces, SE Asia, 1945. Asst Dir-Gen., War Office, 1948; OC The David Bruce Laboratories, 1949–52 and 1955–61; Asst Dir of Pathology, Middle East Land Forces, 1953–55; Editor, Journal RAMC, 1955–61; Dep. Dir of Pathology, Far East Land Forces, 1961–64. CStJ 1968. *Publications:* contribs (jtly) to scientific jls on scrub typhus, immunology and industrial medicine. *Recreations:* gardening, music, cricket, field sports. *Address:* High Trees, Walmer, Kent. *T:* Deal 363526. *Clubs:* Army and Navy; MCC.

See also J. C. O. R. Hopkinson.

SAYERS, Richard Sidney, FBA 1957; Emeritus Professor of Economics with special reference to Money and Banking, University of London (Cassel Professor of Economics, 1947–68); *b* 1908; *s* of S. J. Sayers; *m* 1930, Millicent Hodson; one *s* one *d*. *Educ:* St Catharine's Coll., Cambridge. Asst Lectr in Economics, London Sch. of Economics, 1931–35; Lectr in Economics, Exeter, Corpus Christi and Pembroke Colleges, Oxford, 1935–45; Fellow of Pembroke College, Oxford, 1939–45; Ministry of Supply, 1940–45; Economic Adviser, Cabinet Office, 1945–47. Member: Radcliffe Committee on the Working of the Monetary System, 1957–59; OECD Cttee on Fiscal Measures, 1966–68; Monopolies Commission, 1968. Pres. Section F, Brit. Assoc., 1960; Vice-Pres., Brit. Academy, 1966–67; Pres., Economic Hist. Soc., 1972–74; Vice-Pres., Royal Econ. Soc., 1973–. Hon. Fellow: St Catharine's Coll., Cambridge; LSE; Inst. of Bankers. Hon. DLitt Warwick, 1967; Hon. DCL Kent, 1967. *Publications:* Bank of England Operations, 1890–1914, 1936; Modern Banking, 1938 (7th edn 1967); American Banking System, 1948; (ed) Banking in the British Commonwealth, 1952; (jt editor with T. S. Ashton) Papers in English Monetary History, 1953; Financial Policy, 1939–45, 1956; Central Banking after Bagehot, 1957; Lloyds Bank in the History of English Banking, 1957; (ed) Banking in Western Europe, 1962; (ed) Economic Writings of James Pennington, 1963; A History of Economic Change in England, 1880–1939, 1967; Gilletts in the London Money Market, 1867–1967, 1968; The Bank of England 1891–1944, 1976.

SAYLES, Prof. George Osborne, LittD, DLitt, LLD; FBA 1962; MRIA; *b* 20 April 1901; *s* of Rev. L. P. Sayles and Margaret Brown, Glasgow; *m* 1936, Agnes, *d* of George Sutherland, Glasgow; one *s* one *d*. *Educ:* Ilkeston Grammar Sch.; Glasgow Univ.; University Coll., London. Open Bursar, Ewing Gold Medallist, First Cl. Hons History, Glasgow Univ., 1923; Carnegie Res. Schol., University Coll., London, 1923–24. Asst. 1924, Lectr, 1925 and Sen. Lectr, 1934–45, in History, Glasgow Univ.; Leverhulme Res. Fellow, 1939; Professor of Modern History in the Queen's University, Belfast, 1945–53; Burnett-Fletcher Professor of History in the Univ. of Aberdeen, 1953–62; first Kenan Prof. of History, New York Univ., 1967; Vis. Prof., Louvain Univ., Belgium, 1951; Woodward Lectr, Yale Univ., USA, 1952; Fellow, Folger Library, Washington, 1960–61; Corr. Fellow, American Soc. for Legal History, 1971; Hon. Fellow, Medieval Acad. of America, 1980. Vis. Mem., Inst. for Advanced Study, Princeton, NJ, 1969. Hon. LittD Trinity Coll. Dublin, 1965; Hon. LLD Glasgow, 1979. James Barr Ames Medal, Fac. of Law, Harvard Univ., 1958. Hon. Mem., Selden Soc., London, 1985. Chm. Advisory Cttee, Official War History of Northern Ireland, 1949; Member: Commission Internationale pour l'Histoire des Assemblées d'Etats; Advisory Historical Committee, Official Histories of War (Gt Brit.), 1950; Irish Manuscripts Commn, Dublin, 1949; Scottish Cttee on History of Scottish Parliament, 1937; Council of Stair Soc. (Scotland). Intelligence Officer (voluntary) to District Commissioner for Civil Defence SW Scotland, 1939–44; HG, Glasgow 12th Bn 1940. *Publications:* Author, Editor or Joint Editor (with H. G. Richardson) of: The Early Statutes, 1934; Rotuli Parliamentorum Anglie Hactenus Inediti, 1935; Select Cases in Court of King's Bench: under Edward I (3 vols), 1936–39; Edward II (1 vol.), 1956; Edward III (2 vols), 1958, 1965; Richard II, Henry IV, Henry V (1 vol.), 1972; Select Cases in Procedure without Writ, 1943; Parliaments and Councils of Medieval Ireland, 1947; Medieval Foundations of England, 1948, 3rd edn 1964, American edn, 1950; Irish Parliament in the Middle Ages, 1952, 2nd edn 1964; The Irish Parliament in 1782, 1954; Fleta, vol. I, 1955, vol. II, 1972, vol. III, 1984; Parliaments and Great Councils in Medieval England, 1961; Governance of Medieval England, 1963; The Administration of Ireland, 1172–1377, 1964; Law and Legislation in Medieval England, 1966; The King's Parliament of England, 1974; Documents on the Affairs of Ireland before the King's Council, 1979; The English Parliament in the Middle Ages, 1981; Scripta Diversa, 1983; articles and reviews in Eng. Hist. Review, Scot. Hist. Review, Law Quarterly Review, Proc. RIA, etc. *Recreations:* travel, motoring. *Address:* Warren Hill, Crowborough, East Sussex. *T:* 61439.

SCADDING, John Guyett, MD (London), FRCP; Emeritus Professor of Medicine in the University of London; Hon. Consulting Physician, Brompton and Hammersmith Hospitals; *b* 30 August 1907; *e s* of late John William Scadding and Jessima Alice Guyett; *m* 1940, Mabel Pennington; one *s* two *d*. *Educ:* Mercers' School; Middlesex Hospital Medical School, University of London. MRCS, LRCP, 1929; MB, BS (London), 1930. Resident appts, Middx Hosp., Connaught Hosp., Walthamstow, and Brompton Hosp., 1930–35; MRCP 1932; MD (London, Univ. gold medal), 1932; First Asst, Dept of Med., Brit. Postgrad. Med. Sch., 1935; FRCP 1941; RAMC 1940–45 (Lt-Col, O i/c Med. Div.); Phys., Hammersmith Hosp., Postgrad. Med. Sch. of London, 1946–72; Physician, Brompton Hosp., 1939–72; Inst. of Diseases of the Chest: Dean, 1946–60; Dir of Studies, 1950–62; Prof. of Medicine, 1962–72; Hon. Cons. in Diseases of the Chest to the Army at Home, 1953–72 (Guthrie Medal, 1973). Visiting Professor: Univ. Oklahoma, 1963; Stanford Univ. and Univ. Colorado, 1965; McMaster Univ., 1973; Univ. Manitoba, 1974; Univ. Chicago, 1976; Dalhousie Univ., 1977. Mem. Central Health Services Council, and Standing Medical Advisory Cttee, 1954–66; Mem. Clinical Research Board, 1960–65. Royal College of Physicians: Bradshaw Lectr, 1949; Mitchell Lectr, 1960; Tudor Edwards Lectr, 1970; Lumleian Lectr, 1973; Councillor, 1949–52; Censor, 1968–70; Second Vice-Pres., 1971–72; Moxon Medal, 1975; Lettsomian Lectr, Med. Soc. of London, 1955. Editor, Thorax, 1946–59. President: British Tuberculosis Assoc., 1959–61; Section of Medicine, RSM, 1969–71; Thoracic Soc., 1971–72. Dr *hc* Reims, 1978. *Publications:* Sarcoidosis, 1967, 2nd edn 1985; contributions to textbooks and articles, mainly on respiratory diseases, in medical journals. *Recreations:* music, pottering about. *Address:* 18 Seagrave Road, Beaconsfield, Bucks HP9 1SU. *T:* Beaconsfield 6033. *Club:* Athenæum.

SCALES, Prof. John Tracey, OBE 1986; FRCS, LRCP; CIMechE; Professor of Biomedical Engineering, Institute of Orthopaedics, University of London, 1974–Oct. 87; Consultant in Orthopaedic Prosthetics, since 1958, and in Biomedical Engineering, since 1968, Royal National Orthopaedic Hospital, Stanmore and London; Consultant, Royal Orthopaedic Hospital, Birmingham, since 1978; *b* 2 July 1920; *s* of late W. L. Scales and E. M. Scales (*née* Tracey); *m* 1945, Cecilia May, *d* of late A. W. Sparrow; two *d*. *Educ:* Haberdashers' Aske's Sch., Hampstead; King's Coll., London (evacuated to Glasgow and Birmingham Univs); Charing Cross Hosp. Med. Sch. MRCS, LRCP 1944; Hon. FRCS 1969. CIMechE 1966. Captain RAMC, 1945–47. Casualty Officer and Resident Anaesthetist, Charing Cross Hosp., 1944; Royal National Orthopaedic Hosp., Stanmore: House Surgeon, 1944–45 and 1947–49; MO i/c Plastics Res. Unit, 1949–50; Hon. Registrar, 1950–52; Hon. Sen Registrar, 1952–57; Lectr i/c Plastics Res. Unit, Inst. of Orth., Stanmore, 1951–52; Sen. Lectr i/c Plastics Res. Unit (re-named Dept. of Biomechanics and Surg. Materials, 1956; re-named Dept of Biomed. Engrg, 1968), Inst.

of Orth., Univ. of London, 1952–68; Consultant in Orthopaedic Prosthetics, Royal Nat. Orthopaedic Hosp., Stanmore and London, 1958–68; Reader in Biomed. Engrg, Dept of Biomed. Engrg, Inst. of Orth., Univ. of London, 1968–74; Consultant in Biomed. Engrg, Mt Vernon Hosp., Northwood, 1972–85. Chairman: BSI Cttee on Orthopaedic Joint-replacements, 1981–; ISO Cttee on Bone and Joint Replacements; Member: IMechE Engrg in Medicine Gp, 1966– (Founder Mem.); British Orthopaedic Res. Engrg in Medicine Gp, 1966– (Founder Mem.); Adv. Panel on Med. Engrg, National Fund for Res. into Crippling Diseases; British Orth. Res. Soc., 1962–; Biol Engrg Soc., 1960– (Founder Mem.); Eur. Soc. of Biomaterials, 1974– (Founder Mem.); Hon. Mem., Eur. Soc. of Biomechanics, 1976– (Former Pres., Founder Mem.). Ext. Examiner, Univ. of Surrey, 1969–84, and other univs. FRSocMed 1950; Companion Fellow, British Orth. Assoc., 1959. Thomas Henry Green Prize in Surgery, Charing Cross Hosp. Med. Sch., 1943; Robert Danis Prize, Internat. Soc. of Surgery, Brussels, 1969; James Berrie Prize, RCS, 1973; Clemson Univ. Award, USA, 1974; S. G. Brown Award, Royal Soc., 1974; A. A. Griffith Silver Medal, Materials Science Club, 1980; Jackson Burrows Medal, Royal Nat. Orthopaedic Hosp., Stanmore, 1985. Mem. Editorial Bd, Engineering in Medicine. *Publications: chapters in:* Modern Trends in Surgical Materials, ed Gillis, 1958; Aspects of Medical Physics, ed Rotblat, 1966; Surgical Dressings and Wound Healing, ed Harkiss, 1971; (and ed jtly) Bed Sore Biomechanics, 1976; Surgical Dressings in the Hospital Environment, ed Turner and Brain; Treatment of Burns, ed Donati, Burke and Bertelli, 1976; Scientific Foundations of Orthopaedics and Traumatology, ed Owen, Goodfellow and Bullough, 1980; also jt author of chapters in med. books; contrib. Proc. RSM, Proc. IMechE, Proc. Physiol Soc., BMJ, Jl of Bone and Jt Surg., Lancet, Nature, and other med. and scientific jls; contrib. conf. and symposia reports. *Recreations:* walking dogs, Goss china. *Address:* 17 Brockley Avenue, Stanmore, Mddx HA7 4LX. *T:* 01–958 8773. *Club:* Army and Navy.

SCALES, Prunella, (Prunella Margaret Rumney West); actress; *d* of John Richardson Illingworth and Catherine Scales; *m* 1963, Timothy Lancaster West, *qv*; two *s*. *Educ:* Moira House, Eastbourne; Old Vic Theatre School, London; Herbert Berghof Studio, New York (with Uta Hagen). Repertory in Huddersfield, Salisbury, Oxford, Bristol Old Vic, etc; seasons at Stratford-on-Avon and Chichester Festival Theatre, 1967–68; plays on London Stage include: The Promise, 1967; Hay Fever, 1968; It's a Two-Foot-Six-Inches-Above-The-Ground-World, 1970; The Wolf, 1975; Breezeblock Park, 1978; Make and Break, 1980; An Evening with Queen Victoria, 1980; The Merchant of Venice, 1981; Quartermaine's Terms, 1981; Big in Brazil, 1984; When We Are Married, 1986; *television:* Fawlty Towers (series), 1975–79; Grand Duo, The Merry Wives of Windsor, 1982; Mapp and Lucia (series), 1985–86; Absurd Person Singular, 1985; frequent broadcasts, readings, poetry recitals and fringe productions. Has directed plays at Bristol Old Vic, Arts Theatre, Cambridge, Billingham Forum, Almost Free Theatre, London, Nottingham Playhouse, Palace Theatre, Watford, Nat. Theatre of WA, Perth, and taught at several drama schools. *Recreation:* growing vegetables. *Address:* c/o Jeremy Conway, Eagle House, 109 Jermyn Street, SW1Y 6HB. *Club:* BBC.

SCANLON, family name of **Baron Scanlon.**

SCANLON, Baron *cr* 1979 (Life Peer), of Davyhulme in the County of Greater Manchester; **Hugh Parr Scanlon**; President, Amalgamated Union of Engineering Workers, 1968–78; Member, British Gas Corporation, 1976–82; *b* 26 Oct. 1913; *m* 1943, Nora; two *d*. *Educ:* Stretford Elem. Sch.; NCLC. Apprentice, Instrument Maker, Shop Steward-Convener, AEI, Trafford Park; Divisional Organiser, AEU, Manchester, 1947–63; Member: Exec. Council, AEU, London, 1963–67; TUC Gen. Council, 1968–78; TUC Econ. Cttee, 1968–78. Member: NEDC, 1971–; Metrication Bd, 1973–78; NEB, 1977–79; Govt Cttee of Inquiry into Teaching of Maths in Primary and Secondary Schs in England and Wales, 1978–; Chm., Engineering Industry Training Bd, 1975–82. Vice-Pres., Internat. Metalworkers' Fedn, 1969–78; Pres., European Metal Workers' Fedn, 1974–78. *Recreations:* golf, swimming, gardening. *Address:* 23 Seven Stones Drive, Broadstairs, Kent. *Club:* Eltham Warren Golf.

SCANNELL, Vernon, FRSL; free-lance author, poet and broadcaster, since 1962; *b* 23 Jan. 1922. *Educ:* elementary schools; Leeds Univ. Served with Gordon Highlanders (51st Highland Div.), ME and Normandy, 1940–45; Leeds Univ. (reading Eng. Lit.), 1946–47; various jobs incl. professional boxer, 1945–46, English Master at Hazelwood Prep. Sch., 1955–62. Southern Arts Assoc. Writing Fellowship, 1975–76; Vis. Poet, Shrewsbury Sch., 1978–79; Res. Poet, King's Sch. Canterbury, Michaelmas Term 1979. FRSL 1960. Granted a civil list pension, 1981, for services to literature. *Publications: novels:* The Fight, 1953; The Wound and the Scar, 1953; The Big Chance, 1960; The Face of the Enemy, 1961; The Shadowed Place, 1961; The Dividing Night, 1962; The Big Time, 1965; The Dangerous Ones, 1970; A Lonely Game (for younger readers), 1979; Ring of Truth, 1983; *poetry:* The Masks of Love, 1960 (Heinemann Award, 1960); A Sense of Danger, 1962; (ed, with Ted Hughes and Patricia Beer) New Poems: a PEN anthology, 1962; Walking Wounded: poems 1962–65, 1968; Epithets of War: poems 1965–69, 1969; Mastering the Craft (Poets Today Series), 1970; (with J. Silkin) Pergamon Poets, No 8, 1970; Selected Poems, 1971; The Winter Man: new poems, 1973; The Apple Raid and other poems, 1974 (Cholmondeley Poetry Prize, 1974); The Loving Game, 1975 (also in paperback); New and Collected Poems 1950–80, 1980; Winterlude and other poems, 1982; *criticism:* Not Without Glory: poets of World War II, 1976; How to Enjoy Poetry, 1982; How to Enjoy Novels, 1984; *autobiography:* The Tiger and the Rose, 1971; A Proper Gentleman, 1977. *Recreations:* listening to radio (mainly music), drink, boxing (as a spectator), films, reading. *Address:* 51 North Street, Otley, W Yorks LS21 1AH. *T:* Otley 467176.

SCARASCIA-MUGNOZZA, Carlo; President, International Centre for Advanced Mediterranean Agronomic Studies, Paris, since 1983; *b* Rome, 19 Jan. 1920. Mem., Italian Chamber of Deputies, for Lecce-Brindisi-Taranto, 1953; Vice-Pres., Christian Democrat Parly Gp, 1958–62; Leader, Italian Delegn to UNESCO, 1962; Secretary of State: for Educn, 1962–63; for Justice, June 1963–Dec. 1963; Mem., European Parliament, 1961, Chm., Political Cttee, 1971–72; a Vice-Pres., EEC, 1972–77. *Address:* Via Proba Petronia 43, 00136 Rome, Italy. *T:* 345.31.14; International Centre for Advanced Mediterranean Agronomic Studies, 11 rue Newton, 75116 Paris, France.

SCARBOROUGH, Prof. Harold, CBE 1976; Professor, Department of Medicine, and Provost, College of Medical Sciences, University of Maiduguri, Nigeria, and Chief Medical Director, University of Maiduguri Teaching Hospital, 1979–84, retired; *b* 27 March 1909; British; unmarried. *Educ:* Bridlington School, Yorks; Edinburgh University; St Mary's Hospital Medical School; Harvard University. Clinical Tutor, Royal Infirmary of Edinburgh and Assistant, Dept of Therapeutics, Edinburgh Univ., 1933–38; Beit Memorial Research Fellow and Demonstrator in Pharmacology, Edinburgh Univ., 1938–39; Beit Memorial Research Fellow, Medical Unit, St Mary's Hosp., London, 1945–47; Rockefeller Travelling Fellow at Harvard Medical School, 1947–48; Reader in Medicine, University of Birmingham, 1949–50; Prof. of Medicine in Welsh Nat. Sch. of Medicine, Univ. of Wales, 1950–70; formerly: Dir, Med. Unit, Cardiff Royal Infirmary; Chm., Div. of Medicine, United Cardiff Hosps; Prof. of Medicine and Dean of the Faculty of Medicine, Ahmadu Bello Univ., Zaria, Nigeria, 1970–76; Visiting Professor of Medicine: Garyounis Univ., Libya, 1978–; Faculty of Health Sciences, Univ. of Ilorin, Nigeria, 1978–79. Hon. Fellow, Univ. of Wales Coll. of Medicine, 1986. *Publications:* (part author) Textbook of Physiology and Biochemistry, 1950; papers in BMJ, Lancet, Quart. Jl Med., and other medical and scientific journals. *Recreations:* gardening, the theatre. *Address:* c/o Barclays Bank, 170 Whitchurch Road, Cardiff CF4 3YG.

SCARBROUGH, 12th Earl of, *cr* 1690; **Richard Aldred Lumley,** DL; Viscount Lumley (Ire.), 1628; Baron Lumley, 1681; Viscount Lumley, 1690; *b* 5 Dec. 1932; *o s* of 11th Earl of Scarbrough, KG, PC, GCSI, GCIE, GCVO, and Katharine Isobel, Dowager Countess of Scarbrough, DCVO (*d* 1979), *d* of late R. F. McEwen; *S* father, 1969; *m* 1970, Lady Elizabeth Ramsay, *d* of Earl of Dalhousie, *qv*; two *s* one *d*. *Educ:* Eton; Magdalen College, Oxford. 2nd Lt 11th Hussars, 1951–52; formerly Lt Queen's Own Yorkshire Dragoons. ADC to Governor and C-in-C, Cyprus, 1956. Hon. Col, 1st Bn The Yorkshire Volunteers, 1975–. President: Northern Area, Royal British Legion, 1984–; York Georgian Soc., 1985–; Yorkshire and North Western Assoc. of Building Socs, 1985–. Mem. Council, Univ. of Sheffield, 1974–79. Hon. RIBA, Yorks Region. DL S Yorks, 1974. *Heir: s* Viscount Lumley, *qv*. *Address:* Sandbeck Park, Maltby, Rotherham, S Yorks S66 8PF. *T:* Doncaster 742210. *Clubs:* White's, Pratt's; Jockey (Newmarket).

See also Lady Grimthorpe.

SCARFE, Gerald; artist; *b* 1 June 1936; *m* Jane Asher. *Educ:* scattered (due to chronic asthma as a child). Punch, 1960; Private Eye, 1961; Daily Mail, 1966; Sunday Times, 1967; cover artist to illustrator, Time Magazine, 1967; animation and film directing for BBC, 1969–. Has taken part in exhibitions: Grosvenor Gall., 1969 and 1970; Pavillon d'Humour, Montreal, 1967 and 1971; Expo '70, Osaka, 1970. One-man exhibitions of sculptures and lithographs: Waddell Gall., New York, 1968 and 1970; Grosvenor Gall., 1969; Vincent Price Gall., Chicago, 1969; National Portrait Gall., 1971; retrospective exhibn, Royal Festival Hall, 1983. Animated film for BBC, Long Drawn Out Trip, 1973 (prizewinner, Zagreb); Designer and Dir, animated sequences in film, The Wall, 1982; designer: Who's A Lucky Boy?, Royal Exchange, Manchester, 1984; Orpheus in the Underworld, ENO, 1985. *Publications:* Gerald Scarfe's People, 1966; Indecent Exposure (ltd edn), 1973; Expletive Deleted: the life and times of Richard Nixon (ltd edn), 1974; Gerald Scarfe, 1982; Father Kissmass and Mother Claws, 1985. *Recreations:* drawing, painting and sculpting. *Address:* 10 Cheyne Walk, SW3.

SCARGILL, Arthur; President, National Union of Mineworkers, since 1981; *b* 11 Jan. 1938; *o c* of Harold and Alice Scargill; *m* 1961, Anne, *d* of Elliott Harper; one *d*. *Educ:* Worsbrough Dale School; White Cross Secondary School; Leeds Univ. Miner, Woolley Colliery, 1953; Mem., NUM branch cttee, 1960; Woolley branch deleg. to Yorks NUM Council, 1964; Mem., Nat. Exec., 1972, Pres., 1973, Yorks NUM. Mem., TUC Gen. Council, 1986–. Member: Young Communists' League, 1955–62; Co-op Party, 1963; Labour Party, 1966; CND. *Address:* National Union of Mineworkers, St James' House, Vicar Lane, Sheffield S1 2EX.

SCARLETT, family name of **Baron Abinger.**

SCARLETT, James Harvey Anglin; His Honour Judge Scarlett; a Circuit Judge, since 1974; *b* 27 Jan. 1924; *s* of Lt-Col James Alexander Scarlett, DSO, RA, and Muriel Scarlett, *d* of Walter Blease; unmarried. *Educ:* Shrewsbury Sch.; Christ Church, Oxford (MA). Barrister-at-law. Served War, Royal Artillery (Lieut), 1943–47. Called to the Bar, Inner Temple, 1950. A Recorder of the Crown Court, 1972–74. Malayan Civil Service, 1955–58. *Recreation:* fell walking. *Address:* Chilmington Green, Great Chart, near Ashford, Kent TN23 3DP. *Club:* Athenæum; Athenæum (Liverpool); Border County (Carlisle).

SCARLETT, Hon. John Leopold Campbell, CBE 1973; Deputy to Health Service Commissioner, 1973–76; *b* 18 Dec. 1916; 2nd *s* of 7th Baron Abinger and Marjorie, 2nd *d* of John McPhillamy, Bathurst, NSW; *m* 1947, Bridget Valerie, *d* of late H. B. Crook; two *s* one *d*. *Educ:* Eton; Magdalene Coll., Cambridge (MA). Served War of 1939–45, France, Madagascar, Burma (despatches); 2nd Lieut 1940; Major 1944, RA. House Governor, London Hosp., 1962–72. *Address:* Bramblewood, Castle Walk, Wadhurst, Sussex TN5 6DB. *T:* Wadhurst 2642. *Club:* Royal Automobile.

SCARLETT, Sir Peter (William Shelley Yorke), KCMG 1958 (CMG 1949); KCVO 1955; *b* 30 March 1905; *s* of late William James Yorke Scarlett, Fyfield House, Andover; *m* 1934, Elisabeth, *d* of late Sir John Dearman Birchall, TD, MP, Cotswold Farm, Cirencester; one *s* three *d*. *Educ:* Eton; Christ Church, Oxford. Apptd to Foreign Office as a Third Secretary, 1929; Cairo, 1930; Bagdad, 1932; Lisbon, 1934; promoted a Second Secretary, 1934; acted as Chargé d'Affaires, Riga, 1937 and 1938. Attached to representative of Latvia at coronation of King George VI, 1937; Brussels, 1938; promoted actg First Sec., 1940; captured by enemy forces, 1940; returned to UK and resumed duties at Foreign Office, 1941; Paris, 1944; Allied Forces Headquarters, Caserta, 1946; Counsellor, Foreign Office, 1947; Inspector of HM Diplomatic Service Establishments, 1950; British Permanent Representative on the Council of Europe, Strasbourg, 1952; HM Ambassador to Norway, 1955; HM Minister to the Holy See, 1960–65, retired. Chairman, Cathedrals Advisory Committee, 1967–81. *Address:* 35 Tivoli Road, Cheltenham, Glos. *Club:* Carlton.

SCARMAN, family name of **Baron Scarman.**

SCARMAN, Baron *cr* 1977 (Life Peer), of Quatt in the county of Salop; **Leslie George Scarman,** PC 1973; Kt 1961; OBE 1944; a Lord of Appeal in Ordinary, 1977–86; *b* 29 July 1911; *s* of late George Charles and Ida Irene Scarman; *m* 1947, Ruth Clement Wright; one *s*. *Educ:* Radley College; Brasenose College, Oxford. Classical Scholar, Radley, 1925; Open Classical Scholar, Brasenose Coll., 1930; Hon. Mods 1st cl., 1932; Lit. Hum. 1st cl., 1934; Harmsworth Law Scholar, Middle Temple, 1936, Barrister, 1936; QC 1957. A Judge of the High Court of Justice, Probate, Divorce, and Admiralty Div., later Family Div., 1961–73; a Lord Justice of Appeal, 1973–77. Chairman: Law Commn, 1965–73; Council of Legal Educn, 1973–76; Pres., Constitutional Reform Centre, 1984–. Chm., Univ. of London Court, 1970– (Dep. Chm., 1966–70); Chancellor, Univ. of Warwick, 1977–. Vice-Chm., Statute Law Cttee, 1967–72. Pres., Senate of Inns of Court and Bar, 1976–79. Mem. Arts Council, 1968–70, 1972–73; Vice-chm., ENO, 1976–81. Pres., RIPA, 1981–. Hon. Fellow: Brasenose College, Oxford, 1966; Imperial Coll., Univ. of London, 1975; UCL, 1985; LSE, 1985. Hon. LLD: Exeter, 1965; Glasgow, 1969; London, 1971; Keele, 1972; Freiburg, 1973; Warwick, 1974; Bristol, 1976; Manchester, 1977; Kent, 1981; Wales, 1985; Hon. DCL: City, 1980; Oxon, 1982. RAFVR, 1940–45; Chm., Malcolm Clubs, RAF. Order of Battle Merit (Russia), 1945. *Publications:* Pattern of Law Reform, 1967; English Law—The New Dimension, 1975. *Recreations:* gardening, walking. *Address:* House of Lords, SW1A 0PW. *Club:* Athenæum.

SCARSDALE, 3rd Viscount *cr* 1911; **Francis John Nathaniel Curzon**; Bt (Scotland) 1636, (England) 1641; Baron Scarsdale 1761; late Captain, Scots Guards; *b* 28 July 1924; *o s* of late Hon. Francis Nathaniel Curzon, 3rd *s* of 4th Baron Scarsdale, and late Winifred Phyllis (*née* Combe); *S* cousin, 1977; *m* 1st, 1948, Solange (marr. diss. 1967, she *d* 1974), *yr d* of late Oscar Hanse, Mont-sur-Marchienne, Belgium; two *s* one *d*; 2nd, 1968, Helene Gladys Frances, *o d* of late Maj. William Ferguson Thomson, Kinellar, Aberdeenshire; two *s*. *Educ:* Eton. *Recreations:* shooting, piping, photography. *Heir:* *s* Hon. Peter Ghislain Nathaniel Curzon [*b* 6 March 1949; *m* 1983, Mrs Karen Osborne; one *d*]. *Address:* Kedleston Hall, Derby. *T:* Derby 840386. *Club:* County (Derby).

SCATCHARD, Vice-Adm. John Percival, CB 1963; DSC 1941; first Bar, 1944; second Bar, 1945; *b* 5 Sept. 1910; *s* of Dr James P. Scatchard, MB, BS, Tadcaster, Yorks; *m* 1943, Edith Margaret Niven; one *d*. *Educ:* Aysgarth School, Yorkshire; RNC Dartmouth. Joined RN, 1924; served War of 1939–45, in HMS Kashmir-Garth and Termagent; Captain (D) Portsmouth, 1951–52; Captain 5th Destroyer Squadron, 1957–58; Director Naval Equipment, Admiralty, 1959–60; Commandant, Joint Services Staff College, Latimer, Bucks, 1960–62; Flag Officer, Second-in-Command, Far East Fleet, 1962–64; retd list, 1964. *Recreations:* gardening, sailing. *Address:* Reachfar, Warsash, near Southampton, Hants.

SCHAFFTER, Ernest Merill James; Secretary, Royal Aeronautical Society, 1973–82 (Deputy Secretary, 1970–73); Director, Engineering Sciences Data Unit Ltd, 1975–82; *b* 1922; *er s* of late Dr Charles Merill Schaffter and of Bertha Grace Brownrigg, of the CMS in Isfahan, Iran; *m* 1951, Barbara Joy, *o c* of Alfred Bennett Wallis and Hilda Frances Hammond; three *d*. *Educ:* Trent Coll., Nottinghamshire; King's Coll., Cambridge. BA 1950, MA 1955. Served War: RAF, as Pilot with Coastal and Transport Command, Flt Lt, 1941–46. De Havilland Aircraft Co., Hatfield, as Aerodynamicist and Engr, 1950–54; Marshall's Flying Sch., Cambridge, as Engr, 1954–60; Marshall of Cambridge (Eng) Ltd, as Personal Asst to Chief Designer and later as Design Office Manager, 1960–70. Freeman, GAPAN, 1978. FRAeS, AFAIAA, AFCASI, FBIM. *Address:* 43 Speldhurst Road, W4 1BX. *T:* 01–995 0708. *Clubs:* Royal Air Force, Les Ambassadeurs.

SCHALLY, Dr Andrew Victor; Chief of Endocrine Polypeptide and Cancer Institute, since 1962 and Senior Medical Investigator, since 1973, Veterans Administration Medical Center, New Orleans; Professor of Medicine, Department of Medicine, Tulane University School of Medicine, New Orleans, since 1967 (Associate Professor, 1962–67); *b* Wilno, Poland, 30 Nov. 1926; US Citizen (formerly Canadian Citizen); *s* of Casimir and Maria Schally; *m* 1st, 1956, Margaret White (marr. diss.); one *s* one *d*; 2nd, 1976, Ana Maria Comaru. *Educ:* Bridge of Allan, Scotland (Higher Learning Cert.); London (studied chemistry); McGill Univ., Montreal, Canada (BSc Biochem., 1955; PhD Biochem., 1957). Res. Assistant: Dept of Biochem., Nat. Inst. for Med. Res., MRC, Mill Hill, 1949–52; Endocrine Unit, Allan Meml Inst. for Psych., McGill Univ., Montreal, 1952–57; Baylor University Coll. of Medicine, Texas Med. Center: Res. Associate, Dept of Physiol., 1957–60; Asst Prof. of Physiol., Dept of Physiol., and Asst Prof. of Biochem., Dept of Biochem., 1960–62. Member: Endocrine Soc., USA; AAAS; Soc. of Biol Chemists; Amer. Physiol Soc.; Soc. for Experimental Biol. and Med.; Internat. Soc. for Res. in Biol. of Reprodn; Internat. Brain Res. Org.; Nat. Acad. of Medicine, Mexico; Nat. Acad. of Medicine, Brazil; Nat. Acad. of Medicine, Venezuela; Nat. Acad. of Scis (US). Hon. Member: Internat. Family Planning Res. Assoc., Inc.; Chilean Endocrine Soc.; Mexican Assoc. for Study of Human Fertility and Reprodn; Mexican Soc. of Nutrition and Endocrinol.; Acad. of Med. Sciences of Cataluna and Baleares; Endocrine Soc. of Madrid; Polish Soc. of Internal Med.; Endocrine Soc. of Ecuador; Endocrine Soc. of Peru. Dr *hc* State Univ. of Rio de Janeiro, 1977; Rosario, Argentina, 1979; Univ. Peruana Cayetano Heredia, Lima, 1979; Univ. Nat. de San Marcos, Lima, 1979; MD *hc*: Tulane, 1978; Cadiz, 1979; Univ. Villareal-Lima, 1979; Copernicus Med. Acad., Cracow, 1979; Chile, 1979; Buenos Aires, 1980; Salamanca, 1981; Complutense Univ., Madrid, 1984; Hon. DSc McGill, 1979. Nobel Prize in Physiology or Medicine, 1977. Veterans Administration: William S. Middleton Award, 1970; Exceptional Service Award and Medal, 1978. Van Meter Prize, Amer. Thyroid Assoc., 1969; Ayerst-Squibb Award, US Endocrine Soc., 1970; Charles Mickle Award, Faculty of Med., Univ. of Toronto, 1974; Gairdner Foundn Internat. Award, Toronto, 1974; Edward T. Tyler Award, 1975; Borden Award, Assoc. of Amer. Med. Colls, 1975; Albert Lasker Basic Med. Res. Award, 1975; Laude Award 1975, Spanish Pharmaceutical Soc., 1977; Medal of Scientific Merit, Fed. Univ. of Ceara, Brazil, 1977; 1st Dip. of Merit of St Luke, Foundn of Social Pioneers, Rio de Janeiro, 1977. Mem. Editorial Bd, Proc. of Society for Experimental Biology and Medicine, 1973–. *Publications:* (compiled and ed with William Locke) The Hypothalamus and Pituitary in Health and Disease, 1972; over 1400 other pubns (papers, revs, books, abstracts). *Address:* Quadrant F, 7th Floor Veterans Administration Medical Center, 1601 Perdido Street, New Orleans, La 70146, USA. *T:* (504) 589–5230.

SCHAPERA, Prof. Isaac, MA (Cape Town) 1925; PhD (London) 1929; DSc (London) 1939; FBA 1958; FRSSAf 1934; Emeritus Professor, University of London (London School of Economics), 1969; *b* Garies, South Africa, 23 June 1905; 3rd *s* of late Herman and Rose Schapera. *Educ:* S African Coll. Sch., Cape Town; Universities of Cape Town and London. Prof. of Social Anthropology, Univ. of Cape Town, 1935–50; Prof. of Anthropology, Univ. of London (LSE), 1950–69, now Emeritus; Hon. Fellow, 1974. Many anthropological field expeditions to Bechuanaland Protectorate, 1929–50. Chairman Association of Social Anthropologists of the British Commonwealth, 1954–57; President, Royal Anthropological Inst., 1961–63. Hon. DLitt: Cape Town, 1975; Botswana, 1985; Hon. LLD Witwatersrand, 1979. *Publications:* The Khoisan Peoples of South Africa, 1930; A Handbook of Tswana Law and Custom, 1938; Married Life in an African Tribe, 1940; Native Land Tenure in the Bechuanaland Protectorate, 1943; Migrant Labour and Tribal Life, 1948; The Ethnic Composition of Tswana Tribes, 1952; The Tswana, 1953; Government and Politics in Tribal Societies, 1956; Praise Poems of Tswana Chiefs, 1965; Tribal Innovators, 1970; Rainmaking Rites of Tswana Tribes, 1971; Kinship Terminology in Jane Austen's Novels, 1977; Editor: Western Civilization and the Natives of South Africa, 1934; The Bantu-speaking Tribes of South Africa, 1937; David Livingstone's Journals and Letters, 1841–56 (6 vols), 1959–63; David Livingstone: South African Papers 1849–1853, 1974; contrib. to many learned journals. *Address:* 457 White House, Albany Street, NW1 3UP.

SCHAPIRO, Meyer; University Professor, Columbia University, 1965–73, now Emeritus Professor; *b* Shavly, Lithuania, 23 Sept. 1904; *s* of Nathan Menahem Schapiro and Fege Edelman; *m* 1928, Dr Lillian Milgram; one *s* one *d*. *Educ:* Boys' High Sch., Brooklyn; Columbia University. PhD Columbia, 1929. Columbia University: Lectr, Dept of Art History and Archæology, 1928; Asst Prof., 1936; Assoc. Prof., 1948; Prof., 1952; University Prof., 1965. Visiting Lecturer: Institute of Fine Arts, NY University, 1931–36; New School for Social Research, NY, 1938–50; Vis. Prof.: Univ. of London, 1947, 1957; Univ. of Jerusalem, 1961; Messenger Lectr, Cornell Univ., 1960; Patten Lectr, Indiana Univ., 1961; Charles Eliot Norton Prof., Harvard Univ., 1966–67; Slade Prof. of Fine Art, Oxford Univ., 1968; Vis. Lectr, Collège de France, 1974. Guggenheim Fellow, 1939, 1943; Fellow: Amer. Acad. of Arts and Sciences, 1952; Inst. for Advanced Study in Behavioral Sciences, Palo Alto, 1962–63; Amer. Philosophical Soc., 1969; Mediaeval Acad., 1970; Amer. Inst. of Arts and Letters, 1976. Hon. degrees: Columbia Univ.; Harvard Univ.; Yale Univ.; Jewish Theological Seminary, NY, etc. Bd of Editors: Jl of History of Ideas; Semiotica; Dissent. Award for Distinction, Amer. Council of Learned Socs, 1960; Mitchell Prize, 1979; Aby M. Warburg Prize, Hamburg, 1985. *Publications:* The Romanesque Sculpture of Moissac, 1931; Van Gogh, 1950; Cézanne, 1952; The Parma Ildefonsus, 1964; Words and Pictures, 1973; Selected Papers, vol. I, Romanesque Art, 1976, vol. II, Modern Art, 1978; vol. III, Late Antique, Early Christian and Medieval Art, 1980; Style, Artiste et Société, 1983; articles in collective books and in Art Bulletin, Gazette des Beaux-Arts, Jl Warburg and Courtauld Insts, Jl History of Ideas, Jl Architectural Historians, Kritische Berichte, Amer. Jl Sociology, Partisan Review, Encounter, etc. *Address:* 279 West 4th Street, New York, NY 10014, USA.

SCHAUFUSS, Peter; ballet dancer, producer, choreographer; Artistic Director, London Festival Ballet, since 1984; *b* 26 April 1950; *s* of Frank Schaufuss and Mona Vangsaae, former solo dancers with Royal Danish Ballet. *Educ:* Royal Danish Ballet School. Apprentice, Royal Danish Ballet, 1965; soloist, Nat. Ballet of Canada, 1967–68; Royal Danish Ballet, 1969–70; Principal, London Festival Ballet, 1970–74; NY City Ballet, 1974–77; Principal, National Ballet of Canada, 1977–83. Guest appearances in Austria, Canada, Denmark, France, Germany, Greece, Israel, Italy, Japan, Norway, S America, Turkey, UK, USA, USSR; Presenter, Dancer, BBC, 1984; numerous TV appearances. Roles created for him in: Phantom of the Opera; Orpheus; Verdi Variations; The Steadfast Tin Soldier; Rhapsodie Espagnole. Produced Bournonville ballets: La Sylphide (London Fest. Ballet, Stuttgart Ballet, Roland Petit's Ballet de Marseille, Deutsche Oper Berlin, Teatro Comunale, Florence); Napoli (Nat. Ballet of Canada); Folktale (Deutsche Oper Berlin); Dances from Napoli (London Fest. Ballet); Bournonville (Aterballetto). Solo award, 2nd Internat. Ballet Competition, Moscow, 1973; Star of the Year, Munich Abendzeitung, 1978; Evening Standard and SWET ballet award, 1979. *Recreation:* boxing. *Address:* c/o Papoutsis Representation Ltd, 18 Sundial Avenue, SE25 4BX.

SCHAWLOW, Prof. Arthur Leonard, PhD; J. G. Jackson—C. J. Wood Professor of Physics, Stanford University, since 1961; *b* Mt Vernon, New York, 5 May 1921; *s* of Arthur Schawlow and Helen Schawlow (*née* Mason); *m* 1951, Aurelia Keith Townes; one *s* two *d*. *Educ:* Univ. of Toronto, Canada. BA 1941, MA 1942, PhD 1949. Postdoctoral Fellow and Research Associate, Columbia Univ., 1949–51; Research Physicist, Bell Telephone Laboratories, 1951–61; Visiting Assoc. Prof., Columbia Univ., 1960. Hon. DSc: Ghent, 1968; Bradford, 1970; Alabama, 1984; TCD, 1986; Hon. LLD, Toronto, 1970. Ballantine Medal, Franklin Inst., 1962; Liebmann Prize, Inst. of Electrical and Electronic Engrs, 1963; Thomas Young Medal and Prize (GB), 1963; California Scientist of the Year, 1973; Ives Medal, Optical Soc. of America, 1975; Marconi Internat. Fellowship, 1977; (jtly) Nobel Prize in Physics, 1981; Arthur L. Schawlow Medal, Laser Inst. of America, 1982. *Publications:* (with C. H. Townes) Microwave Spectroscopy, 1955; many contribs to learned journals. *Recreation:* jazz music. *Address:* Department of Physics, Stanford University, Stanford, California 94305, USA. *T:* (415) 723–4356.

SCHEEL, Walter; President of the Federal Republic of Germany, 1974–79; *b* 8 July 1919; *m* 1969, Dr Mildred Scheel (*d* 1985); one *s* two *d* (and one *s* of previous *m*). *Educ:* Reform Gymnasium, Solingen. Served in German Air Force, War of 1939–45. At one time head of market research organization. Mem. of Bundestag, 1953–74; Federal Minister for Economic Co-operation, 1961–Oct. 1966, Vice-President of Bundestag, 1967–69; Vice-Chancellor and Foreign Minister, 1969–74. Former Mem., Landtag North Rhine Westphalia. Chm., Free Democrats, 1968–74. *Publications:* Konturen einer neuen Welt, 1965; Reden und Interviews, 1–5, 1972–79; Vom Recht des anderen, 1977; Die Zukunft der Freiheit, 1979. *Address:* Lindenallee 23, D 5000 Köln 51, West Germany.

SCHEMBRI, His Honour Carmelo; Chief Justice of Malta and President of the Constitutional Court, Court of Appeal and Court of Criminal Appeal, since 1981; *b* 2 Sept. 1922; *s* of Joseph Schembri and Lucia (*née* Tabone Adami); *m* 1949, Helen (*née* Holland); six *s* five *d*. *Educ:* The Lyceum, Malta; Royal Univ. of Malta (LLD 1946). Called to the Bar, 1947; elected Mem., Malta Legislative Assembly (Nationalist Party), 1950; Dep. Speaker and Chm., Cttees until dissolution of Assembly, 1951; returned to Parliament in General Election, 1951 and re-elected Dep. Speaker and Chm. Cttees; Minister of Educn, 1952–53; Asst Crown Counsel and Officer i/c Inland Revenue Dept, Gozo, 1954–62; Magistrate: for Gozo, 1962–68; Malta, 1968–78; Judge of Superior Courts, 1978–81. Coronation Medal 1953. *Recreations:* football, woodwork, collecting match boxes. *Address:* 2 Holland Court, Bisazza Street, Sliema, Malta; Chief Justice's Chambers, Law Courts, Malta. *T:* 38569. *Club:* Union (Malta).

SCHERER, Prof. Jacques, DèsL; Professor, University of Paris-III, 1979–83, now Emeritus; *b* 24 Feb. 1912; *s* of Maurice Scherer and Madeleine Franck; *m* 1965, Colette Bié. *Educ:* Ecole Normale Supérieure; Sorbonne Univ., Paris (Agrégé des Lettres, Docteur ès Lettres). Prof. of French Literature, Univ. of Nancy, 1946–54; Prof. of French Literature and Theatre, Sorbonne Univ., 1954–73; Marshal Foch Prof. of French Literature and Fellow of All Souls Coll., Univ. of Oxford, 1973–79. *Publications:* L'expression littéraire dans l'œuvre de Mallarmé, 1947; La dramaturgie classique en France, 1950; La dramaturgie de Beaumarchais, 1954; Le 'Livre' de Mallarmé, 1957 (new edn 1977); Structures de Tartuffe, 1966; Sur le Dom Juan de Molière, 1967; Le cardinal et l'orang-outang, essai sur Diderot, 1972; Théâtre du XVIIe siècle, 1975; Grammaire de Mallarmé, 1977; Racine et/ou la cérémonie, 1982; Le théâtre de Corneille, 1984. *Address:* 11 rue de la Colonie, 75013 Paris, France.

SCHIEMANN, Hon. Sir Konrad Hermann Theodor, Kt 1986; **Hon. Mr Justice Schiemann;** a Justice of the High Court, Queen's Bench Division, since 1986; *b* 15 Sept. 1937; *s* of Helmuth and Beate Schiemann; *m* 1965, Elisabeth Hanna Eleonore Holroyd-Reece; one *d*. *Educ:* King Edward's Sch., Birmingham; Pembroke Coll., Cambridge (Schol.; MA, LLB). Called to Bar, Inner Temple, 1962 (Bencher, 1985); Junior Counsel to the Crown, Common Law, 1978–80; QC 1980; a Recorder of the Crown Court, 1985–86. Chairman of panel conducting Examinations in Public of: North-East Hants and Mid Hants Structure Plans, 1979; Merseyside Structure Plan, 1980; Oxfordshire Structure Plan, 1984. *Recreations:* music, reading. *Address:* c/o Royal Courts of Justice, Strand, WC2.

SCHIFF, András; concert pianist; *b* 21 Dec. 1953; *s* of Odon Schiff and Klara Schiff (Csengeri). *Educ:* Franz Liszt Academy of Music, Budapest; with Prof. Paul Kadosa and Ferenc Rados; private study with George Malcolm. Prizewinner, Tchaikovsky competition, Moscow, 1974 and Leeds comp., 1975; Liszt Prize, 1977. Regular orch. engagements include: NY Philharmonic, Chicago Symphony, Vienna Phil., Concertgebouw, Orch. de Paris, London Phil., London Symph., Royal Phil., Israel Phil., Philadelphia, Washington Nat. Symph.; major festival performances include: Salzburg, Edinburgh, Aldeburgh, Tanglewood. Numerous recordings. *Recreations:* literature, languages, soccer. *Address:* c/o Harrison/Parrott Ltd, 12 Penzance Place, W11 4PA. *T:* 01–229 9166.

SCHILLER, Prof. Dr Karl; Member of Deutscher Bundestag, 1965–72; Professor of Political Economy, University of Hamburg, and Director of Institute for Foreign Trade and Overseas Economy, 1947–72; Member, Ford European Advisory Council, since 1976; *b* 24 April 1911; *s* of Carl and Maria Schiller; *m*; one *s* three *d*. *Educ:* Univs of Kiel, Frankfurt, Berlin, Heidelberg. Research Asst, Institut für Weltwirtschaft, Kiel, 1935–39;

Lectr, Univ. of Kiel, 1945–46; Rector, Univ. of Hamburg, 1956–58. Senator for Economic Affairs and Transportation, Hamburg, 1948–53; Mem., Bürgerschaft Hamburg, 1949–57; Senator for Economics, West Berlin, 1961–65; Federal Minister of Economics, 1966–71, of Economics and Finance, 1971–72. Pres., EDESA, 1973–79. *Publications:* Sozialismus und Wettbewerb, 1955; Neuere Entwicklungen in der Theorie der Wirtschaftspolitik, 1958; Zur Wachstumsproblematik der Entwicklungsländer, 1960; Der Ökonom und die Gesellschaft, 1964; Reden zur Wirtschaft und Finanzpolitik (10 vols), 1966–72; Betrachtungen zur Geld- und Konjunkturpolitik, 1984, etc. *Address:* 2112 Jesteburg, Reindorferstrasse 84, West Germany.

SCHILLING, Prof. Richard Selwyn Francis, CBE 1975; MD (London); DSc (London); FRCP; FFCM, FFOM; DPH; DIH; Professor of Occupational Health, London School of Hygiene and Tropical Medicine, University of London, 1960–76, now Emeritus, Hon. Fellow 1979; Director, TUC Centenary Institute of Occupational Health, 1968–76; *b* 9 Jan. 1911; *s* of late George Schilling and of Florence Louise Schilling, Kessingland, Suffolk; *m* 1937, Heather Maude Elinore Norman; one *s* two *d*. *Educ:* Epsom College; St Thomas' Hospital. Obstetric house physician, St Thomas' Hosp., 1935; house physician, Addenbrooke's Hosp., Cambridge, 1936; Asst Industrial MO, ICI (metals) Ltd, Birmingham, 1937; Medical Inspector of Factories, 1939–42. Served War of 1939–45, Captain RAMC, France and Belgium, 1939–40. Sec. Industrial Health Research Board of Med. Research Council, 1942–46; Nuffield Fellow in Industrial Health, 1946–47; Reader in Occupational Health, Univ. of Manchester, 1947–56; WHO Consultant, 1956–69. Lectures: Milroy, RCP, 1956; Mackenzie, BMA, 1956; Cantor, RSA, 1963; C.-E. A. Winslow, Yale Univ., 1963; Ernestine Henry, RCP, 1970. Former Vice-Pres., Perm. Commn, Internat. Assoc. Occupational Health. Former President: Assoc. of Industrial Medical Officers; British Occupational Hygiene Soc.; Occup. Med. Sect. of Roy. Soc. Med. Member: Committee of Inquiry into Trawler Safety, 1968; Royal Commn on Civil Liability and Compensation for Personal Injury, 1973–78. Hon. Mem., Amer. Occupational Med. Assoc., 1986. Hon. FRSM 1976. *Publications:* (ed) Modern Trends in Occupational Health, 1960; (ed) Occupational Health Practice, 1973, 2nd edn 1980; original papers on Byssinosis (respiratory disease of textile workers) and other subjects in occupational health in BMJ, Lancet, Brit. Jl of Industrial Medicine, and foreign journals. *Recreations:* fishing, gardening. *Address:* 11c Prior Bolton Street, N1. *T:* 01–359 1627.

SCHLESINGER, Arthur (Meier), Jr; writer; educator; Schweitzer Professor of the Humanities, City University of New York since 1966; *b* Columbus, Ohio, 15 Oct. 1917; *s* of late Arthur Meier and of Elizabeth Bancroft Schlesinger; *m* 1st, 1940, Marian Cannon (marr. diss. 1970); two *s* two *d*; 2nd, 1971, Alexandra Emmet; one *s*. *Educ:* Phillips Exeter Acad. AB (Harvard), 1938; Henry Fellow, Peterhouse, Cambridge, 1938–39. Soc. of Fellows, Harvard, 1939–42; US Office of War Information, 1942–43; US Office of Strategic Services, 1943–45; US Army, 1945. Mem. Adlai Stevenson Campaign Staff, 1952, 1956. Professor of History, Harvard University, 1954–61 (Associate, 1946–54); Special Assistant to President Kennedy, 1961–63. Film Reviewer: Show, 1962–65; Vogue (US), 1966–70; Saturday Review, 1977–80; Amer. Heritage, 1981. Member of Jury, Cannes Film Festival, 1964. Holds Hon. Doctorates, 1950–. Mem. of numerous Socs and Instns; Pres., Amer. Inst. of Arts and Letters, 1981–84; Chancellor, Amer. Acad., 1985–. Pulitzer Prize: History, 1946; Biography, 1966; Nat. Book Award for Biog., 1966 (for A Thousand Days: John F. Kennedy in the White House), 1979 (for Robert Kennedy and His Times); Amer. Inst. of Arts and Letters, Gold Medal for History, 1967. *Publications:* Orestes A. Brownson: a Pilgrim's Progress, 1939; The Age of Jackson, 1945; The Vital Center, 1949, (in UK) The Politics of Freedom, 1950; The General and the President (with R. H. Rovere), 1951; (co-editor) Harvard Guide to American History, 1954; The Age of Roosevelt: I: The Crisis of the Old Order, 1957; II: The Coming of the New Deal, 1958; III: The Politics of Upheaval, 1960; Kennedy or Nixon, 1960; The Politics of Hope, 1963; (ed with Morton White) Paths of American Thought, 1963; A Thousand Days: John F. Kennedy in the White House, 1965; The Bitter Heritage: Vietnam and American Democracy 1941–1966, 1967; The Crisis of Confidence: ideas, power & violence in America, 1969; (ed with F. L. Israel) History of American Presidential Elections, 1971; The Imperial Presidency, 1973; (ed) History of US Political Parties, 1973; Robert Kennedy and His Times, 1978; The Cycles of American History, 1986; articles to magazines and newspapers. *Address:* (office) 33 W 42nd Street, New York, NY 10036, USA. *T:* 790–4261. *Clubs:* Century (New York), Federal City (Washington).

SCHLESINGER, John Richard, CBE 1970; film director; Associate Director, National Theatre, since 1973; *b* 16 Feb. 1926; *s* of late Bernard Schlesinger, OBE, MD, FRCP and Winifred Henrietta (*née* Regensburg). *Educ:* Uppingham; Balliol Coll., Oxford (BA; Hon. Fellow 1981). Mem., Theatre Dirs' Guild of GB, 1983–. Directed: *films:* for Monitor and Tonight (BBC TV), 1958–60; Terminus, for British Transport Films, 1960 (Golden Lion Award, Venice Film Fest., 1961); A Kind of Loving, 1961 (Golden Bear Award, Berlin Film Festival, 1962); Billy Liar, 1962–63; Darling, 1964–65 (NY Critics Award); Far from the Madding Crowd, 1966–67; Midnight Cowboy, 1968–69 (Soc. of TV and Film Acad. Award for Best Dir; Dir's Guild of America Award; American Oscar); Sunday, Bloody Sunday, 1971 (Soc. of TV and Film Acad. Award for Best Dir; David di Donatello Award); contrib. Visions of Eight, 1973; Day of the Locust, 1975; Marathon Man, 1976; Yanks, 1978 (New Evening Standard Award, 1980); Honky Tonk Freeway, 1980; The Falcon and the Snowman, 1984; *television:* Separate Tables, 1982; An Englishman Abroad, 1983 (BAFTA Award, Broadcasting Press Guild Award, Barcelona Film Fest. Award and Nat. Bd of Review Award, 1984); *plays:* No, Why, for RSC, 1964; Timon of Athens, and Days in the Trees, for RSC, 1964–66; I and Albert, Piccadilly, 1972; Heartbreak House, 1975, Julius Caesar, 1977, and True West, 1981, for Nat. Theatre; Les Contes d'Hoffmann, 1980 (SWET Award, 1981), and Der Rosenkavalier, 1984, for Covent Garden. David di Donatello Special Award, 1980; Shakespeare Prize, FVS Foundn of Hamburg, 1981. *Recreations:* gardening, travel, music, antiques. *Address:* c/o DHAL, Paramount House, 162 Wardour Street, W1.

SCHMIDT, Helmut H. W.; Member of Bundestag, Federal Republic of Germany, 1953–62, and 1965–86; Senior Editor, Die Zeit, since 1983; *b* 23 Dec. 1918; *s* of Gustav L. and Ludovica Schmidt; *m* 1942, Hannelore Glaser; one *d*. *Educ:* Univ. of Hamburg. Diplom-Volkswirt, 1948. Manager of Transport Administration, State of Hamburg, 1949–53; Social Democratic Party: Member, 1946–; Chm., Parly Gp, 1967–69; Vice-Chm. of Party, 1968–84; Senator (Minister) for Domestic Affairs in Hamburg, 1961–65; Minister of Defence, 1969–72; Minister of Finance and Econs, 1972; Minister of Finance, 1972–74; Chancellor, Federal Republic of Germany, 1974–82. Hon LLD: Newberry Coll., S Carolina, 1973; Johns Hopkins Univ., 1976; Cambridge, 1983; Hon. DCL Oxford, 1979; Hon. Doctorate: Harvard, 1979; Sorbonne, 1981.; Georgetown, 1986. Athinai Prize for Man and Mankind, Onassis Foundn, Greece, 1986. *Publications:* Defence or Retaliation, 1962; Beiträge, 1967; Balance of Power, 1971; Auf dem Fundament des Godesberger Programms, 1973; Bundestagsreden, 1975; Kontinuität und Konzentration, 1975; Als Christ in der politischen Entscheidung, 1976; (with Willy Brandt) Deutschland 1976—Zwei Sozialdemokraten im Gespräch, 1976; Der Kurs heisst Frieden, 1979; Pflicht zur Menschlichkeit, 1981; A Grand Strategy for the West, 1985. *Recreations:* sailing, chess, playing the organ. *Address:* c/o Deutscher Bundestag, Görresstrasse 15, Bundeshaus, 5300 Bonn 1, West Germany.

SCHMITTHOFF, Clive Macmillan, Dr jur, LLD; barrister; *b* 24 March 1903; *s* of Hermann and Anna Schmitthoff; *m* 1940, Twinkie (Ilse) (*née* Auerbach). *Educ:* Univs of Berlin and London. Dr jur Berlin 1927; LLM 1936, LLD 1953, London. Called to Bar, Gray's Inn, 1936. Lectr, 1948–58, Sen. Lectr, 1958–63, Principal Lectr, 1963–71, Prof. Emeritus, 1982, City of London Polytechnic. Served HM Army, 1940–45: Normandy, War Office, CCG, Warrant Officer (France and Germany Star, Def. and War medals). Legal Advr to UN, 1966. Visiting Professor: City Univ., 1971–87; Louisiana State Univ., 1964, 1965; Univ. of Manitoba Law Sch., 1965, 1969, 1971, 1978; Univ. of Kent, 1971–84; Gresham Prof. in Law, 1976–86. Jt Vice-Chm., Centre for Commercial Law Studies, QMC, Univ. of London, 1985–. Vice-President: Assoc. of Law Teachers, 1965–; Inst. of Export, 1979–; Mansfield Law Club, 1985– (Founder 1948); Founder and Gen. Editor, Journal of Business Law, 1957–. Hon. Professor of Law: Ruhr Univ., Bochum, 1968; Univ. of Kent, 1978; Hon. Djur: Marburg and Berne, 1977; Bielefeld, 1983; Hon. DLitt Heriot-Watt, 1978; Hon. LLD Kent, 1982. FIEx 1974. Grand Cross of Merit, German Fed. Republic, 1974. *Publications:* The English Conflict of Laws, 1945, 3rd edn 1954; Schmitthoff's Export Trade, 1948, 8th edn 1986; The Sale of Goods, 1951, 2nd edn 1966; ed, Palmer's Company Law, 1959–, 24th edn 1986; jt ed, Charlesworth's Mercantile Law, 1960–, 14th edn 1984; (ed jtly) International Commercial Arbitration, 1976, 3rd edn 1985; Commercial Law in a Changing Economic Climate, 1977, 2nd edn 1981; Extrajudicial Dispute Settlement, Forum Internationale No 6, 1985; contrib. many legal jls, UK and abroad; *relevant publications:* Law and International Trade, ed Fritz Fabricius, 1973; Essays for Clive Schmitthoff, ed John Adams, 1983. *Recreations:* history, literature, music, modern art. *Address:* 29 Blenheim Road, Bedford Park, W4 1ET.

SCHNEIDER, Rt. Hon. Sir Lancelot Raymond A.; *see* Adams-Schneider.

SCHNEIDER, Dr William George, OC 1977; FRS 1962; FRSC 1951; Research Consultant, National Research Council of Canada, Ottawa, since 1980 (President, 1967–80); *b* Wolseley, Saskatchewan, 1 June 1915; *s* of Michael Schneider and Phillipina Schneider (*née* Kraushaar); *m* 1940, Jean Frances Purves; two *d*. *Educ:* University of Saskatchewan; McGill University; Harvard University. BSc 1937, MSc 1939, University of Saskatchewan; PhD (in physical chem.), 1941, McGill Univ. Research physicist at Woods Hole Oceanographic Inst., Woods Hole, Mass, USA, 1943–46 (US Navy Certificate of Merit, 1946). Joined Nat. Research Council, Division of Pure Chemistry, Ottawa, 1946; Vice-President (Scientific), 1965–67. Pres., Internat. Union of Pure and Applied Chemistry, 1983–85. Chemical Inst. of Canada Medal, 1961, Montreal Medal, 1973; Henry Marshall Tory Medal, RSC, 1969. Hon. DSc: York, 1966; Memorial, 1968; Saskatchewan, 1969; Moncton, 1969; McMaster, 1969; Laval, 1969; New Brunswick, 1970; Montreal, 1970; McGill, 1970; Acadia, 1976; Regina, 1976; Ottawa, 1978; Hon. LLD: Alberta, 1968; Laurentian, 1968. *Publications:* (with J. A. Pople and H. J. Bernstein) High Resolution Nuclear Magnetic Resonance, 1959; scientific papers in chemistry and physics research jls. *Recreations:* tennis, ski-ing. *Address:* #2–65 Whitemarl Drive, Ottawa, Ontario K1L 8J9, Canada. *T:* (613) 748–9742.

SCHNEIDERHAN, Frau Wolfgang; *see* Seefried, Irmgard.

SCHNYDER, Félix; Ambassador of Switzerland to the United States, 1966–75; *b* 5 March 1910; Swiss; *s* of Maximilian Schnyder and Louise (*née* Steiner); *m* 1941, Sigrid Bucher; one *d*. *Educ:* University of Berne. Barrister, 1938; activities in private enterprise, 1938–40; joined Federal Political Dept, 1940; assigned to Swiss Legation in Moscow, 1947–49; Counsellor of Legation, Head of Swiss Delegation in Berlin, 1949–54; First Counsellor, Swiss Legation in Washington, 1954–57; Swiss Minister in Israel, 1957; Permanent Observer for Switzerland at UN in New York, 1958–61; Swiss Delegate to Technical Assistance Cttee; Swiss Delegate to Exec. Board of UNICEF (Chm. 1960); UN High Comr for Refugees, 1961–65. President: Swiss Nat. Cttee for UNESCO, 1976–80; Swiss Foreign Policy Assoc., 1976–84. *Recreations:* ski-ing, mountaineering, reading (history and politics), chess and bridge. *Address:* Via Navegna 25, 6648 Minusio-Locarno, Switzerland.

SCHOFIELD, Alfred, FCBSI; Director, Leeds Permanent Building Society, 1970–86; *b* 18 Feb. 1913; *s* of James Henry and Alice Schofield; *m* 1939, Kathleen Risingham; one *d*. *Educ:* Queen Elizabeth's Grammar Sch., Wakefield. Apptd General Manager, Leeds Permanent Bldg Soc., 1967; retd, 1973; Pres., 1975–78. Dir, Homeowners Friendly Soc., 1983–. *Recreation:* orchid growing. *Address:* The Cottage, Rudding, Harrogate, N Yorks HG3 1DH. *T:* Harrogate 872037.

SCHOFIELD, Prof. Andrew Noel, MA, PhD (Cantab); FEng 1986; FICE; Professor of Engineering, Cambridge University, since 1974; Fellow of Churchill College, Cambridge, 1963–66 and since 1974; *b* 1 Nov. 1930; *s* of Rev. John Noel Schofield and Winifred Jane Mary (*née* Eyles); *m* 1961, Margaret Eileen Green; two *s* two *d*. *Educ:* Mill Hill Sch.; Christ's Coll., Cambridge. John Winbolt Prize, 1954. Asst Engr, in Malawi, with Scott Wilson Kirkpatrick and Partners, 1951. Cambridge Univ.: Demonstrator, 1955, Lectr, 1959, Dept of Engrg. Research Fellow, California Inst. of Technology, 1963–64. Univ. of Manchester Inst. of Science and Technology: Prof. of Civil Engrg, 1968; Head of Dept of Civil and Structural Engrg, 1973. Formed Andrew N. Schofield and Associates Ltd (ANS&A), 1984. Rankine Lecture, ICE British Geotechnical Soc., 1980. Chm., Cttee on Centrifuges, Int. Soc. for Soil Mech. and Foundn Engrg, 1982–85. US Army Outstanding Civilian Service Medal, 1979. *Publications:* (with C. P. Wroth) Critical State Soil Mechanics, 1968; papers on soil mechanics and civil engrg. *Address:* 9 Little St Mary's Lane, Cambridge CB2 1RR. *T:* Cambridge 314536.

SCHOFIELD, Bertram, CBE 1959; MA, PhD, LittD; Keeper of Manuscripts and Egerton Librarian, British Museum, 1956–61; *b* 13 June 1896; *m* 1928, Edith (*d* 1981), *d* of Arthur William and Edith Emily Thomas; one *s* two *d*. *Educ:* University Sch., Southport; University of Liverpool (Charles Beard and University Fellow); Sorbonne, Ecole des Chartes and Ecole des Hautes Etudes, Paris; Emmanuel College, Cambridge (Open Research Student). Served European War, with Roy. Wilts Yeomanry, 1917–19. Asst Keeper, Dept of MSS, British Museum, 1922; Deputy-Keeper, 1947; Keeper, 1956. Seconded to Min. of Economic Warfare, 1940–42, and for special duties with Inter-Services Intelligence and Combined Ops, HQ, 1942–44. Member: Bd of Studies in Palæography, University of London; Committee of Inst. of Historical Research, 1951–61; Council of Royal Historical Society, 1956–59; Canterbury and York Society; Vice-Pres. British Records Assoc., 1956–61; Governor: North London Collegiate School and Camden High Sch. for Girls, 1955–64. *Publications:* Muchelney Memoranda (Somerset Record Soc.), 1927; (with A. J. Collins) Legal and Manorial Formularies, 1933; The Knyvett Letters, 1949; contrib. to Musical Quarterly, Music Review, Music and Letters. British Museum Quarterly, Studies presented to Sir Hilary Jenkinson, 1957; Musik in Geschichte und Gegenwart, etc. *Recreations:* gardening and music. *Address:* 4 Farm Close, Kidlington, Oxford. *T:* Kidlington 4110.

SCHOFIELD, (Edward) Guy; FJI; Journalist; *b* 10 July 1902; *s* of Frank Garside Schofield and Fanny Atkinson; *m* 1st, Norah Ellett (*d* 1935); one *d*; 2nd, Ellen Clark (*d* 1977). *Educ:* Leeds Modern School. Leeds Mercury, 1918–25; Daily Dispatch, Manchester, 1925–27; Evening Chronicle, Manchester, 1929–30; Chief Sub-Editor, Evening Standard, London,

1931–38; Editor: Yorkshire Evening News, 1938–42; The Evening News, London, 1942–50; Daily Mail, London, 1950–55; Director: Associated Newspapers Ltd, 1947–55; United Newspapers Ltd, 1960–79; Sheffield Newspapers Ltd, 1963–79; Yorkshire Post Newspapers Ltd, 1969–82. Member of Press Council, 1953–55; Chairman British Committee, International Press Institute, 1953–55; Director of Publicity, Conservative Party Headquarters, 1955–57. *Publications:* The Purple and the Scarlet, 1959; Crime Before Calvary, 1960; In the Year 62, 1962; Why Was He Killed?, 1965; The Men that Carry the News, 1975. *Address:* Pear Tree Cottage, Sinnington, York YO6 6RZ.

SCHOFIELD, Grace Florence; Regional Nursing Officer to the South West Thames Regional Health Authority, 1974–82, retired; *b* 24 Feb. 1925; *d* of Percy and Matilda Schofield. *Educ:* Mayfield Sch., Putney; University College Hosp. (SRN, SCM); Univ. of London (Dip. in Nursing); Royal College of Nursing (Dip. in Nursing Admin. (Hosp.)). Asst Matron, Guy's Hosp., 1960–61; Dep. Matron, Hammersmith Hosp., 1962–66; Matron, Mount Vernon Hosp. Northwood, and Harefield Hosp., Harefield, 1966–69; Chief Nursing Officer, University Coll. Hosp., 1969–73. *Address:* 42 Briarwood Road, Stoneleigh, Epsom, Surrey.

SCHOLAR, Michael Charles; Under Secretary, Fiscal Policy Group, HM Treasury, since 1986; *b* 3 Jan. 1942; *s* of Richard Herbert Scholar and Mary Blodwen Scholar; *m* 1964, Angela Mary (*née* Sweet); three *s* (one *d* decd). *Educ:* St Olave's Grammar School, Bermondsey; St John's College, Cambridge (PhD, MA); Univ. of California at Berkeley. ARCO. Loeb Fellow, Harvard Univ., 1967; Asst Lectr, Leicester Univ., 1968; Fellow, St John's College, Cambridge, 1969; HM Treasury, 1969; Private Sec. to Chief Sec., 1974–76; Barclays Bank International, 1979–81; Private Sec. to Prime Minister, 1981–83; Under Secretary, HM Treasury, 1983; Central Unit, 1985. *Publications:* contribs to Mind and other philosophical jls. *Recreations:* music, walking. *Address:* HM Treasury, Parliament Street, SW1. *T:* 01–233 3016.

SCHOLEFIELD, Charles Edward, QC 1959; *b* 15 July 1902; *e s* of Edward Scholefield, Castleford, Yorks; *m* 1966, Catherine Helène (formerly Childs), *o d* of Reginald and Marguerite Blyth; one step *s*; one step *d*. *Educ:* St Peter's School, York. Admitted a Solicitor, 1925; Barrister, Middle Temple, 1934; North Eastern Circuit. Served in Royal Army Pay Corps, 1940–45; Captain, 1943–45. Chm., Council of Professions supplementary to Medicine, 1966–73. Master of the Bench of the Middle Temple, 1966. *Publications:* (ed) 11th and 12th edns, Lumley's Public Health. *Recreations:* watching cricket and Rugby football; Sherlock Holmes Society of London; Society of Yorkshiremen in London (Past Chairman). *Address:* 4 Gray's Inn Square, WC1; c/o Mrs Pattison, Brampton Lodge, 20 Fiddicroft Avenue, Banstead, Surrey.

SCHOLES, Alwyn Denton; Senior Puisne Judge, Hong Kong, 1970–71 (Acting Chief Justice, 1970); *b* 16 Dec. 1910; *s* of Denton Scholes and Mrs Scholes (*née* Birch); *m* 1939, Juliet Angela Ierne Pyne; one *s* four *d*. *Educ:* Cheltenham College; Selwyn College, Cambridge. Legal Tripos Parts I and II, Cantab, 1932, 1933; MA 1933. Called to the Bar, 1934; practised at the Bar in London and on Midland Circuit, 1934–38; apptd District Magistrate, Gold Coast, 1938; Acting Crown Counsel and Solicitor General, Gold Coast, 1941; apptd Magistrate, Hong Kong, 1948; First Magistrate: Kowloon, 1949; Hong Kong, 1949. Appointed District Judge, Hong Kong, 1953, Puisne Judge, Hong Kong, 1958. Comr, Supreme Ct of State of Brunei, 1964–67, 1968–71. Pres. or Mem., Hong Kong Full Ct of Appeal, on occasions, 1949–71. Member: Sidmouth Parochial Church Council, 1972–82; Ottery Deanery Synod, 1973–82. Governor, St Nicholas Sch., Sidmouth, 1984–. *Recreations:* walking, swimming, gardening. *Address:* West Hayes, Convent Road, Sidmouth, Devon EX10 8RL. *Club:* Royal Commonwealth Society.

SCHOLES, Gordon Glen Denton; MHR for Corio (Victoria), Australia, since 1967; Minister for Territories, since 1984; *b* 7 June 1931; *s* of Glen Scholes and Mary Scholes; *m* 1957, Della Kathleen Robinson; two *d*. *Educ:* various schs. Loco-engine driver, Victorian Railways, 1949–67. Councillor, Geelong City, 1965–67; Pres., Geelong Trades Hall Council, 1965–66. House of Representatives: Chm. cttees, 1973–75; Speaker, 1975–76; Shadow Minister for Defence, 1977–83; Minister for Defence, 1983–84. Amateur Boxing Champion (Heavyweight), Vic, 1949. *Recreations:* golf, reading. *Address:* 20 Stephen Street, Newtown, Vic 3220, Australia.

SCHOLES, Hubert, CB 1977; Specialist Adviser to House of Commons Employment Committee, 1981–82; *b* 22 March 1921; *s* of late Hubert Scholes and Lucy (*née* Carter); *m* 1949, Patricia Caldwell; one *s*. *Educ:* Shrewsbury Sch.; Balliol Coll., Oxford. Served RA, 1940–45. Asst Principal, Min. of Fuel and Power, 1946; Principal, 1950; Ministry of Housing and Local Govt, 1956–57; Principal Private Sec. to Minister of Power, 1959–62; Asst Sec., 1962; Under-Sec., Min. of Power, subseq. Min. of Technol., DTI and Dept of Industry, 1968–78; a Comr of Customs and Excise, 1978–81. *Address:* 5A Lancaster Avenue, Farnham, Surrey. *T:* Farnham 723992.

SCHOLES, Mary Elizabeth, (Mrs A. I. M. Haggart), OBE 1983; SRN; Chief Area Nursing Officer, Tayside Health Board, 1973–83; *b* 8 April 1924; *d* of late John Neville Carpenter Scholes and Margaret Elizabeth (*née* Hines); *m* 1983, Most Rev. Alastair Iain Macdonald Haggart, *qv*. *Educ:* Wyggeston Grammar Sch. for Girls, Leicester; Leicester Royal Infirmary and Children's Hosp. (SRN 1946); Guy's Hosp., London (CMB Pt I Cert. 1947); Royal Coll. of Nursing, London (Nursing Admin (Hosp.) Cert. 1962). Leicester Royal Infirmary and Children's Hospital: Staff Nurse, 1947–48; Night Sister, 1948–50; Ward Sister, 1950–56; Night Supt, 1956–58; Asst Matron, 1958–61; Asst Matron, Memorial/Brook Gen. Hosp., London, 1962–64; Matron, Dundee Royal Infirm. and Matron Designate, Ninewells Hosp., Dundee, 1964–68; Chief Nursing Officer, Bd of Management for Dundee Gen. Hosps and Bd of Man. for Ninewells and Associated Hosps, 1968–73. Pres., Scottish Assoc. of Nurse Administrators, 1973–77. Member: Scottish Bd, Royal Coll. of Nursing, 1965–70; Gen. Nursing Council for Scotland, 1966–70, 1979–; Standing Nursing and Midwifery Cttee, Scotland, 1971–74 (Vice-Chm., 1973–74); UK Central Council for Nursing, Midwifery and Health Visiting, 1980–; Management Cttee, State Hosp., Carstairs, 1983; Scottish Hosp. Endowments Res. Trust, 1986; Chm., Scottish National Bd for Nursing, Midwifery and Health Visiting, 1980–. *Recreations:* travel, music. *Address:* 19 Eglinton Crescent, Edinburgh EH12 5BY. *Club:* Royal Commonwealth Society.

SCHOLEY, David Gerald, CBE 1976; Chairman, Mercury International Group, since 1984; Joint Chairman, S. G. Warburg & Co. Ltd, Bankers, since 1980; a Director, Bank of England, since 1981; *b* 28 June 1935; *s* of Dudley and Lois Scholey; *m* 1960, Alexandra Beatrix, *d* of Hon. George and Fiorenza Drew, Canada; one *s* one *d*. *Educ:* Wellington Coll., Berks; Christ Church, Oxford. Joined S. G. Warburg & Co. Ltd, 1965, Dir 1967, Dep. Chm., 1977; Director: Mercury Securities plc, 1969 (Chm., 1984–86); Orion Insurance Co. Ltd, 1963; Stewart Wrightson Holdings Ltd, 1972–81; Union Discount Co. of London, Ltd, 1976–81; British Telecom plc, 1985–. Mem., Export Guarantees Adv. Council, 1970–75, Dep. Chm. 1974–75; Chm., Construction Exports Adv. Bd, 1975–78; Mem., Cttee on Finance for Industry, NEDO, 1980–. Hon. Treasurer, IISS, 1984–. Governor: Wellington Coll., 1977–; NIESR, 1984–. *Address:* Heath End House, Spaniards Road, NW3 7JE. *T:* 01–455 4795.

SCHOLEY, Robert, CBE 1982; Chairman, British Steel Corporation, since 1986; *b* 8 Oct. 1921; *s* of Harold and Eveline Scholey; *m* 1946, Joan Methley; two *d*. *Educ:* King Edward VII Sch. and Sheffield Univ. Associateship in Mech Engrg. United Steel Companies, 1947–68; British Steel Corporation, 1968–: Mem. and Chief Executive, 1973–86; Dep. Chm., 1976–86. *Recreations:* outdoor life, history. *Address:* The Coach House, Much Hadham, Herts. *T:* Much Hadham 2908.

SCHOLTENS, Sir James (Henry), KCVO 1977 (CVO 1963); consultant; Director, Office of Government Ceremonial and Hospitality, Department of the Prime Minister and Cabinet, Canberra, 1973–80, retired; Extra Gentleman Usher to the Queen, since 1981; *b* 12 June 1920; *s* of late Theo F. J. Scholtens and late Grace M. E. (*née* Nolan); *m* 1945, Mary Maguire, Brisbane; one *s* five *d*. *Educ:* St Patrick's Marist Brothers' Coll., Sale, Vic. Served War, RAAF, 1943–45. Joined Aust. Public Service, 1935; PMG's Dept, Melbourne, 1935; Dept of Commerce, Melb., 1938; transf. to Dept of Commerce, Canberra, 1941; Dept of Prime Minister, Canberra: Accountant, 1949; Ceremonial Officer, 1954; Asst Sec., Ceremonial and Hospitality Br., 1967. Dir of visits to Australia by the Sovereign and Members of the Royal Family, Heads of State, Monarchs and Presidents, and by Heads of Govt and Ministers of State. *Address:* 74 Boldrewood Street, Turner, Canberra, ACT 2601, Australia. *T:* 48 6639. *Clubs:* Canberra, Southern Cross, National Press (Canberra); Royal Automobile of Australia (Sydney).

SCHON, family name of **Baron Schon.**

SCHON, Baron *cr* 1976 (Life Peer), of Whitehaven, Cumbria; **Frank Schon,** Kt 1966; Chairman, National Research Development Corporation, 1969–79 (Member, 1967–79); *b* 18 May 1912; *o s* of Dr Frederick Schon and Henriette (*née* Nettel); *m* 1936, Gertrude Secher; two *d*. *Educ:* Rainer Gymnasium, Vienna II; University of Prague; University of Vienna (studied law externally). Co-founder: Marchon Products Ltd, 1939; Solway Chemicals Ltd, 1943; Chm. and Man. Dir of both until May 1967; Dir, Albright & Wilson Ltd, 1956–67; Non-exec. Dir, Blue Circle Industries PLC (formerly Associated Portland Cement Manufacturers Ltd), 1967–82. Mem. Council, King's College, Durham, 1959–63; Mem. Council, 1963–66, Mem. Court, 1963–78, Univ. of Newcastle upon Tyne. Chm. Cumberland Development Council, 1964–68; Member: Northern Economic Planning Council, 1965–68; Industrial Reorganisation Corp., 1966–71; Adv. Council of Technology, 1968–70; part-time Mem., Northern Gas Bd, 1963–66. Hon. Freeman of Whitehaven, 1961. Hon. DCL Durham, 1961. *Recreations:* golf, reading. *Address:* Flat 82, Prince Albert Court, 33 Prince Albert Road, NW8 7LU. *T:* 01–586 1461.

SCHOPPER, Prof. Herwig Franz; Director-General, European Organization for Nuclear Research, since 1981; Professor of Physics, University of Hamburg, since 1973; *b* 28 Feb. 1928; *s* of Franz Schopper and Margarete Hartmann; *m* 1949, Dora Klara Ingeborg (*née* Stieler); one *s* one *d*. *Educ:* Univ. of Hamburg. Dip. Phys. 1949, Dr rer nat 1951. Asst Prof. and Univ. Lectr, Univ. of Erlangen, 1954–57; Prof., Univ. of Mainz, 1957–60; Prof., Univ. of Karlsruhe and Dir of Inst. for Nuclear Physics, 1961–73; Research Associate, CERN, 1966–67; Chm., Scientific Council, Kerforschungszentrum, Karlsruhe, 1967–69; Head of Dept of particle physics, CERN and Mem., Directorate for experimental programme, 1970–73; Chm., Deutsches Elektronen Synchrotron particle physics Lab., Hamburg, 1973–80. Chm., CERN Intersecting Storage Ring Cttee, 1973–76; Mem., CERN Sci. Policy Cttee, 1979–80; Chm., Assoc. of German Nat. Research Centres, 1978–80; Mem., Scientific Council, IN2P3, Paris. Member: Akad. der Wissenschaften Leopoldina, Halle; Joachim Jungius Gesellschaft, Hamburg; Corresp. Mem., Bavarian Acad. of Scis, 1981; Sudetendeutsche Akad. der Wissenschaft, 1979. Dr *hc* Univ. of Erlangen, 1982. Physics Award, Göttinger Akad. der Wissenschaft, 1957; Carus Medal, Akad. Leopoldina, 1958; Ritter von Gerstner Medal, 1978; Sudetendeutscher Kulturpreis, 1984; Golden Plate Award, Amer. Acad. of Achievement, 1984. *Publications:* Weak Interactions and Nuclear Beta Decay, 1966; papers on elementary particle physics, high energy accelerators, relation of science and society. *Recreations:* reading, music, gardening. *Address:* CERN, CH 1211 Geneva, Switzerland. *T:* 832300.

SCHOUVALOFF, Alexander, MA; Curator, Theatre Museum, Victoria and Albert Museum, since 1974; *b* 4 May 1934; *s* of Paul Schouvaloff (professional name Paul Sheriff) and Anna Schouvaloff (*née* Raevsky); *m* 1st, Gillian Baker; one *s*; 2nd, 1971, Daria Chorley (*née* de Mérindol). *Educ:* Harrow Sch.; Jesus Coll., Oxford (MA). Asst Director, Edinburgh Festival, 1965–67; Dir, North West Arts Assoc., 1967–74; Director: Rochdale Festival, 1971; Chester Festival, 1973. Sec. Gen., Société Internat. des Bibliothèques et des Musées des Arts du Spectacle, 1980–. BBC Radio plays: Summer of the Bullshine Boys, 1981; No Saleable Value, 1982. FRSA. Cross of Polonia Restituta, 1971. *Publications:* Place for the Arts, 1971; Summer of the Bullshine Boys, 1979; (with Victor Borovsky) Stravinsky on Stage, 1982; (with April FitzLyon) A Month in the Country, 1983; Thyssen-Bornemisza Collection: catalogue of set and costume designs, 1986. *Recreation:* celebrating birthdays. *Address:* 59 Lyndhurst Grove, SE15 5AW. *T:* 01–703 3671. *Club:* Garrick.

SCHRAM, Emil; Chairman of Board, Peru Trust Co.; *b* Peru, Indiana, 23 November 1893; *s* of Emil Alexander Schram and Katharine Graf; *m* 1914, Mabel Miller (decd); three *s*; *m* 1971, Margaret Beauchamp Percy. *Educ:* Peru High School. Book-keeper, J. O. Cole, Peru, Ind., 1910–15; manager Hartwell Land Trust, Hillview, Ill., 1915–33; Chairman National Drainage Assoc., 1931–33; chief, drainage, levee and irrigation div., Reconstruction Finance Corp., 1933–36; Director, 1936–41; Chm., 1939–41; President, New York Stock Exchange, 1941–51; Director: Cities Service Co.; Associates Investment Co.; Home Insce Co.; Indiana National Bank; CTS Corp. Valley Farms, Inc.; Hon. Mem. Business Council. Hon. degrees: Dr of Law: New York Univ.; Univ. of Vermont; Franklin College; Indiana Univ. *Recreations:* golf and fishing. *Address:* Hillcrest, RR1, Peru, Ind 46970, USA. *T:* 473 9100. *Club:* Columbia (Indianapolis).

SCHRAM, Prof. Stuart Reynolds; Professor of Politics (with reference to China) in the University of London, School of Oriental and African Studies, since 1968; *b* Excelsior, Minn, 27 Feb. 1924; *s* of Warren R. Schram and Nada Stedman Schram; *m* 1972, Marie-Annick Lancelot; one *s*. *Educ:* West High Sch., Minneapolis, Minn; Univ. of Minnesota (BA, 1944); Columbia Univ. (PhD 1954). Dir, Soviet and Chinese Section, Centre d'Etude des Relations Internationales, Fondation Nationale des Sciences Politiques, Paris, 1954–67; Head, Contemporary China Inst., SOAS, 1968–72. *Publications:* Protestantism and Politics in France, 1954; La théorie de la "révolution permanente" en Chine, 1963; The Political Thought of Mao Tse-Tung, 1963, rev. edn 1969; Le marxisme et l'Asie 1853–1964, 1965, rev. and enl. English edn 1969; Mao Tse-tung, 1966; (ed) Authority, Participation and Cultural Change in China, 1973; Mao Zedong: a preliminary re-assessment, 1983; Ideology and Policy in China since the Third Plenum, 1978–84, 1984; (ed) The Scope of State Power in China, 1985; *translations:* Mao Ze-dong, Une étude de l'éducation physique, 1962; Mao Tse-tung Unrehearsed, 1974. *Recreations:* concert- and theatre-going, walking in the country, fishing. *Address:* 4 Regal Lane, NW1.

SCHRAMEK, Sir Eric von; *see* von Schramek.

SCHREIBER, Mrs Gaby, FSIAD; General Consultant Designer for Industry; specialist in Colour Consultancy and Interiors; Adviser on purchases of works of art; Chairman, Gaby Schreiber & Associates; *d* of Gunther George Peter Wolff; *m* Leopold Schreiber. *Educ:* studied art and stage and interior design in Vienna, Florence, Berlin and Paris. Interior Design Consultant to: William Clark & Sons Ltd, NI, 1981–; National Westminster Bank Ltd; Westminster Foreign Bank, Brussels, 1972–73; Chm.'s offices, GHP Gp Ltd, 1974; Pres.'s offices, Gulf Oil-Eastern Hemisphere, 1973–74; Lythe Hill Hotel, Haslemere, Surrey; Anglo-Continental Investment & Finance Co. and Continental Bankers Agents, London; Myers & Co.; Peter Robinson Ltd; David Morgan, Cardiff; W Cumberland Hosp.; Newcastle Regnl Hosp. Bd; Fine Fare Ltd (Queensway Store, Crawley); Gen. Consultant and Designer to: Cunard Steamship Co. Ltd (QE2); Zarach Ltd; Marquess of Londonderry; Crown Agents; Allen and Hanbury (Surgical Engineering) Limited; BOAC (whole fleet of aeroplanes, 1957–63); Divs of Dunlop Rubber Gp; Bartrev Gp of Cos; Hawker Siddeley Aviation Ltd (for the Queen's Flight and RAF); Rank Organisation Ltd; Design Consultant on Plastics to Marks & Spencer Ltd. Yachts: Sir Gerard d'Erlanger; Whitney Straight, and others. Designed Exhibn Stands in Britain, Europe and USA. Member CoID, 1960–62 (Mem. Design Awards Cttee, 1961); Judge on Indep. Panel, to select Duke of Edinburgh's Prize for Elegant Design, 1960 and 1961. Fellow, Soc. of Industrial Artists and Designers (Past Chm., Consultant Designers Gp and Internat. Relations Cttee; Mem. Council; UK delegate at Gen. Assembly of Internat. Council of Soc. of Ind. Design, Venice, 1961); Mem., Panel of Judges for newspaper and magazine competitions on ind. design. Has broadcast and appeared on TV. *Publications:* her work has appeared in internat. books and jls on design. *Recreations:* gardening, farming, golf, arts and crafts. *Address:* 26 Kylestrome House, Cundy Street, SW1W 9JT. *T:* 01–235 4656.

SCHREIBER, Mark Shuldham; political consultant, farmer and journalist; Editorial Staff of The Economist, since 1974, lobby correspondent, since 1976; *b* 11 Sept. 1931; *s* of late John Shuldham Schreiber, DL, Marlesford Hall, Suffolk and Maureen Schreiber (*née* Dent); *m* 1969, Gabriella Federica, *d* of Conte Teodoro Veglio di Castelletto d'Uzzone; two *d*. *Educ:* Eton; Trinity Coll., Cambridge. Nat. Service in Coldstream Guards, 1950–51. Fisons Ltd, 1957–63; Conservative Research Dept, 1963–67; Dir, Conservative Party Public Sector Research Unit, 1967–70; Special Advr to the Govt, 1970–74; Special Adviser to Leader of the Opposition, 1974–75; Member: Royal Ordnance Factories Bd, 1972–74; Govt Computer Agency Council, 1973–74; Countryside Commn, 1980–; Development Commn, 1985–; Mem., East Suffolk CC, 1968–70. *Recreation:* countryside conservation. *Address:* Marlesford Hall, Woodbridge, Suffolk. *T:* Wickham Market 310; 5 Kersley Street, SW11. *Club:* Pratt's.

SCHREYER, Rt. Hon. Edward Richard, CC (Canada) 1979; CMM 1979; CD 1979; PC 1984; High Commissioner for Canada in Australia, since 1984; *b* Beausejour, Man., 21 Dec. 1935; *s* of John and Elizabeth Schreyer, a pioneer family of the district; *m* 1960, Lily, *d* of Jacob Schulz, MP; two *s* two *d*. *Educ:* United Coll., Winnipeg; St John's Coll., Winnipeg, Univ. of Manitoba (BA, BEd, MA). While at university served as 2nd Lieut, COTC, Royal Canadian Armored Corps, 1954–56. Member, Legislative Assembly of Manitoba, 1958; re-elected, 1959 and 1962; MP: for Springfield, 1965, for Selkirk, 1968; chosen as Leader of New Democratic Party in Manitoba, 1969, and resigned seat in House of Commons; MLA for Rossmere and Premier of Manitoba, 1969; re-elected MLA, 1977; Governor-Gen. and C-in-C of Canada, 1979–84. Prof. of Political Science and Internat. Relns, St John's Coll., Univ. of Manitoba, 1962–65. Member, Commonwealth Parly Assoc., Interparly Union, 1960–78. Hon. LLD: Manitoba, 1979; Ottawa 1980; ME Allison, 1983; McGill, 1984; Simon Fraser, 1984; Lakehead, 1985. Chancellor and Principal Companion of the Order of Canada, 1979; Chancellor and Commander of the Order of Military Merit, 1979. Vanier Award as Outstanding Young Canadian, 1975. *Recreations:* curling, golf, canoeing. *Address:* 32 Mugga Way, Red Hill, Canberra, ACT 2603, Australia. *Clubs:* Royal Canberra; Commonwealth.

SCHRIEFFER, Prof. John Robert, PhD; Professor of Physics, since 1980, and Essam Khashoggi Professor and Director, Institute for Theoretical Physics, since 1984, University of California, Santa Barbara; *b* Oak Park, Ill, 31 May 1931; *s* of John Henry Schrieffer and Louise Anderson; *m* 1960, Anne Grete Thomsen; one *s* two *d*. *Educ:* MIT(BS); Univ. of Illinois (MS, PhD). Nat. Sci. Foundn Fellow, Univ. of Birmingham, and Niels Bohr Inst. for Theoretical Physics, Copenhagen, 1957–58; Asst Prof., Univ. of Chicago, 1957–59; Asst Prof., Univ. of Illinois, 1959–60, Associate Prof., 1960–62; Univ. of Pennsylvania: Mem. Faculty, 1962–79; Mary Amanda Wood Prof. of Physics, 1964–79. Guggenheim Fellow, Copenhagen, 1967. Member: Nat. Acad. Scis; Amer. Acad. of Arts and Scis; Amer. Philos. Soc.; Amer. Phys Soc.; Danish Royal Acad. Sci. Hon. ScD: Technische Hoschschule, Munich, 1968; Univ. of Geneva, 1968; Univ. of Pennsylvania, 1973; Illinois Univ., 1974; Univ. of Cincinnati, 1977. Buckley Prize, Amer. Phys Soc., 1968; Comstock Prize, Nat. Acad. Scis, 1968; (jtly) Nobel Prize for Physics, 1972; John Ericsson Medal, Amer. Soc. of Swedish Engineers, 1976; Nat. Medal of Science, USA, 1985. *Publications:* Theory of Superconductivity, 1964; articles on solid state physics and chemistry. *Recreations:* painting, gardening, wood working. *Address:* Institute for Theoretical Physics, University of California, Santa Barbara, Calif 93106, USA.

SCHRODER, Ernest Melville, CMG 1970; *b* 23 Aug. 1901; *s* of Harold Schroder and Florence L. A. Schroder (*née* Stimson); *m* 1928, Winsome Dawson; two *s* one *d*. *Educ:* Newcastle (NSW) High Sch.; Newcastle Techn. College. Chief Chemist: Kandos Cement Co., Sydney, 1927–30; Australian Cement Ltd, Geelong, 1930–44; Man. Dir, Adelaide Cement Ltd, Adelaide, 1944–68, Chm., 1970–77; Dir, Quarry Industries Ltd, 1965–77. Pres., SA Chamber of Manufacturers, 1963–64, 1964–65; Vice-Pres., Assoc. Chamber of Manufrs of Aust., 1964–65; Pres., Cement and Concrete Assoc. of Aust., 1953–54, 1960–61; State Cttee Mem., CSIRO, 1954–71; Mem., CSIRO Adv. Council, 1955–61. FRACI; AIEAust. *Recreation:* gardening. *Address:* 23 Coreega Avenue, Springfield, South Australia 5062. *T:* Adelaide 796452. *Club:* Adelaide.

SCHUBERT, Sir Sydney, Kt 1985; Co-ordinator General, Premier's Department, Government of Queensland, Australia, since 1977; *b* 22 March 1928; *s* of Wilhelm F. Schubert and Mary A. Price; *m* 1961, Maureen Kistle; two *d*. *Educ:* Univ. of Queensland; Univ. of Durham. Queensland Government: Main Roads Dept, 1950–69; Dep. Co-ordinator General, 1969–77. *Recreations:* golf, fishing. *Address:* 15 Apex Street, Clayfield, Brisbane, Qld 4011, Australia. *T:* 07 2623907. *Club:* Queensland.

SCHULTZ, Rt. Rev. Bruce Allan; *see* Grafton, NSW, Bishop of.

SCHULTZ, Prof. Donald Lorimer, OBE 1984; Professor of Mechanical Engineering, and Fellow of St Hugh's College, Oxford, since 1984; *b* 20 Dec. 1926; *s* of William Alexander and Olga Schultz; *m* 1954, June (*née* Matheson); three *s* one *d*. *Educ:* Canterbury University College, NZ (BE (Hons) Elec.); Oriel College, Oxford (MA 1961, DPhil 1954). National Physical Laboratory, 1955–61; Tutor and Fellow, St Catherine's College, Oxford, 1961–84; Donald Pollock Reader in Engineering Sci., Oxford, 1973–84. *Publications:* contribs to Jl Fluid Mech., ASME; papers on physiological fluid dynamics. *Recreation:* carpentry. *Address:* The Bakehouse, Stanton St John, Oxford. *T:* Stanton St John 396.

SCHULTZ, Sir Leo, (Joseph Leopold), Kt 1966; OBE 1945; Member, Kingston upon Hull District Council, 1973–83; *b* 4 Feb. 1900; *s* of Solomon Schultz; *m* 1928, Kate, *d* of George Pickersgill; one *s*. *Educ:* Hull. Alderman, City of Kingston upon Hull, 1962–74. Chm., Humberside Local Govt Reorganisation Jt Cttee, 1973; Mem., Humberside County Council, 1973–76. *Recreation:* cricket. *Address:* 6 Newland Park, Kingston upon Hull HU5 2DW. *T:* Hull 42253.

SCHULTZ, Prof. Theodore W., PhD; Charles L. Hutchinson Distinguished Service Professor of Economics, University of Chicago, since 1952; *b* 30 April 1902; *s* of Henry E. Schultz and Anna Elizabeth Weiss; *m* Esther Florence Werth; one *s* two *d*. *Educ:* South Dakota State Coll. (BS); Univ. of Wisconsin (MS, PhD). Iowa State College: Faculty of Economics, 1930–43; Head, Dept of Economics and Sociology, 1934–43; University of Chicago: Prof. of Economics, from 1943; Chairman, Dept of Economics, 1946–61. Hon. LLD: Grinnell Coll. 1949; Michigan State 1962; Illinois 1968; Wisconsin 1968; Catholic Univ. of Chile 1979; Dijon 1981; N Carolina State Univ. 1984. Francis A. Walker Medal, Amer. Econ. Assoc., 1972; Leonard Elmhirst Medal, Internat. Agricl Econ. Assoc., 1976; Nobel Prize for Economic Science, 1979. *Publications:* Redirecting Farm Policy, 1943; Agriculture in an Unstable Economy, 1945; The Economic Organization of Agriculture, 1953; The Economic Value of Education, 1963; Transforming Traditional Agriculture, 1964; Economic Growth and Agriculture, 1968; Investment in Human Capital: role of education and research, 1971; Human Resources: policy issues and research opportunities, 1972; (ed) Distortions of Agricultural Incentives, 1978; Investing in People: the economics of population quality, 1981. *Address:* 5620 South Kimbark Avenue, Chicago, Illinois 60637, USA. *T:* (312) 493–6083.

SCHUMANN, Maurice; Chevalier de la Légion d'Honneur; Compagnon de la Libération; Croix de Guerre (1939–45); Senator from the Department of the Nord, since 1974; Vice-President of the Senate, since 1977; Member, Académie Française, since 1974; writer and broadcaster; *b* Paris, 10 April 1911; *s* of Julien Schumann and Thérèse Michel; *m* 1944, Lucie Daniel; three *d*. *Educ:* Lycées of Janson-de-Sailly and Henry IV; Faculty of Letters, Univ. of Paris (Licencié ès Lettres). Attached to l'Agence Havas in London and later Paris, 1935–39; Chief Official Broadcaster, BBC French Service, 1940–44; Liaison Officer with Allied Expeditionary Forces at end of war; Mem. Provisional Consultative Assembly, Nov. 1944–July 1945; Deputy for Nord, 1945–67 and 1968–73; Mem. Constituent Assemblies, Oct. 1945–May 1946 and June-Nov. 1946. Chm., Popular Republican Movement (MRP); Deputy of this group, 1945–73 (Pres., 1945–49; Hon. Pres., 1949–); Dep. Minister for Foreign Affairs, 1951–54; Pres., For. Affairs Cttee of Nat. Assembly, 1959; Minister of State (Prime Minister's Office), April-May 1962; Minister of State, in charge of scientific res. and atomic and spacial questions, 1967–68; Minister of State for Social Affairs, 1968–69; Minister for Foreign Affairs, 1969–73. Has been Pres. of various organisations, incl. Internat. Movement for Atlantic Union, 1966–. Associate Prof., Faculté Catholique de Lille, 1975–. Pres., Assoc. des Ecrivains catholiques, 1980–. Hon. LLD: Cantab, 1972; St Andrews, 1974. *Publications:* Le Germanisme en marche, 1938; Mussolini, 1939; Les problèmes Ukrainiens et la paix européenne, 1939; Honneur et Patrie, 1945; Le vrai malaise des intellectuels de gauche, 1957; La Mort née de leur propre vie: essai sur Péguy, Simone Weil et Gandhi, 1974; Un Certain 18 Juin, 1980 (Prix Aujourd'hui); Qui a tué le duc d'Enghien?, 1984; Une grande Imprudence, 1986; *novels:* Le Rendezvous avec quelqu'un, 1962; Les Flots roulant au loin, 1973; La Communication, 1974; Angoisse et Certitude, 1978 (Grand Prix de Littérature Catholique); Le Concerto en Ut Majeur, 1982; chapters in: Mazarin, 1960; Talleyrand, 1962; Clemenceau, 1974; many articles etc (under pseudonym of André Sidobre) to L'Aube (Paris daily), Le Temps présent and La Vie catholique, etc. *Address:* 53 avenue du Maréchal-Lyautey, Paris 16e, France.

SCHUSTER, Sir (Felix) James (Moncrieff), 3rd Bt, *cr* 1906; OBE 1955; TD; Senior Partner, Sheppards and Chase, 1970–75, retired; *b* 8 January 1913; *o s* of Sir Victor Schuster, 2nd Bt, and Lucy, *d* of W. B. Skene, Pitlour-Halyards, Fife; *S* father, 1962; *m* 1937, Ragna, *er d* of late Direktor Sundt, Copenhagen; two *d*. *Educ:* Winchester. Served War of 1939–45, with The Rifle Brigade (Middle East and Combined Operations). Lt-Col comdg London Rifle Brigade. Rangers (RB), TA, 1952; Bt-Colonel, 1955. Hon. Col, 5th Bn Royal Green Jackets, 1970–75. *Heir:* none. *Address:* Piltdown Cottage, Piltdown, Uckfield, East Sussex TN22 3XB. *T:* Newick 2916. *Clubs:* Naval and Military, Lansdowne.

SCHUSTER, Sir James; *see* Schuster, Sir F. J. M.

SCHUSTER, Rt. Rev. James Leo; Rector of Swellendam, since 1980; *b* 18 July 1912; *s* of Rev. Harold Vernon Schuster and Elsie Jane (*née* Roberton); *m* 1951, Ilse Henriette Emmy Gottschalk; three *s* two *d* (and one *s* decd). *Educ:* Lancing; Keble Coll., Oxford. Deacon, 1937; Priest, 1938; Asst Missioner, Clare Coll. Mission, Rotherhithe, 1937–38; Chaplain St Stephen's House, Oxford, 1938–40; CF (EC), 1940–46; wounded, 1942; despatches, 1943. Chaplain, St Stephen's House, Oxford, 1946–49; Principal St Bede's Coll., Umtata, 1949–56; Bishop of St John's, 1956–79; Archdeacon of Riversdale, 1980–86. *Address:* PO Box 285, Swellendam 6740, South Africa.

SCHWARZ, Rudolf, CBE 1973; Conductor Laureate, Northern Sinfonia of England (formerly Northern Sinfonia Orchestra, Newcastle upon Tyne), since 1982 (Principal Guest Conductor, 1973–82); *b* 29 April 1905; Austrian (British subject, 1952); *m* 1950, Greta Ohlson (*d* 1984); one *s* (and one step *d* and one step *s*). *Educ:* Vienna. Conductor, Opera House, Düsseldorf, 1923–27; Conductor, Opera House, Karlsruhe, 1927–33; Musical Director, Jewish Cultural Organisation, Berlin, 1936–41; Conductor, Bournemouth Municipal Orchestra, 1947–51; Conductor, City of Birmingham Symphony Orchestra, 1951–57; Chief Conductor of the BBC Symphony Orchestra, 1957–62; Principal Conductor, Northern Sinfonia Orchestra, Newcastle upon Tyne, 1964–73; Guest Conductor, Bergen Orchestra, Norway, 1964–71; Principal Guest Conductor, Bournemouth Symphony Orchestra, 1970–79. Hon. RAM; Hon. GSM; DMus (*hc*) Newcastle upon Tyne, 1972. *Address:* 24 Wildcroft Manor, SW15 3TS.

SCHWARZ-BART, André; French writer; *b* Metz, Lorraine, France, 1928; 2nd *s* of parents from Poland; *m* Simone Schwarz-Bart. *Educ:* self-educated; Sorbonne. Joined French Resistance at 15. Has worked in a factory and in Les Halles, Paris, while writing. *Publications:* Le Dernier des Justes, 1959 (Prix Goncourt, 1959; Eng. trans., 1960); (with Simone Schwarz-Bart) Un plat de porc aux bananes vertes, 1967 (Jerusalem Prize, 1967); A Woman Named Solitude, 1973. *Address:* c/o Editions du Seuil, 27 rue Jacob, 75261 Paris Cedex 06, France.

SCHWARZENBERGER, Prof. Georg; Professor of International Law in the University of London, 1962–75, now Emeritus; Dean, Faculty of Laws, University College, London, 1965–67 (Vice-Dean, 1949–55 and 1963–65); Director, London Institute of World Affairs since 1943; Barrister-at-Law, Gray's Inn, since 1955; *b* 20 May 1908; *o s* of Ludwig and Ferry Schwarzenberger; *m* 1931, Suse Schwarz; one *s*. *Educ:* Karls-Gymnasium,

Heilbronn aN; Univs of Heidelberg, Frankfurt, Berlin, Tübingen, Paris and London. Dr Jur. (Tübingen) 1930; PhD (London) 1936. Sec. London Inst. of World Affairs (formerly New Commonwealth Inst.) 1934–43; Lectr in Internat. Law and Relations, University Coll., London, 1938–45; Sub-Dean and Tutor, Faculty of Laws, 1942–49; Reader in Internat. Law, 1945–62. Co-Editor (with G. W. Keeton) of: The Library of World Affairs, 1946–; The Year Book of World Affairs, 1947–84; Current Legal Problems, 1948–72. Member, Permanent Finnish-Netherlands Conciliation Commission. Hon. LLD Dalhousie, 1979. *Publications:* The League of Nations and World Order, 1936; Power Politics: A Study of World Society (1st edn 1941, 3rd edn 1964); International Law and Totalitarian Lawlessness, 1943; International Law as Applied by International Court and Tribunals, 1945 (Vol. I, 3rd edn 1957, Vol. II, 1968, Vol. III, 1976, Vol. IV, 1986); A Manual of International Law, 1947 (6th edn (with E. D. Brown) 1976); The Fundamental Principles of International Law, Hague Academy of Internat. Law (Recueil, Vol. 87), 1955; The Legality of Nuclear Weapons, 1958; The Frontiers of International Law, 1962; The Inductive Approach to International Law, 1965; The Principles and Standards of International Economic Law, Hague Acad. of Internat. Law (Recueil, Vol. 117), 1966; Foreign Investments and International Law, 1969; International Law and Order, 1971; The Dynamics of International Law, 1976. *Recreations:* gardening, swimming. *Address:* 4 Bowers Way, Harpenden, Herts AL5 4EW. *T:* Harpenden 3497.

SCHWARZKOPF, Elisabeth; Opera and Concert Singer; *b* 9 Dec. 1915; *o d* of Gymnasial-direktor Friedrich Schwarzkopf and Elisabeth (*née* Fröhlich); *m* Walter Legge (*d* 1979). *Educ:* High School for Music, Berlin. Sang at Vienna State Opera, Royal Opera House, Covent Garden, La Scala, Milan, 1948–64 (inc. inauguration Piccolo Teatro della Scala, 1955), Metropolitan Opera, NY, San Francisco Opera, Bayreuth, Aix-en-Provence (first Cigale d'Or, 1974), and other internat. festivals. Made film, Der Rosenkavalier, 1961. Mem., Royal Swedish Acad. for Arts and Sciences; Hon. mem., Accad. S Cecilia, Roma; Corres. mem., Bayerischer Akad. der Künste. MusD (*hc*) Cambridge, 1976; Hon. Dr Amer. Univ. Washington, DC, 1982. Lilli Lehmann Medal, Salzburg, 1950; first Premio Orfeo d'oro, Mantua; Lily Pons Medal, Paris; Hugo Wolf Verein Medal, Vienna, 1973. Grosse Verdienstkreuz, Germany, 1974; 1st class Order of Dannebrog, Denmark. Hon. RAM. *Publication:* (ed) On and Off the Record: a memoir of Walter Legge, 1982. *Recreations:* music, theatre, tennis, gardening, ski-ing, mountain walking.

SCHWEITZER, Prof. Miguel; Minister for Foreign Affairs, Chile, 1983; *b* 22 July 1940; *s* of Miguel Schweitzer and Cora Walters; *m* 1964, Maria Luisa Fernándes; two *s* one *d*. *Educ:* The Grange School, Santiago (preparatory and secondary schooling); Law School, Univ. of Chile (law degree). Doctorate in Penal Law, Rome, 1964–65; Professor of Penal Law: Law Sch., Univ. of Chile, 1966; High Sch. of Carabineros (Police), 1968, 1970 and from 1974; Director, Dept of Penal Sciences, Univ. of Chile, 1974–76; Chile's Alternate Representative with the Chilean Delegn to UN, 1975, 1976, 1978; Ambassador on special missions, 1975–80; Chilean Delegate to OAS, 1976–78; Ambassador to the Court of St James's, 1980–83. *Publications:* El Error de Derecho en Materia Penal (Chile), 1964; Sull elemento soggettivo nel reato di bancarotta del l'imprenditore (Rome), 1965; Prospectus for a Course on the Special Part of Penal Law (USA), 1969. *Recreations:* music, reading, golf, tennis, Rugby. *Address:* Moneda 1040, Of. 703, Santiago, Chile. *Clubs:* Temple Golf; Prince of Wales Country (Santiago).

SCHWEITZER, Pierre-Paul; Grand Croix de la Légion d'Honneur; Croix de Guerre (1939–45); Médaille de la Résistance avec rosette; Inspecteur Général des Finances Honoraire, 1974; Director: Compagnie de Participations et d'Investissements Holding SA, Luxembourg, since 1975 (Chairman, 1975–84); Société Financière Internationale de Participations, Paris, since 1976 (Chairman, 1976–84); Compagnie Monégasque de Banque, Monaco, since 1978; *b* 29 May 1912; *s* of Paul Schweitzer and Emma Munch; *m* 1941, Catherine Hatt; one *s* one *d*. *Educ:* Univs of Strasbourg and Paris; Ecole Libre des Sciences Politiques. Joined French Treasury as Inspecteur des Finances, 1936; Dep. Dir for Internat. Finance, French Treasury, Paris, 1946; Alternate Exec. Dir, IMF, Washington, 1947; Sec.-Gen. for European Economic Cooperation in the French Administration, Paris, 1948; Financial Counsellor, French Embassy, Washington, 1949; Director, Treasury, Paris, 1953; Dep. Governor of the Banque de France, Paris, 1960–63; Inspecteur Général des Finances, 1963; Man. Dir and Chm. Exec. Bd, IMF, 1963–73. Chm., Bank of America International, Luxembourg, 1974–77; Director: Banque Pétrofigaz, Paris, 1974– (Chm., 1974–79); Robeco Gp, Rotterdam, 1974–82; Adv. Dir, Bank of America, NY, 1974–77, and Unilever NV, Rotterdam, 1974–84. Hon. LLD: Yale, 1966; Harvard 1966; Leeds, 1968; New York, 1968; George Washington Univ., 1972; Wales, 1972; Williams, 1973. *Address:* 19 rue de Valois, 75001 Paris, France. *T:* 42.61.48.85.

SCHWINGER, Prof. Julian, AB, PhD; University Professor, University of California at Los Angeles, since 1980 (Professor of Physics, 1972–80); *b* 12 Feb. 1918; *s* of Benjamin Schwinger and Belle Schwinger (*née* Rosenfeld); *m* 1947, Clarice Carrol. *Educ:* Columbia University. Nat. Research Council Fellow, 1939–40; Research Associate, University of California at Berkeley, 1940–41; Instructor, later Assistant Professor, Purdue University, 1941–43; Member Staff: Radiation Laboratory, MIT, 1943–46; Metallurgy Laboratory, University of Chicago, 1943; Associate Professor of Physics, Harvard University, 1945–47, Prof., 1947–72, Higgins Prof. of Physics, 1966–72. Writer and presenter of series Understanding Space and Time, BBC (jt Univ. of Calif and Open Univ. prodn). Member, Board of Sponsors, Bulletin of the Atomic Scientists. Member: Nat. Acad. of Scis; Amer. Acad. of Arts and Scis; Amer. Phys. Soc.; Amer. Assoc. for Advancement of Science; NY Acad. of Sciences; Bd of Sponsors, Amer. Fedn of Scientists; Royal Instn of GB; Civil Liberties Union. Guggenheim Fellow, 1970. Awarded Nobel Prize for Physics (with R. Feynman and S. Tomonaga), 1965; Humboldt Prize, 1981; many other awards and medals. Hon. DSc: Purdue, 1961; Harvard, 1962; Columbia, 1966; Brandeis, 1973; Gustavus Adolphus Coll., 1975; Hon. LLD City Univ. of NY, 1972. *Publications:* Quantum Electrodynamics (editor), 1958; (with D. Saxon) Discontinuities in Wave Guides, 1968; Particles and Sources, 1969; Quantum Kinematics and Dynamics, 1970; Particles, Sources and Fields, vol I, 1970, vol II, 1973. *Recreations:* tennis, swimming, ski-ing, driving, and being one of the world's worst pianists. *Address:* Department of Physics, University of California at Los Angeles, Calif 90024, USA; 10727 Stradella Court, Los Angeles, Calif 90077.

SCIAMA, Prof. Dennis William, PhD; FRS 1983; Extraordinary Fellow, Churchill College, Cambridge, since 1986; Professor of Astrophysics, International School of Advanced Studies, Trieste, since 1983; Consultant, International Centre for Theoretical Physics, Trieste, since 1986; *b* 18 Nov. 1926; *s* of Abraham and Nelly Sciama; *m* 1959, Lidia Dina; two *d*. *Educ:* Malvern Coll.; Trinity Coll., Cambridge (MA, PhD). Fellow, Trinity Coll., Cambridge, 1952–56; Mem., Inst. for Advanced Study, Princeton, 1954–55; Agassiz Fellow, Harvard Univ., 1955–56; Res. Associate, KCL, 1958–60; Lectr in Maths, 1961–70, and Fellow of Peterhouse, 1963–70, Cambridge Univ.; Sen. Res. Fellow, All Souls Coll., Oxford, 1970–85. Vis. Prof., Cornell Univ., 1960–61; Luce Prof., Mount Holyoke Coll., 1977–78; Prof. of Physics, Univ. of Texas at Austin, 1978–83. Foreign Member: Amer. Philosophical Soc., 1981; Amer. Acad. of Arts and Scis, 1982; Accademia Nazionale dei Linzei, 1984. *Publications:* The Unity of the Universe, 1959; The Physical Foundations of General Relativity, 1969; Modern Cosmology, 1971, 2nd edn 1975; contribs to physics and astronomy jls. *Address:* 7 Park Town, Oxford. *T:* Oxford 59441.

SCLATER, Prof. John George, PhD; FRS 1982; Professor, Department of Geological Sciences, Shell Distinguished Chair in Geophysics, and Assistant Director, Institute for Geophysics, University of Texas at Austin, since 1983; *b* 17 June 1940; *s* of John George Sclater and Margaret Bennett Glen; *m* 1st, 1968, Fredrica Rose Felcyn; two *s*; 2nd, 1985, Paula Ann Edwards. *Educ:* Carlekemp Priory School; Stonyhurst College; Edinburgh Univ. (BSc); Cambridge Univ. (PhD 1966). Research Scientist, Scripps Instn of Oceanography, 1965; Massachusetts Institute of Technology: Associate Prof., 1972; Professor, 1977; Dir, Jt Prog. in Oceanography and Oceanographic Engrg with Woods Hole Oceanographic Instn, 1981. Fellow Geological Soc. of America; Fellow Amer. Geophysical Union. Rosenstiel Award in Oceanography, Rosenstiel Sch., Univ. of Miami, 1979; Bucher Medal, Amer. Geophysical Union, 1985. *Recreations:* running, swimming, golf. *Address:* Institute for Geophysics, University of Texas at Austin, PO Box 7456, Austin, Texas 78712, USA. *T:* 512–471–6156.

SCLATER, John Richard; Deputy Chairman, Guinness Mahon & Co. Ltd, since 1985 (Director, since 1985); Chairman: Foreign & Colonial Investment Trust PLC, since 1985 (Director, since 1981); F & C Enterprise Trust PLC, since 1986; Deputy Chairman, Union Discount Co. of London PLC, since 1986 (Director, since 1981); *b* 14 July 1940; *s* of Arthur William Sclater and Alice Sclater (*née* Collett); *m* 1st, 1967, Nicola Mary Gloria Cropper (marr. diss.); one *s* one *d*; 2nd, 1985, Grizel Elizabeth Catherine Dawson. *Educ:* Charterhouse; Gonville and Caius Coll., Cambridge (schol., 1st Cl. Hons History Tripos, BA, MA); Commonwealth Fellow, 1962–64; Yale Univ. (MA 1963); Harvard Univ. (MBA 1968). Glyn, Mills & Co., 1964–70; Dir, Williams, Glyn & Co., 1970–76; Man. Dir, Nordic Bank, 1976–85 (Chm., 1985); Director: James Cropper PLC, 1972–; Holker Estates Co. Ltd, 1974–; Guinness Peat Gp PLC, 1985–; Equitable Life Assurance Soc., 1985–; Yamaichi International (Europe) Ltd, 1985–; S & W Berisford PLC, 1986–; Billingsgate City Securities PLC, 1986–; Member, London Bd of Halifax Building Soc., 1983–. Trustee, Grosvenor Estate, 1973–; Mem., City Taxation Cttee, 1973–76. Governor: Internat. Students Trust, 1976–; Brambletye Sch. Trust, 1976–. Chm., Assoc. of Consortium Banks, 1980–82. *Recreations:* shooting, fishing, gardening, forestry. *Address:* Sutton Hall, Barcombe, near Lewes, Sussex BN8 5EB. *T:* Barcombe 400450. *Clubs:* Brooks's; University Pitt (Cambridge).

SCLATER-BOOTH, family name of **Baron Basing.**

SCOBLE, (Arthur William) John; Chairman, Economic Planning Board, South West Region (Bristol), 1965–71, retired; *er s* of Arthur Scoble; *m* 1935, Constance Aveline, *d* of Samuel Robbins; three *d*. Min. of Nat. Insce, 1945–50; jssc 1950; Min. of Works, 1951–59; UN, Buenos Aires, 1960–61; Min. of Works, 1962–64; Dept of Economic Affairs, 1965–70; Dept of the Environment, 1970–71, 1972–73. Chm., Agricl Housing Adv. Cttee, 1977–. Dir, Bath Preservation Trust, 1973–74. Regional Advisor, Employment Fellowship, 1975–79. Clerk to Bathampton Council, 1980–86. *Address:* Cross Deep, Bathampton Lane, Bath BA2 6ST. *T:* Bath 60525.

SCOFIELD, (David) Paul, CBE 1956; Actor; *b* 21 Jan. 1922; *s* of Edward H. and M. Scofield; *m* 1943, Joy Parker (actress); one *s* one *d*. *Educ:* Varndean Sch. for Boys, Brighton. Theatre training, Croydon Repertory, 1939; London Mask Theatre School, 1940. Shakespeare with ENSA, 1940–41; Birmingham Repertory Theatre, 1942; CEMA Factory tours, 1942–43; Whitehall Theatre, 1943; Birmingham Repertory, 1943–44–45; Stratford-upon-Avon, 1946–47–48. Mem., Royal Shakespeare Directorate, 1966–68. Associate Dir, Nat. Theatre, 1970–71. London theatres: Arts, 1946; Phoenix, 1947; Adventure Story, and The Seagull, St James's, 1949; Ring Round the Moon, Globe, 1950; Much Ado About Nothing, Phœnix, 1952; The River Line, Edin. Fest., Lyric (Hammersmith), Strand, 1952; John Gielgud's Company, 1952–53: Richard II, The Way of the World, Venice Preserved, etc; A Question of Fact, Piccadilly, 1953–54; Time Remembered, Lyric, Hammersmith, New Theatre, 1954–55; Hamlet, Moscow, 1955; Paul Scofield-Peter Brook Season, Phœnix Theatre, 1956; Hamlet, The Power and the Glory, Family Reunion; A Dead Secret, Piccadilly Theatre, 1957; Expresso Bongo, Saville Theatre, 1958; The Complaisant Lover, Globe Theatre, 1959; A Man For All Seasons, Globe Theatre, 1960, New York, 1961–62; Coriolanus and Love's Labour's Lost, at Shakespeare Festival Season, Stratford, Ont., 1961; King Lear: Stratford-on-Avon, Aldwych Theatre, 1962–63, Europe and US, 1964; Timon of Athens, Stratford-on-Avon, 1965; The Government Inspector, also Staircase, Aldwych, 1966; Macbeth, Stratford-on-Avon, 1967, Russia, Finland, 1967, Aldwych, 1968; The Hotel in Amsterdam, Royal Court, 1968; Uncle Vanya, Royal Court, 1970; Savages, Royal Court and Comedy, 1973; The Tempest, Wyndhams, 1975; Dimetos, Comedy, 1976; The Family, Royal Exchange, Manchester, and Haymarket, 1978; I am Not Rappaport, Apollo, 1986; *National Theatre:* The Captain of Kopenick, The Rules of the Game, 1971; Volpone, The Madras House, 1977; Amadeus, 1979; Othello, 1980; Don Quixote, A Midsummer Night's Dream, 1982. *Films:* The Train, 1964; A Man for All Seasons, 1966 (from the play); Bartleby, King Lear, 1971; Scorpio, 1973; A Delicate Balance, 1974; Anna Karenina, 1985; Nineteen Nineteen, 1985. Hon. LLD Glasgow, 1968; Hon. DLit Kent, 1973; Hon. DLitt Sussex, 1985. Shakespeare prize, Hamburg, 1972. *Relevant publication:* Paul Scofield, by J. C. Trewin, 1956. *Address:* The Gables, Balcombe, Sussex. *T:* 378. *Club:* Athenæum.

SCOON, Sir Paul, GCMG 1979; GCVO 1985; OBE 1970; Governor General of Grenada, since 1978; *b* 4 July 1935; *m* 1970, Esmai Monica McNeilly (*née* Lumsden); two step *s* one step *d*. *Educ:* St John's Anglican Sch., Grenada; Grenada Boys' Secondary Sch.; Inst. of Education, Leeds; Toronto Univ. BA, MEd. Teacher, Grenada Boys' Secondary Sch., 1953–67. Chief Educn Officer, 1967–68, Permanent Sec., 1969, Secretary to the Cabinet, 1970–72, Grenada; Dep. Director, Commonwealth Foundn, 1973–78. Governor, Centre for Internat. Briefing, Farnham Castle, 1973–78; Vice-Pres., Civil Service Assoc., Grenada, 1968; Co-founder and former Pres., Assoc. of Masters and Mistresses, Grenada. *Recreations:* reading, tennis. *Address:* Governor General's House, St George's, Grenada. *T:* 2401.

SCOONES, Major-General Sir Reginald (Laurence), KBE 1955 (OBE 1941); CB 1951; DSO 1945; late Royal Armoured Corps; Director, The Brewers' Society, 1957–69; *b* 18 Dec. 1900; *s* of late Major Fitzmaurice Scoones, Royal Fusiliers; *m* 1933, Isabella Bowie, *d* of John Nisbet, Cumbrae Isles, Scotland; one *d*. *Educ:* Wellington College; RMC, Sandhurst. 2nd Lt R Fus., 1920; transferred Royal Tank Corps, 1923; attd Sudan Defence Force, 1926–34; Adj. 1 RTR, 1935; GSO3 Mobile Div., 1938; served War of 1939–45, Middle East and Burma; Brigade Major, Cavalry Brigade, Cairo, 1939; GSO2 Western Desert Corps, 1940; CO 42 RTR, 1941; GSO1 War Office, 1941; Brig. Dep. Dir Military Trng, 1942; Comdr, 254 Tank Brigade, Burma, 1943; Dep. Dir Military Trng, 1945; Asst Kaid, Sudan Defence Force, 1947–50; Maj.-Gen. 1950; Major-General Commanding British Troops Sudan and Commandant Sudan Defence Force, 1950–54. *Address:* 7 Court Royal Mansions, 1 Eastern Terrace, Brighton BN2 1DJ. *T:* Brighton 697141.

SCOPES, Sir Leonard Arthur, KCVO 1961; CMG 1957; OBE 1946; *b* 19 March 1912; *s* of late Arthur Edward Scopes and Jessie Russell Hendry; *m* 1938, Brunhilde Slater Rolfe;

two *s* two *d*. *Educ:* St Dunstan's College; Gonville and Caius College, Cambridge (MA). Joined HM Consular Service, 1933; Vice-Consul: Antwerp, 1933, Saigon, 1935; Canton, 1937; Acting Consul, Surabaya, 1941; Vice-Consul, Lourenço Marques, 1942; Consul, Skoplje and Ljubljana, 1945; Commercial Secretary, Bogota, 1947; Assistant in United Nations (Economic and Social) Department of Foreign Office, 1950; Counsellor, Djakarta, 1952; Foreign Service Inspector, 1954; HM Ambassador to Nepal, 1957–62; HM Ambassador to Paraguay, 1962–67; Mem., UN Jt Inspection Unit, Geneva, 1968–71. *Recreation:* retirement. *Address:* 2 Whaddon Hall Mews, Milton Keynes, Bucks MK17 0NA.

SCORER, Philip Segar; a Recorder of the Crown Court, since 1976; *b* 11 March 1916; *s* of Eric W. Scorer and Maud Scorer (*née* Segar); *m* 1950, Monica Smith; one *s* three *d*. *Educ:* Repton. Admitted Solicitor, 1938; London County Council Legal Dept, 1938–40. Served War, Army (Royal Signals: War Office, SHAEF and BAS, Paris), 1940–46. Solicitors' Dept, New Scotland Yard, 1947–51; Partner in Burton & Co., Solicitors, Lincoln, 1952–; Clerk of the Peace, City of Lincoln, 1952–71; Under-Sheriff of Lincolnshire, 1954–; Pres., Under Sheriffs Assoc., 1978–. *Address:* Stonebow, Lincoln LN2 1DA. *T:* Lincoln 23215. *Club:* National Liberal.

SCOTFORD, John Edward; Treasurer, Hampshire County Council, since 1983; *b* 15 Aug. 1939; *s* of Albert and Louisa Scotford; *m* 1962, Marjorie Clare Wells; one *s*. *Educ:* Reading Grammar Sch. IPFA. Reading County Borough Council, 1955–62; Coventry County Borough Council, 1962–65; Hampshire CC, 1965–; Dep. County Treasurer, 1977–83. *Address:* Hampshire County Council, The Castle, Winchester SO23 8UJ.

SCOTHORNE, Prof. Raymond John, BSc, MD Leeds; MD Chicago; FRSE; FRCSGlas; Regius Professor of Anatomy, University of Glasgow, since 1972; *b* 1920; *s* of late John Scothorne and of Lavinia Scothorne; *m* 1948, Audrey, *o d* of late Rev. Selwyn and Winifred Gillott; one *s* two *d*. *Educ:* Royal Grammar School, Newcastle upon Tyne; Universities of Leeds and Chicago, BSc (Hons) 1st cl. (Leeds), 1941; MD (Chicago), Rockefeller Student, 1941–43; MB (Hons) 1st cl. (Leeds), 1944; MD (with Distinction) (Leeds), 1951. Demonstrator and Lecturer in Anatomy, 1944–50, Univ. of Leeds; Sen. Lecturer in Anatomy, 1950–60, Univ. of Glasgow; Prof., Univ. of Newcastle upon Tyne, 1960–72. Hon. Sec., Anat. Soc. of Great Britain and Ireland, 1967–71, Pres., 1971–73; Fellow, British Assoc. of Clinical Anatomists (Pres., 1986–); Mem., Med. Sub-Cttee, UGC, 1967–76. Hon. Mem., Assoc. des Anatomistes. Struthers Prize and Gold Medal in Anatomy, Univ. of Glasgow, 1957. Anatomical Editor, Companion to Medical Studies. *Publications:* chapter on Peripheral Nervous System in Hamilton's Textbook of Anatomy, 2nd edn, 1975; chapters on Early Development, on Tissue and Organ Growth, on Skin and on the Nervous System in Companion to Medical Studies, 3rd edn, 1985; chapter on Development and Structure of Liver in Pathology of Liver, 1979, 2nd edn 1986; chapter on Respiratory System in Cunningham's Textbook, 12th edn, 1981; papers on embryology, histology and tissue transplantation. *Address:* Department of Anatomy, University of Glasgow, Glasgow G12 8QQ; Southernknowe, Linlithgow, West Lothian. *T:* Linlithgow 2463.

SCOTT, family name of **Earl of Eldon.**

SCOTT; *see* Hepburn-Scott, family name of Lord Polwarth.

SCOTT; *see* Maxwell-Scott.

SCOTT; *see* Montagu Douglas Scott, family name of Duke of Buccleuch.

SCOTT, Alan James, CBE 1982; Deputy Chief Secretary, Hong Kong Government, since 1985; *b* 14 Jan. 1934; *s* of Rev. Harold James Scott and Mary Phyllis Barbara Scott; *m* 1st, 1958, Mary Elizabeth Ireland (*d* 1969); one *s* two *d*; 2nd, 1971, Joan Hall; one step *s* two step *d*. *Educ:* King's Sch., Ely; Cambridge Univ. Suffolk Regt, Italy and Germany, 1952–54. HMOCS, 1958–: Fiji: Dist Officer, 1958; Estabt Officer, 1960; Registrar, Univ. of S Pacific, 1968; Controller, Organisation and Estabts, 1969; Hong Kong: Asst Financial Sec., 1971; Principal Asst Financial Sec., 1972; Sec. for Civil Service, 1973; MLC 1976–85; Sec. for Housing, and Chm., Hong Kong Housing Authority, 1977; Sec. for Information, 1980; Sec. for Transport, 1982. President: Fiji AAA, 1964–69; Hong Kong AAA, 1978–; Vice-President: Dante Aligheri Soc., Hong Kong; Assoc. Physically Handicapped, Hong Kong; Chm., Chateau de Bon Vivant, Hong Kong. Fellow HKIPM. JP Hong Kong, 1971. *Recreations:* mild athletic sports, music (passive), wine bottling, dilatory travel. *Address:* Petraea, 30 Severn Road, Hong Kong; Free Union, Buck Mountain, Virginia, USA. *Clubs:* Farmers', Royal Commonwealth Soc.; Royal Hong Kong Jockey (Hong Kong).

SCOTT, Prof. Alastair Ian, FRS 1978; FRSE 1981; Davidson Professor of Chemistry and Biochemistry, Texas A & M University, since 1981; *b* 10 April 1928; *s* of William Scott and Nell Florence (*née* Newton); *m* 1950, Elizabeth Wilson (*née* Walters); one *s* one *d*. *Educ:* Glasgow Univ. (BSc, PhD, DSc). Postdoctoral Fellow, Ohio State Univ., 1952–53; Technical Officer, ICI (Nobel Div.), 1953–54; Postdoctoral Fellow, London and Glasgow Univs, 1954–57; Lectr, Glasgow Univ., 1957–62; Professor: Univ. of British Columbia, 1962–65; Univ. of Sussex, 1965–68; Yale Univ., 1968–77; Texas A&M Univ., 1977–80; Edinburgh Univ., 1980–83 (Forbes Prof., 1980–81). Lectures: Karl Folkers, Wisconsin Univ., 1964; Burger, Virginia Univ., 1975; Benjamin Rush, Pennsylvania Univ., 1975; 5 colls, Mass, 1977; Andrews, NSW Univ., 1979; Dreyfus, Indiana Univ., 1983. Hon. Mem., Pharmaceutical Soc. of Japan, 1985. Hon. MA, Yale Univ., 1968; Corday-Morgan Medallist, Chemical Soc., 1964; Ernest Guenther Medallist, Amer. Chem. Soc., 1976. *Publications:* Interpretation of Ultraviolet Spectra of Natural Products, 1964; (with T. K. Devon) Handbook of Naturally Occurring Compounds, 1972; numerous pubns in learned jls. *Recreations:* music, gardening. *Address:* Department of Chemistry, Texas A & M University, College Station, Texas 77843, USA. *T:* 409–845 3243. *Club:* Athenæum.

SCOTT, Prof. Alexander Whiteford, CBE 1960; Professor of Chemical Engineering, University of Strathclyde, Glasgow, 1955–71; Hon. Engineering Consultant to Ministry of Agriculture, Fisheries and Food, 1946–62; *b* 28 January 1904; *s* of Alexander Scott, Glasgow; *m* 1933, Rowena Christianna (*d* 1970), *d* of John Craig, Glasgow; one *s*. *Educ:* Royal College of Science and Technology, Glasgow. BSc, PhD, ARCST, Glasgow. Pres., Instn of Engineers and Shipbuilders in Scotland, 1975–76 and 1976–77. FIMechE, FIChemE, Hon. FCIBS. Hon. LLD Strathclyde, 1980. *Address:* 9 Rowallan Road, Thornliebank, Glasgow G46 7EP. *T:* 041–638 2968.

SCOTT, Anthony Douglas, TD 1972; Chief Executive and Director, Council for Small Industries in Rural Areas, since 1981; *b* 6 Nov. 1933; *o s* of Douglas Ernest and Mary Gladys Scott; *m* 1962, Irene Robson; one *s* one *d*. *Educ:* Gateshead Central Technical Secondary Sch. Articled to Middleton & Middleton, also J. Stanley Armstrong, Chartered Accountants, Newcastle upon Tyne, 1952–57; National Service, WO Selection Bd, 1957–59; Accountant with Commercial Plastics Ltd, 1959; joined ICI Ltd (Agricl Div), 1961; seconded by ICI to Hargreaves Fertilisers Ltd, as Chief Accountant, 1966; ICI Ltd (Nobel Div.) as Asst Chief Acct, 1970; seconded by ICI to MoD as Dir-Gen. Internal Audit, 1972–74. Dir of Consumer Credit, Office of Fair Trading, 1974–80. Chm., Teesside Soc. of Chartered Accts, 1969–70; Mem. Cttee, London Chartered Accountants, 1974–79. Chm., Jt Working Party on Students' Societies (ICAE&W), 1979–80. *Publications:* Accountants Digests on Consumer Credit Act 1974, 1980; Accountants Digest on Estate Agents Act 1979, 1982. *Recreations:* antiquary, walking, gardening; TA, 1959–. *Address:* 33 Barlings Road, Harpenden, Herts. *T:* Harpenden 63067.

SCOTT, Sir Anthony (Percy), 3rd Bt *cr* 1913; Chairman and Managing Director, L. M. (Moneybrokers) Ltd, since 1986; *b* 1 May 1937; *s* of Sir Douglas Winchester Scott, 2nd Bt, and of Elizabeth Joyce, *d* of W. N. C. Grant; *S* father, 1984; *m* 1962, Caroline Theresa Anne, *er d* of Edward Bacon; two *s* one *d*. *Educ:* Harrow; Christ Church, Oxford. Barrister, Inner Temple, 1960. *Recreation:* racing. *Heir:* *s* Henry Douglas Edward Scott, *b* 26 March 1964. *Address:* North Park Farm, Fernhurst, Haslemere, Surrey. *T:* Haslemere 52826.

SCOTT, Audrey; *see* Scott, M. Audrey.

SCOTT, Sir Bernard (Francis William), Kt 1979; CBE 1974; TD; FIMechE; FEng; Deputy Chairman, 1969–73, Managing Director, 1972–74, and Chairman, 1974–80, Lucas Industries Ltd; Deputy Chairman: Lloyds Bank, 1980–85 (Director, 1975–85); Lloyds Bank UK Management, 1980–85; Vice-Chairman, Lloyds Bank International, 1980–85 (Director, 1978–85); *b* Kings Norton, 19 Nov. 1914; *s* of Francis William Robert Scott and Agnes Edith Kett; *m* 1st, 1942, Charlotte Kathleen (marr. diss. 1980), *d* of Charles and Charlotte Laidlow, Monkseaton; one *s* two *d*; 2nd, 1980, Nicole Henriette, *d* of Gustave and Sophy Douchet, Douai. *Educ:* Bishop Vesey's Grammar Sch.; Epsom College. FRSA. Served War of 1939–45 (despatches, 1944): mobilised as TA Officer in 45th Bn Royal Warwicks Regt, 1939; Major, RA, 1946. Joined Joseph Lucas Ltd as apprentice, 1931; Personal Asst to Oliver Lucas, 1936; Sales Dir, Joseph Lucas (Electrical) Ltd, 1947; Vice-Chm. and Gen. Man., CAV Ltd and dir of various Lucas subsids at home and abroad, 1959; Dir, Joseph Lucas (Industries) Ltd, 1968; Vice-Chm., Boots Co., 1983–85 (Dir, 1976–85); Director: Thomas Tilling Ltd, 1979–83; Grindlays Bank, 1981–83. Mem., Export Council for Europe, 1966–71; Chm., European Components Service (BNEC), 1967–71; President: Birmingham Chamber of Commerce, 1972–73 (Vice-Pres. 1970); Motor Industry Res. Assoc. Council, 1975–77; Engineering Industries Council, 1975–81; Fellowship of the Motor Industry, 1984–86; Vice-President: ABCC; Instn of Motor Industry, 1976; EEF, 1976–80; Member: Council, CBI, 1974–80; British Overseas Trade Bd, 1973–77; British Overseas Trade Adv. Council, 1975–77; Nat. Defence Industries Council, 1976–80; Council, SMM&T, 1971 (Exec. Cttee, 1974, Vice-Pres., 1976–80; Pres., 1980–81); Council on Internat. Development, 1977–79. Trustee: Anglo-German Foundn for Study of Industrial Society, 1978–; Duke of Edinburgh Award Scheme, 1980–; Globe Theatre Trust, 1981–; Chm., Berks Council Boys' Clubs, 1950–70; Vice-Chm., Nat. Assoc. of Boys' Clubs, 1974; Pres., Birmingham Fedn of Boys' Clubs, 1977–81. Hon. LLD Birmingham, 1977; Hon. DSc Aston in Birmingham, 1979. Belgian Croix de Guerre, 1945; Chevalier, Order of Leopold with palm, 1945. *Recreations:* sailing, gardening. *Address:* Grove Corner, Grove Road, Lymington, Hants. *T:* Lymington 78154. *Clubs:* Boodle's, Royal Automobile, Royal Cruising; Royal Yacht Squadron, Royal Lymington Yacht; Cercle de l'Union Interalliée.

SCOTT, Dame Catherine Margaret Mary; *see* Scott, Dame M.

SCOTT, Sir (Charles) Hilary, Kt 1967; *b* Bradford, 27 March 1906; *s* of late Lieutenant-Colonel C. E. Scott and Mrs M. E. M. Scott, of Bradford; *m* 1932, Beatrice Margery, *d* of late Reverend Canon Garrad; one *s* two *d*. *Educ:* Sedbergh Sch. Articled with Wade & Co., Bradford. Qual. as Solicitor (Class 2 Hons) 1930; Partner Slaughter & May, London, 1937–74. Served in RNVR, 1940–45 (Lieut-Comdr); President of the Law Society, 1966–67 (Mem. Council, 1948–71; Vice-Pres. 1965–66); Member: Nat. Film Finance Corp., 1948–70 (Chm. 1964–69); Jenkins Cttee on Company Law, 1959–62; Panel of Judges of The Accountant Awards for company accounts, 1961–69; London Adv. Bd of Salvation Army, 1968–82; Noise Adv. Council, 1971–75; Council, Royal Sch. of Church Music, 1974–85; Chm., Cttee on Property Bonds and Equity-linked Life Assurance, 1971–73. Trustee, Glyndebourne Arts Trust, 1961–76. Director: Tarmac Ltd, 1968–76; Equity & Law Life Assurance Society Ltd, 1955–81; London Board, Bank of Scotland, 1966–76. FRSA. *Recreations:* travel, music. *Address:* Knowle House, Bishop's Walk, Addington, Surrey CR0 5BA. *T:* 01–654 3638.

See also M. Audrey Scott, G. M. C. Thornely.

SCOTT, Sir (Charles) Peter, KBE 1978 (OBE 1948); CMG 1964; HM Diplomatic Service, retired; Chairman: Council of Anglo-Norse Society, since 1979 (Member since 1978); Norfolk Branch of the European Movement, since 1984; *b* 30 Dec. 1917; *er s* of late Rev. John Joseph Scott and late Dorothea Scott (*née* Senior); *m* 1954, Rachael, *yr d* of C. W. Lloyd Jones, CIE; one *s* two *d*. *Educ:* Weymouth Coll.; Pembroke Coll., Cambridge. Indian Civil Service: Probationer, 1939; appointed to Madras Presidency, 1940; Asst Private Sec. to Viceroy, 1946–47. Entered HM Diplomatic Service, 1947, Second Sec., Tokyo, 1948; First Sec., 1949; Foreign Office, 1950; Private Sec. to Gen. Lord Ismay at NATO, Paris, 1952; First Sec., Vienna, 1954; First Sec. at British Information Services, NY, 1956; Counsellor and Consul-General, Washington, 1959; Student at IDC, 1962; Head of UK Mission to European Office of the United Nations, Geneva, 1963; Minister at HM Embassy, Rome, 1966–69; Temp. Vis. Fellow at Centre for Contemporary European Studies, Univ. of Sussex, 1969–70; Asst Under-Sec. of State, FCO, 1970–75; Ambassador to Norway, 1975–77. Private Sec., 1978–79, Treasurer, 1979–81, to HRH Prince Michael of Kent. Mem., Council of Internat. Social Service of GB, 1978– (Chm., 1979–85). *Recreations:* walking, and such as offer. *Address:* Bisley Farmhouse, Irstead, near Norwich, Norfolk NR12 8XT. *T:* Horning 630413. *Clubs:* United Oxford & Cambridge University; Norfolk (Norwich).

SCOTT, Rt. Rev. Colin John Fraser; *see* Hulme, Bishop Suffragan of.

SCOTT, Prof. Dana Stewart, FBA 1976; University Professor of Computer Science and Mathematical Logic, Carnegie-Mellon University, since 1981; *b* Berkeley, Calif, 11 Oct. 1932; *m* 1959, Irene Schreier; one *d*. *Educ:* Univ. of Calif, Berkeley (BA); Princeton Univ. (PhD). Instructor, Univ. of Chicago, 1958–60; Asst Prof., Univ. of Calif, Berkeley, 1960–63; Associate Prof. and Prof., Stanford Univ., 1963–69; Prof., Princeton, 1969–72; Prof. of Mathematical Logic, Oxford Univ., 1972–81. Visiting Prof., Amsterdam, 1968–69; Guggenheim Fellow, 1978–79. *Publications:* papers on logic and mathematics in technical jls. *Address:* Department of Computer Science, Carnegie-Mellon University, Schenley Park, Pittsburgh, Pa 15213, USA.

SCOTT, Sir David; *see* Scott, Sir W. D. S.

SCOTT, David; *b* 6 Sept. 1916; *er s* of late Sir Basil Scott and late Gertrude, MBE, 2nd *d* of Henry Villiers Stuart of Dromana, MP; *m* 1951, Hester Mary, MA, *y d* of late Gilbert Ogilvy of Winton and Pencaitland; one *s* three *d*. *Educ:* Stowe; New College, Oxford (MA). War Service 1939–45: Argyll and Sutherland Highlanders (SR), Reconnaissance Corps and Highland Light Infantry; T/Capt., 1941; Asst to Political Adviser for Khuzistan, Iran, 1944; Actg Vice Consul, Ahwaz, 1944–45. Clerk, House of Commons, 1946; Deputy Principal Clerk, 1962; Clerk of Standing Cttees, 1966–70; Clerk of Select Cttees,

1970–73; Clerk of Private Bills, an Examiner of Petitions for Private Bills and Taxing Officer, House of Commons, 1974–77; retired 1977. Mem., Cttee on Canons, General Synod, Scottish Episcopal Church, 1983. *Recreation:* fishing. *Address:* Glenaros, Aros, Isle of Mull. *T:* Aros 337; 6a Stafford House, Maida Avenue, W2. *T:* 01–723 8398. *Clubs:* New, Puffin's (Edinburgh).

SCOTT, Ven. David; Archdeacon of Stow, since 1975; Vicar of Hackthorn with Cold Hanworth, since 1975; also Priest-in-charge of North and South Carlton, since 1978; Chaplain to the Queen, since 1983; *b* 19 June 1924; *m;* two *c. Educ:* Trinity Hall, Cambridge (BA 1950, MA 1954); Cuddesdon Theological College. Deacon 1952, priest 1953, dio. Portsmouth, Curate of St Mark, Portsea, 1952–58; Asst Chaplain, Univ. of London, 1958–59; PC, Old Brumby, 1959–66; Vicar of Boston, Lincs, 1966–75; Rural Dean of Holland East, 1971–75; Surrogate, 1972–75; Canon and Prebendary of Lincoln Cathedral, 1971. Mem. Gen. Synod, 1978–80, 1983–85. *Address:* The Vicarage, Hackthorn, Lincoln LN2 3PF.

SCOTT, Sir David (Aubrey), GCMG 1979 (KCMG 1974; CMG 1966); HM Diplomatic Service, retired 1979; Chairman, Nuclear Resources Ltd, since 1984; Director, Mitchell Cotts plc; Consultant to Thomas De La Rue & Co. Ltd, since 1986; Governor, Sadler's Wells Theatre, and Chairman, Appeal Committee, since 1984; *b* 3 Aug. 1919; *s* of late Hugh Sumner Scott and of Barbara E. Scott, JP; *m* 1941, Vera Kathleen, *d* of late Major G. H. Ibbitson, MBE, RA; two *s* one *d. Educ:* Charterhouse; Birmingham University (Mining Engrg). Served War of 1939–45, Royal Artillery, 1939–47; Chief Radar Adviser, British Military Mission to Egyptian Army, 1945–47, Major. Appointed to CRO, 1948; Asst Private Secretary to Secretary of State, 1949; Cape Town/Pretoria, 1951–53; Cabinet Office, 1954–56; Malta Round Table Conf., 1955; Secretary-General, Malaya and Caribbean Constitutional Confs, 1956; Singapore, 1956–58; Monckton Commn, 1960; Dep. High Comr, Fedn of Rhodesia and Nyasaland, 1961–63; Imperial Defence College, 1964; Dep. High Comr, India, 1965–67; British High Comr in Uganda, and Ambassador (non-resident) to Rwanda, 1967–70; Asst Under-Sec. of State, FCO, 1970–72; British High Comr to New Zealand, and Governor, Pitcairn Is., 1973–75; HM Ambassador to Republic of S Africa, 1976–79. Chm., Ellerman Lines plc, 1982–83; Director: Barclays Bank International Ltd, 1979–85; Delta Metal Overseas Ltd, 1980–83; Bradbury Wilkinson plc, 1984–86. Pres., Ugandan Soc. for Disabled Children, 1984–; Vice-Pres., UK South Africa Trade Assoc., 1980–85. *Publication:* Ambassador in Black and White, 1981. *Recreations:* music, birdwatching. *Address:* Wayside, Moushill Lane, Milford, Surrey. *Club:* Royal Over-Seas League (Chm., 1981–86).

See also J. B. Unwin.

SCOTT, Donald; *see* Scott, W. D.

SCOTT, Douglas, RDI 1974; FSIAD; Profesor Titular, Universidad Nacional Autonoma de Mexico, 1977–80; Profesor and Presidente de la Carrera, Universidad Anahuac, Mexico, 1977–80; *b* 4 April 1913; *s* of Edward Scott and Lilian Scott; *m* 1939, Kathleen Tierney; one *s* one *d. Educ:* Central Sch. of Art and Design, London (trained as silversmith and jeweller). Joined Osler & Faraday, 1929, and subseq. other lighting cos, as designer and illuminating engr; Raymond Loewy's London Office, 1936–39; opened own office, 1946; MSIAD 1946, elected FSIAD 1960. Lectr, Central Sch. of Art and Design, 1945; founded Industrial Design course, first in UK, 1946; started postgrad. course; trained Mexican designers from Universidad Nacional Autonoma de Mexico, and helped set up course. Designed for many clients in UK, Europe and USA. Profesor Honorario, Universitario Autonoma de Guadalajara, Mexico, 1977. Wash basin designed for Ideal Standard, Italy, on perm. exhibn in Museum of Modern Art, New York. Gold Medal for Design, Instituto Mexicano de Comercio Exterior, Mexico, 1973; three Design Council awards; Medal for Design, SIAD, 1983; 2nd Internat. Design Award, Osaka, Japan, 1985. *Publications:* (with James Pilditch) The Business of Product Design, 1964; articles in periodicals. *Recreations:* listening to music, gardening, walking, photography. *Address:* 12 Lentune Way, Lymington, Hants SO4 9PF. *T:* Lymington 77311.

SCOTT, Prof. Douglas Frederick Schumacher; Professor of German in the University of Durham (late Durham Colleges), 1958–75, now Emeritus Professor; *b* Newcastle under Lyme, Staffs, 17 Sept. 1910; *o s* of Frederick Scott and Magdalena (*née* Gronbach); *m* 1942, Margaret (*d* 1972), *o d* of late Owen Gray Ellis, Beaumaris, Anglesey, and Helen (*née* Gibbs); two *d. Educ:* Queen Mary's Grammar School, Walsall, Staffs; Dillman-Realgymnasium Stuttgart, Germany; University of Tübingen, Göttingen (Dr phil.); University College, London (MA). Part-time Assistant, German Dept, University Coll., London, 1935–37; Lecturer in charge German Dept, Huddersfield Technical Coll. 1937–38; Lecturer in German, King's Coll., Newcastle, 1938–46; released for service with Friends' Ambulance Unit, 1940–46; Lecturer in German, King's Coll., London, 1946–49; Reader and Head of Dept of German, The Durham Colls, 1949–58. *Publications:* Some English Correspondents of Goethe, 1949; W. v. Humboldt and the Idea of a University, 1960; Luke Howard: his correspondence with Goethe and his continental journey of 1816, 1976; articles and reviews on German lit. and Anglo-German literary relations in various English and German journals. *Recreations:* music, travel. *Address:* 6 Fieldhouse Terrace, Durham DH1 4NA. *T:* Durham 3864518. *Club:* Penn.

SCOTT, Douglas Keith, (Doug Scott); *b* Nottingham, 29 May 1941; *s* of George Douglas Scott and Edith Joyce Scott; *m* 1962, Janice Elaine Brook; one *s* two *d. Educ:* Cottesmore Secondary Modern Sch.; Mundella Grammar Sch., Nottingham; Loughborough Teachers' Trng Coll. (Teaching Certificate). Began climbing age of 12, British crag climbing, and most weekends thereafter; visited the Alps age of 17 and every year thereafter; first ascent, Tarso Teiroko, Tibest Mts, Sahara, 1965; first ascents, Cilo Dag Mts, SE Turkey, 1966; first ascent, S face Koh-i-Bandaka (6837 m), Hindu Kush, Afghanistan, 1967; first British ascent, Salathé Wall, El Capitain, Yosemite, 1971; 1972: Spring, Mem., European Mt Everest Expedn to SW face; Summer, first ascent, E Pillar of Mt Asgard, Baffin Island Expedn; Autumn, Mem., British Mt Everest Expedn to SW face; 1974: first ascent, Changabang; first ascent, SE spur, Pic Lenin (7189 m); reached summit of Mt Everest, via SW face, with Dougal Haston, as Members, British Everest Expedn, 24th Sept. 1975; first Alpine ascent of S face, Mt McKinley (6226 m), via new route, British Direct, with Dougal Haston, 1976; first ascent, East Face Direct, Mt Kenya, 1976; first ascent, Ogre (7330 m), Karakoram Mountains, 1977; first ascent, N Ridge route, Kangchenjunga (8593 m), without oxygen, 1979; first ascent, N Summit, Kussum Kangguru, 1979; first ascent, N Face, Nuptse, 1979; Alpine style, Kangchungtse (7640 m), 1980; E Pillar, Shivling, 1981; Chamlang (7366 m), North Face to Centre Summit, 1981; first ascent, Pungpa Ri (7445 m), 1982; Xixabangma South Face (8046 m), 1982; first ascent, Lobsang Spire (Karakoram), and ascent Broad Peak (8047 m), 1983; Mt Baruntse (7143 m), first ascent, East Summit Mt Chamlang (7287 m), 1984; first Alpine style ascent, Diran (7260 m), 1985. Pres., Alpine Climbing Gp, 1976–82. A vegetarian, 1978–. *Publications:* Big Wall Climbing, 1974; (with Alex MacIntyre) Shishapangma, Tibet, 1984; contrib. to Alpine Jl, Amer. Alpine Jl and Mountain Magazine. *Recreations:* mountaineering, Nottingham Moderns Rugby Football Club. *Address:* Pasture Lane, Hesket Newmarket, Wigton, Cumbria. *T:* Caldbeck 303. *Clubs:* Alpine; Alpine Climbing Group, Nottingham Climbers'.

SCOTT, Edward McM.; *see* McMillan-Scott.

SCOTT, Most Rev. Edward Walter, CC 1978; Archbishop, and Primate of All Canada, 1971–86; *b* Edmonton, Alberta; *s* of Tom Walter Scott and Kathleen Frances Ford; *m* 1942, Isabel Florence Brannan; one *s* three *d. Educ:* Univ. of British Columbia; Anglican Theological Coll. of BC. Vicar of St Peter's, Seal Cove, 1943–45; SCM Secretary, Univ. of Manitoba, 1945–59; Staff of St John's Coll., Winnipeg, 1947–48; Rector: St John the Baptist, Fort Garry, 1949–55; St Jude's, Winnipeg, 1955–60; Dir, Diocesan Council for Social Service, Diocese of Rupert's Land, and Priest Dir of Indian Work, 1960–64; Associate Sec., Council for Social Service, Anglican Church of Canada, 1964–66; Bishop of Kootenay, 1966–71. Moderator of Executive and Central Cttees, WCC, 1975–83; Pres., Canadian Council of Churches, 1985–. Mem. Commonwealth Eminent Persons Gp on South Africa, Dec. 1985–June 1986. DD Lambeth, 1986; Hon. DD: Anglican Theol Coll., BC, 1966; Trinity Coll., Toronto, 1971; Wycliffe Coll., Toronto, 1971; Huron Coll., Ont., 1973; United Theol Coll., Montreal, 1971; Renison Coll., Waterloo; Coll. of Emmanuel & St Chad, Saskatoon, 1979; Univ. of Victoria Coll., Toronto, 1986; Hon. DCL St John's Coll., Winnipeg, 1971; Hon. STD: Dio. Theol Coll., Montreal, 1973; Thorneloe Coll., Ont., 1974. *Recreation:* carpentry. *Address:* 29 Hawthorn Avenue, Toronto, Ont M4W 2Z1, Canada.

SCOTT, George Barclay; consultant; *b* 10 Aug. 1928; *s* of late Joseph Scott and Margaret Gardner Crawford Barclay Scott; *m* 1955, Janette Margaret Forrester Lindsay; one *s* one *d* (twins). *Educ:* Whitehill Senior Secondary School, Glasgow; Univ. of Strathclyde. BSc (Hons) Mech. Eng. Scottish Gas Board: Distribution Engineer, 1962–70; Member of Board, 1970–72; Dir of Distribution and Service, 1970–73; British Gas Corporation: Commercial Dir, Scottish Region, 1973–74; Dep. Chairman, 1974–82, Chairman, 1982–85, North Western Region. Pres., Instn of Gas Engineers, 1982–83. Mem. Regl Bd, BIM. Mem. Council, Univ. of Salford, 1983–. *Recreations:* gardening, golf, walking, music. *Address:* The Belfry, Chapel Drive, Hale Barns, Altrincham, Cheshire WA15 0BL.

SCOTT, Sir George (Edward), Kt 1967; CBE 1963 (OBE 1941); KPM; Chief Constable of the West Riding Constabulary, 1959–68, and of the West Yorkshire Constabulary, 1968–69, retired; *b* 6 June 1903; *s* of late Frederick William Scott; *m* 1926, Lilian, *d* of Matthew Brown, Norwich; one *s* one *d. Educ:* City of Norwich School. Joined Norwich City Police, as Cadet, 1918; Dep. Chief Constable, Norwich, 1933–36; Chief Constable: Luton, 1936–44; Newcastle upon Tyne, 1944–48; Sheffield, 1948–59. Vice-President: Royal Life Saving Soc.; RoSPA. King's Police Medal, 1949; KStJ 1966 (CStJ 1957). *Recreation:* golf. *Address:* White Lodge, Barham Close, Weybridge, Surrey.

SCOTT, George Edwin; author, television commentator, broadcaster, journalist; Head of UK Offices, Commission of the European Communities, since 1979; *b* 22 June 1925; *s* of late George Benjamin Scott and Florence Hilda Scott; *m* 1947, Shelagh Maud Isobel Maw; two *s* (one *d* decd). *Educ:* Middlesbrough High School; New College, Oxford. Northern Echo, 1941–42; Yorkshire Post, 1942–43; RNVR, 1943–46; New College, Oxford, 1946–48 (Founder and Editor of Oxford Viewpoint); Daily Express, 1948–53; Truth, 1953–57 (Deputy Editor, 1954; Editor, 1954–57, when ceased publication); The Economist, 1970–74; Editor, The Listener, 1974–79. Contested (L): Middlesbrough East, March 1962; Middlesbrough West, June 1962; Wimbledon, 1964; Surrey South West, 1983. Chm., Political Div., Liberal Party, 1962–63. Mem., Panorama team, 1958–59; Chairman/Interviewer: TWW, 1959–67; Rediffusion, 1966–68; Tyne-Tees, 1970–74; Presenter, The Editors, BBC, 1976–79. *Publications:* Time and Place (auto-biographical), 1956; The RCs, 1967; Reporter Anonymous, 1968; Rise and Fall of the League of Nations, 1973; contrib. column, Liberal View, Daily Mirror, 1962–64; contribs to Punch and other jls. *Recreations:* theatre, cricket and watching others gardening. *Address:* (office) 8 Storey's Gate, SW1P 3AT. *T:* 01–222 8122. *Club:* Reform.

SCOTT, Prof. George Ian, CBE 1968; FRCSE; FRCPE; FRSE; Surgeon Oculist to the Queen in Scotland, 1965–78; Professor of Ophthalmology, University of Edinburgh, 1954–72, now Emeritus Professor; Ophthalmic Surgeon, Royal Infirmary, Edinburgh, 1953–72, now Hon. Ophthalmic Surgeon; *b* 15 March 1907; *s* of late George John Scott; *m* 1946, Maxine, *d* of late A. D. Vandamm; one *s. Educ:* Edinburgh Acad.; Univ. of Edinburgh. MA 1929; MB, ChB 1933; FRCS Edin. 1937; FRS Edin. 1954. Served War of 1939–45, RAMC; Command Ophthalmologist, Scottish Command, 1939; Mem. Advisory Ophthalmic Panel, Ministry of Supply, 1941; Consultant Ophthalmologist, MEF, 1942; Brig. RAMC, 1942. Asst Ophthalmic Surgeon, Royal Infirmary, Edinburgh, 1946; Mem. Vision Cttee, MRC, 1946; Visiting Consultant, Western General and Bangour Hosps, 1949; Consultant in Neuro-Ophthalmology to Department of Neuro-Surgery, Edinburgh, 1954. Member, International Council of Ophthalmology, 1963–70; Past President: Faculty of Ophthalmologists; RCSE; Ophthalmological Soc. of UK; Member Association of British Neurologists; FRSoc.Med. (former Vice-President Section of Ophthalmology); Hon. Col RAMC. *Publications:* papers in British Journal of Ophthalmology, Nature, Lancet, British Medical Journal, British Journal of Radiology, Proc. Roy. Soc. Med., Trans. Ophthalmological Soc., United Kingdom, and The American Journal of Ophthalmology. *Address:* 4 Moray Place, Edinburgh EH3 6DS. *T:* 031–225 6943. *Club:* New (Edinburgh).

SCOTT, Dr Graham Alexander; Deputy Chief Medical Officer, Scottish Home and Health Department, since 1975; *b* 26 Nov. 1927; *s* of Alexander Scott and Jessie Scott; *m* 1951, Helena Patricia Margaret Cavanagh; two *s* one *d. Educ:* Daniel Stewart's Coll., Edinburgh; Edinburgh Univ. (MB, ChB). FRCPE, FFCM, DPH. RAAMC, 1951–56 (Dep. Asst Dir, Army Health, 1st Commonwealth Div., Korea, 1953–54). Sen. Asst MO, Stirling CC, 1957–62, Dep. County MO, 1962–65; Scottish Home and Health Department: MO, 1965–68; SMO, 1968–74; PMO, 1974–75. *Recreations:* curling and walking. *Address:* Rosemains, Pathhead, Midlothian EH37 5UQ. *Club:* Royal Commonwealth Society.

SCOTT, Hardiman; *see* Scott, J. P. H.

SCOTT, Sir Hilary; *see* Scott, Sir C. H.

SCOTT, Sir Ian Dixon, KCMG 1962 (CMG 1959); KCVO 1965; CIE 1947; *b* Inverness, 6 March 1909; *s* of Thomas Henderson Scott, OBE, MICE, and Mary Agnes Dixon, Selkirk; *m* 1937, Hon. Anna Drusilla Lindsay, *d* of 1st Baron Lindsay of Birker, CBE, LLD; one *s* four *d. Educ:* Queen's Royal College, Trinidad; Balliol College, Oxford (MA); London School of Economics. Entered Indian Civil Service, 1932; Indian Political Service, 1935; Assistant Director of Intelligence, Peshawar, 1941; Principal, Islamia College, Peshawar, 1943; Deputy Private Secretary to the Viceroy of India, 1945–47. Dep. Dir of Personnel, John Lewis & Co. Ltd, 1948–50. Appointed to Foreign Service, 1950; First Secretary, Foreign Office, 1950–51; British Legation, Helsinki, 1952; British Embassy, Beirut, 1954; Counsellor, 1956; Chargé d'Affaires, 1956, 1957, 1958; idc 1959; Consul-General, then Ambassador to the Congo, 1960–61; Ambassador to Sudan, 1961–65, to Norway, 1965–68. Chm., Clarksons Holidays Ltd, 1972–73 (Dir, 1968–73). Chm., Suffolk AHA, 1973–77; Member: Council, Dr Barnardo's, 1970–84 (Chm., 1972–78; elected Vice-Pres., 1984–); Bd of Governors, Felixstowe Coll., 1971–84 (Chm., 1972–78);

Chm., Indian Civil Service (retd) Assoc., 1977–. *Publication:* Tumbled House, 1969. *Recreation:* sailing. *Address:* Ash House, Alde Lane, Aldeburgh, Suffolk.

SCOTT, Prof. Ian Richard, PhD; Barber Professor of Law, since 1978, and Dean of the Faculty of Law, since 1985, University of Birmingham; *b* 8 Jan. 1940; *s* of Ernest and Edith Scott; *m* 1971, Ecce Cole; two *d*. *Educ:* Geelong Coll.; Queen's Coll., Univ. of Melbourne (LLB); King's Coll., Univ. of London (PhD). Barrister and Solicitor, Supreme Court of Victoria. Dir, Inst. of Judicial Admin, 1975–82. *Recreation:* law. *Address:* Faculty of Law, University of Birmingham, Birmingham B15 2TT. *T:* 021–472 1301.

SCOTT, Jack, (Peter), Hardiman; Chief Assistant to Director General BBC, 1975–80; *b* King's Lynn, 2 April 1920; *s* of Thomas Hardiman Scott and Dorothy Constance Smith; *m* 1st, 1942, Sheilah Stewart Roberts (marr. diss.); two *s*; 2nd, Patricia Mary (Sue) Windle. *Educ:* Grammar Sch.; privately. Northampton Chronicle and Echo series, 1939; then various provincial newspapers; Associated Press, and finally Hants and Sussex News, when began freelance broadcasting, 1948. Joined BBC; Asst News Editor Midland Region, 1950; gen. reporting staff, London, 1954; various foreign assignments, incl. Suez war; BBC's first Polit. Corresp., 1960; subseq. first Polit. Editor until 1975. Member: Study Gp on Future of Broadcasting in Zimbabwe, 1980; Broadcasting Complaints Commn, 1981–. Pres., Suffolk Poetry Soc., 1979–. *Publications:* Secret Sussex, 1949; (ed) How Shall I Vote?, 1976; *poems:* Adam and Eve and Us, 1946; When the Words are Gone, 1972; Part of Silence, 1984; *novels:* Within the Centre, 1946; The Lonely River, 1950; Text for Murder, 1951; Operation 10, 1982; No Exit, 1984; Deadly Nature, 1985; (with Becky Allan) Bait of Lies, 1986; contribs to: TV and Elections, 1977; BBC Guide to Parliament, 1979; Politics and the Media, 1980. *Recreations:* poetry, paintings, listening to music, conservation, East Anglia. *Address:* 4 Butchers Lane, Boxford, via Colchester CO6 5DZ. *T:* Boxford (Suffolk) 210320.

SCOTT, Prof. James Alexander, CBE 1986; Regional Medical Officer, Trent Regional Health Authority, since 1973; Special Professor of Health Care Planning, Nottingham University, since 1974; *b* 3 July 1931; *s* of Thomas Scott, MA Oxon and Margaret L. Scott; *m* 1957, Margaret Olive Slinger, BA, SRN; one *s* two *d*. *Educ:* Doncaster Grammar Sch.; Trinity Coll., Dublin Univ. BA 1953; MB, BCh, BAO 1955; MA, MD 1965; FFCM 1974; FRCP 1985. Pathologist, Sir Patrick Dun's Hosp., Dublin, 1957–59; Registrar in Clinical Pathology, United Sheffield Hosps, 1959–61; Trainee, later Asst and Principal Asst Sen. MO, Sheffield RHB, 1961–70; Sen. Lectr in Community Medicine, Nottingham Univ., 1967–71; Sen. Admin. MO, Sheffield RHB, 1971–73. Chm., English Regional MOs Gp, 1978–80; Pres., Hospital Cttee, EEC, 1980–86; Treas., Fac. of Community Medicine, RCP, 1984–86; Mem., Health Services Res. Cttee, MRC, 1986–. Masur Fellow, National Provincial Hospitals Trust, 1983. QHP, 1980–83. Hon. LLD Sheffield, 1983. *Publications:* contrib. Lancet. *Recreation:* stamp collecting. *Address:* 5 Slayleigh Lane, Sheffield S10 3RE. *T:* Sheffield 302238; La Gardelle, 24260 Le Bugue, Dordogne, France.

SCOTT, James Archibald, LVO 1961; Secretary, Scottish Education Department, since 1984; *b* 5 March 1932; *s* of late James Scott, MBE, and Agnes Bone Howie; *m* 1957, Elizabeth Agnes Joyce Buchan-Hepburn; three *s* one *d*. *Educ:* Dollar Acad.; Queen's Univ. of Ont.; Univ. of St Andrews (MA Hons). RAF aircrew, 1954–56. Asst Principal, CRO, 1956; served in New Delhi, 1958–62, and UK Mission to UN, New York, 1962–65; transf. to Scottish Office, 1965; Private Sec. to Sec. of State for Scotland, 1969–71; Asst Sec., Scottish Office, 1971; Under-Sec., Scottish Economic Planning Dept, later Industry Dept for Scotland, 1976–84. *Recreations:* music, golf. *Address:* 38 Queen's Crescent, Edinburgh EH9 2BA. *T:* 031–667 8417. *Club:* Travellers'.

SCOTT, James Steel, MD, FRCSEd; Professor of Obstetrics and Gynæcology, since 1961, and Dean of Faculty of Medicine, since 1986, University of Leeds; *b* 18 April 1924; *s* of late Dr Angus M. Scott and late Margaret Scott; *m* 1958, Olive Sharpe; two *s*. *Educ:* Glasgow Academy; University of Glasgow. MB, ChB 1946. Service in RAMC, 1947–49. MRCOG 1953, FRCOG 1962. Obstetric Tutor, Liverpool University, 1954; Lecturer, 1958; Senior Lecturer, 1960. MD, FRCSEd 1959, FRCS (*ad eund*) 1986. *Publications:* contrib. to Lancet, Brit. Med. Jl, Jl of Obst. and Gynæc. of Brit. Empire, Amer. Jl of Obstetrics and Gynæcology. *Recreation:* skiing. *Address:* Byards Lodge, Boroughbridge Road, Knaresborough, N Yorks HG5 0LT.

SCOTT, Sir James (Walter), 2nd Bt, *cr* 1962; JP; Lord-Lieutenant of Hampshire, since 1982; a Member of HM Body Guard, Hon. Corps of Gentlemen-at-Arms, since 1977; *b* 26 Oct. 1924; *e s* of Col Sir Jervoise Bolitho Scott, 1st Bt, and Kathleen Isabel, *yr d* of late Godfrey Walter, Malshanger, Basingstoke; *S* father 1965; *m* 1951, Anne Constantia, *e d* of late Lt-Col Clive Austin, Roundwood, Micheldever, Hants and the Lady Lilian Austin, *d* of late Brig. Lumley; three *s* one *d* (and one *d* decd). *Educ:* Eton. Lt-Col The Life Guards, formerly Grenadier Guards, retired 1969. Served War of 1939–45: NW Europe, 1944–45. Palestine, 1945–46; ADC to Viceroy and Gov.-Gen. of India, 1946–48; Malaya, 1948–49; Cyprus, 1958, 1960, 1964; Malaysia, 1966. Hon Col, 2nd Bn Wessex Regt (Volunteers) TA, 1985–. Underwriting Member of Lloyd's; Mem., Inst. of Dirs. Master, Mercers' Co., 1976. Chm. Hants Branch, Country Landowners' Assoc., 1981–84. Councillor, Hants CC, 1973–83. DL 1978, High Sheriff 1981–82, JP 1982, Hants. KStJ 1983. *Heir: s* James Jervoise Scott [*b* 12 Oct. 1952; *m* 1982, Mrs Judy Lyndon-Skeggs, *d* of Brian Trafford; one *s* one *d* and two step *d*]. *Address:* Rotherfield Park, Alton, Hampshire GU34 3QL. *T:* Tisted 204. *Clubs:* Cavalry and Guards, Farmers'.

SCOTT, Prof. John Fraser; Vice-Chancellor, La Trobe University, Melbourne, since 1977; *b* 10 Oct. 1928; *s* of Douglas Fraser Scott and Cecilia Louise Scott; *m* 1956, Dorothea Elizabeth Paton Scott; one *s* three *d*. *Educ:* Bristol Grammar Sch.; Trinity Coll., Cambridge. MA, FIS. Research Asst, Univ. of Sheffield, 1950–53; Asst, Univ. of Aberdeen, 1953–55; Lectr in Biometry, Univ. of Oxford, 1955–65; Univ. of Sussex: Reader in Statistics, 1965–67; Prof. of Applied Statistics, 1967–77; Pro-Vice-Chancellor, 1971–77. Visiting Consultant in Statistics: Nigeria, 1961, 1965; Sweden, 1969; Kuwait, 1973, 1976; Iraq, 1973; Malaysia, 1976. Reader, Church of England, 1971–77; Examining Chaplain to Bp of Chichester, 1974–77; Diocesan Lay Reader, Anglican Dio. of Melbourne, 1977–. Chairman: Jt Cttee on Univ. Statistics; Cttee of Review of Student Finances, 1983; Aust. Univs Industrial Assoc., 1986–; Dep. Chm., AVCC, 1986– (Chm., Working Party on Attrition); Mem., Grad. Careers Council of Aust. Mem., ABC Victorian State Adv. Cttee, 1978–81. Editor, Applied Statistics, 1971–76. *Publications:* The Comparability of Grade Standards in Mathematics, 1975; Report of Committee of Review of Student Finances, 1983; papers in JRSS, Lancet, BMJ, Chemistry and Industry, Statistician, etc. *Recreations:* wine, women and song; canals. *Address:* La Trobe University, Bundoora, Victoria 3083, Australia. *T:* 478 3122. *Club:* Melbourne.

SCOTT, John Hamilton; Vice Lord-Lieutenant for Shetland, since 1983; farming in Bressay and Noss, since 1964; *b* 30 Nov. 1936; *s* of Dr Thomas Gilbert Scott and Elizabeth M. B. Scott; *m* 1965, Wendy Ronald; one *s* one *d*. *Educ:* Bryanston; Cambridge Univ.; Guy's Hosp., London. Shepherd, Scrabster, Caithness, 1961–64. Chm., Woolgrowers of Shetland Ltd, 1981–; Dir, Reawick (Shetland) Lamb Co. Ltd, 1976–. Pres., Shetland NFU, 1976; Chairman: Radio Shetland Adv. Cttee, 1982–; Shetland Crofting, Farming and Wildlife Adv. Gp, 1984–; Mem., Nature Conservancy Council Adv. Cttee for Scotland, 1984–. *Recreations:* mountain climbing, Up-Helly-Aa, music. *Address:* Gardie House, Bressay, Shetland. *T:* Bressay 281. *Club:* Alpine.

SCOTT, John James; Financial Planning Consultant and Managing Director, Dudmass Ltd, since 1983; *b* 4 Sept. 1924; *s* of late Col John Creagh Scott, DSO, OBE and Mary Elizabeth Marjory (*née* Murray of Polmaise); *m* 1st, Katherine Mary (*née* Bruce); twin *d*; 2nd, Heather Marguerite (*née* Douglas Brown); 3rd, June Rose (*née* Mackie); twin *s*. *Educ:* Radley (Schol.); Corpus Christi Coll., Cambridge (Schol.); National Inst. for Medical Research, London. War Service, Captain, Argyll and Sutherland Highlanders, 1944–47. BA 1st cl. hons Nat. Sci. Tripos, Pts I and II, 1950, MA 1953, Cantab; PhD London 1954. Senior Lectr in Chem. Pathology, St Mary's Hosp., 1955–61; Mem. Editorial Bd, Biochem. Jl, 1956–61; Mem. Cttee of Biochem. Soc., 1961; Vis. Scientist, Nat. Insts of Health, Bethesda, Md, 1961. Entered Diplomatic Service, 1961; Office of Comr Gen. for SE Asia, Singapore, 1962; Office of Political Adviser to C-in-C, Singapore, 1963; FO, 1966; Counsellor, Rio de Janeiro and Brasilia, 1971; seconded to NI Office as Asst Sec., Stormont, 1974–76; Asst Under-Sec., FCO, 1978–80; Asst Managing Dir, later Commercial Dir, Industrial Engines (Sales) Ltd, Elbar Group, 1980. Francis Bacon Prize, Cambridge, 1950. *Publications:* papers in Biochem. Jl, Proc. Royal Soc. and other learned jls. *Recreations:* botany, photography, music. *Address:* The Cottage, South Rauceby, Sleaford, Lincs NG34 7QG. *T:* South Rauceby 254. *Clubs:* Carlton, Institute of Directors; Leander (Henley-on-Thames); Hawks (Cambridge); Ski Club of GB.

SCOTT, Kenneth Bertram Adam, CMG 1980; HM Diplomatic Service; Assistant Private Secretary to the Queen, since 1985; *b* 23 Jan. 1931; *s* of late Adam Scott, OBE, and Lena Kaye; *m* 1966, Gabrielle Justine (*d* 1977), *d* of R. W. Smart, Christchurch, New Zealand; one *s* one *d*. *Educ:* George Watson's Coll., Edinburgh; Edinburgh Univ. MA Hons 1952. Foreign Office, 1954; Third Sec., Moscow 1956; Second Sec., (Commercial), Bonn, 1958; FO, 1961; First Sec., Washington, 1964; Head of Chancery and Consul, Vientiane, 1968; Counsellor and Head of Chancery, Moscow, 1971; Sen. Officers' War Course, RNC, Greenwich, 1973; Dep. Head, Personnel Ops Dept, FCO, 1973; Counsellor and Head of Chancery, Washington, 1975; Head of E European and Soviet Dept, FCO, 1977; Minister and Dep. UK Perm. Rep. to NATO, 1979–82; Ambassador to Yugoslavia, 1982–85. *Address:* c/o Buckingham Palace, SW1. *Clubs:* Royal Automobile; New (Edinburgh).

SCOTT, Kenneth Farish, MC 1943 and Bar, 1944; FEng 1979, FICE; Senior Consultant, Sir Alexander Gibb & Partners, since 1984 (Senior Partner, 1977–84); *b* 21 Dec. 1918; *s* of Norman James Stewart and Ethel May Scott; *m* 1945, Elizabeth Mary Barrowcliff; one *s* one *d*. *Educ:* Stockton Grammar School; Constantine Tech. Coll. Served Royal Engineers, 1939–46. Joined Sir Alexander Gibb & Partners, 1946; Resident Engineer, Hydro-Electric Works, Scotland, 1946–52; Chief Rep., NZ, 1952–55, Scotland, 1955–59; Partner 1959, Senior Partner 1977; responsible for design and supervision of construction of major water resource develt projects, incl. Latiyan Dam, 1959–67, Lar Dam 1968–82, Greater Tehran Water Supply, 1959–82; major maritime works incl. modernisation Devonport Dockyard, 1970–80; internat. airports at Tripoli, 1966–70, Bahrain, 1970–72. Pres., Soc. des Ingénieurs et Scientifiques de France (British Section), 1975; Vice-Pres., ICE, 1985–86. Chm., Assoc. of Consulting Engineers, 1976. Hon. Mem., Instn of RE, 1982. *Publications:* papers to ICE and International Congress of Large Dams. *Recreations:* sailing, golf, wood working. *Address:* Forest House, Brookside Road, Brockenhurst, Hants SO42 7SS. *T:* Lymington 23531. *Clubs:* Special Forces, Royal Over-Seas League; RE Yacht, Cowes Island Sailing.

SCOTT, M. Audrey; Headmistress of the Perse School for Girls, Cambridge, 1947–67, retired; *b* 22 Oct. 1904; *d* of late Lieutenant-Colonel C. E. Scott, solicitor, and Mrs M. E. M. Scott, Bradford. *Educ:* Queen Margaret's School, Scarborough (now at Escrick); Newnham College, Cambridge. Teaching at Benenden School, Kent, 1926–29; Atherley School, Southampton, 1929–31; Edgbaston Church College, 1931–40; Thornbury Grammar School, Glos, 1941–43; Headmistress, Yeovil High School, Jan. 1944–Aug. 1947. Association of Headmistresses: Exec. Cttee, 1956–62; Chm., Foreign and Commonwealth Education Cttee, 1960–62; Pres., Six Counties Branch, 1959–61. *Publication:* The First Hundred Years 1881–1981: a history of the Perse School for Girls, 1981. *Address:* 24 Gretton Court, Girton, Cambridge CB3 0QN. *T:* Cambridge 276646.
See also Sir Hilary Scott.

SCOTT, Dame Margaret, (Dame Catherine Margaret Mary Denton), DBE 1981 (OBE 1977); Founding Director of the Australian Ballet School, since 1964; *b* 26 April 1922; *d* of John and Marjorie Douglas-Scott; *m* 1953, Prof. Derek Ashworth Denton, FAA, FRACP; two *s*. *Educ:* Parktown Convent, Johannesburg, S Africa. Sadler's Wells Ballet, London, 1940–43; Ballet Rambert, London and Australia, 1944–49; National Ballet, Australia, 1949–50; Ballet Rambert, and John Cranko Group, London, 1951–53; private ballet teaching, Australia, 1953–61; planned and prepared the founding of the Aust. Ballet Sch., 1962–64. *Recreations:* music, theatre, garden. *Address:* 816 Orrong Road, Toorak, Melbourne, Vic 3142, Australia. *T:* 241–2640. *Club:* Alexandra (Melbourne).

SCOTT, Maurice FitzGerald; Official Fellow in Economics, Nuffield College, Oxford, since 1968; *b* 6 Dec. 1924; *s* of Colonel G. C. Scott, OBE and H. M. G. Scott; *m* 1953, Eleanor Warren (*née* Dawson); three *d*. *Educ:* Wadham Coll., Oxford (MA); Nuffield Coll., Oxford (BLitt). Served RE, 1943–46. OEEC, Paris, 1949–51; Paymaster-General's Office (Lord Cherwell), 1951–53; Cabinet Office, 1953–54; NIESR, London, 1954–57; Tutor in Economics and Student of Christ Church, Oxford, 1957–68; NEDO, London, 1962–63; OECD, Paris, 1967–68. *Publications:* A Study of U.K. Imports, 1963; (with I. M. D. Little and T. Scitovsky) Industry and Trade in Some Developing Countries, 1970; (with J. D. MacArthur and D. M. G. Newbery) Project Appraisal in Practice, 1976; (with R. A. Laslett) Can We get back to Full Employment?, 1978; (with W. M. Corden and I. M. D. Little) The Case against General Import Restrictions, 1980. *Recreation:* walking. *Address:* 11 Blandford Avenue, Oxford OX2 8EA. *T:* Oxford 59115. *Club:* Political Economy (Oxford).

SCOTT, Sir Michael, KCVO 1979 (MVO 1961); CMG 1977; HM Diplomatic Service, retired; Secretary-General, Royal Commonwealth Society, since 1983; *b* 19 May 1923; *yr s* of late John Scott and Kathleen Scott; *m* 1st, 1944, Vivienne Sylvia Vincent-Barwood (marr. diss. 1967); three *s*; 2nd, 1971, Jennifer Slawikowski (*née* Cameron Smith), *widow* of Dr George J. M. Slawikowski. *Educ:* Dame Allan's School; Durham Univ. Durham Light Infantry, 1941; 1st Gurkha Rifles, 1943–47. Colonial Office, 1949; CRO, 1957; First Secretary, Karachi, 1958–59; Deputy High Commissioner, Peshawar, 1959–62; Counsellor and Director, British Information Services in India, New Delhi, 1963–65; Head of E and Central Africa Dept, FCO, 1965–68; Counsellor, British High Commn, Nicosia, 1968–72; RCDS, 1973; Ambassador to Nepal, 1974–77; High Comr in Malaŵi, 1977–79; High Comr in Bangladesh, 1980–81. Mem. Governing Council, ODI, 1983–. *Address:* 87A Cornwall Gardens, SW7 4AY. *T:* 01–589 6794. *Clubs:* Oriental, Royal Commonwealth Society.

SCOTT, Maj.-Gen. Michael Frederick, JP; Farmer; *b* 25 Oct. 1911; *s* of Col F. W. Scott, Romsey, Hants; *m* 1961, Laila Wallis (*née* Tatchell). *Educ:* Harrow. Apprenticed as Mechanical Engr to John I. Thornycroft Co. Basingstoke, 1932–35; commnd Lieut, RAOC, 1935; transf. REME 1942. Served: India, 1938–44; Palestine, 1947–48; Germany, 1951–54; Cyprus, 1955–58. Inspector, REME, 1960–63; Commandant Technical Group, REME, 1963–65 (retd); Col Comdt, REME, 1968–73. CEng; FIMechE. JP Somerset, 1967. *Recreations:* sailing, shooting, country pursuits. *Address:* Parsonage Farm, South Barrow, Yeovil, Somerset. *T:* North Cadbury 40417. *Club:* Royal Ocean Racing.

SCOTT, Michael John; Programme Controller, Granada TV, since 1979; *b* 8 Dec. 1932; *s* of Tony and Pam Scott; *m* 1956, Sylvia Hudson; one *d*. *Educ:* Latymer Upper Sch., Hammersmith; Clayesmore, Iwerne Minster, Dorset. National Service, RAOC, 1951–53. Stagehand with Festival Ballet, and film extra, 1954; TV production trainee, Rank Organization, 1955; Granada TV: joined as floormanager, 1956; Programme Director, 1957; Producer/Performer, daily magazine programme, 1963–65; Presenter, Cinema, 1965–68; Executive Producer, local programmes, 1968–73; World in Action interviewer, and producer/performer of other programmes, 1974–75; Executive Producer and Reporter, Nuts and Bolts of the Economy, 1975–78; Dep. Programme Controller, 1978–79. Dir, Channel 4 Television Co., 1984–. *Recreations:* watching the box, jogging, a 1932 Lagonda, a garden. *Address:* Flat 1, 39 Gloucester Walk, W8. *T:* 01–937 3962; Flat 1, Scottish Life House, Bridge Street, Manchester. *T:* 061–832 9061.

SCOTT, Most Rev. Moses Nathanael Christopher Omobiala, Commander of the Rokel, 1974; CBE 1970; Hon. DD Durham; *b* 18 Aug. 1911; *s* of late Christopher Columbus Scott, Hastings Village, Sierra Leone, and Cleopatra Eliza Scott, York Village; *m* 1941, Cordelia Elizabeth Deborah Maddy, Gloucester Village; three *s* two *d*. *Educ:* CMS Grammar School and Fourah Bay Coll., Freetown, Sierra Leone. Deacon 1943; Priest, 1946. Curate of: Lunsar, 1943–44; Yongro, Bullom, 1944–46; Missionary-in-charge of Makeni, 1946–48, of Bo, 1948–50; studied at London College of Divinity for DipTheol, 1950–51; Curate of Grappenhall, Cheshire, 1951–53; returned to Bo, 1954; Priest in charge, Bo District, 1954–57 (Educn Sec. to the Diocese, 1955–61); Archdeacon of Missions, Sierra Leone, 1957–59; Archdeacon of Bonthe and Bo, 1959–61; Bishop of Sierra Leone, 1961–81; Archbishop of West Africa, 1969–81. Hon. DD Durham, 1962. *Recreations:* playwriting, croquet. *Address:* c/o PO Box 128, Freetown, Sierra Leone.

SCOTT, Nicholas Paul, MBE 1964; JP; MP (C) Chelsea, since Oct. 1974; Minister of State, Northern Ireland Office, since 1986; *b* 1933; *e s* of late Percival John Scott; *m* 1st, 1964, Elizabeth Robinson (marr. diss. 1976); one *s* two *d*; 2nd, 1979, Hon. Mrs Cecilia Anne Tapsell, *d* of 9th Baron Hawke; one *s*. *Educ:* Clapham College. Served Holborn Borough Coun., 1956–59 and 1962–65; contested (C) SW Islington, 1959 and 1964; MP (C) Paddington S, 1966–Feb. 1974; PPS to: Chancellor of the Exchequer, Rt Hon. Iain Macleod, 1970; Home Sec., Rt. Hon. Robert Carr, 1972–74; Parly Under-Sec. of State, Dept of Employment, 1974; Opposition spokesman on housing, 1974–75; Parly Under Sec. of State, Northern Ireland Office, 1981–86. Mem., 1922 Exec. Cttee, 1978–81; Dir, London Office, European Cons. Gp in European Parlt, 1974. Nat. Chm., Young Conservatives, 1963; Chm., Conservative Parly Employment Cttee, 1979–81 (Vice-Chm., 1967–72). Chairman: Westminster Community Relations Council, 1967–72; Paddington Churches Housing Assoc., 1970–76; British Atlantic Gp Younger Politicians, 1970–73; Nat. Pres., Tory Reform Gp. Dep. Chm., British Caribbean Assoc.; Mem. Council, Community Service Volunteers; Governor, British Inst. of Human Rights; Dep. Chm., Youthaid, 1977–79. Mem., Cttee, MCC, 1972–75. Churchwarden, St Margaret's, Westminster, 1971–73. Man. Dir, E. Allom & Co., 1968–70; Chm., Creative Consultants Ltd, 1969–79; Director: A. S. Kerswill Ltd, 1970–81; Eastbourne Printers Ltd, 1970–81; Juniper Studios Ltd, 1970–81; Midhurst White Holdings Ltd, 1977–78; Bonusbond Hldgs Ltd, 1980–81; Bonusplan Ltd, 1977–81; Cleveland Offshore Fund Inc., 1970–81; Throgmorton Securities Ltd, 1970–74; Ede & Townsend, 1977–80; Learplan Ltd, 1978–81; Consultant: Campbell-Johnson Ltd, 1970–76; Roulston & Co. Inc., 1970–78; Lombard North Central Ltd, 1971–74; Clevebourne Investments Ltd, 1974–76; Claremont Textiles Ltd, 1974–76; Procter & Gamble Ltd, 1974–78; Hill & Knowlton (UK) Ltd, 1981; VSO, 1974–76; Council, Bank Staff Assocs, 1968–77. Mem., GAPAN, 1979–. JP London, 1961. *Recreations:* cricket, tennis, golf, flying. *Address:* House of Commons, SW1A 0AA. *Clubs:* Pratt's, Buck's, MCC.

SCOTT, Sir Oliver (Christopher Anderson), 3rd Bt, of Yews, Westmorland, *cr* 1909; Radiobiologist, Richard Dimbleby Cancer Research Department, St Thomas' Hospital, since 1982; Radiobiologist, 1954–66, Director, 1966–69, British Empire Cancer Campaign Research Unit in Radiobiology; *b* 6 November 1922; *s* of Sir Samuel H. Scott, 2nd Bt and Nancy Lilian (*née* Anderson); *S* father 1960; *m* 1951, Phoebe Ann Tolhurst; one *s* two *d*. *Educ:* Charterhouse; King's College, Cambridge. Clinical training at St Thomas' Hosp., 1943–46; MRCS, LRCP, 1946; MB, BCh, Cambridge, 1946; MD Cambridge, 1976; Surgeon-Lieutenant RNVR, 1947–49. Dir, Provincial Insurance Co., 1955–64. Hon. Consultant, Inst. of Cancer Res., Sutton, 1974–82. Mem. Council, Cancer Res. Campaign, 1978–. High Sheriff of Westmorland, 1966. *Publications:* contributions to scientific books and journals. *Recreations:* music, walking. *Heir: s* Christopher James Scott, *b* 16 Jan. 1955. *Address:* 31 Kensington Square, W8. *T:* 01–937 8556. *Club:* Brooks's.

SCOTT, Oliver Lester Schreiner; Honorary Consultant, Skin Department, Charing Cross Hospital, since 1978 (formerly Physician-in-Charge); Consultant Dermatologist: South West Metropolitan Regional Hospital Board, since 1951; Dispensaire Française, London, since 1958; King Edward VII Hospital for Officers, London, since 1979; *b* London, 16 June 1919; *s* of Ralph Lester Scott, FRCSE, and Ursula Hester Schreiner; *m* 1943, Katherine Ogle Branfoot; two *d*. *Educ:* Diocesan College, Cape Town; Trinity College, Cambridge; St Thomas's Hospital, London. MRCS, LRCP 1942; MA, MB, BChir, (Cantab) 1943; MRCP (London) 1944. FRCP 1964, FRSM. Med. Specialist, RAF Med. Branch, 1943–46. Consultant, Medical Insurance Agency, 1976–. Pres., Dermatology Section, RSocMed, 1977–78; Hon. Treas., Royal Medical Foundn of Epsom Coll.; Hon. Mem., British Assoc. of Dermatologists, (Pres., 1982–83). Chevalier, l'Ordre National du Mérite, France. *Publications:* section on skin disorders in Clinical Genetics, ed A. Sorsby; medical articles in Lancet, British Journal of Dermatology, etc. *Recreations:* fishing, gardening. *Address:* 114 Harley Street, W1. *T:* 01–935 0621; South Lodge, South Side, Wimbledon Common, SW19. *T:* 01–946 6662.

SCOTT, Paul Henderson, CMG 1974; writer; HM Diplomatic Service, retired 1980; *b* 7 Nov. 1920; *s* of Alan Scott and Catherine Scott (*née* Henderson), Edinburgh; *m* 1953, Beatrice Celia Sharpe; one *s* one *d*. *Educ:* Royal High School, Edinburgh; Edinburgh University (MA). HM Forces, 1941–47 (Major RA). Foreign Office, 1947–53; First Secretary, Warsaw, 1953–55; First Secretary, La Paz, 1955–59; Foreign Office, 1959–62; Counsellor, Havana, 1962–64; Canadian National Defence College, 1964–65; British Deputy Commissioner General for Montreal Exhibition, 1965–67; Counsellor and Consul-General, Vienna, 1968–71; Head of British Govt Office, 1971, Consul-Gen., 1974–75, Montreal; Research Associate, IISS, 1975–76; Asst Under Sec., FO (negotiator on behalf of EEC Presidency for negotiations with USSR, Poland and East Germany), 1977; Minister and Consul General, Milan, 1977–80. Chm., Adv. Council for the Arts in Scotland, 1981–; Dep. Chm., Saltire Soc., 1981–; Member: Council, Nat. Trust for Scotland, 1981–; Assoc. for Scottish Literary Studies, 1981–; Scots Language Soc., 1981; Cockburn Assoc., 1982–85; Council, Edinburgh Internat. Fest., 1984. Grosse Goldene Ehrenzeichen, Austria, 1969. *Publications:* 1707: The Union of Scotland and England, 1979; (ed with A. C. Davis) The Age of MacDiarmid, 1980; Walter Scott and Scotland, 1981; (ed) Walter Scott's Letters of Malachi Malagrowther, 1981; (ed) Andrew Fletcher's United and Separate Parliaments, 1982; John Galt, 1985; In Bed with an Elephant, 1985; (ed with George Bruce) A Scottish Letter Book, 1986; articles and book reviews esp. in Economist, Scotsman and other periodicals. *Recreations:* ski-ing, sailing. *Address:* 33 Drumsheugh Gardens, Edinburgh. *T:* 031–225 1038. *Club:* New (Edinburgh)

SCOTT, Rev. Dr Percy; Warden of Hartley Hall, Manchester, 1973–77, retired; *b* 14 Nov. 1910; *s* of Herbert and Emma Scott; *m* 1937, Christa Schleining; one *s* two *d*. *Educ:* Lincoln City School; London and Marburg Universities. Richmond College, London, 1931–35; Marburg, 1935–37; Minister at: Exeter, 1937–39; Stockton-on-Tees, 1939–45; Leeds, 1945–47; Tutor in Systematic Theology at Hartley Victoria College, 1947–73; Member, Faculty of Theology, Manchester Univ., 1953–77, Principal, Hartley Victoria Coll., Manchester, 1959–73. *Publications:* John Wesley's Lehre von der Heiligung, 1938; (trans.) Day by Day we Magnify Thee (Luther), 1950; other translations from German; signed reviews in The Expository Times and London Quarterly; articles. *Recreation:* sport. *Address:* 53 Alexandra Road South, Manchester M16 8GH. *T:* 061–226 7311. *Club:* Rotarian (Manchester South).

SCOTT, Sir Peter; *see* Scott, Sir C. P.

SCOTT, Peter Denys John, QC 1978; *b* 19 April 1935; *s* of John Ernest Dudley Scott and Joan G. Steinberg. *Educ:* Monroe High Sch., Rochester, NY, USA; Balliol Coll., Oxford (BA Hons). Second Lieut, RHA, Lieut (TA), National Service, 1955. Called to the Bar, Middle Temple (Harmsworth Scholar), 1960, Bencher, 1984; Standing Counsel: to Dir, Gen. of Fair Trading, 1973–78; to Dept of Employment, 1974–78. Member: Home Sec's Cttee on Prison Disciplinary System, 1984; Interception of Communications Tribunal, 1986–. Vice-Chm., Senate of the Inns of Court and the Bar, 1985–86; Chm., Bar Council, 1987; Mem., Senate and Bar Council, 1981–; Chm., London Common Law Bar Assoc., 1983–85. Chm., N Kensington Amenity Trust, 1981–85. *Recreations:* walking, theatre. *Address:* 4 Eldon Road, W8. *T:* 01–937 3301.

SCOTT, Peter Hardiman; *see* Scott, J. P. H.

SCOTT, Sir Peter (Markham), Kt 1973; CBE 1953 (MBE 1942); DSC 1943; Artist; Ornithologist; Hon. Chairman of Council, World Wildlife Fund International, since 1985 (Chairman, 1961–82; Chairman of Council, 1983–85); Hon. Director: Wildfowl Trust; Survival Anglia Ltd; Lt Comdr RNVR, retired; *b* 14 Sept. 1909; *s* of Captain Robert Falcon Scott, CVO, RN, and Kathleen Bruce (she *m* 2nd, 1922, Edward Hilton Young, later 1st Baron Kennet, PC, GBE, DSO, DSC, who *d* 1960; she *d* 1947); *m* 1st, 1942, Elizabeth Jane (marr. diss. 1951), *d* of David Howard; one *d*; 2nd, 1951, Philippa, *d* of late Comdr F. W. Talbot-Ponsonby, RN; one *s* one *d*. *Educ:* Oundle; Trinity College, Cambridge (MA); Munich State Academy; Royal Academy Schools, London. Exhibited paintings Royal Acad. since 1933; held Exhibitions of oil paintings at Ackermann's Galleries, Bond Street, also New York; specialises in bird-painting and portraits; lectures and nature feature programmes on television. Won international 14-foot Dinghy Championship for Prince of Wales Cup, 1937, 1938, and 1946. Represented Great Britain at Olympic Games, 1936 in single-handed sailing (bronze medal). Served in destroyers in Battle of Atlantic, and Light Coastal Forces in Channel, 1939–45 (despatches thrice, MBE, DSC and Bar). President: Soc. of Wildlife Artists, 1964–78; Fauna and Flora Preservation Soc., 1981–; Glos Assoc. of Youth Clubs; Internat. Yacht Racing Union, 1955–69; The Otter Trust; Glos Trust for Nature Conservation; British Butterfly Conservation Soc.; Vice-President: British Gliding Assoc.; Inland Waterways Assoc.; Camping Club of Great Britain; Bristol Gliding Club; Chairman: Survival Service Commn, IUCN, 1962–81 (now Chm. Emeritus); Falkland Islands Foundn, 1979–; Trustee Emeritus, WWF UK. Chm., Olympic Yachting Cttee, 1947–48; Internat. Jury for Yachting, Olympic Games: 1956, Melbourne; 1960, Naples; 1964, Tokyo. Member Council: Boy Scout Assoc., 1945–73; Winston Churchill Meml Trust. Rector, Aberdeen Univ., 1960–63; Chancellor, Birmingham Univ., 1974–83. Admiral, Manx Herring Fleet, 1962–65. Explored unmapped Perry River area in Canadian Arctic, May-August 1949; Leader of ornithological expeditions to Central Highlands, Iceland, to mark wild geese, 1951, 1953; Expeditions to Australasia Galapagos Is, Seychelles and Antarctic (thrice). Gliding: International Gold Badge, 1958; International Diamond badge, 1963; National Gliding Champion, 1963; Chm., British Gliding Assoc., 1968–70. Hon. Fellow, UMIST, 1974. Hon. LLD: Exeter, 1963; Aberdeen, 1963; Birmingham, 1974; Bristol, 1974; Liverpool, 1984; Hon. DSc Bath, 1979; Guelph, 1981. Cherry Kearton Medal, 1967, Founder's Medal, 1983, RGS; Albert Medal, RSA, 1970; Bernard Tucker Medal, BOU, 1970; Arthur Allen Medal, Cornell Univ., 1971; Gold Medal, NY Zoological Soc., 1975; IUCN John Phillips Medal, 1981; World Wildlife Fund Twentieth Anniversary Special Award, 1981; Gold Medal, Philadelphia Acad. of Natural Scis, 1983; RSPB Gold Award, 1986; J. P. Getty Prize, 1986; WWF Gold Award, 1986. Icelandic Order of the Falcon, 1969; Commander, Dutch Order of Golden Ark, 1976; Internat. Pahlavi Environment Prize (UN), 1977. *Publications:* Morning Flight, 1935; Wild Chorus, 1938; The Battle of the Narrow Seas, 1945; Portrait Drawings, 1949; Key to Wildfowl of the World, 1949 (Coloured Key, 1958); Wild Geese and Eskimos, 1951; (with James Fisher) A Thousand Geese, 1953; (with Hugh Boyd) Wildfowl of the British Isles, 1957; The Eye of the Wind (autobiography), 1961; (with Philippa Scott) Animals in Africa, 1962; (with the Wildfowl Trust) The Swans, 1972; Fishwatchers' Guide to West Atlantic Coral Reefs, 1972; Observations of Wildlife, 1980; Travel Diaries of a Naturalist, vol. I, 1983, vol. II, 1985, vol. III, 1987; illustrated: Lord Kennet's A Bird in the Bush, Michael Bratby's Grey Goose and Through the Air, Paul Gallico's The Snow Goose, Adventures Among Birds, Handbook of British Birds, Vol. III, Jean Delacour's Waterfowl of the World, Birds of the Western Palearctic, vol. 1, Malcolm Ogilvie's The Wildfowl of Britain and Europe. *Recreations:* exploring, bird-watching, fish-watching, scuba diving. *Address:* New Grounds, Slimbridge, Glos GL2 7BT. *Clubs:* Royal Thames Yacht; Explorers (New York) (Hon. Mem.).

SCOTT, Sheriff Richard John Dinwoodie; Sheriff of Lothian and Borders at Edinburgh, since 1986; *b* 28 May 1939; *s* of late Prof. Richard Scott and of Mary Ellen Maclachlan; *m* 1969, Josephine Moretta Blake; two *d*. *Educ:* Edinburgh Academy; Univ. of Edinburgh (MA, LLB) (Vans Dunlop Schol. in Evidence and Pleading, 1963). Lektor in English, British Centre, Sweden, 1960–61; Tutor, Faculty of Law, Univ. of Edinburgh, 1964–72; admitted to Faculty of Advocates, 1965; Standing Jun. Counsel to Min. of Defence (Air) in Scotland, 1968–77. Sheriff of Grampian, Highland and Islands, at Aberdeen and Stonehaven, 1977–86. Hon. Lectr, Univ. of Aberdeen, 1980–. *Publications:* various articles in legal jls. *Address:* Sheriff Court House, Lawnmarket, Edinburgh EH1 2NS.

SCOTT, Hon. Sir Richard (Rashleigh Folliott), Kt 1983; **Hon. Mr Justice Scott;** a Judge of the High Court of Justice, Chancery Division, since 1983; *b* 2 Oct. 1934; *s* of Lt-

Col C. W. F. Scott, 2/9th Gurkha Rifles and Katharine Scott (*née* Rashleigh); *m* 1959, Rima Elisa, *d* of Salvador Ripoll and Blanca Korsi de Ripoll, Panama City; two *s* two *d*. *Educ:* Michaelhouse Coll., Natal; Univ. of Cape Town (BA); Trinity Coll., Cambridge (BA, LLB). Bigelow Fellow, Univ. of Chicago, 1958–59. Called to Bar, Inner Temple, 1959, Bencher, 1981. QC 1975; Attorney Gen., Duchy of Lancaster, 1980–83. Chm. of the Bar, 1982–83 (Vice-Chm., 1981–82). *Recreations:* hunting, tennis, bridge; formerly Rugby (Cambridge Blue, 1957). *Address:* Royal Courts of Justice, Strand, WC2. *Club:* Hawks (Cambridge).

SCOTT, Robert, CBE 1976; Director, Polytechnic, Wolverhampton, 1969–77, retired; *b* 7 July 1913; 2nd *s* of H. Scott, Westhoughton, Bolton; *m* 1940, Dorothy M. Howell, Westhoughton; one *s* one *d*. *Educ:* Hindley and Abram Grammar Sch., Lancs; Univ. of Liverpool; St John's Coll., Cambridge (Wrangler; MA). BSc 1st cl. hons 1934, DipEd 1937, Liverpool; BA Cantab, 1936; FIMA. Asst Master, Newton-le-Willows Grammar Sch., 1937–41; Army and WO Staff, 1941–46; Scientific Civil Service at RMCS Shrivenham, 1946–54; Vice-Principal, Bolton Techn. Coll., 1954–57; Principal, Wolverhampton and Staffs Coll. of Technology, 1958–69. *Recreations:* motoring, reading. *Address:* 4 Wrekin Lane, The Wergs, Wolverhampton WV6 8UL. *T:* Wolverhampton 752107.

SCOTT, Maj.-Gen. Robert, FRCS; Commandant and Post-Graduate Dean, Royal Army Medical College, since 1986; *b* 16 Aug. 1929; *s* of late Thomas Montgomery Scott and of Margaret Scott; *m* 1957, Rosemary Stott Sunderland; one *s* two *d*. *Educ:* Campbell College; University College, Oxford (MA, MCh); King's College Hospital. Joined RAMC 1956; Consultant surgeon, mil. hospitals at home and overseas, and BAOR, 1956–86. FRSocMed. *Publications:* chapters and papers on military surgery. *Recreations:* golf, sailing, bagpiping. *Address:* Aish Barton, Aish, Stoke Gabriel, South Devon. *T:* Stoke Gabriel 477.

SCOTT, Col Robert Edmond Gabriel, MBE 1959; MC 1953; Director General, Engineering Industries Association, since 1981; *b* 3 Aug. 1920; *s* of Edmond James and Lilian Kate Scott; *m* 1942, Anna Maria Larkin; two *s*. *Educ:* Roan, Greenwich. Commissioned into Durham Light Inf., 1942; regimental service with this regt in Western Desert, Italy, Korea and Rhine Army, 1942–52; Staff duties, MoD and Eastern Comd, 1952–56; service with W African Frontier Force, 1956–60; comd inf. batt., Home Service, 1960–66; seconded to Diplomatic Service, as Defence Adviser, Lagos, 1966–70; Dep. Comd, W. Midland Dist, 1970–72; retired, 1972. Engineering Industries Association: Export Sec. and Dep. Dir, 1973–77; Dir, 1977–81. *Recreations:* rough shooting, country pursuits, philately. *Address:* Melsbury, 13 Sandhurst Road, Wokingham, Berks RG11 3JG. *T:* Wokingham 738426. *Club:* Army and Navy.

SCOTT, Robin; *see* Scutt, R. H.

SCOTT, Ronald, OBE 1981; musician; *b* 28 Jan. 1927. *Educ:* Jews' Infant Sch., Aldgate, E1; Benthal Road Elementary Sch., N16; Central Foundation Sch., Cowper St, E1. Musician (Tenor Saxophone), 1943–. Opened Ronnie Scott's Club, 1959 (Director, with Pete King). *Publication:* (with Michael Hennessey) Some of My Best Friends are Blues, 1979. *Recreation:* motor sport. *Address:* 47 Frith Street, W1. *T:* 01–439 0747. *Club:* just his own.

SCOTT, Sheila (Christine), OBE 1968; aviator; lecturer; actress; writer; *b* 27 April 1927; *d* of Harold R. Hopkins, Worcester, and Edith Hopkins (*née* Kenward); *m* 1945, Rupert Leaman Bellamy (marr. diss. 1950). *Educ:* Alice Ottley School, Worcs. VAD, RN, 1945; acting, 1946–59, with Repertory Companies at Watford, Aldershot and Windsor; small parts in films, TV and West End Stage. Started flying, 1959; obtained British and USA commercial licences; Racing Pilot: first race won 1960 national air races (De Havilland Trophy, etc); Holder of 100 World Class Records (Aviation), incl. Round the World in class CIc and in open feminine classes; London to Capetown and Capetown to London; N Atlantic (western and eastern crossings direct); S Atlantic, Brazil to W Africa; has flown solo three times round world, including first world flight via North Pole in a light aircraft, 1971; winner of many air races; won female Light Aircraft prize, Transatlantic Air Race London-New York May 1969; won Ford Woman's Prize, London-Sydney Air Race, Dec. 1969. Founder and 1st Gov., Brit. Section, Ninety Nines Inc., 1964. Founder British Balloon and Airships Club. Life Mem. and Hon. Diploma, Academia Romana vel Sodalitis Quirinale. Silver Award of Merit, Brit. Guild of Air Pilots and Navigators, 1966, Liveryman, 1968; Isabella D'Este Award (Italy), 1966; Silver Medal, Royal Aero Club, 1967, Gold Medal, 1972; Harmon Trophy, USA, 1967; Britannia Trophy, 1968. *Publications:* I Must Fly, 1968; On Top of the World, 1973; Barefoot in the Sky, 1974. *Recreation:* sailing. *Address:* c/o Ravenscroft, Highcliffe Lane, Turnditch, Derbyshire DE5 2EA. *T:* Ripley 89362; 01–821 0889. *Club:* Naval and Military.

SCOTT, Sir Terence Charles Stuart M.; *see* Morrison-Scott.

SCOTT, Prof. Thomas Frederick McNair, MA Cantab, MD Cantab, MRCS; FRCP; Associate Director of Ambulatory Pediatrics, 1983–85, now Emeritus Professor of Paediatrics, Hahnemann University (Professor of Paediatrics, 1974, Co-ordinator of Ambulatory Care Teaching, 1974–75, and Co-Director of Ambulatory Paediatrics, 1975–83, Hahnemann Medical College and Hospital); Senior Physician, The Children's Hospital of Philadelphia, 1940–69, now Physician Emeritus; *b* 18 June 1901; *e s* of Robert Frederick McNair Scott, MB, ChB (Edin.), and Alice Nystrom; *m* 1936, Mary Dwight Baker, PhD (Radcliffe), *o d* of late Clarence Dwight Baker, Wisconsin, USA; one *s* one *d*. *Educ:* Cheltenham College; Caius College, Cambridge (Scholar). Natural Science Tripos Pt I Class I, Part II (Physiology) Class II; Junior University Entrance Scholarship to St George's Hospital, 1924; Brackenbury Prize in Medicine, 1926; Qualified conjoint board, 1927; MRCP 1928; FRCP 1953; MD (Cantab) 1938; Casualty Officer, House Surgeon, House Physn, Resident Obst. Asst, Medical Registrar, at St George's Hospital, 1927–29; House Physician Queens Hospital for Children, 1930; Research Fellow of Medicine, Harvard University, Mass, USA, 1930–31; Instructor in Pædiatrics Johns Hopkins University, Baltimore, Md, USA, 1931–34; Assistant Resident Physician at Hospital of Rockefeller Institute for Medical Research, New York, USA, working on Virus diseases, 1934–36; Assistant Physician i/c of Children's Out-patients, Lecturer in Children's Diseases, at St George's Hospital, SW1, Assistant Physician at Queens Hospital for Children, E2, 1936–38; Prof. of Pediatrics, Temple Univ. Med. Sch., Philadelphia, 1938–40; Research Prof. of Pediatrics, Univ. of Pennsylvania, 1940–66, Prof. of Paediatrics, 1966–69, now Emeritus. Corp. medal, Hahnemann Med. Coll., 1978. Elected Faculty Mem., Medical Students' Honor Soc. (AOA), 1981. *Publications:* Papers on Cytology and Blood diseases, Lead poisoning in children, Virus diseases of the central nervous system, Herpes simplex infections, Common exanthemata, History of measles and herpes. *Address:* 2 Franklin Town Boulevard 1605, Philadelphia, Philadelphia 19103, USA.

SCOTT, Sir Walter, 4th Bt, *cr* 1907; DL; *b* 29 July 1918; *s* of Sir Walter Scott, 3rd Bt, and Nancie Margot, *d* of S. H. March; *S* father, 1967; *m* 1945, Diana Mary, *d* of J. R. Owen; one *s* one *d*. *Educ:* Eton; Jesus College, Cambridge. Served 1st Royal Dragoons, 1939–46; Temp. Major, 1945. JP East Sussex, 1963; DL East Sussex, 1975. *Recreations:* field sports. *Heir:* *s* Walter John Scott, *b* 24 Feb. 1948. *Address:* Newhouse Farm, Chalvington, Hailsham, Sussex.

See also Duke of Hamilton and Brandon.

SCOTT, William Clifford Munro, MD; Consulting Psychiatrist, Montreal Children's Hospital, and Montreal General Hospital; *b* 11 March 1903; *o s* of late Rev. Robert Smyth Scott and late Katherine Munro Hopper; *m* 1934, Emmy Luise (marr. diss.), *er d* of late Hugo Böcking; two *s*; *m* 1970, Evelyn Freeman Fitch. *Educ:* Parkdale Collegiate, Toronto; University of Toronto. BSc (Med.), MD (Tor.), DPM (London), LMSSA. James H. Richardson Fellow, Department of Anat., 1922–24; Lectr in Anat. and Physiol., Margaret Eaton Sch. of Phys. Educ., Toronto, 1923–25; Post-Grad. Educ. in Psychiatry: Johns Hopkins Med. Sch., 1928–29; Boston Psychopathic Hosp., Harvard Univ. Med. Sch., 1929–30; Commonwealth Fund Fellow, Dept of Psychiatry, Harvard Univ., 1930–33; studied at Nat. Hosp., Queen Sq., London, 1931–32, and at Inst of Psycho-Analysis, London, 1931–33. Staff positions Maudsley Hosp., 1933–35, Cassel Hosp., 1935–38; private practice, 1938–. EMS Psychiatrist, Min. of Health, London, Sheffield and S Wales, 1939–46; Psychiatric Cons. to St Dunstan's, 1945. Mem. Cttee of Management, Inst. of Psychiatry (Univ. of London), 1951–53; Med. Dir London Clinic of Psycho-Analysis, 1947–53; Senior Psychotherapist, Bethlem Royal Hosp. and Maudsley Hosp., 1948–54; Teacher Inst. of Psychiatry (Univ. of London), 1948–54; Associate Professor in charge of Training in Psycho-Analysis, Department of Psychiatry, McGill University, Montreal, 1954–59; Post-Grad. Teacher (Psychiatry and Psycho-Analysis), 1945–. Chm. Psychotherapy and Social Psychiatry Section, Roy. Medico-Psychological Assoc., 1952–54; Pres. Brit. Psycho-Analytical Soc., 1953–54; Mem. Bd Dirs, Inst. of Psycho-Analysis, 1947–54 (Chm. 1954); Director of Canadian Inst. of Psycho-Analysis, 1965–67. FRCPsych; FBPsS; ex-Chm. Med. Sect. and Mem. Council, Brit. Psychological Soc.; ex-Mem. Cttee Sect. Psychiatry; Roy. Soc. Med.; Amer. Psychiatric Assoc.; Vice-Pres., Psychiatric Sect., BMA, 1952 and 1955; ex-Asst Ed. Internat. Jl Psycho-Analysis; ex-Asst Ed., Brit. Jl Med. Psychology. Mem., Montreal AAA. *Publications:* chiefly in Brit. Jl of Med. Psychol. and Internat. Jl of Psycho-Analysis. *Recreations:* people and books. *Address:* 488 Mount Pleasant, Westmount, Quebec, Canada H3Y 3H3.

SCOTT, Rear-Adm. Sir (William) David (Stewart), KBE 1977; CB 1974; Chief Polaris Executive, 1976–80; *b* 5 April 1921; *y s* of Brig. H. St G. Scott, CB, DSO and Ida Christabel Trower Scott (*née* Hogg); *m* 1952, Pamela Dorothy Whitlock; one *s* two *d*. *Educ:* Tonbridge. Naval Cadet, 1938; comd HM Submarines: Umbra, 1944; Satyr, 1945; Andrew, 1953; Thermopylae, 1955; comd HM Ships: Gateshead, 1951; Surprise, 1960; Adamant, 1963; Fife, 1969; Chief of British Navy Staff, Washington, UK Rep. to SACLANT, and Naval Attaché to USA, 1971–73; Deputy Controller, Polaris, 1973–76; Comdr 1956; Captain 1962; Rear-Adm. 1971. FInstD 1979. *Address:* c/o Lloyds Bank, 6 Pall Mall, SW1.

SCOTT, (William) Donald, CBE 1968; MA (Oxon); BSc (Yale); *b* 22 May 1903; *s* of late Reverend William Scott and Sara Jane (*née* Platt); *m* 1928, Muriel Barbara, *d* of late Louis F. Rothschild, NYC; two *s* one *d*. *Educ:* Taunton Sch., Taunton; Univ. College, Oxford (open scholar); Yale University, USA (Henry P. Davison Scholar). Hercules Powder Co., USA and Rotterdam, 1926–28; British Paint & Lacquer Co., Cowley, Oxford, 1928–35; ICI Ltd: Nobel Div., 1935–41; Dyestuffs Div., 1941–43; Southern Sales Region, Dep. Regional Manager, 1943–45; Regional Manager, 1945–51; Billingham Div., Jt Man. Dir, 1951–55; Main Board Director, 1954–65. Director, 1952–60, and Chairman, 1956–60, Scottish Agricultural Industries Ltd; Chm., Home Grown Cereals Authority, 1965–68; Director: Canadian Industries Ltd, 1957–62; Glaxo Group Ltd, 1965–68; Laporte Industries Ltd, 1965–68. Mem., Western Hemisphere Exports Council, 1961–64. FRSA 1968. *Recreations:* cricket, golf. *Address:* 42 Cumberland Terrace, Regent's Park, NW1 4HP.

SCOTT, Rev. W(illiam) G.; *see* Gardiner-Scott.

SCOTT, William (George), CBE 1966; RA 1984 (ARA 1977); painter; *b* 15 Feb. 1913; *e s* of William John and Agnes Scott; *m* 1937, Hilda Mary Lucas; two *s*. *Educ:* Enniskillen; Belfast Sch. of Art; Roy. Acad. Schools, London. Hon. Dr RCA, 1975; Hon. DLit: Belfast, 1976; Dublin, 1977. *Exhibitions:* Leger Gall., 1942, 1944, 1946; Leicester Gall., 1948, 1951; Hanover Gall., 1953, 1956, 1961, 1963, 1965, 1967; Martha Jackson Gall., NY, 1954, 1958, 1973; Venice Biennale, 1958; VIth Sao Paulo Biennial, 1953 and 1961, Brazil; Tate Gall., 1972; Gimpel Fils Gall., 1974, 1980, 1985 (retrospective); Martha Jackson Gall., NY, 1974; Moos Gall., Toronto, 1975, 1982; Kasahara Gall., Japan, 1976; Arts Council, Ulster (retrospectives), 1979, 1986; War Paintings 1942–46, Imperial War Mus., 1981; Gimpel Weidenhofer Gall., NY, 1983; Nat. Galleries of Scotland (retrospective), 1986; in British Council Exhibns in Europe; *works exhibited in:* Tate Gall.; Victoria and Albert Museum; Paris; New York; Toledo, USA; S Africa; Canada; Australia; S America. Feature film, Every Picture Tells a Story. Major prizewinner: RA Summer exhibns, 1985, 1986. *Address:* 13 Edith Terrace, Chelsea, SW10. *T:* 01–352 8044.

SCOTT, William Wootton; Under Secretary, Industry Department for Scotland, since 1985; *b* 20 May 1930; *s* of Dr Archibald C. Scott and Barbara R. Scott; *m* 1958, Margaret Chandler, SRN; three *s* one *d*. *Educ:* Kilmarnock Academy; Dollar Academy; Glasgow Univ. (MA, 1st Cl. Hons History). National Service in Royal Artillery, 1952–54. Assistant Principal, 1954, Principal, 1958, Min. of Transport and Civil Aviation; Principal Private Sec. to Minister of Transport, 1965–66; Asst Sec., 1966; Regional Controller (Housing and Planning), Northern Regional Office of DoE, 1971–74; joined Scottish Development Dept, 1974, Under Sec., 1978. *Publications:* occasional historical notes. *Recreations:* historical research, music, gardening, reading. *Address:* 13A Merchiston Place, Edinburgh EH10 4PL. *T:* 031–229 6768. *Club:* Royal Commonwealth Society.

SCOTT-BARRETT, Lt-Gen. Sir David (William), KBE 1976 (MBE 1956); MC 1945; GOC Scotland and Governor of Edinburgh Castle, 1976–79; Chairman, Army Cadet Force Association, since 1982; *b* 16 Dec. 1922; 2nd *s* of late Brig. Rev. H. Scott-Barrett, CB, CBE; *m* 1948, Marie Elise (*d* 1985), *d* of late Norman Morris; three *s*. *Educ:* Westminster School. Commnd Scots Guards, 1942; served NW Europe, 3rd Armd Bn Scots Guards; GSO3 Gds Div., 1948; Co. Comdr 2nd Bn Malaya, 1951; GSO2, 1st Div., 1955; DS Camberley, 1961; Comdt Gds Depot, 1963; GSO1, 4th Div. BAOR, 1965; comd 6 Inf. Bde BAOR, 1967; idc 1970; GOC Eastern District, 1971–73; GOC Berlin, 1973–75. Col Comdt, Scottish Div., 1976–79; Hon. Col, 205 (Scottish) Gen. Hosp., RAMC, TAVR, 1981–. *Address:* Hall House, Kersey, Ipswich, Suffolk IP7 6DZ. *T:* Hadleigh 822365. *Club:* Cavalry and Guards.

SCOTT BLAIR, George William, MA (Oxon), DSc (London); FRSC; FInstP; *b* 23 July 1902; *s* of late James and Jessie Scott Blair; *m* 1927, Margaret Florence Riddelsdell; no *c*. *Educ:* Charterhouse; Trinity College, Oxford. Ten years on Research Staff at Rothamsted Experimental Station; sometime Fellow on Rockefeller Foundation at University of Cornell; Head of Chemistry, later Physics Department National Institute for Research in Dairying, University of Reading, 1937–67; retired. Herbert Freundlich Medal, Deutsche

Rheol. Ges., 1954; Poiseuille Gold Medal, Internat. Soc. of Biorheology, 1969; Gold Medal, Brit. Soc. of Rheology, 1970. Membre d'honneur, Groupe français de Rhéologie, 1970. *Publications*: An Introduction to Industrial Rheology, 1938; A Survey of General and Applied Rheology, 1943, 2nd edn 1949; Measurements of Mind and Matter, 1950; (ed) Foodstuffs: their Plasticity, Fluidity, and Consistency, 1953; (with Prof. M. Reiner) Agricultural Rheology, 1957; Elementary Rheology, 1969; An Introduction to Biorheology, 1974; many papers in various scientific journals, 1925–82. *Recreations*: music, modern languages, philosophy of science. *Address*: Grist Cottage, Iffley, Oxford. *T*: Oxford 777462.

SCOTT-BOWDEN, Maj.-Gen. Logan, CBE 1972 (OBE 1964); DSO 1944; MC 1944 and Bar 1946; *b* 21 Feb. 1920; *s* of late Lt-Col Jonathan Scott-Bowden, OBE, TD, and Mary Scott-Bowden (*née* Logan); *m* 1950, Helen Jocelyn, *d* of late Major Sir Francis Caradoc Rose Price, 5th Bt, and late Marjorie Lady Price; three *s* three *d*. *Educ*: Malvern Coll.; RMA Woolwich. Commissioned Royal Engineers, 1939; served in War of 1939–45: Norway, 1940; Adjt, 53rd (Welsh) Div. RE, 1941; Liaison Duties in Canada and USA, 1942; Normandy Beach Reconnaissance Team (Major), 1943; OC 17 Fd Co RE, NW Europe, 1944; psc 1945; Singapore, Burma (Bde Maj. 98 Indian Inf. Bde), Palestine, Libya, 1946–51; Korea, 1953; jssc 1956; Arabia, 1958–60 (Lt-Col 1959); CRE 1st Div., BAOR, 1960; Head, UK Land Forces Planning Staff, 1963; Asst Dir, Def. Plans MoD (Col), 1964; Comd Trg Bde RE (Brig.), 1966; Nat. Defence Coll. (India), 1969; Comd Ulster Defence Regiment, 1970–71; Head of British Defence Liaison Staff, India, 1971–74, retd 1974. Col Comdt RE, 1975–80. *Recreations*: riding, ski-ing, travel. *Address*: c/o Lloyds Bank, 6 Pall Mall, SW1A 2AH.

SCOTT-BROWN, Walter Graham, CVO 1945; BA (Hon. Nat. Sci. Tripos), MD, BCh Cambridge; FRCS, FRCSE; Consulting Surgeon, Throat, Nose and Ear Department, Royal Free Hospital, and late Surgeon and Lecturer Royal National Throat, Nose and Ear Hospital; late Consulting Aurist and Laryngologist at East Grinstead Cottage Hospital and at the Maxillo-facial unit; and Lecturer to University of London; Fellow Royal Society Medicine and Member Otological and Laryngological Section; Fellow Medical Society of London; formerly engaged in consulting practice in London as oto-rhino-laryngologist; *e s* of late George A. Brown; *m* 1926, Margaret Affleck, *d* of G. K. Bannerman, High Wycombe; one *s* three *d*. *Educ*: Whitgift Sch.; Corpus Christi College, Cambridge; St Bartholomew's Hospital, London. Served European War, 1916–18 (despatches, wounded); France and Italy T Battery RHA and Captain and Adjutant 14th Brigade RHA 1918; Exhibitioner Corpus Christi College, Cambridge, 1919; Shuter Scholar St Bartholomew's Hospital, 1922; House Surgeon and Clinical Assistant in Ear, Nose and Throat Dept St Barts; Copeman Medallist for Scientific Research, Cambridge, 1932; Dorothy Temple Cross Research Fellowship (travelling), 1932, Berlin, Vienna, Stockholm, Copenhagen, etc. Mem., Pastel Soc. (former Hon. Sec.); exhibitions of paintings in London, Edinburgh and abroad; work in many private collections. *Publications*: Allergic affections of the Nose, 1945; (ed and contrib.) Diseases of the Ear, Nose and Throat, 2nd edn 1965; Methods of Examination in Ear, Nose and Throat, 1953; Broncho-oesophageal fistula, Cavernous sinus thrombosis: a fatal complication of minor facial sepsis, and other scientific and clinical publications. *Recreations*: fishing, painting. *Address*: Little Down, Monkwood, near Alresford, Hants SO24 0HB. *T*: Ropley 2314.

See also Earl of Orkney.

SCOTT-ELLIOT, Aydua Helen, CVO 1970 (MVO 1958); FSA; retired 1970; *b* 1909; *d* of late Lewis Alexander Scott-Elliot and of Princess Eydua Odescalchi. *Educ*: St Paul's Girls' School and abroad. Temp. Asst Civilian Officer, Admty, 1941–46; Keeper of Prints and Drawings, Royal Library, Windsor Castle, 1946–69. *Publications*: articles in Burlington Magazine, Apollo, etc. *Address*: Shaldon, Station Road, Mayfield, East Sussex. *T*: Mayfield 872079. *Club*: University Women's.

SCOTT ELLIOT, Major-General James, CB 1954; CBE 1945 (OBE 1940); DSO 1943, Bar 1944; HM Lieutenant of the County of Dumfries, 1962–67; *b* 6 Nov. 1902; *s* of late Lt-Col W. Scott Elliot, DSO and Marie Theresa Scott Elliot (*née* Lyon); *m* 1st, 1932, Cecil Margaret Du Buisson; one *s* two *d*; 2nd, 1971, Mrs Fay Courtauld. *Educ*: Wellington College; Sandhurst. 2nd Lieut KOSB, 1923; Capt. Argyll and Sutherland Highlanders, 1936; psc 1937–38; Major, 1940; served in Egypt, China, India, Malta, Palestine. War of 1939–45: France, N Africa, Sicily, Italy; Temp. Lt-Col 1941; Temp. Brig. 1944; despatches, 1945; Germany, 1946–47; War Office, 1948–49; Maj.-Gen., 1954; GOC 51st (Highland) Division and Highland Dist, 1952–56; retd, 1956. Colonel King's Own Scottish Borderers, 1954–61. President: Dumfries and Galloway Natural History and Antiquarian Soc., 1962–65; Soc. of Antiquaries of Scotland, 1965–67; Brit. Soc. of Dowsers, 1966–75. *Publication*: Dowsing One Man's Way, 1977. *Address*: 14 King Street, Emsworth, Hants PO10 7AZ. *T*: Emsworth 372401. *Club*: Army and Navy.

SCOTT-ELLIS, family name of **Baron Howard de Walden.**

SCOTT-HOPKINS, Major Sir James (Sidney Rawdon), Kt 1981; Member (C) European Parliament, since 1973, elected Member for Hereford and Worcester, since 1979; *b* 29 Nov. 1921; *s* of late Col R. Scott-Hopkins, DSO, MC and late Mrs Scott-Hopkins; *m* 1946, Geraldine Elizabeth Mary Hargreaves, CBE; three *s* one *d*. *Educ*: Eton; Oxford. Army, 1939–50; farming, 1950–59. MP (C) North Cornwall, 1959–66, Derbyshire West, Nov. 1967–1979; Joint Parliamentary Secretary, Ministry of Agriculture, Fisheries and Food, 1962–64. European Parliament: Dep. Leader Cons. Gp and Spokesman on Agric., 1973–79; Vice-Pres., 1976–79; Chm., European Democratic Gp, 1979–82. *Recreations*: riding, shooting. *Address*: 602 Nelson House, Dolphin Square, SW1; Bicknor House, English Bicknor, Coleford, Glos GL16 7PF. *Club*: Carlton.

See also T. J. Smith.

SCOTT-JAMES, Anne Eleanor, (Lady Lancaster); journalist; *b* 5 April 1913; *d* of R. A. Scott-James and Violet Brooks; *m* 1st, 1944, Macdonald Hastings (*d* 1982); one *s* one *d*; 2nd, 1967, Sir Osbert Lancaster, CBE (*d* 1986). *Educ*: St Paul's Girls' Sch.; Somerville Coll., Oxford (Class. Schol.). Editorial staff of Vogue, 1934–41; Woman's Editor, Picture Post, 1941–45; Editor, Harper's Bazaar, 1945–51; Woman's Editor, Sunday Express, 1953–57; Woman's Adviser to Beaverbrook Newspapers, 1959–60; Columnist, Daily Mail, 1960–68; freelance journalist, broadcasting, TV, 1968–. Member: Council, RCA, 1948–51, 1954–56; Council, RHS, 1978–82. *Publications*: In the Mink, 1952; Down to Earth, 1971; Sissinghurst: The Making of a Garden, 1975; (with Osbert Lancaster) The Pleasure Garden, 1977; The Cottage Garden, 1981; (with Christopher Lloyd) Glyndebourne—the Gardens, 1983; The Language of the Garden: a personal anthology, 1984. *Recreations*: reading, gardening, travelling looking at churches and flowers. *Address*: Rose Cottage, Aldworth, Reading, Berks.

See also M. M. Hastings.

SCOTT-MALDEN, (Charles) Peter, CB 1966; Member, Transport Tribunal, since 1978; *b* 29 June 1918; *e s* of late Gilbert Scott Scott-Malden and Phyllis Dorothy Scott-Malden (*née* Wilkinson); *m* 1941, Jean Honor Chamberlain Silver, *yr d* of late Lt-Col J. P. Silver, CBE, DSO, RAMC; two *s* two *d*. *Educ*: Winchester Coll. (Schol.); King's College, Cambridge (major Scholar). Entered Ministry of Transport, 1939. War of 1939–45; RAMC 1940–41; Glider Pilot Regiment, 1942–45. Min. of Transport (later DoE): Asst Sec., 1949; Under-Sec., 1959; Dep. Sec., 1968, retired, 1976. Member: Management Cttee, Hanover Housing Assoc., 1978–; Nat. Exec. Cttee, Abbeyfield Soc., 1983–. *Recreations*: music, golf. *Address*: 23 Burdon Lane, Cheam, Surrey. *T*: 01-642 7086.

SCOTT-MALDEN, Air Vice-Marshal (Francis) David (Stephen), DSO 1942; DFC 1941; RAF (Retd); *b* 26 Dec. 1919; *s* of late Gilbert Scott Scott-Malden and Phyllis Dorothy Wilkinson; *m* 1955, Anne Elizabeth Watson; two *s* two *d*. *Educ*: Winchester Coll. (Scholar; Goddard Scholar, 1938); King's Coll., Cambridge (Scholar, Sir William Browne Medal for Greek Verse, 1939). Joined Cambridge University Air Squadron, Nov. 1938; called up into RAFVR as Pilot Officer, Oct 1939; flying on operations, 1940–42, as Pilot Officer, Flight Lt, Squadron Leader, and Wing Comdr (DFC and Bar, DSO, Norwegian War Cross; Commander, Order of Orange Nassau, 1945). Visited International Youth Assembly at Washington, DC, as rep. of English Universities, and toured USA as member of United Nations delegation, Sept.-Nov. 1942. RAF Selection Board (Dep. Pres.), 1946; on staff of RAF College, 1946–48; Central Fighter Establishment, 1948; RAF Staff Coll., Bracknell, 1951; psa; RAF Flying Coll., 1954–55; pfc; Jt Planning Staff, Min. of Defence, 1955–57; Group Capt. 1958; Imperial Defence College, 1957–59; idc. Dep. Dir Plans, Air Ministry, 1959–61; Air Cdre 1962; Air Vice-Marshal, 1965. Department of Transport, 1966–78. *Recreations*: shooting, fishing, sailing. *Address*: Roughwood, 1 White House Gardens, Upgate, Poringland, Norwich, Norfolk NR14 7RU. *T*: Framingham Earl 4779.

SCOTT-MALDEN, Peter; *see* Scott-Malden, C. P.

SCOTT-MILLER, Commander Ronald, VRD 1942; RNVR (Retired); *b* 1 Nov. 1904; *s* of late Colonel Walter Scott-Miller, DL; *m* 1932, Stella Louise Farquhar, *d* of late Farquhar Deuchar, Shortridge Hall, Northumberland. *Educ*: Aldro School, Eastbourne; Uppingham. Joined London Division, RNVR, as Midshipman, 1924; War of 1939–45 (despatches): HMS Dunedin, Northern Patrol, 1939; HMS London, Atlantic, Russian Convoys, 1940–43; Combined Operations, Mediterranean, NW Europe, 1943–45. Commander, 1943; retired, 1946. MP (C) King's Lynn Division of Norfolk, 1951–59; Parliamentary Private Secretary: to Financial Secretary to Treasury, Dec. 1953–July 1954; to Minister of Transport, 1954–56; to Minister of Pensions and National Insurance, 1956–59. Trustee of Uppingham School, 1954–59. Freeman of the City of London, and Liveryman of Worshipful Company of Butchers, 1926. US Legion of Merit (Legionaire), 1943. *Recreations*: shooting, sailing. *Club*: Naval.

SCOTT-MONCRIEFF, William; Under-Secretary for Finance (Health), Department of Health and Social Security, 1977–82; *b* 22 Aug. 1922; *s* of Major R. Scott-Moncrieff and Mrs R. Scott-Moncrieff; *m* 1950, Dora Rosemary Knollys; two *d*. *Educ*: Trinity Coll., Glenalmond; Emmanuel Coll., Cambridge (BA Mech. Sciences). Served RE, 1941–65 (Lt-Col); DHSS (formerly Min. of Social Security), 1965–82. *Recreations*: golf, fishing. *Address*: Combe Cottage, Chiddingfold, Surrey. *T*: Wormley 2937.

SCOTT-SMITH, Catharine Mary, MA Cantab; Principal of Beechlawn Tutorial College, Oxford, 1966–71, retired; *b* 4 April 1912; *d* of Edward Montagu Scott-Smith and Catharine Lorance (*née* Garland). *Educ*: Wycombe Abbey School, Bucks; Girton College, Cambridge. Classics Mistress: St Katharine's School, Wantage, 1933–37; Godolphin School, Salisbury 1937–41; Classics Mistress and house-mistress, Headington School, Oxford, 1941–47, Second Mistress, 1946–47; Classics Mistress and house-mistress, Wycombe Abbey School, Bucks, 1947–55, Second Mistress, 1951–54; Headmistress of Westonbirt School, Tetbury, Gloucestershire, 1955–64. Member Council: Berkhamsted School for Girls; Berkhamsted School; Mem. Exec. Cttee, GBGSA, 1975–78. Pres., Wycombe Abbey School Seniors, 1974–79. *Address*: Graystones, Lower Waites Lane, Fairlight, Hastings, East Sussex. *T*: Hastings 813071. *Club*: University Women's.

SCOTT WHYTE, Stuart; *see* Whyte, J. S. S.

SCOTT WRIGHT, Prof. Margaret, PhD; Dean, 1979–84, and Professor, 1979–86, now Emeritus, Faculty of Nursing, University of Calgary; *b* 10 Sept. 1923; *d* of Ebenezer Wright and Margaret Greig Masson. *Educ*: Wallington County Grammar Sch.; Univ. of Edinburgh; St George's and Queen Charlotte's Hosps, London. MA Hons Hist., PhD and Dipl. Med. Services Admin, Edinburgh; SRN and SCM. Research Asst, Unilever Ltd, 1947–50; Staff Nurse and Sister, St George's Hosp., London, 1953–57; Boots Research Fellow in Nursing, Dept of Social Medicine, Univ. of Edinburgh, 1957–61; Rockefeller Fellow, USA, 1961–62; Deputy Matron, St George's Hosp., 1962–64; Matron, Middlesex Hosp., 1965–68; Dir, Dept of Nursing Studies, Univ. of Edinburgh, 1968–71; Prof. of Nursing Studies, Univ. of Edinburgh, 1972–76; Dir and Prof. of Sch. of Nursing, Dalhousie Univ., Nova Scotia, 1976–79. Second Vice-Pres., Internat. Council of Nurses, 1973–77. Margaret Scott Wright Annual Lecture in Nursing Research established in Faculty of Nursing, Univ. of Alberta, 1984. Silver Jubilee Medal, 1977. *Publications*: Experimental Nurse Training at Glasgow Royal Infirmary, 1963; Student Nurses in Scotland, 1968. *Recreations*: walking, music, reading, travel. *Address*: 25 The Walnuts, Branksome Road, Norwich, Norfolk. *Club*: University Women's.

SCOULLER, (John) Alan; Head of Group Employee Relations, Midland Bank, since 1986; *b* 23 Sept. 1929; *e s* of late Charles James Scouller and Mary Helena Scouller; *m* 1954, Angela Geneste Ambrose; two *s* five *d*. *Educ*: John Fisher Sch., Purley. Army service, Queen's Own Royal W Kent Regt, 1948–58 (Captain). Joined Unilever as management trainee, 1958; Personnel Man., Wall's Ice Cream, 1959–62; Domestos, 1963–66; Holpak, 1966–68; Commercial Plastics and Holpak, 1968–69; left Unilever to join Commn on Industrial Relations, 1969; Dir of Industrial Relations until 1973, full-time Comr, 1973–74; Asst Gen. Manager (Personnel) Industrial Relations, Midland Bank, 1975–85. Mem., Employment Appeal Tribunal, 1976–. *Address*: Shortlands, 32 Sollershott West, Letchworth, Herts. *T*: Letchworth 2781.

SCOURFIELD, Edward Grismond Beaumont D.; *see* Davies-Scourfield.

SCOWEN, Sir Eric (Frank), Kt 1973; MD, DSc, LLD; FRCP, FRCS, FRCPE; FRCPath; Director, Medical Professorial Unit, 1955–75; Physician to St Bartholomew's Hospital, 1946–75; Professor of Medicine, University of London, 1961–75 (Reader in Medicine, 1938–61); *b* 22 April 1910; *s* of late Frank Edward Scowen and Eleanor Betsy (*née* Barnes) (*d* 1969). *Educ*: City of London School; St Bartholomew's Hospital Medical College. St Bartholomew's Hospital: House Physician, 1931, Second Assistant, 1933, to Medical Professorial Unit; Baly Research Fell. in Clin. Med., 1933; First Asst to Med. Professorial Unit, 1935; Asst Dir of Med. Prof. Unit, and Asst Phys, 1937; Rockefeller Research Fell. to Columbia Univ., New York, 1937. Chairman: Council, Imperial Cancer Research Fund, 1967–82 (Vice-Pres., 1982); Cttee on Safety of Drugs, 1969– (Mem., 1963); British Pharmacopœia Commission, 1963–69; Cttee on Safety of Medicines, 1970–80; Cttee on the Review of Medicines, 1975–78; Poisons Bd (Home Office), 1976–83. Chm. Council, Sch. of Pharmacy, Univ. of London, 1979–. Hon. FPS 1984; Hon. Fellow, Sch. of Pharmacy, Univ. of London, 1986. *Publications*: various in medical and scientific journals. *Address*: Flat 77, 6/9 Charterhouse Square, EC1M 6EX. *T*: 01-251 3212. *Club*: Athenæum.

SCRAGG, Air Vice-Marshal Sir Colin, KBE 1963 (CBE 1953; MBE 1940); CB 1960; AFC 1942, Bar to AFC 1949; retired; *b* 8 Sept. 1908; *s* of late Lt A. Scragg, KRRC; *m* 1932, Phyllis Kathleen Rayner, Southampton; one *s* two *d*. *Educ:* King Edward VI School, Southampton. No 1 (Fighter) Squadron, 1931–34; served in a succession of flying training schools, including 34 FTS Canada, until 1943; War of 1939–45, Comd No 166 (Bomber) Squadron, 1944–45 (PoW, Germany). Transport Command Development Unit, 1946–49; Dep. Director, Operational Requirements, Air Min., 1950–53, Director, 1955–58; idc 1954; AOC No 23 Training Group, 1958–60; Deputy Controller Aircraft (RAF), Ministry of Aviation, 1960–64. Order of Orange Nassau (Netherlands), 1945. *Address:* Wedgwood, Pine Walk, Chilworth, Southampton. *T:* Southampton 769110.
See also R. K. Stott.

SCREECH, Michael Andrew, FBA 1981; Senior Research Fellow, All Souls College, Oxford, since 1984; *b* 2 May 1926; 3rd *s* of Richard John Screech, MM and Nellie Screech (*née* Maunder); *m* 1956, Anne (*née* Reeve); three *s*. *Educ:* Sutton High Sch., Plymouth; University Coll. London (BA 1950; Fellow, 1982); University of Montpellier, France. DLitt (Birmingham), 1958; DLit (London), 1982. Other Rank, Intelligence Corps (Far East), 1944–48. Asst, UCL, 1950–51; Birmingham Univ.: Lectr, 1951–58; Sen. Lectr., 1959–61; UCL: Reader, 1961–66; Personal Chair of French, 1966–71; Fielden Prof. of French Language and Lit., London Univ., 1971–84. Visiting Professor: Univ. of Western Ontario, 1964–65; Univ. of New York, Albany, 1968–69; Johnson Prof., Inst. for Research in the Humanities, Wisconsin, USA, 1978–79; Vis. Fellow, All Souls, Oxford, 1981; Edmund Campion Lectr, Regina, 1985; Wiley Visiting Prof., N Carolina, 1986. Member: Cttee, Warburg Inst., 1970–84; Comité d'Humanisme et Renaissance, 1971–. Chevalier dans l'Ordre National du Mérite, 1983; Hon. Citizen of the Ville de Tours, 1984. *Publications:* The Rabelaisian Marriage, 1958; L'Evangélisme de Rabelais, 1959; Tiers Livre de Pantagruel, 1964, repr. 1975; Les épistres et évangiles de Lefèvre d'Etaples, 1964; (with John Jollife) Les Regrets et autres oeuvres poëtiques (Du Bellay), 1966, repr. 1975; Marot évangélique, 1967; (with R. M. Calder) Gargantua, 1970; La Pantagrueline Prognostication, 1975; Rabelais, 1980; Ecstasy and the Praise of Folly, 1981; Montaigne and Melancholy, 1983; (with Anne Screech) Erasmus' Annotations on the New Testament: The Gospels, 1986; *edited reprints:* Le Nouveau Testament de Lefèvre d'Etaples, 1970; F. de Billon: Le Fort inexpugnable de l'Honneur du Sexe Femenin, 1970; Opuscules d'Amour par Héroët et autres divins poëtes, 1970; Amyot: Les œuvres morales et meslées de Plutarque, 1971; articles on Renaissance, Reformation, and the history of the classical and Christian tradition in: Bibliothèque d'Humanisme et Renaissance, Etudes rabelaisiennes, Jl of Warburg Inst., Bulletins des Colloques de Loches, etc.; contribs to several collective volumes. *Recreation:* walking. *Address:* 5 Swanston-field, Whitchurch-on-Thames RG8 7HP. *T:* Pangbourne 2513.

SCRIMGEOUR, James, CMG 1959; OBE 1944; *b* 8 June 1903; *s* of late Alexander Carron Scrimgeour and Helen May Scrimgeour (*née* Bird); *m* 1928, Winifred (*d* 1984), *d* of late Stephen Ward Giles; one *s*. *Educ:* Loretto School; Clare College, Cambridge. Member of Stock Exchange, 1929–69. Auxiliary Air Force, 1938–45; Air staff, Air Ministry, 1942–45. Senior Partner, J. & A. Scrimgeour, 1949–69; Chm., Hume Holdings Ltd, 1953–75; Dir, MEPC Ltd, 1946–69 (Vice Chm., 1965–69). Orig. Mem., Council of White Ensign Assoc., 1958–75. *Address:* c/o Royal Bank of Scotland, Burlington Gardens, W1. *Club:* Hawks (Cambridge).

SCRIMSHAW, Frank Herbert; *b* 25 Dec. 1917; *s* of late John Leonard Scrimshaw and Jessie Scrimshaw (*née* Sewell), Lincoln; *m* 1950, Joan Olive, *d* of Leslie Stephen Paskall, Felixstowe; one *s*. *Educ:* The City Sch., Lincoln; University Coll., Nottingham. BSc London. Joined Scientific Civil Service, 1939; various posts at RAE, Farnborough, and Blind Landing Experimental Unit, RAF Martlesham Heath, 1939–58; Dir of Scientific Research (Electronics), Min. of Aviation, 1959–61; RRE, Malvern: Head of Guided Weapons Group, 1961–65; Head of Mil. and Civil Systems Dept, 1965–67; Dir Gen., Electronics R&D, Min. of Technology, later MoD, 1967–72; Dep. Dir, RAE, Farnborough, 1972–78, retired. *Address:* 53 Feoffees Road, Somersham, near Huntingdon, Cambs. *T:* Ramsey (Cambs) 840143.

SCRIVEN, Wilton Maxwell, AO 1983; Chairman, State Clothing Corporation; *b* 10 Dec. 1924; *m* 1948, Marjorie Reta Shaw; two *s* two *d*. *Educ:* Univ. of Adelaide. BSc; FIEAust. Flying Officer RAAF; served with RAF Sqdn 622 Mildenhall, 1943–45. Engr, PMG's Dept, 1946–64; Regional Dir, Dept of Trade, 1965–66; Chm., Australian Industrial Research and Develt Grants Bd, 1967–68; Dir of Industrial Develt, S Australian Govt, 1969–76; Agent General for S Australia in London, 1977–80; Dir Gen., S Aust. Dept of Premier and Cabinet, 1980–83; Dir Gen., Dept of Lands, SA, 1983–84. *Recreations:* tennis, golf, flute. *Address:* 7 Knightsbridge Road, Leabrook, SA 5068, Australia. *Clubs:* Adelaide Rotary; Royal Wimbledon Golf, Mount Osmond Golf.

SCRIVENER, Anthony Frank Bertram, QC 1975; a Recorder of the Crown Court, since 1976; *b* 31 July 1935; *s* of Frank Bertram Scrivener and Edna Scrivener; *m* 1964, Irén Becze; one *s* one *d*. *Educ:* Kent Coll., Canterbury; University Coll. London (LLB). Called to Bar, Gray's Inn, 1958; Bencher, Lincoln's Inn, 1985. Lectr in Law, Ghana, 1959–61; practice as Junior, 1961–75. *Recreations:* tennis, chess, cricket. *Address:* 4 Willow Dene, Uxbridge Road, Pinner, Mddx HA5 3LT. *T:* 01–868 7678; 8 New Square, Lincoln's Inn, WC2A 3QP.

SCRIVENER, Ronald Stratford, CMG 1965; HM Diplomatic Service, retired; *b* 29 Dec. 1919; *s* of Sir Patrick Scrivener, KCMG; *m* 1st, 1947, Elizabeth Drake-Brockman (marr. diss., 1952); 2nd, 1962, Mary Alice Olga Sofia Jane Hohler, *d* of late Squadron-Leader Robert Charlton Lane; two step-*s* two step-*d*. *Educ:* Westminster School; St Catharine's College, Cambridge. Served with Royal Air Force Volunteer Reserve, 1940–45. Appointed HM Diplomatic Service, Dec. 1945. Served in Berlin, Buenos Aires, Vienna, Caracas, Berne, Bangkok; Ambassador to: Panama, 1969–70; Czechoslovakia, 1971–74; Asst Under-Sec. of State, FCO, 1974–76. Freeman of City of London, 1984; Liveryman, Scriveners' Co., 1984–. *Recreations:* travel, fishing. *Address:* 38 Lysia Street, SW6 6NG. *T:* 01–385 3013. *Clubs:* White's, Beefsteak.

SCRIVENOR, Sir Thomas (Vaisey), Kt 1960; CMG 1956; *b* 28 Aug. 1908; *e s* of late John Brooke Scrivenor, ISO, formerly Dir of Geological Survey, Malaya; *m* 1934, Mary Elizabeth Neatby; one *s* three *d*. *Educ:* King's School, Canterbury; Oriel College, Oxford (MA). Temp. Assistant Principal, Colonial Office, 1930–33; Assistant District Officer, Tanganyika, 1934–37; Assistant District Commissioner, Palestine, 1937–43; Assistant Lt-Governor, Malta, 1943–44; Principal, Colonial Office, 1944–46; Principal Asst Sec., Palestine, 1946–48; Civil Service Comr, Nigeria, 1948–53; Deputy High Commissioner for Basutoland, the Bechuanaland Protectorate, and Swaziland, 1953–60. Sec. to Exec. Council of Commonwealth Agric. Bureaux, 1961–73. *Address:* Vine Cottage, Minster Lovell, Oxon. *T:* Witney 75620.

SCROGGIE, Alan Ure Reith, CBE 1973 (OBE 1961); QPM 1968; one of HM's Inspectors of Constabulary 1963–75; *b* 1912; *s* of late Col W. R. J. Scroggie, CIE, IMS, Callander, Perthshire; *m* 1940, Shiela Catherine, *d* of late Finlay Mackenzie, Elgin, Morayshire; two *s*. *Educ:* Cargilfield Preparatory Sch.; Fettes Coll.; Edinburgh Univ. (BL). Joined Edinburgh City Police, 1930; Asst Chief Constable of Bucks, 1947–53; Chief Constable of Northumberland, 1953–63. OStJ 1955. *Recreations:* golf, fishing, shooting. *Address:* Fowler's Cottage, Abercrombie, by St Monan's, Fife. *Clubs:* Royal and Ancient (St Andrews); Golf House (Elie).

SCRUBY, Ven. Ronald Victor, MA; Archdeacon of Portsmouth, 1977–85, now Emeritus; *b* 23 Dec. 1919; 6th *s* of late Thomas Henry Scruby and late Florence Jane Scruby, Norwood Green, Southall, Middx; *m* 1955, Sylvia Tremayne Miles, *e d* of late Rear-Adm. Roderic B. T. Miles, Trotton, Sussex; two *s* one *d*. *Educ:* Southall Technical Coll.; Trinity Hall, Cambridge. Engineering Apprentice, London Transport, 1936–39. Royal Engineers, 1939–45; Capt. 1943. Trinity Hall, Cambridge, 1945–48; Cuddesdon Coll., Oxford, 1948–50. Asst Curate, Rogate, Sussex, 1950–53; Chaplain, King Edward VII Hosp., Midhurst, 1950–53; Chaplain, Saunders-Roe, Osborne, E Cowes, 1953–58; Vicar of Eastney, Portsmouth, 1958–65; Rural Dean of Portsmouth, 1960–65; Archdeacon of the Isle of Wight, 1965–77. *Address:* The Dower House, Rogate, Petersfield, Hants GU31 5EG. *T:* Rogate 325.

SCRUTON, Prof. Roger Vernon; Professor of Aesthetics, Birkbeck College, London, since 1985; *b* 27 Feb. 1944; *s* of John Scruton and Beryl C. Haynes; *m* 1973, Danielle Laffitte (marr. diss.). *Educ:* Jesus Coll., Cambridge (MA, PhD). Called to the Bar, Inner Temple, 1978. Res. Fellow, Peterhouse, 1969–71; Lectr in Philosophy, Birkbeck Coll., London, 1971–79, Reader, 1979–85. Editor, Salisbury Review, 1982–. *Publications:* Art and Imagination, 1974, 2nd edn 1982; The Aesthetics of Architecture, 1979; The Meaning of Conservatism, 1980; From Descartes to Wittgenstein, 1981; Fortnight's Anger (novel), 1981; The Politics of Culture, 1981; Kant, 1982; A Dictionary of Political Thought, 1982; The Aesthetic Understanding, 1983; (with Baroness Cox) Peace Studies: A Critical Survey, 1984; Thinkers of the New Left, 1985; (jtly) Education and Indoctrination, 1985; Sexual Desire, 1986; contribs to The Times, Guardian, etc. *Recreations:* music, architecture, literature. *Address:* Department of Philosophy, Birkbeck College, Malet Street, WC1. *Club:* Athenæum.

SCRUTTON, (Thomas) Hugh, CBE 1967; *b* 8 June 1917; *s* of late Rev. Canon Tom Burton Scrutton and Lesley Hay; *m* 1st, 1941, Helen Greeves (who obtd a divorce, 1952); one *d*; 2nd, 1960, Elizabeth Quayle. *Educ:* Charterhouse; King's Coll., Cambridge (MA). War Service, 1940–45, Army. Temporary Asst Keeper, Print Room, British Museum, 1946; Asst, 1947, and Director, 1948, Whitechapel Art Gallery; Director: Walker Art Gallery, Liverpool, 1952–70; Nat. Galls of Scotland, Edinburgh, 1971–77, retired; Penwith Galleries, St Ives, 1978–80. Pres., Museums Assoc., 1970–71. Hon. DLitt Liverpool, 1971. *Address:* Gwelmor, Venton Road, St Ives, Cornwall TR26 2AQ. *T:* Penzance 795735.

SCRYMGEOUR, family name of **Earl of Dundee.**

SCRYMGEOUR, Lord; Henry David; *b* 20 June 1982; *s* and *heir* of 12th Earl of Dundee, *qv*.

SCULLARD, Geoffrey Layton, OBE 1971; HM Diplomatic Service, retired; Head of Accommodation and Services Department, Foreign and Commonwealth Office, 1978–80; *b* 5 July 1922; *s* of late William Harold Scullard and late Eleanor Mary Scullard (*née* Tomkin); *m* 1945, Catherine Margaret Pinington; three *d*. *Educ:* St Olave's Grammar Sch. Joined Foreign Office, 1939. Served War (RAF Signals), 1942–46. Diplomatic service at: Stockholm, Washington, Baghdad, Los Angeles, Moscow. *Recreations:* fishing, golf. *Address:* 2 Albury Heights, 8 Albury Road, Guildford, Surrey GU1 2BT. *T:* Guildford 39915. *Club:* Bramley Golf.

SCULLY, Prof. Crispian Michael, FDS RCPSG; Professor of Stomatology, University of Bristol, since 1982; *b* 24 May 1945; *s* of Patrick and Rosaleen Scully; *m* Zoitsa; one *d*. *Educ:* Univ. of London; Univ. of Glasgow (BSc, BDS, MB BS, PhD). MRCS; LRCP; LDS RCS; MRCPath. MRC Research Fellow, Guy's Hosp., 1975–78; Lectr, 1979–81, Sen. Lectr, 1981–82, Univ. of Glasgow. Consultant Adviser in Dental Research, DHSS, 1986–. Mem., GDC, 1984–. *Publications:* Medical Problems in Dentistry, 1982; (jtly) Multiple Choice Questions in Dentistry, 1985; Handbook for Hospital Dental Surgeons, 1985; (jtly) Slide Interpretation in Oral Disease, 1986; contribs to learned jls. *Recreation:* music. *Address:* University Department of Oral Medicine and Oral Surgery, Bristol Dental Hospital and School, Lower Maudlin Street, Bristol BS1 2LY. *T:* Bristol 276201.

SCUPHAM, John, OBE 1961; retired as Controller of Educational Broadcasting, British Broadcasting Corporation, 1963–65; *b* 7 Sept. 1904; *s* of Roger Scupham and Kate Whittingham; *m* 1932, Dorothy Lacey Clark; one *s* one *d*. *Educ:* Market Rasen Gram. Sch.; Emmanuel Coll., Cambridge (Scholar). BA 1st Cl., History, 1926, 1st Cl. English, 1927 (Cantab). Various teaching posts, 1927–46. Joined staff of BBC as Educn Officer, 1946; Head of Educational Broadcasting, 1954. Member, Central Advisory Council for Education (England), 1961–63; Member, Church of England Board of Education, 1960–72. President, Educational Section of British Association, 1965–66. Mem. Council, Open Univ., 1969–78. DUniv, Open Univ., 1975. *Publications:* Broadcasting and the Community, 1967; The Revolution in Communications, 1970; Open Learning, 1976. *Recreations:* reading, gardening. *Address:* 9 Hillside Road, Thorpe St Andrew, Norwich. *T:* Norwich 35834.
See also A. R. H. Glover.

SCURR, Dr Cyril Frederick, CBE 1980; LVO 1952; FRCS, FFARCS; Consultant Anaesthetist, Westminster Hospital, since 1949; Hon. Anaesthetist, Hospital of SS John and Elizabeth, since 1952; *b* 14 July 1920; *s* of Cyril Albert Scurr and Mabel Rose Scurr; *m* 1947, Isabel Jean Spiller; three *s* one *d*. *Educ:* King's Coll., London; Westminster Hosp. MB, BS. Served War of 1939–45: RAMC, 1942–47, Major, Specialist Anaesthetist. Faculty of Anaesthetists: Mem. Bd, 1961–77; Dean, 1970–73; Mem. Council, RCS, 1970–73; Pres., Assoc. of Anaesthetists of GB and Ireland, 1976–78; Mem. Health Services Bd, 1977–80; Chm., Scientific Programme, World Congress of Anaesthetists, London, 1968; Pres., Anaesthetics Section, RSocMed, 1978–79; Mem. Adv. Cttee on Distinction Awards, 1973–84; Vice-Chm., Jt Consultants Cttee, 1979–81; past Member: Cttee, Competence to Practise; Standing Med. Adv. Cttee, DHSS. Hon. Mem., Société Française d'Anesthésie et de Réanimation; Academician, European Acad. of Anaesthesiology. Frederick Hewitt Lectr, RCS, 1971; Dudley Buxton Prize, RCS, 1977; Gold Medal, Faculty of Anaesthetists, 1983; John Snow Medal, Assoc. of Anaesthetists of GB and Ireland, 1984. Fellow, RSocMed; Hon. FFARCSI 1977. *Publication:* Scientific Foundations of Anaesthesia, 1970, 3rd edn 1982. *Recreations:* photography, gardening. *Address:* 16 Grange Avenue, Totteridge Common, N20 8AD. *T:* 01–445 7188.

SCUSE, Dennis George, MBE 1957; TD 1946; Consultant, Hanson Trust, since 1984; Managing Director, Dennis Scuse Ltd, PR, TV and Radio Consultants, since 1976; *b* 19 May 1921; *yr s* of late Charles H. and Katherine Scuse; *m* 1948, Joyce Evelyn, *yr d* of late Frank and Frances Burt; one *s*. *Educ:* Park Sch., Ilford; Mercers' Sch., London. Joined Martins Bank, 1937. TA (RA), 1938; mobilised, Sept. 1939. Served War, commissioned 78th (HyAA) Regt, RA, 1940. Air Defence of Gt Britain, 1940–41; Command Entertainment Officer, Ceylon Army Comd, 1942; subseq. 65th (HyAA) Regt, in MELF and CMF, 1943–44; joined Army Broadcasting Service, CMF: commanded stations in Bari, Rome and Athens, 1945–46; demobilised, Sept. 1946. Joined Overseas Div. BBC and seconded to War Office for Forces Broadcasting Service in Benghasi and Canal Zone; Chief Programme Officer, 1947–48; Asst Dir, British Forces Network, Germany, 1949–50; Dir, 1950–57. Introduced "Two-Way Family Favourites", 1952–57; Sen. Planning Asst, BBC-TV, 1958–59; Chief Asst (Light Entertainment), BBC-TV, 1960; Chief Asst (TV), BBC New York Office, Sept. 1960; BBC Rep. in USA, July 1962; Gen. Manager, BBC-TV Enterprises, 1963–72, and BBC Radio Enterprises, 1968–72. Trident Management Ltd, 1972; Man. Dir, Trident Internat. TV Enterprises Ltd, 1972–76. *Publications:* numerous articles on broadcasting, television programme exports, etc. *Recreations:* wine making, watching television. *Address:* 2 York House, Courtlands, Sheen Road, Richmond, Surrey. *T:* 01–948 4737. *Club:* Royal Greenjackets.

SCUTT, Robin Hugh, CBE 1976; Chairman, United Media Ltd, since 1983; Director: National Video Corporation, since 1981; London Weekend Television Ltd, since 1981; Lella Productions plc, since 1980; Suffolk Group Radio plc, since 1981; Turner Programme Services, since 1985; Chairman, Saxon Radio, Bury St Edmunds, since 1981; *b* Sandgate, Kent, 24 Oct. 1920; *s* of late Rev. A. O. Scutt, MA and Freda M. Scutt (*née* Palmer); *m* 1st, 1943, Judy Watson (marr. diss. 1960); two *s*; 2nd, 1961, Patricia A. M. Smith. *Educ:* Fonthill; Bryanston; Jesus Coll., Cambridge (MA Mod. Lang.). Served Intell. Corps, 1941–42 (invalided out). BBC Eur. Service (French Section), 1942; BBC TV Outside Broadcasts Producer, 1955; BBC Paris Rep., 1958; Gen. Man., Trans Europe Television, 1962; rejoined BBC TV Outside Broadcasts, 1963; Asst Head of BBC TV Presentation (BBC1), 1966; Controller: BBC Radio 1 and 2, 1967–68; BBC 2, 1969–74; Development TV, 1974–77; Dep. Man. Dir, BBC TV, 1977–80. Chm., New Technologies Working Party, Broadcast Res. Unit, BFI, 1981–83. TV Exec. Producer for National Video Corp.: Tales of Hoffmann, Peter Grimes, La Bohème, Fanciulla del West, Manon Lescaut, Die Fledermaus, Der Rosenkavalier, Nutcracker and Don Carlo, Covent Gdn, 1981–85; Ernani, Il Trittico, I Lombardi, Andrea Chenier, Aida and Madame Butterfly, La Scala, 1982–86; Otello, Turandot, Madame Butterfly, Tosca, Il Trovatore and Attila, Verona, 1982–85; Don Quixote, and ABT at the Met, and at San Francisco, Amer. Ballet Theatre, 1983–85; Natasha (Natalia Makarova), and Carols for Christmas, 1985. Producer, Napoli, Royal Theatre Copenhagen. Mem., BAFTA. Fellow, Royal TV Soc., 1978, and Gold Medallist, 1980; FRSA 1984. Officier de la Légion d'Honneur, France, 1983. *Recreations:* music, theatre, gardening. *Address:* The Abbey Cottage, Cockfield, Suffolk. *Clubs:* Garrick, St James.

SEABORG, Glenn Theodore; University Professor of Chemistry, University of California, Berkeley, since 1971; *b* 19 April 1912; *s* of Herman Theodore and Selma Erickson Seaborg; *m* 1942, Helen Lucille Griggs; four *s* two *d*. *Educ:* Univ. of Calif, Los Angeles (BA); Univ. of Calif, Berkeley (PhD). University of California, Berkeley: Res. Associate (with Prof. Gilbert N. Lewis), Coll. of Chem., 1937–39; Instr, Dept of Chem., 1939–41, Asst Prof., 1941–45, Prof., 1945–71; Chancellor, 1958–61; Lawrence Berkeley Laboratory: Associate Dir, 1954–61, and 1972–; Dir, Nuclear Chem. Div., 1946–58, and 1972–75; Dir, Lawrence Hall of Science, 1982–; Head, Plutonium Chem. Metall. Lab., Univ. of Chicago, 1942–46; Chm., US Atomic Energy Commn, 1961–71. Member, US Delegns to: 3rd (Chm.) and 4th (Chm. and Pres.) UN Internat. Confs on Peaceful Uses of Atomic Energy, Geneva, 1964 and 1971; 5–15th annual Gen. Confs of Internat. Atomic Energy Agency, 1961–71; USSR, for signing of Memorandum on Cooperation in the Field of Utilization of Atomic Energy for Peaceful Purposes (Chm.), 1963; USSR, for signing of Limited Test Ban Treaty, 1963. Member: Nat. Council on Marine Resources and Engineering Development, 1966–71; Nat. Aeronautics and Space Council, 1961–71; Fed. Council for Science and Tech., 1961–71; Pres.'s Cttee on Manpower, 1964–69; Fed. Radiation Council, 1961–69; Nat. Sci. Bd, Nat. Sci. Foundn, 1960–61; Pres.'s Science Adv. Cttee, 1959–61; 1st Gen. Adv. Cttee, US Atomic Energy Commn, 1946–50; Commn on the Humanities, 1962–65; Scientific Adv. Bd, Robert A. Welch Foundn, 1957–; Bd of Dirs, Nat. Educnl TV and Radio Centre, 1958–64, 1967–70; Bd of Dirs, World Future Soc., 1969–; Nat. Programming Council for Public TV, 1970–72; Bd of Governors, Amer.-Swedish Hist. Foundn, 1972–; Steering Cttee, Chem. Educn Material Study (Chm.), 1959–74; Nat. Cttee on America's Goals and Resources, Nat. Planning Assoc., 1962–64; Electoral Coll. Hall of Fame for Great Americans, 1969–; California Inventors' Hall of Fame, 1983–; Council on Foreign Relations, 1965–; Bd of Trustees: Pacific Science Centre Foundn, 1962–; Science Service, 1965– (Pres., 1966–); Amer.-Scandinavian Foundn, 1968–; Educnl Broadcasting Corp., 1970–73; Amer. Assoc. for the Advancement of Science (Pres. 1972, Chm. 1973); Amer. Chem. Soc. (Pres., 1976); Chm. Bd, Swedish Council of America, 1978–. Mem. and Hon. Mem., Fellow and Hon. Fellow, numerous scientific and professional socs and instns, Argentina, German Dem. Republic., German Fed. Republic, Japan, Poland, Spain, Sweden, UK, USA, USSR; Foreign Mem., Royal Society, 1985. Holds over 49 hon. doctorates from univs and colls. Named one of America's 10 Outstanding Young Men, 1947. Awards (1947–) include: Nobel Prize for Chemistry (jtly), 1951; Perkin Medal (Amer. Sect. Soc. Chem. Ind.), 1957; USAEC Enrico Fermi Award, 1959; Priestley Meml Award, 1960; Franklin Medal (Franklin Inst. of Philadelphia), 1963; Award in Pure Chem., 1947, Charles Lathrop Parsons Award, (Amer. Chem. Soc.), 1964; Chem. Pioneer Award, 1968, Gold Medal Award, (Am. Inst. of Chemists), 1973; Arches of Science Award (Pacific Science Centre, Seattle), 1968; John R. Kuebler Award, Alpha Chi Sigma, 1978; Priestley Medal, Amer. Chem. Soc., 1979; Henry DeWolf Smyth Award, Amer. Nuclear Soc., 1982; Actinide Award, 1984; Great Swedish Heritage Award, 1984. Officer, French Legion of Honour, 1973. Co-discoverer of: nuclear energy source isotopes Pu-239 and U-233; elements (1940–74): 94, plutonium; 95, americium; 96, curium; 97, berkelium; 98, californium; 99, einsteinium; 100, fermium; 101, mendelevium; 102, nobelium; element 106. *Publications:* (jtly) The Chemistry of the Actinide Elements, 1958; The Transuranium Elements (Silliman Lectures), 1958; (jtly) Elements of the Universe, 1958; Man-made Transuranium Elements, 1963; (jtly) Education and the Atom, 1964; (jtly) The Nuclear Properties of the Heavy Elements, 1964; (jtly) Oppenheimer, 1969; (jtly) Man and Atom, 1971; Nuclear Milestones, 1972; (ed) Transuranium Elements—Products of Modern Alchemy, 1978; Kennedy, Khrushchev and the Test Ban, 1981; (jtly) Nuclear Chemistry; contrib. numerous papers on nuclear chem. and nuclear physics, transuranium elements, high energy nuclear reactions and educn in Physical Rev., Jl Amer. Chm. Soc., Annual Rev. of Nuclear Science, etc. *Recreations:* golf, reading, hiking. *Address:* (business) Lawrence Berkeley Laboratory, University of California, Berkeley, Calif 94720, USA; (home) 1154 Glen Road, Lafayette, Calif 94549, USA. *Clubs:* Faculty (Univ. Calif, Berkeley); Commonwealth Club of California, Bohemian (San Francisco); Chemists (NY); Cosmos, University (Washington).

SEABORN, Most Rev. Robert Lowder; Chancellor, University of Trinity College, Toronto, since 1983; *b* 9 July 1911; *s* of Rev. Richard Seaborn and Muriel Kathleen Reid; *m* 1938, Mary Elizabeth Gilchrist; four *s* one *d*. *Educ:* Univ. of Toronto Schs; Trinity Coll., Univ. of Toronto (MA); Oxford Univ. Deacon, 1934; Priest, 1935; Asst Curate, St Simon's, Toronto, 1934–36; Asst Curate, St James's Cathedral, Toronto, 1937–41; Rector, St Peter's, Cobourg, Ont., 1941–48; Chaplain, Canadian Army, 1942–45 (Padre Canadian Scottish Regt); Dean of Quebec and Rector of Parish of Quebec, 1948–57; Rector, St Mary's, Kerrisdale, Vancouver, BC, 1957–58; Asst Bishop of Newfoundland, 1958–65, Coadjutor, June-Dec. 1965; Bishop of Newfoundland, 1965–75, of Eastern Newfoundland and Labrador, 1975–80; Archbishop of Newfoundland and Metropolitan of Ecclesiastical Province of Canada, 1975–80; Bishop Ordinary (Anglican) to Canadian Forces, 1980–86. Croix de Guerre avec étoile de vermeil (French), 1945. DD, (*jure dignitatis*), Trinity Coll., 1948; DCL (*hc*), Bishop's Univ., 1962; Hon. LLD Meml Univ. of Newfoundland, 1972; Hon. DD Montreal Diocesan Theological Coll., 1980. *Publication:* Faith in our Time, 1963. *Recreations:* camping, golf. *Address:* 247 Lake Street, Cobourg, Ont K9A 1R6, Canada.

SEABROOK, Air Vice-Marshal Geoffrey Leonard, CB 1965; *b* 25 Aug. 1909; *s* of late Robert Leonard Seabrook; *m* 1949, Beryl Mary (*née* Hughes); one *s* one *d*. *Educ:* King's Sch., Canterbury. Commissioned in RAF (Accountant Branch), 1933; served in: Middle East, 1935–43; Bomber Command, 1943–45; Transport Command, 1945–47; Iraq, 1947–49; Signals Command, 1949–51; Air Ministry Organisation and Methods, 1951–53; Home Command Group Captain Organisation, 1953–56; Far East Air Force, 1957–59; idc 1960; Director of Personnel, Air Ministry, 1961–63; Air Officer Administration, HQ, RAF Tech. Trg Comd, 1963–66; retired June 1966. Air Cdre 1961; Air Vice-Marshal, 1964. Head of Secretarial Branch, Royal Air Force, 1963–66. FCA 1957 (Associate, 1932). *Recreations:* sailing, golf. *Address:* Long Pightle, Piltdown, Uckfield, E Sussex. *T:* Newick 2322. *Clubs:* Royal Air Force; Piltdown Golf.

SEABROOK, Robert John; QC 1983; a Recorder, since 1985; *b* 6 Oct. 1941; *s* of Alan Thomas Pertwee Seabrook, MBE and late Mary Seabrook (*née* Parker); *m* 1965, Liv Karin Djupvik, Bergen, Norway; two *s* one *d*. *Educ:* St George's Coll., Salisbury, Southern Rhodesia; University Coll., London (LLB). Called to the Bar, Middle Temple, 1964. The Recorder, SE Circuit Bar Mess, 1982–84. Liveryman, Curriers' Co., 1972. *Recreations:* travel, listening to music, wine, riding. *Address:* (chambers) 1 Crown Office Row, Temple, EC4Y 7HH. *T:* 01–353 1801; (home) 41 Surrenden Road, Brighton, East Sussex BN1 6PQ. *T:* Brighton 505491.

SEABROOKE, George Alfred; Director, The Polytechnic, Wolverhampton, 1977–85; *b* 8 Dec. 1923; *s* of late John Arthur Seabrooke and Elsie Seabrooke; *m* 1945, Evelyn Sargent; two *s*. *Educ:* Keighley Boys' Grammar Sch.; Bradford Technical Coll.; Stoke-on-Trent Tech. Coll.; King's Coll., London Univ. FBIM 1978. National Service, 1946–48. Post Office Engrg Dept, 1940–50; Estate Duty Office, Comrs of Inland Revenue, 1950–56; SW London Coll. of Commerce, 1956–60; Trent Polytechnic, Nottingham (and precursor Colls), 1960–73; Dep. Dir, NE London Polytechnic, 1974–77. *Publications:* Air Law, 1964; contrib. learned jls. *Recreations:* music, cricket, rugby. *Address:* 45 Codsall Road, Tettenhall, Wolverhampton WV6 9QD. *T:* Wolverhampton 751515.

SEABY, Wilfred Arthur; retired museum official; Director, Ulster Museum (previously Belfast Museum and Art Gallery), 1953–70; Numismatic Section, Department of Technology and Local History, 1970–73; *b* 16 Sept. 1910; *y s* of late Allen W. Seaby, sometime Prof. of Art, Univ. of Reading; *m* 1937, Nora, *d* of late A. E. Pecover, Reading; two *s* one *d*. *Educ:* Wycliffe College; Reading University, College of Art. Dip. Museums Assoc., 1939. Served War of 1939–45, Royal Air Force, 1940–46 (Flt-Lt). B. A. Seaby Ltd, 1927–30; Reading, Birmingham, and Taunton Museums, 1931–53. FSA 1948. Hon. MA QUB, 1971. *Publication:* Hiberno-Norse Coins in the Ulster Museum, 1984. *Recreation:* water colour painting. *Address:* 36 Ladbrook Road, Solihull, West Midlands.

SEAFIELD, 13th Earl of, *cr* 1701; **Ian Derek Francis Ogilvie-Grant;** Viscount Seafield, Baron Ogilvy of Cullen, 1698; Viscount Reidhaven, Baron Ogilvy of Deskford and Cullen, 1701; *b* 20 March 1939; *s* of Countess of Seafield (12th in line), and Derek Studley-Herbert (who assumed by deed poll, 1939, the additional surnames of Ogilvie-Grant; he *d* 1960); *S* mother, 1969; *m* 1st, 1960, Mary Dawn Mackenzie (marr. diss., 1971), *er d* of Henry Illingworth; two *s*; 2nd, 1971, Leila, *d* of Mahmoud Refaat, Cairo. *Educ:* Eton. *Recreations:* shooting, fishing, tennis. *Heir:* *s* Viscount Reidhaven, *qv*. *Address:* Old Cullen, Cullen, Banffshire. *T:* Cullen 40221. *Club:* White's.

SEAGA, Rt. Hon. Edward Philip George, PC 1982; Prime Minister of Jamaica, and Minister of Finance and Planning, Mining and Energy, and Culture, since 1980; MP for Western Kingston, since 1962; Leader of the Jamaica Labour Party, since 1974; *b* 28 May 1930; *s* of late Philip Seaga and of Erna (*née* Maxwell); *m* 1965, Marie Elizabeth (*née* Constantine) (Miss Jamaica, 1964); two *s* one *d*. *Educ:* Wolmers Boys' Sch., Kingston, Jamaica; Harvard Univ., USA (BA Social Science, 1952). Did field research in connection with Inst. of Social and Econ. Res., University Coll. of the West Indies (now Univ. of the WI), Jamaica, on develt of the child, and revival spirit cults, by living in rural villages and urban slums; proposed estabt of Unesco Internat. Fund for Promotion of Culture, 1971, and is founding mem. of its Administrative Council. Nominated to Upper House (Legislative Council), 1959 (youngest mem. in its history); Asst Sec., Jamaica Labour Party, 1960–62, Sec., 1962; Minister of Develt and Social Welfare, 1962–67; Minister of Finance and Planning, 1967–72; Leader of Opposition, 1974–80. Director: Consulting Services Ltd, to 1979; Capital Finance Co. Ltd, to 1979. Hon. LLD Miami, 1981. Grand Collar, and Golden Mercury Internat. Award, Venezuela, 1981; Gold Key Award, Avenue of the Americas, NYC, 1981; Grand Cross, Order of Merit of Fed. Rep. of Germany, 1982. Religion Anglican. *Publications:* The Development of the Child; Revival Spirit Cults. *Recreations:* classical music, reading, shooting, hockey, football, cricket, tennis, swimming. *Address:* (office) Jamaica House, Kingston, Jamaica, West Indies. *T:* 927–7854; (home) Vale Royal, Kingston. *Clubs:* Kingston Cricket, Jamaica Gun (Jamaica).

SEAGER, family name of **Baron Leighton of Saint Mellons.**

SEAGER, Major Ronald Frank, RA, retired; Executive Director, RSPCA, 1971–78 (Secretary, 1966–71); Advisory Director, International Society for Protection of Animals; *b* 27 May 1918; *s* of Frank Seager and Lilias K. (*née* Parr); *m* 1941, Josephine, *d* of Rev. R. M. Chadwick; one *s* one *d*. *Educ:* St Albans School. Royal Artillery (HAC), 1939; commnd, 1941; Italy, 1944–45; seconded Royal Pakistan Artillery, 1949–50; served Korean War, 1953–54; Perm. Pres. Courts Martial, Eastern Command, 1960–63. Joined RSPCA, 1963. *Recreations:* golf, gardening. *Address:* Merle Cottage, Church Street, Yetminster, Sherborne, Dorset DT9 6LG. *T:* Yetminster 872111.

SEAGROATT, Conrad; QC 1983; barrister-at-law; a Recorder of the Crown Court, since 1980; *b* 17 Aug. 1938; *s* of E. G. Seagroatt, Solicitor of the Supreme Court, and Barbara C. Seagroatt; *m* Cornelia Mary Anne Verdegaal; five *d*. *Educ:* Solihull Sch., Warwicks; Pembroke Coll., Oxford (MA Hons). Admitted Solicitor of the Supreme Court, 1967; called to the Bar, Gray's Inn, 1970; Mem., Senate of the Inns of Court and the Bar, 1980–83. *Recreations:* running, hockey. *Address:* 1 King's Bench Walk, Temple, EC4Y 7DB. *T:* 01–353 8436.

SEAL, Dr Barry Herbert; Member (Lab) Yorkshire West, European Parliament, since 1979; Chairman, Economic, Monetary and Industrial Policy Committee, European Parliament, since 1984; *b* 28 Oct. 1937; *s* of Herbert Seal and Rose Anne Seal; *m* 1963, Frances Catherine Wilkinson; one *s* one *d*. *Educ:* Heath Grammar Sch., Halifax; Univ. of Bradford (MSc, PhD); European Business Sch., Fontainebleau. CEng, MIChemE; FBIM.

Served RAF, 1955–58. Lab. Asst, finally Chem. Engr, ICI Ltd, 1958–64; Develt Engr, subseq. Div. Chem. Engr, Murex Ltd, 1964–68; Sen. Engr, BOC Internat., 1968–71; Principal Lectr in Systems, Huddersfield Polytechnic, 1971–79; consultant on microprocessors. Parly Candidate (Lab), Harrogate, 1974; Leader, Bradford Met. Dist Council Labour Gp, 1976–79. *Publications:* papers on computer and microprocessor applications. *Recreations:* running, reading, tv. *Address:* (office) City Hall, Bradford, West Yorks BD1 1HY. *T:* Bradford 752091; (home) 5 Paddock Close, Wyke, Bradford, West Yorks. *T:* Bradford 671888.

SEAL, Richard Godfrey, FRCO; Organist of Salisbury Cathedral, since 1968; *b* 4 Dec. 1935; *s* of William Godfrey Seal and Shelagh Seal (*née* Bagshaw); *m* 1975, Dr Sarah Helen Hamilton; two *s*. *Educ:* New Coll. Choir Sch., Oxford; Cranleigh Sch., Surrey; Christ's Coll., Cambridge (MA). FRCO 1958. Asst Organist: St Bartholomews the Great, London, 1960–61; Chichester Cathedral (and Dir of Music, Prebendal Sch.) Sussex, 1961–68. *Address:* 5 The Close, Salisbury, Wilts. *T:* Salisbury 336828. *Club:* Crudgemens (Godalming).

SEALE, Douglas (Robert); producer, actor and director (stage); *b* 28 Oct. 1913; *s* of Robert Henry Seale and Margaret Seale (*née* Law). *Educ:* Rutlish. Studied for stage at Royal Academy of Dramatic Art and became an actor. First appeared as Starling in The Drums Begin, Embassy, 1934; subseq. in Repertory. Served in Army, 1940–46, commissioned in Royal Signals. Joined Shakespeare Memorial Theatre Company, Stratford-on-Avon season's 1946 and 1947. From 1948 produced at Birmingham Repertory Theatre, at The Bedford, Camden Town (under Donald Wolfit), and again at Birmingham where he became Director of Productions, 1950. Later Productions include: Figaro and Fidelio, Sadler's Wells; Shaw's Caesar and Cleopatra at Birmingham Rep. Theatre, 1956 (later presented at Théâtre Sarah Bernhardt, Paris, and Old Vic). Season 1957: The Tempest, at Univ. of BC, Vancouver; King John, Stratford-on-Avon; Richard III, Old Vic; Trilogy of Henry VI, Old Vic; Season 1958; The World of the Wonderful Dark, for first Vancouver Festival; King Lear, Old Vic; Much Ado about Nothing, Stratford-on-Avon. Old Vic productions as Associate Director, 1958: Julius Caesar; Macbeth; 1959: Molière's Tartuffe; Pinero's The Magistrate; Dryden-Davenant-Purcell version of Shakespeare's The Tempest; St Joan; She Stoops to Conquer, 1960, Landscape with Figures, by Cecil Beaton, Dublin Festival, 1960: King John, Festival Theatre, Stratford, Ontario, 1960; Director of tours in Russia and Poland for Old Vic Theatre Co., 1961: prod. The Importance of Being Earnest, New York, 1962; The Comedy of Errors, Henry V, Stratford, Connecticut, 1963; Regent's Prof., Univ. of Calif. at Santa Barbara, Jan.-June 1965; Artistic Director, Center Stage, Baltimore, Maryland, USA, 1965–67; directed and acted, Meadowbrook Theater, Rochester, Mich, 1968; co-producing Director, Goodman Theater, Chicago, 1969–72 (productions incl.: Soldiers, Marching Song, Heartbreak House (Jefferson award), The Tempest, Twelfth Night, own musical adaptation of Lady Audley's Secret); directed and acted in Lady Audley's Secret, Washington and New York, 1972; Giovani, in Pirandello's Henry IV, New York, 1973; directed: King Lear, Marin Shakespeare Festival, San Francisco; Doll's House and Look Back in Anger, Cleveland, Getting Married, New Haven, 1973; Sorin in The Seagull, Seattle; Artistic Dir, Philadelphia Drama Guild, 1974–80; The Last Few Days of Willie Callendar, Philadelphia, 1979; Summer, Philadelphia, 1980; directed at Shaw Festival, Ont.: Too True to be Good, 1974; Caesar and Cleopatra, 1975; Lady Audley's Secret, 1978; Director: The Winslow Boy, NY, 1980, and tour; The Dresser, Witness for the Prosecution, Miami, 1982; acted in: Frankenstein, NY, 1980; The Dresser, NY, 1981; (film) Amadeus, 1983; Noises Off, 1983; (film) Heaven Help Us, 1984; (TV series) Lucy Arnaz Show, 1985; (TV) Amazing Stories, 1985. Has also produced for TV. Hon. DFA Washington Coll., Md, 1967. Mensa Annual Achievement Award, 1979. *Address:* Apt 14c, One University Place, New York, NY 10003, USA.

SEALE, Sir John Henry, 5th Bt, *cr* 1838; RIBA; *b* 3 March 1921; *s* of 4th Bt; *S* father, 1964; *m* 1953, Ray Josephine, *d* of Robert Gordon Charters, MC, Christchurch, New Zealand; one *s* one *d*. *Educ:* Eton; Christ Church, Oxford. Served War of 1939–45: Royal Artillery, North Africa and Italy; Captain, 1945. ARIBA 1951. *Heir: s* John Robert Charters Seale, *b* 17 Aug. 1954. *Address:* Slade, Kingsbridge, Devon TQ7 4BL. *T:* Kingsbridge 550226.

SEALES, Peter Clinton; Consultant to Saatchi & Saatchi Compton Plc, since 1984; Chairman, PSL Associates, since 1978; *b* 1 Nov. 1929; *s* of James Seales, Solicitor, and Angela Seales; *m* 1955, Bernadette Rogers; one *d* (and one *d* decd). Called to the Bar, King's Inns, 1953. Group Marketing Dir, Raleigh Industries Ltd, 1962–74; Dir, E Midlands Electricity Board, 1972–74; Man. Dir, Potterton International, and Chm. overseas subsidiaries in France, Belgium, Germany, Holland and Japan, 1974–76; International Marketing Dir, Ever Ready Holdings, 1977. Chief Executive: Sea Fish Industry Authority, 1982–83; Operation Raleigh, 1984–85. *Publications:* various articles on commercial matters. *Recreations:* daughter's riding, sailing, music. *Address:* 78 Northumberland Road, Leamington Spa, Warwickshire. *T:* Leamington Spa 315624. *Clubs:* White Elephant, Wig and Pen, Institute of Directors; Leamington Real Tennis.

SEAMAN, Christopher; international conductor; Principal Conductor, BBC Robert Mayer concerts, since 1978; *b* 7 March 1942; *s* of late Albert Edward Seaman and Ethel Margery Seaman (*née* Chambers). *Educ:* Canterbury Cathedral Choir Sch.; The King's Sch., Canterbury; King's Coll., Cambridge. MA, double first cl. Hons in Music; ARCM, ARCO. Principal Timpanist, London Philharmonic Orch., 1964–68 (Mem., LPO Bd of Dirs, 1965–68); Asst Conductor, 1968–70, Principal Conductor, 1971–77, BBC Scottish Symphony Orchestra; Princ. Conductor and Artistic Dir, Northern Sinfonia Orch., 1974–79; Principal Guest Conductor, Utrecht Symphony Orch., 1979–83; now works widely as a guest conductor, and has appeared in America, Holland, France, Germany, Belgium, Italy, Norway, Spain, Portugal, Czechoslovakia, Hong Kong, Australia, New Zealand and all parts of UK. FGSM 1972. *Recreations:* people, reading, walking, theology. *Address:* 2 The Paddox, Banbury Road, Oxford OX2 7PN.

SEAMAN, Dick; *see* Seaman, R. J.

SEAMAN, Gilbert Frederick, AO 1981; CMG 1967; Chairman, State Bank of South Australia, 1963–83; Deputy Chairman, Electricity Trust of SA, 1970–84; Trustee, Savings Bank of SA, 1973–81; *b* 7 Sept. 1912; *s* of Eli S. Seaman, McLaren Vale, South Australia; *m* 1935, Avenal Essie Fong; one *s* one *d*. *Educ:* University of Adelaide. BEc, Associate of University of Adelaide, 1935, High School Teacher, Port Pirie and Unley, 1932–35; South Australian Public Service, 1936–41; Seconded to Commonwealth of Australia as Assistant Director of Manpower for SA, 1941–46; Economist, SA Treasury, 1946–60; Under Treasurer for SA, 1960–72. *Address:* 27 William Street, Hawthorn, SA 5062, Australia. *T:* 271–4271.

See also Sir K. D. Seaman.

SEAMAN, Sir Keith (Douglas), KCVO 1981; OBE 1976; Governor of South Australia, 1977–82; *b* 11 June 1920; *s* of late E. S. and E. M. Seaman; *m* 1946, Joan, *d* of F. Birbeck; one *s* one *d*. *Educ:* Unley High Sch.; Univ. of Adelaide (BA, LLB). South Australian Public Service, 1937–54; RAAF Overseas HQ, London, 1941–45, Flt-Lieut. Entered Methodist Ministry, 1954: Renmark, 1954–58; Adelaide Central Methodist Mission, 1958–77 (Supt, 1971–77). Sec., Christian Television Assoc. of S Australia, 1959–73; Mem. Executive, World Assoc. of Christian Broadcasting, 1963–70; Director, 5KA, 5AU and 5RM Broadcasting Companies, 1960–77; Chm., 5KA, 5AU and 5RM, 1971–77. Mem., Australian Govt Social Welfare Commn, 1973–76. KStJ 1978. *Recreations:* reading, gardening. *Address:* Victor Harbor, SA 5211, Australia.

See also G. F. Seaman.

SEAMAN, Reginald Jaspar, (Dick Seaman); Director of Information, Department of Employment, 1978–80; *b* 19 March 1923; *o s* of Jaspar and Flora Seaman, Wandsworth; *m* 1950, Marian, *o d* of Henry and Ethel Sarah Moser. *Educ:* West Hill Elem. Sch., Wandsworth, SW18. Served War, 1940–46, RAF aircrew. Entered Civil Service as Post Office Messenger, 1937; Clerical Officer, HM Treasury, 1950; Asst Inf. Officer, Treasury, 1959–61; Inf. Officer, MAFF, 1961–64; Sen. Inf. Officer, DEA, 1964–67; Principal Inf. Officer, 1967–69; Chief Press Officer, DEP, 1969–72; Chief Inf. Officer, Northern Ireland Office, 1972–78. Silver Jubilee Medal, 1977. *Recreations:* orchids, horticulture (Chm., Caterham Horticultural Soc.). *Address:* 9 Ninehams Road, Caterham, Surrey.

SEARBY, Philip James, CBE 1981; Secretary and Authority Finance Officer, UK Atomic Energy Authority, 1976–84; *b* 20 Sept. 1924; *s* of Leonard James and Lillian Mary Searby; *m* 1955, Mary Brent Dudley; two *s*. *Educ:* Bedford Sch.; Wadham Coll., Oxford (MA). Entered Civil Service, Min. of Nat. Insurance, 1949; Prime Minister's Statistical Branch, 1951; Private Sec. to Paymaster Gen. (Lord Cherwell), 1952; Principal, Atomic Energy Office, 1954. Joined UK Atomic Energy Authority, 1956; Dep. Gen. Sec., Harwell, 1959; Principal Economics and Programmes Officer, 1965; Authority Finance and Programmes Officer, 1971. St Albans Diocesan Reader, 1950. *Recreation:* gardening. *Address:* 35 Wordsworth Road, Harpenden, Herts AL5 4AG. *T:* Harpenden 60837. *Club:* United Oxford & Cambridge University.

SEARLE, Rear-Adm. (retd) Malcolm Walter St Leger, CB 1955; CBE 1945; *b* Cape Colony, S Africa, 23 Dec. 1900; *e s* of late Sir Malcolm William Searle; *m* 1930, Betty Margaret Crampton; one *s* two *d*. *Educ:* accepted as Dominion candidate to enter RN by Gen. Jan Smuts, 1912; RN Colleges Osborne and Dartmouth, 1914–17. Served European War, 1914–19 (Grand Fleet and Baltic, 1917–1919); specialised in Gunnery, 1927; Comdr 1936 (Anti-aircraft Comdr); served War of 1939–45 (Fleet Gunnery Officer, Home Fleet, 1939–41; HMS Sheffield, Mediterranean and Arctic, 1941–43); Capt. 1943; CSO to Vice-Adm., E Fleet, 1943–44; COS to C-in-C East Indies Fleet, 1944–46; Dir of Plans (Q), Naval Staff, 1948–51; Commodore, RN Barracks, Portsmouth, 1951; Rear-Adm. 1952; Deputy Chief of Naval Personnel, 1953–55; retired, 1956. *Recreations:* small boat sailing, mountaineering, ski-ing. *Address:* Lindens, Kithurst Park, Storrington, Pulborough, West Sussex RH20 4JH.

SEARLE, Ronald William Fordham, AGI; artist; *b* Cambridge, 3 March 1920; *s* of late William James Searle and of Nellie Hunt; *m* 1st, Kaye Webb (marr. diss. 1967); one *s* one *d*; 2nd, 1967, Monica Koenig. *Educ:* Cambridge School of Art. Humorous work first published in Cambridge Daily News and Granta, 1935–39. Served with 287 Field Co. RE, 1939–46; captured by the Japanese at fall of Singapore, 1942; Prisoner of War in Siam and Malaya, 1942–45; Allied Force HQ Port Said Ops, 1956. Began contributing widely to nat. publications from 1946; creator of the schoolgirls of St Trinian's, 1941 (abandoned them in 1953); Cartoonist to Tribune, 1949–51; to Sunday Express, 1950–51; Special Feature artist, News Chronicle, 1951–53; Weekly Cartoonist, News Chronicle, 1954; Punch Theatre artist, 1949–62; Contributor, New Yorker. Designer of commemorative medals for: the French Mint, 1974–; British Art Medal Soc., 1983–. *Awards:* Art Dirs Club, Philadelphia, Medal, 1959; Nat. Cartoonists Soc. of America, Awards, 1959, 1960, 1966; Art Dirs Club, LA, Medal, 1959; Gold Medal, III Biennale Tolentino, 1965; Prix de la Critique Belge, 1968; Médaille de la ville d'Avignon, 1971; Prix d'Humour du Festival d'Avignon, 1971; Grand Prix de l'Humour noir "Grandville", 1971; Prix Internationale Charles Huard de dessin de presse, 1972. *One Man Exhibitions:* Batsford Gall., 1947; Leicester Galls, 1948, 1950, 1954, 1957; New York, 1959, 1963, 1969, 1976; Hannover, Tolentino (Italy), Stuttgart, Berlin, 1965; Bremerhaven, Basle, Linz, 1966; Galerie La Pochade, Paris, 1966, 1967, 1968, 1969, 1971; Galerie Gurlitt, Munich, 1967, 1968, 1969, 1970, 1971, 1973, 1976; Grosvenor Gall., London, Brussels, 1968; Frankfurt, 1969; Konstanz, Würzburg, 1970; Salzburg, 1971; Lausanne, Poncey, 1972; Paris, Vienna, 1973; Lausanne, 1974; Paris, 1975; Berlin, Hannover, Stuttgart, Mainz, Recklinghausen, New York, Stuttgart, Paris, 1976; Brussels, London, Paris, 1977; London, Vienna, Lausanne, Berlin, 1978; Graz, Tübingen, Salzburg, 1979; Bonn, Heidelberg, 1980; Rizzoli Gall., NY, Gal. Bartsch & Chariau, Munich, 1981; Cooper-Hewitt Museum, NY, 1984; Neve Galerie Wien, Vienna, 1985; Imperial War Museum, BM, 1986. *Works in permanent collections:* V&A, BM, Imperial War Museum; Bibliothèque Nat., Paris; Kunsthalle, Bremen; Wilhelm-Busch Museum, Hanover; Stadtmuseum, Munich; Art Museum, Dallas, Texas; Staatlische Mus., Berlin-Dahlem; Cooper-Hewitt Museum, NY; Univ. of Texas, Austin. *Films based on the characters of St Trinian's:* The Belles of St Trinian's, 1954; Blue Murder at St Trinian's, 1957; The Pure Hell of St Trinian's, 1960; The Great St Trinian's Train Robbery, 1966; The Wildcats of St Trinian's, 1980. *Films designed:* John Gilpin, 1951; On the Twelfth Day, 1954 (Acad. Award Nomination); Energetically Yours (USA), 1957; Germany, 1960 (for Suddeutschen RTV); The King's Breakfast, 1962; Those Magnificent Men in their Flying Machines (Animation Sequence), 1965; Monte Carlo or Bust (Animation Sequence), 1969; Scrooge (Animation Sequence), 1970; Dick Deadeye, 1975. *Publications:* Forty Drawings, 1946; Le Nouveau Ballet Anglais, 1947; Hurrah for St Trinian's!, 1948; The Female Approach, 1949; Back to the Slaughterhouse, 1951; John Gilpin, 1952; Souls in Torment, 1953; Rake's Progress, 1955; Merry England, etc, 1956; A Christmas Carol, 1961; Which Way Did He Go, 1961; Searle in the Sixties, 1964; From Frozen North to Filthy Lucre, 1964; Pardong M'sieur, 1965; Searle's Cats, 1967; The Square Egg, 1968; Take one Toad, 1968; Baron Munchausen, 1960; Hello—where did all the people go?, 1969; Hommage à Toulouse-Lautrec, 1969; Secret Sketchbook, 1970; The Addict, 1971; More Cats, 1975; Drawings from Gilbert and Sullivan, 1975; The Zoodiac, 1977; Ronald Searle (Monograph), 1978; The King of Beasts, 1980; The Big Fat Cat Book, 1982; Illustrated Winespeak, 1983; Ronald Searle in Perspective (monograph), 1984; Ronald Searle's Golden Oldies 1941–61, 1985; To the Kwai—and Back, 1986; Something in the Cellar, 1986; *in collaboration:* (with D. B. Wyndham Lewis) The Terror of St Trinian's, 1952; (with Geoffrey Willans) Down with Skool, 1953; How to be Topp, 1954; Whizz for Atomms, 1956; The Compleet Molesworth, 1958; The Dog's Ear Book, 1958; Back in the Jug Agane, 1959; (with Kaye Webb) Paris Sketchbook, 1950 and 1957; Looking at London, 1953; The St Trinian's Story, 1959; Refugees 1960, 1960; (with Alex Atkinson) The Big City, 1958; USA for Beginners, 1959; Russia for Beginners, 1960; Escape from the Amazon!, 1964; (with A. Andrews & B. Richardson) Those Magnificent Men in their Flying Machines, 1965; (with Heinz Huber) Haven't We Met Before Somewhere?, 1966; (with Kildare Dobbs) The Great Fur Opera, 1970; (with Irwin Shaw) Paris! Paris!, 1977. *Address:* c/o Tessa Sayle, 11 Jubilee Place, SW3 3TE. *T:* 01–352 4311. *Club:* Garrick.

SEARS, Hon. Raymond Arthur William; Hon. Mr Justice Sears; Judge of the Supreme Court of Hong Kong, since 1986; *b* 10 March 1933; *s* of William Arthur and

Lillian Sears; *m* 1960 (marr. diss. 1981); one *s* one *d*. *Educ:* Epsom Coll.; Jesus Coll., Cambridge. BA 1956. Lieut RA (TA) Airborne, 1953. Called to Bar, Gray's Inn, 1957. QC 1975; Recorder of the Crown Court, 1977–86. *Recreations:* watching horse-racing; music. *Address:* Supreme Court, Hong Kong. *Clubs:* Royal Automobile; Royal Hong Kong Jockey.

SEATON, Colin Robert; Under Secretary, Lord Chancellor's Department, since 1974, Head of Legislation Group, since 1983; Barrister-at-Law; *b* 21 Nov. 1928; 2nd *s* of late Arthur William Robert Seaton and Helen Amelia Seaton (*née* Stone); *m* 1952, Betty (*née* Gosling); two *s*. *Educ:* Wallington County Grammar Sch. for Boys; Worcester Coll., Oxford. BA 1953; MA 1956. Royal Air Force, 1947–49. Called to Bar, Inner Temple, 1956 (Profumo Prize, 1953, 1954); Schoolmaster for LCC (now GLC), 1953–57; Solicitor's Dept, Ministries of Health and Housing and Local Govt, also Dept of the Environment, 1957–71; Sec. (Master) of Nat. Industrial Relations Court, 1971–74; Circuit Administrator (Under Secretary): Northern Circuit, 1974–82; SE Circuit, 1982–83. Sec., Lord Chancellor's Law Reform Cttee, 1983–. *Publication:* Aspects of the National Health Service Acts, 1966. *Recreations:* golf, reading. *Address:* Tree Tops, The Drive, Coulsdon, Surrey. *T:* 01–668 5538. *Club:* Civil Service.

See also M. J. Seaton.

SEATON, Prof. Michael John, FRS 1967; Professor of Physics, Department of Physics and Astronomy, University College London, since 1963; Senior Fellow, Science and Engineering Research Council, since 1984; *b* 16 Jan. 1923; *s* of late Arthur William Robert Seaton and Helen Amelia Seaton; *m* 1st, 1943, Olive May (*d* 1959), *d* of Charles Edward Singleton; one *s* one *d*; 2nd, 1960, Joy Clarice, *d* of Harry Albert Balchin; one *s*. *Educ:* Wallington Co. Sch., Surrey; University Coll., London (Fellow, 1972). BSc 1948, PhD 1951, London. Dept of Physics, UCL: Asst Lectr, 1950; Lectr, 1953; Reader, 1959; Prof., 1963. Chargé de Recherche, Institut d'Astrophysique, Paris, 1954–55; Univ. of Colorado, 1961; Fellow-Adjoint, Jt Inst. for Laboratory Astrophysics (Nat. Bureau of Standards and Univ. of Colorado), Boulder, Colo, 1964–. Hon. Mem., Amer. Astronomical Soc., 1983; For. Associate, Amer. Nat. Acad. of Scis. Pres., RAS, 1979–81, Gold Medal, 1983; Guthrie Medal and Prize, Inst. of Physics, 1984. Dr *hc* Observatoire de Paris, 1976; Hon. DSc QUB, 1982. *Publications:* papers on atomic physics and astrophysics in various jls. *Address:* 51 Hall Drive, Sydenham, SE26 6XL. *T:* 01–778 7121.

See also C. R. Seaton.

SEAWARD, Colin Hugh; HM Diplomatic Service, retired; London Correspondent of Jornal do Brasil, since 1986; *b* 16 Sept. 1926; *s* of late Sydney W. Seaward and Molly W. Seaward; *m* 1st, 1949, Jean Bugler (decd); three *s* one *d*; 2nd, 1973, Judith Margaret Hinkley; two *d*. *Educ:* RNC, Dartmouth. Served Royal Navy, 1944–65. Joined HM Diplomatic Service, 1965; served: Accra, 1965; Bathurst (Banjul), 1966, FO, 1968; Rio de Janeiro, 1971; Prague, 1972; FCO, 1973; RNC, Greenwich (sowc), 1976; Counsellor (Econ. and Comm.), Islamabad, 1977–80; Consul-General, Rio de Janeiro, 1980–86. Hon. Sec., Anglo-Brazilian Soc., 1986–. *Address:* Brasted House, Brasted, Westerham, Kent TN16 1JA.

SEBAG-MONTEFIORE, Harold Henry; Barrister-at-law; Deputy Circuit Judge, 1973–83; *b* 5 Dec. 1924; *e s* of late John Sebag-Montefiore and Violet, *o c* of late James Henry Solomon; *m* 1968, Harriet, *o d* of Benjamin Harrison Paley, New York; one step *d*. *Educ:* Stowe; Lower Canada Coll., Montreal; Pembroke Coll., Cambridge (MA). Served War of 1939–45, RAF. Called to Bar, Lincoln's Inn, 1951. Contested (C) North Paddington, Gen. Elec., 1959; Chm., Conservative Parly Candidates Assoc., 1960–64. Member: LCC, 1955–65; GLC, for Cities of London and Westminster, 1964–73, First Chm., GLC Arts and Recreation Cttee, 1968–73; Sports Council, 1972–74. Pres., Anglo-Jewish Assoc., 1966–71. Freeman, City of London, and Liveryman, Spectacle Makers' Co. Trustee: Nat. Theatre Foundn; Internat. Festival of Youth Orchestras; Whitechapel Art Gall.; Mem., Cttee of Honour: RAH Centenary; "Fanfare for Europe"; William and Mary Tercentenary; Montefiore Hosp. (NY) Centenary. Chevalier, Légion d'Honneur, 1973. *Publications:* book reviews and articles on Polo under *nom-de-plume* of "Marco II". *Recreation:* looking for Lord Lucan. *Address:* 2 Paper Buildings, Temple, EC4. *T:* 01–353 5835. *Clubs:* Carlton, Hurlingham, Pegasus (Pres., 1979).

SEBRIGHT, Sir Peter Giles Vivian, 15th Bt *cr* 1626, of Besford, Worcs; *b* 2 Aug. 1953; *s* of Sir Hugo Giles Edmund Sebright, 14th Bt and of Deirdre Ann, *d* of late Major Vivian Lionel Slingsby Bethell; *S* father, 1985; *m* 1977, Regina Maria, *d* of Francis Steven Clarebrough, Melbourne; one *s*. *Heir:* *s* Rufus Hugo Giles Sebright, *b* 31 July 1978.

SECCOMBE, Hugh Digorie, CBE 1976; Chairman, Seccombe Marshall & Campion Ltd, 1962–77; *b* 3 June 1917; *s* of Lawrence Henry Seccombe, CBE and Norah (*née* Wood); *m* 1947, Eirene Rosemary Banister, *d* of Richard Whittow and Eirene, and *widow* of Lieut P. C. McC. Banister, DSC, RN; one *s* one *d*. *Educ:* Stowe; Sidney Sussex Coll., Cambridge (BA 1938, MA 1942). RNVR, 1939–50; retd, Lt-Comdr. Joined Seccombe Marshall & Campion, 1938; Dir, 1947. Chm., YWCA Central Club, 1971–86. Fellow, Inst. of Bankers, 1964. *Recreations:* gardening, fishing, shooting, hill-walking. *Address:* Sparkes Place, Wonersh, Guildford, Surrey GU5 0PH. *T:* Guildford 893296; Benmore Lodge, Isle of Mull, Argyllshire. *T:* Aros 351. *Club:* Army and Navy.

SECCOMBE, Dame Joan Anna Dalziel, DBE 1984; JP; Vice Chairman, Conservative National Union Executive, since 1984 (Member, since 1975); Chairman, Conservative Women's National Committee, 1981–84; *b* 3 May 1930; *d* of Robert John Owen and Olive Barlow Owen; *m* 1950, Henry Lawrence Seccombe; two *s*. *Educ:* St Martin's Sch., Solihull. Member: Heart of England Tourist Bd, 1977–81 (Chm., Marketing Sub-Cttee, 1979–81); Women's Nat. Commn. Chairman: W Midlands Area Cons. Women's Cttee, 1975–78; Cons. Women's Nat. Cttee, 1981–84; Cons. Party Social Affairs Forum, 1985–; Dep. Chm., W Midlands Area Cons. Council, 1979–81. Mem., W Midlands CC, 1979–81 (Chm., Trading Standards Cttee, 1979–81). JP Solihull, 1968 (Chm., 1981–84). *Recreations:* golf, ski-ing. *Address:* Tythe Barn, Walsal End Lane, Hampton-in-Arden, Solihull, West Midlands B92 0HX. *T:* Hampton-in-Arden 3252.

See also Hon. Sir J. A. D. Owen.

SECCOMBE, (William) Vernon (Stephen); JP; Chairman, South Western Regional Health Authority, since 1983; founded Secco Electric, 1965; *b* 14 Jan. 1928; *s* of Stephen Seccombe and Edith Violet (*née* Henbry-Smith); *m* 1950, Margaret Vera Profit; four *s*. *Educ:* Saltash Grammar Sch.; Plymouth and Devonport Tech. Coll. Mem., E Cornwall Water Bd, 1960–74 (Vice-Chm., 1963–66; Chm., 1966–69); Chm., Cornwall and Isles of Scilly DHA, late AHA, 1981–82; Dep. Comr, 1970–79, Comr, 1979–82, Western Area Traffic Comrs. Member: Saltash BC, 1953–74 (Chairman: Works Cttee, 1956–62; Finance and Estabs Cttee, 1963–74; Mayor, 1962–63); Caradon DC, 1973–79 (Vice-Chm., 1973–76; Chm., 1976–78). Governor, Saltash Comprehensive Sch., 1970–81 (Chm., 1974–78). JP Cornwall East South Bench, 1970. *Recreations:* industrial and local archaeology, genealogy, watching Association football, listening to military music. *Address:* King Square House, 26/27 King Square, Bristol BS2 8EF. *T:* Bristol 423271. *Club:* Saltash Sailing (Cornwall).

SECOMBE, Sir Harry (Donald), Kt 1981; CBE 1963; Actor, Comedian and Singer; *b* 8 Sept. 1921; *m* 1948, Myra Joan Atherton, Swansea; two *s* two *d*. *Educ:* Dynevor School, Swansea. Served with Royal Artillery, 1939–46. Windmill Theatre, 1947–48; General Variety since 1948. Appearances include: at London Palladium, 1956, 1958, 1959, 1961, 1966; in Roy. Command Perfs, 1955, 1957, 1958, 1963, 1966, 1969, 1975, 1978; (musical) Pickwick, Saville, 1963; (musical) The Four Musketeers, Drury Lane, 1967; The Plumber's Progress, Prince of Wales, 1975. Radio: Goon Show, 1949–60, and special performance of Goon Show for 50th Anniversary of BBC, 1972. Television: BBC, ITV, CBS (New York), Yorkshire TV, 1950–. Films: Davy, for Ealing Films, 1957; Jetstorm, 1959; Bed-Sitting Room, 1968; Mr Bumble in Oliver!, 1968; Bjornsen in Song of Norway, 1969; Rhubarb, 1969; Doctor in Trouble, 1970; The Magnificent Seven Deadly Sins, 1971; Sunstruck, 1972. Has made recordings for HMV, 1953–54, Philips Records, 1955–80, Celebrity Records, 1980–. FRSA 1971. *Publications:* Twice Brightly, 1974; Goon for Lunch, 1975; Katy and the Nurgla, 1978; Welsh Fargo, 1981; Goon Abroad, 1982; The Harry Secombe Diet Book, 1983. *Recreations:* film photography, literature, travel, golf, cricket. *Address:* 46 St James's Place, SW1. *T:* 01–629 2768. *Clubs:* Savage, Royal Automobile, Lord's Taverners, Variety Club of Great Britain.

SECONDÉ, Sir Reginald (Louis), KCMG 1981 (CMG 1972); CVO 1968 (MVO 1957); HM Diplomatic Service, retired; Ambassador to Venezuela, 1979–82; *b* 28 July 1922; *s* of late Lt-Col Emile Charles Secondé and Doreen Secondé (*née* Sutherland); *m* 1951, Catherine Penelope, *d* of late Thomas Ralph Sneyd-Kynnersley, OBE, MC and late Alice Sneyd-Kynnersley; one *s* two *d*. *Educ:* Beaumont; King's Coll., Cambridge. Served, 1941–47, in Coldstream Guards: N Africa and Italy (despatches); Major. Entered Diplomatic Service, 1949; UK Delegn to the UN, New York, 1951–55; British Embassy: Lisbon, 1955–57; Cambodia, 1957–59; FO, 1959–62; British Embassy, Warsaw, 1962–64; First Secretary and later Political Counsellor, Rio de Janeiro, 1964–69; Head of S European Dept, FCO, 1969–72; Royal Coll. of Defence Studies, 1972–73; Ambassador to Chile, 1973–76, to Romania, 1977–79. Comdr, Order of the Southern Cross (Brazil), 1968. *Recreations:* gardening, shooting. *Address:* Wamil Hall, near Mildenhall, Suffolk. *T:* Mildenhall 714160. *Club:* Cavalry and Guards.

SECRETAN, Lance H.; consultant, lecturer, journalist, author and entrepreneur, since 1981; Professor of Entrepreneurship, York University, Toronto, Ont, since 1983; President: The Thaler Corporation Inc., since 1980; Thaler Resources Ltd, since 1981; Chief Executive Officer, The Kenyon Corporation SA, since 1972; Director, Televent Canada Ltd, since 1982; *b* 1 Aug. 1939; *s* of late Kenyon and of Marie-Therese Secretan; *m* 1961, Gloria Christina (separated, 1985); two *d* (and one *d* decd). *Educ:* Los Cocos, Argentina; Italia Conti, London; St Peters, Bournemouth; Univ. of Waterloo, Canada; Univ. of Southern California (MA in International Relations, *cum laude*); LSE (PhD in International Relations). Toronto Stock Exchange, 1958–59; Office Overload Co. Ltd, 1959–67; Man. Dir, Manpower Ltd Gp of Cos, UK, Ireland, Middle East and Africa, 1967–81. FIEC 1969; FRSA 1981. *Publications:* How to be an Effective Secretary, 1972; Managerial Moxie, 1985; The State of Small Business in Ontario, 1986. *Recreations:* skiing, scuba-diving, cycling, walking, playing guitar, writing poetry, interesting people. *Address:* RR2, Alton, Ontario, L0N 1A0, Canada; 25a Bryanston Square, W1H 7FI. *Clubs:* Mensa, White Elephant; University (Toronto).

SEDCOLE, Cecil Frazer, FCA; Deputy Chairman, Reed International PLC, since 1985; *b* 15 March 1927; *s* of late William John Sedcole and Georgina Irene Kathleen Bluett (*née* Moffatt); *m* 1962, Jennifer Bennett Riggall; one *s* one *d*. *Educ:* Uppingham Sch., Rutland. FCA 1952; CBIM 1982. Joined Unilever Group of Cos, 1952: Dir, Birds Eye Foods, 1960–67; Vice-Chm., Langnese-Iglo, Germany, 1966–67; Vice-Chm., Frozen Products Gp, Rotterdam, 1967–71; Dir, Unilever PLC and Unilever NV, 1974–85; Chm., UAC International, 1976–79; Vice Chm., Unilever PLC, 1982–85; Mem., 1971–75, Chm., 1979–85, Overseas Cttee, Unilever; Dir, Tate & Lyle, 1982–. Mem., BOTB, 1982–86; Mem. Bd, Commonwealth Devlt Corp., 1984–. Trustee, Leverhulme Trust, 1982–. Governor, Bedales, 1983–. *Recreation:* golf. *Address:* c/o Reed International PLC, Reed House, 83 Piccadilly, W1A 1EJ. *Club:* Royal Air Force.

SEDDON, Dr John; Aeronautical Consultant; *b* 29 Sept. 1915; *m* 1940, Barbara Mary Mackintosh; one *s* two *d*. *Educ:* Leeds Modern Sch.; Univ. of Leeds. BSc 1937, PhD 1939; DSc Bristol, 1982. Scientific Officer, RAE, Farnborough, 1939–55; Harkness Fund Fellow, California Inst. of Technology, 1955–56; Head of Experimental Supersonics, RAE, Farnborough, 1957–59; Supt, Tunnels II Div., RAE, Bedford, 1959–66; Dir, Scientific Research (Air), Min. of Technology, 1966–68; Dir-Gen. Research, Aircraft, MoD, 1969–75. Consultant: Westland Helicopters, 1976–84; Rolls-Royce, 1985–86. Sen. Res. Fellow, Bristol Univ., 1976–82; Visiting Professor: Nanjing Aeronautical Inst., China, 1980 and 1984 (Hon. Prof., 1984); Middle East Technological Univ., Ankara, Turkey, 1985 and 1986. *Publications:* (with E. L. Goldsmith) Intake Aerodynamics, 1985; papers on air intakes and other aerodynamic subjects, in ARC Reports and Memoranda Series and other scientific media. *Recreation:* music. *Address:* 7 Vicarage Hill, The Bourne, Farnham, Surrey GU9 8HG. *T:* Farnham 723680.

SEDDON, Richard Harding, PhD; RWS 1976 (ARWS 1972); ARCA; artist and writer; *b* 1 May 1915; *s* of Cyril Harding Seddon; *m* 1946, Audrey Madeline Wareham. *Educ:* King Edward VII School; Roy. Coll. of Art; Univ. of Reading (PhD 1946). Demonstrator in Fine Art, Univ. of Reading, 1944; Extra-Mural Staff Tutor in Fine Art, Univ. of Birmingham, 1947; Director, Sheffield City Art Galleries, 1948–63; Curator, Ruskin Collection, 1948–63; Dir of Art History and Liberal Studies, Sch. of Design and Furniture, Buckinghamshire Coll. of Higher Educn, 1963–80. Hon. Advisory Panel, Hereford Art Galls, 1948; Arts Council Selection Bd (Art Students Exhib.), 1947; Pres. Ludlow Art Soc., 1947–67; Hon. Member: Sheffield Soc. of Artists; Oxford Folk Art Soc.; Sheffield Photographic Soc.; Mem., Oxford Bureau for Artists in War-time, 1940; Chm. Selection Cttee, Nottingham Artists Exhibition, 1953; Guest Speaker Educational Centres Association Annual Conference, 1951; West Riding Artists Exhibition Selection Committee, 1956; Northern Young Artists Exhibition Selection Committee, 1958; Member Sheffield Univ. Court; Sheffield Diocesan Advisory Cttee, 1948. Exhibitor at: RA; NEAC; RI; RBA; Internat. Artists; Architectural Assoc.; RIBA; National Gallery (War Artists) 1943; Leicester Galleries; Redfern Galleries. Official acquisitions: V. & A. Museum, 1939; Pilgrim Trust, 1942; Imperial War Museum (War Artists), 1943, 1956 (ten paintings); Graves Gall., Sheffield, 1943 and 1956; Atkinson Gall., Southport, 1953; Reading Art Gall., 1956; Leeds Education Cttee Collection, 1956. Extra Mural and Univ. Extension lectr on art to Univs of Oxford, Birmingham, London and Sheffield, 1948–; initiated Sheffield Conference on Nation's Art Treasures, 1958; FMA, 1951–74; Mem. Yorkshire Fed. Museums and Art Galls, 1948 (Committee 1952 and 1957, President, 1954–55, Vice-President, 1955–56); Secretary Yorks Museums Regional Fact Finding Committee, 1959; National Art Collections Fund Rep. for Yorks, 1954–63; Judge for Wakefield Art Galls Open Art Competition, 1984. Hon. Adviser to Co. of Cutlers in Hallamshire, 1950–64; Dep. Chm., Sheffield Design Council for Gold, Silver and Jewelry Trades, 1960; Mem. BBC '51 Soc., 1960; Mem. Govg Council, Design and Res. Centre, 1960; Mem. Art Adv. Cttee Yorks Area Scheme for Museums and Art Galleries, 1963;

Art Critic: Birmingham Post, 1963–71; Yorkshire Post, 1974–; Jl Fedn of British Artists, 1975–83; Mem. Recognised Panel of London Univ. Extension Lectrs, 1964; Mem. Council and Hon. Treasurer, 1976, Trustee, 1983–86, RWS; Hon. Treas., Artists' League of GB, 1984–86. Hon. Mem., Mark Twain Soc., USA, 1976. War Service with RAOC Field Park, France, 1940 (King's Badge); facilities by War Office Order to make war drawings in Maginot Line, 1940. *Publications:* The Technical Methods of Paul Nash (Memorial Vol.), 1949; The Artist's Vision, 1949; The Academic Technique of Oil Painting, 1960; A Hand Uplifted (war memoirs), 1962; Art Collecting for Amateurs, 1964; (ed) Dictionary of Art Terms, 1981; The Artist's Studio Book, 1983; articles on fine art for Jl of Aesthetics (USA), Burlington Magazine, Apollo, The Studio, The Connoisseur, Arch. Review, The Artist, The Antique Collector and daily press; lectures on art in England and abroad; criticisms; book reviews; broadcasts. *Recreation:* gardening. *Address:* 6 Arlesey Close, Putney, SW15 2EX. *T:* 01–788 5899.

SEDGEMORE, Brian Charles John; MP (Lab) Hackney South and Shoreditch, since 1983; *b* 17 March 1937; *s* of Charles John Sedgemore, fisherman; *m* 1964 (marr. diss.); one *s*. *Educ:* Newtown Primary Sch.; Heles Sch.; Oxford Univ. (MA). Diploma in public and social administration. Called to Bar, Middle Temple, 1966. RAF, 1956–58; Oxford, 1958–62. Administrative Class, Civil Service, Min. of Housing and Local Govt, 1962–66 (Private Sec. to R. J. Mellish, MP, then junior Minister of Housing, 1964–66). Practising barrister, 1966–74. MP (Lab) Luton West, Feb. 1974–1979; PPS to Tony Benn, MP, 1977–78. Researcher, Granada TV, 1980–83. *Publications:* The How and Why of Socialism, 1977; Mr Secretary of State (fiction), 1979; The Secret Constitution, 1980; Power Failure (fiction), 1985; contributor to Tribune, one time contributor to Britain's top satirical magazine. *Recreation:* sleeping on the grass. *Address:* 21 Pitfield Street, N1; House of Commons, SW1.

SEDGMAN, Francis Arthur, AM 1980; Lawn Tennis Champion: Australia, 1949, 1950; USA, 1951, 1952; Wimbledon, 1952; Italy, 1952; Asia, 1952; Professional Tennis Player since 1953; *b* Victoria, Australia, 29 Oct. 1927; *m* 1952, Jean Margaret Spence; four *d*. *Educ:* Box Hill High School, Vic, Australia. First played in the Australian Davis Cup team, 1949; also played in winning Australian Davis Cup team, 1950, 1951, 1952. With John Bromwich, won Wimbledon doubles title, 1948; with Kenneth McGregor, won the Australian, French, Wimbledon and American doubles titles in the same year (1951), the only pair ever to do so; with Kenneth McGregor also won Australian, French and Wimbledon doubles titles, 1952; with Doris Hart, won French, Wimbledon and US mixed doubles titles, 1952. Last male player to win three titles at Wimbledon in one year, 1952. Director of many private companies including: Tennis Camps of Australia Pty Ltd; Reelco Industries Pty Ltd; Polytray Pty Ltd. *Publication:* Winning Tennis, 1955. *Recreation:* golfing. *Address:* 28 Bolton Avenue, Hampton, Victoria 3188, Australia. *T:* 98 6341. *Clubs:* All England Tennis and Croquet, Queen's; Melbourne Cricket (Melbourne); Kooyong Tennis; Grace Park Tennis; Victoria Amateur Turf, Victoria Racing; Royal Melbourne Golf.

SEDGWICK, Mrs A. R. M.; *see* Milkina, Nina.

SEDGWICK, Peter Norman; Under Secretary, HM Treasury, since 1984; *b* 4 Dec. 1943; *s* of Norman Victor Sedgwick and Lorna Clara (*née* Burton); *m* 1984, Catherine Jane, *d* of B. D. T. Saunders. *Educ:* Westminster Cathedral Choir Sch.; Downside; Lincoln Coll., Oxford (MA PPE, BPhilEcon). HM Treasury: Economic Asst, 1969; Economic Adviser, 1971; Sen. Economic Adviser, 1977. Chm. 1979–84, Mem. Develt Cttee 1984–, London Symphony Chorus. *Recreation:* singing. *Address:* 75 Elsenham Street, SW18 5NX. *T:* 01–874 6595. *Club:* Royal Automobile.

SEDLEY, Stephen John; QC 1983; *b* 9 Oct. 1939; *s* of William and Rachel Sedley; *m* 1968, Ann Tate; one *s* two *d*. *Educ:* Mill Hill Sch.; Queens' Coll., Cambridge (BA Hons 1961). Freelance writer, interpreter, musician, translator, 1961–64; called to the Bar, Inner Temple, 1964; a Pres., Nat. Reference Tribunals for the Coalmining Industry, 1983–. Vis. Professorial Fellow, Warwick Univ., 1981. Mem., Internat. Commn on Mercenaries, Angola, 1976. Sec., Haldane Soc., 1964–69. *Publications:* (trans.) From Burgos Jail, by Marcos Ana and Vidal de Nicolas, 1964; (ed) Seeds of Love (anthology), 1967; (contrib.) Orwell: inside the myth, 1984; (contrib.) Civil Liberty, 1984; (contrib.) Police, the Constitution and the Community, 1986. *Recreations:* carpentry, music, cycling, walking, changing the world. *Address:* 3 Torriano Cottages, NW5 2TA. *T:* 01–485 3660.

SEDOV, Leonid I.; 5 Orders of Lenin, Hero of Socialist Labour, USSR; Professor, Moscow University, since 1937; Chief of Department of Hydrodynamics, since 1941; Member, USSR Academy of Sciences; *b* 14 Nov. 1907; *m* 1931, Galya Tolstova; one *s* one *d*. *Educ:* Moscow University. Chief Engineer, Associate Chief lab., N.E. Zhukovsky Aerohydrodynamic Inst., Moscow, 1930–47; Vice-President, International Astronautical Federation, 1962–80 (Pres., 1959–61); Internat. Astronautical Acad., 1980–. Hon. Member: American Academy of Arts and Sciences; Internat. Astronautical Acad.; Serbian Academy, Belgrade; Tech. Academy, Finland; For. Associate, Acad. of Sciences, Paris; Academia Leopoldina. Hon. doctorates from many foreign universities. Medal of Obert; State Prize; Chaplygin Prize; Lomonosov Prize; Lyapunov Medal; Guggenheim Award; Van Allen Award. Commandeur de la Légion d'Honneur (France). *Publications:* Theory of Plane Flow of Liquids, 1939; Plane Problems of Hydrodynamics and Aerodynamics, 1950, 1966, 1980; Similarity and Dimensional Methods in Mechanics, 1944, 1951, 1953, 1957, 1960, 1965, 1967, 1977; Introduction into the Mechanics of Continua, 1962; Mechanics of Continuous Media, 2 vols, 1970, 1973, 1976, 1983–84; Thoughts about Science and Scientists, 1980; numerous articles. *Address:* Moscow University, Zone U, kv 84 Leninskie Gory, Moscow B-234, USSR.

SEEAR, family name of **Baroness Seear.**

SEEAR, Baroness *cr* 1971 (Life Peer), of Paddington; **Beatrice Nancy Seear,** PC 1985; formerly Reader in Personnel Management, University of London, The London School of Economics, retired 1978, Hon. Fellow, 1980; Liberal Leader, House of Lords, since 1984; *b* 7 Aug. 1913; *d* of late Herbert Charles Seear and Beatrice Maud Catchpole. *Educ:* Croydon High Sch.; Newnham Coll., Cambridge (Hon. Fellow, 1983); London Sch. of Economics and Political Science. BA (Cambridge Hist. Tripos). Personnel Officer, C. & J. Clark Ltd, shoe manufacturers, 1936–46; seconded as Mem. (pt-time), staff of Production Efficiency Bd at Min. of Aircraft Production, 1943–45; Teacher at London School of Economics, 1946–78. Vis. Prof. of Personnel Management, City Univ., 1980–July 1987. Member: Hansard Soc. Commn on Electoral Reform, 1975–76; Top Salaries Review Body, 1971–84. Chairman: Nat. Council for Carers and their Elderly Dependants; Council, Morley Coll. President: BSI, 1974–77; Women's Liberal Fedn, 1974; Fawcett Soc., 1970–85; Inst. of Personnel Management, 1977–79. Mem. Council, Industrial Soc. Hon. LLD Leeds, 1979; Hon. DLit Bath, 1982. *Publications:* (with P. Jephcott and J. H. Smith) Married Women Working, 1962; (with V. Roberts and J. Brock) A Career for Women in Industry?, 1964; Industrial Social Services, 1964; The Position of Women in Industry, 1967; The Re-Entry of Women into Employment, 1971. *Recreations:* travel, gardening. *Address:* The Garden Flat, 44 Blomfield Road, W9. *T:* 01–286 5701. *Club:* Royal Commonwealth Society.

SEEBOHM, family name of **Baron Seebohm.**

SEEBOHM, Baron *cr* 1972 (Life Peer), of Hertford; **Frederic Seebohm,** Kt 1970; TD; psc; Lt-Col (Retd); *b* 18 Jan. 1909; *s* of late H. E. Seebohm, Poynders End, Hitchin, Herts; *m* 1932, Evangeline, *d* of late Sir Gerald Hurst, QC; one *s* two *d*. *Educ:* Leighton Park School; Trinity Coll., Cambridge. Joined Staff of Barclays Bank Ltd, 1929; Director: Barclays Bank Ltd, 1947–79 (Dep. Chm., 1968–74); Barclays Bank International Ltd, 1951–79 (formerly Barclays Bank DCO) (Vice-Chm., 1955–59, Dep. Chm., 1959–65, Chm., 1965–72; Vice-Chm., Barclays Bank SA, 1968–73); Friends' Provident Life Office, 1952–79 (Chm., 1962–68); ICFC, 1969–80 (Chm., 1974–79); Finance for Industry Ltd, 1974–80 (Chm., 1974–79); Finance Corp. for Industry Ltd, 1974–80 (Chm., 1974–79). Chairman: Joseph Rowntree Memorial Trust, 1966–81; London House, 1970–83; Seebohm Cttee on Local Authority and Allied Personal Social Services, 1965–68; Export Guarantees Adv. Council, 1967–72; President: Age Concern; Nat. Inst. for Social Work; Royal African Soc., 1978–84 (Hon. Vice Pres., 1984–); Project Fullemploy, 1982–; Vice Chm., Volunteer Centre, 1983–. Mem., Overseas Develt Inst. (Chm., 1972–77). Governor: London School of Economics; Haileybury Imperial Service Coll., 1970; Fellow, Inst. of Bankers (Pres., 1966–68). Served with Royal Artillery, 1939–45 (despatches). High Sheriff, Herts, 1970–71. Hon. LLD Nottingham, 1970; Hon. DSc Aston, 1976. Bronze Star of America, 1945. *Recreations:* gardening, painting. *Address:* 28 Marsham Court, Marsham Street, SW1. *T:* 01–828 2168. *Clubs:* Carlton, Royal Commonwealth Society; Hurlingham.

See also Hon. V. Glendinning.

SEEFRIED, Irmgard Maria Theresia; Austrian opera and concert singer; Kammersängerin at Vienna State Opera since 1943; *b* Koengetried, Bavaria; *m* 1948, Wolfgang Schneiderhan; two *d*. *Educ:* Augsburg Conservatory, Germany. First engagement under von Karajan, at Aachen, Germany, 1940. Concert tours all over the world; appeared: Metropolitan Opera, New York; Covent Garden, London; La Scala, Milan; also festivals at Salzburg, Lucerne, Edinburgh, San Francisco. Honorary Member: Boston Symphony Orch.; Vienna Philharmonic Orch. Hon. Mem., Austrian-German Culture Soc., 1980. Recipient various Mozart Medals; Lilly-Lehmann Medal; Golden Cross of merit for Culture and Science; Decoration of Chevalier I, Denmark; Grosses Verdienstkreuz des Verdienstordens der Bundesrepublik Deutschland, 1963; Schubert Medal; Hugo Wolf Medal; Culture Prize, Luxemburg; Culture Prize, Donauwörth, Germany, 1979; Gold Medal of Honour, Vienna, 1979; Werner Egg Prize, 1979; Silver Decoration of merit, Austria, 1979; Gold Burgher Medal, Bad Wörishofen, 1980. *Publications:* articles on Mozart, Bartók, Hindemith, Hugo Wolf. *Address:* Vienna State Opera, Austria.

SEELY, family name of **Baron Mottistone.**

SEELY, Sir Nigel (Edward), 5th Bt *cr* 1896; Dorland DFS International; *b* 28 July 1923; *s* of Sir Victor Basil John Seely, 4th Bt and of Sybil Helen, *d* of late Sills Clifford Gibbons; *S* father, 1980; *m* 1949, Loraine, *d* of late W. W. Lindley-Travis; three *d*; *m* 1984, Trudi Pacter, *d* of Sydney Pacter. *Educ:* Stowe. *Heir:* half-*b* Victor Ronald Seely [*b* 1 Aug. 1941; *m* 1972, Annette Bruce, *d* of Lt-Col J. A. D. McEwen; one *s* one *d*]. *Address:* 3 Craven Hill Mews, W2. *Clubs:* Buck's; Royal Solent.

SEENEY, Leslie Elon Sidney, OBE 1978; Director General (formerly General Secretary), National Chamber of Trade, since 1971; *b* 19 Jan. 1922; *s* of Sidney Leonard and Daisy Seeney, Forest Hill; *m* 1947, Marjory Doreen Greenwood, Spalding; one *s*. *Educ:* St Matthews, Camberwell. RAFVR, 1941–46 (Flt Lt, Pilot). Man. Dir, family manufrg business (clothing), 1946–63, with other interests in insce and advertising. Mem., West Lewisham Chamber of Commerce, 1951, subseq. Sec. and Chm.; Delegate to Nat. Chamber of Trade, 1960; joined NCT staff, 1966. Mem., Home Office Standing Cttee on Crime Prevention, 1971–. Council Member: (founding) Retail Consortium, 1971–; Assoc. for Prevention of Theft from Shops, 1976–. Fellow, Soc. of Assoc. Executives, 1970. *Publications:* various articles. *Recreations:* reading, writing, travel, photography. *Address:* 16 Barn Close, Southcote, Reading, Berks. *T:* Reading 55478.

SEENEY, Noel Conway; Commissioner of Stamp Duties, Queensland, 1975–86; *b* 7 April 1926; *s* of Percy Matthew Mark Seeney and Wilhelmina Augusta Zanow; *m* 1949, Valrae Muriel Uhlmann; two *d*. *Educ:* Teachers' Coll., Brisbane; Univ. of Queensland (BCom). Assoc. Accountancy, Assoc. Coll. of Preceptors, London. Teacher, 1944; Dep. Principal, Secondary Sch., 1960; Principal 1964; Official Sec., Office of Agent-General for Qld in London, 1969; Agent-General for Qld in London, 1973. *Recreations:* golf, tennis. *Address:* 20 Nawarra Street, Indooroopilly, Qld 4068, Australia. *Clubs:* United Service (Brisbane); Indooroopilly Golf.

SEEYAVE, Sir René (Sow Choung), Kt 1985; CBE 1979; Group Managing Director and Chief Executive, Happy World Ltd, since 1968; *b* 15 March 1935; *s* of Antoine Seeyave, CBE and Lam Tung Ying; *m* 1961, Thérèse How Hong; one *s* four *d*. *Educ:* Royal College, Port Louis, Mauritius. Founder, Floreal Knitwear Ltd, pioneers in export of woollen knitwear, 1971; Chm., Mauritius Farms Ltd, 1974–85. Board Mem., Mauritius Marine Authority, 1980–85. Vice-Chm. Council, Univ. of Mauritius, 1985. *Recreations:* photography, jogging, table tennis, swimming. *Address:* 29 bis Mgr Gonin Street, Port Louis, Mauritius. *T:* 2–1391. *Clubs:* Hua Lien, Mauritius Gymkhana, Port Louis City.

SEFTON, family name of **Baron Sefton of Garston.**

SEFTON OF GARSTON, Baron *cr* 1978 (Life Peer), of Garston in the County of Merseyside; **William Henry Sefton;** Chairman, North West Economic Planning Council, since 1975; Vice-Chairman and Board Member, Warrington and Runcorn Development Corporation, 1981–85 (Chairman, 1974–81, Board Member, 1964–81, Runcorn Development Corporation); *b* 5 Aug. 1915; *s* of George and Emma Sefton; *m* 1940, Phyllis Kerr. *Educ:* Duncombe Road Sch., Liverpool. Joined Liverpool CC, 1953, Leader 1964; Chm. and Leader, Merseyside CC, 1974–77, Opposition Leader, 1977–79. Joined Runcorn Develt Corp., 1964, Dep. Chm. 1967. Member: New Towns Commn, 1978–85; SSRC, 1978–. *Recreations:* gardening, woodwork. *Address:* House of Lords, SW1.

SEGAL, Prof. Erich; Adjunct Professor of Classics, Yale University, since 1981; Hon. Research Fellow, Classics, University College London, since 1982; *b* 16 June 1937; *s* of Samuel M. Segal, PhD, DHL and Cynthia Shapiro Segal; *m* 1975, Karen James; one *d*. *Educ:* Harvard (Boylston Prize 1957, AB 1958, AM 1959, PhD 1965). Teaching Fellow, Harvard, 1959–64; Lectr in Classics, Yale, 1964, Asst Prof., 1965–68, Associate Prof., 1968–73; Vis. Prof. in Classics: Munich, 1973; Princeton, 1974–75; Tel Aviv, 1976–77; Vis. Prof. in Comp. Lit., Dartmouth, 1976–78; Vis. Fellow, Wolfson Coll., Oxford, 1979–80, Mem. Common Room, 1984–. Mem., Acad. of Literary Studies, USA, 1981. Lectures: Amer. Philological Assoc., 1971; Amer. Comparative Lit. Assoc., 1971; German Classical Assoc., 1974; Boston Psychoanalytic Inst., 1974; Instituto Nazionale del Dramma Antico, Sicily, 1975; Brit. Classical Assoc., 1977; William Kelley Prentice Meml, Princeton, 1981. Screenplays include: The Beatles' Yellow Submarine, 1968; The Games, 1969; Love Story, 1970; Oliver's Story, 1978; Man, Woman and Child, 1983. *Publications:*

Roman Laughter: the comedy of Plautus, 1968, rev. edn 1985; (ed) Euripides: a collection of critical essays, 1968; (ed and trans.) Plautus: Three Comedies, 1969, rev. edn 1985; (ed) Oxford Readings in Greek Tragedy, 1983; (ed with Fergus Millar) Caesar Augustus, 1984; (ed) Plato's Dialogues, 1985; *novels:* Love Story, 1970; Fairy Tale (for children), 1973; Oliver's Story, 1977; Man, Woman and Child, 1980; The Class, 1985; articles and reviews in Amer. Jl of Philology, Classical World, Harvard Studies in Classical Philology, Greek, Roman and Byzantine Studies, TLS, New York Times Book Review, New Republic. *Recreations:* swimming, athletics. *Address:* Wolfson College, Oxford OX2 6UD. *T:* Oxford 56711. *Clubs:* Harvard (New York and Boston); Yale (New York).

SEGAL, Graeme Bryce, DPhil; FRS 1982; Reader in Mathematics, Oxford University, since 1978; Fellow of St Catherine's College, since 1966; *b* 21 Dec. 1941; *s* of Reuben Segal and Iza Joan Harris; *m* 1962, Desley Rae Cheetham (marr. diss. 1972). *Educ:* Sydney Grammar School; Univ. of Sydney (BSc 1962); Univ. of Cambridge; Univ. of Oxford (MA, DPhil 1967). Junior Res. Fellow, Worcester Coll., Oxford, 1964–66; Junior Lectr in Mathematics, Oxford Univ., 1965–66. Mem., Inst. for Advanced Study, Princeton, 1969–70. Editor, Topology, 1970–. *Publications:* articles in learned jls. *Address:* 2 Abberbury Road, Iffley, Oxford. *T:* Oxford 777027.

SEGAL, Prof. Judah Benzion, MC 1942; FBA 1968; Professor of Semitic Languages in the University of London, School of Oriental and African Studies, 1961–79; now Emeritus; *b* 21 June 1912; *s* of Prof. Moses H. Segal and Hannah Leah Segal; *m* 1946, Leah (*née* Seidemann); two *d. Educ:* Magdalen College School, Oxford; St Catharine's College, Cambridge. Jarrett Schol., 1932; John Stewart of Rannoch Schol., in Hebrew, 1933; 1st Cl. Oriental Langs Tripos, 1935; Tyrwhitt Schol. and Mason Prizeman, 1936; BA (Cambridge), 1935; MA 1938. Colours, Cambridge Univ. Boxing Club, 1935, 1936. Mansel Research Exhibitioner, St John's Coll., Oxford, 1936–39; James Mew Schol., 1937; DPhil (Oxon.), 1939. Deputy Assistant Director, Public Security, Sudan Government, 1939–41; served War of 1939–45, GHQ, MEF, 1942–44, Captain; Education Officer, British Military Administration, Tripolitania, 1945–46. Head of Dept of Near and Middle East, Sch. of Oriental and African Studies, 1961–68 (Hon. Fellow 1983); Visiting Lectr, Ain Shams Univ., Cairo, 1979; Res. Fellow, Hebrew Univ., Jerusalem, 1980; Leverhulme Emeritus Fellowship, S India, 1981. Principal, Leo Baeck Coll., 1982–85, Pres., 1985–. Dir, Jewish Chronicle Trust. Mem., Council of Christians and Jews; President: North Western Reform Synagogue; British Assoc. for Jewish Studies, 1980; Vice-Pres., Reform Synagogues of GB, 1985–. Freedom, City of Urfa, Turkey, 1973. *Publications:* The Diacritical Point and the Accents in Syriac, 1953; The Hebrew Passover, 1963; Edessa, 1970; Aramaic Texts From North Saqqara, 1983; articles in learned periodicals. *Recreations:* walking, meditation. *Address:* 17 Hillersdon Avenue, Edgware, Mddx. *T:* 01-958 4993.

SEGAL, Michael John; Registrar, Principal Registry, Family Division, since 1985; *b* 20 Sept. 1937; *s* of Abraham Charles Segal and Iris Muriel (*née* Parsons); *m* 1963, Barbara Gina Fluxman; one *d. Educ:* Strode's Sch., Egham. Called to the Bar, Middle Temple, 1962. Practiced at Bar, Midland and Oxford Circuit, 1962–84. *Recreations:* reading, music. *Address:* 28 Grange Road, N6 4AP. *T:* 01–348 0680.

SEGOVIA, Andrés; Marquis of Salobreña, 1981; Grand Cross: Order of Alfonso X el Sabio, 1953; Order of Isabel la Católica, 1958; Spanish concert-guitarist; *b* Linares, Spain, 21 Feb. 1893; *m* 1962, Emilia; one *s* (and one *s* one *d* by former marr.). Brought up in Granada; has been playing the guitar since the age of ten; gave first recital, Granada, 1909; since 1919 has performed in Europe, USA, Japan, Russia, Australia and Canada; first came to England in 1926; has often returned on concert tours since 1952; has had many pupils and has taught at Santiago de Compostela and Academia Musicale Chigiana, Siena, and other schools; has adapted works of Bach, Haydn, Mozart and other classical composers for the guitar; has had many works composed especially for him by Casella, Castelnuovo-Tedesco, Falla, Moreno Torroba, Ponce, Roussel, Tansman, Turina, Villa-Lobos and others. Mem., Spanish Royal Acad. of Fine Arts, 1978. Hon. DMus Oxon, 1972. Gold Medal for Meritorious Work (Spain), 1967; Albert Schweitzer Award, 1981; Ernst Von Siemens Prize, 1985; Gold Medal, Royal Philharmonic Soc., 1986. Order of Rising Sun (Japan), 1985. *Publications:* Segovia: an autobiography of the years 1893–1920, trans. W. F. O'Brien, 1977; (with George Mendoza) Segovia: My Book of the Guitar, 1979. *Address:* c/o Ibbs & Tillett, 450–452 Edgware Road, W2 1EG.

SEGRÈ, Prof. Emilio; Grande Ufficiale, Merito della Repubblica (Italy); Professor of Physics, University of California, Berkeley, 1946–72, now Emeritus; *b* 1 Feb. 1905; *s* of Giuseppe Segrè and Amelia Treves-Segrè; *m* 1936, Elfriede Spiro (*d* 1970); one *s* two *d*; *m* 1972, Rosa Mines Segrè. *Educ:* University of Rome, Italy. Asst Prof. of Physics, Rome, 1929–35; Dir, Physics Inst., Univ. of Palermo, Italy, 1936–38; Research Associate and Lectr, Univ. of Calif., Berkeley, 1938–42; Group Leader, Los Alamos Scientific Lab., 1942–46. Hon. Prof. S Marcos Univ., Lima, 1954; Prof. of Nuclear Physics, Univ. of Rome, 1974–75. Codiscoverer of: slow neutrons, 1934; (chemical elements) technetium, 1937, astatine, 1940, plutonium, 1941; the antiproton, 1955. Hon. DSc Palermo, 1958; Hon. Dr Tel Aviv Univ. Nobel laureate (joint) for physics, 1959. Member: Nat. Acad. Sciences, USA, 1952; Accad. Nazionale Lincei, Roma, 1959; Accad. Nationale de XL, Roma; Heidelberg Akad. der Wissenschaften; Amer. Phil. Soc.; Amer. Acad. of Arts and Sciences; Indian Acad. of Sciences. *Publications:* Nuclei and Particles, 1964, new edn 1977; Enrico Fermi, Physicist, 1970; From X-rays to Quarks: modern physicists and their discoveries, 1980; From Falling Bodies to Radio Waves: classical physicists and their discoveries, 1984; contrib. to Physical Review, Proc. Roy. Soc. London, Nature, Nuovo Cimento. *Recreation:* hiking. *Address:* 3802 Quail Ridge Road, Lafayette, Calif 94549, USA; Department of Physics, University of California, Berkeley, Calif 94720. *Club:* University of California Faculty (Berkeley).

SEIFERT, Robin (also known as **Richard**); JP; FRIBA; Principal R. Seifert and Partners, Architects, since 1934; *b* 25 Nov. 1910; *s* of William Seifert; *m* 1939, Josephine Jeanette Harding; two *s* one *d. Educ:* Central Foundation Sch., City of London; University College, London (DipArch), Fellow, 1971. Commenced architectural practice, 1934. Corps of Royal Engineers, 1940–44; Indian Army, 1944–46; Hon. Lt-Col, 1946; Certif. for Meritorious Services Home Forces, 1943. Returned to private practice, 1948. Designed: ICI Laboratories, Dyestuffs Div., Blackley, Manchester; The Times Newspapers building, Printing House Square; Centre Point, St Giles Circus; Drapers Gardens, Nat. West. Bank Tower, City; The Royal Garden Hotel, Kensington; Tolworth Towers, Surbiton; Guiness Mahon Bank, Gracechurch Street; HQ of ICT, Putney; Kellogg House, Baker Street; Dunlop House, King Street, St James's; BSC Res. Labs, Middlesbrough; Britannia Hotel; Park Tower Hotel; London Heathrow Hotel; Sobell Sports Centre; ATV Centre, Birmingham; Central Television Complex, Nottingham; International Press Centre; Metropolitan Police HQ, Putney; Wembley Conference Centre; Princess Grace Hospital, Marylebone Road; Princess Grace Hospital, Windsor; Princess Margaret Hospital, Windsor; Churchill Hospital, Harrow; BUPA Hospital, Bushey; The Pirate Castle, Camden; British Rail HQ Offices, Euston Station. RIBA Architectural Exhibition (depicting 50 years of practice), Heinz Gall., 1984. Member, MoT Road Safety Council, 1969 (now disbanded); Home Office Cttee of Management, Housing Assoc. for Discharged Offenders; (part-time) British Waterways Bd, 1971–74; Council, RIBA, 1971–74. FRSA 1976. Liveryman, Glaziers' Co. City of London. JP Barnet, 1969. *Recreations:* chess, violin. *Address:* Eleventrees, Milespit Hill, Mill Hill, NW7. *T:* 01–959 3397. *Clubs:* Army and Navy, City Livery, Arts.

SEIGNORET, Eustace Edward; High Commissioner for Trinidad and Tobago in Georgetown, Guyana, since 1982; *b* 16 Feb. 1925; *m*; two *s* one *d. Educ:* Howard Univ., Washington; Univ. of Wales, Bangor. BSc. Agricultural Officer, Dept of Agriculture, Trinidad and Tobago, 1953–58; West Indies Fedn Public Service, 1958–62; Asst Sec., Trinidad and Tobago Public Service, 1962; First Sec., 1962–65, Counsellor, 1965–68, Trinidad and Tobago Perm. Mission to UN; Dep. High Comr in London, 1969–71; Perm. Rep. to UN, 1971–75; High Comr in London, 1977–82. *Address:* Trinidad and Tobago High Commission, 91 Middle Street, Georgetown, Guyana.

SEITZ, Raymond George Hardenbergh; Minister and Deputy Chief of Mission, United States Embassy in London, since 1984; *b* Hawaii, 8 Dec. 1940; *s* of Maj.-Gen. John Francis Regis Seitz and Helen Johnson Hardenbergh; two *s* one *d*; *m* 1985, Caroline Richardson. *Educ:* Yale University (BA History 1963). Joined Foreign Service, Dept of State, 1966; served Montreal, Nairobi, Bukavu, Zaire, 1966–72; Staff Officer, later Director, Secretariat Staff, Washington, Special Asst to Dir Gen., Foreign Service, 1972–75; Political Officer, London, 1975–79; Dep. Exec. Sec., Washington, 1979–81; Senior Dep. Asst Sec., Public Affairs, Washington, 1981–82; Exec. Asst to Secretary George P. Shultz, Washington, 1982–84. *Address:* Wychwood House, 1 Cottesmore Gardens, W8. *T:* 01–499 9000.

SEKYI, Henry Van Hien; Permanent Representative of Ghana to the United Nations, 1979–80; *b* 15 Jan. 1928; *s* of W. E. G. Sekyi, MA London, BL, and Lily Anna Sekyi (*née* Cleland); *m* 1958, Maria Joyce Sekyi (*née* Tachie-Menson); one *s* one *d. Educ:* Adisadel Coll., Cape Coast; Univ. of Ghana; King's Coll., Cambridge; LSE. BA London 1953; BA Cantab 1955. Third Sec., Second Sec., and First Sec., in succession, Ghana Embassy, Washington, DC, USA, 1958–61; First Sec., later Counsellor, Ghana Embassy, Rome, 1961–62; Director, Min. Foreign Affairs, 1962–65, in charge of Divisions of: Eastern Europe and China; Middle East and Asia; UN Affairs; Personnel and Administration; Acting Principal Sec., Min. of Foreign Affairs, 1965–66; Ghana High Comr to Australia, 1966–70; Ghana Ambassador to Italy, 1970–72; High Comr in UK, 1972–75; Supervising Dir, Political Dept, Min. of Foreign Affairs, Ghana, 1975–76, Senior Principal Secretary 1976–79. *Recreations:* classics, music, Africana and gymnastics. *Address:* c/o Ministry of Foreign Affairs, Accra, Ghana.

SELBORNE, 4th Earl of, *cr* 1882; **John Roundell Palmer;** DL; Baron Selborne, 1872; Viscount Wolmer, 1882; Chairman, Agricultural and Food Research Council, since 1983 (Member, since 1975, Vice-Chairman, 1980–83); *b* 24 March 1940; *er s* of William Matthew, Viscount Wolmer (killed on active service, 1942), and of Priscilla (who *m* 1948, Hon. Peter Legh, now 4th Baron Newton, *qv*), *d* of late Captain John Egerton-Warburton; *S* grandfather, 1971; *m* 1969, Joanna Van Antwerp, *yr d* of Evan Maitland James, *qv*; three *s* one *d. Educ:* Eton; Christ Church, Oxford (MA). Vice-Chm., Apple and Pear Develt Council, 1969–73; Mem., Hops Mkting Bd, 1972–82 (Chm., 1978–82); Pres., South of England Agric. Soc., 1984. Treas., Bridewell Royal Hosp. (King Edward's Sch., Witley), 1972–83; Mem., Hampshire County Council, 1967–74. JP Hants 1971–78; DL Hants 1982. *Heir: s* Viscount Wolmer, *qv. Address:* Temple Manor, Selborne, Alton, Hants. *T:* Bordon 3646. *Club:* Brooks's.

SELBY, 4th Viscount, *cr* 1905; **Michael Guy John Gully;** Director: Kames Fish Farming Ltd; Ledger Selby Ltd; Verden Properties Ltd; *b* 15 Aug. 1942; *s* of 3rd Viscount and of Veronica, *er d* of late J. George and of Mrs Briscoe-George; *S* father, 1959; *m* 1965, Mary Theresa, *d* of late Capt. Thomas Powell, London, SW7; one *s* one *d. Educ:* Harrow. FCA. *Recreations:* shooting, fishing, sailing. *Heir: s* Hon. Edward Thomas William Gully, *b* 21 Sept. 1967. *Address:* Ardfern House, by Lochgilphead, Argyll PA31 8QN.

SELBY, Bishop Suffragan of, since 1983; **Rt. Rev. Clifford Conder Barker,** TD 1970; *b* 22 April 1926; *s* of Sidney and Kathleen Alice Barker; *m* 1952, Marie Edwards (*d* 1982); one *s* two *d*; 2nd, 1983, Mrs Audrey Gregson; two step *s* one step *d. Educ:* Oriel Coll., Oxford (BA 1950, MA 1955); St Chad's Coll., Durham (Dip. in Theol. 1952). Emergency Commn, The Green Howards, 1944–48; deacon 1952, priest 1953; Curate: All Saints', Scarborough, 1952–55; Redcar, 1955–57; Vicar: All Saints', Sculcoates, Hull, 1957–63; Rudby-in-Cleveland, 1963–70; RD of Stokesley, 1965–70; Vicar, St Olave with St Giles, York, 1970–76; RD of York, 1971–76; Canon of York, 1973–76; Bishop Suffragan of Whitby, 1976–83. CF (TA), 1958–74. *Recreations:* golf, gardening, music. *Address:* Greenriggs, 8 Bankside Close, Upper Poppleton, York YO2 6LH. *T:* York 795342. *Club:* Yorkshire (York).

SELBY, Sir Kenneth, Kt 1970; FCMA, FCCA, CBIM, FIQ; President, Bath & Portland Group plc, 1983–86; *b* 16 Feb. 1914; *s* of Thomas William Selby; *m* 1937, Elma Gertrude, *d* of Johnstone Sleator; two *s. Educ:* High School for Boys, Worthing. Bath & Portland Group Ltd: Managing Director, 1963–81; Chm., 1969–82. Governor, Wells Cathedral Sch., 1976–; Mem., Ct and Council, 1975–, Chm. Council, 1975–84, Pro Chancellor, 1975–, Bath Univ. Chm., Air Travel Reserve Fund Agency, 1975–86. Hon. LLD Bath, 1985. *Address:* Hartham Park, Corsham, Wilts. *T:* Corsham 713176. *Clubs:* Reform; Savages (Bristol).

SELBY, Rt. Rev. Peter Stephen Maurice; *see* Kingston-upon-Thames, Bishop of.

SELBY, Ralph Walford, CMG 1961; HM Diplomatic Service, retired; *b* 20 March 1915; *e s* of late Sir Walford Selby, KCMG, CB, CVO; *m* 1947, Julianna Snell; three *d. Educ:* Eton; Christ Church, Oxford. Entered HM Diplomatic Service, Sept. 1938; served in Foreign Office until Oct. 1939. Enlisted in Army and served with Grenadier Guards, March 1940–Feb. 1945, when returned to Foreign Office; seconded to Treasury for service in India as First Secretary in Office of High Commissioner for UK, Sept. 1947; transferred to The Hague, 1950; returned to FO, 1953–56; transf. to Tokyo as Counsellor, 1956, to Copenhagen in 1958, to Djakarta in 1961, to Warsaw in 1964; Chargé d'Affaires in 1952, 1958, 1959, 1960, 1961, 1962, 1964, 1965, 1969, 1970; Consul-Gen., Boston, 1966–69; Minister, British Embassy, Rome, 1969–72; Ambassador to Norway, 1972–75. *Recreation:* sports as available. *Address:* Mengeham House, Mengham Lane, Hayling Island, Hants PO11 9JX. *Clubs:* MCC; Royal Yacht Squadron (Cowes).

SELBY, Rear-Adm. William Halford, CB 1955; DSC 1942; *b* 29 April 1902; *s* of E. H. Selby; *m* 1926, Hilary Elizabeth Salter (*d* 1960); two *d*; *m* 1961, Mrs R. Milne. *Educ:* Royal Naval Colleges, Osborne and Dartmouth. Entered Royal Navy, 1916; Midshipman, HMS Royal Oak, Black Sea and Dardanelles, 1920; Sub.-Lt HMS Vendetta and HMY Victoria and Albert, 1924. Destroyers, Medit and China Station between 1927 and 1936; Naval Staff Coll., 1939; War of 1939–45: in comd HMS Wren, Mashona (despatches), Onslaught (despatches). Capt. 1943; Chief of Staff, Londonderry, 1944–45; Capt. 'D' Third Flotilla in comd HMS Saumarez, 1946–47; Dep. Dir Ops Div., Admty, 1948–50; Capt-in-Charge, Simonstown, 1950–52; Rear-Adm. 1953; Head of British Naval Mission to Greece, 1953–55; retired, 1956. *Address:* The Old Cottage, Chittoe, Chippenham, Wilts.

SELBY WRIGHT, Very Rev. Ronald (William Vernon); *see* Wright.

SELDON, Arthur, CBE 1983; economist and writer; Consultant, Institute of Economic Affairs, since 1981; Economic Consultant, since 1981; Editor, Economic Affairs, since 1980; *b* 29 May 1916; *m* Audrey Marjorie, *d* of Wilfred Willett and Eileen Willett (*née* Stenhouse) three *s*. *Educ:* Dempsey St Elementary Sch., Stepney; Raine's Foundation Sch. (State Scholar); LSE. BCom 1937 (1st cl. hons). Editor, Store, 1946–49; economist in industry, 1949–1959; Editorial Dir, Inst. of Economic Affairs, 1959–81. Chm., Liberal Party Cttee on the Aged, 1948–49; Mem., BMA Cttee on Health Financing, 1968–70; Adviser, Australian Cabinet Cttee on Welfare, 1968; Vice-Pres., Mont Pèlerin Soc., 1984–86; Founder Trustee, Social Affairs Unit, 1980. Member of advisory board: Jl of Post-Misesian Economics (Washington), 1983–; Inst für Bildungs- und Forschungspolitik (Cologne), 1983–; Libertaviansk Allianse (Oslo), 1983–; Ludwig von Mises Institut (Brussels), 1983–. *Publications:* Advertising in a Free Society (with Lord Harris of High Cross), 1959; Pensions for Prosperity, 1960; Everyman's Dictionary of Economics (with F. G. Pennance), 1965, 2nd edn 1976; After the NHS, 1968; The Great Pensions Swindle, 1970; Charge, 1977; (with Lord Harris of High Cross) Over-ruled on Welfare 1963–78, 1979; Wither the Welfare State, 1981; Socialism Explained, 1983 (US edn as Socialism: the grand delusion, 1986); The Riddle of the Voucher, 1986; (with C. K. Rowley and G. Tullock) A Primer on Public Choice, 1987. *Recreations:* work, cricket, opera, parties for non-conformists. *Address:* The Thatched Cottage, Godden Green, Sevenoaks, Kent. *T:* Sevenoaks 61499.

SELDON TRUSS, Leslie; author; *b* 21 Aug. 1892; *s* of George Marquand Truss and Ann Blanche, *d* of Samuel Seldon, CB; *m* 1st, 1918, Gwendolen, *d* of Charles Kershaw, Cooden Mount, Sussex; one *d*; 2nd, 1925, Kathleen Mary (*d* 1981), *d* of Charles Hornung, of Oaklands, Hookwood, Surrey; one *s* one *d*. Scenario Editor, Gaumont Co., 1914. Lieut Scots Guards, Special Reserve, 1915–19, Flanders and the Somme; Major Home Guard, 1940–44. *Publications:* Gallows Bait, 1928; The Stolen Millionaire, 1929; The Man Without Pity, 1930; The Hunterstone Outrage, 1931; Turmoil at Brede, 1932; Mr Coroner Presides, 1932; They Came by Night, 1933; The Daughters of Belial, 1934; Murder Paves the Way, Escort to Danger, 1935; Draw the Blinds, Rooksmiths, 1936; The Man who Played Patience, She Could Take Care, Footsteps Behind Them, 1937; Foreign Bodies, 1938; The Disappearance of Julie Hints, 1940; Sweeter for his Going, Where's Mr Chumley?, 1949; Ladies Always Talk, 1950; Never Fight a Lady, 1951; Death of No Lady, 1952; Always Ask a Policeman, 1953; Put Out The Light, The High Wall, 1954; The Long Night, The Barberton Intrigue, 1956; The Truth About Claire Veryan, 1957; In Secret Places, 1958; The Hidden Men, 1959; One Man's Death, 1960; Seven Years Dead, 1961; A Time to Hate, 1962; Technique for Treachery, 1963; Walk a Crooked Mile, 1964; The Town That Went Sick, 1965; Eyes at the Window, 1966; The Bride That Got Away, 1967; The Hands of the Shadow, 1968; The Corpse That Got Away, 1969; under *pseudonym* of George Selmark, Murder in Silence, 1939; various short stories and serials; novels translated in 18 countries. *Recreations:* anything but writing. *Address:* Dale Hill House, Ticehurst, Sussex. *T:* Ticehurst 251.

SELF, Hugh Michael, QC 1973; a Recorder of the Crown Court, since 1975; *b* 19 March 1921; *s* of Sir (Albert) Henry Self, KCB, KCMG, KBE; *m* 1950, Penelope Ann, *d* of late John Drinkwater, poet and dramatist and Daisy (*née* Kennedy), violinist; two *d*. *Educ:* Lancing Coll.; Worcester Coll., Oxford (BA). Royal Navy, 1942–46, Lieut RNVR 1946. Called to Bar, Lincoln's Inn, 1951, Bencher, 1980. *Recreations:* golf, walking in England, literature. *Address:* 59 Maresfield Gardens, Hampstead, NW3 5TE. *T:* 01–435 8311. *Club:* Savile.
See also Prof. P. J. O. Self.

SELF, Prof. Peter John Otter; Emeritus Professor of Public Administration, University of London; Visiting Fellow, Australian National University, since 1984; *b* 7 June 1919; *s* of Sir (Albert) Henry Self, KCB, KCMG, KBE; *m* 1st, 1950, Diana Mary Pitt (marr. diss.); 2nd, 1959, Elaine Rosenbloom Adams (marr. diss.); two *s*; 3rd, 1981, Sandra Guerita Gough (*née* Moiseiwitsch). *Educ:* Lancing Coll.; Balliol Coll., Oxford (MA). Editorial staff of The Economist, 1944–62; Extra-mural Lectr, London Univ., 1944–49; Lectr in Public Administration, LSE, 1948–61; Reader in Political Science, LSE, 1961–63; Prof. of Public Admin, Univ. of London, 1963–82; Sen. Res. Fellow, ANU, 1982–84. Dir of Studies (Administration), Civil Service Dept, 1969–70. Chm., Australian Govt Inquiry into Local Govt Finance, 1984–85. Mem. Exec. and Coun., 1954, Vice-Chm. Exec., 1955, Chm. Exec., 1961–69, Chm. Council, 1979–82, Town and Country Planning Assoc.; Mem., SE Regional Economic Planning Coun., 1966–79. Hon. Mem., RTPI. *Publications:* Regionalism, 1949; Cities in Flood: The Problems of Urban Growth, 1957; (with H. Storing) The State and the Farmer, 1962; Administrative Theories and Politics, 1972; Econocrats and the Policy Process, 1976; Planning the Urban Region, 1982; Political Theories of Modern Government, 1985; numerous articles on administration, politics and planning. *Recreations:* walking, golf, story-telling. *Address:* 17 Temple Street, Brill, Bucks. *T:* Brill 237443. *Club:* Reform.
See also H. M. Self.

SELIGMAN, Henry, OBE 1958; PhD; President, EXEC AG, Basle, 1975–85; Scientific Consultant (part-time) to International Atomic Energy Agency, Vienna, since 1969; Scientific Adviser to various industries, since 1970; *b* Frankfurt am Main, 25 Feb. 1909; *s* of Milton Seligman and Marie (*née* Gans); *m* 1941, Lesley Bradley; two *s*. *Educ:* Liebigschule Frankfurt; Sorbonne; Universities of Lausanne and of Zürich. Staff, DSIR, Cavendish Lab., Cambridge, 1942–43. Joined British-Canadian Research Project at Montreal, 1943, Chalk River, Ontario, 1944–; Staff, Brit. Atomic Energy Project, 1946; Head of Isotope Div., Atomic Energy Research Establishment, Harwell, UK, 1947–58; Dep. Dir Gen., Dept of Research and Isotopes, Internat. Atomic Energy Agency, Vienna, 1958–69. Austrian Decoration for Science and Art, 1979. Editor-in-Chief: Scientific Jl; Internat. Jl of Applied Radiation and Isotopes, 1973–. *Publications:* papers on: physical constants necessary for reactor development; waste disposal; production and uses of radioisotopes; contrib. scientific journals. *Address:* Scherpegasse 8/6/3, 1190 Vienna, Austria. *T:* Vienna 323225.

SELIGMAN, Madron; *see* Seligman, R. M.

SELIGMAN, Sir Peter (Wendel), Kt 1978; CBE 1969; BA; FIMechE; *b* 16 Jan. 1913; *s* of late Dr Richard Joseph Simon Seligman and of Hilda Mary Seligman; *m* 1937, Elizabeth Lavinia Mary Wheatley; two *s* four *d*. *Educ:* King's Coll. Sch., Wimbledon; Harrow Sch.; Kantonschule, Zürich; Caius Coll., Cambridge. Joined APV Co. Ltd, as Asst to Man. Dir, 1936; appointed Dir, 1939; Man. Dir, 1947; Dep. Chm., 1961; Chm., APV Holdings Ltd, 1966–77. Director: St Regis International Ltd, 1973–83 (Vice-Chm., 1981–83); EIBIS International Ltd, 1980–; Bell Bryant Pty Ltd, 1976–80; St Regis ACI Pty Ltd, 1980–84. Mem., Engineering Industries Council, 1975–77. Chm., Nat. Ski Fedn of GB, 1977–81. *Recreations:* ski-ing, yachting, carpentry. *Address:* Kings Lea, Kings Saltern Road, Lymington, Hants SO4 9QF. *T:* Lymington 76569. *Clubs:* Royal Over-Seas League; Royal Lymington Yacht; Hawks (Cambridge); Ski of Great Britain (Invitation Life Mem.); Kandahar Ski (Chm., 1972–77; Invitation Life Mem.).
See also R. M. Seligman.

SELIGMAN, (Richard) Madron; Member (C) Sussex West, European Parliament, since 1979; *b* 10 Nov. 1918; 4th *s* of late Dr Richard Seligman, FCGI, FIM, and Hilda Mary (*née* MacDowell); *m* 1947, Nancy-Joan, *d* of Julian Marks; three *s* one *d*. *Educ:* Rokeby Sch., Wimbledon; Harrow Sch.; Balliol Coll., Oxford (BA (Hons) PPE). Oxford Univ. ski team, 1938–39; President, Oxford Union, 1940. Served war, 6th Armoured Divisional Signals, N Africa and Italy, 1941–46, Major 1945. Dir, St Regis Internat., 1983–; Chm., Incinerator Company, Eaton Socon, 1960–. *Recreations:* tennis, skiing, gardening, piano, sailing. *Address:* Micklepage House, Nuthurst, near Horsham, Sussex. *T:* Lower Beeding 259 or 533. *Clubs:* Royal Thames Yacht, Royal Institute of International Affairs, MCC.
See also Sir Peter Seligman.

SELKIRK, 10th Earl of, *cr* 1646; **George Nigel Douglas-Hamilton,** KT 1976; GCMG 1959; GBE 1963 (OBE 1941); AFC; AE; PC 1955; QC(Scot.), 1959; late Gp Capt. Auxiliary Air Force; Scottish Representative Peer, 1945–63; *b* Merly, Wimborne, Dorset, 4 Jan. 1906; 2nd *s* of 13th Duke of Hamilton and Brandon; *S* to earldom of father under terms of special remainder, 1940; *m* 1949, Audrey Durell, *o d* of late Maurice Drummond-Sale-Barker and of Mrs H. S. Brooks. *Educ:* Eton; Balliol College, Oxford, MA; Edinburgh University, LLB. Admitted to Faculty of Advocates, 1935; Commanded 603 Squadron AAF, 1934–38; Captain, 44th Co., Boys' Brigade, 1932–38; Member of Edinburgh Town Council, 1935–40; Commisssioner of General Board of Control (Scotland), 1936–39; Commissioner for Special Areas in Scotland, 1937–39. Served War of 1939–45 (OBE, despatches twice). A Lord-in-Waiting to the Queen, 1952–53 (to King George VI, 1951–52); Paymaster-General, Nov. 1953–Dec. 1955; Chancellor of the Duchy of Lancaster, Dec. 1955–Jan. 1957; First Lord of the Admiralty, 1957–Oct. 1959; UK Commissioner for Singapore and Comr Gen. for SE Asia, 1959–63; also UK Council Representative to SEATO, 1960–63; Chm., Cons. Commonwealth Council, 1965–72. Freeman of Hamilton. President: National Ski Fedn of Great Britain, 1964–68; Anglo-Swiss Society, 1965–74; Building Societies Assoc., 1965–82; Royal Soc. for Asian Affairs, 1966–76; Assoc. of Independent Unionist Peers, 1967–79. Chm., Victoria League, 1971–77. Hon. Chief, Saulteaux Indians, 1967. Hon. Citizen of the City of Winnipeg and of the Town of Selkirk in Manitoba. *Address:* Rose Lawn Coppice, Wimborne, Dorset. *T:* Wimborne 883160; 60 Eaton Place, SW1. *T:* 01–235 6926. *Clubs:* Athenæum, Caledonian; New (Edinburgh).

SELLARS, John Ernest, CEng; FIMA, FRSA; MRAeS; Chief Executive, Business and Technician Education Council, since 1983; *b* 5 Feb. 1936; *s* of Ernest Buttle Sellars and Edna Grace Sellars; *m* 1958, Dorothy Beatrice (*née* Morrison); three *d*. *Educ:* Wintringham Grammar Sch., Grimsby; Manchester Univ. (BSc, MSc). Research Engineer, English Electric (GW) Ltd, 1958–61; Lectr, Royal College of Advanced Technology (now Univ. of Salford), 1961–67; Head of Mathematics, Lanchester College of Technology, Coventry, 1967–71; Head of Computer Science, Lanchester Polytechnic, Coventry/Rugby, 1971–74; Chief Officer, Business Educn Council, 1974–83. Member: Bd, Nat. Adv. Body for Public Sector Higher Educn, 1982–; BBC School Broadcasting Council for UK, 1982–. *Publications:* papers on mathematics, computer science and business educn. *Recreation:* walking. *Address:* 306 Cassiobury Drive, Watford, Herts WD1 3AW. *T:* Watford 33055. *Club:* Reform.

SELLERS, Norman William Malin, VRD; DL; **His Honour Judge Sellers;** a Circuit Judge, since 1974; *b* 29 Aug. 1919; *e s* of late Rt Hon. Sir Frederic Sellers, MC, and of Grace (*née* Malin); *m* 1946, Angela Laurie, *er d* of Sidney Jukes, Barnet; four *d*. *Educ:* Merchant Taylors' Sch., Crosby; Silcoates Sch., Wakefield; Hertford Coll., Oxford (MA). Officer, RNVR, 1940–65 (despatches, HMS Nelson, 1942); Lt Cdr 1953, comd HMS Mersey. Called to Bar, Gray's Inn, 1947; Northern Circuit; Asst Recorder of Blackpool, 1962–71; Recorder of Crown Court, 1972–74. Contested (L) Crosby Div. of Lancs, 1964. DL Lancs, 1986. *Recreation:* sailing. *Address:* Hillside, Lower Road, Longridge, Preston PR3 2YN. *T:* Longridge 3222. *Clubs:* Bar Yacht, Ribble Cruising.

SELLERS, Philip Edward; Board Member for Corporate and Finance Planning (formerly for Finance), The Post Office, since 1984; *b* 20 March 1937; *s* of George Edward and Helen Sellers; *m* 1962, Brenda Anne Bell; two *s*. *Educ:* Ernest Bailey Grammar School, Matlock; CIPFA. Local Govt, 1953–72; Controller of Audit, British Gas Corp., 1972–76; Finance Dir, North Thames Gas, 1976–80; Dir of Finance and Planning, British Rail Board, 1980–84. Pres., CIPFA, 1985–86. *Recreations:* The Institute (CIPFA), tennis. *Address:* Yarrimba, 31 Howards Thicket, Gerrards Cross, Bucks. *T:* Gerrards Cross 884669.

SELLERS, Robert Firth, ScD; FRSE; MRCVS; Consultant, Foreign Animal Disease Unit, Agriculture, Canada, since 1985; *b* 9 June 1924; *s* of Frederick Sellers and Janet Walkinshaw Shiels; *m* 1951, Margaret Peterkin; one *s* one *d*. *Educ:* Christ's Hospital; Gonville and Caius Coll., Cambridge (MA, ScD); Royal (Dick) School of Veterinary Studies, Edinburgh (PhD, BSc). Served War, Royal Artillery, 1943–46. Research Institute (Animal Virus Diseases), Pirbright, 1953–58; Wellcome Research Laboratories, Beckenham, 1958–62; Instituto Venezolano de Investigaciones Cientificas, Venezuela, 1962–64; Animal Virus Research Institute, Pirbright, 1964–84, Dep. Dir, 1964–79, Dir, 1979–84. J. T. Edwards Meml Medal, 1976. *Publications:* papers on animal viruses in scientific jls. *Recreation:* archaeology. *Address:* Animal Diseases Research Institute, PO Box 11300, Station H, Nepean, Ontario, Canada; 4 Pewley Way, Guildford, Surrey GU1 3PY.

SELLORS, Patrick John Holmes, FRCS; Surgeon-Oculist to the Queen, since 1980; Surgeon, King Edward VIIth Hospital for Officers, since 1975; Ophthalmic Surgeon, Croydon Eye Unit, since 1970; *b* 11 Feb. 1934; *s* of Sir Thomas Holmes Sellors, *qv*; *m* 1961, Gillian Gratton Swallow; two *s* one *d*. *Educ:* Rugby Sch.; Oriel Coll., Oxford; Middlesex Hosp. Med. School. MA Oxon; BM, BCh Oxon 1958; FRCS 1965. Registrar, Moorfields Eye Hosp., 1962–65; recognised teacher in Ophthalmology, St George's Hosp., 1966; Ophthalmic Surgeon, St George's Hosp., 1965–82 (Hon., 1983); Surgeon-Oculist to HM Household, 1974–80; Hon. Consultant Ophthalmic Surgeon, St Luke's Hosp. for the Clergy, 1983–. Sec. to Ophthalmic Soc. of UK, 1970–72; Examr for Diploma of Ophthalmology, 1974–77; Member: Council, Faculty of Ophthalmologists, 1977–; Council, Gen. Optical Council, 1978–. Vice-Pres., Med. Defence Union, 1977–. *Publications:* articles in BMJ and Trans OSUK. *Recreations:* gardening, golf. *Address:* 149 Harley Street, W1N 2DE. *T:* 01–935 4444.

SELLORS, Sir Thomas Holmes, Kt 1963; DM, MCh; FRCP; FRCS; Consultant Surgeon, London Chest Hospital, since 1934; Emeritus Thoracic Surgeon, Middlesex Hospital, since 1947; Consultant Surgeon, National Heart and Harefield Hospitals, since 1957; Consulting Surgeon, Aylesbury Group of Hospitals; *b* 7 April 1902; *s* of Dr T. B. Sellors; *m* 1st, Brenda Lyell (*d* 1928); 2nd, 1932, Dorothy Elizabeth Chesshire (*d* 1953); one *s* one *d*; 3rd, 1955, Marie Hobson (*d* 1986). *Educ:* Loretto School; Oriel Coll., Oxford, Hon. Fellow 1973. BA Oxon 1923, MA 1927; MRCS, LRCP 1926; BM, BCh Oxon 1926; G. H. Hunt Travelling Scholarship, Univ. of Oxford, 1928; MCh 1931, DM 1933.

Held various appts in London hosps; FRCS 1930; Member of Council, RCS, 1957–73, Vice-Pres., 1968–69, President 1969–72; FRCP 1963; Chairman of Joint Consultants Committee, 1958–67; President: Thoracic Society, 1960; Soc. of Thoracic Surgeons of Great Britain and Ireland, 1961–62; BMA, 1972; Royal Med. Benevolent Fund; Pres., Internat. Soc. Surg., 1977–79, Pres. Congress 1977; Chm. Council, British Heart Foundn. Surgeon to Royal Waterloo and Queen Mary's Hospitals; Regional Adviser in Thoracic Surgery, 1940–45. Hunterian Prof. RCS, 1944; Chm., Hunterian Trustees, 1981– (Trustee, 1978). Lectures: Carey Coombs, Univ. of Bristol, 1956; G. A. Gibson, RCPE, 1959; Strickland Goodall, Society Apothecaries, 1960; Entwhistle Meml and W. W. Hamburger, Chicago, 1961; St Cyre's, 1965; Grey-Turner, Internat. Soc. Surg., 1967; Gordon-Taylor, RCS, 1968; Tudor Edwards Meml, RCS, 1968; Bradshaw, RCS, 1969; Colles, RCSI, 1975. Hunterian Orator, RCS, 1973. Examiner in Surgery, Univ. of Oxford. Member: Acad. of Medicine, Rome; Royal Acad. of Medicine, Belgium; Membre d'Honneur, Europe Cardiol. Soc.; Hon. Fellow: Amer. Coll. Surgeons, 1971; Coll. of Med., S Africa; RCSE, 1972; RCSI; Faculty of Dental Surgeons, RCS, 1974. MD (*hc*) Groningen, 1964; Hon. DSc Liverpool, 1970; Hon. MS Southampton, 1972; BMA Gold Medal, 1979; Médaille de la Reconnaissance Française. Officer of the Order of Carlos Finlay, Cuba. *Publications:* Surgery of the Thorax, 1933. Editor and contributor in current text books. Articles in English and foreign medical publications. *Recreations:* water-colour painting, gardening. *Address:* Spring Coppice Farm, Speen, Aylesbury, Bucks. *T:* Hampden Row 379.

See also P. J. H. Sellors.

SELLS, Sir David (Perronet), Kt 1980; *b* 23 June 1918; *s* of late Edward Perronet Sells; *m* 1948, Beryl Cecilia, *er d* of late C. E. W. Charrington, MC; three *s*. *Educ:* Sandroyd Sch.; Repton Sch.; Christ Church, Oxford. Commissioned, Coldstream Guards, 1941; active service, N Africa and Italy. Called to Bar, Inner Temple, 1947. Chairman: Cambridgeshire Conservative and Unionist Assoc., 1962–67; Conservative Council for Europ. Constit. of Cambs, 1978–85; Mem. Executive Cttee, Nat. Union of Conservative and Unionist Assocs, 1965–81; Chairman, Conservative Central Council and Conservative Party Conf., 1977–78. *Recreations:* fishing, painting, shooting. *Address:* Tadlow House, Tadlow, Royston, Herts SG8 0EL. *T:* Wrestlingworth 228. *Club:* Savile.

SELLY, Susan, (Mrs Clifford Selly); *see* Strange, S.

SELSDON, 3rd Baron, *cr* 1932, of Croydon; **Malcolm McEacharn Mitchell-Thomson;** Bt 1900; banker; *b* 27 Oct. 1937; *s* of 2nd Baron Selsdon (3rd Bt, *cr* 1900), DSC; *S* father, 1963; *m* 1965, Patricia Anne, *d* of Donald Smith; one *s*. *Educ:* Winchester College. Sub-Lieut, RNVR. Deleg. to Council of Europe and WEU, 1972–78. Midland Bank Group, 1976–: EEC Advr, 1979–, Group Public Finance Advr, 1985–. Dir of various companies. Chm., Committee for Middle East Trade (COMET), 1979–86; Mem., BOTB, 1983–. Chairman: Greater London and SE Regional Council for Sport and Recreation, 1977–83; London Docklands Arena Trust, 1984–. *Recreations:* rackets, squash, tennis, lawn tennis, cricket, ski-ing, sailing. *Heir: s* Hon. Callum Malcolm McEacharn Mitchell-Thomson, *b* 7 Nov. 1969. *Address:* c/o House of Lords, SW1. *Club:* MCC.

SELVON, Samuel Dickson; author since 1954; *b* Trinidad, West Indies, 20 May 1923; *m* 1st, 1947, Draupadi Persaud; one *d*; 2nd, 1963, Althea Nesta Daroux; two *s* one *d*. *Educ:* Naparima College, Trinidad. Wireless Operator, 1940–45; Journalist, 1946–50; Civil Servant, 1950–53. Fellow, John Simon Guggenheim Memorial Foundn (USA), 1954 and 1968; Travelling Schol., Soc. of Authors (London), 1958; Trinidad Govt Schol., 1962. Hon. DLitt Univ. of West Indies, 1985. Humming Bird Medal (Trinidad), 1969. *Publications:* A Brighter Sun, 1952; An Island is a World, 1954; The Lonely Londoners, 1956; Ways of Sunlight, 1957; Turn Again Tiger, 1959; I Hear Thunder, 1963; The Housing Lark, 1965; The Plains of Caroni, 1970; Those Who Eat the Cascadura, 1972; Moses Ascending, 1975; Moses Migrating, 1983; contribs to London Magazine, New Statesman and Nation, Sunday Times, also Evergreen Review (USA). *Recreations:* tennis, swimming, gardening, cooking.

SELWOOD, Brig. David Henry Deering; Brigadier, Legal, HQ British Army of the Rhine, since 1986; a Recorder of the Crown Court, since 1985; *b* 27 June 1934; *s* of Comdr George Deering Selwood, RN, and Enid Marguerite Selwood (*née* Rowlinson); *m* 1973, Barbara Dorothea (*née* Hütter); three *s* one *d*. *Educ:* Kelly Coll., Tavistock; University College of the South-West; Law Society's School of Law. Articled to G. C. Aldhouse, Esq., Plymouth, 1952–57; admitted Solicitor 1957; National Service, RASC 2/Lieut, 1957–59; private practice, Plymouth, 1959–61; TA 4 Devons, Lieut, 1959–61; commnd Army Legal Services Staff List, 1961; service on legal staffs, MoD, Headquarters: BAOR, MELF, FARELF, UKLF, Land Forces Cyprus, 1961–85; Asst Recorder, SE Circuit, 1980. Hon. Advocate, US Court of Military Appeals, 1972–. *Address:* HQ BAOR, BFPO 40. *Club:* Lansdowne.

SELWYN, John Sidney Augustus, OBE 1962 (MBE 1939); HM Diplomatic Service, retired; *b* 17 Oct. 1908; *s* of Rev. A. L. H. Selwyn; *m* 1932, Cicely Georgina Armour (marr. diss.); one *s* one *d* (and one *d* decd); *m* 1952, Janette Bruce Mullin (*d* 1968); one *s*; *m* 1971, Sonja Fischer; one *d*. *Educ:* St Lawrence College, Ramsgate; Royal Military Coll., Sandhurst. Entered the Indian Police, 1928. Served in NWF Campaigns, 1930, 1937 and 1941. Major, 12th Frontier Force Regt, active service in Burma, 1942–46, Allied Control Commission, Germany, 1946–48. Entered Diplomatic Service, 1948. Served in Bucharest, Lisbon, London, Lima, Santos, Beirut; Consul-General: Berlin, 1963; Strasbourg, 1964–68; Vice-Consul, Calais, 1969–73. *Recreation:* walking. *Address:* Erlaufstrasse 35/2/6, A-2344 Maria Enzersdorf-Südstadt, Austria. *Club:* Civil Service.

SEMEGA-JANNEH, Bocar Ousman, MBE 1954; High Commissioner for The Gambia in London and Ambassador to Western Germany, Belgium, Sweden, Switzerland, France and Austria, 1971–80, to The Holy See, 1979–80; *b* 21 July 1910; *s* of late Ousman Semega-Janneh, merchant and late Koumba Tunkara, The Gambia; *m* 1936, and other Muslim marriages; several *c*. *Educ:* Mohammedan Primary Sch.; Methodist Boys' High School. Air Raid Warden, Bathurst, 1939–45. Gambia Surveys Dept: Surveys Asst 1931; Surveyor 1937; Sen. Surveyor 1948; Dir 1953; retd 1966. Gambian High Comr, Senegal, 1967; Ambassador to Mauritania, Mali, Guinea and Liberia, and High Comr, Sierra Leone, 1969; rep. Gambia at Gen. Assembly of UN, 1968–; rep. at meetings of Ministers of Foreign Affairs and Heads of State and Govt of members of Organisation of African Unity, 1968–. Rep. Gambia, triennial Survey Officers' Conf., Cambridge, 1955–65. Boy Scout, 1925; District Scout-master, 1938–42; Chief Comr of Scouts, The Gambia, 1947–66 (Silver Acorn 1954). Bathurst City Council: Councillor, 1951; Dep. Chm., 1957; Chm., 1960; first Mayor 1965; resigned 1967. Vice-Pres. 1955–56, Pres. 1957–67, Gambia Football Assoc.; formerly: Mem. Kombo Rural Authority; Governor, Gambia High Sch.; Actg Mem. Gambia Oilseeds Marketing Bd; Mem. Bathurst Colony Team and Town Planning Bd; Mem. Consultative Cttee for foundation of Constitution; Mem., Mohammedan Sch. Man. Cttee. Grand Officer, Order of Merit: Senegal, 1971; Mauritania, 1971; Officer of Republic of The Gambia. *Recreations:* football, cricket, golf, lawn tennis (singles champion, Gambia, 1932–50). *Address:* 15 Hagan Street, Banjul, Republic of The Gambia.

SEMENOV, Prof. Nikolai Nikolaevich; Orders of Lenin; State awards; Director, Institute of Chemical Physics of the USSR Academy of Sciences since 1931; Professor, Moscow State University; *b* 16 April 1896; *s* of a state employee; *m* Lidiya Grigorievna Scherbakova; one *s* one *d*. *Educ:* Leningrad State University. Chief of Electronic Phenomena Laboratory of Physico-Technical Institute in Leningrad, 1920; Assistant Professor and then Professor, Leningrad Polytechnic Institute, 1920–41. (Jointly) Nobel Prize for Chemistry, 1956. Foreign Member: Royal Society, 1958; Acad. of Sciences of French Inst., 1978–; Member: USSR Academy of Sciences, 1932–; Chem. Soc. of England, 1949–; Naturalists' Soc., Leopoldina (Halle DDR), 1959; Polish Acad. of Scis, 1974; Amer. Chem. Soc., 1976; Hon. Fellow: Indian Academy of Sciences, 1959; Hungarian Academy of Sciences, 1961; New York Academy of Sciences, 1962; Roumanian Acad. Sci., 1965; Czechoslovakian Acad. Sci., 1965; Roy. Soc. of Edinburgh, 1966; For. Associate, Nat. Acad. of Sciences (USA), 1963; Corresp. Member: Akademie der Wissenschaften, Berlin, DDR, 1966; Bulgarian Acad. of Sciences, 1969; Hon. DSc: Oxford, 1960; Bruxelles, 1962; London, 1965; Hon. DrSci: Milan, 1964; Prague, 1965; Budapest, 1965; Humboldt-Universität zu Berlin, 1973; Vroclav Univ., 1976. *Publications:* several textbooks and scientific monographs, notably: Chain reactions, 1934 (Russia), 1935 (Oxford); Some Problems on Chemical Kinetics and Reactivity, 1954 (Russia), enlarged 2nd edn 1958 (Russia), (Eng. trans. 1959); Science and Community, 1973, 2nd edn 1981 (Russia); Science et société, 1981 (France); numerous articles in the field of chemical physics. *Address:* Kosygin str. 4, Institute of Chemical Physics, USSR Academy of Sciences, Moscow 117977, USSR.

SEMKEN, John Douglas, CB 1980; MC 1944; Legal Adviser to the Home Office, 1977–83; *b* 9 Jan. 1921; *s* of Wm R. Semken and Mrs B. R. Semken (*née* Craymer); *m* 1952, Edna Margaret, *yr d* of T. R. Poole; three *s*. *Educ:* St Albans Sch.; Pembroke Coll., Oxford (MA, BCL). Solicitor's articled clerk, 1938–39. Commnd in Sherwood Rangers Yeo., 1940; 1st Lieut 1941, Captain 1942, Major 1944; 8th Armd Bde, N Africa, 1942–43; Normandy beaches to Germany, 1944. Called to Bar, Lincoln's Inn, 1949; practised at Chancery Bar, 1949–54; joined Legal Adviser's Br., Home Office, 1954; Mem., Criminal Law Revision Cttee, 1980–83. Silver Star Medal (USA), 1944. *Address:* 2 The Ridgeway, Mill Hill, NW7 1RS. *T:* 01–346 3092. *Club:* Lawrenny Yacht.

SEMMENCE, Dr Adrian Murdoch, CB 1986; Civil Service Medical Adviser, since 1979, and Acting Director, Civil Service Occupational Health Service, Cabinet Office, Management and Personnel Office, since 1986; *b* 5 April 1926; *s* of Adrian George Semmence, MA, and Henrietta Scorgie (*née* Murdoch), MA; *m* 1949, Joan, *d* of Hugh and Bobbie Wood; four *s* one *d*. *Educ:* Robert Gordon's Coll.; Univ. of Aberdeen (MB, ChB 1953; MD 1957); Univ. of London (MSc 1972); DObstRCOG, FRCGP, DIH, FFOM, FRSM. Served War, RN, 1943–47. General Practitioner, E Yorks, Berks and Oxon, 1954–76; Nuffield Travelling Fellow, 1969–70; Unit of Clinical Epidemiology, Univ. of Oxford, 1970–76; Principal MO, CSD, 1976–79. Pres. Sect. of Occupational Med., RSM, 1985–86. *Address:* Stone Cottage, Steventon, Abingdon OX13 6RZ. *T:* Abingdon 831527. *Club:* Athenæum.

SEMPER, Very Rev. Colin (Douglas); Provost of Coventry Cathedral, since 1982; *b* 5 Feb. 1938; *s* of William Frederick and Dorothy Anne Semper; *m* 1962, Janet Louise Greaves; two *s*. *Educ:* Lincoln School; Keble College, Oxford (BA); Westcott House, Cambridge. Curate of Holy Trinity with St Mary, Guildford, 1963–66; Recruitment and Selection Sec., ACCM, 1966–69; Head of Religious Programmes, BBC Radio, and Deputy Head of Religious Broadcasting, BBC, 1969–82. *Recreations:* travel, reading modern novels, canals. *Address:* Provost's Lodge, Priory Row, Coventry, West Midlands CV1 5ES. *T:* Coventry 27597.

SEMPILL, family name of **Lady Sempill** (*née* Forbes-Sempill).

SEMPILL, Lady (20th in line, of the Lordship *cr* 1489); **Ann Moira Sempill** (*née* Forbes-Sempill); *b* 19 March 1920; *d* of 19th Lord Sempill, AFC; *S* father, 1965; *m* 1st, 1941, Captain Eric Holt (marr. diss., 1945); one *d*; 2nd, 1948, Lt-Col Stuart Whitemore Chant, OBE, MC (who assumed by decree of Lyon Court, 1966, the additional surname of Sempill), now Chant-Sempill; two *s*. *Educ:* Austrian, German and English Convents. Served War, 1939–42 (Petty Officer, WRNS). Mem. Cttee, Anglo Austrian Soc., 1966–. *Heir: s* The Master of Sempill, *qv*. *Address:* East Lodge, Druminnor, Rhynie, Aberdeenshire; 15 Onslow Court, Drayton Gardens, SW10.

See also Hon. Sir Ewan Forbes of Brux, Bt.

SEMPILL, Master of; Hon. James William Stuart Whitemore Sempill; Account Director, Bates Wells (Pty) Ltd, Advertising Agency, since 1986; Marketing Manager, South African Breweries, since 1983; *b* 25 Feb 1949; *s* and *heir* of Lady Sempill, *qv*, and of Lt-Col Stuart Whitemore Chant-Sempill; *m* 1977, Josephine Ann Edith, *e d* of J. Norman Rees, Johannesburg; one *s* one *d*. *Educ:* The Oratory School; St Clare's Hall, Oxford (BA Hons History, 1971); Hertford Coll., Oxford. Gallaher Ltd, 1972–80; PA to Managing Director, Sentinel Engineering Pty Ltd, Johannesburg, 1980–81; Manager, TWS Public Relations Company, Johannesburg, 1981–83; investment manager, Alan Clarke and Partners, 1982–83. *Address:* 50 Fort Street, Birnam, Johannesburg, 2193, South Africa. *Clubs:* Vincent's, Carlton (Oxford); Wanderers' (Johannesburg).

SEMPLE, Prof. Andrew Best, CBE 1966; VRD 1953; QHP 1962; Professor of Community and Environmental Health (formerly of Public Health), University of Liverpool, 1953–77, now Professor Emeritus; *b* 3 May 1912; *m* 1941, Jean (*née* Sweet); one *d*. *Educ:* Allan Glen's School, Glasgow; Glasgow Univ. MB, ChB 1934, MD 1947, DPH 1936, Glasgow. FFCM 1972. Various hospital appointments, 1934–38; Asst MOH and Deputy Medical Superintendent, Infectious Diseases Hosp., Portsmouth, 1938–39; Asst MOH and Asst School Medical Officer, Blackburn, 1939–47 (interrupted by War Service); Senior Asst MOH, Manchester, 1947–48; Deputy MOH, City and Port of Liverpool, 1948–53, MOH and Principal Sch. Med. Officer, 1953–74; Area MO (teaching), Liverpool AHA, 1974–77. Served War of 1939–46; Surgeon Commander, RNVR; Naval MOH, Western Approaches, Malta and Central Mediterranean. Chm. Council and Hon. Treasurer, RSH, 1963. *Publications:* various regarding infectious disease, port health, hygiene, etc. *Address:* Kelvin, 433 Woolton Road, Gateacre, Liverpool L25 4SY. *T:* 051–428 2081.

SEMPLE, Andrew Greenlees; Secretary, Water Authorities Association, since 1983; *b* 16 Jan. 1934; *s* of late William Hugh Semple and Madeline, *d* of late E. H. Wood, Malvern, Worcs; *m* 1961, Janet Elizabeth, *d* of late H. R. G. Whates and of Mrs Whates, Ludlow, Salop; one *s* one *d*. *Educ:* Winchester Coll.; St John's Coll., Cambridge (MA). Entered Min. of Transport and Civil Aviation, 1957; Private Sec. to Permanent Sec., 1960–62; Principal, 1962; Asst Sec., 1970; Private Sec. to successive Secs of State for the Environment, 1972–74; Under Sec., DoE, 1976; Principal Finance Officer, PSA, DoE, 1980–83. CompIWES 1984. *Recreations:* walking, reading, gardening, occasional golf. *Address:* 83 Burbage Road, SE24 9HB. *T:* 01–274 6550.

SEMPLE, John Laughlin; Under Secretary, Department of Finance and Personnel for Northern Ireland, since 1983; *b* 10 Aug. 1940; *s* of late James E. Semple and of Violet E.

G. Semple; *m* 1970, Maureen Anne Kerr; two *s* one *d*. *Educ:* Campbell Coll., Belfast; Corpus Christi Coll., Cambridge (MA). BScEcon London. Joined Home CS as Asst Principal, Min. of Aviation, 1961; transf. to NI CS, 1962; Asst Principal, Mins of Health and Local Govt, Finance, and Health and Social Services, 1962–65; Dep. Principal, Min. of Health and Social Services, 1965; Principal: Min. of Finance, 1968; Min. of Community Relations, 1970–72; Asst Sec. (Planning), Min. of Develt, 1972; Asst Sec. (Housing), DoE, 1977–79; Under Sec. (Housing), DoE for N Ireland, 1979–83. *Recreations:* golf, tennis, gardening. *Club:* Royal Belfast Golf.

SEMPLE, Prof. Stephen John Greenhill, MD, FRCP; Professor of Medicine, University College, London, and The Middlesex Hospital Medical School, since 1985; *b* 4 Aug. 1926; *s* of late John Edward Stewart and Janet Semple; *m* 1961, Penelope Ann, *y d* of Sir Geoffrey Aldington, *qv*; three *s*. *Educ:* Westminster; London Univ. MB, BS, 1950, MD 1952, FRCP 1968. Research Asst, St Thomas' Hosp. Med. Sch., 1952; Jun. Med. Specialist, RAMC, Malaya, 1953–55; Instr, Med. Sch., Univ. of Pennsylvania, USA, 1957–59; St Thomas' Hosp. Medical Sch.: Lectr, 1959; Sen. Lectr, 1961; Reader, 1965; Prof. in Medicine, 1969; Prof. of Medicine, The Middlesex Hosp. Medical Sch., 1970–84. *Publications:* Disorders of Respiration, 1972; articles in: Lancet, Jl Physiol. (London), Jl Applied Physiol. *Recreations:* tennis, music. *Address:* White Lodge, 3 Claremont Park Road, Esher, Surrey KT10 9LT. *T:* Esher 65057. *Club:* Queen's.

SEMPLE, William David Crowe; Director of Education, Lothian Region, since 1974; *b* 11 June 1933; *s* of late George Crowe and Helen Davidson Semple (*née* Paterson); *m* 1958, Margaret Bain Donald; one *s* one *d*. *Educ:* Glasgow Univ.; Jordanhill Coll. of Educn; London Univ. BSc Hons, DipEd. FBIM. Educn Officer, Northern Rhodesia, 1958–64; Zambia: Dep. Chief Educn Officer, 1964–66; Chief Educn Officer, 1966–67; Actg Dir of Techn. Educn, 1967–68; Edinburgh: Asst Dir of Educn, 1968–72; Depute Dir of Educn, 1972–74. Member: Sec. of State (Scot.) Wkg Party on Educnl Catering, 1971–73; Council for Tertiary Educn in Scotland, 1979–83; STV Educn Adv. Cttee, 1979–85; UK Nat. Cttee for UNESCO, 1981–85; UGC, 1983–. *Publications:* contrib. various journals. *Recreations:* gardening, reading, gastronomy. *Address:* 15 Essex Park, Edinburgh EH4 6LH. *T:* 031-339 6157.

SEN, Prof. Amartya Kumar, FBA 1977; Drummond Professor of Political Economy, Oxford University, since 1980 (Professor of Economics, 1977–80); Fellow of All Souls College, since 1980; *b* 3 Nov. 1933; *s* of late Dr Ashutosh Sen, Dacca, and of Amita Sen, Santiniketan, India; *m* 1st, 1960, Nabaneeta Dev (marr. diss. 1975); two *d*; 2nd, 1978, Eva Colorni (*d* 1985); one *s* one *d*. *Educ:* Calcutta Univ.; Cambridge Univ. MA, PhD. Prof. of Economics, Jadavpur Univ., Calcutta, 1956–58; Trinity Coll., Cambridge: Prize Fellow, 1957–61; Staff Fellow, 1961–63; Professor of Economics: Delhi Univ., 1963–71 (Chm., Dept of Economics, 1966–68, Hon. Prof., 1971–); LSE, 1971–77; Fellow, Nuffield College, Oxford, 1977–80 (Associate Mem., 1980–). Hon. Dir, Agricultural Economics Research Centre, Delhi, 1966–68 and 1969–71. Res. Advr, World Inst. for Develt Econ. Res., Helsinki, Finland, 1985–. Vis. Professor: MIT, 1960–61; Univ. of Calif at Berkeley, 1964–65; Harvard Univ., 1968–69; Andrew D. White Professor-at-large, Cornell Univ., 1978–84. Chm., UN Expert Gp Meeting on Role of Advanced Skill and Technology, New York, 1967; Pres., Econometric Soc., 1984 (Fellow 1968–, Vice-Pres. 1982–83); Mem. Council, Royal Economic Soc., 1977–; Pres., Development Studies Assoc., 1980–82. Foreign Hon. Mem., Amer. Acad. of Arts and Sciences, 1981; Hon. Mem., Amer. Econ. Assoc., 1981. Hon. Fellow: Inst. of Social Studies, The Hague, 1982; LSE, 1984; IDS, Sussex Univ., 1984. Hon. DLitt: Saskatchewan, 1980; Visva-Bharati Univ., 1983; Hon. DSc Bath, 1984; DU Essex, 1984. *Publications:* Choice of Techniques: an aspect of planned economic development, 1960 (3rd edn, 1968); Growth Economics, 1970; Collective Choice and Social Welfare, 1971; On Economic Inequality, 1973; Employment, Technology and Development, 1975; Poverty and Famines: an essay on entitlement and deprivation, 1981; (ed with Bernard Williams) Utilitarianism and Beyond, 1982; Choice, Welfare and Measurement, 1982; Resources, Values and Development, 1984; Commodities and Capabilities, 1985; On Ethics and Economics, 1987; articles in various jls in economics, philosophy and political science. *Address:* All Souls College, Oxford OX1 4AL. *T:* Oxford 722251.

SEN, Shri Binay Ranjan, Padmavibhusan 1970; CIE 1944; ICS; Director-General of the United Nations Food and Agriculture Organisation, Rome, 1956–67; *b* 1 Jan. 1898; *s* of Dr K. M. Sen; *m* 1931, Chiroprova Chatterjee. *Educ:* Calcutta and Oxford Universities. Secretary to Govt of Bengal, Political and Appointment Departments, and Press Officer, 1931–34; District Magistrate, Midnapore, 1937–40; Revenue Secretary to Government of Bengal, 1940–43; Director of Civil Evacuation, Bengal, 1942–43; Relief Commissioner, 1942–43; Director-General of Food, Government of India, 1943–46; Sec. to Food Dept, Govt of India, 1946; Minister of the Embassy of India, at Washington, 1947–50; Indian Ambassador to: Italy and Yugoslavia, 1950–51; US and Mexico, 1951–52; Italy and Yugoslavia, 1952–55; Japan, 1955–56. Member Indian Delegation to General Assembly of United Nations, 1947; India's Rep. to United Nations Security Council, 1947; Agriculture Sec. to Govt of India, 1948; Head of Jt Mission of FAO and ECAFE (Economic Commn for Asia and the Far East) in Far East to study Agricultural Development plans; Head of Ind. Deleg. to: ECOSOC (Economic and Social Council of the UN), 1949 and 1953; Annual Conf. of FAO, 1949, and FAO Coun., 1950, 1951, 1953. Hon. Fellow, St Catherine's Coll., Oxford. Several Hon. degrees and decorations, incl. Kt Comdr Piani Ordinis, and Kt Grand Cross Ordinis Sancti Silvetri Papae. *Address:* 14/2 Palm Avenue, Calcutta 19, India.

SEN, K. Chandra; late Indian CS; *b* 5 Oct. 1888; *s* of Durgadas Sen and Mokshada Sundari Devi; *m* 1916, Lilavati Das-Gupta; one *s* two *d*. *Educ:* Hindu Sch., Calcutta; Presidency College, Calcutta; Trinity Hall, Cambridge (BA in Moral Sciences Tripos, 1913). Joined Indian Civil Service, 1913; Assistant Collector, Bombay Presidency, 1913–21; service in Judicial department of Government of Bombay since 1921; acted as a puisne judge of Bombay High Court, various times 1934–38; Secretary to Government of Bombay, Legal Department and Remembrancer of Legal Affairs, 1935–37; Additional Judge of High Court, 1939–41; Judge, High Court of Bombay, 1941–48; Pres. Industrial Court, Bombay, 1948–53; Pres. Bombay Co-op, Revenue, and Sales Tax Tribunals, between 1953 and 1959; Constitutional Adviser to Govt of West Bengal and Chm., State Law Commn, 1959–64; Chm., Police Commn, W Bengal, and Mem. Hindu Religious Endowments Commn, 1960–62. *Address:* A-12, Sea Face Park, Bombay 26, India. *T:* 82–4368.

SEN, Prof. Satyendra Nath, MA, PhD (Econ) London; Chairman, Board of Governors, Indian Institute of Technology, Kharagpur, since 1981; President, Calcutta Local Board and Member, Central Board of Directors, State Bank of India, since 1979; Vice-Chancellor, 1968–76, Professor of Economics, 1958–76, Calcutta University; *b* April 1909. Visited UK and other parts of Europe, 1949–51; Vis. Prof., Princeton and Stanford Univs (sponsored Ford Foundn), 1962–63; subseq. Dean, Faculties of Arts and Commerce, and Head of Dept of Econs, Calcutta University. Mem. Bd of Trustees: Indian Museum, Calcutta; Victoria Memorial, Calcutta; Mahajati Sadan, Calcutta; Mem. Research Programmes Cttee, Planning Commn, Govt of India (Chm. East Regional Cttee); Mem. Pay Commn, Govt of W Bengal, 1967–69; Discussion Leader, Section on Medium and Longterm Credit, Internat. Conf. on Agricultural Credit, Lahore (FAO and ECAFE), 1956; Mem. Industrial Tribunal adjudicating dispute between United Bank of India Ltd and its employees, 1954–55. Mem., Nat. Co-operative Union, Delhi; Vice-Pres., State Co-operative Union, W Bengal. Mem. Adv. Cttee of Vice-Chancellors, New Delhi, and Chm., Cttee on salary scales of univ. and coll. teachers, 1974, Univ. Grants Commn; Mem. Exec. Cttee, Assoc. of Commonwealth Univs, 1974; Pres., Assoc. of Indian Univs, 1976; Mem., Central Adv. Commn on Educn, Govt of India, 1976. Pres., Asiatic Soc., Calcutta, 1983– (Hon. Fellow, 1982). *Publications:* Central Banking in Undeveloped Money Markets, 1952; The City of Calcutta: a socio-economic survey, 1954–55 to 1957–58, 1960; The Co-operative Movement in West Bengal, 1966; (with T. Piplai) Industrial Relations in Jute Industry in West Bengal, 1968. *Address:* 18c Lake View Road, Calcutta, West Bengal, 700029, India.

SENDAK, Maurice Bernard; writer and illustrator of children's books; theatrical designer; *b* 10 June 1928; *yr s* of Philip Sendak and Sarah (*née* Schindler). *Educ:* Lafayette High School, Brooklyn; Art Students' League, NY. Worked part-time at All American Comics; window display work with Timely Service, 1946–48, F. A. O. Schwartz, 1948–50; illustrated over 50 books by other writers, 1951–. Retrospective one-man exhibitions: Sch. of Visual Arts, NY, 1964; Ashmolean, Oxford, 1975; Amer. Cultural Center, Paris, 1978. *Stage designs:* The Magic Flute, Houston, 1980; The Cunning Little Vixen, NY, 1981; The Love of Three Oranges, Glyndebourne, 1982; Where the Wild Things Are, NT, 1984. *Publications:* Kenny's Window, 1956; Very Far Away, 1957; The Sign on Rosie's Door, 1960; Nutshell Library set, 1962; Where the Wild Things Are, 1963 (Amer. Liby Assoc. Caldecott Medal, 1964); Higglety Pigglety Pop!, 1967; Hector Protector, 1967; In the Night Kitchen, 1971; (with Charlotte Zolotow) Rabbit and the Lovely Present, 1971; Pictures, 1972; Maxfield Parrish Poster Book, 1974; (with Matthelo Margolis) Some Swell Pup, 1976; Charlotte and the White Horse, 1977; (ed) Disney Poster Book, 1977; Seven Little Monsters, 1977; (with Doris Orgel) Sarah's Room, 1977; Very Far Away, 1978; Outside Over There, 1981; (with Frank Corsaro) The Love for Three Oranges, 1984; (with Ralph Manheim) Nutcracker, 1984. *Address:* c/o Harper & Row, 10 East 53rd Street, New York, NY 10022, USA.

SENDALL, Bernard Charles, CBE 1952; Deputy Director-General, Independent Broadcasting Authority (formerly Independent Television Authority), 1955–77; *b* 30 April 1913; *s* of late William Sendall, Malvern, Worcestershire; *m* 1963, Barbara Mary, *d* of late Ambrose Coviello, DCM, FRAM. *Educ:* Magdalen College, Oxford; Harvard University. Entered Civil Service in the Admiralty, 1935; Principal Private Secretary to Minister of Information 1941–45; Controller (Home), Central Office of Information, 1946–49; Controller, Festival of Britain Office, 1949–51; Assistant Secretary, Admiralty, 1951–55. *Publication:* Independent Television in Britain, vol. I, 1982, vol. II, 1983. *Address:* 144 Montagu Mansions, York Street, W1.

SENIOR, (Alan) Gordon, CBE 1981; CEng, FICE, FIStructE; Managing Partner, Gordon Senior Associates, Consulting Engineers, since 1980; Director, Armstrong Technology Services Ltd, since 1986; *b* 1 Jan. 1928; *s* of late Oscar Senior and Helen Senior (*née* Cooper); *m* 1st, 1955, Sheila Lockyer (marr. diss. 1961); 2nd, 1968, Lawmary Mitchell (marr. diss. 1978); one *s*. *Educ:* Normanton Grammar School; Leeds Univ. (BSc 1948, MSc 1949). J. B. Edwards (Whyteleafe) Ltd, 1949–51; Oscar Faber & Partners, Consulting Engineers, 1951–54; W. S. Atkins & Partners, Consulting Engineers, 1954–80: Technical Dir, 1967; Man. Dir of Atkins Research and Development, 1972; Director, W. S. Atkins & Partners, 1976. Chm., Surface Engineering and Inspection Ltd, 1983–86; Dir, Ansen Offshore Consultants Ltd and McMillan Sloan & Partners, 1981–84. Member, Navy Dept Advisory Cttee on Structural Steels, 1967–71. Science and Engineering Research Council: Mem., Engineering Bd, 1974–78; Chm., Transport and Civil Engineering Cttee, 1974–78; Chm., Marine Technology Management Cttee, 1980–83. Department of Trade and Industry: Mem., Ship and Marine Technology Requirements Bd, and Chm., Marine Technology Cttee, 1976–81; Mem., Maritime Technology Cttee, 1981–86; Chm., Adv. Cttee on Resources from the Sea, 1983–86. Member: Programme Cttee, Offshore Energy Technology Bd, 1978–85; Offshore Safety and Tech. Bd, 1985–. Vice-Pres. and Chm. of Council, Soc. for Underwater Technology, 1979–81. *Publications:* (co-author) Brittle Fracture of Steel Structures, 1970; papers on welding, fatigue, brittle fracture, design of steel structures and future developments offshore and in the oceans. *Recreations:* food and wine, travel, water ski-ing. *Address:* Deanlands, Guildford Road, Normandy, Surrey GU3 2AR. *T:* Worplesdon 235496. *Club:* Athenæum.

SENIOR, Derek; free-lance writer; *b* 4 May 1912; *s* of Oliver and Sally G. Senior; *m* 1st, 1942, Edith Frances Bentley; one *s* two *d*; 2nd, 1959, Helen Elizabeth Mair; one *d*. *Educ:* six elementary schools; Manchester Grammar Sch.; Balliol Coll., Oxford (BA). Joined editorial staff of Manchester Guardian, 1937; turned free-lance, 1960. Member, Royal Commission on Local Government in England, 1966–69. Mem., Basildon Develt Corp., 1975–79. Hon. MRTPI (Hon. AMTPI 1956). *Publications:* Guide to the Cambridge Plan, 1956; Your Architect, 1964; The Regional City, 1966; Memorandum of Dissent from Redcliffe-Maud Report, 1969; Skopje Resurgent, 1971; numerous planning publications. *Recreation:* gardening. *Address:* Birling House, Birling, Maidstone, Kent. *T:* West Malling 842229.

SENIOR, Sir Edward (Walters), Kt 1970; CMG 1955; Chairman, Ransome Hoffman Pollard Ltd, 1953–72; Chairman, George Senior & Sons Ltd, since 1930 (Managing Director, 1929); *b* 29 March 1902; *s* of Albert Senior; *m* 1928, Stephanie Vera Heald; one *s* one *d*. *Educ:* Repton School; Sheffield University. Vice-Consul for Sweden, in Sheffield, 1930; RA, TA, Major, 1938; General Director of Alloy and Special Steels, Iron and Steel Control, 1941; Director, Steel Division of Raw Materials Mission, Washington, DC, 1942; Controller of Ball and Roller Bearings, 1944; British Iron and Steel Federation: Commercial Dir, 1949–61; Dir, 1961–62; Dir-Gen., 1962–66; retd, Dec. 1966; Exec. Chm., Derbyshire Stone Ltd, 1967–68; Dep. Chm., Tarmac Derby Ltd, 1968–71. Master of Cutlers' Company of Hallamshire in County of York, 1947; Vice-President of the Sheffield Chamber of Commerce, 1948; Chairman of Steel Re-Armament Panel, 1951. FBIM, 1971. JP Sheffield, 1937–50. *Recreations:* normal country activities. *Address:* Hollies, Church Close, Brenchley, Tonbridge, Kent TN12 7AA. *T:* Brenchley 2359. *Clubs:* Naval and Military; Sheffield (Sheffield).

SENIOR, Gordon; *see* Senior, A. G.

SENIOR, Olive Edith, JP, MPhil, SRN; Regional Nursing Officer, Trent Regional Health Authority, since Nov. 1973; *b* 26 April 1934; *d* of Harold and Doris Senior, Mansfield, Notts. *Educ:* Harlow Wood Orthopaedic Hosp., 1949–52; St George's Hosp., Hyde Park Corner, 1952–56; City Hosp., Nottingham (Pt I, CMB 1956); Nottingham Univ. (HV Cert. 1957, MPhil 1978). Health Visitor, Notts CC, 1958–60; St George's Hosp., London (Ward Sister), 1960–63; S Africa, June-Dec. 1963; Forest Gate Hosp., London (SCM), 1964; St Mary's Hosp., Portsmouth (Asst Matron/Night Supt), 1964–66; NE Metropolitan Regional Hosp. Bd (Management Services), 1966–71; Chief Nursing Officer, Nottingham and Dist. Hosp. Management Cttee, 1971–73. Secretary of State Fellow, 1973. JP

Nottingham Guildhall, 1973. *Publications:* An Analysis of Nurse Staffing Levels in Hospitals in the Trent Region (1977 Data), 1978; Dependency and Establishments, 1979; contrib. to Nursing Times (Determining Nursing Establishments). *Address:* Trent Regional Health Authority, Fulwood House, Old Fulwood Road, Sheffield S10 3TH. *T:* Sheffield 306511. *Club:* Nottingham Univ. (Nottingham).

SENIOR, Ronald Henry, DSO 1940, Bar 1943; TD; *b* 3 July 1904; *e s* of Lawrence Henry Senior and Emmadonna Shuttleworth, *d* of Reverend J. S. Holden, Aston-on-Trent, Derbyshire; *m* 1932, Hon. Norah Marguerite Joicey, *e d* of 2nd Baron Joicey; two *d. Educ:* Cheltenham College. Chairman, Nat. Assoc. of Port Employers, 1954–59. Joined TA 1924; served France, 1940; Middle East; Sicily, NW Europe. Hon. Rank Brigadier. *Recreation:* golf. *Address:* 110 Eaton Square, SW1. *Club:* Carlton.

SENOUSSI, Badreddine; Officer, Order of Ouissame Alaouite, Morocco; Ambassador of the Kingdom of Morocco to the Court of St James's, 1977–80; *b* 30 March 1933; *m* 1958; three *s. Educ:* Univ. of Bordeaux, France (Lic. (MA) en Droit); Univ. Mohamed V Rabat, Morocco (Lic. ès Lettres). Counsellor, High Cherifian Tribunal, 1956; in charge of: State Min. of Public Functions, Mar. 1957; Nat. Defense Min., Mar.-Sept. 1958; Gen. Sec., Tobacco Management, Oct. 1958–Feb. 1963; Chief, Royal Cabinet, 1963–64; Under-Sec. of State for Commerce, Industry, Mines and Merchant Navy, Dec. 1964–June 1965; Under-Sec. of State for Admin. Affairs, June 1965–Feb. 1966; Post and Telecommunications Minister, Feb. 1966–Mar. 1970; Benslimane Dep., Mem. Representative Chamber, Aug. 1970; Youth, Sports and Social Affairs Minister, Mar. 1970–Aug. 1971; Ambassador of Kingdom of Morocco: in Washington, Sept 1971–Dec. 1974; in Teheran, Mar. 1974–Sept. 1976. Holds many foreign honours. *Address:* Km 5, Route des Zaers, Rabat, Morocco. *Clubs:* Les Ambassadeurs, Mark's.

SENSI, His Eminence Cardinal (Giuseppe M.); *b* 27 May 1907. Ordained, 1929; Sec. of Apostolic Nunciature in Roumania, 1934–38; Secretary and Auditor of Apostolic Nunciature in Switzerland, 1938–46; Councillor of Apostolic Nunciature in Belgium, 1946–47; Chargé d'Affaires of the Holy See in Prague, 1948–49; Councillor in the Secretariat of State of His Holiness, 1949–53; Permanent Observer of the Holy See at UNESCO in Paris, 1953–55; apptd Nuncio Apostolic to Costa Rica, May 1955, and consecrated Titular Archbishop of Sardi, July 1955; Apostolic Delegate to Jerusalem, 1957; Apostolic Nuncio to Ireland, 1962–67; Apostolic Nuncio to Portugal, 1967–76; Cardinal, 1976. Hon. Mem., Accademia Cosentiria, 1976. *Address:* Piazza S Calisto 16, 00153 Rome, Italy.

SERBY, John Edward, CB 1958; CBE 1951; FRAeS; Consultant; *b* 15 March 1902; *m* 1933, Clarice Lilian (*née* Hawes); one *d. Educ:* Haberdashers' Aske's School; Emmanuel College, Cambridge (BA). Junior Scientific Officer, Admiralty, 1927–30; Scientific Officer, RAE, 1930–38; Headquarters, MAP, 1938–50; Deputy Director, Royal Aircraft Establishment, Farnborough, 1950–54; Dir-Gen. of Guided Weapons, Min. of Aviation, 1954–61. Dep. Controller Guided Weapons, Ministry of Aviation, 1961–63. *Recreation:* gardening. *Address:* Overwey, Bishopsmead, Farnham, Surrey. *T:* Farnham 713526.

SERGEANT, (Herbert) Howard, MBE 1978; Founder, and Editor, Outposts (quarterly poetry magazine), since 1943; *b* 6 May 1914; *s* of Edwin Sergeant and Edith Alice Sergeant (*née* Crowther); *m* 1954, Jean Crabtree; one *s* three *d. Educ:* Hull Grammar Sch.; Hull Coll. of Commerce, and privately. FCCA, FCIS, MBIM, FSCA. Dist Chief Accountant, Broadcast Relay Services, 1935–41; Travelling Accountant, Air Min., 1941–48; Co. Sec. and Accountant, Jordan & Sons Ltd, 1949–54; Co. Sec. and Gp Accountant, E. Austin & Sons (London) Ltd, 1954–63; Lectr, Norwood Tech. Coll., 1963–65; Sen. Lectr, Wandsworth Tech. Coll., 1965–68; Sen. Lectr, 1969–72, Head of Sch. of Management, 1972–78, Brooklands Tech. Coll., Weybridge; Creative Writing Fellow, Queen Mary's Coll., Basingstoke, 1978–79. Dorothy Tutin Award, 1980; Henry Shore Award, 1980. *Publications: poetry:* The Leavening Air, 1946; The Headlands, 1954; Selected Poems, 1980; Travelling Without a Valid Ticket, 1982; Fairground Familiars, 1985; A Question of Respect, 1986; *criticism:* The Cumberland Wordsworth, 1950; Tradition in the Making of Modern Poetry, 1952; A Critical Survey of South African Poetry (Cape Town), 1958; compiled selections from the poetry of Milton, 1953, and from Milton and Wordsworth, 1970; *ed anthologies of poetry:* For Those Who Are Alive, 1946; An Anthology of Contemporary Northern Poetry, 1947; These Years (for schools), 1950; (jtly) New Poems, a PEN anthology, 1953; (jtly) Mavericks, 1957; Commonwealth Poems of Today, 1967; New Voices of the Commonwealth, 1968; Poems from Hospital, 1968; Universities' Poetry 8, 1968; Poetry from Africa, 1968; Poetry from Australia, 1969; The Swinging Rainbow, for children, 1969; Poetry from India, 1970; Poetry of the 1940s, 1970; Happy Landings, for children, 1971; Evans Book of Children's Verse, 1972; African Voices, 1973; For Today and Tomorrow, 1974; Poetry South East I, 1976; New Poems 1976/77, a PEN anthology, 1976; Two Continents Book of Children's Verse, 1977; Candles and Lamps, 1979; Poems from The Medical World, 1979; How Strong the Roots, 1981; (jtly) The Gregory Awards Anthology 1980, 1981; (jtly) The Gregory Awards Anthology 1981–82, 1982; Independent Voices (Public School Verse), 1983; Independent Voices, 2, 1984; A Package of Poems, 1984; (jtly) Gregory Awards Anthology 1983–84, 1985; Independent Voices, 3, 1985; (jtly) annual Borestone Mountain Poetry Award anthologies, Best Poems of 1949–78. *Recreations:* walking, writing, poetry workshops. *Address:* 72 Burwood Road, Walton-on-Thames, Surrey KT12 4AL. *T:* Walton-on-Thames 240712. *Clubs:* PEN, Society of Authors, Poetry Society; Ver Poets (St Albans) (Vice Pres.); Kent & Sussex Poetry Society (Vice Pres.).

SERGEANT, Sir Patrick (John Rushton), Kt 1984; City Editor, Daily Mail, 1960–84; Founder, 1969, and Chairman, since 1985, Euromoney Publications (Managing Director, 1969–85); *b* 17 March 1924; *s* of George and Rene Sergeant; *m* 1952, Gillian Anne Wilks, Cape Town; two *d. Educ:* Beaumont Coll. Served as Lieut, RNVR, 1945. Asst City Editor, News Chronicle, 1948; Dep. City Editor, Daily Mail, 1953. Director: Associated Newspapers Group, 1971–83; Daily Mail General Trust, 1983–. Wincott Award, Financial Journalist of the Year, 1979. *Publications:* Another Road to Samarkand, 1955; Money Matters, 1967; Inflation Fighters Handbook, 1976. *Recreations:* skiing, tennis, swimming, talking. *Address:* One The Grove, Highgate Village, N6 6JU. *T:* 01–340 1245. *Clubs:* Royal Automobile, Annabelle's; Cumberland Lawn Tennis.

SERIES, Sir Emile; *see* Seriès, Sir J. M. E.

SERIES, Prof. George William, FRS 1971; Hon. Research Fellow, Clarendon Laboratory, Oxford, since 1983; Professor of Physics, University of Reading, 1968, Emeritus 1982; *b* 22 Feb. 1920; *s* of William Series and Alice (*née* Crosthwaite); *m* 1948, Annette (*née* Pepper); three *s* one *d. Educ:* Reading Sch.; St John's Coll., Oxford. MA 1946, DPhil 1950, DSc 1969, Oxford. Served with Friends' Ambulance Unit, 1942–46. Open Schol., Oxford, 1938; 1st cl. hons Physics, Oxford, 1947; Nuffield Research Fellow, 1950. University Demonstrator, Oxford, 1951; St Edmund Hall, Oxford: Lectr, 1953; Fellow, 1954; Emeritus Fellow, 1969. William Evans Vis. Prof., Univ. of Otago, 1972; Raman Vis. Prof., Indian Acad. of Sci., 1982–83. Hon. Fellow, Indian Acad. of Science, 1984. Hon. Editor, Jl of Physics B (Atomic and Molecular Physics), 1975–79; Editor, Europ. Jl Physics, 1980–85. William F. Meggers Award, Optical Soc. Amer., 1982. *Publications:* Spectrum of Atomic Hydrogen, 1957; Laser Spectroscopy and other topics, 1985. *Recreation:* family. *Address:* Clarendon Laboratory, Oxford OX1 3PU. *T:* Oxford 59291.

SERIES, Sir (Joseph Michel) Emile, Kt 1978; CBE 1974; FCIS, FAIA, FSCA, FREconS; Chairman and General Manager, Flacq United Estates Ltd and WEAL Group (West East Ltd), since 1968; *b* 29 Sept. 1918; *s* of late Emile Seriès and Julie (*née* Langlois); *m* 1942, Rose-Aimée Jullienne; two *s* two *d. Educ:* Royal Coll., Mauritius; London Univ. MCom Delhi Commercial Univ., 1967. FBIM; FCCS 1958. Accounts Dept, General Electric Supply Co. of Mauritius Ltd, 1936–52 (final position, Chief Acct); Chief Acct and Econ. Adviser, Union Flacq Sugar Estate Ltd and Flacq United Estates Ltd, 1952–61; Manager, Union Flacq Sugar Estate Ltd, 1961–68. Chairman. Rogers & Co. Ltd; Alcohol & Molasses Co. Ltd; Compagnie Mauricienne de Commerce Ltd. Director: Maur. Commercial Bank Ltd; Maur. Oil Refineries Co. Ltd; La Nouvelle Quincaillerie Mauricienne Ltd; Anglo-Maur. Assurance Society Ltd; Maur. Farms Ltd, and other cos in Mauritius. Past President: Maur. Chamber of Agriculture; Maur. Sugar Industry Research Inst. Member: Maur. Sugar Producers' Assoc.; Maur. Sugar Syndicate; Amer. Management Assoc., New York; National Assoc. of Accts, New York. FRSA. Chevalier de l'Ordre National du Mérite (France), 1978. *Recreations:* sailing, shooting, photography, classical music, horse racing. *Address:* Flacq United Estates Ltd, Union Flacq, Mauritius. *T:* 532–583 and 535535. *Clubs:* Dodo, Mauritius Turf, Grand'Baie Yacht (Mauritius).

SERJEANT, Graham Roger, CMG 1981; MD; FRCP; Director, Medical Research Council Laboratories, Jamaica, since 1974; *b* 26 Oct. 1938; *s* of Ewart Egbert and Violet Elizabeth Serjeant; *m* 1965, Beryl Elizabeth, *d* of late Ivor Edward King, CB, CBE. *Educ:* Sibford Sch., Banbury; Bootham Sch., York; Clare Coll., Cambridge (BA 1960, MA 1965); London Hosp. Med. Sch.; Makerere Coll., Kampala. MB BChir 1963, MD 1971, Cantab; MRCP 1966, FRCP 1977. House Physician: London Hosp., 1963–64; Royal United Hosp., Bath, 1965–66; RPMS, 1966; Med. Registrar, University Hosp. of WI, 1966–67; Wellcome Res. Fellow, Dept of Medicine, Univ. of WI, 1967–71; Medical Research Council: Mem., Scientific Staff, Abnormal Haemoglobin Unit, Cambridge, 1971–72; Epidemiology Res. Unit, Jamaica, 1972–74. Hon. Prof. Faculty of Medicine, Univ. of WI, 1981. *Publications:* The Clinical Features of Sickle Cell Disease, 1974; Sickle Cell Disease, 1985; numerous papers on the nat. hist. of sickle cell disease, in med. jls. *Recreation:* squash. *Address:* Medical Research Council Laboratories, University of the West Indies, Mona, Kingston 7, Jamaica, WI. *T:* (809) 927–0687. *Club:* Liguanea (Kingston).

SERJEANT, Robert Bertram, FBA 1986; Sir Thomas Adams's Professor of Arabic, 1970–82, and Director, Middle East Centre, 1965–82, University of Cambridge; *b* 23 March 1915; *er s* of R. T. R. and A. B. Serjeant; *m* Marion Keith Serjeant (*née* Robertson), MB, ChB; one *s* one *d. Educ:* Edinburgh; Trinity Coll., Cambridge. Vans Dunlop Schol. 1935; Visit to Syria, 1935; MA 1st Cl. Hons Semitic Langs, Edinburgh Univ., 1936; PhD Cambridge 1939; Tweedie Fellow Edinburgh, 1939; Studentship, SOAS, for research in S Arabia, 1940; Governor's Commn in Aden Prot. G Guards, 1940–41. Attached Mission 106. Lectr, SOAS, 1941; Seconded to BBC Eastern Service, 1942; Editor, Arabic Listener, 1943–45; Min. of Inf., Editor Arabic pubns, 1944. Colonial Research Fell., in Hadramawt, 1947–48; Reader in Arabic, 1948; Research in S Arabia and Persian Gulf, 1953–54; in N Nigeria, Minister of Education's mission to examine instruction in Arabic, 1956; Sec. of State for Colonies' mission to examine Muslim Education in E Africa, 1957; Inter-University Council's Advisory Delegation on University of N Nigeria, 1961; Research in Trucial States, Yemen, Aden, 1963–64 and 1966; Professor of Arabic, 1955–64, Middle East Department, SOAS, University of London; Lectr in Islamic History, ME Centre, Univ. of Cambridge, 1964–66, Reader in Arabic Studies, 1966–70. Member: ME Comd Expedition to Socotra, 1967; Cambridge expedn to San'ā' and N Yemen, 1972. Member: Royal Soc. for Asian Affairs; Royal Asiatic Soc.; Mem., Arab Acad., Cairo, 1976. Hon. DLitt Edinburgh, 1985. Lawrence of Arabia Meml Medal, RCAS, 1974; Sir Richard Burton Meml Medal, RAS, 1981. Co-editor, Arabian Studies, 1973–; Mem. Editl Bd, Cambridge History of Arabic Literature, 1983–. *Publications:* Cat. Arabic, Persian & Hindustani MSS in New College, Edinburgh, 1942; Materials for a History of Islamic Textiles, 1942–51; Prose and Poetry from Hadramawt, I, 1950; Saiyids of Hadramawt, 1957; Portuguese off the South Arabian Coast, 1961; The South Arabian Hunt, 1976; (ed) The Islamic City, 1980; Studies in Arabic History and Civilisation, 1981; (ed with R. Lewcock) San'ā': an Arabian Islamic city, 1983; articles in BSOAS, RAS, Le Muséon, Rivista d. Studi Orientali, Islamic Culture, etc. *Address:* Summerhill Cottage, Denhead, near St Andrews, Fife.

SERJEANT, William Ronald, FRHistS; County Archivist, Suffolk, 1974–82, retired; President, Society of Archivists, since 1982; *b* 5 March 1921; *s* of Frederick William and Louisa (*née* Wood); *m* 1961, Ruth Kneale (*née* Bridson); one *s. Educ:* Univ. of Manchester (BA Hons History); Univ. of Liverpool (Dip. Archive Admin. and Study of Records). Archivist/Librarian: Univ. of Sheffield, Sheffield City Library, Liverpool Record Office, 1952–56; Librarian/Archivist, Manx Nat. Library and Archives, Dep. Dir, Manx Mus. and Nat. Trust, 1957–62; County Archivist, Notts, 1962–70; Jt County Bor. and County Archivist, Ipswich and E Suffolk, 1970–74. Mem., Lord Chancellor's Adv. Council on Public Records, 1982–. Editor: Jl of the Manx Museum, 1957–62; The Suffolk Review, 1970–82; The Blazon (Suffolk Heraldry Soc.), 1984–. *Publications:* The History of Tuxford Grammar School, 1969; (ed) Index to the Probate Records of the Court of the Archdeacon of Suffolk 1444–1700, 1979–80; (ed) Index to the Probate Records of the Court of the Archdeacon of Sudbury 1354–1700, 1984; articles in county and other local history periodicals. *Recreations:* walking, participation in local historical and heraldic studies and activities, theatre and cinema going; any gaps filled by reading novels. *Address:* 51 Derwent Road, Ipswich, Suffolk IP3 0QR. *T:* Ipswich 78997.

SERKIN, Rudolf, Presidential Medal of Freedom, 1963; pianist; Director, Curtis Institute of Music, Philadelphia, Pa, 1968–76, Head of Piano Department, 1939–76; *b* 28 March 1903; *s* of Mordko Serkin and Augusta Schargl; *m* 1935, Irene Busch; two *s* four *d. Educ:* Vienna, Austria. Concert Pianist: Début, Vienna, 1915; USA since 1933; New York Philharmonic with Arturo Toscanini, 1936. President and Artistic Director of Marlboro School of Music, Marlboro, Vermont. Former Mem., Nat. Council on the Arts, Carnegie Commn Report. Fellow, Amer. Acad. of Arts and Scis; Hon. Member: Accademia Nationale di Santa Cecilia; Verein Beethoven Haus, Bonn; Philharmonic-Symphony Soc. of NY; Amer. Philosophical Soc.; Riemenschneider Bach Inst.; Konzertverein, Vienna; Neue Bachgesellschaft, Bonn. Dr *hc*: Curtis Inst., Philadelphia; Temple Univ., Philadelphia; Univ. of Vermont; Williams Coll., Williamstown, Mass; Oberlin Coll.; Rochester Univ.; Harvard; Marlboro Coll. Kennedy Center Honors, 1981; Ernst von Siemens Musikpreis. Grand Officiale del Ordina, Italy; Cross of Honor for Scis and Art, Austria; Commander's Cross, Icelandic Order of Falcon; Chevalier de l'Ordre National de la Legion d'Honneur; Orden pour le Mérite für Wissenschaften und Künste, W Germany, 1981. *Address:* RFD 3, Brattleboro, Vermont 05301, USA.

SEROTA, family name of **Baroness Serota.**

SEROTA, Baroness, *cr* 1967 (Life Peer), of Hampstead in Greater London; **Beatrice Serota,** JP, Chairman, Commission for Local Administration, 1974–82; Governor, BBC,

1977–82; *b* 15 Oct. 1919; *m* 1942, Stanley Serota, BSc (Eng), FICE; one *s* one *d*. *Educ:* John Howard School; London School of Economics (BSc (Econ)); Hon. Fellow, 1976. Member: Hampstead Borough Council, 1945–49; LCC for Brixton, 1954–65 (Chm., Children's Cttee, 1958–65); GLC for Lambeth, 1964–67 (Chief Whip). Baroness in Waiting, 1968–69; Minister of State (Health), Dept of Health and Social Security, 1969–70. Member: Adv. Council in Child Care, and Central Training Council in Child Care, 1958–68; Adv. Council on Treatment of Offenders, 1960–64; Longford Cttee on "Crime—A Challenge to us all", 1964; Royal Commn on Penal System, 1964–66; Latey Cttee on Age of Majority, 1965–67; Adv. Council on Penal System, 1966–68, 1974–79 (Chm., 1976–79); Seebohm Cttee on Organization of Local Authority Personal Social Services, 1966–68; Community Relations Commn, 1970–76; BBC Complaints Commn, 1975–77. Pres., Volunteer Centre. JP Inner London (West Central Division). Peerage conferred for services to children. Hon. DLitt Loughborough, 1983. *Recreations:* crochet, gardening, collecting shells. *Address:* The Coach House, 15 Lyndhurst Terrace, NW3.
See also N. A. Serota.

SEROTA, Nicholas Andrew; Director of the Whitechapel Art Gallery, since 1976; *b* 27 April 1946; *s* of Stanley Serota and Beatrice Serota (*see* Baroness Serota); *m* 1973, Angela Mary Beveridge; two *d*. *Educ:* Haberdashers' Askes Sch., Hampstead and Elstree; Christ's Coll., Cambridge (BA); Courtauld Inst. of Art, London (MA). Regional Art Officer and Exhibn Organiser, Arts Council of GB, 1970–73; Dir, Museum of Modern Art, Oxford, 1973–76. Mem., Fine Arts Adv. Cttee, British Council, 1976–; Trustee, Public Art Develt Trust, 1983–. *Address:* Whitechapel Art Gallery, 80–82 Whitechapel High Street, E1 7QX. *T:* 01–377 5015.

SERPELL, Sir David Radford, KCB 1968 (CB 1962); CMG 1952; OBE 1944; FCIT; Member, British Railways Board, 1974–82; *b* 10 Nov. 1911; 2nd *s* of Charles Robert and Elsie Leila Serpell, Plymouth; *m* 1st, Ann Dooley (marr. diss.); three *s*; 2nd, Doris Farr. *Educ:* Plymouth Coll.; Exeter Coll., Oxford; Univ. of Toulouse (DèsL); Syracuse University, USA; Fletcher School of Law and Diplomacy, USA. (Fell.) Imp. Economic Cttee, 1937–39; Min. of Food, 1939–42; Min. of Fuel and Power, 1942–45; Under-Sec., HM Treasury, 1954–60; Dep. Sec., MoT, 1960–63; Second Sec., BoT, 1963–66; Second Permanent Sec., 1966–68; Second Sec., Treasury, 1968; Permanent Secretary: MoT, 1968–70; DoE, 1970–72. Private Sec. to Parly Sec., Ministry of Food, 1941–42; Principal Private Sec. to Minister of Fuel and Power, 1942–45. Chairman: Nature Conservancy Council, 1973–77; Ordnance Survey Review Cttee, 1978–79; Cttee on the Review of Railway Finances, 1982; Member: NERC, 1973–76; Council, National Trust, 1973–80. *Recreations:* walking, golf. *Address:* 25 Crossparks, Dartmouth, Devon TQ6 9HP. *T:* Dartmouth 2073. *Club:* United Oxford & Cambridge University.

SERVAN-SCHREIBER, Jean-Jacques; engineer, author, politician; *b* Paris, 13 Feb. 1924; *s* of late Emile Servan-Schreiber, journalist, and of Denise Bresard; *m* 1960, Sabine de Fouquières; four *s*. *Educ:* Ecole Polytechnique. Served as fighter pilot, Free French Air Force, World War II. Diplomatic Editor of Le Monde, 1948–53; Founder and Director of weekly news-magazine, L'Express, 1953–73. Deputy for Lorraine, French National Assembly, 1970–78; Minister of Reforms, June 1974. Pres., Region of Lorraine, 1976–78. President: Radical Party, 1971–79; "Paris Group", 1979–84; Chm., World Center for Computer Literacy, 1981–85. Chm., Internat. Cttee, Carnegie-Mellon Univ., 1986–. Holds military cross for valour. *Publications:* Lieutenant en Algérie, 1957 (Lieutenant in Algeria); Le Défi américain, 1967 (The American Challenge); Le Manifeste Radical, 1970 (The Radical Alternative); Le Défi mondial, 1980 (The World Challenge). *Address:* 623 Morewood Avenue, Pittsburgh, Pa 15213, USA.

SERVICE, Alastair Stanley Douglas; General Secretary, Family Planning Association, since 1980; writer and publisher; *b* 8 May 1933; *s* of Douglas William Service and late Evelyn Caroline (*née* Sharp); *m* 1959, Louisa Anne (*née* Hemming), *qv* (marr. diss. 1984); one *s* one *d*. *Educ:* Westminster Sch.; Queen's Coll., Oxford. Midshipman, RNR, 1952–54. Director: McKinlay, Watson and Co. Ltd, Brazil, USA and London, 1959–64 (export finance); Seeley, Service and Co. Ltd (publishers), 1965–79; Municipal Journal Ltd, 1970–78. Hon. Parly Officer: Abortion Law Reform Assoc., during passage of Abortion Act, 1964–67; Divorce Law Reform Union, during passage of Divorce Reform Act, 1967–69; Chm., Birth Control Campaign, during passage of NHS (Family Planning) Amendment Act, 1972, and NHS Reorganisation Act, 1973 (made vasectomy and contraception available free from NHS); involved in other parly campaigns, incl.: Town and Country Amenities Act, 1974; Children's Act, 1975; Public Lending Right for Authors; One-Parent Families. Member: cttees, FPA, 1964– (Mem. Nat. Exec. Cttee, 1972–80, Chm., 1975–80); Health Educn Council (Sec. of State appointee), 1976– (Vice-Chm., 1979–); Cttee, Nat. Council for One-Parent Families, 1979–84; Cttee, Victorian Soc., 1976–; Cttee, Family Forum, 1981–82. *Publications:* A Birth Control Plan for Britain (with Dr John Dunwoody and Dr Tom Stuttaford), 1972; The Benefits of Birth Control—Aberdeen's Experience, 1973; Edwardian Architecture and its Origins, 1975; Edwardian Architecture, 1977; The Architects of London from 1066 to Present Day, 1979; London 1900, 1979; (with Jean Bradbery) Megaliths of Europe, 1979; Lost Worlds, 1981; Edwardian Interiors, 1982; series editor, The Buildings of Britain, 1981–84, and author, Anglo-Saxon and Norman Buildings vol., 1982; Victorian and Edwardian Hampstead, 1987; articles in Arch. Rev., Arch. Assoc. Qly, Guardian, etc. *Recreations:* looking at buildings, opera, cycling et al. *Address:* 49 Maresfield Gardens, NW3; Swan House, Avebury, Wilts. *Club:* Garrick.

SERVICE, Louisa Anne, JP; Joint Chairman, The Municipal Group of Companies, since 1976; *d* of late Henry Harold Hemming, OBE, MC, and of Alice Louisa Weaver, OBE; *m* 1959, Alastair Stanley Douglas Service, *qv* (marr. diss. 1984); one *s* one *d*. *Educ:* private and state schs, Canada, USA and Britain; Ecole des Sciences Politiques, Paris; St Hilda's Coll., Oxford (BA and MA, PPE). Export Dir, Ladybird Appliances Ltd, 1957–59; Municipal Journal Ltd and associated cos: Financial Dir, 1966; Dep. Chm., 1974; Chm., Merchant Printers Ltd, 1975–80; Dir, Brintex Ltd, 1965–; Dir, Glass's Guides Services Ltd, 1971, Dep. Chm. 1976–81, Chm., 1982–. Member: Dept of Trade Consumer Credit Act Appeals Panel, 1981–; Cttee of Magistrates, 1985–. JP Inner London Juvenile Courts, 1969; Chm., Hackney Juvenile Court, 1975–82, Westminster Juvenile Ct, 1982–; JP Inner London (5) PSD, 1980–; Chm., Exec. Cttee, Inner London Juvenile Courts, 1977–79; Mem., working party on re-org. of London Juvenile Courts, 1975; Vice-Chm., Paddington Probation Hostel, 1976–. Corres. mem., SDP Policy Gp on Citizens' Rights, 1982–. Chm. Council, Mayer-Lismann Opera Workshop; Hon. Sec., Women's India Assoc. of UK, 1967–74. Dir, Arts Club Ltd, 1981–84; Mem. Council, Friends of Covent Garden, 1982–. *Publications:* articles on a variety of subjects. *Recreations:* travel, and attractive and witty people including my family. *Address:* c/o The Municipal Journal Ltd, 178–202 Great Portland Street, W1N 6NH. *T:* 01–637 2400. *Club:* Arts.
See also J. H. Hemming.

SESSFORD, Rt. Rev. George Minshull; *see* Moray, Ross and Caithness, Bishop of.

SETH, Prof. George; Professor of Psychology, 1958–71, Head of Department of Psychology, 1946–71, The Queen's University, Belfast; now Professor Emeritus; *b* 23 April 1905; *s* of George Seth and Jane Steven Loudon; *m* 1936, May, *er d* of John Dods, Edinburgh, and late Lily Anderson; three *s* one *d*. *Educ:* Royal High School and University of Edinburgh. MA (Edin.) 1928; BEd (Edin.) 1930; PhD (Edin.) 1933. Assistant in Psychology, Edinburgh University and University Psychological Clinic, 1930–34; Research Fellow, Yale Univ., USA, 1934–35; Lecturer in Education, University College, Cardiff, and Psychologist, Cardiff Child Guidance Clinic, 1935–46; Senior Psychologist, Welsh Board of Health, (Evacuation Service), 1941–45. Vans Dunlop Scholar (Psychology), Edinburgh, 1930–33; Rockefeller Fellow, USA, 1935–36. Fellow, British Psychological Soc., President, 1967, Vice-Pres., 1968; President, Psychology Section, British Association, 1961. Member: Psychology Bd, CNAA, 1968–75; N Ireland Council for Educnl Research. Fellow, Psychological Soc. of Ireland, 1970, Lectr 1975. *Publications:* (with Douglas Guthrie) Speech in Childhood, 1934; articles in various psychological and educational jls. *Address:* 24 Osborne Park, Belfast BT9 6JN.

SETON, Lady, (Alice Ida), CBE 1949; Group Officer, WRAF, retired; *d* of late P. C. Hodge, Port Elizabeth, South Africa; *m* 1923, Capt. Sir John Hastings Seton, 10th Bt (from whom she obtained a divorce, 1950); one *s* (*see* Sir Robert Seton, 11th Bt) one *d*. Joined WAAF as Assistant Section Officer, 1939. *Address:* 3 Maddison Close, Teddington, Mddx.

SETON, Anya, (Anya Seton Chase); Author; *b* as British subject, New York City, USA; *d* of late Ernest Thompson Seton and late Grace Gallatin Thompson Seton. *Educ:* private tutors in England. *Publications:* (in USA, UK and 20 foreign countries) My Theodosia, 1941; Dragonwyck, 1944; The Turquoise, 1946; The Hearth and the Eagle, 1948; Foxfire, 1951; Katherine, 1954; The Mistletoe and Sword (juvenile), 1956; The Winthrop Woman, 1958; Washington Irving (juvenile), 1960; Devil Water, 1962; Avalon, 1966; Green Darkness, 1972; Smouldering Fires (juvenile), 1975. *Recreations:* swimming, croquet, bridge, cooking. *Address:* Binney Lane, Old Greenwich, Conn 06870, USA. *Clubs:* (Hon.) Pen and Brush (New York); PEN.

SETON, Sir (Christopher) Bruce, 12th Bt *cr* 1663, of Abercorn; farmer; *b* 3 Oct. 1909; *s* of Charles Henry Seton (*d* 1917), and Mrs V. A. Neilson (*d* 1973), Greys, Kelvedon, Essex; *S* cousin, 1969; *m* 1939, Joyce Vivien, *e d* of late O. G. Barnard, Stowmarket; two *s* two *d*. *Educ:* Marlborough; Univ. of Cambridge (BA Agric. 1931). Farming since 1931. *Heir:* *s* Iain Bruce Seton [*b* 27 Aug. 1942; *m* 1963, Margaret Ann, *o d* of Walter Charles Faulkner; one *s* one *d*]. *Address:* Bay Laurel, 3 Larkfield Road, Great Bentley, Colchester, Essex. *T:* Colchester 250723.

SETON, Lady, (Julia), VMH; (Julia Clements, professionally); author, speaker, international floral art judge; flower arrangement judge for RHS and National Association of Flower Arrangement Societies; *d* of late Frank Clements; *m* 1962, Sir Alexander Hay Seton, 10th Bt, of Abercorn (*d* 1963); no *c*. *Educ:* Isle of Wight; Zwicker College, Belgium. Organised and conducted first Judges' School in England at Royal Horticultural Society Halls; has since conducted many other courses for judges all over Britain. VMH, RHS, 1974. *Publications:* Fun with Flowers; Fun without Flowers; 101 Ideas for Flower Arrangement; Party Pieces; The Julia Clements Colour Book of Flower Arrangements; Flower Arrangements in Stately Homes; Julia Clements' Gift Book of Flower Arranging; Flowers in Praise; The Art of Arranging a Flower, etc. *Address:* 122 Swan Court, SW3. *T:* 01–352 9039. *Clubs:* Women's Press, Anglo-Belge.

SETON, Sir Robert (James), 11th Bt, *cr* 1683; *b* 20 April 1926; *s* of Captain Sir John Hastings Seton, 10th Bt and Alice (*see* Lady Seton), *d* of Percy Hodge, Cape Civil Service; *S* father 1956; unmarried. *Educ:* HMS Worcester (Thames Nautical Training College). Midshipman RNVR (invalided), 1943–44. Banker, with Hong Kong and Shanghai Banking Corpn, 1946–61 (retd). *Heir:* *kinsman* James Christall Seton [*b* 21 Jan. 1913; *m* 1939, Evelyn, *d* of Ray Hafer]. *Address:* c/o The Hongkong and Shanghai Banking Corporation, 99 Bishopsgate, EC2P 2LA.

SETSHOGO, Boithoko Moonwa; Founding Partner and Managing Director, Media Productions (Pty) Ltd, Gaborone, since 1980; *b* Serowe, 16 June 1941; *m* 1971, Jennifer Tlalane; two *d*. *Educ:* Moeng Coll.; Univ. of Botswana, Lesotho and Swaziland (BA). District Officer, Kanye, 1969–70; First Sec., High Commn, London, 1970–72; Clerk to the Cabinet, 1972–73; Under-Sec., Min. of Commerce and Industry, 1973–75; High Comr of Botswana in London, 1975–78; Dir of Inf. and Broadcasting, 1978–80. *Address:* PO Box 20645, Bontleng, Gaborone, Botswana.

SETTRINGTON, Lord; Charles Henry Gordon-Lennox; *b* 8 Jan. 1955; *s* and *heir* of Earl of March and Kinrara, *qv*; *m* 1976, Sally, *d* of late Maurice Clayton and of Mrs Denis Irwin; one *d*. *Educ:* Eton. *Address:* Goodwood House, Chichester, West Sussex.

SEVER, (Eric) John; *b* 1 April 1943; *s* of Eric and Clara Sever. *Educ:* Sparkhill Commercial School. Travel Executive with tour operator, 1970–77. MP (Lab) Birmingham, Ladywood, Aug. 1977–1983; PPS to the Solicitor General, 1978–79. Contested (Lab) Meriden, 1983. *Recreations:* theatre, cinema, reading.

SEVERIN, Prof. Dorothy Virginia Sherman, PhD; Gilmour Professor of Spanish, University of Liverpool, since 1982; *b* 24 March 1942; *d* of Wilbur B. and Virginia L. Sherman; marr. diss.; one *d*. *Educ:* Harvard Univ. AB 1963; AM 1964; PhD 1967. Teaching Fellow and Tutor, Harvard Univ., 1964–66; Vis. Lectr, Univ. of W Indies, 1967–68; Asst Prof., Vassar Coll., 1968; Lectr, Westfield Coll., London Univ., 1969–82. Vis. Associate Prof., Harvard Univ., 1982; Visiting Professor: Columbia Univ., 1985; Yale Univ., 1985. Editor, Bulletin of Hispanic Studies, 1982–. *Publications:* (ed) de Rojas, La Celestina, 1969, 12th edn 1985; Memory in La Celestina, 1970; (ed) Diego de San Pedro, La pasión trobada, 1973; (ed) La Lengua de Erasmo romançada por muy elegante estilo, 1975; The Cancionero de Martínez de Burgos, 1976; (ed with K. Whinnom) Diego de San Pedro, Poesía (Obras completas III), 1979; (ed with Angus MacKay) Cosas sacadas de la Historia del rey Juan el Segundo, 1982; contribs to learned jls incl. Hispanic Rev., Romance Philology, Medium Aevum, MLR and THES. *Address:* Department of Hispanic Studies, The University, PO Box 147, Liverpool L69 3BX. *T:* 051–709 6022, ext 3055.

SEVERIN, (Giles) Timothy; author, traveller and historian; *b* 25 Sept. 1940; *s* of Maurice Watkins and Inge Severin; *m* 1966, Dorothy Virginia Sherman (marr. diss. 1979); one *d*. *Educ:* Tonbridge School; Keble Coll., Oxford. MA, BLitt. Commonwealth Fellow, USA, 1964–66. Expeditions: led motorcycle team along Marco Polo route, 1961; R Mississippi by canoe and launch, 1965; Brendan Voyage from W Ireland to N America, 1977; Sindbad Voyage from Oman to China, 1980–81; Jason Voyage from Iolkos to Colchis, 1984; Ulysses Voyage from Troy to Ithaca, 1985. *Publications:* Tracking Marco Polo, 1964; Explorers of the Mississippi, 1967; The Golden Antilles, 1970; The African Adventure, 1973; Vanishing Primitive Man, 1973; The Oriental Adventure, 1976; The Brendan Voyage, 1978; The Sindbad Voyage, 1982; The Jason Voyage, 1985. *Address:* Courtmacsherry, Co. Cork, Eire. *T:* Bandon 46127. *Club:* United Oxford & Cambridge University.

SEVERN, David; *see* Unwin, David Storr.

SEVERN, Prof. Roy Thomas, FEng 1981; FICE; Professor and Head of Department of Civil Engineering, Bristol University, since 1968; *b* 6 Sept. 1929; *s* of Ernest Severn and Muriel Woollatt; *m* 1957, Hilary Irene Saxton; two *d*. *Educ:* Deacons School, Peterborough; Imperial College (DSc). Demonstrator, Imperial College, 1949–54; Royal Engineers (Survey), 1954–56; Bristol University: Lectr, 1956–65; Reader, 1965–68. *Publications:* (ed) Engineering Structures: developments in the twentieth century, 1983; contribs to Procs of ICE, Jl Earthquake Eng. and Structural Dynamics. *Recreations:* sailing, gardening, cricket. *Address:* 49 Gloucester Road, Rudgeway, Bristol BS12 2SF. *T:* Thornbury 412027.

SEVERNE, Air Vice-Marshal John de Milt, LVO 1961; OBE 1968; AFC 1955; Captain of the Queen's Flight, since 1982; Extra Equerry to the Queen, since 1984; *b* 15 Aug. 1925; *s* of late Dr A. de M. Severne, Wateringbury, Kent; *m* 1951, Katharine Veronica, *d* of late Captain V. E. Kemball, RN (Retd); three *d*. *Educ:* Marlborough. Joined RAF, 1944; Flying Instr, Cranwell, 1948; Staff Instr and PA to Comdt CFS, 1950–53; Flt Comdr No 98 Sqdn, Germany, 1954–55; Sqdn Comdr No 26 Sqdn, Germany, 1956–57; Air Min., 1958; Equerry to Duke of Edinburgh, 1958–61; psa 1962; Chief Instr No 226 Operational Conversion Unit (Lightning), 1963–65; jssc 1965; Jt HQ, ME Comd, Aden, and Air Adviser to the South Arabian Govt, 1966–67; Dirg Staff, Jt Services Staff Coll., 1968; Gp Captain Organisation, HQ Strike Comd, 1968–70; Stn Comdr, RAF Kinloss, 1971–72; RCDS 1973; Comdt, Central Flying School, RAF, 1974–76; Air Cdre Flying Training, HQ RAF Support Comd, 1976–78; Comdr, Southern Maritime Air Region, Central Sub-Area Eastern Atlantic Command, and Plymouth Sub-Area Channel Command, 1978–80. ADC to The Queen, 1972–73. Pres., SW Area, RAFA, 1981–. Won Kings Cup Air Race, British Air Racing Champion, 1960. Pres., RAF Equitation Assoc., 1976–79 (Chm. 1973); Chm., Combined Services Equitation Assoc., 1977–79 (Vice-Chm., 1976). *Address:* The Queen's Flight, RAF Benson, Oxon OX9 6AA. *Club:* Royal Air Force.

SEWARD, Guy William, QC 1982; FRVA; *b* 10 June 1916; *s* of late William Guy Seward and Maud Peacock; *m* 1946, Peggy Dearman. *Educ:* Stationers' Sch. Called to the Bar, Inner Temple, 1956. FRVA 1948. Chairman: Examination in Public, Devon Structure Plan, 1980; E Herts Health Authority, 1982–; Member: Mid-Herts HMC, 1966–70; Napsbury HMC, 1970–74 (Chm., 1972–74); Bd of Governors, UCH, 1970–74; Herts AHA, 1974–82 (Vice Chm., 1980–82); Council, Rating and Valuation Assoc., 1983. Freeman, City of London, 1949. *Publications:* (jtly) Enforcement of Planning Control, 1956; (jtly) Local Government Act, 1958; Howard Roberts Law of Town and Country Planning, 1963; (jtly) Rent Act, 1965; (jtly) Land Commission Act, 1967; (jtly) Leasehold Reform, 1967. *Recreations:* National Health Service, gardening. *Address:* Stocking Lane Cottage, Ayot St Lawrence, Welwyn, Herts AL6. *Club:* Garrick.

SEWARD, William Richard, RCNC; General Manager, HM Dockyard, Portsmouth, 1975–79, retired; *b* 7 Feb. 1922; *s* of William and Gertrude Seward, Portsmouth; *m* 1946, Mary Deas Ritchie; one *d*. *Educ:* Portsmouth Dockyard Techn. Coll.; RNC Greenwich; Royal Corps of Naval Constructors. Asst Constructor, HM Dockyard, Rosyth, 1945–47; Constructor, Naval Construction Dept, Admty, 1947–58; Admty Constructor Overseer, Birkenhead, 1958–63; Chief Constructor, MoD (N), 1963–70; Prodn Man., HM Dockyard, Chatham, 1970–73, Gen. Manager, 1973–75. *Recreations:* reading, music, caravanning, walking. *Address:* Willowfalls Cottage, 166A London Road West, Bath BA1 7QU. *Club:* Civil Service.

SEWELL, Sir (John) Allan, Kt 1977; ISO 1968; company director; *b* 23 July 1915; *s* of George Allan Sewell and Francis Doris Sewell; *m* 1st, 1939, Thelma Edith Buchholz (*d* 1965); one *s* one *d*; 2nd, 1978, Yoko Fukano, *d* of I. Fukano, Kyoto, Japan. *Educ:* Brisbane Grammar Sch. Dir of Local Govt, 1948–60; Under Treasurer of Qld, 1960–70; Auditor-General of Qld, 1970–78; Chm., State Govt Insurance Office, Qld, 1979–81. *Recreation:* game fishing. *Address:* 63 Ryans Road, St Lucia, Brisbane, Queensland, Australia. *Clubs:* Queensland (Brisbane); Cairns Game Fishing (Cairns); Moreton Bay Game Fishing (Brisbane).

SEWELL, Thomas Robert McKie; HM Diplomatic Service, retired; international grains consultant; *b* 18 Aug. 1921; *s* of late O. B. Fane Sewell and late Frances M. Sewell (*née* Sharp); *m* 1955, Jennifer Mary Sandeman; one *d* (and one *d* decd). *Educ:* Eastbourne Coll.; Trinity Coll., Oxford (Schol., Heath Harrison Prize, MA); Lausanne and Stockholm Univs (Schol.). HM Forces, 1940–45 (despatches); Major. Entered Foreign Service, 1949; Second Sec., Moscow, 1950–52; FO, 1952–55; First Sec., 1954; Madrid, 1955–59; Lima, 1959–61; Chargé d'Affaires, 1960; FO, 1961–63; Counsellor and Head of Chancery, Moscow, 1964–66; Diplomatic Service Rep. at IDC, 1966; Head of Associated States, West Indies and Swaziland Depts, Commonwealth Office, 1967–68; Head of N American and Caribbean Dept, FCO, 1968–70; Asst Sec., MAFF, 1970–81; UK Rep. to Internat. Wheat Council, 1972–81. Contested (C) Greater Manchester Central, Europ. Parly elecn, 1984. Vis. Fellow, Hubert H. Humphrey Inst. of Public Affairs and Dept of Agricl and Applied Econs, Univ. of Minnesota, 1985. *Publication:* (with John de Courcy Ling) Famine and Surplus, 1985. *Recreations:* ski-ing, inland waterways cruising. *Address:* c/o Barclays Bank, 16 Whitehall, SW1. *Clubs:* Farmers', Airborne.

SEXTON, Maj.-Gen. (Francis) Michael, CB 1980; OBE 1966; retired; Director of Military Survey and Chief of Geographic Section of General Staff, Ministry of Defence, 1970–80; *b* 15 July 1923; *s* of Timothy and Catherine Sexton; *m* 1947, Naomi, *d* of Bertram Alonzo and Dorothy May Middleton; one *s* one *d*. *Educ:* Wanstead County High Sch.; Birmingham Univ. Commnd Kirkee India into RE, 1943; Royal Bombay Sappers and Miners and 5th/16th Punjab Regt, India, Assam and Burma, 1943–46; RE units, UK, Egypt and Cyprus, 1946–53; Dept of Mines and Surveys, Canada, 1953–56; Asst Dir, MoD, 1964–65; Dep. Dir, Ordnance Survey, 1966–70; Chief Geographic Officer, SHAPE, Belgium, 1970–73; Brig. (Survey), 1973–77. Bursar and Fellow, St Peter's Coll., Oxford, 1980–85. Mem., Panel of Indep. Inspectors, 1980–. MA Oxon, 1980. *Clubs:* Army and Navy, MCC; Geographical.

SEYCHELLES, Bishop of; *see* Indian Ocean, Archbishop of.

SEYLER, Athene, CBE 1959; Actress on the London stage; *b* London, 31 May 1889; *d* of Clara Thies and Clarence H. Seyler; *m* 1st, James Bury Sterndale-Bennett; one *d*; 2nd, Nicholas James Hannen, OBE (mil.) (*d* 1972). *Educ:* Coombe Hill School; Bedford College. Gold Medallist, Royal Academy of Dramatic Art, 1908; first appearance on the stage at Kingsway Theatre, 1909; specialised in comedy acting; served on the Drama Panel of CEMA, 1943 and subsequently of the Arts Council of Great Britain. Pres. of RADA, 1950; Pres. of Theatrical Ladies Guild. Principal successes as Madame Ranevska in The Cherry Orchard, Fanny Farrelli in Watch on the Rhine, the Duchess of Berwick in Lady Windermere's Fan, Vita Louise in Harvey, Mrs Malaprop in The Rivals, The Nurse in Romeo and Juliet. Has appeared in films, 1932–. Hon. Treasurer of British Actors Equity Association, 1944. *Publication:* The Craft of Comedy, 1944. *Recreations:* walking, talking. *Address:* Coach House, 26 Upper Mall, Hammersmith, W6.

SEYMOUR, family name of **Marquess of Hertford** and **Duke of Somerset.**

SEYMOUR, Lord; Sebastian Edward Seymour; *b* 3 Feb. 1982; *s* and *heir* of 19th Duke of Somerset, *qv*.

SEYMOUR, Dr Francis, FFCM; Director of Clinical and Scientific Services (formerly Regional Medical Officer), North West Thames Regional Health Authority, since 1982; *b* 29 June 1928; *s* of Francis Reginald and Drusilla Seymour; *m* 1953, Ivy Esther; two *d*. *Educ:* Wallasey Grammar School; Liverpool University. MB ChB 1951; DPH 1955; MFCM 1972. Dep. MOH, N Bucks, 1955–58; MOH, Mid Bucks Districts, 1958–62; Div. MO, Runcorn and Mid Cheshire, 1962–70; Dep. County MO, Herts, 1970–74; Area MO, Herts AHA, 1974–82. FRSA 1984. *Recreations:* walking, sailing, theatre. *Address:* 66A Hempstead Road, Watford, Herts WD1 3ER.

SEYMOUR, Lynn, CBE 1976; Ballerina; Artistic Director, Ballet of the Bavarian State Opera, Munich, 1979–80; *b* Wainwright, Alberta, 8 March 1939; *d* of E. V. Springbett; *m* 1st, 1963, Colin Jones, photo-journalist (marr. diss.); 2nd, 1974, Philip Pace; three *s*; 3rd, 1983, Vanya Hackel. *Educ:* Vancouver; Sadler's Wells Ballet School. Joined Sadler's Wells Ballet Company, 1957; Deutsche Oper, Berlin, 1966. *Roles created:* Adolescent, in The Burrow, Royal Opera House, 1958; Bride, in Le Baiser de la Fée, 1960; Girl, in The Invitation, 1960; Young Girl, in Les Deux Pigeons, 1961; Principal, in Symphony, 1963; Principal, in Images of Love, 1964; Juliet, in Romeo and Juliet, 1964; Albertine, BBC TV, 1966; Concerto, 1966; Anastasia, 1966; Flowers, 1972; Side Show, 1972; A Month in the Country, 1976; Five Brahms Waltzes in the manner of Isadora Duncan, 1976; mother, in Fourth Symphony, 1977; Mary Vetsera, in Mayerling, 1978; Take Five, 1978. *Other appearances include:* Danses Concertantes; Solitaire; La Fête Etrange; Sleeping Beauty; Swan Lake; Giselle (title-role); Cinderella; Das Lied von der Erde; The Four Seasons; Voluntaries; Manon, Sleeping Beauty, Dances at a Gathering, The Concert, Pillar of Fire, Romeo and Juliet (Tudor, Nureyev and Cranko), Las Hermañas, Moor's Pavane, Auriole, Apollon, Le Corsaire, Flower Festival, La Sylphide (Sylph and Madge). *Choreography for:* Rashomon, 1976; The Court of Love, 1977; Intimate Letters, 1978; Mac and Polly, 1979, Boreas, 1980; Tattooed Lady, 1980. *Publication:* Lynn: leaps and boundaries (autobiog.), 1984. *Address:* c/o Granada Publishing Ltd, 8 Grafton Street, W1X 3LE.

SEYMOUR, Commander Sir Michael Culme-, 5th Bt, *cr* 1809; Royal Navy (retired); *b* 26 April 1909; *o s* of Vice-Admiral Sir M. Culme-Seymour, 4th Bt, and Florence Agnes Louisa (*d* 1956), *y d* of late A. L. Nugent; *S* father, 1925; *m* 1948, Lady (Mary) Faith Nesbitt (*d* 1983), *er d* of 9th Earl of Sandwich; one *step-d* (two *s* decd). Succeeded Rev. Wentworth Watson to the Rockingham Castle estates, 1925, and transferred them to his nephew, Cmdr L. M. M. Saunders Watson, RN, 1967; is a farmer and a landowner. ADC to Governor-General of Canada, 1933–35; served War of 1939–45 (despatches); served Imperial Defence College, 1946–47; retired from RN 1947. JP Northants, 1949; Mem. Northants CC 1948–55; DL Northants, 1958–71; High Sheriff of Northants, 1966. Bledisloe Gold Medal for Landowners, 1972. *Heir to baronetcy: cousin* Mark Charles Culme-Seymour [*b* 20 Dec. 1910; *m*; one *s* two *d*]. *Address:* Wytherston, Powerstock, Bridport, Dorset. *T:* Powerstock 211. *Club:* Brooks's.

SEYMOUR, Rosalind; *see* Wade, R. (H.).

SHACKLE, Prof. George Lennox Sharman, FBA 1967; Brunner Professor of Economic Science in the University of Liverpool, 1951–69, now Professor Emeritus; *b* 14 July 1903; *s* of Robert Walker Shackle, MA (Cambridge) and of Fanny Shackle (*née* Sharman); *m* 1st, 1939, Gertrude Courtney Susan Rowe (*d* 1978); two *s* one *d* (and one *d* decd); 2nd, 1979, Catherine Squarey Gibb (*née* Weldsmith). *Educ:* The Perse School, Cambridge; The London School of Economics; New College, Oxford. BA (London) 1931; Leverhulme Research Schol., 1934; PhD (Econ) (London), 1937; DPhil (Oxford), 1940. Oxford University Institute of Statistics, 1937; University of St Andrews, 1939; Admiralty and Cabinet Office; Sir Winston Churchill's Statistical Branch, 1939; Economic Section of Cabinet Secretariat, 1945; Reader in Economic Theory, Univ. of Leeds, 1950. F. de Vries Lecturer, Amsterdam, 1957; Visiting Professor: Columbia University, 1957–58; of Economics and Philosophy, Univ. of Pittsburgh, 1967; Keynes Lectr, British Acad., 1976. Mem. Council, Royal Economic Society, 1955–69; Pres., Section F, BAAS, 1966. Fellow of Econometric Society, 1960; Distinguished Fellow, Amer. Hist. of Econs Soc., 1985. Hon. DSc NUU, 1974; Hon. DSocSc Birmingham, 1978. *Publications:* Expectations, Investment, and Income, 1938, 2nd edn 1968; Expectation in Economics, 1949, 2nd edn 1952; Mathematics at the Fireside, 1952 (French edn 1967); Uncertainty in Economics and Other Reflections, 1955; Time in Economics, 1957; Economics for Pleasure, 1959, 2nd edn 1968 (also foreign editions); Decision, Order and Time in Human Affairs, 1961, 2nd edn 1969 (also foreign editions); A Scheme of Economic Theory, 1965 (also Portuguese edn); The Nature of Economic Thought, 1966 (also Spanish edn); The Years of High Theory, 1967 (Italian edn 1985); Expectation, Enterprise and Profit, 1970 (Spanish edn 1976); Epistemics and Economics, 1973 (Spanish edn 1976); An Economic Querist, 1973 (Spanish edn 1976); Keynesian Kaleidics, 1974; Imagination and the Nature of Choice, 1979; (ed and contrib.) Uncertainty and Business Decisions, 1954, 2nd edn, 1957; The Theory of General Static Equilibrium, 1957; A New Prospect of Economics, 1958; On the Nature of Business Success, 1968; articles in Chambers's Encyclopædia, 1950, 1967, Internat. Encyclopedia of the Social Sciences, 1968, and in other books; sixty or more main articles in learned jls. *Address:* Rudloe, Alde House Drive, Aldeburgh, Suffolk IP15 5EE. *T:* Aldeburgh 2227 and 2003.

SHACKLETON, family name of **Baron Shackleton.**

SHACKLETON, Baron *cr* 1958 (Life Peer), of Burley; **Edward Arthur Alexander Shackleton,** KG 1974; PC 1966; OBE 1945; an Adviser to RTZ Corporation, since 1982 (Director, 1973–82, Deputy Chairman 1975–82); Chairman: RTZ Development Enterprises, 1973–83; Anglesey Aluminium Ltd, since 1981; *b* 15 July 1911; *s* of late Sir Ernest Shackleton, CVO, OBE; *m* 1938, Betty Homan; one *d* (and one *s* decd). *Educ:* Radley College; Magdalen College, Oxford (MA; Hon. Fellow, 1986). Surveyor, Oxford University Expedition to Sarawak, 1932; first ascent of Mt Mulu; Organiser and Surveyor, Oxford University Expedition to Ellesmereland, 1934–35; Lecture tours in Europe and America; BBC talks producer, MOI. Served War of 1939–45, 1940–45; RAF Station Intelligence Officer, St Eval; Anti-U-Boat Planner and Intelligence Officer, Coastal Command; Naval and Military Intelligence, Air Ministry; Wing Cdr (despatches twice, OBE). Contested (Lab) Epsom, General Election, and Bournemouth by-election, 1945; MP (Lab), Preston (by-election), 1946–50, Preston South, 1950–55. Parliamentary Private Secretary to Minister of Supply, 1949–50; Parliamentary Private Sec. to Foreign Sec., March-Oct. 1951 (to Lord President of the Council, 1950–51); Minister of Defence for the RAF, 1964–67; Mission to S Arabia, 1967; Minister Without Portfolio and Deputy Leader, House of Lords, 1967–68; Lord Privy Seal, Jan.-April, 1968; Paymaster-General, April-Oct. 1968; Leader of the House of Lords, April 1968–70; Lord Privy Seal, Oct. 1968–1970; Minister in charge, Civil Service Dept, Nov. 1968–70; Opposition Leader, House of Lords, 1970–74. Sen. Executive and Director, J. Lewis Partnership, 1955–64; Dir, Personnel and Admin, RTZ Corp. Ltd, 1974–82. Chairman: Adv. Council on Oil Pollution, 1962–64; Political Honours Scrutiny Committee, 1976–; East European Trade

Council, 1977–86 (Hon. Pres., 1986–); Vice-Chm., H of L Select Cttee on Sci. and Tech. Mem., BOTB, 1975–78. Member, Council: Industrial Soc., 1963–83; RIIA, 1980–86; President: British Assoc. of Industrial Editors, 1960–64; ASLIB, 1963–65; Royal Geographical Society, 1971–74 (formerly Vice-Pres.); Parly and Scientific Cttee, 1976–80 (formerly Vice-Pres.); British Standards Inst., 1977–80. Chm., Arctic Club, 1960, 1979. Pro-Chancellor, Southampton Univ. Vice-Pres., YHA. Governor: London Chest Hosps, 1947–51; Imperial Coll. of Science, 1950–53. Mem. Council, SSAFA, 1951–55. Hon. Elder Brother, Trinity Hse, 1980; Hon. Fellow, St Hugh's Coll., Oxford; Hon. Mem., RICS. CBIM. Hon. LLD Univ. of Newfoundland, 1970; Hon. DSc: Warwick, 1978; Southampton, 1986. Cuthbert Peek Award (Royal Geographical Society), 1933; Ludwig Medallist (Munich Geog. Soc.), 1938. *Publications:* Arctic Journeys; Nansen, the Explorer; (part-author) Borneo Jungle; Economic Survey of Falkland Is, 1976, updated 1982; Review of UK Anti-Terrorist Legislation, 1978; articles, broadcasts, etc. on geographical and political subjects and personnel and general administration. *Address:* c/o RTZ Corporation, 6 St James's Square, SW1Y 4LD. *T:* 01–930 2399.

SHACKLETON, Keith Hope; artist and naturalist; President, Society of Wildlife Artists, 1978–83; Chairman, Artists League of Great Britain; *b* 16 Jan. 1923; *s* of W. S. Shackleton; *m* 1951, Jacqueline Tate; two *s* one *d*. *Educ:* Oundle. Served RAF, 1941–46. Civil Pilot and Dir, Shackleton Aviation Ltd, 1948–63; natural history programmes for television, 1964–68; joined naturalist team aboard MS Lindblad Explorer, 1969. Pres., Royal Soc. of Marine Artists, 1973–78. Member: RGS; Zool Soc. of London; NZ Antarctic Soc. Hon. LLD Birmingham, 1983. *Publications:* Tidelines, 1951; Wake, 1953; Wild Animals in Britain, 1959; Ship in the Wilderness, 1986; Wildlife and Wilderness, 1986; illustrations for books. *Recreations:* small Boat Sailing, exploration field work. *Address:* 28 Ladbroke Square, W11 3NB. *T:* 01–727 7320. *Club:* Itchenor Sailing.

SHACKLETON, Nicholas John, PhD; FRS 1985; Assistant Director of Research Sub-Department of Quaternary Research, University of Cambridge, since 1972; Fellow of Clare Hall, since 1980; *b* 23 June 1937; *s* of Prof. Robert Millner Shackleton, *qv*. *Educ:* Cranbrook Sch.; Clare Coll., Cambridge (BA, PhD); ScD Cantab 1984. Senior Asst in Research, sub-dept of Quaternary Res., Univ. of Cambridge, 1965–72; Research Fellow, Clare Hall, 1974–80, Official Fellow, 1980–. Sen. Vis. Res. Fellow, Lamont Doherty Geol Observatory of Columbia Univ., 1974–75. Carus Medal, Deutsche Akad. der Naturforscher Leopoldina, 1985; Sheppard Medal, SEPM, 1985. *Publications:* numerous articles on marine geology, geological history of climate, etc; articles in New Grove Dictionary of Music and Musicians. *Recreations:* clarinet playing, researching history of clarinet, Thai food. *Address:* 12 Tenison Avenue, Cambridge CB1 2DY. *T:* Cambridge 311938.

SHACKLETON, Prof. Robert Millner, BSc, PhD; FRS 1971; FGS; Hon. Research Professor, Open University, since 1977, Senior Research Fellow since 1979; Visiting Professor, Imperial College, University of London, 1985–87; Professor of Geology, University of Leeds, 1962–75, now Emeritus; Director, Research Institute of African Geology, University of Leeds, 1966–75; *b* 30 Dec. 1909; *m* 1st, 1934, Gwen Isabel Harland; one *s* two *d*; 2nd, 1949, Judith Wyndham Jeffreys (marr. diss. 1978); one *s* one *d*; 3rd, 1984, Peigi Wallace. *Educ:* Sidcot School; University of Liverpool. BSc (Hons) 1931, PhD 1934, Liverpool; Beit Fellow, Imperial College, 1932–34; Chief Geologist to Whitehall Explorations Ltd in Fiji, 1935–36; on teaching staff, Imperial College, 1936–40 and 1945–48; Geologist, Mining and Geological Dept, Kenya, 1940–45; Herdman Professor of Geology, University of Liverpool, 1948–62. Royal Society Leverhulme Vis. Prof., Haile Sellassie I Univ., 1970–71; Trevelyan Coll. Fellow, Durham Univ., 1984–85. Vice-Pres., Geolog. Soc. of London, 1966. Murchison Medal, 1970. *Publications:* Mining and Geological Dept of Kenya Reports 10, 11, 12; papers in geological journals, etc. *Address:* The Croft Barn, Church Street, East Hendred, Oxon OX12 8LA. *T:* (home) Abingdon 834802; (office) Milton Keynes 653002.

See also N. J. Shackleton.

SHACKLETON BAILEY, D. R.; *see* Bailey.

SHACKLOCK, Constance, OBE 1971; LRAM 1940; FRAM 1953; International Opera and Concert Singer; Professor, Royal Academy of Music, 1968–84; *b* 16 April 1913; *e d* of Randolph and Hilda Shacklock, Nottingham; *m* 1947, Eric Mitchell (*d* 1965). *Educ:* Huntingdon Street Secondary School, Nottingham; RAM. Principal mezzo-soprano, Covent Garden, 1946–56. Outstanding rôles: Carmen, Amneris (Aida), Octavian (Der Rosenkavalier), Brangaene (Tristan und Isolde). Guest artist: Wagner Society, Holland, 1949; Berlin State Opera, 1951; Edinburgh Festival, 1954; Berlin Festival, 1956; Teatro Colon, Buenos Aires, 1956; Bolshoi Theatre, Moscow, 1957; Kirov Theatre, Leningrad, 1957; Elizabethan Theatre Trust, Sydney, 1958; Liège Opera, 1960; London production of The Sound of Music, 1961–66. President: English Singers and Speakers, 1978–79; Royal Acad. of Music, 1979–80. *Recreations:* gardening, reading, tapestry. *Address:* East Dorincourt, Kingston Vale, SW15 3RN.

SHAFER, Prof. Byron Edwin; Andrew W. Mellon Professor of American Government, Oxford, since 1985; *b* 8 Jan. 1947; *s* of Byron Henry Shafer and Doris Marguerite (Von Bergen) Shafer; *m* 1981, Wanda K. Green; one *s*. *Educ:* Yale Univ. (BA Magna Cum Laude, Deptl Hons in Pol. Sci. with Excep. Dist. 1968); Univ. of California at Berkeley (PhD Pol. Sci. 1979). Resident Scholar, Russell Sage Foundn, USA, 1977–84; Associate Prof. of Pol. Sci., Florida State Univ., 1984–85. Hon. MA Oxford, 1985. E. E. Schattschneider Prize, Amer. Pol. Sci. Assoc., 1980. *Publications:* Quiet Revolution: the struggle for the Democratic Party and the shaping of post-reform politics, 1983; Presidential Politics: readings on nominations and elections, 1980; articles in learned jls. *Recreations:* furniture restoration, gardening, travel. *Address:* Nuffield College, Oxford OX1 1NF. *T:* Oxford 248014; 55 Stapleton Road, Headington, Oxford OX3 7LX. *T:* Oxford 64705.

SHAFFER, Peter Levin; playwright; critic; *b* 15 May 1926; *s* of Jack Shaffer and Reka Shaffer (*née* Fredman). *Educ:* St Paul's School, London; Trinity College, Cambridge. Literary Critic, Truth, 1956–57; Music Critic, Time and Tide, 1961–62. Awards: Evening Standard Drama Award, 1958; New York Drama Critics Circle Award (best foreign play), 1959–60. *Stage Plays:* Five Finger Exercise, prod. Comedy, London, 1958–60, and Music Box Theatre, New York, 1960–61; (double bill) The Private Ear (filmed 1966) and The Public Eye, produced, Globe, London, 1962, Morosco Theater, New York 1963 (filmed 1972); The Merry Roosters Panto (with Joan Littlewood and Theatre Workshop) prod. Wyndham's Theatre, Christmas, 1963; The Royal Hunt of the Sun, Nat. Theatre, Chichester Festival, 1964, The Old Vic, and Queen's Theatres, 1964–67, NY, 1965–66 (filmed 1969); Black Comedy, Nat. Theatre, Chichester Fest., 1965, The Old Vic and Queen's Theatres, 1965–67; as double bill with White Lies, NY, 1967, Shaw, 1976; The White Liars, Lyric, 1968; The Battle of Shrivings, Lyric, 1970; Equus, Nat. Theatre, 1973–74, NY, 1976, Albery Theatre, 1976–77 (NY Drama Critics' and Antoinette Perry Awards) (filmed 1977); Amadeus, Nat. Theatre, 1979 (Evening Standard Drama Award, Plays and Players Award, London Theatre Critics Award), NY, 1980 (Antoinette Perry Award, Drama Desk Award), Her Majesty's, 1981 (filmed 1984, Acad. Award, Golden Globe Award, Los Angeles Film Critics Assoc. Award, 1985); Yonadab, Nat. Theatre, 1985. Plays produced on television and sound include: Salt Land (ITV), 1955; Balance of Terror (BBC TV), 1957; The Prodigal Father (Radio), etc. *Recreations:* music, architecture. *Address:* c/o McNaughton-Lowe Representation, 200 Fulham Road, SW10.

SHAFTESBURY, 10th Earl of, *cr* 1672; **Anthony Ashley-Cooper;** Bt 1622; Baron Ashley 1661; Baron Cooper of Paulet, 1672; *b* 22 May 1938; *o s* of Major Lord Ashley (*d* 1947; *e s* of 9th Earl of Shaftesbury, KP, PC, GCVO, CBE) and of Françoise Soulier; *S* grandfather, 1961; *m* 1st, 1966, Bianca Maria (marr. diss. 1976), *o d* of late Gino de Paolis; 2nd, 1976, Christina Eva, *o d* of Ambassador Nils Montan; two *s*. *Educ:* Eton; Christchurch, Oxford. Chm., London Philharmonic Orchestra Council, 1966–80. Hon. Citizen, South Carolina, USA, 1967. Patron of seven livings. *Recreations:* ski-ing, music, shooting. *Heir:* *s* Lord Ashley, *qv*. *Address:* St Giles, Wimborne, Dorset BH21 5NH. *T:* Cranborne 312. *Clubs:* Pratt's, Turf.

SHAGARI, Alhaji Shehu Usman Aliyu; President of Nigeria and Commander-in-Chief of the Armed Forces, 1979–83; *b* April 1925; *s* of Magaji Aliyu; *m* 1946; three *s* three *d*. *Educ:* Middle Sch., Sokoto; Barewa Coll., Kaduna; Teacher Trg Coll., Zaria. Teacher of science, Sokoto Middle Sch., 1945–50; Headmaster, Argungu Sen. Primary Sch., 1951–52; Sen. Visiting Teacher, Sokoto Prov., 1953–58. Entered politics as Mem. Federal Parl., 1954–58; Parly Sec. to Prime Minister, 1958–59; Federal Minister: Economic Develt, 1959–60; Establishments, 1960–62; Internal Affairs, 1962–65; Works, 1965–66; Sec., Sokoto Prov. Educl Develt Fund, 1966–68; State Comr for Educn, Sokoto Province, 1968–70; Fed. Comr for Econ. Develt and Reconstruction, 1970–71; for Finance, 1971–75. Mem., Constituent Assembly, Oct. 1977–; Mem., Nat. Party of Nigeria. *Publications:* (poetry) Wakar Nijeriya, 1948; Dun Fodia, 1978; (collected speeches) My Vision of Nigeria, 1981. *Recreations:* Hausa poetry, reading, farming, indoor games.

SHAKERLEY, Sir Geoffrey (Adam), 6th Bt *cr* 1838; Director, Photographic Records Ltd, since 1970; *b* 9 Dec. 1932; *s* of Sir Cyril Holland Shakerley, 5th Bt, and of Elizabeth Averil (MBE 1955), *d* of late Edward Gwynne Eardley-Wilmot; *S* father, 1970; *m* 1st, 1962, Virginia Elizabeth (*d* 1968), *d* of W. E. Maskell; two *s*; 2nd, 1972, Lady Elizabeth Georgiana, *d* of late Viscount Anson and Princess Georg of Denmark; one *d*. *Educ:* Harrow; Trinity College, Oxford. *Heir:* *s* Nicholas Simon Adam Shakerley, *b* 20 Dec. 1963. *Address:* 56 Ladbroke Grove, W11 2PB.

SHAKESPEARE, John William Richmond, CMG 1985; LVO 1968; HM Diplomatic Service; Ambassador to Peru, since 1983; *b* 11 June 1930; *s* of late Dr W. G. Shakespeare; *m* 1955, Lalage Ann, *d* of late S. P. B. Mais; three *s* one *d*. *Educ:* Winchester; Trinity Coll., Oxford (Scholar, MA). 2nd Lieut Irish Guards, 1949–50. Lectr in English, Ecole Normale Supérieure, Paris, 1953–54; on editorial staff, Times Educational Supplement, 1955–56 and Times, 1956–59; entered Diplomatic Service, 1959; Private Sec. to Ambassador in Paris, 1959–61; FO, 1961–63; 1st Sec., Phnom-Penh, 1963–64; 1st Sec., Office of Polit. Adviser to C-in-C Far East, Singapore, 1964–66; Dir of British Information Service in Brazil, 1966–69; FCO, 1969–73; Counsellor and Consul-Gen., Buenos Aires, 1973–75; Chargé d'Affaires, Buenos Aires, 1976–77; Head of Mexico and Caribbean Dept, FCO, 1977–79; Counsellor, Lisbon, 1979–83. Officer, Order of Southern Cross (Brazil), 1968. *Recreations:* tennis, sailing, bicycling, gardening, sun-bathing, music (light), poetry. *Address:* c/o Foreign and Commonwealth Office, SW1A 2AH.

SHAKESPEARE, Sir William (Geoffrey), 2nd Bt *cr* 1942; General Practitioner, Aylesbury, and Clinical Assistant, Mental Subnormality, Manor House Hospital, Aylesbury; *b* 12 Oct. 1927; *s* of Rt Hon. Sir Geoffrey Hithersay Shakespeare, 1st Bt, and Aimée Constance (*d* 1950), *d* of Walter Loveridge; *S* father, 1980; *m* 1964, Susan Mary, *d* of A. D. Raffel, Colombo, Ceylon; two *s*. *Educ:* Radley; Clare Coll., Cambridge (BA Hons Nat. Scis, MA 1957); St George's Hospital. MB BChir Camb. 1958; DCH Eng. 1961. Boston Children's Hosp., USA, 1963–64; Paediatric Registrar, Stoke Mandeville Hosp., 1964–66. Mem., Snowdon Working Party, Integration of Handicapped, 1974–76. Vice-President: Physically Handicapped & Able-Bodied (PHAB), 1977–; Assoc. for Res. into Restricted Growth (ARRG), 1982–. Member BMA. *Heir:* *s* Thomas William Shakespeare, *b* 11 May 1966. *Address:* Manor Cottage, Stoke Mandeville, Bucks. *Clubs:* MCC; Leander.

SHAMOYA, Leonard Hantebele; High Commissioner for Zambia in London, 1975–77; *b* 20 Dec. 1936; *s* of Chiyupa Shamoya and Kavumbu Shamoya; *m* 1964; two *s* three *d*. *Educ:* London Univ. (BA); Brunel Univ. (MTech). RCM, Zambia: Secretarial Asst, 1964–67; Personnel Officer, 1967–69; Chief Personnel Officer, 1969–75. Director: Bank of Zambia, 1964–75; Zambia Trade Fair, 1966–68 and 1970–75; Zambia Nat. Building Soc., 1974–75; Shell and BP, 1975. Mayor, City of Ndola, 1966–68 and 1970–75; Constituency Sec., UNIP, 1970–75. *Recreations:* football, sports. *Address:* c/o Ministry of Foreign Affairs, PO Box RW69, Lusaka, Zambia.

SHAMS-UD DOHA, Aminur Rahman; Minister for Foreign Affairs, Government of the People's Republic of Bangladesh, since 1982; *b* 1929; *m*; two *s*; *m* 1981, Wajiha Moukaddem. *Educ:* Calcutta and Dacca Univs (BSc Hons; BA). Commnd 2nd Lieut, Pakistan Artillery, 1952; Sch. of Artillery and Guided Missiles, Ft Sill, Okla, USA, 1957–58; Gen. Staff Coll., Quetta, 1962; GS Inf. Bde HQ, 1963; RMCS, Shrivenham, 1964–65; Sen. Instr, Gunnery, 1965; GS GHQ, 1965–66, retired. Editor and Publisher, Inter-Wing, Rawalpindi, 1968–71; Gen. Sec., Awami League, Rawalpindi, 1969–71, and Mem. Working Cttee; Ambassador of Bangladesh to: Yugoslavia and Roumania, 1972–74; Iran and Turkey, 1974–77; High Comr for Bangladesh in UK, 1977–82; Minister for Information, Bangladesh, March–June 1982. Member and Leader of Bangladesh delegns to numerous internat., Islamic and Commonwealth meetings. Associate Mem., Inst. of Strategic Studies, London. C-in-C's Commendation, 1964; several military awards and decorations. Order of the Lance and Flag, Cl. 1 (Yugoslavia). *Publications:* Arab-Israeli War, 1967; The Emergence of South Asia's First Nation State; Aryans on the Indus (MS). *Recreations:* sport (selected for London Olympics, 1948), writing, gardening. *Address:* Ministry of Foreign Affairs, Government of People's Republic of Bangladesh, Segunbagicha, Dhaka, Bangladesh; Farm View, Indra Road, Tejgaon, Dhaka 15, Bangladesh. *Clubs:* Grosvenor House, Royal Automobile, Hurlingham; Dacca; Chittagong; Diplomatic (Belgrade); Imperial, Iran (Tehran), etc.

SHAND, Major Bruce Middleton Hope, MC 1940, and Bar 1942; Vice Lord Lieutenant, East Sussex, since 1974; *b* 22 Jan. 1917; *s* of late P. Morton Shand; *m* 1946, Rosalind Maud, *d* of 3rd Baron Ashcombe; one *s* two *d*. *Educ:* Rugby; RMC, Sandhurst. 2nd Lieut 12th Royal Lancers, 1937; Major 1942; wounded and PoW 1942; retd 1947. Exon, Queen's Body Guard of the Yeomen of the Guard, 1971, Ensign, 1978–85, Adjutant and Clerk of the Cheque, 1985–. Joint or Acting Master, Southdown Fox Hounds, 1956–75. DL Sussex, 1962. *Recreations:* hunting, gardening. *Address:* The Laines, Plumpton, near Lewes, East Sussex BN7 3AJ. *T:* Plumpton 890248. *Club:* Cavalry and Guards.

See also E. R. M. Howe.

SHAND, Rt. Rev. David Hubert Warner; Assistant Bishop and Bishop in Geelong, Diocese of Melbourne, Archbishop's Provincial Assistant, since 1985; *b* 6 April 1921; *s* of late Rev. Canon Rupert Warner Shand and Madeleine Ethel Warner Shand; *m* 1946, Muriel Jean Horwood Bennett; one *s* three *d*. *Educ:* The Southport Sch., Queensland; St Francis' Theological Coll., Brisbane (ThL, 2nd Cl. Hons); Univ. of Queensland (BA, 2nd Cl. Hons). Served War, AIF, 1941–45: Lieut, 1942. St Francis' Coll., Brisbane, 1946–48. Deacon, 1948; Priest, 1949; Asst Curate, Lutwyche. Served in Parishes: Moorooka, Inglewood, Nambour, Ipswich; Org. Sec., Home Mission Fund, 1960–63; Rural Dean of Ipswich, 1963–66; Dio. of Brisbane: Chaplain CMF, 1950–57; Vicar, Christ Church, South Yarra, 1966–69; St Andrew's, Brighton, 1969–73; Rural Dean of St Kilda, 1972–73; Dio. of Melbourne: consecrated Bishop, St Paul's Cathedral, Melbourne, Nov. 1973; Bishop of St Arnaud, 1973–76 (when diocese amalgamated with that of Bendigo); Vicar of St Stephen's, Mt Waverley, 1976–78; Bishop of the Southern Region, 1978–85. Chm., Gen. Bd of Religious Educn, 1974–84. *Recreation:* carpentry. *Address:* 27 Shoubra Drive, Highton, Victoria 3216, Australia.

SHAND, John Alexander Ogilvie; Chairman of Industrial Tribunals (Birmingham Region), since 1981; a Recorder of the Crown Court, since 1981; *b* 6 Nov. 1942; *s* of late Alexander Shand and Marguerite Marie Shand; *m* 1965, Patricia Margaret (*née* Toynbee); two *s* one *d*. *Educ:* Nottingham High Sch.; Queens' Coll., Cambridge (MA, LLB; Chancellor's Medal for Law 1965). Called to the Bar, Middle Temple, 1965 (Harmsworth Scholarship); practised on Midland and Oxford Circuit (Birmingham), 1965–71 and 1973–81 (Dep. Circuit Judge, 1979); Fellow and Tutor, Queens' Coll., Cambridge, 1971–73. Chancellor, Dio. Southwell, 1981–. *Publications:* (with P. G. Stein) Legal Values in Western Society, 1974; contrib. various articles in Cambridge Law Jl. *Address:* 21 Prince Rupert Mews, Beacon Street, Lichfield, Staffs SW13 7DD. *T:* Lichfield 58589.

SHANKAR, Pandit Ravi; Presidential Padma Vibhushan Award, 1980; MP; Member of Rajya Sabha, since 1986; musician and composer; *b* 7 April 1920. Studied with brother Uday Shankar in Paris, 1930, with Ustad Allaudin Khan in Maihar, 1936. Music Dir, All-India Radio, 1949–56; music and choreography for ASIAD 82 (Asian Games, New Delhi, 1982). Fellow, Sangeet Natak Akademi, 1977 (President's Award, 1962); Member, Nat. Acad. for Recording Arts and Sciences, 1966. Has received hon. doctorates in letters and arts from California, 1968; Colgate, NY, 1972; Rabindra Bharati, Calcutta; Benares Hindu Univ. Deshikottam Award, 1982. *Compositions:* Indian ragas; music for ballet, and films incl. Gandhi, 1983; Concertos for sitar and orch., No 1, 1971, No 2, 1981. *Publication:* My Music My Life, 1968. *Recreations:* films, people. *Address:* c/o Basil Douglas Artists Management, 8 St George's Terrace, NW1 8XJ.

SHANKS, Ernest Pattison, CBE 1975; QC (Singapore) 1958; Deputy Bailiff of Guernsey, 1973–76; *b* 11 Jan. 1911; *e s* of late Hugh P. Shanks and Mary E. Shanks; *m* 1st, 1937, Audrey E. Moore; one *s*; 2nd, 1947, Betty Katherine Battersby; two *s* one *d*. *Educ:* Mill Hill Sch.; Downing Coll., Cambridge (MA); Inner Temple; Staff Coll., Camberley. Called to the Bar, Inner Temple, 1936; N Eastern Circuit. SRO, Mddx Regt, 1939–44: Princess Louise's Kensington Regt, France (despatches); Sicily, Italy, 1944; Staff Coll., Camberley, 1944–46; Sen. Legal Officer, Schleswig-Holstein, Milit. Govt, Germany, 1946; Lt-Col RARO, 1946. Colonial Legal Service: Dist Judge, Trengganu, Malaya, 1946; Singapore: Dist Judge and First Magistrate, 1947; Crown Counsel and Solicitor-Gen.; Attorney-Gen. and Minister of Legal Affairs, 1957–59. HM Comptroller, Guernsey, 1960; HM Procureur, 1969. *Address:* Le Petit Mas, Clos des Fosses, St Martin's, Guernsey. *T:* Guernsey 38300. *Clubs:* Old Millhillians (Pres., 1979–80), Royal Commonwealth Society; Royal Channel Islands Yacht, Royal Guernsey Golf.

SHANKS, Ian Alexander, PhD; FRS 1984; Chief Scientist, THORN EMI plc, since 1986; *b* 22 June 1948; *s* of Alexander and Isabella Affleck (*née* Beaton); *m* 1971, Janice Smillie Coulter; one *d*. *Educ:* Dumbarton Acad.; Glasgow Univ. (BSc); Glasgow Coll. of Technology (PhD); CEng, MIEE 1983. Projects Manager, Scottish Colorfoto Labs, 1970–72; Research Student, Portsmouth Polytechnic, 1972–73 (liquid crystal displays); RSRE, Malvern, 1973–82 (displays and L-B films); Unilever Research, 1982, Principal Scientist, 1984–86 (electronic biosensors). Vis. Prof. of Electrical and Electronic Engrg, Univ. of Glasgow, 1985. Paterson Medal and Prize, Inst. of Physics, 1984; Best Paper Award, Soc. for Inf. Display, 1983. *Publications:* numerous sci. and tech. papers; numerous patents. *Recreations:* music, home computing. *Address:* Flintwood Cottage, Channer Drive, Penn, Bucks HP10 8AQ.

SHANN, Sir Keith (Charles Owen), Kt 1980; CBE 1964; retired Australian public servant and diplomat; *b* 22 Nov. 1917; *s* of late F. Shann, Melbourne; *m* 1944, Betty, *d* of late C. L. Evans; two *s* one *d*. *Educ:* Trinity Grammar Sch., Kew, Vic; Trinity Coll., Melbourne Univ. (BA). Commonwealth Treasury Dept, 1939; Dept of Labour and Nat. Service, 1940; joined Dept of External Affairs: 2nd Sec., UN Div., 1946; 1st Sec., Acting Counsellor i/c UN Div., 1948; Aust. Mission to UN, New York, 1949–52; Head, UN Branch, 1952–55; Head, Americas and Pacific Branch, 1955; Minister, later Ambassador, to the Philippines, 1955–59; External Affairs Officer, London, 1959–62; Ambassador to Indonesia, 1962–66; First Asst Sec., 1966–70, Dep. Sec., 1970–74, Dept of External (later Foreign) Affairs; Ambassador to Japan, 1974–77; Chm., Aust. Public Service Board, 1977–78. Dir, Mount Isa Mines Ltd, 1978–; Chm., Burns Philp Trustee Co. (Canberra), 1982–. Mem. Delegns to UN Gen. Assembly, Paris, 1948, 1951, NY 1949, 1950, 1952, 1953, 1957, 1967, 1974; Aust. Observer Bandoeng Conf., 1955; *Rapporteur*, UN Special Cttee on Hungary, 1957; Leader, Aust. Delegn to Develt Assistance Cttee of OECD, 1966–67, 1968–69; Commonwealth Observer, Zimbabwe Elections, 1980. *Recreations:* golf, gardening, music. *Address:* 11 Grey Street, Deakin, Canberra 2600, Australia. *Clubs:* Commonwealth (Canberra); Melbourne Cricket, Royal Canberra Golf.

SHANNON, 9th Earl of, *cr* 1756; **Richard Bentinck Boyle;** Viscount Boyle, Baron of Castle-Martyr, 1756; Baron Carleton (GB), 1786; late Captain Irish Guards; Director of companies; Secretary and Treasurer, Federation of European Industrial Co-operative Research Organisations; *b* 23 Oct. 1924; *o s* of 8th Earl of Shannon; *S* father, 1963; *m* 1st, 1947, Catherine Irene Helen (marr. diss. 1955), *d* of the Marquis Demetrio Imperiali di Francavilla; 2nd, 1957, Susan Margaret (marr. diss. 1979), *d* of late J. P. R. Hogg; one *s* two *d*. *Educ:* Eton College. A Dep. Speaker and Dep. Chm. of Cttees, House of Lords, 1968–78. Dir, Cttee of Dirs of Res. Assocs, 1969–85. Vice-President: Inland Waterways Assoc.; Brit. Hydromechanics Research Assoc.; Pres., Kent Br., BIM; Hon. Pres., Foundn for Education of Underachieving and Dyslexic Pres., Architectural Metalwork Assoc., 1966–74; Vice-Pres., Aslib, 1974; Chm., Foundn for Sci. and Tech., 1977–83. FRSA, FBIM, MBHI. *Heir: s* Viscount Boyle, *qv. Address:* Pimm's Cottage, Man's Hill, Burghfield Common, Berks RG7 3BD. *Club:* White's.

SHANNON, Godfrey Eccleston Boyd, CMG 1951; Assistant Under-Secretary of State, in the Commonwealth Office, 1956–68, retired 1968; *b* 14 Dec. 1907; *s* of late W. B. Shannon. *Educ:* Wellington; St John's College, Cambridge. Appointed to Dominions Office, 1930; visited Australia and New Zealand, as Private Sec., with 10th Duke of Devonshire, 1936; Official Sec., UK High Commissioner's Office, New Zealand, 1939–41; served on UK Delegation to various international conferences in London, Geneva, New York, Chicago and Moscow, 1944–48, to UNCTAD, 1964, and to Commonwealth Finance Ministers' meetings, Jamaica, Montreal and Trinidad, 1965–67; Deputy United Kingdom High Commissioner in Canada, 1948–50, in Calcutta, 1952–56. Member, Cttee for Exports: to Canada, 1964–68; to Australia, 1965–68. Renter Warden, Dyers' Co., 1967–68, Prime Warden, 1968–69. *Address:* 18 Lamont Road, SW10 0JE. *T:* 01–351 1585. *Club:* Travellers'.

SHAPCOTT, Sidney Edward, CEng, FIEE, FInstP; consulting engineer; *b* 20 June 1920; *s* of late Percy Thomas and Beatrice Shapcott; *m* 1943, Betty Jean Richens; two *s* one *d*. *Educ:* Hele's School, Exeter; King's College, London. BSc. Joined Air Defence Experimental Establishment, 1941; various appointments in Min. of Supply and Min. of Aviation, 1941–62; DCSO, 1963; Dir of Projects, ESRO, 1963–65; Min. of Defence, Navy Dept, 1965–75; CSO, 1968; Dep. Dir, Admiralty Surface Weapons Establishment, 1968–72; Dir, Underwater Weapon Projects, Admiralty Underwater Weapons Establishment, Portland, 1972–75; Dir-Gen., Airborne Weapons and Electronic Systems, MoD, 1976–80. *Address:* 23 Upper Churston Rise, Seaton, Devon EX12 2HD. *T:* Seaton 21545.

SHAPIRO, Erin Patria Margaret; Founder of first Shelter for Battered Wives and their children, 1971; therapeutic consultant and fund-raiser, Women's Aid Ltd; *b* 19 Feb. 1939; *d* of Cyril Edward Antony Carney and Ruth Patricia Balfour-Last; *m* 1st, 1961, John Leo Pizzey (marr. diss. 1979); one *s* one *d*; 2nd, 1980, Jeffrey Scott Shapiro. *Educ:* St Antony's; Leweston Manor, Sherborne, Dorset. Somewhat chequered career as pioneering attracts frequent clashes with the law; appearances at such places as Acton Magistrates Court and the House of Lords could be considered milestones in the fulfilment of a career dedicated to defending women and children. Member: Soc. of Authors; AFI; Smithsonian Instn. *Publications:* (as Erin Pizzey) Scream Quietly or the Neighbours Will Hear, 1974 (paperback), 2nd edn 1978; Infernal Child (autobiog.), 1978; The Slut's Cookbook, 1981; (with Jeff Shapiro) Prone to Violence, 1982; Erin Pizzey Collects, 1983; *novels:* The Watershed, 1983; In the Shadow of the Castle, 1984; The Pleasure Palace, 1986; First Lady; poems and short stories. *Recreations:* wine, books, travel. *Address:* 10 Conchas Loop, Eldorado, Santa Fe, New Mexico 87505, USA.

SHAPLAND, Maj.-Gen. Peter Charles, CB 1977; MBE 1960; MA; Planning Inspector, Department of the Environment, since 1980; *b* 14 July 1923; *s* of late F. C. Shapland, Merton Park, Surrey; *m* 1954, Joyce Barbara Shapland (*née* Peradon); two *s*. *Educ:* Rutlish Sch., Merton Park; St Catharine's Coll., Cambridge. Served War: commissioned Royal Engineers, 1944; QVO Madras Sappers and Miners, Indian Army, 1944–47. Served United Kingdom, Middle East (Canal Zone) and Cyprus, 1948–63. Attended Staff Coll., 1952; jssc, 1960. Lt-Col, 1965; comd in Aden, 1965–67; Brig., Dec. 1968; comd 30 Engineer Bde. Attended Royal Coll. of Defence Studies, 1971. Dep. Comdr and Chief of Staff, HQ SE Dist, 1972–74; Maj.-Gen. 1974; Dir, Volunteers Territorials and Cadets, MoD (Army), 1974–78, retired. Hon. Col, 73 Engineer Regt, TA, 1979–; Col Comdt, RE, 1981–86. Chm., Combined Cadet Forces Assoc., 1982–; Pres., Instn of Royal Engrs, 1982–. Mem., Worshipful Co. of Painter-Stainers, 1983–. *Publications:* contribs to Royal Engineers' Jl. *Recreations:* sailing, swimming, golf. *Address:* c/o Royal Bank of Scotland, Holts Branch, Kirkland House, Whitehall, SW1A 2EB. *Clubs:* Royal Ocean Racing, Lansdowne; Royal Engineer Yacht (Chatham).

SHAPLAND, Sir William (Arthur), Kt 1982; Trustee, Bernard Sunley Charitable Foundation; *b* 20 Oct. 1912; *s* of late Arthur Frederick Shapland and of Alice Maud (*née* Jackson); *m* 1943; Madeline Annie (*née* Amiss); two *d*. *Educ:* Tollington Sch., Muswell Hill. Incorporated Accountant, 1936; Chartered Accountant, 1946. Allan Charlesworth & Co, Chartered Accountants, London, Cambridge and Rangoon, 1929–55; Blackwood Hodge, 1955–83 (Chm., 1965–83). Waynflete Fellow, Magdalen Coll., Oxford, 1981–; Hon. Fellow, St Catherine's College, Oxford, 1982. Hon. FRCS 1978. Past Master, Paviors' Co. OStJ 1981. Hon. DSc Buckingham, 1983; Hon. DLitt Leicester, 1985. *Recreations:* golf, gardening, travel. *Address:* 44 Beech Drive, N2 9NY. *T:* 01–883 5073.

SHARKEY, Colum John, CMG 1984; MBE 1973; HM Diplomatic Service; Head of British Interests Section, Buenos Aires, since 1984; *b* 9 June 1931; *s* of late Andrew Sharkey and late Sarah Josephine Sharkey (*née* Whelan); *m* 1962, Olivia Anne (*née* Brassil); two *s* one *d*. Commonwealth Relations Office, 1954; served in New Delhi, 1955, Calcutta, 1956–58; Second Secretary: Dacca, 1959–61; Melbourne, 1962–66; Montevideo, 1967–68 (joined HM Diplomatic Service, 1968); First Sec. and Consul, Asuncion, 1969; First Sec., Montevideo, 1971; seconded to Dept of Trade, 1972–74; Consul, Vancouver, 1974–78; Consul-Gen., Bilbao, 1978–81; Ambassador to Honduras, 1981–84 and non-resident Ambassador to El Salvador, 1982–84. *Recreations:* reading, tennis, golf. *Address:* c/o Foreign and Commonwealth Office, SW1. *Club:* Hurlingham (Buenos Aires).

SHARLAND, Edward John; HM Diplomatic Service; Consul-General, Perth, since 1982; *b* 25 Dec. 1937; *s* of William Rex Sharland and Phyllis Eileen Sharland (*née* Pitts); *m* 1970, Susan Mary Rodway Millard; four *d*. *Educ:* Monmouth Sch.; Jesus Coll., Oxford. BA Hons History; MA. FO, 1961–62; Bangkok, 1962–67; Far Eastern Dept, FCO, 1967–69; Dep. Perm. Rep. to UNIDO and Dep. Resident Rep. to IAEA, Vienna, 1969–72; Bangkok, 1972–75; Montevideo, 1976–79; Cultural Relations Dept, FCO, 1979–82. *Recreations:* tennis, bridge, stamp collecting. *Address:* c/o Foreign and Commonwealth Office, SW1A 2AH. *Club:* Royal Bangkok Sports.

SHARMA, Usha Kumari, (Mrs V. K. Sharma); *see* Prashar, U. K.

SHARMA, Vishnu Datt; Senior Supervisor, Ealing Community Relations Council, since 1981; Member, Executive Committee, National Council for Civil Liberties, since 1982 (Race Relations Officer, 1979–80); *b* 19 Oct. 1921; *s* of late Pandit Girdhari Lal Kaushik and Shrimati Ganga Devi; *m* 1960, Krishna Sharma; one *d*. *Educ:* High Sch. in India. Came to UK from India, 1957; worked in factories until 1967; apptd Mem. Nat. Cttee for Commonwealth Immigrants (by the Prime Minister, Rt Hon. Harold Wilson); twice elected Gen. Sec. of Indian Workers' Assoc., Southall, 1961–63 and 1965–67, and once Pres., 1977–79; Nat. Organiser, Campaign Against Racial Discrimination (later Vice-Chm.); Chm., Jt Council for the Welfare of Immigrants (Gen. Sec., Exec. Sec. and again Gen. Sec., 1967–77); Vice-Chm., Steering Cttee, Anti-Nazi League. Mem., Adv. Cttee BBC, Asian Magazine; Chief Editor, Charcha (Punjabi journal). Has attended five internat. confs on migrant workers and race relns. *Recreations:* cinema, watching television, sightseeing, etc. *Address:* 43 Lady Margaret Road, Southall, Mddx UB1 2PJ. *T:* 01–843 0518.

SHARMAN, Peter William, CBE 1984; Director since 1974 and Chief General Manager, 1975–84, Norwich Union Insurance Group; *b* 1 June 1924; *s* of William Charles Sharman and Olive Mabel (*née* Burl); *m* 1946, Eileen Barbara Crix; one *s* two *d*. *Educ:* Northgate Grammar Sch., Ipswich; Edinburgh Univ. MA 1950; FIA 1956. War service as Pilot, RAF. Joined Norwich Union Insce Gp, 1950; Gen. Man. and Actuary, 1969. Chairman: Life Offices' Assoc., 1977–78; British Insurance Assoc., 1982–83. *Recreations:* tennis, badminton, golf. *Address:* 28B Eaton Road, Norwich NR4 6PZ. *T:* Norwich 51230.

SHARMAN, Thomas Charles, OBE 1960; HM Diplomatic Service, retired; *b* 12 April 1912; *s* of Thomas Sharman and Mary Ward; *m* 1935, Paulette Elisabeth Padioleau; one *d*. *Educ:* Long Eaton County Secondary Sch.; Clare Coll., Cambridge. HM Consular

Service, 1934; Paris, 1935; Saigon, 1937; Milan, 1939; British Embassy, Lisbon, 1940, and Moscow, 1945; HM Foreign Service, 1945; Batavia, 1946; São Paulo, 1947; Superintending Trade Consul, New Orleans, 1949; HM Consul, Luanda, 1952; Consul (Commercial) Hamburg, 1953; Counsellor (Commercial) Lisbon, 1960; Consul-General, Atlanta, Georgia, USA, 1965–68; Consul-General, Oporto, 1968–70. *Address:* 103 Résidence Jeanne Hachette, 60000 Beauvais, France.

SHARP, Sir Adrian, 4th Bt *cr* 1922, of Warden Court, Maidstone, Kent; *b* 17 Sept. 1951; *s* of Sir Edward Herbert Sharp, 3rd Bt and of Beryl Kathleen, *d* of Leonard Simmons-Green; *S* father, 1986; *m* 1976, Hazel Patricia Bothwell, *o d* of James Trevor Wallace. *Heir: b* Owen Sharp [*b* 17 Sept. 1956; *m*; one *s*].

SHARP, His Honour Alastair George, MBE 1945; QC 1961; DL; a Circuit Judge (formerly Judge of County Courts), 1962–84; Liaison Judge, Durham County Magistrates Courts, 1972–84; *b* 25 May 1911; *s* of late Alexander Sharp, Advocate in Aberdeen, and of late Mrs Isabella Sharp, OBE; *m* 1940, Daphne Sybil, *d* of late Maj. Harold Smithers, RGA, and late Mrs Connor; one *s* two *d*. *Educ:* Aberdeen Grammar School; Fettes; Clare College, Cambridge (Archdeacon Johnson Exhibitioner in Classics). BA 1933, 1st Class Hons Classical Tripos Part II, Aegrotat Part I. Boxed Cambridge Univ., 1931–32; Cambridge Union Debating Team in America, 1933. On staff of Bonar Law College, Ashridge, 1934–35; Barrister, Middle Temple, 1935; Harmsworth Law Scholar; North Eastern Circuit, 1936. Dep. Chm. of Agricultural Land Tribunal, Northern Area, 1958–62; Asst Recorder of Huddersfield, 1958–60; Recorder of Rotherham, 1960–62; Dep. Chm., N Riding Yorks QS, 1959–65; Dep. Chm., 1965–70, Chm., 1970–71, Durham QS. Chm., Washington New Town Licensed Premises Cttee, 1966–78; Jt Pres., Council of Circuit Judges, 1979. Commissioned, The Gordon Highlanders, Feb. 1939; served War of 1939–45: Staff Coll., 1943; 2nd Bn The London Scottish, 1943; Gen. Staff, War Office, 1944–45, Temp. Major. Governor, Sherburn Hosp. Charity, 1972–81. Mem. Board, Faculty of Law, Durham Univ., 1976–84. DL Co. Durham, 1973. *Recreations:* golf, gardening, music, hill walking, fishing. *Address:* 49 South Street, Durham DH1 4QP; The Old Kennels, Tomintoul, Banffshire. *Clubs:* Durham County; Brancepeth Castle Golf.

See also Baron Mackie of Benshie, Sir R. L. Sharp.

SHARP, Sir Angus; *see* Sharp, Sir W. H. A.

SHARP, Derek Joseph; British Council Representative, Italy, 1981–85; *b* 12 June 1925; *s* of Joseph Frank Sharp and Sylvia May (*née* Allen); *m* 1957, Hilda Francesca Cernigoj; two *s*. *Educ:* Preston Grammar School; Queen's Coll., Oxford; MA, DipEd. Lectr, British Inst., Milan, 1956–58; British Council, 1958; served Indonesia, Bristol, Bangkok, Addis Ababa, Pretoria and London, 1958–77; Controller, Africa and Middle East Div., 1977–81. *Address:* 3 Hartley Close, Bickley, Kent BR1 2TP.

SHARP, Sir Eric, Kt 1984; CBE 1980; Chairman since 1980 and Chief Executive since 1981, Cable and Wireless PLC; *b* 17 Aug. 1916; *s* of Isaac and Martha Sharp; *m* 1950, Marion (*née* Freeman); one *s* one *d* (and one *d* decd). *Educ:* London School of Economics (BScEcon Hons). CBIM. Served Army, 1940–46, Staff Captain SOIII Southern Comd, 1944. Principal, Min. of Power, 1948; UK Delegate, Coal and Petroleum Cttees of OEEC, 1948–50; Vice-Chm., Electricity Cttee, OEEC, 1951–54; Sec. to Herbert Cttee of Inquiry into Electricity Supply Industry, 1955–56; British Nylon Spinners Ltd, 1957–64; Director, ICI Fibres Ltd, 1964–68; Mem. Board, Monsanto Europe, 1969; Resident USA, Mem. Management Bd, 1970–72; Dep. Chm., 1973–74, Chm., 1975–81, Monsanto Ltd; Chm., Polyamide Intermediates Ltd, 1975–81. Chm., Chemical Industry Safety and Health Council, 1977–79; President: Chemical Industries Assoc., 1979–80; Sino-British Trade Council, 1985–; part-time Mem., London Electricity Bd, 1969–78; Member: EDC for Chemical Industry, 1980–82; Central Electricity Generating Board, 1980–86. Freeman, City of London, 1982. Officer, Order of Merit (Cameroon). *Recreations:* music, wine, gardening. *Address:* c/o Cable and Wireless PLC, Mercury House, Theobalds Road, WC1. *Club:* Athenæum.

SHARP, Sir George, Kt 1976; OBE 1969; JP; DL; Chairman, Glenrothes Development Corporation, since 1978 (Vice-Chairman, 1973–78); commercial manager, since 1969; *b* 8 April 1919; *s* of Angus Sharp and Mary S. McNee; *m* 1948, Elsie May Rodger, *o d* of David Porter Rodger and Williamina S. Young; one *s*. *Educ:* Thornton Public Sch.; Buckhaven High Sch. Engine driver, 1962; PRO, 1962–69. Fife County Council: Mem., 1945–75; Chm., Water and Drainage Cttee, 1955–61; Chm., Finance Cttee, 1961–72; Convener, 1972–75; Convener, Fife Regional Council, 1974–78. Managing Trustee, Municipal Mutual Insurance Co. Ltd, 1979–. President: Assoc. of County Councils, 1972–74; Convention of Scottish Local Authorities, 1975–78. Chairman: Kirkcaldy Dist Council, 1958–75; Fife and Kinross Water Bd, 1967–75; Forth River Purification Bd, 1955–67 and 1975–78; Scottish River Purification Adv. Cttee, 1967–75; Scottish Tourist Consultative Council, 1979–83. Vice-Chm., Forth Road Bridge Cttee, 1972–78. Member: Scottish Water Adv. Cttee, 1962–69; Cttee of Enquiry into Salmon and Trout Fishing, 1963; Scottish Valuation Adv. Cttee, 1972; Cttee of Enquiry into Local Govt Finance, 1974–76; Scottish Develt Agency, 1975–80; Royal Commn on Legal Services in Scotland, 1978–80; Econ. and Soc. Cttee, EEC, 1982–. Director: Grampian Television, 1975–; National Girobank Scotland. JP Fife, 1975; DL Fife, 1978. *Recreation:* golf. *Address:* Strathlea, 56 Station Road, Thornton, Fife. *T:* Thornton 347.

SHARP, Lt-Col Granville Maynard, MA (Cantab); *b* 5 Jan. 1906; *s* of Walter Sharp, Cleckheaton, Yorks; *m* 1935, Margaret, *d* of Dr J. H. Vincent, Wembley Hill; two *d*. *Educ:* Cleckheaton Grammar School; Ashville College, Harrogate; St John's College, Cambridge, MA (Hons) (Economics). Lecturer in Economics at West Riding Technical Institutes, 1929–34; Chairman, Spenborough Housing and Town Planning Committee, 1935–39; Hon. Secretary, Spen Valley Divisional Labour Party, 1936–39; Battery Capt. 68 Anti-Tank Regt RA, 1939–42; Staff Capt. and DAQMG Belfast Area, 1942–43; Senior British Staff Officer, Economics Section, Allied Control Commission, Italy, 1943–44; Chief Economics and Supply Officer, Military Govt, Austria, 1944–45. MP (Lab) for Spen Valley Div. of West Riding of Yorks, 1945–50; PPS Min. of Civil Aviation, 1946; Chairman, Select Cttee of Estimates Sub-Cttee, 1946–48; Parliamentary Private Sec. to Minister of Works, 1947–50. Keymer Parish Councillor, 1969–83 (Vice-Chm., 1976–80); CC E Sussex, 1970–74; CC W Sussex, 1973–85 (Chm., Rts of Way Cttee, 1974–83); Member: Cuckfield RDC, 1971–74; Mid-Sussex DC, 1973–76. *Recreations:* swimming, singing, scything, Sussex Downs; attempting to preserve the local rural environment by every practical means, from collecting litter and clearing Rights of Way to chivvying authority. *Address:* 31 Wilmington Close, Hassocks, West Sussex. *T:* Hassocks 2294.

SHARP, Dr John; Headmaster of Rossall School, 1973–Sept. 1987; *b* 18 Dec. 1927; *o s* of late Alfred and May Sharp, North Ives, Oxenhope, Keighley; *m* 1950, Jean Prosser; one *s* two *d*. *Educ:* Boys' Grammar Sch., Keighley; Brasenose Coll., Oxford. MA, MSc, DPhil Oxon. RAF Educn Br., 1950–52; research at Oxford, 1952–54; Asst Master, Marlborough Coll., 1954–62; Senior Chemistry Master, 1956–62; Senior Science Master, 1959–62; Headmaster, Christ Coll., Brecon, 1962–72. Co-opted Mem., Oxford and Cambridge Schools Examn Bd, 1966–74; Selected Mem., Breconshire Educn Cttee, 1966–72; Co-opted Mem., Lancs Educn Cttee, 1974–81; Divisional Chm., HMC, SW 1971 and NW 1977–78; Chm., HMC Acad. Policy Sub-Cttee, 1982–85. *Publications:* contrib. Anal. Chim. Acta. *Recreations:* fishing, photography, roses and shrubs. *Address:* (until Sept. 1987) The Hall, Rossall School, Fleetwood, Lancs FY7 8JW. *T:* Fleetwood 3849; (from Sept. 1987) Wood End Cottage, St Michael's, Tenbury Wells, Worcs WR15 8TG. *Club:* East India, Devonshire, Sports and Public Schools.

SHARP, J(ohn) M(ichael) Cartwright; Secretary of Law Commission, 1968–78; Chairman, Leche Trust, since 1982; *b* 11 Aug. 1918; *s* of W. H. Cartwright Sharp, KC, and Dorothy (*née* Shelton). *Educ:* Rossall Sch.; Lincoln Coll., Oxford. Royal Artillery, 1940–46. Called to Bar, Middle Temple, 1947. Lord Chancellor's Office, 1951–65; Legal Sec. to Law Officers, 1965; Asst Solicitor, Law Commn, 1966. *Recreations:* travel, reading. *Address:* 15 Bolton Gardens, SW5. *T:* 01–370 1896. *Clubs:* Reform, Beefsteak.

SHARP, Sir Kenneth (Johnston), Kt 1984; TD 1960; Partner, Howard, Tilly & Co., Chartered Accountants, since 1983; Chairman, T. M. Hunter Ltd, since 1983; several directorships; *b* 29 Dec. 1926; *s* of Johnston Sharp and late Ann Sharp (*née* Routledge); *m* 1955, Barbara Maud Keating; one *s*. *Educ:* Shrewsbury Sch.; St John's Coll., Cambridge (MA). ACA 1955, FCA 1960. Partner, Armstrong, Watson & Co., Chartered Accountants, 1955–75; Head, Govt Accountancy Service and Accountancy Advr to DoI, 1975–83. Indian Army, 1945–48; TA, 251st (Westmorland and Cumberland Yeo.) Field Regt RA, 1948–62; 2nd-in-Comd, 1959–62. Inst. of Chartered Accountants: Mem. Council, 1966–83; Vice-Pres., 1972–73; Dep. Pres., 1973–74; Pres., 1974–75. Master, Co. of Chartered Accountants in England and Wales, 1979–80. Mem., Governing Body, Shrewsbury Sch., 1976–. JP Carlisle, 1957–73. *Publications:* The Family Business and the Companies Act 1967, 1967; articles in professional accountancy press. *Recreations:* messing about in boats, DIY, gardening. *Address:* Flat 1, Coker House, East Coker, Yeovil, Somerset BA22 9HS. *T:* West Coker 2527; Tavern Rocks, 25 Lower Castle Road, St Mawes, Cornwall TR2 5DR. *Club:* United Oxford & Cambridge University.

SHARP, Brig. Mainwaring Cato Ensor, CBE 1945; *b* 1 March 1897; *s* of late Rev. Cato Ensor Sharp; *m* 1949, Betty Yolande Constance, *o d* of late Col M. H. Knaggs, CMG. *Educ:* Trinity College School, Port Hope; RMC, Kingston, Canada. Commissioned, 1915, 5th RI Lancers; transfd Leinster Regt 1916; S Lanc. Regt 1922. Staff College, Camberley, 1928–29; retired, 1935; Insurance Broker, 1937–39; rejoined, 1939; Lt-Col 1941; Brig. 1944. Served European War and War of 1939–45 (despatches twice). Director of Maintenance, Control Commission, Germany, 1946–51; employed by War Office, 1951–58. Croix de Guerre (France); Officer, Legion of Merit (USA). *Recreations:* golf, ornithology. *Address:* 11 Maple Road, Walberton, Arundel, West Sussex. *T:* Yapton 551563.

SHARP, Margery; novelist and playwright; *m* 1938, Major G. L. Castle, RA. *Educ:* Streatham Hill High School; London University. French Honours BA. *Publications:* Rhododendron Pie; Fanfare for Tin Trumpets; The Flowering Thorn; Four Gardens; The Nymph and the Nobleman; Sophy Cassmajor; Meeting at Night (play); The Nutmeg Tree, 1937 (play: USA 1940, England 1941, filmed as Julia Misbehaves, 1948); The Stone of Chastity, 1940; Cluny Brown, 1944 (filmed 1946); Britannia Mews, 1946 (filmed 1949); The Foolish Gentlewoman, 1948 (Play, London, 1949); Lise Lillywhite, 1951; The Gipsy in the Parlour, 1953; The Tigress on the Hearth, 1955; The Eye of Love, 1957; The Rescuers, 1959; Something Light, 1960; Martha in Paris, 1962; Martha, Eric and George, 1964; The Sun in Scorpio, 1965; In Pious Memory, 1968; Rosa, 1969; The Innocents, 1971; The Faithful Servants, 1975; *books for children:* Miss Bianca, 1962; The Turret, 1964 (USA 1963); Miss Bianca in the Salt Mines, 1966; Lost at the Fair, 1967; Miss Bianca in the Orient, 1970; Miss Bianca in the Antarctic, 1971; Miss Bianca and the Bridesmaid, 1972; The Magical Cockatoo, 1974; The Children Next Door, 1974; Bernard the Brave, 1976; Summer Visits, 1977; *short stories:* The Lost Chapel Picnic, 1973. *Address:* c/o William Heinemann Ltd, 10 Upper Grosvenor Street, W1X 9PA.

SHARP, Michael Cartwright; *see* Sharp, J. M. C.

SHARP, Sir Milton Reginald, 3rd Bt, *cr* 1920; Capt. REME, TA; *b* 21 Nov. 1909; *s* of Sir Milton Sharp, 2nd Bt, and Gertrude (*d* 1940), *d* of John Earl, of London; *S* father, 1941; *m* 1951, Marie-Louise de Vignon, Paris. *Educ:* Shrewsbury; Trinity Hall, Cambridge.

SHARP, Hon. Mitchell William, OC 1983; PC (Can.); Commissioner, Northern Pipeline Agency, since 1978; *b* 11 May 1911; *s* of Thomas Sharp and Elizabeth (*née* Little); *m* 1938, Daisy Boyd (decd); one *s*; *m* 1976, Jeannette Dugal. *Educ:* University of Manitoba; London School of Economics. Statistician, Sanford Evans Statistical Service, 1926–36; Economist, James Richardson & Sons Ltd, 1937–42; Officer, Canadian Dept of Finance, Ottawa, 1942–51; Director Economic Policy Division, 1947–51; Associate Deputy Minister, Canadian Dept Trade and Commerce, 1951–57; Dep. Minister, 1957–58; Minister, 1963–65; elected to Canadian House of Commons, 1963; Minister of Finance, 1965–68; Sec. of State for External Affairs, 1968–74; Pres., Privy Council, 1974–76; Govt Leader in House of Commons, 1974–76; MP for Eglinton, 1976–78, resigned. Vice-Pres., Brazilian Traction, Light & Power Co., Toronto, 1958–62. Hon. LLD: Univ. of Manitoba, 1965; Univ. of Western Ontario, 1977; Hon. DrSocSci Ottawa, 1970. *Recreations:* music, walking, skating. *Address:* Station 210, Centennial Towers, 200 Kent Street, Ottawa, Ont K1A 0E6, Canada. *T:* (613) 993–7466.

SHARP, Rear-Adm. Philip Graham, CB 1967; DSC 1942; *b* 23 Nov. 1913; *e s* of late Rev. Douglas Simmonds Sharp and Mrs Sharp; *m* 1940, Dilys Mary Aldwyth, *er d* of late David Roberts and Mrs Roberts, Welford-on-Avon, Warwicks; one *s*. *Educ:* Northampton Sch.; Tynemouth High Sch. Sub-Lt, RNVR, 1937: War Service in destroyers (despatches 1943); Capt. 1956; comdg HMS Defender, 1956–58; NATO, 1958–60; Capt. of Fleet, Home Fleet, 1960–62; comdg HMS Centaur 1962–63; Cdre RN Barracks, Portsmouth, 1963–65; Rear-Adm. 1965; Flag Officer Sea Training, Portland, 1965–67; retired 1967. ADC to the Queen, 1965. County Pres. for Sussex, Royal British Legion, 1983–; Past President: Inter-Allied Confedn of Reserve Officers; Reserve Forces Assoc. Freeman, City of London, 1978. Silver Medal, City of Paris, 1983. *Recreations:* golf, fishing, music, model-making. *Address:* Dolphin House, Old Shoreham Road, Hove, East Sussex. *T:* Brighton 736545. *Clubs:* Naval and Military; Brighton and Hove Golf; Sussex County Cricket.

SHARP, Sir Richard (Lyall), KCVO 1982; CB 1977; Ceremonial Officer, Management and Personnel Office (formerly Civil Service Department), 1977–82; *b* 27 March 1915; *s* of late Alexander Sharp, Advocate, Aberdeen, and late Mrs Isabella Sharp, OBE; *m* 1950, Jean Helen, *er d* of late Sir James Crombie, KCB, KBE, CMG; two *s* two *d* (and one *d* decd). *Educ:* Fettes Coll.; Aberdeen Univ.; Clare Coll., Cambridge. MA with 1st Class Hons Classics, Aberdeen 1937; BA with 1st Class in Classical Tripos pt II, Cambridge 1939. Served Royal Northumberland Fusiliers, 1939–46 (POW, Singapore and Siam, 1942–45). Principal, HM Treasury, 1946; Private Sec. to Chancellor of Exchequer, 1948–50 and to Minister of State for Economic Affairs, 1950; UK Treasury and Supply

Delegn, Washington, 1952–56; Asst Sec., 1954; IDC, 1961; Under-Secretary: Nat. Bd for Prices and Incomes, 1966–68; HM Treasury, 1968–77. *Recreations:* playing the viola, gardening. *Address:* Home Farm House, Briston, Melton Constable, Norfolk. *T:* Melton Constable 860445.

See also Baron Mackie of Benshie, A. G. Sharp.

SHARP, Robert Charles, CMG 1971; Director of Public Works, Tasmania, 1949–71; *b* 20 Sept. 1907; *s* of Robert George Sharp and Gertrude Coral (*née* Bellette); *m* 1st, 1935, Margaret Fairbrass Andrewartha (*d* 1975); one *d*; 2nd, 1978, Marie, widow of Alan C. Wharton, St Albans, Herts. *Educ:* Univ. of Tasmania. BE 1929. Bridge Engr, Public Works, 1935. Enlisted RAE (Major): comd 2/4 Aust. Field Sqdn RAE, 1942; 1 Aust. Port Mtce Co. RAE, 1943; HQ Docks Ops Gp, 1944. Chief Engr, Public Works, 1946; State Co-ordinator of Works, 1949–71. *Recreation:* golf. *Address:* The Coach House, Wickwood Court, Sandpit Lane, St Albans, Herts AL1 4BP; 594 Sandy Bay Road, Hobart, Tasmania 7005, Australia. *T:* Hobart 344.612. *Clubs:* Athenæum, Kingston Beach Golf.

SHARP, Thomas; Department of Trade and Industry; *b* 19 June 1931; *s* of William Douglas Sharp and Margaret Sharp (*née* Tout); *m* 1962, Margaret Lucy Hailstone; two *d*. *Educ:* Brown Sch., Toronto; Abbotsholme Sch., Derbs; Jesus Coll., Oxford. BoT and DTI (with short interval HM Treasury), 1954–73; Counsellor (Commercial), British Embassy, Washington, 1973–76; Dept of Trade, 1976–79; Dept of Industry, 1979–83. *Address:* 96 London Road, Guildford, Surrey GU1 1TH. *T:* Guildford 572669.

SHARP, Sir (William Harold) Angus, KBE 1974; QPM 1969; *b* Auckland, 1915. *Educ:* Cathedral Grammar School, Christchurch. Graduated Imperial Defence College, 1966. Joined New Zealand Police Force, 1937; Commissioner of Police, 1970; retd NZ Police, 1975; Commissioner, Police and Prisons Dept, Western Samoa, 1977–78. *Address:* Rural Delivery 4, Rotorua, New Zealand.

SHARP, William Johnstone, CB 1983; Controller and Chief Executive, Her Majesty's Stationery Office and Queen's Printer of Acts of Parliament, 1981–86; *b* 30 May 1926; *s* of Frederick Matthew and Gladys Evelyn Sharp; *m* 1952, Joan Alice Clark, MBE, *d* of Arnold and Violet Clark. *Educ:* Queen Elizabeth Grammar Sch., Hexham; Emmanuel Coll., Cambridge (MA). Army Service, Reconnaissance Corps, Durham LI and Staff, 1944–48. Entered Min. of Transport, 1949; Private Sec. to Perm. Sec., 1951–53; Principal, Min. of Civil Aviation, 1953; Asst Sec., Min. of Transport, 1962; Under-Sec., DoE, 1970; Controller of Supplies, PSA, 1976–80. FRSA 1984. *Recreation:* the Turf. *Address:* 43 Friars Quay, Norwich NR3 1ES. *T:* Norwich 624258.

SHARPE, Brian Sidney; Consultant, financial and marketing presentation; Chief Tutor, Wadlow Grosvenor Presentation Training; *b* 12 Feb. 1927; *s* of S. H. Sharpe and Norah Sharpe; *m* 1967, Susan Lillywhite; two *s*. *Educ:* Haberdashers' Aske's Sch., Hampstead; Guildhall Sch. of Music and Drama. Royal Fusiliers (att. Forces Broadcasting Service), 1945–48; BBC: Announcer, Midland Region, 1955; Television Presentation, 1956; Producer, African Service, External Services, 1957; Senior Producer: Overseas Talks and Features, 1965; The Financial World Tonight, Radio 4, 1974; Money Programme, Sept-Dec. 1979; on secondment as Exec. Dir, City Communications Centre, 1976–79; Director: Charles Barker Lyons, 1980–85; Charles Barker City, 1983–85. *Publications:* How Money Works (with A. Wilson), 1975; several articles on corporate and other forms of communication. *Recreations:* offshore fishing, music. *Address:* 26 Hallam Road, Godalming, Surrey GU7 3HW. *T:* Godalming 21551.

SHARPE, Sir Frank (Victor), Kt 1978; CMG 1972; OBE (mil.) 1943; ED 1942; Australian representative, Bell Helicopter Company, Fort Worth, USA, 1955–72; Helicopter Consultant to Bell Helicopter Australia Pty Ltd, Brisbane International Airport, 1972–74; Avocado consultant and farm adviser since 1946; Director of several companies; *b* 21 Jan. 1903; *s* of Frederick Robert Sharpe, Avening, Glos, and Elizabeth Matilda Glassop, Sydney (third generation); *m* 1947, Millicent Adelaide Gardner; one *s* one *d*. *Educ:* Rudd's Clayfield Coll.; Queensland Univ. Became dir, family merchant tool business, 1923 (Chm. and Man. Dir and sole proprietor, 1946–). Commissioned Aust. Army, 1921 (Militia); served War of 1939–45, AIF, Australia and SW Pacific; Lt-Col, retd 1955. Built and operated first commercial broadcasting station in Queensland, 1925. FAIM; Fellow, Australian Inst. Dirs. JP Brisbane 1947. *Recreations:* flying, farming, amateur radio. *Address:* 138 Adelaide Street, Clayfield, Brisbane, Qld 4011, Australia. *T:* 262.4842. *Clubs:* Athenæum (Melbourne); Queensland, Brisbane, United Service, Royal Queensland Yacht Squadron, Royal Queensland Aero, Queensland Turf, Tattersalls (Brisbane).

SHARPE, Hon. Sir John (Henry), Kt 1977; CBE 1972; JP; MP for Warwick West, Bermuda, since 1963; *b* 8 Nov. 1921; *s* of Harry Sharpe; *m* 1948, Eileen Margaret, *d* of George Morrow, BC, Canada; one *s* one *d*. *Educ:* Warwick Acad., Warwick, Bermuda; Mount Allison Commercial Coll., Sackville, New Brunswick. Served War of 1939–45: Pilot Officer, with Bomber Comd, NW Europe, RCAF, attached RAF. Chm., Purvis Ltd (Importers), Bermuda. MHA for Warwick, Bermuda, 1963–; Minister of Finance, 1968–75; Dep. Leader of Govt, 1971–75; Premier of Bermuda, 1975–77, resigned; Minister of Transport, May-Dec. 1980; Minister of Marine and Air Services, 1980–82; Minister of Home Affairs, 1982–. Formerly Member several Parliamentary Select Cttees, and of Bd of Educn, Bermuda; also Dep. Chm., Central Planning Authority and Defence Bd. Delegate to Constitutional Conf., London, 1966. Mem., War Veterans Assoc., Bermuda; Warden, Anglican Church. *Address:* Uplands, Harbour Road, Warwick West, Bermuda.

SHARPE, John Herbert S.; *see* Subak-Sharpe.

SHARPE, Sir Reginald (Taaffe), Kt 1947; QC; *b* 20 November 1898; *o s* of late Herbert Sharpe, Lindfield, Sussex; *m* 1st, 1922, Phyllis Maude (marr. diss. 1929), *d* of late Major Edward Whinney, Haywards Heath, Sussex; one *d* (and one *d* decd); 2nd, 1930, Eileen Kate (*d* 1946), *d* of Thomas Howarth Usherwood, Christ's Hospital, Sussex; 3rd, 1947, Vivien Travers (*d* 1971), *d* of late Rev. Herbert Seddon Rowley, Wretham, Norfolk; 4th, 1976, Mary Millicent, *d* of late Maj.-Gen. Patrick Barclay Sangster, CB, CMG, DSO, Roehampton. *Educ:* Westminster School. Served European War: enlisted in Army, 1916; 2nd Lieut Grenadier Guards (SR), Jan. 1917; Lt, 1918; served with 2nd Bn in France (wounded). Called to Bar at Gray's Inn, Easter, 1920. Went South-Eastern Circuit and Sussex Sessions. Judge of High Court, Rangoon, 1937–48; Director of Supply, Burma (at Calcutta), 1942–44; Trustee of Rangoon University Endowment Fund, 1946–48; KC Feb. 1949; HM Comr of Assize: Western and Northern Circuits, 1949; Midland and Western Circuits, 1950; South-Eastern Circuit, 1952; North-Eastern Circuit, 1954; Birmingham October Assize, 1954; Midland Circuit, 1960. Special Comr for Divorce Causes, 1948–67. Chm., Nat. Health Service Tribunal for England and Wales, 1948–71. Deputy Chairman QS: E Sussex, 1949–69; W Kent, 1949–62; Kent, 1962–69; Mddx, 1963–65 (Asst Chm. 1951–63); Mddx area of Greater London, 1965–71; Asst Chm., W Sussex QS, 1950–70; Dep. Chm., Hailsham Petty Sessional Div., 1950–57 and 1959–70 (Chm., 1957–58). Mem. Standing Jt Cttee for E Sussex, 1958–65, for W Sussex, 1953–65. Mem., Nat. Arbitration Tribunal, 1951, and of Industrial Disputes Tribunal, 1951;

Chairman, 1951–54, of Joint Council, and Independent Chairman, 1955–57, of Conciliation Board set up by Assoc. of Health and Pleasure Resorts and the Musicians' Union; Sole Commissioner to hold British Honduras Inquiry at Belize, March 1954; Chm., Departmental Cttee on Summary Trial of Minor Offences in Magistrates' Courts, 1954–55. Mem., Governing Body, Westminster Sch., 1955–83. JP East Sussex. *Address:* The Old Post Office, Rushlake Green, Sussex. *T:* Rushlake Green 830253.

SHARPE, Thomas Ridley; novelist; *b* 30 March 1928; *s* of Rev. George Coverdale Sharpe and Grace Egerton Sharpe; *m* 1969, Nancy Anne Looper; three *d*. *Educ:* Lancing College; Pembroke Coll., Cambridge (MA). National service, Royal Marines, 1946–48. Social worker 1952, teacher 1952–56, photographer 1956–61, in S Africa; Lecturer in History, Cambridge Coll. of Arts and Technology, 1963–71; full time novelist, 1971–. *Publications:* Riotous Assembly, 1971; Indecent Exposure, 1973; Porterhouse Blue, 1974; Blott on the Landscape, 1975 (televised, 1985); Wilt, 1976; The Great Pursuit, 1977; The Throwback, 1978; The Wilt Alternative, 1979; Ancestral Vices, 1980; Vintage Stuff, 1982; Wilt on High, 1984. *Recreations:* gardening, photography. *Address:* c/o Martin Secker & Warburg Ltd, 54 Poland Street, W1V 3DF.

SHARPE, William, OBE 1967; HM Diplomatic Service, retired; Overseas Relations Adviser, Potato Marketing Board, since 1979; *b* 9 Dec. 1923; *s* of late William Joseph Sharpe and of Phoebe Irene (*née* Standen); *m* 1959, Marie-Antoinette Rodesch; one *s*. *Educ:* High Sch., Chichester; London Univ. BA (Hons), MA, BSc Econ (Hons). Served RAF, 1943–47. Joined Foreign (subseq. Diplomatic) Service, 1947; Foreign Office 1947–52; Cologne and Bonn, 1952–54; Leopoldville, 1954–57; UK Mission to UN, New York, 1957–61; Foreign Office, 1961–66; Milan, 1966–70; FCO, 1971–72; Kuwait, 1972–75; Consul-Gen., Berlin, 1975–78. *Recreations:* reading, music, golf. *Address:* 15 Regis Avenue, Aldwick Bay, Bognor Regis, Sussex PO21 4HQ.

SHARPE, William James, CBE 1967 (OBE 1950); Director of Communications, Foreign and Commonwealth Office (formerly Foreign Office), 1965–69, retired; *b* 3 Jan. 1908; *s* of James Sharpe; *m* 1940, Doreen Winifred Cockell; three *s*. *Educ:* Aldershot Grammar School. 1927–39: Merchant Navy; Marconi International; Marine Communications Company. Commissioned Royal Corps of Signals, 1940; Served in France and South East Asia; Lt-Col 1945. Diplomatic Wireless Service, 1947; Deputy Director of Communications, 1959. *Address:* The Mount, Tingewick, Buckingham. *T:* Finmere 291.

SHARPLES, family name of **Baroness Sharples.**

SHARPLES, Baroness *cr* 1973 (Life Peer); **Pamela Sharples;** Director, TVS, since 1981; *b* 11 Feb. 1923; *o d* of late Lt-Comdr K. W. Newall and of Violet (who *m* 2nd, Lord Claud Hamilton, GCVO, CMG, DSO); *m* 1st, 1946, Major R. C. Sharples, MC, Welsh Guards (later Sir Richard Sharples, KCMG, OBE, MC, assassinated 1973); two *s* two *d*; 2nd, 1977, Patrick D. de Laszlo (*d* 1980); 3rd, 1983, Robert Douglas Swan. *Educ:* Southover Manor, Lewes; Florence. WAAF, 1941–46. Mem., Review Body on Armed Forces Pay, 1979–81. *Recreations:* sailing, riding, fishing, tennis, golf. *Address:* Byron's Chambers, Albany, Piccadilly, W1. *T:* 01–434 2621; Nunswell, Higher Coombe, Shaftesbury, Dorset SP7 9LR. *T:* Shaftesbury 2971.

SHARPLES, Florence Elizabeth; National General Secretary, Young Women's Christian Association of Great Britain, since 1978; *b* 27 May 1931; *d* of late Flying Officer Albert Sharples, RAFVR, and Kathleen (*née* Evans). *Educ:* Alice Ottley Sch., Worcester; Homerton Coll., Cambridge (Teachers' Cert.); King's Coll., London (Cert. Prof. in Religious Knowledge). Head of Religious Education: Bruton Sch. for Girls, Somerset, 1953–57; Loughton High Sch., Essex, 1957–60; Housemistress, Headington Sch., Oxford, 1960–66; Headmistress, Ancaster House, Bexhill, Sussex, 1966–78. Former Mem., New Philharmonia Chorus. *Recreation:* the theatre. *Address:* The Forge, Aston Upthorpe, Oxon.

SHARPLEY, Ven. Roger Ernest Dion; Archdeacon of Hackney and Vicar of Guild Church of St Andrew, Holborn, since 1981; *b* 19 Dec. 1928; *s* of Frederick Charles and Doris Irene Sharpley; unmarried. *Educ:* Dulwich College; Christ Church, Oxford (MA); St Stephen's House, Oxford. Deacon, 1954; Priest, 1955; Curate of St Columba, Southwick, 1954–60; Vicar of All Saints', Middlesbrough, 1960–81; Curate-in-charge, St Hilda with St Peter, Middlesbrough, 1964–72; RD of Middlesbrough, 1970–81; Canon and Prebendary of York Minster, 1974–81; Priest-in-charge, St Aidan, Middlesbrough, 1979–81. *Recreations:* hill and country walking. *Address:* St Andrew's Vicarage, 5 St Andrew Street, EC4A 3AB. *T:* 01–353 3544.

SHARROCK, Prof. Roger Ian; Professor of English Language and Literature, University of London, King's College, 1968–81, now Emeritus; *b* Robin Hood's Bay, 23 Aug. 1919; *s* of Arthur and Iva France Sharrock; *m* 1940, Gertrude Elizabeth Adams, *d* of Edgar Leenie Adams, Bradford; one *s* two *d*. *Educ:* Queen Elizabeth's Sch., Wakefield; St John's Coll., Oxford (Open Exhibr). 1st cl. Hon. Sch. of Eng. Lang. and Lit., 1943; BLitt 1947. Served with King's Own Yorks LI, 1939–41; Nat. Buildings Record, 1942–44; Asst Master, Rugby Sch., 1944–46; Lectr, Univ. of Southampton, 1946; Reader, 1962; Prof. of English, Univ. of Durham, 1963. Editor, Durham Univ. Jl, 1964–68; Fulbright Vis. Prof., Univ. of Virginia, 1972; Warton Lectr of British Academy, 1972; Trustee, Dove Cottage Trust, 1968–; Dir, Shakespeare Globe Centre, 1970–; Chm., English Assoc., 1972–79. Gen. Editor, Oxford Bunyan. *Publications:* Songs and Comments, 1946; John Bunyan, 1954; (ed) Selected Poems of Wordsworth, 1958; (ed) Bunyan, The Pilgrim's Progress, 1960; (ed) Bunyan, Grace Abounding, 1962; (ed) Selected Poems of Dryden, 1963; (ed) Keats, Selected Poems and Letters, 1964; The Pilgrim's Progress, 1966; (ed) Oxford Standard Authors Bunyan, 1966; Solitude and Community in Wordsworth's Poetry, 1969; (ed) Pelican Book of English Prose, 1970; (ed) Casebook on Pilgrim's Progress, 1976; (ed) English Short Stories of Today, 1976; (ed) The Holy War, 1980; Saints, Sinners and Comedians: the novels of Graham Greene, 1984; contrib. Encycl. Britannica, Essays in Criticism, Mod. Lang. Review, Review of English Studies, Tablet, etc. *Recreations:* walking, chess. *Address:* 12 Plough Lane, Purley, Surrey. *T:* 01–660 3248. *Club:* United Oxford & Cambridge University.

SHATTOCK, Sir Gordon, Kt 1985; Director, Veterinary Drug Co., since 1982; *b* 12 May 1928; *s* of Frederick Thomas and Rose May Irene Shattock; *m* 1952, Jeanne Mary Watkins; one *s* one *d*. *Educ:* Hele's Sch., Exeter; Royal Veterinary Coll., London. MRCVS. Senior Partner, St David's Vet. Hosp., Exeter, 1954–84. Fellow of Woodard Corp., 1973–; Executive Member: Animal Health Trust, 1978–; GBA, 1986–; Chm., Grenville Coll., 1982–. Liveryman, 1978–, Mem. Ct of Assistants, 1986–, Farriers' Company. *Publications:* contrib. to Jl Small Animal Practice; papers to British Veterinary Assoc. *Recreation:* gardening. *Address:* Lewishill, Dunsford, Exeter EX6 7AA. *T:* Christow 52385.

SHATTOCK, John Swithun Harvey, CMG 1952; OBE 1946; HM Diplomatic Service, 1947–67; *b* 21 Nov. 1907; *s* of late Rev. E. A. Shattock, Kingston St Mary, Nr Taunton; unmarried. *Educ:* Westminster School; Christ Church, Oxford. Entered ICS, 1931; served in Bengal, 1931–36; Under Sec., Govt of India (Defence Dept), 1936–39; joined Indian Political Service, 1939; served in Kathiawar, Baroda, and Kashmir Residencies, 1939–44; Dep. Sec. to Crown Representative (Political Dept), New Delhi, 1944–46; Chief Minister, Chamba State, 1946–47; apptd HM Diplomatic Service, 1947; served in UK High

Commission, New Delhi, 1947–49; Head of Far Eastern Dept, Foreign Office, London, 1950–51; Head of China and Korea Dept, FO 1951; FO Rep. at Imperial Defence Coll., London, 1952; Head of China and Korea Dept, FO, 1953; Counsellor, British Embassy, Belgrade, Dec. 1953–Nov. 1955; Political Representative, Middle East Forces, Cyprus, Jan. 1956–Nov. 1958. Deputy to UK Permanent Representative on North Atlantic Council, Paris, 1959–61; Minister, UK Delegation to Disarmament Conference, Geneva, 1961–63; FO, 1963–67. *Recreation:* travel. *Address:* St Mary's Cottage, Kingston St Mary, near Taunton, Somerset; Grindlay's Bank, 13 St James's Square, SW1. *Clubs:* Travellers', Royal Commonwealth Society.

SHATWELL, Prof. Kenneth Owen; Emeritus Professor in the University of Sydney; New South Wales Liaison Officer (Recruitment) for Government of Hong Kong, since 1962; *b* 16 Oct. 1909; *m* 1936, Betty, *d* of Thomas Rae Hogarth, Tasmania; one *s* one *d* (and one *d* decd). *Educ:* Lincoln College, Oxford. Served War of 1939–45: Lieut RANVR, on active service in Atlantic and Pacific. Prof. of Law and Dean of the Faculty of Law, Univ. of Tasmania, 1934–47; Challis Prof. of Law, Univ. of Sydney, 1947–74; Dean of the Faculty of Law, Univ. of Sydney, 1947–73; Dir, Inst. of Criminology, Sydney Univ., 1962–74. Vis. Prof., The Queen's Univ., Belfast, 1951; Australian Comr, S Pacific Commn, 1950–52; Sen. Research Fellow, Yale Univ., 1958–59, 1962; Visiting Professor: New York Univ. Law School Summer Workshop on Contracts, 1962; Temple Univ. Law School, 1968. Aust. Mem., Permanent Court of Arbitration under the Hague Convention, 1960–84; Ministerial Cnsltnt to NSW Dept of Corrective Services, and Mem., NSW Corrective Services Adv. Council, 1972–79. FASSA. *Publications:* various articles in legal jls. *Recreation:* criminology. *Address:* 36 Chilton Parade, Turramurra, NSW 2074, Australia. *T:* Sydney 48–1189. *Clubs:* Athenæum; Tasmanian (Hobart).

SHAUGHNESSY, family name of **Baron Shaughnessy.**

SHAUGHNESSY, 3rd Baron, *cr* 1916, of Montreal; **William Graham Shaughnessy;** Director, Arbor Capital Inc., Toronto, since 1972; *b* 28 March 1922; *s* of 2nd Baron and Marion (*d* 1936), *d* of late R. K. Graham, Montreal; *S* father, 1938; *m* 1944, Mary Whitley, *o d* of late John Whitley, Copthorne House, Letchworth; one *s* two *d* (and one *s* decd). *Educ:* Bishop's Univ., Lennoxville, Canada; BA 1941; MSc Columbia Univ., NY, 1947. Dir, Canada-UK Chamber of Commerce. Trustee, The Last Post Fund Inc., Canada. Major, Canadian Grenadier Guards, R of O. *Heir: s* Hon. Michael James Shaughnessy, *b* 12 Nov. 1946. *Address:* 27 Melton Court, Old Brompton Road, SW7 3JQ. *Clubs:* Cavalry and Guards; Ranchmen's (Calgary); University (Montreal).

SHAVE, Kenneth George, CEng, FIMechE; Member, London Transport Executive, 1967–73, retired; *b* 25 June 1908; *s* of George Shave and Frances Larkin; *m* 1935, Doris May Stone; one *s* one *d*. *Educ:* St Paul's School. Apprenticed London General Omnibus Company, 1925; Rolling Stock Engineer, East Surrey Traction Company, 1930; London Transport: Asst Divisional Engineer, 1935; Divisional Engineer, 1948; Rolling Stock Engineer, 1956; Chief Mechanical Engineer, 1965. CStJ 1971 (OStJ 1963). *Recreations:* golf, bridge, gardening. *Address:* 5 St Katherine's Road, Henley on Thames, Oxon RG9 7PJ. *T:* Henley 3379.

SHAW; *see* Byam Shaw.

SHAW, family name of **Baron Craigmyle** and **Baron Kilbrandon.**

SHAW, Maj.-Gen. Anthony John, CBE 1985; QHP 1983; Commander Medical Services, UK Land Forces, since 1984; *b* 13 July 1930; *s* of late Lt Col W. A. Shaw, MC and Mrs E. Shaw (*née* Malley); *m* 1961, Gillian Shaw (*née* Best); one *s* one *d*. *Educ:* Epsom College; Clare College, Cambridge (MA; MB BChir); Westminster Hosp. MRCS; LRCP 1954; D(Obst)RCOG 1956; DTM&H 1961; FFCM 1983. Casualty Officer, Westminster Hosp.; House Surgeon and Obst. House Officer, Kingston Hosp., 1955–56; Commissioned Lieut RAMC, 1956; Staff College, 1963; served in UK, Malta, Berlin, BAOR, MoD, Malaya, Nepal, Penang, Cameron Highlands; CO Field Ambulance, 1969–70; Chief Instructor, RAMC Training Centre, 1970–72; Nat. Defence Coll., 1973; ADGMS, MoD, 1973–76; CO Cambridge Mil. Hosp., 1977–79; Comdr Med. 2 Armd Div., BAOR, 1979–81; Comdr Med. SE Dist., 1981; Dir of Med. Supply, MoD, 1981–83; DDGAMS, 1983–84; Dir, Army Community and Occupational Medicine, 1983–. Member: BMA; Board of Faculty of Community Medicine, 1983–. FRSocMed. OStJ 1975. *Recreations:* sailing, squash, lawn tennis, skiing, gardening, music, military history. *Clubs:* Lansdowne; Jesters, Escorts Squash Rackets.

SHAW, Rev. Arthur; *see* Shaw, Rev. B. A.

SHAW, Sir Barry; *see* Shaw, Sir C. B.

SHAW, Benjamin, CBE 1986; Councillor (Lab), Liverpool City Council, 1957–74; Merseyside County Council, 1974–86 (Chairman, 1984–85); *b* 3 Oct. 1906; *s* of Nathan and Esther Shaw; *m* 1946, Paulette Weinstein; three *s* one *d*. *Educ:* Liverpool. Served in Royal Engineers, 1940–46. Textile wholesaler, now retired. Mem. Cttee, Royal Liverpool Philharmonic Society, 1967–84 (Chm., 1974–77 and 1981–84; Vice-Pres., 1984–); First Chm., Liverpool Heritage Bureau, 1972; Founder, Chm., 1973–79, Pres., 1981–, Friends of Merseyside Museums and Art Galleries; Mem. Cttee, Playhouse Theatre, 1974–84; Chm., Merseyside Arts and Culture Cttee, 1974–77 and 1981–83; Vice-Chm., King David High Sch., Liverpool, 1976–; Member: Merseyside Maritime Trust, 1979–; Merseyside Enterprise Forum, 1984–; Chm., Nat. Cttee, Area Services for Museums and Chm., NW Museum and Art Gallery Service, 1981–; Vice-Pres., Museums' Assoc. of GB, 1981; Chm., Empire Theatre Trust (Liverpool), 1981–83. *Recreations:* reading, music, watching sports. *Address:* 63 Childwall Priory Road, Liverpool L16 7PD. *T:* 051–722 6333.

SHAW, Rev. (Bernard) Arthur; Chairman of the Chester and Stoke on Trent District of the Methodist Church, 1962–80; President of the Methodist Conference, 1977–78; *b* 12 Sept. 1914; *s* of John and Lillie Shaw; *m* 1944, Alma Kirk (*d* 1977); two *s* one *d*. *Educ:* Queen Elizabeth Grammar Sch., Wakefield; Lancaster Royal Grammar Sch.; Richmond Coll. (Theological: London Univ.), Surrey. Filton, Bristol, 1941–43; RAF Chaplain, 1943–46; Stoke on Trent, 1946–51; Hinde Street Methodist Church, London Univ. Methodist Chaplaincy, 1951–57; Leeds Mission, 1957–62. DUniv Keele, 1977. *Recreations:* gardening, reading, walking. *Address:* 10 Rope Bank Avenue, Wistaston, Crewe, Cheshire CW2 6RZ. *T:* Crewe 68255.

SHAW, Prof. Bernard Leslie, FRS 1978; Professor of Chemistry, University of Leeds, since 1971; *b* Springhead, Yorks, 28 March 1930; *s* of Thomas Shaw and Vera Shaw (*née* Dale); *m* 1951, Mary Elizabeth Neild; two *s* (and one *s* decd). *Educ:* Hulme Grammar Sch., Oldham; Univ. of Manchester (BSc, PhD). Sen. DSIR Fellow, Torry Research Station, Aberdeen, 1953–55; Scientific Officer, CDEE, Porton, 1955–56; Technical Officer, ICI Ltd, Akers Research Labs, Welwyn, 1956–61; Lectr, Reader, and Prof., Univ. of Leeds, 1962–. Visiting Professor: Univ. of Western Ontario, 1969; Carnegie Mellon Univ., 1969; ANU, 1983. Member: Royal Soc. Cttees; Royal Chem. Soc. Cttees; SERC (formerly SRC) Chem. Cttee, 1975–78, 1981– (and Inorganic Panel, 1977–78, Co-

operative Grants Panel, 1982–); Tilden Lectr and Prizewinner, 1975; Chem. Soc. Medal and Prize for Transition Metal Chem., 1975. *Publications:* Transition Metal Hydrides, 1967; (with N. Tucker) Organotransition Metal Chemistry, and Related Aspects of Homogeneous Catalysis, 1973; numerous original papers and reviews in chem. jls. *Recreations:* squash, tennis, pottery, music, walking, gardening. *Address:* School of Chemistry, The University of Leeds, Leeds LS2 9JT. *T:* Leeds 431751.

SHAW, Sir Brian (Piers), Kt 1986; Chairman and Managing Director, Furness Withy & Co. Ltd, since 1979 (Managing Director since 1977); *b* 21 March 1933; *s* of Percy Augustus Shaw; *m* 1962, Penelope Reece; three *s*. *Educ:* Wrekin Coll.; Corpus Christi Coll., Cambridge (MA). National Service (2nd Lieut, Cheshire Regt), 1951–53. Called to Bar, Gray's Inn, 1957. Joined Pacific Steam Navigation Co., Liverpool, 1957; Company Secretary, 1960; Company Sec., Royal Mail Lines, London, 1961–67; Dir, Royal Mail Lines, 1968–; Manager, Furness Withy & Co., 1969–73; Chairman, Shaw Savill & Albion Co., 1973–; Director: Furness Withy & Co., 1973–; other Furness Withy Group cos; Overseas Containers Ltd, 1972–80; Nat. Bank of NZ, 1973–77 (London Board, 1977–80; Chm., London Adv. Cttee, 1980–84); New Zealand Line, 1974–79; Grindlays Bank, 1977–85; Orient Overseas (Holdings), 1980–; ANZ Holdings (UK), 1985–; Enterprise Oil, 1986–. Member: Gen. Cttee, Lloyd's Register of Shipping, 1974–; Exec. Cttee, Internat Chamber of Shipping, 1983–; Chm., Council of European and Japanese Nat. Shipowners' Assocs (CENSA), 1979–84; Pres., Gen. Council of British Shipping, 1985–86. Pres., New Zealand Soc., 1979–80. Mem. Ct of Assts, Shipwrights' Co., 1979–. *Recreations:* golf, music, theatre. *Address:* 42 Norland Square, W11. *T:* 01–221 4066. *Clubs:* MCC; Denham Golf.

SHAW, Very Rev. Charles Allan; Rector of Alcester with Arrow, Diocese of Coventry, since 1984; *b* 16 Feb. 1927; *s* of Henry and Anne Shaw. *Educ:* Bolton School; Christ's Coll., Cambridge (MA 1952); Westcott House, Cambridge. Assistant Master, Tonbridge School, 1949; ordained, 1951; Curate of Swinton, Manchester, 1951–54; Chaplain and Asst Master, Malvern Coll., 1954–58; Vicar of St Ambrose, Pendleton, 1958–62; Domestic Chaplain to Bishop of Birmingham and Succentor of Birmingham Cathedral, 1962–67; Dean of Bulawayo, 1967–75; Archdeacon of Bulawayo, 1969–75; Vicar General of Matabeleland, 1972–75; Dean Emeritus, 1975–; Residentiary Canon, Prebendary de Warham and Precentor of Hereford Cathedral, 1975–82; Dean of Ely, 1982–84. *Recreations:* theatre, music and people. *Address:* The Rectory, Alcester, Warwickshire B49 5AL. *T:* Alcester 764261; 3 The Parks, Burwarton, Shropshire. *T:* Burwarton 622. *Club:* Junior Carlton.

SHAW, Sir (Charles) Barry, Kt 1980; CB 1974; QC 1964; Director of Public Prosecutions for Northern Ireland, since 1972; *b* 12 April 1923; *s* of late Ernest Hunter Shaw and Sarah Gertrude Shaw, Mayfield, Balmoral, Belfast; *m* 1964, Jane (*née* Phillips). *Educ:* Inchmarlo House, Belfast; Pannal Ash Coll., Harrogate; The Queen's Univ. of Belfast (LLB). Served War: commissioned RA, 97 A/Tk Regt RA, 15th (Scottish) Div., 1942–46. Called to Bar of Northern Ireland, 1948; called to Bar, Middle Temple, 1970 (Hon. Bencher, 1986). *Address:* Royal Courts of Justice, Belfast, Northern Ireland BT1 3NX.

SHAW, Prof. C(harles) Thurstan, CBE 1972; Professor of Archaeology, University of Ibadan, 1963–74; *b* 27 June 1914; 2nd *s* of late Rev. John Herbert Shaw and Grace Irene (*née* Woollatt); *m* Gilian Ione Maud, *e d* of late Edward John Penberthy Magor and Gilian Sarah (*née* Westmacott); two *s* three *d*. *Educ:* Blundell's Sch.; Sidney Sussex Coll., Cambridge; Univ. of London Inst. of Education. 1st cl. hons Arch. and Anthrop. Tripos 1936, MA, PhD Cantab; DipEd London. FRAI 1938; FSA 1947. Curator, Anthropology Museum, Achimota Coll., Gold Coast, 1937–45; Cambs Educn Cttee, 1945–51; Cambridge Inst. of Educn, 1951–63; Dir of Studies, Archaeol. and Anthrop., Magdalene Coll., Cambridge, 1976–79. Vis. Fellow, Clare Hall, Cambridge, 1973; Vis. Prof., Northwestern Univ., USA, 1969; Vis. Res. Prof., Ahmadu Bello Univ., 1975–78; Visiting Lecturer: Harvard, 1975; Yale, 1979; Calgary, 1980; Hans Wolf Meml Lectr, Indiana Univ., 1984. Founder and Editor: W African Archaeological Newsletter, 1964–70; W African Jl of Archaeology, 1971–75. Mem. Perm. Council, Internat. Union of Pre- and Proto-historic Sciences, 1965–74; Vice-Pres., Panafrican Congress on Prehistory and Study of Quaternary, 1966–77; Dir, and Mem. Exec. Cttee, World Archaeol Congress, 1986. Founder, and Chm., Icknield Way Assoc., 1984–; Pres., Prehistoric Soc., 1986–. Mem. Council, Univ. of Ibadan, 1969–71. Hon. DSc Univ. of Nigeria, 1982. Amaury Talbot Prize, Royal Anthrop. Inst., 1970 and 1978. Onuna-Ekwulu Ora of Igbo-Ukwu, 1972. *Publications:* Excavation at Dawu, 1961; Archaeology and Nigeria, 1964; (with J. Vanderburg) Bibliography of Nigerian Archaeology, 1969; (ed) Nigerian Prehistory and Archaeology, 1969; Igbo-Ukwu: an account of archaeological discoveries in eastern Nigeria, 2 vols, 1970; Discovering Nigeria's Past, 1975; Why 'Darkest' Africa?, 1975; Unearthing Igbo-Ukwu, 1977; Ancient People and Places: Nigeria, 1978; numerous articles on African archaeology and prehistory in jls. *Recreations:* walking, music. *Address:* Silver Ley, 37 Hawthorne Road, Stapleford, Cambridge CB2 5DU. *T:* Cambridge 842283. *Clubs:* Athenæum; Explorers' (New York).

SHAW, Prof. Charles Timothy, CEng; Professor of Mining, Royal School of Mines, since 1980 (Head of Department of Mineral Resources Engineering, 1980–85); *b* 4 Oct. 1934; *s* of Charles John and Constance Olive Shaw (*née* Scotton); *m* 1962, Tuulike Raili Linari-Linholm; one *s* two *d*. *Educ:* Univ. of Witwatersrand (BSc(Mining) 1956); McGill Univ. (MSc(Applied) (Mineral Exploration) 1959). Mine Manager's, Mine Overseer's and Mine Surveyor's Certs of SA; Chartered Engineer. Johannesburg Consolidated Investment Co. Ltd (JCI): numerous positions at various levels, 1960–67; Head of Computer Div., 1967–70; Manager, 1970–72 (as such an appointed dir of 14 cos incl. Consolidated Murchison Ltd and Alternate Dir of 9 cos); Consulting Engr, Consolidated Murchison Ltd, Randfontein Estates Gold Mining Co. (Wits.) Ltd and Shangani Mining Corp. (Zimbabwe), 1972–74; Consulting Engr and Alternate Dir, Rustenburg Platinum Mines Ltd, 1974–76; Chief Consulting Engr and Alternate Dir, Johannesburg Consolidated Investment Co. Ltd, also Man. Dir, Western Areas Gold Mining Co. Ltd, 1976–77; Associate Prof., Virginia Polytechnic Inst. and State Univ., 1977–80. Rep. for JCI on Technical Adv. Cttee of SA Chamber of Mines, 1974–77; Alternate Mem. for Gold Producers Cttee, 1976–77. Mem. Council, InstnMM, 1981–. *Publications:* (with J. R. Lucas) The Coal Industry: Industry Guides for Accountants, Auditors and Financial Executives, 1980; papers both in technical literature and in house at Johannesburg Consolidated Investment Co. Ltd. *Recreations:* golf, mining history. *Address:* Department of Mineral Resources Engineering, Royal School of Mines, SW7 2BP. *T:* 01–589 5111.

SHAW, Colin Don; Director, Programme Planning Secretariat, Independent Television Companies' Association, since 1983; *b* 2 Nov. 1928; *s* of late Rupert M. Shaw and Enid F. Shaw (*née* Smith); *m* 1955, Elizabeth Ann, *d* of Paul Bowker; one *s* two *d*. *Educ:* Liverpool Coll.; St Peter's Hall, Oxford (MA). Called to the Bar, Inner Temple, 1960. Nat. Service, RAF, 1947–49. Joined BBC as Radio Drama Producer, North Region, 1953; Asst, BBC Secretariat, 1957–59; Asst Head of Programme Contracts Dept, 1959–60; Sen. Asst, BBC Secretariat, 1960–63; special duties in connection with recruitment for BBC2, 1963; Asst Head of Programmes, BBC North Region, 1963–66; various posts in TV Programme

Planning, ending as Head of Group, 1966–69; Secretary to the BBC, 1969–72, Chief Secretary, 1972–76; Dir of Television, IBA, 1977–83. Vis. Fellow, Europ. Inst. for the Media, Manchester, 1985–. Mem., Arts Council of GB, 1978–80 (Chairman: Arts Council Research Adv. Gp, 1978–80; Housing the Arts Cttee, 1979–80; Touring Cttee, 1980). Trustee, Internat. Inst. of Communications, 1983–; Governor, E-SU of the Commonwealth, 1976–83; Chm., Bd of Governors, Hampden House Sch., 1972–77. FRSA 1978. *Publications:* several radio plays and a stage-play for children. *Recreations:* going to the theatre, reading. *Address:* Lesters, Little Ickford, Aylesbury, Bucks. *T:* Ickford 225. *Club:* Reform.

SHAW, David; General Secretary, Independent Television Companies Association, since 1981; *b* 19 Oct. 1936; *s* of Thomas Young Boyd Shaw and Elizabeth Shaw; *m* 1961, Margaret Esmé Bagnall; one *s* one *d. Educ:* Univ. of Birmingham (BA (Hons) Geography); Univ. of Sussex (Adv. Dip. Educnl Technology). Education Officer in Royal Air Force, final rank Sqdn Ldr, 1960–76; Training Adviser to North Western Provincial Councils, 1976–78; Gen. Sec., British Amateur Athletic Bd, 1978–81. Represented Great Britain in Athletics (3000 metres steeplechase), 1958; British Universities Cross-Country Champion, 1959. *Recreations:* reading, hill-climbing, sketching. *Address:* (business) Independent Television Companies Association, 56 Mortimer Street, W1N 8AN. *Club:* Royal Air Force.

SHAW, Prof. David Aitken, FRCP, FRCPE; Professor of Clinical Neurology since 1976, and Dean of Medicine since 1981, University of Newcastle upon Tyne; *b* 11 April 1924; *s* of John James McIntosh Shaw and Mina Draper; *m* 1960, Jill Parry; one *s* two *d. Educ:* Edinburgh Academy; Edinburgh Univ. MB ChB (Edin) 1951; FRCP (Edin.) 1968; FRCP (Lond.) 1976. Served as Lieut RNVR, 1943–46. Hospital appts, Edinburgh Royal Infirmary, 1951–57; Lectr, Inst. of Neurology, Univ. of London, 1957–64; Mayo Foundation Fellow, 1962–63; Sen. Lectr, Univ. of Newcastle upon Tyne, 1964–76; Public Orator, Univ. of Newcastle upon Tyne, 1976–79. Mem., GMC, 1984–. *Publications:* (with N. E. F. Cartlidge) Head Injury, 1981; chapters in books and scientific articles in medical jls. *Recreations:* golf and fishing. *Address:* 4 Adderstone Crescent, Newcastle upon Tyne NE2 2HH. *T:* Newcastle upon Tyne 814146. *Club:* Athenæum.

SHAW, Dr Dennis Frederick, CBE 1974; Fellow of Keble College, since 1957, Professorial Fellow, 1978; Keeper of Scientific Books, Bodleian Library, Oxford, since 1975; *b* 20 April 1924; 2nd *s* of Albert Shaw and Lily (*née* Hill), Teddington; *m* 1949, Joan Irene, *er d* of Sidney and Maud Chandler; one *s* three *d. Educ:* Harrow County Sch.; Christ Church, Oxford. BA 1945, MA 1950, DPhil 1950. FInstP 1971, CPhys; FZS. Jun. Sci. Officer, MAP, 1944–46; Res. Officer in Physics, Clarendon Lab., Oxford, 1950–57, Sen. Res. Officer 1957–64; Univ. Lectr in Physics, Oxford, 1964–75. Vis. Prof. of Physics and Brown Foundn Fellow, Univ. of the South, Tennessee, 1974. Pres., Internat. Assoc. of Technol Univ. Libraries, 1986– (Sec., 1983 85); Mem., Cttee for Sci. and Technol. Libys, IFLA, 1985–. Mem., Oxford City Council, 1963–67; Chm., Oxford City Civil Emergency Cttee, 1966–67; Member: Home Office Sci. Adv. Council, 1966–78; Home Defence Sci. Adv. Cttee, 1978–; Hebdomadal Council, 1980–; Chairman: Oxford Univ. Delegacy for Educnl Studies, 1969–73; Home Office Police Equipment Cttee, 1969–70; Home Office Police Sci. Develt Cttee, 1971–74. Member: Amer. Phys. Soc., 1957; NY Acad. of Scis, 1981. Almoner, Christ's Hosp., 1980–. *Publications:* An Introduction to Electronics, 1962, 2nd edn 1970; A Review of Oxford University Science Libraries, 1977, 2nd edn 1981; (ed) Information Sources in Physics, 1985; papers in sci. jls. *Recreations:* riding, gardening, enjoying music. *Address:* Keble College, Oxford. *T:* Oxford 59201. *Club:* United Oxford & Cambridge University.

SHAW, Rev. Douglas William David; Professor of Divinity, since 1979, and Principal, St Mary's College, since 1986, University of St Andrews; *b* 25 June 1928; *s* of William David Shaw and Nansie Smart. *Educ:* Edinburgh Acad.; Loretto; Ashbury Coll., Ottawa; Univs of Cambridge and Edinburgh. MA (Cantab), BD (Edin.), LLB (Edin.). WS. Practised law as Partner of Davidson and Syme, WS, Edinburgh, 1953–57. Ordained Minister of Church of Scotland, 1960; Asst Minister, St George's West Church, Edinburgh, 1960–63; Official Observer of World Alliance of Reformed Churches at Second Vatican Council, Rome, 1962. University of Edinburgh: Dean, Faculty of Divinity, and Principal, New College, 1974–78; Lectr in Divinity, 1963–79; Dean, Faculty of Divinity, Univ. of St Andrews, 1983–86. Croall Lectr, New Coll., Edinburgh, 1983. *Publications:* Who is God? 1968, 2nd edn 1970; The Dissuaders, 1978; trans. from German: F. Heyer: The Catholic Church from 1648 to 1870, 1969; various articles in theological jls. *Recreations:* squash (Scottish Amateur Champion, 1950–51–52), golf. *Address:* St Mary's College, St Andrews, Fife. *T:* St Andrews 76161. *Clubs:* New (Edinburgh); Royal and Ancient (St Andrews); Luffness New; Edinburgh Sports.

SHAW, Frank Howard, MBE 1945; TD; MA; JP; Headmaster, King's College School, Wimbledon, 1960–75; *b* 13 June 1913; *s* of E. H. Shaw; *m* 1950, Harriette Alice, *d* of late His Honour Robert Peel; one *s* two *d. Educ:* Altrincham Grammar School; Hertford College, Oxford. Asst master: King's Coll. School, 1935–39; Marlborough College (and Housemaster), 1939–52; first Headmaster of Pakistan Air Force Public School, Murree Hills, 1952–58; Principal, Aden Coll., Aden, 1958–60. Chm., HMC, 1972. Served War of 1939–45 in Devonshire Regt; Jt Planning Staff, 1943–45. Lt-Col. JP, SW London, 1966–76. *Publications:* textbooks for teaching of English in Pakistan. *Recreation:* golf. *Address:* Medstead House, Medstead, near Alton, Hants. *T:* Alton 62195. *Clubs:* East India, Devonshire, Sports and Public Schools, MCC.

SHAW, Dr Gavin Brown, CBE 1981; FRCP, FRCPE, FRCPGlas; Consultant Physician, Southern General Hospital, Glasgow, 1956–84, Hon. Consultant, since 1984; *b* 24 May 1919; *s* of Gavin Shaw and Christian Douglas Cormack; *m* 1943, Margaret Mabon Henderson; one *s* two *d. Educ:* Glasgow Academy; Glasgow Univ., 1936–42 (BSc, MB ChB). President, Students' Representative Council, 1940–41. House Phys. to Sir J. W. McNee, 1942; Temporary Surg.-Lieut, RNVR, 1942–45; Asst Phys., Southern Gen. Hosp., Glasgow, 1948–56. Actg post-Grad. Dean., Glasgow Univ., 1983–84. Royal College of Physicians and Surgeons of Glasgow: Hon. Sec., 1957–65; Visitor, 1977–78; Pres., 1978–80. Mem., West Regional Hosp. Bd, 1971–74; Chairman: Greater Glasgow Med. Adv. Cttee, 1973–76; Jt Cttee for Higher Med. Trng, 1979–83; Specialty Adviser in Medicine, W of Scotland Post-Graduate Cttee, 1971–. Mem., GMC, 1982–87. Hon. FACP 1979; Hon. FRCPI 1979; Hon. FRCPsych 1980; Hon. FRCGP 1980. *Publications:* (ed jtly) Cardiac Resuscitation and Pacing, 1964; occasional contributor to BMJ, Brit. Heart Jl, Lancet, Practitioner, Amer. Heart Jl, Scottish Med. Jl. *Recreations:* walking, gardening, bird watching and one-time sailor, listening to music, reading. *Address:* 4 Horseshoe Road, Bearsden, Glasgow G61 2ST. *T:* 041–942 4553. *Clubs:* Royal Scottish Automobile; College, Glasgow University.

SHAW, Rev. Canon Geoffrey Norman; Principal, Wycliffe Hall, Oxford, since 1979; *b* 15 April 1926; *s* of Samuel Norman Shaw and Maud Shaw; *m* 1948, Cynthia Brown; one *s* two *d. Educ:* Holgate Grammar Sch., Barnsley; Jesus Coll., Oxford (MA); Wycliffe Hall, Oxford. Asst Curate, St Mary, Rushden, 1951–54; Vicar of St Paul, Woking, 1954–62; Rector of St Leonards-on-Sea, Sussex, 1962–68; Asst Master, Ecclesfield

Grammar Sch., Sheffield, 1968–69; Head of Religious Educn and Classics, Silverdale Sch., Sheffield, 1969–72; Vice-Principal, Oak Hill Theol Coll., Southgate, 1972–79. Hon. Canon of Christ Church Cathedral, Oxford, 1985–. *Recreations:* caravanning, tennis, music. *Address:* The Principal's Lodge, 2 Norham Gardens, Oxford OX2 6PW. *T:* Oxford 57539.

SHAW, George Anthony Theodore, CBE 1965; *b* 25 Oct. 1917; *s* of late G. E. Shaw, CMG, OBE, LLB; *m* 1st, Suzanne Alexandra Barber (marr. diss.), *d* of late H. C. Barber; one *s* one *d*; 2nd, Joan Margaret (*d* 1984), *d* of late Rev. N. M. Livingstone, DCL, RN; two *d*; 3rd, 1985, Mrs Hilary Aileen Reynolds, *d* of late R. H. Parker. *Educ:* Marlborough Coll.; Clare Coll., Cambridge (MA). Intell. Corps, Army, 1941 46, Indian Civil Service, 1944–45; HM Overseas Civil Service, 1940–67: Malaya, Singapore, Sarawak, Brunei, Malaysia; State Sec., Sarawak, 1963–67; Milton Keynes Develt Corp., 1967–74; Severn Trent Water Auth., 1974–79. Order of Star of Sarawak (PNBS), 1966. *Recreations:* wide. *Address:* Fircroft, Kivernall Road, Milford-on-Sea, Lymington, Hants. *Clubs:* East India; Royal Lymington Yacht.

SHAW, Sir (George) Neville B.; *see* Bowman-Shaw.

SHAW, Giles; *see* Shaw, J. G. D.

SHAW, James John Sutherland, CB 1970; Chairman, Civil Service Appeal Board, 1973–77 (Deputy Chairman, 1972–73); *b* 5 Jan. 1912; *s* of Robert Shaw and Christina Macallum Sutherland; *m* 1947, Rosamond Chisholm Sharman; no *c. Educ:* Ardrossan Academy, Ayrshire; Glasgow and London Universities. Glasgow University: MA 1st Class Hons History, 1932, PhD 1935; Lecturer in History, 1936–40. Served War with RAF, 1940–45, Navigator, AC2 to Sqdn Leader (despatches). Senior Lecturer in History, Glasgow Univ., 1945–46; HM Treasury, 1946–68: Principal, Asst Sec., Under-Sec.; Under-Sec., 1968–69, Dep. Sec., 1969–72, CSD. OECD Consltnt on Greek CS, 1973; Chm., Internat. Commn on Reform, Sudan CS, 1973–74; consultant to Commn on Structure and Functions, Ghana CS, 1974, to States of Jersey on Jersey CS, 1975. *Recreations:* talking, walking and gardening. *Address:* North Field, Neaves Lane, Stradbroke, Eye, Suffolk IP21 5JP. *T:* Stradbroke 535.

SHAW, Prof. John Calman, CA; Executive Director, Scottish Financial Enterprise, since 1986; *b* 10 July 1932; *m* 1960, Shirley Botterill; three *d. Educ:* Strathallan Sch.; Edinburgh Univ. BL; FCMA, MBCS, JDipMA. Qualified Chartered Accountant, 1955. National Service, RAF, 1955–57. Resumed accountancy career in London; became a partner in Edinburgh accountancy firm of Graham, Smart & Annan (later Deloitte, Haskins & Sells), 1960, Sen. Edinburgh Partner, 1980–87. Johnstone Smith Prof. of Accountancy (pt-time appt), Glasgow Univ., 1977–82. Director: Scottish Mortgage and Trust PLC, 1982–; Scottish American Investment Co PLC, 1986–. Pres., Inst. of Chartered Accountants of Scotland, 1983–84 (Vice-Pres., 1981–83). Commander of The Priory of Scotland of Most Venerable Order of St John, 1970; CStJ. *Publications:* ed, Bogie on Group Accounts (3rd edn), 1973; The Audit Report, 1980; (jtly) Information Disclosure and the Multinational Corporation, 1984; numerous articles in Accountant's Magazine and Accounting and Business Research and Accountancy, etc. *Recreations:* opera, theatre, walking. *Address:* 10 Belgrave Crescent, Edinburgh EH4 3AH. *T:* 031–332 5697. *Clubs:* Caledonian; New (Edinburgh); Western (Glasgow).

SHAW, John Dennis Bolton, MVO 1961; HM Diplomatic Service, retired; *b* 5 July 1920; *er s* of William Bolton Shaw and Margaret Bolton Shaw, Manchester; *m* 1955, Isabel Loewy; two *s. Educ:* Manchester Grammar Sch.; Balliol Coll., Oxford (MA). Served War: in North Africa, Italy and India, Lieut RA and RWAFF, 1940–46. Colonial Office, 1948–55; District Comr and Dep. Financial Sec., Sierra Leone, 1955–57; Commonwealth Relations Office, 1957–58 and 1962–65; Karachi, 1958–61; Washington, 1961–62; apptd Counsellor, 1962; Nairobi, 1965–67; Counsellor for Trusteeship Affairs, UK Mission to the UN, 1967–71; Head of Gibraltar and General Dept, FCO, 1971–73; Ambassador to Somali Democratic Republic, 1973–76; Dep. High Comr, Kuala Lumpur, 1976–77. *Recreations:* travel, archaeology, music. *Address:* West Beeches, Ashurst Wood, W Sussex RH19 3RQ.

SHAW, (John) Giles (Dunkerley); MP (C) Pudsey since Feb. 1974; Minister of State, Department of Trade and Industry, since 1986; *b* 16 Nov. 1931; *y s* of Hugh D. Shaw; *m* 1962, Dione Patricia Crosthwaite Ellison; one *s* two *d. Educ:* Sedbergh Sch.; St. John's Coll., Cambridge (MA). President of the Union, Cambridge, 1954. Past Rural District Councillor; served on Flaxton RDC, 1957–64. Marketing Dir, Confectionery Div., Rowntree Mackintosh Ltd, 1970–74. Contested (C) Kingston upon Hull West, 1966. Parliamentary Under-Secretary of State: NI Office, 1979–81; DoE, 1981–83; Dept of Energy, 1983–84; Minister of State, Home Office, 1984–86. Mem., House of Commons Select Cttee on Nationalised Industries, 1976–79; Vice-Chm., Cons. Prices and Consumer Affairs Cttee, 1976–78; Joint-Sec., All Party Wool Textile Group, 1978–79; Treasurer Yorks Cons. Members' Group, 1974–79. *Recreations:* ornithology, fishing, tennis. *Address:* 20 Parkside, Horsforth, Leeds; House of Commons, SW1.

SHAW, John Michael, MC 1940; QC 1967; Barrister-at-Law; Regional Chairman of Industrial Tribunals, 1972–84; *b* 14 Nov. 1914; *yr s* of late M. J. Shaw (killed in action, 1916); *m* 1940, Margaret L. *yr d* of Robert T. D. Stoneham, CBE; two *s* two *d. Educ:* Rugby; Worcester Coll., Oxford. Called to the Bar, Gray's Inn, 1937. Served War of 1939–45 (Major): commissioned Royal Fusiliers, 1940. *Recreations:* fishing, gardening. *Address:* South Knighton House, South Knighton, near Newton Abbot, Devon.

SHAW, Sir John Michael Robert B.; *see* Best-Shaw.

SHAW, Dr Mark Robert; Keeper of Natural History, Royal Scottish Museum, since 1983; *b* 11 May 1945; *s* of William Shaw and Mabel Courtenay Shaw (*née* Bower); *m* 1970, Francesca Dennis Wilkinson; two *d. Educ:* Dartington Hall Sch.; Oriel Coll., Oxford (BA 1968; MA, DPhil 1972). Res. Assistant, Manchester Univ., 1973–76; Univ. Res. Fellow, Reading Univ., 1977–80; Asst Keeper, Dept of Natural History, Royal Scottish Museum, 1980–83. *Publications:* contribs to chemical jls and (mainly on parasitic wasps) entomological jls. *Recreations:* field entomology, family life, gardening. *Address:* 48 St Alban's Road, Edinburgh EH9 2LU. *T:* 031–667 0577. *Club:* University of Edinburgh Staff (Edinburgh).

SHAW, Group Captain Mary Michal; RRC 1981; QHNS 1985; Director and Matron-in-Chief, Princess Mary's Royal Air Force Nursing Service, and Deputy Director, Defence Nursing Services (Org), since 1985; *b* 7 April 1933; *d* of Ven. Archdeacon Thorndike Shaw and Violet Rosario Shaw. *Educ:* Wokingham Grammar School for Girls. SRN 1955, Royal Berkshire Hosp., Reading; SCM 1957, Central Middlesex Hosp., London and Battle Hosp., Reading; PMRAFNS, 1963–. OStJ 1974. *Recreations:* gardening, home crafts. *Address:* 5 William Barnaby Yard, College Street, Bury St Edmunds, Suffolk IP33 1PQ. *T:* Bury St Edmunds 705836. *Club:* Royal Air Force.

SHAW, Max S.; *see* Stuart-Shaw.

SHAW, Michael Hewitt; HM Diplomatic Service; Counsellor, Foreign and Commonwealth Office, since 1986; *b* 5 Jan. 1935; *s* of late Donald Shaw and of Marion (*née* Hewitt); *m* 1963, Elizabeth Rance; three *d* (and one *d* decd). *Educ:* Sedbergh; Clare College, Cambridge (MA). HM Forces, 1953. HMOCS Tanganyika, 1959–62; joined Diplomatic Service, 1963; served The Hague, FCO and Vientiane, 1964–68; First Sec., FCO, 1968–72, Valletta, 1972–76, FCO, 1976–82, Brussels, 1982–84; Counsellor, Brussels, 1984–86. *Recreations:* cricket, theatre, walking. *Address:* c/o Foreign and Commonwealth Office, SW1A 2AH. *Clubs:* Army and Navy, MCC.

SHAW, Sir Michael (Norman), Kt 1982; JP; DL; MP (C) Scarborough, since 1974 (Scarborough and Whitby, 1966–74); *b* 9 Oct. 1920; *e s* of late Norman Shaw; *m* 1951, Joan Mary Louise, *o d* of Sir Alfred L. Mowat, 2nd Bt; three *s. Educ:* Sedbergh. Chartered Accountant. MP (L and C) Brighouse and Spenborough, March 1960–Oct. 1964; PPS: to Minister of Labour, 1962–63; to Sec. of State, Dept of Trade and Industry, 1970–72; to Chancellor of the Duchy of Lancaster, 1973. Mem., UK Delegn to European Parlt, 1974–79. FCA. JP Dewsbury, 1953; DL W Yorks, 1977. *Address:* Duxbury Hall, Liversedge, W Yorkshire. *T:* Heckmondwike 402270. *Club:* Carlton.

SHAW, Neil McGowan; Chairman and Chief Executive, Tate & Lyle plc, London, since 1986 (Group Managing Director, 1980–86); Chairman: Tate & Lyle Inc. (New York), since 1980; Tate & Lyle Hldgs, since 1981; Tate & Lyle Industries, since 1981; Tunnel Refineries, since 1982; Vice-Chairman, Redpath Industries, since 1981 (Director, since 1972); *b* 31 May 1929; *s* of Harold LeRoy Shaw and Fabiola Marie Shaw; *m* 1952, Audrey Robinson (marr. diss.); two *s* three *d*; *m* 1985, Elizabeth Fern Mudge-Massey. *Educ:* Knowlton High Sch.; Lower Canada Coll., Canada. Trust Officer, Crown Trust Co., Montreal, 1947–54; Merchandising Manager, Canada & Dominion Sugar Co. (later Redpath Industries Ltd), Montreal, 1954–66; Vice Pres., Canada & Dominion Sugar Co., Toronto, 1967–72; Vice-Pres., 1967–72, Pres., 1972–80, Redpath Industries Ltd. Director: Mid Industries & Explorations, 1973–; Texaco Canada Inc., 1974–; Americare Corp., 1980–; G. R. Amylum nv, 1982–; Touche Remnant N America Trust, 1982–; Alcantara, 1983–; Canadian Imperial Bank of Commerce (Canada), 1986–; Canadian Imperial Bank of Commerce (Toronto), 1986–; Smiths Industries, 1986–. Director, World Sugar Res. Orgn, 1982–. Mem. Resources Cttee, Food and Drink Fedn, 1985–. Member, Advisory Council: YES, 1986–; London Enterprise Agency, 1986–. Governor: Montreal Gen. Hosp.; Reddy Meml Hosp. *Recreations:* sailing, skiing, golfing. *Address:* 10 Sydney Place, SW7 3NL. *Clubs:* Brooks's; Toronto (Toronto); Mount Royal (Montreal).

SHAW, Sir Neville B.; *see* Bowman-Shaw.

SHAW, Captain Peter Jack, RN (retd); General Secretary, British Group Inter-Parliamentary Union, since 1979; *b* Geelong, Australia, 27 Oct. 1924; *s* of late Jack and Betty Shaw; *m* 1951, Pauline, *e d* of Sir Frank Madge, 2nd Bt, and Lady (Doris) Madge, East Grinstead; one *s* one *d. Educ:* Watford Grammar School; RNC Dartmouth; RN Staff Coll. Greenwich; NATO Defence Coll., Paris. FIL 1957. War service in HM Ships Kenya, Resolution, Quadrant, Kelvin, incl. Malta and Russian Convoys and Normandy invasion; comd HM Ships Venus, Carron, Vigilant, 1958–61; Staff, C-in-C Portsmouth and MoD, 1961–65; SHAPE, Paris and Mons, 1966–68; Comdr, RN Coll. Greenwich, 1968–70; Defence and Naval Attaché, The Hague, 1971–73; Captain of Port and Queen's Harbourmaster, Plymouth, 1973–76; Captain of Port, Chatham, 1976–79. MBIM. *Recreations:* international relations, foreign languages, domestic pursuits. *Address:* Woodside, Rogate, Petersfield, Hants. *T:* Rogate 344.

SHAW, Sir Robert, 7th Bt *cr* 1821; Design Engineer, T. Lamb, McManus & Associates Ltd, Calgary, Alberta; *b* Nairobi, Kenya, 31 Jan. 1925; *s* of Sir Robert de Vere Shaw, 6th Bt, MC, and Joan (*d* 1967), *d* of Thomas Cross; *S* father, 1969; *m* 1954, Jocelyn, *d* of late Andrew McGuffie, Swaziland; two *d. Educ:* Harrow; Univs of Oklahoma and Missouri, USA. RN, 1943–47 (Lieut RN retd). BS Civil Eng. Oklahoma, 1962; MS Civil Eng. Missouri, 1964; Professional Engineer, Alberta; Mem. Engineering Inst. of Canada. *Recreation:* sailing. *Heir: n* Charles de Vere Shaw, *b* 1 March 1957. *Address:* 234 40th Avenue SW, Calgary, Alberta T2S 0X3, Canada. *Club:* Alberta United Services Inst. (Calgary, Alberta).

SHAW, Dr Robert Macdonald, CB 1968; Deputy Chief Medical Officer, Department of Health and Social Security (formerly Ministry of Health), 1965–77; *b* 16 Sept. 1912; *s* of late Peter Macdonald and late Ellen Shaw; *m* 1941, Grace Helen Stringfellow; two *s* one *d. Educ:* Mill Hill School; Victoria Univ. of Manchester. Miscellaneous hospital appointments, etc, 1936–39. Emergency Commission, RAMC, 1939–45. Asst County MOH, Essex, 1945–48; Department of Health and Social Security (formerly Ministry of Health), 1948–77. QHP 1971–74. *Address:* The Lodge, Tor Bryan, Ingatestone, Essex CM4 9HN.

SHAW, Sir Roy, Kt 1979; Secretary General of the Arts Council of Great Britain, 1975–83; *b* 8 July 1918; *s* of Frederick and Elsie Shaw; *m* 1946, Gwenyth Baron; five *s* two *d. Educ:* Firth Park Grammar School, Sheffield; Manchester Univ. BA(Hons). Newspaper printing department 'copy-holder', 1937; newspaper publicity, 1938; Library Asst, Sheffield City Library, 1939; Cataloguer, Manchester Univ. Library, 1945; Organizing Tutor, WEA, 1946; Adult Educn Lectr, Leeds Univ., 1947; Warden, Leeds Univ. Adult Educn Centre, Bradford, 1959; Professor and Dir of Adult Educn, Keele Univ., 1962. Vis. Prof., Centre for Arts, City Univ., London, 1977–83. Vice-Pres., Coleg Harlech, 1983. Hon. DLitt: City, 1978; Southampton, 1984; DUniv Open, 1981. *Publications:* The Arts and the people, 1986; contrib. chapters to: Trends in English Adult Education, 1959; The Committed Church, 1966; Your Sunday Paper, 1967; over 150 articles on cultural policy, adult education and the mass media. *Recreations:* reading, theatre, opera, films, concerts and art galleries, swimming, watching the best of television—and sometimes, for clinical reasons, the worst. *Address:* 48 Farrer Road, N8 8LB. *Club:* Arts.

SHAW, Roy Edwin; Council Member, London Borough of Camden, since 1964; *b* 21 July 1925; *s* of Edwin Victor and Edith Lily Shaw. Hampstead Borough Council, 1956–62; St Pancras Borough, 1962–65; Camden Borough Council: Chm., Planning Cttee, 1967–68; Chm., Finance Cttee, 1971–74; Chief Whip and Dep. Leader, 1965–73; Leader, 1975–82. Vice-Chm., AMA, 1979–83; Dep. Chm. and Leader of Labour Party, London Boroughs Assoc. Part-time Mem., London Electricity Bd, 1977–83; Member: Transport Users Consultative Cttee for London, 1974–80; Adv. Cttee on Local Govt Audit, 1979–82; Audit Commn, 1983–; Consult. Council on Local Govt Finances, 1978–84. *Recreations:* listening to music; entertaining attractive women. *Address:* Town Hall, Euston Road, NW1 2RU. *T:* 01–278 4444.

SHAW, Sir Run Run, Kt 1977; CBE 1974; President, Shaw Organisation, since 1963; *b* 14 Oct. 1907; *m* 1932, Lily Wong Mee Chun; two *s* two *d*. Left China for Singapore and began making films and operating cinemas, 1927; left Singapore for Hong Kong and built Shaw Movietown, making and distributing films, 1959. Pres., Hong Kong Red Cross Soc., 1972–. Chairman: Hong Kong Arts Festival, 1974–; Bd of Governors, Hong Kong Arts Centre, 1978–; Hong Kong Television Broadcasts Ltd (TVB), 1980–; Bd of Trustees,

United Coll., Hong Kong, 1983–. Mem. Council, Chinese Univ. of Hong Kong, 1977–. Founder, Shaw Coll., Univ. of Hong Kong, 1986. Hon. LLD Hong Kong Univ., 1980; Hon. Dr Soc. Scis Chinese Univ. of Hong Kong, 1981. *Recreations:* shadow-boxing, golf. *Address:* Shaw House, Lot 220 Clearwater Bay Road, Kowloon, Hong Kong. *T:* 3–7198371.

SHAW, Sydney Herbert, CMG 1963; OBE 1958; *b* 6 Nov. 1903; 2nd *s* of John Beaumont and Gertrude Shaw; *m* 1930, Mary Louise, *e d* of Ernest Lewin Chapman; one *s* one *d. Educ:* King's College School; Royal School of Mines, London University. BSc Hons 1st cl. Mining Engineering, 1925 and Mining Geology, 1926; MSc (Birm.) 1937; PhD (Lond.) 1949. Geophys. prospecting N and S Rhodesia, 1926–28; Imperial Geophys. Experimental Survey, Aust., 1928–30; geophys. prospecting, Cyprus, 1930. Demonstrator, Geolog. Dept, Roy. Sch. of Mines, 1931; Lectr in Geology, Birmingham Univ., 1932–37; Govt Geologist, Palestine, 1937–48 (seconded as Dep. Controller Heavy Industries, Palestine, 1942–45); Colonial (later Overseas) Geological Surveys, London, 1949, Deputy Director, 1950, Dir, 1959–65; Head, Overseas Div., Inst. of Geological Sciences, 1965–68. Geological Adviser, Colonial Office (subseq. Dept of Tech. Co-op., then Min. of Overseas Develt), 1959–68. Retd, 1968. FIMM (Pres., 1968–69); FGS. *Publications:* scientific papers in various jls. *Recreation:* gardening. *Address:* Bisham Edge, Stoney Ware, Marlow, Bucks SL7 1RN. *T:* Marlow 4951.

SHAW, Thomas Richard, CMG 1960; HM Diplomatic Service, retired; *b* 5 Sept. 1912; *s* of Colin R. and Ida L. Shaw, Bolton, Lancs; *m* 1939, Evelyn Frances Young; four *s. Educ:* Repton; Clare Coll., Cambridge. Appointed probationer vice-consul at Istanbul, Nov. 1934; transferred to Bushire, December 1937; acting Consul, Grade 2, Tientsin, 1938–39; transferred to Trieste, Jan. 1940, to Leopoldville, Oct. 1940, to Elisabethville, 1942; served at Casablanca, 1943; vice-consul, Rabat, Dec. 1943; appointed one of HM vice-consuls serving in Foreign Office, 1944; promoted to consul, 1945; transferred to Bremen as consul, 1949; Deputy Consul-General, New York, 1953; actg Consul-General, 1953; Consul-General, Izmir, 1955; Inspector of Foreign Service Establishments, 1957, Senior Inspector, 1961; Ambassador to the Republics of Niger, Upper Volta and the Ivory Coast, 1964–67 (also to the Republic of Dahomey, 1964–65); Minister, Tokyo, 1967–69; Ambassador to Morocco, 1969–71. *Address:* Upton, Harrow Road West, Dorking, Surrey.

SHAW, Thurstan; *see* Shaw, C. T.

SHAW, Prof. William V., MD; Professor of Biochemistry, University of Leicester, since 1974; *b* Philadelphia, Pennsylvania, 13 May 1933. *Educ:* Williams Coll., Williamstown, Mass (BA Chemistry 1955); Columbia Univ., New York (MD 1959). Diplomate: Amer. Bd of Med. Examrs, 1960; Amer. Bd of Internal Med., 1968 (Examiner, 1970). Appts, Presbyterian Hosp., New York, Nat. Heart Inst., Bethesda, Maryland, and Columbia Univ., New York, until 1966; Asst Prof. of Medicine, Columbia Univ., New York, 1966–68; University of Miami School of Medicine, Miami, Florida: Associate Prof. of Medicine and Biochemistry, 1968–73; Chief, Infectious Diseases, 1971–74; Prof. of Medicine, 1973–74. Vis. Scientist, MRC Lab. of Molecular Biology, Cambridge, Eng., 1972–74. Member: MRC Cell Biology and Disorders Bd, 1976–80 (Bd Chm. and Mem. Council, 1978–80); Science Council, Celltech Ltd, 1980– (Chm., 1983–); Lister Inst. Sci. Adv. Council, 1981–85. Member: Amer. Soc. for Clinical Investigation, 1971; Infectious Disease Soc. of Amer., 1969; Amer. Soc. of Biol Chemists; Biochem. Soc. (UK); Amer. Soc. for Microbiology; Soc. for Gen. Microbiology (UK). *Publications:* contribs to professional works and jls in microbial biochem. and molecular biology. *Address:* Department of Biochemistry, University of Leicester, University Road, Leicester LE1 7RH. *T:* Leicester 551234.

SHAW-STEWART, Sir Houston (Mark), 11th Bt *cr* 1667; MC 1950; TD; Vice Lord-Lieutenant, Strathclyde Region (Eastwood, Renfrew and Inverclyde Districts), since 1980; *b* 24 April 1931; *s* of Sir Guy Shaw-Stewart, 9th Bt, MC, and Diana (*d* 1931), *d* of late George Bulteel; *S* brother, 1980; *m* 1982, Lucinda Victoria, *yr d* of Alexander Fletcher, Old Vicarage, Wighill, near Tadcaster. *Educ:* Eton. Joined Coldstream Guards, 1949; served as 2/Lt Royal Ulster Rifles, Korea, 1950 (MC); joined Ayrshire Yeomanry, 1952; retired, 1969; Hon. Col A (Ayrshire Yeomanry) Sqdn, Queen's Own Yeomanry RAC, TA, 1984–. Member of the Royal Company of Archers, Queen's Body Guard for Scotland. Joint Master, Lanark and Renfrewshire Foxhounds, 1974–79. DL Renfrewshire, 1970. *Recreations:* hunting, shooting and racing. *Heir: kinsman* Donald Erskine Stewart [*b* 1905; *m* 1936, Ailsa Violet Annie (*d* 1970), *d* of John Forbes; one *s*]. *Address:* Ardgowan, Inverkip, Renfrewshire. *T:* Wemyss Bay 521226. *Clubs:* White's, Turf, Pratt's; Greenock (Greenock).

SHAWCROSS, family name of **Baron Shawcross.**

SHAWCROSS, Baron, *cr* 1959 (Life Peer), of Friston; **Hartley William Shawcross,** PC 1946; GBE 1974; Kt 1945; QC 1939; Special Adviser, Morgan Guaranty Trust of New York, since 1965 (Chairman, International Advisory Council, 1967–74); Director, Hawker Siddeley Group, 1968–82, now Consultant; Director, The Observer, since 1981; *b* 4 Feb. 1902; *s* of John Shawcross, MA, and Hilda Shawcross; *m* 1st, 1924, Rosita Alberta Shyvers (*d* 1943); 2nd, 1944, Joan Winifred Mather (*d* 1974); two *s* one *d. Educ:* Dulwich Coll.; abroad. Certificate of Honour for 1st place in Bar Final; called to Bar, Gray's Inn, 1925 (Bencher, 1939); practised on Northern Circuit. Sen. Law Lectr, Liverpool Univ., 1927–34. Chm., Enemy Aliens Tribunal, 1939–40; left practice at Bar for War Service, 1940; Chief Prosecutor for UK before Internat. Military Tribunal at Nuremberg. Asst Chm. of E Sussex QS, 1941; Recorder of Salford, 1941–45; Dep. Regional Comr, South-Eastern Region, 1941; Regional Comr, North-Western Region, 1942–45; Recorder of Kingston-upon-Thames, 1946–61; retired from practice at Bar, 1958. MP (Lab) St Helens, 1945–58; Attorney-General, 1945–51; Pres., BoT, April-Oct. 1951. A Principal Deleg. for UK to Assemblies of UN, 1945–49; a UK Mem., Permanent Court of Arbitration at The Hague, 1950–67. Independent Chm., Kent District Coal Mining Board, 1940–45; Chairman: Catering Wages Commn, 1943–45; Bar Council, 1952–57; Royal Commn on the Press, 1961–62; MRC, 1961–65; Internat. Law Section of British Inst. of Internat. and Comparative Law; Justice (British Br. of Internat. Commn of Jurists), 1956–72; Panel on Take-overs and Mergers, 1969–80; Press Council, 1974–78; ICC Commn on Unethical Practices, 1976. President: Rainer Foundn (formerly London Police Court Mission), 1951–71; British Hotels and Restaurants Assoc., 1959–71. Member: Home Secretary's Adv. Council on Treatment of Offenders, 1944–45; Council, Internat. Law Assoc., 1958–74; Exec. Cttee, Internat. Commn of Jurists, 1959. Hon. Member: Bar Council; Amer. and New York Bar Assoc.; Fellow, Amer. Bar Foundn. Director: Shell Transport and Trading Co., 1961–72; EMI Ltd, 1965–81; Rank-Hovis-McDougall Ltd, 1965–79; Caffyns Motors Ltd, 1965–; Morgan et Cie International SA, 1966–77; Morgan et Cie SA, 1967–; Times Newspapers Ltd, 1967–74; Upjohn & Co Ltd, 1967–76 (Chm.); Birmingham Small Arms Co. Ltd, 1968–73 (Chm., 1971–73); European Enterprises Development Co. SA, 1970–78 (Chm., 1973–78); Chairman: Dominion Lincoln Assurance Co. Ltd, 1969–76; Thames Television Ltd, 1969–74; London and Continental Bankers, 1974–80 (now Consultant); Chm. Bd of Governors, Dulwich Coll.; Member:

Court, London Univ., 1958–74; Council and Exec. Cttee, Sussex Univ., 1959– (Pro-Chancellor, 1960–65; Chancellor, 1965–85); Council, Eastbourne Coll., 1965–70. Hon. FRCS 1981; Hon. FRCOG 1978. Hon. Degrees from Universities of Bristol, Columbia, Hull, Lehigh, Liverpool, London, Massachusetts (Ann Arbor), Michigan, Sussex. JP Sussex, 1941–68. Chm., Soc. of Sussex Downsmen, 1962–75. Knight Grand Cross, Imperial Iranian Order of Homayoon, 1st Cl., 1974. *Recreations:* sailing, riding. *Address:* Friston Place, Sussex BN20 0AH. *Clubs:* White's, Buck's; Travellers' (Paris); Royal Cornwall Yacht (Falmouth); Royal Yacht Squadron (Cowes); New York Yacht (US).

SHAWE-TAYLOR, Desmond (Christopher), CBE 1965; Music Critic, The Sunday Times, since 1958; *b* 29 May 1907; *s* of Frank Shawe-Taylor and Agnes Ussher. *Educ:* Shrewsbury Sch.; Oriel Coll., Oxford. Literary and occasional musical criticism, New Statesman, etc until 1939. Served War of 1939–45 with the Royal Artillery. Music Critic, New Statesman, 1945–58; Guest Music Critic, New Yorker, 1973–74. *Publications:* Covent Garden, 1948; (with Edward Sackville-West, later Lord Sackville), The Record Guide (with supplements and revisions, 1951–56). *Recreations:* travel, croquet, gramophone. *Address:* Long Crichel House, Wimborne, Dorset. *T:* Tarrant Hinton 250; 15 Furlong Road, N7. *T:* 01–607 4854. *Club:* Brooks's.

SHAWYER, Robert Cort, MA, PhD; *b* 9 Oct. 1913; *e s* of late Arthur Frederic Shawyer, sometime Gen. Manager, Martins Bank; *m* 1939, Isabel Jessie Rogers (*d* 1986); two *d*. *Educ:* Charterhouse; Corpus Christi Coll., Oxford; Birkbeck Coll., Univ. of London. Bank of England, 1935–37. Commissioned RAEC, 1938 (Lt-Col 1945). Princ., Min. of Nat. Insce, 1948; Admty, 1951; Asst Sec., 1957; seconded to NATO, 1960; Nat. Def. Coll., Canada, 1961–62; Commonwealth Office, 1967; Consul-Gen., Buenos Aires, 1967–70; FCO, Cultural Relations Dept, 1970–72; retired. FRGS. *Publications:* articles in professional, etc, jls. *Recreation:* archaeology. *Address:* Southfield, 3 South Road, Taunton, Somerset; (winter) Apartamentos Damara, Calpe, Spain. *Clubs:* Army and Navy; Royal Commonwealth Society (Bristol).

SHEA, Michael Sinclair MacAuslan, LVO 1985; PhD; Press Secretary to the Queen, since 1978; *b* 10 May 1938; *s* of late James Michael Shea and of Mary Dalrymple Davidson MacAuslan, North Berwick; *m* 1968, Mona Grec Stensen, Oslo; two *d*. *Educ:* Gordonstoun Sch.; Edinburgh Univ. (MA, PhD Econs). FO, 1963; Inst. of African Studies, Accra, Ghana, 1963; FO, 1964; Third, later Second Sec., CRO, 1965; Second, later First Sec. (Econ.), Bonn, 1966; seconded to Cabinet Office, 1969; FO, 1971; Head of Chancery, Bucharest, 1973; Dep. Dir Gen., Brit. Inf. Services, New York, 1976. *Publications:* Britain's Offshore Islands, 1981; Maritime England, 1981; Tomorrow's Men, 1982; (as Michael Sinclair): Sonntag, 1971; Folio Forty-One, 1972; The Dollar Covenant, 1974; A Long Time Sleeping, 1976; The Master Players, 1978; (with David Frost) The Mid-Atlantic Companion, 1986; The Rich Tide, 1986. *Recreations:* writing, sailing. *Address:* Buckingham Palace, SW1. *T:* 01–930 4832.

SHEALS, Dr John Gordon; Keeper of Zoology, British Museum (Natural History), 1971–85; *b* 19 Dec. 1923; *o s* of late John Joseph Sheals and Anne (*née* Ffoulkes); *m* 1945, Blodwen M. Davies (*d* 1972); two *s*. *Educ:* Caernarvon County Sch.; UC North Wales; Glasgow Univ. BSc, PhD, FIBiol. Asst Lectr, West of Scotland Agricultural Coll., Glasgow, 1948–56; Asst Advisory Entomologist, Min. of Agric., Fisheries and Food, 1956–58; Asst Keeper, 1958–68, and Dep. Keeper, 1968–71, Dept of Zoology, British Museum (Natural History). Mem. Council, Freshwater Biological Assoc., 1976–85; Trustee, Percy Sladen Meml Fund, 1978–85. *Publications:* (with G. O. Evans and D. Macfarlane) The Terrestrial Acari of the British Isles: Introduction and Biology, 1961; papers on taxonomy and ecology of mites in scientific jls. *Recreation:* music. *Address:* 6 The Mount, Rickmansworth, Herts. *T:* Rickmansworth 720250.

SHEARER, Rt. Hon. Hugh Lawson, PC 1969; MP South-east Clarendon, since 1976 (South Clarendon, 1967–76); Deputy Prime Minister of Jamaica, and Minister of Foreign Affairs and Foreign Trade, since 1980; President, Bustamante Industrial Trade Union, since 1977; *b* 18 May 1923. *Educ:* St Simons Coll., Jamaica. Journalist on weekly newspaper, Jamaica Worker, 1941–44, subseq. Editor. Apptd Asst Gen. Sec., Bustamante Industrial TU, 1947, Island Supervisor, 1953–67, Vice-Pres., 1960–79 (on leave of absence, 1967–72). Mem. Kingston and St Andrew Corp. Council, 1947; MHR for West Kingston, 1955–59; MLC, later Senator, 1962–67; Leader of Govt Business in Senate, 1962–67; Prime Minister of Jamaica, 1967–72; Minister of Defence and of External Affairs, 1967–72; Leader of the Opposition, 1972–74; Leader, Jamaica Labour Party, 1967–74. Hon. Dr of Laws, Howard Univ., Washington, DC, 1968. *Address:* House of Representatives, Kingston, Jamaica.

SHEARER, Rt. Hon. Ian Hamilton; *see* Avonside, Rt Hon. Lord.

SHEARER, Janet Sutherland; *see* Avonside, Lady.

SHEARER, Magnus MacDonald; JP; Lord Lieutenant of Shetland since 1982; Managing Director, J. & M. Shearer Ltd (Est. 1919), 1960–85; *b* 27 Feb. 1924; *s* of late Lt-Col Magnus Shearer, OBE, TD, JP, and of Flora MacDonald Stephen; *m* 1949, Martha Nicolson Henderson, *d* of late Captain John Henderson, DSM, and late Martha Nicolson; one *s*. *Educ:* Anderson Educational Institute, Shetland; George Watson's Coll., Edinburgh. Served RN in Atlantic, Mediterranean and Far East, 1942–46. 2nd Lieut, RA (TA), 1949; Captain, TARO, 1959. Hon. Consul: for Sweden in Shetland and Orkney, 1958–; for Federal Republic of Germany in Shetland, 1972–. Mem., Lerwick Harbour Trust, 1960–75 (Chm., 1967–72); Hon. Sec., RNLI Lerwick Branch, 1968–; Mem. Lerwick Town Council, 1963–69; JP 1969, DL 1973, Shetland. Knight 1st Class, Royal Order of Vasa (Sweden), 1969; Officer 1st Class, Order of Merit (Federal Republic of Germany), 1983; Officer 1st Class, Order of Polar Star (Sweden), 1983. *Recreations:* reading, bird watching and ships. *Address:* Birka, Cruester, Bressay, Shetland ZE2 9EL. *T:* Bressay 363.

SHEARER, Moira, (Mrs L. Kennedy); lecturer; *b* Dunfermline, Fifeshire, 17 Jan. 1926; *d* of Harold King; *m* 1950, Ludovic Kennedy, *qv*; one *s* three *d*. *Educ:* Dunfermline High School; Ndola, N Rhodesia; Bearsden, Scotland. Professional training: Mayfair Sch.; Legat Sch. Début with International Ballet, 1941; joined Sadler's Wells Ballet, 1942, during following ten years danced all major classic roles and full repertoire of revivals and new ballets; first ballerina rôle in Sleeping Beauty, 1946; created rôle of Cinderella, 1948; Titania in Old Vic production of A Midsummer Night's Dream (Edin. Festival, 1954, and tour of US and Canada); American tours with Sadler's Wells Ballet, 1949, 1950–51. Toured as Sally Bowles in I am a Camera, 1955; joined Bristol Old Vic, 1955; played in Man of Distinction, Edin. Fest., 1957; played Madame Ranevskaya in The Cherry Orchard, Royal Lyceum, Edin., 1977; Judith Bliss in Hay Fever, Royal Lyceum, 1978. Recorded: Thomas Hardy's Tess of the D'Urbervilles, 1977; Muriel Spark's The Ballad of Peckham Rye, BBC Radio 4, 1982. Member: Scottish Arts Council, 1971–73; BBC Gen. Adv. Council, 1970–77; Dir, Border TV, 1977–82. Toured US, lecturing on history of ballet, March-April 1973; regular lecturing in England and Wales. Lectured and gave recitals on three world cruises, Queen Elizabeth II. Poetry and prose recitals, Edinburgh Festivals, 1974 and 1975. *Films:* Ballerina in The Red Shoes (première, 1948); Tales of Hoffmann, 1950; Story of Three Loves, 1952; The Man Who Loved Redheads, 1954; Peeping Tom, 1960; Black Tights, 1961. *Publication:* Balletmaster: a dancer's view of George Balanchine, 1986. *Address:* c/o A. D. Peters, 10 Buckingham Street, WC2H 6BU.

SHEARER, Thomas Hamilton, CB 1974; a Controller, Royal Opera House Development Land Trust, since 1981; *b* 7 Nov. 1923; *o s* of late Thomas Appleby Shearer, OBE; *m* 1945, Sybil Mary Robinson, Stratford-on-Avon; one *s* one *d*. *Educ:* Haberdashers' Aske's, Hatcham; Emmanuel Coll., Cambridge (open exhibition in English). Served RAF, 1942–45 (despatches). Entered Air Ministry, as Asst Principal, 1948; Principal, 1951; Sec. to Grigg Cttee on Recruitment to Armed Forces, 1958; Asst Sec., 1959; transf. Min. of Public Building and Works, 1963; student, IDC, 1965; Under-Sec., 1967; Dir of Establishments, MPBW, 1967–70, DoE, 1970; Dir of Personnel Management, DoE, 1970–72; Dep. Chief Exec. II, PSA, DoE, 1972–73; Deputy Secretary, 1973–81. Chairman: Maplin Develt Authority, 1974–77; British Channel Tunnel Company, 1975–77; Location of Offices Bureau, 1980. *Recreations:* opera, claret. *Address:* 9 Denny Crescent, SE11. *T:* 01–587 0921.

SHEARER, Rev. W(illiam) Russell; *b* 12 Oct. 1898; *s* of Henry S. and Jessie A. Shearer; *m* 1934, Phyllis Mary Wigfield (*d* 1986). *Educ:* Harrogate Grammar School; Leeds University; Wesley House, Cambridge. Served European War, 1914–18, in Tank Corps. Since 1923 has been Methodist Minister at: Tunstall, Staffs; Manchester; Muswell Hill; Sutton, Surrey; Hanley. Chairman, Stoke-on-Trent Methodist District, 1943–50; Chairman, Birmingham Methodist District, 1950–63. Pres. of Methodist Conference, 1954–55; Moderator, National Free Church Federal Council, 1959–60. Pres. UK Bd, Hope Union, 1960–74. *Address:* 32 Layton Lane, Shaftesbury, Dorset SP7 8EY. *T:* Shaftesbury 2678. *Club:* National Liberal.

SHEARLOCK, Very Rev. David John; Dean of Truro, since 1982; *b* 1 July 1932; *s* of Arthur John Shearlock and Honora Frances Hawkins; *m* 1959, Jean Margaret Marr; one *s* one *d*. *Educ:* Univ. of Birmingham (BA); Westcott House, Cambridge. Assistant Curate: Guisborough, Yorks, 1957–60; Christchurch Priory, Hants, 1960–64; Vicar: Kingsclere, 1964–71; Romsey Abbey, 1971–82; Diocesan Director of Ordinands (Winchester), 1977–82; Hon. Canon of Winchester, 1978–82. *Recreations:* model railways, music, walking the Cornish coastal footpath. *Address:* The Deanery, Lemon Street, Truro, Cornwall TR1 2PE. *T:* Truro 72661.

SHEARMAN, Rt. Rev. Donald Norman, OBE 1978; *b* 6 Feb. 1926; *s* of late S. F. Shearman, Sydney; *m* 1952, Stuart Fay, *d* of late Chap. F. H. Bashford; three *s* three *d*. *Educ:* Fort St and Orange High Schools; St John's Theological College, Morpeth, NSW. Served War of 1939–45: air crew, 1944–46. Theological College, 1948–50. Deacon, 1950; Priest, 1951. Curate: of Dubbo, 1950–52; of Forbes, and Warden of St John's Hostel, 1953–56; Rector of Coonabarabran, 1957–59; Director of Promotion and Adult Christian Education 1959–62; Canon, All Saints Cathedral, Bathurst, 1962; Archdeacon of Mildura and Rector of St. Margaret's, 1963; Bishop of Rockhampton, 1963–71; Chairman, Australian Board of Missions, Sydney, 1971–73; Bishop of Grafton, 1973–85. *Address:* 123 Turner Street, Scarborough, Qld 4020, Australia.

SHEARMAN, Prof. John Kinder Gowran, PhD; FBA 1976; Chairman, Department of Art and Archaeology, Princeton University, since 1979; *b* 24 June 1931; *s* of Brig. C. E. G. Shearman; *m* 1957, Jane Dalrymple Smith; one *s* three *d*; *m* 1983, Deirdre Raskill. *Educ:* St Edmund's, Hindhead; Felsted; Courtauld Inst., London Univ.; BA, PhD 1957. Lectr, Courtauld Inst., 1957–67; Research Fellow, Inst. for Advanced Study, Princeton, 1964; Reader, Courtauld Inst., 1967–74, Prof. of the History of Art, 1974–79 (Dep. Dir, 1974–78). Mem., Accademia del Disegno, Florence, 1979. Serena Medal, British Acad., 1979. *Publications:* Andrea del Sarto, 1965; Mannerism, 1967, 4th edn 1977; Raphael's Cartoons, 1972; Catalogue of the Early Italian Paintings in the Collection of HM the Queen, 1983; Funzione e Illusione, 1983; contribs to British, French, German, American jls. *Recreations:* sailing, music. *Address:* 5 Yar Quay, St Helen's, Isle of Wight. *Clubs:* Bembridge Sailing, Island Sailing (Cowes).

SHEEHAN, Albert Vincent; Sheriff of Tayside, Central and Fife, since 1983; *b* 23 Aug. 1936; *s* of Richard Greig Sheehan and May Moffat; *m* 1965, Edna Georgina Scott Hastings; two *d*. *Educ:* Bo'ness Acad.; Edinburgh Univ. (MA 1957; LLB 1959). Admitted as Solicitor, 1959. 2nd Lieut, 1st Bn The Royal Scots (The Royal Regt), 1960; Captain, Directorate of Army Legal Services, 1961. Depute Procurator Fiscal, Hamilton, 1961–71; Sen. Depute Procurator Fiscal, Glasgow, 1971–74; Depute Crown Agent for Scotland, 1974–79; Asst Solicitor, Scottish Law Commn, 1979–81; Sheriff of Lothian and Borders, 1981–83. Leverhulme Fellow, 1971. *Publication:* Criminal Procedure in Scotland and France, 1975. *Recreations:* naval history, travel, legal history, boating. *Address:* Sheriff's Chambers, Sheriff Court House, Falkirk. *Club:* East Lodge Yacht.

SHEEHAN, Harold Leeming, MD, DSc, FRCP, FRCOG, FRCPath; Professor of Pathology, University of Liverpool, 1946–65 (Professor Emeritus since 1965); *b* 4 Aug. 1900; *s* of Dr P. Sheehan, Carlisle; *m* 1934, E. S. G. Potter; no *c*. *Educ:* University of Manchester. Demonstrator and Lecturer in Pathology, University of Manchester, 1927–34; Rockefeller Medical Fellow in USA, 1934–35; Director of Research, Glasgow Royal Maternity Hosp., 1935–46; Hon. Lecturer in Pathology, Univ. of Glasgow, 1943–46. Served in RAMC, 1939–45; Colonel, Deputy Director of Pathology, AFHQ, Italy, 1945 (despatches, TD). Hon. Member: Fac. Med., Univ. of Chile; Fac. Med., Univ. of Concepcion; Soc. Roy. Belge Gyn. Obst.; Soc. Chil. Obst. Gyn.; Soc. Argent. Neurol.; Soc. Med. Hop. Paris; Socs Endocrinology: Chile, Argentine, Roumania, Hungary; Hon. Fellow, Amer. Assoc. Obst. Gyn.; Foreign Associate, Académie Nationale de Médecine, Paris; Foreign Corresp., Acad. Nat. Méd., France. Hon. MD Szeged (Hungary), 1982. *Publications:* papers on pathology, endocrinology and renal physiology in various med. jls. *Address:* 18 Knowsley Road, Liverpool L19 0PG. *T:* 051–427 2936.

SHEEHY, Patrick; Chairman, BAT Industries, since 1982 (Vice-Chairman, 1981–82); *b* 2 Sept. 1930; *s* of Sir John Francis Sheehy, CSI and Jean Newton Simpson; *m* 1964, Jill Patricia Tindall; one *s* one *d*. *Educ:* Australia; Ampleforth Coll., Yorks. Served Irish Guards, 1948–50; rank on leaving 2nd Lieut. Joined British-American Tobacco Co., 1950, first appt in Nigeria; Ghana, 1951; Reg. Sales Manager, Nigeria, 1953; Ethiopian Tobacco Monopoly, 1954; Marketing Dir, Jamaica, 1957; General Manager: Barbados, 1961; Holland, 1967; Dir, 1970–81, Chm., 1976–81, British-American Tobacco Co.; Dir, 1976–, Mem., Chm's Policy Cttee, 1976–, Dep. Chm., 1976–81, BAT Industries; Chm., BATUS, 1986–; Director: Batus Inc., 1979–82; BP, 1984–; Eagle Star Hldgs, 1984–. *Recreations:* golf, reading. *Address:* BAT Industries plc, Windsor House, 50 Victoria Street, SW1H 0NL. *T:* 01–222–7979.

SHEEHY, Terence Joseph; Editor, Catholic Herald, since 1983; *b* 12 May 1918; 2nd *s* of Michael Sheehy and Mary (*née* O'Sullivan); *m* 1955, Margaret Patricia Barry, *y d* of Dr T. St John Barry; one *s* three *d*. *Educ:* by Jesuits in London and Dublin. Editorial staff, Irish Catholic, Dublin, 1942–46; publisher and Editor, Irish Cinema Quarterly, Editor, Irish Hotelier, and Editor, Irish Licensing World, 1946–50; Gen. Manager and Dir, Ron Harris (Ireland), film distributors, 1950–52; Bord Fáilte Éireann (Irish Tourist Board): Asst Gen. Manager, N America, 1952–56; Gen. Manager (Britain), and Dir of Publicity,

1956–82; Editor, Irish Observer, 1982. Allied Irish Banks' Irish Post Community Award, 1977. *Publications:* Ireland in Colour, 1975; Ireland, 1978; Ireland and Her People, 1980; Journey through Ireland, 1986. *Recreations:* reading, writing, conversation. *Address:* Ballinona, 7 Tower Road, Tadworth, Surrey KT20 5QY. *T:* Tadworth 4241. *Club:* Garrick.

SHEEN, Hon. Sir Barry (Cross), Kt 1978; **Hon. Mr Justice Sheen;** a Judge of the High Court of Justice, Queen's Bench Division, since~1978; *b* 31 Aug. 1918; 2nd *s* of late Ronald Sheen, FCA, St John's Wood; *m* 1946, Diane (*d* 1986), *d* of late C. L. Donne, MD; three *s. Educ:* Haileybury College, Hill School (USA); Trinity Hall, Cambridge (MA). Served in RNVR, 1939–46; Commanding Officer, HMS Kilkenzie, 1943–45. Called to Bar, Middle Temple, 1947, Master of the Bench, 1971; Member Bar Council, 1959–63; QC 1966. Junior Counsel to Admiralty, 1961–66; a Recorder of the Crown Court, 1972–78. On Panel of Wreck Comrs (Eng.) under Merchant Shipping Acts, 1966–78; Mem., Panel of Lloyd's Arbitrators in Salvage Cases, 1966–78; Appeal Arbitrator, 1977–78. Vice-Pres., British Maritime Law Assoc., 1979–. Life Governor, Haileybury (Pres., Haileybury Soc., 1982); Hon. Mem., Assoc. of Average Adjusters, 1979– (Chm., 1986). Freeman, Shipwrights' Co. *Recreations:* bridge, golf. *Address:* Royal Courts of Justice, WC2. *T:* 01–946 8534. *Clubs:* Hurlingham; Royal Wimbledon Golf.

SHEERIN, John Declan; His Honour Judge Sheerin; a Circuit Judge, since 1982; *b* 29 Nov. 1932; *s* of late John Patrick Sheerin and Agnes Mary Sheerin; *m* 1958, Helen Suzanne (*née* LeRoux); two *s* two *d. Educ:* Wimbledon Coll.; London Sch. of Econs and Polit Science (LLB 1954). Served RAF, 1958–60 (Flying Officer). Admitted solicitor, 1957; Partner, Greene & Greene, 1962–82; a Recorder of the Crown Court, 1979–82. Councillor (Ind.), W Suffolk CC, 1964–76 (Chm., Library and Museums Cttee). *Recreations:* golf, cooking. *Address:* Kings Hall Farmhouse, Rougham, Bury St Edmunds, Suffolk IP30 9LG; Rue du Château, Viviers 07220, France. *T:* Beyton 70309. *Club:* Flempton Golf.

SHEERMAN, Barry John; MP (Lab and Co-Op) Huddersfield, since 1983 (Huddersfield East, 1979–83); *b* 17 Aug. 1940; *s* of Albert William Sheerman and Florence Sheerman (*née* Pike); *m* 1965 Pamela Elizabeth (*née* Brenchley); one *s* three *d. Educ:* Hampton Grammar Sch.; Kingston Technical Coll.; LSE. BSc (Economics) Hons; MSc Hons. Chemical worker, laboratory assistant, technical sales trainee, etc., 1958–61; Lectr, Univ. Coll. of Swansea, 1966–79. An opposition front bench spokesman on education and employment dealing with training and youth affairs, small business and tourism; Chairman: Parly Adv. Cttee on Transport Safety, 1981–; PLP Trade Cttee, 1981–83; Mem., Public Accounts Cttee, 1981–83. *Publications:* various. *Address:* House of Commons, SW1A 0AA.

SHEFFIELD, 8th Baron; *see under* Stanley of Alderley, 8th Baron.

SHEFFIELD, Bishop of, since 1980; **Rt. Rev. David Ramsay Lunn;** *b* 1930. *Educ:* King's College, Cambridge (BA 1953, MA 1957); Cuddesdon College, Oxford. Deacon 1955, priest 1956, Newcastle upon Tyne; Curate of Sugley, 1955–59; N Gosforth, 1959–63; Chaplain, Lincoln Theological College, 1963–66; Sub-Warden, 1966–70; Vicar of St George, Cullercoats, 1970–75, Rector, 1975–80; Rural Dean of Tynemouth, 1975–80. *Address:* Bishopscroft, Snaithing Lane, Sheffield, S Yorks S10 3LG.

SHEFFIELD, Provost of; *see* Curtis, Very Rev. W. F.

SHEFFIELD, Archdeacon of; *see* Paton, Ven. M. J. M.

SHEFFIELD, Maj.-Gen. John, CB 1967; CBE 1961; Commandant of the Star and Garter Home, Richmond, 1975–77, a Governor, since 1977; *b* 28 April 1910; *s* of late Major W. G. F. Sheffield, DSO, and Mrs C. G. A. Sheffield (*née* Wing); *m* 1936, Mary Patience Vere (*née* Nicoll); one *s* one *d* (and one *s* decd). *Educ:* Winchester; RMA, Woolwich. Commd, 1930; served RA and RHA; transferred RAOC, 1939. Served War of 1939–45: BEF, 1939–40; MEF, 1944–48. Egypt, 1954–56; Cyprus, 1959–62; Comdr Base Organization, RAOC, 1964–67. Col Comdt, RAOC, 1970–74. *Recreations:* athletics (British Olympic Team, 1936), golf, sailing, numismatics. *Address:* Tuns Arch House, Odiham, Hants. *T:* Odiham 2436. *Club:* Royal Automobile.

SHEFFIELD, John Vincent, CBE 1984; Chairman, Norcros Ltd, 1956–81; *b* 11 Nov. 1913; *y s* of Sir Berkeley Sheffield, 6th Bt; *m* 1st, 1936, Anne (*d* 1969), *d* of Sir Lionel Faudel-Phillips, 3rd Bt; one *s* three *d*; 2nd, 1971, Mrs France Crosthwaite, *d* of Brig.-Gen. Goland Clarke. *Educ:* Eton; Magdalene College, Cambridge (MA). Private Secretary to Minister of Works, 1943–44; Chairman: Portals Ltd, 1968–78; Atlantic Assets Trust Ltd, 1972–83. Chm., BEC, 1980–83; Vice-Chm., BTEC, 1983. High Sheriff of Lincolnshire, 1944–45. *Address:* New Barn House, Laverstoke, Whitchurch, Hants RG28 7PF. *T:* Whitchurch (Hants) 893187. *Club:* White's.

SHEFFIELD, Sir Reginald (Adrian Berkeley), 8th Bt *cr* 1755; DL; Chairman: Aylesford Holdings Ltd, since 1979; Alpwood Holdings plc, since 1984; Director, Normanby Estate Co. Ltd, and other companies; Member of Lloyd's, since 1977; *b* 9 May 1946; *s* of Edmund Charles Reginald Sheffield, JP, DL (*d* 1977) and of Nancie Miriel Denise, *d* of Edward Roland Soames; *S* uncle, 1977; *m* 1st, 1969, Annabel Lucy Veronica (marr. diss.), *d* of T. A. Jones; two *d*; 2nd, 1977, Victoria, *d* of late R. C. Walker, DFC; one *s* two *d. Educ:* Eton. Member of Stock Exchange, 1973–75. Vice-Chm., S Humberside Business Advice Centre Ltd. Pres., S Humberside CPRE. Mem. for Ermine Ward, Humberside County Council, 1985–. Pres., Scunthorpe United Football Club, 1982–. DL Humberside, 1985. *Heir: s* Robert Charles Berkeley Sheffield, *b* 1 Sept. 1984. *Address:* Estate Office, Normanby, Scunthorpe, S Humberside DN15 9HS. *T:* Scunthorpe 720618. *Club:* White's.

SHEFTON, Prof. Brian Benjamin, FBA 1985; FSA 1980; Professor of Greek Art and Archaeology, University of Newcastle upon Tyne, 1979–84, now Emeritus; *b* 11 Aug. 1919; *yr s* of late Prof. I. Scheftelowitz (Cologne, Germany, until 1933 and Oxford) and Frieda (*née* Kohn); *m* 1960, Jutta Ebel of Alingsås, Sweden; one *d. Educ:* Apostelngymnasium, Cologne; St Lawrence Coll., Ramsgate; Magdalen Coll. Sch., Oxford; Oriel Coll., Oxford (Open Scholar, 1938; Hon. Mods Greek and Latin Lit. 1940; Lit Hum 1947, Class I). War service, HM Forces (change of name), 1940–45. Sch. Student, British Sch. at Athens, 1947; Derby Scholar, Oxford, 1948; Bishop Fraser Scholar, Oriel Coll., Oxford, 1949, in Aegean to 1950; excavated at Old Smyrna; Lectr in Classics, University Coll., Exeter, 1950–55; Lectr in Greek Archaeology and Ancient History, 1955, Sen. Lectr, 1960, Reader, 1974–79, King's Coll., Univ. of Durham (later Univ. of Newcastle upon Tyne). Established and directed Univ.'s Greek Museum, 1956–84, Hon. Advr, 1985–. Vis. Res. Fellow, Merton Coll., Oxford, 1969; British Acad. Vis. Scholar to Albania, 1973; Munro Lectr, Edinburgh Univ., 1974; British Acad. European Exchange Fellow, Marburg Univ., 1975; German Academic Exchange Fellow, Marburg and Cologne, 1976; Leverhulme Res. Fellow, 1977; Webster Meml Lectr, Stanford Univ., 1981; Vis. Prof. of Classical Archaeology, Vienna Univ. (winter), 1981–82; British Council Vis. Scholar to Soviet Union, 1982, to Spain, 1985; Jackson Knight Meml Lectr, Exeter Univ., 1983; Leverhulme Emeritus Fellow, 1984–86; Balsdon Sen. Fellow, British

Sch. at Rome, 1985. Mem., German Archaeological Inst., 1961. Aylwin Cotton Award, 1977. *Publications:* History of Greek Vase Painting (with P. Arias and M. Hirmer), 1962; Die rhodischen Bronzekannen, 1979; chapters in: Perachora II, 1962; Phoenizier im Westen, 1982; The Eye of Greece, 1982; articles in British and foreign periodicals. *Recreations:* music, travel. *Address:* 24 Holly Avenue, Newcastle upon Tyne NE2 2PY. *T:* 091–281 4184.

SHEHADIE, Sir Nicholas (Michael), Kt 1976; OBE 1971; Managing Director, Nicholas Shehadie Pty Ltd, since 1959; *b* 15 Nov. 1926; *s* of Michael and Hannah Shehadie; *m* 1957, Dr Marie Roslyn Bashir; one *s* two *d. Educ:* Sydney. Elected Alderman, City of Sydney, Dec. 1962; Dep. Lord Mayor, Sept. 1969–Sept. 1973; Lord Mayor of Sydney, Sept. 1973–Sept. 1975. Director: Rothmans Pall Mall (Aust.) Ltd; Wormald International Ltd; Mercantile Credits Ltd; Chm., Special Broadcasting Services. Rugby Union career: Captained NSW and Australia; played 30 Internationals and 6 overseas tours; Pres., Aust. Rugby Football Union; Mem., Barbarians'. Trustee, Sydney Cricket Ground. *Recreations:* Rugby, surfing, horse racing, bowls. *Address:* 118 Old Canterbury Road, Lewisham, Sydney, NSW, Australia. *Clubs:* Randwick Rugby, Tattersall's (Sydney).

SHELBOURNE, Sir Philip, Kt 1984; Chairman, Britoil plc, since 1982; *b* 15 June 1924; *s* of late Leslie John Shelbourne. *Educ:* Radley Coll.; Corpus Christi Coll., Oxford (MA); Harvard Law School. Called to Bar, Inner Temple, Hon. Bencher 1984. Barrister specialising in taxation, 1951–62; Partner, N. M. Rothschild & Sons, 1962–70; Chief Exec., Drayton Corp., 1971–72; Chm., Drayton Gp and Drayton Corp., 1973–74; Chm. and Chief Exec., Samuel Montagu & Co., 1974–80; Chm. and Chief Exec., BNOC, 1980–82. *Recreation:* music. *Address:* Britoil plc, Stornoway House, Cleveland Row, SW1A 1DH. *Club:* Brooks's.

SHELBURNE, Earl of; Charles Maurice Petty-Fitzmaurice; *b* 21 Feb. 1941; *s* and heir of 8th Marquess of Lansdowne, *qv; m* 1965, Lady Frances Eliot, *o d* of 9th Earl of St Germans, *qv;* two *s* two *d. Educ:* Eton. Page of Honour to The Queen, 1956–57. Served with Kenya Regt, 1960–61; with Wiltshire Yeomanry (TA), amalgamated with Royal Yeomanry Regt, 1963–73. Pres., Wiltshire Playing Fields Assoc., 1965–74; Wiltshire County Councillor, 1970–85; Mem., South West Economic Planning Council, 1972–77; Chairman: Working Committee Population & Settlement Pattern (SWEPC), 1972–77; North Wiltshire DC, 1973–76; Mem., Calne and Chippenham RDC, 1964–73. Mem., Historic Bldgs and Monuments Commn, 1983–. President: Wiltshire Assocs Boys Clubs and Youth Clubs, 1976–; North-West Wiltshire District Scout Council, 1977–. Contested (C) Coventry North East, 1979. *Heir: s* Viscount Calne and Calstone, *qv. Address:* Bowood House, Calne, Wiltshire SN11 0LZ. *T:* Calne 813343; Flat 2, 99 Lexham Gardens, W8. *Clubs:* Turf, White's.

SHELDON, Hon. Sir Gervase; *see* Sheldon, Hon. Sir J. G. K.

SHELDON, Harold; County Councillor; *b* 22 June 1918; *s* of Charles Edwin Sheldon and Lily Sheldon (*née* Taylor); *m* 1941, Bessie Sheldon (*née* Barratt); two *s* one *d*. HM Forces, 1939–45 (Sgt; wounded D Day landings). Local Government: elected Batley Borough Council, 1953; Mayor of Batley, 1962–63; W Yorkshire County Council, 1973– (Chm., May 1976–May 1977); re-elected 1977, 1981. Chairman: Batley Sports Develt Council, 1965–; Kirklees Dist Sports Council, 1974–; Mem., Yorks and Humberside Council for Sport and Recreation, 1977–86; Pres., Batley Boys' Club (Founder Mem.). *Address:* 5 Norfolk Avenue, Carlton Grange, Batley, West Yorkshire. *T:* Batley 473619.

SHELDON, John Denby; General Secretary, Civil Service Union, since 1982; *b* 31 Jan. 1941; *s* of Frank and Doreen Sheldon; *m* 1976; two *s. Educ:* Wingate County Primary and West Leeds High School. Oxford Univ. Diploma in Social Studies. Post Office Engineer, 1957–68; student, Ruskin Coll., 1968–70; full time Trade Union Official, Instn of Professional Civil Servants, 1970–72; National Officer, Civil Service Union, 1972–78; Deputy Gen. Sec., 1978–82. *Recreations:* cricket; Rugby League as spectator; family; representing the working man. *Address:* 2 Wincroft Road, Reading, Berks RG4 7HH. *T:* Reading 477810.

SHELDON, Hon. Sir (John) Gervase (Kensington), Kt 1978; **Hon. Mr Justice Sheldon;** a Judge of the High Court, Family Division, since 1978; *b* 4 Oct. 1913; *s* of John Henry Sheldon, MD, DPH, and Eleanor Gladys Sheldon, MB, BS; *m* 1st, 1940, Patricia Mary Mardon; one *s*; 2nd, 1960, Janet Marguerite Seager; two *s* one *d. Educ:* Winchester Coll.; Trinity Coll., Cambridge (MA; 1st Cl. Hons Law). Barrister-at-Law, called Lincoln's Inn, 1939 (Cert. of Honour, Cholmeley Schol.), Bencher, 1978. Served RA (TA), 1939–45 (despatches twice): Egypt, N Africa, Italy; Major, RA, 1943. A Circuit Judge (formerly a County Court Judge), 1968–78; Presiding Judge, Western Circuit, 1980–84. *Recreation:* family and home. *Address:* Hopton, Churt, Surrey GU10 2LD. *T:* Frensham 2035. *Club:* United Oxford & Cambridge University.

SHELDON, Rt. Hon. Robert (Edward), PC 1977; MP (Lab) Ashton-under-Lyne, since 1964; *b* 13 Sept. 1923; *m* 1st, 1945, Eileen Shamash (*d* 1969); one *s* one *d*; 2nd 1971, Mary Shield. *Educ:* Elementary and Grammar Schools; Engineering Apprenticeship; Technical Colleges in Stockport, Burnley and Salford; WhSch 1944. Engineering diplomas; external graduate, London University. Contested Withington, Manchester, 1959; Chm., Labour Parly Economic Affairs and Finance Group, 1967–68; Opposition Front Bench Spokesman on Civil Service and Machinery of Govt, also on Treasury matters, 1970–74; Minister of State, CSD, March-Oct. 1974; Minister of State, HM Treasury, Oct. 1974–June 1975; Financial Sec. to the Treasury, 1975–79; Opposition front bench spokesman on Treasury matters, 1981–83; Chm., Public Accounts Cttee, 1983– (Mem., 1965–70, 1975–79); Member: Public Expenditure Cttee (Chm. Gen. Sub-Cttee), 1972–74; Select Cttee on Treasury and Civil Service, 1979–81 (Chm., Sub-Cttee); Fulton Cttee on the Civil Service, 1966–68. Chm., NW Gp of Labour MPs, 1970–74. Dir, Manchester Chamber of Commerce, 1964–74, 1979–. *Recreations:* various crafts. *Address:* 27 Darley Avenue, Manchester M20 8ZD; 2 Ryder Street, SW1.

SHELFORD, Cornelius William, DL; retired; *b* 6 July 1908; *s* of William Heard Shelford and Maud Ethel Shelford, Horncastle, Sharpthorne, Sussex, and Singapore; *m* 1934, Helen Beatrice Hilda Schuster; one *s* two *d. Educ:* private tutor and Trinity College, Cambridge. Chartered Accountant, 1934; Partner, Rowley Pemberton & Co., 1940 (retd 1960); Chm., Mills & Allen Ltd, 1964 (retd 1969); Chm., London County Freehold & Leasehold Properties Ltd, 1964 (retd 1970). East Sussex CC, 1952 (CA, 1957; Chm., 1964–67; Chm., Finance Cttee, 1970–74); High Sheriff of Sussex, 1954; DL Sussex, 1968–. *Recreations:* travelling, walking, gardening. *Address:* Chailey Place, near Lewes, E Sussex BN8 4DA. *T:* Newick 2881. *Club:* Carlton.

SHELLEY, Alan John; Senior Partner, Knight, Frank & Rutley, since 1983; *b* 7 Aug. 1931; *s* of Stanley and Ivy Shelley; *m* 1958, Josephine (*née* Flood); one *s* one *d. Educ:* People's College, Nottingham. FRICS. Senior Partner, Knight, Frank & Rutley (Nigeria), 1965; Dir, JHI Ltd, 1981. General Commissioner of Income Tax, 1984–. Chm., W Africa Cttee, 1985–. *Recreations:* theatre, squash. *Address:* 54 Bathurst Mews, W2. *T:* 01–262 1991; Thatch Farm, Glaston, Rutland, Leics. *T:* Uppingham 2396. *Clubs:* Oriental, MCC.

SHELLEY, Charles William Evans; Charity Commissioner, 1968–74; *b* 15 Aug. 1912; *s* of George Shelley and Frances Mary Anne Shelley (*née* Dain); *m* 1939, Patricia May Dolby; three *d* (and one *d* decd). *Educ:* Alleyn's Sch., Dulwich; Fitzwilliam House, Cambridge. Called to Bar, Inner Temple, 1937; practised at the Bar, to 1940. Served in Army: first in RAPC and later in Dept of Judge Advocate-General, rank Major, 1940–47. Joined Charity Commn as Legal Asst, 1947; Sen. Legal Asst, 1958; Dep. Comr, 1964. *Recreations:* English literature, listening to music, mountaineering. *Address:* Pen y Bryn, Llansilin, Oswestry, Salop. *T:* Llansilin 273. *Club:* Camping.

SHELLEY, James Edward; Secretary to Church Commissioners, since 1985; *b* 1932; *s* of Vice-Adm. Richard Shelley and Eve Cecil; *m* 1956, Judy Grubb; two *s* two *d. Educ:* Eton; University College, Oxford (MA). Joined Church Commissioners' staff, 1954; Under Secretary General, 1976–81; Assets Secretary, 1981–85. *Recreations:* country pursuits. *Address:* Church Commissioners, 1 Millbank, SW1P 3JZ. *T:* 01-222 7010; Mays Farm House, Ramsdell, Basingstoke, Hants RG27 5RE. *T:* Basingstoke 850770. *Club:* Naval and Military.

SHELLEY, Sir John (Richard), 11th Bt *cr* 1611; (professionally Dr J. R. Shelley); general medical practitioner; Partner, Drs Shelley, Newth and Doddington (formerly Durstan-Smith, Shelley and Newth), Health Centre, South Molton, Devon, since 1974; *b* 18 Jan. 1943; *s* of John Shelley (*d* 1974), and of Dorothy, *d* of Arthur Irvine Ingram; *S* grandfather, 1976; *m* 1965, Clare, *d* of Claud Bicknell, *qv;* two *d. Educ:* King's Sch., Bruton; Trinity Coll., Cambridge (BA 1964, MA 1967); St Mary's Hosp., London Univ. MB, BChir 1967; DObstRCOG 1969; MRCGP 1978. Partner in Drs Harris, Barkworth, Savile, Shelley and Gurney, Eastbourne, Sx, 1969–74. Member: Exeter Diocesan Synod for South Molton Deanery, 1976–79; BMA; CLA; NFU. *Heir: b* Thomas Henry Shelley [*b* 3 Feb. 1945; *m* 1970, Katherine Mary Holton; three *d*]. *Address:* Molford House, 27 South Street, South Molton, Devon EX36 4AA. *T:* South Molton 3101.

SHELLEY, Ursula, MD, FRCP; retired 1971; Physician to Royal Free Hospital's Children's Department, 1940–71 (Assistant Physician, 1935–40), to Princess Louise (Kensington) Hospital for Children, 1944–71 (Assistant Physician, 1937–44), and to Queen Elizabeth Hospital for Children, 1946–71; *b* 11 Apr. 1906; *d* of Frederick Farey Shelley, FIC, and Rachel Hicks Shelley, MB, BS. *Educ:* St Paul's Girls' School; Royal Free Hospital School of Medicine. MB, BS Lond., Univ. Gold Medal, 1930; MD Lond., 1932; FRCP 1948. Examiner: Coll. of Physicians, 1960–70; Univ. of London, 1965–70. Vice-Pres., Nat. Assoc. of Family Life and Child Care (formerly Nat. Assoc. of Nursery Matrons), 1968– (Pres., 1960–65); Member: Medical Women's Fedn, 1936–; British Pædiatric Assoc., 1946–85. Liveryman, Worshipful Soc. of Apothecaries; Freeman of City of London, 1950. *Publications:* numerous articles in medical journals. *Recreations:* gardening, lion dogs. *Address:* 15 Hyde Park Gate, SW7 5DG. *T:* 01-584 7941; Threeways, 2 Mincing Lane, Chobham GU24 8RX.

SHELTON, Shirley Megan, (Mrs W. T. Shelton); Editor, What's Cooking?, since 1985; *b* 8 March 1934; *d* of Lt-Col T. F. Goodwin; *m* 1960, William Timothy Shelton; one *s* two *d. Educ:* various institutions. Home Editor, 1970–75, Assistant Editor, 1975–78, Editor, 1978–82, Woman and Home magazine. *Address:* 59 Croftdown Road, NW5 1EL. *T:* 01-485 4936.

SHELTON, William Jeremy Masefield, MA Oxon; MP (C) Streatham, since 1974 (Clapham, 1970–74); *b* 30 Oct. 1929; *s* of late Lt-Col R. C. M. Shelton, MBE, St Saviour's, Guernsey, and Mrs R. E. P. Shelton (*née* Coode), London Place, Oxford; *m* 1960, Anne Patricia, *o d* of John Arthur Warder, *qv;* one *s* one *d. Educ:* Radley Coll.; Tabor Academy, Marion, Mass; Worcester Coll., Oxford; Univ. of Texas, Austin, Texas. Colman, Prentis & Varley Ltd, 1952–55; Corpa, Caracas, Venezuela, 1955–60; Managing Director: CPV (Colombiana) Ltd, Bogota, Colombia, 1960–64; CPV (International) Ltd, 1967–74 (Dir, 1964); Grosvenor Advertising Ltd, 1969–74 (Dir, 1964); Chairman: Fletcher, Shelton, Delaney & Reynolds Ltd, 1974–81; GGK London Ltd, 1984–86. Member for Wandsworth, GLC, 1967–70; Chief Whip, on ILEA, 1968–70. PPS to Minister of Posts and Telecommunications, 1972–74; PPS to Rt Hon. Margaret Thatcher, MP, 1975; Parly Under-Sec. of State, DES, 1981–83. *Recreations:* golf, reading, painting. *Address:* 27 Ponsonby Terrace, SW1. *T:* 01-821 8204; The Manor House, Long Crendon, Bucks. *T:* Long Crendon 208748. *Club:* Carlton.

SHENFIELD, Dame Barbara (Estelle), DBE 1986; Chairman, Women's Royal Voluntary Service, since 1981 (Vice Chairman, 1976–81); *d* of George and Jane Farrow, Bearwood, Staffs; *m* 1st, Flt-Lt Gwilym Ivor Lewis, RAF (killed in action); one *s;* 2nd, Arthur A. Shenfield; one *s. Educ:* Langley High Sch., Worcs; Univ. of Birmingham (Hons Social and Political Science). Lectr in Soc. Studies, Univ. of Birmingham, 1945–56; Lectr, Dept of Econs and Soc. Studies, Bedford Coll., London Univ., 1959–65; Academic Dir, UC at Buckingham, 1972–73. Visiting Professor: Michigan State Univ., 1960; Temple Univ., Philadelphia, 1974; Distinguished Vis. Prof., Rockford Coll., Ill, 1969–71, 1974. Consultant, US Dept of Labor, 1964; Dir, PEP Study of Co. Bds' Soc. Responsibilities, 1965–68. Member: UK Govt Cttee on Local Taxation, 1965–66; UK Govt Cttee on Abuse of Welfare Services, 1971–73; Govt Review Team on Social Security, 1984–85. Chm., Nat Exec., Nat. Old People's Welfare Council (now Age Concern), 1971–73. *Publications:* Social Policies for Old Age, 1957; The Social Responsibilities of Company Boards, 1971; The Organisation of a Voluntary Service, 1972; monographs and articles on gerontological and other social subjects. *Recreations:* gardening, music, viticulture. *Address:* 1 Albert Court, Prince Consort Road, SW7 2BE. *T:* 01-581 0363.

SHEPARD, Giles Richard Carless; Managing Director, Savoy Hotel plc, since 1979; *b* 1 April 1937; *er s* of Richard S. H. Shepard, MC, TD; *m* 1966, Peter Carolyn Fern Keighley; one *s* one *d. Educ:* Heatherdown, Ascot; Eton (King's Scholar); Harvard Business School (PMD 1967). Commissioned Coldstream Guards, 1955–60. Director: Charrington & Co., 1960–64; H. P. Bulmer & Co., 1964–70; Managing Director: Findlater Mackie, Todd, 1967–70; Westminster & Country Properties, 1970–76; Director: Dorchester Hotel, 1972–76; Savoy Hotel, 1976–79. Mem., Court of Assistants, Fishmongers' Co. (Renter Warden, 1986–87); High Sheriff of Greater London, 1986–87. Governor, Gresham's School, Holt, 1980–. *Recreations:* gardening, shooting, tennis. *Address:* 1 Savoy Hill, WC2R 0BP. *T:* 01-836 1533. *Clubs:* White's, Pratt's.

SHEPHARD, George Clifford, CBE 1979; retired as NCB Board Member for Industrial Relations, 1969–80, now Consultant; Member, Paul Finet Foundation, since 1974; *b* 2 Aug. 1915; British; *m* 1942, Mollie Dorothy Mansfield; one *s* (one *d* decd). *Educ:* Chesterfield Grammar School. Bolsover Colliery Co. Ltd, Head Office, 1933–40. Served in Army, N Africa, various Comd HQs, 1940–45, commnd 1942. Official, National Union of Mineworkers, 1945–69. Director, 1969–80: Coal Products Div., NCB; Associated Heat Services Ltd; Compower Ltd; British Investment; former Dir, Inst. of Occupational Medicine. Member: CBI Cttees; ECSC. Jt Hon. Sec., Coal Industry Social Welfare Organisation; Chm., Mineworkers' Pension Scheme. Editor, various bulletins and tracts, FCIS, ACMA, CBIM. *Recreations:* golf, music. *Address:* 27 Chiswick Quay, Hartington Road, W4. *T:* 01-995 7137. *Club:* Grimsdyke Golf.

SHEPHARD, Air Cdre Harold Montague, CBE 1974 (OBE 1959); Provost Marshal (RAF) and Director of Security, 1971–74, retired; *b* 15 Aug. 1918; *s* of late Rev. Leonard B. Shephard; *m* 1939, Margaret Isobel (*née* Girdlestone); one *s* one *d. Educ:* St John's, Leatherhead. Metropolitan Police (CID), 1937–41. Served War, RAF, 1941; commissioned for Provost duties, 1943. Seconded Public Safety Br., CCG, 1945; Wing Comdr, SIB, BAFO, 1947–50; OC, RAF Police Sch., 1951–52; DAPM, Hong Kong; PMI, Air Ministry; Command Provost Marshal, Cyprus; OC, 4 RAF Police District; PM4, Air Ministry; Comdt, RAF Police Depot, Debden, 1963–64; CPM, FEAF, 1964–67; Comdt, Police Depot, 1967–69; Comd Provost and Security Officer, RAF Germany, 1969–71; Air Cdre, 1971. MBIM. *Recreations:* watching all sports, reading. *Address:* 6 Bennetts Mews, Tenterden, Kent. *Club:* Royal Air Force.

SHEPHEARD, Major-General Joseph Kenneth, CB 1962; DSO 1943, and Bar, 1945; OBE 1949; *b* 15 Nov. 1908; *s* of late J. D. Shepheard, Poole and Bournemouth; *m* 1939, Maureen, *d* of late Capt. R. McG. Bowen-Colthurst, Oak Grove, County Cork; three *d. Educ:* Monmouth School; RMA Woolwich; Christ's Coll., Cambridge (BA Hons). Commissioned RE, 1928; served in India with King George V's Own Bengal Sappers and Miners, 1933–38; served in France with BEF as Adjt 4 Div. RE, 1939–40; Staff College, Camberley, 1940; Bde Major 161 (Essex) Inf. Bde in UK, Sierra Leone and Western Desert, 1940–41; Bde Major 18 Indian Inf. Bde in Iraq, 1941; GSO1 4 Indian Div. in N Africa and Italy, 1942–44; Comd 6 Assault Regt RE, Normandy to Baltic, 1944–46; JSSC, Latimer, Bucks, 1947; GSO1, FarELF, 1948–49; Staff Officer to Dir of Operations, Malaya, 1950; Comd 27 Fd Enrg Regt and CRE 6 Armd Div., 1951–53; Defence Research Policy Staff, 1953–56; Imperial Defence Coll., 1957; CCRE 1 (Br.) Corps in Germany, 1958–60; Chief of Staff, Northern Comd, 1960–62; Chief Engineer, Northern Army Group and BAOR, 1962–64. Col Comdt, RE, 1967–72. Gen. Sec., The Officers' Assoc., 1966–74. *Address:* Comfrey Cottage, Fields Farm Lane, Layer-de-la-Haye, Colchester, Essex.

SHEPHEARD, Sir Peter (Faulkner), Kt 1980; CBE 1972; PPRIBA, MRTPI, PPILA; Architect, town planner and landscape architect in private practice since 1948 (Shepheard, Epstein & Hunter); Professor of Architecture and Environmental Design, Graduate School of Fine Arts, University of Pennsylvania, since 1971; *b* 11 Nov. 1913; *s* of Thomas Faulkner Shepheard, FRIBA, Liverpool; *m* 1943, Mary Bailey; one *s* one *d. Educ:* Birkenhead Sch.; Liverpool Sch. of Architecture. BArch. (1st Cl. Hons) Liverpool, 1936; Univ. Grad. Scholar in Civic Design, 1936–37. Asst to Derek Bridgwater, 1937–40; Min. of Supply, Royal Ordnance Factories, 1940–43; Min. of Town and Country Planning: technical officer, first on Greater London Plan (Sir Patrick Abercrombie's staff), later on research and master plan for Stevenage New Town, 1943–47. Dep. Chief Architect and Planner, Stevenage Develt Corp., 1947–48. Vis. Prof., Landscape Architecture, 1959 and 1962–71, and Dean of Fine Arts, 1971–79, Univ. of Pennsylvania. Member: Nat. Parks Commn, 1966–68; Countryside Commn, 1968–71; Royal Fine Art Commn, 1968–71; Environmental Bd, 1977–. Artistic Advr, Commonwealth War Graves Commn, 1977–. Works include: housing and schools for GLC and other authorities; Landscape of part of Festival of Britain South Bank Exhibition, London, 1951; Master plan and buildings for University of Lancaster; work for the Universities of Keele, Liverpool, Oxford, and Ghana, and for Winchester College; gardens in England and USA. President: RIBA, 1969–71; Architectural Association, 1954–55; Inst. of Landscape Architects, 1965–66. RIBA Distinction in Town Planning, 1956. Hon. FRAIC; Hon. FAIA. *Publications:* Modern Gardens, 1953; Gardens, 1969; various articles, lectures and broadcasts on architecture and landscape; drawings and illustrations of architecture and other things; illustr. A Book of Ducks, and Woodland Birds (King Penguins). *Recreations:* music and poetry; drawing, gardening and the study of natural history. *Address:* 60 Kingly Street, W1R 6EY. *T:* 01-734 8577. *Clubs:* Athenæum, Savile.

SHEPHEARD, Sir Victor (George), KCB 1954 (CB 1950); FEng 1976; Director: William Denny & Brothers Ltd, Shipbuilders and Engineers, Dumbarton, 1959–63; Marinite Ltd, 1961–73; Director of Research, British Ship Research Association, 1959–63; *b* 21 March 1893; *e s* of late V. G. Shepheard, Shortlands, Kent; *m* 1924, Florence (*d* 1984), *d* of late Capt. James Wood, Bridgwater. *Educ:* HM Dockyard School, Devonport; Royal Naval Coll., Greenwich. Royal Corps of Naval Constructors, 1915; Constructor Lieut, Grand Fleet, 1915–17; present at Battle of Jutland. Professor of Naval Architecture, RN College, Greenwich, 1934–39; Chief Constructor, 1939–42; Asst Director of Naval Construction, 1942–47; Deputy Director 1947–51; Director of Naval Construction, Admiralty, and Head of RCNC, 1951–58. Member Council Royal Inst. of Naval Architects, 1944–; Vice-Pres. 1952–; Hon. Vice-Pres., 1961; Treasurer, 1960–69. Hon. Vice-Pres., Soc. for Nautical Research; Member: Admty Adv. Cttee on Structural Steel; Cttee on application of Nuclear Power to Marine Purposes, 1961–63; HMS Victory Advisory Technical Cttee. Hon. Fell., NEC Inst.; Mem., Smeatonian Soc. of Civil Engineers, Pres., 1976; Liveryman of Worshipful Company of Shipwrights, Prime Warden, 1968; Board of Governors Cutty Sark Society; formerly Trustee, Nat. Maritime Museum. Froude Gold Medal for services to Naval Architecture and Shipbuilding, 1963. Chev. de la Légion d'Honneur, 1947. *Publications:* various papers to Professional Institutions. *Recreations:* gardening, music. *Address:* Manor Place, Manor Park, Chislehurst, Kent. *T:* 01-467 5455.

SHEPHERD, family name of **Baron Shepherd.**

SHEPHERD, 2nd Baron, *cr* 1946, of Spalding; **Malcolm Newton Shepherd,** PC 1965; Deputy Chairman, Sterling Group of Companies, since 1976; *b* 27 Sept. 1918; *s* of 1st Baron Shepherd, PC, and Ada Newton (*d* 1975); *S* father, 1954; *m* 1941, Allison Wilson Redmond; two *s. Educ:* Lower Sch. of John Lyon; Friends' Sch., Saffron Walden. War of 1939–45: commissioned RASC, 1941; served in Desert, N Africa, Sicily, Italy. Deputy Opposition Chief Whip, House of Lords, 1960. Member Parly Labour Party Exec., 1964; Deputy Speaker, House of Lords, subseq. Opposition Chief Whip, 1964; Captain of the Hon. Corps of Gentlemen-at-Arms and Government Chief Whip, House of Lords, 1964–67; Minister of State, FCO, 1967–70; Deputy Leader of the House of Lords, 1968–70; Opposition Dep. Leader, House of Lords, 1970–74; Lord Privy Seal and Leader, House of Lords, 1974–76, resigned. First Chm., CS Pay Res. Unit Bd, 1978–81; Chairman: MRC, 1978–82; Packaging Council, 1978–82; Nat. Bus Co., 1979–84; Pres., Centre Européen de l'Enterprise Publique, 1985–. *Recreation:* golf. *Heir: s* Hon. Graeme George Shepherd, *b* 6 January 1949. *Address:* 29 Kennington Palace Court, Sancroft Street, SE11. *T:* 01-582 6772. *Clubs:* Singapore, Tanglin, Royal Singapore Golf (Singapore).

SHEPHERD, Alan Arthur, CBE 1984; PhD; FEng 1986; FIEE; FInstP; Managing Director, Ferranti Electronics Ltd, since 1978; *b* 6 Sept. 1927; *s* of Arthur and Hannah Shepherd; *m* 1953, Edith Hudson; two *d. Educ:* Univ. of Manchester (BSc, MSc, PhD). Lectr, Physics Dept, Univ. of Keele, 1950–54; Ferranti Ltd: Chief Engineer, Electronic Components Div., 1954–67; Gen. Manager, Instrument Dept, 1967–70; Gen. Manager, Electronic Components Div., 1970–78; Mem. Main Board, Ferranti plc, 1981; Chm., Ferranti California Group of Cos. *Publication:* The Physics of Semiconductors, 1957. *Recreations:* golf, swimming, photography. *Address:* 53 Broadway, Bramhall, Cheshire SK7 3BU. *T:* 061-439 2824. *Club:* St James's (Manchester).

SHEPHERD, Archie; HM Diplomatic Service, retired; Counsellor and Head of Migration and Visa Department, Foreign and Commonwealth Office, 1977–80; *b* 2 Nov. 1922; *s* of William Shepherd and Edith (*née* Browning); *m* 1959, Dorothy Annette Walker; one *s. Educ:* Torquay Grammar Sch. Prison Commission, 1939; served War, RAF, 1942–46. Foreign Office, 1949; Asst Political Agent and Vice Consul, Muscat, 1951–53; FO, 1954–55; Second Sec., UK Delegn to United Nations, Geneva, 1956–57; HM Consul: Warsaw, 1958–60; Rabat, 1960–62; FO, 1963–67; Consul, Cape Town, 1968–72; First Sec. (Commercial), Beirut, 1973–75. *Recreations:* tennis, gardening. *Address:* 9 Oaks Way, Kenley, Surrey. *T:* 01–660 1299. *Clubs:* Civil Service, Royal Commonwealth Society.

SHEPHERD, Rear-Adm. Charles William Haimes, CB 1972; CBE 1968 (OBE 1958); *b* 10 Dec. 1917; *s* of William Henry Haimes Shepherd and Florence (*née* Hayter); *m* 1940, Myra Betty Joan Major; one *s. Educ:* Public Central Sch., Plymouth; HMS Fisgard and RNC Greenwich. Entered RN as Artificer Apprentice, 1933; specialised Engrg Officer, 1940; served War of 1939–45 in HMS: Repulse; Hero; Royal Sovereign; Gambia (RNZN); Staff of C-in-C Pacific (Sydney); R&D, Guided Weapons, 1946–49 and 1954–58 incl. Flotilla Eng Officer 3rd Trng Flotilla (HMS Crispin), 1949–51; Sen. Officers War Course, 1961–62; Tech. Dir, UK Polaris Weapon System, 1962–68; Dir Project Teams (Submarines), and Dep. Asst Controller (Polaris), MoD (Navy), 1968–71; Dep. Controller (Polaris), MoD, 1971–73. Sub-Lt 1940; Lieut 1941; Lt-Comdr 1949; Comdr 1952; Captain 1960; Rear-Adm. 1970; retired 1974. Pres., Plymouth Albion RFC. *Address:* 5 Underhill Road, Stoke, Plymouth PL3 4BP. *T:* Plymouth 556888. *Clubs:* Royal Western Yacht; Royal Plymouth Corinthian Yacht.

SHEPHERD, Colin; MP (C) Hereford, since Oct. 1974; *b* 13 Jan. 1938; *s* of late T. C. R. Shepherd, MBE; *m* 1966, Louise, *d* of late Lt-Col E. A. M. Cleveland, MC. *Educ:* Oundle; Caius Coll., Cambridge; McGill Univ., Montreal. RCN, 1959–63. Dir, Haigh Engineering Co. Ltd, 1963–. Jt Sec., Cons. Parly Agr. Fish. and Food Cttee, 1975–79, Vice-Chm., 1979–; Mem., Select Cttee on H of C Services, 1979–; Sec., Cons. Parly Hort. Sub-Cttee, 1976–; Chm., Library Sub-Cttee, 1983–. *Address:* House of Commons, SW1A 0AA; Manor House, Ganarew, near Monmouth, Gwent. *T:* Symonds Yat 890220. *Club:* Naval.

SHEPHERD, David; *see* Shepherd, R. D.

SHEPHERD, Eric William, CB 1967; *b* London, 17 May 1913; *s* of late Charles Thomas Shepherd; *m* 1938, Marie Noele Carpenter; two *d. Educ:* Hackney Downs School; The Polytechnic, Regent Street. BSc 1st Class Hons (Maths and Physics) London 1932. Entered Post Office as Executive Officer, 1932. Served War of 1939–45, with Royal Engineers (Postal Section), 1940–46. Principal, Post Office, 1948; Treasury, 1949–52; Asst Accountant General, Post Office, 1952; Dep. Comptroller and Accountant General, 1953; Assistant Secretary, 1956; Director of Finance and Accounts, 1960; Senior Director, 1967–73. *Recreations:* music, especially choral singing, golf. *Address:* 2 Arkley View, Arkley, Barnet, Herts. *T:* 01–449 9316.

SHEPHERD, Geoffrey Thomas, CBE 1979; FIMechE, FIEE; management and engineering consultant, since 1982; *b* 1922; *s* of Thomas Henry and Louise Shepherd; *m* Irene Wilkes; one *d. Educ:* King Edward's Sch., Birmingham; Coll. of Technology, Birmingham. BSc (Hons). GEC Ltd; British Electricity Authority (several positions in power stations); Nuclear Ops Engr, CEGB, 1958–61; Asst Regional Dir (Western Div.), 1962–65; South of Scotland Electricity Bd, 1965, becoming Dir of Engineering, 1968–69; Dep. Chm., LEB, 1969–72; Chm., Midlands Electricity Bd, 1972–82; part-time Mem., CEGB, 1977–82. Chm., Worcestershire Cttee, VSO, 1975–81. Pres., IEE, 1986–87. Hon. DSc Aston, 1986. *Recreations:* fair weather sailing, railways. *Address:* Avon Reach, Church Street, Wyre Piddle, Pershore, Worcs. *T:* Pershore 553076.

SHEPHERD, George Anthony, CMG 1986; HM Diplomatic Service; Counsellor, British High Commission, New Delhi, 1982–86; *b* 8 Sept. 1931; *m* 1961, Sarah Eirlys Adamson; one *s* two *d. Educ:* Blundell's School; RMA Sandhurst. Served 4th Royal Tank Regt, in Egypt and BAOR, 1951–57; Trucial Oman Scouts, 1957–59; 2nd RTR, 1959–60; Durham Univ., 1960–61; Federal Regular Army, Aden, 1961–64; 2nd RTR, 1965; Asst Defence Adviser, British High Commission, Lagos, 1967–69; retd as Major RTR, 1969. 1st Secretary, FCO, Bahrain, Dubai and Islamabad, 1969–82. Life Member, Fauna Preservation Soc., 1964. *Publications:* Arabian Adventure, 1961; Flight of the Unicorns, 1964. *Recreations:* walking, bird watching, poetry. *Address:* c/o Foreign and Commonwealth Office, SW1. *Club:* Army and Navy.

SHEPHERD, James Rodney; Under-Secretary, Department of Trade and Industry (formerly Department of Industry), since 1980; *b* 27 Nov. 1935; *s* of Richard James Shepherd and Winifred Mary Shepherd. *Educ:* Blundell's; Magdalen Coll., Oxford (PPE; Diploma in Statistics). National Inst. of Economic and Social Res., 1960–64; Consultant to OECD, 1964; HM Treasury, 1965–80 (Under-Sec., 1975–80). *Publications:* articles in technical jls. *Address:* 32 Addison Grove, Bedford Park, W4. *T:* 01–995 7577.

SHEPHERD, John Alan; HM Diplomatic Service; Head of European Community Department (External), Foreign and Commonwealth Office, since 1985; *b* 27 April 1943; *s* of William (Mathieson) Shepherd and (Elsie) Rae Shepherd; *m* 1969, Jessica Mary Nichols; one *d. Educ:* Charterhouse; Selwyn Coll., Cambridge (MA); Stanford Univ., Calif (MA). Merchant Navy, 1961; HM Diplomatic Service, 1965–: CO, 1965–66; MECAS, Lebanon, 1966–68; 3rd Sec., Amman, 1968–70; 2nd Sec., Rome, 1970–73; 1st Secretary: FCO, 1973–76; The Hague, 1977–80; First Sec., 1980–82, Counsellor and Hd of Chancery, 1982–84, Office of UK Rep. to EEC , Brussels. *Recreations:* hills, birds, books, maps.

SHEPHERD, John Dodson, CBE 1979; Regional Administrator, Yorkshire Regional Health Authority, 1977–82, retired; *b* 24 Dec. 1920; *s* of Norman and Elizabeth Ellen Shepherd; *m* 1948, Marjorie Nettleton; one *s* two *d. Educ:* Barrow Grammar School. RAF, 1940–46: N Africa, Italy, Middle East, 1943–46. Asst Sec., Oxford RHB, 1956–58; Dep. Sec., Newcastle upon Tyne HMC, 1958–62; Sec., East Cumberland HMC, 1962–67; Sec., Liverpool RHB, 1967–73; Reg. Administrator, Mersey RHA, 1973–77. Pres., Inst. of Health Service Administrators, 1974–75 (Mem. Council, 1969–78). *Recreations:* golf, music. *Address:* 14 Leconfield Garth, Follifoot, Harrogate HG3 1NF. *T:* Harrogate 870520. *Clubs:* Harrogate Golf, Harrogate Rotary.

SHEPHERD, Dame Margaret (Alice), DBE 1964 (CBE 1962); Chairman, Haigh Engineering Co. Ltd, Ross-on-Wye; *b* 1910; *d* of Percy S. Turner, Redcourt, Pyrford; *m* 1935, Thomas Cropper Ryley Shepherd (*d* 1975); three *s* one *d. Educ:* Wimbledon, Lausanne and London Univ. Chairman: Conservative and Unionist Women's National Advisory Cttee, 1960–63; Conservative Political Centre National Advisory Cttee, 1966–69; Chm., 1963–64, Pres., 1972–73, Nat. Union of Conservative and Unionist Assocs. Mem. House of Laity, Gen. Synod of C of E, 1980–85. *Recreations:* swimming, gardening. *Address:* Moraston House, Bridstow, Ross-on-Wye, Herefordshire. *T:* Ross-on-Wye 62370.

SHEPHERD, Air Vice-Marshal Melvin Clifford Seymour, CB 1975; OBE 1953; Chief Executive, Wine and Spirit Trades Benevolent Society, since 1980; *b* 22 Oct. 1922; *s* of Clifford Charles Golding Shepherd and Isabella Davidson Shepherd (*née* Kemp); *m* 1949; one *s. Educ:* in South Africa. Commnd SAAF 1942; war service N Africa, Sicily, Burma, 1942–45; joined RAF, 1947; comd No 73 (F) Sqdn Malta, 1950–53 psa 1954; Chief Ops Officer, Western Sector UK, 1954–57; Comdr No 15 MU Wroughton, 1957–60; Air Min. Air Plans, 1960–63; Dirg Staff, Jt Services Staff Coll., 1963–65; Chief Ops Officer, Far East Comd, 1966; ACOS (Intell.) 2ATAF, 1967–69; comd RAF Binbrook, 1969–72; SASO No 38 Gp, 1972–74; Dir of Ops (Air Defence and Overseas), 1974–75; AOA Strike Command, 1976–78. *Recreations:* golf, shooting, fishing, reading. *Club:* Royal Air Force.

SHEPHERD, Sir Peter (Malcolm), Kt 1976; CBE 1967; DL; FCIOB; Director: Shepherd Building Group Ltd (Chairman, 1958–86); Shepherd Construction Ltd, since 1940 (Chairman since 1958); *b* 18 Oct. 1916; *s* of Alderman Frederick Welton Shepherd and Mrs Martha Eleanor Shepherd; *m* 1940, Patricia Mary Welton; four *s. Educ:* Nunthorpe and Rossall Schs. Chairman: Wool, Jute and Flax ITB, 1964–74; Jt Cttee, Textile ITBs, 1966–74; Construction ITB, 1973–76; Mem. Council, CBI, 1976–. Chartered Inst. of Building: Pres., 1964–65; Mem., Nat. Council, 1956–; Vice-Chm., Professional Practice Bd, 1975– (Chm. 1963–75); Mem., Bd of Bldg Educn, 1957–75 (Chm. 1965–68). British Inst. of Management: Mem., Nat. Council, 1965–71; Mem., Bd of Fellows, 1969–73; Founder Chm., Yorks and N Lincs Adv. Bd, 1969–71. Mem., President's Consult. Cttee, Building Employers Confedn (formerly Nat. Fedn of Building Trades Employers), 1956–; Mem. Council, Fedn of Civil Eng Contractors, 1952–60; Founder Mem., TEC, 1973–79. Chm., York and N Yorks Scanner Trust, 1979–. Member: Co. of Merchant Adventurers of City of York (Governor, 1984–85); York Rotary Club. Mem. Court, York Univ., 1976–; Governor, St Peter's Sch., York, 1970–. DL N Yorks, 1981. FCIOB; CBIM; Hon. DSc Heriot-Watt, 1979; DUniv York, 1981. *Recreation:* sailing. *Address:* Galtres House, Rawcliffe Lane, York. *T:* York 24250. *Club:* Yorkshire (York).

SHEPHERD, Richard Charles Scrimgeour; MP (C) Aldridge-Brownhills, since 1979; *b* 6 Dec. 1942; *s* of late Alfred Reginald Shepherd and of Davida Sophia Wallace. *Educ:* LSE; Johns Hopkins Univ. (Sch. of Advanced Internat. Studies). Director: Shepherd Foods (London) Ltd, 1970–; Partridges of Sloane Street Ltd, 1972–. Mem., SE Econ. Planning Council, 1970–74. Underwriting Mem. of Lloyds, 1974–. Mem., Treasury and Civil Service Select Cttee, 1979–83; Secretary: Cons. Parly Industry Cttee, 1980–81; Cons. Parly European Cttee, 1980–81. *Recreations:* book collecting; searching for the Home Service on the wireless. *Address:* 14 Addison Road, W14. *T:* 01–603 7108. *Clubs:* Carlton, Beefsteak, Chelsea Arts.

SHEPHERD, (Richard) David, OBE 1980; artist; *b* 25 April 1931; *s* of Raymond Oxley Shepherd and Margaret Joyce Shepherd (*née* Williamson); *m* 1957, Avril Shirley Gaywood; four *d. Educ:* Stowe. Art trng under Robin Goodwin, 1950–53; started career as aviation artist (Founder Mem., Soc. of Aviation Artists). Frequent worldwide trips for aviation and paintings for Services. Exhibited, RA, 1956; began painting African wild life, 1960. First London one-man show, 1962; painted 15 ft reredos of Christ for army garrison church, Bordon, 1964; 2nd London exhibn, 1965; Johannesburg exhibns, 1966 and 1969; exhibn, Tryon Gall., London, 1978. Painted: HE Dr Kaunda, President of Zambia, 1967; HM the Queen Mother for King's Regt, 1969; HE Sheikh Zaid of Abu Dhabi, 1970; 3rd London exhibn, 1971. BBC made 50-minute colour life documentary, The Man Who Loves Giants, for worldwide TV, 1970; auctioned 5 wildlife paintings in USA and raised sufficient to purchase Bell Jet Ranger helicopter to combat game poaching in Zambia, 1971; painted Tiger Fire (raised £127,500 for Operation Tiger), 1973; presented with 1896 steam locomotive by Pres. of Zambia (its return to Britain subject of BBC TV documentary, Last Train to Mulobezi); purchased 2 main line steam locomotives from BR, 1967 (92203 Black Prince, 75209 The Green Knight; ambition, to drive Black Prince into Waterloo); Founder Chm., E Somerset Railway. Mem. of Honour, World Wildlife Fund, 1979. Hon. DFA, Pratt Inst., New York, for services to wildlife conservation, 1971; Order of the Golden Ark, Netherlands, for services to wildlife conservation (Zambia, Operation Tiger, etc), 1973. *Publications:* Artist in Africa, 1967; (autobiog.) The Man who Loves Giants, 1975; Paintings of Africa and India, 1978; A Brush with Steam, 1983; David Shepherd: the man and his paintings, 1985. *Recreations:* driving steam engines, raising money for wildlife. *Address:* Winkworth Farm, Hascombe, Godalming, Surrey GU8 4JW. *T:* Hascombe 220.

SHEPHERD, Rt. Rev. Ronald Francis; *see* British Columbia, Bishop of.

SHEPHERD, Prof. William Morgan, DSc (London); Professor of Theoretical Mechanics in Faculty of Engineering, University of Bristol, 1959–71, Emeritus, 1971; *b* 19 Dec. 1905; *s* of Charles Henry and Elizabeth Shepherd; *m* 1932, Brenda Coulson; two *d. Educ:* Wellington School; University College of the South West, Exeter; University College, London. Asst lecturer and lecturer in mathematics, University College of North Wales, Bangor, 1928–35; Lecturer in mathematics in Faculty of Engineering, University of Bristol, 1935–44; Reader in Elasticity, University of Bristol, 1944–59; Head of Department of Theoretical Mechanics, 1951–71. *Publications:* various publications, mainly on applied mathematics, in Proceedings of the Royal Society and other scientific journals. *Recreations:* gardening, cricket. *Address:* 1 Thorpe Lodge, Cotham Side, Bristol BS6 5TJ. *T:* Bristol 426284.

SHEPHERD, William Stanley; *b* 1918; *s* of W. D. Shepherd; *m* 1942, Betty, *d* of late T. F. Howard, MP for Islington South, 1931–35; two *s.* Served in Army, War of 1939–45. A managing director of businesses which he has established; MP (C) for Cheadle Division of Cheshire, 1950–66 (Bucklow Division of Cheshire, 1945–50); Member of the Select Committee on Estimates; Joint Hon. Sec. Conservative Parliamentary Committee in Trade and Industry, 1945–51. Joined SDP, 1982. Hon. Mem., Valuers Institution. FREconS. *Address:* (office) 77 George Street, W1. *T:* 01–935 0753; (home) 33 Queens Grove, St John's Wood, NW8. *T:* 01–722 7526. *Club:* Savile.

SHEPPARD, Allen John George; Group Managing Director, Grand Metropolitan plc, since 1982; *b* 25 Dec. 1932; *s* of John Baggott Sheppard and Lily Marjorie Sheppard (*née* Palmer); *m* 1st, 1959, Peggy Damaris (*née* Jones) (marr. diss. 1980); 2nd, 1980, Mary (*née* Stewart). *Educ:* Ilford County School; London School of Economics (BSc Econ). FCMA, FCIS, ATII. Ford of Britain and Ford of Europe, 1958–68; Roots/Chrysler, 1968–71; British Leyland, 1971–75; Grand Metropolitan, 1975–; Non. Exec. Dir, later Chm., UBM Group, 1981–85; Chm., Mallinson-Denny Group, 1985–. Part time Mem., BR Board, 1985–. CBIM. *Publications:* Your Business Matters, 1958; articles in professional jls. *Recreations:* gardening, reading, red setter dogs. *Address:* Didgemere Hall, Low Hill Road, Roydon, near Harlow, Essex. *T:* 01–791 1233.

SHEPPARD, Rt. Rev. David Stuart; *see* Liverpool, Bishop of.

SHEPPARD, Francis Henry Wollaston; General Editor, Survey of London, 1954–82, retired; *b* 10 Sept. 1921; *s* of late Leslie Alfred Sheppard; *m* 1st, 1949, Pamela Gordon

Davies (*d* 1954); one *s* one *d*; 2nd, 1957, Elizabeth Fleur Lees; one *d*. *Educ:* Bradfield; King's Coll., Cambridge (MA); PhD London. FRHistS. Asst Archivist, West Sussex CC, Chichester, 1947–48; Asst Keeper, London Museum, 1948–53. Mayor of Henley on Thames, 1970–71; Pres., Henley Symphony Orchestra, 1973–76. Visiting Fellow, Leicester Univ., 1977–78; Alice Davis Hitchcock Medallion of Soc. of Architectural Historians of Gt Britain, 1964. *Publications:* Local Government in St Marylebone 1688–1835, 1958; London 1808–1870: The Infernal Wen, 1971; Brakspear's Brewery, Henley on Thames, 1779–1979, 1979; (ed) Survey of London, Vols XXVI-XLI, 1956–83. *Recreation:* music. *Address:* 55 New Street, Henley on Thames, Oxon RG9 2BP. *T:* Henley on Thames 574658.

SHEPPARD, Maurice Raymond, RWS; painter; President, Royal Society of Painters in Water-Colours, since 1984; *b* 25 Feb. 1947; *s* of late Wilfred Ernest Sheppard and of Florence Hilda (*née* Morris). *Educ:* Loughborough; Kingston upon Thames (Dip AD Hons 1970); Royal College of Art (MA 1973). ARWS 1974, RWS 1977, Vice-Pres., 1978–83. One man exhibition, New Grafton Gallery, 1979; works in: Royal Library, Windsor; V&A; Nat. Museum of Wales; Beecroft Museum and Art Gallery, Southend. *Relevant publication:* Maurice Sheppard, RWS, by Felicity Owen (Old Watercolour Society Club, vol. 59, 1984). *Recreations:* cycling, a small garden, the pursuit of quiet. *Address:* 8 Adelaide Road, Chislehurst, Kent BR7 6BB. *T:* Haverfordwest 2659.

SHEPPARD, Tan Sri Dato Mervyn Cecil ffranck, PSM (Malaysia) 1969; DPMS 1982; DJPD (Malaysia), 1967; JMN (Malaysia), 1963; CMG 1957; MBE 1946; ED 1947; Vice-President and Editor, Malaysian Branch, Royal Asiatic Society; *b* 1905; *s* of late Canon J. W. ff. Sheppard; *m* 1940, Rosemary, *d* of late Major Edward Oakeley; one *d*. *Educ:* Marlborough; Magdalene Coll., Cambridge (MA). Cadet, Federated Malay States, 1928; Private Sec. to Chief Sec., 1929. Interned by Japanese, 1942–45; Major, FMS Volunteer Force, retd 1946. Director of Public Relations, 1946; District Officer, Klang, 1947–50; British Adviser, Negri Sembilan, 1952; Head of the Emergency Food Denial Organisation, Federation of Malaya, 1956. First Keeper of Public Records, 1957–62, and Director of Museums, 1958–63, Federation of Malaya. Co-Founder and Vice-Pres., Heritage of Malaysia Trust, 1985. Hon. Curator, Nat. Museum, Kuala Lumpur. Hon. DLitt Univ. Sains Malaysia, 1984. Biennial Award, Tun Abdul Razak Foundn, 1983. Panglima Setia Mahkota, 1969; Dato Jasa Purba Di-Raja, Negri Sembilan, 1967; Dato Paduka Mahkota Selangor, 1982. *Publications:* Taman Indera, 1972; The Living Crafts of Malaysia, 1978; Memoirs of an Unorthodox Civil Servant, 1979; Tunku: a pictorial biography, 1984; Historic Malaysia, 1985. *Address:* Flat 7C, Crescent Court, Brickfields, Kuala Lumpur, Malaysia. *Clubs:* United Oxford & Cambridge University; Royal Selangor (Kuala Lumpur).

SHEPPARD, Prof. Norman, FRS 1967; Professor of Chemical Sciences, University of East Anglia, Norwich, 1964–86; *b* 16 May 1921; *s* of Walter Sheppard and Anne Clarges Sheppard (*née* Finding); *m* 1949, Kathleen Margery McLean; two *s* one *d* (and one *s* decd). *Educ:* Hymers Coll., Hull; St Catharine's Coll., Cambridge. BA Cantab 1st cl. hons 1943; PhD and MA Cantab 1947. Vis. Asst Prof., Pennsylvania State Univ., 1947–48; Ramsay Memorial Fellow, 1948–49; Senior 1851 Exhibn, 1949–51; Fellow of Trinity Coll., Cambridge and Asst Dir of Research in Spectroscopy, Cambridge Univ., 1957–64. *Publications:* scientific papers on spectroscopy in Proc. Roy. Soc., Trans. Faraday Soc., Jl Chem. Soc., Spectrochimica Acta, etc. *Recreations:* architecture, classical music, walking. *Address:* 5 Hornor Close, Norwich NR2 2LY. *T:* Norwich 53052.

SHEPPARD FIDLER, Alwyn G.; *see* Fidler.

SHEPPERD, Alfred Joseph; Chairman and Chief Executive: Wellcome plc, since 1986; The Wellcome Foundation Ltd, since 1977; Chairman, Burroughs Wellcome Co., since 1986; *b* 19 June 1925; *s* of Alfred Charles Shepperd and Mary Ann Williams; *m* 1950, Gabrielle Marie Yvette Bouloux; two *d*. *Educ:* Archbishop Tenison's Sch.; University Coll., London (BSc Econ; Fellow, 1986). Rank Organisation, 1949; Selincourt & Sons Ltd, 1963; Chamberlain Group, 1965; Managing Director, Keyser Ullmann Industries Ltd, 1967; Dir, Keyser Ullmann Ltd, 1967; Financial Dir, Laporte Industries Ltd, 1971, Wellcome Foundation Ltd, 1972; Dir, Anglia Maltings (Holdings) Ltd, 1972–. *Address:* The Wellcome Foundation Ltd, PO Box 129, 183 Euston Road, NW1 2BP. *Clubs:* Athenæum, Naval, Oriental.

SHEPPERSON, Prof. George Albert; William Robertson Professor of Commonwealth and American History, University of Edinburgh, 1963–86, now Emeritus; Visiting Scholar, W. E. B. DuBois Institute for Afro American Research, Harvard University, Oct. 1986–87; *b* 7 Jan. 1922; *s* of late Albert Edward Shepperson and Bertha Agnes (*née* Jennings); *m* 1952, Joyce Irene (*née* Cooper); one *d*. *Educ:* King's Sch., Peterborough; St John's Coll., Cambridge (Schol.; 1st Class Hons: English Tripos, Pt I, 1942; Historical Tripos, Pt II, 1947); 1st Cl. CertEd (Cantab), 1948. Served War, commnd Northamptonshire Regt, seconded to KAR, 1942–46. Edinburgh University: Lectr in Imperial and American History, 1948, Sen. Lectr, 1960, Reader, 1961; Dean of Faculty of Arts, 1974–77. Visiting Professor: Roosevelt and Chicago Univs, 1959; Makerere Coll., Uganda, 1962; Dalhousie Univ., 1968–69; Rhode Is Coll., 1984; Lectures: Herskovits Meml, Northwestern Univ., 1966 and 1972; Livingstone Centenary, RGS, 1973; Soc. of the Cincinnati, State of Virginia, 1976; Sarah Tryphena Phillips, in Amer. Lit. and Hist., British Acad., 1979; Rhodes Commem., Rhodes Univ., 1981. Chairman: British Assoc. for American Studies, 1971–74; Mungo Park Bicentenary Cttee, 1971; David Livingstone Documentation Project, 1973–; Commonwealth Inst., Scotland, 1973–. Jt Editor, Oxford Studies in African Affairs, 1969–85. *Publications:* Independent African: John Chilembwe, 1958, 3rd edn 1969; David Livingstone and the Rovuma, 1964; many articles and chapters in learned jls, collaborative vols and encycs. *Recreations:* theatre; collecting African and Afro-American documents. *Address:* 23 Ormidale Terrace, Edinburgh EH12 6DY. *T:* 031-337 4424.

SHER, Samuel Julius; QC 1981; *b* 22 Oct. 1941; *s* of Philip and Isa Phyllis Sher; *m* 1965, Sandra Maris; one *s* two *d*. *Educ:* Athlone High Sch., Johannesburg; Univ. of the Witwatersrand (BComm, LLB); New Coll., Oxford (BCL). Called to the Bar, Inner Temple, 1968. *Recreation:* tennis. *Address:* 12 Constable Close, NW11 6TY. *T:* 01–455 2753.

SHERBORNE, Area Bishop of; Rt. Rev. John Dudley Galtrey Kirkham; appointed Bishop Suffragan of Sherborne, 1976; Canon and Prebendary of Salisbury Cathedral, since 1977; *b* 20 Sept. 1935; *s* of Canon Charles Dudley Kirkham and Doreen Betty Galtrey; *m* 1986, Mrs Hester Gregory. *Educ:* Lancing Coll.; Trinity Coll., Cambridge (BA 1959, MA 1963). Commnd, Royal Hampshire Regt and seconded to 23 (K) Bn, King's African Rifles, 1954–56. Trinity Coll., Cambridge, 1956–59; Westcott House, 1960–62; Curate, St Mary-Le-Tower, Ipswich, 1962–65; Chaplain to Bishop of Norwich, 1965–69; Priest in Charge, Rockland St Mary w. Hellington, 1967–69; Chaplain to Bishop of New Guinea, 1969; Asst Priest, St Martin in the Fields and St Margaret's, Westminster, 1970–72; Domestic Chaplain to Archbishop of Canterbury, 1972–76; Canterbury Diocesan Director of Ordinands, 1972–76. Serving Brother Chaplain of the Order of St John of Jerusalem; Chaplain to the Guild of the Nineteen Lubricators. Croix d'Argent de Saint-Rombaut, 1973. *Recreations:* skiing, walking, wood-work, reading. *Address:* Little Bailie, Sturminster Marshall, Wimborne, Dorset BH21 4AD. *Clubs:* Army and Navy, Ski of Great Britain, Kandahar.

SHERBORNE, Archdeacon of; *see* Oliver, Ven. J. K.

SHERBOURNE, Stephen Ashley; Political Secretary to the Prime Minister, since 1983; *b* 15 Oct. 1945; *s* of Jack and Blanche Sherbourne. *Educ:* Burnage Grammar Sch., Manchester; St Edmund Hall, Oxford (BA PPE). Hill Samuel, 1968–70; Conservative Research Dept, 1970–75: Head of Economic Section, 1973–74; Asst Dir, 1974–75; Head of Rt Hon. Edward Heath's Office, 1975–76; Gallaher, 1978–82; Special Adviser to Rt Hon. Patrick Jenkin, (then) Sec. of State for Industry, 1982–83. *Recreations:* cinema, tennis. *Address:* 139 Hurlingham Road, SW6 3NH. *T:* 01–736 5192. *Club:* Reform.

SHERBROOKE, Archbishop of, (RC), since 1968; **Most Rev. Jean-Marie Fortier;** *b* 1 July 1920. *Educ:* Laval University, Quebec. Bishop Auxiliary, La Pocatière, PQ, 1961–65; Bishop of Gaspé, PQ, 1965–68. Elected Pres., Canadian Catholic Conference, 1973–75. *Publication:* contrib. to Dictionnaire d'Histoire et de Géographie. *Address:* 130 rue de la Cathédrale, Sherbrooke, PQ J1H 4M1, Canada. *T:* 569–6070.

SHERFIELD, 1st Baron, *cr* 1964; **Roger Mellor Makins,** GCB 1960 (KCB 1953); GCMG 1955 (KCMG 1949; CMG 1944); FRS 1986; DL; Chancellor of Reading University, since 1970; President, Centre for International Briefing; Member of Council, Royal Albert Hall; *b* 3 Feb. 1904; *e s* of late Brigadier-General Sir Ernest Makins, KBE, CB, DSO; *m* 1934, Alice (*d* 1985), *e d* of late Hon. Dwight F. Davis; two *s* four *d*. *Educ:* Winchester; Christ Church, Oxford. First Class Honours in History, 1925; Fellow of All Souls College, 1925–39 and 1957–; called to Bar, Inner Temple, 1927; Foreign Office, 1928; served Washington, 1931–34, Oslo, 1934; Foreign Office, 1934; Assistant Adviser on League of Nations Affairs, 1937; Sec. Intergovernmental Cttee on Refugees from Germany, 1938–39; Adviser on League of Nations Affairs, 1939; Acting First Secretary, 1939; Acting Counsellor, 1940; Adviser to British Delegation, International Labour Conference, New York, 1941; served on Staff of Resident Minister in West Africa, 1942; Counsellor, 1942; Asst to Resident Minister at Allied Force Headquarters, Mediterranean, 1943–44; Minister at British Embassy, Washington, 1945–47; UK rep. on United Nations Interim Commission for Food and Agriculture, 1945; Asst Under-Sec. of State, FO, 1947–48, Dep. Under-Sec. of State, 1948–52; British Ambassador to the United States, 1953–56; Joint Permanent Secretary of the Treasury, 1956–59; Chm., UKAEA, 1960–64. Chairman: Hill, Samuel Group, 1966–70; Finance for Industry Ltd, 1973–74; Finance Corp. for Industry Ltd, 1973–74; Industrial & Commercial Finance Corp., 1964–74; Estate Duties Investment Trust, 1966–73; Ship Mortgage Finance Co., 1966–74; Technical Develt Capital, 1966–74; A. C. Cossor, 1968–82; Raytheon Europe Internat. Co., 1970–82; Wells Fargo Ltd, 1972–84, and other companies; Director: Times Publishing Co., 1964–67; Badger Ltd, 1981–83. Pres., BSI, 1970–73. Pres., Parly and Scientific Cttee, 1969–73; Chm., H of L Select Cttee on Science and Technology, 1984–. Vice-Chm., The Ditchley Foundn, 1965–74 (Chm., 1962–65); Pres., Centre for Internat. Briefing, 1972–85. Chm., Governing Body and Fellow of Imperial Coll. of Science and Technology, 1962–74. Fellow, Winchester College, 1962–79 (Warden, 1974–79). Chairman: Marshall Aid Commemoration Commn, 1965–73; Lindemann Trust Fellowship Cttee, 1973–83; Trustee, The Times Trust, 1968–73. DL Hants, 1978. Hon. Student, Christ Church, Oxford, 1973; Hon. FICE 1964; Hon. DCL Oxford; Hon. DLitt Reading; Hon. LLD: Sheffield; London; Hon. DL North Carolina; and other American universities and colleges. Benjamin Franklin Medal, RSA, 1982. *Publication:* (ed) Economic and Social Consequences of Nuclear Energy, 1972. *Recreations:* shooting, gardening. *Heir:* *s* Hon. Christopher James Makins [*b* 23 July 1942; *m* 1976, Wendy Cortesi]. *Address:* 81 Onslow Square, SW7; Ham Farm House, Ramsdell, near Basingstoke, Hants. *Clubs:* Boodle's, Pratt's, MCC.

See also Baron Milford.

SHERGOLD, Harold Taplin, CMG 1963; OBE 1958 (MBE 1945); served in Foreign and Commonwealth Office (formerly Foreign Office), 1954–80; *b* 5 Dec. 1915; *s* of late Ernest Henry Shergold; *m* 1949, Bevis Anael, *d* of late William Bernard Reid; no *c*. *Educ:* Peter Symonds' School, Winchester; St Edmund Hall, Oxford; Corpus Christi Coll., Cambridge. Asst Master, Cheltenham Grammar Sch., 1937–40. Joined Hampshire Regt, 1940; transferred to Intelligence Corps, 1941; served in Middle East and Italy, 1941–46 (despatches). Joined Foreign Office, 1947; served in Germany, 1947–54. Chm., Richmond, Twickenham & Dist Br., Guide Dogs for the Blind Assoc., 1983–. *Address:* 1 Ancaster Court, Queens Road, Richmond, Surrey TW10 6JJ. *T:* 01–948 2048.

SHERIDAN, Cecil Majella, CMG 1961; *b* 9 Dec. 1911; *s* of late J. P. Sheridan, Liverpool, and Mrs Sheridan (*née* Myerscough), Preston, Lancs; *m* 1949, Monica, *d* of H. F. Ereaut, MBE, Jersey, CI; two *s* one *d*. *Educ:* Ampleforth College, York. Admitted Solicitor, England, 1934; called to Bar, Innner Temple, 1952. Practised as solicitor in Liverpool (Messrs Yates, Sheridan & Co.), 1934–40. Served in RAFVR, General Duties Pilot, 1940–46; resigned with hon. rank of Squadron Leader. Joined Colonial Legal Service, 1946; Crown Counsel and Dep. Public Prosecutor, Malayan Union, 1946–48; Legal Adviser, Malay States of Pahang, Kelantan, Trengganu and Selangor and Settlement of Penang, 1948–55; Legal Draftsman, Fedn of Malaya, 1955–57; Solicitor-General, Fedn of Malaya, 1957–59; Attorney-General, Fedn of Malaya, 1959–63; Attorney-General, Malaysia, retd. Mem. (Fedn of Malaya) Inter-Governmental Cttees for Borneo Territories and Singapore, 1962–63; Chm. Traffic Comrs, E Midland Traffic Area, 1965–81, Dep. Chm., 1981–; Pres., British Assoc. of Malaysia, 1964–65. Chm., Malaysia Housing Soc., 1964–65. Hon. PMN (Malaysia), 1963. Associate Mem., Commonwealth Parly Assoc. (UK Branch). *Address:* 18 Private Road, Sherwood, Nottingham NG5 4DB. *Clubs:* East India, Devonshire, Sports and Public Schools; Nottinghamshire.

SHERIDAN, Peter, QC 1977; *b* 29 May 1927; *s* of Hugo and Marie Sheridan. *Educ:* eight schools; Lincoln Coll., Oxford Univ. BA Hons, 1950. Called to the Bar, Middle Temple, 1955. *Recreations:* motor cars, archery. *Address:* 17 Brompton Square, SW3. *T:* 01–584 7250; Pile Oak Lodge, Donhead St Andrew, Wilts. *T:* Donhead 484.

SHERIDAN, Roderick Gerald, OBE 1978; MVO 1968; HM Diplomatic Service, retired; Consul-General, Barcelona and Andorra, 1977–80; Hon. Vice-Consul, Menorca, since 1983; *b* 24 Jan. 1921; *s* of late Sir Joseph Sheridan; *m* 1942, Lois Mary (*née* Greene); one *s* one *d*. *Educ:* Downside Sch.; Pembroke Coll., Cambridge. Served War, Coldstream Guards, N Africa and Italy, 1940–46. HM Overseas Colonial Service: Zanzibar and Cyprus, 1946–60; retd as District Comr, Nicosia; HM Diplomatic Service, 1960–: First Sec., Cyprus, 1960–63; Foreign Office, 1964–66; First Sec., Brasilia, 1966–69; FO, 1969–70; Head of Chancery, Oslo, 1970–73; Consul, Algeciras, 1973–77. *Recreations:* tennis, golf, skiing. *Address:* Torret 28, San Luis, Menorca, Spain. *T:* (971) 36 64 39.

SHERLOCK, Dr Alexander; Member (C) South West Essex, European Parliament, since 1979; Member of Environment Committee (European Democratic (Conservative) Leader) and Development Committee; medical practitioner; *b* 14 Feb. 1922; *s* of Thomas Sherlock, MM, and Evelyn M. Sherlock (*née* Alexander); *m* 1st, 1945, Clarice C. Scarff;

one s two d; 2nd, 1976, Eileen Hall; one step d. *Educ:* Magdalen College Sch., Oxford; Stowmarket Grammar Sch.; London Hospital. MB BS (Hons) 1945. Ho. Phys., Ho. Surg., London Hosp.; RAF, 1946–48; Medical Practitioner, Felixstowe, and Consultant/Adviser to many organisations in matters of occupational health, safety and welfare. Called to the Bar, Gray's Inn, 1961. Member: Felixstowe UDC, 1960–74; E Suffolk CC, 1966–74; Suffolk CC, 1974–79 (Chairman, Fire and Public Protection Cttee, 1977–79). Spokesman on Environment, Health and Consumer Protection, Eur. Parlt, 1979–. OStJ 1974. *Recreation:* gardening. *Address:* 58 Orwell Road, Felixstowe IP11 7PS. *T:* Felixstowe 284503. *Club:* Royal Air Force.

SHERLOCK, Sir Philip (Manderson), KBE 1967 (CBE 1953); Vice President, Caribbean Resources Development Foundation Inc., since 1983; *b* Jamaica, 25 Feb. 1902; *s* of Rev. Terence Sherlock, Methodist Minister, and Adina Sherlock; *m* 1942, Grace Marjorye Verity; two *s* one *d. Educ:* Calabar High Sch., Jamaica. Headmaster, Wolmer's Boys' Sch., Jamaica, 1933–38; Sec., Inst. of Jamaica, 1939–44; Educn Officer, Jamaica Welfare, 1944–47; Dir, Extra-Mural Dept, University Coll. of West Indies, 1947–60, also Vice-Principal, University Coll. of W Indies, 1952–62; Pro-Vice-Chancellor, Univ. of West Indies, 1962, Vice-Chancellor, 1963–69; Sec.-Gen., Assoc. of Caribbean Univs & Res. Insts, 1969–79; Sec., Assoc. of Caribbean Univs Foundn, 1979–83. Hon. LLD: Leeds, 1959; Carleton, 1967; St Andrews, 1968; Hon. DCL New Brunswick, 1966; Hon. DLitt: Acadia, 1966; Miami, 1971; Univ. of WI, 1972. Order of Andres Bello with collar (Venezuela), 1978. *Publications:* Anansi the Spider Man, 1956; (with John Parry) Short History of the West Indies, 1956; Caribbean Citizen, 1957; West Indian Story, 1960; Three Finger Jack, 1961; Jamaica, A Junior History, 1966; West Indian Folk Tales, 1966; West Indies, 1966; Land and People of the West Indies, 1967; Belize, a Junior History, 1969; The Iguana's Tail, 1969; West Indian Nations, 1973; Ears and Tails and Common Sense, 1974; Shout for Freedom, 1976; Norman Manley, a biography, 1980; Keeping Company with Jamaica, 1984; educational books and articles. *Recreations:* reading, writing, cooking. *Address:* 7855 NW 12th Street, Suite 217, Miami, Florida 33126, USA. *T:* (305) 594–0564. *Club:* National Liberal.

SHERLOCK, Prof. Dame Sheila (Patricia Violet), DBE 1978; MD; FRCP; FRCPEd; Professor of Medicine, University of London, at the Royal Free Hospital School of Medicine, since 1959; *b* 31 March 1918; *d* of late Samuel Philip Sherlock and Violet Mary Catherine Beckett; *m* 1951, David Geraint James, *qv*; two *d. Educ:* Folkestone County Sch.; Edinburgh Univ. Ettles Scholar, 1941; Beit Memorial Research Fellow, 1942–47; Rockefeller Fellow, Yale University, USA, 1948. Physician and Lecturer in Medicine, Postgraduate Medical School of London, 1948–59. RCP Lectures: Bradshaw, 1961; Rolleston, 1968; Lumleian, 1978; Harveian, 1985. RCP: Councillor, 1964–68; Censor, 1970–72; Senior Censor and Vice-Pres., 1976–77. Mem. Senate, Univ. of London, 1976–81. Hon. Member: Gastro-enterological Societies of America, 1963, Australasia, 1965, Mexico, 1968, Czechoslovakia, 1968, Yugoslavia, 1981, Sweden, 1983; Assoc. of Amer. Physicians, 1973; Assoc. of Alimentary Surgeons, 1973. Hon. FACP; Hon. FRCPC; Hon. FRACP 1984; Hon. FRCPI; Hon. FRCPS 1986. Hon. DSc: City Univ. of NY, 1977; Yale Univ., USA, 1983; Edinburgh, 1985; Hon. MD: Lisbon, 1981; Oslo, 1981; Leuven, 1984; Hon. LLD Aberdeen, 1982. William Cullen Prize, 1962 (shared); Jimenez-Diaz Prize, 1980; Thannhauser Prize, 1980; Fothergillian Gold Medal, Med. Soc. of London, 1983; Gold Medal, BMA, 1985. *Publications:* Diseases of the Liver and Biliary System, 1955, 7th edn 1985; papers on liver structure and function in various medical journals, since 1943. *Recreations:* cricket, travel. *Address:* 41 York Terrace East, NW1 4PT. *T:* 01–486 4560.

SHERMAN, Sir Alfred, Kt 1983; journalist; public affairs advisor in private practice as Interthought; co-founder, Centre for Policy Studies, 1974 (Director of Studies until 1984); Chairman, Policy-Search Ltd, since 1985; *b* 10 Nov. 1919; *m* 1958, Zahava (*née* Levin); one *s.* Served in International Brigade, Spanish Civil War, 1937–38; war of 1939–45 in field security and occupied enemy territory administration. Leader writer, Jewish Chronicle; various appts with Daily Telegraph, 1965–86, as leader writer 1977–86. Vis. Fellow, LSE, 1983–85. Member, economic advisory staff of Israeli Govt, in 1950's. Broadcaster. Councillor, RBK&C, 1971–78. Member: West End Synagogue; Council, Anglo-Jewish Assoc. *Publications:* Local Government Reorganisation and Industry, 1970; Councils, Councillors and Public Relations, 1973; Local Government Reorganization and the Salary Bill, 1974; (with D. Mallam) Waste in Wandsworth, 1976; Crisis Calls for a Minister for Denationalization, 1980; The Scott Report, 1981; (contrib.) Revisionism, 1961; Communism and Arab Nationalism: a reappraisal; Capitalism and Liberty; Our Complacent Satirists; Political Violence in Britain; contribs to newspapers and periodicals. *Address:* 10 Gerald Road, SW1. *T:* 01–730 2838; (office) 16 Great College Street, SW1. *T:* 01–222 1019. *Cables:* SHERMANIA LONDON SW1; (business) RESPUBLICA LONDON SW1. *Clubs:* Reform, Hurlingham.

SHERMAN, Sir Louis, (Sir Lou Sherman), Kt 1975; OBE 1967; JP; Chairman, Housing Corporation, 1977–80; Deputy Chairman, Harlow Development Corporation. Initiated Lea Valley Regional Park Authority. JP Inner London Area. *Recreations:* politics, reading, talking. *Club:* Reform.

SHERRARD, Michael David, QC 1968; a Recorder of the Crown Court, since 1974; *b* 23 June 1928; *er s* of late Morris and Ethel Sherrard; *m* 1952, Shirley (C. B. Piper, writer), *d* of late Maurice and Lucy Bagrit; two *s. Educ:* King's Coll., London. LLB 1949. Called to Bar, Middle Temple, 1949 (Bencher 1977); Mem., Inner Temple, 1980; Mem. Senate, 1977–80. Mem., SE Circuit, 1950. Mem., Winn Cttee on Personal Injury Litigation, 1966; Mem. Council and Exec. Cttee, Justice, British Section, Internat. Commn of Jurists, 1974–; Dept of Trade Inspector, London Capital Group, 1975–77; Chm., Normansfield Hosp. Inquiry, 1977–78; Comr for trial of local govt election petitions (under Representation of the People Act 1949), 1978–80. *Recreations:* oil painting, listening to opera. *Address:* 2 Crown Office Row, Temple, EC4. *T:* 01–583 2681; 14 Burgess Hill, Hampstead, NW2. *T:* 01–435 7828. *Club:* Oriental.

SHERRIN, Ned, (Edward George Sherrin); film, theatre and television producer, director and writer; *b* Low Ham, Som, 18 Feb. 1931; *s* of late T. A. Sherrin and D. F. Sherrin (*née* Drewett). *Educ:* Sexey's Sch., Bruton; Exeter Coll., Oxford; Gray's Inn. Producer: ATV, Birmingham, 1955–57; BBC TV, 1957–66 (prod. and dir. That Was The Week That Was). Produced films: The Virgin Soldiers (with Leslie Gilliat) 1968; Every Home Should Have One, 1969; (with Terry Glinwood) Up Pompeii, 1971; Up the Chastity Belt, 1971; Girl Stroke Boy, 1971; Rentadick, 1971; Up the Front, 1972; The National Health, 1972; TV plays (with Caryl Brahms) include: Little Beggars; Benbow was his Name; Take a Sapphire; The Great Inimitable Mr Dickens; Feydeau Farces; plays (with Caryl Brahms): No Bed for Bacon; Cindy-Ella or I Gotta Shoe, 1962–63; The Spoils, 1968; Nicholas Nickleby, 1969; Sing a Rude Song, 1970; Fish out of Water, 1971; Liberty Ranch, 1972; Nickleby and Me, 1975; Beecham, 1980; The Mitford Girls, 1981; Oh, Kay! (new book with Tony Geiss), 1984; directed: Come Spy with Me, Whitehall, 1967; (and appeared in) Side by Side by Sondheim, Mermaid, 1976, NY 1977; Only in America (with D. Yakir), Roundhouse, 1980; Noël, Goodspeed, USA, 1981; directed and co-adapted: The Ratepayers' Iolanthe, QEH, 1984 (Olivier Award);

The Metropolitan Mikado, QEH, 1985; Small Expectations, QEH, 1986; dir, The Sloane Ranger Revue, Duchess, 1985. TV appearances include: Song by Song, BBC and Yorkshire TV series; Quiz of the Week, BBC; The Rather Reassuring Programme, BBC; We Interrupt this Week, PBS, NY; Friday Night Saturday Morning, BBC-2; Countdown, Channel 4; radio appearances: Midweek (host), Medium Dry Sherrin, Extra Dry Sherrin, And So to Ned; Loose Ends; Counterpoint. Governor, BFI, 1980–84. Guild of TV Producers and Directors' Awards; Ivor Novello Award, 1966. *Publications:* (with Caryl Brahms) Cindy-Ella or I Gotta Shoe, 1962; Rappell 1910, 1964; Benbow was his Name, 1967; Ooh la! la! (short stories), 1973; After You Mr Feydeau, 1975; A Small Thing—Like an Earthquake (memoirs), 1983; (with Caryl Brahms) Song by Song, 1984; Cutting Edge, 1984; (with Neil Shand) 1956 and all that, 1984; (with Caryl Brahms) Too Dirty for the Windmill, 1986; many songs. *Address:* c/o Margaret Ramsay Ltd, 14a Goodwin's Court, WC2. *T:* 01–240 0691.

SHERRY, Prof. Norman, FRSL 1985; Mitchell Distinguished Professor of Literature, Trinity University, San Antonio, Texas, since 1983; *b* 6 July 1935; *m* 1960, Sylvia Brunt. *Educ:* Univ. of Durham (BA Eng Lit); Univ. of Singapore (PhD). Lectr, Univ. of Singapore, 1961–66; Lectr and Sen. Lectr, Univ. of Liverpool, 1966–70; Prof. of English, Univ. of Lancaster, 1970–82. Fellow, Humanities Research Center, N Carolina, 1982. *Publications:* Conrad's Eastern World, 1966; The Novels of Jane Austen, 1966; Charlotte and Emily Bronte, 1969; Conrad's Western World, 1971; Conrad and his World, 1972; (ed) Conrad: the Critical Heritage, 1973; (ed) An Outpost of Progress and Heart of Darkness, 1973; (ed) Lord Jim, 1974; (ed) Nostromo, 1974; (ed) The Secret Agent, 1974; (ed) The Nigger of Narcissus, Typhoon, Falk and Other Stories, 1975; (ed) Joseph Conrad: a commemoration, 1976; contribs to Review of English Studies, Notes & Queries, Modern Language Review, TLS, Observer. *Recreations:* reading, writing, jogging, talking. *Address:* 6 Gillison Close, Melling, Carnforth, Lancs. *T:* Hornby 21686. *Club:* Savile.

SHERRY, Mrs Vincent; *see* Robinson, Kathleen M.

SHERSBY, (Julian) Michael; MP (C) Uxbridge, since Dec. 1972; *b* Ickenham, 17 Feb. 1933; *s* of William Henry and Elinor Shersby; *m* 1958, Barbara Joan, *d* of John Henry Barrow; one *s* one *d. Educ:* John Lyon Sch., Harrow-on-the-Hill. Mem., Paddington Borough Council, 1959–64; Mem., Westminster City Council, 1964–71; Deputy Lord Mayor of Westminster, 1967–68. Chm., Uxbridge Div. Young Conservatives, 1951–52; Conservative and Unionist Party Organisation, 1952–58; Sec., Assoc. of Specialised Film Producers, 1958–62; Dir, British Industrial Film Assoc., 1962–66; Dir, 1966–77, Dir-Gen., 1977–, Sugar Bureau (formerly British Sugar Bureau); Sec., UK Sugar Industry Assoc., 1978. PPS to Minister of Aerospace and Shipping, DTI, 1974; Mem., Speaker's Panel of Chairmen, 1983–. Mem., Public Accounts Cttee, 1983–; Jt Sec., Conservative Party Parly Industry Cttee, 1972–74; Chairman: Cons. Party Trade Cttee, 1974–76 (Vice-Chm., 1977–79); Cons. Party Parly Food and Drink Industries Sub-Cttee, 1979–; Vice-Chairman: Cons. Party Parly Environment Cttee, 1979–83; Cons. Party Parly Small Businesses Cttee, 1979–80 and 1983; Member: CPA Delegn to Caribbean, 1975; British Parly delegn to UN, 1978; CPA Delegn to Falkland Islands, 1981 and 1983; deleg., CPA Annual Conf., Canada, 1985; promoted Private Member's Bills: Town and Country Amenities Act, 1974; Parks Regulation (Amendment) Act, 1974; Stock Exchange (Completion of Bargains) Act, 1976; Gaming (Amendment) Act, 1980; Copyright Act (1956) Amendment Act, 1982; British Nationality (Falkland Islands) Act, 1983. Jt Sec., 1977–80, Vice-Pres., 1980–83, Parly and Scientific Cttee. Mem. Court, Brunel Univ., 1975–; Pres., Abbeyfield Uxbridge Soc., 1975–. *Recreations:* theatre, travel. *Address:* Anvil House, Park Road, Stoke Poges, Bucks. *T:* Farnham Common 4548. *Club:* Conservative (Uxbridge).

SHERSTON-BAKER, Sir Humphrey Dodington Benedict, 6th Bt, *cr* 1796; *b* 13 Oct. 1907; *s* of Lt-Col Sir Dodington Sherston-Baker, 5th Bt, and Irene Roper (*d* 1950), *yr d* of Sir Roper Parkington; *S* father, 1944; *m* 1938, Margaret Alice (Bobby) (marriage dissolved, 1953), *o d* of H. W. Binns, 9 Campden Street, W, and Blythburgh, Suffolk; one *s* three *d. Educ:* Downside; Christ's College, Cambridge. *Heir: s* Robert George Humphrey Sherston-Baker, *b* 3 April 1951. *Address:* 22 Frognal Court, NW3 5HP.

SHERVAL, Rear-Adm. David Robert; Chief Staff Officer (Engineering) to Comander-in-Chief Fleet, since 1985; *b* 4 July 1933; *s* of William Robert Sherval and Florence Margaret Sherval (*née* Luke); *m* 1961, Patricia Ann Phillips; one *s* one *d. Educ:* Portsmouth Southern Grammar School. MIMechE. Artificer Apprentice, 1950; BRNC Dartmouth, 1951; Training: at sea, HM Ships Devonshire, Forth and Glasgow, 1951–52 and 1955; RNEC, 1952–53, 1956; served: HM Ships Eagle, Tiger, Hampshire, HM Dockyard Gibraltar and HMY Britannia, 1957–68; BRNC, 1968–70; HMS Juno, 1970–72; NDC, 1972–73; Naval Plans, MoD, 1973–75; Staff of FO Sea Training, 1975–76; Naval Op. Requirements, MoD, 1976–77; NATO Defence Coll., Rome, 1979; ACOS (Intell.) to SACLANT, 1979–82; Fleet Marine Engineer Officer, 1982–84; Dir, Naval Logistic Planning, 1984–85. *Recreation:* music. *Address:* CSO(E), C-in-C Fleet, Northwood, Middx HA6 3HP.

SHERWIN-WHITE, Adrian Nicholas, MA; FBA 1956; Reader in Ancient History, University of Oxford, 1966–79; Fellow and Tutor of St John's College, Oxford, 1936–79, Fellow Emeritus 1979; Keeper of the Groves, 1970; *b* 1911; *s* of H. N. Sherwin-White, Solicitors' Dept of LCC. *Educ:* Merchant Taylors' School; St John's College, Oxford (Derby Scholar, 1935; Arnold Historical Essay Prize, 1935; MA, 1937). War Service in RN and Admiralty, 1942–45. Conington Prize, 1947. Sarum Lecturer, Oxford Univ., 1960–61; Gray Lecturer, Cambridge Univ., 1965–66; Special Lectr, Open Univ., 1973–81. Pres., Soc. for Promotion of Roman Studies, 1974–77. Corresp. Fellow, Bayerische Akademie der Wissenschaften, 1977. *Publications:* Roman Citizenship, 1939, enlarged edn 1973; Ancient Rome (Then and There Series), 1959; Roman Society and Roman Law in the New Testament, 1963; Historical Commentary on the Letters of Pliny the Younger, 1966; Racial Prejudice in Imperial Rome, 1967; Roman Foreign Policy in the East 167BC-AD1, 1983; (contrib.) Cambridge Ancient History, 1985; ed Geographical Handbook Series, Admiralty; contrib. Jl Roman Studies. *Recreations:* watching horses and growing hardy plants. *Address:* St John's College, Oxford. *T:* Frilford Heath 390496.

SHERWOOD, Bishop Suffragan of, since 1975; **Rt. Rev. Harold Richard Darby;** *b* 28 Feb. 1919; *s* of late William and Miriam Darby; *m* 1949, Audrey Elizabeth Lesley Green; two *s* three *d. Educ:* Cathedral School, Shanghai; St John's Coll., Durham (BA). Military service, 1939–45; Durham Univ., 1946–50. Deacon 1950; priest 1951; Curate of Leyton, 1950–51; Curate of Harlow, 1951–53; Vicar of Shrub End, Colchester, 1953–59; Vicar of Waltham Abbey, 1959–70; Dean of Battle, 1970–75. *Recreation:* vintage cars. *Address:* Applegarth, Halam, Notts. *T:* Southwell 814041.

SHERWOOD, James Blair; Founder and Chairman, Sea Containers Group, London, since 1965; Chairman, Sealink British Ferries, since 1984; *b* 8 Aug. 1933; *s* of William Earl Sherwood and Florence Balph Sherwood; *m* 1977, Shirley Angela Masser Cross; two step *s. Educ:* Yale Univ. (BA Economics 1955). Lieut US Naval Reserve, Far East service, afloat and ashore, 1955–58 (Korean Service Medal, US Navy, 1956). Manager, French Ports, later Asst General Freight Traffic Manager, United States Lines Co., Le Havre and

NY, 1959–62; Gen. Manager, Container Transport Internat. Inc., NY and Paris, 1963–64. In partnership with Mark Birley, established Harry's Bar Club in London, 1979. Restored, and brought into regular service, the Venice Simplon-Orient-Express, 1982. *Publication:* James Sherwood's Discriminating Guide to London, 1975, 2nd edn 1977. *Recreations:* sailing, tennis, skiing. *Address:* Hinton Manor, Hinton Waldrist, Oxon. *T:* Oxford 820260. *Clubs:* Hurlingham, Mark's.

SHERWOOD, (Robert) Antony (Frank), CMG 1981; Assistant Director-General, British Council, 1977–81, retired; *b* 29 May 1923; *s* of Frank Henry Sherwood and Mollie Sherwood (*née* Moore); *m* 1953, Margaret Elizabeth Simpson; two *s* two *d*. *Educ:* Christ's Hospital; St John's Coll., Oxford (BA 1949, MA 1953). War service, RAF, 1942–46. Apptd to British Council, 1949; Lectr, Turkey, 1949–50; Asst Dir, Ibadan, Nigeria, 1950–55; Lectr, Syria, 1955–56; Fellowships Dept, 1957; Asst Rep., Uganda, 1957–59; Representative: Somaliland Protectorate, 1959–60; Somali Republic, 1960–63; Dir, Commonwealth Dept, 1963–66; Dep. Controller, Home Div., 1966–69; Representative, Nigeria, 1969–72; Controller, Africa and Middle East Div., 1972–77. Vice-Chm., Overseas Grants Cttee, Help The Aged, 1982–; Mem. Exec. Cttee, HelpAge Internat., 1983–; Hon. PRO, Surrey Voluntary Service Council, 1982–. *Recreations:* travel, genealogy, family history. *Address:* 18 Rivermount Gardens, Guildford, Surrey GU2 5DN. *T:* Guildford 38277.

SHERWOOD, Prof. Thomas, FRCP, FRCR; Professor of Radiology, since 1978, and Clinical Dean, since 1984, University of Cambridge; Fellow of Girton College, Cambridge, since 1982; *b* 25 Sept. 1934; *m* 1961, Margaret Gooch; two *s* one *d*. *Educ:* Frensham Heights Sch.; Guy's Hospital, London. MA; DCH. Consultant Radiologist, Hammersmith Hospital and St Peter's Hospitals, 1969–77. *Publications:* Uroradiology, 1980; Roads to Radiology, 1983; papers in medical and radiological jls, 1964–. *Recreations:* music, reading and writing. *Address:* Department of Radiology, Addenbrooke's Hospital, Hills Road, Cambridge CB2 2QQ. *T:* Cambridge 336891.

SHESTOPAL, Dawn Angela, (Mrs N. J. Shestopal); *see* Freedman, D. A.

SHETH, Pranlal; Director: Abbey Life Assurance Co. Ltd, since 1974; Ambassador Life Assurance Co. Ltd, since 1980; Secretary and Legal Adviser, Abbey Life Group plc, since 1985; *b* 20 Dec. 1924; *s* of Purashotam Virji Sheth and Sakarben Sheth; *m* 1951, Indumati Sheth; one *s* one *d*. Called to the Bar, Lincoln's Inn, 1962. Journalist, Kenya, 1943–52; Chm., Nyanza Farmers' Cooperative Soc., 1954–60; Mem., Central Agriculture Bd, Kenya, 1963–66; Dep. Chm., Asian Hosp. Authority, 1964–66; Mem., Economic Planning and Develt Council, Kenya, 1964–66. Group Sec., Abbey Life Gp of Cos, 1971; Legal Dir, Hartford Europe Gp of Cos, 1977–86; Dir, Abbey Life Assurance (Ireland), 1981–85; Gp Sec., ITT cos in UK, 1983–86. Dir, Round House Arts Centre, 1986–; Mem., BBC Consultative Gp on Industry and Business Affairs, 1986–. Chief Editor, Gujaret Samachar Weekly, 1972–73; Mem., N Metropolitan Conciliation Cttee, Race Relations Bd, 1973–77; a Dep. Chm., CRE, 1977–80; Trustee, Project Fullemploy (Charitable Trust), 1977–; Vice-Patron, UK Assoc., Internat. Year of the Child, 1978–80. Fellow, Inst. of Directors, 1977; FBIM 1980. Mem., Court of Governors, Polytech. of N London, 1979–. Mem. Editorial Adv. Panel, Equal Opportunities Review, 1984. *Address:* (home) 70 Howberry Road, Edgware, Mddx. *T:* 01–952 2413; (business) Abbey Life House, 80 Holdenhurst Road, Bournemouth BH8 8AL. *T:* Bournemouth 292373.

SHEVARDNADZE, Eduard Amvrosiyevich; Minister of Foreign Affairs, USSR, since 1985; Member of the Politburo, since 1985; *b* Georgia, 25 Jan. 1928. *Educ:* Pedagogical Institute, Kutaisi. Mem., CPSU, 1948–; Sec., Komsomol Cttee in Kutaisi, 1952–56, of Georgia, 1956–61; 1st Sec., Regional Party Cttee, Mtsheta, 1961–63, Tbilisi, 1963–64; Minister of Internal Affairs, Georgia, 1964–72; 1st Sec., Republican Party Cttee, Georgia, 1972–85. Order of Lenin (four times); Hero of Socialist Labour (twice); Order of Red Banner of Labour. *Address:* Ministry of Foreign Affairs, Smolenskaya, Moscow, USSR.

SHEVILL, Rt. Rev. Ian (Wotton Allnutt), AO 1976; MA (Sydney); *b* 11 May 1917; *s* of Erson James Shevill; *m* 1st, 1959, Dr June (*d* 1970), *d* of Basil Stephenson, Worthing; two *s*; 2nd, 1974, Ann, *d* of A. Brabazon, Winton, Queensland. *Educ:* Scot's Coll., Sydney; Sydney Univ.; School of Oriental and African Studies, London Univ.; Moore Theological Coll., Sydney, BA, 1939, MA, 1945, Sydney; ThL, ThD, 1953, Moore Theol Coll. Deacon, 1940; Priest, 1941; Curate of St Paul, Burwood, 1940–45; Organising Secretary of the Australian Board of Missions, for Province of Queensland, 1946–47; Education Secretary, Society for the Propagation of Gospel, 1948–51; Bishop of North Queensland, 1953–70; Secretary, United Society for the Propagation of the Gospel, 1970–73; Asst Bishop, Diocese of London, 1971–73; Bishop of Newcastle, NSW, 1973–77. *Publications:* New Dawn in Papua, 1946; Pacific Conquest, 1948; God's World at Prayer, 1951; Orthodox and other Eastern Churches in Australia, 1964; Half Time, 1966; Going it with God, 1969; One Man's Meditations, 1982; O, My God, 1982. *Address:* 13 Cottesmore Street, Fig Tree Pocket, Brisbane, Qld 4069, Australia. *Club:* Athenæum.

SHEWAN, Henry Alexander, CB 1974; OBE (mil.) 1946; QC (Scotland) 1949; Commissioner of Social Security (formerly National Insurance), 1955–81 (part time 1979–81); *b* 7 November 1906; *s* of late James Smith Shewan, Advocate in Aberdeen; *m* 1937, Ann Fraser Thomson (*d* 1977), Aberdeen; two *s*. *Educ:* Robert Gordon's Coll., Aberdeen; Aberdeen Univ.; Emmanuel College, Cambridge. Advocate, 1933. Served War of 1939–45, RAF, 1940–45, Sqdn Leader. Member Scottish Medical Practices Cttee, 1948–55; Member Court of Session Rules Council, 1948–55; Dep. Chm. Panel of Arbiters and Referee under Coal Industry Nationalisation Act, 1949–55; Chm., Medical Appeal Tribunal National Insurance (Industrial Injuries) Act, 1950–55; Chairman General Nursing Council for Scot., 1960–62. Referee under Child Benefit Act 1975, 1976–79. *Address:* 7 Winton Loan, Edinburgh EH10 7AN. *T:* 031–445 3239. *Club:* New (Edinburgh).

SHIACH, Sheriff Gordon Iain Wilson; Sheriff of Lothian and Borders, at Edinburgh, since 1984; *b* 15 Oct. 1935; *o s* of late Dr John Crawford Shiach, FDS, QHDS, and of Florence Bygott Wilson; *m* 1962, Margaret Grant Smith; two *d*. *Educ:* Lathallan Sch.; Gordonstoun Sch.; Edinburgh Univ. (MA, LLB); Open Univ. (BA Hons). Admitted to Faculty of Advocates, 1960; practised as Advocate, 1960–72; Tutor, Dept of Evidence and Pleading, Univ. of Edinburgh, 1963–66; Clerk to Rules Council of Court of Session, 1963–72; Standing Jun. Counsel in Scotland to Post Office, 1969–72, Sheriff of: Fife and Kinross, later Tayside, Central and Fife, at Dunfermline, 1972–79; Lothian and Borders at Linlithgow, 1979–84; Hon. Sheriff at Elgin, 1986–. *Recreations:* orienteering, music, theatre. *Address:* Sheriffs' Chambers, Sheriff Court House, Lawnmarket, Edinburgh EH1 2NS. *Club:* New (Edinburgh).

SHIELD, Leslie, TD; DL; a Recorder of the Crown Court, since 1980; *b* 8 May 1916; *s* of Tom Shield and Annie Maud Shield; *m* 1941, Doris Leather; one *s*. *Educ:* Cowley Sch., St Helens; Univ. of Liverpool (LLB 1936, LLM 1938). Qualified solicitor, 1939, admitted 1945. Served War, 1939–46: commnd 5th Bn Prince of Wales' Volunteers (S Lancs) Regt; demob., Major. Entered into gen. practice as solicitor, 1946. DL Merseyside, 1976. *Recreations:* gardening (particular interest, orchids), music. *Address:* 185 Higher Lane, Rainford, St Helens, Merseyside WA11 8NF. *T:* Rainford 2708.

SHIELDS, Elizabeth Lois; MP (L) Ryedale, since May 1986; *b* 27 Feb. 1928; *d* of Thomas Henry Teare and Dorothy Emma Elizabeth Roberts-Lawrence; *m* 1961, David Cathro Shields. *Educ:* Whyteleafe Girls' Grammar School; UCL (BA Hons Classics); Avery Hill College of Education (Cert Ed). Asst Teacher, St Philomena's Sch., Carshalton, 1954–59; Head of Department: Jersey Coll. for Girls, 1959–61; Whyteleafe Girls' Grammar Sch., 1961–62; Trowbridge Girls' High Sch., 1962–64; St Swithun's, Winchester, 1964–65; Queen Ethelburga's, Harrogate, 1967–69; Malton Sch., N Yorks, 1976–86; Univ. of York (on secondment), 1985–86 (Medieval Studies). Contested (L) Howden, 1979, Ryedale, 1983; Mem., Ryedale Dist. Council, 1980–. *Recreations:* gardening, music, theatre. *Address:* Firby Hall, Kirkham Abbey, Westow, York YO6 7LH. *T:* Whitwell-on-the-Hill 474. *Clubs:* National Liberal; Ryedale House.

SHIELDS, John Sinclair; *b* 4 Feb. 1903; *s* of Rev. W. H. Shields and Margaret Louisa (*née* Sinclair); *m* 1st, 1924, Norah Fane Smith; three *d*; 2nd, 1963, Mrs Noreen Moultrie, *widow* of Comdr John Moultrie. *Educ:* Charterhouse; Lincoln Coll., Oxford (MA). Headmaster: Wem Grammar School, 1934–47; Queen Mary's School, Basingstoke, 1947–56; Headmaster, Peter Symonds' School, Winchester, 1957–63; Vice-Pres. Classical Assoc., 1958; Mem., Broadcasting Cttee, 1960. *Recreation:* golf. *Address:* North End House, Hursley, Winchester, Hants.

SHIELDS, (Leslie) Stuart, QC 1970; a Recorder of the Crown Court, since 1972; *b* 15 May 1919; *m* 1941, Maureen Margaret McKinstry; two *s* two *d* (and one *s* decd). *Educ:* St Paul's School; Corpus Christi College, Oxford. Paid Local Serjeant, Oxford and Buckinghamshire Light Infantry, 1945–47. Called to the Bar, Middle Temple, 1948; Bencher, 1977. Member: Criminal Injuries Compensation Bd, 1981–; Independent Review Body for Coal Industry, 1985–. *Recreations:* music, travel. *Address:* Devereux Chambers, Devereux Court, Temple, WC2R 3JJ.

SHIELDS, Sir Neil (Stanley), Kt 1964; MC 1946; management consultant and company director; Chairman, Commission for New Towns, since 1982 (Member, since 1981); *b* 7 September 1919; *o s* of late Archie Shields and Mrs Hannah Shields; *m* 1970, Gloria Dawn Wilson. Member of Honourable Artillery Company 1939–. Served in Royal Artillery, 1939–46; commnd 1940; Major 1943. Chairman: Anglo Continental Investment & Finance Co., 1965–74; Standard Catalogue Co., 1976–84; Holcombe Hldgs, 1978–84; Trianco Redfyre, 1979–84; Director: Chesham Amalgamations & Investments, 1964–84; Continental Bankers Agents, 1965–74; Central and Sheerwood, 1969–84; Newton Chambers & Co., 1972–84; Paxall Engineering, 1976–79. Mem. Bd, LRT, 1986–; Chm., LRT Property Bd, 1986–. Prospective candidate (C) North St Pancras 1947 and contested by election 1949. Chairman: Camden Conservative Cttee, 1965–67; Hampstead Conservative Assoc., 1954–65 (Vice-Chm., 1951–54); Hon. Treas. 1965–67; National Union of Conservative and Unionist Assocs: Chm. of London Area, 1961–63 (Vice-Chm., 1959–61); Mem. of National Executive, 1955–59, 1961–67, 1968–69; Hampstead Borough Council: Mem. 1947–65; Deputy Leader, 1952–61; Chm. of Works Cttee, 1951–55; Chm. of Finance Cttee, 1955–59. Mem. Council, Aims of Industry, 1976–. Governor, Bedford Coll., London Univ., 1983–85. *Recreations:* reading, music, motoring, wining and dining. *Address:* 12 London House, Avenue Road, NW8 7PX. *T:* 01–586 4155. *Clubs:* Carlton, HAC.

SHIELDS, Prof. Robert, MD, FRCS, FRCSE; Professor of Surgery, University of Liverpool, since 1969; Consultant Surgeon, Royal Liverpool Hospital and Broadgreen Hospital, since 1969; *b* 8 Nov. 1930; *o s* of late Robert Alexander Shields and Isobel Dougall Shields; *m* 1957, Grace Marianne Swinburn; one *s* two *d*. *Educ:* John Neilson Institution, Paisley; Univ. of Glasgow. MB, ChB 1953 (Asher-Asher Medal and MacLeod Medal); MD (Hons and Bellahouston Medal) 1965; FRCSE 1959; FRCS 1966. House appts, Western Infirmary, Glasgow, 1953–54; RAMC, Captain attached 1 Bn Argyll and Sutherland Highlanders, 1954–56; RAMC (TA), Major (Surg. Specialist) attached 7 Bn A & S H, 1956–61. Hall Fellow, Univ. of Glasgow, 1957–58; Mayo Foundn Fellow, 1959–60; Lectr in Surgery, Univ. of Glasgow, 1960–63; Sen. Lectr and Reader in Surgery, Welsh Nat. Sch. of Medicine, 1963–69; Dean, Faculty of Medicine, Univ. of Liverpool, 1982–85. General Medical Council: Mem., 1982–; Member: Educn Cttee, 1984–85, 1986–87; Exec. Cttee, 1985–86; Prof. Conduct Cttee, 1986–87; Royal College of Surgeons: Mem., Ct of Examrs, 1980–86; Mem. Bd, Hunterian Inst., 1986–; Regl Advr to Mersey RHA, 1986–; Member: Surgical Research Soc. (Hon. Sec. 1972–76 and Pres. 1983–85); British Soc. of Gastroenterology (Mem. Council, 1984–86); N of England Gastroent. Soc. (Pres., 1981–83); Internat. Surgical Gp; Assoc. of Surgs of GB and Ire. (Mem. Council 1966–69; Pres., 1986–87); Cell Bd, MRC, 1974–77; Liverpool AHA(T) (Chm. Area/Univ. Liaison Cttee), 1974–78; Mersey RHA, 1982–85 (Vice-Chm., 1985); Council, RCSE, 1985–; Liverpool Med. Instn (Vice-Pres., 1983–84); Panel of Assesssors, Nat. Health and Med. Res. Council of Commonwealth and Australia, 1983–; List of Assessors for Cancer Grants, Anti-Cancer Council of Vic, Australia, 1986–. Mem., Editorial Bd of Brit. Jl of Surgery, 1970–85, and of Gut, 1969–76. Marjorie Budd Prof., Univ. of Bristol, 1983. Former Visiting Prof., Univs of Toronto, Virginia, Witwatersrand, Rochester (NY), Hong Kong, and Examiner in Surgery, Univs of Glasgow, Edinburgh, Dundee, Leicester, Sheffield, Lagos, Amman, Riyadh, Malta. Mem. Bd of Advrs in Surgery, London Univ., 1983–. Moynihan Medal, Assoc. of Surgs of GB and Ire. *Publications:* (ed jtly): Surgical Emergencies II, 1979; Textbook of Surgery, 1983; contribs to medical and surgical jls relating to surgery and gastroenterology. *Recreations:* sailing and walking. *Address:* 81 Meols Drive, West Kirby, Wirral L48 5DF. *T:* 051–632 3588. *Clubs:* Army and Navy; Racquets (Liverpool).

SHIELDS, Maj.-Gen. Ronald Frederick, OBE 1943; BSc (Eng); CEng; FIEE; *b* 4 November 1912; *s* of late John Benjamin Frederick Shields, Chichester; *m* 1944, Lorna, *d* of late Frederick Murgatroyd, Manchester; one *s* one *d*. *Educ:* Portsmouth Grammar School. Lieut RAOC 1936. Served War of 1939–45 in Middle East and NW Europe; transferred to REME, 1942; Staff College Camberley, 1945; MELF, 1948–51; AQMG, HQ Northern Comd, 1952–55; War Office, 1956–59; REME Training Centre, 1959–62; DEME, HQ, BAOR, 1962–65; Comdt, Technical Group, REME, 1965–68; retd 1968. Col, 1955; Brig. 1962; Maj.-Gen. 1965. Col Comdt, REME, 1968–73. *Address:* 58 Petersfield Road, Midhurst, West Sussex.

SHIELDS, Ronald McGregor Pollock; Managing Director, since 1970, and Deputy Chairman, since 1986, Associated Newspapers Group; *b* 30 July 1921; *s* of Thomas Shields and Beatrice Gordon; *m* 1948, Jacqueline (*née* Cowan); one *s* one *d*. *Educ:* Swanage Grammar Sch.; London Univ. (BSc (Econ)). Served War of 1939–45, Royal Artillery. Joined Associated Newspapers Gp, 1948; spent several years in various depts of the Co. and a year at Associated Rediffusion in charge of Audience Research. Set up the research co. National Opinion Polls, and was made Advertisement Dir of Associated Newspapers, 1963. Director: AmLaw Publishing Corp. (USA); Angus Ltd (USA); Associated Investments Harmsworth Ltd; Associated Magazines Ltd; Associated Newspapers N America Inc.; Associated Newspapers Property Ltd; Consolidated-Bathurst Ltd (Canada);

Blackfriars Oil Refining Co. Inc.; Continental Daily Mail SA (France); Brighton Brook Realty Inc. (USA); CB Pak Inc. (Can.); Crowvale Properties Ltd; Daily Mail Ltd; Daily Mail & General Trust plc; Ely Mine Forest Inc. (USA); English National Opera Ltd; Esquire Magazine Gp Inc (USA); Euromoney Publications Ltd; Evening Standard Co. Ltd; Harmsworth Holdings Ltd (Canada); Harmsworth Pension Funds Trustees Ltd; Harmsworth Press Ltd and Inc. (USA); Harmsworth Publications Ltd; Harmsworth Publishing Ltd; Harmsworth SARL (France); Les Investissements Bouverie (Canada); London Cab Co.; The Mail on Sunday; Mickfield Hall Farms; John M. Newton & Sons Ltd; NOP Market Research Ltd; Purfleet Deep Wharf & Storage; Reuters Hldgs plc; Southern Television; Stiles Brook Forest Inc. (USA); Trevian Hldgs plc; Weekend Publications Ltd; 13–30 Corp. (USA). FSS. *Recreations:* golf, music, the theatre. *Address:* New Carmelite House, Carmelite Street, EC4. *T:* 01–353 6000.

SHIELDS, Stuart; *see* Shields, L. S.

SHIELL, James Wyllie, BSc, FICE, FIWES; chartered civil engineer, retired; *b* 20 Aug. 1912; *yr s* of late George Douglas Shiell, farmer, Rennieston, Jedburgh and Janet Gladstone Wyllie; *m* 1941, Maureen Cameron Macpherson Hunter, *d* of late Thomas Hunter, Leeds; two *s*. *Educ:* Jedburgh Grammar and Kelso High Schools; Edinburgh Univ. Municipal Engrg posts in Edinburgh, Southampton, Sunderland and Leeds, 1934–39; Sen. Engr on Staff of J. D. & D. M. Watson, Consulting Engrs, Westminster, 1939–43 and 1945–47; Civil Engr on wartime service with Admty, 1943–45; Sen. Engr, Min. of Agriculture, 1947–49; Engrg Inspector, Dept of Health for Scotland, 1949–62; Dep. Chief Engr, Scottish Development Dept, 1962–68; Under Sec. and Chief Engr, Scottish Development Dept, 1968–75. Hon. FInstWPC. *Recreations:* bowling, photography. *Address:* 25 Mortonhall Road, Edinburgh EH9 2HS. *T:* 031–667 8528.

SHIERLAW, Norman Craig; Senior Partner, N. C. Shierlaw & Associates (Stock and Sharebrokers), since 1968; *b* 17 Aug. 1921; *s* of Howard Alison Shierlaw and Margaret Bruce; *m* 1944, Patricia Yates; two *d*. *Educ:* Pulteney Grammar Sch., Adelaide; St Peter's Coll., Adelaide; Univ. of Adelaide (BE). Assoc. Mem. Australian Inst. Mining and Metallurgy; FSASM; Mining Manager's Certificate. War Service, AIF, 1941–45 (War Service medals). Mining Engr with North Broken Hill Ltd, 1949–58; Sharebroker's Clerk, 1959–60; Partner, F. W. Porter & Co. (Sharebrokers), 1960–68. Director: Australian Development Ltd, 1959–; Poseidon Ltd, 1968–77; North Flinders Mines Ltd, 1969–77; Nobelex NL, 1974–. FAIM 1971. *Recreations:* golf, tennis. *Address:* N. C. Shierlaw & Associates, 28 Grenfell Street, Adelaide, SA 5000, Australia. *T:* Adelaide 51–7468. *Clubs:* Royal Automobile (Sydney); Naval, Military and Air Force, Stock Exchange, Kooyonga Golf (Adelaide); West Australian (Perth).

SHIFFNER, Sir Henry David, 8th Bt, *cr* 1818; Company Director; *b* 2 Feb. 1930; *s* of Major Sir Henry Shiffner, 7th Bt, and Margaret Mary, *er d* of late Sir Ernest Gowers, GCB, GBE; *S* father, 1941; *m* 1st, 1949, Dorothy Jackson (marr. diss. 1956); one *d* (and one *d* decd); 2nd, 1957, Beryl (marr. diss. 1970), *d* of George Milburn, Saltdean, Sussex; one *d*; 3rd, 1970, Joaquina Ramos Lopez. *Educ:* Rugby; Trinity Hall, Cambridge. *Heir: cousin* George Frederick Shiffner [*b* 3 August 1936; *m* 1961, Dorothea Helena Cynthia, *d* of late T. H. McLean; one *s* one *d*]. *Club:* Royal Automobile.

SHILLINGFORD, Arden; *see* Shillingford, R. A. C.

SHILLINGFORD, Prof. John Parsons, MD (Harvard and London), FRCP, FACP; FACC; Sir John McMichael Professor of Cardiovascular Medicine, Royal Postgraduate Medical School, London University, 1976–79, now Emeritus Professor (Director, Cardiovascular Research Unit, and Professor of Angiocardiology, 1966–76); Consultant Medical Director, British Heart Foundation, 1981–86; *b* 15 April 1914; *s* of Victor Shillingford and Ethel Eugenie Parsons; *m* 1947, Doris Margaret Franklin; two *s* one *d*. *Educ:* Bishops Stortford; Harvard Univ.; London Hosp. Med. Sch. Rockefeller Student, Harvard Med. Sch., 1939–42; House appts, Presbyterian Hosp., New York, and London Hosp., 1943–45; Med. First Asst, London Hosp., 1945–52; Sen. Lectr Royal Postgrad. Med. Sch., 1958–62. Pres., Sect. Experimental Med., Royal Soc. Med., 1968; Sec., Brit. Cardiac Soc., 1963–70; Chm. Org. Cttee, Sixth World Congress Cardiology, 1970; Lumleian Lectr, RCP, 1972. Member: Assoc. Physicians Gt Brit.; Med. Res. Soc.; Med. Soc. London; Royal Soc. Med.; Comité Recherche Médicale, EEC; various cttees, Brit. Heart Foundn. Hon. Mem.: Hellenic Cardiac Soc.; Cardiac Soc. of Yugoslavia; Polish Cardiac Soc.; Cardiological Soc. of India; French Cardiac Soc.; Corr. Mem., Australian Cardiac Soc.; Fellow, Amer. Coll. of Cardiology; Hon. FACP; Editor, Cardiovascular Research. Visiting Prof., Australian Heart Foundn, 1965; lectured extensively in Europe, USA, S America, Africa, Middle East. James Berry Prize, RCS. *Publications:* numerous scientific papers, mainly on heart disease and coronary thrombosis. *Recreation:* sailing. *Address:* Crohamhurst, Hesworth Lane, Fittleworth, W Sussex RH20 1EW. *T:* Fittleworth 290. *Club:* Hurlingham.

SHILLINGFORD, (Romeo) Arden (Coleridge), MBE 1977; Permanent Secretary, Ministry of Community Development, Housing and Social Affairs, Commonwealth of Dominica, since 1985; *b* 11 Feb. 1936; *s* of Stafford Shillingford and Ophelia Thomas, step *d* of Hosford Samuel O'Brien and *d* of Clarita (*née* Hunt), Roseau, Dominica; *m* 1st, Evelyn Blanche Hart; one *s* one *d*; 2nd, Maudline Joan Green; three *s*. *Educ:* Wesley High Sch., Roseau Boys' Sch., Dominica; grammar school; School of Law. Member, Hon. Soc. Inner Temple. Joined Dominican Civil Service, 1957, after brief period as solicitor's clerk; junior clerk, various Govt Depts, Dominica, 1957–59; Clerk of Court, then Chief Clerk, Magistrates' Office, 1960–61; joined staff, Eastern Caribbean Commn, London, on secondment from Dominican CS, 1965; served variously as Migrants' Welfare Officer, Students' Officer, Asst Trade Sec. and PA to Comr, 1968–71; Admin. Asst, Consular and Protocol Affairs, 1973–78 (actg Comr, several occasions, 1975–78); High Comr in UK, 1978–85 (concurrently non-resident Ambassador to France, Spain, Belgium, W Germany and EEC, Brussels). Past Member, numerous cttees and ad hoc bodies for West Indian Immigrant Welfare and Education; Dep. Chm., Bd of Governors, W Indian Students' Centre, 1970–75, Chm., 1976–79; Member, West India Cttee (Vice-Pres. 1979–). Liaison Officer, Victoria League for Commonwealth Friendship; Founder-Mem. and Vice-Chm., Jaycees (Dominica Jun. Chamber of Commerce). *Recreations:* cricket, collecting authentic folk music, swimming. *Address:* Ministry of Community Development, Housing and Social Affairs, Government Headquarters, Roseau, Commonwealth of Dominica, W Indies.

SHILLINGTON, Sir (Robert Edward) Graham, Kt 1972; CBE 1970 (OBE 1959; MBE 1951); DL; Chief Constable, Royal Ulster Constabulary, 1970–73; *b* 2 April 1911; *s* of Major D. Graham Shillington, DL, MP, and Mrs Louisa Shillington (*née* Collen); *m* 1935, Mary E. R. Bulloch (*d* 1977), Holywood, Co. Down; two *s* one *d*. *Educ:* Sedbergh Sch., Yorks; Clare Coll., Cambridge. Royal Ulster Constabulary: Officer Cadet, 1933; 3rd Class District Inspector, 1934; 2nd Class District Inspector, 1936; 1st Class District Inspector, 1944; County Inspector, 1953; Commissioner, Belfast, 1961; Deputy Inspector General (Deputy Chief Constable), 1969–70. Chm., Belfast Voluntary Welfare Soc., 1976–81. DL Co. Down, 1975. King's Coronation Medal, 1937; Queen's Coronation Medal, 1953; Police Long Service and Good Conduct Medal, 1955; RUC Service Medal, 1985. *Recreations:* golf, gardening. *Address:* Ardeevin, 184 Bangor Road, Holywood, Co. Down. *T:* Holywood 3471. *Clubs:* Royal Over-Seas League; Royal Belfast Golf, Royal County Down Golf.

SHILLITO, Charles Henry; Under-Secretary, Ministry of Agriculture, Fisheries and Food, 1974–82; *b* 8 Jan. 1922; *s* of Charles Cawthorne and Florence Shillito; *m* 1947, Elizabeth Jean (*née* Bull); two *d*. *Educ:* Hugh Bell Sch., Middlesbrough. Clerk, Min. of Agriculture and Fisheries, 1938; War Service, Lieut RNVR, 1941–46; Principal, MAFF, 1957; Asst Sec. 1966; Section Head, Nat. Econ. Develt Office, 1966–69 (on secondment). Hon. ARCVS 1986. *Recreations:* gardening, nautical pursuits. *Address:* 62 Downs Road, Coulsdon, Surrey CR3 1AB. *T:* Downland 53392.

SHILLITO, Edward Alan, CB 1964; retired Civil Servant; *b* 13 May 1910; *s* of late Rev. Edward and Mrs Annie Shillito, Buckhurst Hill, Essex; *m* 1934, Dorothy Jean, *d* of late Robert J. Davies, Buckhurst Hill, Essex; two *s* three *d*. *Educ:* Chigwell School; Oriel College, Oxford (Exhibitioner). Litt Hum 2nd Class, 1933; MA 1985. Customs and Excise, 1934–36; HM Treas., 1936–57; Under-Secretary, 1951; Admiralty, and MoD, 1957–69; Dir, Greenwich Hosp., 1969–71; a Gen. Comr of Income Tax, 1972–82. Imperial Defence College course, 1953. *Recreations:* music, lacrosse (Oxford Univ., 1931–33). *Address:* 8 Baldwins Hill, Loughton, Essex. *T:* 01–508 1988.

SHINDLER, George John, QC 1970; **His Honour Judge Shindler;** a Circuit Judge, since 1980; *b* 27 Oct. 1922; *yr s* of late Dr Bruno and Mrs Alma Schindler; *m* 1955, Eva Muller; three *s*. *Educ:* Regent's Park Sch.; University Coll. Sch., Hampstead. Served in Royal Tank Regt, NW Europe, 1942–47. Called to Bar, Inner Temple, 1952; Bencher 1978. Standing Counsel to Inland Revenue at Central Criminal Court and all London sessions, 1965–70; a Recorder of the Crown Court, 1972–80. Legal Mem., Mental Health Review Tribunal, 1983–. *Recreations:* theatre, music, reading, watching soccer and cricket, travel. *Address:* c/o Queen Elizabeth Building, Temple, EC4Y 9BS. *T:* 01–353 6453. *Club:* MCC.

SHINNIE, Prof. Peter Lewis; Professor of Archæology, in the University of Calgary, 1970–80, now Emeritus; *b* 1915; *s* of late Andrew James Shinnie, OBE; *m* 1st, 1940, Margaret Blanche Elizabeth Cloake; two *s* one *d*; 2nd, Ama Nantwi. *Educ:* Westminster Sch.; Christ Church, Oxford. Served War with RAF, 1939–45. Temp. Asst Keeper, Ashmolean Museum, 1945; Asst Commissioner for Archæology, Sudan Government, 1946; Commissioner for Archæology, Sudan Govt, 1948; Director of Antiquities, Uganda, 1956; Prof. of Archæology: Univ. of Ghana, 1958–66; Univ. of Khartoum, 1966–70. FSA. Hon. LLD Calgary, 1983. *Publications:* Excavation at Soba, 1955; Medieval Nubia, 1954; Ghazali: A Monastery in Northern Sudan, 1960; Meroe-Civilization of the Sudan, 1967; The African Iron Age, 1971; Debeira West, 1978; (with R. J. Bradley) The Capital of Kush, 1980; articles in Journal of Egyptian Archæology, Sudan Notes and Records, Kush. *Recreations:* reading, photography, travelling in Greece. *Address:* Department of Archæology, University of Calgary, Calgary, T2N 1N4 Canada. *T:* 403–284–5227. *Club:* Athenæum.

SHIRER, William Lawrence; broadcaster, journalist; author; *b* Chicago, 23 Feb. 1904; *s* of Seward Smith Shirer; *m* 1931, Theresa Stiberitz; two *d*. *Educ:* Coe College. DLitt (Hon.). Légion d'Honneur. *Publications:* Berlin Diary, 1941; End of a Berlin Diary, 1947; The Traitor, 1950; Mid-Century Journey, 1953; Stranger Come Home, 1954; The Challenge of Scandinavia, 1955; The Consul's Wife, 1956; The Rise and Fall of The Third Reich, 1960; The Rise and Fall of Adolf Hitler, 1961; The Sinking of the Bismarck, 1962; The Collapse of the Third Republic, 1970; 20th Century Journey: a memoir of a Life and the Times, vol. I, The Start 1904–1930, 1976, vol. II, The Nightmare Years 1930–1940, 1984; Gandhi, a Memoir, 1979. *Recreations:* walking, sailing. *Address:* Box 487, 34 Sunset Avenue, Lenox, Massachusetts 01240, USA. *Club:* Century (New York).

SHIRLEY, family name of **Earl Ferrers.**

SHIRLEY, Philip Hammond; retired; *b* 4 Oct. 1912; *s* of Frank Shillito Shirley and Annie Lucy (*née* Hammond); *m* 1st, 1936, Marie Edna Walsh (*d* 1972); one *s* one *d*; 2nd, 1973, Norma Jones. *Educ:* Sydney Church of England Grammar School (Shore). Qualified in Australia as Chartered Accountant, 1934; with Peat Marwick Mitchell & Co., Chartered Accountants, London, 1937–49; with Unilever from 1951; Dep. Chief Accountant, 1951–52; Chief Accountant, 1952–58; Chm. Batchelors Foods Ltd 1958–61; Mem. BTC (Oct. 1961–Nov. 1962); Mem. BR Bd, 1962–67 (Vice-Chm. Bd, 1964–67); Dep. Chm., Cunard Steamship Co., 1968–71; Chief Commissioner of Public Transport, NSW, 1972–75. *Recreation:* bowls. *Address:* 11, 25 Belmont Avenue, Wollstonecraft, NSW 2065, Australia.

SHIRLEY, Mrs Stephanie; *see* Shirley, Mrs V. S.

SHIRLEY, Mrs (Vera) Stephanie, (Steve), OBE 1980; CBIM, FBCS; Founder and Group Managing Director, F International Group plc, since 1984 (Director, since 1962); *b* 16 Sept. 1933; *d* of late Arnold Buchthal and of Mrs Margaret Brook (formerly Buchthal, *née* Schick); *m* 1959, Derek George Millington Shirley; one *s*. *Educ:* Sir John Cass Coll., London. BSc (Spec.) London 1956. CBIM 1984; FBCS 1971. PO Res. Stn, Dollis Hill, 1951–59; CDL (subsid. of ICL), 1959–62; F International Group and its overseas subsids, 1962–. Vice Pres. (Professional), British Computer Soc., 1979–82; Member: Computer, Systems and Electronics Requirements Bd, 1979–81; Electronics and Avionics Requirements Bd, 1981–83; Open Tech, MSC, 1983–; Council, Industrial Soc., 1984–; BBC Consultative Group on Industrial and Business Affairs, 1985–. Consulting Editor on information processing, J. Wiley & Sons, 1978–. Mem. Council, City Univ. Business Sch., 1986–. FRSA 1985. *Publications:* articles in prof. jls, reviews, proc. of confs, and papers. *Recreation:* sleep. *Address:* c/o F International Group plc, The Bury, Church Street, Chesham, Bucks HP5 1JE. *T:* Chesham 773232.

SHIRLEY-QUIRK, John Stanton, CBE 1975; bass-baritone singer; *b* 28 Aug. 1931; *s* of Joseph Stanley and Amelia Shirley-Quirk; *m* 1st, 1955, Patricia Hastie (*d* 1981); one *s* one *d*; 2nd, 1981, Sara V. Watkins; one *s* one *d*. *Educ:* Holt School, Liverpool; Liverpool University. Violin Scholarship, 1945; read Chemistry, Liverpool Univ., 1948–53; BSc (Hons), 1952; Dipl. in Educn 1953; became professional singer, 1961. Officer in Education Br., RAF, 1953–57. Asst Lectr in Chemistry, Acton Technical Coll., 1957–61; Lay-clerk in St Paul's Cathedral, 1961–62. First Appearance Glyndebourne Opera in Elegy for Young Lovers, 1961; subseq. 1962, 1963. Sang in first performance of Curlew River, 1964, The Burning Fiery Furnace, 1966, The Prodigal Son, 1968, Owen Wingrave, 1970, Death in Venice, 1973, Confessions of a Justified Sinner, 1976, The Ice Break, 1977. Has sung world wide. First American tour, 1966; Australian tour, 1967; first appearance Metropolitan Opera, NY, 1974. Has made numerous recordings: operas, songs, cantatas, etc. Mem. Court, Brunel Univ., 1977–. Hon. RAM 1972; Hon. DMus Liverpool, 1976; DUniv Brunel, 1981. Liverpool Univ. Chem. Soc. Medal, 1965; Sir Charles Santley Meml Gift, Worshipful Co. of Musicians, 1969. *Recreations:* trees, canals, clocks. *Address:* 51 Wellesley Road, Twickenham, Middlesex TW2 5RX. *T:* 01–894 1714.

SHIRRAS, Ven. Edward Scott; Archdeacon of Northolt, since 1985; *b* 23 April 1937; *s* of Edward Shirras and Alice Emma Shirras (*née* Morten); *m* 1962, Pamela Susan Mackenzie; two *s* two *d*. *Educ:* Sevenoaks School; St Andrews Univ. (BSc); Union Coll., Schenectady, NY, USA; Clifton Theolog. Coll., Bristol. Curate: Christ Church, Surbiton Hill, 1963–66; Jesmond Parish Church, Newcastle upon Tyne, 1966–68; Church Pastoral Aid Society: Youth Sec., 1968–71; Publications Sec., 1971–74; Asst Gen. Sec., 1974–75; Vicar of Christ Church, Roxeth, dio. London, 1975–85; Area Dean of Harrow, 1982–85. *Recreations:* transport photography (Scottish), Aberdeen FC. *Address:* 71 Gayton Road, Harrow, Middx HA1 2LY. *T:* 01–863 1530.

SHOCK, Maurice; Vice-Chancellor of Leicester University, 1977–Aug. 1987; Rector, Lincoln College, Oxford, from Aug. 1987; Chairman, Committee of Vice-Chancellors and Principals, 1985–87 (Vice-Chairman, 1983–85); *b* 15 April 1926; *o s* of Alfred and Ellen Shock; *m* 1947, Dorothy Donald; one *s* three *d*. *Educ:* King Edward's Sch., Birmingham; Balliol Coll., Oxford (MA); St Antony's Coll., Oxford. Served Intell. Corps, 1945–48. Lectr in Politics, Christ Church and Trinity Coll., Oxford, 1955–56; Fellow and Praelector in Politics, University Coll., Oxford, 1956–77; Estates Bursar, 1959–74; Sen. Treasurer, Oxford Union Soc., 1954–72; Member: Franks Commn of Inquiry into the University of Oxford, 1964–66; Hebdomadal Council, Oxford Univ., 1969–75; Chm., Univ. Authorities Panel, 1980–85. Vis. Prof. of Govt, Pomona Coll., 1961–62, 1968–69. Mem., ESRC, 1981–85; a Governing Trustee, Nuffield Provincial Hosps Trust, 1980–. *Publications:* The Liberal Tradition; articles on politics and recent history. *Recreations:* gardening, theatre. *Address:* Knighton Hall, Leicester LE2 3WG. *T:* Leicester 706677; (from Aug. 1987) Lincoln College, Oxford.

SHOCKLEY, Dr William (Bradford); Medal of Merit (US) 1946; Alexander M. Poniatoff Professor of Engineering Science, Stanford University, 1963–75, Professor Emeritus 1975; Executive Consultant, Bell Telephone Laboratories, 1965–75; *b* 13 Feb. 1910; *s* of William Hillman Shockley and May (*née* Bradford); *m* 1933, Jean Alberta Bailey; two *s* one *d*; *m* 1955, Emmy I. Lanning. *Educ:* Calif. Inst. of Technology (BS); Mass Inst. Tech. (PhD). Teaching Fellow, Mass. Inst. Tech., 1932–36; Mem. Technical Staff, Bell Teleph. Laboratories, 1936–42 and 1945–54; Director Transistor Physics Department, 1954–55. Dir of Research, Anti-submarine Warfare Ops Research Gp, US Navy, 1942–44; Expert Consultant, Office of Secretary of War, 1944–45. Visiting Lectr, Princeton Univ., 1946; Scientific Advisor, Policy Council, Jt Research and Development Bd, 1947–49; Visiting Prof., Calif. Inst. Tech., 1954; Dep. Dir and Dir of Research, Weapons Systems Evaluation Gp, Dept of Defense, 1954–55; Dir, Shockley Semiconductor Lab. of Beckman Instruments, Inc., 1955–58; Pres. Shockley Transistor Corp., 1958–60; Director, Shockley Transistor, Unit of Clevite Transistor, 1960–63; Consultant, 1963–65. Member: US Army Science Advisory Panel, 1951–63, 1964–; USAF Science Advisory Board, 1959–63; National Academy of Science, 1951–; Sigma Xi; Tau Beta Pi. National Inventors' Hall of Fame, 1974; more than 90 US Patents. Inventor of junction transistor; research on energy bands of solids, ferromagnetic domains, plastic properties of metals, theory of grain boundaries, order and disorder in alloys; semi-conductor theory and electromagnetic theory; mental tools for sci. thinking, ops res. on human quality statistics. Fellowship fund established in his name with Bardeen and Brattain, SEMI, 1977. Fellow AAAS. Hon. DSc: Pennsylvania, 1955; Rutgers 1956; Gustavus Adolphus Coll., 1963. Morris Liebmann Prize, 1951, Gold Medal, 1972, Medal of Honour, 1980, Centennial Medal and Certificate, 1984, IEEE. Air Force Citation of Honour, 1951; O. E. Buckley Prize (Amer. Physical Soc.), 1953; US Army Cert. of Appreciation, 1953; Comstock Prize (Nat. Acad. of Science), 1954; (jtly) Nobel Prize in Physics, 1956; Wilhelm Exner Medal (Oesterreichischer Gewerberein), 1963; Holley Medal (Amer. Soc. Mech. Engrs), 1963; Caltech Alumni Distinguished Service Award, 1966; NASA Certificate of Appreciation (Apollo 8), 1969; Public Service Group Achievement Award, NASA, 1969; California Inventors Hall of Fame, 1983. *Publications:* Electrons and Holes in Semiconductors, 1950; Mechanics (with W. A. Gong), 1966; (ed) Imperfections of Nearly Perfect Crystals; over 100 articles in sci. and tech. jls. *Recreations:* mountain climbing, swimming, sailing. *Address:* 797 Esplanada Way, Stanford, Calif 94305, USA. *Clubs:* Cosmos, University (Washington, DC); Bohemian (San Francisco); Stanford Faculty; Palo Alto Yacht.

SHOENBERG, Prof. David, MBE 1944; FRS 1953; Professor of Physics, Cambridge University and Head of Low Temperature Physics Group, Cavendish Laboratory, 1973–78, now Emeritus; Life Fellow of Gonville and Caius College; *b* 4 Jan. 1911; *s* of Isaac and Esther Shoenberg; *m* 1940, Catherine Felicitée Fischmann; one *s* two *d*. *Educ:* Latymer Upper School, W6; Trinity College, Cambridge (Scholar). PhD 1935; Exhibition of 1851 Senior Student, 1936–39; Research in low temperature physics, 1932–, in charge of Royal Soc. Mond Laboratory, 1947–73; Univ. Lectr in Physics, 1944–52; Univ. Reader in Physics, 1952–73; UNESCO Adviser on Low Temperature Physics, NPL of India, 1953–54. Guthrie Lectr, 1961; Mellon Prof., Univ. of Pittsburgh, 1962; Gauss Prof., Univ. of Göttingen, 1964; Visiting Professor: Univ. of Maryland, 1968; Univ. of Toronto, 1974; Univ. of Waterloo, 1977; Rutherford Meml Lectr, India and Sri Lanka, 1980. Hon. Foreign Mem., Amer. Acad. of Arts and Sciences, 1982. Dr (*hc*) Univ. of Lausanne, 1973. Fritz London Award for Low Temperature Physics, 1964. *Publications:* Superconductivity, 1938, revised edn, 1952; Magnetism, 1949; Magnetic Oscillations in Metals, 1984; scientific papers on low temperature physics and magnetism. *Address:* 2 Long Road, Cambridge CB2 2PS; Cavendish Laboratory, Madingley Road, Cambridge CB3 0HE. *T:* Cambridge 337733.

SHOLL, Hon. Sir Reginald (Richard), Kt 1962; MA, BCL, Oxon; MA Melbourne; QC; retired Judge; former legal consultant and company director, Melbourne and Queensland; *b* 8 Oct. 1902; *e s* of late Reginald Frank and Alice Maud Sholl (*née* Mumby), Melbourne; *m* 1st, 1927, Hazel Ethel (*d* 1962), *yr d* of late Alfred L. and Fanny Bradshaw, Melbourne; two *s* two *d*; 2nd, 1964, Anna Campbell, *widow* of Alister Bruce McLean, Melbourne, and *e d* of late Campbell Colin and Edith Carpenter, Indiana, USA. *Educ:* Melbourne Church of England Grammar Sch.; Trinity Coll., Univ. of Melbourne; New Coll., Oxford. 1st Cl. Final Hons and exhibn, Sch. of Classical Philology, and Wyselaskie Schol. in Classical and Comparative Philology and Logic, Melbourne Univ., 1922; Rhodes Schol., Victoria, 1924; 1st Cl. Final Hons, School of Jurisprudence, Oxford, 1926, Bar Finals, London, 1926 and BCL, Oxford, 1927; Official Law Fellow, Brasenose Coll., Oxford, 1927. Called to Bar, Middle Temple, 1927; journalist, London, 1927; Tutor in Classics, Melbourne Univ., 1928–29; Lectr in law, 1928–38; Barrister, Melbourne, 1929–49; admitted to Bars of NSW and Tasmania, 1935. Served Aust. Army, 1940–44; Capt. retd. Chm. various Commonwealth Bds of Inquiry into Army contracts, 1941–42; KC Vic. and Tas., 1947, NSW 1948; Justice of the Supreme Court of Victoria, 1950–66; Australian Consul-Gen. in New York, 1966–69; Chm., Western Australian Parly Salaries Tribunal, 1971–77. Consultant: to Russell, Kennedy & Cook, solicitors, Melbourne, 1969–79; to Nat. Trustees Executors and Agency Co. of Australasia Ltd; Chm., Sperry Rand Corp. (Australia), 1969–74, and Mem. Internat. Adv. Bd, Sperry Rand Corp. (USA), 1971–74. Pres. ESU (Vic. Br.) 1961–66; Fed. Chm., ESU in Aust., 1961–63, 1969–73; Trustee, Northcote Trust Fund, 1978–; Member: Aust. Bd of Trustees, Northcote Children's Emigration Fund for Aust., 1950–78; Bd, US Educnl Foundn in Aust., 1961–64; Archbishop-in-Council, Dio. Melbourne, 1958–66, 1969–79; Advocate of Diocese of Melbourne, 1969–79; Mem. Councils: Trinity Coll., Melbourne, 1939–66; C of E Grammar Sch., Melbourne, 1960–66; Peninsula Sch., Mt Eliza, 1960–63; Toorak Coll., 1969–71; C of E Girls' Grammar Sch., Melbourne, 1969–75; Aust. Adv. Council of Elders, 1983–; Hon. Life Mem., Nat. Gall. of Vic., 1975 (Trustee, 1950–63, Dep. Chm. 1958). Pres. Somers Area, Boy Scouts Assoc. (Vic. Br.), 1955–64, 1972–76; Member: State Exec. Boy Scouts Assoc., 1958–66, (Vice-Pres., 1964–66); Nat. Council Australian Boy Scouts Assoc., 1959–69, 1975–; Cttee, Overseas Service Bureau (Australia), 1970–71; Foundn Dir, Winston Churchill Memorial Trust in Australia, 1965–66, Dep. Nat. Chm., 1969–75, Dep. Nat. Pres., 1975–81; Chm., Nat. Fellowship Cttee, 1965–66, 1969–75; Mem., Victoria Cttee, Duke of Edinburgh's Award in Australia, 1964–66; Chairman, Vict. Supreme Court Rules Cttee, 1960–66; Chm., Royal Commn, Western Australia Inquiry into the airline system, 1974–75. Stawell Orator, 1970; Fellow, Trinity Coll., Melbourne, 1981. *Publications:* contrib. to legal periodicals. *Recreations:* golf, bowls, sailing, gardening; formerly football (Melbourne Univ. blue) and lacrosse (Oxford half-blue). *Address:* 11/168 Toorak Road West, South Yarra, Vic 3141, Australia. *Clubs:* Melbourne, Australian (Melbourne); Peninsula Country (Victoria); Queensland (Brisbane); Melbourne Cricket (1918–), Surfers Paradise Bridge (Qld).

SHONE, Very Rev. John Terence; Dean of the United Diocese of St Andrews, Dunkeld and Dunblane, since 1982; Diocesan Research and Development Officer, since 1986; *b* 15 May 1935; *s* of late Arthur Shone and of E. B. Shone; *m* 1958, Ursula Ruth Buss; three *s*. *Educ:* St Dunstan's College; Selwyn Coll., Cambridge (BA 1958, MA 1962); Lincoln Theological Coll. Deacon 1960, priest 1961, London; Curate, St Pancras Parish Church, 1960–62; Chaplain, St Andrew's Cathedral, Aberdeen, 1962–65; Chaplain to Anglican Students, Aberdeen, 1962–68; Lectr, Aberdeen Coll. of Education, 1965–68; Exam. Chaplain to Bishop of Aberdeen, 1966–68; Vicar, St Andrew and St Luke, Grimsby, 1968–69; Rector, St Saviour, Bridge of Allan, 1969–86; Chaplain, Stirling Univ., 1969–80; Priest i/c, St John's, Alloa, 1977–85, and St James', Dollar, 1981–86; Canon, St Ninian's Cathedral, Perth, 1980–82. *Address:* 66 Jeanfield Road, Perth PH1 1NZ. *T:* Perth 21373.

SHONE, Sir Robert Minshull, Kt 1955; CBE 1949; *b* 27 May 1906; *s* of Robert Harold Shone. *Educ:* Sedbergh School; Liverpool University (MEng); Chicago Univ. (MA Economics). Commonwealth Fellow, USA, 1932–34; Lecturer, London School of Economics, 1935–36; British Iron and Steel Federation, 1936–39 and 1946–53, Director 1950–53; Iron and Steel Control, 1940–45, Gen. Dir, 1943–45; Executive Member, Iron and Steel Board, 1953–62; Joint Chairman, UK and ECSC Steel Committee, 1954–62; Dir-Gen., Nat. Economic Develt Council, 1962–66; Research Fellow, Nuffield Coll., Oxford, 1966–67; Special Prof., Nottingham Univ., 1971–73; Vis. Prof., City Univ., 1967–83. Director: M & G Gp, 1966–84; Rank Orgn, 1968–78; A. P. V. Holdings Ltd, 1969–75. Hon. Fellow, LSE. Pres., Soc. of Business Economists, 1963–68. *Publications:* Problems of Investment, 1971; Price and Investment Relationships, 1975; contributions to: Some Modern Business Problems, 1937; The Industrial Future of Great Britain, 1948; Large Scale Organisation, 1950; Models for Decision, 1965; Britain and the Common Market, 1967; Financial Management Handbook, 1978; articles in journals. *Recreation:* golf. *Address:* 7 Windmill Hill, Hampstead, NW3. *T:* 01–435 1930.

SHOOTER, Prof. Reginald Arthur, CBE 1980; Emeritus Professor of Medical Microbiology, London University, since 1981; *b* 1916; *s* of Rev. A. E. Shooter, TD and M. K. Shooter; *m* 1946, Jean Wallace, MB, ChB; one *s* three *d*. *Educ:* Mill Hill Sch.; Caius Coll., Cambridge; St Bartholomew's Hosp. BA 1937; MB, BChir 1940; MRCS, LRCP 1940; MA 1941; MD 1945; MRCP 1961; FRCP 1968; FRCS 1977; FRCPath 1963 (Vice-Pres., 1971–74). After various Hosp. appts became Surgeon Lieut, RNVR. Appointments at St Bartholomew's Hospital from 1946; Rockefeller Travelling Fellow in Medicine, 1950–51; Reader in Bacteriology, 1953–61, Prof. of Medical Microbiology, 1961–81, Univ. of London; Bacteriologist to St Bartholomew's Hosp., 1961–81 and Dean, Medical Coll., 1972–81. Member: City and E London AHA (T), 1974–81; Gloucester HA, 1982–85; Chm., Regional Computing Policy Steering Gp, SW RHA, 1983–85. Mem., Public Health Lab. Service Bd, 1970–82; Chm., Dangerous Pathogens Adv. Gp, 1975–81. Mem., Scientific Adv. Council, Stress Foundn, 1981–. Governor: St Bartholomew's Hosp., 1972–74; Queen Mary Coll., 1972–81; Trustee, Mitchell City of London Trust, 1958–82; Mem. Court, City Univ., 1972–81. Pybus Medal, N of England Surg. Soc., 1979. Asst Editor, British Jl of Exp. Pathology, 1953–58; Hon. Editor, RSocMed, 1960–65. *Publications:* books, and articles in medical journals. *Recreations:* archaeology, gardening, fishing. *Address:* Eastlea, Back Edge Lane, The Edge, Stroud, Glos GL6 6PE. *T:* Painswick 812408.

SHOPPEE, Prof. Charles William, FRS 1956; FAA 1958; Emeritus Professor of Chemistry, University of Sydney; *b* London, 24 Feb. 1904; *er s* of J. W. and Elizabeth Shoppee, Totteridge; *m* 1929, Eileen Alice West; one *d*. *Educ:* Stationers' Company's Sch.; Univs of London and Leeds. PhD, DSc (London); MA, DPhil (Basle). Sen. Student of Royal Commn for Exhibition of 1851, 1926–28; Asst Lecturer and Lecturer in Organic Chemistry, Univ. of Leeds, 1929–39; Rockefeller Research Fellow, Univ. of Basle, 1939–45; Reader in Chemistry, Univ. of London, at Royal Cancer Hosp., 1945–48; Prof. of Chemistry, Univ. of Wales, at University Coll., Swansea, 1948–56; Prof. of Organic Chemistry, Univ. of Sydney, 1956–70; Foundation Welch Prof. of Chemistry, Texas Tech. Univ., 1970–75. Visiting Professor of Chemistry: Duke Univ., N Carolina, USA, 1963; Univ. of Georgia, USA, 1966; Univ. of Mississippi, USA, 1968; Hon. Professorial Fellow in Chem., Macquarie Univ., 1976–79; Hon. Vis. Prof. of Organic Chem., La Trobe Univ., 1980–. *Publications:* Scientific papers in Jl Chem. Soc. and Helvetica Chimica Acta. *Recreations:* bowls, music, bridge. *Address:* Unit 1, 75 Normanby Road, Kew, Vic 3101, Australia. *T:* 817–2644. *Club:* Royal Automobile of Victoria.

SHORE, David Teignmouth, OBE 1982; FEng 1979; Director (Technical), APV Holdings PLC, since 1984; *b* 15 Nov. 1928; *e s* of Geoffrey and Cecilia Mary Shore; *m* 1950, Pamela Goodge; one *s* two *d*. *Educ:* Tiffin Boys' Sch., Kingston; Imperial Coll., London (MSc(Eng)). FIMechE 1967; FIChemE 1970; FIFST 1970; FCGI 1979. Engrg apprenticeship, 1944–47; Thermal Engr, Foster Wheeler Ltd, 1953–54; APV Co. Ltd: Research Engr, 1950–52; Process Develt Engr, 1954–65; Research Dir, 1965–77; Man. Dir, 1977–82; Chm., 1982–84; Divisional Dir, APV Holdings PLC, 1982–84. Chm., British Food Manufg Industries Res. Assoc., 1984–; Chm. Engrg Bd, 1985– and Mem. Council, 1985–, SERC; Member: Bd of Advisers in Chemical Engrg, Univ. of London, 1983–; Bd of Food Studies, Univ. of Reading, 1984–; Jt Delegacy for Food Res. Inst., Reading, 1985–. *Publications:* technical articles on rheology, heat transfer and food process engrg in learned jls. *Recreations:* walking, astronomy, wine-making. *Address:* Hembury, Garratts Lane, Banstead, Surrey. *T:* Burgh Heath 53721. *Club:* National Liberal.

SHORE, Dr Elizabeth Catherine, CB 1980; Postgraduate Medical Dean, North West Thames Region, since 1985; *b* 1927; *d* of Edward Murray Wrong and Rosalind Grace Smith; *m* 1948, Rt Hon. Peter David Shore, *qv*; one *s* two *d* (and one *s* decd). *Educ:* Newnham Coll., Cambridge; St Bartholomew's Hospital. MRCP, FRCP; MRCS, FFCM, DRCOG. Joined Medical Civil Service, 1962, Dep. Chief Medical Officer, DHSS,

1977–85. Chm., Council, Child Accident Prevention Trust. *Recreations:* reading, cookery, swimming in rough seas. *Address:* 33 Millman Street, WC1N 3EJ.

SHORE, Jack; Head of Chester School of Art, 1960–81; President, Royal Cambrian Academy of Art, 1977–83; *b* 17 July 1922; *s* of Frank and Maggie Shore; *m* 1970, Olive Brenda Williams; one *s* one *d*. *Educ:* Accrington and Manchester Schools of Art. Lectr, Blackpool School of Art, 1945–60. RCamA 1962 (ARCamA 1961). Jubilee Medal, 1977. *Recreations:* gardening, enjoyment of music. *Address:* 11 St George's Crescent, Queens Park, Chester CH4 7AR. *T:* Chester 675017.

SHORE, Rt. Hon. Peter (David), PC 1967; MP (Lab) Bethnal Green and Stepney, since 1983 (Stepney, 1964–74; Stepney and Poplar, 1974–83); *b* 20 May 1924; *m* 1948, Elizabeth Catherine Wrong (*see* E. C. Shore); one *s* two *d* (and one *s* decd). *Educ:* Quarry Bank High Sch., Liverpool; King's Coll., Cambridge. Political economist. Joined Labour Party, 1948; Head of Research Dept, Labour Party, 1959–64. Member of Fabian Society. Contested (Lab) St Ives, Cornwall, 1950, Halifax, 1959. PPS to the Prime Minister, 1965–66; Jt Parly Sec.: Min. of Technology, 1966–67; Dept of Economic Affairs, 1967; Sec. of State for Economic Affairs, 1967–69; Minister without Portfolio, 1969–70; Dep. Leader of House of Commons, 1969–70; Opposition Spokesman on Europe, 1971–74; Sec. of State for Trade, 1974–76; Sec. of State for the Environment, 1976–79; Opposition Spokesman on Foreign Affairs, 1979–80, on Treasury and Economic Affairs, 1980–83; Opposition Spokesman on Trade and Industry, 1983–84; Shadow Leader of the House of Commons, 1984–. *Publication:* Entitled to Know, 1966. *Recreation:* swimming. *Address:* House of Commons, SW1; 23 Dryburgh Road, SW15.

SHORROCK, James Godby; Barrister-at-Law, retired 1972; Recorder of Barrow-in-Furness, 1963–71; *b* 10 Dec. 1910; *s* of late William Gordon Shorrock, JP, Morland, Westmorland; *m* 1936, Mary Patricia, *d* of late George Herbert Lings, Burnage, Manchester; two *s* two *d*. *Educ:* Clifton; Hertford College, Oxford. Called to Bar, Inner Temple, 1934. Served War of 1939–45: Major RA (TA) and Judge Advocate General's Department. Dep. Chm., Westmorland QS, 1955–71. Legal Member, Mental Health Review Tribunal, 1960–63; Legal Chm., Manchester City Licensing Planning Cttee, 1964. *Recreations:* walking, fishing, gardening.

See also J. M. Shorrock.

SHORROCK, John Michael; a Recorder of the Crown Court, since 1982; *b* 25 May 1943; *s* of James Godby Shorrock, *qv*; *m* 1971, Marianne (*née* Mills); two *d*. *Educ:* Clifton College, Bristol; Pembroke College, Cambridge. MA. Called to the Bar, Inner Temple, 1966; practising on Northern Circuit, 1966–: Junior, 1968; Sec., Exec. Cttee, 1981–85. *Recreations:* squash, gardening, opera, theatre, films. *Address:* 2 Old Bank Street, Manchester. *T:* 061–832 3791; 5 Essex Court, Temple, EC4.

SHORT, family name of **Baron Glenamara.**

SHORT, Clare; MP (Lab) Birmingham Ladywood, since 1983; *b* 15 Feb. 1946; *d* of Frank and Joan Short; *m* 1981, Alexander Ward Lyon, *qv*. *Educ:* Keele Univ.; Leeds Univ. (BA Hons Political Sci.). Home Office, 1970–75; Dir, All Faiths for One Race, Birmingham, 1976–78; Dir, Youth Aid and the Unemployment Unit, 1979–83. Chm., All Party Parly Gp on Race Relations, 1985–86; Mem., Home Affairs Select Cttee, 1983–85; front bench spokesperson on employment, 1985–. *Publications:* Talking Blues: a study of young West Indians' views of policing, 1978; Handbook of Immigration Law, 1978. *Recreations:* family and friends, swimming, and dog. *Address:* House of Commons, SW1. *T:* 01–219 3000.

SHORT, Prof. David Somerset, MD, FRCP, FRCPE; Clinical Professor in Medicine, University of Aberdeen, since 1983; Hon. Consultant Physician, Aberdeen Royal Infirmary, since 1983 (Consultant Physician, 1960–83); *b* 6 Aug. 1918; *s* of Latimer James Short, MD, DPH, Bristol, and Mabel Annie Wood, SRN, Nottingham; *m* 1948, Joan Anne McLay, BSc, MB, ChB, Cardiff; one *s* four *d*. *Educ:* Bristol Grammar Sch.; Cambridge Univ.; Bristol Royal Hospitals. MD 1948; PhD 1957; FRCP 1964; FRCPE 1966. Served with RAMC, 1944–47; Registrar, Southmead Hosp., Bristol, 1947–49; Sen. Registrar, National Heart Hosp. and London Hosp., 1950–54; Lecturer in Medicine, Middlesex Hosp., 1955–59. Physician to the Queen in Scotland, 1977–83. *Publications:* contribs to medical journals, mainly on cardiovascular and pulmonary diseases. *Recreations:* walking, music. *Address:* 48 Victoria Street, Aberdeen, Scotland AB9 2PL. *T:* Aberdeen 645853.

SHORT, Rt. Rev. Hedley Vicars Roycraft; *b* 24 Jan. 1914; *s* of Hedley Vicars Short and Martha Hallam Parke; *m* 1953, Elizabeth Frances Louise Shirley; one *s* four *d*. *Educ:* Trinity College, Univ. of Toronto (BA, LTh, BD). Deacon, 1943, priest, 1944, Assistant Curate St Michael and All Angels, Toronto; Junior Chaplain, Coventry Cathedral, England, 1946–47; Lecturer, Trinity Coll., Toronto, 1947–51; Dean of Residence, 1949–51; Rector, Cochrane, Ont, 1951–56; Rector, St Barnabas, St Catharines, Ont, 1956–63; Canon, Christ's Church Cathedral, Hamilton, Ont, 1962; Dean of Saskatchewan, 1963–70; Archdeacon of Prince Albert, 1966–70; Bishop of Saskatchewan, 1970–85. Member of General Synod, 1955–; Examining Chaplain successively to Bishops of Moosonee, Niagara and Saskatchewan. Pres. Council, Coll. of Emmanuel and St Chad, Saskatoon, 1974–80; Chm., Natonum Community Coll., Prince Albert, 1974–76; Chancellor, 1975–80, Hon. Fellow, 1980, Univ. of Emmanuel Coll. Hon. DD: Trinity Coll., Toronto, 1964; Emmanuel Coll., Saskatoon, 1983. *Publication:* (contrib.) Eucharistic Dimensions, 1977. *Recreations:* music, sketching, reading. *Address:* 355 19th Street W, Prince Albert, Saskatchewan S6V 4C8, Canada.

SHORT, Rev. John, MA (Edinburgh); PhD (Edinburgh); Hon. DD (St Andrews); Minister of St George's United Church, Toronto, Canada, 1951–64; *b* Berwickshire, 27 March 1896; *m* 1st; one *s* one *d*; 2nd, 1939, Anneliese, 2nd *d* of Dr C. J. F. Bechler, Danzig; two *s*. *Educ:* Edinburgh University. Trained for a business career but attracted by religious convictions to the Christian ministry; began to study for same just before the war of 1914–18, joined army and served for 3 years and 6 months; commenced studies at Edinburgh; graduated MA. First class honours in Philosophy; awarded John Edward Baxter Scholarship in Philosophy for 3 years; received University Diploma in Education and Medal; trained for Teacher's Certificate; awarded Doctorate in Philosophy for a thesis on the Philosophic Character of English XIVth Century Mysticism; medallist in class of Moral Philosophy, and in Metaphysics; Prizeman in Psychology; trained in Scottish Congregational College for Ministry under Principal T. Hywel Hughes, DLitt, DD; called to Bathgate E. U. Congregational Church, 1924; Minister of Lyndhurst Road Congregational Church, Hampstead, 1930–37. Minister of Richmond Hill Congregational Church, Bournemouth, 1937–51; Chairman of the Congregational Union of England and Wales, 1949–50. Mason: 3° Home Lodge Amity, Poole, Dorset, 18° Downend Chapter Rose Croix, Gloucester, 1953; affiliated Ashlar Lodge, 247 GRC, Toronto, 1952; 32° Moore Sovereign Consistory, Hamilton, Ont, 1964; 33° Supreme Council A&ASR, Dominion of Canada (Hon. Inspector Gen.), 1967. DD (hc): St Andrews Univ., 1950; McMaster Univ., Hamilton, Ontario, 1964. *Publications:* Can I Find Faith?, 1937; All Things are Yours (book of sermons), 1939; The Interpreter's Bible Exposition of I Corinthians; Triumphant Believing, 1952. *Recreations:* gardening, reading, and travel. *Address:* 162 Coldstream Avenue, Toronto M5N 1X9, Canada. *T:* 489–8614.

SHORT, Rt. Rev. Kenneth Herbert; Anglican Bishop to the Australian Defence Force (Army, Navy and Air Force), since 1979; an Assistant Bishop, Diocese of Sydney (Bishop of Parramatta), since 1982; *b* 6 July 1927; *s* of Cecil Charles Short and Joyce Ellen Begbie; *m* 1950, Gloria Noelle Funnell; one *s* two *d*. *Educ:* Moore Theological Coll. (ThL and Moore Coll. Dipl.). Commissioned AIF, 1946; with BCOF, 1946–48; theological training, 1949–52; ordained Anglican Ministry, 1952; Minister in Charge, Provisional Parish of Pittwater, 1952–54; with CMS in Tanzania, E Africa, 1955–64; Chaplain, Tabora 1955, Mwanza 1955–59; first Principal, Msalato Bible School, 1961–64; Gen. Secretary, CMS NSW Branch, 1964–71, including Sec. for S America. Canon of St Andrew's Cathedral, Sydney, 1970–75; Exam. Chaplain to Archbishop of Sydney, 1971–82; Rector of St Michael's, Vaucluse, 1971–75; Archdeacon of Wollongong and Camden, 1975–79; Chaplain General (CE), Australian Army, 1979–81; Bishop in Wollongong, Diocese of Sydney, 1975–82. *Publication:* Guidance, 1969. *Recreations:* fishing, reading, walking. *Address:* 5 Keith Place, Baulkham Hills, NSW 2153, Australia. *T:* (02) 6399878.

SHORT, Sir Noel (Edward Vivian), Kt 1977; MBE 1951; MC 1945; Speaker's Secretary, House of Commons, 1970–82; *b* 19 Jan. 1916; *s* of late Vivian A. Short, CIE, Indian Police, and late Annie W. Short; *m* 1st, 1949, Diana Hester Morison (*d* 1951); one *s*; 2nd, 1957, Karin Margarete Anders; one *s* one *d*. *Educ:* Radley College; RMA Sandhurst. Commissioned Indian Army, 1936; joined 6th Gurkha Rifles, 1937. Active service: NW Frontier of India, 1937, 1940–41; Assam and Burma, 1942, 1944–45; New Guinea, 1943–44; Malaysia, 1950–51, 1952–53, 1956–57. Staff College, 1946–47; jssc, 1953; Comdr, 63 Gurkha Bde, Malaysia, 1960–61; Comdr, 51 Infty Bde, Tidworth, 1962–63. Principal, Home Office, 1964–70. Col, 6th Queen Elizabeth's Own Gurkha Rifles, 1978–83. *Publications:* contribs: Jl of RUSI; Army Quarterly. *Recreations:* ski-ing, photography.

SHORT, Peter, BA; IPFA; City Treasurer, Manchester City Council, since 1983; *b* 21 June 1945; *s* of Christopher John Grewcock Short and Isabella Short; *m* 1967, Eileen Short (*née* Makin); one *s* one *d*. *Educ:* South Shields Grammar Sch.; Univ. of Exeter (2nd Cl. Hons, Div. 1, Modern Economic History). IPFA (1st place Final, 1970). Local Govt Accountant with Manchester City Council, 1967–73; Leeds City Council, 1973–78; Dir of Finance, South Tyneside MDC, 1978–83. *Recreations:* reading, walking, caravanning, avoiding household maintenance, planning to walk the Pennine Way. *Address:* 2 Netherwood Road, Northenden, Manchester M22 4BQ.

SHORT, Mrs Renee; MP (Lab) Wolverhampton North-East, since 1964; *m*; two *d*. *Educ:* Nottingham County Grammar Sch.; Manchester Univ. Freelance journalist. Member: Herts County Council, 1952–67; Watford RDC, 1952–64; West Herts Group Hosp. Management Cttee; former Chm. Shrodell's Hosp., Watford. Governor: Watford Coll. of Technology; Watford Grammar Sch. Contested (Lab) St Albans, 1955, Watford, 1959. TGWU sponsored Member of Parliament. Member: Delegation to Council of Europe, 1964–68; Expenditure Cttee, 1970–79 (Chm., Social Services and Employment Sub-Cttee); Chm., Select Cttee for Social Services, 1979–; Chm., Parly and Scientific Cttee, 1982–; Vice-Chm., Parly East-West Trade Gp, 1968–; Chm., British-GDR Parly Gp; Sec., British-Soviet Parly Gp; Pres., British-Romanian Friendship Assoc. Mem., Nat. Exec. Cttee of Labour Party, 1970–81, 1983–. National President: Nursery Schools Assoc., 1970–80; Campaign for Nursery Educn, 1970–83. Mem., Roundhouse Theatre Council; Chm., Theatres' Advisory Council, 1974–80. *Publication:* The Care of Long Term Prisoners, 1979. *Address:* House of Commons, SW1A 0AA.

SHORT, Prof. Roger Valentine, FRS 1974; FRSE 1974; FRCVS 1976; FAA 1984; Professor of Reproductive Biology, Monash University, Australia, since 1982; *b* 31 July 1930; *s* of F. A. and M. C. Short, Weybridge; *m* 1st, 1958, Dr Mary Bowen Wilson (marr. diss. 1981); one *s* three *d*; 2nd, 1982, Dr Marilyn Bernice Renfree; one *d*. *Educ:* Sherborne Sch.; Univs of Bristol (BVSc, MRCVS), Wisconsin (MSc) and Cambridge (PhD, ScD). Mem., ARC Unit of Reproductive Physiology and Biochemistry, Cambridge, 1956–72; Fellow, Magdalene Coll., Cambridge, 1962–72; Lectr, then Reader, Dept of Veterinary Clinical Studies, Cambridge, 1961–72; Dir, MRC Unit of Reproductive Biology, Edinburgh, 1972–82. Hon. Prof., Univ. of Edinburgh, 1976–82. *Publications:* (ed, with C. R. Austin) Reproduction in Mammals, vols 1–8, 1972–80, 2nd edn vols 1–5, 1982–86; (ed, with D. T. Baird) Contraceptives of the Future, 1976; contrib. Jl Endocrinology, Jl Reproduction and Fertility, Jl Zoology. *Recreations:* gardening, wildlife, history of biology. *Address:* Department of Physiology, Monash University, Clayton, Victoria 3168, Australia.

SHORTIS, Maj.-Gen. Colin Terry, CBE 1980 (OBE 1977; MBE 1974); General Officer Commanding North West District, since 1986; *b* 18 Jan. 1934; *s* of late Tom Richardson Shortis and Marna Evelyn Shortis (*née* Kenworthy); *m* 1957, Sylvia Mary, *o d* of H. C. A. Jenkinson; two *s* two *d*. *Educ:* Bedford School. Enlisted Army 1951; 2nd Lieut Royal Fusiliers, 1953; transf. to Dorset Regt, 1955; served Hong Kong, Korea, Suez Canal Zone, Sudan, BAOR, Aden, Singapore and British Guiana, 1953–63; Instructor, Sch. of Infantry, 1964–65; Staff Coll., 1966; Co. Comdr, 1st Devonshire and Dorset, 1967–73; served Malta, NI, Belize, Cyprus, BAOR, CO 1974–77; Directing Staff, Staff Coll., 1977; Comdr, 8 Infantry Brigade, 1978–80; RCDS 1981; Comdr, British Mil. Adv. and Training Team, Zimbabwe, 1982–83; Dir of Infantry, 1983–86. Col Comdt, The Prince of Wales Div., 1983–; Col, Devonshire and Dorset Regt, 1984–. *Recreations:* sailing, manual work. *Address:* c/o Barclays Bank, 137 Brompton Road, SW3 1QF. *Club:* Army and Navy.

SHORTT, Colonel Henry Edward, CIE 1941; FRS 1950; LLD 1952; Colonel IMS, retired; formerly Professor of Medical Protozoology, University of London, and Head of Department of Parasitology, London School of Hygiene and Tropical Medicine; *b* 15 April 1887; *m* 1921, Eleanor M. Hobson; one *s* one *d*. *Educ:* Univ. of Aberdeen. MB, ChB 1910; MD 1936; DSc 1938; KHP 1941–44; Inspector-Gen. of Civil Hospitals and Prisons, Assam, 1941–44; retired, 1944. President, Royal Society of Tropical Medicine and Hygiene, 1949–51; Technical Expert under Colombo Plan in E Pakistan, 1952–55. Straits Settlements Gold Medal, 1938; Kaisar-i-Hind Gold Medal, 1945; Laveran Prize, 1948; Mary Kingsley medal, 1949; Darling medal and prize, 1951; Stewart prize, 1954; Manson Medal, 1959; Gaspar Vianna Medal, 1962. *Publications:* over 130 scientific papers. *Recreations:* shooting and fishing. *Address:* Rivenhall, 39 Lenten Street, Alton, Hants. *T:* Alton 83252.

SHOTTON, Prof. Edward; Professor of Pharmaceutics, University of London, 1956–77, now Emeritus; *b* 15 July 1910; *s* of Ernest Richard and Maud Shotton; *m* 1943, Mary Constance Louise Marchant; one *d*. *Educ:* Smethwick (Junior) Technical School; Birkbeck College, University of London. Pharmaceutical Chemist (PhC), 1933; BSc (London), 1939; PhD (London), 1955; Hon. ACT (Birmingham), 1961. FRIC 1949. Pharmaceutical research and development work at Burroughs, Wellcome & Co., Dartford, 1939–48. Sen. Lecturer in Pharmaceutics, Univ. of London, 1948–56. Chairman, British Pharmaceutical Conference, 1966. *Publications:* (with K. Ridgway) Physical Pharmaceutics, 1974; research papers, mainly in Jl of Pharmacy and Pharmacology. *Recreations:* gardening, cricket, fly-fishing. *Address:* 10 Winston Gardens, Berkhamsted, Herts. *T:* Berkhamsted 6402. *Club:* Athenæum.

SHOTTON, Prof. Frederick William, MBE (mil.) 1945; MA, ScD; FRS 1956; FEng 1976; FGS; FIMinE; MIWES; Professor of Geology, University of Birmingham, 1949–74, Emeritus Professor 1975 (Pro-Vice-Chancellor and Vice-Principal, 1965–71); *b* 8 Oct. 1906; *s* of F. J. and Ada Shotton, Coventry; *m* 1930, Alice L. Linnett; two *d*; *m* 1983, Mrs Lucille F. Bailey, *widow*, Portland, Oregon, USA. *Educ:* Bablake, Coventry; Sidney Sussex College, Cambridge. Wiltshire Prizeman, 1926, Harkness Scholar, 1927, Cambridge. Assistant Lecturer and Lecturer, University of Birmingham, 1928–36; Lecturer, Cambridge University, 1936–45. Served War of 1939–45, MEF and 21 Army Group, 1940–45. Prof. of Geology, Sheffield Univ., 1945–49. Mem., NERC, 1969–72. Pres., Geological Soc., 1964–66, Vice-Pres., 1966–68. Founder Fellow, Fellowship of Engineering, 1976. Hon. Mem., Royal Irish Acad., 1970. Prestwich Medal, Geological Soc. of London, 1954; Stopes Medal, Geologists' Assoc., 1967. *Publications:* (ed and contrib.) British Quaternary Studies, 1977; numerous scientific. *Recreations:* archæology and natural history; gardening. *Address:* 111 Dorridge Road, Dorridge, West Midlands B93 8BP. *T:* Knowle 2820.

SHOVELTON, Prof. David Scott, FDSRCS; Professor of Conservative Dentistry, University of Birmingham, since 1964; Consultant Dental Surgeon, United Birmingham Hospitals, now Central Birmingham Health Authority, since 1960; *b* 12 Sept. 1925; *s* of Leslie Shovelton, LDSRCS, and Marion de Winton (*née* Scott); *m* 1949, Pearl Holland; two *s*. *Educ:* The Downs Sch., Colwall; King's Sch., Worcester; Univ. of Birmingham (BSc, LDS, BDS). House Surg., Birmingham Dental Hosp., 1951; gen. dental practice, Evesham, Worcs, 1951; Dental Officer, RAF, 1951–53; Birmingham University: Lectr in Operative Dental Surg., 1953–60; Sen. Lectr, 1960–64; Dir, 1974–78, Dep. Dir, 1982–84, Dental Sch. Vis. Asst Prof. of Clin. Dentistry, Univ. of Alabama, 1959–60. Hon. Cons. Dental Surg., Birmingham Reg. Hosp. Bd, 1962–74. Pres., British Soc. for Restorative Dentistry, 1970–71 (Vice-Pres., 1968–70 and 1971–72). Consultant, Commn on Dental Practice, Fédn Dentaire Internat., 1972–79; Consultant Adviser in Restorative Dentistry, DHSS, 1983–. Member: Gen. Dental Council, 1974–; Birmingham Area Health Authority (Teaching), 1973–79; Cttee of Management, Sch. for Dental Therapists, 1977–80; Jt Cttee for Higher Trng in Dentistry, 1979–84 (Chm., Specialist Adv. Cttee in Restorative Dentistry, 1979–84); Standing Dental Adv. Cttee, 1982–; Bd, Faculty of Dental Surgery, RCS, 1983–; Cttee of Enquiry into unnecessary dental treatment, 1984–85. Ext. Examnr in dental subjects, univs and colls, 1968–. *Publications:* Inlays, Crowns and Bridges (jtly), 1963, 4th edn 1985; articles in med. and dental jls, 1957–. *Recreations:* music, learning about wine, gardening, caravanning. *Address:* 86 Broad Oaks Road, Solihull, West Midlands B91 1HZ. *T:* 021–705 3026. *Club:* Royal Air Force.

SHOVELTON, (Walter) Patrick, CB 1976; CMG 1972; FCIT; Director, Maersk Co., since 1985; *b* 18 Aug. 1919; *s* of late S. T. Shovelton, CBE, and M. C. Kelly, cousin of Patrick and Willie Pearse; *m* 1st, 1942, Marjorie Lucy Joan Manners (marr. diss. 1967); one *d*; 2nd, Helena Richards, 3rd *d* of D. G. Richards, *qv*. *Educ:* Charterhouse; Keble Coll., Oxford (scholar of both). Rep. Oxford Univ. at Eton Fives. Served in RA and RHA, 1940–46; DAAG, War Office, 1945–46. Entered Administrative Civil Service as Asst Principal, Min. of Transport, 1946; Principal 1947; Admin. Staff College, 1951; Private Sec. to Secretary of State for Co-ordination of Transport, Fuel and Power, 1951–53; Asst Sec., Road Transport, 1957; transferred to Min. of Aviation, 1959; IDC, 1962; Under Secretary, 1966; transferred to Min. of Technology, 1966, and to DTI, 1970; Mem., UK Negotiating Team for entry into EEC, 1970–72; Deputy Secretary: DTI, 1972–74; Dept of Prices and Consumer Protection, 1974–76; Dept of Trade, 1976–78; Dir-Gen., Gen. Council of British Shipping, 1978–85; Dir, British Airports Authy, 1982–85. Led UK Negotiating Team for Bermuda 2, 1977. Council, CIT, 1982–85; Advr, H of L Inquiry into EEC Maritime Transport Policy, 1985–86. Brancker Lectr (civil aviation), 1979; Grout Lectr (shipping), 1985. *Recreations:* competitive golf, gardening, reading, opera. *Address:* 63 London Road, Tunbridge Wells, Kent TN1 1DP. *T:* Tunbridge Wells 27885. *Clubs:* Royal Ashdown Forest, Rye, Hampstead, Seniors' Golf, Jesters.

SHRAPNEL, Norman; Parliamentary Correspondent of the Guardian, 1958–75; *b* 5 Oct. 1912; *yr s* of Arthur Edward Scrope Shrapnel and Rosa Brosy; *m* 1940, Mary Lilian Myfanwy Edwards; two *s*. *Educ:* King's School, Grantham. Various weekly, evening and morning newspapers from 1930; Manchester Guardian (later the Guardian) from 1947, as reporter, theatre critic and reviewer; contributor to various journals. Political Writer of the Year Award (the Political Companion), 1969. *Publications:* A View of the Thames, 1977; The Performers: politics as theatre, 1978; The Seventies, 1980. *Recreations:* walking, music. *Address:* 27A Shooters Hill Road, Blackheath, SE3. *T:* 01–858 7123.

SHREEVE, Ven. David Herbert; Archdeacon of Bradford, since 1984; *b* 18 Jan. 1934; *s* of Hubert Ernest and Ivy Eleanor Shreeve; *m* 1957, Barbara (*née* Fogden); one *s* one *d*. *Educ:* Southfield School, Oxford; St Peter's Coll., Oxford (MA); Ridley Hall, Cambridge. Asst Curate, St Andrew's Church, Plymouth, 1959–64; Vicar: St Anne's, Bermondsey, 1964–71; St Luke's, Eccleshill, 1971–84; RD of Calverley, 1978–84. Mem., Gen. Synod and Proctor in Convocation, 1977–. Hon. Canon of Bradford Cathedral, 1983–84. *Recreations:* walking, camping, jogging, photography. *Address:* Rowan House, 11 The Rowans, Baildon, Shipley, W Yorks BD17 5DB. *T:* Bradford 583735.

SHREWSBURY, Bishop Suffragan of; *no new appointment at time of going to press.*

SHREWSBURY, Bishop of, (RC), since 1980; **Rt. Rev. Joseph Gray,** DCL; *b* 20 Oct. 1919; *s* of Terence Gray and Mary Gray (*née* Alwill). *Educ:* Patrick's Coll., Cavan, Eire; St Mary's Seminary, Oscott, Birmingham; Dunboyne House, St Patrick's Coll., Maynooth, Eire; Pontifical Univ. of St Thomas Aquinas, Rome. Priest, 1943; Asst Priest, Sacred Heart, Aston, Birmingham, 1943–48; Dunboyne House, 1948–50 (Licentiate in Canon Law, 1950); Sec. to Archbp of Birmingham, 1950–55. Diocesan Chancellor, Birmingham, 1951–69; Pontifical Univ., 1959–60 (Doctorate in Canon Law, 1960); Vicar-Gen., Birmingham, 1960–69; Parish Priest, St Michael's, Birmingham, 1955–69. Papal Chamberlain, 1960; Domestic Prelate, 1966. Episcopal Ordination, Cathedral of Christ the King, Liverpool, Feb. 1969; Titular Bishop of Mercia and Auxiliary Bishop of Liverpool, 1969–80. Pres., Liturgy Commn of Bishops' Conf. of England and Wales, 1976–84; Chm., Commn for Religious Life, 1984–. *Recreations:* music, reading, travel. *Address:* Bishop's House, Eleanor Road, Birkenhead L43 7QW. *T:* 051–653 3600.

SHREWSBURY AND WATERFORD, 22nd Earl of, *cr* 1442 and 1446; **Charles Henry John Benedict Crofton Chetwynd Chetwynd-Talbot;** Baron Talbot, 1733; 7th Earl Talbot, Viscount Ingestre, 1784; Premier Earl on the Rolls of England and Ireland, Hereditary Great Seneschal or Lord High Steward of Ireland; farmer and director; *b* 18 Dec. 1952; *s* of 21st Earl of Shrewsbury and Waterford, and of Nadine, *yr d* of late Brig.-Gen. C. R. Crofton, CBE; *S* father, 1980; *m* 1974, Deborah, *o d* of Noel Hutchinson; two *s* one *d*. *Educ:* Harrow. Pres., Burslem Festival, 1979–; Hon. Pres., Shropshire Hospice, 1983–. Patron of 11 livings. *Recreations:* hunting, racing, shooting. *Heir:* *s* Viscount Ingestre, *qv*. *Address:* Wanfield Hall, Kingstone, Uttoxeter, Staffs.

SHRIMSLEY, Bernard; journalist; Associate Editor, Daily Express; *b* 13 Jan. 1931; *er s* of John and Alice Shrimsley, London; *m* 1952, Norma Jessie Alexandra, *d* of Albert and Maude Porter, Southport; one *d*. *Educ:* Kilburn Grammar School. Press Association, 1947; Southport Guardian, 1948; RAF, 1949–51; Daily Mirror, 1953; Sunday Express, 1958; Northern Editor, Daily Mirror, 1963; Editor, Liverpool Daily Post, 1968; Editor, The Sun, 1972; Editor, News of the World, and Dir, News Group Newspapers Ltd, 1975; Editor, The Mail on Sunday, and Vice-Chm., The Mail on Sunday Ltd, 1982. *Publications:* The Candidates, 1968; Lion Rampant, 1984. *Address:* Daily Express, Fleet Street, EC4P 4JT. *T:* 01–353 8000.

SHRIVER, (Robert) Sargent; Lawyer, of Counsel, Fried, Frank, Harris, Shriver & Jacobson, since 1971; *b* Westminster, Md, 9 Nov. 1915; *s* of Robert Sargent and Hilda Shriver; *m* 1953, Eunice Mary Kennedy; four *s* one *d*. *Educ:* parochial schools, Baltimore; Canterbury School, New Milford, Conn.; Yale College; Yale University. BA (*cum laude*) 1938; LLB 1941; LLD 1964. Apprentice Seaman, USNR, 1940; Ensign, 1941. Served War of 1941–45: Atlantic and Pacific Ocean Areas aboard battleships and submarines; Lt-Comdr, USNR. Admitted to: New York Bar, 1941; Illinois Bar, (retd) 1959; US Supreme Court, 1966; District of Columbia Bar, 1971. With legal firm of Winthrop, Stimson, Putnam & Roberts, NYC, 1940–41; Asst Editor, Newsweek, 1945–46; associated with Joseph P. Kennedy Enterprises, 1946–48; Asst Gen. Man., Merchandise Mart, 1948–61; President: Chicago Bd of Educn, 1955–60; Catholic Interracial Council of Chicago, 1954–59; Dir, Peace Corps, Washington, 1961–66; Dir, Office of Economic Opportunity and Special Asst to Pres. Johnson, 1964–68; US Ambassador to France, 1968–70. Pres., Special Olympics Internat., 1984–. Vice-Presidential candidate (Democrat), Nov. 1972. Democrat; Roman Catholic. *Address:* 1350 New York Avenue NW, Washington, DC 20005, USA.

SHRUBSOLE, Alison Cheveley, CBE 1982; Principal, Homerton College, Cambridge, 1971–85; Fellow of Hughes Hall, Cambridge, 1974; *b* 7 April 1925; *d* of Rev. Stanley and Mrs Margaret Shrubsole. *Educ:* Milton Mount Coll.; Royal Holloway Coll.; Inst. of Education. BA Hons London; MA Cantab; Postgraduate Cert. in Educn. FCP. Teaching in schools in South London, 1946–50; Lectr and Sen. Lectr, Stockwell Coll., 1950–57; Principal: Machakos Training Coll., Kenya, 1957–62; Philippa Fawcett Coll., London SW16, 1963–71. DUniv. Open, 1985. *Publications:* articles in TES, THES, Dialogue, Learning for Teaching. *Recreations:* music, architecture, travel, mountaineering, gardening, cooking. *Address:* 4 Chancellor House, Mount Ephraim, Tunbridge Wells, Kent TN4 8BT; Cortijo Abulagar, Rubite, Granada, Spain. *Club:* English-Speaking Union.

SHTEREV, Kiril; Order of Georgi Dimitrov; Order of Narodna Republica Bulgaria, 2nd Degree; Ambassador of the People's Republic of Bulgaria to the Court of St James's, since 1980; *b* 17 Feb. 1918; *s* of Shteriu Georgiev Gotchev and Dobra Shtereva; *m* 1945, Anna Shtereva; one *d* (and one *d* decd). *Educ:* Univ. of Sofia (degree in Economics). Joined Min. of Foreign Affairs, Sofia, 1947; Secretary: Bulgarian Embassy, Prague, 1950–54; Min. of Foreign Affairs, Sofia, 1954–56; Counsellor, Bulgarian Delegn to UN, 1956–59; Counsellor and Chargé d'Affaires, Bulgarian Embassy, Washington, 1959–63; Counsellor and Head of Dept, Min. of For. Affairs, Sofia, 1963–67; Ambassador to Ottawa, 1967–71; Head of State Protocol, Sofia, 1971–73; Ambassador to Teheran, 1973–79; Ambassador, Min. of For. Affairs, Sofia, 1979–80. Foreign Orders awarded by Govts of Czechoslovakia, Egypt, Ethiopia and Afghanistan. *Recreations:* reading, collection of postage stamps. *Address:* 29 Hyde Park Gate, SW7. *T:* 01–589 4694.

SHUCKBURGH, Sir (Charles Arthur) Evelyn, GCMG 1967 (KCMG 1959; CMG 1949); CB 1954; HM Diplomatic Service, retired; Chairman, Executive Committee, British Red Cross Society, 1970–80; Chairman, Council, 1976–80 (Vice-Chairman, 1980–81); Member, Standing Commission, International Red Cross, 1974–81 (Chairman, 1977–81); *b* 26 May 1909; *e s* of late Sir John Shuckburgh, KCMG, CB; *m* 1937, Nancy Brett, 2nd *d* of 3rd Viscount Esher, GBE; two *s* one *d*. *Educ:* Winchester; King's College, Cambridge. Entered Diplomatic Service, 1933; served at HM Embassy, Cairo, 1937–39; seconded for service on staff of UK High Comr in Ottawa, 1940; transferred to Buenos Aires, 1942; Chargé d'Affaires there in 1944; First Secretary at HM Embassy, Prague, 1945–47. Head of South American Department, FO, 1947–48; Western Dept, 1949–50; Western Organizations Dept, 1950–51; Principal Private Secretary to Secretary of State for Foreign Affairs, 1951–54; Assistant Under-Secretary, Foreign Office, 1954–56; Senior Civilian Instructor, IDC, 1956–58; Asst Sec.-Gen. (Polit.) of NATO, Paris, 1958–60; Dep. Under-Sec., FO, 1960–62; Perm. Brit. Rep. to N Atlantic Council, in Paris, 1962–66; Ambassador to Italy, 1966–69. Dir, Commercial Union Assurance, 1971–80. Chm., N Home Counties Regional Cttee, National Trust, 1975–79. *Address:* High Wood House, Watlington, Oxon.

SHUCKBURGH, Sir Charles Gerald Stewkley, 12th Bt, *cr* 1660; TD; DL; JP; Major, late 11th (City of London Yeomanry) LAA; *b* 28 Feb. 1911; *s* of 11th Bt and Honour Zoë, OBE (*d* 1979), *d* of Neville Thursby, of Harlestone, Northamptonshire; *S* father, 1939; *m* 1st, 1935, Remony (*d* 1936), *o d* of late F. N. Bell, Buenos Aires; 2nd, 1937, Nancy Diana Mary (OBE 1970) (*d* 1984), *o d* of late Capt. Rupert Lubbock, RN; one *s* two *d*. *Educ:* Harrow; Trinity College, Oxford. JP 1946, DL 1965, Warwickshire; High Sheriff, Warwickshire, 1965. *Heir:* *s* Rupert Charles Gerald Shuckburgh [*b* 12 Feb. 1949; *m* 1976, Judith, *d* of W. G. Mackaness; two *s*]. *Address:* The Gate House, White Colne, Colchester, Essex.

SHUCKBURGH, Sir Evelyn; *see* Shuckburgh, Sir C. A. E.

SHUFFREY, Ralph Frederick Dendy, CB 1983; CVO 1981; Deputy Under-Secretary of State and Principal Establishment Officer, Home Office, 1980–84; *b* 9 Dec. 1925; *s* of late Frederick Arthur Shuffrey, MC and Mary Shuffrey (*née* Dendy) *m* 1953, Sheila, *d* of late Brig. John Lingham, CB, DSO, MC, and Juliet Judd; one *s* one *d*. *Educ:* Shrewsbury; Balliol Coll., Oxford. Served Army, 1944–47 (Captain). Entered Home Office, 1951; Private Sec. to Parly Under-Sec. of State, 1956–57; Private Sec. to Home Sec., 1965–66; Asst Sec., 1966–72; Asst Under-Sec. of State, 1972–80. Hon. Sec., Soc. for Individual Freedom, 1985–. *Address:* 21 Claremont Road, Claygate, Surrey. *T:* Esher 65123. *Club:* Reform.

SHULMAN, Drusilla Norman; *see* Beyfus, Drusilla N.

SHULMAN, Milton; writer, journalist, critic; *b* Toronto; *s* of late Samuel Shulman, merchant, and of Ethel Shulman; *m* 1956, Drusilla Beyfus, *qv*; one *s* two *d*. *Educ:* Univ. of Toronto (BA); Osgoode Hall, Toronto. Barrister, Toronto, 1937–40. Armoured Corps and Intelligence, Canadian Army, 1940–46 (despatches, Normandy, 1945); Major. Film critic, Evening Standard and Sunday Express, 1948–58; book critic, Sunday Express, 1957–58; theatre critic, Evening Standard, 1953–; TV critic, Evening Standard, 1964–73; columnist, social and political affairs, Daily Express, 1973–75; film critic, Vogue Magazine, 1975–. Executive producer and producer, Granada TV, 1958–62; Asst Controller of Programmes, Rediffusion TV, 1962–64. Mem., Adv. Council, British Theatre Museum, 1981–83. Regular panel mem., Stop the Week, BBC Radio 4. IPC Award, Critic of the Year, 1966. *Publications:* Defeat in the West, 1948; How To Be a Celebrity, 1950; The

Ravenous Eye, 1973; The Least Worst Television in the World, 1973; *children's books:* Preep, 1964; Preep in Paris, 1967; Preep and The Queen, 1970; *novel:* Kill Three, 1967; *novel and film story:* (with Herbert Kretzmer) Every Home Should Have One, 1970. *Recreations:* modern art, history, tennis. *Address:* 51 Eaton Square, SW1. *T:* 01–235 7162. *Clubs:* Garrick, Hurlingham.

SHULTZ, George Pratt; Secretary of State, United States of America, since July 1982; *b* New York City, 13 Dec. 1920; *s* of Birl E. Shultz and Margaret Pratt; *m* 1946, Helena Maria O'Brien; two *s* three *d*. *Educ:* Princeton Univ., 1942 (BA Econ); Massachusetts Inst. of Technology, 1949 (PhD Industrial Econ). Served War, US Marine Corps, Pacific, 1942; Major, 1945. Faculty, MIT, 1948–57; Sen. staff economist, President's Council of Economic Advisers, 1955–56 (on leave, MIT); Univ. of Chicago, Graduate Sch. of Business: Prof. of Industrial Relations, 1957–62; Dean, 1962–69; Prof. of Management and Public Policy, Stanford Univ., Graduate Sch. of Business, 1974. Secretary of Labor, 1969–July 1, 1970; Dir, Office of Management and Budget, 1970–72; Secretary of the Treasury, 1972–74; Exec. Vice-Pres., Bechtel Corp., 1974–75, Pres. 1975–79; Vice-Chm., Bechtel Group, 1980; Pres., Bechtel Group Inc., San Francisco, 1981–82. Chm., President's Economic Policy Adv. Bd, 1981–82. Director: General Motors Corp.; Dillon, Read & Co. Inc. Hon. Dr of Laws: Notre Dame Univ., 1969; Loyola Univ., 1972; Pennsylvania, 1973; Rochester, 1973; Princeton, 1973; Carnegie-Mellon Univ., 1975. *Publications:* Pressures on Wage Decisions, 1951; The Dynamics of a Labor Market (with C. A. Myers), 1951; Management Organization and the Computer (with T. A. Whisler), 1960; Strategies for the Displaced Worker (with Arnold R. Weber), 1966; Guidelines, Informal Controls, and the Market Place (with Rober Z. Aliber), 1966; Workers and Wages in the Urban Labor Market (with Albert Rees), 1970; Economic Policy Beyond the Headlines (with Kenneth W. Dam), 1978. *Recreations:* golf, tennis. *Address:* (office) Secretary of State, 2201 C Street NW, Washington, DC 20520, USA. *T:* (202) 647–4910; (home) Bethesda, Md, USA.

SHUTE, Prof. Charles Cameron Donald, MD; Professor of Histology, Cambridge University, 1969–84, now Emeritus; Fellow of Christ's College, Cambridge, 1957–84; *b* 23 May 1917; *s* of late Cameron Deane Shute; *m* 1st, 1947, Patricia Cameron (*d* 1952), *d* of F. H. Doran; 2nd, 1954, Lydia May (Wendy) (*née* Harwood) (marr diss. 1980); one *s* three *d*; 3rd, 1980, Rosemary Gay Robins. *Educ:* Eton; King's Coll., Cambridge; Middlesex Hosp., London. MA, MB, BChir Cambridge, 1945; MD Cambridge 1958. Resident posts at Middlesex Hosp., 1945–47; RAMC (otologist), 1947–49; Demonstrator and Lectr in Anatomy, London Hosp. Med. Coll., 1951; Univ. Demonstrator and Lectr, Cambridge, 1952–69; Univ. Reader in Neuroanatomy, Cambridge, 1969. *Publications:* The McCollough Effect, 1979; papers in biological and egyptological jls. *Recreation:* Egyptology. *Address:* Milton House, Christ's Pieces, Cambridge. *T:* Cambridge 62035.

SHUTE, John Lawson, CMG 1970; OBE 1959; Member: Council of Egg Marketing Authorities of Australia, 1970–79; Egg Marketing Board of New South Wales, 1970–79; Director, Arthur Yates & Co. Pty Ltd, 1970–80; *b* Mudgee, NSW, 31 Jan. 1901; *s* of J. Shute, Mudgee; *m* 1937, Constance W. M., *d* of J. Douglas; two *s*. *Educ:* Parramatta High Sch. Asst Sec., Primary Producers' Union, NSW, 1923–33; Gen.-Sec., 1933–42; Sec., Federated Co-operative Bacon Factories, 1927–42; Member: NSW Dairy Products Bd, 1934–46; Commonwealth Air Beef Panel, 1962; Dir, Commonwealth Dairy Produce Equalisation Cttee, 1941–46; 1st Sec. Aust. Dairy Farmers' Fedn, 1942; Mem. Exec. and Asst Sec., Empire Producers' Conf., 1938; Mem. Special Dairy Industry Cttee apptd by Commonwealth Govt, 1942; Dep. Controller, Meat Supplies, NSW, 1942–46. Chairman: Aust. Meat Bd, 1946–70; Aust. Cttee of Animal Production, 1947–70; Aust. Cattle and Beef Research Cttee, 1960–66; Belmont-Brian Pastures Res. Cttee, 1962–76; Aust. Meat Research Cttee, 1966–70; Aust. Frozen Cargo Shippers' Cttee, 1967–70; Member: Export Development Council, 1958–66; Overseas Trade Publicity Cttee, 1955–70; Australia Japan Business Co-operation Cttee, 1962–70; Industry Co-operative Programme, FAO, 1973–78 (Chm., Working Gp on Integrated Meat Develt, 1975–78); NSW Rural Reconstruction Bd, 1942–71. Life Mem., Rural Youth Orgn of NSW, 1961. Life Mem., Australia-Britain Soc., 1979; Hon. Life Mem., Australian Veterinary Assoc., 1970–. Mem., Worshipful Co. of Butchers, 1950. Freedom, City of London, 1951. *Recreations:* Rugby Union (former Internat. rep.), cricket. *Address:* 5/2 Woonona Avenue, Wahroonga, NSW 2076, Australia. *Clubs:* Commercial Travellers' (NSW); Eastwood Rugby Union (NSW).

SHUTLER, Ronald Rex Barry, FRICS; CAAV; Deputy Chief Valuer, Valuation Office (Inland Revenue), since 1984; *b* 27 June 1933; *s* of Ronald Edgar Coggin Shutler and Helena Emily Shutler (*née* Lawes); *m* 1958, Patricia Elizabeth Longman; two *s*. *Educ:* Hardye's, Dorchester. Articled pupil and assistant, chartered surveyors, Dorchester, 1952–59; joined Valuation Office, 1959; District Valuer, Hereford and Worcester, 1970; Superintending Valuer, Wales, 1976; Asst Chief Valuer, 1979. *Recreations:* golf, country pursuits, gardening. *Address:* Chief Valuer's Office, New Court, Carey Street, WC2A 2JE. *T:* 01–831 6111, ext. 2102. *Clubs:* Hereford Golf, Boxmoor Golf.

SHUTTLE, Penelope (Diane); writer and poet; *b* 12 May 1947; *d* of Jack Frederick Shuttle and Joan Shepherdess Lipscombe; *m* Peter Redgrove, *qv*; one *d*. *Educ:* Staines Grammar Sch.; Matthew Arnold County Secondary Sch., Mddx. Radio plays: The Girl who Lost her Glove, 1975 (Jt 3rd Prize Winner, Radio Times Drama Bursaries Comp., 1974); The Dauntless Girl, 1978. Poetry recorded for Poetry Room, Harvard Univ. Arts Council Awards, 1969, 1972 and 1985; Greenwood Poetry Prize, 1972; E. C. Gregory Award for Poetry, 1974. *Publications: novels:* An Excusable Vengeance, 1967; All the Usual Hours of Sleeping, 1969; Wailing Monkey Embracing a Tree, 1974; Rainsplitter in the Zodiac Garden, 1976; Mirror of the Giant, 1979; *poetry:* Nostalgia Neurosis, 1968; Midwinter Mandala, 1973; Photographs of Persephone, 1973; Autumn Piano, 1973; Songbook of the Snow, 1973; Webs on Fire, 1977; The Orchard Upstairs, 1981; The Child-Stealer, 1983; The Lion from Rio, 1986; *with Peter Redgrove:* The Hermaphrodite Album (poems), 1973; The Terrors of Dr Treviles (novel), 1974; The Wise Wound (psychology), 1978. *Recreations:* listening to music, Hatha Yoga, walking. *Address:* c/o David Higham Associates Ltd, 5–8 Lower John Street, Golden Square, W1R 4HA.

SHUTTLEWORTH, 5th Baron *cr* 1902, of Gawthorpe; **Charles Geoffrey Nicholas Kay-Shuttleworth;** Bt 1850; DL; Partner, Burton, Barnes & Vigers, Chartered Surveyors, since 1977; *b* 2 Aug. 1948; *s* of 4th Baron Shuttleworth, MC, and of Anne Elizabeth, *er d* of late Col Geoffrey Phillips, CBE, DSO; *S* father, 1975; *m* 1975, Mrs Ann Mary Barclay, *d* of James Whatman; three *s*. *Educ:* Eton. Dir and Dep. Chm., National & Provincial Bldg Soc., 1983–; Dir, Burnley Bldg Soc., 1978–82 (Vice-Chm., 1982). Chairman: Lancs Small Industries Cttee, COSIRA, 1978–83; Lancs Youth Clubs Assoc., 1980–; Member: Skelmersdale Develt Corp., 1982–85; NW Regional Cttee, National Trust, 1980– (Vice Chm., 1983–); President: Royal Lancashire Agricl Soc., 1985–86; Assoc. of Lancastrians in London, 1986–87; Governor, Giggleswick Sch., 1981– (Chm., 1984–). FRICS. DL Lancs, 1986. *Heir: s* Hon. Thomas Edward Kay-Shuttleworth, *b* 29 Sept. 1976. *Address:* 14 Sloane Avenue, SW3 3JE; Leck Hall, Carnforth, Lancs. *Clubs:* Brooks's, MCC.

SIBBALD, Maj.-Gen. Peter Frank Aubrey, CB 1982; OBE 1972; consultant in defence industries; *b* 24 March 1928; *s* of Major Francis Victor Sibbald, MBE, MM, BEM, and Mrs Alice Emma Hawking, The Hoe, Plymouth; *m* 1957, Margaret Maureen Entwistle; one *s* one *d*. *Educ:* ISC, Haileybury. Commnd, 1948; served with 1 KOYLI, 1948–53; Malayan Emergency, 1948–51 (mentioned in despatches); Korea, 1953–54; Kenya Emergency, 1954–55; Instr, Sch. of Inf., 1955–57; psc 1961; Aden, 1965–66; Bde Maj., 151 Inf. Bde, 1962–64; jssc 1964; GSO2 HQ FARELF, 1966–68; CO 2 LI, 1968–71; Col GS HQ BAOR, 1972; Comdr 51 Inf. Bde, 1972–74; Div. Brig., Light Div., 1975–77; GOC NW District, 1977–80; Dir of Infantry, 1980–83. Dep. Col, Light Infantry (Yorks), 1977–80; Col Comdt, The Light Div., 1980–83. *Recreations:* game shooting, fishing, squash, swimming. *Address:* c/o Lloyds Bank, 8 Royal Parade, Plymouth, Devon. *Club:* Army and Navy.

SIBERRY, John William Morgan; Under-Secretary, Welsh Office, 1964–73, retired; Secretary to Local Government Staff Commission for Wales, and NHS Staff Commission for Wales, 1973–75; *b* 26 Feb. 1913; *s* of late John William and Martha (*née* Morgan) Siberry; *m* 1949, Florence Jane Davies; one *s* one *d*. *Educ:* Porth County School, Rhondda; Univ. Coll. Cardiff. Entered Civil Service as Asst Principal, Unemployment Assistance Board (later Nat. Assistance Board), 1935; Principal, 1941; Asst Sec., 1947; transferred to Min. of Housing and Local Govt as Under-Sec., 1963; Welsh Secretary, Welsh Office and Office for Wales of the Ministry of Housing and Local Government, 1963–64. Chm., Working Party on Fourth Television Service in Wales, 1975. *Recreation:* golf. *Address:* Northgates, Pwllmelin Road, Llandaff, Cardiff CF5 2NG. *T:* Cardiff 564666. *Club:* Cardiff and County.

SIBLEY, Antoinette, CBE 1973; Prima Ballerina, The Royal Ballet, Covent Garden; *b* 27 Feb. 1939; *d* of Edward G. Sibley and Winifred M. Sibley (*née* Smith); *m* 1964, M. G. Somes, CBE (marr. diss. 1973); *m* 1974, Panton Corbett; one *s* one *d*. *Educ:* Arts Educational Sch. and Royal Ballet Sch. 1st performance on stage as Student with Royal Ballet at Covent Garden, a swan, Jan. 1956; joined company, July 1956; has appeared with the company or as guest artist in many countries around the world. Leading role in: Swan Lake, Sleeping Beauty, Giselle, Coppelia, Cinderella, The Nutcracker, La Fille Mal Gardée, Romeo and Juliet, Harlequin in April, Les Rendezvous, Jabez and the Devil (created the role of Mary), La Fête Etrange, The Rakes Progress, Hamlet, Ballet Imperial, Two Pigeons, La Bayadère, Symphonic Variations, Scènes de Ballet, Lilac Garden, Daphnis and Chloe, Pas de Quatre (Dolin's), Konservatoriett, A Month in the Country, The Dream (created Titania), Laurentia, Good Humoured Ladies, Aristocrat in Mam'zelle Angot, Façade, Song of the Earth, Monotones (created role), Jazz Calendar (created Friday's Child), Enigma Variations (created Dorabella), Thais (created pas de deux), Anastasia (created Kshessinska), Afternoon of a Faun, Triad (created the Girl), Pavanne, Manon (created title role), Soupirs (created pas de deux), L'invitation au voyage (created), Impromptu (created pas de deux), Varii Capricci (created La Capricciosa), Fleeting Figures. *Film:* The Turning Point, 1978. *Relevant publications:* Sibley and Dowell, by Nicholas Dromgoole and Leslie Spatt, 1976; Antoinette Sibley, 1981, photographs with text by Mary Clarke. *Recreations:* doing nothing; opera and books. *Address:* Royal Opera House, WC2.

SICH, Sir Rupert (Leigh), Kt 1968; CB 1953; Registrar of Restrictive Trading Agreements, 1956–73; *b* 3 Aug. 1908; *s* of late A. E. Sich, Caterham, Surrey; *m* 1933, Elizabeth Mary, *d* of late R. W. Hutchison, Gerrards Cross; one *s* two *d*. *Educ:* Radley College; Merton College, Oxford. Called to Bar, Inner Temple, 1930. Board of Trade Solicitor's Dept, 1932–48; Treasury Solicitor's Dept, 1948–56. *Recreations:* J. S. Bach; gardening. *Address:* Norfolk House, The Mall, Chiswick, W4. *T:* 01–994 2133. *Clubs:* United Oxford & Cambridge University, MCC.

SIDDALL, Sir Norman, Kt 1983; CBE 1975; FEng; mining consultant; Member of the National Coal Board, 1971–83, Deputy Chairman 1973–82, Chairman 1982–83; *b* 4 May 1918; *s* of late Frederick and Mabel Siddall; *m* 1943, Pauline, *d* of late John Alexander and Edith Arthur; two *s* one *d*. *Educ:* King Edward VII School, Sheffield; Sheffield Univ. (BEng). National Coal Board: Production Manager, No 5 Area, East Midlands Div., 1951–56; General Manager, No 5 Area, East Midlands Div., 1956–57; General Manager, No 1 Area, East Midlands Div., 1957–66; Chief Mining Engineer, 1966–67; Dir Gen. of Production, 1967–71. Chartered Engineer; FRSA; FIMinE; CBIM; 1st Vice-Chm., Organising Cttee, World Mining Congress, 1977; Member: Midland Counties Institution of Engineers (Silver Medal, 1951; Past President); Amer. Inst. Mining Engrs. National Association of Colliery Managers: Silver Medal, 1955; Bronze Medal, 1960; Coal Science Lecture Medal, 1972; CGLI Insignia Award in Technology (*hc*), 1978; Instn Medal, IME, 1982. Hon. DSc Nottingham, 1982. Krupinski Medal, 1982. *Publications:* articles in professional journals. *Address:* Brentwood, High Oakham Road, Mansfield, Notts NG18 5AJ.

SIDDELEY, family name of **Baron Kenilworth.**

SIDDELEY, Randle; *see* Kenilworth, 4th Baron.

SIDDIQI, Prof. Obaid, Padma Bhushan 1984; FRS 1984; FIASc 1968; FNA 1977; Professor of Molecular Biology, Tata Institute of Fundamental Research, Bombay, since 1972; *b* 7 Jan. 1932; *s* of M. A. Qadeer Siddiqi and Umme Kulsum; *m* 1955, Asiya Siddiqi; two *s* two *d*. *Educ:* Univ. of Aligarh (MSc); Univ. of Glasgow (PhD). Lecturer, Aligarh Univ., 1954–57; Indian Agricl Res. Inst., 1957–58; Dept of Genetics, Glasgow Univ., 1958–61; Cold Spring Harbor Lab., NY, 1961; Univ. of Pennsylvania, 1961–62; joined Tata Inst. of Fundamental Research as Fellow, 1962. Vis. Associate, Yale Univ., 1966; Vis. Prof., MIT, 1970–71; CIT Gosney Fellow, 1971–72; Sherman Fairchild Distinguished Scholar, 1981–82. Hon. DSc Aligarh, 1984. *Publications:* (co-ed) Development and Neurobiology of Drosophila, 1981; several papers in learned jls on genetics and neurobiology. *Recreations:* music, tennis, photography. *Address:* Molecular Biology Unit, Tata Institute of Fundamental Research, Bombay 400 005, India. *T:* (office) 219111/337, (residence) 211340. *Club:* Bombay Gymkhana.

SIDDIQUI, Dr Salimuzzaman, MBE 1946; Tamgha-i-Pakistan 1958; Sitara-i-Imtiaz (Pakistan) 1962; Hilal-e-Imtiaz, 1980; FRS 1961; DPhil; Hon DMed; Director, H. E. J. Research Institute of Chemistry, University of Karachi, since 1966; *b* 19 Oct. 1897. *Educ:* Lucknow; MAO College, Aligarh, UP; University College, London; Univ. of Frankfurt-on-Main. Returned to India, 1928; planned and directed Research Inst. at Ayurvedic and Unani Tibbi Coll., Delhi, 1928–40. Joined Council of Scientific and Industrial Research (India): Organic Chemist, 1940; Actg Dir of Chemical Laboratories, 1944. Director of Scientific and Industrial Research, Pakistan, 1951; Director and Chairman of Pakistan Council of Scientific and Industrial Research, 1953–66; Chairman, Nat. Science Council, 1962–66; Pres., Pakistan Acad. of Sciences, 1968. A chemist, working on the chemistry of natural products; has led the promotion of scientific and industrial research in Pakistan; has rep. Pakistan at internat. scientific confs, etc. Gold Medal, Russian Acad.; President's Pride of Performance Medal (Pakistan), 1966. Elected Mem., Vatican Acad. of Sciences, 1964. Hon. DSc. *Address:* Director, H. E. J. Research Institute of Chemistry, University of Karachi, Karachi, Pakistan. *T:* 463414.

SIDDONS, Arthur Harold Makins, MChir Cantab; FRCS; FRCP; Hon. Consulting Surgeon, St George's Hospital; *b* 17 Jan. 1911; *s* of late A. W. Siddons, Housemaster, Harrow School; *m* 1st, 1939, Joan Richardson Anderson (*née* McConnell) (*d* 1949); one *s* one *d*; 2nd, 1956, Eleanor Mary Oliver (*née* Hunter) (*d* 1970); 3rd, 1971, Margaret Christine Beardmore (*née* Smith). *Educ:* Harrow; Jesus College, Cambridge; St George's Hospital. MB, BCh Cantab 1935. Surgeon, St George's Hospital, 1941; Consultant General and Thoracic Surgeon, St George's Hosp. and others, 1948–76. Served RAF Medical Branch, 1942–46. Member of Court of Examiners, Royal College of Surgeons of England, 1958–63. *Publications:* Cardiac Pacemakers, 1967; sections on lung surgery in various textbooks. *Recreations:* travel, gardens, birds. *Address:* Robin Hey, Tilford Road, Farnham, Surrey GU9 8HX. *T:* Farnham 715667.

SIDEBOTHAM, John Biddulph, CMG 1946; MA Cantab; retired as Assistant Secretary, Colonial Office (1941–54); *b* 23 Nov. 1891; *er s* of late Rev. Frederick William Gilbert Sidebotham, MA, Rector of Weeting, Norfolk; *m* 1st, 1917, Hilda, *d* of late F. Haviland; one *d*; 2nd, 1941, Mary, *d* of late A. Blascheck; 3rd, 1971, Audrey (*née* Sidebotham), *widow* of Major D. B. Williams. *Educ:* King's School, Canterbury; Gonville and Caius Coll., Cambridge (Stanhope Exhibitioner, Open Class Exhibitioner, Scholar). 1st cl. theolog. tripos, pt 1, 1914; BA 1914, MA 1920; 2nd Lieut Home Counties RE (TF), 1914; Lieut 1916; served in France, 1914–15 (wounded); Inland Revenue, Somerset House, 1920; transferred to Colonial Office as asst prin. under reconstruction scheme, Dec. 1922; sec. managing cttee, Bureau of Hygiene and Tropical Diseases, 1925; sec., East African guaranteed loan advisory cttee, 1927; pte sec. to Parliamentary Under-Sec. of State for Dominion Affairs, 1928; pte sec. Permt Under-Sec. for the Colonies, 1929, principal, 1930; accompanied Permt Under-Secretary of State for the Colonies (Sir J. Maffey) to W Indies, 1936. Visited St Helena, 1939 and 1955; also visited Ceylon, Borneo, Sarawak, Hong Kong, Fiji and Mauritius. Mem. managing cttee of Bureau of Hygiene and Tropical Diseases, 1941–73. *Address:* Nantwatcyn, Cwmystwyth, Aberystwyth, Dyfed SY23 4AG. *T:* Pontrhydygroes 217.

SIDEBOTTOM, Edward John; a Chief Inspector, Department of Education and Science, 1973–80 (Divisional Inspector, 1969–73); *b* 1918; *s* of late Ernest Sidebottom, Wylam, Northumberland; *m* 1949, Brenda Millicent, *d* of late Alec H. Sadler, Wandsworth. *Educ:* Queen Elizabeth Grammar School, Hexham; Hatfield College, Durham (BSc). Entered Iraq Government education service, 1939; lecturer, Leavesden Green Emergency Training College, 1946; County Youth Organiser for Hampshire, 1947; HM Inspector of Schools, 1949–80. Sec. to Albemarle Cttee on the Youth Service in England and Wales, 1958–59; seconded as first Principal, Nat. Coll. for the Training of Youth Leaders, 1960–64. Chm., Jt Working Gp on Training for Staff Working with Mentally Handicapped People, 1981–83. *Address:* 3 Queen's Court, Marlborough Road, West Cliff, Bournemouth, Dorset BH4 8DB.

SIDEY, Air Marshal Sir Ernest (Shaw), KBE 1972; CB 1965; MD, ChB, FFCM, DPH; Director-General, Chest, Heart and Stroke Association, 1974–85; *b* 2 Jan. 1913; *s* of Thomas Sidey, Alyth, Perthshire; *m* 1946, Doreen Florence, *y d* of late Cecil Ronald Lurring, Dalkey, Ireland; one *d* (and one *d* decd). *Educ:* Morgan Acad., Dundee; St Andrews Univ. Commissioned in RAF, 1937. Served in Burma Campaign during War of 1939–45. Recent appts include: Chief, Med. Adv. Staff, Allied Air Forces Central Europe, 1957–59; PMO: Flying Trg Comd, 1961–63; Middle East Comd, 1963–65; Transport Command, 1965–66; DDGMS, RAF, 1966–68. PMO, Strike Command, 1968–70; Dir-Gen., RAF Med. Services, 1971–74; QHS 1966–74. Governor, Royal Star and Garter Home, 1974–86. *Recreations:* racing, golf, bridge. *Address:* Callums, Tugwood Common, Cookham Dean, Berks. *T:* Marlow 3006. *Club:* Royal Air Force.

SIDEY, John MacNaughton, DSO 1945; Founder of Ferrymasters Ltd, European hauliers, 1954; Director, P&O Steam Navigation Co., 1970–77, retired; *b* 11 July 1914; *e c* of John and Florence Sidey; *m* 1941, Eileen, *o d* of Sir George Wilkinson, 1st Bt, KCVO; one *s* (one *d* decd). *Educ:* Exeter School. Served War, 1939–45, with Royal Tank Regiment and Westminster Dragoons, finishing as Lt-Col commanding 22nd Dragoons. Mem., Southern Area Board, BTC, 1955–61 (Chm. Jan.–Dec. 1962); part-time Mem., British Railways Bd, 1962–68; Chm., Eastern Region Bd, British Railways, 1963–65. Council Mem. and Chm., Transport Policy Cttee, CBI, 1967–79; Mem., Nat. Docks Labour Bd, 1977–83. Pres., London Chapter, Nat. Defence Transportation Assoc. of America, 1961–62. *Recreations:* fishing, gardening, golf. *Address:* Brook Furlong, Station Road, Chipping Campden, Glos GL55 6HY. *T:* Evesham 840789; 275A Park Street, New Canaan, Conn 06840, USA. *T:* (203)–966–5080.

SIDEY, Thomas Kay Stuart, CMG 1968; Executive Chairman, Wickliffe Press Ltd, since 1983 (Managing Director, 1961–83); Barrister and Solicitor, NZ, since 1932; *b* 8 Oct. 1908; *s* of Sir Thomas Kay Sidey; *m* 1933, Beryl, *d* of Harvey Richardson Thomas, Wellington, NZ; one *s* one *d*. *Educ:* Otago Boys' High School; Univ. of Otago (LLM; Hon LLD, 1978). Served War of 1939–45 (despatches): 2nd NZEF; 4 years, Middle East and Italy, rank of Major. Dunedin City Council, 1947–50, 1953–65, 1968–83; Dep. Mayor, 1956–59, 1968–77; Mayor, 1959–65. Mem., Univ. of Otago Council, 1947–83, Pro-Chancellor, 1959–70, Chancellor, 1970–76. Past President: Dunedin Chamber of Commerce; Automobile Assoc., Otago; Trusteebank Otago; NZ Library Assoc.; Otago Old People's Welfare Council; Otago Boys' High Sch. Old Boys' Soc. *Recreations:* fishing, boating, ski-ing. *Address:* 16 Tolcarne Avenue, Dunedin, New Zealand. *T:* 775–694. *Club:* Dunedin (Dunedin, NZ).

SIDMOUTH, 7th Viscount *cr* 1805; **John Tonge Anthony Pellew Addington;** *b* 3 Oct. 1914; *s* of 6th Viscount Sidmouth and of Gladys Mary Dever (*d* 1983), *d* of late Thomas Francis Hughes; *S* father, 1976; *m* 1940, Barbara Mary, *d* of Bernard Rochford, OBE; one *s* five *d* (and one *s* decd). *Educ:* Downside School (Scholar); Brasenose Coll., Oxford (Scholar). Colonial Service, E Africa, 1938–54. Director, Joseph Rochford & Sons Ltd and other cos. Mem. Council and Chm. Glasshouse Cttee, Nat. Farmers Union, 1962–69; Member: Agricultural Research Council, 1964–74; Central Council for Agricultural Cooperation, 1970–73. Mem., Select Cttee on European Communities, 1984–. Pres., Nat. Council on Inland Transport, 1978–84. Trustee, John Innes Foundation, 1974–. Chm. of Governing Body, Glasshouse Crops Research Inst., 1981–84. Knight of Malta, 1962. *Recreations:* sailing, gardening. *Heir: s* Hon. Jeremy Francis Addington [*b* 29 July 1947; *m* 1970, Grete Henningsen; one *s* one *d*]. *Address:* Highway Manor, near Calne, Wilts SN11 8SR. *T:* Hilmarton 390; 16 Westminster Palace Gardens, Artillery Row, SW1P 1RL. *T:* 01–222 2445.

SIDNEY, family name of **Viscount De L'Isle.**

SIDNEY-WILMOT, Air Vice-Marshal Aubrey, CB 1977; OBE 1948; Director of Legal Services (Royal Air Force), 1970–79; a Chairman of Industrial Tribunals, since 1979; *b* 4 Jan. 1915; *s* of Alfred Robert Sidney-Wilmot and Harriet Sidney-Wilmot; *m* 1968, Ursula Hartmann; one *s* by former marriage. *Educ:* Framlingham College. Admitted Solicitor, 1938; practised, 1938–40. Commnd in Administrative Br., RAF, 1940; transf. to Office of JAG, 1942; DJAG (Army and RAF), Far East, 1948–50; transf. to Directorate of Legal Services (RAF), 1950; Dep. Dir of Legal Services (RAF), 1969.

Recreations: travel, swimming, gardening. *Address:* Grove House, Great Horkesley, Colchester, Essex CO6 4AG. *Club:* Royal Air Force.

SIDWELL, Martindale, FRAM; FRCO; Organist and Choirmaster, Hampstead Parish Church, since 1945; Organist and Director of Music, St Clement Danes (Central Church of the RAF), since 1957; Conductor: Martindale Sidwell Choir, since 1956; St Clement Danes Chorale and Martindale Sidwell Sinfonia, since 1983; St Clement's Orchestra, since 1984; *b* 23 Feb. 1916; *s* of John William Sidwell, Little Packington, Warwicks, and Mary Martindale, Liverpool; *m* 1944, Barbara Anne (*née* Hill) (pianist, harpsichordist and Prof. of Piano and Harpsichord, Royal Coll. of Music, under the name Barbara Hill); two *s*. *Educ:* Wells Cathedral Sch., Somerset; Royal Academy of Music. Sub-Organist, Wells Cathedral, 1932. Served War of 1939–45, Royal Engineers. Organist, Holy Trinity Church, Leamington Spa, and Director of Music, Warwick School, 1943, also at same time Conductor of Royal Leamington Spa Bach Choir; Conductor, Hampstead Choral Soc., 1946–81; Founder 1967, and Director and Conductor, 1967–81, London Bach Orch. Prof., RSCM, 1958–66; Prof. of Organ, RAM, 1963–84. Mem. Council, RCO, 1966–. Harriet Cohen International Bach Medal, 1967. Frequent broadcasts as Conductor and as Organ Recitalist, 1944–. *Address:* 1 Frognal Gardens, Hampstead, NW3. *T:* 01–435 9210. *Clubs:* Savage, Wig and Pen.

SIE, Sir Banja T.; see Tejan-Sie.

SIEFF, family name of **Baron Sieff of Brimpton** and of Sieff barony (extinct).

SIEFF OF BRIMPTON, Baron *cr* 1980 (Life Peer), of Brimpton in the Royal County of Berkshire; **Marcus Joseph Sieff;** Kt 1971; OBE 1944; Chairman, First International Bank of Israel Financial Trust Ltd, since 1983; Non-Executive Chairman, The Independent, since 1986; Director, N. M. Rothschild & Sons, since 1983; *b* 2 July 1913; *yr s* of late Baron Sieff; *m* 1st, 1937, Rosalie Fromson (marr. diss., 1947); one *s*; 2nd, 1951, Elsa Florence Gosen (marr. diss., 1953); 3rd, 1956, Brenda Mary Beith (marr. diss., 1962); one *d*; 4th, 1963, Mrs Pauline Lily Moretzki (*née* Spatz); one *d*. *Educ:* Manchester Grammar School; St Paul's; Corpus Christi College, Cambridge (MA), Hon. Fellow, 1975. Served War 1939–45, Royal Artillery. Joined Marks and Spencer Ltd, 1935; Dir, 1954; Asst Man. Dir, 1963; Vice-Chm., 1965; Jt Man. Dir, 1967–83; Dep. Chm., 1971; Chm., 1972–84; Pres., 1984–85; Hon. Pres., 1985–. Mem., BNEC, 1965–71 (Chm., Export Cttee for Israel, 1965–68). Hon. Pres., Joint Israel Appeal, 1984–. Vice Pres., Policy Studies Institute (formerly PEP) Exec., 1975–; Pres., Anglo-Israel Chamber of Commerce, 1975–. Trustee, Nat. Portrait Gallery, 1986–. Hon. FRCS 1984. Hon. LLD St Andrews, 1983; Hon. Dr Babson Coll., Mass, 1984; Hon. DLitt Reading; DUniv Stirling, 1986. Hambro Award, Businessman of the Year, 1977; Aims National Free Enterprise Award, 1978; B'nai B'rith Internat. gold medallion for humanitarianism, 1982; Retailer of the Year Award, National Retail Merchants' Assoc., USA, 1982; BIM Gold Medal, 1983. *Address:* Michael House, Baker Street, W1A 1DN.

See also Hon. D. D. Sieff, Hon. M. D. Sieff.

SIEFF, Hon. David Daniel; Director, Marks and Spencer plc, since 1972; *b* 22 March 1939; *s* of Baron Sieff of Brimpton, *qv*, and late Rosalie Cottage; *m* 1962, Jennifer Walton; two *s*. *Educ:* Repton. Joined Marks & Spencer, 1957; Alternate Director, 1968; Full Director, 1972. Chairman, North Metropolitan Conciliation Cttee of Race Relations Board, 1969–71; Vice-Chm., Inst. of Race Relations, 1971–72; part-time Member, National Freight Corp., 1972–78; Mem., Policy Studies Inst. (formerly PEP), 1976–84. Governor: Weizmann Inst. of Science, Rehovot, Israel, 1978– (Chm. Exec. Cttee, UK Foundn, 1984–); Shenkar Coll. of Textile Technology (Israel), 1980–; Hon. Pres., British ORT, 1983–. Trustee, Glyndebourne Arts Trust, 1971–. Pres., Racehorse Owners Assoc., 1975–78; Member, Jockey Club, 1977–. *Address:* Michael House, 47 Baker Street, W1A 1DN. *T:* 01–935 4422. *Club:* Saints and Sinners.

SIEFF, Hon. Michael David, CBE 1975; Director, Marks & Spencer, 1950–78 (Joint Managing Director, 1971–76; Joint Vice-Chairman, 1972–76); *b* 12 March 1911; *er s* of late Baron Sieff; *m* 1st, 1932, Daphne Madge Kerin Michael (marr. diss. 1975); one *s*; 2nd, 1975, Elizabeth Pitt; one *s* one *d*. *Educ:* Manchester Grammar School. Served War of 1939–45, Col RAOC 1944; Hon. Col, TA, 1956. Joined Marks & Spencer Ltd, 1929; Asst Man. Dir, 1965–71. Member: European Trade Cttee, British Overseas Trade Bd, 1974–; British Overseas Trade Adv. Council, 1975–; Pres., British Overseas Trade Gp for Israel, 1979–83 (Chm., 1972–78); Vice-Chm., British-Israel Chamber of Commerce, 1969–. Founder Fellow, Royal Post-Grad. Med. Sch. (Hammersmith Hosp.), 1972 (formerly Mem. Council). *Address:* Michael House, Baker Street, W1A 1DN. *T:* 01–935 4422.

See also Baron Sieff of Brimpton.

SIEGBAHN, Prof. Kai Manne Börje; Professor of Physics, University of Uppsala, since 1954; *b* 20 April 1918; *s* of Manne Siegbahn and Karin Siegbahn (*née* Högbom); *m* 1944, Anna-Brita (*née* Rhedin); three *s*. *Educ:* Univ. of Uppsala (BSc 1939); Licentiate of Philosophy 1942); Univ. of Stockholm (Dr of Philosophy 1944). Research Associate, Nobel Inst. of Physics, 1942–51; Prof. of Physics, Royal Inst. of Technology, Stockholm, 1951–54. Member: Roy. Swedish Acad. of Sci.; Roy. Swedish Acad. of Engrg Scis; Roy. Soc. of Sci.; Roy. Acad. of Arts and Sci. of Uppsala; Roy. Physiographical Soc. of Lund; Societas Scientiarum Fennica; Norwegian Acad. of Sci.; Roy. Norwegian Soc. of Scis and Letters; Nat. Acad. of Sciences. Hon. Mem. Amer. Acad. of Arts and Scis; Membre de Comité des Poids et Mesures, Paris; Pres., Internat. Union of Pure and Applied Physics (IUPAP). Dr of Science, *hc*: Durham, 1972; Basel, 1980; Liège, 1980; Upsala Coll., East Orange, NJ, 1982; Sussex, 1983. Lindblom Prize, 1945; Björkén Prize, 1955, 1977; Celsius Medal, 1962; Sixten Heyman Award, 1971; Harrison Howe Award, 1973; Maurice F. Hasler Award, 1975; Charles Frederick Chandler Medal, 1976; Torbern Bergman Medal, 1979; Pittsburgh Award of Spectroscopy, 1982. (Jtly) Nobel Prize for Physics, 1981. *Publications:* Beta- and Gamma-Ray Spectroscopy, 1955; Alpha-, Beta- and Gamma-Ray Spectroscopy, 1965; ESCA—Atomic, Molecular and Solid State Structure Studied by Means of Electron Spectroscopy, 1967; ESCA Applied to Free Molecules, 1969; around 400 scientific papers. *Recreations:* tennis, skiing and music. *Address:* Institute of Physics, University of Uppsala, Box 530, S-751 21 Uppsala, Sweden. *T:* 018/146963.

SIEGERT, Air Vice-Marshal Cyril Laurence, CB 1979; CBE 1975; MVO 1954; DFC 1944; AFC 1954; *b* 14 March 1923; *s* of Lawrence Siegert and Julia Ann Siegert; *m* 1948, Shirley Berenice Dick; two *s* two *d*. *Educ:* Fairlie High School; St Kevin's Coll., Oamaru; Victoria Univ. of Wellington. Joined RNZAF, 1942; served in UK with Nos 299 and 190 Sqdns, on loan to BOAC, 1945–47; Berlin airlift, 1949; NZ, 1952–54; NZ Defence Staff, Washington, 1954–56; RAF Staff Coll., 1957; NZ, 1958–62; Comdt, RNZAF's Command and Staff Sch., 1962; RAF Coll. of Air Warfare, 1963; Singapore, 1963–65; CO, No 3 Battlefield Support Sqdn and RNZAF Transport Wing, 1965–69; AOC RNZAF Ops Group, 1969–70; IDC 1970; RNZAF Air Staff, 1971; Chief of Staff, ANZUK Joint Force HQ, Singapore, 1971–73; Dep. Chief of Defence Staff (Policy), 1973–76; Chief of Air Staff, RNZAF, 1976–79. Gen. Manager, Marine Air Systems, 1980–84, Mem., Air Services Licensing Authority, 1980 . *Recreations:* fishing, tramping, gardening. *Address:* 46 Wyndrum Avenue, Lower Hutt, New Zealand. *Clubs:* United Services (Wellington); Wellington Racing.

SIEGHART, Paul; law reformer, international arbitrator and consultant, writer and broadcaster; Chairman, Executive Committee, Justice (British Section of International Commission of Jurists), since 1978; *b* 22 Feb. 1927; *s* of Ernest and Marguerite Alexander Sieghart; *m* 1st, 1954, Rosemary (*d* 1956), *d* of Comdr C. E. Aglionby, DSO, RN; one *s* one *d*; 2nd, 1959, Felicity Ann, *d* of A. M. Baer; one *s* one *d*. *Educ:* Harrow; Berkhamsted Sch.; University Coll. London. FRSA; FCIArb. Called to the Bar, Gray's Inn, 1953; retired from practice, 1966. Chm., Professions Jt Working Party on Statutory Registration of Psychotherapists, 1975–81; Vice-Chm., Arbitration Cttee, CIArb, 1983–84; Member: Home Office Data Protection Cttee, 1976–78; Gpe de Bellerive, Geneva, 1977–; Gorleben Internat. Rev., 1978–79; Commn for Internat. Justice and Peace of England and Wales, 1976–80; Council, Catholic Union of GB, 1981–. Founder, Council for Sci. and Society, 1972 (Vice-Chm., 1972–78); Governor, British Inst. of Human Rights, 1974–; Trustee: European Human Rights Foundn, 1980– (Chm., 1986–); The Tablet Trust, 1976–; Monteverdi Trust, 1980–; Justice Educnl and Res. Trust, 1981–; Tavistock Clinic Foundn, 1982–. Jt recipient, Airey Neave Meml Scholarship for research into freedom under national laws, 1981. Lectures: Cantor, RSA, 1977; Lucas, RCP, 1981; Shaw Meml, Oxford, 1981; Trueman Wood, RSA, 1983. Draftsman: Right of Privacy Bill 1970; Rehabilitation of Offenders Act 1974. Freeman, City of London. *Publications:* (ed) Chalmers' Sale of Goods, 13th edn 1957, 14th edn 1963; (with J. B. Whalley) Slaughterhouses, 1960; Privacy and Computers, 1976; (ed) Microchips with Everything, 1982; The International Law of Human Rights, 1983; The Lawful Rights of Mankind, 1985; The World of Science and the Rule of Law, 1986; contribs to learned jls. *Recreations:* travel, music, ski-ing, sailing, shooting. *Address:* 6 Gray's Inn Square, WC1R 5AZ. *T:* 01–405 1351. *Clubs:* Brooks's; Bar Yacht.

SIEVE, James Ezekiel Balfour, PhD, FCA; *b* 31 July 1922; *s* of Isaac and Rachel Sieve; *m* 1953, Yvonne Manley; two *s*. *Educ:* London Sch. of Economics. BSc Econ, PhD. With Urwick Orr & Partners, 1950–54; Aquascutum & Associated Cos Ltd, 1954–68, Finance Dir, 1957–68; Metal Box Ltd, 1968, Finance Dir, 1970–80; Hacker Young, Chartered Accountants, 1981–83. Governor, Home Farm Trust (residential care of mentally handicapped), 1974–83; Member: Tax Reform Cttee, 1975–83; Nat. Freight Consortium, 1982–83 (Nat. Freight Corp., later Nat. Freight Co., 1977–82). *Publication:* Income Redistribution and the Welfare State (with Adrian Webb), 1971. *Recreation:* relaxing with family. *Address:* 56 Hampstead Lane, NW3 7JP.

SIGMON, Robert Leland; lawyer; *b* Roanoke, Va, 3 April 1929; *s* of Ottis Leland Sigmon and Aubrey Virginia (née Bishop); *m* 1963, Marianne Rita Gellner. *Educ:* Univ. of Virginia; Sorbonne; London Sch. of Economics. BA, DrJur. Member of the Bar: US Supreme Court; Court of Appeals, Second and District of Columbia Circuits; Virginia; District of Columbia. Chairman, Exec. Cttee, Pilgrims Soc. of Gt Britain, 1977–; Director and Founder Mem., Associates of the Victoria and Albert Museum; Mem., Council of Management, British Inst. of Internat. and Comparative Law, 1982–. Trustee: American Sch. in London, 1977–; Magna Carta Trust, 1984–; Vice-Chm., Mid-Atlantic Club of London, 1977–; Vice-Pres., European-Atlantic Gp, 1978–; Member: Exec. Cttee, Amer. Soc. in London, 1969– (Chm. 1974); Amer. Soc. of Internat. Law; Selden Soc.; Guild of St Bride's Church, Fleet Street; Ends of the Earth; Gov., E-SU, 1984–. Chevalier du Tastevin. *Publications:* contribs to legal periodicals. *Recreations:* collecting antiquarian books, oenology. *Address:* 2 Plowden Buildings, Middle Temple, EC4Y 9AS. *T:* 01–583 4851. *Club:* Reform.

SIGURDSSON, Niels P.; Ambassador of Iceland to Norway, since 1985; *b* Reykjavik, 10 Feb. 1926; *s* of Sigurdur B. Sigurdsson and Karitas Einarsdóttir; *m* 1953, Olafia Rafnsdóttir; two *s* one *d*. *Educ:* Univ. of Iceland (Law). Joined Diplomatic Service 1952; First Sec., Paris Embassy, 1956–60; Dep. Permanent Rep. to NATO and OECD, 1957–60; Dir, Internat. Policy Div., Min. of Foreign Affairs, Reykjavik, 1961–67; Delegate to UN Gen. Assembly, 1965; Ambassador and Permanent Rep. of Iceland to N Atlantic Council, 1967–71. Ambassador: to Belgium and EEC, 1968–71; to UK, 1971–76; to Fed. Republic of Germany, 1976–78; Ministry of Foreign Affairs, Reykjavik, 1979–84. *Recreations:* swimming, riding. *Address:* Langviksveien 6, Bygdöy, Oslo 2, Norway; Safamýri 83, 108 Reykjavik, Iceland.

SIKRI, Sarv Mittra; *b* 26 April 1908; *s* of late Dr Nihal Chand; *m* 1937, Mrs Leila Sikri; one *s*. *Educ:* Trinity Hall, Cambridge (BA). Barrister-at-Law (Lincoln's Inn). Started practice in Lahore High Court, 1930; Asst Advocate Gen., Punjab, 1949; Advocate Gen., Punjab, 1951–64; Judge, Supreme Ct of India, 1964–71; Chief Justice of India, 1971–73. Chm., Railway Accidents Enquiry Cttee, 1978–80; Chm., Jammu and Kashmir Enquiry Cttee, 1979–80. Alternate rep., UN Cttee on Codification and Develt of Internat. Law, 1947; Legal Adviser to Min. of Irrigation and Power, Govt of India, 1949; Mem. Internat. Law Assoc. Cttee on Internat. Rivers, 1955; Mem., Indian Law Commn, 1955–58. Delegate to: Law of the Sea Conf., Geneva, 1958; World Peace Through Law Conf., Tokyo, 1961, Athens, 1963; Accra Assembly, Accra, 1962. Pres., Indian Br. of Internat. Law Assoc., 1971–73; Member: Indian Commn of Jurists; Univ. Grants Commn, 1979–82; Chm., Sir Ganga Ram Hosp. Trust; Hon. Mem., Acad. of Political Sci., NY; Vice-Pres., Delhi Public School Soc. *Recreations:* golf, tennis, bridge. *Address:* 3 Nizam-ud-din East, New Delhi 110013, India. *T:* 692327. *Clubs:* Delhi Golf, Delhi Gymkhana (both in New Delhi).

SILBERSTON, Prof. (Zangwill) Aubrey; Professor of Economics, Imperial College of Science and Technology, University of London, since 1978, and Head of Department of Social and Economic Studies, since 1981; *b* 26 Jan. 1922; *s* of Louis and Polly Silberston; *m* 1st, 1945, Dorothy Marion (marr. diss. 1985), *d* of A. S. Nicholls; one *s* (one *d* decd); 2nd, 1985, Michèle, *d* of Vitomir and Nelly Ledić, Zagreb. *Educ:* Hackney Downs Sch., London; Jesus Coll., Cambridge. Econs Tripos Pt II, Cambridge, 1946. Courtaulds Ltd, 1946–50; Kenward Res. Fellow in Industrial Admin, St Catharine's Coll., Cambridge, 1950–53; University Lectr in Economics, Cambridge, 1953–71; Fellow, 1958–71, Dir of Studies in Econs, 1965–71, St John's Coll., Cambridge; Chm., Faculty Bd of Econs and Politics, 1966–70; Official Fellow in Econs, 1971–78, and Dean, 1972–78, Nuffield Coll., Oxford. Visiting Professor: Queensland Univ., 1977; Univ. of the South, Sewanee, 1984. Member: Monopolies Commn, 1965–68; Board of British Steel Corp., 1967–76; Departmental Cttee on Patent System, 1967–70; Royal Commn on the Press, 1974–77; Restrictive Practices Ct, 1986–; Royal Commn on Environmental Pollution, 1986–; Econs Cttee, SSRC, 1969–73; Chm., Assoc. of Learned Societies in the Social Sciences, 1985–. Economic Adviser, CBI, 1972–74. Sec.-Gen., Royal Economic Soc., 1979–; Pres., Section F, British Assoc., 1987. *Publications:* Education and Training for Industrial Management, 1955; (with G. Maxcy) The Motor Industry, 1959; (in collaboration with C. Pratten and R. M. Dean) Economies of Large-scale Production in British Industry, 1965; (in collaboration with K. H. Boehm) The Patent System, 1967; (with C. T. Taylor) The Economic Impact of the Patent System, 1973; (ed, with Francis Seton) Industrial Management: East and West, 1973; (with A. Cockerill) The Steel Industry, 1974; (ed, with D. Shepherd and J. Turk) Microeconomic Efficiency and Macroeconomic

Performance, 1983; The Multi-Fibre Arrangement and the UK Economy, 1984; (with D. Shepherd and R. Strange) British Manufacturing Investment Overseas, 1985; articles in Econ. Jl, Bulletin of Oxford Inst. of Statistics, Oxford Economic Papers, Jl of Royal Statistical Society. *Recreations:* music, ballet. *Address:* 53 Prince's Gate, SW7 2PG. *T:* 01–589 5111. *Club:* Travellers'.

SILK, Ven. David; *see* Silk, Ven. R. D.

SILK, Dennis Raoul Whitehall; Warden of Radley College, since 1968; *b* 8 Oct. 1931; 2nd *s* of late Rev. Dr Claude Whitehall Silk and Mrs Louise Silk; *m* 1963, Diana Merilyn, 2nd *d* of W. F. Milton, Pitminster, Somerset; two *s* two *d*. *Educ:* Christ's Hosp.; Sidney Sussex Coll., Cambridge (Exhibr). MA (History) Cantab. Asst Master, Marlborough Coll., 1955–68 (Housemaster, 1957–68). *Publications:* Cricket for Schools, 1964; Attacking Cricket, 1965. *Recreations:* antiquarian, literary, sporting (Blues in cricket (Capt. Cambridge Univ. CC, 1955) and Rugby football). *Address:* The Warden's House, Radley College, Abingdon, Oxon OX14 2HR. *T:* Abingdon 20585. *Clubs:* East India, Devonshire, Sports and Public Schools; Hawks (Cambridge).

SILK, Ven. (Robert) David; Archdeacon of Leicester, since 1980; Team Rector, Holy Spirit, Leicester, since 1982; *b* 23 Aug. 1936; *s* of Robert Reeve Silk and Winifred Patience Silk; *m* 1957, Joyce Irene Bracey; one *s* one *d*. *Educ:* Gillingham Grammar School; Univ. of Exeter (BA Hons Theology 1958); St Stephen's House, Oxford. Deacon 1959, priest 1960, Rochester; Curate: St Barnabas, Gillingham, 1959–63; Holy Redeemer, Lamorbey, 1963–69; Priest-in-Charge of the Good Shepherd, Blackfen, 1967–69; Rector of Swanscombe, 1969–75; Rector of Beckenham, St George, 1975–80. Proctor in Convocation, 1970–; Prolocutor of Lower House of Convocation of Canterbury, 1980–; Member of Liturgical Commission, 1976–; Chm., Leicester Council of Faiths, 1986–. *Publications:* Prayers for Use at the Alternative Services, 1980; Compline—an Alternative Order, 1980. *Recreations:* Richard III, tennis, squash. *Address:* 13 Stoneygate Avenue, Stoneygate, Leicester. *T:* Leicester 704441. *Club:* Leicestershire (Leicester).

SILK, Robert K.; *see* Kilroy-Silk.

SILKE, Hon. William James; Hon. Mr Justice Silke; Justice of Appeal, Supreme Court of Hong Kong, since 1981; *b* 21 Sept. 1929; *s* of William Joseph Silke and Gertrude (née Delany). *Educ:* Dominican Convent, Wicklow; Xavier Sch., Donnybrook; King's Inns, Dublin. Called to Irish Bar (South Eastern Circuit, Leinster Bar), 1955; Magistrate, North Borneo/Malaysia, 1959; Registrar, High Court in Borneo (Sabah-Sarawak), 1965; Puisne Judge, 1966; retired under compensation scheme during Malaysianisation, 1969; Hong Kong: Magistrate, 1969; President, Tenancy Tribunal, 1971; Acting Asst Registrar, High Court, 1972; President, Lands Tribunal, 1974; Judge, District Court, 1975; Judicial Commissioner, State of Brunei, 1978; Judge of the High Court, 1979. *Recreations:* horse racing/breeding, music, travel. *Address:* Supreme Court, Hong Kong. *T:* 5–8214606. *Clubs:* Stephen's Green (Dublin); Royal Sabah Turf (Sabah, Malaysia); Hong Kong, Royal Hong Kong Jockey (Hong Kong).

SILKIN, family name of **Baron Silkin of Dulwich.**

SILKIN, 2nd Baron, *cr* 1950, of Dulwich [disclaimed his peerage for life, 1972]; *see under* Silkin, Arthur.

SILKIN OF DULWICH, Baron *cr* 1985 (Life Peer), of North Leigh in the County of Oxfordshire; **Samuel Charles Silkin;** PC 1974; QC 1963; Deputy Chairman, BPCC plc, since 1982 (Director since 1981); Partner (with Rt Hon. John Silkin) in Silkin Brothers (consultancy to advise on governmental, international, EEC and local government problems), since 1986; *b* 6 March 1918; 2nd *s* of 1st Baron Silkin, PC, CH; *m* 1941, Elaine Violet (née Stamp) (*d* 1984); two *s* two *d*; *m* 1985, Sheila Marian Swanston, widow. *Educ:* Dulwich College (Schol.); Trinity Hall, Cambridge (Schol.; BA 1st cl. hons Parts I and II of Law Tripos; Law Studentship, 1939). Called to Bar, Middle Temple, 1941 (Cert. of Honour 1940, Harmsworth Law Schol., 1946), Bencher 1969. Served War of 1939–45, Lt-Col RA (despatches). Member, Royal Commission on the Penal System for England and Wales, 1965–66. MP (Lab) Camberwell, Dulwich, 1964–74, Southwark, Dulwich, 1974–83; Chairman: Parly Labour Party's Group on Common Market and European Affairs, 1966–70; Select Cttee on Parly Privilege, 1967; Leader, UK Delegn to Assembly of Council of Europe, 1968–70; Chm. Council of Europe Legal Cttee, 1966–70; Opposition front-bench spokesman on Law Officer matters, 1970–74; Attorney General, 1974–79. Recorder of Bedford, 1966–71. Chairman: Waterlow Publishers Ltd, 1981–; Solicitors Law Stationery Soc., 1985–; Dir, Pergamon Press Ltd, 1984–. Society of Labour Lawyers: Foundn Mem.; Chm., 1964–71; Vice Pres., 1971–. Governor, Royal Bethlem and Maudsley Hosps, 1970–74; Chm., British Inst. of Human Rights, 1972–74; Pres., Alcohol Educn Centre, 1973–. Mem., CIArb., 1979–. MacDermott Lectr, QUB, 1976. Hon. Freeman, London Borough of Southwark, 1982. Hon. Mem., Amer. Bar Assoc., 1976–. *Address:* 4 Dean's Yard, SW1. *Club:* Athenæum.
See also Arthur Silkin, Rt Hon. J. E. Silkin.

SILKIN, Arthur; Lecturer in Public Administration, Civil Service College, Sunningdale, 1971–76, on secondment from Department of Employment; retired 1976; *b* 20 Oct. 1916; *e s* of 1st Baron Silkin, PC, CH; *S* father, 1972, as 2nd Baron Silkin, but disclaimed his peerage for life; *m* 1969, Audrey Bennett. *Educ:* Dulwich College; Peterhouse, Cambridge. BA 1938; Diploma in Govt Administration, 1959. Served 1940–45, Royal Air Force (A and SD Branch), Pilot Officer, 1941, subsequently Flying Officer. Entered Ministry of Labour and National Service, 1939; formerly 2nd Secretary, British Embassy, Paris. First Secretary: High Commissioner's Office, Calcutta, 1960–61; British Embassy, Dakar, May 1962–Mar. 1964; British Embassy, Kinshasa, 1964–66. *Publications:* contrib. to Public Administration, Political Qly. *Address:* Cuzco, 33 Woodnook Road, SW16. *T:* 01–677 8733.
See also Baron Silkin of Dulwich, Rt Hon. J. E. Silkin.

SILKIN, Rt. Hon. John Ernest, PC 1966; MP (Lab) Lewisham, Deptford, since 1974 (Deptford, July 1963–1974); Partner (with Lord Silkin of Dulwich) in Silkin Brothers, consultants on national, international, EEC and local politics and administration, since 1986; *b* 18 March 1923; *y s* of 1st Baron Silkin, PC, CH; *m* 1950, Rosamund John (actress), *d* of Frederick Jones; one *s*. *Educ:* Dulwich College; University of Wales (Fellow, University College, Cardiff, 1981); Trinity Hall, Cambridge. BA 1944; LLM (LLB 1946); MA 1949. Royal Navy, 1941–46. Admitted a Solicitor, 1950. Contested (Lab): St Marylebone, 1950; West Woolwich, 1951; South Nottingham, 1959. Govt Chief Whip, 1966–69; Dep. Leader, House of Commons, 1968–69; Minister of Public Building and Works, 1969–70; Minister for Planning and Local Govt, DoE, 1974–76; Minister of Agric., Fisheries and Food, 1976–79; Opposition spokesman on industry, 1979–80, on defence and disarmament, 1981–83; Shadow Leader of House of Commons, 1980–83. *Address:* 4 Dean's Yard, SW1P 3NL. *T:* 01–222 2213. *Clubs:* Garrick, Royal Automobile, Naval.
See also Baron Silkin of Dulwich, Arthur Silkin.

SILKIN, Jon; poet; *b* 2 Dec. 1930; *s* of Dora Rubenstein and Joseph Silkin, solicitor (retd); three *s* one *d* (and one *s* decd); *m* Lorna Tracy (American writer and co-editor of Stand). *Educ:* Wycliffe Coll.; Dulwich Coll.; Univ. of Leeds. BA Hons Eng. Lit. 1962. Journalist, 1947; Nat. Service, teaching in Educn Corps, Army; subseq. six years as manual labourer, London and two years teaching English to foreign students. Founded magazine Stand, 1952. Several poetry-reading tours, USA; Vis. Lectr, Denison Univ., Ohio; taught at Writers' Workshop, Univ. of Iowa, 1968–69; Visiting writer: for Australian Council for the Arts, 1974; College of Idaho, Caldwell, 1978; Mishkenot Sha'ananim, Jerusalem, 1980; Bingham Vis. Poet, Univ. of Louisville, 1981; Elliston Poet-in-Residence, Univ. of Cincinnati, 1983. C. Day Lewis Fellowship, 1976–77. Vis. Speaker, World Congress of Poets: Korea, 1979; Madrid, 1982; Corfu, 1985; Florence, 1986. *Publications:* The Peaceable Kingdom, 1954, reprint 1976; The Two Freedoms, 1958; The Re-ordering of the Stones, 1961; Nature with Man, 1965 (Geoffrey Faber Meml Prize, 1966); (with Murphy and Tarn) Penguin Modern Poets 7, 1965; Poems New and Selected, 1966; Killhope Wheel, 1971; Amana Grass, 1971; Out of Battle: the poetry of the Great War, 1972; (ed) Poetry of the Committed Individual, 1973; The Principle of Water, 1974; The Little Time-keeper, 1976; (ed) Penguin Book of First World War Poetry, 1979; (ed with Peter Redgrove) New Poetry, 1979; The Psalms with Their Spoils, 1980; Selected Poems, 1980; (ed jtly) Stand One, 1984; Gurney (verse play), 1985; (ed) Wilfred Owen: the Collected Poems, 1985; The Ship's Pasture (poems), 1986; (with Jon Glover) The Penguin Book of First World War Prose, 1987. *Recreation:* travelling. *Address:* 19 Haldane Terrace, Newcastle upon Tyne NE2 3AN. *T:* Tyneside 2812614.

SILLARS, James; management consultant; *b* Ayr, 4 Oct. 1937; *s* of Matthew Sillars; *m* 1st, 1957; one *s* one *d*; 2nd, 1981, Mrs Margo MacDonald, *qv*. *Educ:* Newton Park Sch., Ayr; Ayr Academy. Former official, Fire Brigades Union; Past Member Ayr Town Council and Ayr County Council Educn Cttee; Mem., T&GWU. Head of Organization and Social Services Dept, Scottish TUC, 1968–70. Full-time Labour Party agent, 1964 and 1966 elections. MP (Lab) South Ayrshire, March 1970–1976, (SLP) 1976–79. Among the founders of the Scottish Labour Party, Jan. 1976. Man. Dir, Scoted Ltd, 1980–83. Especially interested in education, social services, industrial relations, development policies. *Publications:* Scotland—the Case for Optimism, 1986; Labour Party pamphlets on Scottish Nationalism; Tribune Gp pamphlet on Democracy within the Labour Party. *Recreations:* reading, camping, tennis, swimming.

SILLARS, Margo; *see* MacDonald, M.

SILLERY, William Moore; Headmaster, Belfast Royal Academy, since 1980; *b* 14 March 1941; *s* of William and Adeline Sillery; *m* 1963, Elizabeth Margaret Dunwoody; two *d*. *Educ:* Methodist Coll., Belfast; St Catharine's Coll., Cambridge. Head of Modern Languages, Belfast Royal Academy, 1968, Vice-Principal 1974, Deputy Headmaster 1976. *Recreations:* golf, bridge. *Address:* Ardmore, 15 Saintfield Road, Belfast BT8 4AE. *T:* Belfast 645260. *Club:* Belvoir Park (Belfast).

SILLITOE, Alan; writer since 1948; *b* 4 March 1928; *s* of Christopher Archibald Sillitoe and Sylvina (*née* Burton); *m* 1959, Ruth Fainlight; one *s* one *d*. *Educ:* various elementary schools in Nottingham. Raleigh Bicycle Factory, 1942; wireless operator, RAF, 1946–49. Lived in France and Spain, 1952–58. FRGS; Hon. Fellow, Manchester Polytechnic, 1977. *Publications: novels:* Saturday Night and Sunday Morning, 1958 (Authors' Club Award for best first novel of 1958; filmed, 1960, play, 1964); The General, 1960 (filmed 1967 as Counterpoint); Key to the Door, 1961; The Death of William Posters, 1965; A Tree on Fire, 1967; A Start in Life, 1970; Travels in Nihilon, 1971; Raw Material, 1972; The Flame of Life, 1974; The Widower's Son, 1976; The Storyteller, 1979; Her Victory, 1982; The Lost Flying Boat, 1983; Down from the Hill, 1984; Life Goes On, 1985; *stories:* The Loneliness of the Long Distance Runner, 1959 (Hawthornden Prize; filmed, 1962); The Ragman's Daughter, 1963 (filmed, 1972); Guzman, Go Home, 1968; Men, Women and Children, 1973; The Second Chance, 1981; *poetry:* The Rats and Other Poems, 1960; A Falling Out of Love, 1964; Love in the Environs of Voronezh, 1968; Storm and Other Poems, 1974; Snow on the North Side of Lucifer, 1979; Sun before Departure, 1984; Tides and Stone Walls, 1986; *for children:* The City Adventures of Marmalade Jim, 1967; Big John and the Stars, 1977; The Incredible Fencing Fleas, 1978; Marmalade Jim at the Farm, 1980; Marmalade Jim and the Fox, 1985; *travel:* Road to Volgograd, 1964; (with Fay Godwin) The Saxon Shore Way, 1983; (with David Sillitoe) Nottinghamshire, 1987; *plays:* (with Ruth Fainlight) All Citizens are Soldiers, 1969; Three Plays, 1978; *essays:* Mountains and Caverns, 1975. *Recreation:* travel. *Address:* 21 The Street, Wittersham, Kent. *Club:* Savage.

SILLITOE, Leslie Richard, OBE 1977; JP; General Secretary, Ceramic and Allied Trades Union, 1975–80, now Life Member; *b* 30 Aug. 1915; *s* of Leonard Richard Sillitoe and Ellen (*née* Sutton); *m* 1939, Lucy (*née* Goulding); two *d*. *Educ:* St George's and St Giles' Sch., Newcastle, Staffs; Stoke-on-Trent School of Art; WEA, N Staffs Technical Coll. Modeller and mouldmaker on leaving school. Served War, Royal Artillery, sen. non-commnd officer, 1939–46. Ceramic and Allied Trades Union: General President, 1961–63; Organiser, 1963; Asst Gen. Sec., 1967. Dep. Chm., Ceramics, Glass and Mineral Products Industry Trng Bd, 1977–82; Chm., Nat. Jt Council for Ceramic Industry, 1975–81. Chm., N Staffs Manpower Services Cttee, 1975–83; Life Mem., N Staffs Trades Council (Pres., 1963–81); Member: Staffs Develt Assoc.; N Staffs Tourist Assoc.; N Staffs Medical Inst.; Staffordshire Soc.; Pottery & Glass Benevolent Inst. (Vice-Pres., 1980–); N Staffs Community Health Council, 1975–85; Staffordshire War Pensions Cttee, 1980–; Council, Univ. of Keele, 1976–; BBC Local Radio Council, 1978–81; Mem. Bd of Management, and Custodian Trustee, N Staffs Trustee Savings Bank; Vice-President: N Staffs District WEA, 1976–86; Muscular Dystrophy N Staffs Gp, 1978–; Pres., Staffordshire Lads and Dads Assoc., 1981–82, Vice-Pres. 1982–; Sec. and Treas., Ceramic Ind. Welfare Soc., 1971–81. Mem., Magistrates' Assoc.; Gideons Internat. Mem., Stoke-on-Trent District Council, 1953–83, 1986– (Vice-Chm., Museums Cttee); Lord Mayor, Stoke-on-Trent, 1981–82, Dep. Lord Mayor 1982–83. Governor: St Peters High Sch., Penkhull, 1975–; Cauldon Coll. of Further Educn, Stoke-on-Trent, 1976–; Thistley Hough High Sch., Penkhull, 1982–. Mem., W Midland TAVRA, 1979–83; Chm., Friends of the Staffordshire Regt (N Staffs), 1982–. Gov., Stoke Harpfield Primary Sch., 1982–. Territorial Efficient Service Medal, 1944. JP Stoke-on-Trent 1963–. *Publication:* foreword to The History of the Potters Union, 1977. *Recreations:* walking, photography, swimming, history. *Address:* 19 Sillitoe Place, Penkhull, Stoke-on-Trent ST4 5DQ. *T:* Stoke-on-Trent 47866.

SILLS, Beverly, (Mrs P. B. Greenough); Director, New York City Opera, since 1979; former leading soprano, New York City Opera and Metropolitan Opera; *b* 25 May 1929; *d* of late Morris Silverman and of Sonia Bahn; *m* 1956, Peter B. Greenough; one *s* one *d*. *Educ:* Professional Children's Sch., NYC; privately. Vocal studies with Estelle Liebling, piano with Paulo Gallico. Operatic debut, Philadelphia Civic Opera, 1947; San Francisco Opera, 1953; New York City Opera, 1955; Vienna State Opera, 1967; Teatro Colon, Buenos Aires, 1968; La Scala, Milan, 1969; Teatro San Carlo, Naples, 1970; Royal Opera, Covent Garden, London, 1970; Deutsche Oper, W Berlin, 1971; NY Metropolitan Opera, 1975, etc. Repeated appearances as soloist with major US symphony orchestras; English orchestral debut with London Symphony Orch., London, 1971; Paris debut, orchestral concert, Salle Pleyel, 1971. Repertoire includes title roles of Norma, Manon, Lucia di Lammermoor, Maria Stuarda, Daughter of Regiment, Anna Bolena, Traviata, Lucrezia Borgia, Thais, Louise, Cleopatra in Giulio Cesare, Elizabeth in Roberto Devereux, Tales of Hoffmann, Elvira in Puritani, Rosina in Barber of Seville, Norina in Don Pasquale; created title role, La Loca, San Diego Opera, 1979. Subject of BBC-TV's Profile in Music (Nat. Acad. of TV Arts and Sciences Emmy Award, 1975); other TV includes: Sills and Burnett at the Met, 1976; Hostess/Commentator for Young People's Concerts, NY Philharmonic, 1977; Moderator/Hostess, Lifestyles with Beverly Sills, 1976, 1977 (Emmy 1978). Hon. DMus: Temple Univ., 1972; New York Univ., 1973; New England Conservatory, 1973; Harvard Univ., 1974. Woman of the Year, Hasty Pudding Club, Harvard, 1974. *Publication:* Bubbles: a self-portrait, 1976. *Recreations:* fishing, bridge. *Address:* c/o Edgar Vincent Associates, 124 East 40 Street, New York, NY 10016, USA. *T:* 212–687–5105.

SILSOE, 2nd Baron *cr* 1963; **David Malcolm Trustram Eve,** Bt 1943; QC 1972; Barrister, Inner Temple, since 1955; *b* 2 May 1930; *er* twin *s* of 1st Baron Silsoe, GBE, MC, TD, QC, and Marguerite (*d* 1945), *d* of late Sir Augustus Meredith Nanton, Winnipeg; *S* father, 1976; *m* 1963, Bridget Min, *d* of Sir Rupert Hart-Davis, *qv*; one *s* one *d*. *Educ:* Winchester; Christ Church, Oxford (MA); Columbia Univ., New York. 2nd Lt, Royal Welch Fusiliers, 1949–50; Lieut, Queen Victoria's Rifles (TA), 1950–53. Bar Auditor, Inner Temple, 1965–70; Bencher, 1970. *Recreation:* ski-ing. *Heir:* *s* Hon. Simon Rupert Trustram Eve, *b* 17 April 1966. *Address:* Neals Farm, Wyfold, Reading, Berks RG4 9JB. *Club:* Ski of Great Britain.

SILVER, Prof. Ian Adair; Professor of Comparative Pathology since 1970, and Head of Department of Pathology, since 1982, University of Bristol; Adjunct Professor of Neurology, University of Pennsylvania, since 1977; *b* 28 Dec. 1927; *s* of Captain George James Silver and Nora Adair Silver; *m* 1950, Dr Marian Scrase, *d* of Dr F. J. Scrase; two *s* two *d*. *Educ:* Rugby School; Corpus Christi Coll., Cambridge (BA, MA); Royal Veterinary Coll. MRCVS. University of Cambridge: Univ. Demonstrator, Zoology, 1952–57; Univ. Lectr, Anatomy, 1957–70; Official Fellow and Coll. Lectr, Churchill Coll., 1965–70; Sen. Tutor for Advanced Students, Churchill Coll., 1966–70. Vis. Fellow, Weitzmann Inst., Rehovot, 1963; Vis. Prof., Louisiana Tech. Univ., 1973; Royal Soc. Vis. Prof., Fed. Univ. of Rio de Janeiro, 1977. Mem., SERC Biol. Scis Cttee, 1975–80; President: Internat. Soc. for O_2 Transport to Tissue, 1976 and 1986; RCVS, 1985–86 (Sen. Vice-Pres., 1986–87). RAgS Silver Medal, 1952; Sir Frederick Hobday Meml Medal, British Equine Vet. Assoc., 1982; Dalrymple-Champneys Medal, BVA, 1984. *Publications:* Editor of scientific books, 1971–; numerous articles in scientific jls. *Recreations:* farming, exploring, fishing, DIY. *Address:* Department of Pathology, Medical School, University of Bristol, Bristol BS8 1TD. *T:* Bristol 303446.

SILVER, Prof. Peter Hele S.; *see* Spencer-Silver.

SILVER, Prof. Robert Simpson, CBE 1967; FRSE; FIMechE; FInstP; James Watt Professor of Mechanical Engineering, University of Glasgow, 1967–79; *b* Montrose, Angus, 13 March 1913; *s* of Alexander Clark Silver and Isabella Simpson; *m* 1937, Jean McIntyre Bruce, *er d* of Alexander and Elizabeth Bruce (*née* Livingstone); two *s*. *Educ:* Montrose Academy; University of Glasgow. MA, 1932; BSc (1st Class Hons Nat. Phil) 1934; PhD 1938; DSc 1945. Research Physicist, ICI (Explosives), 1936–39; Head of Research, G. & J. Weir Ltd, 1939–46; Asst Director, Gas Research Board, 1947–48; Director of Research, Federated Founderies Ltd, 1948–54; Chief Designer, John Brown Land Boilers Ltd, 1954–56; Chief of Development and Research, G. & J. Weir Ltd, 1956–62 (Director 1958–); Prof. of Mech. Engrng, Heriot-Watt Coll. (now Univ.), 1962–66. FInstP 1942; MIMechE 1953; FRSE 1963. Hon. DSc Strathclyde, 1984. Foreign Associate, Nat. Acad. of Engineering, USA, 1979. Unesco Prize for Science, 1968. *Publications:* An Introduction to Thermodynamics, 1971; The Bruce, Robert I King of Scots (play), 1986; papers on physics and engineering, with special emphasis on thermodynamics, desalination, combustion, phase-change, and heat transfer; also on philosophy of science and education; a few poems, as Robert Simpson. *Recreations:* fishing, music, theatre, Scottish history and affairs. *Address:* Oakbank, Tobermory, Isle of Mull. *T:* Tobermory 2024.

SILVERLEAF, Alexander, CB 1980; FEng; FRINA; FICE; FCIT; Co-ordinator, International Transport Group (INTRA), since 1981; *b* 29 Oct. 1920; *m* 1950, Helen Marion Scott; two *d*. *Educ:* Kilburn Grammar Sch., London; Glasgow Univ. (BSc 1941). Wm Denny and Bros Ltd, Shipbuilders, Dumbarton, 1937–51: Student apprentice, 1937–41; Head, Design Office, 1947–51; National Physical Laboratory, 1951–71: Superintendent, Ship Div., 1962–67; Dep. Dir, 1966–71; Dir, Transport and Road Res. Lab., 1971–80. Chm., UK Council for Computing Develt, 1981–86. Hon. FIHT. *Publications:* papers in Trans. Royal Instn Naval Architects and other technical jls. *Address:* 64 Fairfax Road, Teddington, Mddx. *T:* 01–977 6261. *Club:* Athenæum.

SILVERMAN, Julius; Barrister-at-law; *b* Leeds, 8 Dec. 1905; *s* of Nathan Silverman; *m* 1959, Eva Price. *Educ:* Central High School, Leeds (Matriculated). Entered Gray's Inn as student in 1928; called to Bar, 1931; joined Midland Circuit, 1933, practised in Birmingham. Birmingham City Councillor, 1934–45. Contested Moseley Division, 1935. MP (Lab) Birmingham, Erdington, 1945–55 and 1974–83, Birmingham, Aston, 1955–74. Apptd Chm., by Birmingham City Council, of Handsworth Inquiry (into disturbances in Handsworth), 1985 (report published by Council, 1986). Chm., India League, 1971–. Freeman, City of Birmingham, 1982. *Address:* c/o 132A Croxted Road, SE21 8NR.

SILVERWOOD-COPE, Maclachlan Alan Carl, CBE 1959; FCA 1960; ATII 1978; Chartered Accountant; HM Diplomatic Service, retired; *b* 15 Dec. 1915; *s* of late Alan Lachlan Silverwood-Cope and late Elizabeth Masters; *m* 1st, 1940, Hilkka (*née* Halme) (marr. diss. 1970); one *s* one *d*; 2nd, 1971, Jane (*née* Monier-Williams); one *s* one *d*. *Educ:* Malvern College. ACA 1939. HM Forces, 1939–45 (Major, RA). Foreign (later Diplomatic) Service, 1939–71: served as 3rd Sec., Stockholm, 1945–50; 1st Sec., Washington, 1951 and 1956–57; Tokyo, 1952–55; Copenhagen, 1960–64; Counsellor, Buenos Aires, 1966–68; FCO, 1968–71. Finance appts with Aspro-Nicholas Ltd, 1971–78. Home Front Medal (Finland), 1940; Freedom Cross (Norway), 1945. *Recreations:* tennis, bridge, music. *Address:* Brock Hill, Winkfield Row, Berks RG12 6LS. *T:* Winkfield Row 882746.

SILVESTER, Frederick John; MP (C) Manchester, Withington, since Feb. 1974; Senior Associate Director, J. Walter Thompson; *b* 20 Sept. 1933; *s* of William Thomas Silvester and Kathleen Gertrude (*née* Jones); *m* 1971, Victoria Ann, *d* of James Harold and Mary Lloyd Davies; two *d*. *Educ:* Sir George Monoux Grammar Sch.; Sidney Sussex Coll., Cambridge. Called to the Bar, Gray's Inn, 1957. Teacher, Wolstanton Grammar School, 1955–57; Political Education Officer, Conservative Political Centre, 1957–60. Member, Walthamstow Borough Council, 1961–64; Chairman, Walthamstow West Conservative Association, 1961–64. MP (C) Walthamstow West, Sept. 1967–70; an Opposition Whip, 1974–76; PPS to Sec. of State for Employment, 1979–81, to Sec. of State for NI, 1981–83. Member: Public Accounts Cttee, 1983–; Procedure Cttee, 1983–; Exec., 1922 Cttee,

1985–; Vice-Chm., Cons. Employment Cttee, 1976–79. *Address:* House of Commons, SW1A 0AA.

SIM, David, CMG 1946; retired; Commissioner of Excise, 1934–43 and Deputy Minister of National Revenue for Customs and Excise, Canada, 1943–65; *b* Glasgow, Scotland, 4 May 1899; *s* of David Sim, and Cora Lilian Angus; *m* 1924, Ada Helen Inrig (*d* 1958); one *s* one *d*; *m* 1960, Winnifred Emily Blois. *Educ:* Haghill Public School, Glasgow; Kitchener-Waterloo Collegiate. Served European War, Canadian Army in Canada and Overseas with the 1st Canadian Infantry Battalion (wounded at Passchendaele). Bank of Nova Scotia, 1919–25; Waterloo Trust & Savings Co., 1926; Secretary to Minister of National Revenue, 1927–33; Administrator of Alcoholic Beverages, 1942–45; Administrator of Tobacco, 1942–46; Dir Commodity Prices Stabilization Corporation; Member of External Trade Advisory Cttee and Nat. Joint Council of the Public Service of Canada; Member, Board of Broadcast Governors, 1966–68. Past President: Rotary Club; Canadian Club. Mem. Canadian delegation to: 1st Session of Preparatory Cttee for Internat. Conf. on Trade and Employment, London, 1946; 2nd Session of Preparatory Cttee for UN Conf. on Trade and Employment, Geneva, 1947. General Service, Victory, Jubilee and Coronation Medals. *Address:* 1833 Riverside Drive, Apt 414, Ottawa, Ontario, Canada.

SIM, John Mackay, MBE 1945; Deputy Chairman, Inchcape & Co. Ltd, 1975–82 (Deputy Chairman/Managing Director, 1965–75); *b* 4 Oct. 1917; *s* of William Aberdeen Mackay Sim and Zoe Sim; *m* 1st, Dora Cecilia Plumridge Levita (*d* 1951); two *d*; 2nd, Mrs Muriel Harvard (Peggie) Norman. *Educ:* Glenalmond; Pembroke Coll., Cambridge (MA). Lieut RA, 1940, Captain 1942; served NW Europe (despatches). Smith Mackenzie & Co. Ltd (East Africa), 1946–62, Chm. 1960–62; Dir, subseq. Man. Dir, Inchcape & Co. Ltd, 1962. *Recreation:* gardening. *Address:* 6 Bryanston Mews West, W1H 7FR. *T:* 01–262 7673. *Club:* MCC.

SIMCOX, Richard Alfred, CBE 1975 (MBE 1956); Hon. Member of the British Council; *b* 29 March 1915; *s* of Alfred William and Alice Simcox; *m* 1951, Patricia Elisabeth Gutteridge; one *s* two *d*. *Educ:* Gonville and Caius Coll., Cambridge. BA Class. Tripos. Served with N Staffs Regt, 1939–43; British Council from 1943: Rep. in Jordan, 1957–60; in Libya, 1960; in Jordan (again), 1960; Cultural Attaché, British Embassy, Cairo, 1968–71; British Council Representative, Iran, 1971–75. Governor, Gabbitas-Thring Educnl Trust. *Recreations:* gardening, philately. *Address:* Little Brockhurst, Lye Green Road, Chesham, Bucks HP5 3NH. *T:* Chesham 783797.

SIMENON, Georges; Novelist; *b* Liège, Belgium, 13 February 1903; *s* of Désiré Simenon and Henriette Brull; *m* Denise Ouimet; three *s* (and one *d* decd). *Educ:* Collège St Servais, Liège, Belgium. His books are translated into 55 Languages and have been published in 39 countries. *Publications:* 212 novels, including the 80 titles of the Maigret series; autobiographical works: Letter to my Mother, 1976; Un Homme comme un autre, 1975; Des traces de pas, 1975; Les petits hommes, 1976; Vent du nord vent du sud, 1976; Un banc au soleil, 1977; De la cave au grenier, 1977; A l'abri de notre arbre, 1977; Tant que je suis vivant, 1978; Vacances obligatoires, 1978; La main dans la main, 1978; Au-delà de ma porte-fenêtre, 1978; Je suis resté un enfant de choeur, 1979; A quoi bon jurer?, 1979; Point-virgule, 1979; Le prix d'un homme, 1980; On dit que j'ai soixante quinze ans, 1980; Quand vient le froid, 1980; Les libertés qu'il nous reste, 1980; La femme endormie, 1981; Jour et nuit, 1981; Destinées, 1981; Mémoires Intimes suivis du livre du Marie-Jo, 1981 (Intimate Memoirs, 1984). *Address:* Secretariat de Georges Simenon, avenue du Temple 19B, 1012 Lausanne, Switzerland. *T:* 33 39 79; 155 avenue de Cour, 1007 Lausanne.

SIMEON, Sir John Edmund Barrington, 7th Bt, *cr* 1815; Civil Servant in Department of Social Welfare, Provincial Government, British Columbia, retired 1975; lately in Real Estate business; *b* 1 March 1911; *s* of Sir John Walter Barrington Simeon, 6th Bt, and Adelaide Emily (*d* 1934), *e d* of late Col Hon. E. A. Holmes-à-Court; *S* father 1957; *m* 1937, Anne Robina Mary Dean; one *s* two *d*. *Educ:* Eton; Christ Church, Oxford. Motor business, 1931–39. Served with RAF, 1939–43; invalided, rank of Flight Lt, 1943. Civil Servant, Ministry of Agriculture, 1943–51. Took up residence in Vancouver, Canada, 1951. *Recreations:* sailing, painting. *Heir: s* Richard Edmund Barrington Simeon, PhD Yale; Professor of Political Science, Queen's Univ., Kingston, Ont [*b* 2 March 1943; *m* 1966, Agnes Joan, *d* of George Frederick Weld; one *s* one *d*]. *Address:* c/o Jerome & Co., Solicitors, 98 High Street, Newport, Isle of Wight PO3 1BD; 987 Wavertree Road, N Vancouver, BC V7R 1S6, Canada.

SIMEON, John Power Barrington, OBE 1978; HM Diplomatic Service, retired; *b* 15 Nov. 1929; *o s* of late Cornwall Barrington Simeon and Ellaline Margery Mary (*née* Le Poer Power, Clonmel, Co. Tipperary); *m* 1970, Carina Renate Elisabeth Schüller; one *s*. *Educ:* Beaumont Coll.; RMA, Sandhurst. Commnd 2nd Lieut Royal Corps of Signals, 1949; Lieut 1951; resigned, 1952. Ferrous and non-ferrous metal broker, London and Europe, 1953–57; Rank Organisation: served in Germany, Thailand, Singapore, India, ME, N Africa, Hong Kong and London, 1957–65; entered HM Diplomatic Service, 1965; First Sec. (Commercial): Colombo, 1967; Bonn, 1968–70; First Sec., and sometime Actg High Comr, Port of Spain, 1970–73; FCO, 1973–75; Dep. High Comr and Head of Post, Ibadan, Nigeria, 1975–79. Counsellor, 1978; HM Consul-General: Berlin, 1979–81; Hamburg, 1981–84. *Recreations:* travel, photography, shooting, riding. *Address:* The Old School House, Burnham-on-Crouch, Essex CM0 8AH. *T:* Maldon 784274. *Club:* Burnham Golf.

SIMEONE, Reginald Nicola, CBE 1985; Comptroller of Finance and Administration, United Kingdom Atomic Energy Authority, since 1984; *b* 12 July 1927; *s* of late Nicola Francisco Simeone, FCIS, and Phyllis Simeone (*née* Iles); *m* 1954, Josephine Frances, *d* of late Robert Hope and of Marjorie Hope; two *s*. *Educ:* Raynes Park Grammar Sch.; St John's Coll., Cambridge (Schol.; MA). Instr Lieut, Royal Navy, 1947–50; Admiralty: Asst Principal, 1950–55; Principal, 1955–59; UKAEA: Finance Br., 1959–61; Economics and Programmes Br., 1961–65; Chief Personnel Officer, AWRE, 1965–69; Principal Estabts Officer, 1970–76; Authority Personnel Officer, 1976–84. *Recreations:* travel and music. *Club:* United Oxford & Cambridge University.

SIMEONS, Charles Fitzmaurice Creighton, MA; Consultant: Environmental Control, Market and Behavioural Studies, Health and Safety at Work, Electronic Information Technology, Communications with Government, technical programmes for conferences; Director, Action Learning Trust, 1978–82; *b* 22 Sept. 1921; *s* of Charles Albert Simeons and Vera Hildegarde Simeons; *m* 1945, Rosemary (*née* Tabrum); one *s* one *d*. *Educ:* Oundle; Queens' Coll., Cambridge. Royal Artillery with 8th Indian Div., 1942–45. Man. Dir, supplier to photographic industry, 1957–70. MP (C) Luton, 1970–Feb. 1974. Chm., Luton Cons. Assoc., 1960–63. Pres., Luton, Dunstable and District Chamber of Commerce, 1967–68; District Gov., Rotary International, 1967–68; Chm. of cttees raising funds for disabled and cancer research and for National Children's Homes; Mem., Nat. Appeals Cttee, Cancer Res. Campaign, 1977–78. Chm., Adv. Cttee, Rotary Internat. Bd on Environmental Research and Resources, 1973–74 (Chm., Children in Danger campaign); Vice Pres., Nat. Industrial Material Recovery Assoc.; Member: Internat. Cttee, Water Pollution Control Federation, Washington, DC, 1974–77; Customer Consultative Cttee, Anglia Water Authority, 1984–; Council, Smaller Business Assoc., 1974–76; ABCC Small Firms Panel; Chm., Central Govt Cttee, Union of Independent Cos. Hon. Mem., Inst. of Water Pollution Control. Liveryman: Worshipful Co. of Feltmakers (Upper Warden, 1985–86); Guild of Freemen of City of London. FIIM; FRSA. Pres., Old Oundelian Club, 1976–77; Hon. Sec., 8th Indian Clover Club, 1984–. JP Luton, 1959–74. *Publications:* Energy Research in Western Europe, 1976; Coal: its role in tomorrow's technology, 1978; Water as a Source of Energy, 1980; A Review of Chemical Response Data Bases in Europe and the United States, 1985; Studies on Incidents Involving Chemicals on Board Ship, in Port, and at Sea in Europe and the United States, 1985; Data Bases capable of response to Chemical Incidents Worldwide. *Recreations:* watching football, cricket, gardening. *Address:* 21 Ludlow Avenue, Luton, Beds. *T:* Luton 30965. *Club:* City Livery.

SIMINOVITCH, Prof. Louis, OC 1980; FRS 1980; FRSC 1965; Director, Mount Sinai Hospital Research Institute, University of Toronto; *b* Montreal, PQ, 1 May 1920; *s* of Nathan Siminovitch and Goldie Watchman; *m* 1944, Elinore, *d* of late Harry Faierman; three *d*. *Educ:* McGill Univ. (BSc 1941, PhD 1944; Arts and Sci. schol. 1939, Sir William McDonald schol. 1940, Anne Molson prize in Chem. 1941). With NRC at Ottawa and Chalk River, Ont., 1944–47; NRC Studentship and Fellowship, 1942–44; with Centre Nat. de la Recherche Scientifique, Paris, 1949–53; Nat. Cancer Inst. Canadian Fellowships, 1953–55; Connaught Med. Res. Labs, Univ. of Toronto, 1953–56. Head of Div. of Biolog. Research, Ontario Cancer Inst., Toronto, 1963–69; Chm., Dept of Med. Cell Biology, Univ. of Toronto, 1969–79; Chm., Dept of Med. Genetics, 1974–86, Univ. Prof., 1976–86, Toronto Univ.; Dir of Res., Mount Sinai Hosp., Toronto, 1983–. Founding Mem. and Pres., Editorial Bd, Science Forum, 1966–79; Pres., Canadian Cell Biology Soc., 1967. Member: Bd of Dirs, Nat. Cancer Inst. of Canada, 1975–85 (Pres., 1982–84); Nat. Bd of Dirs, Canadian Cancer Soc., 1981–84; Bd, Ontario Cancer Treatment and Res. Foundn, 1979–; Scientific Adv. Cttee, Connaught Res. Inst., 1980–84; Alfred P. Sloan, Jr, Selection Cttee, General Motors Cancer Res. Foundn, 1980–81, 1983–84; Health Res. and Develt Council of Ont, 1983–. Editor: Cell; Somatic Cell Genetics; Jl de Microscopie et de Biologie Cellulaire; Annales de Microbiologie; Jl of Molecular and Cellular Biology; Jl Cancer Surveys (London). Jubilee Silver Medal, 1977; Flavelle Gold Medal, RSC, 1978; Univ. of Toronto Alumni Assoc. Award, 1978; Izaak Walton Killam Meml Prize, 1981; Gairdner Foundn Wightman Award, 1981; Medal of Achievement Award, Institut de Recherches Cliniques de Montreal, 1985; Environmental Mutagen Society Award, Baltimore, Maryland, 1986; R. P. Taylor Award, Canadian Cancer Soc., Nat. Cancer Inst., 1986. Has specialised in the study of bacterial and somatic cell genetics. Hon. degrees: Memorial Univ., Newfoundland, 1978; McMaster Univ., 1978. *Publications:* many contribs to scientific and learned journals. *Address:* Mount Sinai Hospital, 600 University Avenue, Toronto, Ont M5G 1X5, Canada; 106 Wembley Road, Toronto, Ont., Canada.

SIMKINS, Charles Anthony Goodall, CB 1968; CBE 1963; *b* 2 March 1912; *s* of Charles Wyckens Simkins; *m* 1938, Sylvia, *d* of Thomas Hartley, Silchester, Hants; two *s* one *d*. *Educ:* Marlborough; New Coll., Oxford (1st Class Hons Mod. Hist.). Barrister, Lincoln's Inn, 1936; served 1939–45 as Captain, Rifle Bde (POW); attached War Office (later MoD), 1945–71. *Address:* The Cottage, 94 Broad Street, near Guildford, Surrey. *T:* Guildford 572456. *Clubs:* Naval and Military, MCC.

SIMMONDS, Rt. Hon. Dr Kennedy Alphonse, PC 1984; Prime Minister, Federation of St Christopher (St Kitts) and Nevis, since 1983; *b* 12 April 1936; *s* of Bronte Clarke and Arthur Simmonds; *m* 1976, Mary Camella (*née* Matthew); three *s* two *d*. *Educ:* St Kitts and Nevis Grammar School; Leeward Islands Scholar, 1954; Univ. of West Indies (studies in Medicine), 1955–62. Senior Bench Chemist, Sugar Assoc. Res. Lab., St Kitts, 1955; Internship, Kingston Public Hosp., 1963; medical practice, St Kitts, Anguilla and Nevis, 1964–66; postgrad. studies, Princess Margaret Hosp., Bahamas, 1966; Resident in Anaesthesiology, Pittsburgh, 1968–69; medical practice, St Kitts, 1969–80; Premier of St Christopher (St Kitts) and Nevis, 1980–83. Foundn Mem., People's Action Movement Opposition Party, 1965, Pres., People's Action Movement, 1976. Fellow, Amer. Coll. of Anaesthesiology, 1970. *Recreations:* tennis, cricket, football, video taping. *Address:* PO Box 186, Government Headquarters, Basseterre, St Kitts, West Indies. *T:* 809–465 2103.

SIMMONDS, Prof. Kenneth Royston; Professor of International Law in the University of London, at Queen Mary College, since 1976; Gresham Professor of Law, City University, London, since 1986; *b* 11 Nov. 1927; *s* of Frederick John Simmonds and Maude (*née* Coxhill) *m* 1958, Gloria Mary (*née* Tatchell); one *s* one *d*. *Educ:* Watford Grammar Sch.; Exeter Coll., Oxford. BA, MA, DPhil (Oxon). Amelia Jackson Sen. Fellow, Exeter Coll., Oxford, 1951–53. Director, British Inst. of Internat. and Comparative Law, 1965–76, Hon. Dir, 1976–82; Dean, Faculty of Law, QMC, 1980–84. Gen. Editor, International and Comparative Law Qly, 1966–86; Editor, Common Market Law Review, 1967–; Gen. Editor, Encyclopedia of European Community Law, 1972–; Mem. Editorial Cttee, British Year Book of International Law, 1967–. Visiting Professor: McGill Univ., 1963; Univ. of Wyoming, 1969; Free Univ. of Brussels, 1972 and 1973; Univ. of Amsterdam, annually, 1979–; Univ. of Kentucky, 1985; Univ. of Texas at Austin, 1986–87. Mem., Legal Adv. Cttee, British Council, 1966–; Chm., UK Nat. Cttee of Comparative Law, 1973–76; Pres., Internat. Assoc. of Legal Science, 1975–76. Consultant, EEC, 1983–84. Chevalier, l'Ordre de Mérite, 1973; Comdr's Cross of Order of Merit, Federal Republic of Germany, 1983. *Publications:* Resources of the Ocean Bed, 1970; New Directions in the Law of the Sea, 1972–; (ed) Legal Problems of an Enlarged European Community, 1972; (Gen. Editor) Encyclopedia of European Community Law, 1972–; (ed) Sweet and Maxwell's European Community Treaties, 1972, 4th edn 1980; Cases on the Law of the Sea, 1976–84; (ed, with C. M. Schmitthoff) International Economic and Trade Law, 1976; Legal Problems of Multinational Corporations, 1978; (ed, with R. M. Goode) Commercial Operations in Europe, 1978; Multinational Corporations Law, 1979–; The UN Convention on the Law of the Sea, 1982; numerous articles in Internat. and Comparative Law Qly, Common Market Law Rev., Europarecht. *Recreations:* travel (espec. in the Americas), classical music, cats. *Address:* The Oast Barn, Bell's Forstal, Throwley, near Faversham, Kent.

SIMMONDS, Kenneth Willison, CMG 1956; FRSA; *b* Carmacoup, Douglas, Lanarkshire, 13 May 1912; *s* of late William Henry Simmonds, Civil Servant, and late Ida, *d* of John Willison, Acharn, Killin, Perthshire; *m* 1st, 1939, Ruth Constance Sargant (marr. diss. 1974); two *s*; 2nd, 1974, Mrs Catherine Clare Lewis, *y d* of late Col F. J. Brakenridge, CMG, Chew Magna. *Educ:* Bedford Sch.; Humberstone Sch.; St Catharine's Coll., Cambridge (MA). District Officer, Colonial Administrative Service, Kenya, 1935–48; Deputy Financial Secretary, Uganda, 1948–51; Financial Secretary, Nyasaland Protectorate, 1951–57; Chief Secretary, Aden, 1957–63. Exhibited paintings: Southern Arts Open Field, 1972–73; Royal Acad., 1973, 1974, 1977, 1978; Royal West of England Acad., 1976, 1978; Bladon, Andover (one-man show), 1977; Westward Open, 1977, 1979; Royal Bath and West, 1979 (awards); group and collective exhbns. *Address:* North Close, Milverton, Taunton, Somerset TA4 1QZ. *T:* Milverton 400235.

SIMMONDS, Posy; cartoonist, The Guardian, since 1977; *b* 9 Aug. 1945; *d* of Reginald A. C. Simmonds and Betty Cahusac; *m* 1974, Richard Hollis. *Educ:* Queen Anne's Sch., Caversham; L'Ecole des Beaux Arts, Paris; Central Sch. of Art and Design, London (BA Art and Design). Freelance illustrator/cartoonist, 1969–. Exhibitions: The Cartoon Gall. (formerly the Workshop), 1974, 1976, 1979, 1981, 1982, 1984; Mus. of Modern Art, Oxford, 1981; Manor House Mus. & Art Gall., Ilkley, 1985. Cartoonist of the Year: Granada TV/What The Papers Say, 1980; British Press Awards, 1981. *Publications:* Bear Book, 1969; Mrs Weber's Diary, 1979; True Love, 1981; Pick of Posy, 1982; (illustrator) Daisy Ashford, The Young Visiters, 1984; Very Posy, 1985; Fred, 1987. *Address:* c/o A. D. Peters & Co. Ltd, 10 Buckingham Street, WC2N 6BU. *T:* 01-839 2556.
See also R. J. Simmonds.

SIMMONDS, Richard James; Member (C) Wight and Hampshire East, European Parliament, since 1984 (Midlands West, 1979–84); farmer of free range poultry and breeder of Jersey cattle; consultant surveyor; *b* 2 Aug. 1944; *s* of Reginald A. C. Simmonds and Betty Cahusac; *m* 1967, Mary (*née* Stewart); one *s* two *d*. *Educ:* Trinity Coll., Glenalmond. Councillor, Berkshire CC (Chm. of Environment, Property, Transport, and Development Cttees), 1973–79. National Vice-Chm. of Young Conservatives, 1973–75; Founding Vice-Chm. of Young European Democrats, 1974; Personal Asst to Rt Hon. Edward Heath, 1973–75; PPS to Sir James Scott-Hopkins, Leader of European Democratic Gp, European Parlt, 1979–82; Cons. spokesman on youth and educn, European Parlt, 1982–84, on budget control, 1984–. Chm. of Governors, Berkshire Coll. of Agriculture, 1979–. *Publications:* The Common Agricultural Policy—a sad misnomer, 1979; An A to Z of Myths and Misunderstandings of the European Community, 1981; European Parliamentary report on farm animal welfare, 1985. *Recreation:* resisting bureaucracy. *Address:* Woodlands Farm, Cookham Dean, Berkshire SL6 9PJ. *Clubs:* Carlton, United & Cecil, Ancient Britons, Tamworth.
See also Posy Simmonds.

SIMMONS, Fr Eric, CR; Superior of the Community of the Resurrection, Mirfield, Yorkshire, 1974–87; *b* 1930. *Educ:* Univ. of Leeds. BA (Phil) 1951. Coll. of the Resurrection, Mirfield, 1951; deacon, 1953, priest, 1954; Curate of St Luke, Chesterton, 1953–57; Chaplain, University Coll. of N Staffordshire, 1957–61; licensed to officiate: Dio. Wakefield, 1963–65 and 1967–; Dio. Ripon, 1965–67; Warden and Prior of Hostel of the Resurrection, Leeds, 1966–67; subseq. Novice Guardian, looking after young Community members; the Community is an Anglican foundation engaged in evangelism and teaching work, based in Yorkshire but with work in Southern Africa. *Address:* House of the Resurrection, Mirfield, West Yorks WF14 0BN. *T:* Mirfield 494318.

SIMMONS, Ernest Bernard; QC (Seychelles) 1949; *b* 7 Sept. 1913; *o s* of Bernard Simmons and Ethel (*née* Booth); *m* 1940, Edna Muriel Tomlinson; one *s* three *d*. Barrister-at-Law, Gray's Inn, 1936; Asst Attorney-Gen., Gibraltar, 1946; Attorney-Gen., Seychelles, 1949; Judge of the Supreme Court, Mauritius, 1952–58; Judge of the High Court, Tanganyika, 1958–61; retired. *Address:* The Gate House, 27 Middleton Road, Brentwood, Essex CM15 8DL.

SIMMONS, Guy Lintorn, MVO 1961; HM Diplomatic Service, retired; *b* 27 Feb. 1925; *s* of late Captain Geoffrey Larpent Simmons, RN and Frances Gladys Simmons (*née* Wright); *m* 1951, Sheila Jacob; three *d*. *Educ:* Bradfield Coll.; Oriel Coll., Oxford. RAF, 1943–46; CRO, 1949; 2nd Sec., British High Commn: Lahore, 1950; Dacca, 1952; CRO, 1954–58 and 1964–66; 1st Sec.: Bombay, 1958; New Delhi, 1961; Commercial Counsellor: New Delhi, 1966–68; Cairo, 1968–71; Head of Trade Policy Dept, FCO, 1971–73; Diplomatic Service Inspectorate, 1973–76; Commercial Counsellor, Copenhagen, 1975–79; Consul-General: Karachi, 1979–82; Montreal, 1982–84. *Recreations:* the arts, travel, country pursuits. *Address:* c/o Bank of Scotland, EC2P 2EH. *Clubs:* Oriental, Royal Commonwealth Society.

SIMMONS, Jack; Professor of History, University of Leicester, 1947–75, now Professor Emeritus; Pro-Vice-Chancellor, 1960–63; Public Orator, 1965–68; *b* 30 Aug. 1915; *o c* of Seymour Francis Simmons and Katharine Lillias, *d* of Thomas Finch, MB, Babbacombe, Devon. *Educ:* Westminster Sch.; Christ Church, Oxford. Beit Lectr in the History of the British Empire, Oxford Univ., 1943–47. FSA. Mem., Adv. Council, Science Museum, 1969–84; Chm., Nat. Railway Museum Cttee, York, 1981–84; Leicestershire Archæological and Historical Society: Hon. Editor, 1948–61; Pres. 1966–77. Chm., Leicester Local Broadcasting Council, 1967–70. Jt Editor, The Journal of Transport History, 1953–73. Editor: A Visual History of Modern Britain; Classical County Histories. *Publications:* African Discovery: An Anthology of Exploration (edited with Margery Perham), 1942; Southey, 1945; Edition of Southey's Letters from England, 1951; Journeys in England: an Anthology, 1951; Parish and Empire, 1952; Livingstone and Africa, 1955; New University, 1958; The Railways of Britain, 1961, 3rd edn, 1986; Transport, 1962; Britain and the World, 1965; St Pancras Station, 1968; Transport Museums, 1970; A Devon Anthology, 1971; (ed) Memoirs of a Station Master, 1973; Leicester Past and Present (2 vols), 1974; (ed) Rail 150: The Stockton and Darlington Railway and What Followed, 1975; The Railway in England and Wales 1830–1914, 1978; A Selective Guide to England, 1979; Dandy Cart to Diesel: the National Railway Museum, 1981; (ed) F. R. Conder, The Men who Built Railways, 1983; The Railway in Town and Country 1830–1914, 1986. *Address:* Flat 6, 36 Victoria Park Road, Leicester LE2 1XB. *Club:* United Oxford & Cambridge University.

SIMMONS, Jean; film actress; *b* London, 31 Jan. 1929; *m* 1950, Stewart Granger, *qv* (marr. diss. 1960); one *d*; *m* 1960, Richard Brooks; one *d*. *Educ:* Orange Hill Sch.; Aida Foster School of Dancing. First film appearance in Give Us the Moon, 1942; minor parts in Cæsar and Cleopatra, The Way to the Stars, etc., 1942–44; since then has appeared in numerous British films, including: Great Expectations, Black Narcissus, Hungry Hill, Uncle Silas, Hamlet, So Long at the Fair, The Blue Lagoon, Trio, Adam and Evalyn, Clouded Yellow; The Grass is Greener, 1960; Life at the Top, 1965; Say Hello to Yesterday, 1971; began American film career, 1950; American films include: Androcles and the Lion, Young Bess, The Actress, Desirée, Footsteps in the Fog, Guys and Dolls, This Could be the Night, Spartacus, Elmer Gantry, All the Way Home; Divorce, American Style, 1967; The Happy Ending, 1970; The Thorn Birds, 1982 (Emmy award, 1983); television includes: Down at the Hydro, 1982. Musical: A Little Night Music, Adelphi, 1975. *Address:* c/o A. Morgan Maree, Jr & Assoc., Inc., 6363 Wilshire Boulevard, Los Angeles, California 90048, USA.

SIMMONS, Air Vice-Marshal Michael George, AFC 1976; Air Officer Commanding No 1 Group, RAF, since 1985; *b* 8 May 1937; *s* of George and Thelma Simmons; *m* 1964, Jean Aliwell; two *d*. *Educ:* Shrewsbury Sch.; RAF Coll., Cranwell. Commissioned 1958; No 6 Squadron, Cyprus, 1959–61; ADC to AOC-in-C FTC, 1961–64; No 39 Sqdn, Malta, 1964–66; No 13 Sqdn, Malta, 1966–67; No 51 Sqdn, Wyton, 1967–69; RN Staff Coll., 1970; MoD, 1971–72; OC No XV Sqdn, Germany, 1973–76; MoD, 1976–79; OC RAF Cottesmore, 1980–82; MoD, 1982–84; SASO, HQ Strike Comd, 1984–85. ADC to the Queen, 1980–81. *Recreations:* walking, gardening, languages, cricket, golf. *Address:* c/o Royal Bank of Scotland, Kirkland House, Whitehall, SW1A 2EB. *Club:* Royal Air Force.

SIMMS, Most Rev. George Otto, DD; MRIA 1957; *b* 4 July 1910; 3rd *s* of John F. A. Simms, Crown Solicitor, County Tyrone, and Mrs Simms, Combermore, Lifford, County Donegal; *m* 1941, Mercy Felicia, *o d* of Brian James Gwynn, Temple Hill, Terenure, Dublin; three *s* two *d*. *Educ:* St Edmund's School, Hindhead; Cheltenham College; Trinity College, Dublin; Scholar, 1930; Moderator in Classics, and History and Political Science, 1932; Berkeley Medallist; Vice-Chancellor's Latin Medallist; Theological Exhibnr; Hon. Fellow, 1978. MA 1935; BD 1936; PhD 1950; DD (*jure dignitatis*, Dublin), 1952; DD (*hc* Huron), 1963; Hon. DCL Kent, 1978. Deacon, 1935; Priest, 1936; Curate-asst, St Bartholomew's Church, Dublin, 1935–38; Chaplain Lincoln Theol. Coll., 1938–39; Dean of Residence, Trinity Coll., Dublin, 1939–52; Asst Lectr to Archbishop King's Prof. of Divinity, Dublin Univ., 1939–52; Chaplain-Secretary, Church of Ireland Training Coll., 1943–52; Hon. Clerical Vicar, Christ Church Cathedral, Dublin, 1937–52; Dean of Cork, 1952; Bishop of Cork, Cloyne, and Ross, 1952–56; Archbishop of Dublin and Primate of Ireland, 1956–69; also Bishop of Glendalough and Bishop of Kildare; Archbishop of Armagh and Primate of All Ireland, 1969–80. Member Governing Body, University College, Cork, 1953–57; President: The Leprosy Mission, 1964–; APCK, 1983–. Hon. Life Mem., Royal Dublin Soc., 1984. Hon. DLitt New Univ. of Ulster, 1981. *Publications:* joint-editor (with E. H. Alton and P. Meyer), The Book of Kells (fac. edn), Berne, 1951; For Better, for Worse, 1945; The Book of Kells: a short description, 1950; The Bible in Perspective, 1953; contributor, The Book of Durrow (fac. edn), 1960; Memoir of Michael Lloyd Ferrar, 1962; Christ within Me, 1975; Irish Illuminated Manuscripts, 1980; In My Understanding, 1982; Tullow's Story, 1983; (with R. G. F. Jenkins) Pioneers and Partners, 1985; (contrib.) Treasures of the Library of Trinity College Dublin, 1986; articles in Hermathena, Theology, and Dublin Magazine, JTS; contrib. to New Divinity, Booklore, Search, Newman Review. *Address:* 62 Cypress Grove Road, Dublin 6. *T:* Dublin 905594.

SIMOGUN, Sir Petar, Kt 1981; MBE 1971; BEM 1945; a Chief of Arapesh Clan; landowner; engaged in business and farming, Dagua, Papua New Guinea; *b* 1900; *s* of Hajuta Matahek and Samare Mainoken; *m* 1946, Berta Barai; three *s* seven *d* (and two *s* decd). Self-educated. Plantation worker, Manup Is, Manus Prov., 1920–34; Police Force, 1936–42; Coastwatcher with RAN, 1942–45 (War Service Medals); Supervisor, Angau, 1945–46; Police Force, 1946–47; business promotion, development and organisation of food and cash crops, transport, etc, Dagua Area, 1947–; instrumental in starting Oil Palm industry, Hoskins, 1967–77. One of first 3 New Guineans nominated to Legislative Council, 1951–60; Mem., PNG House of Assembly, 1960–65; Vice Pres., But-Boikin Local Govt Council, 1957–59. Coronation Medal, 1953. *Recreation:* hunting. *Address:* N. V. Urip, c/o Catholic Mission, Dagua, via Wewak, East Sepik Province, Papua New Guinea.

SIMON, family name of **Viscount Simon,** of **Baron Simon of Glaisdale** and of **Baron Simon of Wythenshawe.**

SIMON, 2nd Viscount, *cr* 1940, of Stackpole Elidor; **John Gilbert Simon,** CMG 1947; *b* 2 Sept. 1902; *o s* of 1st Viscount Simon, PC, GCSI, GCVO, and of Ethel Mary (*d* 1902), *d* of Gilbert Venables; *S* father, 1954; *m* 1930, Christie, *d* of William Stanley Hunt; one *s* one *d*. *Educ:* Winchester; Balliol College, Oxford (Scholar). With Ministry of War Transport, 1940–47. Man. Dir, 1947–58, Dep. Chm., 1951–58, Peninsular and Oriental Steam Navigation Co. Chm., PLA, 1958–71; Mem., Nat. Ports Council, 1967–71. President: Chamber of Shipping of UK, 1957–58; Inst. of Marine Engineers, 1960–61; RINA, 1961–71; British Hydromechanics Res. Assoc., 1968–80. Officer Order of Orange Nassau, Netherlands. *Heir:* *s* Hon. Jan David Simon [*b* 20 July 1940; *m* 1969, Mary Elizabeth Burns, Sydney; one *d*]. *Address:* 2 Church Cottages, Abbotskerswell, Newton Abbot, Devon TQ12 5NY. *T:* Newton Abbot 65573.

SIMON OF GLAISDALE, Baron *cr* 1971 (Life Peer), of Glaisdale, Yorks; **Jocelyn Edward Salis Simon,** PC 1961; Kt 1959; DL; a Lord of Appeal in Ordinary, 1971–77; *b* 15 Jan. 1911; *s* of Frank Cecil and Claire Evelyn Simon, 51 Belsize Pk, NW3; *m* 1st, 1934, Gwendolen Helen (*d* 1937), *d* of E. J. Evans; 2nd, 1948, Fay Elizabeth Leicester, JP, *d* of Brig. H. G. A. Pearson; three *s*. *Educ:* Gresham's School, Holt; Trinity Hall, Cambridge (Exhibitioner). Called to Bar, Middle Temple, 1934 (Blackstone Prizeman). Served War of 1939–45; commissioned RTR, 1939; comd Spec. Service Sqn, RAC, Madagascar, 1942; Burma Campaign, 1944; Lieut-Col. 1945. Resumed practice at Bar, 1946; QC 1951. MP (C) Middlesbrough West, 1951–62; Mem. of the Royal Commission on the Law relating to Mental Illness and Mental Deficiency, 1954–57. Jt Parly Under-Sec. of State, Home Office, 1957–58; Financial Sec. to the Treasury, 1958–59; Solicitor-General, 1959–62. President, Probate, Divorce and Admiralty Div. of the High Court of Justice, 1962–71. Hon. Elder Brother, Trinity House, 1975. Hon. Fellow, Trinity Hall, Cambridge, 1963. DL NR (now North) Yorks, 1973. *Publications:* Change is Our Ally, 1954 (part); Rule of Law, 1955 (part); The Church and the Law of Nullity, 1955 (part); articles in learned jls. *Address:* Midge Hall, Glaisdale Head, Whitby, North Yorks.

SIMON OF WYTHENSHAWE, 2nd Baron, *cr* 1947, of Didsbury; **Roger Simon;** *b* 16 Oct. 1913; *S* father, 1960 (but does not use the title and wishes to be known as Roger Simon); *m* 1951 (Anthea) Daphne May; one *s* one *d*. *Educ:* Gresham's School; Gonville and Caius College, Cambridge. *Heir:* *s* Hon. Matthew Simon, *b* 10 April 1955. *Address:* Oakhill, Chester Avenue, Richmond, Surrey.
See also B. Simon.

SIMON, Prof. Brian; Emeritus Professor of Education, University of Leicester; *b* 26 March 1915; *yr s* of 1st Baron Simon of Wythenshawe and Shena D. Potter; *m* 1941, Joan Home Peel; two *s*. *Educ:* Gresham's Sch., Holt; Schloss Schule, Salem; Trinity Coll., Cambridge; Inst. of Educn, Univ. of London. MA. Pres., Nat. Union of Students, 1939–40; Royal Corps of Signals, GHQ Liaison Regt (Phantom), 1940–45; teaching Manchester and Salford schs, 1945–50; Univ. of Leicester: Lectr in Educn, 1950–64; Reader, 1964–66; Professor, 1966–80; Dir, Sch. of Educn, 1968–70, 1974–77. Chairman: History of Educn Soc., 1976–79; Internat. Standing Conf. for Hist. of Educn, 1979–82; Pres., British Educn Res. Assoc., 1977–78. Editor, Forum (for discussion of new trends in educn), 1958–; Jt Editor, Students Library of Education, 1966–77. Dr *hc* Cath. Univ. of Leuven, 1980. DUniv Open Univ., 1981. *Publications:* A Student's View of the Universities, 1943; Intelligence Testing and the Comprehensive School, 1953; The Common Secondary School, 1955; (ed) New Trends in English Education, 1957; (ed) Psychology in the Soviet Union, 1957; Studies in the History of Education 1780–1870, 1960; (ed, with Joan Simon) Educational Psychology in the USSR, 1963; (ed) The Challenge of Marxism, 1963; (ed) Non-streaming in the Junior School, 1964; Education and the Labour Movement 1870–1920, 1965; (ed) Education in Leicestershire 1540–1940, 1968; (with D. Rubinstein) The Evolution of the Comprehensive School 1926–66, 1969 (revised edn 1973); (with Caroline Benn) Half-Way There: Report on the British Comprehensive School Reform, 1970 (revised edn 1972); Intelligence, Psychology and Education, 1971 (revised edn 1978); (ed) The Radical Tradition in Education in Britain, 1972; The Politics of Educational Reform 1920–1940, 1974; (ed with Ian Bradley) The

Victorian Public School, 1975; (with Maurice Galton) Inside the Primary Classroom, 1980; Progress and Performance in the Primary Classroom, 1980; (ed with William Taylor) Education in the Eighties, the central issues, 1981; (ed with John Willcocks) Research and Practice in the Primary Classroom, 1981; Does Education Matter?, 1985; (ed with Detlef Müller and Fritz Ringer) The Rise of the Modern Educational System, 1986. *Address:* 11 Pendene Road, Leicester LE2 3DQ. *T:* Leicester 705176.

SIMON, Claude (Henri Eugène); French writer and vine grower; *b* Madagascar, 10 Oct. 1913; *s* of Antoine Simon and Suzanne (*née* Denamiel); *m* Yvonne Ducuing. *Educ:* Collège Stanislas, Paris. Jury Mem., Prix Médicis, 1968–70. Nobel Prize for Literature, 1985. *Publications:* Le tricheur, 1945; La corde raide, 1947; Gulliver, 1952; Le sacre du printemps, 1954; Le vent, 1957; L'herbe, 1958 (trans. The Grass, 1961); La route des Flandres (Prix de l'Express), 1960 (trans. The Flanders Road, 1962); Le palace, 1962 (trans. 1964); Histoire (Prix Médicis), 1967 (trans. 1969); La bataille de Pharsale, 1969 (trans. The Battle of Pharsalus, 1971); Orion aveugle, 1970; Les corps conducteurs, 1971 (trans. Conducting Bodies, 1975); Triptyque, 1973 (trans. 1977); Leçon de choses, 1975; Les Géorgiques, 1981 (trans. 1985); articles in journals. *Address:* c/o Editions de Minuit, 7 rue Bernard-Palissy, 75006 Paris, France.

SIMON, David Alec Gwyn; Managing Director, British Petroleum Co. plc, since 1986; *b* 24 July 1939; *s* of Roger Albert Damas Jules Simon and Barbara (*née* Hudd); *m* 1964, Hanne (*née* Mohn); two *s*. *Educ:* Christ's Hospital; Gonville and Caius College, Cambridge (MA Hons); MBA INSEAD. Joined BP 1961; Marketing Co-ordinator, European Region, 1975–80; Dir, BP Oil UK and Chm., National Benzole Co., 1980–82; Man. Dir, BP Oil International, 1982–85; Chairman: BP Nutritions; BP Detergents; BP Finance International. Mem., International Council and UK Adv. Bd, INSEAD. *Recreations:* golf, tennis, books, music. *Address:* c/o The British Petroleum Co. plc, Britannic House, Moor Lane, EC2Y 9BU. *Clubs:* Groucho; Hampstead Cricket, Cumberland Lawn Tennis, Highgate Golf.

SIMON, Prof. Herbert A(lexander), PhD; Richard King Mellon University Professor of Computer Science and Psychology, Carnegie-Mellon University, since 1967; *b* 15 June 1916; *s* of Arthur Simon and Edna Merkel Simon; *m* 1937, Dorothea Pye; one *s* two *d*. *Educ:* University of Chicago (BA, PhD). Staff member, Internat. City Managers' Assoc., 1936–39; Study Director, Bureau of Public Admin., Univ. of California (Berkeley), 1939–42; Asst Prof. to Professor, Illinois Inst. of Technology, 1942–49 (Head, Dept of Pol. and Social Sci., 1947–49); Professor of Administration, Carnegie-Mellon Univ., 1949–67 (Associate Dean, Graduate Sch. of Industrial Admin., 1957–73). Mem., Nat. Acad. of Scis, 1967 (Mem. Council, 1978–81, 1983–86). Hon. degrees: DSc: Case Inst. of Technol., 1963; Yale, 1963; Marquette, 1981; Columbia, 1983; Université Paul-Valéry, 1984; Gustavus Adolphus, 1985; LLD: Chicago, 1964; McGill, 1970; Michigan, 1978; Pittsburgh, 1979; FilDr, Lund, 1968; DrEconSci, Erasmus (Rotterdam), 1973. Hon. Professor: Tianjin Univ., 1980; Beijing Univ., 1986; Hon. Res. Fellow, Inst. of Psych., Chinese Acad. of Sciences, 1985. Nobel Prize in Economics, 1978; Dist. Sci. Contrib. Award, Amer. Psych. Assoc., 1969; Turing Award, Assoc. for Computing Machinery, 1975; James Madison Award, Amer. Political Science Assoc., 1984; National Medal of Science, 1986. *Publications:* Administrative Behavior, 1947, 3rd edn 1976; Models of Man, 1957; (with J. G. March) Organizations, 1958; The New Science of Management Decision, 1960, rev. edn 1977; The Sciences of the Artificial, 1969, 2nd edn 1981; (with A. Newell) Human Problem Solving, 1972; Models of Discovery, 1977; (with Y. Ijiri) Skew Distributions and the Sizes of Business Firms, 1977; Models of Thought, 1979; Models of Bounded Rationality (2 vols), 1982; Reason in Human Affairs, 1983; (with K. A. Ericsson) Protocol Analysis, 1984; (with P. Langley *et al*) Scientific Discovery, 1986; other books, and articles in sci. jls. *Recreations:* walking, piano, painting. *Address:* Department of Psychology, Carnegie-Mellon University, Pittsburgh, Pa 15213, USA. *T:* 412–268–2787. *Clubs:* University (Pittsburgh); Cosmos (Washington).

SIMON, Neil; playwright; *b* NYC, 4 July 1927; *s* of Irving and Mamie Simon; *m* 1st, 1953, Joan Baim (decd); two *d*; 2nd, 1973, Marsha Mason. *Educ:* De Witt Clinton High Sch.; entered Army Air Force Reserve training programme as an engineering student at New York University; discharged with rank of corporal, 1946. Went to New York Offices of Warner Brothers Pictures to work in mail room. Hon. LHD Hofstra Univ., 1981. *Screenplays include:* After The Fox (produced 1966); The Heartbreak Kid, 1973; The Prisoner of 2nd Avenue, 1975; The Sunshine Boys, 1976; Murder by Death, 1976; The Goodbye Girl, 1977; The Cheap Detective, 1978; California Suite, 1979; Chapter Two, 1979; Seems Like Old Times, 1980; Only When I Laugh, 1981; I Ought To Be In Pictures, 1982; Max Dugan Returns, 1983; The Slugger's Wife, 1985. *Plays produced:* Come Blow Your Horn, 1961 (publ. 1961); (jtly) Little Me, 1962 (publ. 1979), revival 1982, West End 1984; Barefoot in the Park, 1963 (publ. 1964); The Odd Couple, 1965 (publ. 1966); (jtly) Sweet Charity, 1966 (publ. 1966); The Star-Spangled Girl, 1966 (publ. 1967); Plaza Suite, 1968 (publ. 1969); (jtly) Promises, Promises, 1968 (publ. 1969); Last of the Red Hot Lovers, 1969 (publ. 1970), Criterion, 1979; The Gingerbread Lady, 1970 (publ. 1971); The Prisoner of Second Avenue, 1971 (publ. 1972); The Sunshine Boys, 1972 (publ. 1973); The Good Doctor, 1973 (publ. 1974); God's Favorite, 1974 (publ. 1975); California Suite, 1976 (publ. 1977); Chapter Two, 1977 (publ. 1978); (jtly) They're Playing Our Song, 1978 (publ. 1980); I Ought To Be In Pictures, 1980 (publ. 1981); Fools, 1981 (publ. 1982); Brighton Beach Memoirs, 1983 (publ. 1984); Biloxi Blues, 1985 (Tony Award for Best Play, 1985); The Odd Couple (female version), 1985. *Address:* c/o A. DaSilva, 502 Park Avenue, New York, NY 10022, USA.

SIMON, Roger; *see* Simon of Wythenshawe barony.

SIMON, Prof. Ulrich Ernst, DD; Professor of Christian Literature, 1972–80, Dean, 1978–80, King's College, London; *b* 21 Sept. 1913; *s* of James and Anna Simon; *m* 1949, Joan Edith Raynor Westlake; two *s* one *d*. *Educ:* Grunewald Gymnasium, Berlin; King's Coll., London. BD, MTh, DD, FKC. Ordained in Church of England, 1938; Univ. Lectr, 1945; Reader, 1960. *Publications:* Theology of Crisis, 1948; Theology of Salvation, 1953; Heaven in the Christian Tradition, 1958; The Ascent to Heaven, 1961; The End is not Yet, 1964; Theology Observed, 1966; A Theology of Auschwitz, 1967 (paperback 1978); The Trial of Man, 1973; Story and Faith, 1975; Sitting in Judgment, 1978. *Recreations:* gardening, chamber music, walking. *Address:* 22 Collingwood Avenue, N10 3ED. *T:* 01–883 4852.

SIMON, William Edward; Chairman of Boards of Wesray Corp. and Gibson Greeting Cards Inc.; Member of the Board of Directors: Xerox Corporation; Dart & Kraft, Inc.; Halliburton Co. Power Corp., Canada; United Technologies; President, John M. Olin Foundation; *b* 27 Nov. 1927; *s* of Charles Simon and Eleanor Kearns; *m* 1950, Carol Girard; two *s* five *d*. *Educ:* Newark Academy, NJ; Lafayette Coll. (BA). Joined Union Securities, NYC 1952, Asst Vice-Pres. and Manager of firm's Municipal Trading Dept, 1955; Vice Pres., Weeden & Co., 1957–64; Sen. Partner, Salomon Brothers, NYC, 1964–72. Dep. Sec., US Treasury Dept, and Administrator, Federal Energy Office, 1973–74; Secretary of the Treasury, May 1974–Jan. 1977. Chm., Wilson Council, Woodrow Wilson Internat. Center of Scholars; Pres., US Olympic Cttee (former Treasurer); Trustee: Lafayette Coll.; Hudson Inst. Hon. Dr of Laws: Lafayette Coll., 1973; Pepperdine Univ., 1975; Hon. DCL Jacksonville Univ., 1976; Hon. PhD Tel Aviv, 1976; Hon. Scriptural Degree, Israel Torah Res. Inst., 1976; Hon. DSc New England Coll., 1977. *Publications:* A Time for Truth, 1978; A Time for Action, 1980. *Address:* Wesray Corp., 330 South Street, CN 1975, Morristown, NJ 07960, USA; Sand Spring Road, New Vernon, NJ 07976, USA. *Clubs:* River, Links, Union League, Pilgrims of US (New York, NY); Maidstone (East Hampton, NY); Alfalfa (Washington, DC); Balboa Bay (Calif); Morris County Golf (Convent Station, NJ).

SIMONET, Henri François; Member, Belgian Parliament, since 1966; *b* Brussels, 10 May 1931; *m* 1960, Marie-Louise Angenent; one *s* one *d*. *Educ:* Univ. Libre de Bruxelles (DenD, DèsSc); Columbia Univ., USA. Assistant, Univ. Libre de Bruxelles, 1956–58, now Prof.; Financial Adv., Inst. Nat. d'Etudes pour le Développement du Bas-Congo, 1958–59; Legal Adv., Commn of Brussels Stock Exchange, 1956–60; Dep. Dir, Office of Econ. Programming, 1961; Director of Cabinet: of Min. of Econ. Affairs and Power, 1961–65; of Dep. Prime Minister responsible for co-ordination of Econ. Policy, 1965; Minister of Econ. Affairs, 1972; Vice-Pres., Commn of the European Communities, 1973–77; Foreign Minister, Belgium, 1977–80; Sec. of State, Brussels Regional Economy, 1977–79. Mayor of Anderlecht, 1966–84. Commander, Order of Leopold. *Publications:* various books and articles on economics, financial and political topics. *Address:* 34 avenue Franklin Roosevelt, 1050 Brussels, Belgium.

SIMONET, Sir (Louis Marcel) Pierre, Kt 1985; CBE 1980 (OBE 1972); Director and Proprietor, Pharmacie Simonet, since 1955 (founded by father, 1926); *b* 6 March 1934; *s* of Marcel Simonet and Marguerite Simonet. *Educ:* Collège du St Esprit up to Higher School Certificate. Town Council of Curepipe: Mem., 1960; Vice-Chm., 1962; Chm., 1964; 1st Mem. for Curepipe, Legislative Assembly, 1976; Pres., Mauritian Social Democratic Party, 1981. Judge Assessor, Permt Arbitration Tribunal, 1984. Dir, Central Electricity Bd, 1972. Mem., Ex-servicemen's Assoc., 1977; Pres., Widows and Orphans Pension Fund, 1978; Vice-Chm., Lions Club of Curepipe, 1985; Vice-Chm., Centre Culturel d'Expressions Française (Founder Mem., 1960). Pres., Soc. of St Vincent de Paul. Testimonial, Royal Humane Soc. for life saving, 1962; Chevalier de l'Ordre National du Mérite (France), 1980. *Adddress:* Queen Mary Avenue, Floreal, Mauritius. *T:* (office) 6/3532, (residence) 86/5240. *Club:* Mauritius Racing.

SIMONS, (Alfred) Murray, CMG 1983; HM Diplomatic Service, retired; Head of UK Delegation to Negotiations on Mutual Reduction of Forces and Armaments and Associated Measures in Central Europe, at Vienna, 1982–85, with personal rank of Ambassador; *b* 9 Aug. 1927; *s* of late Louis Simons and of Fay Simons; *m* 1975, Patricia Jill, *d* of late David and May Barclay, Westbury on Trym, Bristol; two *s*. *Educ:* City of London Sch.; Magdalen Coll., Oxford (MA). FO, 1951; 3rd Sec., Moscow, 1952–55; FO, 1955–56; Columbia Univ., 1956; 2nd Sec., Bogota, 1957; 1st Sec., Office of Comr-Gen. for SE Asia, Singapore, 1958–61; FO, 1961–64; 1st Sec., British High Commn, New Delhi, 1964–68; FCO, 1968–71; Counsellor, 1969; British Embassy, Washington, 1971–75; Head of SE Asia Dept, FCO, 1975–79; Consul General, Montreal, 1980–82. International Institute of Strategic Studies. *Recreations:* tennis, theatre. *Address:* 128 Longland Drive, Totteridge, N20 8HL. *T:* 01–445 0896. *Club:* Royal Over-Seas League.

SIMPLE, Peter; *see* Wharton, Michael B.

SIMPSON, Alan, MA, DPhil Oxon, LHD, LLD; President and Professor of History, Vassar College, Poughkeepsie, NY, 1964–77; *b* Gateshead, Durham, England, 23 July 1912; *s* of George Hardwick Simpson and Isabella Simpson (*née* Graham); *m* 1938, Mary McQueen McEldowney, Chicago Heights, Ill; one *s* two *d*. *Educ:* Worcester Coll., Oxford (BA); Merton Coll., Oxford (MA, DPhil); Harvard Univ. (Commonwealth Fellow). Served War of 1939–45, RA, Major. Sen. Lectr in Modern British History and American History, Univ. of St Andrews, and Lectr in Constitutional Law, Law Sch., University Coll., Dundee, 1938–46; Asst Prof. of History, Univ. of Chicago, 1946–54; Associate Prof., 1954–59; Thomas E. Donnelley Prof. of History and Dean of the College, Univ. of Chicago, 1959–64. Member Board of Trustees: Colonial Williamsburg; Salve Regina Coll., Newport; Old Dartmouth Hist. Soc.; Mem., Amer. Antiquarian Soc.; Former Member: Council of the Inst. of Early Amer. History and Culture, Williamsburg, Va, 1957–60; Midwest Conf. of British Historians (Co-Founder, 1954; Sec., 1954–61); Commn on Academic Affairs and Bd of Dirs, Amer. Council on Educn; Commn on Liberal Learning, Assoc. of Amer. Colls; Hudson River Valley Commn. *Publications:* (Co-Editor) The People Shall Judge: Readings in the Formation of American Policy, 1949; Puritanism in Old and New England, 1955; The Wealth of the Gentry, 1540–1660: East Anglian Studies, 1961; (co-ed with Mary Simpson): Diary of King Philip's War by Benjamin Church, 1975; (with Mary Simpson) I Too Am Here: selections from the letters of Jane Welsh Carlyle, 1977; (with Mary Simpson) Jean Webster, Storyteller, 1984; The Mysteries of the "Frenchman's Map" of Williamsburg, Virginia, 1984. *Address:* Yellow Gate Farm, Little Compton, RI, USA. *Club:* Century (New York).

SIMPSON, Alan; author and scriptwriter since 1951 (in collaboration with Ray Galton, *qv*); *b* 27 Nov. 1929; *s* of Francis and Lilian Simpson; *m* 1958, Kathleen Phillips (*d* 1978). *Educ:* Mitcham Grammar Sch. *Television:* Hancock's Half Hour, 1954–61 (adaptation and trans., Fleksnes, Scandinavian TV, film and stage); Comedy Playhouse, 1962–63; Steptoe and Son, 1962–74 (US TV Version, Sanford and Son, Dutch TV, Stiefbeen And Zoon, Scandinavian TV, Albert Och Herbert); Galton-Simpson Comedy, 1969; Clochemerle, 1971; Casanova '74, 1974; Dawson's Weekly, 1975; The Galton and Simpson Playhouse, 1976–77; *films:* The Rebel, 1960; The Bargee, 1963; The Wrong Arm of the Law, 1963; The Spy with a Cold Nose, 1966; Loot, 1969; Steptoe and Son, 1971; Steptoe and Son Ride Again, 1973; Den Siste Fleksnes (Scandinavia), 1974; Skraphandlarne (Scandinavia), 1975; *theatre:* Way Out in Piccadilly, 1966; The Wind in the Sassafras Trees, 1968; Albert och Herbert (Sweden), 1981; Fleksnes (Norway), 1983; Mordet pa Skölgatan 15 (Sweden), 1984. Awards: Scriptwriters of the Year, 1959 (Guild of TV Producers and Directors); Best TV Comedy Series (Steptoe and Son, 1962, 1963, 1964, 1965 (Screenwriters Guild)); John Logie Baird Award (for outstanding contribution to Television), 1964; Best Comedy Series (Stiefbeen And Zoon, Dutch TV), 1966; Best Comedy Screenplay, (Steptoe and Son) Screenwriters Guild, 1972. *Publications:* (jointly with Ray Galton, *qv*): Hancock, 1961; Steptoe and Son, 1963; The Reunion and Other Plays, 1966; Hancock Scripts, 1974; The Best of Hancock, 1986. *Recreations:* Hampton FC (Pres.), gourmet travelling, guest speaking. *Address:* c/o Tessa Le Bars Management, 18 Queen Anne Street, W1. *T:* 01–636 3191.

SIMPSON, Alan; His Honour Judge Simpson; a Circuit Judge, since 1985; *b* 17 April 1937; *s* of William Henry Simpson and Gladys Simpson; *m* 1965, Maureen O'Shea; one *s* one *d*. *Educ:* Leeds Grammar Sch.; Corpus Christi Coll., Oxford (MA). Called to the Bar, Inner Temple, 1962; a Recorder, 1975–85. Prosecuting Counsel to DHSS, North Eastern Circuit, 1977–85. *Recreations:* music, books, sport (especially cricket and boxing). *Address:* The Keep, 41 Colton Road, Whitkirk, Leeds LS15 9AA. *T:* Leeds 605448. *Club:* St Anne's (Leeds).

SIMPSON, Sir Alfred (Henry), Kt 1985; Chief Justice of Kenya, 1982–85; *b* 29 Oct. 1914; *s* of John Robertson Simpson, Dundee; *m* 1941, Hilda Corson Rodgers; one *d*. *Educ:* Grove Academy; St Andrews University; Edinburgh University. MA St Andrews, 1935; LLB Edinburgh, 1938 and Solicitor. Served in RASC, 1940–46, Middle East and Italy; Military Mission to the Italian Army and Allied Commission, Austria. Legal Officer, BMA, Cyrenaica, 1946–48. Member of the Faculty of Advocates, 1952. Crown Counsel, Singapore, 1948–56; Legal Draftsman, Gold Coast, 1956; Solicitor-General, Ghana, 1957, then Puisne Judge, Supreme Court, 1957–61; Puisne Judge, Combined Judiciary of Sarawak, North Borneo and Brunei, 1962; Senior Puisne Judge, Fedn of Malaysia High Court in Borneo, 1964; Reader, Faculty of Law, ANU, Canberra, 1965; Barrister-at-Law, NSW, 1967; Puisne Judge, High Court of Kenya, 1967–82. *Publication:* (with others) The Laws of Singapore, revised edn, 1955. *Recreation:* golf. *Address:* 23 Downes Place, Hughes, ACT 2605, Australia. *Clubs:* Royal Commonwealth Society; Royal Canberra Golf.

SIMPSON, Alfred Moxon, AC 1978; CMG 1959; Chairman: Simpson Holdings Ltd, 1939–83; SA Telecasters Ltd, since 1964 (Director since 1962); *b* 17 Nov. 1910; *s* of late A. A. Simpson, CMG, CBE; *m* 1938, Elizabeth Robson Cleland; one *s*. *Educ:* St Peter's College; University of Adelaide, (BSc). Associate (Commerce) of Univ. of Adelaide, 1940. Pres. Adelaide Chamber of Commerce, 1950–52; Sen. Vice-Pres. Associated Chambers of Commerce of Aust., 1953–55; Pres. SA Chamber of Manufrs, 1956–58; Pres. Associated Chambers of Manufrs of Aust., 1957–58. Director: Bank of Adelaide, 1952–79; Elder Smith Goldsbrough Mort Ltd, 1954–81; Adelaide Steamship Co. Ltd, 1960–83; QBE Insurance Group Ltd, 1975–83 (Local Dir, 1935). Mem. Hulme Cttee on Rates of Depreciation, 1956; reported on early retirement of expatriate staff in Papua-New Guinea, 1972. Mem. Council, Flinders Univ., 1965–76. *Recreations:* carpentry, skiing. *Address:* 31 Heatherbank Terrace, Stonyfell, SA 5066, Australia. *T:* 31 12 85. *Clubs:* Adelaide, Mt Lofty Ski (Adelaide).

SIMPSON, Prof. (Alfred William) Brian, DCL; FBA 1983; JP; Professor of Law: University of Chicago, since 1984; University of Kent, 1973–85, now Emeritus; *b* 17 Aug. 1931; *s* of Rev. Canon Bernard W. Simpson and Mary E. Simpson; *m* 1st, 1954, Kathleen Anne Seston (marr. diss. 1968); one *s* one *d*; 2nd, 1969, Caroline Elizabeth Ann Brown; one *s* two *d*. *Educ:* Oakham Sch., Rutland; The Queen's Coll., Oxford (MA 1958, DCL 1976). Nat. Service with RWAFF, 1950–51. Junior Research Fellow, St Edmund Hall, Oxford, 1954–55; Fellow and Tutor, Lincoln Coll., Oxford, 1955–73. Dean: Faculty of Law, Univ. of Ghana, 1968–69; Faculty of Social Sciences, Univ. of Kent, 1975–78; Visiting Professor: Dalhousie Univ., 1964; Univ. of Chicago, 1979, 1980, 1982, 1984; Univ. of Michigan, 1985; Hon. Dep. District Attorney, Denver City, 1982. Member, Deptl Cttee on Obscenity and Film Censorship, 1977–79. JP Canterbury and St Augustine's, 1968–. *Publications:* Introduction to the History of the Land Law, 1961, new edn as A History of the Land Law, 1986; (ed) Oxford Essays in Jurisprudence, 2nd Series, 1973; A History of the Common Law of Contract, 1975; Pornography and Politics, 1983; Cannibalism and the Common Law, 1984; (ed) A Biographical Dictionary of the Common Law, 1984; articles in legal jls. *Recreation:* sailing. *Address:* 36 High Street, Wingham, Canterbury, Kent CT3 1AB. *T:* Canterbury 720979; The Law School, University of Chicago, 1111 E 60th Street, Chicago, Illinois 60637, USA.

SIMPSON, Anthony Maurice Herbert, TD 1973; Member (C) Northamptonshire, European Parliament, since 1979; *b* 28 Oct. 1935; *y s* of late Lt-Col Maurice Rowton Simpson, OBE, TD, DL and Mrs Renée Claire Simpson; *m* 1961, Penelope Gillian, *d* of late Howard Dixon Spackman; one *s* two *d*. *Educ:* Rugby; Magdalene College, Cambridge. BA 1959, LLM (LLB 1961), MA 1963. Leics and Derbys (PAO) Yeomanry, 1956–59; 21st SAS Regt (Artists Rifles) (V), 1959–68; 23rd SAS Regt (V), 1968–74; Major 1968. Called to Bar, Inner Temple, 1961; practised Midland and Oxford Circuit, 1961–75; Mem., Legal Service of European Commn, Brussels, 1975–79; Quaestor of the European Parlt, 1979. Contested (C) West Leicester, Feb. and Oct. 1974. Common Market Law Editor, Current Law, 1965–72. *Recreations:* walking, travelling. *Address:* Bassets, Great Glen, Leicestershire. *T:* Great Glen 2386; Avenue Michel-Ange 57, 1040 Brussels, Belgium. *T:* (02) 736–4219. *Club:* Special Forces.

SIMPSON, Athol John Dundas, OBE 1976; Director of Technical Services, Crown Agents for Oversea Governments and Administrations, since 1983; *b* 4 May 1932; *s* of John Simpson and Helen Murray Simpson (*née* Cubie); *m* 1956, Ricki Ellen Carter; one *s* two *d*. *Educ:* Reigate Grammar Sch. Joined Crown Agents, 1950; served, Royal Air Force, 1951–53; Crown Agents' Representative in E Africa, 1965–69; seconded as Managing Director, Millbank Technical Services (Iran) Ltd, 1973–77; returned to Bd appt as Dir of Marketing and Development with Crown Agents, Nov. 1977; Dir, Crown Agents, 1978–83. *Recreations:* Rugby football, golf, reading. *Address:* 7 Chelsea Embankment, SW3. *T:* 01–351 5751. *Club:* Travellers'.

SIMPSON, Prof. Brian; *see* Simpson, Prof. A. W. B.

SIMPSON, Air Vice-Marshal Charles Ednam, QHS 1985; Principal Medical Officer, HQ RAF Strike Command, since 1986; *b* 24 Sept. 1929; *s* of Charles and Margaret Simpson; *m* 1955, Margaret Riddell; two *s* one *d*. *Educ:* Stirling and Falkirk High Schools; Univ. of Glasgow (MB ChB); University of London (MSc). MFOM, MFCM. British Defence Staff, Washington DC, 1975; Dep. Dir, Aviation Medicine, RAF, 1978; CO, RAF Hosp., Wegberg, 1981; CO, Princess Alexandra Hosp., Wroughton, 1982; Dir of Health and Research, RAF, 1984; Asst Surgeon General (Envtl Medicine and Res.), 1985. *Recreations:* golf, birdwatching. *Address:* RAF High Wycombe, Bucks HP14 4UE. *T:* High Wycombe 26200. *Club:* Royal Air Force.

SIMPSON, Charles Valentine George; former Director: Wigham Poland Midlands Ltd; Walker, Moate, Simpson & Co. Ltd, Birmingham, since 1960; Wigham-Richardson and Bevingtons (Midlands) Ltd; *b* 14 Feb. 1900; 2nd *s* of Alexander Simpson, Ayrshire; *m*; two *s* one *d*; 2nd, Muriel Edwina, *e d* of Rev. Edwin Jones, Montgomeryshire; one *s*. *Educ:* Tindal Street Elementary Sch., Birmingham. RMLI, 1915–19; RNVR, 1939–45, rank of Lt-Comdr; served China, Med., Iceland, Germany. Councillor, Birmingham, 1935, Alderman, 1949–74; Chairman, Airports Cttee, 1950, Public Works Cttee, 1966–68; Lord Mayor, City of Birmingham, 1968–69. President: RN Assoc., City of Birmingham; Handsworth Wood Residents Assoc.; Birmingham Br., RNLI; County Pres., Birmingham Royal British Legion; Vice-Pres., Birmingham Bn, Boys' Brigade; Life Mem., Court of Governors, Birmingham Univ. Successfully inaugurated appeal, 1969, for a new lifeboat to be called City of Birmingham. *Recreations:* bowls, foreign travel (preferably by caravan). *Address:* 16 Knowle Wood Road, Dorridge, W Midlands B93 8JJ. *T:* Knowle 2427.

SIMPSON, Commander Cortlandt James Woore, CBE 1956; DSC 1945; retired 1961; *b* 2 Sept. 1911; *s* of late Rear-Admiral C. H. Simpson, CBE, and, Edith Octavia (*née* Busby); *m* 1st, Lettice Mary Johnstone; 2nd, Ann Margaret Cubitt (*née* Tooth); 3rd, Joan Mary Watson; one *d*; 4th, Vanessa Ann Stainton (*née* Heald). *Educ:* St Ronans, Worthing; RN College, Dartmouth; London Univ. (BSc Engineering, Hons). Joined RN (Dartmouth), 1925; Lieut, 1934. Served War of 1939–45 in Home and Mediterranean Fleets; Commander, 1948. Summer expeditions to Greenland, 1950, 1951; Leader of British North Greenland Expedition, 1952–54. Polar Medal, 1954; Royal Geographical Society, Founder's Medal, 1955. *Publication:* North Ice, 1957. *Recreations:* mountaineering, sailing, walking. *Address:* Lower Lambie, Luxborough, Watchet, Somerset. *Club:* Alpine.

SIMPSON, Prof. David Rae Fisher; Research Professor, Department of Economics, University of Strathclyde, since 1985; *b* 29 Nov. 1936; *s* of David Ebenezer Simpson and Roberta Muriel Wilson; *m* 1980, Barbara Dianne Goalen, *d* of Mrs G. Inglis, Edinburgh; one *s* (and one step *s* one step *d*). *Educ:* Skerry's Coll.; Edinburgh and Harvard Univs. MA 1st cl. hons Econs Edinburgh; PhD Econs Harvard. Instr in Econs, Harvard Univ., 1963–64; Assoc. Statistician, UN Hdqtrs, NY, 1964–65; Res. Officer, Econ. Res. Inst., Dublin, 1965–67; Lectr in Polit. Economy, UCL, 1967–69; Sen. Lectr in Econs, Univ. of Stirling, 1969–74; Prof. and Dir, Fraser of Allander Inst., Univ. of Strathclyde, 1975–80, Res. Prof., 1980–85. Contested (SNP) Berwick and E Lothian Division, 1970 and Feb. 1974. *Publications:* Problems of Input-Output Tables and Analysis, 1966; General Equilibrium Analysis, 1975; The Political Economy of Growth, 1983; The Challenge of New Technology, 1986; articles in Econometrica, Rev. Econs and Statistics, Scientific American. *Recreations:* golf, reading. *Address:* 11 Kingsburgh Road, Edinburgh.

SIMPSON, David Richard Salisbury; Director, Action on Smoking and Health, since 1979; *b* 1 Oct. 1945; *s* of Richard Salisbury Simpson and Joan Margaret Simpson (*née* Braund). *Educ:* Merchiston Castle School, Edinburgh. ACA 1969; FCA 1979 (but resigned from Institute, 1981). Teacher at Cadet College, Hasan Abdal, West Pakistan, 1963–64 (VSO). Peat, Marwick, Mitchell & Co., Chartered Accountants, 1964–72; Scottish Director, Shelter, Campaign for the Homeless, 1972–74; Director, Amnesty International (British Section), 1974–79. Sundry journalism, broadcasting and public lectures. Consultant, Internat. Union Against Cancer Special Project on Smoking and Cancer (responsibility for Indian Sub-Continent), 1980–. *Publications:* contribs to national newspapers and magazines. *Recreations:* friends, reading, music, hill-walking, Orkney. *Address:* c/o ASH, 5–11 Mortimer Street, W1N 7RH. *T:* 01–637 9843.

SIMPSON, Lt-Col (Retd) David Sackville Bruce; Chief Executive, Civil Service Catering Organisation, since 1981; *b* 18 March 1930; *s* of Henry and Violet Simpson; *m* 1956, Margaret Elizabeth Goslin; two *s* three *d*. *Educ:* Brockley Grammar Sch.; Westminster Technical Coll. FHCIMA. Regular Officer, Army Catering Corps (retd in rank of Lt-Col), 1950–75; Principal Education Catering Organiser, Inner London Education Authority, 1975–81. *Recreations:* golf, squash. *Address:* 65 Gally Hill Road, Church Crookham, Hants. *T:* Fleet 3754.

SIMPSON, Dennis Charles; business consultant; Business Development Director, Neath Development Partnership Enterprise Ltd, since 1985; *b* 24 Oct. 1931; *s* of late Arthur and Helen Simpson; *m* 1st, 1964, Margery Bruce Anderson (marr. diss.); three *s* one *d*; 2nd, 1983, Susan Gaynor Conway-Williams. *Educ:* Manchester Univ. (BA). FInstPS. 2nd Lieut Royal Signals, 1952–54; commercial appts, Philips Electrical Industries, 1956–63; Group Purchasing Manager: STC Ltd, 1963–66; Rank Organisation, 1966–69; Gen. Man., Cam Gears (S Wales) Ltd, 1969–72; Industrial Dir for Wales, Dept of Industry, 1972–75; Industrial Dir for Wales, Welsh Office, 1975–76; Business Agent, Welsh Develt Agency, 1983–85. Chairman: Spencer Harris Ltd, 1976–81; Grainger Hydraulics Ltd, 1976–81; Wellfield Engineering, 1976–81; Director: Beechwood Holdings, 1976–81; Gower Technology Ltd, 1983–; Video Interactive Systems Ltd, 1983–; Gower Alarms Ltd, 1985–; Video Interactive Teaching Aids Ltd, 1985–. *Recreations:* golf, bridge, reading war histories. *Address:* 9 Langland Bay Road, Langland, Swansea, West Glamorgan SA3 4QQ. *T:* Swansea 66648. *Club:* Langland Bay Golf.

SIMPSON, Edward Hugh, CB 1976; FSS 1947; Senior Hon. Research Fellow, Birmingham University; Deputy Secretary, Department of Education and Science, 1973–82, retired; *b* 10 Dec. 1922; *o s* of Hugh and Mary Simpson, of Brookfield, Ballymena, Co. Antrim; *m* 1947, Gladys Rebecca, *er d* of Sam and Elizabeth Gibson, Ernevale, Kesh, Co. Fermanagh; one *s* one *d*. *Educ:* Coleraine Academical Institution; Queen's Univ., Belfast (BSc (1st cl. Hons Mathematics), 1942); Christ's Coll., Cambridge (Scholar). Foreign Office, Bletchley Park, 1942–45; Min. of Education, 1947–50 and 1952–56; HM Treasury, 1950–52; Commonwealth Fund Fellow, USA, 1956–57; Private Sec. to Lord President of Council and Lord Privy Seal, 1957–60; Dep. Dir, Commonwealth Educn Liaison Unit, 1960–62; Sec., Commonwealth Educn Conf., New Delhi, 1962; Asst Sec., DES, 1962–68; Under-Sec., Civil Service Dept, 1968–71, DES, 1971–73. Chm., Nat. Assessment Panel, Schools Curriculum Award. Governor: Bishop Grosseteste Coll., Lincoln; Regent's Coll., London. *Publications:* articles in statistical and educn journals. *Address:* 40 Frays Avenue, West Drayton, Mddx UB7 7AG. *T:* West Drayton 443417. *Club:* Athenæum.

SIMPSON, Ernest Smith, CEng, FIMechE; Chairman, Jonas Woodhead & Sons PLC, Leeds, since 1973 (Managing Director, 1966–84); *b* 7 Nov. 1921; *s* of Leonard and Gladys Simpson; *m* 1961, Janet (*née* Wright); one *s* one *d*. *Educ:* Leeds City School of Commerce; Hendon Technical Coll. Junior draughtsman, Woodhead Group, 1936; Director of Holding Company, Woodhead Group, 1964. Member, Monopolies Commission, 1978–81. MSAE. *Recreations:* golf, painting. *Address:* Old Smithy Cottage, Kearby, Wetherby, W Yorks LS22 3BR.

SIMPSON, Esther Eleanor, MD, FRCP, FFCM, DPH, DCH; former Senior Principal Medical Officer, Department of Education and Science, and Department of Health and Social Security, retired 1979; *b* 28 May 1919. *Educ:* Kendal High Sch.; London Univ. Medical Officer, London County Council, then to Province of Natal Centre, Inst. of Child Health; joined Medical Br., Min. of Education, 1961. *Recreations:* music, reading, walking. *Address:* 19 Belsize Lane, NW3 5AG. *T:* 01–794 4400.

SIMPSON, Ffreebairn Liddon, CMG 1967; General Manager, Central Water Authority, Mauritius, 1976–78; *b* 11 July 1916; *s* of late James Liddon Simpson and Dorothy (*née* Blyth); *m* 1947, Dorina Laura Magda, MBE (*née* Ilieva); one *s*. *Educ:* Westminster School; Trinity College, Cambridge. HM Diplomatic/Foreign Service, 1939–48; HM Treasury, 1948–50; Administrative Officer, Gold Coast, 1950–55; Dep. Colonial Sec., Mauritius, 1955; Perm. Secretary: Min. of Works and Internal Communications, 1961; Premier's Office, 1966; Sec. to the Cabinet, Mauritius, 1967–76. *Recreations:* reading, philately. *Address:* c/o Lloyds Bank (G Section), 6 Pall Mall, SW1Y 5NH. *Club:* United Oxford & Cambridge University.

SIMPSON, Gordon Russell, DSO 1944 and Bar 1945; LVO 1979; TD; DL; stockbroker; Partner, Bell, Cowan & Co. (now Bell, Lawrie Ltd), 1938–82; *b* 2 Jan. 1917; *s* of A. Russell Simpson, WS; *m* 1943, Marion Elizabeth King (*d* 1976); two *s*. *Educ:* Rugby School. Served with 2nd Lothians and Border Horse, 1939–46 (comd 1944–46). Chm., Edinburgh Stock Exchange, 1961–63; Chm., Scottish Stock Exchange, 1965–66; Pres., Council of Associated Stock Exchanges, 1971–73; Dep. Chm., Stock Exchange, 1973–78. Chm., General Accident Fire & Life Assurance Corporation Ltd, 1979– (Dir, 1967–). Brigadier, Queen's Body Guard for Scotland (Royal Company of Archers). Mem. Court, Stirling Univ., 1980–; Comr, Queen Victoria Sch., 1982–. DL Stirling and Falkirk Dists

(Central Region), 1981. *Recreations:* music, ski-ing, archery. *Address:* c/o Bell, Lawrie Ltd, Erskine House, 68/73 Queen Street, Edinburgh EH2 4AE. *Club:* New (Edinburgh).

SIMPSON, Henry George, CBE 1980 (OBE 1968); Controller of Housing and Technical Services to Greater London Council, 1974–82; *b* 27 April 1917; *s* of late William James and late Alice Simpson; *m* 1938, Gladys Lee; one *s*. *Educ:* Enfield Grammar School. FIH, FSVA. War Service 1940–46, Royal Fusiliers. Dir of Housing and Property Services, London Borough of Lambeth, 1962–72; Dir-Gen., Northern Ireland Housing Exec., 1972–74. Member: Social Services Adv. Cttee, 1982–; Adv. Gp, Urban Housing Renewal Unit, 1985–; Dep. Chm., Hanover Housing Assoc., 1985– (Mem. Management Cttee, 1982–85); Pres., Housing Centre Trust, 1982–; Trustee, Shelter Housing Aid Centre, 1982–. FRSA 1977. *Recreations:* gardening, hi-fi, clay pigeon shooting. *Address:* 19 Abbotswood, Guildford, Surrey GU1 1UX. *T:* Guildford 570384.

SIMPSON, Ian; Assistant Rector, The London Institute, since 1986; Head of St Martin's School of Art, since 1986; *b* 12 Nov. 1933; *s* of Herbert William and Elsie Simpson; *m* 1st, 1958, Joan (*née* Charlton) (marr. diss. 1982); two *s* one *d*; 2nd, 1982, Birgitta Willcocks (*née* Brädde). *Educ:* Bede Grammar Sch., Sunderland; Sunderland Coll. of Art; Royal Coll. of Art. ARCA 1958. Freelance artist and illustrator, 1958–63; Hornsey Coll. of Art: Lectr, 1963–66; Head, Dept of Visual Research, 1966–69; Head, Dept of Co-ordinated Studies, 1969–72; Principal, St Martin's Sch. of Art, 1972–86. Exhibited various exhibns, Britain, USA, etc; one-man exhibn, Cambridge, 1975, Durham, 1977, Blandford, 1985. Mem. Council, CNAA, 1974–80 (Chm., Fine Art Bd, 1976–81). Pres., Nat. Soc. for Art Educn, 1976. Consultant, Leisure Study Group Ltd, 1986. FSAE 1976; FRSA 1983. *Publications:* Eyeline, 1968; Drawing: seeing and observation, 1973; Picture Making, 1973; Guide to Painting and Composition, 1979; Painters Progress, 1983; *Television Programmes:* Eyeline (10 programmes), 1968, 1969; Picture Making (10 programmes), 1973, 1976; Reading the Signs (5 programmes), 1977–78. *Recreations:* reading, music. *Address:* St Martin's School of Art, 107 Charing Cross Road, WC2H 0DU. *T:* 01–437 0611.

SIMPSON, James Joseph Trevor, KBE (Hon.) 1965 (CBE 1957); (forename James added by deed poll, 1965); Chairman, James Simpson & Co. Ltd; retired as Chairman, Uganda Development Corporation, Ltd (1952–64); *b* 9 Jan. 1908; 2nd *s* of late Lieut-Colonel Herbert Simpson, OBE, MC, and of Mrs Henrietta Augusta Simpson; *m* 1940, Enid Florence (*née* Danzelman) (*d* 1979). *Educ:* Ardingly College, Sussex. Branch Manager, Vacuum Oil Co., Nakuru, Nairobi, Dar es Salaam, Mombasa, Kampala, 1932–46; General Manager, The Uganda Company Ltd, 1947–52; President, Uganda Chamber of Commerce, 1941, 1946–50. Member: Uganda Executive Council, 1952–55; Uganda Legislative Council, 1950–58 (Chm. Representative Members Organization 1951–58); E African Legislative Assembly, 1957–60, 1962–63; E African Railways and Harbours, Transport Advisory Council, 1948–61; E African Industrial Council, 1947–61; Uganda Electricity Bd, 1955–60; East African Airways Corporation, 1958–73; Minister of Economic Affairs, Uganda, 1962–63. *Recreation:* bridge. *Address:* PO Box 48816, Nairobi, Kenya; c/o PO Box 4343, Kampala, Uganda. *Club:* Muthaiga (Kenya).

SIMPSON, Very Rev. John Arthur; Dean of Canterbury, since 1986; *b* 7 June 1933; *s* of Arthur Simpson and Mary Esther Simpson; *m* 1968, Ruth Marian (*née* Dibbens); one *s* two *d*. *Educ:* Cathays High School, Cardiff; Keble Coll., Oxford (BA, 2nd cl. Mod. History 1956, MA 1960); Clifton Theological Coll. Deacon 1958, priest 1959; Curate: Leyton, 1958–59; Christ Church, Orpington, 1959–62; Tutor, Oak Hill Coll., Southgate N14, 1962–72; Vicar of Ridge, Herts, 1972–79; Director of Ordinands and Post-Ordination Training, Diocese of St Albans, 1975–81; Hon. Canon of St Albans Cathedral, 1977–79; Residentiary Canon, St Albans, and Priest-in-charge of Ridge, 1979–81; Archdeacon of Canterbury and Canon Res. of Canterbury Cathedral, 1981–86. Dir, Ecclesiastical Insurance Office, 1983–. *Recreations:* travel, theatre, opera. *Address:* The Deanery, Canterbury, Kent CT1 2EP. *T:* Canterbury 65983. *Club:* Athenæum.

SIMPSON, John (Cody Fidler-); Diplomatic Editor, BBC-TV, since 1982; *b* 9 Aug. 1944; *s* of Roy Simpson Fidler-Simpson and Joyce Leila Vivienne Cody; *m* 1965, Diane Jean Petteys (separated), El Cajon, California; two *d*. *Educ:* St Paul's School; Magdalene Coll., Cambridge (MA). Reporter, BBC Radio News, 1970; BBC correspondent, Dublin, 1972; Common Market correspondent (based in Brussels), 1975; Southern Africa correspondent (based in Johannesburg), 1977; Diplomatic correspondent, BBC Television News, 1978; BBC Political Editor, 1980; Presenter and Correspondent, BBC-TV News, 1981. Reporting assignments from 51 countries include: wars and uprisings in Angola, Rhodesia, Soweto, Iran, Iraq, Chile, Lebanon, Nicaragua; dissent in USSR and Czechoslovakia; causes célèbres in Angola (mercenary trials), Iran (return of the Ayatollah), Lebanon (massacre in Sabra/Chatila), Argentina (disappearances); treaties and summits at Sunningdale, 1973, Vienna (SALT II), 1979, Lancaster House, 1980, Hillsborough, 1985, Geneva, 1985; interviews with Ayatollah Khomeini, Col Ghaddafi, Dr Andrei Sakharov, and 42 presidents or prime ministers. *Publications:* (ed jtly) The Best of Granta, 1966; The Disappeared: voices from a secret war, 1985; *novels:* Moscow Requiem, 1981; A Fine And Private Place, 1983. *Recreations:* collecting obscure books, travelling to obscure places, and returning to Suffolk. *Address:* BBC Television Centre, Wood Lane, W12. *T:* 01–743 8000. *Club:* Chelsea Arts.

SIMPSON, John Ferguson, FRCS; Consulting Surgeon to Ear, Nose and Throat Department, St Mary's Hospital, retired; formerly Civil Consultant, Ministry of Aviation; *b* 10 Oct. 1902; *s* of late Col P. J. Simpson, DSO, FRCVS, Maidenhead; *m* 1947, Winifred Beatrice Rood; one *s* one *d*. *Educ:* Reading Sch.; St Mary's Hosp. FRCS 1929; MRCS, LRCP 1926. Formerly: Lectr in Diseases of the Ear, Nose and Throat, Univ. of London; Specialist in Otorhino-laryngology, RAF; Hon. Surg. Royal Nat. Throat, Nose and Ear Hosp. FRSocMed (ex-President Section of Otology; Hon. Life Mem., Section of Laryngology). Liveryman, Farriers' Co. *Publications:* A Synopsis of Otorhinolaryngology (jointly), 1957; chapters: Operative Surgery, 1957; ENT Diseases, 1965. *Recreations:* entomology; formerly Rugby football. *Address:* Waverley Cottage, Upton Grey, Basingstoke, Hants RG25 2RA. *T:* Basingstoke 862433.

SIMPSON, John Liddle, CMG 1958; TD 1950; QC 1980; *b* 9 Oct. 1912; *s* of late James Simpson; *m* 1st, 1939, Nellie Lavender Mussett (*d* 1944); 2nd, 1959, Ursula Vaughan Washington (*nee* Rigby). *Educ:* George Watson's Coll.; Edinburgh Univ. (MA, DLitt). Barrister, Middle Temple, 1937. Served War of 1939–45; GSO1, 1945. Principal, Control Office for Germany and Austria, 1946; Senior legal assistant, FO (German Section), 1948; transferred to Foreign (now Diplomatic) Service and promoted Counsellor, 1954; Legal Counsellor, FO, 1954–59 and 1961–68; Legal Adviser, United Kingdom Mission to the United Nations, New York, 1959–61; Dep. Legal Adviser, 1968–71, Second Legal Adviser, 1971–72, FCO; returned to practice, 1973; elected alternate Pres. of Arbitral Tribunals, Internat. Telecommunications Satellite Org., 1974 and 1976. Mem., Dubai/Sharjah Boundary Court of Arbitration, 1978–81; Chm., UNESCO Appeals Bd, 1980–85. Freeman, City of London, 1976. *Publications:* Germany and the North Atlantic Community: A Legal Survey (with M. E. Bathurst), 1956; International Arbitration; Law and Practice (with Hazel Fox), 1959; articles and notes in legal journals. *Address:* 137a Ashley Gardens, Thirleby Road, SW1P 1HN. *T:* 01–834 4814; 5 Paper Buildings, Temple, EC4Y 7HB. *T:* 01–353 8494.

SIMPSON, Kenneth John, CMG 1961; HM Diplomatic Service, retired; *b* 5 Feb. 1914; *s* of Bernard and Ann Simpson, Millhouses, Sheffield; *m* 1939, Harriet (Shan) Hughes; three *s*. *Educ:* Downing College, Cambridge. Entered HM Foreign (now Diplomatic) Service, 1937; lastly Consul-Gen., Hanoi and Stuttgart, Inspector, Diplomatic Service and Counsellor, FCO. *Address:* 76 Wood Ride, Petts Wood, Kent BR5 1PY. *T:* Orpington 24710.

SIMPSON, Malcolm Carter; Director of Finance, Leeds City Council, 1978–82, retired; Member of Board, Yorkshire Water Authority, since 1983; *b* 15 June 1929; *s* of Arthur and Rhoda Simpson; *m* 1st, 1952, Doreen Patricia Wooler; two *d*; 2nd, 1980, Andrea Gillian Blythe. *Educ:* Stanningley Council Sch. DPA; CIPFA. Employed by Leeds CC for whole of working life, 1943–82: Asst Dir of Finance, 1968; Dep. Dir of Finance, 1973. Bd Mem., S Yorks Residuary Body, 1985–. *Recreations:* golf, bridge. *Address:* Swiss Cottage, 44 Millbeck Green, Collingham Bridge, Leeds. *T:* Collingham Bridge 73917.

SIMPSON, Rear-Adm. Michael Frank, CB 1985; CEng, FIMechE; FRAeS; Director General Aircraft (Naval), 1983–85; Director and General Manager, Field Aircraft Services (Croydon) Ltd, since 1985; *b* 27 Sept. 1928; *s* of Robert Michael Simpson and Florence Mabel Simpson; *m* 1973, Sandra MacDonald (*née* Clift); two *s* one *d*. *Educ:* King Edward VI Sch., Bath; RN Engrg Coll., Manadon. CEng, FIMechE 1983; FRAeS 1983. Joined RN, 1944; qual. as Air Engr Officer, 1956; served in FAA Sqdns, cruisers and carriers; served with US Navy on exchange, 1964–66; Air Engr Officer, HMS Ark Royal, 1970–72; MoD appts, 1972–78; Supt, RN Aircraft Yard, Fleetlands, 1978–80; Cdre, RN Barracks, Portsmouth, 1981–83. Chairman: RN/RM Children's Home Management Cttee, 1980–83; RN Athletics Assoc., 1981–83. Mem. Court, Cranfield Inst. of Technology, 1983–86. *Publications:* articles on helicopter engrg in Jl of Naval Engrg; symposium paper on helicopter design, 1975. *Recreations:* sailing, ski-ing, shooting, making things, military history, swimming. *Address:* c/o Barclays Bank, 9 High Street, Colchester CO1 1DD. *Clubs:* Army and Navy; Royal Naval Sailing Association (Captain, Portsmouth Br., 1981–83); Royal Navy Ski.

SIMPSON, Oliver, CB 1977; MA, PhD, FInstP; Chief Scientist, Deputy Under-Secretary of State, Home Office, 1974–83; *b* 28 Oct. 1924; *y s* of late Sir George C. Simpson, KCB, FRS, and Dorothy (*née* Stephen); *m* 1946, Joan, *d* of late Walter and Maud Morgan; one *s* (and one *s* decd). *Educ:* Highgate Sch.; Trinity Coll., Cambridge. War Service: Admiralty Research Laboratory, Teddington, on submarine detection, 1944–46. Research Scholar, 1946–49, Fellow of Trinity Coll., Cambridge, 1949–53; Asst Prof. of Physics, Univ. of Michigan, USA, 1949–52; Imperial Chemical Industries Fellow in Dept. of Theoretical Chemistry, Cambridge, 1952–53; joined Services Electronics Research Laboratory, Admty, 1953, Head of Solid State Physics, 1956–63; Supt, Basic Physics Div., Nat. Physical Laboratory, 1964–66; Dep. Dir, Nat. Physical Laboratory, 1966–69; Under-Sec., Cabinet Office, 1969–74. *Publications:* articles in scientific jls on infra-red detectors, semiconductors, fluorescence and standards of measurement. *Address:* 4 Highbury Road, Wimbledon, SW19. *T:* 01–946 3871. *Club:* Athenæum.

SIMPSON, Peter Miller, RDI 1974; FSIA; company director; Director: Bute Looms Ltd, since 1973; Bute Fabrics Ltd, since 1977; *b* 5 April 1921; *s* of David Simpson and Annie Simpson; *m* 1964, Orma Macallum; one *s* one *d*. *Educ:* Perth High Sch.; Dundee Coll. of Art (DA 1950). MSIA 1956, FSIA 1974. Study and work, USA, 1950–53. Mem. Scottish Cttee, Design Council. Governor, Duncan of Jordanstone Coll. of Art, Dundee, 1978–. *Recreations:* gardening, pottery, walking. *Address:* 35 Lovers Lane, Scone, Perth. *T:* Perth 51573. *Clubs:* Caledonian; Arts (Edinburgh).

SIMPSON, Ven. Rennie, LVO 1974; MA Lambeth 1970; Archdeacon of Macclesfield, 1978–85, Emeritus since 1986; Rector of Gawsworth, 1978–85; Chaplain to the Queen, since 1982; *b* 13 Jan. 1920; *o s* of late Doctor Taylor Simpson and late May Simpson, Rishton; *m* 1949, Margaret, *er d* of late Herbert Hardy and Olive Hardy, South Kirkby; one *s* one *d*. *Educ:* Blackburn Tech. Coll.; Kelham Theol College. Curate of S Elmsall, Yorks, 1945–49; Succentor of Blackburn Cath., 1949–52; Sacrist and Minor Canon of St Paul's Cath., 1952–58, Hon. Minor Canon, 1958–, Jun. Cardinal, 1954–55, Sen. Cardinal, 1955–58; Vicar of John Keble Church, Mill Hill, 1958–63; Precentor, 1963–74, Acting Sacrist, 1973–74, Westminster Abbey; Canon Residentiary, 1974–78, Vice-Dean, 1975–78, Chester Cathedral. Chaplain, RNVR, 1953–55; Dep. Chaplain, Gt Ormond St Hosp., 1954–58; Asst Chaplain, 1956–64, Officiating Chaplain, 1964–, Sub-Prelate, 1973–, Order of St John of Jerusalem; Deputy Priest to the Queen, 1956–67; Priest-in-Ordinary to the Queen, 1967–74. Life Governor, Imperial Cancer Research Fund, 1963. Liveryman of Waxchandlers' Co. and Freeman of City of London, 1955. Jt Hon. Treas., Corp. Sons of the Clergy, 1967–74; Governor: King's School, Chester, 1974–78; King's Sch., Macclesfield, 1979–85. *Recreations:* football, cricket, theatre. *Address:* 18 Roseberry Green, North Stainley, Ripon, N Yorks HG4 3HZ.

SIMPSON, Rt. Hon. Dr Robert, PC (N Ireland) 1970; *b* 3 July 1923; *er s* of Samuel and Agnes Simpson, Craigbilly, Ballymena; *m* 1954, Dorothy Isobel, 2nd *d* of Dr Robert Strawbridge, MA, DD, and Anne Strawbridge; two *s* one *d*. *Educ:* Ballymena Academy; Queen's University, Belfast. MB, BCh, BAO, 1946; Founder Mem., RCGP; LRCPI (Occupational Medicine), 1980. House Surgeon, Belfast City Hosp., 1947; Resident Anaesthetist, Royal Infirmary, Leicester, 1948; GP, Ballymena, Co. Antrim, 1949–; Medical Correspondent, Belfast Telegraph and Leicester Mercury; Medical Representative, NI, Europ Assistance; Medical Officer, Flexibox Ltd, Ballymena, Northern Dairies Ltd. Founder Chm., Ballymena Round Table, 1951. NI Deleg. to CPA Conf. in NZ and Australia, 1965. Minister of Community Relations, N Ireland, 1969–71; MP (U) Mid-Antrim, Parlt of N Ireland, 1953–72. Director, John Atkinson & Co., etc. Vice-Pres., Co. Antrim Agricl Assoc., 1960–. *Publications:* contribs to newspapers and magazines on medical, country and travel subjects. *Recreations:* the country, writing, music, France, food, travel. *Address:* Random Cottage, Craigbilly, Ballymena, Co. Antrim. *T:* Ballymena 3105. *Club:* Royal Over-Seas League.

SIMPSON, Robert Watson; Under Secretary, and North East Regional Director, Department of Trade and Industry, since 1986; *b* 14 June 1940; *s* of Robert Watson Simpson and Susan Gourlay Thomson Simpson (*née* Rolland). *Educ:* Perth Academy; University of St Andrews (BSc Hons). Board of Trade (Patent Office), 1962; Dept of Trade (Aviation), 1973; Dept of Industry (Indust. Develt Unit), 1976; Dept of Trade (Shipping), 1979; Dept of Trade and Industry (Management Services and Manpower), 1982. *Recreatins:* history, bridge. *Address:* 17 Eslington Terrace, Newcastle upn Tyne. *Club:* Reform.

SIMPSON, Robert Wilfred Levick, DMus; composer; BBC Music Producer, 1951–80; *b* Leamington, Warwickshire, 2 March 1921; *s* of Robert Warren Simpson (British) and Helena Hendrika Govaars (Dutch); *m* 1946, Bessie Fraser (*d* 1981); *m* 1982, Angela Musgrave. *Educ:* Westminster City Sch.; studied with Herbert Howells. DMus (Dunelm) 1952. Holder of: Carl Nielsen Gold Medal (Denmark), 1956; Medal of Honor of

Bruckner Soc. of America, 1962. Mem., British Astronomical Assoc.; FRAS. *Compositions*: Symphonies: No 1, 1951 (recorded); No 2, 1956; No 3, 1962 (recorded); No 4, 1972; No 5, 1972; Nos 6 and 7, 1977; No 8, 1981; No 9, 1986; Concertos: Violin, 1959; Piano, 1967; String Quartets: No 1, 1952 (recorded); No 2, 1953; No 3, 1954; No 4, 1973; No 5, 1974; No 6, 1975; No 7, 1977 (recorded); No 8, 1979 (recorded); No 9, 1982 (recorded); No 10 (For Peace), 1983 (recorded); No 11, 1984 (recorded); Piano Sonata, 1946; Variations and Finale on a Theme of Haydn, for piano, 1948; Allegro Deciso, for string orchestra (from String Quartet No 3); Canzona for Brass, 1958 (recorded); Variations and Fugue for recorder and string quartet, 1959; Incidental Music to Ibsen's The Pretenders, 1965; Trio for clarinet, cello and piano, 1967; Quintet for clarinet, and strings, 1968 (recorded); Energy, Symphonic Study for brass band (test piece for 1971 World Championship); Incidental Music to Milton's Samson Agonistes, 1974; *Media morte in vita sumus* (Motet for choir, brass, and timpani), 1975; Quartet for horn, violin, cello and piano, 1976; Volcano, for brass band, 1979 (test piece for Nat. Championship, 1979); Sonata for two pianos, 1980; Quintet for double basses, clarinet and bass clarinet, 1981 (also for string trio, clarinet and bass clarinet); The Four Temperaments, for brass band, 1982; Variations on a theme of Carl Nielsen, for orchestra, 1983; Trio for horn, violin and piano, 1984; Sonata for violin and piano, 1984; Eppur si muove, for organ, 1985. *Publications*: Carl Nielsen, Symphonist, 1952, rev. edn 1977; The Essence of Bruckner, 1966; The Proms and Natural Justice, 1981; numerous articles in various jls and three BBC booklets (Bruckner and the Symphony, Sibelius and Nielsen, and The Beethoven Symphonies); contrib. to: Encycl. Brit.; Musik in Geschichte und Gegenwart; (ed) The Symphony (Pelican), 1966. *Recreation*: astronomy. *Address*: Síocháin, Killelton, near Camp, Tralee, Co. Kerry, Eire. *T*: Tralee 30213.

SIMPSON, Robin Muschamp Garry; QC 1971; *b* 19 June 1927; *s* of Ronald Maitland Simpson, actor and Lila Maravan Simpson (*née* Muschamp); *m* 1st, 1956, Avril Carolyn Harrisson; one *s* one *d*; 2nd, 1968, Mary Faith Laughton-Scott; one *s* one *d*. *Educ*: Charterhouse; Peterhouse, Cambridge (BA). Called to Bar, Middle Temple, 1951, Bencher, 1979; SE Circuit; former Mem., Surrey and S London Sessions; a Recorder, 1976–86. Mem., CCC Bar Mess. Appeal Steward, British Boxing Bd of Control. *Recreations*: real tennis, sailing. *Address*: 9 Drayton Gardens, SW10. *T*: 01–373 3284. *Clubs*: Garrick, MCC.

SIMPSON, Sir William (James), Kt 1984; Chairman, Health and Safety Commission, 1974–83; *b* Falkirk, 20 May 1920; *s* of William Simpson and Margaret Nimmo; *m* 1942, Catherine McEwan Nicol; one *s*. *Educ*: Victoria Sch. and Falkirk Techn. Sch., Falkirk. Served War of 1939–45, Argyll and Sutherland Highlanders (Sgt). Apprenticed to moulding trade, 1935; returned to foundry, 1946. Mem. Nat. Exec. Council, Amalgamated Union of Foundry Workers, 1955–67; Gen. Sec., AUEW (Foundry Section), 1967–75. Chm. of Labour Party, 1972–73; Member: Race Relations Board; Ct of Inquiry into Flixborough explosion, 1974; Chm., Adv. Cttee on Asbestos, 1976–79. *Publication*: Labour: The Unions and the Party, 1973.

SIMPSON, William Wynn, OBE 1967; MA; FRSA; Hon. Life Vice-President, International Council of Christians and Jews, since 1981 (Hon. Chairman, 1978); *b* 11 July 1907; *m* 1933; one *s* one *d*. *Educ*: King Edward VI Grammar School, Camp Hill, Birmingham; Birmingham University; Wesley House and Fitzwilliam House, Cambridge. Asst Minister, Leysian Mission, London, 1929–32; Oxford Methodist Circuit, 1932–33; Vis. Student, Jews' College, London and research into contemp. Jewish problems, 1933–35; Minister, Amhurst Park Methodist Church, N London, 1935–38; General Secretary: Christian Council for Refugees, 1938–42; Council of Christians and Jews, 1942–74. Vice-President: Greater London Assoc. for the Disabled; Pestalozzi Children's Village Trust. Member: Soc. for Old Testament Study; London Soc. for Study of Religion. *Publications*: Readings in the Old Testament, 1932; Youth and Antisemitism, 1938; Christians and Jews Today (Beckly Social Service Lecture), 1942; (with A. I. Polack) Jesus in the Background of History, 1957; Jewish Prayer and Worship, 1965; Mini-Commentary on Pentateuch (Jerusalem Bible), 1969; Light and Rejoicing: a Christian's understanding of Jewish worship, 1976; pamphlets and articles on various aspects Jewish-Christian relations. *Recreation*: being alive. *Address*: 20 Sentis Court, 8 Carew Road, Northwood, Mddx HA6 3NG. *Club*: Athenæum.

SIMPSON-JONES, Peter Trevor, CBE 1971; Président d'Honneur, Société Française des Industries Lucas, since 1980 (Président-Directeur Général, 1957–80); *b* 20 March 1914; *s* of Frederick Henry Jones and Constance Agnès Simpson; *m* 1948, Marie-Lucy Sylvain; one *s* one *d*. *Educ*: Royal Navy School. British Chamber of Commerce, France: Vice-Pres., 1967–68 and 1970–72; Pres., 1968–70. Chevalier de la Légion d'Honneur, 1948, Officier 1973. *Recreation*: yachting. *Address*: 50 rue du Château, 92 Boulogne-sur-Seine, France. *T*: 825–01–20. *Clubs*: Special Forces; Polo (Paris).

SIMPSON-ORLEBAR, Michael Keith Orlebar, CMG 1982; HM Diplomatic Service; Ambassador to Portugal, since 1986; *b* 5 Feb. 1932; *s* of Aubrey Orlebar Simpson, Royal Artillery and Laura Violet, *d* of Captain Frederick Keith-Jones; *m* 1964, Rosita Duarte Triana; two *s* one *d*. *Educ*: Eton; Christ Church, Oxford (MA). 2nd Lieut, KRRC, 1950–51. Joined Foreign Service, 1954; 3rd Sec., Tehran, 1955–57; FO, 1957–62; Private Sec. to Parly Under-Sec. of State, 1960–62; 1st Sec. (Commercial) and Consul, Bogotá, 1962–65; seconded to Urwick, Orr and Partners Ltd, 1966; FO, 1966–68; 1st Sec., Paris, 1969–72; Counsellor (Commercial), Tehran, 1972–76; Head of UN Dept, FCO, 1977–80; Minister, HM Embassy, Rome, 1980–83; Head of British Interests Section, Tehran, 1983–85. *Recreations*: gardening, fishing. *Address*: c/o Foreign and Commonwealth Office, SW1A 2AH. *Club*: Travellers'.

SIMS, Prof. Geoffrey Donald, OBE 1971; FEng 1980; Vice-Chancellor, University of Sheffield, since 1974; *b* 13 Dec. 1926; *s* of Albert Edward Hope Sims and Jessie Elizabeth Sims; *m* 1949, Pamela Audrey Richings; one *s* two *d*. *Educ*: Wembley County Grammar School; Imperial College of Science and Technology, London. Research physicist, GEC, 1948–54; Sen. Scientific Officer, UKAEA, 1954–56; Lecturer/Senior Lecturer, University College, London, 1956–63; University of Southampton: Prof. and Head of Dept of Electronics, 1963–74; Dean, Faculty of Engrg, 1967–70; Senior Dep. Vice-Chancellor, 1970–72. Member: Council, British Association for the Advancement of Science, 1965–69 (Chm., Sheffield Area Council, 1974–); EDC for Electronics Industry, 1966–75; Adv. Cttee for Scientific and Technical Information, 1969–74; CNAA Electrical Engineering Bd, 1970–73; Planning Cttee for British Library, 1971–73 (Chm., British Library R&D Adv. Cttee, 1975–81); Adv. Council, Science Museum, 1972–84; British Nat. Cttee for Physics, 1972–78; Royal Soc. Cttee on Sci. Information, 1972–81; Electronics Res. Council, 1973–74; Annan Cttee on Future of Broadcasting, 1974–77; Naval Educn Adv. Cttee, 1974–79; Trent RHA, 1975–84; British Council Engrg and Tech. Adv. Cttee, 1976–84 (Chm.); Interim Action Cttee on British Film Industry, 1977–81; EEC Adv. Cttee on Scientific and Technical Trng, 1977–81; Univs Council for Adult and Continuing Educn, 1978–84 (Chm., 1980–84); CNAA, 1979–83; Liaison Cttee on Highly Qualified Technol Manpower, 1979–82; Council, Nat. Inst. of Adult Educn, 1980–84; SRC, later SERC Engrg Bd, 1980–84; Inter Univ. and Polytechnic Council, 1981– (IUC and Exec. Cttee, 1974–81; Vice-Chm., IUPC, 1985–); Cttee for Internat. Co operation in Higher Educn, 1981– (Vice-Chm., 1985–); EEC Adv. Cttee on Programme Management, 1981–; BBC Engrg Adv. Cttee, 1981– (Chm.); Council, Fellowship of Engrg, 1986–; Museums and Galleries Commn, 1983–; Hong Kong City Polytechnic Sub-cttee, 1984–; Hon. Dep. Treas., ACU, 1984–. UK rep. on Perm. Cttee of Conf. of European Rectors, 1981–84; *ad personem* rep. on Perm. Cttee and Bureau of Conf. of European Rectors, 1984–. Chairman of Governors: Southampton College of Technology, 1967–69; Southampton Sch. of Navigation, 1972–74; Sheffield High Sch., 1978–85; Fellow, Midland Chapter, Woodard Schools, 1977–; Custos, Worksop Coll., 1984–. FIEE 1963; FIERE 1966; FCGI 1980. Hon. DSc Southampton, 1979. Founder Mem., 1966, Reviews Editor, 1969–, Jl of Materials Science Bd. *Publications*: Microwave Tubes and Semiconductor Devices (with I. M. Stephenson), 1963; Variational Techniques in Electromagnetism (trans.), 1965; numerous papers on microwaves, electronics and education in learned jls. *Recreations*: golf, travel, music. *Address*: The Vice-Chancellor's Office, Sheffield University, Sheffield S10 2TN. *Club*: Athenæum.

SIMS, Monica Louie, OBE 1971; MA, LRAM, LGSM; Director of Production, Children's Film and Television Foundation, since 1985; *d* of late Albert Charles Sims and Eva Elizabeth Preen, both of Gloucester. *Educ*: Girls' High School, Gloucester; St Hugh's College, Oxford. Tutor in Literature and Drama, Dept of Adult Educn, Hull Univ., 1947–50; Educn Tutor, Nat. Fedn of Women's Institutes, 1950–53; BBC Sound Talks Producer, 1953–55; BBC Television Producer, 1955–64; Editor of Woman's Hour, BBC, 1964–67; Head of Children's Programmes, BBC TV, 1967–78; Controller, BBC Radio 4, 1978–83; Dir of Programmes, BBC Radio, 1983–84. Vice-Pres., British Bd of Film Classification, 1985–. *Address*: 97 Gloucester Terrace, W2.

SIMS, Roger Edward, JP; MP (C) Chislehurst since Feb. 1974; *b* 27 Jan. 1930; *s* of late Herbert William Sims and of Annie Amy Savidge; *m* 1957, Angela Mathews; two *s* one *d*. *Educ*: City Boys' Grammar Sch., Leicester; St Olave's Grammar Sch., London. MInstM. National Service, 1948–50. Coutts & Co., 1950–51; Campbell Booker Carter Ltd, 1953–62; Dept Man., Dodwell & Co. Ltd, 1962–; Dir, Inchcape International Ltd, 1981–. Contested (C) Shoreditch and Finsbury, 1966 and 1970; PPS to Home Sec., 1979–83. Mem., Central Exec. Cttee, NSPCC, 1980–. Mem. Chislehurst and Sidcup UDC, 1956–62; JP Bromley, 1960–72 (Dep. Chm. 1970–72); Chm., Juvenile Panel, 1971–72. *Recreations*: swimming; music, especially singing (Mem. Royal Choral Soc. from 1950). *Address*: 68 Towncourt Crescent, Petts Wood, Orpington, Kent BR5 1PJ. *T*: Orpington 25676; House of Commons, SW1A 0AA. *Club*: Bromley Conservative (Bromley).

SIMSON, Michael Ronald Fraser, OBE 1966; Secretary of the National Corporation for the Care of Old People, 1948–73; *b* 9 Oct. 1913; *er s* of Ronald Stuart Fraser Simson and Ethel Alice Henderson; *m* 1939, Elizabeth Joan Wilkinson; one *s*. *Educ*: Winchester Coll.; Christ Church, Oxford. OUAFC 1936 and 1937. Asst Master, West Downs Sch., 1938–40; RNVR, 1941–46; Asst Sec., Nat. Fedn of Housing Socs, 1946–48. Member: Min. of Labour Cttee on Employment of Older Men and Women, 1953–55; Cttee on Local Authority and Allied Personal Social Services (Seebohm Cttee), 1966–68; Supplementary Benefits Commn, 1967–76; Adv. Cttee on Rent Rebates and Rent Allowances, 1973–75, resigned 1975; Personal Social Services Council, 1973–78. *Recreations*: gardening, interested in all forms of sport. *Address*: Summerhill, Kingsdon, Somerton, Somerset. *T*: Ilchester 840858.

SINATRA, Francis Albert, (Frank); singer, actor, film producer, publisher; *b* Hoboken, New Jersey, USA, 12 Dec. 1915; *s* of late Natalie and Martin Sinatra; *m* 1st, 1939, Nancy Barbato (marr. diss.); one *s* two *d*; 2nd 1951, Ava Gardner (marr. diss.); 3rd, 1966, Mia Farrow (marr. diss.); 4th, 1976, Barbara Marx. *Educ*: Demarest High School, New Jersey. Started in radio, 1936; then became band singer with orchestras. First appearance in films, 1943. *Films include*: From Here to Eternity (Oscar for best supporting actor, 1953), Anchors Aweigh, On the Town, The Tender Trap, High Society, Guys and Dolls, The Man with the Golden Arm, Johnny Concho, The Joker is Wild, Kings Go Forth, Some Came Running, A Hole in the Head, Ocean's 11, The Devil at Four O'Clock, Sergeants Three, Manchurian Candidate, Come Blow Your Horn, Four for Texas, Robin and the Seven Hoods, None But the Brave, Marriage on the Rocks, Von Ryan's Express, Assault on a Queen, The Naked Runner, Tony Rome, The Detective, Lady in Cement, Dirty Dingus Magee, The First Deadly Sin, Cannonball Run II. Owner music publishing companies, etc. Jean Hersholt Humanitarian Award, 1971. *Publications*: composed numerous popular songs. *Address*: Sinatra Enterprises, Goldwyn Studios, 1041 N Formosa, Los Angeles, Calif 90046, USA.

SINCLAIR; see Alexander-Sinclair.

SINCLAIR, family name of **Earl of Caithness**, **Viscount Thurso**, and **Baron Sinclair of Cleeve**.

SINCLAIR, 17th Lord, *cr* 1449 (Scotland); **Charles Murray Kennedy St Clair**, LVO 1953; Major, late Coldstream Guards; Extra Equerry to Queen Elizabeth the Queen Mother since 1953; Lord-Lieutenant, Dumfries and Galloway Region (District of Stewartry), since 1982 (Vice-Lord-Lieutenant, 1977–82); Member Queen's Body Guard for Scotland (Royal Company of Archers); *b* 21 June 1914; *o s* of 16th Lord Sinclair, MVO, and Violet (*d* 1953), *d* of Col J. Murray Kennedy, MVO; *S* father, 1957; *m* 1968, Anne Lettice, *yr d* of Sir Richard Cotterell, 5th Bt, CBE; one *s* two *d*. *Educ*: Eton; Magdalene Coll., Cambridge. Served War of 1939–45, Palestine, 1939 (wounded, despatches). Retired as Major Coldstream Guards, 1947. Portcullis Pursuivant of Arms, 1949–57; York Herald, 1957–68, retired. A Representative Peer for Scotland, 1959–63. DL Kirkcudbrightshire, 1969. *Heir*: *s* Master of Sinclair, *qv*. *Address*: Knocknalling, St John's Town of Dalry, Castle Douglas, Kirkcudbrightshire, Scotland. *T*: 221. *Club*: New (Edinburgh).

SINCLAIR, Master of; Hon. Matthew Murray Kennedy St Clair; *b* 9 Dec. 1968; *s* and *heir* of 17th Lord Sinclair, *qv*.

SINCLAIR OF CLEEVE, 3rd Baron *cr* 1957, of Cleeve, Somerset; **John Lawrence Robert Sinclair**; Teaching Support Staff Governor at an Inner London comprehensive school, since 1985; *b* 6 Jan. 1953; *s* of 2nd Baron Sinclair of Cleeve, OBE, and of Patricia, *d* of late Major Lawrence Hellyer; *S* father, 1985. *Educ*: Winchester College; Manchester Univ. *Recreations*: motor cycling, mime, music. *Address*: c/o Toppinghoe Hall, Hatfield Peverel, Essex CM3 2EX.

SINCLAIR, Alexander Riddell; HM Diplomatic Service, retired; *b* 28 Aug. 1917; *s* of Henry W. Sinclair and Mary Turner; *m* 1948, Alice Evelyn Nottingham; three *d*. *Educ*: Greenock High School. DipCAM. Inland Revenue, 1935–37; Admty, 1938–47 (Comdr RNVR, 1945–46); 2nd Sec., HM Embassy, Moscow, 1947–48; Vice-Consul: Detroit, 1949; Mosul, 1950; FO, 1952; 1st Secretary, HM Embassy: Saigon, 1953–56; Amman, 1957–58; FO, 1959; 1st Sec. (Cultural), Budapest, 1962; FO, 1964; 1st Secretary (Information): Beirut, 1967–70; Rome, 1970–71; Consul-Gen., Genoa, 1972–76; FCO Library, 1977–85. Silver Jubilee Medal, 1977. *Publications*: literary articles in learned jls. *Recreations*: reading, book browsing, walking. *Address*: 7 Berry Walk, Ashtead, Surrey KT21 1DT. *Club*: Civil Service.

SINCLAIR, Andrew Annandale; author; Managing Director, Lorrimer Publishing, Timon Films, since 1967; *b* 21 Jan. 1935; *m* 1960, Marianne, *d* of Mr and Mrs Arsène Alexandre; *m* 1972, Miranda, *o d* of Mr and Hon. Mrs George Seymour; two *s*; *m* 1984, Sonia Lady Melchett, *d* of Dr and Mrs Roland Graham. *Educ:* Eton Coll.; Trinity Coll., Cambridge (BA, PhD); Harvard. Ensign, Coldstream Guards, 1953–55. Harkness Fellow of the Commonwealth Fund, 1959–61; Dir of Historical Studies, Churchill Coll., Cambridge, 1961–63; Fellow of American Council of Learned Societies, 1963–64; Lectr in American History, University Coll., London, 1965–67. Dir/Writer Mem., ACTT. FRSL 1973; Fellow Soc. of American Historians, 1974. Somerset Maugham Literary Prize, 1966. *Film:* (dir) Under Milk Wood, 1971. *Publications:* The Breaking of Bumbo, 1958; My Friend Judas, 1959; The Project, 1960; Prohibition, 1962; The Hallelujah Bum, 1963; The Available Man: Warren E. Harding, 1964; The Better Half, 1964; The Raker, 1965; Concise History of the United States, 1966; Gog, 1967; The Greek Anthology, 1967; Adventures in the Skin Trade, 1968; The Last of the Best, 1969; Guevara, 1970; Magog, 1972; Dylan Thomas: poet of his people, 1975; The Surrey Cat, 1976; The Savage, 1977; Jack: the biography of Jack London, 1977; A Patriot for Hire, 1978; John Ford, 1979; The Facts in the Case of E. A. Poe, 1979; Corsair, 1981; The Other Victoria, 1981; Sir Walter Raleigh and the Age of Discovery, 1984; Beau Bumbo, 1985; The Red and the Blue, 1986. *Recreations:* old cities, old movies. *Address:* 16 Tite Street, SW3.

SINCLAIR, Sir Clive (Marles), Kt 1983; Chairman: Sinclair Research Ltd, since 1979; Sinclair Browne Ltd, since 1981; *b* 30 July 1940; *s* of George William Carter Sinclair and Thora Edith Ella (*née* Marles); *m* 1962, Ann (*née* Trevor Briscoe) (marr. diss. 1985); two *s* one *d*. *Educ:* Boxgrove Prep. Sch., Guildford; Highgate; Reading; St George's Coll., Weybridge. Editor, Bernards Publishers Ltd, 1958–61; Chm., Sinclair Radionics Ltd, 1962–79. Vis. Fellow, Robinson Coll., Cambridge, 1982–; Vis. Prof., Dept of Elec. Engrg, Imperial Coll. of Science and Technol., London, 1984– (Hon. Fellow, 1984). Chm., British Mensa, 1980–. Hon. Fellow UMIST, 1984. Hon. DSc: Bath, 1983; Warwick, 1983; Heriot-Watt, 1983. Mullard Award, Royal Soc., 1984. *Publications:* Practical Transistor Receivers, 1959; British Semiconductor Survey, 1963. *Recreations:* music, poetry, mathematics, science. *Address:* 32 Donne Place, SW3 2NH. *T:* 01–589 7907. *Club:* Carlton.

SINCLAIR, Prof. David Cecil; Emeritus Professor, University of Western Australia; Director of Postgraduate Medical Education, Queen Elizabeth II Medical Centre, Western Australia, 1975–80; *b* 28 Aug. 1915; *s* of Norman James Sinclair and Annie Smart Sinclair; *m* 1945, Grace Elizabeth Simondson, Melbourne, Vic.; one *s* one *d*. *Educ:* Merchiston Castle Sch.; St Andrews University. MB, ChB (Commendation) St Andrews, 1937; MD (Hons and Rutherford Gold Medal) St Andrews, 1947; MA Oxon, 1948; DSc Western Australia, 1965. Served in RAMC, 1940–46: AMF, 1943–45; Head of Physiology Sect., Aust. Chem. Warfare Research and Experimental Stn, 1943–44; Dep. Chief Supt, Aust. Field Experimental Stn, 1944–45. Sen. Res. Off., Dept of Human Anatomy, Oxford, 1946–49; Univ. Demonstrator in Anatomy, Oxford, 1949–56; Lectr in Anatomy, Pembroke Coll., Oxford, 1950–56; Lectr in Anatomy, Ruskin Sch. of Fine Art, 1950–56; first Prof. of Anatomy, Univ. of W Australia, 1957–64, Dean of Med. Sch., 1964; Regius Prof. of Anatomy, Univ. of Aberdeen, 1965–75. FRCSE 1966. Life Governor, Aust. Postgrad. Fedn in Medicine, 1983. *Publications:* Medical Students and Medical Sciences, 1955; An Introduction to Functional Anatomy, 1957 (5th edn 1975); A Student's Guide to Anatomy, 1961; Cutaneous Sensation, 1967, Japanese edn 1969; Human Growth after Birth, 1969 (4th edn 1985); Muscles and Fascia (section in Cunningham's Anatomy), 11th edn, 1972, 12th edn, 1981; Basic Medical Education, 1972; The Nerves of the Skin (section in Physiology and Pathophysiology of the Skin, ed Jarrett), 1973; Growth, section in Textbook of Human Anatomy (ed Hamilton), 1976; Mechanisms of Cutaneous Sensation, 1981; papers on chemical warfare, neurological anatomy, experimental psychology, and medical education; Editor, Jl of Anatomy, 1970–73. *Recreations:* reading, writing, photography, chess problems. *Address:* Four Winds, Barclay Park, Aboyne AB3 5JF.

SINCLAIR, Ernest Keith, CMG 1966; OBE 1946; DFC 1943; journalist-consultant; Commissioner, Australian Heritage Commission, 1976–81; Associate Commissioner, Industries Assistance Commission, 1974–81; *b* 13 November 1914; 2nd *s* of Ernest and Florence Sinclair, Victoria, Australia; *m* 1949, Jill, *d* of John and Muriel Nelder, Pangbourne; one *s*. *Educ:* Melbourne High School, Australia. Literary staff, The Age, 1932–38. Served War of 1939–45, RAF, 1940–45 (despatches, 1944). Associate Editor, The Age, Melbourne, 1946–59, Editor, 1959–66. Consultant to Dept of Prime Minister and Cabinet, 1967–74 and 1977–81 (to Prime Minister of Australia, 1967–72). Dep. Chm., Australian Tourist Commn, 1969–75 (Mem. 1966). Director: Australian Assoc. Press, 1959–66 (Chm., 1965–66); Gen. Television Corp. (Melbourne), 1959–66; Australian Paper Manufacturers Ltd, 1966–86; Member: Australian Council, Internat. Press Inst., 1959–66; Schools Bd for the Humanities, Victoria Inst. of Colleges, 1969–72 (Chm.); Library Council of Victoria, 1966–78 (Dep. Pres., 1969–78); Council, Royal Historical Soc. of Victoria, 1981– (Hon. Editor, Jl, 1982–); Observer, Nat. Capital Planning Cttee, 1967–72; Dep. Chm., Building Trustees Library Council, Nat. Museum and Sci. Museum of Victoria, 1976–78. *Recreations:* gardening, reading. *Address:* 138 Toorak Road West, South Yarra, Victoria 3141, Australia. *T:* 267–1405. *Clubs:* Press (London); Melbourne (Melbourne).

SINCLAIR, Rear-Adm. Erroll Norman, CB 1963; DSC 1944; retired; *b* 6 Mar. 1909; *s* of late Col John Norman Sinclair, RHA; *m* 1940, Frances Elinor Knox-Gore; two *s*. *Educ:* RNC Dartmouth. Served HMS Cairo, 1936–38; HMS Gallant, 1938–40 (Dunkirk); in comd HMS Fortune, 1940, HMS Antelope, 1941–43, N African Landings; in comd HMS Eskimo, 10th Destroyer Flotilla, 1943–45 (DSC); First Lieut, RN Barracks, Chatham, 1946, Comdr 1946; Exec. Officer, RN Air Station, Eglinton, 1947; Staff Officer Ops to C-in-C, S Atlantic Station, Simonstown, and UK Liaison Officer to S Af. Naval Forces, until 1951. In comd HMS St Kitts, 5th Destroyer Sqdn, Home Fleet, 1951–53; Capt. 1952; Pres. Second Admiralty Interview Board, 1953–54; Naval Attaché at Ankara, Teheran and Tel Aviv, 1955; Capt. (D) 4th Destroyer Sqdn, HMS Agincourt, 1957–59; in comd HMS Sea Eagle and Sen. Naval Officer N Ireland, and Naval Director, Joint A/S School, Londonderry, 1959–61; Flag Officer, Gibraltar, and Admiral Superintendent, HM Dockyard, Gibraltar, also NATO Commander of Gibraltar sub areas, 1962–64; retd list, 1964; Naval Regional Officer (North), 1964–68. *Address:* Island Cottage, Wittersham, Kent. *T:* Wittersham 354. *Club:* Rye Golf.

SINCLAIR, Maj.-Gen. George Brian, CB 1983; CBE 1975; FIHE; Engineer-in-Chief (Army), 1980–83; *b* 21 July 1928; *s* of Thomas S. Sinclair and Blanche Sinclair; *m* 1953, Edna Margaret Richardson; two *s* one *d*. *Educ:* Christ's College, Finchley; RMA Sandhurst. Commissioned, Royal Engineers, 1948; served UK, BAOR, Korea, and Christmas Island, 1948–66; Directing Staff, Staff College, Camberley, 1967–69; CRE, Near East, 1970–71; Col GS, HQ 1st British Corps, 1972–74; Nat. Defence Coll., India, 1975; Commandant Royal School of Military Engineering, 1976–77; BGS, Military Operations, MoD, 1978–80. Col Comdt, RE, 1983–; Hon. Col, Airfield Damage Repair Sqdns, RE(Vols)TA, 1984–. Governor, King's Sch., Rochester, 1984–. *Recreations:* hill walking, running, bird watching and discussion. *Address:* 6 Prospect Row, Brompton, Gillingham, Kent. *T:* Medway 42364. *Club:* Army and Navy.

SINCLAIR, Sir George (Evelyn), Kt 1960; CMG 1956; OBE 1950; engaged in voluntary work on behalf of independent schools in UK and on population and development worldwide; *b* Cornwall, 6 November 1912; 2nd *s* of late F. Sinclair, Chynance, St Buryan, Cornwall; *m* 1st, 1941, Katharine Jane Burdekin (*d* 1971); one *s* three *d*; 2nd, 1972, Mary Violet, *widow* of George Lester Sawday, Saxmundham, Suffolk. *Educ:* Abingdon School; Pembroke College, Oxford (MA; Hon. Fellow, 1986). Entered Colonial Administrative Service, 1936; appointed to Gold Coast Administration; Asst District Comr, 1937. Military service, 1940–43. District Commissioner, Gold Coast, 1943; seconded to Colonial Office, 1943–45; Sec. to Commn on Higher Education in West Africa, 1943–45; returned to Gold Coast, 1945; Senior Assistant Colonial Secretary, 1947; Principal Assistant Secretary, 1950; Regional Officer, Trans-Volta Togoland Region, 1952; Deputy Governor, Cyprus, 1955–60; retired, 1961. MP (C) Dorking, Surrey, Oct. 1964–1979. Member, Parly Select Committees on: Procedure, 1965–66; Race Relations, 1969–70; Overseas Aid, 1969–70; Race Relations and Immigration, 1970–74; Members Interests, 1975; Abortion Act (Amendment) Bill; Joint Secretary: Cons. Parly Commonwealth Affairs Cttee, 1966–68; Cons. Parly Educn Cttee, 1974–79, Vice-Chm., 1974; Member: Intermediate Technology Develt Gp (Vice-Pres., 1966–79; Dir, 1979–82); Nat. Exec. Cttee, UNA (UK Branch), 1968–70; Council, Overseas Services Resettlement Bureau; Council of PDSA, 1964–70; Council, Christian Aid, 1973–78; Steering Cttee, UN/FPA World Conf. of Parliamentarians on population and develt, 1978–79; Vice-Chm., Family Planning Assoc., 1979–81; Consultant: UN Fund for Population Affairs, 1979–82; IPPF, 1979–; special advr to Global Cttee on Population and Develt, 1982–. Trustee: Runnymede Trust, 1969–75; Human Rights Trust, 1971–74; Physically Handicapped and Able Bodied (Foundn Trustee), 1973–81; Wyndham Place Trust. Mem., Wimbledon Borough Council, 1962–65; Chm., Bd of Governors, Abingdon School, 1971–79; Member, Board of Governors: Felixstowe Coll., 1980–; Campion Sch., Athens, 1983–; Chm., Assoc. of Governing Bodies of Independent Schools, 1979–84 (Mem., 1973–); Member: Direct Grant Jt Cttee, 1974–80; Indep. Schools Jt Council, 1979–84 (Chm. 1980–83, Dep. Chm., 1984); Council, Oxford Soc., 1982–. *Recreations:* golf, fishing. *Address:* Carlton Rookery, Saxmundham, Suffolk; South Minack, Porthcurno, Cornwall. *Clubs:* Athenæum, Royal Commonwealth Society; Aldeburgh Golf, Aldeburgh Yacht.

SINCLAIR, Hugh Macdonald, DM, MA, DSc, FRCP, LMSSA; Director, International Institute of Human Nutrition, since 1972; Fellow, Magdalen College, Oxford, 1937–80, now Emeritus Fellow (Vice-President, 1956–58); *b* Duddingston House, Edinburgh, 4 Feb. 1910; 2nd *s* of late Col H. M. Sinclair, CB, CMG, CBE, RE, and late Rosalie, *d* of Sir John Jackson, CVO, LLD; unmarried. *Educ:* Winchester (Senior Science Prize); Oriel College, Oxford. First Cl. Hons Animal Physiology, 1932; Gotch Prize, 1933; Senior Demy, Magdalen College, 1932–34; University Coll. Hosp. 1933–36 (Gold and Silver Medals for Clinical Medicine); Radcliffe Schol. in Pharmacology, 1934; Radcliffe Travelling Fellow, 1937–38; Rolleston Prize, 1938. University Demonstrator and Lectr in Biochemistry, Oxford, 1937–47; Director, Oxford Nutrition Survey, 1942–47; Hon. Nutrition Consultant (with rank of Brig.), CCG, 1945–47; Lectr in Physiology and Biochemistry, Magdalen College, Oxford, 1937–76; Reader in Human Nutrition and Dir, Lab. of Human Nutrition, Oxford, 1951–58; Vis. Prof. in Food Science, Univ. of Reading, 1970–80. Lectures: Cutter, Harvard, 1951; Schuman, Los Angeles, 1962; Golden Acres, Dallas, 1963; Bergami, Pisa, 1985. Member: Physiological Soc.; Biochemical Soc.; Med. Research Soc.; Soc. for Experimental Biology; Soc. Philomathique; Fellow: Royal Soc. of Chem.; Inst. Biol.; Amer. Public Health Soc.; Hollywood Acad. Med. Master, Apothecaries Co., 1967–68. Hon. DSc Baldwin-Wallace, USA, 1968. US Medal of Freedom with Silver Palm; Officer of Order of Orange Nassau, Holland. Editor-in-Chief, Internat. Encyclopedia of Food and Nutrition (24 vols), 1969–. *Publications:* papers on Human Nutrition and on Brain Metabolism in scientific and med. jls; Use of Vitamins in Medicine, in Whitla's Pharmacy, Materia Medica and Therapeutics (13th edn), 1939; Vitamins in Treatment, in Modern Therapeutics (Practitioner Handbooks), 1941; Nutrition, in Aspects of Modern Science, 1951; A Short History of Anatomical Teaching in Oxford (with A. H. T. Robb-Smith), 1950; (ed) The Work of Sir Robert McCarrison, 1953; (with McCarrison) Nutrition and Health, 1953 and 1961; (with Prof. Jelliffe) Nicholl's Tropical Nutrition, 1961; (with F. C. Rodger) Metabolic and Nutritional Eye Diseases, 1968; (with D. Hollingsworth) Hutchison's Food and Principles of Nutrition, 1969; (with G. R. Howat) World Nutrition and Nutrition Education, 1980; articles on med. educn. *Recreations:* tennis, cricket, and gardening. *Address:* International Nutrition Foundation, High Street, Sutton Courtenay, Oxon OX14 4AW. *T:* Abingdon 848246; Lady Place, Sutton Courtenay, Oxon. *Clubs:* Athenæum, MCC.

SINCLAIR, Hon. Ian David, OC 1979; QC (Can.) 1961; Member, Senate of Canada, since 1983; *b* Winnipeg, 27 Dec. 1913; *s* of late John David Sinclair and late Lillian Sinclair; *m* 1942, Ruth Beatrice, *d* of Robert Parsons Drennan, Winnipeg; two *s* two *d*. *Educ:* public schs, Winnipeg; Univ. of Manitoba (BA Econs 1937); Manitoba Law School (LLB 1941). Barrister, Guy Chappell & Co., Winnipeg, 1937–41; Lectr in Torts, Univ. of Manitoba, 1942–43; joined Canadian Pacific Law Dept as Asst Solicitor, Winnipeg, 1942; Solicitor, Montreal, 1946; Asst to General Counsel, 1951; General Solicitor, 1953; Vice-Pres. and Gen. Counsel, 1960; Vice-Pres., Law, 1960; Canadian Pacific Railway Co.: Vice-Pres., Dir and Mem. Exec. Cttee, 1961; Pres., 1966; Chief Exec. Officer, 1969; Chm. and Chief Exec. Officer: Canadian Pacific Ltd, 1972–81; Canadian Pacific Enterprises Ltd, 1972–82 (Chm., 1982–84); Director: Canadian Fund, Inc.; Canadian Investment Fund, Ltd; Canadian Marconi Co.; Union Carbide Canada Ltd; Public Dir, Investment Dealers Assoc. of Canada; Mem., Internat. Adv. Cttee, Chase Manhattan Bank, N America. Hon. LLD Manitoba, 1967; Hon. DBA Laval, 1981; Hon. DCL Acadia, 1982. *Address:* Suite 1100, University Place, 123 Front Street West, Toronto, Ont M5J 2M2, Canada. *T:* (416) 860–0144. *Clubs:* Toronto (Toronto); Rideau (Ottawa).

SINCLAIR, Rt. Hon. Ian (McCahon), PC 1977; MHR; Leader, National Party of Australia, since 1984 (Deputy Leader, 1971–84); Leader of the Opposition in the House, and Shadow Minister for Defence, since 1983; *b* 10 June 1929; *s* of George McCahon Sinclair and Gertrude Hazel Sinclair; *m* 1st, 1956, Margaret Tarrant (*d* 1967); one *s* two *d*; 2nd, 1970, Rosemary Fenton; one *s*. *Educ:* Knox Grammar Sch., Wahroonga, NSW; Sydney Univ. BA, LLB. Mem. Legislative Council, NSW, 1961–63; MHR for New England, 1963–; Minister for: Social Services, 1965–68; Shipping and Transport, 1968–71; Trade and Industry (Minister Assisting Minister), 1966–71; Primary Industry, 1971–72; Leader of House for Opposition, 1972–75; Country Party spokesman for Defence, Foreign Affairs, Law and Agriculture, 1973; Opposition spokesman on primary industry, 1974–75; Minister for Agriculture and Minister for N Territory, Nov.-Dec. 1975; Govt Leader in the House of Representatives, 1975–82; Minister for: Primary Industry, 1975–80; Communications, 1980–82; Defence, 1982–83. *Address:* Parliament House, Canberra, ACT 2600, Australia. *T:* (062) 726661. *Clubs:* Australian, American, Union (Sydney); Tamworth; Killara Golf.

SINCLAIR, Sir Ian (McTaggart), KCMG 1977 (CMG 1972); QC 1979; Barrister-at-Law; *b* 14 Jan. 1926; *s* of late John Sinclair, company director; *m* 1954, Barbara Elizabeth (*née* Lenton); two *s* one *d*. *Educ*: Merchiston Castle Sch. (Scholar); King's Coll., Cambridge; BA 1948, LLB 1949 (1st cl. hons). Served Intelligence Corps, 1944–47. Called to the Bar, Middle Temple, 1952; Bencher, 1980. Asst Legal Adviser, Foreign Office, 1950–56; Legal Adviser, HM Embassy, Bonn, 1957–60; Asst Legal Adviser, FO, 1960–64; Legal Adviser, UK Mission to the UN, New York, and HM Embassy, Washington, 1964–67; Foreign and Commonwealth Office: Legal Counsellor, 1967–71; Dep. Legal Advr, 1971–72; Second Legal Advr, 1973–75; Legal Advr, 1976–84. Has been Legal Adviser to UK delegn at numerous internat. confs, incl. Geneva Conf. on Korea and Indo-China, 1954, and Brussels negotiations for UK entry into the EEC, 1961–63, Dep. Chm., UK delegn to Law of Treaties Conf., Vienna, 1968–69; Legal Adviser to UK delegn on negotiations for UK entry into EEC, 1970–72; Member: Bureau of European Cttee on Legal Co-operation, Council of Europe, 1979–81; Panel of Conciliators, Annex to Vienna Convention on Law of Treaties, 1981–; Internat. Law Commn, 1981–. Mem., Committee of Management: British Inst. of Internat. and Comparative Law, 1976–; Inst. of Advanced Legal Studies, 1980–84. Associate Mem., Inst de Droit Internat., 1983. *Publications*: Vienna Convention on the Law of Treaties, 1973, 2nd edn 1984; articles in British Yearbook of International Law, International and Comparative Law Qly and other legal jls. *Recreations*: golf, fishing, watching sea-birds. *Address*: Lassington, Chithurst, Petersfield, Hants GU31 5EU. *T*: Midhurst 5370; 10B South Park Road, Wimbledon, SW19 8ST. *T*: 01–543 1843; (chambers) 2 Hare Court, Temple, EC4. *T*: 01–583 1770. *Club*: Athenæum.

SINCLAIR, Isabel Lillias, (Mrs J. G. MacDonald), QC (Scotland) 1964; Sheriff of Lothian and Borders (formerly Roxburgh, Berwick, and Selkirk), 1968–79, now Honorary Sheriff; Honorary Sheriff of Bute; *d* of William Sinclair, Glasgow, and Isabella (*née* Thomson), Glasgow; *m* 1938, J. Gordon MacDonald, BL, Solicitor, Glasgow. *Educ*: Shawlands Academy; Glasgow Univ.; Edinburgh Univ. MA 1932; BL 1946. Worked as a newspaper-woman from 1932. Admitted to Faculty of Advocates, Edinburgh, 1949. Sheriff-Substitute of Lanarkshire at Airdrie, 1966–68. *Address*: 30 Ravelston Garden, Edinburgh EH4 3LE. *T*: 031–337 7979; Ambrisbeg by Rothesay, Isle of Bute. *T*: Rothesay 83202. *Club*: Royal Scottish Automobile (Glasgow).

SINCLAIR, Sir John (Rollo Norman Blair), 9th Bt, *cr* 1704; *b* 4 Nov. 1928; *s* of Sir Ronald Norman John Charles Udny Sinclair, 8th Bt, TD, and Reba Blair (Company Comdt, Auxiliary Territorial Service, 1938–41) (*d* 1985), *d* of Anthony Inglis, MS, Lismore, Ayrshire; *S* father 1952. *Educ*: Wellington College. Lt Intelligence Corps, 1948–49. Director: The Lucis Trust, 1957–61; The Human Development Trust, 1970–; Natural Health Foundn, 1982–. *Publications*: The Mystical Ladder, 1968; The Other Universe, 1972; The Alice Bailey Inheritance, 1984. *Heir*: *cousin* Patrick Robert Richard Sinclair [*b* 21 May 1936; *m* 1974, Susan Catherine Beresford, *e d* of Geoffrey Clive Davies; one *s* one *d*]. *Address*: (seat) Barrock House, Wick, Caithness.
See also Baroness Masham of Ilton.

SINCLAIR, Prof. Sir Keith, Kt 1985; CBE 1983; Professor of History, University of Auckland, since 1963; *b* 5 Dec. 1922; *s* of Ernest Duncan and Florence Sinclair; *m* 1st, 1947, Mary Edith Land; four *s*; 2nd, 1976, Raewyn Mary Dalziel. *Educ*: Mount Albert Grammar Sch.; Auckland University Coll.; MA, PhD (NZ); LittD (Auckland); Univ. of London. War service, NZ Army, 1941–43; RNZNVR, in UK, 1944–45; Lectr in History, 1947, Senior Lectr, 1952, Associate Prof., 1960, Auckland University Coll. Carnegie Commonwealth Fellow, Inst. of Commonwealth Studies, London, 1954–55; Carnegie Travelling Grant, USA, 1955; Vis. Fellow, Inst. of Advanced Studies, ANU, 1967, 1978, 1983; Smuts Vis. Fellow, Cambridge, 1968–69. Labour candidate, Eden electorate, 1969 (elected for 3 weeks, defeated on postal ballot). Chm., NZ Authors' Fund Cttee, 1973–85; Trustee, NZ Nat. Library, 1981–. *Publications*: Maori Land League, 1950; Songs for a Summer, 1952; Strangers or Beasts, 1954; Imperial Federation, 1955; Origins of the Maori Wars, 1957; A History of New Zealand, 1959, rev. edn 1980; (ed) The Maori King, by J. E. Gorst, 1959; (with W. F. Mandle) The Bank of New South Wales in New Zealand, 1961; (ed) Distance Looks Our Way, 1961; A Time to Embrace, 1963; (ed with R. M. Chapman) Studies of a Small Democracy, 1963; William Pember Reeves, 1965; The Firewheel Tree, 1973; Walter Nash, 1977; The Reefs of Fire, 1977; (with Wendy Harrex) Looking Back: a photographic history of New Zealand, 1978; History of the University of Auckland, 1983; (with Judith Bassett and Marcia Stenson) The Story of New Zealand, 1985; A Destiny Apart: New Zealand's search for national identity, 1986; articles in learned jls. *Recreations*: fishing, gardening. *Address*: 13 Mariposa Crescent, Birkenhead, Auckland 10, New Zealand. *T*: 485–057.

SINCLAIR, Air Vice-Marshal Sir Laurence (Frank), GC 1941; KCB 1957 (CB 1946); CBE 1943; DSO 1940 (and Bar, 1943); *b* 1908; *m* 1941, Valerie, *d* of Lt-Col Joseph Dalton White; one *s* one *d*. *Educ*: Imperial Service Coll.; RAF Coll. Cranwell. Comd No 110 Sqdn in 1940; Comd RAF Watton, 1941; Comd Tactical Light Bomber Force in North Africa and Italy, 1943–44; ADC to King George VI, 1943–44; subsequently Sen. Air Staff Officer, Balkan Air Force; Imperial Defence Coll., 1947; commanded No 2 Light Bomber Group (Germany), 1948–49; Assistant Commandant RAF Staff College, 1949–50; Commandant, Royal Air Force College Cranwell, 1950–52; Commandant, School of Land/Air Warfare, 1952–53; Asst Chief of the Air Staff (Operations), 1953–55; Comdr British Forces, Arabian Peninsula, 1955–57; Commandant Joint Services Staff College, 1958–60, retired from RAF. Controller of Ground Services, Min. of Aviation, 1960–61; Controller, Nat. Air Traffic Control Services, Min. of Aviation, and MoD, 1962–66. Legion of Merit (American), 1943; Legion of Honour, 1944; Partisan Star (Yugoslavia). *Address*: Haines Land, Great Brickhill, Milton Keynes MK17 9AQ.

SINCLAIR, Michael; *see* Shea, M. S. MacA.

SINCLAIR, Sir Ronald Ormiston, KBE 1963; Kt 1956; President, Court of Appeal: for the Bahamas and for Bermuda, 1965–70; for British Honduras, 1968–70; Chairman, Industrial Tribunals (England and Wales), 1966–69; *b* 2 May 1903; *yr s* of Rev. W. A. Sinclair, Auckland, NZ; *m* 1935, Ellen Isabel Entrican; two *s*. *Educ*: New Plymouth Boys' High School, NZ; Auckland University College, NZ; Balliol College, Oxford. Barrister and Solicitor of Supreme Court of New Zealand, 1924; LLM (NZ) (Hons) 1925; Administrative Service, Nigeria, 1931; Magistrate, Nigeria, 1936; Resident Magistrate, Northern Rhodesia, 1938; Barrister-at-Law, Middle Temple, 1939; Puisne Judge, Tanganyika, 1946; Chief Justice, Nyasaland, 1953–55; Vice-President, East African Court of Appeal, 1956–57, Pres., 1962–64; Chief Justice of Kenya, 1957–62. *Address*: 158 Victoria Avenue, Remuera, Auckland, New Zealand.

SINCLAIR-LOCKHART, Sir Simon (John Edward Francis), 15th Bt *cr* 1636 (NS); *b* 22 July 1941; *s* of Sir Muir Edward Sinclair-Lockhart, 14th Bt, and of Olga Ann, *d* of late Claude Victor White-Parsons, Hawkes Bay, NZ; *S* father, 1985; *m* 1973, Felicity Edith, *d* of late I. L. C. Stewart, NZ; twin *s* one *d*. *Heir*: *er* twin *s* Robert Muir Sinclair-Lockhart, *b* 12 Sept. 1973. *Address*: PO Box 215, Waipukurau, New Zealand.

SINDALL, Adrian John; HM Diplomatic Service; Consul-General, Sydney, since 1985; *b* 5 Oct. 1937; *s* of Stephen Sindall and Clare Mallet; *m* 1st, 1958; one *s* one *d*; 2nd, 1978, Jill Margaret Cowley. *Educ*: Battersea Grammar Sch. FO, 1956–58; ME Centre for Arab Studies, 1958–60; Third Sec. (Commercial), Baghdad, 1960–62; Second Sec., British Embassy, Rabat, 1962–67; First Secretary: FCO, 1967–70; Beirut, 1970–72; First Sec. and Head of Chancery, British Embassy, Lima, 1972–76; FCO, 1976–79; Counsellor, Head of Chancery and Consul-Gen., Amman, 1979–82; Hd of S America Dept, FCO, 1982–85. *Address*: c/o Foreign and Commonwealth Office, SW1A 2AH.

SINDELL, Marion Harwood; Chief Executive, Equal Opportunities Commission, 1979–85; *b* 23 June 1925; *d* of Arthur Barrett Sindell and Ethel Maude Sindell. *Educ*: Lincoln Girls' High Sch.; St Hilda's Coll., Oxford (MA). Solicitor. Deputy Town Clerk: Workington, 1959–64; Nuneaton, 1964–66; Town Clerk, Goole, 1966–74; Chief Exec., Boothferry Bor. Council, 1974–79. *Address*: The Granary, Skelton, Penrith, Cumbria.

SINDEN, Donald Alfred, CBE 1979; actor; *b* 9 Oct. 1923; *s* of Alfred Edward Sinden and Mabel Agnes (*née* Fuller), Sussex; *m* 1948, Diana, *d* of Daniel and Muriel Mahony; two *s*. *Educ*: Webber-Douglas Sch. of Dramatic Art. First appearance on stage, 1942, in Charles F. Smith's Co., Mobile Entertainments Southern Area; Leicester Repertory Co., 1945; Memorial Theatre Co., Stratford upon Avon, 1946 and 1947; Old Vic and Bristol Old Vic, 1948; The Heiress, Haymarket, 1949–50; Bristol Old Vic, 1950; Red Letter Day, Garrick, 1951. Under contract to Rank Organisation, 1952–60, appearing in 23 films including The Cruel Sea, Doctor in the House, etc. Returned to theatre, appearing in Odd Man In, St Martin's, 1957; Peter Pan, Scala, 1960; Guilty Party, St Martin's, 1961; Royal Shakespeare Co., playing Richard Plantagenet in Henry VI (The Wars of the Roses), Price in Eh!, etc, 1963 and 1964; British Council tour of S America in Dear Liar and Happy Days, 1965; There's a Girl in my Soup, Globe, 1966; Lord Foppington in The Relapse, RSC, Aldwych, 1967; Not Now Darling, Strand, 1968; RSC, Stratford, 1969 and Aldwych, 1970 playing Malvolio; Henry VIII; Sir Harcourt Courtly in London Assurance, revived at New Theatre, 1972, tour of the USA, 1974 (Drama Desk Award); In Praise of Love, Duchess, 1973; Stockmann in An Enemy of the People, Chichester, 1975; Habeas Corpus, USA, 1975; Benedick in Much Ado About Nothing, King Lear, RSC, Stratford, 1976, Aldwych, 1977 (Variety Club of GB Stage Actor of 1976; Evening Standard Drama Award, Best Actor, 1977); Shut Your Eyes and Think of England, Apollo, 1977; Othello, RSC, Stratford, 1979, Aldwych, 1980; Present Laughter, Vaudeville, 1981 (TV film, 1981); Uncle Vanya, Haymarket, 1982; The School for Scandal, Haymarket and Duke of York's (Eur. tour, 1984), and Ariadne auf Naxos, Coliseum, 1983; Two Into One, Shaftesbury, 1984; The Scarlet Pimpernel, Chichester transf. to Her Majesty's, 1985; *television series include*: Our Man from St Marks; Two's Company; Discovering English Churches; Never the Twain; has appeared in many films. Assoc. Artist, RSC, 1967–. Member: Council, British Actors Equity Assoc., 1966–77; Council, RSA, 1972; Adv. Council, V&A Museum, 1973–80; Arts Council Drama Panel, 1973–77; Leicestershire Educn Arts Cttee, 1974–; BBC Archives Adv. Cttee, 1975–78; London Acad. of Music and Dramatic Art Council, 1976–; Kent and E Sussex Reg. Cttee, National Trust, 1978–82; Arts Council of GB, 1982–86; Chairman: British Theatre Museum Assoc., 1971–77; Theatre Museum Adv. Council, 1973–80; President: Fedn of Playgoers Socs, 1968–; Royal Gen. Theatrical Fund, 1983–; Vice-Pres., London Appreciation Soc., 1960–. FRSA 1966. *Publications*: A Touch of the Memoirs (autobiog.), 1982; Laughter in the Second Act (autobiog.), 1985. *Recreations*: theatrical history, French history, architecture, ecclesiology, genealogy, serendipity, London. *Address*: 60 Temple Fortune Lane, NW11; Rats Castle, Isle of Oxney, Kent. *Clubs*: Garrick (Trustee, 1980–), Beefsteak, MCC.

SINGER, Alfred Ernst; Chairman: FKB Group PLC; Hugin Group PLC; London Trust PLC; Pearce Technology Ltd; Director: Ansbacher PLC; Equity Capital for Industry Ltd; Gestetner Holdings Ltd; Tiptop Drugstores PLC; *b* 15 Nov. 1924; *s* of late Dr Robert Singer and Mrs Charlotte Singer; *m* 1951, Gwendoline Doris Barnett (*d* 1985); one *s* one *d*. *Educ*: Halesowen Grammar Sch. FCCA, FBCS. Served War of 1939–45: Army, 1943–47. Subseq. professional and exec. posts with: Callingham, Brown & Co, Bunzl Pulp & Paper Ltd, David Brown Tractors Ltd; Rank Xerox Ltd, 1963–70 (Dir, 1967); Tesco Stores (Holdings) Ltd, 1970–73 (Dep. Managing Dir); Man. Dir (Giro), PO Corp., 1973–76; Chairman: PO Staff Superannuation Fund, 1977–79; Cannon Assurance Ltd, 1980–86. Chairman: Long Range Planning Soc., 1970–73; Council, Assoc. of Certified Accountants, 1972–81 (Vice-Pres., 1979–80); Member: Cttee for Industrial Technologies, DTI, 1972–76; National Economic Develt Council: Chm., Electronic Computers Sector Working Party; Member: Electronics EDC; Food and Drink Manufacturing Industry EDC, 1976–77. Governor, Centre for Environmental Studies, 1979–85 (Chm., 1981–85). *Address*: 7 Bacon's Lane, Highgate Village, N6 6BL. *T*: 01–340 0189. *Clubs*: Athenæum, MCC.

SINGER, Aubrey Edward, CBE 1984; Chairman and Managing Director, White City Films, since 1984; Chairman, Screen Sport, since 1984; *b* 21 Jan. 1927; *s* of Louis Henry Singer and Elizabeth (*née* Walton); *m* 1949, Cynthia Hilda Adams; one *s* three *d*. *Educ*: Giggleswick; Bradford Grammar School. Joined film industry, 1944; directed various films teaching armed forces to shoot; worked extensively in Africa, 1946–48; worked on children's films in Austria, 1948–49; joined BBC TV Outside Broadcasts, 1949; TV Producer Scotland, 1951; BBC New York Office, 1953; returned to London as Producer, 1956; produced many scientific programmes; Asst Head of Outside Broadcasts, 1959; Head of Science and Features, 1961; Head of Features Gp, BBC TV, 1967; Controller, BBC 2, 1974–78; Man. Dir, BBC Radio, 1978–82; Dep. Dir-Gen., and Man. Dir, Television, BBC, 1982–84. Chm., Soc. of Film and Television Arts, 1971–73. President: TV and Radio Industries Club, 1984–85; Nat. Mus. of Photography, Film and TV, 1984–. Fellow, Royal TV Soc., 1978, a Vice-Pres., 1982–. Hon. DLitt Bradford, 1984. *Recreations*: walking, talking, archery. *Address*: 79 Sutton Court Road, Chiswick, W4 3EQ. *T*: 01–994 6795. *Club*: Savile.

SINGER, Harold Samuel; His Honour Judge Singer; a Circuit Judge, since 1984; *b* 17 July 1935; *s* of Ellis and Minnie Singer; *m* 1966, Adèle Berenice Emanuel; one *s* two *d*. *Educ*: Salford Grammar School; Fitzwilliam House, Cambridge. BA Cantab. Called to the Bar, Gray's Inn, 1957; a Recorder, 1981–84. *Recreations*: music, oil painting, books, photography, golf. *Address*: 229 Kingsway, Gatley, Cheadle, Cheshire SK8 1LA. *T*: 061–491 3836.

SINGER, Harry Bruce, TD 1955; DL; FCA; Senior Partner, Singer & Partners, Chartered Accountants, since 1968; *b* 21 June 1921; *er s* of Geoffrey and Agnes Singer; *m* 1945, Betty Alison Brittan; one *s*. *Educ*: Cathedral Sch., Hereford. FCA 1960 (Mem., 1953). Served War: commnd 99th (London Welsh) HAA Regt, RA, 1941; served in UK and NW Europe; Instr, Sch. of AA Artillery, 1945; joined 281 (Glam Yeomanry) Field Regt, RA (TA), 1947; in comd, 1959–62. Pres., S Wales Soc. of Chartered Accountants, 1970–71; Inst. of Chartered Accountants in England and Wales: Mem. Council, 1973–85; Vice Pres., 1979–80; Dep. Pres., 1980–81; Pres., 1981–82. Liveryman, Worshipful Co. of Chartered Accountants, 1978; Freeman, City of London, 1978. Vice Chm. Wales, TA&VRA, 1984–. DL Mid Glamorgan, 1985. *Recreations*: golf, foreign travel, Rugby football (originally as player). *Address*: 8 Windsor House, Castle Court, Cardiff CF1 1DG. *Clubs*: Army and Navy; Cardiff and County, Cardiff Golf (Cardiff).

SINGER, Isaac Bashevis; writer; *b* Poland, 14 July 1904; *s* of Pinchos Menachem Singer and Bathsheba Singer (*née* Zylberman); *m* 1940, Alma Haimann; one *s*. *Educ:* Tachkemoni Rabbinical Seminary, Warsaw. Worked for publishing firms, Poland, 1926–35; with Jewish Daily Forward, NY, 1935–. Fellow: Jewish Acad. of Arts and Scis; Amer. Acad. and Inst. of Arts and Letters, NY; Mem., Amer. Acad. of Arts and Sciences, Boston; Nat. Book Award, 1970, 1974; Nobel Prize for Literature, 1978. DHL Hebrew Union Coll., LA, 1963. *Publications:* The Family Moskal, 1950; Satan in Goray, 1955; Gimpel the Fool and Other Stories, 1957; The Magician of Lublin, 1959; The Spinoza of Market Street, 1961; The Slave, 1962; Short Friday, 1964; Zlateh the Goat and Other Stories, 1966; In My Father's Court, 1966; The Manor, 1967; The Seance, 1968; The Estate, 1969; A Friend of Kafka and Other Stories, 1970; A Day of Pleasure (for children), 1970; Enemies, A Love Story, 1972; Crown of Feathers, 1973; When Shlemiel Went to War and Other Stories, 1974; Passions, 1976; Shosha, 1979; Old Love, 1980; The Collected Stories of Isaac Bashevis Singer, 1982; The Penitent, 1984; Love and Exile (memoirs), 1985; The Image and Other Stories, 1986. *Address:* 209 West 86th Street, New York, NY 10024, USA. *T:* 212–877–5968.

SINGER, Norbert, PhD, FRSC; Director, Thames Polytechnic, since 1978; *b* 3 May 1931; *s* of late Salomon Singer and late Mina Korn; *m* Brenda Margaret Walter, *e d* of Richard and Gladys Walter, Tunbridge Wells, Kent. *Educ:* Highbury County School; Queen Mary Coll., London. BSc, PhD, CChem, FRSC. Research Chemist and Project Leader, Morgan Crucible Co. Ltd, 1954–57; Lecturer, Senior Lectr, Principal Lectr and Dep. Head of Department, Dept of Chemistry, Northern Polytechnic, 1958–70; Head of Dept of Life Sciences 1971–74, Professor of Life Sciences 1972–74, Polytechnic of Central London; Asst Director, then Dep. Director, Polytechnic of North London, 1974–78. Mem., CNAA, 1982– (Chm., Reviews Co-ordination Sub-Cttee, 1984–; Vice Chm., Cttee for Academic and Institutional Policy, 1985–). *Publications:* research papers in electrochemistry, theoretical chemistry and surface chemistry in scientific jls. *Recreation:* squash. *Address:* Croft Lodge, Bayhall Road, Tunbridge Wells, Kent TN2 4TP. *T:* Tunbridge Wells 23821.

SINGER, Very Rev. Samuel Stanfield; Dean of Diocese of Glasgow and Galloway, since 1974; Rector of Holy Trinity, Ayr, since 1975; *b* 1920; *m* 1942, Helen Audrey Naughton, *o c* of Rev. and Mrs Michael William Naughton; three *s* one *d*. *Educ:* Trinity College, Dublin (BA 1942, MA 1961). Deacon 1943, priest, 1944, Dio. Down; Curate of Derriaghy, 1943–45; Minor Canon of Down Cathedral and Curate of Down, 1945–46; Curate of Wirksworth, 1946–49; Vicar of Middleton-by-Wirksworth, 1949–52; Rector: St George, Maryhill, Glasgow, 1952–62; All Saints, Jordanhill, Glasgow, 1962–75; Synod Clerk and Canon of Glasgow, 1966–74. *Address:* 12 Barns Terrace, Ayr, Ayrshire.

SINGH, Kanwar N.; *see* Natwar-Singh.

SINGH, Khushwant; Padma Bhushan, 1974; Member of Parliament, India, since 1980; Barrister-at-Law; *b* Feb. 1915; *m* Kaval (*née* Malik); one *s* one *d*. *Educ:* Univ. of London (LLB); called to Bar. Practising Lawyer, High Court, Lahore, 1939–47; Min. of External Affairs, of India; PRO Ottawa and London, 1947–51; UNESCO, 1954–56. Visiting Lectr: Oxford (Spalding Trust); USA: Rochester, Princeton, Hawaii, Swarthmore; led Indian Delegn to Writers' Conf., Manila, Philippines, 1965; Guest Speaker at Montreal 'Expo 67'. Has written for many nat. dailies and foreign jls: New York Times; Observer and New Statesman (London); Harper's (USA); Evergreen Review (USA); London Magazine. Editor, The Illustrated Weekly of India, Bombay, 1969–78; Chief Editor, New Delhi, 1979–80; increased circulation of Illustrated Weekly of India from 80,000 to 410,000 in 9 yrs; Editor-in-chief, The Hindustan Times and Contour, New Delhi, 1980–83. *Broadcasting and Television:* All India Radio, BBC, CBC; LP recordings. Awards include: from Punjab Govt: 5,000 rupees and Robe of Honour, for contrib. to Sikh literature; Mohan Singh Award: 1,500 rupees for trans. of Sikh hymns, etc. *Publications: Sikh History and Religion:* The Sikhs, 1953; A History of the Sikhs: vol. i, 1469–1839, 1964; vol. ii, 1839–1964, 1967; Ranjit Singh, Maharajah of the Punjab, 1780–1839, 1963; Fall of the Kingdom of the Punjab; Sikhs Today; (ed) Sunset of the Sikh Empire, by Dr Sita Ram Kohli (posthumous); Hymns of Nanak The Guru. *Fiction:* The Mark of Vishnu and other stories, 1951; Train to Pakistan, 1956; I Shall Not Hear the Nightingales, 1961; *stories:* The Voice of God and other stories; Black Jasmine and other stories; A Bride for the Sahib and other stories. (*Co-author*): Sacred Writing of the Sikhs; (with Arun Joshi) Shri Ram: a biog., 1969; (with Satindra Singh) Ghadr Rebellion; (with Suneet Veer Singh) Homage to Guru Gobind Singh; *miscellaneous:* Love and Friendship (editor of anthology); Khushwant Singh's India—collection of articles (ed Rahul Singh); Shri Ram—a biography; Delhi—a Profile, 1982; The Sikhs, 1984; (with Kuldip Nayar) Punjab Tragedy, 1984; *translations:* Umrao Jan Ada, Courtesan of Lucknow, by Mohammed Ruswa (with M. A. Husaini); The Skeleton (by Amrita Pritam); Land of the Five Rivers; I Take This Woman, by Rajinder Singh Bedi; Iqbal's Dialogue with Allah (Shikwah and Jawab-e-Shikwah); We Indians. *Recreation:* bird watching. *Address:* 49E Sujan Singh Park, New Delhi 110003, India. *T:* 690159. *Clubs:* Authors'; Imperial Gymkhana (New Delhi); Bombay Gymkhana (Bombay 1).

SINGH, Mota; QC 1978; **His Honour Judge Mota Singh;** a Circuit Judge, since 1982; *b* 26 July 1930; *s* of Dalip Singh and Harnam Kaur; *m* 1950, Swaran Kaur; two *s* two *d*. *Educ:* Duke of Gloucester Sch., Nairobi, Kenya; Hon. Soc. of Lincoln's Inn. Called to the Bar, 1956. Left school, 1947; Solicitor's Clerk, Nairobi, 1948–54; Lincoln's Inn, London, 1954–56; Advocate, High Court of Kenya, 1957–65; Alderman, City of Nairobi, 1958–63; Vice-Chm., Kenya Justice; Sec., Law Soc. of Kenya, 1963–64. A Deputy Circuit Judge, 1976–82; a Recorder of the Crown Court, 1979–82. Member: London Rent Assessment Panel, 1965–67; Race Relations Bd, 1968–77. Hon. LLD Guru Nanak Dev Univ., Amritsar, 1981. *Recreations:* reading; formerly cricket (represented Kenya). *Address:* Cedarwood, 3 Somerset Road, Wimbledon SW19 5JU. *T:* 01–947 2271.

SINGH, Judge Nagendra; Padma Vibhushan 1973; Member, International Court of Justice, since 1973, President, since 1985 (Vice-President, 1976–79); Ambassador rank, since 1972; *b* 18 March 1914; *s* of late HH Mahawawal Bijaya Singiji of Dungarpur and Maharani Devendra Kunwer; *m* 1940, Pushpa Kumari Devi. *Educ:* Mayo Coll.; Agra Univ. (Pinhey Medal, BA); St John's Coll., Cambridge (MA, LLD; Fellow, 1974). Called to the Bar, Gray's Inn, 1942, Hon. Bencher 1975; Bencher, Kings Inn, Dublin, 1985. Entered ICS, 1937; Mem. Constituent Assembly of India, 1947–48; Dist. Magistrate and Collector, Madhya Pradesh, 1938–46; Jt Sec., Defence Min., India, 1946–56; Regional Comr, Eastern States, 1948; IDC London, 1950; Dir-Gen. Shipping, 1956–64 and Sec. to Govt of India, Min. of Transport, to 1965; Special Sec., Min. of Inf. and Broadcasting, 1964; Sec. to Pres. of India, 1966–72; Constitutional Advr to Govt of Bhutan, 1970; Chief Election Comr, India, 1972. Chancellor, Univ. of Goa, 1985–. President: UN Internat. Law Commn; UNCITRAL; UN World Commn on Environment and Develt. Mem. Indian, European, American and other foreign learned Socs; Corresp. FBA, 1986. Lectures include: Andhra Univ., 1959; Acad. of Internat Law, The Hague, 1962; Bombay Univ., 1968; Grad. Inst. of Internat. Studies, Geneva, 1969; Univ. of Nepal, 1969; Univ. of Cambridge, 1978; Univ. of Thessaloniki, 1985. JP Bombay, 1958. Numerous hon. degrees and awards from Indian and foreign Univs. *Publications:* Termination of Membership of International Organisations, 1958; Nuclear Weapons and International Law, 1959; Defence Mechanism of the Modern State, 1963; British Shipping Law series: vol. 8, Shipowners, 1967, vol. 13, International Conventions of Merchant Shipping, 1973, revised 1983 as vol. 1, Navigation, vol. 2, Safety, vol. 3, Training and Employment, vol. 4, Maritime Law; The Concept of Force and Organization of Defence in the Constitutional History of India, 1969; Achievements of UNCTAD I and II in the Field of Invisibles, 1969; India and International Law, 1969; The State Practice of India in the Field of International Law, vol. 1, Ancient and Mediaeval, 1973; Commercial Law of India, 1975; Bhutan, 1978; Maritime Flag and International Law, 1978; articles to law jls, India and overseas. *Recreation:* cricket. *Address:* International Court of Justice, Peace Palace, The Hague, Netherlands. *T:* The Hague 924 441; 6 Akbar Road, New Delhi 110011, India. *T:* New Delhi 3013258. *Clubs:* Athenæum, Lansdowne, MCC; Imperial Gymkhana (New Delhi).

SINGH, Preetam, QC 1976; *b* 1 Oct. 1914; *s* of Waryam Singh and late Balwant Kaur; *m* 1934, Rattan Kaur (*née* Bura); three *s* one *d*. *Educ:* A. V. High Sch., Mombasa, Kenya; King's Coll., London. Called to the Bar, Gray's Inn, 1951; Mem. Bar Council and Senate of Inns of Court. Dep. Official Receiver, Kenya, 1960–64; Barrister, N Eastern Circuit, 1964–77; Advocate: Supreme Court, Kenya; High Court (Punjab and Haryana), India. Member: Commn for Racial Equality, 1977–78; BBC Adv. Cttee on Asian programmes, 1979–. Contested (L) Hallam (Sheffield), 1970. Hon. LLD Punjab, 1977. *Recreations:* hunting, politics, religion, Indian classical music. *Club:* Liberal.

SINGH, Sardar Swaran; President, Indian Council of World Affairs; *b* 19 Aug. 1907. *Educ:* Government College, Lahore; Lahore Law College. MSc (Physics) 1930; LLB 1932. Elected to Punjab Legislative Assembly, 1946; Punjab State Government: Minister for Development, Food and Civil Supplies, 1946–47; Member, Partition Committee, 1947; Minister: of Home, General Administration, Revenue, Irrigation and Electricity, 1947–49; of Capital Projects and Electricity, 1952; for Works, Housing and Supply, 1952–57, Govt of India; Member, Upper House of Indian Legislature, 1952–57; Member, Lower House of Indian Legislature, 1957; Minister: for Steel, Mines and Fuel, 1957–62; for Railways, 1962–63; for Food and Agriculture, 1963–64; for Industry and Supply, 1964; for External Affairs, 1964–66; Foreign Minister, 1970–74, Minister of Defence, 1966–70 and 1974–75. Has led many Indian delegations to the United Nations, its agencies, foreign countries and international conferences. *Address:* c/o Indian National Congress, 5 Dr Rajendra Prasad Road, New Delhi, India.

SINGH, Giani Zail; President of India, since 1982; *b* Faridkot, 5 May 1916; *s* of Kishan Singh and Ind Kaur; *m* Pardan Kaur; one *s* three *d*. Founded Faridkot State Congress, 1946; formed govt in Faridkot State, 1948; Pres., State Praja Mandal, 1946–48; Government of Patiala and E Punjab States Union: Revenue Minister, 1948–49; Minister for Public Works and Agric., 1951–52; Pres., Provincial Congress Cttee, 1955–56; Member: Rajya Sabha, 1956–62; Punjab Assembly, 1962; Minister of State, and Pres. Punjab Provincial Congress Cttee, 1966–72; Chief Minister of Punjab, 1972–77; Minister of Home Affairs, 1980–82. *Address:* Rashtrapati Bhavan, New Delhi 110004, India.

SINGH BAHADUR, Maharawal Shri Sir Lakshman, GCIE 1947; KCSI 1935; *b* 7 March 1908; *S* father as Maharawal of Dungapur, 1918; title no longer recognised by the Government of India, 1971; *m* grand-daughter of Raja Saheb of Bhinga, and *d* of Lieut-Col His late Highness Maharajadhiraj Sir Madan Singh Bahadur, KCSI, KCIE, of Kishengarh (wife decd); four *s* four *d*. *Educ:* Mayo Coll., Ajmer. Visited England, Scotland, Switzerland, France, and other European countries, 1927; invested with full ruling powers, 1928; Mem., Standing Cttee of Chamber of Princes, 1931–47; one of the select Princes chosen by his order to meet Cabinet Mission, 1946; elected Mem., Rajya Sabha, 1952–58; Leader, Rajasthan Assembly Swatantra Party and Leader of Opposition, 1962; Leader of Assembly Swatantra Party, Leader of SVD, and Leader of Opposition, 1967; President: Swatantra Party in Rajasthan, 1961–69; All-India Kshatriya Mahasabha, 1962–. Patron: Rajputana Cricket Assoc.; Cricket Club of India; Mem., MCC; captained Rajputana XI against MCC and Australian XI on four occasions. Is a keen naturalist and is interested in agriculture and study of wild life. *Address:* Udai Bilas Palace, Dungarpur, Rajasthan, India.
See also Maharaja of Bikaner.

SINGHANIA, Sir Padampat, Kt 1943; President of the JK Organisation, India; *b* 1905; *s* of late Lala Kamlapat Singhania; *m* Srimati Anusiya Devi; four *s* one *d*. *Educ:* Home. A pioneer of Cotton, Rayon, Nylon, Jute, Woollen Textiles, Sugar, Aluminium, Steel and Engineering, Plastic, Strawboard, Paper, Chemicals, Oil Industries, Shipping, Cement, Tyres and Tubes, Dry Cell Batteries, Banking; Patron, large number of social, educational, political, and literary institutions. Founder of the Merchants' Chamber of UP: ex-Pres. of Federation of Indian Chambers of Commerce and Industry; ex-Pres., Employers' Assoc. of Northern India; Member 1st Indian Parliament, 1947–52, and many government and semi-govt bodies; formerly Chairman, Board of Governors, IIT Kanpur. Dr of Letters, Kanpur Univ., 1968. *Recreations:* riding, music, buildings, and studies. *Address:* Kamla Tower, Kanpur 208001, India. *TA:* Laljuggi, Kanpur. *T:* 69854, 51147 and 62988. *Telex* KP215.

SINGHATEH, Alhaji Sir Farimang (Mohamadu), GCMG 1966; JP; Governor-General of The Gambia, 1965–70; *b* 30 Nov. 1912; *m* 1939; three *s* six *d* (and two *s* one *d* decd). *Educ:* Armitage Secondary School, Georgetown, The Gambia. Career as Druggist and Chemist. *Address:* 48 Grant Street, Banjul, The Gambia.

SINGHJI BAHADUR, Dr Karni; *see* Bikaner, Maharaja of.

SINGHVI, Dr Laxmi Mall; Senior Advocate, Supreme Court of India, since 1967; *b* 9 Nov. 1931; *s* of D. M. Singhvi and Akal Kaur Singhvi; *m* 1957, Kamla Singhvi; one *s* one *d*. *Educ:* Allahabad Univ. (BA); Rajasthan Univ. (LLB); Harvard Univ. Law Sch. (LLM); Cornell Univ. Law Sch. (SJD). MP, Independent, Lok Sabha, 1962–67; Senior Standing Counsel, State of UP, Union of India, 1967–71; Advocate-Gen., 1972–77. Dep. Leader, Indian Parly Delegn to CPA, 1964, Leader Parly Delegn, 1966; Chm. and Founder, Inst. of Constitutional and Parly Studies, 1964–. Chairman: Indian Fedn of Unesco Assocs, 1974–; World Colloquim on Legal Aid, 1975; State Bar Council, 1975–77; Indian Nat. Cttee for Abolition of Death Penalty, 1977–; Nat. Sch. of Drama, 1978–82; Supreme Court Law Reforms Cttee, 1981–82; Founder Chm., 1972, Hon. Patron, 1983, Commonwealth Legal Educn Assoc.; Member: UN Human Rights Sub-Commn, Geneva, 1978–82 (Vice-Chm.); Nat. Commn for Unesco; Govt of India Expert Cttee on Legal Aid, 1971–73; Commn on Inf. and Broadcasting, 1964–68; Internat. Forum on Freedoms and Rights of Man, Paris, 1985–. President: Supreme Court Bar Assoc., 1977, 1978, 1980, 1982 (Pres., Trust, 1981–); Nat. Legal Aid Assoc.; Indian Centre for Independence of Judges and Lawyers, 1979–; UN Special Rapporteur on Independence of Judges and Lawyers, 1979–. Life Trustee, India Internat. Centre. Hon. Tagore Law Prof., 1975–. Pres., Authors Guild of India, 1986–. Hon. LLD: Banaras Hindu Univ. 1984; Jabalpur, 1983. Hon. Nyayavacaspati, Gurukul, 1968. *Publications:* Horizons of Freedom, 1969; (ed) Law and Poverty, 1970; Indian Federalism, 1974; Legal Aid, 1985; Law Day, 1985; Independence of Justice, 1985. *Recreations:* theatre, poetry, chess, gardening, classical Indian dance appreciation, archaeology. *Address:* B-8 South Extension II, New Delhi 110049, India. *T:* 6440308, 6444831.

SINGLETON, Sir Edward (Henry Sibbald), Kt 1975; solicitor; Member of Council, The Law Society, 1961–80 (Vice-President of the Society, 1973, President, 1974); *b* 7 April 1921; *s* of W. P. Singleton, Colwall, and Florence, *d* of Sir Francis Sibbald Scott, 5th Bt; *m* 1943, Margaret Vere Hutton; three *s* one *d*. *Educ:* Shrewsbury; BNC, Oxford. MA 1946. Served War, as Pilot, Fleet Air Arm, 1941–45. Solicitor, 1949; Partner in Macfarlanes, 1954, consultant 1977–86; FCIArb 1982; Companion, Instn of Civil Engrs, 1982. Chairman: Solicitors' Law Stationery Soc. plc, 1980–85; Anglo-Swedish Construction Co. Ltd. Dir, Abbey National Bldg Soc. and various cos. Member: Council for the Securities Industry, 1978–83; Council of Management, The White Ensign Assoc. Ltd; Trustee: Fleet Air Arm Museum; Temple Bar Trust; Westminster Hospital, 1978–84. *Recreation:* relaxing. *Address:* 57 Victoria Road, W8 5RH. *T:* 01–937 2277. *Clubs:* City of London; Vincent's (Oxford).

SINGLETON, Norman, CB 1966; Arbitrator and Mediator, Advisory, Conciliation and Arbitration Service; *b* 21 March 1913; *s* of Charles and Alice Singleton, Bolton, Lancs; *m* 1936, Cicely Margaret Lucas, Claverdon, Warwick; one *s* two *d*. *Educ:* Bolton School; Emmanuel College, Cambridge. Min. of Labour, 1935; Under-Secretary: Civil Service Pay Research Unit, 1956–60; Min. of Labour (now Dept of Employment), 1960–69; Sec., 1969–72, Dep. Chm., 1973–74, Commn on Industrial Relns; Dep. Chm., Central Arbitration Cttee, 1976–85. *Publication:* Industrial Relations Procedures, 1976. *Address:* 34 Willoughby Road, Hampstead, NW3. *T:* 01–435 1504.

SINGLETON, William Brian, CBE 1974; FRCVS; Director, Animal Health Trust, since 1977; *b* 23 Feb. 1923; *s* of William Max Singleton and Blanche May Singleton; *m* 1950, Hilda Stott; two *s* one *d* (and one *s* decd). *Educ:* Queen Elizabeth Grammar Sch., Darlington; Royal (Dick) Sch. of Vet. Medicine, Edinburgh. Vis. Prof. Surgery, Ontario Vet. Coll., Guelph, Canada, 1973–74; Hon. Vet. Advr to Jockey Club, 1977–. Mem., Govt Cttee of Inquiry into Future Role of Veterinary Profession in GB (Chm., Sir Michael Swann), 1971–75. President: British Small Animal Vet. Assoc., 1960–61; RCVS, 1969–70; World Small Animal Vet. Assoc., 1975–77. Hon. Diplomate, Amer. Coll. of Vet. Surgeons, 1973. *Publications:* (ed jtly) Canine Medicine and Therapeutics, 1979; chapter in International Encyclopaedia of Veterinary Medicine, 1966; chapters in Animal Nursing Part II, 1966; numerous papers in veterinary and comparative pathology jls. *Recreations:* gardening, sailing, bird watching, horse riding. *Address:* Lanwades Hall, Kennett, Newmarket, Suffolk CB8 7PN. *T:* Newmarket 750448. *Club:* Farmers'.

SINHA, 3rd Baron *cr* 1919, of Raipur; **Sudhindro Prosanno Sinha;** Chairman and Managing Director, MacNeill and Barry Ltd, Calcutta; *b* 29 Oct. 1920; *s* of Aroon Kumar, 2nd Baron Sinha (*s* of Satyendra Prasanna, 1st Baron Sinha, the first Indian to be created a peer) and Nirupama, *yr d* of Rai Bahadur Lalit Mohan Chatterjee; *S* father, 1967; *m* 1945, Madhabi, *d* of late Monoranjan Chatterjee, Calcutta; one *s* two *d* (and one *s* decd). *Educ:* Bryanston School, Blandford. *Heir:* *s* Hon. Sushanto Sinha, *b* 1953. *Address:* 7 Lord Sinha Road, Calcutta, India.

SINKER, Rev. Canon Michael Roy; Canon Emeritus of Lincoln Cathedral, 1969; *b* 28 Sept. 1908; 3rd *s* of late Rev. Francis Sinker, sometime Vicar of Ilkley; *m* 1939, Edith Watt Applegate; one *s* two *d*. *Educ:* Haileybury; Clare College, Cambridge (MA); Cuddesdon College, Oxford. Curate of Dalston, Cumberland, 1932–34; Chaplain to South African Church Railway Mission, 1935–38; Curate of Bishop's Hatfield 1938–39; Vicar of Dalton-in-Furness, 1939–46; Vicar of Saffron Walden, 1946–63; Hon. Canon of Chelmsford Cathedral, 1955–63; Rural Dean of Saffron Walden, 1948–63; Archdeacon of Stow, 1963–67; Rector of St Matthew, Ipswich, 1967–77. *Address:* 8 White Horse Way, Westbury, Wilts.

SINNAMON, Sir Hercules Vincent, Kt 1985; OBE 1980; *b* 13 Nov. 1899; *s* of James Sinnamon and Janie Sinnamon (*née* Jackson). *Educ:* Taringa State School; Stott's Business College, Brisbane. Joined National Mutual Life Association, 1914; Manager, Townsville, Sub Accountant, and other executive positions; retired as Executive Officer, 1965. Retirement is happily spent furthering community projects and breeding beef and dairy cattle. *Publication:* The Gentleman Farmer's Paradise, 1980. *Recreations:* outdoors, riding, surfing. *Address:* Glen Ross, 619 Sinnamon Road, 17 Mile Rocks, Qld 4073, Australia. *T:* 07/3761540. *Club:* National Mutual Life 25 Years' and Retired Officers' (Brisbane).

SINNATT, Maj.-Gen. Martin Henry, CB 1984; Senior Executive and Secretary, Kennel Club, since 1984; *b* 28 Jan. 1928; *s* of Dr O. S. Sinnatt and Mrs M. H. Sinnatt (*née* Randall); *m* 1957, Susan Rosemary Clarke; four *d*. *Educ:* Hitchin Grammar School; Hertford College, Oxford (1 Year Army Short Course); RMA Sandhurst. Commissioned RTR, 1948; served Germany, Korea, UK, Hong Kong, 1948–58; psc 1959; Aden, 1959–62; Germany and UK, 1962–64; MA to C-in-C AFNE, Norway, 1964–66; jssc 1967; Germany and UK, 1967–69; CO 4 RTR, BAOR, 1969–71; Nat. Defence Coll., 1971–72; Comdr RAC, 1 (BR) Corps, BAOR, 1972–74; Dir Operational Requirements MoD, 1974–77; rcds 1978; Dir, Combat Development (Army), 1979–81; Chief of Staff to Live Oak, SHAPE, 1982–84; completed service, 1984. *Recreations:* medieval history, gardening and swimming; also, when time and finances permit, skiing and golf. *Address:* East Highlands, Three Gates Lane, Haslemere, Surrey GU27 2ET. *Clubs:* Army and Navy, Kennel.

SINNOTT, Ernest; Chairman, South Eastern Electricity Board, 1966–74; *b* 10 March 1909; *s* of John Sinnott and Emily (*née* Currie); *m* 1934, Simone Marie (*née* Petitjean); two *s*. *Educ:* Salford Grammar School. City Treasurer's Dept, Salford, 1924–31; City Accountant's Dept, Chester, 1931; Borough Treasurer's Dept, Warrington, 1931–32; Dep. Borough Treasurer, Middleton 1932–35, Worthing 1935–37; Borough Treasurer, Worthing, 1937–48; Chief Accountant, SE Electricity Bd, 1948–62, Dep. Chairman, 1962–66. Chartered Accountant (hons) 1935; FIMTA (Collins gold medal), 1932, now IPFA; Pres. 1956–57. *Publications:* (jointly) Brown's Municipal Book-keeping and Accounts; contribs to learned journals on local government finance. *Recreations:* music, reading and walking. *Address:* Little Court, 6 West Parade, Worthing, West Sussex.

SIRS, William, JP; General Secretary, Iron and Steel Trades Confederation, 1975–85, retired; *b* 6 Jan. 1920; *s* of Frederick Sirs and Margaret (*née* Powell); *m* 1941, Joan (*née* Clark); one *s* one *d*. *Educ:* Middleton St Johns, Hartlepool; WEA. Steel Industry, 1937–63; Iron and Steel Trades Confedn: Organiser, 1963; Divisional Officer, Manchester, 1970; Asst Gen. Sec., 1973. Member: Iron and Steel Industry Trng Bd, 1973; TUC Gen. Council, 1975–85; Trade Union Steel Industry Cons. Cttee, 1973– (Chm., 1975–) and Jt Accident Prevention Adv. Cttee, 1973; Employment Appeal Tribunal, 1976–; Jt Sec., Jt Industrial Council for Slag Industry, 1973; Exec. Mem., Paul Finet Foundn, European Coal and Steel Community, 1974; Hon. Sec. (British Section), Internat. Metalworkers Fedn, 1975. Mem., Management Cttee, BSC (Industry) Ltd, 1975–. Pres., Northern Home Counties Productivity Assoc.; Mem. RIIA, 1973. JP Hartlepool, Co. Durham, Knutsford, Cheshire, Herts, 1963. Freeman, City of London, 1984. *Publication:* Hard Labour (autobiog.), 1985. *Recreations:* sailing, squash, swimming, running. *Address:* Hatfield, Hertfordshire.

SISSON, Charles Hubert; writer; *b* 22 April 1914; *s* of late Richard Percy Sisson and Ellen Minnie Sisson (*née* Worlock); *m* 1937, Nora Gilbertson; two *d*. *Educ:* University of Bristol, and in France and Germany. Entered Ministry of Labour as Assistant Principal, 1936; HM Forces, in the ranks, mainly in India, 1942–45; Simon Senior Research Fellow, 1956–57; Dir of Establishments, Min. of Labour, 1962–68; Dir of Occupational Safety and Health, Dept of Employment, 1972. FRSL 1975. Hon. DLitt Bristol, 1980. Jt Editor, PN Review, 1976–84. *Publications:* An Asiatic Romance, 1953; Versions and Perversions of Heine, 1955; The Spirit of British Administration, 1959; The London Zoo (poems), 1961; Numbers (poems), 1965; Christopher Homm, 1965; Art and Action, 1965; The Discarnation (poem), 1967; Essays, 1967; Metamorphoses (poems), 1968; English Poetry 1900–1950, 1971, rev. edn 1981; The Case of Walter Bagehot, 1972; In the Trojan Ditch (poems), 1974; The Poetic Art, 1975; The Corridor (poem), 1975; (ed) The English Sermon, Vol. II 1650–1750, 1976; David Hume, 1976; Anchises (poems), 1976; (ed) Selected Poems of Jonathan Swift, 1977; The Avoidance of Literature, 1978; Exactions (poems), 1980; (ed) Autobiographical and Other Papers of Philip Mairet, 1981; Selected Poems, 1981; Anglican Essays, 1983; Collected Poems, 1984; (ed) Selected Poems of Christina Rossetti, 1984; *translations:* Catullus, 1966; The Poem on Nature, 1976; Some Tales of La Fontaine, 1979; The Divine Comedy, 1980; The Song of Roland, 1983; Les Regrets of Joachim du Bellay, 1983; The Aeneid of Virgil, 1986; Three Plays of Racine, 1987. *Address:* Moorfield Cottage, The Hill, Langport, Somerset TA10 9PU. *T:* Langport 250845.

SISSON, Rosemary Anne; writer since 1929; *b* 13 Oct. 1923; *d* of Prof. C. J. Sisson, MA, DèsL and Vera Kathleen (*née* Ginn). *Educ:* Cheltenham Ladies' Coll.; University Coll., London (BA Hons English); Newnham Coll., Cambridge (MLit). Served War, Royal Observer Corps, 1943–45. Instr in English, Univ. of Wisconsin, 1949; Lecturer in English: UCL, 1950–53; Univ. of Birmingham, 1953–54; Dramatic Critic, Stratford-upon-Avon Herald, 1954–57; after prodn of first play, The Queen and the Welshman, became full-time writer, 1957. Co-Chm., Writers Guild of GB, 1979 and 1980; Mem., Dramatists' Club. *Plays:* The Queen and the Welshman, 1957; Fear Came to Supper, 1958; The Splendid Outcast, 1959; The Royal Captivity, 1960; Bitter Sanctuary, 1963; Ghost on Tiptoe (with Robert Morley), 1974; The Dark Horse, 1978. Contributed to *TV series:* Catherine of Aragon, in The Six Wives of Henry VIII; The Marriage Game, in Elizabeth R; Upstairs, Downstairs; A Town Like Alice; Irish RM; Seal Morning; The Bretts. *Film scripts* include: Ride a Wild Pony; Escape from the Dark; Candleshoe; Watcher in the Woods; The Black Cauldron (full-length animation film) (all for Walt Disney); The Wind in the Willows (animation film), 1983 (also TV series, 1984). *Other scripts:* Heart of a Nation (Son-et-Lumière), Horse Guards Parade, 1983; Dawn to Dusk, Royal Tournament, 1984. *Publications:* children's books: The Adventures of Ambrose, 1951; The Young Shakespeare, 1959; The Young Jane Austen, 1962; The Young Shaftesbury, 1964; novels: The Exciseman, 1972; The Killer of Horseman's Flats, 1973; The Stratford Story, 1975; Escape from the Dark, 1976; The Queen and the Welshman, 1979; The Manions of America, 1982; Bury Love Deep, 1985; Beneath the Visiting Moon, 1986. *Recreations:* travel, walking, riding, writing poetry. *Address:* 167 New King's Road, Parson's Green, SW6.

SISSON, Sir Roy, Kt 1980; CEng, FRAeS; Chairman, Smiths Industries Ltd, 1976–85; *b* 17 June 1914; *s* of Bernard Sisson and Violet (*née* Hagg); *m* 1943, Constance Mary Cutchey; two *s* two *d*. *Educ:* Regent Street Polytechnic. De Havilland Aircraft Co. Ltd, 1933–37; Flight Engineer and Station Engineer, BOAC, 1944–47; BOAC rep. at de Havilland Aircraft Co., 1948; Smiths Industries: joined, 1955; Divl Dir, 1964; Chief Exec., Aviation Div., 1966; Managing Dir, 1973; Chm., 1976 (Chief Exec., 1976–81). Pres., SBAC, 1973–74. FBIM. *Recreations:* sailing, tennis. *Address:* Gustard Wood House, Gustard Wood, near Wheathampstead, Herts. *Club:* Royal Dart Yacht.

SISSONS, (Thomas) Michael (Beswick); Chairman and Managing Director, A. D. Peters & Co. Ltd, since 1973 (Director since 1965); *b* 13 Oct. 1934; *s* of Captain T. E. B. Sissons (killed in action, 1940) and Marjorie (*née* Shepherd) *m* 1st, 1960, Nicola Ann Fowler; one *s* one *d*; 2nd, 1974, Ilze Kadegis; two *d*. *Educ:* Winchester Coll.; Exeter Coll., Oxford (BA 1958, MA 1964). National Service, 2nd Lieut 13/18 Royal Hussars, 1953–55. Lectr in History, Tulane Univ., New Orleans, USA, 1958–59; freelance writer and journalist, 1958–60; joined A.D. Peters, Literary Agent, 1959. Pres., Assoc. of Authors' Agents, 1978–81; Dir, London Broadcasting Co., 1973–75; Mem. Council, Consumers Assoc., 1974–77. *Publication:* (ed with Philip French) The Age of Austerity, 1963, new edn 1986. *Recreations:* riding, gardening, cricket, music. *Address:* Flinty, Clanville, Andover, Hants SP11 9HZ. *T:* Weyhill 2197. *Clubs:* Garrick, Groucho, MCC (Mem. Cttee, 1984–87).

SITWELL, Rev. Francis Gerard, OSB, MA; *b* 22 Dec. 1906; *s* of late Major Francis Sitwell and Margaret Elizabeth, *d* of late Matthew Culley, Coupland Castle, Northumberland. *Educ:* Ampleforth; St Benet's Hall, Oxford. Received Benedictine Habit, 1924; Professed, 1925; Priest, 1933; Assistant Master at Ampleforth, 1933–39; Assistant Procurator at Ampleforth, 1939–47; Subprior of Ampleforth, 1946–47; Master of St Benet's Hall, Oxford, 1947–64; Priest of Our Lady and St Wilfrid, Warwick Bridge, Carlisle, 1966–69. *Publications:* Walter Hilton, Scale of Perfection (trans. and ed); St Odo of Cluny; Medieval Spirituality; articles in Ampleforth Journal, Downside Review, Clergy Review, Month, etc. *Address:* Ampleforth Abbey, York YO6 4EN.

SITWELL, Peter Sacheverell W.; *see* Wilmot-Sitwell.

SITWELL, Sir Sacheverell, 6th Bt *cr* 1808; CH 1984; *b* Scarborough, 15 Nov. 1897; *s* of Sir George Sitwell, 4th Bt, and Lady Ida Emily Augusta Denison (*d* 1937), *d* of 1st Earl of Londesborough; *S* brother, 1969; *m* 1925, Georgia (*d* 1980), *yr d* of Arthur Doble, Montreal; two *s*. *Educ:* Eton College. High Sheriff of Northamptonshire, 1948–49. Freedom of City of Lima (Peru), 1960; Benson Silver Medal, RSL, 1981. *Publications:* Southern Baroque Art, 1924; All Summer in a Day, 1926; The Gothick North, 1929; Mozart, 1932; Life of Liszt, 1936; Dance of the Quick and the Dead, 1936; Conversation Pieces, 1936; La Vie Parisienne, 1937; Narrative Pictures, 1937; Roumanian Journey, 1938; Old Fashioned Flowers, 1939; Mauretania, 1939; Poltergeists, 1940; Sacred and Profane Love, 1940; Valse des Fleurs, 1941; Primitive Scenes and Festivals, 1942; The Homing of the Winds, 1942; Splendours and Miseries, 1943; British Architects and Craftsmen, 1945; The Hunters and the Hunted, 1947; The Netherlands, 1948; Selected Poems, 1948; Morning, Noon, and Night in London, 1948; Spain, 1950, new edn 1975; Cupid and the Jacaranda, 1952; Truffle Hunt with Sacheverell Sitwell, 1953: Portugal and Madeira, 1954; Denmark, 1956; Arabesque and Honeycomb, 1957; Malta, 1958; Bridge of the Brocade Sash, 1959; Journey to the Ends of Time: Vol. I, Lost in the Dark Wood, 1959; Golden Wall and Mirador, 1961; The Red Chapels of Banteai Srei, 1962; Monks, Nuns and Monasteries, 1965; Forty-eight Poems (in Poetry Review), 1967; Southern Baroque Revisited, 1968; Gothic Europe, 1969; For Want of the Golden City, 1973; An Indian Summer, one hundred recent poems, 1982; (jtly) Hortus Sitwellianus,

1985; Sacheverell Sitwell's England, ed Michael Raeburn, 1986; and 15 books of Poetry, 1918–36, with a further 40 small books of Poems, 1972–76. *Recreation:* 'Westerns'. *Heir:* s Sacheverell Reresby Sitwell [b 15 April 1927; m 1952, Penelope, yr d of late Col Hon. Donald Alexander Forbes, DSO, MVO; one d. DL Derbys]. *Address:* Weston Hall, Towcester, Northants.

SIVEWRIGHT, Col Robert Charles Townsend, CB 1983; MC 1945; DL; Joint Principal (with Molly Sivewright) of the Talland School of Equitation, since 1959; b 7 Sept. 1923; s of late Captain R. H. V. Sivewright, DSC, RN and of Sylvia Townsend (née Cobbold); m 1951, (Pamela) Molly Ryder-Richardson, FIH, FBHS (as Molly Sivewright, author of Thinking Riding); three d. *Educ:* Repton; Royal Agricultural Coll., Cirencester. Served Regular Army, 11th Hussars (PAO), 1943–52; TA, Royal Glos Hussars, 1959–67 (CO, 1964–67); Chm., Western Wessex TA&VRA, 1970–83; Vice-Chm., Council of TA&VRAs, 1979–83. DL 1965, High Sheriff 1977, Glos. *Recreation:* National Hunt racing. *Address:* Talland House, South Cerney, Cirencester, Glos GL7 6HU. *T:* Cirencester 860209. *Club:* Cavalry and Guards.

SIZER, Prof. John; Professor of Financial Management, Loughborough University of Technology, since 1970; b 14 Sept. 1938; s of Mary and John Robert Sizer; m 1965, Valerie Davies; three s. *Educ:* Grimsby Coll. of Technology; Univ. of Nottingham (BA). FCMA. Teaching Fellow, later Lectr, Univ. of Edinburgh, 1965; Sen. Lectr, London Graduate Sch. of Business Studies, 1968; Loughborough University of Technology: Founding Head of Dept of Management Studies, 1971–84; Dean of Sch. of Human and Environmental Studies, 1973–76; Sen. Pro Vice-Chancellor, 1980–82. Chm., Directing Group, OECD/CERI Programme on Institutional Management in Higher Educn, 1980–84; Mem., UGC, 1984– (Chm., Business and Management Studies Sub-Cttee). FBIM; FRSA. *Publications:* An Insight into Management Accounting, 1969; Case Studies in Management Accounting, 1974; Perspectives in Management Accounting, 1981; (jtly) A Casebook of British Management Accounting, vol. 1, 1984, vol. 2, 1985; (ed jtly) Resources and Higher Education, 1983; numerous articles in accounting, higher educn and management jls. *Recreations:* table tennis, walking. *Address:* Department of Management Studies, Loughborough University of Technology, Loughborough, Leics LE11 3TU. *T:* Loughborough 263171.

SKAN, Peter Henry O.; see Ogle-Skan.

SKEAT, Theodore Cressy, BA; Keeper of Manuscripts and Egerton Librarian, British Museum, 1961–72; b 15 Feb. 1907; s of Walter William Skeat, MA; m 1942, Olive Martin; one s. *Educ:* Whitgift School, Croydon; Christ's College, Cambridge. Student at British School of Archaeology, Athens, 1929–31; Asst Keeper, Dept of Manuscripts, British Museum, 1931; Deputy Keeper, 1948. FBA, 1963–80. *Publications:* (with H. I. Bell) Fragments of an Unknown Gospel, 1935; (with H. J. M. Milne) Scribes and Correctors of the Codex Sinaiticus, 1938; The Reigns of the Ptolemies, 1954; Papyri from Panopolis, 1964; Catalogue of Greek Papyri in the British Museum, vol. VII, 1974; (with C. H. Roberts) The Birth of the Codex, 1983; articles in papyrological journals. *Address:* 63 Ashbourne Road, W5 3DH. *T:* 01–998 1246.

SKEATES, Basil George; Director, Ashdown Gallery; Under Secretary, Department of the Environment, 1980–85; b 19 May 1929; s of George William Skeates and Florence Rachel Skeates; m 1957, Irene Margaret (née Hughes); four s. *Educ:* Hampton Grammar Sch. RIBA 1955. Mil. Service with RE, W Africa, 1947–49. Architect with LCC schs and special works, 1949–61; Principal Architect: NE Metrop. Reg. Hosp. Bd, 1961–64; MPBW, 1964–71; Superintending Architect, CSD, 1971–73; Asst Dir, Architectural Services, PSA, 1973–75; Dir of Works, PO Services, 1975–80; Dir of Def. Services II, DoE, 1980–85. *Publications:* articles in prof. and technical jls. *Recreation:* designing and making things.

SKEET, Muriel Harvey; Health Services adviser and consultant, World Health Organisation Headquarters and other international agencies and organisations, since 1978; b 12 July 1926; y d of late Col F. W. C. Harvey-Skeet, Suffolk. *Educ:* privately; Endsleigh House; Middlesex Hosp. SRN, MRSH; FRCN. Gen. Nursing Trg at Middx Hosp., 1946–49; also London Sch. of Hygiene and Tropical Med.; Ward Sister and Admin. Sister, Middx Hosp., 1949–60; Field Work Organiser, Opl Res. Unit, Nuffield Provincial Hosps Trust, 1961–64; Res. Org., Dan Mason Nursing Res. Cttee of Nat. Florence Nightingale Memorial Cttee of Gt Britain and N Ire., 1965–70; Chief Nursing Officer and Nursing Advr, BRCS, and St John of Jerusalem and BRCS Jt Cttee, 1970–78. WHO Res. Consultant, SE Asia, 1970; European Deleg. and First Chm. of Bd of Commonwealth Nurses' Fed., 1971. Leverhulme Fellowship, 1974–75. Member: Hosp. and Med. Services Cttee, 1970; Ex-Services War Disabled Help Cttee, 1970; British Commonwealth Nurses War Memorial Fund Cttee and Council, 1970; Council of Management of Nat. Florence Nightingale Memorial Cttee, 1970; Council of Queen's Inst. of District Nursing, 1970; Royal Coll. of Nursing and Nat. Council of Nurses; RSM, 1980. Fellow RCN, 1977. *Publications:* Waiting in Outpatient Departments (Nuffield Provincial Hospitals Trust), 1965; Marriage and Nursing (Dan Mason NRC), 1968; Home from Hospital (Dan Mason NRC), 1970; Home Nursing, 1975; Manual: Disaster Relief Work, 1977; Back to Our Basic Skills, 1977; Health needs Help, 1977; (jtly) Health Auxiliaries in the Health Team, 1978; Self Care for the People of Developing Countries, 1979; Discharge Procedures, 1980; Notes on Nursing 1860 and 1980, 1980; Emergency Procedures and First Aid for Nurses, 1981; The Third Age, 1982; Providing Continuing Care for Elderly People, 1983; First Aid for Developing Countries, 1983; various articles in professional jls. *Recreations:* music, opera, painting, reading. *Address:* Oakford House, Nether Stowey, Som. *T:* Nether Stowey 303. *Clubs:* Arts, New Cavendish.

SKEET, Sir Trevor (Herbert Harry), Kt 1986; MP (C) Bedfordshire North, since 1983 (Bedford, 1970–83); Barrister, Writer and Consultant; b 28 Jan. 1918; British; m 1st, 1958, Elizabeth Margaret Gilling (d 1973); two s; 2nd, 1985, Mrs Valerie Anita Edwina Benson. *Educ:* King's College, Auckland; University of New Zealand, Auckland (LLB). Served War of 1939–45, with NZ Engineers (sergeant); 2nd Lieut, NZ Anti-Aircraft (Heavy); Sub-Lieutenant, NZ Roy. Naval Volunteer Reserve; demobilised, 1945. Formerly Barrister and Solicitor of Supreme Court of New Zealand; Barrister, Inner Temple, 1947. Has considerable experience in public speaking. Contested (C): Stoke Newington and Hackney, North, Gen. Election, 1951; Llanelly Div. of Carmarthenshire, Gen. Election, 1955; MP (C) Willesden East, 1959–64. Formerly associated with Commonwealth and Empire Industries Assoc.; Mem. Council, Royal Commonwealth Soc., 1952–55, and 1956–69. Vice-Chairman: Cons. Party Power Cttee, 1959–64; Energy Cttee, 1974–77; Chairman: Oil Sub-Cttee, 1959–64; Cons. Party Trade Cttee, 1971–74; Cons. Party Middle East Cttee (Foreign and Commonwealth Affairs), 1973–78; Secretary: All-Party Cttee on Airships, 1971–78; All-Party Gp on Minerals, 1971– (Co-Chm., 1979–); Chm., Steering Cttee, Parly and Scientific Cttee, 1985– (Mem., 1982–; Sec., 1983–85); Vice-Chm., British-Japanese and British-Brazilian Gps; Sec., British-Nigerian Gp. Mem., Econ. Cttee, Machine Tool Trades Association for several years; Member Technical Legislation Cttee, CBI. *Publications:* contrib. to numerous journals including New Commonwealth and Mining World, on oil, atomic energy, metals, commodities,

finance, and Imperial and Commonwealth development. *Address:* (home) The Gables, Milton Ernest, Bedfordshire MK44 1RS. *T:* Oakley 2307. *Clubs:* Army and Navy, Royal Commonwealth Society.

SKEFFINGTON, family name of **Viscount Massereene and Ferrard.**

SKEFFINGTON-LODGE, Thomas Cecil; b 15 Jan. 1905; s of late Thomas Robert Lodge and late Winifred Marian Skeffington; unmarried. *Educ:* privately; Giggleswick and Westminster Schools. For some years engaged in Advertising and Publicity both in London and the North of England; later did Public Relations and administrative work in the Coal Trade as Northern Area Organiser for the Coal Utilisation Council, in which he served Cttees of Coal Trade in North-East, North-West and Yorkshire; on the outbreak of war, became a Mines Dept official; then volunteered for the Navy; from early 1941 a Naval Officer. Mem., Parly Delegn, Nüremberg Trials. Lecture tour in USA under auspices of Anglo-American Parly Gp, 1949. MP (Lab) Bedford, 1945–50; contested (Lab) York, 1951, Mid-Bedfordshire, 1955; Grantham, 1959; Brighton (Pavilion), March 1969; Personal Asst to Chm., Colonial Development Corp., 1950–52. Mem. of post-war Parly Delegns to Eire, Belgium, Luxembourg and USA; formerly Mem., Parly Ecclesiastical Cttee, and served on Parochial Church Council, St Margaret's, Westminster. Past-Pres. and Chm., Pudsey Divisional Labour Party; Pres., Brighton and Hove Fabian Soc.; Member: Labour Party many years; Socialist Christian Movement (Vice-Pres.); IPU; Exec. Cttee, Brighton and Hove Br. UNA; German-British Christian Fellowship (past Chm.); Union of Shop, Distributive and Allied Workers; Conservation Soc.; CPRE (Chm., Brighton Dist Cttee, Sussex Branch); RSPB; Georgian Group; Friends of the Lake District; Amnesty Internat.; British-Soviet Friendship Soc.; Anglo-German Assoc.; Anglo-Belgian Assoc.; former Chm., Socialist Christian League and Parly Socialist Christian Group. *Recreations:* travel, gardening, politics and associating Christianity with them, in the hope of erecting fairer national and international living conditions for mankind. *Address:* 5 Powis Grove, Brighton, East Sussex. *T:* Brighton 25472. *Club:* Savile.

SKEHEL, John James, PhD; FRS 1984; Head of Division of Virology, National Institute for Medical Research, since 1984; Co-Director, World Influenza Centre, since 1975; b 27 Feb. 1941; s of Joseph and Ann Josephine Skehel; m 1962, Anita Varley; two s. *Educ:* St Mary's Coll., Blackburn; University College of Wales, Aberystwyth (BSc); UMIST (PhD). Post-doctoral Fellow, Marischal Coll., Aberdeen, 1965–68; Fellow, Helen Hay Whitney Foundn, 1968–71; Mem., Scientific Staff, Nat. Inst. for Med. Res. 1971–. *Publications:* scientific articles in various jls. *Address:* 49 Homewood Road, St Albans, Herts. *T:* St Albans 60603.

SKELHORN, Sir Norman John, KBE 1966; QC 1954; Director of Public Prosecutions, 1964–77; b Glossop, Derbyshire, 10 Sept. 1909; s of late Rev. Samuel and late Bertha Skelhorn; m 1937, Rosamund, d of late Prof. James Swain, CB, CBE; no c. *Educ:* Shrewsbury School. Called to Bar, Middle Temple, 1931, Master of the Bench, 1962. Member of Western Circuit; employed in Trading with the Enemy Dept (Treasury and Board of Trade), 1940–42; in Admiralty, 1942–45, latterly as head of Naval Law Branch. Recorder, Bridgwater, 1945–54; Plymouth, 1954–62; Portsmouth, 1962–64; a Recorder of the Crown Court, 1977–81. Chairman, Isle of Wight County Quarter Sessions, 1951–64. Member, Departmental Cttee on Probation Service, 1959–61; appointed Member of Home Secretary's Advisory Council on Treatment of Offenders, 1962; Member Home Secretary's: Probation Advisory and Training Board, 1962–73; Criminal Law Revision Cttee, 1964–80. *Publication:* Public Prosecutor: the Memoirs of Sir Norman Skelhorn, Director of Public Prosecutions 1964–1977, 1981. *Clubs:* Athenæum, Royal Automobile.

SKELLERUP, Sir Valdemar (Reid), Kt 1979; CBE 1973; Chairman and Joint Managing Director, Skellerup Industries Ltd, since 1961; b 22 Dec. 1907; s of George Waldemar Skjellerup and Elizabeth Skjellerup; m 1933, Marion Caroline Bates; one s three d. *Educ:* Ashburton High Sch.; Canterbury University Coll. *Address:* 110 North Parade, Shirley, Christchurch 1, New Zealand. *T:* 852–245.

SKELMERSDALE, 7th Baron cr 1828; **Roger Bootle-Wilbraham;** Parliamentary Under-Secretary of State, Department of the Environment, since 1986; b 2 April 1945; o s of 6th Baron Skelmersdale, DSO, MC, and Ann (d 1974), d of late Percy Cuthbert Quilter; S father, 1973; m 1972, Christine Joan, o d of Roy Morgan; one s one d. *Educ:* Eton; Lord Wandsworth Coll., Basingstoke; Somerset Farm Institute; Hadlow Coll. VSO (Zambia), 1969–71; Proprietor, Broadleigh Gardens, 1972; Man. Dir, Broadleigh Nurseries Ltd, 1973–81; Vice-Chm., Co En Co, 1979–81. A Lord in Waiting (Govt Whip), 1981–86. President: Somerset Trust for Nature Conservation, 1980–; British Naturalists Trust, 1980–. *Recreations:* gardening, reading, bridge playing. *Heir:* s Hon. Andrew Bootle-Wilbraham, b 9 Aug. 1977. *Address:* Barr House, Bishops Hull, Taunton, Somerset. *T:* Taunton 70655.

SKELTON, Rt. Rev. Kenneth John Fraser, CBE 1972; an Assistant Bishop, Dioceses of Sheffield and Derby; b 16 May 1918; s of Henry Edmund and Kate Elizabeth Skelton; m 1945, Phyllis Barbara, y d of James Emerton; two s one d. *Educ:* Dulwich Coll.; Corpus Christi Coll., Cambridge; Wells Theological Coll. 1st Cl. Class. Tripos, Pt 1, 1939; 1st Cl. Theol. Tripos, Pt 1, 1940; BA 1940, MA 1944. Deacon, 1941; Priest, 1942; Curate: Normanton-by-Derby, 1941–43; Bakewell, 1943–45; Bolsover, 1945–46; Tutor, Wells Theol Coll., and Priest-Vicar, Wells Cathedral, 1946–50; Vicar of Howe Bridge, Atherton, 1950–55; Rector, Walton-on-the-Hill, Liverpool, 1955–62; Exam. Chap. to Bp of Liverpool, 1957–62; Bishop of Matabeleland, 1962–70; Asst Bishop, Dio. Durham, Rural Dean of Wearmouth and Rector of Bishopwearmouth, 1970–75; Bishop of Lichfield, 1975–84. Select Preacher, Cambridge Univ., 1971, 1973. *Publication:* Bishop in Smith's Rhodesia, 1985. *Recreation:* music. *Address:* 65 Crescent Road, Sheffield S7 1HN. *T:* Sheffield 551260.

SKELTON, Rear-Adm. Peter, CB 1956; b 27 Dec. 1901; s of Peter John and Selina Frances Skelton; m 1928, Janice Brown Clark; two d. *Educ:* RN Colleges, Osborne and Dartmouth; Trinity Hall, Cambridge. Cadet, 1915; Midshipman, HMS Valiant, 1918; Commander, 1936; Capt. 1944; Rear-Adm., 1953. Served War of 1939–45, as Staff Officer in HMS Aurora, later at Admiralty in Torpedo Division; Commander and Actg Capt. in HMS Royal Sovereign, 1942; Director of Trade Div., Admiralty, 1944; Supt of Torpedo Experimental Establishment, 1946; Sen. Naval Officer, Persian Gulf, 1949; Captain of Dockyard, Portsmouth, 1951; Admiral Superintendent, Rosyth, 1953–56; retired. Bucks CC, 1958. *Recreations:* golf, tennis, shooting. *Address:* Craigie Barns, Kippen, Stirlingshire.

SKELTON, Robert William; Keeper, Indian Department, Victoria and Albert Museum, since 1978; b 11 June 1929; s of John William Skelton and Victoria (née Wright); m 1954, Frances Aird; three s. *Educ:* Tiffin Boys' Sch., Kingston-upon-Thames. Joined Indian Section of Victoria and Albert Museum, 1950; Asst Keeper, 1960; Dep. Keeper, 1972; Nuffield Travelling Fellow in India, 1962. Mem. Council: Royal Asiatic Soc., 1970–73, 1975–78; Soc. for S Asian Studies, 1984–; Trustee, Asia House Trust (London), 1977–. *Publications:* Indian Miniatures from the XVth to XIXth Centuries, 1961; Rajasthani

Temple Hangings of the Krishna Cult, 1973; (jtly) Islamic Painting and Arts of the Book, 1976; (jtly) Indian Painting, 1978; (jtly) Arts of Bengal, 1979; (jtly) The Indian Heritage, 1982; various contribs to art periodicals and conf. proc., 1956–. *Recreations:* chamber music, walking. *Address:* 10 Spencer Road, South Croydon CR2 7EH. *T:* 01–688 7187.

SKELTON, Prof. Robin, FRSL; author; Professor of English, since 1966, and Chairman of Department of Creative Writing, 1973–76, University of Victoria, British Columbia; *b* 12 Oct. 1925; *o s* of Cyril Frederick William and Eliza Skelton; *m* 1957, Sylvia Mary Jarrett; one *s* two *d. Educ:* Pocklington Grammar Sch., 1936–43; Christ's Coll., Cambridge, 1943–44; Univ. of Leeds, 1947–51. BA 1950, MA 1951. Served RAF, 1944–47. Asst Lectr in English, Univ. of Manchester, 1951; Lectr, 1954. Managing Dir, The Lotus Press, 1950–52; Examiner for NUJMB, 1954–58; Chm. of Examrs in English, 'O' Level, 1958–60; Co-founder and Chm., Peterloo Gp, Manchester, 1957–60; Founding Mem. and Hon. Sec., Manchester Inst. of Contemporary Arts, 1960–63; Centenary Lectr at Univ. of Massachusetts, 1962–63; Gen. Editor, OUP edn of Works of J. M. Synge, 1962–68; Associate Prof. of English, Univ. of Victoria, BC, 1963–66. Visiting Prof., Univ. of Michigan, Ann Arbor, 1967; Dir, Creative Writing Programme, Univ. of Victoria, 1967–73; Founder and co-Editor, Malahat Review, 1967–71, Editor 1972–83. Mem. Bd of Dirs, Art Gall. of Greater Victoria, BC, 1968–69, 1970–73; Dir, Pharos Press, 1972–; Editor, Sono Nis Press, 1976–83. FRSL 1966. Chm., Writers' Union of Canada, 1982 (first Vice-Chm., 1981). *Publications: poetry* Patmos and Other Poems, 1955; Third Day Lucky, 1958; Two Ballads of the Muse, 1960; Begging the Dialect, 1960; The Dark Window, 1962; A Valedictory Poem, 1963; An Irish Gathering, 1964; A Ballad of Billy Barker, 1965; Inscriptions, 1967; Because of This, 1968; The Hold of Our Hands, 1968; Selected Poems, 1947–67, 1968; An Irish Album, 1969; Georges Zuk, Selected Verse, 1969; Answers, 1969; The Hunting Dark, 1971; Two Hundred Poems from the Greek Anthology, 1971; A Different Mountain, 1971; A Private Speech, 1971; Remembering Synge, 1971; Three for Herself, 1972; Musebook, 1972; Country Songs, 1973; Timelight, 1974; Georges Zuk: The Underwear of the Unicorn, 1975; Callsigns, 1976; Because of Love, 1977; Landmarks, 1979; Collected Shorter Poems 1947–1977, 1981; Limits, 1981; De Nihilo, 1982; Zuk, 1982; Wordsong, 1983; Distances, 1985; The Collected Longer Poems 1947–1977, 1985; *prose:* John Ruskin: The Final Years, 1955; The Poetic Pattern, 1956; Cavalier Poets, 1960; Poetry (in Teach Yourself series), 1963; The Writings of J. M. Synge, 1971; J. M. Synge and His World, 1971; The Practice of Poetry, 1971; J. M. Synge (Irish Writers series), 1972; The Poet's Calling, 1975; Poetic Truth, 1978; Spellcraft, 1978; They Call It The Cariboo, 1980; Talismanic Magic, 1985; *fiction:* The Man who sang in his Sleep, 1984; *drama:* The Paper Cage, 1982; *edited texts:* J. M. Synge: Translations, 1961; J. M. Synge, Four Plays and the Aran Islands, 1962; J. M. Synge, Collected Poems, 1962; Edward Thomas, Selected Poems, 1962; Selected Poems of Byron, 1965; David Gascoyne, Collected Poems, 1965; J. M. Synge, Riders to the Sea, 1969; David Gascoyne, Collected Verse Translations (with Alan Clodd), 1970; J. M. Synge, Translations of Petrarch, 1971; Jack B. Yeats, Collected Plays, 1971; (also trans.) George Faludy: selected poems, 1985; *anthologies:* Leeds University Poetry, 1949, 1950; Viewpoint, 1962; Six Irish Poets, 1962; Poetry of the Thirties, 1964; Five Poets of the Pacific Northwest, 1964; Poetry of the Forties, 1968; The Cavalier Poets, 1970; Six Poets of British Columbia, 1980; *symposia:* The World of W. B. Yeats (with Ann Saddlemyer), 1965; Irish Renaissance (with David R. Clark), 1965; Herbert Read: a memorial symposium, 1970. *Recreations:* book collecting, art collecting, making collages, stone carving, philately. *Address:* 1255 Victoria Avenue, Victoria, BC V8S 4P3, Canada. *T:* (604) 592–7032.

SKEMP, Prof. Joseph Bright, MA Cantab, PhD Edinburgh; Emeritus Professor of Greek, in the University of Durham; *b* 10 May 1910; *s* of late Thomas William Widlake Skemp, solicitor and local government officer, and Caroline (*née* Southall); *m* 1941, Ruby James; no *c. Educ:* Wolverhampton Grammar School; Gonville and Caius College, Cambridge. Unofficial Drosier Fellow, Gonville and Caius College, Cambridge, 1936–47; Warden of Refugee Club and Asst Sec. to Refugee Cttee, Cambridge, 1940–46; Sec., Soc. for the Protection of Science and Learning, 1944–46; Lecturer in Greek and Latin, Univ. of Manchester, 1946–49; Reader in Greek, Univ. of Durham (Newcastle Div.), 1949–50; Prof. of Greek, Univ. of Durham, 1950–73; Vis. Prof., Univ. of Alexandria, 1977. Editor, Durham University Journal, 1953–57; Joint Editor, Phronesis, 1955–64. *Publications:* The Theory of Motion in Plato's Later Dialogues, 1942 (enlarged 1967); Plato's Statesman, 1952; The Greeks and the Gospel, 1964; Plato (supplementary vol. periodical Greece and Rome), 1976. *Recreations:* walking, history of railways. *Address:* 6A Westfield Park, Bristol BS6 6LT. *T:* Bristol 739402.

SKEMP, Terence Rowland Frazer, CB 1973; QC 1984; Barrister-at-Law; *b* 14 Feb. 1915; *s* of Frank Whittingham Skemp and Dorothy Frazer; *m* 1939, Dorothy Norman Pringle; one *s* two *d. Educ:* Charterhouse; Christ Church, Oxford. Called to Bar, Gray's Inn, 1938. Served War, Army, 1939–46. Entered Parliamentary Counsel Office, 1946; Parliamentary Counsel, 1964; Second Parly Counsel, 1973–80; Counsel to the Speaker, 1980–85. *Address:* 997 Finchley Road, NW11.

SKEMPTON, Prof. Alec Westley, DSc London 1949; FRS 1961; FEng; FICE; Professor of Civil Engineering in the University of London (Imperial College), 1957–81, now Emeritus; Senior Research Fellow, Imperial College, since 1981; *b* 4 June 1914; *o c* of late A. W. Skempton, Northampton, and Beatrice Edridge Payne; *m* 1940, Mary, *d* of E. R. Wood, Brighouse, Yorks; two *d. Educ:* Northampton Grammar School; Imperial College, University of London (Goldsmiths' Bursar). Building Research Station, 1936–46; University Reader in Soil Mechanics, Imperial College, 1946–54; Professor of Soil Mechanics, Imperial College, 1955–57. Vice-Pres., 1974–76 (Member Council, 1949–54), Institute Civil Engineers; Pres., Internat. Soc. Soil Mechanics and Foundn Eng, 1957–61; Chm. Jt Cttee on Soils, Min. of Supply and Road Research Bd, 1954–59; Mem., Cathedrals Advisory Cttee, 1964–70; Mem., NERC, 1973–76; President: Newcomen Soc., 1977–79; Smeatonian Soc., 1981. Hitchcock Foundn Prof., Univ. of Calif, Berkeley, 1978; Lectures: Copenhagen, Paris, Harvard, Univ. of Illinois, Oslo, Stockholm, Madrid, Florence, Sydney, Quebec, Mexico City, Tokyo, Berkeley; Special Lectr, Architectural Assoc., 1948–57; Vis. Lectr Cambridge Univ. School of Architecture, 1962–66; Consultant to Binnie & Partners, John Mowlem & Co., etc. For. Associate, Nat. Acad. of Engineering, USA, 1976. Hon. DSc: Durham, 1968; Aston, 1980; Chalmers, 1982. Ewing Medal, 1968; Lyell Medal, 1972; Dickinson Medal, 1974; Karl Terzaghi Award, 1981; IStructE Gold Medal, 1981. Silver Jubilee Medal, 1977. *Publications:* Early Printed Reports in the Institution of Civil Engineers, 1977; (with C. Hadfield) William Jessop, Engineer, 1979; John Smeaton, FRS, 1981; Selected Papers on Soil Mechanics, 1984; numerous contribs on soil mechanics, engineering geology and history of construction. *Recreations:* field and archive research on 18th cent. civil engineering and engineers, croquet. *Address:* Imperial College, SW7. *T:* 01–589 5111; 16 The Boltons, SW10. *T:* 01–370 3457. *Clubs:* Athenæum, Hurlingham.

SKERMAN, Ronald Sidney, CBE 1974; Deputy Chairman, Prudential Corporation plc, since 1985 (Director, since 1980; Group Chief Actuary, 1979); *b* 1 June 1914; *s* of S. H. Skerman; *m* 1939, Gladys Mary Fosdike; no *c. Educ:* Hertford Grammar School. FIA.

Actuarial Trainee with Prudential Assurance Co., 1932; Chief Actuary, 1968–79. Pres., Inst. Actuaries, 1970–72; Chm., Life Offices Assoc., 1973–74; Chm., British Insurers European Cttee, 1972–82; Mem., Royal Commn on Civil Liability, 1973–78. Gold Medal, Inst. of Actuaries, 1980. *Publications:* contrib. Jl Inst. Actuaries. *Recreations:* walking, travel, music. *Address:* 30 Springfields, Broxbourne, Herts EN10 7LX. *T:* Hoddesdon 463257.

SKEWIS, (William) Iain, PhD; Chief Executive, Development Board for Rural Wales, since 1977; *b* 1 May 1936; *s* of John Jamieson and Margaret Middlemass Skewis; *m* 1963, Jessie Frame Weir; two *s* one *d. Educ:* Hamilton Academy; Univ. of Glasgow (BSc, PhD). MCIT. British Rail, 1961–63; Transport Holding Co., 1963–66; Highlands and Islands Development Bd, 1966–72; Yorkshire and Humberside Development Assoc., 1973–77. *Recreation:* soccer. *Address:* Rock House, The Square, Montgomery, Powys SY15 6RA. *T:* Montgomery 276.

SKIDELSKY, Prof. Robert Jacob Alexander, DPhil; FRHistS, FRSL; Professor of International Studies, Warwick University, since 1978; *b* 25 April 1939; *s* of Boris Skidelsky and Galia Sapelkin; *m* 1970, Augusta Mary Clarissa Hope; two *s* one *d. Educ:* Brighton Coll.; Jesus Coll., Oxford (BA and MA Mod. Hist.; DPhil). FRHistS 1973; FRSL 1978. Res. Fellow: Nuffield Coll., Oxford, 1965–68; British Acad., 1968–70; Associate Prof. of History, Sch. of Advanced Internat. Studies, Johns Hopkins Univ., Washington, DC, 1970–76; Head, Dept of History, Philosophy and Eur. Studies, Polytechnic of N London, 1976–78. *Publications:* Politicians and the Slump, 1967; English Progressive Schools, 1969; Oswald Mosley, 1975, 2nd edn 1980; (ed) The End of the Keynesian Era, 1977; (ed, with Michael Holroyd) William Gerhardie's God's Fifth Column, 1981; John Maynard Keynes, vol. 1 1883–1920, Hopes Betrayed, 1983; contrib. Encounter, Spectator, TLS, New Soc. *Recreations:* opera, ballet, cinema, squash (with Michael Holroyd), tennis, table tennis. *Address:* Tilton House, Firle, East Sussex BN8 6LL. *T:* Ripe 570. *Club:* United Oxford & Cambridge University.

SKILBECK, Diana Margaret; Headmistress, Sheffield High School, GPDST, since 1983; *b* 14 Nov. 1942; *d* of late William Allen Skilbeck and Elsie Almond Skilbeck. *Educ:* Wirral County Grammar School for Girls, Cheshire; Furzedown Coll., London (Teacher's Cert.); BA Hons London (External). Assistant Teacher: Mendell Primary Sch., 1964–67; Gayton Primary Sch., 1967–69; Wirral County Grammar Sch., 1969–74; Head of Geography, Wirral County Grammar Sch., 1974–78; Dep. Headmistress, West Kirby Grammar Sch., 1978–83. *Recreations:* inland waterways, walking, singing, squash, skating, reading, industrial archaeology. *Address:* 21 Arkwood Close, Bebington, Wirral, Merseyside L62 2AU. *T:* 051–334 4432; (term-time) Sheffield 660324.

SKILBECK, Dunstan, CBE 1957; MA Oxon; FIBiol; Principal, Wye College, University of London, 1945–68; Hon. Fellow, Wye College; *b* 13 June 1904; 2nd *s* of Clement Oswald Skilbeck, FSA, and Elizabeth Bertha Skilbeck; *m* 1934, Elspeth Irene Jomini, *d* of Edward Carruthers, MD, and Mary Carruthers; two *s* one *d. Educ:* University College School, London; St John's College, Oxford. Agricultural Economics Res. Inst., University of Oxford, 1927–30; Univ. Demonstrator in School of Rural Economy, University of Oxford; Director of St John's College Farm; Lecturer and Tutor in Rural Economy, St John's College, Oxford, 1930–40. Served with RAF Home and Middle East, Air Staff HQ, Middle East, 1940–45; as Wing Comdr, appointed Asst Director, Middle East Supply Centre (Food Production), 1942–45 (despatches). Vice-Chm. Imperial Coll. of Tropical Agric., 1958–60; Liaison Officer to Minister of Agriculture, for SE England, 1952–60; Mem., Ghana Commn on Univ. Educn., 1961. Team Leader, Near East Res. Review Mission for Consultative Gp on Internat. Agricl Research, 1973. Chairman: Collegiate Council, Univ. of London, 1962–65 (Mem., Senate, 1959–68); Canterbury Diocesan Adv. Cttee, 1970–81. Member Council: Voluntary Service Overseas, 1964–68; England and Wales Nature Conservancy, 1968–73; Vice-Chm., CPRE, 1974–80, Vice-Pres., 1980–. Trustee, Ernest Cook Trust, 1966–. Liveryman, Worshipful Co. of Fruiterers, 1960. *Publications:* contribs to scientific and agricultural jls. *Address:* Mount Bottom, Elham, near Canterbury, Kent. *T:* Elham 258. *Club:* Farmers'.

SKILBECK, Prof. Malcolm; Professor and Vice-Chancellor, Deakin University, Australia, since 1986; *b* 22 Sept. 1932; *s* of Charles Harrison Skilbeck and Elsie Muriel Nash Skilbeck; *m* Helen Connell. *Educ:* Univ. of Sydney (BA); Acad. DipEd London, PhD London; MA Illinois. Secondary school teacher and adult educn teacher, 1958–63; Lectr. Univ. of Bristol, 1963–71; Prof., New Univ. of Ulster, 1971–75; Dir, Australian Curriculum Develt Centre, 1975–81; Dir of Studies, Schs Council for Curriculum and Exams for England and Wales, 1981–83; Prof. of Education, Univ. of London, 1981–85. Consultancies for Unesco, British Council, OECD, etc, intermittently, 1967–; active in voluntary organizations concerned with educn for internat. understanding, eg, Chm., World Educn Fellowship, 1981–85. *Publications:* John Dewey, 1970; (jtly) Classroom and Culture, 1976; (jtly) Inservice Education and Training, 1977; A Core Curriculum for the Common School 1984, 1982; (ed) Evaluating the Curriculum in the Eighties, 1984; School Based Curriculum Development, 1984; Readings in School-Based Curriculum Development, 1984; numerous contribs to jls, project reports, etc. *Recreations:* gardening, travelling, walking, reading. *Address:* Deakin University, Victoria 3217, Australia.

SKILLINGTON, William Patrick Denny, CB 1964; a Deputy Secretary, Department of the Environment (formerly Ministry of Public Building and Works), 1966–73; Housing Commissioner, for Clay Cross UDC, 1973–74; *b* 13 Feb. 1913; *s* of late S. J. Skillington, Leicester; *m* 1941, Dorin Kahn, Sydney, Australia; two *d. Educ:* Malvern College; Exeter College, Oxford. BA 1935, MA 1939, Oxford. Articled to Clerk of Leicestershire CC, 1936–39. Commissioned in R Welch Fusiliers (SR), 1933; served War of 1939–45 (despatches); regimental officer in France and Belgium, and on staff in Sicily, Italy and Greece; AA and QMG; Lt-Col. Entered Min. of Works as Principal, 1946; Asst Sec., 1952; Under-Sec. (Dir of Establishments), Min. of Public Building and Works, 1956–64; Asst Under-Sec. of State, Home Office, 1964–66. *Address:* 95a S Mark's Road, Henley-on-Thames, Oxon. *T:* Henley 573756. *Clubs:* United Oxford & Cambridge University; Phyllis Court (Henley).

SKINGSLEY, Air Marshal Sir Anthony (Gerald), KCB 1986 (CB 1983); Air Member for Personnel, since 1986; *b* 19 Oct. 1933; *s* of Edward Roberts Skingsley; *m* 1957, Lilwen; two *s* one *d. Educ:* St Bartholomew's, Newbury; Cambridge Univ. (BA, MA). Commissioned RAFVR 1954, RAF 1955; several flying appointments, then Flt Comdr 13 Sqdn, 1961–62; OC Ops Sqdn, RAF Akrotiri, 1962–63; RAF Staff Coll., Bracknell, 1964; OC 45 Sqdn, RAF Tengah, Singapore, 1965–67; jssc Latimer, 1968; RAF Project Officer for Tornado in MoD, 1968–71; OC 214 Sqdn, RAF Marham, 1972–74; Station Comdr, RAF Laarbruch, Germany, 1974–76; Hon. ADC to the Queen, 1976–78; Asst Chief of Staff, Offensive Ops, HQ 2nd ATAF, 1977; RCDS 1978; Director of Air Staff Plans, MoD, 1978–80; Asst Chief of Staff, Plans and Policy, SHAPE, 1980–83; Comdt, RAF Staff Coll., Bracknell, 1983–84; ACAS, 1985–86. Mem., Allgemeine Rheinlaendische Industrie Gesellschaft, 1975. *Recreations:* travel, off-shore sailing, music, walking, golf. *Address:* c/o National Westminster Bank, 30 Market Place, Newbury, Berks. *Clubs:* Royal Air Force, Royal Thames Yacht.

SKINNER, Prof. Andrew Forrester, MA, BSc, PhD (St Andrews); MA (Columbia); FEIS; Professor of Education, Ontario College of Education, University of Toronto, 1954–70, now Emeritus Professor; *b* 21 May 1902; *s* of Alexander H. and Jessie F. Skinner, Kingskettle, Scotland; *m* 1932, Elizabeth Balmer Lockhart (*d* 1983), Manchester. *Educ:* Bell-Baxter School, Cupar, Fife; University of St Andrews. MA, BSc, 1st Cl. Hons Maths and Phys Sci., 1925; Carnegie Research Fellow in Chemistry, PhD, 1928; Commonwealth Fund Fellow, Columbia, New York, 1929–31 (Educ. MA); Teacher in various schools, 1931–37; Asst Dir of Education, Co. of Aberdeen, 1937–39; Principal Lecturer in Methods, Dundee Trg Coll., 1939–41; Prof. of Education, Univ. of St Andrews, and Principal, Dundee Trg Coll., 1941–54. Vis. Prof. Ontario Coll. of Educ., Univ. of Toronto, 1950 and 1954; Visiting Professor: E Tennessee State Coll., 1951; State Univ. of Iowa, 1951–52; Univ. of British Columbia, 1962; Univ. of Victoria, 1964; Queen's Univ., Kingston, 1971. Former Member: Scottish Council for Research in Education; Scottish Universities Entrance Bd; School Broadcasting Council for Scotland; Mem., Bd of Directors, Comparative Educn Soc. of USA; Mem. Exec., Comparative and Internat. Educn Soc. of Canada, Vice-Pres., 1968–69, Pres., 1969–70, now Hon. Mem. *Publications:* (Booklet) Scottish Education in Schools, 1942; (Booklet) Introductory Course on Education in Scotland, 1944; Citizenship in the Training of Teachers, 1948; Teachers' Heritage: an introduction to the study of education, 1979; articles in Jl of Amer. Chem. Soc.; Trans Chem. Soc.; Scottish Educnl Jl; The Year Book of Education; Educnl Forum: Educational Record of Quebec; The American People's Encyclopedia; Canadian and International Education; Canadian Education and Research Digest. *Recreations:* golf, gardening and walking. *Address:* 296 Ferry Road, Edinburgh EH5 3NP. *T:* 031–552 4907.

SKINNER, Burrhus Frederic; Emeritus Professor, Harvard University, since 1975; *b* Susquehanna, 20 March 1904; *s* of William Arthur Skinner and Grace (*née* Burrhus); *m* 1936, Yvonne Blue; two *d. Educ:* Hamilton Coll.; Harvard Univ. AB Hamilton 1926; MA 1930, PhD 1931, Harvard. Res. Fellow NRC, Harvard, 1931–33; Jr Fellow, Harvard Soc. Fellows, 1933–36; Minnesota Univ.: Instr Psychol., 1936–37; Asst Prof., 1937–39; Assoc. Prof., 1939–45; conducted war research sponsored by Gen. Mills, Inc., 1942–43; Guggenheim Fellow, 1944–45; Prof. Psychol., Chm. Dept, Indiana Univ., 1945–48; Harvard Univ.: William James Lectr, 1947; Prof. Psychol., 1948–57; Edgar Pierce Prof., 1958–75. FRSA; Member: Brit. and Swedish Psychol Socs; Amer. Psychol Assoc.; AAAS; Nat. Acad. Sci.; Amer. Acad. Arts and Scis; Amer. Phil Soc.; Phi Beta Kappa; Sigma Xi. Holds numerous hon. degrees; has won many awards. *Publications:* Behavior of Organisms, 1938; Walden Two, 1948; Science and Human Behavior, 1953; Verbal Behavior, 1957; (with C. B. Ferster) Schedules of Reinforcement, 1957; Cumulative Record, 1959, 3rd edn 1972; (with J. G. Holland) The Analysis of Behavior, 1961; The Technology of Teaching, 1968; Contingencies of Reinforcement: A Theoretical Analysis, 1969; Beyond Freedom and Dignity, 1971; About Behaviorism, 1974; Reflections on Behaviorism and Society, 1978; Notebooks, 1980; Skinner for the Classroom, 1982; (with Margaret E. Vaughan) Enjoy Old Age, 1983; *autobiography:* Particulars of My Life, 1976; The Shaping of a Behaviorist, 1979; A Matter of Consequences, 1983; Upon Further Reflection, 1986. *Address:* 11 Old Dee Road, Cambridge, Mass 02138, USA. *T:* 864–0848.

SKINNER, Dennis Edward; MP (Lab) Bolsover since 1970; Miner at Glapwell Colliery; *b* 11 Feb. 1932; good working-class mining stock; *m* 1960; one *s* two *d. Educ:* Tupton Hall Grammar Sch.; Ruskin Coll., Oxford. Miner, 1949–70. Mem., Nat. Exec. Cttee of Labour Party, 1978–. Pres., Derbyshire Miners (NUM), 1966–70; Pres., NE Derbs Constituency Labour Party, 1968–71; Derbyshire CC, 1964–70; Clay Cross UDC, 1960–70. *Recreations:* tennis, cycling, walking. *Address:* House of Commons, SW1; 86 Thanet Street, Clay Cross, Chesterfield, Derbyshire. *T:* Clay Cross 863429. *Clubs:* Miners' Welfares in Derbyshire; Bestwood Working Men's.

SKINNER, James John; QC; Social Security Commissioner, since 1986; *b* 24 July 1923; *o s* of late William Skinner, Solicitor, Clonmel, Ireland; *m* 1950, Regina Brigitte Reiss; three *s* two *d. Educ:* Clongowes Wood Coll.; Trinity Coll., Dublin; King's Inns, Dublin. Called to Irish Bar, 1946; joined Leinster Circuit; called to English Bar, Gray's Inn, 1950; called to Bar of Northern Rhodesia, 1951; QC (Northern Rhodesia) 1964; MP (UNIP) Lusaka East, 1964–68; Minister of Justice, 1964–65; Attorney-General, 1965–69 (in addition, Minister of Legal Affairs, 1967–68); Chief Justice of Zambia, March-Sept. 1969; Chief Justice of Malaŵi, 1970–85. Grand Comdr, Order of Menelik II of Ethiopia, 1965. *Recreation:* reading. *Address:* 65 Castelnau, SW13. *T:* 01–748 1228. *Club:* Royal Commonwealth Society.

SKINNER, Joyce Eva, CBE 1975; retired; *b* 20 Sept. 1920; *d* of Matthew and Ruth Eva Skinner. *Educ:* Christ's Hosp.; Girls' High Sch., Lincoln; Somerville Coll., Oxford. BA 1941, MA 1945. Bridlington Girls' High Sch., 1942–45; Perse Girls' Sch., 1946–50; Keswick Sch., 1950–52; Homerton Coll., Cambridge, 1952–64; Vis. Prof., Queen's Coll., NY, 1955–56; Principal, Bishop Grosseteste Coll., Lincoln, 1964–74; Dir, Cambridge Inst. of Educn, 1974–80; Academic Sec., Universities' Council for Educn of Teachers, 1979–84. Fellow: Hughes Hall, Cambridge, 1974–85; Worcester Coll. of Higher Educn, 1985. Hon. Fellow, Coll. of Preceptors, 1971. *Recreations:* walking, reading, conversation. *Address:* 26 Rasen Lane, Lincoln. *T:* Lincoln 29483.

SKINNER, Sir Keith; *see* Skinner, Sir T. K. H.

SKINNER, Martyn; *b* 1906; *s* of late Sir Sydney Skinner; *m* 1938, Pauline Giles; three *s* one *d* (and one *s* one *d* decd). *Educ:* two well-known Public Schools; Magdalen College, Oxford (no degree taken). Hawthornden prize, 1943; Heinemann Award, 1947; Runner-up, Barley Championship, Brewers' Exhibition, 1949. *Publications:* Sir Elfadore and Mabyna, 1935; Letters to Malaya I and II, 1941; III and IV, 1943; V, 1947; Two Colloquies, 1949; The Return of Arthur, 1966; Old Rectory (Prologue), 1970; Old Rectory (The Session), 1973; Old Rectory (Epilogue), 1977; (with R. C. Hutchinson) Two Men of Letters, 1979; Alms for Oblivion, 1983. *Address:* Fitzhead, Taunton, Somerset. *T:* Milverton 400337.

SKINNER, Maj.-Gen. Michael Timothy, CB 1986; Director General Weapons (Army), since 1986; *b* 5 Aug. 1931; *s* of Wilfred Skinner, MBE, FCIS and Ethel Skinner (*née* Jones); *m* 1959, Anne Kathleen Perry; three *s. Educ:* Merchant Taylors' School; RMA Sandhurst; psc, ptsc. Commissioned Royal Regt of Artillery, 1953; Malaya, 1955–58 (despatches); Parachute Brigade, UK, and Commando Brigade, Malta, 1958–62; RMCS and Staff Coll.; staff (weapon locating), RRE, 1967–68; GSO2 (future equipment), HQ Dir RA, 1971–72; CO 4th Regt RA, 1972–75, Germany and UK (despatches); MGO Secretariat, 1975–78; GS Op. Requirements and Dir, Heavy Weapons Projects, MoD, 1978–84; Vice Master-General of the Ordnance, 1984–86. Hon. Col, 4th Regt RA, 1985–. FBIM. *Recreations:* travel, opera, roses, campaign medals. *Address:* c/o Lloyds Bank, 18 Week Street, Maidstone, Kent ME14 1RW. *Club:* Royal Commonwealth Society.

SKINNER, Most Rev. Patrick James, CJM; *b* 1904. *Educ:* St Bonaventure's College, St John's; Holy Heart Seminary, Halifax; Eudist Seminary, Gros Pin, PQ; Laval University, Quebec. Priest, 1929; consecrated, as Auxiliary to Archbishop of St John's, Newfoundland, 1950; Archbishop of St John's, Newfoundland, 1951–79. *Address:* The Deanery, St Patrick's Parish, Patrick Street, St John's, Newfoundland A1E 2S7, Canada.

SKINNER, Prof. Quentin Robert Duthie, FBA 1981; Professor of Political Science, University of Cambridge, since 1978; Fellow of Christ's College, Cambridge, since 1962; *b* 26 Nov. 1940; 2nd *s* of late Alexander Skinner, CBE, and Winifred Skinner, MA; *m* 1979, Susan Deborah Thorpe James, MA, PhD; one *s* one *d. Educ:* Bedford Sch.; Gonville and Caius Coll., Cambridge (BA 1962, MA 1965). Lecturer in History, Univ. of Cambridge, 1967–78. Visiting Fellow, Research Sch. of Social Science, ANU, 1970; Institute for Advanced Study, Princeton: Mem., School of Historical Studies, 1974–75; longer-term Mem., School of Social Science, 1976–79; Gauss Seminars, Princeton Univ., 1980. Carlyle Vis. Lectr, Univ. of Oxford, 1980–81; Lectures: Messenger, Cornell Univ., 1983; Tanner, Harvard Univ., 1984; James Ford, Univ. of Oxford, 1985; Raleigh, British Acad., 1986. Foreign Hon. Mem., Amer. Acad. of Arts and Sciences, 1986. *Publications:* Philosophy, Politics and Society, Series 4 (ed jtly and contrib.), 1972; The Foundations of Modern Political Thought, Vol. 1, The Renaissance, 1978; Vol. 2, The Age of Reformation, 1978 (Wolfson Prize, 1979); Machiavelli, 1981; (ed jtly and contrib.) Philosophy in History, 1984; (ed and contrib.) The Return of Grand Theory in the Human Sciences, 1985. *Address:* c/o Christ's College, Cambridge CB2 3BU. *T:* Cambridge 334974.

SKINNER, Sir Thomas (Edward), KBE 1976; JP; Chairman, New Zealand Shipping Line, 1973–82; *b* 18 April 1909; *s* of Thomas Edward Skinner and Alice Skinner; *m* 1942, Mary Ethel Yardley; two *s* one *d. Educ:* Bayfield District Sch. Pres., NZ Fedn of Labour, 1963–79. Chairman: The Shipping Corp. of New Zealand Ltd, 1973–82; Container Terminals Ltd, 1975–82. Chm., St John Ambulance Trust Bd, Auckland, 1973–; KStJ 1970. JP New Zealand, 1943. *Recreations:* racing, boating, fishing. *Address:* 164 Kohimarama Road, St Heliers, Auckland 5, New Zealand. *T:* 587–571. *Clubs:* Avondale Jockey (New Zealand); Auckland Branch, International Lions.

SKINNER, Sir (Thomas) Keith (Hewitt), 4th Bt *cr* 1912; Director, Reed International, since 1980; Chairman and Chief Executive, Reed Publishing and Reed Regional Publishing, since 1982, and other companies; *b* 6 Dec. 1927; *s* of Sir (Thomas) Gordon Skinner, 3rd Bt, and Mollie Barbara (*d* 1965), *d* of Herbert William Girling; *S* father, 1972; *m* 1959, Jill, *d* of Cedric Ivor Tuckett; two *s. Educ:* Charterhouse. Managing Director, Thomas Skinner & Co. (Publishers) Ltd, 1952–60; also Director, Iliffe & Co. Ltd, 1958–65; Director, Iliffe-NTP Ltd; Chairman: Industrial Trade Fairs Holdings Ltd, 1977–; Business Press Internat., 1970–84. *Recreations:* publishing, shooting, fishing, gardening, golf. *Heir: s* Thomas James Hewitt Skinner, *b* 11 Sept. 1962. *Address:* Wood Farm, Reydon, near Southwold, Suffolk. *Clubs:* Royal Automobile; Aldeburgh Golf.

SKINNER, Thomas Monier, CMG 1958; MBE; MA Oxon; Company Chairman; *b* 2 Feb. 1913; *s* of Lt-Col and Mrs T. B. Skinner; *m* 1st, 1935, Margaret Adeline (*née* Pope) (*d* 1969); two *s*; 2nd, 1981, Elizabeth Jane Hardie, *d* of late Mr and Mrs P. L. Hardie. *Educ:* Cheltenham Coll.; Lincoln Coll., Oxford. Asst District Officer (Cadet), Tanganyika, 1935; Asst District Officer, 1937; District Officer, 1947; Senior Asst Secretary, East Africa High Commission, 1952; Director of Establishments (Kenya), 1955–62, retired 1962. Member, Civil Service Commission, East Caribbean Territories, 1962–63; Chairman, Nyasaland Local Civil Service Commission, 1963; Salaries Commissioner, Basutoland, The Bechuanaland Protectorate and Swaziland, 1964. Reports on Localisation of Civil Service, Gilbert and Ellice Islands Colony and of British National Service, New Hebrides, 1968. *Recreation:* fishing. *Address:* Innerpeffray Lodge, by Crieff, Perthshire PH7 3QW.

SKIPPER, David John; Headmaster, Merchant Taylors' School, Northwood, since 1982; *b* 14 April 1931; *s* of Herbert G. and Edna Skipper; *m* 1955, Brenda Ann Williams; three *s* one *d. Educ:* Watford Grammar Sch.; Brasenose Coll., Oxford (2nd Cl. Hons Nat. Science (Chemistry)). Royal Air Force (Short Service Commn) (Education), 1954–57; Assistant Master: Radley Coll., 1957–63; Rugby Sch., 1963–69; Headmaster, Ellesmere Coll., Shropshire, 1969–81. *Recreations:* golf, hill-walking, drawing, music. *Address:* Headmaster's House, Merchant Taylors' School, Sandy Lodge, Northwood, Mddx HA6 2AT. *T:* Northwood 21850. *Club:* East India, Devonshire, Sports and Public Schools.

SKIPWITH, Sir Patrick Alexander d'Estoteville, 12th Bt, *cr* 1622; The Editor, Bureau de Recherches Géologiques et Minières, Jiddah, since 1973; *b* 1 Sept. 1938; *o s* of Grey d'Estoteville Townsend Skipwith (killed in action, 1942), Flying Officer, RAFVR, and Sofka, *d* of late Prince Peter Dolgorouky; *S* grandfather, 1950; *m* 1st, 1964, Gillian Patricia (marr. diss. 1970), *d* of late Charles F. Harwood; one *s* one *d*; 2nd, 1972, Ashkhain, *d* of Bedros Atikian, Calgary, Alta. *Educ:* Harrow; Dublin (MA); London (DIC, PhD). With Ocean Mining Inc., in Tasmania, 1966–67, Malaysia, 1967–69, W Africa, 1969–70; with Min. of Petroleum and Mineral Resources, Saudi Arabia, 1970–71 and 1972–73. *Heir: s* Alexander Sebastian Grey d'Estoteville Skipwith, *b* 9 April 1969. *Address:* c/o BRGM, PO Box 1492, Jiddah, Kingdom of Saudi Arabia. *Clubs:* Zanzibar, Chelsea Arts.

SKONE JAMES, Edmund Purcell; barrister; *b* 14 June 1927; *s* of Francis Edmund Skone James and Kate Eve Skone James; *m* 1952, Jean Norah Knight; one *s* one *d. Educ:* Westminster Sch.; New Coll., Oxford (MA). Served RASC, 2nd Lieut, 1946–48. Called to the Bar, Middle Temple, 1951; Bencher, Middle Temple, 1977. Mem., Whitford Cttee to Consider the Law on Copyright and Designs, 1973 (Report 1977). *Publication:* Copinger and Skone James on Copyright, 9th edn 1958–12th edn 1980. *Recreations:* gardening, walking, reading fiction. *Address:* 5 New Square, Lincoln's Inn, WC2A 3RJ. *T:* 01–404 0404.

SKUTSCH, Prof. Otto; Professor of Latin, University College London, 1951–72, now Emeritus Professor; *b* 6 Dec. 1906; *yr s* of Latinist Franz Skutsch and Selma Dorff; *m* 1938, Gillian Mary, *e d* of late Sir Findlater Stewart, GCB, GCIE, CSI; one *s* three *d. Educ:* Friedrichs-Gymnasium, Breslau; Univs of Breslau, Kiel, Berlin, Göttingen. DrPhil, Göttingen, 1934; Asst Thesaurus Linguae Latinae, 1932; Sen. Asst, Latin Dept, Queen's Univ., Belfast, 1938; Asst Lectr, Lectr, Sen. Lectr, Univ. of Manchester, 1939, 1946, 1949; Guest Lectr, Harvard Univ., 1958, Loeb Fellow, 1973; Vis. Andrew Mellon Prof. of Classics, Univ. of Pittsburgh, 1972–73, 1981; Guest Mem., Inst. for Advanced Study, Princeton, 1963, 1968, 1974; Vice-Pres., Soc. for Promotion of Roman Studies; For. Mem., Kungl. Vetenskaps- och Vitterhets- Samhället i Göteborg. Hon. DLitt Padua, 1986. *Publications:* Prosodische und metrische Gesetze der Iambenkürzung, 1934; Studia Enniana, 1968; The Annals of Q. Ennius, Text and Commentary, 1985; articles in classical journals, etc. *Address:* 3 Wild Hatch, NW11 7LD. *T:* 01–455 4876.

SKYRME, Sir (William) Thomas (Charles), KCVO 1974; CB 1966; CBE 1953; TD 1949; JP, DL; Chairman, Broadcasting Complaints Commission, 1985–87 (Member, 1981–87); Secretary of Commissions, 1948–77; Vice-President, Magistrates' Association of England and Wales, since 1981 (Member of Council, since 1974; Deputy Chairman, 1977–79; Chairman, 1979–81); *b* 20 March 1913; *s* of Charles G. Skyrme, Hereford, and of Katherine (*née* Smith), Maryland, USA; *m* 1st, 1938, Hon. Barbara Suzanne Lyle (marr. diss. 1953), *yr d* of 1st Baron Lyle of Westbourne; one *s* two *d*; 2nd, 1957, Mary, *d* of Dr R. C. Leaning. *Educ:* Rugby School; New College, Oxford (MA); Universities of Dresden and Paris. Called to the Bar, Inner Temple, 1935. Practised in London and on Western

Circuit. Served War of 1939–45 in Royal Artillery in Middle East, North Africa and Italy (wounded twice). Lt-Col. Secretary to the Lord Chancellor, 1944. Governor and Member of Committee of Management of Queen Mary's Hosp., London, 1938–48. Mem., Magistrates' Courts Rule Cttee, 1950–66; Chm., Interdepartmental Working Party on Legal Proceedings against Justices and Clerks, 1960; Mem., Interdepartmental Cttee on Magistrates Courts in London, 1961; Life Vice-Pres., Commonwealth Magistrates' Assoc., 1979 (Pres., 1970–79); Chm., Commonwealth Magistrates' Confs, London, 1970, Bermuda, 1972, Nairobi, 1973, Kuala Lumpur, 1975, Tonga, 1976, Jamaica, 1977, Oxford, 1979; Vice-Chm., Adv. Cttee on Training of Magistrates, 1974–80. Hon. Life Mem., Justices' Clerks' Soc., 1979–. A General Comr of Income Tax, 1977–; Mem., Top Salaries Review Body, 1981–; Chm., Judicial Salaries Cttee, 1983–. Freeman of City of London, 1970; HM Lieut for City of London, 1977–. DL Glos 1983. FRGS. JP (Oxfordshire), 1948, (London), 1952, (Gloucestershire), 1976. *Publications:* The Changing Image of the Magistracy, 1979; contribs to legal jls. *Recreations:* travel; rifle shooting (captained Oxford University, 1934). *Address:* Elm Barns, Blockley, Gloucestershire; Casa Larissa, Klosters, Switzerland. *Clubs:* Garrick; Royal Solent Yacht.

See also Sir J. G. Waterlow, Bt.

SLABBERT, Dr Frederik Van Zyl; *b* 2 March 1940; *s* of Petrus Johannes and Barbara Zacharia Slabbert; *m* 1965, Marié Jordaan (marr. diss. 1983); one *s* one *d*. *Educ:* Univ. of Stellenbosch. BA, BA (Hons), MA 1964, DPhil 1967. Lectr in Sociology, Stellenbosch Univ., 1964–68; Senior Lecturer: Rhodes Univ., 1969; Stellenbosch Univ., 1970–71; Cape Town Univ., 1972–73; Prof. of Sociology, Univ. of the Witwatersrand, 1973–74. MP (Progressive Federal Party) Claremont, 1974–86; Leader, Official Opposition, S African Parlt, 1979–86. *Publications:* South African Society: its central perspectives, 1972; (jtly) South Africa's Options: strategies for sharing power, 1979; The Last White Parliament (autobiog.), 1986; contributions to: Change in Contemporary South Africa, 1975; Explorations in Social Theory, 1976; various SPROCAS (Study Project of a Christian in an Apartheid Society) publications. *Recreations:* jogging, swimming, squash, chess. *Address:* 33 Albion Road, Rondebosch, 7700, South Africa. *T:* Cape Town 699468.

SLACK, Prof. Geoffrey Layton, CBE 1974 (OBE (mil.) 1944); TD 1946; Emeritus Professor, University of London, since 1977; Professor of Community Dental Health, 1976–77 (formerly Professor of Dental Surgery, 1959–76), The London Hospital Medical College; *b* 27 March 1912; *er s* of late Charles Garrett Slack and Gertrude Wild, Southport; *m* Doreen Percival Ball, *d* of late Walter Knight Ball and Mary Percival, Birkdale; two *d*. *Educ:* Preparatory school, Croxton and Terra Nova; Leys School, Cambridge. LDS (with distinction) Univ. of Liverpool, 1934; DDS Northwestern Univ., Chicago, 1947; FDSRCS, 1948; Nuffield Fellow, 1949; Dipl. in Bacteriology, Manchester Univ. 1950; FFDRCSI 1978; FDSRCPS (Glas) 1979. Private practice, 1934–39, 1945–46; House Surg., Liverpool Dental Hosp. 1934. TA, RASC, 1934–39; served in RASC, 1939–45; Major, DADST (T) Eastern Comd HQ, 1941–43; Lieut-Col ADST (T) HQ Second Army, 1943–44; Lieut-Col ADST (T) HQ 21 Army Gp, 1944–45; demobilized 1945. Lectr in Preventive Dentistry, Univ. of Liverpool, 1948–51; Sen. Lectr, 1951–59; Head of Dept of Preventive and Children's Dentistry, 1948–59; Consultant Dental Surgeon 1948–59, United Liverpool Hosps; Dean of Dental Studies, The London Hosp. Med. Coll. Dental Sch., 1965–69. Mem., Central Health Services Council, 1969–80; Mem., 1956–80, Chm., 1974–80, Standing Dental Adv. Cttee to DHSS; Mem. General Dental Council, 1974–79; Consultant Adviser, DHSS, 1974–77; Vice-Chm. Dental Health Cttee, British Dental Assoc., 1959. Hon. Dir, MRC Dental Epidemiology Unit, 1971–77; Hon. Consultant in Dental Surgery to the Army, 1975–77; Civilian Consultant in Community Dentistry to the RAF, 1975–83. Mem. Council, RCS, 1971–77; Mem. Board of Faculty of Dental Surgery, RCS, 1961–77 (Vice-Dean, 1968–69, Dean, 1971–74); Governor: The London Hosp. Med. Coll., 1963–69 (Fellow, 1986); The London Hospital, 1963–69. WHO Consultant, 1963–84. Fellow Am. College of Dentists, 1963. RCS John Tomes Prize, 1960–62; RCS Charles Tomes Lectr, 1965. Hon. Dr of Odontology, Goteborg, 1974. *Publications:* (part-author) Dental Health, 1957; World Survey of Teaching Methods in Children's Dentistry, 1958; (with T. H. Melville) Bacteriology for Dental Students, 1960; (part-author) Demand and Need for Dental Care (Report to Nuffield Foundation), 1968; (part-author) Child Dental Health, 1969; (jt author) GSS Adult Dental Health in England and Wales in 1968, 1970; (ed) Dental Public Health, 1973, 2nd rev. edn, 1981; many contribs to medical and dental journals. *Recreations:* golf, sailing, fishing; formerly hockey (played Lancashire 1933–39, 1945–52 (57 Caps), North of England, 1935–39, 1945–52, England XI 1938–39). *Address:* 1 Treesdale Close, Birkdale, Southport PR8 2EL. *T:* Southport 64007. *Clubs:* Royal Commonwealth Society; Union (Pres., 1986) (Southport); Royal Birkdale Golf, Royal Liverpool Golf.

SLACK, His Honour George Granville; a Circuit Judge (formerly a County Court Judge), 1966–81; *b* 11 July 1906; *s* of George Edwin and Amy Beatrice Slack; *m* 1st, 1935, Ella Kathleen (*d* 1957), *d* of Henry Alexander Eason; one *d*; 2nd, 1958, Vera Gertrude, *d* of Reginald Ackland Spencer; one *s* one *d*. *Educ:* Accrington Grammar School; London University. BA (Hons History) 1926; LLB 1929; LLM 1932. Called to Bar, Gray's Inn, 1929. Served RAFVR, 1943–46. Judge of Croydon County Court, 1969–75, of Willesden County Court, 1976–81. Contested (L): Twickenham, 1945; Dewsbury, 1950; Chairman: London Liberal Party, 1947–48, 1950–53; Liberal Party Organisation, 1956–57. Sec., Acton Baptist Church, 1954–77. Chm., West Gp Housing Soc. Ltd (West Haven), 1961–. *Publications:* Slack on War Damage, 1941; Liabilities (War Time Adjustment) Act, 1941; Liability for National Service, 1942. *Address:* 10 Baronsmede, Ealing, W5. *T:* 01-567 8164. *Club:* National Liberal.

SLACK, John Kenneth Edward, TD 1964; **His Honour Judge John Slack;** a Circuit Judge, since 1977; *b* 23 Dec. 1930; *o s* of late Ernest Edward Slack, formerly Chief Clerk Westminster County Court, and late Beatrice Mary Slack (*née* Shorten), Broadstairs; *m* 1959, Patricia Helen, MA Cantab, *o d* of late William Keith Metcalfe, Southport; two *s*. *Educ:* University College Sch., Hampstead; St John's Coll., Cambridge (MA). Captain, RAEC, 1950. Admitted Solicitor, 1957; Partner, Freeborough Slack & Co., 1958–76; Mem. No 1 (later No 14) Legal Aid Area, 1966–69; Deputy Registrar, County Courts, 1969–72; a Recorder of the Crown Court, 1972–77; Pres., Wireless Telegraphy Appeals Tribunal, 1974–77. Captain Club Cricket Conf., 1962–66; Captain Bucks County Cricket Club, 1967–69 (Minor County Champions 1969); Active Vice-Pres., Club Cricket Conf., 1969–77, Pres., 1978. Chm. Council, University Coll. Sch., 1980– (Mem., 1974–). *Recreations:* cricket (Cambridge Blue 1954); golf. *Address:* c/o Crown Court, St Albans, Herts AL1 3XE. *Clubs:* Hawks (Cambridge); Beaconsfield Cricket, Beaconsfield Golf.

SLACK, Rev. Dr Kenneth, MBE 1946; Minister, Kensington United Reformed Church, since 1982; Moderator, Free Church Federal Council, 1983–84; *b* 20 July 1917; *s* of late Reginald Slack and late Nellie (*née* Bennett); *m* 1941, Barbara Millicent Blake; two *s* one *d*. *Educ:* Wallasey Grammar School; Liverpool Univ., BA Liverpool, 1937; Westminster College, Cambridge. Ordained to ministry of Presbyterian Church of England, 1941. Minister, St Nicholas', Shrewsbury, 1941–45. Chaplain, RAFVR, 1942–46, serving Air Command, South East Asia, 1943–46 (MBE). Minister, St James's, Edgware, 1946–55; General Secretary, 1955–65, British Council of Churches; Minister, St Andrew's Church, Cheam, 1965–67; Minister of the City Temple, London, 1967–75; Moderator, Gen. Assembly, United Reformed Church, 1973–74; Dir, Christian Aid Div., British Council of Churches, 1975–82. Member: Adv. Cttee, Conf. of European Churches, 1960–67; WCC's Commn on Inter-Church Aid, Refugee and World Service, 1975–82. Vice-President, Churches' Council for Health and Healing and United Soc. for Christian Literature. Chm., Editorial Board, New Christian, 1965–70; British Correspondent, Christian Century, Chicago, 1982–; Free Church Correspondent, Church Times, 1975–. Regular contributor, Thought for the Day, BBC Radio 4, 1982–. Select Preacher, Cambridge, 1961, Oxford, 1982. Hon. LLD Southampton, 1971. *Publications:* The Christian Conflict, 1960; The British Churches Today, 1961, 2nd edn 1970; Despatch from New Delhi, 1962; Is Sacrifice Outmoded?, 1966; Uppsala Report, 1968, Martin Luther King, 1970; George Bell, 1971; Praying the Lord's Prayer Today, 1973; New Light on Old Songs, 1975; Nairobi Narrative, 1976; Seven Deadly Sins, 1985; (ed) Hope in the Desert, 1986. *Recreations:* reading, journalism. *Address:* The Manse, Allen Street, Kensington, W8 6BL. *T:* 01–937 8826; 3 High Busk, Blue Hill Road, Ambleside, Cumbria LA22 0AW. *T:* Ambleside 33670.

SLACK, Timothy Willatt, MA; Principal, St Catherine's Foundation at Cumberland Lodge, since 1985; *b* 18 April 1928; *yr s* of late Cecil Moorhouse Slack, MC, and Dora Willatt, Beverley, Yorks; *m* 1957, Katharine, 2nd *d* of Walter Norman Hughes, MA, and Jean Sorsbie, Chepstow, Mon.; one *s* three *d*. *Educ:* Winchester Coll.; New Coll., Oxford. Hons. PPE, 1951. Asst, Lycée de Rennes, France, 1951; Asst master, the Salem School, Baden, Germany, 1952; Assistant master, Repton School, 1953–59; Headmaster of Kambawsa College, Taunggyi, Shan State, Burma, 1959–62; Headmaster, Bedales Sch., 1962–74. Chairman, Society of Headmasters of Independent Schools, 1968–70. Dep. Dir, 1975–77, Dir, 1977–83, Wiston House FCO Conf. Centre (incorp. Wilton Park Confs), Steyning; Headmaster, Hellenic Coll. of London, 1983–84. Kurt Hahn Meml Lectr, 1982. Contested (L): Petersfield, Feb. and Oct. 1974; Enfield, Southgate, Dec. 1984. *Address:* Hamlet House, Hambledon, Portsmouth PO7 6RY; Cumberland Lodge, The Great Park, Windsor, Berks SL4 2HP.

See also W. W. Slack.

SLACK, William Willatt, MA, MCh, BM, FRCS; Serjeant Surgeon to the Queen, since 1983; Consultant Surgeon, Middlesex Hospital, since 1962; Senior Lecturer in Surgery, since 1962, and Dean, 1983–86, Middlesex Hospital Medical School; also Surgeon: Hospital of St John and St Elizabeth, since 1970; King Edward VII Hospital for Officers, since 1975; *b* 22 Feb. 1925; *s* of late Cecil Moorhouse Slack, MC, and Dora Slack (*née* Willatt); *m* 1951, Joan, 4th *d* of late Lt-Col Talbot H. Wheelwright, OBE; two *s* two *d*. *Educ:* Winchester Coll.; New Coll., Oxford; Middlesex Hosp. Med. Sch. Ho. Surg., Surgical Registrar and Sen. Surgical Registrar, Mddx Hosp., 1950–59; Jun. Registrar, St Bartholomew's Hosp., 1953; Fulbright Scholar, R. & E. Hosp., Univ. of Illinois, Chicago, 1959. Surgeon to the Queen, 1975–83. *Publications:* various surgical articles in med. jls and textbooks. *Recreations:* skiing, gardening; Oxford blue for Association football, 1946. *Address:* 58 Harley House, Marylebone Road, NW1 5HL. *T:* 01–486 1191; 22 Platts Lane, NW3. *T:* 01–435 5887.

See also T. W. Slack.

SLADE, (Sir) Benjamin Julian Alfred, (7th Bt *cr* 1831, but does not use the title); Chairman: Shirlstar Container Transport Ltd; Shirlstar Container Brokers Ltd; Shirlstar Aviation Ltd; Director: Shirlstar Norway SA; Shirlstar Conteneurs France SARL; Shirlstar Container Transport GmbH; Pyman Bell Ltd; *b* 22 May 1946; *s* of Sir Michael Slade, 6th Bt and Angela (*d* 1959), *d* of Captain Orlando Chichester; *S* father, 1962; *m* 1977, Pauline Carol, *er d* of Major Claude Myburgh. *Educ:* Millfield Sch. Chairman: Transair Freight Ltd; Flipper Watches UK Ltd; W. M. Drummonds Ltd; Modern Securities Ltd; Imperial Finance Ltd; Pyman Bell (Holding) Ltd. Mem., Worshipful Co. of Ironmongers. Freeman, City of London, 1979. *Recreations:* hunting, shooting, racing, polo, bridge. *Heir:* none. *Address:* 164 Ashley Gardens, Emery Hill Street, SW1. *T:* 01–828 2809; Maunsel, North Newton, Bridgwater, Somerset. *T:* Bridgwater 663413, (Estate Office) Bridgwater 662387; *Telex:* (office) 917760; Shirlstar House, 37 St John's Road, Uxbridge, Mddx. *T:* Uxbridge 72929; *Telex:* 885639. *Clubs:* Turf, Institute of Directors; Old Somerset Dining (Taunton).

SLADE, Brian John; Director General of Defence Contracts, Ministry of Defence, since 1986; *b* 28 April 1931; *s* of Albert Edward Victor Slade and Florence Elizabeth (*née* Eveleigh); *m* 1955, Grace, *d* of late W. McK. Murray and Mary Murray, Ayr; one *s* one *d*. *Educ:* Portsmouth Northern Grammar School; London University. Joined Min. of Supply, 1951; Private Sec. to Permanent Sec., Min. of Aviation, 1962–64; Head of Industrial Personnel Branch, Min. of Technology, 1968–73; Principal Dir of Contracts, Air, MoD, 1982–86. Mem. Synod, Methodist Church, 1981–. *Recreations:* cricket, downs walking. *Address:* Doonbank, 16 Greenway, Great Bookham, Surrey. *T:* Bookham 54359.

SLADE, Rt. Hon. Sir Christopher John, Kt 1975; PC 1982; **Rt. Hon. Lord Justice Slade;** a Lord Justice of Appeal, since 1982; *b* 2 June 1927; *s* of late George Penkivil Slade, KC, and Mary Albinia Alice Slade; *m* 1958, Jane Gwenllian Armstrong Buckley; one *s* three *d*. *Educ:* Eton (Scholar); New Coll., Oxford (Scholar). Eldon Law Scholar, 1950. Called to Bar, Inner Temple, 1951; in practice at Chancery Bar, 1951–75; QC 1965; Bencher, Lincoln's Inn, 1973. Attorney General, Duchy of Lancaster and Attorney and Serjeant Within the County Palatine of Lancaster, 1972–75; a Judge of the High Ct, Chancery Division, 1975–82; a Judge of Restrictive Practices Ct, 1980–82, Pres., 1981–82. Member: Gen. Council of the Bar, 1958–62, 1965–69; Senate of Four Inns of Court, 1966–69; Lord Chancellor's Legal Educn Cttee, 1969–71. Master, Ironmongers' Co., 1973. *Address:* Royal Courts of Justice, Strand, WC2. *Club:* Garrick.

SLADE, Julian Penkivil; author and composer since 1951; *b* 28 May 1930; *s* of G. P. Slade, KC. *Educ:* Eton College; Trinity College, Cambridge (BA). Went to Bristol Old Vic Theatre School, 1951; wrote incidental music for Bristol Old Vic production of Two Gentlemen of Verona, 1952; joined Bristol Old Vic Co. as musical director, 1952. Wrote and composed Christmas in King St (with Dorothy Reynolds and James Cairncross) Bristol, 1952; composed music for Sheridan's The Duenna, Bristol, 1953; transferred to Westminster Theatre, London, 1954; wrote and composed The Merry Gentleman (with Dorothy Reynolds), Bristol, 1953; composed incidental music for The Merchant of Venice (1953 Stratford season). Wrote musical version of The Comedy of Errors for TV, 1954, and for Arts Theatre, London, 1956; wrote (with Dorothy Reynolds) Salad Days, Bristol, 1954, Vaudeville, London, 1954, Duke of York's, 1976; Free as Air, Savoy, London, 1957; Hooray for Daisy!, Bristol, 1959, Lyric, Hammersmith, 1960; Follow that Girl, Vaudeville, London, 1960; Wildest Dreams, 1960; Vanity Fair (with Alan Pryce-Jones and Robin Miller), Queen's Theatre, London, 1962; Nutmeg and Ginger, Cheltenham, 1963; Sixty Thousand Nights (with George Rowell), Bristol, 1966; The Pursuit of Love, Bristol, 1967; composed music for songs in: As You Like It, Bristol, 1970; A Midsummer Night's Dream and Much Ado About Nothing, Regent's Park, 1970; adapted A. A. Milne's Winnie The Pooh, Phoenix Theatre, 1970, 1975; (music and lyrics) Trelawny, Bristol, then London West End, 1972; Out of Bounds (book, music and lyrics, based on Pinero's The Schoolmistress), 1973. Composed incidental music for Nancy

Mitford's Love in a Cold Climate, Thames TV, 1980; adapted Salad Days for Yorkshire TV, 1983; (with Veronica Flint-Shipman and Kit Harvey) musical adaptation of J. M. Barrie's Dear Brutus, 1985; (with Gyles Brandreth) Now We Are Sixty (musical play based on works of A. A. Milne), Arts Theatre, Cambridge, 1986. Played and sang for solo record album of own songs, Looking for a Piano, 1981; played for vocal album, Salad Days, 1982. *Publications*: Nibble the Squirrel (children's book), 1946; music of: The Duenna, 1954; Salad Days, 1954; Free as Air, 1957; Follow That Girl, 1967; Trelawny, 1974; The Merry Gentleman, 1985. *Recreations*: drawing, going to theatres and cinemas, listening to music. *Address*: 3 Priory Walk, SW10. *T*: 01–370 4859.

SLADE, Leslie William, JP; Agent General for Western Australia in London, 1978–82; *b* 17 July 1915; *s* of Leonard Barrington Slade and Gwendoline (*née* Fraser); *m* 1942, Marion Joan, *d* of V. J. Devitt, Perth, WA; one *d* decd. *Educ*: Scotch Coll., Melbourne, Australia. Accountant, Myer Emporium Ltd, Melbourne, 1933–39; served RAN (Lieut-Comdr), 1939–46; Proprietor of import/export business, Perth, WA, 1947–61; Export Consultant, W Australian Govt, Perth, 1962–68; Official Rep., Govt of W Australia for Far East, Tokyo, 1968–78. Freedom of City of London, 1978. JP WA, 1978. *Recreations*: golf, cricket, fishing, sailing. *Address*: Unit 8, Kyamala, 19 Broome Street, Mosman Park, WA 6012, Australia. *Clubs*: Weld, West Australian Cricket Association, Royal Perth Yacht, Nedlands Golf (Perth); Tokyo (Tokyo).

SLADE, Patrick Buxton M.; *see* Mitford-Slade.

SLANE, Viscount; Alexander Burton Conyngham; *b* 30 Jan. 1975; *s* and *heir* of Earl of Mount Charles, *qv*.

SLANEY, Prof. Sir Geoffrey, KBE 1984; FRCS; Barling Professor, Head of Department of Surgery, Queen Elizabeth Hospital, Birmingham, 1971–86; Hon. Consultant Surgeon: United Birmingham Hospitals and Regional Hospital Board, since 1959; Royal Prince Alfred Hospital, Sydney, since 1981; President, Royal College of Surgeons of England, 1982–86; Hon. Consulting Surgeon Emeritus, City of London and Hackney Health Authority, since 1983; *b* 19 Sept. 1922; *er s* of Richard and Gladys Lois Slaney; *m* 1956, Josephine Mary Davy; one *s* two *d*. *Educ*: Brewood Grammar Sch.; Univs of Birmingham, London and Illinois, USA. MB, ChB (Birmingham) 1947, FRCS 1953, MS (Ill) 1956, ChM (Birmingham) 1961; Hon. FRCSI 1983; Hon. FRACS 1983; Hon. FCSSL 1984; Hon. FACS 1985; Hon. FCSSA 1986; Hon. FRCSCan 1986. Ho. Surg. and Surgical Registrar, Gen. Hosp. Birmingham, 1947–48. Captain RAMC, 1948–50. Surgical Registrar, Coventry, London and Hackney Hosps, 1950–53; Surgical Registrar, Lectr in Surgery and Surgical Research Fellow, Queen Elizabeth Hosp., Birmingham, 1953–59; Hunterian Prof., RCS, 1961–62; Prof. of Surgery, Univ. of Birmingham, 1966–. Member: London Adv. Group to Sec. of State, DHSS, 1980–81; Ministerial Adv. Gp on Med. Manpower, 1985–86; Res. Liaison Gp, DHSS, 1979–85; Midlands Med. Appeals Tribunal, 1964–. External Examr in Surgery to Univs of: Newcastle upon Tyne, London, Cambridge, Oxford, Liverpool, Nat. Univ. of Ireland, Lagos, Zimbabwe, and Licentiate Cttee, Hong Kong; Advisor in Surgery, Univs of Bristol and London. Lectures: Richardson Meml, Massachusetts Gen. Hosp., Boston, USA, 1975; Pybus Meml, Newcastle, 1978; Simpson Smith Meml, London, 1979; Legg Meml, KCH, London, 1982; Chesledon, St Thomas' Hosp., London, 1983; Miles Meml, London, 1983; Berrill Meml, Coventry, 1984; Sandblom, Lund, Sweden, 1984; Sir John Frazer Meml, Edinburgh, 1984; Tung Wah Inaugural, Hong Kong, 1986. Visiting Professor: Durban, Cape Town, Witwatersrand, 1970; Sir Logan Campbell and RACS, NZ, 1977; Univ. of Calif and Cedars-Sinai Hosp., LA, 1978; Pearce Gould, Middlesex Hosp., 1980; McIlrath Guest, Sydney, 1981; G. B. Ong, Univ. of Hong Kong, 1983 (Ong Inaugural Lecture); Foundn Culpepper Prof., Univ. of California, 1984; Madras Med. Coll., and Univ. of Istanbul, 1986. Mem. Council, RCS, 1975–; Member: Moynihan Chirurgical Club; James IV Assoc. of Surgeons (Pres., 1985–86); Internat. Surgical Gp (Pres., 1985–86); Surgical Research Soc.; Internat. Soc. of Cardio-Vascular Surgeons; Vascular Surgical Soc., GB (Pres., 1974–75); Chm., Assoc. of Profs of Surgery of GB and Ireland, 1979–82. Mem. Council, Univ. of Zimbabwe, 1973–82. Fellow: RSM; Assoc. of Surgeons GB and Ire. (Mem. Council, 1966–76, Treasurer, 1970–76); Assoc. Clinical Anatomists; Amer. Surgical Assoc.; Hon. FCS Sri Lanka, 1984. Hon. Life Mem., Los Angeles Surgical Soc.; Hon. Member: Grey Turner Surgical Club; Assoc. of Surgeons of India. Jacksonian Prize and Medal, RCS, 1959; Pybus Meml Medal, NE Surgical Soc., 1978; Miles Medal, Royal Marsden Hosp., 1983. *Publications*: Metabolic Derangements in Gastrointestinal Surgery (with B. N. Brooke), 1967 (USA); numerous contribs to med. and surg. jls. *Recreations*: fishing and family. *Address*: 23 Aston Bury, Edgbaston, Birmingham B15 3QB. *T*: 021–454 0261.

SLATCHER, William Kenneth, CMG 1983; CVO 1975; HM Diplomatic Service, retired; High Commissioner in Guyana and non-resident Ambassador to Suriname, 1982–85; *b* 12 April 1926; *s* of John William and Ada Slatcher; *m* 1948, Erica Marjorie Konigs; one *s* one *d*. *Educ*: St John's Coll., Oxford. Royal Artillery, 1950–57; HM Diplomatic Service, 1958: Peking, 1959–60; Tokyo, 1961–63; Paris, 1965–68; New Delhi, 1968–71; Tokyo, 1974–77; Consul-Gen., Osaka, 1977–80; Head of Consular Dept, FCO, 1980–82. *Recreations*: travelling, oriental art and history, reading. *Address*: 90 Drayton Gardens, SW10 9RG. *Club*: Royal Commonwealth Society.

SLATER, Bill; *see* Slater, W. J.

SLATER, Duncan, CMG 1982; HM Diplomatic Service; Assistant Under Secretary of State, Foreign and Commonwealth Office, since 1986; *b* 15 July 1934; *m* 1972, Candida Coralie Anne Wheatley; one *s* two *d*. Joined FO, 1958; Asst Polit. Agent, Abu Dhabi, 1962–66; First Secretary: Islamabad, 1966; New Delhi, 1966–68; Head of Chancery, Aden, 1968–69; FO, 1969; Special Asst to Sir William Luce, 1970–71; First Sec., UK Representation to EEC, Brussels, 1973–75; UK Resident Rep. to IAEA and UK Perm. Rep. to UNIDO, Vienna, 1975–78; on staff of Government House, Salisbury, Dec. 1979–April 1980; Counsellor and Head of Chancery, Lagos, 1978–81; Ambassador to Oman, 1981–86. *Recreations*: walking, sailing, skiing, studying Islamic art. *Address*: c/o Foreign and Commonwealth Office, SW1.

SLATER, Prof. Edward Charles, ScD; FRS 1975; Professor of Physiological Chemistry, University of Amsterdam, The Netherlands, 1955–85; Hon. Professor, University of Southampton, since 1985; *b* 16 Jan. 1917; *s* of Edward Brunton Slater and Violet Podmore; *m* 1940, Marion Winifred Hutley; one *d*. *Educ*: Melbourne Univ. (BSc, MSc); Cambridge Univ. (PhD, ScD). Biochemist, Australian Inst. of Anatomy, Canberra, Aust., 1939–46; Research Fellow, Molteno Inst., Univ. of Cambridge, UK, 1946–55. Member: Royal Netherlands Acad. of Science and Letters, 1964; Hollandsche Maatschappij van Wetenschappen, 1970; Hon. Member: Amer. Soc. of Biological Chemists, 1971; Academie Nacional de Ciencias Exactas, Fisicas y Naturales, Argentina, 1973; Japanese Biochemical Soc., 1973; For. Mem., Royal Swedish Acad. of Sciences, 1975; Hon. For. Mem., Académie Royal de Méd., Belgium, 1982; Corresp. Mem., Australian Acad. of Science, 1985. Kt, Order of the Netherlands Lion. *Publications*: about 400 contribs to learned jls. *Recreations*: yachting, skiing. *Address*: 9 Oaklands, Lymington, Hants SO41 9TH. *T*: (home) Lymington 79455, (work) Southampton 559122.

SLATER, Gordon Charles Henry, CMG 1964; CBE 1956; Director, Branch Office in London of International Labour Office, 1964–70; Under-Secretary, Ministry of Labour, in the Overseas Department, 1960–64, retired; *b* 14 Dec. 1903; *s* of Matthew and Florence Slater; *m* 1928, Doris Primrose Hammond; one *s* one *d*. Entered Ministry of Labour, 1928, as Third Class Officer; Assistant Secretary, Organisation and Establishments, 1945, Disabled Persons Branch, 1949; Secretary of National Advisory Council on Employment of Disabled Persons, 1949–56; Sec. of Piercy Committee on Rehabilitation of Disabled, 1953–56; Under-Sec., Ministry of Labour, 1958. Member Governing Body, ILO, 1961–64; UK Govt delegate, IL Conf., 1961–64. Mem. Berkshire CC, 1970–81, Vice-Chm., 1977–79. *Address*: White House, Altwood Road, Maidenhead, Berks. *T*: Maidenhead 27463.

SLATER, Gordon James Augustus; HM Diplomatic Service, retired; Secretary to Government, and Adviser to Foreign Affairs Department, Tuvalu, 1985–86; *b* 8 July 1922; *s* of William Augustus Slater and Edith Garden; *m* 1st, 1952, Beryl Ruth Oliver (marr. diss. 1968); one *s* one *d*; 2nd, 1976, Gina Michelle Lambert; one *d*. *Educ*: Sydney, Australia. Foreign and Commonwealth Office (formerly Commonwealth Relations Office), 1958–82; High Comr, Honiara, Solomon Is, 1978–82. *Recreations*: sailing, diving, golf.

SLATER, James Derrick, FCA; *b* 13 March 1929; *o s* of Hubert and Jessica Slater; *m* 1965, Helen Wyndham Goodwyn; two *s* two *d*. *Educ*: Preston Manor County Sch. Accountant and then Gen. Man. to a gp of metal finishing cos, 1953–55; Sec., Park Royal Vehicles Ltd, 1955–58; Dep. Sales Dir, Leyland Motor Corp. Ltd, 1963; Chm., Slater Walker Securities Ltd, 1964–75; Dir, BLMC, 1969–75. FCA 1963 (ACA 1953). *Publications*: Return to Go, 1977; *for children*: Goldenrod, 1978; A. Mazing Monsters, 1979; Grasshopper and the Unwise Owl, 1979; The Boy Who Saved Earth, 1979. *Recreations*: chess, bridge, salmon fishing, table tennis. *Address*: High Beeches, Blackhills, Esher, Surrey.

SLATER, Rear-Adm. John Cunningham Kirkwood, LVO 1971; Assistant Chief of Defence Staff (Policy and Nuclear), since 1985; *b* 27 March 1938; *s* of late Dr James K. Slater, OBE, MD, FRCPE and M. C. B. Slater (*née* Bramwell); *m* 1972, Ann Frances, *d* of W. P. Scott of Orkney; two *s*. *Educ*: Edinburgh Academy; Sedbergh. BRNC Dartmouth, 1956–58; served HM Ships Troubridge, Yaxham, HM Yacht Britannia, Cassandra and Soberton, 1959–65; specialised in navigation, HMS Dryad, 1965–66; HM Ships Victorious and Scarborough (Dartmouth Training Sqdn), 1966–68; Equerry to HM the Queen, 1968–71; Comd, HMS Jupiter, 1972–73; Directorate of Naval Ops, MoD, 1973–75; Comd, HMS Kent, 1976–77; RCDS 1978; Asst Dir of Naval Warfare, MoD, 1979–81; Comd, HMS Illustrious, 1982–83; Captain, Sch. of Maritime Ops and Comd, HMS Dryad, 1983–85. Mem. Bd of Management, British Nat. Space Centre, 1986–. *Address*: c/o Royal Bank of Scotland, 142/144 Princes Street, Edinburgh EH2 4EQ. *Club*: Army and Navy.
See also P. J. B. Slater.

SLATER, John Fell, CMG 1972; Assistant Secretary, HM Treasury, 1968–83; *b* 3 July 1924; *s* of J. Alan Slater, FRIBA, and Freide R. Slater (*née* Flight); *m* 1951, Susan Baron; two *s* two *d* (and one *d* decd). *Educ*: Abinger Hill Preparatory Sch.; Leighton Park Sch.; New Coll., Oxford (BA). *Recreations*: fly-fishing, photography. *Address*: 50 Cathcart Road, SW10. *T*: 01–352 8686.

SLATER, Kenneth Frederick, FEng 1985; FIEE; Director of Engineering, Marconi Underwater Systems Ltd, since 1984; *b* 31 July 1925; *s* of Charles Frederick and Emily Gertrude Slater; *m* 1965, Marjorie Gladys Beadsworth, Northampton. *Educ*: Hull Grammar Sch.; Manchester Univ. BSc Tech (Hons). Admiralty Signal Estab. Extension, 1943–46; RRE, 1949–63; UK Mem., NATO Air Defence Planning Team, 1964; Supt, Radar Div., RRE, 1965–68; Asst Dir of Electronics R&D, Min. of Technology, 1968–70; Dir, 1970–71; Head of Ground Radar Gp, 1971–75, of Electronics Gp, 1975, of Applied Physics Dept, and Dep. Dir, 1976, RRE; Head of Military and Civil Systems Dept and Dep. Dir, RSRE, 1977; Dir, Admiralty Surface Weapons Estab., 1978–84. *Publications*: specialist contribs on Radar to Encyclopaedia Britannica and Encyclopaedic Dictionary of Physics; technical articles. *Recreations*: photography, music. *Address*: Wessenden, Biddenfield Lane, Wickham, Hants PO17 5NU. *T*: 833495.

SLATER, Leonard, CBE 1976; JP; DL; *b* 23 July 1908; *s* of S. M. Slater, Oldham, and Heysham, Lancs; *m* 1943, Olga Patricia George (*d* 1983); two *s*. *Educ*: Hulme Grammar School, Oldham; St Catharine's College, Cambridge (MA). British Guiana Exped. 1929; Research at Cambridge, 1930–32; MA 1932. Lecturer in Geography, Univ. of Rangoon, 1932–37; Geography Master, Repton School, 1937. Served War, 1940–45; RE (Survey) in UK, India and SE Asia; Lieut-Col, 1944 and Hon. Lieut-Col, 1946. Univ. of Durham: Geography Dept, Lectr, 1939; Reader, 1948; Pro-Vice-Chancellor, 1969–73; Master, University Coll., Durham, 1953–73. Mem. Peterlee Develt Corp., 1956–63; Chairman: Durham Hosp. Management Cttee, 1961–73; Durham AHA, 1973–77; Mem., Newcastle Regional Hosp. Bd, 1965–69 and 1971–74. JP 1961, DL 1978, Durham. *Publications*: articles in geographical periodicals. *Recreation*: travel. *Address*: 8 Farnley Ridge, Durham DH1 4HB. *T*: Durham 63319.

SLATER, Prof. Peter James Bramwell; Kennedy Professor of Natural History, University of St Andrews, since 1984; *b* 26 Dec. 1942; *s* of Dr James Kirkwood Slater, OBE and Margaret Claire Byrom Slater (*née* Bramwell); *m* 1968, Elisabeth Priscilla Vernon Smith; two *s*. *Educ*: Edinburgh Academy; Glenalmond; Univ. of Edinburgh (BSc 1964; PhD 1968; DSc 1983). Shaw Macfie Lang Fellow, 1964–66, Demonstrator in Zoology, 1966–68, Univ. of Edinburgh; Lectr in Biology, Univ. of Sussex, 1968–84. Hon. Sec., Assoc. for Study of Animal Behaviour, 1973–78, Hon. Pres., 1986–. European Editor, Animal Behaviour, 1979–82; Associate Editor, Advances in the Study of Behavior, 1982–; Editor, Science Progress, 1983–. *Publications*: Sex Hormones and Behaviour, 1978; (ed with T. R. Halliday) Animal Behaviour, 1983; An Introduction to Ethology, 1985; (ed) Collins Encyclopaedia of Animal Behaviour, 1986; numerous articles in learned jls. *Recreations*: ornithology, writing, listening to music. *Address*: Department of Zoology and Marine Biology, University of St Andrews, Fife KY16 9TS. *T*: St Andrews 76161.
See also J. C. K. Slater.

SLATER, Richard Mercer Keene, CMG 1962; *b* 27 May 1915; *s* of late Samuel Henry Slater, CMG, CIE; *m* 1939, Barbara Janet Murdoch; four *s*. *Educ*: Eton; Magdalene Coll., Cambridge. Indian Civil Service (Punjab Commission), 1939–47; joined HM Diplomatic Service, 1947; served in Karachi (on secondment to Commonwealth Relations Office), Lima, Moscow, Rangoon and Foreign Office; Ambassador to Cuba, 1966–70; High Comr in Uganda and Ambassador to Rwanda, 1970–72; Asst Under-Sec. of State, FCO, 1973. Adviser to Commercial Union Assurance Co., 1973–81. Chm., Hampshire Br., CPRE, 1974–85. *Address*: Vicary's, Odiham, Hants.

SLATER, William Bell, CBE 1982; VRD 1959; FCIT; Managing Director, The Cunard Steam-Ship Co. plc, 1974–85 (Director, 1971–85 and since 1986); Director, Trafalgar

House plc, since 1975; *b* 7 Jan. 1925; *s* of William Bell and Mamie Slater; *m* 1950, Jean Mary Kiernan; two *s*. *Educ:* Lancaster Royal Grammar Sch. FCIT 1970. National Service, RM, 1943–47 (Captain, 3rd Commando Bde); RM Reserve, 1949–63 (Lt-Col and CO Merseyside Unit). Trainee, Thos & Jno Brocklebank Ltd, 1947, Dir 1966–85, also Chm.; Ops Dir, 1968, Dep. Man. Dir, 1969, Man. Dir, 1971–72, Chm. 1972–85, Cunard Brocklebank Ltd. Director: Atlantic Container Line Ltd, 1968–85 (Chm., 1977–78 and 1982–83); Associated Container Transportation (Australia) Ltd, 1974–85 (Chm., 1982–85); Associated Container Transportation Ltd, 1974–85 (Chm., 1982–85); The Mersey Docks & Harbour Co., 1980– (Dep. Chm., 1985–). Vice-Pres., CIT, 1984–. Hon. Col, RM Reserve, Merseyside, 1986–. Order of El Istiqlal (2nd Cl.), Jordan, 1972. *Recreations:* Rugby and cricket (formerly Senior Club player). *Address:* Gayton Court, 419 Woodham Lane, Woodham, Weybridge, Surrey KT15 3PP. *T:* Byfleet 49389. *Club:* Naval.

SLATER, William John, (Bill Slater), OBE 1982; Director of Development Services, Sports Council, since 1984; *b* 29 April 1927; *s* of John Rothwell Slater and Ethel May Slater; *m* 1952, Marion Warr; two *s* two *d*. *Educ:* Clitheroe Royal Grammar Sch.; Carnegie Coll. of Physical Educn (Dip. in Phys. Educn); Univ. of Birmingham (BSc). FPEA 1984. Dep. Dir, Crystal Palace Nat. Sports Centre, 1963–64; Dir of Phys. Educn, Univ. of Liverpool, 1964–70 (Warden, McNair Hall, 1966–69); Dir of Phys. Educn, Univ. of Birmingham, 1970–83. Member: Central Adv. Council for Educn (Newsom Cttee), 1961–63; Cttee of Enquiry into Association Football (Chester Cttee), 1966–68; Exec. Cttee, Internat. Council of Sport and Physical Educn, 1980–; Sports Council, 1974–83 (Chm., Nat. Resources Cttee, 1982–83). Chairman: Cttee of Advrs, Sports Aid Foundn, 1978–; Management Cttee, Lilleshall Nat. Sports Centre, 1979–83; West Midlands Council for Sport and Recreation, 1979–83. Wolverhampton Wanderers Football Club, 1951–62; rep. England in Association Football, 1951–60; Olympic Games, Helsinki, 1952; World Cup (Assoc. Football), Sweden, 1958. Footballer of the Year, 1960. *Recreations:* games and sports of all kinds. *Address:* 55 Green Meadow Road, Birmingham B29 4DD. *T:* 021–475 1858.

SLATTERY, Rear-Adm. Sir Matthew (Sausse), KBE 1960; Kt 1955; CB 1946; FRAeS 1946; *b* 12 May 1902; 3rd *s* of late H. F. Slattery, one-time Chairman of National Bank Ltd; *m* 1925, Mica Mary, *d* of Col G. D. Swain, CMG; two *s* one *d*. *Educ:* Stonyhurst Coll.; RN Colls, Osborne and Dartmouth. Joined RN, 1916; Director Air Material, Admiralty, 1939–41; commanded HMS Cleopatra, 1941–42; appointed Director-General of Naval Aircraft Development and Production, Ministry of Aircraft Production, 1941, and Chief Naval Representative, 1943; Vice-Controller (Air) and Chief of Naval Air Equipment at Admiralty, and Chief Naval Representative on Supply Council, Ministry of Supply, 1945–48; retd list, Royal Navy, 1948. Vice-Chm., Air Requirements Bd, 1960–74. Man. Dir, Short Brothers & Harland, Ltd, 1948–52, Chm. and Man. Dir, 1952–60; Chairman: (SB Realisations) Ltd, 1952–60; Bristol Aircraft Ltd, 1957–60; Dir Bristol Aeroplane Co. Ltd, 1957–60. Special Adviser to Prime Minister on Transport of Middle East Oil, 1957–59; Dir National Bank Ltd, 1959–60, 1963–69; Chairman: BOAC, 1960–63; BOAC-Cunard Ltd, 1962–63; R. & W. Hawthorn, Leslie & Co., 1966–73. Commander Legion of Merit (USA). DSc(*hc*) Queen's Univ., Belfast, 1954. *Recreations:* country pursuits. *Address:* Harvey's Farm, Warninglid, West Sussex.

SLATYER, Prof. Ralph Owen, AO 1982; FRS 1975; Chairman, Australian Science and Technology Council (ASTEC), since 1982; Ambassador of Australia to UNESCO, 1978–81; Professor, Institute of Advanced Studies, since 1967, and Director, Research School of Biological Sciences, since 1984, Australian National University, Canberra; *b* 16 April 1929; *s* of Thomas Henry and Jean Slatyer; *m* 1953, June Helen Wade; one *s* two *d*. *Educ:* Univ. of Western Australia. BSc (Agric.), MSc, DSc. CSIRO Res. Scientist, subseq. Chief Res. Scientist, 1951–67. Member: Australian Res. Grants Cttee, 1969–72; Nat. Capital Planning Cttee, 1973–76; Aust. Nat. Commn for UNESCO, 1975–78 (Chm., 1976–78); Policy Adv. Council and Bd of Management, Aust. Centre for Internat. Agricl Research, 1981–85; President: Ecol Soc. of Austr., 1969–71; UNESCO Man and the Biosphere Programme, 1977–81; UNESCO World Heritage Cttee, 1981–83; ICSU Sci. Cttee on Problems of the Environment, 1982–85; ANZAAS, 1983; Chm., Aust. Biol. Resources Study, 1981–84. FAA 1967. Hon. DSc: Univ. of WA, 1983; Duke Univ., 1986. Edgeworth David Medal, 1960; Austr. Medal of Agric. Sci., 1968. For. Associate, US Nat. Acad. of Sciences, 1976; Hon. For. Mem., Amer. Acad. of Arts and Scis, 1981. *Publications:* (with I. C. McIlroy) Practical Microclimatology, 1961 (Russian edn 1964); Plant-Water Relationships, 1967 (Russian edn 1970); (ed with R. A. Perry) Arid Lands of Australia, 1969; (ed jtly) Photosynthesis and Photorespiration, 1971; (ed) Plant Response to Climatic Factors, 1974; papers in learned jls. *Recreations:* ski-ing, bushwalking. *Address:* 10 Tennyson Crescent, Forrest, ACT 2603, Australia. *T:* (062) 95–2347.

SLAUGHTER, Audrey Cecelia, (Mrs C. V. Wintour); Chairman, Wintour Productions, since 1983; Life style Editor, The Independent, since 1986; *b* 17 Jan. 1930; *d* of Frederick George Smith and Ethel Louise Smith; *m* 1st, 1950, W. A. Slaughter (marr. diss.); one *s* one *d*; 2nd, 1979, Charles Vere Wintour, *qv*. *Educ:* Chislehurst High Sch., Stand Grammar Sch., Manchester. Editor, Honey magazine, 1960; founded Petticoat magazine, 1964; columnist, Evening News, 1968; joined National Magazine Co., to edit Vanity Fair, 1969; founded and funded own magazine, Over 21, 1970; after sale to Morgan Grampian, 1972, remained as Dir and Editor until 1979; Associate Editor, Sunday Times, 1979; with husband founded Sunday Express colour magazine, 1981; Founder Editor, Working Woman magazine, 1984–86. *Publications:* Every Man Should Have One (with Margaret Goodman), 1969; Getting Through . . ., 1981; Your Brilliant Career, 1987. *Recreations:* classical music, theatre, painting, gardening, entertaining. *Address:* 5 Alwyne Road, N1 2HH. *T:* 01–359 4590. *Clubs:* Institute of Directors, Network, City Women's Network.

SLAUGHTER, Frank Gill, MC; MD, FACS; novelist (self-employed); physician and surgeon (retd); *b* Washington, USA, 25 Feb. 1908; *s* of Stephen Lucius Slaughter and Sallie Nicholson Gill; *m* 1933, Jane Mundy; two *s*. *Educ:* Duke Univ. (AB); Johns Hopkins (MD). Served War, 1942–46 (MC): Major to Lt-Col, US Army Med. Corps. Intern, asst resident, and resident surgeon, Jefferson Hosp., Roanoke, Va, 1930–34; practice, specializing in surgery, Jacksonville, Fla, 1934–42; retired, 1946; Lectr, W. Colston Leigh, Inc., NY City, 1947–49. Res. Diplomate, Amer. Bd of Surgery. Mem., Sons of Amer. Revolution. Presbyterian (Elder). Hon. DHL Jacksonville Univ., 1978. *Publications:* That None Should Die, 1941; Spencer Brade, MD, 1942; Air Surgeon, 1943; Battle Surgeon, 1944; A Touch of Glory, 1945; In a Dark Garden, 1946; The New Science of Surgery, 1946; The Golden Isle, 1947; Sangaree, 1948; Medicine for Moderns, 1948; Divine Mistress, 1949; The Stubborn Heart, 1950; Immortal Magyar, 1950; Fort Everglades, 1951; The Road to Bithynia, 1951; East Side General, 1952; The Galileans, 1953; Storm Haven, 1953; The Song of Ruth, 1954; Apalachee Gold, 1954; The Healer, 1955; Flight from Natchez, 1955; The Scarlet Cord, 1956; The Warrior, 1956; Sword and Scalpel, 1957; The Mapmaker, 1957; Daybreak, 1958; The Thorn of Arimathea, 1958; The Crown and the Cross, 1959; Lorena, 1959; The Land and the Promise, 1960; Pilgrims in Paradise, 1960; Epidemic, 1961; The Curse of Jezebel, 1961; David: Warrior and King, 1962; Tomorrow's Miracle, 1962; Devil's Harvest, 1963; Upon This Rock, 1963; A Savage Place, 1964; The Purple Quest, 1965; Constantine: The Miracle of the Flaming Cross, 1965; Surgeon, USA, 1966; God's Warrior, 1967; Doctor's Wives, 1967; The Sins of Herod, 1968; Surgeon's Choice, 1969; Countdown, 1970; Code Five, 1971; Convention, MD, 1972; Life blood, 1974; Stonewall Brigade, 1975; Plague Ship, 1977; Devil's Gamble, 1978; The Passionate Rebel, 1979; Gospel Fever, 1980; Doctor's Daughters, 1981; Doctors At Risk, 1983; No Greater Love, 1985. *Recreations:* boating, hiking, reading. *Address:* 5051 Yacht Club Road, Jacksonville, Fla 32210, USA. *T:* 904–389–7677. *Club:* Timuquana Country (Jacksonville, Fla).

SLAUGHTER, Giles David, MA; Headmaster, University College School, since 1983; *b* 11 July 1937; *s* of Gerald Slaughter and Enid Lillian Slaughter (*née* Crane); *m* 1965, Gillian Rothwell Shepherd; three *d*. *Educ:* Royal Masonic School; King's College, Cambridge. MA. Pierrepont School, Frensham, 1961–65; Campbell College, Belfast, 1965–68; Stockport Grammar School, 1968–70; Housemaster, Ormiston House, 1970–73; Headmaster, Solihull School, 1973–82. JP Solihull, 1977–82. FRSA 1985. *Recreations:* gardening, cricket, golf, theatre. *Address:* 5 Redington Road, Hampstead, NW3 7QX. *Club:* East India, Devonshire, Sports and Public Schools.

SLEDGE, Ven. Richard Kitson; Archdeacon of Huntingdon and Rector of Hemingford Abbots, since 1978; *b* 13 April 1930; *s* of Sydney Kitson and Mary Sylvia Sledge; *m* 1958, Patricia Henley (*née* Sear); one *s* two *d* (and one *s* decd). *Educ:* Epsom College; Peterhouse, Cambridge (MA). Curate of Emmanuel, Plymouth, 1954–57; Curate-in-charge of St Stephen's, Exeter, 1957–63; Rector of Dronfield, 1963–78. *Address:* The Rectory, Hemingford Abbots, Huntingdon, Cambs PE18 9AN. *T:* St Ives 69856.

SLEEMAN, His Honour (Stuart) Colin; a Circuit Judge, 1976–86; *s* of Stuart Bertram Sleeman and Phyllis Grace (*née* Pitt); *m* 1944, Margaret Emily, *d* of late William Joseph Farmer; two *s* one *d*. *Educ:* Clifton Coll.; Merton Coll., Oxford (BA 1936, MA 1963). Called to the Bar, Gray's Inn, 1938; Bencher, 1974. World War II: Admin. Officer, Prize Dept, Min. of Economic Warfare, 1939–40; Lt-Col 16th-5th Lancers; Staff Captain: RAC Wing, Combined Trng Centre, 1941; 6th Armoured Div., 1942; Adjt, RAC Range, Minehead, 1942–44; Asst Judge Advocate Gen., HQ Allied Land Forces, SE Asia, 1945. London Corresp., Scottish Law Rev., 1949–54; a Recorder, 1975–76. *Publications:* The Trial of Gozawa Sadaichi and Nine Others, 1948; (with S. C. Silkin) The 'Double Tenth' Trial, 1950. *Recreations:* travel, genealogy. *Address:* West Walls, Cotmandene, Dorking, Surrey RH4 2BL. *T:* Dorking 883616; 1 Gray's Inn Square, WC1R 5AA. *T:* 01–404 0763.

SLEEP, Wayne; dancer, actor, choreographer; formed own company, DASH, 1980; *b* Plymouth, 17 July 1948. *Educ:* Hartlepool; Royal Ballet Sch. (Leverhulme Scholar). Graduated into Royal Ballet, 1966; Soloist, 1970; Principal, 1973; roles in: Giselle; Dancers at a Gathering; The Nutcracker; Romeo and Juliet; The Grand Tour; Elite Syncopations; Swan Lake; The Four Seasons; Les Patineurs; Petroushka (title role); Cinderella; The Dream; Pineapple Poll; Mam'zelle Angot; 4th Symphony; La Fille mal gardée; A Month in the Country; A Good Night's Sleep (gala); chor., with Robert North, David & Goliath; also roles in operas, A Midsummer Night's Dream and Aida; roles created for him by Sir Frederick Ashton, Dame Ninette de Valois, Sir Kenneth MacMillan, Rudolf Nureyev, John Neumeier, Joe Layton and many others. *Theatre:* Ariel in The Tempest, New Shakespeare Co.; title role in Pinocchio, Birmingham Rep.; genie in Aladdin, Palladium; soldier in The Soldier's Tale, QEH, 1980 and 1981; Truffaldino in The Servant of Two Masters; chor. and played lead in The Point, Mermaid; Mr Mistoffelees in Cats, New London, 1981; co-starred in Song and Dance, Palace, 1982 (video, 1984). DASH, Chichester Fest., 1980, national tour and Sadler's Wells, 1982, Apollo Victoria and national tour, Christmas season, Dominion, 1983. *Films:* The Virgin Soldiers; The First Great Train Robbery; The Tales of Beatrix Potter, 1971. Chor. films and television, inc. Adam's Rib, and appeared in many television progs inc. Dizzy Feet and series, The Hot Shoe Show, 1983, 1984; Tony Lumpkin in She Stoops to Conquer, radio. Show Business Personality of the Year, 1983. *Publication:* Variations on Wayne Sleep, 1983. *Recreation:* entertaining. *Address:* c/o London Management, 235 Regent Street, W1. *Clubs:* YMCA, Zanzibar.

SLEIGHT, Sir John Frederick, 3rd Bt, *cr* 1920; *b* 13 April 1909; *s* of Major Sir Ernest Sleight, 2nd Bt and Margaret (*d* 1976), *d* of C. F. Carter, JP, The Limes, Grimsby; *S* father 1946; *m* 1942, Jacqueline Margaret Mundell, *widow* of Ronald Mundell and *o d* of late Major H. R. Carter of Brisbane, Queensland; one *s*. *Heir:* *s* Richard Sleight [*b* 27 May 1946; *m* 1978, Marie-Thérèse, *o d* of O. M. Stepan, Bromley, Kent]. *Address:* c/o National Westminster Bank, 58 High Street, Watford, Herts.

SLEIGHT, Prof. Peter, MD (Cantab), DM (Oxon), FRCP; FACC; Field-Marshal Alexander Professor of Cardiovascular Medicine in the University of Oxford, and Fellow of Exeter College, Oxford, since 1973; *b* 27 June 1929; *s* of William and Mary Sleight, Boston Spa, Yorks; *m* 1953, Gillian France; two *s*. *Educ:* Leeds Grammar Sch.; Gonville and Caius Coll., Cambridge; St Bartholomew's Hosp., London. Ho. Phys. and Ho. Surg., Med. and Surg. Professorial Units, Bart's, 1953; Sen. Registrar, St George's Hosp., London, 1959–64; Bissinger Fellow, Cardiovascular Research Unit, Univ. of California, San Francisco, 1961–63; MRC Scientific Officer, Depts of Physiology and Medicine, Univ. of Oxford, 1964–66; Consultant Physician, Radcliffe Infirmary, Oxford, 1966–73; Visiting Prof., Univ. of Sydney (Warren McDonald Sen. Overseas Fellow of Aust. Heart Foundn), 1972–73; Hon. Prof. of Medicine, Federal Univ. of Pernambuco, 1975. Civil Consultant in Medicine, RAF, 1985–. Member Council: Internat. Soc. of Hypertension, 1978–; European Soc. of Cardiology, 1983–. Chm., ASH, 1982–. Mem. Editorial Bd, British Heart Jl, 1976–; Editor, Jl of Cardiovascular Res., 1983–. Young Investigators Award, Amer. Coll. of Cardiology, 1963. *Films:* Control of Circulation; History of Hypertension (Medal, BMA Scientific Film Competition, 1981). *Publications:* Modern Trends in Cardiology, 1976; (ed) Arterial Baroreceptors and Hypertension, 1981; Hypertension, 1982; (ed) Scientific Foundations of Cardiology, 1983; contribs on nervous control of the circulation and hypertension in: Circulation Research; Jl Physiol; Lancet (Chm., Internat. Studies of Infant Survival). *Recreations:* sailing, golf, travel. *Address:* Wayside, 32 Crown Road, Wheatley, Oxon. *Club:* Royal Air Force.

SLEIGHTHOLME, Derek; Member of Tyne and Wear County Council, 1974–86 (Chairman, 1975–76); *b* 4 June 1935; *s* of George Henry Sleightholme and Evelyn Sleightholme; *m* 1957, Norma; one *s* one *d*. *Educ:* Washington Glebe. RAF, 1953–57; miner, 1957–75. Former Member, Washington Develt Corp. *Recreations:* sport, agriculture. *Address:* 28 Woburn, Biddick Village, Washington NE38 7JX. *Club:* Celtic (Washington).

SLEMON, Air Marshal Charles Roy, CB 1946; CBE 1943; retired from RCAF, 1964; *b* Winnipeg, Manitoba, Canada, 7 November 1904; *s* of Samuel Slemon and Mary Bonser; *m* 1935, Marion Pamela Slemon, Bowmanville, Ont; one *s* two *d*. *Educ:* University of Manitoba (BSc). Lieut COTC (Army), Canada, 1923; Cadet Royal Canadian Air Force, 1923; Royal Air Force Staff College Course, England, 1938; Senior Air Staff Officer at Western Air Command Headquarters, Canada, 1939–41; commanded

Western Air Command, Canada, for 5 months in 1941; Director of Operations at RCAF HQ Ottawa, 1941–42; Senior Air Staff Officer, No. 6 (RCAF) Bomber Group, England, 1942–44; Air Vice-Marshal, 1945; Deputy AOC-in-C, RCAF Overseas, March 1945; Commanded Canadian Air Forces preparing for the Pacific, 1945; Air Council Member for Supply and Organization, 1946; Air Council Member for Operations and Training, 1947–48; AOC Trg Comd, RCAF, 1949–53; Chief of the Air Staff, Canada, 1953–57; Dep. C-in-C, N American Defence Comd (Canada-USA), 1957–64, retd. Exec. Vice-Pres., US Air Force Acad. Foundn Inc., 1964–81. Hon. LLD (Univ. of Manitoba), 1953; Hon. DMSc (RMC), Kingston, Ont, 1965. USA Legion of Merit, 1946; French Legion of Honour and Croix de Guerre with Palm, 1947. *Recreations:* golf, swimming. *Address:* 8 Thayer Road, Broadmoor Heights, Colorado Springs, Colorado 80906, USA.

SLEVIN, Brian Francis Patrick, CMG 1975; OBE 1973; QPM 1968; CPM 1965; *b* 13 Aug. 1926; *s* of late Thomas and Helen Slevin; *m* 1972, Constance Gay, *e d* of Major Ronald Moody and Amy Moody; one *s. Educ:* Blackrock Coll., Ireland. Palestine Police, 1946–48; Hong Kong Police, 1949–79; Directing Staff, Overseas Police Courses, Metropolitan Police Coll., Hendon, London, 1955–57; Director, Special Branch, 1966–69; Sen. Asst Comr of Police, Comdg Kowloon Dist, 1969–70; Dir, Criminal Investigation Dept, 1971; Dep. Comr of Police, 1971, Comr of Police, 1974–79, Hong Kong; retired 1979. *Recreations:* walking, golf, reading, painting. *Address:* Lantau Lodge, 152 Coonanbarra Road, Wahroonga, Sydney, NSW 2076, Australia. *T:* 48661. *Clubs:* East India, Royal Automobile; Hong Kong, Royal Hong Kong Golf, Royal Hong Kong Jockey (Hong Kong).

SLIGO, 10th Marquess of, *cr* 1800; **Denis Edward Browne;** Baron Mount Eagle, 1760; Viscount Westport, 1768; Earl of Altamont, 1771; Earl of Clanricarde, 1543 and 1800 (special remainder); Baron Monteagle (UK), 1806; *b* 13 Dec. 1908; *er s* of late Lt-Col Lord Alfred Eden Browne, DSO (5th *s* of 5th Marquess) and late Cicely, *d* of Edward Wormald, 15 Berkeley Square, W; *S* uncle, 1952; *m* 1930, José Gauche; one *s. Educ:* Eton. *Heir: s* Earl of Altamont, *qv. Address:* c/o Messrs Trower, Still and Keeling, 5 New Square, Lincoln's Inn, WC2.
See also Baron Brabourne.

SLIM, family name of **Viscount Slim.**

SLIM, 2nd Viscount *cr* 1960, of Yarralumla and Bishopston; **John Douglas Slim,** OBE 1973; Chairman: Peek Holdings Ltd, since 1976; Royal Gulf Group; Royal Gulf Security Services Ltd; Director: Runcorda Ltd, since 1974; F.O.'s (Trade Advisory Services) Ltd, since 1975; *b* 20 July 1927; *s* of Field Marshal the 1st Viscount Slim, KG, GCB, GCMG, GCVO, GBE, DSO, MC, and of Aileen, *d* of Rev. J. A. Robertson, MA, Edinburgh; *S* father, 1970; *m* 1958, Elisabeth, *d* of Arthur Rawdon Spinney, CBE; two *s* one *d. Educ:* Prince of Wales Royal Indian Military College, Dehra Dun. Indian Army, 6 Gurkha Rifles, 1945–48; Argyll and Sutherland Highlanders, 1948; SAS, 1952; Staff. Coll. Camberley, 1961; Brigade Major, HQ Infantry Bde (TA), 1962–64; JSSC 1964; Lt-Col 1967; Comdr, 22 Special Air Service Regt, 1967–70; GSO1 (Special Forces) HQ UK Land Forces, 1970–72; retired 1972. President, Burma Star Association, 1971–. Chm., Britain-Australia Soc., 1978–84. FRGS 1983. *Heir: s* Hon. Mark William Rawdon Slim, *b* 13 Feb. 1960. *Address:* c/o Lloyds Bank, 6 Pall Mall, SW1. *Clubs:* White's, Special Forces.

SLIMMINGS, Sir William Kenneth MacLeod, Kt 1966; CBE 1960; *b* 15 Dec. 1912; *s* of George and Robina Slimmings; *m* 1943, Lilian Ellen Willis; one *s* one *d. Educ:* Dunfermline High School. Chartered Accountant: Partner in Thomson McLintock & Co., Chartered Accountants, London, etc, 1946–78. Member: Committee of Inquiry on the Cost of Housebuilding, 1947–53; Committee on Tax-paid Stocks, 1952–53; Committee on Cheque Endorsement, 1955–56; Performing Right Tribunal, 1963–77; Crown Agents Tribunal, 1978–82; Chairman: Board of Trade Advisory Committee, 1957–66; Review Bd for Govt Contracts, 1971–81; Accounting Standards Cttee, 1976–78. Member: Council, Inst. Chartered Accountants of Scotland, 1962–66 (Pres., 1969–70); Scottish Tourist Bd, 1969–76; Review Body on Doctors' and Dentists' Pay, 1976–83. Independent Chm., Cement Makers' Fedn, 1977–80. Hon. DLitt, Heriot-Watt, 1970. *Recreation:* gardening. *Address:* 62 The Avenue, Worcester Park, Surrey KT4 7HH. *T:* 01–337 2579. *Club:* Caledonian.

SLINGER, William; *b* 27 Oct. 1917; *yr s* of late William Slinger and Maud Slinger, Newcastle, Co. Down; *m* 1944, Muriel, *o d* of late R. J. Johnston, Belfast; three *d. Educ:* Methodist Coll., Belfast; Queen's Univ., Belfast (BComSc). Entered Northern Ireland Civil Service, 1937; Private Secretary: to Minister of Labour, 1942–43 and 1945–46; to Minister of Public Security, 1944; Sec. to Nat. Arbitration Tribunal (NI), 1946–48; Principal, Min. of Labour and Nat. Insurance, Industrial Relations Div., 1954–60; Asst Sec. and Head of Industrial Relations Div., 1961–69; Sec., Dept of Community Relations, 1969–75; Dep. Sec., Dept of Educn for NI, 1975–77. CBIM. *Recreations:* gardening, walking. *Address:* Cairnfield, Circular Road, Belfast BT4 2GD. *T:* Belfast 768240. *Clubs:* East India, Devonshire, Sports and Public Schools; Civil Service (N Ireland).

SLIPMAN, Sue; Director, National Council for One Parent Families, since 1985; *b* 3 Aug. 1949; *d* of Marks Slipman and Doris Barham. *Educ:* Stockwell Manor Comprehensive School; Univ. of Wales (BA Hons 1st Class English; Post Graduate Cert Ed); Univs of Leeds and London. Sec. and Nat. Pres., Nat. Union of Students, 1975–78; Mem., Adv. Council for Adult and Continuing Educn, 1978–79; Area Officer, Nat. Union of Public Employees, 1979–85. Mem. Exec., NCCL, 1974–75; Vice-Chair, British Youth Council, 1977–78; Chair, Women for Social Democracy, 1983–86; Mem. Exec. and Chair of Training, 300 Group, 1985–86; Mem. Exec., London Voluntary Service Council, 1986–. *Publications:* Chapter in The Re-Birth of Britain, 1983; Help Yourself to Power: a handbook for women on the skills of public life, 1986. *Address:* c/o National Council for One Parent Families, 255 Kentish Town Road, NW5 2LX. *T:* 01–267 1361.

SLIVE, Prof. Seymour; Gleason Professor of Fine Arts at Harvard University since 1973; Director, Fogg Art Museum, 1975–82, sometime Elizabeth and John Moors Cabot Director of Harvard Art Museums; *b* Chicago, 15 Sept. 1920; *s* of Daniel Slive and Sonia (*née* Rapoport); *m* 1946, Zoya Gregorovna Sandomirsky; one *s* two *d. Educ:* Univ. of Chicago. BA 1943; PhD 1952. Served US Navy, Lieut, CO Small Craft, 1943–46. Instructor in Art History, Oberlin Coll., 1950–51; Asst Prof. and Chm. of Art Dept, Pomona Coll., 1952–54; Asst Prof. 1954–57, Assoc. Prof. 1957–61, Prof., 1961–73, Chm. of Dept 1968–71, Fine Arts, Harvard Univ.; Exchange Prof., Univ. of Leningrad, 1961. Ryerson Lectr, Yale, 1962. Slade Prof. of Fine Art, Univ. of Oxford, 1972–73. Trustee, Solomon R. Guggenheim Foundn, 1978–. FAAAS 1964. For. Mem., Netherlands Soc. of Sciences, 1971. Hon. MA Harvard, 1958; Hon. MA Oxford, 1972. Officer, Order of Orange Nassau, 1962. *Publications:* Rembrandt and His Critics: 1630–1730, 1953; Drawings of Rembrandt, 1965; (with J. Rosenberg) Dutch Art and Architecture: 1600–1800, 1965, 2nd edn (with J. Rosenberg and E. H. ter Kuile), 1978; Frans Hals, 3 vols, 1970–74; Jacob van Ruisdael, 1981; contribs to learned jls. *Address:* 1 Walker Street Place, Cambridge, Mass 02138, USA.

SLOAN, Andrew Kirkpatrick, QPM 1983; Chief Constable of Strathclyde, since 1985; *b* 27 Feb. 1931; *s* of Andrew Kirkpatrick Sloan and Amelia Sarah (*née* Vernon), Kirkcudbright; *m* 1953, Agnes Sofie Storvik, Trondheim, Norway; three *d. Educ:* Kirkcudbright Acad.; Dumfries Acad.; Open Univ. (BA). Joined RN as boy seaman, 1947; served at home and abroad in cruisers and submarines, and worked in industry in Norway, 1947–55; joined W Riding Constab., 1955; apptd to CID, 1963; Det. Sgt, Barnsley, 1964; Det. Insp., Reg. Crime Squad, Leeds, 1966; Det. Chief Insp., Goole and Pontefract, 1969; Det. Supt, Reg. Crime Squad, Wakefield, 1970; Chief Supt, Toller Lane Div., Bradford, 1975; Asst Chief Constable, Operations, Lincolnshire Police, 1976–79; National Co-ordinator, Regional Crime Squads of England and Wales, 1979–81; Dep. Chief Constable, Lincs, 1981–83; Chief Constable, Beds, 1983–85. *Recreations:* reading, travel, walking, conversation. *Address:* Police HQ, 173 Pitt Street, Glasgow G2 4JS.

SLOAN, Norman Alexander; QC (Scot.) 1953; Legal Adviser, British Shipbuilders, 1978–81; *b* 27 Jan. 1914; *s* of George Scott Sloan and Margaret Hutcheson Smith; *m* 1st, 1944, Peggy Perry (*d* 1982); two *s* one *d*; 2nd, 1983, Norma Olsen (*d* 1985). *Educ:* Glasgow Academy; Glasgow University (BL). Solicitor, 1935; Admitted to Faculty of Advocates, 1939; Served in RNVR 1940–46. Lecturer in Industrial Law, Edinburgh University, 1946–51; Standing Counsel to Department of Health for Scotland, 1946–51; Advocate-Depute, 1951–53. Director: The Shipbuilding Employers' Federation, 1955–68; Shipbuilders and Repairers Nat. Assoc., 1968–72; Swan Hunter Group Ltd, 1973–77; Swan Hunter Shipbuilders Ltd, 1973–78. *Recreations:* golf, gardening. *Address:* Ardyne, Felton, Morpeth, Northumberland NE65 9HN. *T:* Felton 496.

SLOANE, Maj.-Gen. John Bramley Malet, CB 1967; CBE 1962 (OBE 1951); DL; Director of Manning (Army), Ministry of Defence, 1964–67; retired; *b* 17 Sept. 1912; *s* of late James Kay Sloane, Penpont; *m* 1939, Marjorie (*née* Crowley); three *s.* Served 1934–39, London Scottish; commnd Argyll and Sutherland Highlanders, 1940; served Paiforce, ME, Burma, 1939–45, India, Aug. 1945–Dec. 1947, Korea, 1950–51, Malayan Campaign, 1951–53; War Office Staff, 1953–56; SHAPE, 1956–58; MoD, 1958–60; Brig. AQ, Western Comd, 1960–63. DL Beds, 1976. *Recreations:* golf, walking. *Address:* Jordans, Newton Blossomville, near Turvey, Beds. *T:* Turvey 392. *Club:* Army and Navy.

SLOANE, Peter James, PhD; Jaffrey Professor of Political Economy, University of Aberdeen, 1984–86; *b* 6 Aug. 1942; *s* of John Joseph Sloane and Elizabeth (*née* Clarke); *m* 1969, Avril Mary Urquhart; one *s. Educ:* Cheadle Hulme Sch.; Univ. of Sheffield (BAEcon Hons 1964); Univ. of Strathclyde (PhD 1966). Asst Lectr in Pol. Econ., Univ. of Aberdeen, 1966–67, Lectr in Pol. Econ., 1967–69; Lectr in Indust. Econs, Univ. of Nottingham, 1969–75; Economic Adviser, Unit for Manpower Studies, Dept of Employment (on secondment), 1973–74; Prof. of Econs and Management, Paisley Coll., 1975–84. Vis. Prof. (Commonwealth Fellow), Faculty of Business, McMaster Univ., Canada, 1978. Member: ESRC (formerly SSRC), 1979–85; Council, Scottish Economic Soc., 1983–. *Publications:* (with B. Chiplin) Sex Discrimination in the Labour Market, 1976; (ed) Women and Low Pay, 1980; (with H. C. Jain) Equal Employment Issues, 1981; (with B. Chiplin) Tackling Discrimination, 1982; (with D. Carline et al) Labour Economics, 1985; papers on changing patterns of working hours and on sport in the market; articles in learned jls, incl. Econ. Jl, Economica, Applied Econs, Bull. Econ. Res., Jl of Econ. Studies, Scottish Jl of Pol. Econ., British Jl of Indust. Relations, Indust. Relations Jl, Internat. Labour Rev., Internat. Jl of Social Econs, Managerial and Decision Econs, Internat. Jl of Manpower, and Leisure Studies. *Recreation:* sport. *Address:* The Eaves, Kincardine Road, Torphins, Banchory, Aberdeenshire AB3 4HH. *T:* Torphins 553. *Clubs:* Royal Commonwealth Society; Aboyne Golf.

SLOGGETT, Jolyon Edward, CEng, FRINA, FIMarE, FICS; Secretary, Institute of Marine Engineers, since 1986; *b* 30 May 1933; *s* of Edward Cornelius Sloggett and Lena May (*née* Norton); *m* 1970, Patricia Marjorie Iverson Ward; two *d. Educ:* John Lyon Sch.; Univ. of Glasgow (BSc). CDipAF. William Denny & Brothers Ltd, Leven Shipyard, Dumbarton, 1951–57 and 1959–60. Served, Royal Navy, TA Sub Lieut (E), RNVR, 1957–58; Houlder Brothers & Co. Ltd, 1960–78, Director, 1972–78; Man. Dir, Offshore, British Shipbuilders Corp., 1978–81; Dir, Vickers Shipbuilding Group, 1979–80; Chm., Vickers Offshore (Projects & Development) Ltd, 1979–81; Consultant to Marine and Offshore Industries, 1981–86. Liveryman, Shipwrights' Co. *Publication:* Shipping Finance, 1984. *Recreations:* sailing, gardening, woodwork. *Address:* Annington House, Steyning, West Sussex BN4 3WA. *T:* Steyning 812259.

SLOMAN, Albert Edward, CBE 1980; DPhil; Vice-Chancellor of University of Essex, 1962–Sept. 1987; *b* Launceston, Cornwall, 14 Feb. 1921; *y s* of Albert Sloman; *m* 1948, Marie Bernadette, *d* of Leo Bergeron, Cognac, France; three *d. Educ:* Launceston Coll., Cornwall; Wadham Coll., Oxford (Pope Exhibitioner, 1939; Hon. Fellow, 1982). Mediæval and Mod. Langs, 1941; MA (Oxon and Dublin); DPhil (Oxon). Served War of 1939–45 (despatches): night-fighter pilot with 219 and 68 squadrons; Flight-Lieut. Lecturer in Spanish, Univ. of California, Berkeley, USA, 1946–47; Reader in Spanish, in charge of Spanish studies, Univ. of Dublin, 1947–53; Fellow TCD, 1950–53; Gilmour Professor of Spanish, University of Liverpool, 1953–62; Dean, Faculty of Arts, 1961–62. Editor of Bulletin of Hispanic Studies, 1953–62. Reith Lecturer, 1963. Chairman: Dept of Education State Studentship Cttee (Humanities), 1965–; Cttee of Vice-Chancellors and Principals of UK Univs, 1981–83 (Vice-Chm., 1979–81); Overseas Research Students Fees Support Scheme, 1980–; Univs' Council for Adult and Continuing Educn, 1984–; Inter-Univ. and Polytechnic Council, 1985–; Cttee for Internat. Co-operation in Higher Educn, 1985–; Selection Cttee of Commonwealth Scholarship Commn, 1986–; Member: Council of Europe Cttee for Higher Educn and Research, 1963–72; Inter-univ. Council for Higher Educn Overseas, 1964–81; Conf. of European Rectors and Vice-Chancellors, 1965–85 (Pres., 1969–74); Admin. Bd, Internat. Assoc. of Univs, 1965–75 (Vice-Pres., 1970–75); Economic and Social Cttee, EEC, 1973–82; Council, ACU, 1981– (Vice-Chm., 1985–); Commonwealth Scholarship Commn, 1984–; Bd, British Council, 1985–. Chm. Bd of Governors, Centre for Inf. on Lang. Teaching and Res., 1979–; Member: Bd of Governors, Guyana Univ., 1966–; Cttee of Management, British Inst. in Paris, 1982–; Internat. Bd, United World Colleges, 1985–. Hon. Doctorate, Nice, 1974. *Publications:* The Sources of Calderón's El Principe constante, 1950; The Dramatic Craftsmanship of Calderón, 1958; A University in the Making, 1964; articles and reviews in Modern Language Review, Bulletin of Hispanic Studies, Hispanic Review, Romance Philology and other journals. *Recreation:* travel. *Address:* The University of Essex, Colchester CO4 3SQ. *Club:* Savile.

SLOMAN, Mrs (Margaret) Barbara; Under Secretary, Management and Personnel Office (formerly Civil Service Department), 1975–84, retired; *b* 29 June 1925; *d* of Charles and Margaret Pilkington-Rogers; *m* 1950, Peter Sloman, *qv*; one *s* one *d. Educ:* Cheltenham Ladies' Coll.; Girton Coll., Cambridge. BA Hons Classics. FBIM. Asst Principal, Treasury, 1947, Principal 1954–65; Asst Sec., DES, 1965–69; Asst Sec., Civil Service Dept, 1970–75. *Address:* 26 Glebe Road, SW13 0EA.

SLOMAN, Peter; Education Officer, Association of Metropolitan Authorities, 1974–79; *b* Oct. 1919; *s* of H. N. P. and Mary Sloman (*née* Trinder); *m* 1950, Barbara (see M. B.

Sloman); one s one d. *Educ:* Winchester Coll.; New Coll., Oxford (BA, MA 1945). War Service (RA), 1939–46. Home Civil Service, 1946–74: Under-Secretary, 1968; Min. (later Dept) of Education; Treasury; Ministries of Defence, Land and Natural Resources, Housing and Local Govt; IDC 1960. Principal Admin. Officer: Newham, 1980–83; Surrey CC, 1985; Principal Administrator, ACC, 1983–86. *Address:* 26 Glebe Road, SW13 0EA.

SLOSS; *see* Butler-Sloss.

SLOT, Peter Maurice Joseph; His Honour Judge Slot; a Circuit Judge, since 1980; *b* 3 Dec. 1932; *s* of Joseph and Marie Slot; *m* 1962, Mary Eiluned Lewis; two s three d. *Educ:* Bradfield Coll.; St John's Coll., Oxford (MA). Called to Bar, Inner Temple, 1957. A Recorder of the Crown Court, 1974–80. *Recreations:* golf, madrigals, argument. *Address:* The Red House, Betchworth, Surrey RH3 7DR. *T:* Betchworth 2010. *Club:* Walton Heath Golf.

SLYNN, Hon. Sir Gordon, Kt 1976; an Advocate-General, Court of Justice of the European Communities, since 1981; *b* 17 Feb. 1930; *er s* of John and Edith Slynn; *m* 1962, Odile Marie Henriette Boutin. *Educ:* Sandbach Sch.; Goldsmiths' Coll.; Trinity Coll., Cambridge (Sen. Schol.; MA, LLB; Sub-Lector, 1956–61). Commnd RAF, 1951–54. Called to Bar, Gray's Inn, 1956, Bencher, 1970. Jun. Counsel, Min. of Labour, 1967–68; Jun. Counsel to the Treasury (Common Law), 1968–74; QC 1974; Leading Counsel to the Treasury, 1974–76. Recorder of Hereford, 1971; a Recorder, and Hon. Recorder of Hereford, 1972–76; a Judge of the High Ct of Justice, QBD, 1976–81. Pres., Employment Appeal Tribunal, 1978–81. Lecturer in Air Law, LSE, 1958–61; Vis. Professor in Law: Univ. of Durham, 1981–; Cornell, 1983; Irvine Lectr, Cornell, 1984. Chief Steward of Hereford, 1978– (Dep. Chief Steward, 1977–78). Hon. Vice-Pres., Union Internat. des Avocats, 1976– (Vice-Pres., 1973–76); Governor, Internat. Students' Trust, 1979–85; Fellow, Internat. Soc. of Barristers, USA. Mem. Ct, Broderers' Company. Hon. Member: Canadian Bar Assoc.; Georgia Trial Lawyers' Assoc.; Florida Defense Lawyers' Assoc. Hon. Fellow, UC at Buckingham, 1982. Hon. LLD: Birmingham, 1983; Buckingham, 1983; Exeter, 1985; Hon. Decanus Juris, Mercer Univ., Ga, USA, 1986. Chevalier du Tastevin. *Publications:* (contrib.) Halsbury's Laws of England; (contrib.) Atkin's Court Forms; lectures published in legal jls. *Address:* Court of Justice of the European Communities, Kirchberg, Luxembourg. *Club:* Beefsteak.

SLYTH, Arthur Roy, CB 1966; OBE 1957; *b* 30 May 1910; *s* of Thomas Slyth; *m* 1938, Anne Mary Muir Grieve (d 1973). *Educ:* Lincoln School. Entered Exchequer and Audit Department, 1929; Dep. Sec., 1961; Sec., 1963–73. *Recreation:* golf. *Address:* 4 Broadlands Road, N6 4AS. *T:* 01–340 2366.

SMAILES, George Mason; retired barrister; *b* 23 Jan. 1916; *s* of late Thomas and Kate Smailes; *m* 1939, Evelyn Mabel Jones; one s two d. *Educ:* The Leys Sch., Cambridge; Leeds Univ. (LLB); Metropolitan Police College. Solicitor's articled clerk, 1933–37; Station Inspector, Metropolitan Police, 1937–47; served RAF, 1944–45. Called to Bar, Gray's Inn, 1946; practised on North-Eastern Circuit, 1947–67; acted as Deputy County Court Judge and Deputy and Asst Recorder of various boroughs, 1961–68. Part-time legal member of tribunals: Mental Health Review, 1960–67; National Insurance, Local, 1962–65; Medical Appeal (Industrial Injuries), 1965–67; Industrial, 1966–67; Regional Chm. of Industrial Tribunals, Leeds, 1967–82. Associate, Wellington Dist Law Soc. (NZ). *Recreations:* listening to music, gardening. *Address:* 24 Liverpool Street, Masterton, New Zealand. *T:* Masterton 84610. *Clubs:* Leeds (Leeds), Masterton (Masterton).

SMALE, John Arthur, CBE 1953; AFC 1919; Technical consultant, Marconi's Wireless Telegraph Co. Ltd, 1957–62, retd; *b* 16 Feb. 1895; *s* of Charles Blackwell and Ann Smale; *m* 1920, Hilda Marguerita Watts; one d (one s killed on active service, RAF, 1941). *Educ:* Wycliffe Coll., Stonehouse; Bristol Univ. (BSc). Apprentice British Thompson Houston, Rugby, 1914; served European War, 1914–18, in RNAS; RAF, 1918–19. Engineer, Marconi's Wireless Telegraph Co. Ltd, 1919–29; Cable & Wireless Ltd, 1929–57, retired (Asst Engineer-in-Chief, 1935–48; Engineer-in-Chief, 1948–57). Chairman Cyprus Inland Telecommunications Authority, 1955–60, retired. FIEE 1941; Chairman, Radio Section of IEE, 1953; FIEEE 1958. *Recreations:* sport, music. *Address:* Cotswold, 21 Ilex Way, Goring-By-Sea, W Sussex BN12 4UZ.

SMALL, (Charles) John; consultant, since 1985; Canadian High Commissioner to Malaysia and concurrently to Brunei, 1983–84; economist; *b* Chengtu, Szechuan, China, 19 Dec. 1919; *s* of Rev. and Mrs Walter Small; *m* 1946, Jean McNeel; four d. *Educ:* Ontario Agricultural Coll. (BSA); Univ. of Toronto (BA). LLD *hc* Univ. of Guelph, 1975. Royal Canadian Navy service, 1941–46, in N Atlantic, Mediterranean, Normandy and Australia. Mem., Dept of Trade and Commerce, 1949–55; serving in The Hague as Commercial Sec. (Agriculture), 1950–55; Dept of External Affairs, 1955–; Chinese studies at Univ. of Toronto, 1956–57; seconded to Dept of Trade and Commerce, and apptd Canadian Govt Trade Comr, Hong Kong, 1958–61; Ottawa, 1961–63; Counsellor, Canadian High Commn, Karachi, 1963–65; Perm. Rep. of Canada to OECD, Paris, concurrently Canadian observer, Council of Europe, Strasbourg, 1965–69; Amb. to Pakistan, 1969–72, concurrently Amb. to Afghanistan; Amb. to People's Repub. of China, 1972–76, concurrently to Socialist Repub. of Viet-Nam, 1975–76; Dep. Sec.-Gen. of the Commonwealth, 1978–83. Member: RIIA; CIIA; Agricl Inst. of Canada. *Recreations:* tennis, golf, swimming.

SMALL, David Purvis, MBE 1966; HM Diplomatic Service; Counsellor (Commercial), Copenhagen, since 1982; *b* 17 Oct. 1930; *s* of Joseph Small and Ann (*née* Purvis); *m* 1957, Patricia Kennedy; three s. *Educ:* Our Lady's High Sch., Motherwell. National Service, RAF Transport Comd, 1949–51. Metropolitan Vickers, 1951–53; Admiralty, Bath, 1953–55; HM Dockyard, Rosyth, 1955–58 and Singapore, 1958–60; Admiralty, London, 1960–61; CRO, 1961; Madras, 1962–64; Ibadan, 1964–68; Quito, 1968–73; FCO, 1973–76; Dacca, 1976–80; Stockholm, 1980–82. *Recreations:* golf, soccer. *Address:* c/o Foreign and Commonwealth Office, SW1. *Clubs:* Royal Commonwealth Society; Royal Copenhagen Golf.

SMALL, John; *see* Small, C. J.

SMALL, Prof. John Rankin; Professor and Head of Department of Accountancy and Finance, Heriot-Watt University, since 1967; *b* 28 Feb. 1933; *s* of David and Annie Small; *m* 1957, Catherine Wood; one s two d. *Educ:* Harris Academy, Dundee; Dundee Sch. of Econs. BScEcon London; FCCA, FCMA, JDipMA. Dunlop Rubber Co., 1956–60; Lectr, Univ. of Edinburgh, 1960–64; Sen. Lectr, Univ. of Glasgow, 1964–67; Dean of Faculty of Econ. and Social Studies, Heriot-Watt Univ., 1972–74; Vice-Principal, Heriot-Watt Univ., 1974–78. Dir, Edinburgh Instruments Ltd, 1976–; Mem. Adv. Bd, Douglas Llambias Associates Ltd, Scotland, 1979–. Pres., Assoc. of Certified Accountants, 1982 (Mem. Council, 1971–); Member: Educn Cttee, Internat. Fedn of Accountants, 1978–85 (Chm., 1978–82); Commn for Local Authority Accounts in Scotland, 1982– (Chm., 1983–). *Publications:* (jtly) Introduction to Managerial Economics, 1966; (contrib.) Business and Accounting in Europe, 1973; articles in accounting and financial jls on

accounting and financial management. *Recreation:* golf. *Address:* 39 Caiystane Terrace, Edinburgh EH10 6ST. *T:* 031–445 2638. *Club:* New (Edinburgh).

SMALL, Very Rev. Robert Leonard, CBE 1975 (OBE 1958); DD; Minister of St Cuthbert's Parish Church, Edinburgh, 1956–75; Chaplain to the Queen in Scotland, 1967–75, Extra Chaplain since 1975; *b* N Berwick, 12 May 1905; *s* of Rev. Robert Small, MA, and Marion C. McEwen; *m* 1931, Jane Hay McGregor; three s one d. *Educ:* N Berwick High Sch.; Edinburgh Univ.; New Coll., Edinburgh. MA 1st cl. hons Classics; Sen. Cunningham Fellowship; studied in Rome, Berlin and Zurich; DD 1957. Ordained, 1931, to St John's, Bathgate; W High Church, Kilmarnock, 1935–44; Cramond Church, Edinburgh 1944–56. Convener: C of S Cttee on Huts and Canteens for HM Forces, 1946–58; Cttee on Temperance and Morals, 1958–63; Social and Moral Welfare Bd, 1963–64; Stewardship and Budget Ctee, 1964–69; Mem., Scottish Adv. Cttee on Treatment of Offenders; Regional Chaplain (Scotland), Air Trng Corps; Hon. Vice-Pres., Boys' Brigade; awarded Silver Acorn by Chief Scout, 1978. Warrack Lectr on Preaching, 1959. Guest Preacher: Knox Church, Dunedin, 1950; Fifth Ave., Presbyterian Church, NY, 1960; St Stephen's Presbyterian Church, Sydney, 1962, 1971, 1976, 1981; Scots Church, Melbourne, 1971, 1976, 1979; St Columba's C of S, London, 1983–84. Moderator of the General Assembly of the Church of Scotland, 1966–67; First Chm., Scottish Parole Bd, 1967–73; Chm., Parkinson's Disease Soc., Edinburgh; Chm., Age Concern, Scotland, 1980–83. TV Series, What I Believe, 1970. *Publications:* With Ardour and Accuracy (Warrack Lectures), 1959; No Uncertain Sound (Scholar as Preacher Series), 1964; No Other Name, 1966; contribs to The Expository Times. *Recreations:* boating, walking; formerly Association football (Edinburgh Univ. Blue, captained team, 1927–28; played as amateur for St Bernard's FC, 1928–29; capped *v* England (Amateur), 1929). *Address:* 5 Craighill Gardens, Edinburgh EH10 5PY. *T:* 031–447 4243. *Club:* Royal Over-Seas League.

SMALLBONE, Graham; Headmaster, Oakham School, since 1985; *b* 5 April 1934; *s* of Dr E. G. Smallbone and Jane Mann; *m* 1959, Dorothea Ruth Löw; two s two d. *Educ:* Uppingham School (music scholar); Worcester College, Oxford (Hadow Scholar; MA); Pres., Oxford Univ. Music Club, 1957). ARCO, ARCM. 2nd Lieut, RA, 1952–54. Asst Master, Oundle Sch., 1958–61; Director of Music: Dean Close Sch., 1961–66; Marlborough Coll., 1967–71; Precentor and Director of Music, Eton, 1971–85. Pres., Music Masters' Assoc., 1975; Warden, Music in Educn Section, ISM, 1977; Pres., International Cello Centre, 1985. Conductor: Cheltenham Chamber Orch., 1963–66; N Wilts Orch., 1966–71; Windsor and Eton Choral Soc., 1971–85. *Recreations:* music, golf, photography. *Address:* Headmaster's House, Oakham School, Station Road, Oakham, Rutland LE15 6QY. *T:* Oakham 2179. *Club:* East India.

SMALLEY, Very Rev. Stephen Stewart; Dean of Chester since 1987; *b* 11 May 1931; *s* of Arthur Thomas Smalley and May Elizabeth Selina Smalley; *m* 1974, Susan Jane Paterson; one s one d. *Educ:* Jesus Coll., Cambridge (MA, PhD); Eden Theological Seminary, USA (BD). Assistant Curate, St Paul's, Portman Square, London, 1958–60; Chaplain of Peterhouse, Cambridge, 1960–63; Lectr and Sen. Lectr in Religious Studies, Univ. of Ibadan, Nigeria, 1963–69; Lectr in New Testament, Univ. of Manchester, 1970–77, Sen. Lectr, 1977 (also Warden of St Anselm Hall, 1972–77); Canon Residentiary and Precentor of Coventry Cathedral, 1977–86, Vice-Provost 1986. Mem., C of E Doctrine Commn, 1981–86. Mem., Studiorum Novi Testamenti Soc., 1965–. *Publications:* Building for Worship, 1967; Heaven and Hell (Ibadan), 1968; The Spirit's Power (Achimota), 1972; ed, Christ and Spirit in the New Testament, 1973; John: Evangelist and Interpreter, 1978, USA 1984; 1, 2, 3 John, USA 1984; numerous articles in learned jls, incl. New Testament Studies, Novum Testamentum, Jl of Biblical Lit. *Recreations:* literature, music, drama, travel. *Address:* The Deanery, 7 Abbey Street, Chester CH1 2JF. *T:* Chester 25920; Hadrians, Bourton-on-the-Hill, Moreton-in-Marsh, Gloucestershire. *T:* Blockley 700564.

SMALLMAN, Barry Granger, CMG 1976; CVO 1972; HM Diplomatic Service, retired; Founder, Granger Consultancies, 1984; *b* 22 Feb. 1924; *s* of late C. Stanley Smallman, CBE, ARCM, and Ruby Marian Granger; *m* 1952, Sheila Knight; two s one d. *Educ:* St Paul's School; Trinity College, Cambridge (Major Scholar, MA). Served War of 1939–45, Intelligence Corps, Australia 1944–46. Joined Colonial Office, 1947; Assistant Private Secretary to Secretary of State, 1951–52; Principal, 1953; attached to United Kingdom Delegation to United Nations, New York, 1956–57, 1958, 1961, 1962; seconded to Government of Western Nigeria, Senior Assistant Secretary, Governor's Office, Ibadan, 1959–60; transferred to CRO, 1961; British Deputy High Comr in Sierra Leone, 1963–64; British Dep. High Comr in NZ, 1964–67; Imp. Defence Coll., 1968; FCO, 1969–71; Counsellor and Consul-Gen., British Embassy, Bangkok, 1971–74; British High Comr to Bangladesh, 1975–78; Resident Diplomatic Service Chm., Civil Service Selection Bd, 1978–81; High Comr to Jamaica and non-resident Ambassador to Haiti, 1982–84. Mem. Governing Council: SPCK, 1984–; Leprosy Mission, 1985–; St Lawrence Coll., Ramsgate, 1984–; Benenden Sch., 1985– (Chm., 1986–). *Recreations:* tennis, golf, making and listening to music, light verse, bird watching. *Address:* Beacon Shaw, Benenden, Kent. *T:* Cranbrook 240625.

SMALLMAN, Prof. Raymond Edward, FRS 1986; Feeney Professor of Metallurgy, since 1969, and Head of Department of Metallurgy and Materials, since 1981, University of Birmingham; *b* 4 Aug. 1929; *s* of David Smallman and Edith French; *m* 1952, Joan Doreen Faulkner; one s one d. *Educ:* Rugeley Grammar Sch.; Univ. of Birmingham (BSc, PhD, DSc). CEng, FIM. AERE Harwell, 1953–58; University of Birmingham: Lectr in Dept of Physical Metallurgy, 1958, Sen Lectr, 1963; Prof. of Phys. Metall., 1964; Head of Dept of Phys. Metall. and Sci. of Materials, 1969; Dean of Faculty of Sci. and Eng., 1984–85, of Faculty of Eng., 1985–. Visiting Professor: Pennsylvania, 1961; Stanford, 1962; NSW, 1974; UCLA Berkeley, 1978; Cape Town, 1982; Van Horn Dist. Lectr, Case Western Reserve Univ., 1978. IUC Consultant, Hong Kong, 1979. Member: Inter-Services Cttee, MoD, 1965; Metals and Materials Cttee, SRC, 1968; Materials Adv. Cttee, MoD, 1971; Cttee, Engrg Profs Conf., 1985. Pres., Birmingham Metallurgical Assoc., 1972–73; Vice-Pres., Metals Soc., 1980–84 (Chm., Metals Sci Cttee, 1974). Sir George Beilby Gold Medal, Inst. of Metals and Chem. Soc., 1969; Rosenhain Medal, Inst. Metals, 1972; Elegant Work Prize, Metals Soc., 1979. *Publications:* Modern Physical Metallurgy, 1962, 4th edn 1985; (jtly) Modern Metallography, 1966; (jtly) Structure of Metal and Alloys, 1969; (jtly) Defect Analysis in Electron Microscopy, 1975; sci. papers on relationship of microstructure of materials to their properties in learned jls. *Recreations:* writing, travel, friendly golf, bridge. *Address:* 59 Woodthorne Road South, Tettenhall, Wolverhampton WV6 8SN. *T:* Wolverhampton 752545. *Club:* South Staffordshire Golf.

SMALLPEICE, Sir Basil, KCVO 1961; chartered accountant and air/sea transport executive, retired; *b* Rio de Janeiro, Brazil, 18 Sept. 1906; *s* of Herbert Charles Smallpeice, bank manager, and Georgina Ruth (*née* Rust); *m* 1931, Kathleen Ivey Singleton Brame (d 1973), d of late Edwin Singleton Brame; *m* 1973, Rita Burns, yr d of late Major William Burns, MBE. *Educ:* Shrewsbury. BComm London. Articled to Bullimore & Co., Chartered Accts, 1925–30. Accountant of Hoover Ltd, 1930–37; Chief Accountant and later Sec. of Doulton & Co. Ltd, 1937–48; Dir of Costs and Statistics, British Transport Commission, 1948–50; BOAC: Financial Comptroller, 1950–56; Member of Board, 1953–63; Deputy Chief Executive, 1954–56; Man. Dir, 1956–63; Chm., Nat. Jt Council for Civil Air Transport, 1960–61; Man. Dir, BOAC-Cunard Ltd, from its inception in 1962 till end of 1963; Administrative Adviser in HM Household, 1964–80; Chairman: Cunard Steam-Ship Co. Ltd, 1965–71 (Dir, 1964; a Dep. Chm., 1965); Cunard Line Ltd, 1965–71; Cunard-Brocklebank, 1967–70; Cunard Cargo Shipping, 1970–71; ACT (Australia)/Australian Nat. Line Co-ordinating Bd, 1969–79; Associated Container Transportation (Australia), 1971–79; a Dep. Chm., Lonrho Ltd, April 1972–May 1973; Director: Martins Bank Ltd, 1966–69; London Local Bd, Barclays Bank, 1969–74. Member Council: Inst. of Chartered Accountants, 1948–57; Inst. of Transport, 1958–61; Brit. Inst. of Management, 1959–64 and 1965–75 (Chm., 1970–72; a Vice-Pres., 1972–); Pres., Inst. of Freight Forwarders, 1977–78. Mem., Cttee for Exports to the US, 1964–66. Chairman: The English Speaking Union of the Commonwealth, 1965–68; Leatherhead New Theatre (Thorndike) Trust, 1966–74; Air League, 1971–74. Companion, RAeS, 1960–75; Liveryman: Guild of Air Pilots and Air Navigators, 1960; Coachmakers and Coach Harness Makers, 1961. Key to the City of San Francisco, 1959. Order of the Cedar, Lebanon, 1955. Pioneers Award for contribs to develt of containerization, Containerization Inst., NY, 1981. Publications: various articles in the 1940s on the development of industrial and management accounting; Of Comets and Queens (autobiog.), 1981. Recreations: gardening, golf. Address: Bridge House, 45 Leigh Hill Road, Cobham, Surrey KT11 2HU. T: Cobham 65425. Clubs: Athenæum, Boodle's; Melbourne (Melbourne, Australia).

SMALLWOOD, Anne Hunter, CMG 1976; Commissioner, Board of Inland Revenue, 1973–81; b 20 June 1922; d of Martin Wilkinson McNicol and Elizabeth Straiton Harper; m 1972, Peter Basil Smallwood (d 1977). Educ: High Sch. for Girls, Glasgow; Glasgow Univ. Entered Inland Revenue, 1943; Dep. Comptroller (Scotland), 1956–58; Min. of Land and Natural Resources, 1964–66; Min. of Housing and Local Govt, 1966; Under-Sec., Inland Revenue, 1971–73. Address: 83 Lyncombe Hill, Bath BA2 4PJ. Club: United Oxford & Cambridge University.
See also G. P. McNicol.

SMALLWOOD, Air Chief Marshal Sir Denis (Graham), GBE 1975 (CBE 1961; MBE 1951); KCB 1969 (CB 1966); DSO 1944; DFC 1942; idc; jssc; psc; aws; FRSA; FRAeS; Military Adviser to Chairman and Chief Executive, Aircraft Group, British Aerospace, 1977–83; b 13 Aug. 1918; s of Frederick William Smallwood, Moseley, Birmingham; m 1940, Frances Jeanne, d of Walter Needham; one s one d. Educ: King Edward VI School, Birmingham. Joined Royal Air Force, 1938. Served War of 1939–45, Fighter Command. Group Captain, 1957; commanded RAF Guided Missiles Station, Lincs, 1959–61; AOC and Commandant, RAF Coll. of Air Warfare, Manby, 1961–62; ACAS (Ops), 1962–65; AOC No 3 Gp, RAF Bomber Comd, 1965–67; SASO, Bomber Comd, 1967–68; Dep. C-in-C, Strike Comd, 1968–69; AOC-in-C, NEAF, Comdr, British Forces Near East, and Administrator, Sovereign Base Area, Cyprus, 1969–70; Vice-Chief of the Air Staff, 1970–74; C-in-C, RAF Strike Command, 1974–76, and C-in-C, UK Air Forces, 1975–76. ADC to the Queen, 1959–64. Life Vice-Pres., Air League, 1984 (Pres., 1981–84). Freeman, City of London, 1976; Liveryman, Guild of Air Pilots and Navigators, 1975. Address: The Flint House, Owlswick, Bucks. Clubs: Royal Air Force, Les Ambassadeurs, Belfry.

SMALLWOOD, John Frank Monton; a Church Commissioner, since 1966 (Board of Governors and General Purposes Committee); b 12 April 1926; s of late Frank Theodore and Edith Smallwood; m 1952, Jean Margaret Lovell; one s two d. Educ: City of London Sch.; Peterhouse, Cambridge, 1948–51 (MA Classics). Served RAF, 1944–48 (Japanese translation and interrogation). Joined Bank of England, 1951; Private Sec. to Governors, 1959–62; Adviser, 1967; Auditor, 1969; Dep. Chief Accountant, 1974–79. Member: Church Assembly/General Synod, 1965– (Standing Cttee, 1971–); numerous ad hoc Cttees, etc, over years; Central Bd of Finance, 1965– (Dep. Vice-Chm. 1972–82); Pensions Bd, 1985–; Anglican Consultative Council, 1975–83 (Trinidad, 1976, Lambeth Conf., 1978, Canada, 1979, Newcastle, 1981). A Trustee: City Parochial Foundn, 1969– (Vice-Chm., 1977–81; Chm., 1981–); Overseas Bishoprics Fund, 1977–; Lambeth Palace Library, 1978–. Member: Southwark Dio. Bd of Finance, 1962– (Chm. 1975–); Southwark Ordination Course Council, 1960–74 and 1980– (Vice-Chm., 1980–); Lee Abbey Council, 1969–74. Recreations: church finances (incl. various financial pamphlets), family, music, cathedrals, old churches, historic houses, gardens. Address: Downsview, 32 Brockham Lane, Brockham, Betchworth, Surrey RH3 7EL. T: Betchworth 2032.

SMART, (Alexander Basil) Peter; HM Diplomatic Service; High Commissioner to Seychelles, since 1986; b 19 Feb. 1932; s of late Henry Prescott Smart and Mary Gertrude Todd; m 1955, Joan Mary Cumming; three s (incl. twin s). Educ: Ryhope Grammar Sch., Co. Durham. Commnd RAEC, 1951; Supervising Officer, Educn, Gibraltar Comd, 1951–52; entered HM Foreign (later Diplomatic) Service, 1953; Vice Consul, Duala, 1955; Polit. Office, ME Forces, Cyprus, 1956; 2nd Sec. (Information), Seoul, 1959; News Dept, FO, 1964; Head of Chancery, Rangoon, 1968; FCO, 1971; Head of Communications Technical Services Dept, 1975; Counsellor, 1977–82, and Dep. High Comr, 1981–82, Canberra; Counsellor and Head of Chancery, Prague, 1983–86. FRSA. Recreations: wild nature, the arts; looking and listening. Address: c/o Foreign and Commonwealth Office, SW1A 2AL.

SMART, Andrew, CB 1981; Director, Royal Signals and Radar Establishment, Malvern, 1978–84; b 12 Feb. 1924; s of late Mr and Mrs William S. Smart; m 1949, Pamela Kathleen Stephens; two s two d. Educ: Denny; High Sch. of Stirling; Glasgow Univ. MA 1944. TRE Malvern, 1943; Science 2 Air Min., 1950–53; Guided Weapons Gp, RRE, Malvern, 1953–70 (Head, 1968–70); Dep. Dir (Scientific B), DOAE, 1970; RAE, Farnborough: Head of Weapons Res. Gp, 1972; Head of Weapons Dept, 1973; Dep. Dir (W), 1974–77. Recreations: gardening, caravanning. Address: Hill Orchard, Shelsley Drive, Colwall, Malvern, Worcs. T: Colwall 40664.

SMART, Prof. (Arthur David) Gerald, FRTPI; Emeritus Professor of Urban Planning, University of London, since 1984; Professor of Urban Planning at University College London, 1975–84 and part-time, 1984–86 (Head of Bartlett School of Architecture and Planning, University College London, 1975–80); b 19 March 1925; s of Dr A. H. J. Smart and A. O. M. Smart (née Evans); m 1955, Anne Patience Smart (née Baxter); two d. Educ: Rugby Sch.; King's Coll., Cambridge; Polytechnic of Central London. MA, DipTP; ARICS, FRSA. Served in The Rifle Brigade, 1943–47 (Captain). Appts in local govt (planning), London, NE England, E Midlands, 1950–63; County Planning Officer, Hants CC, 1963–75; Member: Planning Adv. Gp, 1964–65, Cttee on Public Participation in Planning, 1968–69, Min. of Housing and Local Govt; Planning and Transportation Res. Adv. Council, DoE, 1975–79; Working Party on alternative uses of Historic Buildings, Historic Bldgs Council and BTA, 1979–81; Exec., TCPA, 1983–; Council, RSPB, 1985–; Governing Body, GB/E Europe Centre, 1985–; occasional Chm., Structure Plans Exams in Public for DoE. Publications: articles, conf. papers, in books, professional and other jls. Recreations: sailing, ornithology, music, walking. Address: 10 Harewood Green, Keyhaven,

Lymington, Hants SO41 0TZ. T: Lymington 45475. Clubs: Athenæum; Royal Lymington Yacht, Keyhaven Yacht (Lymington).

SMART, Edwin; see Smart, L. E.

SMART, Professor Sir George (Algernon), Kt 1978; MD, FRCP; Director, British Postgraduate Medical Federation, 1971–78, retired; b 16 Dec. 1913; er s of A. Smart, Alnwick, Northumb; m 1939, Monica Helen Carrick; two s one d. Educ: Uppingham; Durham Univ., BSc 1935, MB, BS 1937. MD 1939 (Durham); MRCP 1940, FRCP 1952. Commonwealth Fund Fellow, 1948–49. Lectr in Med., Univ. of Bristol, 1946–50; Reader in Medicine, Univ. of Durham, 1950–56; Prof. of Medicine, Univ. of Durham, 1956–68, Univ. of Newcastle upon Tyne, 1968–71 (Post-graduate Sub-Dean, 1962–68, Dean of Medicine, 1968–71). Censor, 1965–67, Senior Censor and Senior Vice-Pres., 1972–73, RCP. Chairman: Review Bd for Overseas Qualified Practitioners, GMC, 1979–82; Cttee of Management, and Med. and Survival Cttee, RNLI, 1979–. Hon. Fellow, Coll. of Physicians and Surgeons, Pakistan, 1976. Publications: contrib. to Price's Textbook of Medicine, and Progress in Clinical Medicine (Daley and Miller); (ed) Metabolic Disturbances in Clinical Medicine, 1958; (co-author) Fundamentals of Clinical Endocrinology, 1969, 2nd edn 1974. Recreation: photography. Address: Taffrail, Crede Lane, Old Bosham, Chichester, Sussex PO18 8NX.

SMART, Gerald; see Smart, A. D. G.

SMART, Henry Walter, CB 1966; formerly Director of Savings, GPO (1958–68); b 7 Sept. 1908; m; two s. Educ: Sir Thomas Rich's School, Gloucester. Address: 24 Gumstool Hill, Tetbury, Glos GL8 8DG. T: Tetbury 53979.

SMART, Sir Jack, Kt 1982; CBE 1976; JP; Chairman, Wakefield District Health Authority, since 1982; b 25 April 1920; s of James and Emily Smart; m 1941, Ethel King; one d. Educ: Altofts Colliery Sch. Miner, 1934–59; Branch Sec., Glasshoughton Colliery, NUM, 1949–59; Mem., Castleford Municipal Borough Council, 1949–74; Mayor of Castleford, 1962–63; Mem., Wakefield Metropolitan Dist Council, 1973–, Leader, 1973–86. Chm., Assoc. of Metropolitan Authorities, 1977–78, 1980–84; Leader of the Opposition Group, AMA, 1978–80. Chm., Wakefield AHA, 1977–81; Mem., Layfield Cttee of Enquiry into Local Govt Finance, 1974–76. Hon. Fellow, Bretton Coll., 1983. Hon. Freeman, City of Wakefield, 1985. JP Castleford, 1960. FRSA. Recreations: golf, music. Address: Churchside, Weetworth, Pontefract Road, Castleford, West Yorks. T: Castleford 554880.

SMART, Jack; see Smart, R. J.

SMART, (Louis) Edwin, JD; Chairman and Chief Executive Officer, Trans World Corporation, since 1978; Chairman of Executive Committee, Hilton International Co., since 1986 (Chairman of Board, 1978–86); b Columbus, Ohio, 17 Nov. 1923; s of Louis Edwin Smart and Esther Guthery; m 1st, 1944, Virginia Alice Knouff (marr. diss. 1958); one s one d; 2nd, 1964, Jeanie Alberta Milone; one s. Educ: Harvard Coll. (AB magna cum laude 1947); Harvard Law Sch. (JD magna cum laude 1949). Served to Lieut, USNR, 1943–46. Admitted to NY Bar, 1950; Associate, Hughes, Hubbard & Ewing, NYC, 1949–56; Partner, Hughes, Hubbard & Reed, NYC, 1957–64; Pres., Bendix Internat. and Dir, Bendix Corp. and foreign subsids, 1964–67; Trans World Airlines Inc.: Sen. Vice Pres., External Affairs, 1967–71; Corp. Affairs, 1971–75; Vice Chm. 1976; Chief Exec. Officer, 1977–78; Chm. of Bd, 1977–85; also Dir, Mem. Exec., and Mem. Finance Cttee. Chairman: Canteen Corp., 1973–; Spartan Food Systems Inc., 1979–; Director: Sonat Inc.; The Continental Corp.; NY Stock Exchange; Trustee, Cttee for Econ. Develt, 1977–. Member: Conf. Bd, 1977–; Amer. Bar Assoc.; NY County Lawyers Assoc.; Phi Beta Kappa; Sigma Alpha Epsilon. Address: (office) 605 Third Avenue, New York, NY 10158, USA. T: (212) 972–4700; (home) 535 E 86th Street, New York, NY 10028; Coakley Bay, Christiansted, St Croix 00820, Virgin Islands. Clubs: Economic of New York, Presidents, Marco Polo, Sky (NYC); St Croix Yacht.

SMART, Ninian; see Smart, R. N.

SMART, Peter; see Smart, A. B. P.

SMART, (Raymond) Jack; retired; b 1 Aug. 1917; s of Frank Smart and Emily Rose Smart; m 1942, Jessie Alice Tyrrell; one s one d. Educ: Redhill Technical Coll. (HNC). Apprentice Prodn Engr, Lanston Monotype Corp., 1933–38; Aeronautical Inspection Directorate, Air Min., 1939–40; Rotol Airscrews/Dowty Rotol, 1940–59: successively Chief Inspector, Prodn Controller, Works Manager; Man. Dir, British Light Steel Pressings (subsidiary of Rootes Motors Ltd), 1960–65; British Leyland (formerly BM Corp.): Man. Dir, Truck Div., 1966–72; Gp Manufg Dir, 1972–76; Gp Exec. Dir and Dep. Man. Dir, 1976–79; Man. Dir, Aveling Barford Holdings Ltd, 1979–80; formerly non-exec. Dir, Marshall Sons & Co. Ltd. Recreations: Rugby Union, gardening. Address: 228 Heyhouses Lane, St Annes, Lancs FY8 3RG. T: St Annes 724571.

SMART, Maj.-Gen. Robert Arthur, CBE 1958; FRCP; Chief Medical Officer, Esso Petroleum Co., 1975–79, Senior Medical Officer, 1972–75; b 29 April 1914; s of Arthur Francis Smart and Roberta Teresa Farquhar; m 1947, Josephine von Oepen; one d. Educ: Aberdeen Gram. Sch.; Aberdeen University. MB, ChB 1936; DPH (Eng.) 1948; MRCP 1965, FRCP 1977; AFOM 1978. Lt, RAMC, 1936; Capt. 1937; Maj. 1946; Lt-Col 1951; Col 1960; Brig. 1964; Maj.-Gen. 1967. Served in Palestine, Egypt, Western Desert, Eritrea, France and Germany, 1939–45; N Africa and E Africa, 1951–55; Asst Dir of Army Health, E Africa, 1952–55; Leader, Royal Society's Internat. Geophysical Year Expedn to Antarctica, 1956–57; Dep. Chief Med. Off., Supreme HQ Allied Powers Europe, 1960–62; Dep. Dir of Army Health, BAOR, 1962–64; Dir of Army Health, MoD, 1964–68; DMS, FARELF, 1968–70; DMS, BAOR, 1970–71; DDMS, HQ Army Strategic Comd, 1971–72, retired 1972. Polar Medal, 1958. QHS 1968–72. Address: 186 Forest Avenue, Aberdeen AB1 6UY. Clubs: Army and Navy; Royal Northern and University (Aberdeen).

SMART, Prof. (Roderick) Ninian; Professor of Religious Studies, University of California, Santa Barbara, since 1976; Hon. Professor, University of Lancaster (Professor of Religious Studies, 1967–82); b 6 May 1927; s of late Prof. W. M. Smart, FRSE, and Isabel (née Carswell); m 1954, Libushka Clementina Baruffaldi; one s two d. Educ: Glasgow Academy; The Queen's College, Oxford. Army service with Intelligence Corps, 1945–48, 2nd Lt, Captain, 1947; overseas service in Ceylon. Oxford: Mods (shortened), Class II, 1949; Lit. Hum. Class I, 1951; BPhil 1954. Asst Lecturer in Philosophy, Univ. Coll. of Wales, Aberystwyth, 1952–55, Lecturer, 1955; Vis. Lecturer in Philosophy, Yale Univ., 1955–56; Lecturer in History and Philosophy of Religion, Univ. of London, King's College, 1956–61; H. G. Wood Professor of Theology, University of Birmingham, 1961–66. Pro-Vice-Chancellor, Univ. of Lancaster, 1969–72. Lectures: Banaras Hindu Univ., Summer, 1960; Teape, Univ. Delhi, 1964; Gifford, Univ. of Edinburgh, 1979–80; Visiting Professor: Univ. Wisconsin, 1965; Princeton and Otago, 1971; Queensland, 1980 and 1985; Univ. of Cape Town, 1982; Harvard, 1983. President: Inst. of Religion and Theology, 1980–85 (first Gen. Sec., 1973–77); British Assoc. History of Religions,

1981–85; Amer. Soc. for Study of Religion, 1984–. Hon. LHD Loyola, 1968; Hon. DLitt Glasgow, 1984; DUniv Stirling, 1986. *Publications*: Reasons and Faiths, 1958; A Dialogue of Religions, 1960; Historical Selections in the Philosophy of Religion, 1962; Philosophers and Religious Truth, 1964; Doctrine and Argument in Indian Philosophy, 1964; The Teacher and Christian Belief, 1966; The Yogi and the Devotee, 1968; Secular Education and the Logic of Religion, 1968; The Religious Experience of Mankind, 1969; Philosophy of Religion, 1970; The Concept of Worship, 1972; The Phenomenon of Religion, 1973; The Science of Religion and the Sociology of Knowledge, 1973; Mao, 1974; A Companion to the Long Search, 1977; The Phenomenon of Christianity, 1979; Beyond Ideology, 1982; (with R. Hecht) Sacred Texts of the World, 1982; Worldviews, 1983; (with Swami Purnananda) Prophet of a New Hindu Age, 1985; Concept and Empathy, 1986; Religion and the Western Mind, 1986, contrib. to Mind, Philosophy, Philosophical Quarterly, Review of Metaphysics, Religion, Religious Studies. *Recreations*: cricket, tennis, poetry. *Address*: Department of Religious Studies, University of Lancaster, Bailrigg, Lancaster LA1 4YG; Department of Religious Studies, University of California at Santa Barbara, Calif 93106, USA. *Club*: Athenæum.

SMART, William Norman H.; *see* Hunter Smart.

SMEALL, James Leathley, MA, JP; Principal, Saint Luke's College, Exeter, 1945–72; *b* 16 June 1907; *s* of late William Francis Smeall, MB, BCh (Edin.), and late Ethel Mary Leathley; *m* 1936, Joan Rachel Harris (*d* 1984); one *d*. *Educ*: Sorbonne; Queens' College, Cambridge (Scholar). Class I English Tripos, Class II Division 1 Anthropological and Archæological Tripos; Assistant Master, Merchiston, 1929–30; Staff, Royal Naval College, Dartmouth, 1930–34; Housemaster, Bradfield College, 1934–36; Head of the English Department, Epsom College, 1936–39; Headmaster, Chesterfield Grammar School, 1939–45; Commissioned RAFVR, 1941–44. Mayor of Exeter, 1965–66; President: Exeter Civic Soc., 1980–; Exeter and Dist Br., E-SU, 1983–. *Publication*: English Satire, Parody and Burlesque, 1952. *Recreations*: gardening and travel. *Address*: Follett Orchard, Topsham, Exeter. *T*: Topsham 3892.

SMEDDLES, Thomas Henry; Chief General Manager, Royal Insurance Group, 1963–69; *b* 18 Dec. 1904; *s* of late T. H. Smeddles; *m* 1931, Dorothy Boardman; one *s*. Joined The Liverpool & London & Globe Insurance Co. Ltd, 1924. *Recreation*: gardening. *Address*: 6 Abbotts Close, Abbotts Ann, Andover, Hants.

SMEDLEY, (Frank) Brian, QC 1977; Barrister-at-Law; *b* 28 Nov. 1934. *Educ*: West Bridgford Grammar Sch.; London Univ. LLB Hons, 1957. Called to the Bar, Gray's Inn, 1960; Midland Circuit; a Recorder, 1972. Mem., Senate of the Inns of Court and the Bar, 1973–77. *Recreations*: travel, music. *Address*: 4 Hale Court, Lincoln's Inn, WC2. *T*: 01–242 4552. *Club*: Garrick.

SMEDLEY, George; *see* Smedley, R. R. G. B.

SMEDLEY, Sir Harold, KCMG 1978 (CMG 1965); MBE 1946; HM Diplomatic Service, retired; *b* 19 June 1920; *s* of late Dr R. D. Smedley, MA, MD, DPH, Worthing; *m* 1950, Beryl Mary Harley Brown, Wellington, New Zealand; two *s* two *d*. *Educ*: Aldenham School; Pembroke College, Cambridge. Served War of 1939–45, Royal Marines. Entered Dominions Office (later Commonwealth Relations Office), 1946; Private Secretary to Permanent Under-Secretary of State, 1947–48; British High Commissioner's Office: Wellington, NZ, 1948–50; Salisbury, Southern Rhodesia, 1951–53; Principal Private Sec. to Sec. of State for Commonwealth Relations, 1954–57; Counsellor, British High Comr's Office: Calcutta, 1957; New Delhi, 1958–60; British High Comr in Ghana, 1964–67; Ambassador to Laos, 1967–70; Asst Under-Sec. of State, FCO, 1970–72; Sec. Gen., Commn on Rhodesian opinion, 1971–72; High Comr in Sri Lanka, and Ambassador to Republic of Maldives, 1972–75; High Comr in NZ and concurrently Governor of Pitcairn Island, 1976–80; High Comr in Western Samoa (non-resident), 1977–80. Chm., London Bd, Bank of NZ, 1983–. Vice Chm., Victoria League, 1981–. *Address*: Sherwood, Oak End Way, Woodham, Weybridge, Surrey KT15 3DX. *Clubs*: United Oxford & Cambridge University, Royal Commonwealth Society.

SMEDLEY, (Roscoe Relph) George (Boleyne); Barrister; Counsellor, HM Diplomatic Service, retired; *b* 3 Sept. 1919; *o s* of late Charles Boleyne Smedley and Aimie Blaine Smedley (*née* Relph); *m* 1st, 1947, Muriel Hallaway Murray (*d* 1975), *o d* of late Arthur Stanley Murray; one *s*; 2nd, 1979, Margaret Gerrard Gourlay, *o c* of late Augustus Thorburn Hallaway and *widow* of Dr John Stewart Gourlay. *Educ*: King's Sch., Ely; King's Coll., London (LLB). Called to Bar, Inner Temple. Artists Rifles TA; commnd S Lancs Regt, 1940; Indian Army, 1942–46 (Captain); Foreign Office, 1937 and 1946; Foreign Service (subsecq. Diplomatic Service): Rangoon, 1947; Maymyo, 1950; Brussels, 1952; Baghdad, 1954; FO, 1958; Beirut, 1963; Kuwait, 1965; FCO, 1969; Consul-Gen., Lubumbashi, 1972–74; British Mil. Govt, Berlin, 1974–76; FCO 1976; Head of Nationality and Treaty Dept, 1977–79. Part-time appointments (since retirement): Legal Mem., Mental Health Review Tribunal; Chm., Rent Assessment Cttee; Adjudicator under Immigration Act 1971; Inspector, Planning Inspectorate, Depts of the Environment and Transport; Dep. Traffic Comr for N Eastern Traffic Area; Mem., No 2 Dip. Service Appeal Bd. Churchwarden. *Address*: Garden House, Whorlton, Barnard Castle, Co. Durham DL12 8XQ. *T*: Teesdale 27381. *Clubs*: Royal Automobile, Royal Over-Seas League.

SMEDLEY, Susan M.; *see* Marsden.

SMEE, Clive Harrod; Chief Economic Adviser to Department of Health and Social Security, since 1984; *b* 29 April 1942; *s* of Victor Woolley Smee and Leila Olive Smee (*née* Harrod); *m* 1975, Denise Eileen Sell; one *s* two *d*. *Educ*: Royal Grammar Sch., Guildford; LSE (BSc Econ); Indiana Univ. (MBA); Inst. of Commonwealth Studies, Oxford. British Council, Nigeria, 1966–68; Economic Advr, ODM, 1969–75; Sen. Economic Advr, DHSS, 1975–82; Nuffield and Leverhulme Travelling Fellow, USA and Canada, 1978–79; Advr, Central Policy Review Staff, 1982–83; Sen. Economic Advr, HM Treasury, 1983–84. *Publications*: articles on economics in learned jls. *Recreations*: running, gardening; Anna, David and Elizabeth. *Address*: c/o Department of Health and Social Security, Friars House, Blackfriars Road, SE1. *T*: 01–703 6380.

SMEE, John Charles O.; *see* Odling-Smee, J. C.

SMEETON, Vice-Adm. Sir Richard Michael, KCB 1964 (CB 1961); MBE 1942; FRAeS 1973; DL; aerospace and defence consultant; *b* 24 Sept. 1912; *s* of Edward Leaf Smeeton and Charlotte Mildred Leighton; *m* 1940, Maria Elizabeth Hawkins; no *c*. *Educ*: RNC, Dartmouth. 800 Squadron i/c HMS Ark Royal, 1940–41; Assistant Naval Attaché (Air), Washington, DC, 1941–43; staff of Admiral Nimitz, USN 1943–44; Air Plans Officer, British Pacific Fleet, 1944–45; Captain (Air) Med., 1952–54; Imperial Defence College, 1955; Captain, HMS Albion, 1956–57; Director of Plans, Admiralty, 1958–59; Flag Officer Aircraft Carriers, 1960–62; NATO Deputy Supreme Allied Commander, Atlantic, 1962–64; Flag Officer, Naval Air Command, 1964–65. Rear-Admiral, 1959; Vice-Admiral, 1962. Retired Nov. 1965, at own request. Dir and Chief Exec., Soc. of British Aerospace Cos, 1966–79; Sec., Defence Industries Council, 1970–79. Mem. Council, Inst. of Dirs. DL Surrey 1976. *Address*: St Mary's Cottage, Shamley Green, Guildford, Surrey GU5 0SP. *T*: Guildford 893478. *Club*: Army and Navy.

SMELLIE, Kingsley Bryce Speakman; Professor Emeritus of Political Science, London School of Economics, since 1965; Professor, 1949–65, Hon. Fellow, 1977; *b* 22 Nov. 1897; *o s* of late John and Elizabeth Smellie; *m* 1931, Stephanie, *o d* of late Anthony E. and Stephanie Narlian. *Educ*: Mrs Bolwell, 15 Mall Road, Hammersmith; Latymer Upper School, Hammersmith; St John's College, Cambridge. Served European War, 1914–18, as private in London Scottish. Staff of London School of Economics, 1921–65. Laura Spelman Rockefeller Student in USA (Harvard Law School), 1925–26; Research Assistant, propaganda research unit of BBC, 1940; temp. principal: Ministry of Home Security, 1940–42, Board of Trade, 1942–45. *Publications*: The American Federal System, 1928; A Hundred Years of English Government, 1937; Civics, 1939; Reason in Politics, 1939; Our Two Democracies at Work, 1944; A History of Local Government, 1946; Why We Read History, 1948; British Way of Life, 1955; Great Britain since 1688, 1962. *Address*: 24 Parkside Gardens, SW19 5EU. *T*: 01–946 7869.

SMELLIE, Prof. R(obert) Martin S(tuart), PhD, DSc; FRSE 1964; FIBiol; Cathcart Professor of Biochemistry, since 1966, Director of the Biochemical Laboratories, since 1972, University of Glasgow; *b* Rothesay, Bute, 1 April 1927; *s* of Rev. W. T. Smellie, OBE, MA and Jean (*née* Craig); *m* 1954, Florence Mary Devlin Adams, MB ChB; two *s*. *Educ*: Dundee High Sch.; Glasgow Acad.; Univ. of St Andrews (BSc 1947); Univ. of Glasgow (PhD 1952, DSc 1963). FIBiol 1964. National Service, 1947–49: commnd Royal Scots Fusiliers; served with 2nd Bn Royal Scots and at CDEE, Porton. University of Glasgow: Asst Lectr in Biochemistry, 1949–52; Beit Memorial Res. Fellow, 1952–53; Lectr in Biochem., 1953–55 and 1956–59, Sen. Lectr, 1959–63; Reader in Molecular Biol., 1963–65. Res. Fellow, NY Univ. Coll. of Med., 1955–56. Biochemical Society: Mem. Cttee, 1967–71; Symposium Organiser, 1970–75. Member: EMBO, 1964; MRC Physiol. Systems and Disorders Bd, 1977–82; Brit. Biophys. Soc., 1968; Brit. Assoc. for Cancer Res., 1961; Soc. for Endocrinology, 1968; Council, Trinity Coll., Glenalmond, 1976–. Governor, Glasgow Academicals War Meml Trust, 1976–79. Mem. Court, Glasgow Univ., 1986–. Hon. Gen. Sec., RSE, 1976–86. Bicentenary Medal, 1986. *Publications*: A Matter of Life: DNA, 1969; (contrib.) The Biochemistry of the Nucleic Acids, 8th edn 1976, 9th edn 1981; (ed) Biochemical Society Symposia Nos 31–41; papers in scientific jls on nucleic acid biosynthesis and hormone control mechanisms. *Recreations*: fishing, walking, music, foreign travel. *Address*: 39 Falkland Street, Glasgow G12 9QZ. *T*: 041–334 4255. *Club*: New (Edinburgh).

SMETHAM, Andrew James, MA; Headmaster, The Purbeck School, Wareham, Dorset, since 1985; *b* 22 Feb. 1937; *s* of Arthur James Smetham and Eunice (*née* Jones); *m* 1964, Sandra Mary (*née* Owen); two *s*. *Educ*: Vaynor and Penderyn Grammar Sch., Cefn Coed, Breconshire; King's Coll., Univ. of London (BA (Hons German) 1959, DipEd 1964, MA (Educn) 1968). Assistant Master: Wandsworth Sch., 1960–66; Sedgehill Sch., 1966–70; Dep. Headmaster, Holloway Sch., 1970–74; Headmaster, Wandsworth Sch., 1974–84. *Recreations*: music, walking. *Address*: The Water Barn, East Burton, Wareham, Dorset BH20 6HE. *T*: Bindon Abbey 463727.

SMETHURST, John Michael; Director-General, Humanities and Social Sciences, British Library, since 1986; *b* 25 April 1934; *s* of Albert Smethurst and Nelly Smethurst (*née* Kitchin); *m* 1960, Mary Clayworth; one *s* one *d*. *Educ*: William Hulme's Grammar School, Manchester; Manchester Univ. (BA). ALA. Librarian: Bede Coll., Durham Univ., 1964–66; Inst. of Educn, Newcastle upon Tyne, 1966–69; Dep. Librarian, Univ. of Glasgow, 1969–72; Univ. Librarian, Univ. of Aberdeen, 1972–86. Trustee, Nat. Library of Scotland, 1976–86; Chairman: Library and Inf. Services Cttee (Scotland), 1982–86; SCONUL, 1984–86 (Mem. Council, 1977–80); Member: British Liby Lending Div. Adv. Cttee, 1976–80; British Liby Adv. Council, 1982–86 (Chm., Bibliog. Services Adv. Cttee, 1983–). Pres., Scottish Liby Assoc., 1983. FRSA. *Publications*: papers and articles in professional jls. *Recreations*: music, art, travel, gardening. *Address*: British Library, Great Russell Street, WC1B 3DG. *Club*: Athenæum.

SMETHURST, Richard Good, MA; Director, Department for External Studies, University of Oxford, since 1976; Professorial Fellow of Worcester College, Oxford; *b* 17 Jan. 1941; *s* of Thomas Good Smethurst and Madeleine Nora Foulkes; *m* 1964, Dorothy Joan (*née* Mitchenall); two *s* two *d*. *Educ*: Liverpool Coll.; Worcester Coll., Oxford; Nuffield Coll., Oxford. Webb Medley Jun. Schol. 1962; BA 1st Cl. 1963; MA Oxon. Research Fellow, Inst. for Commonwealth Studies, Oxford, 1966 (Consultant, UN/FAO World Food Program); Fellow and Tutor in Economics, St Edmund Hall, Oxford, 1966–67; Fellow and Tutor in Economics, Worcester Coll., Oxford, and Univ. Lectr in Economics, 1967–76; Economic Adviser, HM Treasury, 1969–71; Policy Adviser, Prime Minister's Policy Unit, 1975–76. Member: Adv. Council for Adult and Continuing Educn, DES, 1977–83; Monopolies and Mergers Commn, 1978– (Dep. Chm., 1986–). Governor, Liverpool Coll. *Publications*: Impact of Food Aid on Donor Countries (with G. R. Allen), 1967; contribs to New Thinking About Welfare, 1969; Economic System in the UK, 1977, 2nd edn 1979; New Directions in Adult and Continuing Education, 1979; contrib. Jl of Development Studies, Studies in Adult Education. *Recreation*: good food. *Address*: Beckett House, Wallingford Street, Wantage, Oxfordshire OX12 8AZ. *T*: Wantage 4334.

SMETTEM, Colin William; Chairman, North Eastern Region, British Gas Corporation, 1973–76; *b* 1 June 1916; *s* of William Home Smettem and Agnes Grace; *m* 1945, Sylvia Elisabeth (*née* Alcock); two *s* two *d*. *Educ*: Scarborough High Sch. Solicitor (Hons). Asst Solicitor, Scarborough Corp., 1938. Served War, 1939–45: UK, India, Assam; GII at Tactical Trng Centre, India Command, 1944. Asst Town Clerk, Wallasey, 1948; Solicitor, North Western Gas Bd, 1950; Commercial Manager, North Western Gas Bd, 1961, and Mem. Bd, 1965–68; Dep. Chm., Eastern Gas Bd, 1968. *Recreation*: DIY. *Address*: The Rookery, Tinwell, via Stamford, Lincs PE9 3UJ. *T*: Stamford 53168. *Club*: Naval and Military.

SMIETON, Dame Mary Guillan, DBE 1949; MA Oxon; Permanent Secretary, Ministry of Education, 1959–63, retired; *b* 5 Dec. 1902; *d* of John Guillan Smieton, late librarian and bursar Westminster Coll., Cambridge, and of Maria Judith Toop. *Educ*: Perse Sch., Cambridge; Wimbledon High Sch.; Bedford Coll., London (1 year) (Hon. Fellow, 1971); Lady Margaret Hall. Assistant Keeper, Public Record Office, 1925–28; Ministry of Labour and National Service, 1928–46; on loan to Home Office as General Secretary, Women's Voluntary Services, 1938–40, and to UN as Director of Personnel, 1946–48; Deputy Secretary, Ministry of Labour and National Service, 1955–59 (Under-Secretary, 1946–55). UK representative, Unesco Executive Board, 1962–68. Trustee, British Museum, 1963–73; Chm., Bedford Coll. Council, 1964–70. Member: Advisory Council on Public Records, 1965–73; Standing Commn on Museums and Galleries, 1970–73; Vice Pres., Museums Assoc., 1974–77. Hon. Fellow, Lady Margaret Hall, Oxford, 1959. *Address*: 14 St George's Road, St Margaret's on Thames, Middlesex. *T*: 01–892 9279. *Club*: United Oxford & Cambridge University.

SMIJTH-WINDHAM, Brig. William Russell, CBE 1946; DSO 1942; *b* 21 Oct. 1907; *s* of late Arthur Russell Smijth-Windham; *m* 1934, Helen Teresa, *d* of late Brig. H. Clementi Smith, DSO; one *s* three *d*. *Educ:* Wellington College; Royal Military Academy, Woolwich. Commissioned Royal Corps of Signals, 1927; Mount Everest Expedition, 1933 and 1936; Mohmand Ops, 1935; Army Revolver VIII, 1937–39; British Pistol VIII, 1939. Served War of 1939–45, Greece and Crete, 1941; Western Desert and Tunisia, 1942–43; France and Germany, 1944–45 (despatches); British Mil. Mission to Greece during Greek Civil War, 1948–49; Chief Signal Officer, Eastern Command, 1957–60, retd 1960; ADC to the Queen, 1957–60. FIEE. *Recreations:* shooting, fishing. *Address:* Icentown House, Pitney, Langport, Somerset. *T:* Langport 250525.

SMILEY, Sir Hugh Houston, 3rd Bt, *cr* 1903; late Grenadier Guards; JP; Vice Lord-Lieutenant of Hampshire, 1973–82; *b* 14 Nov. 1905; *s* of 2nd Bt and Valerie (*d* 1978), *y d* of late Sir Claude Champion de Crespigny, 4th Bt; *S* father, 1930; *m* 1933, Nancy, *er d* of E. W. H. Beaton; one *s*. *Educ:* Eton; RMC, Sandhurst. Served with 1st Bn Grenadier Guards NW Europe, 1944–45. JP 1952, DL 1962, Hampshire; High Sheriff, 1959. Chm., Jane Austen Society, 1969– (Hon. Sec., 1953–85). *Heir: s* Lt-Col John Philip Smiley [*b* 24 Feb. 1934; *m* 1963, Davina Elizabeth, *e d* of late Denis Griffiths; two *s* one *d*. *Educ:* Eton; RMA, Sandhurst; Lt-Col late Grenadier Guards]. *Address:* Ivalls, Bentworth, Alton, Hants GU34 5JU. *T:* Alton 63193. *Club:* Cavalry and Guards.

SMILEY, Prof. Timothy John, PhD; FBA 1984; Knightbridge Professor of Philosophy, University of Cambridge, since 1980; Fellow of Clare College, Cambridge, since 1955; *b* 13 Nov. 1930; *s* of Prof. M. T. Smiley and Mrs T. M. Smiley (*née* Browne); *m* 1955, Benita Mary Bentley; four *d*. *Educ:* Ardwyn Grammar Sch., Aberystwyth; Ampleforth Coll.; Fribourg Univ.; Clare Coll., Cambridge (BA 1952, Math. Tripos; MA, PhD 1956). Holt Scholarship, Gray's Inn, 1954; called to the Bar, 1956. Pilot Officer, RAFVR, 1954. Scientific Officer, Air Min., 1955–56; Clare Coll., Cambridge: Res. Fellow, 1955–59; Asst Tutor, 1959–65; Sen. Tutor, 1966–69; Asst Lectr in Phil., Cambridge Univ., 1957–62, Lectr, 1962–79. Vis. Professor: Cornell Univ., 1964; Univ. of Virginia, 1972; Yale Univ., 1975; Univ. of Notre Dame, 1986. *Publications:* (with D. J. Shoesmith) Multiple-conclusion Logic, 1978; articles in phil and math. jls. *Recreation:* orienteering. *Address:* Clare College, Cambridge. *T:* Cambridge 247106.

SMILLIE, William John Jones; Head of the Refreshment Department, House of Commons, since 1980; *b* 18 Feb. 1940; *s* of late John Smillie and Emily Mary Caroline (*née* Jones). *Educ:* Lauriston Sch., Falkirk; Territorial Sch., Stirling; Stirling High Sch. Scottish hotel family background; trained in all hotel depts in Scotland and Paris, with extensive kitchen work; progressed to management with Edward R. Barnett & Co. Ltd, industrial caterers (now taken over by Grand Metropolitan Gp), resp. for 50 outlets throughout Scotland, England and Wales (Asst Gen. Man., 1964–67); joined House of Commons Catering Dept as Personnel Manager, 1967; Personnel Manager and Asst to Catering Manager, 1970; Gen. Man., Refreshment Dept, 1971. Member: British Inst. of Cleaning Science, 1976–; Hine Soc., 1979–; FHCIMA 1979; Fellow, Cookery and Food Assoc., 1967; Founder Mem., Wine Guild of UK, 1984–; Mem., Restaurateurs Assoc. of GB, 1983–; Hon. Mem., Assoc. Culinaire Française, 1972. Vice Pres., British Epilepsy Assoc., 1981; Mem., League Against Cruel Sports, 1983. *Publications:* articles for catering trade papers. *Recreations:* theatre, ballet, music, piano, motoring, boating, disc-jockey, travel, gourmandise, intervals at the opera. *Address:* Kingsmere House, 1 Kingsmere Road, Wimbledon Common, SW19 6PY. *Clubs:* Preston Cross Country; Jaguar Drivers (Luton).

SMIRK, Sir (Frederick) Horace, KBE 1958; Emeritus Professor, University of Otago, Dunedin, New Zealand (Professor of Medicine, 1940–61); Director, Wellcome Research Institute, 1962–68, engaged in honororary research 1969–76; *b* 12 December 1902; *s* of Thomas Smirk and Betsy Ann (*née* Cunliffe); *m* 1931, Aileen Winifrede, *d* of Rev. Arthur Bamforth and Martha Bamforth; three *s* one *d*. *Educ:* Haslingden Gram. Sch.; Univ. of Manchester. Gaskill mathematical schol., 1919; MB, ChB 1st Cl. Hons 1925; MD Gold Medallist, 1927; FRCP 1940; FRACP (Hon.) 1940. Med. Registrar, Manchester Royal Infirmary, 1926–29; RMO 1929; Dickenson Travelling Scholar, University of Vienna, 1930; Beit Memorial Fell., successively Asst Depts of Pharmacology, and Medicine, Univ. Coll. London, 1930–34; Prof. of Pharmacology and Physician Postgrad. Dept, Egyptian Univ., 1935–39. Visiting Prof., Brit. Postgrad. Med. Sch., London, 1949; McIlraith Visiting Prof., Roy. Prince Alfred Hosp., Sydney, 1953; Holme Lectr Univ. Coll. Hosp. Med. Sch., 1949; Alexander Gibson Lectr, Edinburgh Coll. of Physicians, 1956; Dr N. D. Patel Inaugural lecture, Bombay, 1959; Member Board of Censors, later Senior Censor, 1940–58; Vice-President RACP, 1958–60; Chairman Clinical Reseach Committee, 1942–, Psychiatric Research Cttee, 1957–60; Mem. Council Med. Research Council of NZ, 1944–60; Mem. Expert Cttee on Hypertension and Ischaemic Heart Disease, of WHO; Life Member, New York Acad. of Science, 1961; formerly Councillor, International Society of Cardiology (Mem. Hypertension Research Sub-Cttee); Hon. overseas Mem. Assoc. of Physicians of GB, 1967. Hon. DSc: Hahneman Coll., Pa, 1961; Otago, 1975. Gairdner Foundn International Award for Research in Medicine, 1965. *Publications:* Hypotensive Drugs, 1956; Arterial Hypertension, 1957; jointly: Modern Trends in Geriatrics, 1956, Current Therapy, 1956, Annual Reviews of Medicine, 1955; Antihypertensive Agents, 1967; contrib. to med. jls, mainly on disorders of the heart. *Recreations:* reading, writing, travel. *Address:* 68 Cannington Road, Dunedin, New Zealand. *T:* 741.046.

SMIRNOVSKY, Mikhail Nikolaevich; Soviet Ambassador to the Court of St James's, 1966–73; non-resident Ambassador to Malta, 1967–73; *b* 7 Aug. 1921; *m* Liudmila A.; one *s* two *d*. *Educ:* Moscow Aviation Institute. Mem. Soviet Foreign Service, 1948; Assistant, 1955, Deputy Head of American Div., Ministry for Foreign Affairs, 1957–58; Counsellor, 1958, Minister-Counsellor, Soviet Embassy in Washington, 1960–62; Head of US Div. and Mem. Collegium, Ministry for Foreign Affairs, 1962–66. Member: Central Auditing Commn of CPSU, 1966–76; Soviet Delegations to several International Conferences. *Address:* Ministry of Foreign Affairs, 32–34 Smolenskaya Sennaya Ploshchad, Moscow, USSR.

SMITH; *see* Abel Smith and Abel-Smith.

SMITH; *see* Buchanan-Smith.

SMITH; *see* Delacourt-Smith.

SMITH; *see* Gordon-Smith.

SMITH; *see* Hamilton-Smith, family name of Baron Colwyn.

SMITH; *see* Llewellyn Smith and Llewellyn-Smith.

SMITH; *see* Macdonald-Smith.

SMITH; *see* Nowell-Smith.

SMITH; *see* Spencer Smith and Spencer-Smith.

SMITH; *see* Stewart-Smith.

SMITH; *see* Stuart-Smith.

SMITH; *see* Walker-Smith.

SMITH; *see* Wenban-Smith.

SMITH, family name of **Viscount Hambleden, Barons Bicester, Kirkhill** and **Smith.**

SMITH, Baron *cr* 1978 (Life Peer), of Marlow in the County of Buckinghamshire; **Rodney Smith,** KBE 1975; MS, FRCS; Hon. Consulting Surgeon: St George's Hospital London, 1978; Royal Prince Alfred Hospital, Sydney, NSW; Wimbledon Hospital; Examiner in Surgery, University of London; External Examiner in Surgery, Universities of Cambridge, Birmingham and Hong Kong; former Advisor in Surgery to Department of Health and Social Security; Hon. Consultant in Surgery to the Army, 1972, Emeritus Consultant, 1980; *b* 10 May 1914; *o s* of Dr Edwin Smith and Edith Catherine (*née* Dyer); *m* 1st, 1938, Mary Rodwell (marr. diss. 1971); three *s* one *d*; 2nd, 1971, Susan Fry. *Educ:* Westminster Sch.; London Univ. (St Thomas's Hospital). MB, BS London, MRCS, LRCP 1937; FRCS 1939; MS London 1941. Surgical Registrar, Middlesex Hospital, 1939–41; Surgeon RAMC, 1941–45; appointed Surgeon, St George's Hospital 1946. Royal College of Surgeons: Hunterian Professor, 1947 and 1952; Arris and Gale Lecturer, 1959; Jacksonian Prizewinner, 1951; Penrose May Tutor in Surgery, 1957–63; Dean, Inst. of Basic Medical Sciences, 1966–71; Mem., Ct of Examiners, 1963–69, Chm. Feb.-July 1969; Mem. Council, 1965–78; Pres., 1973–77; Mem. Ct of Patrons; Hunterian Orator, 1975. President: Brit. Assoc. Surg. Oncologists; Harveian Soc., 1965; Pancreatic Soc., GB and Ire., 1976; Roy. Soc. Med., 1978–80; London Med. Orchestra. Chairman: ASCAB; Conf. of Med. Roy. Coll. UK, 1976–78; Armed Forces Med. Adv. Bd, 1980–84. Member: Council, Brit. Empire Cancer Campaign; Exec., Internat. Fedn Surg. Colls. Trustee, Wolfson Foundn; Governor, Motability. Vis. Lectr to S Africa Assoc. of Surgeons, 1957; McIlrath Guest Prof. in Surgery, Royal Prince Alfred Hosp., Sydney, NSW, 1966; Vis. Prof., Surg. Unit, Univ. of Illinois, Chicago, 1978; Visiting Professor of Surgery: Jackson Univ., Miss, 1979; Johns Hopkins Hosp., Baltimore, 1979; Flint Univ., Mich, 1979. Lectures: First Datuk Abdul Majid Ismail Oration and Gold Medal, Malaysian Assoc. of Surgeons, 1972; Robert Whitmarsh Oration, Providence, 1972; Cheselden, St Thomas's Hosp., 1975; Philip Mitchiner, 1976; Balfour, Toronto, 1976; Colles, RCSI, 1976; Faltin (and Medal), Helsinki, 1976; Bradshaw, RCP, 1977; Sir Robert Bradlaw, Faculty of Dental Surgery, RCS, 1978; Sir Ernest Finch Meml, Sheffield, 1978; Telford Meml, Manchester, 1978; Annual Oration Med. Soc. of London, 1978; Sir William MacEwen Meml, Glasgow, 1978; Eisenberg, Boston, 1978; Judd, Minneapolis, 1979; first Samuel Jason Mixter, New England Surgical Soc., 1985. Hon. Member: Soc. of Grad. Surgeons of LA County Hosp., 1965; Finnish Surgical Soc., 1976; Surgical Res. Soc., 1976; Surgical Soc. of Phoenix, Arizona; Soc. Surg. Alimentary Tract; Hellenic Surg. Soc.; Kentucky Surg. Soc., 1979; Internat. Biliary Assoc., 1977. Hon. Fellow: Amer. Assoc. Surg.; Assoc. Clin. Anat.; Surgical Res. Soc., 1977; Assoc. of Surgeons of France, 1979; Philadelphia Acad. of Surg., 1979; Acad. de Chirurgie de Paris, 1981; Hon. FRACS 1957; Hon. FRCSEd 1975; Hon. FACS 1975; Hon. FRCSCan 1976; Hon. FRCSI 1976; Hon. FRCS S Africa 1976; Hon. FDS; Hon. FRSocMed 1981; Hon. FRCSGlas 1982. Hon. DSc: Exeter, 1974; Leeds, 1976; Hon. MD Zürich Univ., 1979. Biennial Prize, Internat. Soc. of Surgery, 1975; Gimbernat Surg. Prize, Surg. Soc. of Barcelona, 1980; Gold Medal, BMA, 1982. Hon. Freeman, Worshipful Co. of Barbers. *Publications:* Acute Intestinal Obstruction, 1947; Surgery of Pancreatic Neoplasms, 1951; Progress in Clinical Surgery, 1953, 1961, 1969; (ed with C. G. Rob) Operative Surgery (8 Vols) 1956–57 (14 Vols) 1968–69; Surgery of the Gallbladder and Bile Ducts, 1965; Clinical Surgery (Vols 1–14), 1965–67; papers in learned journals on pancreatic surgery, general abdominal surgery, intestinal obstruction. *Recreations:* music, painting, cricket, golf, bridge. *Address:* 135 Harley Street, W1. *T:* 01–935 1714. *Club:* MCC.

SMITH, Agnes Lawrie Addie, (Laura); Sheriff of Glasgow and Strathkelvin, since 1982; *b* 17 June 1947; *d* of late William Smith, District Clerk, and of Mary Marshall Smith McClure. *Educ:* Hamilton Acad.; Glasgow Univ. (LLB 1967). Admitted Solicitor, 1969; called to the Scottish Bar, 1976. Solicitor, private practice, 1969–71; Procurator Fiscal Depute, 1971–75; Standing Junior Counsel to Dept of Employment, 1982. *Recreations:* sailing, various sports. *Address:* Glasgow Sheriff Court, 1 Carlton Place, Glasgow G1 1SY. *Club:* Western (Glasgow).

SMITH, Alan; Chartered Mining Engineer; *b* 19 Jan. 1930; *s* of John Smith and Alice (*née* Williams); *m* 1958, Adele Marguerite (*née* Buckle) (marr. diss. 1986); two *s* two *d*. *Educ:* Rossall; St Catherine's Soc., Oxford. BSc Leeds 1957. MIMinE 1958. NCB, 1957–64; Principal Sci. Officer, Min. of Power, 1964; Sci. Counsellor, HM Embassy, Paris, 1965–70; Cabinet Secretariat, 1970–71; DTI, 1971–73; Dept of Industry, 1973–74; Sci. and Technol. Counsellor, HM Embassy, Washington, 1975–77; Head of Sci. and Technol. Div., OECD, 1977–80. De Laune Lectr, Apothecaries' Soc., 1980. *Publications:* learned articles on steam engines. *Recreation:* engineering history.

SMITH, Sir Alan, Kt 1982; CBE 1976; DFC 1941, and Bar 1942; DL; President, Dawson International plc, since 1982; *b* 14 March 1917; *s* of Alfred and Lilian Smith; *m* 1st, 1943, Margaret Stewart Todd (*d* 1971); three *s* two *d*; 2nd, 1977, Alice Elizabeth Moncur. *Educ:* Bede College, Sunderland. Self employed, 1931–36; Unilever Ltd, 1937–39; RAF, 1939–45; Man. Dir, Todd & Duncan Ltd, 1946–60; Chm. and Chief Exec., Dawson International, 1960–82. DL Kinross, 1967. *Recreations:* sailing, swimming. *Address:* Ardgairney House, Cleish, by Kinross, Scotland. *T:* Cleish Hills 265. *Club:* Lansdowne.

SMITH, Alan Christopher; Chief Executive, Test and County Cricket Board, since 1987; *b* 25 Oct. 1936; *s* of Herbert Sidney and Elsie Smith; *m* 1963, Anne Elizabeth Boddy; one *s* one *d*. *Educ:* King Edward's Sch., Birmingham; Brasenose Coll., Oxford (BA). Played cricket: Oxford Univ. CC, 1958–60 (Captain, 1959 and 1960); Warwicks CCC, 1958–74 (Captain, 1968–74); rep. England in six Test Matches, Australia and NZ, 1962–63. Gen. Sec., Warwicks CCC, 1976–86; England overseas cricket tours: Asst Manager, Australia, 1974–75; Manager: West Indies, 1981; Fiji, NZ and Pakistan, 1984. Mem., England Cricket Selection Cttee, 1969–73, 1982–86. Director: Royds Advertising and Marketing, 1971–86; Aston Villa Football Club plc, 1972–78. *Recreations:* both football codes, golf, bridge, motoring. *Address:* (office) TCCB, Lord's Ground, NW8 8QN. *T:* 01–286 4405; The Bridge House, Oversley Green, Alcester, Warwicks B49 6LE. *T:* Alcester 762847. *Clubs:* MCC, I Zingari; Vincent's (Oxford).

SMITH, Alan Guy E.; *see* Elliot-Smith.

SMITH, Alan Oliver, QPM 1986; Chief Constable of Derbyshire, since 1985; *b* 9 Sept. 1929; *s* of Thomas Allen and Lily Oliver; *m* 1950, Jane (*née* Elliott); one *d*. *Educ:* elementary schools, Birmingham; Guiseley and Bradford Tech. Coll.; courses at Police Staff Coll., 1964, 1973, 1979. Constable to Supt, Bradford City Police, 1952–74; Supt and Chief Supt, W Yorks Metropolitan Police, 1974–79; Comdt, Bishopgarth Detective Training Sch., 1977–79; Asst Chief Constable, W Yorks, 1979–83; Dep. Chief Constable, Derbyshire Constabulary, 1983–84 (Acting Chief Constable, June 1984–Dec. 1985).

Formerly Mem., NE Consultative Cttee, Commn for Racial Equality; Mem., Professional Adv. Cttee, NSPCC, 1980–; Mem., St John Council for Derbyshire, 1986– (formerly Hon. County Dir, St John Ambulance, S and W Yorks). *Recreations:* landscape artist (various exhibns; works in permt collections, Calderdale Authy, Leeds City Council, Bradford Univ.). *Address:* Constabulary HQ, Butterley Hall, Ripley, Derbyshire DE5 3RS. *T:* Ripley 46161.

SMITH, Alastair Macleod M.; *see* Macleod-Smith.

SMITH, Sir Alex; *see* Smith, Sir Alexander M.

SMITH, Prof. Alexander Crampton, (Alex. Crampton Smith); Nuffield Professor of Anaesthetics, Oxford University, and Fellow of Pembroke College, Oxford, 1965–79; now Emeritus Professor; *b* 15 June 1917; *s* of William and Mary Elizabeth Crampton Smith; *m* 1953, Marjorie (*née* Mason); three *s*; two *d* by a former marriage. *Educ:* Inverness Royal Acad.; Edinburgh University. Edinburgh Univ., 1935–41. Served War of 1939–45 (Croix de Guerre, despatches), RNVR, 1942–46. Consultant Anaesthetist, United Oxford Hospitals, 1951; Clinical Lectr in Anaesthetics, Oxford Univ., 1961. FFARCS 1953; MA Oxon 1961. Civilian Consultant Anaesthetist to Royal Navy, 1968. Mem. Bd, Faculty of Anaesthetists, 1965–80. Mem. Trustees, Nuffield Medical Benefaction, 1973. *Publications:* Clinical Practice and Physiology of Artificial Respiration (with J. M. K. Spalding), 1963; contribs to anaesthetic, medical and physiological jls. *Recreations:* sailing, fishing. *Address:* 10 Horwood Close, Headington, Oxford OX3 7RF. *T:* Oxford 69593.

SMITH, Sir Alexander Mair, (Sir Alex), Kt 1975; Director of various companies; *b* 15 Oct. 1922; *s* of late John S. and Anne M. Smith; *m* 1st, 1944, Muriel (*née* Harris) (*d* 1950); one *d*; 2nd, 1956, Doris Neil (*née* Patrick) (*d* 1980); two *d*; 3rd, 1984, Jennifer Lewis (*née* Pearce); two step *s*. *Educ:* Univ. of Aberdeen. MA (Maths and Nat. Phil.), PhD, FInstP. Physicist, UKAEA, 1952–56; Head of Advanced Research, Rolls Royce Ltd, 1956–67; Dir and Chief Scientist, Rolls Royce & Associates Ltd, 1967–69; Dir, Manchester Polytechnic, 1969–81. Vis. Prof., Internat. Management Centre from Buckingham, 1986–. Chairman: Cttee of Dirs of Polytechnics, 1974–76; Schools Council, 1975–78; Member: UGC, 1974–76; BBC Gen. Adv. Council, 1978–81; Council, RSA, 1979–84; Vice-Pres., CGLI, 1981–; Patron, Educnl Inst. of Design, Craft and Technology, 1977–83. *Publications:* papers in learned jls. *Recreation:* golf. *Address:* 33 Parkway, Wilmslow, Cheshire. *T:* Wilmslow 522011. *Club:* Athenæum.

SMITH, Sir (Alexander) Rowland, Kt 1944; formerly Chairman and Managing Director, Ford Motor Co. Ltd; formerly Director, National Provincial Bank Ltd; Ex-Member, UK Atomic Energy Authority and National Research Corp.; *b* Gillingham, Kent, 25 Jan. 1888; *s* of late Alexander James Frederick Smith, Gillingham, Kent; *m* 1913, Janet Lucretia (*d* 1972), *d* of late George Henry Baker, Gillingham, Kent; one *s* one *d*. *Educ:* Mathematical School, Rochester. Freeman, City of London; Livery Cos: Glaziers (Past Master); Coachmakers and Coach Harness Makers; Member: Ministry of Aircraft Production Mission to USA, 1941; Ministry of Pensions Standing Advisory Cttee on Artificial Limbs, 1948; Cttee on Procedure for ordering Civil Aircraft, 1948. FIB; FRSA; CEng; FIMechE; Fell. Inst. of Bankers. *Recreation:* sailing. *Address:* The Manor House, Maresfield, W Sussex. *Clubs:* Athenæum; Royal Southern Yacht.

SMITH, Alistair; *see* Smith, E. A.

SMITH, Prof. Alwyn, CBE 1986; PhD; Professor of Epidemiology and Social Oncology, University of Manchester, since 1979; *b* 9 Nov. 1925; *s* of Ernest Smith and Constance Barbara Smith; *m* 1950, Doreen Preston; one *s* one *d*. *Educ:* Queen Mary's Sch., Walsall; Birmingham Univ. MB, PhD; FRCP 1970; FRCGP 1973; FFCM 1974. Served War, RM, 1943–46. Res. Fellow in Social Medicine, Birmingham Univ., 1952–55; WHO Vis. Lectr, Univ. of Malaya, 1956–58; Lectr, Univ. of St Andrews, 1959–61; Sen. Lectr, Univ. of Edinburgh, 1961–66; First Dir, Social Paediatric Res. Gp, Glasgow, 1966–67; Prof. of Community Medicine, Univ. of Manchester, 1967–79. Pres., FCM, 1981–. *Publications:* Genetics in Medicine, 1966; The Science of Social Medicine, 1968; (ed) Cancer Control, 1979; (ed) Recent Advances in Community Medicine, 1982; papers on epidemiological subjects in Lancet, British Jl of Epidemiol., etc. *Recreations:* music, bird watching, fishing. *Address:* 66 Kingston Road, Manchester M20 8SB. *T:* 061–434 1395.

SMITH, Andreas W.; *see* Whittam Smith.

SMITH, Anthony David; Director, British Film Institute, since 1979; *b* 14 March 1938; *s* of Henry and Esther Smith. *Educ:* Brasenose Coll., Oxford (BA). BBC TV Current Affairs Producer, 1960–71; Fellow, St Antony's Coll., Oxford, 1971–76. Bd Mem., Channel Four Television Co., 1980–84. Member: Acton Soc. Trust, 1978–; Writers and Scholars Educnl Trust, 1982–. *Publications:* The Shadow in the Cave: the broadcaster, the audience and the state, 1973, 2nd edn 1976; British Broadcasting, 1974; The British Press since the War, 1976; Subsidies and the Press in Europe, 1977; The Politics of Information, 1978; Television and Political Life, 1979; The Newspaper: an international history, 1979; Newspapers and Democracy, 1980; Goodbye Gutenberg—the newspaper revolution of the 1980's, 1980; The Geopolitics of Information, 1980. *Address:* Albany, Piccadilly, W1V 9RP. *T:* 01–734 5494; Bridge Cottage, Old Minster Lovell, Oxford OX8 5RN. *T:* Witney 75629. *Club:* British Academy of Film and Television Arts.

SMITH, Prof. (Anthony) David, DPhil; Professor and Head of the Department of Pharmacology, University of Oxford, since 1984; Hon. Director, MRC Anatomical Neuropharmacology Unit, Oxford, since 1985; Fellow, Lady Margaret Hall, Oxford, since 1984; *b* 16 Sept. 1938; *s* of Rev. William Beddard Smith and Evelyn Smith; *m* 1st, 1962, Wendy Diana Lee (marr. diss. 1974); one *s* one *d*; 2nd, 1975, Dr Ingegerd Östman. *Educ:* Kingswood Sch., Bath; Christ Church, Oxford (Bostock Exhibnr; BA 1963, MA 1966, DPhil 1966). Royal Soc. Stothert Res. Fellow, Oxford, 1966–70; Res. Lectr, Christ Church, Oxford, 1966–71; Wellcome Res. Fellow, Oxford, 1970–71; Univ. Lectr in Pharmacology and Student of Christ Church, 1971–84. Member: Gen. Bd of the Faculties, Oxford, 1980–84; Neurosciences Bd, MRC, 1983–; Physiol Soc.; Pharmacol Soc. Dir of Pubns, IBRO, 1977–; Editor: Methods in the Neurosciences (IBRO Handbook Series), 1981–; Neuroscience, 1976–; Mem., editorial bds of various scientific jls. (Seventh) Gaddum Meml Prize, British Pharmacol Soc., 1979. *Publications:* (ed) Handbook of Physiology, Section 7 Vol. 6, 1974; (ed) Commentaries in the Neurosciences, 1980; articles on neuropharmacology in jls. *Recreations:* music, travel, birds. *Address:* University Department of Pharmacology, South Parks Road, Oxford OX1 3QT. *T:* Oxford 512323.

SMITH, Anthony (John Francis); writer, broadcaster; *b* 30 March 1926; 2nd *s* of late Hubert Smith (formerly Chief Agent, National Trust) and of Diana Watkin; *m* 1st, 1956, Barbara Dorothy Newman (marr. diss. 1983); one *s* two *d*; 2nd, 1984, Margaret Ann Holloway. *Educ:* Dragon School, Oxford; Blundell's School, Devon; Balliol College, Oxford. MA Oxon., 1951. Served with RAF, 1944–48. Oxford University, 1948–51. Manchester Guardian, 1953 and 1956–57; Drum, Africa, 1954–55; Science Correspondent, Daily Telegraph, 1957–63. Founded British Balloon and Airship Club, 1965 (Pres., 1970–). Scientific Fellow of Zoological Society. Glaxo Award for Science Writers, 1977; Cherry Kearton Medal and Award, RGS, 1978. TV series include: Balloon Safari, Balloons over the Alps, Great Zoos of the World, Great Parks of the World, Wilderness; radio series include: A Sideways Look, 1977–; High Street Africa Revisited, 1983–84. *Publications:* Blind White Fish in Persia, 1953; Sea Never Dry, 1958; High Street Africa, 1961; Throw Out Two Hands, 1963; The Body, 1968, new edn 1985; The Seasons, 1970; The Dangerous Sort, 1970; Mato Grosso, 1971; Beside the Seaside, 1972; Good Beach Guide, 1973; The Human Pedigree, 1975; Animals on View, 1977; Wilderness, 1978; A Persian Quarter Century, 1979; A Sideways Look, 1983; The Mind, 1984; Smith & Son, 1984. *Recreations:* travel, lighter-than-air flying. *Address:* 10 Aldbourne Road, W12. *T:* 01–743 6935.

SMITH, Ven. (Anthony Michael) Percival; Archdeacon of Maidstone, since 1979; Diocesan Director of Ordinands, since 1980; *b* 5 Sept. 1924; *s* of Kenneth and Audrey Smith; *m* 1950, Mildred Elizabeth; two *d*. *Educ:* Shrewsbury; Gonville and Caius Coll., Cambridge (MA); Westcott House Theological Coll. Served Army, Rifle Brigade, 1942–46. Cambridge, 1946–48; Westcott House, 1948–50. Deacon 1950, priest 1951; Curate, Holy Trinity, Leamington, 1950–53; Domestic Chaplain to Archbishop of Canterbury, 1953–57; Vicar of All Saints, Upper Norwood, 1957–66; Vicar of Yeovil, 1966–72; Prebendary of Wells Cathedral, 1968–72; RD of Murston, 1968–72; Vicar of St Mildred's, Addiscombe, Croydon, 1972–80; Hon. Canon of Canterbury Cathedral, 1980–. *Recreations:* reading, walking. *Address:* Archdeacon's House, Charing, Ashford, Kent TN27 0LU. *T:* Charing 2294.

SMITH, Anthony Robert; Director of Statistics and Research, Department of Health and Social Security, 1976–86; *b* 29 March 1926; *s* of late Ernest George Smith and Mildred Smith (*née* Murphy); *m* 1949, Helen Elizabeth Mary Morgan; two *d*. *Educ:* De La Salle Coll., Pendleton; Peterhouse, Cambridge; London Sch. of Economics (BScEcon). Royal Marines and Army, 1944–47. Various appts in Admty, 1950–64; Defence, 1964–68; Treasury, 1968; Civil Service Dept, 1968–76; Under-Sec., 1970. Actively involved in Manpower Planning Study Gp, 1967–70; Member: Manpower Soc., 1970–75 (Hon. Vice-Pres., 1975–); Inst. of Manpower Studies, 1968–; Inst. of Personnel Management, 1972–79; Consultant, Organisation for Economic Co-operation and Development, 1970–78. *Publications:* Models of Manpower Systems (ed), 1970; Manpower and Management Science (with D. J. Bartholomew), 1971; (ed) Manpower Planning in the Civil Service, 1976; Corporate Manpower Planning, 1980; contributor to related books and jls. *Recreation:* dabbling. *Address:* 16 Carlton Road, Redhill RH1 2BX. *T:* Redhill 62258.

SMITH, Anthony Thomas, QC 1977; a Recorder of the Crown Court, since 1977; *b* 21 June 1935; *s* of Sydney Ernest Smith and Winston Victoria Smith; *m* 1959, Letitia Ann Wheldon Griffith; one *s* two *d*. *Educ:* Northampton, Stafford, and Hinckley Grammar Schs; King's Coll., Cambridge (Exhibnr; MA). Called to the Bar, Inner Temple, 1958, Bencher, 1985. Flying Officer, RAF, 1958–60. *Recreations:* music, reading, hunting, farming. *Address:* Skeffington House, Skeffington, Leics. *T:* Billesdon 445.

SMITH, Arnold Cantwell, OC 1985; CH 1975; *b* 18 Jan. 1915; *m* 1938, Evelyn Hardwick Stewart; two *s* one *d*. *Educ:* Upper Canada Coll., Toronto; Lycée Champoléon, Grenoble; Univ. of Toronto; Christ Church, Oxford (Rhodes Scholar for Ont), BA Toronto, 1935; BA (Juris) Oxon 1937 (MA 1968); BCL 1938. Editor, The Baltic Times, Tallinn, Estonia, and Assoc. Prof. of Polit. Econ., Univ. of Tartu, Estonia, 1939–40; Attaché, British Legation, Tallinn, 1940; Attaché, British Embassy, Cairo, 1940–43; part-time Lectr in Polit. Sci. and Econs, Egyptian State Univ., Cairo, 1940–42; transf. to Canadian Diplomatic Service, 1943; Sec., Canadian Legation, Kuibyshev, USSR, 1943; Sec., Canadian Embassy, Moscow, 1943–45; Dept of External Affairs, Ottawa, 1946–47; Assoc. Dir, Nat. Def. Coll. of Canada, Kingston, Ont, 1947–49; Mem. Canadian Delegns to various UN Confs, 1947–51; Alternate Perm. Deleg. of Canada to UN Security Coun. and Atomic Energy Commn, 1949–50; Counsellor, Canadian Embassy, Brussels, and Head of Canadian Delegn to Inter-Allied Reparations Agency, 1950–53; Special Asst to Sec. of State for External Affairs, 1953–55; Internat. Truce Comr in Indochina, 1955–56; Canadian Minister to UK, 1956–58; Canadian Ambassador to UAR, 1958–61; Canadian Ambassador to USSR, 1961–63; Asst Under-Sec. of State for External Affairs, Ottawa, 1963–65; Secretary-General of the Commonwealth, 1965–75; Lester B. Pearson Prof. of Internat. Affairs, Carleton Univ., Ottawa, 1975–81; Montague Burton Lectr in Internat. Relations, Leeds Univ., 1982, 75th Anniv. Lectr, Univ. of Alberta, 1983. Chairman: North-South Inst.; Hudson Inst. of Canada; Internat. Peace Acad., NY; Hon. Pres., Canadian Mediterranean Inst., 1981–; Trustee: Hudson Inst., Croton, NJ, 1976–81; Cambridge Univ. Commonwealth Trust, 1982–; Governor, Newsconcern Internat. Foundn; Mem. Univ. College Cttee, Univ. of Toronto, 1982–; Life Vice-Pres., Royal Commonwealth Soc. Hon. Fellow, Lady Eaton Coll., Trent Univ. R. B. Bennett Commonwealth Prize, RSA, 1975. Hon. LLD: Ricker Coll., 1964; Queen's Univ., Kingston, Ont, 1966; Univ. of New Brunswick, 1968; Univ. of BC, 1969; Univ. of Toronto, 1969; Leeds Univ., 1975; Trent Univ., 1979; Hon. DCL: Michigan, 1966; Oxon, 1975; Bishop's Univ., 1978. Zimbabwe Independence Medal, 1980. *Publications:* Stitches in Time—the Commonwealth in World Politics, 1981; The We-They Frontier: from international relations to world politics, 1983; (with Arthur Lall) Multilateral Negotiation and Mediation—Instruments and Methods, 1985; reports; articles in learned jls. *Recreations:* fishing, reading, travelling, farming in France. *Address:* 260 Metcalfe Street, Apt 4–B, Ottawa K2P 1R6, Canada. *T:* (613) 235.3073; (summer) Aux Anjeaux, Gavaudun, 47150 Monflanquin, France. *T:* (53) 711316. *Clubs:* Athenæum; Cercle Universitaire (Ottawa).

SMITH, Arnold Terence, MBE 1963; HM Diplomatic Service, retired; *b* 7 Oct. 1922; *s* of Thomas Smith and Minnie Louisa (*née* Mole); *m* 1st, 1944, Mary James (*d* 1983), Preston, Yorks; one *s* one *d*; 2nd, 1985, Brenda Day (*née* Edwards), Edmonton; one step *s*. *Educ:* Christ Church, Dover; Coll. of Technol., Dover. Enlisted HM Forces, Army, 1939; served War, 1939–45; released, 1947. Joined CRO, 1948; Attaché, Karachi, 1952–56; Second Sec., Madras, 1956–60; CRO, 1960–61; First Sec., Kuala Lumpur, 1961–65; Consul, Oslo, 1965–69; FCO, 1969–73; Head of Chancery, Mbabane, 1973–77; Head of Admin, Nairobi, 1977–78; Counsellor and Consul-Gen., Lagos, Nigeria, 1978–80. *Recreations:* hiking, gardening, golf, swimming. *Address:* Flowers Cottage, Streetly End, West Wickham, Cambridgeshire CB1 6RP. *T:* Cambridge 891247.

SMITH, Ven. Arthur Cyril, VRD 1955; MA; Archdeacon of Lincoln, 1960–76, now Archdeacon Emeritus; Rector of Algarkirk, 1960–76, now Canon Emeritus; *b* 26 Jan. 1909; *s* of late Arthur Smith and of Margaret Ryde, Manchester; *m* 1940, Patricia Marion Greenwood, *d* of late Lt-Col Ranolf Nelson Greenwood, MC, and Beatrice Marion, *d* of late Rev. Llewellyn L. Montford Bebb, DD; two *s* two *d*. *Educ:* St John's College, Winnipeg, Canada; Sheffield University; Westcott House, Cambridge. Curate of: Keighley, 1934–36; Bishop's Hatfield, 1936–40. Chaplain RNVR, 1940; HMS Hawkins, 1940–41; 13th Destroyer Flotilla Gibraltar, 1941–43; HMS Eaglet, 1943–44; Senior Chaplain, Liverpool 1945–46. Rector, South Ormsby Group of Parishes, 1946–60; Rural Dean, Hill North, 1955; Canon and Prebendary of Centum Solidorum, 1960. Member: Standing Cttee, House of Clergy, Church Assembly, 1966–70; General Synod, 1970–76;

Inspections Cttee, Adv. Council for Churches Ministry, 1967. Church Comr, 1968. Dir, Ecclesiastical Insurance Office Ltd. *Publications:* The South Ormsby Experiment, 1960; Deaneries: Dead or Alive, 1963; Team and Group Ministry, 1965; contributor: to Mission and Communication, 1963; to Theology; to The Caring Church, 1964. *Address:* Farthings, Church End, Great Rollright, Chipping Norton, Oxon OX7 5RX. *T:* Hook Norton 737769. *Club:* Army and Navy.

SMITH, Sir Arthur (Henry), Kt 1968; Chairman, United Africa Co. Ltd, 1955–69; Director of Unilever Ltd, 1948–69; retired; *b* 18 Jan. 1905; *s* of Frederick Smith; *m* 1930, Dorothy Percy; two *s. Educ:* Bolton School. Specialised in Company's interests in French and Belgian Africa, incl. several years' residence in those territories. Econ. Adviser to Brit. Govt's Econ. Mission to French W Africa, 1943. Officer, Legion of Honour, 1957 (Cross 1951); Commander, National Order of the Ivory Coast, 1969. *Recreations:* reading, theatre. *Address:* The Coach House, 31 Withdean Road, Brighton, East Sussex.

SMITH, Arthur Norman E.; *see* Exton-Smith.

SMITH, Basil Gerald P.; *see* Parsons-Smith.

SMITH, Basil Gerrard, TD 1950; *b* 29 January 1911; *m* 1938, Marjorie Elizabeth Artz; one *s* two *d. Educ:* Epsom College, Surrey; Merton College, Oxford (MA). Solicitor (England), 1938. War Service, 1939–46; Hon. Lt.-Col. District Judge, Pahang, 1946; joined Colonial Legal Service, 1946; District Judge: Selangor, 1947; Perak, 1948; President, Sessions Court: Ipoh, 1949; Georgetown, Penang, 1950; Barrister (Gray's Inn), 1950; Federal Counsel and Deputy Public Prosecutor, 1953; Asst Legal Draftsman, 1954; Actg Legal Draftsman, 1955; Judge, Supreme Court, Federation of Malaya, 1956–60; Attorney-General, Southern Cameroons, 1960–61; Legal Adviser to the UK Commissioner, Malta, 1962–64; Legal Asst, Solicitor's Dept, Post Office, 1964, Senior Legal Assistant, 1967–69; Treasury Solicitor's Office, 1969–77; Adjudicator, Immigration Act, 1977–81. Law Reviser, Kiribati and Tuvalu, 1970, 1976, 1980 and 1981. *Address:* 7 Langley Grove, New Malden, Surrey KT3 3AL. *T:* 01–949 4366.
  See also S. A. Goldstein.

SMITH, Dr Brian; *see* Smith, Dr N. B.

SMITH, Brian, OBE 1975; HM Diplomatic Service; Counsellor (Commercial), Bonn, 1982–86; *b* 15 Sept. 1935; *s* of Charles Francis Smith and Grace Amelia (*née* Pope); *m* 1955, Joan Patricia Rivers; one *s* two *d. Educ:* Hull Grammar School. Foreign Office, 1952; HM Forces, 1954–57; Bahrain, 1957; Doha, 1959; Vice-Consul, Luxembourg, 1960, Casablanca, 1962; Tehran, 1964; Berne, 1967; FCO, 1969; Kampala, 1973; Tehran, 1975; FCO, 1977; New York, 1979. *Recreations:* riding, photography, music, handicrafts. *Address:* c/o Foreign and Commonwealth Office, SW1A 2AH.

SMITH, Brian, IPFA; County Treasurer, Staffordshire County Council, since 1983; *b* 16 May 1947; *s* of Albert Frederick and Gladys Smith; *m* 1972, Susan Jane Lund; two *s. Educ:* Bristol Univ. (BA Hons). Graduate trainee accountant, Derbyshire CC, 1968; Accountancy Asst, Berkshire CC, 1972; Group Technical Officer, South Yorkshire CC, 1974; Asst County Treasurer, Dorset CC, 1976; Sen. Asst County Treasurer, Avon CC, 1979; Dep. County Treasurer, Staffordshire CC, 1981. *Publications:* various articles in local govt finance jls. *Recreations:* music, gardening, travel. *T:* (office) Stafford 3121, ext. 6300; (home) Stafford 660085.

SMITH, Ven. Brian Arthur; Archdeacon of Craven, since 1987; *b* 15 Aug. 1943; *s* of Arthur and Doris Marion Smith; *m* 1970, Elizabeth Berring (*née* Hutchinson); two *d. Educ:* George Heriot's School, Edinburgh; Edinburgh Univ. (MA Mental Philosophy 1966); Fitzwilliam Coll., Cambridge (BA Theology 1968, MA 1972); Westcott House, Cambridge; Jesus Coll., Cambridge (MLitt 1973). Curate of Cuddesdon, 1972–79; Tutor in Doctrine, Cuddesdon Coll., Oxford, 1972–75; Dir of Studies, Ripon Coll., Cuddesdon, 1975–78, Senior Tutor 1978–79. Diocese of Wakefield: Priest-in-charge of Cragg Vale, 1979–85; Dir of In-Service Training, 1979–81; Dir of Ministerial Trng, 1981–87; Warden of Readers, 1981–87; Sec. of Dio. Board of Ministry, 1979–87; Hon. Canon of Wakefield, 1981–87; Proctor in Convocation, 1985–87. Vice-Chairman, Northern Ordination Course, 1985–. A Director, Scottish Jl of Theology, 1977–81. *Recreations:* browsing in junk shops, walking, reading, music, short-wave radio listening. *Address:* Brooklands, Bridge End, Long Preston, Skipton BD23 4RD. *T:* Long Preston 334. *Club:* National Liberal.

SMITH, Ven. Brian John; Archdeacon of Wilts, since 1980; *b* 21 Sept. 1933; *s* of Stanley and Doris Jessie Smith; *m* 1965, Jean Margaret, *d* of Frank and Beryl Hanning; one *s* two *d. Educ:* St Marylebone Grammar School; Mill Hill School; St John's Coll., Durham; Salisbury Theological Coll. Army, 1952–55; professional photographer, 1956–62. Ordained, 1965; Curate of All Saints', Whitstable, 1965–69; Vicar of Woodford, Wilsford and Durnford, and Religious Drama Adviser to Diocese of Salisbury, 1969–76; Vicar of Mere, West Knoyle and Maiden Bradley, 1976–80; RD of Heytesbury, 1977–80; Vicar of Bishop's Cannings, All Cannings and Etchilhampton, 1980–83; Non-residentiary Canon, Salisbury Cath., 1980–. Member: Gen. Synod of C of E, 1985–; Council of RADIUS (Religious Drama Soc. of GB), 1971–76; various cttees, Diocese of Salisbury, 1969–; Chm., Diocesan Christian Giving Cttee, 1983–. Author of a number of plays. *Publication:* contrib. to Religious Drama. *Recreations:* drama, photography, canals. *Address:* The Vicarage, White Street, West Lavington, Devizes, Wilts SN10 4LW. *T:* Lavington 8388.

SMITH, Brian Percival, CEng, FIProdE; CBIM; independent business consultant; Associate, PA Management Consultants, since 1984; *b* 3 Oct. 1919; *s* of Percival Smith and Hilda Judge; *m* 1943, Phoebe (Tina) Ginno; one *s. Educ:* Erith, Woolwich; London Univ. (BSc). Apprentice, 1936–41, Manager, 1941–46, Royal Ordnance Factories; Gen. Manager, Cumbrian Tool Co., 1946–49; PA Management Consultants: Consultant, 1949–59; Dir, R&D, 1959–66; Man. Dir, 1966–72; Chm. of Bd, 1972–76. Mem., CAA, 1981–84. Mem., Design Council, 1975–80; Vice-Pres., Royal Soc. of Arts, 1976–80. Prof. of Design Management, RCA, 1977–81. Member Council: BIM, 1972–74; Instn of Prod. Engrs, 1972– (Pres., 1973–74). *Publications:* Leadership in Management, 1968; Bureaucracy in Management, 1969; Management Style, 1973; Going into Europe, Why and How, 1975; The Morality and Management of Design, 1977. *Recreations:* painting, writing, listening to music. *Address:* 4 Cliff Road, Eastbourne, East Sussex BN20 7RU. *T:* Eastbourne 31870.

SMITH, Brian Stanley, FSA, FRHistS; Secretary, Royal Commission on Historical Manuscripts, since 1982; *b* 15 May 1932; *s* of late Ernest Stanley Smith and Dorothy (*née* Palmer); *m* 1963, Alison Margaret Hemming; two *d. Educ:* Bloxham; Keble College, Oxford (Holroyd Scholar). MA 1957. FSA 1972, FRHistS 1980. Assistant Archivist, Worcestershire, 1956–58, Essex, 1958–60, Gloucestershire, 1961–68; County Archivist, Gloucestershire, 1968–79; Asst Sec., Royal Commn on Historical Manuscripts, 1980–81. Part-time Editor, Victoria County History of Gloucestershire, 1968–70; Editor, 1971–79, Pres., 1986–, Bristol and Gloucestershire Archaeological Soc. Chm., Soc. of Archivists, 1979–80. Mem., Cttee of Management, Inst. of Historical Res., London Univ., 1982–.

Lay Mem., Gloucester Diocesan Synod, 1972–76. *Publications:* History of Malvern, 1964, 2nd edn 1978; (with Elizabeth Ralph) History of Bristol and Gloucestershire, 1972, 2nd edn 1982; The Cotswolds, 1976; History of Bloxham School, 1978; articles in learned jls on local history and archives. *Recreations:* mountaineering, gardening. *Address:* Midwoods, Shire Lane, Cholesbury, Tring, Herts HP23 6NA.

SMITH, Maj.-Gen. Sir Brian W.; *see* Wyldbore-Smith.

SMITH, Brian William, PhD, FIEAust; Director, Royal Melbourne Institute of Technology, since 1979; *b* 24 June 1938; *s* of William Lyle Smith and Grace Ellen Smith; *m* 1961, Josephine Peden; two *d* (one *s* decd). *Educ:* Univ. of Melbourne (BEng); Univ. of Cambridge (PhD). MIEE, SMIREE Aust. Australian Paper Manufacturers Ltd, 1964–70; Consolidated Electronic Industries Ltd, 1971–73; Head, School of Electrical Engineering, 1973–77, Dean, Faculty of Engineering, 1977–79, Royal Melbourne Inst. of Technology. *Recreations:* golf, model railway. *Address:* 60 Faraday Street, Carlton, Victoria 3093, Australia. *T:* 347 9341. *Clubs:* Athenæum; Greenacres Golf, Melbourne Cricket.

SMITH, Bryan Crossley, CBE 1982; CEng, FIGasE; Member for Marketing, British Gas Corporation, 1977–82; Chairman: C.S.E. (Wendover) Ltd, Business Consultants, since 1985; Sports & Fitness Assessment (Harley Street) Ltd, since 1985; *b* 28 Feb. 1925; *s* of Frank Riley Smith and Fanny Smith; *m* 1948, Patricia Mabbott; one *s* one *d. Educ:* Hipperholme Grammar Sch.; Bradford Technical Coll. CEng, FIGasE 1944. Articled pupil to John Corrigan, 1941; Operating Engr, Humphreys & Glasgow, 1944; Works Engr, Middlesbrough Corp. Gas Dept, 1948; N Eastern Gas Board: Asst Works Manager, Huddersfield, 1952; Engr and Man., Dewsbury, 1956; Group Sales Man., Wakefield, 1961; Conversion Man., 1966; Dep. Commercial Man., 1968; Chief Service Man., Gas Council, 1970; Service Dir, British Gas Corp., 1973. Senior Vice-Pres., IGasE, 1980–81. Chm., Wendover Soc., 1985–. *Recreations:* golf, gardening. *Address:* Heron Path House, Wendover, Aylesbury, Bucks HP22 6NN. *T:* Wendover 622742.

SMITH, Campbell (Sherston); retired; *b* 24 April 1906; *s* of Herbert Smith and Carlotta Amelia Smith (*née* Newbury); *m* 1st, 1936, Leonora Florence Beeney (marr. diss., 1948); one *s*; 2nd, 1948, Gwenllian Elizabeth Anne Williams (marr. diss., 1963); one *s*; 3rd, 1964, Barbara Irene Winstone. *Educ:* City of London School. General Departmental Manager, Keith Prowse & Co. Ltd, 1932, Director and General Manager, 1936. Squadron Leader, RAF, 1939–45 (Defence Medal). Assistant Managing Director, Keith Prowse & Co. Ltd, 1945; Managing Director, 1951–54; Managing Director: Mechanical Copyright Protection Soc., 1945–57; Campbell Williams Ltd, 1960–75; Director: Performing Right Society, 1951–54; MEEC Productions Ltd, 1953–62; Proprietor, Mayfair Hotel, Worthing, 1964–75. Administrator of the Arts Theatre Club, 1954–62: *principal productions:* Saint Joan, 1954; The Immoralist, 1954; South, 1955; Waiting for Godot, 1955; Waltz of the Toreadors, 1956; The Bald Prima Donna, 1956; No Laughing Matter, 1957; The Balcony, 1957; The Iceman Cometh, 1958; The Imperial Nightingale, 1958; Madame de . . . . ., 1959; Traveller without Luggage, 1959; Ulysses in Nighttown, 1959; A Moon for the Misbegotten, 1959; The Caretaker, 1959; The Naked Island, 1960; Three, 1961; Stop It Whoever You Are, 1961; The Knacker's Yard, 1962; Everything in the Garden, 1962. *Recreation:* theatre. *Address:* 32 Wordsworth Road, Worthing, West Sussex. *Clubs:* Garrick, Arts Theatre.

SMITH, Catharine Mary S.; *see* Scott-Smith.

SMITH, Maj.-Gen. Sir Cecil (Miller), KBE 1951 (CBE 1944; OBE 1941); CB 1947; MC; CEng, MIMechE; psc; late RASC; *b* 17 June 1896; *s* of John Smith, Dromore, Co. Down; *m* 1930, Isabel Buswell; two *d. Educ:* Royal Belfast Academical Institution; Royal Military College, Sandhurst; Staff College, Camberley. Served European War, 1914–19, ASC and Royal Inniskilling Fusiliers. France and Belgium, 1916–18 (wounded, MC, two medals); Served War, 1939–45: ME, 1939–44; NW Europe, 1944–45; Maj.-Gen., 1943; DQMG (Army Equipment) ME, 1943–44; DACOS, SHAEF, 1944–45; Maj.-Gen. in charge of Administration, Northern Command, 1945–47; Chief of Staff, Northern Command, 1947–48; Director of Supplies and Transport, War Office, 1948–51; retired pay, 1951. Col Comdt, RASC, 1950–60. Chm. Ulster Society in London, 1964–73. Commander, Legion of Merit, US; Officier de la Légion d'Honneur (France). *Address:* Crosh, Southfield Place, Weybridge, Surrey. *T:* Weybridge 42199.

SMITH, Sheriff Charles; Sheriff of Glasgow and Strathkelvin (floating appointment), since 1982; *b* 15 Aug. 1930; *s* of late Charles Smith and of Mary Allan Hunter or Smith; *m* 1959, Janet Elizabeth Hurst; one *s* one *d. Educ:* Kinnoull Primary Sch.; Perth Academy; St Andrews University. MA, LLB. Solicitor 1956. Practised as principal in Perth, 1961–82; Temporary Sheriff, 1977–82. Hon. Tutor, Dept of Law, Dundee Univ., 1982–. Mem. Council, Law Soc. of Scotland, 1977–82 (Convener, various cttees). Mem., Perth Town Council, 1966–68. *Recreations:* tennis, golf, croquet. *Address:* c/o Sheriff Court, Ingram Street, Glasgow G1 1SY. *T:* 041–552 3434. *Clubs:* Western (Glasgow); Kinnoull LTC.

SMITH, Sir Charles B.; *see* Bracewell-Smith.

SMITH, Charles Edward Gordon, CB 1970; MD, FRCP, FRCPath; Dean, London School of Hygiene and Tropical Medicine, since 1971; *b* 12 May 1924; *s* of late John A. and Margaret Smith, Lundin Links, Fife; *m* 1948, Elsie, *d* of late S. S. McClellan, Lorton, Cumberland; one *s* two *d. Educ:* Forfar Academy; St Andrews University. MB, ChB (with commendation) 1947; MD (with hons and Singapore Gold Medal) 1956. House Surgeon and Physician, Cumberland Infirmary, Carlisle, 1947–48; HM Colonial Medical Service, 1948–57; Clinical appts Malacca, Kuala Lumpur, 1949–51; Virologist, Inst. for Med. Research, Kuala Lumpur, 1952–57; Sen. Lectr in Bacteriology, London Sch. of Hygiene and Trop. Med., 1957–61; Reader in Virology, London Sch. of Hygiene and Trop. Med., 1961–64; Director, Microbiological Research Estab., MoD, 1964–70. Chairman: Public Health Lab. Service Bd, 1972–; Independent Commn on the Onchocerciasis Control Programme, 1979–81. A Wellcome Trustee, 1972– (Dep. Chm., 1983–); Pres., Royal Soc. of Tropical Medicine and Hygiene, 1975–77; Pres., Assoc. of Schs of Public Health in the European Region, 1979–81 (Pres.-elect 1977–79); Vice-Pres., Zoological Soc. of London, 1974–76, 1978–82, 1985–86. Chalmers Medal, Royal Soc. of Trop. Med. and Hygiene, 1961; Stewart Prize, BMA, 1973; Tulloch Award, Dundee, 1982. Hon. DSc St Andrews, 1975. *Publications:* papers mainly on tropical diseases and third world development. *Recreations:* gardening, golf. *Address:* London School of Hygiene and Tropical Medicine, Keppel Street, WC1E 7HT. *Clubs:* Savile; Bramshaw Golf.

SMITH, Charles Nugent C.; *see* Close-Smith.

SMITH, Charles Russell, CBE 1984; Chief Executive since 1963, and Chairman since 1983, Allied Textile Companies PLC; Regional Chairman, Yorkshire and Humberside, Lloyds Bank plc, since 1984 (Regional Director, since 1973); *b* 19 Aug. 1925; *m* 1951, Jean Rita Thomas; one *s* three *d. Educ:* Rastrick Grammar Sch., Brighouse, W Yorks. Served War, RNVR, 1943–46 (commnd). Armitage and Norton, Chartered Accountants, Huddersfield, 1941–50; Dir, subseq. Man. Dir, R. Beanland and Co. Ltd, 1950–63.

Director: Yorkshire Bank PLC, 1978–84; Lloyds Bank UK Management Ltd, 1984–85; Lloyds & Scottish PLC, 1985–; Lloyds Bank PLC, 1985–. Pres., British Textile Confedn, 1982 and 1983; Chm., Wakefield Diocesan Bd of Finance, 1974–; Mem., Yorks and Humberside Regional Develt Bd, 1975–79. Liveryman, Co. of Woolmen, 1982. *Recreations:* travel, caravanning, walking. *Address:* Broom House, West Bretton, Wakefield, West Yorks WF4 4LE. *T:* Bretton 232. *Clubs:* Naval and Military; Huddersfield and Borough (Huddersfield).

SMITH, Dr Charles Stuart, FEng 1985; FRINA; Head of Structures Research, Admiralty Research Establishment, since 1982; *b* 21 April 1936; *s* of Ebenezer and Mary Smith; *m* 1962, Colette Marie Claude Paulicand; one *s* three *d*. *Educ:* George Watson's College; Glasgow University (BSc, PhD, DSc). MIStructE. Joined Naval Construction Research Establishment, 1962; Head of Ship Structures Division, 1974. *Recreations:* squash, sailing, ski-ing. *Address:* Broomrigg, Dollar, Clackmannanshire FK14 7PT. *T:* Dollar 2703.

SMITH, Prof. (Christopher) Colin; Professor of Spanish, University of Cambridge, since 1975; *b* 17 Sept. 1927; *s* of Alfred Edward Smith and Dorothy May Berry; *m* 1954, Ruth Margaret Barnes; three *d* (one *s* decd). *Educ:* Varndean Grammar Sch., Brighton; St Catharine's Coll., Cambridge (MA, PhD; LittD). BA 1st cl. hons 1950. Dept of Spanish, Univ. of Leeds: Asst Lectr 1953; Lectr 1956; Sen. Lectr 1964; Sub-Dean of Arts, etc, 1963–67; Cambridge Univ.: Univ. Lectr in Spanish, 1968; Fellow, St Catharine's Coll., 1968–, Professorial Fellow, 1975–, Tutor 1970; Chm. Faculty of Mod. and Med. Langs, 1973. General Editor, Modern Language Review, 1976–81 (Hispanic Editor, 1974–81). *Publications:* Spanish Ballads, 1964; (ed) Poema de mio Cid, 1972, Spanish edn, 1976; Collins' Spanish-English, English-Spanish Dictionary, 1971, Spanish edn 1972; Estudios cidianos, 1977; (with A. L. F. Rivet) Place-names of Roman Britain, 1979; The Making of the Poema de mio Cid, 1983; contrib. Bull. Hispanic Studies, Mod. Lang. Rev., Bull. Hispanique, etc. *Recreations:* theatre, opera, squash, natural history (especially entomology), archaeology. *Address:* 56 Girton Road, Cambridge. *T:* Cambridge 276214.

SMITH, Rev. Christopher Hughes; Chairman of Birmingham Methodist District, since 1974; President of the Methodist Conference, 1985–86; *b* 30 Nov. 1929; *s* of Rev. Bernard Hughes Smith and Dorothy Lucy Smith; *m* 1956, Margaret Jean Smith; three *s* and one foster *s*. *Educ:* Bolton School; Emmanuel College and Wesley House, Cambridge. MA Cantab. Intercollegiate Sec., SCM, 1955–58; ordained at Methodist Conf., Newcastle upon Tyne, 1958; Leicester South Methodist Circuit, 1958–65; Birmingham South-West Methodist Circuit, 1965–74. Hon. MA Birmingham. *Publications:* contribs to Birmingham Post, Methodist Recorder, Epworth Review. *Recreations:* gardening, music, books, walking. *Address:* 36 Amesbury Road, Moseley, Birmingham B13 8LE. *T:* 021–449 0131. *Club:* Royal Commonwealth Society.

SMITH, Christopher Robert, PhD; MP (Lab) Islington South and Finsbury, since 1983; *b* 24 July 1951; *s* of Colin Smith and Gladys (*née* Luscombe). *Educ:* Cassiobury Primary Sch., Watford; George Watson's Coll., Edinburgh; Pembroke Coll., Cambridge Univ. (BA 1st Cl. Hons 1972, PhD 1979); Harvard Univ., Mass (Kennedy Scholar, 1975–76). Develt Sec., Shaftesbury Soc. Housing Assoc., 1977–80; Develt Co-ordinator, Soc. for Co-operative Dwellings, 1980–83. Councillor, London Bor. of Islington, 1978–83 (Chief Whip, 1978–79; Chm., Housing Cttee, 1981–83). Sec., Tribune Gp of MPs, 1985–; Chm., Labour Campaign for Criminal Justice, 1985–. Pres., Cambridge Union, 1972; Vice-Chm., Young Fabian Gp, 1974–75; Chm., Charing Cross Br., ASTMS, 1980–83; Exec., NCCL, 1986–. *Recreations:* mountaineering, literature, theatre, music. *Address:* Top Flat, 78 Barnsbury Road, N1 0ES. *T:* 01–837 1884.

SMITH, Sir Christopher Sydney Winwood, 5th Bt, *cr* 1809; *b* 20 Sept. 1906; *s* of Sir William Sydney Winwood Smith, 4th Bt, and Caroline, *o d* of James Harris, County Cork; *S* father 1953; *m* 1932, Phyllis Berenice, *y d* of late Thomas Robert O'Grady, Grafton, New South Wales, and County Waterford, Ireland; three *s* two *d*. *Heir:* *s* Robert Sydney Winwood Smith, *b* 1939. *Address:* Junction Road, via Grafton, New South Wales 2460, Australia.

SMITH, Claude C.; *see* Croxton-Smith.

SMITH, Clifford Bertram Bruce H.; *see* Heathcote-Smith.

SMITH, Colin; *see* Smith, Christopher C.

SMITH, Colin; International Executive Director, National Anti-Vivisection Society Ltd, since 1981; *b* 4 July 1941; *s* of Henry E. Smith and A. E. Smith. *Educ:* Upton House Sch., London. Asst Sec., National Anti-Vivisection Soc., 1962–71, Gen. Sec., 1971–81. Hon. Sec., Internat. Assoc. Against Painful Experiments on Animals, 1969–; Dir, American Fund for Alternatives to Animal Res., 1977–. Mem., Hon. Nederlandse Laureat van de Arbeid, 1981. Editor, Animals' Defender and Anti-Vivisection News, 1967–72, 1982–. *Publications:* Progress without Pain, 1973; Animal Experiments: steps towards reform, 1975; Moral and Social Aspects of Vivisection, 1981; numerous contribs to med. and scientific jls on the anti-vivisection case. *Recreations:* music, travel, gardening. *Address:* 51 Harley Street, W1N 1DD. *T:* 01–580 4034; (home) 29 College Place, St Albans, Herts.

SMITH, Colin Milner; QC 1985; *b* 2 Nov. 1936; *s* of Alan Milner Smith and late Vera Ivy Smith; *m* 1979, Moira Soraya, *d* of Reginald Braybrooke; one *s*. *Educ:* Tonbridge; Brasenose College, Oxford (BA); Univ. of Chicago (JD). Called to the Bar, Gray's Inn, 1962. *Recreations:* cricket, skiing, reading. *Address:* 3 Gray's Inn Place, Gray's Inn, WC1R 5DU. *T:* 01–831 8441. *Club:* MCC.

SMITH, Colin Roderick, CVO 1984; Chief Constable, Thames Valley Police, since 1985; *b* 26 March 1941; *s* of Humphrey and Marie Smith; *m* 1961, Patricia Joan Coppin. *Educ:* Dorking County and Bexhill Grammar Schools; Univ. of Birmingham (BSocSc, Hons Social Admin.); rcds 1981. Royal Army Service Corps (Lieut), 18 Co. (Amph), 1959–62; East Sussex Constabulary, later Sussex Police, from Constable to Chief Supt, 1962–77; Asst Chief Constable, Thames Valley Police, 1977–82; Dep. Asst Comr, Metropolitan Police, 1982–85 (incl. founder, Royalty and Diplomatic Protection Dept). *Recreation:* horse riding. *Address:* Thames Valley Police Headquarters, Kidlington, Oxford OX5 2NX. *T:* Kidlington 4343. *Club:* Naval and Military.

SMITH, Cyril, MBE 1966; MP (L) Rochdale, since Oct. 1972; Liberal Chief Whip, 1975–76; Managing Director, Smith Springs (Rochdale) Ltd, since 1963; *b* 28 June 1928; unmarried. *Educ:* Rochdale Grammar Sch. for Boys. Civil Service, 1944–45; Wages Clerk, 1945–48; Liberal Party Agent, Stockport, 1948–50; Labour Party Agent, Ashton-under-Lyne, 1950–53, Heywood and Royton 1953–55; rejoined Liberal Party, 1967. Newsagent (own account), 1955–58; Production Controller, Spring Manufacturing, 1958–63; founded Smith Springs (Rochdale) Ltd, 1963. Councillor, 1952–66, Alderman, 1966–74, Mayor, 1966–67, Co. Borough of Rochdale (Chm., Education Cttee, 1966–72); Councillor, Rochdale Metropolitan DC, 1973–75. A Dep. Pro-Chancellor, Lancaster Univ., 1978–86. OStJ 1976. *Publications:* Big Cyril (autobiog.), 1977; Industrial Participation, 1977. *Recreations:* music (listener), reading, charitable work, local government. *Address:* 14 Emma Street, Rochdale, Lancs. *T:* Rochdale 48840.

SMITH, Cyril Robert, OBE 1945; consultant and lecturer; *b* 28 Dec. 1907; *s* of late Robert Smith and Rose Smith (*née* Sommerville); *m* 1933, Margaret Jane Kathleen Gwladys Hughes; two *s*. *Educ:* Whitgift; Queen Mary's Coll., Univ. of London. Served in Army, Europe, N Africa, 1939–45 (despatches, OBE; Col). Entered PO as Asst Traffic Supt Telephones, 1927; Asst Inspector, Telephone Traffic PO Headquarters, 1930; Asst Surveyor, Postal Services, 1935; Asst Principal, PO Headquarters, 1936; Asst Postal Controller, 1941; Instructor, PO Management Training Centre, 1954; Postal Controller, 1955; Asst Sec. i/c of Central Organisation and Methods Br., PO Headquarters, 1958; Director, Computer Development, 1965–67; Dir, National Data Processing, GPO, 1967–68. UN Advisor to Greek Govt on computers in public service, 1971–74. FBCS; FBIM. *Publications:* various papers on computer matters in Computer Jl, etc. *Address:* 64 Copse Avenue, West Wickham, Kent. *T:* 01–777 1100.

SMITH, Cyril Stanley, CBE 1985; MSc, PhD; Managing Director, ReStrat, since 1985; Secretary to Economic and Social Research Council (formerly Social Science Research Council), 1975–85; *b* 21 July 1925; *s* of Walter and Beatrice May Smith; *m* 1968, Eileen Cameron; two *d* (by first marr.). *Educ:* Plaistow Municipal Secondary Sch.; London Sch. of Economics. HM Forces, Dorset Regt, 1943–47. Univ. of Birmingham, 1950–51; Univ. of Sheffield, 1951–52; Dulwich Coll. Mission, 1952–56; Nat. Coal Board, 1956–61; Univ. of Manchester, 1961–71; Civil Service Coll., 1971–75. Visiting Prof., Univ. of Virginia, 1965; Academic Visitor, Nuffield Coll., Oxford, 1980–81, 1985–86. British Nat. Expert, European Poverty Prog., 1977–82. Mem., Sec. of State's Cttee on Inequalities in Health, DHSS, 1977–80. Chm., British Sociological Assoc., 1972–74; Pres., Sociol. Sect., British Assoc., 1979. *Publications:* Adolescence, 1968; (sen. author) The Wincroft Youth Project, 1972; (ed jtly) Society and Leisure in Britain, 1973; numerous articles on youth, leisure and developments in social science. *Recreations:* gardening, domestic technology. *Address:* Cornwall House, Cornwall Gardens, SW7 4AE.

SMITH, Dan; *see* Smith, T. D.

SMITH, Prof. David; *see* Smith, Prof. A. D.

SMITH, Prof. David; *see* Smith, Prof. N. J. D.

SMITH, David, PhD, FInstPet; Chairman and Managing Director, Esso Chemical Ltd, since 1978; *b* 18 July 1927; *s* of Walter and Annie Smith; *m* 1951, Nancy Elizabeth (*née* Hawley); two *s* three *d*. *Educ:* Burton Grammar School; Univ. of Sheffield. BSc, PhD. Lectr in Fuel Technology and Chemical Engineering, Univ. of Sheffield, 1951–55; Esso Research Ltd, 1955–65; Dir, Products Research Div., Esso Research and Engineering, USA, 1966–68; Marketing Dir and Man. Dir, Esso Chemical Ltd, 1968–71; Vice-Pres., Essochem Europe Inc., Brussels, 1971–73; Vice-Pres., Exxon Chemical Inc., USA, 1973–78. *Recreation:* golf. *Address:* Meadowlands, Stockbridge Road, Winchester, Hants SO22 5JH. *T:* Winchester 64880. *Clubs:* MCC; Royal Southampton Yacht; Royal Winchester Golf.

SMITH, David Arthur, QC 1982; **His Honour Judge David Smith;** a Circuit Judge, since 1986; *b* 7 May 1938; *s* of late Arthur Heber Smith and of Marjorie Edith Pounds Smith; *m* 1967, Clementine Smith (*née* Urquhart); two *s*. *Educ:* Lancing College; Merton Coll., Oxford (MA Hons Jurisprudence). Called to Bar, Middle Temple, 1962; Official Principal of Archdeaconry of Hackney, 1973–; a Recorder, 1978–86. Wine Treasurer, Western Circuit, 1980–85. *Publications:* John Evelyn's Manuscript on Bees from Elysium Britannicum, 1966; Bibliography of British Bee Books, 1979. *Recreations:* bees (Sec. of Internat. Bee Research Assoc., 1963–), books, canals, Rossini. *Address:* Bristol Crown Court, Guildhall, Bristol.

SMITH, David Arthur George, JP; Headmaster of Bradford Grammar School, since 1974; *b* 17 Dec. 1934; *o s* of Stanley George and Winifred Smith, Bath, Somerset; *m* 1957, Jennifer, *e d* of John and Rhoda Anning, Launceston, Cornwall; one *s* two *d*. *Educ:* City of Bath Boys' Sch.; Balliol Coll., Oxford. MA, Dip. Ed (Oxon). Assistant Master, Manchester Grammar Sch., 1957–62; Head of History, Rossall School, 1963–70; Headmaster, The King's School, Peterborough, 1970–74. JP West Yorks, 1975. FRSA 1985. *Publications:* (with John Thorn and Roger Lockyer) A History of England, 1961; Left and Right in Twentieth Century Europe, 1970; Russia of the Tsars, 1971. *Recreations:* writing, cricket. *Address:* Bradford Grammar School, Bradford, West Yorks. *T:* Bradford 45461. *Club:* Bradford Athenæum (Bradford).

SMITH, David Buchanan; Sheriff of North Strathclyde at Kilmarnock, since 1975; *b* 31 Oct. 1936; *s* of William Adam Smith and Irene Mary Calderwood Hogarth; *m* 1961, Hazel Mary Sinclair; two *s* one *d*. *Educ:* Paisley Grammar Sch.; Glasgow Univ. (MA); Edinburgh Univ. (LLB). Advocate, 1961; Standing Junior Counsel to Scottish Educn Dept, 1968–75. Trustee, The Scottish Curling Museum Trust, 1980–. *Publications:* Curling: an illustrated history, 1981; The Roaring Game: memories of Scottish curling, 1985; articles in Scots Law Times, Juridical Rev. and newspapers. *Recreations:* Scottish and legal history, curling, music. *Address:* 72 South Beach, Troon, Ayrshire. *T:* Troon 312130; Sheriff's Chambers, Sheriff Court House, Kilmarnock. *T:* Kilmarnock 20211.

SMITH, Sir David (Cecil), Kt 1986; FRS 1975; Sibthorpian Professor of Rural Economy, Oxford University, since 1980; Fellow of St John's College, Oxford, since 1980; *b* 21 May 1930; *s* of William John Smith and Elva Emily Smith; *m* 1965, Lesley Margaret Mollison Mutch; two *s* one *d*. *Educ:* Colston's Sch., Bristol; St Paul's Sch., London; Queen's Coll., Oxford (Browne Schol., MA, DPhil). Christopher Welch Res. Schol., Oxford, 1951–54; Swedish Inst. Schol., Uppsala Univ., 1951–52; Browne Res. Fellow, Queen's Coll., Oxford, 1956–59; Harkness Fellow, Univ. Calif, Berkeley, 1959–60; Univ. Lectr, Dept Agric., Oxford Univ., 1960–74; Royal Soc. Res. Fellow, Wadham Coll., 1964–71; Tutorial Fellow and Tutor for Admissions, Wadham Coll., Oxford, 1971–74; Melville Wills Prof. of Botany, 1974–80, and Dir of Biological Studies, 1977–79, Bristol Univ. Vis. Prof., Univ. Calif, Los Angeles, 1968. Chairman: NERC Aquatic Life Scis Cttee, 1978–81; Subject Area Rev. Cttee in Biol. Sci., London Univ., 1982–; Member: NERC Terrestrial Life Scis Cttee, 1975–78; AFRC (formerly ARC), 1982– (Mem. Plants and Soils Cttee, 1976– (Chm., 1983–)); Consultative Bd, JCO for Res. in Agric. and Food, 1981–83; SERC Science Board, 1983–85 (Chm., SERC Biol Scis Cttee, 1981–83); Royal Soc. Assessor, ARC, 1978–80. President: British Lichen Soc., 1972–74; British Mycological Soc., 1980; Soc. for Experimental Biol., 1983–85 (Vice-Pres., 1981–83); Royal Society: a Vice-Pres., 1978–80, 1983–; Biological Sec., 1983–. Bidder Lecture, Soc. for Experimental Biology, 1985. Editor and Trustee, New Phytologist, 1965–. Hon. DSc: Liverpool, 1986; Exeter, 1986. *Publications:* (with A. Douglas) The Biology of Symbiosis, 1987; various articles on symbiosis, in New Phytol., Proc. Royal Soc., Biol. Rev., etc. *Address:* The Old Dog, 18 School Road, Kidlington, Oxford OX5 2HB. *T:* Kidlington 3126.

SMITH, David Douglas R.; *see* Rae Smith, D. D.

SMITH, David Dury H.; *see* Hindley-Smith.

SMITH, David Grahame G.; *see* Grahame-Smith.

SMITH, Air Marshal Sir David H.; *see* Harcourt-Smith.

SMITH, David Iser, AO 1986; CVO 1977; BA; Official Secretary to the Governor-General of Australia, since 1973; Secretary of the Order of Australia, since 1975; *b* 9 Aug. 1933; *s* of late W. M. Smith; *m* 1955, June F., *d* of M. A. W. Forestier; three *s*. *Educ:* Scotch Coll., Melbourne; Melbourne Univ.; Australian National Univ., Canberra (BA). Commnd CMF, Melb. Univ. Regt, 1956. Entered Aust. Public Service, 1954; Dept of Customs and Excise, Melb., 1954–57; Trng Officer, Dept of the Interior, Canberra, 1957–58; Private Sec. to Minister for the Interior and Minister for Works, 1958–63; Exec. Asst to Sec., Dept of the Interior, 1963–66; Exec. Officer (Govt), Dept of the Interior, 1966–69; Sen. Adviser, Govt Br., Prime Minister's Dept, 1969–71; Sec., Federal Exec. Council, 1971–73; Asst Sec., Govt Br., Dept of the Prime Minister and Cabinet, 1972–73. Attached to The Queen's Household, Buckingham Palace, June-July 1975. Dist Comr, Capital Hill Dist, Scout Assoc. of Australia, 1971–74. CStJ 1974. *Recreations:* music, reading. *Address:* Government House, Canberra, ACT 2600, Australia. *T:* 81.1211. *Club:* Commonwealth (Canberra).

SMITH, Ven. David James; Archdeacon of Lindisfarne, since 1981; *b* 14 July 1935; *s* of Stanley James and Gwendolen Emie Smith; *m* 1961, Mary Hunter Moult; one *s* one *d*. *Educ:* Hertford Grammar School; King's College, London (AKC). Assistant Curate: All Saints, Gosforth, 1959–62; St Francis, High Heaton, 1962–64; Long Benton, 1964–68; Vicar: Longhirst with Hebron, 1968–75; St Mary, Monkseaton, 1975–81; Felton, 1982–83. *Recreations:* fell walking, reading science fiction. *Address:* 12 Rectory Park, Morpeth, Northumberland NE61 2SZ. *T:* Morpeth 513207.

SMITH, David John Leslie, PhD; CEng, FRAeS; Deputy Director (Planning), Admiralty Research Establishment, since 1986; *b* 8 Oct. 1938; *s* of Gertrude Mary and late Arthur George Smith; *m* 1962, Wendy Lavinia (*née* Smith); two *d*. *Educ:* Cinderford Tech. Coll.; N Glos Tech. Coll.; Coll. of Aeronautics (MSc); Univ. of London; rcds. Mech. Engrg Apprentice, Rotol Ltd, 1954–59; Nat. Gas Turbine Estabt, Min. of Aviation, 1961, Head of Turbomachinery Dept, 1973; RCDS 1979; Ministry of Defence (PE): Dir, Aircraft Mech. and Elect. Equipment, Controllerate of Aircraft, 1980–81; Head of Aero. Dept, RAE, 1981–84; Dep. Dir (Marine Technology), Admiralty Res. Estabt, 1984–85. *Publications:* contribs to learned jls on gas turbine technology and fluid mechanics. *Recreation:* garden, including exhibiting flowers. *Address:* Admiralty Research Establishment, Procurement Executive, Ministry of Defence, Portsdown, Portsmouth, Hants PO6 4AA. *T:* Cosham 379411.

SMITH, Very Rev. David MacIntyre Bell Armour; Minister at Logie Kirk, Stirling, since 1965; Moderator of the General Assembly of the Church of Scotland, 1985–86; *b* 5 April 1923; *s* of Frederick Smith and Matilda Shearer; *m* 1960, Mary Kulvear Cumming; three *s*. *Educ:* Monkton Combe School; Peebles High School; St Andrews Univ. (MA 1947, BD 1950; Cook and Macfarlan Scholar). Served as Pilot, RAF, 1942–45. Warrender Church, Edinburgh, 1951–60; Old Partick Parish, Glasgow, 1960–65. Member: Stirlingshire Education Cttee, 1969–79; Central Region Educn Cttee, 1986–; Chm., Church of Scotland Bd of Education, 1979–83. DUniv Stirling, 1983. *Recreations:* gardening, philately. *Address:* 34 Airthrey Road, Stirling FK9 5JS. *T:* Stirling 75085.

SMITH, Delia; cookery writer and broadcaster; *m* Michael Wynn Jones. Several BBC TV series; cookery writer, Evening Standard, later the Standard, 1972–85; columnist, Radio Times. Is a Roman Catholic. *Publications:* How to Cheat at Cooking, 1973; Country Fare, 1973; Recipes from Country Inns and Restaurants, 1973; Family Fare, book 1, 1973, book 2, 1974; Evening Standard Cook Book, 1974; Country recipes from "Look East", 1975; More Country Recipes from "Look East", 1976; Frugal Food, 1976; Book of Cakes, 1977; Recipes from "Look East", 1977; Food for our Times, 1978; Cookery Course, part 1, 1978, part 2, 1979, part 3, 1981, The Complete Cookery Course, 1982; A Feast for Lent, 1983; A Feast for Advent, 1983; One is Fun, 1985; (ed) Food Aid Cookery Book, 1986. *Address:* c/o BBC Publications, 35 Marylebone High Street, W1M 4AA.

SMITH, Denis M.; *see* Mack Smith.

SMITH, Derek B.; *see* Bryce-Smith.

SMITH, Derek Cyril; Under-Secretary, Export Credits Guarantee Department, 1974–87, retired; *b* 29 Jan. 1927; *s* of Albert Cyril and Edith Mary Elizabeth Smith; *m* 1st, 1949, Ursula Kulich (marr. diss. 1967); two *d*; 2nd, 1967, Nina Munday; one *s*. *Educ:* Pinner Grammar Sch.; St Catherine's Soc., Oxford. BA Mod. History 1951. Asst Principal, Min. of Materials, 1952–55; BoT, 1955–57: Asst Private Sec., Minister of State; Private Sec., Parly Sec.; Principal, ECGD, 1958–67; Asst Sec., BoT and DTI, 1967–72: Sec. to Lord Cromer's Survey of Capital Projects Contracting Overseas; Asst Sec., ECGD, 1972–74. *Recreations:* walking, reading, model-building.

SMITH, Derek Edward H.; *see* Hill-Smith.

SMITH, Derek Frank; Consultant, World Bank, 1986; *b* 11 Feb. 1929; *s* of Frank H. and late Rose V. Smith; *m* 1954, Anne Carpenter; one *s* one *d*. *Educ:* Chatham House Sch., Ramsgate. Served RAF, 1947–49. Colonial Office, 1949–66: Sec., Develt and Welfare Org. in WI, 1956–58; transf. to Min. of Overseas Develt, 1966; Financial Adviser, British Develt Div. in the Caribbean, 1966–68; Principal, India Sect., ODA, 1968–72; Asst Sec., 1972; Head of Southern African Develt Div., 1972–75; Establishment Officer, 1976–78, Head of UN Dept B, 1978–79, ODA; Counsellor (Overseas Develt), Washington, and Alternate Exec. Dir of the World Bank, 1979–84. Consultant, ODA, 1985. *Address:* 3 The Close, Montreal Park, Sevenoaks, Kent TN13 2HE. *T:* Sevenoaks 452534.

SMITH, Maj.-Gen. Desmond; *see* Smith, Maj.-Gen. J. D. B.

SMITH, Desmond; *see* Smith, S. D.

SMITH, Dodie, (wrote under the name of C. L. Anthony up to 1935); Dramatist and Novelist; *b* 3 May 1896; *d* of Ernest Walter Smith and Ella Furber; *m* 1939, Alec Macbeth Beesley. *Educ:* St Paul's School for Girls. Studied at Royal Academy of Dramatic Art; on the stage for several years; gave up the stage and became a buyer at Heal and Son, Tottenham Court Road; wrote Autumn Crocus in 1930; produced Lyric Theatre, 1931; gave up business, 1931; wrote Service, 1932; produced Wyndham's Theatre, 1932; wrote Touch Wood, 1933; produced Theatre Royal, Haymarket, 1934; wrote Call It A Day, 1935; produced Globe Theatre, 1935; Bonnet Over the Windmill; produced New Theatre, 1937; wrote Dear Octopus, 1938; produced Queen's Theatre, 1938, revived Theatre Royal, Haymarket, 1967; wrote Lovers and Friends, 1942; prod. Plymouth Theatre, New York, 1943; Letter from Paris (adapted from novel, The Reverberator, by Henry James), Aldwych, 1952; wrote I Capture the Castle, 1952 (adapted from own novel of same name), prod. Aldwych Theatre, 1953; wrote These People-Those Books, 1957; prod. Leeds, 1958; wrote Amateur Means Lover, 1956; prod. Liverpool, 1961. *Publications: Plays by C. L. Anthony:* Autumn Crocus; Service; Touch Wood; *Plays by Dodie Smith:* Call It A Day; Bonnet Over the Windmill; Dear Octopus; Lovers and Friends; Letter from Paris; I Capture the Castle; *novels:* I Capture the Castle, 1949 (US 1948); The New Moon with the Old, 1963 (US 1963); The Town in Bloom, 1965 (US 1965); It Ends with Revelations, 1967 (US 1967); A Tale of Two Families, 1970 (US 1970); The Girl from the Candle-lit Bath, 1978; *children's books:* The Hundred and One Dalmatians, 1956 (US 1957); The Starlight Barking, 1967 (US 1968); The Midnight Kittens, 1978; *autobiography:* Look Back With Love, 1974; Look Back With Mixed Feelings, 1978; Look Back With Astonishment, 1979; Look Back with Gratitude, 1985. *Recreations:* reading, music, dogs, donkeys. *Address:* The Barretts, Finchingfield, Essex. *T:* Great Dunmow 810260.

SMITH, Donald Charles; a Master of the Supreme Court of Judicature (Chancery Division), 1969–73; *b* 23 Jan. 1910; *o s* of Charles Frederic Smith and Cecilia Anastasia Smith (*née* Toomey); *m* 1941, Joan Rowsell, twin *d* of Richard Norman Rowsell Blaker, MC. *Educ:* Stonyhurst College. Articled, Peacock & Goddard, Gray's Inn, 1927–31; admitted Solicitor, 1932; Solicitor with Thorold, Brodie & Bonham-Carter, Westminster, 1931–34; Legal Staff of Public Trustee Office, 1934–39; joined Chancery Registrars' Office, 1939; Chancery Registrar, 1952; Chief Registrar, 1963; first Chancery Registrar to be appointed a Master. Pres., Stonyhurst Assoc., 1969. Served in RNVR, Fleet Air Arm, 1943–46; Lieut, 1944–46. *Publications:* (Revising Editor) Atkin's Encyclopaedia of Court Forms, 1st edn, (Advisory Editor) 2nd edn; contribs to Law Jl. *Recreations:* cricket, walking, theatre, philately. *Address:* Reading Hall, Denham, Eye, Suffolk IP21 5DR. *T:* Eye 870500. *Club:* MCC.

SMITH, Ven. Donald John; Archdeacon of Sudbury, since 1984; Hon. Canon of St Edmundsbury and Ipswich, since 1973; *b* 10 April 1926; *m* 1948, Violet Olive Goss; two *s* one *d*. *Educ:* Clifton Theological Coll. Asst Curate: Edgware, 1953–56; St Margaret's, Ipswich, 1956–58; Vicar of St Mary, Hornsey Rise, Islington, 1958–62; Rector of Whitton, Ipswich, 1962–75; Rector of Redgrave cum Botesdale with The Rickinghalls, 1975–79; Archdeacon of Suffolk, 1975–84. HCF 1964. *Publications:* A Confirmation Course, 1974; Covenanting for Disunity, 1981. *Recreations:* driving, foreign travel, chess, collecting Meerschaum and antiques, drama, reading, photography, gardening, caravanning, good food, dining out, pastoral reorganisation, redundant churches. *Address:* 84 Southgate Street, Bury St Edmunds, Suffolk IP33 2BJ. *T:* Bury St Edmunds 66796.

SMITH, Donald MacKeen; Agent General of Nova Scotia, in London, since 1980; *b* 26 Nov. 1923; *s* of Leonard Vernard and Lena Smith (*née* MacKeen); *m* 1949, Helen Elizabeth, *d* of late Lt-Col David Guildford; three *d*. *Educ:* Halifax Public Schs; King's College Sch.; Dalhousie Univ., Nova Scotia. Served Canadian Armored Corps, 1942–45; 18th Armored Car Regt, 1944–45. J. E. Morse and Co. Ltd, Halifax: salesman, 1946; Vice-Pres., Director, 1951; Pres., 1956–. Pres., Tea Council of Canada, 1975–78; Vice-Pres. and Dir, Tea and Coffee Assoc. of Canada, 1960–78. Member, Executive Council of Nova Scotia, 1960–69; MLA Nova Scotia (Halifax Citadel), 1960–70; Minister of Mines, Minister in Charge of Liquor Control Act, 1960–69. Mem., Rotary Club. *Recreations:* swimming, sailing, fishing, walking. *Address:* Nova Scotia House, 14 Pall Mall, SW1Y 5LU. *T:* 01-930 6864; Sunnywood Road, Head of St Margaret's Bay, Halifax County, Nova Scotia, Canada. *Clubs:* East India, Devonshire, Sports and Public Schools; Royal Automobile; Saraguay; Halifax; Royal Nova Scotia Yacht Squadron.

SMITH, Douglas; *see* Smith, I. D.

SMITH, Douglas Alexander; Commissioner of Inland Revenue, 1968–75; *b* 15 June 1915; *m* 1941, Mary Eileen Lyon; one *s* one *d*. *Educ:* Glasgow High Sch.; Glasgow Univ. MA, BSc 1937. Entered Inland Revenue, 1938; Asst Secretary: Inland Revenue, 1952–59; Office of Minister for Science, 1959–61; Under-Sec., Medical Research Council, 1964–67. *Recreations:* hockey, golf, bridge, gardening. *Address:* 66 Eastwick Drive, Great Bookham, Surrey. *T:* Bookham 54274. *Club:* Civil Service.

SMITH, Douglas Boucher, CB 1982; Deputy Secretary, Department of Employment, since 1979; *b* 9 June 1932; *m* 1956, Mary Barbara Tarran. *Educ:* Leeds Modern Sch.; Leeds Univ. Entered Ministry of Labour, 1953; successively: Private Sec. to Minister of Labour, 1967–68; to First Sec. of State and Sec. of State for Employment and Productivity, 1968–70; to Sec. of State for Employment, 1970–71; Chief Conciliation Officer, 1971–74, Under Secretary: Dept. of Employment, 1974–77; Cabinet Office, 1977–79. *Address:* 17 Dundas Close, Bracknell, Berkshire. *T:* Bracknell 54573. *Club:* Athenæum.

SMITH, Ven. Douglas Leslie B.; *see* Bartles-Smith.

SMITH, Drew; *see* Smith, F. D.

SMITH, Sir Dudley (Gordon), Kt 1983; MP (C) Warwick and Leamington, since 1968 (Brentford and Chiswick, 1959–66); *b* 14 Nov. 1926; *o s* of late Hugh William and Florence Elizabeth Smith, Cambridge; 1st marr. diss.; one *s* two *d*; *m* 2nd, 1976, Catherine Amos, *o d* of late Mr and Mrs Thomas Amos, Liverpool. *Educ:* Chichester High Sch., Sussex. Worked for various provincial and national newspapers, as journalist and senior executive, 1943–66; Asst News Editor, Sunday Express, 1953–59. Vice-Chm. Southgate Conservative Assoc., 1958–59; CC Middlesex, 1958–65. Chief Whip of Majority Group, 1961–63. A Divl Dir, Beecham Group, 1966–70; Management Consultant. Contested (C) Camberwell-Peckham, General Election, 1955. PPS to Sec. for Tech. Co-operation, 1963–64; an Opposition Whip, 1964–66; an Opposition Spokesman on Employment and Productivity, 1969–70; Parliamentary Under-Secretary of State: Dept of Employment, 1970–74; (Army) MoD, 1974; UK delegate to Council of Europe and WEU, 1979– (Sec.-Gen. and Sen. Vice-Pres., European Democratic Group, 1983–). Vice Chm., Parly Select Cttee on Race Relations and Immigration, 1974–79. Promoted Town and Country Planning (Amendment) Act, 1977, as a private member. Governor, Mill Hill Sch.; Chm., United & Cecil Club, 1975–80. *Publications:* Harold Wilson: A Critical Biography, 1964; etc. *Recreations:* books, travel, music, wild life and wilderness preservation. *Address:* Church Farm, Weston-under-Wetherley, Warwicks. *T:* Marton 632 352.

SMITH, Dugal N.; *see* Nisbet-Smith.

SMITH, Dr Edgar Charles B.; *see* Bate-Smith.

SMITH, Dr (Edward) Alistair, CBE 1982; Director, University of Aberdeen Development Trust, since 1982; Chairman, Northern Antiquities Ltd, since 1984; *b* 16 Jan. 1939; *s* of Archibald Smith and Jean Milne Johnston. *Educ:* Aberdeen Grammar Sch.; Univ. of Aberdeen (MA, PhD); Univ. of Uppsala, Sweden. Lectr, Univ. of Aberdeen, 1963–. Mem., Grampian Health Bd, 1983–. Pres., Scottish Conservative and Unionist Assoc., 1979–81; Dep. Chm., Scottish Conservative Party, 1981–85. Member: Exec., Aberdeen and NE Council on Disability; Exec., Grampian ASH. *Publications:* (with R. E. H. Mellor) Europe: a geographical survey of the Continent, 1979; articles on Scandinavia, Europe and Scotland. *Recreations:* travel, photography, music. *Address:* 68A Beaconsfield Place, Aberdeen AB2 4AJ. *T:* Aberdeen 642932.

SMITH, Edward John Gregg, CB 1982; Deputy Secretary, Ministry of Agriculture, Fisheries and Food, since 1979; *b* 1 Oct. 1930; *o s* of late Major J. W. Smith and Mrs V. H. E. Smith; *m* 1956, Jean Margaret Clayton; one *s* two *d*. *Educ:* Churcher's Coll., Petersfield; Queens' Coll., Cambridge (MA). FRGS. MAFF, 1953–68: Private Sec. to Minister, 1964–66; Head of Economic Policy Div., 1966–68; Principal Private Sec. to Lord President of Council and Leader of House of Commons, 1968–70; returned to MAFF:

Head of Meat Div., 1970–71; Under-Sec., 1971–74, 1976–79; Under-Sec., Cabinet Office, 1974–76. Mem., AFRC (formerly ARC), 1979–; Mem., Guildford Diocesan Synod, 1976– (Chm., House of Laity, 1985–). FRSA. *Recreations:* choral music, Christian activities. *Address:* The Holme, Oakfield Road, Ashtead, Surrey. *T:* Ashtead 72311. *Club:* Reform.

SMITH, Eileen S.; *see* Stamers-Smith.

SMITH, Emma; Author; *b* 1923; *m* 1951, Richard Stewart-Jones (*d* 1957); one *s* one *d*. *Publications:* Maidens' Trip, 1948 (awarded John Llewellyn Rhys Memorial Prize, 1948); The Far Cry, 1949 (awarded James Tait Black Memorial Prize, 1949); Emily, 1959; Out of Hand, 1963, Emily's Voyage, 1966; No Way of Telling, 1972; The Opportunity of a Lifetime, 1978. *Address:* c/o Curtis Brown, 162–168 Regent Street, W1R 5TB.

SMITH, Dame Enid Mary R. R.; *see* Russell-Smith.

SMITH, Sir Eric; *see* Smith, Sir J. E.

SMITH, Eric John R.; *see* Radley-Smith.

SMITH, Eric Norman, CMG 1976; HM Diplomatic Service, retired; British High Commissioner in The Gambia, 1979–81; *b* 28 Jan. 1922; *s* of late Arthur Sidney David Smith; *m* 1955, Mary Gillian Horrocks. *Educ:* Colfe's Sch., London. Served War, Royal Corps of Signals, 1941–46. Foreign Office, 1947–53; HM Embassy, Cairo, 1953–55; UK Delegn to the UN, New York, 1955–57; FO, 1957–60; HM Embassy, Tehran, 1960–64; FO, 1964–68; British Information Services, New York, 1968–71; FCO, 1971–75; Singapore, 1975–79. *Recreations:* music, photography. *Address:* Kilsby, Llanwrtyd Wells, Powys LD5 4TL.

SMITH, E(rnest) Lester, DSc; FRS 1957; formerly Consultant, Glaxo Laboratories, Greenford; *b* 7 August 1904; *s* of Lester and Rose Smith; *m* 1931, Winifred R. Fitch; no *c. Educ:* Wood Green County School; Chelsea Polytechnic. Joined Glaxo Laboratories, 1926, as first post after graduation. Various posts in development, Fine Chemical Production (Head), then Biochemical Research. Shared responsibility for production of penicillin during War of 1939–45; isolation of vitamin B_{12} accomplished, 1948. *Publications:* Vitamin B_{12} (in series of Biochemical Monographs), 1960, 3rd edn 1965; numerous research papers in various scientific journals, 1927–. *Recreation:* horticulture. *Address:* Quarry Wood, 23 Grange Road, Hastings, East Sussex TN34 2RL.

SMITH, Sir Ewart; *see* Smith, Sir Frank Ewart.

SMITH, Maj.-Gen. Sir (Francis) Brian W.; *see* Wyldbore-Smith.

SMITH, Sir Francis Graham-, Kt 1986; FRS 1970; Professor of Radio Astronomy, Manchester University, 1964–74 and since 1981; Director, Nuffield Radio Astronomy Laboratories, since 1981; Astronomer Royal, since 1982; *b* 25 April 1923; *s* of Claud Henry and Cicely Winifred Smith; *m* 1945, Dorothy Elizabeth (*née* Palmer); three *s* one *d*. *Educ:* Epsom Coll.; Rossall Sch.; Downing Coll., Cambridge. Nat. Sci. Tripos, Downing Coll., 1941–43 and 1946–47; PhD Cantab 1952. Telecommunications Research Estab., Malvern, 1943–46; Cavendish Lab., 1947–64; 1851 Exhibr 1951–52; Warren Research Fellow of Royal Soc., 1959–64; Fellow of Downing Coll., 1953–64, Hon. Fellow 1970; Dir-Designate, 1974–75, Dir, 1976–81, Royal Greenwich Observatory. Vis. Prof. of Astronomy, Univ. of Sussex, 1975. Sec., Royal Astronomical Soc., 1964–71, Pres., 1975–77. Hon. DSc QUB, 1986. *Publications:* Radio Astronomy, 1960; (with J. H. Thomson) Optics, 1971; Pulsars, 1977; papers in Monthly Notices of RAS, Nature and other scientific jls. *Recreations:* sailing, walking. *Address:* Nuffield Radio Astronomy Laboratories, Jodrell Bank, Macclesfield, Cheshire SK11 9DL; Old School House, Henbury, Macclesfield, Cheshire SK11 9PH.

SMITH, Rev. Francis Taylor; Minister of St Paul's Parish Church, Dunfermline, since 1964; *b* 22 Jan. 1933; *s* of James William Smith and Jeannie Moir Catto Cockburn; *m* 1957, Jean Millar Wallace; three *s* one *d*. *Educ:* Aberdeen Grammar Sch.; Aberdeen Univ. (MA); Christ's Coll., Aberdeen (Licence to Preach). Student Assistant: Queen's Cross Church, Aberdeen, 1954–56; North Church, Aberdeen, 1956–57; Sen. Asst, Govan Old Church, Glasgow, 1957–58; Parish Minister, Aberlour, Banffshire, 1958–64. Chaplain, Dunfermline and West Fife Hosp., 1964–; Moderator of Presbytery, 1973–74. Councillor, Banff CC, 1964; Chairman, West Fife Local Health Council, 1975–; Vice-Pres., Assoc. of Scottish Local Health Councils, 1978–79, Pres., 1980, 1981; Crown Lay Nominee, General Medical Council, 1979–. Chm., Fife Marriage Counselling Service, 1984–85. Governor, Aberlour Orphanage, 1964. *Recreations:* work, music, fishing, shooting, reading. *Address:* St Paul's Manse, 6 Park Avenue, Dunfermline, Fife KY12 7HX. *T:* Dunfermline 721124. *Club:* Caledonian.

SMITH, Sir (Frank) Ewart, Kt 1946; MA; FRS 1957; FEng; Hon. FIMechE; FIChemE; a past Deputy Chairman, Imperial Chemical Industries, Ltd; *b* 31 May 1897; *s* of late Richard Sidney Smith; *m* 1924, Kathleen Winifred (*d* 1978), *d* of late H. Rudd Dawes; one *d* (one *s* decd). *Educ:* Christ's Hospital; Sidney Sussex College, Cambridge (Scholar, 1st Class Mech. Science Tripos, John Winbolt Prizeman). War service, 1916–19, RA; ICI Ltd, Billingham Works in various engineering and managerial posts, 1923–42; chief engineer, 1932–42; Chief Engineer and Supt of Armament Design, Ministry of Supply, 1942–45; Formerly Member: Advisory Council on Scientific Policy; Scientific Advisory Council of Ministry of Works and Ministry of Fuel and Power; British Productivity Council, Cttee on Scientific Manpower; Chairman, National Health Service Advisory Council for Management Efficiency (England and Wales), etc. Hon. Fellow Sidney Sussex College; Hon. Member, City and Guilds of London Institute; Hon. FIMS; Hon. Associate, Univ. of Aston. James Clayton Prize, IMechE. American Medal of Freedom with Palm, 1946. *Publications:* various technical papers. *Recreations:* cabinet making, gardening. *Address:* Parkhill Cottage, Sandy Lane, Watersfield, Pulborough, W Sussex. *T:* Bury 354.

SMITH, Prof. Frank Thomas, FRS 1984; Goldsmid Professor of Applied Mathematics in the University of London, at University College London, since 1984; *b* 24 Feb. 1948; *s* of Leslie Maxwell Smith and Catherine Matilda Smith; *m* 1972, Valerie Sheila (*née* Hearn); two *d*. *Educ:* Bournemouth Grammar Sch.; Jesus Coll., Oxford (BA; DPhil); University College London. Research Fellow in Theoretical Aerodynamics Unit, Southampton, 1972–73; Lectr in Maths Dept, Imperial Coll., London, 1973–78; Vis. Scientist, Applied Mathematics Dept, Univ. of Western Ontario, Canada, 1978–79; Reader in Maths Dept, 1979–83, Prof. in Maths, 1983–84, Imperial Coll., London. *Publications:* on applied mathematics, fluid mechanics, computing and natural sciences, in jls. *Recreations:* the family, reading, music, sport. *Address:* Mathematics Department, University College, Gower Street, WC1E 6BT. *T:* 01–387 7050.

SMITH, Frank William G.; *see* Glaves-Smith.

SMITH, (Fraser) Drew; Editor, Good Food Guide, since 1982; *b* 30 March 1950; *s* of Frank and Beatrice Smith. *Educ:* Westminster School. Worked on student magazine, 1967; IPC magazines, 1969–72; Westminster Press Newspapers, 1972–81. *Recreations:* walking, music, cooking, people.

SMITH, Frederick Llewellyn, CBE 1964; MSc, DPhil, CEng, FIMechE; *b* 25 July 1909; *s* of late James Brooksbank Smith; *m* 1943, Alice Mary McMurdo; one *s* two *d*. *Educ:* Rochdale High Sch.; Univ. of Manchester; Balliol Coll., Oxford. Joined Rolls-Royce Ltd, 1933; Dir, 1947; Group Man. Dir, Automotive and subsidiary cos, 1970; Chm., Rolls-Royce Motors Ltd, 1971; retired 1972. Pres. Soc. of Motor Manufacturers & Traders Ltd, 1955–56. Mem. Nat. Research Development Corp., 1959–73. Pres., Motor Industry Research Assoc., 1963–65. *Address:* 4 Raglan Close, Reigate, Surrey RH2 0EU.

SMITH, Prof. Frederick Viggers; Professor of Psychology, University of Durham, 1950–77, now Emeritus; *b* Hamilton, New South Wales, 24 Jan. 1912; *s* of Frederick Thomas Smith and Agnes (*née* Viggers); unmarried. *Educ:* Newcastle (NSW) High School; Sydney and London Universities. BA 1938, MA 1941, Lithgow Schol., Sydney; PhD London 1948. FBPsS, 1950 (Pres., British Psychological Society, 1959–60). Research Office, Dept of Educ., NSW, 1936; Lecturer in Psychology, The Teachers' Coll., Sydney, 1938; Lectr, Birkbeck Coll., Univ. of London, 1946; Lectr, Univ. of Aberdeen, 1948. Visiting Prof., Cornell Univ., USA, 1957, Christchurch and Wellington Univs, NZ, 1960. Consultant, Council of Europe Sub-Cttee on Crime Problems, 1973; Unesco Consultant, Univ. of Riyadh, 1973. Hon. Research Associate, Univ. of Newcastle, NSW, 1980. *Publications:* The Child's Point of View (Sydney), 1946 (under pseudonym Victor Southward); Explanation of Human Behaviour (London), 1951, 1960; Attachment of the Young: Imprinting and Other Developments, 1969; Purpose in Animal Behaviour, 1971; papers to psychological and philosophical jls. *Recreations:* mountain walking, swimming, photography, music, golf. *Address:* 58 Harbourside Haven, Shoal Bay, Port Stephens, NSW 2315, Australia.

SMITH, Geoffrey Ellrington Fane, CMG 1955; Senior Provincial Commissioner, Northern Rhodesia, 1951–55, retired; Colonial Office, 1956–61, Department of Technical Co-operation (later Ministry of Overseas Development), 1961–66; *b* 1903; *m* 1933, Olga Smith. *Educ:* King Edward VI Grammar School, Louth; Lincoln College, Oxford. Cadet, Northern Rhodesia, 1926–29; District Officer, 1929; Provincial Commissioner, Northern Rhodesia, 1947–51. *Address:* 26 Vincent Road, Stoke D'Abernon, Cobham, Surrey.

SMITH, Sir Geoffrey J.; *see* Johnson Smith.

SMITH, Geoffrey M.; *see* Maitland Smith.

SMITH, Vice-Adm. Sir Geoffrey T.; *see* Thistleton-Smith.

SMITH, Prof. George, MBE 1945; FRSE 1979; Chief of Surgery, Veterans' Administration Hospital, Fayetteville, North Carolina, since 1982; Clinical Professor of Surgery, Duke University Medical Centre, since 1986; Regius Professor of Surgery, University of Aberdeen, 1962–82, now Emeritus; *b* 4 June 1919; *s* of late John Shand Smith and Lilimina Myles Mathers Smith; *m* 1951, Vivienne Marie Tuck, BA, Wooster, Ohio, USA, *d* of Rev. Robert Sidney Tuck, DD; two *s* one *d*. *Educ:* Grove Academy; Queen's College, Univ. of St Andrews. MB, ChB (St Andrews) 1942; MD (Hons) 1957, ChM (Hons) 1959; DSc (Glasgow) 1964; FRFP&S (Glasgow) 1949; FRCS (Edinburgh) 1949; FACS 1958; FACCP 1963; FInstBiol 1963. Commonwealth Fund Fellow, 1949–51 (Johns Hopkins, Columbia and Western Reserve Medical Schools). Formerly Reader in Cardiovascular Surgery, Univ. of Glasgow; Dean of Medicine, Aberdeen Univ., 1974–76, Dir, Inst. of Environmental and Offshore Med., 1975–78. Chm., NE Region Med. Postgrad. Cttee; Civil Consultant in surgery to RN; Governor: Robert Gordon's Colleges; Amer. Coll. of Chest Physicians. Mason: Scottish Rite, 32°; York Rite; Knight Templar; Sudan Shrine. *Publications:* (ed jtly) Resuscitation and Cardiac Pacing, 1965; The Biology of Affluence, 1972; The Staphylococci, 1981; (ed) Proceedings, 6th International Congress on Hyperbaric Medicine, 1979; sections in books and some 300 papers, mainly on cardiovascular, respiratory, bacteriological and educnl topics. *Recreations:* sailing, gardening, golf. *Address:* 212 Thorncliff Drive, Fayetteville, N Carolina 28303, USA. *T:* 919 484 1284. *Clubs:* Naval; RNVR (Glasgow); Fort Bragg Officers (Fayetteville).

SMITH, George; formerly Director-General of Ordnance Factories (Finance), 1972–76; *b* 13 Dec. 1914; *s* of George Smith and Catherine Annie Smith (*née* Ashby); *m* 1939, Alice May Smith; two *s*. *Educ:* Alderman Newton's Sch., Leicester. FCCA. Various posts in industry, 1929–40; joined Min. of Supply, 1940, various posts in Royal Ordnance factories, 1940–52; Asst Dir of Ordnance Factories (Accounts), 1952; Civil Asst, ROF Woolwich, 1958; Dir of Ordnance Factories (Accounts), 1962. *Recreations:* gardening, walking, bowls. *Address:* 14 Blenheim Gardens, Sanderstead, Surrey. *T:* 01–657 5826.

SMITH, George Neil; HM Diplomatic Service; Head of Trade Relations and Exports Department, Foreign and Commonwealth Office, since 1985; *b* 12 July 1936; *s* of George Smith and Ena (*née* Hill); *m* 1956, Elvi Vappu Hämäläinen; one *s* one *d*. *Educ:* King Edward VII Sch., Sheffield. Joined HM Foreign (subseq. Diplomatic) Service, 1953; served RAF, 1954–56; Foreign Office, 1957; Rangoon, 1958–61; 2nd Sec., Berne, 1961–65; Diplomatic Service Administration, 1965–66; 1st Sec., CO, 1966–68; British Mil. Govt, Berlin, 1969–73; FCO, 1973–77; Counsellor (Commercial), Helsinki, 1977–80; Consul-Gen., Zürich and Principality of Liechtenstein, 1980–85. *Recreations:* music, tennis. *Address:* c/o Foreign and Commonwealth Office, SW1. *Club:* Travellers'.

SMITH, Gerard Thomas C.; *see* Corley Smith.

SMITH, Sir Gilbert; *see* Smith, Sir T. G.

SMITH, Gordon E.; *see* Etherington-Smith.

SMITH, Gordon Edward C.; *see* Connell-Smith.

SMITH, Prof. Hamilton Othanel; Professor of Molecular Biology and Genetics, Johns Hopkins University School of Medicine, Maryland, USA, since 1981; *b* 23 Aug. 1931; *s* of Bunnie Othanel Smith and Tommie Harkey Smith; *m* 1957, Elizabeth Anne Bolton; four *s* one *d*. *Educ:* Univ. of Illinois; Univ. of California (AB); Johns Hopkins Univ. Sch. of Medicine (MD). Research Associate, Dept of Human Genetics, Univ. of Michigan, 1964–67; Asst Prof. of Microbiology, 1967–69, Associate Prof. of Microbiology, 1969–73, Prof. of Microbiology, 1973–81, Johns Hopkins Univ. Sch. of Medicine. During sabbatical leave in Zürich, worked in collaboration with Prof. Dr M. L. Birnstiel, Inst. für Molekularbiologie II der Univ. Zürich, July 1975–June 1976. Nobel Prize in Medicine (jtly), 1978. *Publications:* A restriction enzyme from *Hemophilus influenzae:* I. Purification and general properties (with K. W. Wilcox), in Jl Mol. Biol. *51*, 379, 1970; A restriction enzyme from *Hemophilus influenzae:* II. Base sequence of the recognition site (with T. J. Kelly), in Jl Mol. Biol. *51*, 393, 1970. *Recreations:* piano, classical music. *Address:* Department of Molecular Biology and Genetics, Johns Hopkins University School of Medicine, 725 N Wolfe Street, Baltimore, Maryland 21205, USA. *T:* (301) 955–3650.

SMITH, Prof. Harry, PhD, DSc; FRCPath; FRS 1979; FIBiol; Professor and Head, Department of Microbiology, University of Birmingham, since 1965; *b* 7 Aug. 1921; *s* of Harry and Annie Smith; *m* 1947, Janet Mary Holmes; one *s* one *d*. *Educ:* Northampton Grammar Sch.; University Coll. (of London) at Nottingham. BPharm, BScChem (1st Cl. Hons), PhD, DSc London. Analyst, Boots Pure Drug Co., Nottingham, 1942–45; Asst

Lectr, then Lectr, Dept of Chemistry, UCL at Nottingham, 1945–47; Microbiological Research Establishment, Porton: Sen. Scientific Officer, 1947; Principal Sci. Officer, 1951; Sen. Prin. Sci. Officer (Research Merit), 1956; Dep. Chief Sci. Officer (Res. Merit), 1964. Visiting Professor: Dept of Bacteriology, Univ. of Calif, Berkeley, USA, 1964, UCLA, 1972; (summer) Dept of Microbiol., Univ. of Washington, Seattle, USA, 1977, Univ. of Michigan, Ann Arbor, 1981. Society for General Microbiology: Mem. Council, 1960–64; Meetings Sec., 1964–68; Treas., 1968–75; Pres., 1975–78; Treas., Fedn of Europ. Microbiol Socs, 1975–82; Pres. and Chm., Organising Cttee, 14th (1986) Internat. Congress of Microbiology, Manchester. Lectures: Amer. Soc. for Microbiol., 1984; Australian Soc. for Microbiol., 1985. *Publications:* over 250 papers in jls and books, mainly on mechanisms of microbial (bacterial, viral and fungal) pathogenicity. *Recreation:* farming 52 hectares, Melton Mowbray, Leics. *Address:* Department of Microbiology, University of Birmingham, PO Box 363, Birmingham B15 2TT. *T:* 021–472 1301 (ext. 3124). *Club:* Athenæum.

SMITH, Harvey; *see* Smith, R. H.

SMITH, Hedworth Cunningham, CBE 1972; Chairman, Medical Appeal Tribunals and Pensions Appeals Tribunals, England; Judge of the Supreme Court of the Bahama Islands 1965–72, retired; *b* 12 May 1912; *s* of James Smith and Elizabeth (*née* Brown); unmarried. *Educ:* George Watson's Coll., Edinburgh; Edinburgh University. MA 1933; LLB 1936. Solicitor, Scotland, 1937–40; Barrister-at-Law, Gray's Inn, London, 1950. Served War of 1939–45: commnd 1940; Staff Officer, GHQ India Command, 1943–46 (Major). District Magistrate, 1946, Senior District Magistrate, 1950, Gold Coast; Judge of Supreme Court of Ghana, 1957; retd from Ghana Govt service, 1961; Legal Adviser, Unilever Ltd Gp of Cos in Ghana, 1962–64. *Recreation:* golf. *Address:* c/o 40 Thorne Road, Doncaster, Yorks. *T:* Doncaster 62819. *Club:* East India, Devonshire, Sports and Public Schools.

SMITH, Lt-Col Henry Owen H.; *see* Hugh Smith.

SMITH, Prof. Henry Sidney, FBA 1985; Edwards Professor of Egyptology, University College London, 1970–86, now Professor Emeritus and Head of Department of Egyptology; *b* 14 June 1928; *s* of Prof. Sidney Smith, FBA, and of Mary, *d* of H. W. Parker; *m* 1961, Hazel Flory Leeper. *Educ:* Merchant Taylors' Sch., Northwood; Christ's Coll., Cambridge (MA). Lectr in Egyptology, Univ. of Cambridge, 1954–63; Budge Fellow in Egyptology, Christ's Coll., Cambridge, 1955–63; Reader in Egyptian Archaeology, University Coll. London, 1963–70. Field Dir for Egypt Exploration Soc. in Nubia, 1961, 1964–65, and at Saqqara and Memphis, Egypt, 1970–. *Publications:* Preliminary Reports of the Egypt Exploration Society's Nubian Survey, 1962; A Visit to Ancient Egypt, 1974; The Fortress of Buhen: the inscriptions, 1976; The Fortress of Buhen: the archaeological report, 1979; (with W. J. Tait) Saqqara Demotic Papyri I, 1983; articles in Kush, Jl of Egyptian Arch., Orientalia, Rev. d'Egyptologie, Bull. Inst. Français d'Arch. Or., Z für Äg. Sprache und Altertümskunde, etc. *Address:* Ailwyn House, Upwood, Huntingdon, Cambs.

SMITH, Dr Herbert Williams, FRS 1980; FRCVS, FRCPath; Wellcome Trust Visiting Research Worker, Department of Microbiology, Houghton Poultry Research Station, Cambridgeshire, since 1971 (Head of Department 1971–84); *b* 3 May 1919; *s* of Herbert Harry Smith and Ida Elizabeth Williams; *m* 1942, Kathleen Margaret Mary Bezant; one *s* two *d*. *Educ:* Pontypridd Grammar Sch.; London Univ. (PhD 1947; DSc 1957; DipBact 1948). FRCVS 1953; FRCPath 1970. Wellcome Res. Fellow, London Sch. of Hygiene and Trop. Medicine, 1945–49; Head, Dept of Pathology and Bacteriology, Livestock Res. Stn of Animal Health Trust, 1949–71. *Recreations:* gardening, work. *Address:* 7 Quaker Close, Kings Ripton, Huntingdon, Cambs PE17 2NP. *T:* Abbots Ripton 294.

SMITH, Sir Howard (Frank Trayton), GCMG 1981 (KCMG 1976; CMG 1966); HM Diplomatic Service, retired; *b* 15 Oct. 1919; *m* 1st, 1943, Winifred Mary Cropper (*d* 1982); one *d*; 2nd, 1983, Mary Penney. *Educ:* Sidney Sussex Coll., Cambridge. Employed in FO, 1939; apptd Foreign Service, 1946. Served Oslo; transf. Washington, 2nd Sec. (Inf.) 1950; 1st Sec., Dec. 1950; 1st Sec. and Consul, Caracas, 1953; FO, 1956; Counsellor: Moscow, 1961–63; Foreign Office, 1964–68; Ambassador to Czechoslovakia, 1968–71; UK Rep. in NI, 1971–72; Dep. Sec., Cabinet Office, on secondment, 1972–75; Ambassador in Moscow, 1976–78. *Address:* Coromandel, Cross in Hand, Heathfield, E Sussex. *T:* Heathfield 4420. *Club:* Travellers'.

SMITH, Captain Hugh D.; *see* Dalrymple-Smith.

SMITH, Captain Humphry Gilbert B.; *see* Boys-Smith.

SMITH, Iain-Mór L.; *see* Lindsay-Smith.

SMITH, Ian Douglas, GCLM 1979; ID 1970; MP (Cons. Alliance, formerly Republican Front), Zimbabwe, since 1980; *b* 8 April 1919; *m* Janet Watt; two *s* one *d*. *Educ:* Selukwe Sch.; Chaplin Sch., Gwelo, S Rhodesia (now Zimbabwe); Rhodes Univ., Grahamstown, S Africa. Served War of 1939–45 in 237 (Rhodesia) Sqdn and 130 Sqdn, RAF. Farmer. Member: Southern Rhodesia Legislative Assembly, 1948–53; Parliament of Fedn of Rhodesia & Nyasaland, 1953–61; former Chief Whip (United Federal Party), 1958; resigned from United Federal Party, 1961; Foundn Mem. and Vice-Pres., Republican Front (formerly Rhodesian Front), 1962, President, 1964–; Dep. Prime Minister and Minister of the Treasury, S Rhodesia, 1962–64; Prime Minister of Rhodesia, 1964–79; delivered Rhodesia's Unilateral Declaration of Independence, Nov. 1965; Minister Without Portfolio in Bishop Muzorewa's Govt, 1979; Mem., Transitional Exec. Council to prepare for transfer of power in Rhodesia, 1978–79. *Address:* Gwenoro Farm, Shurugwi, Zimbabwe; Box 8198, Causeway, Harare, Zimbabwe; (office) House of Assembly, Harare, Zimbabwe. *Clubs:* Harare, Harare Sports (Zimbabwe).

SMITH, Ivor Otterbein, CMG 1963; OBE 1952; retired as Chairman of Public Service and Police Service Commissions and Member of Judicial Service Commission, British Guiana (1961–66); *b* Georgetown, British Guiana, 13 Dec. 1907; *s* of Bryce Otterbein Smith and late Florette Maud Smith (*née* Chapman); *m* 1936, Leila Muriel Fowler; one *s* two *d*. *Educ:* Queen's Coll., British Guiana; Pitman's Commercial Coll., London. Joined Brit. Guiana CS, as Clerical Asst, Treas., 1925; Sec. Commissioners of Currency, 1933; Asst Dist. Comr, 1941; Private Sec. to Gov., 1943; Dist Comr, 1945; Comr, Cayman Is, 1946–52; Dep. Comr of Local Govt, Brit. Guiana, 1953; Governor's Sec., and Clerk Exec. Coun., 1956; Dep. Chief Sec., 1960; Acted as Chief Sec. on several occasions and was Officer Administering the Govt, Sept.-Oct. 1960. Served with S Caribbean Force, 1941–43; Major, Staff Officer, Brit. Guiana Garrison. Hon. Col, British Guiana Volunteer Force, 1962–66. Chm., Nat. Sports Coun, 1962–66. *Recreations:* tennis; interested in sports of all kinds; rep. Brit. Guiana at Association and Rugby football, cricket, hockey. *Address:* Suite No 606, 460 Westview Street, Coquitlam, BC V3K 3W4, Canada.

SMITH, Jack, ARCA 1952; artist; *b* 18 June 1928; *s* of John Edward and Laura Smith; *m* 1956, Susan Craigie Halkett. *Educ:* Sheffield College of Art; St Martin's School of Art; Royal College of Art. Exhibitions: Whitechapel Art Gallery, 1959, 1971; Beaux Arts Gallery, 1952–58; Matthiesen Gallery, 1960, 1963; Catherine Viviano Gallery, New York, 1958, 1961; Pittsburgh International, 1955, 1957, 1964; Grosvenor Gallery, 1965; Marlborough Gallery, 1968; Konsthallen, Gothenburg, Sweden, 1968; Hull Univ., 1969; Bear Lane Gallery, Oxford, 1970; Whitechapel Gall., 1970; Redfern Gall., 1973 and 1976; Serpentine Gall., 1978; Fischer Fine Art, London, 1981, 1983; British Painting, Museo Municipal, Madrid, 1983. Designer, sets and costumes, Carmen Arcadiae Mechanicae Perpetuum, Ballet Rambert, 1986. Guggenheim Award (Nat.), 1960. Work in permanent collections: Tate Gallery; Arts Council of Great Britain; Contemporary Art Society; British Council. *Address:* 29 Seafield Road, Hove, Sussex. *T:* Brighton 738312.

SMITH, Jack Stanley, CMG 1970; Professor, and Chairman, Graduate School of Business Administration, University of Melbourne, 1973–77, retired; *b* 13 July 1916; *s* of C. P. T. Smith, Avoca, Victoria; *m* 1940, Nancy, *d* of J. C. Beckley, Melbourne; one *s* two *d*. *Educ:* Ballarat Grammar Sch.; Melbourne Univ. Construction Engineer, Australasian Petroleum Co., 1938–41. Served in Australian Imperial Forces, 1942–45, Lieut. Project Engineer, Melbourne & Metropolitan Bd of Works, 1946–48. P.A. Management Consultants, UK and Australia, 1949–72, Managing Dir, 1964–72. *Recreations:* golf, tennis. *Address:* 15 Glyndebourne Avenue, Toorak, Victoria 3142, Australia. *T:* 20 4581. *Clubs:* Melbourne (Melbourne); Lawn Tennis Association of Victoria, Metropolitan Golf (Vic.).

SMITH, James Aikman, TD; Sheriff of Lothian and Borders (formerly the Lothians and Peebles) at Edinburgh, 1968–76; Hon. Sheriff, 1976; *b* 13 June 1914; *s* of Rev. W. J. Smith, DD; *m* 1947, Ann, *d* of Norman A. Millar, FRICS, Glasgow; three *d*. *Educ:* Glasgow Academy; The Queen's Coll., Oxford; Edinburgh Univ. BA (Oxford) 1936; LLB (Edinburgh) 1939; Mem. of Faculty of Advocates, 1939. Served War of 1939–45 (despatches): Royal Artillery, 1939–46; Lt-Col 1944. Sheriff-Substitute: of Renfrew and Argyll, 1948–52; of Roxburgh, Berwick and Selkirk, 1952–57; of Aberdeen, Kincardine and Banff, 1957–68. Pres., Sheriffs-Substitute Assoc., 1969; Pres., Sheriffs' Assoc., 1971–72. Member Departmental Cttee on Probation Service, 1959–62. Chm., Edinburgh and E of Scotland Br., English-Speaking Union, 1971. Bronze Star (US), 1945. *Publications:* occasional articles in legal journals. *Address:* 16 Murrayfield Avenue, Edinburgh EH12 6AX. *Club:* New (Edinburgh).

SMITH, Hon. Sir James (Alfred), Kt 1979; CBE 1964; TD; President of Court of Appeal for Belize, since 1984; Member of the Court of Appeal for Turks and Caicos Islands, since 1981; *b* Llandyssul, Cardiganshire, 11 May 1913; *s* of late Charles Silas and Elizabeth Smith (*née* Williams), Timberdine, Lampeter, Cardiganshire. *Educ:* Christ Coll., Brecon. Solicitor of the Supreme Court, 1937; called to the Bar, Lincoln's Inn, 1949. Served War of 1939–45: various Army Staff appointments; on staff of Supreme Allied Commander, South-East Asia, with rank of Major, 1944–45. Appointed to Colonial Legal Service, as Resident Magistrate, Nigeria, 1946; Chief Magistrate, 1951; Chief Registrar of the Supreme Court, Nigeria, 1953; Puisne Judge, Nigeria, 1955; Judge, High Court, Northern Nigeria, 1955; Senior Puisne Judge, High Court, N Nigeria, 1960–65; Puisne Judge, Supreme Court, Bahamas, 1965–75, Sen. Justice, 1975–78, Chief Justice, 1978–80; Justice of Appeal: for Bermuda, 1980–84; for Bahamas, 1981–83; for Belize, 1981–84. Pres., Commn of Inquiry into transshipment of drugs through Bahamas to USA, 1983–84. *Address:* c/o Court of Appeal for the Bahamas, Nassau, Bahamas. *Clubs:* Naval and Military, Royal Commonwealth Society; Lyford Cay (Nassau).

SMITH, James Andrew Buchan, CBE 1959; DSc; FRSE 1952; retired as Director of the Hannah Dairy Research Institute, Ayr, Scotland, 1951–70 (Acting Director, 1948–51); *b* 26 May 1906; *yr s* of late Dr James Fleming Smith, JP, MB, CM, Whithorn, Wigtownshire; *m* 1933, Elizabeth Marion, *d* of James Kerr, Wallasey, Cheshire; four *d*. *Educ:* Leamington College, Warwicks; Univ. of Birmingham. PhD (Birmingham) 1929; DSc (London) 1940. Graduate Research Asst: at UCL, 1929–30; at Imperial College, London, 1930–32; Lectr in Biochemistry, Univ. of Liverpool, 1932–36; Biochemist, Hannah Dairy Research Inst., 1936–46; Lectr in Biochemistry, Univ. of Glasgow, 1946–47. President: Society of Dairy Technology, 1951–52; Nutrition Society, 1968–71; Treasurer, Internat. Union of Nutritional Sciences, 1969–75. Hon. LLD Glasgow, 1972. *Publications:* scientific papers in Biochemical Jl, Jl of Dairy Research, Proc. Nutrition Soc., etc. *Recreation:* gardening. *Address:* Flaxton House, 1 St Leonard's Road, Ayr KA7 2PR. *T:* Ayr 264865. *Club:* Farmers'.

SMITH, James Archibald Bruce, CBE 1981; British Council Representative, Indonesia, 1978–83; *b* 12 Sept. 1929; *s* of James Thom Smith and Anna Tyrie; *m* 1957, Anne Elizabeth Whittle; three *d*. *Educ:* Forfar Acad.; Edinburgh Univ. (MA 1952); Sch. of Econs, Dundee (BScEcon 1953); Jesus Coll., Cambridge. RAF, 1953–55. HMOCS, Dist Officer, Kenya, 1956–62; British Council, 1962–: Asst, Edinburgh, 1962–65; Asst Rep., Tanzania, 1965–66; Reg. Dir, Kumasi, Ghana, 1966–69; Rep., Sierra Leone, 1969–72; seconded to ODM, 1973–75; Dir, Personnel Dept, 1975–77; Controller, Personnel and Staff Recruitment Div., 1977–78. *Recreations:* Angusiana, reading, walking, collecting. *Address:* Calluna, West Hemming Street, Letham, Angus. *T:* Forfar 81212.

SMITH, James Cadzow, DRC; CEng; FIMechE, FIEE, FIMarE; FRSE 1981; Chairman, Eastern Electricity Board, since 1982; *b* 28 Nov. 1927; *s* of James Smith and Margaret Ann Cadzow; *m* 1954, Moira Barrie Hogg; one *s* one *d*. *Educ:* Bellvue Secondary Sch.; Heriot-Watt Coll.; Strathclyde Univ. Diploma of Royal Coll. of Science and Technology, Glasgow. CBIM. Engineer Officer, Mercantile Marine, 1948–53; various positions in Fossil and Nuclear Power Generation, 1953–73; Director of Engineering, N Ireland Electricity Service, 1973–74; Deputy Chairman and Chief Executive, 1974–77; Chm., E Midlands Electricity Bd, 1977–82. *Recreations:* music, drama, mountaineering. *Address:* c/o Eastern Electricity Board, PO Box 40, Wherstead, Ipswich IP9 2AQ. *T:* Ipswich 55841.

SMITH, Maj.-Gen. (James) Desmond (Blaise), CBE 1944; DSO 1944; CD 1948; Chairman: Blaise Investments Ltd; Desmond Smith Investments Ltd; Dashabel Properties and Interiors Ltd; WMT Holdings Ltd; Seasalv Marine Ltd; Combined Industrial Properties Plc; Damar Properties Ltd; Member, Commonwealth War Graves Commission, since 1986; *b* 7 Oct. 1911; *s* of William George Smith, Ottawa, Canada; *m* 1st, 1937, Miriam Irene Blackburn (*d* 1969); two *s*; 2nd, 1979, Mrs Belle Shenkman, Ottawa. *Educ:* Ottawa University, Canada; Royal Military College, Canada. Joined Canadian Army, Royal Canadian Dragoons, 1933; National Defence HQ, Ottawa, as Assistant Field Officer in Bde Waiting to Governor-General of Canada, 1939. Served War of 1939–45, in England, Italy and N W Europe holding following commands and appts: CO Royal Canadian Dragoons; Comdr: 4th Cdn Armoured Bde; 5th Cdn Armoured Bde; 1st Cdn Inf. Bde: 5th Cdn Armoured Div.; 1st Cdn Inf. Div.; Chief of Staff, 1st Cdn Corps. Comdt Canadian Army Staff Coll., 1946; Imp. Defence Coll., 1947; Sec. Chiefs of Staff Cttee, 1948–50; Military Sec. Cdn Cabinet Defence Cttee, 1948–50; QMG, Canadian Army, 1951; Chairman, Canadian Joint Staff, London, 1951–54; Commandant, National Defence College of Canada, 1954–58; Adjutant-General of the Canadian Army, 1958–62. Colonel, HM Regt of Canadian Guards, 1961–66. Director: Indal Technologies Ltd, Canada; Teron Construction Ltd, Canada; MEKO Holdings Ltd, Hong Kong, and numerous other cos. Freedom, City of London, 1954. Croix de Guerre, 1944, Chevalier,

Legion of Honour, 1944 (France); Comdr Military Order of Italy, 1944; Officer Legion of Merit (USA), 1944; Order of Valour (Greece), 1945. KStJ 1961 (CStJ 1952); KLJ 1985. *Recreations*: shooting, tennis, ski-ing, painting. *Address*: 50 Albert Court, SW7 2HB. *Clubs*: Carlton, Mark's; Queen's Tennis.

SMITH, Sir (James) Eric, Kt 1977; CBE 1972; FRS 1958; ScD; Secretary, Marine Biological Association of the UK, and Director Plymouth Laboratory, 1965–74; *b* 23 Feb. 1909; *er s* of Walter Smith and Elsie Kate Smith (*née* Pickett); *m* 1934, Thelma Audrey Cornish; one *s* one *d*. *Educ*: Hull Grammar School; King's College, London. Student Probat., Plymouth Marine Biol Lab., 1930–32; Asst Lecturer: Univ. of Manchester, 1932–35; Univ. of Sheffield, 1935–38; Univ. of Cambridge, 1938–50; Prof. of Zoology, Queen Mary Coll., Univ. of London, 1950–65 (Vice-Principal, 1963–65). Trustee, British Museum (Natural History), 1963–74, Chm. Trustees, 1969–74. Pres., Soc. for History of Nat. History, 1984–; Member: Council, Royal Soc., 1962–63 and 1972–74 (Vice-Pres., 1973–74); Senate, Univ. of London, 1963–65; Scientific Advisory Committee, British Council; Science Research Council, 1965–67; Nature Conservancy, 1969–71; Royal Commn, Barrier Reef, 1970; Adv. Bd for the Research Councils, 1974–77. Pres., Devonshire Assoc., 1980–81. Fellow: King's Coll., London, 1964; Queen Mary College, 1967; Plymouth Polytechnic, 1977. Hon. Associate, Natural Hist. Mus., 1981. Hon. DSc Exeter, 1968. Gold Medal, Linnean Soc., 1971; Frink Medal, Zoological Soc., 1981. *Publications*: various on marine biology, embryology, nervous anatomy and behaviour. *Recreations*: walking, gardening. *Address*: Wellesley House, 7 Coombe Road, Saltash, Cornwall PL12 4ER. *Club*: Royal Western Yacht.

SMITH, James Ian, CB 1974; Member: Potato Marketing Bd, since 1985; Panel of Chairmen, Civil Service Selection Board, since 1984; *b* 22 April 1924; *s* of late James Smith, Ballater, Aberdeenshire, and of Agnes Michie; *m* 1947, Pearl Myra Fraser; one *s*. *Educ*: Alderman Newton's Sch., Leicester; St Andrews Univ. Served War of 1939–45: India and Burma; RA (attached Indian Mountain Artillery), Lieut, 1943–46. Entered Dept of Agriculture for Scotland, 1949; Private Sec. to Parly Under-Sec. of State, Scottish Office, 1953; Dept of Agriculture for Scotland: Principal, 1953; Asst Sec., 1959; Asst Sec., Scottish Development Dept, 1965–67; Under-Sec., Dept of Agriculture and Fisheries for Scotland, 1967–72; Sec., Dept of Agriculture and Fisheries for Scotland, 1972–84. Mem., ARC, 1967–72, 1983–84. Mem., St Andrews Links Trust, 1985–. *Recreation*: golf. *Address*: 7 Hillpark Loan, Edinburgh EH4 7ST. *T*: 031–336 4652. *Club*: Royal Commonwealth Society.

SMITH, James Stewart, CMG 1955; Nigerian Administrative Service, retired; *b* 15 Aug. 1900; 4th *s* of late Charles Stewart Smith, HM Consul-General at Odessa; *m* 1955, Rosemary Stella Middlemore, *er d* of late Dr and Mrs P. T. Hughes, Bromsgrove, Worcs. *Educ*: Marlborough; King's College, Cambridge. Entered Nigerian Administrative Service, 1924; Senior District Officer 1943; Resident 1945; Senior Resident 1951; retired 1955. Papal Order of Knight Commander of Order of St Gregory the Great, 1953. *Recreations*: gardening, watching cricket, chess. *Address*: Davenham, Graham Road, Malvern, Worcs. *T*: Malvern 68667. *Club*: United Oxford & Cambridge University.

SMITH, Janet (B.) A.; *see* Adam Smith.

SMITH, Janet Hilary, (Mrs R. E. A. Mathieson); QC 1986; *b* 29 Nov. 1940; *d* of Alexander Roe and Margaret Holt; *m* 1st, 1959, Edward Stuart Smith; two *s* one *d*; 2nd, 1984, Robin Edward Alexander Mathieson. *Educ*: Bolton School. Called to the Bar, Lincoln's Inn, 1972. *Recreations*: gardening, music, keeping house. *Address*: (chambers) 5 Essex Court, Temple, EC4; 25 Byrom Street, Manchester. *T*: 061–834 5238.

SMITH, Jeremy Fox Eric; Chairman, Smith St Aubyn (Holdings) plc, 1973–86; *b* 17 Nov. 1928; *s* of Captain E. C. E. Smith, MC, and B. H. Smith (*née* Williams); *m* 1953, Julia Mary Rona, *d* of Sir Walter Burrell, 8th Bt, CBE, TD; two *s* two *d*. *Educ*: Eton; New College, Oxford. Chairman, Transparent Paper Ltd, 1965–76. Chairman, London Discount Market Assoc., 1978–80. *Recreations*: hunting, shooting, stalking, skiing. *Address*: Balcombe House, Balcombe, Sussex RH17 6PB. *T*: Balcombe 811267. *Clubs*: Beefsteak; Leander (Henley on Thames).

SMITH, Dr John, OBE 1945; TD 1950; Deputy Chief Medical Officer, Scottish Home and Health Department, 1963–75, retired; *b* 13 July 1913; *e s* of late John Smith, DL, JP, Glasgow and Symington, and Agnes Smith; *m* 1942, Elizabeth Fleming (*d* 1981), twin *d* of late A. F. Wylie, Giffnock; three *s* one *d* (and one *s* decd). *Educ*: High Sch., Glasgow; Sedbergh Sch.; Christ's Coll., Cambridge; Glasgow Univ. BA 1935; MA 1943; MB, BChir Cantab 1938; MB, ChB Glasgow 1938; MRCPG 1965; FRCPG 1967; FRCPE 1969; FFCM 1972. TA (RA from 1935, RAMC from 1940); War Service, 1939–46; ADMS Second Army, DDMS (Ops and Plans) 21 Army Group (despatches); OC 155 (Lowland) Fd Amb., 1950–53; ADMS 52 (Lowland) Div., 1953–56; Hon. Col 52 Div. Medical Service, 1961–67. House appts Glasgow Victoria and Western Infirmaries; joined Dept of Health for Scotland, 1947; Medical Supt, Glasgow Victoria Hosps, 1955–58; rejoined Dept of Health for Scotland, 1958; specialised in hospital planning. QHP 1971–74. Officier, Ordre de Leopold I (Belgium), 1947. *Publications*: articles on medical administration and hospital services in various medical jls. *Recreations*: rifle shooting (shot in Scottish and TA representative teams); hill walking, gardening. *Address*: Murrayfield, Biggar, Lanarkshire. *T*: Biggar 20036. *Clubs*: Naval and Military; New (Edinburgh).
See also R. C. Smith, Sir T. B. Smith.

SMITH, Rt. Hon. John, PC 1978; QC (Scot.) 1983; MP (Lab) Monklands East, since 1983 (Lanarkshire North, 1970–83); *b* 13 Sept. 1938; *s* of late Archibald Leitch Smith and of Sarah Cameron Smith; *m* 1967, Elizabeth Margaret Bennett; three *d*. *Educ*: Dunoon Grammar Sch.; Glasgow Univ. (MA, LLB). Advocate, Scottish Bar, 1967–. Contested East Fife, 1961 by-election and 1964. PPS to Sec. of State for Scotland, Feb.-Oct. 1974; Parly Under-Sec. of State, 1974–75, Minister of State, 1975–76, Dept of Energy; Minister of State, Privy Council Office, 1976–78; Sec. of State for Trade, 1978–79; principal Opposition Spokesman on Trade, Prices and Consumer Protection, 1979–82, on Energy, 1982–83, on Employment, 1983–84, on Trade and Industry, 1984–. Winner, Observer Mace, Nat. Debating Tournament, 1962. *Recreations*: tennis, hill-walking. *Address*: 21 Cluny Drive, Edinburgh EH10 6DW. *T*: 031–447 3667.

SMITH, Professor John Cyril, CBE 1983; QC 1979; FBA 1973; Professor of Law in the University of Nottingham 1958–Aug. 1987, and Head of Department of Law 1956–74, and 1977–86; *b* 15 Jan. 1922; 2nd *s* of Bernard and Madeline Smith; *m* 1957, Shirley Ann Walters; two *s* one *d*. *Educ*: St Mary's Grammar Sch., Darlington; Downing Coll., Cambridge (Hon. Fellow, 1977). Served Royal Artillery, 1942–47 (Captain). BA 1949, LLB 1950, MA 1954, LLD 1975 Cantab. Called to Bar, Lincoln's Inn, 1950; Hon. Bencher, 1977; Hon. Mem., Midland and Oxford Circuit Bar Mess. Nottingham University: Assistant Lecturer in Law, 1950–52; Lecturer, 1952–56; Reader, 1956–57; Pro-Vice-Chancellor, 1973–77; Hon. Pres. of Convocation, 1978–. Commonwealth Fund Fellow, Harvard Law Sch., 1952–53. Member: Criminal Law Revision Cttee, 1977– (co-opted, 1960–66 (theft reference) and 1970–77); Policy Adv. Cttee, 1975–85. Pres., Soc. of Public Teachers of Law, 1979–80. Hon. LLD Sheffield, 1984. *Publications*: (with J. A. C. Thomas) A Casebook on Contract, 1957, 7th edn 1982; (with Brian Hogan) Criminal Law, 1965, 5th edn 1983; Law of Theft, 1968, 5th edn 1984; Criminal Law, Cases and Materials, 1975, 2nd edn 1980; (with I. H. Dennis and E. J. Griew) Codification of the Criminal Law, 1985. *Recreations*: walking, gardening. *Address*: 445 Derby Road, Lenton, Nottingham NG7 2EB. *T*: Nottingham 782323.

SMITH, John Derek, MA, PhD; FRS 1976; Member of Scientific Staff, Medical Research Council, Laboratory of Molecular Biology, Cambridge, since 1962; *b* 8 Dec. 1924; *s* of Richard Ernest Smith and Winifred Strickland Smith (*née* Davis); *m* 1955, Ruth Irwin Aney (marr. diss. 1968). *Educ*: King James' Grammar Sch., Knaresborough; Clare Coll., Cambridge. Mem., Scientific Staff, Agric Research Council Virus Research Unit, Cambridge, 1945–59; Research Fellow, Clare Coll., 1949–52; with Institut Pasteur, Paris, 1952–53; Rockefeller Foundn Fellow, Univ. of California, Berkeley, 1955–57; California Institute of Technology: Sen. Research Fellow, 1959–62; Sherman Fairchild Scholar, 1974–75. *Publications*: numerous papers in scientific jls on biochemistry and molecular biology. *Recreation*: travel. *Address*: MRC Laboratory of Molecular Biology, Hills Road, Cambridge CB2 2QH. *T*: Cambridge 248011; 12 Stansgate Avenue, Cambridge. *T*: Cambridge 247841.

SMITH, Air Vice-Marshal John Edward, CB 1979; CBE 1972; AFC 1967; Air Officer Administration, Headquarters Strike Command, 1977–81; retired; *b* 8 June 1924; *m* 1944, Roseanne Margurite (*née* Eriksson); four *s* two *d* (and one *s* decd). *Educ*: Tonbridge Sch. Served in Far East, ME, USA and Germany as well as UK Stations since joining the Service in Nov. 1941. *Recreations*: sailing, travel. *Address*: 1 Butlers Grove, Great Linford, Bucks MK14 5DT. *Club*: Royal Air Force.

SMITH, Rear-Adm. John Edward D.; *see* Dyer-Smith.

SMITH, (John) Edward (McKenzie) L.; *see* Lucie-Smith.

SMITH, John Herbert, CBE 1977; FCA, IPFA, CIGasE; Member, Management Committee, since 1975, Deputy Chairman, since 1984, Pension Funds Property Unit Trust; *b* 30 April 1918; *s* of Thomas Arthur Smith and Pattie Lord; *m* 1945, Phyllis Mary Baxter; two *s* three *d*. *Educ*: Salt High Sch., Shipley, Yorks. Articled Clerk, Bradford and Otley, 1934–39. Served War: RAMC, 1940–46. Dep. Clerk and Chief Financial Officer, Littleborough, Lancs, 1946–49; West Midlands Gas Bd, 1949–61 (various posts, finishing as Asst Chief Accountant); Chief Accountant, Southern Gas Bd, 1961–65; Director of Finance and Administration, East Midlands Gas Bd, 1965–68; Mem. (full-time), East Midlands Gas Bd, 1968 (Dep. Chm., 1968–72); Mem. for Finance, Gas Council, June-Dec. 1972; British Gas Corporation: Mem. for Finance, 1973–76; Dep. Chm. and Chief Exec., 1976–83. Chm., Nationalised Industries Finance Panel, 1978–83. Chairman: Moracrest Investments, 1977–85; United Property Unit Trust (formerly Industrial and Commercial Property Unit Trust), 1985– (Mem., 1983–84; Mem., Management Cttee, 1985–); Member, Management Committee: Lazard American Exempt Fund, 1976–; British American Property Unit Trust, 1982–. Mem. Council, Inst. of Chartered Accountants, 1977–81. FRSA 1985. *Recreations*: music, piano playing, choral activities. *Address*: 81 Albany, Manor Road, East Cliff, Bournemouth, Dorset BH1 3EJ. *T*: Bournemouth 298157.

SMITH, John Hilary, CBE 1970 (OBE 1964); Secretary, Imperial College of Science and Technology, and Clerk to the Governors, since 1979; *b* 20 March 1928; 2nd *s* of late P. R. Smith, OBE and Edith Prince; *m* 1964, Mary Sylvester Head; two *s* one *d*. *Educ*: Cardinal Vaughan Sch., London; University Coll. London; University Coll., Oxford. BA Hons London 1948. Mil. service, 1948–50, commnd Queen's Own Royal W Kent Regt. Cadet, Northern Nigerian Administration, 1951; Supervisor, Admin. Service Trng, 1960; Dep. Sec. to Premier, 1963; Dir Staff, Develt Centre, 1964; Perm. Sec., Min. of Finance, Benue Plateau State, 1968; Vis. Lectr, Duke Univ., 1970; Financial Sec., British Solomon Is, 1970; Governor of Gilbert and Ellice Islands, 1973–76, of Gilbert Islands, 1976–78. Mem. Council, Scout Assoc., 1980– (Chm., Cttee of Council, 1984–); Pres., Pacific Is Soc. of UK and Ireland, 1981–85. Governor: St Mary's Coll., Strawberry Hill, 1980–; Cardinal Vaughan School, 1982–. *Publications*: How to Write Letters that get Results, 1965; Colonial Cadet in Nigeria, 1968; articles in S Atlantic Quarterly, Administration, Jl of Overseas Administration, Nigeria. *Recreations*: walking, writing, music. *Address*: 47B Princes Gardens, SW7 1LU. *Club*: Royal Commonwealth Society.

SMITH, Sir John Kenneth N.; *see* Newson-Smith.

SMITH, John (Lindsay Eric), CBE 1975; *b* 3 April 1923; *s* of Captain E. C. E. Smith, MC, LLD; *m* 1952, Christian, *d* of late Col U. E. C. Carnegy of Lour, DSO, MC; two *s* two *d* (and one *d* decd). *Educ*: Eton (Fellow, 1974–); New Coll., Oxford (MA; Hon. Fellow, 1979). Served Fleet Air Arm 1942–46 (Lieut RNVR). MP (C) Cities of London and Westminster, Nov. 1965–1970; Mem., Public Accounts Cttee, 1968–69. National Trust: Mem., Historic Bldgs Cttee, 1952–61; Mem. Exec. Cttee, 1961–85; Mem. Council, 1961–; Dep. Chm., 1980–85. Member: Standing Commission on Museums and Galleries, 1958–66; Inland Waterways Redevelopment Cttee, 1959–62; Historic Buildings Council, 1971–78; Redundant Churches Fund, 1972–74; Nat. Heritage Memorial Fund, 1980–82. Director: Coutts & Co., 1950–; Financial Times Ltd, 1959–68; Rolls Royce Ltd, 1955–75; Dep. Governor, Royal Exchange Assurance, 1961–66. Founder, Manifold and Landmark Charitable Trusts. High Steward of Maidenhead, 1966–75. Freeman of Windsor and Maidenhead, 1975. FSA; Hon. FRIBA, 1973. JP Berks, 1964; DL 1978, Lord-Lieut, 1975–78, Berks. *Address*: Shottesbrooke Park, Maidenhead, Berks; 1 Smith Square, SW1. *Clubs*: Pratt's, Beefsteak, Brooks's.

SMITH, John M.; *see* Maynard Smith, J.

SMITH, John Roger B.; *see* Bickford Smith.

SMITH, Rev. John Sandwith B.; *see* Boys Smith.

SMITH, John Wilson, CBE 1982; JP; DL; Chairman: Liverpool Football Club, since 1973; Sports Council, since 1985 (Member, since 1980); *b* 6 Nov. 1920; *m* 1946, Doris Mabel Parfitt; one *s*. *Educ*: Oulton High School, Liverpool. Director: Tetley Walker Ltd, 1966–77; First Castle Electronics plc, 1978–. Member: Football Trust, 1980–; Restructuring Cttee, Football League, 1982–; Chairman: Duke of Edinburgh's Merseyside Industrial Award Council, 1977–; Cttee of Inquiry into Lawn Tennis (report, 1980); Anfield Foundn, 1984–. JP Liverpool, 1971; DL Merseyside, 1983. *Recreation*: golf. *Address*: Pine Close, Mill Lane, Gayton, Wirral, Merseyside. *T*: 051–342 5362. *Club*: Reform.

SMITH, Jonathan A.; *see* Ashley-Smith.

SMITH, Prof. Joseph Victor, FRS 1978; Louis Block Professor of Physical Sciences, University of Chicago, since 1977 (Professor of Mineralogy and Crystallography, 1960–76); *b* 30 July 1928; *s* of Henry Victor Smith and Edith (*née* Robinson); *m* 1951, Brenda Florence Wallis; two *d*. *Educ*: Cambridge Univ. (MA, PhD). Fellow, Carnegie Instn of Washington, 1951–54; Demonstrator in Mineralogy and Petrology, Cambridge

Univ., 1954–56; Asst then Associate Prof., Pennsylvania State Univ., 1956–60. Editor, Power Diffraction File, 1959–69. Visiting Prof., California Inst. of Technology, 1965; Consultant, Union Carbide Corp., 1956–. Murchison Medal, 1980; Roebling Medal, 1982. US Nat. Acad. of Scis, 1986. *Publications:* Feldspar Minerals, Vols 1 and 2, 1975; Geometrical and Structural Crystallography, 1982; numerous articles on crystallography, mineralogy, petrology and planetology. *Recreations:* music, painting. *Address:* Department of the Geophysical Sciences, University of Chicago, 5734 S Ellis Avenue, Chicago, Ill 60637, USA. *T:* 312–962 8110. *Club:* Quadrangle (Chicago).

SMITH, Dr Joseph William Grenville, MD; FRCPath; FFCM; FIBiol; Director, Public Health Laboratory Service, since 1985; *b* 14 Nov. 1930; *s* of Douglas Ralph and Hannah Letitia Margaret Smith; *m* 1954, Nira Jean (*née* Davies); one *s. Educ:* Cathays High School, Cardiff; Welsh Nat. Sch. of Medicine (MD); Dip. Bact. Sen. Lectr, Dept of Bacteriology and Immunology, LSHTM, 1960–65; Consultant Clinical Bacteriologist, Radcliffe Infirmary, Oxford, 1965–69; Gen. Practitioner, Islington, 1970–71; Consultant Epidemiologist, Dep. Dir, Epidemiological Res. Lab., PHLS, 1971–76; Dir, Nat. Inst. for Biological Standards and Control, 1976–85. Member: Cttee on Safety of Medicines, 1978–; Jt Cttee on Vaccination and Immunisation, 1976–; British Pharmacopoea Commn, 1976–85; Chairman: Cttee on Vaccination and Immunization Procedures, MRC, 1976–; Simian Virus Cttee, MRC, 1982–. *Publications:* (with E. B. Adams and D. R. Laurence) Tetanus, 1969; papers on tetanus, immunization, and epidemiology of infections in scientific and med. jls. *Recreation:* the arts. *Address:* Public Health Laboratory Service Board, 61 Colindale Avenue, NW9 5DF. *T:* 01–200 1295. *Club:* Athenæum.

SMITH, Hon. Kenneth George, OJ 1973; **Hon. Mr Justice Smith;** Justice of Appeal, Bahamas, since 1985; *b* 25 July 1920; *s* of Franklin C. Smith; *m* 1942, Hyacinth Whitfield Connell; two *d. Educ:* Primary schs; Cornwall Coll., Jamaica; Inns of Court Sch. of Law, London. Barrister-at-Law, Lincoln's Inn. Asst Clerk of Courts, 1940–48; Dep. Clerk of Courts, 1948–53; Clerk of Courts, 1953–56; Crown Counsel, 1956–62; Asst Attorney-Gen., 1962–65; Supreme Court Judge, 1965–70; Judge of Appeal, Jamaica, 1970–73; Chief Justice of Jamaica, 1973–85. *Recreations:* swimming, gardening. *Address:* 5 Wagner Avenue, Kingston 8, Jamaica.

SMITH, Kenneth Graeme Stewart, CMG 1958; JP; retired as Civil Secretary, The Gambia, West Africa, 1962; *b* 26 July 1918; 3rd *s* of late Prof. H. A. Smith, DCL; unmarried. *Educ:* Bradfield; Magdalen College, Oxford. Cadet, Colonial Administrative Service, Tanganyika, 1940; appointments in Colonial Service, 1945–62. JP Dorset, 1967. *Address:* The Old House, Newland, Sherborne, Dorset DT9 3AQ. *T:* Sherborne 812754.

SMITH, Kenneth Shirley, MD, BSc London, FRCP; Lieutenant-Colonel RAMC 1942; Hon. Physician and Cardiologist, Charing Cross Hospital and to the London Chest Hospital; formerly: Chief Medical Officer Marine and General Mutual Life Assurance Society; Consulting Physician, Samaritan Free Hospital for Women; Staff Examiner in Medicine, University of London; Examiner in Medicine, Conjoint Board; *b* 23 Jan. 1900; *s* of E. Shirley Smith; *m* 1929, Alice Mary Hoogewerf; one *s* two *d. Educ:* London University; Middlesex Hospital (Senior Scholar). BSc, 1st Class Hons in Physiology, London, 1923; formerly House Physician, Casualty Medical Officer and Medical Registrar Middlesex Hospital; also Resident Medical Officer, Nat. Hosp. for Diseases of the Heart, 1927; Pres., British Cardiac Soc. Member, Assoc. of Physicians of Great Britain. Editor, British Heart Journal. Organizing Secretary, First European Congress of Cardiology, London, 1952. Served with 1st Army in N Africa, later with CMF in Italy, Greece and Austria (despatches 1943). Gold Staff Officer, Coronation of King George VI. *Publications:* Contributor to British Encyclopædia of Medical Practice, 1937; Papers on cardiological and pulmonary subjects in British Heart Journal, American Heart Journal, Quarterly Journal of Medicine, Lancet, British Medical Journal, Practitioner, etc. *Recreation:* water colour. *Address:* 5 Asmun's Hill, Hampstead Garden Suburb, NW11. *T:* 01–455 2706.

SMITH, Laura; *see* Smith, A. L. A.

SMITH, Sir Laurence Barton G.; *see* Grafftey-Smith.

SMITH, Lawrence Delpré; Senior Puisne Judge of the Supreme Court of Sarawak, North Borneo and Brunei, 1951–64, retired; *b* 29 October 1905; *m*; one *s* three *d. Educ:* Christ's Hospital; Hertford College, Oxford; Gray's Inn. Colonial Administrative Service, 1929; Colonial Legal Service, 1934; Tanganyika, 1929; Palestine, 1946; Gambia, 1948. *Address:* 34 The Avenue, Muswell Hill, N10 2QL. *T:* 01–883 7198.

SMITH, Lawrence Joseph, OBE 1976; Executive Officer with Transport and General Workers Union, since 1979; two *d.* Served in HM Forces, 1941–47; joined London Transport, 1947; District Officer, TGWU, 1961, London District Secretary, 1965, National Officer, 1966, National Secretary, Passenger Services Group, 1971. Part-time Mem., London Transport Bd, 1983–. Mem., TUC Gen. Council, 1979–. *Recreations:* gardening, football. *Address:* Transport House, Smith Square, SW1P 3JB. *T:* 01–828 7788.

SMITH, Lawrence Roger Hines, FSA; Keeper of Oriental Antiquities, British Museum, since 1977; *b* 19 Feb. 1941; *s* of Frank Ernest Smith and Eva Lilian Smith (*née* Hines); *m* 1965, Louise Geraldine Gallini (marr. diss. 1986); one *s* five *d. Educ:* Collyer's Grammar Sch., Horsham; Queens' Coll., Cambridge (BA). British Museum: Asst Keeper, Dept of Manuscripts, 1962; Dept of Oriental Antiquities, 1965; Dep. Keeper, 1976. Academic adviser, Great Japan Exhibn, RA, 1981–82, and contrib. to catalogue. Uchiyama Prize, Ukiyoe Soc. of Japan, 1986. *Publications:* Netsuke: the miniature sculpture of Japan (with R. Barker), 1976; Flowers in Art from East and West (with P. Hulton), 1979; Japanese Prints: 300 years of albums and books (with J. Hillier), 1980; Japanese Decorative Arts 1600–1900 (with V. Harris), 1982; The Japanese Print since 1900, 1983; Contemporary Japanese Prints, 1985; articles and reviews in learned jls. *Recreations:* walking, running, bellringing, music. *Address:* Department of Oriental Antiquities, British Museum, WC1B 3DG. *T:* 01–636 1555, ext. 314.

SMITH, Sir Leonard (Herbert), Kt 1982; CBE 1977 (MBE 1963); Deputy Treasurer, Liberal Party, since 1972; *b* 28 May 1907; *s* of Herbert Thomas and Harriett Smith; *m* 1943, Ruth Pauline Lees; two *d. Educ:* King's Sch., Chester. Active member of Liberal Party, 1922–; Sec. and Agent, Chester Div., 1929–39; Chief Agent, 1949–51; Foundn Officer, Liberal Party Orgn, 1946–49; Sec., Campaign Fund, 1948–50; Mem., Party Council, 1952–67 (Hon. Mem., 1967–); Hon. Treasurer, 1967–68; Vice-Pres., 1968; Dep. Chm., Fund Raising Cttee, 1980–; Pres., Eastern Reg., 1982– (Hon. Treasurer, 1972–80). Social Policy Exec., Booker McConnell Ltd, 1957–72. Member: Exec. and Council, Royal Commonwealth Soc. for the Blind, 1957– (Appeal Dir, 1951–57); British Cttee, World Prevention of Blindness Campaign, 1975–82; Exec. Cttee, West India Cttee, 1959–71; Hon. Sec., British Caribbean Assoc., 1958–; Hon. Secretary and Treasurer: London Cttee, English Harbour Restoration Fund, 1959–67; Sir Frank Worrell Commonwealth Meml Fund, 1968–; Hon. Treasurer, Women Caring Trust, 1972–; Jt Chm., Appeal Cttee, E-SU, 1975–. Mem. Council, Football Assoc., 1970–. JP Middlesex, subseq. City of London, 1963–77; Mem., City of London Adv. Cttee, 1965–77, Inner London Adv. Cttee, 1968–77, for appointment of magistrates. *Address:* Fen Farmhouse,

Buxhall, Stowmarket, Suffolk IP14 5DG. *T:* Rattlesden 370. *Clubs:* National Liberal (Chm., 1972–), English-Speaking Union, MCC.

SMITH, Leslie Charles, OBE 1968; Founder Director, Eastway Zinc Alloy Co. Ltd, 1965–82; *b* 6 March 1918; *s* of Edward A. Smith and Elizabeth Smith; *m* 1948, Nancy Smith; two *s* one *d. Educ:* Enfield Central School. Export Buyer, 1938–40; Lieut, RNVR, 1940–46. Founder Dir, Lesney Products, 1947, Jt Man. Dir 1947–73, Man. Dir 1973–80; Chief Exec. Officer, 1980–81, Vice-Chm., 1981–82. FInstM; FBIM 1976; FInstD 1979. *Recreations:* ski-ing, sailing, golf. *Address:* White Timbers, 9a Broad Walk, N21 3DA. *T:* 01–886 1656. *Clubs:* Naval; Royal Thames Yacht, Royal Ocean Racing, Royal Motor Yacht, Parkstone Yacht, Poole Harbour Yacht; Parkstone Golf, Hadley Wood Golf.

SMITH, Sir Leslie (Edward George), Kt 1977; Chairman, The BOC Group plc (formerly The British Oxygen Co. Ltd), 1972–85; *b* 15 April 1919; *m* 1st, 1943, Lorna Bell Pickworth; two *d*; 2nd, 1964, Cynthia Barbara Holmes; one *s* one *d. Educ:* Christ's Hospital, Horsham, Sussex. Served War, Army (Royal Artillery, Royal Fusiliers), 1940–46. Variety of activities, 1946–55. Joined British Oxygen as Accountant, 1956, Group Man. Dir, 1969–72, Group Chm. and Chief Exec., 1972–79, Chm., 1979–85. Dir, Cadbury Schweppes, 1977–. Member: Exec. Cttee, King Edward VII Hospital for Officers, 1978–; British Gas Corp., 1982–; Adv. Council, European Banking Co., 1984–. FCA. *Recreations:* unremarkable. *Address:* Cookley House, Cookley Green, Swyncombe, near Henley-on-Thames, Oxon RG9 6EN.

SMITH, Llewellyn; Member (Lab) South East Wales, European Parliament, since 1984; *b* 16 April 1944; *m*; two *s* one *d. Educ:* Cardiff University. Formerly with Pilkington Glass, George Wimpey and Workers' Educational Assoc. Mem., CND. *Address:* The Mount, Uplands, Tynewydd, Newbridge, Gwent.

SMITH, Maggie, (Mrs Margaret Natalie Cross), CBE 1970; Actress; Director, United British Artists, since 1982; *b* 28 Dec. 1934; *d* of Nathaniel Smith and Margaret Little (*née* Hutton); *m* 1st, 1967, Robert Stephens, *qv* (marr. diss. 1975); two *s*; 2nd, 1975, Beverley Cross, *qv. Educ:* Oxford High School for Girls. Studied at Oxford Playhouse School under Isabel van Beers. Hon. DLitt St Andrews, 1971; Hon. DLitt Leicester, 1982. First appearance, June 1952, as Viola in OUDS Twelfth Night; 1st New York appearance, Ethel Barrymore Theatre, June 1956, as comedienne in New Faces. Played in Share My Lettuce, Lyric, Hammersmith, 1957; The Stepmother, St Martin's, 1958. Old Vic Co., 1959–60 season: The Double Dealer; As You Like It; Richard II; The Merry Wives of Windsor; What Every Woman Knows; Rhinoceros, Strand, 1960; Strip the Willow, Cambridge, 1960; The Rehearsal, Globe, 1961; The Private Ear and The Public Eye (Evening Standard Drama Award, best actress of 1962), Globe, 1962; Mary, Mary, Queen's, 1963 (Variety Club of Gt Britain, best actress of the year); The Country Wife, Chichester, 1969; Design for Living, LA, 1971; Private Lives, Queen's, 1972, Globe, 1973, NY, 1975 (Variety Club of GB Stage Actress Award, 1972); Peter Pan, Coliseum, 1973; Snap, Vaudeville, 1974; Night and Day, Phoenix, 1979; Virginia, Haymarket, 1981 (Standard Best Actress Award, 1982); The Way of the World, Chichester and Haymarket, 1984 (Standard Best Actress Award, 1985); Interpreters, Queen's, 1985; *at National Theatre:* The Recruiting Officer, 1963; Othello, The Master Builder, Hay Fever, 1964; Much Ado About Nothing, Miss Julie, 1965; A Bond Honoured, 1966; The Beaux' Stratagem, 1970 (also USA); Hedda Gabler, 1970 (Evening Standard Best Actress award); War Plays, 1985; *at Festival Theatre, Stratford, Ontario:* 1976: Antony and Cleopatra, The Way of the World, Measure for Measure, The Three Sisters; 1977: Midsummer Night's Dream, Richard III, The Guardsman, As You Like It, Hay Fever; 1978: As You Like It, Macbeth, Private Lives; 1980: Virginia; Much Ado About Nothing. *Films:* The VIP's, 1963; The Pumpkin Eater, 1964; Young Cassidy, 1965; Othello, 1966; The Honey Pot, 1967; Hot Millions, 1968 (Variety Club of GB Award); The Prime of Miss Jean Brodie, 1968 (Oscar; SFTA award); Oh! What a Lovely War, 1968; Love and Pain (and the Whole Damned Thing), 1973; Travels with my Aunt, 1973; Murder by Death, 1976; California Suite, 1977 (Oscar); Death on the Nile, 1978; Quartet, 1981; Clash of the Titans, 1981; Evil Under the Sun, 1982; The Missionary, 1982; A Private Function, 1984 (BAFTA award, Best Actress, 1985); The Loves of Lily, 1985; A Room with a View, 1986. *Recreation:* reading. *Address:* c/o ICM Ltd, 388 Oxford Street, W1N 9HE. *T:* 01–629 8080.

SMITH, Malcolm Andrew F.; *see* Ferguson-Smith.

SMITH, Dame Margôt, DBE 1974; *b* 5 Sept. 1918; *d* of Leonard Graham Brown, MC, FRCS, and Margaret Jane Menzies; *m* 1947, Roy Smith, MC, TD (*d* 1983); two *s* one *d. Educ:* Westonbirt. Chm., Nat. Conservative Women's Adv. Cttee, 1969–72; Chm., Nat. Union of Conservative and Unionist Assocs, 1973–74. Mem., NSPCC Central Exec. Cttee. *Address:* Howden Lodge, Spennithorne, Leyburn, N Yorks DL8 5PR. *T:* Wensleydale 23621.

SMITH, Mark Barnet; His Honour Judge Mark Smith; a Circuit Judge since 1972; *b* 11 Feb. 1917; *s* of David Smith and Sophie Smith (*née* Abrahams); *m* 1943, Edith Winifred Harrison; two *d. Educ:* Freehold Council Sch., Oldham; Manchester Grammar Sch.; Sidney Sussex Coll., Cambridge. MA (Hons) Natural Sci.). Asst Examr in HM Patent Office, 1939 (and promoted Examr in 1944, while on war service). Served War, RA (Staff Sergt), 1940–46. Returned to Patent Office, 1946. Called to Bar, Middle Temple, 1948. Left Patent Office, end of 1948; pupil at the Bar, 1949. Temp. Recorder of Folkestone, 1971; a Recorder of the Crown Court, Jan.-Apr. 1972.

SMITH, Maurice George; retired; Under-Secretary, Ministry of Overseas Development, 1968–76; *b* 4 Sept. 1915; *s* of Alfred Graham and Laura Maria Smith; *m* 1940, Eva Margaret Vanstone; two *s. Educ:* Sir Walter St John's School, Battersea. Examiner, Estate Duty Office, 1939. Flt Lieut RAF, 1942–46. Asst Principal, Min. of Civil Aviation, 1947; Principal, 1948; transferred to Colonial Office, 1950; seconded Commonwealth Office, 1954–55; Asst Secretary, Colonial Office, 1959; transferred to Dept of Technical Co-operation, 1961; Min. of Overseas Development, 1964; Under-Sec. and Principal Finance Officer, ODM, 1968. Chairman, Knights' Assoc. of Christian Youth Clubs, Lambeth, 1970– (Hon. Sec., 1950–70). *Recreations:* voluntary work in youth service, travel. *Address:* 52 Woodfield Avenue, SW16. *T:* 01–769 5356.

SMITH, Prof. Michael, FRS 1986; FRSC 1981; Professor, Department of Biochemistry, University of British Columbia, since 1970; *b* 26 April 1932; *s* of Rowland Smith and Mary Agnes Smith; *m* 1960, Helen Wood Smith; two *s* one *d. Educ:* Arnold Sch., Blackpool, England; Manchester Univ. (BSc Chemistry, PhD). Post-doctoral fellowship, Brit. Columbia Res. Council, 1956–60; Res. Associate, Inst. for Enzyme Res., Univ. of Wisconsin, 1960–61; Hd, Chemistry Sect., Vancouver Lab., Fisheries Res. Bd of Canada, 1961–66; Associate Prof., Dept of Biochem., Univ. of Brit. Columbia, 1966–70. Career Investigator, MRC of Canada, 1966–. *Recreations:* ski-ing, hiking, sailing. *Address:* Department of Biochemistry, Faculty of Medicine, University of British Columbia, 2146 Health Sciences Mall, Vancouver, BC V6T 1W5, Canada. *T:* (604) 228 3179. *Club:* Faculty (Univ. of British Columbia).

SMITH, Michael Edward C.; *see* Carleton-Smith.

SMITH, Prof. Michael G.; Crosby Professor of Human Environment, Department of Anthropology, Yale University, since 1978; *b* 18 Aug. 1921; *m*; three *s*. *Educ:* University College London. BA 1948, PhD 1951; Fellow, 1985. Research Fellow, Inst. of Social and Economic Research, University Coll. of the West Indies, 1952–56, Sen. Research Fellow, there, 1956–58; Sen. Research Fellow, Nigerian Inst. of Social and Economic Research, Ibadan, 1958–60; Sen. Lectr (Sociology), Univ. Coll. of the WI, 1960–61; Prof. of Anthropology: Univ. of California, Los Angeles, 1961–69; University Coll. London, 1969–75. Special Advr to Prime Minister of Jamaica, 1975–78. Hon. LLD McGill, 1976. Order of Merit (Jamaica), 1973. *Publications:* The Economy of Hausa Communities of Zaria, 1955; Labour Supply in Rural Jamaica, 1956; (with G. J. Kruijer) A Sociological Manual for Caribbean Extension Workers, 1957; Government in Zazzau, 1800–1950, 1960; Kinship and Community in Carriacou, 1962; West Indian Family Structure, 1962; Dark Puritan, 1963; The Plural Society in the British West Indies, 1965; Stratification in Grenada, 1965; (ed, with Leo Kuper) Pluralism in Africa, 1969; Corporations and Society, 1974; The Affairs of Daura, 1978. *Address:* Department of Anthropology, Yale University, New Haven, Conn 06520, USA.

SMITH, Michael K.; *see* Kinchin Smith.

SMITH, Michael Wharton; food journalist, television presenter and cookery book writer, since 1970; *b* 24 April 1927; *s* of Fred and Helena Smith; *m* 1952, Elisabeth Hamilton Downs; one *s* one *d*. *Educ:* Wakefield Grammar School; Ecole Hotelière, Lausanne (School diploma in Hotel Admin.). Food journalist, broadcaster and TV presenter with BBC Pebble Mill at One, 1976–86; Food Correspondent, Homes and Gardens, 1980–87; participator in numerous TV films; restaurateur and designer. Glenfiddich Award for Man contributing most to educn in food and wine, 1982. *Publications:* Fine English Cookery, 1973; Best of British Cookware, 1975; Cooking with Michael Smith, 1981; Michael Smith's Complete Recipe Collection from BBC Pebble Mill, 1982; The Homes and Gardens Cook Book, 1983; A Cook's Tour of Britain, 1984; New English Cookery, 1985; Michael Smith Entertains, 1986; The Afternoon Tea Book, 1986; The Glyndebourne Picnic Book, 1987; articles in magazines. *Recreation:* classical music. *Address:* 4 Woodside Road, Kingston upon Thames KT2 5AT. *T:* 01–546 0603. *Club:* Guild of Food Writers.

SMITH, Dr (Norman) Brian, CBE 1980; Chairman, Metal Box plc, since 1986 (Deputy Chairman, 1985–86); Director: Lister & Co. plc, since 1985; Davy Corporation, since 1986; *b* 10 Sept. 1928; *s* of late Vincent and Louise Smith; *m* 1955, Phyllis Crossley; one *s* one *d* (and one *s* decd). *Educ:* Sir John Deane's Grammar Sch., Northwich; Manchester Univ. (PhD Phys. Chemistry, 1954). FTI 1981. Joined ICI Ltd, Terylene Council, 1954; Fibres Division: Textile Develt Dir, 1969; Dep. Chm., 1972; Chm., 1975–78; ICI Main Bd, 1978–85; Director: Fiber Industries Inc., 1972–83; Canadian Industries Ltd, 1981–85; Territorial Dir for the Americas, and Chm., ICI Americas Inc., 1981–85 (Dir, 1980–85); Non-Exec. Dir, Carrington Viyella Ltd, 1979–81. Pres., British Textile Confedn, 1977–79; Chairman: Man-Made Fibres Producers Cttee, 1976–78; EDC for Wool Textile Industry, 1979–81; Mem., BOTB, 1980–81, 1983– (Chm., N American Adv. Group, 1983–). *Recreations:* cricket, sailing, tennis, gardening, watching football. *Address:* Metal Box plc, Queens House, Forbury Road, Reading RG1 3JH. *T:* Reading 581177.

SMITH, Norman Jack, MA, MPhil; Managing Director, Smith Rea Energy Associates Ltd, since 1981; Director: SAI Tubular Services Ltd, since 1983; Smith Rea Energy Analysts, since 1985; Atkins Oil and Gas Engineering, since 1985; *b* 14 April 1936; *s* of late Maurice Leslie and Ellen Dorothy Smith; *m* 1967, Valerie Ann, *o d* of late A. E. Frost; one *s* one *d*. *Educ:* Grammar Sch., Henley-on-Thames; Oriel Coll., Oxford (MA); City Univ. (MPhil). Dexion Ltd, 1957; Vickers Ltd, 1960; Baring Brothers & Co. Ltd, 1969; seconded as Industrial Director, 1977, Dir-Gen., 1978–80, Offshore Supplies Office, Dept of Energy; Chm., British Underwater Engineering Ltd, 1980–83. Member: Soc. of Business Economists, 1958–; Offshore Energy Technology Bd, 1978–80. *Publications:* sundry articles in economic and similar jls. *Recreations:* walking, swimming, photography, history. *Address:* c/o Smith Rea Energy Associates Ltd, 3 Beer Cart Lane, Canterbury, Kent CT1 2NJ. *T:* Canterbury 459441. *Club:* United Oxford & Cambridge University.

SMITH, Prof. (Norman John) David; Head of Department of Dental Radiology, King's College School of Medicine and Dentistry (formerly King's College Hospital Dental School), since 1972, and Professor of Dental Radiology, University of London, since 1978; *b* 2 Feb. 1931; *s* of late Norman S. Smith; *m* 1st, 1954, Regina Eileen Lugg (marr. diss.); one *s*; 2nd, 1983, Mary Christine Pocock; one *d*. *Educ:* King's Coll. Sch., Wimbledon; King's Coll., London; KCH Dental Sch. (BDS 1963; MPhil 1969); Royal Free Hosp. Sch. of Medicine (MSc 1966). Apprenticed to Pacific Steam Navigation Co., 1948–51; Officer Service, Royal Mail Lines, 1952–58 (Master Mariner, 1957); part-time posts at KCH Dental Sch., Guy's Hosp. Dental Sch. and in gen. dental practice, 1966–69; Sen. Lectr in Dental Surg., KCH Dental Sch., 1969–72; Reader in Dental Radiol., Univ. of London, 1973. Member: Southwark Bor. Council, 1974–78; GLC for Norwood, 1977–86 (Leader of Opposition, ILEA, 1979–86); Thames Water Authority, 1977–83; SE Thames RHA, 1978–; Council, Open Univ., 1978–81, 1982–; Court, Univ. of London, 1982–; Governor, Bethlem Royal and Maudsley Hosps, 1980–82; Mem., Bethlem Royal and Maudsley SHA, 1982–86. Visiting Professor: Univ. of Garyounis, 1980–84; Univ. of Stellenbosch, 1982; Univ. of Alexandria, 1984. Liveryman, Hon. Co. of Master Mariners. Sir Charlton Briscoe Res. Prize, KCH Med. Sch., 1969. *Publications:* Simple Navigation by the Sun, 1974; Dental Radiography, 1980; articles in dental jls. *Recreations:* sailing, nature photography. *Address:* c/o King's College School of Medicine and Dentistry, Denmark Hill, SE5 8RX. *T:* 01–274 6222, ext. 2863.

SMITH, Ven. Percival; *see* Smith, Ven. A. M. P.

SMITH, Peter, FSA; Secretary, Royal Commission on Ancient Monuments in Wales, since 1973; *b* 15 June 1926; *s* of late L. W. Smith, HMI, and Mrs H. Smith (*née* Halsted); *m* 1954, Joyce Evelyn, *d* of late J. W. Abbott and of Alice Abbott (*née* Lloyd); two *s* one *d*. *Educ:* Peter Symonds' Sch., Winchester; Oriel Coll. and Lincoln Coll. (Open Scholar), Oxford (BA, Hons Mod. Hist. 1947); Hammersmith Sch. of Building (Inter ARIBA 1950). Royal Commission on Ancient Monuments in Wales: Jun. Investigator, 1949; Sen. Investigator, 1954; Investigator in Charge of Nat. Monuments Record, 1963. President: Cambrian Archaeological Assoc., 1979; Vernacular Architecture Gp, 1983–86. G. T. Clark Prize, 1969; Alice Davis Hitchcock Medallion, Soc. of Architectural Historians of GB, 1978. *Publications:* Houses of the Welsh Countryside, 1975; contribs to Agrarian History of England; periodical literature on historic domestic architecture. *Recreations:* reading, drawing, learning Welsh. *Address:* Tŷ-coch, Lluest, Llanbadarn Fawr, Aberystwyth, Dyfed SY23 3AU. *T:* Aberystwyth 3556.

SMITH, Peter Alexander Charles, OBE 1981; Chairman: Securicor Group plc, since 1974; Security Services plc, since 1974; *b* 18 Aug. 1920; *s* of Alexander Alfred Smith and Gwendoline Mary (*née* Beer); *m* 1945, Marjorie May Humphrey; one *s*. *Educ:* St Paul's Sch., London. Admitted solicitor, 1948. Served RA, 1941–46: Captain; Adjt, 17th Medium Regt. Partner, Hextall, Erskine & Co., 1953–79. Chairman: British Security Industry Assoc. Ltd, 1977–81; Metal Closures Gp plc, 1983– (Dir, 1972, Dep. Chm., 1981); Dir, Fitch Lovell plc. Mem. Council, Royal Warrant Holders Assoc., 1976–, Vice-Pres., 1981–82, Pres., 1982–83. CBIM. FRSA. *Recreations:* golf, music, photography. *Address:* Vigilant House, 24 Gillingham Street, SW1V 1HZ. *T:* 01–828 5611. *Club:* British Racing Drivers (Hon. Life Mem.).

SMITH, Peter Bruce; Head Master, Bradfield College, since 1985; *b* 18 March 1944; *s* of Alexander D. Smith and Grace Smith; *m* 1968, Diana Margaret Morgan; two *d*. *Educ:* Magdalen College School, Oxford; Lincoln College, Oxford (Old Members Scholar; MA). Asst Master, Rugby Sch., 1967–85 (Head of Hist. Dept, 1973–77, Housemaster of School Field, 1977–85). Mem. Governing Body, Downe House Sch., 1985–. Captain Oxfordshire County Cricket Club, 1971–77 (Minor Counties Champions, 1974). *Recreations:* antiquarian, sporting, literary. *Address:* Headmaster's House, Bradfield College, Bradfield, Reading RG7 6AR. *Club:* Vincent's (Oxford).

SMITH, Peter Claudius G.; *see* Gautier-Smith.

SMITH, Dr Peter Graham; Director General Guided Weapons and Electronics, Ministry of Defence (Procurement Executive), since 1982; *b* 12 June 1929; *s* of James A. and Florence L. Smith; *m* 1952, Doreen Millicent (*née* Wyatt); two *d*. *Educ:* Wellington Grammar Sch., Shropshire; Birmingham Univ. (BSc, PhD). Radar Res. Estab., 1953–75: seconded to British Defence Staff, Washington, 1966–68; Supt, Airborne Defensive Radar Div., 1970–75; Dir Defence Science 8, MoD, 1975–78; Dir Surveillance and Instrument Projs, MoD (PE), 1978–82. *Recreations:* gardening, reading, modelling. *Address:* c/o Fleetbank House, Salisbury Square, EC4Y 8AT. *T:* 01–632 3835.

SMITH, Peter John, IPFA; General Manager, Tyne and Wear Residuary Body, since 1985; County Treasurer, Tyne and Wear County Council, 1980–86; *b* 31 Dec. 1936; *s* of Frank and Sarah Ann Smith; *m* 1959, Marie Louise Smith; one *s* one *d*. *Educ:* Rastrick Grammar Sch., Brighouse, W Yorkshire. Trainee Accountant, Huddersfield CBC, 1953–59; Accountancy Asst, Bradford CBC, 1959–61; Asst Chief Accountant, Chester CBC, 1961–63; Computer Manager, Keighley BC, 1963–66; Asst City Treasurer, Gloucester CBC, 1966–69; Dep. Borough Treasurer, Gateshead CBC, 1969–73; Asst County Treasurer, Tyne and Wear CC, 1973–74, Dep. County Treasurer, 1974–80. Treasurer: NE Regional Airport Jt Cttee, 1980–86; Northumbria Police Authority, 1980–86; Northumbria Probation and After Care Cttee, 1980–86; Mem., Tyne and Wear Passenger Transport Exec. Bd, 1981–86. Director: N American Property Unit Trust; Northern Investors Co. *Recreations:* fell walking, jogging. *Address:* Wheatsheaf House, Station Road, Beamish, Co. Durham DH9 0QU. *T:* Durham 700481. *Club:* Beamish Park Golf.

SMITH, Peter Vivian Henworth; Solicitor, HM Customs and Excise, since 1986; *b* 5 Dec. 1928; *s* of Vivian and Dorothea Smith; *m* 1955, Mary Marjorie, *d* of Frank John Willsher and Sybil Marjorie Willsher; five *d*. *Educ:* Clacton County High Sch.; Brasenose Coll., Oxford (MA, BCL). Called to the Bar, Lincoln's Inn, 1953. HM Overseas Civil Service: Resident Magistrate, Nyasaland, 1955–63; Registrar, High Court, Nyasaland, 1963–64; Sen. Resident Magistrate, Malaŵi, 1964–69; Puisne Judge, Malaŵi, 1969–70; HM Customs and Excise: Legal Asst, 1970–72; Sen. Legal Asst, 1972–76; Asst Solicitor, 1976–82; Prin. Asst Solicitor, 1982–85. *Recreations:* classical music, walking, bridge. *Address:* Likabula, 14 St Albans Road, Clacton-on-Sea CO15 6BA. *T:* Clacton-on-Sea 422053.

SMITH, Philip; Deputy Director Warship Design (Electrical), Ministry of Defence (Navy), 1969–73, retired; *b* 19 May 1913; *m* 1940, Joan Mary Harker; one *s* one *d*. *Educ:* Bishop Wordsworth's Sch., Salisbury; Bristol Univ. BSc (First Cl. Hons). Graduate Trainee Apprentice, BTH Co., 1934–37; Outside Construction Engrg, BTH Co., 1937–38; Central Electricity Bd, 1938–39; Admty (Electrical Engrg Dept) (now MoD Navy), 1939–: past service at Chatham Dockyard and Dockyard Dept, HQ; Electrical Engrg Design Divs; Head of Electrical Dept, Admty Engrg Laboratory, West Drayton. CEng, FIEE, FIMechE; RCNC. *Recreations:* horticulture, golf, oil painting. *Address:* Myrfield, Summer Lane, Combe Down, Bath. *T:* Combe Down 833408. *Club:* Bath Golf.

SMITH, Philip George, CBE 1973; Director, Metal Market & Exchange Co. Ltd, since 1954 (Chairman, 1967–84); Adviser, Triland Metals Ltd, since 1984. *Educ:* St Lawrence Coll., Ramsgate; Royal School of Mines, London. ARSM, BSc (Eng). Director: Bassett Smith & Co. Ltd, 1946–75; Bardyke Chemicals Ltd, 1968–; (non-exec.), Comfin (Commodity & Finance) Co. Ltd, 1978–82. Mem. Inst. Exports; Mem. Cttee, London Metal Exchange, 1949–64 (Chm. 1954–64). Adviser to Dept of Trade and Industry; part-time Mem. Sugar Bd, 1967–76. *Address:* 67B Camlet Way, Hadley Wood, Barnet EN4 0NL.

SMITH, Ralph E. K. T.; *see* Taylor-Smith.

SMITH, (Raymond) Gordon (Antony); *see* Etherington-Smith.

SMITH, Sir Raymond (Horace), KBE 1967 (CBE 1960); Chairman of Hawker Siddeley and other British companies in Venezuela; Consultant to: Rolls-Royce Ltd; The Economist; *b* 1917; *s* of Horace P. Smith and Mabelle (*née* Osborne-Couzens); *m* 1943, Dorothy, *d* of Robert Cheney Hart. *Educ:* Salesian College, London; Barcelona University. Served War of 1939–45, with British Security Co-ordination, NY, and with Intelligence Corps, in France, India, Burma, Malaya, Indonesia. Civil Attaché British Embassy, Caracas, 1941; Negotiator, sale of British owned railway cos to Venezuelan Govt and other S American govts, 1946–50; Rep., London Reinsurers in Venezuela, 1954–60; Consultant: Cammell Laird; Mirrlees; British Aerospace, 1952–82; Provincial Insurance Co. Ltd; Fairey Engrg Ltd, etc; Director: Daily Journal; Anglo-Venezuelan Cultural Inst., 1946–80; Board Dir, Anglo-Venezuelan Trade Assoc.; Pres. British Commonwealth Assoc. of Venezuela, 1955–57. Companion of Royal Aeronautical Society. Knight Grand Cross, St Lazarus of Jerusalem; Venezuelan Air Force Cross. *Recreations:* tennis, water ski-ing, winter sports (Cresta Run and ski-ing). *Address:* Edificio Fedecámaras, Oficinas GH, Piso 4, Avenida El Empalme, El Bosque, Caracas 1050, Venezuela; Carlton Ledge, 37 Lowndes Street, SW1. *Clubs:* White's, Naval and Military; Caracas Country, Jockey (Caracas); St Moritz Tobogganing (Switzerland).

SMITH, Sir Reginald Verdon; *see* Verdon-Smith.

SMITH, Richard; *see* Smith, W. R.

SMITH, Richard H. S.; *see* Sandford Smith.

SMITH, Richard Maybury H.; *see* Hastie-Smith.

SMITH, Sir Richard P.; *see* Prince-Smith, Sir (William) Richard.

SMITH, Sir Richard Robert L.; *see* Law-Smith.

SMITH, Sir Richard R. V.; *see* Vassar-Smith.

SMITH, Prof. R(ichard) Selby, OBE 1981; MA (Oxon), MA (Harvard); Professor of Education and Head of Department of Education, University of Tasmania, 1973–79, now Professor Emeritus; b 1914; s of Selby Smith, Hall Place, Barming, Maidstone, Kent, and Annie Rachel Smith (née Rawlins); m 1940, Rachel Hebe Philippa Pease, Rounton, Northallerton, Yorks; two s. Educ: Rugby Sch.; Magdalen Coll., Oxford; Harvard Univ. Asst Master, Milton Acad., Milton, Mass, USA, 1938–39; House Tutor and Sixth Form Master, Sedbergh Sch., 1939–40; War of 1939–45: Royal Navy, 1940–46; final rank of Lt-Comdr, RNVR. Administrative Asst, Kent Education Cttee, 1946–48; Asst Education Officer, Kent, 1948–50; Dep. Chief Education Officer, Warwickshire, 1950–53; Principal, Scotch Coll., Melbourne, 1953–64; Foundation Prof. of Educn, Monash Univ., 1964, Dean of Faculty of Educn, 1965–71; Principal, Tasmanian Coll. of Advanced Education, 1971–73. Chairman: Victorian Univs and Schools Examinations Bd, 1967–71; State Planning and Finance Cttee, Australian Schools Commn, 1974–77, 1980–83; Vice-Pres., Australian Council for Educnl Research, 1976–79. Publications: Towards an Australian Philosophy of Education, 1965; (ed jtly) Fundamental Issues in Australian Education, 1971; The Education Policy Process in Tasmania, 1980; Australian Independent Schools: yesterday, today and tomorrow, 1983. Recreations: fishing, shooting, gardening, sailing, riding and ornithology. Address: 297 Nelson Road, Mount Nelson, Tasmania 7007, Australia. Clubs: Naval; Melbourne (Melbourne).

SMITH, Robert Carr, PhD; Director, Kingston Polytechnic, since 1982; b 19 Nov. 1935; s of Edward Albert Smith and Olive Winifred Smith; m 1960, Rosalie Mary (née Spencer); one s one d. Educ: Queen Elizabeth's School, Barnet; Southampton Univ. (BSc); London Univ. (PhD). Research Asst, Guy's Hosp. Med. Sch., 1957–61; Lectr, Senior Lectr, Reader, Prof. of Electronics, Southampton Univ., 1961–82. Seconded to DoE, 1973–74. Chm., Engineering Profs' Conf., 1980–82; Member: Design Council, 1983–; Council for Industry and Higher Educn, 1985–. Publications: research papers on radiation physics, laser physics, technological change. Recreations: visual arts. Address: 22 Astor Close, Kingston Hill, Kingston-upon-Thames, Surrey KT2 7LT. T: 01–541 1534.

SMITH, Robert Courtney, CBE 1980; MA, CA; Chairman: Sidlaw Group, since 1980; Standard Life Assurance, since 1982; Alliance and Second Alliance Trust, since 1984; b 10 Sept. 1927; 4th s of late John Smith, DL, JP, and Agnes Smith, Glasgow and Symington; m 1954, Moira Rose, d of late Wilfred H. Macdougall, CA, Glasgow; one s two d (and one s decd). Educ: Kelvinside Academy, Glasgow; Sedbergh Sch.; Trinity Coll., Cambridge. BA 1950, MA 1957. Served, Royal Marines, 1945–47, and RMFVR, 1951–57. Partner, Arthur Young McClelland Moores & Co., Chartered Accountants, 1957–78. Director: Wm Collins (Vice-Chm.), 1978–; Volvo Trucks (GB), 1979–; Edinburgh Investment Trust, 1983–; British Alcan Aluminium, 1983–; Bank of Scotland, 1985–. Chm., Scottish Industrial Develt Adv. Bd (Mem. 1972–); Pres., Business Archives Council of Scotland; Dir, Nat. Register of Archives (Scotland); Chancellor's Assessor, Glasgow Univ., 1984–. Mem., Horserace Betting Levy Bd, 1977–82; Deacon Convener, Trades House of Glasgow, 1976–78. Mem. Council, Inst. of Chartered Accountants of Scotland, 1974–79. Trustee, Carnegie Trust for Univs of Scotland. Hon. LLD Glasgow, 1978. OStJ. Recreations: racing, gardening. Address: North Lodge, Dunkeld, Perthshire. T: Dunkeld 574; (professional) 50 George Square, Glasgow G2 1RR. Clubs: East India; Western (Glasgow); Hawks (Cambridge).
See also John Smith, Sir T. B. Smith.

SMITH, (Robert) Harvey; show jumper, farmer; b 29 Dec. 1938; m Irene Shuttleworth (marr. diss. 1986); two s. First major win with Farmer's Boy. Leading Show Jumper of the Year; other major wins include: King George V Cup, Royal Internat. Horse Show, 1958; has won the John Player Trophy 7 times, King George V Gold Cup once, and the British Jumping Derby 4 times; Grand Prix and Prix des Nations wins in UK, Ireland, Europe and USA; took part in Olympic Games, 1968 and 1972; best-known mounts: Farmer's Boy, Mattie Brown, Olympic Star, O'Malley, Salvador, Harvester. BBC TV Commentator, Los Angeles Olympics, 1984. Publications: Show Jumping with Harvey Smith, 1979; Bedside Jumping, 1985.

SMITH, Sir Robert Hill, 3rd Bt cr 1945, of Crowmallie, Co. Aberdeen; b 15 April 1958; s of Sir (William) Gordon Smith, 2nd Bt, VRD, and of Diana (née Goodchild); S father, 1983. Educ: Merchant Taylors' School; Aberdeen Univ. Heir: b Charles Gordon Smith, b 21 April 1959. Address: 5 Elmfield Avenue, Aberdeen AB2 3NU.

SMITH, Roger Bonham; Chairman and Chief Executive Officer, General Motors, since 1981; b Columbus, Ohio, 12 July 1925. Educ: Detroit University Sch.; Univ. of Michigan (BBA, MBA). Served US Navy, 1944–46. General Motors: Sen. Clerk, subseq. Director, general accounting, Detroit Central Office, 1949–58; Dir, financial analysis sect., NY Central Office, 1960, later Asst Treas.; transf. to Detroit as Gen. Asst Comptroller, then Gen. Asst Treas., 1968; Treasurer, 1970; Vice-Pres. i/c Financial Staff, 1971, also Mem. Admin Cttee, 1971–; Vice-Pres. and Gp Exec. i/c Nonautomotive and Defense Gp, 1972; Exec. Vice-Pres., Mem. Bd of Dirs and Mem. Finance Cttee, 1974, also Mem. Exec. Cttee, 1974–; Vice-Chm. Finance Cttee, 1975–80, Chm., 1981–. Conceived GM Cancer Res. Awards, 1978 (Chm., administering Foundn); Trustee, Cranbrook Schs and Mich Colls Foundn Inc., 1981–; Chm., United Foundn, Detroit, 1975–; Member: Policy Cttee, Business Roundtable, 1981–; Business Council, 1981–; Motor Vehicle Manufrs Assoc., 1981–82; Soc. of Automotive Engrs, 1978–. Hon. Dr DePauw, 1979; Hon. Dr Albion Coll., 1982. Address: General Motors, 3044 West Grand Boulevard, Detroit, Michigan 48202, USA; (home) Bloomfield Hills, Michigan 48013. Clubs: Economic, Detroit, Detroit Athletic (Detroit); Links (NY).

SMITH, Roger C.; see Castle-Smith.

SMITH, Roger John; Deputy Chairman and Managing Director, Tricentrol plc, since 1983; b 20 April 1939; s of Horace W. Smith and Marjorie E. Pummery; m 1962, Margaret R. Campbell; one s two d. Educ: Bedford School. Nat. Service, Subaltern, RCT, 1958–60. Dir, Family Group business, incl. Lea Heating Merchants (later part of Tricentrol), 1960–70; Man. Dir, Commercial Div., 1971–75, Dir, Special Projects, 1976–78, Tricentrol International; Dir, Group Co-ordination, Tricentrol, 1978–81; Man. Dir, Commercial Div., 1981–83. Director: Combined Technologies Corp. plc; Brengreen Hldgs plc, and other cos. Sloan Fellow, Stanford Univ., 1976. Liveryman: Founders' Co.; Coach and Harnessmakers' Co. Recreations: Methodist church activities, sailing, squash, tennis, reading; Dir of Luton Town Football Club. Address: Gilvers, Markyate, Herts. T: Luton 840536. Clubs: City of London; Salcombe Yacht.

SMITH, Prof. Roland; Professor of Marketing (part-time), University of Manchester Institute of Science and Technology, since 1966; b 1 Oct. 1928; s of late Joshua Smith and of Mrs Hannah Smith; m 1954, Joan (née Shaw); no c. Educ: Univs of Birmingham and Manchester. BA, MSc, PhD (Econ). Flying Officer, RAF, 1953. Asst Dir, Footwear Manufacturers' Fedn, 1955; Lectr in Econs, Univ. of Liverpool, 1960; Dir, Univ. of Liverpool Business Sch., 1963. Non-Executive Chairman: Senior Engineering Ltd, 1973; Barrow Hepburn Group, 1974; Chairman: Temple Bar Investment Trust Ltd, 1980–; House of Fraser, 1981–86 (Dep. Chm., 1980–81); Readicut International, 1984– (Dep. Chm., 1982–84); Hepworth Ceramic Holdings, 1986–; Phoenix Properties and Finance,

1986–; Stakis, 1986–; Dir-Consultant to a number of public companies. Recreation: walking. Address: Branksome, Enville Road, Bowdon, Cheshire.

SMITH, Roland Hedley; HM Diplomatic Service; Political Adviser and Head of Chancery, British Military Government, Berlin, since 1984; b 11 April 1943; s of Alan Hedley Smith and Elizabeth Louise Smith; m 1971, Katherine Jane Lawrence; two d. Educ: King Edward VII School, Sheffield; Keble College, Oxford (BA 1st cl. hons 1965, MA 1981). Third Sec., Foreign Office, 1967; Second Sec., Moscow, 1969; Second, later First Sec., UK Delegn to NATO, Brussels, 1971; First Sec., FCO, 1974; First Sec. and Cultural Attaché, Moscow, 1978; FCO, 1980; attached to Internat. Inst. for Strategic Studies, 1983. Publication: Soviet Policy Towards West Germany, 1985. Recreation: music, esp. choral singing. Address: c/o Foreign and Commonwealth Office, SW1A 2AH. Club: Royal Commonwealth Society.

SMITH, Ron, CBE 1973; Member, British Steel Corporation, 1967–77 (Managing Director (Personnel and Social Policy), 1967–72); b 15 July 1915; s of Henry Sidney Smith and Bertha Clara (née Barnwell); m 1940, Daisy Hope (d 1974), d of Herbert Leggatt Nicholson; one d. Educ: Workers' Education Association. Post Office Messenger, 1929; Postman, 1934; Postal and Telegraph Officer, 1951; Treasurer, Union of Post Office Workers, 1953; Gen. Sec., Union of Post Office Workers, 1957–66. General Council, TUC, 1957–66; Civil Service National Whitley Council, 1957–66; Exec. Cttee, Postal, Telegraph and Telephone International, 1957–66; Vice-Chairman, Post Office Dept, Whitley Council, 1959–66. Member: Cttee on Grants to Students, 1958–60; Development Areas, Treasury Advisory Cttee, 1959–60; Cttee on Company Law, 1960–62; National Economic Development Council, 1962–66; Court of Enquiry into Ford Motor Co. Dispute, 1963; Cttee of Enquiry into Pay, etc, of London Transport Bus Staff, 1963–64; Organising Cttee for Nat. Steel Corp., 1966; (part-time) Associated British Ports Hldgs plc (formerly BTDB), 1978–86. President, Postal, Telegraph and Telephone Internat., 1966. Director, BOAC, 1964–70. Recreations: photography, golf. Address: 3 Beech Grove, Epsom, Surrey. Club: Tyrrells Wood Golf.

SMITH, Ronald A. D.; see Dingwall-Smith.

SMITH, Ronald Good; Sheriff of North Strathclyde, since 1984; b 24 July 1933; s of Adam Smith and Selina Spence Smith; m 1962, Joan Robertson Beharrie; two s. Educ: Glasgow University (BL 1962). Private practice to 1984. Recreations: philately, photography, gardening, reading. Address: 369 Mearns Road, Newton Mearns, Glasgow G77 5LZ. T: 041–639 3904.

SMITH, Rosemary Ann, (Mrs G. F. Smith); Headmistress, Wimbledon High School, GPDST, since 1982; b 10 Feb. 1932; d of late Harold Edward Wincott, CBE, editor of the Investors Chronicle, and of Joyce Mary Wincott; m 1954, Rev. Canon Graham Francis Smith; two s two d. Educ: Brighton and Hove High School, GPDST; Westfield College, Univ. of London (BA Hons); London Univ. Inst. of Education (post grad. Cert. in Education). Assistant Teacher: Central Foundation Girls' School, 1964–69; Rosa Bassett Girls' School, 1970–77; Furzedown Secondary School, 1977–80; Deputy Head, Rowan High School, 1980–82. Recreations: theatre, gardening, dressmaking, reading, walking, camping. Address: 30 Gorringe Park Avenue, Mitcham, Surrey CR4 2DG. T: 01–685 0772.

SMITH, Sir Rowland; see Smith, Sir Alexander R.

SMITH, Air Marshal Sir Roy David A.; see Austen-Smith.

SMITH, Sidney William; Regional Administrator, East Anglian Regional Health Authority, 1975–83; b 17 May 1920; s of late Sidney John and Harriet May Smith; m 1943, Doreen Kelly; one s one d. Educ: Wirral Grammar Sch., Cheshire. FHA, ACIS. Dep. Group Sec.: Mansfield Hosp. Management Cttee, 1948–61; Wolverhampton Hosp. Management Cttee, 1961–63; Group Sec., Wakefield Hosp. Management Cttee, 1963–73; Area Administrator, Wakefield Area Health Authority, 1973–75. Member: Management Side, Ancillary Staff, Whitley Council, 1969–83 (Chm., 1982–83); Assoc. of Chief Administrators of Health Authorities, 1974–84 (Chm., 1974–76); Health Services Panel, Inst. of Chartered Secretaries and Administrators, 1978–84 (Chm., 1978–83); Vice Chm., Cambs FPC, 1985–. Dir, Sketchley Hosp. Services Ltd, 1983–84. Recreations: gardening, walking. Address: 77 Gough Way, Cambridge CB3 9LN. T: Cambridge 62307.

SMITH, Prof. (Stanley) Desmond, FRS 1976; FRSE 1972; Professor of Physics, Heriot-Watt University, Edinburgh, since 1970 (Dean of the Faculty of Science, 1981–84); b 3 March 1931; s of Henry George Stanley Smith and Sarah Emily Ruth Smith; m 1956, Gillian Anne Parish; one s one d. Educ: Cotham Grammar Sch., Bristol; Bristol Univ. (BSc, DSc); Reading Univ. (PhD). SSO, RAE, Farnborough, 1956–58; Research Asst, Dept of Meteorology, Imperial Coll., London, 1958–59; Lectr, then Reader, Univ. of Reading, 1960–70; Hd, Dept of Physics, Heriot-Watt Univ., 1970–84. Chm., Edinburgh Instruments Ltd, 1971–. Member: ACARD; Defence Scientific Adv. Cttee; Astronomy Bd, Space & Radio Bd, Engrg Bd, SERC; Council, Inst. of Physics; Educn in Partnership with Industry or Commerce; Technical or Business Innovation in Engrg. C. V. Boys Prizeman, Inst. of Physics, 1976. Publications: Infra-red Physics, 1966; numerous papers on semi-conductor and laser physics, satellite meteorology, nonlinear optics and optical computing. Recreations: tennis, skiing, mountaineering, golf. Address: 4 Cherry Tree View, Balerno, Edinburgh EH14 5AP. T: 031–449 4520.

SMITH, Stanley Frank, MA; CEng, FIMechE, FCIT; Vice-President (Technology), Urban Transport Development Company, Kingston, Ontario, since 1985; b 15 Dec. 1924; s of Frederick and Edith Maria Smith; m 1946, Margaret (née Garrett); two s three d. Educ: Purley Sch.; Hertford Coll., Oxford (MA). Served War, RAF Pilot, 1943–46. Oxford Univ., 1946–49. Rolls-Royce Ltd, 1949–65 (Chief Research Engineer, 1963); British Railways, 1965–71 (Dir of Engineering Research, 1965; Dir of Research, 1966); joined London Transport, 1971: Dir-Gen. of Research and Develt, 1971–72; Chief Mech. Engr, 1972–81, retired; Gen. Manager, Res. Develt, Urban Transport Development Co., 1981–85. Recreations: tennis, sailing. Address: Rural Road 1, Bath, Ontario K0H 1G0, Canada. T: 613–352–7429.

SMITH, Stanley G.; see Graham Smith.

SMITH, Stewart Ranson, CBE 1986; British Council Representative, Spain, since 1980; b 16 Feb. 1931; s of John Smith and Elizabeth Smith; m 1960, Lee Tjam Mui, Singapore. Educ: Bedlington Grammar Sch., Northumberland; Nottingham Univ. (BA, MA); Yale Univ., USA (MA). British Council: Asst Rep., Singapore, 1957–59; Reg. Officer, Overseas A, 1959–61; Dir, Curitiba, Brazil, 1961–65; Asst Rep., Sri Lanka, 1965–69; Planning Officer, London, 1969–70; seconded Min. of Overseas Develt, 1970–73; Rep., Kenya, 1973–76; Controller, Overseas B, British Council, 1976–80. Recreations: music, cricket. Address: c/o British Council, 10 Spring Gardens, SW1A 2BN. Club: Royal Commonwealth Society.

SMITH, Prof. Sir Thomas (Broun), Kt 1981; QC Scotland 1956; DCL Oxon, 1956; LLD Edinburgh, 1963; FRSE 1977; FBA 1958; Professor Emeritus of Edinburgh

University, 1980; General Editor, The Laws of Scotland, Stair Memorial Encyclopædia, since 1981; *b* 3 Dec. 1915; 2nd *s* of late J. Smith, DL, JP, and Agnes Smith, Symington, Lanarkshire; *m* 1940, Ann Dorothea, *d* of late Christian Tindall, CIE, ICS, Exmouth, Devon; one *d* (one *s* one *d* decd). *Educ:* High Sch. of Glasgow; Sedbergh Sch.; Christ Church, Oxford (MA). Boulter Exhibitioner, 1st Class Hons School of Jurisprudence, 1937; Eldon Scholar, 1937; Edinburgh Univ.; 1st Class and Certificate of Honour English Bar Final, Called to English Bar by Grays Inn, 1938. Served TA from 1937; War Service, 1939–46; BEF, Home Forces, Middle East and Central Mediterranean; London Scottish (Gordon Highlanders) and RA (Fd.); variously employed on regimental and intelligence duties and at School of Infantry; Lieut-Colonel (despatches); Lieut-Colonel (TA) Gordon Highlanders, 1950; OC Aberdeen University Contingent, Officers Training Corps, 1950–55; Hon. Colonel, 1964–73. Attached to Foreign Office, 1946–47. Examined by and admitted to Faculty of Advocates in Scotland, 1947. Professor of Scots Law, University of Aberdeen, 1949–58; Dean of Faculty of Law, 1950–53 and 1956–58; Prof. of Civil Law, University of Edinburgh, 1958–68, of Scots Law, 1968–72; Hon. Prof., 1972–80. Hon. Sheriff of Aberdeen, 1950 and of Lothians and Peebles, 1964; Member: Scottish Law Reform Cttee, 1954; Scottish Law Commn, part-time 1965–72, full-time, 1972–80. Director Scottish Universities Law Inst., 1960–72; Hon. Member: Council Louisiana State Law Inst., 1960; Law Soc. of Scotland, 1986; Mem., Academic Advisory Cttee, Universities of St Andrews and Dundee, 1964–; Ford Visiting Professor, Tulane Univ. (Louisiana), 1957–58; Visiting Lecturer, Cape Town and Witwatersrand Universities, 1958; Visiting Prof., Harvard Law Sch., 1962–63; Tagore Prof., Calcutta, 1977. Hon. Foreign Mem., Amer. Acad. of Arts and Sciences, 1969. Hon. LLD: Cape Town, 1959; Aberdeen, 1969; Glasgow, 1978. *Publications:* Doctrines of Judicial Precedent in Scots Law, 1952; Scotland: The Development of its Laws and Constitution, 1955; British Justice: The Scottish Contribution, 1961; Studies Critical and Comparative, 1962; A Short Commentary on the Law of Scotland, 1962; Property Problems in Sale, 1978; Basic Rights and their Enforcement, 1979; contribs to legal publications on Scottish, historical and comparative law. *Recreations:* reading, foreign travel. *Address:* 18 Royal Circus, Edinburgh EH3 6SS. *T:* 031–225 8306. *Clubs:* Naval and Military; New (Edinburgh).
See also John Smith, R. C. Smith.

SMITH, T(homas) Dan; Founder, New Directions, projects to assist ex-offenders, 1978; *b* 11 May 1915; *m* 1939; one *s* two *d.* City Councillor, Newcastle upon Tyne, 1950–65 (Chairman, Finance Cttee); Member: Nat. Sports Council, 1965–69; Royal Commission on Local Government, 1966–69; Shakespeare Theatre Trust, 1968–. Chairman: Northern Economic Planning Council, 1965–70; Peterlee and Aycliffe Develt Corp., 1968–70. Researcher for Amber Films, 1982–85. Consultant on the develt of an internat. science and technology paper, Change, 1982–86. Hon. DCL Newcastle University, 1966. *Publications:* Essays in Local Government, 1965; contrib. to Which Way, 1970; Education, Science and Technology (paper to British Assoc. for Advancement of Science), 1970; An Autobiography, 1971. *Recreations:* painting, music, writing, sport. *Address:* 92 Millhouse, 5 Hunters Road, Spital Tongues, Newcastle upon Tyne NE2 4AQ.

SMITH, Sir (Thomas) Gilbert, 4th Bt, *cr* 1897; Area Manager; *b* 2 July 1937; *er s* of Sir Thomas Turner Smith, 3rd Bt, and Agnes, *o d* of Bernard Page, Wellington, New Zealand; *S* father, 1961; *m* 1962, Patricia Christine Cooper; two *s* one *d. Educ:* Huntley Sch.; Nelson Coll. *Recreation:* skiing. *Heir: s* Andrew Thomas Smith, *b* 17 Oct. 1965.

SMITH, Rt. Rev. Timothy D.; *see* Thetford, Bishop Suffragan of.

SMITH, Timothy John; MP (C) Beaconsfield, since May 1982; *b* 5 Oct. 1947; *s* of late Captain Norman Wesley Smith, CBE and of Nancy Phyllis Smith; *m* 1980, Jennifer Jane Scott-Hopkins, *d* of Sir James Scott-Hopkins, *qv*; two *s. Educ:* Harrow Sch.; St Peter's Coll., Oxford (MA). FCA. Articled with Gibson, Harris & Turnbull, 1969; Audit Sen., Peat, Marwick, Mitchell & Co., 1971; Company Sec., Coubro & Scrutton (Hldgs) Ltd, 1973. Sec., Parly and Law Cttee, ICA, 1979–82. Pres., Oxford Univ. Conservative Assoc., 1968; Chm., Coningsby Club, 1977–78. MP (C) Ashfield, April 1977–1979; PPS to Chief Sec. HM Treasury, 1983, to Sec. of State for Home Dept, 1983–85. Secretary: Conservative Trade and Industry Cttee, 1985–; Conservative Finance Cttee, 1985–. *Recreations:* theatre, gardening. *Address:* 27 Rosenau Crescent, SW11. *T:* 01–223 3378.

SMITH, Adm. Sir Victor (Alfred Trumper), AC 1975; KBE 1969 (CBE 1963); CB 1968; DSC 1941; Chairman, Australian Chiefs of Staff Committee, 1970–75; Military Adviser to SEATO, 1970–74; *b* 9 May 1913; *s* of George Smith; *m* 1944, Nanette Suzanne Harrison; three *s. Educ:* Royal Australian Naval College. Sub-Lieut, 1935; Lieut, 1936; Lieut-Commander, 1944; Commander, 1947; Captain, 1953; Rear-Admiral, 1963; Vice Admiral, 1968; Chief of Naval Staff and First Naval Member, Austr. Commonwealth Naval Bd, 1968–70; Admiral, 1970. *Recreation:* walking. *Address:* Fishburn Street, Red Hill, ACT 2603, Australia. *T:* Canberra 958942.

SMITH, Walter Campbell, CBE 1949; MC; TD; MA, ScD; *b* 30 Nov. 1887; 2nd *s* of late George Hamilton Smith, Solihull, Warwickshire; *m* 1936, Susan, *y d* of late John Finnegan, Belfast; one *s* one *d. Educ:* Solihull; Corpus Christi, Cambridge. Wiltshire Prize, Cambridge Univ., 1909; Assistant, Dept of Minerals, British Museum, 1910; Deputy Keeper, 1931–37; Deputy Chief Scientific Officer, British Museum (Natural History), 1948–52; also Keeper of Minerals, 1937–52; Non-resident Fellow Corpus Christi, Cambridge, 1921–24; Honorary Secretary, Geological Society of London, 1921–33 (Murchison Medallist, 1945), President, 1955–56, Hon. Mem., 1982; General Secretary, Mineralogical Society, 1927–38, President, 1945–48; President, geological section, British Assoc., 1950; Governor, Royal Holloway Coll., 1922–43, representing Cambridge University; served in the Artists' Rifles, 1910–35 and 1939–42; European War, France, 1914–18 (MC, despatches twice, 1914 Star); Acting Lieut-Colonel, 1918; Brevet Lieut-Colonel, 1935; Second-in-Command, 163 OCTU (The Artists' Rifles), 1939–41. *Publications:* numerous papers on minerals, rocks and meteorites. *Address:* Roof Tops, Back Lane, Goudhurst, Kent.

SMITH, Walter Purvis, CB 1982; OBE 1960 (MBE 1945); Director General, Ordnance Survey, 1977–85; Director, Sys Scan (UK) Ltd, since 1985; *b* 8 March 1920; *s* of John William Smith and Margaret Jane (*née* Purvis); *m* 1946, Bettie Cox; one *s* one *d. Educ:* Wellfield Grammar Sch., Co. Durham; St Edmund Hall, Oxford (MA). FRICS 1951. Commnd RE (Survey), 1940; served War, UK and Europe, 1940–46; CO 135 Survey Engr Regt (TA), 1957–60. Directorate of Colonial (later Overseas) Surveys: served in Ghana, Tanzania, Malawi, 1946–50; Gen. Man., Air Survey Co. of Rhodesia Ltd, 1950–54; Fairey Surveys Ltd, 1954–75 (Man. Dir, 1969–75); Adviser: Surveying and Mapping, UN, NY, 1975–77; Ordnance Survey Review Cttee, 1978–79. Mem., Field Mission, Argentine-Chile Frontier Case, 1965. 15th British Commonwealth Lectr, RAeS, 1968. President: Photogrammetric Soc., 1972–73; European Council of Heads of National Mapping Agencies, 1982–84; Eur. Orgn for Photogrammetric Res., 1984–85; Guild of Surveyors, 1985–; Chm., National Cttee for Photogrammetry and Remote Sensing, 1985–; Dep. Chm., Govt Cttee of Enquiry into Handling of Geographical Information, 1985–; Mem., Gen. Council, RICS, 1967–70 (Chm., Land Survey Cttee, 1963–64). Patron's Medal, RGS, 1985. *Publications:* papers and technical jls. *Recreations:* music, walking, golf. *Address:* 15 Forest Gardens, Lyndhurst, Hants. *T:* Lyndhurst 2566. *Club:* Oriental.

SMITH, (Walter) Richard; Regional Chairman of Industrial Tribunals, since 1976; *b* 12 Oct. 1926; *s* of Walter Richard and Ivy Millicent Smith; *m* 1959, Jean Monica Law; one *s* one *d. Educ:* Bromsgrove Sch.; Birmingham Univ. (LLB). Called to the Bar, Gray's Inn, 1954. A Chairman of Industrial Tribunals, 1971. *Address:* Punter's Hill, Moorwood, near Cirencester, Glos GL7 7EA. *T:* North Cerney 340.

SMITH, Wilbur Addison; author; *b* 1933; *m*; two *s* one *d. Educ:* Michaelhouse, Natal; Rhodes Univ. (BCom). Business executive, 1954–58; factory owner, 1958–64; full-time author, 1964–. *Publications:* When the Lion Feeds, 1964, Dark of the Sun, 1965; Sound of Thunder, 1966; Shout at the Devil, 1968; Gold Mine, 1970; Diamond Hunters, 1971; The Sunbird, 1972; Eagle in the Sky, 1974; Eye of the Tiger, 1975; Cry Wolf, 1976; Sparrow Falls, 1977; Hungry as the Sea, 1978; Wild Justice, 1979; A Falcon Flies, 1980; Men of Men, 1981; The Angels Weep, 1982; The Leopard hunts in Darkness, 1984; The Burning Shore, 1985; Power of the Sword, 1986. *Recreations:* fly fishing, big game angling. *Address:* c/o Heinemann, 10 Upper Grosvenor Street, W1X 9PA.

SMITH, William Austin N.; *see* Nimmo Smith.

SMITH, William Frederick Bottrill, CBE 1964; Accountant and Comptroller General of Inland Revenue, 1958–68; Principal, Uganda Resettlement Board, 1972–74; *b* 29 Oct. 1903; *s* of late Arthur and Harriet Frances Smith; *m* 1926, Edyth Kilbourne (*d* 1970). *Educ:* Newton's, Leicester. Entered the Inland Revenue Dept, Civil Service, 1934. President, Inland Revenue Staff Federation, 1945–47. Vice-Pres., CS Fedn Drama Socs. Church Warden, All Saints Church, Las Palmas. *Address:* 11 Preston Avenue, Rustington-on-Sea, Littlehampton, W Sussex; Los Frailes, Tafira Alta, Gran Canaria, Canary Islands.

SMITH, William French; Partner, Gibson, Dunn & Crutcher, 1946–80 and since 1985; Attorney General of the United States of America, 1981–85; *b* 26 Aug. 1917; *s* of William and Margaret Smith; *m* 1964, Jean Webb. *Educ:* Univ. of Calif (AB); Harvard Univ. (LLB). Served USNR, 1942–46 (Lieut). Barrister, 1942. Member: US Adv. Commn on Internat. Educnl and Cultural Affairs, 1971–78; Stanton Panel on Internat. Inf., Educn and Cultural Relns, 1974–75. Mem., LA Cttee on For. Relns, 1954–74; Pres., LA World Affairs Council, 1975–76 (Mem., Bd of Dirs, 1970–81). Mem., Bd of Dirs, Legal Aid Foundn, LA, 1963–72; Trustee, Henry E. Huntington Library and Art Gall., 1971–. Golden Plate Award, Amer. Acad. of Achievement, 1984; Franklin Soc. Award, Fedn for Amer. Immigrations Reform, 1986. *Address:* Gibson, Dunn & Crutcher, 333 South Grand Avenue, Los Angeles, Calif 90071, USA.

SMITH, William Jeffrey, CB 1976; Under-Secretary, Northern Ireland Office, 1972–76; *b* 14 Oct. 1916; 2nd *s* of Frederick Smith, Sheffield, and Ellen Hickinson, Ringinglow, Derbyshire; *m* 1942, Marie Hughes; one *s* one *d. Educ:* King Edward VII Sch., Sheffield; University Coll., Oxford (Schol.) (MA). Employed by Calico Printers' Assoc., Manchester, 1938–40 and in 1946. Served War, Army: enlisted Sept. 1939, embodied, 1940; RA and York and Lancaster Regt (Captain), 1940–46. Dominions Office (subseq. CRO), 1946; Principal, 1948; Office of UK High Commissioner in South Africa, 1953–56; Asst Sec., 1959; sundry internat. confs; Dept of Technical Co-operation, 1961–64; Min. of Overseas Development, 1964–70; Overseas Develt Admin., 1970–72; UK Rep. to UNESCO, 1969–72. Sec. to Widgery Tribunal on loss of life in Londonderry, 1972; Northern Ireland Office, 1972. *Recreations:* theatre, scrambling up mountains, walking. *Address:* Salmons, 121 Salmons Lane, Whyteleafe, Surrey CR3 0HB. *T:* 01–660 5493.

SMITH, William McGregor, OBE 1970; HM Inspector of Constabulary for Scotland, 1970–75, retired; *b* 14 April 1910; *s* of John Smith, Milngavie and Agnes Smith (*née* Haldane); *m* 1939, Alice Mary Ewen, Montrose; one *s* one *d. Educ:* Bearsden Academy and Glasgow University (MA 1930). Joined City of Glasgow Police, 1933; Deputy Commandant, Scottish Police College, 1951; Chief Constable of Aberdeen, 1963. *Recreations:* golf, bridge. *Address:* Sherwood, 2 Cherry Tree Park, Balerno, Midlothian. *Clubs:* Luffness New Golf, Baberton Golf.

SMITH, Sir William Reardon Reardon-, 3rd Bt, *cr* 1920; Major, RA (TA); *b* 12 March 1911; *e s* of Sir Willie Reardon-Smith, 2nd Bt, and Elizabeth Ann (*d* 1986), *d* of John and Mary Wakely; *S* father, 1950; *m* 1st, 1935, Nesta (marr. diss., 1954; she *d* 1959), *d* of late Frederick J. Phillips; three *s* one *d*; 2nd, 1954, Beryl, *d* of William H. Powell; one *s* three *d. Educ:* Blundell's Sch., Tiverton. Served War of 1939–45. *Heir: s* (William) Antony (John) Reardon-Smith [*b* 20 June 1937; *m* 1962, Susan, *d* of H. W. Gibson, Cardiff; three *s* one *d. Educ:* Wycliffe Coll., Glos]. *Address:* Rhode Farm, Romansleigh, South Molton, Devon EX36 4JW. *T:* Bishops Nympton 371. *Club:* Cardiff and County (Cardiff).

SMITH, Sir William Reginald Verdon; *see* Verdon-Smith.

SMITH-DODSWORTH, Sir John (Christopher), 8th Bt, *cr* 1784; *b* 4 March 1935; *s* of Sir Claude Smith-Dodsworth, 7th Bt, and Cyrilla Marie Louise von Sobbe, (*d* 1984), 3rd *d* of William Ernest Taylor, Linnet Lane, Liverpool; *S* father, 1940; *m* 1st, 1961, Margaret Anne (*née* Jones) (marr. diss. 1971); one *s* one *d*; 2nd, 1972, Margaret Theresa (*née* Grey), Auckland, NZ; one *s. Educ:* Ampleforth Coll., Yorks. Now resident in Coromandel, New Zealand. *Heir: s* David John Smith-Dodsworth, *b* 23 Oct. 1963.

SMITH-GORDON, Sir (Lionel) Eldred (Peter), 5th Bt *cr* 1838; engaged in book publishing, since 1960; *b* 7 May 1935; *s* of Sir Lionel Eldred Pottinger Smith-Gordon, 4th Bt, and Eileen Laura (*d* 1979), *d* of late Captain H. G. Adams-Connor, CVO; *S* father, 1976; *m* 1962, Sandra Rosamund Ann, *d* of late Wing Commander Walter Farley, DFC and of Mrs Dennis Poore; one *s* one *d. Educ:* Eton College; Trinity College, Oxford. Director: John Libbey (Publishers) Ltd, 1978–; John Libbey Eurotext, 1978–. *Heir: s* Lionel George Eldred Smith-Gordon [*b* 1 July 1964. *Educ:* Eton]. *Address:* 13 Shalcomb Street, SW10. *T:* 01–352 8506.

SMITH-MARRIOTT, Sir Ralph George Cavendish, 10th Bt, *cr* 1774; retired Bank Official; *b* 16 Dec. 1900; *s* of late George Rudolph Wyldbore Smith-Marriott and of Dorothy Magdalene, *d* of Rev. John Parry; *S* uncle, 1944; *m* 1st, Phyllis Elizabeth (*d* 1932), *d* of Richard Kemp (late Governor HM Prison, Bristol); two *s* one *d*; 2nd, 1933, Doris Mary (*d* 1951), *d* of R. L. C. Morrison, Tenby, Pembs; 3rd, 1966, Mrs Barbara Mary Cantlay. *Educ:* Cranleigh Sch., Surrey. Bristol Univ. OTC, 1918. *Recreations:* tennis, golf, cricket. *Heir: s* Hugh Cavendish Smith-Marriott [*b* 22 March 1925; *m* 1953, Pauline Anne, *d* of F. F. Holt, Bristol; one *d*]. *Address:* 28a Westover Road, Westbury-on-Trym, Bristol. *T:* Bristol 503797.

SMITH-RYLAND, Charles Mortimer Tollemache; Lord-Lieutenant of Warwickshire since 1968; *b* 24 May 1927; *s* of Charles Ivor Phipson Smith-Ryland and Leila Mary Tollemache; *m* 1952, Hon. Jeryl Marcia Sarah Gurdon, *d* of Hon. Robin Gurdon; two *s* three *d. Educ:* Eton. Lt, Coldstream Guards, 1945–48; Reserve, Warwickshire Yeomanry. Warwickshire: CC, 1949; DL, 1955; Alderman, 1958; Vice-Chm. CC, 1963; Chm. CC, 1964–67; Vice-Chm. Police Authority, 1966–68; Chm., Warwickshire and Coventry Police Authority, 1969–74; High Sheriff, 1967–68. Chm. Council, RASE, 1976–. KStJ

1968. *Recreations:* hunting, shooting, golf. *Address:* Sherbourne Park, Warwick. *T:* Barford 624255. *Clubs:* White's; Leamington Tennis.
See also Baron Cranworth.

SMITHERMAN, Frank, MBE 1951; HM Diplomatic Service, retired; *b* 13 Oct. 1913; *s* of Lt-Col H. C. Smitherman and Mildred E. Holten; *m* 1937, Frances Ellen Rivers Calvert; one *s* one *d*. *Educ:* Sir Joseph Williamson's Mathematical Sch., Rochester. Indian Police, Burma, 1933; served in: Yenangyaung; Rangoon; Myitkyina; Sagaing; Thayetmyo; Thaton. Served War of 1939–45 (despatches, 1945), Burma Army Reserve of Officers; Maj. 1945. Joined Civil Affairs Service; Foreign Office, 1949; subseq. service in: Amoy; Cairo; Rome; Khartoum; Miami; Consul-General, Bordeaux, 1967–69; Counsellor, Moscow, 1969–70; Ambassador to Togo and Dahomey, 1970–73. *Recreations:* fishing, gardening. *Address:* Pickwick Cottage, New Buckenham, Norfolk. *T:* Attleborough 860388.
See also Sir T. F. V. Buxton, Bt.

SMITHERS, Prof. Sir David (Waldron), Kt 1969; MD, FRCP, FRCS, FRCR; Professor of Radiotherapy in the University of London, 1943–73, now Emeritus; Director of the Radiotherapy Department at the Royal Marsden Hospital, 1943–73; *b* 17 Jan. 1908; *s* of late Sir Waldron Smithers, MP; *m* 1933, Gwladys Margaret (Marjorie), *d* of Harry Reeve Angel, Officer (1st class) Order of White Rose of Finland; one *s* one *d*. *Educ:* Boxgrove School, Guildford; Charterhouse; Clare College, Cambridge; St Thomas's Hospital. MRCS, LRCP 1933; MB, BChir (Cantab) 1934; MD (Cantab) 1937; DMR (London) 1937; MRCP 1946; FRCP 1952; FFR 1953, now FRCR; FRCS 1963. Pres. British Inst. of Radiology, 1946–47; President, Faculty of Radiologists, 1959–61; Kt Comdr, Order of St John of Jerusalem, Kts of Malta, 1973. *Publications:* Dickens's Doctors, 1979; Castles in Kent, 1980; Jane Austen in Kent, 1981; papers on cancer and radiotherapy. *Recreations:* growing roses, book collecting. *Address:* Ringfield, Knockholt, Kent. *T:* Knockholt 32122. *Club:* Arts.
See also Maj.-Gen. B. C. Webster.

SMITHERS, Professor Geoffrey Victor; Professor of English Language, University of Durham, 1960–74, now Emeritus; *b* 5 May 1909; *s* of William Henry and Agnes Madeline Smithers; *m* 1953, Jean Buglass Hay McDonald; three *s* one *d*. *Educ:* Durban High School; Natal University College; Hertford College, Oxford. Rhodes Schol. for Natal, 1930; 1st Cl. in Final Hon. School of English, Oxford, 1933. Asst Lecturer: King's Coll., London, 1936; University Coll., London, 1938; Lectr in English Language, 1940, Senior Lecturer in English Language, 1950, Reader in Medieval English, 1954, Univ. of Oxford, and professorial Fellow of Merton Coll., 1954. *Publications:* 2nd edn of C. Brown's Religious Lyrics of the Fourteenth Century, 1952; Kyng Alisaunder, Vol. I 1952, Vol. II 1957; (with J. A. W. Bennett and N. Davis) Early Middle English Verse and Prose, 1966 (rev. edn 1974); contribs to vols in honour of M. Schlauch, G. N. Garmonsway, D. Meritt, A. McIntosh and N. Davis; papers in Med. Æv., English and Germanic Studies, Archivum Linguisticum, Rev. Eng. Studies, Durham Univ. Jl. *Recreation:* music. *Address:* 6 Manor Close, Shincliffe, Durham. *T:* 61094.

SMITHERS, Sir Peter (Henry Berry Otway), Kt 1970; VRD with clasp; DPhil Oxon; Lt-Comdr RNR, retired; *b* 9 Dec. 1913; *o s* of late Lt-Col H. O. Smithers, JP, Hants, and Ethel Berry; *m* 1943, Dojean, *d* of late T. M. Sayman, St Louis, Mo; two *d*. *Educ:* Hawtrey's; Harrow Sch.; Magdalen Coll., Oxford. Demyship in History, 1931; 1st cl. Hons Modern History, 1934. Called to Bar, Inner Temple, 1936; joined Lincoln's Inn, 1937. Commn, London Div. RNVR, 1939; British Staff, Paris, 1940; Naval Intelligence Div., Admiralty; Asst Naval Attaché, British Embassy, Washington; Actg Naval Attaché, Mexico, Central Amer. Republics and Panama. RD Councillor, Winchester, 1946–49. MP (C) Winchester Div. of Hampshire, 1950–64; PPS to Minister of State for Colonies, 1952–56 and to Sec. of State for Colonies, 1956–59; Deleg., Consultative Assembly of Council of Europe, 1952–56 and 1960; UK Deleg. to UN Gen. Assembly, 1960–62; Parly Under-Sec. of State, FO, 1962–64; Sec.-Gen., Council of Europe, 1964–69; Senior Research Fellow, UN Inst. for Trng and Research, 1969–72; General Rapporteur, European Conf. of Parliamentarians and Scientists, 1970–77. Chairman: British-Mexican Soc., 1952–55; Conservative Overseas Bureau, 1956–59; Vice-Chm., Conservative Parly Foreign Affairs Cttee, 1958–62; Vice-Pres., European Assembly of Local Authorities, 1959–62. Master, Turners' Co., 1955; Liveryman, Goldsmiths' Co. Dr of Law *hc* Zürich, 1969. Alexander von Humboldt Gold Medal, 1969; Medal of Honour, Parly Assembly, Council of Europe, 1984; Gold Medal (for photography), RHS, 1981 and 1983, Gold Medal and Grenfell Medal, 1985. One-man shows of photography: Oklahoma Art Center, 1984; Musée Cernuschi, Paris, Norton Museum, Palm Beach, Brooklyn Botanic Garden, and Bois des Moutiers, Dieppe, 1985; Minneapolis, Pasadena, Philadelphia, Oklahoma City and Atlanta, 1986. Chevalier de la Légion d'Honneur; Orden Mexicana del Aguila Azteca. *Publication:* Life of Joseph Addison, 1954, 2nd edn, 1966. *Recreation:* gardening. *Address:* CH-6911 Vico Morcote, Switzerland. *Clubs:* Carlton; The Everglades.

SMITHERS, Hon. Sir Reginald (Allfree), Kt 1980; **Hon. Mr Justice Smithers;** Judge of Federal Court of Australia, since 1977 (Judge, Australian Industrial Court, 1965–77); Additional Judge, Supreme Court of ACT and Supreme Court of NT, since 1964; *b* Echuca, 3 Feb. 1903; *s* of F. Smithers, Hove, Brighton, England; *m* 1932, Dorothy, *d* of J. Smalley, Bendigo; two *s* one *d*. *Educ:* Melbourne Grammar School; Melbourne Univ. (LLB 1924). Admitted to Victorian Bar, 1929; QC 1951. Served War, RAAF, 1942–45 (Sqdn Ldr); Censorship Liaison Officer to Gen. MacArthur, 1944–45, New Guinea and Philippines. Judge of Supreme Court of Papua and NG, 1962–64; Dep. Pres., Administrative Appeals Tribunal, 1977–80. Chancellor, La Trobe Univ., 1972–80 (DUniv); Pres., Australian Assoc. of Youth Clubs, 1967–. *Address:* 11 Florence Avenue, Kew, Victoria 3101, Australia.

SMITHIES, Frederick Albert; General Secretary, National Association of Schoolmasters and Union of Women Teachers, since 1983; *b* 12 May 1929; *s* of Frederick Albert and Lilian Smithies; *m* 1960, Olga Margaret Yates. *Educ:* St Mary's Coll., Blackburn, Lancs; St Mary's Coll., Twickenham, Mddx. Schoolteacher: Accrington, Lancs, 1948–60; Northampton, 1960–76. NAS/UWT (before 1975, NAS): Nat. Executive Member, 1966–76; Chm. of Education Cttee, 1972–76; Vice-President, 1976; Asst Gen. Secretary, 1976–81; Dep. Gen. Secretary, 1981–82; Gen. Sec. Designate, 1982–83. Member: TUC Gen. Council, 1983–; Exec. Bd, European Trade Union Cttee for Educn, 1985–; Exec. Bd, Internat. Fedn of Free Teachers' Unions, 1985–. *Recreations:* reading, music, theatre, fell-walking. *Address:* 22 Upper Brook Street, Mayfair, W1. *T:* 01–629 3916.

SMITHIES, Kenneth Charles Lester; His Honour Judge Smithies; a Circuit Judge, since 1975; *b* 15 Aug. 1927; *s* of late Harold King Smithies and Kathleen Margaret (*née* Walsh); *m* 1950, Joan Winifred (*née* Ellis) (*d* 1983); one *s* two *d*. *Educ:* City of London Sch. (Corporation Scholar); University College London (LLB). Volunteered 60th Rifles, 1945, later commnd in Royal Artillery, in India; demobilised, 1948. Called to Bar, Gray's Inn, 1955. *Recreation:* music. *Address:* c/o Courts Administrator, Law Courts, Winchester, Hants SO23 9EL.

SMITHSON, Peter Denham; architect in private practice since 1950; *b* 18 Sept. 1923; *s* of William Blenkiron Smithson and Elizabeth Smithson; *m* 1949, Alison Margaret (*née* Gill); one *s* two *d*. *Educ:* The Grammar School, Stockton-on-Tees; King's College, Univ. of Durham. Served War of 1939–45: Queen Victoria's Own Madras Sappers and Miners, India and Burma, 1942–45. Asst in Schools Div. LCC, 1949–50; subseq. in private practice with wife. Banister Fletcher Prof. of Architecture, UCL, 1976–77; Vis. Prof. of Architecture: Bath Univ., 1978–; Univ. of Delft, 1982–83; Univ. of Munich, 1984–85; Univ. of Barcelona, 1985–86. *Buildings:* Hunstanton School, 1950–54; The Economist Building, St James's, 1959–64, Porch 1983; Robin Hood Gardens, Tower Hamlets, 1963–72; Garden Bldg, St Hilda's Coll., Oxford, 1968–70; for Bath University: Amenity Bldg, 1979–80, 1984; Second Arts Bldg, 1980–81; Architecture and Building Engrg, 1986–87; *furniture:* for Tecta, Germany (with A. Smithson), 1982–. *Publications:* (all with A. Smithson) Uppercase 3, 1960; The Heroic Period of Modern Architecture, 1965, rev. edn 1981; Urban Structuring Studies of Alison and Peter Smithson, 1967; Team 10 Primer, 1968; The Euston Arch, 1968; Ordinariness and Light, 1970; Without Rhetoric, 1973; Bath: Walks Within the Walls, 1980; The Shift, 1982; AS in DS, 1983; The 1930s, 1985; Upper Lawn, 1986; theoretical work on town structuring in ILAUD Year Book, Spazio e Società and other periodicals; *relevant publications:* synopsis of professional life in Arch. Assoc.'s Arena, Feb. 1966; selective bibliography in The Shift, 1982. *Address:* 24 Gilston Road, SW10. *T:* 01–373 7423.

SMOUT, David Arthur Lister, QC 1975; **His Honour Judge Smout;** a Circuit Judge (Official Referee), since 1983; *b* 17 Dec. 1923; *s* of Sir Arthur Smout and Hilda Smout (*née* Follows); *m* 1957, Kathleen Sally, *d* of Dr J. L. and Mrs N. M. Potts, Salisbury; two *s* two *d*. *Educ:* Leys Sch.; Clare Coll., Cambridge (MA, LLB); Birmingham Univ. (LLM). Served War, F/O, RAFVR, 1943–45. Cecil Peace Prize, 1948. Admitted solicitor, 1949; called to Ontario Bar, 1949. Lectr, Osgoode Hall, Toronto, 1949–53, Vis. Prof., 1977. Called to English Bar, Gray's Inn, 1953; Midland and Oxford Circuit, 1953–83. Dir, Murex Ltd and associated cos, 1954–67. Bar Council, 1958–62; prosecuting counsel, DTI, 1967–75; Dep.-Chm., Lines QS (parts of Holland), 1968–71; a Recorder of the Crown Court, 1972–83. *Publications:* Chalmers, Bills of Exchange, 13th edn, 1964; (with B. E. Basden) Department of Trade Investigations: Bernard Russell Ltd, 1975; Blane Ltd, 1975. *Recreations:* walking the Chilterns and Cotswolds, gardening, Canadiana. *Address:* Long Swan Cottage, Haddenham, Aylesbury HP17 8AB. *Club:* Garrick.

SMYTH, Rev. Canon Charles Hugh Egerton, MA, FRHistS; Fellow of Corpus Christi College, Cambridge, 1925–32 and since 1937; *b* Ningpo, China, 31 March 1903; *s* of Richard Smyth, MD; *m* 1934, Violet, *e d* of Rev. Canon Alexander Copland, Forfar. *Educ:* Repton; Corpus Christi College, Cambridge (Scholar); Wells Theological Coll. 1st class, Historical Tripos, Part 1, 1923, and Part 2, 1924; Thirlwall Medal and Gladstone Prize, 1925. Tutor and Lectr in History, Harvard Univ., USA, 1926–27; Deacon, 1929; Priest, 1930; University Lecturer in History, Cambridge, 1929–32 and 1944–46; Curate of St Clement's, Barnsbury, Islington, 1933–34; of St Saviour's, Upper Chelsea, 1934–36; of St Giles', Cambridge, 1936–37. Birkbeck Lecturer in Ecclesiastical History, Trinity College, Cambridge, 1937–38; Dean of Chapel, Corpus Christi College, 1937–46; Hon. Canon of Derby and Chaplain to Bishop of Derby at the University of Cambridge, 1938–46; Select Preacher, Oxford, 1941–43 and 1965; Canon of Westminster and Rector of St Margaret's, Westminster, 1946–56; Hon. Canon and Prebendary of Nassington in Lincoln Cathedral, 1965–79; Canon Emeritus of Derby Cathedral, 1977–, of Lincoln Cathedral, 1979–. Editor of the Cambridge Review, 1925 and 1940–41. *Publications:* Cranmer and the Reformation under Edward VI, 1926; The Art of Preaching (747–1939), 1940; Simeon and Church Order (Birkbeck Lectures), 1940; Religion and Politics, 1943; The Friendship of Christ, 1945; Dean Milman, 1949; Church and Parish (Bishop Paddock Lectures), 1955; Good Friday at St Margaret's, 1957; Cyril Forster Garbett, Archbishop of York, 1959; The Two Families, 1962; The Church and the Nation, 1962. *Address:* Corpus Christi College, Cambridge.

SMYTH, Desmond; *see* Smyth, J.D.

SMYTH, (James) Robert Staples; Stipendiary Magistrate, West Midlands, since 1978; a Recorder of the Crown Court, since 1983; *b* 11 July 1926; *s* of late Major Robert Smyth, Gaybrook, Co. Westmeath, and Mabel Anne Georgiana (*née* MacGeough-Bond) *m* 1971, Fenella Joan Mowat; one *s*. *Educ:* St Columba's, Dublin; Merton Coll., Oxford (BA 1948, MA). Served RAF, 1944–46. Called to Bar, Inner Temple, 1949. Resident Magistrate, Northern Rhodesia, 1951–55; a Dep. Circuit Judge, 1974. Dep. Chairman, Agricultural Land Tribunal, 1974. *Recreations:* shooting, fishing, English literature. *Address:* Leys, Shelsley Beauchamp, Worcs WR6 6RB.

SMYTH, John Jackson; QC 1979; barrister-at-law; Director of Zambesi Ministries, African Enterprise, Zimbabwe, since 1986; *b* 27 June 1941; *e s* of Col Edward Hugh Jackson Smyth, FRCSEd, and late Ursula Helen Lucie (*née* Ross) *m* 1968, Josephine Anne, *er d* of late Walter Leggott and Miriam Moss Leggott, Manor Farm, Burtoft, Lincs; one *s* three *d*. *Educ:* Strathcona Sch., Calgary, Alberta; St Lawrence Coll.; Trinity Hall, Cambridge. MA, LLB (Cantab). Called to Bar, Inner Temple (Major Schol.), 1965. A Recorder, 1978–84. *Publication:* Discovering Christianity Today, 1985. *Recreations:* skiing, sailing, trout fishing, real tennis. *Address:* 2 Crown Office Row, Temple, EC4; PO Box HG 167, Highlands, Harare, Zimbabwe. *T:* 42561.

SMYTH, (Joseph) Desmond, FCA; Managing Director, Ulster Television, since 1983; *b* 20 April 1950; *s* of Andrew and Annie Elizabeth Smyth; *m* 1975, Irene Janette (*née* Dale); one *s* one *d*. *Educ:* Limavady Grammar School; Queen's University, Belfast. BSc (Jt Hons Pure Maths and Statistics). Accountancy articles, Coopers and Lybrand, 1971–75; Ulster Television: Chief Accountant, 1975–76; Financial Controller and Company Secretary, 1976–83. *Recreations:* fishing, gardening. *Address:* Ulster Television plc, Havelock House, Ormeau Road, Belfast BT7 1EB.

SMYTH, Margaret Jane, CBE 1959 (OBE 1955); retired; *b* 23 Sept. 1897; *d* of late Colonel John Smyth, IMS. *Educ:* Uplands School (Church Education Corporation); Clifton High School. Trained at Univ. Settlement, Bristol; Health Visitors Certificate. Roy. Sanitary Inst., 1918; Central Midwives Board, SCM, 1920; Maternity and Child Welfare Certificate, RSI, 1921; SRN, 1925, trained in Nightingale Trng School, St Thomas Hosp.; Sister, St Thomas Hosp., 1926–34; Matron, St Thomas Babies' Hostel, 1934–37; Warden, St Christopher's Nursery Trng College, 1937–39; Dep. Matron, St Thomas Hosp., 1939–45, Supt, Nightingale Trng School and Matron, St Thomas Hospital, 1945–55; Chairman of the General Nursing Council for England and Wales, 1955–60; President Royal College of Nursing, 1960–62; Chairman, South West Metropolitan Area, Nurse Training Cttee, 1952–64, Mem., 1964–66; Vice-Chm., Long Grove Hospital Management Cttee, 1964–67; Mem., Kingston and Long Grove Hosp. Management Cttee, 1967–69. *Address:* 9 Stockbridge Gardens, Chichester, West Sussex.

SMYTH, Rev. Martin; *see* Smyth, Rev. W. M.

SMYTH, Robert Staples; *see* Smyth, J. R. S.

SMYTH, Sir Thomas Weyland Bowyer-, 15th Bt *cr* 1661; *b* 25 June 1960; *s* of Captain Sir Philip Weyland Bowyer-Smyth, 14th Bt, RN, and of Veronica Mary, *d* of Captain C. W. Bower, DSC, RN; *S* father, 1978. *Heir: kinsman* John Jeremy Windham [*b* 22 Nov. 1948; *m* 1976, Rachel Mary Finney; two *d*]. *Address:* 3 Lillian Road, Barnes, SW13.

SMYTH, Dr Sir Timothy (John), 2nd Bt *cr* 1956, of Teignmouth, Co. Devon; Medical Administrator, Prince Henry Hospital, Prince of Wales Hospital Group, Sydney, Australia, since 1980; *b* 16 April 1953; *s* of Julian Smyth (*d* 1974) and of Phyllis, *d* of John Francis Cannon; *S* grandfather, Brig. Rt Hon. Sir John Smyth, 1st Bt, VC, MC, 1983; *m* 1981, Bernadette Mary, *d* of Leo Askew; one *s* one *d*. *Educ:* Univ. of New South Wales. MB, BS 1977; MBA (AGSM) 1985. Resident Medical Officer, 1977–79. *Heir: s* Brendan Julian Smyth, *b* 4 Oct. 1981. *Address:* 31/16 Alma Road, Padstow, NSW 2211, Australia.

SMYTH, Rev. (William) Martin; MP (UU) Belfast South, since March 1982 (resigned seat Dec. 1985 in protest against Anglo-Irish Agreement; re-elected Jan. 1986); *b* 15 June 1931; *s* of James Smyth, JP, and Minnie Kane; *m* 1957, Kathleen Jean Johnston, BA; two *d* (and one *d* decd). *Educ:* Methodist Coll., Belfast; Magee University Coll., Londonderry; Trinity Coll., Dublin (BA 1953, BD 1961); Assembly's Coll., Belfast. Assistant Minister, Lowe Memorial, Finaghy, 1953–57; Raffrey Presbyterian Church, Crossgar, 1957–63; Alexandra Presbyterian Church, Belfast, 1963–82. Member, Northern Ireland Convention, 1975; Vice-Chm., Parly Cttee for Soviet Jewry, 1983–; Mem., Select Cttee for Social Services, 1983–; Mem. (UU) Belfast S, NI Assembly, 1982–86 (Chm., Health and Social Services Cttee, 1983–84; Chm., Finance and Personnel Cttee, 1984–86). Chm. of Executive 1974–76, Vice-Pres. 1974–, Ulster Unionist Council. Governor, Belfast City Mission. Grand Master, Grand Orange Lodge of Ireland, 1972–; Grand Master of World Orange Council, 1974–82, Pres., 1985–; Hon. Past Grand Master, Canada, and Hon. Deputy Grand Master, USA, NZ, NSW, of Orange Order. *Publications:* (ed) Faith for Today, 1961; pamphlets: Why Presbyterian?, 1963; Till Death Us Do Part, 1965; In Defence of Ulster, 1970; The Battle for Northern Ireland, 1972; occasional papers, and articles in Christian Irishman, Evangelical Quarterly, Biblical Theology. *Recreations:* reading, photography; former Rugby player (capped for Magee University College). *Address:* 117 Cregagh Road, Belfast BT6 0LA. *T:* Belfast 57009.

SMYTHE, Clifford Anthony, (Tony); consultant; *b* 2 Aug. 1938; *s* of Clifford John and Florence May Smythe; *m*; four *d*. *Educ:* University College School. Conscientious Objector, 1958; General Secretary, War Resisters' International, 1959–64, Treasurer, 1982–86; Council Member, Internat. Confederation for Disarmament and Peace, 1963–71; Gen. Sec., Nat. Council for Civil Liberties, 1966–72; Field Dir, American Civil Liberties Union, 1973; Director: Mind (Nat. Assoc. for Mental Health), 1973–81; SHAC, 1986–. Board Member: Volunteer Centre, 1977–81; Retired Execs Clearing Hse (REACH), 1978–; Member: Nat. Adv. Council on Employment of Disabled People, 1975–81; Nat. Develt Council for Mentally Handicapped People, 1981; (co-opted), Mddx Area Probation Cttee, 1984–. Chairman: Campaign for Homeless Single People, 1982–84; National Peace Council, 1982–; Dir, Assoc. of Community Health Councils for England and Wales. *Publications:* Conscription: a World Survey, 1968; (with D. Madgwick) The Invasion of Privacy, 1974. *Address:* 136 Stapleton Hall Road, N4 4QB.

SMYTHE, Captain George Quentin Murray, VC 1942; Officer Instructor, Department of Defence, South Africa, 1970–81, retired; *b* 6 Aug. 1916; *s* of Edric Murray Smythe and *g s* of 1st Administrator of Natal (Hon. Charles Smythe, Methven Castle, Perthshire, Scotland); *m* 1945, Dale Griffiths (marr. diss. 1970), Capetown; three *s* one *d*; *m* 1970, Margaret Joan Shatwell (*d* 1980); *m* 1984, Patricia Stamper. *Educ:* Estcourt High Sch. Went through Abyssinian Campaign with Regt, Natal Carabineers; Sgt at Alem Hanza, Egypt (VC). *Recreations:* bowls, fishing, shooting. *Address:* 54 Seadoone Road, Amanzimtoti, Natal, Republic of South Africa.

SMYTHE, Patricia Rosemary K.; *see* Koechlin-Smythe.

SMYTHE, Tony; *see* Smythe, C. A.

SNAGGE, John Derrick Mordaunt, OBE 1944; *b* 1904; 2nd *s* of late Judge Sir Mordaunt Snagge; *m* 1st, 1936, Eileen Mary (*d* 1980), *e d* of late H. P. Joscelyne; 2nd, 1983, Joan Mary, *e d* of late William Wilson. *Educ:* Winchester College; Pembroke College, Oxford. Assistant Station Director BBC, Stoke-on-Trent, 1924; Announcer London (Savoy Hill), 1928; Assistant Outside Broadcast Department 1933; Commentator Oxford and Cambridge Boat Race, 1931–80; Assistant Director Outside Broadcasts, 1939; Presentation Director BBC, 1939–45; Head of Presentation (Home Service), 1945–57; Head of Presentation (Sound) BBC, 1957–63; Special Duties, BBC, 1963–65. Retired from BBC 1965. Chairman of the Lord's Taverners, 1956, 1960, 1961; President, 1952, 1964; Secretary, 1965–67; Trustee, 1970–76. *Publication:* (with Michael Barsley) Those Vintage Years of Radio, 1972. *Recreation:* fishing. *Address:* Delgaty, Village Road, Dorney, near Windsor, Berks SL4 6QJ. *T:* Burnham 61303. *Clubs:* MCC, Leander, Lord's Taverners, Sportsman's.

SNAGGE, Dame Nancy (Marion), DBE 1955 (OBE 1945); *b* 2 May 1906; *d* of late Henry Thomas Salmon; *m* 1962, Thomas Geoffrey Mordaunt Snagge, DSC (*d* 1984), *e s* of late His Hon. Sir Mordaunt Snagge. *Educ:* Notting Hill, High Sch. Joined the WAAF on its inception, March 1939; served as a commnd officer in the WAAF and WRAF from Sept. 1939. ADC to King George VI, 1950–52; ADC to the Queen, 1952–56; Director Women's Royal Air Force, 1950–56, retired as Air Commandant. *Address:* Test Lodge, Longstock, Stockbridge, Hampshire.

SNAITH, George Robert, FRINA; Director, Worldwide Marine Marketing Computervision Ltd, since 1985; *b* 9 July 1930; *s* of late Robert and Clara Snaith; *m* 1953, Verna Patricia (*née* Codling); one *s* one *d*. *Educ:* University of Durham. BSc Applied Science (Naval Architecture), 1952. A. Kari & Co., Consulting Naval Architects, Newcastle, 1952–57; Northern Aluminium Co. Ltd, Banbury, 1957–59; Burness, Corlett & Partners, Consulting Naval Architects, Basingstoke, 1959–64; British Ship Research Association, 1964–77, Dir of Research, 1976–77; British Shipbuilders: Dir of Research, 1977–81; Technol. and Systems Adviser (formerly Production Systems Adviser), 1981–85. Vis. Prof., Dept of Naval Architecture and Shipbldg, Univ. of Newcastle upon Tyne, 1980–. Vice-Pres., NE Coast Instn of Engrs and Shipbuilders, 1979; Member: Council, RINA, 1977–; Ship and Marine Technol. Requirements Bd, Dept of Industry, 1978–81; Bd, National Maritime Inst., 1978–82. *Recreations:* ships and shipbuilding, technology, reading, literature and discussion. *Address:* 10 Fieldhouse Close, Hepscott, Morpeth, Northumberland NE61 6LU. *T:* Morpeth 515319. *Club:* Athenæum.

SNAPE, Peter Charles; MP (Lab) West Bromwich East since Feb. 1974; *b* 12 Feb. 1942; *s* of Thomas and Kathleen Snape; *m* 1963, Winifred Grimshaw (marr. diss. 1980); two *d*. *Educ:* St Joseph's RC Sch., Stockport; St Winifred's Sch., Stockport. Railway signalman, 1957–61; regular soldier, RE & RCT, 1961–67; goods guard, 1967–70; clerical officer BR, 1970–74. Mem., Council of Europe and WEU, May-Nov. 1975. An Asst Govt Whip, 1975–77; a Lord Comr, HM Treasury, 1977–79; opposition spokesman for Defence, 1979–82, for Home Affairs, 1982–83, for Transport, 1983–. Mem., Bredbury and Romiley UDC, 1971–74 (Chm., Finance Cttee). *Address:* c/o House of Commons, SW1A 0AA.

SNAPE, Royden Eric; a Recorder of the Crown Court, since 1979; *b* 20 April 1922; *s* of John Robert and Gwladys Constance Snape; *m* 1949, Unity Frances Money; one *s* one *d*. *Educ:* Bromsgrove Sch. Served War, Royal Regt of Artillery (Field), 1940–46; Adjt, 80th Field Regt, 1945. Admitted Solicitor, 1949; a Deputy Circuit Judge, 1975. Chm., Med. Appeal Tribunal, 1985–. Governor, St John's Sch., Porthcawl, 1971–. *Recreations:* golf, Rugby Union football, cricket. *Address:* West Winds, Llanblethian, Cowbridge, South Glamorgan, Wales CF7 7JQ. *T:* Cowbridge 2362. *Clubs:* Royal Porthcawl Golf; Cardiff Athletic; Glamorgan CCC.

SNAPE, Thomas Peter; General Secretary, Secondary Heads Association and Headmasters' Conference, since 1983; *b* 4 June 1925; *s* of Charles Snape and Jane Elizabeth Middleton; *m* 1951, Anne Christina McColl; one *s* three *d*. *Educ:* Cockburn High Sch., Leeds; Exeter Coll., Oxford (MA). PCE London Univ. Asst Master, grammar and comprehensive schs, 1950–60; Headmaster: Settle High Sch., Yorks, 1960–64; King Edward VI Grammar Sch., Totnes, 1964–66; King Edward VI Comprehensive Sch., Totnes, 1966–83; Warden, Totnes Community Coll., 1971–83. Leverhulme Res. Fellow, USA, 1970. Chm., Educn Cttee, HMA and SHA, 1977–79; Additional Mem., Headmasters' Conf., 1975–83; Member: Exams Cttee, SW Exam. Bd, 1976–78; Consultative Cttee, Assessment of Performance Unit, 1975–84; Teacher Educn Accreditation Council, 1984–86. Consultant to Faculty of Educnl Studies, Open Univ., 1970–75. JP Devon, 1975, Inner London 1983. *Publications:* chapters in edited works; sections of Open University readers; contrib. learned jls. *Recreations:* family life, the arts, reading newspapers, travel. *Address:* 10 Chalcot Square, NW1 8YB.

SNEDDEN, Rt. Hon. Sir Billy (Mackie), KCMG 1978; PC 1972; QC (Australia); barrister and company director; Federal Member of Parliament for Bruce (Victoria), Commonwealth of Australia, 1955–83; Speaker, House of Representatives, 1976–83; *b* 31 Dec. 1926; *s* of A. Snedden, Scotland; *m* 1950, Joy; two *s* two *d*. *Educ:* Univ. of Western Australia (LLB). Barrister, admitted Supreme Ct of Western Australia, 1951; admitted Victorian Bar, 1955. Australian Govt: Attorney-General, 1963–66; Minister for Immigration, 1966–69; Leader of the House, 1966–71; Minister for Labour and Nat. Service, 1969–71; Treasurer, 1971–72; Leader of the Opposition, 1972–75; Leader, Parliamentary Liberal Party, 1972–75 (Dep. Leader, 1971–72). Chm., Standing Cttee of Conf. of Commonwealth Speakers and Presiding Officers, 1978–81. National Patron, Young Liberal Movement, 1980–82. *Recreation:* tennis. *Address:* Owen Dixon Chambers, 205 William Street, Melbourne, Victoria 3000, Australia. *Clubs:* Melbourne, Melbourne Scots.

SNEDDEN, David King, CA; Chief Executive and Managing Director, Trinity International Holdings plc, since 1982; Chairman, Liverpool Daily Post and Echo, since 1985; *b* 23 Feb. 1933; *s* of David King Snedden and Isabella (*née* Martin); *m* 1958, Jean Swan Smith; two *s* one *d*. *Educ:* Daniel Stewart's College, Edinburgh. CA 1956. Flying Officer, RAF, 1956–57. Investment Adviser, Guinness Mahon, 1958–59; Chief Accountant, Scotsman Publications Ltd, Thomson British Publications Ltd, Thomson Scottish Associates Ltd, 1959–64; Commercial Controller, The Scotsman Publications Ltd, 1964–66; Managing Director: Belfast Telegraph Newspapers Ltd, 1967–70 (Director, 1979–82); The Scotsman Publications Ltd, 1970–78 (Director, 1970–82). Thomson Regional Newspapers Ltd: Dir, 1974–82; Gp Asst Man. Dir, 1979–80; Jt Man. Dir, 1980–82. Director: Radio Forth Ltd, 1973–77; Scottish Council Research Inst. Ltd, 1975–77; The Press Association Ltd, 1984–. Pres., Scottish Daily Newspaper Soc., 1975–78; Member: Press Council, 1976–80; Council, Newspaper Soc., 1983–; Regional Council, CBI, NI, 1968–70. Organiser, Ulster Innocent Victims Appeal Fund, 1969. *Recreations:* golf, shooting, fishing. *Address:* Fairleigh, Hinderton Lane, Neston, Cheshire; 15 Great King Street, Edinburgh. *Clubs:* Caledonian; Bruntsfield Links Golfing Society.

SNEDDON, Hutchison Burt, CBE 1983 (OBE 1968); JP; Regional Sales Manager (Special Projects), Scottish Gas, since 1983; Scottish Divisional Director, Nationwide Building Society, since 1983; *b* 17 April 1929; *s* of Robert and Catherine Sneddon; *m* 1960, Elizabeth Jardine; one *s* two *d*. *Educ:* Wishaw High School. Chm., Cumbernauld Develt Corp., 1979–83; Dir, National Bldg Agency, 1973–82; Vice-Chm., Scottish National Housing and Town Planning Council,1965–71; Member: Bd, Housing Corp., 1977–83; Consultative Cttee, Scottish Develt Agency, 1979–83; Scottish Adv. Commn on Housing Rents, 1973–74; Anderson Cttee on Commercial Rating, 1972–74; Western Regional Hosp. Bd, 1968–70; Scottish Tourist Bd, 1969–83; Chm., Burns Heritage Trail, 1971–83. Dep. Pres., Convention of Scottish Local Authorities, 1974–76; Chm., Gas Higher Managers Assoc., Scotland, 1984–. Motherwell District Council: Councillor, 1958–77; Bailie, 1960–64; Chm., Housing Cttee, 1960–71; Chm., Policy and Resources Cttee, 1974–77; Leader, 1960–77; Chm., 1974–77; Provost, Burgh of Motherwell and Wishaw, 1971–75. JP Motherwell District, 1974 (Mem. JP Adv. Cttee). Gold Medal of Schweinfurt, Bavaria, 1977 (Internat. Relations). *Recreations:* football (watching), philately. *Address:* 36 Shand Street, Wishaw, Lanarks.

SNEDDON, Prof. Ian Naismith, OBE 1969; MA Cantab, DSc Glasgow; FRS 1983; FRSE; FIMA; Member of the Polish Academy of Sciences; Emeritus Professor of Mathematics, University of Glasgow, 1985; Visiting Professor of Mathematics, University of Strathclyde, since 1985; *b* 8 Dec. 1919; *o s* of Naismith Sneddon and Mary Ann Cameron; *m* 1943, Mary Campbell Macgregor; two *s* one *d*. *Educ:* Hyndland School, Glasgow; The University of Glasgow; Trinity College, Cambridge (Senior Scholar, 1941). Scientific Officer, Ministry of Supply, 1942–45; Research Worker, H. H. Wills Physical Lab., Univ. of Bristol, 1945–46; Lecturer in Natural Philosophy, Univ. of Glasgow, 1946–50; Professor of Mathematics in University Coll. of N Staffordshire, 1950–56 (Senior Tutor of the College, 1954–56); Simson Prof. of Mathematics, Univ. of Glasgow, 1956–85 (Dean of Faculty of Science, 1970–72, Senate Assessor on Univ. Court, 1973–77); Visiting Professor: Duke Univ., North Carolina, 1959 and 1960; Michigan State Univ., 1967; Univ. of California, Berkeley, 1979; La Trobe Univ., 1984; Georgia Inst of Technol., 1986; Adjunct Prof., North Carolina State Univ., 1965–72; Visiting Lecturer: Univ. of Palermo, 1953 and 1980; Serbian Acad. of Sciences, 1958; Univ. of Warsaw, 1959, 1973, 1975; Canadian Mathematical Congress, 1961; Polish Acad. of Sciences, 1962; US Midwest Mechanics Research Seminar, 1963 and 1981; Univ. of Zagreb, 1964; Univ. of Calgary, 1968; Indiana Univ., 1970–80; Kuwait Univ., 1972; CISM, Udine, 1972, 1974; Britton Lectr, McMaster Univ., 1979; Huber Lectr, Polish Acad. of Sciences, 1980. NSF Distinguished Vis. Scientist, State Univ., New York, 1969. Member: various govt scientific cttees, 1950–; Adv. Council on Scientific Research and Tech. Development, Min. of Supply, 1953–56, Min. of Defence, 1965–68; Univs Science and Technology Bd (SRC), 1965–69; Adv. Council of Scottish Opera, 1972–; Bd of Scottish Nat. Orch., 1976–83; Bd of Citizens Theatre, Glasgow, 1975–; BBC Central Music Adv. Cttee, 1978–85; Chm., BBC Scottish Music Adv. Cttee, 1978–85; Mem. Council, Scottish Soc. of Composers, 1981–83; Vice-Pres., RSE, 1966–69 and 1979–82. Kelvin Medal, Univ. of Glasgow, 1948; Makdougall-Brisbane Prize, RSE, 1956–58; Soc. of Engrg Sci. Medal, 1979. FRSA. Mem., Order of Long-Leaf Pine, USA, 1964; Hon.

Fellow, Soc. of Engng Sci., USA, 1977; Foreign Mem., Acad. of Scis, Turin. Hon. DSc: Warsaw, 1973; Heriot-Watt, 1982; Hull, 1983. Comdr's Cross, Order of Polonia Restituta, 1969; Comdr, Order of Merit (Poland), 1979; Medal of Cultural Merit, Poland, 1983. *Publications:* (with N. F. Mott) Wave Mechanics and Its Applications, 1948; Fourier Transforms, 1951; Special Functions of Mathematical Physics and Chemistry, 1956; The Elements of Partial Differential Equations, 1956; Introduction to the Mathematics of Biology and Medicine (with J. G. Defares), 1960; Fourier Series, 1961; Zagadnienie Szczelin w Teorii Sprezystasci, 1962; Mixed Boundary Value Problems in Potential Theory, 1966; Crack Problems in the Mathematical Theory of Elasticity (with M. Lowengrub), 1969; An Introduction to the Use of Integral Transforms, 1972; Metoda Transformacji Calkowych w Mieszanych Zogadnieniach Brzegowych, 1974; The Linear Theory of Thermoelasticity, 1974; (ed) Encyclopedic Dictionary of Mathematics for Engineers, 1976; (with G. Eason, W. Nowacki and Z. Olesiak) Integral Transform Methods in Elasticity, 1977; (with E. L. Ince) The Solution of Ordinary Differential Equations, 1987; articles in Handbuch der Physik, 1956–58; scientific papers on quantum theory of nuclei, theory of elasticity, and boundary value problems in jls. *Recreations:* music, painting and photography. *Address:* 19 Crown Terrace, Glasgow G12 9ES. *T:* 041–339 4114. *Club:* Glasgow Art.

SNEDDON, Robert, CMG 1976; MBE 1945; HM Diplomatic Service, retired; *b* 8 June 1920; *m* 1945, Kathleen Margaret Smith; two *d. Educ:* Dalziel High Sch., Motherwell; Kettering Grammar Sch.; University Coll., Nottingham. HM Forces, 1940–46: 8th Army, ME and Italy, 1942–45; 30 Corps, Germany (Major), 1945–46. Joined Foreign (subseq. Diplomatic) Service, 1946; 3rd Sec., Warsaw, 1946; 2nd Sec., Stockholm, 1950; FO, 1954; 1st Sec., Oslo, 1956; 1st Sec., Berlin, 1961; FO, 1963; Counsellor, Bonn, 1969; FCO, 1971, retired 1977. *Recreations:* tennis, golf, music. *Address:* Windrose, Church Road, Horsell, Woking, Surrey. *T:* Woking 4335. *Clubs:* Woking Lawn Tennis and Croquet, Westhill Golf.

SNELGROVE, Rt. Rev. Donald George; *see* Hull, Bishop Suffragan of.

SNELL, Frederick Rowlandson, MA, BSc; *b* 18 Sept. 1903; *s* of Rev. C. D. Snell; *m* 1928, Margaret Lucy Sidebottom; one *s* three *d. Educ:* Winchester College (Scholar); Oriel College, Oxford (Scholar). BA, 1925; BSc, 1927; Lecturer in Chemistry, St John's College, Agra, UP, India, 1927–32; Senior Science Master, Eastbourne College, 1932–38; Rector of Michaelhouse, Natal, SA, 1939–52; Founder and first Rector of Peterhouse, Rhodesia, 1953–67; Treasurer, Anglican Church in Central Africa, 1968–82. *Recreations:* walking and music. *Address:* 5 5th Street, Marondera, Zimbabwe.

SNELL, Rt. Rev. Geoffrey Stuart; *b* 25 Oct. 1920; *s* of Charles James and Ellen Snell; *m* 1948, Margaret Lonsdale Geary; two *s* one *d. Educ:* Exeter School; St Peter's College, Oxford (MA 2nd cl. Hons PPE). Called to the Bar, Inner Temple, 1957. UK Civil Service, 1937–39. Served Army, 1939–46, Major, Supplies and Transport. University, 1946–49; Overseas Admin. Civil Service, 1950–54; Managing Governor, Gabbitas-Thring Educational Trust, 1954–61. Deacon and priest, Church of England, 1962; Curate, Emmanuel Church, Northwood; Fellow, Central College of the Anglican Communion, Canterbury, 1964–67; Founder/Director, Christian Organisations Research and Advisory Trust, 1968–75, of Africa, 1975–77; Bishop Suffragan of Croydon, 1977–85; Bishop to the Forces, 1977–84. *Publication:* Nandi Customary Law, 1955. *Recreations:* music, travel. *Address:* 34 Wychwood Avenue, Luton, Beds LU2 7HU.

SNELL, Rt. Rev. George Boyd, DD, PhD; *b* Toronto, Ontario, 17 June 1907; *s* of John George Snell and Minnie Alice Boyd; *m* 1934, Esther Mary. *Educ:* Trinity College, Toronto. BA 1929, MA 1930, PhD 1937, DD 1948. Deacon, Toronto, 1931; Priest, Niagara (for Tor.), 1932; Curate of St Michael and All Angels, Tor., 1931–39; Rector, 1940–48; Private Chaplain to Bp of Tor., 1945–48; Rector of Pro-Cathedral, Calgary, and Dean of Calgary, 1948–51; Exam. Chaplain to Bp of Calgary, 1948–51; Rector of St Clem. Eglinton, Tor., 1951–56; Archdeacon of Toronto, 1953–56; Exam. Chaplain to Bp of Toronto, 1953–55. Consecrated Bp Suffragan of Toronto, 1956; elected Bp-Coadjutor of Toronto, 1959; Bishop of Toronto, 1966–72. Hon. DD: Wycliffe Coll., Toronto, 1959; Huron Coll., Ontario, 1968. *Address:* 1210 Glen Road, Mississauga, Ont., Canada. *Club:* National (Toronto).

SNELL, Dr George Davis; geneticist; *b* Bradford, Mass, 19 Dec. 1903; *s* of Cullen Bryant and Katharine Davis Snell; *m* 1937, Rhoda Carson; three *s. Educ:* Dartmouth Coll. (BS 1926); Harvard Univ. (MS 1928; ScD 1930). Instr in Zoology, Dartmouth Coll., 1929–30, Brown Univ., 1930–31; Res. Fellow, Texas Univ., 1931–33; Asst Prof., Washington Univ., St Louis, 1933–34; Jackson Laboratory: Res. Associate, 1935–56; Sen. Staff Scientist, 1957–69, now Emeritus. Guggenheim Fellow, Texas Univ., 1953–54. Mem., Allergy and Immunology Study Sect., NIH, 1958–62. Member: Amer. Acad. of Arts and Sci; Nat. Acad. of Scis; French Acad. of Scis (foreign associate); Amer. Philosophical Soc., 1982; Hon. Member: British Transplantation Soc.; British Soc. for Immunology, 1983. Hon. MD Charles Univ., Prague, 1967; Hon. DSc: Dartmouth, 1974; Gustavus Adolphus Coll., 1981; Bates Coll., 1981; Ohio State Univ., 1984; Hon. LLD: Univ. of Maine, 1981; Colby Coll., 1981. Bertner Foundn Award, 1962; Gregor Mendel Medal, Czechoslovak Acad. of Scis, 1967; Gairdner Foundn Award, 1976; Prize in Medicine, Wolf Foundn, 1978; (jt) Nobel Prize for Physiology or Medicine, 1980. *Publications:* (ed) The Biology of the Laboratory Mouse, 1941; (jtly) Histocompatibility, 1976; contribs to learned jls. *Address:* The Jackson Laboratory, Bar Harbor, Maine 04609, USA; 21 Atlantic Avenue, Bar Harbor, Maine 04609, USA.

SNELL, John Nicholas B.; *see* Blashford-Snell.

SNELL, Philip D.; Member (Lab), Tyne and Wear County Council, since 1974, Chairman, General Services Committee, since 1981; *b* 14 Oct. 1915; *s* of Alfred William Snell and Jane Herdman; *m* 1939, Selina Waite; two *d. Educ:* Causey Road Council Sch., Gateshead. Miner, Marley Hill Colliery, Gateshead, 1929–57; Industrial Relations Advr, NCB, 1957–61; Education and Welfare Officer: Durham CC, 1961–73; Gateshead MDC, 1973. Chm., Tyne and Wear CC, 1980–81. Trustee, Whickham Glebe Sports Club. *Recreation:* enjoying Northern Federation Brewery Beer. *Address:* School House, Marley Hill, Whickham, Gateshead, Tyne and Wear. *T:* Gateshead 887006. *Club:* Sunniside Social (Gateshead).

SNELL, William Edward, MD; FRCP; Consultant Physician Superintendent, Colindale Chest Hospital, 1938–67; Demonstrator in Tuberculosis, St Bartholomew's Hospital Medical College, 1948–67; Consultant Chest Physician, Napsbury and Shenley Hospitals, 1963–67; *b* 16 Aug. 1902; *er s* of late S. H. Snell, MD; *m* 1934, Yvonne Creagh Brown; two *s* one *d. Educ:* Stubbington House; Bradfield College; Corpus Christi College, Cambridge (Exhibitioner and Prizeman); University College Hospital. MA Cambridge; BSc Hons London; MD; FRCP; DPH. Tuberculosis Scholarship Tour, Canada and USA, 1930. Formerly: Pres. Brit. Tuberculosis Assoc., 1955–57; Chairman: NW Metropolitan Thoracic Soc.; Metropolitan Branch, Soc. of Med. Supts; Editorial Cttee TB Index; Member: Management Cttees, Hendon and Chelsea Groups of Hosps; Brit. Tuberculosis Research Cttee; Examiner to Gen. Nursing Council. Mem. Council (twice Vice-Pres.), History of Medicine Section, RSM. *Publications:* articles in medical press relating to tuberculosis and chest disease, accidents to patients and history of medicine. *Recreations:* gardening, sailing, collecting ship models and prints; late part owner 15 ton ketch Craignair. *Address:* Yewden Manor, Hambleden, Henley-on-Thames, Oxon. *T:* Hambleden 351. *Clubs:* Keyhaven Yacht, Cambridge University Cruising, etc.

SNELLGROVE, David Llewellyn, LittD, PhD; FBA 1969; Professor of Tibetan in the University of London, 1974–82, now Emeritus Professor (Reader, 1960–74, Lecturer, 1950–60); Founder Director of Institute of Tibetan Studies, Tring, 1966–82; *b* Portsmouth, 29 June 1920; *s* of Lt-Comdr Clifford Snellgrove, RN, and Eleanor Maud Snellgrove. *Educ:* Christ's Hospital, Horsham; Southampton Univ.; Queens' Coll., Cambridge. Served War of 1939–45: commissioned in Infantry, 1942; Intell. Officer in India until 1946. Then started seriously on oriental studies at Cambridge, 1946, cont. Rome, 1949–50. BA Cantab 1949, MA Cantab 1953; PhD London 1954; LittD Cantab 1969. Made expedns to India and the Himalayas, 1953–54, 1956, 1960, 1964, 1967, 1974–75, 1978–80, 1982; founded with Mr Hugh E. Richardson an Inst. of Tibetan Studies, 1966. Apptd Consultant to Vatican in new Secretariat for non-Christian Religions, 1967. Many professional visits abroad, mainly to W Europe and USA. *Publications:* Buddhist Himalaya, 1957; The Hevajra Tantra, 1959; Himalayan Pilgrimage, 1961, 2nd edn 1981; Four Lamas of Dolpo, 1967; The Nine Ways of Bon, 1967, repr. 1980; (with H. E. Richardson) A Cultural History of Tibet, 1968, 2nd edn 1980; (with T. Skorupski) The Cultural Heritage of Ladakh, vol. I, 1977, vol. II, 1980; (ed) The Image of the Buddha, 1978; Indo-Tibetan Buddhism, 1986; articles in Arts Asiatiques (Paris), Bulletin of the Secretariat for non-Christian Religions (Rome), etc. *Address:* Via Matteo Gay 26/7, 10066 Torre Pellice, Italy.

SNELLGROVE, John Anthony; HM Diplomatic Service, retired; Secretary, British Brush Manufacturers' Association, since 1977; *b* 29 Jan. 1922; *s* of late John Snellgrove and of Anne Mary Priscilla (*née* Brown); *m* 1956, Rose Jeanne Marie Suzanne (*née* Paris); two *d. Educ:* Wimbledon Coll.; Stonyhurst Coll.; Peterhouse, Cambridge (1940–41 and 1945–48; BA and MA). Served War, Royal Navy, latterly as temp. actg Lieut, RNVR, 1941–45. Asst Principal, Colonial Office, 1948–49; joined Foreign Service, Oct. 1949; 2nd Sec., Prague, 1950–51; FO (Econ. Relations Dept), 1951–53; HM Vice-Consul, Tamsui (Formosa), 1953–56; 1st Sec., 1954; FO (SE Asia Dept and UN (E&S) Dept), 1956–59; 1st Sec., Bangkok, 1959–62; 1st Sec. and Consul, Mogadishu (Somali Republic), 1962–63; FO (Arabian and European Econ. Org. Depts), 1963–66; 1st Sec., Holy See, 1967–71; Counsellor, 1971; Dep. Sec.-Gen. (Economic), CENTO, 1971–73; Counsellor and Head of Chancery, Carácas, 1973–75, retired, 1976. *Recreations:* music, bridge. *Address:* 13 Chantry Hurst, Woodcote, Epsom, Surrey KT18 7BN.

SNELLING, Sir Arthur (Wendell), KCMG 1960 (CMG 1954); KCVO 1962; HM Diplomatic Service, retired; *b* 7 May 1914; *s* of Arthur and Ellen Snelling; *m* 1939, Frieda, *d* of late Lt-Col F. C. Barnes; one *s. Educ:* Ackworth Sch., Yorks; University Coll., London (BSc Econ.). Study Gp Sec., Royal Inst. of Internat. Affairs, 1934–36; Dominions Office, 1936; Private Sec. to Parl. Under-Sec., 1939; Joint Sec. to UK Delegn to Internat. Monetary Conference, Bretton Woods, USA, 1944; accompanied Lord Keynes on missions to USA and Canada, 1943 and 1944; Dep. High Comr for UK in New Zealand, 1947–50, in S Africa, 1953–55; Assistant Under-Secretary of State, Commonwealth Relations Office, 1956–59; British High Comr in Ghana, 1959–61; Dep. Under-Sec. of State, FCO (formerly CRO), 1961–69; Ambassador to South Africa, 1970–72. Dir, Gordon and Gotch Holdings Ltd, 1973–81. Fellow, UCL, 1970; Mem., College Council, UCL, 1976–86. Vice-Pres., UK-S Africa Trade Assoc., 1974–80; Mem., Ciskei Commn, 1978–80. *Address:* 19 Albany Park Road, Kingston-upon-Thames, Surrey KT2 5SW. *T:* 01–549 4160. *Club:* Reform.

SNELSON, Sir Edward Alec Abbott, KBE 1954 (OBE 1946); Justice, Supreme Restitution Court, Herford, German Federal Republic, since 1962; Judge, Arbitral Tribunal for Agreement on German External Debts and Mixed Commission, Koblenz, 1969–77; *b* 31 Oct. 1904; *er s* of Thomas Edward and Alice Martha Snelson; *m* 1956, Prof. Jean Johnston Mackay, MA, 3rd *d* of Donald and Isabella Mackay; two *s. Educ:* St Olave's; Gonville and Caius Coll., Cambridge. Called to Bar, Gray's Inn, 1929; entered ICS 1929; served in Central Provinces, District and Sessions Judge, 1936; Registrar, High Court, 1941; Legal Secretary, 1946; Joint Secretary, Govt of India, 1947; retired, 1947; Official Draftsman, Govt of Pakistan, 1948; Sec. Min. of Law, 1951–61, also of Parliamentary Affairs, 1952–58. Mem. Exec. Cttee, Arts Council of Pakistan, 1953–61. *Publication:* Father Damien, 1938. *Recreations:* sailing, music, theatre. *Address:* c/o Barclays Bank, Piccadilly Circus, W1A 3BJ. *Clubs:* United Oxford & Cambridge University; Challoner.

SNELUS, Alan Roe, CMG 1960; retired as Deputy Chief Secretary, Sarawak (1955–64); *b* 19 May 1911; *s* of John Ernest Snelus, late of Ennerdale Hall, Cumberland; *m* 1947, Margaret Bird Deacon-Elliott; one *s* one *d. Educ:* Haileybury Coll.; St Catharine's Coll., Cambridge. Barrister, Gray's Inn, 1934. Joined Sarawak Civil Service as an Administrative Officer, 1934; Actg Chief Sec., 1958–59; Officer Administering the Government of Sarawak, March-April 1959. *Recreations:* gardening and contemplation. *Address:* 115A Hansford Square, Combe Down, Bath, Avon.

SNODGRASS, Prof. Anthony McElrea, FSA; FBA 1979; Laurence Professor of Classical Archaeology, University of Cambridge, since 1976; Fellow of Clare College, Cambridge, since 1977; *b* 7 July 1934; *s* of William McElrea Snodgrass, MC (Major, RAMC), and Kathleen Mabel (*née* Owen); *m* 1st, 1959, Ann Elizabeth Vaughan (marr. diss.); three *d*; 2nd, 1983, Annemarie Künzl; one *s. Educ:* Marlborough Coll.; Worcester Coll., Oxford (BA 1959, MA, DPhil 1963). FSA 1978. Served with RAF in Iraq, 1953–55 (National Service). Student of the British School, Athens, 1959–60; University of Edinburgh: Lectr in Classical Archaeology, 1961; Reader, 1969; Prof., 1975. Myres Meml Lectr, Oxford, 1981. Corresp. Mem., German Archaeol. Inst., 1977. *Publications:* Early Greek Armour and Weapons, 1964; Arms and Armour of the Greeks, 1967; The Dark Age of Greece, 1971; Archaic Greece, 1980; Narration and Allusion in Early Greek Art, 1982; contrib. Jl of Hellenic Studies, Proc. of Prehistoric Soc., Gnomon, etc. *Recreations:* mountaineering, skiing. *Address:* Museum of Classical Archaeology, Sidgwick Avenue, Cambridge CB3 9DA. *T:* Cambridge 62253. *Club:* Alpine Ski.

See also J. M. O. Snodgrass.

SNODGRASS, John Michael Owen, CMG 1981; HM Diplomatic Service, retired; *b* 12 Aug. 1928; *e s* of Major W. M. Snodgrass, MC, RAMC; *m* 1957, Jennifer James; three *s. Educ:* Marlborough Coll.; Trinity Hall, Cambridge (MA, Maths and Moral Scis). Diplomatic Service: 3rd Sec., Rome, 1953–56; FO, 1956–60; 1st Sec., Beirut, 1960–63; S Africa, 1964–67; FCO, 1967–70; Consul-Gen., Jerusalem, 1970–74; Counsellor, South Africa, 1974–77; Hd of South Pacific Dept, FCO, 1977–80; Ambassador: to Zaire, 1980–83 (also to Burundi, Rwanda and Congo); to Bulgaria, 1983–86. CStJ 1975. *Recreations:* ski-ing, tennis, travel. *Address:* 3 Ovington Gardens, SW3. *Clubs:* Royal Commonwealth Society, Ski Club of Great Britain.

See also A. McE. Snodgrass.

SNOW, Adrian John, MA, MEd; Headmaster, The Oratory School, since 1973; *b* 20 March 1939; *e s* of Edward Percy John Snow and Marjory Ellen Nicholls; *m* 1963, Alessina Teresa Kilkelly; one *s* one *d*. *Educ:* Hurstpierpoint Coll.; Trinity Coll., Dublin (BA, MA, HDipEd); Reading Univ. (MEd). Asst Master, The New Beacon, Sevenoaks, 1958–59; RAF Pilot Officer, 1963; Assistant Master: King's Sch., Sherborne, 1964; High Sch., Dublin, 1964–65 (part-time); Brighton Coll., 1965–66; The Oratory School: Head of Econ. and Pol Studies, 1966–73; Head of Hist., 1967–73; Housemaster, 1967–73; acting Headmaster, Sept. 1972–Mar. 1973. Governor: Prior Park Coll., 1981– (Mem., Action Cttee, 1980–81); Moreton Hall Prep. Sch., 1984–. Mem., RYA. *Recreations:* athletics (univ. colour), cricket, farming, hockey (Jun. Internat. trialist), Rugby (Combined Univs), sailing, squash. *Address:* The Oratory School, Woodcote, near Reading RG8 0PJ. *T:* Checkendon 680207. *Clubs:* Leander (Henley); Emeriti CC, Sussex Martlets CC.

SNOW, Antony Edmund, MIPA, FIPR; Chairman and Chief Executive, Charles Barker PLC, since 1983; *b* 5 Dec. 1932; 2nd *s* of Thomas Maitland Snow, *qv*; *m* 1961, Caroline Wilson; one *s* two *d*. *Educ:* Sherborne Sch.; New College, Oxford. National Service, commnd in 10th Royal Hussars, 1952–53; Royal Wiltshire Yeomanry, TA, 1953–63. W. S. Crawford, 1958; Charles Barker & Sons, 1961, Dep. Chairman, 1975. Vice-Pres., Market Planning, Steuben Glass, 1976; Dep. Dir, Corning Museum of Glass, 1978 (Trustee, 1983–); Dir, Rockwell Museum, 1979. Member: Cttee of Management, Courtauld Institute of Art, 1984–; Exec. Cttee, Nat. Art-Collections Fund, 1985–. *Recreations:* windsurfing, ski-ing, tennis, English watercolours. *Address:* 16 Rumbold Road, SW6. *Clubs:* Cavalry and Guards, City of London; The Pilgrims (New York).
See also Thomas Snow.

SNOW, Jonathan George; Television Reporter, Independent Television News, since 1976, Diplomatic Correspondent, since 1986; *b* 28 Sept. 1947; *s* of late Rt Rev. George Snow, sometime Bishop of Whitby, and of Joan Snow; two *d*. *Educ:* St Edward's School, Oxford; Liverpool Univ. (no degree; sent down following political disturbances, 1970). VSO, Uganda, 1967–68; Co-ordinator, New Horizon Youth Centre, Covent Garden, 1970–73; Journalist, Independent Radio News, LBC, 1973–76; Washington Correspondent, ITN, 1983–86. TV Journalist of the Year (Royal Television Soc.), 1981; Valiant for Truth Media Award, 1982. Member, NUJ. *Address:* ITN, 48 Wells Street, W1. *T:* (office) 01–637 2424, (home) 01–485 3513.

SNOW, Rear-Adm. Kenneth Arthur; Deputy Assistant Chief of Staff (Operations) to Supreme Allied Commander Europe, 1984–July 1987, retired; *b* 14 April 1934; *s* of Arthur Chandos Pole Snow and Evelyn (*née* Joyce); *m* 1956, Pamela Elizabeth Terry (*née* Sorrell); one *s* two *d*. *Educ:* St Andrews College, Grahamstown; South African Nautical College. Joined RN, 1952; commanded HMS Kirkliston, 1962; qualified navigation specialist, 1963; commanded: HMS Llandaff, 1970; HMS Arethusa, 1979; HMS Hermes, 1983. *Recreations:* gardening, painting. *Address:* c/o Naval Secretary, Ministry of Defence (Navy), Whitehall, SW1.

SNOW, Philip Albert, OBE 1985 (MBE 1979); JP; MA; FRSA; FRAI; author; *b* 7 Aug. 1915; *s* of William Edward Snow, FRCO and Ada Sophia Robinson; *m* 1940, Anne Harris; one *d*. *Educ:* Newton's Sch., Leicester; Christ's Coll., Cambridge (MA Hons). FRAI 1952. Provincial Comr, Magistrate and Asst Colonial Sec., Fiji and Western Pacific, 1938–52; ADC to Governor and C-in-C, Fiji, 1939; Fiji Govt Liaison Officer, US and NZ Forces, 1942–44; Bursar, Rugby Sch., 1952–76. President: Public Schs Bursars' Assoc., 1962–65; The Worthing Soc., 1983–; Vice-Pres., Fiji Soc., 1944–52. Founder, Fiji Cricket Assoc., 1946, Vice-Patron, 1952–; Captain, Fiji Cricket Team, NZ tour, 1948. Internat. Cricket Conference: Perm. Rep. of Fiji, 1965–; Mem., first World Cup Cttee, 1971–75; Chm., Associate Member Countries, 1982–. Literary Executor and Executor of Lord Snow. JP Warwicks, 1967–76, and W Sussex, 1976–. FRSA 1984. Foreign Specialist Award, USA Govt, 1964. *Publications:* Cricket in the Fiji Islands, 1949; Report on the Visit of Three Bursars to the United States of America in 1964, 1965; Best Stories of the South Seas, 1967; Bibliography of Fiji, Tonga and Rotuma, 1969; (with Stefanie Waine) The People from the Horizon: an illustrated history of the Europeans among the South Sea Islanders, 1979; Stranger and Brother: a portrait of C. P. Snow, 1982; contrib. TLS, Sunday Times, Daily Telegraph, The Times, Jls of RAI, RGS and Polynesian Soc., Jl de la Société des Océanistes, Amer. Anthropologist, Wisden's Almanack, Barclays World of Cricket, Dictionary of Nat. Biog; numerous reviews of, and introductions to, Pacific books. *Recreations:* taming robins; formerly cricket (Leics 2nd XI, Cambridge Crusaders, Googlies, MCC, Authors, Fiji), chess (Half-Blue), table-tennis (Half-Blue), deck-tennis, tennis. *Address:* Gables, Station Road, Angmering, West Sussex BN16 4HY. *T:* Rustington 773594. *Clubs:* MCC (Hon. Life Mem. for distinguished services to internat. cricket, 1970); Hawks (Cambridge).

SNOW, Surg. Rear-Adm. Ronald Edward, LVO 1972; OBE 1977; QHP 1984; Surgeon Rear Admiral (Support Medical Services), since 1987; *b* 17 May 1933; *s* of Arthur Chandos Pole Snow (formerly Soppitt) and Evelyn Dorothea Snow (*née* Joyce); *m* 1959, Valerie Melian French; two *d*. *Educ:* St Andrew's Coll., Grahamstown, S Africa; Trinity Coll., Dublin (MA, MB, BCh, BAO); MFOM, DA, LMCC. HMS Victorious, 1966; HMS Dolphin, 1967; HMY Britannia, 1970; MoD, 1973 and 1977; Inst. of Naval Medicine, 1975 and 1984; Staff of Surg. Rear Adm. (Naval Hosps), 1980; Staff of C-in-C Fleet, 1982; Asst Surg. Gen. (Service Hosps), 1985. *Recreations:* National Hunt racing, cruising. *Address:* 22 Sheep Street, Petersfield, Hants GU32 3JX. *Clubs:* Army and Navy; Royal Naval Sailing Association (Portsmouth).
See also Rear-Adm. K. A. Snow.

SNOW, Thomas; Secretary to Oxford University Appointments Committee, since 1970; Fellow, New College, Oxford, since 1973; *b* 16 June 1929; *e s* of Thomas Maitland Snow, *qv*; *m* 1961, Elena Tidmarsh; two *s* one *d*. *Educ:* Winchester Coll. (Fellow, 1985); New Coll., Oxford. Joined Crittall Manufacturing Co. Ltd as Management Trainee, 1952; Dir 1966; Director: Crittall Hope Ltd, Darlington Simpson Rolling Mills, Minex Metals Ltd, 1968. Dep. Chm., Assoc. of Graduate Careers Adv. Services, 1985–. Held various positions in local govt; Marriage Counsellor, 1964–70; Chm., Oxford Marriage Guidance Council, 1974–. JP 1964–69. *Address:* 157 Woodstock Road, Oxford.
See also A. E. Snow.

SNOW, Thomas Maitland, CMG 1934; *b* 21 May 1890; *s* of Thomas Snow, Cleve, Exeter, and Edith Banbury; *m* 1st, 1927, Phyllis Annette Malcolmson; three *s*; 2nd, 1949, Sylvia, *d* of W. Delmar, Buda-Pest. *Educ:* Winchester; New Coll., Oxford. 1st Secretary, HM Diplomatic Service, 1923; Counsellor, 1930; Minister: to Cuba, 1935–37; to Finland, 1937–40; to Colombia, 1941–44 (Ambassador, 1944–45); to Switzerland, 1946–49. Retired, 1950. *Recreation:* metaphysics. *Address:* Maison du Bailli, 1816 Chailly-sur-Clarens, Switzerland.
See also A. E. Snow, Thomas Snow.

SNOWDEN, Rt. Rev. John Samuel Philip; *see* Cariboo, Bishop of.

SNOWDON, 1st Earl of, *cr* 1961; **Antony Charles Robert Armstrong-Jones,** GCVO 1969; RDI 1978; FSIAD; Viscount Linley, 1961; an Artistic Adviser to the Sunday Times and Sunday Times Publications Ltd, since 1962; Constable of Caernarfon Castle since 1963; *b* 7 March 1930; *s* of Ronald Owen Lloyd Armstrong-Jones, MBE, QC, DL (*d* 1966), and of Anne, *o d* of Lt-Col Leonard Messel, OBE (later Countess of Rosse); *m* 1st, 1960, HRH The Princess Margaret (marr. diss. 1978); one *s* one *d*; 2nd, 1978, Lucy Lindsay-Hogg, *d* of Donald Davies; one *d*. *Educ:* Eton; Jesus Coll., Cambridge. Joined Staff of Council of Industrial Design, 1961, continuing on a consultative basis, 1962, also an Editorial Adviser of Design Magazine. Designed: Snowdon Aviary, London Zoo, 1965; Chairmobile, 1972. Mem. Council, National Fund for Research for Crippling Diseases; Patron, Circle of Guide Dog Owners; Chm., Working Party on Integrating the Disabled (Report 1976); Pres. for England, Cttee, International Year for Disabled People, 1981. Hon. Fellow: Institute of British Photographers; Royal Photographic Soc.; Manchester College of Art and Design; Hon. Member: North Wales Society of Architects; South Wales Institute of Architects; Royal Welsh Yacht Club; Patron: Welsh Nat. Rowing Club; Metropolitan Union of YMCAs; British Water Ski Federation. President: Contemp. Art Society for Wales; Civic Trust for Wales; Welsh Theatre Company; Mem. Council, English Stage Co., 1978–82. Senior Fellow, RCA, 1986. FRSA. Silver Progress Medal, RPS, 1985. *Television films:* Don't Count the Candles, 1968 (2 Hollywood Emmy Awards; St George Prize, Venice; awards at Prague and Barcelona film festivals); Love of a Kind, 1969; Born to be Small, 1971 (Chicago Hugo Award); Happy being Happy, 1973; Mary Kingsley, 1975; Burke and Wills, 1975; Peter, Tina and Steve, 1977; Snowdon on Camera, BBC (presenter), 1981. *Exhibitions include:* Photocall, London, 1958; Assignments, Cologne, London, Brussels, USA, 1972, Japan, Canada, Denmark, Holland, 1975, Australia, 1976, France, 1977. *Publications:* London, 1958; Malta (in collaboration), 1958; Private View (in collaboration), 1965; A View of Venice, 1972; Assignments, 1972; Inchcape Review, 1977; (jtly) Pride of the Shires, 1979; Personal View, 1979; Sittings, 1983; Israel: a first view, 1986. *Heir: s* Viscount Linley, *qv*. *Address:* 22 Launceston Place, W8 5RL. *Clubs:* Buck's, United Oxford & Cambridge University; Leander (Henley-on-Thames); Hawks (Cambridge).
See also under Royal Family, and Earl of Rosse.

SNOY ET d'OPPUERS, Comte Jean-Charles, Hon. KBE 1975 (OBE 1948); Grand Officier de l'Ordre de Léopold, Belgium; Grand Officier de l'Ordre de la Couronne, Belgium; Member of Belgian Parliament, 1968–71; Minister of Finance, Belgium, 1968–72; *b* 2 July 1907; *s* of 9th Baron and of Claire de Beughem de Houtem; created Count, 1982; *m* 1935, Nathalie, Countess d'Alcantara; two *s* five *d*. *Educ:* Collège Saint-Pierre, Uccle; University of Louvain; Harvard Univ. Secretary Société Belge de Banque, 1932; Attaché Cabinet Minister of Economic Affairs, 1934; Directeur Ministry Econ. Aff., 1936; Secrétaire Général, Ministère des Affaires Economiques, 1939–60; Président du Conseil de l'Union Benelux, 1945–60. War Service: Services de Renseignements et d'Action, 1940–44. Chairman, Four Party Supply Cttee, Belgium, 1945; Président du Conseil, Organisation Européenne de Coopération Economique, 1948–50 (OEEC in English); Chm., Steering Board for Trade, OEEC, 1952–61; Chef de la délégation Belge pour la négociation des Traités de Rome, 1957; Président, Comité Intérimaire du Marché Commun et de l'Euratom, 1957–58; Representant Permanent de la Belgique, Communauté Economique Européenne, 1958–59; Administrateur-Délégué de la Compagnie Lambert pour l'Industrie et la Finance, Brussels, 1960–68. Holds several foreign decorations. *Publications:* La Commission des Douanes, 1932; L'Aristocratie de Demain, 1936; La Profession et l'Organisation de la Production, 1942; Revue Générale Belge; La Libre Belgique. *Recreations:* shooting, tennis. *Heir: s* Bernard, Baron Snoy, *b* 11 March 1945. *Address:* Château de Bois-Seigneur-Isaac, 1421 Braine l'Alleud, Belgium. *T:* Nivelles 21.22.27. *Club:* Club de la Fondation Universitaire (Brussels).

SOAME, Sir Charles (John) Buckworth-Herne-, 12th Bt *cr* 1697; *b* 28 May 1932; *s* of Sir Charles Burnett Buckworth-Herne-Soame, 11th Bt, and Elsie May (*d* 1972), *d* of Walter Alfred Lloyd; *S* father, 1977; *m* 1958, Eileen Margaret Mary, *d* of Leonard Minton; one *s*. *Heir: s* Richard John Buckworth-Herne-Soame, *b* 17 Aug. 1970. *Address:* Sheen Cottage, Coalbrookdale, Telford, Salop.

SOAMES, family name of **Baron Soames.**

SOAMES, Baron *cr* 1978 (Life Peer), of Fletching in the County of E Sussex; **Arthur Christopher John Soames,** PC 1958; GCMG 1972; GCVO 1972; CH 1980; CBE 1955; *b* 12 Oct. 1920; *m* 1947, Mary Churchill (*see* Lady Soames); three *s* two *d*. *Educ:* Eton; Royal Military Coll., Sandhurst. 2nd Lieut, Coldstream Guards, 1939; Captain, 1942; served Middle East, Italy and France. Assistant Military Attaché British Embassy, Paris, 1946–47, MP (C) Bedford Division of Bedfordshire, 1950–66. Parliamentary Private Secretary to the Prime Minister, 1952–55; Parliamentary Under-Secretary of State, Air Ministry, Dec. 1955–Jan. 1957; Parliamentary and Financial Secretary, Admiralty, 1957–58; Secretary of State for War, Jan. 1958–July 1960; Minister of Agriculture, Fisheries and Food, 1960–64. Director: Decca Ltd, 1964–68; James Hole & Co. Ltd, 1964–68. Ambassador to France, 1968–72. A Vice-Pres., Commn of the European Communities, 1973–Jan. 1977. Chm., ICL (UK) Ltd, 1984–; Director: N. M. Rothschild & Sons Ltd, 1977–79; Nat. Westminster Bank Ltd, 1978–79. Governor of Southern Rhodesia, 1979–80. Lord President of the Council and Leader of the House of Lords, 1979–81. Pres., RASE, 1973. Hon. LLD St Andrews, 1974; Hon. DCL Oxon, 1981. Croix de Guerre (France), 1942; Grand Officier de la Légion d'honneur, 1972; Grand Cross of St Olav (Norway), 1974. Medal of the City of Paris, 1972. *Address:* House of Lords, SW1A 0PW. *Clubs:* White's, Portland.
See also Hon. A. N. W. Soames.

SOAMES, Lady; Mary Soames, DBE 1980 (MBE (mil.) 1945); President, National Benevolent Fund for the Aged, since 1978; Member, Winston Churchill Memorial Trust Council, since 1978; Governor, Harrow School, since 1980; *b* 15 Sept. 1922; *y d* of late Rt Hon. Sir Winston Churchill, KG, OM, CH, FRS, and late Baroness Spencer-Churchill, GBE; *m* 1947, Captain Christopher Soames, Coldstream Guards (now Baron Soames, *qv*); three *s* two *d*. *Educ:* privately. Served War: Red Cross and WVS, 1939–41; ATS, 1941–46, with mixed anti-aircraft batteries in UK and Europe (Jun. Comdr). Accompanied father on various journeys; campaigned with husband through six elections whilst he was Conservative MP for Bedford, 1950–66; accompanied husband to Paris where he was Ambassador, 1968–72, and to Brussels where he was first British Vice Pres. of Eur. Commn, 1973–76; accompanied husband when he was appointed last British Governor of Southern Rhodesia, Dec. 1979–April 1980. Associated with Church Army, 1945–77, esp. in connection with scheme for housing old people (Churchill Houses) and with their work for delinquent girls; Chm., UK Assoc. for Internat. Year of the Child, 1979. Hon. Fellow, Churchill Coll., Cambridge, 1983. JP E Sussex, 1960–74. *Publications:* Clementine Churchill by Her Daughter Mary Soames, 1979 (a Wolfson Prize for History, and Yorkshire Post Prize for Best First Work, 1979); A Churchill Family Album—A Personal Anthology Selected by Mary Soames, 1982; The Profligate Duke: George Spencer-Churchill 5th Duke of Marlborough and his Duchess, 1987. *Recreations:* reading, sight-seeing, gardening.
See also Hon. A. N. W. Soames.

SOAMES, Hon. (Arthur) Nicholas (Winston); MP (C) Crawley, since 1983; *b* 12 Feb. 1948; *s* of Baron Soames, *qv* and of Lady Soames, *qv*; *m* 1981, Catherine Weatherall; one *s. Educ:* Eton. Served 11th Hussars (PAO), 1967–70 (2nd Lieut); Equerry to the Prince of Wales, 1970–72; Asst Dir, Sedgwick Group, 1976–82. PPS to Minister of State for Employment, 1984–. *Recreation:* country pursuits. *Address:* House of Commons, SW1A 0AA. *T:* 01-219 3000. *Clubs:* White's, Turf.

SOANE, Leslie James, OBE 1985; CEng, MICE; FCIT, FBIM; FRSA; Member of Board and Director, Railway Heritage Trust, since 1985; *b* 15 Jan. 1926; *s* of Arthur Edward Soane and Florence May Herring; *m* 1950, Joan Edith Mayo; one *s* one *d. Educ:* Watford Central Sch.; London Univ. Civil Engineer posts: London Midland Region, 1948–55; Eastern Region, 1955–62; LMR, 1962–71; Chief Civil Engr, Western Region, 1971–75; Dep. Gen. Manager, WR, 1975–77; Gen. Manager, Scottish Region, 1977–83; Man. Dir (Reorganisation), BRB, 1983–85. Lt-Col Engr and Transport Staff Corps, RE (TA), 1985–. *Recreations:* theatre, reading, golf. *Address:* St Michael's Croft, Woodcock Hill, Berkhamsted, Herts HP4 3PJ. *T:* Berkhamsted 75831.

SOBELL, Sir Michael, Kt 1972; Chairman, GEC (Radio & Television) Ltd; *b* 1 Nov. 1892; *s* of Lewis and Esther Sobell; *m* 1917, Anne Rakusen; two *d. Educ:* Central London Foundation Sch. Freeman and Liveryman, Carmen Co. Hon. FRCPath, 1981; Hon. Fellow: Bar Ilan Univ.; Jews' Coll.; Hon. Dr Science and Technol., Technion Inst., Haifa, 1980; Hon. Dr Bar-Ilan Univ. *Recreations:* racing, charitable work. *Address:* Bakeham House, Englefield Green, Surrey. *Clubs:* City Livery; Jockey (Newmarket).

See also Baron Weinstock.

SOBER, Phillip, FCA; Senior Partner since 1985, and International Partner since 1975, Stoy Hayward, Chartered Accountants; *b* 1 April 1931; *s* of Abraham and Sandra Sober; *m* 1957, Vivien Louise Oppenheimer; three *d. Educ:* Haberdashers' Aske's. Qual. as Chartered Accountant, 1953; FCA 1963. Partner, Stoy Hayward, 1958. Crown Estate Comr, 1983–. Mem. Council, UK Central Council for Nursing, Midwifery and Health Visiting, 1980–83. Trustee, Royal Opera House Trust, 1985–. *Publications:* articles in prof. press on various subjects but primarily on property co. accounting. *Recreations:* interested in all the arts, partic. music; golf main sporting activity. *Address:* 10 Longwood Drive, Roehampton, SW15 5DL. *T:* 01-789 0437. *Clubs:* Savile, Royal Automobile, Hurlingham, Roehampton.

SOBERS, Sir Garfield (St Auburn), (Sir Garry Sobers), Kt 1975; cricketer; *b* Bridgetown, Barbados, 28 July 1936; *m* 1969, Prudence Kirby; two *s* one *d. Educ:* Bay Street Sch., Barbados. First major match, 1953, for Barbados; played in 93 Test Matches for West Indies, 39 as Captain, 1953–74 (made world record Test Match score, Kingston, 1958); captained West Indies and Barbados teams, 1965–74; Captain of Nottinghamshire CCC, 1968–74. On retirement from Test cricket held the following world records in Test Matches: 365 not out; 26 centuries; 235 wickets; 110 catches. *Publications:* Cricket Advance, 1965; Cricket Crusader, 1966; King Cricket, 1967; (with J. S. Barker) Cricket in the Sun, 1967; Bonaventure and the Flashing Blade, 1967; *relevant publication:* Sir Gary: a biography by Trevor Bailey, 1976.

SOBHI, Mohamed Ibrahim; Order of Merit, 1st Class, Egypt, 1974; Director General, International Bureau of Universal Postal Union, Berne, 1975–84, retired; *b* Alexandria, 28 March 1925; *s* of Gen. Ibrahim Sobhi and Mrs Zenab Affifi; *m* 1950, Laila Ahmed Sobhi; two *s* one *d. Educ:* Cairo Univ. (BE 1949). Construction of roads and airports, Engr Corps, 1950; Technical Sec., Communications Commn, Permanent Council for Develt and National Prodn, Cairo, 1954; Fellow, Vanderbilt Univ., Nashville, Tenn (studying transport and communications services in USA), 1955–56; Tech. Dir, Office of Minister of Communications for Posts, Railways and Coordination between means of transp. and communications, Cairo, 1956–61; Dir-Gen., Sea Transp. Authority (remaining Mem. Tech. Cttees, Postal Org.), 1961–64; Under Sec. of State for Communications and Mem. Bd, Postal Org., Cairo, 1964–68; Chm. Bd, Postal Org., and Sec.-Gen., African Postal Union, Cairo, 1968–74. Universal Postal Union: attended Congress, Ottawa, 1957; attended Cons. Council for Postal Studies session, Brussels, 1958; Head of Egyptian Delegn, Tokyo and Lausanne Congresses, and sessions of CCPS (set up by Tokyo Congress), 1969–74; Dir, Exec. Bureau i/c Egyptian projects in Africa, incl. construction of Hôtel de l'Amitié, Bamako, Mali, and roads, Republic of Mali, 1963–74; as Director-General of UPU, acts as Sec.-Gen. of the Congress, Exec. Council, and Cons. Council for Postal Studies; acts as intermediary between UPU and Restricted Unions, UN and internat. orgns; visits member countries and attends many meetings and congresses, inc. those of Restricted Unions, in all continents. Heinrich von Stephan Medal (Germany), 1979; Order of Postal Merit (Gran Placa) (Spain), 1979. *Recreations:* croquet, philately, music. *Address:* 4 Sheik Zakaria El-Ansary Street, Heliopolis, Cairo, Egypt.

SODOR AND MAN, Bishop of, since 1983; **Rt. Rev. Arthur Henry Attwell;** *b* 5 Aug. 1920; *s* of Henry John and Kate Attwell; *m* 1982, Muriel Isobel Hesson. *Educ:* Wilson School, Reading; Leeds Univ. (BA 1941); College of the Resurrection, Mirfield. BD 1947, MTh 1958, MA 1972 all London. Deacon 1943, priest 1944; Curate of St George, Wolverton, 1943–45; Curate of Wigan, 1945–51; Sub-warden of St Paul's Coll., Grahamstown, S Africa, 1951–52; Dean of Kimberley, S Africa, 1952–60; Rector of Workington, Cumberland, 1960–72; Hon. Canon of Carlisle, 1964–72, 1978–83; Rural Dean of Cockermouth and Workington, 1966–70; Canon Residentiary of Carlisle Cathedral, 1972–78; Vicar of St John's, Windermere, 1978–82; Archdeacon of Westmorland and Furness, 1978–83; Dir, Carlisle Discesen Training Inst., 1978–83. Proctor in Convocation, 1965–78; Exam. Chaplain to Bishop of Carlisle, 1972–83. *Recreation:* travel. *Address:* The Bishop's House, Quarterbridge Road, Douglas, Isle of Man. *T:* Douglas 22108.

SOFER, Mrs Anne Hallowell; Member (SDP), GLC/ILEA for St Pancras North, Oct. 1981–1986 (by-election) (Labour, 1977–81); *b* 19 April 1937; *d* of Geoffrey Crowther (later Baron Crowther) and Margaret Worth; *m* 1958, Jonathan Sofer; two *s* one *d. Educ:* St Paul's Sch.; Swarthmore Coll., USA; Somerville Coll., Oxford (MA); DipEd London. Secretary, National Assoc. of Governors and Managers, 1972–75; Additional Member, ILEA Education Cttee, 1974–77; Chairman, ILEA Schools Sub-Cttee, 1978–81. Mem., SDP Nat. Cttee, 1982–. Dir, Channel Four Television Co. Ltd, 1981–83. Contested (SDP) Hampstead and Highgate, 1983. *Publication:* (with Tyrrell Burgess) The School Governors and Managers Handbook and Training Guide, 1978. *Address:* 46 Regent's Park Road, NW1 7SX. *T:* 01-722 8970.

SOLANKI, Ramniklal Chhaganlal; Editor, Garavi Gujarat, London, since 1968; Editor-in-Chief, Asian Trader, since 1985; Correspondent, Janmabhoomi Group, Bombay, since 1968; *b* 12 July 1931; *s* of Chhaganlal Kalidas and Mrs Ichchhaben Solanki, Surat, Gujarat, India; *m* 1955, Mrs Parvatiben, *d* of Makanji Dullabhji Chavda, Nani Pethan, India; two *s* two *d. Educ:* Irish Presbyterian Mission Sch., Surat (Matriculation Gold Medal, 1949); MTB Coll., Gujarat Univ. (BA(Econ)); Sarvajanik Law Coll., Surat, Gujarat (LLB). Pres., Rander Student Union, 1950–54; Sec., Surat Dist Students' Assoc., 1954–55. Sub-Editor, Nutan Bharat and Lok Vani, Surat, 1954–56; freelance columnist for several newspapers, while serving State Govt in India, 1956–63; London correspondent, Gujarat Mitra Surat, 1964–68; European Correspondent, Janmabhoomi Gp of Newspapers, 1968–; Managing Director: Garavi Gujarat Publications Ltd and Garavi Gujarat Property Ltd; Asian Trade Publications Ltd. Member: Guild of British Newspaper Editors, 1976–; Asian Adv. Cttee, BBC, 1976–80; Nat. Centre for Ind. Language Trng Steering Gp, 1976–; Exec. Cttee, Gujarati Arya Kshtriya Maha Sabha UK, 1979–84; Exec. Cttee, Gujarati Arya Assoc., 1974–84 (Vice-Pres., 1980–81, 1982–83); CPU, 1964–; Foreign Press Assoc., 1984–; Parly Press Gallery, House of Commons; Sec., Indian Journalists Assoc. of Europe, 1978–79. Best Reporter of the Year in Gujarati, 1970. *Publications:* contrib. many articles. *Recreations:* reading, writing. *Address:* 74 Harrowdene Road, N Wembley, Mddx. *T:* 01-902 2879; *(office):* Garavi Gujarat House, 1/2 Silex Street, SE1 0DW. *T:* 01-928 1234; *Telex:* 8955335 Gujrat G; *Telefax:* 01-261 0055.

SOLDATOV, Aleksandr Alekseyevich; Rector, Moscow State Institute of International Relations, since 1970; *b* 27 Aug. 1915; *m* Rufina B.; two *d. Educ:* Moscow Teachers' Training Inst. (grad. Hist. Sciences, 1939). Member Soviet Foreign Service, 1941; Senior Counsellor of Soviet Delegation to the UN and Representative on Trusteeship Council, 1948–53; Head of UN Div., 1953–54, of American Div., 1954–60, Soviet Foreign Ministry; Soviet Ambassador to the Court of St James's, 1960–66; Deputy Foreign Minister, 1966–68; Ambassador in Cuba, 1968–70; Ambassador to Lebanon, 1974–86. Member Soviet Delegation to Geneva Conferences: on Germany, 1959; on Laos, 1961. Mem., CPSU Central Auditing Commn, 1966–71. *Address:* Moscow State Institute of International Relations, Ulitsa Metrostroevskaya 53, Moscow, USSR.

SOLER, Antonio R.; *see* Ruiz Soler, A.

SOLESBY, Tessa Audrey Hilda, CMG 1986; HM Diplomatic Service; Minister, Pretoria, since 1986; *b* 1932; *d* of Charles Solesby and Hilda Solesby (*née* Willis). *Educ:* Clifton High School; St Hugh's College, Oxford. MA. Min. of Labour and Nat. Service, 1954–55; joined Diplomatic Service, 1956; FO, 1956; Manila, 1957–59; Lisbon, 1959–62; FO, 1962–64; First Sec., UK Mission to UN, Geneva, 1964–68; FO, 1968–70; First Sec., UK Mission to UN, NY, 1970–72; FCO, 1972–75, Counsellor, 1975; on secondment to NATO Internat. Staff, Brussels, 1975–78; Counsellor, East Berlin, 1978–81; temp. Minister, UK Mission to UN, NY, 1981–82; Head of Central African Dept, FCO, 1982–86. *Recreations:* hill-walking, music. *Address:* c/o Foreign and Commonwealth Office, SW1A 2AH.

SOLEY, Clive Stafford; MP (Lab) Hammersmith, since 1983 (Hammersmith North, 1979–83); *b* 7 May 1939. *Educ:* Downshall Sec. Modern School; Newbattle Abbey Coll.; Strathclyde Univ. (BA Hons); Southampton Univ. (Dip. in Applied Social Studies). Various appointments; Probation Officer, 1970–75; Senior Probation Officer, 1975–79. Chm., Alcohol Educn Centre, 1977–83. Opposition front bench spokesman on N Ireland, 1981–84, on Home Affairs, 1984–. *Address:* House of Commons, SW1.

SOLLBERGER, Edmond, FBA 1973; Keeper of Western Asiatic Antiquities, The British Museum, 1974–83 (Deputy Keeper, 1970–74); *b* 12 Oct. 1920; *s* of W. Sollberger and M.-A. Calavassy; *m* 1949, Ariane Zender; two *d. Educ:* Univ. of Geneva, LicLitt 1945; DLitt 1952. Asst Keeper of Archæology, Musée d'art et d'histoire, Geneva, 1949; Keeper, 1952; Principal Keeper, 1958; Actg-Dir, 1959; Privat-Docent for Sumerian and Akkadian, Faculty of Letters, Univ. of Geneva, 1956–61; Asst Keeper of Western Asiatic Antiquities, The British Museum, 1961. Member: Council and Exec. Cttee, British Sch. of Archaeology in Iraq, 1961; Council of Management, British Inst. of Archæology at Ankara, 1961–70, 1976–82; British Sch. of Archæology, Jerusalem, 1974–82; Governing Body, SOAS, 1975–80; Governing Council, British Inst. of Persian Studies, 1977–82. Corresp. Mem., German Archæological Inst., 1961. Hon. Mem., American Oriental Soc., 1977. Mem., Internat. Cttee for study of the texts from Ebla, Rome Univ., 1978–. *Publications:* Le Système verbal dans les inscriptions royales présargoniques de Lagash, 1952 (Geneva); Corpus des inscriptions royales présargoniques de Lagash, 1956 (Geneva); Ur Excavations Texts VIII: Royal Inscriptions, 1965 (London); The Business and Administrative Correspondence under the Kings of Ur, 1966 (New York); (with J. R. Kupper) Inscriptions royales sumériennes et akkadiennes, 1971 (Paris); Pre-Sargonic and Sargonic Economic Texts, 1972 (London); The Pinches Manuscript, 1978 (Rome); numerous articles on Cuneiform and related studies in learned jls; jt editor: Littératures anciennes du Proche Orient, 1963–82 (Paris); Texts from Cuneiform Sources, 1965– (New York); Cambridge Ancient History, vols I-III (rev. edn), 1969–82; editor-in-chief, Royal Inscriptions of Mesopotamia, Toronto Univ., 1981–85. *Address:* 20 Manor Road, Richmond, Surrey TW9 1YB. *T:* 01-940 7698.

SOLOMON, CBE 1946; pianist; *b* London, 9 Aug. 1902; *m* 1970, Gwendoline Byrne. First public appearance at Queen's Hall at age of eight, June 1910; frequent appearances till 1916 then studied in London and Paris; reappeared in London at Wigmore Hall, Oct. 1921, and has since toured in the British Isles, America, France, Germany, Holland, Italy, Australia, and New Zealand. Hon. LLD St Andrews; Hon. MusD Cantab. *Recreations:* golf, bridge, motoring. *Address:* 16 Blenheim Road, NW8.

SOLOMON, His Honour (Alan) Peter; a Circuit Judge, 1973–86; *b* 6 July 1923; *s* of late Jacob Ovid Solomon, Manchester; *m* 1st, 1954; one *d*; 2nd, 1973; one *d*; 3rd, 1981, Susan Jennifer Hunter. *Educ:* Mill Hill Sch.; Lincoln College, Oxford; MA. Served War 1942–46, Fleet Air Arm, Petty Officer Airman. Called to Bar, Inner Temple, 1949; practised South-Eastern circuit. *Publications: poetry:* The Lunatic, Balance, in Keats Prize Poems, 1973. *Recreations:* the turf, travel, poetry, burgundy. *Club:* Garrick.

SOLOMON, Sir David (Arnold), Kt 1973; MBE 1944; *b* 13 Nov. 1907; *s* of Richard Solomon and Sarah Annie Solomon (*née* Simpson); *m* 1935, Marjorie Miles; two *s* one *d. Educ:* Leys Sch., Cambridge; Liverpool Univ. Qualified a Solicitor, 1933; became Mem. Liverpool Stock Exchange, 1935. Served War of 1939–45, RAF (MBE). Practised as a Stockbroker until retirement, March 1969. Chairman: Liverpool RHB, 1968–73; Community Health Council, SE Cumbria, 1973–76. *Recreation:* music. *Address:* Tithe Barn, Cartmel, Grange over Sands, Cumbria LA11 6PP. *T:* Cartmel 558.

SOLOMON, Jonathan Hilali Moïse; Director of Special Projects, Cable and Wireless PLC, since 1985; *b* 3 March 1939; *s* of Samuel and Moselle Solomon; *m* 1966, Hester McFarland; one *s. Educ:* Clifton College; King's College, Cambridge. BA Hons, MA. Research worker, Supervisor and Tutor, Cambridge and London Univs, 1960–63, 1965. Entered Home Civil Service, 1963; Asst Private Sec. to Pres. of Board of Trade, 1966–67; Principal, Companies Div., BoT, transferred to DTI, 1970; to Treasury, 1972; Asst Sec., Dept of Prices and Consumer Protection, 1974; returned to Dept of Industry, Electronics Divs, 1977–80; Under-Sec., Telecomns (formerly Posts and Telecomns) Div., DoI, 1980–84; Under Sec., Quality and Educn Div., DTI, 1984–85. Head UK Delegn, ITU Plenipotentiary Conf., Nairobi, 1982. *Publications:* contribs to journals such as Platon, Contemporary Review, New Outlook, Frontier, Tablet, Telecomunications Policy. *Recreations:* sport, futurology, writing. *Address:* 53 Hollycroft Avenue, NW3. *T:* 01-794 6230. *Club:* English-Speaking Union.

SOLOMON, Dr Patrick Vincent Joseph, TC 1978; retired from Trinidad and Tobago Diplomatic Service, 1977; High Commissioner for Trinidad and Tobago in London, 1971–76, concurrently Ambassador for Trinidad and Tobago to Switzerland, France, Germany, Austria, Luxembourg, Denmark, Norway, Sweden, Italy, Netherlands and

Finland; Chairman, Crown Life (Caribbean) Ltd, since 1977; *b* 12 April 1910; *s* of late Charles William Solomon and late Euphemia Alexia (*née* Payne); *m*; two *s*; *m* 1974, Mrs Leslie Richardson, *widow* of late William A. Richardson, Trinidad and Tobago. *Educ*: Tranquility Boys' Sch.; St Mary's Coll., Trinidad; Island Science Scholar, 1928; studied Medicine at Belfast and Edinburgh Univs, graduating in 1934. Practised medicine in Scotland, Ireland and Wales, to 1939; Leeward Island Medical Service, 1939–42; practised medicine in Trinidad, 1943–. Entered Politics, 1944. Elected: MLC, 1946–50 and 1956; MP (MHR) 1961; Minister of: Education, 1956–60; Home Affairs, 1960–64; External Affairs, 1964–66; Dep. Prime Minister, 1962–66; Dep. Political Leader of People's Nat. Movement, 1956–66; Permanent Rep. of Trinidad and Tobago to the United Nations, NY, 1966–71; Vice-Pres., UN General Assembly, 21st Session, 1966; Chm., UN Fourth Cttee, 23rd Session, 1968; Trinidad and Tobago Rep., Special Cttee on Apartheid, 1966–71, and Special Cttee of 24 on question of Decolonization; Mem. Preparatory Cttees concerning: celebration of Tenth Anniversary of Declaration on granting of Independence to Colonial Countries and Peoples (Resolution 1514, xv), 1968 and 1969; Commemoration of 25th Anniversary of United Nations. Pres. of Assembly, IMCO, 1976–77. Chm., Trinidad Assoc. in Aid of the Deaf. Kt Great Band, Most Humane order of African Redemption, Liberia, 1963; Gran Cordon del Libertador, Venezuela, 1963; Grand Croix de l'Ordre de Mérite, Luxembourg, 1977. Is a Roman Catholic. *Publication*: Solomon: an autobiography, 1981. *Recreations*: bridge, fishing. *Address*: 8 Woodlands Road, Valsayn Park, Trinidad and Tobago, West Indies.

SOLOMON, Peter; *see* Solomon, A. P.

SOLOMONS, Hon. Sir Adrian; *see* Solomons, Hon. Sir L. A.

SOLOMONS, Anthony Nathan, FCA; Chairman since 1976, and Chief Executive since 1973, Singer & Friedlander Ltd; Director, Bullough Ltd, since 1983; Deputy Chairman, Britannia Arrow Holdings PLC, since 1984; Director, Milton Keynes Development Corporation, since 1985; *b* 26 Jan. 1930; *s* of Leslie Emanuel Solomons and Susie Schneiders; *m* 1957, Jean Golding; two *d*. Qual. as chartered accountant, 1953; FCA 1963. National Service, 1953–54: commnd Dorset Regt. Accountant, Kennedy & Fox Oldfield & Co., 1955; Asst Accountant, then Chief Accountant, Lobitos Oilfields Ltd, 1955–58; Singer & Friedlander Ltd, 1958–: successively Exec. Dir, Man. Dir, and Jt Chief Exec. *Address*: 21 New Street, EC2M 4HR. *T*: 01–623 3000. *Club*: Carlton.

SOLOMONS, Prof. David; Professor of Accounting in the University of Pennsylvania (Wharton School), USA, 1959–83, now Professor Emeritus; Chairman of Accounting Department, 1969–75, designated Arthur Young Professor, 1974; *b* London, 11 Oct. 1912; *e s* of Louis Solomons and Hannah Solomons (*née* Isaacs); *m* 1945, Kate Miriam (*née* Goldschmidt); one *s* one *d*. *Educ*: Hackney Downs Sch., London, E8; London School of Economics. BCom (London) 1932; DSc (Econ.) (London), 1966. Chartered accountant, 1936; engaged in professional accountancy until Sept. 1939. Enlisted in ranks on outbreak of war; 2nd Lieut, RASC, 1941; Temp. Captain, 1942; Petrol Supply Officer, HQ 88 Area (Tobruk), 1942; prisoner-of-war in Italy and Germany, 1942–45. Lectr in Accounting, LSE, 1946; Reader in Accounting, Univ. of London, 1948–55; Prof. of Accounting, University of Bristol, 1955–59. Visiting Assoc. Prof., University of California, 1954; Prof. at Institut pour l'Etude des Méthodes de Direction de l'Entreprise (IMEDE), Lausanne, 1963–64; Visiting Professor: Nat. Univ. of Singapore, 1984; Graduate Inst. of Business Admin, Chulalongkorn Univ., Bangkok, 1985 and 1986. Vis. Erskine Fellow, Univ. of Canterbury, NZ, 1976. AAA Distinguished Internat. Lectr, 1984. Mem., AICPA Study on Establishment of Accounting Principles, 1971–72; directed (UK) Adv. Bd of Accountancy Educn Long-range Enquiry into Educn and Trng for Accountancy Profession, 1972–74; Dir of Res., Amer. Accounting Assoc., 1968–70, Pres., 1977–78. Mem., Financial Accounting Standards Adv. Council, 1982–86. AICPA Award for Notable Contribution to Accounting Literature, 1969; Jl of Accountancy Literary Award, 1979; AAA Outstanding Accounting Educator Award, 1980; Walter Taplin Prize, Accounting and Business Research, 1984. *Publications*: Divisional Performance: Measurement and Control, 1965; ed and contrib. to Studies in Cost Analysis, 1968; Prospectus for a Profession, 1974; Collected Papers on Accounting and Accounting Education (2 vols), 1984; Making Accountancy Policy: the quest for credibility in financial reporting, 1986. *Address*: 205 Elm Avenue, Swarthmore, Pa 19081, USA. *T*: 215–544–8193.

SOLOMONS, Hon. Sir (Louis) Adrian, Kt 1982; Member, Legislative Council of New South Wales, since 1969; Senior Partner, Messrs Everingham, Solomons & Co., Solicitors, since 1975; *b* 9 June 1922; *s* of George Albert Solomons and Katie Isabel (*née* Rowland); *m* 1944 (whilst on War Service), Olwyn Ainslie Bishop; two *s*. *Educ*: New England University Coll.; Sydney Univ. (BA *in absentia* 1945, LLB 1949). Admitted solicitor, 1949. National Country Party of Australia (now National Party), NSW: Mem., Central Exec., 1964–67; Vice Chm., 1967–69; Chm., 1969–74; National Pres., 1974–80. Mem., Bd of Governors, Law Foundn of NSW, 1984–. *Recreation*: deep sea fishing. *Address*: Fairview, 17 Campbell Road, Calala, Tamworth, NSW 2340, Australia. *T*: (067) 65–9899. *Clubs*: National Liberal, Lansdowne; Tattersall's (Sydney); Tamworth (NSW).

SOLOW, Prof. Robert Merton; Professor of Economics, Massachusetts Institute of Technology, since 1949; *b* 23 Aug. 1924; *s* of Milton H. Solow and Hannah Solow (*née* Sarney); *m* 1945, Barbara Lewis; two *s* one *d*. *Educ*: New York City schools; Harvard College (BA 1947); Harvard University (MA 1949, PhD 1951). Served US forces, 1942–45 (Bronze Star, 1944). Joined MIT Faculty as Asst Prof. of Statistics, 1949, Inst. Prof. of Economics, 1974–. Senior Economist, Council of Economic Advisers, 1961–62. Eastman Prof. and Fellow of Balliol Coll., Oxford, 1968–69; Overseas Fellow, Churchill Coll., Cambridge, 1984. President: Econometric Soc., 1965; Amer. Econ. Assoc., 1976; Mem., Nat. Acad. of Sciences, USA, 1972; Corr. Mem., British Acad., 1975. Hon. degrees: Chicago, 1967; Brown, 1972; Williams, 1974; Warwick, 1976; Paris I, 1975; Lehigh, 1977; Geneva, 1982; Wesleyan, 1982; Tulane, 1983; Yale, 1986. *Publications*: Linear Programming and Economic Analysis (with P. Samuelson and R. Dorfman), 1958; Capital Theory and the Rate of Return, 1964; The Sources of Unemployment in the US, 1964; Growth Theory: an exposition, 1970; articles in learned jls. *Recreation*: sailing. *Address*: 528 Lewis Wharf, Boston, Mass 02110, USA. *T*: (617) 227 4436.

SOLTI, Sir Georg, KBE 1971 (CBE (Hon.) 1968); Music Director, Chicago Symphony Orchestra, since 1969; Principal Conductor and Artistic Director, London Philharmonic Orchestra, 1979–Sept. 1983, then Conductor Emeritus; *b* Budapest, 21 Oct. 1912; adopted British nationality, 1972; *m* 1st, 1946, Hedwig Oeschli; 2nd, 1967, Anne Valerie Pitts; two *d*. *Educ*: High School of Music, Budapest. Studied with Kodály, Bartók, and Dohnányi. Conductor and pianist, State Opera, Budapest, 1930–39; first prize, as pianist, Concours Internationale, Geneva, 1942; Musical Director, Bavarian State Opera, 1946–52; Musical Director, Frankfurt Opera, and Permanent Conductor, Museums Concerts, Frankfurt, 1952–61; Musical Director: Covent Garden Opera Co., 1961–71; Orchestre de Paris, 1972–75. Guest Conductor: Berlin, Salzburg, Vienna, Munich, Paris, London (first conducted London Philharmonic Orchestra, 1947; Covent Garden début, 1959), Glyndebourne Festival, Edinburgh Festival, Bayreuth Festival, San Francisco, New York,

Los Angeles, Chicago, etc. Has made numerous recordings (many of which have received international awards or prizes, incl. Grand Prix Mondiale du Disque (14 times), and 25 Grammy Awards (incl. special Trustees Grammy Award for recording of The Ring Cycle), Nat. Acad. of Recorded Arts and Scis). Hon. FRCM, 1980; Hon. Prof., Baden-Württemberg, 1985. Hon. DMus: Leeds, 1971; Oxon, 1972; Yale Univ., 1974; Harvard, 1979; Furman, 1983; Surrey, 1983; Hon. Dr DePaul, 1975. *Address*: Chalet Haut Pré, Villars s. Ollon, Switzerland. *Club*: Athenæum.

SOLZHENITSYN, Alexander Isayevitch; author; Hon. Fellow, Hoover Institution on War, Revolution and Peace, 1975; *b* 11 Dec. 1918; *m*; three *s*. *Educ*: Univ. of Rostov (degree in maths and physics); Moscow Inst. of History, Philosophy and Literature (correspondence course). Joined Army, 1941; grad. from Artillery School, 1942; in comd artillery battery and served at front until 1945 (twice decorated); sentenced to eight years' imprisonment, 1945, released, 1953; exile in Siberia, 1953–56; officially rehabilitated, 1957; taught and wrote in Ryazan and Moscow; expelled from Soviet Union, 1974. Member Union of Soviet writers, 1962, expelled 1969; Member Amer. Acad. of Arts and Sciences, 1969. Awarded Nobel Prize for Literature, 1970; Templeton Prize for Progress in Religion, 1983. *Publications*: One Day in the Life of Ivan Denisovich, 1962, new edn 1970, filmed 1971; An Incident at Krechetovka Station, and Matryona's House (publ. US as We Never Make Mistakes, 1969), 1963; For the Good of the Cause, 1964; The First Circle, 1968; Cancer Ward, part 1, 1968, part 2, 1969 (Prix du Meilleur Livre Etranger, Paris); Stories and Prose Poems, 1970; August 1914, 1972; One Word of Truth: the Nobel speech on literature, 1972; The Gulag Archipelago: an experiment in literary investigation, vol. 1, 1973, vol. 2, 1974, vol. 3, 1976; The Oak and the Calf, (autobiog.), 1975; Lenin in Zurich, 1975; Prussian Nights (poem), 1977; The Red Wheel: August 1914, 1983 (revd edn of 1972 publication); October 1916, 1985; *plays*: trilogy: The Love Girl and the Innocent, 1969, Victory Celebrations, Prisoners, 1983. *Address*: c/o Harper & Row Inc., 10 East 53rd Street, New York, NY 10022, USA.

SOMARE, Rt. Hon. Michael Thomas, CH 1978; PC 1977; MP; first Prime Minister of Papua New Guinea, 1975–80, and again 1982–85; *b* 9 April 1936; *m* 1965, Veronica Somare; three *s* two *d*. *Educ*: Sogeri Secondary Sch.; Admin. Coll. Teaching, 1956–62; Asst Area Educn Officer, Madang, 1962–63; Broadcasts Officer, Dept of Information and Extension Services, Wewack, 1963–66; Journalism, 1966–68. Member for E Sepik Region (Nat. Parl.) House of Assembly, 1968–; Parly Leader, Pangu Pati, 1968–; First Chief Minister, 1972–75; Leader of Opposition in House of Assembly, 1980–82. Dep. Chm., Exec. Council, 1972–73, Chm., 1973–75. Mem., Second Select Cttee on Constitutional Develt, 1968–72; Mem. Adv. Cttee, Australian Broadcasting Commission. *Address*: House of Assembly, Port Moresby, Papua New Guinea; (home) Karan, Murik Lakes, East Sepik, Papua New Guinea.

SOMERFIELD, Stafford William; editorial consultant, since 1970, *b* 9 Jan. 1911; *m* 1st, 1933, Gertrude Camfield (marr. diss. 1951); two *d*; 2nd, 1951, Elizabeth Montgomery (*d* 1977); 3rd, 1977, Ferelith Hamilton. *Educ*: Ashleigh Road School, Barnstaple. Exeter Express and Echo, Bristol Evening World, Daily Telegraph, 1934–39; News Chronicle, 1939, until outbreak of War. Rifleman, Queen's Westminsters, 1939–40; Major, Gloucestershire Regt. 1945. News of the World: Features Editor, Asst Editor, Northern Editor, Dep. Editor; Editor, 1960–70; Chm., Dog World, 1982. *Publications*: John George Haigh, 1950; Banner Headlines, 1979; The Boxer, 1985. *Recreation*: pedigree dogs. *Address*: Ivy Lodge, Ivychurch, Romney Marsh, Kent TN29 0AL. *T*: Brookland 240. *Club*: Kennel.

SOMERLEYTON, 3rd Baron *cr* 1916; **Savile William Francis Crossley;** Bt 1863; DL; farmer; a Lord in Waiting to the Queen, since 1978; *b* 17 Sept. 1928; *er s* of 2nd Baron Somerleyton, MC; *S* father, 1959; *m* 1963, Belinda Maris Loyd, *d* of late Vivian Loyd and of Mrs Gerald Critchley; one *s* four *d*. *Educ*: Eton Coll. Captain Coldstream Guards, 1948; retired, 1956. Royal Agricultural Coll., Cirencester, 1958–59; farming, 1959–. Dir, E Anglian Water Co., 1961–. DL Suffolk, 1964. *Heir: s* Hon. Hugh Francis Savile Crossley, *b* 27 Sept. 1971. *Address*: Somerleyton Hall, Lowestoft, Suffolk. *T*: Lowestoft 730308. *Club*: White's.

SOMERS, 8th Baron *cr* 1784; **John Patrick Somers Cocks;** Bt 1772; *b* 30 April 1907; *o s* of 7th Baron and Mary Benita (*d* 1950), *d* of late Major Luther M. Sabin, United States Army; *S* father, 1953; *m* 1st, 1935, Barbara Marianne (*d* 1959), *d* of Charles Henry Southall, Norwich; 2nd, 1961, Dora Helen, *d* of late John Mountfort. *Educ*: privately; Royal College of Music, London. 2nd Music Master, Westonbirt School, 1935–38; Director of Music, Epsom Coll., 1949–53; Prof. of Composition and Theory, RCM, 1967–77. BMus, ARCM. *Heir: cousin* Philip Sebastian Somers-Cocks, *b* 4 Jan. 1948. *Address*: 35 Links Road, Epsom, Surrey KT17 3PP.

SOMERS, Rt Hon. Edward Jonathan, PC 1981; **Rt. Hon. Mr Justice Somers;** Judge of the Court of Appeal, New Zealand, since 1981; *b* 9 Sept. 1928; *s* of Ewart Somers and Muriel Ann Crossley; *m* 1953, Mollie Louise Morison; one *s* two *d*. *Educ*: Christ's Coll., Christchurch; Canterbury University Coll., Christchurch, NZ (BA, LLB). Practised as barrister and solicitor, 1952–71; practised as barrister, 1971; QC (NZ) 1973; Judge of Supreme Court of New Zealand, 1974. *Recreation*: gardening. *Address*: Waverley, Kaiapoi, RD2, New Zealand. *T*: Kaiapoi 7094. *Club*: Christchurch (New Zealand).

SOMERSCALES, Thomas Lawrence, CBE 1970; General Secretary, Joint Committee of the Order of St John of Jerusalem and the British Red Cross Society, 1960–78; *b* 1 July 1913; *s* of Wilfred Somerscales; *m* 1941, Ann Teresa, *d* of Robert Victor Kearney; three *s* one *d*. *Educ*: Riley High Sch., Hull. FCA 1939. KStJ 1978. Finance Sec., Jt Cttee, OStJ and BRCS, 1953–60. Mem., Adv. Council, ITA, 1964–67. *Address*: The Dormer House, The Rookery, Alveston, Stratford-upon-Avon.

SOMERSET, family name of **Duke of Beaufort** and of **Baron Raglan.**

SOMERSET, 19th Duke of, *cr* 1547; **John Michael Edward Seymour,** ARICS; Baron Seymour 1547; Bt 1611; *b* 30 Dec. 1952; *s* of 18th Duke of Somerset and of Gwendoline Collette (Jane), 2nd *d* of Major J. C. C. Thomas; *S* father, 1984; *m* 1978, Judith-Rose, *d* of J. F. C. Hull, *qv*; one *s*. *Educ*: Eton. *Heir: s* Lord Seymour, *qv*. *Address*: Maiden Bradley, Warminster, Wilts; Berry Pomeroy, Totnes, Devon. *Club*: MCC.

SOMERSET, David Henry Fitzroy, FIB; Chief of the Banking Department and Chief Cashier of the Bank of England, since 1980; *b* 19 June 1930; *s* of Brig. Hon. Nigel Somerset, *qv*; *m* 1955, Ruth Ivy, *d* of late W. R. Wildbur; one *s* one *d*. *Educ*: Wellington Coll.; Peterhouse, Cambridge (MA). CBIM; FCT 1983. Entered Bank of England, 1952; Personal Asst to Managing Director, International Monetary Fund, Washington DC, 1959–62; Private Secretary to Governor of Bank of England, 1962–63; Asst Chief Cashier, 1968–69; Asst Chief of Establishments, 1969–73; Dep. Chief Cashier, 1973–80. Chm., EBS Investments, 1977–; Dir, Securities Management Trust, 1980–. Member: Court of Governors, City of London Polytechnic, 1980–; Council, Friends of Peterhouse, 1982–. *Recreations*: gardening, tennis, shooting. *Address*: Bank of England, Threadneedle Street, EC2R 8AH. *T*: 01–601 4444.

SOMERSET, Sir Henry Beaufort, Kt 1966; CBE 1961; *b* 21 May 1906; *s* of Henry St John Somerset; *m* 1930, Patricia Agnes Strickland; two *d. Educ:* St Peter's Coll., Adelaide; Trinity Coll., University of Melbourne; MSc 1928. Director: Humes Ltd, 1957–82 (Chm., 1961–82); Goliath Cement Hldgs Ltd, 1947–82 (Chm., 1967–82); Associated Pulp & Paper Mills Ltd, 1937–81 (Man. Dir, 1948–70; Dep. Chm., 1970–81); Electrolytic Zinc Co. of Australasia Ltd, 1953–78; Perpetual Exors Trustees Ltd, 1971–81 (Chm., 1973–81); Tioxide Australia Pty Ltd, 1949–82 (Chm., 1953–76); Central Norseman Gold Corp. Ltd, 1977–82. Chancellor, University of Tasmania, 1964–72; Member: Council, Australasian Inst. of Mining and Metallurgy, 1956– (President, 1958 and 1966); Exec., CSIRO, 1965–74; Council, Nat. Museum of Victoria, 1968–77; Pres., Australian Mineral Foundn, 1972–83. FRACI; FTS. Hon. DSc Tasmania, 1973. *Address:* 193 Domain Road, South Yarra, Victoria 3141, Australia. *Clubs:* Melbourne, Australian (Melbourne).

SOMERSET, Brigadier Hon. Nigel FitzRoy, CBE 1945; DSO; MC; *b* Cefntilla Court, Usk, Monmouthshire, 27 July 1893; 3rd *s* of 3rd Baron Raglan, GBE, CB; *m* 1922, Phyllis Marion Offley Irwin (*d* 1979), Western Australia; one *s* one *d. Educ:* King William's Coll., IOM; RMC Sandhurst. Served France with 1st Bn Gloucestershire Regt, 12 Aug. 1914 till wounded at the Battle of the Aisne, 15 Sept. 1914; 3 Dec. 1914, till wounded at Cuinchy, 12 May 1915; Mesopotamia, Oct. 1916–May 1919, comdg 14th Light Armoured Motor Battery (despatches thrice, DSO, MC); Bt Majority on promotion to Subst. Captain, 1918; Afghan War, 1919, with Armoured Motor Brigade (Medal and Clasp); ADC to Governor of South Australia, 1920–22; Assistant Military Secretary, Headquarters, Southern Command, India, 1926–30; Major 1933; Lieut-Colonel Comdg 2nd Bn The Gloucestershire Regt, 1938; served War of 1939–45 comdg 145 Inf. Bde (PoW 1940–45; despatches; CBE); Comdg Kent Sub District, 1946–47; Brig. Special Appt Germany, 1947–48; retired pay, 1949. *Address:* 8 Regency Close, Uckfield, East Sussex TN22 1DS.
See also D. H. F. Somerset.

SOMERSET FRY, Peter George Robin Plantagenet; author and journalist, since 1955; *b* 3 Jan. 1931; *s* of late Comdr Peter K. Ll. Fry, OBE, RN, and Ruth Emily (*née* Marriott), LRAM; *m* 1st, 1958, Daphne Diana Elizabeth Caroline Yorke (*d* 1961); 2nd, 1961, Hon. Mrs Leri Butler (marr. diss. 1973, she *d* 1985); 3rd, 1974, Pamela Fiona Ileene (author, Horses, 1981), *d* of late Col H. M. Whitcombe, MBE. *Educ:* Lancing; St Thomas's Hosp. Med. Sch., London; St Catherine's Coll., Oxford (Sec. Oxford Union, Hilary 1956). Mem. editorial staff: Atomics and Nuclear Energy, 1957–58; The Tatler and Bystander, 1958; public relations, 1960–64; Information Officer: Incorp. Assoc. of Architects and Surveyors, 1965–67; MPBW, 1967–70; Head of Inf. Services, COSIRA, 1970–74; Editor of Books, HM Stationery Office, 1975–80. Gen. Editor, Macmillan History in Pictures Series, 1977–. Vis. Scholar, 1980–84, Sen. Mem., 1984–, Wolfson Coll., Cambridge. Mem. Council, East Anglian Writers, 1977–82; Co-founder, Congress of Indep. Archaeologists, 1985; Founder and Hon. Secretary: Little Bardfield Village Community Trust, 1971–74; Daphne Somerset Fry Meml Trust for Kidney Disease Res., 1961–; Burgh Soc., 1978–80. FRSA 1966. *Publications:* Mysteries of History, 1957; The Cankered Rose, 1959; Rulers of Britain, 1967 (3rd edn 1973); They Made History, 1970 (2nd edn 1973); The World of Antiques, 1970 (4th edn 1972); Antique Furniture, 1971 (2nd edn 1972); Constantinople, 1970; The Wonderful Story of the Jews, 1970; Children's History of the World, 1972 (10th edn 1983); Answer Book of History, 1972 (2nd edn 1973); Zebra Book of Famous Men, 1972; Zebra Book of Famous Women, 1972; Collecting Inexpensive Antiques, 1973 (5th edn 1980); Zebra Book of Castles, 1974; Great Caesar, 1974; British Mediaeval Castles, 1974; 1000 Great Lives, 1975 (8th edn 1984); Questions, 1976; 2,000 Years of British Life, 1976; Chequers: the country home of Britain's Prime Ministers, 1977 (official history); 3,000 Questions and Answers, 1977 (12th edn 1984); Boudicca, 1978; David & Charles Book of Castles, 1980; Fountains Abbey (official souvenir guide), 1980; Beautiful Britain, 1981; (with Fiona Somerset Fry) History of Scotland, 1982; Revolt Against Rome, 1982; Great Cathedrals, 1982; (ed) Longman Pocket History Dictionary, 1983; Roman Britain: history and sites, 1984; Battle Abbey and the Battle of Hastings (official souvenir guide), 1984; 3,000 More Questions and Answers, 1984; Antiques, 1984; Rievaulx Abbey (official souvenir guide), 1986. *Recreations:* studying 18th Century French furniture, Roman history, visiting British castles, promoting freedom of information. *Address:* Wood Cottage, Wattisfield, Bury St Edmunds, Suffolk. *T:* Stanton 51324.

SOMERSET JONES, Eric, QC 1978; a Recorder of the Crown Court, since 1975; *b* 21 Nov. 1925; *s* of late Daniel Jones and of Florence Somerset Jones; *m* 1966, Brenda Marion, *yr d* of late Hedley Shimmin and Doris Shimmin (*née* Beacroft) two *d. Educ:* Birkenhead Institute; Lincoln College, Oxford. MA Oxon. Served with RAF, 1944–47; RAF Coll., Cranwell; Link Trainer Instructor, SEAC. Oxford Univ., 1947–50. Called to Bar, Middle Temple, 1952; Mem., Northern Circuit; Member, Lord Chancellor's County Courts Rule Cttee, 1975–78. *Recreations:* family pursuits; travel; listening to music; photography. *Address:* Southmead, Mill Lane, Willaston, Wirral, Cheshire L64 1RL. *T:* 051–327 5138. *Clubs:* United Oxford & Cambridge University; Royal Chester Rowing (Chester).

SOMERTON, Viscount; James Shaun Christian Welbore Ellis Agar; *b* 7 Sept. 1982; *s* and *heir* of 6th Earl of Normanton, *qv.*

SOMERVILLE, David, CB 1971; Under-Secretary, Department of Health and Social Security, 1968–77; *b* 27 Feb. 1917; *e s* of late Rev. David Somerville and of Euphemia Somerville; *m* 1950, Patricia Amy Johnston; two *s* two *d. Educ:* George Watson's Coll.; Fettes Coll.; Edinburgh Univ.; Christ Church, Oxford. Served with Army, 1940–45; Major, Royal Artillery. Entered Civil Service as Asst Principal, Ministry of Health, 1946; Under-Secretary, Min. of Health, 1963–67. *Recreations:* golf, gardening, adult education. *Address:* Wyndley, Deepdene Park Road, Dorking, Surrey RH5 4AW. *T:* Dorking 885102. *Club:* Betchworth Park Golf.
See also R. M. Somerville.

SOMERVILLE, Jane, MD; FRCP; Consultant Physician, National Heart Hospital, since 1974; Hon. Consultant Physician, Hospital for Sick Children, Great Ormond Street, since 1968; *b* 24 Jan. 1933; *d* of Joseph Bertram Platnauer and Pearl Ashton; *m* 1957, Dr Walter Somerville, *qv*; three *s* one *d. Educ:* Queen's Coll., London; Guy's Hosp., London Univ. MB, BS (Treasurer's Gold Medal for Clin. Surg.) 1955; MD 1966. MRCS 1955; FRCP 1973 (LRCP 1955, MRCP 1957). FACC 1972. Med. Registrar, Guy's Hosp., 1956–58; Registrar, Nat. Heart Hosp., 1958–59; First Asst to Dr Paul Wood, 1959–63, Sen. Lectr 1964–74, Inst. of Cardiol.; Hon. Cons. Phys., Nat. Heart Hosp., 1967–74. Lectr in Cardiovascular Disease, Turin Univ., 1973. Vis. Prof. and Guest Lectr, Europe, ME, USA, Mexico, S America, USSR; St Cyres Lectr, Imperial Coll., London, 1976; first Mahboubian Lectr, NY, 1981; World Congress Gold Medal Lectr, Bombay, 1982. Sci. Sec., World Congress, Ped. Cardiol., 1980. Member: Assoc. Europ. Pæd. Cardiol.; British Cardiac Soc.; British Ped. Assoc., 1977; Anglo-Argentine Soc.; RSocMed; Council, Harveian Soc.; Council, Stonham Housing Assoc. Hon. Member: Argentine Pæd. Soc.; Chilean Cardiol. Soc.; Argentine Soc. of Cardiol. Governor: Queen's Coll., London; Nat. Heart and Chest Hosp. Woman of the Year, 1968. *Publications:* numerous contribs to med. lit. on heart disease in children, congenital heart disease and results of cardiac surgery; chapters in Paul Wood's Diseases of Heart and Circulation (3rd edn). *Recreations:* collecting stone eggs, pictures, porcelain soldiers; chess, orchid culture. *Address:* 30 York House, Upper Montagu Street, W1H 1FR. *T:* 01–262 2144.

SOMERVILLE, John Arthur Fownes, CB 1977; CBE 1964; DL; an Under-Secretary, Government Communications Headquarters, 1969–78; *b* 5 Dec. 1917; *s* of late Admiral of the Fleet Sir James Fownes Somerville, GCB, GBE, DSO; *m* 1945, Julia Elizabeth Payne; one *s* two *d. Educ:* RNC Dartmouth. Midshipman 1936; Sub-Lieut 1938; Lieut 1940; Lieut-Comdr 1945; retd 1950. Govt Communications Headquarters, 1950–78. DL Somerset, 1985. *Recreation:* walking. *Address:* The Old Rectory, Dinder, Wells, Som. *T:* Wells 74900. *Club:* Army and Navy.

SOMERVILLE, Brig. Sir (John) Nicholas, Kt 1985; CBE 1975; self employed consultant, personnel selection, since 1984; *b* 16 Jan. 1924; *s* of Brig. Desmond Henry Sykes Somerville and Moira Burke Somerville; *m* 1951, Jenifer Dorothea Nash; one *s* two *d. Educ:* Winchester College. Commissioned, The South Wales Borderers, 24th Regt, 1943; served: France and Germany, D-day—VE day, 1944–45 (despatches 1945); BAOR, War Office, FARELF, Aden, 1967–68 (despatches 1968); Directing Staff, JSSC, 1967–69; Comdt, Junior Div., Staff Coll., 1969–72; Dir of Army Recruiting, 1973–75; retired, 1978. Managing Director, Saladin Security Ltd, 1981–84; voluntary consultant responsible for designing Cons. Party Parly selection board procedure, 1980–85. *Recreations:* sailing, gardening, house designing. *Address:* Deptford Cottage, Greywell, near Basingstoke, Hants RG25 1BS. *T:* Odiham 2796. *Club:* Lansdowne.

SOMERVILLE, Brig. Sir Nicholas; *see* Somerville, Sir J. N.

SOMERVILLE, Sir Robert, KCVO 1961 (CVO 1953); MA; FSA; FRHistS; Clerk of the Council of the Duchy of Lancaster, 1952–70; *b* 5 June 1906; *s* of late Robert Somerville, FRSE, Dunfermline; *m* 1st, 1932, Marie-Louise Cornelia Bergené (*d* 1976); one *d*; 2nd, 1981, Mrs Jessie B. Warburton. *Educ:* Fettes; St John's Coll., Cambridge (1st cl. Class. Tripos, 1929); Edinburgh Univ. Entered Duchy of Lancaster Office, 1930; Ministry of Shipping, 1940; Chief Clerk, Duchy of Lancaster, 1945; Hon. Research Asst, History of Medicine, UCL, 1935–38; Chairman: Council, British Records Assoc., 1957–67 (Hon. Secretary, 1947–56); London Record Soc., 1964–84; Member: Advisory Council on Public Records, 1959–64; Royal Commn on Historical MSS, 1966–; Corr. Member, Indian Historical Records Commn. Alexander Medallist, Royal Historical Society, 1940. *Publications:* History of the Duchy of Lancaster, 2 vols, 1953, 1970; The Savoy, 1960; Handlist of Record Publications, 1951; Duchy of Lancaster Office-Holders from 1603, 1972; (joint editor) John of Gaunt's Register, 1937; contribs to Chambers's Encyclopædia, historical journals, etc. *Address:* 3 Hunt's Close, Morden Road, SE3 0AH.

SOMERVILLE, Maj.-Gen. Ronald Macaulay, CB 1974; OBE 1963; Chairman of Directors, Buildings Investigation Centre Ltd, since 1985; *b* 2 July 1919; 2nd *s* of late Rev. David Somerville and of Euphemia Somerville; *m* 1947, Jean McEwen Balderston; no *c. Educ:* George Watson's Coll., Edinburgh. Joined TA, 1939; commnd RA, 1940; regtl and Staff War Service in UK, NW Europe and Far East, 1939–45 (MBE, despatches, 1945); psc 1944; jssc 1956; comd Maiwand Battery, Cyprus Emergency, 1957–59 (despatches, 1958); Bt Lt-Col, 1960; CO 4th Light Regt RA, 1963–65; Borneo Emergency, 1965; CRA 51st (H) Div., 1965–66; idc 1967; DQMG, BAOR, 1968–70; GOC Yorks District, 1970–72; Vice-QMG, MoD, 1972–74; Chm., Logistic Reorganisation Cttee, 1974–75; retd 1975. Gen. Manager, Scottish Special Housing Assoc., 1975–83. Hon. Col, 3rd Bn Yorkshire Volunteers, 1972–77; Col Comdt, RA, 1974–79. Comr, Royal Hospital, Chelsea, 1972–74; Chm., RA Council for Scotland, 1975–79; President: RA Assoc., Scotland, 1978–; Scottish Union Jack Assoc., 1982–; Vice-Chm., Officers Assoc., Scotland, 1985–. Chm., West End Community Council, Edinburgh, 1980–83. CBIM 1984; MIH 1980. Kt Officer, Order of Orange Nassau, with Swords, 1946. *Recreations:* painting, golf, gardening, fishing. *Address:* 6 Magdala Mews, Edinburgh EH12 5BX. *T:* 031–346 0371; Bynack Mhor, Boat of Garten, Inverness-shire PH24 3BP. *T:* Boat of Garten 245. *Club:* New (Edinburgh).
See also David Somerville.

SOMERVILLE, Most Rev. Thomas David; Archbishop of New Westminster and Metropolitan of Ecclesiastical Province of British Columbia, 1975–80, retired; Anglican Chaplain, Vancouver School of Theology, 1981–84; *b* 11 Nov. 1915; *s* of Thomas Alexander Somerville and Martha Stephenson Scott; *m* 1985, Frances Best. *Educ:* King George High Sch., Vancouver; Univ. of British Columbia (BA 1937); Anglican Theological Coll. of BC (LTh 1939, BD 1951). Deacon, 1939; priest, 1940; Incumbent of: Princeton, 1940–44; Sardis with Rosedale, 1944–49; Curate of St James, Vancouver, 1949–52, Rector, 1952–60; Chapter Canon, Dio. of New Westminster, 1957; Dean of Residence, Anglican Theological Coll. of BC, 1960–65; Gen. Sec., Gen. Bd of Religious Education, Anglican Church of Canada, 1965–66; Director of Planning and Research, Anglican Church of Canada, 1966–69; Coadjutor Bishop of New Westminster, 1969–71; Bishop of New Westminster, 1971. Hon. DD: Anglican Theol. Coll. of BC, 1969; Vancouver Sch. of Theology, 1981. *Recreations:* music, botany. *Address:* 3485 Capilano Road, North Vancouver, BC V7R 4H9, Canada.

SOMERVILLE, Walter, CBE 1979; MD, FRCP; Hon. Physician to Department of Cardiology, Middlesex Hospital, since 1979 (Physician, 1954–79); to Cardiac Surgical Unit, Harefield Hospital, 1952–78; Lecturer in Cardiology, Middlesex Hospital Medical School, 1954–79; Consultant in Cardiology to the Army, 1963–79, Hon. Consultant, 1980–85, Emeritus Consultant, 1985; Hon. Civil Consultant in Cardiology to Royal Air Force, Civil Aviation Authority, and Royal Hospital, Chelsea, since 1963, to Association of Naval Officers, since 1960; to King Edward VII Convalescent Home for Officers, Osborne, since 1970; *b* 2 Oct. 1913; *s* of late Patrick and Catherine Somerville, Dublin; *m* 1957, Jane Platnauer (*see* Jane Somerville); three *s* one *d. Educ:* Belvedere Coll., Dublin; University College, Dublin. House appts, Mater Hosp., Dublin, 1937; out-patients Assistant, Brompton Hosp. and Chelsea Chest Clinic, 1938–39. Served in War 1939–45; attached: Canadian Dept of Defense, 1942; US Army, 1943; Lt-Col RAMC 1944. Fellow in Med., Mass General Hosp., Boston, 1946; Registrar, British Postgraduate Med. School, Hammersmith, 1947; studied in Paris, Stockholm and Univ. of Michigan, 1948; Fellow in Medicine, Peter Bent Brigham Hosp. Boston and Harvard Med. Sch., 1949; Med. Registrar, Nat. Heart Hosp. and Inst. of Cardiology, 1951; Sen. Med. Registrar, Middlesex Hosp., 1951–54. Lectures: Carey Coombs, Bristol Univ., 1977; St Cyres, Nat. Heart Hosp., 1978; William Stokes, Irish Cardiac Soc., Belfast, 1983. Editor, British Heart Journal, 1973–80; Editorial Board: American Heart Journal, 1975–; Revista Portuguesa de cardiologia, 1982–. Pres., British Cardiac Soc., 1976–80; former Pres., British Acad. of Forensic Sciences; Mem., Assoc. of Physicians of Great Britain and Ireland and other socs; Corr. Member: Colombian Soc. of Cardiology; Chilean Soc. of Cardiology; Fellow, Amer. Coll. of Cardiology. Vis. Prof., Cleveland Clinic, Cleveland, Ohio, 1980. Purkyne Medal, Czechoslovakian Cardiac Soc., 1981. Officer, Legion of Merit, USA, 1945. *Publications:* (ed) Paul Wood's Diseases of the Heart and Circulation (3rd edn), 1968; various articles on cardiovascular subjects in British, continental European and American journals. *Address:* 149 Harley Street, W1. *T:* 01–935 4444; 30 York House, Upper Montagu Street, W1H 1FR. *T:* 01–262 2144.

SOMES, Michael (George), CBE 1959; Principal Repetiteur, Royal Ballet, Covent Garden 1970–84; *b* 28 Sept. 1917; British; *m* 1956, Deirdre Annette Dixon (*d* 1959). *Educ:* Huish's Grammar Sch., Taunton, Somerset. Started dancing at Sadler's Wells, 1934; first important rôle in Horoscope, 1938; Leading Male Dancer, Royal Ballet, Covent Garden, 1951–68; Asst Director, 1963–70. *Recreation:* music.

SONDES, 5th Earl *cr* 1880; **Henry George Herbert Milles-Lade;** Baron Sondes, 1760; Viscount Throwley, 1880; *b* 1 May 1940; *o s* of 4th Earl Sondes, and Pamela (*d* 1967), *d* of Col H. McDougall; *S* father, 1970; *m* 1968, Primrose Creswell (marr. diss. 1969), *d* of late Lawrence Stopford Llewellyn Cotter; *m* 1976, Sissy Fürstin zu Salm-Reifferscheidt-Raitz (marr. diss. 1981). *Recreations:* shooting, skiing. *Address:* Stringman's Farm, Faversham, Kent. *T:* Chilham 336.

SONDHEIM, Stephen Joshua; composer-lyricist; *b* 22 March 1930; *s* of Herbert Sondheim and Janet (*née* Fox). *Educ:* Williams Coll. (BA 1950). Lyrics: West Side Story, 1957; Gypsy, 1959; Do I Hear a Waltz?, 1965; (additional lyrics) Candide, 1973; music and lyrics: A Funny Thing Happened on the Way to the Forum, 1962; Anyone Can Whistle, 1964; Company, 1970; Follies, 1971; A Little Night Music, 1973 (filmed, 1976); The Frogs, 1974; Pacific Overtures, 1976; Sweeney Todd, 1979; Merrily We Roll Along, 1981; Sunday in the Park with George, 1983 (Pulitzer Prize, 1985); incidental music: Girls of Summer, 1956; Invitation to a March, 1961; Twigs, 1971; film scores: Stavisky, 1974; Reds, 1981; co-author, The Last of Sheila (film); songs for Evening Primrose (TV), 1966; anthologies: Side By Side By Sondheim, 1976; Marry Me A Little, 1981; You're Gonna Love Tomorrow. Mem. Council, Dramatists Guild (Pres., 1973–81); Mem., AAIL, 1983. Hon. Doctorate, Williams Coll., 1971. Tony Awards and New York Drama Critics' Circle Award for Sweeney Todd, A Little Night Music, Follies and Company; New York Drama Critics' Circle Award for Pacific Overtures and Sunday in the Park with George. *Publications:* (book and vocal score): West Side Story, 1958; Gypsy, 1960; A Funny Thing Happened on the Way to the Forum, 1963; Anyone Can Whistle, 1965; Do I Hear a Waltz?, 1966; Company, 1971; Follies, 1972; A Little Night Music, 1974; Pacific Overtures, 1977; Sweeney Todd, 1979; Sunday in the Park with George, 1986. *Address:* c/o Flora Roberts, 157 West 57th Street, New York, NY 10019, USA.

SONDHEIMER, Professor Ernst Helmut, MA, ScD; Professor Emeritus of Mathematics, University of London; *b* 8 Sept. 1923; *er s* of late Max and of Ida Sondheimer; *m* 1950, Janet Harrington Matthews, PhD; one *s* one *d*. *Educ:* University College School; Trinity Coll., Cambridge. Smith's Prize, 1947; Fellow of Trinity Coll., 1948–52; Research Fellow, H. H. Wills Physical Lab., University of Bristol, 1948–49; Research Associate, Massachusetts Inst. of Technology, 1949–50; London University: Lecturer in Mathematics, Imperial College of Science and Technology, 1951–54; Reader in Applied Mathematics, Queen Mary Coll., 1954–60; Prof. of Mathematics, Westfield Coll., 1960–82. Vis. Research Asst Prof. of Physics, Univ. of Illinois, USA, 1958–59; Vis. Prof. of Theoretical Physics, University of Cologne, 1967. FKC 1985. Editor, Alpine Journal, 1986–. *Publications:* (with S. Doniach) Green's Functions for Solid State Physicists, 1974; (with A. Rogerson) Numbers and Infinity, 1981; papers on the electron theory of metals. *Recreations:* mountaineering, photography, books, growing alpines. *Address:* 51 Cholmeley Crescent, Highgate, N6 5EX. *T:* 01–340 6607. *Club:* Alpine.

SONTAG, Susan; writer; *b* 16 Jan. 1933; one *s*. *Educ:* Univ. of Chicago (BA 1952); Harvard Univ. (MA 1955). Mem., AAIL. Writer and director for films and stage; *films:* Duet for Cannibals, 1969; Brother Carl, 1971; Promised Lands, 1974; Unguided Tour, 1983. *Publications:* The Benefactor, 1963; Against Interpretation, 1966; Death Kit, 1967; Styles of Radical Will, 1969; On Photography, 1977; Illness as Metaphor, 1978; I, Etcetera, 1978; Under the Sign of Saturn, 1980. *Address:* c/o Farrar, Straus & Giroux, 19 Union Square West, New York, NY 10003, USA.

SOPER, family name of **Baron Soper.**

SOPER, Baron, *cr* 1965 (Life Peer); **Rev. Donald Oliver Soper,** MA Cantab; PhD (London); Methodist Minister; President of the Methodist Conference, 1953, Superintendent West London Mission, Kingsway Hall, 1936–78; *b* 31 Jan. 1903; *s* of late Ernest and Caroline Soper; *m* 1929, Marie Dean, *d* of late Arthur Dean, Norbury; four *d*. *Educ:* Aske's School, Hatcham; St Catharine's College, Cambridge University; Wesley House, Cambridge; London School of Economics, London University. Hon. Fellow, St Catharine's Coll., Cambridge, 1966. Minister, South London Mission, 1926–29; Central London Mission, 1929–36. Chm., Shelter, 1974–78. President, League against Cruel Sports. Peace Award, World Methodist Council, 1981. *Publications:* Christianity and its Critics; Popular Fallacies about the Christian Faith; Will Christianity Work?; Practical Christianity To-day; Questions and Answers in Ceylon; All His Grace (Methodist Lent Book for 1957); It is hard to work for God; The Advocacy of the Gospel; Tower Hill 12.30; Aflame with Faith; Christian Politics; Calling for Action, 1984. *Recreations:* music, golf. *Address:* 19 Thayer Street, W1M 5LJ.

SOPWITH, Sir Charles (Ronald), Kt 1966; Second Counsel to Chairman of Committees, House of Lords, 1974–82; *b* 12 Nov. 1905; *s* of Alfred Sopwith, S Shields, Co. Durham; *m* 1946, Ivy Violet (*d* 1968), *d* of Frederick Leonard Yeates, Gidea Park, Essex. *Educ:* S Shields High School. Chartered Accountant, 1928; Solicitor, 1938. Assistant Director, Press Censorship, 1943–45; Assistant Solicitor, 1952–56, Principal Asst Solicitor, 1956–61, Solicitor, 1963–70, Board of Inland Revenue; Public Trustee, 1961–63; Deputy Sec., Cabinet Office, 1970–72. Hon. FRAM, 1984. *Recreations:* music, reading history, golf. *Address:* 18 Moor Lane, Rickmansworth, Herts. *Club:* Reform.

SOPWITH, Sir Thomas Octave Murdoch, Kt 1953; CBE 1918; Founder President, Hawker Siddeley Group Ltd (Chairman, 1935–63); *s* of Thomas Sopwith, MICE; *b* 1888; *m* 1st, 1914, Hon. Beatrix Mary Leslie Hore-Ruthven (*d* 1930), *d* of 8th Baron Ruthven; no *c*; 2nd, 1932, Phyllis Brodie (*d* 1978), 2nd *d* of late F. P. A. Gordon; one *s*. Founded the Sopwith Aviation Co. Ltd, Kingston-on-Thames, 1912; Chairman, 1925–27, Society of British Aircraft Constructors. *Recreations:* yachting, shooting, fishing. *Address:* Compton Manor, Kings Somborne, Hampshire. *Club:* Royal Yacht Squadron.

SOREF, Harold Benjamin; *b* 18 Dec. 1916; *o s* of late Paul Soref and Zelma Soref (*née* Goodman), Hampstead. *Educ:* Hall Sch., Hampstead; St Paul's Sch.; Queen's Coll., Oxford. Served with Royal Scots and Intell. Corps, 1940–46. Contested (C): Dudley, 1951; Rugby, 1955. MP (C) Lancashire, Ormskirk, 1970–Feb. 1974. Delegate, first all-British Africa Conf. held Bulawayo, 1938, to form Africa Defence Fedn; formerly Vice-Chm., Monday Club and Chm., Africa Cttee, Monday Club; Mem. Council, Anglo-Jewish Assoc.; Founder Mem., Conservative Commonwealth Council. *Publications:* (jtly) The War of 1939, 1940; (with Ian Greig) The Puppeteers, 1965; numerous articles in press and periodicals. *Recreations:* research, reading, writing. *Address:* 20 Meriden Court, Chelsea Manor Street, SW3 3TT. *T:* 01–352 0691, (office) 01–248 7435. *Clubs:* Carlton, PEN, 1900.

SORINJ, Dr L. T.; *see* Tončić-Sorinj.

SOROKOS, Lt-Gen. John A., Greek Gold Medal for Gallantry (3 times); Greek Military Cross (twice); Medal for Distinguished Services (3 times); Silver and Gold Cross (with swords) of Order of George I; Comdr, Order of George I and Order of Phoenix; Military Medal of Merit (1st Class); Ambassador of Greece to the United States of America, 1972–74; *b* 1917; *s* of A. and P. Sorokos; *m* 1954, Pia Madaros; one *s*. *Educ:* Mil. Acad. of Greece; Staff and Nat. Defence Colls, Greece; British Staff Coll., Camberley; US Mil. Schools. Company Comdr: in Second World War in Greece, 1940–41; in El Alamein Campaign, N Africa, 1942–43; Div. Staff Officer and Bn Comdr, 1947–49; served as Staff Officer: in Mil. Units in Army HQ and Armed Forces HQ, 1952–63; in NATO Allied Forces Southern Europe, 1957–59; Instructor, Nat. Defence Coll., Greece, 1963–64; Regt Comdr, 1965; Mil. Attaché to Greek Embassies in Washington and Ottawa, 1966–68; Div. Comdr, 1968–69; Dep. Comdr, Greek Armed Forces, 1969; Ambassador to UK, 1969–72. Officer, Legion of Merit (US). *Recreations:* horses, boating, fishing. *Address:* Mimnermou 2, Athens 106 74, Greece.

SORRELL, Alec Albert; Director of Statistics, Department of the Environment, 1981–83, retired; *b* 20 July 1925; *s* of Albert Edward Sorrell and Jessie (*née* Morris); *m* 1962, Eileen Joan Orchard; one *s*. *Educ:* George Gascoigne Sch., Walthamstow; SW Essex Technical College. BSc (Econ). Statistical Officer, MAP, 1945; Board of Trade: Asst Statistician, 1950; Statistician, 1954; Chief Statistician, 1966; Chief Statistician: Min. of Technology, 1969; Dept of Trade and Industry, 1970; Central Statistical Office, 1971; Asst Dir, Central Statistical Office, Cabinet Office, 1972–78; Principal Dir of Statistics, Depts of the Environment and Transport, 1978–81. *Publications:* various articles in trade, professional and learned jls. *Recreations:* walking, reading, beachcombing. *Address:* 8 Ravensmere, Epping, Essex. *T:* Epping 73961; River Cottage, West Putford, Devon.

SORSBIE, Sir Malin, Kt 1965; CBE 1956 (OBE 1942); *b* 25 May 1906; *s* of late Rev. William Frances Sorsbie and late Blanche Georgina Sorsbie; *m* 1955, Constantine Eugenie, *d* of late Albert Wheeler Johnston, Greenwich, Connecticut, USA; one step *d*. *Educ:* Brighton College; Manitoba University. Royal Canadian Mounted Police, 1926–29; RAF, 1930–35; Imperial Airways, 1936–39; BOAC, 1940–47; East African Airways (Gen. Manager), 1947–56. Chm., Munitalp Foundn, 1960–75. Life Fellow, RGS. KStJ. *Publications:* Dragonfly, 1971; Brandy for Breakfast, 1972. *Address:* PO Box 45337, Nairobi, Kenya. *T:* 65331 and 65343. *Clubs:* Carlton, Royal Air Force; RAF Yacht; Muthaiga Country, Nairobi (Nairobi); Mombasa (Mombasa).

SOTERIADES, Antis Georghios; Ambassador of Cyprus to Yugoslavia, concurrently accredited to Algeria and Sudan, since 1979; *b* 10 Sept. 1924; *m* 1962, Mona, *yr d* of Petros Petrides, Nicosia; one *s* one *d*. *Educ:* London Univ.; Inns of Court, London. Practising lawyer until 1956, joined patriotic Organization EOKA and fought British Colonialism in Cyprus, 1956–59; President of the first political party formed in Cyprus after independence, 1959; High Commissioner for Cyprus in the UK, 1960–66; Ambassador to Egypt, concurrently to Syrian Arab Republic, Iraq and Lebanon, 1966–78. Kt Order of St Gregory the Great (Vatican), 1963. *Address:* Diplomatska Koloniya No 9, Belgrade, Yugoslavia.

SOUKOP, Wilhelm Josef, RA 1969 (ARA 1963); RBA 1950; FRBS 1956; freelance sculptor; Master of Sculpture, Royal Academy Schools, 1969–82; *b* 5 Jan. 1907; *s* of Karl Soukop and Anna Soukop (*née* Vogel); *m* 1945, Simone (*née* Moser), Paris; one *s* one *d*. *Educ:* Vienna State School; apprenticed to an engraver; Academy of Fine Art, Vienna. Arrived in England, Dartington Hall, 1934; taught at Dartington Hall, Bryanston and Blundell's Schools, 1935–45; moved to London, 1945, and taught at Bromley Sch. of Art, 1945–46, Guildford Sch. of Art, 1945–47; sculpture teacher, Chelsea Sch. of Art, 1947–72. Examr for Scotland, 1959–62. Sculptures for new schools in Herts, Leics, Derbs, Staffs, LCC. Work for housing estates. Sculptures in museums: USA; Cordova Mus., Boston; Chantry Bequest; Tate Gallery; Cheltenham Mus. and Gall.; Collection of LCC Educn Cttee. Work in many private collections England, America, Canada, Europe. Archibald McIndoe Award, 1964. *Recreation:* gardening. *Address:* 26 Greville Road, NW6. *T:* 01–624 5987.

SOULBURY, 2nd Viscount *cr* 1954, of Soulbury; **James Herwald Ramsbotham;** Baron 1941; *b* 21 March 1915; *s* of 1st Viscount Soulbury, PC, GCMG, GCVO, OBE, MC, and Doris Violet (*d* 1954), *d* of late S. de Stein; *S* father, 1971; *m* 1949, Anthea Margaret (*d* 1950), *d* of late David Wilton. *Educ:* Eton; Magdalen College, Oxford. *Heir:* *b* Hon. Sir Peter Edward Ramsbotham, *qv*.

SOULSBY, Prof. Ernest Jackson Lawson; Professor of Animal Pathology, University of Cambridge, since 1978; Fellow, Wolfson College, Cambridge, since 1978; *b* 23 June 1926; *s* of William George Lawson Soulsby and Agnes Soulsby; *m* 1962, Georgina Elizabeth Annette Williams; one *s* one *d*. *Educ:* Queen Elizabeth Grammar Sch., Penrith; Univ. of Edinburgh. MRCVS; DVSM; PhD; MA (Cantab). Veterinary Officer, City of Edinburgh, 1949–52; Lectr in Clinical Parasitology, Univ. of Bristol, 1952–54; Univ. Lectr in Animal Pathology, Univ. of Cambridge, 1954–63; Prof. of Parasitology, Univ. of Pennsylvania, 1964–78. Ford Foundn Visiting Prof., Univ. of Ibadan, 1964; Richard Merton Guest Prof., Justus Liebig Univ., 1974–75. Lectures: Hume Meml Univ. Fedn Animal Welfare, 1985; Wooldridge Meml, BVA, 1986; Sir Frederick Hobday Meml, British Equine Vet. Assoc., 1986. Member: AFRC, 1984– (Chm., Animal Res. Grants Bd, 1986–); Vet. Adv. Cttee, Horserace Betting Levy Bd, 1984– (Chm., 1985–); EEC Adv. Cttee on Vet. Trng, 1981–86. Royal College of Veterinary Surgeons: Mem. Council, 1978–; Jun. Vice-Pres., 1983; Pres., 1984; Sen. Vice-Pres., 1985. President: Cambridge Soc. for Comp. Medicine, 1984–85; Vet. Res. Club, 1985–86. Corresp. Mem., German Parasitology Soc.; Hon. Member: Mexican Parasitology Soc.; Argentinian Parasitological Soc.; Expert Advisor and Consultant, and Member, Scientific Groups: various internat. agencies and govts. Hon. AM 1972, Hon. DSc 1984, Univ. of Pennsylvania. R. N. Chaudhury Gold Medal, Calcutta Sch. of Tropical Med., Calcutta, 1976; Behring-Bilharz Prize, Cairo, 1977; Ludwig-Schunk Prize, Justus-Liebig Universität, Giessen, 1979. *Publications:* Textbook of Veterinary Clinical Parasitology, 1965; Biology of Parasites, 1966; Reaction of the Host to Parasitism, 1968; Helminths, Arthropods and Protozoa of Domesticated Animals, 6th edn 1968, 7th edn 1982; Immunity to Animal Parasites, 1972; Parasitic Zoonoses, 1974; Pathophysiology of Parasitic Infections, 1976; Epidemiology and Control of Nematodiasis in Cattle, 1981; Immunology, Immunopathology and Immunoprophylaxis of Parasitic Infections, Vols I, II & III, 1986; articles in jls of parasitology, immunology and pathology. *Recreations:* travel, gardening, photography. *Address:* Old Barn House, Swaffham Prior, Cambridge CB5 0LD. *T:* Newmarket 741304. *Clubs:* Farmers', United Oxford & Cambridge University.

SOUROZH, Metropolitan of; *see* Anthony, Archbishop.

SOUSTELLE, Jacques; Commandeur, Légion d'Honneur, 1981; Hon. CBE; Member of French Academy, 1983; *b* 3 Feb. 1912. *Educ:* Ecole Normale supérieure, Paris; Univ. of Lyon. Agrégé de l'Université 1932, PhD 1937. Asst Dir, Musée de l'Homme, 1937; Nat. Comr for Information in London, 1942; Head of French special services, Algiers,

1943–44; Governor of Bordeaux, 1945; Minister of Information and Colonies, 1945–46. Prof. of Sociology, Ecole des Hautes Etudes, 1951. Mem., Lyon Municipal Council, 1954–62, 1971–77. Mem. Nat. Assembly, 1945–46, 1951–59, 1973–78. Gov.-Gen. of Algeria, 1955–56; Minister of Information, 1958; Minister delegate to the Prime Minister, France, 1959–60. President: PACT Gp, Council of Europe, Strasbourg, 1983; Centro Universitario Europe, Ravello, Member: NY Acad. of Scis; Instituto Mexicano de Cultura. FRAI. Order of Polonia Restituta, 1944; US Medal of Freedom, 1945; Hon. CBE, Great Britain, 1946; Comdr, Aztec Eagle (Mexico), 1978; Comdr, Nat. Order of Merit (Paraguay), 1984. *Publications*: Mexique, terre indienne, 1935; Envers et contre tout, 1947; La Vie quotidienne des Aztèques, 1955 (Daily Life of the Aztecs, 1962); Aimée et souffrante Algérie, 1956; L'espérance trahie, 1962; Sur une route nouvelle, 1964; L'Art du Mexique ancien, 1966 (Arts of Ancient Mexico, 1967); Archæologia Mundi: Mexique, 1967 (Archæologia Mundi: Mexico, 1967, repr. as The Ancient Civilizations of Mexico, 1969); Les quatre soleils, 1967 (The Four Suns, 1971); La longue marche d'Israël, 1968 (The Long March of Israel, 1969); Vingt-huit ans de Gaullisme, 1968; Les Aztèques, 1970; Lettre ouverte aux victimes de la décolonisation, 1973; L'Univers des Aztèques, 1979; Les Olmèques, 1979; Les Maya, 1982; papers and memoirs on anthropology and ethnology, in learned jls. *Address*: 209 Boulevard St-Germain, 75007 Paris, France. *T*: 45 44 07 35.

SOUTAR, Air Marshal Sir Charles (John Williamson), KBE 1978 (MBE 1958); Director-General, Medical Services (RAF), 1978–81; *b* 12 June 1920; *s* of Charles Alexander Soutar and Mary Helen (*née* Watson); *m* 1944, Joy Dorée Upton; *s two d. Educ*: Brentwood Sch.; London Hosp. MB, BS, LMSSA, FFCM, DPH, DIH. Commissioned RAF, 1946. Various appts, then PMO, Middle East Command, 1967–68; Dep. Dir, Med. Organisation, RAF, 1968–70; OC, PMRAF Hosp., Halton, 1970–73; Comdt, RAF Inst. of Aviation Medicine, 1973–75; PMO, Strike Command, 1975–78. QHS 1974–81. CStJ 1972. *Recreations*: sport, gardening, ornithology, music. *Address*: Oak Cottage, High Street, Aldeburgh, Suffolk IP15 5DT. *T*: Aldeburgh 2201. *Club*: Royal Air Force.

SOUTER, family name of **Baron Audley.**

SOUTH, Sir Arthur, Kt 1974; JP; Senior Partner, Norwich Fur Company, since 1947; *b* 29 Oct. 1914; *s* of Arthur and Violet South, Norwich; *m* 1st, 1937, May Adamson (marr. diss. 1976); two *s*; 2nd, 1976, Mary June (*d* 1982), widow of Robert Edward Carter, JP, DL. *Educ*: City of Norwich Sch. RAF and MAP, 1941–46. Mem., Norwich, Lowestoft, Gt Yarmouth Hosp. Management Cttee, 1948–74 (Vice-Chm., 1954–66, Chm., 1966–74); Chairman: Norfolk Area Health Authority, 1974–78; E Anglian RHA, 1978–; Mem., E Anglia Regional Hosp. Bd, 1969–74. Member: Assoc. of Educn Cttees, 1963–74; Assoc. of Municipal Corporations, 1965–74; E Anglia Econ. Planning Council, 1966–80; E Anglia Rent Assessment Panel, 1967–74; E Anglia Adv. Cttee to BBC, 1970–74; Univ. of E Anglia Council, 1964–80 (Life Mem., Court, 1964). Norwich: City Councillor, 1935–41 and 1946–61; Alderman, 1961–74; Sheriff, 1953–54; Lord Mayor, 1956–57, Dep. Lord Mayor, 1959–60; JP 1949; Dep. Leader, Norwich City Council, 1959–60; Chm., Labour Party Gp and Leader Norwich City Council, 1960–78. Norwich City Football Club: Vice-Pres., 1957–66; Dir, 1966–73; Chm., 1973–85; Member: FA Council, 1981–86; Football League: Mem., Management Cttee, 1981–85; Life Vice-Pres., 1985. *Recreations*: football, bowls, cricket. *Address*: The Lowlands, Drayton, Norfolk NR8 6HA. *T*: Norwich 867 355 ext. 207. *Clubs*: MCC; Mitre Bowls, Norfolk Cricket, Norwich City Football.

SOUTHALL, Kenneth Charles; Under-Secretary, Inland Revenue, 1975–82; *b* 3 Aug. 1922; *s* of Arthur and Margarette Jane Southall; *m* 1947, Audrey Kathleen Skeels; one *s. Educ*: Queen Elizabeth's Grammar Sch., Hartlebury, Worcs. Inland Revenue, 1939; RAF, 1942–46; Administrative Staff College, 1962. *Address*: The Green, Brill, Bucks HP13 9RU.

SOUTHAM, Gordon Ronald, BSc; AInstP; Headmaster, Ashville College, 1958–77; *b* 20 March 1918; *s* of G. H. Southam, Brackley; *m* 1948, Joan, *d* of W. Thompson; one *d. Educ*: Magdalen College School, Brackley; Westminster College, and King's College, London. BSc (Gen. Hons) 1938, BSc (Special Physics) 1st Class Hons 1939. Teacher's diploma, 1947, AInstP 1947. Served Royal Air Force, 1940–46: Bomber Comd, 1940–43; Staff Officer in HQ, ACSEA, 1943–46 (Sqdn Ldr). Senior Physics Master, Culford School, 1947–49; Lecturer, Royal Military Academy, Sandhurst, 1950–52; Head of Department of Science, Royal Military Academy, Sandhurst, 1953–57. *Recreations*: motoring, electronics; formerly Rugby football, athletics. *Address*: Culford, 20 Oak Tree Drive, Bedale, N Yorks DL8 1UL.

SOUTHAMPTON, Barony of (*cr* 1780); title disclaimed by 5th Baron; *see under* FitzRoy, Charles.

SOUTHAMPTON, Bishop Suffragan of, since 1984; **Rt. Rev. (Edward) David Cartwright;** Hon. Canon of Winchester Cathedral, since 1973; *b* 15 July 1920; *o c* of John Edward Cartwright and Gertrude Cartwright (*née* Lusby), North Somercotes and Grimsby, Lincs; *m* 1946, Elsie Irene, *o c* of Walter and Jane Elizabeth Rogers, Grimsby; one *s* two *d. Educ*: Grimsby Parish Church Choir Sch.; Lincoln Sch.; Selwyn Coll. and Westcott House, Cambridge. 2nd Cl. Hons Hist. Tripos Pt 1, 1940; 2nd Cl. Hons Theol Tripos Pt 1, 1942; Steel Univ. Student in Divinity, 1941; BA 1941, MA 1945; Pres., SCM in Cambridge, 1941–42. Deacon, 1943; Priest, 1944; Curate of Boston, 1943–48; Vicar: St Leonard's, Redfield, Bristol, 1948–52; Olveston with Aust, 1952–60; Bishopston, 1960–73; Secretary, Bristol Diocesan Synod, 1967–73; Hon. Canon of Bristol Cathedral, 1970–73; Archdeacon of Winchester and Vicar of Sparsholt with Lainston, 1973–84. Dir of Studies, Bristol Lay Readers, 1956–72; Proctor in Convocation, Mem. of Church Assembly and General Synod, 1956–73, 1975–83. Member: Central Bd of Finance of C of E, 1970–73; C of E Pensions Bd, 1980–84. Church Commissioner, 1973–83 (Mem. Board of Governors, 1978–83); Member: Dilapidations Legislation Commn, 1958–64; Working Party on Housing of Retired Clergy, 1972–73; Differential Payment of Clergy, 1976–77. Secretary, Bristol Council of Christian Churches, 1950–61; Chm., Winchester Christian Council, 1976–77; Pres., Southampton Council of Churches, 1984–. Chm., Christian Aid Cttee: Bristol, 1956–73; Winchester, 1974–81. Anglican-Presbyterian Conversations, 1962–66; Convocations Jt Cttees on Anglican-Methodist Union Scheme, 1965. *Recreations*: book-hunting and rose-growing. *Address*: Jollers, Sparsholt, Winchester SO21 2NS. *T*: Sparsholt 265.

SOUTHAN, Robert Joseph; His Honour Judge Southan; a Circuit Judge, since 1986; *b* 13 July 1928; *s* of late Thomas Southan and of Kathleen Southan; *m* 1960, Elizabeth Andreas (*née* Evatt); one *d* (one *s* decd). *Educ*: Rugby; St Edmund Hall, Oxford (MA); University Coll., London (LLM). Called to the Bar, Inner Temple, 1953; called to the Bar of NSW, 1976; a Recorder, 1983–86. *Recreations*: theatre, opera, sailing, ski-ing, squash, tennis. *Address*: 16 Hillside Court, 409 Finchley Road, Hampstead, NW3 6HG. *T*: 01–794 4935; 15 Old Square, Lincoln's Inn, WC2A 3UH. *T*: 01–831 0801. *Clubs*: Naval; Royal Corinthian Yacht, Bar Yacht; Cumberland Lawn Tennis.

SOUTHBOROUGH, 4th Baron *cr* 1917; **Francis Michael Hopwood;** *b* 3 May 1922; *s* of 3rd Baron Southborough and of Audrey, Baroness Southborough (Audrey Evelyn Dorothy, *d* of late Edgar George Money); *S* father, 1982; *m* 1945, Moyna Kemp, *d* of Robert John Kemp Chattey; one *d. Educ*: Wellington College; Christ Church, Oxford. An Underwriting Member of Lloyd's, 1949–; Dep. Chairman, Glanvill, Enthoven & Co. Ltd, 1977–80 (Director, 1954); Chairman, Robert Woodson Ltd, 1970–72 (Director, 1950). Served War of 1939–45 as Lieut, The Rifle Brigade. *Heir*: none. *Address*: 50A Eaton Square, SW1W 9BE. *Clubs*: Brooks's, City of London.

SOUTHBY, Sir (Archibald) Richard (Charles), 2nd Bt *cr* 1937; OBE 1945; Lt-Col (retd), Rifle Brigade; *b* 18 June 1910; *s* of Sir Archibald Richard James Southby, 1st Bt, and Phyllis Mary (*d* 1974), *er d* of late Charles Henry Garton, Banstead Wood, Surrey; *S* father, 1969; *m* 1st, 1935, Joan Alice (marr. diss. 1947), *o d* of Reginald Balston; 2nd, 1947, Olive Marion (marr. diss. 1964), *d* of late Sir Thomas Bilbe-Robinson; one *s*; 3rd, 1964, Hon. Ethel Peggy (*d* 1978), *d* of 1st Baron Cunliffe and *widow* of Brig. Bernard Lorenzo de Robeck, MC, RA; 4th, 1979, Iris Mackay Robertson, *d* of late Lt-Col G. Mackay Heriot, DSO, RM, and *widow* of Brig. I. C. A. Robertson. *Educ*: Eton; Magdalen Coll., Oxford (MA). Medal of Freedom (US). *Heir*: *s* John Richard Bilbe Southby [*b* 2 April 1948; *m* 1971, Victoria, *d* of William James Sturrock; two *s* one *d*]. *Address*: 7 Bolus Avenue, Kenilworth, Cape, 7700, Republic of South Africa; Greystone House, Stone, Tenterden, Kent TN30 7JT. *T*: Appledore 400.

SOUTHEND, Archdeacon of; *see* Bailey, Ven. J. S.

SOUTHERN, Michael William; Adviser to HE the Minister of Health, Kingdom of Saudi Arabia, 1978, now retired; Regional Administrator, South West Thames Regional Health Authority, 1973–77; *b* 22 June 1918; *s* of William Southern and Ida Frances Southern; *m* 1945, Nancy Russell Golsworthy; three *d. Educ*: Tiffin Boys' Sch., Kingston-upon-Thames; London Univ. (DPA); Open Univ. (BA Humanities). FHSM. Surrey CC Public Health Dept, 1934–39 and 1945–48; served with RAMC (NCO), 1939–45: Technician in No 1 Malaria Field Lab., 1940–41; POW Germany, 1941–44; Planning Officer and later Sec. of SW Metropolitan Regional Hosp. Bd, 1948–73. Chm., Surrey Council, Royal British Legion, 1985–. *Publications*: various articles in Hospital and Health Services Review, Health and Social Service Jl. *Recreations*: music, travel, philately. *Address*: 14 Poole Road, West Ewell, Epsom, Surrey KT19 9RY. *T*: 01–393 5096.

SOUTHERN, Richard; Theatre Consultant (private) since 1947; *b* 5 Oct. 1903; *o s* of Harry Southern and Edith (*née* Hockney); *m* 1933, Grace Kathleen Loosemore; two *d. Educ*: St Dunstan's College; Goldsmiths' Art School; Royal Academy of Art. Designed scenery, 1928–, for over fifty shows (Everyman Theatre, Cambridge Festival Theatre and various London theatres); also acted and stage-managed; specialized in study of stage technique and theatre architecture. Technical Lectr, Goldsmiths' College, 1932, London Theatre Studio, 1937, Royal Academy of Dramatic Art, 1945, Old Vic Theatre Centre, 1947; Theatre planning adviser to Arts Council, 1947; Director, Nuffield Theatre, Univ. of Southampton, 1964–66; Lectr, Drama Dept, Bristol Univ., 1959–60, and Special Lectr in Theatre Architecture, 1961–69, retired. Has planned various modern theatres and stages includ. Bristol Univ., 1951, Royal College of Art, 1952, Glasgow, 1953, Reading University, 1957, Nottingham, 1961, Southampton University, 1961, University Coll., London, 1967, also various reconstructions of historical theatres, Richmond, Yorkshire, 1950, King's Lynn, 1951, Williamsburg, Virginia, 1953. Hon. DLitt (Bristol), 1956. *Publications*: Stage Setting, 1937; Proscenium and Sightlines, 1939; The Georgian Playhouse, 1948; The Essentials of Stage Planning (with Stanley Bell and Norman Marshall), 1949; Changeable Scenery, 1952; The Open Stage, 1953; The Medieval Theatre in the Round, 1957; The Seven Ages of the Theatre, 1961; The Victorian Theatre, 1970; The Staging of Plays before Shakespeare, 1973; contrib. to specialist journals and encyclopædias. *Recreation*: figure drawing. *Address*: 37 Langham Road, Teddington TW11 9HF. *T*: 01–943 1979.

SOUTHERN, Sir Richard (William), Kt 1974; FBA 1960; FRSL 1973; President of St John's College, Oxford, 1969–81, Honorary Fellow, 1981; *b* 8 Feb. 1912; 2nd *s* of Matthew Henry Southern, Newcastle upon Tyne; *m* 1944, Sheila (*née* Cobley), *widow* of Sqdn Ldr C. Crichton-Miller; two *s. Educ*: Royal Grammar Sch., Newcastle upon Tyne; Balliol College, Oxford (Domus Exhibr). 1st Class Hons Modern History, 1932. Junior Research Fellow, Exeter College, Oxford, 1933–37; studied in Paris, 1933–34 and Munich, 1935; Fellow and Tutor, Balliol Coll., Oxford, 1937–61 (Hon. Fellow 1966). Served Oxford and Bucks LI, 1940; 2nd Lt Durham LI 1941; 155th Regt RAC, 1942; Captain 1943; Major 1944; Political Intelligence Dept, Foreign Office, 1943–45. Junior Proctor, Oxford Univ., 1948–49; Birkbeck Lectr in Ecclesiastical History, Trinity College, Cambridge, 1959–60; Chichele Prof. of Modern History, Oxford, 1961–69; President: Royal Historical Soc., 1968–72; Selden Soc., 1973–76. Lectures: Raleigh, British Academy, 1962; David Murray, Glasgow Univ., 1963; Gifford, Glasgow Univ., 1970–72; G. M. Trevelyan, Cambridge Univ., 1980–81. Corresponding Fellow: Medieval Academy of America, 1965; Monumenta Germaniae Historica, 1982; For. Hon. Mem., Amer. Acad. of Arts and Scis, 1972. Hon. Fellow, Sidney Sussex Coll., Cambridge, 1971; Hon. DLitt: Glasgow, 1964; Durham, 1969; Cantab, 1971; Bristol, 1974; Newcastle, 1977; Warwick, 1978; St Anselm's Coll., 1981; Columbia, 1982; Hon. LLD Harvard, 1977. *Publications*: The Making of the Middle Ages, 1953 (numerous foreign translations); (ed) Eadmer's Vita Anselmi, 1963; St Anselm and his Biographer, 1963; Western Views of Islam in the Middle Ages, 1962; (ed with F. S. Schmitt) Memorials of St Anselm, 1969; Medieval Humanism and other studies, 1970 (RSL award 1970); Western Society and the Church in the Middle Ages, 1970; Robert Grosseteste, 1986; articles in English Historical Review, Medieval and Renaissance Studies, etc. *Address*: 40 St John Street, Oxford OX1 2LH.

SOUTHERN, Sir Robert, Kt 1970; CBE 1953; General Secretary, Co-operative Union Ltd, 1948–72; *b* 17 March 1907; *s* of Job Southern and Margaret (*née* Tonge); *m* 1933, Lena Chapman; one *s* one *d. Educ*: Stand Grammar Sch.; Co-operative Coll.; Manchester University. Co-operative Wholesale Soc., Bank Dept, 1925–29; Co-operative Union Ltd, 1929. *Publication*: Handbook to the Industrial and Provident Societies' Act, 1938. *Recreations*: photography, gardening. *Address*: 22 Glebelands Road, Prestwich, Manchester M25 5NE. *T*: 061–773 2699.

SOUTHERTON, Thomas Henry, BSc (Eng); CEng, MIEE; *b* 1 July 1917; *s* of C. H. Southerton, Birmingham; *m* 1st, 1945, Marjorie Elizabeth Sheen (*d* 1979); one *s*; 2nd, 1981, Joyce Try. *Educ*: Bemrose Sch., Derby; Northampton Coll., London (BSc(Eng)). PO Apprentice, Derby, 1933–36; Engineering Workman, Derby and Nottingham, 1936–40; Inspector, Engineer-in-Chief's Office, 1940–45; Engineer, 1945–50; Sen. Exec. Engr, 1950–53; Factory Manager, PO Provinces, 1953–56; Dep. Controller, Factories Dept, 1956–64; Controller, Factories Dept, 1964–67; Dir, Telecommunications Management Services, 1967–73; Sen. Dir Telecommunications Personnel, 1973–75; Sen. Dir Data Processing, 1975–78. Mem., Industrial Tribunals, 1978–86. *Recreations*: art, architecture, music. *Address*: 92 Greenways, Hinchley Wood, Esher, Surrey. *T*: 01–398 1985.

SOUTHESK, 11th Earl of *cr* 1633; **Charles Alexander Carnegie,** KCVO 1926; Major late Scots Guards; Baron Carnegie, 1616; Baron Balinhard (UK), 1869; Bt of Nova Scotia, 1663; *b* 23 Sept. 1893; *e s* of 10th Earl of Southesk and Ethel (*d* 1947), *o c* of Sir Alexander Bannerman, 9th Bt of Elsick; *S* father, 1941; *m* 1st, 1923, HH Princess Maud (*d* 1945), 2nd *d* of HRH Princess Louise, Princess Royal and late Duke of Fife; one *s*; 2nd, 1952, Evelyn, *e d* of Lieut-Colonel A. P. Williams-Freeman, and *widow* of Major Ion E. F. Campbell, DCLI. *Educ:* Eton; Sandhurst. *Heir: s* Duke of Fife, *qv*. *Address:* Kinnaird Castle, Brechin, Angus. *T:* Bridge of Dun 209.

SOUTHEY, Sir Robert (John), Kt 1976; CMG 1970; Chairman, Wm Haughton & Co. Ltd, 1968–80; Federal President, Liberal Party of Australia, 1970–75; Chairman, Australian Ballet Foundation, since 1980; *b* 20 March 1922; *s* of Allen Hope Southey and Ethel Thorpe McComas, MBE; *m* 1st, 1946, Valerie Janet Cotton (*d* 1977), *y d* of late Hon. Sir Francis Grenville Clarke, KBE, MLC; five *s*; 2nd, 1982, Marigold Merlyn Baillieu, *yr d* of late Sidney and Dame Merlyn Myer, DBE, and *widow* of Ross Shelmerdine, CMG, OBE. *Educ:* Geelong Grammar Sch.; Magdalen Coll., Oxford (MA). Coldstream Guards, 1941–46 (Captain 1944, served N Africa, Italy). BA, 1st cl. PPE Oxon, 1948. Wm Haughton & Co. Ltd: Dir 1953; Man. Dir, 1959–75; Chm. 1968; Director: British Petroleum Co. of Australia Ltd; ICL Australia Pty Ltd; Kinnears Ltd, 1975–84; National Westminster Finance Australia Ltd, 1983–85; Nat West Australia Bank Ltd, 1985–; Kawasaki (Australia) Pty Ltd, 1986–; Chairman: McArthur Shipping (Vic.) Pty Ltd, 1974–81; Australian Adv. Council, General Accident Assurance Corp. PLC; Computer Benefits (Aust.) Pty Ltd, 1982–. Mem. Executive, Liberal Party, 1966–82; Victorian State Pres., Liberal Party, 1966–70; Chm. of Council, Geelong Grammar Sch., 1966–72; Pres., Geelong Grammar Foundn, 1975–; Chm. Australian Adv. Cttee, Nuffield Foundn, 1970–81; Mem., Rhodes Scholarship Selection Cttee, Victoria, 1973–76. *Publication:* (with C. J. Puplick) Liberal Thinking, 1980. *Recreations:* fishing, golf, music. *Address:* Denistoun Avenue, Mount Eliza, Victoria 3930, Australia. *T:* 7871701. *Clubs:* Cavalry and Guards, MCC; Melbourne, Australian (Melbourne); Union (Sydney); Vincent's (Oxford); Leander.

SOUTHGATE, Air Vice-Marshal Harry Charles, CB 1976; CBE 1973 (MBE 1950); Director General of Engineering and Supply Policy and Planning, Ministry of Defence (Air), 1973–76, retired; *b* 30 Oct. 1921; *s* of George Harry Southgate and Lily Maud (*née* Clarke); *m* 1945, Violet Louise Davies; one *s*. *Educ:* St Saviour's Sch., Walthamstow. Entered RAF, 1941; India, 1942–45; HQ 90 Gp, 1946–50; RAF Stafford, 1950–52; Air Min., 1952–53; transf. to Equipment Br., 1953; RAF Tangmere, 1953–55; Singapore, 1955–57; psc 1957; Air Min., 1958–60; jssc 1961; Dirg Staff, RAF Staff Coll., Bracknell, 1961–64; CO 35 MU RAF Heywood, 1965–66; SESO, RAF Germany, 1967–68; idc 1969; Dir Supply Management, MoD Air, 1970–73. *Recreations:* travel, golf, painting, bird-watching. *Address:* The Rushings, Winksley, near Ripon, North Yorkshire HG4 3NR. *T:* Kirkby Malzeard 582. *Club:* Royal Air Force.

SOUTHGATE, Very Rev. John Eliot; Dean of York, since 1984; *b* 2 Sept. 1926; *m* 1958, Patricia Mary Plumb; two *s* one *d*. *Educ:* City of Norwich Sch.; Durham Univ. BA 1953, DipTh 1955. Ordained 1955; Vicar of Plumstead, 1962; Rector of Old Charlton, 1966; Dean of Greenwich, 1968; York Diocesan Sec. for Mission and Evangelism, 1972–81, and Vicar of Harome, 1972–77; Archdeacon of Cleveland, 1974–84. *Recreations:* music, sailing, Egyptology. *Address:* The Deanery, York, N Yorks YO1 2JD.

SOUTHGATE, Malcolm John; Director, Channel Tunnel, British Railways Board, since 1986; *b* 11 Nov. 1933; *s* of Harold Edwin Southgate and Mary (*née* Kelleher); *m* 1959, Anne Margaret Yeoman; two *s*. *Educ:* Royal Grammar Sch., Colchester; Corpus Christi Coll., Cambridge (BA). British Railways: Divl Manager, S Eastern Div., 1972; Chief Operating Manager, 1975, Dep. Gen. Man., 1977, Southern Region; Dir of Ops, 1980, Dir of Policy Unit, 1983, BR Board; Gen. Man., LMR, 1983. *Recreations:* Rugby, education administration, transport affairs. *Address:* 4 Langdale Rise, Maidstone, Kent ME16 0EU. *T:* Maidstone 53792.

SOUTHWARD, Sir Leonard (Bingley), (Sir Len), Kt 1986; OBE 1978; Founder (with Lady Southward) of Southward Museum Trust Inc., Paraparaumu, New Zealand, 1972; *b* 20 Sept. 1905; *s* of Philip Edmund Southward and Elizabeth Sarah Southward; *m* 2nd, 1954, Vera Thelma Bellamore; two *s* of former marriage. *Educ:* Te Aro Sch., Wellington, NZ. Started motorcycle repair business, 1926; changed to car repairs, 1935; started prodn engrg and manufacture of steel tubing, 1939; Governing Dir, Southward Engrg Co. Ltd, 1957–. The Southward Museum, which was opened to the public in 1979, contains one of the largest and most varied privately owned collection of veteran and vintage cars in the Southern Hemisphere. *Recreations:* veteran and vintage cars, rallies, etc; formerly speed boat racing, Australasia (first man in region to travel at over 100 mph on water). *Address:* Main Road North, Paraparaumu, New Zealand. *T:* 84–627.

SOUTHWARD, Dr Nigel Ralph, LVO 1985; Apothecary to the Queen, Apothecary to the Household and to the Households of Princess Margaret Countess of Snowdon, Princess Alice Duchess of Gloucester and the Duke and Duchess of Gloucester, since 1975; *b* 8 Feb. 1941; *s* of Sir Ralph Southward, *qv*; *m* 1965, Annette, *d* of J. H. Hoffmann; one *s* two *d*. *Educ:* Rugby Sch.; Trinity Hall, Cambridge; Middlesex Hosp. Med. Sch. MA, MB, BChir, 1965; MRCP 1969. Ho. Surg., Mddx Hosp., 1965; Ho. Phys., Royal Berkshire Hosp., Reading, 1966; Ho. Phys., Central Mddx Hosp., 1966; Casualty MO, Mddx Hosp., 1967; Vis. MO, King Edward VII Hosp. for Officers, 1972–. *Recreations:* sailing, golf, skiing. *Address:* 9 Devonshire Place, W1N 1PB. *T:* 01–935 8425; 56 Primrose Gardens, NW3 4TP. *Club:* Royal Yacht Squadron.

SOUTHWARD, Sir Ralph, KCVO 1975; Apothecary to the Household of Queen Elizabeth the Queen Mother, since 1966 (Apothecary to Household of HRH the Duke of Gloucester, 1966–75, to HM Household, 1964–74, to HM the Queen, 1972–74); *b* 2 Jan. 1908; *s* of Henry Stalker Southward; *m* 1935, Evelyn, *d* of J. G. Tassell; four *s*. *Educ:* High School of Glasgow; Glasgow Univ. MB, ChB (Glasgow) 1930; MRCP 1939; FRCP 1970. Western Infirmary, and Royal Hospital for Sick Children, Glasgow; Postgraduate Medical School, Hammersmith, London. Served War of 1939–45: Medical Officer, 215 Field Ambulance, North Africa, 1940–41; Medical Specialist, Egypt, India and Ceylon, and Lieut-Colonel in charge Medical Division, 1942–43; Colonel Comdg Combined General Hospital, 1944–45. Hon. Freeman, Worshipful Soc. of Apothecaries of London, 1975. *Recreations:* trout and salmon fishing, golf, travel. *Address:* 9 Devonshire Place, W1. *T:* 01–935 7969; Amerden Priory, Taplow, Bucks. *T:* Maidenhead 23525.

See also N. R. Southward.

SOUTHWARK, Archbishop and Metropolitan of, (RC), since 1977; **Most Rev. Michael George Bowen;** *b* 23 April 1930; *s* of late Major C. L. J. Bowen and Lady Makins (who *m* 1945, Sir Paul Makins, Bt, *qv*). *Educ:* Downside; Trinity Coll., Cambridge; Gregorian Univ., Rome. Army, 1948–49, 2nd Lieut Irish Guards; Wine Trade, 1951–52; English Coll., Rome, 1952–59; ordained 1958; Curate at Earlsfield and at Walworth, South London, 1959–63; taught theology, Beda Coll., Rome, 1963–66; Chancellor of Diocese of Arundel and Brighton, 1966–70; Coadjutor Bishop with right of succession to See of Arundel and Brighton, 1970–71; Bishop of Arundel and Brighton, 1971–77. *Recreations:* golf, tennis. *Address:* Archbishop's House, St George's Road, Southwark, SE1 6HX. *T:* 01–928 2495/5592.

SOUTHWARK, Bishop of, since 1980; **Rt. Rev. Ronald Oliver Bowlby;** *b* 16 August 1926; *s* of Oliver and Helena Bowlby; *m* 1956, Elizabeth Trevelyan Monro; three *s* two *d*. *Educ:* Eton Coll.; Trinity College, Oxford (MA); Westcott House, Cambridge. Curate of St Luke's, Pallion, Sunderland, 1952–56; Priest-in-charge and Vicar of St Aidan, Billingham, 1956–66; Vicar of Croydon, 1966–72; Bishop of Newcastle, 1973–80. Hon. Fellow, Newcastle upon Tyne Polytechnic, 1980. *Publications:* contrib. Church without Walls, ed Lindars, 1969; contrib. Church and Politics Today, ed Moyser, 1985. *Recreations:* walking, gardening, music. *Address:* Bishop's House, 38 Tooting Bec Gardens, SW16 1QZ.

SOUTHWARK, Auxiliary Bishops in, (RC); *see* Henderson, Rt Rev. C. J.; Jukes, Rt Rev. J.; Tripp, Rt Rev. H. G.

SOUTHWARK, Provost of; *see* Edwards, Very Rev. D. L.

SOUTHWARK, Archdeacon of; *see* Bartles-Smith, Ven. D. L.

SOUTHWELL, family name of **Viscount Southwell.**

SOUTHWELL, 7th Viscount, *cr* 1776; **Pyers Anthony Joseph Southwell;** Bt 1662; Baron Southwell, 1717; International Management and Marketing Consultant; *b* 14 Sept. 1930; *s* of Hon. Francis Joseph Southwell (2nd *s* of 5th Viscount) and Agnes Mary Annette Southwell (*née* Clifford); *S* uncle, 1960; *m* 1955, Barbara Jacqueline Raynes; two *s*. *Educ:* Beaumont Coll., Old Windsor, Berks; Royal Military Academy, Sandhurst. Commissioned into 8th King's Royal Irish Hussars, 1951; resigned commission, 1955. *Recreation:* golf. *Heir: s* Hon. Richard Andrew Pyers Southwell, *b* 15 June 1956. *Address:* 4 Rosebery Avenue, Harpenden, Herts AL5 2QP. *T:* Harpenden 5831. *Clubs:* Army and Navy, MCC.

SOUTHWELL, Bishop of, since 1985; **Rt. Rev. Michael Humphrey Dickens Whinney;** *b* 8 July 1930; *s* of late Humphrey Charles Dickens Whinney and Evelyn Lawrence Revell Whinney (*née* Low); great-great-grandson of Charles Dickens; *m* 1958, Veronica (*née* Webster); two *s* one *d*. *Educ:* Charterhouse; Pembroke Coll., Cambridge (BA 1955, MA 1958); Ridley Hall, Cambridge. National Service commission, RA, 1949 (served in 5th Regt, RHA and Surrey Yeo. Queen Mary's Regt). Articled clerk to Chartered Accountants, Whinney Smith & Whinney (now Ernst Whinney), 1950–52. Curate, Rainham Parish Church, Essex, 1957–60; Head, Cambridge University Mission Settlement, Bermondsey, 1960–67, Chaplain, 1967–72; Vicar, St James' with Christ Church, Bermondsey, 1967–73; Archdeacon and Borough Dean of Southwark, 1973–82; Bishop Suffragan of Aston, 1982 85. *Address:* Bishop's Manor, Southwell, Notts NG25 0JR.

SOUTHWELL, Provost of; *see* Irvine, Very Rev. J. M.

SOUTHWELL, Richard Charles; QC 1977; *s* of late Sir Philip Southwell, CBE, MC and Mary Burnett, *d* of Thomas Scarratt, Belmont Hall, Ipstones, Staffs; *m* 1962, Belinda Mary, *d* of Col F. H. Pownall, MC; two *s* one *d*. *Address:* 1 Hare Court, Temple, EC4. *T:* 01–353 3171.

SOUTHWELL, Ven. Roy; Archdeacon of Northolt, 1970–80, Archdeacon Emeritus, since 1980; Warden of the Community of All Hallows, Ditchingham, Norfolk, since 1983; *b* 3 Dec. 1914; *s* of William Thomas and Lilian Southwell; *m* 1948, Nancy Elizabeth Lindsay Sharp; two *d*. *Educ:* Sudbury Grammar Sch.; King's Coll., London (AKC 1942). Curate: St Michael's, Wigan, 1942–44; St John the Divine, Kennington, 1944–48; Vicar of Ixworth, 1948–51; Vicar of St John's, Bury St Edmunds, 1951–56; Rector of Bucklesham with Brightwell and Foxhall, 1956–59; Asst Director of Religious Education, Diocese of St Edmundsbury and Ipswich, 1956–58, Director, 1959–67. Hon. Canon of St Edmundsbury, 1959–68; Vicar of Hendon, 1968–71. *Recreations:* reading, singing and watching TV. *Address:* 397 Sprowston Road, Norwich NR3 4HY. *T:* Norwich 405977.

SOUTHWOOD, Captain Horace Gerald, CBE 1966; DSC 1941; Royal Navy; Managing Director, Silley, Cox & Co. Ltd, Falmouth Docks, 1974–78; Chairman, Falmouth Group, 1976–78; *b* 19 April 1912; *s* of late Horace George Southwood; *m* 1936, Ruby Edith Hayes; two *s* one *d*. *Educ:* HMS Fisgard, RN Coll., Greenwich. Joined RN, 1927; HMS Resolution, Medit. Stn, 1932–34; HMS Barham, 1934–35; RN Coll., Greenwich, 1935–36; HMS Royal Oak, Home Fleet, 1936–38; specialised in Submarines, 1938; HMS Lucia, 1938–39. HM Submarine, Regent, 1939–41, China and Medit. (despatches, DSC); HMS Medway, Medit., 1941–42; HM Submarine, Amphion (first of Class), 1943–45. HMS Dolphin, 1946–48; HMS Vengeance, 1948–49; Comdr, 1948; HMS Glory, 1949–51; HMS Forth, 1951–52; Admty, Whitehall, 1952–54; HM Dockyard, Portsmouth (Dep. Man.), 1954–58; jssc, 1958–59; Capt., 1958. Chief Engr, Singapore, 1959–62; Sen. Officers' War Course, 1962; Manager, Engrg Dept, HM Dockyard, Portsmouth, 1963–67; Gen. Manager, HM Dockyard, Devonport, 1967–72, retd. Management Consultant, Productivity and Management Services Ltd, 1972–74. CEng, FIMechE. *Recreations:* sailing, fishing, golf, caravanning. *Address:* Dolphin Cottage, Riverside, Newton Ferrers, Devon. *T:* Plymouth 872401. *Clubs:* Royal Western Yacht (Plymouth); Yealm Yacht (Newton Ferrers).

SOUTHWOOD, Prof. Sir (Thomas) Richard (Edmund), Kt 1984; FRS 1977; Linacre Professor of Zoology, University of Oxford and Fellow of Merton College, Oxford, since 1979; Chairman, National Radiological Protection Board, since 1985 (Member, since 1980); *b* 20 June 1931; *s* of Edmund W. Southwood and late A. Mary, *d* of Archdeacon T. R. Regg, and *g s* of W. E. W. Southwood; *m* 1955, Alison Langley, *d* of late A. L. Harden, Harpenden, Herts; two *s*. *Educ:* Gravesend Grammar Sch.; Imperial Coll., London. BSc, ARCS 1952; PhD London, 1955; DSc London, 1963; MA Oxon 1979. FIBiol 1968. ARC Research Schol., Rothamsted Experimental Station, 1952–55; Res. Asst and Lecturer, Zoology Dept, Imperial Coll., London, 1955–64; Vis. Prof., Dept. of Entomology, University of California, Berkeley, 1964–65; Reader in Insect Ecology, University of London, 1964–67; Prof. of Zoology and Applied Entomology, London Univ., Head of Dept of Zoology and Applied Entomol., and Dir of Field Station, Imperial Coll., 1967–79; Dean, Royal Coll. of Science, 1971–72; Chm., Division of Life Sciences, Imperial Coll., 1974–77. A. D. White Prof.-at-Large, Cornell Univ., 1985–. Member: ARC Adv. Cttee on Plants and Soils, 1970–72; ARC Res. Grants Bd, 1972–; JCO Arable and Forage Crops Bd, 1972–79; NERC Terrestrial Life Sciences (formerly Nature Conservancy) Grants Cttee, 1971–76 (Chm., 1972–76); Council, St George's House, Windsor, 1974–80; Adv. Bd Research Councils, 1977–80; Trop. Medicine Panel, Wellcome Trust, 1977–79; Chm., Royal Commn on Environmental Pollution, 1981–86 (Mem., 1974–86). Vice-Pres., Royal Soc., 1982–84; President: British Ecological Soc., 1976–78 (Hon. Treas., 1960–64 and 1967–68); Royal Entomological Soc., 1983 (Vice-Pres., 1963–64); Vice Pres., Game Conservancy, 1986–. Hon. Vice-Pres., Inst. of Environmental Health Offices, 1984–. Governor, Glasshouse Crops Research Inst., 1969–81; Trustee: British Museum (Natural History), 1974–83 (Chm., 1980–83);

Rhodes Trust, 1986–; Delegate, OUP, 1980–; Mem., Hebdomadal Council, 1981–. Plenary speaker, 15th Internat. Congress on Entomology, Washington, 1976; Spencer Lectr, Univ. of British Columbia, 1978; Bawden Lectr, British Crop Protection Conf., 1979. Foreign Hon. Mem., Amer. Acad. of Arts and Sciences, 1981; Hon. Mem., Ecol Soc. of America, 1986. Hon. Fellow, Imperial Coll., 1984. Hon. DSc Griffith, 1983; Fil. Doc. *hc* Lund, 1986. Scientific Medal, Zool. Soc., London, 1969. *Publications:* (with D. Leston) Land and Water Bugs of the British Isles, 1959; Life of the Wayside and Woodland, 1963; Ecological Methods, 1966, 2nd edn 1978; (jtly) Insects on Plants, 1984; (ed with B. J. Juniper) Insects and the Plant Surface, 1986; many papers in entomological and ecological jls. *Recreations:* natural history, gardening. *Address:* Merton College, Oxford. *Club:* Athenæum.
See also W. F. W. Southwood.

SOUTHWOOD, William Frederick Walter, MD; MChir; FRCS; Consultant Surgeon, Bath Health District, since 1966; *b* 8 June 1925; *s* of late Stuart W. Southwood, MC, and of Mildred M. Southwood, and *g s* of W. E. W. Southwood; *m* 1965, Margaret Carleton Holderness, *d* of late Sir Ernest Holderness, Bt, CBE, and Lady Holderness; two *s*. *Educ:* Charterhouse; Trinity Coll., Cambridge (MA 1951, MD 1964, MChir 1956); Guy's Hosp. FRCS 1954. Captain, RAMC, 1949–51. Surg. Registrar, West London Hosp. and St Mark's Hosp. for Diseases of the Rectum, 1954–60; Sen. Surg. Registrar, Royal Infirmary, Bristol, 1960–66. Hunterian Prof., RCS, 1961. Chm., Professional and Linguistic Assessment Bd, 1984– (Mem., 1976–; Vice-Chm., 1983–84). Member: Court of Assts, Worshipful Soc. of Apothecaries of London, 1975– (Chm., Exams Cttee, 1981–85; Jun. Warden, 1984–85; Sen. Warden, 1985–86; Master, 1986–87); Cttee, Non-Univ. Medical Licencing Bodies, 1979–. Examr in Anatomy and Surgery to GNC, 1957–72. *Publications:* articles in surgical jls. *Recreations:* fishing, snooker. *Address:* Upton House, Bathwick Hill, Bath, Avon. *T:* Bath 65152. *Clubs:* East India; Bath and County (Bath).

SOUTHWORTH, Sir Frederick, Kt 1965; QC; Chief Justice, Malawi, 1964–70, retired 1970; *b* Blackburn, Lancashire, 9 May 1910; *s* of late Harper Southworth, Blackburn, Lancs; *m* 1942, Margaret, *d* of James Rice, Monaghan, Ireland; three *d*. *Educ:* Queen Elizabeth's Grammar Sch., Blackburn; Exeter Coll., Oxford. Called to the Bar, Gray's Inn, 1936. War of 1939–45; commissioned 1939; served with South Lancashire Regiment and Lancashire Fusiliers, and with Department of the Judge Advocate General in India, 1939–46; Hon. Colonel, Crown Counsel, Palestine, 1946–47; Crown Counsel, Tanganyika, 1947–51; Attorney-General, Bahamas, 1951–55; QC Bahamas, 1952; Acting Governor, July–Aug. 1952; Acting Chief Justice, July–Oct. 1954; Puisne Judge, Nyasaland, 1955–64; Acting Governor-General, Malawi, 1964 and 1965. *Publications:* Specimen Charges, in use in the courts of Tanzania, Zanzibar, Kenya and Uganda; The Southworth Commission Report: an inquiry into allegations made by the international press against the Nyasaland Police, 1960. *Address:* c/o Barclays Bank, Darwen Street, Blackburn, Lancs.

SOUTHWORTH, Jean May, QC 1973; a Recorder of the Crown Court, since 1972; *b* 20 April 1926; *o c* of late Edgar and Jane Southworth, Clitheroe. *Educ:* Queen Ethelburga's Sch., Harrogate; St Anne's Coll., Oxford (MA). Served in WRNS, 1944–45. Called to Bar, Gray's Inn, 1954; Bencher, 1980. Standing Counsel to Dept of Trade and Industry for Central Criminal Court and Inner London Sessions, 1969–73. Fellow, Woodard Corporation (Northern Div.), 1974. *Recreations:* music, watching cricket. *Address:* 21 Caroline Place, W2 4AN; Queen Elizabeth Building, Temple, EC4Y 9BS.

SOUYAVE, Sir (Louis) Georges, Kt 1971; **His Honour Judge Souyave;** District Judge, Hong Kong, since 1980; *b* 29 May 1926; *m* 1953, Mona de Chermont; two *s* four *d*. *Educ:* St Louis Coll., Seychelles; Gray's Inn, London. Barrister-at-Law, Gray's Inn, 1949. In private practice, Seychelles, 1949–56; Asst Attorney-Gen., Seychelles, 1956–62; Supreme Court, Seychelles: Additional Judge, 1962–64; Puisne Judge, 1964–70; Chief Justice, 1970–76; New Hebrides: Resident Judge of the High Court (British jurisdiction) and British Judge of the Supreme Ct of the Condominium, 1976–80. *Recreations:* walking, swimming. *Address:* District Court, Victoria, Hong Kong.

SOUZAY, Gérard, (*né* Gérard Marcel Tisserand), Chevalier, Légion d'Honneur; Chevalier de l'Ordre des Arts et Lettres; French baritone; *b* 8 Dec. 1921. *Educ:* Paris Conservatoire Musique. World Première, Stravinsky's Canticum Sacrum, Venice Festival, 1956; Bach B Minor Mass at Salzburg Festival; Pelléas et Mélisande, Rome Opera, Opera Comique, 1962, Scala, Milan, 1973; Don Giovanni, Paris Opera, 1963; second tour of Australia and New Zealand, 1964. Also tours in US, South America, Japan, Africa, Europe. Annual Lieder recitals, Salzburg Festival. Has made recordings; Grand Prix du Disque, for Ravel Recital, etc. *Recreations:* tennis, painting. *Address:* 26 rue Freycinet, 75116 Paris, France.

SOWDEN, John Percival; Chairman, Costain Group Ltd (formerly Richard Costain Ltd), 1972–80 (Director, 1967–82); Regional Director, Central London Regional Board, Lloyds Bank, since 1980; *b* 6 Jan. 1917; *s* of Percy Sowden and Gertrude Sowden (*née* Moss); *m* 1st, 1940, Ruth Dorothy Keane (marr. diss. 1969); one *s*; 2nd, 1969, Joyce Diana Timson. *Educ:* Silcoates Sch., Wakefield, Yorks; The Grammar Sch., Hebden Bridge, Yorks; City and Guilds Coll., Imperial Coll. of Science (BScEng, ACGI; FCGI 1973). FIStructE. Served War: commnd RE, with service in UK, ME and Italy, 1939–46 (despatches, 1943). Joined Richard Costain Ltd, 1948; Site Project Manager on various construction projects, incl. Festival of Britain, Apapa Wharf, Nigeria, and Bridgetown Harbour, Barbados, 1948–60; Joint Managing Director: Richard Costain (Associates) Ltd, 1961–62; Costain-Blankevoort Internat. Dredging Co. Ltd, 1963–65; Richard Costain Ltd: Manager, Civil Engrg Div., 1965–69; Board Member, 1967; Chief Executive, Internat. Area, 1969–70; Group Chief Executive, 1970–75. Member, Governing Body, Imperial Coll. of Science and Technology, 1971–, Fellow, 1980. FRSA 1983. *Recreations:* reading, joinery. *Address:* Below Star Cottage, East Tytherley Road, Lockerley, Romsey, Hants SO5 0LW. *T:* Romsey 41172. *Club:* Royal Automobile.

SOWREY, Air Marshal Sir Frederick (Beresford), KCB 1978 (CB 1968); CBE 1965; AFC 1954; *b* 14 Sept. 1922; *s* of late Group Captain Frederick Sowrey, DSO, MC, AFC; *m* 1946, Anne Margaret, *d* of late Captain C. T. A. Bunbury, OBE, RN; one *s* one *d*. *Educ:* Charterhouse. Joined RAF 1940; flying training in Canada, 1941; Fighter-reconnaissance Squadron, European theatre, 1942–44; Flying Instructors Sch., 1944; Airborne Forces, 1945; No 615 (Co. of Surrey) Squadron, RAuxAF ('Winston Churchill's Own'), 1946–48; Fighter Gunnery Sch., 1949–50, comdg 615 Sqdn, 1951–54; RAF Staff Coll., Bracknell, 1954; Chiefs of Staff Secretariat, 1955–58; comdg No 46 Sqdn, 1958–60; Personal Staff Officer to CAS, 1960–62; comdg RAF Abingdon, 1962–64; IDC 1965; SASO, Middle East Comd (Aden), 1966–67; Dir Defence Policy, MoD, 1968–70; SASO, RAF Trng Comd, 1970–72; Comdt, Nat. Defence Coll., 1972–75; Dir-Gen. RAF Training, 1975–77; UK Representative, Permanent Military Deputies Group CENTO, 1977–79. Research Fellow, IISS, 1980–81. Chm., Sussex Indust. Archaeology Soc., 1981–; Mem., Bd of Conservators, Ashdown Forest, 1984–; Chm., Victory Services Assoc., 1985–. *Publications:* contribs and book reviews for defence jls. *Recreations:* motoring sport (world class records 1956), veteran aircraft and cars, mechanical devices of any kind and age. *Address:* 40 Adam and Eve Mews, W8. *Club:* Royal Air Force.

SOWRY, Dr (George Stephen) Clive, FRCP; Physician, Edgware General Hospital, 1953–82; *b* 26 Dec. 1917; *s* of Dr George H. Sowry and Mrs Stella Sowry; *m* 1943, Jeanne (*née* Adams); one *s* one *d*. *Educ:* Bilton Grange, near Rugby; Epsom Coll., Surrey; St Mary's Hosp. Med. Sch., London (MB, BS 1940; MD 1947). FRCP 1963 (MRCP 1946). Served War, RNVR, 1941–45 (Surg. Lieut). Med. appts, St Mary's Hosp., Brompton Hosp. and Hammersmith Hosp., until 1953; med. admin, Edgware Gen. Hosp., 1957–73. Royal College of Physicians: Pro Censor, 1975; Censor, 1976; Sen. Censor and Vice-Pres., 1978–79; Mem. Qualification Cttee, 1981–; Examnr, Faculty of Occupational Medicine, 1981–. Med. Sec., MRCP (UK) Pt 2 Exam. Bd., 1983–; Member: Jt Academic Cttee, Conjoint Bd, 1983– (Chm., 1985–); Med. Adv. Cttee, HSE, 1983–. Silver Jubilee Medal, 1977. *Publication:* (jtly) article on aetiology of essential hypertension in Clin. Science. *Recreations:* sailing, singing. *Address:* 53 Aldenham Avenue, Radlett, Herts. *T:* Radlett 6046.

SOYSA, Sir Warusahennedige Abraham Bastian, Kt 1954; CBE 1953 (MBE 1950); JP; formerly Mayor of Kandy, Sri Lanka. *Address:* 32/36 Sangaraja Mawatha, Kandy, Sri Lanka.

SPACIE, Maj.-Gen. Keith, OBE 1974; Director of Army Training, since 1984; *b* 21 June 1935; *s* of Frederick and Kathleen Spacie; *m* 1961, Valerie Rich; one *s*. *Educ:* Queen Elizabeth Sch., Gainsborough; RMA, Sandhurst. Commnd Royal Lincolns, 1955; transf. Parachute Regt, 1959; Staff Coll., Camberley, 1966; DAA&QMG 16 Parachute Bde, 1968–70; Staff, RMA, Sandhurst, 1970–72; Comd, 3rd Bn Parachute Regt, 1973–75; SHAPE, 1976–78; Comdr 7 Field Force, 1979–81; RCDS, 1982; Mil. Comr and Comdr, British Forces Falkland Is, 1983–84. *Recreations:* cross-country running, athletics, walking, battlefield touring, Victorian paintings. *Address:* c/o Lloyds Bank, Obelisk Way, Camberley, Surrey GU15 3SE. *Clubs:* Army and Navy; Thames Hare and Hounds.

SPACKMAN, Brig. John William Charles, PhD; Under Secretary, and Director of Social Security Operational Strategy, Department of Health and Social Security, since 1983; *b* 12 May 1932; *s* of Lt-Col Robert Thomas Spackman, MBE and Ann (*née* Rees); *m* 1955, Jeanette Vera; two *s* one *d*. *Educ:* Cyfarthfa Castle Grammar School, Merthyr Tydfil; Wellington Grammar School; RMCS. BSc 1st cl. Hons London (external) 1960, PhD 1964; MSc (Management Sci.) UMIST, 1968. Nat. Service, 1950–52; Regular Commission, RAOC, 1952; Regtl appts, 1952–72; Project Wavell, 1969–72; RARDE, 1972–75; Senior Mil. Officer, Chem. Defence and Microbiological Defence Estab., Porton Down, 1975–78; Branch Chief, Inf. Systems Div., SHAPE, 1978–80; Dir, Supply Computer Services, 1980–83; retired from Army, 1983 (Brig.); Mem., Nat. Electronics Council. MInstD. *Recreations:* gardening, tennis, hill walking, opera. *Address:* 4 The Green, Evenley, Brackley, Northants. *T:* Brackley 703317. *Club:* Naval and Military.

SPACKMAN, Michael John; Under Secretary, and Head of Public Expenditure Economics and Operational Research Group, HM Treasury, since 1985; *b* 8 Oct. 1936; *s* of late Geoffrey Spackman and Audrey (*née* Morecombe); *m* 1965, Judith Ann Leathem; two *s* one *d*. *Educ:* Malvern Coll.; Clare Coll., Cambridge (MA); Queen Mary Coll., London (MScEcon). Served RA (2nd Lieut), 1955–57; Physicist, UKAEA, Capenhurst, 1960–69; Sen. Physicist/Engr, Nuclear Power Gp Ltd, 1969–71; PSO, then Economic Advr, Dept of Energy, 1971–77; Economic Advr, HM Treasury, 1977–79; Dir of Econs and Accountancy, CS Coll., 1979–80; Hd of Public Services Econs Div., HM Treasury, 1980–85. *Recreations:* walking, children. *Address:* 44 Gibson Square, Islington, N1 0RA. *T:* 01–359 1053.

SPAFFORD, Very Rev. Christopher Garnett Howsin; Provost and Vicar of Newcastle, since 1976; *b* 10 Sept. 1924; *s* of late Rev. Canon Douglas Norman Spafford and Frances Alison Spafford; *m* 1953, Stephanie Peel; three *s*. *Educ:* Marlborough Coll.; St John's Coll., Oxford (MA 2nd Cl. Hons Modern History); Wells Theological Coll. Curate of Brighouse, 1950; Curate of Huddersfield Parish Church, 1953; Vicar of Hebden Bridge, 1955; Rector of Thornhill, Dewsbury, 1961; Vicar of St Chad's, Shrewsbury, 1969. *Recreations:* reading, gardening, walking. *Address:* The Cathedral Vicarage, 23 Montagu Avenue, Newcastle upon Tyne NE3 4HY. *T:* Tyneside 2853472.

SPAFFORD, George Christopher Howsin; a Recorder of the Crown Court, since 1975; Chancellor, Manchester Diocese, since 1976; *b* 1 Sept. 1921; *s* of Christopher Howsin Spafford and Clara Margaret Spafford; *m* 1959, Iola Margaret, 3rd *d* of Bertrand Leslie Hallward, *qv*; one *s* one *d*. *Educ:* Rugby; Brasenose Coll., Oxford (MA, BCL Hons). Served RA, 1939–46 (Captain). Called to Bar, Middle Temple, 1948. Mem., Legal Adv. Commn of Gen. Synod, 1981–. Treasurer, Friends of the Manchester City Art Gall., 1986–; Former Treasurer: Parish and People; Red Rose Guild of Designer Craftsmen. ARCamA. *Recreation:* painting pictures. *Address:* 57 Hawthorn Lane, Wilmslow, Cheshire SK9 5DQ.

SPAGHT, Monroe E., MA, PhD; retired Director, Royal Dutch/Shell companies; Director: Shell Oil Co., USA, 1953–80 (Chairman, 1965–70); Royal Dutch Petroleum Co., 1965–80; various Royal Dutch/Shell companies, 1965–80; *b* Eureka, California, 9 Dec. 1909; *s* of Fred E. and Alpha L. Spaght; *m* two *s* one *d*. *Educ:* Humboldt State Univ.; Stanford Univ.; University of Leipzig. AB 1929, MA 1930, PhD 1933, Stanford Univ. (Chemistry). Research scientist and technologist, Shell Oil Co., 1933–45; Vice-President, Shell Development Co., 1945–48, President, 1949–52; Exec. Vice-President, Shell Oil Co., 1953–60, President, 1961–65; Man. Dir, Royal Dutch/Shell Group, 1965–70; Director: Stanford Research Inst., 1953–70; Inst. of International Education, 1953– (Chm., 1971–74); American Petroleum Inst. 1953–; American Standard, 1972–82; Mem. Adv. Bd, The Boston Co., 1979–80 (Dir, 1971–79). Chm., Internat. Adv. Bd of Chemical Bank, 1977–80; Mem., Internat. Adv. Cttee, Wells Fargo Bank, 1977–84. Trustee, Stanford Univ., 1955–65. President, Economic Club of New York, 1964–65. Mem., Nat. Acad. of Engrg, USA, 1969. Hon. DSc: Rensselaer Polytechnic Inst., 1958; Drexel Inst. of Technology, 1962; Hon. LLD: Manchester, 1964; California State Colleges, 1965; Millikin Univ., Illinois, 1967; Wesleyan Univ., Middletown, Conn, 1968; Hon. DEng, Colorado Sch. of Mines, 1971. Order of Francisco de Miranda, Venezuela, 1968; Comdr, Order of Oranje–Nassau, Netherlands, 1970. *Publications:* The Bright Key, 1965; Minding My Own Business, 1971; Here's What I Said, 1977; The Multinational Corporation, its Manners, Methods and Myths, 1977; The Long Road from Eureka, 1986; contribs to scientific journals. *Address:* 2 Lyall Mews, Belgravia, SW1X 8DJ. *Clubs:* Athenæum; Sunningdale; Blind Brook Country (New York).

SPALDING, Prof. (Dudley) Brian, MA, ScD; FRS 1983; FIMechE, FInstF; Professor of Heat Transfer, London University, since 1958, and Head, Computational Fluid Dynamics Unit, Imperial College of Science and Technology, since 1981; *b* New Malden, Surrey, 9 Jan. 1923; *s* of H. A. Spalding; *m* 1st, Eda Ilse-Lotte (*née* Goericke); two *s* two *d*; 2nd, Colleen (*née* King); two *s*. *Educ:* King's College Sch., Wimbledon; The Queen's Coll., Oxford; Pembroke Coll., Cambridge. BA (Oxon) 1944; MA (Cantab) 1948, PhD (Cantab) 1951. Bataafsche Petroleum Matschapij, 1944–45; Ministry of Supply, 1945–47; National Physical Laboratory, 1947–48; ICI Research Fellow at Cambridge Univ., 1948–50; Cambridge University Demonstrator in Engineering, 1950–54; Reader in Applied Heat, Imperial College of Science and Technology, 1954–58. Managing Director:

Combustion, Heat and Mass Transfer Ltd, 1970–; Concentration, Heat and Momentum Ltd, 1975–; Chm., CHAM of N America Inc., 1977–. *Publications:* Some Fundamentals of Combustion, 1955; (with E. H. Cole) Engineering Thermodynamics, 1958; Convective Mass Transfer, 1963; (with S. V. Patankar) Heat and Mass Transfer in Boundary Layers, 1967, rev. edn 1970; (co-author) Heat and Mass Transfer in Recirculating Flows, 1969; (with B. E. Launder) Mathematical Models of Turbulence, 1972; GENMIX: a general computer program for two-dimensional parabolic phenomena, 1978; Combustion and Mass Transfer: a textbook with multiple choice exercises for engineering students, 1979; (jtly) Heat Exchanger Design Handbook, 1982; Numerical Prediction of Flow, Heat Transfer, Turbulence and Combustion (selected works), 1983; numerous scientific papers. *Recreations:* squash, poetry. *Address:* Imperial College, Exhibition Road, SW7. *T:* 01–589 5111.

SPALDING, Rear-Adm. Ian Jaffery L.; *see* Lees-Spalding.

SPALDING, John Oliver, MA; Director and Chief Executive, Halifax Building Society, since 1982; *b* 4 Aug. 1924; *m* 1952. *Educ:* William Hulme's Grammar School, Manchester; Jesus College, Cambridge (MA). Admitted a Solicitor, 1952; service with Manchester Corporation and Hampshire CC, 1952–62; Assistant Solicitor, Halifax Building Soc., 1962–64; Head Office Solicitor, 1964–74; General Manager, 1970; Director, 1975; Deputy Chief General Manager, 1981; Chief Gen. Man., 1982. Mem., BSA Legal Adv. Panel, 1965–80; Halifax rep., Council of BSA, 1981; Chairman: Future Constitution and Powers of Bldg Socs Working Party, 1981–83; Calderdale Small Business Advice Centre (Mem., Calderdale Adv. Cttee); Mem., Farrand Cttee investigating Conveyancing, 1984. *Recreations:* boats and bird-watching. *Address:* Halifax Building Society, Trinity Road, Halifax HX1 2RG.

SPALDING, Julian, FMA; Director, Manchester City Art Galleries, since 1985; *b* 15 June 1947; *s* of Eric Peter Spalding and Margaret Grace Savager; *m* 1974, Frances (*née* Crabtree), author; one *s*. *Educ:* Chislehurst and Sidcup Grammar Sch. for Boys; Univ. of Nottingham (BA Hons Fine Art). Dip. Museums Assoc., 1973; FMA 1983. Art Assistant: Leicester Museum and Art Gall., 1970; Duham Light Infantry Mus. and Arts Centre, 1971; Sheffield City Art Galleries: Keeper, Mappin Art Gall., 1972–76; Dep. Dir, 1976–82; Dir of Arts, Sheffield City Council, 1982–85. Art Panel Mem., Arts Council of GB, 1978–82 (Chm., Exhibns Sub-Cttee, 1981–82 and 1986–); Founder, Art Galleries Assoc., 1976 (also Mem. Cttee); Dir, Guild of St George (John Ruskin's Guild), 1983– (Companion, 1978); Mem. Projects and Orgn Cttee, Crafts Council, 1985–. BBC broadcaster (talks and reviews). *Publications:* L. S. Lowry, 1979; Three Little Books on Painting, 1984; exhibition catalogues, including: Modern British Painting 1900–1960, 1975; Fragments against Ruin, 1981; Francis Davison, 1983; George Fullard Drawings, 1984; The Forgotten Fifties, 1984; contrib. Burlington Magazine. *Recreations:* painting, cycling, gardening. *Address:* Manchester City Art Galleries, Mosley Street, Manchester M2 3JL. *T:* 061–236 9422.

SPANKIE, Hugh Oliver; HM Diplomatic Service, retired 1986; *b* 11 Dec. 1936; *s* of late Col Hugh Vernon Spankie and Elizabeth Ursula (*née* Hills); *m* 1963, Anne Bridget Colville (marr. diss. 1981); one *s* one *d*. *Educ:* Tonbridge Sch. RM Officer, 1955–66; HM Diplomatic Service, 1967–: Helsinki, 1968–71; FCO, 1971–74; Helsinki, 1974–77; FCO and CSD, 1977–81; Counsellor, Copenhagen, 1981–85. *Address:* c/o Barclays Bank plc, 29 Stone Street, Cranbrook, Kent TN17 3HH.

SPANN, Keith, CB 1980; CVO 1977; Secretary, Premier's Department, Queensland, 1978–82; retired; *b* 8 Nov. 1922; *s* of late G. F. A. Spann; *m* 1946, Marjorie, *d* of W. R. Golding, CMG, MBE; three *s*. *Educ:* State High School, Gympie. Joined Queensland Public Service, 1938; Dept of Auditor-Gen., 1948–61; Sec. to Cabinet, 1961–64; Asst Under Sec., Premier's Dept, 1964–70, Under Sec., 1970–78. *Recreations:* fishing, golf, gemmology. *Address:* 2 Quaver Court, Bridgeman Downs, Queensland 4035, Australia.

SPANTON, (Harry) Merrik, OBE 1975; CEng, FIMinE; CBIM; Chairman, British Coal Enterprise Ltd (formerly NCB (Enterprise) Ltd), since 1984; *b* 27 Nov. 1924; *s* of late Henry Broadley Spanton and Edith Jane Spanton; *m* 1945, Mary Margaret Hawkins; one *s*. *Educ:* Eastbourne Coll.; Royal Sch. of Mines (BSc (Min) (Eng) 1945; ARSM). CEng, FIMinE 1957; CBIM 1979. Colliery Manager, 1950; Agent, 1954; Gp Man., 1956; Dep. Prodn Man., 1958; Dep. Prodn Dir, 1960; Asst Gen. Man., 1962; Gen. Man., 1964; Area Dir, 1967–80; Mem., NCB, 1980–85. Chairman: J. H. Sankey & Son, 1982–83; Coal Industry (Patents) Ltd, 1982–85; Director: British Mining Consultants Ltd, 1980– (Chm., 1981–83); Overseas Coal Develts Ltd, 1980–83; Compower, 1981–85 (Chm., 1984–85); NCB (Coal Products) Ltd, 1981–83; Coal Processing Consultants, 1981–83; Staveley Chemicals Ltd, 1981–83; NCB (Ancillaries) Ltd, 1982–85; British Fuel Co., 1983–; Berry Hill Investments Ltd, 1984–85; CIBT Insurance Services Ltd, 1984–85; CIBT Developments Ltd, 1984–85; Coal Industry Social Welfare Orgn, 1983–85. Member: W European Coal Producers Assoc., 1980–85; CBI Overseas Cttee, 1981–85. Vice-Pres., Coal Trade Benevolent Assoc., 1979– (Chm., 1978). *Publications:* articles in prof. jls. *Recreations:* travel, shooting. *Address:* 4 Roselands Gardens, Canterbury, Kent CT2 7LP. *T:* Canterbury 69356.

SPAREY, John Raymond, MA; Director (Association of Municipal Engineers), Institution of Civil Engineers, 1984–85; Secretary-General, International Federation of Municipal Engineers, since 1979; *b* 28 July 1924; *s* of late Henry Sparey and Lilian May (*née* Coles); *m* 1950, Audrie Kathleen, *d* of late Col E. J. W. Porter, OBE, TD, Portsmouth; two *s* one *d*. *Educ:* City of Bath Sch.; King's Coll., London; Trinity Coll., Cambridge (BA 1950, MA 1954). Royal Naval Scientific Service, 1944–47; Asst Secretary, Assoc. of Certified Accountants, 1952–69; Royal Institution of Chartered Surveyors: Dep. Sec., 1969–70; Sec. for Educn and Membership, 1970–74; Sec., Planning and Development Div., 1976; Sec., Instn of Municipal Engrs, 1977–84. *Recreations:* gardening, sailing. *Address:* Oakdene, 21 Broomfield Ride, Oxshott KT22 0LP. *T:* Oxshott 2587. *Clubs:* Reform; Seaview Yacht (Seaview, IoW).

SPARK, Mrs Muriel Sarah, OBE 1967; writer; *b* Edinburgh; *d* of Bernard Camberg and Sarah Elizabeth Maud (*née* Uezzell); *m* 1937 (marr. diss.); one *s*. *Educ:* James Gillespie's School for Girls, Edinburgh; Heriot Watt Coll., Edinburgh. FO, 1944; General Secretary, The Poetry Society, Editor, The Poetry Review, 1947–49. FRSL 1963. Hon. Mem., Amer. Acad. of Arts and Letters, 1978. Hon. DLitt Strathclyde, 1971. *Publications: critical and biographical:* (ed jtly) Tribute to Wordsworth, 1950; (ed) Selected Poems of Emily Brontë, 1952; Child of Light: a Reassessment of Mary Shelley, 1951; (ed jtly) My Best Mary: the letters of Mary Shelley, 1953; John Masefield, 1953; (joint) Emily Brontë: her Life and Work, 1953; (ed) The Brontë Letters, 1954; (ed jointly) Letters of John Henry Newman, 1957; *poems:* The Fanfarlo and Other Verse, 1952; Collected Poems I, 1967; Going Up to Sotheby's and other poems, 1982; *fiction:* The Comforters, 1957; Robinson, 1958; The Go-Away Bird, 1958; Memento Mori, 1959 (adapted for stage, 1964); The Ballad of Peckham Rye, 1960 (Italia prize, for dramatic radio, 1962); The Bachelors, 1960; Voices at Play, 1961; The Prime of Miss Jean Brodie, 1961 (adapted for stage, 1966, filmed 1969, and BBC TV, 1978); Doctors of Philosophy (play), 1963; The Girls of Slender Means, 1963 (adapted for radio, 1964, and BBC TV, 1975); The Mandelbaum Gate, 1965 (James Tait Black Memorial Prize); Collected Stories I, 1967; The Public Image, 1968; The Very Fine Clock (for children), 1969; The Driver's Seat, 1970 (filmed 1974); Not to Disturb, 1971; The Hothouse by the East River, 1973; The Abbess of Crewe, 1974 (filmed 1977); The Takeover, 1976; Territorial Rights, 1979; Loitering with Intent, 1981; Bang-Bang You're Dead and other stories, 1982; The Only Problem, 1984; The Stories of Muriel Spark, 1985. *Recreations:* reading, travel. *Address:* c/o Macmillan & Co. Ltd, Little Essex Street, WC2.

SPARKES, Sir Robert Lyndley, Kt 1979; State President, National Party of Australia (formerly Country Party), Queensland, since 1970; Managing Partner, Lyndley Pastoral Co., since 1974; *b* 30 May 1929; *s* of late Sir James Sparkes, Jandowae, Queensland; *m* 1953, June, *d* of M. Morgan; two *s*. *Educ:* Southport Sch., Queensland. Chairman: National Party (formerly Country Party) Lands Cttee, Queensland, 1966–; NPA Nominees Pty Ltd; Wambo Shire Council, 1967– (Mem., 1952–55 and 1964–). *Recreation:* reading. *Address:* Dundonald, PO Box 117, Jandowae, Queensland 4410, Australia. *T:* (074) 68 5196.

SPARKS, Arthur Charles, BSc (Econ); Under-Secretary, Ministry of Agriculture, Fisheries and Food, 1959–74; *b* 1914; *s* of late Charles Herbert and Kate Dorothy Sparks; *m* 1939, Betty Joan (*d* 1978), *d* of late Harry Oswald and Lilian Mary Simmons; three *d*. *Educ:* Selhurst Grammar Sch.; London School of Economics. Clerk, Ministry of Agriculture and Fisheries, 1931; Administrative Grade, 1936; National Fire Service, 1942–44; Principal Private Secretary to Minister of Agriculture and Fisheries, 1946–47; Asst Secretary, Ministry of Agriculture and Fisheries, 1947–49 and 1951–59; Asst Secretary, Treasury, 1949–51. Chm., Internat. Wheat Council, 1968–69. *Recreations:* reading, walking. *Address:* 2 Stratton Close, Merton Park, SW19 3JF. *T:* 01–542 4827.

SPARKS, Rev. Hedley Frederick Davis, DD Oxon, 1949; FBA 1959; ATCL 1927; Oriel Professor of the Interpretation of Holy Scripture, University of Oxford, 1952–76; *b* 14 Nov. 1908; *s* of late Rev. Frederick Sparks and late Blanche Barnes Sparks (formerly Jackson); *m* 1953, Margaret Joan, *d* of late C. H. Davy; two *s* one *d*. *Educ:* St Edmund's Sch., Canterbury; BNC, Oxford; Ripon Hall, Oxford. Hon. DD: St Andrews, 1963; Birmingham, 1983. Hon. Fellow, Oriel Coll., Oxford, 1980. *Publications:* The Old Testament in the Christian Church, 1944; The Formation of the New Testament, 1952; A Synopsis of the Gospels, part I: The Synoptic Gospels with the Johannine Parallels, 1964, 2nd edn 1970; part II: The Gospel according to St John with the Synoptic Parallels, 1974, combined volume edn, 1977; *Editor:* The Apocryphal Old Testament, 1984; *Joint Editor:* Novum Testamentum Domini Nostri Iesu Christi Latine secundum editionem Sancti Hieronymi, Part ii, fasc. 5, 1937, fasc. 6, 1939, fasc. 7, 1941, Part iii, fasc. 2, 1949, fasc. 3, 1953; Biblia Sacra iuxta Vulgatam versionem, 1969, 3rd edn 1983; *Contributor:* The Bible in its Ancient and English Versions, 1940, 2nd edn 1954; Studies in the Gospels, 1955; The Cambridge History of the Bible, vol. 1, 1970, 2nd edn, 1975. *Recreations:* music and railways. *Address:* 14 Longport, Canterbury, Kent. *T:* Canterbury 66265.

SPARROW, (Albert) Charles; QC 1966; DL; barrister; *b* Kasauli, India, 16 Sept. 1925; *e s* of Captain Charles Thomas Sparrow, sometime Essex Regt, and Antonia Sparrow; *m* 1949, Edith Rosalie Taylor (*d* 1985); two *s* one *d*. *Educ:* Royal Grammar Sch., Colchester. Served Civil Defence, 1939–43; joined Army, 1943; posted as cadet to India, commnd into Royal Signals and served in Far East, 1944–47; OC, GHQ Signals, Simla, 1947. Admitted to Gray's Inn, 1947 (Holker Senior Scholar, Atkin Scholar, Lee Prizeman and Richards Prizeman); called to Bar, 1950, Master of the Bench, 1976; LLB London Univ., 1951; admitted to Lincoln's Inn, 1967; in practice in Chancery and before Parliament, 1950–. Member: General Council of the Bar, 1969–73; Senate of the Four Inns of Court, 1970–73; Incorp. Council of Law Reporting, 1977–83. Hon. Legal Adviser to Council for British Archæology (concerned notably with legal protection of antiquities and reform of treasure trove; produced two draft Antiquities Bills), 1966–. Chairman: independent Panel of Inquiry for affairs of RSPCA, 1973–74; independent Cttee of Inquiry for Girl Guides Rally at Crystal Palace, 1985. FSA 1972; Pres., Essex Archaeological Soc., 1975–78. Chm., Stock Branch, British Legion, 1970–75. Advr to assocs of customary freemen, 1972–; Hon. Counsellor to Freemen of England, 1978; Freeman, City of London; Hon. Life Mem., Gild of Freemen of City of York. OStJ 1982; Comr for Essex, St John Ambulance Bde, 1983–. DL Essex, 1985. *Recreation:* Romano-British archæology. *Address:* 13 Old Square, Lincoln's Inn, WC2A 3UA. *T:* 01–242 6105; Croyde Lodge, Stock, Essex.

SPARROW, Bryan; HM Diplomatic Service; Consul-General, Toronto, since 1985; *b* 8 June 1933; *m* 1958, Fiona Mary Mylechreest; one *s* one *d*. *Educ:* Hemel Hempstead Grammar Sch.; Pembroke Coll., Oxford (BA Hons). Served Army, 1951–53. Belgrade, 1958–61; FO, 1961–64; Moscow, 1964–66; Tunis, 1967–68; Casablanca, 1968–70; FO, 1970–72; Kinshasa, 1972–76; Prague, 1976–78; Counsellor (Commercial), Belgrade, 1978–81; Ambassador, United Republic of Cameroon, 1981–84, and concurrently to Republic of Equatorial Guinea and Central African Republic, 1982–84; Canadian Nat. Defence Coll., 1984–85. *Recreations:* fishing, gardening, travel. *Address:* c/o Foreign and Commonwealth Office, SW1; 35 Linton Street, N1.

SPARROW, Charles; *see* Sparrow, A. C.

SPARROW, Sir John, Kt 1984; FCA; Director, Morgan Grenfell Group PLC (formerly Morgan Grenfell Holdings), since 1971 (on secondment, 1982–83); Chairman: Morgan Grenfell Asset Management Ltd, since 1985; Morgan Grenfell Laurie Holdings Ltd, since 1985; *b* 4 June 1933; *s* of Richard A. and Winifred R. Sparrow; *m* 1967, Cynthia Whitehouse. *Educ:* Stationers' Company's School; London School of Economics (BSc Econ). FCA 1957. With Rawlinson & Hunter, Chartered Accountants, 1954–59; Ford Motor Co. Ltd, 1960; AEI-Hotpoint Ltd, 1960–63; United Leasing Corporation, 1963–64; Morgan Grenfell Group (formerly Morgan Grenfell & Co.), 1964–. Director: Coalite Group plc, 1974–82, 1984–; Peterborough Develt Corp., 1981–; Short Brothers plc, 1984– (Dep. Chm., 1985–); Mem., London Adv. Bd, National and Provincial Building Society, 1986–. Seconded as Head of Central Policy Review Staff, Cabinet Office, 1982–83. Vice-Chm., Governors, LSE, 1984–. *Recreations:* cricket, crosswords, horse-racing. *Address:* 46 New Broad Street, EC2M 1NB. *Club:* MCC.

SPARROW, John Hanbury Angus, OBE 1946; Warden of All Souls College, Oxford, 1952–77; *b* New Oxley, near Wolverhampton, 13 Nov. 1906; *e s* of I. S. Sparrow and Margaret Macgregor; unmarried. *Educ:* Winchester (Scholar); New Coll., Oxford (Scholar). 1st Class, Hon. Mods, 1927, 1st Class, Lit Hum, 1929; Fellow of All Souls Coll., 1929 (re-elected 1937, 1946); Chancellor's Prize for Latin Verse, 1929; Eldon Scholar, 1929; called to Bar, Middle Temple, 1931; practised in Chancery Division, 1931–39; enlisted in Oxford and Bucks LI, 1939; Commnd Coldstream Guards, 1940; Military Asst to Lt-Gen. Sir H. C. B. Wemyss in War Office and on Military Mission in Washington, Feb.-Dec. 1941; rejoined regt in England, 1942; DAAG and AAG, War Office, 1942–45; resumed practice at Bar, 1946; ceased to practise on appointment as Warden of All Souls Coll., 1952; Hon. Bencher, Middle Temple, 1952; Fellow of Winchester Coll., 1951–81; Hon. Fellow, New Coll., 1956. Hon. DLitt, Univ. of Warwick, 1967. *Publications:* various; mostly reviews and essays in periodicals, some of which were collected in Independent Essays, 1963, and Controversial Essays, 1966; Half-lines and Repetitions in Virgil, 1931; Sense and Poetry: essays on the place of meaning in contemporary verse, 1934; Mark Pattison and the Idea of a University (Clark Lectures), 1967; After the Assassination, 1968; Visible Words (Sandars Lectures), 1969; (with A. Perosa) Renaissance Latin Verse: an anthology, 1979; Grave Epigrams and Other Verses, 1981; Words on the Air, 1981; (ed with John Gere) Geoffrey Madan's Notebooks, 1981; Leaves from a Victorian Diary, 1985. *Address:* Beechwood House, Iffley Turn, Oxford. *Clubs:* Garrick, Reform, Beefsteak.

SPAWFORTH, David Meredith, MA; Headmaster, Merchiston Castle School, Edinburgh, since April 1981; *b* 2 Jan. 1938; *s* of Lawrence and Gwen Spawforth, Wakefield, Yorks; *m* 1963, Yvonne Mary Gude; one *s* one *d. Educ:* Silcoates School; Hertford Coll., Oxford (Heath Harrison Travelling Schol.; MA ModLang). Assistant Master: Winchester Coll., 1961–64; Wellington Coll., 1964–80; Housemaster, Wellington Coll., 1968–80. British Petroleum Education Fellow, Keble Coll., Oxford, 1977. *Publications:* articles in Conference and Teaching about Europe. *Recreations:* gardening, France, history, theatre, walking. *Address:* Castle Gates, Merchiston Castle School, Colinton, Edinburgh EH13 0PU. *T:* 031–441 3468.

SPEAKMAN-PITT, William, VC 1951; *b* 21 Sept. 1927; *m* 1st, 1956, Rachel Snitch; one *s*; 2nd, Jill; one *d. Educ:* Wellington Road Senior Boys' Sch., Altrincham. Entered Army as Private. Served Korean War, 1950–53 (VC), King's Own Scottish Borderers. *Recreations:* swimming, and ski-ing.

SPEAR, Harold Cumming, CBE 1976; Member, Electricity Council, 1972–76; *b* 26 Oct. 1909; *yr s* of late Rev. Edwin A. and Elizabeth Spear; *m* 1935, Gwendolen (*née* Richards); one *s* one *d. Educ:* Kingswood Sch., Bath. Asst to Employment Manager, Gramophone Co. Ltd, 1928–33; Labour and Welfare Supervisor, Mitcham Works Ltd, 1933–35; Employment Supervisor, Hoover Ltd, 1935–38; Personnel Manager, Sperry Gyroscope Co. Ltd, 1938–40; appts with British Overseas Airways Corp., finally as Chief Personnel Officer, 1941–59; Dir of Personnel Management, Central Electricity Generating Bd, 1959–72; Mem., Central Arbitration Cttee, 1976–85. Pres., Inst. of Personnel Management, 1969–71; CIPM. *Recreation:* golf. *Address:* The Almonry, Newlands, Pershore, Worcs WR10 1BW. *Clubs:* Roehampton; Cotswold Hills Golf.

SPEAR, Ruskin, CBE 1979; RA 1954 (ARA 1944); artist; *b* 30 June 1911; *s* of Augustus and Jane Spear; *m* 1935, Mary Hill; one *s. Educ:* Brook Green School; Hammersmith School of Art; Royal College of Art, Kensington, under Sir William Rothenstein. Diploma, 1934; first exhibited Royal Academy, 1932; elected London Group, 1942; President London Group, 1949–50; Visiting teacher, Royal College of Art, 1952–77. Pictures purchased by Chantrey Bequest, Contemporary Art Society, Arts Council of Great Britain, and British Council. Exhibited work in Pushkin Museum, Moscow, 1957; has also exhibited in Paris, USA, Belgium, S Africa, Australia, NZ. Commissions include: Altar Piece for RAF Memorial Church, St Clement Danes, 1959; four mural panels for P&O Liner Canberra. Portraits include: Lord Adrian; Herbert Butterfield; Sir Stewart Duke-Elder; Sir Laurence Olivier as Macbeth (Stratford Memorial Theatre); Lord Chandos; Sir Ian Jacob; Sir Robin Darwin; Miss Ruth Cohen; Sir Eric Ashby; S. S. Eriks, KBE; Dr Ramsey, Archbishop of Canterbury; Sir Aubrey Lewis; Arthur Armitage; 5th Duke of Westminster; Sir Hugh Greene; Lord Goodman; Dr Charles Bosanquet; Sir James Tait; Sir John Mellor; Sir Geoffrey Taylor; Sir Peter Allen; Sir Maurice Bridgemen; Lord Butler of Saffron Walden; Sir Geoffrey Howe; Sir David Willcocks, CBE, MC; Prof. Dame Sheila Sherlock; Sir Cyril Clarke; Edward Ardizzone; Lucien Ercolani; Sir Ralph Richardson as Falstaff for NT (posthumous); portraits in National Portrait Gallery: Francis Bacon; Lord Wilson of Rievaulx; Lord Redcliffe-Maud; Sir Alan Herbert; self-portrait. Visiting teacher, RCA, until 1976. *Relevant publication:* Ruskin Spear, by Mervyn Levy, 1985. *Address:* 60 British Grove, Hammersmith, W4. *T:* 01–741 2894.

SPEAR, Prof. Walter Eric, PhD, DSc; FRS 1980, FRSE; Harris Professor of Physics, University of Dundee, since 1968; *b* 20 Jan. 1921; *s* of David and Eva Spear; *m* 1952, Hilda Doris King; two *d. Educ:* Musterschule, Frankfurt/Main; Univ. of London (BSc 1947, PhD 1950, DSc 1967). Lecturer, 1953, Reader, 1967, in Physics, Univ. of Leicester; Vis. Professor, Purdue Univ., 1957–58. FRSE 1972; FInstP 1962. Max Born Prize and Medal, 1977; Europhysics Prize, 1977; Makdougal-Brisbane Medal, RSE, 1981. *Publications:* numerous research papers on electronic and transport properties in crystalline solids, liquids and amorphous semiconductors. *Recreations:* literature, music (particularly chamber music), languages. *Address:* Carnegie Laboratory of Physics, University of Dundee, Dundee DD1 4HN. *T:* Dundee 23181; 323 Blackness Road, Dundee DD2 1SH. *T:* Dundee 67649.

SPEARING, George David; Technical Adviser, Institution of Highways and Transportation, 1984–86, retired; *b* 16 Dec. 1927; *s* of late George Thomas and Edith Lydia Anna Spearing; *m* 1951, Josephine Mary Newbould; two *s* one *d. Educ:* Rotherham Grammar Sch.; Sheffield Univ. BEng; MICE, FIHE. RAF, Airfield Construction Br., 1948. Asst Divl Surveyor, Somerset CC, 1951; Asst Civil Engr, W Riding of Yorks CC, 1953; Asst Engr, MoT, 1957; Supt. Engr, Midland Road Construction Unit, 1967; Asst Chief Engr, MoT, 1969; Regional Controller (Roads and Transportation), West Midlands, 1972; Dep. Chief Engr, DoE, 1973; Under Sec., DoE, 1974; Under Sec., Dept of Transport, and Dir Highways Planning and Management, 1974–78; Regional Dir, Eastern Reg., Depts of the Environment and Transport, and Chm., E Anglia Regional Bd, 1978–83. *Publications:* papers in Proc. Instn CE and Jl Instn HE. *Address:* 23 Colburn Avenue, Caterham, Surrey CR3 6HW. *T:* Caterham 47472.

SPEARING, Nigel John; MP (Lab) Newham South, since May 1974; *b* 8 Oct. 1930; *s* of late Austen and of May Spearing; *m* 1956, Wendy, *d* of Percy and Molly Newman, Newport, Mon; one *s* two *d. Educ:* Latymer Upper School, Hammersmith. Ranks and commission, Royal Signals, 1950–52; St Catharine's Coll., Cambridge, 1953–56. Tutor, Wandsworth School, 1956–68 (Sen. Geography Master, 1967–68); Director, Thameside Research and Development Group, Inst. of Community Studies, 1968–69; Housemaster, Elliott School, Putney, 1969–70. Chairman: Barons Court Labour Party, 1961–63; Hammersmith Local Govt Cttee of the Labour Party, 1966–68. Contested (Lab) Warwick and Leamington, 1964. MP (Lab) Acton, 1970–74; Secretary: Parly Lab. Party Educn Gp, 1971–74; Parly Inland Waterways Gp, 1970–74; Member Select Cttee: Overseas Develt, 1973–74, 1977–79; Members' Interests, 1974–75; Procedure, 1975–79; EEC Legislation, 1979– (Chm., 1983–); Foreign and Commonwealth Affairs, 1980–86. Vice-Pres., River Thames Soc.; Pres., Socialist Envt and Resources Assoc., 1977–; Chm., British Anti-Common Market Campaign, 1977–83. Co-opted Mem. GLC Cttees, 1966–73. *Publication:* The Thames Barrier-Barrage Controversy (Inst. of Community Studies), 1969. *Recreations:* rowing, reading. *Address:* House of Commons, SW1. *T:* 01–219 3000.

SPEARMAN, Sir Alexander Young Richard Mainwaring, 5th Bt *cr* 1840; *b* 3 Feb. 1969; *s* of Sir Alexander Bowyer Spearman, 4th Bt, and Martha, *d* of John Green, Naauwpoort, S Africa; *S* father, 1977. *Heir: uncle* Dr Richard Ian Campbell Spearman, FLS, FZS, *b* 14 Aug. 1926. *Address:* Windwards, Klein Constantia Road, Constantia, Cape Town, 7800, S Africa.

SPEARMAN, Clement, CBE 1979; HM Diplomatic Service, retired; Ambassador and Consul-General to the Dominican Republic, 1975–79; *b* 10 Sept. 1919; *y s* of late Edward and Clara Spearman; *m* 1950, Olwen Regina Morgan; one *s* two *d. Educ:* Cardiff High School. RN (Air Arm), 1942–46. Entered Foreign (subseq. Diplomatic) Service, 1947; 3rd Sec., Brussels, 1948–49; 2nd Sec., FO, 1949–51; HM Consul, Skoplje, 1951–53; FO, 1953–56; 1st Sec., Buenos Aires, 1956–60; FO, 1960–62; Counsellor, CENTO, Ankara, 1962–65; Reykjavik, 1965–69; FCO, 1969–71; Manila, 1971–74; Toronto, 1974–75. *Recreations:* tennis, swimming. *Address:* 56 Riverview Gardens, SW13 9QZ. *T:* 01–748 9339. *Clubs:* Naval, Roehampton.

SPECTOR, Prof. Roy Geoffrey, MD, PhD; FRCP, FRCPath; Professor of Applied Pharmacology, Guy's Hospital Medical School, since 1972; Chairman, Division of Pharmacology, United Medical and Dental Schools of Guy's and St Thomas's Hospitals, since 1985; *b* 27 Aug. 1931; *s* of Paul Spector and Esther Cohen; *m* 1960, Evie Joan Freeman (marr. diss. 1979); two *s* one *d. Educ:* Roundhay Sch., Leeds; Sch. of Medicine, Leeds Univ. (MB, ChB, MD); PhD Lond 1964, Dip. in Biochem. 1966. FRCP 1971; FRCPath 1976; FRSM. Lectr in Paediatric Res. Unit, Guy's Hosp., 1961–67; Guy's Hosp. Medical School: Reader in Pharmacology, 1968–71; Sub Dean for Admissions, 1975–. Vis. Prof. in Clin. Pharmacology, West China Med. Univ., Chengdu, 1986–87. Vice Chm., British Univs' Film Council, 1976–. *Publications:* (jtly) The Nerve Cell, 1964, 2nd edn 1986; (jtly) Clinical Pharmacology in Dentistry, 1975, 4th edn 1985; (jtly) Mechanisms in Pharmacology and Therapeutics, 1976; (jtly) Aids to Pharmacology, 1980, 2nd edn 1986; (jtly) Textbook of Clinical Pharmacology, 1981, 2nd edn 1986; (jtly) Aids to Clinical Pharmacology and Therapeutics, 1984; (jtly) Common Drug Treatments in Psychiatry, 1984; Catechism in Clinical Pharmacology Therapeutics, 1986; contribs to jls on pathology, gen. science, and applied pharmacology. *Recreations:* music, walking. *Address:* Department of Pharmacology, United Medical Schools, Guy's Hospital Campus, London Bridge, SE1 9RT. *T:* 01–407 7600, ext. 3651.

SPEDDING, Prof. Colin Raymond William; Professor of Agriculture Systems, since 1975, and Pro-Vice-Chancellor since 1986, University of Reading; *b* 22 March 1925; *s* of Robert Kewley Spedding and Ilynn Spedding; *m* 1952, Betty Noreen George; one *s* one *d* (and one *s* decd). *Educ:* London Univ. (External) (BSc 1951; MSc 1953; PhD 1955; DSc 1967). FIBiol 1967, CBiol 1984; FRASE 1984; FIHort 1986. Ilford Ltd, 1940–43; RNVR, 1943–46; Allen & Hanbury, 1947; Grassland Research Institute: joined 1949; Head of Ecology Div., 1967–75; Assit Dir, 1969–72; Dep. Dir, 1972–75; Univ. of Reading: Visiting, then part-time Prof. of Agric. Systems, 1970–75; Head of Dept of Agric. and Horticl., 1975–83; Dean, Faculty of Agriculture and Food, 1983–86; Dir, Centre for Agricl. Strategy, 1981–. Mem., Programme Cttee, Internat. Livestock Centre for Africa, Addis Ababa, 1976–80, Vice Chm., 1980–83; Special Advr, H of C Select Cttee on Agric., 1980–83. President: European Assoc. of Animal Production Study Commn for Sheep and Goat Production, 1970–76; British Soc. for Animal Production, 1979–80; Chm., Agricl Scis Div., Inst. Biol., 1980. Governor, Royal Agricl Coll., 1982–; Vice-Chm. of Governors, Animal and Grassland Res. Inst., 1985–. Editor, Agricultural Systems, 1976–. *Publications:* Sheep Production and Grazing Management, 1965, 2nd edn 1970; Grassland Ecology, 1971; (ed with E. C. Diekmahns) Grasses and Legumes in British Agriculture, 1972; The Biology of Agriculture Systems, 1975; An Introduction to Agricultural Systems, 1979; (ed) Vegetable Productivity, 1981; (with J. M. Walsingham and A. M. Hoxey) Biological Efficiency in Agriculture, 1981; (ed) Fream's Agriculture, 1983; numerous sci papers in learned jls. *Address:* Vine Cottage, Orchard Road, Hurst, Berks RG10 0SD. *Clubs:* Athenæum, Farmers'.

SPEDDING, David Rolland, CVO 1984; OBE 1980; HM Diplomatic Service; Counsellor, Foreign and Commonwealth Office, since 1987; *b* 7 March 1943; *s* of Lt Col Carlisle Montagu Rodney Spedding and Gwynfydd Joan Llewellyn; *m* 1970, Gillian Leslie Kinnear; two *s. Educ:* Sherborne School; Hertford College, Oxford (MA). Third Sec., FO, 1967; Middle East Centre for Arabic Studies, 1968; Second Sec., Beirut, 1970; Santiago, 1972; First Sec., FCO, 1974; Abu Dhabi, 1978; FCO, 1981–83; Counsellor, Amman, 1983–86. *Recreations:* golf, tennis, reading, walking. *Address:* c/o Foreign and Commonwealth Office, King Charles Street, SW1A 2AH. *Clubs:* Royal Commonwealth Society; Huntercombe Golf.

SPEED, (Herbert) Keith, RD 1967; MP (C) Ashford, since Oct. 1974; *b* 11 March 1934; *s* of late Herbert Victor Speed and of Dorothy Barbara (*née* Mumford); *m* 1961, Peggy Voss Clarke; two *s* one *d* (and one *s* decd). *Educ:* Greenhill Sch., Evesham; Bedford Modern Sch.; RNC, Dartmouth and Greenwich. Officer, RN, 1947–56; Lt-Comdr RNR, 1964–79. Sales Man., Amos (Electronics) Ltd, 1957–60; Marketing Man., Plysu Products Ltd, 1960–65; Officer, Conservative Res. Dept, 1965–68. MP (C) Meriden, March 1968–Feb. 1974; An Asst Govt Whip, 1970–71; a Lord Comr of HM Treasury, 1971–72; Parly Under-Sec. of State, DoE, 1972–74; Opposition spokesman on local govt, 1976–77, on home affairs, 1977–79; Parly Under Sec. of State for Defence for RN, 1979–81; Mem., Parly Select Cttee on Defence, 1983–. Parly Consultant, Professional Assoc. of Teachers, 1982–. Chm., Westminster Communications Ltd, 1982–; Dir, Folkestone and District Water Co., 1986–. *Publications:* Blue Print for Britain, 1965; Sea Change, 1982; contribs to various political and defence jls. *Recreations:* classical music, motor cycling, reading. *Address:* Strood House, Rolvenden, Cranbrook, Kent.

SPEED, Sir Robert (William Arney), Kt 1954; CB 1946; QC 1963; Counsel to the Speaker, 1960–80; *b* 1905; *s* of late Sir Edwin Arney Speed; *m* 1929, Phyllis, *d* of Rev. P. Armitage; one *s* one *d. Educ:* Rugby; Trinity College, Cambridge. Called to Bar, Inner Temple, 1928; Bencher, 1961; Principal Assistant Solicitor, Office of HM Procurator-General and Treasury Solicitor, 1945–48; Solicitor to the Board of Trade, 1948–60. *Address:* Upper Culham, Wargrave, Berks RG10 8NR. *T:* Henley-on-Thames 574271. *Club:* United Oxford & Cambridge University.

SPEELMAN, Sir Cornelis Jacob, 8th Bt *cr* 1686; BA; *b* 17 March 1917; *s* of Sir Cornelis Jacob Speelman, 7th Bt and Maria Catharina Helena, Castendijk; *S* father, 1949; *m* 1972, Julia Mona Le Besque (*d* 1978); *m* 1986, Irene Agnes van Leeuwen; two step *c.* Education Dept, Royal Dutch Army, 1947–49; with The Shell Company (Marketing Service Dept), 1950. Student, Univ. of Western Australia, 1952; formerly Master of Modern Languages at Clifton Coll., Geelong Grammar Sch.; Exeter Tutorial Coll. *Address:* Lake's Edge Villas No 3, Wembley, Perth, WA, Australia.

SPEIGHT, Hon. Sir Graham (Davies), Kt 1983; Judge of the High Court of New Zealand, since 1966; Justice of Appeal, Fiji, since 1980; Chief Justice of the Cook Islands, since 1982; *b* 21 July 1921; *s* of Henry Baxter and Anna May Speight; *m* 1947, Elisabeth Muriel Booth; one *s* one *d. Educ:* Auckland Grammar Sch.; Univ. of Auckland (LLB). Qualified barrister and solicitor, 1942; served 2nd NZ Expeditionary Force, Middle East and Italy, 1943–46; Lieut Royal NZ Artillery, 1943–46; Aide-de-Camp, General B. C. Freyberg, VC (later 1st Baron Freyberg), 1944–45; practising barrister, 1946–66. Chairman: Winston Churchill Meml Trust, NZ; Eden Park Bd. Chancellor, Univ. of Auckland, 1973–79; Hon. LLD Auckland, 1983. *Publication:* (jt ed) Adams: Criminal Law in New Zealand, 1986. *Recreations:* golf, yachting. *Address:* 94A Arney Road,

Auckland 5, New Zealand. *T:* 544 464. *Clubs:* Northern, Auckland Golf, Royal New Zealand Yacht Squadron (Auckland) (Cdre 1961–63).

SPEIGHT, Johnny; writer; *b* 2 June 1920; *s* of John and Johanna Speight; *m* 1956, Constance Beatrice Barrett; two *s* one *d. Educ:* St Helen's RC School. Has written for: Arthur Haynes Show; Morecambe and Wise Show; Peter Sellers; Till Death Us Do Part (Screenwriters Guild Award, 1966, 1967, 1968); The Lady is a Tramp (Pye TV Award, 1982); In Sickness and in Health; with Ray Galton: Tea Ladies, 1979; Spooner's Patch, 1979. *Plays:* Compartment (Screenwriters Guild Award, 1962); Playmates; Salesman; Knackers Yard; If There Weren't any Blacks You Would Have to Invent Them (Prague Festival Award, 1969). Evening Standard Drama Award for Best Comedy. *Publications:* It Stands to Reason, 1974; The Thoughts of Chairman Alf, 1974; various scripts. *Recreation:* golf. *Address:* Fouracres, Heronsgate, Chorleywood, Herts. *T:* Chorleywood 2463. *Clubs:* 21; White Elephant; Stage Golf, Variety Golf, Pinner Hill Golf.

SPEIR, Sir Rupert (Malise), Kt 1964; *b* 10 Sept. 1910; *y s* of late Guy Thomas Speir and late Mary Lucy Fletcher, of Saltoun. *Educ:* Eton Coll.; Pembroke Coll., Cambridge (BA). Admitted Solicitor, 1936. Special Mem., Hops Marketing Board, 1958. Served in Army throughout War of 1939–45; commissioned in Intelligence Corps, Sept. 1939; retired with rank of Lt-Col, 1945. Contested (C) Linlithgow, 1945, Leek, 1950; MP (C) Hexham Div. of Northumberland, 1951–66, retired. Sponsor of: Litter Act, 1958; Noise Abatement Act, 1960; Local Government (Financial Provisions) Act, 1963; Parliamentary Private Secretary: to Minister of State for Foreign Affairs and to Parly Sec., CRO, 1956–59; to Parly and Fin. Sec., Admty and to Civil Lord of Admty, 1952–56. Hon. Fellow, Inst. of Public Cleansing; Vice-Pres., Keep Britain Tidy Group. *Recreations:* golf, shooting. *Address:* Birtley Hall, Hexham, Northumberland. *T:* Bellingham 30275.

SPEIRS, Graham Hamilton; Hon. Research Fellow, Faculty of Social Sciences, University of Edinburgh, since 1986; *b* 9 Jan. 1927; *s* of Graham Mushet Speirs and Jane (*née* McChesney) *m* 1954, Myra Reid (*née* Mills); one *s* one *d. Educ:* High Sch. of Glasgow Glasgow Univ. (MA 1950, LLB 1952). Anderson, Young and Dickson, Writers, Glasgow, 1950–52; Legal Asst, Dunbarton CC, 1952–54; Sen. Legal Asst, Stirling CC, 1954–59; Depute Sec., then Sec., Assoc. of County Councils in Scotland, 1959–75; Sec.; Convention of Scottish Local Authorities, 1975–86, retd. Sec. Gen., Council of European Municipalities (British Section), 1980–84. Mem., UK delegn to Economic and Social Cttee of EC, 1986–. Mem. Bd, Bield Housing Assoc., 1986–. *Recreation:* golf. *Address:* 3 Dirleton Avenue, North Berwick EH39 4AX. *T:* North Berwick 2801. *Clubs:* Royal Scottish Automobile (Glasgow); North Berwick Golf (North Berwick).

SPEIRS, William James McLaren; HM Diplomatic Service, retired; Adviser, Sultanate of Oman; *b* 22 Nov. 1924; *s* of Alec McLaren Speirs and Olivia (*née* Petersen) *m* 1952, Jane Downing; two *s* one *d* (and one *d* decd). *Educ:* Clifton Coll.; Jesus Coll., Cambridge. Served Royal Signals, 1943–47; ADC to Governor of Singapore, 1946–47. HM Diplomatic Service, 1948–79: Rangoon, 1950; Jakarta, 1953; Berlin, 1957; Munich, 1963; Tel Aviv, 1970; Counsellor, FCO, 1979. Gp Security Adviser, Gallaher Ltd, 1979–85. *Recreations:* walking, collecting topographical books. *Address:* 24 Kingswood Firs, Grayshott, Hindhead, Surrey GU26 6ET. *T:* Hindhead 4112. *Clubs:* Army and Navy, Special Forces.

SPELLER, Antony; MP (C) North Devon, since 1979; *b* 12 June 1929; *s* of late John and Ethel Speller; *m* 1960, Maureen R. McLellan; one *s* one *d. Educ:* Univ. of London (BScEcon); Univ. of Exeter (BA Social Studies); FHCIMA; MIRT. Subaltern, Devonshire Regt, 1951; Major, Devonshire Regt TA, 1965. Nigerian Produce Marketing Boards, 1951; Director: Atlas Ltd, Nigeria, 1953; Copyshops of SW England, 1963–. Councillor, Exeter CC, 1963–74 (Chairman: Public Works Cttee, 1965–69; Education Cttee, 1971–72). Mem., Select Cttee on Energy, 1982–; Chm., Parly Liaison Cttee for Alternative Energy Strategies, 1983; Pres., Catering Industry Liaison Cttee, 1982–. Chm., W Country Cons. MPs. *Address:* House of Commons, SW1A 0AA. *T:* 01–219 4589. *Clubs:* Carlton; North Devon (Barnstaple); Lagos Motor Boat (Nigeria).

SPELLER, Maj.-Gen. Norman Henry, CB 1976; Government Relations Adviser, ICL, 1976–86, retired; *b* 5 March 1921; *s* of late Col Norman Speller and Emily Florence Speller (*née* Lambert); *m* 1950, Barbara Eleanor (*née* Earle); two *s. Educ:* Wallingford Grammar School. Commnd RA, 1940; War Service N Africa; transf. to RAOC, 1945; psc 1952; DAA&QMG 39 Inf. Bde, 1953–55; Dirg Staff, Staff Coll., 1955–58; OC 20 Ordnance Field Park, 1958–60; Admin. Staff Coll., 1961; AA&QMG N Ireland, 1961–63; D/SPO COD Donnington, 1964–65; Col AQ 54 (EA) Div./District, 1965–66; AAG AG9, MoD, 1967; DDOS 1 British Corps, 1968–69; idc 1970; Dir of Systems Coordination, MoD, 1971–73; Dir of Ordnance Services, MoD, 1973–76, retired. Col Comdt, RAOC, 1978–83. *Recreations:* sailing, golf. *Address:* 1 Steeple Close, SW6. *Club:* Roehampton.

SPENCE, Allan William, MA, MD Cantab; FRCP; Hon. Consultant Physician: St Bartholomew's Hospital, since 1965; Luton and Dunstable Hospital, since 1965; King George Hospital, Ilford, since 1967; *b* 4 Aug. 1900; *s* of late William Ritchie Spence and Emma (*née* Allan), Bath; *m* 1930, Martha Lena (*d* 1981), *d* of late Hugh Hamilton Hutchison, JP, Girvan, Ayrshire; two *s. Educ:* King Edward's VI School, Bath; Gonville and Caius College, Cambridge; St Bartholomew's Hospital, London. Brackenbury Schol. in Medicine, 1926, Lawrence Research Schol. and Gold Medal, 1929–30, Cattlin Research Fell., 1938, St Bartholomew's Hosp.; Rockefeller Travelling Fellow, USA, 1931–32. House Phys., 1927, Demonstrator of Physiology, 1928–30, of Pathology, 1930–31, First Asst, 1933–36, Asst Dir of Med. Unit, 1936–37, St Bartholomew's Hospital; Physician St Bartholomew's Hosp., London, 1937–65; King George Hospital, Ilford, 1938–67; Luton and Dunstable Hospital, 1946–65; Hon. Consultant in Endocrinology to Army at Home, 1954–65; Med. Referee to Civil Service Commn, 1952–70; Physician on Med. Appeal Tribunal, DHSS, 1965–72; Member Medical Research Coun. Adv. Cttee: on Iodine Deficiency and Thyroid Disease, 1933–39; and on Hormones, 1937–41. Hon. Lt-Col, RAMC; service in North Africa and Greece as OC Med. Div., 97th Gen. Hosp., 1943–45. Mem. Assoc. of Physicians of Gt Brit.; Foundation Mem. Soc. for Endocrinology, to 1965; Fellow RSM, 1926–72 (Vice-Pres., Section of Med., 1949, Pres. Section of Endocrinology, 1951–52, Councillor, 1958–61); Foundn Mem. Internat. Soc. of Internal Medicine; Fellow Medical Soc. of London, 1937–72 (Councillor, 1957–60); Foundn Mem., London Thyroid Club; Mem., Physiological Soc., 1935–52; Emeritus Mem., Endocrine Society, USA, 1966. Examr in Medicine: Univ. of Cambridge, 1946–50; to Society of Apothecaries of London, 1947–52; in Therapeutics to University of London, 1953–57; to the Conjoint Examining Bd in England, 1955–59; to Fellowship of Faculty of Anæsthetists, RCS, 1964–66. Trustee, Peel Med. Res. Trust, 1961–85. Mem. of Editorial Bd, Jl of Endocrinology, 1956–63. Freeman of City of London; Member of Livery, Society of Apothecaries of London. *Publications:* Clinical Endocrinology, 1953 (translated into Spanish); articles to medical and scientific journals on endocrinological and general medical subjects. *Recreations:* reading, gardening; formerly rowing (Pres. Caius Boat Club, 1922–23). *Address:* Oak Spinney, 60 Liphook Road, Lindford, Bordon, Hants GU35

0PN. *T:* Bordon 2450. *Club:* Hawks (Cambridge).
See also M. H. Spence.

SPENCE, Most Rev. Francis John; *see* Kingston (Ontario), Archbishop of.

SPENCE, Captain (Frederick) Michael (Alexander) T.; *see* Torrens-Spence.

SPENCE, Gabriel John; Under Secretary, Department of Education and Science, retired; *b* 5 April 1924; *s* of G. S. and D. A. Spence, Hope, Flints; *m* 1950, Averil Kingston (*née* Beresford); one *s* decd. *Educ:* Arnold House; King's Sch., Chester (King's Schol., Head of School); Wadham Coll., Oxon (Schol.). MA 1949; Stanhope Prize and Proxime, Gibbs Schol., Oxon, 1947; Haldane Essay Prize, Inst. Public Admin, 1959. Civil Service from 1949 (Min. of Works, Science Office, Min. of Housing and Local Govt, DES); Jt Sec., Adv. Council on Scientific Policy, 1959–62; Asst Sec., DES, 1964–73; Sec., Council for Scientific Policy, 1964–67; Under Sec., DES, 1973–81; Dep. Sec., UGC, 1978–81. Admin. Staff Coll., Henley, 1957. Trustee, The Oates Meml and Gilbert White Library and Museum, 1982–. *Recreations:* natural history, photography. *Address:* Old Heath, Hillbrow Road, Liss, Hants. *T:* Liss 893235.

SPENCE, Malcolm Hugh; QC 1979; a Recorder, since 1985; barrister-at-law, since 1958; *b* 23 March 1934; *s* of Allan William Spence, *qv; m* 1967, Jennifer Jane, *d* of Lt-Gen. Sir George Cole, KCB, CBE; one *s* one *d. Educ:* Summer Fields, Oxford; Stowe Sch.; Gonville and Caius Coll., Cambridge (MA, LLM). James Mould Schol., Holker Sen. Exhibnr, Lee Prizeman, Gray's Inn, called to the Bar, 1958. Worcester Regt, First Lieut, 1954. Marshal to Mr Justice McNair, 1957; Pupil to Mr Nigel Bridge (now Lord Bridge of Harwich), 1958; entered chambers of Mr John Widgery, QC, 1958; practises mainly in Town and Country Planning and Compensation for Compulsory Purchase. Assistant Recorder, 1982–85. Chairman of Panel, Examination-in-Public of Hartlepool and Cleveland Structure Plans, 1979–. *Publication:* (jtly) Rating Law and Valuation, 1961. *Recreations:* trout fishing, forestry and golf (Captain: Cambridge University Stymies, 1957; Old Stoic Golfing Soc., 1972; Semi-finalist, Scandinavian Amateur Championship, 1964). *Address:* 23 Ennerdale Road, Kew, Surrey TW9 3PE. *T:* 01–940 9884; Scamadale, Arisaig, Inverness-shire. *T:* Arisaig 698; 8 New Square, Lincoln's Inn, WC2. *T:* 01–242 4986. *Club:* Hawks (Cambridge).

SPENCER, family name of **Viscount Churchill** and of **Earl Spencer.**

SPENCER, 8th Earl *cr* 1765; **Edward John Spencer,** LVO 1954; DL; Baron and Viscount Spencer, 1761; Viscount Althorp, 1765; Viscount Althorp (UK), 1905; President, Northamptonshire Association of Boys' Clubs; Deputy President, National Association of Boys' Clubs, since 1980 (Chairman, 1962–80); *b* 24 Jan. 1924; *o s* of 7th Earl Spencer, TD, and Lady Cynthia Elinor Beatrix Hamilton, DCVO, OBE (*d* 1972), *d* of 3rd Duke of Abercorn; *S* father, 1975; *m* 1st, 1954, Hon. Frances Ruth Burke Roche (marr. diss. 1969), *yr d* of 4th Baron Fermoy; one *s* three *d* (and one *s* decd); 2nd, 1976, Raine (*see* Countess Spencer). *Educ:* Eton; RMC Sandhurst and RAC, Cirencester. ADC to Gov. of South Australia, 1947–50; Equerry to the Queen, 1952–54 (to King George VI, 1950–52). Formerly Capt RS Greys. Hon. Col The Northamptonshire Regt (Territorials), T&AVR, 1967–71; a Dep. Hon. Col, The Royal Anglian Regt, 1971–79. Chairman: SGBI, 1962–; The Nene Foundn, 1978–. Trustee: King George's Jubilee Trust; Queen's Silver Jubilee Appeal; Mem. UK Council European Architectural Heritage Year, 1975. CC Northants, 1952–81; High Sheriff of Northants, 1959; DL Northants, 1961; JP Norfolk, 1970. *Publications:* photographs for The Spencers on Spas, by Countess Spencer, 1983; Japan and the East (book of photographs), 1986. *Heir:* *s* Viscount Althorp, *qv. Address:* Althorp, Northampton NN7 4HG. *T:* (estate office) Northampton 770006. *Clubs:* Turf, Brooks's, MCC, Royal Over-Seas League.
See also under Royal Family, and R. Fellowes.

SPENCER, Countess; Raine Spencer; *b* 9 Sept. 1929; *d* of late Alexander George McCorquodale and of Barbara Cartland, *qv; m* 1st, 1948, Earl of Dartmouth (marr. diss. 1976), *qv;* three *s* one *d;* 2nd, 1976, Earl Spencer, *qv.* Westminster City Councillor, 1954–65 (served on various cttees); Member: for Lewisham West, LCC, 1958–65 (served on Town Planning, Parks, Staff Appeals Cttees); for Richmond upon Thames, GLC, 1967–73; GLC, Gen. Purposes Cttee, 1971–73; Chm., GLC Historic Buildings Bd, 1968–71; Mem., Environmental Planning Cttee, 1967–71; Chm., Covent Garden Develt Cttee, 1971–72; Chm., Govt working party on Human Habitat in connection with UN Conf. on Environment, Stockholm (June 1972), 1971–72 (report: How Do You Want to Live?); Chm., UK Exec., European Architectural Heritage Year, 1975. British Tourist Authority: Member: Infrastructure Cttee, 1972–; Board, 1982–; Chairman: Spas Cttee, 1982–83; Hotels and Restaurants Cttee, 1983–; Commended Hotels Panel; Member: English Tourist Bd, 1971–75; Adv. Council, V&A Museum, 1980–83; Cttee of Honour, Business Sponsorship of the Arts, 1980–. Formerly LCC Voluntary Care Cttee Worker, Wandsworth and Vauxhall. Hon. Dr Laws, Dartmouth Coll., USA. *Publications:* What Is Our Heritage?, 1975; The Spencers on Spas (with photographs by Earl Spencer), 1983. *Address:* Althorp, Northampton NN7 4HG. *T:* (estate office) Northampton 770006.

SPENCER, Alan Douglas, CBIM; Director: Owen Owen plc, 1980–86; Johnson Wax (UK) Ltd, since 1981; Member, East Midlands Electricity Board, 1976–86; *b* 22 Aug. 1920; *s* of Thomas Spencer and late Laura Spencer; *m* 1944, Dorothy Joan Harper; two *d. Educ:* Prince Henry's Grammar Sch., Evesham. FBIM 1975. Commnd Gloucester Regt, 1940; served War with Green Howards, 1940–45; Instr, Sch. of Infantry, 1945–47. Joined Boots Co., 1938; rejoined 1947; Dir, 1963–81, Man. Dir, 1975, Vice-Chm., 1978–80, Boots Co. Ltd; Man. Dir, 1977–79, Chm., 1977–80, Boots The Chemist Ltd. Pres., British Retailers' Assoc., 1983–84 (British Multiple Retailers Assoc., 1981–83). Governor, Trent Coll. *Recreation:* shooting. *Address:* Oakwood, Grange Road, Edwalton, Nottingham. *T:* Nottingham 231722. *Club:* Naval and Military.
See also Sir G. M. Brown.

SPENCER, Cyril; Chairman: Waring and Gillow, since 1985; Youngs Franchise Ltd, since 1985; Tectonic Products Ltd, since 1986; Deputy Chairman, First Computer Ltd, since 1984; *b* 31 Aug. 1924; *s* of Isaac and Lily Spencer; *m* 1971, Wendy Lois Sutton; two *s* one *d* and two step *s* one step *d. Educ:* Christ Coll., Finchley; London Univ. (BSc). Joined Evans (Outsizes) Ltd, 1946: Managing Director, 1956; Chairman, 1969; Take Over of Evans by Burton Group Ltd, 1971; Head of Womenswear, 1972; Group Man. Dir and Chief Exec., 1976; Chairman, Burton Menswear, 1977; Exec. Chm., Burton Group Ltd, 1979–81. *Recreations:* tennis, swimming, golf. *Address:* Eliot House, The Bishops Avenue, N2 0BA. *Club:* Royal Automobile.

SPENCER, Cyril Charles, CMG 1951; First Deputy Executive Director, International Coffee Organisation, London, 1964–68; *b* 1 Feb. 1912; *s* of late Albert Edward Spencer, CBE, and Elsie Maud Spencer; *m* 1st, 1938; one *d* 2nd, 1949, Catherine Dewar Robertson. *Educ:* Royal Grammar Sch., Worcester; St John's Coll., Cambridge (BA 1934). Uganda: Asst Treas., 1935; Asst District Officer, 1937; Asst Financial Sec., 1946; Economic Sec., E Africa High Commission, 1948; Financial Sec., 1948; Acting Chief Sec. at various dates; Acting Governor, July 1951; Chairman: Uganda Lint Marketing Bd; Uganda Coffee Marketing Board; Member: Uganda Electricity Board; Uganda Development Corp.;

Comr on Special Duty, Uganda, 1953–61; Sec.-Gen., Inter-African Coffee Organisation, Paris, 1961–64. *Recreations:* golf, fishing. *Address:* Flat No 2, Norton Garth, Sidmouth, Devon. *Club:* MCC.

SPENCER, Derek Harold, QC 1980; MP (C) Leicester South, since 1983; a Recorder of the Crown Court, since 1979; *b* 31 March 1936; *s* of Thomas Harold Spencer and Gladys Spencer (*née* Heslop); *m* 1960, Joan (*née* Nutter); two *s* one *d. Educ:* Clitheroe Royal Grammar Sch.; Keble Coll., Oxford (MA, BCL). 2nd/Lieut King's Own Royal Regt, 1954–56; served in Nigeria. Called to Bar, Gray's Inn, 1961. (Holt Scholar; Arden Scholar); in practice SE Circuit. Councillor, London Borough of Camden, 1978–83; Dep. Leader, Conservative Party, London Borough of Camden, 1979–81. Joint Sec. Cons. Parly Legal Affairs Cttee, 1985–. Vice-Chm., St Pancras North Cons. Assoc., 1977–78. *Recreations:* reading, swimming, golf. *Address:* 2D Oakford Road, NW5. *T:* 01–482 1876; 22 Waldale Drive, Leicester. *T:* Leicester 701527. *Club:* Highgate Golf.

SPENCER, Prof. Herbert, MD London, PhD; FRCP, FRCS, FRCPath; Professor of Morbid Anatomy, St Thomas's Hospital Medical School, 1965–80, now Emeritus Professor; Visiting Professor of Pathology, St Mary's Hospital Medical School; *b* 8 Feb. 1915; *s* of Hubert and Edith Maude Spencer; *m* 1940, Eileen Mabel Morgan; one *s* three *d. Educ:* Highgate Sch.; St Mary's Hosp. Med. Sch. Served War of 1939–45: Specialist Pathologist, RAMC, 1942–47. Reader in Pathology, St Thomas's Hosp. Med. Sch., 1954–65; Visiting Associate Prof. of Pathology, Yale Univ. Sch. of Med., 1961. Examiner: RCS, 1958–70; Univ. of London, 1974–77; Univ. of Liverpool, 1972–76; RCP, 1973–. *Publications:* Pathology of the Lung, 1962, 4th edn 1985; Tropical Pathology, 1973; contribs to numerous British and foreign med. jls and books. *Recreation:* woodwork. *Address:* Uplands Cottage, Barnet Road, Arkley, Barnet, Herts EN5 3ET. *T:* 01–449 7030.

SPENCER, Herbert, RDI 1965; DrRCA; Professor of Graphic Arts, Royal College of Art, 1978–85; *b* 22 June 1924; *m* 1954, Marianne Möls, Dordrecht; one *d.* DrRCA 1970; FSIA 1947. Sen. Res. Fellow, RCA, 1966–78, Hon. Fellow, 1985. Internat. Pres., Alliance Graphique Internat., 1971–74; Mem., PO Stamp Adv. Cttee, 1968–; External advr to Design Cttee, British Telecom, 1981–83. Dir, Lund Humphries Publishers Ltd, 1970–. Consultant: W. H. Smith & Son Ltd, 1973–; Tate Gall., 1981–; British Rail, 1984–. Master, Faculty of Royal Designers for Industry, 1979–81; Vice-Pres., RSA, 1979–81. Governor, Bath Acad. of Art, Corsham, 1982–83. Editor: Typographica, 1949–67; Penrose Annual, 1964–73. *Publications:* Design in Business Printing, 1952; London's Canal, 1961, 2nd edn 1976; Traces of Man, 1967; The Visible Word, 1968, 2nd edn 1969; Pioneers of Modern Typography, 1969, 2nd edn 1982, German edn 1970, Dutch edn 1983; (with Colin Forbes) New Alphabets A-Z, 1973, French edn 1974; (with Mafalda Spencer) The Book of Numbers, 1975. *Address:* 75 Deodar Road, Putney, SW15 2NU. *T:* 01–874 6352. *Club:* Chelsea Arts.

SPENCER, Air Vice-Marshal Ian James, CB 1963; DFC 1941 (Bar 1943); *b* 6 June 1916; *s* of late Percival James Spencer; *m* 1940, Kathleen Jeune Follis, *d* of late Canon Charles Follis; two *s.* Commissioned 1937. War of 1939–45: bomber sqdns of No 2 Gp (despatches). RAF Staff College, 1948; Air Attaché, Berne, 1950–53; CO, Univ. of London Air Sqdn, 1954–56; Director of Plans Second Allied TAF, 1956–59; commanded RAF Benson, 1959–61; AOA, Transport Command, 1961–64; Dir of Personnel, MoD, 1964–65; AOA, Far East Air Force, 1965–67; retired 1968. Member: CPRE; Franco-British Soc.; Anglo-Swiss Soc.; BIM. Croix de Guerre, 1944; Légion d'Honneur 1945. Interests: internat. affairs, the countryside.

SPENCER, Mrs Joanna Miriam, CB 1971; CBE 1961; CompIGasE; *b* 26 July 1910; *d* of late Rev. R. S. Franks; *m* 1954, Frank Woolley Sim Spencer (*d* 1975). *Educ:* Redland High School for Girls, Bristol; Girton College, Cambridge (MA). Asst, Lancs County Library, 1934–35; Asst Librarian: Hull Univ. Coll., 1936–37; Regent Street Polytechnic, 1938; Librarian, Selly Oak Colls, 1938–42. Temp. Civil Servant, Min. of Aircraft Production, 1942–45. Principal, Min. of Supply, 1946; Assistant Secretary, Min. of Supply, 1949–55, Board of Trade, 1955–56, Min. of Power, 1957–64; Under-Secretary: Min. of Power, 1964–69; Min. of Technology, 1969–70; DTI, 1970–72. *Address:* 4 Rostrevor Road, SW19 7AP. *T:* 01–946 4969.

SPENCER, John Loraine, TD; Headmaster, Berkhamsted School, 1972–83; Assistant Director, GAP Activity Projects Ltd, since 1985; *b* 19 Jan. 1923; *s* of late Arthur Loraine Spencer, OBE, and Emily Maude Spencer, OBE, Woodford Green; *m* 1954, Brenda Elizabeth (*née* Loft); two *s* one *d. Educ:* Bancroft's Sch.; Gonville and Caius Coll., Cambridge (MA). 1st cl. hons Class. Tripos Pts I and II. War Service in Essex Regt, 1942–45 (Captain, despatches). Asst Master, Housemaster and Sixth Form Classics Master, Haileybury Coll., 1947–61; Headmaster, Lancaster Royal Grammar Sch., 1961–72. Pres., Soc. of Schoolmasters, 1985–. Mem. Council, Lancaster Univ., 1968–72. *Address:* Crofts Close, 7 Aston Road, Haddenham, Bucks HP17 8AF. *T:* Haddenham 291235.

SPENCER, Sir Kelvin (Tallent), Kt 1959; CBE 1950; MC 1918; Chief Scientist, Ministry of Power, 1954–59, retired; *b* 7 July 1898; *s* of Charles Tallent and Edith Ælfrida Spencer; *m* 1927, Phœbe Mary Wills; one *s. Educ:* University College School, Hampstead; City and Guilds Engineering Coll., London Univ. Founder Mem., Scientific and Medical Network. FCGI 1959. Formerly MICE, FRAeS. Hon. LLD Exeter, 1981. *Address:* Wootans, Branscombe, Seaton, Devon EX12 3DN. *T:* Branscombe 242. *Clubs:* Farmers'; University of Exeter Staff.

SPENCER, Oscar Alan, CMG 1957; economic consultant; Economic Adviser to Government of Seychelles, 1976–83; *b* Eastleigh, Hants, 12 Dec. 1913; *m* 1952, Diana Mary, *d* of late Edmund Walker, Henley-on-Thames; two *s* one *d. Educ:* Mayfield Coll., Sussex; London Sch. of Economics. BCom (Hons) 1936. Premchand Prize in Banking and Currency, 1936; John Coleman Postgraduate Scholar in Business Administration, 1936–37. Served War of 1939–45, Lt-Col (despatches twice). Economic Adviser and Development Comr, British Guiana, 1945; also Comr, Interior, 1949; Economic Sec., Malaya, 1950; Member, 1951, Minister, 1955, for Economic Affairs, Economic Adviser, and Head of Economic Secretariat, Fedn of Malaya, 1956–60. UN Tech. Assistance Service, 1960–76: Econ. Adviser to Govt of Sudan, 1960–64; Sen. Regl Adviser on Public Finance and Head of Fiscal Sect., UN Econ. Commn for Africa, 1964–66; Financial Adviser to Govt of Ethiopia, 1966–76; Dep. Chm., Seychelles Nat. Investment Corp., 1979–81. Chm., Central Electricity Board, Malaya, 1952–55, 1956–60; British Guiana Delegate, Caribbean Commn, 1948; Malayan Adviser to Sec. of State. Commonwealth Finance Ministers' Conf., 1951; Leader of Malayan Reps, Internat. Rubber Study Gp, London, 1952, Copenhagen, 1953; Malayan Deleg., Internat. Tin Conf., Geneva, 1953; Adviser to Malayan Delegation, London Constitutional and Financial Confs, 1956 and 1957. Comdr, Order of St Agatha, San Marino, 1944; Knight of the Order of Defenders of the Realm (PMN), Malaya, 1958. *Publications:* The Finances of British Guiana, 1920–45, 1946; The Development Plan of British Guiana, 1947. *Recreation:* swimming. *Address:* Gatehurst, Pett, near Hastings, East Sussex. *T:* Hastings 812197. *Club:* East India, Devonshire, Sports and Public Schools.

SPENCER, Rosemary Jane; HM Diplomatic Service; Counsellor (External Relations), Office of UK Permanent Representative to European Community, Brussels, since 1984; *b* 1 April 1941; *d* of Air Vice-Marshal Geoffrey Roger Cole Spencer, CB, CBE, and Juliet Mary Spencer (*née* Warwick). *Educ:* Upper Chine Sch., Shanklin, IoW; St Hilda's Coll., Oxford (BA Hons Modern Langs). Joined Foreign Office, 1962; FO, 1962–65; Third Secretary, Nairobi, 1965–67; Second Sec., FCO, 1967–70; Second Sec., UK Delegn to EEC, and Private Sec. to Hon. Sir Con O'Neill, Official Leader of UK negotiating team, 1970–71; First Sec., Office of UK Permanent Representative to EEC, Brussels, 1972–73; First Sec. (Economic), Lagos, 1974–77; First Sec., Asst Head of Rhodesia Dept, FCO, 1977–80; RCDS 1980; Counsellor (Agric. and Economic Affairs), Paris, 1980–84. Mem., Governing Bd, Upper Chine Sch., 1984–. *Recreations:* country walking, travel, riding, domestic arts. *Address:* c/o Foreign and Commonwealth Office, SW1. *Club:* Royal Commonwealth Society.

SPENCER, Sarah Ann; General Secretary, National Council for Civil Liberties, since 1985; *b* 11 Dec. 1952; *d* of late Dr I. O. B. Spencer and of Dr Elspeth Wilkinson; *m* 1978, Brian Hackland. *Educ:* Nottingham Univ. (BA Hons); University Coll. London (MPhil). Researcher, Law Faculty, UCL, 1977–79; Res. Officer, Cobden Trust (Civil Liberties Charity), 1979–84, Dir 1984–85. Trustee: Cobden Trust, 1985–; Prisoners' Legal Services Foundn, 1985–. Editor, Rights Jl, 1979–84. *Publications:* Called to Account: police accountability in England and Wales, 1985; (jtly) The New Prevention of Terrorism Act, 1985; The Role of Police Authorities during the Miners' Strike, 1985. *Recreations:* reading, walking, opera. *Address:* (office) 21 Tabard Street, SE1. *T:* 01–403 3888.

SPENCER, Thomas Newnham Bayley, (Tom Spencer); Associate Dean, Templeton College, Oxford; *b* 10 April 1948; *s* of Captain Thomas Henry Newnham Spencer and Anne Hester (*née* Readett-Bayley); *m* 1979, Elizabeth Nan Maltby, *er d* of late Captain Ronald Edgar Bath and of Doreen Lester (*née* Bush); two *d* and one step *d. Educ:* Nautical Coll., Pangbourne; Southampton Univ. (BSc Social Sciences). Peat, Marwick, Mitchell & Co., 1972–75; Asst to Dir, Britain-in-Europe Campaign, 1975; J. Walter Thompson & Co., 1975–79. Mem. (C) Derbyshire, European Parlt, 1979–84, contested same seat, 1984; European Democratic Gp spokesman on: Social Affairs and Employment, 1979–81; External Econ. Relations, 1982–84. Chm., European Union Cons. and Christian-Democratic Students, 1971–73. *Recreations:* gardening, swimming, opera. *Address:* The Manor House, Doveridge, Derbyshire. *Clubs:* Carlton, Brass Monkey.

SPENCER-CHURCHILL, family name of **Duke of Marlborough.**

SPENCER CHURCHILL, John George; see Churchill, J. G. S.

SPENCER-NAIRN, Sir Robert (Arnold), 3rd Bt *cr* 1933; *b* 11 Oct. 1933; *s* of Sir Douglas Spencer-Nairn, 2nd Bt, TD, and Elizabeth Livingston (*d* 1985), *d* of late Arnold J. Henderson; *S* father, 1970; *m* 1963, Joanna Elizabeth, *d* of late Lt-Comdr G. S. Salt, RN; two *s* one *d. Educ:* Eton College; Trinity Hall, Cambridge (MA). *Heir: s* James Robert Spencer-Nairn, *b* 7 Dec. 1966. *Address:* Barham, Cupar, Fife KY15 5RG. *Clubs:* New (Edinburgh); Royal and Ancient Golf (St Andrews).

SPENCER PATERSON, Arthur; see Paterson, A. S.

SPENCER-SILVER, Prof. Peter Hele; S. A. Courtauld Professor of Anatomy in the University of London, at the Middlesex Hospital Medical School, 1974–82, now Emeritus; *b* 29 Oct. 1922; 2nd *s* of late Lt-Col J. H. Spencer Silver; *m* 1948, Patricia Anne, *e d* of late Col J. A. F. Cuffe, CMG, DSO, Wyke Mark, Winchester; two *s* one *d. Educ:* Harrow School; Middlesex Hosp. Med. School, Univ. of London. MRCS, LRCP; MB, BS London 1945; PhD London 1952. Res., Middlesex Hosp., 1945–46. RAF, 1946–48. Demonstrator in Anatomy, Middlesex Hosp. Med. Sch., 1948–57; Mem. 2nd Internat. Team in Embryology, Hübrecht Laboratory, Utrecht, Netherlands Govt Fellowship, 1956; Reader in Anatomy, Univ. of London, 1957; US Nat. Inst. of Health Post-doctoral Travelling Fellowship, 1961; Carnegie Inst. of Washington, Dept of Embryology, Baltimore, 1961–62; Prof. of Embryology, Mddx Hosp. Medical Sch., 1964–74, Sub-Dean, 1976–81. WHO Vis. Prof., 1976, 1979, 1981; Chm., Dept of Anatomy, King Saud Univ. (Abha Br.), Saudi Arabia, 1984–86. FRSM. *Publications:* An Introduction to Human Anatomy, 1981; contribs to Jl Embryology and Experimental Morphology, Jl Physiol., Jl Anat., Lancet, etc. *Recreation:* music. *Address:* c/o Barclays Bank, Jewry Street, Winchester, Hants SO23 8RG.

SPENCER SMITH, Prof. David, PhD; Hope Professor of Entomology, University of Oxford, and Fellow of Jesus College, Oxford, since 1980; *b* 10 April 1934; *s* of Rev. Harry Chadwick Smith and Mary Edith (*née* Lupton); *m* 1st, 1964, Una Scully; one *d;* 2nd, 1974, Sylvia Hyder. *Educ:* Kingswood Sch.; Cambridge Univ. (BA, MA, PhD). Research Fellow: Rockefeller Univ., NY, 1958–61; St Catharine's Coll., Cambridge, 1961–63 (Res. Fellow); Asst Prof., Univ. of Virginia, 1963–66; Associate Prof. of Medicine and Biology, Univ. of Miami, Fla, 1966–70; Prof. of Medicine, Pharmacology and Biology, Univ. of Miami, 1970–80. Trustee, BM (Natural Hist.), 1984–. Editor, Tissue & Cell, 1969–. *Publications:* Insect Cells: their structure and function, 1968; Muscle: a monograph, 1972; contrib. Standard Catalog of World Coins; papers and chapters in books and jls. *Recreations:* the ceramics and coinage of China; the coinage of the Indian subcontinent; the history of entomology; cricket, American football (spectator). *Address:* Jesus College, Oxford.

SPENCER-SMITH, Sir John Hamilton-, 7th Bt, *cr* 1804; quarantine kennel owner; *b* 18 March 1947; *s* of Sir Thomas Cospatric Hamilton-Spencer-Smith, 6th Bt, and Lucy Ashton, *o d* of late Thomas Ashton Ingram, Hopes, Norton-sub-Hamdon, Somerset; *S* father, 1959; *m* 1980, Christine, *d* of late John Theodore Charles Osborne, Durrington, Worthing, Sussex; one *d. Educ:* Milton Abbey; Lackham College of Agriculture, Wilts. *Recreation:* watching polo. *Heir: cousin* Peter Compton Hamilton-Spencer-Smith [*b* 12 Nov. 1912; *m* 1950, Philippa Mary, *yr d* of late Captain Richard Ford; two *s*]. *Address:* Dairy Cottage, Elsted, Midhurst, West Sussex; Hazel House Quarantine Kennels, Midhurst, West Sussex GU29 0JT. *T:* Midhurst 3616.

SPENCER WILLS, Sir John; see Wills.

SPENDER, Sir Stephen (Harold), Kt 1983; CBE 1962; CLit 1977; FRSL; poet and critic; Professor of English, University College, London University, 1970–77, now Emeritus; *b* 28 Feb. 1909; *s* of Edward Harold Spender and Violet Hilda Schuster; *m* 1st, 1936, Agnes Marie (Inez), *o d* of late William Henry Pearn; 2nd, 1941, Natasha Litvin; one *s* one *d. Educ:* University College Sch.; University College, Oxford (Hon. Fellow, 1973). Co-editor Horizon Magazine, 1939–41; Counsellor, Section of Letters, Unesco, 1947; Co-Editor, Encounter, 1953–67. Fireman in NFS, 1941–44. Hon. Mem. Phi Beta Kappa (Harvard Univ.); Elliston Chair of Poetry, Univ. of Cincinnati, 1953; Beckman Prof., Univ. of California, 1959; Visiting Lecturer, Northwestern Univ., Illinois, 1963; Consultant in Poetry in English, Library of Congress, Washington, 1965; Clark Lectures (Cambridge), 1966; Mellon Lectures, Washington, DC, 1968; Northcliffe Lectures (London Univ.), 1969. Pres., English Centre, PEN Internat., 1975–. Fellow, Inst. of Advanced Studies, Wesleyan Univ., 1967. Visiting Professor: Univ. of Connecticut,

1969; Vanderbilt Univ., 1979; Emory Univ. Hon. Mem. Amer. Acad. of Arts and Letters and Nat. Inst. of Arts and Letters, 1969. Queen's Gold Medal for Poetry for 1971. Hon. DLitt: Montpellier Univ.; Cornell Coll.; Loyola Univ. *Publications:* 20 Poems; Poems, the Destructive Element, 1934; Vienna, 1934; The Burning Cactus, 1936; Forward from Liberalism, 1937; Trial of a Judge (verse play), 1937; Poems for Spain, 1939; The Still Centre, 1939; Ruins and Visions, 1941; Life and the Poet, 1942; Citizens in War and After, 1945; Poems of Dedication, 1946; European Witness, 1946; The Edge of Being, 1949; essay, in The God that Failed, 1949; World Within World (autobiog.), 1951; Learning Laughter (travels in Israel), 1952; The Creative Element, 1953; Collected Poems, 1954; The Making of a Poem, 1955; Engaged in Writing (stories), 1958; Schiller's Mary Stuart (trans.), 1958 (staged at Old Vic, 1961); The Struggle of the Modern, 1963; Selected Poems, 1965; The Year of the Young Rebels, 1969; The Generous Days (poems), 1971; (ed) A Choice of Shelley's Verse, 1971; (ed) D. H. Lawrence: novelist, poet, prophet, 1973; Love-Hate Relations, 1974; T. S. Eliot, 1975; (ed) W. H. Auden: a tribute, 1975; The Thirties and After, 1978; (with David Hockney) China Diary, 1982; Oedipus Trilogy (trans.), 1983 (staged, Oxford Playhouse, 1983); Journals 1939–1982, 1985; Collected Poems 1930–1985, 1985. *Address:* 15 Loudoun Road, NW8. *Clubs:* Savile, Beefsteak.

SPENDLOVE, Peter Roy, CVO 1981; HM Diplomatic Service, retired; Deputy Chief Administrator, Broads Authority (East Anglia), since 1983; *b* 11 Nov. 1925; *s* of H. A. Spendlove and Florence (*née* Jackson) *m* 1952, Wendy Margaret Valentine; two *s* three *d*. *Educ:* Chichester High Sch.; London Sch. of Economics; Edinburgh and Cambridge Univs. BScEcon Hons 1951. Called to Bar, Middle Temple, 1964. Served HM Forces, 1943–47: commnd, Indian Army/Royal Indian Artillery. LSE, 1948–51; Internat. Law Scholar at The Hague, 1951; Univ. of Cambridge, 1951–52. Apptd District Officer, Kenya, 1952; retired after serving in Provincial Admin and Central Govt, 1964. First Secretary, FCO, 1964; served in E Malaysia, Washington, Manila, FO, Jamaica; Counsellor, Economic, Commercial and Aid, Jakarta, 1977–80; Deputy High Comr, Sri Lanka, 1981–82. *Recreations:* riding, skiing, hill walking. *Address:* 120 Newmarket Road, Norwich NR4 6SA.

SPENS, family name of **Baron Spens.**

SPENS, 3rd Baron *cr* 1959, of Blairsanquhar, Co. Fife; **Patrick Michael Rex Spens,** FCA; Managing Director, Henry Ansbacher & Co. Ltd, since 1983; Director: London & Midland Industries; Arlington Securities; *b* 22 July 1942; *s* of 2nd Baron Spens and of Joan Elizabeth, *d* of late Reginald Goodall; *S* father, 1984; *m* 1966, Barbara Janet Lindsay, *d* of Rear-Adm. Ralph Lindsay Fisher, *qv*; one *s* one *d*. *Educ:* Rugby; Corpus Christi Coll., Cambridge (MA). FCA 1967. Director of Morgan Grenfell & Co. Ltd, 1972–82. *Heir: s* Hon. Patrick Nathaniel George Spens, *b* 14 Oct 1968. *Address:* Gould, Frittenden, Kent. *Clubs:* Carlton, City of London.

SPENS, Colin Hope, CB 1962; FICE, FIWES, FInstWPC; *b* 22 May 1906; *er s* of late Archibald Hope Spens, Lathallan, Fifeshire and Hilda Constance Hooper; *m* 1941, Josephine, *d* of late Septimus Simond; two *s* one *d*. *Educ:* Lancing Coll.; Imperial College of Science and Technology. Consulting engineering experience, 1928–39. Served War of 1939–45 with Royal Signals, 1939–41; PA to Director of Works in Ministry of Works, 1941–44; Engineering Inspectorate of Min. of Health, 1944–51, Min. of Housing and Local Govt, 1951–60; Chief Engineer, Min. of Housing and Local Govt, 1960–67. Senior Consultant, Rofe, Kennard and Lapworth, 1967–76; Dep. Chm., Sutton District Water Co., 1971–83. Pres., IWES, 1974–75. Hon. FInstPHE. *Address:* 10 Ashbourne Court, Burlington Place, Eastbourne BN21 4AX. *T:* Eastbourne 638742.

SPENS, John Alexander, RD 1970; Partner, Maclay, Murray & Spens, Solicitors, Glasgow and Edinburgh, since 1960; *b* 7 June 1933; *s* of Thomas Patrick Spens and Nancy F. Spens (*née* Anderson); *m* 1961, Finella Jane, *d* of Donald Duff Gilroy; two *s* one *d* (and one *s* decd). *Educ:* Cargilfield; Rugby School; Corpus Christi College, Cambridge (BA); Glasgow Univ. (LLB). Director: Scottish Amicable Life Assurance Soc., 1963– (Chairman, 1978–81); Standard Property Investment PLC, 1977–. Carrick Pursuivant, 1974–85; Albany Herald, 1985–. *Recreations:* sailing, countryside and opera. *Address:* The Old Manse, Gartocharn, Dunbartonshire G83 8RX. *T:* Gartocharn 329. *Clubs:* Naval; Western (Glasgow).

SPENSLEY, Philip Calvert, DPhil; CChem, FRSC; Editor, Tropical Science, since 1984; Consultant in Post-Harvest Science and Technology and the Organisation of Research and Development; Director, Tropical Products Institute, Overseas Development Administration, Foreign and Commonwealth Office, 1966–81; *b* 7 May 1920; *s* of late Kent and Mary Spensley, Ealing; *m* 1957, Sheila Ross Fraser, *d* of late Alexander and Annie Fraser, Forres, Scotland; one *s* three *d*. *Educ:* St Paul's Sch., London; Keble Coll., Oxford (MA, BSc). Technical Officer, Royal Ordnance Factories, Ministry of Supply, 1940–45; Research Chemist, Nat. Inst. for Medical Research, MRC, 1950–54; Scientific Secretary, Colonial Products Council, Colonial Office, 1954–58; Asst Director, Tropical Products Inst., DSIR, 1958–61, Dep. Director, 1961–66, Director, 1966. Mem. Council, Royal Institution, 1985– (Chm., Cttee of Visitors, 1959). Member: FAO/WHO/Unicef Protein Adv. Gp, 1968–71; Cttee on Needs of Developing Countries, Internat. Union of Food Science and Technology, 1970–78; Food Science and Technol. Bd, MAFF/ARC/Dept of Agric. and Fisheries for Scotland Jt Consultative Organisation, 1973–79; UK Rep., CENTO Council for Scientific Educn and Research, 1970–78. Member: Internat. Cttee, RSC, 1982–; British Nat. Cttee for Chemistry, Royal Soc., 1986–. Received MRC/NRDC Inventors Awards, 1963 and 1971. Freeman, City of London, 1951. *Publications:* Tropical Products Institute Crop and Product Digests, vol. 1, 1971; various research and review papers, particularly in the fields of chemotherapeutic substances, plant sources of drugs, aflatoxin, food losses, and work of Tropical Products Inst.; patents on extraction of hecogenin from sisal. *Recreations:* house design and building, gardening, boating. *Address:* 96 Laurel Way, Totteridge, N20. *T:* 01–445 7895. *Clubs:* Athenæum, Royal Automobile; Island Cruising (Salcombe).

SPERRY, Rt. Rev. John Reginald; *see* Arctic, Bishop of The.

SPERRY, Prof. Roger Wolcott, PhD; Hixon Professor of Psychobiology, 1954–84, Trustee Professor, since 1984, California Institute of Technology; *b* 20 Aug. 1913; *s* of Francis Bushnell Sperry and Florence Kraemer Sperry; *m* 1949, Norma Gay Deupree; one *s* one *d*. *Educ:* Oberlin Coll. (Amos C. Miller Schol.; AB English 1935; MA Psych. 1937); Univ. of Chicago (PhD Zoology 1941). Nat. Research Council Fellow, Harvard Univ., 1941–42; Biology Research Fellow, Harvard Univ. at Yerkes Labs of Primate Biology, 1942–46; Asst Prof., Dept of Anatomy, Univ. of Chicago, 1946–52; Section Chief, Neurolog. Diseases and Blindness, NIH, 1952–53; Assoc. Prof. of Psychology, Univ. of Chicago, 1952–53. For. Mem. of Royal Soc., 1976–; Fellow: Amer. Psycholog. Assoc. (Distinguished Scientific Contribn Award, 1971); Amer. Assoc. for Advancement of Sci.; Member: Nat. Acad. of Scis, 1960–; Pontifical Acad. of Scis, 1978–; Amer. Philosophical Soc., 1974– (Karl Lashley Award, 1976); Amer. Acad. of Arts and Scis, 1963–; (Hon.) Amer. Neurolog. Assoc., 1974–; Internat. Neuropsychology Soc.; Amer. Assoc. for Anatomists; Soc. for Developmental Biology; Amer. Physiological Soc.; Psychonomic Soc.; Soc. for Neuroscience (Ralph Gerard Award, 1979); Internat. Brain Res. Org.; Internat. Soc. of Developmental Biologists; Soc. of Sigma XI; Amer. Assoc. of Univ. Profs. Hon. Dr of Science: Cambridge, 1972; Chicago, 1976; Kenyon Coll., 1979; Rockefeller, 1980; Oberlin Coll., 1982; Howard Crosby Warren Medal, Soc. of Exper. Psychologists, 1969; Calif. Scientist of the Year Award, Calif. Mus. of Sci. and Industry, 1972; (jtly) William Thomson Wakeman Res. Award, Nat. Paraplegia Foundn, 1972; Passano Award in Med. Sci., 1973; Claude Bernard Science Journalism Award, 1975; (jtly) Wolf Prize in Medicine, 1979; Internat. Visual Literacy Assoc. Special Award, 1979; Albert Lasker Med. Res. Award, 1979; Golden Plate Award of Amer. Acad. of Achievement, 1980; (jtly) Nobel Prize in Physiology or Medicine, 1981. *Publications:* Science and Moral Priority, 1982; many contribs to scientific jls, chapters in books, and scattered theoretical, philosophical and humanistic articles. *Recreations:* paleontology, camping, ceramics and sculpture. *Address:* 3625 Lombardy Road, Pasadena, California 91107, USA. *T:* (213) 793–0117. *Club:* Athenæum of Pasadena (Calif.).

SPERRYN, Simon George; Chief Executive, Manchester Chamber of Commerce and Industry, since 1986; *b* 7 April 1946; *s* of George Roland Neville Sperryn and Wendy Sperryn (*née* King). *Educ:* Rydal School; Pembroke College, Cambridge (MA); Cranfield School of Management (MBA). Birmingham Chamber of Commerce and Industry, 1967–77; Chief Exec., Northants Chamber of Commerce and Industry, 1979–85. Director: Northants Enterprise Agency, 1983–85; English Heritage Orchestra, 1984–85; Member: E Midlands Adv. Cttee, Understanding British Industry, 1983–85; Management Cttee, Northampton Inf. Tech. Centre, 1982–85; Management Cttee, Croyland Workcentre, 1981–85; Northants Business Educn Liaison Cttee, 1979–85 (Chm., 1984–85); Local Govt Cttee, 1984–, Nat. Council, 1986–, ABCC; Exec. Cttee, British Chambers of Commerce Execs, 1984–; Exec. Cttee, Manchester Business Venture, 1986–; Regional Sec., NW Region Chambers of Commerce Council, 1986–. Chm., Business Secretarial Studies Consultative Cttee, Nene Coll., 1982–85; Member: Court, Nottingham Univ., 1979–85; Governing Body, Tresham Coll., 1984–85; Wellingborough Coll. Business Studies Adv. Cttee, 1983–85; Governing Body, Kingsthorpe Upper Sch., 1983–85 (Chm., 1984–85). FBIM. *Recreations:* singing, reading, walking. *Address:* Manchester Chamber of Commerce and Industry, 56 Oxford Street, Manchester M60 7HJ. *T:* 061–236 4160; Lilac Cottage, Wincle, Macclesfield, Cheshire SK11 0QE. *T:* Wincle 620. *Club:* St James's (Manchester).

SPICER, Clive Colquhoun; Honorary Research Fellow, Exeter University; Director, Medical Research Council Computer Unit, 1967–79; *b* 5 Nov. 1917; *s* of John Bishop Spicer and Marion Isobel Spicer; *m* 1st, 1941, Faith Haughton James, MB (marr. diss. 1979); one *s* two *d*; 2nd, 1979, Anne Nolan. *Educ:* Charterhouse Sch.; Guy's Hospital. Operational research on war casualties, 1941–46; Hon. Sqdn Leader, RAF; Staff, Imperial Cancer Research Fund, 1946–49; Dept of Biometry, University Coll., London, 1946–47; Public Health Laboratory Service, 1949–59; WHO Fellow, Univ. of Wisconsin, 1952–53; Vis. Scientist, US Nat. Insts of Health, 1959–60; Statistician, Imperial Cancer Research Fund, 1960–62; Chief Medical Statistician, General Register Office, 1962–66. Main interest has been in application of mathematical methods to medical problems. *Publications:* papers in scientific journals on epidemiology and medical statistics. *Recreations:* sailing, reading. *Address:* Churchtown, Michaelstow, St Tudy, Bodmin PL30 3PD.

SPICER, James Wilton; MP (C) Dorset West since Feb. 1974; a Vice Chairman, Conservative Party Organisation, since 1985; company director; *b* 4 Oct. 1925; *s* of James and Florence Clara Spicer; *m* 1954, Winifred Douglas Shanks; two *d*. *Educ:* Latymer. Regular army, 1943–57, retd (Major); commnd Royal Fusiliers, 1944; Para. Regt, 1951–57. Nat. Chm., CPC, 1968–71. Mem., Select Cttee on Agriculture, 1984–85. Mem. (C) European Parlt, 1975–84 (elected Mem. for Wessex, 1979–84); Chief Whip, European Democratic Gp, 1975–79; Dir, Cons. Group for Europe, 1972–74, Chm., 1975–78. *Recreations:* swimming, tennis. *Address:* Whatley, Beaminster, Dorset. *T:* Beaminster 862337. *Club:* Naval and Military.

SPICER, Michael; *see* Spicer, W. M. H.

SPICER, (Sir) Peter James, 4th Bt *cr* 1906 (but does not use the title); retired; *b* 20 May 1921; *s* of Captain Sir Stewart Dykes Spicer, 3rd Bt, RN, and Margaret Grace (*née* Gillespie) (*d* 1967); *S* father, 1968; *m* 1949, Margaret, *e d* of Sir Steuart Wilson (*d* 1966), and Ann Mary Grace, now Lady Boult; one *s* three *d* (and one *d* decd). *Educ:* Winchester Coll. (Schol.); Trinity Coll., Cambridge (Exhibr); Christ Church, Oxford (MA). Served War of 1939–45 (despatches, 1944); Royal Sussex Regt, then RN (Temp. Lieut, RNVR). Trinity Coll., Cambridge, 1939–40; Christ Church, Oxford, 1945–47. Member of publishing staff, Oxford University Press, 1947–81. Co-opted Member, Educn Cttee of Oxfordshire CC, 1959–74 (Chairman, Libraries Sub-Cttee, 1961–74). Congregational Rep., British Council of Churches, 1963–72; Chm., Educational Publishers' Council, 1976–78. *Recreations:* theology, gardening, walking, sailing, music, large family gatherings. *Heir: s* Dr Nicholas Adrian Albert Spicer, *b* 28 Oct. 1953. *Address:* Salt Mill House, Fishbourne, Chichester PO19 3JN. *T:* Chichester 782825.

SPICER, (William) Michael (Hardy); MP (C) South Worcestershire since Feb. 1974; Parliamentary Under Secretary of State, since 1984 and Minister for Aviation, 1985, Department of Transport; *b* 22 Jan. 1943; *s* of late Brig. L. H. Spicer; *m* 1967, Patricia Ann Hunter; one *s* two *d*. *Educ:* Wellington Coll.; Emmanuel Coll., Cambridge (MA Econs). Asst to Editor, The Statist, 1964–66; Conservative Research Dept, 1966–68; Dir, Conservative Systems Research Centre, 1968–70; Man. Dir, Economic Models Ltd, 1970–80. PPS, Dept of Trade, 1979–81; a Vice-Chm., 1981–83, Dep. Chm., 1983–84, Conservative Party. *Publications:* Final Act (political novel), 1981; contrib. Jl Royal Inst. Public Admin. *Recreations:* painting, tennis, writing, travelling. *Address:* House of Commons, SW1. *T:* 01–219 3000.

SPICKERNELL, Rear-Adm. Derek Garland, CB 1974; CEng, FIMechE, FIProdE, MIPM, CBIM, MIMarE; Chairman, Ocean Control PLC; Director General, British Standards Institution, 1981–86 (Technical Director, 1976–81); *b* 1 June 1921; *s* of late Comdr Sidney Garland Spickernell, RN, and Florence Elizabeth (*née* March); *m* 1946, Ursula Rosemary Sheila Money; one *s* one *d* (and one *s* decd). *Educ:* RNEC, Keyham. Served War, HM Ships Abdiel, Wayland, and Engr Officer HM Submarine Statesman, 1943–45. Engr Officer HM Submarines Telemachus, Tudor and Alcide, 1945–50; Submarine Trials Officer, 1950–51; Engrg Dept, HM Dockyard, Portsmouth, 1951–53; SEO: Portsmouth Frigate Sqdn, 1954–55; 2nd Submarine Sqdn, 1956–57; Supt, ULE, Bournemouth, 1958–59; Dep. Captain Supt, AUWE, Portland, 1959–62; Dep. Manager, Engrg Dept, HM Dockyard, Portsmouth, 1962–64; in command, HMS Fisgard, 1965–66; Dep. Dir, Naval Ship Production, 1967–70; Dep. Chief Exec., Defence Quality Assurance Bd, 1970–71; Dir-Gen., Quality Assurance, MoD (PE), 1972–75. Director: Bolton House Investments PLC; James Martin Associates PLC. Chm., Nat. Council for Quality and Reliability, 1973–75; A Vice-Pres., Inst. of Quality Assurance, 1974– (Hon. FIQA); Vice-Pres., Internat. Orgn for Standardisation, 1985–; Bd Mem. for Internat. Affairs, BSI; Member: Internat. Acad. of Quality Assurance, 1977–; Agrément Bd, 1980–; Design Council, 1984–; Council, Cranfield Inst. of Technol. FRSA. *Publications:* papers on

Quality Assurance. *Recreation*: golf. *Address*: Ridgefield, Shawford, Hants. *T*: Twyford 712157. *Clubs*: Naval and Military, English-Speaking Union; Royal Fowey Yacht.

SPIEGL, Fritz; musician, writer, broadcaster; *b* 27 Jan. 1926; *s* of Rudolf Spiegl and Josefine Geiringer; *m* 1st, 1952, Bridget Katharine Fry (marr. diss. 1970); three *d*; 2nd, 1976, Ingrid Frances Romnes. *Educ*: Magdalen College Sch.; Royal Academy of Music (ARAM). Designer/typographer, Colman Prentis & Varley, 1941–46; Principal Flautist, Royal Liverpool Philharmonic, 1948–63; occasional spare flautist: RPO; CBSO; Hallé; BBC NSO; Founder/Conductor, Liverpool Music Group, Liverpool Wind Ensemble, 1949–; Director, The Spieglers, 1975–. Columnist: Liverpool Daily Post, 1970–; Classical Music, 1979–81; The Listener; broadcaster in various capacities. *Publications*: various edns of music; What the Papers Didn't Mean to Say, 1964; Lern Yerself Scouse, 1965; ABZ of Scouse, 1967; The Growth of a City, 1967; Liverpool Ballads, 1967; The Liverpool Manchester Railway, 1970; Slavers and Privateers, 1970; A Small Book of Grave Humour, 1971; Dead Funny, 1982; Keep Taking the Tabloids, 1983; Music Through the Looking-Glass, 1984; The Joy of Words, 1986; contrib. Grove's Dictionary of Music. *Recreations*: printing, cooking, inventing and several deadly sins. *Address*: 4 Windermere Terrace, Liverpool L8 3SB. *T*: 051–727 2727.

SPIERS, Donald Maurice, TD 1966; Controller of Research and Development Establishments, Research and Nuclear Programmes, Ministry of Defence, since 1986; *b* 27 Jan. 1934; *s* of Harold Herbert Spiers and Emma (*née* Foster); *m* 1958, Sylvia Mary Lowman; two *s* *Educ*: Raynes Park County Grammar Sch.; Trinity Coll., Cambridge (MA). CEng, MRAeS 1966. Commnd RE, 1952–54. de Havilland Engine Co., Hatfield, 1957–60; joined Air Min. as SSO, 1960; operational res. on deterrence, 1960–63; trials and analysis, Aden and Radfan, 1964; Kestrel evaluation trial, 1965; Scientific Adviser to FEAF, Singapore, 1967–70; Asst Chief Scientist (RAF), MoD, 1972–77; Asst Dir, Mil. Aircraft Projs, MoD (PE), 1978; Dir of Aircraft Post Design Services, MoD (PE), 1979–81; Dir Gen. Aircraft 1, MoD (PE), 1981–84; Dep. Controller Aircraft, MoD (PE), 1984–86; Head of Profession, Defence Engrg Service, 1986. *Recreation*: keeping old cars and lawnmowers working. *Address*: Ministry of Defence, Whitehall, SW1.

SPIERS, Prof. Frederick William, CBE 1962; Part-time Director, Bone Dosimetry Research, University of Leeds, 1972–78; Professor of Medical Physics, University of Leeds, 1950–72; *b* 29 July 1907; *er s* of Charles Edward and Annie Spiers; *m* 1936, Kathleen M. Brown; one *d*. *Educ*: Prince Henry's Grammar Sch., Evesham; University of Birmingham. 1st Class Hons Physics, 1929; PhD 1932; DSc 1952. Anglo-German Exchange Scholar, Univ. of Munich, 1930. Demonstrator in Physics, University of Leeds, 1931; Senior Physicist, General Infirmary, Leeds, 1935; Vis. Lecturer, Washington Univ., St Louis, USA, 1950. Hon. Director: MRC Environmental Radiation Unit, 1959–72; MRC Regional Radiological Protection Service, Leeds, 1963–70; Consultant to the Dir, NRPB, 1972–; Chief Regional Scientific Adviser for Civil Defence, NE Region, 1952–77; President, British Inst. of Radiology, 1955–56; Chairman: Hospital Physicists Assoc., 1944–45; British Cttee on Radiation Units and Measurements, 1967–77; Home Defence Scientific Adv. Standing Conference, 1972–77; Hon. Mem., Royal Coll. of Radiologists; Member: MRC Protection Cttee; Radio-active Substances Adv. Cttee, 1960–70; Internat. Commn on Radiation Units and Measurements, 1969–73; Statutory Adv. Cttee to National Radiological Protection Bd; Adv. Council on Calibration and Measurement, 1973–77. Silvanus Thompson Meml Lectr, British Inst. Radiology, 1973; Vis. Scientist, Argonne Nat. Laboratory, Univ. of Chicago, 1979. Röntgen Prize, 1950; Barclay Medal, 1970; Silver Jubilee Medal, 1977. FInstP 1970. *Publications*: Radioisotopes in the Human Body, 1968; articles on radiation physics and radiobiology in scientific journals; contribs in: British Practice in Radiotherapy, 1955; Radiation Dosimetry, 1956, 1969; Encyclopedia of Medical Radiology, 1968; Manual on Radiation Haematology, 1971. *Recreations*: photography, music, gardening. *Address*: Lanesfield House, Old Lane, Bramhope, near Leeds LS16 9AZ. *T*: Arthington 842680.

SPIERS, Ven. Graeme Hendry Gordon; Archdeacon of Liverpool, since 1979; *b* 15 Jan. 1925; *s* of Gordon and Mary Spiers; *m* 1958, Ann Chadwick; two *s*. *Educ*: Mercers Sch.; London College of Divinity. Westminster Bank, 1941–49; served RNVR, 1943–47. Deacon 1952, Priest 1953; Curate of Addiscombe, 1952–56; Succentor of Bradford Cathedral, 1956–58; Vicar of Speke, 1958–66; Vicar of Aigburth, 1966–80 and Rural Dean of Childwall, 1975–79. Hon. Canon, Liverpool Cathedral, 1977. *Recreation*: gardening. *Address*: 40 Sinclair Drive, Liverpool L18 0HW. *T*: 051–722 6675.

SPIERS, Air Cdre Reginald James, OBE 1972; FRAeS; Marketing Executive, GEC (formerly Marconi) Avionics, since 1984; *b* 8 Nov. 1928; *s* of Alfred James Oscar and Rose Emma Alice Spiers; *m* 1956, Cynthia Jeanette Williams; two *d*. *Educ*: Haberdashers' Aske's Sch.; RAF Coll., Cranwell. FRAeS 1975. Commissioned 1949; 247 and 64 Fighter Sqdns, 1950–54; Graduate, Empire Test Pilots' Sch., 1955; Fighter Test Sqdn, A&AEE, 1955–58; CO 4 Fighter Sqdn, 1958–61; PSO to C-in-C RAF Germany, 1961–63; RAF Staff Coll., 1964; FCO, 1965–67; CO RAF Masirah, 1967–68; Chief Test Flying Instructor, ETPS, 1968–71; Air Warfare Course, 1972; Air Secretary's Dept, MoD, 1972–73; MA to Governor of Gibraltar, 1973–75; CO Experimental Flying Dept, RAE Farnborough, 1975–78; Director, Defence Operational Requirements Staff, MoD, 1978–79; Comdt, A&AEE, Boscombe Down, 1979–83, retd. *Recreations*: shooting, aviation. *Address*: Barnside, Chalkcroft Lane, Penton Mewsey, near Andover, Hants SP11 0RQ. *T*: Weyhill 2376. *Club*: Royal Air Force.

SPIERS, Ronald Ian; Under Secretary of State for Management, United States, since 1983; *b* 9 July 1925; *s* of Tomas H. and Blanca De P. Spiers; *m* 1949, Patience Baker; one *s* three *d*. *Educ*: Dartmouth Coll., New Hampshire (BA); Princeton Univ. (Master in Public Affairs, PhD). Mem., US Delegn to UN, 1956–60; US Department of State: Dir, Office of Disarmament and Arms Control, 1960–62; Dir, Office of NATO Affairs, 1962–66; Political Counsellor, London, 1966–69; Asst Sec. of State, Politico-Military Affairs, 1969–73; Ambassador to the Bahamas, 1973–74; Minister, London, 1974–77; Ambassador to Turkey, 1977–80; Dir, Bureau of Intelligence and Research, Dept of State, 1980–81; Ambassador to Pakistan, 1981–83. *Recreations*: swimming, music, theatre-going, gardening. *Address*: c/o Department of State, Washington, DC 20520, USA.

SPIKINGS, Barry Peter; President, Nelson Holdings International; Chairman and Chief Executive: Galactic Films Inc.; Barry Spikings Productions Inc., since 1983; Chairman: Elstree Studios Ltd, since 1979; EMI TV Programms Inc., since 1979; Director: EMI Cinemas, since 1979; Pacific Vending Technology Ltd; Autovend Technology Corp., since 1986; *b* 23 Nov. 1939; *m* 1st, 1962, Judith Anne Spikings; one *s* one *d*; 2nd, 1978, Dorothy Spikings; two step *d*. *Educ*: Boston Grammar School. Managing Director, British Lion Films Ltd, 1973–75; Chairman, Shepperton Studios Ltd, 1973–75; Managing Director, EMI Films Ltd, Director, EMI Films Inc., 1975; Chm. and Chief Exec., Thorn EMI Films Worldwide, 1980–82. Oscar award as Producer of Best Picture of the Year, for The Deer Hunter, Acad. of Motion Picture Arts and Sciences, 1979. *Recreations*: making films. *Address*: B. Spikings Productions Inc., c/o Finley Kumble Wagner, 9100 Wilshire Boulevard, Beverly Hills, Calif 90212, USA. *Clubs*: Mark's, White Elephant, Burkes.

SPILLER, John Anthony Walsh, MBE 1979; Secretary General, Liberal Party, 1983–85; *b* 29 Dec. 1942; *s* of C. H. Spiller and Sarah (*née* Walsh), Moycullen, Co. Galway, Eire; *m* 1972, Angela, *d* of Surtees Gleghorn; one *s* one *d*. *Educ*: County Secondary Sch., Bideford; North Devon College. Member Executive, Nat. League of Young Liberals, 1960–61; Organiser, Torrington Constituency Liberal Assoc., 1962–64; Divl Liberal Agent, Cornwall (Northern) Parly Constituency, 1965–71; Northern Regional Organiser (Election Agent, Rochdale By-Elec. 1972 and Berwick-upon-Tweed By-Elec. 1973), 1972–74; Nat. Agent, Liberal Central Assoc., 1974–76; Mem., Liberal Party Gen. Elec. Campaign Cttee, and Press Officer, Gen. Elections Feb. and Oct. 1974; Western Area Agent, 1977–80; Advisor, African Peoples Union, Independence Elections, Zimbabwe, 1980; By-Elec. and Marginal Seats Agent, Liberal Party Org. Headquarters, 1981–82. *Recreation*: growing old roses. *Address*: Marine House, 4 North Street, Northam, by Bideford, Devonshire EX39 1DH. *Clubs*: National Liberal; Royal North Devon Golf (Westward Ho!).

SPIRO, Sidney, MC 1945; Consultant, Hambros Bank Ltd, since 1985; Chairman, Landor Associates (Europe) Ltd; *b* 27 July 1914; *m* 1949, Diana Susskind; two *d*. Law degree. RA in Middle East, Italy, 1939–45. Joined Anglo American Corp., 1953, Exec. Dir 1961–77; International Banking Consultant, 1977–; Man. Dir and Dep. Chm., Charter Consolidated, 1969, Chm. 1971–76; Director: De Beers Consolidated Mines Ltd; Minerals & Resources Corp., 1984–; Hambros plc, 1977–84. *Recreations*: shooting, golf, tennis, music. *Address*: 9 Cedar House, Marloes Road, W8. *Clubs*: White's, MCC; Swinley Forest Golf.

SPITZ, Kathleen Emily, (Mrs Heinz Spitz); *see* Gales, Kathleen Emily.

SPITZ, Prof. Lewis, PhD; FRCS, FRCSE; Nuffield Professor of Paediatric Surgery, Institute of Child Health, London, since 1979; Hon. Consultant Surgeon, Hospital for Sick Children, Great Ormond Street, and Queen Elizabeth Hospital for Children, London, since 1979; *b* 25 Aug. 1939; *s* of Woolf and Selma Spitz; *m* 1972, Louise Ruth Dyzenhaus; one *s* one *d*. *Educ*: Univ. of Pretoria (MB, ChB); Univ. of the Witwatersrand (PhD). FRCS (*ad eundem*) 1980; FRCSE 1969. Smith and Nephew Fellow, Liverpool and London, 1971; Paediatric Surgeon, Johannesburg, 1971–74; Consultant Paediatric Surgeon, Sheffield Children's Hosp., 1974–79. Hon. Consultant in Paediatric Surgery to the Army, 1983–. Member: British Assoc. of Paediatric Surgeons; Assoc. of Surgeons of GB and Ireland; British Paediatric Assoc.; British Soc. of Gastroenterology; MRSocMed. Exec. Editor, Progress in Paediatric Surgery, 1982; Member, Editorial Board: Jl of Paediatric Surgery, 1980–; Archives of Diseases in Childhood, 1984–; Annals of Paediatric Surgery, 1984–; Associate Editor, Pediatric Surgery International, 1986–. *Publications*: A Colour Atlas of Paediatric Surgical Diagnosis, 1981; A Colour Atlas of Surgery for Undescended Testes, 1984; chapters in books on paediatrics and surgery; articles on pyloric stenosis, biliary atresia and choledochal cyst, gastro-oesophageal reflux, and neonatal surgery. *Recreation*: tennis. *Address*: 78 Wood Vale, N10 3DN. *T*: 01–444 9985.

SPITZER, Prof. Lyman, (Jr), BA; PhD; Professor of Astronomy, 1947–82 (Charles A. Young Professor, 1952–82), Princeton University; Chairman of Astrophysical Sciences Department, and Director of Observatory, Princeton University, 1947–79; Chairman, Research Board, 1967–72; *b* 26 June 1914; *s* of Lyman Spitzer and Blanche B. (*née* Brumback); *m* 1940, Doreen D. Canaday; one *s* three *d*. *Educ*: Phillips Academy, Andover; Yale Univ. (BA); Cambridge Univ., England; Princeton Univ. (PhD). Instructor in Physics and Astronomy, Yale Univ., 1939–42; Scientist, Special Studies Group, Columbia Univ. Div. of War Research, 1942–44; Dir, Sonar Analysis Group, Columbia Univ. Div. of War Research, 1944–46; Assoc. Prof. of Astrophysics, Yale Univ., 1946–47. Dir Project Matterhorn, Princeton Univ., 1953–61; Chm. Exec. Cttee, Plasma Physics Lab., Princeton Univ., 1961–66; Principal Investigator, Princeton telescope on Copernicus satellite; Chm., Space Telescope Inst. Council, 1981–. Member: Nat. Acad. of Sciences; American Academy of Arts and Sciences; American Philosophical Society; Internat. Acad. of Astronautics; Corr. Member, Société Royale des Sciences, Liège; Foreign Associate, Royal Astronomical Soc.; Pres., American Astronomical Soc., 1959–61. Hon. Dr of Science: Yale Univ., 1958; Case Inst. of Technology, 1961; Harvard, 1975; Princeton, 1984; Hon. Dr of Laws, Toledo Univ., 1963. Rittenhouse Medal, 1957; NASA Medal, 1972; Bruce Medal, 1973; Draper Medal, 1974; Maxwell Prize, 1975; Dist. Public Service Medal, NASA, 1976; Gold Medal, RAS, 1978; Nat. Medal of Science, 1980; Janssen Medal, Soc. Astron. de France, 1980; Franklin Medal, Franklin Inst., 1980; Crafoord Prize, Royal Swedish Acad. Sci., 1985. *Publications*: (ed) Physics of Sound in the Sea, 1946; Physics of Fully Ionized Gases, 1956 (2nd edn 1962); Diffuse Matter in Space, 1968; Physical Processes in the Interstellar Medium, 1978; Searching between the Stars, 1982; papers in Astrophysical Jl, Monthly Notices of Royal Astronomical Soc., Physical Review, Physics of Fluids, on interstellar matter, stellar dynamics, plasma physics, etc. *Recreations*: ski-ing, mountain climbing. *Address*: 659 Lake Drive, Princeton, NJ 08540, USA. *T*: 609–924 3007. *Clubs*: Alpine; American Alpine.

SPOCK, Dr Benjamin McLane; Professor of Child Development, Western Reserve University, USA, 1955–67, now lecturing, writing and working for peace; *b* New Haven, Connecticut, 2 May 1903; *s* of Benjamin Ives Spock and Mildred Louise (*née* Stoughton); *m* 1st, 1927, Jane Davenport Cheney (marr. diss.); two *s*; 2nd, 1976, Mary Morgan. *Educ*: Yale Univ. (BA); Yale Medical Sch.; Coll. Physicians and Surgeons, Columbia Univ. (MD). In practice (Pediatrics) from 1933; Cornell Med. Coll.; NY Hospital; NYC Health Dept. Served, 1944–46 in US Navy. Subseq. on Staff of: Rochester (Minn) Child Health Inst., Mayo Clinic, University of Minnesota; Prof. of Child Development, University of Pittsburgh, 1951–55. *Publications*: Baby and Child Care, 1946; (with John Reinhart and Wayne Miller) A Baby's First Year, 1955; (with Miriam E. Lowenberg) Feeding Your Baby and Child, 1955; Dr Spock Talks with Mothers, 1961; Problems of Parents, 1962; (with Marion Lerrigo) Caring for Your Disabled Child, 1964; (with Mitchell Zimmerman) Dr Spock on Vietnam, 1968; Decent and Indecent: our personal and political behaviour, 1970; A Young Person's Guide to Life and Love, 1971; Raising Children in a Difficult Time, 1974 (UK as Bringing Up Children in a Difficult Time, 1974). *Relevant publications*: The Trial of Doctor Spock, by Jessica Mitford, 1969; Dr Spock: biography of a conservative radical, by Lynn Z. Bloom, 1972. *Address*: PO Box 1890, St Thomas, USVI 00801, USA.

SPOFFORD, Charles Merville, CBE (Hon.) 1945; DSM and Purple Heart (US), 1945; Lawyer (US); Trustee: Carnegie Corporation of New York; Juillard Musical Foundation; Director Emeritus: Council on Foreign Relations; Metropolitan Opera Association (Chairman Exec. Cttee, 1956–71, Member since 1971, President, 1946–50); Vice-Chairman and Director Emeritus, Lincoln Center for the Performing Arts, Inc.; Member Exec. Cttee, American Branch, International Law Association; former Member Exec. Council, American Society International Law, etc.; Trustee, The Mutual Life Insurance Co. of New York; *b* 17 Nov. 1902; *s* of Charles W. and Beulah Merville Spofford; *m* 1st, 1930, Margaret Mercer Walker (marr. diss. 1960); two *s* two *d*; 2nd, 1960, Carolyn Storrs Andre (*d* 1970); 3rd, 1970, Sydney Brewster Luddy. *Educ*: Northwest Univ.; University of Grenoble; Yale Univ. (AB 1924; Hon. MA 1956); Harvard Law Sch. JD 1928. Instructor, European History, Yale Univ., 1924–25, and sometime Alumni Fellow; practised Law, Chicago, 1929–30, New York (Davis Polk & Wardwell), 1930–40;

member of firm, 1940–50 and 1952–. Lieut-Colonel 1942, AFHQ Algiers; adv. on econ. and supply, French N Africa and French W Africa, 1942–43; Chief of Planning Staff (for AMG Sicily and Italy); Dep. Chief Civil Affairs Officer for Sicily and S Italy, 1943–44; AFHQ, Asst Chief of Staff, (G-5) Med. Theatre, 1944–45; War Dept as Military Adv. to State Dept, 1945; Colonel, 1943; Brig-General, 1944. Asst to President and Special Counsel to American National Red Cross, 1946–50; also other former civic activities. Deputy US Representative, North Atlantic Council, and Chairman, North Atlantic Council Deputies, 1950–52; Member European Co-ordinating Cttee (US); resigned 1952, to rejoin law firm. Formerly Director: American Univ. in Beirut, 1957–63; Nat. Council, English-Speaking Union, 1955–64; The Distillers Co. Ltd, 1952–76; subsid. CIBA Corp., 1957–71; Inst. for Defense Analyses, 1960–70. Carnegie Lectr, Hague Acad. of Internat. Law, 1964. Hon. LLD Northwestern Univ., 1959. Comdr, Order of Nishan Iftikhar, Tunisia, 1943; Croix de Guerre with palm, France, 1945; Commander, Order of SS Maurice and Lazarus, Italy, 1945; Commander, Legion of Honour, France, 1952; Commander with Star, Order of the Falcon, Iceland, 1953; Grand Officer, Order of the Crown, Belgium. *Recreation:* golf. *Publications:* articles in journals. *Address:* (business) 1 Chase Manhattan Plaza, New York, NY 10005, USA; (residence) Windmill Lane, East Hampton, New York, NY 11937. *Clubs:* Century Association, Links (New York); Maidstone (East Hampton).

SPOKES, Ann; *see* Spokes Symonds, A. H.

SPOKES, John Arthur Clayton, QC 1973; a Recorder of the Crown Court, since 1972; *b* 6 Feb. 1931; 2nd *s* of late Peter Spencer Spokes and Lilla Jane Spokes (*née* Clayton), Oxford; *m* 1961, Jean, *yr d* of late Dr Robert McLean, Carluke, and Jean Symington McLean (*née* Barr); one *s* one *d. Educ:* Westminster Sch.; Brasenose Coll., Oxford. BA 1954; MA 1959. Nat. Service, Royal Artillery, 1949–51 (commnd 1950). Called to Bar, Gray's Inn, 1955, Bencher, 1985. Chm., Data Protection Tribunal, 1985–. Chancellor, Dio. of Winchester, 1985–. *Recreations:* gardening, walking. *Address:* 3 Pump Court, Temple, EC4Y 7AJ. *T:* 01-353 0711. *Club:* Leander (Henley-on-Thames).
See also A. H. Spokes Symonds.

SPOKES SYMONDS, Ann (Hazel); Chairman, Age Concern England, 1983–86; *b* 10 Nov. 1925; *d* of Peter Spencer Spokes and Lilla Jane Spokes (*née* Clayton); *m* 1980, (John) Richard (Charters) Symonds, *qv*. *Educ:* Wychwood Sch., Oxford; Masters Sch., Dobbs Ferry, NY, USA; St Anne's Coll., Oxford (BA 1947; MA). Organising Secretary: Oxford Council of Social Service, 1959–74; Age Concern Oxford, 1958–80. Dir, ATV, 1978–81; Mem. W Midlands Bd, Central Indep. Television plc, 1981–. Mem., Thames Valley Police Authy, 1973–85; Chm., No 5 Police Dist. Authy Cttee, 1982–85; Vice-Chm., Personal Social Services Council, 1978–80; Chm., Social Services Cttee, ACC, 1978–82; Mem. Bd, Anchor Housing Assoc., 1976–83, 1985–; Member: Prince of Wales' Adv. Gp on Disability, 1983–; Oftel Adv. Cttee for Disabled and Elderly People, 1985–; Trustee, CERT, 1986–. Member: Oxford City Council, 1957– (Lord Mayor, 1976–77); Oxfordshire CC, 1974–85 (Chm., 1981–83). Contested (C) NE Leicester, 1959, Brigg, 1966 and 1970. *Recreations:* lawn tennis, photography, enjoying cats. *Address:* 43 Davenant Road, Oxford OX2 8BU. *T:* Oxford 55661. *Club:* Royal Over-Seas League.
See also J. A. C. Spokes.

SPOONER, Edward Tenney Casswell, CMG 1966; MD, MA, MRCS, LRCP; FRCP; *b* 22 May 1904; *s* of William Casswell Spooner, MB, and Edith Maud Spooner, Blandford, Dorset; *m* 1948, Colin Mary Stewart. *Educ:* Epsom Coll.; Clare Coll., Cambridge; St Bartholomew's Hospital. Foundation Scholar of Clare Coll., 1923; House Physician, St Bartholomew's Hospital, 1927–28; Commonwealth Fellow, Harvard Medical Sch., 1929–31; Fellow of Clare Coll., 1929–47; Tutor of Clare Coll., 1939–47; University Demonstrator and Lecturer, Dept of Pathology, University of Cambridge, 1931–46; Professor of Bacteriology and Immunology, London School of Hygiene and Tropical Medicine, 1947–60, Dean, 1960–70. Temporary Major, RAMC, in No 1 Medical Research Section, 1942–43; Director, Emergency Public Health Laboratory, Cambridge, 1943–44; Editor, Journal of Hygiene, 1949–55; Member Medical Research Council, 1953–57; Member Council Epsom Coll., 1955–65; Chm., Public Health Lab. Service Bd, 1963–72. *Publications:* papers on tetanus, certain virus diseases and wound infection. *Address:* Ellergarth, Dalditch Lane, Knowle, Budleigh Salterton, Devon EX9 7AH.

SPOONER, Prof. Frank Clyffurde, MA, PhD, LittD; Professor of Economic History, University of Durham, 1966–85, now Emeritus; *b* 5 March 1924; *s* of Harry Gordon Morrison Spooner. *Educ:* Bromley Grammar Sch.; Christ's Coll., Cambridge. Hist. Tripos, 1st cl., Pt I 1947 and Pt II 1948; MA 1949, PhD 1953; LittD 1985. War Service, Sub-Lt (S) RNVR, 1943–46; Bachelor Research Scholar, 1948; Chargé de Recherches, CNRS, Paris, 1949–50; Allen Scholar, 1951; Fellow, Christ's Coll., Cambridge, 1951–57; Commonwealth Fund Fellow, 1955–57 at Chicago, Columbia, New York, and Harvard Univs; Ecole Pratique des Hautes Etudes, VI Section, Sorbonne, 1957–61; Lectr, Univ. of Oxford, 1958–59; Vis. Lectr in Econs, Harvard Univ., 1961–62; Irving Fisher Research Prof. of Econs, Yale Univ., 1962–63; Univ. of Durham: Lectr, 1963; Reader, 1964; Resident Tutor-in-charge, Lumley Castle, 1965–70; Dir, Inst. of European Studies, 1969–76; Leverhulme Fellow, 1976–78; Leverhulme Emeritus Fellow, 1985–86. FRHistS 1970; FSA 1983. Prix Limantour de l'Académie des Sciences Morales et Politiques, 1957; West European Award, British Academy, 1979; Ernst Meyer Award, 1983. *Publications:* L'économie mondiale et les frappes monétaires en France, 1493–1680, 1956, revised edn The International Economy and Monetary Movements in France, 1493–1725, 1972; Risks at Sea: Amsterdam insurance and maritime Europe 1766–1780, 1983; contribs to joint works and to jls. *Recreations:* music, photography, walking. *Address:* 31 Chatsworth Avenue, Bromley, Kent BR1 5DP. *Club:* United Oxford & Cambridge University.

SPOONER, Sir James (Douglas), Kt 1981; Chairman: Coats Viyella (formerly Vantona Viyella), since 1969; Morgan Crucible, since 1983 (Director, since 1978); Director, John Swire & Sons, since 1970; *b* 11 July 1932; *s* of late Vice-Adm. E. J. Spooner, DSO, and Megan Spooner (*née* Megan Foster, the singer); *m* 1958, Jane Alyson, *d* of Sir Gerald Glover, *qv*; two *s* one *d. Educ:* Eton Coll.; Christ Church, Oxford. Chartered Accountant 1962; Partner, Dixon Wilson & Co., Chartered Accountants, 1963–72. Chm., NAAFI, 1973–86; Director: Abingworth, 1973–; J. Sainsbury, 1981–; Barclays Bank, 1983–; Hogg Robinson Gp, 1971–85 (Dep. Chm., 1971–85). Chm., Council KCL, 1986–. *Recreations:* music, history, shooting. *Address:* Regis House, 43–46 King William Street, EC4R 9BE. *Clubs:* White's, Beefsteak.

SPOTSWOOD, Marshal of the Royal Air Force Sir Denis (Frank), GCB 1971 (KCB 1966; CB 1961); CBE 1946; DSO 1943; DFC 1942; Director: Smiths Industries International Aerospace and Defence Companies, since 1982 (Chairman, 1980–82); Dowty Group, since 1980; *b* 26 Sept. 1916; *s* of late F. H. Spotswood and M. C. Spotswood; *m* 1942, Ann (*née* Child); one *s*. Commissioned in RAF, 1936; UK Service in Squadrons, 1937–41; No 209 Squadron, 1939–41. Served War of 1939–45 (despatches twice, DSO). Chief Instructor, Operation Training Unit, 1941–42; Officer Commanding No 500 (County of Kent) Squadron, RAuxAF, 1942–43; Director of Plans, HQ Supreme Allied Commander, South East Asia, 1944–46; Directing Staff, RAF Staff Coll., 1946–48; Officer Commanding RAF (Fighter) Stations, Horsham St Faith and Coltishall, 1948–50; Directing Staff, Imperial Defence Coll., 1950–52; Exchange Duties, HQUSAF in USA, 1952–54; Officer Commanding RAF (Fighter) Station, Linton-on-Ouse, 1954–56; Deputy Director of Plans, Air Ministry, 1956–58; AOC and Commandant, RAF Coll., Cranwell, 1958–61; Assistant Chief of Staff (Air Defence), SHAPE, 1961–63; AOC No 3 Group, RAF Bomber Command, 1964–65; C-in-C RAF Germany, 1965–68; Commander, 2nd Allied Tactical Air Force, 1966–68; AOC-in-C, RAF Strike Command, 1968–71; Comdr, UK Air Defence Region, 1968–71; Chief of the Air Staff, 1971–74. Group Captain, 1954; Air Commodore, 1958; Air Vice-Marshal, 1961; Air Marshal, 1965; Air Chief Marshal, 1968; Marshal of the RAF, 1974. ADC to the Queen, 1957–61, Air ADC to the Queen, 1970–74. Vice-Chm. and Dir, Rolls Royce Ltd, 1974–80; Chm., Turbo Union Ltd, 1975–80; Dir, RR/Turbomeca Ltd. Pres., SBAC, 1978–79. Chm. of Governors, Royal Star and Garter Home, 1981–85 (Gov., 1974–80); Vice-Patron, RAF Museum (Chm. of Trustees, 1974–80). FRAeS 1975. Officer of the Legion of Merit (USA). *Recreations:* golf, sailing, shooting, bridge. *Address:* c/o Royal Bank of Scotland, Whitehall, SW1. *Clubs:* Royal Air Force; Phyllis Court (Henley); Huntercombe Golf.

SPOTTISWOOD, Air Vice-Marshal James Donald, CVO 1977; AFC 1971; Air Officer Training, RAF Support Command, since 1986; *b* 27 May 1934; *s* of James Thomas Spottiswood and Caroline Margaret Spottiswood; *m* 1957, Margaret Maxwell (*née* Harrison); two *s* one *d. Educ:* West Hartlepool Grammar School; Boston Univ., USA (MA). Enlisted RAF, 1951, commissioned, 1952; 617 Sqn, 1962–64; Royal Naval Staff Coll., 1965; PSO to C-in-C Middle East, 1966–67; Commanded 53 Sqn, 1968–70; JSSC, 1970; Commanded: RAF Thorney Island, 1972–75; RAF Benson, 1975–76; Dep. Captain, the Queen's Flight, 1975–76; RCDS, 1978; Secretary to IMS, HQ NATO, 1980–83; DG of Trng, RAF, 1983–85. *Recreations:* gliding, sailing, golf. *Address:* Royal Bank of Scotland, High Street, Oxford. *Club:* Royal Air Force.

SPRAGGS, Rear-Adm. Trevor Owen Keith, CB 1983; CEng, FIEE; Chief of Staff to Commander-in-Chief, Naval Home Command, 1981–83; *b* 17 June 1926; *s* of Cecil James Spraggs and Gladys Maude (*née* Morey); *m* 1955, Mary Patricia Light (*d* 1983); two *s*; *m* 1986, Gwynedd Kate Green (*née* Adams). *Educ:* Portsmouth Grammar Sch.; St John's Coll., Southsea; Imperial College of Science and Technology, London (BScEng, ACGI). Joined Royal Navy, 1945; courses: HM Ships: King Alfred, Leander, Harrier, 1945–47; Admiralty Compass Obs., Slough, 1948; BRNC, Dartmouth, 1948–50; HM Ships: Dryad, Vanguard, Vernon, Collingwood, Ariel, Falcon, 1950–61; AEI, Manchester, 1962; RNEC, 1962–66; HMS Collingwood, 1966–69 and 1972–75; RNEC, 1969–72, and, as Dean, 1979–80; Dean, RNC, Greenwich, 1975–77; Dir of Naval Trng Support, Dir of Naval Educn and Trng Support, 1977–79; Chief Naval Instr Officer, 1981–83. ADC to the Queen, 1979. Member: Nautical Studies Bd of CNAA, 1975–80; Maritime Studies Adv. Cttee of Plymouth Polytech., 1979–80; Cttee of Management, Royal Hosp. Sch., Holbrook, 1981–83; Governor: Fareham Technical Coll., 1972–75; RN Sch. for Officers' Daughters, Haslemere, 1975–77. Pres., Combined Services and RN Amateur Athletic Assocs, 1981–83. *Recreations:* golf, sailing, rifle shooting, gardening. *Address:* c/o Lloyds Bank, 46 Station Road, Hayling Island, Hants. *Clubs:* Royal Naval Sailing Association; Hayling Golf.

SPRATT, Col Greville Douglas, TD 1962, Bar 1968; DL; JP; Underwriting Member of Lloyd's, 1950; *b* 1 May 1927; *e s* of Hugh Douglas Spratt and Sheelah Ivy (*née* Stace); *m* 1954, Sheila Farrow Wade; three *d. Educ:* Leighton Park; Charterhouse. Served Coldstream Guards, 1945–46; commnd Oxfordshire and Bucks LI, 1946; seconded to Arab Legion; served Palestine, Trans Jordan and Egypt, 1946–48; GSO III (Ops and Intell.), 1948. Lloyd's, 1948–61; Joined J. & N. Wade Gp of Electrical Distributors, 1961; Dir, 1969–76 and Man. Dir, 1972–76. Lieut of the City of London, 1972; Life Mem., Guild of Freemen, 1977 (Mem. Court, 1982–); Liveryman, Ironmongers' Co., 1977– (Mem. Ct, 1982–); Alderman, Castle Baynard Ward, 1978–; JP 1978; Sheriff of the City of London, 1984–85; DL Greater London, 1986. Joined HAC Infantry Bn as private, 1950; re-commnd 1950; CO, 1962–65; Regtl Col, 1966–70; Mem., Ct of Assts, HAC, 1960–70 and 1978–; ADC to the Queen, 1973–78; Mem., City TA&VRA, 1960– (Vice Chm., 1973–77, Chm., 1977–82); Vice Chm., TA&VRA for Greater London, 1980– (Mem., Exec. and Finance Cttee, 1977–); Hon. Col, City and NE sector, London ACF. Pres., London Fedn of Old Comrades Assocs, 1983–; Dep. Pres., London, British Red Cross, 1983–; Member Council: Reserve Forces Assoc., 1981–84; Action Res. for the Crippled Child, 1982– (Mem. Haslemere Cttee, 1971–82). Member: Cttee, Guildhall Sch. of Music and Drama, 1978–80; Court, City Univ., 1981–; Governing Bodies of Girls' Schs Assoc., 1982–; Governor: St Ives Sch., 1976– (Vice Chm., 1977–86; Chm., 1986–); King Edward's Sch., Witley, 1978–; Christ's Hosp., 1978–; Bridewell Royal Hosp., 1978–; City of London Sch. for Girls, 1981–82; Malvern Girls' Coll., 1982–; St Paul's Cathedral Choir Sch., 1985–; Charterhouse, 1985–; Life Governor, Corp. of the Sons of the Clergy, 1985–; Patron, Internat. Centre for Child Studies, 1985–. Blackdown Cttee, Nat. Trust, 1977–. Trustee: Chichester Theatre; Endowment of St Paul's Cathedral; Childrens' Research Internat. Carthusian Trust; Castle Baynard Educnl Trust. FRSA. OStJ 1985. Chevalier de la Légion d'Honneur, 1961; Commandeur de l'Ordre National du Mérite, 1984; Commander, Order of the Lion, Malaŵi, 1985; Mem., Nat. Order of Aztec Eagle, Mexico, 1985. *Recreations:* tennis, music, military history, forestry. *Address:* Grayswood Place, Haslemere, Surrey GU27 2ET. *T:* Haslemere 4367. *Clubs:* City Livery, Guildhall, United Wards, City Pickwick; Cowdray Park Golf and Polo.

SPRECKLEY, (John) Nicholas (Teague), CMG 1983; HM Diplomatic Service; British High Commissioner in Kuala Lumpur, since 1986; *b* 6 Dec. 1934; *s* of late Air Marshal Sir Herbert Spreckley, KBE, CB, and Winifred Emery Teague; *m* 1958, Margaret Paula Jane, *er d* of Prof. W. McC. Stewart, *qv*; one *s* one *d. Educ:* Winchester Coll.; Magdalene Coll., Cambridge (BA). Tokyo, 1957–62; American Dept, FO, 1962–64; Asst Private Sec. to Lord Carrington and Mr Padley, 1964; Defence Dept, FO, 1964–66; Head of Chancery, Dakar, 1966–70; Paris, 1970–75; Head of Referendum Unit, FCO, 1975; Counsellor and Head of Chancery, Tokyo, 1976–78; Fellow, Center for Internat. Affairs, Harvard Univ., 1978–79; Head of European Community Dept (Internal), FCO, 1979–83; Ambassador to Republic of Korea, 1983–86. *Address:* c/o Foreign and Commonwealth Office, SW1A 2AL. *Club:* Army and Navy.

SPREULL, Professor James (Spreull Andrew); William Dick Professor of Veterinary Surgery, at the University of Edinburgh, 1959–78, now Emeritus; *b* 2 May 1908; *s* of late Lt-Col Andrew Spreull, DSO, TD, MRCVS, and Effie Andrew Spreull; *m* 1951, Kirsten Brummerstedt-Hansen; three *s. Educ:* Dundee High Sch.; Edinburgh Univ. (PhD); Royal Dick Veterinary Coll. (MRCVS). Royal Dick Veterinary College: Demonstrator of Anatomy, 1930–34, Lecturer in Applied Anatomy, 1931–34. Engaged in general practice in Dundee, 1934–59. FRSE 1965. *Publications:* various contributions to Veterinary Journals. *Recreations:* agriculture, fishing, badminton, antiques. *Address:* Spencerfield House, Hillend, Fife KY11 5LA. *T:* Inverkeithing 414255.

SPRIDDELL, Peter Henry; Director, Marks & Spencer, since 1970; *b* 18 Aug. 1928; *s* of Thomas Henry Spriddell and Eva Florence Spriddell; *m* 1952, Joyce Patricia (*née* Haycock); two *s* one *d. Educ:* Plymouth Coll.; Exeter Coll., Oxford (MA); Harvard

Business Sch. Joined Marks & Spencer Ltd, 1951: Alternate Dir Store Ops, 1970, full Dir, 1972; Dir of Personnel, 1972–75; Dir Estates, Bldg, Store Ops, Physical Distribution, 1975–. Dir, NFC, 1978–82. Member Council: Templeton Coll; Oxford (formerly Oxford Centre for Management Studies), 1978–; Town and Country Planning Assoc.; Vice-Pres., Devon Historic Bldgs Trust, 1978–. FRSA. Freeman, City of London; Liveryman, Worshipful Co. of Paviors, 1984. *Recreations*: music, golf. *Address*: 37 Main Avenue, Moor Park Estate, Northwood, Mddx. *T*: Northwood 29654. *Club*: Moor Park Golf.

SPRIGGE, Prof. Timothy Lauro Squire, PhD; Professor of Logic and Metaphysics, University of Edinburgh, since 1979; *b* 14 Jan. 1932; *s* of Cecil and Katriona Sprigge; *m* 1959, Giglia Gordon; one *s* twin *d. Educ*: Gonville and Caius Coll., Cambridge (MA, PhD). Lecturer in Philosophy, University Coll. London, 1961–63; Lectr in Philosophy, 1963–70, Reader in Philosophy, 1970–79, Univ. of Sussex. Visiting Associate Professor, Univ. of Cincinnati, 1968–69. Member: Aristotelian Soc., 1960–; Mind Assoc., 1955–; Assoc. for the Advancement of Amer. Philosophy, 1978–; Scots Philosophical Club, 1979–. *Publications*: ed, Correspondence of Jeremy Bentham, vols 1 and 2, 1968; Facts, Words and Beliefs, 1970; Santayana: an examination of his philosophy, 1974; The Vindication of Absolute Idealism, 1983; Theories of Existence, 1985; contribs to various vols of philosophical essays and to periodicals, incl. Mind, Philosophy, Inquiry, Nous. *Recreation*: backgammon. *Address*: David Hume Tower, University of Edinburgh, George Square, Edinburgh EH8 9JX. *T*: 031–667 1011.

SPRIGGS, Leslie, JP; *b* 22 April 1910; British; *m* 1931, Elfrida Mary Brindle Parkinson. *Educ*: Council Sch.; Trade Union Adult Schools. TU Scholarship to Belgium, 1951. Merchant Service, then Railwayman until 1958. Formerly: President, NW (NUR) District Council, Political Section, 1954; Vice-President, Industrial Section, 1955. Served as Auditor to Lancs and Cheshire Region of the Labour Party. Formerly Lecturer, National Council of Labour Colleges on Industrial Law, Economics, Foreign Affairs, Local Government, Trade Union History. MP (Lab) St Helens, June 1958–1983; Member Parliamentary Groups: Employment, Environment, Health, Industry, Transport, and Trade, incl. aviation, shipping, textiles, clothing and footwear. JP N Fylde, 1955. *Recreations*: Rugby League, athletics, water polo, soccer, bowls, gardening. *Address*: 38 Knowle Avenue, Cleveleys, Lancs FY5 3PP. *T*: Cleveleys 852746.

SPRING, Frank Stuart, FRS 1952; DSc (Manchester), PhD (Liverpool), FRSC; Director, Laporte Industries Ltd, London, W1, 1959–71; retired; *b* 5 Sept. 1907; 3rd *s* of John Spring and Isabella Spring, Crosby, Liverpool; *m* 1932, Mary, 2nd *d* of Rev. John Mackintosh, MA, Heswall; one *s* one *d. Educ*: Waterloo Grammar Sch.; University of Liverpool. United Alkali Research Scholar, University of Liverpool, 1928–29; University Fellow, Liverpool, 1929–30. Assistant Lecturer, Lecturer and Senior Lecturer in Chemistry, University of Manchester, 1930–46; Freeland Professor of Chemistry, The Royal College of Science and Technology, Glasgow, 1946–59. Chemical Society, Tilden Lecturer, 1950. Hon. DSc: Salford, 1967; Strathclyde, 1981. *Publications*: papers (mostly jtly) in chemical journals. *Address*: Flat 26, 1 Hyde Park Square, W2 2JZ. *T*: 01–262 8174.

SPRING, Richard, (Dick Spring); Member of the Dáil (TD) (Lab), North Kerry, since 1981; Deputy Prime Minister, since 1982; Minister for Energy, since 1983; Leader of the Irish Labour Party, since 1982; *b* 29 Aug. 1950; *s* of Daniel and Anne Spring; *m* 1977, Kristi Lee Hutcheson; one *s* one *d. Educ*: Mt St Joseph Coll., Roscrea; Trinity Coll., Dublin (BA 1972). Called to the Bar, King's Inns, Dublin, 1975; in practice on Munster Circuit, 1977–81. Minister of State, Dept of Justice, 1981–82; Minister for the Environment, 1982–83. *Recreations*: swimming, reading. *Address*: Dunroamin, Cloonanorig, Tralee, Co. Kerry, Ireland. *T*: Tralee 25337.

SPRING RICE, family name of **Baron Monteagle of Brandon**.

SPRINGER, Sir Hugh (Worrell), GCMG 1984 (KCMG 1971); GCVO 1985; KA 1984; CBE 1961 (OBE 1954); Governor-General, Barbados, since 1984; Barrister-at-Law; *b* 1913; 2nd *s* of late Charles W. Springer, Barbados, and late Florence Springer; *m* 1942, Dorothy Drinan, 3rd *d* of late Lionel Gittens, Barbados, and Cora Gittens; three *s* one *d. Educ*: Harrison Coll., Barbados; Hertford Coll., Oxford (Hon. Fellow 1974). BA 1936, MA 1944. Called to Bar, Inner Temple, 1938. Practice at the Bar, Barbados, 1938–47; MCP, 1940–47, MEC 1944–47, Barbados; Gen.-Sec., Barbados Lab. Party, 1940–47; Organiser and first Gen.-Sec., Workers' Union, 1940–47; Mem., West Indies Cttee of the Asquith Commn on Higher Educn, 1944; Mem., Provisional Council, University Coll. of the West Indies, 1947; first Registrar, Univ. Coll. of WI, 1947–63; John Simon Guggenheim Fellow and Fellow of Harvard Center for Internat. Affairs, 1961–62; first Dir, Univ. of WI Inst. of Educn, 1963–66; Commonwealth Asst Sec.-Gen., 1966–70; Sec.-Gen., ACU, 1970–80. Past Mem., Public Service and other Commns and Cttees in Barbados, Jamaica and W Indies; Sen. Vis. Fellow of All Souls Coll., Oxford, 1962–63; Actg Governor of Barbados, 1964; Mem., Bermuda Civil Disorder Commn, 1968. Chm., Commonwealth Caribbean Med. Res. Council (formerly Brit. Caribbean Med. Research Cttee), 1965–84; Vice-Pres., British Caribbean Assoc., 1974–80; Trustee, Bernard Van Leer Foundn, 1967–78; Barbados Trustee, Commonwealth Foundn, 1967–80, and Chm., 1974–77; Member, Court of Governors: LSE, 1970–80; Exeter Univ., 1970–80; Hull Univ., 1970–80; London Sch. of Hygiene and Tropical Medicine, 1974–77; Inst. of Commonwealth Studies, 1974–80. Trustee, Harlow Campus, Meml Univ. of Newfoundland, 1975–79. Jt Sec., UK Commonwealth Scholarships Commn, 1970–80; Exec. Sec., Marshall Scholarships Commn, 1970–80; Sec., Kennedy Memorial Trust, 1970–80; Chm., Commonwealth Human Ecology Council, 1971–84 (Hon. Pres., 1984–); Member: Council, USPG, 1972–79; Adv. Cttee, Sci. Policy Foundn, 1977–; Bd of Dirs, United World Colleges, 1978–; Bd of Trustees, Sir Ernest Cassel Educational Trust, 1978–81; Pres., Educn Section, British Assoc., 1974–75; Chm., Jt Commonwealth Socs Council, 1978–80. Hon. Prof. of Educn, Mauritius, 1981. Hon. DSc Soc Laval, 1958; Hon. LLD: Victoria, BC, 1972; Univ. of WI, 1973; City, 1978; Manchester, 1979; York, Ontario, 1980; Zimbabwe, 1981; Bristol, 1982; Birmingham, 1983; Hon. DLitt: Warwick, 1974; Ulster, 1974; Heriot-Watt, 1976; Hong Kong, 1977; St Andrews, 1977; Hon. DCL: New Brunswick, 1980; Oxon, 1980; East Anglia, 1980. KStJ 1985. *Publications*: Reflections on the Failure of the First West Indian Federation, 1962 (USA); articles and lectures on West Indian and Commonwealth Educn and Development, in: The Round Table, Commonwealth, RSA Jl, Caribbean Quarterly, Internat. Organisation, Jl of Negro History, etc. *Recreations*: walking, talking. *Address*: Government House, Barbados; Gibbes, St Peter, Barbados. *T*: 22591. *Clubs*: Athenæum, Royal Commonwealth Society.

SPRINGER, Tobias; a Metropolitan Stipendiary Magistrate, 1963–82; Barrister-at-law; *b* 3 April 1907; *o c* of late Samuel Springer, MBE; *m* 1937, Stella Rauchwerger. *Educ*: Mill Hill Sch.; Caius Coll., Cambridge. Law Tripos 1928; called to Bar, Gray's Inn, 1929. Practised London and SE Circuit. Served War of 1939–45: 60th Rifles, 1940–45; Lt-Col GSO1, GHQ, H Forces, 1944. Returned to practise at Bar, 1945. Actg Dep. Chm., Co. London Sessions, periods 1962, 1963; sometime Dep. Circuit Judge. Life Governor: Mill Hill School; Metropolitan Hosp. Freedom, City of London, 1982. *Recreations*: travel, golf,

reading. *Address*: 82 Cholmley Gardens, Fortune Green Road, NW6 1UN. *T*: 01–435 0817. *Clubs*: Hurlingham, Old Mill Hillians; Porters Park Golf.

SPRINGETT, Jack Allan, CBE 1978; MA (Cantab); Education Officer, Association of Metropolitan Authorities, 1980–82; *b* 1 Feb. 1916; *s* of Arthur John and Agnes Springett; *m* 1950, Patricia Winifred Singleton; three *s* one *d. Educ*: Windsor Grammar Sch.; Fitzwilliam House, Cambridge. Asst Master, Christ's Hospital, Horsham, 1938–47. Served War, Royal Signals and Gen. Staff, 1940–46. Administrative Asst, North Riding, 1947–52; Asst Educn Officer, Birmingham, 1952–62; Dep. Educn Officer, Essex, 1962–73; County Educn Officer, Essex, 1973–80. *Address*: 3 Roxwell Road, Chelmsford, Essex CM1 2LY. *T*: Chelmsford 58669.

SPRINGFORD, John Frederick Charles, CBE 1980 (OBE 1970); retired British Council Officer; *b* 6 June 1919; *s* of Frederick Charles Springford and Bertha Agnes Springford (*née* Trenery); *m* 1945, Phyllis Wharton; one *s* two *d. Educ*: Latymer Upper Sch.; Christ's College, Cambridge (MA). Served War 1940–46, RAC; seconded Indian Armoured Corps, 1942; Asst Political Agent II in Mekran, 1945. British Council Service, Baghdad and Mosul, Iraq, 1947–51, Isfahan, Iran, 1951–52; British Council Representative: Tanzania, 1952–57; Sudan, 1957–62; Dir, Overseas Students Dept, 1962–66; Representative: Jordan, 1966–69; Iraq, 1969–74; Canada, 1974–79, and Counsellor, Cultural Affairs, British High Commission, Ottawa. Mem. Council, British Sch. of Archaeology in Iraq, 1980–86. Hon. Sec., Sussex Heritage Trust, 1980–83; Chm., Sussex Eastern Sub-Area, RSCM, 1981–85, Chm., Sussex Area, 1985–. *Recreations*: archaeology, organ music. *Address*: Precinct, Crowhurst, Battle, East Sussex TN33 9AA. *T*: Crowhurst 200.

SPRINGMAN, Dame Ann (Marcella), DBE 1980 (OBE 1974); Hon. Vice-President, National Union of Conservative and Unionist Associations, since 1981 (Chairman, 1980–81; Vice-Chairman, 1978–80; Member, Executive Committee, 1970–84); *b* 5 Jan. 1933; *d* of late Lt-Col Noel Mulloy, MC, The Scinde Horse, and Marcella Mulloy; *m* 1955, Michael Springman; three *s* one *d. Educ*: St George's Sch., Ascot; Harcombe House, Uplyme, Lyme Regis. Founder secretary, Bracknell and District Br., RNLI, 1960–63. Councillor, Easthampstead, subseq. Bracknell District Council, 1968–76 (Chm., Planning Cttee, 1970–72); Council Representative, Bracknell Development Corp. Jt Consultative Cttee, 1968–71. Chairman: Wessex Conservative Women's Adv. Cttee, 1970–73; Wokingham Conservative Assoc., 1972–75; Conservative Women's Nat. Adv. Cttee, 1975–78; E Sussex FPC, 1985–; District Commissioner, Bracknell West Girl Guides, 1970–72; Governor, Easthampstead Park Sch. and Adult Educn Centre, 1975–77. Member: Women's National Commn, 1978–84; ESRC (formerly SSRC), 1979–85; Thomas Coram Res. Unit Adv. Cttee, 1981–85. *Recreation*: family life. *Address*: The Old Farmhouse, Horstedpond Farm, Uckfield, Sussex TN22 5TR. *T*: Uckfield 5406.

SPROAT, Iain Mac Donald; Consultant, N. M. Rothschild and Sons Ltd, merchant bankers, since 1983; *b* Dollar, Clackmannanshire, 8 Nov. 1938; *s* of late William Bigham Sproat and of Lydia Bain Sproat (*née* MacDonald); *m* 1979, Judith Mary Kernot (*née* King); one step *s. Educ*: Melrose; Winchester; Oxford. MP (C) Aberdeen South, 1970–83; Parly Under-Sec. of State, Dept of Trade, 1981–83. Contested (C) Roxburgh and Berwickshire, 1983. *Publications*: (ed) Cricketers' Who's Who, annually 1980–; Wodehouse at War, 1981. *Recreations*: collecting books, cricket. *Address*: Hedenham Hall, Hedenham, Norfolk NR35 2LE.

SPROT, Lt-Col Aidan Mark, MC 1944; JP; Lord-Lieutenant of Tweeddale, since 1980; landed proprietor and farmer (Haystoun Estate); *b* 17 June 1919; *s* of Major Mark Sprot of Riddell. *Educ*: Stowe. Commissioned Royal Scots Greys, 1940; served: Middle East, 1941–43; Italy, 1943–44; NW Europe, 1944–45, and after the war in Germany, Libya, Egypt, Jordan and UK; Adjt 1945–46; CO, 1959–62, retired. Councillor, Peeblesshire CC, 1963–75; JP 1966, DL 1966–80, Peeblesshire. Member, Royal Company of Archers (Queen's Body Guard for Scotland), 1950–; Pres., Lowlands of Scotland, TAVRA, 1986–. *Recreations*: country pursuits, motor cycle touring. *Address*: Crookston, Peebles. *T*: Kirkton Manor 209. *Club*: New (Edinburgh).

SPRY, Brig. Sir Charles Chambers Fowell, Kt 1964; CBE 1956; DSO 1943; retired as Director-General, Australian Security Intelligence Organization, 1950–70; *b* 26 June 1910; *s* of A. F. Spry, Brisbane; *m* 1939, Kathleen Edith Hull, *d* of Rev. Godfrey Smith; one *s* two *d. Educ*: Brisbane Grammar School. Graduated Royal Military College, Duntroon. Served War of 1939–45 as Col, Australian Imperial Force in SW Pacific (DSO) and Middle East. Director of Military Intelligence, 1946–50. Hon. ADC to Gov. Gen., 1946. *Recreation*: golf. *Address*: 2 Mandeville Crescent, Toorak, Victoria 3142, Australia. *Clubs*: Melbourne; Royal Melbourne Golf.

SPRY, Maj.-Gen. Daniel Charles, CBE 1945; DSO 1944; CD; *b* Winnipeg, Man, 4 Feb. 1913; *s* of Major-General Daniel William Bigelow Spry and Ethelyn Alma (*née* Rich); *m* 1939, Elisabeth, *d* of Roy Fletcher Forbes, Halifax, NS; one *s* one *d. Educ*: Public Schools, Calgary and Halifax; Ashford School, England; Dalhousie University. Served with Canadian Militia; 2nd Lt, Princess Louise Fusiliers, 1932; Royal Canadian Regt (permanent force), 1934. Served War, 1939–46 (CBE, DSO, CD, despatches twice); Captain 1939, Major 1940, Lt-Col 1943, Brig. 1943, Maj.-Gen. 1944; GOC 3rd Canadian Infantry Div., 1944–45; retired as Vice-Chief of Gen. Staff, 1946. Col, The Royal Canadian Regt, 1965–78. Chief Exec. Comr, The Boy Scouts' Assoc. of Canada, 1946–51; Dep. Dir, Boy Scouts World Bureau, 1951–53, Dir, 1953–65. Commander, Order of the Crown of Belgium, 1945; Croix de Guerre, Belgium, 1945. *Recreations*: sailing, gardening, fishing. *Address*: 4 Rock Avenue, Ottawa, Ontario K1M 1A6, Canada. *Club*: Rideau (Ottawa).

SPRY, Sir John (Farley), Kt 1975; President, Gibraltar Court of Appeal, since 1983; Chief Justice: British Indian Ocean Territory, since 1981; St Helena and its Dependencies, since 1983; *b* 11 March 1910; *s* of Joseph Farley Spry and Fanny Seagrave Treloar Spry; *m* 1st (marr. diss. 1940); one *s* one *d*; 2nd, Stella Marie (*née* Fichat). *Educ*: Perse School and Peterhouse, Cambridge (MA). Solicitor, 1935; Asst Registrar of Titles and Conveyancer, Uganda, 1936–44; Chief Inspector of Land Registration, Palestine, 1944; Asst Director of Land Registration, Palestine, 1944–48; Registrar-General, Tanganyika 1948–50, Kenya 1950–52; Tanganyika: Registrar-Gen., 1952–56; Legal Draftsman, 1956–60; Principal Sec., Public Service Commn, 1960–61; Puisne Judge, 1961–64; Justice of Appeal, Court of Appeal for Eastern Africa, 1964–70; Vice-President, 1970–75; Chm., Pensions Appeal Tribunals, 1975–76; Chief Justice of Gibraltar, 1976–80, Justice of Appeal, 1980–83. Comr for Revision of Laws of Gibraltar, 1981–85. *Publications*: Sea Shells of Dar es Salaam, Part I, 1961 (3rd edn 1968), Part II, 1964; Civil Procedure in East Africa, 1969; Civil Law of Defamation in East Africa, 1976. *Recreation*: conchology. *Address*: 15 De Vere Gardens, W8 5AN.

SPURGEON, Maj.-Gen. Peter Lester, CB 1980; Chief Executive, Royal Agricultural Benevolent Institution, since 1982; *b* 27 Aug. 1927; *s* of Harold Sidney Spurgeon and Emily Anne (*née* Bolton); *m* 1959, Susan Ann (*née* Aylward); one *s* one *d. Educ*: Merchant Taylors' Sch., Northwood. Commnd, 1946; 1949–66: HMS Glory; Depot, RM Deal; 40 Commando RM; ADC to Maj.-Gen. Plymouth Gp RM; DS Officers' Sch., RM; RAF

Staff Coll., Bracknell; Staff of Comdt Gen. RM; 40 Commando RM; Jt Warfare Estab.; GS02 HQ: ME Comd, Aden, 1967; Army Strategic Comd, 1968–69; Second-in-Comd, 41 Commando RM, 1969–71; DS National Defence Coll., Latimer, 1971–73; CO RM Poole, 1973–75; Dir of Drafting and Records, RM, 1975–76; Comdr, Training Gp, RM, 1977–79 and Training and Reserve Forces, RM, 1979–80; retd 1980. Col Comdt, RM, 1987–. Pres., RM Assoc., 1986–. *Recreations:* golf, dinghy sailing, tennis. *Address:* Shaw House, 27 West Way, Oxford OX2 0QH. *T:* Oxford 724931. *Club:* Army and Navy.

SPURLING, (Susan) Hilary; writer and critic; *b* 25 Dec. 1940; *d* of Gilbert Alexander Forrest and Emily Maureen Forrest; *m* 1961, John Spurling; two *s* one *d. Educ:* Somerville Coll., Oxford (BA). Theatre Critic of the Spectator, 1964–70, Literary Editor, 1966–70. *Publications;* Ivy When Young: the early life of I. Compton-Burnett 1884–1919, 1974; Handbook to Anthony Powell's Music of Time, 1977; Secrets of a Woman's Heart: the later life of I. Compton-Burnett 1920–1969, 1984 (Duff Cooper Meml Prize, 1985; Heinemann Literary Award (jtly), 1985); Elinor Fettiplace's Receipt Book, 1986. *Recreations:* reading, ratting, country walks. *Address:* c/o David Higham Associates, 5–8 Lower John Street, Golden Square, W1R 4HA.

SQUAIR, George Alexander; Chairman, South Eastern Electricity Board, since 1983; *b* 26 July 1929; *s* of Alexander Squair and Elizabeth (*née* Macdonald); *m* 1953, Joy Honeybone; two *s* one *d. Educ:* Woolwich Polytechnic; Oxford Technical Coll.; Southampton Univ. CEng, FIEE 1986; CBIM 1984. Gen. distribution engrg posts, 1950–68; Southern Electricity Board: 1st Asst Dist Engr, 1968–69; Dist Engr, Swindon, 1969–70; Area Engr, Newbury, 1970–73; Dist Manager, Oxford, 1973–74; Area Manager, Newbury, 1974–78; Mem., Exec. Bd, 1976–78; Dep. Chm., 1978–83. *Recreations:* reading, golf. *Address:* South Eastern Electricity Board, Grand Avenue, Hove BN3 2LS. *T:* Brighton 724522.

SQUIBB, George Drewry, LVO 1982; QC 1956; Norfolk Herald Extraordinary since 1959; Earl Marshal's Lieutenant, Assessor and Surrogate in the Court of Chivalry, since 1976; *b* 1 Dec. 1906; *o s* of Reginald Augustus Hodder Squibb, Chester; *m* 1st, 1936, Bessie (*d* 1954), *d* of George Whittaker, Burley, Hants; one *d*; 2nd, 1955, Evelyn May, *d* of Frederick Richard Higgins, of Overleigh Manor, Chester. *Educ:* King's School, Chester; Queen's College, Oxford (BCL, MA). Barrister-at-Law, Inner Temple, 1930; Bencher, 1951; Reader, 1975; Treasurer, 1976. Army Officers' Emergency Reserve, 1938. Deputy Chairman Dorset Quarter Sessions, 1950–53, Chairman, 1953–71; Junior Counsel to the Crown in Peerage and Baronetcy Cases, 1954–56; Hon. Historical Adviser in Peerage Cases to the Attorney-General, 1965–; Pres., Transport Tribunal, 1962–81; Chief Commons Commissioner, 1971–85. Member: Cttee on Rating of Charities, 1958–59; Adv. Council on Public Records, 1964–81; Council, Selden Soc., 1961– (Vice-Pres., 1969–72). FSA 1946; FSG 1973; FRHistS 1978. Master, Scriveners' Co., 1979–80. JP Dorset, 1943. *Publications:* The Law of Arms in England, 1953; Wiltshire Visitation Pedigrees, 1623, 1955; Reports of Heraldic Cases in the Court of Chivalry, 1956; The High Court of Chivalry, 1959; Visitation Pedigrees and the Genealogist, 1964, 2nd edn 1978; Founders' Kin, 1972; Doctors' Commons, 1977; Visitation of Dorset 1677, 1977; Precedence in England and Wales, 1981; Munimenta Heraldica, 1985; papers in legal and antiquarian journals. *Recreation:* genealogical and heraldic research. *Address:* The Old House, Cerne Abbas, Dorset DT2 7JQ. *T:* Cerne Abbas 272. *Clubs:* Athenæum, United Oxford & Cambridge University.

SQUIRE, Clifford William, CMG 1978; LVO 1972; HM Diplomatic Service; Ambassador to Israel, since 1984; *b* 7 Oct. 1928; *s* of Clifford John Squire and Eleanor Eliza Harpley; *m* 1st, 1959, Marie José Carlier (*d* 1973); one *s* two *d* (and one *s* decd); 2nd, 1976, Sara Laetitia Hutchison; one *s* one *d. Educ:* Royal Masonic Sch., Bushey; St John's Coll., Oxford; Coll. of Europe, Bruges. PhD London 1979. British Army, 1947–49. Nigerian Admin. Service, 1953–59; FO, 1959–60; British Legation, Bucharest, 1961–63; FO, 1963–65; UK Mission to UN, New York, 1965–69; Head of Chancery, Bangkok, 1969–72; Head of SE Asian Dept, FCO, 1972–75; Extramural Fellow, Sch. of Oriental and African Studies, London Univ., 1975–76; Counsellor, later Head of Chancery, Washington, 1976–79; Ambassador to Senegal, 1979–82, concurrently to Cape Verde Is, Guinea (Bissau), Guinea (Conakry), Mali and Mauritania; Asst Under-Sec. of State, FCO, 1982–84. *Address:* c/o Foreign and Commonwealth Office, SW1. *Clubs:* Travellers'; Cosmos (Washington, DC).

SQUIRE, Peter John; Headmaster, Bedford Modern School, since 1977; *b* 15 Feb. 1937; *s* of Leslie Ernest Squire and Doris Eileen Squire; *m* 1965, Susan Elizabeth (*née* Edwards); one *s* one *d. Educ:* King Edward's Sch., Birmingham; Jesus Coll., Oxford (BA 1960, MA 1964); Pembroke Coll. and Dept of Educn, Cambridge (Cert. in Educn 1961). Asst Master, Monkton Combe Sch., Bath, 1961–65; Haberdashers' Aske's Sch., Elstree, 1965–77: Sen. Boarding Housemaster, 1968–77; Sen. History Master, 1970–77. *Recreations:* Rugby, squash, gardening, antique collecting. *Address:* Bedford Modern School, Manton Lane, Bedford MK41 7NT. *T:* Bedford 64331.

SQUIRE, Raglan, FRIBA, MSIA; Consultant, Raglan Squire & Partners, Consultants in Architecture, Engineering, Town Planning, etc, since 1981 (Senior Partner, 1948–81); *b* 30 Jan. 1912; *e s* of late Sir John Squire, Kt; *m* 1st, 1938, Rachel, (*d* 1968), *d* of James Atkey, Oxshott, Surrey; two *s*; 2nd, 1968, Bridget Lawless. *Educ:* Blundell's; St John's Coll., Cambridge. Private practice in London, 1935–. War service with Royal Engineers, 1942–45. Founded firm of Raglan Squire & Partners, 1948. Principal projects: housing, educational and industrial work, 1935–41; pre-fabricated bldgs and industrial design, 1945–48; Eaton Sq. Conversion Scheme, 1945–56; Rangoon Univ. Engineering Coll., 1953–56; Associated Architect, Transport Pavilion, Festival of Britain Exhib., 1951; Town Planning Scheme for Mosul, Iraq, 1955; Bagdad airport report, 1955; factories at Weybridge, Huddersfield, etc; office buildings London, Eastbourne, Bournemouth, etc; gen. practice at home and over-seas incl. major hotels at Teheran, Tunis, Nicosia, Malta and Singapore, Gibraltar, Caribbean and Middle East, 1955–81, retired from active practice. Sec. RIBA Reconstruction Cttee, 1941–42; Council of Architectural Assoc., 1951–52; Guest Editor Architects' Journal, 1947. *Publications:* Portrait of an Architect (autobiog.), 1985; articles in technical press on organisation of Building Industry, Architectural Education, etc. *Recreations:* gardening, chess, ocean racing and designing small yachts. *Address:* 1 Chester Row, SW1. *T:* 01–730 7225. *Clubs:* Royal Thames Yacht, Royal Ocean Racing.

SQUIRE, Robin Clifford; MP (C) Hornchurch, since 1979; *b* 12 July 1944; *s* of late Sidney John Squire and Mabel Alice Squire (*née* Gilmore); *m* 1981 Susan Margaret Fey, *d* of Arthur Frederick Branch and Mahala Branch (*née* Parker); one step *s* one step *d. Educ:* Tiffin School, Kingston-upon-Thames. FCA. Qualified as Chartered Accountant, 1966; joined Lombard Banking Ltd (subsequently Lombard North Central Ltd) as Accountant, 1968, becoming Dep. Chief Accountant, 1972–79. Councillor, London Borough of Sutton, 1968–82; Chm., Finance Cttee, 1972–76; Leader of Council, 1976–79. Chm., Greater London Young Conservatives, 1973; Vice-Chm., Nat. Young Conservatives, 1974–75. Personal Asst to Rt Hon. Robert Carr, Gen. Election, Feb. 1974; contested (C) Havering, Hornchurch, Oct. 1974. PPS to Minister of State for Transport, 1983–85;

Mem., Commons Select Cttee on Environment, 1979–83, on European Legislation, 1985–; Sec., Cons. Parly European Affairs Cttee, 1979–80; Vice-Chm., Cons. Parly Trade Cttee, 1980–83; Jt Vice-Chm., Cons. Parly Environment Cttee, 1985–; Originator of Local Govt (Access to Information) Act, 1985. Chm., Cons. Action for Electoral Reform, 1983–86 (Vice-Chm., 1982–83); Dep. Chm., Anglo-Asian Cons. Soc., 1982–83; Mem. Bd, Shelter, 1982–. *Publication:* (jtly) Set the Party Free, 1969. *Recreations:* films, bridge, modern music. *Address:* House of Commons, SW1A 0AA. *T:* 01–219 4526.

SQUIRE, Warwick Nevison, CBE 1982; FRAeS; aviation and defence consultant; Chairman: D. Ellwood Ltd, since 1985; Holdcount Ltd, since 1985; *b* 19 July 1921; *s* of late Alfred Squire and Elizabeth Timms; *m* 1947, Adelheid Elli Behrendt; one *d. Educ:* Cheltenham Higher Technical Sch. Apprenticeship, H. H. Martyn, Cheltenham, 1936–40; Aircraft Components Ltd (now Dowty Gp), 1940–42; HM Forces and German Control Commn, 1942–46; Dowty Group Plc: Gen. Management, 1946–75; Group Dir and Man. Dir, 1975–83 and Chm., 1983–84, Aerospace and Defence Div. FRAeS 1980; FRSA 1982. *Recreations:* gardening, golf, cricket. *Address:* Highlands, Daisy Bank Road, Leckhampton Hill, Cheltenham, Glos GL53 9QQ. *T:* Cheltenham 521038.

SRISKANDAN, Kanagaretnam, CEng, FICE, FIStructE, FIHT; Chief Highway Engineer, Department of Transport, since 1980; *b* 12 Aug. 1930; *s* of Kanagaretnam Kathiravelu and Kanmanyammal Kumaraswamy; *m* 1956, Dorothy (*née* Harley); two *s* one *d. Educ:* Royal College, Colombo; Univ. of Ceylon. BSc Hons London 1952. Junior Asst Engineer, PWD, Ceylon, 1953; Asst Engr, Sir William Halcrow and Partners, Cons. Engrs, London, 1956; Section Engr, Tarmac Civil Engineering Ltd, 1958; Asst Engr, West Riding of Yorkshire CC, 1959, left as Principal Engr; Dept of Transport: Superintending Engr, Midland Road Construction Unit, 1968; Asst Chief Engr, 1971; Deputy Chief Highway Engr, 1976. *Publications:* papers on various engrg topics. *Recreation:* squash. *Address:* Department of Transport, Room P2/046, 2 Marsham Street, SW1. *T:* 01–212 4426.

SRIVASTAVA, Chandrika Prasad, Padma Bhushan 1972; Secretary-General, International Maritime Organization (formerly IMCO), since 1974; Chancellor, World Maritime University, since 1983; *b* 8 July 1920; *s* of B. B. Srivastava; *m* 1947, Nirmala Salve; two *d. Educ:* Lucknow, India. 1st cl. BA 1940, 1st cl. BA Hons 1941, 1st cl. MA 1942, 1st cl. LLB 1944; gold medals for proficiency in Eng. Lit. and Polit. Science. Under-Sec., Min. of Commerce, India, 1948–49; City Magistrate, Lucknow, 1950; Addtl Dist. Magistrate, Meerut, 1951–52; Directorate-Gen. of Shipping, 1953; Dep. Dir-Gen. of Shipping, 1954–57; Dep. Sec., Min. of Transport, and Pvte Sec. to Minister of Transport and Communications, 1958; Sen. Dep. Dir-Gen. of Shipping, 1959–60; Man. Dir, Shipping Corp. of India, 1961–64; Jt Sec. to Prime Minister, 1964–66; Chm. and Man. Dir, Shipping Corp. of India, 1966–73; Director: Central Inland Water Transport Corp., 1967; Central Bd, Reserve Bank of India, 1972–73; Chm., Mogul Line Ltd, 1967–73. Vice-Pres., Sea Cadet Council, 1970–73. President: Indian Nat. Shipowners' Assoc., 1971–73; Inst. Mar. Technologists, India, 1972 (Hon. Mem., 1981); UN Conf. on Code of Conduct for Liner Confs, 1973–74; Internat. Maritime Lectrs' Assoc., 1980–; Chm., Cttee of Invisibles, 3rd UN Conf. on Trade and Develt, 1972; Member: Nat. Shipping Bd, 1959–73; Merchant Navy Trng Bd, 1959–73; Nat. Welfare Bd for Seafarers, 1966–73; Amer. Bureau of Shipping, 1969; Governing Body, Indian Inst. of Foreign Trade, 1970; State Bd of Tourism, 1970; Nat. Harbour Bd, 1970–73; Gen. Cttee, Bombay Chamber of Commerce and Ind., 1971; Governing Body Indian Inst. of Management, 1972–73; Adv. Bd, Seatrade Acad., 1978–; Europort Internat. Cttee of Honour, 1980–; Internat. Chamber of Commerce Internat. Maritime Bureau, 1981–; Bd of Dirs, ICC Centre for Maritime Co-operation, 1985; Marine Soc., 1984. FRSA 1981. Hon. Member: Master Mariners' Co., 1978; Royal Inst. of Navigation, 1984; Internat. Fedn of Shipmasters' Assocs, 1985; Hon. Fellow: Plymouth Polytech., 1979; Nautical Inst., 1985. Hon. LLD Bhopal, 1984. Admiral Padilla Award, Colombia, 1978; Gran Amigo del Mar Award, Colombia, 1978; Commandeur du Mérite Maritime, France, 1982; Comdr, Order of St Olav, Norway, 1982; Grande Ufficiale dell'Ordine al Merito, Italy, 1983; Comdr, Order of Prince Henry the Navigator, Portugal, 1983; Gold Order of Distinguished Seafarers, Poland, 1983; Nautical Medal, 1st cl., Greece, 1983; Gold Mercury Internat. Award Ad Personam, 1984; Gran Cruz Distintivo Blanco, Orden Cruz Peruana al Mérito Naval, Peru, 1984; Gran Cruz, Orden de Manuel Amador Guerrero, Panama, 1985. *Publications:* articles on shipping in newspapers and jls. *Recreation:* music. *Address:* Secretary-General, International Maritime Organization, 4 Albert Embankment, SE1 7SR. *Clubs:* Athenæum, Anglo-Belgian; Willingdon (Bombay).

STABB, His Honour Sir William (Walter), Kt 1981; QC 1968; retired; a Circuit Judge (formerly Official Referee, Supreme Court of Judicature), 1969–78; Senior Official Referee, 1978–85; *b* 6 Oct. 1913; 2nd *s* of late Sir Newton Stabb, OBE and late Lady E. M. Stabb; *m* 1940, Dorothy Margaret Leckie; four *d. Educ:* Rugby; University Coll., Oxford. Called to the Bar, 1936; Master of the Bench, Inner Temple, 1964, Treasurer, 1985. Served with RAF, 1940–46, attaining rank of Sqdn Ldr. Junior Counsel to Ministry of Labour, 1960; Prosecuting Counsel to BoT, 1962–68. Chm. 1961–69, Dep. Chm. 1969–71, Bedfordshire QS. *Recreations:* fishing, golf. *Address:* The Pale Farm, Chipperfield, Kings Langley, Herts. *T:* Kings Langley 63124; 8 King's Bench Walk, Temple, EC4. *T:* 01–583 4306.

STABLE, (Rondle) Owen (Charles), QC 1963; **His Honour Judge Stable;** a Circuit Judge, since 1979; Senior Circuit Judge, Snaresbrook Crown Court, since 1982; *b* 1923; *yr s* of late Rt Hon. Sir Wintringham Norton Stable, MC, and Lucie Haden (*née* Freeman); *m* 1949, Yvonne Brook, *y d* of late Maj. L. B. Holliday, OBE; two *d. Educ:* Winchester. Served with Rifle Bde, 1940–46 (Captain). Barrister, Middle Temple, 1948; Bencher, 1969. Dep. Chm., QS, Herts, 1963–71; a Recorder of the Crown Court, 1972–79. Board of Trade Inspector: Cadco Group of Cos, 1963–64; H. S. Whiteside & Co Ltd, 1965–67; International Learning Systems Corp. Ltd, 1969–71; Pergamon Press, 1969–73. Sec. National Reference Tribunal for the Coal Mining Industry, 1953–64; Chancellor of Diocese of Bangor, 1959–; Member, Governing Body of the Church in Wales, 1960–; Licensed Parochial Lay Reader, Diocese of St Albans, 1961–; Member: General Council of the Bar, 1962–66; Senate of 4 Inns of Court, 1971–74; Senate of the Inns of Court and the Bar, 1974–75. Chm., Horserace Betting Levy Appeal Tribunal, 1969–74. JP Hertfordshire, 1963–71. *Publication:* (with R. M. Stuttard) A Review of Coursing, 1971. *Recreations:* shooting, listening to music. *Address:* Buckler's Hall, Much Hadham, Hertfordshire. *T:* Much Hadham 2604; Snaresbrook Crown Court, Hollybush Hill, E11 1QW. *Clubs:* Boodle's, Pratt's.

See also P. L. W. Owen.

STABLER, Arthur Fletcher; District Councillor, Newcastle upon Tyne; Member, Supplementary Benefits Commission, 1976–79; *b* 1919; *s* of Edward and Maggie Stabler; *m* 1948, Margaret Stabler; two *s. Educ:* Cruddas Park Sch. Engineer apprenticeship, Vickers Armstrong, 1935–39. Served War, Royal Northumberland Fusiliers, 1939–46. With Vickers Armstrong, 1946–78. Newcastle upon Tyne: City Councillor, 1963–74; District Councillor, 1973–; Dep. Lord Mayor, 1982–83; Lord Mayor, 1983–84; Chairman: Housing Renewals, 1975–76; Arts and Recreation, 1976–77; Case Work Sub-

Cttee, 1974–77; Tenancy Relations Sub-Cttee, 1975–77; Community Develt Sub-Cttee, 1975–76; Town Moor Sub-Cttee, 1976–77; Personnel Sub-Cttee, 1982–; Area Housing Cttee, 1984–85; Priority Area Sub-Cttee, 1984–85; Health Adv. Cttee, 1985–87; District HA Jt Consultative; Vice-Chairman: Social Services Cttee, 1974–76; Housing Management Cttee, 1975–76; Tyneside Summer Exhibn Cttee, 1982–. Chm., Axwell Park Community Homes, 1978–79; Mem., numerous Tenants' Assocs. Chm., Newcastle upon Tyne Central Labour Party, 1965–78. Pres., No 6 Br., AUEW. Chm., Westerhope Golf Club Jt Sub-Cttee, 1976–77. President: Newcastle upon Tyne and District Allotments and Garden Council, 1980–; Elswick Park Bowling Club, 1980–; Cttee, Tyne Wear Polish Solidarity Club, 1981–. Hon. Member: Casino Royal Club, 1980; St Joseph's Club, 1983; Royal British Legion Club, 1983. *Publication:* Gannin Along the Scotswood Road, 1976. *Recreations:* social work, local history. *Address:* 10 Whitebeam Place, Elswick, Newcastle upon Tyne NE4 7EJ. *T:* Newcastle upon Tyne 732362. *Clubs:* Pineapple CIU, Polish White Eagle, Tyneside Irish (Hon.), Maddison's (Hon.) (Newcastle upon Tyne).

STACEY, Air Vice-Marshal John Nichol, CBE 1971; DSO 1945; DFC 1942; *b* 14 Sept. 1920; *s* of Captain Herbert Chambers Stacey and Mrs May Stacey; *m* 1950, Veronica Satterly; two *d. Educ:* Whitgift Middle Sch., Croydon. Merchant Marine Apprentice, 1937–38; joined RAF, 1938; flying throughout War of 1939–45; comd No 160 Sqdn, 1944–45; Asst Air Attaché, Washington, 1947–48; psc 1949; on staff at Staff Coll., 1958–60; Chief of Air Staff, Royal Malayan Air Force, 1960–63 (JMN); comd RAF Laarbruch, Germany, 1963–66; AOC, Air Cadets, 1968–71; Dir, Orgn and Admin. Planning (RAF), MoD, 1971–74; AOA, Support Comd, 1974–75, retired. Dir, Stonham Housing Assoc., 1976–81; Mem., Tunbridge Wells HA. Pres., Headcorn Br., RAFA; Vice-Pres., RAF Gliding and Soaring Assoc.; Trustee: Housing Assocs Charitable Trust; Bedgebury Sch., 1983–. *Recreations:* sailing, golf. *Address:* Riseden Cottage, Riseden, Goudhurst, Cranbrook, Kent. *T:* Goudhurst 211239. *Clubs:* Royal Air Force; Dale Hill Golf.

STACEY, Prof. Margaret; Professor of Sociology, University of Warwick, since 1974; *b* 27 March 1922; *d* of Conrad Eugene Petrie and Grace Priscilla Boyce; *m* 1945, Frank Arthur Stacey (*d* 1977); three *s* two *d. Educ:* City of London Sch. for Girls; London Sch. of Econs (BScEcon, 1st Cl. Hons Sociology). Labour Officer, Royal Ordnance Factory, 1943–44; Tutor, Oxford Univ., 1944–51; University Coll. of Swansea: Res. Officer and Fellow, 1961–63; Lectr in Sociol., 1963–70; Sen. Lectr in Sociol., 1970–74; Dir, Medical Sociol. Res. Centre, 1972–74. British Sociol Association: Mem. Exec. Cttee, 1965–70, 1975–79; Hon. Gen. Sec., 1968–70; Chairperson, 1977–79; Pres., 1981–83; Mem. Women's Caucus, 1974–. Scientific Advr to DHSS; Temp. Advr to Reg. Dir, WHO EURO. Pres., Assoc. for Welfare of Children in Hosp. (Wales), 1974–; Member: Assoc. for Welfare of Children in Hosp., 1960–; Welsh Hosp. Bd, 1970–74; Davies Cttee on Hosp. Complaints Procedure, 1971–73; GMC, 1976–84; Sociol. Cttee, SSRC, 1969–71; Health and Health Policy Cttee, SSRC, 1976–77. FRSM. *Publications:* Tradition and Change: a study of Banbury, 1960, paperback 1970; (ed) Comparability in Social Research, 1969; (ed and jt author) Hospitals, Children and their Families: a study of the welfare of children in hospital, 1970; Methods of Social Research, 1970; (jtly) Power, Persistence and Change: a second study of Banbury, 1975; (ed) The Sociology of the NHS, 1976; (ed jtly and contrib.) Beyond Separation: further studies of children in hospital, 1979; (jtly) Women, Politics and Power, 1981 (Fawcett Book Prize, 1982); (ed jtly) Concepts of Health, Illness and Disease: a comparative perspective, 1986; contrib. to Sociol Rev., Sociol., Brit. Jl of Sociol., Social Science and Med., Jl of Med. Ethics, and Sociol. of Health and Illness. *Recreations:* walking, gardening. *Address:* 8 Lansdowne Circus, Leamington Spa, Warwicks CV32 4SW. *T:* Leamington Spa 312094.

STACEY, Prof. Maurice, CBE 1966; FRS 1950; Mason Professor of Chemistry, 1956–74, now Emeritus, and Head of Department, 1956–74, University of Birmingham; Dean of Faculty of Science, 1963–66; Hon. Senior Research Fellow, 1974–76; *b* 8 April 1907; *s* of J. H. Stacey, Bromstead, Newport, Shropshire; *m* 1937, Constance Mary, *d* of Wm Pugh, Birmingham; two *s* two *d. Educ:* Adam's School, Newport, Shropshire; Universities of Birmingham, London and Columbia (New York). BSc (Hons) Birmingham Univ., 1929; Demonstrator, Chemistry, Birmingham Univ., 1929–32; PhD 1932; Meldola Medal, 1933; Beit Memorial Fellow for Medical Research, School of Tropical Medicine, London Univ., 1933–37 (DSc 1939); Travelling Fellow, Columbia Univ., New York, 1937; Lecturer in Chemistry, Univ. of Birmingham, 1937–44, Reader in Biological Chemistry, 1944–46, Prof. of Chemistry, 1946–56. Tilden Lecturer of Chemical Society, 1946; P. F. Frankland Lectr, Roy. Inst. of Chemistry, 1955; Ivan Levinstein Lectr, 1956, Jubilee Meml Lectr, 1973, Soc. Chem. Industry; Vice-Pres. Chemical Society, 1950–53, 1955–58, 1960–63, 1968–71; Associate Editor, Advances in Carbohydrate Chem., 1950–; Editor, Advances in Fluorine Chem., 1960–73; Founder Editor, European Polymer Jl. Chief Scientific Adviser for Civil Defence, Midland Region, 1957–78; Vice-Pres., Home Office Sci. Council, 1974– (Mem., 1963–74); Governor, National Vegetable Research Institute, 1961–73. Former Member, Court of Governors: Univ. of Keele; Univ. of Warwick; Univ. of Loughborough; Gov., Adam's Sch., 1956–74; Mem. Council, Edgbaston High Sch. for Girls, 1963–84 (Vice-Pres., 1984–). Sugar Research Prize of National Academy of Science, New York, 1950; John Scott Medal and Award, 1969; Haworth Meml Medal, 1970. Captain, 2nd in Command Birmingham Home Guard, Chemical Warfare School, 1942–44. Defence Medal, 1945. Visiting Lecturer, Universities of Oslo, Stockholm, Uppsala and Lund, 1949, Helsinki, 1955. Has foreign Hon. doctorate and medals. Hon. DSc Keele, 1977. *Publications:* (with S. A. Barker) Polysaccharides of Micro-organisms, 1961, and Carbohydrates of Living Tissues; about 400 scientific contribs to Jl of Chem. Soc., Proc. Royal Soc., etc., on organic and biological chemistry subjects. *Recreations:* foreign travel, athletics (Hon. Life Mem. AAA), horticulture, science antiques. *Address:* 12 Bryony Road, Weoley Hill, Birmingham B29 4BU. *T:* 021–475 2065; The University, Birmingham. *T:* 021–472 1301. *Club:* Athenæum.

STACEY, Rear-Adm. Michael Lawrence, CB 1979; Director, Marine Emergency Operations, Marine Division, Department of Transport (formerly Department of Trade), since 1979; *b* 6 July 1924; *s* of Maurice Stacey and Dorice Evelyn (*née* Bulling); *m* 1955, Penelope Leana (*née* Riddoch); two *s. Educ:* Epsom Coll. Entered RN as Cadet, 1942; Normandy landings, HMS Hawkins, 1944; served on HM Ships Rotherham, Cambrian, Shoreham, Hornet, Vernon, Euryalus, Bermuda, Vigilant; Comdr 1958; staff of RN Staff Coll.; in comd HMS Blackpool, 1960–62; JSSC; Captain 1966; Chief Staff Officer to Admiral Commanding Reserves, 1966–68; in comd HMS Andromeda and Captain (F) Sixth Frigate Sqdn, 1968–70; Dep. Dir of Naval Warfare, 1970–73; in comd HMS Tiger, 1973–75; Asst Chief of Naval Staff (Policy), 1975–76; Flag Officer, Gibraltar, 1976–78. ADC to the Queen, 1975. MNI; FBIM. Younger Brother, Trinity House, 1979. *Recreations:* fishing, yachting. *Address:* Little Hintock, 40 Lynch Road, Farnham, Surrey. *T:* Farnham 713032. *Clubs:* Army and Navy, Royal Naval Sailing Association.

STACEY, Morna Dorothy, (Mrs W. D. Stacey); *see* Hooker, Prof. M. D.

STACEY, Rev. Nicolas David; *b* 27 Nov. 1927; *s* of David and Gwen Stacey; *m* 1955, Hon. Anne Bridgeman, *er d* of 2nd Viscount Bridgeman, KBE, CB, DSO, MC; one *s* two *d. Educ:* RNC, Dartmouth; St Edmund Hall, Oxford (hons degree Mod. Hist.); Cuddesdon Theol Coll., Oxford. Midshipman, HMS Anson, 1945–46; Sub-Lt, 1946–48. Asst Curate, St Mark's, Portsea, 1953–58; Domestic Chap. to Bp of Birmingham, 1958–60; Rector of Woolwich, 1960–68; Dean of London Borough of Greenwich, 1965–68; Dep. Dir of Oxfam, 1968–70; Director of Social Services: London Borough of Ealing, 1971–74; Kent County Council, 1974–85. Chm., Youth Call, 1981–. Six Preacher, Canterbury Cathedral, 1984–. Sporting career: internat. sprinter, 1948–52, incl. British Empire Games, 1949, and Olympic Games, 1952 (semi-finalist 200 metres and finalist 4 × 400 metres relay); Pres., OUAC, 1951; winner, Oxf. v Cambridge 220 yds, 1948–51; Captain, Combined Oxf. and Camb. Athletic Team, 1951. *Publication:* Who Cares (autobiog.), 1971. *Address:* The Old Vicarage, Selling, Faversham, Kent ME13 9RD. *T:* Canterbury 752833. *Clubs:* Beefsteak; Royal St George's Golf (Sandwich, Kent).

STACK, (Ann) Prunella, (Mrs Brian St Quentin Power), OBE 1980; President, The Women's League of Health and Beauty, since 1982 (Member of Council, since 1950); *b* 28 July 1914; *d* of Capt. Hugh Bagot Stack, 8th Ghurka Rifles, and Mary Meta Bagot Stack, Founder of The Women's League of Health and Beauty; *m* 1st, 1938, Lord David Douglas-Hamilton (*d* 1944); two *s*; 2nd, 1950, Alfred G. Albers, FRCS (*d* 1951), Cape Town, S Africa; 3rd, 1964, Brian St Quentin Power. *Educ:* The Abbey, Malvern Wells. Mem. of the National Fitness Council, 1937–39. Vice-Pres., Outward Bound Trust, 1980–. *Publications:* The Way to Health and Beauty, 1938; Movement is Life, 1973; Island Quest, 1979. *Recreations:* poetry, music, travel. *Address:* 14 Gertrude Street, SW10.

STACK, Air Chief Marshal Sir Neville; *see* Stack, Air Chief Marshal Sir T. N.

STACK, Neville; Editor, Leicester Mercury, since 1974; Director, F. Hewitt and Son (1927) Ltd, since 1982; *b* 2 Sept. 1928; *m* 1953, Molly Rowe; one *s* one *d. Educ:* Arnold School. Reporter: Ashton-under-Lyne Reporter, 1948; Express & Star, 1950; Sheffield Telegraph, and Kemsley National Papers, 1955; Northern News Editor, IPC national papers, 1971; Sub-editor, Daily Express, 1973; Editor, Stockport Advertiser, 1974. *Publication:* The Empty Palace, 1976. *Recreations:* writing, sailing, riding, flying. *Address:* 34 Main Street, Belton-in-Rutland, Leicestershire. *T:* Belton 645. *Clubs:* The Leicestershire (Leicester); Rutland Sailing, Leicestershire Aero.

STACK, Prunella; *see* Stack, A. P.

STACK, Air Chief Marshal Sir (Thomas) Neville, KCB 1972 (CB 1969); CVO 1963; CBE 1965; AFC 1957; Director-General, Asbestos International Association, since 1978; Gentleman Usher to the Queen, since 1978; *b* 19 Oct. 1919; *s* of late T. Neville Stack, AFC, and Edythe Neville Stack; *m* 1955, Diana Virginia, *d* of late Oliver Stuart Todd, MBE; one *s* one *d. Educ:* St Edmund's College, Ware; RAF College, Cranwell. Served on flying boats, 1939–45; Coastal Command, 1945–52; Transport Support flying in Far East and UK, 1954–59; Dep. Captain of The Queen's Flight, 1960–62; Transport Support in Far East, 1963–64; Comdt, RAF Coll., Cranwell, 1967–70; UK Perm. Mil. Deputy, CENTO, Ankara, 1970–72; AOC-in-C, RAF Trng Comd, 1973–75; Air Sec., 1976–78. Air ADC to the Queen, 1976–78. Mem. Council, CRC, 1978–. Pres., Old Cranwellian Assoc., 1984–. Freeman, City of London; Liveryman, Guild of Air Pilots and Air Navigators; Governor, Wellington Coll. FRMetS; FBIM. *Recreations:* various outdoor sports; undergardening. *Address:* 4 Perrymead Street, Fulham, SW6. *Clubs:* Royal Air Force, Boodle's.

STACPOOLE, John Wentworth; Deputy Secretary, Department of Health and Social Security, 1979–82; *b* 16 June 1926; *s* of late G. W. Stacpoole and of Mrs M. G. Butt; *m* 1954, Charmian, *d* of late J. P. Bishop and Mrs E. M. Bishop; one *s* one *d. Educ:* Sedbergh; Magdalen Coll., Oxford (Demy; MA). Army, 1944–47 (Lieut, Assam Regt). Colonial Office, 1951–68, Private Sec. to Sec. of State, 1964–65; transf. to Min. of Social Security, 1968; Under-Sec., DHSS, 1973. *Recreations:* reading, walking, sketching. *Address:* Fairseat Lodge, Fairseat, near Sevenoaks, Kent. *T:* Fairseat 822201.

STAFFORD, 15th Baron *cr* 1640; **Francis Melfort William Fitzherbert;** *b* 13 March 1954; *s* of 14th Baron Stafford and of Morag Nada, *yr d* of late Lt-Col Alastair Campbell; *S* father, 1986; *m* 1980, Katharine Mary Codrington; two *s. Educ:* Ampleforth College; Reading Univ.; RAC, Cirencester. President: Stone Cricket Club, 1982–; North Staffs Sporting Club, 1984–; Staffs Assoc. of Boys Clubs, 1986–; Stafford Rugby Club, 1986–; Swynnerton Park Cricket Club, 1986–; Patron, City of Stoke-on-Trent Amateur Operatic Soc., 1986–. *Recreations:* shooting, cricket, golf. *Heir: s* Hon. Benjamin John Basil Fitzherbert, *b* 8 Nov. 1983. *Address:* Swynnerton Park, Stone, Staffordshire. *T:* Swynnerton 228. *Clubs:* Farmers'; Lord's Taverners, I Zingari, Free Foresters.

STAFFORD, Bishop Suffragan of, since 1979; **Rt. Rev. John Stevens Waller;** *b* 18 April 1924; *m* 1951, Pamela Peregrine; two *s* three *d. Educ:* St Edward's School, Oxford; Peterhouse, Cambridge (MA); Wells Theol Coll. War service with RNVR, 1942–46. Deacon 1950, priest 1951, London. Leader, Strood Gp of Parishes, 1967–72, Team Rector of Strood 1972–73; Rector of St Nicholas, Harpenden, Herts, 1973–79. *Recreations:* gardening, DIY. *Address:* Ash Garth, Broughton Crescent, Barlaston, Stoke-on-Trent ST12 9DD. *T:* Barlaston 3308.

STAFFORD, Archdeaconry of; *see* Lichfield.

STAFFORD, Frank Edmund, CMG 1951; CBE 1946 (OBE 1931); Malayan CS, retired 1951; *b* 24 Aug. 1895; *s* of late Frank Stafford and Marie Stafford; *m* 1943, Ida Wadham (marr. diss., 1950), *d* of late Conway Burton-Durham; one *s*; *m* 1953, Catherine Rolfe (*d* 1984); *m* 1985, Mrs Doreen Voll. *Educ:* Royal Gram. School, Guildford. Served World War I, 1914–19, India and Mesopotamia, Queen's Royal West Surrey Regt. Joined staff of Civil Commissioner, Iraq, 1919; appointed to High Commission, Iraq, 1921; Financial Secretary, 1924; Financial Adviser, British Embassy, Baghdad, 1931; Colonial Service, Nigeria, 1936 (Asst Treasurer, Principal Asst Sec., Actg Financial Sec.). War of 1939–45, commissioned in Army (Lt-Col) for service with Occupied Enemy Territory Administration, 1941; Financial Adviser, Ethiopian Govt, 1942; attached LHQ Australia, 1944; Col, Military Administration, British Borneo, 1945; demobilized, 1946 (Brig.); seconded to Foreign Office, 1946; Member UK Delegn Italian Peace Conference and Council of Foreign Ministers; Head UK Delegn Four Power Commission, 1947; Member UK Delegn to UN, 1948, 1949, 1950, 1952; Foreign Office Adviser (Minister) to Chief Administrator, Eritrea, 1951–53; Adviser to Ethiopian Govt, 1953–60. Chm. Council, Royal Soc. of St George, 1978. FRAS, FRGS. Order Star of Ethiopia, 1944; Grand Officer, Star of Honour, 1955. *Publications:* contributions to Encyc. Britannica and to Kipling Jl, and International Affairs. *Recreations:* horticulture, hagiology. *Address:* 3 Holbrook Park, Horsham, West Sussex RH12 4PW. *T:* Horsham 52497. *Clubs:* Travellers', National Liberal.

STAFFORD, Godfrey Harry, CBE 1976; PhD; FRS 1979; FInstP; Master of St Cross College, Oxford, since 1979; *b* 15 April 1920; *s* of Henry and Sarah Stafford; *m* 1950, Helen Goldthorp (*née* Clark); one *s* twin *d. Educ:* Rondebosch Boys High Sch., S Africa; Univ. of Cape Town; Gonville and Caius Coll., Cambridge. MSc Cape Town, 1941; South African Naval Forces, 1941–46; Ebden Scholar, PhD Cantab 1950; Harwell, 1949–51; Head of Biophysics Subdiv., CSIR, Pretoria, 1951–54; Cyclotron Gp, AERE,

1954–57; Rutherford Laboratory: Head of Proton Linear Accelerator Gp, 1957; Head of High Energy Physics Div., 1963; Dep. Dir, 1966; Dir, Rutherford Lab., Chilton, 1969–79; Dir Gen., Rutherford and Appleton Laboratories, 1979–81. Fellow, St Cross Coll., Oxford, MA, 1971. CERN appointments: UK deleg. to Council, 1973; Vice-Pres., Council, 1973; Scientific Policy Cttee, 1973, Vice-Chm., 1976, Chm., 1978. Vice-Pres. for meetings, Inst. of Physics, 1976; President: European Physical Soc., 1984–86 (Vice-Pres., 1982–84); Inst. of Physics, 1986–. Glazebrook Prize and Medal, Inst. of Physics, 1981. Hon. DSc Birmingham, 1980. *Publications:* papers and articles in learned jls on: biophysics, nuclear physics, high energy physics. *Recreations:* walking, foreign travel, music. *Address:* Ferry Cottage, North Hinksey Village, Oxford OX2 0NA. *T:* (home) Oxford 47621, (office) Oxford 512411. *Club:* United Oxford & Cambridge University.

STAFFORD, John, OBE 1977; HM Diplomatic Service, retired; *b* 15 June 1920; *s* of late Frank and Gertrude Stafford, Sheffield; *m* 1949, Mary Jocelyn Goodwin, *d* of late Capt. J. G. Budge, RN. *Educ:* High Storrs Grammar Sch. Exchequer and Audit Dept, 1939. RAF, W/O Pilot, 1940. Board of Trade, 1946; Assistant Trade Commissioner, Delhi, Karachi, Bulawayo, 1946–56; Trade Commissioner, Karachi, Lahore, Bombay, Madras, Lahore, 1956–65; Dep. High Comr, Lahore, 1965–69; Consul, Houston, Texas, 1969–71; First Sec. (Commercial), New Delhi, 1974–77; Consul Gen., Brisbane, 1978–80. *Recreations:* cricket, tennis, theatre, music. *Address:* Leacroft, 268 Brooklands Road, Weybridge, Surrey. *Clubs:* East India, Devonshire, Sports and Public Schools; Royal Bombay Yacht; Punjab (Lahore).

STAFFORD-CLARK, Dr David, DPM; FRCP; FRCPsych; Consultant Emeritus, Guy's Hospital; formerly Physician in Charge, Department of Psychological Medicine, and Director of The York Clinic, Guy's Hospital, 1954–73; Chairman, Psychiatric Division, Guy's Group, 1973–74; Consultant Physician, Bethlem Royal and Maudsley Hospitals and the Institute of Psychiatry, 1954–73; retired; *b* 17 March 1916; *s* of Francis and Cordelia Susan Stafford Clark; *m* 1941, Dorothy Stewart (*née* Oldfield); three *s* one *d*. *Educ:* Felsted; University of London. Guy's Hospital. MRCS, LRCP, 1939; MB, BS, 1939; MD. Served War of 1939–45, RAFVR; trained as Medical Parachutist (despatches twice); demobilised 1945. Guy's Hosp., MRCP, Nuffield Med. Fellow, 1946; 3 years postgrad. trg appts, Inst. of Psychiatry, Maudsley Hosp.; MD London, 1947, DPM London, 1948; Registrar, Nat. Hosp., Queen Sq., 1948. Resident Massachusetts Gen. Hosp., Dept of Psychiatry, and Teaching Clinical Fellow, Harvard Med. School, 1949; First Asst, Professorial Unit, Maudsley Hosp., 1950; Mem. Assoc. for Research in Mental and Nervous Disorders, NY, 1950–53; Consultant Staff, Guy's Hosp., 1950; Lectureship, Psychology (Faculty of Letters), Reading Univ., 1950–54. Gifford Lectr and Vis. Prof., St Andrews Univ., 1978. Member: Archbishop of Canterbury's Commn on Divine Healing; Council, Royal Medico-Psychological Assoc.; Council, Medico-Legal Soc.; Examr, RCP London and Cambridge MD; Editorial Bds, Guy's Hosp. Reports, and Mod. Med. of Gt Britain. Acted as adviser to various motion picture companies (Universal International etc) on medical aspects of their productions; has also acted as adviser and director on a large number of medical programmes on sound radio, and both BBC and Independent Television, including the "Lifeline" series of programmes for the BBC, and documentary programmes for ITV on the emotional and intellectual growth of normal children, and the life and work of Freud; Author of Brain and Behaviour Series in Adult Education Television Programmes on BBC Channel 2; Mind and Motive Series, 1966. FRCP, 1958; Mem., NY Acad. of Sciences; FRSA (Silver Medal), 1959; Hon. RCM, 1966; Foundn Fellow, RCPsych, 1972, Hon. Fellow, 1976. *Publications: poetry:* Autumn Shadow, 1941; Sound in the Sky, 1944; *novel:* Soldier Without a Rifle, 1979; *medical:* Psychiatry Today (Pelican), 1951; Psychiatry for Students, 1964, 6th edn, 1983; What Freud Really Said, 1965; Five Questions in Search of an Answer, 1970, repr. 1972; chapters in: Emergencies in Medical Practice, 1st, 2nd and 3rd edns, 1948, 1950, 1952; Compendium of Emergencies, 1st and 2nd edns; Case Histories in Psychosomatic Medicine, 1952; Taylor's Medical Jurisprudence, 12th edn, 1965; Schizophrenia: Somatic Aspects, 1st edn, 1957; Frontiers in General Hospital Psychiatry, 1961; A Short Textbook of Medicine, 1963; The Pathology and Treatment of Sexual Deviation, 1964; Modern Trends in Psychological Medicine, 1970; Psychiatric Treatment, Concepts of, in Encyclopædia Britannica, 200th anniv. edn, 1973; contributions to various medical textbooks and to medical and scientific jls. *Recreations:* travel, reading, writing, making and watching films, theatre. *Club:* Royal Air Force.

See also M. Stafford-Clark.

STAFFORD-CLARK, Max; artistic director, English Stage Company at Royal Court Theatre, since 1981; *b* 17 March 1941; *s* of David Stafford-Clark, *qv*; *m* 1st, 1971, Carole Hayman; 2nd, 1981, Ann Pennington. *Educ:* Felstead School; Riverdale Country Day School, NY; Trinity College, Dublin. Associate dir, Traverse, 1966, artistic dir, 1968–70; dir, Traverse Workshop Co., 1970–74; co-founder, Joint Stock Theatre Group, 1974; at Abbey Theatre, Dublin, Nottingham Rep. and NY Shakespeare Festival Public Theatre. Best Drama Director Award, British Theatre Assoc., 1981 (for Outskirts and Borderline); Obie Award, 1983 (for Top Girls, NY). *Recreation:* lobbying Arts Council. *Address:* 7 Gloucester Crescent, NW1; Royal Court Theatre, Sloane Square, SW1. *T:* 01–730 5174. *Club:* Groucho.

STAFFORD-KING-HARMAN, Sir Cecil William Francis, 2nd Bt, *cr* 1913; *b* 6 Jan. 1895; *s* of late Rt Hon. Sir Thomas Stafford, Bt, CB, and Frances Agnes King-Harman; *S* father, 1935; assumed additional surname of King-Harman, 1932; *m* 1917, Sarah Beatrice (*d* 1979), *y d* of late Col A. D. Acland, CBE, and Hon. Mrs Acland, Feniton Court, Honiton, Devon; one *d* (one *s* killed in action and one *d* decd). *Educ:* RN Colleges, Osborne and Dartmouth; RMC Sandhurst; Christ Church, Oxford. Formerly Midshipman, Royal Navy, retired, 1912; commissioned 2nd Lt, The King's Royal Rifle Corps, 1914; Captain, 1917; served throughout European War in France and Italy (despatches); after war went to Christ Church, Oxford, MA (Hons) Agriculture; Steward, Irish Turf Club, 1938–40, 1943–46, 1948–51, 1952–55, 1959–62; Mem. of Racing Board, 1945–50. Appointed Member, Council of State for Ireland, 1956. War substantive Captain, 1940; Temporary Major, 1941; Temporary Lt-Col 1942. *Recreations:* shooting, racing, fishing. *Address:* St Catherines Park, Leixlip, Co. Kildare, Ireland. *T:* 280421. *Clubs:* Kildare Street and University, Irish Turf (Dublin).

STAGG, Prof. Geoffrey Leonard, MBE 1945; Professor Emeritus, Department of Spanish and Portuguese, University of Toronto; *b* 10 May 1913; *s* of Henry Percy Stagg and Maude Emily Bradbury; *m* 1948, Amy Southwell, Wellesley Hills, Mass, USA; two *s* one *d*. *Educ:* King Edward's School, Birmingham (Scholar); Trinity Hall, Cambridge (Scholar). BA 1st cl. Hons Modern and Medieval Languages Tripos, 1934; MA 1946; Joseph Hodges Choate Mem. Fellow, Harvard Univ., 1934–36; AM (Harvard), 1935; Modern Languages Master, King Edward's School, Birmingham, 1938–40, 1946–47; served in Intelligence Corps, 1940–46; Lecturer in Spanish and Italian, Nottingham Univ., 1947–53, and Head of Dept of Spanish, 1954–56; Dept of Italian and Hispanic Studies, Toronto Univ.: Prof., 1956–78; Chm., 1956–66, 1969–78. Vice-Pres., Assoc. of Teachers of Spanish and Portuguese of GB and Ireland, 1948–; Pres., Canadian Assoc. of Hispanists, 1964–66, 1972–74; Vice-Pres., Asociación Internacional de Hispanistas, 1977–83. Fellow, New Coll., Univ. of Toronto, 1962–; Senior Fellow, Massey Coll., Univ. of Toronto, 1965–70; Canada Council Senior Fellowship, 1967–68. *Publications:* articles on Spanish literature in learned jls. *Address:* 30 Old Bridle Path, Toronto, Ont M4T 1A7, Canada.

STAHL, Professor Ernest Ludwig, DLitt; Taylor Professor of the German Language and Literature and Fellow of The Queen's College, Oxford, 1959–69, Supernumerary Fellow, since 1969; *b* Senekal, OFS, S Africa, 10 Dec. 1902; *s* of Philip and Theresa Stahl; *m* 1942, Kathleen Mary Hudson; no *c*. *Educ:* Univ. of Capetown (MA 1925); Heidelberg Univ.; Oxford Univ. (First Class Hons, 1927; DLitt 1980); Berne Univ. (PhD *magna cum laude* 1931). Assistant Lecturer in German, Birmingham, 1932; Lecturer in German, Oxford, 1935; Reader in German Literature, Oxford, 1945; Student of Christ Church, Oxford, 1945, Student Emeritus, 1960. Vis. Professor: Cornell, 1956; Princeton, 1958; Yale, 1964; Kansas, 1968; Calif (Davis), 1969–70. Gold Medal, Goethe Gesellschaft, 1966. *Publications:* Die religiöse und die philosophische Bildungsidee und die Entstehung des Bildungsromans, 1934; Hölderlin's Symbolism, 1944; The Dramas of Heinrich von Kleist, 1948 (revised edn, 1961); (trans. with Louis MacNeice) Goethe's Faust pts I and II (abridged), 1951; Schiller's Drama: Theory and Practice, 1954; Goethe's Iphigenie auf Tauris, 1962. Editions of Goethe's Werther, 1942 (new edn, 1972), Lessing's Emilia Galotti, 1946, Goethe's Torquato Tasso, 1962, and R. M. Rilke's Duino Elegies, 1965; revised edn, Oxford Book of German Verse, 1967; (with W. E. Yuill) Introduction to German Literature, vol. III, 1970; The Faust Translation in Time Was Away: the world of Louis MacNeice, 1975; articles in Modern Language Review, Germanic Review, German Life and Letters, Journal of English and Germanic Philology, Oxford German Studies, Yearbook of Comparative Criticism; contrib. to Festschrift for Ralph Farrell. *Address:* 43 Plantation Road, Oxford OX2 6JE. *T:* Oxford 55896.

STAINE, Sir Albert (Llewellyn), Kt 1984; CBE 1979; **Hon. Mr Justice Staine;** Judge of the Court of Appeal, Belize, since 1982; Chief Justice of Belize, 1979–82; *b* 4 July 1928; *s* of Robert George and Beatrice Staine; *m*; one *s*. *Educ:* St Michael's College, Belize; Hull University; LLB (Hons). Clerical Service, 1946; called to the Bar, Middle Temple, 1963; Crown Counsel, 1963; Solicitor General, 1966; Dir of Public Prosecutions, 1969; Acting Puisne Judge, 1971; Puisne Judge, 1973. Pres., Boys Brigade Council, 1975–; Chief Scout of Belize, 1980–. *Recreations:* reading, photography, tape recording. *Address:* 17 Princess Margaret Drive, Belize. *T:* 44385; (chambers) 2053.

STAINFORTH, Maj.-Gen. Charles Herbert, CB 1969; OBE 1955; Editor, Army Quarterly and Defence Journal, since 1974; *b* 12 Dec. 1914; *s* of Lt-Col Stainforth, CMG, 4th Cavalry, IA, and Georgina Helen, *d* of Maj.-Gen. H. Pipon, CB; *m* Elizabeth, *d* of late John Tait Easdale; one *s* one *d*. *Educ:* Wellington Coll.; RMC, Sandhurst. Commnd into 2nd Royal Lancers, IA; transferred British Army, 1947; Chief of Staff, Southern Comd, 1965–66; GOC Aldershot District and SE Dist, 1966–69; Head of UK Future Command Structure, MoD, 1969–72. Col Comdt, RCT, 1970–72. Chm. Combined Cadet Forces, 1970–72. Consultant to Nat. Tourist Bds, 1973–75. *Address:* Powderham House, Dippenhall, near Farnham, Surrey. *Clubs:* Army and Navy, MCC.

See also G. H. Stainforth.

STAINFORTH, Graham Henry; *b* 3 Oct. 1906; *s* of Lt-Col H. G. Stainforth, CMG, Indian Cavalry, and Georgina Helen, *d* of Maj.-Gen. H. Pipon, CB; *m* 1943, Ruth Ellen Douglas-Cooper (*d* 1986); one *s* two *d*. *Educ:* Wellington Coll., Berks; Emmanuel Coll., Cambridge. Assistant Master at Merchant Taylors' Sch., 1928–35, and Assistant Housemaster, 1933–35; Assistant Master and Tutor at Wellington Coll., and Head of the English Department, 1935–45; Hon. Secretary of Wellington College Clubs at Walworth, 1935–45; Headmaster of Oundle and Laxton Grammar Schools, 1945–56; Master of Wellington, 1956–66. Mem., Berks Educn Cttee, 1961–74; Fellow of Woodard Corp., 1966–80; Governor: Ardingly College, 1966–80; Portsmouth Grammar School, 1966–77; Cobham Hall Girls' School, 1969–75; Wallingford Comprehensive School, 1976–82. Hon. Liveryman, Grocers' Co., 1975. *Address:* The Cottage, Winterbrook, Wallingford, Oxon OX10 9EF. *T:* Wallingford 36414.

See also C. H. Stainforth.

STAINTON, Sir Anthony (Nathaniel), KCB 1974 (CB 1967); QC 1975; First Parliamentary Counsel to HM Treasury, 1972–76 (Parliamentary Counsel, 1956–72); *b* 8 Jan. 1913; *s* of Evelyn Stainton, Barham Court, Canterbury; *m* 1st, 1947, Barbara Russell; three *d*; 2nd, 1966, Rachel Frances, *d* of late Col C. E. Coghill, CMG. *Educ:* Eton; Christ Church, Oxford. Called to the Bar, Lincoln's Inn, 1937; Hon. Bencher, 1984. *Club:* United Oxford & Cambridge University.

STAINTON, Sir (John) Ross, Kt 1981; CBE 1971; retired; *b* 27 May 1914; *s* of late George Stainton and Helen Ross; *m* 1939, Doreen Werner; three *d*. *Educ:* Glengorse, Eastbourne; Malvern Coll., Worcestershire. Joined Imperial Airways as Trainee, 1933; served in Italy, Egypt, Sudan. Served with RAF in England, West Indies and USA, 1940–46. Man. N America, BOAC, 1949–53; General Sales Man. BOAC, and other Head Office posts, 1954–68; Dep. Man. Dir, 1968–71; Man. Dir, 1971–72; Mem., BOAC Bd, 1968, Chm. and Chief Exec., 1972, until merged into British Airways, 1974; Mem., 1971–, Dep. Chm. and Chief Exec., 1977–79, Chairman, 1979–80, British Airways Bd. Vice Pres., Private Patients Plan; Dir, DMSSB. FCIT (Pres., 1970–71). *Clubs:* Royal Air Force; Royal and Ancient Golf (St Andrews); Sunningdale Golf.

STAINTON, Keith; Chairman, Hodgson & Faraday, since 1984; *b* 8 Nov. 1921; *m* 1946, Vanessa Ann Heald (marr. diss.); three *s* three *d*; *m* 1980, Frances Easton. *Educ:* Kendal Sch.; Manchester Univ. (BA (Com.) Dist. in Economics). Insurance clerk, 1936–39. Served War of 1939–45: Lieut, RNVR, Submarines and with French Resistance, 1940–46. Manchester Univ., 1946–49; Leader Writer, Financial Times, 1949–52; Industrial Consultant, 1952–57; joined Burton, Son & Sanders, Ltd, 1957, Man. Dir 1961–69, Chm. 1962–69; Chm. Scotia Investments Ltd, 1969–72. MP (C) Sudbury and Woodbridge, Dec. 1963–1983; Mem., House of Commons Select Cttees on Expenditure and Science and Technology. Mem. Council of Europe and WEU, 1979–83. Légion d'Honneur, Croix de Guerre avec Palmes, Ordre de l'Armée, 1943. *Address:* Little Bealings House, near Woodbridge, Suffolk. *T:* Ipswich 624205.

STAINTON, Sir Ross; *see* Stainton, Sir J. R.

STAIR, 13th Earl of, *cr* 1703; **John Aymer Dalrymple,** KCVO 1978 (CVO 1964); MBE 1941; Bt 1664 and (Scot.) 1698; Viscount Stair, Lord Glenluce and Stranraer, 1690; Viscount Dalrymple, Lord Newliston, 1703; Baron Oxenfoord (UK) 1841; Colonel (retired) Scots Guards; Lord-Lieutenant of Wigtown, 1961–81; Captain General of the Queen's Body Guard for Scotland, Royal Company of Archers, since 1973; *b* 9 Oct. 1906; *e s* of 12th Earl of Stair, KT, DSO, and Violet Evelyn (*née* Harford) (*d* 1968); *S* father, 1961; *m* 1960, Davina, *d* of late Hon. Sir David Bowes-Lyon, KCVO; three *s*. *Educ:* Eton; Sandhurst. Bde Major, 3rd (London) Infantry Bde and Regimental Adjt Scots Guards, 1935–38; served Middle East, 1941; Bde Major, 16th Inf. Bde (despatches, MBE); Lieut-Colonel 1942; commanded 1st Scots Guards, 1942–43; AMS Headquarters AAI, 1944; Comd Trg Bn Scots Guards, 1945; Comd 2nd Scots Guards, 1946–49; Comd Scots Guards, Temp. Colonel, 1949–52; retired, 1953; retired as Hon. Colonel Scots Guards,

1953. *Heir: s* Viscount Dalrymple, *qv. Address:* Lochinch Castle, Stranraer, Wigtownshire. *Club:* Cavalry and Guards.
    See also Lady Marion Philipps, Lady Jean Rankin.

STALKER, Prof. Alexander Logie, TD; DL; Regius Professor of Pathology, University of Aberdeen, 1972–82, now Emeritus; Consultant Pathologist, North East Regional Hospital Board, 1955–82; *b* 15 Feb. 1920; *s* of late J. S. Stalker and Jean Logie; *m* 1945, Mary E. C. MacLean, MB, ChB (*d* 1985); one *s* three *d. Educ:* Morrison's Academy, Crieff; Univ. of Aberdeen. MB, ChB 1942; MD 1961; FRCPath 1970. RAMC War Service, 1942–47 and TA Service, 1948–64; ADMS 51 (H) Div., 1958–64; QHS, 1963–65. Univ. of Aberdeen: Sen. Lectr in Pathology, 1948–65; Reader in Pathology, 1965–69; Personal Prof. of Pathology, 1969–72; Dean of Faculty of Medicine, 1979–82. County Comr Scouts, City of Aberdeen, 1965–68. Pres., British Microcirculation Soc., 1968–73; Pres., European Soc. for Microcirculation, 1970–72; Mem., Pathological Soc. of Gt Britain and Ireland. Mem. Court, Univ. of Aberdeen, 1984–. DL Aberdeen, 1967. *Publications:* scientific papers in medical jls, esp. in field of microcirculation. *Recreations:* fishing, hill walking, Norwegian studies. *Address:* Coach End, Banchory, Kincardineshire AB3 3HS. *T:* Banchory 2460.

STALLARD, family name of **Baron Stallard.**

STALLARD, Baron *cr* 1983 (Life Peer), of St Pancras in the London Borough of Camden; **Albert William Stallard;** *b* 5 Nov. 1921; *m* 1944; one *s* one *d. Educ:* Low Waters Public School; Hamilton Academy, Scotland. Engineer, 1937–65; Technical Training Officer, 1965–70. Councillor, St Pancras, 1953–59, Alderman, 1962–65; Councillor, Camden, 1965–70, Alderman, 1971–78. MP (Lab) St Pancras N, 1970–83; PPS to: Minister of State, Agriculture, Fisheries and Food, 1974; Minister of State for Housing and Construction, 1974–76; an Asst Govt Whip, 1976–78; a Lord Comr, HM Treasury, 1978–79. Chairman: Camden Town Disablement Cttee (Mem., 1951–); Camden Assoc. for Mental Health. Mem., Inst. of Training Officers, 1971. AEU Order of Merit, 1968. *Address:* Flat 2, 2 Belmont Street, NW1.

STALLARD, Sir Peter (Hyla Gawne), KCMG 1961 (CMG 1960); CVO 1956; MBE 1945; Secretary to the Prime Minister of the Federation of Nigeria, 1958–61; *b* 6 March 1915; *y c* of Rev. L. B. Stallard and Eleanor, *e d* of Colonel J. M. Gawne; *m* 1941, Mary Elizabeth Kirke, CStJ; one *s* one *d. Educ:* Bromsgrove Sch.; Corpus Christi Coll., Oxford (MA). Cadet, Colonial Administrative Service, Northern Nigeria, 1937. Military Service, Nigeria, Gold Coast, Burma, 1939–45. Governor and Commander-in-Chief of British Honduras, 1961–66; Lt Governor of the Isle of Man, 1966–74. Pres., Devon and Cornwall Rent Assessment Panel, 1976–85. Pres., Somerset Assoc. of Boys Clubs, 1977–; Chm., Dartmoor Steering Gp, 1978–. KStJ 1961; Chapter-Gen., Order of St John, 1976–. *Recreation:* golf. *Address:* 18 Henley Road, Taunton, Somerset. *T:* Taunton 331505. *Club:* Athenæum.
    See also R. D. Wilson.

STALLIBRASS, Geoffrey Ward, CB 1972; OBE 1952; FRAeS; Controller, National Air Traffic Services (Civil Aviation Authority/Ministry of Defence), 1969–74 (Joint Field Commander, 1966–69); *b* 17 Dec. 1911; *s* of Thomas and Ivy Stallibrass, Midhurst; *m* 1940, Alison, *e d* of late James and Rita Scott, Norwich; two *s* three *d. Educ:* Wellingborough Sch. Air Service Training, Hamble (Commercial Pilot/Instrument Rating Course), 1948. Dep. Director, Civil Aviation Ops, Ministry of Civil Aviation, 1946; attached to BOAC, 1949; Dep. Director of Control and Navigation (Development), 1950; Director of Aerodromes (Tech.), Ministry of Transport and Civil Aviation, 1953; Director of Flight Safety, Min. of Aviation, 1962. *Publications:* articles on aviation subjects. *Recreations:* walking, birdwatching, conservation work, music. *Address:* Turkey Island Corner, East Harting, Petersfield, Hants. *T:* Harting 220.

STALLWORTHY, Sir John (Arthur), Kt 1972; Nuffield Professor of Obstetrics and Gynæcology, University of Oxford, 1967–73, now Emeritus; Fellow Emeritus, Oriel College, Oxford, 1973, Hon. Fellow, 1974; *b* 26 July 1906; *s* of Arthur John Stallworthy; *m* 1934, Margaret Wright Howie (*d* 1980); one *s* twin *d. Educ:* Auckland Grammar Sch.; Universities of Auckland and Otago, NZ. Distinction and gold medal in surgery, gynæcology and obstetrics, 1930; travelling med. schol., 1931; obstetrical travelling schol., 1932; postgrad. experience in Melbourne, London and Vienna. MRCOG 1935; FRCS 1936; FRCOG 1951. Joseph Price Orator, US, 1950; McIlrath Guest Prof., Sydney, 1952; Sommer Mem. Lecturer, US, 1958; Hunterian Prof., RCS, 1963; Sims Black Prof. S Africa, 1964. Sometime Examiner in Obstetrics and Gynæcology for RCOG, RCS of S Africa, Universities of Oxford, Birmingham, Leeds, E Africa and Singapore. Hon. Cons., Royal Prince Alfred Hospital, Sydney, 1952; Assoc. Obstetrician, National Maternity Hospital, Dublin, 1959. Vice-Pres., RCOG, 1969; President: RSM, 1974–75, 1980–81 (Hon. Fellow, 1976; Chm. Appeal Cttee); Medical Protection Soc.; BMA, 1975 (Gold Medal, 1981; Chm. Working Party, The Medical Effects of Nuclear War, 1981–83). Hon. Fellow, Surgical, Obstetrical and Gynæcological Societies in US, Wales, Canada, S Africa, Spain and Turkey; Hon. FACS 1954; Hon. FCOG (SA) 1964; Hon. FACOG 1974; Hon. FRCSI 1976. Hon. DSc: Otago, 1975; Leeds, 1975. Victor Bonney Prize, RCS, 1970. Member, Honourable Order of Kentucky Colonels, 1968. *Publications:* (jointly) Problems of Fertility in General Practice, 1948; (jointly) Recent Advances in Obstetrics and Gynæcology, 1966–79; (jointly) Bonney's Gynaecological Surgery, 8th edn; (ed jtly) The Medical Effects of Nuclear War, 1983; (contrib.) Cancer of the Uterine Cervix, 1984; joint contrib. to British Obstetric Practice and British Gynæcological Practice, 1959, and 1963. *Recreations:* formerly Rugby football, tennis, swimming, driving fast cars; now gardening, writing, driving fast cars more slowly. *Address:* Shotover Edge, Headington, Oxford. *T:* Oxford 62481. *Club:* Athenæum.
    See also J. H. Stallworthy.

STALLWORTHY, Jon Howie; Reader in English Literature, and Fellow of Wolfson College, Oxford University, since 1986; *b* 18 Jan. 1935; *s* of Sir John (Arthur) Stallworthy, *qv; m* 1960, Gillian Meredith (*née* Waldock); two *s* one *d. Educ:* The Dragon Sch., Oxford; Rugby Sch.; Magdalen Coll., Oxford (MA, BLitt). Served RWAFF (pre-Oxford). At Oxford won Newdigate Prize, 1958 (runner-up, 1957). Joined Oxford Univ. Press, 1959, Dep. Head, Academic Div., 1975–77; John Wendell Anderson Prof. of English Lit., Cornell Univ., 1977–86. Gave Chatterton Lecture on an English Poet to British Academy, 1970; during a sabbatical year, 1971–72, was a Visiting Fellow at All Souls Coll., Oxford. FRSL, 1971. *Publications: poems:* (8 collections) The Astronomy of Love, 1961; Out of Bounds, 1963; Root and Branch, 1969; Positives, 1969; The Apple Barrel: selected poems, 1955–63, 1974; Hand in Hand, 1974; A Familiar Tree, 1978; The Anzac Sonata: new and selected poems, 1986; *criticism:* Between the Lines, W. B. Yeats's Poetry in the Making, 1963; Vision and Revision in Yeats's Last Poems, 1969; *biography:* Wilfred Owen, 1974 (winner of Duff Cooper Meml Prize, W. H. Smith Literary Award and E. M. Forster Award); *translations:* (with Peter France) Alexander Blok: The Twelve and other poems, 1970; (with Jerzy Peterkiewicz) poems for 2nd edn of Five Centuries of Polish Poetry, 1970; (with Peter France) Boris Pasternak: Selected Poems, 1983; *edited:* The Penguin Book of Love Poetry, 1973; Wilfred Owen: Complete Poems and

Fragments, 1983; The Oxford Book of War Poetry, 1984; The Poems of Wilfred Owen, 1985. *Address:* Wolfson College, Oxford; Long Farm, Elsfield Road, Old Marston, Oxford. *Club:* Vincent's (Oxford).

STAMENKOVIĆ, Dragi; Order of National Hero, Yugoslavia, 1952; Yugoslav Star with ribbon, 1981; Yugoslav Ambassador to the Court of St James's, 1981–85, retired; *b* 29 Feb. 1920; *s* of Todor Stamenković and Darinka Malešević; *m* 1945, Jelica Purić; two *s* one *d. Educ:* Belgrade Univ. Mem., Supreme HQ, Nat. Liberation Army for Serbia, 1941–45. Mem., Liberation Cttee for Belgrade Dist, 1945–48; Minister in Govt of Serbia, 1949–51; Pres., Fedn of Trade Unions of Serbia 1951–62; President: Exec. Council of Serbia, 1964–67; Working People of Serbia, 1967–71; Mem., Presidency of Yugoslavia, 1971–74; Ambassador to Brazil, 1974–78; Ambassador in Federal Secretariat for Foreign Affairs, 1978–81. Mem. Council, Fedn of Yugoslavia, 1985–. Deputy of Fed. Assembly in three convocations, and of Republican Assembly in four; Mem., Presidency of Fed. Conf., Socialist Alliance of Working People of Yugoslavia; sometime head or mem., Yugoslav delegns abroad. Holder of many Yugoslav and foreign decorations. *Publications:* From Travels through China, 1955; contribs to jls and newspapers on economic and political affairs of Yugoslavia, 1945–75. *Recreations:* tennis, football. *Address:* Užička 10, 11040 Beograd, Yugoslavia. *Club:* Hurlingham.

STAMER, Sir (Lovelace) Anthony, 5th Bt, *cr* 1809; MA; AMIMI; *b* 28 Feb. 1917; *s* of Sir Lovelace Stamer, 4th Bt, and Eva Mary (*d* 1974), *e d* of R. C. Otter; *S* father, 1941; *m* 1st, 1948, Stella Huguette (marr. diss., 1953), *d* of Paul Burnell Binnie, Brussels; one *s* one *d*; 2nd, 1955, Margaret Lucy (marr. diss., 1959), *d* of late Major Belben and Mrs Stewart, Marandellas, Zimbabwe; 3rd, 1960, Marjorie June (marr. diss. 1968), *d* of T. C. Noakes, St James, Cape; 4th, 1983, Mrs Elizabeth Graham Smith, *widow* of G. P. H. Smith, Colyton, Devon. *Educ:* Harrow; Trinity Coll., Cambridge; Royal Agricultural Coll., Cirencester. BA 1947; MA 1963; AMIMI 1963. Served RAF 1939–41; Officer in ATA 1941–45. Executive Director: Bentley Drivers Club Ltd, 1969–73; Bugatti & Ferrari Owners Club, 1973–75; Hon. Treasurer, Ferrari Owners' Club, 1975–81. *Heir: s* Peter Tomlinson Stamer, Flight Lieut, RAF [*b* 19 Nov. 1951; *m* 1979, Dinah Louise Berry; one *s* one *d*]. *Address:* White Farm Cottage, White Farm Lane, West Hill, Ottery St Mary, Devon EX11 1XF.

STAMERS-SMITH, Eileen, MA; Headmistress, Malvern Girls' College, 1984–85; *b* 17 April 1929; *d* of Charles and May Fairey; *m* 1970, Henry Arthur Stamers-Smith, CBE, MA (*d* 1982). *Educ:* Castleford Grammar Sch., Yorks; Lady Margaret Hall, Oxford (BA Hons English Lang. and Lit., Cl. II, 1951; MA; DipEd). Asst English Teacher: Abbeydale Girls' Grammar Sch., Sheffield, 1952–57; Cheltenham Ladies' Coll., 1957–67; Headmistress, Bermuda Girls' High Sch., 1967–71. *Publications:* articles in Garden Hist. Soc. Jl and Newsletter. *Recreations:* music, garden history, Venice, photography, calligraphy, writing poetry, sketching, fell walking. *Address:* 8 Mavor Close, Old Woodstock, Oxon OX7 1YL. *T:* Woodstock 811383.

STAMLER, Samuel Aaron, QC 1971; a Recorder of the Crown Court, since 1974; *b* 3 Dec. 1925; *s* of late Herman Stamler and Bronia Stamler; *m* 1953, Honor, *d* of A. G. Brotman; two *s* one *d. Educ:* Berkhamsted; King's College, Cambridge. Called to Bar, Middle Temple, 1949, Bencher, 1979. *Recreations:* walking, grandchildren. *Address:* 1 Essex Court, Temple, EC4. *T:* 01–353 5362. *Club:* Athenæum.

STAMM, Temple Theodore, FRCS; Orthopædic Surgeon Emeritus, Guy's Hospital; *b* 22 Dec. 1905; *s* of Dr Louis Edward Stamm, Streatham, and Louisa Ethel (*née* Perry), Caterham, Surrey; *m* 1945, Pamela, *d* of Charles Russell, Chislehurst, Kent. *Educ:* Rose Hill Sch., Surrey; Haileybury Coll.; Guy's Hospital Medical School. MB, BS (London), 1930, MRCS, LRCP 1928, FRCS 1934. Fellow Royal Society of Medicine; Fellow British Orthopædic Assoc.; Member British Med. Assoc. Formerly: Orthopædic Surgeon, Bromley Hospital, 1941–66; Asst Orthopædic Surgeon and Orthopædic Registrar, Royal Nat. Orthopædic Hospital; Asst Orthopædic Surgeon, Orthopædic Registrar, Asst Anæsthetist and Demonstrator of Anatomy, Guy's Hospital. Major RAMC. *Publications:* Foot Troubles, 1957; Guide to Orthopædics, 1958; Surgery of the Foot, British Surgical Practice, Vol. 4; contributions to Blackburn and Lawrie's Textbook of Surgery, 1958; articles in: Lancet, Guy's Hospital Reports, Journal of Bone and Joint Surgery, Medical Press, etc. *Recreations:* farming, sailing, music. *Address:* Hambrook Lodge, West Ashling, Chichester, West Sussex PO18 8DQ.

STAMP, family name of **Baron Stamp.**

STAMP, 3rd Baron, *cr* 1938, of Shortlands; **Trevor Charles Stamp,** MA, MD, FRCPath; Emeritus Professor of Bacteriology, Royal Postgraduate Medical School, University of London (Reader, 1937–48, Professor, 1948–70); *b* 13 Feb. 1907; *s* of 1st Baron Stamp, GCB, GBE; *S* brother, 1941; *m* 1932, Frances Dawes, *d* of late Charles Henry Bosworth, Evanston, Illinois, USA; two *s. Educ:* The Leys Sch., Cambridge; Gonville and Caius Coll., Cambridge; St Bartholomew's Hospital. MRCS, LRCP, BCh Cambridge, MA Cambridge, 1931; MB Cambridge, 1937. MD 1966. Demonstrator in Bacteriology, 1932–34, Lecturer in Bacteriology, 1934–37, London School of Hygiene and Tropical Medicine; Dir, Emergency Public Health Lab. Service Sect. 9, 1939–41; attached to the Ministry of Supply, 1941–45; Governor: Imperial College of Science and Technology, 1949–79; The Leys School, 1942–77; Pres., Queenswood School, 1981– (Governor, 1941–81; Chm., 1971–81). Mem., Exec. and Scientific Adv. Cttees, Animal Health Trust (formerly Vet. Educnl Trust), 1946–79. Mem., Parly Delegn of IPU to Egypt, 1973, to Tokyo, 1974, to Sofia, 1977, to Prague and Caracas, 1979. Founder Fellow, College of Pathologists, 1963 (now RCPath); Fellow, Royal Postgrad. Med. Sch., 1972. US Medal of Freedom with Silver Palm, 1947. Hon. Freeman, Barbers' Company, 1958. *Publications:* various papers on bacteriological subjects. *Recreations:* music, writing memoirs. *Heir: s* Dr the Hon. Trevor Charles Bosworth Stamp, MD, FRCP [*b* 18 Sept. 1935; *m* 1st, 1963, Anne Carolynn Churchill (marr. diss. 1971); two *d*; 2nd, 1975, Carol Anne, *d* of Keith Russell; one *s* one *d*]. *Address:* Middle House, 7 Hyde Park Street, W2. *T:* 01–723 8363. *Club:* Athenæum.

STAMPER, John Trevor, MA, FEng, Hon. FRAeS, CBIM; Corporate Technical Director, British Aerospace, 1977–85, retired; *b* 12 Oct. 1926; *s* of late Col Horace John Stamper and Clara Jane (*née* Collin); *m* 1950, Cynthia Joan Parsons; two *s* one *d. Educ:* Loughborough Grammar Sch.; Jesus Coll., Cambridge (MA 1951). FRAeS 1965 (Hon. FRAeS 1984); CEng 1966; FEng 1977; CBIM 1983. Blackburn Aircraft Ltd: Post-grad. apprenticeship, 1947; Dep. Head of Aerodynamics, 1955; Head of Structures, 1956; Flight Test Manager, 1960; Chief Designer (Buccaneer), 1961; Dir and Chief Designer, 1963; Hawker Siddeley Aviation Ltd (following merger): Exec. Dir Design (Military), 1966; Exec. Dir and Dep. Chief Engr (Civil), 1968; Tech. Dir, 1968–77. Member: Council, RAeS, 1971–77, 1978– (Pres., 1981–82); Tech. Bd, SBAC, 1966–85 (Chm., 1972–74); Council, SBAC, 1981–84; Council, Aircraft Res. Assoc., 1966–85 (Chm., 1976–78); Aeronautical Res. Council, 1971–74; Air Warfare Adv. Bd, Defence Scientific Adv. Council, 1973–84; Noise Adv. Council, 1975–78; Comité Technique et Industriel, Assoc. Européenne des Constructeurs de Matériel Aerospatial, 1971–81 (Chm., 1974–81); Airworthiness Requirements Bd, CAA, 1976–78. Hon. DSc Loughborough, 1986.

Hodgeson Prize, RAeS, 1975; British Gold Medal for Aeronautics, RAeS, 1976. *Publications:* (contrib.) The Future of Aeronautics, 1970; Air Power in the Next Generation, 1979; papers in Jl RAeS. *Recreations:* sailing, photography. *Address:* 8 Brendon Drive, Esher, Surrey KT10 9EQ. *T:* Esher 66009.

STANAGE, Rt. Rev. Thomas Shaun; *see* Bloemfontein, Bishop of.

STANBRIDGE, Air Vice-Marshal Sir Brian (Gerald Tivy), KCVO 1979 (MVO 1958); CBE 1974; AFC 1952; Director-General, Air Transport Users' Committee, 1979–85; *b* 6 July 1924; *s* of late Gerald Edward and Violet Georgina Stanbridge; *m* 1st, 1949, Kathleen Diana Hayes (marr. diss. 1983); two *d*; 2nd, 1984, Jennifer Anne Jenkins. *Educ:* Thurlestone Coll., Dartmouth. Served War: RAFVR, 1942; commnd, 1944; No 31 Sqdn (SE Asia), 1944–46; No 47 Sqdn, 1947–49; 2FTS/CFS, 1950–52, British Services Mission to Burma, 1952–54; The Queen's Flight (personal pilot and flying instructor to Duke of Edinburgh), 1954–58; Naval Staff Coll., 1958; PSO to AOC-in-C Coastal Comd, 1958–59; W/Cdr, Flying, RAF St Mawgan, 1960–62; jssc, 1962; RAFDS, Army Staff Coll., Camberley, 1962–63; Gp Captain on staff of NATO Standing Gp, Washington, DC, 1963–66; RAF Dir, Jt Anti-Submarine Sch., Londonderry, and Sen. RAF Officer, NI, 1966–68; Gp Captain Ops, HQ Coastal Comd, 1968–70; IDC, 1970; Air Cdre, 1970; Sec., Chiefs of Staff Cttee, MoD, 1971–73; Dep. Comdt, RAF Staff Coll., Bracknell, 1973–75; ADC to the Queen, 1973–75; Air Vice-Marshal, 1975; Defence Services Sec. to the Queen, 1975–79; retired 1979. Vice Pres., RAF Gliding and Soaring Assoc. *Address:* 20 Durrant Way, Sway, Lymington, Hants SO41 6DQ. *Club:* Royal Air Force.

STANBRIDGE, Ven. Leslie Cyril; Archdeacon of York since 1972; *b* 19 May 1920. *Educ:* Bromley County Grammar Sch., Kent; St John's Coll., Durham Univ. (MA, DipTheol). Asst Curate of Erith Parish Church, Kent, 1949–51; Tutor and Chaplain, St John's Coll., Durham, 1951–55; Vicar of St Martin's, Hull, 1955–64; Examining Chaplain to the Archbishop of York, 1962–; Rector of Cottingham, Yorks, 1964–72; Canon of York, 1968–; Rural Dean of Kingston-upon-Hull, 1970–72. *Recreations:* fell walking, cycling. *Address:* 14 St George's Place, York YO2 2DR. *T:* York 23775.

STANBROOK, Ivor Robert; MP (C) Orpington, since 1970; Barrister-at-Law; *b* 13 Jan. 1924; *y s* of Arthur William and Lilian Stanbrook; *m* 1946, Joan (*née* Clement); two *s*. *Educ:* state schools and London and Oxford Universities. Served RAF, 1942–46. Colonial Administrative Service, Nigeria, 1950–60: Asst Sec., Council of Ministers, Lagos, 1956; Dist Officer, N Region, 1957–60. Called to the Bar, Inner Temple, 1960; practising barrister, 1960–; Partner, Stanbrook & Hooper, European Law Office, Brussels, 1980–. *Publications:* Extradition—the Law and Practice, 1979; British Nationality—the New Law, 1981. *Address:* 6 Sevenoaks Road, Orpington, Kent. *T:* Orpington 20347; 42 rue du Taciturne, Brussels 1040, Belgium. *T:* 230 5059. *Club:* Carlton.

STANBURY, Richard Vivian Macaulay; HM Diplomatic Service, retired; *b* 5 Feb. 1916; *s* of late Gilbert Vivian Stanbury and Doris Marguerite (*née* Smythe); *m* 1953, Geraldine Anne, *d* of late R. F. W. Grant and of Winifred Helen Grant; one *s* one *d*. *Educ:* Shrewsbury Sch. (exhibnr); Magdalene Coll., Cambridge (exhibnr, 1st cl. Hons in Classical Tripos). Sudan Political Service, 1937–50 (District Comr in 12 districts, and Magistrate); HM Foreign (subseq. Diplomatic) Service, 1951–71: 2nd Sec., Cairo, 1951; FO 1954; Bahrain, Persian Gulf, 1956; FO 1959; Counsellor, Buenos Aires, 1968. *Recreations:* tennis, golf, and watching cricket (played for Somerset); trying to avoid playing bridge. *Address:* Shepherds House, Peasmarsh, near Rye, East Sussex. *Clubs:* Naval & Military; Hawks (Cambridge); Rye Golf; Hurlingham (Buenos Aires).

STANBURY, Prof. Sydney William, MD, FRCP; Professor of Medicine, University of Manchester, 1965–84, now Emeritus; *b* 21 April 1919; *s* of F. A. W. Stanbury and A. B. Stanbury (*née* Rowe); *m* 1943, Helen, *d* of Harry and Patty Jackson; one *s* four *d*. *Educ:* Hulme Grammar Sch., Oldham; Manchester Univ. MB, ChB (1st Cl. Hons) 1942; MD (Gold Medal) 1948; MRCP 1947, FRCP 1958. Served RAMC, Burma and India, 1944–47. Beit Meml Res. Fellow, 1948–51; Rockefeller Travelling Fellow, 1951–52; Registrar, Lectr and Reader, Dept of Medicine, Manchester Royal Infirmary, 1947–65; Consultant Phys., United Manchester Hosps, 1959–. Member: Assoc. of Physicians; Medical Res. Soc.; Bone and Tooth Soc. Visiting Professor: John Howard Means, Massachusetts Gen. Hosp., Boston, 1958; Henry M. Winans, Univ. of Texas, Dallas, 1958; W. T. Connoll, Queen's Univ., Kingston, Ont, 1978; Weild Lectr, RCP and S, Glasgow, 1958; Vis. Lectr: Univ. of Washington, Mayo Clinic, etc. *Publications:* contrib. European and American med. books and jls on: renal function, electrolyte metabolism, metabolic bone disease and vitamin D metabolism. *Recreation:* gardening. *Address:* Halamana, Gillan, Manaccan, Helston, Cornwall. *T:* Manaccan 586.

STANCLIFFE, Very Rev. David Staffurth; Provost of Portsmouth, since 1982; *b* 1 Oct. 1942; *s* of Very Rev. Michael Staffurth Stancliffe, *qv*; *m* 1965, Sarah Loveday Smith; one *s* two *d*. *Educ:* Westminster School; Trinity College, Oxford (MA); Cuddesdon Theological College. Assistant Curate, St Bartholomew's, Armley, Leeds, 1967–70; Chaplain to Clifton Coll., Bristol, 1970–77; Canon Residentiary of Portsmouth Cathedral, Diocesan Director of Ordinands and Lay Ministry Adviser, 1977–82. Member: Gen. Synod, 1985–; Liturgical Commn, 1986–. *Recreations:* old music, Italy. *Address:* Provost's House, Pembroke Road, Portsmouth PO1 2NS. *T:* Portsmouth 824400.

STANCLIFFE, Very Rev. Michael Staffurth, MA; Dean of Winchester, 1969–86; *b* 8 April 1916; *s* of late Rev. Canon Harold Emmet Stancliffe, Lincoln; *m* 1940, Barbara Elizabeth, *yr d* of late Rev. Canon Tissington Tatlow; two *s* one *d*. *Educ:* Haileybury; Trinity Coll., Oxford. Curate of St James, Southbroom, Devizes, 1940–43; priest-in-charge, Ramsbury, 1943–44; curate of Cirencester and priest-in-charge of Holy Trinity, Watermoor, 1944–49; Chaplain and Master, Westminster School, 1949–57; Canon of Westminster and Rector of St Margaret's, Westminster, 1957–69; Speaker's Chaplain, 1961–69; Preacher to Lincoln's Inn, 1954–57. Mem., General Synod, 1970–80; Chm., Council for Places of Worship, 1972–75; Mem. Cathedrals Advisory Commn for England, 1981–. Fellow, Winchester Coll., 1973. *Publications:* contrib. to A House of Kings, 1966; Symbols and Dances, 1986. *Address:* 36 Potter Hill, Pickering, N Yorks YO18 8AD.

See also Very Rev. D. S. Stancliffe.

STANDARD, Prof. Sir Kenneth (Livingstone), Kt 1982; CD 1976; MD, MPH; FFCM; Professor, since 1968, and Head of Department of Social and Preventive Medicine, since 1966, University of the West Indies at Mona; *b* 8 Dec. 1920; *m* 1955, Evelyn Francis; one *d*. *Educ:* UC of West Indies (MB BS); Univ. of Pittsburgh (MPH); Univ. of London (MD). Schoolmaster, Lynch's Secondary Sch., Barbados, 1940–48 (Headmaster, 1948); Med. House Officer, UCH of WI, 1956; MO, Nutrition Res., Jamaica, 1957–58; MOH, Barbados, 1958–61; MO, MRC Epidemiol. Res. Unit, Jamaica, 1961–66; Lectr, 1961–65, Sen. Lectr, 1965–68, Dept of Social and Preventive Medicine, Univ. of WI, Jamaica. Adjunct Prof. of Public Health, Grad. Sch. Public Health, Univ. of Pittsburgh, 1972–75; Stubenbord Vis. Prof., Cornell Univ. Med. Coll., USA, 1975–. Thomas Parran Lecture, Grad. Sch. of Public Health, Univ. of Pittsburgh, 1984. Member: WHO Adv. Cttee on Med. Res., 1969–72; WHO Expert Adv. Panel on Public Health Admin, 1969–. Jacques Parisot Foundn Medal and Fellowship, WHO, 1980–81. *Publications:* (ed jtly) Manual for Community Health Workers, 1974, rev. edn 1983; Epidemiology and Community Health in Warm Climate Countries, 1976; Alternatives in the Delivery of Health Services, 1976; Four Decades of Advances in Health in the Commonwealth Caribbean, 1979. *Recreations:* reading, poetry, gardening. *Address:* Department of Social and Preventive Medicine, University of the West Indies, Mona, Jamaica. *T:* 092–70773. *Club:* Royal Commonwealth Society.

STANDING, John; *see* Leon, Sir J. R.

STANESBY, Rev. Canon Derek Malcolm, PhD; Canon of St George's Chapel, Windsor, since 1985; *b* 28 March 1931; *s* of Laurence J. C. Stanesby and late Elsie L. Stanesby (*née* Stean); *m* 1958, Christine A. Payne; three *s* one *d*. *Educ:* Orange Hill Central School, London; Northampton Polytechnic, London; Leeds Univ. (BA Hons); Manchester Univ. (MEd, PhD); College of the Resurrection, Mirfield. GPO Radio Research Station, Dollis Hill, 1947–51; RAF (Navigator), 1951–53. Ordained, 1958; Curate: Old Lakenham, Norwich, 1958–61; St Mary, Welling, Dio. Southwark, 1961–63; Vicar, St Mark, Bury, Dio. Manchester, 1963–67; Rector, St Chad, Ladybarn, Manchester, 1967–85. *Publications:* Science, Reason and Religion, 1985; various articles. *Recreations:* hill walking, sailing, woodwork, idling. *Address:* 4 The Cloisters, Windsor Castle, Berks SL4 1NJ. *T:* Windsor 864142.

STANFIELD, Hon. Robert Lorne, PC (Canada) 1967; QC; Chairman, Institute for Research on Public Policy, since 1981; *b* Truro, NS, 11 April 1914; *s* of late Frank Stanfield, sometime MLA and Lieutenant-Governor of NS, and Sarah (*née* Thomas); *m* 1st, 1940, N. Joyce (*d* 1954), *d* of C. W. Frazee, Vancouver; one *s* three *d*; 2nd, 1957, Mary Margaret (*d* 1977), *d* of late Hon. W. L. Hall, Judge of Supreme Court and formerly Attorney-Gen. of NS; 3rd, 1978, Anne Margaret Austin, *d* of Dr D. Nelson, Henderson, Toronto. *Educ:* Colchester County Academy, Truro; Ashbury Coll., Ottawa; Dalhousie Univ.; Harvard Law Sch. Southam Cup, Ashbury Coll.; BA Political Science and Economics 1936, Governor-General's Gold Medal, Dalhousie Univ.; LLB Harvard, 1939. War of 1939–45: attached Halifax Office of Wartime Prices and Trade Bd as Regional Rentals Officer, later as Enforcement Counsel. Admitted Bar of NS, 1940. Practised law, McInnes and Stanfield, Halifax, 1945–56; KC 1950. President, Nova Scotia Progressive Cons. Assoc., 1947–48; Leader, Nova Scotia Progressive Cons. Party, 1948–67; elected to Legislature of NS, 1949, Mem. for Colchester Co.; re-elected Mem., 1953, 1960, 1963, 1967; Premier and Minister of Education, NS, 1956; resigned as Premier of NS, 1967; MP (Progressive C): Colchester-Hants, NS, 1967–68; Halifax, NS, 1968–79; Leader, Progressive Cons. Party of Canada, and of Opposition in House of Commons, 1967–74. Ambassador at Large and special representative of Govt of Canada in Middle East, 1979–80. Hon. LLD: University of New Brunswick, 1958; St Dunstan's Univ., PEI, 1964; McGill Univ., PQ, 1967; St Mary's Univ., NS, 1969; Dalhousie, 1982. Anglican. *Address:* 136 Acacia Avenue, Rockcliffe Park, Ottawa, Ontario K1M 0R1, Canada.

STANFORD, Adm. Sir Peter (Maxwell), GCB 1986 (KCB 1983); LVO 1970; Commander-in-Chief, Naval Home Command, since 1985; Flag Aide-de-Camp to the Queen, since 1985; *b* 11 July 1929; *s* of late Brig. Henry Morrant Stanford, CBE, MC, and of Edith Hamilton Stanford; *m* 1957, Helen Ann Lingard; one *s* two *d*. *Educ:* Britannia Royal Naval College. Midshipman, W Indies Sqdn, 1947–48; HMS Kenya, Korea, 1950–51; HMS Welfare, 1952–54; French Interpreter, 1954; HMS Camberford, 1954–56; Long Signals Course, 1956–57; Staff of C-in-C Mediterranean, 1957–58; Signal Officer, 3rd Destroyer Sqdn, 1958–59; HM Signal Sch., 1960–62; i/c HMS Grafton, 1962–63; Signal Div., Naval Staff, 1963–65; i/c HMS Brighton, 1966–67; HM Signal Sch., 1967–68; HM Yacht Britannia, 1969–70; Asst Dir Naval Plans, 1970–72; RCDS 1973; i/c HMS Hermione and Captain (F) 5, 1974–75; Commodore 1975; Sec., Chiefs of Staff Cttee, 1975–78; Flag Officer, Second Flotilla, 1978–80; Asst Chief of Naval Staff (Op. Req.), 1980–82; VCNS, 1982–85. *Publications:* various papers for Naval Review. *Recreations:* field sports, ornithology. *Address:* c/o Lloyd's Bank, Cox's & King's Branch, 6 Pall Mall, SW1Y 5NH. *Club:* Flyfishers'.

STANFORD-TUCK, Wing Commander Robert Roland, DSO 1940; DFC (2 bars); *b* 1 July 1916; *s* of Stanley Lewis Tuck and Ethel Constance Tuck; *m* 1945; two *s*. *Educ:* St Dunstan's Preparatory School and College, Reading. Left school, 1932, and went to sea as a cadet with Lamport and Holt; joined Royal Air Force, Sept. 1935; posted to No 65 Fighter Sqdn, Aug. 1936, and served with them until outbreak of war; posted to 92 (F) Sqdn, and went through air fighting at Dunkirk, shooting down 8 enemy aircraft (DFC); posted to Comd No 257 Burma Fighter Sqdn, Sept. 1940, till July 1941, when given command of Wing; comd Duxford and Biggin Hill Wings; prisoner 1942, escaped 1945. Record to end July 1941: 27 confirmed victories, 8 probably destroyed, 6 damaged; wounded twice, baled out 4 times. Retired list, 1948. *Relevant publication:* Fly For Your Life (by L. Forrester). *Address:* 2 Whitehall, Sandwich Bay, Kent.

STANGER, David Harry, FFB, FIQA, FBIM; Executive Chairman, Harry Stanger Ltd, since 1972; *b* 14 Feb. 1939; *s* of Charles Harry Stanger, CBE and Florence Bessie Hepworth Stanger; *m* 1963, Jill Patricia (*née* Barnes); one *s* two *d*. *Educ:* Oundle Sch.; Millfield Sch. TEng(CEI) 1971; FFB 1977; FIQA 1982; FBIM 1980. Served Corps of RE, 1960–66; joined R. H. Harry Stanger, 1966; Partner, Al Hoty-Stanger Ltd, 1975. Internat. Exec. Officer, Materials Consultants (Internat.) Ltd, 1983–. Chm., Adv. Cttee, NAMAS, 1985–. Sec. Gen., Union Internationale des Laboratoires Indépendants, 1983. A Vice-Pres., IQA, 1986; Member: Steering Cttee, NATLAS, 1981; Adv. Council for Calibration and Measurement, 1982. MSocIS, France, 1982. Pingat Peringatan, Malaysia, 1966. *Recreation:* collecting vintage wines. *Address:* Summerfield House, Barnet Lane, Elstree, Herts WD6 3HQ. *T:* 01–953 0022. *Clubs:* Carlton, St Stephen's Constitutional.

STANHOPE, family name of **Earl of Harrington.**

STANIER, Brigadier Sir Alexander Beville Gibbons, 2nd Bt, *cr* 1917; DSO 1940 (and Bar, 1945); MC; DL, JP; CStJ; *b* 31 Jan. 1899; *s* of 1st Bt, and Constance (*d* 1948), *d* of late Rev. B. Gibbons; *S* father, 1921; *m* 1927, Dorothy Gladys (*d* 1973), *e d* of late Brig.-Gen. Alfred Douglas Miller, CBE, DSO; one *s* one *d*. *Educ:* Eton; RMC, Sandhurst. Served European War in France, 1918 (MC); served War of 1939–45, in France 1940 and 1944 (despatches, DSO and Bar, American Silver Star, Comdr Order of Leopold of Belgium with palm, Belgian Croix de Guerre with palm). Adjutant 1st Bn Welsh Guards, 1923–26; Military Secretary, Gibraltar, 1927–30; commanded 2nd Battalion Welsh Guards, 1939–40; temp. Brigadier, 1940–45; Lieut-Colonel Commanding Welsh Guards, 1945–48. CC Salop, 1950–58. High Sheriff of Shropshire, 1951. County President of the St John Ambulance Bde, 1950–60. *Heir:* *s* Beville Douglas Stanier [*b* 20 April 1934; *m* 1963, Shelagh, *er d* of late Major and Mrs J. S. Sinnott, Tetbury, Glos; one *s* two *d*]. *Address:* Hill House, Shotover Park, Wheatley, Oxford. *T:* Wheatley 2996; Park Cottage, Ludford, Ludlow. *T:* Ludlow 2675.

STANIER, Field Marshal Sir John (Wilfred), GCB 1982 (KCB 1978); MBE 1961; Chairman, Royal United Services Institute for Defence Studies, since 1986; Director, Royal Ordnance plc, 1986; Chairman, Control Risks (GS), since 1985, *b* 6 Oct. 1925; *s* of late Harold Allan Stanier and Penelope Rose Stanier (*née* Price); *m* 1955, Cicely Constance Lambert; four *d*. *Educ*: Marlborough Coll.; Merton Coll., Oxford. MBIM, FRGS. Commd in 7th Queen's Own Hussars, 1946; served in N Italy, Germany and Hong Kong; comd Royal Scots Greys, 1966–68; comd 20th Armd Bde, 1969–70; GOC 1st Div., 1973–75; Comdt, Staff Coll., Camberley, 1975–78; Vice Chief of the General Staff, 1978–80; C-in-C, UKLF, 1981–82; CGS, 1982–85. ADC General to the Queen, 1981–85. Col, The Royal Scots Dragoon Guards, 1979–84; Col Comdt, RAC, 1982–85. Pres., Hampshire Br., British Red Cross Soc., 1986; Mem. Council, WWF. Comr, Royal Hosp., Chelsea, 1986–. Mem. Council, Marlborough Coll., 1984–. *Recreations*: hunting, fishing, sailing, talking. *Address*: c/o Coutts & Co., Chandos Branch, 440 Strand, WC2R 0QS. *Clubs*: Cavalry and Guards, Pratt's.

STANIFORTH, John Arthur Reginald, CBE 1969; Director: John Brown & Co., Ltd, 1965–84; John Brown Engineering (Clydebank) Ltd, 1968–84 (Chm., 1970–77); St Wilfrid's Hospice (South Coast) Ltd, since 1981; *b* 19 Sept. 1912; *o s* of Captain Staniforth, MC, Anston House, Anston, Yorks; *m* 1936, Penelope Cecile, *y d* of Maj.-Gen. Sir Henry Freeland; one *d* (one *s* decd). *Educ*: Marlborough Coll. With John Brown Group, 1929–84. Mem., Export Guarantees Adv. Council, 1971–76, Dep. Chm., 1975–76. Founder Chm., British Chemical Engrg Contractors Assoc., 1965–68. Governor, Bryanston Sch., 1962–. *Recreations*: golf, fishing. *Address*: 11 The Holdens, Old Bosham, West Sussex PO18 8LN. *T*: Bosham 572401. *Clubs*: MCC; Goodwood Golf.

STANISZEWSKI, Stefan; Officer's Cross, Order of Polonia Restituta, and other orders; with Polish Ministry of Foreign Affairs, since 1986; *b* 11 Feb. 1931; *s* of Andrzej and Katarzyna Staniszewski; *m* 1953, Wanda Szuszkiewicz; one *d*. *Educ*: Warsaw Univ. (BA Philosophy); Jagiellonian Univ. (BA Pol. Sciences). Active in students' and social organizations at university; Chm., Polish Youth Union's Jagiellonian Univ. Bd; official, Warsaw Cttee of Polish United Workers' Party, 1951–58; Head of Editorial Dept, ISKRY state publishing firm, 1958–60; entered foreign service, 1960; Minister's Cabinet, Min. of Foreign Affairs, 1960–63; successively 2nd Sec., 1st Sec. and Counsellor, Polish Embassy, Paris, 1963–69; Head of West European Dept and Mem. of Minister's Council, Min. of Foreign Affairs, 1969–72; Ambassador to Sweden, 1972–77; Head of Press, Cultural and Scientific Co-operation Dept, Min. of Foreign Affairs, 1977–81; Ambassador to UK, 1981–86, and to Ireland, 1984–86. Commander, Légion d'Honneur, 1972; Order of the Star of the North, Sweden, 1977; Commander, Order of the Aztec Eagle, Mexico, 1979. *Recreation*: swimming. *Address*: Ministerstwo Spraw Zagranicznych, Al. I Armii Wojska Polskiego 23, 00–580 Warsawa, Poland. *T*: 28–74–51.

STANLEY, family name of **Earl of Derby** and **Baron Stanley of Alderley.**

STANLEY OF ALDERLEY, 8th Baron (UK) *cr* 1839; **Thomas Henry Oliver Stanley;** Bt 1660; Baron Sheffield (Ire), 1783; Baron Eddisbury, 1848; DL; Captain (retired), Coldstream Guards; Tenant Farmer of New College, Oxford, since 1954; *b* 28 Sept. 1927; *s* of Lt-Col The Hon. Oliver Hugh Stanley, DSO, JP (3rd *s* of 4th Baron) (*d* 1952), and Lady Kathleen Stanley (*d* 1977), *e d* of 5th Marquess of Bath; *S* cousin (known as Baron Sheffield), 1971; *m* 1955, Jane Barrett, *d* of Ernest George Hartley; three *s* one *d*. *Educ*: Wellington College, Berks. Coldstream Guards, 1945–52; Guards Parachute Battalion and Independent Company, 1947–50; Northamptonshire Institute of Agriculture, 1952–53. Director: Thames Valley Cereals, 1976– (Chm., 1979–); Group Cereal Services, 1978–. Mem., Cttee of Management, RNLI, 1981–. Governor, St Edward's Sch., Oxford, 1979–. DL Gwynedd, 1985. *Recreations*: sailing, skiing, fishing. *Heir*: *e s* Hon. Richard Oliver Stanley, BSc [*b* 24 April 1956; *m* 1983, Carla, *er d* of Dr K. T. C. McKenzie, Solihull; one *s*]. *Address*: Trysglwyn Fawr, Amlwch, Anglesey. *T*: Amlwch 830364; Rectory Farm, Stanton St John, Oxford. *T*: Stanton St John 214. *Club*: Farmers'.

STANLEY, Charles Orr, CBE 1945 (OBE 1943); Hon. President, Sunbeam Wolsey Ltd; Director: Arts Theatre Trust; Stanley Foundation Ltd; Orr Investments Ltd; *b* 15 April 1899; *s* of John and Louisa A. Stanley; *m* 1st, 1924, Elsie Florence Gibbs; one *s* decd; 2nd, 1934, Velma Dardis Price (*d* 1970); 3rd, 1971, Lorna Katherine Sheppard (*d* 1977). *Educ*: Bishop Foy School, Waterford; City and Guilds, Finsbury. Served European War, RFC, 1917–18; Civil Engineer, 1922. Chm., Radio Industry Council, 1962–65; Pres., British Radio Equipment Manufrs Assoc., 1962–64. Hon. Pres., Pye of Cambridge Ltd. Hon. LLD Trinity College, Dublin, 1960. FCGI 1961. *Address*: Lisselan, Clonakilty, County Cork, Ireland. *T*: Bandon 33699. *Clubs*: Royal Automobile; Royal Thames Yacht; Royal Cork Yacht.

STANLEY, Prof. Eric Gerald, MA (Oxford and Yale); PhD (Birmingham); FBA 1985; Rawlinson and Bosworth Professor of Anglo-Saxon in the University of Oxford, since Jan. 1977; *b* 19 Oct. 1923; *m* 1959, Mary Bateman, MD, FRCP; one *d*. *Educ*: Queen Elizabeth's Grammar Sch., Blackburn; University Coll., Oxford. Lectr in Eng. Lang. and Lit., Birmingham Univ., 1951–62; Reader in Eng. Lang. and Lit., 1962–64, Prof. of English, 1964–75, Univ. of London at QMC; Prof. of English, Yale Univ., 1975–76. Member: Mediaeval Acad. of America, 1975–; Connecticut Acad. of Arts and Scis, 1976–. Sir Israel Gollancz Meml Lectr, British Acad., 1984. Co-Editor, Notes and Queries, 1963–. *Publications*: academic articles and books. *Recreation*: photography. *Address*: Pembroke College, Oxford.

STANLEY, Henry Sydney Herbert Cloete, CMG 1968; HM Diplomatic Service, retired; British High Commissioner to Trinidad and Tobago and (non-resident) to Grenada, 1977–80; *b* 5 March 1920; *er s* of late Sir Herbert Stanley, GCMG and Reniera (*née* Cloete), DBE; *m* 1941, Margaret, *d* of late Professor H. B. Dixon, CBE, FRS; three *s*. *Educ*: Eton; Balliol College, Oxford. Served with King's Royal Rifle Corps, 1940–46 (Capt.); N-W Europe, 1944–46, also HQ, CCG. Appointed to Commonwealth Relations Office, 1947. Served in Pakistan, 1950–52; Swaziland and South Africa, 1954–57; USA, 1959–61; Tanganyika, 1961–63; Kenya, 1963–65; Inspector, HM Diplomatic Service, 1966–68, Chief Inspector, 1968–70; High Comr, Ghana, 1970–75; Asst Under Sec. of State, FCO, 1975–77; High Comr for the New Hebrides (non-resident), 1976–77. *Address*: Silver How, 7 Harberton Mead, Oxford OX3 0DB.

STANLEY, Dr Herbert Muggleton, FRS 1966; *b* Stratford-upon-Avon, 20 July 1903; *m* 1930, Marjorie Mary (*née* Johnson); two *s* two *d*. *Educ*: King Edward VI Grammar School, Stratford-on-Avon; Birmingham University (1919–29). BSc 1923; MSc 1925; PhD 1930, FRIC; Mem. Council, Royal Soc., 1968. *Publications*: articles in numerous journals, including Jl Chem. Soc., Soc. Chem. Ind. *Recreations*: archæology, gardening. *Address*: West Halse, Bow, Crediton, Devon. *T*: Bow 262.

STANLEY, Rt. Hon. John (Paul); PC 1984; MP (C) Tonbridge and Malling since Feb. 1974; Minister of State for the Armed Forces, Ministry of Defence, since 1983; *b* 19 Jan. 1942; *s* of H. Stanley; *m* 1968, Susan Elizabeth Giles; two *s* one *d*. *Educ*: Repton Sch.; Lincoln Coll., Oxford (MA). Conservative Research Dept with responsibility for Housing, 1967–68; Research Associate, Internat. Inst. for Strategic Studies, 1968–69; Rio Tinto-Zinc Corp. Ltd, 1969–79. PPS to Rt Hon. Margaret Thatcher, 1976–79; Minister of State (Minister for Housing and Construction), DoE, 1979–83. Mem., Parly Select Cttee on Nationalised Industries, 1974. *Publication*: (jtly) The International Trade in Arms, 1972. *Recreations*: music, photography, sailing. *Address*: House of Commons, SW1A 0AA. *Club*: Leander (Henley-on-Thames).

STANLEY, Michael Charles, MBE 1945; Director of The Proprietors of Hay's Wharf Ltd, and various subsidiary companies, 1955–80; *b* 11 Aug. 1921; *s* of late Col Rt Hon. O. F. G. Stanley, PC, MC, MP, and Lady Maureen Stanley (*née* Vane-Tempest-Stewart); *m* 1951, Ailleen Fortune Hugh Smith, *d* of Owen Hugh Smith, Old Hall, Langham, Rutland; two *s*. *Educ*: Eton; Trinity College, Cambridge. Served 1939–46 with Royal Signals (Capt. 1943); N Africa, Sicily and Italy with 78th Infantry Div. Trinity, 1946–49 (Nat. Science and Engineering, MA). Served Engineering Apprenticeship with Metropolitan Vickers Electrical Co. Ltd, 1949–52. CEng 1966; MIEE 1966 (AMIEE 1952). Mem. Court, Lancaster University, 1980–. High Sheriff for Westmorland, 1959; Westmorland County Councillor, 1961–74; Vice-Lieutenant of Westmorland, 1965–74; DL Westmorland, 1964–74, Cumbria, 1974; High Sheriff, Cumbria, 1975. Hon. Col 33rd Signal Regt (V), 1981. *Recreations*: idleness, walking, wine. *Address*: Halecat, Witherslack, Grange-over-Sands, Cumbria LA11 6RU. *T*: Witherslack 229. *Clubs*: White's, Beefsteak, Brooks's; St James's (Manchester); Puffins (Edinburgh).

See also Dame K. E. H. Dugdale.

STANLEY, Oliver Duncan; Chief Executive, Comprehensive Financial Services PLC, since 1972; *b* 5 June 1925; *s* of Bernard Stanley and Mabel Best; *m* 1954, Ruth Brenner, JP, BA; one *s* three *d*. *Educ*: Christ Church, Oxford (MA); Harvard Univ., USA. Called to the Bar, Middle Temple, 1963. Served War, 8 Hussars, 1943–47. HM Inspector of Taxes, 1952–65; Dir, Gray Dawes Bank, 1966–72; founded Comprehensive Financial Services Gp of Cos, 1971. Chief Taxation Adviser, CLA, 1975–83 (Mem., Tax Cttee, 1983–). Mem., Soc. of Authors, 1967–. *Publications*: A Guide to Taxation, 1967; Taxology, 1971; Creation and Protection of Capital, 1974; Taxation of Farmers and Landowners, 1981; Offshore Tax Planning, 1986; contrib. The Times and The Sunday Times, 1966–83; numerous articles in legal and agricultural periodicals. *Recreations*: music, tennis, French civilisation. *Address*: 5 The Park, NW11 7SR. *T*: 01–455 0375. *Club*: Travellers'.

STANLEY, Hon. Pamela Margaret; *b* 6 Sept. 1909; *d* of 5th Lord Stanley of Alderley and Margaret Evans Gordon; *m* 1941, Sir David Cunynghame, 11th Bt (*d* 1978); three *s*. *Educ*: Switzerland; France. Studied at Webber-Douglas School of Acting and Singing; first appearance Lyric, Hammersmith, 1932, in Derby Day; six months at Oxford Repertory, 1933; with Martin Harvey in The Bells, Savoy, 1933; Sydney Carroll's Open Air Theatre, 1934; Wendy in Peter Pan, 1934; Queen Victoria in Victoria Regina, Gate Theatre, 1935; went to USA with Leslie Howard in Hamlet, 1936; Queen Victoria in Victoria Regina, Lyric, 1937–38; Open Air Theatre, 1938; Queen Victoria in The Queen's Highland Servant, Savoy, 1968. *Address*: 83 Clarendon Street, Leamington Spa, Warwickshire.

See also Sir A. D. F. Cunynghame, Bt.

STANLEY PRICE, His Honour Peter, QC 1956; a Circuit Judge (formerly a Judge of the Central Criminal Court), 1969–83; President, National Reference Tribunal for the Coal Mining Industry, 1979–83; Judge of the Chancery Court of York, 1967–83; *b* 27 Nov. 1911; *s* of late Herbert Stanley Price and late Gertrude Rangeley S. P. (*née* Wightman); *m* 1st, 1946, Harriett Ella Theresa (*d* 1948), *o d* of late Rev. R. E. Pownall; two *s*; 2nd, 1950, Margaret Jane, *o d* of late Samuel Milkins (she *m* 1937, William Hebditch, RAF; he *d* 1941); one *d* one step *s*. *Educ*: Cheltenham; Exeter College, Oxford (1st cl. Final Hons Sch. of Jurisprudence, 1933). Barrister, Inner Temple, 1936, Master of the Bench, 1963. Served War of 1939–45, Lieut (S) RNVR. Recorder of Pontefract, 1954, of York, 1955, of Kingston-upon-Hull, 1958, of Sheffield, 1965–69. Dep. Chm., N Riding QS, 1955–58, 1970–71, Chm., 1958–70; Judge of Appeal, Jersey and Guernsey, 1964–69; Solicitor-General, County Palatine of Durham, 1965–69. Pres., Nat. Reference Tribunal, Officials Conciliation Scheme, 1967–79. *Recreations*: birds and trees; gardening, shooting. *Address*: Church Hill, Great Ouseburn, York. *T*: Green Hammerton 30252. *Clubs*: Brooks's; Yorkshire (York).

STANNARD, Ven. Colin Percy, TD 1966; Archdeacon of Carlisle and Residentiary Canon of Carlisle Cathedral, since 1984; *b* 8 Feb. 1924; *s* of Percy and Grace Adelaide Stannard; *m* 1950, Joan Callow; one *s* two *d*. *Educ*: Woodbridge School; Selwyn Coll., Cambridge (BA 1947, MA 1949); Lincoln Theological Coll. Deacon 1949, priest 1950; Curate, St James Cathedral, Bury St Edmunds, 1949–52; Priest-in-charge, St Martin's, Grimsby, 1952–55; CF (TA), 1953–67; Vicar: St James's, Barrow-in-Furness, 1955–64; St John the Baptist's, Upperby, 1964–70; Rector of Gosforth, 1970–75; RD of Calder, 1970–75; Hon. Canon of Carlisle, 1975–84; Priest-in-charge of Natland, 1975–76, Vicar, 1976–84; RD of Kendal, 1975–84. *Recreations*: walking, bringing order out of chaos—especially in gardens. *Address*: 38 Longlands Road, Carlisle, Cumbria CA3 9AE. *T*: Carlisle 27622.

STANNARD, John Anthony; His Honour Judge Stannard; a Circuit Judge, since 1983; *s* of Anthony Stannard and Joan Stannard (*née* Joslin); *m* 1956, Madeline Betty (*née* Limb); two *d*. *Educ*: Quarry Bank High School, Liverpool; Trinity College, Cambridge. Called to the Bar, Lincoln's Inn, 1956; a Recorder of the Crown Court, 1980–83. *Address*: Robinswood, Glenrose Road, Woolton, Liverpool. *T*: 051–428 1187. *Club*: Athenæum (Liverpool).

STANNARD, Rt. Rev. Robert William, MA; *b* 20 Oct. 1895; *s* of late Robert John and Fanny Rebecca Stannard; *m* 1922, Muriel Rose Sylvia Knight (*d* 1985); one *s* (elder son killed in action April 1945). *Educ*: Westminster; Christ Ch., Oxford; Cuddesdon Theological College. ALCM 1910. Served army, 1915–19, Lieut Middlesex Regiment. Oxford: Distinction in Lit. Hum., First in Theology, Liddon Student; Ordained, 1922; Curate Bermondsey Parish Church, 1922–24; Curate-in-Charge S Mary's, Putney, 1924–27; Vicar of St James, Barrow-in-Furness, 1927–34; Rural Dean of Dalton, 1934; Rector of Bishopwearmouth (Sunderland), 1934–41; Rural Dean of Sunderland, 1937–41; Archdeacon of Doncaster, 1941–47; Chaplain to the King, 1944–47; Bishop Suffragan of Woolwich, 1947–59; Dean of Rochester, 1959–66. Grand Chaplain, United Grand Lodge of England, 1948–50. Master, Worshipful Co. of Gardeners, 1972–73. *Recreations*: gardening and music. *Address*: Dendron, Reading Road North, Fleet, Hants. *T*: Fleet 614059.

STANSBY, John; Chairman, UIE (UK) Ltd, since 1974 (UK parent company of UIE Scotland Ltd and part of Bouygues Group); *b* 2 July 1930; *s* of late Dumon Stansby and Vera Margaret Main; *m* 1966, Anna Maria Kruschewsky; one *d* and one step *s* one step *d*. *Educ*: Oundle; Jesus Coll., Cambridge (Schol., MA). FInstPet, FCIT, FRSA, MInstM. Commissioned, Queen's Own Royal Regt, 1949; Service, 1949–50, Somaliland Scouts. Shell Mex & BP Ltd, 1955–62; AIC Ltd, 1962–66; Dir, Rank Leisure Services, Rank Organisation, 1966–70; Dir, P&O Energy, P&OSN Co., 1970–74; Dep. Chm., London Transport Exec., 1978–80; Chairman: Transworld Leisure plc, 1985–; SAUR (UK) Ltd, 1986–; Director: Dumon Stansby & Co. Ltd, 1974–; Cementation–SAUR Water

Development Ltd, 1986–. European Bobsleigh Championship, 1952. *Address:* 19 Brook Green, W6 7BL. *T:* 01–603 0886. *Club:* Travellers'.

STANSFIELD, George Norman, CBE 1985 (OBE 1980); HM Diplomatic Service, retired; High Commissioner to the Solomon Islands, 1982–86; *b* 28 Feb. 1926; *s* of George Stansfield and Martha Alice (*née* Leadbetter); *m* 1947, Elizabeth Margaret Williams. *Educ:* Liscard High Sch. Served War, RAF, 1944–47. Ministries of Food and Supply, 1948–58; Private Sec. to Dir-Gen. of Armament Prodn, 1958–61; CRO, 1961; Second Secretary: Calcutta, 1962–66; Port of Spain, 1966–68; First Secretary: FCO, 1968–71; Singapore, 1971–74; Consul, Durban, 1974–78; FCO, 1978; Counsellor, and Head of Overseas Estate Dept, 1980–82. *Recreations:* sailing, cine-photography, wildlife. *Address:* Deryn's Wood, 80 Westfield Road, Woking, Surrey GU22 9QA. *Club:* Royal Commonwealth Society.

STANSFIELD, His Honour James Warden; a Circuit Judge (formerly County Court Judge), 1963–78; *b* 7 April 1906; *s* of James Hampson Stansfield, Sunny Lea, Wilmslow, Cheshire; *m* 1937, Florence Evelyn, *d* of Arthur Harry Holdcroft, Congleton, Cheshire; two *s* one *d. Educ:* King's School, Macclesfield; Sidney Sussex College, University of Cambridge. Called to the Bar, Inner Temple, 1929; practised Northern Circuit. Contested (C) Platting Division of Manchester, 1935. Served War of 1939–45: Royal Air Force, Middle East, and Staff of Judge Advocate-General; formerly RAFVR (Squadron Leader). Chairman: Manchester Licensing Planning Cttee, 1955–63; Manchester Mental Health Review Tribunal, 1962; Warrington Licensed Premises Cttee, 1970. *Recreations:* golf, walking. *Address:* Oak Lea, Victoria Road, Wilmslow, Cheshire. *T:* Wilmslow 523915.

STANSGATE, Viscountcy of (*cr* 1942, of Stansgate); title disclaimed by 2nd Viscount.

STANTON, Maj.-Gen. Anthony Francis, OBE 1955; *b* 6 Aug. 1915; *s* of Brig.-Gen. F. H. G. Stanton and Hilda Margaret (*née* Parkin); *m* 1943, Elizabeth Mary (*d* 1985), *d* of John Reginald Blackett-Ord, Whitfield Hall, Hexham; one *s* two *d. Educ:* Eton Coll.; RMA Woolwich. Commissioned RA, 1936. Served in: India, 1936–41; ME, 1941–43; NW Europe, 1944–45; subseq. in Germany, Far East and UK; Imp. Def. Coll., 1962; COS, HQ Northern Comd, 1967–70, retired 1970. Col Comdt, RA, 1972–77. *Recreation:* country sporting pursuits. *Address:* Wooperton Hall, Alnwick, Northumberland. *T:* Wooperton 241. *Club:* Army and Navy.

STANTON, Rev. John Maurice, MA; Rector of Chesham Bois, 1973–83; *b* 29 Aug. 1918; *s* of Frederick William Stanton, MInstCE and Maude Lozel (*née* Cole); *m* 1947, Helen Winifred (*née* Bowden); one *s* two *d. Educ:* King's School, Rochester; University College, Oxford. 2nd Class Hons, Final Hon. Sch. of Nat. Science, 1947; MA 1947. Commissioned Royal Artillery, 1940, 92nd Field Regt, RA, 1940–43. ISLD, CMF, 1943–46. Assistant Master, Tonbridge School, 1947–59; Headmaster, Blundell's School, Tiverton, Devon, 1959–71; Curate, St Matthew's, Exeter, 1972. Ordained Deacon, 1952; Priest, 1953. *Recreations:* water colour painting, gardening. *Address:* 37A St Andrew's Road, Old Headington, Oxford OX3 9DL.

STANTON-JONES, Richard, FEng 1984; engineering consultant since 1984; *b* 25 Sept. 1926; *s* of John C. Stanton Jones and Katharine Stanton; *m* 1949, Dorine Mary Watkins; one *s. Educ:* King's College, Cambridge (MA); Cranfield College of Aeronautics (MSc). CEng. Aerodynamicist, de Havilland, Saunders-Roe, Lockheed (USA), 1949–56; Chief Aerodynamicist, Saunders-Roe/British Hovercraft Corp. (SRN series of hovercraft), 1959–66; British Hovercraft Corp.: Technical Dir, 1966–68; Managing Dir, 1968–82; Dep. Chm., 1982–84; established RSJ Engineering, 1984. RAeS Silver Medal, 1965; Elmer A. Sperry Award (Transportation), 1968. *Publications:* numerous papers on hovercraft for tech. instns; author of 31 patents on hovercraft. *Recreations:* sailing, carpentry. *Address:* Doubloon, Springvale, Seaview, Isle of Wight. *T:* Seaview 3363. *Clubs:* Naval and Military; Island Sailing (Cowes).

STANWAY, Rt. Rev. Alfred; President, Australian Christian Literature Society, since 1971; *b* 9 Sept. 1908; *s* of Alfred Stanway, Millicent, S Australia, and Rosa Dawson; *m* 1939, Marjory Dixon Harrison. *Educ:* Melbourne High Sch.; Ridley Coll., Melbourne; Australian Coll. of Theology (ThL (Hons), 1934); Melbourne Teachers Coll. MA (Lamb), 1951. Diocese of Melbourne: Curate of St Albans, 1935–36; Mission of St James and St John, 1936–37; Diocese of Mombasa: Missionary, Giriama District, 1937–44; Principal Kaloleni Sch., 1938–44; Acting Gen. Sec., Victorian Branch, Church Missionary Soc., 1941; Hon. CF, 1942–46; Missionary, Maseno District, 1944–45; Rural Dean of Nyanza, 1945–47; Examining Chaplain to Bishop of Mombasa, 1945–51; Sec. African Council and African Education Board, Diocese of Mombasa, 1948–50; Commissary to Bishop of Mombasa, 1949–51; Archdeacon and Canon of Diocese of Mombasa, 1949–51; Bishop of Central Tanganyika, 1951–71; Dep. Principal, Ridley Coll., Melbourne Univ., 1971–75; Pres., Trinity Episcopal Sch. for Ministry, Pittsburgh, 1975–78. *Recreation:* chess. *Address:* 7 Elm Grove, Mt Waverley, Victoria 3149, Australia.

STANYER, Maj.-Gen. John Turner, CBE 1971 (OBE 1967); *b* 28 July 1920; *s* of late Charles T. Stanyer and late Mrs R. H. Stanyer; *m* 1942, Mary Patricia Pattie; three *s* four *d. Educ:* Latymer Upper Sch., Hammersmith. Served War, 2/Lieut The Middlesex Regt, 1941; Lieut to Captain, The Middlesex Regt, 1941–47: Iceland, France, Germany, Palestine. Captain, Royal Army Ordnance Corps, 1947; Student, Staff Coll., Camberley, 1951; AA&QMG, UN Force in Cyprus, 1966; Dir of Ordnance Services, BAOR, 1968–71; Commandant, Central Ordnance Depot, Bicester, 1971–73; Comdr, Base Orgn, RAOC, 1973–75, retired. Col Comdt, RAOC, 1977–82. Dir Gen., Supply Co-ordination, MoD, 1975–80. Mem., Oxford City Council, 1983–. CBIM. *Recreation:* sailing. *Address:* 36 Jack Straws Lane, Headington, Oxford. *T:* Oxford 68757. *Club:* Army and Navy.

STAPLES, Rev. Canon Edward Eric, CBE 1977 (OBE 1973); Chaplain to the Queen, 1973–80; Chaplain to the Anglican congregations in Helsinki and throughout Finland, in Moscow, Leningrad and elsewhere in the Soviet Union, and in Outer Mongolia, 1964–80; Hon. Chaplain, British Embassy: Helsinki, 1967–80, Moscow, 1968–80, Ulan Bator, 1970–81; Hon. Lecturer, English History, University of Helsinki, 1972–80; Hon. Canon of Gibraltar Cathedral, since 1974; *b* 15 Nov. 1910; *yr s* of Christopher Walter Staples and Esther Jane Staples; *m* 1962, Kate Ethel Thusberg (*née* Rönngren); two step *d. Educ:* Chichester Theol Coll. (earlier opportunities so misused that it is unwise to name the establishments concerned!). MA, PhD. Niger Company, 1932. Served with RNVR, 1939–46. Ordained 1948. Assistant of Court of Russia Company, 1977, Consul 1978. Life Mem., Finnish-British Soc.; Mem., Anglo-Mongolian Soc. Medal of Univ. of Helsinki, 1980. Kt, Order of the Lion (Finland), 1976; Order of St Vladimir (3rd cl.) (Russian Orthodox Church), 1977. *Recreations:* climbing, cricket (no longer actively), fishing, gardening, historical research. *Address:* Coombe Cottage, Templecombe BA8 0HQ. *T:* Templecombe 70340; Suvisaari, Heinävesi as, Finland. *Clubs:* MCC; Helsinki Cricket (Founder Mem.); Moscow Cricket (Founder Mem.); Ulan Bator Golf (Hon. Life Mem.).

STAPLES, (Hubert Anthony) Justin, CMG 1981; HM Diplomatic Service; Ambassador to Finland, since 1986; *b* 14 Nov. 1929; *s* of late Francis Hammond Staples, formerly ICS, and Catherine Margaret Mary Pownall; *m* 1962, Susan Angela Collingwood Carter; one *s* one *d. Educ:* Downside; Oriel Coll., Oxford. Served in RAF 1952–54 (Pilot Officer). Entered Foreign (later Diplomatic) Service, 1954; 3rd Sec., Bangkok, 1955; Foreign Office, 1959; 1st Sec., Berlin (Dep. Political Adviser), 1962; Vientiane, 1965 (acted as Chargé d'Affaires in 1966 and 1967); transf. to FO and seconded to Cabinet Office, 1968; Counsellor, UK Delegn to NATO, Brussels, 1971; Counsellor and Consul-General, Bangkok, 1974 (acted as Chargé d'affaires, 1975 and 1977); Counsellor, Dublin, 1978–81; Ambassador to Thailand, 1981–86 and concurrently to Laos, 1985–86. *Address:* c/o Foreign and Commonwealth Office, SW1. *Clubs:* Travellers'; Kildare Street and University (Dublin); Royal Bangkok Sports (Bangkok).

STAPLES, Sir John (Richard), 14th Bt *cr* 1628; *b* 5 April 1906; *s* of John Molesworth Staples (*d* 1948) and of Helen Lucy Johnstone, *yr d* of late Richard Williams Barrington, *S* kinsman, Sir Robert George Alexander Staples, 13th Bt, 1970; *m* 1933, Sybella, *d* of late Dr Charles Henry Wade; two *d. Heir: cousin* Thomas Staples [*b* 9 Feb. 1905; *m* 1952, Frances Ann Irvine (*d* 1981)]. *Address:* Butter Hill House, Dorking, Surrey.

STAPLES, Justin; *see* Staples, H. A. J.

STAPLETON, Sir Alfred; *see* Stapleton, Sir H. A.

STAPLETON, Air Vice-Marshal Deryck Cameron, CB 1960; CBE 1948; DFC; AFC; psa; *b* 1918; *s* of John Rouse Stapleton, OBE, Sarnia, Natal; *m* 1942, Ethleen Joan Clifford, *d* of late Sir Cuthbert William Whiteside. *Educ:* King Edward VI Sch., Totnes. Joined RAF, 1936; served Transjordan and Palestine (AFC), 1937–39; War of 1939–45 (DFC). Middle East, N Africa, Italy. Asst Sec. (Air), War Cabinet Offices, 1945–46; Secretary, Chiefs of Staff Cttee, Ministry of Defence, 1947–49; OC RAF, Odiham, 1949–51; subsequently, Plans, Fighter Comd HQ and Ops at AFCENT Fontainebleu; then OC, RAF, Oldenburg (Germany); Plans, Bomber Comd HQ, 1957–60; Air Ministry, 1960–62; Dir, Defence Plans, Min. of Defence, 1963–64; AOC No 1 Group, RAF Bomber Command, 1964–66; Comdt, RAF Staff Coll., Bracknell, 1966–68. BAC Area Manager, Libya, 1969–70; BAC Rep. CENTO Area, Tehran, later BAe Chief Exec. Iran, and Man. Dir, Irano-British Dynamics Co. Iran, 1970–79; Rep. BAe, Peking, China, and Chm., British Cos Assoc., Peking, 1979–83. Associate Fellow, British Interplanetary Soc., 1960. *Recreations:* most sports. *Address:* c/o National Westminster Bank, Haymarket, SW1. *Club:* White's.

STAPLETON, Guy; Director of Establishments, Ministry of Agriculture, Fisheries and Food, since 1985; *b* 10 Nov. 1935; *s* of William Algernon Swann Stapleton and Joan Denise Stapleton (*née* Wilson). *Educ:* Malvern Coll. Clerical Officer, Min. of Transport and Civil Aviation, 1954–58; Exec. Officer, 1958; transf. to Min. of Aviation, 1959; Civil Aviation Asst, British Embassy, Rome, 1960–63; Private Sec. to Controller of National Air Traffic Control Services, 1963–65; Asst Principal, MAFF, 1965; Private Sec. to Jt Parly Sec., 1967–68; Principal, 1968; Asst Sec., 1973; Dept of Prices and Consumer Protection, 1974–76; Under Sec., 1981; European Secretariat, Cabinet Office, 1982–85. *Publications:* A Walk of Verse, 1961; (compiled) Poet's England: 2, Gloucestershire, 1977, 2nd edn 1982; 4, Avon and Somerset, 1981; Devon, 1986; articles on history of Moreton in Marsh, Glos. *Recreations:* history of North Cotswolds, genealogy, topographical verse. *Address:* c/o Ministry of Agriculture, Fisheries and Food, Whitehall Place, SW1A 2HH. *T:* 01–233 3000. *Clubs:* Civil Service, Royal Commonwealth Society.

STAPLETON, Sir (Henry) Alfred, 10th Bt *cr* 1679; *b* 2 May 1913; *s* of Brig. Francis Harry Stapleton, CMG (*d* 1956) and *g g s* of 7th Bt, and Maud Ellen (*d* 1958), *d* of late Major Alfred Edward Wrottesley; *S* kinsman, 1977; *m* 1961, Rosslyne Murray, *d* of late Captain H. S. Warren, RN. *Educ:* Marlborough; Christ Church, Oxford. Served War of 1939–45, Oxfordshire and Bucks Light Infantry. *Recreations:* cricket umpiring, campanology. *Heir:* none. *Address:* 7 Ridgeway, Horsecastles Lane, Sherborne, Dorset. *Clubs:* Garrick, MCC.

STAPLETON, Richard Christopher, PhD; Fellow, Churchill College, Cambridge, since 1986; *b* 11 Oct. 1942; *s* of Leonard Stapleton and Rosamund Kathleen May Stapleton; *m* 1968, Linda Cairns; one *s* one *d. Educ:* Univ. of Sheffield (BAEcon, PhD Business Studies); Open Univ. (BA Maths). Lectr in Business Finance, Sheffield Univ., 1965–73; Asst Prof. of Finance, New York Univ., 1973–76; Sen. Res. Fellow, 1976–77, Nat. West. Bank Prof. of Business Finance, 1977–86, Manchester Business Sch., Univ. of Manchester. Hon. MBA Manchester, 1980. *Publications:* The Theory of Corporate Finance, 1970; International Tax Systems and Financing Policy, 1978; Capital Markets and Corporate Financial Decisions, 1980; contrib. Econ. Jl, Jl of Finance, Jl of Financial Econs, Qly Jl of Econs. *Recreations:* golf, reading, travel. *Address:* Churchill College, Cambridge.

STAPLETON-COTTON, family name of **Viscount Combermere.**

STAREWICZ, Artur, 2 Orders of Banner of Labour (1st cl.); Polonia Restituta; and other orders; Ambassador of Poland to the Court of St James's, 1971–78; *b* Warsaw, 20 March 1917; *m* 1947, Maria Rutkiewicz; two *s* two *d. Educ:* Warsaw Univ.; Institut Chimique de Rouen, 1938–39; Lvov Technical Univ., 1940–41; Grad. Engr, Soviet Electrochemical Inst., 1943. Chemical engr. Mem., revolutionary youth orgns incl. Communist Union of Polish Youth; arrested 1935 and 1936; Mem., Polish Workers Party (PPR), 1944–48; worked in PPR Voivoidship Cttees: Rzeszow; Cracow; Warsaw; First Sec., Wroclaw, 1947–48; Polish United Workers Party (PZPR): Mem., 1948–; Head of Propaganda, Central Cttee, 1948–53; Sec., Central Council of Trade Unions, 1954–56; Dep. Editor-in-Chief, daily newspaper Trybuna Ludu, 1956; Alternate Mem., Central Cttee, 1954–59, Mem., 1959–71; Head of Press Office, 1957–63; Sec., Central Cttee, 1963–71. Mem., Seym, 1957–72; Chairman: Polish Gp, Inter-Parly Union; Polish Cttee for Security and Cooperation in Europe, 1978–86; Editor, Polish Perspectives, 1979–86. *Recreation:* aquatic sport. *Address:* Swietojerska 16 m3, Warsaw, Poland.

STARK, Sir Andrew (Alexander Steel), KCMG 1975 (CMG 1964); CVO 1965; DL; HM Diplomatic Service, retired; Chairman, The Maersk Co., since 1978; Director: Scandinavian Bank Ltd, since 1978; Carlsberg Brewery Ltd, since 1980; Adviser on European Affairs, Society of Motor Manufacturers and Traders, since 1977; *b* 30 Dec. 1916; *yr s* of late Thomas Bow Stark and of late Barbara Black Stark (*née* Steel), Fauldhouse, West Lothian; *m* 1944, Helen Rosemary, *er d* of late Lt-Col J. Oxley Parker, TD, and Mary Monica (*née* Hills); two *s* (and one *s* decd). *Educ:* Bathgate Acad.; Edinburgh Univ. MA (Hons), Eng. Lit, Edinburgh, 1938. Served War of 1939–45, Green Howards and Staff appts. Major 1945. Entered Foreign Service, 1948, and served in Foreign Office until 1950; 1st Secretary, Vienna, 1951–53; Asst Private Sec. to Foreign Secretary, 1953–55; Head of Chancery: Belgrade, 1956–58; Rome, 1958–60; Counsellor: FO, 1960–64; Bonn, 1964–68; attached to Mission to UN with rank of Ambassador, Jan. 1968; British Mem., Seven Nation Cttee on Reorganisation of UN Secretariat; seconded to UN, NY, as Under-Secretary-General, Oct. 1968–1971; HM Ambassador to Denmark, 1971–76; Dep. Under-Sec. of State, FCO, 1976–77. Mem., CBI Europe Cttee, 1980–85. Chairman: Anglo-Danish Soc., 1983–; Anglo-Danish Trade Adv. Bd, 1983–. Pres., Essex Physically Handicapped Assoc., 1979–. Chm. Council, Univ. of Essex, 1983– (Mem., 1978–); Pro-Chancellor, Essex Univ., 1983–. DL Essex, 1981. Grosses Verdienstkreuz, German Federal Republic, 1965; Grand Cross, Order of the Dannebrog, Denmark, 1974.

Recreations: ski-ing, tennis, shooting. *Address:* Fambridge Hall, White Notley, Essex. *T:* Silver End 83117. *Clubs:* Travellers' (Chairman 1978–81), MCC.

STARK, Dame Freya (Madeline), DBE 1972 (CBE 1953); *d* of late Robert Stark, sculptor, Ford Park, Chagford, Devon; *m* 1947, Stewart Perowne, *qv*. *Educ:* privately in Italy; Bedford College, London University; School of Oriental Studies, London. Engaged on Govt service in Middle East and elsewhere, 1939–45. Awarded Back Grant, 1933, for travel in Luristan; Triennial Burton Memorial Medal from Royal Asiatic Society, 1934; Mungo Park Medal from Royal Scottish Geographical Society, 1936; Founder's Medal from Royal Geographical Society, 1942; Percy Sykes Memorial Medal from R Central Asian Soc., 1951. Sister of the Order of St John of Jerusalem, 1949, Sister Comdr, 1981. LLD Glasgow Univ., 1951; DLitt Durham, 1971. *Publications:* Bagdad Sketches, 1933, enlarged edition, 1937; The Valleys of the Assassins, 1934; The Southern Gates of Arabia, 1936; Seen in the Hadhramaut, 1938; A Winter in Arabia, 1940; Letters from Syria, 1942; East is West, 1945; Perseus in the Wind, 1948; Traveller's Prelude, 1950; Beyond Euphrates, 1951; The Coast of Incense, 1953; Ionia: a Quest, 1954; The Lycian Shore, 1956; Alexander's Path, 1958; Riding to the Tigris, 1959; Dust in the Lion's Paw, 1961; The Journey's Echo, 1963; Rome on the Euphrates, 1966; The Zodiac Arch, 1968; Space, Time and Movement in Landscape, 1969; The Minaret of Djam, 1970; Turkey: a sketch of Turkish History, 1971; A Peak in Darien, 1976; Letters (ed Lucy Moorehead): vol. 1, The Furnace and the Cup, 1914–1930, 1974; vol. 2, The Open Road, 1930–1935, 1975; vol. 3, The Growth of Danger, 1935–1939, 1976; vol. 4, The Bridge of the Levant, 1940–1943, 1977; vol. 5, New Worlds for Old, 1943–1946, 1978; vol. 6, The Broken Road, 1947–1952, 1981; Rivers of Time, 1982. *Recreations:* travel, mountaineering and embroidery. *Address:* Via Canova, Asolo (Treviso), Italy; c/o John Murray, 50 Albemarle Street, W1.

STARKE, Hon. Sir John Erskine, Kt 1976; **Hon. Mr Justice Starke;** Judge of Supreme Court of Victoria, Australia, since 1964. Admitted to Victorian Bar, 1939; QC 1955; Judge, 1946. *Address:* Supreme Court, Melbourne, Victoria 3000, Australia; Mount Eliza, Victoria, Australia.

STARKER, Janos; concert cellist, recording artist; Distinguished Professor of Music, Indiana University, since 1958; *b* 5 July 1924; *s* of F. Sandor and M. Margit; *m* 1944, Eva Uranyi; one *d*; *m* 1960, Rae D. Busch; one *d*. *Educ:* Franz Liszt Academy of Music, Budapest; Zrinyi Gymnasium, Budapest. Solo cellist: Budapest Opera and Philh., 1945–46; Dallas Symphony, 1948–49; Metropolitan Opera, 1949–53; Chicago Symphony, 1953–58; concert tours on all continents in recitals and as soloist with orchestras; numerous recordings. Grand Prix du Disque, 1948; George Washington Award, 1972; Sanford Fellowship Award, Yale, 1974; Herzl Award, 1978; Ed Press Award, 1983; Kodály Commemorative Medallion, NY, 1983; Arturo Toscanini Award, 1986; Tracy Sonneborn Award, Indiana Univ., 1986. Mem., Amer. Fedn Musicians; Hon. RAM, 1981. Hon. DMus: Chicago Conservatory Coll., 1961; Cornell, 1978; East-West Univ., 1982; Williams Coll., 1983. Invented the Starker Bridge. *Publications:* Cello Method: an organised method of string playing, 1963; Bach Suites, 1971; Concerto Cadenzas, 1976; Beethoven Sonatas, 1978; Beethoven Variations, 1979; Bach Sonatas, 1979; Schubert-Starker Sonatina, 1980; Dvorak Concerto, 1981; Bottermund-Starker Variations, 1982; Encores, 1985; many articles and essays. *Recreations:* writing, swimming. *Address:* Indiana University Music Department, Bloomington, Ind 47401, USA.

STARKEY, Sir John (Philip), 3rd Bt *cr* 1935; JP; DL; *b* 8 May 1938; *s* of Sir William Randle Starkey, 2nd Bt, and Irene Myrtle Starkey (*née* Francklin) (*d* 1965); *S* father, 1977; *m* 1966, Victoria Henrietta Fleetwood, *y d* of Lt-Col Christopher Fuller, TD; one *s* three *d*. *Educ:* Eton College; Christ Church, Oxford. Sloan Fellow, London Business School. A Church Commissioner and Mem. Commissioners' Assets Cttee, 1985–. DL Notts, 1981; JP Newark, 1981. *Recreation:* cricket. *Heir:* *s* Henry John Starkey, *b* 13 Oct. 1973. *Address:* Norwood Park, Southwell, Notts. *T:* Southwell 812762. *Clubs:* Boodle's, MCC.

STASSEN, Harold Edward; lawyer, politician, educator, United States; Partner in law firm Stassen, Kostos and Mason; Chairman, International Law Committee of Philadelphia Bar Association, 1973; *b* W St Paul, Minn, 13 April 1907; *s* of William Andrew Stassen and Elsie Emma Mueller; *m* 1929, Esther G. Glewwe, artist; one *s* one *d*. *Educ:* Univ. of Minnesota Coll. (BA 1927; LLB 1929); Law School. Has several hon. degrees. Admitted to Minnesota Bar, 1929; practised South St Paul; County Attorney, Dakota County, 1930–38; thrice elected Governor of Minnesota, 1939–43; resigned for service with Navy; Lt Comdr, USN; Comdr on staff of Admiral Halsey in South Pacific, 1943–44; Asst Chief of Staff, 1944; Capt., USN; released to inactive duty, 1945. One of US delegates to San Francisco Conference, drafting and signing UN Charter, 1945. Pres., Minnesota Young Republicans; Delegate to Republican Convention, 1936; Temporary Chairman and Keynoter of Republican National Convention and floor manager for Wendell Wilkie, 1940; twice elected National Chairman National Governors' Conference, and of Council of State Governments, 1940–41. President, University of Pennsylvania, 1948–53. President International Council of Religious Education, 1942, 1950; Vice-Pres. and a Founder, Nat. Council of Churches, 1951–52; President, Div. of Christian Educ. of Nat. Council of Churches, 1953–. Director Foreign Operations Admin., 1953–55; Special Assistant to the President for Disarmament, 1955–58; Dep. US Rep. on Disarmament Commn, UN, 1955–58. Chief Consultant to ME Tech. Univ., Ankara, 1958; Mem., Nat. Security Council, 1953–58. Delivered Godkind Lectures on Human Rights, Harvard Univ., 1946; candidate for Republican nomination for President of US, 1948–. Chm., World Law Day, Geneva, 1968. Bronze Star, 1944; Legion of Merit, Six Battle Stars (Western Pacific campaign), 1945. Baptist. Mason. *Publications:* Where I Stand, 1947; Man was meant to be Free, 1951. *Address:* (office) 2300 Two Girard Plaza, Philadelphia, Pennsylvania 19102, USA.

STATHAM, Sir Norman, KCMG 1977 (CMG 1967); CVO 1968; HM Diplomatic Service, retired; Vice-President, British Chamber of Commerce in Germany, since 1981; *b* Stretford, Lancs, 15 Aug. 1922; *s* of Frederick William and Maud Statham; *m* 1948, Hedwig Gerlich; one *s* one *d* (and one *s* decd). *Educ:* Seymour Park Council School, Stretford; Manchester Grammar School; Gonville and Caius College, Cambridge (MA). Intelligence Corps, 1943–47; Manchester Oil Refinery Ltd and Petrochemicals Ltd, 1948–50; Foreign Service, 1951: Foreign Office, 1951; Consul (Commercial), New York, 1954–58; First Secretary (Commercial), Bonn, 1958–63; Administrative Staff College, Henley, 1963; Foreign Office, 1964; Counsellor, Head of European Economic Integration Dept, 1965–68, 1970–71; Consul-General, São Paulo, 1968–70; Minister (Economic), Bonn, 1971–75; Asst Under Sec. of State, FCO, 1975; Dep. Under Sec. of State, FCO, 1975–77; Ambassador to Brazil, 1977–79. Pres., Council of British Chambers of Commerce in Continental Europe, 1982–84. *Recreations:* gardening, reading. *Address:* 11 Underhill Park Road, Reigate, Surrey RH2 9LU. *Clubs:* Travellers'; Lancashire County Cricket.

STATHATOS, Stephanos; Commander, Order of Phoenix; Officer, Order of George I; Greek Ambassador to the Court of St James's, since 1986, and non-resident Ambassador to Iceland; *b* 1922; *s* of Gerassimo and Eugenia Stathatos; *m* 1947, Thalia Mouzina. *Educ:* Law School, Athens Univ.; post graduate studies: Ecole des Sciences Politiques, Paris; LSE. Entered Greek Diplomatic Service, 1953; served NATO, Paris, Athens, Washington; Dep. Perm. Rep. to UN, NY, 1968–72; Dir, Middle East Political Affairs, Min. of Foreign Affairs, 1972–74; Ambassador, Perm. Rep. to EEC, 1974–79; Ambassador, Paris, 1979–82; non-resident Ambassador to Holy See, 1981–82; Dep. Political Dir, 1982–84, Political Dir, 1984–85, Min. of Foreign Affairs. Holds numerous foreign orders and decorations. *Address:* 51 Upper Brook Street, W1. *Club:* Athenæum.

STAUGHTON, Hon. Sir Christopher (Stephen Thomas Jonathan Thayer), Kt 1981; **Hon. Mr Justice Staughton;** Judge of the High Court of Justice, Queen's Bench Division, since 1981; *b* 24 May 1933; *yr s* of Simon Thomas Samuel Staughton and Edith Madeline Jones; *m* 1960, Joanna Susan Elizabeth, *er d* of George Frederick Arthur Burgess; two *d*. *Educ:* Eton Coll. (Scholar); Magdalene Coll., Cambridge (Scholar). 2nd Lieut, 11th Hussars PAO, 1952–53; Lieut, Derbyshire Yeomanry TA, 1954–56. George Long Prize for Roman Law, Cambridge, 1955; BA 1956; MA 1961. Called to Bar, Inner Temple, 1957, Bencher, 1978; QC 1970; a Recorder of the Crown Court, 1972–81. Mem., Senate of the Inns of Court and the Bar, 1974–81; Chm., Code of Conduct sub-cttee, 1979–80. Chm., St Peter's Eaton Square Church of England Sch., 1974–83. *Publications:* (Jt Editor) The Law of General Average (British Shipping Laws vol. 7), 1964, new edn, 1975; (jtly) Profits of Crime and their Recovery, 1984. *Recreations:* bridge, growing dahlias. *Address:* Royal Courts of Justice, Strand, WC2. *T:* 01–936 6000. *Club:* Brooks's.

STAVELEY, Sir John (Malfroy), KBE 1980 (OBE 1972); MC 1941; FRCP; FRACPath; Director, Auckland Blood Transfusion Service, 1965–76; Hon. Medical Director, New Zealand Blood Foundation, since 1978; *b* 30 Aug. 1914; *s* of William Staveley and Annie May Staveley (*née* Malfroy); *m* 1940, Elvira Cliafe Wycherley; one *s* one *d*. *Educ:* Univ. of Dunedin (MB ChB); Univ. of Edinburgh. FRCP 1958; FRACPath 1965. House Surgeon, Auckland Hosp., 1939; war service with 2NZEF, Middle East, 1940–45; post graduate educn, UK, 1946–47; Pathologist, Auckland Hosp., 1948–50; Haematologist, Auckland Hosp. Bd, 1950–64. Landsteiner Award, USA, for medical research, 1980. *Publications:* papers in medical and scientific jls (British, American and NZ). *Recreations:* mountaineering, fishing, music. *Address:* 11 Matanui Street, Northcote, Auckland 9, New Zealand. *Club:* New Zealand Alpine.

STAVELEY, Martin Samuel, CMG 1966; CVO 1966; CBE 1962 (MBE 1955); *b* 3 Oct. 1921; fourth *s* of late Herbert Samuel Staveley and Edith Ellen Staveley (*née* Shepherd); *m* 1942, Edith Eileen Baker; one *s* two *d*. *Educ:* Stamford School; Trinity College, Oxford. Appointed Cadet, Colonial Administrative Service, Nigeria, 1942; Secretary, Development and Welfare Organisation in the West Indies, 1946–57; Secretary to Governor-General, Federation of the West Indies, 1958–62; Administrator, British Virgin Islands, 1962–67; HM Diplomatic Service, 1967–74; Home Civil Service, 1974–84. *Address:* Centre Flat, Monkton Farleigh Manor, Bradford-on-Avon, Wilts.

STAVELEY, Maj.-Gen. Robert; Administrative Controller, Norton Rose Botterell & Roche, solicitors, since 1983; *b* 3 June 1928; *s* of Brig. Robin Staveley, DSO, and Ilys (*née* Sutherland); *m* 1958, Airlie, *d* of Maj.-Gen. W. H. Lambert, CB, CBE; one *s* one *d*. *Educ:* Wellington. RMA, Sandhurst, 1947; commissioned RA, 1948; served BAOR, 1949–51; ADC to GOC Malta, 1951–53; Air OP pilot, Malaya, 1954–57 (despatches); ADC to GOC-in-C Northern Command, 1957–58; Indian Staff Coll., 1959; Staff Officer and Missile Battery Comdr, BAOR, 1960–65; Instructor, Staff Coll., 1966–68; commanded 47 Lt Regt RA, UK and Hong Kong, 1969–71; CRA 2nd Div., BAOR, 1973–74; RCDS 1975; Director of Operational Requirements, MoD, 1976–79; C of S, Logistic Exec. (Army), 1979–82. Col Comdt, RA, 1982–. FBIM 1983. *Recreations:* good food, sailing, skiing, music. *Address:* c/o Lloyds Bank (Cox's & King's Branch), 6 Pall Mall, SW1Y 5NH. *Clubs:* Army and Navy, Royal Ocean Racing; Royal Artillery Yacht (Commodore, 1980–83).

STAVELEY, Adm. Sir William (Doveton Minet), GCB 1984 (KCB 1981); First Sea Lord and Chief of Naval Staff, since 1985; First and Principal Naval Aide-de-Camp to the Queen, since 1985; *b* 10 Nov. 1928; *s* of late Adm. Cecil Minet Staveley, CB, CMG, and Margaret Adela (*née* Sturdee); *m* 1954, Bettina Kirstine Shuter; one *s* one *d*. *Educ:* West Downs, Winchester; RN Colls, Dartmouth and Greenwich. Entered Royal Navy as Cadet, 1942; Midshipman, HMS Ajax, Mediterranean, 1946–47; Sub-Lieut/Lieut, HM Ships Nigeria and Bermuda, S Atlantic, 1949–51; Flag Lieut to Adm. Sir George Creasy, C-in-C Home Fleet, HM Ships Indomitable and Vanguard, 1952–54; Staff, Britannia, RNC, Dartmouth, 1954–56; HM Yacht Britannia, 1957; First Lieut, HMS Cavalier, Far East, 1958–59; Lt-Comdr, 1958; RN Staff Coll., 1959; Staff, C-in-C Nore and Flag Officer Medway, 1959–61; Comdr 1961; Sen. Officer, 104th and 6th Minesweeping Sqdn, HMS Houghton, Far East, 1962–63; Comdr, Sea Trng, Staff of Flag Officer, Sea Trng, Portland, 1964–66; comd HMS Zulu, ME and Home Station, 1967; Captain 1967; Asst Dir, Naval Plans, Naval Staff, 1967–70; Command: HM Ships Intrepid, Far and ME, 1970–72; Albion, Home Station, 1972; RCDS, 1973; Dir of Naval Plans, Naval Staff, 1974–76; Flag Officer, Second Flotilla, 1976–77; Flag Officer, Carriers and Amphibious Ships, and NATO Commander, Carrier Striking Group Two, 1977–78; Chief of Staff to C-in-C Fleet, 1978–80; Vice-Chief of Naval Staff, 1980–82; C-in-C, Fleet, and Allied C-in-C, Channel and E Atlantic, 1982–85. Chairman: Combined Services Equitation Assoc., 1980–82; Council, British Horse Soc., 1982; Member: Royal Naval Sailing Assoc.; Royal Yachting Assoc.; RHS; Royal Nat. Rose Soc. A Younger Brother of Trinity House, 1973. CBIM 1983. *Recreations:* gardening, shooting, fishing, riding, sailing, restoring antiques. *Address:* c/o Ministry of Defence, Main Building, Whitehall, SW1A 2HB. *Club:* Boodle's.

STAWELL, Maj.-Gen. William Arthur Macdonald, CB 1945; CBE 1944; MC 1917; *b* 22 Jan. 1895; *s* of G. C. Stawell, ICS; *m* 1926, Amy (*d* 1986), *d* of C. W. Bowring, New York; one *s*. *Educ:* Clifton College; RMA, Woolwich. Served European War, 1914–21, France, Greek Macedonia, Serbia, Bulgaria, Turkey (wounded, MC); 2nd Lieut 1914; Temp. Captain, 1916–17; Acting Major, Mar.-April 1917 and 1918–19; Captain, 1917; Major 1929; Lieut-Col 1937; Col 1940; Brig. 1940. GSO3 War Office, 1931–32; Brigade Maj., Aldershot, 1932–35; DAAG India, 1935–37; CRE 1937–40; AA and QMG Feb.-July 1940; GSO1 July-Nov. 1940; DDMI War Office, 1940–42; Brig., Comdr Home Forces, Feb.-Nov. 1942; Brig. General Staff, Home Forces, 1942–43; MEF and CMF, 1943–45 (CBE, CB); Temp. Maj.-Gen. 1943–45; Deputy Chief of Operations UNRRA, Nov. 1945–Aug. 1946; Deputy Chief Intelligence Division, CCG, 1947–48; retired. *Recreations:* yachting, golf. *Address:* Crobeg, The Common, Southwold, Suffolk. *Clubs:* Army and Navy; Royal Norfolk and Suffolk Yacht.

STEAD, Rev. Canon (George) Christopher, LittD, FBA 1980; Fellow, King's College, Cambridge, 1938–49 and 1971–85 (Professorial Fellow, 1971–80); Emeritus Fellow, Keble College, Oxford, since 1981; *b* 9 April 1913; *s* of Francis Bernard Stead, CBE, and Rachel Elizabeth, *d* of Rev. Canon G. C. Bell; *m* 1958, Doris Elizabeth Odom; two *s* one *d*. *Educ:* Marlborough Coll.; King's Coll., Cambridge (scholar). 1st cl. Classical Tripos Pt I, 1933; Pitt Scholar, 1934; 1st cl. Moral Science Tripos Pt II, 1935; BA 1935, MA 1938, LittD Cantab 1978; New Coll., Oxford (BA 1935); Cuddesdon Coll., Oxford, 1938. Ordained, 1938; Curate, St John's, Newcastle upon Tyne, 1939; Lectr in Divinity, King's

Coll., Cambridge, 1938–49; Asst Master, Eton Coll., 1940–44; Fellow and Chaplain, Keble Coll., Oxford, 1949–71 (MA Oxon 1949); Ely Professor of Divinity, Cambridge, and Canon Residentiary of Ely Cathedral, 1971–80, Canon Emeritus, 1981. *Publications:* Divine Substance, 1977; Substance and Illusion in the Christian Fathers, 1985; contributor to: Faith and Logic, 1957; New Testament Apocrypha, 1965; The Philosophical Frontiers of Christian Theology, 1981; Platonismus und Christentum, 1983; A New Dictionary of Christian Theology, 1983; Dizionario di Patristica, 1983; about 15 major articles, mostly in Jl of Theol Studies, Vigiliae Christianae. *Recreations:* walking, sailing, music. *Address:* 13 Station Road, Haddenham, Ely, Cambs.

STEAD, Ralph Edmund, FCA, FCMA; retired; Chairman, Eastern Region, British Gas Corporation, 1977–81; *b* 7 Jan. 1917; *s* of Albert Stead and Mabel Stead; *m* 1946, Evelyn Annie Ness; two *s* two *d.* *Educ:* Manchester Grammar Sch.; Ilford County High Sch. FCA 1949; FCMA 1952. Served War, RASC, 1940–46. Asst Divl Accountant, Cambridge Div., Eastern Gas Bd, 1949–50; N Eastern Gas Board: Asst Chief Accountant, 1950–53; Group Accountant, Bradford Gp, 1953–57; N Western Gas Board: Gp Accountant, Manchester Gp, 1957–61; Gen. Man., West Lancs Gp, 1961–65; Head of Management Services, 1966–71; Dir of Finance, 1971–73; Dep. Chm., Eastern Reg., British Gas Corp., 1973–77. Member: Financial Instns Gp, DoE, 1981–82; Management Cttee, Lazards Property Unit Trust, 1979–; Rent Assessment Panel for Scotland, 1983–. *Recreations:* golf, gardening, reading. *Address:* 88 Craiglockhart Road, Edinburgh.

STEAD, Robert, CBE 1965; retired as Controller, BBC North Region, 1958–69; *b* 10 Aug. 1909; *s* of Charles Fearnley Stead and Mary Ellen Taylor; *m* 1932, Constance Ann Sharpley; two *s.* *Educ:* Morley Grammar Sch. In journalism, 1926–40; served in RN, 1940–45. Talks Producer, BBC North Region, 1946–48; Head of North Regional Programmes, 1948–53; BBC Australian Representative, 1953–57. *Recreations:* golf, gardening, theatre. *Address:* 20 Fulshaw Court, Wilmslow, Cheshire. *T:* Wilmslow 525536.

STEADMAN, Ralph Idris; freelance cartoonist, illustrator and writer; *b* 15 May 1936; *s* of Lionel Raphael Steadman (English), and Gwendoline (Welsh); *m* 1st, 1959, Sheila Thwaite (marr. diss. 1971); two *s* two *d*; 2nd, 1972, Anna Deverson; one *d.* *Educ:* Abergele Grammar Sch.; London Coll. of Printing and Graphic Arts. Apprentice, de Havilland Aircraft Co., 1952; Cartoonist, Kemsley (Thomson) Newspapers, 1956–59; freelance for Punch, Private Eye, Telegraph, during 1960s; Political Cartoonist, New Statesman, 1978–80; retired to work on book about Leonardo da Vinci. Retrospective exhibitions: Nat. Theatre, 1977; Royal Festival Hall, 1984. Designed set of stamps of Halley's Comet, 1986. Designers and Art Directors Assoc. Gold Award (for outstanding contribution to illustration), 1977, and Silver Award (for outstanding editorial illustration), 1977. *Publications:* Jelly Book, 1968; Still Life with Raspberry: collected drawings, 1969; The Little Red Computer, 1970; Dogs Bodies, 1971; Bumper to Bumper Book, 1973; Two Donkeys and the Bridge, 1974; Flowers for the Moon, 1974; The Watchdog and the Lazy Dog, 1974; America: drawings, 1975; America: collected drawings, 1977; I, Leonardo, 1983; Between the Eyes, 1984; Paranoids, 1986; *written and illustrated:* Sigmund Freud, 1979 (as The Penguin Sigmund Freud, 1982); A Leg in the Wind and other Canine Curses, 1982; designed and printed, Steam Press Broadsheets; *illustrated:* Frank Dickens, Fly Away Peter, 1961; Mischa Damjan: The Big Squirrel and the Little Rhinoceros, 1962; The False Flamingoes, 1963; The Little Prince and the Tiger Cat, 1964; Richard Ingrams, The Tale of Driver Grope, 1964; Love and Marriage, 1964; Where Love Lies Deepest, 1964; Fiona Saint, The Yellow Flowers, 1965; Alice in Wonderland, 1967; Midnight, 1967; Mischa Damjan, Two Cats in America, 1968; Tariq Ali, The Thoughts of Chairman Harold, 1968; Dr Hunter S. Thompson: Fear and Loathing in Las Vegas, 1972; The Curse of Lono, 1984; Contemporary Poets set to Music series, 1972; Through the Looking Glass, 1972; Night Edge: poems, 1973; The Poor Mouth, 1973; John Letts Limericks, 1974; The Hunting of the Snark, 1975; Dmitri Sidjanski, Cherrywood Cannon, 1978; Bernard Stone: Emergency Mouse, 1978; Inspector Mouse, 1980; Quasimodo Mouse, 1984; Ted Hughes, The Threshold (limited edn), 1979; Adrian Mitchell, For Beauty Douglas, 1982; Flann O'Brien, More of Myles, 1982; Wolf Mankowitz, The Devil in Texas, 1984; Treasure Island, 1985; The Complete Alice and The Hunting of the Snark, 1986. *Recreations:* gardening, collecting, writing, sheep husbandry, fishing, guitar, trumpet. *Club:* Chelsea Arts.

STEAR, Air Vice-Marshal Michael James Douglas, CBE 1982; QCVSA 1969; Air Officer Commanding No 11 Group, since 1985; *b* 11 Oct. 1938; *s* of late Melbourne Douglas Stear and Barbara Jane Stear (*née* Fletcher); *m* 1966, Elizabeth Jane, *d* of late Donald Edward Macrae, FRCS and of Janet Wallace Macpherson Simpson; two *s* one *d.* *Educ:* Monkton Combe Sch.; Emmanuel Coll., Cambridge (MA; CU Air Sqn (RAFVR), 1959–62). Nat. Service, 1957–59. Joined RAF, 1962; served on 1 Sqn, 1964–67, on 208 Sqn, Persian Gulf, 1967–69; exchange tour with USAF, 1969–71; Air Sec.'s Br., MoD, 1972–74; OC 17 Sqn, Germany, 1974–76; OC 56 Sqn, RAF Wattisham, 1976; PSO to CAS, MoD, 1976–79; OC RAF Gutersloh, 1980–82; Asst C of S (Ops), HQ 2 ATAF, 1982; Air Cdre Plans, HQ Strike Command, 1982–85. *Recreations:* Rugby football, gardening, fishing, shooting. *Address:* HQ No 11 Group, Royal Air Force, Bentley Priory, Stanmore, Middlesex HA7 3HH. *T:* 01–950 4000. *Club:* Royal Air Force.

STEARN, Dr William Thomas; botanical consultant; retired as Senior Principal Scientific Officer, Department of Botany, British Museum (Natural History), 1976; Editor, Annales Musei Goulandris, since 1976; *b* 16 April 1911; *e s* of late Thomas Stearn, Cambridge; *m* 1940, Eldwyth Ruth Alford, *d* of late Roger R. Alford, Tavistock; one *s* two *d.* *Educ:* Cambridge High Sch. for Boys; part-time research at Botany Sch., Cambridge; apprentice antiquarian bookseller, Bowes & Bowes, Cambridge, 1929–32. Librarian, Royal Horticultural Soc., 1933–41, 1946–52. Served RAF, in Britain, India and Burma, 1941–46. Botanist, British Museum (Natural History), 1952–76. Hon. Sec., Internat. Cttee for Nomenclature of Cultivated Plants, 1950–53; former Council Member: Botanical Soc. of British Isles (Vice-Pres., 1973–77); British Soc. for History of Science (Vice-Pres., 1969–72); British Soc. for History of Medicine; Field Studies Council; Garden History Soc. (Founder Mem., 1965; Pres., 1977–82); Linnean Soc. (Vice-Pres., 1961–62; Pres., 1979–82; Hon. Botanical Curator, 1959–85); Ray Soc. (Vice-Pres., 1964–67, 1970–73, Pres., 1974–77); Richmond Scientific Soc. (Pres., 1969–71); Soc. for Bibliography of Natural History (Founder Mem., 1936, Hon. Mem., 1976); Systematics Assoc.; Mem., Old Cantabrigian Soc. (Pres., 1984–85). Masters Meml Lectr, 1964; Sandars Reader in Bibliography, Cambridge, 1965; Vis. Prof., Dept of Botany and Agricl Botany, 1977–83, Hon. Res. Fellow, 1983, Univ. of Reading; Wilkins Lectr, Royal Soc., 1985. Has lectured in Australia, Austria, Canada, Germany, Greece, Holland, Jamaica, Papua New Guinea, Sweden, USA; botanical collections made in Europe, Jamaica, USA, Australia. Royal Horticultural Society: Hon. Fellow, 1946; Vice-Pres., 1986; Veitch Meml Medal, 1964; Victoria Medal of Honour, 1965. FLS 1934; FIBiol 1967 (MIBiol 1965); Hon. Member: Kungl. Vetenskaps-Societeten i Uppsala, 1967; Svenska Linnésällskapet, 1971; Botanical Soc. of Amer., 1982; For. Mem., Royal Swedish Acad. of Sci., 1983; Corr. Mem., Amer. Soc. of Plant Taxonomists, 1980. Freeman, Gardeners' Co., 1982. Hon. Fellow, Sidney Sussex Coll., Cambridge, 1968. DSc *hc* Leiden, 1960; Hon. ScD Cantab, 1967; FilDr *hc* Uppsala, 1972. Boerhaave Commem. Medal, Leiden, 1969; Linnaeus Medal, Royal Swedish Acad. of Sciences, 1972; Linnean Gold Medal, Linnean Soc., 1976; Hutchinson Medal, Chicago Horticultural Soc., 1985; Founders Medal, Soc. for the Hist. of Natural Hist., 1986. Comdr, Order of the Star of the North (Sweden), 1980. *Publications:* (with H. B. D. Woodcock) Lilies of the World, 1950; (with E. Blatter and W. S. Millard) Some Beautiful Indian Trees, 1955; Introduction to the *Species Plantarum* of Carl Linnaeus, 1957; Early Leyden Botany, 1961; Botanical Latin, 1966, 3rd edn 1983 (trans. Chinese, 1981); Three Prefaces on Linnaeus and Robert Brown, 1967; Humboldt, Bonpland, Kunth and Tropical American Botany, 1968; (with C. N. Goulimis and N. Goulandris) Wild Flowers of Greece, 1968; (with A. W. Smith) Gardener's Dictionary of Plant Names, 1972; (with W. Blunt) Captain Cook's Florilegium, 1973; (with M. Page) Culinary Herbs, 1974; (with W. Blunt) Australian Flower Paintings of Ferdinand Bauer, 1976; The Wondrous Transformation of Caterpillars: M. S. Merian (Biog.), 1978; (with H. Hara and L. H. J. Williams) Enumeration of Flowering Plants of Nepal, vol. 1, 1978; The Natural History Museum at South Kensington, 1981; Plant Portraits from the *Flora Danica*, 1983; (with E. Roberts and C. Opsomer) Livre des Simples Médicines, English trans. and commentaries, 1984; (with P. H. Davis) Peonies of Greece, 1984; numerous bibliographical, biographical, botanical and horticultural contribs to learned jls (listed in Biological Jl of Linnean Soc. vol. 8, 1976), RHS Dictionary of Gardening, Chambers's Encyclopaedia, Dictionary of Scientific Biography, Flora Europaea, etc. *Recreations:* gardening, talking. *Address:* 17 High Park Road, Kew Gardens, Richmond, Surrey TW9 4BL.

STEBBINGS, Sir John (Chalmer), Kt 1980; Partner, Payne, Hicks Beach, Solicitors, since 1951; *b* 10 Oct. 1924; *s* of late John Morley Stebbings, MC, EM, TD, and of Doris Percy (*née* Chalmer); *m* 1949, Patricia (*née* Strange); two *s* three *d.* *Educ:* Harrow; New Coll., Oxford (MA). Admitted solicitor, 1949. Law Society: Mem. Council, 1964; Treasurer, 1969–75; Vice Pres., 1978–79; Pres., 1979. Mem., Lord Chancellor's Cttee on Age of Majority, 1965–66. *Recreations:* swimming, sailing. *Address:* 435 Fulham Road, Chelsea, SW10 9TX. *T:* 01–352 7190; (office) 10 New Square, Lincoln's Inn, WC2A 3QG. *T:* 01–242 6041. *Clubs:* Hurlingham; Royal Temple Yacht (Ramsgate).

STEDMAN, family name of **Baroness Stedman.**

STEDMAN, Baroness *cr* 1974 (Life Peer), of Longthorpe, Peterborough; **Phyllis Stedman,** OBE 1965; *b* 14 July 1916; *o d* of Percy and Emmie Adams; *m* 1941, Henry William Stedman, OBE 1981. *Educ:* County Grammar Sch., Peterborough. Branch Librarian, Peterborough City Council, 1934–41; Group Officer, National Fire Service, 1942–45. Baroness-in-Waiting (a Govt Whip), 1975–79; Parly Under-Sec. of State, DoE, 1979; Govt spokesman for Transport, the Environment, Educn and Trade, 1975–79; Opposition spokesman on the environment, local govt, new towns and transport, 1979–81; Mem., SDP, 1981–; SDP Whip in House of Lords, 1982–. County Councillor: Soke of Peterborough, 1946–65; Huntingdon and Peterborough, 1965–74; Cambridgeshire, 1974–76; Vice-Chm., Cambridgeshire County Council, 1974–76. Member: Board, Peterborough Development Corp., 1972–76; IBA, 1974–75; Board, Hereward Radio, 1979–85; Vice-Chm., Nat. PHAB, 1978–; Vice-President: Assoc. of District Councils, 1979–; Nat. Assoc. of Local Councils, 1982–; ACC, 1986–; Building Societies Assoc., 1985–. Mem. Exec. Council, Fire Services Nat. Benevolent Fund, 1976–. *Address:* Green Pastures, Grove Lane, Longthorpe, Peterborough PE3 6ND. *T:* Peterborough 266506; 01–219 3229.

STEEDMAN, Air Chief Marshal Sir Alasdair, (Alexander McKay Sinclair), GCB 1980 (KCB 1976; CB 1973); CBE 1965; DFC 1944; Controller, Royal Air Force Benevolent Fund, since 1981; *b* 29 Jan. 1922; *s* of late James Steedman, Hampton-on-Thames, Mddx, and late Anna McKay Steedman (*née* Sinclair), Fulford, York; *m* 1945, Dorothy Isobel (*d* 1983), *d* of late Col Walter Todd, Knockbrex, Kirkcudbright; one *s* two *d.* *Educ:* Hampton Grammar School. Entered RAF, 1941; reconnaissance ops, 1942–45; (241 and 2 Sqns) Air Ministry (DP2), 1945–48; comd 39 Sqdn, Khartoum, 1948–49; comd 8 Sqdn, Aden, 1949–50; CFS Course, 1951; Training Sqn Comdr 201 Advanced Flying Sch., 1951–53; Syndicate Leader Aircrew Selection Centre, Hornchurch, 1953–54; psa 1955; Chief Instructor, CFS (B), 1955–57; Comdr Royal Ceylon Air Force, Katanayake, 1957–59; jssc 1959; Dir Staff, Jt Services Staff Coll., 1960–62; Comdr RAF Lyneham, 1962–65; CAS, Royal Malaysian Air Force, 1965–67; Dir of Defence Plans (Air), 1967–68; Dir Defence Operations Staff, 1968–69; ACAS (Policy), MoD, 1969–71; Comdt, RAF Staff Coll., 1972–75; Air Member for Supply and Organisation, 1976–77; UK Mil. Rep. to NATO, 1977–80. Mem., Security Commn, 1982–. Pres., British Pistol Club, 1986–. Governor, Hampton Sch., 1976–; Mem. Foundn Cttee, Gordon Boys' Sch., 1981–. Patron, Central Flying Sch. Assoc., 1984–; Vice Patron, RAF Small Arms Assoc., 1978–. FRAeS 1981; CBIM 1979. Johan Mangku Negara (Malaysia), 1967. *Recreations:* defence, golf, reading. *Address:* Rutherford, St Chloe Lane, Amberley, Stroud, Glos. *Club:* Royal Air Force.

STEEDMAN, Martha, (Mrs R. R. Steedman); *see* Hamilton, M.

STEEDMAN, Robert Russell, RSA 1979 (ARSA 1973); RIBA; FRIAS; ALI; Partner, Morris and Steedman, Architects and Landscape Architects, Edinburgh, since 1959; *b* 3 Jan. 1929; *s* of late Robert Smith Steedman and Helen Hope Brazier; *m* 1st, 1956, Susan Elizabeth (marr. diss. 1974), *d* of Sir Robert Scott, GCMG, CBE; one *s* two *d*; 2nd, 1977, Martha Hamilton, *qv.* *Educ:* Loretto Sch.; School of Architecture, Edinburgh College of Art (DA); Univ. of Pennsylvania (MLA). RIBA 1955; ALI 1979. Lieut, RWAFF, 1947–48. Worked in office, Alfred Roth, Zürich, 1953. Architectural works include: Principal's House, Univ. of Stirling; Head Offices for Christian Salvesen, Edinburgh; Administration Building for Shell UK Exploration and Production; Moss Morran Fife; Restoration of Old Waterworks, Perth, to form Tourist Information Centre and Offices. Nine Civic Trust Awards, 1963–78; British Steel Award, 1971; Saltire Award, 1971; RIBA Award for Scotland, 1974; European Architectural Heritage Medal, 1975; Assoc. for Preservation of Rural Scotland Award, 1977. Member: Countryside Commn for Scotland, 1980–; Royal Fine Art Commn for Scotland, 1984–; Sec., Royal Scottish Acad., 1983– (Mem. Council 1981–, Dep. Pres. 1982–83); Governor, Edinburgh College of Art, 1974–; Mem., Edinburgh Festival Soc., 1978–; past Mem. Council, RIAS and Soc. of Scottish Artists. *Recreations:* skiing, tennis, shooting, sketching. *Address:* 11B Belford Mews, Edinburgh; (office) 1 Young Street, Edinburgh. *T:* 031–226 6563. *Clubs:* New, Scottish Arts (Edinburgh).

STEEGMULLER, Francis; writer; *b* New Haven, Conn, 3 July 1906; *s* of Joseph Francis Steegmuller and Bertha Tierney; *m* 1st, 1935, Beatrice Stein (decd); 2nd, 1963, Shirley Hazzard. *Educ:* Columbia University, New York. Member, Nat. Inst. of Arts and Letters, 1966. Gold Medal for Biography, 1982. Chevalier de la Légion d'Honneur, 1957; Chevalier de l'Ordre des Arts et des Lettres, 1984. *Publications:* O Rare Ben Jonson (under pseudonym Byron Steel), 1928; Flaubert and Madame Bovary, 1939, reprinted 1947, 1958, 1968; States of Grace, 1947; Maupassant, 1950, repr. 1973; Blue Harpsichord (under pseudonym David Keith), 1950; The Two Lives of James Jackson Jarves, 1953; (trans. and ed) The Selected Letters of Gustave Flaubert, 1954; La Grande Mademoiselle,

1955; The Christening Party, 1961; Le Hibou et la Poussiquette, 1961; Apollinaire, 1963, repr. 1986; Papillot, Clignot et Dodo (with Norbert Guterman), 1965; (trans.) Gustave Flaubert, Intimate Notebook, 1967; Cocteau, 1970, repr. 1986 (Nat. Book Award 1971); Stories and True Stories, 1972; (trans. and ed) Flaubert in Egypt, 1972, repr. 1982; (ed) Your Isadora, 1975; (trans. and ed) The Letters of Gustave Flaubert, 1830–1857, 1980 (American Book Award 1981), 2nd vol. 1983; works published abroad include a translation of Madame Bovary, 1957, Silence at Salerno (novel), 1979, and many short stories and articles in The New Yorker. *Address:* 200 East 66th Street, New York, NY 10021, USA. *Clubs:* Century, University (New York); Circolo del Remo e della Vela "Italia" (Naples).

STEEL, (Anne) Heather, (Mrs D. K.-M. Beattie); a Recorder of the Crown Court, since 1984; *b* 3 July 1940; *d* of late His Honour Edward Steel and of Mary Evelyn Griffith Steel; *m* 1967, David Kerr-Muir Beattie; one *s* one *d*. *Educ:* Howell's School, Denbigh; Liverpool University (LLB). Called to the Bar, Gray's Inn, 1963; practice on N Circuit; Prosecuting Counsel to DHSS on N Circuit, 1984–. *Recreations:* theatre, gardening, art, antiques. *Address:* Peel House, Harrington Street, Liverpool L2 9QA. *T:* 051-236 4321.

STEEL, Byron; *see* Steegmuller, Francis.

STEEL, Brig. Charles Deane, CMG 1957; OBE 1941; *b* 29 May 1901; *s* of Dr Gerard Steel, JP, Leominster, Herefs; *m* 1932, Elizabeth Chenevix-Trench (*d* 1973); two *s*. *Educ:* Bedford; Royal Military Academy, Woolwich. Prize Cadetship, Woolwich, 1919. Armstrong Memorial Prize, 1921. Commissioned 2nd Lieut RE, 1921; served in India (Bengal Sappers and Miners), 1924–29; Staff College, Camberley, 1936–37; War of 1939–45; E Africa and Abyssinia, 1941; Western Desert, 1942; POW, 1942; Switzerland, 1943; Dep. Head, British Mil. Mission to Greece, 1945–49; Dep. Mil. Sec., 1949–52; retd Feb. 1952; Head of Conference and Supply Dept, Foreign Office, 1952–64; Head of Accommodation Department Diplomatic Service, 1965–67. *Recreations:* golf, and gardening. *Address:* Little Hill, Nettlebed, Oxfordshire. *T:* Nettlebed 641287. *Clubs:* Naval and Military, Shikar.

STEEL, Very Rev. David; Minister of St Michael's, Linlithgow, 1959–76, now Minister Emeritus; Moderator of the General Assembly of the Church of Scotland, 1974–75; *b* 5 Oct. 1910; *s* of John S. G. Steel and Jane Scott, Hamilton; *m* 1937, Sheila Martin, Aberdeen; three *s* two *d*. *Educ:* Peterhead Academy; Robert Gordon's Coll., Aberdeen; Aberdeen Univ. MA 1932, BD 1935. Minister of Church of Scotland: Denbeath, Fife, 1936–41; Bridgend, Dumbarton, 1941–46; Home Organisation Foreign Mission Secretary, 1946–49; Minister of Parish of East Africa and of St Andrew's, Nairobi, 1949–57; Associate Minister, St Cuthbert's, Edinburgh, 1957–59. Vis. Prof., Columbia Theol Seminary, Atlanta, 1979–85. Chm. of Governors, Callendar Park Coll. of Educn, 1974–79; Vice-Pres., Boys' Brigade, 1974–79. Hon. DD Aberdeen 1964; Hon. LLD Dundee, 1977. *Publications:* History of St Michael's, Linlithgow, 1961; Preaching Through the Year, 1980; contrib. theological and church jls. *Recreation:* trout fishing. *Address:* 39 Newbattle Terrace, Edinburgh EH10 4SF. *T:* 031-447 2180. *Clubs:* Scottish Liberal (Edinburgh); Edinburgh Amateur Angling.

See also Rt Hon. D. M. S. Steel.

STEEL, Sir David (Edward Charles), Kt 1977; DSO 1940; MC 1945; TD; Chairman, The Wellcome Trust, since 1982; *b* 29 Nov. 1916; *s* of late Gerald Arthur Steel, CB; *m* 1956, Ann Wynne, *d* of Maj.-Gen. C. B. Price, CB, DSO, DCM, VD, CD; one *s* two *d*. *Educ:* Rugby School; University Coll., Oxford (BA; Hon. Fellow, 1981). Inns of Court Regt, 1938; Commissioned 9 QR Lancers, 1940; served 1940–45 France, Middle East, North Africa, Italy (DSO, MC, despatches thrice). Admitted a Solicitor, June 1948; Linklaters and Paines, 1948–50; Legal Dept of The British Petroleum Co. Ltd, 1950–56; Pres. BP (N Amer.) Ltd, 1959–61; Man. Dir, Kuwait Oil Co. Ltd, 1962–65; Man. Dir, 1965–75, a Dep. Chm., 1972–75 and Chm., 1975–81, BP. A Dir, Bank of England, 1978–85; Dir, Kleinwort, Benson, Lonsdale, 1985–. Pres., London Chamber of Commerce and Industry, 1982–85. Trustee, The Economist, 1979–. Chm. of Governors, Rugby Sch., 1984–. Hon. DCL City Univ., 1983. Order of Taj III, Iran, 1974; Comdr, Order of Leopold, Belgium, 1980. *Address:* 51 Onslow Square, SW7 3LR. *Clubs:* Cavalry and Guards; Royal and Ancient (St Andrews).

STEEL, Rt. Hon. David (Martin Scott), PC 1977; MP (L) Tweeddale, Ettrick and Lauderdale, since 1983 (Roxburgh, Selkirk and Peebles, 1965–83); Leader of the Liberal Party, since 1976; journalist and broadcaster; *b* Scotland, March 1938; *s* of Very Rev. Dr David Steel, *qv*; *m* 1962, Judith Mary, *d* of W. D. MacGregor, CBE, Dunblane; two *s* one *d* and one adopted *s*. *Educ:* Prince of Wales School, Nairobi, Kenya; George Watson's College and Edinburgh University. MA 1960; LLB 1962. Rector, Edinburgh Univ., 1982–85. President: Edinburgh University Liberals, 1959; Students' Representative Council, 1960. Visited Soviet Union, 1961. Asst Secretary, Scottish Liberal Party, 1962–64; Youngest Member of 1964–66 Parliament, of Privy Council, 1977; Liberal Chief Whip, 1970–75; Mem. Parly Delegn to UN Gen. Assembly, 1967; Sponsor, Private Member's Bill to reform law on abortion, 1966–67; Pres., Anti-Apartheid Movement of GB, 1966–69; Chm., Shelter, Scotland, 1969–73. Member: Acton Trust, 1970–; British Council of Churches, 1971–75; Council of Management, Centre for Studies in Social Policy, 1971–76; Adv. Council, European Discussion Centre, 1971–76. BBC television interviewer in Scotland, 1964–65; Presenter of STV weekly religious programme, 1966–67, and for Granada, 1969, and BBC, 1971–76. *Publications:* Boost for the Borders, 1964; Out of Control, 1968; No Entry, 1969; The Liberal Way Forward, 1975; A New Political Agenda, 1976; Militant for the Reasonable Man, 1977; New Majority for a New Parliament, 1978; High Ground of Politics, 1979; A House Divided, 1980; Border Country, 1985; (presenter) Partners in One Nation: a new vision of Britain 2000, 1985; contrib. to The Times, The Guardian, The Scotsman, other newspapers and political weeklies. *Recreations:* angling, riding, motoring. *Address:* House of Commons, SW1A 0AA; Cherry Dene, Ettrick Bridge, Selkirkshire.

STEEL, David William, QC 1981; *b* 7 May 1943; *s* of Sir Lincoln Steel and of Barbara (*née* Goldschmidt); *m* 1970, Charlotte Elizabeth Ramsay; two *s*. *Educ:* Eton Coll.; Keble Coll., Oxford (MA Hons Jurisprudence). Called to the Bar, Inner Temple, 1966. With Coudert Bros (Attorneys), New York, 1967–68; commenced practice in England, 1969; Junior Counsel to the Treasury (Common Law) 1978–81; Junior Counsel to the Treasury (Admiralty), 1978–81. Wreck Commissioner for England and Wales, 1982–. *Publications:* Editor: Temperley: Merchant Shipping Acts, 1976–; Forms and Precedents: British Shipping Laws, 1977–; Kennedy: Salvage, 1981–. *Recreations:* shooting, fishing. *Address:* The Bell House, Askett, near Aylesbury, Bucks. *T:* Princes Risborough 3453. *Club:* Turf.

STEEL, Major Sir (Fiennes) William Strang, 2nd Bt, *cr* 1938; DL; JP; Major (retired), 17/21st Lancers; Forestry Commissioner, 1958–73; *b* 24 July 1912; *e s* of Sir Samuel Steel, 1st Bt and of Hon. Vere Mabel (*d* 1964), *d* of 1st Baron Cornwallis; *S* father, 1961; *m* 1941, Joan (*d* 1982), *d* of late Brig.-Gen. Sir Brodie Haldane Henderson, KCMG, CB, Braughing, Ware; two *s* (one *d* decd). *Educ:* Eton; RMC, Sandhurst; joined 17/21st Lancers, 1933; Major, 1941; retired, 1947. Convener, Selkirk CC, 1967–75. DL Selkirkshire, 1955, JP 1965. *Heir:* *s* Major (Fiennes) Michael Strang Steel, 17/21 Lancers [*b* 22 Feb. 1943; *m* 1977, Sarah Russell; two *s* one *d*]. *Address:* Philiphaugh, Selkirk. *T:* Selkirk 21216. *Club:* Cavalry and Guards.

STEEL, Henry, CMG 1976; OBE 1965; Director, Commonwealth Legal Advisory Service, British Institute of International and Comparative Law, since 1986; *b* 13 Jan. 1926; *yr s* of late Raphael Steel; *m* 1960, Jennifer Isobel Margaret, *d* of late Brig. M. M. Simpson, MBE; two *s* two *d*. *Educ:* Christ's Coll., Finchley; New Coll., Oxford. BA Oxon 1950. Military Service, RASC and Intell. Corps, 1944–47. Called to Bar, Lincoln's Inn, 1951; Legal Asst, Colonial Office, 1955; Senior Legal Asst, CO, 1960; Asst Legal Adviser, CRO, 1965; Legal Counsellor, FCO, 1967–73; Legal Adviser, UK Mission to UN, NY, 1973–76; Legal Counsellor, FCO, 1976–79; Asst Under-Sec. of State (on loan to Law Officers' Dept), 1979; Legal Adviser to Governor of Southern Rhodesia, 1979–80; Asst Legal Secretary (Under-Secretary), 1980–83, Legal Sec. (Dep. Sec.), 1983–86, Law Officers' Dept. *Address:* c/o British Institute of International and Comparative Law, Charles Clore House, 17 Russell Square, WC1.

STEEL, Sir James, Kt 1967; CBE 1964; Lord-Lieutenant of Tyne and Wear, 1974–84; Chairman, Furness Withy & Co. Ltd, 1975–79; *b* 19 May 1909; *s* of Alfred Steel and Katharine (*née* Meikle); *m* 1935, Margaret Jean MacLauchlan; two *s* two *d*. *Educ:* Trent College. Mem., Commn on the Constitution, 1969–73. Trustee, Sir John Priestman Charity Trust. Chairman: British Productivity Council, 1966–67; Textile Council, 1968–72; Washington Develt Corp., 1964–77. Pres., TA for N of England, 1979–84; Vice-Pres., Wildfowl Trust. Liveryman, Worshipful Co. of Founders. JP Sunderland, 1964; Durham: DL 1969; Sheriff 1972–73. KStJ 1975. Hon. DCL Dunelm, 1978. *Recreation:* ornithology. *Address:* Fawnlees Hall, Wolsingham, County Durham DL13 3LW. *T:* 527307.

STEEL, Patricia Ann; Secretary, Institution of Highways and Transportation (formerly Institution of Highway Engineers), since 1973; *b* 30 Oct. 1941; *d* of Thomas Norman Steel and Winifred Steel. *Educ:* Hunmanby Hall, near Filey, Yorks; Exeter Univ. (BA). Parly Liaison, Chamber of Shipping of UK and British Shipping Fedn, 1968–71; Sec., Highway and Traffic Technicians Assoc., 1972–73. Member: Occupational Pensions Bd, 1979–84; Jt Bd, Docklands Light Rly, 1984–; part time Dir, LRT, 1984–. *Recreations:* music, travel, politics. *Address:* 7 The Strathmore, 27 Petersham Road, Richmond, Surrey.

STEEL, Robert, CBE 1979; Secretary-General, Royal Institution of Chartered Surveyors, 1968–85 (Fellow, 1961; Hon. Mem., 1985); *b* 7 April 1920; *e s* of late John Thomas Steel, Wooler, Northumberland; *m* 1943, Averal Frances, *d* of Arthur Pettitt; one *s* one *d*. *Educ:* Duke's Sch., Alnwick, Northumb.; Univ. of London (BSc 1945); Gray's Inn (Barrister, 1956). Surveyor, 1937–46; Asst Sec., Under Sec., Royal Instn of Surveyors, 1946–61; Dir of Town Development, Basingstoke, 1962–67. Sec.-Gen., Internat. Fedn of Surveyors, 1967–69, Vice-Pres., 1970–72, Hon. Mem., 1983; Sec., Commonwealth Assoc. of Surveying and Land Economy, 1969–; Sec., Aubrey Barker Trust, 1970–; Member: South East Economic Planning Council, 1974–76; Council, British Consultants Bureau, 1977–85. Chm., Geometers Liaison Cttee, EEC, 1972–86. Hon. Editor, Commonwealth Surveying and Land Economy. Mem. Ct of Assts, 1977–, Jun. Warden, 1986–87, Worshipful Co. of Chartered Surveyors. Organised national networks of beacons for Queen's Silver Jubilee celebrations, 1977, and for the Wedding of Prince Charles and Lady Diana Spencer, 1981. Raised: £71,210 for RICS Benev. Fund by sponsored walk of 1000 miles, John O'Groats to Land's End, 1979 (world record for largest sum raised by a single walker); £66,333 for RICS Benev. Fund and The Prince's Trust by walk of 1100 miles, Cape Wrath to Dover and London, 1985. Hon. Mem., Union Belge des Geomètres Experts, 1976; Hon. Fellow, Inst. of Surveyors, Malaysia, 1983. Hon. LLD Aberdeen, 1985. Distinguished Service Award, Surveyors Inst. of Sri Lanka, 1986. *Publications:* on Property Law; contrib. professional jls and internat. conferences. *Recreations:* mountain walking, travel, music. *Address:* 2 Oaklands Close, Winchester, Hants.

STEEL, Prof. Robert Walter, CBE 1983; BSc, MA Oxon; Principal, University College of Swansea, 1974–82; Vice-Chancellor, 1979–81, Emeritus Professor 1982, University of Wales; *b* 31 July 1915; *er s* of late Frederick Grabham and Winifred Barry Steel; *m* 1940, Eileen Margaret, *er d* of late Arthur Ernest and Evelyn Beatrice Page, Bournemouth; one *s* two *d*. *Educ:* Great Yarmouth Grammar Sch.; Cambridge and County High School for Boys; Jesus College, Oxford (Open Exhibitioner in Geography; Hon. Fellow 1982). RGS Essay Prize, 1936. Drapers' Co. Research Scholarship for Geography, 1937–39, for work in Sierra Leone; Departmental Lectr in Geography, Univ. of Oxford, 1939–47; Naval Intelligence Div., Admiralty, 1940–45; attached to Sociological Dept of W African Inst. of Arts, Industry and Social Science as geographer to Ashanti Social Survey, Gold Coast, 1945–46; University of Oxford: Univ. Lectr in Commonwealth Geography, 1947–56; Lectr in Geography, St Peter's Hall, 1951–56; Official Fellow and Tutor in Geography, Jesus Coll., 1954–56 (Supernumary Welsh Fellow, 1974–75 and 1979–80; Hon. Fellow 1982); Univ. of Liverpool: John Rankin Prof. of Geography, 1957–74; Dean, Faculty of Arts, 1965–68, Pro-Vice-Chancellor, 1971–73. Murchison Grant (RGS), 1948; Council RGS, 1949–53, 1968–71; Inst. of Brit. Geographers: Council, 1947–60; Actg Sec., 1948, Asst Sec., 1949–50; Hon. Editor of Publications, 1950–60; Vice-Pres., 1966–67, Pres. 1968, Hon. Mem. 1974; President: Section E (Geography), BAAS, 1966; African Studies Assoc. of the UK, 1970–71 (Vice-Pres., 1969–70); Geographical Assoc., 1973 (Hon. Mem. 1982); Glamorgan Trust for Nature Conservation, 1982–86. Dir, Commonwealth Geographical Bureau, 1972–81; Member: Inter-Univ. Council for Higher Educn Overseas, 1974–81; Welsh Adv. Cttee, British Council, 1978–; Cttee for Internat. Co-operation in Higher Educn, British Council (Higher Educn Div.), 1981–85; Chairman: Universities Council for Adult Educn, 1976–80; Governors, Westhill Coll., Birmingham, 1981–; Bd, Wales Adv. Body for Local Authority Higher Educn, 1982–; Swansea Festival of Music and the Arts, 1982–; Lower Swansea Valley Develt Gp, 1979–; Mem., ESRC, 1983–86. Mem. Council, National Univ. of Lesotho, 1981–85. Vice-Pres., Royal African Soc., 1977–; Council, Nat. Inst. of Adult Educn, 1977–80. Vis. Prof., Univ. of Ghana, 1964; Canadian Commonwealth Vis. Fellow, Carleton Univ., 1970. Hon. DSc Salford, 1977; Hon. LLD: Wales, 1983; Liverpool, 1985. *Publications:* ed (with A. F. Martin), and contrib. to The Oxford Region: a Scientific and Historical Survey, 1954; ed (with C. A. Fisher), and contrib. to Geographical Essays on British Tropical Lands, 1956; ed (with R. M. Prothero), and contrib. to Geographers and the Tropics: Liverpool Essays, 1964; ed (with R. Lawton), and contrib. to Liverpool Essays on Geography: a Jubilee Collection, 1967; (with Eileen M. Steel) Africa, 1974, 3rd edn 1982; ed, Human Ecology and Hong Kong: report for the Commonwealth Human Ecology Council, 1975; The Institute of British Geographers, the First Fifty Years, 1983; articles, mainly on tropical Africa, in Geographical Jl and other geog. jls. *Recreations:* walking, gardening, music. *Address:* 12 Cambridge Road, Langland, Swansea SA3 4PE. *T:* Swansea 369087. *Club:* Royal Commonwealth Society.

STEEL, Rupert Oliver; Chairman: Black Horse Life Assurance Co. Ltd, since 1979; Lloyds Bank Unit Trust Managers Ltd, since 1979; *b* 30 April 1922; *s* of Joseph Steel and Beatrice Elizabeth Courage; *m* 1st, Marigold Katharine, *d* of Percy Lowe; two *s*; 2nd, Lucinda Evelyn Tennant, *d* of Arthur James; one *s* one *d*. *Educ:* Eton. Served War of 1939–45 (despatches), Pilot, RNVR, Fleet Air Arm, 1941–46. Courage & Co. Ltd,

1946–78; Imperial Group Ltd, 1975–78; Chm., Everards Brewery Ltd, 1978–84; Director: Lloyds Bank Ltd, 1977–79; Lloyds Bank UK Management, 1979–85; Umeco Holdings Ltd, 1979–; South Uist Estates Ltd, 1980–. High Sheriff, Berks, 1985–86. *Recreation:* country. *Address:* Winterbourne Holt, Newbury, Berks RG16 8AP. *T:* Chieveley 220. *Club:* Brooks's.

STEEL, Major Sir William Strang; *see* Steel, Major Sir F. W. S.

STEELE, Prof. Alan John; Professor of French, University of Edinburgh, 1972–80, retired; *b* Bellshill, Lanark, 11 April 1916; *s* of John Steele, MA, BD, and Anne (*née* Lawson); *m* 1947, Claire Alice Louise Belet; one *s* one *d.* *Educ:* Royal Grammar School, Newcastle upon Tyne; Blyth Secondary School, Northumberland; Universities of Edinburgh, Grenoble and Paris. MA 1st Cl. Hons in French Language and Literature, Vans Dunlop Schol., Univ. of Edinburgh, 1938. Served War of 1939–45, at sea with 4th Maritime AA Regt, RA, 1941–42; commissioned, 1942, with 64th LAA Regt RA in Algeria, Italy and Greece. Lecturer in French, University of Edinburgh, 1946, Prof. of French Literature, 1961–72. Chairman: Scottish Central Cttee for Modern Languages, 1972–81; Assoc. of Univ. Profs of French, 1974–75; Consultative Cttee, Institut Français d'Ecosse, 1981–; Vice-Pres., Franco-Scottish Soc., 1961–. Mem., Church of Scotland Panel on Doctrine, 1978–86. Editor, Modern Language Review (French Section), 1971–79. Chevalier, Légion d'Honneur, 1973. *Publications:* (with R. A. Leigh) Contemporary French Translation Passages, 1956; Three Centuries of French Verse, 1956, new edn, 1961; contrib. to Cahiers de l'Assoc. Internat. des Etudes françaises, Modern Language Review. *Recreation:* music. *Address:* 17 Polwarth Grove, Edinburgh EH11 1LY. *T:* 031–337 5092.

STEELE, Dr Bernard Robert; Head, Housing Services, Greater London Council, 1982–86; *b* 21 July 1929; *s* of Robert Walter and late Phyllis Mabel Steele; *m* 1953, Dorothy Anne Newman; one *s* two *d.* *Educ:* Oakham Sch.; Selwyn Coll., Cambridge (MA, PhD). Scientific Officer, Min. of Supply, 1953–55; Section Leader, UKAEA, Springfields, 1955–66; Building Research Station: Head, Materials Div., 1966–69; Asst Dir, 1969–72; Dep. Dir, Building Res. Estabt, 1972–75; Borough Housing Officer, Haringey, 1975–78; Dir, Science and Research Policy, DoE, 1978–82. Chm., Environment Cttee, SRC, later SERC, 1978–81. Pres., RILEM (Internat. Union of Testing and Res. Labs for Materials and Structures), 1974–75. Chm., Watford Churches Housing Assoc., 1975–78. *Publications:* contrib. numerous scientific publications on chemistry, materials science and building. *Recreations:* travelling, photography. *Address:* 1 Broom Grove, Watford WD1 3RY. *T:* Watford 41271.

STEELE, Frank Fenwick, OBE 1969; Director, and Head of Export Finance Department, Kleinwort, Benson, since 1985; Director: Arab British Chamber of Commerce, since 1978; Cluff Group Cos, since 1979; Chairman, Network Television Ltd, since 1981; *b* 11 Feb. 1923; *s* of Frank Robert and Mary Fenwick Steele; *m*; one *s* one *d.* *Educ:* St Peter's Sch., York; Emmanuel Coll., Cambridge (MA). Army, 1943–47. Joined HM Diplomatic Service, 1951; FO, 1951; Vice-Consul, Basra, 1951; Third, later Second Sec., Tripoli, 1953; Foreign Office, 1956; Second Sec., Beirut, 1958; FO, 1961; First Sec.: Amman, 1965; Nairobi, 1968; Counsellor and Dep. UK Rep., Belfast, 1971; FCO, 1973; resigned 1975. Joined Kleinwort, Benson as Adviser, 1975. Mem., Export Promotion Cttee, CBI, 1983–. Member Council: Anglo-Jordanian Soc., 1980–; Royal Soc. for Asian Affairs, 1981– (Vice-Pres., 1985); Royal Asiatic Soc., 1986–; Mem., RGS F and GP Cttee, 1986–87. *Publications:* articles on Tibet. *Recreation:* travel. *Address:* 9 Ashley Gardens, SW1P 1QD. *T:* 01–834 7596. *Clubs:* Travellers', Beefsteak, Shikar.

STEELE, John Ernest, FInstPS; Corporate Managing Director, Procurement, British Shipbuilders, since 1985; Commercial Director, North East Shipbuilders Ltd, since 1986; *b* 4 June 1935; *s* of William Steele and Amelia Steele (*née* Graham); *m* 1958, Lucy Wilkinson; one *s* three *d.* *Educ:* Rutherford College of Technology, Newcastle upon Tyne. MNECInst. Swan Hunter and Wigham Richardson Ltd: apprentice shipbuilder, 1951–56; Management Progression, 1956–68; Swan Hunter Shipbuilders Ltd: Local Dir, 1968–71; Purchasing Dir, 1971–74; Dep. Chm., 1974–78; Chief Exec., 1977–83; Chm. and Chief Exec., 1978–83; Div. Man. Dir, Composite Yards, 1981–83; Chm., Cammell Laird Shipbuilders Ltd, 1981–84; British Shipbuilders: part time Bd Mem., 1979–82; Exec. Bd Mem., Offshore, 1982–84; a Corp. Man. Dir, Offshore, 1982–84; Exec. Bd Mem., Procurement, 1984–85; Chairman: V. O. Offshore Ltd, 1982–84; Scott Lithgow Ltd, 1983–84; Lyon Street Railway Ltd, 1977–84; Vosper Thorneycroft (UK) Ltd, 1984–86. British Cttee Mem., Det Norske Veritas, 1981–. Liveryman, Shipwrights' Co. *Recreations:* rugby football, golf, reading. *Address:* 7 Denebank, Monkseaton, Whitley Bay, NE25 9AE. *T:* Whitley Bay 528373.

STEELE, Dr John Hyslop, FRS 1978; FRSE; Director, Woods Hole Oceanographic Institution, Mass, since 1977 (President, 1986); *b* 15 Nov. 1926; *s* of Adam Steele and Annie Hyslop Steele; *m* 1956, Margaret Evelyn Travis; one *s.* *Educ:* George Watson's Boys' Coll., Edinburgh (Higher Cert. of Educn); University Coll., London Univ. (BSc, DSc). FRSE 1968. Marine Lab., Aberdeen, Scotland: Marine Scientist, 1951–66; Sen. Principal Scientific Officer, 1966–73; Dep. Dir, 1973–77. Fellow, Amer. Acad. of Arts and Sciences, 1980. Agassiz Medal, Nat. Acad. of Sciences, USA, 1973. *Publications:* Structure of Marine Ecosystems, 1974; over 80 pubns in oceanographic and ecological jls. *Recreation:* sailing. *Address:* Woods Hole Oceanographic Institution, Woods Hole, Mass 02543, USA. *T:* (617) 548–1400. *Club:* Cosmos (Washington, DC).

STEELE, John Martin, OBE 1986 (MBE 1979); TD 1970; Director, Northern Ireland Court Service, since 1982; *b* 20 May 1938; *s* of John and Margaret Steele; *m* 1961, Molly Fulton; one *s* two *d.* *Educ:* Belfast High Sch.; Queen's Univ., Belfast. Various posts, NI Civil Service, 1962–66; staff of NI Parlt, 1966–72; Dept of Community Relations, 1972–73; Second Clerk Asst, NI Assembly, 1973–74; Co-Sec., Gardiner Cttee on measures to deal with terrorism in NI, 1974; Second Clerk Asst, NI Constitutional Convention, 1975–76; DoE, NI, 1976–78; DHSS, NI, 1978–82. Mem., TA, 1958–85; formerly Dep. Comd 23 Artillery Bde and CO 102 Air Defence Regt, RA(V). *Recreations:* gardening, cycling, reading, cooking. *Address:* Newtownards, Co. Down, Northern Ireland. *T:* (office) Belfast 228594. *Club:* Army and Navy.

STEELE, John Roderic, CB 1979; transport consultant; *b* 22 Feb. 1929; *s* of late Harold Graham Steele and Doris Steele (*née* Hall); *m* 1956, Margaret Marie, *d* of late Joseph and Alice Stevens; two *s* two *d.* *Educ:* Queen Elizabeth Grammar Sch., Wakefield; Queen's Coll., Oxford (MA). Asst Principal, Min. Civil Aviation, 1951; Private Sec. to Parly Sec., MTCA, 1954; Principal, Road Trans. Div., 1957; Sea Transport, 1960; Shipping Policy, 1962; Asst Sec., Shipping Policy, BoT, 1964; Counsellor (Shipping), British Embassy, Washington, 1967; Asst Sec., Civil Aviation Div., DTI, 1971, Under-Sec., Space Div., 1973, Shipping Policy Div., 1974, Gen. Div., 1975, Dept of Trade; Dep. Sec., Dept of Trade, 1976–80, Dept of Industry, 1980–81; Dir-Gen. for Transport, EEC, 1981–86. *Recreations:* normal. *Address:* 7 Kemerton Road, Beckenham, Kent; Square Ambiorix 30, Bte 30, 1040 Bruxelles, Belgium. *Clubs:* United Oxford & Cambridge University; Philippics.

STEELE, Kenneth Walter Lawrence, CBE 1980 (OBE 1967); KPM 1936; Chief Constable, Avon and Somerset Constabulary, 1974–79; *b* 28 July 1914; *s* of Walter and Susan Steele, Godalming, Surrey. *Educ:* Wellington Sch., Wellington, Somerset. Served War: with Somerset LI and Royal Northumberland Fusiliers, 1942–45. Asst Chief Constable, Buckinghamshire, 1953–55; Chief Constable: Somerset, 1955–66; Somerset and Bath, 1966–74. *Recreations:* badminton, tennis. *Address:* Lloyds Bank Ltd, 31 Fore Street, Taunton, Somerset.

STEELE, Maj.-Gen. Michael Chandos Merrett, MBE 1972; Chief of Joint Services Liaison Organization, Bonn, 1983–86; *s* of late William Chandos Steele and Daisy Steele (*née* Merrett); *m* 1961, Judith Ann Huxford; two *s* one *d.* *Educ:* Westminster School; RMA Sandhurst. Commissioned RA, 1952; Staff Coll., Camberley, 1962; BM RA, 53rd Welsh Div., 1965–67; BM, 8th Inf. Brigade, 1970–72; CO 22nd Light Air Defence Regt, RA, 1972–74; GSO1, HQ DRA, 1974–76; Comdr, 7th Artillery Brigade, 1976–78; Nat. Defence Coll., Canada, 1978–79; BGS, Defence Sales Organization, 1979–82. *Recreations:* lawn tennis, gardening. *Address:* c/o Lloyds Bank PLC, Cox's & King's Branch, 6 Pall Mall, SW1.

STEELE, Sir (Philip John) Rupert, Kt 1980; Director, Union Fidelity Trustee Co. of Australia, since 1984; *b* 3 Nov. 1920; *s* of late C. Steele; *m* 1946, Judith, *d* of Dr Clifford Sharp; one *s* two *d.* *Educ:* Melbourne C of E Grammar School. Served RAAF and 115 Sqdn (Lancaster), RAF; POW 1944. Director. Steele & Co. Ltd, 1949–59; Carlton Brewery Ltd, 1964–73; Carlton and United Breweries, 1973–84. Mem. Council, Royal Agr. Soc. of Victoria, 1961–74. Pres., Prahan Football Club, 1980–85; Mem. Cttee, Victoria Racing Club, 1958–85, Hon. Treasurer, 1971–73, Vice-Chm., 1973–77, Chm., 1977–82; Mem., Racecourses Licensing Board, 1975–81. *Recreation:* racing thoroughbred horses. *Address:* 2/64 Irving Road, Toorak, Victoria 3142, Australia.

STEELE, Richard Charles, FIBiol, FICFor; Director General, Nature Conservancy Council, since 1980; *b* 26 May 1928; *s* of Richard Orson Steele and Helen Curtis Steele (*née* Robertson); *m* 1966, Anne Freda Nelson; two *s* one *d.* *Educ:* Univ. of Wales (BSc Forestry and Botany); Univ. of Oxford. National Service, 1946–48. Assistant Conservator of Forests, Colonial Forest Service (later HMOCS), Tanganyika (later Tanzania), 1951–63; Head: Woodland Management Section, Nature Conservancy, Monks Wood, 1963–73; Terrestrial Life Sciences Section, Natural Environment Research Council, London, 1973–78; Division of Scientific Services, NERC Inst. of Terrestrial Ecology, Cambridge, 1978–80. Past Pres., Inst. of Foresters of Gt Britain. *Publications:* Wildlife Conservation in Woodlands, 1972; ed, Monks Wood: a nature reserve record, 1974; numerous papers on nature conservation, ecology and forestry in professional and scientific jls. *Recreations:* hill-walking, gardening, collecting books on natural history and E African travel. *Address:* Treetops, Deepdene Wood, Dorking, Surrey, RH5 4BQ. *T:* Dorking 883106. *Club:* Athenæum.

STEELE, Sir Rupert; *see* Steele, Sir P. J. R.

STEELE, Tommy, (Thomas Hicks), OBE 1979; Actor; *b* Bermondsey, London, 17 Dec. 1936; *s* of late Thomas Walter Hicks and Elizabeth Ellen (*née* Bennett); *m* 1960, Ann Donoghue; one *d.* *Educ:* Bacon's Sch. for Boys, Bermondsey. First appearance on stage in variety, Empire Theatre, Sunderland, Nov. 1956; first London appearance, variety, Dominion Theatre, 1957; Buttons in Rodgers and Hammerstein's Cinderella, Coliseum, 1958; Tony Lumpkin in She Stoops to Conquer, Old Vic, 1960; Arthur Kipps in Half a Sixpence, Cambridge Theatre, London, 1963–64 and Broadhurst Theatre (first NY appearance), 1965; Truffaldino in The Servant of Two Masters, Queen's, 1969; Dick Whittington, London Palladium, 1969; Meet Me In London, Adelphi, 1971; Jack Point, in The Yeomen of the Guard, City of London Fest., 1978; London Palladium: The Tommy Steele Show, 1973; Hans Andersen, 1974 and 1977; one-man show, Prince of Wales, 1979; Singin' in the Rain (also dir.), 1983; *films:* Kill Me Tomorrow, 1956; The Tommy Steele Story; The Duke Wore Jeans; Tommy the Toreador; Touch It Light; It's All Happening; The Happiest Millionaire; Half a Sixpence; Finian's Rainbow; Where's Jack?; *television:* wrote and acted in Quincy's Quest, 1979. Composed and recorded, My Life, My Song, 1974; composed, A Portrait of Pablo, 1985. *Publications:* Quincy, 1981; The Final Run, 1983. *Recreations:* squash, sculpture. *Address:* c/o Talent Artists Ltd, 37 Hill Street, W1X 8JY. *T:* 01–493 0343.

STEELE-BODGER, Prof. Alasdair, CBE 1980; FRCVS; Professor of Veterinary Clinical Studies, University of Cambridge, since 1979; *b* 1 Jan. 1924; *s* of late Harry Steele-Bodger, MRCVS, and Mrs K. Steele-Bodger (*née* MacDonald); *m* 1948, Anne, 2nd *d* of late Captain A. W. J. Finlayson, RN, and Mrs Nancy Finlayson; three *d.* *Educ:* Shrewsbury Sch.; Caius Coll., Cambridge (BA 1945, MA); Royal (Dick) Veterinary Coll., Edinburgh Univ. (BSc, MRCVS 1948). Hon. FRCVS 1975. Gen. vet. practice, Lichfield, Staffs, 1948–77; consultant practice, Fordingbridge, Hants, 1977–79. Hon. Vet. Consultant to British Agricl Export Council, 1967–. Vis. Prof., Univ. of Toronto, 1973. Pres., British Small Animal Vet. Assoc., 1962; Member: Horserace Scientific Adv. Cttee (formerly Jockey Club's Horserace Anti-Doping Cttee), 1973–; UGC's Agricl and Vet. Sub-Cttee, 1973–81; Council, BVA, 1957–85 (Pres., 1966; Hon. Mem., 1985); RCVS, 1960– (Pres., 1972); Jt RCVS/BVA Cttee on Eur. Vet. Affairs, 1967–; Eur. Liaison Gp for Agriculture, 1972–; Cttee of Inquiry on Experiments on Animals, 1963–65; Council, Royal Agricl Soc. of England, 1967–; former Mem., Animal Feedingstuffs Industry/BVA/ADAS HQ Liaison Cttee. UK Deleg. to Fedn of Veterinarians of EEC, 1967–; EEC Official Vet. Expert, 1974–; Mem., EEC Adv. Cttee on Vet. Trng, 1981–. Hon. Vet. Consultant, Nat. Cattle Breeders' Assoc., 1979–. Mem. Bd of Advisers, Univ. of London, 1984–. Gen. Comr to Bd of Inland Revenue, 1969–81. Chm., Editorial Bd, Veterinary Times (formerly Veterinary Drug), 1978–. Crookes' Prize, 1970; Dalrymple-Champneys Cup and Medal, 1972. Cambridge Triple Blue. *Publications:* Society of Practising Veterinary Surgeons Economics Report, 1961, and papers in vet. jls on clinical subjects and vet. econs. *Recreations:* swimming, fishing, travel. *Address:* The Miller's House, Mill Causeway, Chrishall, near Royston, Herts SG8 8QH. *Clubs:* Farmers'; Hawks (Cambridge).

See also M. R. Steele-Bodger.

STEELE-BODGER, Michael Roland; veterinary surgeon in private practice; *b* 4 Sept. 1925; *s* of late Henry William Steele-Bodger and Kathrine Macdonald; *m* 1955, Violet Mary St Clair Murray; two *s* one *d.* *Educ:* Rugby Sch.; Gonville and Caius Coll., Cambridge. MRCVS. Mem., Sports Council, 1976–82. England Rugby Selector, 1954–70; Pres., RFU, 1973–74; Mem., Internat. Rugby Football Bd, 1974–84; Chm., Four Home Rugby Unions' Tours Cttee, 1976–. Cambridge Univ. Rugby Blue, Captain 1946; England Rugby Internat., 1947–48. *Recreation:* interest in all sport. *Address:* Laxford Lodge, Bonehill, Tamworth, Staffs. *T:* Tamworth 251001. *Clubs:* East India, Devonshire, Sports and Public Schools; Hawks (Cambridge).

See also A. Steele-Bodger.

STEELE-PERKINS, Surgeon Vice-Admiral Sir Derek (Duncombe), KCB 1966 (CB 1963); KCVO 1964 (CVO 1954); FRCS; FRACS; *b* 19 June 1908; *s* of late Dr Duncombe Steele-Perkins, Honiton, Devon, and Sybil Mary Hill-Jones, Edinburgh; *m* 1937, Joan Boddan (*d* 1985), Birkdale, Lancashire; three *d.* *Educ:* Allhallows School,

Rousdon; Edinburgh University and College of Surgeons (Edin.). Entered RN, 1932; RN Hosp., Haslar, 1932; HMS Mantis, China, 1934–36; HMS Ganges, Shotley, 1936–38; HMS Vindictive, 1938–39; RN Hospitals: Haslar, 1939–40; Chatham, 1940–44; Sydney, Australia, 1944–46; Malta, 1946–50; RY Gothic, 1951–52; Chatham, 1952–59; Senior Surgical Specialist, RN Hosp., Bighi, Malta, Oct. 1959–61; Medical Officer-in-Charge, Royal Naval Hospital, Haslar, 1961; Command MO to C-in-C, Portsmouth, 1962–63; Medical Director of the Navy, 1963–66. FRSocMed. Royal Commonwealth Tours, 1953–54, 1959. QHS 1961. CStJ. *Recreations:* sailing, fly-fishing, shooting. *Address:* c/o National Westminster Bank, Lymington, Hants. *Clubs:* Royal Cruising; Royal Lymington Yacht (Cdre 1969–72).

STEEN, Anthony David; MP (C) South Hams, since 1983 (Liverpool Wavertree, Feb. 1974–1983); barrister; youth leader; social worker; underwriter; *b* 22 July 1939; *s* of Stephen Nicholas Steen, *qv*; *m* 1965, Carolyn Padfield, educational psychologist; one *s* one *d. Educ:* Westminster Sch.; occasional student University Coll., London. Called to Bar, Gray's Inn, 1962; practising Barrister, 1962–74, Defence Counsel, MoD (Court Martials). Lectr in Law, Council of Legal Educn, 1964–68; Adv. Tutor, Sch. of Environment, Central London Poly, 1981–83. Founder and First Director: Task Force to help London's old and lonely, with Govt support, 1964; Govt Foundn YVFF, tackling urban deprivation, 1968–74; Consultant to Canadian Govt on student and employment matters, 1970–71. Mem., Select Cttee on Race Relations, 1975–79; Chairman: Cons. Mems Parly Gp, 1974; Cons. Party Back Bench Cttee on Cities, Urban and New Town Affairs, 1979–83; All Party Friends of Cycling, 1979–; Vice-Chm., Health and Social Services, 1979–80; Sec., Parly Caribbean Gp, 1979–; Co-ordinator, Chm's Unit for Marginal and Critical Seats, Cons. Central Office, 1982–; Jt Nat. Chm., Impact 80's Campaign. Vice-Pres., Merseyside Young Conservatives. Member: Exec. Council, NPFA; Board, Community Transport; Council of Reference, Internat. Christian Relief; Council Mem., Anglo-Jewish Assoc.; Chm., Outlandos Charitable Trust; Vice-Chm., Task Force Trust; Vice-President: Ecology Bldg Soc.; Internat. Centre for Child Studies; Bentley Operatic Soc. Patron, Liverpool's Open Circle for Detached Youth Work; Pres., Devon Youth Assoc. *Publications:* New Life for Old Cities, 1981; Tested Ideas for Political Success, 1983. *Recreations:* piano, hill climbing, swimming, cycling. *Address:* House of Commons, SW1; 46 Fore Street, Totnes, South Devon. *T:* Totnes 866069. *Clubs:* Lansdowne; Churchill (Liverpool); Brixham; Totnes Conservative (South Hams).

STEEN, Stephen Nicholas; President, Smith & Nephew Associated Companies Ltd, since 1976 (Chairman, 1968–76); Chairman, British Tissues Limited, 1971–77; *b* 19 July 1907; *m* 1934; one *s* one *d.* Arthur Berton & Co. Ltd, 1943; Director, Smith & Nephew Associated Companies Ltd, 1958, Dep. Chm. 1962. Underwriting Member, Matthews Wrightson Pulbrook Ltd; called to the Bar, Gray's Inn, 1949. Mem., Ct of Patrons, RCS, 1973–. *Recreation:* golf. *Address:* (office) 2 Temple Place, WC2R 3BP. *T:* 01–836 7922.
See also A. D. Steen.

STEER, Prof. John Richardson, FSA 1981; Emeritus Professor of the History of Art, University of London; art-historian and director; *b* 14 Oct. 1928; *s* of Walter Wallis Steer and Elsie Gertrude (*née* Colman). *Educ:* Clayesmore Sch., Dorset; Keble Coll., Oxford (MA); Courtauld Inst. of Art, Univ. of London (BA). Gen. Asst, City Art Gall., Birmingham, 1953–56; Asst Lectr, Dept of Fine Art, Univ. of Glasgow, 1956–59; Lectr in Hist. of European Art, Univ. of Bristol, 1959–67; Prof. of Fine Arts, Univ. of St Andrews, 1967–80; Prof. of Hist. of Art, Birkbeck Coll., Univ. of London, 1980–84. Chm., Adv. Cttee on Validation, Heriot-Watt Univ./Edinburgh Coll. of Art, 1978–; Chm., Art Historians Assoc. of GB, 1980–83; Vice-Chm., Scottish Theatre Ballet, 1969–71; Mem., Cttee for Art and Design, CNAA, 1977–82 (Chm., Hist. of Art/Design and Complementary Studies Bd, 1977–79); Member: Theatre Museum Adv. Council, 1981–83; Theatre Museum Cttee, V & A Mus., 1984–; Exec., Genius of Venice Exhibn, RA, 1983–84. Adjudicator, National Student Drama Festival, 1977. Theatrical prodns include: The Seagull, St Andrews, 1971; And When Love Speaks, Edinburgh, 1975; The Privacy of the Patients, Edinburgh Fringe, 1977, ICA, 1978; Waiting for Godot, St Andrews, 1978. *Publications:* A Concise History of Venetian Painting, 1967; Mr Bacon's Titian (Selwyn Brinton Lecture, RSA), 1977; Alvise Vivarini, 1982; contribs to Burlington Magazine, Art History. *Recreation:* travel. *Address:* 1 Cheriton Square, SW17 8AE.

STEER, Kenneth Arthur, CBE 1978; MA, PhD, FSA, FSAScot; Secretary, Royal Commission on the Ancient and Historical Monuments of Scotland, 1957–78; *b* 12 Nov. 1913; *o s* of Harold Steer and Emily Florence Thompson; *m* 1st, 1941, Rona Mary Mitchell (*d* 1983); one *d*; 2nd, 1985, Eileen Alice Nelson. *Educ:* Wath Grammar School; Durham University. Research Fellowship, 1936–38. Joined staff of Royal Commission on Ancient and Historical Monuments of Scotland, 1938. Intelligence Officer in Army, 1941–45 (despatches twice). Monuments, Fine Arts and Archives Officer, North Rhine Region, 1945–46. Corresponding Member, German Archæological Inst.; Horsley Memorial Lectr, Durham University, 1963; Rhind Lectr, Edinburgh, 1968. Pres., Soc. of Antiquaries of Scotland, 1972–75. Arts Council Literary Award, 1978. *Publications:* Late Medieval Monumental Sculpture in the West Highlands (with J. W. M. Bannerman), 1976; numerous articles in archæological journals. *Address:* 1 Silver Hay, Dumbleton, near Evesham, Worcs. *T:* Evesham 881783.

STEER, Rt. Rev. Stanley Charles; Bishop of Saskatoon, 1950–70; *s* of S. E. and E. G. Steer; *m* 1936, Marjorie Slater. *Educ:* Guildford Gram. Sch.; Univ. of Saskatchewan (B), Oxford Univ. (MA). Hon. DD: Wycliffe Coll., Toronto, 1947, Emmanuel Coll., Saskatoon, 1952; St Chad's Coll., Regina, 1964. Missionary at Vanderhoof, BC, 1929; Chaplain, St Mark's Church, Alexandria, 1931; Chaplain, University Coll., Oxford, 1932–33; St John's Hall, Univ. of London: Tutor, 1933; Vice-Principal, 1936. Chaplain, The Mercers' Company, City of London, 1937; Principal, Emmanuel Coll., Saskatoon, 1941; Hon. Canon of St John's Cathedral, Saskatoon, and CF (R of O), 1943. *Recreation:* tennis. *Address:* 2383 Lincoln Road, Victoria, BC V8R 6A3, Canada. *T:* 592 9888.

STEER, Wilfred Reed, QC 1972; *b* 23 Aug. 1926; *s* of George William and Dorothy Steer; *m* 1953, Jill Park; one *s* one *d*, and two step *s. Educ:* Bede Collegiate Sch., Sunderland, Co. Durham; London Sch. of Economics. LLB (Lond.) 1949. Called to the Bar, Gray's Inn, 1950. *Address:* 51 Westgate Road, Newcastle upon Tyne. *T:* Newcastle upon Tyne 20541.

STEER, William Reed Hornby, MA, LLM; Barrister-at-Law; Recorder of South Molton, 1936–51; Deputy Chairman, London County Council, 1948–49; Lt-Col in the Army (released); *b* 5 April 1899; *s* of late Rev. W. H. Hornby Steer, TD MA, JP; unmarried. *Educ:* Eton; Trinity College, Cambridge. Commissioned in Royal Field Artillery; served European War, France and Belgium; called to Bar, Inner Temple, 1922; joined Western Circuit; Standing Counsel: to Commons, Open Spaces, and Footpaths Preservation Society; to Council for Preservation of Rural England; to National Smoke Abatement Society and to Pure Rivers Society; an Examiner in Law to Chartered Institute of Secretaries; Legal Member of Town Planning Inst.; Fellow of Royal Soc. of Health; Associate of Royal Institution of Chartered Surveyors; a representative for Hampstead on

London County Council, 1931–52; a representative of London County Council on International Union of Local Authorities; Master of Worshipful Company of Turners, 1949–50; a Governor of Haberdashers' Aske's Schools and of Royal Free Hospital; a Governor and an Almoner of Christ's Hospital, Dep. Chm. Council of Almoners, 1970–75; Chairman Children's Hospital, Hampstead; Vice-Chairman London Old Age Pensions Committee; Treasurer, London Soc.; Kt of Justice, Order of St John; Joint Hon. Secretary of League of Mercy; Gold Staff Officer at Coronation of King George VI; Inspector of Metropolitan Special Constabulary; Army Officers Emergency Reserve, 1938; Extra Regimentally Employed, Military Dept, Judge Advocate-General's Office, 1939; Deputy Judge Advocate-General, Malta, 1941–43; graded Assistant Adjutant-General, War Office, 1944; Staff Officer (I), Control Commission for Germany, 1945; Captain, 1939; Major, 1941; Lt-Col 1943; Member of Territorial Army and Air Force Association of the County of London. *Publications:* articles on the law relating to Highways; Assistant Editor of Glen's Public Health Act, 1936; Steer's Law of Smoke Nuisances, 1938, 2nd edn 1948; contributions to Lord Macmillan's Local Government Law and Administration. *Recreation:* sailing. *Address:* 71A Whitehall Court, SW1A 2EL. *T:* 01–930 3160. *Clubs:* United Oxford & Cambridge University, Carlton, Pratt's, MCC; Royal Corinthian Yacht (Burnham-on-Crouch).

STEERE, Sir Ernest H. L.; *see* Lee-Steere, Sir E. H.

STEERS, James Alfred, CBE 1973; MA; Professor Emeritus of Geography and Emeritus Fellow of St Catharine's College, Cambridge; Chairman, National Committee of Geography, 1967–72; Coastal Consultant to Conservation Committee of Council of Europe, 1968; Chairman, Coastal Conferences, 1966–67; *b* 8 Aug. 1899; *s* of J. A. Steers, Bedford; *m* 1942, Harriet, *d* of J. A. Wanklyn, Cambridge; one *s* one *d. Educ:* Elstow (Private) School, Bedford; St Catharine's Coll., Cambridge. Senior Geography Master, Framlingham Coll., 1921–22; elected Fellow of St Catharine's, 1925, subsequently Dean, Tutor and President, Univ. Demonstrator, 1926–27; Univ. Lecturer, 1927–49; Prof. of Geography, 1949–66; Member of the British Expedition to the Great Barrier Reefs, 1928; Leader of Geographical Expedition to the Reefs, 1936; Expedition to the Jamaica Cays, 1939; War Service, 1917–18; Vice-Pres., Royal Geographical Soc., 1959–63, 1967–72, Hon. Vice-Pres., 1972–, Hon. Mem., 1977–; Pres. Norfolk and Norwich Naturalists Soc., 1940–41; Pres., Section E British Association (Oxford), 1954; President, Inst. Brit. Geographers (Reading), 1956; President: Geographical Assoc., 1959; Estuarine and Brackish Water Science Assoc., 1977–80. Corresp. Mem., Royal Dutch Geographical Soc.; Hon. Mem., Ges. für Erdkunde Berlin; Member: Council of Senate, Cambridge, 1941–48; Wild Life Conservation Cttee; Nature Conservancy, 1949–54, 1957–66; Scientific Policy Cttee, 1949–66; Cttee for England, 1949–68, 1970–73; Nat. Parks Commn, 1960–66; Properties Cttee, Nat. Trust, 1969–76; Hon. Adviser on Coastal Preservation to Ministry of Town and Country Planning and to Department of Health, Scotland; Member: Departmental Cttee on Coastal Flooding, 1953; Advisory Committee to improve Sea Defences, 1954–; Hydraulics Research Board, DSIR, 1957–61; Visiting Prof., Berkeley, Calif, 1959; Visiting Fellow, Aust. Nat. Univ., 1967. Hon. LLD Aberdeen, 1971; Hon. DSc East Anglia, 1978. Victoria Medal, RGS, 1960; Scottish Geographical Medal, 1969. *Publications:* Introduction to the Study of Map Projections, 1927, 15th edn 1970; The Unstable Earth, 1932 (new edn 1950); Editor and contrib. to Scolt Head Island, 1934, 2nd rev. edn 1960; The Coastline of England and Wales, 1946, 2nd edn 1969; A Picture Book of the Whole Coast of England and Wales, 1948; The Sea Coast, 1953, 4th edn 1969; The Coast of England and Wales in Pictures, 1960; The English Coast and the Coast of Wales, 1966; Coasts and Beaches, 1969; Introduction to Coastline and Development, 1970; The Coastline of Scotland, 1973; Coastal Features of England and Wales, 1980; Editor: new edns of P. Lake's Physical Geography, 1958; Vol. on Field Studies in the British Isles, Internat. Geog. Union. London meeting, 1964; Brit. Assoc. Advancement of Science, The Cambridge Region, 1965; Engl. edn of V. P. Zenkovitch, Processes of Coastal Development, 1967; papers on Coastal Physiography, Coral Islands, etc, in various scientific publications. *Recreations:* walking, philately, travel. *Address:* 47 Gretton Court, Girton, Cambridge CB3 0QN. *T:* Cambridge 276007. *Clubs:* Travellers', Geographical (Hon. Mem.).

STEGGLE, Terence Harry; HM Diplomatic Service; Consul-General, São Paulo, since 1986; *b* 4 March 1932; *s* of Henry Richard Steggle and Jane Steggle; *m* 1954, Odette Marie (*née* Audisio); two *d. Educ:* Chislehurst and Sidcup County Grammar School. Crown Agents, 1950–57; Lieut RA (TA), 1951–53; seconded to Govt of E Nigeria, 1957–58, 1960–62; FO 1963; served Laos, 1963, France, 1964, Zaire, 1970, Bolivia, 1978–82; Ambassador to Panama, 1983–86. *Recreations:* swimming, philately, bridge. *Address:* c/o Foreign and Commonwealth Office, SW1. *Club:* Rotary.

STEIN, Prof. Peter Gonville, FBA 1974; JP; Regius Professor of Civil Law in the University of Cambridge, and Fellow of Queens' College, since 1968; *b* 29 May 1926; *o s* of late Walter Stein, MA, Solicitor, and Effie Stein (*née* Walker); *m* 1st, 1953, Janet Chamberlain; three *d*; 2nd, 1978, Anne M. Howard; one step *s. Educ:* Liverpool Coll.; Gonville and Caius Coll., Camb. (Classical Exhibitioner); University of Pavia. Served in RN, Sub-lieut (Sp) RNVR, 1944–47. Admitted a Solicitor, 1951; Italian Govt Scholar, 1951–52; Asst Lecturer in Law, Nottingham Univ., 1952–53; Lecturer in Jurisprudence, 1953–56, Prof. of Jurisprudence, 1956–68, Dean of Faculty of Law, 1961–64, Aberdeen Univ.; Chm., Faculty Bd of Law, Cambridge, 1973–76; Vice Pres., Queens' Coll., 1974–81 (Acting Pres., 1976 and 1980–81). Visiting Prof. of Law: Univ. of Virginia, 1965–66, 1978–79; Colorado, 1966; Witwatersrand, 1970; Louisiana State, 1974, 1977, 1983, 1985; Chicago, 1985; Lectures: R. M. Jones, QUB, 1978; Irvine, Cornell, 1979; Sherman, Boston, 1979; Tucker, Louisiana State, 1985. Fellow, Winchester Coll., 1976–. Member: Council, Max Planck Inst. for European Legal History, Frankfurt, 1966–; Council, Internat. Assoc. of Legal History, 1970–; Sec. of State for Scotland's Working Party on Hospital Endowments, 1966–69; Bd of Management, Royal Cornhill and Assoc. (Mental) Hospitals, Aberdeen, 1963–68 (Chm. 1967–68); UGC, 1971–75; US–UK Educnl Commn, 1985–. Pres., Soc. of Public Teachers of Law, 1980–81; Vice-Pres., Selden Soc., 1984–. For. Fellow, Accad. di Scienze morali e politiche, Naples, 1982. Hon. Dr jur, Göttingen, 1980. JP Cambridge, 1970–. *Publications:* Fault in the formation of Contract in Roman Law and Scots Law, 1958; editor, Buckland's Textbook of Roman Law, 3rd edn, 1963; Regulae Iuris: from juristic rules to legal maxims, 1966; Roman Law in Scotland in Ius Romanum Medii Aevi, 1968; Roman Law and English Jurisprudence (inaugural lect.), 1969; (with J. Shand) Legal Values in Western Society, 1974, Italian edn 1981; (ed jtly) Adam Smith's Lectures on Jurisprudence, 1978; Legal Evolution, 1980, Japanese edn 1986; (ed jtly) Studies in Justinian's Institutes, 1983; Legal Institutions: the development of dispute settlement, 1984, Italian edn 1986; articles in legal periodicals mainly on Roman Law and legal history. *Recreations:* hill walking, gardening. *Address:* Queens' College, Cambridge. *T:* Cambridge 335511; Wimpole Cottage, Wimpole Road, Great Eversden, Cambridge. *T:* Cambridge 262349.

STEINBERG, Professor Hannah; Professor of Psychopharmacology in the University of London at University College, since 1970; Head of Psychopharmacology Group, Department of Psychology, University College London, since 1979; *d* of late Michael

Steinberg, doctor of law, and Marie (née Wein). *Educ*: Schwarzwaldschule, Vienna; Putney High School; Queen Anne's School, Caversham; Univ. of Reading (Cert. Comm.); Denton Secretarial Coll., London; University College London (BA 1st cl. Hons Psychology, PhD; Troughton Schol., 1948–50). FBPsS, FZS. Pres., Univ. of London Union, 1947–48; Univ. of London Postgrad. Studentship, 1948–50. Sec. to Man. Dir, Omes Ltd, 1943–44. University College London: Asst Lectr in Pharmacology, 1954–55; Lectr, 1955–62; Reader in Psychopharmacology, 1962–70; Prof. of Psychopharmacology (first in W Europe), 1970–. Hon. consulting Clinical Psychologist, Dept of Psychological Medicine, Royal Free Hosp., 1970. Member MRC working parties on: Biochemistry and Pharmacology of Drug Dependence, 1968–73; Biological Aspects of Drug Dependence, 1971–75. Vice-President: Collegium Internationale Neuro-Psychopharmacologicum (CINP), 1968–74; Brit. Assoc. of Psychopharmacology, 1973–77; Mem., Biological Council, 1977–80. Distinguished Affiliate of Amer. Psychol Assoc., Psychopharmacology Div., 1978; Member: British Pharmacol Soc.; Experimental Psychol. Soc.; Assoc. for Study of Animal Behaviour; Soc. for Study of Addiction, etc. Convener, Academic Women's Achievement Gp, 1979–. *Publications*: (trans. and ed jtly) Animals and Men, 1951; organiser of symposia and editor: Animal Behaviour and Drug Action (jt), 1963; Scientific Basis of Drug Dependence, 1968; Psychopharmacology, Sexual Disorders and Drug Abuse (jt), 1972, etc; articles and reviews on psychopharmacology in scientific jls and books. *Address*: University College London, Gower Street, WC1E 6BT. *T*: 01–387 7050.

STEINBERG, Jack; President, Steinberg Group, since 1982 (Chairman, 1966–81); *b* 23 May 1913; *s* of Alexander and Sophie Steinberg; *m* 1938, Hannah Anne, *d* of late Solomon Wolfson, JP; two *d*. *Educ*: privately, London. Underwriting Member of Lloyd's. Chairman: Horrockes Fashions Ltd; Butte Knit (London) Ltd. Mem., NEDC, 1966–78; Vice-President: British Mantle Manufacturers' Assoc.; Clothing Export Council, 1974– (Chm., 1970–74); Chairman: KCH Res. Trust, 1977–; King's Medical Res. Trust, 1979–. Member of Plumbers' Livery Co.; Freeman, City of London. *Address*: 74 Portland Place, W1. *T*: 01–580 5908. *Clubs*: Brooks's, Portland, Carlton.

STEINBERG, Saul Phillip; Founder, 1961, and Chairman and Chief Executive Officer, since 1961, Reliance Group Holdings Inc.; *b* 13 Aug. 1939; *m* 3rd, 1984, Gayfryd McNabb; one *d* and one step *s*; and three *s* one *d* by previous marriages. *Educ*: Wharton School of Univ. of Pennsylvania (BScEcon). *Address*: Park Avenue Plaza, 55 E 52 Street, New York, NY 10055, USA. *T*: (212) 909–1110. *Clubs*: Glen Oaks, The Board Room (NY).

STEINER, Prof. George, MA, DPhil; Extraordinary Fellow, Churchill College, Cambridge, since 1969; Professor of English and Comparative Literature, University of Geneva, since 1974; *b* 23 April 1929; *s* of Dr F. G. and Mrs E. Steiner; *m* 1955, Zara Steiner (née Shakow); one *s* one *d*. *Educ*: Paris (BèsL); Univ. of Chicago (BA); Harvard (MA); Oxford (DPhil). Member, staff of the Economist, in London, 1952–56; Inst. for Advanced Study, Princeton, 1956–58; Gauss Lectr, Princeton Univ., 1959–60; Fellow of Churchill Coll., Cambridge, 1961–. Massey Lectr, 1974; Leslie Stephen Lectr, Cambridge, 1986; W. P. Ker Lectr, Univ. of Glasgow, 1986. Fulbright Professorship, 1958–69; O. Henry Short Story Award, 1958; Guggenheim Fellowship, 1971–72; Zabel Award of Nat. Inst. of Arts and Letters of the Us, 1970; Faulkner Stipend for Fiction, PEN, 1983. Pres., English Assoc., 1975; Corresp. Mem., (Federal) German Acad. of Literature, 1981. FRSL 1964. Hon. DLitt: East Anglia, 1976; Louvain, 1980; Mount Holyoke Coll., USA, 1983. Chevalier de la Légion d'Honneur, 1984. *Publications*: Tolstoy or Dostoevsky, 1958; The Death of Tragedy, 1960; Anno Domini, 1964; Language and Silence, 1967; Extraterritorial, 1971; In Bluebeard's Castle, 1971; The Sporting Scene: White Knights in Reykjavik, 1973; After Babel, 1975 (adapted for TV as The Tongues of Men, 1977); Heidegger, 1978; On Difficulty and Other Essays, 1978; The Portage to San Cristobal of A. H., 1981; Antigones, 1984; George Steiner: a reader, 1984. *Recreations*: music, chess, mountain walking. *Address*: 32 Barrow Road, Cambridge. *T*: Cambridge 61200. *Clubs*: Athenæum, Savile; Harvard (New York).

STEINER, Rear-Adm. Ottokar Harold Mojmir St John, CB 1967; Assistant Chief of Defence Staff, 1966–68, retired; *b* 8 July 1916; *e s* of late O. F. Steiner; *m* 1st, 1940, Evelyn Mary Young (marr. diss. 1975); one *s* one *d*; 2nd, 1975, Eleanor, widow of Sqdn Leader W. J. H. Powell, RAF. *Educ*: St Paul's School. Special entry cadet, RN, 1935. Served War of 1939–45 (despatches twice), HMS Ilex, Havelock, Frobisher, Superb. Naval Staff Course, 1947; Staff of C-in-C, Far East Fleet, 1948–50; Comdr 1950; jssc 1953; HMS Ceylon, 1953–54; NATO Defence Coll., 1955; HMS Daedalus, 1955–56; Capt. 1956; Admiralty, 1956–58; in comd HMS Saintes and Capt. (D) 3rd Destroyer Squdn, 1958–60; Naval Adviser to UK High Commission, Canada, 1960–62; Senior Offrs War Course, 1962; in comd HMS Centaur, 1963–65; ADC to HM the Queen, 1965; Rear-Adm., 1966. Chm. Council, Shipwrecked Fishermen and Mariners Royal Benevolent Soc. Freeman, City of London; Liveryman, Coachmakers and Coach Harness Makers. *Recreations*: sailing, golf. *Address*: The Cottage, Moons Hill, Totland, IoW. *T*: Isle of Wight 753404. *Clubs*: Royal Cruising, Isle of Wight Motor Yacht (Adm.); Royal Naval Sailing Association; Royal Solent Yacht; Union (Malta).

STEINER, Prof. Robert Emil, CBE 1979; Professor of Diagnostic Radiology, University of London, Royal Postgraduate Medical School, 1961–83, now Emeritus; *b* 1 Feb. 1918; *s* of Rudolf Steiner and Clary (née Nordlinger); *m* 1945, Gertrude Margaret Konirsch; two *d*. *Educ*: University of Vienna; University College, Dublin. Dep. Director, Dept of Radiology, Hammersmith Hosp.; Lecturer Diagnostic Radiology, Postgraduate Med. School of London, 1950, Sen. Lecturer, 1955, Director, 1955–. Vice-Chm., Nat. Radiological Protection Bd, 1972–83. Past Consultant Adviser in Radiology to DHSS; Past Civil Consultant in Radiology to Med. Dir-Gen., Navy. Warden of Fellowship, Faculty of Radiologists. Former Mem. Council, RCS; Past Pres., British Inst. Radiology; Pres., RCR, 1977–80. Hon. Fellow: Amer. Coll. of Radiology; Australian Coll. of Radiology; Faculty of Radiologists, RCSI. Hon. Member: Radiological Soc. of Finland; Radiological Soc. of N America; Amer. Roentgen Ray Soc.; Germany Roentgen Soc. Barclay Medal British Inst. of Radiology. Former Editor, British Jl of Radiology. *Publications*: Clinical Disorders of the Pulmonary Circulation, 1960; Recent Advances of Radiology, 1979; contrib. to British Journal of Radiology, Clinical Radiology, British Heart Jl, Lancet, BMJ, etc. *Address*: 12 Stonehill Road, East Sheen, SW14. *T*: 01–876 4038. *Club*: Hurlingham.

STEINITZ, Dr (Charles) Paul (Joseph), OBE 1985; FRAM 1948; Founder-Conductor, London Bach Society and Steinitz Bach Players; Consultant Professor, Royal Academy of Music, since 1984; *b* 25 Aug. 1909; *s* of Rev. Charles Steinitz and Sarah Jessie Prior; *m* 1st, 1933, Joan Paxton (marr. diss.); two *s*; 2nd, 1946, Margery Still (marr. diss.); one *d*; 3rd, 1976, Margaret Johnson. *Educ*: privately and Royal Acad. of Music (LRAM); FRCO 1930; BMus 1934, DMus 1940 London. Prof., RAM, 1945–84; Lectr, then Principal Lectr, Univ. of London Goldsmiths' Coll., 1948–76; Dir of Music, Priory Church of St Bartholomew-the-Great, W Smithfield, 1949–61. Founder: London Bach Soc., 1947; Steinitz Bach Players, 1969. Ext. Examr in Music, Cambridge Coll. of Arts and Tech., 1976–82. Mem. Senate, Univ. of London, 1968–. BBC broadcasts, 1949–; appearances in

major British festivals, including Bath, Cambridge and City of London; appearances in festivals and concert halls in USA, Israel, W and E Europe, Australia and NZ. Lecture tours to USA, Canada, Australia and NZ, 1965–. Specialist in music of J. S. Bach. Recordings incl. complete Cantiones Sacrae of 1625 by Schütz. *Publications*: chapter on German Church Music, New Oxford History of Music, vol. V, 1975; Bach's Passions, 1979; Bach for Choirs, 1980; Performing Bach's Vocal Music, 1980; edns and books on harmony; contribs to music jls, USA, Australia, Musical Times. *Recreations*: organic gardening, cooking, reading, theatre. *Address*: 73 High Street, Old Oxted, Surrey RH8 9LN. *T*: Oxted 7372. *Club*: Athenæum.

STELL, Prof. Philip Michael, FRCS, FRCSE; Professor of Oto-rhino-laryngology, University of Liverpool, since 1979; *b* 14 Aug. 1934; *s* of Frank Law Stell and Ada Stell; *m* 1959, Shirley Kathleen Mills; four *s* one *d*. *Educ*: Archbishop Holgate's Grammar Sch., York; Edinburgh Univ. (MB, ChB 1958). ChM Liverpool, 1976. FRCS 1966; FRCSE 1962. Jun. hosp. appts, Edinburgh and Liverpool, 1958–63; Fellow, Washington Univ., St Louis, USA, 1964–65; Sen. Lectr, Univ. of Liverpool, 1965–78. Hunterian Prof., RCS, 1976. President: Otorhinolaryngological Res. Soc., 1983–86; Assoc. of Head and Neck Oncologists of GB, 1986–; Liverpool Med. Inst., 1986–87. Yearsley Gold Medal, 1980; Harrison Prize, RSM, 1982; Semon Medal, 1986. *Publications*: approx. 20 books and 80 articles in learned jls on surgery for cancer of head and neck. *Recreations*: squash, rowing, gardening. *Address*: 7 Partridge Road, Blundellsands, Liverpool L23 6UH. *T*: 051–924 2725. *Club*: Royal Artillery Association (Crosby).

STEMBRIDGE, David Harry; a Recorder of the Crown Court, since 1977; *b* 23 Dec. 1932; *s* of Percy G. Stembridge and Emily W. Stembridge; *m* 1956, Therese C. Furer; three *s* one *d*. *Educ*: St Chad's Cathedral Choir Sch., Lichfield; Bromsgrove Sch.; Birmingham Univ. (LLB Hons). Called to the Bar, Gray's Inn, 1955; practising barrister, 1956–. *Recreations*: flute and organ playing, sailing. *Club*: Bar Yacht.

STENHAM, Anthony William Paul, (Cob), FCA; Managing Director, Bankers Trust Company, since 1986 (Executive Chairman, Operations in UK, Europe, etc.; Chairman, Global Policy Committee); *b* 28 Jan. 1932; *s* of Bernard Basil Stenham and Annie Josephine (née Naylor); *m* 1st, 1966, Hon. Sheila Marion Poole (marr. diss.); 2nd, 1983, Anne Martha Mary O'Rawe; one *d*. *Educ*: Eton Coll.; Trinity Coll., Cambridge. MA. Qualified Accountant FCA 1958. Mem., Inner Temple, 1954. Price Waterhouse, 1955–61; Philip Hill Higginson Erlanger, 1962–64; William Baird & Co., 1964–69; Unilever, 1969–86 (Financial Dir, Unilever PLC and Unilever NV, 1970–86). Director: Equity Capital for Industry, 1976–81; Capital Radio, 1982–. Underwriting Mem. of Lloyd's, 1978. Chm., Institute of Contemporary Arts, 1977–; Mem. Council, Architectural Assoc., 1982–84; Royal Coll. of Art: Mem. Court, 1978–; Mem. Council, 1978–81; Chm. Council and Pro-Provost, 1979–81; Hon. Fellow, 1980. Gov., Museum of London, 1986–. FRSA. *Recreations*: cinema, theatre, opera, painting. *Address*: 4 The Grove, Highgate, N6 6JU. *T*: 01–340 2266. *Clubs*: White's, Turf.

STENHOUSE, John Godwyn, TD with bar; FCIB; Chairman, Stenhouse Holdings plc, 1978–80 (Director, 1947–84); retired; *b* 16 Nov. 1908; *s* of Alexander Rennie Stenhouse and Hughina Cowan Stenhouse; *m* 1st, 1936, Margaret Constance Thornton (*d* 1965); two *d*; 2nd, 1967, Jean Ann Bennie (née Finlayson); one step *s*. *Educ*: Warristo Sch., Moffat; Kelvinside Acad., Glasgow. With an insurance co., 1927; joined A. R. Stenhouse & Partners, Ltd, Insurance Brokers (later Stenhouse Holdings Ltd), 1931. *Recreations*: sailing, mechanical engineering. *Address*: 2 St Germains, Bearsden, Glasgow G61 2RS. *T*: 041–942 0151. *Club*: Royal Scottish Automobile (Glasgow).

STENHOUSE, Sir Nicol, Kt 1962; *b* 14 Feb. 1911; 2nd *s* of late John Stenhouse, Shanghai, China, and Tring, Hertfordshire; *m* 1951, Barbara Heath Wilson; two *s* one *d*. *Educ*: Repton. Joined Andrew Yule & Co. Ltd, Calcutta, India, 1937; Managing Director, 1953–59; Chairman and Senior Managing Director, 1959–62; President: Bengal Chamber of Commerce and Industry, Calcutta, 1961–62; Associated Chambers of Commerce of India, Calcutta, 1961–62. *Recreation*: gardening. *Address*: 3 St Mary's Court, Sixpenny Handley, near Salisbury, Wilts SP5 5PH.

STENING, Sir George (Grafton Lees), Kt 1968; ED; Hon. Consultant Gynæcological Surgeon, Royal Prince Alfred Hosp., Sydney; Emeritus Consultant, St Luke's Hospital, Sydney; *b* 16 Feb. 1904; *s* of George Smith Stening and Muriel Grafton Lees; *m* 1935, Kathleen Mary Packer; one *s* one *d*. *Educ*: Sydney High Sch.; Univ. of Sydney. MB, BS (Syd.) 1927 (Hons Cl. II); FRCS (Ed.) 1931; FRACS 1935; FRCOG 1947; Fellow, Aust. Coll. Obst. and Gyn., 1980. Carnegie Trav. Fellow, 1948. Served War of 1939–45: Middle East, New Guinea, Australia; OC, 3rd Aust. Surgical Team, Libyan Desert, 1941; CO, 2/11 Aust. Gen. Hosp., 1941–44; CO, 113 Aust. Gen. Hosp., 1945. Hon. Col, RAAMC. GCStJ 1971; Chancellor, Order of St John, in Australia, 1961–82. Past Pres., Sen. Golfers' Soc. of Aust. *Publication*: A Text Book of Gynæcology (co-author), 1948. *Recreations*: golf, yachting. *Address*: 2/22 Wolseley Road, Point Piper, NSW 2027, Australia. *Clubs*: Royal Sydney Golf (Sydney); Australian Jockey.

STEPHEN, David; *see* Stephen, J. D.

STEPHEN, Derek Ronald James, CB 1975; Assistant Secretary, Royal Hospital Chelsea, since 1982; *b* 22 June 1922; *s* of late Ronald James Stephen; *m* 1948, Gwendolen Margaret, *d* of late William James Heasman, CBE; two *s* one *d* (and one *s* decd). *Educ*: Bec Sch.; Christ's Coll., Cambridge (1st cl. Hons Classics). Served War, 1941–45; 11th Hussars and HQ 7th Armoured Div., N Africa, Italy, NW Europe; Captain. Asst Principal, War Office, 1946; Asst Private Sec. to Sec. of State for War, 1949–50; Principal, 1951; Private Sec. to Sec. of Cabinet, 1958–60; Asst Sec., WO (later Ministry of Defence), 1960; IDC 1966; HM Treasury, 1968; Civil Service Dept (on its formation), 1968; Under-Sec., 1969–71; Asst Under-Sec. of State, MoD, 1972–73; Dep. Under-Sec. of State (Navy), MoD, and Mem. Admiralty Bd, 1973–78; Dep. Under-Sec. of State (Army), MoD, and Mem., Army Bd, 1978–82. *Recreations*: golf, music. *Address*: Light Horse Court, Royal Hospital Chelsea, SW3 4SL.

STEPHEN, Harbourne Mackay, CBE 1985; DSO 1941; DFC and bar 1940; AE 1943; Consultant and Chairman, Daily Telegraph Developments Ltd, since 1986; Director, Daily Telegraph plc; *b* 18 April 1916; *s* of Thomas Milne Stephen, JP, and Kathleen Vincent Park; *m* 1947, Sybil Erica Palmer; two *d*. *Educ*: Shrewsbury. Staff of Allied Newspapers, London, 1931; Evening Standard, 1936–39. RAFVR, 1937; served RAF, 1939–45 (destroyed numerous enemy aircraft): 605 and 74 Sqdns, 1939–40; at MAP, 1941, then joined 130 Sqdn and comd 234 Sqdn; served Far East, 1942–45; Wing Comdr (Flying) Dum Dum; RAF Jessore, Bengal; comd 166 Fighter Wing; then to Fighter Ops, 224 Gp Arakan; Ops "A" Air Comd SEA, 1945. Was OC 602 City of Glasgow (F) Sqdn RAuxAF, 1950–52. Returned to Beaverbrook Newspapers, Oct. 1945; worked on Scottish Daily Express, Scottish Sunday Express, and Evening Citizen in Glasgow, 1945–55. General Manager, Sunday Express, 1958; General Manager, Sunday Graphic, 1960, and thereafter General Manager, Thomson Papers, London; Man. Dir, Daily Telegraph and Sunday Telegraph, 1963–86. Dir, Internat. Newspaper Colour Assoc., Darmstadt, 1964–69. Council Mem., RSPB, 1972–73. *Recreations*: normal, occasionally.

Address: Donnington Fields, Newbury, Berks. *T:* Newbury 40105. *Clubs:* Royal Automobile, Royal Air Force.

STEPHEN, Henrietta Hamilton, (Rita Stephen), MBE 1973; National Secretary, Association of Professional, Executive, Clerical and Computer Staff (formerly the Clerical and Administrative Workers' Union), since 1965; *b* 9 Dec. 1925; *d* of late James Pithie Stephen, engine driver, Montrose and late Mary Hamilton Morton, South Queensferry. *Educ:* Wolseley Street and King's Park Elem. Schs, Glasgow; Queen's Park Sen. Secondary, Glasgow; Glasgow Univ. (extra-mural); LSE (TUC Schol.). McGill Univ. and Canada/US Travel, 1958–59. Law office junior, 1941; Clerk, Labour Exchange (Mem. MLSA), 1941–42; Post Office Telephonist, 1942–60; Officer and delegate, Union of Post Office Workers, Glasgow Br., 1942–60; Member: UPW Parly Panel, 1957; Glasgow City Labour Party; Cathcart Ward Labour Party; Election Agent (Municipal), 1955–60; London and Home Counties Area Organiser, CAWU, 1960–65. Negotiator in public and private sectors of industry, 1960–; Editor, The Clerk, 1965–71; Union Educn Officer, 1965–72; Delegate: TUC; Labour Party Annual Confs; Member: EDC for Food and Drink Manufacturing, 1976–; Food Standards Cttee, 1968–80; Industrial Soc. Council and Exec., 1968–; Mary Macarthur Educnl Trust, 1965; Distributive Industry Trng Bd, 1968–73; Monopolies and Mergers Commn, 1973–83; British Wool Marketing Bd, 1973–; Duke of Edinburgh's Commonwealth Study Conf., UK Trust; LSE Court, 1976–. Mem., TUC Women's Adv. Cttee, 1983–; Chair, Nat. Jt Cttee of Working Women's Organisations, 1983–84. *Publications:* (jtly) Training Shop Stewards, 1968; (with Roy Moore) Statistics for Negotiators, 1973; contrib. Clerk, Industrial Soc. Jl, Target, etc. *Recreations:* food, walking, conversation, theatre, reading. *Address:* 3 Pond Road, SE3. *T:* 01–852 7797, 01–947 3131.

STEPHEN, Sir James Alexander, 4th Bt, *cr* 1891; *b* 25 Feb. 1908; *o c* of 3rd Bt and Barbara, *y d* of late W. Shore-Nightingale of Embley, Hants and Lea Hurst, Derbyshire; *cousin* of Florence Nightingale; *S* father, 1945. *Educ:* Eton; Trinity College, Cambridge. Law Student, Inner Temple; embraced Roman Catholic faith, 1936; Resident, Toynbee Hall, 1936–39; Air Raid Warden, 1940; served RA (AA), 1940–41, discharged unfit; worked on the land as a volunteer, 1941–45; certified insane, 1945; name restored to vote, 1960; discharged from hospital, 1972. FRGS. Interested in exploration; has raised money for Outward Bound Trust. *Heir:* none. *Recreation:* contract bridge. *Address:* 48 Princess Road, Branksome, Poole, Dorset BH12 1BH. *T:* Bournemouth 761665. *Club:* Sloane.

STEPHEN, (John) David; Head of External Relations and Member of General Management Board, Commonwealth Development Corporation, since 1985; *b* 3 April 1942; *s* of late John Stephen and of Anne Eileen Stephen; *m* 1968, Susan Dorothy (*née* Harris); three *s* one *d. Educ:* Denbigh Road Primary Sch., Luton; Luton Grammar Sch.; King's Coll., Cambridge (BA Mod. Langs, 1964); Univ. of San Marcos, Lima, Peru; Univ. of Essex (MA Govt, 1968). Educn Officer, CRC, 1969–70; with Runnymede Trust, 1970–75 (Dir, 1973–75); Latin American Regional Rep., Internat. Univ. Exchange Fund, 1975–77; Special Adviser to Sec. of State for Foreign and Commonwealth Affairs, 1977–79; Editor, International Affairs, 1979–83; Dir, UK Immigrants Advisory Service, 1983–84. Member: Bd of Trustees, Action Aid, 1981–; Latin America and Caribbean Cttee, Christian Aid, 1980–84. Broadcaster in English, French and Spanish, BBC Ext. Services, 1980–. Contested (SDP-Liberal Alliance) N Luton, 1983. *Publications:* The San of the Kalahari, 1982; articles in New Society, The Times and other jls. *Recreations:* the family, music, the countryside. *Address:* 39 Cautley Avenue, SW4 9HX. *T:* 01–675 2397. *Club:* Royal Commonwealth Society.

STEPHEN, John Low, ChM (Aberdeen), FRCSE, FRCS; Surgeon, St Mary's Hospital, W2, since 1958; Senior Surgeon, St Mary's Hospital, W9, 1948–77, retired; *b* 13 May 1912; 2nd *s* of late Dr J. H. Stephen, Aberdeen; *m* 1938, Mary Milne, MA, BSc; one *s* one *d. Educ:* Aberdeen Grammar School; Aberdeen and Edinburgh Universities. MA 1931, MB 1935, Aberd.; FRCSEd, 1937; ChM Aberd., 1945; FRCS (ad eundem), 1968. Various university and hospital appointments in Scotland and England. Associate Teacher in Surgery, St Mary's Hosp. Med. School, 1950–. FRSocMed. *Publications:* chapters in Operative Surgery (Smith and Rob); various articles on abdominal surgery in Brit. Jl of Surgery. *Recreations:* golf, motoring. *Address:* Luibeg, Groombridge, Tunbridge Wells, East Sussex.

STEPHEN, Lessel Bruce; His Honour Judge Stephen, a Circuit Judge, since 1972; *b* 15 Feb. 1920; *s* of L. P. Stephen, FRCS(E); *m* 1949, Brenda (*née* Tinkler). *Educ:* Marlborough; Sydney Sussex Coll., Cambridge (BA). Called to the Bar, Inner Temple, 1948; subsequently practised NE Circuit; Recorder, 1972. *Recreations:* golf, wine. *Address:* 2 Harcourt Buildings, Temple, EC4Y 9DB. *T:* 01–353 2548.

STEPHEN, Rt. Hon. Sir Ninian (Martin), AK 1982; GCMG 1982; GCVO 1982; KBE 1972; PC 1979; Governor-General of Australia, since 1982; *b* 15 June 1923; *o s* of late Frederick Stephen and Barbara Stephen (*née* Cruickshank); *m* 1949, Valery Mary, *d* of late A. Q. Sinclair and of Mrs G. M. Sinclair; five *d. Educ:* George Watson's Sch., Edinburgh; Edinburgh Acad.; St Paul's Sch., London; Chillon Coll., Switzerland; Scotch Coll., Melbourne; Melbourne Univ. (LLB). Served War, HM Forces (Australian Army), 1941–46. Admitted as Barrister and Solicitor, in State of Victoria, 1949; signed Roll of Victorian Bar, 1951; QC 1966. Appointed Judge of Supreme Court of Victoria, 1970; Justice of High Court of Australia, 1972–82. Hon. Bencher Gray's Inn, 1981. KStJ 1982. *Address:* Government House, Canberra, ACT 2600, Australia.

STEPHEN, Rita; see Stephen, H. H.

STEPHENS, Air Commandant Dame Anne, DBE 1961 (MBE 1946); Hon. ADC to the Queen, 1960–63; Director, Women's Royal Air Force, 1960–63; *b* 4 Nov. 1912; *d* of late General Sir Reginald Byng Stephens, KCB, CMG and late Lady Stephens. *Educ:* privately. Joined WAAF, 1939; served in UK, Belgium and Germany, 1939–45. Command WRAF Depot, Hawkinge, 1950–52; promoted Group Officer, 1951; Inspector WRAF, 1952–54; Deputy Director, 1954–57; Staff Officer, HQ 2nd TAF, 1957–59; promoted Air Commandant, 1960. *Address:* The Forge, Sibford Ferris, Banbury, Oxfordshire. *T:* Swalcliffe 452.

STEPHENS, Anthony William, CMG 1976; Deputy Under Secretary of State, Northern Ireland Office, since 1985; *b* 9 Jan. 1930; *s* of late Donald Martyn Stephens and Norah Stephens (*née* Smith-Cleburne); *m* 1954, Mytyl Joy, *d* of late William Gay Burdett; four *d. Educ:* Bradfield Coll.; Bristol Univ. (LLB); Corpus Christi Coll., Cambridge. RM, 1948–50. Colonial Administrative Service, 1953; District Officer, Kenya, 1954–63; Home Civil Service, 1964; Principal, MoD, 1964–70; Asst Private Sec. to successive Secretaries of State for Defence, 1970–71; Asst Sec., 1971; Chief Officer, Sovereign Base Areas, Cyprus, 1974–76; Under Sec., NI Office, 1976–79; Asst Under Sec. of State, General Staff, 1979–83, Ordnance, 1983–84, MoD. *Recreations:* travel and the outdoor life, music, theatre. *Club:* Royal Commonwealth Society.

STEPHENS, Prof. Arthur Veryan, MA Cantab; CEng; FRAeS; Professor of Aeronautical Engineering, The Queen's University, Belfast, 1956–73, now Emeritus Professor; *b* 9 July 1908; *s* of Arthur John Stephens and Mildred, *d* of Robert Fowler Sturge; *m* 1st, 1938,

Jane Dows, *d* of F. W. Lester; three *s* one *d*; 2nd, 1981, Marjorie Phyllis Irene Sprince. *Educ:* Clifton Coll.; St John's Coll., Cambridge (Mechanical Sciences Tripos, John Bernard Seely Prize). Scientific Officer, Royal Aircraft Establishment, 1930–34; Fellow of St John's College, Cambridge, 1934–39; Lawrence Hargrave Professor of Aeronautics, 1939–56, Dean of the Faculty of Engineering, 1947–56, University of Sydney, NSW. Edward Busk Meml Prize of RAeS, 1934; Member: Australian Flying Personnel Research Cttee, 1940–45; Australian Council for Aeronautics, 1941–46; Chairman: Aeronautical Research Consultative Cttee, 1947–54; Australian Aeronautical Research Cttee, 1954–56; Member, Australian Defence Research and Development Policy Cttee, 1953–56; Chairman, Australian Division of Royal Aeronautical Society, 1947–56. Dean of Faculty of Applied Science and Technology, 1961–64; Vice-President (Buildings), 1964–67. *Publications:* numerous papers on applied aerodynamics published by Aeronautical Research Council, Australian Dept of Supply and in Jl of RAeS. *Recreations:* golf, real tennis, antiquarian horology. *Address:* 118 Loudoun Road, NW8. *Club:* Athenæum.

STEPHENS, Cedric John; consultant; retired; *b* 13 Feb. 1921; *s* of late Col J. E. Stephens, Truro, Cornwall. *Educ:* London University (BSc (Eng.) Hons); CEng, FRAeS, FIEE. Entered Scientific Civil Service, 1951; Dir, Space Activities, Min. of Aviation, 1961; Mem. Coun., European Launcher Development Organisation, Paris, 1962; Chm. Technical Cttee, European Coun. on Satellite Communications, 1964; Imperial Defence Coll., 1965; Director, Signals Research and Develt Estabt, Min. of Technology, 1966–67; Chief Scientific Adviser, Home Office, 1968; Dir-Gen. of Research and Chief Scientist, Home Office, 1969–73. Called to Bar, Gray's Inn, 1971. Mem., Electronics Div. Bd, IEE, 1972. *Address:* 6 Newlyn Road, Welling, Kent DA16 3LH. *Club:* Athenæum.

STEPHENS, Christopher Wilson T.; see Stephens, Wilson T.

STEPHENS, Sir David, KCB 1964; CVO 1960; Clerk of the Parliaments, House of Lords, 1963–74; *b* 25 April 1910; *s* of late Berkeley John Byng Stephens, CIE, and Gwendolen Elizabeth (*née* Cripps), Cirencester; *m* 1st, 1941, Mary Clemency, JP (*d* 1966), *er d* of late Colonel Sir Eric Gore Browne, DSO, OBE, TD; three *s* one *d*; 2nd, 1967, Charlotte Evelyn, *widow* of Henry Manisty, *d* of late Rev. A. M. Baird-Smith; three step *s. Educ:* Winchester College; Christ Church. Oxford (2nd cl. Lit. Hum.). Laming Travelling Fellow, the Queen's College, Oxford, 1932–34; Clerk in the Parliament Office, House of Lords, 1935–38; Member Runciman Mission to Czechoslovakia, 1938; transf. HM Treasury, 1938; Political Warfare Executive, 1941–43; Principal Private Sec. to the Lord Pres. of the Council (Mr Herbert Morrison), 1947–49; Asst Sec., HM Treasury, 1949; Secretary for Appointments to two Prime Ministers (Sir Anthony Eden and Mr Harold Macmillan), 1955–61; Reading Clerk and Clerk of the Journals, House of Lords, 1961–63. Chm., Redundant Churches Fund, 1976–81. Chm. of Governors, Maidwell Hall Sch., 1964–70. Mem., Cotswold DC, 1976–83. Pres. Friends of Cirencester Parish Church, 1976–. *Recreations:* gardening, tennis and country life; preserving the Cotswolds. *Address:* The Old Rectory, Coates, near Cirencester, Glos GL7 6NS. *T:* Kemble 258. *Clubs:* Brooks's, MCC.

See also R. A. Ryder.

STEPHENS, Maj.-Gen. Keith Fielding, CB 1970; OBE 1957; Medical Officer, Department of Health and Social Security, 1970–85, retired; *b* Taplow, Bucks, 28 July 1910; *s* of late Edgar Percy and Mary Louise Stephens; *m* 1937, Margaret Ann, *d* of late Alexander MacGregor; two *s. Educ:* Eastbourne College; St Bartholomew's Hospital. MB, BS London 1934; FFARCS 1953; DA 1945. Commissioned into RAMC, 1937; served in India, 1937–43; France and Germany, 1944–46; Cyprus, 1954–56; Adviser in Anæsthetics to the Army, 1949–53 and 1957–66; Commandant and Director of Studies, Royal Army Medical College, 1966–68; DDMS, Southern Command, 1968–70, retired. FRSocMed (Pres., Sect. of Anæsthetics, 1970–71); Hon. Member, Assoc. of Anæsthetists of Gt Brit. and Ireland. Fellow, Med. Soc. of London. Hon. FFARCS (Ireland), 1970; QHS, 1964–70. Hon. Col, 221 (Surrey) Field Ambulance RAMC(V), 1972–76. Mitchiner Medal, 1962. CStJ 1967. *Publications:* numerous articles in medical journals. *Address:* 3 Carnegie Place, Parkside, Wimbledon, SW19. *T:* 01–946 0911. *Club:* Naval and Military.

STEPHENS, Malcolm George; Export Finance Director, Barclays Bank PLC, since 1985; Director, Barclays Export Services, since 1983; *b* 14 July 1937; *s* of Frank Ernest Stephens and Janet (*née* McQueen); *m* 1975, Lynette Marie Caffery, Brisbane, Australia. *Educ:* St Michael's and All Angels; Shooter's Hill Grammar Sch.; St John's Coll., Oxford (Casberd Scholar; BA 1st Cl. Hons PPE). National Service, RAOC, 1956–58. CRO, 1953; British High Commission: Ghana, 1959–62; Kenya, 1963–65; Export Credits Guarantee Dept, 1965–82: Principal, 1970; seconded to Civil Service Coll., 1971–72; Asst Sec., 1973; Estab. Officer, 1977; Under Sec., 1978; Head of Proj. Gp B, 1978–79; Principal Finance Officer, 1979–82; Internat. Finance Dir, Barclays Bank Internat. Ltd, 1982. Member: Inst. of Export, 1984; Overseas Projects Bd, 1985. FIB 1984. *Recreations:* gardening, reading. *Address:* 111 Woolwich Road, Bexleyheath, Kent DA7 4LP. *T:* 01–303 6782. *Club:* Overseas Bankers.

STEPHENS, Martin; see Stephens, S. M.

STEPHENS, Peter Norman Stuart; Director, News Group Newspapers, since 1978, Editorial Director, since 1981; *b* 19 Dec. 1927; *s* of J. G. Stephens; *m* 1950, Constance Mary Ratheram; two *s* one *d. Educ:* Mundella Grammar Sch., Nottingham. Newark Advertiser, 1945–48; Northern Echo, 1948–50; Daily Dispatch, 1950–55; Daily Mirror, Manchester, 1955–57; Asst Editor, Newcastle Journal, 1957–60; Asst Editor, Evening Chronicle, Newcastle, 1960–62, Editor 1962–66; Editor, Newcastle Journal, 1966–70; Asst Editor, The Sun, 1970–72, Dep. Editor 1972; Associate Editor, News of the World, 1973, Editor, 1974–75; Associate Editor, The Sun, 1975–81. *Recreation:* supporting Derby County Football Club. *Address:* 1 Virginia Street, E1 9XP. *T:* 01–481 4100.

STEPHENS, Major Robert, CVO 1964; ERD; Administrative Officer, Hillsborough Castle (formerly Government House), 1973–78; retired; *b* 1909; *s* of late John Samuel Stephens; *m* 1939, Kathleen, *d* of late R. I. Trelford, Helen's Bay, Belfast. *Educ:* Campbell Coll., Belfast. Ulster Bank, 1929–39. Served War of 1939–45: RA, Middle East, 1941–45. Commercial Manager, Newforge Ltd, 1946–55; Private Secretary to the Governor of Northern Ireland, 1955–73; Comptroller to: Lord Wakehurst, 1955–64; Lord Erskine of Rerrick, 1964–68; Lord Grey of Naunton, 1968–73. Hon. Sec., SSAFA (NI), 1979. OStJ 1980. *Recreation:* golf. *Address:* 13 Ballynahinch Street, Hillsborough, Co. Down, Northern Ireland. *T:* Hillsborough 682550.

STEPHENS, Robert; actor; *b* 14 July 1931; *s* of Rueben Stephens and Gladys (*née* Deverell); *m* Tarn Bassett; one *d*; *m* 1967, Maggie Smith, *qv* (marr. diss. 1975); two *s. Educ:* Bradford Civic Theatre School. Started with Caryl Jenner Mobile Theatre Co.; Mem. English Stage Co., Royal Court, 1956. *Stage:* The Crucible, Don Juan, The Death of Satan, Cards of Identity, The Good Woman of Setzuan and The Country Wife (also at Adelphi, 1957); The Apollo de Bellac, Yes-and After, The Making of Moo, How Can We Save Father?, The Waters of Babylon, Royal Court, 1957; The Entertainer, Palace, 1957; Epitaph for George Dillon, Royal Court, Comedy, Golden (NY), 1958 and Henry Miller, 1959; Look After Lulu (also at New) and The Kitchen (also 1961), Royal Court,

1959; The Wrong Side of the Park, Cambridge, 1960; The Sponge Room, Squat Betty, Royal Court, 1962; Chichester and Edinburgh Festival, 1963; Design for Living (Los Angeles), 1971; Private Lives, Queen's, 1972; The Seagull, Chichester, 1973; Apropos The Falling Sleet (dir.), Open Space, 1973; Ghosts, The Seagull, Hamlet, Greenwich, 1974; Sherlock Holmes, NY and Canada, 1975; Murderer, Garrick, 1975; Zoo Story, 1975, Othello, 1976, Open Air, Regent's Park; Pygmalion, Los Angeles, 1979; Othello, Cape Town, SA, 1982; WCPC, Half Moon, 1982; Light Up the Sky, Old Vic, 1985; *National Theatre Company:* Hamlet, St Joan, The Recruiting Officer, 1963; Andorra, Play, The Royal Hunt of the Sun (also Chichester Fest.), Hay Fever, 1964; Much Ado About Nothing, Armstrong's Last Goodnight, Trelawny of the Wells (also Chichester Fest.), 1965; A Bond Honoured, Black Comedy, 1966; The Dance of Death, The Three Sisters (at Los Angeles, 1968), As You Like It, Tartuffe, 1967; Most Unwarrantable Intrusion (also dir.), Home and Beauty, 1968, Macrune's Guevara (also co-dir), 1969; The Beaux' Stratagem (also Los Angeles), Hedda Gabler, 1970; The Cherry Orchard, Brand, The Double Dealer, Has "Washington" Legs?, 1978; A Midsummer Night's Dream, Inner Voices, Cinderella, 1983. *Films:* A Taste of Honey; Cleopatra; The Small World of Sammy Lee; The Prime of Miss Jean Brodie; The Private Life of Sherlock Holmes; Travels with my Aunt; The Asphyx; Luther; QBVIII; Alexander the Great, Ill Fares The Land, etc. TV performances include: Vienna 1900 (6 part series), 1973; Tribute to J. B. Priestley, 1974; Kean, 1978; Voyage of Charles Darwin, 1978; Office Story, 1978; Friends in Space, 1979; Suez, 1979; The Executioner, 1980; Adelaide Bartlett (series), 1980; Winter's Tale, 1980; The Double Dealer, 1980; The Trial of Madame Famay, 1980; Holocaust (USA), 1980; Eden End, 1981; The Year of the French (RTE), 1981; Anyone for Denis?, 1982; Tales Out of School, 1982; Box of Delights, 1984; Puccini, 1984; By the Sword Divided (series), 1984, etc. Radio plays include: The Light Shines in the Darkness (BBC), 1985. Variety Club Award for stage actor, 1965. *Recreations:* cooking, gymnastics, swimming. *Address:* c/o Film Rights Ltd, 4 New Burlington Place, Regent Street, W1X 2AS. *T:* 01-437 7151.

STEPHENS, (Stephen) Martin; QC 1982; **His Honour Judge Martin Stephens;** a Circuit Judge, since 1986; *b* 26 June 1939; *s* of late Abraham Stephens and of Freda Stephens, Swansea; *m* 1965, Patricia Alison, *d* of late Joseph and of Anne Morris, Mapperley, Nottingham; two *s* one *d*. *Educ:* Swansea Grammar Sch.; Wadham Coll., Oxford (BA). Called to the Bar, Middle Temple, 1963; Wales and Chester Circuit; a Recorder, 1979–86. *Recreations:* cricket, tennis, theatre. *Address:* The Red House, 87 Cyncoed Road, Cyncoed, Cardiff. *T:* Cardiff 484553.

STEPHENS, William Henry, CB 1961; DSc, MSc, CEng, FRAeS; FBIS; Senior Executive Director, General Technology Systems Ltd, since 1973; *b* Kilkenny, Ireland, 18 March 1913; *s* of William Henry Stephens, MBE, and Helena Read Stephens (*née* Cantley); *m* 1938, Elizabeth Margaret Brown, BSc; one *s* one *d*. *Educ:* Methodist College and Queen's University, Belfast. Air Ministry, Royal Aircraft Establishment (Aerodynamic Research), 1935–38; War Office, Woolwich (Rocket Research), 1938–39; Ministry of Aircraft Prod., London (Air Defence Research), 1939–44; Asst Scientific Attaché and Asst Director, UK Scientific Mission, British Commonwealth Scientific Office, Washington, USA, 1944–47; Min. of Supply, RAE, Head of Guided Weapons Dept and later Dep. Director, 1947–58; Dir-Gen. Ballistic Missiles, Ministry of Aviation, 1959–62; Technical Dir, European Space Launcher Devélt Organisation, Paris, 1962–69; Minister, Defence R&D, British Embassy, Washington, 1969–72; Special Advr (Internat. Affairs), Controllerate of Res., MoD, 1972–73. Mem., Internat. Acad. of Astronautics; Fellow, British Interplanetary Soc. *Publications:* contrib. to Jl Royal Aeronautical Soc.; Proc. Brit. Assoc.; Proc. Internat. Congress of Aeronautical Sciences. *Recreations:* travel, music, art, theatre. *Address:* Rosebrook House, Oriel Hill, Camberley, Surrey. *Club:* Athenæum.

STEPHENS, Wilson (Treeve); Editor of The Field, 1950–77; *b* 2 June 1912; *s* of Rev. Arthur Treeve Stephens, Shepton Beauchamp, Somerset, and Margaret Wilson; *m* 1st, 1934, Nina, *d* of Arthur Frederick Curzon, Derby; two *d*; 2nd, 1960, Marygold Anne, *o d* of Major-General G. O. Crawford, *qv*; two *d*. *Educ:* Christ's Hosp. Formerly on editorial staffs of several provincial newspapers, and of The Daily Express. Served War of 1939–45, Royal Artillery. *Publications:* The Guinness Guide to Field Sports, 1979; Gundog Sense and Sensibility, 1982; Pigeon Racing, 1983; A Year Observed, 1984; Rivers of Britain (series) 1985–; contribs to The Field and other jls. *Recreation:* fly-fishing. *Address:* c/o Blake, Friedmann, 37–41 Gower Street, WC1E 6HH. *Club:* Kennel.

STEPHENSON, Ashley; *see* Stephenson, R. A. S.

STEPHENSON, Donald, CBE 1957 (OBE 1943); Controller, Overseas and Foreign Relations, BBC, 1966–71; *b* 18 May 1909; *yr s* of late J. V. G. Stephenson; *m* 1st, 1940, Alison (*d* 1965), *yr d* of late Wynn ap H. Thomas, OBE, LLB; three *d* (one *s* decd); 2nd, 1982, Francesca, *yr d* of late Captain Charles Francis Ward, RHA. *Educ:* Denstone College (Scholar); Paris; Baghdad. Banking business, 1925–31; permanent commission, RAF, 1932; Flt Lt, 1936; served France and Middle East, 1935–37; language specialist (interpreter, French and Arabic); Special Duty List, 1938; Arabic Editor, BBC, 1939; Director, BBC, New Delhi, 1944–45; Director, Eastern Services, 1946–47; Asst Controller in Overseas Div., 1948; Controller, North Region, 1948–56; Controller, Overseas Services, BBC, 1956–58; Chief Executive, Anglia Television Ltd, 1959; Head of Overseas and Foreign Relations, BBC, Dec. 1960. A Governor of Manchester Univ., 1950–58. A delegate to 5th Commonwealth Broadcasting Conf., Canada, 1963, to 7th Conf., NZ, 1968, and 8th Conf., Jamaica, 1970. *Recreation:* family life. *Address:* 21 Boulthurst Way, Oxted, Surrey. *T:* Limpsfield Chart 3151.

STEPHENSON, Prof. Gordon, CBE 1967; FRIBA, FRTPI, LFRAIA, LFRAPI, FLI, DistTP; Professor Emeritus of Architecture, University of Western Australia; Member, National Capital Planning Committee, Canberra, 1967–73; *b* 6 June 1908; *s* of Francis E. and Eva E. Stephenson, Liverpool; *m* 1938, Flora Bartlett Crockett (decd), Boston, USA; three *d*. *Educ:* Liverpool Institute; University of Liverpool; University of Paris; Massachusetts Institute of Technology. Elmes Scholar, Univ. of Liverpool, 1925–30; Holt Scholar, 1928; First Cl. Hons in Architecture, 1930; Chadwick Scholar at Brit. Inst. in Paris and Univ. of Paris, 1930–32; BArch; MCP(MIT). Lecturer and Studio Instructor in Architecture, University of Liverpool, 1932–36; Commonwealth Fellow and Medallist, Massachusetts Inst. of Technology, 1936–38; Studio Master, Architectural Assoc., School of Architecture, 1939–40; Lever Professor of Civic Design, School of Architecture, University of Liverpool, 1948–53; Professor of Town and Regional Planning in the University of Toronto, Canada, 1955–60; Prof. of Architecture, Univ. of WA, 1960–72. Architectural and Planning practice: asst to Corbett, Harrison and McMurray, NY City, 1929, asst to Le Corbusier and Pierre Jeanneret, Paris, 1930–32; Div. Architect, with W. G. Holford, on Royal Ordnance Factory work, 1940–42; Research Officer, Sen. Research Officer, and Chief Planning Officer, Min. of Works and Planning, and Min. of Town and Country Planning, 1942–47; seconded to assist Sir Patrick Abercrombie on Greater London Plan, 1943–44; Cnslt Architect, Univ. of WA, 1960–69; in partnership with R. J. Ferguson, as architects and planners for Murdoch Univ., WA, 1972–76; in private practice, houses, militia camp, university bldgs, community centre, housing schemes, town and regional planning studies. Editor, Town Planning Review, 1949–54. Hon. MCIP 1960. Hon. LLD Univ. of WA, 1976; Hon. DArch Univ. of Melbourne, 1984; Hon. DSc Flinders Univ. *Publications:* (with Flora Stephenson) Community Centres, 1941; (with F. R. S. Yorke) Planning for Reconstruction, 1944; (with J. A. Hepburn) Plan for the Metropolitan Region of Perth and Fremantle, 1955; a Redevelopment Study of Halifax, Nova Scotia, 1957; (with G. G. Muirhead) A Planning Study of Kingston, Ontario, 1959; The Design of Central Perth, 1975; Joondalup Regional Centre, 1977; Planning for the University of Western Australia: 1914–70, 1986; articles and papers in British, Australian, Canadian Technical Professional Jls. *Recreations:* architectural practice, drawing and travel. *Address:* 17 Langham Street, Nedlands, WA 6009, Australia. *T:* (09) 386.6699.

STEPHENSON, Henry Shepherd, CEng, FIMinE; Chairman, Mining Qualifications Board, 1970–75; *b* 1 Oct. 1905; *m* 1934, Faith Estelle, 3rd *d* of Tom Edward Arnold, Bolton Old Hall, Bradford; two *d*. *Educ:* Whitehaven Grammar School; Armstrong College, Durham University (BSc). Articled apprentice Mining Engineer, Whitehaven Colliery Co., 1924–28; official posts, Whitehaven Colliery Co., 1928–35; HM Junior Inspector of Mines Northern Div., 1935–39; Mining Agent, Cumberland Coal Co., 1939–41; HM Junior Inspector of Mines and Quarries (Yorkshire), 1941–44; Senior Inspector (Scotland), 1944–47; Senior Dist Inspector (Durham), 1948–52; Senior Dist Inspector (West Midland), 1952–58; Divisional Inspector (East Midland), 1958–62; Deputy Chief Inspector, Jan. 1962; Chief Inspector, 1962–70. Hon. DSc Newcastle upon Tyne, 1971. *Address:* Flat 13, The Redlands, Manor Road, Sidmouth, Devon.

STEPHENSON, Sir Henry Upton, 3rd Bt *cr* 1936; TD; Director: Stephenson, Blake (Holdings) Ltd; Thos Turton and Sons Ltd; *b* 26 Nov. 1926; *s* of Lt-Col Sir Henry Francis Blake Stephenson, 2nd Bt, OBE, TD, and of Joan, *d* of Major John Herbert Upton (formerly Upton Cottrell-Dormer); *S* father, 1982; *m* 1962, Susan, *o d* of Major J. E. Clowes, Ashbourne, Derbyshire; four *d*. *Educ:* Eton. Formerly Major, QO Yorkshire Dragoons. High Sheriff of Derbyshire, 1975. *Heir: cousin* Timothy Hugh Stephenson [*b* 5 Jan. 1930; *m* 1959, Susan Lesley, *yr d* of late George Arthur Harris; two *s*]. *Address:* Tissington Cottage, Rowland, Bakewell, Derbyshire.

STEPHENSON, Hugh; writer and journalist; Professor of Journalism, The City University, since 1986; *b* 18 July 1938; *s* of late Sir Hugh Stephenson, GBE, KCMG, CIE, CVO, and of Lady Stephenson; *m* 1962, Auriol Stevens; two *s* one *d*. *Educ:* Winchester Coll.; New Coll., Oxford (BA); Univ. of Calif, Berkeley. Pres., Oxford Union, 1962. HM Diplomatic Service, 1964–68; joined The Times, 1968; Editor, The Times Business News, 1972–81; Editor, The New Statesman, 1982–86. Mem., Cttee to Review Functioning of Financial Instns, 1977–80. Councillor, London Bor. of Wandsworth, 1971–78. *Publications:* The Coming Clash, 1972; Mrs Thatcher's First Year, 1980; Claret and Chips, 1982. *Address:* Graduate Centre for Journalism, 223–227 St John Street, EC1.

STEPHENSON, (James) Ian (Love), RA 1986 (ARA 1975); painter; Director, Postgraduate Painting, Chelsea School of Art, since 1970; *b* 11 Jan. 1934; *o s* of James Stephenson and May (*née* Emery); *m* 1959, Kate, *o d* of James Brown; one *s* one *d*. *Educ:* King Edward VII School of Art, King's Coll., Univ. of Durham, Newcastle upon Tyne (3 prizes; Hatton Schol.; BA Dunelm 1956, 1st Class Hons in Fine Art). Tutorial Student, 1956–57, Studio Demonstrator, 1957–58, King's Coll., Newcastle upon Tyne (pioneered 1st foundn course in UK dedicated to new creativity in art); Boise Schol. (Italy), Univ. of London, 1958–59; Vis. Lectr, Polytechnic Sch. of Art, London, 1959–62; Vis. Painter, Chelsea Sch. of Art, 1959–66; Dir, Foundn Studies, Dept of Fine Art, Univ. of Newcastle, 1966–70 (introd alternating approach between perceptual and conceptual studies to academic syllabus); Internat. Course Leader, Voss Summer Sch., 1979. Member: Visual Arts Panel, Northern Arts Assoc., Newcastle, 1967–70; Fine Art Panel, NCDAD, 1972–74; Perm. Cttee, New Contemp. Assoc., 1973–75; Fine Art Board, CNAA, 1974–75; Adv. Cttee, Nat. Exhibn of Children's Art, Manchester, 1975–; Working Party, RA Jubilee Exhbn, 1976–77; Selection Cttee, Arts Council Awards, 1977–78; Painting Faculty, Rome and Abbey Major Scholarships, 1978–82; Recommending Cttee, Chantrey Bequest, 1979–80; RA Steward, Artists' Gen. Benevolent Instn, 1979–80. Fine Art Advr, Canterbury Art Coll., 1974–79; Specialist Adviser, CNAA, 1980–83; Vice-Pres., Sunderland Arts Centre, 1982–; Boise Scholarship Cttee, UCL, 1983. Examiner: Birmingham Poly., 1972–73; Portsmouth Poly., 1973–76; London Univ., 1975–83 (Sen. Examiner, 1978–); Leicester Poly., 1976–78; Ulster Poly., 1979–82; Canterbury Art Coll., 1981–83; Newcastle Poly., 1982–85. Hon. Member: CAS, 1980–81; Accademia Italia, 1980–; Mark Twain Soc., 1978–. *Exhibitions include:* British Painting in the Sixties, London, 1963; Mostra di Pittura Contemporanea, Amsterdam and Europe, 1964–65; 9o Biennio, Lugano, 1966; 5e Biennale and 18e Salon, Paris, 1967; Recent British Painting, London and world tour, 1967–75; Junge Generation Grossbritannien, Berlin, 1968; Retrospective, Newcastle, 1970; La Peinture Anglaise Aujourd'hui, Paris, 1973; Elf Englische Zeichner, Baden Baden and Bremen, 1973; Recente Britse Tekenkunst, Antwerp, 1973; 13a Bienal, São Paulo and Latin America, 1975; Arte Inglese Oggi, Milan, 1976; Retrospective, London and Bristol, 1977; Englische Kunst der Gegenwart, Bregenz, 1977; British Painting 1952–77, London, 1977; Color en la Pintura Britanica, Rio de Janeiro and Latin America, 1977–79; Abstract Paintings from UK, Washington, 1978; Retrospective, Birmingham and Cardiff, 1978; Royal Acad. of Arts, Edinburgh, 1979–80; Art Anglais d'Aujourd'hui, Geneva, 1980; British Art 1940–80, London, 1980; Colour in British Painting, Hong Kong and Far East, 1980–81; Contemporary British Drawings, Tel-Aviv and Near East, 1980–82; The Deck of Cards, Athens and Arabia, 1980–82; A Taste of British Art Today, Brussels, 1982; Arteder Muestra Internacional, Bilbao, 1982; La Couleur en la Peinture Britannique, Luxembourg and Bucharest, 1982–83; 7th, 8th and 9th Internat. Print Biennales, Bradford, 1982, 1984 and 1986; 15a Bienale, Ljubljana, 1983; *illustrations include:* Cubism and After (BBC film), 1962; Contemporary British Art, 1965; Private View, 1965; Blow Up (film), 1966; Art of Our Time, 1967; Recent British Painting, 1968; Adventure in Art, 1969; In Vogue, 1975; Painting in Britain 1525–1975, 1976; British Painting, 1976; Contemporary Artists, 1977 and 1982; Contemporary British Artists, 1979; Tendenze e Testimonianze, 1983; *work in collections:* Arnolfini Trust, Arts Council, Birmingham and Bristol City Art Galls, British Council, BP Chemicals and Co., Bury Art Gall., Contemp. Art Soc., Creasey Lit. Museum, DoE, Economist Newspaper, Granada TV, Gulbenkian Foundn, Hatton Gall., Hunterian Museum, Kettle's Yard, Leeds City Art Gall., Leicestershire Educn Authority, Madison Art Center, Marzotto Roma, Nat. West. Bank, Northern Arts Assoc., Nuffield Foundn, Stuyvesant Foundn, Sunderland Art Gall., Tate Gall., Unilever Ltd, Union Bank of Switzerland, V&A Museum, Victoria Nat. Gall., Welsh Nat. Museum, Whitworth Art Gall. *Prizes include:* Junior Section, Moores Exhibn, Liverpool, 1957; European Selection, Premio Marzotto, Valdagno, 1964; First, Northern Painters' Exhibn, 1966. *Address:* Chelsea School of Art, Manresa Road, SW3 6LS. *T:* 01-351 3844.

STEPHENSON, Jim; His Honour Judge Stephenson; a Circuit Judge, since 1983; *b* 17 July 1932; *s* of late Alex Stephenson, Heworth, Co. Durham, and of Mrs Stephenson; *m* 1964, Jill Christine, *d* of Dr Lindeck, Fairwarp, Sussex; three *s*. *Educ:* Royal Grammar Sch. and Dame Allan's Sch., Newcastle; Exeter Coll., Oxford (Exhibnr, BA). Pres., Oxford Univ. Law Society, Michaelmas, 1955. Called to Bar, Gray's Inn, 1957. Mem., General Council of the Bar, 1961–64; Junior, NE Circuit, 1961; a Recorder of the Crown Court,

1974–83. *Recreations:* reading, fell-walking, history. *Address:* 12 Tankerville Terrace, Newcastle upon Tyne NE2 3AH. *T:* Tyneside 2813570.

STEPHENSON, Maj.-Gen. John Aubrey, CB 1982; OBE 1971; Managing Director, Weapon Systems Ltd, since 1982; Director, ATX Ltd, since 1984; Deputy Master General of the Ordnance, 1980–81; *b* 15 May 1929; *s* of Reginald Jack Stephenson and Florence Stephenson; *m* 1953, Sheila Colbeck; two *s* one *d. Educ:* Dorchester Grammar School. Commnd RA, 1948; served Malaya (despatches, 1951), Libya, Canal Zone and Germany, 1949–58 (student pilot, 1953–54); student, RMCS, 1958–60; 39 Missile Regt, 1960–61; student, RMCS and Staff Coll., 1961–62; served UK and Germany, 1962–67; Staff, RMCS, 1967–69; CO 16 Light Air Defence Regt RA, 1969–71; Project Manager, 155mm Systems, Woolwich, 1971–73; student, RCDS, 1974; Comdr, 1st Artillery Bde, Germany, 1975–77; Sen. Mil. Officer, RARDE, 1977–78; Dir Gen. Weapons (Army), 1978–80. Col Comdt, RA, 1984–. Governor, Hardeye's Sch., Dorchester, 1984–. MInstD; FBIM. *Recreations:* fishing, sailing, gardening, bridge, golf, military history. *Address:* Collingwood, 27 Trafalgar Way, Stockbridge, Hants SO20 6ET. *T:* Andover 810458. *Club:* Royal Commonwealth Society.

STEPHENSON, Rt. Hon. Sir John (Frederick Eustace), PC 1971; Kt 1962; a Lord Justice of Appeal, 1971–85; *b* 28 March 1910; 2nd *s* of late Sir Guy Stephenson, CB, and of late Gwendolen, *d* of Rt Hon. J. G. Talbot; *m* 1951, Frances Rose, *yr d* of late Lord Asquith of Bishopstone, PC; two *s* two *d. Educ:* Winchester College (Schol.); New Coll., Oxford (Schol.); Hon. Fellow, 1979. 1st Cl. Hon. Mods. 1930, 1st Cl. Litt Hum. 1932, BA 1932, MA 1956. Called to Bar, Inner Temple (Entrance Scholarship), 1934; Bencher, 1962. Sapper RE (TA), 1938; War Office, 1940; Intelligence Corps, Captain 1943, Major 1944 and Lieut-Col 1946; Middle East and NW Europe; Regional Intelligence Officer, Hamburg, 1946; Recorder of Bridgwater, 1954–59; Recorder of Winchester, 1959–62; Chancellor of the Diocese: of Peterborough, 1956–62; of Winchester, 1958–62; QC 1960; Dep. Chm., Dorset QS, 1962–71; Judge of Queen's Bench Div., High Court of Justice, 1962–71. *Publication:* A Royal Correspondence, 1938. *Address:* 26 Doneraile Street, SW6. *T:* 01–736 6782. *Clubs:* Hurlingham; MCC.

STEPHENSON, Lynne, (Mrs Chaim Stephenson); *see* Banks, L. R.

STEPHENSON, Margaret Maud; *see* Tyzack, M. M.

STEPHENSON, Prof. Patrick Hay, MA, CEng, FIMechE; consultant Mechanical Engineer; research advisor to Institution of Mechanical Engineers; senior industrial advisor to the Design Council; *b* 31 March 1916; *e s* of late Stanley George Stephenson; *m* 1947, Pauline Coupland; two *s* one *d. Educ:* Wyggeston Sch., Leicester; Cambridge Univ. (MA). Apprenticeship and Research Engr, Brit. United Shoe Machinery Co., 1932–39. War Service as Ordnance Mechanical Engr and REME, India and Far East, 1939–45. Chief Mechanical Engr, Pye Ltd, 1949–67; Prof. of Mech. Engrg, Univ. of Strathclyde, 1967–79; Dir, Inst. of Advanced Machine Tool and Control Technology, Min. of Technology, 1967–70; Dir, Birniehill Inst. and Manufacturing Systems Group, DTI, 1970–72; Head of Research Requirements Branch 2, DoI, 1972–77. Mem. Council, IMechE, 1960–68; Member: Bd, UKAC, 1964–73; Engrg Bd, SRC, 1973–. *Publications:* papers and articles in technical press. *Recreations:* music, vintage motoring. *Address:* Toft Lane, Great Wilbraham, Cambridge. *T:* Cambridge 880854. *Clubs:* Army and Navy; Vintage Sports Car.

STEPHENSON, Paul; Senior Liaison Officer, Commission for Racial Equality, since 1980; *b* 6 May 1937; *s* of Olive Stephenson; *m* 1965, Joyce Annikie; one *s* one *d. Educ:* Westhill Coll. of Educn, Selly Oak, Birmingham. MIPR 1978. Youth Tutor, St Paul's, Bristol, 1962–68; Sen. Community Relations Officer, Coventry, 1968–72; National Youth Trng Officer, Community Relations Commn, 1972–77. Chm., Muhammad Ali Sports Develt Assoc., Brixton and Lambeth, 1974–; Member: British Sports Council, 1976–82; Press Council, 1984–. *Recreations:* travel, cinema, reading, international politics. *Address:* 12 Downs Park East, Westbury Park, Bristol. *T:* Bristol 623638.

STEPHENSON, Philip Robert, CMG 1962; OBE 1951; *b* 29 May 1914; *s* of late Robert Barnard Stephenson and Lilian Stephenson (*née* Sharp); *m* 1947, Marianne Hurst Wraith; two *s. Educ:* Berkhamsted School; Imperial College, London; Downing College, Cambridge; Imperial College of Tropical Agriculture, Trinidad. Colonial Agricultural Service, Entomologist, Uganda, 1938. Military Service, 1940–43. East African Anti-Locust Directorate, 1943–47, Director, Desert Locust Survey, 1948–62, HM Overseas Service. Member, British Advisory Mission on Tropical Agriculture in Bolivia, Dept of Technical Co-operation, 1963–64. *Address:* c/o Lloyds Bank, Berkhamsted, Herts. *Club:* MCC.

STEPHENSON, (Robert) Ashley (Shute), MVO 1979; Bailiff of the Royal Parks, since 1980; Gardening Correspondent, The Times, since 1982; *b* 1 Sept. 1927; *s* of late James Stephenson and Agnes Maud Stephenson; *m* 1955, Isabel Dunn; one *s* one *d. Educ:* Walbottle Secondary Sch. Diploma in Horticulture, RHS, Wisley, 1954. Apprenticeship, Newcastle upon Tyne Parks Dept, 1942; served RASC, Palestine and Cyprus, 1946; Landscape Gardener, Donald Ireland Ltd, 1949; Student, RHS's gardens, Wisley, 1952; Royal Parks, 1954–: Supt, Regent's Park, 1969; Supt, Central Royal Parks, 1972. Pres., British Pelargonium and Geranium Soc., 1983–; Member: Cttee, RHS, 1981–; London in Bloom Cttee, English Tourist Bd, 1980–. Contributor to television and radio programmes; gardening correspondent to professional and amateur papers. *Publication:* The Garden Planner, 1981. *Recreations:* sport, judging horticultural shows, natural history, walking. *Address:* Ranger's Lodge, Hyde Park, W2 2UH. *T:* 01–402 7994. *Club:* Arts.

STEPHENSON, Stanley; HM Diplomatic Service, retired; *b* 30 Sept. 1926; *s* of George Stephenson and Margaret Jane (*née* Nicholson); *m* 1957, Grace Claire Lyons; one *s* one *d. Educ:* Bede Sch., Sunderland. Inland Revenue, 1942; Royal Navy, 1944–48; Foreign (later Diplomatic) Service, 1948–: Cairo, Jedda, Damascus, Curaçao, Ciudad Trujillo (now Santo Domingo), San José, Seoul, Santiago de Cuba, Bogotá (twice), Asunción, San Francisco, FCO; Diplomatic Service Inspector, 1978–80; Ambassador to Panama, 1981–83; Consul-Gen., Vancouver, 1983–86. *Recreations:* tennis, cricket, Rugby (non-active!), theatre, gardening. *Address:* Marymount, Raggleswood, Chislehurst, Kent. *Clubs:* Civil Service; Vancouver, Shaughnessy Golf and Country (Vancouver).

STEPHENSON, Air Vice-Marshal Tom Birkett, CB 1982; Assistant Chief of Defence Staff (Signals), 1980–82, retired; *b* 18 Aug. 1926; *s* of Richard and Isabel Stephenson; *m* 1951, Rosemary Patricia (*née* Kaye) (*d* 1984); one *s* three *d. Educ:* Workington Secondary Sch.; Manchester Univ.; Southampton Univ. (DipEl). Commissioned in RAF Engrg Branch, 1945; Staff Coll., 1962; Wing Comdr, Station and Staff appointments, until 1967; Command Electrical Engr, HQASC, 1967–69; Dep. Director Op. Requirements, 1969–72; AOEng, HQ NEAF, 1972–74; RCDS 1975; Director of Signals (Air), 1976–79. *Recreations:* sport, walking, reading. *Address:* c/o National Westminster Bank, 14 Coney Street, York Y01 1YH. *Club:* Royal Air Force.

STEPHENSON, Sir William (Samuel), CC 1980; Kt 1945; MC; DFC and two bars; *b* 1896; *s* of Victor and Christina Stephenson, Canada; *m* 1924, Mary Simmons (*d* 1978). *Educ:* Canada. Served European War, Capt. RFC, 1914–18. Formerly: Personal Representative of Winston Churchill, and Director of British Security Co-ordination in the Western Hemisphere, 1940–46. Patron, CDF Intell. Branch. Hon. Life Mem., Royal Military Inst., Canada. Hon. DSc, Univ. of West Indies, 1950; Hon. DScMil, Royal Military Coll.; Hon. LLD Winnipeg; Hon. DSc Manitoba, 1979; Hon. DSc Winnipeg, 1980. Scholarships established in his name: Univ. of the West Indies, Jamaica; Univ. of Winnipeg, Canada; Bermuda Coll., Bermuda. Croix de Guerre avec Palmes, 1918; French Légion d'Honneur; US Medal for Merit. CC specially invested, in Bermuda, by Governor-Gen. of Canada, 1980. *Relevant publications:* (biography by H. M. Hyde) The Quiet Canadian, 1962 (as Room 3603, in USA); (by William Stevenson): A Man called Intrepid, 1977; Intrepid's Last Case, 1984. *Address:* PO Box 445, Devonshire, Bermuda. *TA:* Inter, Bermuda. *Clubs:* Carlton, Royal Aero; Royal Yacht (Bermuda).

STEPNEY, Area Bishop of; Rt. Rev. James Lawton Thompson; appointed Bishop Suffragan of Stepney, 1978; *b* 11 Aug. 1936; *s* of Bernard Isaac and Marjorie May Thompson; *m* 1965, Sally Patricia Stallworthy; one *s* one *d. Educ:* Dean Close School, Cheltenham; Emmanuel Coll., Cambridge (MA 1964). FCA 1959. 2nd Lt, 3rd Royal Tank Regt, 1960–61. Deacon, 1966; Curate, East Ham, 1966–68; Chaplain, Cuddesdon Coll., Oxford, 1968–71; Rector of Thamesmead and Ecumenical Team Leader, 1971–78. Hon. Fellow, QMC, 1986. *Recreations:* painting, a pony, sport. *Address:* 23 Tredegar Square, E3 5AG. *T:* 01–981 2323.

STEPTOE, Patrick Christopher, FRCSE 1951, FRCOG 1961; Director of Centre for Human Reproduction, Oldham, 1969–79; Medical Director, Bourn Hall Clinic, Bourn, Cambridgeshire, since 1980; *b* 9 June 1913; *s* of Harry Arthur Steptoe and Grace Maud (*née* Minns); *m* 1943, Sheena Macleod Kennedy; one *s* one *d. Educ:* Grammar Sch., Witney; King's Coll., London Univ.; St George's Hosp. Med. Sch. (qual. 1939). MRCS, LRCP; MRCOG 1948. Served War, RNVR, 1939–46: Surg. Lieut, 1939; POW, Italy, 1941–43; seconded to Admiralty, 1943; Surg. Lt-Comdr; demob. 1946. Chief Asst Obstetrician and Gynaecol., St George's Hosp., 1947; Sen. Registrar, Whittington Hosps, 1949; Sen. Obstetrician and Gynaecologist, Oldham Hosps, 1951–78. President: Internat. Fedn of Fertility Socs, 1977–; Brit. Fertility Soc., 1973– (Founder Chm.). Hon. DSc Hull, 1983. Blair Bell Gold Medal, RSM, 1975; Gregory Pincus Award, 1983; Eardley Holland Gold Medal, RCOG, 1985. Commandant du Tastevin de Bourgogne, 1979. *Publications:* Laparoscopy in Gynaecology, 1967; Progress in Fertility, 1976; (contrib.) Recent Advances in Obstetrics and Gynaecology, 1977; A Matter of Life, 1980; contributor, author and jt author of papers in Lancet, Jl of Reprodn, Annals of RSM, and Brit. Med. Bull. (inc. 'In vitro fertilization of human ova'). *Recreations:* music, travel, wine, sailing. *Address:* 38 Caxton End, Bourn, Cambridge.

STERLING, Sir Jeffrey (Maurice), Kt 1985; CBE 1977; Chairman, Peninsular & Oriental Steam Navigation Company, since 1983; Special Adviser to Secretary of State for Trade and Industry, since 1983; *b* 27 Dec. 1934; *s* of Harry and Alice Sterling; *m* 1985, Dorothy Ann Smith; one *d. Educ:* Reigate Grammar Sch.; Preston Manor County Sch.; Guildhall School of Music. Paul Schweder & Co. (Stock Exchange), 1957–63; Fin. Dir, General Guarantee Corp., 1963–64; Man. Dir, Gula Investments Ltd, 1964–69; Chm., Sterling Guarantee Trust plc, 1969–85, when it merged with P&O Steam Navigation Co. Member: British Airways Bd, 1979–82; Bd, European Ferries, 1985–. Special Advr to Sec. of State for Industry, 1982–83. Mem. Exec., 1966–, Chm. Organisation Cttee, 1969–73, World ORT Union; Chm., ORT Technical Services, 1974–; Vice-Pres., British ORT, 1978–. Dep. Chm. and Hon. Treasurer, London Celebrations Cttee, Queen's Silver Jubilee, 1975–83. Chm., Young Vic Co., 1975–83; Chm., of the Governors, Royal Ballet Sch., 1983–; Gov., Royal Ballet, 1986–; Vice-Chm. and Chm. of the Exec., Motability, 1977–. *Recreations:* music, swimming, tennis. *Address:* 17 Brompton Square, SW3. *Clubs:* Garrick, Carlton, Hurlingham.

STERN, Isaac; violinist; *b* Kreminiecz, Russia, 21 July 1920; *s* of Solomon and Clara Stern; *m* 1948, Nora Kaye; *m* 1951, Vera Lindenblit; three *c.* Studied San Francisco Conservatory, 1930–37. First public concert as guest artist San Francisco Symphony Orchestra, 1934; played with Los Angeles Philharmonic Orchestra and in concerts in Pacific Coast cities; New York début, 1937. Has since played in concerts throughout USA, in Europe, Israel, Australia, South America, Japan, China, India, The Philippines, Soviet Union and Iceland; has played with major American and European orchestras. Took part in Prades Festivals, 1950–52; Edinburgh and other major festivals in Europe and US. Film, Mao to Mozart: Isaac Stern in China (Best Full-length Documentary Acad. Award, 1981). Chm., America-Israel Cultural Foundn, NY, 1964–; President, Carnegie Hall, NY, 1960–. Hon. Degrees from Univs of Columbia, Johns Hopkins, Dalhousie, Brown, and San Francisco Conservatory of Music. Albert Schweitzer Music Award, 1975; Kennedy Center Honor, 1984. Officer, Légion d'Honneur. *Address:* c/o ICM Artists Ltd, 40 West 57th Street, New York, NY 10019, USA.

STERN, Prof. Joseph Peter Maria, PhD, LittD; Professor of German, University of London, and Head of Department, University College, 1972–86; *b* 25 Dec. 1920; *s* of Gustav Stern and Louisa (*née* Bondy); *m* 1944, Sheila Frances (*née* McMullan); two *s* two *d. Educ:* Czech schs in Prague and Vienna; Barry County Sch. for Boys, Glam; St John's Coll., Cambridge (MA 1947, PhD 1949, LittD 1975). Wartime service in Czech Army and RAF (VR). Asst Lectr, Bedford Coll., London, 1950–52; Asst Lectr, then Lectr, Cambridge Univ., 1952–72; Fellow, St John's Coll., Cambridge, 1954–72 (Tutor, 1963–70, 1972); Chm. of Bd, Germanic Languages and Literature, Univ. of London, 1978–79; Hon. Dir, Inst. of Germanic Studies, Univ. of London, 1981–85. Prof.-at-Large, Cornell Univ., Ithaca, NY, 1976–82. Vis. Professor: City Coll. of New York, 1958; Univ. of Calif at Berkeley, 1964 and 1967; State Univ. of NY at Buffalo, 1969; Univ. of Va, Charlottesville, 1971. Merton Prof., Univ. of Göttingen, 1965; Bernhard Vis. Prof., Williams Coll., Williamstown, Mass, 1986–87. Fellow, Center for Humanities, Wesleyan Univ., 1972. Lewis Fry Meml Lectr, Univ. of Bristol, 1973; British Academy Master Mind Lectr, 1978. Goethe Medal, Goethe Inst., 1980; Alexander von Humboldt Research Prize, 1980. *Publications:* Ernst Jünger: a writer of our time, 1952; (trans.) R. W. Meyer, Leibnitz and the seventeenth-century revolution, 1952; (trans.) H.-E. Holthusen, R. M. Rilke: a study of his later poetry, 1952; G. C. Lichtenberg: a doctrine of scattered occasions, 1959; Re-Interpretations: seven studies in nineteenth-century German literature, 1964, repr. 1981; (ed) Arthur Schnitzler: Liebelei, Leutnant Gustl, and Die letzten Masken, 1966; Idylls and Realities: studies in nineteenth-century German literature, 1971; On Realism, 1973, rev. German version, 1982; Hitler: the Führer and the People, 1975 (2nd edn 1984, rev. German version 1978, French trans. rev. by S. F. Stern, 1985); Nietzsche (Fontana Modern Masters), 1978; A Study of Nietzsche, 1979, rev. German version, 1982; (with Michael Silk) Nietzsche on Tragedy, 1981; (ed) The World of Franz Kafka, 1981; (ed) London German Studies II, 1984, III, 1986; (ed) Paths and Labyrinths: a Kafka symposium, 1985; contribs (incl. 42 Poems from the Czech, trans. with S. F. Stern) and articles in English and foreign jls and newspapers. *Address:* 83 Barton Road, Cambridge CB3 9LL. *T:* Cambridge 353078.

STERN, Michael Charles, FCA; MP (C) Bristol North West, since 1983; *b* 3 Aug. 1942; *s* of late Maurice Leonard Stern and of Rose Stern; *m* 1976, Jillian Denise Aldridge; one *d.*

Educ: Christ's College Grammar School, Finchley. Mem. ICA 1964; FCA 1969. Partner, Percy Phillips & Co., Accountants, 1964–80; Partner, Halpern & Woolf, Chartered Accountants, 1980–. Chm., The Bow Group, 1977–78; contested (C) Derby South, 1979; coopted Mem., Educn Cttee, Borough of Ealing, 1980–83. *Publications:* papers for the Bow Group. *Recreations:* fell walking, bridge, chess. *Address:* House of Commons, SW1. *Clubs:* United and Cecil, Millbank, London Mountaineering.

STERN, Prof. Nicholas Herbert; Professor of Economics, London School of Economics and Political Science, since 1986; *b* 22 April 1946; *s* of Adalbert Stern and Marion Fatima Stern; *m* 1968, Susan Ruth (*née* Chesterton); two *s* one *d. Educ:* Peterhouse, Cambridge (BA Mathematics); Nuffield Coll., Oxford (DPhilEcon). Jun. Res. Fellow, The Queen's Coll., Oxford, 1969–70; Fellow/Tutor in Econs, St Catherine's Coll., and Univ. Lectr, Oxford, 1970–77; Prof. of Econs, Univ. of Warwick, 1978–85. Research Associate/Vis. Professor: MIT, 1972; Ecole Polytech., 1977; Indian Statistical Inst. (Overseas Vis. Fellow of British Acad., 1974–75, and Ford Foundn Vis. Prof., 1981–82). Fellow, Econometric Soc., 1978. Editor, Journal of Public Economics, 1980–. *Publications:* An Appraisal of Tea Production on Smallholdings in Kenya, 1972; (ed jtly) Theories of Economic Growth, 1973; (jtly) Crime, the Police and Criminal Statistics, 1979; (jtly) Palanpur: the economy of an Indian village, 1982; (jtly) The Theory of Taxation for Developing Countries, 1987; articles in Rev. of Econ. Studies, Jl of Public Econs, Jl of Develt Econs, and others. *Recreations:* reading novels, watching sport. *Address:* London School of Economics, Houghton Street, WC2A 2AE. *T:* 01–405 7686.

STERN, Vivien Helen; Director, National Association for the Care and Resettlement of Offenders (NACRO), since 1977; *b* 25 Sept. 1941; *d* of Frederick Stern and Renate Mills. *Educ:* Kent Coll., Pembury, Kent; Bristol Univ. (BA, MLitt, CertEd). Lectr in Further Educn until 1970; Community Relations Commn, 1970–77. Member: Special Programmes Bd, Manpower Services Commn, 1980–82; Youth Training Bd, 1982–; Gen. Adv. Council, IBA, 1982–; Cttee on the Prison Disciplinary System, 1984–85. Vis. Fellow, Nuffield Coll., Oxford, 1984–. *Address:* National Association for the Care and Resettlement of Offenders, 169 Clapham Road, SW9.

STERNBERG, Sir Sigmund, Kt 1976; JP; Chairman: CRU Holdings, since 1983; Martin Slowe Estates Ltd, since 1971; Director: Commodities Research Unit Ltd, since 1975; Commodities Research Unit (Holdings) Ltd, since 1978; Lloyds Underwriter, since 1969; *b* Budapest, 2 June 1921; *s* of Abraham and Elizabeth Sternberg; *m* 1970, Hazel (*née* Everett Jones); two *s* two *d.* Served War of 1939–45, Civil Defence Corps. Former Ring-Dealing Mem., London Metal Exchange. Co-Chm., Arbitration Cttee, Bureau Internat. de la Récupération, 1966. Instituted Res. Gp for Labour Shadow Cabinet, 1973–74; Econ. and Industry Cttee, Fabian Soc., 1976 (Chm., Appeals Cttee, 1975–77); Dep. Chm., Labour Finance and Industry Gp. Chm., St Charles Gp, HMC, 1974; NW Metrop. RHB, 1974; Member: Camden and Islington AHA, 1974–77; Gen. Purposes Cttee, NAMH, 1972; Vice-President: Coll. of Speech Therapists; Association for all Speech Impaired Children; Chm., Inst. for Archaeo-Metallurgical Studies. Pres., VOCAL (Voluntary Organisation Communications and Language); Hon. Treasurer and Chm. of Friends, CRUSE National Org. for the Widowed and their Children; Hon. Treasurer, Council of Christians and Jews; Chm., Internat. Council of Christians and Jews; Co-Chm., Friends of Keston Coll. Mem., Board of Deputies of British Jews; Chm., Function Cttee, Inst. of Jewish Affairs; Governor, Hebrew Univ. of Jerusalem; Chm., Friends of Oxford Centre of Post-grad. Hebrew Studies; Mem. Bd of Management, Spiro Inst; Trustee, Manor House Trust (Sternberg Centre for Judaism), 1984–. Speaker Chm., Rotary Club of London, 1980–83. Mem., Court, Essex Univ. Liveryman, Co. of Horners; Freeman, City of London. JP Middlesex, 1965 (Middlesex Probation (Case) Cttee, 1973). Hon. FRSM 1981. Brotherhood Award, Nat. Conf. of Christians and Jews Inc., 1980; Silver Pontifical Medal, 1986. KCSG 1985. *Recreations:* golf, swimming. *Address:* 31 Mount Pleasant, WC1X 0AD. *T:* 01–278 0414. *Telex* 264008. *Clubs:* Reform, City Livery.

STERNE, Laurence Henry Gordon, MA; *b* 2 July 1916; *o s* of late Henry Herbert Sterne and late Hilda Davey; *m* 1944, Katharine Clover; two *d. Educ:* Culford Sch.; Jesus Coll. (Open Exhibnr and Hon. Schol.), Oxford (MA). Royal Aircraft Establishment: Structures and Mechanical Engrg Depts, 1940; Aerodynamics Dept, 1949; Head of Naval Air Dept, 1954; Chief Supt at Bedford, 1955. Prof. and Dir, von Karman Inst., Rhode Saint Genèse, Belgium, 1958–62; Aviation Mem., Research Policy Staff, MoD, 1962–64; Dir, Royal Naval Aircraft and Helicopters, 1964–68; Dep. Dir, Nat. Engineering Lab., E Kilbride, 1968–77. Vis. Prof., Strathclyde Univ., 1971–76. *Publications:* reports and memoranda of Aeronautical Research Council; ed jtly, early vols of Progress in Aeronautical Sciences. *Recreation:* gardening. *Address:* 10 Trinity Street, Bungay, Suffolk NR35 1EH.

STEVAS, Norman Antony Francis St J.; *see* St John-Stevas.

STEVEN, Stewart; Editor, The Mail on Sunday, since 1982; *b* 30 Sept. 1938; *s* of Rudolph and Trude Steven; *m* 1965, Inka Sobieniewska; one *s. Educ:* Mayfield Coll., Sussex. Political Reporter, Central Press Features, 1961–63; Political Correspondent, Western Daily Press, 1963–64; Daily Express: Political Reporter, 1964–65; Diplomatic Correspondent, 1965–67; Foreign Editor, 1967–72; Daily Mail: Asst Editor, 1972–74; Associate Editor, 1974–82. *Publications:* Operation Splinter-Factor, 1974; The Spymasters of Israel, 1976; The Poles, 1982. *Recreations:* travel, skiing, writing. *Address:* Carmelite House, Carmelite Street, EC4Y 0JA. *T:* 01–353 6000.

STEVENS, Air Marshal Sir Alick (Charles), KBE 1952; CB 1944; retired; *b* 31 July 1898; *s* of late Charles Edward Russell Stevens, Jersey; *m* 1927, Beryl, *d* of B. J. Gates, Wing, Bucks; one *s. Educ:* Victoria College, Jersey. Joined RNAS 1916; transferred to RAF on formation, 1918; Wing Comdr, 1937; Air Commodore, 1942. Dep. Director, 1940–42, and then Director of Operations (Naval Co-operation) at Air Ministry, 1942–43; SASO, No 18 Group, 1943–44 (despatches); AOC, RAF, Gibraltar, 1944–45; AOC No 47 Group, 1945; AOC No 4 Group, Transport Command, 1946; Air Vice-Marshal, 1947; AOC No 22 Group, Technical Training Comd, 1946–48; AOC British Forces, Aden, 1948–50; SASO, Coastal Comd, 1950–51; AOC-in-C, Coastal Comd, 1951–53; Air C-in-C, Eastern Atlantic Area, Atlantic Comd, 1952–53; Allied Maritime Air C-in-C Channel and Southern North Sea, Channel Comd, 1952–53; retd Dec. 1953; Vice-Chairman, Gloucestershire T&AFA, 1955–63. *Address:* Cherry Tree Cottage, Cadmore End, near High Wycombe, Bucks HP14 3PT. *T:* High Wycombe 881569. *Club:* Royal Air Force.

STEVENS, Anthony John; Director, Veterinary Laboratories, Ministry of Agriculture, Fisheries and Food, 1979–86; *b* 29 July 1926; *s* of John Walker Stevens and Hilda Stevens; *m* 1954, Patricia Frances, *d* of Robert Gill, Ponteland; one *s* two *d. Educ:* Liverpool and Manchester Univs; Magdalene Coll., Cambridge. MA, BVSc, MRCVS, DipBact. Veterinary Investigation Officer, Cambridge, 1956–65; Animal Health Expert for UNO, 1959–63; Suptg Veterinary Investigation Officer, Leeds, 1965–68; Ministry of Agriculture, Fisheries and Food: Dep. Dir, Central Vet. Lab., 1968–71; Asst Chief Vet. Officer, 1971–73; Dep. Chief Vet. Officer, 1973–78. External Examr, Dublin, Liverpool and Edinburgh Univs., 1964–70. Past Pres., Veterinary Research Club. FRSA. *Publications:* UN/FAO Manual of Diagnostic Techniques; regular contributor to Veterinary Record, etc. *Recreations:* industrial archaeology particularly canals, riding, and all forms of livestock. *Address:* Marigold Cottage, Great Halfpenny Farm, Guildford, Surrey. *T:* Guildford 65375.

STEVENS, (Arthur) Edwin, CBE 1979; *b* 17 Oct. 1905; *s* of Arthur Edwin Stevens and Bessie Annie (*née* Dowden); *m* 1933, Kathleen Alberta James; three *s. Educ:* West Monmouth Sch.; University Coll., Cardiff (BSc Hons 1927; Hon. Fellow 1981); Jesus Coll., Oxford (MA Hons 1929). FInstP 1937. Founder, Amplivox Ltd: Chm. and Man. Dir, 1935–75; designed world's first wearable electronic hearing aid, 1935; collector of world's most comprehensive exhibn of aids to hearing covering 400 yrs. Hon. Fellow, Jesus Coll., Oxford, 1973; financed building of Stevens Close, Jesus Coll. Hall of Residence opened by the Queen, 1976; founded RSM Edwin Stevens Lectures for Laity, 1970; Hon. FRSM 1981. Hon. LLD Wales, 1984. *Recreations:* golf, gardening. *Address:* Penates, Littleworth Common Road, Esher, Surrey. *T:* Esher 64829.

See also D. R. Stevens.

STEVENS, David Robert; Chairman: United Newspapers plc, since 1981 (Director, since 1974); Express Newspapers, since 1985; Chairman and Chief Executive, MIM Britannia Ltd (formerly Montagu Investment Management Ltd), since 1980; *b* 26 May 1936; *s* of (Arthur) Edwin Stevens, *qv*; *m* 1977, Melissa, Countess Andrassy; one *s* one *d. Educ:* Stowe Sch.; Sidney Sussex Coll., Cambridge (MA Hons Econ). Management Trainee, Elliott Automation, 1959; Director: Hill Samuel Securities, 1959–68; Drayton Group, 1968–74. Chairman: City & Foreign, 1976–; Drayton Far East, 1976–; English & International, 1976–; Dualvest, 1979–; Consolidated Venture (formerly Montagu Boston), 1979–; Triplevest, 1979–; Drayton Consolidated, 1980–; Drayton Japan, 1980–. Chm., EDC for Civil Engrg, 1984–. *Recreation:* golf. *Address:* 11 Devonshire Square, EC2M 4YR. *Clubs:* White's; Sunningdale Golf.

STEVENS, Prof. Denis William, CBE 1984; President and Artistic Director, Accademia Monteverdiana, since 1961; *b* 2 March 1922; *s* of William J. Stevens and Edith Driver; *m* 1st, 1949, Sheila Elizabeth Holloway; two *s* one *d*; 2nd, 1975, Leocadia Elzbieta Kwasny. *Educ:* Royal Grammar Sch., High Wycombe; Jesus College, Oxford. Served War of 1939–45, RAF Intelligence, India and Burma, 1942–46. Producer, BBC Music Div., 1949–54; Assoc. Founder and Conductor, Ambrosian Singers, 1952; Vis. Professor of Musicology, Cornell Univ., 1955, Columbia Univ., 1956; Secretary, Plainsong and Mediaeval Music Soc., 1958–63; Editor, Grove's Dictionary of Music and Musicians, 1959–63. Professor, Royal Acad. of Music, 1960. Vis. Prof. Univ. of California (Berkeley), 1962; Dist. Vis. Prof., Pennsylvania State Univ., 1962–63; Prof. of Musicology, Columbia Univ., 1964–76; Vis. Prof. Univ. of California (Santa Barbara), 1974–75; Brechemin Dist. Vis. Prof., Univ. of Washington, Seattle, 1976; Vis. Prof., Univ. of Michigan, Ann Arbor, 1977, San Diego State Univ., 1978. Lectures on music, especially British, in England, France, Germany, Italy, USA; concerts, conducting own and ancillary ensembles at internat. festivals in GB, Europe and USA; TV and radio programmes in Europe and N America; cons. for films. FSA; Member Worshipful Company of Musicians. Hon. RAM, 1960. Hon.D, Humane Letters, Fairfield Univ., Connecticut, 1967. *Publications:* The Mulliner Book, 1952; Thomas Tomkins, 1957, rev. edn 1966; A History of Song, 1960, rev. edn, 1971; Tudor Church Music, 1966; A Treasury of English Church Music (I), 1965; (ed) First and Second Penguin Book of English Madrigals, 1967, 1971; Early Tudor Organ Music (II), 1969; Music in Honour of St Thomas of Canterbury, 1970; Monteverdi: sacred, secular and occasional music, 1978; Musicology: a practical guide, 1980; The Letters of Monteverdi, 1980; Renaissance Dialogues, 1981; The Worcester Fragments, 1981; many edns of early music, including Monteverdi Vespers and Orfeo; choral works by Gabrieli, Lassus, Machaut, Tallis, Tomkins; articles in English and foreign journals; also many stereo recordings ranging from plainsong to Beethoven. *Recreations:* travel, photography. *Club:* Garrick.

STEVENS, Edwin; *see* Stevens, A. E.

STEVENS, Frank Leonard; formerly Editor, FBI Review and Publicity Officer, Federation of British Industries; *b* Mexborough, 8 Jan. 1898; *s* of late Frederick Thomas Stevens; *m* 1925, Winifred, 2nd *d* of Alexander Bruce, JP; two *s. Educ:* Mexborough Grammar School; University College, London. After a year as teacher, three years in the Army (1916–19), entered journalism, South Yorkshire Times, Allied Newspapers, Manchester; Manchester Evening News; assistant editor, John O' London's Weekly; Daily News sub-editorial staff; associate editor, Everyman; joint editor, monthly Clarion. *Publications:* Through Merrie England, 1926; On Going to Press, 1928; Under London, 1939. *Recreations:* reading, sketching. *Address:* Barn Cottage, Singleton, Chichester, West Sussex. *T:* Singleton 653.

STEVENS, Handley Michael Gambrell; Under Secretary, International Aviation, Department of Transport (formerly at Department of Trade), since 1983; *b* 29 June 1941; *s* of Ernest Norman Stevens and Kathleen Emily Gambrell; *m* 1966, Anne Frances Ross; three *d. Educ:* The Leys Sch., Cambridge; Phillips Acad., Andover, Mass (E-SU schol.); King's Coll., Cambridge (BA). Translator, Chrysler Internat., 1963; joined Foreign Office, 1964; Third, later Second, Sec., Kuala Lumpur, 1966; Asst Private Sec. to the Lord Privy Seal, 1970; Principal: CSD, 1971; DTI, 1973; Asst Sec., Dept of Trade, 1976. *Recreations:* music, hill walking, travel. *Address:* 13 Powis Square, Brighton, Sussex. *T:* Brighton 26928.

STEVENS, Jocelyn Edward Greville; Rector and Vice-Provost, Royal College of Art, since 1984; *b* 14 Feb. 1932; *s* of Major C. G. B. Stewart-Stevens and of Mrs Greville Stevens; *m* 1956, Jane Armyne Sheffield (marr. diss. 1979); two *s* two *d. Educ:* Eton; Cambridge. Military service in Rifle Bde, 1950–52; Journalist, Hulton Press Ltd, 1955–56; Chairman and Managing Dir, Stevens Press Ltd, and Editor of Queen Magazine, 1957–68; Personal Asst to Chairman of Beaverbrook Newspapers, May-Dec. 1968; Director, 1971–81; Managing Director: Evening Standard Co. Ltd, 1969–72; Daily Express, 1972–74; Beaverbrook Newspapers, 1974–77; Express Newspapers, 1977–81 (Dep. Chm. and Man. Dir); Editor and Publisher, The Magazine, 1982–84; Dir, Centaur Communications, 1982–84. FRSA 1984. *Address:* Testbourne, Longparish, near Andover, Hants. *T:* Longparish 232. *Clubs:* Buck's, Beefsteak, White's.

STEVENS, Prof. John Edgar, CBE 1980; PhD; FBA 1975; President of Magdalene College, Cambridge, since 1983, Fellow since 1950; Professor of Medieval and Renaissance English, University of Cambridge, since 1978; *b* 8 Oct. 1921; *s* of William Charles James and Fanny Stevens; *m* 1946, Charlotte Ethel Mary (*née* Somner); two *s* two *d. Educ:* Christ's Hospital, Horsham; Magdalene College, Cambridge (Schol.; MA, PhD). Served Royal Navy; Temp. Lieut RNVR. Cambridge University: Bye-Fellow 1948, Research Fellow 1950, Fellow 1953 and Tutor 1958–74, Magdalene Coll.; Univ. Lectr in English, 1954–74; Reader in English and Musical History, 1974–78. *Publications:* Medieval Carols (Musica Britannica vol. 4), 1952, 2nd edn 1958; Music and Poetry in the Early Tudor Court, 1961; Music at the Court of Henry VIII (Musica Britannica vol 18), 1962, 2nd edn 1969; (with Richard Axton) Medieval French Plays, 1971; Medieval Romance,

1973; Early Tudor Songs & Carols (Musica Britannica vol. 36), 1975; Words and Music in the Middle Ages, 1986. *Recreations:* viol-playing, sailing, bricklaying. *Address:* 4 & 5 Bell's Court, Cambridge.

STEVENS, Vice-Adm. Sir John (Felgate), KBE 1955 (CBE 1945); CB 1951; *b* 1 June 1900; *o* surv. *s* of late Henry Marshall Stevens, Droveway Corner, Hove; *m* 1928, Mary, *o d* of J. Harry Gilkes, JP, Wychcote, Patcham, Sussex; one *s* two *d*. Midshipman, 1918; King's Coll., Cambridge, 1922, specialised in Navigation, 1924; Staff College, 1930; Commander, 1933; Captain, 1940. Served War of 1939–45 (despatches, CBE); Director of Plans, Admiralty, 1946–47; commanded HMS Implacable, 1948–49; Rear-Admiral, 1949; Director of Naval Training, 1949–50; Chief of Staff to Head of British Joint Services Mission, Washington, 1950–52; Flag Officer, Home Fleet Training Squadron, 1952–53; Commander-in-Chief, America and West Indies Station, and Deputy Supreme Allied Commander, Atlantic, 1953–55; retired list, 1956. *Address:* Withy Springs, Petworth Road, Haslemere, Surrey. *T:* Haslemere 2970. *Club:* Naval and Military.

STEVENS, Hon. John Paul; Associate Justice, Supreme Court of the United States, since 1975; *b* 20 April 1920; *s* of Ernest James Stevens and Elizabeth Stevens (*née* Street); *m* 1st, 1942, Elizabeth Jane Sheeren; one *s* three *d*; 2nd, 1979, Maryan Mulholland Simon. *Educ:* Univ. of Chicago (AB 1941); Northwestern Univ. (JD 1947). Served War, USNR, 1942–45 (Bronze Star). Law Clerk to US Supreme Ct Justice Wiley Rutledge, 1947–48; Associate, Poppenhusen, Johnston, Thompson & Raymond, 1948–50; Associate Counsel, sub-cttee on Study Monopoly Power, Cttee on Judiciary, US House of Reps, 1951; Partner, Rothschild, Hart, Stevens & Barry, 1952–70; US Circuit Judge, 1970–75. Lectr, anti-trust law, Northwestern Univ. Sch. of Law, 1953; Univ. of Chicago Law Sch., 1954–55; Mem., Attorney-Gen.'s Nat. Cttee to study Anti-Trust Laws, 1953–55. Mem., Chicago Bar Assoc. (2nd Vice-Pres. 1970). Order of Coif, Phi Beta Kappa, Psi Upsilon, Phi Delta Phi. *Publications:* chap. in book, Mr Justice (ed Dunham and Kurland); contrib. to Antitrust Developments: a supp. to Report of Attorney-Gen.'s Nat. Cttee to Study the Anti-trust Laws, 1955–68; various articles etc, in Ill. Law Rev., Proc. confs, and reports. *Recreations:* flying, tennis, bridge, reading, travel. *Address:* Supreme Court of the United States, Washington, DC 20543, USA.

STEVENS, John Williams; Principal Establishments and Finance Officer, Cabinet Office, since 1980; *b* 27 Feb. 1929; *s* of John Williams and Kathleen Stevens; *m* 1949, Grace Stevens; one *s* one *d*. *Educ:* St Ives School. Min. of Supply, 1952; UK Defence Res. and Supply Staff, Australia, 1958–61; HM Treasury, 1966; Civil Service Dept, 1969–73; Price Commn, 1973–74; Head of Personnel, Stock Exchange, 1975–76; Principal Private Sec. to Lord Pres. of the Council and Leader of the House of Commons, 1977–79, to Chancellor of Duchy of Lancaster and Leader of the House, 1979–80; Under Sec. 1984. *Recreations:* Cornwall, reading, theatre. *Address:* 14 Highbury Crescent, Camberley, Surrey. *T:* Camberley 23571.

STEVENS, Kenneth Henry, CBE 1983; Chief Executive Commissioner, The Scout Association, since 1970; *b* 8 Oct. 1922; *s* of late Horace J. Stevens, CBE, sometime Senior Principal Inspector of Taxes, and late Nora Stevens (*née* Kauntze); *m* 1947, Yvonne Grace Ruth (*née* Mitchell); one *s* one *d*. *Educ:* Brighton Coll.; Brighton Technical Coll. South Coast Civil Defence, 1941–44. Alliance Assurance Co., 1944–47; Asst Dir of Adult Leader Training, Internat. Scout Training Centre, Gilwell Park, Chingford, 1947–56; Organising Comr, World Scout Jamboree, Indaba and Rover Moot, Sutton Coldfield, 1956–58; Dep. Dir of Adult Leader Training, Internat. Scout Training Centre, 1958–61; Asst Chief Exec. Comr, The Scout Assoc., 1961–63; Dep. Chief Exec. Comr, 1963–70. FBIM. *Publication:* Ceremonies of The Scout Movement, 1958. *Recreations:* motoring, gardening. *Address:* 69 Ashley Road, Epsom, Surrey. *T:* Epsom 25031. *Club:* MCC.

STEVENS, Prof. Kenneth William Harry; Professor of Theoretical Physics, University of Nottingham since 1958; *b* 17 Sept. 1922; *s* of Harry and Rose Stevens; *m* 1949, Audrey A. Gawthrop; one *s* one *d*. *Educ:* Magdalen College School, Oxford; Jesus and Merton Colleges, Oxford. MA 1947, DPhil 1949. Pressed Steel Company Ltd Research Fellow, Oxford University, 1949–53; Research Fellow, Harvard University, 1953–54; Reader in Theoretical Physics, University of Nottingham, 1953–58. Mem., IUPHP Commn on Magnetism, 1984. (Jointly) Maxwell Medal and Prize, 1968. *Publications:* contrib. to learned journals. *Recreations:* music, tennis. *Address:* The University, Nottingham.

STEVENS, Sir Laurence (Houghton), Kt 1983; CBE 1979; company director and business consultant; *b* 9 Jan. 1920; *s* of Laurence Stevens and Annie (*née* Houghton); *m* 1943, Beryl J. Dickson; one *s* two *d*. *Educ:* Auckland Boys' Grammar Sch.; Auckland Univ. (BCom). FCA NZ 1969; CMA 1966. Served War, Pacific (Tonga Defence Force) and ME (2NZEF). Joined Auckland Knitting Mills Ltd, 1946; Man. Dir, 1952; retd 1980. Chairman: Thorn EMI Gp of Cos, NZ, 1980–; Les Mills Fitness Ltd, 1985–; Capital Markets Ltd, 1986–; Director: Guardian Royal Exchange, 1983–; Wormald International NZ Ltd, 1983–; Reserve Bank of New Zealand, 1978–; Petroleum Corp. of New Zealand Ltd, 1984–; R. W. Saunders Ltd, 1984–; Petralgas Chemicals NZ Ltd, 1986–. Past President and Life Member: NZ Knitting Industries Fedn; Textile and Garment Fedn of NZ; Auckland Manufrs' Assoc.; Pres., NZ Manufrs' Fedn, 1970–71 and 1980–81; Chm., Auckland Agricl, Pastoral and Indust. Shows Bd, 1976–86; Mem., Melanesian Trust Bd, 1977–. *Recreation:* tennis (Pres., Auckland Lawn Tennis Assoc., 1983–84). *Address:* 1/1 Watene Crescent, Orakei, Auckland 5, New Zealand. *T:* Auckland 546–672. *Club:* Northern (Auckland).

STEVENS, Lewis David, MBE 1982; MP (C) Nuneaton, since 1983; *b* 13 April 1936; *s* of Richard and Winnifred Stevens; *m* 1959, Margaret Eileen Gibson; two *s* one *d*. *Educ:* Oldbury Grammar Sch.; Liverpool Univ.; Lanchester Coll. RAF 1956–58. Various engrg cos, mainly in industrial engrg and production management positions, 1958–79; management and industrial engrg consultant (self-employed), 1979–. Mem., Nuneaton Borough Council, 1966–72. *Address:* 151 Sherbourne Avenue, Nuneaton, Warwicks CV10 9JN. *T:* Chapel End 396105.

STEVENS, Norman Anthony, ARA 1983; artist (painter/printmaker); *b* 17 June 1937; *s* of Stanley Whitmore Stevens and Elsie May Whitehead; *m* 1961, Jean Mary Warhurst; one *s* one *d*. *Educ:* Bradford Regional Coll. of Art (NDD 1957); RCA (ARCA 1960). Lecturer in Fine Art Departments of: Manchester Polytechnic, 1960–66; Maidstone Coll. of Art, 1966–71; Middlesex Polytechnic, 1971–73; Gregory Fellow (Painting), Univ. of Leeds, 1974–75. Works in the collections of: Tate Gall.; Arts Council of GB; Arts Council NI; V & A Mus.; Govt Art Collection; Bradford City Art Gall.; Leeds City Art Gall.; Carlisle City Art Gall.; Rochdale City Art Gall.; British Council; British Museum; Nat. Trust; Mus. of Modern Art, NY; Musée d'Art et d'Histoire, Geneva; AT&T, Chicago; Yale Univ.; European Parlt. *Address:* 10 Rugby Mansions, Bishop King's Road, W14. *T:* 01–603 0321.

STEVENS, Philip Theodore; Professor of Greek in the University of London (Bedford College), 1950–74, now Emeritus; *b* 11 Nov. 1906; *s* of late Rev. Herbert Stevens, Vicar of Milwich; *m* 1939, Evelyn Grace, 2nd *d* of late G. L. Crickmay, FRIBA, Oatlands Park, Weybridge, Surrey; one *s*. *Educ:* Wolverhampton Grammar School; New Coll., Oxford (Scholar; 1st Cl. Hon. Mods, 1927; 2nd Cl. Lit. Hum., 1929); PhD Aberdeen, 1939. Asst Master, Liverpool Institute, 1929–30; Tutor at Univ. Corresp. Coll., Cambridge, 1930–32; Asst Lecturer in Greek, Univ. of Aberdeen, 1933–38; Lectr in Classics, Univ. of Cape Town, 1938–41. War Service, S African Mil. Intelligence, 1941–45. Lecturer in Latin and Greek, University of Liverpool, 1945–50. Trustee, Hellenic Soc., 1961–. *Publications:* Euripides, Andromache, 1971; Colloquial Expressions in Euripides, 1976; The Society for the Promotion of Hellenic Studies 1879–1979, 1979; contribs to English and foreign classical periodicals. *Recreation:* music. *Address:* Baywell Cottage, Charlbury, Oxon. *Club:* Reform.

STEVENS, Richard William, RDI 1973; BSc; FSIAD, FCIBS; Chartered Designer; *b* 1 Oct. 1924; *s* of William Edward Stevens and Caroline Alice (*née* Mills); *m* 1947, Anne Clara Hammond; one *s* one *d*. *Educ:* Dorking County Grammar Sch.; Regent St Polytechnic (BSc). FSIAD 1960, FCIBS 1977. Designer, then Chief Designer, Atlas Lighting Ltd, 1954–63; Industrial Design Manager, Standard Telephones and Cables Ltd, 1963–69; Design Manager, Post Office Telecommunications (later British Telecom), 1969–83. Pres., SIAD, 1972–73; Treasurer, ICSID, 1975–77. Gold Medal, Milan Triennale, 1957; three Design Centre Awards, London. *Recreations:* gardening, music, photography, walking. *Address:* Hazel Cottage, Ewood Lane, Newdigate, Dorking, Surrey RH5 5AR. *Club:* Arts.

STEVENS, Dr Siaka (Probyn), Hon. GCMG 1980; First Prime Minister and First Executive President, Republic of Sierra Leone, 1971–85; elected Secretary-General of All People's Congress (ruling party), 1979; *b* 24 Aug. 1905; *m* 1940, Rebecca Stevens; seven *s* five *d*. *Educ:* Albert Academy, Freetown; Ruskin Coll., Oxford. Joined Sierra Leone Police Force, 1923, and became 1st Cl. Sergt and Musketry Instr; worked for Sierra Leone Development Co., and became first Gen. Sec. of United Mine Workers Union (co-founder), 1931–46. Member: Moyamba Dist Council; Freetown City Council (rep. Protectorate Assembly); several Govt Cttees, 1946–48; Sec., Sierra Leone TUC, 1948–50; MLC (elec. by Assembly), 1951, and first Minister of Lands, Mines and Labour; Dep. Leader of (the now dissolved) Peoples' National Party, 1958–60; formed Election before Independence Movement (which later became the All Peoples' Congress), 1960; Leader of the Opposition, All Peoples' Congress, 1962; Mayor of Freetown, 1964; sworn in as Prime Minister of Sierra Leone in 1967, re-appointed 1968. Chm., OAU, 1980–81. Hon. DCL Univ. of Sierra Leone, 1969; Hon. DLitt Lincoln Univ., USA, 1979. *Recreation:* walking.

STEVENS, Prof. Thomas Stevens, FRS 1963; FRSE 1964; Emeritus Professor of Chemistry, University of Sheffield; *b* 8 Oct. 1900; *o c* of John Stevens and Jane E. Stevens (*née* Irving); *m* 1949, Janet Wilson Forsyth; no *c*. *Educ:* Paisley Grammar School; Glasgow Academy; Universities of Glasgow and Oxford. DPhil 1925. Assistant in Chemistry, Univ. of Glasgow, 1921–23, Lecturer, 1925–47; Ramsay Memorial Fellow, Oxford, 1923–25; Sen. Lectr in Organic Chemistry, Univ. of Sheffield, 1947–49, Reader, 1949–63, Prof., 1963–66; Visiting Prof. of Chemistry, Univ. of Strathclyde, Oct. 1966–Sept. 1967. Hon. DSc Glasgow, 1985. *Publications:* (with W. E. Watts) Selected Molecular Rearrangements, 1973; contrib. to Elsevier-Rodd, Chemistry of Carbon Compounds, 1957–60. Papers in scientific jls. *Recreation:* unsophisticated bridge. *Address:* 313 Albert Drive, Glasgow G41 5RP.

STEVENS, Thomas Terry Hoar; *see* Terry-Thomas.

STEVENS, Thomas Wilson, CBE 1962; RD 1942; Commodore, Royal Mail Line Fleet, 1961–63, retired; *b* 16 Oct. 1901; *s* of John Wilson Stevens and Susan Eliza Smith; *m* 1939, Mary Doreen Whitington; one *s* one *d*. *Educ:* Sir Walter St John's, Battersea. Joined Royal Mail Steam Packet Co. as a Cadet, 1917; joined Royal Naval Reserve as Sub-Lieut 1927. Active service, Royal Navy, 1939–47. Younger Brother of Trinity House, 1944. Captain Royal Mail Lines, 1947; Captain Royal Naval Reserve, 1950. *Recreation:* golf. *Address:* 79 Offington Lane, Worthing, West Sussex. *T:* Worthing 61100.

STEVENS, Timothy John; Deputy Director, National Museums and Galleries on Merseyside, since 1986; *b* 17 Jan. 1940; *s* of Seymour Stevens; *m* 1969, Caroline Sankey; twin *s*. *Educ:* King's Sch., Canterbury; Hertford Coll., Oxford (MA); Courtauld Inst., Univ. of London (Academic Diploma, History of Art). Walker Art Gallery: Asst Keeper of British Art, 1964–65; Keeper of Foreign Art, 1965–67; Dep. Dir, 1967–70; Dir, 1971–74; Dir, Merseyside CC Art Galls, 1974–86. Hon. LittD Liverpool, 1985. *Recreation:* gardening. *Address:* Walker Art Gallery, William Brown Street, Liverpool L3 8EL. *T:* 051–227 5234.

STEVENS, William David; Executive Vice President, Esso Europe; *b* USA, 18 Sept. 1934; *s* of Walter Gerald and Amy Grace Stevens; *m* 1954, Barbara Ann Duncan; one *s* three *d*. *Educ:* Texas A&I Univ. (BScEng). Joined Humble Oil, 1958: various assignments, US Gulf Coast, 1959–73; Exxon Corporation: Executive Asst to President, 1973–74; various assignments, New York, 1974–77; Vice Pres., Gas, 1977–78. *Recreations:* golf, shooting, hiking. *Address:* Exxon Co. International, Division of Exxon Corporation, 200 Park Avenue, Florham Park, NJ, USA.

STEVENSON, Dr Alan Carruth; *b* 27 Jan. 1909; *s* of Allan Stevenson, CBE, and Christina Kennedy Lawson; *m* 1937, Annie Gordon Sheila Steven; two *s* one *d*. *Educ:* Glasgow Academy; Glasgow University. BSc 1930, MB, ChB 1933, MD 1946, Glasgow; MRCP 1935; FRCP 1955. Appointments: Royal Infirmary, Glasgow; Highgate Hospital, London; London Hospital. Served RAMC 1939–45 (despatches); retired with hon. rank of Lieutenant-Colonel, 1946–48. Professor of Social and Preventive Medicine, The Queen's University, Belfast, 1948–58; Reader in Public Health, London University; Dir, MRC Population Genetics Unit, Oxford, and Lectr in Human Genetics, Oxford Univ., 1958–74. *Publications:* Build your own Enlarger, 1943; Recent Advances in Social Medicine, 1948; Genetic Counselling, 1971; articles on Tropical and Preventive Medicine and human genetics in appropriate scientific journals. *Recreation:* fishing. *Address:* 17 Little Dene Copse, Pennington, Lymington, Hants SO4 8EW. *T:* Lymington 76444.

STEVENSON, Rt. Hon. Sir (Aubrey) Melford (Steed), PC 1973; Kt 1957; Justice of the High Court, 1957–79 (Queen's Bench Division, 1961–79; Probate, Divorce and Admiralty Division, 1957–61); *b* 17 October 1902; *o s* of late Rev. J. G. Stevenson; one *d* (by 1st marriage); *m* 2nd, Rosalind Monica, *d* of late Orlando H. Wagner; one *s* one *d*. *Educ:* Dulwich Coll. LLB (London). Called to Bar, Inner Temple, 1925, Treasurer, 1972; Major and Dep. Judge Advocate, 1940–45; KC 1943; Bencher, 1950. Recorder of Rye, 1944–51, of City of Cambridge, 1952–57; Dep. Chairman, West Kent Quarter Sessions, 1949–55; Presiding Judge, South-Eastern Circuit, 1970–75. Mem. Inter-Departmental Committee on Human Artificial Insemination, 1958–60. *Address:* Truncheons, Winchelsea, East Sussex TN36 4AB. *T:* Rye 226223. *Clubs:* Garrick; Dormy House (Rye).

STEVENSON, Sir David; *see* Stevenson, Sir H. D.

STEVENSON, Dennis; *see* Stevenson, H. D.

STEVENSON, Dr Derek Paul, CBE 1972; MRCS, LRCP; *b* 11 July 1911; *s* of late Frederick Stevenson and Maud Coucher; *m* 1941, Pamela Mary, *d* of late Col C. N. Jervelund, OBE; two *s* one *d*. *Educ:* Epsom College; Guy's Hospital. Lieut RAMC, 1935 (Montefiore Prize, Royal Army Med. Coll., 1935); Capt. RAMC 1936; Maj. 1942; Lt-Col 1943; service in China and Malaya. Asst Director-General Army Medical Service, War Office, 1942–46; Sec. Army Medical Advisory Bd 1943–46. War Office rep. on Central Med., War Cttee, 1943–46. British Medical Association: Asst Sec., 1946–48; Dep. Sec., 1948–58; Sec., 1958–76. Sec. Jt Consultants Cttee, 1958–76; Mem., Health Services Bd, and Scottish Cttee, 1977–80. Vice-Pres. British Medical Students Assoc.; Hon. Sec./Treas., British Commonwealth Med. Conf.; Delegate, Gen. Assembly World Medical Association: Sydney, 1968, Paris, 1969, Oslo, 1970, Ottawa, 1971, Amsterdam, 1972, Munich, 1973, Stockholm, 1974, Chm. Council, 1969, 1970–71 (Mem. Council, 1967–). Medical Sec. to Nat. Ophthalmic Treatment Board Assoc.; Mem. Council of London Hospital Service Plan; Mem. Cttee of Management: Medical Insurance Agency; Medical and Dental Retirement Adv. Service; Vice Pres., Private Patients Plan, 1984–. Adviser: Sterling Winthrop, Mediscope Jl; Mem. Adv. Bd, Allied Investments; Dir, Tavistock Computer Services; Gen. Comr, Inland Revenue. Hon. Sec. and Treas., British Commonwealth Medical Assoc., 1964; Sec. Gen., Permanent Cttee of Doctors, EEC, 1973–76; Member: Chichester HA; West Sussex Gen. Practitioners' Cttee; Hon. Sec., British Life Assurance Trust. Liaison Officer, MoD, 1964. Mem. Bd of Governors, Epsom College; Governor, Midhurst Grammar Sch.; Pres., Old Epsomian Club, 1974–75. Mem., Chichester Dio. Bd; Lay Chm., Rural Deanery. Mem., West Sussex CC, 1980–85. Fellow, Royal Commonwealth Soc., 1968; Fellow, BMA, 1976 (Gold Medal, 1976). Hon. LLD, Manchester, 1964. *Publications:* contrib. Irish Medical Jl; BMA Lecture delivered to Irish Medical Assoc.; contrib. Canadian Med. Assoc. Jl, and address at Centennial meeting, Montreal; NHS Reorganisation (in RSH Jl), address to RSH Congress 1973; regular contribs to Medical Interface. *Recreations:* golf, sailing, gardening. *Address:* Bodrigy, Holycombe, Liphook, Hants. *T:* Liphook 724205. *Clubs:* Athenæum, Garrick, Royal Commonwealth Society; Hindhead Golf.

STEVENSON, Prof. George Telford; Professor of Immunochemistry, Faculty of Medicine, University of Southampton, since 1974; *b* 18 April 1932; *s* of Ernest George Stevenson and Mary Josephine Madden; *m* 1963, Freda Kathryn Hartley; three *s*. *Educ:* North Sydney High Sch.; Univ. of Sydney (MB, BS; MD); Univ. of Oxford (DPhil). Resident MO, 1955–56, Resident Pathologist, 1957, Sydney Hosp.; Research Fellow, Dept of Medicine, Univ. of Sydney, 1958–61; Nuffield Dominions Demonstrator, Dept of Biochemistry, Univ. of Oxford, 1962–64; Sen. Research Fellow, Dept of Biochemistry, Univ. of Sydney, 1965–66; Scientific Staff, MRC Immunochemistry Unit, Univ. of Oxford, 1967–70; Dir, Tenovus Research Lab., Southampton Gen. Hosp., 1970–; Consultant Immunologist, Southampton Univ. Hosps, 1976–. Hammer Prize for Cancer Research (jtly) (Armand Hammer Foundn, LA), 1982. *Publications:* Immunological Investigation of Lymphoid Neoplasms (with J. L. Smith and T. J. Hamblin), 1983; research papers on immunology and cancer, considered mainly at molecular level. *Recreations:* reading, squash rackets. *Address:* 9 Meadowhead Road, Bassett, Southampton. *T:* Southampton 769092.

STEVENSON, George William; Member (Lab) Staffordshire East, European Parliament, since 1984; *b* 30 Aug. 1938; *s* of Harold and Elsie May Stevenson; *m* 1958, Doreen June; two *s* one *d*. *Educ:* Uttoxeter Road Primary School; Queensberry Road Secondary School, Stoke-on-Trent. Pottery caster, 1953–57; coal miner, 1957–64; transport driver, 1964–66; bus driver, 1966–84; shop steward, TGWU 5/24 Branch, 1968–84 (Mem., 1964–; Chm., 1975–81). Member: Stoke-on-Trent City Council, 1972–86; Staffs County Council, 1981–85. *Recreations:* reading, crown green bowling. *Address:* (home) 56 Canberra Crescent, Meir Park, Stoke-on-Trent, Staffs ST3 7RA. *T:* Stoke-on-Trent 393496; (office) Euro-Constituency Office, Pioneer House, 76/80 Lonsdale Street, Stoke-on-Trent, Staffs ST4 4DP. *T:* Stoke-on-Trent 414232. *Club:* Meir Sports and Social.

STEVENSON, Henry Dennistoun, (Dennis Stevenson), CBE 1981; Partner, SRU Group of companies, since 1972; Director, London Docklands Development Corporation, since 1981; Chairman, Intermediate Technology Development Group, since 1983; *b* 19 July 1945; *s* of Alexander James Stevenson and Sylvia Florence Stevenson (*née* Ingleby); *m* 1972, Charlotte Susan, *d* of Hon. Sir Peter Vanneck, *qv*; four *s*. *Educ:* Glenalmond; King's Coll., Cambridge (MA). Chm., Newton Aycliffe and Peterlee New Town Develt Corp., 1971–80. Chairman: govt working party on role of voluntary movements and youth in the environment, 1971, '50 Million Volunteers' (HMSO); Indep. Advisory Cttee on Pop Festivals, 1972–76, 'Pop Festivals, Report and Code of Practice' (HMSO); Adviser on Agricultural Marketing to Minister of Agriculture, 1979–83. Chm., Nat. Assoc. of Youth Clubs, 1973–81. Mem. Admin. Council, Royal Jubilee Trusts, 1978–80. Director: Nat. Building Agency, 1977–81; British Technology Gp, 1979–; Tyne Tees Television, 1982–; Pearson plc, 1986–. *Recreation:* home. *Address:* 20 Surrey Square, SE17 2JX. *T:* 01–703 8316; 320 East 57th Street, New York, NY 10022, USA. *T:* 212–935–9815. *Clubs:* Brooks's, MCC.

STEVENSON, Dame Hilda (Mabel), DBE 1967 (CBE 1963; OBE 1960); Vice-President, Royal Children's Hospital, Melbourne, Victoria, Australia, 1938–72; *b* 1895; *d* of H. V. McKay, CBE, Sunshine, Vic; *m* 1st, Cleveland Kidd (*d* 1925); one *d*; 2nd, Col G. I. Stevenson (*d* 1958), CMG, DSO, VD. *Educ:* Presbyterian Ladies' College. Hon. LLD Melbourne, 1973. *Address:* 17 St George's Road, Toorak, Victoria 3142, Australia. *T:* 24–4628. *Clubs:* International Sportsmen's; Sunningdale Golf; Alexandra (Melbourne).

STEVENSON, Vice-Adm. Sir (Hugh) David, KBE 1977 (CBE 1970); AC 1976; Royal Australian Navy, retired; *b* 24 Aug. 1918; *s* of late Rt Rev. William Henry Webster Stevenson, Bishop of Grafton, NSW, and Mrs Katherine Saumarez Stevenson; *m* 1st, 1944, Myra Joyce Clarke (*d* 1978); one *s* one *d*; 2nd, Margaret Lorraine Wright. *Educ:* Southport Sch., Qld; RAN Coll. psc RN 1956; idc 1966. Commnd, 1938; served War: Mediterranean, East Indies, Pacific; minesweeping post, SW Pacific; specialised in navigation, 1944 (HM Navigation Sch.); Commands: HMAS Tobruk and 10th Destroyer Sqdn, 1959–60; HMNZS Royalist, 1960–61; HMAS Sydney, 1964; HMAS Melbourne, 1965–66; Dir of Plans, 1962–63; Naval Officer i/c W Australian area, 1967; Dep. Chief of Naval Staff, 1968–69; Comdr Aust. Fleet, 1970–71; Chief of: Naval Personnel, 1972–73; Naval Staff, 1973–76; retd 1976. Comdr 1952; Captain 1958; Cdre 1967; Rear-Adm. 1968; Vice-Adm. 1973. Chm. for Territories, Queen Elizabeth Jubilee Fund for Young Australians, 1977. *Publication:* (contrib.) The Use of Radar at Sea, 1952. *Recreations:* golf, fishing, gardening. *Address:* 4 Charlotte Street, Red Hill, ACT 2603, Australia. *T:* Canberra 95–6172. *Clubs:* Royal Commonwealth Society; Canberra Yacht, Federal Golf (Canberra).

STEVENSON, John; Secretary, Association of County Councils, since 1980; *b* 15 June 1927; *s* of John and Harriet Esther Stevenson; *m* 1956, Kathleen Petch; one *s* one *d*. *Educ:* Durham Univ. (LLB); MA Oxon 1982. Solicitor. Legal Asst, Borough of Hartlepool, 1951; Junior Solicitor, County Borough of Sunderland, 1952; Solicitor, Hertfordshire CC, 1953, Asst Clerk, 1964; Clerk of the Peace and County Solicitor, Gloucestershire CC, 1969; Chief Executive, Buckinghamshire CC, 1974. Hon. Fellow, Inst. Local Govt Studies, Birmingham Univ., 1981–; Vis. Fellow, Nuffield Coll., Oxford, 1982–. *Address:* (home) 2 Water's Edge, Port La Salle, Bouldnor Road, Yarmouth, Isle of Wight; 405 Keyes House, Dolphin Square, SW1. *T:* 01–834 2149; (office) Eaton House, 66a Eaton Square, SW1W 9BH. *T:* 01–235 1200.

STEVENSON, Air Vice-Marshal Leigh Forbes, CB 1944; *b* 24 May 1895; *s* of John Henry Stevenson and Mary Ann Irving; *m* 1926, Lillian Myrtle Comber (*d* 1981); two *d*. *Educ:* Richibucto Grammar School, Richibucto, NB, Canada. Canadian Expeditionary Force, 1914–17; Commissioned, 1916; RFC 1917–18; RAF 1918–19; RCAF 1920–45. Air Vice-Marshal, 1942; Graduate Royal Naval Staff College, Greenwich, 1930; AOC, RCAF Overseas, 1940–41; retired, Oct. 1945. MLA of BC, 1946–53. US Commander of Legion of Merit, 1945. *Recreations:* shooting, fishing. *Address:* 1163 Balfour Avenue, Vancouver, BC V6H 1X3, Canada. *Club:* Vancouver (BC).

STEVENSON, Rt. Hon. Sir Melford; *see* Stevenson, Rt Hon. Sir A. M. S.

STEVENSON, Prof. Olive; Professor of Social Work Studies, University of Nottingham, since 1984; *b* 13 Dec. 1930; *d* of John and Evelyn Stevenson. *Educ:* Purley County Grammar Sch. for Girls; Lady Margaret Hall, Oxford (BA EngLitt, MA 1955); London Sch. of Economics (Dip. in Social Studies, Dip. in Child Care). Tavistock Clinic; Child Care Officer, Devon CC, 1954–58; Lecturer in Applied Social Studies: Univ. of Bristol, 1959–61; Univ. of Oxford, 1961–68; Social Work Adviser, Supplementary Benefits Commn, 1968–70; Reader in Applied Social Studies, Univ. of Oxford, and Professorial Fellow, St Anne's Coll., Oxford, 1970–76; Prof. of Social Policy and Social Work: Univ. of Keele, 1976–82; Univ. of Liverpool, 1983–84. Member: Royal Commn on Civil Liability, 1973–78; Social Security Adv. Cttee, 1982–; Registered Homes Tribunal, 1985–; Chairman: Adv. Cttee, Rent Rebates and Rent Allowances, 1977–83; Age Concern England, 1980–83; CVSNA, 1985–. *Publications:* Someone Else's Child, 1965, rev. edn 1977; Claimant or Client?, 1970; Social Service Teams: the practitioner's view, 1978; Child Abuse: interprofessional communication, 1979; Specialisation in Social Service Teams, 1981; (with Fuller) Policies, Programmes and Disadvantage, 1983. *Recreations:* music, cookery, conversation. *Address:* Department of Social Administration, University of Nottingham, Nottingham NG7 2RD.

STEVENSON, Robert Barron Kerr, CBE 1976; MA; FSA; Keeper, National Museum of Antiquities of Scotland, 1946–78, Trustee, 1975–78; *b* 16 July 1913; *s* of late Professor William B. Stevenson; *m* 1950, Elizabeth M. Begg; twin *s*. Member: Ancient Monuments Board for Scotland, 1961–79; Cttees of Inquiry: Field Monuments, 1966–68; Provincial Museums, 1972–73. Pres., Soc. of Antiquaries of Scotland, 1975–78. Fellow, UCL, 1977. Hon. FRNS 1979; Hon. DLitt Edinburgh, 1981. *Address:* 8 Cobden Crescent, Edinburgh EH9 2BG. *T:* 031–667 3164.

STEVENSON, Robert Bryce; General President, National Union of Footwear Leather and Allied Trades, since 1980; *b* 26 June 1926; *s* of Daniel Liddle Stevenson and Christina Stevenson; *m* 1947, Margaret Eugenia; two *d*. *Educ:* Caldercruix Advanced Sch., Airdrie, Lanarks. Full-time Officer NUFLAT, Street, Som. Branch, 1961–80. Member, 1980–: Internat. Textile, Garment and Leather Workers Fedn Exec. Council and Cttee (Brussels); Jt Cttee, Footwear Industry in Europe (Brussels); Footwear Econ. Develt Cttee; TUC Textile, Clothing and Footwear Industries Cttee; Council, Shoe and Allied Trades Res. Assoc.; Boot and Shoe Repairing Wages Council for GB; Bd of Management, Boot Trade Benevolent Soc.; Mem., Footwear Leather and Fur Skin Industry Trng Bd, 1980–82; Mem., TUC Gen. Council, 1984–. JP Wells and Glastonbury 1970 (on Supplementary List, Northants, 1981). *Recreations:* listening to and playing music, all sports. *Address:* 27 Wentworth Avenue, Wellingborough, Northants. *T:* Wellingborough 676959. *Club:* Unity (Street, Som.).

STEVENSON, Sir Simpson, Kt 1976; Chairman, Scottish Health Services Common Service Agency, 1973–77, and since 1983; *b* 18 Aug. 1921; *s* of T. H. Stevenson, Greenock; *m* 1945, Jean Holmes Henry, JP, Port Glasgow. *Educ:* Greenock High Sch. Member: Greenock Town Council, 1949–67 and 1971–; Inverclyde DC, 1974–; Provost of Greenock, 1962–65; Vice-Chm., Clyde Port Authority, 1966–69; Chm., Greater Glasgow Health Bd, 1973–83. Member: Western Regional Hosp. Bd (Scotland), 1959–; Scottish Hosp. Administrative Staffs Cttee, 1965–74 (Chm., 1972–74); Chm., W Regional Hosp. Bd (Scotland), Glasgow, 1967–74; Member: Scottish Hosp. Endowments Commn, 1969–70; Scottish Health Services Planning Council; Royal Commn on the NHS, 1976–79. Chm., Consortium of Local Authorities Special Programme (CLASP), 1974. Hon. LLD Glasgow, 1982. *Recreations:* football, reading, choral singing. *Address:* 64A Reservoir Road, Gourock, Renfrewshire PA19 1YQ.

STEVENSON, William Trevor, CBE 1985; DL; Chairman: Hodgson Martin Ventures, since 1982; Aerotime, since 1978; Alexander Wilkie, since 1977; *b* 21 March 1921; *o s* of late William Houston Stevenson and Mabel Rose Stevenson (*née* Hunt); *m* Alison Wilson (*née* Roy). *Educ:* Edinburgh Acad. Apprentice mechanical engineer, 1937–41; engineer, 1941–45; entered family food manufacturing business, Cottage Rusks, 1945; Man. Dir, 1948–54; Chm., 1954–59; Chief Executive, Cottage Rusks Associates, (following merger with Joseph Rank Ltd), 1959–69; Reg. Dir, Ranks Hovis McDougall, 1969–74; Dir, various cos in food, engrg, medical, hotel and aviation industries, 1974–; Chairman: Gleneagles Hotels, 1981–83; Scottish Transport Gp, 1981–86. Master, Co. of Merchants of City of Edinburgh, 1978–80. DL City of Edinburgh, 1984. *Recreations:* flying, sailing, curling. *Address:* 45 Pentland View, Edinburgh EH10 6PY. *T:* 031–445 1512. *Clubs:* Caledonian; New (Edinburgh).

STEWARD, Rear Adm. Cedric John, CB 1984; Chief of Naval Staff, New Zealand, 1983–86; *b* 31 Jan. 1931; *s* of Ethelbert Harold Steward and Anne Isabelle Steward; *m* 1952, Marie Antoinette Gurr; three *s*. *Educ:* Northcote College, Auckland, NZ; RNC Dartmouth; RNC Greenwich. Served: HMS Devonshire, 1950; HMS Illustrious, 1950; HMS Glory, 1951 (Korean Campaign and UN Medals, 1951); HMAS Australia, HMAS Barcoo, 1952; HM NZ Ships Hawea, 1953, Kaniere, 1954 (Korea), Tamaki, 1955–58, Stawell, 1958–59; HMAS Creswell (RAN College), 1959–62; HM NZ Ships Rotoiti, 1962–63 (Antarctic support), Tamaki, 1963–64, Royalist, 1965–66 (Confrontation), Philomel, 1966, Inverell (in Command), 1966–67; JSSC Latimer, 1968; Dep. Head, NZ Defence Liaison Staff, Canberra, 1969–73; in Command, HMNZS Otago, 1973–74; in Command and Captain F11, HMNZS Canterbury, 1974–75; Defence HQ, 1976–77; RCDS, 1978; Dep. Chief of Naval Staff, NZ, 1979–81; Commodore, Auckland, 1981–83. *Recreations:* rugby, golf, tennis, equestrian events, fishing, boating, philately, farming.

STEWARD, Prof. Frederick Campion, FRS 1957; Charles A. Alexander Professor of Biological Sciences and Director of Laboratory for Cell Physiology and Growth, Cornell University, Ithaca, NY, 1965–72, now Professor Emeritus (Professor of Botany, 1950–65); *b* 16 June 1904; *s* of Frederick Walter and Mary Daglish Steward; *m* 1929, Anne Temple Gordon, Richmond, Va, USA; one *s*. *Educ:* Heckmondwike Gram. Sch., Yorks; Leeds Univ. BSc 1924 (1st Class Hons); PhD 1926. DSc London 1937. Demonstrator in Botany, Leeds Univ., 1926; Rockefeller Fellow; Cornell Univ., 1927, Univ. of California, 1928; Asst Lecturer, Univ. of Leeds (Botany), 1929; Rockefeller Foundation Fellow, 1933–34;

Reader in Botany, Univ. of London (Birkbeck Coll.), 1934; War Service with MAP (Dir of Aircraft Equipment), 1940–45; Prof. of Botany and Chm. of Dept, Univ. of Rochester, Rochester, NY, 1946–50. John Simon Guggenheim Fell., 1963–64; Sir C. V. Raman Vis. Prof., Madras Univ., 1974. Fellow American Academy of Arts and Sciences, 1956. Merit Award, Botanical Society of America, 1961. Hon. DSc: Delhi, 1974; William and Mary, 1982; Guelph, 1983. *Publications:* Plants at Work, 1964; Growth and Organisation in Plants, 1968; Plants, Chemicals and Growth, 1971; (ed) Treatise on Plant Physiology, 6 vols and 11 tomes, 1959–72, Vols 7 and 8, 1983; papers in scientific journals and proceedings of learned societies. *Recreations:* gardening, swimming. *Address:* 1612 Inglewood Drive, Charlottesville, Va 22901, USA.

STEWARD, George Coton, MA, ScD, DSc; Professor of Mathematics, The University, Hull, 1930–61, Emeritus Professor, since 1961; *b* 6 April 1896; *o c* of Joseph Steward and Minnie, *d* of William Coton, Wolverhampton; unmarried. *Educ:* The Grammar School, Wolverhampton; Gonville and Caius College, Cambridge (Senior Scholar). Wrangler, with distinction in schedule b, Mathematical Tripos, 1920; ScD, 1937; First Class Honours in Mathematics in BSc (Honours), Univ. of London, 1917; DSc, 1926; Smith's Prize, Univ. of Cambridge, 1922, for contributions on Geometrical and Physical Optics; Member of Scientific Staff of Optics Department of National Physical Laboratory, 1918; Assistant Lecturer in Applied Mathematics, University of Leeds, 1920; Fellow of Gonville and Caius College, Cambridge, 1922; Fellow and Mathematical Lecturer, Emmanuel College, Cambridge, 1923. *Publications:* The Symmetrical Optical System, Cambridge Mathematical and Physical Tracts, No 25, 1928, 1958; papers on Geometrical and Physical Optics, and Plane Kinematics, in Transactions of Royal Society, of Cambridge Philosophical Society, etc. *Address:* 42 South Street, Cottingham, North Humberside. *T:* Hull 847654.

STEWARD, Nigel Oliver Willoughby, OBE 1946; MA Oxon, BA Cantab; Consul-General, Haifa, 1955–59, retired; *b* 16 October 1899; *s* of Arthur Bennett Steward, ICS, and Alice Willoughby; *m* 1933, Raquel Wyneken, of Viña del Mar, Chile; three *d*. *Educ:* Winchester (Scholar); Trinity College, Oxford. Entered Consular Service, 1924. Vice-Consul at San Francisco, Valparaiso, Guatemala (Second Secretary), and Paris; Consul and First Secretary at Montevideo; Minister (local rank) to Paraguay; First Secretary, Bucharest, 1946; Deputy Consul-Gen., New York, 1946–48; Minister to Nicaragua, 1948–52; Consul-General, Nice and Monaco, 1952–55. *Address:* Church Cottage, 13 Gravel Walk, Cullompton, Devon EX15 1DA. *Club:* United Oxford & Cambridge University.

STEWARD, Stanley Feargus, CBE 1947; CEng; FIProdE; Chairman: George Thurlow and Sons (Holdings) Ltd; ERA Technology Ltd, 1983–84; *b* 9 July 1904; *s* of late Arthur Robert and late Minnie Elizabeth Steward, Mundesley, Norfolk; *m* 1929, Phyllis Winifred, *d* of late J. Thurlow, Stowmarket, Suffolk; one *s* one *d*. *Educ:* The Paston Sch., North Walsham, Norfolk. Was apprenticed to East Anglian Engineering Co. (subseq. Bull Motors Ltd) and subseq. held positions of Chief Designer, Sales Manager and Managing Dir; Min. of Supply Electrical Adviser to Machine Tool Control, 1940; Director of Industrial Electrical Equipment, 1941–44; Dir Gen. of Machine Tools, 1944–45; Chm. Machine Tool Advisory Council, 1946–47; Chm. Gauge & Tool Advisory Council, 1946–47. Director: E. R. & F. Turner, Ltd, Ipswich, 1944–48. Chm., South Western Electricity Board, 1948–55; Man. Dir, Lancashire Dynamo Holdings Ltd, 1956–59 (Chm., 1957–58); Former Chm., Lancashire Dynamo and Crypto Ltd, Lancashire Dynamo Electronic Products Ltd and Lancashire Dynamo Group Sales; Chairman: William Steward (Holdings) Ltd and William Steward & Co. Ltd, 1970–80; Thurlow, Nunn & Sons Ltd, 1970–84; Dir, Bull Motors Ltd, 1981–85. Member: British Electricity Authority, 1952–53; Elect. Engineering EDC, 1962–71; Machine Tool EDC, 1971–80; Chm., British Electrical Development Assoc., 1954; President: Ipswich and District Electrical Assoc., 1964–67, 1972–78; Electrical Industries Club, 1966–67; Assoc. of Supervisory and Exec. Engineers, 1970–74; Electrical and Electronic Industries Benevolent Assoc., 1971–72; Instn of Engineers-in-Charge, 1982–84; Man. Dir, BEAMA, 1959–71; Pres., Exec. Cttee, Organisme de Liaison des Industries Metalliques Europeénes, 1963–67. Freeman of City of London; Master, Worshipful Company of Glaziers and Painters of Glass, 1964. *Publications:* Electricity and Food Production, 1953; British Electrical Manufacture in the National Economy, 1961; Twenty Five Years of South Western Electricity, 1973; The Story of the Dynamicables, 1983; The Story of Electrex, 1984; regular 'Personal View' contribs to Electrical Review and other jls. *Recreations:* books, music, watching cricket. *Address:* 41 Fairacres, Roehampton Lane, SW15 5LX. *T:* 01-876 2457. *Clubs:* Athenæum, MCC.

STEWARD, Sir William Arthur, Kt 1955; Director of food manufacturing companies; *b* 20 Apr. 1901; *s* of late W. A. Steward and of Mrs C. E. Steward, Norwich; *m* 1939. *Educ:* Norwich Model Sch., and privately. Freeman of City of London; Master, Worshipful Co. of Distillers, 1964–65; Liveryman, Worshipful Co. of Fruiterers. Served RAF, 1938–45; Sen. Catering Officer at Air Min., 1943–45; retired with rank of Squadron Leader. MP (C) Woolwich West, 1950–59; Chm. Kitchen Cttee, House of Commons, Nov. 1951–Sept. 1959. Mem. of London County Council for Woolwich West, 1949–52. Chm., London Conservative Union, 1953–55. Pres., Hotel and Catering Trades Benevolent Assoc., 1964. Comdr IoM Commandery, Sword Bearer and Mem. Supreme Council, Mil. and Hospitaller Order of St Lazarus of Jerusalem (GCLJ 1979; KMLJ 1980). *Recreations:* composing music for both organ and piano, and writing. *Address:* Fairway House, 1 Fairway Drive, Ramsey, Isle of Man.

STEWART, family name of **Earl of Galloway,** and **Baron Stewart of Fulham.**

STEWART; *see* Vane-Tempest-Stewart, family name of Marquess of Londonderry.

STEWART, Hon. Lord; Ewan George Francis Stewart, MC 1945; a Senator of the College of Justice in Scotland, since 1975; *b* 9 May 1923; *s* of late George Duncan Stewart, CA, Edinburgh, and late Catherine Wilson Stewart; *m* 1953, Sheila Margaret, *er d* of late Major K. G. Richman, East Lancs Regt; one *s* one *d*. *Educ:* George Watson's Coll., Edinburgh; Edinburgh Univ. Served War of 1939–45 with 7/9 (Highlanders) Bn, The Royal Scots, in 52 (L) Division. Mem. of Faculty of Advocates, 1949; QC (Scotland) 1960; standing junior counsel to Min. of Civil Aviation in Scotland, 1955–60; Hon. Sheriff-Substitute of the Lothians and Peebles, 1961–64; practised at New Zealand Bar, 1962–64; resumed practice at Scottish Bar, 1964; Home Advocate-Depute, 1965–67; Solicitor-General for Scotland, 1967–70; Scottish Law Commissioner, 1971–75. Member: Cttee on Criminal Procedure in Scotland, 1971–77; Cttee on Preparation of Legislation, 1973–75; Chm., Cttee on Alternatives to Prosecution, 1977–83. Governor, St Denis School, Edinburgh, 1967–76; Chm., Court, Univ. of Stirling, 1976–84. DUniv Stirling, 1984. *Address:* 5 Munro Drive, Edinburgh EH13 0EG. *Club:* Caledonian.

STEWART OF FULHAM, Baron *cr* 1979 (Life Peer), of Fulham in Greater London; **Robert Michael Maitland Stewart;** PC 1964; CH 1969; *b* 6 Nov. 1906; *s* of Robert Wallace Stewart, DSc and Eva Stewart; *m* 1941, Mary Elizabeth Henderson Birkinshaw (later Baroness Stewart of Alvechurch) (*d* 1984); no *c*. *Educ:* Christ's Hosp.; St John's Coll., Oxford. Pres. Oxford Union, 1929; Asst Master, Merchant Taylors' Sch., 1930–31; Asst Master, Coopers' Company's School, and Lectr for Workers' Educational Assoc., 1931–42. Joined Army Intelligence Corps, 1942. Trans. to Army Educational Corps, 1943; commissioned and promoted to Capt., 1944. Contested (Lab) West Lewisham, 1931 and 1935; MP (Lab) Fulham East, 1945–55, Fulham, 1955–74, Hammersmith, Fulham, 1974–79; Vice-Chamberlain of HM Household, 1946–47; Comptroller of HM Household, 1946–47; Under-Sec. of State for War, 1947–51; Parly Sec., Min. of Supply, May-Oct. 1951; Sec. of State for Education and Science, Oct. 1964–Jan. 1965; Sec. of State for Foreign Affairs, Jan. 1965–Aug. 1966; First Sec. of State, 1966–68; Sec. of State for Economic Affairs, 1966–67; Secretary of State for Foreign and Commonwealth Affairs, 1968–70. Mem., European Parlt, 1975–76. Pres., H. G. Wells Soc., 1982–. Freeman of Hammersmith, 1967. Hon. Fellow, St John's Coll. Oxford, 1965; Hon. LLD Leeds, 1966; Hon. DSc Benin, 1972. *Publications:* The Forty Hour Week (Fabian Soc.), 1936; Bias and Education for Democracy, 1937; The British Approach to Politics, 1938; Modern Forms of Government, 1959; Life and Labour (autobiog.), 1980; European Security: the case against unilateral nuclear disarmament, 1981. *Recreations:* chess, painting. *Address:* 11 Felden Street, SW6. *T:* 01–736 5194.

STEWART, Sir Alan, KBE 1981 (CBE 1972); Vice-Chancellor of Massey University, 1964–83; *b* 8 Dec. 1917; *s* of Kenneth and Vera Mary Stewart; *m* 1950, Joan Cecily Sisam; one *s* three *d*. *Educ:* Massey Agricultural College; University College, Oxford. Sen. Lectr, Massey Agric. Coll., 1950–54; Chief Consulting Officer, Milk Marketing Board, England and Wales, 1954–58; Principal, Massey Agric. Coll., 1959–63. Hon. DSc Massey, 1984. *Address:* PO Box 3, Whakatane, New Zealand. *T:* Whakatane 86–619.

STEWART, Sir Alan (d'Arcy), 13th Bt *cr* 1623; yachtbuilder; *b* 29 Nov. 1932; *s* of Sir Jocelyn Harry Stewart, 12th Bt, and Constance Mary (*d* 1940), *d* of D'Arcy Shillaber; *S* father, 1982; *m* 1952, Patricia, *d* of Lawrence Turner; two *s* two *d*. *Educ:* All Saints College, Bathurst, NSW. *Heir:* *s* Nicholas Courtney d'Arcy Stewart, BSc, HDipEd, *b* 4 Aug. 1953. *Address:* One Acre House, Ramelton, Co. Donegal. *T:* Ramelton 82.

STEWART, Alastair Lindsay; Sheriff of Grampian, Highland and Islands, at Aberdeen and Stonehaven, since 1979; *b* 28 Nov. 1938; *s* of Alexander Lindsay Stewart and Anna Stewart; *m* 1968, Annabel Claire Stewart, *yr d* of Prof. W. McC. Stewart, *qv*; two *s*. *Educ:* Edinburgh Academy; St Edmund Hall, Oxford (BA); Univ. of Edinburgh (LLB). Admitted to Faculty of Advocates, 1963; Tutor, Faculty of Law, Univ. of Edinburgh, 1963–73; Standing Junior Counsel to Registrar of Restrictive Trading Agreements, 1968–70; Advocate Depute, 1970–73; Sheriff of South Strathclyde, Dumfries and Galloway, at Airdrie, 1973–79. Chm., Aberdeen Family Conciliation Service, 1984–. Governor, Robert Gordon's Inst. of Technology, 1982– (Vice-Chm. of Governors, 1985–). *Publications:* various articles in legal jls. *Recreations:* reading, music. *Address:* 131 Desswood Place, Aberdeen AB2 4DP. *T:* Aberdeen 644683.

STEWART, Allan; *see* Stewart, J. A.

STEWART, Prof. Andrew; *b* 17 Jan. 1904; *s* of Andrew Stewart, Edinburgh, Scotland, and Marcia Sabina (*née* Sprot); *m* 1931, Jessie Christobel Borland; four *s* two *d*. *Educ:* Daniel Stewart's College, Edinburgh, Scotland; East of Scotland College of Agriculture (CDA); University of Manitoba. BSA 1931, MA 1932 (Univ. of Manitoba). Lecturer in Agricultural Economics, Univ. of Manitoba, 1932–33; Lectr, 1935, Prof. 1946, of Political Economy, Dean of Business Affairs, 1949, President, 1950–59, Univ. of Alberta; Chm. Bd of Broadcast Governors, Ottawa, 1958–68; Chm. Alberta Univs Commn, 1968–70; Prof. of Education, Univ. of Ibadan, Nigeria, 1970–72. Member of Royal Commissions: Province of Alberta (Natural Gas), 1948; Canada (Economic Prospects), 1955–57; Canada (Price Spreads of Food Products) (Chairman), 1958–59; Pres. Nat. Conf. of Canadian Univs, 1958; Chm. Assoc. of Univs of British Commonwealth, 1958. Hon. LLD Manitoba, New Brunswick, Melbourne, Alberta; Hon. DEcon Laval; FRSC; Fellow, Agricultural Inst. of Canada. *Address:* 10435 Allbay Road, Sidney, BC, Canada.

STEWART, Andrew, CBE 1954; *b* 23 June 1907; *s* of James Stewart; *m* 1937, Agnes Isabella Burnet, *d* of James McKechnie, JP. *Educ:* Glasgow University (MA). Hon LLD Glasgow, 1970. Joined BBC at Glasgow, 1926; Glasgow Representative, 1931–35; Scottish Programme Director, 1935–48; Controller (N Ire.), 1948–52; Controller (Home Service), 1953–57; Controller, Scotland, 1957–68. Min. of Information, 1939–41. Director, Scottish Television, 1968–77. Chm., Scottish Music Archive, 1972–82; Chm., Films of Scotland Committee. Governor, National Film School, 1971–76. Hon. Pres., Scottish Radio Industries Club, 1972–. *Recreations:* reading, the theatre, mountaineering. *Address:* 36 Sherbrooke Avenue, Glasgow G41 4EP.

STEWART, Andrew Struthers, (Andy); MP (C) Sherwood, since 1983; farmer; *b* 27 May 1937; *s* of late James Stewart and of Elizabeth Stewart; *m* 1961, Louise Melvin (*née* Skimming); one *s* one *d*. *Educ:* Strathaven Acad., Scotland; West of Scotland Agricl Coll. Farming Beesthorpe Manor Farm, 1961–. Mem., Caunton Parish Council, 1973–83; Conservative Mem., Notts CC, 1975–83; Cons. spokesman on leisure services, 1981–83. Chairman: Strathaven Br., Young Conservatives, 1957 and 1958; Caunton, Maplebeck and Kersall Cons. Br., 1970–73 (Founder Mem.). Member: Newark Br., NFU, 1961– (Mem., County Exec. Cttee, 1966–); Newark and Notts Agricl Soc.; Adv. Mem., Nottingham University Coll. of Agriculture, 1977–82 (formerly Chm., Notts Coll. of Agriculture Brackenhurst); formerly Chm., Governing Bd, Rufford Comprehensive Sch. Youth Club Leader, 1965–76; Life Vice President: Southwell Rugby Club; Caunton Cricket Club; Trustee, Southwell Recreation Centre, 1979–83. *Address:* Beesthorpe Manor Farm, Caunton, Newark, Notts NG23 6AX. *T:* Caunton 270. *Clubs:* Farmers'; Bentinck Conservative (Hucknall, Notts).

STEWART, (Bernard Harold) Ian (Halley), RD 1972; FBA 1981; FRSE 1986; MP (C) Hertfordshire North, since 1983 (Hitchin, Feb. 1974–1983); Economic Secretary to HM Treasury, since 1983; *b* 10 Aug. 1935; *s* of Prof. H. C. Stewart, *qv*; *m* 1966, Deborah Charlotte, *d* of Hon. William Buchan and late Barbara Howard Ensor, JP; one *s* two *d*. *Educ:* Haileybury; Jesus Coll., Cambridge (MA; LittD 1978). 1st cl. hons Class. Tripos Cantab. Nat. Service, RNVR, 1954–56; subseq. Lt-Cmdr RNR. Seccombe, Marshall & Campion Ltd, bill brokers, 1959–60; joined Brown, Shipley & Co. Ltd, 1960, Asst Man. 1963, Man. 1966, Dir 1971–83; Director: Brown Shipley Holdings Ltd, 1980–83; Victory Insurance Co. Ltd, 1976–83. Jt Sec., Cons. Parly Finance Cttee, 1975–76, 1977–79; Mem. Public Expenditure Cttee, 1977–79. Opposition spokesman on Banking Bill, 1978–79; PPS to Chancellor of the Exchequer, 1979–83; Parly Under-Sec. of State for Defence Procurement, MoD, Jan.-Oct. 1983. Mem. British Academy Cttee for Sylloge of Coins of British Isles, 1967–; Hon. Treas., Westminster Cttee for Protection of Children, 1960–70, Vice-Chm., 1975–. FSA (Mem. Council 1974–76); FSA Scot; Dir, British Numismatic Soc., 1965–75 (Sanford Saltus Gold Medal 1971); FRNS (Parkes Weber Prize). Vice-Pres., Hertfordshire Soc., 1974–; Mem. Council, British Museum Soc., 1975–76. Life Governor, 1977, Mem. Council, 1980–, Haileybury; Trustee, Sir Halley Stewart Trust, 1978–. County Vice-Pres., St John Ambulance for Herts, 1978–; OStJ 1980. *Publications:* The Scottish Coinage, 1955 (2nd edn 1967); Scottish Mints, 1971; (ed with C. N. L. Brooke and others) Studies in Numismatic Method, 1983; many papers in Proc. Soc. Antiquaries of Scotland, Numismatic Chronicle, British Numismatic Jl, etc. *Recreations:* history; tennis (Captain CU Tennis Club, 1958–59; 1st string v

Oxford, 1958 and 1959; winner Coupe de Bordeaux 1959; led 1st Oxford and Cambridge Tennis and Rackets team to USA, 1958; played squash for Herts); Homer. *Address:* House of Commons, SW1. *Clubs:* MCC; Hawks, Pitt (Cambridge).

STEWART, Brian Thomas Webster, CMG 1969; Special Representative, Rubber Growers Association, Malaysia, since 1979; *b* 27 April 1922; *s* of late Redvers Buller Stewart and Mabel Banks Sparks, Broich, Crieff; *m* 1946, Millicent Peggy Pollock (marr. diss. 1970); two *d*; *m* 1972, Sally Nugent; one *s* one *d*. *Educ:* Trinity Coll., Glenalmond; Worcester Coll., Oxford (MA). Commnd The Black Watch (RHR), 1942; served Europe and Far East (Capt.). Joined Malayan Civil Service, 1946; studying Chinese Macau, 1947; Asst Sec., Chinese Affairs, Singapore, 1949; Devonshire Course, Oxford, 1950; Asst Comr for Labour, Kuala Lumpur, 1951; Sec. for Chinese Affairs, Supt of Chinese Schs, Malacca and Penang, 1952–57; joined HM Diplomatic Service, 1957; served Rangoon, Peking, Shanghai, Manila, Kuala Lumpur, Hanoi; Asst Sec., Cabinet Office, 1968–72; Counsellor, Hong Kong, 1972–74; FCO, 1974–78. *Publication:* All Men's Wisdom (anthology of Chinese Proverbs), 1957. *Recreations:* climbing, sailing, ski-ing, chamber music, orientalia particularly chinoiserie. *Address:* c/o Hongkong and Shanghai Banking Corporation, 9 Waterloo Place, SW1. *Clubs:* Athenæum, Royal Commonwealth Society; Lake (Kuala Lumpur).

STEWART, Charles Cosmo Bruce, CMG 1962; Head of Cultural Relations Department, Foreign and Commonwealth Office (formerly Foreign Office), 1967–72; *b* 29 July 1912; *o s* of late Brig.-Gen. Cosmo Gordon Stewart, CB, CMG, DSO, and Mrs Gladys Berry Stewart (*née* Honeyman). *Educ:* Eton; King's Coll., Cambridge. Barrister-at-law, Middle Temple, 1938. Served War, 1939–46. Foreign Service Officer, 1946; First Sec., Rome, 1949; First Sec. (Commercial), Cologne, 1951; transf. to Foreign Office, 1954; Head of Information Policy Dept, 1955–58; Counsellor and Consul-General, Saigon, Vietnam, 1958–61; Counsellor and Head of Chancery, Copenhagen, 1961–63; Consul-General at Luanda, 1963–68. *Club:* Travellers'.

STEWART, Colin MacDonald, CB 1983; FIA, FSS; Directing Actuary, Government Actuary's Department, London, 1974–84; *b* 26 Dec. 1922; *s* of John Stewart and Lillias Cecilia MacDonald Fraser; *m* 1948, Gladys Edith Thwaites; three *d*. *Educ:* Queen's Park Secondary Sch., Glasgow. Clerical Officer, Rosyth Dockyard, 1939–42. Served War: Fleet Air Arm (Lieut (A) RNVR), 1942–46. Govt Actuary's Dept, London, 1946–84. FIA 1953. *Publications:* The Students' Society Log 1960–85, 1985; numerous articles on actuarial and demographic subjects in British and internat. jls. *Recreations:* genealogical research, foreign travel, grandchilding. *Address:* 8 The Chase, Coulsdon, Surrey CR3 2EG. *T:* 01-660 3966.

STEWART, Air Vice-Marshal Colin Murray, CB 1962; CBE 1952 (OBE 1945); RAF, retired; *b* 17 June 1910; *s* of Archie Stewart, Sherborne, Dorset; *m* 1940, Anthea, *d* of Maynard Loveless, Stockbridge, Hants; four *s*. *Educ:* Wycliffe College, Stonehouse, Glos. Joined RAF, 1932; served in 5 Sqdn, NWF, India, and 16 Sqdn at home; specialised in Signals, 1937. Served War of 1939–45 (despatches, OBE): CSO various formations at home and in Europe. Chairman: British Joint Communications Board, 1952–55; Communications Electronics Cttee of Standing Group, Washington, 1955–57; AOC, No 27 Gp, 1957–58; Comd Electronics Officer, Fighter Comd, 1958–61; Dir-Gen. of Signals, Air Ministry, 1961–64; STSO, Fighter Comd, 1964–67; SASO, Technical Training Comd, 1967–68, retired. Controller, Computing Services, Univ. of London, 1968–73. *Recreations:* fishing, gardening, etc. *Address:* Byelanes, Moult Road, Salcombe, S Devon TQ8 8LG. *T:* Salcombe 2042.

STEWART, Sir David (Brodribb), 2nd Bt *cr* 1960, TD 1948; Managing Director, Francis Price (Fabrics) Ltd, Manchester, 1960–81; retired; *b* 20 Dec. 1913; *s* of Sir Kenneth Dugald Stewart, 1st Bt, GBE, and Noel (*d* 1946), *y d* of Kenric Brodribb, Melbourne; *S* father, 1972; *m* 1963, Barbara Dykes, *widow* of Donald Ian Stewart and *d* of late Harry Dykes Lloyd. *Educ:* Marlborough College; Manchester College of Technology (BSc (Tech), Textile Technology). Joined Stewart Thomson & Co. Ltd, Textile Merchant Converters, 1935; continuously employed in this company, except for six years war service, until absorbed into the Haighton & Dewhurst Group, 1958; Francis Price (Fabrics) Ltd is a subsidiary of this Group. Commissioned 8th Bn Lancashire Fusiliers (TA), 1934; war service, 1939–45; joined Duke of Lancaster's Own Yeomanry (TA) on re-formation of TA, 1947; in comd, 1952–56; retd with rank of Bt Col. *Recreation:* gardening. *Heir:* *b* Robin Alastair Stewart [*b* 26 Sept. 1925; *m* 1953, Patricia Helen, *d* of late J. A. Merrett; one *s* three *d*]. *Address:* Delamere, Heyes Lane, Alderley Edge, Cheshire SK9 7JY. *T:* Alderley Edge 582312.

STEWART, Sir David James H.; *see* Henderson-Stewart.

STEWART, Rt. Hon. Donald James, PC 1977; MP (SNP) Western Isles, since 1970; *b* 17 Oct. 1920; *m* 1955, Christina Macaulay. *Educ:* Nicolson Institute, Stornoway. Provost of Stornoway, 1958–64 and 1968–70; Hon. Sheriff, 1960. Leader, Parly SNP, 1974–; Pres., SNP, 1982–. *Recreations:* fishing, photography, gardening. *Address:* Hillcrest, 41 Goathill Road, Stornoway, Isle of Lewis. *T:* Stornoway 2672.

STEWART, Duncan Montgomery; Principal of Lady Margaret Hall, Oxford, since 1979; *b* 14 Feb. 1930; *s* of William Montgomery Stewart and Mary Pauline (*née* Checkley); *m* 1961, Valerie Mary Grace, *er d* of Major E. H. T. Boileau, Rampisham, Dorset; one *s* one *d*. *Educ:* Greymouth Technical High Sch.; Christ's Coll., NZ; Canterbury University Coll., NZ (MA 1st Cl. French 1951, 1st Cl. Latin 1952); Rhodes Scholar, 1953; Queen's Coll., Oxford (1st Cl. Hons Mod. Langs 1955). Lectr, Wadham Coll., Oxford, 1955, Fellow, 1956–79. Vice-Chm., Oxford Univ. Gen. Bd of Faculties, 1976–78. *Publications:* articles and revs on French Literature, esp. later medieval. *Recreations:* senescent cricket and tennis, opera, wine. *Address:* 6 Fyfield Road, Oxford.

STEWART, Sir Edward (Jackson), Kt 1980; Chairman and Managing Director, Stewarts Hotels Pty Ltd, since 1956; *b* 10 Dec. 1923; *s* of Charles Jackson Stewart and Jessie Stewart (*née* Dobbie); *m* 1956, Shirley Patricia Holmes; four *s*. *Educ:* St Joseph's College, Brisbane. Fellow Catering Inst. of Australia (FCIA); FAIM. Served with Australian Army, RAA, 1942–44. Chairman: Castlemaine Perkins Ltd, 1977–80 (Dir, 1970); Castlemaine Tooheys Ltd, 1980–85; Director: Birch Carroll & Coyle Ltd, 1967–; Roadshow (Qld) Pty Ltd, 1970–; Darwin Cinemas Pty Ltd, 1972–; G. R. E. (Australia) Ltd, 1980–; Besser (Qld) Ltd, 1981–. President: Queensland Hotels Assoc., 1963–69; Aust. Hotels Assoc., 1966–69; QUF Industries Ltd, 1986–. Mem. Totalisator Administration Bd of Queensland, 1977–81. Chm., Queensland Inst. of Medical Research Trust, 1980– *Recreations:* reading, fishing and thoroughbred breeding. *Address:* Box 456, GPO, Brisbane, Qld 4001, Australia. *Clubs:* Australian (Sydney); Brisbane, Tattersall's (Past Pres.) (Brisbane); Queensland Turf, Victorian Racing.

STEWART, Ewan George Francis; *see* Stewart, Hon. Lord.

STEWART, Ewen; Sheriff at Wick, Caithness, since 1962 and at Dornoch, Sutherland and Tain, Ross and Cromarty, since 1977; *b* 22 April 1926; *o s* of late Duncan Stewart and Kate Blunt, and *gs* of late Ewen Stewart, Kinlocheil; *m* 1959, Norma Porteous Hollands, *d* of late William Charteris Hollands, Earlston; one *d*. *Educ:* Edinburgh University. BSc (Agric.) 1946; MA (Econ.) 1950; LLB 1952. Asst Agricultural Economist, East of Scotland Coll. of Agriculture, 1946–49; practised at Scottish Bar, 1952–62; lectr on Agricultural Law, Univ. of Edinburgh, 1957–62; former standing junior counsel, Min. of Fuel and Power. Parly Cand. (Lab.) Banffshire, 1962. *Address:* Rose Cottage, Swiney, Lybster, Caithness KW3 6BT.

STEWART, Prof. Sir Frederick (Henry), Kt 1974; FRS 1964; PhD Cantab; FRSE; FGS; Regius Professor of Geology, 1956–82, now Emeritus, Dean of Science Faculty, 1966–68, and Member, University Court, 1969–70, Edinburgh University; *b* 16 Jan. 1916; *o s* of Frederick Robert Stewart and Hester Alexander, Aberdeen; *m* 1945, Mary Florence Elinor Rainbow (*see* Mary Stewart); no *c*. *Educ:* Fettes Coll.; Univ. of Aberdeen (BSc); Emmanuel Coll., Cambridge. Mineralogist in Research Dept of ICI Ltd (Billingham Div.), 1941–43; Lectr in Geology, Durham Colls in the Univ. of Durham, 1943–56. Vice-Pres., Geological Soc. of London, 1965–66; Member: Council for Scientific Policy, 1967–71; Adv. Council for Applied R&D, 1976–79; Chairman: NERC, 1971–73 (Mem., Geol. Geophysics Cttee, 1967–70); Adv. Bd for Res. Councils, 1973–79 (Mem., 1972–73); Mem. Council, Royal Soc., 1969–70; Trustee, BM (Nat. Hist.), 1983–; Mem. Council, Scottish Marine Biol Assoc., 1983–. Lyell Fund Award, 1951, J. B. Tyrrell Fund, 1952, Geological Soc. of London; Mineralogical Soc. of America Award, 1952; Lyell Medal, Geological Soc. of London, 1970; Clough Medal, Edinburgh Geol. Soc., 1971; Sorby Medal, Yorks Geol. Soc., 1975. Hon. DSc: Aberdeen, 1975; Leicester, 1977; Heriot-Watt, 1978; Durham, 1983. *Publications:* The British Caledonides (ed with M. R. W. Johnson), 1963; Marine Evaporites, 1963; papers in Mineralogical Magazine, Jl of Geol. Soc. of London, etc., dealing with igneous and metamorphic petrology and salt deposits. *Recreation:* fishing. *Address:* 79 Morningside Park, Edinburgh EH10 5EZ. *T:* 031–447 2620. *Club:* New (Edinburgh).

STEWART, George Girdwood, CB 1979; MC 1945; TD 1954; Regional Representative, Central and Tayside, National Trust for Scotland, since 1984; *b* 12 Dec. 1919; *o s* of late Herbert A. Stewart, BSc, and of Janetta Dunlop Girdwood; *m* 1950, Shelagh Jean Morven Murray; one *s* one *d*. *Educ:* Kelvinside Academy, Glasgow; Glasgow Univ.; Edinburgh Univ. (BSc). Served RA, 1940–46 (MC, despatches); CO 278 (Lowland) Field Regt RA (TA), 1957–60. Dist Officer, Forestry Commn, 1949; Asst Conservator, 1961; Conservator, West Scotland, 1966; Comr for Forest and Estate Management, 1969–79; Rep., Branklyn Garden, Perth, NT for Scotland, 1980–84. Member: BR Bd Envt Panel, 1980–; Countryside Commn for Scotland, 1981–; Chm., Scottish Wildlife Trust, 1981–. FRSA; FICFor; Hon. FLI. Pres., Scottish Ski Club, 1971–75; Vice-Pres., Nat. Ski Fedn of GB; Chm., Alpine Racing Cttee, 1975–78. *Recreations:* ski-ing, tennis, studying Scottish painting. *Address:* Branklyn House, Dundee Road, Perth. *T:* Perth 25535. *Club:* Ski Club of Great Britain.

STEWART, (George Robert) Gordon, OBE 1984; Legal Adviser, Institute of Chartered Accountants of Scotland, since 1983 (Secretary, 1976–83); *b* 13 Oct. 1924; *s* of David Gordon Stewart and Mary Grant Thompson or Stewart; *m* 1952, Rachel Jean Morrison; two *s* one *d*. *Educ:* George Watson's Coll., Edinburgh; Edinburgh Univ. (MA 1947, LLB 1949). WS and Mem., Law Soc. of Scotland, 1949. Served War, 1943–46: Captain, Royal Signals; Burma and SEAC. In practice as WS, Melville & Lindesay, WS, Edinburgh, 1950–59; Asst Sec., subseq. Sec., and Dir, Ideal-Standard Ltd, Hull, 1959–75. *Recreation:* golf. *Address:* 15 Hillpark Loan, Edinburgh EH4 7BH. *T:* 031–336 7079. *Club:* Royal Scots (Edinburgh).

STEWART, Prof. Gordon Thallon, MD; Mechan Professor of Public Health, University of Glasgow, 1972–84; Hon. Consultant in Epidemiology and Preventive Medicine, Glasgow Area Health Board; *b* 5 Feb. 1919; *s* of John Stewart and Mary L. Thallon; *m* 1946, Joan Kego; two *s* two *d*; *m* 1975, Neena Walker. *Educ:* Paisley Grammar Sch.; Univs of Glasgow and Liverpool. BSc 1939; MB, ChB 1942; DTM&H 1947; MD (High Commendation) 1949; FRCPath 1964; FFCM 1972; MRCPGlas 1972; FRCPGlas 1975. House Phys. and House Surg., 1942–43; Surg. Lieut RNVR, 1943–46; Res. Fellow (MRC), Univ. of Liverpool, 1946–48; Sen. Registrar and Tutor, Wright-Fleming Inst., St Mary's Hosp., London, 1948–52; Cons. Pathologist, SW Metrop. Regional Hosp. Bd, 1954–63; Res. Worker at MRC Labs Carshalton, 1955–63; Prof. of Epidem. and Path., Univ. of N Carolina, 1964–68; Watkins Prof. of Epidem., Tulane Univ. Med. Center, New Orleans, 1968–72. Vis. Prof., Dow Med. Coll., Karachi, 1952–53 and Cornell Univ. Med. Coll., 1970–71; Cons. to WHO, and to NYC Dept of Health; Vis. Lectr and Examr, various univs in UK and overseas. Sen. Fellow, Nat. Science Foundn, Washington, 1964; Delta omega, 1969. *Publications:* (ed) Trends in Epidemiology, 1972; (ed jtly) Penicillin Allergy, 1970; Penicillin Group of Drugs, 1965; papers on chemotherapy of infectious diseases, drug allergy and epidemiology in various med. and sci. jls. *Recreations:* sailing, drawing, music. *Address:* Springwell, High Down, Totland, Isle of Wight. *T:* Isle of Wight 752658.

STEWART, Gordon William, CVO 1964; Chairman and General Manager, Scottish Region, British Railways, 1967–71; Chairman and Managing Director, British Transport Ship Management (Scotland) Ltd, 1967–71; Director, British Transport Hotels Ltd, 1968–71, retired; *b* 13 April 1906; *s* of James E. Stewart and Margaret Stewart; *m* 1935, Dorothy Swan Taylor, MA. *Educ:* Daniel Stewart's Coll.; George Heriot Sch., Edinburgh. L&NER: Traffic Apprentice, 1929; appts in London, Lincoln and Manchester, 1942–52; Prin. Asst to Gen. Man., Eastern Region, 1952; Asst Gen. Man., Scottish Region, 1956. Member: Stirling CC, 1972–75; Bridge of Allan Town Council, 1972–75. *Recreations:* golf, shooting. *Address:* 34 Keir Street, Bridge of Allan, Stirlingshire. *T:* Bridge of Allan 832266.

STEWART, Prof. Harold Charles, CBE 1975; FRCP; FRSE; DL; Head of Pharmacology Department, St Mary's Hospital Medical School, 1950–74; Professor of Pharmacology in the University of London 1965–74, now Emeritus Professor (Reader, 1949–64); Consultant in Pharmacology to: St Mary's Hospital, 1946; Ministry of Defence (Army), since 1961; *b* 23 Nov. 1906; *s* of Bernard Halley Stewart, MA, MD, FRSE, FKC, Pres. of Sir Halley Stewart Trust, and Mabel Florence Wyatt; *m* 1st, 1929, Dorothy Irene Lowen (*d* 1969); one *s* one *d*; 2nd, 1970, Audrey Patricia Nicolle. *Educ:* Mill Hill Sch.; University Coll. London; Jesus Coll., Cambridge; University Coll. Hospital. Cambridge Univ.: BA 1928, MA 1934; MB, BCh 1931, MD 1935. London Univ.: PhD 1941, MRCP 1949. Gen. practice, Barnet, Herts, 1932–36. Sub-Dean, St Mary's Hospital Med. Sch., 1950–52; Gresham Prof. in Physic, City Univ., 1968–70. Examr now or formerly, Univs of London, Cambridge, Birmingham, Bristol and Wales, RCS, Soc. of Apothecaries. Research work, mainly on fat absorption and transport in the human subject, and on problems of pain and analgesia. Cons. in Pharmacology to Army; Med. Adviser and Mem. Commonwealth Council, Brit. Commonwealth Ex-Services League; Pres., Sir Halley Stewart Trust for Research and Buttle Trust for Children, 1986– (Chm., 1979–86); Mem. Asthma Research Council; Dir-Gen., St John Ambulance Assoc., 1976–78 (Dep Dir-Gen., 1973–76; Dist Surg. for London, SJAB, 1950–64); Mem. Chapter-Gen., Order of St John (KStJ); Mem. Council, Stewart Soc.; Vice-Chairman: Med. Council of Alcoholism; St Christopher's Hospice for terminal cases; Sen. Vice-Pres. and British Rep., Assoc. Internat.

de Sauvetage et de Premiers Secours en Cas d'Accidents, 1974–. Liveryman, Soc. of Apothecaries of London; Freeman, City of London: Mem. Physiolog., Brit. Pharmacolog., Nutrition and Genealog. Socs. FFA, RCS, 1969. FRSE 1974. RAMC, T, 1935; Mem. LDV, later Major and Med. Adviser, HG; comd and reformed Med. Unit, Univ. of London STC as Major RAMC, 1942–46. Defence Medal; Gen. Serv. Medal, 1939–46; Coronation Medal, 1953; Guthrie Meml Medal, 1974. DL Greater London, 1967–82. *Publications:* Drugs in Anæsthetic Practice (with F. G. Wood-Smith), 1962; (with W. H. Hughes) Concise Antibiotic Treatment, 2nd edn 1973; contribs to jls. *Recreations:* voluntary service; sport (lacrosse: Cambridge Half-Blue 1928; lawn tennis); genealogy and heraldry. *Address:* 41 The Glen, Green Lane, Northwood, Mddx. *T:* Northwood 24893. *Club:* Athenæum.

See also B. H. I. H. Stewart.

STEWART, Sir Herbert (Ray), Kt 1946; CIE 1939; FRCScI, DIC, NDA, MSc; international consultant on agriculture, retired 1962; *b* 10 July 1890; *s* of Hugh Stewart, Ballyward, Co. Down; *m* 1917, Eva (*d* 1955), *d* of William Rea, JP, Ballygawley, Co. Tyrone; one *d*; *m* 1957, Elsie, *d* of Walter J. Pyne, London. *Educ:* Excelsior Academy, Banbridge; Royal College of Science, Dublin; Imperial College of Science and Technology, London. Military Service, 1915–19; entered the Indian Agricultural Service as Deputy Director of Agriculture, 1920; Professor of Agriculture, Punjab, 1921–27; Assistant Director of Agriculture, 1928–32; Agricultural Expert, Imperial Council of Agricultural Research, Government of India, 1938; Director of Agriculture, Punjab, 1932–43; Nominated Member of the Punjab Legislative Council from time to time, 1927–36; Fellow of the University of the Punjab, 1929–43; Dean of the Faculty of Agriculture, 1933–43; Agriculture Commissioner with Government of India, 1943–46; Vice-Chairman, Imperial Council of Agricultural Research, 1944–46; Agricultural Adviser to British Middle East Office, Cairo, 1946–51; Principal Consultant, Agriculture, to UN Economic Survey Mission for Middle East, 1949; Agricultural Adviser to UN Relief and Works Agency for Palestine Refugees, 1950–51; Chief, Agricultural Mission to Colombia of Internat. Bank for Reconstruction and Development, 1955–56; Agricultural Consultant to Bank Missions to Pakistan, 1956, 1958, Italy, 1957, Yugoslavia and Uganda, 1960 and Kenya, 1961–62. *Publications:* various pamphlets and reports on agriculture and farm accounts in India, and on agriculture in Middle East. *Address:* 29 Alyth Road, Bournemouth, Dorset BH3 7DG. *T:* Bournemouth 764782.

See also Sir E. J. W. Barnes.

STEWART, Sir Houston Mark S.; *see* Shaw-Stewart.

STEWART, Sir Hugh Charlie Godfray, 6th Bt, *cr* 1803, of Athenree; Major; DL; High Sheriff, Co. Tyrone, 1955; *b* 13 April 1897; *s* of Colonel Sir George Powell Stewart, 5th Bt, and Florence Maria Georgina, *d* of Sir James Godfray; *S* father, 1945; *m* 1st, 1929 (marr. diss. 1942); one *s* one *d*; 2nd, 1948, Diana Margaret, *d* of late Capt. J. E. Hibbert, MC, DFC, and late Mrs R. B. Bannon, Jersey; one *s* one *d*. *Educ:* Bradfield Coll., Berkshire; RMC, Sandhurst. Served European War, Royal Inniskilling Fusiliers, 1916; Arras, 1917 (wounded); France, 1939–40. Foreign Service has included India, Iraq, China, Malaya, South Africa and Syria; retired. DL Co. Tyrone, 1971. *Heir: s* David John Christopher Stewart [*b* 19 June 1935; *m* 1959, Bridget Anne, *er d* of late Patrick W. Sim and of Mrs Leslie Parkhouse; three *d*]. *Address:* Cottesbrook, Sandy Pluck Lane, Bentham, near Cheltenham, Glos.

STEWART, Ian; *see* Stewart, B. H. I. H.

STEWART, Prof. Ian George; Professor of Economics, University of Edinburgh, 1967–84; *b* 24 June 1923; *s* of David Tweedie Stewart, MA and Ada Doris Montgomery Haldane; *m* 1949, Mary Katharine Oddie; one *s* two *d*. *Educ:* Fettes Coll.; Univ. of St Andrews (MA 1st Class Hons); MA Cantab 1954. Pilot, RAF, 1942–46. Commonwealth Fund Fellow, 1948–50. Research Officer, Dept of Applied Economics, Univ. of Cambridge, 1950–57; University of Edinburgh: Lectr in Economics, 1957–58; Sen. Lectr, 1958–61; Reader, 1961–67; Curator of Patronage, 1979–84. Vis. Associate Prof., Univ. of Michigan, 1962; Vis. Prof., Univ. of S Carolina, 1975. Dir, Scottish Provident Instn, 1980–, Dep. Chm., 1983–85. Mem., British Library Bd, 1980–. Governor, Fettes Coll., 1976–. *Publications:* National Income of Nigeria (with A. R. Prest), 1953; (ed) Economic Development and Structural Change, 1969; articles in jls and bank reviews. *Recreations:* golf, fishing, gardening. *Address:* 571 Lanark Road West, Edinburgh EH14. *Club:* New (Edinburgh).

STEWART, Jackie; *see* Stewart, John Young.

STEWART, James Cecil Campbell, CBE 1960; Consultant; Chairman: British Nuclear Forum, since 1974; Nuclear Power Company Pension Trustee Ltd, since 1979; *b* 1916; *s* of late James Stewart and Mary Campbell Stewart; *m* 1946, Pamela Rouselle, *d* of William King-Smith; one *d*. *Educ:* Armstrong College and King's College, Durham University (BSc Physics). Telecommunications Research Establishment, 1939–46; Atomic Energy Research Establishment, Harwell, 1946–49; Industrial Group, UKAEA, 1949–63; Dep. Chm., British Nuclear Design and Construction, 1969–75; Member: UKAEA, 1963–69; Central Electricity Generating Bd, 1965–69; Dep. Chm., Nuclear Power Co. Ltd, 1975–80; Dir, National Nuclear Corp. Ltd, 1980–82. *Recreation:* tending a garden. *Address:* Whitethorns, Higher Whitley, Cheshire WA4 4QJ. *T:* Norcott Brook 377; 901 Keyes House, Dolphin Square, SW1V 3NB. *T:* 01–798 8395. *Club:* East India, Devonshire, Sports and Public Schools.

STEWART, Sir James (Douglas), Kt 1983; agricultural consultant; Principal, Lincoln University College of Agriculture, 1974–84, retired; Chairman, New Zealand Wheat Board, since 1984; *b* 11 Aug. 1925; *s* of Charles Edward Stewart and Edith May Stewart (*née* Caldwell); *m* 1953, Nancy Elizabeth Dunbar; one *s* three *d*. *Educ:* Lincoln UC (Dip. Valuation and Farm Management); Canterbury Univ. (MA); Reading Univ. (DPhil). Lectr in Farm Management, Lincoln Coll., NZ, 1951–59; Research Fellow, Reading Univ., 1959–61; Sen. Lectr, Lincoln Coll., 1962–64; Prof. of Farm Management, Lincoln Coll., 1964–74. Chm., NZ Vice-Chancellors Cttee, 1981–82; Mem., Govt Adv. Cttee on External Aid and Develt, 1975–. Director: China NZ Agricultural Consultants, 1979–; Pyne Gould Guinness Ltd, 1980–; Asian NZ Development Consultants Ltd. Chm., Canterbury Develt Corp., 1983–; Dep. Chm., Christchurch Clinical Sch. of Medicine, 1983–. Queen's Jubilee Medal, 1977. *Publications:* contrib. Jl Agricl Econs, Jl Farm Econs, Econ. Record, etc. *Recreations:* swimming, Rugby coaching, part-time farming. *Address:* Marshs Road, Halswell, Christchurch, New Zealand.

STEWART, James Gill, CB 1958; CBE 1952; Hon. FITO; *b* 13 March 1907; *s* of John Stewart (builder) and Isabella Stewart, late of Edinburgh; *m* 1936, Jessie Dodd; one *s* one *d*. *Educ:* George Watson's College, Edinburgh; Edinburgh University. Passed Home Civil Service Administrative Class Competition, 1929; entered Min. of Labour, Asst Principal, 1930; Private Sec. to Permanent Sec., 1934; Principal, 1936; Asst Sec., 1941; on loan to Min. of Works, 1941–43; on loan to UN (Bureau of Personnel), 1946–47; on loan to Cabinet Office, 1947–49; Industrial Relations Dept, 1950–53; Under-Sec., Employment Dept, 1953; Training Dept, 1960, retired, 1967. *Recreations:* choral singing, hill walking. *Address:* 19 Shirelake Close, Oxford. *T:* Oxford 251543.

STEWART, James Harvey; District General Manager, Barking, Havering and Brentwood Health Authority, since 1985; *b* 15 Aug. 1939; *s* of Harvey Stewart and Annie (*née* Gray); *m* 1965, Fiona Maria Maclay Reid; three *s* one *d*. *Educ:* Peterhead Acad.; Aberdeen Univ. (MA 1962); Manchester Univ. (DSA 1964). Pres., Jun. Common Room, Crombie Hall, Aberdeen Univ., 1961–62. Hosp. Sec., Princess Margaret Rose Orthopaedic Hosp., Edinburgh, 1965–67; Principal Admin. Asst, 1967–68, and Dep. Gp Sec. and sometime Acting Gp Sec., 1968–73, York A HMC; Area Administrator, 1973–82, and Dist Administrator, 1982–83, Northumberland AHA; Regional Administrator, East Anglian RHA, 1983–85. Mem., National Staff Cttee for NHS Admin. and Clerical Staff, 1981–85; Hon. Treasurer, Assoc. of Chief Administrators of Health Authorities in England and Wales, 1982–85 (Mem. Council, 1975–82). Associate Mem., Inst. of Health Service Administrators, 1966. *Recreations:* music, reading, walking, gardening, playing squash, watching Rugby and soccer. *Address:* Barking, Havering and Brentwood Health Authority, The Grange, Harold Wood Hospital, Romford, Essex RM3 0BE; White Cottage, Hardwick, Cambridge CB3 7QU. *T:* Madingley 210961. *Clubs:* Rotary (Cambridge); Cambridge Rugby Union Football.

STEWART, James Lablache; *see* Granger, Stewart.

STEWART, James (Maitland), DFC with 2 oak leaf clusters (US); Air Medal with 3 oak leaf clusters; DSM (US); actor, stage and film; *b* Indiana, Pa, 20 May 1908; *s* of Alexander Maitland Stewart and Elizabeth Ruth (*née* Jackson); *m* 1949, Gloria McLean; two *s* twin *d*. *Educ:* Mercersburg Academy, Pa; Princeton University (BS Arch.). War Service, 1942–45: Lt-Col Air Corps; Europe, 1943–45 (Air Medal, DFC); Colonel, 1945. USAF Reserve; Brig.-Gen. 1959. Dir, Air Force Assoc. First New York appearance, Carry Nation, 1932; subseq. played in Goodbye Again, Spring in Autumn, All Good Americans, Yellow Jack, Divided by Three, Page Miss Glory, A Journey by Night. Entered films, 1935; *films include:* Murder Man, Next Time We Love, Seventh Heaven, You Can't Take It With You, Made for Each Other, Vivacious Lady, The Shopworn Angel, Mr Smith Goes to Washington, Destry Rides Again, No Time for Comedy, Philadelphia Story, The Shop around the Corner, Pot o' Gold, Ziegfeld Girl, Come Live with Me, It's a Wonderful Life, Magic Town, On Our Merry Way, You Gotta Stay Happy, Call Northside 777, Rope, The Stratton Story, Malaya, The Jackpot, Harvey, Winchester '73, Broken Arrow, No Highway in the Sky, Bend of the River, Carbine Williams, The Greatest Show on Earth, Thunder Bay, Naked Spur, The Glenn Miller Story, Rear Window, The Man from Laramie, The Far Country, Strategic Air Command, The Man Who Knew Too Much, Night Passage, Spirit of St Louis, Midnight Story, Vertigo, Bell, Book and Candle, Anatomy of a Murder, The FBI Story, The Mountain Road, The Man Who Shot Liberty Valance, Mr Hobbs Takes a Vacation, Take her, She's Mine, Cheyenne Autumn, Shenandoah, The Rare Breed, Firecreek, Bandalero, The Cheyenne Social Club, Fool's Parade, Dynamite Man from Glory Jail, The Shootist, Airport 77, The Big Sleep, Magic of Lassie. *Play:* Harvey (Broadway), 1970, (Prince of Wales), 1975. Holds many awards including: five Academy Award nominations; Oscar award as best actor of the year; Hon. Oscar Award; two NY Film Critics best actor awards; Venice Film Festival best actor award; France's Victoire Trophy for best actor; Screen Actors Guild award. Hon. degrees include: DLitt, Pennsylvania; MA, Princeton. *Address:* PO Box 90, Beverly Hills, Calif 90213, USA.

STEWART, James Moray; Deputy Under Secretary of State, Ministry of Defence, since 1986; *b* 21 June 1938; third *s* of James and Evelyn Stewart; *m* 1963, Dorothy May Batey, *o d* of Alan and Maud Batey; three *s*. *Educ:* Marlborough Coll.; Univ. of Keele (BA First Cl. Hons History and Econs). Sec., Univ. of Keele Union, 1960–61. Breakdown and Information Service Operator, AA, 1956–57; Asst Master, Northcliffe Sch., Bognor Regis, 1957–58; Asst Principal, Air Min., 1962–65; Private Sec. to 2nd Permanent Under Sec. of State (RAF), MoD, 1965–66; Principal, MoD, 1966–70; First Sec. (Defence), UK Delegn to NATO, 1970–73; Asst Sec., MoD, 1974–75; Private Sec. to successive Secs of State for NI, 1975–77; Dir, Naval Manpower Requirements, MoD, 1977; Dir, Defence Policy Staff, MoD, 1978–80; Asst Under Sec. of State, MoD, 1980–84; Asst Sec. Gen. for Defence Planning and Policy, NATO, 1984–86. *Recreations:* reading, listening to music, walking. *Address:* Ministry of Defence, Whitehall, SW1A 2HB. *Club:* Royal Commonwealth Society.

STEWART, James Robertson, CBE 1971 (OBE 1964); Principal, University of London, 1978–83; *b* 1917; *s* of James and Isabella Stewart; *m* 1941, Grace Margaret Kirsop; two *s* one *d*. *Educ:* Perth Acad.; Whitley and Monkseaton High Sch.; Armstrong Coll. (later King's Coll.), Newcastle, Univ. of Durham. BA Dunelm (1st cl. hons Mod. History) 1937; DThPT (1st cl.) 1938; research in Canada (Canada Co.), 1938–39; awarded Holland Rose Studentship, Cambridge, and William Black Noble Fellowship, Durham, 1939; admitted to Christ's Coll., Cambridge, 1939; MA Dunelm 1941. Served Army, 1939–46: Royal Artillery (BEF); Combined Ops HQ; Directorate of Combined Ops, India and SE Asia; Major (Actg Lt-Col); Certif. of Good Service. Dep. Clerk of Court, Univ. of London, 1946–49, Clerk of Court, 1950–82. Member, governing bodies: RPMS, 1983; Sch. of Pharmacy, London Univ., 1983–; Wye Coll., 1983–; Inst. of Educn, 1983–; RVC, 1983– (Hon. Treasurer); LSE, 1984–; Brunel Univ., 1984–; Inst. of Germanic Studies, 1984– (Chm.); Roedean Sch., 1984–; Sussex Univ., 1985–; Westfield Coll., London, 1985–. Hon. Fellow: Westfield Coll., London, 1981; KCL, 1982; Sch. of Pharmacy, London Univ., 1982; Birkbeck Coll., London, 1982; LSE, 1982; UCL, 1982. Hon. LLD: London, 1983; Western Ontario, 1984. Symons Medal, ACU, 1983. *Recreations:* golf, gardening, watching soccer and cricket. *Address:* 2 Hilltop, Dyke Road Avenue, Brighton, Sussex BN1 5LY. *T:* Brighton 551039. *Clubs:* Athenæum; Cuddington (Banstead) Golf, Dyke Golf (Brighton).

STEWART, James Simeon Hamilton, QC 1982; barrister; a Recorder of the Crown Court, since 1982; *b* 2 May 1943; *s* of late Henry Hamilton Stewart, MD, FRCS and of Edna Mary Hamilton Stewart; *m* 1972, Helen Margaret Whiteley; two *d*. *Educ:* Cheltenham Coll.; Univ. of Leeds (LLB Hons). Called to the Bar, Inner Temple, 1966. *Recreations:* cricket, golf, gardening. *Address:* Shaftesbury House, Chellow Dene, Bradford BD9 6BD. *T:* Bradford 493043. *Clubs:* Bradford (Bradford); Leeds Taverners (Leeds).

STEWART, Very Rev. James Stuart, MA, Hon. DD; Professor Emeritus of New Testament Language, Literature and Theology, University of Edinburgh, New College (retired 1966); Extra Chaplain to the Queen in Scotland (Chaplain, 1952–66); *b* 21 July 1896; *s* of William Stewart, Dundee, and Katharine Jane Stuart Duke; *m* 1931, Rosamund Anne Barron, Berkeley Lodge, Blandford, Dorset; two *s*. *Educ:* High School, Dundee; St Andrews University (MA, BD); New College, Edinburgh; University of Bonn, Germany. Minister of following Church of Scotland Congregations: St Andrews, Auchterarder, 1924–28; Beechgrove, Aberdeen, 1928–35; North Morningside, Edinburgh, 1935–46. Hon. DD, St Andrews Univ., 1945. Held following special lectureships: Cunningham Lectures, New Coll., Edinburgh, 1934; Warrack Lectures, Edinburgh and St Andrews Univs, 1944; Hoyt Lectures, Union Seminary, New York, 1949; Lyman Beecher

Lectures, Yale University, USA, 1952; Duff Missionary Lectures, 1953; Turnbull Trust Preacher, Scots Church, Melbourne, 1959; Stone Lectures, Princeton, 1962; Earl Lectures, Berkeley, California, 1967. Moderator of General Assembly of Church of Scotland, May 1963–64. *Publications:* The Life and Teaching of Jesus Christ, 1932; A Man in Christ: St Paul's Theology, 1935; The Gates of New Life, 1937; The Strong Name, 1941; Heralds of God, 1945; A Faith To Proclaim, 1953; Thine Is The Kingdom, 1956; The Wind of the Spirit, 1968; River of Life, 1972; King for Ever, 1975; Joint Editor, English Trans. of Schleiermacher, The Christian Faith, 1928. *Address:* St Raphael's Home, 6 Blackford Avenue, Edinburgh EH9 2LB.

STEWART, Sir James Watson, 4th Bt, *cr* 1920; *b* 8 Nov. 1922; *s* of Sir James Watson Stewart, 3rd Bt and Janie Steuart Stewart (*née* Sim) (she *m* 2nd, 1961, Neil Charteris Riddell); *S* father 1955; *m* 1st, 1946, Anne Elizabeth Glaister (*d* 1979); no *c*; 2nd, 1980, Avril Veronica Gibb, FRSA, Hon. FBID, Hon. MASC, *o d* of late Andrew Adamson Gibb. *Educ:* Uppingham; Aberdeen University. Served 1940–47: Royal Artillery; 1st Special Air Service: Parachute Regiment. Administrator, Ardgowan Hospice, Greenock. *Heir: brother* John Keith Watson Stewart [*b* 25 Feb. 1929; *m* 1954, Mary Elizabeth, *d* of John Francis Moxon; two *s* one *d*]. *Address:* Balgownie, Kilcreggan, Dumbartonshire G84 0JY. *T:* Kilcreggan 2455.

STEWART, (John) Allan; MP (C) Eastwood, since 1983 (East Renfrewshire, 1979–83); *b* 1 June 1942; *s* of Edward MacPherson Stewart and Eadie Barrie Stewart; *m* 1973, Marjorie Sally (Susie); one *s* one *d*. *Educ:* Bell Baxter High Sch., Cupar; St Andrews Univ. (1st Cl. Hons MA 1964); Harvard Univ. (Rotary Internat. Foundn Fellow, 1964–65). Lectr in Polit. Economy, St Andrews Univ., 1965–70 (Warden, John Burnet Hall, 1968–70); Confederation of British Industry: Head of Regional Develt Dept, 1971–73; Dep. Dir (Econs), 1973–76; Scottish Sec., 1976–78; Scottish Dir, 1978–79. Conservative Parly Candidate, Dundee E, 1970; Councillor, London Bor. of Bromley, 1975–76. PPS to Minister of State for Energy, 1981; Parly Under Sec. of State, Scottish Office, 1981–86. Mem., Select Cttee on Scottish Affairs, 1979–81. *Publications:* articles in academic and gen. pubns on econ. and polit. affairs. *Recreation:* bridge. *Address:* 34 Rowan Road, Dumbreck, Glasgow G41 5BZ. *T:* 041–427 2178.

STEWART, John Anthony Benedict, CMG 1979; OBE 1973; HM Diplomatic Service; High Commissioner to Sri Lanka, since 1984; *b* 24 May 1927; *e s* of late Edward Vincent Stewart and Emily Veronica (*née* Jones); *m* 1960, Geraldine Margaret, *o d* of late Captain G. C. Clifton; one *s* one *d* (and one *s* decd). *Educ:* St Illtyd's Coll.; Univ. of Wales; Cambridge Univ.; Imperial Coll. of Science and Technology; Cox Gold medal for Geology, 1950. RNVR Ordinary Seaman, later Midshipman, 1944–47. Colonial Geol. Survey Service, Somaliland Protectorate, 1952–56; Dist Officer, 1956–57; seconded to Anglo-Ethiopian Liaison Service, 1957–60 (Sen. Liaison Officer, 1960); transf. N Rhodesia as Dist Officer, 1960, Dist Comr, 1962–64; Resident Local Govt Officer, Barotseland, 1964–67. Entered HM Diplomatic Service, 1968; served FCO, Barbados, Uganda; RCDS, 1974; Ambassador to Democratic Republic of Vietnam, 1975–76; Head of Hong Kong Dept, FCO, 1976–78; Ambassador: to Laos, 1978–80; to Mozambique, 1980–84. *Publications:* The Geology of the Mait Area, 1955; papers in geological jls. *Recreations:* shooting, fishing. *Address:* c/o Foreign and Commonwealth Office, SW1. *Club:* Travellers'.

STEWART, John Hall; Sheriff of South Strathclyde Dumfries and Galloway at Airdrie, since 1985; *b* 15 March 1944; *s* of Cecil Francis Wilson Stewart and Mary Fyfe Hall or Stewart; *m* 1968, Marion MacCalman; one *s* two *d*. *Educ:* Airdrie Acad.; St Andrews Univ. (LLB). Advocate. Enrolled solicitor, 1970–77; Mem. Faculty of Advocates, 1978–. *Recreations:* golf, spectator sports, his children. *Address:* 3 Fife Crescent, Bothwell, Glasgow G76 8DG. *T:* Bothwell 853854. *Club:* Caledonian (Edinburgh).

STEWART, John Innes Mackintosh; Reader in English Literature, Oxford University, 1969–73; Student of Christ Church, Oxford, 1949–73, now Emeritus; *b* 30 Sept. 1906; *s* of late John Stewart, Director of Education in the City of Edinburgh, and Eliza Jane, *d* of James Clark, Golford, Nairn; *m* 1932, Margaret Hardwick (*d* 1979); three *s* two *d*. *Educ:* Edinburgh Academy; Oriel College, Oxford. Bishop Fraser's Scholar, 1930; 1st class Eng. Lang. and Lit. 1928; Matthew Arnold Memorial Prize, 1929; Lectr in English in Univ. of Leeds, 1930–35; Jury Professor of English in Univ. of Adelaide, 1935–45; Lectr in Queen's Univ., Belfast, 1946–48; Walker-Ames Prof., Univ. of Washington, 1961. Hon. DLitt: New Brunswick, 1962; Leicester, 1979; St Andrews, 1980. *Publications:* Montaigne's Essays: John Florio's Translation, 1931; Character and Motive in Shakespeare, 1949; Eight Modern Writers, 1963; Rudyard Kipling, 1966; Joseph Conrad, 1968; Thomas Hardy, 1971; Shakespeare's Lofty Scene (Shakespeare Lectr, British Acad.), 1971. Detective novels and broadcast scripts (under pseudonym of Michael Innes) Death at the President's Lodging, 1936; Hamlet Revenge!, 1937; Lament for a Maker, 1938; Stop Press, 1939; There Came Both Mist and Snow, 1940; The Secret Vanguard, 1940; Appleby on Ararat, 1941; The Daffodil Affair, 1942; The Weight of the Evidence, 1944; Appleby's End, 1945; From London Far, 1946; What Happened at Hazelwood, 1947; A Night of Errors, 1948; The Hawk and the Handsaw, 1948; The Journeying Boy, 1949; Operation Pax, 1951; A Private View, 1952; Christmas at Candleshoe, 1953; Appleby Talking, 1954; The Man From the Sea, 1955; Old Hall, New Hall, 1956; Appleby Talks Again, 1956; Appleby Plays Chicken, 1956; The Long Farewell, 1958; Hare Sitting Up, 1959; The New Sonia Wayward, 1960; Silence Observed, 1961; A Connoisseur's Case, 1962; Money from Holme, 1964; The Bloody Wood, 1966; A Change of Heir, 1966; Appleby at Allington, 1968; A Family Affair, 1969; Death at the Chase, 1970; An Awkward Lie, 1971; The Open House, 1972; Appleby's Answer, 1973; Appleby's Other Story, 1974; The Mysterious Commission, 1974; The Appleby File, 1975; The Gay Phoenix, 1976; Honeybath's Haven, 1977; The Ampersand Papers, 1978; Going It Alone, 1980; Lord Mullion's Secret, 1981; Sheiks and Adders, 1982; Appleby and Honeybath, 1983; Carson's Conspiracy, 1984; Appleby and the Ospreys, 1986; *novels* (as J. I. M. Stewart): Mark Lambert's Supper, 1954; The Guardians, 1955; A Use of Riches, 1957; The Man Who Wrote Detective Stories, 1959; The Man Who Won the Pools, 1961; The Last Tresilians, 1963; An Acre of Grass, 1965; The Aylwins, 1966; Vanderlyn's Kingdom, 1967; Cucumber Sandwiches, 1969; Avery's Mission, 1971; A Palace of Art, 1972; Mungo's Dream, 1973; quintet, A Staircase in Surrey, 1974–78 (The Gaudy, 1974; Young Pattullo, 1975; A Memorial Service, 1976; The Madonna of the Astrolabe, 1977; Full Term, 1978); Our England is a Garden and other stories, 1979; Andrew and Tobias, 1981; The Bridge at Arta and other stories, 1981; A Villa in France, 1982; My Aunt Christine and Other Stories, 1983; An Open Prison, 1984; The Naylors, 1985; Parlour 4 and other stories, 1986. *Recreation:* walking *Address:* Fawler Copse, Fawler, Wantage, Oxon.

See also M. J. Stewart.

STEWART, John Young, (Jackie Stewart), OBE 1972; racing driver, retired 1973; *b* 11 June 1939; *s* of late Robert Paul Stewart and of Jean Clark Young; *m* 1962, Helen McGregor; two *s*. *Educ:* Dumbarton Academy. First raced, 1961; competed in 4 meetings, 1961–62, driving for Barry Filer, Glasgow; drove for Ecurie Ecosse and Barry Filer, winning 14 out of 23 starts, 1963; 28 wins out of 53 starts, 1964; drove Formula 1 for BRM, 1965–67 and for Ken Tyrrell, 1968–73; has won Australian, New Zealand, Swedish, Mediterranean, Japanese and many other non-championship, major internat. Motor Races; set up new world record by winning his 26th World Championship Grand Prix (Zandvoort), July 1973, and 27th (Nurburgring), Aug. 1973; 3rd in World Championship, 1965; 2nd in 1968 and 1972; World Champion, 1969, 1971, 1973. BARC Gold Medal, 1971, 1973. Daily Express Sportsman of the Year, 1971, 1973; BBC Sports Personality of the Year, 1973; Scottish Sportsman of the Year, 1973; US Sportsman of the Year, 1973; Segrave Trophy, 1973. *Film:* Weekend of a Champion, 1972. *Publications:* World Champion, 1970 (with Eric Dymock); Faster!, 1972 (with Peter Manso); On the Road, 1983. *Recreations:* golf, fishing, tennis, shooting (Mem. British Team for Clay Pigeon shooting; former Scottish, English, Irish, Welsh and British Champion; won Coupe des Nations, 1959 and 1960; reserve for two-man team, 1960 Olympics). *Address:* 24 route de Divonne, 1260 Nyon, Vaud, Switzerland. *T:* Geneva 61.01.52. *Clubs:* (Hon.) Royal Automobile, British Racing Drivers' (Vice-Pres.); (Hon.) Royal Scottish Automobile; (Pres.) Scottish Motor Racing (Duns); Royal and Ancient (St Andrews); Prestwick Golf; Geneva Golf.

STEWART, Kenneth; Member (Lab) Merseyside West, European Parliament, since 1984. Parachute Regt (Sgt). Former joiner. Member: Merseyside CC; Liverpool CC (Chm., Housing Cttee); former Chm. and Sec., Liverpool West Derby Labour Party. *Address:* 62 Ballantyne Road, Liverpool L13 9AL.

STEWART, Kenneth Hope, PhD; Director of Research, Meteorological Office, 1976–82; *b* 29 March 1922; *s* of Harry Sinclair Stewart and Nora Hassan Parry; *m* 1950, Hilary Guest; four *s* four *d*. *Educ:* Trinity Coll., Cambridge (MA, PhD). Entered Meteorol Office, 1949; Dep. Dir, Physical Res., 1974. *Publications:* Ferromagnetic Domains, 1951; contrib. physical and meteorol jls. *Address:* 33 Ravenswood Avenue, Crowthorne, Berks.

STEWART, Hon. Kevin James; Agent General for New South Wales, since 1986; *b* 20 Sept. 1928; *m* 1952, Jean, *d* of late F. I. Keating; two *s* five *d*. *Educ:* Christian Brothers School, Lewisham, NSW; De La Salle College, NSW. Officer, NSW Govt Rlys, 1944–62 (Regional Pres., Aust. Transport Officers' Assoc. and Fedn, 1959–62). MLA for Canterbury, NSW, 1962–85; Exec., NSW Parly Labor Party and Spokesman on Health Matters, 1967; NSW State Exec., Aust. Labor Party, 1968; Minister, NSW: for Health, 1976–81; for Youth and Community Services, 1981–83; for Mineral Resources, 1983–84; for Local Govt, 1984–85. Mem., Labor Transport Cttee, 1965–76; Chm., Labor Health Cttee, 1968–76; Mem., Jt Cttee, Legislative Council upon Drugs. Chm., Bd of Canterbury Hosp., 1955–76 (Dir, 1954). Hon. Citizen of Tokyo, Japan. *Recreations:* supporter of community services, Rugby Football League, swimming, bowls. *Address:* New South Wales House, 66 Strand, WC2. *T:* 01–839 6651. *Clubs:* East India, Royal Automobile; NSW Leagues, Canterbury Brankstown League (Patron).

STEWART, Mary (Florence Elinor), (Lady Stewart); *b* 17 Sept. 1916; *d* of Rev. Frederick A. Rainbow, Durham Diocese, and Mary Edith (*née* Matthews), NZ; *m* 1945, Sir Frederick Henry Stewart, *qv*; no *c*. *Educ:* Eden Hall, Penrith, Cumberland; Skellfield School, Ripon, Yorks; St Hild's Coll., Durham Univ. BA 1938; MA 1941. Asst Lectr in English, Durham Univ., 1941–45; Part-time Lectr in English, St Hild's Training Coll., Durham, and Durham Univ., 1948–56. FRSA 1968. Hon. Fellow, Newnham Coll., Cambridge, 1986. *Publications: novels:* Madam, Will You Talk?, 1954; Wildfire at Midnight, 1956; Thunder on the Right, 1957; Nine Coaches Waiting, 1958; My Brother Michael, 1959; The Ivy Tree, 1961; The Moonspinners, 1962; This Rough Magic, 1964; Airs Above the Ground, 1965; The Gabriel Hounds, 1967; The Wind Off The Small Isles, 1968; The Crystal Cave, 1970 (Frederick Niven Award); The Little Broomstick, 1971; The Hollow Hills, 1973; Ludo and the Star Horse, 1974 (Scottish Arts Council Award); Touch Not the Cat, 1976; The Last Enchantment, 1979; A Walk in Wolf Wood, 1980; The Wicked Day, 1983; also articles, poems, radio plays. *Recreations:* gardening, music, painting. *Address:* 79 Morningside Park, Edinburgh EH10 5EZ. *T:* 031–447 2620.

STEWART, Michael James; Reader in Political Economy, University College, London University, since 1969; *b* 6 Feb. 1933; *s* of John Innes Mackintosh Stewart, *qv*; *m* 1962, Frances Kaldor, *d* of Baron Kaldor, FBA; one *s* two *d* (and one *d* decd). *Educ:* Campbell Coll., Belfast; St Edward's Sch., Oxford; Magdalen Coll., Oxford. 1st cl. PPE (Oxon), 1955. Asst Res. Officer, Oxford Univ. Inst. of Statistics, 1955–56; Barnett Fellow, Cornell Univ., 1956–57; Econ. Asst, HM Treasury, 1957–60; Sec. to Council on Prices, Productivity and Incomes, 1960–61; Econ. Adviser, HM Treasury, 1961–62, Cabinet Office, 1964–67 (Senior Econ. Advr, 1967), Kenya Treasury, 1967–69; Special Adviser to Sec. of State for Trade, Apr.–Oct. 1974; Economic Adviser to Malta Labour Party, 1970–73; Special Econ. Advr to Foreign Sec., 1977–78. Guest Scholar, Brookings Instn, Washington, DC, 1978–79. Mem., Acad. Adv. Panel, Bank of England, 1977–83. Contested (Lab): Folkestone and Hythe, 1964; Croydon North-West, 1966. Asst Editor, Nat. Inst. Econ. Review, 1962–64. Consultant to various UN agencies, 1971–. *Publications:* Keynes and After, 1967; The Jekyll and Hyde Years: politics and economic policy since 1964, 1977; Controlling the Economic Future: policy dilemmas in a shrinking world, 1983. *Recreations:* looking at paintings, eating in restaurants. *Address:* 79 South Hill Park, NW3 2SS. *T:* 01–435 3686. *Club:* United Oxford & Cambridge University.

STEWART, Sir Michael (Norman Francis), KCMG 1966 (CMG 1957); OBE 1948; HM Diplomatic Service, retired; Director, Sotheby's, since 1977; *b* 18 Jan. 1911; *s* of late Sir Francis Stewart, CIE, and of Lady Stewart; *m* 1951, Katharine Damaris Houssemayne du Boulay; one *s* two *d*. *Educ:* Shrewsbury; Trinity College, Cambridge. Assistant Keeper, Victoria and Albert Museum, 1935–39; Ministry of Information, 1939–41; Press Attaché: HM Embassy, Lisbon, 1941–44; HM Embassy, Rome, 1944–48; employed in Foreign Office, 1948–51; Counsellor: Office of Comr-Gen. for UK in SE Asia, 1951–54; HM Embassy, Ankara, 1954–59; HM Chargé d'Affaires, Peking, 1959–62; Senior Civilian Instructor, IDC, 1962–64; HM Minister, British Embassy, Washington, 1964–67; Ambassador to Greece, 1967–71. Dir, Ditchley Foundn, 1971–76. *Recreation:* country life. *Address:* Combe, near Newbury, Berks. *Club:* Buck's.

STEWART, Dame Muriel (Acadia), DBE 1968; Headmistress, Northumberland LEA, 1940–70; *b* 22 Oct. 1905; *d* of late James Edmund Stewart. *Educ:* Gateshead Grammar Sch.; Durham Univ. BA Hons 1926; MA 1929. Teacher: Newcastle upon Tyne, 1927–29; Northumberland, 1929–70 (a headteacher of Secondary Schools, 1940–69); Headmistress, Shiremoor Middle School, 1969–70. Nat. Pres., Nat. Union of Teachers, 1964–65; Chm., Schools Council, 1969–72. Vice-Chm., Bullock Cttee, 1972–74. Hon. MEd, Newcastle Univ., 1965. *Recreation:* music. *Address:* 44 Caldwell Road, Gosforth, Newcastle upon Tyne NE3 2AX. *T:* Newcastle upon Tyne 2853400.

STEWART, Norman MacLeod; Senior Partner, Allan, Black & McCaskie; President, The Law Society of Scotland, May 1985–86; *b* 2 Dec. 1934; *s* of George and Elspeth Stewart; *m* 1959, Mary Slater Campbell; four *d*. *Educ:* Elgin Acad.; Univ. of Edinburgh (BL); SSC. Alex. Morison & Co., WS, Edinburgh, 1954–58; Allan, Black & McCaskie, Solicitors, Elgin, 1959–; Partner, 1961–. Law Society of Scotland: Mem. Council, 1976–; Convener: Public Relations Cttee, 1979–81; Professional Practice Cttee, 1981–84; Vice-Pres., 1984–85. Hon. Mem., American Bar Assoc., 1985–. *Recreations:* walking, golf, music, Spanish culture. *Address:* Argyll Lodge, Lossiemouth, Moray. *T:* Lossiemouth 3150. *Club:* New (Edinburgh).

STEWART, Richard, CBE 1976; JP; Leader of Council, Strathclyde Regional Council, 1974–86; *b* 27 May 1920; *s* of Richard Stewart and Agnes (*née* Cunningham); *m* 1942, Elizabeth Peat; one *d. Educ:* Harthill Sch., Harthill. Mem., Lanark CC for 15 years (Chm. several cttees, finally Chm., Social Work Cttee). Full-time Sec./Organiser, Labour Party, 1950–82; Agent for: Rt Hon. Miss Margaret Herbison for 20 years; Rt Hon. John Smith, MP, 1970–82. Mem., Bd of Dirs, Scottish Transport Group, 1975–. Pres., Convention of Scottish Local Authorities, 1984–86. Past Chairman: Scottish Council of Labour Party; Nat. Union of Labour Organisers. Dir, Scottish Exhibition Centre, 1983–86. JP Lanark County Council 1964. Hon. LLB Strathclyde Univ., 1986. *Recreations:* music, chess. *Address:* 28 Hawthorn Drive, Harthill, Shotts ML7 5SG. *T:* Harthill 51303.

STEWART, Lt-Col Robert Christie, CBE 1983; TD 1962; Lord Lieutenant of Kinross-shire, 1966–74; *b* 3 Aug. 1926; *m* 1953, Ann Grizel Cochrane; three *s* two *d. Educ:* Eton; University College, Oxford. Lt Scots Guards, 1945–49. Oxford Univ., 1949–51 (BA Agric.). TA, 7 Argyll and Sutherland Highlanders, 1948–66; Lt-Col Comdg 7 A & SH, 1963–66. Hon. Col, 1/51 Highland Volunteers, 1972–75. Chm. and Pres., Bd of Governors, E of Scotland Coll. of Agric., 1970–83. DL Kinross 1956, VL 1958; Chairman Kinross County Council, 1963–73. *Address:* Arndean, By Dollar, Kinross-shire. *T:* Dollar 2527. *Club:* New (Edinburgh).

STEWART, Dr Robert William, OC 1979; FRS 1970; FRSC 1967; President, Alberta Research Council, Edmonton, Alberta, since 1984; Hon. Professor of Physics and Oceanography, University of British Columbia; Hon. Professor of Science, University of Alberta, since 1985; *b* 21 Aug. 1923; *m* 1st, 1948, V. Brande (marr. diss. 1972); two *s* one *d*; 2nd, 1973, Anne-Marie Robert; one *s. Educ:* Queen's Univ., Ontario. BSc 1945, MSc 1947, Queen's; PhD Cantab 1952. Canadian Defence Research Bd, 1950–61; Prof. of Physics and Oceanography, Univ. of British Columbia, 1961–70; Dir, Marine Scis Br., Pacific Reg., Environment Canada, 1970–74; Dir-Gen., Ocean and Aquatic Scis, Pacific Reg., Fisheries and Marine Service, Dept of Fisheries and Oceans, Canada, 1974–79; Dep. Minister, Ministry of Univs, Science and Communications, BC, Canada, 1979–84; Vis. Professor: Dalhousie Univ., 1960–61; Harvard Univ., 1964; Pennsylvania State Univ., 1964; Commonwealth Vis. Prof., Cambridge Univ., 1967–68. Vice-Chm., 1968–72, Chm., 1972–76, Jt Organizing Cttee, Global Atmospheric Res. Program; Pres., Internat. Assoc. of Physical Scis of Ocean, 1975–79; Chm., Cttee on Climatic Changes and the Ocean, 1983– (Pres., 1980–83). *Publications:* numerous, on turbulence, oceanography and meteorology. *Address:* Alberta Research Council, Box 8330, Station F, Edmonton, Alberta T6H 5X2, Canada. *T:* (403) 450–5111. *Telex:* 037–2147 (RESEARCH EDM).

STEWART, Sir Robertson (Huntly), Kt 1979; CBE 1970; CEng, FIProdE, FPRI, FNZIM, FInstD; Executive Chairman: PDL Holdings Ltd (manufacturers of electrical and plastic products), since 1982 (Chairman and Managing Director, 1957–82); PDL (Asia), since 1975; *b* 21 Sept. 1913; *s* of Robert McGregor Stewart and Ivy Emily (*née* Grigg); *m* 1st, 1937, Ada Gladys Gunter; two *s* one *d*; 2nd, 1970, Ellen Adrienne Cansdale; two *s. Educ:* Christchurch Boys' High Sch.; Christchurch Technical Inst. CEng, FIProdE 1967, FPRI 1960, FNZIM 1962, FInstD 1970. Introd plastics industry to NZ, 1936; commenced manuf. of electrical products in NZ, 1937; estabd PDL Gp of Cos, 1947. Led NZ Trade Missions, 1962, 1964, 1966, 1967, 1970 and 1972. Pres., NZ Manufrs Fedn, 1963–64. Hon. Malaysian Consul. *Recreations:* motor racing, tennis, fishing. *Address:* 10 Coldstream Court, Christchurch 4, New Zealand. *T:* Christchurch 515831. *Club:* Canterbury (Christchurch).

STEWART, Robin Milton, QC 1978; a Recorder of the Crown Court, since 1978; *b* 5 Aug. 1938; *s* of late Brig. Guy Milton Stewart and of Dr Elaine Oenone Stewart, MD, BS; *m* 1962, Lynda Grace Medhurst; three *s. Educ:* Winchester; New Coll., Oxford (MA). Called to the Bar, Middle Temple, 1963; called to the Irish Bar, King's Inns, Dublin, 1975. Prosecuting Counsel to Inland Revenue, NE Circuit, 1976–78. *Recreations:* pictures, gardening, Scottish family history. *Address:* 2 Harcourt Buildings, Temple, EC4Y 9DB. *T:* 01–353 1394; 17 Blake Street, York YO1 2QJ. *T:* York 20048; South Garth, Tockwith, York YO5 8PY. *T:* Tockwith 754; 58G Pembridge Villas, W11 3ET. *T:* 01–221 5179. *Clubs:* Oriental; Durham County (Durham).

STEWART, Sir Ronald (Compton), 2nd Bt, *cr* 1937; DL; Chairman, London Brick Co. Ltd, 1966–79; *b* 14 Aug. 1903; *s* of Sir (Percy) Malcolm Stewart, 1st Bt, OBE, and Cordelia (*d* 1906,) *d* of late Rt Hon. Sir Joseph Compton Rickett, DL, MP; *S* father, 1951; *m* 1936, Cynthia, OBE, JP, *d* of Harold Farmiloe. *Educ:* Rugby; Jesus College, Cambridge. High Sheriff of Bedfordshire, 1954, DL 1974. *Heir: half-b* Malcolm Stewart [*b* 20 Dec. 1909; *m* 1935, Mary Stephanie (marr. diss. 1957), *d* of Frederick Ramon de Bertodano, 8th Marquis del Moral (Spain)]. *Address:* Maulden Grange, Maulden, Bedfordshire.

STEWART, Stanley Toft, CMG 1958; PJG Singapore, 1962; *b* 13 June 1910; *s* of Charles Campbell Stewart and Jeanette Matilda Doral; *m* 1935, Therese Zelie de Souza; seven *d. Educ:* St Xavier's Instn, Penang; Raffles Coll., Singapore. Straits Settlements CS, 1934–46; Overseas Civil Service, 1946–55; District Officer, Butterworth, Province Wellesley, 1947–52; Dep. Chm., Rural Board, Singapore, 1952–54; Chm., Rural Board, Singapore, 1954; Dep. Sec., Ministry of Local Government, Lands and Housing, Singapore, 1955, Actg Permanent Sec., 1955; Actg Chief Sec., Singapore, Oct. 1957–Jan. 1958; Permanent Secretary: Home Affairs, 1959–63; to Prime Minister, 1961–66; Singapore High Comr in Australia, 1966–69; Permanent Sec., Min. of Foreign Affairs, Singapore, 1969–72; Exec. Sec., Nat. Stadium Corp., 1973. *Recreations:* tennis, gardening. *Address:* 49 Jalan Jelita, Singapore 1027, Republic of Singapore. *Clubs:* Singapore Recreation, Club 200 (Singapore).

STEWART, Stephen Malcolm, CBE 1986; QC 1979; Chairman, Common Law Institute of Intellectual Property, since 1981; *b* 22 April 1914; *s* of Dr Siegmund and Helen Strauss; *m* 1946, Marie Josephine (*née* Bere); two *s. Educ:* Univ. of Vienna (LLD 1936); Ecole des Sciences Politiques, Paris (Diploma 1938); Univ. of London. Overseas Service, BBC, 1939; served Army, 1940–47; Captain, Liaison Officer, Free French Forces and Belgian Army, 1944–45; Major JAG's Branch, 21 Army Group, 1945; Chief Prosecuting Officer, War Crimes Trials, 1946–47; UN War Crimes Commn, 1947–48; called to the Bar, Inner Temple, 1948; practice at the Bar, 1948–61; Director General, IFPI, 1961–79. Mem., Gen. Council of the Bar, 1969–71; Vice-Chm., Bar Assoc. for Commerce, Finance and Industry, 1974–76, Chm., 1976–78; Member of Senate of the Inns of Court and Bar, 1976–81. Governor: Polytechnic of the South Bank, 1967–70; Sevenoaks School, 1968–83. Golden Cross of the Republic, Austria, 1983. *Publications:* The Clearinghouse System for Copyright Licences, 1966; 200 Years of English Copyright Law, 1976; International Copyright in the 1980s (Geiringer Meml Lecture, NY), 1980; International Copyright and Neighbouring Rights, 1983. *Recreations:* music, skiing, tennis. *Address:* Oakwood, Chittoe, Wilts. *T:* Devizes (0380) 850066. *Club:* Reform.

STEWART, Mrs Suzanne Freda; *see* Norwood, S. F.

STEWART, Victor Colvin, FCA; Registrar General for Scotland, 1978–82; *b* 12 April 1921; *s* of Victor Stewart and Jean Cameron; *m* 1949, Aileen Laurie; one *s. Educ:* Selkirk High Sch.; Edinburgh Univ. (BCom). FCA 1954. Served War in RAF, Africa and ME, 1942–46. Joined Dept of Health for Scotland, 1938; Chief Exec. Officer, 1959; Principal, SHHD, 1963, Asst Sec. 1971; Dep. Registrar Gen. for Scotland, 1976. *Recreations:* golf, walking, bridge. *Address:* Tynet, Lodgehill Road, Nairn IV12 4QL. *T:* Nairn 52050. *Club:* Royal Commonwealth Society.

STEWART, Dr William, CB 1977; DSc; aerospace consultant, since 1983; *b* Hamilton, 29 Aug. 1921; *m* 1955, Helen Cairney; two *d. Educ:* St John's Grammar Sch.; Hamilton Acad.; Glasgow Univ. BSc Hons (engin.); DSc 1958. RAE, Farnborough, 1942–53; British Jt Services Mission, Washington, 1953–56; Dep. Head of Naval Air Dept, RAE, Bedford, 1956–63; Imperial Defence College, 1964; Asst Dir, Project Time and Cost Analysis, 1965–66; Dir, Anglo-French Combat Trainer Aircraft Projects, 1966–70; Dir-Gen., Multi-Role Combat Aircraft, 1970–73; Dep. Controller, Aircraft A, 1973–78, Aircraft, 1978–81, MoD (PE). Silver Medal, RAeS, 1981. *Address:* 25 Brickhill Drive, Bedford MK41 7QA.

STEWART, Prof. William Alexander Campbell, MA, PhD; DL; Vice-Chancellor, University of Keele, 1967–79; *b* Glasgow, 17 Dec. 1915; *s* of late Thomas Stewart, Glasgow, and Helen Fraser, Elgin, Morayshire; *m* 1947, Ella Elizabeth Burnett, of Edinburgh; one *s* one *d. Educ:* Colfe's Grammar Sch., London; University Coll., and Inst. of Education, Univ. of London. Exhibitioner, University Coll., London., 1934–37; BA 1937; MA 1941; PhD 1947; Diploma in Education, 1938; Fellow, UCL, 1975. Sen. English Master: (and Housemaster), Friends' School, Saffron Walden, Essex, 1938–43; Abbotsholme School, Derbyshire, 1943–44 (Member of Governing Body, 1960–80; Chm., Council, 1974–80); Asst Lectr and Lectr in Education, University Coll., Nottingham, 1944–47; Lectr in Education, Univ. of Wales (Cardiff), 1947–50; Prof. of Education, Univ. of Keele, 1950–67. Vis. Prof., McGill Univ., 1957, Univ. of Calif., Los Angeles 1959; Simon Vis. Prof., Univ. of Manchester, 1962–63; Prestige Fellow, NZ Univs, 1969; Vis. Professorial Fellow, Univ. of Sussex, 1979–84. Chairman: YMCA Educn Cttee, 1962–67; Nat. Adv. Council for Child Care, 1968–71; Univs Council for Adult Educn, 1969–73; Council, Roehampton Inst. of Higher Educn, 1979–; Member: Inter-Univ. and Polytech. Council for Higher Education Overseas; Commonwealth Univ. Interchange Council, 1968–80; Council, Univ. of Sierra Leone, 1968–83; Adv. Council, Supply and Training of Teachers, 1974–78; US-UK Educnl Commn, 1977–81. Fellow, Internat. Inst. of Art and Letters. DL Stafford, 1973. Hon. DLitt: Ulster, 1973; Keele, 1981. *Publications:* Quakers and Education, 1953; (ed with J. Eros) Systematic Sociology of Karl Mannheim, 1957; (with K. Mannheim) An Introduction to the Sociology of Education, 1962; contrib. to The American College (ed Sanford), 1962; The Educational Innovators, Vol. 1, with W. P. McCann, 1967, Vol. 2, 1968; Progressives and Radicals in English Education 1750–1970, 1972. *Recreations:* formerly most games; travelling, talking, theatre, music. *Address:* 42 Dean Court Road, Rottingdean, Brighton, Sussex. *Clubs:* Oriental; Federation House (Stoke on Trent).

STEWART, Prof. William Duncan Paterson, PhD, DSc; FRS 1977; FRSE; Boyd-Baxter Professor of Biology, since 1968, and Vice-Principal, since 1985, University of Dundee (Head of Department of Biological Sciences, 1968–83); *b* 7 June 1935; *s* of John Stewart and Margaret (*née* Paterson); *m* 1958, Catherine MacLeod; one *s. Educ:* Bowmore Junior Secondary Sch., Isle-of-Islay; Dunoon Grammar Sch.; Glasgow Univ. (BSc, PhD, DSc). FRSE 1973. Asst Lectr, Univ. of Nottingham, 1961–63; Lectr, Westfield Coll., Univ. of London, 1963–68. Vis. Res. Worker, Univ. of Wisconsin, 1966 and 1968; Vis. Professor: Univ. of Kuwait, 1980; Univ. of Otago, 1984. Chairman: Royal Soc. Biological Educn Cttee, 1977–80; Aquatic Life Sciences Grants Cttee, NERC, 1973–78; Sci. Adv. Cttee, Freshwater Biol. Assoc., 1974–85; Royal Soc. Study Group on Nitrogen Cycle, 1979–84; Internat. Cttee on Microbial Ecology, 1983–86 (Sec., 1980–83); Royal Soc. Biotechnology and Educn Wkg Gp, 1980–81; Independent Adv. Gp on Gruinard Is., 1986–; Vice-Pres., 1973–75, Pres., 1975–77, British Phycological Soc.; President: Section K, BAAS, 1984; Council, Scottish Marine Biol. Assoc., 1985– (Mem, 1969–74, 1982–); Vice-Pres., Freshwater Biol. Assoc., 1984–. Trustee, Estuarine and Brackish-Water Sciences Assoc., 1978–; Member: Council, RSE, 1976–79; Council, Marine Biol. Assoc., 1973–76, 1977–80, 1981–84; Plants and Soils Res. Grants Bd, ARC, 1978–84; Governing Body, Scottish Hort. Res. Inst., 1971–80; British Nat. Cttee for problems of environment, Royal Soc., 1979–85; UNESCO Panel on Microbiology, 1975–81; Council, NERC, 1979–85 (Chm., Marine Life Scis Preparatory Gp, 1982–85); Internat. Cell Res. Org., 1979–84; Governing Body, Scottish Crop Res. Inst., 1980–; Royal Soc. Study Gp on Science Educn, 1981–82; Council, Royal Soc., 1984–86; Royal Commn on Environmental Pollution, 1986–. Royal Soc. Assessor, AFRC, 1985–. Lectures: Phycological Soc. of America Dist., 1977; Barton-Wright, Inst. Biol., 1977; Sir David Martin Royal Soc.-BAYS, 1979; Plenary, 2nd Internat. Symp. on Microbial Ecology, 1980; Holden, Nottingham Univ., 1983; Leeuwenhoek, Royal Soc., 1984; Plenary, 2nd Internat. Phycological Congress, Copenhagen, 1985. *Publications:* Nitrogen Fixation in Plants, 1966; (jtly) The Blue-Green Algae, 1973; Algal Physiology and Biochemistry, 1974; (ed) Nitrogen Fixation by Free-living Organisms, 1975; (ed jtly) Nitrogen Fixation, 1980; (ed jtly) The Nitrogen Cycle of the United Kingdom, 1984; papers in learned jls of repute. *Recreations:* watching soccer, playing the bagpipes (occasionally). *Address:* Department of Biological Sciences, University of Dundee, Dundee DD1 4HN. *T:* Dundee 23181, ext. 324; 45 Fairfield Road, West Ferry, Dundee. *T:* Dundee 76702.

STEWART, William Ian; *see* Allanbridge, Hon. Lord.

STEWART, William McCausland; Professor of French, University of Bristol, 1945–66; Emeritus, 1966; *b* 17 Sept. 1900; *yr s* of late Abraham McCausland Stewart, Londonderry, and Alexandrina Catherine Margaret Elsner, Dublin; *m* 1933, Ann Cecilia Selo (*d* 1969); two *d. Educ:* Foyle Coll., Londonderry; Trinity Coll., Dublin (Sizar, Schol. and Sen. Moderator in Mod. Literature-French and German; Prizeman in Old and Middle English; Vice-Chancellor's Prizeman in English Verse). BA 1922; MA 1926; Lecteur d'Anglais, Univ. of Montpellier, 1922–23 (Certificat de Licence en Phonétique, 1923). Resident Lecteur d'Anglais at Ecole Normale Supérieure, Paris, 1923–26; also studied Sorbonne (Diplôme d'Etudes Supérieures de Lettres: Langues Classiques, 1925) and Ecole des Hautes Etudes, Paris, and taught Collège Sainte-Barbe, Paris; Lectr in French, Univ. of Sheffield, 1927 and 1928; Lectr in French and Joint Head of French Dept, Univ. of St Andrews and University College, Dundee, from 1928 onwards. Seconded for War Service in Foreign Research and Press Service (Chatham House), Balliol College, Oxford, Sept. 1939; Head of French Section of same, 1940–43; Head of French Section, Research Dept of Foreign Office, 1943–45. Chairman, University of Bristol Art Lectures Committee, 1946–66; Dean of Faculty of Arts, 1960–62; Visiting Professor, Univ. of Auckland, 1967. Member Council, RWA; Pres., Clifton Arts Club; Governor, Bath Academy of Art, Corsham Court; Chairman, Bristol-Bordeaux Assoc., 1953–76; Corr. Mem. Acad. des Sciences, Belles Lettres et Arts de Bordeaux and of Acad. Montesquieu. Chevalier de la Légion d'Honneur, 1950. Officier des Palmes Académiques, 1957, Commandeur, 1966. DLitt (*hc*), Nat. Univ. of Ireland, 1963. *Publications:* Les Etudes Françaises en Grand Bretagne,

Paris, 1929 (with G. T. Clapton); translation of Paul Valéry's Eupalinos, with Preface, Oxford, 1932, and of his Dialogues, Bollingen Series XLV, New York, 1956 and London, 1958; Les Chœurs d'Athalie (record), 1958; Aspects of the French Classical Ideal, 1967; Tokens in Time (poems), 1968; Alcaics for our Age, 1976; Bristol-Bordeaux: The First Thirty Years, 1977; contribs to literary reviews and learned periodicals, mainly on Classical and Modern France (incl. Descartes, Racine, Montesquieu, Valéry). *Recreations:* promoting Community Service for All (CSA), and proportional representation (PR/STV). *Address:* 5 Cotham Park, Bristol BS6 6BZ. *T:* Bristol 48156. *Club:* Europe House.

See also J. N. T. Spreckley, A. L. Stewart.

STEWART-CLARK, Sir John, 3rd Bt *cr* 1918; Member (C) Sussex East, European Parliament, since 1979; *b* 17 Sept. 1929; *e s* of Sir Stewart Stewart-Clark, 2nd Bt, and of Jane Pamela, *d* of late Major Arundell Clarke; *S* father, 1971; *m* 1958, Lydia Frederike, *d* of J. W. Loudon, Holland; one *s* four *d. Educ:* Eton; Balliol College, Oxford; Harvard Business School. Commissioned with HM Coldstream Guards, 1948–49. Oxford, 1949–52. With J. & P. Coats Ltd, 1952–69; Managing Director: J. & P. Coats, Pakistan, Ltd, 1961–67; J. A. Carp's Garenfabrieken, Holland, 1967–69; Philips Electrical Ltd, London, 1971–75; Pye of Cambridge Ltd, 1975–79. Director: Low and Bonar plc; Oppenheimer Internat.; A. T. Kearwey Ltd. Pres. Supervisory Bd, Eur. Inst. for Security, 1984–; Mem. Council, RUSI, 1979–83. Dir and Trustee, Eur. Centre for Work and Society. Treas., Eur. Democratic Group, 1979–. Member Royal Company of Archers, Queen's Body Guard for Scotland. Contested (U) North Aberdeen, Gen. Election, 1959. *Recreations:* golf, tennis, shooting, photography, vintage cars. *Heir: s* Alexander Dudley Stewart-Clark, *b* 21 Nov. 1960. *Address:* Holmsley House, near Cowden, Kent. *T:* Cowden 541. *Clubs:* White's; Royal Ashdown Golf.

STEWART COX, Maj.-Gen. Arthur George Ernest, DFC 1952; General Officer Commanding Wales, 1978–80; *b* 11 April 1925; *s* of Lt-Col Arthur Stewart Cox and Mrs Dorothea Stewart Cox, *d* of Maj.-Gen. Sir Edward May; *m* 1953, Mary Pamela, *d* of Hon. George Lyttelton; three *s* one *d. Educ:* Marlborough Coll.; Aberdeen Univ. Commissioned RA, 1944; parachutist, RA regts, 1945–50; army pilot, Far East and Korea, 1950–52; ADC to Comdt, RMA Sandhurst, 1954–56; Staff Coll., 1956; SO 99 Gurkha Inf. Bde, 1957–58; SO MoD, Malaya, 1963–65; CO 29 Commando Light Regt, RA, 1965–68; SO Sch. of Artillery, 1968–69; Comdr RA 4th Div., 1969–72; RCDS, 1973; Dep. Dir of Manning (Army), MoD, 1974–76. Col Comdt, RA, 1980–; Hon. Colonel: 3rd Bn RWF, TAVR, 1980–85; 289 Commando Battery, RA, TAVR, 1983–. *Recreations:* shooting, fishing, lepidoptery, gardening. *Address:* The Old Rectory, Bishopstrow, Warminster, Wilts. *T:* Warminster 214584.

STEWART-JONES, Mrs Richard; *see* Smith, Emma.

STEWART-MOORE, Alexander Wyndham Hume; DL; Chairman, Gallaher Ltd, 1975–79 (Managing Director, 1966–75); Director, American Brands Inc., 1975–79; *b* 14 Feb. 1915; 2nd *s* of late James Stewart-Moore, DL, Ballydivity, Dervock, Co. Antrim, and of Katherine Marion (*née* Jackson); *m* 1948, Magdalene Clare, *y d* of Sir David Richard Llewellyn, 1st Bt, LLD, JP; three *s* one *d. Educ:* Shrewsbury. Joined Gallaher Ltd, Nov. 1934. Served War, Royal Artillery (Middle East and Italy), 1939–46. *Recreations:* farming, fishing, gardening. *Address:* Seaport, Portballintrae, Bushmills, Co. Antrim, NI. *T:* Bushmills 31361. *Club:* Ulster.

STEWART-RICHARDSON, Sir Simon (Alaisdair), 17th Bt *cr* 1630; *b* 9 June 1947; *er s* of Sir Ian Rorie Hay Stewart-Richardson, 16th Bt, and of Audrey Meryl (who *m* 1975, P. A. P. Robertson, *qv*), *e d* of late Claude Odlum; *S* father, 1969. *Educ:* Trinity College, Glenalmond. *Heir: b* Ninian Rorie Stewart-Richardson [*b* 20 Jan. 1949; *m* 1983, Joan Kristina, *d* of Howard Smee]. *Address:* Lynedale, Longcross, near Chertsey, Surrey KT16 0DP. *T:* Ottershaw 2329.

STEWART-SMITH, Rev. Canon David Cree, MA; *b* 22 May 1913; 3rd *s* of late Thomas Stewart Stewart-Smith, JP, Heathlands, Kinver, Staffs, and Mabel (*née* McDougall); *m* 1943, Kathleen Georgiana Maule Ffinch, *d* of Rev. K. M. Ffinch, Ifield, Kent. *Educ:* Marlborough; King's Coll., Cambridge; Cuddesdon Theol. College. BA 1939, MA 1943. Vicar-Choral and Sacrist, York Minster, 1944–49; Vicar of Shadwell, Leeds, 1949–52; Warden, Brasted Place Coll., 1952–63; Dean of St George's Cath., Jerusalem, and Administrator of St George's Coll., 1964–67; Commissary for Archbishop in Jerusalem, 1968–76; Archdeacon of Bromley and Hon. Canon of Rochester, 1968–69; Archdeacon of Rochester and Canon Residentiary of Rochester Cathedral, 1969–76; Hon. Canon of Rochester, 1976–78, Canon Emeritus, 1978–; Director of Ordinands, dio. Rochester, 1968–74; Mem., C of E Pensions Bd, 1970–84; a Church Commissioner, 1973–78; Home Sec., Jerusalem and Middle East Church Assoc., 1976–78; Fellow of Woodard Corp.: Northern Div., 1949–52; Southern Div., 1959–64. *Recreations:* architecture, music, travel. *Address:* 16 Capel Court, Prestbury, near Cheltenham GL52 3EL. *T:* Cheltenham 510972. *Club:* United Oxford & Cambridge University.

STEWART-SMITH, (Dudley) Geoffrey; Director, Foreign Affairs Research Institute, since 1976; *b* 28 Dec. 1933; *s* of Dudley Cautley Stewart-Smith; *m* 1956, Kay Mary; three *s. Educ:* Winchester; RMA Sandhurst. Regular Officer, The Black Watch, 1952–60. Director: Foreign Affairs Circle; Freedom Communications Internat. News Agency; Editor, East-West Digest; Dir, Foreign Affairs Publishing Co.; Financial Times, 1968. MP (C) Derbyshire, Belper, 1970–Feb 1974. *Publications:* The Defeat of Communism, 1964; No Vision Here: Non-Military Warfare in Britain, 1966; (ed) Brandt and the Destruction of NATO, 1973; The Struggle for Freedom, 1980; contribs to various foreign, defence and communist affairs jls at home and overseas. *Recreations:* walking, swimming, shooting and stalking. *Address:* Church House, Petersham, Surrey. *T:* 01–940 2885.

STEWART-WILSON, Lt-Col Blair Aubyn, LVO 1983; Deputy Master of the Household and Equerry to Her Majesty, since 1976; *b* 17 July 1929; *s* of late Aubyn Wilson and late Muriel Stewart Stevens; *m* 1962, Helen Mary Fox; three *d. Educ:* Eton; Sandhurst. Commnd Scots Guards, 1949; served with Regt in UK, Germany and Far East; Adjutant 2nd Bn, 1955–57; ADC to Viscount Cobham, Governor General and C-in-C, New Zealand, 1957–59; Equerry to late Duke of Gloucester, 1960–62; Regtl Adjutant, 1966–68; GSO1, Foreign Liaison Sect. (Army), MoD, 1970–73; Defence, Military and Air Attaché, British Embassy, Vienna, 1975–76. *Address:* 3 Browning Close, W9 1BW. *T:* 01–286 9891; The Old Brewery, North Curry, near Taunton, Somerset. *Clubs:* Turf, Pratt's, White's.

STEYN, Hon. Sir Johan, Kt 1985; **Hon. Mr Justice Steyn;** a Judge of the High Court, Queen's Bench Division, since 1985; *b* 15 Aug. 1932; *m* Susan Leonore (*née* Lewis); two *s* two *d* by previous *m. Educ:* Jan van Riebeeck Sch., Cape Town, S Africa; Univ. of Stellenbosch, S Africa (BA, LLB); University Coll., Oxford (MA). Cape Province Rhodes Scholar, 1955; commenced practice at S African Bar, 1958; Sen. Counsel of Supreme Court of SA, 1970; settled in UK; commenced practice at English Bar, 1973 (Bencher, Lincoln's Inn, 1985); QC 1979. Member: Supreme Court Rule Cttee, 1985–; Deptl Adv. Cttee on Arbitration Law, 1986–. *Address:* c/o Royal Courts of Justice, WC2.

STEYN, Hon. (Stephanus Jacobus) Marais, DMS 1981; South African Ambassador to Transkei, since 1984; *b* 25 Dec. 1914; *m* 1940, Susanne Moolman; two *s* two *d. Educ:* Univ. of Cape Town (BA); Univ. of the Witwatersrand (LLB). Journalist, various newspapers and on staff of State Information Office, 1938–42; Sec., United Party, Witwatersrand, 1942–48 (Asst Chief Sec., 1946–48); Opposition MP representing consecutively constituencies of Alberton, Vereeniging and Yeoville, specialising in labour and transport matters, 1948–73; National Party MP for Turffontein, 1974–79; Minister of: Indian Affairs and Tourism, 1975; Community Develt, 1976–79; Community Develt, Coloured Relations and Indian Affairs, 1979; Ambassador to UK, 1980–84. *Recreations:* bowls, chess, grandchildren. *Address:* Private Bag 5022, Umtata, Republic of Transkei, Southern Africa. *Club:* City and Civil Service (Cape Town).

STIBBARD, Peter Jack; Under Secretary, Statistics Division 2, Department of Trade and Industry, since 1985; *b* 15 May 1936; *s* of Frederick Stibbard and Gladys Stibbard (*née* Daines); *m* 1964, Christine Fuller; two *d. Educ:* City of Norwich Grammar School; Hull Univ. (BSc Econ; MIS). Served RAF, 1954–56. Kodak Ltd, 1959–64; Thos Potterton Ltd, 1964–66; Greater London Council, 1966–68; Central Statistical Office, 1968–82 (Chief Statistician 1973); HM Treasury, 1982–85. *Publications:* articles in official and trade jls. *Address:* Department of Trade and Industry, 1–19 Victoria Street, SW1H 0ET. *T:* 01–215 4872.

STIBBE, Philip Godfrey, MA; Head Master of Norwich School, 1975–84; *b* 20 July 1921; *m* 1956, Mary Joy, *d* of late Canon C. G. Thornton; two *s* one *d. Educ:* Mill Hill Sch.; Merton Coll., Oxford (MA). Served War of 1939–45; joined Royal Sussex Regt, 1941; seconded King's (Liverpool) Regt, 1942; 1st Wingate Expedn into Burma (wounded, despatches), 1943; POW, 1943–45. Asst Master, 1948–75, Housemaster, 1953–74, Bradfield Coll. JP Norwich, 1979–84. *Publication:* Return via Rangoon, 1947. *Recreations:* people, places, books. *Address:* Foundry House, Letheringsett, Holt, Norfolk NR25 7JL. *T:* Holt 712329.

STIBBON, Maj.-Gen. John James, OBE 1979; Assistant Chief of Defence Staff Operational Requirements, (Land Systems), since 1985; *b* 5 Jan. 1935; *s* of Jack Stibbon and Elizabeth Matilda Stibbon (*née* Dixon); *m* 1957, Jean Fergusson Skeggs, *d* of John Robert Skeggs and Florence Skeggs (*née* Hayes); two *d. Educ:* Portsmouth Southern Grammar School; Royal Military Academy; Royal Military College of Science. BSc (Eng). Commissioned RE, 1954; CO 28 Amphibious Engineer Regt, 1975–77; Asst Military Secretary, 1977–79; Comd 20 Armoured Brigade, 1979–81; Comdt, RMCS, 1983–85. Colonel Commandant: RAPC, 1985–; RPC, 1986–. *Recreations:* Association football, athletics, painting, palaeontology. *Address:* Lloyds Bank, 6 Pall Mall, SW1.

STIBBS, Prof. Douglas Walter Noble, MSc Sydney, DPhil Oxon; FRAS, FRSE; Napier Professor of Astronomy and Director of the University Observatory, University of St Andrews, since 1959; *b* 17 Feb. 1919; 2nd *s* of Edward John Stibbs, Sydney, NSW; *m* 1949, Margaret Lilian Calvert, BSc, DipEd (Sydney), AID, *er d* of Rev. John Calvert, Sydney, NSW; two *d. Educ:* Sydney High Sch.; Univ. of Sydney; New College, Oxford. Deas Thomson Scholar, Sch. of Physics, Univ. of Sydney, 1940; BSc (Sydney), 1st Class Hons, Univ. Medal in Physics, 1942; MSc (Sydney), 1943; DPhil (Oxon), 1954. Johnson Memorial Prize and Gold Medal for Advancement of Astronomy and Meteorology, Oxford Univ., 1956. Res. Asst, Commonwealth Solar Observatory, Canberra, ACT, 1940–42; Asst Lectr, Dept of Mathematics and Physics, New England University Coll., Armidale, NSW (now the Univ. of New England), 1942–45; Scientific Officer and Sen. Scientific Officer, Commonwealth Observatory, Canberra, ACT, 1945–51; Radcliffe Travelling Fellow in Astronomy, Radcliffe Observatory, Pretoria, S Africa, and Univ. Observatory, Oxford, 1951–54; PSO, UKAEA, 1955–59; Vis. Prof. of Astrophysics, Yale Univ. Observatory, 1966–67; British Council Vis. Prof., Univ. of Utrecht, 1968; Prof., Collège de France, 1975–76. Member: Internat. Astronomical Union, 1951– (Chm. Finance Cttee, 1964–67, 1973–76, 1976–79); Amer. Astronomical Soc., 1956–73; Adv. Cttee on Meteorology for Scotland, 1960–69, 1972–75, 1978–80; Board of Visitors, Royal Greenwich Observatory, 1963–65; Council RAS, 1964–67, 1970–73 (Vice-Pres., 1972–73), Editorial Board, 1970–73; Council, RSE, 1970–72; National Cttee for Astronomy, 1964–76; SRC Cttees for Royal Greenwich Observatory, 1966–70, and Royal Observatory, Edinburgh, 1966–76, Chm., 1970–76; SRC Astronomy, Space and Radio Bd, 1970–76; SRC, 1972–76; S African Astron. Obs. Adv. Cttee, 1972–76; Chairman: Astronomy Policy and Grants Cttee, 1972–74; Northern Hemisphere Observatory Planning Cttee, 1972–75; Astronomy II Cttee, 1974–75; Mem., Centre National de la Recherche Scientifique Cttee, Obs. de Haute Provence, 1973–82. Life Member: Sydney Univ. Union, 1942; New Coll. Soc., 1953; New England Univ. Union, NSW, 1957. Member: Western Province Masters Athletics Assoc., Cape Town, 1983–; British Marathon Runners Club, 1983–; St Andrews Astronomy City-to-Surf Runners Club, 1983–. Marathon Medals: Paris, Caithness, and Edinburgh (3hrs 59mins), 1983; Flying Fox (British Veterans Championships), Honolulu, 1983; London, Loch Rannoch, and Aberdeen (Veterans Trophy Winner), 1984; Stoke-on-Trent (Potteries), Athens, Honolulu, 1985; London, Edinburgh (Commonwealth Games Peoples Marathon), Stoke-on-Trent (Potteries), 1986. *Publications:* The Outer Layers of a Star (with Sir Richard Woolley), 1953; contrib. Theoretical Astrophysics and Astronomy in Monthly Notices of RAS and other jls. *Recreations:* music, ornithology, photography, golf, long-distance running. *Address:* University Observatory, Buchanan Gardens, St Andrews, Fife KY16 9LZ. *T:* St Andrews 72643. *Club:* Royal and Ancient (St Andrews).

STIFF, Rt. Rev. Hugh Vernon; Rector of St James Cathedral and Dean of Toronto, since 1974; Assistant Bishop, Diocese of Toronto, since 1977; *b* 15 Sept. 1916; unmarried. *Educ:* Univ. of Toronto (BA); Trinity Coll., Toronto (LTh). BD General Synod; Hon. DD, Trinity Coll., Toronto. Bishop of Keewatin, 1969–74. *Address:* 65 Church Street, Toronto, Ontario, Canada.

STIGLER, Prof. George Joseph, PhD; economist; Charles R. Walgreen Distinguished Service Professor Emeritus of American Institutions, University of Chicago, since 1981; *b* 17 Jan. 1911; *s* of Joseph Stigler and Elizabeth Stigler (*née* Hungler); *m* 1936, Margaret Mack (*d* 1970); three *s. Educ:* Seattle schools; Univ. of Washington (BBA); Northwestern Univ. (MBA); Univ. of Chicago (PhD 1938). Asst Prof., Iowa State Univ., 1936–38; Asst Prof., later Prof., Univ. of Minnesota, 1938–46 (war-time Mem., Stats Res. Group, Columbia Univ.); Professor: Brown Univ., 1946–47; Columbia Univ., 1947–58; Charles R. Walgreen Prof. of Amer. Instns, Graduate Sch. of Business, Univ. of Chicago, 1958, Dist. Service Prof., 1963; Founder, Center for Study of the Economy and the States, Univ. of Chicago, 1977. Member: Nat. Acad. of Sciences, 1975; Amer. Economic Assoc. (Pres., 1964); Guggenheim Fellow, 1955. Nobel Prize for Economic Science, 1982. Editor, Jl of Political Economy, 1974–. *Publications:* Production and Distribution Theories, 1940; The Theory of Competitive Price, 1942; The Theory of Price, 1946 (numerous rev. edns); Trends in Employment in the Service Industries, 1956; The Intellectual and the Market Place, 1964, rev. edn 1984; Essays in the History of Economics, 1965; The Organization of Industry, 1968; The Citizen and the State, 1975; The Economist as Preacher, 1982; essays and articles for Nat. Bureau of Economic Research, Fortune, Jl of Political Economy (The Economics of Information, 1961), Jl of Business, Jl of Law and Economics, Bell Jl of

Economics and Management Science, Antitrust Bulletin and other learned jls. *Recreations:* book collecting, golf, photography, wood working. *Address:* University of Chicago Graduate School of Business, 1101 East 58th Street, Chicago, Ill 60637, USA; 2621 Brassie Avenue, Flossmoor, Ill 60422, USA.

STIGLITZ, Prof. Joseph Eugene, PhD; Professor of Economics, Princeton University, since 1979; *b* 9 Feb. 1943; *m* M. J. Hannaway; two *s* two *d*. *Educ:* Amherst Coll. (BA 1964); MIT (PhD 1966); Cambridge Univ. (MA 1970). Professor of Economics: Yale Univ. 1970–74; Stanford Univ., 1974–76; Drummond Prof. of Political Economy, Oxford Univ. and All Souls Coll., 1976–79. Fellowships: Nat. Sci. Foundn, 1964–65; Fulbright, 1965–66; SSRC Faculty, 1969–70; Guggenheim, 1969–70; Oskar Morgenstern Distinguished Fellowship, Mathematica and Inst. for Advanced Study, Princeton, 1978–79. Consultant: Nat. Sci. Foundn, 1972–75; Ford Foundn Energy Policy Study, 1973; Dept of Labor (Pensions and Labor Turnover), 1974; Dept of Interior (Offshore Oil Leasing Programs), 1975; Federal Energy Admin (Intertemporal Biases in Market Allocation of Natural Resources), 1975–79; World Bank (Cost Benefit Analysis; Urban Rural Migration; Natural Resources), 1975–; Electric Power Res. Inst., 1976–; OECD; Office of Fair Trading; Federal Trade Commn; Treasury (Office of Tax Analysis), 1980; US AID (commodity price stabilization), 1977; Inter-American Development Bank; Bell Laboratories; Bell Communications Research. Gen. Editor, Econometric Soc. Reprint Series; Associate Editor: Jl of Economic Theory, 1968–73; American Economic Rev., 1972–75; Co-editor, Jl of Public Economics, 1968–83; American Editor, Rev. of Economic Studies, 1968–76; Editorial Bd, World Bank Economic Review. Vice-Pres., American Econ. Assoc., 1985. Fellow: Econometric Soc., 1972 (Sec./Treasurer, 1972–75); Amer. Acad. of Arts and Scis. Hon. MA Yale, 1970; Hon. DHL Amherst, 1974. John Bates Clark Medal, Amer. Econ. Assoc. *Publications:* (ed) Collected Scientific Papers of P. A. Samuelson, 1965; (ed with H. Uzawa) Readings in Modern Theory of Economic Growth, 1969; (with A. B. Atkinson) Lectures in Public Finance, 1980; (with D. Newbery) The Economic Impact of Price Stabilization, 1980; Economics of the Public Sector, 1986; contribs on economics of growth, development, natural resources, information, uncertainty, imperfect competition, corporate finance and public finance in Amer. Econ. Rev., Qly Jl of Econs, Jl of Pol. Econ., Econometrica, Internat. Econ. Rev., Econ. Jl, Rev. of Econ. Studies, Jl of Public Econs, Jl of Econ. Theory, Oxford Econ. Papers. *Address:* 139 Broadmead, Princeton, NJ 08540, USA.

STIMSON, Robert Frederick; HM Diplomatic Service; Counsellor and Head of Chancery, Dublin, since 1984; *b* 16 May 1939; *s* of Frederick Henry and Gladys Alma Stimson (*née* Joel); *m* 1961, Margaret Faith Kerry; two *s* one *d*. *Educ:* Rendcomb Coll.; Queen Mary Coll., London (BSc First Cl. Hons; MSc (by thesis) mathematical physics). HM Diplomatic Service: FO, 1966–67; Saigon, 1967–68; Singapore, 1968–70; Cabinet Office, 1970–73; Mexico City, 1973–75; FCO, 1975–80; Counsellor, East Berlin, 1980–81; Head of Home Inspectorate, 1982–83. Order of Aztec Eagle, Mexico, 1975. *Publications:* contrib. Jl Physics and Chemistry of Solids. *Address:* c/o Foreign and Commonwealth Office, SW1A 2AH.

STINSON, Sir Charles (Alexander), KBE 1979 (OBE 1962); Minister of Finance, Fiji, 1972–79, retired; *b* 22 June 1919; *s* of William John Bolton Stinson and Ella Josephine (*née* Griffiths); *m* 1946, Mollie, *d* of Albert Dean; two *s* one *d*. *Educ:* Levuka Public Sch.; Suva Grammar Sch. Morris Hedstrom Ltd, Fiji, 1935–38; Emperor Gold Mining Co. Ltd, Fiji, 1939–40; Fiji RNVR, 1940–45; Man. Dir, Stinsons Ltd, 1946–66. Elected to Suva City Council, 1952; Mayor of Suva, 1959–66; elected Gen. Mem. for Suva, 1964; Mem. for Communications, Works and Tourism, 1966–70; Minister for Communications, Works and Tourism, 1970–72. *Recreations:* fishing, flying, boating, golf. *Address:* 31 Blair Athol Crescent, Sorrento, Gold Coast, Queensland 4217, Australia.

STINSON, His Honour David John; a Circuit Judge (formerly County Court Judge), 1969–86; Chancellor, Diocese of Carlisle, since 1971; *b* 22 Feb. 1921; *s* of late Henry John Edwin Stinson, MC, MA, LLB, Beckenham, Kent (sometime Chief Commoner of City of London, solicitor), and late Margaret Stinson (*née* Little); *m* 1950, Eleanor Judith (*née* Chance); two *s* two *d* (and one *s* decd). *Educ:* Eastbourne Coll.; Emmanuel Coll., Cambridge. MA 1946; Jesters Club, 1949 (Rugby Fives). Served War of 1939–45: Essex Yeomanry, Captain, RA, and Air OP, 1941–46 (despatches). Called to Bar, Middle Temple, 1947; Dep. Chm., Herts QS, 1965–71; Suffolk and Essex County Court Circuit, 1973–86. *Recreations:* bird-watching, sailing. *Address:* Barrack Row, Waldringfield, Woodbridge, Suffolk IP12 4QX. *T:* Waldringfield 280. *Clubs:* Army and Navy; Waldringfield Sailing.

STIRLING, Sir Alexander (John Dickson), KBE 1981; CMG 1976; HM Diplomatic Service; Ambassador to Sudan, 1984–86; *b* 20 Oct. 1926; *e s* of late Brig. A. Dickson Stirling, DSO, MB, ChB, DPH, and Isobel Stirling, MA, DipEd, DipPsych, *d* of late Rev. J. C. Matthew (former senior Presidency Chaplain, Bombay); *m* 1955, Alison Mary, *y d* of Gp Capt. A. P. Campbell, CBE; two *s* two *d*. *Educ:* Edinburgh Academy; Lincoln Coll., Oxford (MA). RAFVR, 1945–48 (Egypt, 1945–47). Entered Foreign Office, 1951; Lebanon, 1952; British Embassy, Cairo, 1952–56 (Oriental Sec., 1955–56); FO, 1956–59; First Sec., British Embassy, Baghdad, 1959–62; First Sec. and Consul, Amman, 1962–64; First Sec., British Embassy, Santiago, 1965–67; FO, 1967–69; British Political Agent, Bahrain, 1969–71, Ambassador, 1971–72; Counsellor, Beirut, 1972–75; RCDS 1976; Ambassador to Iraq, 1977–80, to the Tunisian Republic, 1981–84.
See also C. J. M. Stirling.

STIRLING, Angus Duncan Æneas; Director-General, The National Trust, since 1983 (Deputy Director-General, 1979–83); *b* 10 Dec. 1933; *s* of Duncan Alexander Stirling, *qv*; *m* 1959, Armyne Morar Helen Schofield, *e d* of W. G. B. Schofield; one *s* two *d*. *Educ:* Eton Coll.; Trinity Coll., Cambridge; London Univ. (Extra Mural) (Dip. History of Art). Christie, Manson and Woods Ltd, 1954–57; Lazard Bros and Co. Ltd, 1957–66; Asst Dir, Paul Mellon Foundn for British Art, 1966–69 (Jt Dir, 1969–70); Dep. Sec.-General, Arts Council of GB, 1971–79. Dir, Royal Opera House, Covent Garden, 1979–; Chm., Friends of Covent Garden, 1981–; Member: Crafts Council, 1980–; Council of Management, Byam Shaw Sch. of Art, 1965–; Management Cttee, Courtauld Inst. of Art, 1981–83; Exec. Cttee, London Symphony Orchestra, 1979–; Bd of Dirs, Old Vic Theatre Co. (Prospect), 1980–81; Bd of Governors, Live Music Now, 1982–; Bd of Trustees, The Theatres Trust, 1983–. *Recreations:* music, travel, walking. *Address:* 25 Ladbroke Grove, W11. *T:* 01–727 8500. *Clubs:* Garrick, Brooks's.

STIRLING, (Archibald) David, DSO 1942; OBE 1946; Chairman, Television International Enterprises Ltd; *b* 15 Nov. 1915; *s* of late Brigadier-General Archibald Stirling of Keir, and Hon. Mrs Margaret Stirling, OBE, 4th *d* of 13th Baron Lovat. *Educ:* Ampleforth College, Yorks; (for a brief period) Cambridge University. In Sept. 1939 was Mem. SRO, Scots Guards and served with that Regt for first six months of War when he was transferred to No 3 Commando (Brigade of Guards) and went out with this unit to Middle East; subseq. served with First SAS Regt (POW, 1943–45). President, Capricorn Africa Society, 1947–59, living at that time in Africa based on Salisbury and Nairobi. Officer, Légion d'Honneur; Officer, Orange Nassau. *Address:* 22 South Audley Street, W1. *T:* 01–499 9252. *Clubs:* White's, Turf, Pratt's.

STIRLING, Prof. Charles James Matthew, FRS 1986; CChem, FRSC; Professor of Organic Chemistry since 1969, and Head of Department of Chemistry since 1981, University College of North Wales, Bangor; *b* 8 Dec. 1930; *s* of Brig. Alexander Dickson Stirling, DSO, MB, ChB, DPH, RAMC, and Isobel Millicent Stirling, MA, DipPsych; *m* 1956, Eileen Gibson Powell, BA, MEd, *yr d* of William Leslie and Elsie May Powell; three *d*. *Educ:* Edinburgh Acad.; Univ. of St Andrews (Harkness Exhibn; BSc; Biochem. Medal 1951); Univ. of London (PhD, DSc). FRSC, CChem 1967. Civil Service Jun. Res. Fellowship, Porton, 1955, Sen. Fellowship, 1956; ICI Fellowship, Univ. of Edinburgh, 1957; Lectr, QUB, 1959; Reader in Org. Chem., KCL, 1965; Dean of Faculty of Science, Bangor, 1977–79. Vis. Prof., Hebrew Univ. of Jerusalem, 1981. Mem., Perkin Council, 1971; Vice-Pres., 1985–. *Publications:* Radicals in Organic Chemistry, 1965; (ed) Organic Sulphur Chemistry, 1975; (ed) The Chemistry of the Sulphonium Group, 1981; numerous res. papers mainly in Jls of RSC. *Recreations:* choral music, travel, furniture restoration. *Address:* Department of Chemistry, University College of North Wales, Bangor, Gwynedd LL57 2UW. *T:* Bangor (N Wales) 351151; (home) Cae Maen, Druid Road, Menai Bridge, Gwynedd. *T:* Menai Bridge 712819.
See also Sir A. J. D. Stirling.

STIRLING, David; *see* Stirling, Archibald D.

STIRLING, Duncan Alexander; *b* 6 Oct. 1899; 4th *s* of late Major William Stirling, JP, DL, of Fairburn, Ross-shire, and Charlotte Eva, *d* of late Æneas Mackintosh, Daviot, Inverness-shire; *m* 1926, Lady Marjorie Murray, *e d* of 8th Earl of Dunmore, VC, DSO, MVO; two *s*. *Educ:* Harrow; New College, Oxford. Coldstream Guards, 1918 and again 1940–43. Partner, H. S. Lefevre & Co., Merchant Bankers, 1929–49; Director: Westminster Bank, and Westminster Foreign Bank, 1935–69 (Chm. 1962–69); National Westminster Bank, 1968–74 (Chm., 1968–69); London Life Association, 1935–80 (Pres., 1951–65). Pres., Inst. of Bankers, 1964–66; Chm., Cttee of London Clearing Bankers and Pres., British Bankers' Assoc., 1966–68. Prime Warden, Fishmongers Co., 1954–55. Mem. Council, Baring Foundn, 1969–79; Trustee, Thalidomide Trust, 1973–81. *Address:* 28 St James's Place, SW1; Lake House, Avington, Winchester, Hants. *Club:* Brooks's.
See also A. D. Æ. Stirling.

STIRLING of Garden, Col James, TD; FRICS; Lord-Lieutenant of Stirling and Falkirk (Central Region), since 1983; *b* 8 Sept. 1930; *s* of Col Archibald Stirling of Garden, OBE; *m* 1958, Fiona Janetta Sophia Wood Parker; two *s* two *d*. *Educ:* Rugby; Trinity Coll., Cambridge. BA; Dip. Estate Management. Partner, K. Ryden and Partners, Chartered Surveyors, 1962–; Director: Local Bd, Scotland and N Ireland, Woolwich Building Soc., 1973–; Scottish Widows and Life Insurance Fund, 1975–. Chm., Highland TAVR Assoc., 1982. DL 1970, Vice-Lieutenant 1979–83, Stirling. Hon. Col, 3/51st Highland Volunteers, TA, 1979. *Address:* Garden, Buchlyvie, Stirlingshire. *T:* Buchlyvie 212. *Club:* New (Edinburgh).

STIRLING, James Frazer, ARA 1985; ARIBA 1950; Architect; *b* 1926; *s* of Joseph Stirling and Louisa Frazer; *m* 1966, Mary, *d* of Morton Shand and Sybil Sissons; one *s* two *d*. *Educ:* Quarry Bank High Sch., Liverpool; Liverpool Sch. of Art, 1942. Served War of 1939–45: Lieut, Black Watch and Paratroops (D-Day Landing). Sch. of Architecture, Liverpool Univ., 1945–50. With Assoc. of Town Planning and Regional Research, London, 1950–52; worked for Lyons, Israel and Ellis, London, 1953–56; entered a series of architectural competitions, and Mem. ICA Indep. Gp, 1952–56. Private practice, 1956– (Partners: James Gowan until 1963 and Michael Wilford, 1971–). Projects include: Flats at Ham Common, 1955–58; Churchill Coll. Comp., 1958 (finalist); Selwyn Coll., Cambridge, 1959; Leicester Univ. Engrg Bldg, 1959–63 (USA Reynolds Award); History Faculty, Cambridge Univ., 1964–67; Andrew Melville Hall, St Andrews Univ., 1964–68; Dorman Long Steel Co. HQ, 1965; Runcorn New Town Housing, 1968–; Florey Bldg at Queen's Coll., Oxford, 1967–71; Olivetti Trng Sch., Surrey, 1969–; Clore Gall., Tate, 1983. Visiting teacher at: Architectural Assoc., London, 1955; Regent Street Polytechnic, London, 1956–57; Cambridge Univ. Sch. of Architecture, 1958; RIBA Lecture (An Architect's Approach to Architecture), 1965; lectures in Europe and USA, 1960–; Charles Davenport Visiting Prof., Yale Univ. Sch. of Architecture, USA, 1970. Re-development plan of West Mid-Town Manhatten, for New York City Planning Commn, USA, 1968–69; invited UK Architect, in internat. limited competitions for Govt/United Nations low cost housing for Peru, 1969, and Siemens AG Computer Centre Munich, 1970; buildings in Iran, Berlin and Stuttgart, 1977; Museum buildings for Univs of Harvard, Columbia and Rice, Houston, 1979. Hon. Mem., Akademie der Kunst, Berlin, 1969; Hon. FAIA, 1976; Hon. Dr RCA, 1979. Exhibitions: "James Stirling—Three Buildings", at Museum of Modern Art, NY, USA, 1969; (drawings) RIBA Heinz Gall., 1974 (associated pubn, James Stirling, 1974); Venice, 1976; Minneapolis and NY, 1977. BBC/Arts Council film, James Stirling's Architecture, 1973. Brunner Award, USA, 1976; Aalto Medal, Finland, 1978; Royal Gold Medal, RIBA, 1980; Pritzker Prize, 1981. *Relevant publication:* James Stirling: Buildings and Projects, 1985. *Address:* 75 Gloucester Place, W1H 3PF.

STIRLING, John Bertram, OC 1970; Chancellor, Queen's University, Kingston, Ontario, 1960–73; *b* 29 Nov. 1888; *s* of Dr James A. Stirling and Jessie Bertram, Picton, Ont; *m* 1928, Emily P., *d* of Col and Mrs E. T. Sturdee, Saint John, NB; one *d*. *Educ:* Queen's University, Kingston, Canada. BA 1909, BSc 1911, Queen's Univ., Kingston. Resident Engineer, Chipman and Power, Cons. Engineers, Toronto, 1911–15; with E. G. M. Cape and Co. Ltd from 1915; Field Engineer, 1915; Supt 1924; Gen. Supt, 1930; Vice-Pres., 1940; Chm., 1960–65. President: Canadian Construction Assoc., 1942; Montreal Board of Trade, 1950; Engineering Inst. of Canada, 1952 (Chm., Nat. Honours and Awards Cttee, to 1981). Hon. LLD: Queen's, Kingston, 1951; Toronto, 1961; Hon. DSc: Royal Mil. Coll., Canada, 1962; McGill, 1963. Hon. Col 3rd Field Regt Royal Can. Engrs. Sir John Kennedy Medal of Eng. Inst. of Canada, 1954; Montreal Medal, Queen's Univ. Alumni Assoc., 1955; Julian Smith Medal, Eng. Inst. of Canada, 1963. *Recreations:* sailing, country life, music. *Address:* 10 Richelieu Place, Montreal, Quebec H3G 1E7, Canada. *Club:* Saint James's (Montreal).

STIRLING, Rear-Adm. Michael Grote; Agent-General for British Columbia in the United Kingdom and Europe, 1968–75; *b* 29 June 1915; *s* of late Hon. Grote Stirling and late Mabel Katherine (*née* Brigstocke), Kelowna, British Columbia; *m* 1942, Sheelagh Kathleen Russell; two *s* one *d*. *Educ:* Shawnigan Lake School, BC; RNC Greenwich. Cadet, RCN, 1933; HMS Frobisher for training till 1934, then as Midshipman and Sub-Lt in RN, returning Canada Jan. 1938; Ships of RCN until 1941; specialized in Signals at HM Signal School, Portsmouth, then Home Fleet; Deputy Director, Signal Div., Naval Service HQ, Ottawa, 1942–43; SSO to C-in-C, Canadian North-West Atlantic, 1943–44; Commanded destroyers, 1944–46; Director Naval Communications, rank of Commander, 1949–51; promoted Captain and staff of Supreme Allied Commander Atlantic, Norfolk, Va, 1953–55; Commanded HMCS Cornwallis, 1955–57; 2nd Cdn Escort Sqdn, 1957–58; Naval Member of Directing Staff, Nat. Defence College as Commodore, 1958–61; Senior

Canadian Officer Afloat, 1961–62; Chief of Naval Personnel, 1962–64; Maritime Comdr, Pacific, 1964–66. Rear-Adm. 1962. Dir, Univ. of Victoria Foundation, 1967–68. *Recreations:* golf, ski-ing. *Address:* 302–1280 Newport Avenue, Victoria, BC V8S 5E7, Canada. *Club:* Victoria Golf (Victoria, BC).

STIRLING, Viola Henrietta Christian, CBE 1947; TD 1951; DL; *b* 3 June 1907; *d* of late Charles Stirling of Gargunnock, landowner and farmer. *Educ:* Queen Ethelburga's Sch., Harrogate; Lady Margaret Hall, Oxford (BA). Joined Auxiliary Territorial Service, 1939; Deputy Director ATS Scottish Command, 1945; released 1949. Member: Finance Committee, ATS Benevolent Fund, 1948–64; of Stirling and Clackmannan Hospitals Board of Management, 1948–64; selected military member TA&AFA, County of Stirling, 1948–68; Hon. Colonel 317 (Scottish Comd) Bn WRAC/TA, 1959–62. Member of Stirling County Council, 1958–67; DL Co. of Stirling, 1965–84. *Address:* Gargunnock, Stirlingshire. *T:* Gargunnock 202.

STIRLING-HAMILTON, Sir Bruce, 13th Bt *cr* 1673; Managing Director, Glasgow Business Services Ltd, since 1985; *b* 5 Aug. 1940; *s* of Captain Sir Robert William Stirling-Hamilton, 12th Bt, JP, DL, RN (retd), and of Eileen, *d* of late Rt Rev. H. K. Southwell, CMG; *S* father, 1982; *m* 1968, Stephanie, *d* of Dr William Campbell, LRCP, LRCS; one *s* two *d*. *Educ:* Nautical College, Pangbourne; RMA Sandhurst. Commissioned, Queen's Own Highlanders (Seaforth and Camerons), 1961; ADC to GOC 51st (Highland) Div., 1964; resigned commn, 1971. Kimberly-Clark Ltd, 1971; Seismograph Service (England) Ltd, 1974–83; MAST (Scotland), 1983–85. *Heir: s* Malcolm William Bruce Stirling-Hamilton, *b* 6 Aug. 1979. *Address:* Afton Lodge, Mossblown, by Ayr, Ayrshire KA6 5AS.

STIRRAT, Prof. Gordon Macmillan, MD, FRCOG; Professor of Obstetrics and Gynaecology, University of Bristol, since 1982; *b* 12 March 1940; *s* of Alexander and Caroline Mary Stirrat; *m* 1965, Janeen Mary (*née* Brown); three *d*. *Educ:* Hutcheson's Boys' Grammar Sch., Glasgow; Glasgow Univ. (MB, ChB). MA Oxon, MD London. FRCOG 1981. Jun. hosp. doctor appts, Glasgow and environs, and London, 1964–71; Lectr, St Mary's Hosp. Med. Sch., London, 1971–75; Clinical Reader, Univ. of Oxford, 1975–81. *Publications:* Legalised Abortion—the Continuing Dilemma, 1979; Obstetrics Pocket Consultant, 1981, 2nd edn 1986; (jtly) You and Your Baby—a Mother's Guide to Health, 1982; Aids to Reproductive Biology, 1982; Aids to Obstetrics and Gynaecology, 1983, 2nd edn 1986. *Recreations:* fly-fishing, model galleons, family. *Address:* Malpas Lodge, 24 Henbury Road, Westbury-on-Trym, Bristol BS9 3HJ. *T:* Bristol 505310. *Club:* Royal Society of Medicine.

STOATE, Isabel Dorothy; HM Diplomatic Service, retired; Counsellor, Foreign and Commonwealth Office, 1980–82; *b* 31 May 1927; *d* of William Maurice Stoate and Dorothy Evelyn Stoate (*née* French). *Educ:* Talbot Heath Sch., Bournemouth; St Andrews Univ. Athlone Press, London Univ., 1950–52; joined HM Diplomatic Service, 1952; served Cyprus, Vienna, Buenos Aires, Tokyo, Athens, Rio de Janeiro and FCO, 1952–80. *Recreations:* travel, tapestry. *Address:* 177 Gloucester Street, Cirencester, Glos.

STOBART, Patrick Desmond, CBE 1976 (MBE 1950); HM Diplomatic Service, retired; Member of Secretariat, International Primary Aluminium Institute, since 1979; *b* 14 Feb. 1920; *s* of late Reginald and Eva Stobart; *m* 1951, Sheila (marr. diss. 1973), *d* of late A. W. Brown, Belfast; three *s* one *d*. *Educ:* Cathedral and Cleveland House Schools, Salisbury; St Edmund Hall, Oxford. Served Royal Artillery and Wilts Regiment, 1940–46. Tübingen University, 1946; Political Officer, Trucial Oman, 1947; Chancery, Bonn, 1951–53; FO, 1953–54; Consul, Benghazi, 1954–58; FO, 1958–60; Commercial Counsellor, British Embassy, Helsinki, 1960–64, Copenhagen, 1964–66; Consul-General, Gothenburg, 1966–68; seconded to Aero-Engine Div., Rolls-Royce Ltd, 1968–69; Gwilym Gibbon Research Fellow, Nuffield College, Oxford, 1969–70; Head of Export Promotion Dept, FCO, 1970–71; Consul-Gen., Zürich, 1971–75; seconded to Commercial Relations and Exports Div., DoT, 1976–79. *Publication:* (also ed) The Centenary Book of the Hall and Héroult Processes for the Production of Aluminium, 1986. *Recreations:* history, fishing. *Address:* 44B Manor View, Finchley, N3. *T:* 01–346 7322.

STOBY, Sir Kenneth Sievewright, Kt 1961; Chairman, Guyana Match Co. Ltd; Director, Shawinigan Engineering (Guyana) Co. Ltd; *b* 19 Oct. 1903; *s* of late Mr and Mrs W. S. Stoby; *m* 1935, Eunice Badley; one *s* one *d*. *Educ:* Christ Church Sch., Georgetown; Queen's Coll., Georgetown. Called to Bar, Lincoln's Inn, 1930; private practice until 1940; seconded Dep. Controller of Prices, 1944; seconded again, 1947, Controller Supplies and Prices; acted Legal Draftsman; Chairman several Boards and Committees; Magistrate Nigeria, 1948; Registrar of Deeds and Supreme Court, British Guiana, 1950; Puisne Judge, 1953; Chief Justice, Barbados, 1959–65; Chancellor of the Judiciary, Guyana, 1966–68. Pro-Chancellor, Univ. of Guyana, 1966–75.

STOCK, Prof. Francis Edgar, CBE 1977 (OBE 1961); FRCS, FACS; Principal and Vice-Chancellor of the University of Natal, South Africa, 1970–77; now Emeritus Professor; *b* 5 July 1914; *o s* of late Edgar Stephen and Olive Blanche Stock; *m* 1939, Gwendoline Mary Thomas; two *s* one *d*. *Educ:* Colfe's Grammar Sch., Lewisham; King's Coll., London (Sambrooke schol.); King's Coll. Hosp., London (Jelf medal, Todd medal and prize in clin. med.; Hygiene and Psychological med. prizes); Univ. of Edinburgh. AKC, MB, BS (Lond.), FRCS, FACS, DTMH (Edin.). Ho. Surg., Cancer Research Registrar, Radium Registrar, King's Coll. Hosp., 1938–39; MO, Colonial Med. Service, Nigeria, 1940–45; Lectr and Asst to Prof. of Surg., Univ. of Liverpool, 1946–48; Prof. of Surgery, Univ. of Hong Kong, 1948–63; Cons. in Surg. to Hong Kong Govt, Brit. Mil. Hosps in Hong Kong, and Ruttonjee Sanatorium, 1948–63; Cons. Surg., RN, 1949–70; Dean, Fac. of Med., Univ. of Hong Kong, 1957–62; Med. Coun., Hong Kong, 1957–60; Pro-Vice-Chancellor, Univ. of Hong Kong, 1959–63; McIlrath Guest Prof., Royal Prince Alfred Hosp., Sydney, NSW, 1960 (Hon. Cons. Surg., 1960–); Prof. of Surg., Univ. of Liverpool, 1964–70; Cons. Surg., Liverpool Royal Infirmary and Liverpool Regional Hosp. Bd, 1964–70; Dean, Fac. of Med., Univ. of Liverpool, 1969–70. Visiting Prof. or Lectr: Univs of Alberta, Edinburgh, Qld, Singapore, W Australia, QUB, State Univ. of NY. Brit. Council Lectr: in Thailand, Burma, Fiji, Mauritius; Hunterian Prof., RCS London, 1948 and 1951. Member: BMA (Council 1964–69; Bd of Science and Educn, 1978–80); Bd of Governors, United Liverpool Hosps, 1967–70; Med. Adv. Council and Chm. Techn. Adv. Cttee on Surg., Liverpool Reg. Hosp. Bd, 1964–70; Gen. Med. Council, 1969–70; Med. Appeals Tribunals, Liverpool and N Wales, 1966–70; Council, Edgewood Coll. of Education, 1976–77; Univs Adv. Council, 1976–; Cttee of Univ. Principals, 1970–77 (Chm., 1976–77). Examr in Surgery: to Univs of Edinburgh, Glasgow, Liverpool, Hong Kong, Malaya, Singapore and NUI, at various times, 1949–70; to Soc. of Apothecaries, 1958–60; Mem. Ct of Examrs, RCS, 1965–69. Sen. Fellow, Assoc. of Surgeons of GB and Ire.; Sen. Mem. Pan Pacific Surg. Assoc. (past Mem. Coun. and Bd of Trustees). Mem., Board of Control, Nat. Inst. of Metallurgy, 1975–77. Liveryman, Soc. of Apothecaries. Hon. FACCP. *Publications:* Surgical Principles (with J. Moroney), 1968; chapters in: Surgery of Liver and Bile Ducts (ed Smith and Sherlock); Clinical Surgery (ed Rob and Smith); Scientific Foundations of Surgery (ed Wells and Kyle); Abdominal Operations (ed Maingot), and others; numerous articles in scientific jls. *Recreations:* swimming (Univ. of London colours, 1934, Kent Co. colours, 1935), sailing (Pres., Hong Kong Yacht Racing Assoc., 1961–63, Vice-Pres., Far East Yacht Racing Fedn, 1961–62), gardening, photography, music (Dep. Organist, Grouville Parish Church, Jersey, 1978–82). *Address:* Hebe Haven, 7 Old Forge Lane, Fauvic, Jersey, CI. *T:* Jersey 53269. *Clubs:* Royal Over-Seas League; Royal Hong Kong Yacht (Cdre, 1957–63).

STOCK, Keith L(ievesley), CB 1957; Under Secretary, Department of Economic Affairs, 1965–68, retired; *b* 24 Oct. 1911; *s* of late Cyril Lievesley Stock and Irene Mary Stock (*née* Tomkins); *m* 1937, Joan Katherine Stock (*née* Milne); two *s* one *d*. *Educ:* Charterhouse; New College, Oxford. Petroleum Department, Board of Trade, 1935; Ministry of Fuel and Power, 1942; Imperial Defence College, 1951; Cabinet Office, 1954; Ministry of Fuel and Power, 1955; Min. of Technology, 1964. *Publication:* Rose Books (bibliog.), 1984. *Address:* c/o Barclays Bank, Millbank, SW1.

STOCK, Raymond, QC 1964; **His Honour Judge Stock;** a Circuit Judge (formerly Judge of County Courts), since 1971; *b* 1913; *s* of late A. E. and M. E. Stock; *m* 1969, E. Dorothy Thorpe, JP. *Educ:* West Monmouth School; Balliol College, Oxford. Barrister-at-law, Gray's Inn, 1936, Bencher, 1969. Royal Artillery, 1939–45. Recorder: Penzance, 1962–64; Exeter, 1964–66; Southampton, 1966–71; Dep. Chm., Dorset QS, 1964–71. *Address:* Brambridge House, Bishopstoke, Hants. *Club:* Athenæum.

STOCKDALE, Sir (Arthur) Noel, Kt 1986; DFM 1942; Chairman, ASDA–MFI; *b* 25 Dec. 1920; *s* of Arthur and Florence Stockdale; *m* 1944, Betty Monica Shaw; two *s*. *Educ:* Woodhouse Grove School; Reading University. Joined Hindells Dairy Farmers, 1939; RAF, 1940–46; rejoined Hindells Dairy Farmers, 1946, subseq. Associated Dairies & Farm Stores (Leeds) Ltd, 1949, Associated Dairies Group PLC, 1977 and ASDA–MFI Group PLC, 1985; Chm., 1969–. Hon. LLD Leeds, 1986. *Recreations:* fishing, garden. *Address:* Granary Gap, Main Street, Linton, Wetherby, Yorks LS22 4HT. *T:* Wetherby 62970.

STOCKDALE, Sir Edmund (Villiers Minshull), 1st Bt *cr* 1960; Kt 1955; JP; *b* 16 April 1903; 2nd *s* of late Major H. M. Stockdale, JP, and Mrs Stockdale, Mears Ashby Hall, Northants; *m* 1937, Hon. Louise Fermor-Hesketh, *er d* of 1st Lord Hesketh; two *s* (one *d* decd). *Educ:* Wellington College. Entered Bank of England, 1921; Assistant to Governors, Reserve Bank of India, 1935; Asst Principal, Bank of England, 1937, Dep. Principal, 1941; pensioned, 1945. Elected Court of Common Council, City of London, 1946, Alderman, Ward of Cornhill, 1948; one of HM Lieuts, City of London, Comr of Assize, 1948–63; Sheriff, City of London 1953; Lord Mayor of London, 1959–60; Chm., Lord Mayor's Appeal Fund, King George's Jubilee Trust, 1960; Mem., Adv. Bd, etc, Holloway Prison, 1948–60 (Chairman, 1951–53); Member, Holloway Discharged Prisoners Aid Society Cttee, 1964; Vice-President, The Griffins (formerly Holloway DPAS), 1965; Member, Boards: Bridewell, Royal Bethlem and Maudsley Hosps, 1948–63, Christ's, 1962–; Mem., Emerg. Bed Service Cttee, King Edward Hosp. Fund, 1963–69; Vice-Pres. King Edward's School, Witley, 1960–63; Governor: United Westminster Schools, 1948–54; Wellington College, 1955–74; Eagle House Preparatory, 1964–74. Director, Embankment Trust Ltd, 1948–74, and other cos. A Church Comr for England, 1962; Mem. Winchester Dioc. Bd of Finance (Exec. Cttee), 1963. Junior Grand Warden (Acting), Grand Lodge of England, 1960–61. Partner, Read Hurst-Brown and Co.; Member: London Stock Exchange, 1946–60; Court of Assistants, Carpenters' Co. (Master, 1970), Glaziers' Co. (Master 1973). JP London (Inner London Sessions), 1968. Grand Officer, Legion of Honour; Grand Cross, Order of Merit, Peru; Grand Official, Order of Mayo, Argentina; Knight Comdr, Order of Crown, Thailand; Order of Triple Power, Nepal; Comdr, Royal Order of North Star, Sweden; KStJ. Gold Medal, Madrid. *Publications:* The Bank of England in 1934, 1966; "Ptolemy Tortoise", 1979. *Recreations:* shooting, drawing. *Heir: er s* Thomas Minshull Stockdale [*b* 7 Jan. 1940; *m* 1965, Jacqueline Ha-Van-Vuong; one *s* one *d*]. *Address:* Hoddington House, Upton Grey, Basingstoke. *T:* Long Sutton 437. *Clubs:* Buck's, City Livery.

See also C. M. Edwards.

STOCKDALE, Eric; His Honour Judge Eric Stockdale; a Circuit Judge since 1972; *b* 8 Feb. 1929; *m* 1952, Joan (*née* Berry); two *s*. *Educ:* Collyers Sch., Horsham; London Sch. of Economics. LLB, BSc(Econ.), LLM, PhD (Lond.); MSc (Cranfield). 2nd Lieut, RA, 1947–49. Called to the Bar, Middle Temple, 1950; practised in London and on Midland Circuit until 1972; admitted to State Bar, Calif, 1983. Mem., Supreme Court Procedure Cttee, 1982–. Tech. Advr, Central Council of Probation Cttees, 1979–84; Mem. Council, Inst. for the Study and Treatment of Delinquency (ISTD), 1966–78; Vice-Pres., NACRO, 1980– (Mem. Council, 1970–80); President: British Soc. of Criminology, 1978–81; Soc. of English and Amer. Lawyers, 1986– (Chm., 1984–86). Member: Central Council for Educn and Trng in Social Work, 1984–; Parole Board, 1985–. Sen. Fellow, Amer. Univ., Washington DC, 1985. Governor, 1977–, Vis. Fellow, 1985–, Hatfield Polytechnic. *Publications:* The Court and the Offender, 1967; A Study of Bedford Prison 1660–1877, 1977; Law and Order in Georgian Bedfordshire, 1982; The Probation Volunteer, 1985. *Address:* 20 Lyonsdown Road, New Barnet, Barnet EN5 1JE. *T:* 01–449 7181.

STOCKDALE, His Honour Frank Alleyne, MA; a Circuit Judge (formerly County Court Judge, Ilford and Westminster Courts), 1964–79; *b* 16 Oct. 1910; *er s* of late Sir Frank Stockdale, GCMG, CBE, MA; *m* 1942, Frances Jean, *er d* of late Sir FitzRoy Anstruther-Gough-Calthorpe, Bt; one *s* two *d*. *Educ:* Repton; Magdalene College, Cambridge. Called to Bar, Gray's Inn, 1934; Bencher, 1964. Served War of 1939–45: 5th Royal Inniskilling Dragoon Guards, BEF, 1939–40; North Africa, 1942–43 (despatches); psc; Lt-Col. Dep. Chm., Hampshire QS, 1954–66; Dep. Chm., Greater London QS, 1966–71. Mem., Inter-Deptl Cttee on Adoption Law, 1969–72, Chm. 1971–72. *Address:* Victoria Place, Monmouth, Gwent NP5 3BR. *T:* Monmouth 5039. *Club:* Garrick.

STOCKDALE, Group Captain George William; Secretary-General, Plastics and Rubber Institute, since 1985; *b* 17 Dec. 1932; *s* of William and Lilian Stockdale; *m* 1957, Ann (*née* Caldon); two *s* two *d*. *Educ:* RMA Sandhurst. Royal Air Force, 1951–81: Policy and Planning Div, 1976–79; Command Regt Officer, Germany, 1979–81. MITD, FBIM. *Recreations:* fell walking, painting, international affairs, travel, people. *Address:* The Plastics and Rubber Institute, 11 Hobart Place, SW1W 0HL. *T:* 01–245 9555. *Club:* Royal Air Force.

STOCKDALE, Sir Noel; *see* Stockdale, Sir A. N.

STOCKER, Prof. Bruce Arnold Dunbar, FRS 1966; MD; Professor of Medical Microbiology in Stanford University, since 1966; *b* 26 May 1917. *Educ:* King's College, London; Westminster Hosp. Med. Sch. MB, BS, 1940, MRCS, LRCP, 1940; MD 1947. Guinness Prof. of Microbiology, Univ. of London, and Dir of Guinness-Lister Microbiological Research Unit, Lister Inst. of Preventive Med., until Dec. 1965. *Publications:* articles in scientific jls. *Address:* Department of Medical Microbiology, Stanford University, Stanford, Calif 94305, USA. *T:* 415–723 2006.

STOCKER, Rt. Hon. Sir John (Dexter), Kt 1973; MC; TD; PC 1986; **Rt. Hon. Lord Justice Stocker;** a Lord Justice of Appeal, since 1986; *b* 7 Oct. 1918; *s* of late John Augustus Stocker and Emma Eyre Stocker (*née* Kettle), Hampstead; *m* 1956, Margaret Mary Hegarty; no *c*. *Educ:* Westminster Sch.; London University. 2nd Lt, QO Royal West Kent Regt, 1939; France, 1940; Middle East, 1942–43; Italy, 1943–46; Maj. 1943;

Lt-Col 1945. LLB London 1947. Called to Bar, Middle Temple, 1948, Master of the Bench, 1971. QC 1965; a Recorder, 1972–73; Judge of the High Court, Queen's Bench Div., 1973–86; Presiding Judge, SE Circuit, 1976–79. *Recreations:* golf, cricket. *Address:* Royal Courts of Justice, Strand, WC2. *Clubs:* Naval and Military, MCC; Royal Wimbledon Golf.

STOCKHAUSEN, Karlheinz; composer and conductor; *b* 22 Aug. 1928; *s* of late Simon and Gertrud Stockhausen; *m* 1st, 1951, Doris Andreae; four *c*; 2nd, 1967, Mary Bauermeister; two *c*. *Educ:* Hochschule für Musik, and Univ., Cologne, 1947–51; studied with: Messaien, 1952–53; Prof. Werner Meyer-Eppler, Bonn Univ., 1954–56. With Westdeutscher Rundfunk Electronic Music Studio, 1953–, Artistic Dir, 1963–. Lectr, Internat. Summer Sch. for New Music, Darmstadt, 1953–; Dir, Interpretation Group for live electronic music, 1964–; Founder, and Artistic Dir, Kölner Kurse für Neue Musik, 1963–68; Visiting Professor: Univ. of Pa, 1965; Univ. of Calif, 1966–67; Cologne State Conservatory, 1971–. Co-Editor, Die Reihe, 1954–59. First annual tour of 30 concert-lectures, 1958, USA and Canada, since then throughout world. Has composed numerous works and made many records of his own works. Member or Foreign Member: Akad. der Künste, Hamburg, 1968; Kungl. Musikaliska Akad., Sweden, 1970; Akad. der Künste, Berlin, 1973; Amer. Acad. and Inst. of Arts and Letters, 1977; Acad. Filarmonica Romana, 1979; Acad. Européenne des Sciences, des Arts et des Lettres, 1980. Awards and Prizes from France, Germany, Italy and USA; Bundesverdienstkreuz 1st class, 1974. *Publications:* Texte, 4 vols, 1963–77; *compositions:* Chöre für Doris, Drei Lieder, Choral, 1950–51; Sonatine, Kreuzspiel, Formel, 1951; Schlagtrio, Spiel für Orchester, Etude, 1952; Punkte, 1952, rev. 1962, Klavierstücke I-XI, 1952–56, 1961; Kontra-Punkte, 1953; Elektronische Studien I and II, 1953–54; Zeitmasze, Gesang der Jünglinge, 1956; Gruppen, 1957; Zyklus, Refrain, 1959; Carré, Kontakte, 1960; Originale (musical play), 1961; Plus Minus, 1963; Momente, 1962–64; Mixtur (new arr. 1967), Mikrophonie I, 1964; Mikrophonie II, Stop (new arr. 1969), 1965; Telemusik, Solo, Adieu, 1966; Hymnen, Prozession, Ensemble, 1967; Kurzwellen, Stimmung, Aus den sieben Tagen, Spiral, Musik für ein Haus, 1968; Hymnen mit Orchester, Fresco, Dr K-Sextett, 1969; Pole, Expo, Mantra, Für Kommende Zeiten, 1970; Sternklang, Trans, 1971; Alphabet für Liège, Am Himmel wandre ich, (Indianerlieder), Ylem, 1972; Vortrag über Hu, Inori, 1973–74; Herbstmusik, Atmen gibt das Leben..., 1974; Musik im Bauch, Tierkreis, Harlekin, Der Kleine Harlekin, 1975; Sirius, 1975–76; Amour, 1976; Jubiläum, In Freundschaft, 1977; Licht, the seven days of the week (for solo voices, solo instruments, solo dancers/choirs, orchestras, ballet and mimes/electronic and concrete music), 1977–; an operatic cycle with Dienstag aus Licht, 1977 (Der Jahreslauf, scene from Dienstag, 1977); Donnerstag aus Licht (opera), 1978–80 (Donnerstags-Gruss, or Michaels-Gruss, 1978; Michaels Jugend, 1979; Michaels Reise um die Erde, 1978; Michaels Heimkehr, 1980; Donnerstags-Abschied, 1980); Samstag aus Licht (opera), 1981–83 (Luzifers Traum or Klavierstück XIII, 1981; Luzifers Abschied, 1982; Kathinkas Gesang als Luzifers Requiem, 1982–83; Luzifers Tanz, 1983; Samstags-Gruss, 1983); Montag aus Licht (opera), 1985 (Botschaft, 1985, Evas Lied, 1986, Evas Zauber, 1986). *Address:* Stockhausen-Verlag, 5067 Kürten, West Germany.

STOCKPORT, Bishop Suffragan of, since 1984; **Rt. Rev. Frank Pilkington Sargeant;** *b* 12 Sept. 1932; *s* of John Stanley and Grace Sargeant; *m* 1958, Sally Jeanette McDermott; three *s* two *d*. *Educ:* Boston Grammar School; Durham Univ., St John's Coll. and Cranmer Hall (BA, Dip Theol); Nottingham Univ. (Diploma in Adult Education). National Service Commission, RA (20th Field Regt), 1955–57. Assistant Curate: Gainsborough Parish Church, 1958–62; Grimsby Parish Church, and Priest-in-Charge of St Martin's, Grimsby, 1962–67; Vicar of North Hykeham and Rector of South Hykeham, 1967–73; Residentiary Canon, Bradford Cathedral, 1973–77; Archdeacon of Bradford, 1977–84. *Address:* 32 Park Gates Drive, Cheadle Hulme, Cheadle, Stockport, Cheshire SK8 7DF. *T:* 061–486 9715.

STOCKS, Alfred James, CBE 1981; DL; Chief Executive, Liverpool City Council, 1973–86; *b* 24 March 1926; *s* of James and Mary Stocks; *m* 1958, Jillian Margery Gedye; one *s* one *d*. *Educ:* Bootham Sch., York; Clare Coll., Cambridge (MA). Admitted solicitor, 1949. Appointed Dep. Town Clerk, Liverpool, 1968. Pres., Soc. of Local Authority Chief Execs, 1983–84. DL Merseyside, 1982. Hon. LLD Liverpool, 1980. *Address:* 38 Glendyke Road, Liverpool L18 6JR. *T:* 051–724 2448. *Club:* Athenæum (Liverpool).

STOCKTON, 1st Earl of, *cr* 1984, of Chelwood Gate in the County of East Sussex and of Stockton-on-Tees in the County of Cleveland; **Maurice Harold Macmillan,** OM 1976; PC 1942; FRS 1962; Viscount Macmillan of Ovenden, 1984; Chancellor, University of Oxford, since 1960; President, Macmillan Ltd, since 1974 (Chairman, 1963–74; Chairman, Macmillan & Co. and Macmillan (Journals), 1963–67); Prime Minister and First Lord of The Treasury, Jan. 1957–Oct. 1963; MP (C) Bromley, Nov. 1945–Sept. 1964; *b* 10 Feb. 1894; *s* of late Maurice Crawford Macmillan; *m* 1920, Lady Dorothy Evelyn Cavendish, GBE 1964 (*d* 1966), *d* of 9th Duke of Devonshire; two *d* (and one *s* one *d* decd). *Educ:* Eton (Scholar); Balliol Coll., Oxford (Exhibitioner). 1st Class Hon. Moderations, 1919; served during war, 1914–18, in Special Reserve Grenadier Guards (wounded 3 times). ADC to Gov.-Gen. of Canada, 1919–20; retired, 1920; MP (U) Stockton-on-Tees, 1924–29 and 1931–45; contested Stockton-on-Tees, 1923 and 1945; Parliamentary Sec., Ministry of Supply, 1940–42; Parliamentary Under-Sec. of State, Colonies, 1942; Minister Resident at Allied HQ in North-West Africa, 1942–45; Sec. for Air, 1945; Minister of Housing and Local Government, 1951–54; Minister of Defence, Oct. 1954–April 1955; Sec. of State for Foreign Affairs, April-Dec. 1955; Chancellor of the Exchequer, Dec. 1955–Jan. 1957. First Pres., Game Research Assoc., 1960–65. A Vice-Pres., Franco-British Soc., 1955; A Trustee, Historic Churches Preservation Fund, 1957–. Freeman of: City of London (Stationers' and Newspaper Makers' Company, 1957), 1957; Bromley, Kent, 1957; Hon. Freedom of City of London, 1961; Toronto, 1962; Stockton-on-Tees, 1968. Hon. Fellow, Balliol Coll., Oxford, 1957; Hon. FBA, 1981. Hon. DCL Oxford, 1958; DCL Oxford (by diploma), 1960; LLD Cambridge, 1961, Sussex, 1963. Benjamin Franklin Medal, RSA, 1976; Olympia Prize, 1979. *Publications:* Industry and the State (jtly), 1927; Reconstruction: A Plea for a National Policy, 1933; Planning for Employment, 1935; The Next Five Years, 1935; The Middle Way, 1938 (re-issued 1966); Economic Aspects of Defence, 1939; Memoirs: Vol. I, Winds of Change, 1966; Vol. II, The Blast of War, 1967; Vol. III, Tides of Fortune, 1969; Vol. IV, Riding the Storm 1956–59, 1971; Vol. V, Pointing the Way 1959–61, 1972; Vol. VI, At the end of the Day 1961–63, 1973; Past Masters, 1975; War Diaries: politics and war in the Mediterranean January 1943–May 1945, 1984. *Heir: g s* Viscount Macmillan of Ovenden, *qv*. *Address:* Macmillan & Co. Ltd, 4 Little Essex Street, WC2; Birch Grove House, Chelwood Gate, Haywards Heath, West Sussex. *Clubs:* Carlton, Beefsteak, Buck's.

See also Rt Hon. Julia Amery, J. T. Faber.

STOCKWELL, Air Cdre Edmund Arthur, CB 1967; MA; Command Education Officer, Training Command, 1968–72 (Flying Training Command, 1964–68); retired 1972; *b* 15 Dec. 1911; *e s* of Arthur Davenport Stockwell, Dewsbury; *m* 1937, Pearl Arber; one *s* two *d*; *m* 1955, Lillian Gertrude Moore (*d* 1965), OBE, MRCP; two *s*; *m* 1970, Mrs Kathleen (Betty) Clarke, Chesham. *Educ:* Wheelwright Grammar School; Balliol Coll., Oxford. Entered RAF Educational Service, Cranwell, 1935; RAF Educn in India, 1936; Punjab and NW Frontier, 1936–38; RAFVR (Admin and Special Duties), 1939; Lahore, Simla, Delhi, 1939–44; Group Educn Officer, No 6 (RCAF) Group, 1944; Air Min., 1944–48; OC, RAF Sch. of Educn, 1948–51; Comd Educn Officer, Coastal Comd, 1951–53; Comd Educn Officer, Far East Air Force, 1953–55; Principal Educn Officer, Halton, 1956–59; Comd Educn Officer, Maintenance Comd, 1959–62; Dep. Dir of Educational Services, Air Min., 1962–64. Group Captain, 1954; Air Commodore, 1964. *Recreations:* golf, gardening. *Address:* Trendles, Ryme Intrinseca, Sherborne, Dorset DT9 6JX. *T:* Yetminster 872085.

STOCKWELL, Gen. Sir Hugh Charles, GCB 1959 (KCB 1954; CB 1946); KBE 1949 (CBE 1945); DSO 1940 and Bar 1957; late Infantry; Chairman: Inland Waterways Amenity Advisory Council, 1971–74; Kennet and Avon Canal Trust, 1966–75; Member: British Waterways Board, 1971–74; Water Space Amenity Commission, 1973–74; *b* 16 June 1903; *s* of late Lt-Col H. C. Stockwell, OBE, late Highland Light Infantry, Chief Constable of Colchester, and Gertrude Forrest; *m* 1931, Joan Rickman Garrard, *d* of Charles and Marion Garrard, Kingston Lisle, Berkshire; two *d*. *Educ:* Cothill House, Abingdon; Marlborough; Royal Military Coll., Sandhurst. Joined 2/Royal Welch Fusiliers, 1923; served West Africa, 1929–35; Instructor, Small Arms School, Netheravon, 1935–38; Brigade-Major, Royal Welch Brigade, 1938–40; served in Norway (DSO); 30 East African Bde, 1942–43; 29th Independent Bde, 1943–45; Burma (CB); Commander 82 (WA) Division, Jan. 1945–June 1946; Commander, Home Counties District, UK, July 1946–47; Commander Sixth Airborne Division, Palestine, 1947–48; Commandant, RMA, Sandhurst, 1948–50; Comdr, 3rd Inf. Div., and Comdr, East Anglian Dist, 1951–52; General Officer Commanding: Malaya, 1952–54; 1 Corps, BAOR, 1954–56; Ground Forces, Suez Operation, 1956; Military Secretary to the Secretary of State for War, 1957–59; Adjutant-General to the Forces, 1959–60; Deputy Supreme Allied Commander, Europe, 1960–64, retired. Gen., 1957. Col, The Royal Welch Fusiliers, 1952–65; Col, The Royal Malay Regt 1954–59; Col Commandant, Army Air Corps, 1957–63; Col Commandant, Royal Army Educational Corps October 1959–64. ADC General to the Queen, 1959–62. Governor, Felsted School, 1954–65. Grand Officier, Légion d'Honneur (France), 1958. *Recreations:* conservation, painting, travel. *Address:* Horton, near Devizes, Wilts. *T:* Cannings 617; Midland Bank plc, The Market Place, Devizes, Wilts. *Clubs:* MCC, Army and Navy.

STOCKWIN, Prof. James Arthur Ainscow; Nissan Professor of Modern Japanese Studies, University of Oxford and Fellow, St Antony's College, Oxford, since 1982; *b* 28 Nov. 1935; *s* of Wilfred Arthur Stockwin and Edith Mary Stockwin; *m* 1960, Audrey Lucretia Hobson Stockwin (*née* Wood); two *s* two *d*. *Educ:* Exeter Coll., Oxford Univ. (MA); Australian Nat. Univ. (PhD). Australian National University: Lectr, Dept of Political Science, 1964–66; Sen. Lectr, 1966–72; Reader, 1972–81. *Publications:* The Japanese Socialist Party and Neutralism, 1968; (ed) Japan and Australia in the Seventies, 1972; Japan, Divided Politics in a Growth Economy, 1975, 2nd edn 1982; Why Japan Matters, 1983; articles, largely on Japanese politics and foreign policy, in Pacific Affairs, Aust. Outlook, Aust. Jl Politics and History, Japan Interpreter, East Asia, Asian and African Studies, Asian Survey, etc. *Recreations:* sailing, languages, bushwalking, skiing. *Address:* Nissan Institute of Japanese Studies, 1 Church Walk, Oxford. *T:* Oxford 59651.

STOCKWOOD, Rt. Rev. (Arthur) Mervyn, DD; *b* 27 May 1913; *s* of late Arthur Stockwood, solicitor, and Beatrice Ethel Stockwood; unmarried. *Educ:* Kelly Coll., Tavistock; Christ's Coll., Cambridge (MA). Curate of St Matthew, Moorfields, Bristol, 1936–41; Blundell's Sch., Missioner, 1936–41; Vicar, St Matthew, Moorfields, Bristol, 1941–55; Hon. Canon of Bristol, 1952–55; Vicar of the University Church, Cambridge, 1955–59; Bishop of Southwark, 1959–80. Member: Bristol CC, 1946–55; Cambridge CC, 1956–59; House of Lords, 1963–80. Mem. Council, Bath Univ., 1980–. Freeman of City of London, 1976. DD Lambeth, 1959; Hon. DLitt Sussex, 1963; Hon. DD Bucharest, 1977. *Publications:* There is a Tide, 1946; Whom They Pierced, 1948; Christianity and Marxism, 1949; I Went to Moscow, 1955; The Faith To-day, 1959; Cambridge Sermons, 1959; Bishop's Journal, 1965; The Cross and the Sickle, 1978; From Strength to Strength, 1980; Chanctonbury Ring (autobiog.), 1982. *Address:* 15 Sydney Buildings, Bath, Avon BA2 6BZ. *T:* Bath 62788.

STODART, family name of **Baron Stodart of Leaston.**

STODART OF LEASTON, Baron *cr* 1981 (Life Peer), of Humbie in the District of East Lothian; **James Anthony Stodart;** PC 1974; *b* 6 June 1916; *yr s* of late Col Thomas Stodart, CIE, IMS, and of Mary Alice Coullie; *m* 1940, Hazel Jean Usher. *Educ:* Wellington. Farming at Kingston, North Berwick, 1934–58, and now at Leaston, Humbie, East Lothian. Hon. Pres., Edinburgh Univ. Agricultural Soc., 1952; Pres. East Lothian Boy Scouts' Assoc., 1960–63. Contested: (L) Berwick and East Lothian, 1950; (C) Midlothian and Peebles, 1951; Midlothian, 1955; MP (C) Edinburgh West, 1959–Oct. 1974; Jt Parly Under-Sec. of State, Scottish Office, Sept. 1963–Oct. 1964; An Opposition spokesman on Agriculture and on Scottish Affairs, 1966–69; Parly Sec., MAFF, 1970–72; Minister of State, MAFF, 1972–74; Vice-Chm., Conservative Agric. Cttee, House of Commons, 1962–63, 1964–65, 1966–70. Led Parly Delegns to Canada, 1974, 1983. Dir, FMC, 1980–82; Chm., Agricultural Credit Corp. Ltd, 1975–. Chairman: Cttee of Inquiry into Local Govt in Scotland, 1980; Manpower Review of Vet. Profession in UK, 1984–85. *Publications:* (jt author) Land of Abundance, a study of Scottish Agriculture in the 20th Century, 1962; contrib. on farming topics to agricultural journals and newspapers. *Recreations:* music, playing golf and preserving a sense of humour. *Address:* Lorimers, North Berwick, East Lothian. *T:* North Berwick 2457. *Clubs:* New (Edinburgh); Hon. Company of Edinburgh Golfers.

STODDART, family name of **Baron Stoddart of Swindon.**

STODDART OF SWINDON, Baron *cr* 1983 (Life Peer), of Reading in the Royal County of Berkshire; **David Leonard Stoddart;** *b* 4 May 1926; *s* of Arthur Leonard Stoddart, coal miner, and Queenie Victoria Stoddart (*née* Price); *m* 1961, Jennifer Percival-Alwyn; two *s* (one *d* by previous marr.). *Educ:* elementary; St Clement Danes and Henley Grammar Schools. Youth in training, PO Telephones, 1942–44; business on own account, 1944–46; Railway Clerk, 1947–49; Hospital Clerk, 1949–51; Power Station Clerical Worker, 1951–70. Joined Labour Party, 1947; Member Reading County Borough Council, 1954–72; served at various times as Chairman of Housing, Transport and Finance Cttees; Leader of the Reading Labour Group of Councillors, 1962–70. Contested (Lab) Newbury, 1959 and 1964, Swindon, 1969, 1983. MP (Lab) Swindon, 1970–83; PPS to Minister for Housing and Construction, 1974–75; an Asst Govt Whip, 1975; a Lord Comr, HM Treasury, 1976–77; an opposition whip, and opposition spokesman on energy, House of Lords, 1983–. *Recreations:* gardening, music. *Address:* Sintra, 37A Bath Road, Reading, Berks. *T:* Reading 56726.

STODDART, Anne Elizabeth; HM Diplomatic Service; Deputy Permanent UK Representative to Council of Europe, Strasbourg, since 1981; *b* 29 March 1937; *d* of late James Stoddart and Ann Jack Stoddart (*née* Inglis). *Educ:* Kirby Grammar School, Middlesbrough; Somerville College, Oxford. MA. Entered Foreign Office, 1960; British

Military Govt, Berlin, 1963–67; FCO, 1967–70; First Secretary (Economic), Ankara, 1970–73; Head of Chancery, Colombo, 1974–76; FCO, 1977–81. *Address:* c/o Foreign and Commonwealth Office, SW1A 2AH; 18 rue Gottfried, 67000 Strasbourg, France. *T:* 8835.00.78.

STODDART, John Maurice; Principal, Sheffield City Polytechnic, since 1983; *b* 18 Sept. 1938; *s* of Gordon Stoddart and May (*née* Ledder); *m* 1st, 1960, Patricia Tyrer (marr. diss. 1975); two *s* two *d*; 2nd, 1976, Jenny Quinlin (marr. diss. 1980); one *s*. *Educ:* Wallasey Grammar Sch.; Univ of Reading (BA Pol Econ.). FBIM 1977. Teacher, Wallasey GS, 1960–62; Lectr, Mid Cheshire Coll. of Further Educn, 1962–64; Lectr, Enfield Coll., 1964–70; Head, Dept of Econs and Business Studies, Sheffield Polytechnic, 1970–72; Asst Dir, NE London Polytechnic, 1972–76; Dir, Hull Coll. of Higher Educn (now Humberside Coll.), 1976–83. Chm., CNAA Cttee for Business and Management, 1985– (Chm., Undergrad. Courses Bd, 1976–83); Member: CNAA, 1982–; CNAA Cttee for Academic Policy, 1979–84; Architects Registration Council, UK, 1979–; Sea Fisheries Trng Council, 1976–80. Mem., Bd of Management, Crucible Theatre, 1986–. Member: Court, Univ. of Hull, 1976–83; Council, Univ. of Sheffield, 1983–; Editorial Adv. Bd, Business Education, 1980–. Companion, British Business Graduates Soc., 1983; Hon. Fellow, Humberside Coll., 1983; FRSA 1977. *Publications:* articles on business and management educn. *Address:* 58 Riverdale Road, Sheffield S10 3FB. *T:* Sheffield 683636. *Club:* Reform.

STODDART, Wing Comdr Kenneth Maxwell, AE 1942; JP; Lord-Lieutenant, Metropolitan County of Merseyside, since 1979; *b* 26 May 1914; *s* of late Wilfrid Bowring Stoddart and Mary Hyslop Stoddart (*née* Maxwell); *m* 1940, Jean Roberta Benson Young; two *d*. *Educ:* Sedbergh; Clare Coll., Cambridge. Chairman: Cearns and Brown Ltd, 1973–84; United Mersey Supply Co. Ltd, 1978–81. Commissioned No 611 (West Lancashire) Sqdn, Auxiliary Air Force, 1936; served War, UK and Europe; comd W Lancashire Wing, Air Trng Corps, 1946–54; Vice-Chm. (Air) W Lancashire T&AFA, 1954–64. Chairman, Liverpool Child Welfare Assoc., 1965–81. DL Lancashire 1958 (transf. to Metropolitan County of Merseyside, 1974); JP Liverpool 1952; High Sheriff of Merseyside, 1974. Hon. LLD Liverpool, 1986. KStJ 1979. *Recreations:* gardening, walking. *Address:* The Spinney, Overdale Road, Willaston, South Wirral L64 1SY. *T:* 051–327 5183. *Clubs:* Royal Commonwealth Society; Liverpool Racquet.

STOESSEL, Walter J., Jr; Chairman, Parallel Studies Program with the Soviet Union of the United Nations Association of the US, since 1982; *b* 24 Jan. 1920; *s* of Walter John Stoessel and Katherine Stoessel (*née* Haston); *m* 1946, Mary Ann (*née* Ferrandou); three *d*. *Educ:* Lausanne Univ.; Stanford Univ. (BA); Russian Inst., Columbia Univ.; Center for Internat. Affairs, Harvard Univ. US Foreign Service, 1942–82; Polit. Officer, Caracas, 1942–46; Dept of State, 1946–47; Moscow, 1947–49; Bad-Nauheim, 1950–52; Officer i/c Soviet Affairs, Dept of State, 1952–56; White House, 1956; Paris, 1956–59; Dir, Exec. Secretariat, Dept of State, 1960–61; Polit. Adviser to SHAPE, Paris, 1961–63; Moscow, 1963–65; Dep. Asst Sec. for European Affairs, Dept of State, 1965–68; US Ambassador to Poland, 1968–72; Asst Sec. for European Affairs, Dept of State, 1972–74; US Ambassador to: USSR, 1974–76; Fed. Rep. of Germany, 1976–81; Under Sec. of State for Political Affairs, 1981–82; Dep. Sec. of State, 1982. Vis. Prof., Amer. Univ., Washington, 1982–84. Director: Lockheed Corp.; Hartford Group; Allen Group. Chairman: President's Commn on Chemical Warfare, 1985; US Delegn to Budapest Cultural Forum, 1985. Dir, German Marshall Fund, Atlantic Council. *Recreations:* tennis, ski-ing, swimming, painting. *Address:* 5155 Rockwood Parkway NW, Washington, DC 20016, USA.

STOGDON, Norman Francis; a Recorder of the Crown Court, 1972–83; *b* 14 June 1909; *s* of late F. R. Stogdon and late L. Stogdon (*née* Reynolds); *m* 1959, Yvonne (*née* Jaques). *Educ:* Harrow; Brasenose Coll., Oxford (BA, BCL). Called to Bar, Middle Temple, 1932. War Service, Army, 1939–45: served with Royal Fusiliers, King's African Rifles, 1941–45; Staff Officer; sc Middle East 1944. *Publications:* contrib. 2nd and 3rd edns Halsbury's Laws of England. *Recreations:* golf, ski-ing. *Address:* 2 Harcourt Buildings, Temple, EC4Y 9DB. *T:* 01–353 2548. *Club:* Moor Park Golf.

STOICHEFF, Prof. Boris Peter, OC 1982; FRS 1975; FRSC 1965; Professor of Physics, since 1964 and University Professor, since 1977, University of Toronto; *b* 1 June 1924; *s* of Peter and Vasilka Stoicheff; *m* 1954, Lillian Joan Ambridge; one *s* one *d*. *Educ:* Univ. of Toronto, Faculty of Applied Science and Engineering (BASc), Dept of Physics (MA, PhD). McKee-Gilchrist Fellowship, Univ. of Toronto, 1950–51; National Research Council of Canada: Fellowship, Ottawa, 1952–53; Res. Officer in Div. of Pure Physics, 1953–64; Member, 1978–83. Visiting Scientist, Mass Inst. of Technology, 1963–64. Chm., Engrg Science, Univ. of Toronto, 1972–77. Izaak Walton Killam Meml Scholarship, 1977–79; Senior Fellow, Massey Coll., Univ. of Toronto, 1979. H. L. Welsh Lecture, Univ. of Toronto, 1984; Elizabeth Laird Meml Lecture, Univ. Western Ontario, 1985. Fellow, Optical Soc. of America, 1965 (Pres. 1976); Fellow, Amer. Phys. Soc., 1969; Geoffrey Frew Fellow, Australian Acad. of Science, 1980. Pres., Canadian Assoc. of Physicists, 1983–84. Hon. Fellow: Indian Acad. of Scis, 1971; Macedonian Acad. of Sci. and Arts, 1981. Hon. DSc: York, Canada, 1982; Skopje, Yugoslavia, 1982. Gold Medal for Achievement in Physics of Canadian Assoc. of Physicists, 1974; William F. Meggers Award, Optical Soc. of America, 1981; Frederic Ives Medal, Optical Soc. of America, 1983. Centennial Medal of Canada, 1967. *Publications:* numerous scientific contribs to phys. and chem. jls. *Address:* Department of Physics, University of Toronto, Toronto, Ontario M5S 1A7, Canada. *T:* (416) 978–2948.

STOKE-UPON-TRENT, Archdeacon of; *see* Delight, Ven. J. D.

STOKER, Sir Michael (George Parke), Kt 1980; CBE 1974; FRCP 1979; FRS 1968, FRSE 1960; President of Clare Hall, Cambridge, since 1980 (Fellow, 1978); *b* 4 July 1918; *e s* of Dr S. P. Stoker, Maypole, Monmouth; *m* 1942, Veronica Mary English; three *s* two *d*. *Educ:* Oakham Sch.; Sidney Sussex Coll., Cambridge (Hon. Fellow 1981); St Thomas' Hosp., London. MRCS, LRCP 1942; MB, BChir 1943; MD 1947. RAMC, 1942–47; Demonstrator in Pathology, Cambridge Univ., 1947–48; Univ. Lecturer in Pathology, 1948–50; Huddersfield Lecturer in Special Pathology, 1950–58; Asst Tutor and Dir of Medical Studies, Clare Coll., 1949–58; Fellow of Clare College, 1948–58, Hon. Fellow, 1976; Prof. of Virology, Glasgow Univ., and Hon. Dir, MRC Experimental Virus Research Unit, 1959–68; Dir, Imperial Cancer Res. Fund Laboratories, 1968–79. WHO Travel Fellow, 1951; Rockefeller Foundn Travel Fellow, 1958; Vis. Prof., UCL, 1968–79. Leeuwenhoek Lecture, Royal Soc., 1971. For. Sec., 1977–81, and a Vice-Pres., 1977–81, Royal Soc. Dir, Celltech Ltd, 1980–86. Member: European Molecular Biology Organisation; Council for Scientific Policy, DES, 1970–73; Gen. Cttee, Internat. Council of Scientific Unions, 1977–81; Eur. Acad. of Arts, Scis and Humanities, 1980; Med. Res. Council, 1982–86; Chairman: UK Co-ordinating Cttee, Cancer Res., 1983–86; Scientific Adv. Cttee, Ludwig Inst. Foreign Hon. Member: Amer. Acad. of Arts and Scis, 1973; Czech Acad. of Scis, 1980. Chairman: Governing Body, Strangeways Lab., Cambridge; Livingstone Trust; Exec. Cttee, Cambridge Commonwealth Trust. Hon. DSc Glasgow, 1982. *Publications:* various articles on cell biology and virology. *Address:* Clare Hall, Cambridge CB3 9AL.

STOKES, family name of **Baron Stokes.**

STOKES, Baron *cr* 1969 (Life Peer), of Leyland; **Donald Gresham Stokes,** Kt 1965; TD; DL; FEng, FIMechE; MSAE; FIMI; FCIT; FICE; Chairman: Dutton Forshaw Motor Group Ltd, since 1980; Jack Barclay Ltd, since 1980; Chairman and Managing Director, 1968–75, Chief Executive, 1973–75, British Leyland Motor Corporation Ltd; President, BL Ltd, 1975–79; Consultant to Leyland Vehicles, 1979–81; *b* 22 March 1914; *o s* of Harry Potts Stokes; *m* 1939, Laura Elizabeth Courteney Lamb; one *s*. *Educ:* Blundell's School; Harris Institute of Technology, Preston. Started Student Apprenticeship, Leyland Motors Ltd, 1930. Served War of 1939–45: REME (Lt-Col). Re-joined Leyland as Exports Manager, 1946; General Sales and Service Manager, 1950; Director, 1954; Managing Director, and Deputy Chairman, Leyland Motor Corp., 1963, Chm. 1967; Chm. and Man. Dir, British Leyland Ltd, 1973. Director: National Westminster Bank, 1969–81; London Weekend Television Ltd, 1967–71; Opus Public Relations Ltd, 1979–84; Scottish & Universal Investments Ltd, 1980–; Dovercourt Motor Co. Ltd, 1982–; Ragheno Beherman Auto-Transports NV, 1983–; KBH Communications, 1985–. Vice-President, Empresa Nacional de Autocamiones SA, Spain, 1959–73. Chairman: British Arabian Adv. Co. Ltd, 1977–85; Two Counties Radio Ltd, 1978–84 (Pres., 1984–); British Arabian Technical Co-operation Ltd, 1981–85. Vice-Pres., Engineering Employers Fedn, 1967–75; President: SMMT, 1961–62; Motor Industry Res. Assoc., 1965–66; Manchester Univ. Inst. of Science and Technology, 1972–76 (Vice-Pres., 1967–71); Vice-Pres., IMechE, 1971, Pres., 1972; Chm., EDC for Electronics Industry, 1966–67; Member: NW Economic Planning Council, 1965–70; IRC, 1966–71 (Dep. Chm. 1969); EDC for the Motor Manufacturing Industry, 1967–; Council, Public Transport Assoc.; Worshipful Co. of Carmen. Fellow, IRTE (Pres., 1983–84), Hon. FIRTE. DL Lancs 1968. Hon. Fellow, Keble Coll., Oxford, 1968. Hon. LLD Lancaster, 1967; Hon. DTech Loughborough, 1968; Hon. DSc: Southampton, 1969; Salford, 1971. Officier de l'Ordre de la Couronne (Belgium), 1964; Commandeur de l'ordre de Leopold II (Belgium), 1972. *Recreation:* sailing. *Address:* Jack Barclay Ltd, 18 Berkeley Square, W1X 6AE. *Clubs:* Beefsteak; Royal Motor Yacht (Commodore, 1979–81).

STOKES, Dr Adrian Victor, OBE 1983; CChem; FBCS; FInstD; MRSC; MBIM; Director of Computing, St Thomas' Hospital, since 1981; *b* 25 June 1945; *s* of Alfred Samuel and Edna Stokes; *m* (marr. diss.). *Educ:* Orange Hill Grammar School, Edgware; University College London. BSc 1966 (1st cl. Hons), PhD 1970; FBCS 1978; MBIM 1986. Research Programmer, GEC-Computers Ltd, 1969–71; Research Asst, Inst. of Computer Science, 1971–73; Research Fellow, UCL, 1973–77; Sen. Research Fellow and Sen. Lectr, Hatfield Polytechnic, 1977–81. Member: Silver Jubilee Cttee on Improving Access for Disabled People, 1977–78; Cttee on Restrictions Against Disabled People, 1979–81; Social Security Adv. Cttee, 1980–; Dept of Transport Panel of Advisers on Disability, 1983–85; Disabled Persons' Transport Adv. Cttee, 1986–; Chm., Disabled Drivers' Motor Club, 1972–82, Vice-Pres., 1982–; Chm., Exec. Cttee, RADAR, 1985–. Governor, Motability, 1978–; Trustee, PHAB, 1982–. *Publications:* An Introduction to Data Processing Networks, 1978; Viewdata: a public information utility, 1979, 2nd edn 1980; The Concise Encyclopaedia of Computer Terminology, 1981; Networks, 1981; (with C. Saiady) What to Read in Microcomputing, 1982; Concise Encyclopaedia of Information Technology, 1982, 3rd edn 1986, USA edn 1983; Integrated Office Systems, 1982; (with M. D. Bacon and J. M. Bacon) Computer Networks: fundamentals and practice, 1984; Overview of Data Communications, 1985; The A to Z of Business Computing, 1986; Communications Standards, 1986; numerous papers and articles, mainly concerned with computer technology. *Recreations:* philately, science fiction, computer programming. *Address:* 97 Millway, Mill Hill, NW7 3JL. *T:* 01–959 6665.

STOKES, David Mayhew Allen; a Recorder of the Crown Court, since 1985; *b* 12 Feb. 1944; *s* of Henry Pauntley Allen Stokes and Marjorie Joan Stokes; *m* 1970, Ruth Elizabeth, *d* of late Charles Tunstall Evans, CMG, Haywards Heath; one *s* one *d*. *Educ:* Radley College; Inst. de Touraine (Tours); Churchill College, Cambridge (MA History/Law). Admitted Student, Gray's Inn, 1964; Holt Scholar, 1966; called to the Bar, 1968. *Recreations:* amateur dramatics, badminton, madrigals. *Address:* 5 Paper Buildings, Temple, EC4Y 7HB. *T:* 01–583 6117. *Club:* Norfolk (Norwich).

STOKES, Harry Michael; HM Diplomatic Service, retired; Counsellor, Foreign and Commonwealth Office, 1979–81; *b* 22 July 1926; *s* of late Wing Comdr Henry Alban Stokes, RAF, and Lilian Frances (*née* Ede); *m* 1951, Prudence Mary Watling two *s* one *d*. *Educ:* Rossall Sch.; Worcester Coll., Oxford (BA, Dip. Slavonic Studies). Served RAF, 1944–47. Joined Foreign Service, 1951; attached Control Commission, Germany, 1952–55; Foreign Office, 1955; Singapore, 1958; FO, 1959; Washington, 1961; Copenhagen, 1963; FO 1965; New Delhi, 1976; FO, 1977. Chm., British Assoc. for Cemeteries in S Asia, 1985. *Recreations:* walking, racquet games, photography, music. *Club:* Royal Commonwealth Society.

STOKES, John Fisher, MA, MD, FRCP; Physician, University College Hospital, since 1947; *b* 19 Sept. 1912; *e s* of late Dr Kenneth Stokes and Mary (*née* Fisher); *m* 1940, Elizabeth Joan, *d* of Thomas Rooke and Elizabeth Frances (*née* Pearce); one *s* one *d*. *Educ:* Haileybury (exhibitioner); Gonville and Caius Coll., Cambridge (exhibitioner); University Coll. Hosp. (Fellowes Silver Medal for clinical medicine). MB BChir (Cambridge) 1937; MRCP 1939; MD (Cambridge) 1947 (proxime accessit, Horton Smith prize); FRCP 1947; FRCPE 1975; Thruston Medal, Gonville and Caius Coll., 1948. Appointments on junior staff University Coll. Hosp. and Victoria Hosp. for Children, Tite St, 1937–42; RAMC 1942–46; served in Far East, 1943–46, Lt-Col (despatches). Examiner in Medicine, various Univs, 1949–70. Member of Council, Royal Soc. of Med., 1951–54, 1967–69. Vice-Pres., RCP, 1968–69; Harveian Orator, RCP, 1981. Trustee, Leeds Castle Foundn, 1984–. Amateur Squash Rackets Champion of Surrey, 1935, of East of England, 1936, Runner-up of British Isles, 1937; English International, 1938; Technical Adviser to Squash Rackets Assoc., 1948–52; Chm. Jesters Club, 1953–59. *Publications:* Examinations in Medicine (jtly), 1976; contrib. on liver disease and general medicine in medical journals. *Recreations:* music, tennis, painting. *Address:* Ossicles, Newnham Hill, near Henley-on-Thames, Oxon RG9 5TL. *Clubs:* Athenæum, Savile.

See also Prof. Sir W. D. M. Paton.

STOKES, John Heydon Romaine; MP (C) Halesowen and Stourbridge, since 1974 (Oldbury and Halesowen, 1970–74); *b* 23 July 1917; *o surv. s* of late Victor Romaine Stokes, Hitchin; *m* 1939, Barbara Esmée, *y d* of late R. E. Yorke, Wellingborough; one *s* two *d*. *Educ:* Temple Grove; Haileybury Coll.; Queen's Coll., Oxford. BA 1938; MA 1946. Hon. Agent and Treas., Oxford Univ. Conservative Assoc., 1937; Pres., Monarchist Soc., 1937; Pres., Mermaid Club, 1937. Asst Master, Prep. Sch., 1938–39. Served War, 1939–46: Dakar Expedn, 1940; wounded in N Africa, 1943; Mil. Asst to HM Minister Beirut and Damascus, 1944–46; Major, Royal Fusiliers. Personnel Officer, Imperial Chemical Industries, 1946–51; Personnel Manager, British Celanese, 1951–59; Dep. Personnel Manager, Courtaulds, 1957–59; Dir, Clive & Stokes, Personnel Consultants, 1959–80. Mem., Gen. Synod of C of E, 1985–. Contested (C): Gloucester, 1964; Hitchin, 1966. Mem., Select Cttee on Parly Commn for Admin (Ombudsman), 1979–83. Leader, Parly delegations: to Portugal, 1980; to Falkland Islands, 1985. Mem., Delegn to Council of Europe and WEU, 1983–. Pres., W Midlands Cons. Clubs, 1971–84. Mem. Exec. Cttee, Oxford Soc.; Chm., Gen. Purposes Cttee, Primrose League, 1971–85; Vice-Pres., Royal Stuart Soc. *Publications:* articles on political and personnel subjects. *Recreations:* gardening, travel, English history, church affairs. *Address:* College Farm House, Oakley, near Aylesbury, Bucks. *Clubs:* Carlton, Buck's.

STOLLERY, Prof. John Leslie, DScEng; FRAeS; FCGI; Professor of Aerodynamics since 1973, and Head, College of Aeronautics, 1976–86, Cranfield Institute of Technology; *b* 21 April 1930; *s* of George and Emma Stollery; *m* 1956, Jane Elizabeth, *d* of Walter and Mildred Reynolds; four *s*. *Educ:* East Barnet Grammar Sch.; Imperial Coll. of Science and Technol., London Univ. (BScEng 1951, MScEng 1953, DScEng 1973). DIC; CEng; FRAeS 1975; FCGI 1984. Aerodynamics Dept, De Havilland Aircraft Co., 1952–56; Lectr, 1956, Reader, 1962, Aeronautics Dept, Imperial Coll., London; Dean, Faculty of Engrg, 1976–79, Pro Vice-Chancellor, 1982–85, Cranfield Inst. of Technol. Chairman: Aerospace Technology Bd, MoD; Aviation Cttee, DTI. Visiting Professor: Cornell Aeronautical Labs, Buffalo, USA, 1964; Aeronaut. Res. Lab., Wright Patterson Air Force Base, 1971; Nat. Aeronaut. Lab., Bangalore, India, 1977; Peking Inst. of Aeronautics and Astronautics, 1979; Univ. of Queensland, 1983. *Publications:* (Chief Editor) Shock Tube Research, 1971; papers in Jl of Fluid Mechanics, and Aeronaut. Qly. *Recreations:* playing tennis, watching football, travelling. *Address:* 28 The Embankment, Bedford. *T:* Bedford 55087.

STONE, Evan David Robert, QC 1979; a Recorder of the Crown Court, since 1979; *b* 26 Aug. 1928; *s* of Laurence George and Lillian Stone; *m* 1959, Gisela Bridget Mann; one *s*. *Educ:* Berkhamsted; Worcester Coll., Oxford (MA). National Service (commnd, Army), 1947–49; served Middle East and UK. Called to Bar, Inner Temple, 1954, Bencher, 1985; sometime HM Deputy Coroner: Inner West London; West Middlesex; City of London. Mem. Senate of Inns of Court and the Bar, 1985. Formerly Associate Editor, Medico-Legal Journal. Councillor, later Alderman, London Borough of Islington, 1969–74 (Dep. Leader, later Leader of Opposition). Chm., City and Hackney HA, 1984–. Governor: Moorfields Eye Hosp., 1970–79; Highbury Grove Sch., 1971– (Chm. of Governors, 1978–83). *Publications:* contrib. Social Welfare and the Citizen (paperback), 1957; contribs to Medico-Legal Jl and other professional jls. *Recreations:* reading, writing, sport, listening to music. *Address:* 60 Canonbury Park South, N1 2JG. *T:* 01-226 6820; The Mill House, Ridgewell, Halstead, Essex. *T:* Ridgewell 338; (chambers) 2 Dr Johnson's Buildings, Temple, EC4. *T:* 01-353 7291. *Clubs:* Garrick, MCC; Norfolk (Norwich).

STONE, Prof. Francis Gordon Albert, FRS 1976; Head of Department of Inorganic Chemistry, and Professor since 1963, Bristol University; *b* 19 May 1925; *s* of Sidney Charles and Florence Stone; *m* 1956, Judith M. Hislop, Sydney, Australia; three *s*. *Educ:* Exeter Sch.; Christ's Coll., Cambridge. BA 1948, MA and PhD 1952, ScD 1963, Cambridge. Fulbright Schol., Univ. of Southern Calif., 1952–54; Instructor and Asst Prof., Harvard Univ., 1954–62; Reader, Queen Mary Coll., London, 1962–63. Vis. Professor: Monash Univ., 1966; Princeton Univ., 1967; Univ. of Arizona, 1970; Carnegie-Mellon Univ., 1972; Texas A&M Univ., 1980; ANU, 1982; Guggenheim Fellow, 1961; Sen. Vis. Fellow, Australian Acad. of Sciences, 1966; A. R. Gordon Distinguished Lectr, Univ. of Toronto, 1977; Misha Strassberg Vis. Lectr, Univ. of WA, 1982. Lectures: Boomer, Univ. of Alberta, 1965; Firestone, Univ. of Wisconsin, 1970; Tilden, Chem. Soc., 1971; Ludwig Mond, RSC, 1982; Reilly, Univ. of Notre Dame, 1983; Waddington, Univ. of Durham, 1984. Member: Council, Royal Soc. of Chemistry (formerly Chemical Soc.), 1968–70, 1981–83; Dalton Div. Council, 1971–74, 1981–85 (Vice-Pres. 1973 and 1984–85; Pres., 1981–83); Chemistry Cttee, SERC, 1982–85 (Mem., Chem. Cttee, SRC, 1971–74). Organometallic Chemistry Medal, 1972, Transition Metal Chemistry Medal, 1979, RSC; Chugaev Medal, Inst. of Inorganic Chem., USSR Acad. of Sciences, 1978; Amer. Chem. Soc. Award in Inorg. Chem., 1985. *Publications:* (Editor) Inorganic Polymers, 1962; (Editor) Advances in Organometallic Chemistry, vols 1–25, 1964–87; (ed) Comprehensive Organometallic Chemistry, 1984; numerous papers in Jl Chem. Soc., Jl Amer. Chem. Soc., etc. *Recreation:* world travel. *Address:* 6 Rylestone Grove, Bristol BS9 3UT. *T:* Bristol 622127.

STONE, Frederick Alistair; solicitor; Clerk and Chief Executive, Surrey County Council, since 1973; *b* 13 Sept. 1927; *s* of Cyril Jackson and Elsie May Stone; *m* 1963, Anne Teresa Connor; one *s* one *d*. *Educ:* William Hulme's Grammar Sch.; Dulwich Coll.; Brasenose Coll., Oxford (BCL, MA). Asst Solicitor: Norwich City Council, 1954–58; Hampshire CC, 1958–60; Sen. Solicitor, CC of Lincoln (Parts of Lindsey), 1960–63; Asst Clerk, Hampshire CC, 1963–65; Dep. Clerk, Cheshire CC, 1965–73. Chairman: RIPA, 1979–81; Assoc. of County Chief Executives, 1986–87; Mem. Council, Industrial Soc. *Recreations:* music, walking, gardening. *Address:* (office) County Hall, Kingston upon Thames, Surrey. *T:* 01-541 9000; (home) North Lodge, Brockham Green, Betchworth RH3 7JS. *T:* Betchworth 2178.

STONE, Gilbert Seymour, FCA; *b* 4 Feb. 1915; *s* of J. Stone; *m* 1941, Josephine Tolhurst; one *s*. *Educ:* Clifton College. War service as Air Gunner with RAF, 1939–45 (Sqdn-Ldr); with Industrial & Commercial Finance Corp. Ltd, 1945–59, latterly Asst Gen. Manager; Dir, Gresham Trust Ltd, 1959–61; practised on own account, 1961–72 and 1974–85; Dir, Industrial Develt Unit, DTI, 1972–74. Director: Babcock International plc; The Frizzell Group Ltd; New Shakespeare Co. Ltd; Manganese Bronze Holdings plc; Smith New Court plc; Household Mortgage Corp. plc. *Recreations:* golf, travel. *Address:* Rose Place, Sunninghill, Berks. *Clubs:* Garrick; Sunningdale Golf.

STONE, Sir (John) Richard (Nicholas), Kt 1978; CBE 1946; ScD; FBA 1956; P. D. Leake Professor of Finance and Accounting, University of Cambridge, 1955–80, retired; Fellow of King's College, Cambridge, since 1945; *b* 30 Aug. 1913; *o c* of late Sir Gilbert Stone; *m* 1941, Feodora Leontinoff (*d* 1956); one *d*; *m* 1960, Mrs Giovanna Croft-Murray, *d* of Count Aurelio Saffi. *Educ:* Westminster School; Gonville and Caius College, Cambridge (Hon. Fellow, 1976). MA 1938; ScD 1957. With C. E. Heath and Co., Lloyd's Brokers, 1936–39; Ministry of Economic Warfare, 1939–40; Offices of the War Cabinet, Central Statistical Office, 1940–45; Dir Dept of Applied Economics, Cambridge, 1945–55. Mem., Internat. Statistical Inst. President: Econometric Soc., 1955; Royal Econ. Soc., 1978–80; Hon. Member: Soc. of Incorp. Accountants, 1954; Amer. Economic Assoc., 1976; For. Hon. Mem., Amer. Acad. of Arts and Sciences, 1968. Hon. doctorates, Univs of Oslo and Brussels, 1965, Geneva, 1971, Warwick, 1975, Paris, 1977, Bristol, 1978. Nobel Prize for Economics, 1984. *Publications:* National Income and Expenditure, 1st edn (with J. E. Meade), 1944, 10th edn (with G. Stone), 1977; The Role of Measurement in Economics, 1951; (with others) The Measurement of Consumers' Expenditure and Behaviour in the United Kingdom 1920–1938, vol. 1 1954, vol. 2 1966; Quantity and Price Indexes in National Accounts, 1956; Input-Output and National Accounts, 1961; Mathematics in the Social Sciences, and Other Essays, 1966; Mathematical Models of the Economy, and Other Essays, 1970; Demographic Accounting and Model Building, 1971; Aspects of Economic and Social Modelling, 1980; gen. editor and pt author series A Programme for Growth, 1962–74; numerous articles in learned journals, particularly on social accounting and econometrics, 1936–. *Recreation:* staying at home. *Address:* 13 Millington Road, Cambridge.

STONE, Prof. Lawrence, MA Oxon; Dodge Professor of History, since 1963, and Director, Shelby Cullom Davis Center for Historical Studies, since 1968, Princeton University; *b* 4 Dec. 1919; *s* of Lawrence Frederick Stone and Mabel Julia Annie Stone; *m* 1943, Jeanne Caecilia, *d* of Prof. Robert Fawtier, Membre de l'Institut, Paris; one *s* one *d*. *Educ:* Charterhouse School, 1933–38; Sorbonne, Paris, 1938; Christ Church, Oxford, 1938–40, 1945–46. Lieut RNVR 1940–45. Bryce Research Student, Oxford Univ., 1946–47; Lectr, University Coll. Oxford, 1947–50; Fellow, Wadham Coll., Oxford, 1950–63 (Hon. Fellow, 1983); Mem. Inst. for Advanced Study, Princeton, 1960–61; Chm., Dept of History, 1967–70. Mem., Amer. Philosophical Soc., 1970. Fellow, Amer. Acad. of Arts and Sciences, 1968; Corresp. FBA 1983. Hon. DHL: Chicago, 1979; Pennsylvania; Hon. DLitt Edinburgh, 1983. *Publications:* Sculpture in Britain: The Middle Ages, 1955; An Elizabethan: Sir Horatio Palavicino, 1956; The Crisis of the Aristocracy, 1558–1641, 1965; The Causes of the English Revolution, 1529–1642, 1972; Family and Fortune: Studies in Aristocratic Finance in the 16th and 17th Centuries, 1973; (ed) The University in Society, 1975; (ed) Schooling and Society, 1977; Family, Sex and Marriage in England 1500–1800, 1977; The Past and the Present, 1981; An Open Elite? England 1540–1880, 1984; numerous articles in History, Economic History Review, Past and Present, Archæological Jl, English Historical Review, Bulletin of the Inst. for Historical Research, Malone Soc., Comparative Studies in Society and History, History Today, etc. *Address:* 266 Moore Street, Princeton, NJ 08540, USA. *T:* 609 921.2717; 231A Woodstock Road, Oxford. *T:* Oxford 59174.

STONE, Marcus; Sheriff of Lothian and Borders, since 1984; Advocate; *b* 22 March 1921; *s* of Morris and Reva Stone; *m* 1956, Jacqueline Barnoin; three *s* two *d*. *Educ:* High Sch. of Glasgow; Univ. of Glasgow (MA 1940, LLB 1948). Served War of 1939–45, RASC: overseas service, West Africa, att. RWAFF. Admitted Solicitor, 1949; Post Grad. Dip., Psychology, Univ. of Glasgow, 1953; admitted Faculty of Advocates, 1965; apptd Hon. Sheriff Substitute, 1967, Sheriff, 1971–76, of Stirling, Dunbarton and Clackmannan, later N Strathclyde at Dumbarton; Sheriff of Glasgow and Strathkelvin, 1976–84. *Publication:* Proof of Fact in Criminal Trials, 1984. *Recreations:* swimming, music. *Address:* Sheriff's Chambers, Sheriff Court House, Court Square, Linlithgow EH49 7EQ.

STONE, Prof. Norman; Professor of Modern History, and Fellow of Worcester College, University of Oxford, since 1984; *b* 8 March 1941; *s* of Norman Stone and Mary Stone (*née* Pettigrew); *m* 1982, Christi Margaret Booker (*née* Verity); one *s*. *Educ:* Glasgow Acad.; Gonville and Caius Coll., Cambridge (MA). Research student in Austria and Hungary, 1962–65; University of Cambridge: Research Fellow, Gonville and Caius Coll., 1965–67; Univ. Lectr in Russian History, 1967–84; Fellow and Dir of Studies in History, Jesus Coll., 1971–79; Fellow of Trinity Coll., 1979–84. Vis. Lectr, Sydney Univ., 1978. *Publications:* The Eastern Front 1914–1917, 1975, 3rd edn 1978 (Wolfson Prize for History, 1976); Hitler, 1980; Europe Transformed 1878–1919 (Fontana History of Europe), 1983; articles in learned jls, reviews. *Recreations:* Eastern Europe, music, languages. *Address:* The Grey Barn, Queen Street, Bampton, Oxon. *T:* Bampton Castle 850214; Garden Flat, 16 Thurlow Road, NW3. *T:* 01-435 5417. *Clubs:* Savile, United Oxford & Cambridge University, Ognisko Polskie.

STONE, Sir Richard; *see* Stone, Sir J. R. N.

STONE, Richard Frederick, QC 1968; *b* 11 March 1928; *s* of Sir Leonard Stone, OBE, QC, and Madeleine Marie (*née* Scheffler); *m* 1st, 1957, Georgina Maxwell Morris (decd); two *d*; 2nd, 1964, Susan van Heel; two *d*. *Educ:* Lakefield College Sch., Canada; Rugby; Trinity Hall, Cambridge (MA). Lt, Worcs Regt, 1946–48. Called to Bar, Gray's Inn, 1952, Bencher, 1974; Mem., Bar Council, 1957–61; Member: Panel of Lloyd's Arbitrators in Salvage Cases; Panel of Wreck Comrs. *Recreation:* sailing. *Address:* 5 Raymond Buildings, Gray's Inn, WC1. *T:* 01-242 2697; Orchard Gap, Wittering Road, Hayling Island, Hants.

STONEFROST, Maurice Frank, CBE 1983; DL; Chief Executive, British Rail Pension Fund; *b* 1 Sept. 1927; *s* of Arthur and Anne Stonefrost, Bristol; *m* 1953, Audrey Jean Fishlock; one *s* one *d*. *Educ:* Merrywood Grammar Sch., Bristol (DPA). IPFA, FBCS, FRSS, MBIM. Nat. Service, RAF, 1948–51; local govt finance: Bristol County Borough, 1951–54; Slough Borough, 1954–56; Coventry County Borough, 1956–61; W Sussex CC, 1961–64; Sec., Inst. of Municipal Treasurers and Accountants, 1964–73; Comptroller of Financial Services, GLC, 1973–84; Dir Gen. and Clerk, GLC, 1984–85. President: Soc. of County Treasurers, 1982–83; CIPFA, 1984–85. DL Greater London, 1986. *Recreation:* gardening. *Address:* 33 Birdham Road, Chichester, Sussex. *T:* Chichester 783304.

STONEHOUSE, John Thomson; *b* 28 July 1925; *m* 1st, 1948, Barbara Joan Smith (marr. diss. 1978); one *s* two *d*; 2nd, 1981, Mrs Sheila Buckley; one *s*. *Educ:* Elementary Sch. and Tauntons Sch., Southampton; Univ. of London (London Sch. of Econs and Political Science). Asst to Senior Probation Officer, Southampton, 1941–44. Served in RAF as pilot and education officer, 1944–47. Studied at LSE, 1947–51 (Chm., Labour Soc., 1950–51); BSc (Econ.) Hons, 1951. Man. for African Co-op. Socs in Uganda, 1952–54; Sec., Kampala Mutual Co-op Soc. Ltd (Uganda), 1953–54; Dir of London Co-operative Soc. Ltd, 1956–62 (Pres., 1962–64); Mem. until 1962 of Development Cttee of the Co-operative Union; Dir of Society Footwear Ltd until 1963. Contested Norwood, London CC Election, 1949; contested (Lab): Twickenham, General Election, 1950; Burton, General Election, 1951; MP (Lab Co-op): Wednesbury, Feb. 1957–74; Walsall N, 1974–76, (English Nat. Party, April-Aug. 1976); Parly Sec., Min. of Aviation, 1964–66; Parly Under-Sec. of State for the Colonies, 1966–67; Minister of Aviation, 1967; Minister of State, Technology, 1967–68; Postmaster-General, 1968–69; Minister of Posts and Telecommunications, 1969–70. Chm., Parly Cttee of ASTMS, 1974–75; Mem. Exec. Cttee, UK Br. IPU. UK Deleg. to Council of Europe and WEU, 1962–64; Leader, UK Govt Delegns, Independence Ceremonies in Botswana and Lesotho, 1966; attended Independence Ceremonies in Uganda, 1962, Kenya, 1963, Zambia, 1964, and Mauritius, 1968, as special guest of Independence Governments. Granted citizenship of Bangladesh, 1972. Councillor, Islington Borough Council, 1956–59. Member, RIIA, 1955–65. *Publications:* (jtly) Gangrene, 1959; Prohibited Immigrant, 1960; Death of an Idealist, 1975; The Ultimate (as James Lund), 1976; My Trial, 1976; Ralph, 1982; The Baring Fault, 1986. *Recreations:* music, learning to ski, desmology. *Address:* c/o Jonathan Cape Ltd, 32 Bedford Square, WC1B 3EL. *Club:* Royal Automobile.

STONES, Prof. Edward Lionel Gregory, MA, PhD; FBA 1979; Professor of Mediæval History, University of Glasgow, 1956–78, now Emeritus Professor; *b* Croydon, 4 March 1914; *s* of Edward Edison Stones, Elland, Yorks, and Eleanor Gregory; *m* 1947, Jeanne Marie Beatrice, *d* of A. J. Fradin and Florence B. Timbury; one *s* one *d*. *Educ:* Glasgow High Sch.; Glasgow Univ.; Balliol Coll., Oxford. 1st Cl. English Lang. and Lit. (Glasgow), 1936; 1st Class Modern History (Oxford), 1939; PhD (Glasgow), 1950; FRHistS, 1950; FSA, 1962. Asst Lectr in History, Glasgow Univ., 1939. War of 1939–45: joined Royal Signals, 1940; Major 1943; GSO2, GHQ, New Delhi (Signals Directorate), 1943–45. Lectr in History, Glasgow, 1945–56. Vis. Res. Fellow, Westfield Coll., London Univ., 1972–73. Lay Mem., Provincial Synod, Episcopal Church of Scotland, 1963–66. Pres., Glasgow Archaeological Soc., 1969–72; Member: Ancient Monuments Board for

Scotland, 1964–79 (Chm. 1968–73); Council, Royal Hist. Soc., 1968–72; Council, Soc. Antiquaries, London, 1972–74. Corresp. Fellow, Mediaeval Acad. of America, 1980. *Publications:* Anglo-Scottish Relations, 1174–1328, 1965; Edward I, 1968; (ed) Maitland's Letters to Neilson, 1976; (with G. G. Simpson) Edward I and the Throne of Scotland, 1978; and articles in various historical journals. *Recreations:* books, music. *Address:* 34 Alexandra Road, Parkstone, Poole, Dorset BH14 9EN. *T:* Poole 742803. *Club:* United Oxford & Cambridge University.

STONES, (Elsie) Margaret, MBE 1977; botanical artist; Visiting Artist, Louisiana State University, Baton Rouge, since 1977; *b* 28 Aug. 1920; *d* of Frederick Stones and Agnes Kirkwood (*née* Fleming). *Educ:* Swinburne Technical Coll., Melbourne; Melbourne National Gall. Art Sch. Came to England, 1951; working independently as botanical artist, 1951–: at Royal Botanic Gardens, Kew; Nat. Hist. Museum; Royal Horticultural Soc., and at other botanical instns; Contrib. Artist to Curtis's Botanical Magazine, 1957–82. Drawings (water-colour): 20, Aust. plants, National Library, Canberra, 1962–63; 250, Tasmanian endemic plants, 1962–77; Basalt Plains flora, Melbourne Univ., 1975–76; to spend 3–4 months annually for 10 years at Louisiana State Univ. doing 200 water-colour drawings of Louisiana flora, 1977–. Exhibitions: Colnaghi's, London, 1967–; Retrospective Exhibn, Melbourne Univ., 1976; Louisiana Drawings, Smithsonian, USA, 1980, Louisiana State Mus., 1985; Baskett & Day, 1984. Hon. DSc Louisiana State Univ. Bâton Rouge, 1986. *Publications:* The Endemic Flora of Tasmania (text by W. M. Curtis), 6 Parts, 1967–78; illus. various books. *Recreations:* gardening, reading. *Address:* 1 Bushwood Road, Kew, Richmond, Surrey. *T:* 01–940 6183.

STONEY, Brigadier Ralph Francis Ewart, CBE 1952 (OBE, 1943); Director-General, The Royal Society for the Prevention of Accidents, 1959–68; *b* 28 June 1903; *o s* of late Col R. D. S. Stoney, The Downs, Delgany, Co. Wicklow and Mrs E. M. M. Stoney; *m* 1st, 1939, Kathleen Nina (*née* Kirkland) (*d* 1973); one *d*; 2nd, 1979, Bridget Mary St John Browne. *Educ:* Royal Naval Colleges, Osborne and Dartmouth; Royal Military Academy, Woolwich. Commissioned Royal Engineers, 1923; Staff College, Camberley, 1937–38. Served War of 1939–45 as GSO, 1939–43 (OBE) and as CRE, 82 Div., 1943–46, in Burma (despatches twice). CRE 5th Div. and 2nd Div., 1947–48; Col GS (Intelligence), War Office, 1949–51; Brig. GS (Intelligence), Middle East, 1952–54. Retired, 1954. *Recreations:* sailing; workshop practice. *Address:* Kinsale, Hook Heath Avenue, Woking, Surrey.

STONHOUSE, Sir Philip (Allan), 18th Bt, *cr* 1628, and 14th Bt *cr* 1670; Assessor and Land Appraiser, Government of Alberta; *b* 24 Oct. 1916; *s* of Sir Arthur Allan Stonhouse, 17th Bt, and Beatrice C. Féron; *S* father, 1967; *m* 1946, Winnifred Emily Shield; two *s*. *Educ:* Western Canada Coll.; Queen's Univ., Kingston, Ontario. Gold Mining, 1936–40; General Construction, 1940–42; Ranching, 1942–54; Assessing, 1954–68. Is a Freemason. *Recreations:* water-fowl and upland game hunting, tennis, ski-ing. *Heir:* *s* Rev. Michael Philip Stonhouse, BA, LTh [*b* 4 Sept. 1948; *m* 1977, Colleen Coueill, Toronto; two *s*. *Educ:* Wycliffe Coll., Toronto]. *Address:* 521–12 Street SW, Medicine Hat, Alberta, Canada. *T:* 526–5832. *Club:* Medicine Hat Ski.

STONHOUSE-GOSTLING, Maj.-Gen. Philip Le Marchant Stonhouse, CB 1955; CBE 1953; retired; *b* 28 August 1899; *s* of Colonel Charles Henry Stonhouse-Gostling and Alice Seton (*née* Fraser-Tytler); *m* 1946, Helen Rimington Myra (*née* Pereira), Ottawa, Ontario, Canada. *Educ:* Cheltenham College; RMA Woolwich. Entered RA, 1919; served India with RA, 1920–26; Mil. Coll. of Science, 1927–29; i/c Technical Intelligence, WO, 1930; Woolwich Arsenal: Asst Inspector Guns and Carriages, 1931–38; Supt Carriage Design, 1939; Technical Adviser to Canadian Govt and British Purchasing Commn for Armaments, 1939–40; Dep. Dir of Supply, British Supply Mission, Washington, 1941–44; Director of Supply (Armaments), 1944–46; Dep. Dir Technical Services, British Jt Staff Mission, 1942–46; Director, 1946–50; Dep. Chief Engineer, Armaments Design Establishment in UK, 1951; President, Ordnance Board, Feb. 1954–Feb. 1955; Retired from Army, March 1955. Exec. Engineer, Beemer Engineering Co., Philadelphia, 1955–64. Legion of Merit (Officer), USA 1944. *Recreations:* sailing, photography. *Address:* Island House West, 325 Beach Road, Tequesta, Florida 33469, USA; c/o Lloyds Bank, Cox's and King's Branch, 6 Pall Mall, SW1.

STONOR, family name of **Baron Camoys.**

STOODLEY, Peter Ernest William; County Treasurer of Kent, 1972–80; *b* 27 July 1925; *s* of Ernest and Esther Stoodley; *m* 1970, June (*née* Bennett). *Educ:* Weymouth Grammar Sch.; Administrative Staff Coll.; Inst. of Public Finance Accountants. Accountant with County Council of: Dorset, 1947–56; Staffordshire, 1956–61; Kent, 1961–65; Asst Co. Treasurer of Kent, 1965–69; Dep. Co. Treasurer of Kent, 1969–72. *Recreations:* ornithology, cricket. *Address:* Cranby, Horseshoe Lane, Leeds, Maidstone, Kent. *T:* Maidstone 861287.

STOPFORD, family name of **Earl of Courtown.**

STOPFORD, Maj.-Gen. Stephen Robert Anthony, MBE 1971; Director General Fighting Vehicles and Engineer Equipment, Ministry of Defence (Procurement Executive), since 1985; *b* 1 April 1934; *s* of Comdr Robert Stopford, RN, and Elsie Stopford; *m* 1963, Vanessa (*née* Baron). *Educ:* Downside; Millfield. Graduate MIERE. Commissioned Royal Scots Greys, 1954; regimental service and various staff appts until 1977; Project Manager, MBT80, 1977–80; Military Attaché, Washington, 1983–85. *Recreations:* sailing, scuba diving, shooting. *Address:* 18 Thornton Avenue, SW2 4HG. *T:* 01–674 1416. *Club:* Cavalry and Guards.

STOPPARD, Miriam, MD, MRCP; writer and broadcaster; *b* 12 May 1937; *d* of Sydney and Jenny Stern; *m* 1972, Tom Stoppard, *qv*; two *s* and two step *s*. *Educ:* Newcastle upon Tyne Central High Sch. (State Scholar, 1955); Royal Free Hosp. Sch. of Medicine, Univ. of London (Prize for Experimental Physiol., 1958); King's Coll. Med. Sch. (Univ. of Durham), Newcastle upon Tyne (MB, BS Durham, 1961; MD Newcastle, 1966). MRCP 1964. Royal Victoria Infirmary, King's Coll. Hosp., Newcastle upon Tyne: House Surg., 1961; House Phys., 1962; Sen. House Officer in Medicine, 1962–63; Univ. of Bristol: Res. Fellow, Dept of Chem. Pathol., 1963–65 (MRC Scholar in Chem. Pathol.); Registrar in Dermatol., 1965–66 (MRC Scholar in Dermatol.); Sen. Registrar in Dermatol., 1966–68; Syntex Pharmaceuticals Ltd: Associate Med. Dir, 1968; Dep. Med. Dir, 1971; Med. Dir, 1974; Dep. Man. Dir, 1976; Man. Dir, 1977–81. TV series: Where There's Life (5 series), 1981–; Baby & Co. (2 series), 1984–; Woman to Woman, 1985–. MRSocMed (Mem. Dermatol. Sect., Endocrinol. Sect.); Member: Heberden Soc.; Brit. Assoc. of Rheumatology and Rehabilitation. *Publications:* Miriam Stoppard's Book of Baby Care, 1977; (contrib). My Medical School, 1978; Miriam Stoppard's Book of Health Care, 1979; The Face and Body Book, 1980; Everywoman's Lifeguide, 1982; Your Baby, 1982; Fifty Plus Lifeguide, 1982; Your Growing Child, 1983; Baby Care Book, 1983; Pregnancy and Birth Book, 1984; Baby and Child Medical Handbook, 1986; over 40 pubns in med. jls. *Recreations:* my family, gardening. *Address:* Iver Grove, Iver, Bucks.

STOPPARD, Tom, CBE 1978; FRSL; playwright and novelist; *b* 3 July 1937; *yr s* of late Eugene Straussler and of Mrs Martha Stoppard; *m* 1st, 1965, Jose (marr. diss. 1972), *yr d*

of John and Alice Ingle; two *s*; 2nd, 1972, Dr Miriam Moore-Robinson (*see* Miriam Stoppard); two *s*. *Educ:* abroad; Dolphin Sch., Notts; Pocklington, Yorks. Journalist: Western Daily Press, Bristol, 1954–58; Bristol Evening World, 1958–60; freelance, 1960–63. Hon. degrees: Bristol, 1976; Brunel, 1979; Leeds, 1980; Sussex, 1980; London, 1982; Kenyon Coll., 1984; York, 1984. Shakespeare Prize, 1979. *Plays:* Enter a Free Man, London, 1968 (TV play, A Walk on the Water, 1963); Rosencrantz and Guildenstern are Dead, Nat. Theatre, 1967, subseq. NY, etc (Tony Award, NY, 1968; NY Drama Critics Circle Award, 1968); The Real Inspector Hound, London, 1968; After Magritte, Ambiance Theatre, 1970; Dogg's Our Pet, Ambiance Theatre, 1972; Jumpers, National Theatre, 1972 (Evening Standard Award); Travesties, Aldwych, 1974 (Evening Standard Award; Tony Award, NY, 1976); Dirty Linen, Newfoundland, Ambiance Theatre, 1976; Every Good Boy Deserves Favour (music-theatre), 1977; Night and Day, Phoenix, 1978 (Evening Standard Award); Dogg's Hamlet and Cahoot's Macbeth, Collegiate, 1979; Undiscovered Country (adaptation), NT, 1979; On the Razzle, NT, 1981; The Real Thing, Strand, 1982 (Standard Award), subseq. NY (Tony Award, 1984); Rough Crossing, NT, 1984; Dalliance (adaptation), NT, 1986; *radio:* The Dissolution of Dominic Boot, 1964; M is for Moon Among Other Things, 1964; If You're Glad I'll be Frank, 1965; Albert's Bridge, 1967 (Prix Italia); Where Are They Now?, 1970; Artist Descending a Staircase, 1972; The Dog it was That Died, 1982 (Giles Cooper Award); *television:* A Separate Peace, 1966; Teeth, 1967; Another Moon Called Earth, 1967; Neutral Ground, 1968; (with Clive Exton) Boundaries, 1975; (adapted) Three Men in a Boat, 1976; Professional Foul, 1977; Squaring the Circle, 1984. *film scripts:* (with T. Wiseman) The Romantic Englishwoman, 1975; Despair, 1978; The Human Factor, 1979; (with Terry Gilliam and Charles McKeown) Brazil, 1985. John Whiting Award, Arts Council, 1967; Evening Standard Award for Most Promising Playwright, 1968. *Publications:* (short stories) Introduction 2, 1964; (novel) Lord Malquist and Mr Moon, 1965; *plays:* Rosencrantz and Guildenstern are Dead, 1967; The Real Inspector Hound, 1968; Albert's Bridge, 1968; Enter a Free Man, 1968; After Magritte, 1971; Jumpers, 1972; Artists Descending a Staircase, and, Where Are They Now?, 1973; Travesties, 1975; Dirty Linen, and New-Found-Land, 1976; Every Good Boy Deserves Favour, 1978; Professional Foul, 1978; Night and Day, 1978; Undiscovered Country, 1980; Dogg's Hamlet, Cahoot's Macbeth, 1980; On the Razzle, 1982; The Real Thing, 1983; The Dog it was that Died, 1983; Squaring the Circle, 1984; Four plays for radio, 1984; Rough Crossing, 1985. *Address:* Iver Grove, Iver, Bucks.

STORAR, John Robert Allan Montague, CA; Chairman, Mitchell Cotts PLC, since 1985 (Director, since 1973; Deputy Chairman, 1978); *b* 6 Nov. 1925; *s* of James and Leonore Storar; *m* 1952, Catherine Swanson Henderson; two *s* one *d*. *Educ:* Dollar Academy. Dir 1960–74, Dep. Chief Exec. 1972–74, Drayton Corporation Ltd; Dir 1974–85, Dep. Chm. 1974–81, Man. Dir 1981–82, Samuel Montagu & Co. Ltd; Dir, Consolidated Gold Fields PLC, 1969–. Chm., Assoc. of Investment Trust Cos, 1979–81. *Recreation:* fly fishing. *Address:* Cotts House, Camomile Street, EC3A 7BJ. *Club:* Caledonian.

See also L. E. T. Storar.

STORAR, Leonore Elizabeth Therese; retired; *b* 3 May 1920. Served HM Forces, 1942–46. Min. of Labour, 1941; Min. of Works, 1947; joined CRO, 1948; First Sec., Delhi and Calcutta, 1951–53; Salisbury, 1956–58; Colombo, 1960–62; Counsellor, 1963; Head of General and Migration Dept, CRO, 1962; Dep. Consul-Gen., NY, 1967; Consul-Gen., Boston, 1969; Head of Commonwealth Co-ordination Dept, FCO, 1971–75; Dir, Colombo Plan Bureau, Colombo, Sri Lanka, 1976–78. *Address:* Lavender Cottage, Dippenhall Street, Crondall, Farnham, Surrey GU10 5PF.

STORER, David George; Under Secretary, Department of Health and Social Security, since 1984; *b* 27 June 1929; *s* of Herbert Edwards Storer; *m* 1960, Jean Mary Isobel Jenkin; one *s* two *d*. *Educ:* Monmouth School; St John's Coll., Cambridge (MA). Assistant Principal, Min. of Labour, 1952; Principal, 1957; Cabinet Office, 1963–66; Asst Secretary, Dept of Employment, 1966–73; Director, Training Opportunities Scheme, 1973–77; Dir of Corporate Services, MSC, 1977–84. *Recreations:* walking, squash, sailing. *Address:* 5a Carlton Road, Redhill, Surrey RH1 2BY.

STORER, James Donald, CEng, MRAeS; Keeper, Department of Science, Technology and Working Life, Royal Museum of Scotland, Edinburgh, since 1985; *b* 11 Jan. 1928; *s* of James Arthur Storer and Elizabeth May Gartshore (*née* Pirie); *m* 1955, Shirley Anne (*née* Kent); one *s* one *d*. *Educ:* Hemsworth Grammar Sch., Yorks; Imperial Coll., London (BSc Hons, ACGI). Design Office, Vickers Armstrongs (Aircraft) Ltd, and British Aircraft Corporation, Weybridge, 1948–66; Dept of Technology, Royal Scottish Museum, 1966–85. MRAeS (AFRAeS 1958). *Publications:* Steel and Engineering, 1959; Behind the Scenes in an Aircraft Factory, 1965; It's Made Like This: Cars, 1967; The World We Are Making: Aviation, 1968; A Simple History of the Steam Engine, 1969; How to Run An Airport, 1971; How We Find Out About Flight, 1973; Flying Feats, 1977; Book of the Air, 1979; Great Inventions, 1980; (jtly) Encyclopedia of Transport, 1983; (jtly) East Fortune: Museum of Flight and history of the airfield, 1983; The Silver Burdett Encyclopedia of Transport: Air, 1984. *Recreation:* aircraft preservation. *Address:* 52 Thomson Road, Currie, Edinburgh EH14 5HW. *T:* 031–449 2843. *Club:* University of Edinburgh Staff (Edinburgh).

STORER, Prof. Roy; Professor of Prosthodontics since 1968 and Dean of Dentistry since 1977 (Clinical Sub-Dean, 1970–77) The Dental School, University of Newcastle upon Tyne; *b* 21 Feb. 1928; *s* of late Harry and Jessie Storer; *m* 1953, Kathleen Mary Frances Pitman; one *s* two *d*. *Educ:* Wallasey Grammar Sch.; Univ. of Liverpool. LDS (Liverpool) 1950; FDSRCS 1954; MSc (Liverpool) 1960; DRD RCS Ed, 1978. House Surg., 1950, and Registrar, 1952–54, United Liverpool Hosps; Lieut (later Captain) Royal Army Dental Corps, 1950–52; Lectr in Dental Prosthetics, Univ. of Liverpool, 1954–61; Visiting Associate Prof., Northwestern Univ., Chicago, 1961–62; Sen. Lectr in Dental Prosthetics, Univ. of Liverpool, 1962–67; Hon. Cons. Dental Surgeon: United Liverpool Hosps, 1962–67; United Newcastle Hosps (now Newcastle Health Authority), 1968–. Mem. Council and Sec., British Soc. for the Study of Prosthetic Dentistry, 1960–69 (Pres., 1968–69); Mem., Bd of Faculty, RCS, 1982–. Pres., Med. Rugby Football Club (Newcastle), 1968–82; Mem., Northern Sports Council, 1973–; Chm., Div. of Dentistry, Newcastle Univ. Hosps, 1972–75. External Examiner in Dental Subjects: Univs of Belfast, Birmingham, Bristol, Dublin, Dundee, Leeds, London, Newcastle upon Tyne, and Royal Coll. of Surgeons of England. *Publications:* A Laboratory Course in Dental Materials for Dental Hygienists (with D. C. Smith), 1963; Immediate and Replacement Dentures (with J. N. Anderson), 3rd edn, 1981; papers on sci. and clin. subjects in dental and med. jls. *Recreations:* Rugby football, cricket, gardening. *Address:* The Dental School, Framlington Place, Newcastle upon Tyne NE2 4BW; 164 Eastern Way, Darras Hall, Ponteland, Newcastle upon Tyne NE20 9RH. *T:* Ponteland 24399. *Clubs:* Athenæum, MCC, East India.

STOREY, Christopher, MA, PhD; Headmaster, Culford School, Bury St Edmunds, 1951–71; *b* 23 July 1908; *s* of William Storey and Margaret T. B. Cowan, Newcastle upon Tyne; *m* 1937, Gertrude Appleby, Scarborough; four *s*. *Educ:* Rutherford Coll.,

Newcastle upon Tyne; King's Coll., Univ. of Durham (BA Hons French, cl. I); Univ. of Strasbourg (PhD). Modern Languages Master, Mundella Sch., Nottingham, 1931–34; French Master: Scarborough High Sch. for Boys, 1934–36; City of London Sch., 1936–42. Headmaster, Johnston Grammar Sch., Durham, 1942–51. Officier d'Académie, 1947. *Publications:* Etude critique de la Vie de St Alexis, 1934; Apprenons le mot juste!, 1939; (ed) La Vie de St Alexis, 1946, 2nd rev. edn, 1968; Sprechen und Schreiben (with C. E. Bond), 1950; articles in Modern Language Review, French Studies, and Medium Aevum. *Address:* 13 The Paddox, Oxford OX2 7PN. *T:* Oxford 52328.

STOREY, David Malcolm; writer and dramatist; *b* 13 July 1933; *s* of Frank Richmond Storey and Lily (*née* Cartwright); *m* 1956, Barbara Rudd Hamilton; two *s* two *d. Educ:* Queen Elizabeth Grammar Sch., Wakefield, Yorks; Slade School of Fine Art, London; Fellow, UCL, 1974. *Plays:* The Restoration of Arnold Middleton, 1967 (Evening Standard Award); In Celebration, 1969 (Los Angeles Critics' Award); The Contractor, 1969 (Writer of the Year Award, Variety Club of GB, NY Critics' Award); Home, 1970 (Evening Standard Award, Critics' Award, NY); The Changing Room, 1971 (Critics' Award, NY); Cromwell, 1973; The Farm, 1973; Life Class, 1974; Mother's Day, 1976; Sisters, 1978; Early Days, 1980. *Publications:* This Sporting Life, 1960 (Macmillan Fiction Award, US); Flight into Camden, 1960 (John Llewellyn Meml Prize, Somerset Maugham award); Radcliffe, 1963; Pasmore, 1972 (Geoffrey Faber Meml Prize, 1973); A Temporary Life, 1973; Edward, 1973; Saville, 1976 (Booker Prize, 1976); A Prodigal Child, 1982; Present Times, 1984. *Address:* c/o Jonathan Cape Ltd, 32 Bedford Square, WC1B 3EL.

STOREY, Graham; Reader in English, since 1981, and Fellow of Trinity Hall, since 1949, Cambridge University; *b* 8 Nov. 1920; *o* surv. *s* of late Stanley Runton Storey, LDS RCS and Winifred Storey (*née* Graham). *Educ:* St Edward's Sch., Oxford; Trinity Hall, Cambridge (MA 1944). Served War, RA, 1941–45; Lieut 1942; mentioned in despatches. Called to the Bar, Middle Temple, 1950, but did not practise. Sen. Tutor, 1958–68, Vice-Master, 1970–74, Trinity Hall, Cambridge; Univ. Lectr in English, 1965–81; Chm., Faculty Bd of English, 1972–74. Vis. Fellow, All Souls Coll., Oxford, 1968. Warton Lectr, British Acad., 1984; Lecture tours for British Council overseas. Syndic, CUP, 1983. Vice-Pres., G. M. Hopkins Soc., 1971; Pres., Dickens Soc. of America, 1983–84. Governor: St Edward's, Oxford, 1959–69; Eastbourne Coll., 1965–69. Jt Gen. Editor, Letters of Dickens, Pilgrim edn, 1965–; General Editor: Cambridge Renaissance and Restoration Dramatists, 1975–; Cambridge English Prose Texts, 1980–. *Publications:* Reuters' Century, 1951; Journals and Papers of G. M. Hopkins, 1959 (completed edn on death of Humphry House); (ed) A. P. Rossiter, Angel with Horns, 1961; (ed) Selected Verse and Prose of G. M. Hopkins, 1966; Letters of Charles Dickens, vol. I, 1965, vol. II, 1969, vol. III, 1974, vol. V, 1981 (ed jtly); A Preface to Hopkins, 1981; (ed with Howard Erskine-Hill) Revolutionary Prose of the English Civil War, 1983; contributions to: New Cambridge Bibliography, 1967; Writers and their Work, 1982; periodicals. *Recreations:* theatre, gardening, travel, tennis. *Address:* Trinity Hall, Cambridge. *T:* Cambridge 332500; Crown House, Caxton, Cambs. *T:* Caxton 316. *Club:* Beefsteak.

STOREY, Maude; Registrar and Chief Executive, United Kingdom Central Council for Nursing, Midwifery and Health Visiting, 1981–June 1987; *b* 24 March 1930; *d* of late Henry Storey and of Sarah Farrimond Storey. *Educ:* Wigan and District Mining and Techn. Coll.; St Mary's Hosp., Manchester; Lancaster Royal Infirmary; Paddington Gen. Hosp.; Royal Coll. of Nursing, Edinburgh; Queen Elizabeth Coll., London. SRN 1952; SCM 1953; RCI (Edin.) 1962; RNT 1965. Domiciliary Midwife, Wigan County Borough, 1953–56; Midwifery Sister, St Mary's Hosp., Manchester, 1956–57; Charge Nurse, Intensive Therapy, Mayo Clinic, USA, 1957–59; Theatre Sister, Clinical Instructor, 1959–63, subseq. Nurse Tutor, 1965–68, Royal Albert Edward Infirmary, Wigan; Lectr in Community Nursing, Manchester Univ., 1968–71; Asst, subseq. Principal Regional Nursing Officer, Liverpool Regional Hosp. Bd, 1971–73; Regional Nursing Officer, Mersey RHA, 1973–77; Registrar, GNC for England and Wales, 1977–81. Member: Standing Nursing and Midwifery Adv. Cttee, 1977–; West Berks DHA, 1982–. FBIM. *Recreations:* travel, theatre, amateur dramatics. *Address:* 14 Conifer Drive, Long Lane, Tilehurst, Berks. *T:* Reading 412082.

STOREY, Hon. Sir Richard, 2nd Bt *cr* 1960; Chairman of Portsmouth and Sunderland Newspapers plc, since 1973; Member, Press Council, since 1980; *b* 23 Jan. 1937; *s* of Baron Buckton (Life Peer) and Elisabeth (*d* 1951), *d* of late Brig.-Gen. W. J. Woodcock, DSO; *S* to baronetcy of father, 1978; *m* 1961, Virginia Anne, 3rd *d* of Sir Kenelm Cayley, 10th Bt; one *s* two *d. Educ:* Winchester; Trinity Coll., Cambridge (BA, LLB). National service commission, RNVR, 1956. Called to the Bar, Inner Temple, 1962. Director: Portsmouth and Sunderland Newspapers plc, 1962; Croydon Cable Television Ltd, 1985–; Reuters Hldgs PLC, 1986–. Member: Nat. Council and Exec., CLA, 1980–84, Yorks Exec., CLA (Chm., 1974–76); Employment Policy Cttee, CBI, 1984–, CBI Regl Council, Yorks and Humberside, 1974–76; Bd, Press Assoc., 1986–; Newspaper Soc. Council and some cttees. Mem. Council, INCA-FIEJ Res. Assoc., 1983–. *Recreations:* sport and silviculture, farms and administers land in Yorkshire. *Heir:* *s* Kenelm Storey, *b* 4 Jan. 1963. *Address:* Settrington House, Malton, North Yorks. *T:* North Grimston 200; 7 Douro Place, W8 5PH. *T:* 01–937 8823.

STORIE-PUGH, Col Peter David, CBE 1981 (MBE 1945); MC 1940; TD 1945 and 3 clasps; DL; Member, Economic and Social Committee of the European Communities, since 1982; Lecturer, University of Cambridge, 1953–82; Fellow of Wolfson College, Cambridge, since 1967; *b* 1 Nov. 1919; *s* of late Prof. Leslie Pugh, CBE, FRCVS and Paula Storie; *m* 1st, 1946, Alison (marr. diss. 1971), *d* of late Sir Oliver Lyle, OBE; one *s* two *d*; 2nd, 1971, Leslie Helen, *d* of Earl Striegel; three *s* one *d. Educ:* Malvern; Queens' Coll., Cambridge (Hon. Foundn Scholar); Royal Veterinary Coll., Univ. of London. MA, PhD, FRCVS, CChem, FRSC. Served War of 1939–45, Queen's Own Royal W Kent Regt (escaped from Spangenberg and Colditz); comd 1st Bn, Cambs Regt, comd 1st Bn Suffolk and Cambs Regt; Col, Dep. Comdr, 161 Inf. Bde, ACF County Comdt. Wellcome Res. Fellow, Cambridge, 1950–52. Mem. Council, RCVS, 1956–84 (Chm. Parly Cttee, 1962–67; Pres., 1977–78); President: Cambridge Soc. for Study of Comparative Medicine, 1966–67; Internat. Pig Vet. Soc., 1967–69 (Life Pres., 1969); British Veterinary Assoc., 1968–69 and 1970–71; Mem. Exec. Cttee, Cambridgeshire Farmers Union, 1960–65; UK delegate, EEC Vet. Liaison Cttee, 1962–75 (Pres., 1973–75); UK Rep., Fedn of Veterinarians of EEC, 1975–83 (Pres. of Fedn, 1975–79); Chm., Eurovet, 1971–73; Mem. Jt RCVS/BVA Cttee on European Vet. Affairs, 1971–; Observer, European Liaison Gp for Agric., 1972–80; Jt Pres., 1st European Vet. Congress, Wiesbaden, 1972; Permanent Mem. EEC Adv. Vet. Cttee, 1976–82; Mem. Council, Secrétariat Européen des Professions Libérales, Intellectuelles et Sociales, 1976–80; Mem. Permanent Cttee, World Vet. Assoc., 1964–75. Member: Parly and Sci. Cttee, 1962–67; Home Sec.'s Adv. Cttee (Cruelty to Animals Act, 1876), 1963–80; Nat. Agric. Centre Adv. Bd, 1966–69; Production Cttee, Meat and Livestock Commn, 1967–70; Min. of Agriculture's Farm Animal Adv. Cttee, 1970–73. Chm., Nat. Sheep Breeders' Assoc., 1964–68; Vice-Pres., Agric. Section, British Assocn, 1970–71. Corresp. Mem., Bund Deutscher Veterinäroffiziere, 1979–. Robert von Ostertag Medal, German Vet. Assoc., 1972. DL Cambs, 1963. *Publications:* (and ed jtly) Eurovet: an Anatomy of Veterinary Europe, 1972; Eurovet-2, 1975. *Address:* Duxford

Grange, Duxford, Cambridge CB2 4QF. *T:* Fowlmere 403. *Club:* United Oxford & Cambridge University.

STORK, Joseph Whiteley, CB 1959; CBE 1949; retired as Director of Studies, Britannia Royal Naval College, Dartmouth (1955–59) (Headmaster, 1942–55); *b* Huddersfield, 9 Aug. 1902; *s* of John Arthur Stork, Huddersfield; *m* 1927, Kathleen, *d* of Alderman J. H. Waddington, JP, Halifax; one *s* three *d. Educ:* Uppingham; Downing Coll., Cambridge (scholar). 1st Class Nat. Sci. Tripos Pt 1, 2nd Class Nat. Sci. Tripos Pt II (Zoology); Senior Biology Master, Cambridge and County School, 1926; Head of Biological Dept, Charterhouse School, 1926–36; Headmaster, Portsmouth Grammar School, 1936–42. *Publications:* Joint Author of: Fundamentals of Biology, 1932, Junior Biology, 1933, Plant and Animal Ecology, 1933. *Address:* 15 Cautley Drive, Killinghall, Harrogate HG3 2DJ.

STORMONT, Viscount; Alexander David Mungo Murray; *b* 17 Oct. 1956; *s* and heir of 8th Earl of Mansfield and Mansfield, *qv; m* 1985, Sophia Mary Veronica, *o d* of Biden Ashbrooke, St John, Jersey. *Educ:* Eton. *Address:* 26 Garfield Road, SW11.

STORMONTH DARLING, Sir James Carlisle, (Sir Jamie Stormonth Darling), Kt 1983; CBE 1972; MC 1945; TD; Director, 1971–83, Vice-President Emeritus, since 1986, The National Trust for Scotland (Secretary, as Chief Executive, 1949–71); *b* 18 July 1918; *s* of late Robert Stormonth Darling, Writer to the Signet, Rosebank, Kelso, Roxburghshire, and late Beryl Madeleine Sayer, Battle, Sussex; *m* 1948, Mary Finella, BEM 1945, DL, *d* of late Lt.-Gen. Sir James Gammell, KCB, DSO, MC; one *s* two *d. Educ:* Winchester Coll.; Christ Church, Oxford; BA 1939, MA 1972; Edinburgh Univ.; LLB 1949. 2nd Lt KOSB (TA), 1938; War Service, 1939–46, in KOSB and 52nd (L) Reconnaissance Regt, RAC, of which Lt-Col comdg in 1945 (TD). Admitted Writer to the Signet, 1949. Member, Queen's Body Guard for Scotland (Royal Company of Archers), 1958–. Mem., Ancient Monuments Bd for Scotland, 1983–. Pres., Scottish Conservation Projects Trust, 1984–; Chm., Edinburgh Old Town Enterprise Trust, 1986–. Hon. FRIAS 1982. DUniv Stirling, 1983; Hon. LLD Aberdeen, 1984. *Address:* Chapelhill House, Dirleton, East Lothian. *T:* Dirleton 296. *Clubs:* New, Puffins (Edinburgh).

STORMONTH-DARLING, Robin Andrew; Chairman, Laing & Cruickshank, since 1980; *b* 1 Oct. 1926; *s* of Patrick Stormonth-Darling and Edith Mary Ormston Lamb; *m* 1st, 1956, Susan Marion Clifford-Turner (marr. diss. 1970); three *s* one *d*; 2nd, 1974, Harriet Heathcoat-Amory (*née* Nye) (marr. diss. 1978); 3rd, 1981, Carola Marion Brooke, *er d* of Sir Robert Erskine-Hill, Bt, *qv. Educ:* Abberley Hall; Winchester Coll. Served Fleet Air Arm (Pilot), 1945; 9th Queen's Royal Lancers, 1946–54: ADC to GOC-in-C Scotland, 1950–52; Officer Cadet Instr, 1952–54. Laing & Cruickshank, 1954–; Director: Austin Motor Co., 1959; British Motor Corp., 1960–68; British Leyland, 1968–75. Director: London Scottish Finance Corp., 1984–; Mercantile House Holdings, 1984–. Stock Exchange: Mem., 1956–; Mem. Council, 1978–; Chairman: Quotations Cttee, 1981–85; Disciplinary Appeals Cttee, 1985–. Dep. Chm., Panel on Take-Overs and Mergers, 1985–; Mem., Securities and Investments Bd, 1985–. *Recreations:* shooting, ski-ing, flying, swimming. *Address:* Balvarran, Enochdhu, Blairgowrie, Perthshire. *T:* Strathardle 248; 21 Paradise Walk, SW3. *T:* 01–352 4161. *Clubs:* White's, City of London, MCC, Hurlingham; Perth Hunt.

STORR, (Charles) Anthony, FRCP, FRCPsych; writer and psychiatrist; Clinical Lecturer in Psychiatry, Faculty of Medicine, University of Oxford, 1974–84; Fellow, Green College, Oxford, 1979–84, now Emeritus; *b* 18 May 1920; *y s* of Vernon Faithfull Storr, Subdean of Westminster and Katherine Cecilia Storr; *m* 1st, 1942, Catherine Cole; three *d*; 2nd, 1970, Catherine Barton (*née* Peters). *Educ:* Winchester Coll.; Christ's Coll., Cambridge; Westminster Hosp. Medical School. MB, BChir Cantab; Qual. in medicine, 1944; postgrad. trng in psychiatry, Maudsley Hosp., 1947–50; held various positions as psychiatrist in different hospitals; Consltnt Psychotherapist, Oxford AHA, 1974–84. Member: Parole Bd, 1976–77; Cttee on Obscenity and Film Censorship, 1977–79. *Publications:* The Integrity of the Personality, 1960; Sexual Deviation, 1964; Human Aggression, 1968; Human Destructiveness, 1972; The Dynamics of Creation, 1972; Jung, 1973; The Art of Psychotherapy, 1979; (ed) Jung: selected writings, 1983; contrib. several books and jls. *Recreations:* music, broadcasting, journalism. *Address:* 45 Chalfont Road, Oxford OX2 6TJ. *T:* Oxford 53348. *Club:* Savile.

STOTESBURY, Herbert Wentworth; Assistant Under-Secretary of State, Home Office, 1966–75; Probation and Aftercare Department, 1969–75; *b* 22 Jan. 1916; *s* of Charles and Ada Stotesbury; *m* 1944, Berenice Mary Simpson; one *s* two *d. Educ:* Christ's Hospital; Emmanuel College, Cambridge. Home Office, 1939; Army, 1940–45. Lecturer, Military Coll. of Science, 1941–45. Home Office, 1945–75; Asst Secretary, 1953. Chm., Working Party on Marriage Guidance, 1976–78 (consultative document: Marriage Matters). *Recreations:* music, gardening, travel. *Address:* 65 Woodside, Wimbledon, SW19. *T:* 01–946 9523.

STOTT, Rt. Hon. Lord; George Gordon Stott, PC 1964; Senator of College of Justice in Scotland, 1967–84; *b* 22 Dec. 1909; *s* of Rev. Dr G. Gordon Stott; *m* 1947, Nancy, *d* of A. D. Braggins; one *s* one *d. Educ:* Cramond Sch.; Edinburgh Acad.; Edinburgh Univ. Advocate 1936; QC (Scotland) 1950; Advocate-Depute, 1947–51; Editor, Edinburgh Clarion, 1939–44; Member, Monopolies Commission, 1949–56; Sheriff of Roxburgh, Berwick and Selkirk, 1961–64; Lord Advocate, 1964–67. *Address:* 12 Midmar Gardens, Edinburgh. *T:* 031–447 4251.

STOTT, Sir Adrian (George Ellingham), 4th Bt *cr* 1920; property development, general management and town planning consultant, 1977–85; real property investment manager, since 1980; *b* 7 Oct. 1948; *s* of Sir Philip Sidney Stott, 3rd Bt, and of Cicely Florence, *o d* of Bertram Ellingham; *S* father, 1979. *Educ:* Univ. of British Columbia (BSc (Maths) 1968, MSc (Town Planning) 1974); Univ. of Waterloo, Ont (MMaths (Computer Science) 1971). Mem. Cdn Inst. of Planners (MCIP). Dir of Planning for a rural region of BC, 1974; formed own consulting practice, 1977; Manager: BC Govt Real Estate Portfolio, 1980; Islands Trust (coastal conservation and property develt control agency), 1985. Member: Assoc. for Computing Machinery; MENSA. *Recreations:* music, inland waterways, computers, politics. *Heir:* *b* Vyvyan Philip Stott, *b* 5 Aug. 1952. *Address:* 45 Knoll Wood, Victoria, BC V9B 1E4, Canada. *T:* (604) 479–8652.

STOTT, Rt. Hon. George Gordon; *see* Stott, Rt Hon. Lord.

STOTT, Rev. John Robert Walmsley, MA Cantab; DD Lambeth; Director, London Institute for Contemporary Christianity, 1982–86, now President; Chaplain to the Queen, since 1959; *b* 27 April 1921; *s* of late Sir Arnold W. Stott, KBE, physician, and late Emily Caroline Holland. *Educ:* Rugby Sch.; Trinity Coll., Cambridge; Ridley Hall, Cambridge. Curate of All Souls, Langham Place, 1945; Rector of All Souls, 1950–75 (with St Peter's, Vere Street, 1952), now Rector Emeritus. Hon. DD, Trinity Evangelical Divinity Sch., Deerfield, USA, 1971. *Publications:* Men with a Message, 1954; What Christ Thinks of the Church, 1958; Basic Christianity, 1958; Your Confirmation, 1958; Fundamentalism and Evangelism, 1959; The Preacher's Portrait, 1961; Confess Your Sins, 1964; The Epistles of John, 1964; Canticles and Selected Psalms, 1966; Men Made New, 1966; Our

Guilty Silence, 1967; The Message of Galatians, 1968; One People, 1969; Christ the Controversialist, 1970; Understanding the Bible, 1972; Guard the Gospel, 1973; Balanced Christianity, 1975; Christian Mission in the Modern World, 1975; Baptism and Fullness, 1975; The Lausanne Covenant, 1975; Christian Counter-Culture, 1978; Focus on Christ, 1979; God's New Society, 1979; I Believe in Preaching, 1982; The Bible Book for Today, 1982; Issues Facing Christians Today, 1984; The Authentic Jesus, 1985; The Cross of Christ, 1986. *Recreations:* bird watching and photography. *Address:* 13 Bridford Mews, Devonshire Street, W1N 1LQ.

STOTT, Prof. Peter Frank, CBE 1978; MA, FEng, FICE, FIHT, FIEAust, FCIT; Nash Professor of Civil Engineering, King's College, London University, since 1983; *b* 8 Aug. 1927; *s* of late Clarence Stott and of Mabel Sutcliffe; *m* 1953, Vera Watkins; two *s*. *Educ:* Bradford Grammar Sch.; Clare Coll., Cambridge. Partner, G. Maunsell & Partners, Consulting Engineers, 1955–63; Deputy Chief Engineer (Roads) and later Chief Engineer, London County Council, 1963–65; Dir of Highways and Transportation, GLC, 1964–67; Traffic Comr and Dir of Transportation, GLC, 1967–69; Controller of Planning and Transportation, GLC, 1969–73; Dir-Gen., Nat. Water Council, 1973–83. Sec.-Gen., Internat. Water Supply Assoc., 1980–83. President: Reinforced Concrete Assoc., 1964; Concrete Soc., 1967; Instn of Highway Engineers, 1971–72; Mem. Council, ICE, 1966–71, 1972–75 and 1976–79. Chm., Quality Scheme for Ready Mixed Concrete Ltd, 1984–. *Address:* 7 Frank Dixon Way, SE21. *T:* 01–693 5121. *Club:* Athenæum.

STOTT, Richard Keith; Editor, Daily Mirror, since 1985; *b* 17 Aug. 1943; *s* of late Fred B. Stott and of Bertha Stott; *m* 1970, Penny, *yr d* of Air Vice-Marshal Sir Colin Scragg, *qv*; one *s* two *d*. *Educ:* Clifton College, Bristol. Bucks Herald, 1963–65; Ferrari Press Agency, 1965–68; Daily Mirror: Reporter, 1968–79; Features Editor, 1979–81; Asst Editor, 1981; Editor, 1984, Sunday People. Reporter of the Year, British Press Awards, 1977. *Recreations:* theatre, reading. *Address:* Daily Mirror, 33 Holborn, EC1 PDQ.

STOTT, Roger, CBE 1979; MP (Lab) Wigan, since 1983 (Westhoughton, May 1973–1983); *b* 7 Aug. 1943; *s* of Richard and Edith Stott; *m* 1st, 1969, Irene Mills (marr. diss. 1982); two *s*; 2nd, 1985, Gillian Pye, Wigan. *Educ:* Rochdale Tech. Coll. Served in Merchant Navy, 1959–64. Post Office Telephone Engineer, 1964–73. PPS to Sec. of State for Industry, 1975–76; PPS to the Prime Minister, 1976–79, to Leader of the Opposition, 1979; opposition spokesman on transport, 1980–83, 1984–, on trade and industry, with special responsibility for IT, 1983–. Mem., Select Cttee on Agriculture, 1980–. Pres., Bass Wingates Band, 1980–. *Recreations:* cricket, gardening. *Address:* House of Commons, SW1A 0AA; 24 Highgate Crescent, Appley Bridge, Wigan.

STOUGHTON-HARRIS, Anthony Geoffrey, FCA; Chief General Manager, Anglia Building Society, since 1983; *b* 5 June 1932; *s* of Geoffrey Stoughton-Harris and Kathleen Mary (*née* Baker Brown); *m* 1959, Elizabeth Thackery (*née* White); one *s* two *d*. *Educ:* Sherborne Sch., Dorset. FCA 1956. Partner, Norton Keen & Co., chartered accountants, 1958–74; Dir, Maidenhead & Berkshire Building Soc., subseq. re-named South of England, London & South of England, then Anglia Building Soc., 1967–; Man. Dir, London & South of England Building Soc., 1975. Part-time Treasurer, W Herts Main Drainage Authority, 1964–70; part-time Mem., Southern Electricity Bd, 1981–. Chm., Metropolitan Assoc. of Building Socs, 1979–80; Mem. Council, Building Societies' Association, 1979– (Dep. Chm., 1985–); Exec. Cttee Mem., Midland Assoc. of Building Societies, 1983–; Chm., Electronic Funds Transfer Ltd, 1984–. Gen. Comr, Inland Revenue, 1982–. *Recreations:* sport, gardening, DIY. *Address:* Old Farm House, Blackmile Lane, Grendon, Northants NN7 1JR. *T:* Wellingborough 664235.

STOURTON, family name of **Baron Mowbray, Segrave and Stourton.**

STOURTON, Hon. John Joseph, TD; *b* 5 March 1899; *yr s* of 24th Lord Mowbray; *m* 1st, 1923, Kathleen Alice (marr. diss. 1933), *d* of late Robert Louis George Gunther, of 8 Princes Gardens and Park Wood, Englefield Green, Surrey; two *s* two *d*; 2nd, 1934, Gladys Leila (marr. diss. 1947), *d* of late Col Sir W. J. Waldron. *Educ:* Downside School. MP (C) South Salford, 1931–45. Served N Russian Relief Force at Archangel, 1919; and in European War, 1939–43; late Lt 10th Royal Hussars; Major The Royal Norfolk Regiment.

See also Earl of Gainsborough, H. L. C. Greig.

STOUT, Prof. David Ker; Head of Economics, Unilever plc, since 1982; Visiting Professor of Economics, Leicester University, since 1982 (Professor of Economics, 1980–81); *b* Bangor, N Wales, 27 Jan. 1932; *s* of late Prof. Alan Ker Stout, FAHA, FASSA and of Evelyn Roberts; *m* 1956, Margaret Sugden; two *s* two *d*. *Educ:* Sydney High Sch.; Sydney Univ., NSW (BA 1st Cl. English Lit, Econs, and University Medal in Econs, 1953); NSW Rhodes Scholar 1954; Magdalen Coll., Oxford; George Webb Medley Jun. Scholar 1955, Sen. Scholar 1956; PPE 1st Cl. 1956; Nuffield Coll., Oxford (Studentship 1956); Magdalen Prize Fellow by Examination, 1958–59. Fellow and Lectr in Econs, University Coll., Oxford, 1959–76; Economic Dir, NEDO, 1971–72 and 1976–80. Adviser on tax structure to Syrian Govt, 1965, and New Hebrides Condominium, 1966; Sen. Econ. Adviser to Monopolies Commn, 1969; Consultant on VAT, Nat. Bureau of Econ. Res., NY, 1970; Adviser to Australian Govt on Prices Justification, 1973, and on Wage Indexation, 1975–76. Member: Management Cttee, NIESR, 1974–; EEC Expert Gp on Community Planning, 1976–78, and on Adjustment Policy, 1979–80; Econ. Affairs Cttee, ESRC, 1980–; Board of Trustees: Strategic Planning Inst., Cambridge, Mass, 1983–; Centre for Econ. Policy Res., 1984–. Mem. Council, REconS, 1984–. *Publications:* papers on taxation policy, VAT, investment, incomes policy, trade performance, indust. policy, de-industrialisation, and European planning. *Recreations:* music, chess. *Address:* Unilever Ltd, PO Box 68, EC4P 4BQ. *T:* 01–822 6557.

STOUT, Samuel Coredon; HM Diplomatic Service, retired; *b* 17 Feb. 1913; *m* 1st, Mary Finn (*d* 1965); two *s* one *d*; 2nd, 1966, Jill Emery. Ministry of National Insurance, 1937–40; Admiralty, 1940–46; Board of Trade, 1946–65 (Trade Commissioner, Singapore, Bombay and Melbourne); Counsellor (Commercial), Canberra, 1966–68; Dep. High Comr and Minister (Commercial), Karachi, 1968–70; Consul-Gen., St Louis, USA, 1970–72. *Address:* Richmond House, Alverston Avenue, Woodhall Spa, Lincs.

STOUT, William Ferguson, CB 1964; Security Adviser to Government of Northern Ireland, 1971–72, retired; *b* Holywood, Co. Down, 22 Feb. 1907; *s* of late Robert and Amelia Stout; *m* 1938, Muriel Kilner; one *s* one *d*. *Educ:* Sullivan Upper Sch., Holywood; Queen's Univ., Belfast. Ministry of Home Affairs: Principal, 1943; Asst Sec., 1954; Senior Asst Sec., 1959; Permanent Sec., 1961–64; Permanent Secretary: Min. of Health and Local Govt, 1964; Min. of Development, 1965–71. *Recreation:* golf.

STOW, Archdeacon of; *see* Scott, Ven. David.

STOW, Sir Christopher P.; *see* Philipson-Stow.

STOW, Sir John Montague, GCMG 1966 (KCMG 1959; CMG 1950); KCVO 1966; Governor-General of Barbados, 1966–67; retired, 1967; *b* 3 Oct. 1911; *s* of late Sir Alexander Stow, KCIE; *m* 1939, Beatrice Tryhorne; two *s*. *Educ:* Harrow School; Pembroke College, Cambridge. Administrative Officer, Nigeria, 1934; Secretariat, Gambia, 1938; Chief Sec., Windward Islands, 1944; Administrator, St Lucia, BWI, 1947; Dir of Establishments, Kenya, 1952–55; Chief Sec., Jamaica, 1955–59; Governor and C-in-C Barbados, 1959–66. Chm., Commonwealth Soc. for Deaf, 1983–85. KStJ 1959. *Recreations:* cricket, tennis. *Address:* 26a Tregunter Road, SW10. *T:* 01–370 1921. *Clubs:* Caledonian, MCC.

STOW, (Julian) Randolph; writer; *b* Geraldton, W Australia, 28 Nov. 1935; *s* of Cedric Ernest Stow, barrister and Mary Stow (*née* Sewell). *Educ:* Guildford Grammar Sch., W Australia; Univ. of Western Australia. Lecturer in English Literature: Univ. of Leeds, 1962; Univ. of Western Australia, 1963–64; Harkness Fellow, United States, 1964–66; Lectr in English and Commonwealth Lit., Univ. of Leeds, 1968–69. Miles Franklin Award, 1958; Britannica Australia Award, 1966; Patrick White Award, 1979. *Publications: poems:* Outrider, 1962; A Counterfeit Silence, 1969; *novels:* To The Islands, 1958, rev. edn 1981; Tourmaline, 1963; The Merry-go-round in the Sea, 1965; Visitants, 1979; The Girl Green as Elderflower, 1980; The Suburbs of Hell, 1984; *music theatre* (with Peter Maxwell Davies): Eight Songs for a Mad King, 1969; Miss Donnithorne's Maggot, 1974; *for children:* Midnite, 1967. *Address:* c/o Richard Scott Simon Ltd, 32 College Cross, N1 1PR.

STOW, Ralph Conyers, CBE 1981; FCIS, FCBSI; President and Chairman, Cheltenham & Gloucester Building Society, since 1982 (Managing Director, 1973–82); Chairman, Cheltenham District Health Authority, since 1981; *b* 19 Dec. 1916; *s* of Albert Conyers Stow and Mabel Louise Bourlet; *m* 1943, Eleanor Joyce Appleby; one *s* one *d*. *Educ:* Woodhouse Sch., Finchley. FCIS 1959; FBS 1952. Supt of Branches, Temperance Permanent Bldg Soc., 1950, Asst Manager 1958; Gen. Man. and Sec., Cheltenham & Gloucester Bldg Soc., 1962, Dir 1967. Pres., Bldg Socs Inst., 1971–72; Chm., Midland Assoc. of Bldg Socs, 1973–74; Chm., Bldg Socs Assoc., 1977–79. Mem., Glos AHA, 1973–81. Mem. Council, Cheltenham Coll.; Governor, Bournside Sch., Cheltenham. *Recreations:* photography, oil painting. *Address:* Shepherds Fold, Charlton Hill, Charlton Kings, Cheltenham, Glos. *T:* Cheltenham 87305. *Club:* Rotary (Cheltenham).

STOW, Randolph; *see* Stow, J. R.

STOWE, Sir Kenneth (Ronald), GCB 1986 (KCB 1980; CB 1977); CVO 1979; Permanent Secretary, Department of Health and Social Security, since 1981; *b* 17 July 1927; *er s* of Arthur and Emily Stowe; *m* 1949, Joan Frances Cullen; two *s* one *d*. *Educ:* County High Sch., Dagenham; Exeter Coll., Oxford (MA). Asst Principal, Nat. Assistance Board, 1951; Principal, 1956; seconded UN Secretariat, New York, 1958; Asst Sec., 1964; Asst Under-Sec. of State, DHSS, 1970–73; Under Sec., Cabinet Office, 1973–75, Dep. Sec., 1976; Principal Private Sec. to the Prime Minister, 1975–79; Permanent Under Sec. of State, NI Office, 1979–81. *Recreations:* opera, theatre, hill walking. *Club:* Athenæum.

STOWELL, Dr Michael James, FRS 1984; Research Manager, Materials and Processes Department, TI Research, since 1978; *b* 10 July 1935; *s* of Albert James Stowell and Kathleen Maude (*née* Poole); *m* 1962, Rosemary Allen; one *s* one *d*. *Educ:* St Julian's High Sch., Newport; Bristol Univ. (BSc 1957, PhD 1961). Res. Scientist and Gp Leader, Tube Investments Research Labs, 1960–78; Post-doctoral Res. Fellow, Ohio State Univ., 1962–63; Res. Fellow, Univ. of Minnesota, 1970. L. B. Pfeil Medal, Metals Soc., 1976; Sir Robert Hadfield Medal, Metals Soc., 1981. *Publications:* papers on electron microscopy, epitaxy, nucleation theory, super plasticity and physical metallurgy, in various jls. *Recreation:* music. *Address:* TI Research, Hinxton, Saffron Walden, Essex CB10 1RH. *T:* Cambridge 832381; 14 Maypole Close, Saffron Walden CB11 4DB. *T:* Saffron Walden 23718.

STOY, Prof. Philip Joseph; Professor of Dentistry, Queen's University of Belfast, 1948–73, now Professor Emeritus; *b* 19 Jan. 1906; *m* 1945, Isabella Mary Beatrice Crispin; two *s*. *Educ:* Wolverhampton School. Queen's Scholar, Birmingham Univ., 1929; LDS, RCS, 1931; BDS (Hons), Birmingham 1932; FDS, RCS, 1947; Fellow of the Faculty of Dentistry, RCSI, 1963 (FFDRCSI). Lectr in Dental Mechanics, Univ. of Bristol, 1934; Lectr in Dental Surgery, Univ. of Bristol, 1940. *Publications:* articles in British Dental Journal, Dental Record. *Recreations:* reading, walking, painting, dental history, chess. *Address:* Westward Ho!, 57 Imperial Road, Exmouth, Devon EX8 1DQ. *T:* Exmouth 5113.

STOYLE, Roger John B.; *see* Blin-Stoyle.

STRABOLGI, 11th Baron of England, *cr* 1318; **David Montague de Burgh Kenworthy;** a Deputy Speaker and Deputy Chairman of Committees, House of Lords, since 1986; *b* 1 Nov. 1914; *e s* of 10th Baron Strabolgi and Doris Whitley, *o c* of late Sir Frederick Whitley-Thomson, MP; *S* father, 1953; *m* 1961, Doreen Margaret, *e d* of late Alexander Morgan, Ashton-under-Lyne, and Emma Morgan (*née* Mellor). *Educ:* Gresham's School; Chelsea Sch. of Art; Paris. Served with HM Forces, BEF, 1939–40; MEF, 1940–45, as Lt-Col RAOC. Mem. Parly Delegations to USSR, 1954, SHAPE, 1955, and France, 1981, 1983 and 1985; PPS to Minister of State, Home Office, 1968–69; PPS to Leader of the House of Lords and Lord Privy Seal, 1969–70; Asst Opposition Whip, and spokesman on the Arts, House of Lords, 1970–74; Captain of the Yeomen of the Guard (Dep. Govt Chief Whip), and Govt spokesman on Energy and Agriculture, 1974–79; opposition spokesman on arts and libraries, 1979–85. Member: Franco-British Parly Relations Cttee; British Sect., Franco-British Council, 1981; Council, Franco-British Soc.; Council, Alliance Française in GB; Labour Party. Dir, Bolton Building Soc., 1958–74, 1979– (Dep. Chm., 1983, Chm., 1986–). Hon. Life Mem., RPO, 1977. Freeman, City of London, 1960. Officier de la Légion d'Honneur, 1981. *Recreations:* books, music, travel. *Heir-pres:* *b* Rev. Hon. Jonathan Malcolm Atholl Kenworthy, MA; retired; Chaplain HM's Forces in World War II [*b* 16 Sept. 1916; *m* 1st, 1943, Joan Gaster (*d* 1963); two *d*; 2nd, 1963, Victoria Hewitt; two *s* one *d*]. *Address:* House of Lords, SW1A 0PW.

See also Sir Harold Hood, Bt.

STRACEY, Sir John (Simon), 9th Bt *cr* 1818; *b* 30 Nov. 1938; *s* of Captain Algernon Augustus Henry Stracey (2nd *s* of 6th Bt) (*d* 1940) and Olive Beryl (*d* 1972), *d* of late Major Charles Robert Eustace Radclyffe; *S* cousin, 1971; *m* 1968, Martha Maria, *d* of late Johann Egger; two *d*. *Heir:* *cousin* Henry Mounteney Stracey [*b* 24 April 1920; *m* 1st, 1943, Susanna, *d* of Adair Tracey; one *d*; 2nd, 1950, Lysbeth, *o d* of Charles Ashford, NZ; one *s* one *d*; 3rd, 1961, Jeltje, *y d* of Scholte de Boer]. *Address:* 32 Park Road, Southborough, near Tunbridge Wells, Kent TN4 0NX. *T:* Tunbridge Wells 20771.

STRACHAN, Alan Lockhart Thomson; Artistic Director, Greenwich Theatre, since 1978; *b* 3 Sept. 1946; *s* of Roualeyn Robert Scott Strachan and Ellen Strachan (*née* Graham); *m* 1977, Jennifer Piercey-Thompson. *Educ:* Morgan Acad., Dundee; St Andrews Univ. (MA); Merton Coll., Oxford (B.Litt). Associate Dir, Mermaid Theatre, 1970–75; freelance director, 1975–78. Productions include: Mermaid: The Watched Pot, 1970; John Bull's Other Island, The Old Boys, 1971; (co-deviser) Cowardy Custard, 1972; Misalliance, 1973; Children, (co-deviser and dir) Cole, 1974; The Immortal Haydon, 1977 (Greenwich, 1978); Greenwich: An Audience Called Edouard, 1978; The Play's the

Thing, I Sent a Letter to my Love, 1979; Private Lives (transf. Duchess), Time and the Conways, 1980; Present Laughter (transf. Vaudeville), The Golden Age, The Doctor's Dilemma, 1981; Design for Living (transf. Globe), The Paranormalist, French Without Tears, 1982; The Dining Room, An Inspector Calls, A Streetcar Named Desire, 1983 (transf. Mermaid, 1984); The Glass Menagerie, Biography, 1985; One of Us, Relatively Speaking, For King and Country, 1986; Family and a Fortune, Apollo, 1975; (deviser and dir) Shakespeare's People, world tours, 1975–78; Confusions, Apollo, 1976; (also jt author) Yahoo, Queen's, 1976; Just Between Ourselves, Queen's, 1977; Bedroom Farce, Amsterdam, 1978; Noël and Gertie, King's Head, 1983. *Publications:* contribs to periodicals. *Recreations:* music, tennis, travelling. *Address:* 11 Garlies Road, SE23 2RU. *T:* 01–699 3360.

STRACHAN, Alexander William Bruce, OBE 1971; HM Diplomatic Service, retired; *b* 2 July 1917; *s* of William Fyfe and Winifred Orchar Strachan; *m* 1940, Rebecca Prince MacFarlane; one *s* one *d. Educ:* Daniel Stewart's Coll., Edinburgh; Allen Glen's High Sch., Glasgow. GPO, 1935; Army, 1939–46; Asst Postal Controller, 1949–64; Postal Adviser to Iraq Govt, 1964–66; First Sec., FCO, 1967–68; Jordan, 1968–72; Addis Ababa, 1972–73; Consul General, Lahore, 1973–74; Counsellor (Economic and Commercial) and Consul General, Islamabad, 1975–77. Order of Istiqlal, Hashemite Kingdom of Jordan, 1971. *Address:* 24 St Margarets, London Road, Guildford, Surrey GU1 1TJ.

STRACHAN, Major Benjamin Leckie, CMG 1978; HM Diplomatic Service, retired; Principal, Mill of Strachan Language Institute, since 1984; Director, Rhalys International Ltd, since 1985; *b* 4 Jan. 1924; *e s* of late Dr C. G. Strachan, MC FRCPE and Annie Primrose (*née* Leckie); *m* 1958, Lize Lund; three *s* and one step *s* one step *d. Educ:* Rossall Sch. (Scholar); RMCS. Royal Dragoons, 1944; France and Germany Campaign, 1944–45 (despatches); 4th QO Hussars, Malayan Campaign, 1948–51; Middle East Centre for Arab Studies, 1952–53; GSO2, HQ British Troops Egypt, 1954–55; Technical Staff Course, RMCS, 1956–58; 10th Royal Hussars, 1959–61; GSO2, WO, 1961; retd from Army and joined Foreign (subseq. Diplomatic) Service, 1961; 1st Sec., FO, 1961–62; Information Adviser to Governor of Aden, 1962–63; FO, 1964–66; Commercial Sec., Kuwait, 1966–69; Counsellor, Amman, 1969–71; Trade Comr, Toronto, 1971–74; Consul General, Vancouver, 1974–76; Ambassador to Yemen Arab Republic, 1977–78, and to Republic of Jibuti (non-resident), 1978, to the Lebanon, 1978–81, to Algeria, 1981–84. *Recreations:* golf, tennis, writing, fishing. *Address:* Mill of Strachan, Strachan, Kincardineshire. *T:* Feughside 663. *Club:* Lansdowne.

STRACHAN, Graham Robert, CBE 1977; DL; FEng, FIMechE, FIMarE; Director, Scott Lithgow Ltd, since 1984; *b* 1 Nov. 1931; *o c* of late George Strachan and of Lily Elizabeth (*née* Ayres); *m* 1960, Catherine Nicol Liston, *o d* of late John and of Eileen Vivian; two *s. Educ:* Trinity Coll., Glenalmond; Trinity Coll., Cambridge (MA, 3rd Cl. Hons Mech. Scis Tripos). Apprentice Engineer: Alexander Stephen and Sons Ltd, 1950–52; John Brown & Co. (Clydebank) Ltd, 1952–55. National Service, RNVR, Actg Sub-Lieut (E), 1955–57. John Brown & Co. (Clydebank) Ltd: Design Engr, 1957; Develt Engr, 1959; Engrg Dir, 1963; John Brown Engineering Ltd: Dir and Gen. Manager, 1966, Man. Dir, 1968, Gp Man. Dir, 1975, Dep. Chm., 1983–84; Director: British Smelter Constructions Ltd, 1968–73; CJB Offshore Ltd, 1975–80; John Brown & Co. (Overseas), 1976–84; Chairman: JBE Offshore Ltd, 1976–81 (Dep. Chm., 1974); JBE Gas Turbines, 1976–84; Stephens of Linthouse Ltd, 1982–84. Member: CBI Oil Steering Gp, 1975–79; Exec. Cttee, Scottish Engrg Employers' Assoc., 1966–82; Hon. Vice Pres., Scottish Council (Develt and Industry), 1983– (Mem., W of Scotland Cttee, 1977–). Dir, Glasgow Chamber of Commerce, 1978–. Mem. Court, Univ. of Strathclyde, 1979–83. DL Dumbarton, 1979. *Recreations:* skiing, golf, early jazz. *Address:* The Mill House, Strathblane, Stirlingshire. *T:* Blanefield 70220. *Clubs:* Caledonian; Buchananan Castle Golf (Drymen).

STRACHAN, Michael Francis, CBE 1980 (MBE 1945); FRSE 1979; Chairman, Ben Line Steamers Ltd and Ben Line Containers Ltd, 1970–82; Director, Bank of Scotland; *b* 23 Oct. 1919; *s* of Francis William Strachan and Violet Blackwell (*née* Palmer); *m* 1948, Iris Hemingway; two *s* two *d. Educ:* Rugby Sch. (Scholar); Corpus Christi Coll., Cambridge (Exhibnr, MA). Served in Army, 1939–46; demobilised 1946 (Lt-Col). Joined Wm Thomson & Co., Edinburgh, Managers of Ben Line, 1946; Partner, 1950–64; Jt Man. Dir, Ben Line Steamers Ltd, 1964. Chm., Associated Container Transportation Ltd, 1971–75. Trustee: Nat. Galleries of Scotland, 1972–74; Carnegie Trust for Univs of Scotland, 1976–; Hakluyt Soc., 1984–; Chm. Bd of Trustees, Nat. Library of Scotland, 1974–. Member of Queen's Body Guard for Scotland. *Publications:* The Life and Adventures of Thomas Coryate, 1962; (ed jtly) The East India Company Journals of Captain William Keeling and Master Thomas Bonner, 1615–1617, 1971; articles in Blackwood's, Hakluyt Society's Hakluyt Handbook, History Today, Jl Soc. for Nautical Research. *Recreations:* country pursuits, silviculture. *Address:* 33 St Mary's Street, Edinburgh EH1 1TN. *Clubs:* Naval and Military; New (Edinburgh).

STRACHAN, Robert Martin; Agent-General for British Columbia in the United Kingdom and Europe, 1975–77; *b* 1 Dec. 1913; *s* of Alexander Strachan and Sarah Martin; *m* 1937, Anne Elsie Paget; two *s* one *d. Educ:* schools in Glasgow, Scotland. Mem., British Columbia Legislature, 1952–75; Leader of Opposition, 1956–69; Minister: of Highways, 1972–73; of Transport and Communications, 1973–75; resigned seat Oct. 1975, to accept appointment as Agent-General. *Recreations:* swimming, fishing, painting. *Address:* RR2, Cedar Road, Nanaimo, Vancouver Island, British Columbia. *Club:* Royal Over-Seas League.

STRACHAN, Mrs Valerie Patricia Marie; Head, Joint Management Unit, HM Treasury/Cabinet Office, since 1985; *b* 10 Jan. 1940; *d* of John Jonas Nicholls and Louise Nicholls; *m* 1965, John Strachan; one *s* one *d. Educ:* Newland High Sch., Hull; Manchester Univ. (BA). Joined Customs and Excise, 1961; Dept of Economic Affairs, 1964; Home Office, 1966; Principal, Customs and Excise, 1966; Treasury, 1972; Asst Secretary, Customs and Excise, 1974, Comr, 1980. *Address:* 9 College Gardens, SE21 7BE. *T:* 01–693 5335.

STRACHAN, Walter, CBE 1967; CEng, FRAeS; Consulting Engineer since 1971; *b* 14 Oct. 1910; *s* of William John Strachan, Rothes, Morayshire, and Eva Hitchins, Bristol; *m* 1937, Elizabeth Dora Bradshaw, Aldershot; two *s. Educ:* Newfoundland Road Sch., Bristol; Merchant Venturers Technical Coll., Bristol. Bristol Aeroplane Co.: Apprentice, 1925; Aircraft Ground Engr, 1932; RAE, Farnborough, 1934; Inspector: Bristol Aeroplane Co., 1937. BAC Service Engr, RAF Martlesham Heath, 1938; BAC: Asst Service Manager, 1940; Asst Works Manager, 1942; Manager, Banwell, building Beaufort and Tempest aircraft, 1943; Gen.-Manager, Banwell and Weston Factories, manufrg Aluminium Houses, 1945; Gen. Manager, Banwell and Weston Factories, building helicopters and aircraft components, 1951; Managing Dir, Bristol Aerojet, Banwell, Rocket Motor Develt and Prod., 1958. *Recreations:* golf, music, ornithology. *Address:* 18 Clarence Road East, Weston-super-Mare, Somerset. *T:* Weston-super-Mare 23878. *Clubs:* Naval and Military; Royal Automobile.

STRACHEY, family name of **Baron O'Hagan.**

STRACHEY, Charles, (6th Bt *cr* 1801, but does not use the title); *b* 20 June 1934; *s* of Rt Hon. Evelyn John St Loe Strachey (*d* 1963) and Celia (*d* 1980), 3rd *d* of late Rev. Arthur Hume Simpson; *S* to baronetcy of cousin, 2nd Baron Strachie, 1973; *m* 1973, Janet Megan, *d* of Alexander Miller; one *d. Heir:* kinsman Henry Leofric Benvenuto Strachey, *b* 17 April 1947. *Address:* 30 Gibson Square, N1 0RD. *T:* 01–226 8216.

STRADBROKE, 6th Earl of, *cr* 1821; **Robert Keith Rous;** Bt 1660; Baron Rous 1796; Viscount Dunwich 1821; *b* 25 March 1937; *s* of 5th Earl of Stradbroke and Pamela Catherine Mabell (*d* 1972), *d* of Captain Hon. Edward James Kay-Shuttleworth; *S* father, 1983; *m* 1960, Dawn Antoinette (marr. diss. 1976), *d* of Thomas Edward Beverley, Brisbane; two *s* five *d*; 2nd, 1977, Roseanna Mary Blanche, *d* of late Francis Reitman, MD; four *s* one *d. Educ:* Harrow. *Heir: s* Viscount Dunwich, *qv. Address:* Fleetwood Station, The Old Booralong Road, Armidale, NSW 2350, Australia.
See also Hon. W. E. Rous.

STRADLING, Donald George; Group Personnel Director, John Laing plc, since 1978; *b* 7 Sept. 1929; *s* of George Frederic and Olive Emily Stradling; *m* 1955, Mary Anne Hartridge; two *d. Educ:* Clifton Coll.; Magdalen Coll., Oxford (Open Exhibnr; MA). CIPM. School Master, St Albans Sch., 1954–55; Group Trng and Educn Officer, John Laing & Son Ltd, Building and Civil Engrg Contractors, 1955; Group Personnel Director, John Laing & Son Ltd, 1969. Comr, Manpower Services Commn, 1980–82; Mem. Council, Inst. of Manpower Studies, 1975–81; Member: Employment Policy Cttee, CBI, 1978–84, 1986; Council, CBI, 1982–86; FCEC Wages and Industrial Cttee, 1978–; National Steering Gp, New Technical and Vocational Educn Initiative, 1983–. Director: Building and Civil Engrg Benefits Scheme (Trustee, 1984–); Building and Civil Engrg Holidays Scheme Management, 1984–; Construction Industry Trng Bd, 1985–. Vice-Pres., Inst. of Personnel Management, 1974–76. Vice-Chm. of Governors, St Albans High Sch., 1977–; Mem. Council, Tyndale House, 1977–. Liveryman, Glaziers' and Painters of Glass Co., 1983–. *Publications:* contribs on music and musical instruments, et al. to New Bible Dictionary, 1962. *Recreations:* singing (choral music), listening to music (espec. opera), walking. *Address:* Courts Edge, 12 The Warren, Harpenden, Herts AL5 2NH. *T:* Harpenden 2744. *Clubs:* Institute of Directors, English-Speaking Union.

STRADLING, Rt. Rev. Leslie Edward, MA; *b* 11 Feb. 1908; *er s* of late Rev. W. H. Stradling; unmarried. *Educ:* King Edward VII Sch., Sheffield; The Queen's Coll., Oxford; Westcott House, Cambridge. Curate of St Paul's, Lorrimore Square, 1933–38; Vicar of St Luke's Camberwell, 1938–43; of St Anne's, Wandsworth, 1943–45; Bishop of Masasi, 1945–52; Bishop of South West Tanganyika, 1952–61; Bishop of Johannesburg, 1961–74. Hon. DCL Bishops' Univ., Lennoxville, Canada, 1968. *Publications:* A Bishop on Safari, 1960; The Acts through Modern Eyes, 1963; An Open Door, 1966; A Bishop at Prayer, 1971; Praying Now, 1976; Praying the Psalms, 1977. *Address:* 36 Alexandra Road, Wynberg, 7800, South Africa. *Club:* City and Civil Service (Cape Town).

STRADLING THOMAS, Sir John, Kt 1985; MP (C) Monmouth, since 1970; farmer; *b* 10 June 1925; *s* of Thomas Roger Thomas and Catherine Thomas (*née* Delahay); *m* 1957, Freda Rhys Evans (marr. diss.); one *s* two *d. Educ:* Rugby School. Contested (C) Aberavon, 1964; Cardigan, 1966. Asst Govt Whip, 1971–73; a Lord Comr, HM Treasury, 1973–74; an Opposition Whip, 1974–79; Treasurer of HM Household and Dep. Chief Whip, 1979–83; Minister of State, Welsh Office, 1983–85; Mem., Select Cttee on the Civil List, 1971. Pres., Fedn of Cons. Clubs, 1984. Member Council, NFU, 1963–70. Hon. ARCVS, 1984; Hon. Associate, BVA. *Address:* House of Commons, SW1A 0AA. *Club:* White's.

STRAFFORD, 8th Earl of, *cr* 1847; **Thomas Edmund Byng;** Baron Strafford, 1835; Viscount Enfield, 1847; *b* 26 Sept. 1936; *s* of 7th Earl of Strafford, and Maria Magdalena Elizabeth, *d* of late Henry Cloete, CMG, Alphen, S Africa; *S* father, 1984; *m* 1963, Jennifer Mary (marr. diss. 1981), *er d* of late Rt Hon. W. M. May, FCA, PC, MP, and of Mrs May, Mertoun Hall, Holywood, Co. Down; two *s* two *d*; 2nd, 1981, Mrs Julia Mary Howard, (Judy), *d* of Sir Dennis Pilcher, *qv*, and of Lady Pilcher. *Educ:* Eton; Clare Coll., Cambridge. Lieut, Royal Sussex Regt (National Service). *Recreation:* gardening. *Heir: s* Viscount Enfield, *qv. Address:* 11 St James Terrace, Winchester, Hants SO22 4PP. *T:* Winchester 53905.

STRAKER, Rear-Adm. Bryan John, CB 1980; OBE 1966; Head of Personnel Services, Imperial Cancer Research Fund, since 1981; *b* 26 May 1929; *s* of late George Straker and Marjorie Straker; *m* 1954, Elizabeth Rosemary, *d* of Maj.-Gen. C. W. Greenway, CB, CBE, and Mrs C. W. Greenway; two *d. Educ:* St Albans Sch. FBIM 1978. Cadet, RNC Dartmouth, 1946; Flag Lieut to Flag Officer, Malayan Area, 1952–53; qual. in communications, 1955; Flag Lieut and Staff Ops Officer to Sen. Naval Officer, WI, 1960–62; CO: HMS Malcolm, 1962–63; HMS Defender, 1966–67; Asst Dir, Naval Operational Requirements, MoD, 1968–70; CO HMS Fearless, 1970–72; Dir of Naval Plans, MoD, 1972–74; Sen. Naval Officer, WI, and Island Comdr, Bermuda, 1974–76; Asst Chief of Naval Staff (Policy), 1976–78; Sen. Naval Mem., DS, RCDS, 1978–80; RN retd, 1981. Freeman, City of London. *Recreations:* tennis, cricket, gardening. *Address:* c/o National Westminster Bank, Petersfield, Hants. *Clubs:* Farmers', Forty, West India.

STRAKER, Major Ivan Charles; Chairman since 1984, and Chief Executive since 1983, Seagram Distillers plc; *b* 17 June 1928; *s* of Arthur Coppin Straker and Cicely Longueville Straker; *m* 1st, 1954, Gillian Elizabeth Grant (marr. diss. 1971); two *s* one *d*; 2nd, 1976, Sally Jane Hastings (marr. diss. 1986); one *s. Educ:* Harrow; RMA, Sandhurst. Commissioned 11th Hussars (PAO), 1948; served Germany, N Ireland, Middle East and Mil. Intell. Staff, War Office; left HM Armed Forces, 1962. Man. Dir, D. Rintoul & Co., 1964; Man. Dir, The Glenlivet and Glen Grant Agencies, 1964–71; apptd Main Board, The Glenlivet and Glen Grant Distillers, 1967; Chief Exec., The Glenlivet Distillers Ltd, 1971. Dir, Lothians Racing Syndicate Ltd, 1986–. Council Mem., Scotch Whisky Assoc., 1978– (Chm., Public Affairs Cttee, 1986–). *Recreations:* fishing, shooting, golf, gardening. *Address:* 33 Cluny Drive, Edinburgh. *T:* 031–447 6621. *Club:* Cavalry and Guards.

STRAKER, Sir Michael (Ian Bowstead), Kt 1984; CBE 1973; JP; farmer, since 1951; Chairman: Aycliffe and Peterlee Development Corporations, since 1980; Northumbrian Water Authority, since 1982; *b* 10 March 1928; *s* of late Edward Charles Straker and of Margaret Alice Bridget Straker. *Educ:* Eton. Served in Coldstream Guards, 1946–50. Dir, Newcastle and Gateshead Water Co., 1975–82 (Chm., 1979–82); Bd, Port of Tyne Authority, 1986. Chairman: Newcastle upon Tyne AHA(T), 1973–81; Newcastle Univ. HMC, 1971; Mem. Newcastle Univ. Court and Council, 1972– (Chm. Council, 1983–). Mem. Council, RASE, 1970–86. Chm., Northern Area Conservative Assoc., 1969–72. High Sheriff of Northumberland, 1977; JP Northumberland, 1962. *Address:* High Warden, Hexham, Northumberland NE46 4SR. *T:* Hexham 602083. *Clubs:* Brooks's; Northern Counties (Newcastle upon Tyne).

STRAND, Prof. Kenneth T.; Professor, Department of Economics, Simon Fraser University, 1968–86, now Emeritus; *b* Yakima, Wash, 30 June 1931; Canadian citizen since 1974; *m* 1960, Elna K. Tomaske; no *c. Educ:* Washington State Coll. (BA); Univ. of Wisconsin (PhD, MS). Woodrow Wilson Fellow, 1955–56; Ford Foundn Fellow,

1957–58; Herfurth Award, Univ. of Wisconsin, 1961 (for PhD thesis). Asst Exec. Sec., Hanford Contractors Negotiation Cttee, Richland, Wash, 1953–55; Asst Prof., Washington State Univ., 1959–60; Asst Prof., Oberlin Coll., 1960–65 (on leave, 1963–65); Economist, Manpower and Social Affairs Div., OECD, Paris, 1964–66; Assoc. Prof., Dept of Econs, Simon Fraser Univ., 1966–68; Pres., Simon Fraser Univ., 1969–74 (Acting Pres., 1968–69). Member: Industrial Relations Research Assoc.; Internat. Industrial Relations Assoc.; Canadian Industrial Relations Assoc. (Pres., 1983). Hon. LLD Simon Fraser Univ., 1983. FRSA 1972. *Publications:* Jurisdictional Disputes in Construction: The Causes, The Joint Board and the NLRB, 1961; contribs to Review of Econs and Statistics, Amer. Econ. Review, Industrial Relations, Sociaal Mannblad Arbeid. *Recreations:* sailing, ski-ing. *Address:* RR1, Box 9C, Port Moody, BC V3H 3C8, Canada.

STRANG, family name of **Baron Strang.**

STRANG, 2nd Baron *cr* 1954, of Stonesfield; **Colin Strang;** Professor of Philosophy, University of Newcastle upon Tyne, 1975–82; Dean of the Faculty of Arts, 1976–79; *b* 12 June 1922; *s* of 1st Baron Strang, GCB, GCMG, MBE, and Elsie Wynne (*d* 1974), *d* of late J. E. Jones; *S* father, 1978; *m* 1st, 1948, Patricia Marie, *d* of Meiert C. Avis, Johannesburg; 2nd, 1955, Barbara Mary Hope Carr (*d* 1982); one *d*; 3rd, 1984, Mary Shewell. *Educ:* Merchant Taylors' School; St John's Coll., Oxford (MA, BPhil). *Heir:* none. *Address:* Le Serre, Les Aires, 34600 Bédarieux, France.

STRANG, Gavin Steel; MP (Lab) Edinburgh East since 1970; *b* 10 July 1943; *s* of James Steel Strang and Marie Strang (*née* Finkle); *m*. *Educ:* Univs of Edinburgh and Cambridge. BSc Hons Edinburgh, 1964; DipAgricSci Cambridge, 1965; PhD Edinburgh, 1968. Mem., Tayside Econ. Planning Consultative Group, 1966–68; Scientist with ARC, 1968–70. Parly Under-Sec. of State, Dept of Energy, March-Oct. 1974; Parly Sec., MAFF, 1974–79. Chm., PLP Defence Group, 1984–. *Publications:* articles in Animal Production. *Recreations:* golf, swimming, films. *Address:* 80 Argyle Crescent, Edinburgh EH15 2QD. *T:* 031–669 5999. *Club:* Newcraighall Miners' Welfare (Edinburgh).

STRANG, William John, CBE 1973; PhD; FRS 1977, FEng, FRAeS; Deputy Technical Director, British Aerospace, Aircraft Group, 1978–83, retired; *b* 29 June 1921; *s* of late John F. Strang and Violet Strang (*née* Terrell); *m* 1946, Margaret Nicholas Howells; three *s* one *d*. *Educ:* Torquay Grammar Sch.; King's Coll., London Univ. (BSc). Bristol Aeroplane Co., Ltd, Stress Office, 1939–46; King's Coll., London Univ., 1946–48; Aeronautical Research Lab., Melbourne, Aust., 1948–51; Bristol Aeroplane Co. Ltd: Dep. Head, Guided Weapons Dept, 1951–52; Head of Aerodynamics and Flight Research, 1952–55; Chief Designer, 1955–60; British Aircraft Corporation: Dir and Chief Engr, 1960–67, Technical Dir, 1967–71, Filton Div.; Technical Dir, 1971–77, Commercial Aircraft Div. Chm., Airworthiness Requirements Bd, 1983– (Mem., 1979–). Fellow, Fellowship of Engineering, 1977. *Recreation:* sailing. *Address:* April Cottage, Castle Combe, Wilts. *T:* Castle Combe 782220. *Clubs:* Royal Yachting Association; Island Cruising (Salcombe), Salcombe Yacht.

STRANG STEEL, Major Sir (Fiennes) William; *see* Steel, Major Sir F. W. S.

STRANGE, Prof. Susan, (Mrs Clifford Selly); Montague Burton Professor of International Relations, London School of Economics and Political Science, since 1978; *b* 9 June 1923; *d* of Col Louis Strange and Marjorie Beath; *m* 1st, 1942, Dr Denis Merritt (marr. diss. 1955); one *s* one *d*; 2nd, 1955, Clifford Selly; three *s* one *d*. *Educ:* Royal Sch., Bath; Université de Caen; London Sch. of Econs (BScEcon). The Economist, 1944–46; The Observer, 1946–57 (Washington, UN, and Econ. Corresp.); Lectr in Internat. Relations, University Coll., London, 1949–64; Res. Fellow, RIIA, 1965–76; German Marshall Fund Fellow, 1976–78; Vis. Prof., Univ. of Southern Calif, 1978. *Publications:* Sterling and British Policy, 1971; International Monetary Relations, 1976; (ed with R. Tooze) The International Politics of Surplus Capacity, 1981; (ed) Paths to International Political Economy, 1984; Casino Capitalism, 1986. *Recreations:* cooking, gardening, tennis, canoeing. *Address:* Weedon Hill House, Aylesbury, Bucks. *T:* Aylesbury 22236.

STRANGWAYS; *see* Fox-Strangways, family name of Earl of Ilchester.

STRASSER, Sir Paul, Kt 1973; Director: Walden Properties Ltd; Nicron Resources NL; Petrocarb Exploration NL; *b* 22 Sept. 1911; *s* of Eugene Strasser and Elizabeth Klein de Ney; *m* 1935, Veronica Gero; one *s*. *Educ:* Univ. of Budapest. Dr of Law, 1933; practised in Hungary for 10 yrs; emigrated to Australia, 1948. Career in fields of construction, mining and oil exploration, hotel and motel chains, meat processing and exporting, merchant banking. Associated with and promoter of several charitable foundns, etc, incl. Jewish Residential Coll. at Univ. of NSW, Children's Surgical Research Fund and Australian Youth Ballet. *Recreations:* playing bridge, swimming, reading. *Address:* Suite 106, Edgecliff Centre, Edgecliff, NSW 2027, Australia. *Clubs:* American, Sydney Turf (Sydney).

STRATFORD, Neil Martin; Keeper of Medieval and Later Antiquities, British Museum, since 1975; *b* 26 April 1938; *s* of Dr Martin Gould Stratford and Dr Mavis Stratford (*née* Beddall); *m* 1966, Anita Jennifer Lewis; two *d*. *Educ:* Marlborough Coll.; Magdalene Coll., Cambridge (BA Hons English 1961, MA); Courtauld Inst., London Univ. (BA Hons History of Art 1966). 2nd Lieut Coldstream Guards, 1956–58; Trainee Kleinwort, Benson, Lonsdale Ltd, 1961–63; Lecturer, Westfield Coll., London Univ., 1969–75. Liveryman, Haberdashers' Company 1959–. Hon. Mem., Académie de Dijon, 1975; For. Mem., Société Nationale des Antiquaires de France, 1985. FSA 1976. *Publications:* La Sculpture Oubliée de Vézelay, 1984; articles in French and English periodicals. *Recreations:* opera, food and wine, cricket and football. *Address:* 17 Church Row, NW3. *T:* 01–794 5688. *Clubs:* Beefsteak, Garrick, MCC, I Zingari; University Pitt, Hawks (Cambridge).

STRATHALLAN, Viscount; John Eric Drummond; *b* 7 July 1935; *e s* of 17th Earl of Perth, *qv*; *m* 1963, Margaret Ann (marr. diss.), *o d* of Robin Gordon; two *s*. *Heir:* *s* Hon. James David Drummond, *b* 24 Oct. 1965. *Address:* Stobhall, by Perth.

STRATHALMOND, 3rd Baron *cr* 1955; **William Roberton Fraser,** CA; *b* 22 July 1947; *s* of 2nd Baron Strathalmond, CMG, OBE, TD, and of Letitia, *d* of late Walter Krementz, New Jersey, USA; *S* father, 1976; *m* 1973, Amanda Rose, *yr d* of Rev. Gordon Clifford Taylor; two *s* one *d*. *Educ:* Loretto. Man. Dir, London Wall (Members Agency) Ltd (formerly Bain Dawes (Underwriting Agency) Ltd), 1986– (Dir, 1985–); Dir, London Wall Hldgs plc, 1986–. *Heir:* *s* Hon. William Gordon Fraser, *b* 24 Sept. 1976. *Address:* Holt House, Elstead, near Godalming, Surrey.

STRATHCARRON, 2nd Baron, *cr* 1936, of Banchor; **David William Anthony Blyth Macpherson;** Bt, *cr* 1933; Partner, Strathcarron & Co.; Director: Kirchhoff (London) Ltd; Seabourne Express Ltd; Seabourne Aviation; Forster and Hales Ltd; *b* 23 Jan. 1924; *s* of 1st Baron and Jill (*d* 1956), *o d* of Sir George Rhodes, 1st Bt; *S* father, 1937; *m* 1st, 1947, Valerie Cole (marr. annulled on his petition, 1947); 2nd, 1948, Mrs Diana Hawtrey Curle (*d* 1973), *o d* of Comdr R. H. Deane; two *s*; 3rd 1974, Mrs Eve Samuel, *o d* of late J. C. Higgins, CIE. *Educ:* Eton; Jesus College, Cambridge. Served War of 1939–45, RAFVR, 1942–47. Motoring Correspondent of The Field, 1954–. Member, British Parly Delegn to Austria, 1964. Pres., Inst. of Freight Forwarders, 1974–75. Member Council: Inst. of Advanced Motorists, 1972–; Order of the Road, 1974–. President: Guild of Motoring Writers, 1971–; Guild of Experienced Motorists, 1980–; National Breakdown Recovery Club, 1982–; Driving Instructors' Assoc., 1982–; Vehicle Builders' and Repairers' Assoc., 1983–. *Publication:* Motoring for Pleasure, 1963. *Recreations:* motor-racing, flying, golf. *Heir:* *s* Hon. Ian David Patrick Macpherson, *b* 31 March 1949. *Address:* 22 Rutland Gate, SW7 1BB. *T:* 01–584 1240; Otterwood, Beaulieu, Hants. *T:* Beaulieu 612334. *Clubs:* Boodle's, Royal Air Force.

STRATHCLYDE, 2nd Baron *cr* 1955, of Barskimming; **Thomas Galloway Dunlop du Roy de Blicquy Galbraith;** Insurance Broker, Bain Dawes PLC, since 1982; *b* 22 Feb. 1960; *s* of Hon. Sir Thomas Galloway Dunlop Galbraith, KBE (*d* 1982) (*e s* of 1st Baron) and of Simone Clothilde Fernande Marie Ghislaine, *e d* of late Jean du Roy de Blicquy; *S* grandfather, 1985. *Educ:* Wellington College; Univ. of East Anglia (BA 1982); Université d'Aix-en-Provence. *Heir:* *b* Charles William du Roy de Blicquy Galbraith, *b* 20 May 1962. *Address:* Old Barskimming, Mauchline, Ayrshire. *T:* Mauchline 50334.

STRATHCONA AND MOUNT ROYAL, 4th Baron, *cr* 1900; **Donald Euan Palmer Howard;** *b* 26 Nov. 1923; *s* of 3rd Baron Strathcona and Mount Royal and Diana Evelyn (*d* 1985), twin *d* of 1st Baron Wakehurst; *S* father 1959; *m* 1st, 1954, Lady Jane Mary Waldegrave (marr. diss. 1977), 2nd *d* of Earl Waldegrave, *qv*; two *s* four *d*; 2nd, 1978, Patricia (*née* Thomas), *widow* of John Middleton. *Educ:* King's Mead, Seaford; Eton; Trinity Coll., Cambridge; McGill University, Montreal (1947–50). Served War of 1939–45: RN, 1942–47: Midshipman, RNVR, 1943; Lieutenant, 1945. With Urwick, Orr and Partners (Industrial Consultants), 1950–56. Lord in Waiting (Govt Whip), 1973–74; Parly Under-Sec. of State for Defence (RAF), MoD, 1974; Jt Dep. Leader of the Opposition, House of Lords, 1976–79; Minister of State, MoD, 1979–81. Director: Dominion International plc (formerly Dundonian plc), 1981–; Computing Devices, Hastings, 1981–; Chm., Hall-Russell Shipyard, 1986–. Chairman, Bath Festival Society, 1966–70. Dep. Chm., SS Great Britain Project, 1970–73; Pres., Falkland Is Trust, 1982–. *Recreations:* gardening, sailing. *Heir:* *s* Hon. Donald Alexander Smith Howard, *b* 24 June 1961. *Address:* 5 Ridgeway Gardens, Wimbledon, SW19. *T:* 01–947 8157; Kiloran, Isle of Colonsay, Scotland. *T:* Colonsay 301. *Clubs:* Brooks's, Pratt's; Royal Yacht Squadron.

STRATHEDEN, 5th Baron *cr* 1836, **AND CAMPBELL,** 5th Baron *cr* 1841; **Gavin Campbell;** Major (retired) KRRC and Lt-Col 19th (Kenya) Bn, KAR; *b* 28 Aug. 1901; *s* of Hon. John Beresford Campbell, DSO (killed in action, 1915) (*s* of 3rd Baron) and Hon. Alice Susan Hamilton (*d* 1949), *d* of 1st Baron Hamilton of Dalzell; *S* brother, 1981; *m* 1933, Evelyn Mary Austen, *d* of late Col Herbert Austen Smith, CIE; one *s*. *Educ:* Eton; RMC Sandhurst. Served War of 1939–45, Abyssinia and Madagascar. *Heir:* *s* Hon. Donald Campbell [*b* 4 April 1934; *m* 1957, Hilary Ann Holland, *d* of Lt-Col W. D. Turner; one *s* three *d*]. *Address:* 7 Denway Grove, South Norwood, Launceston, Tasmania 7250, Australia.

STRATHERN, Prof. Andrew Jamieson, PhD; Andrew Mellon Professor of Anthropology, University of Pittsburgh, since 1987; Emeritus Professor of Anthropology, University of London; Hon. Research Fellow, Institute of Papua New Guinea Studies, Port Moresby (Director, 1981–86); *b* 19 Jan. 1939; *s* of Robert Strathern and Mary Strathern (*née* Sharp); *m* 1963, Ann Marilyn Evans (marr. diss. 1985); two *s* one *d*; *m* Gomb-Minembi. *Educ:* Colchester Royal Grammar Sch.; Trinity Coll., Cambridge (BA, PhD). Research Fellow, Trinity Coll., Cambridge, 1965–68; Research Fellow, then Fellow, Australian National Univ., 1969–72; Professor, later Vis. Professor, Dept of Anthropology and Sociology, Univ. of Papua New Guinea, 1973–77; Prof. of Anthropology and Hd of Dept of Anthropology, UCL, 1976–83. Rivers Memorial Medal, RAI, 1976. *Publications:* The Rope of Moka, 1971; One Father, One Blood, 1972; (with M. Strathern) Self-decoration in Mount Hagen, 1972; Melpa Amb Kenan, 1974; Myths and Legends from Mt Hagen, 1977; Beneath the Andaiya Tree, 1977; Ongka, 1979; (with Malcolm Kirk) Man as Art, 1981; Inequality in New Guinea Highlands Societies, 1982; Wiru Laa, 1983; A line of power, 1984; Kintu Songs, 1985; articles in Man, Oceania, Ethnology, Jl Polyn Soc., Amer. Anthropology, Amer. Ethnology, Mankind, Bijdragen, Jl de la Soc. des Océanistes, Oral History, Bikmaus. *Address:* Department of Anthropology, University of Pittsburgh, Pittsburgh, Penn 15260, USA. *T:* (office) 412–624–4200.

STRATHMORE AND KINGHORNE, 17th Earl of, *cr* 1677; Earl (UK), *cr* 1937; **Fergus Michael Claude Bowes Lyon;** Lord Glamis, 1445; Earl of Kinghorne, Lord Lyon and Glamis, 1606; Viscount Lyon, Lord Glamis, Tannadyce, Sidlaw, and Strathdichtie, 1677; Baron Bowes (UK), 1887; Vice Lord-Lieutenant, County of Angus, since 1981; *b* 31 Dec. 1928; *e s* of Hon. Michael Claude Hamilton Bowes Lyon (5th *s* of 14th Earl) (*d* 1953), and Elizabeth Margaret (*d* 1959), *d* of late John Cator; *S* cousin, 1972; *m* 1956, Mary Pamela, *d* of Brig. Norman Duncan McCorquodale, MC; one *s* two *d*. *Educ:* Eton; RMA, Sandhurst. Commissioned Scots Guards, 1949; Captain 1953; transferred to RARO, 1961. Member of Edinburgh Stock Exchange, 1963. Dir, T. Cowie, 1978–. Member of Royal Company of Archers, Queen's Body Guard for Scotland; Hon. Col, Tayforth Univs OTC, 1974–81. DL Angus, 1973. *Recreations:* shooting, fishing. *Heir:* *s* Lord Glamis, *qv*. *Address:* Glamis Castle, Forfar, Angus. *T:* Glamis 244. *Clubs:* White's, Pratt's; New (Edinburgh).

STRATHNAVER, Lord; Alistair Charles St Clair Sutherland; Master of Sutherland; with Sutherland Estates, since 1978; *b* 7 Jan. 1947; *e s* of Charles Noel Janson, DL, and the Countess of Sutherland, *qv*; *heir* to mother's titles; *m* 1st, 1968, Eileen Elizabeth, *o d* of Richard Wheeler Baker, Jr, Princeton, NJ; two *d*; 2nd, 1980, Gillian, *er d* of Robert Murray, Gourock, Renfrewshire; one *s* one *d*. *Educ:* Eton; Christ Church, Oxford. BA. Metropolitan Police, 1969–74; with IBM UK Ltd, 1975–78. *Heir:* *s* Hon. Alexander Charles Robert Sutherland, *b* 1 Oct. 1981. *Address:* Sutherland Estates Office, Golspie, Sutherland. *T:* Golspie 3268.

STRATHON, Eric Colwill, FRICS; Member of the Lands Tribunal, 1969–80, retired; *b* 20 Feb. 1908; *s* of Daniel Millward Strathon and Ann Colwill; *m* 1932, Margaret Mary Cocks (*d* 1973); one *s* one *d*. *Educ:* Taunton Sch. Chartered Surveyor, election 1929. Served War, 1944–46: Major RA; 14th Army HQ. Articled to chartered surveyors, 1925–28; partner, private practice in London, 1934–69. Crown Estate Comr, 1965–69. Pres., RICS, 1961. *Publication:* Compensation (Defence), 1943. *Recreation:* fishing. *Address:* 106 Rivermead Court, Hurlingham, SW6 3SB. *T:* 01–736 3192. *Clubs:* Naval and Military, Hurlingham.

STRATHSPEY, 5th Baron, *cr* 1884; **Donald Patrick Trevor Grant of Grant,** 17th Bt, of Nova Scotia, *cr* 1625; 32nd Chief of Grant; Lieutenant-Colonel retired; *b* 18 March 1912; *s* of 4th Baron and Alice Louisa (*d* 1945), *d* of T. M. Hardy-Johnston, MICE London, of Christchurch, NZ; *S* father, 1948; *m* 1st, 1938, Alice (marr. diss. 1951), *o c* of late Francis Bowe, Timaru, NZ; one *s* two *d*; 2nd, 1951, Olive, *d* of W. H. Grant, Norwich; one *s* one *d*. *Educ:* Stowe Sch.; South Eastern Agricultural Coll. War Dept Land Agent and Valuer, Portsmouth, 1944–48; Command Land Agent, HQ Scottish Command,

1948–60; Asst Chief Land Agent and Valuer, War Office, 1960–63; Command Land Agent, HQ Cyprus District, 1963–64; Asst Director of Lands, NW Europe, 1964–66; Asst Chief Land Agent, MoD HQ, 1966–72. Associate, Land Agents' Soc. Fellow, Royal Institution of Chartered Surveyors, retd 1972. Member: Standing Council of Scottish Chiefs; Highland Soc. of London; Pres., Clan Grant Socs of Australia, Canada, Nova Scotia, UK and USA. Hon. Mem., Los Angeles Saint Andrew's Soc.; Knight, Mark Twain Soc., Missouri; Patron: American Scottish Foundn; Soc. for Protection of Endangered Species. Defence Medal; Coronation medal. *Publication:* A History of Clan Grant, 1983. *Recreations:* yachting, gardening, carpentry. *Heir: s* Hon. James Patrick Grant of Grant, *b* 9 Sept. 1943. *Address:* Elms Cottage, Elms Ride, West Wittering, West Sussex. *Clubs:* Lancia Motor, House of Lords Motor, House of Lords Sailing, Civil Service Motoring Association (Pres.), West Wittering Sailing; West Wittering Horticultural and Produce Assoc.

STRATTON, Andrew, MSc, FInstP, CEng, FIEE, FInstNav, FIMA; consulting engineer; applied systems analyst; Technical Director, Terrafix Ltd, since 1983; *b* 5 Sept. 1918; *m* 1949, Ruth Deutsch; one *s* one *d. Educ:* Skinners' Company Sch., Tunbridge Wells; University Coll. of the South West, Exeter; Univ. of London (BSc 1st cl. Hons Physics). RAE Farnborough: Air Defence and Armament Depts, 1939–54; Supt, Instruments and Inertial Navigation Div., 1954–62; Head of Weapon Research and Assessment Group, 1962–66; Prof. and Head of Maths Dept, Coll. of Aeronautics, Cranfield, 1966–68; Dir, Defence Operational Analysis Estabt, 1968–76; Under Sec., MoD, on secondment as Consultant, 1977, Senior Consultant, 1978–81, ICI Ltd. Pt-time Mem., CAA, 1980–83; Chm., Civil Aviation R&D Prog. Bd, 1981–84. Faraday Lecture, IEE, 1972–73. Former Chm. and Mem. of Cttees, Aeronautical and Electronics Research Councils; former Mem., Home Office Scientific Adv. Council. Pres., Inst. of Navigation, 1967–70; Chm. of Convocation, Univ. of Exeter, 1959–83. Hon. DSc Exeter, 1972. Hodgson Prize, RAeS, 1969; Bronze Medal, 1971 and 1975, Gold Medal, 1973, Royal Inst of Navigation. US Medal of Freedom with Bronze Palm, 1947. *Publications:* (ed) Energy and Feedstocks in the Chemical Industry, 1983; contrib. to Unless Peace Comes, 1968; to The Future of Aeronautics, 1970; papers on: aircraft instruments, navigation, air traffic, operational analysis in Jl IEE, Jl IMechE, Jl RAeS, Jl Inst. Navigation; energy, and chemical feedstock in Chem. and Ind., Omega, Process Econ. Internat. *Recreations:* painting, rambling. *Address:* Chartley, 39 Salisbury Road, Farnborough, Hants. *T:* Farnborough 542514.

STRATTON, Ven. Basil; Archdeacon of Stafford and Canon Residentiary of Lichfield Cathedral, 1959–April 1974; Archdeacon Emeritus, since 1974; Chaplain to the Queen, 1965–76; *b* 1906; *s* of Reverend Samuel Henry Stratton and Kate Mabel Stratton; *m* 1934, Euphemia Frances Stuart; one *s* three *d. Educ:* Lincoln School; Hatfield College, Durham University. BA 1929, MA 1932. Deacon 1930; Priest 1931; Curate, St Stephen's, Grimsby, 1930–32; SPG Missionary, India, 1932–34; Indian Ecclesiastical Establishment, 1935–47. Chaplain to the Forces on service in Iraq, India, Burma and Malaya, 1941–46 (despatches); officiated as Chaplain-General in India, 1946. Vicar of Figheldean with Milston, Wilts, 1948–53; Vicar of Market Drayton, Shropshire, 1953–59. *Address:* Woodlands Cottage, Mere, Wilts. *T:* Mere 860235.

STRATTON, Julius Adams, ScD; President Emeritus, Massachusetts Institute of Technology; *b* Seattle, 18 May 1901; *s* of Julius A. Stratton and Laura (*née* Adams); *m* 1935, Catherine N. Coffman; three *d. Educ:* Univ. of Washington; Mass Inst. of Technology (SB, SM); Eidgenössische Technische Hochschule, Zurich (ScD). Expert Consultant, Sec. of War, 1942–46. MIT: Res. Assistant, Elect. Engrg, 1924–26; Asst Prof., Electrical Engrg, 1928–30; Asst Prof., Physics, 1930–35; Assoc. Prof., Physics, 1935–41; Prof., Physics, 1941–51; Mem. Staff, Radiation Lab., 1940–45; Dir, Res. Lab. of Electronics, 1945–49; Provost, 1949–56; Vice-Pres., 1951–56; Chancellor, 1956–59; Actg Pres., 1957–59; Pres., 1959–66; Pres. Emer., 1966–. Trustee, Ford Foundn, 1955–71 (Chm. of Board, 1966–71). Chm., Commn on Marine Science, Engrg and Resources, 1967–69; Member: National Adv. Cttee on Oceans and Atmosphere, 1971–73; National Science Bd, 1956–62 and 1964–67; Naval Res. Adv. Cttee, 1954–59 (Chm., 1956–57). Life Mem. Corp., MIT; Life Trustee, Boston Museum of Science. Hon. Life FIEEE; FAAAS; Fellow: Amer. Acad. of Arts and Scis; Amer. Phys. Soc.; Founding Mem., National Acad. of Engrg; Member: Council on For. Relations; Amer. Philos. Soc.; Nat. Acad. of Scis (Vice-Pres., 1961–65); Sigma Xi; Tau Beta Pi; Eminent Mem., Eta Kappa Nu. Hon. Fellow, Coll. of Science and Technology, Manchester, England, 1963; Hon. Mem. Senate, Technical Univ. of Berlin, 1966. Holds numerous hon. doctorates of Engrg, Humane Letters, Laws and Science incl. DSc: Leeds, 1967; Heriot-Watt, 1971; ScD Cantab 1972. Medal for Merit, 1946; Distinguished Public Service Award, US Navy, 1957; Medal of Honor, Inst. Radio Engrs, 1957; Faraday Medal, IEE (England), 1961; Boston Medal for Distinguished Achievement, 1966. Officer, Legion of Honour, France, 1961; Orden de Boyacá, Colombia, 1964; Kt Comdr, Order of Merit, Germany, 1966. *Publications:* Electromagnetic Theory, 1941; Science and the Educated Man, 1966; numerous papers in scientific and professional jls. *Address:* (home) 100 Memorial Drive, Cambridge, Mass 02142, USA; (office) Massachusetts Institute of Technology, Cambridge, Mass 02139. *Clubs:* Century Association (New York); St Botolph (Boston).

STRATTON, Sir Richard (James), KCMG 1982 (CMG 1974); HM Diplomatic Service, retired; High Commissioner to New Zealand, 1980–84, and concurrently to Western Samoa (non-resident); Governor of Pitcairn Island, 1980–84; *b* 16 July 1924; *s* of William Henry and Cicely Muriel Stratton. *Educ:* The King's Sch., Rochester; Merton Coll., Oxford. Served in Coldstream Guards, 1943–46. Joined Foreign Service, Oct. 1947; British Embassy, Rio de Janeiro, 1948–50; FO, 1951–53; British Embassy, Tokyo, March-Aug. 1953; British Legation, Seoul, 1953–55; Private Sec. to Parly Under-Sec. of State, FO, Nov. 1955–Feb. 1958; NATO Defence Coll., Paris, Feb.-Aug. 1958; British Embassy, Bonn, Sept. 1958–July 1960; British Embassy, Abidjan, Ivory Coast, Aug. 1960–Feb. 1962; Private Sec. to Lord Carrington, as Minister without Portfolio, FO, 1963–64; to Minister of State for Foreign Affairs, 1964–66; Counsellor, British High Commn, Rawalpindi, 1966–69; IDC, 1970; FCO, 1971–72; Political Adviser to Govt of Hong Kong, 1972–74; HM Ambassador: to Republic of Zaire and People's Republic of the Congo, 1974–77; to Republic of Burundi, 1975–77; to Rwandan Republic, 1977; Assistant Under-Sec. of State, FCO, 1977–80. *Recreations:* music, bridge. *Address:* 16 Clareville Court, Clareville Grove, SW7 5AT. *T:* 01–373 2764. *Clubs:* Travellers', Royal Commonwealth Society.

STRATTON, Mrs Roy Olin; *see* Dickens, Monica Enid.

STRATTON, Air Vice-Marshal William Hector, CB 1970; CBE 1963; DFC 1939 and Bar 1944; company director; Chief of the Air Staff, RNZAF, 1969–71, retired 1971; *b* 22 July 1916; *s* of V. J. Stratton; *m* 1954, Dorothy M., *d* of J. D. Whyte; one *s* two *d. Educ:* Hawera Tech. High School, and privately. RAF, 1937–44. Appointments include: in comd RNZAF, Ohakea; Air Member for Personnel; assistant chief of Air Staff; Head NZ Defence Staff, Canberra; Head NZ Defence Staff, London. *Address:* 41 Goldsworthy Road, Claremont, Perth, WA 6010, Australia.

STRATTON, Lt-Gen. Sir William (Henry), KCB 1957 (CB 1948); CVO 1944; CBE 1943; DSO 1945; *b* 1903; *o s* of late Lt-Col H. W. Stratton, OBE; *m* 1930, Noreen Mabel Brabazon, *d* of late Dr and Mrs F. H. B. Noble, Sittingbourne, Kent; no *c. Educ:* Dulwich Coll.; RMA, Woolwich. 2nd Lieut RE 1924; psc; Lt-Col, 1940; Brig., 1941; Comdr 169 Inf. Bde, 1944–45; Col 1945; idc 1946; Maj.-Gen. 1947; Chief of Staff, BAOR, 1947–49; Comdt Joint Services Staff Coll., 1949–52; Commander British Army Staff, and Military Member British Joint Services Mission, Washington, 1952–53; Comdr 42 (Lancs) Inf. Div. (TA), 1953–55; Lt-Gen. 1955; Commander, British Forces, Hong Kong, 1955–57; Vice-Chief of the Imperial General Staff, 1957–60, retired. Col Comdt RE, 1960–68; Inspector-General of Civil Defence, Home Office, 1960–62. Chairman: Edwin Danks (Oldbury) Ltd, 1961–71; Penman & Co. Ltd, 1961–71; Babcock-Moxey Ltd, 1965–71.

STRAUB, Marianne, OBE 1985; RDI 1972; textile designer; *b* 23 Sept. 1909; *d* of Karl Straub and Cécile (*née* Kappeler). *Educ:* in Switzerland. Dip. Kunstgewerbeschule Zürich. Textile Designer: Rural Industries Bureau, 1934–37; Helios Ltd, Bolton, 1937–50; Warner & Sons Ltd, Braintree, 1950–69. Teaching posts: Central School of Art and Design, 1958–63; Hornsey College of Art, 1963–68; Royal College of Art, 1968–74. Now retired, but working freelance and teaching by invitation at various colleges. Hon. Fellow, RCA, 1981. *Publication:* Hand Weaving and Cloth Design, 1977. *Address:* 67 Highsett, Hills Road, Cambridge CB2 1NZ. *T:* Cambridge 61947.

STRAUSS, family name of **Baron Strauss.**

STRAUSS, Baron *cr* 1979 (Life Peer), of Vauxhall in the London Borough of Lambeth; **George Russell Strauss;** PC 1947; *b* 18 July 1901; *s* of Arthur Strauss, formerly MP (C) Camborne Div. of Cornwall and N Paddington; *m* 1932, Patricia O'Flynn (*see* Lady Strauss); two *s* one *d. Educ:* Rugby. MP (Lab) Lambeth North, 1929–31 and 1934–50, Lambeth, Vauxhall, 1950–79; PPS to Minister of Transport, 1929–31, to Lord Privy Seal, and later Minister of Aircraft Production, 1942–45; Parly Sec., Min. of Transport, 1945–47; Minister of Supply, 1947–51 (introd. Iron and Steel Nationalisation Bill, 1949). LCC Representative: N Lambeth, 1925–31; SE Southwark, 1932–46; LCC: Chm. Highways Cttee, 1934–37; Vice-Chm. Finance Cttee, 1934–37; Chm. Supplies Cttee, 1937–39; Mem. London and Home Counties Traffic Advisory Cttee, 1934–39. Introduced Theatres Bill for the abolition of stage censorship, 1968. Father of the House of Commons, 1974. *Recreations:* painting and chess. *Address:* 1 Palace Green, W8. *T:* 01–937 1630; Naylands, Slaugham, West Sussex. *T:* Handcross 400270.

STRAUSS, Lady; Patricia Frances Strauss; Governor: St Martin's School of Art, since 1952; Whitechapel Art Gallery since 1957; John Cass School of Art, since 1982; *b* 21 Oct. 1909; *m* 1932, Rt Hon. Lord Strauss, *qv*; two *s* one *d*. Member of London County Council, 1946–58; Chairman: Parks Cttee (LCC), 1947–49; Supplies Cttee (LCC), 1949–52. Contested (Lab) South Kensington, Parliamentary General Election, 1945. Governor: Royal Ballet Sch., 1951–72; The Old Vic, 1951–85; Sadler's Wells Theatre, 1951–85; Royal Ballet, 1957–85; Ballet Rambert, 1958–85; London Opera Centre, 1965–79; Sadler's Wells Opera (Coliseum), 1968–78; Goldsmith Sch. of Art, 1969–85. *Publications:* Bevin and Co., 1941; Cripps, Advocate and Rebel, 1942. *Recreations:* painting, chess, foreign travel. *Address:* 1 Palace Green, W8. *T:* 01–937 1630; Naylands, Slaugham, Sussex. *T:* Handcross 400270.

STRAUSS, Claude L.; *see* Levi-Strauss.

STRAUSS, Franz Josef; Grand Cross, Order of Merit, Federal Republic of Germany; Prime Minister of Bavaria, since 1978; President, Christian Social Union (CSU), since 1961; *b* Munich, 6 Sept. 1915; *s* of Franz Josef Strauss and Walburga (*née* Schiessl); *m* 1957, Marianne (*née* Zwicknagl) (*d* 1984); two *s* one *d. Educ:* Gymnasium, Munich; Munich Univ. Served in War of 1939–45, 1st Lieut. In Bavarian State Govt, 1946–49; Pres., Govt Cttee on Youth in Bavaria, 1946–48; Member of Bundestag, Fed. Republic of Germany, 1949–78; Minister for Special Tasks, 1953–55; Minister for Nuclear Issues, 1955–56; Minister of Defence, 1956–62; Minister of Finance, 1966–69. President: Landrat (County Commissioner) of Schongau, 1946–49; Committee on Questions of European Security. Dr *hc*: Detroit University, USA, 1956; Kalamazoo College, 1962; Case Institute of Technology, Cleveland (Ohio), 1962; De Paul University, Chicago, 1964; Univ. Santiago de Chile, 1977; Dallas Univ., 1980; Maryland Univ., 1983; Ludwig Maxmilians Univ., München, 1985. Holds decorations from other European countries. *Publications:* The Grand Design, 1965; Herausforderung und Antwort, 1968; Challenge and Response: A programme for Europe, 1969; Finanzpolitik: Theorie und Wirklichkeit, 1969; Deutschland Deine Zukunft, 1975; Bundestagsreden, 1975; Signale, 1978; Gebote der Freiheit, 1980; many articles on political affairs in newspapers and periodicals. *Address:* Nymphenburger Strasse 64, Munich 2, Germany. *T:* 1243–215.

STRAUSS, Hon. Jacobus Gideon Nel, QC (South Africa) 1944; Leader of the South African United Party, 1950–56; MP for Germiston District 1932–57; *b* Calvinia CP, 17 Dec. 1900; *s* of late H. J. Strauss; *m* 1928, Joy Carpenter; two *s* two *d* (and one *s* decd). *Educ:* Calvinia High Sch.; Univ. of Cape Town; Univ. of South Africa. Private Sec. to the Prime Minister (General J. C. Smuts), 1923–24; practice at Johannesburg Bar, 1926–53; Minister of Agriculture and Forestry in Smuts Cabinet, 1944; succeeded Field Marshal J. C. Smuts as Leader of the Opposition, 1950. *Recreations:* riding, mountaineering and golf. *Address:* PO Box 67398, Bryanston, Transvaal 2021, South Africa. *Clubs:* Rand, Royal Johannesburg Golf (Johannesburg).

STRAUSS, Nicholas Albert; QC 1984; *b* 29 July 1942; *s* of late Walter Strauss and of Ilse Strauss (*née* Leon); *m* 1972, Christine M. MacColl; two *d. Educ:* Highgate School; Jesus College, Cambridge. BA 1964; LLB 1965. Called to the Bar, Middle Temple, 1965; Harmsworth Scholar, 1965. *Address:* 1 Essex Court, Temple, EC4Y 9AR. *T:* 01–353 5362.

STRAW, Jack, (John Whitaker Straw); MP (Lab) Blackburn, since 1979; Barrister; *b* 3 Aug. 1946; *s* of Walter Arthur Whitaker Straw and of Joan Sylvia Straw; *m* 1st, 1968, Anthea Lilian Weston (marr. diss. 1978); one *d* (decd); 2nd, 1978, Alice Elizabeth Perkins; one *s* one *d. Educ:* Brentwood Sch., Essex; Univ. of Leeds. LLB 1967. Called to Bar, Inner Temple, 1972. Political Advr to Sec. of State for Social Services, 1974–76; Special Advr to Sec. of State for Environment, 1976–77; on staff of Granada TV (World in Action), 1977–79. Pres., Leeds Univ. Union, 1967–68; Pres., Nat. Union of Students, 1969–71; Mem., Islington Borough Council, 1971–78; Dep. Leader, Inner London Educn Authority, 1973–74; Mem., Labour Party's Nat. Exec. Sub-Cttee on Educn and Science, 1970–; Chm., Jt Adv. Cttee on Polytechnic of N London, 1973–75. Vice-Pres., Assoc. of District Councils, 1984–. Contested (Lab) Tonbridge and Malling, Feb. 1974. Opposition spokesman on the Treasury, 1980–83, on the environment, 1983–. Mem. Council, Inst. for Fiscal Studies, 1983–. *Publications:* Granada Guildhall Lecture, 1969; University of Leeds Convocation Lecture, 1978; contrib. pamphlets, articles. *Recreations:* fell-walking, cooking puddings, music. *Address:* House of Commons, SW1A 0AA; Union House, Freckleton Street, Blackburn BB2 2HL. *T:* Blackburn 52317.

STRAWSON, Maj.-Gen. John Michael, CB 1975; OBE 1964; idc, jssc, psc; Senior Military Adviser, Westland Aircraft Ltd, 1978–85 (Head of Cairo Office, 1976–78); *b* 1 Jan. 1921; *s* of late Cyril Walter and Nellie Dora Strawson; *m* 1960, Baroness Wilfried von Schellersheim; two *d. Educ:* Christ's Coll., Finchley. Joined Army, 1940; commnd,

1942; served with 4th QO Hussars in Middle East, Italy, Germany, Malaya, 1942–50, 1953–54, 1956–58; Staff Coll., Camberley, 1950; Bde Major, 1951–53; Instructor, Staff Coll. and Master of Drag Hounds, 1958–60; GSO1 and Col GS in WO and MoD, 1961–62 and 1965–66; comd QR Irish Hussars, Malaysia and BAOR, 1963–65; comd 39 Inf. Bde, 1967–68; idc 1969; COS, Live Oak, SHAPE, 1970–72; COS, HQ UKLF, 1972–76. Col, Queen's Royal Irish Hussars, 1975–85. US Bronze Star, 1945. *Publications:* The Battle for North Africa, 1969; Hitler as Military Commander, 1971; The Battle for the Ardennes, 1972; The Battle for Berlin, 1974; (jtly) The Third World War, 1978; El Alamein, 1981; (jtly) The Third World War: the untold story, 1982; A History of the SAS Regiment, 1984. *Recreations:* equitation, shooting, reading. *Address:* The Old Rectory, Boyton, Warminster, Wilts BA12 0SS. *Club:* Cavalry and Guards.

See also Sir P. F. Strawson.

STRAWSON, Sir Peter (Frederick), Kt 1977; FBA 1960; Fellow of Magdalen College, and Waynflete Professor of Metaphysical Philosophy in the University of Oxford, 1968–Sept. 1987 (Reader, 1966–68); Fellow of University College, Oxford, 1948–68, Honorary Fellow since 1979; *b* 23 November 1919; *s* of late Cyril Walter and Nellie Dora Strawson; *m* 1945, Grace Hall Martin; two *s* two *d*. *Educ:* Christ's College, Finchley; St John's College, Oxford (scholar; Hon. Fellow, 1973). Served War of 1939–45, RA, REME, Capt. Asst Lecturer in Philosophy, University Coll. of N. Wales, 1946; John Locke Schol., Univ. of Oxford, 1946; Lecturer in Philosophy, 1947, Fellow and Praelector, 1948, University Coll., Oxford. Vis. Prof., Duke Univ., N Carolina, 1955–56; Fellow of Humanities Council and Vis. Associate Prof., Princeton Univ., 1960–61, Vis. Prof., 1972; Woodbridge Lectr, Columbia Univ., NY, 1983; Immanuel Kant Lectr, Munich, 1985; Vis. Prof., Collège de France, 1985. For. Hon. Mem., Amer. Acad. Arts and Scis, 1971. *Publications:* Introduction to Logical Theory, 1952; Individuals, 1959; The Bounds of Sense, 1966; (ed) Philosophical Logic, 1967; (ed) Studies in the Philosophy of Thought and Action, 1968; Logico-Linguistic Papers, 1971; Freedom and Resentment, 1974; Subject and Predicate in Logic and Grammar, 1974; Scepticism and Naturalism: some varieties, 1985; Analyse et Métaphysique, 1985; contrib. to Mind, Philosophy, Proc. Aristotelian Soc., Philosophical Review, etc. *Address:* 25 Farndon Road, Oxford. *T:* Oxford 515026. *Club:* Athenæum.

See also J. M. Strawson.

STREAMS, Peter John, CMG 1986; HM Diplomatic Service; Counsellor, Stockholm, since 1985; *b* 8 March 1935; *s* of Horace Stanley Streams and Isabel Esther (*née Ellaway); m* 1956, Margareta Decker; two *s* one *d*. *Educ:* Wallington County Grammar Sch. BoT, 1953; Bombay, 1960, Calcutta, 1962, Oslo, 1966; FCO, 1970; Mexico, 1973; FCO, 1977, Counsellor, 1979; Consul-Gen., Karachi, 1982. *Recreations:* walking, golf. *Address:* c/o Foreign and Commonwealth Office, SW1.

STREATFEILD, Maj.-Gen. Timothy Stuart Champion, CB 1980; MBE 1960; Director, Royal Artillery, 1978–81; *b* 9 Sept. 1926; *s* of Henry Grey Champion and Edythe Streatfeild; *m* 1951, Annette Catherine, *d* of Sir John Clague, CMG, CIE, and Lady Clague; two *s* one *d*. *Educ:* Eton; Christ Church, Oxford. FBIM. Commnd into RA, 1946; Instructor, Staff Coll., Camberley, 1963–65; Chief Instructor, Sudan Armed Forces Staff Coll., 1965–67; Commander, 7th Parachute Regt, RHA, 1967–69; Col Adjt and QMG, 4 Div., 1969–70; Commander, RA 2 Div., 1971–72; RCDS, 1973; Brigadier Adjt and QMG, 1st Corps, 1974–75; COS, Logistic Exec., MoD, 1976–78. Col. Commandant: RA, 1980–; RHA, 1981–. *Recreations:* fishing, sporting, the countryside, music. *Address:* Toatley Farm, Chawleigh, Chulmleigh, N Devon. *T:* Lapford 363. *Clubs:* Army and Navy, MCC.

STREATFEILD-JAMES, Captain John Jocelyn, RN retired; *b* 14 April 1929; *s* of Comdr Rev. Eric Cardew Streatfeild-James, OBE, and Elizabeth Ann (*né Kirby); m* 1962, Sally Madeline (*née* Stewart); three *s* (one *d* decd). *Educ:* RNC, Dartmouth. Specialist in Undersea Warfare. FBIM; MNI 1982. Naval Cadet, 1943–47; Midshipman, 1947–49; Sub-Lt, 1949–51; Lieutenant: Minesweeping, Diving and Anti-Bandit Ops, Far East Stn, 1951; Officer and Rating Trng, Home Stn, 1952–53; specialised in Undersea Warfare, 1954–55; Ship and Staff Duties, Far East Stn, 1955–57; Exchange Service, RAN, 1957–59; Lieutenant-Commander: instructed Officers specialising in Undersea Warfare, 1960–61; Sea Duty, Staff Home Stn, 1962–63; Sen. Instr, Jt Anti-Submarine Sch., HMS Sea Eagle, 1964–65; Commander: Staff of C-in-C Western Fleet and C-in-C Eastern Atlantic Area, 1965–67; Jt Services Staff Coll., 1968; Staff of Comdr Allied Naval Forces, Southern Europe, Malta, 1968–71; HMS Dryad, 1971–73; Captain: Sen. Officers' War Course, RNC, Greenwich, 1974; Dir, OPCON Proj., 1974–77; HMS Howard (i/c), Head of British Defence Liaison Staff, Ottawa, and Defence Advr to British High Comr in Canada, 1978–80 (as Cdre); HMS Excellent (i/c), 1981–82; ADC to the Queen, 1982–83. *Recreations:* sailing, carpentry, painting. *Address:* South Lodge, Tower Road, Hindhead, Surrey. *T:* Hindhead 6064. *Club:* Naval.

STREATOR, Edward James; United States Ambassador to OECD, since 1984; *b* 12 Dec. 1930; *s* of Edward J. and Ella S. Streator; *m* 1957, Priscilla Craig Kenney; one *s* two *d*. *Educ:* Princeton Univ. (AB). US Naval Reserve, served to Lieut (jg), 1952–56; entered Foreign Service, 1956; Third Sec., US Embassy, Addis Ababa, 1958–60; Second Sec., Lome, 1960–62; Office of Intelligence and Research, Dept of State, 1962–64; Staff Asst to Sec. of State, 1964–66; First Sec., US Mission to NATO, 1966–69; Dep. Director, then Director, Office of NATO Affairs, Dept of State, 1969–75; Dep. US Permanent Representative to NATO, Brussels, 1975–77; Minister, US Embassy, London, 1977–84. *Recreation:* swimming. *Address:* US Mission to OECD, 19 rue de Franqueville, 75016 Paris, France. *Clubs:* Brooks's, Beefsteak, Buck's, Garrick; Travellers' (Paris); Metropolitan (Washington); Mill Reef (Antigua).

STREDDER, James Cecil; Headmaster, Wellington School, Somerset, 1957–73; *b* 22 Sept. 1912; 4th *s* of late Rev. J. Clifton Stredder and late Mrs Stredder; *m* 1938, Catherine Jane, *er d* of late Rev. A. R. Price, RN (Retd), Paignton, Devon; one *d*. *Educ:* King Edward VI School, Stratford-on-Avon; Jesus College, Oxford. Senior Chemistry Master at: Victoria College, Alexandria, Egypt, 1935; St Lawrence Coll., Ramsgate, 1936; Fettes Coll., Edinburgh, 1940; Tonbridge School, 1942–57. BA (Hons) Natural Science (Chemistry) Oxon 1935, MA 1943. *Recreation:* walking. *Address:* 21 Crouch Cross Lane, Boxgrove, near Chichester, Sussex.

STREET, Hon. Anthony Austin; manager and company director; *b* 8 Feb. 1926; *s* of late Brig. the Hon. G. A. Street, MC, MHR; *m* 1951, Valerie Erica, *d* of J. A. Rickard; three *s*. *Educ:* Melbourne C of E Grammar Sch. RAN, 1945–46. MP (L) Corangamite, Vic, 1966–84 (resigned); Mem., various Govt Mems Cttees, 1967–71; Mem., Fed. Exec. Council, 1971–; Asst Minister for Labour and Nat. Service, 1971–72; Mem., Opposition Exec., 1973–75 (Special Asst to Leader of Opposition and Shadow Minister for Labour and Immigration, March-Nov. 1975); Minister for Labour and Immigration, Caretaker Ministry after dissolution of Parliament, Nov. 1975; Minister for Employment and Industrial Relations and Minister Assisting Prime Minister in Public Service Matters, 1975–78; Minister for: Industrial Relations, 1978–80; Foreign Affairs, 1980–83. Chm., Fed. Rural Cttee, Liberal Party, 1970–74. *Recreations:* cricket, golf, tennis, flying. *Address:* 153 The Terrace, Ocean Grove, Vic 3226, Australia. *Clubs:* MCC; Royal Melbourne Golf, Barwon Heads Golf.

STREET, John Edmund Dudley, CMG 1966; retired; *b* 21 April 1918; *er s* of late Philip Edmund Wells Street and of Elinor Gladys Whittington-Ince; *m* 1st, 1940, Noreen Mary (*d* 1981), *o d* of Edward John Griffin Comerford and Mary Elizabeth Winstone; three *s* one *d*; 2nd, 1983, Mrs Patricia Curzon. *Educ:* Tonbridge School; Exeter College, Oxford. Served War of 1939–45, HM Forces, 1940–46. Entered Foreign Service, 1947; First Secretary: British Embassy, Oslo, 1950; British Embassy, Lisbon, 1952; Foreign Office, 1954; First Secretary and Head of Chancery, British Legation, Budapest, 1957–60; HM Ambassador to Malagasy Republic, 1961–62, also Consul-General for the Island of Réunion and the Comoro Islands, 1961–62; Asst Sec., MoD, 1967–76; Asst Under-Sec. of State, MoD, 1976–78. *Recreations:* reading, golf, bridge. *Address:* Cornerways, High Street, Old Woking, Surrey. *T:* Woking 64371.

STREET, Hon. Sir Laurence (Whistler), KCMG 1976; Lieutenant-Governor of New South Wales since 1974; Chief Justice of New South Wales since 1974; *b* Sydney, 3 July 1926; *s* of Hon. Sir Kenneth Street, KCMG; *m* 1952, Susan Gai, AM, *d* of E. A. S. Watt; two *s* two *d*. *Educ:* Cranbrook Sch.; Univ. of Sydney (LLB Hons). Ord. Seaman, RANR, 1943–44; Midshipman, RANVR, 1944–45; Sub-Lt 1945–47; Comdr, Sen. Officer RANR Legal Br., 1964–65. Admitted to NSW Bar, 1951; QC 1963; Judge, Supreme Court of NSW, 1965; Judge of Appeal, 1972–74; Chief Judge in Equity, 1972–74. Lectr in Procedure, Univ. of Sydney, 1962–63, Lectr in Bankruptcy, 1964–65; Mem., Public Accountants Regn Bd, 1962–65; Mem., Companies Auditors Bd, 1962–65; Pres., Courts-Martial Appeal Tribunal, 1971–74; Pres., Cranbrook Sch. Council, 1966–74. Hon. Col, 1st/15th Royal NSW Lancers, 1986. KStJ 1976. Hon. LLD Sydney, 1984. Grand Officer of Merit, SMO Malta, 1977. *Address:* Supreme Court, Queen's Square, Sydney, NSW, Australia. *Clubs:* Union (Sydney); Royal Sydney Golf.

STREET, Prof. Robert, AO 1985; DSc; Vice-Chancellor, University of Western Australia, 1978–86; *b* 16 Dec. 1920; *s* of late J. Street, Allerton Bywater, Yorkshire, UK; *m* 1943, Joan Marjorie Bere; one *s* one *d*. *Educ:* Hanley High Sch.; King's Coll., London. BSc, MSc, PhD, DSc (London). MIEE, FInstP, FAIP, FAA. Scientific Officer, Dept of Supply, UK, 1942–45; Lectr, Dept of Physics, Univ. of Nottingham, 1945–54; Sen. Lectr, Dept of Physics, Univ. of Sheffield, 1954–60; Foundn Prof. of Physics, Monash Univ., Melbourne, Vic., 1960–74; Dir, Research Sch. of Physical Sciences, Aust. Nat. Univ., 1974–78. Former President: Aust. Inst. of Nuclear Science and Engrg; Aust. Inst. of Physics; Mem. and Chm., Aust. Research Grants Cttee, 1970–76; Chm., Nat. Standards Commn, 1967–78; Member: State Energy Adv. Council, WA, 1981–86; Australian Science and Technology Council, 1977–80; Council, Univ. of Technology, Lae, Papua New Guinea, 1982–84; Bd of Management, Royal Perth Hosp., 1978–85. Fellow, Aust. Acad. of Science, 1973 (Treas., 1976–77). Hon. DSc Sheffield, 1986. *Publications:* research papers in scientific jls. *Recreation:* swimming. *Address:* Department of Physics, University of Western Australia, Nedlands, WA 6009, Australia. *Club:* Weld (Perth).

STREETEN, Frank; *see* Streeten, R. H.

STREETEN, Paul Patrick, DLitt; Director, World Development Institute, since 1984, Professor, since 1980, Boston University (Director, Center for Asian Development Studies, 1980–84); *b* 18 July 1917; *e s* of Wilhelm Hornig, Vienna; changed name to Streeten under Army Council Instruction, 1943; *m* 1951, Ann Hilary Palmer, *d* of Edgar Higgins, Woodstock, Vermont; two *d* (and one step *s*). *Educ:* Vienna; Aberdeen Univ.; Balliol Coll., Oxford (Hon. Schol.); 1st cl. PPE, 1947; Student, Nuffield Coll., Oxford, 1947–48. DLitt Oxon, 1976. Mil. service in Commandos, 1941–43; wounded in Sicily, 1943. Fellow, Balliol Coll., Oxford, 1948–66 (Hon. Fellow, 1986); Associate, Oxford Univ. Inst. of Econs and Statistics, 1960–64; Dep. Dir-Gen., Econ. Planning Staff, Min. of Overseas Develt, 1964–66; Prof. of Econs, Fellow and Dep. Dir of Inst. of Develt Studies, Sussex Univ., 1966–68; Warden of Queen Elizabeth House, Dir, Inst. of Commonwealth Studies, Univ. of Oxford, and Fellow of Balliol Coll., 1968–78; Special Adviser, World Bank, 1976–79; Dir of Studies, Overseas Develt Council, 1979–80. Rockefeller Fellow, USA, 1950–51; Fellow, Johns Hopkins Univ., Baltimore, 1955–56; Fellow, Center for Advanced Studies, Wesleyan Univ., Conn.; Vis. Prof., Econ. Develt Inst. of World Bank, 1984–86. Sec., Oxford Econ. Papers, until 1961, Mem. Edit. Bd, 1971–78; Editor, Bulletin of Oxford Univ. Inst. of Econs and Statistics, 1961–64; Member: UK Nat. Commn of Unesco, 1966; Provisional Council of Univ. of Mauritius, 1966–72; Commonwealth Develt Corp., 1967–72; Statutory Commn, Royal Univ. of Malta, 1972–; Royal Commn on Environmental Pollution, 1974–76. Mem., Internat. Adv. Panel, Canadian Univ. Service Overseas. Vice-Chm., Social Sciences Adv. Cttee, 1971; Member, Governing Body: Queen Elizabeth House, Oxford, 1966–68; Inst. of Develt Studies, Univ. of Sussex, 1968–80 (Vice-Chm.); Dominion Students' Hall Trust, London House; Mem. Council, Overseas Develt Institute, until 1979. Pres., UK Chapter, Soc. for Internat. Develt until 1976. Hon. Fellow, Inst. of Develt Studies, Sussex, 1980; Hon. LLD Aberdeen, 1980. Chm. Editorial Bd, World Develt, 1972–. *Publications:* (ed) Value in Social Theory, 1958; Economic Integration, 1961, 2nd edn 1964; (contrib.) Economic Growth in Britain, 1966; The Teaching of Development Economics, 1967; (ed with M. Lipton) Crisis in Indian Planning, 1968; (contrib. to) Gunnar Myrdal, Asian Drama, 1968; (ed) Unfashionable Economics, 1970; (ed, with Hugh Corbet) Commonwealth Policy in a Global Context, 1971; Frontiers of Development Studies, 1972; (ed) Trade Strategies for Development, 1973; The Limits of Development Research, 1975; (with S. Lall) Foreign Investment, Transnationals and Developing Countries, 1977; Development Perspectives, 1981; First Things First, 1981; (ed with Richard Jolly) Recent Issues in World Development, 1981; (ed with H. Maier) Human Resources, Employment and Development, 1983; What Price Food?, 1987; contribs to learned journals. *Address:* World Development Institute, Boston University, 270 Bay State Road, Boston, Mass 02215, USA. *Club:* United Oxford & Cambridge University.

STREETEN, Reginald Hawkins, (Frank); Assistant Solicitor, Law Commission, since 1967 (Secretary, 1981–82); *b* 19 March 1928; *s* of late Reginald Craufurd Streeten, BA, LLB and Olive Gladys Streeten (*née* Palmer); *m* 1962, Bodile Westergren, Lappland, Sweden; two *s*. *Educ:* Grey Coll., S Africa; Rhodes University Coll. (BA, LLB). Called to the Bar, S Rhodesia, 1959. Crown Counsel and Legal Draftsman, S Rhodesia and Fedn of Rhodesia and Nyasaland, 1952–63; Jun. Counsel for Fed. Govt at inquiry into aircraft accident involving late Dag Hammarskjöld, 1961; Parly Draftsman, Zambia, 1964–66. Legal Mem., Med. Council of S Rhodesia, 1959–63. *Address:* 32 Holme Chase, St George's Avenue, Weybridge, Surrey KT13 0BZ.

STREETER, His Honour John Stuart; DL; a Circuit Judge, 1972–86 (Deputy Chairman 1967–71, Chairman 1971, Kent Quarter Sessions); *b* 20 May 1920; *yr s* of late Wilfrid A. Streeter, osteopath, and late Mrs R. L. Streeter; *m* 1956, (Margaret) Nancy Richardson; one *s* two *d*. *Educ:* Sherborne. Served War of 1939–45 (despatches): Captain, Royal Scots Fusiliers, 1940–46. Called to Bar, Gray's Inn, Nov. 1947. Post Office Counsel SE Circuit, 1957; Treasury Counsel, London Sessions, 1959; Part-time Dep. Chm., Kent Quarter

Sessions, 1963. DL Kent, 1986. *Recreation:* gardening. *Address:* Playstole, Sissinghurst, Cranbrook, Kent TN17 2JN. *T:* Cranbrook 712847.

STREETON, Terence George, CMG 1981; MBE 1969; HM Diplomatic Service; High Commissioner to Bangladesh, since 1983; *b* 12 Jan. 1930; *er s* of Alfred Victor Streeton and Edith Streeton (*née* Deiton); *m* 1962, Molly Horsburgh; two *s* two *d. Educ:* Wellingborough Grammar School. Inland Revenue, 1946; Prison Commission, 1947; Government Communications Headquarters, 1952; Foreign Office (Diplomatic Wireless Service), 1953; Diplomatic Service, 1965–: First Secretary, Bonn, 1966; FCO, 1970; First Secretary and Head of Chancery, Bombay, 1972; Counsellor and Head of Joint Admin Office, Brussels, 1975; Head of Finance Dept, FCO, 1979; Asst Under-Sec. of State and Prin. Finance Officer, FCO, 1982–83. *Recreations:* motor boating, walking. *Address:* c/o Foreign and Commonwealth Office, SW1A 2AH.

STRETTON, Eric Hugh Alexander, CB 1972; Deputy Chief Executive in Property Services Agency, Department of the Environment, 1972–76, Deputy Chairman, 1973–76; *b* 22 June 1916; *y s* of Major S. G. Stretton, Wigston, Leicester; *m* 1946, Sheila Woodroffe Anderson, MB, BS, *d* of Dr A. W. Anderson, Cardiff (formerly of Ogmore Vale); one *s* one *d. Educ:* Wyggeston Sch; Pembroke Coll., Oxford. BA 1939, MA 1942. Leics Regt and 2/4 PWO Gurkha Rifles (Major), 1939–46. Asst Sec., Birmingham Univ. Appointments Board, 1946. Entered Ministry of Works, 1947; Prin. Private Sec. to Minister of Works, 1952–54; Asst Sec., 1954; Under-Secretary: MPBW, 1962–70; DoE, 1970–72; Dep. Sec., 1972. Chm., Structure Plan Examns in Public, Salop, 1979, Lincs, 1980, Central and N Lancs, 1981. *Address:* Dacre Castle, Penrith, Cumbria. *T:* Pooley Bridge 375. *Club:* United Oxford & Cambridge University.

STRETTON, Peter John; a Recorder of the Crown Court, since 1982; *b* 14 June 1938; *s* of Frank and Ella Stretton; *m* 1973, Eleanor Anne Wait; two *s* one *d. Educ:* Bedford Modern Sch. Called to the Bar, Middle Temple, 1962; Head of Chambers, 1985. *Recreations:* squash, gardening. *Address:* 1 Fountain Court, Steelhouse Lane, Birmingham. *T:* 021–236 5721.

STREVENS, Peter Derek, MA; FIL; Director-General, Bell Educational Trust, since 1978; Fellow of Wolfson College, Cambridge, since 1976; *b* 1922; *s* of late William Strevens and Dorothie Strevens; *m* 1946, Gwyneth Moore; one *s. Educ:* Ackworth Sch.; University Coll. London (BA); MA Cantab 1979. FIL 1971. Lectr in Phonetics, University Coll. of the Gold Coast, 1949–56; Lectr in Phonetics and Applied Linguistics, Univ. of Edinburgh, 1957–61; Prof. of Contemporary English, Univ. of Leeds, 1961–64; Prof of Applied Linguistics, Univ. of Essex, 1964–74. Sec., Internat. Assoc. of Applied Linguistics, 1966–70; Chairman: British Assoc. of Applied Linguistics, 1972–75; Internat. Assoc. of Teachers of English as a Foreign Language, 1983–86. Gen. Editor, Special English Series, 1962–77; Joint Editor: Language and Language Learning, 1964–76; New Directions in Language Teaching, 1977–. FRSA 1978. *Publications:* The Linguistic Sciences and Language Teaching (jtly), 1964; British and American English, 1972; New Orientations in the Teaching of English, 1977; Teaching English as an International Language, 1980; (jtly) International English for Maritime Communication: Seaspeak, 1984. *Recreations:* travel, the sea. *Address:* Bell Educational Trust, Hillscross, Red Cross Lane, Cambridge CB2 2QX. *T:* Cambridge 212333. *Clubs:* English-Speaking Union, Royal Commonwealth Society.

STRICK, Robert Charles Gordon; Clerk to the Drapers' Company, since 1980; *b* 23 March 1931; *s* of late Charles Gordon Strick and Doris Gwendoline Strick; *m* 1960, Jennifer Mary Hathway; one *s* one *d. Educ:* Royal Grammar Sch., Guildford; Sidney Sussex Coll., Cambridge. MA. Served RA, 1949–51; TA, 1951–55. Spicers Ltd, 1954–55; joined HMOCS, 1955; Dist Officer, Fiji, 1955–59; Sec., Burns Commn into Natural Resources and Population Trends, 1959–60; Asst Sec., Suva, 1960–61; Sec. to Govt, Tonga, 1961–63; Develt Officer and Divl Comr, 1963–67, Sec. for Natural Resources, 1967–71, Fiji; retired 1971; Under Sec., ICA, 1971–72; Asst Sec.-Gen., RICS, 1972–80; Clerk, Chartered Surveyors' Co., 1977–80. Clerk to Governors, Howells Sch., Denbigh, 1980–; Governor, QMC, London Univ., 1980–. *Recreations:* the countryside, walking, cycling, gardening. *Address:* Monkston Barns, Lickfold, West Sussex GU28 9DX. *T:* Lodsworth 367.

STRICKLAND, Hon. Mabel Edeline, OBE 1944; Leader of the Progressive Constitutional Party in Malta, since 1953; *b* Malta, 8 Jan. 1899; 3rd *d* of 1st and last Baron Strickland, of Sizergh Castle, Kendal (and 6th Count della Catena in the Island of Malta) and of late Lady Edeline Sackville. *Educ:* privately in Australia. Attached Naval HQ, Malta, 1917–18; War Correspondent, attached 21st Army Group, BAOR, Aug. 1945. Asst Sec., Constitutional Party, 1921–45; Editor: Times of Malta, 1935–50; Sunday Times of Malta, 1935–56; Member: Malta Legislative Assembly, 1950, 1951–53, 1962–66; Malta Chamber of Commerce; Man. Dir, Allied Malta Newspapers Ltd, 1940–55; Chairman: Xara Palace Hotel Co. Ltd, 1949–61, 1966–; Allied Malta Newspapers Ltd, 1950–55, 1966–; Director, Progress Press Co. Ltd, 1957–61, 1966–. Life Member: Commonwealth Parliamentary Assoc.; Air League; RSA; Mem. Royal Horticultural Soc.; Hon. Corresp. Sec. (Malta), Royal Commonwealth Soc. Astor Award, CPU, 1971. CStJ 1969. Coronation medal, 1953. *Publications:* A Collection of Essays on Malta, 1923–54; Maltese Constitutional and Economic Issue, 1955–59. *Recreations:* gardening, reading. *Address:* Villa Parisio, Lija, Malta. *T:* 41286. *Clubs:* Lansdowne; Marsa Sports.

STRICKLAND-CONSTABLE, Sir Robert (Frederick), 11th Bt *cr* 1641; *b* 22 Oct. 1903; 2nd *s* of Lt-Col Frederick Charles Strickland-Constable (*d* 1917) (*g g s* of 7th Bt) and Margaret Elizabeth (*d* 1961), *d* of late Rear-Adm. Hon. Thomas Alexander Pakenham; *S* brother, 1975; *m* 1936, Lettice, *y d* of late Major Frederick Strickland; two *s* two *d. Educ:* Magdalen Coll., Oxford (BA 1925, MA 1936, DPhil 1940). Served War of 1939–45, Lieut Comdr RNVR. Teaching Staff, Chem. Engineering Dept, Imperial Coll., Univ. of London, 1948–71, Readership 1963–71. Mem. Faraday Soc. *Publications:* Kinetics and Mechanism of Crystallization, 1968; approx. 50 contribs to scientific jls. *Recreations:* music, mountains, bird-watching. *Heir: s* Frederick Strickland-Constable [*b* 21 Oct. 1944; *m* 1982, Pauline Margaret Harding; one *s* one *d*]. *Address:* Combe Wood, Brasted, Westerham, Kent TN16 1NJ.

STRINGER, Donald Arthur, OBE 1975; Deputy Chairman, Associated British Ports (formerly British Transport Docks Board), 1982–85 (Member, 1969–85; Deputy Managing Director, 1967–71 and 1978–82; Joint Managing Director, 1982–85); *b* 15 June 1922; *s* of late Harry William Stringer and Helen Stringer; *m* 1945, Hazel Handley; one *s* one *d. Educ:* Dorking High Sch.; Borden Grammar Sch. FCIT; CBIM. Joined Southern Railway Co., 1938; service with RAF, 1941–46; Docks Manager: Fleetwood, 1957–58; East Coast Scottish Ports, 1958–62; Chief Docks Man., Southampton, 1963–67, Port Director, 1970–77. Chairman: ABP (formerly BTDB) Bds: Southampton, 1972–85; Humber, 1978–85; Southampton Cargo Handling Co. Ltd, 1968–85; Nat. Assoc. of Port Employers, 1982–85 (Mem. Exec. Cttee, 1964–85); Mem., National Dock Labour Bd, 1976–85; Past Pres., Southampton Chamber of Commerce. Col, Engr and Transport Staff Corps, RE(TA). *Recreation:* gardening. *Address:* Hillcrest, Pinehurst Road, Bassett, Southampton SO1 7FZ. *T:* Southampton 768887. *Clubs:* Army and Navy; Royal Southampton Yacht.

STRINGER, Pamela Mary; Headmistress, Clifton High School for Girls, 1965–85; *b* 30 Aug. 1928; *e d* of late E. Allen Stringer. *Educ:* Worcester Grammar Sch. for Girls; St Hugh's Coll., Oxford. MA (Hons Lit Hum). Asst Classics Mistress, Sherborne Sch. for Girls, 1950–59; Head of Classics Dept, Pate's Grammar Sch. for Girls, Cheltenham, 1959–64 (Dep. Head, 1963–64). Member: Exec. Cttee, Assoc. of Headmistresses, 1975–; Exec. Cttee, Girls Schools Assoc., 1975– (Pres., 1978–79; Chm., Educn Cttee, 1981–84); Council, Secondary Heads Assoc., 1978–79 (Pres. Area 7, 1978–79). *Recreations:* travel in Tuscany and Umbria, reading, arctophily, cooking. *Address:* 36 Henleaze Gardens, Bristol BS9 4HJ.

STRONACH, David Brian, OBE 1975; FSA; Professor of Near Eastern Studies, University of California, Berkeley, since 1981; Curator of Near Eastern Archaeology, Lowie Museum of Anthropology, Berkeley, since 1982; *b* 10 June 1931; *s* of Ian David Stronach, MB, FRCSE, and Marjorie Jessie Duncan (*née* Minto); *m* 1966, Ruth Vaadia; two *d. Educ:* Gordonstoun; St John's Coll., Cambridge (MA). Pres., Cambridge Univ. Archaeological Field Club, 1954. British Inst. of Archaeology at Ankara: Scholar, 1955–56; Fellow, 1957–58; Fellow, British Sch. of Archaeology in Iraq, 1957–60; Brit. Acad. Archaeological Attaché in Iran, 1960–61; Dir, British Inst. of Persian Studies, 1961–80, Hon. Vice Pres., 1981–. Asst on excavations at: Istanbul, 1954; Tell Rifa'at, 1956; Beycesultan, 1956–57; Hacilar, 1957–59; Nimrud, 1957–60; Charsada, 1958. Dir, excavations at: Ras al'Amiya, 1960; Yarim Tepe, 1960–62; Pasargadae, 1961–63; Tepe Nush-i Jan, 1967–; Co-dir, excavs at Shahr-i Qumis, 1967–. Mem., Internat. Cttee of Internat. Congresses of Iranian Art and Archaeology, 1968–. Hagop Kevorkian Visiting Lectr in Iranian Art and Archaeology, Univ. of Pennsylvania, 1967; Rhind Lectr, Edin., 1973; Norton Lectr, Amer. Inst. of Archaeology, 1980; Columbia Lectr in Iranian Studies, Columbia Univ., 1986. Vis. Prof. of Archaeology, Hebrew Univ., Jerusalem, 1977; Vis. Prof. of Archaeology and Iranian Studies, Univ. of Arizona, Tucson, 1980–81. Mem., German Archaeological Inst., 1973 (Corr. Mem., 1966). Ghirshman Prize, Académie des Inscriptions et Belles-Lettres, Paris, 1979; Sir Percy Sykes Meml Medal, Royal Soc. for Asian Affairs, 1980. Adv. Editor: Jl of Mithraic Studies, 1976–79; Iran, 1980–; Iranica Antiqua, 1984–; Bulletin of Asia Inst., 1986–. *Publications:* Pasargadae, a Report on the Excavations conducted by the British Institute of Persian Studies, 1978; archaeological articles in: Jl of Near Eastern Studies; Iran; Iraq; Anatolian Studies, etc. *Recreations:* fly fishing, mediaeval architecture, tribal carpets; repr. Cambridge in athletics, 1953. *Address:* Department of Near Eastern Studies, University of California, Berkeley, Calif 94720, USA. *Clubs:* Achilles; Hawks (Cambridge); Explorers' (New York).

STRONG, Sir Charles Love, KCVO 1974 (MVO 1962); chartered physiotherapist in private practice in London, 1938–83; *b* 16 April 1908; *o s* of late Alfred Strong; *m* 1st, 1933, Ivy Maud (*d* 1976), *yr d* of late Arthur Stockley; one *d*; 2nd, 1977, Ruth Mary, *d* of late Charles Hermon Smith. *Educ:* privately (Bailey Sch., Durham). Miner and merchant seaman, 1924–26; RN (Sick Berth Br.), qualified MCSP; Physiotherapist, RN Hosps, Haslar and Malta. Devised new apparatus and technique for treatment of injury to humans by faradism; developed manipulative techniques, 1926–38; running parallel with human practice designed special apparatus and technique for treatment of injuries to horses by faradism with outstanding success; under observation of leading equine veterinarian treated 100 cases of lameness in horses which had failed to respond to previous treatment, curing 88 per cent; some hundreds of races have now been won by horses cured of lameness by this method and which had failed to respond to other treatments. Formed firm of 'Transeva' for development, manufacture and marketing of horse apparatus, which is now supplied to many parts of the world. Served War, RAF Marine Section, 1st cl. Coxwain, 1940–44 (invalided). *Publications:* Common-Sense Therapy for Horses' Injuries, 1956; Horses' Injuries, 1967. *Recreation:* racing. *Address:* 115A Harley Street, W1N 1DG. *T:* 01–935 4523.

STRONG, Air Cdre David Malcolm, CB 1964; AFC 1941; *b* 30 Sept. 1913; *s* of Theo Strong; *m* 1941, Daphne Irene Warren-Brown; two *s* one *d. Educ:* Cardiff High School. Pilot, under trng, 1936; Bomber Sqdn, 1937–41; POW, 1941–45. Station Commander, RAF Jurby, RAF Driffield, 1946–48; Staff Coll. (psa), 1949; Staff Officer, Rhodesian Air Trng Grp, 1949–51; Directing Staff, Staff Coll., 1952–55; Air Warfare Coll. (pfc), 1956; Station Comdr, RAF Coningsby, 1957–59; Dir of Personnel, Air Min., 1959–61; Senior Air Staff Officer, RAF Germany, 1962–63; Officer Commanding, RAF Halton, 1964–66. Retired, 1966. Chairman: RAF Rugby Union, 1954–56; RAF Golf Soc., 1964–66. *Recreation:* golf. *Address:* Old Coach House, Wendover, Bucks. *T:* Wendover 624724. *Clubs:* Royal Air Force; Ashridge Golf.

STRONG, Dr John Anderson, CBE 1978 (MBE (mil.) 1942); MD; FRCP; FRCPE; FRSE; President, Royal College of Physicians of Edinburgh, 1979–82; *b* 18 Feb. 1915; *s* of Charles James Strong and Mabel Emma Strong (*née* Anderson); *m* 1939, Anne Frances Moira Heaney; one *s* two *d. Educ:* Monkton Combe Sch., Bath; Trinity Coll., Dublin (MB 1937, MA, MD). Served RAMC, UK, India and Burma, 1939–46 (despatches, Burma, 1945); Hon. Lt-Col RAMC, 1946. Senior Lecturer, Dept of Medicine, Univ. of Edinburgh, 1949; Hon. Cons. Phys., Western General Hosp., Edinburgh, 1949; Hon. Physician, MRC Clinical and Population Cytogenetics Unit, 1959–80; Professor of Medicine, Univ. of Edinburgh, 1966–80, Professor Emeritus, 1981. Mem., Medicines Commn, 1976–83; Chm., Scottish Health Educn Co-ordinating Cttee, 1986–. Hon. FACP 1980; Hon. FRCPI 1980; Hon. Fellow: Coll. of Physicians of Philadelphia, 1981; TCD, 1982; Coll. of Physicians of S Africa, 1982; Fellow *ad eundem*, RCGP, 1982; Mem., Acad. of Medicine, Singapore, 1982. *Publications:* chapter on Endocrinology in Principles and Practice of Medicine, ed L. S. P. Davidson, 1952, 12th edn 1977; articles in general medical and endocrinological jls. *Recreations:* fishing, golf, stalking, natural history. *Address:* 6 York Road, Edinburgh EH5 3EH. *T:* 031–552 2865. *Clubs:* New (Edinburgh); Hon. Company of Edinburgh Golfers (Muirfield).

STRONG, John Clifford, CBE 1980; HM Diplomatic Service, retired; Governor, Turks and Caicos Islands, 1978–82; *b* 14 Jan. 1922; *m* 1942, Janet Browning; three *d. Educ:* Beckenham Grammar Sch.; London Sch. of Economics and Political Science. LLB 1953. Served RN, 1942–46; HMOCS Tanzania, 1946–63; CRO, 1963; First Sec., Nairobi, 1964–68; FCO, 1968–73; Counsellor and Head of Chancery, Dar es Salaam, 1973–78. *Address:* Oakover, 24 Crescent Road, Beckenham BR3 2NE. *Club:* Royal Over-Seas League.

STRONG, Julia Trevelyan; *see* Oman, J. T.

STRONG, Maurice F., OC 1976; Executive Co-ordinator, UN Office for Emergency Operations in Africa, New York; President, Strovest Holdings Inc., Vancouver; Director, Teron International, Ottawa; Vice-Chairman and Director, Société Générale pour l'Energie et les Ressources, Geneva; *b* 29 April 1929; *s* of Frederick Milton Strong and late Mary Fyfe Strong; *m* 1st, 1950 (marr. diss. 1980); two *s* two *d*; 2nd, 1981, Hanne Marstrand; one foster *d. Educ:* Public and High Sch., Oak Lake, Manitoba, Canada. Served in UN Secretariat, 1947; worked in industry and Pres. or Dir, various Canadian and internat. corporations, 1948–66; Dir-Gen., External Aid Office (later Canadian Internat. Develt Agency), Canadian Govt, 1966–71; Under-Sec.-Gen. with responsibility for environmental affairs, and Sec.-Gen. of 1972 Conf. on the Human Environment, Stockholm, 1971–72; Exec. Dir, UN Environmental Programme, 1972–75; Special Rep. of Sec.-Gen. for UN Financing System for Science and Technol. for Develt; Member: Internat. Adv. Bd, Burroughs Corp., USA; Bd, Bretton Woods Cttee, Washington; Dir, Massey Ferguson, Canada. Chairman: Bd, AZL Resources Inc., USA, 1978–83; Centre for Internat. Management Studies, Geneva, 1971–78; Internat. Energy Develt Corp., Geneva (also Special Advr); Canada Develt Investment Corp., Vancouver; Bd of Governors, Internat. Develt Res. Centre, 1977–78; Mem., World Commn on Environment and Develt; Co-Chm., Interaction Policy Bd, Vienna; Pres., Chm. of Bd and Chm. of Exec. Cttee, Petro-Canada, 1976–78; Alt. Governor, IBRD, ADB, Caribbean Develt Bank. Chairman: North South Energy Roundtable, Washington, DC; North South Energy Roundtable, Rome; Adv. Cttee, UN Univ., Tokyo, Japan; Director: (also Mem. Exec. Cttee) Canada Develt Corp., Toronto (Vice-Chm.); Lindisfarne Assoc.; Mem., Internat. Asia Soc., New York. Trustee: Rockefeller Foundn, 1971–78; Aspen Inst., 1971–; Internat. Foundn for Develt Alternatives. Holds numerous hon. degrees from univs and colls in Canada, USA and UK. *Publications:* articles in various journals, including Foreign Affairs Magazine, Natural History Magazine. *Recreations:* swimming, skin-diving, farming, reading. *Address:* Suite 1800, 999 W Hastings Street, Vancouver, BC V6C 2W2, Canada. *Clubs:* Farmers'; Mount Royal (Montreal); Canadian, Yale, Century (New York); Rideau (Ottawa); Ranchmen's (Calgary).

STRONG, Sir Roy (Colin), Kt 1982; PhD, FSA; Director, Victoria and Albert Museum, since 1974; *b* 23 Aug. 1935; *s* of G. E. C. Strong; *m* 1971, Julia Trevelyan Oman, *qv. Educ:* Edmonton Co. Grammar Sch.; Queen Mary Coll., London (Fellow, 1976); Warburg Inst., London. Asst Keeper, 1959, Director, Keeper and Secretary 1967–73, Nat. Portrait Gallery. Ferens Prof. of Fine Art, Univ. of Hull, 1972. Walls Lectures, Pierpont Morgan Library, 1974. Lecturer, critic, columnist, contributor to radio and TV and organiser of exhibitions. Member: Fine Arts Adv. Cttee, British Council, 1974–; Westminster Abbey Architectl Panel, 1975–; Council, RCA, 1979–; Arts Council of GB, 1983– (Chm., Arts Panel, 1983–); Vice-Chm., South Bank Bd, 1985–. Trustee: Arundel Castle, 1974–86; Chevening, 1974–; Sutton Place, 1982–84; Patron, Pallant House, Chichester, 1986– (Trustee, 1980–86). Hon. DLitt: Leeds, 1983; Keele, 1984. Sen. Fellow, RCA, 1983. Shakespeare Prize, FVS Foundn, Hamburg, 1980. *Publications:* Portraits of Queen Elizabeth I, 1963; (with J. A. van Dorsten) Leicester's Triumph, 1964; Holbein and Henry VIII, 1967; Tudor and Jacobean Portraits, 1969; The English Icon: Elizabethan and Jacobean Portraiture, 1969; (with Julia Trevelyan Oman) Elizabeth R, 1971; Van Dyck: Charles I on Horseback, 1972; (with Julia Trevelyan Oman) Mary Queen of Scots, 1972; (with Stephen Orgel) Inigo Jones: the theatre of the Stuart court, 1973; contrib. Burke's Guide to the Royal Family, 1973; Splendour at Court: Renaissance Spectacle and the Theatre of Power, 1973; (with Colin Ford) An Early Victorian Album: the Hill-Adamson collection, 1974; Nicholas Hilliard, 1975; (contrib.) Spirit of the Age, 1975; The Cult of Elizabeth: Elizabethan Portraiture and Pageantry, 1977; And When Did You Last See Your Father?, 1978; The Renaissance Garden in England, 1979; (contrib.) The Garden, 1979; Britannia Triumphans: Inigo Jones, Rubens and Whitehall Palace, 1980; (introd.) Holbein, 1980; (contrib.) Designing for the Dancer, 1981; (jtly) The English Miniature, 1981; (with Julia Trevelyan Oman) The English Year, 1982; (contrib.) Pelican Guide to English Literature vol. 3, 1982; (with J. Murrell) Artists of the Tudor Court, 1983; The English Renaissance Miniature, 1983; (contrib.) Glyndebourne: a celebration, 1984; Art & Power, 1984; Strong Points, 1985; Henry, Prince of Wales and England's Lost Renaissance, 1986; (contrib.) For Veronica Wedgwood These, 1986; Creating Small Gardens, 1986; Gloriana, Portraits of Queen Elizabeth I, 1987; contributor to learned jls. *Recreations:* gardening, cooking, country life. *Address:* c/o Victoria and Albert Museum, South Kensington, SW7 2RL. *Clubs:* Garrick, Grillions.

STRONGE, Sir James Anselan Maxwell, 10th Bt *cr* 1803; *b* 17 July 1946; *s* of Maxwell Du Pré James Stronge (*d* 1973) (*g g s* of 2nd Bt) and Eileen Mary (*d* 1976), *d* of Rt Hon. Maurice Marcus McCausland, PC, Drenagh, Limavady, Co. Londonderry; *S* cousin, 1981. *Heir:* none. *Address:* Shannagh Camphill Community, Kilkeel, Co. Down; c/o Helen Allen-Morgan, Manor South, Bishopstone, Sussex BN25 2UD.

STROUD, Prof. (Charles) Eric, FRCP; Professor of Child Health, King's College School of Medicine and Dentistry (formerly King's College Hospital Medical School), and Director, Department of Child Health, since 1968; Paediatric Consultant to RAF, since 1976; *b* 15 May 1924; *s* of Frank Edmund and Lavinia May Stroud; *m* 1950, June, *d* of Harold Neep; one *s* two *d. Educ:* Cardiff High Sch. for Boys; Welsh National Sch. of Medicine. BSc 1945, MB, BCh 1948 (Wales); MRCP 1955, DCH 1955, FRCP 1968 (London). Sqdn Ldr, RAF, 1950–52. Med. Qual., 1948; Paediatric Registrar, Welsh Nat. Sch. of Med.; Sen. Registrar, Great Ormond Street Children's Hosp., 1957–61; Paediatrician, Uganda Govt, 1958–60; Asst to Dir, Dept of Child Health, Guy's Hosp., 1961–62; Cons. Paediatrician, King's Coll. Hosp., 1962–68. Med. Advr, Eastern Hemisphere, Variety Clubs Internat., 1985–; Hon. Med. Dir, Children Nationwide Med. Res. Fund. *Publications:* chapters in Textbook of Obstetrics, 1958; Childhealth in the Tropics, 1961; various articles in med. jls, mainly on sickle cell anaemia, nutrition and health of ethnic minorities. *Recreations:* bad golf, good fishing, cheap antiques, planning for retirement. *Address:* Variety Club Children's Hospital, King's College School of Medicine and Dentistry, Denmark Hill, SE5 8RX; 84 Copse Hill, Wimbledon, SW20. *T:* 01-947 1336.

STROUD, Derek H.; *see* Hammond-Stroud.

STROUD, Dorothy Nancy, MBE 1968; Assistant Curator, Sir John Soane's Museum, 1945–84; *b* London, 11 Jan. 1910; *o c* of late Nancy and Alfred Stroud, London. *Educ:* Claremont, Eastbourne; Edgbaston High Sch. On staff of: Country Life, 1930–41; National Monuments Record, 1941–45. Vice-Pres., Garden History Soc., 1982–; Mem., Historic Buildings Council, 1974–82. FSA 1951; Hon. RIBA, 1975. *Publications:* Capability Brown, 1950, new edn 1975; The Thurloe Estate, 1959; The Architecture of Sir John Soane, 1961; Humphry Repton, 1962; Henry Holland, 1966; George Dance, 1971; The South Kensington Estate of Henry Smith's Charity, 1975; Sir John Soane, Architect, 1984. *Address:* 24 Onslow Square, SW7 3NS.

STROUD, Prof. Eric; *see* Stroud, Prof. C. E.

STROUD, Ven. Ernest Charles Frederick; Archdeacon of Colchester, since 1983; *b* 20 May 1931; *s* of Charles Henry and Irene Doris Stroud; *m* 1959, Jeanne Marguerite Evans; two *d. Educ:* Merrywood Grammar School; Merchant Venturers' Technical College; St Chad's Coll., Univ. of Durham. BA (Hons Theology), Diploma in Theology. Esso Petroleum Co. Ltd, 1947–55. Deacon 1960, priest 1961, dio. Wakefield; Asst Curate, All Saints, S Kirby, Yorks, 1960–63; Priest-in-Charge, St Ninian, Whitby, 1963–66; Minister of Conventional District, and first Vicar, All Saints, Chelmsford, 1966–75; Vicar of St Margaret of Antioch, Leigh on Sea, 1976–83; Asst RD of Southend, 1976–79; RD of Hadleigh, 1979–83; Mem. General Synod, 1981–; Hon. Canon of Chelmsford, 1982–.

Publication: contrib. on ministry of healing to Christian. *Recreations:* travel, music, theatre. *Address:* 63 Powers Hall End, Witham, Essex. *T:* Witham 513130.

STROWGER, Gaston Jack, CBE 1976; Managing Director, Thorn Electrical Industries, 1970–79; Chairman: Hornby Hobbies, since 1981; Wiltminster Ltd, since 1981; Director, Harland Simon; *b* 8 Feb. 1916; *s* of Alfred Henry Strowger, Lowestoft boat-owner, and Lily Ellen Tripp; *m* 1939, Katherine Ellen Gilbert; two *s* one *d. Educ:* Lowestoft Grammar School. Joined London Electrical Supply Co., 1934; HM Forces, 1939–43. Joined TEI, as an Accountant, 1943; Group Chief Accountant, 1952; joined Tricity Finance Corp. as Dir, 1959; Exec. Dir, TEI, 1961; full Dir 1966; Financial Dir 1967; Dep. Chm., Tricity Finance Corp., 1968; Chm., Thorn-Ericsson, 1974–81. FBIM 1971. *Recreations:* gardening, bowling. *Address:* The Penthouse, 46 Maplin Close, Eversley Park Road, Winchmore Hill, N21 1NB.

STROYAN, Ronald Angus Ropner, QC 1972; **His Honour Judge Stroyan;** a Circuit Judge, since 1975; *b* 27 Nov. 1924; *e s* of Ronald S. Stroyan of Boreland, Killin; *m* 1st, 1952, Elisabeth Anna Grant (marr. diss. 1965), *y d* of Col J. P. Grant of Rothiemurchus; one *s* two *d*; 2nd, 1967, Jill Annette Johnston, *d* of late Sir Douglas Marshall; one *s* (and two step *s* two step *d*). *Educ:* Harrow School; Trinity College, Cambridge; BA(Hons). Served 1943–45 with The Black Watch (NW Europe); attd Argyll and Sutherland Highlanders, Palestine, 1945–47 (despatches); Captain; later with Black Watch TA. Barrister-at-Law, 1950, Inner Temple. Dep. Chm., North Riding QS, 1962–70, Chm., 1970–71; a Recorder of the Crown Court, 1972–75. Mem. Gen. Council of the Bar, 1963–67, 1969–73 and 1975. *Recreations:* shooting, stalking, fishing. *Address:* Chapel Cottage, Whashton, near Richmond, Yorks; Boreland, Killin, Perthshire. *T:* Killin 252. *Clubs:* Caledonian; Yorkshire (York).

STRUDWICK, Air Cdre Arthur Sidney Ronald, CB 1976; DFC 1945; Defence Liaison Officer, The Singer Co., Link-Miles Division, since 1976; *b* 16 April 1921; *s* of Percival and Mary Strudwick; *m* 1941, Cissily (*d* 1983); two *s* one *d. Educ:* Guildford Tech. Coll.; RAF Colls. Joined RAF 1940; War Service as Fighter Pilot, 1941–43; POW Germany, 1944; Test Flying, Canada, 1948–50; CO No 98 Sqdn, 1951–53; Staff Coll., Camberley, 1954; Commanded Jt Services Trials Unit, Woomera, 1956–59; JSSC, 1959–60; MoD Planning Staff, 1960–62; Dir of Plans, Far East, 1962–64; Commanded RAF Leuchars, 1965–67; Air Cdre Plans, Strategic Comd, 1967–69; IDC 1969; Dir of Flying (R&D), MoD PE, 1970–73; AOC Central Tactics and Trials Orgn, 1973–76, retired 1976. *Recreations:* golf and gardening. *Address:* 37 Upper Brighton Road, Worthing, Sussex. *Club:* Royal Air Force.

STRUDWICK, John Philip, CBE 1970; CVO 1973; Assistant Secretary, Board of Inland Revenue, 1950–74, retired; *b* 30 May 1914; *s* of Philip Strudwick, FRICS and Marjorie Strudwick (*née* Clements); *m* 1942, Elizabeth Marion Stemson; two *s* three *d* (and one *d* decd). *Educ:* Eltham Coll.; St John's Coll., Cambridge. BA 1936, MA 1973. Asst Principal, Bd of Inland Revenue, 1937; Principal 1942. Sec., Millard Tucker Cttee on Taxation Treatment of Provisions for Retirement, 1951–53. KSG 1977. *Recreations:* music, gardening, voluntary social work (Chm. of Univ. of Sussex Catholic Chaplaincy Assoc., 1972–76 and Edenbridge Volunteer Bureau, 1978–82). *Address:* The Moat, Cowden, Edenbridge, Kent TN8 7DP. *T:* Cowden 441.

STRUTT, family name of **Barons Belper** and **Rayleigh.**

STRUTT, Sir Nigel (Edward), Kt 1972; TD; DL; Chairman, Strutt & Parker (Farms) Ltd; Managing Director, Lord Rayleigh's Farms Inc.; *b* 18 Jan. 1916; *yr s* of late Edward Jolliffe Strutt. *Educ:* Winchester; Wye Agricultural College (Fellow, 1970). Essex Yeomanry (Major), 1937–56. Member: Eastern Electricity Bd, 1964–76; Agricultural Advisory Council, 1963– (Chm. 1969–73; Chm., Adv. Council for Agriculture and Horticulture, 1973–80); NEDC for Agriculture, 1967–82. President: Country Landowners' Association, 1967–69; British Friesian Cattle Soc., 1974–75; Royal Agricultural Soc. of England, 1982–83. Master, Farmers' Co., 1976–77. DL Essex 1954; High Sheriff of Essex, 1966. Hon. FRASE, 1971. Hon. DSc Cranfield, 1979; DU Essex, 1981. Massey Ferguson Award, 1976. Von Thünen Gold Medal, Kiel Univ., 1974. *Recreations:* shooting, ski-ing. *Address:* Sparrows, Terling, Essex. *T:* Terling 213. *Clubs:* Brooks's, Farmers'.

STUART, family name of **Earl Castle Stewart, Earl of Moray** and **Viscount Stuart of Findhorn.**

STUART; *see* Crichton-Stuart, family name of Marquess of Bute.

STUART, Viscount; Andrew Richard Charles Stuart; *b* 7 Oct. 1953; *s* and *heir* of 8th Earl Castle Stewart, *qv; m* 1973, Annie Le Poulain, St Malo, France; one *d. Educ:* Wynstones, Glos; Millfield, Som. *Recreation:* flying. *Address:* Combe Hayes Farm, Buckerell, near Honiton, Devon.

STUART OF FINDHORN, 2nd Viscount *cr* 1959; **David Randolph Moray Stuart;** *b* 20 June 1924; *s* of 1st Viscount Stuart of Findhorn, PC, CH, MVO, MC, and Lady Rachel Cavendish, OBE (*d* 1977), 4th *d* of 9th Duke of Devonshire; *S* father, 1971; *m* 1st, 1945, Grizel Mary Wilfreda (*d* 1948), *d* of D. T. Fyfe and *widow* of Michael Gillilan; one *s*; 2nd, 1951, Marian Emelia (marr. diss. 1979), *d* of Gerald H. Wilson; one *s* three *d*; 3rd, 1979, Margaret Anne, *yr d* of Comdr Peter Du Cane, CBE, RN. *Educ:* Eton; Cirencester Agricultural College. FRICS. Partner, Bernard Thorpe & Partners. *Heir:* *s* Hon. James Dominic Stuart [*b* 25 March 1948; *m* 1979, Yvonne Lucienne, *d* of Edgar Després, Ottawa]. *Address:* 63 Winchenden Road, SW6. *T:* 01–736 8760. *Clubs:* White's, Buck's.

STUART, Alexander John Mackenzie; *see* Mackenzie Stuart, Hon. Lord.

STUART, Andrew Christopher, CMG 1979; CPM 1961; Principal, United World College of the Atlantic, since 1983; *b* 30 Nov. 1928; *s* of late Rt Rev. Cyril Edgar Stuart and Mary Summerhayes; *m* 1959, Patricia Kelly; two *s* one *d. Educ:* Bryanston; Clare Coll., Cambridge (MA). Royal Navy, 1947–49. Colonial Admin. Service, Uganda, 1953; retd from HMOCS as Judicial Adviser, 1965. Called to Bar, Middle Temple, 1965. Entered HM Diplomatic Service, 1965; 1st Sec. and Head of Chancery, Helsinki, 1968; Asst, S Asian Dept, FCO, 1971; Head of Hong Kong and Indian Ocean Dept, FCO, 1972–75; Counsellor, Jakarta, 1975–78; British Resident Comr, New Hebrides, 1978–80; Ambassador to Finland, 1980–83. *Recreations:* sailing, gliding, squash, diving, mountaineering. *Address:* United World College of the Atlantic, Llantwit Major, South Glamorgan CF6 9WF. *Clubs:* United Oxford & Cambridge University, Alpine; Jesters; Royal Naval Sailing Association.

STUART, Duncan; HM Diplomatic Service; Counsellor, British Embassy, Washington, since 1986; *b* 1 July 1934; *s* of Ian Cameron Stuart and Patricia Forbes; *m* 1961, Leonore Luise Liederwald; one *s* one *d. Educ:* Rugby Sch.; Brasenose Coll., Oxford (MA). Served 1st Bn Oxfordshire and Bucks LI, 1955–57 (2nd Lieut). Joined Foreign, later Diplomatic, Service, 1959; Office of Political Advr, Berlin, 1960–61; FO, 1961–64; Helsinki, 1964–66; Head of Chancery, Dar-es-Salaam, 1966–69; FCO, 1969–70; Helsinki, 1970–74; FCO, 1974–80; Bonn, 1980–83; FCO, 1983–86. *Address:* c/o Foreign and

Commonwealth Office, SW1A 2AH. *Clubs:* United Oxford & Cambridge University, MCC.

STUART, Francis; *b* Queensland, Australia, 1902; *s* of Henry and Elizabeth Stuart, Co. Antrim, Ireland; *m* 1st, 1920, Iseult Gonne; one *s* one *d*; 2nd, 1954, Gertrude Meiszner. *Educ:* Rugby. First book, poems, which received an American prize and also award of the Royal Irish Academy, published at age of 21; first novel published in 1931 at age of 29; contributor to various newspapers and periodicals. *Publications: novels:* Women and God, 1931; Pigeon Irish, 1932; The Coloured Dome, 1933; Try the Sky, 1933; Glory, 1934; The Pillar of Cloud, 1948; Redemption, 1949; The Flowering Cross, 1950; Good Friday's Daughter, 1951; The Chariot, 1953; The Pilgrimage, 1955; Victors and Vanquished, 1958; Angels of Providence, 1959; Black List, Section H, 1971; Memorial, 1973; A Hole in the Head, 1977; The High Consistory, 1980; Faillandia, 1985; *short stories:* Selected Stories, 1983; *poetry:* We Have Kept the Faith; *autobiography:* Things to Live For, 1936. *Recreations:* horse-racing, golf. *Address:* 2 Highfield Park, Dublin 14, Ireland.

STUART, Rev. Canon Herbert James, CB 1983; Rector of Cherbury, since 1983; Canon Emeritus of Lincoln Cathedral, since 1983 (Canon, 1980–83); *b* 16 Nov. 1926; *s* of Joseph and Jane Stuart; *m* 1955, Adrienne Le Fanu; two *s* one *d*. *Educ:* Mountjoy School, Dublin; Trinity Coll., Dublin (BA Hons, MA). Priest, 1950; served in Church of Ireland, 1950–55; Chaplain, RAF, 1955; Asst Chaplain-in-Chief, RAF, 1973; Chaplain-in-Chief and Archdeacon, RAF, 1980–83; QHC, 1978–83. *Recreations:* gardening, travel, books. *Address:* The Rectory, Longworth, Abingdon, Oxfordshire OX13 5DX. *T:* Longworth 820213. *Club:* Royal Air Force.

STUART, Sir (James) Keith, Kt 1986; Chairman, Associated British Ports Holdings PLC, since 1983; *b* 4 March 1940; *s* of James and Marjorie Stuart; *m* 1966, Kathleen Anne Pinder (*née* Woodman); three *s* one *d*. *Educ:* King George V School, Southport; Gonville and Caius College, Cambridge (MA). FCIT, CBIM, FRSA. District Manager, South Western Electricity Bd, 1970–72; British Transport Docks Board: Sec., 1972–75; Gen. Manager, 1976–77; Man. Dir, 1977–82; Dep. Chm., 1980–82; Chm., 1982–83. Dir, Internat. Assoc. of Ports and Harbors, 1983; Vice-Pres., Cttee on Internat. Port Develt, 1985– (Chm., 1979–85); Pres., Inst. of Freight Forwarders, 1983–84. Dir, Royal Ordnance Factories, 1983–85. Chartered Inst. of Transport: Mem. Council, 1979–; Vice-Pres., 1982–83; Pres., 1985–86. Freeman, Clockmakers' Co., 1985–. *Recreation:* music. *Address:* Associated British Ports Holdings PLC, 150 Holborn, EC1N 2LR. *T:* 01–430 1177. *Clubs:* Brooks's, United Oxford & Cambridge University.

STUART, Prof. John Trevor, FRS 1974; Professor of Theoretical Fluid Mechanics since 1966, Head of Mathematics Department, 1974–79 and 1983–86, Imperial College of Science and Technology, University of London; *b* 28 Jan. 1929; *s* of Horace Stuart and Phyllis Emily Stuart (*née* Potter); *m* 1957, Christine Mary (*née* Tracy); two *s* one *d*. *Educ:* Gateway Sch., Leicester; Imperial Coll., London. BSc 1949, PhD 1951. Aerodynamics Div., Nat. Physical Lab., Teddington, 1951–66; Sen. Principal Scientific Officer (Special Merit), 1961. Vis. Lectr, Dept of Maths, MIT, 1956–57; Vis. Prof. of Maths, MIT, 1965–66; Vis. Prof. of Theoretical Fluid Mechanics, Brown Univ., 1978–; Hon. Prof., Tianjin Univ., China, 1983–. Mem. Council, Royal Soc., 1982–84; Chm., Mathematics Cttee, SERC, 1985–. 1st Stewartson Meml Lectr, Long Beach, Calif., 1985; 1st DiPrima Meml Lectr, Troy, NY, 1985; Ludwig Prandtl Meml Lectr, Dortmund, 1986. Hon. DSc Brown Univ., 1986. Senior Whitehead Prize, London Mathematical Soc., 1984. *Publications:* (contrib.) Laminar Boundary Layers, ed L. Rosenhead, 1963; articles in Proc. Royal Soc., Phil. Trans Royal Soc., Jl Fluid Mech., Proc. 10th Int. Cong. Appl. Mech., Jl Lub. Tech. (ASME). *Recreations:* theatre, music, gardening, reading, do-it-yourself, ornithology. *Address:* Mathematics Department, Imperial College, SW7 2AZ. *T:* 01–589 5111; 3 Steeple Close, Wimbledon, SW19 5AD. *T:* 01–946 7019.

STUART, Joseph B.; *see* Burnett-Stuart.

STUART, Sir Keith; *see* Stuart, Sir J. K.

STUART, Prof. Sir Kenneth (Lamonte), Kt 1977; MD, FRCP, FRCPE, FACP, DTM&H; Consultant Adviser, The Wellcome Trust, since 1984; *b* 16 June 1920; *s* of Egbert and Louise Stuart; *m* 1958, Barbara Cecille Ashby; one *s* two *d*. *Educ:* Harrison Coll., Barbados; Queen's Univ., Belfast (MB, BCh, BAO 1948). Consultant Physician, University Coll. Hospital of the West Indies, 1954–76; University of the West Indies: Prof. of Medicine, 1966–76; Dean, Medical Faculty, 1969–71; Head, Dept of Medicine, 1972–76; Mem. Council, 1971–76; Medical Adviser, Commonwealth Secretariat, 1976–84. Rockefeller Foundation Fellow in Cardiology, Massachusetts Gen. Hosp., Boston, 1956–57; Wellcome Foundation Research Fellow, Harvard Univ., Boston, 1960–61; Consultant to WHO on Cardiovascular Disorders, 1969–. Chm., Court of Governors, LSHTM, 1982–; Mem., Court of Governors, Internat. Develt Res. Centre of Canada, 1985–. *Publications:* articles on hepatic and cardiovascular disorders in medical journals. *Recreations:* tennis, music. *Address:* The Wellcome Trust, 1 Park Square West, NW1 4LJ.

STUART, Malcolm Moncrieff, CIE 1947; OBE 1944; ICS retired; Recorder to Council of Lord High Commissioners to the General Assembly of the Church of Scotland; *b* 21 May 1903; *s* of George Malcolm Stuart and Mary Elizabeth Scott Moncrieff; *m* 1928, Grizel Graham Balfour Paul; one *s* one *d*. *Educ:* Sedbergh; St John's College, Cambridge; Queen's Coll., Oxford. Entered ICS 1927; served as Dist Magistrate of various districts and was on special duty for Govt Estates, 1938; during War of 1939–45 was mostly Dist Magistrate of Chittagong and also Comr there. Served in Pakistan until 1950, as additional Member, Board of Revenue. Hon. MA Edinburgh, 1978. *Publications:* Bob Potts at Murshedabad (Bengal Past and Present), 1933; Handbook to Bengal Records, 1948; and other stories. *Recreations:* golf, shooting, bridge. *Address:* Old Manse, Pilmuir, Haddington, East Lothian. *Clubs:* New (Edinburgh); Muirfield Golf.

STUART, Michael Francis Harvey; Treasury Adviser, UK Mission to the United Nations, 1974–82; *b* 3 Oct. 1926; *s* of late Willoughby Stuart and Ethel Candy; *m* 1961, Ruth Tennyson-d'Eyncourt; one *s* one *d*. *Educ:* Harrow; Magdalen Coll., Oxford. Air Min., 1950–65; DEA, 1965–69; HM Treasury, 1969–74. Mem., UN Adv. Cttee on Administrative and Budgetary Questions, 1975–80. *Recreations:* music, tennis. *Address:* Bourne House, Chertsey Road, Chobham, Woking, Surrey. *T:* Chobham 7954.

STUART, Nicholas Willoughby; Accountant General, Department of Education and Science, since 1984; *b* 2 Oct. 1942; *s* of Douglas Willoughby Stuart and Margaret Eileen Stuart; *m* 1st, 1963, Sarah Mustard (marr. diss. 1974); one *d* (one *s* decd); 2nd, 1975, Susan Jane Fletcher; one *d*. *Educ:* Harrow Sch.; Christ Church Coll., Oxford (MA). Asst Principal, DES, 1964–68; Private Sec. to Minister for the Arts, 1968–69; Principal, DES, 1969–73; Private Secretary to: Head of the Civil Service, 1973; Prime Minister, 1973–76; Asst Sec., DES, 1976–78; Advr, Cabinet of Pres. of EEC, 1978–80; Under Sec., DES, 1981–. *Recreation:* collecting Tunbridgeware. *Address:* 15 Brooksville Avenue, Queen's Park, NW6. *T:* 01–968 7567.

STUART, Sir Phillip (Luttrell), 9th Bt *cr* 1660; late F/O RCAF; President, Agassiz Industries Ltd; *b* 7 September 1937; *s* of late Luttrell Hamilton Stuart and late Irene Ethel Jackman; *S* uncle, Sir Houlton John Stuart, 8th Bt, 1959; *m* 1st, 1962, Marlene Rose Muth (marr. diss. 1968); two *d*; 2nd, 1969, Beverley Clare Pieri; one *s* one *d*. *Educ:* Vancouver. Enlisted RCAF, Nov. 1955; commnd FO (1957–62). *Heir:* *s* Geoffrey Phillip Stuart, *b* 5 July 1973. *Address:* 3 Windermere Bay, Winnipeg, Manitoba R3T 1B1, Canada.

[*But his name does not, at the time of going to press, appear on the official Roll of Baronets.*]

STUART-COLE, James; DL; Chairman, Merseyside Region, Co-operative Retail Services Ltd, since 1974; *b* 6 March 1916; *s* of Charles Albert Stuart-Cole and Gertrude Mary Stuart-Cole; *m* 1937, Margaret Evelyn Robb; one *s* two *d*. *Educ:* Birley Street Central Sch., Manchester. Engr, 1930–55; Political Organiser, Labour Party, 1955–60; Political Sec., Co-operative Soc., 1960–81. Mem. Bd, Merseyside Development Corp, 1981–. Merseyside County Council: Mem., 1973–86; Leader, 1981–82; Chm., 1983–84. DL Merseyside, 1983. *Recreations:* sport, grandchildren. *Address:* 85 Kylemore Drive, Pensby, Wirral, Merseyside L61 6XZ. *T:* 051–342 6180.

STUART-FORBES, Sir Charles Edward; *see* Forbes.

STUART-HARRIS, Sir Charles (Herbert), Kt 1970; CBE 1961; MD; FRCP; Fogarty Scholar-in-Residence, National Institutes of Health, Bethesda, Maryland, USA, 1979–80; Postgraduate Dean of Medicine, University of Sheffield, 1972–77, Professor of Medicine, 1946–72, now Emeritus Professor; Physician, United Sheffield Hospitals, 1946–74; *b* 12 July 1909; *s* of late Dr and Mrs Herbert Harris, Birmingham; *m* 1937, Marjorie, *y d* of late Mr and Mrs F. Robinson, Dulwich; two *s* one *d*. *Educ:* King Edward's School, Birmingham; St Bartholomew's Hospital Medical School. MB, BS London 1931 (Gold Medal); MD 1933 (Gold Medal); FRCP 1944. House-Physician and Demonstrator in Pathology, St Bartholomew's Hosp.; First Asst, Dept of Medicine, Brit. Postgrad. Medical Sch., 1935; Sir Henry Royce Research Fellow. Univ. of London, 1935; Foulerton Research Fellow, Royal Society, 1938. War Service, 1939–46; Specialist Pathologist Comdg Mobile Bacteriological, Command and Field Laboratories; Colonel RAMC, 1945. Goulstonian Lectr, Royal College of Physicians, 1945; Visiting Prof. of Medicine, Albany Medical Coll., New York, 1953; Sir Arthur Sims Commonwealth Travelling Prof., 1962. Vis. Professor of Medicine: Vanderbilt Univ., Tennessee, 1961; Univ. of Southern California, Los Angeles, 1962; Croonian Lectr, Royal Coll. of Physicians, 1962; Henry Cohen Lectr, Hebrew Univ. of Jerusalem, 1966; Waring Prof., Univ. of Colorado and Stanford Univ., Calif., 1967; Harveian Orator, RCP, 1974. Member: MRC, 1957–61; Public Health Lab. Service Bd, 1954–66; UGC 1968–77 (Chm., Med. Sub-Cttee, 1973–77); UPGC, Hong Kong, 1978–84. Pres., Assoc. of Physicians of GB and Ireland, 1971. Hon. Member: Assoc. of Amer. Physicians; Infectious Diseases Soc. of Amer. Hon. DSc: Hull, 1973; Sheffield, 1978. *Publications:* (co-author) Chronic bronchitis emphysema and cor pulmonale, 1957; Influenza and other virus infections of the respiratory tract, 1965; (co-author) Virus and Rickettsial Diseases, 1967; (co-author) Influenza—the Viruses and the Disease, 1976; papers in med. and scientific jls on influenza, typhus and bronchitis. *Recreation:* music. *Address:* 28 Whitworth Road, Sheffield S10 3HD. *T:* Sheffield 301200.

STUART-MENTETH, Sir James; *see* Menteth.

STUART-MOORE, Michael; a Recorder of the Crown Court, since 1985; *b* 7 July 1944; *s* of (Kenneth) Basil Moore and Marjorie (Elizabeth) Moore; *m* 1973, Katherine Ann, *d* of William and Ruth Scott; one *s* one *d*. *Educ:* Cranleigh School. Called to the Bar, Middle Temple, 1966. *Recreations:* cine photography, travel to outlandish places, music, tennis. *Address:* 1 Hare Court, Temple, EC4Y 7BE. *T:* 01–353 5324.

STUART-PAUL, Air Vice-Marshal Ronald Ian, MBE 1967; Director General, Saudi Export Project, since 1985; *b* 7 Nov. 1934; *s* of Dr J. G. Stuart-Paul and Mary (*née* McDonald); *m* 1963, Priscilla Frances (*née* Kay); one *s* one *d*. *Educ:* Dollar Acad.; RAF Coll., Cranwell. Served 14, 19, 56 and 92 Sqns and 11 and 12 Groups, 1957–73; Defence Attaché, Saudi Arabia, 1974–75; Stn Comdr, RAF Lossiemouth, 1976–78; RCDS, 1979; Dep. Comdr, NAEW Force, SHAPE, 1980–82; Dir of Ops Air Defence, RAF, 1982–83; AO Training, RAF Support Command, 1984–85. *Recreations:* golf, campanology, sailing, rug-making. *Address:* 27 Church Way, Little Stukeley, Huntingdon, Cambs PE17 5BQ. *Club:* Royal Air Force.

STUART-SHAW, Max, CBE 1963; Executive Director, Olympic Airways, 1969–71; *b* 20 Dec. 1912; *e s* of Herman and Anne Louise Stuart-Shaw; *m* 1967, Janna Job, *d* of C. W. Howard. *Educ:* Belmont School, Sussex; St Paul's, London. Imperial Airways/BOAC, 1931–46; Aer Lingus Irish Airlines; Traffic Manager, Commercial Manager, Asst Gen. Manager, 1947–57; Chief Exec. and Gen. Manager Central African Airways, Salisbury, Rhodesia, 1958–65; Man. Dir, BUA, 1966–67; Vice-Chairman, British United Airways, 1967–68. FCIT. *Recreation:* air transport. *Address:* c/o Barclays Bank, 160 Piccadilly, W1A 2AB. *Club:* Harare (Zimbabwe).

STUART-SMITH, James, CB 1986; Judge Advocate General, since 1984 (Vice Judge Advocate General, 1979–84); a Recorder, since 1985; *b* 13 Sept. 1919; *s* of James Stuart-Smith and Florence Emma (*née* Armfield); *m* 1957, Jean Marie Therese Young Groundsell, *d* of Hubert Young Groundsell, Newport, IoW; one *s* one *d*. *Educ:* Brighton Coll.; London Hospital. Medical student, 1938. Served War of 1939–45: commnd KRRC, 1940; served ME and Italy, and staff appointments in UK; demobilised 1947. Called to Bar, Middle Temple, 1948; practised in London, 1948–55; Legal Asst, JAG's Office, 1955; Dep. Judge Advocate, 1957; Asst Judge Advocate General, 1968; Dep. Judge Advocate, Middle East Comd (Aden), 1964–65; Dep. Judge Advocate General, British Forces Germany, 1976–79. Pres., Internat. Soc. for Military Law and the Law of War, 1985– (Vice-Pres., 1979–85). *Publications:* contribs to Internat. Soc. for Military Law and Law of War Rev. and Law Qly Rev., on history and practice of British military law. *Recreations:* composing letters, lawn tennis, mowing lawns. *Address:* The Firs, Copthorne, Sussex RH10 4HH. *T:* Copthorne 712395. *Club:* Royal Air Force.

STUART-SMITH, Hon. Sir Murray, Kt 1981; **Hon. Mr Justice Stuart-Smith;** Judge of the High Court of Justice, Queen's Bench Division, since 1981; *b* 18 Nov. 1927; *s* of Edward Stuart-Smith and Doris Mary Laughland; *m* 1953, Joan Elizabeth Mary Motion, BA, JP (High Sheriff of Herts, 1983); three *s* three *d*. *Educ:* Radley; Corpus Christi Coll., Cambridge (Foundn Scholar; 1st Cl. Hons Law Tripos, Pts I and II; 1st Cl. Hons LLM; MA). Commnd 5th Royal Inniskilling Dragoon Guards, 1947. Called to the Bar, Gray's Inn, 1952 (Atkin Scholar), Bencher 1977; QC 1970; a Recorder of the Crown Court, 1972–81; Presiding Judge, Western Circuit, 1983–87. Jt Inspector into Grays Bldg Soc., 1979. Mem., Criminal Injuries Compensation Bd, 1980–81. *Recreations:* playing 'cello, shooting, building, playing bridge. *Address:* Royal Courts of Justice, Strand, WC2.

STUART TAYLOR, Sir Nicholas (Richard), 4th Bt *cr* 1917; *b* 14 Jan. 1952; *s* of Sir Richard Laurence Stuart Taylor, 3rd Bt, and of Iris Mary, *d* of Rev. Edwin John Gargery; *S* father, 1978; *m* 1984, Malvena Elizabeth Sullivan, BSc, MB, BS, FFARCS, *d* of Daniel David Charles Sullivan and late Kathleen Sullivan. *Educ:* Bradfield. Admitted Solicitor, 1977. *Recreation:* ski-ing. *Heir:* none. *Address:* White Lodge, Hambrook, Chichester, West Sussex. *Club:* Ski Club of Great Britain.

STUART-WHITE, Christopher Stuart; His Honour Judge Stuart-White; a Circuit Judge, since 1978; *b* 18 Dec. 1933; *s* of Reginald Stuart-White and Catherine Mary Wigmore Stuart-White (*née* Higginson); *m* 1957, Pamela (*née* Grant); one *s* two *d*. *Educ:* Winchester; Trinity Coll., Oxford (BA). Called to Bar, Inner Temple, 1957. Practising Barrister on the Midland and Oxford Circuit, 1958–78; a Recorder of the Crown Court, 1974–78. *Recreation:* gardening.

STUBBLEFIELD, Sir (Cyril) James, Kt 1965; FRS 1944; FGS; FZS; DSc (London); ARCS; formerly Director, Geological Survey of Great Britain and Museum of Practical Geology, 1960–66; Director, Geological Survey in Northern Ireland, 1960–66; *b* Cambridge, 6 Sept. 1901; *s* of James Stubblefield; *m* 1932, Muriel Elizabeth, *d* of L. R. Yakchee; two *s*. *Educ:* The Perse Sch.; Chelsea Polytechnic; Royal College of Science, London (Royal Scholar); London Univ. Geology Scholar, 1921. Demonstrator in Geology, Imperial College of Science and Technology, 1923–28; Warden of pioneer Imperial Coll. Hostel, 1926–28. Apptd Geological Survey as Geologist, 1928; Chief Palæontologist, 1947–53; Asst Director, 1953–60. Mem., Anglo-French Commn of Surveillance, Channel Tunnel, 1964–67. Pres. Geological Soc. of London, 1958–60; Bigsby Medallist, 1941; Murchison Medallist, 1955. Sec. of Palæontographical Soc., 1934–48; Pres., 1966–71, Hon. Mem., 1974. Member Council Brit. Assoc. for Advancement of Science, 1946–52, 1958–63; Pres. Section C (Geology), Oxford, 1954. Pres. Cambrian Subcommn, Internat. Geol. Union's Commn on Stratigraphy, 1964–72. Pres. Internat. Congress Carboniferous Stratigraphy and Geology, 6th Session, Sheffield, 1967, and Editor, 4 vol. Compte rendu, 1968–72. Vice-Pres. International Paleontological Union, 1948–56. Corresp. Paleont. Soc. (USA), 1950–; Corresp. Mem. Geol. Soc. Stockholm, 1952–; Senckenbergische Naturforschende Gesellschaft, 1957–. Member: Gov. Body (later Council), Chelsea Coll. of Science and Technology, 1958–82; Council, Royal Soc., 1960–62. Hon. Fellow: Pal. Soc. India, 1961–; Chelsea Coll., 1985; KCL, 1985–. Fellow Imperial Coll., 1962–; Hon. Member: Geologists' Assoc., 1973–; Liverpool Geol. Soc., 1960–; For. Corr., Geol. Soc., France, 1963–, For. Vice-Pres., 1966. Hon. DSc Southampton, 1965. *Publications:* papers in journals, on Palæozoic fossils and rocks; also contributions to: Geological Survey Memoirs; Trilobita, Zoological Record, 1938–51, 1965–77. Joint Editor of the Handbook of the Geology of Great Britain, 1929; Reviser, Introduction to Palæontology (A. Morley Davies), 3rd edn, 1961. *Address:* 35 Kent Avenue, Ealing, W13 8BE. *T:* 01–997 5051.

STUBBS, Sir James (Wilfrid), KCVO 1979; TD 1946; Grand Secretary, United Grand Lodge of England, 1958–80; *b* 13 Aug. 1910; *s* of Rev. Wilfrid Thomas Stubbs and Muriel Elizabeth (*née* Pope); *m* Richenda Katherine Theodora Streatfeild; one *s* (and one *d* decd). *Educ:* Charterhouse (Junior and Senior Scholar); Brasenose Coll., Oxford (Scholar; MA). Assistant Master, St Paul's Sch., London, 1934–46. Served War, Royal Signals, 1941–46: Captain 1941, Major 1945, Lt-Col 1946 (2nd Lieut, SR, 1932, Lieut 1935). Asst Grand Sec., United Grand Lodge of England, 1948–54; Dep. Grand Sec., 1954–58. *Publications:* Grand Lodge 1717–1967, 1967; The Four Corners, 1983; Freemasonry in My Life, 1985. *Recreations:* family history, travel. *Address:* 5 Pensioners Court, The Charterhouse, EC1. *T:* 01–253 1982. *Club:* Athenæum.

STUBBS, John F. A. H.; *see* Heath-Stubbs.

STUBBS, Thomas, OBE 1980; HM Diplomatic Service, retired; *b* 12 July 1926; *s* of Thomas Stubbs and Lillian Marguerite (*née* Rumball, formerly Bell); *m* 1951, Dorothy Miller; one *s* one *d*. *Educ:* Heaton Tech. Sch., Newcastle upon Tyne. Served in Army, 1944–48. Joined Min. of Nat. Insce, later Min. of Pensions and Nat. Insce, 1948; transf. to CRO, 1960; New Delhi, 1962; CRO, 1964; Wellington, NZ, 1965; Vice-Consul, Düsseldorf, 1970; seconded to BOTB, 1974; First Sec. (Commercial) and Consul, Addis Ababa, 1977; Consul, Hannover, 1980; Dep. High Comr, Madras, 1983–86. *Recreations:* reading, golf. *Address:* 17 Chester Close, Ashford Common, Middlesex TW15 1PH. *Club:* Madras (Madras).

STUBBS, William Frederick, CMG 1955; CBE 1952 (OBE 1941); HMOCS, retired; *b* 19 June 1902; *e s* of late Lawrence Morley Stubbs, CSI, CIE, ICS (retd); *m* 1929, Eileen Mary (*d* 1963), *y d* of late Sir W. E. Stanford, KBE, CB, CMG, Rondebosch, S Africa; one *d*. *Educ:* Winchester, Joined British S Africa Police, S Rhodesia, 1921; N Rhodesia Police on transfer, 1924; Colonial Administrative Service, Northern Rhodesia, 1926; Labour Comr, 1944–48; Provincial Comr, 1949; acted as Secretary for Native Affairs, 1951 and 1953; Secretary for Native Affairs, 1954–57; *Ex-officio* member of Executive and Legislative Councils (Speaker, Legislative Council, and Chm. Public Service Commn Somaliland Protectorate, 1960, until Union with Somalia). Associate Commonwealth Parliamentary Association. *Address:* Nash Barn, Marnhull, Dorset. *Club:* Royal Commonwealth Society.

STUBBS, William Frederick, QC 1978; *b* 27 Nov. 1934; *s* of William John Stubbs and Winifred Hilda (*née* Johnson); *m* 1961, Anne Katharine (*d* 1966), *d* of late Prof. W. K. C. Guthrie, FBA; one *s* one *d*. *Educ:* The High Sch., Newcastle-under-Lyme, Staffs; Gonville and Caius Coll., Cambridge; Harvard Law Sch. Open Minor Scholar in Nat. Sci., Gonville and Caius Coll., 1951; Student, Gray's Inn, 1953; 1st Cl. Hons Law Tripos Pt I, and George Long Prize for Roman Law, Cambridge, 1954; Major Scholar, Gonville and Caius Coll., 1954; 1st Cl. Hons with Distinction Law Tripos Pt II, Cambridge, 1955; LLB 1st Cl. Hons with Dist., and Chancellor's Medal for English Law, Cambridge, 1956; Tapp Post-Grad. Law Scholar, Gonville and Caius Coll., 1956 (also awarded Schuldham Plate); Joseph Hodges Choate Meml Fellow, Harvard Coll., 1957; Bar Final Exam., 2nd Cl. Hons Div. 1, 1957; Holker Sen. Scholar and Macaskie Scholar, Gray's Inn, 1957; called to the Bar, Gray's Inn, 1957. *Recreations:* reading, walking, natural history. *Address:* 24 Old Buildings, Lincoln's Inn, WC2A 3UJ. *T:* 01–242 5532; 3 Atherton Drive, SW19 5LB. *T:* 01–947 3986. *Club:* MCC.

STUBBS, William Hamilton; Education Officer and Chief Executive, Inner London Education Authority, since 1982; *b* 5 Nov. 1937; *s* of Joseph Stubbs and Mary Stubbs (*née* McNicol); *m* 1963, Marie Margaret Pierce; three *d*. *Educ:* Workington Grammar Sch.; St Aloysius Coll., Glasgow; Glasgow Univ. (BSc, PhD). Res. Associate, Univ. of Arizona, 1963–64; with Shell Oil Co., San Francisco, 1964–67; teaching, 1967–72; Asst Dir of Educn, Carlisle, 1972–74; Asst Dir of Educn, 1974–76, Second Dep. Dir of Educn, 1976–77, Cumbria; Second Dep. Educn Officer, 1977–79, Dir of Educn (Schools), 1979–82, ILEA. Mem, Nat. Adv. Body for Local Authy Higher Educn; Advr, AMA and Council of Local Educn Authorities. *Address:* 122 Cromwell Tower, Barbican, EC2.

STÜCKLEN, Richard; Grosskreuz des Verdienstordens der Bundesrepublik Deutschland; Bayerischer Verdienstorden; Vice-President of the Bundestag, Federal Republic of Germany, since 1983 (President, 1979–83); *b* 20 Aug. 1916; *s* of Georg Stücklen and Mathilde (*née* Bach); *m* 1943, Ruth Stücklen (*née* Geissler); one *s* one *d*. *Educ:* primary sch.; technical sch.; engineering sch. Industrial Dept Manager and Manager in family business, 1945–49. Mem. of Bundestag, 1949–; Dep. Chm., CDU/Christian Social Union and Parly Leader, Christian Social Union, 1953–57 and 1967–76; Federal Minister of Posts and Telegraphs, 1957–66; Vice-Pres. of Bundestag, 1976–79. *Publications:* Bundestagsreden und Zeitdokumente, 1979; and others. *Recreations:* skating, chess, soccer. *Address:* Bundeshaus, 5300 Bonn, Germany. *T:* Bonn 16 29 12. *Club:* Lions.

STUCLEY, Sir Hugh (George Coplestone Bampfylde), 6th Bt *cr* 1859; Lieut Royal Horse Guards, retired; *b* 8 Jan. 1945; *s* of Major Sir Dennis Frederic Bankes Stucley, 5th Bt, and of Hon. Sheila Bampfylde, *o d* of 4th Baron Poltimore; *S* father, 1983; *m* 1969, Angela Caroline, *e d* of Richard Charles Robertson Toller, MC, Theale, Berks; two *s* two *d*. *Educ:* Milton Abbey School; Royal Agricultural College, Cirencester. *Heir:* *s* George Dennis Bampfylde Stucley, *b* 26 Dec. 1970. *Address:* Affeton Castle, Worlington, Crediton, Devon. *Clubs:* Cavalry and Guards, Sloane.

STUCLEY, John Humphrey Albert, DSC 1945; **His Honour Judge Stucley;** a Circuit Judge, since 1974; *b* 12 July 1916; 2nd *s* of Sir Hugh Stucley, 4th Bt, Affeton Castle, Devon; *m* 1941, Natalia, *d* of Don Alberto Jiménez, CBE and Natalia Cossío de Jiménez; no *c*. *Educ:* RN Colls, Dartmouth and Greenwich. Cadet, RN, 1930; served China, Mediterranean and Home stns and throughout War of 1939–45; Lt-Comdr 1945. Called to Bar, Middle Temple, 1957. A Recorder of the Crown Court, 1972–74. Dep. Chm., SE England Agricultural Land Tribunal, 1971. *Publications:* Affeton Castle: a lost Devon village, 1967; Sir Bevill Grenvile and his times, 1983. *Recreations:* gardening, travel. *Address:* 14 Chester Row, SW1W 9JH.

STUDD, Sir Edward (Fairfax), 4th Bt *cr* 1929; Director, Inchcape plc and other Inchcape Group Companies, 1974–86; *b* 3 May 1929; *s* of Sir Eric Studd, 2nd Bt, OBE, and Stephana (*d* 1976), *o d* of L. J. Langmead; *S* brother, 1977; *m* 1960, Prudence Janet, *o d* of Alastair Douglas Fyfe, OBE, Riding Mill, Northumberland; two *s* one *d*. *Educ:* Winchester College. Lieutenant Coldstream Guards, London and Malaya, 1947–49; Macneill & Barry Ltd, Calcutta, 1951–62; Inchcape & Co. Ltd, London, 1962–86. *Recreations:* walking, shooting, fishing. *Heir:* *s* Philip Alastair Fairfax Studd, *b* 27 Oct. 1961. *Address:* Danceys, Clavering, near Saffron Walden, Essex. *T:* Clavering 444. *Clubs:* Boodle's, MCC, City of London; Royal Calcutta Turf (Calcutta).

STUDD, Sir Peter Malden, GBE 1971; KCVO 1979; Kt 1969; DL; MA, DSc; *b* 15 Sept. 1916; *s* of late Brig. Malden Augustus Studd, DSO, MC and Netta Cramsie; *m* 1943, Angela Mary Hamilton (*née* Garnier); two *s*. *Educ:* Harrow; Clare Coll., Cambridge (MA). Served War of 1939–45, Royal Artillery, ME and European campaigns. De La Rue Co., 1939–81. Alderman, Cripplegate Ward, City of London, 1959–76; Sheriff, 1967–68; Lord Mayor of London, 1970–71; Hon. DSc City Univ., 1971. Chm., King George's Jubilee Trust, 1972; Dep. Chm., Queen's Silver Jubilee Trust, 1976–80; Vice-Pres., Britain-Australia Bicentennial Cttee '88, 1985–; Trustee, Royal Jubilee Trusts, 1980–. Patron, Lady Eleanor Holles Sch., Hampton. Liveryman, Merchant Taylors' Co., 1959 (Asst, 1959–, Master, 1973–74); Hon. Liveryman, Worshipful Cos of Fruiterers and Plaisterers. DL Wilts, 1983. KStJ. *Recreations:* gardening, fishing, shooting, 'lighting up the Thames'. *Address:* c/o Messrs C. Hoare & Co., 37 Fleet Street, EC4P 4DQ. *Clubs:* City Livery, MCC, I Zingari.

STUDHOLME, Sir Henry (Gray), 1st Bt, *cr* 1956; CVO 1953; DL; *b* 13 June 1899; *s* of late William Paul Studholme, Perridge House, Exeter; *m* 1929, Judith, *d* of Henry William Whitbread, Norton Bavant Manor, Warminster; two *s* one *d*. *Educ:* Eton; Magdalen Coll., Oxford (MA). Served European War with Scots Guards, 1917–19; Member LCC, 1931–45; rejoined Scots Guards, 1940; Staff appointments, 1941–44. MP (C) Tavistock Division, 1942–66. PPS to late Comdr R. Brabner, Under-Sec. of State for Air, Nov. 1944–March 1945; Conservative Whip, 1945–56; Joint Treas. of the Conservative Party, 1956–62. Vice-Chamberlain of King George VI's Household, 1951–52, of the Queen's Household, 1952–56. DL Devon, 1969. *Heir:* *s* Paul Henry William Studholme, late Capt. Coldstream Guards [*b* 16 Jan. 1930; *m* 1957, Virginia Katherine, *yr d* of late Sir Richmond Palmer, KCMG; two *s* one *d*]. *Address:* Wembury House, Wembury, Plymouth. *T:* Plymouth 862210. *Club:* MCC.

STURDEE, Rear-Adm. Arthur Rodney Barry, CB 1971; DSC 1945; *b* 6 Dec. 1919; *s* of Comdr Barry V. Sturdee, RN, and Barbara (*née* Sturdee); *m* 1953, Marie-Claire Amstoutz, Mulhouse, France; one *s* one *d*. *Educ:* Canford Sch. Entered Royal Navy as Special Entry Cadet, 1937. Served War of 1939–45: Midshipman in HMS Exeter at Battle of the River Plate, 1939; Lieut, 1941; specialised in Navigation, 1944; minesweeping in Mediterranean, 1944–45 (DSC). Lt-Comdr, 1949; RN Staff Coll., 1950–51; Staff of Navigation Sch., 1951–52; Comdr, 1952; JSSC, 1953; BJSM, Washington, 1953–55; Fleet Navigating Officer, Medit., 1955–57; Exec. Officer, RNAS, Culdrose, 1958–59; Captain 1960; NATO Defence Coll., 1960–63; Queen's Harbour-Master, Singapore, 1963–65; Staff of Chief of Defence Staff, 1965–67; Chief of Staff to C-in-C, Portsmouth (as Cdre), 1967–69; Rear-Adm. 1969; Flag Officer, Gibraltar, 1969–72; retired 1972. ADC to the Queen, 1969. *Address:* 3 Tibberton Mews, Tibberton Road, Malvern, Worcestershire. *T:* Malvern 5402.

STURDY, Henry William, OBE 1975 (MBE 1968); HM Diplomatic Service, retired; Deputy Consul General and Counsellor Commercial, Chicago, 1976–78; *b* 17 Feb. 1919; *s* of late Henry William Dawson Sturdy and Jemima Aixill; *m* 1945, Anne Jamieson Marr; one *s* one *d*. *Educ:* Woolwich Polytechnic (Mechanical Engineering). Served War in Middle East, 1939–45; Allied Control Commission, Germany, 1946. Executive Branch of Civil Service and Board of Trade, 1951; tour in Trade Commission Service, 1953; appointments: Pakistan, Bangladesh, Sri Lanka, Canada. First Secretary, Diplomatic Service, 1965; Counsellor, Korea, 1976. Defence Medal; 1939–45 Medal; General Service Medal, 1939, with Palestine Clasp, 1945. *Recreations:* squash, bridge, reading, argument, international cuisine. *Address:* 17 Clock Tower Court, West Parade, Bexhill-on-Sea, E Sussex.

STURGE, Harold Francis Ralph; Metropolitan Magistrate, 1947–68; *b* 15 May 1902; *y s* of Ernest Harold Sturge; *m* 1936, Doreen, *e d* of Sir Percy Greenaway, 1st Bt; two *s* (and one *s* decd). *Educ:* Highgate Sch.; Oriel Coll., Oxford, MA (Lit. Hum.). Called to Bar, Inner Temple, 1925; Midland Circuit. War of 1939–45, served on staff of Judge Advocate-General. Mem., Departmental Cttee on the Probation Service, 1959–62; President, Old Cholmelian Society, 1962–63. *Publications:* The Road Haulage Wages Act, 1938; (with T. D. Corpe, OBE) Road Haulage Law and Compensation, 1947; (with C. A. Reston, LLB) The Main Rules of Evidence in Criminal Cases, 1972. *Recreation:* painting. *Address:* 10 Tilney Court, Catherine Road, Surbiton, Surrey KT6 4HA.

STURGE, Maj.-Gen. Henry Arthur John, CB 1978; Principal Consultant, Logica Space and Defence Systems Ltd, since 1986; *b* 27 April 1925; *s* of Henry George Arthur Sturge and Lilian Beatrice Sturge; *m* 1953, Jean Ailsa Mountain; two *s* one *d*. *Educ:* Wilson's Sch., (formerly) Camberwell, London; Queen Mary Coll., London. Commissioned, Royal Signals, 1946; UK, 1946–50; Egypt, 1950–53; UK, incl. psc, 1953–59; Far East, 1959–62; jssc, 1962; BAOR, 1963–64; RMA, Sandhurst, 1965–66; BAOR, incl. Command, 1966–69; Min. of Defence, 1970–75; Chief Signal Officer, BAOR, 1975–77; ACDS (Signals), 1977–80. Col Comdt, Royal Corps of Signals, 1977–85. Colonel, Queen's Gurkha Signals, 1980–86. Gen. Manager, 1981–84, Dir, 1983–84, Marconi Space and Defence Systems; Man. Dir, 1984–85, Chm., 1985–86, Marconi Secure Radio Systems.

Vice Chm., Governors, Wilson's Sch., 1979–. *Recreations:* sailing, (formerly) Rugby. *Address:* Border Hill, Dippenhall, Farnham, Surrey. *Club:* Army and Navy.

STUTTAFORD, Dr (Irving) Thomas; medical practitioner; *b* 4 May 1931; 2nd *s* of late Dr W. J. E. Stuttaford, MC, Horning, Norfolk; *m* 1957, Pamela, *d* of late Col Richard Ropner, TD, DL, Tain; three *s*. *Educ:* Gresham's Sch.; Brasenose Coll., Oxford; West London Hosp. 2nd Lieut, 10th Royal Hussars (PWO), 1953–55; Lieut, Scottish Horse (TA), 1955–59. Qualif. MRCS, LRCP, 1959; junior hosp. appts, 1959 and 1960. Gen. Med. practice, 1960–70. Mem. Blofield and Flegg RDC, 1964–66; Mem., Norwich City Council, 1969–71. MP (C) Norwich S, 1970–Feb. 1974; Mem. Select Cttee Science and Technology, 1970–74. Contested (C) Isle of Ely, Oct. 1974, 1979. Physician, BUPA Medical Centre; Clinical Assistant to: The London Hosp.; Queen Mary's Hosp. for East End, 1974–79; Moorfields Eye Hosp., 1975–79. Member: Council, Research Defence Soc., 1970–79; Birth Control Campaign Cttee, 1970–79; British Cancer Council, 1970–79. Medical Adviser, Rank Organisation, 1980–; Medical Corresp. to The Times, 1982–. *Recreation:* country life. *Address:* Worstead Manor, Worstead, North Walsham, Norfolk. *Clubs:* Athenæum, Reform, Cavalry and Guards; Norfolk (Norwich).

STYLE, Lt-Comdr Sir Godfrey (William), Kt 1973; CBE 1961; DSC 1941; RN; Governor, Queen Elizabeth's Foundation, since 1975; Director, Star Centre for Youth, Cheltenham, since 1967; also Member of a number of allied advisory bodies and panels; a Member of Lloyd's, since 1945; *b* 3 April 1915; *er s* of Brig.-Gen. R. C. Style (*y s* of Sir William Henry Marsham Style, 9th Bt), and Hélène Pauline, *d* of Herman Greverus Kleinwort; *m* 1st, 1942, Jill Elizabeth Caruth (marr. diss. 1951); one *s* two *d*; 2nd, 1951, Sigrid Elisabeth Julin (*née* Carlberg) (*d* 1985); one *s*; 3rd, 1986, Valerie Beauclerk (*née* Hulton-Sams), *widow* of W. D. McClure. *Educ:* Eton. Joined Royal Navy as a Regular Officer, 1933; served in Royal Yacht Victoria and Albert, 1938. Served War, Flag-Lieut to C-in-C, Home Fleet, 1939–41 (despatches, DSC, 1941; wounded, 1942, in Mediterranean); despatches, 1943; invalided from Royal Navy, due to war wounds and injuries, 1945. Dep. Underwriter at Lloyd's, 1945–55; Mem., National Advisory Council on Employment of Disabled People, 1944– (Chm., 1963–74). Mem. Council, Sir Oswald Stoll Foundn, 1975–84. *Recreations:* the field sports, horticulture, lapidary work. *Address:* Rocklands, Norton-sub-Hamdon, Somerset TA14 6SR. *T:* Chiselborough 279; 62 Whitelands House, Cheltenham Terrace, SW3. *Club:* Naval and Military.

STYLE, Sir William Frederick, 13th Bt *cr* 1627, of Wateringbury, Kent; *b* 13 May 1945; *s* of Sir William Montague Style, 12th Bt, and of La Verne, *d* of late T. M. Comstock; *S* father, 1981; *m* 1968, Wendy Gay, *d* of Gene Wittenberger, Sussex, Wisconsin, USA; two *d*; *m* 1986, Linnea L., *d* of Dann Erikson, Sussex, Wisconsin. *Heir:* *b* Frederick Montague Style [*b* 5 Nov. 1947; *m* 1971, Sharon, *d* of William H. Kurz; two *d*]. *Address:* 2430 N 3rd Lane, Oconomowoc, Wisconsin 53066, USA.

STYLES, (Frank) Showell, FRGS; author; *b* 14 March 1908; *s* of Frank Styles and Edith (*née* Showell); *m* 1954, Kathleen Jane Humphreys; one *s* two *d*. *Educ:* Bishop Vesey's Grammar Sch., Sutton Coldfield. Served Royal Navy, 1939; retd (Comdr), 1946. Professional author, 1946–76, retd. Led two private Arctic expedns, 1952–53; led private Himalayan expedn, 1954. FRGS 1954. *Publications:* 117 books on travel, fiction, children's fiction, biography, mountain guidebooks, instructional books (including, recently, Mutiny in the Caribbean, Stella and the Fireships, The Lee Shore); detective works under pen-name Glyn Carr. *Recreations:* mountaineering, gardening, music. *Address:* Trwyn Cae Iago, Borth-y-Gest, Porthmadog, Gwynedd. *T:* Porthmadog 2849. *Club:* Midland Association of Mountaineers (Birmingham).

STYLES, Fredrick William, BEM 1943; Director, Royal Arsenal Co-operative Society, 1968–84 (Chairman, 1975–79); *b* 18 Dec. 1914; *s* of Henry Albert Styles and Mabel Louise (*née* Sherwood); *m* 1942, Mary Gwendoline Harrison; one *s* three *d*. *Educ:* LCC elementary sch.; London Univ. (Dipl. economics); NCLC (Dipls Local and Central Govt). Salesman, Co-op, 1929–39. RAFVR Air Sea Rescue Service, 1939–46. Royal Humane Soc. Silver Medal, 1939; BEM for gallantry, 1943. Trade union official, NUPE (London divisional officer), 1946–52; social worker, hospital, 1952–58; social worker, LCC and GLC, 1958–68. Mem. Exec., 1973, Vice-Chm., 1974–79, Chm., 1979–80, Bexley and Greenwich AHA. Mem. for Greenwich, GLC, 1974–81; Mem., Greenwich Borough Council, 1971–78; Mem., 1971–81, Vice-Chm., 1974–75, Chm., 1975–76, ILEA; Chm. Staff and General Cttee, ILEA, 1977–81; Chm., ILEA schools, 1983– (Vice Chm., 1976–83): Nansen (partially sighted), Hawthorn Cottage (physically handicapped), and Rose Cottage (educationally sub-normal). Chm., Co-operative Metropolitan Industrial Relations Cttee, 1979– (Exec. Mem., 1970; Vice-Chm., 1973); first Chm., Heronsgate Community Centre, Thamesmead, 1982–; Governor: Avery Hill Teachers Trng Coll. (now incorporated in Thames Polytechnic), 1971– (Chm., 1983–; Senior Vice-Chm.); Woolwich Coll., 1971– (Vice-Chm., 1983–84); Thameside Inst., 1971– (Vice Chm., 1983–). *Recreations:* problems, people, pensioners, politics. *Address:* 49 Court Farm Road, Mottingham, SE9 4JN. *T:* 01–857 1508.

STYLES, Showell; *see* Styles, F. S.

STYLES, Lt-Col Stephen George, GC 1972; retired; company director, since 1974; *b* 16 March 1928; *s* of Stephen Styles and Grace Lily Styles (*née* Preston) *m* 1952, Mary Rose Styles (*née* Woolgar); one *s* two *d*. *Educ:* Collyers Sch., Horsham; Royal Military Coll. of Science. Ammunition Technical Officer, commissioned RAOC, Nov. 1947; seconded to 1 Bn KOYLI, 1949–51 (despatches, 1952); RMCS, 1952–56; HQ Ammunition Organisation, 1956–58; OC 28 Commonwealth Bde, Ordnance Field Park, Malaya, 1958–61; 2i/c 16 Bn RAOC, Bicester, 1961–64; OC Eastern Command Ammunition Inspectorate, 1964–67; Sen. Ammo Tech. Officer, 3 BAPD, BAOR, 1967–68; OC 1(BR) Corps Vehicle Company, 1968–69; Sen. Ammo Tech. Officer, Northern Ireland, 1969–72; Chief Ammo Tech. Officer (EOD), HQ DOS (CILSA), 1972–74. Member: Royal Soc. of St George, NRA, NSRA. *Publications:* Bombs Have No Pity, 1975; contrib. Proc. ICE, Jl of Forensic Science Soc. *Recreation:* rifle and game shooting, cartridge collector. *Address:* c/o Barclays Bank, Wantage.

SUAREZ, Juan L.; *see* Lechin-Suarez.

SUBAK-SHARPE, Prof. John Herbert, FRSE 1970; Professor of Virology, University of Glasgow, since 1968; Hon. Director, Medical Research Council Virology Unit, since 1968; *b* 14 Feb. 1924; *s* of late Robert Subak and late Nelly (*née* Bruell), Vienna, Austria; *m* 1953, Barbara Naomi Morris; two *s* one *d*. *Educ:* Humanistic Gymnasium, Vienna; Univ. of Birmingham. BSc (Genetics) (1st Cl. Hons) 1952; PhD 1956. Refugee from Nazi oppression, 1939; farm pupil, 1939–44; HM Forces (Parachute Regt), 1944–47. Asst Lectr in Genetics, Glasgow Univ., 1954–56; Mem. scientific staff, ARC Animal Virus Research Inst., Pirbright, 1956–60; Nat. Foundn Fellow, California Inst. of Technology, 1961; Mem. Scientific staff of MRC, in Experimental Virus Research Unit, Glasgow, 1961–68. Visiting Professor: US Nat. Insts of Health, Bethesda, Md, 1967; US Univ. of Health Services, Bethesda, Md, 1985; Vis. Fellow, Clare Hall, Cambridge, 1986–87. Sec., Genetical Soc., 1966–72, Vice-Pres. 1972–75, Trustee 1971–. Member: European Molecular Biology Orgn, 1969– (Chm., Course and Workshops Cttee, 1976–78); Genetic Manipulation Adv. Gp, 1976–80; Biomed. Res. Cttee, SHHD Chief Scientist Orgn, 1979–84; British Nat. Cttee of Biophysics, 1970–76; Governing Body, W of Scotland Oncological Orgn, 1974–; Scientific Adv. Body, W German Cancer Res. Centre, 1977–82; Governing Body, Animal Virus Res. Inst., Pirbright, 1986–. *Publications:* articles in scientific jls on genetic studies with viruses and cells. *Recreations:* travel, mountain walking, bridge. *Address:* 17 Kingsborough Gardens, Glasgow G12 9NH. *T:* 041–334 1863. *Club:* Athenæum.

SUBBA ROW, Raman; Managing Director, Management Public Relations Ltd, since 1969; Chairman, Test and County Cricket Board, since 1985; *b* 29 Jan. 1932; *s* of Panguluri Venkata Subba Row and Doris Mildred Subba Row; *m* 1960, Anne Dorothy (*née* Harrison); two *s* one *d*. *Educ:* Whitgift Sch., Croydon; Trinity Hall, Cambridge (MA Hons). Associate Dir, W. S. Crawford Ltd, 1963–69. *Recreation:* golf. *Address:* Leeward, Manor Way, South Croydon, Surrey CR2 7BT. *T:* 01–688 3388. *Clubs:* Institute of Directors, MCC, Surrey County Cricket.

SUBRAMANIAM, Chidambaram; President, International Institute of Public Enterprises, Ljubljana, Yugoslavia, since 1985; Chairman, Rajaji International Institute of Public Affairs and Administration, since 1980; *b* 30 Jan. 1910; *s* of Chidambara Gounder and Valliammal; *m* 1945, Sakuntala; one *s* two *d*. *Educ:* Madras (BA, LLB). Set up legal practice, Coimbatore, 1936; took active part in freedom movt, imprisoned 1932, 1941 and again 1942; Pres., District Congress Committee, Coimbatore; Mem. Working Cttee of State Congress Cttee; Mem. Constituent Assembly; Minister of Finance, Educn and Law, Govt of Madras, 1952; MP 1962; Minister of Steel, 1962–63; Minister of Steel, Mines and Heavy Engrg, 1963–64; Minister of Food and Agric., 1964–66; Minister of Food and Agriculture, CD and Coopn, 1966–67; Chm. Cttee on Aeronautics Industry, 1967–69; Interim Pres., Indian Nat. Congress, July-Dec. 1969; Chm. Nat. Commn on Agric., 1970; Minister of Planning and Dep. Chm., Planning Commn, 1971; also i/c Dept of Science and Technology; Minister of Industrial Develt and Science and Technology, 1972 (also Agric., temp., 1974); Minister of Finance, 1974–77; Minister of Defence, 1979. Hon. DLitt: Wattair; Sri Venkateswara; Madurai; Hon. LLD Andhra. *Publications:* Nan Sendra Sila Nadugal (Travelogues); War on Poverty; Ulagam Sutrinen (in Tamil); India of My Dreams (in English); Strategy Statement for Fighting Protein Hunger in Developing Countries; The New Strategy in Indian Agriculture. *Recreation:* yoga. *Address:* River View, Madras 85, India. *T:* 414298. *Clubs:* Cosmopolitan, Gymkhana (Madras); Cosmopolitan (Coimbatore).

SUCH, Frederick Rudolph Charles; a Recorder of the Crown Court, since 1979; *b* 19 June 1936; *s* of Frederick Sidney Such and Anne Marie Louise (*née* Martin); *m* 1961, Elizabeth, *d* of late Judge Norman and Mrs Harper, Cloughton, Yorkshire; one *s* one *d*. *Educ:* Mbeya Sch., Tanganyika Territory, E Africa (Tanzania); Taunton Sch.; Keble Coll., Oxford (MA). Called to the Bar, Gray's Inn, 1960; practised: London, 1960–69, then North Eastern Circuit, 1969–. *Recreations:* theatre, opera, hockey, squash, tennis. *Address:* The Rift Barns, Wylam, Northumberland NE41 8BL. *T:* Wylam 2763. *Club:* Northern Counties (Newcastle upon Tyne).

SUCKLING, Dr Charles Walter, FRS 1978; FRSC; Chairman, Bradbury, Suckling and Partners Ltd, since 1982; Non-Executive Director, Albright and Wilson, since 1982; *b* 24 July 1920; *s* of Edward Ernest and Barbara Suckling (*née* Thomson); *m* 1946, (Eleanor) Margaret Watterson; two *s* one *d*. *Educ:* Oldershaw Grammar Sch., Wallasey; Liverpool Univ. (BSc, PhD). ICI: joined Gen. Chemicals Div., 1942; R&D Director, Mond Div., 1967; Dep. Chairman, Mond Div., 1969; Chairman, Paints Div., 1972; Gen. Man., Res. and Technol., 1977–82. Hon. Vis. Prof., Univ. of Stirling. Member: BBC Science Consultative Gp, 1980–85; Royal Commn on Environmental Pollution, 1982–; Council, RCA, 1981– (Treasurer, 1984–). Bicentennial Lecture, Washington Coll., Maryland, 1981. Senior Fellow, RCA, 1986. Hon. DSc Liverpool, 1980; DUniv Stirling, 1985. Liverpool Univ. Chem. Soc. Medal, 1964; John Scott Medal, City of Philadelphia, 1973. *Publications:* (with A. Baines and F. R. Bradbury) Research in the Chemical Industry, 1969; (with C. J. Suckling and K. E. Suckling) Chemistry through Models, 1978; papers on industrial research and strategy in journals. *Recreations:* music, gardening, languages, writing. *Address:* Willowhay, Shoppenhangers Road, Maidenhead, Berks SL6 2QA. *T:* Maidenhead 27502.

SUCKSDORFF, Mrs Åke; *see* Jonzen, Mrs Karin.

SUDBURY, Archdeacon of; *see* Smith, Ven. D. J.

SUDDABY, Arthur, CBE 1980; PhD, MSc; CChem, FRSC; CEng, MIChemE; scientific consultant on the carriage of goods by sea; Provost, City of London Polytechnic, 1970–81; *b* 26 Feb. 1919; *e s* of George Suddaby, Kingston-upon-Hull, Yorks; *m* 1944, Elizabeth Bullin Vyse (decd), *d* of Charles Vyse; two *s*. *Educ:* Riley High Sch., Kingston-upon-Hull; Hull Technical Coll.; Chelsea Polytechnic; Queen Mary Coll. London. Chemist and Chemical Engr, in industry, 1937–47; Lectr in Physical Chemistry, and later Sen. Lectr in Chem. Engrg, West Ham Coll. of Technology, 1947–50; Sir John Cass Coll.: Sen. Lectr in Physics, 1950–61; Head of Dept of Physics, 1961–66; Principal, 1966–70. Chm., Cttee of Directors of Polytechnics, 1976–78; Member: Chem. Engrg Cttee, 1948–51; London and Home Counties Regional Adv. Council, 1971–; Bd of Examrs and Educn Cttee, Inst. of Chem. Engrs, 1948–51; CNAA: Chem. Engrg Bd, 1969–75; Nautical Studies Bd, 1972–75; Chm., Standing Conf. of Approved Coll. Res. Deg. Cttees, 1979–81; Court of the City University, 1967–81; Vis. Cttee, Cranfield Inst. of Technology, 1979–85; Chm., Assoc. of Navigation Schs, 1972. *Publications:* various original research papers in theoretical physics, in scientific jls; review articles. *Recreations:* fishing, occasional hunting. *Address:* Flat 3, 16 Elm Park Gardens, Chelsea, SW10. *T:* 01–352 9164; Castle Hill House, Woodgreen, near Fordingbridge, Hants. *T:* Fordingbridge 52234. *Club:* Athenæum.

SUDDARDS, His Honour (Henry) Gaunt; a Circuit Judge (formerly Judge of County Courts), 1963–80; *b* 30 July 1910; *s* of Fred Suddards and Agnes Suddards (*née* Gaunt); unmarried. *Educ:* Cheltenham College; Trinity College, Cambridge (MA). Barrister, Inner Temple, 1932; joined NE Circuit, 1933. Served War of 1939–45, RAFVR, 1940–46. Recorder of Pontefract, 1960–61; Recorder of Middlesbrough, 1961–63; Dep. Chm., West Riding QS, 1961–71; Chairman, Agricultural Land Tribunal, Northern Area, 1961–63, Dep. Chairman 1960. *Recreations:* fishing, shooting, sailing. *Address:* Rockville, Frizinghall, Shipley, West Yorkshire. *Club:* Bradford (Bradford).

SUDELEY, 7th Baron *cr* 1838; **Merlin Charles Sainthill Hanbury-Tracy;** *b* 17 June 1939; *o c* of late Captain Michael David Charles Hanbury-Tracy, Scots Guards, and Colline Ammabel (*d* 1985), *d* of late Lt-Col C. G. H. St Hill and *widow* of Lt-Col Frank King, DSO, OBE; *S* cousin, 1941; *m* 1980, Hon. Mrs Elizabeth Villiers, *d* of late Viscount Bury (*s* of 9th Earl of Albemarle). *Educ:* at Eton and in the ranks of the Scots Guards. Patron: Prayer Book Soc.; Anglican Assoc.; St Peter's, Petersham, Richmond, Surrey. *Publications:* contribs to Quarterly Review, Contemporary Review, Family History, Trans of Bristol and Gloucestershire Archaeol. Soc., Montgomeryshire Collections, Bull. of Manorial Soc., Die Waage (Zeitschrift der Chemie Grünenthal). *Recreations:* ancestor worship; cultivating his sensibility. *Heir:* *kinsman* Claud Edward Frederick Hanbury-

Tracy-Domvile, TD [*b* 11 Jan. 1904; assumed by deed poll, 1961, additional surname of Domvile; *m* 1st, 1927, Veronica May (marr. diss. 1948; she *d* 1985), *d* of late Cyril Grant Cunard; two *s* one *d*; 2nd, 1954, Marcella Elizabeth Willis (*d* 1983), *er d* of late Rev. Canon John Willis Price]. *Address:* c/o Royal Bank of Scotland, 21 Grosvenor Gardens, SW1. *Clubs:* Brooks's, (as Member of Parliament) House of Lords.

SUENENS, His Eminence Cardinal Leo Joseph, DTheol, DPhil; Cardinal since 1962; Archbishop of Malines-Brussels and Primate of Belgium, 1961–79; *b* Ixelles (Brussels), 16 July 1904. *Educ:* primary sch., Inst. of Marist Brothers, Brussels; secondary sch., St Mary's High Sch., Brussels; Gregorian Univ., Rome (BCL, DPhil, DrTheol). Priest, 1927; Teacher, St Mary's High Sch., Brussels, 1929, Prof. of Philosophy, Diocesan Seminary, Malines, 1930; Vice-Rector, Cath. Univ. of Louvain, 1940; Vicar-Gen., Archdio. of Malines, 1945; Auxiliary Bp to Archbp of Malines, 1945. Moderator of Second Vatican Council, 1962–65; Pres., Belgian Bishops' Conf.; Internat. Pastoral Delegate for Catholic Charismatic Renewal. Templeton Prize for Religion, 1976. *Publications:* Theology of the Apostolate of the Legion of Mary, 1951 (Cork); Edel Quinn, 1952 (Dublin); (ed) The Right View on Moral Rearmament, 1953 (London); (ed) The Gospel to Every Creature, 1955 (London); (ed) Mary the Mother of God, 1957 (New York); (ed) Love and Control, 1959 (London); (ed) Christian Life Day by Day, 1961 (London); (ed) The Nun in the World, 1962 (London); (ed) Co-responsibility in the Church, 1968 (New York), 1969 (London); (ed, with Archbp Ramsey) The Future of the Christian Church, 1971 (New York); A New Pentecost?, 1975 (New York); Open the Frontiers, 1980; Renewal and Powers of Darkness, 1982; Nature and Grace, 1986. *Address:* Boulevard de Smet de Mayer 570, 1020 Bruxelles, Belgium. *T:* 02/4791950.

SUENSON-TAYLOR, family name of **Baron Grantchester.**

SUFFIAN, Tun Mohamed, SSM 1975 (PSM 1967); SPCM 1978; DIMP 1969; JMN 1961; PJK 1963; Adviser, Standard Chartered Bank in Malaysia, since 1982; Member, Administrative Tribunal, World Bank, Washington DC, since 1985; Judge, International Labour Organisation Administrative Tribunal, Geneva, since 1986; *b* 12 Nov. 1917; *s* of late Haji Mohamed Hashim and Zaharah binti Ibrahim; *m* 1946, Dora Evelina Grange. *Educ:* Gonville and Caius Coll., Cambridge (BA Hons, LLB); SOAS; LSE. Called to the Bar, Middle Temple, 1941 (Hon. Bencher, 1984). All India Radio, New Delhi, 1942–45; BBC, London, 1945–46; Malayan Civil Service, 1948; Malayan Judicial and Legal Service, 1949–61; Solicitor General, 1959; High Court Judge, 1961; Federal Judge, 1968; Chief Justice of Malaya, 1973; Lord Pres., Federal Court, 1974–82. Pro-Chancellor, Univ. of Malaya, 1963–. President: Commonwealth Magistrates Assoc., 1979–85; Asean Law Assoc., 1982–84. Pres., Malaysian Br., Royal Asiatic Soc., 1978–. Fellow, Univ. Coll. at Buckingham, 1979. Hon. LLD: Singapore, 1975; Buckingham, 1983; Hon. DLitt Malaya, 1975. Ramon Magsaysay Foundn Award for Government Service, 1975. SMB (Brunei), 1959. *Publications:* Malayan Constitution (official trans.), 1963; An Introduction to the Constitution of Malaysia, 1972, 2nd edn 1976; (ed jtly) The Constitution of Malaysia: its development 1957–1977, 1978. *Recreations:* gardening, swimming, reading. *Address:* The Standard Chartered Bank, 9th Floor, 2 Jalan Ampang, Kuala Lumpur, Malaysia. *T:* 03–223 090; *telex:* MA 32947. *Club:* Lake (Kuala Lumpur).

SUFFIELD, 11th Baron *cr* 1786; **Anthony Philip Harbord-Hamond,** Bt, *cr* 1745; MC 1950; Major, retired, 1961; *b* 19 June 1922; *o s* of 10th Baron and Nina Annette Mary Crawfuird (*d* 1955), *e d* of John Hutchison of Laurieston and Edingham, Stewartry of Kirkcudbright; *S* father 1951; *m* 1952, Elizabeth Eve, *er d* of late Judge Edgedale; three *s* one *d*. *Educ:* Eton. Commission, Coldstream Guards, 1942; served War of 1939–45, in North African and Italian campaigns, 1942–45; Malaya, 1948–50. One of HM Hon. Corps of Gentlemen-at-Arms, 1973–. *Recreations:* normal. *Heir:* *s* Hon. Charles Anthony Assheton Harbord-Hamond [*b* 3 Dec. 1953; *m* 1983, Lucy, *yr d* of Comdr A. S. Hutchinson. Commissioned Coldstream Guards, 1972, RARO 1979]. *Address:* Wood Norton Grange, Dereham, Norfolk NR20 5BD. *T:* Foulsham 235. *Clubs:* Army and Navy, Pratt's.

SUFFIELD, Sir (Henry John) Lester, Kt 1973; Head of Defence Sales, Ministry of Defence, 1969–76; *b* 28 April 1911; *m* 1940, Elizabeth Mary White (*d* 1985); one *s* one *d*. *Educ:* Camberwell Central, LCC. Served with RASC, 1939–45 (Major). LNER, 1926–35; Morris Motors, 1935–38 and 1945–52; Pres., British Motor Corp., Canada and USA, 1952–64; Dep. Man. Dir, British Motor Corp., Birmingham, 1964–68; Sales Dir, British Leyland Motor Corp., 1968–69. Freeman of City of London, 1978; Liveryman, Coachmakers and Coach Harness Makers Co. *Recreation:* golf. *Address:* 16 Glebe Court, Fleet, Hants. *T:* Fleet 616861. *Clubs:* Royal Automobile; Royal Wimbledon Golf.

SUFFOLK AND BERKSHIRE, 21st Earl of, *cr* 1603; **Michael John James George Robert Howard;** Viscount Andover and Baron Howard, 1622; Earl of Berkshire, 1626; *b* 27 March 1935; *s* of 20th Earl (killed by enemy action, 1941) and Mimi (*d* 1966), *yr d* of late A. G. Forde Pigott; *S* father 1941; *m* 1st, 1960, Mme Simone Paulmier (marr. diss. 1967), *d* of late Georges Litman, Paris; (one *d* decd); 2nd, 1973, Anita (marr. diss. 1980), *d* of R. R. Fuglesang, Haywards Heath, Sussex; one *s* one *d*; 3rd, 1983, Linda Viscountess Bridport; one *d*. Owns 5,000 acres. *Heir:* *s* Viscount Andover, *qv*. *Address:* Charlton Park, Malmesbury, Wilts.

See also Hon. G. R. Howard.

SUFFOLK, Archdeacon of; *see* Gibson, Ven. T.A.

SUGAR, Alan Michael; Chairman, Amstrad plc, since 1968; *b* 24 March 1947; *s* of Nathan and Fay Sugar; *m* 1968, Ann Simons; two *s* one *d*. *Educ:* Brooke House School, London. Chm. and owner of Amstrad since formation in 1968. *Recreation:* tennis. *Address:* 169 King's Road, Brentwood, Essex. *T:* Brentwood 228888.

SUGDEN, family name of **Baron St Leonards.**

SUGDEN, Sir Arthur, Kt 1978; Director, Manchester Ship Canal Limited, since 1978; Chief Executive Officer, Co-operative Wholesale Society Ltd, 1974–80; Chairman: Co-operative Bank Ltd, 1974–80; Co-operative Commercial Bank Ltd, 1974–80; *b* 12 Sept. 1918; *s* of late Arthur and Elizabeth Ann Sugden; *m* 1946, Agnes Grayston; two *s*. *Educ:* Thomas Street, Manchester. Certified Accountant, Chartered Secretary. FIB 1975. Served War of 1939–45, Royal Artillery; CPO 6th Super Heavy Battery; Adjt 12th Medium Regt; Staff Captain 16th Army Group. CWS Ltd: Accountancy Asst, 1946; Office Man., 1950; Factory Man., 1954; Group Man., Edible Oils and Fats Factories, 1964; Controller, Food Div., 1967; Dep. Chief Exec. Officer, 1971. Chairman, 1974–80: FC Finance Ltd; CWS (Longburn) Ltd; CWS (New Zealand) Holdings Ltd; CWS Marketing Ltd; CWS (India) Ltd; Ocean Beach Freezing Co. Ltd; Shaw's Smokers' Products Ltd; Former Director: Co-operative City Investments Ltd; Co-operative Pension Funds Unit Trust Managers' Ltd; Associated Co-operative Creameries Ltd; CWS Svineslagterier A/S Denmark; CWS (Overseas) Ltd; Tukuyu Tea Estates Ltd; Spillers French Holdings Ltd; J. W. French (Milling & Baking Holdings) Ltd; North Eastern Co-operative Soc. Ltd; Manchester Chamber of Commerce. Former Vice-President: Inst. of Bankers; Inst. of Grocery Distribution Ltd. Member: Central Cttee, Internat. Co-operative Alliance; Management Bds, Euro-Coop and Inter-Coop (Pres., 1979–80). Pres., Co-operative Congress, 1978. CBIM; FIGD. *Recreations:* music, reading, walking. *Address:* 56 Old Wool Lane, Cheadle Hulme, Cheadle, Cheshire.

SUGDEN, John Goldthorp, MA; ARCM; Headmaster, Wellingborough School, 1965–73; *b* 22 July 1921; *s* of A. G. Sugden, Brighouse, Yorkshire; *m* 1954, Jane Machin; two *s*. *Educ:* Radley; Magdalene College, Cambridge. War Service, Royal Signals, 1941–46. Asst Master, Bilton Grange Prep. School, 1948–52; Asst Master, The King's School, Canterbury, 1952–59; Headmaster, Foster's School, Sherborne, 1959–64. *Publication:* Niccolo Paganini, 1980. *Recreations:* music, golf. *Address:* Woodlands, 2 Linksview Avenue, Parkstone, Poole, Dorset BH14 9QT. *T:* Parkstone 707497.

SUGG, Aldhelm St John, CMG 1963; retired as Provincial Commissioner, Southern Province of Northern Rhodesia, August 1963; *b* 21 Oct. 1909; *s* of H. G. St J. Sugg; *m* 1935, Jessie May Parker; one *s* one *d*. *Educ:* Colchester Royal Grammar School. Palestine Police, 1930–31; Northern Rhodesia Police, 1932–43; Colonial Administrative Service, in N Rhodesia, 1943–63. Retired to England, 1963. *Recreations:* sailing, field sports. *Address:* Bushbury, Blackboys, Uckfield, East Sussex. *T:* Framfield 282. *Club:* Royal Commonwealth Society.

SUIRDALE, Viscount; John Michael James Hely-Hutchinson; company director since 1981; *b* 7 Aug. 1952; *s* and *heir* of 8th Earl of Donoughmore, *qv*; *m* 1976, Marie-Claire Carola Etienne van den Driessche; one *s* two *d*. *Educ:* Harrow. *Recreations:* shooting, ski-ing, fishing, etc. *Heir:* *s* Hon. Richard Gregory Hely-Hutchinson, *b* 3 July 1980. *Address:* 15 Rue de Luzarches, 60580 Coye-la-Forêt, France. *T:* 4/458 7117.

SULLIVAN, David Douglas Hooper, QC 1975; barrister-at-law; *b* 10 April 1926; *s* of Michael and Maude Sullivan; *m* 1st, 1951, Sheila, *d* of Henry and Georgina Bathurst; three *d*; 2nd, 1981, Ann Munro, *d* of Malcolm and Eva Betten. *Educ:* Haileybury (schol.); Christ Church, Oxford (schol.). MA 1949, BCL 1951. Served War, with RNVR (Sub-Lieut), 1944–46. Called to Bar, Inner Temple, 1951, Bencher, 1984. Mem., Central Policy Cttee, Mental Health Act Commn, 1983–. *Recreations:* painting, walking, geology. *Address:* 9 Gayton Road, NW3 1TX. *T:* 01–431 3433.

SULLIVAN, Sir Desmond (John), Kt 1985; Chief District Court Judge, New Zealand, 1979–85, retired; Executive Director, 1987 World Rugby Tournament, since 1985; *b* 3 March 1920; *s* of Patrick James Sullivan and Annie Sullivan; *m* 1947, Phyllis Maude Mahon; two *s* four *d* (and one *s* decd). *Educ:* Timaru Marist; Timaru Boys' High Sch.; Canterbury Univ. (LLB). Served NZ Army and Navy, 1940–45. Barrister and solicitor: Westport, 1949–59; Palmerston North, 1960–66; Stipendiary Magistrate, Wellington, 1966–79. Member, Westport Bor. Council, 1955–59; Chairman: NZ Council for Recreation and Sport, 1973–76; Film Industry Board, 1962–85. *Publication:* (jtly) Violence in the Community, 1975. *Recreations:* golf, swimming, reading. *Address:* 208 Whites Line East, Lower Hutt, New Zealand. *T:* 695–440. *Club:* Wellington.

SULLIVAN, Prof. (Donovan) Michael; Professor of Oriental Art, 1966–85, Christensen Professor, 1975–85, Stanford University, California; Fellow, St Catherine's College, Oxford, since 1979; *b* 29 Oct. 1916; *s* of Alan Sullivan and Elisabeth Hees; *m* 1943, Khoan, *d* of Ngo Eng-lim, Kulangsu, Amoy, China; no *c*. *Educ:* Rugby School; Corpus Christi College, Cambridge (MA); Univ. of London (BA Hons); Harvard Univ. (PhD); LittD Cambridge, 1966; MA, DLitt Oxon, 1973. Chinese Govt Scholarship, Univ. of London, 1947–50; Rockefeller Foundn Travelling Fellowship in USA, 1950–51; Bollingen Foundn Research Fellowship, 1952–54; Curator of Art Museum and Lectr in the History of Art, Univ. of Malaya (now Univ. of Singapore), Singapore, 1954–60; Lectr in Asian Art, Sch. of Oriental and African Studies, Univ. of London, 1960–66. Vis. Prof. of Far Eastern Art, Univ. of Michigan (Spring Semester), 1964; Slade Prof. of Fine Art, Oxford Univ., 1973–74, Cambridge Univ., 1983–84; Guggenheim Foundn Fellowship, 1974; Vis. Fellow, St Antony's Coll., Oxford, 1976–77; Nat. Endowment for the Humanities Fellowship, 1976–77; Professorial Fellow, Corpus Christi Coll., Cambridge, 1983–84. Fellow, Amer. Acad. of Arts and Sciences, 1977. *Publications:* Chinese Art in the Twentieth Century, 1959; An Introduction to Chinese Art, 1961; The Birth of Landscape Painting in China, 1962; Chinese Ceramics, Bronzes and Jades in the Collection of Sir Alan and Lady Barlow, 1963; Chinese and Japanese Art, 1965; A Short History of Chinese Art, 1967, 3rd edn as The Arts of China, 1973, rev. edns 1977, 1984, 1986; The Cave Temples of Maichishan, 1969; The Meeting of Eastern and Western Art, 1973; Chinese Art: recent discoveries, 1973; The Three Perfections, 1975; Chinese Landscape Painting, vol. II, The Sui and T'ang Dynasties, 1979; Symbols of Eternity: the art of landscape painting in China, 1979; contrib. to learned journals, Encyclopedia Britannica, Chambers's Encyclopædia, etc. *Address:* St Catherine's College, Oxford OX1 3UJ. *Club:* Athenæum.

SULLIVAN, Edmund Wendell; Chief Veterinary Officer, Department of Agriculture for Northern Ireland, since 1983; *b* 21 March 1925; *s* of Thomas Llewellyn Sullivan and Letitia Sullivan; *m* 1957, Elinor Wilson Melville; two *s* one *d*. *Educ:* Portadown College; Queen's University, Belfast; Royal (Dick) Veterinary College. MRCVS. General Veterinary Practice, Appleby, Westmoreland, 1947; joined staff of State Veterinary Service, Dept. of Agriculture for N Ireland, 1948; Headquarters staff, 1966–. *Recreations:* hill walking, wood craft, following rugby and cricket. *Address:* Kinfauns, 26 Dillon's Avenue, Newtownabbey, Co. Antrim BT37 0SX. *T:* Whiteabbey 62323.

SULLIVAN, Jeremy Mirth; QC 1982; *b* 17 Sept. 1945; *s* of Arthur Brian and Pamela Jean Sullivan; *m* 1970, Ursula Klara Marie Hildenbrock; two *s*. *Educ:* Framlingham Coll.; King's Coll., London. LLB 1967, LLM 1968; LAMTPI 1970, LMRTPI 1976. 2nd Lieut, Suffolk & Cambs Regt (TA), 1963–65. Called to the Bar, Inner Temple, 1968; Lectr in Law, City of London Polytechnic, 1968–71; in practice, Planning and Local Govt Bar, 1971–; Mem., Supplemental Panel of Junior Counsel to Crown (Common Law), 1978–82. Mem. Council, RTPI, 1984–. *Publications:* contribs to Jl of Planning Law. *Recreations:* walking, railways, canals, reading history. *Address:* 4–5 Gray's Inn Square, WC1R 5JA. *T:* 01–404 5252.

SULLIVAN, Prof. Michael; *see* Sullivan, D. M.

SULLIVAN, Richard Arthur, (9th Bt *cr* 1804, but does not use the title); General Manager, Geocon of Lavalin; *b* 9 Aug. 1931; *s* of Sir Richard Benjamin Magniac Sullivan, 8th Bt, and Muriel Mary Paget, *d* of late Francis Charles Trayler Pineo; *S* father, 1977; *m* 1962, Elenor Mary, *e d* of late K. M. Thorpe; one *s* three *d*. *Educ:* Univ. of Cape Town (BSc); Massachusetts Inst. of Technology (SM). Chartered Engineer, UK; Professional Engineer, Ontario, Texas and Louisiana. *Publications:* technical papers to international conferences and geotechnical journals. *Recreation:* tennis. *Heir:* *s* Charles Merson Sullivan, *b* 15 Dec. 1962. *Address:* 1060 Royal York Road, Toronto, Ontario M8X 2G7, Canada.

SULLIVAN, Tod; National Secretary, Association of Clerical, Technical and Supervisory Staffs, Transport and General Workers' Union, since 1974; *b* 3 Jan. 1934; *s* of Timothy William and Elizabeth Sullivan; *m* 1963, Patricia Norma Roughsedge; one *s* three *d*. *Educ:* Fanshawe Crescent Sch., Dagenham. Merchant Navy, 1950–52; RAF, 1952–55; Electrician, 1955–60; Children's Journalist, 1960–68; Industrial Relations Officer: ATV,

1968–71; CIR, 1971–72; Gen. Sec., Union of Kodak Workers, 1973–74 (until transfer of engagements to TGWU). *Recreations:* reading, music, golf. *Address:* 267 Luton Road, Harpenden, Herts. *T:* Harpenden 5034.

SULLY, Leonard Thomas George, CBE 1963; Covent Garden Market Authority, 1967–80; Member, Industrial Tribunals Panel, 1976–80; *b* 25 June 1909; British; *m* 1935, Phyllis Emily Phipps, Bristol; one *d. Educ:* elementary schs; Fairfield Grammar Sch., Bristol. Public Health Dept, Bristol Corp., 1927; Assistance Officer, Unemployment Assistance Board, Bristol District, 1934; subseq. served in Bath, Weston-super-Mare, etc.; Staff Officer, Air Ministry, London, 1943; Principal, and allocated to Air Ministry, 1949; Asst Sec., 1954, Dir of Contracts, 1960; Dir of Contracts (Air) MoD, 1964. *Recreation:* gardening. *Address:* Coppins, 20 Brackendale Close, Camberley, Surrey. *T:* Camberley 63604.

SULSTON, John Edward, PhD; FRS 1986; Staff Scientist, Laboratory of Molecular Biology, Cambridge, since 1969; *b* 27 March 1942; *s* of late Rev. Canon Arthur Edward Aubrey Sulston and of Josephine Muriel Frearson (*née* Blocksidge); *m* 1966, Daphne Edith Bate; one *s* one *d. Educ:* Merchant Taylors' School; Pembroke College, Cambridge (BA, PhD). Postdoctoral Fellow, Salk Inst., San Diego, 1966–69. *Publications:* articles on organic chemistry, molecular and developmental biology in sci. jls. *Recreations:* gardening, walking, avoiding people. *Address:* 39 Mingle Lane, Stapleford, Cambridge CB2 5BG. *T:* Cambridge 842248.

SULTAN, Syed Abdus; *b* 1 Feb. 1917; Bengali Muslim; lawyer, Supreme Court of Bangladesh, Dacca, since 1976; *m* 1938, Begum Kulsum Sultan; two *s* two *d. Educ:* Calcutta and Dacca Univs. Grad. Calcutta 1936, LLB Dacca 1949. Joined Dacca High Court Bar, 1949; Mem. Nat. Assembly of Pakistan, 1962; Delegate Inter-Parly Union Conf., Belgrade, 1963; toured Europe and Middle East; Mem. Pakistan Bar Council, 1967; Mem. Pakistan Nat. Assembly, 1970 with Sheikh Mujibur Rahman (Mem. Constitution Drafting Cttee); joined Bangladesh liberation movt, 1971; visited India, UK, USA and Canada to project cause of Bangladesh; Mem. Unofficial Delegn of Govt of Bangladesh to UN; Ambassador, later High Comr, for Bangladesh in UK, 1972–75. Member: Bangladesh Inst. of Law and Internat. Affairs; Bangla Academy. *Publications:* (in Bengali): Biography of M. A. Jinnah, 1948; Pancha Nadir Palimati, 1953; Ibne Sina, 1955; Man Over the Ages (history), 1969; Manirag (Belles Lettres), 1969; Byati Kramer Ek Adhyaya (One Chapter of Difference), 1981; Ar Rakta Nay (No more Blood), 1982; translations of short stories. *Recreations:* tennis, cricket, literature, literary and cultural activities. *Address:* Supreme Court Bar Association, Dacca, Bangladesh.

SULZBERGER, Arthur Ochs; Chairman, New York Times Co. and Publisher of The New York Times since 1963; *b* 5 Feb. 1926; *s* of late Arthur Hays Sulzberger; *m* 1st, 1948, Barbara Grant (marr. diss. 1956); one *s* one *d*; 2nd, 1956, Carol Fox Fuhrman; one *d* (and one adopted *d*). *Educ:* Browning School, New York City; Loomis School, Windsor, Conn; Columbia University, NYC. Reporter, Milwaukee Journal, 1953–54; Foreign Correspondent, New York Times, 1954–55; Asst to the Publisher, New York Times, 1956–57; Asst Treasurer, New York Times, 1957–63. Trustee: Metropolitan Mus. of Art; Columbia Univ. Hon. LLD: Dartmouth, 1964; Bard, 1967; Hon LHD: Montclair State Coll.; Tufts Univ., 1984. *Recreation:* golf. *Address:* 229 West 43rd Street, New York, NY 10036, USA. *T:* 556–1771. *Clubs:* Overseas Press, Century Country, Explorers (New York); Metropolitan, Federal City (Washington, DC).

SUMBERG, David Anthony Gerald; MP (C) Bury South, since 1983; *b* 2 June 1941; *s* of Joshua and Lorna Sumberg; *m* 1972, Carolyn Ann Rae Franks; one *s* one *d. Educ:* Tettenhall Coll., Staffs; Coll. of Law, London. Qualified as a Solicitor, 1959; Partner, Price Bieber & Co., solicitors, 1985–. Mem. (C) Manchester City Council, 1982–84. Contested (C) Manchester, Wythenshawe, 1979. PPS to Solicitor-General, 1986. *Recreation:* family. *Address:* 27 Burndale Drive, Bury, Lancs. *T:* 061–766 5052.

SUMMERFIELD, Prof. Arthur, BSc Tech; BSc; FBPsS; Professor of Psychology, University of London, and Head of the Department of Psychology at Birkbeck College since 1961; *b* 31 March 1923; *s* of late Arthur and Dora Gertrude Summerfield; *m* 1st, 1946, Aline Whalley; one *s* one *d*; 2nd, 1974, Angela Barbara, MA Cantab, PhD London, *d* of late George Frederick Steer and of Estelle Steer. *Educ:* Manchester Grammar Sch.; Manchester Univ.; University Coll. London (1st cl. hons Psychology). Served War of 1939–45, Electrical Officer, RNVR, 1943–46: Naval Air Stations, 1943–46; Dept of Sen. Psychologist to the Admiralty, 1946. Asst Lectr in Psychology, University Coll. London, 1949–51, Lectr, 1951–61, Hon. Research Associate, 1961–70, Hon. Research Fellow, 1970–; first Dean, Fac. of Econs, Birkbeck Coll., 1971–72, Governor, 1982–; Hon. Lectr in Psychology, Westminster Med. Sch., 1974–76. Mem. Council, British Psychological Soc., 1953–65, 1967–75, 1977–84 (Hon. Gen. Sec., 1954–59; Pres., 1963–64; Vice-Pres., 1964–65); first Chm., Scientific Affairs Bd, 1974–75); Member: Cttee on Internat. Relations in Psychology, Amer. Psychological Assoc., 1977–79; Bd of Dirs, European Coordination Centre for Res. and Documentation in Social Scis (Vienna Centre), 1977–81; ICSU Study Gp on biol, med. and physical effects of large scale use of nuclear weapons, 1983–; Pres., International Union of Psychological Science, 1976–80 (Mem., Exec. Cttee, 1963–84, Assembly, 1957–84; Vice-Pres., 1972–76); Pres., Section J (Psychology) BAAS, 1976–77; Pres., Internat. Soc. Sci. Council, 1977–81 (Mem. Prog. Cttee, 1973–83; Mem. Exec. Cttee, 1977–83); Chm., DES Working Party on Psychologists in Educn Services, 1965–68. Member: DSIR Human Sciences Res. Grants Cttee, 1962–65; SSRC, 1979–81; Psychology Cttee, SSRC, 1979–81. Vis. Prof., Univ. of California (at Dept of Psychobiology, Irvine Campus), 1968. Governor, Enfield Coll. of Technology, 1968–72. Asst Editor, Brit. Jl Psychology (Statistical Section), 1950–54; Editor, British Journal of Psychology, 1964–67; Scientific Editor, British Med. Bulletin issues on Experimental Psychology, 1964, Cognitive Psychology, 1971, (with D. M. Warburton) Psychobiology, 1981. *Publications:* articles on perception, memory, statistical methods and psycho-pharmacology in scientific periodicals. *Address:* Birkbeck College, Malet Street, WC1E 7HX; 14 Colonels Walk, The Ridgeway, Enfield EN2 8HN. *Club:* Athenæum.

SUMMERFIELD, Hon. Sir John (Crampton), Kt 1973; CBE 1966 (OBE 1961); **Hon. Mr Justice Summerfield;** Judge of the Grand Court and Chief Justice of the Cayman Islands, since 1977; Justice of Appeal of the Court of Appeal for Bermuda, since 1979; *b* 20 Sept. 1920; *s* of late Arthur Fred Summerfield and late Lilian Winifred Summerfield (*née* Staas); *m* 1945, Patricia Sandra Musgrave; two *s* two *d. Educ:* Lucton Sch., Herefordshire. Called to Bar, Gray's Inn, 1949. Served War, 1939–46: East Africa, Abyssinia, Somaliland, Madagascar; Captain, Royal Signals. Crown Counsel, Tanganyika (now Tanzania), 1949; Legal Draftsman, 1953; Dep. Legal Sec., EA High Commission, 1958. Attorney-Gen., Bermuda, 1962; QC (Bermuda) 1963; MEC, 1962–68, and MLC, 1962–68 (Bermuda); Chief Justice of Bermuda, 1972–77; Judge of Supreme Court, Turks and Caicos Islands, 1977–82; Pres., Ct of Appeal for Belize, 1982–84. *Publications:* Preparation of Revised Laws of Bermuda, 1963 and 1971 edns. *Recreations:* photography, chess, sailing. *Address:* c/o The Grand Court, Grand Cayman, Cayman Islands, West Indies. *Clubs:* Naval and Military, Royal Commonwealth Society.

SUMMERHAYES, Sir Christopher (Henry), KBE 1955 (MBE 1929); CMG 1949; *b* 8 March 1896; *s* of late Rev. H. Summerhayes; *m* 1921, Anna (Johnson) (*d* 1972); two *s* two *d*. Served HM Forces, 1914–19 and 1940–45, Gloucestershire Regt (despatches). HM Foreign Service; Consul-General at Alexandria, 1946–51; Ambassador to Nepal, 1951–55. *Address:* Tara, Limpsfield Chart, Oxted, Surrey.
See also D. M. Summerhayes.

SUMMERHAYES, David Michael, CMG 1975; HM Diplomatic Service, retired; Ambassador and Leader, UK Delegation to Committee on Disarmament, Geneva, 1979–82; *b* 29 Sept. 1922; *s* of Sir Christopher Summerhayes, *qv*; *m* 1959, June van der Hardt Aberson; two *s* one *d. Educ:* Marlborough; Emmanuel Coll., Cambridge. Served War of 1939–45 in Royal Artillery (Capt.) N Africa and Italy. 3rd Sec., FO, 1948; Baghdad, 1949; Brussels, 1950–53; 2nd Sec., FO, 1953–56; 1st Sec. (Commercial), The Hague, 1956–59; 1st Sec. and Consul, Reykjavik, 1959–61; FO, 1961–65; Consul-General and Counsellor, Buenos Aires, 1965–70; Head of Arms Control and Disarmament Dept, FCO, 1970–74; Minister, Pretoria/Cape Town, 1974–78. Disarmament Advr, FCO, 1983–86. Hon. Officer, Order of Orange Nassau. *Recreations:* tennis, golf, wildlife. *Address:* 6 Kingsmere Road, Wimbledon, SW19 6PX. *Clubs:* United Oxford & Cambridge University; Royal Wimbledon Golf.

SUMMERHAYES, Gerald Victor, CMG 1979; OBE 1969; *b* 28 Jan. 1928; *s* of Victor Samuel and Florence A. V. Summerhayes. Administrative Service, Nigeria, 1952–81; Permanent Secretary: Local Govt, North Western State, 1975–76, Sokoto State, 1976–77; Cabinet Office (Political and Trng), 1977–79; Dir of Trng, Cabinet Office, Sokoto, 1979–81. *Address:* Bridge Cottage, Bridge Street, Sidbury, Devon EX10 0RU. *T:* Sidbury 311; PO Box 172, Sokoto, Nigeria.

SUMMERS, (Sir) Felix Roland Brattan, 2nd Bt *cr* 1952; does not use the title and his name is not on the Official Roll of Baronets.

SUMMERS, Henry Forbes, CB 1961; Under-Secretary, Department of the Environment (formerly Ministry of Housing and Local Government), 1955–71; *b* 18 August 1911; *s* of late Rev. H. H. Summers, Harrogate, Yorks; *m* 1937, Rosemary, *d* of late Robert L. Roberts, CBE; two *s* one *d. Educ:* Fettes Coll., Edinburgh; Trinity College, Oxford. *Publications:* Smoke After Flame, 1944; Hinterland, 1947; Tomorrow is my Love, 1978; The Burning Book, 1982. *Address:* Folly Fields, Tunbridge Wells, Kent. *T:* 27671.
See also N. Summers.

SUMMERS, Janet Margaret, (Mrs L. J. Summers); see Bately, J. M.

SUMMERS, Nicholas; Under Secretary, Department of Education and Science, since 1981; *b* 11 July 1939; *s* of Henry Forbes Summers, *qv*; *m* 1964, Marian Elizabeth Ottley; four *s. Educ:* Tonbridge Sch.; Corpus Christi Coll., Oxford. Min. of Educn, 1961–64; DES, 1964–74; Private Sec. to Minister for the Arts, 1965–66; Cabinet Office, 1974–76; DES, 1976–. *Recreations:* family, music. *Address:* c/o Department of Education and Science, Elizabeth House, York Road, SE1 7PH.

SUMMERSCALE, David Michael, MA; Head Master of Westminster School, since 1986; *b* 22 April 1937; *s* of Noel Tynwald Summerscale and Beatrice (*née* Wilson); *m* 1975, Pauline, *d* of Prof. Michel Fleury, Président de l'Ecole des Hautes Etudes, Paris, Directeur des Antiquités Historiques de l'Ile-de-France; one *s* one *d. Educ:* Northaw; Sherborne Sch.; Trinity Hall, Cambridge. Lectr in English Literature and Tutor, St Stephen's Coll., Univ. of Delhi, 1959–63; Charterhouse, 1963–75 (Head of English, Housemaster); Master of Haileybury, 1976–86. Oxford and Cambridge Schs Examination Bd Awarder and Reviser in English. Vice-Chm., E-SU Scholarship Cttee, 1982–; Member: Managing Cttee of Cambridge Mission to Delhi, 1965; C. F. Andrews Centenary Appeal Cttee, 1970; HMC Academic Policy Sub-Cttee, 1982–. FRSA 1984. *Publications:* articles on English and Indian literature; dramatisations of novels and verse. *Recreations:* music, play production, reading, mountaineering, games (squash (Mem. SRA), cricket, tennis, rackets (Mem. Tennis and Rackets Assoc.), golf, football, cross-country, hockey). *Address:* 17 Dean's Yard, SE1P 3PB. *Clubs:* Athenæum, I Zingari, Free Foresters, Jesters; Club Alpin Suisse.

SUMMERSCALE, Peter Wayne; HM Diplomatic Service; Deputy Leader, UK Delegation to Conference on Security and Co-operation in Europe, Vienna, since 1986; *b* 22 April 1935; *s* of Sir John Summerscale, KBE; *m* 1st, 1964, Valerie Turner (marr. diss. 1983); one *s* two *d*; 2nd, 1985, Cristina Fournier. *Educ:* Rugby Sch.; New Coll., Oxford Univ. (Exhibnr; 1st Cl. Hons Modern History); Russian Res. Centre, Harvard Univ. FO, 1960–62; Polit. Residency, Bahrain, 1962–65; 1st Sec., Tokyo, 1965–68; FCO, 1968–69; Cabinet Office, 1969–71; 1st Sec. and Head of Chancery, Santiago, Chile, 1971–75; Head of CSCE Unit, FCO, 1976–77; Dep. Leader, UK Delegn, Belgrade Rev. Conf., 1977–78; Counsellor and Head of Chancery, Brussels, 1978–79; Vis. FCO Res. Fellow, RIIA, Chatham House, 1979–81; Head of Civilian Faculty, Nat. Defence Coll., 1981–82; Ambassador to Costa Rica, 1982–86, and concurrently (non-resident) to Nicaragua. *Publications:* (jtly) Soviet—East European Dilemmas, 1981; The East European Predicament, 1982; articles on E Europe and communism. *Recreations:* sailing, skiing, walking. *Address:* c/o Foreign and Commonwealth Office, SW1; 5 Grove Terrace, NW5. *Club:* Royal Automobile.

SUMMERSKILL, Dr the Hon. Shirley Catherine Wynne; Medical Practitioner since 1959; *b* London, 9 Sept. 1931; *d* of late Dr E. J. Samuel and Baroness Summerskill, CH, PC. *Educ:* St Paul's Girls' Sch.; Somerville Coll., Oxford; St Thomas' Hospital. MA, BM, BCh., 1958. Treas., Oxford Univ. Labour Club. 1952. Resident House Surgeon, later House Physician, St Helier Hosp., Carshalton, 1959. Contested (Lab): Blackpool North by-election, 1962; Halifax, 1983. MP (Lab) Halifax, 1964–83; opposition spokesman on health, 1970–74; Parly Under-Sec. of State, Home Office, 1974–79; opposition spokesman on home affairs, 1979–83. Vice-Chm., PLP Health Gp, 1964–69, Chm., 1969–70; Mem., Labour Party NEC, 1981–83. UK delegate, UN Status of Women Commn, 1968 and 1969; Mem. British delegn, Council of Europe and WEU, 1968, 1969. *Publication:* A Surgical Affair (novel), 1963.

SUMMERSON, Sir John (Newenham), Kt 1958; CBE 1952; FBA 1954; BA(Arch); FSA; ARIBA; Curator of Sir John Soane's Museum, 1945–84; *b* 25 Nov. 1904; *o s* of late Samuel James Summerson of Darlington and Dorothea Worth Newenham; *m* 1938, Elizabeth Alison, *d* of H. R. Hepworth, CBE, Leeds; three *s. Educ:* Harrow; University College, London. From 1926 worked in architects' offices, including those of late W. D. Caröe and Sir Giles Gilbert Scott, OM. Instructor in Sch. of Architecture, Edinburgh Coll. of Art, 1929–30. Asst Editor, Architect and Building News, 1934–41; Dep. Dir, National Buildings Record, 1941–45. Lectr in History of Architecture: Architectural Assoc., 1949–62; Birkbeck Coll., 1950–67; Slade Prof. of Fine Art, Oxford, 1958–59; Ferens Prof. of Fine Art, Hull, 1960–61 and 1970–71; Slade Prof. of Fine Art, Cambridge, 1966–67; Bampton Lectr, Columbia Univ., 1968; Page-Barbour Lectr, Virginia Univ., 1972; Banister Fletcher Prof., UCL, 1981. Member: Royal Fine Art Commn, 1947–54; Royal Commn on Historical Monuments (England), 1953–74; Historic Buildings Council, 1953–78; Arts Council Art Panel, 1953–56; Historical Manuscripts Commn,

1959–83; Listed Buildings Cttee Min. of Housing and Local Govt, 1944–66 (Chm., 1960–62); Adv. Council on Public Records, 1968–74; Council, Architectural Assoc., 1940–45; Trustee, National Portrait Gallery, 1966–73. Hon. Fellow, Trinity Hall, Cambridge, 1968; Fellow, UCL. Foreign Hon. Mem., Amer. Acad. of Arts and Sciences, 1967; Chairman, National Council for Diplomas in Art and Design, 1961–70. Hon. DLitt: Leicester, 1959; Oxford, 1963; Hull, 1971; Newcastle, 1973; Hon. DSc Edinburgh, 1968; Hon. Dr, RCA, 1975. Hon. RSA 1982. RIBA Silver Medal (Essay), 1937; RIBA Royal Gold Medal for Architecture, 1976. *Publications:* Architecture Here and Now (with C. Williams-Ellis), 1934; John Nash, Architect to George IV, 1935; The Bombed Buildings of Britain (with J. M. Richards), 1942 and 1945; Georgian London, 1946, rev. edn 1970; The Architectural Association (Centenary History), 1947; Ben Nicholson (Penguin Modern Painters), 1948; Heavenly Mansions (essays), 1949; Sir John Soane, 1952; Sir Christopher Wren, 1953; Architecture in Britain, 1530–1830 (Pelican History of Art), 1953, 7th edn 1983; New Description of Sir J. Soane's Museum, 1955; The Classical Language of Architecture, 1964, rev. edn 1980; The Book of John Thorpe (Walpole Soc., vol. 40), 1966; Inigo Jones, 1966; Victorian Architecture (four studies in evaluation), 1969; (ed) Concerning Architecture, 1969; The London Building World of the Eighteen-Sixties, 1974; (jt author) The History of the King's Works (ed H. M. Colvin), vol. 3, 1976, vol. 4, 1982; The Life and Work of John Nash, Architect, 1981; The Architecture of the Eighteenth Century, 1986. *Address:* 1 Eton Villas, NW3. *T:* 01–722 6247. *Club:* Athenæum.

SUMMERTON, Dr Neil William; Under Secretary, Planning Land-Use Policy Directorate, Department of the Environment, since 1985; *b* 5 April 1942; *s* of H. E. W. Summerton and Nancy Summerton; *m* 1965, Pauline Webb; two *s*. *Educ:* Wellington Grammar Sch., Shropshire; King's Coll., London (BA History 1963; PhD War Studies 1970). Min. of Transport, 1966–69; PA to Principal, 1969–71, Asst Sec. (Co-ordination), 1971–74, KCL; DoE, 1974–; Asst Sec., heading various housing Divs, 1978–85. Attended HM Treasury Centre for Admin. Studies, 1968–69; Civil Service Top Management Programme, 1985. Elder of a Christian congregation; other Christian activities; Hon. Sec., Council on Christian Approaches to Defence and Disarmament, 1984–. *Publications:* A Noble Task: eldership and ministry in the local church, 1987; articles and essays on historical, theological and ethical matters. *Address:* 52 Hornsey Lane, N6 5LU. *T:* 01–272 0643.

SUMNER, Donald; *see* Sumner, W. D. M.

SUMNER, Victor Emmanuel, MRSL 1983; High Commissioner for Sierra Leone in the United Kingdom and Ambassador to Sweden, Denmark and Norway, since 1980 and to Spain, Portugal, Greece and Algeria, since 1983; *b* 17 April 1929; *s* of D. R. Sumner; *m* 1962, Gladys Victoria Small; two *s* one *d*. *Educ:* Fourah Bay Coll., Sierra Leone; Otterbein Coll., Ohio, USA; Laval Univ., Canada. BA, MA. School teacher, 1949–55; Sierra Leone Commonwealth and Foreign Service: Asst Sec., 1961; Sen. Asst Sec., 1965; Dep. Sec., 1968; Counsellor: Washington, 1969; Bonn, 1970; Permanent Secretary: Min. of For. Affairs, 1971; Min. of Health, 1974–76; Asst to Sec. to Pres., 1976–77; Permanent Sec., Min. of For. Affairs, 1977–80. *Recreations:* fishing, walking, volleyball, football. *Address:* 33 Portland Place, W1N 3AG. *T:* 01–636 6483.

SUMNER, His Honour (William) Donald (Massey), OBE (mil.) 1945; QC 1960; a Circuit Judge (formerly Judge of County Courts), 1961–82; *b* 13 Aug. 1913; *s* of Harold Sumner, OBE, Standish, Lancs. *Educ:* Charterhouse; Sidney Sussex Coll., Cambridge. Called to the Bar, Lincoln's Inn, 1937. Served War of 1939–45 with Royal Artillery (despatches); Lt-Col and Asst Adjutant-General, 21st Army Group. Mem. Orpington UDC, 1950–53. Acted as Asst Recorder of Plymouth frequently, 1954–61. MP (C) Orpington Div. of Kent, Jan. 1955–Oct. 1961; formerly PPS to Under Secs of State, Home Office, and to Solicitor-General. Officier, Ordre de la Couronne and Croix de Guerre (Belgian); Bronze Star Medal (American). *Address:* 2 Harcourt Buildings, Temple, EC4; Duxbury, Church Hill, High Halden, Ashford, Kent.

SUMPTION, Anthony James Chadwick, DSC 1944; *b* 15 May 1919; *s* of late John Chadwick Sumption and late Winifred Fanny Sumption; *m* 1946, Hedy Hedigan (marr. diss. 1979); two *s* two *d*. *Educ:* Cheltenham; London Sch. of Economics. Served RNVR, 1939–46; HM Submarines, 1941–45: comd Varangian, 1944; Upright, 1945. Solicitor, 1946; called to the Bar, Lincoln's Inn, 1971; a Recorder of the Crown Court, 1980–84. Member (C): LCC, 1949–52; Westminster City Council, 1953–56. Contested (C): Hayes and Harlington, March 1953; Middlesbrough W, 1964. *Publications:* Taxation of Overseas Income and Gains, 1973, 4th edn 1982, Tax Planning, (with Philip Lawton) 6th edn 1973–8th edn 1979, (with Giles Clarke) 9th edn 1981–10th edn 1982; Capital Gains Tax, 1981. *Recreations:* painting, angling. *Address:* c/o Coutts & Co., 188 Fleet Street, EC4. *Club:* Garrick.

See also J. P. C. Sumption.

SUMPTION, Jonathan Philip Chadwick; QC 1986; *b* 9 Dec. 1948; *s* of Anthony James Chadwick Sumption, *qv*; *m* 1971, Teresa Mary (*née* Whelan); one *s* two *d*. *Educ:* Eton; Magdalen College, Oxford (BA). Fellow (in History) of Magdalen College, Oxford, 1971–75; called to the Bar, Inner Temple, 1975. *Publications:* Pilgrimage: an image of medieval religion, 1975; The Albigensian Crusade, 1978. *Recreations:* music, history. *Address:* 34 Crooms Hill, Greenwich, SE10. *T:* 01–858 4444.

SUMSION, Herbert Whitton, CBE 1961; DMus Lambeth; FRCM, Hon. RAM, FRCO, FRSCM; Organist of Gloucester Cathedral, 1928–67; Director of Music, Ladies' College, Cheltenham, 1935–68; *b* Gloucester, 19 Jan. 1899; *m* 1927, Alice Hartley Garlichs, BA; three *s*. *Educ:* Durham Univ. (MusBac 1920). DMus Lambeth, 1947. Organist and Choirmaster at Christ Church, Lancaster Gate; Director of Music, Bishop's Stortford College; Asst Instructor in Music at Morley Coll., London; Teacher of Harmony and Counterpoint, Curtis Institute, Philadelphia, 1926–28; Conductor Three Choirs Fest., 1928, 1931, 1934, 1937, 1947, 1950, 1953, 1956, 1959, 1962, 1965. *Publications:* Introduction and Theme for Organ, 1935; Morning and Evening Service in G, 1935; Two pieces for Cello and Piano, 1939 (No 1 arranged for String Orchestra); Magnificat and Nunc Dimittis in G for Boys' Voices, 1953, for Men's Voices, 1953, for Boys' Voices in D, 1973; Cradle Song for Organ, 1953; Benedicite in B flat, 1955; Four Carol Preludes for Organ, 1956; Festival Benedicite in D, 1971; They That Go Down to the Sea in Ships (anthem), 1979; Transposition Exercises, 1980; Piano Technique, a Book of Exercises, 1980; There is a Green Hill Far Away (anthem), 1981; Two Anthems for Holy Communion, 1981; In Exile (By the Waters of Babylon) (anthem), 1981. *Address:* Hartley, Private Road, Rodborough Common, Stroud, Glos GL5 5BT. *T:* Amberley 3528.

See also J. W. Sumsion.

SUMSION, John Walbridge; Registrar of Public Lending Right, since 1981; *b* 16 Aug. 1928; *s* of Dr Herbert Sumsion, *qv*; *m* 1st, 1961, Annette Dorothea Wilson (marr. diss. 1979); two *s* two *d*; 2nd, 1979, Hazel Mary Jones (*née* English). *Educ:* St George's Choir Sch., Windsor Castle; St Thomas' Choir Sch., New York City; Rendcomb Coll., Cirencester; Clare Coll., Cambridge (BA (Hons) History); Yale Univ., USA (MA Economics); Cornell Univ., USA (Teaching Fellow). FBIM. Somervell Brothers (K Shoemakers) Ltd: Graduate trainee, 1954; Production Manager (Women's Shoes), 1959; Director, 1962–81. *Recreations:* music (flute, singing), tennis. *Address:* Stoneway, Appleton Wiske, Northallerton, N Yorks DL6 2AF. *T:* Great Smeaton 408. *Clubs:* United Oxford & Cambridge University; Stockton-on-Tees Rotary.

SUNDARAVADIVELU, Neyyadupakkam Duraiswamy; Vice President, Madras State Board for Adult Education; Vice-Chancellor, University of Madras, 1969–75; *b* 15 Oct. 1912. *Educ:* Univ. of Madras (MA, Licentiate in Teaching). Asst Panchayat Officer (organising and directing village panchayats), 1935–40; Madras Educnl Subordinate Service, inspection of primary schs, 1940–42; Madras Educnl Service, inspection of secondary schs and gen. direction of primary schs, 1942–51; Dep. Dir of Public Instruction, 1951–56 and Comr for Public Examns, 1954–65, Tamil Nadu; Dir of Higher Educn, Tamil Nadu, 1965–66; Dir of Public Libraries, Tamil Nadu, 1954–65; Jt Educnl Adviser to Govt of India, Min. of Educn, New Delhi, 1966–68; Chief Educnl Adviser and Additional Sec. to Govt of Tamil Nadu, Educn Dept, 1968–69; Dir of Collegiate Educn, Tamil Nadu, 1968–69. Visited: UK, 1951, 1962, 1973; USSR, 1961, 1967, 1971, 1973; USA, 1964, 1970; France, 1951, 1968, 1970, 1971, 1973; Malaysia, 1966, 1975; Philippines, 1971, 1972; Ghana, 1971; Canada, 1970; Singapore, 1966, 1975; Hong Kong, 1970, 1975; German Dem. Republic, 1973; participated in various confs, meetings, etc. Past Member: Nat. Council of Educnl Research and Trng, New Delhi; Nat. Commn on UNESCO; Mem., Nat. Council for Rural Higher Educn; Pres., Madras Cttee of World Univ. Service (Vice-Pres., Indian Nat. Cttee); Mem., Nat. Bd of Adult Educn; Chm., Southern Languages Book Trust; Mem., Standing Cttee of Inter-Univ. Bd of India and Ceylon, New Delhi; Vice-Pres., Indian Adult Educn Assoc.; Mem., Central Cttee of Tamil Nadu Tuberculosis Assoc.; Chm., Kendriya Vidyalaya, Gill Nagar, Madras. Originator of schemes, Free Mid-day Meals, School Improvement, and Free Supply of Uniforms to School Children, recommended to all Asian countries for adoption (personally commended by Pres. of India, 1960). Hon. DLitt Madras, 1983. Padma Shri (presidential award), 1961. *Publications:* 45 books in Tamil, incl. 13 for children and Autobiography, part I, 1983; State awards for best travelogue, 1968, 1981. *Address:* 90C Shenoynagar, Madras 600030, India. *T:* Madras 612516.

SUNDERLAND, Eric, PhD; FIBiol; Principal, University College of North Wales, Bangor, since 1984; *b* 18 March 1930; *s* of Leonard Sunderland and Mary Agnes (*née* Davies); *m* 1957, Jean Patricia (*née* Watson); two *d*. *Educ:* Amman Valley Grammar Sch.; Univ. of Wales (BA, MA); Univ. of London (PhD). Commnd Officer, RA, 1955–56. Res. Asst, UCL, 1953–54; Res. Scientist, NCB, 1957–58; Univ. of Durham: Lectr, 1958–66; Sen. Lectr, 1966–71; Prof. of Anthropology, 1971–84; Pro Vice Chancellor, 1979–84. Sec.-Gen., Internat. Union of Anthropol and Ethnol Sciences, 1978–; Hon. Treasurer, Royal Anthropol Inst., 1985– (Hon. Sec., 1978–85); Chm., Biosocial Soc., 1981–85. Hon. Mem., The Gorsedd, 1985. *Publications:* Elements of Human and Social Geography: some anthropological perspectives, 1973; (ed jtly) Genetic Variation in Britain, 1973; (ed jtly) The Operation of Intelligence: biological preconditions for the operation of intelligence, 1980; (ed jtly) Genetic and Population Studies in Wales, 1986; contrib. Annals of Human Biol., Human Heredity, Man, Human Biol., Nature, and Amer. Jl of Phys. Anthropol. *Recreations:* travel, gardening, book collecting, reading. *Address:* University College of North Wales, Bangor, Gwynedd. *T:* Bangor 351151. *Club:* Athenæum.

SUNDERLAND, (Godfrey) Russell; Director of Shipping Policy, Department of Transport, since 1984; *b* 28 July 1936; *s* of Allan and Laura Sunderland; *m* 1965, Greta Jones; one *s* one *d*. *Educ:* Heath Grammar Sch., Halifax; The Queen's College, Oxford (MA). Ministry of Aviation: Asst Principal, 1962; Asst Private Sec. to Minister, 1964; Principal, 1965; HM Diplomatic Service: First Sec. (Civil Air), Beirut, and other Middle East posts, 1969; Principal, Board of Trade, 1971; Asst Sec., DTI, 1973; Under Sec., DTI, 1979. Chairman, Consultative Shipping Group, 1984–. *Address:* Windrush, Silkmore Lane, West Horsley, Leatherhead, Surrey KT24 6JQ. *T:* East Horsley 2660.

SUNDERLAND, Prof. Sir Sydney, Kt 1971; CMG 1961; FAA 1954; Professor of Experimental Neurology, 1961–75, now Emeritus Professor, and Dean of the Faculty of Medicine 1953–71, University of Melbourne; *b* Brisbane, Aust., 31 Dec. 1910; *s* of Harry and Anne Sunderland; *m* 1939, Nina Gwendoline Johnston, LLB; one *s*. *Educ:* University of Melbourne. BM, BS 1935, DSc 1945, DMed 1946, Melbourne. FRACP 1941; FRACS 1952. Sen. Lectr in Anatomy, Univ. of Melbourne, 1936–37; Demonstrator in Human Anatomy, Oxford, 1938–39; Prof. of Anatomy, Univ. of Melbourne, 1940–61. Visiting Specialist (Hon. Major) 115 Aust. Gen. Mil. Hosp., 1941–45. Mem. Zool Bd of Vict., 1944–65 (Chm. Scientific Cttee, 1958–62); Dep. Chm., Adv. Cttee to Mental Hygiene Dept, Vict., 1952–63; Mem. Nat. Health and MRC, 1953–69; Chm., Med. Research Adv. Cttee of Nat. Health and MRC, 1964–69. Visiting Prof. of Anatomy, Johns Hopkins Univ., 1953–54; Sec., Div. of Biol Sciences, Aust. Acad. Sci., 1955–58; Member: Nat. Radiation Adv. Cttee, 1957–64 (Chm. 1958–64); Defence Research and Development Policy Cttee, 1957–75; Med. Services Cttee, Dept of Defence, 1957–78; Council, AMA, Victorian Branch, 1960–68; Safety Review Cttee, Aust. Atomic Energy Commn, 1961–74 (Chm.); Aust. Univs Commn, 1962–76; Cttee of Management, Royal Melbourne Hosp., 1963–71; Protective Chemistry Research Adv. Cttee, Dept of Supply, 1964–73 (Chm.); Victorian Med. Adv. Cttee, 1962–71; Board of Walter and Eliza Hall Inst. of Med. Research, 1968–75. Governor, Ian Potter Foundn, 1964–. Trustee: National Museum, 1954–82; Van Cleef Foundn, 1971–. Fogarty Scholar in residence, Nat. Inst. of Health, Bethesda, USA, 1972–73. Foundn Fellow, Aust. Acad. of Science, 1954, and rep. on Pacific Science Council, 1957–69. Hon. MD: Tasmania, 1970; Queensland, 1975; Hon. LLD: Melbourne, 1975; Monash, 1977. *Publications:* Nerves and Nerve Injuries, 1968, 2nd edn 1978; about 100 articles in scientific jls in Gt Britain, Europe, US and Australia. *Address:* 72 Kingstoun, 461 St Kilda Road, Melbourne, Victoria 3004, Australia. *T:* 2665858. *Club:* Melbourne.

SUPHAMONGKHON, Dr Konthi, Kt Grand Cordon of the White Elephant, Kt Grand Cordon, Order of the Crown of Thailand; Kt Grand Commander, Order of Chula Chom Klao; Hon. GCVO 1972; Ambassador of Thailand to the Court of St James's, 1970–76; *b* 3 Aug. 1916; *m* 1951, Dootsdi Atthakravi; two *s* one *d*. *Educ:* Univ. of Moral and Political Sciences, Bangkok (LLB); Univ. of Paris (Dr-en-Droit). Joined Min. of Foreign Affairs, 1940; Second Sec., Tokyo, 1942–44; Chief of Polit. Div., 1944–48; Dir-Gen., Western Affairs Dept, 1948–50; UN Affairs Dept, 1950–52; Minister to Australia, 1952–56, Ambassador, June 1956–59, and to New Zealand, Oct. 1956–59; Dir-Gen. of Internat. Organizations, 1959–63; Adviser on Foreign Affairs to the Prime Minister, 1962–64; Sec.-Gen., SEATO, 1964–65; Ambassador to Federal Republic of Germany, 1965–70, and to Finland, 1967–70. Frequent Lecturer, 1944–; notably at Thammasat Univ., 1944–52, at National Defence Coll., 1960–62, and at Army War Coll., Bangkok, 1960–63. Holds foreign decorations. *Publication:* Thailand and her relations with France, 1940 (in French). *Recreations:* tennis, golf, swimming. *Address:* c/o Ministry of Foreign Affairs, Bangkok, Thailand. *Clubs:* Travellers', Hurlingham; Royal Wimbledon Golf, Cuddington Golf.

SUPPLE, Prof. Barry Emanuel, FRHistS; Professor of Economic History, University of Cambridge, since 1981; Master of St Catharine's College, Cambridge, since 1984; *b* 27

Oct. 1930; *s* of Solomon and Rose Supple; *m* 1958, Sonia (*née* Caller); two *s* one *d*. *Educ:* Hackney Downs Grammar Sch.; London Sch. of Econs and Polit. Science (BScEcon 1952); Christ's Coll., Cambridge (PhD 1955). FRHistS 1972. Asst Prof. of Business History, Grad. Sch. of Business Admin, Harvard Univ., 1955–60; Associate Prof. of Econ. Hist., McGill Univ., 1960–62; University of Sussex: Lectr, Reader, then Prof. of Econ. and Social Hist., 1962–78; Dean, Sch. of Social Sciences, 1965–68; Pro-Vice-Chancellor (Arts and Social Studies), 1968–72; Pro-Vice-Chancellor, 1978; University of Oxford: Reader in Recent Social and Econ. Hist., 1978–81; Professorial Fellow, Nuffield Coll., 1978–81; Professorial Fellow, 1981–83, Hon. Fellow, 1984, Christ's Coll., Cambridge. Hon. Fellow, Worcester Coll., 1986. Chm., Consultative Cttee of Assessment of Performance Unit, DES, 1975–80; Member: Council, SSRC, 1972–77; Social Science Fellowship Cttee, Nuffield Foundn, 1974–. Co-editor, Econ. Hist. Rev., 1973–82. *Publications:* Commercial Crisis and Change in England, 1600–42, 1959; (ed) The Experience of Economic Growth, 1963; Boston Capitalists and Western Railroads, 1967; The Royal Exchange Assurance: a history of British insurance, 1720–1970, 1970; (ed) Essays in Business History, 1977; articles and revs in learned jls. *Recreations:* tennis, photography. *Address:* The Master's Lodge, St Catharine's College, Cambridge. *T:* Cambridge 338347. *Club:* United Oxford & Cambridge University.

SURREY, Archdeacon of; *see* Barber, Ven. P. E.

SURRIDGE, Sir (Ernest) Rex (Edward), Kt 1951; CMG 1946; retired; *b* 21 Feb. 1899; *s* of late E. E. Surridge, Coggeshall, Essex; *m* Roy (*d* 1982), *d* of late Major F. E. Bradstock, DSO, MC; two *s*. *Educ:* Felsted; St John's College, Oxford. European War, 1917–20, Lieut 7th Bn DCLI; St John's College, Oxford, 1920–22, Mod. Hist. (Hons); Colonial Admin. Service, 1924, Tanganyika; Assistant Chief Secretary, Tanganyika, 1936; Deputy Chief Secretary, Kenya, 1940; Chief Secretary to Govt of Tanganyika, 1946–51; Salaries Comr, Cyprus, 1953–54; Financial Comr, Seychelles, 1957–58; Salaries Comr, High Commn Territories (South Africa), 1958–59; Salaries Comr, Gibraltar, 1959–60. *Address:* 10 Park Manor, St Aldhelm's Road, Branksome Park, Poole, Dorset. *T:* Bournemouth 766638.

SURTEES, John, MBE 1961; controls companies in automotive research and development and property development; *b* 11 Feb. 1934; *s* of late John Norman and Dorothy Surtees; *m* 1962, Patricia Phyllis Burke (marr. diss. 1979); no *c*. *Educ:* Ashburton School, Croydon. 5 year engineering apprenticeship, Vincent Engrs, Stevenage, Herts. Motorcycle racing, 1952–60; British Champion, 1954, 1955; World 500 cc Motorcycle Champion, 1956; World 350 and 500 cc Motorcycle Champion, 1958, 1959, 1960. At end of 1960 he retd from motorcycling; motor racing, 1961–72; with Ferrari Co., won World Motor Racing title, 1964; 5th in World Championship, 1965 (following accident in Canada due to suspension failure); in 1966 left Ferrari in mid-season and joined Cooper, finishing 2nd in World Championship; in 1967 with Honda Motor Co. as first driver and develt engr (1967–68); 3rd in World Championship; with BRM as No 1 driver, 1969; designed and built own Formula 1 car, 1970. *Publications:* Motorcycle Racing and Preparation, 1958; John Surtees Book of Motorcycling, 1960; Speed, 1963; Six Days in August, 1968. *Recreations:* music, architecture; interested in most sports. *Address:* c/o John Surtees Developments Ltd, Station Road, Edenbridge, Kent. *T:* Edenbridge 863773.

SUSMAN, Maurice Philip, MB, ChM Sydney; FRCS; FRACS; AAMC; Hon. Consulting Surgeon, Sydney Hospital, 1958; Hon. Consulting Thoracic Surgeon, Royal North Shore Hospital, Sydney, 1958; *b* 4 Aug. 1898; *s* of Philip Tasman Susman and Gertrude Lehane; *m* 1934, Ina May Shanahan; one *d*. *Educ:* Sydney Church of England Grammar School; University of Sydney. *Publications:* some ephemeral light verse, essays and medical and surgical articles. *Recreations:* chess, flying light aircraft, meditating, reading books enjoyed in the past and an occasional new one. *Address:* 22 Bathurst Street, Woollahra, NSW 2025, Australia. *T:* 389 6053. *Club:* Royal Aero (NSW).

SUTCLIFF, Rosemary, OBE 1975 (for services to children's literature); writer of historical novels for adults and children; *b* 14 Dec. 1920; *d* of George Ernest Sutcliff and Elizabeth Sutcliff (*née* Lawton). *Educ:* privately. Carne Medal, 1959; The Other Award, 1978; Phoenix Award, 1985. *Publications:* Chronicles of Robin Hood, 1950; The Queen Elizabeth Story, 1950; The Armourer's House, 1951; Brother Dusty-feet, 1952; Simon, 1953; The Eagle of the Ninth, 1954; Outcast, 1955; Lady in Waiting, 1956; The Shield Ring, 1956; The Silver Branch, 1957; Warrior Scarlet, 1958; Rider of the White Horse, 1959; Lantern Bearers, 1959; Houses and History, 1960; Knights Fee, 1960; Rudyard Kipling, 1960; Beowulf, 1961; Dawn Wind, 1961; Sword at Sunset, 1963; The Hound of Ulster, 1963; The Mark of the Horse Lord, 1965; Heroes and History, 1965; The Chief's Daughter, 1967; The High Deeds of Finn McCool, 1967; A Circlet of Oak Leaves, 1968; The Flowers of Adonis, 1969; The Witches' Brat, 1970; Tristan and Iseult, 1971; The Capricorn Bracelet, 1973; The Changeling, 1974; Blood Feud, 1977; Sun Horse, Moon Horse, 1977; Shifting Sands, 1977; Song for a Dark Queen, 1978; The Light Beyond the Forest, 1979; Frontier Wolf, 1980; The Sword and the Circle: King Arthur and the Knights of the Round Table, 1981; Eagle's Egg, 1981; The Road to Camlann, 1981; Blue Remembered Hills (childhood memoir), 1982; Bonnie Dundee, 1983; Flame Coloured Taffeta, 1985; The Roundabout Horse, 1986. *Recreations:* painting, needlework, dogs, travel. *Address:* Swallowshaw, Walberton, Arundel, West Sussex BN18 0PQ. *T:* Yapton 551316.

SUTCLIFFE, His Honour Edward Davis, QC 1959; a Circuit Judge and Additional Judge of the Central Criminal Court, 1969–84; *b* 25 Aug. 1917; 3rd *s* of late Richard Joseph and Anne Sutcliffe; *m* 1939, Elsie Eileen Brooks; two *d*. *Educ:* University College School, Hampstead; Wadham College, Oxford (MA). Served Royal Artillery, 1939–46 (despatches). Called to Bar, Inner Temple, 1946; Bencher, 1966. Recorder of Canterbury, 1968–69, and Hon. Recorder, 1974–84. Mem., Criminal Injuries Compensation Board, 1964–69; Legal Assessor, GMC and GDC, 1967–69; Chm., Statutory Cttee, Pharmaceutical Soc., 1986–. Governor: Bedford Coll., London, 1968–76; St Michael's Sch., Otford, 1973–83. Hon. Freedom of Canterbury, 1983. Liveryman, Needlemakers' Co. *Address:* 41 West Hill Park, Highgate, N6 6ND.

See also A. J. C. Britton.

SUTCLIFFE, Geoffrey Scott, OBE 1944; TD 1952; *b* 12 June 1912; *o s* of late John Walton Sutcliffe and late Alice Mary Sutcliffe (*née* Scott); *m* 1946, Mary Sylvia, *d* of late George Herbert Kay; two *s* one *d*. *Educ:* Repton. TA 2nd Lieut, 1939; Lt-Col, 1943; GSO1, AFHQ, N Africa and Italy; served France and Belgium, 1940; N Africa and Italy, 1943–45 (despatches, OBE). Ferodo Ltd, 1932: Works Dir, 1947; Home Sales Dir, 1952; Man. Dir, 1955; Chm., 1956–67; Turner & Newall Ltd: Dir, 1957–75; Jt Man. Dir, 1963–74; Dep. Chm., 1967–74. *Recreations:* cricket, gardening, reading. *Address:* Hill Farm House, Inkpen Road, Kintbury, Berks RG15 0TX. *T:* Kintbury 58681. *Clubs:* Army and Navy, MCC.

SUTCLIFFE, John Harold Vick; DL; landowner; company director; Member, Housing Corporation, since 1982; *b* 30 April 1931; *o s* of late Sir Harold Sutcliffe and Emily Theodora Cochrane; *m* 1959, Cecilia Mary, *e d* of Ralph Meredyth Turton; three *s* one *d*. *Educ:* Winchester Coll.; New Coll., Oxford (MA). 2nd Lieut RA, 1950–51. Called to Bar, Inner Temple, 1956; practised until 1960, Midland Circuit. Chairman: Great Fosters (1931) Ltd, 1958–; Northern Heritage Trust Ltd, 1981–; North Housing Assoc., 1985–; North Housing Ltd, 1985–; Vice-Chm., Civic Trust North East, 1977–; Director: Allied Investors Trusts Ltd, 1958–69; Norton Junction Sand & Gravel Ltd, 1958–64; Tyne Tees Waste Disposal Ltd, 1964–71. Contested (C): Oldham West, 1959; Chorley, Lancs, 1964; Middlesbrough West, 1966. MP (C) Middlesbrough W, 1970–Feb. 1974. Contested (C) Teesside Thornaby, Oct. 1974. Mem., N Yorks Moors Nat. Park Cttee, 1982–. DL Cleveland, 1983. *Recreations:* gardening, travel, shooting. *Address:* Chapelgarth, Great Broughton, Middlesbrough, Cleveland. *T:* Stokesley 712228.

SUTCLIFFE, Kenneth Edward; Headmaster, Latymer Upper School, Hammersmith, W6, 1958–71; *b* 24 March 1911; *s* of late Rev. James Sutcliffe; *m* 1937, Nora, *d* of late Charles Herbert Burcham; two *d*. *Educ:* Manchester Grammar School; King's College, Cambridge (Scholar). BA Modern and Medieval Languages Tripos 1932; MA 1936. Assistant Master, Stockport Grammar School, 1933–38; Assistant Master, Liverpool Institute High School, 1938–46; Headmaster, Cockburn High School, Leeds, 1946–57. Served with Royal Armoured Corps and Intelligence Corps, 1940–46, Captain (General Staff). Lay Reader, dios of Ripon, Guildford, Bath and Wells, 1953–81. *Publications:* German Translation and Composition, 1948; French Translation and Composition, 1951; Fahrt ins Blaue (a German course for schools), 1960. *Address:* Hatherlow, Springfield Drive, Wedmore, Somerset.

SUTCLIFFE, Prof. Reginald Cockcroft, CB 1961; OBE 1942; FRS 1957; BSc, PhD Leeds; Professor of Meteorology, Reading University, 1965–70, now Emeritus Professor; *b* 16 Nov. 1904; 2nd *s* of late O. G. Sutcliffe and late Jessie Sutcliffe (*née* Cockcroft), Cleckheaton, Yorkshire; *m* 1929, Evelyn, *d* of late Rev. William Williams, Halkyn; two *d*. *Educ:* Whitcliffe Mount Grammar Sch., Cleckheaton; Leeds Univ.; University Coll., Bangor. Professional Asst, Meteorological Office, 1927; Meteorological Office appointments: Malta, 1928–32, Felixstowe, 1932–35; Air Ministry, 1935–37; Thorney Island, 1937–39. Squadron Leader RAFVR, France, 1939–40; Sen. Meteorological Officer, No. 3 Bomber Group RAF, 1941–44; Group Capt., Chief Meteorological Officer AEAF, later BAFO, Germany, 1944–46. Research in Meteorological Office, 1946–65; Director of Research, 1957–65. President, Commission for Aerology of World Meteorological Organization, 1957–61; Mem. Adv. Cttee, World Meteorological Organization, 1964–68; Mem. Council, Royal Soc., 1968–70; Pres., Internat. Assoc. of Meteorology, 1967–71; Hon. Mem., Amer. Meteorological Soc., 1975–; Royal Meteorological Society: Pres., 1955–57; Hon. Mem., 1976; Editor, Quarterly Jl, 1970–73; Buchan Prize, 1950; Symons Gold Medal, 1955. Charles Chree Medal, Physical Soc., 1959; Internat. Meteorological Organization Prize, 1963. *Publications:* Meteorology for Aviators, 1938; Weather and Climate, 1966; meteorological papers in jls. *Address:* Pound Farm, Cadmore End, near High Wycombe, Bucks HP14 3PF. *T:* High Wycombe 881315.

SUTCLIFFE, Air Cdre Walter Philip, CB 1958; DFC 1940; *b* 15 Aug. 1910; *s* of late W. Sutcliffe, Brampton, Cumberland; *m* 1947, Margery Anne Taylor, *d* of W. L. Taylor, Tulse Hill, SW2; one *s*. *Educ:* Durham School; Royal Air Force Coll., Cranwell. Fleet Air Arm, 1933–35 and 1937–39; Central Flying Sch., 1936. War of 1939–45: Bomber Command, 1939–42, India and Burma, 1942–45 (despatches). RAF Staff College, 1946; Director of Operational Training, Air Ministry, 1948–50; Standing Group, NATO, 1950–51; RAF Station, Wittering, 1953–55; SHAPE, 1955–56; Atomic Weapon Trials, Australia, 1957; Director of Intelligence, Air Ministry, 1958–61; retd April 1961; Officers' Association, 1961–75. Officer, Legion of Merit (USA), 1945. *Address:* The Pond House, Pluckley, Kent. *T:* Pluckley 209.

SUTHERLAND, family name of **Countess of Sutherland.**

SUTHERLAND, 6th Duke of, *cr* 1833; **John Sutherland Egerton,** TD; DL; Bt 1620; Baron Gower, 1703; Earl Gower, Viscount Trentham, 1746; Marquis of Stafford (county), 1786; Viscount Brackley and Earl of Ellesmere, 1846; *b* 10 May 1915; *o s* of 4th Earl of Ellesmere and Violet (*d* 1976), *e d* of 4th Earl of Durham; *S* father, 1944; *S* kinsman as Duke of Sutherland, 1963; *m* 1st, 1939, Lady Diana Percy (*d* 1978), *yr d* of 8th Duke of Northumberland; 2nd, 1979, Evelyn, *e d* of late Maj. Robert Moubray. Served War of 1939–45 (prisoner). DL Berwickshire, 1955. *Heir: c* Cyril Reginald Egerton [*b* 7 Sept. 1905; *m* 1st, 1934, Mary (*d* 1949), *d* of late Rt Hon. Sir Ronald Hugh Campbell, PC, GCMG; one *s* three *d*; 2nd, 1954, Mary (*d* 1982), *d* of late Sir Sydney Lea, Dunley Hall, Worcestershire]. *Address:* Mertoun, St Boswell's, Roxburghshire; Lingay Cottage, Hall Farm, Newmarket. *Clubs:* White's, Turf; Jockey (Newmarket).

See also J. M. E. Askew, Lady M. Colville, Baron Home of the Hirsel, Viscount Rochdale.

SUTHERLAND, Countess of (24th in line) *cr* (*c*) 1235; **Elizabeth Millicent Sutherland;** Lady Strathnaver (*c*) 1235; Chief of Clan Sutherland; *b* 30 March 1921; *o c* of Lord Alastair St Clair Sutherland-Leveson-Gower, MC (*d* 1921; 2nd *s* of 4th Duke), and Baroness Osten Driesen (*d* 1931); *niece* of 5th Duke of Sutherland, KT, PC; *S* (to uncle's Earldom of Sutherland and Lordship of Strathnaver), 1963; *m* 1946, Charles Noel Janson, DL, late Welsh Guards; two *s* one *d* (and one *s* decd). *Educ:* Queen's College, Harley Street, W1, and abroad. Land Army, 1939–41; Laboratory Technician: Raigmore Hospital, Inverness, 1941–43; St Thomas' Hospital, SE1, 1943–45. Chairman: Dunrobin Castle Ltd; The Northern Times Ltd. *Recreations:* reading, swimming. *Heir: e s* Lord Strathnaver, *qv*. *Address:* Dunrobin Castle, Sutherland; House of Tongue, by Lairg, Sutherland; 39 Edwardes Square, W8. *T:* 01–603 0659.

SUTHERLAND, Hon. Lord; Ranald Iain Sutherland; a Senator of the College of Justice in Scotland, since 1985; *b* 23 Jan. 1932; *s* of J. W. and A. K. Sutherland, Edinburgh; *m* 1964, Janice Mary, *d* of W. S. Miller, Edinburgh; two *s*. *Educ:* Edinburgh Academy; Edinburgh University. MA 1951, LLB 1953. Admitted to Faculty of Advocates, 1956; QC (Scot.) 1969. Advocate Depute, 1962–64, 1971–77; Standing Junior Counsel to Min. of Defence (Army Dept), 1964–69. Mem., Criminal Injuries Compensation Bd, 1977–85. *Recreations:* sailing, shooting. *Address:* 38 Lauder Road, Edinburgh. *T:* 031–667 5280. *Club:* New (Edinburgh).

SUTHERLAND, Anthony (Frederic Arthur); Under-Secretary, Department of Employment, retired; *b* 19 Oct. 1916; *e s* of Bertram and Grace Sutherland; *m* 1940, Betty Josephine Glass; one *s* two *d*. *Educ:* Christ's Hosp.; Gonville and Caius Coll., Cambridge (Classical Schol.). 1st cl. hons Classics, 1938; MA 1944. HM Forces, 1940–45 (Major, Mddx Regt). Asst Prin., Min. of Labour, 1938; Prin., 1943; Prin. Private Sec. to Ministers of Labour, 1948–53; Counsellor (Labour), British Embassy, Rome, 1953–55; Asst Sec., 1955; Imp. Def. Coll., 1960; Under-Sec., 1967. Coronation Medal, 1953; Silver Jubilee Medal, 1977. *Recreations:* philately, bird watching. *Address:* 53 Wieland Road, Northwood, Mddx. *T:* Northwood 22078. *Club:* Civil Service.

SUTHERLAND, Sir (Frederick) Neil, Kt 1969; CBE 1955; MA; Chairman, The Marconi Co. (formerly Marconi's Wireless Telegraph Co. Ltd), and of Marconi Instruments, 1965–69, retired; Director, English Electric Co. Ltd, 1965; *b* 4 March 1900; *s* of late Neil Hugh Sutherland; *m* 1st, 1931, Naruna d'Amorim Jordan (*d* 1970); one *s*; 2nd, 1973, Gladys Jackman (*d* 1986). *Educ:* St Catharine's College, Cambridge. MA 1922.

Served apprenticeship with English Electric Co. Ltd; Gen. Manager, English Electric Co. in Brazil, 1928; Man. Dir, English Electric (South Africa) Ltd, 1937; Gen. Manager, Marconi's Wireless Telegraph Co. Ltd, 1948; Man. Dir, Marconi Co. Ltd, 1958–65. *Recreation:* golf. *Address:* Conifers, 45 High Street, Wickham Market, Woodbridge, Suffolk IP13 0HE.

SUTHERLAND, Ian, MA; Director of Education and Training to Health Education Council, 1971–85; *b* 7 July 1926; *m* 1951, Virginia Scovil Bliss (marr. diss. 1978); one *s* one *d*. *Educ:* Wyggeston Grammar School, Leicester; Sidney Sussex College, Cambridge. Assistant Professor of Classics, Univ. of New Brunswick, NB, Canada, 1949–50; Asst Master: Christ's Hospital, 1951–52; Harrow School, 1952–60; Head Master, St John's School, Leatherhead, 1960–70; Dir of Educn, Health Educn Council, 1970–71. Mem., Wandsworth HA, 1986. Governor, Reeds Sch., 1980–. *Publications:* From Pericles to Cleophon, 1954; (ed) Health Education: perspectives and choices, 1979. *Recreations:* painting, cricket. *Address:* 57 Burntwood Grange Road, Wandsworth Common, SW18 3JY. *Clubs:* United Oxford & Cambridge University, MCC, Free Foresters'.

SUTHERLAND, Dr Ian Boyd; Research Fellow, Department of Clinical Surgery, University of Edinburgh, since 1986; *b* 19 Oct. 1926; *s* of William Sutherland and Grace Alexandra Campbell; *m* 1950, Charlotte Winifred Cordin; two *d*. *Educ:* Bradford Grammar Sch.; Edinburgh Univ. MB, ChB; FRCPE, FFCM, DPH. Medical Officer, RAF, 1950–52; Asst MOH, Counties of Roxburgh and Selkirk, 1953–55; Dep. MOH, County and Borough of Inverness, 1955–59; Dep. County MOH, Oxfordshire CC, 1959–60; Asst SMO, Leeds Regional Hosp. Bd, 1960–63; South Western Regional Hosp. Bd: Dep. Sen. Admin. MO, 1963–70; Sen. Admin. MO, 1970–73; Regional MO, S Western RHA, 1973–80; Community Medicine Specialist, Lothian Health Bd, 1980–86. *Recreations:* golf, reading, archaeology. *Address:* 11 Belford Terrace, Edinburgh EH4 3DQ.

SUTHERLAND, James, CBE 1974; Partner, McClure Naismith, Anderson & Gardiner (formerly McClure Naismith), Solicitors, Glasgow and Edinburgh, since 1951; *b* 15 Feb. 1920; *s* of James Sutherland, JP and Agnes Walker; *m* 1st, 1948, Elizabeth Kelly Barr; two *s*; 2nd, 1984, Grace Williamson Dawson. *Educ:* Queens Park Secondary Sch., Glasgow; Glasgow Univ. MA 1940, LLB 1948; Hon. LLD 1985. Served Royal Signals, 1940–46. Examr in Scots Law, 1951–55 and Mercantile Law and Industrial Law, 1968–69, Glasgow Univ.; Chm., Glasgow South Nat. Insce Tribunal, 1964–66; Member: Bd of Management, Glasgow Maternity and Women's Hosps, 1964–74 (Chm. 1966–74); Council, Law Soc. of Scotland, 1959–77 (Vice-Pres. 1969–70; Pres. 1972–74); Council, Internat. Bar Assoc., 1972– (Chm., Gen. Practice Section, 1978–80; Sec.-Gen., 1980–84; Pres., 1984–); GDC, 1975–; Scottish Dental Estimates Bd, 1982–; Vice-Chm., Glasgow Eastern Health Council, 1975–77; Deacon, Incorporation of Barbers, Glasgow, 1962–63; Sec., Local Dental Cttee, City of Glasgow, 1955–65; Dean, Royal Faculty of Procurators in Glasgow, 1977–80. Mem. Court, Univ. of Strathclyde, 1977–. *Recreation:* golf. *Address:* Greenacres, 20/1 Easter Belmont Road, Edinburgh EH12 6EX. *T:* 031–337 1888. *Clubs:* Western, Royal Scottish Automobile (Glasgow); Royal and Ancient.

SUTHERLAND, Prof. James Runcieman, FBA 1953; MA, BLitt; Emeritus Professor of Modern English Literature, University College, London (Lord Northcliffe Professor, 1951–67); *b* Aberdeen, 26 April 1900; *s* of Henry Edward Sutherland, Stockbroker; *m* 1st, 1931, Helen (*d* 1975) *d* of Will H. Dircks; 2nd, 1977, Eve Betts, *widow* of Ernest Betts. *Educ:* Aberdeen Grammar Sch.; Univ. of Aberdeen; Oxford Univ. BLitt Oxford, 1927. Lecturer in English, Univ. of Saskatchewan, 1921–23; Merton Coll., Oxford, 1923–25; Chancellor's English Essay Prize, Oxford, 1925; Lecturer in English, University College, Southampton, 1925; Lecturer in English, University of Glasgow, 1925–30; Senior Lecturer in English, University College, London, 1930–36; Professor of English Literature, Birkbeck College, London, 1936–44; Prof. of English Language and Literature, Queen Mary College, London, 1944–51. Warton lecturer on English Poetry to the British Academy, 1944; editor of The Review of English Studies, 1940–47. Visiting Professor: Harvard Univ., 1947; Indiana Univ., 1950–51; Univ. California, Los Angeles, 1967–68; Mellon Prof., Univ. of Pittsburgh, 1965; Berg Prof., NY Univ., 1969–70. Sir Walter Scott Lectures, Edinburgh University, 1952; Clark Lectures, Cambridge University, 1956; Alexander Lectures, Toronto University, 1956; Public Orator, University of London, 1957–62; W. P. Ker Memorial Lecture, Glasgow Univ., 1962; Clark Library Fellow, Univ. of California, Los Angeles, 1962–63. Hon. Mem. Modern Language Assoc. of America, 1960. Hon. LLD Aberdeen, 1955; Hon. DLitt Edinburgh, 1968; Hon. Doctor, Liège, 1974. *Publications:* Leucocholy (Poems), 1926; Jasper Weeple, 1930; The Medium of Poetry, 1934; Defoe, 1937; Background for Queen Anne, 1939; The Dunciad, 1943; English in the Universities, 1945; A Preface to Eighteenth Century Poetry, 1948; The English Critic, 1952; The Oxford Book of English Talk, 1953; On English Prose, 1957; English Satire, 1958; English Literature of the late Seventeenth Century, 1969; Daniel Defoe: a critical study, 1971; editions of plays by Nicholas Rowe, Thomas Dekker, John Dryden, William Shakespeare, and of Lucy Hutchinson's Memoirs of the Life of Colonel Hutchinson, 1973; (ed) The Oxford Book of Literary Anecdotes, 1975; The Restoration Newspaper and its Development, 1986; contributions to various literary journals. *Recreations:* fishing, second-hand book catalogues. *Address:* 16 Murray Court, 80 Banbury Road, Oxford OX2 6LQ. *T:* Oxford 510469.

SUTHERLAND, Dame Joan, AC 1975; DBE 1979 (CBE 1961); soprano; *b* 7 Nov. 1926; *d* of McDonald Sutherland, Sydney, NSW, and Muriel Alston Sutherland; *m* 1954, Richard Bonynge, *qv*; one *s*. *Educ:* St Catherine's, Waverley, Sydney. DMus. Début as Dido in Purcell's Dido and Aeneas, Sydney, 1947; subsequently concerts, oratorios and broadcasts throughout Australia. Came to London, 1951; joined Covent Garden, 1952, where she remained resident soprano for 7 years; won international fame with début as Lucia di Lammermoor, Covent Garden, 1959, and by early 1960s had sung throughout the Americas and Europe. Has specialised throughout her career in the popular and lesser-known bel canto operatic repertoire of 18th and 19th centuries, and has made many recordings. *Relevant publications:* Joan Sutherland, by R. Braddon, 1962; Joan Sutherland, by E. Greenfield, 1972; La Stupenda, by B. Adams, 1980. *Recreations:* reading, gardening, needlepoint. *Address:* c/o Ingpen & Williams, 14 Kensington Court, W8 5DN.

SUTHERLAND, John Alexander Muir; Chief Executive, Celtic Films Ltd, since 1986; *b* 5 April 1933; *m* 1970, Mercedes Gonzalez; two *s*. *Educ:* India; Trinity Coll., Glenalmond; Hertford Coll., Oxford (MA). 2nd Lieut, HLI, 1952–53. Economist, Fed. Govt of Nigeria, 1957–58; film production, Spain and Portugal, 1958–62; Head of Presentation and Programme Planning, Border TV, 1963–66; Programme Co-Ordinator: ABC TV, 1966–68; Thames TV, 1968–72; Controller of Programme Sales, Thames TV, 1973–74; Man. Dir, 1975–82, Dep Chm., 1982–86, Thames TV Internat.; Dir of Programmes, Thames TV, 1982–86. *Address:* Celtic Films Ltd, 10A Bedford Square, WC1B 3RA. *T:* 01–637 7651.

SUTHERLAND, John Brewer; (3rd Bt *cr* 1921, but does not use the title); *b* 19 Oct. 1931; *s* of Sir (Benjamin) Ivan Sutherland, 2nd Bt, and Marjorie Constance Daniel (*d* 1980), *yr d* of Frederic William Brewer, OBE; *S* father, 1980; *m* 1958, Alice Muireall (*d* 1984), *d* of late W. Stamford Henderson, Kelso; three *s* one *d*. *Educ:* Sedbergh; St Catharine's Coll., Cambridge. *Heir:* *s* Peter William Sutherland, *b* 18 May 1963. *Address:* Ross Farm, Belford, Northumberland.

SUTHERLAND, Sir Maurice, Kt 1976; Leader of Cleveland County Council, 1973–77 and 1981–85 (Leader of Opposition, 1977–81); *b* 12 July 1915; *s* of Thomas Daniel and Ada Sutherland; *m* 1st, 1941, Beatrice (*née* Skinner); one *s*; 2nd, 1960, Jane Ellen (*née* Bell); one step-*d*; 3rd, Ellen Margaret (*née* Guy). *Educ:* Stockton Secondary Sch. War service with Green Howards and RCS, N Africa and NW Europe. Solicitor, 1937–. Mem. Stockton Borough Council, 1957–67; Chm., Teesside Steering Cttee, 1966–67; Leader of Labour Party, Teesside County Borough Council, 1967–74; Mayor of Teesside, 1972–73. Chm., Northern Econ. Planning Council, 1977–79. *Recreations:* cricket, walking, chess, politics. *Address:* 8 Manor Close, Low Worsall, Yarm, Cleveland. *T:* Eaglescliffe 782799.

SUTHERLAND, Muir; *see* Sutherland, J. A. M.

SUTHERLAND, Sir Neil; *see* Sutherland, Sir F. N.

SUTHERLAND, Prof. (Norman) Stuart, MA, DPhil; Professor of Experimental Psychology, University of Sussex, since 1965; *b* 26 March 1927; *s* of Norman McLeod Sutherland; *m* 1966, Jose Louise Fogden; two *d*. *Educ:* Magdalen Coll., Oxford. BA Hons Lit. Hum. 1949 and PPP 1953; John Locke Scholar 1953. Fellow; Magdalen Coll., 1954–58; Merton Coll., 1962–64; Oxford Univ. Lectr in Exper. Psychol., 1960–64. Vis. Prof., MIT, 1961–62, 1964–65. Dir, William Schlackman Ltd, 1968–81. *Publications:* Shape Discrimination by Animals, 1959; (ed jtly) Animal Discrimination Learning, 1969; (with N. J. Mackintosh) Mechanisms of Animal Discrimination Learning, 1971; Breakdown: a personal crisis and a medical dilemma, 1976; (ed) Tutorial Essays in Psychology, vol. 1, 1977, vol. 2, 1979; Discovering the Human Mind, 1982; The Price of Everything, 1986; scientific papers mainly on perception and learning. *Address:* Centre for Research on Perception and Cognition, Sussex University, Brighton BN1 9QG. *T:* Brighton 678304.

SUTHERLAND, Peter Denis, SC; Commissioner for Competition and Relations with European Parliament, European Communities, since 1985; *b* 25 April 1946; *s* of W. G. Sutherland and Barbara Sutherland (*née* Neahon); *m* 1971, Maria Del Pilar Cabria Valcarcel; two *s* one *d*. *Educ:* Gonzaga Coll.; University Coll. Dublin (BCL). Called to Bar: King's Inns, 1968; Middle Temple, 1976; Attorney of New York Bar. Tutor in Law, University Coll., Dublin, 1968–71; practising member of Irish Bar, 1968–81, and 1981–82; Senior Counsel 1980; Attorney General of Ireland, June 1981–Feb. 1982 and Dec. 1982–Dec. 1984; Mem. Council of State, 1981–82 and 1982–84. Hon. LLD St Louis, 1985. *Publications:* contribs to law jls. *Recreations:* sports generally, reading. *Address:* 200 Rue de la Loi, 1049 Brussels, Belgium. *T:* 235 85 37. *Clubs:* Hibernian United Service, Fitzwilliam (Dublin); Lansdowne FC.

SUTHERLAND, Ranald Iain; *see* Sutherland, Hon. Lord.

SUTHERLAND, Prof. Stewart Ross; Principal, King's College London, since 1985; *b* 25 Feb. 1941; *s* of late George A. C. Sutherland and of Ethel (*née* Masson); *m* 1964, Sheena Robertson; one *s* two *d*. *Educ:* Woodside Sch.; Robert Gordon's Coll.; Univ. of Aberdeen (MA); Corpus Christi Coll., Cambridge (Hon. Schol.; MA). Asst Lectr in Philosophy, UCNW, 1965; Lectr in Philosophy, 1968, Sen. Lectr, 1972, Reader, 1976, Univ. of Stirling; King's College London: Prof. of Hist. and Philos. of Religion, 1977–85, Titular Prof., 1985–; Vice-Principal, 1981–85; FKC 1983. Vis. Fellow, ANU, 1974; Gillespie Vis. Prof., Wooster Ohio, 1975. Lectures: Hope, Stirling, 1979; Ferguson, Manchester, 1982; Wilde, Oxford, 1981–84. Member: C of E Bd of Educn, 1980–84; Arts Sub-Cttee, UGC, 1983–85. Pres., Soc. for the Study of Theology, 1985, 1986. Editor, Religious Studies, 1984–; Member, Editorial Board: Scottish Jl of Religious Studies, 1980–; Modern Theology, 1984–. Associate Fellow, Warwick Univ., 1986–. Hon. LHD Wooster, Ohio, 1986. *Publications:* Atheism and the Rejection of God, 1977, 2nd edn 1980; (ed with B. L. Hebblethwaite) The Philosophical Frontiers of Christian Theology, 1983; God, Jesus and Belief, 1984; Faith and Ambiguity, 1984; articles in books and learned jls. *Recreations:* Tassie medallions, theatre, jazz. *Address:* King's College London, Strand, WC2R 2LS. *T:* 01–836 5454. *Club:* Athenæum.

SUTHERLAND, Prof. Stuart; *see* Sutherland, Prof. N. S.

SUTHERLAND, Veronica Evelyn, (Mrs A. J. Sutherland); HM Diplomatic Service; Counsellor, Foreign and Commonwealth Office, since 1984; *b* 25 April 1939; *d* of late Lt-Col Maurice George Beckett, KOYLI, and of Constance Mary Cavenagh-Mainwaring; *m* 1981, Alex James Sutherland. *Educ:* Royal Sch., Bath; London Univ. (BA); Southampton Univ. (MA). Joined HM Diplomatic Service, 1965; Second, later First Sec., Copenhagen, 1967–70; FCO, 1970–75; First Sec., New Delhi, 1975–78; FCO, 1978–80; Counsellor, 1981; Perm. UK Deleg. to UNESCO, 1981–84. *Address:* c/o Foreign and Commonwealth Office, SW1.

SUTHERLAND, William George MacKenzie, QPM 1981; Chief Constable, Lothian and Borders Police, since 1983; *b* 12 Nov. 1933; *m* 1957, Jennie Abbott; two *d*. *Educ:* Inverness Technical High Sch. Cheshire Police, 1954–73; Surrey Police, 1973–75; Hertfordshire Police, 1975–79; Chief Constable of Bedfordshire, 1979–83. *Recreations:* squash, hill walking. *Address:* Police Headquarters, Fettes Avenue, Edinburgh EH4 1RB. *T:* 031–311 3131.

SUTHERLAND-HARRIS, Sir Jack (Alexander), KCVO 1968; CB 1959; Second Crown Estate Commissioner, 1960–68; *b* 8 May 1908; *s* of late Lieut-Colonel A. S. Sutherland-Harris, DL, JP, Burwash, Sussex; *m* 1934, Rachel Owen Jones, *yr d* of late Capt. Owen Jones, CBE, Worplesdon, Surrey; two *s* two *d*. *Educ:* Winchester Coll.; New Coll., Oxford. Entered Min. of Agriculture and Fisheries as Asst Principal, 1932; Principal Private Secretary to Minister of Agriculture and Fisheries, 1941–43; Asst Sec., 1943–50; Under-Sec., 1950–60. *Address:* Old Well Cottage, Bury, Pulborough, West Sussex. *T:* Bury 465. *Club:* Royal Commonwealth Society.

SUTHIWART-NARUEPUT, Dr Owart; Kt Grand Cordon: Order of Crown of Thailand, 1981; Order of White Elephant, 1985; Hon. CMG 1972; Ambassador of Thailand to the Court of St James's, 1984–86, concurrently to Ireland, 1985–86; *b* 19 Sept. 1926; *s* of Luang Suthiwart-Narueput and Mrs Khae; *m* 1959, Angkana (*née* Sthapitanond); one *s* one *d*. *Educ:* Thammasat Univ., Thailand (BA Law); Fletcher Sch. of Law and Diplomacy, Tufts Univ., USA (MA, PhD); Nat. Defence Coll. Joined Min. of For. Affairs, 1945; Asst Sec. to Minister, 1958; SEATO Res. Asst, 1959; Protocol Dept, 1963; Econ. Dept, 1964; Counsellor, Thai Embassy, Canberra, 1965; Dir-Gen. of Inf. Dept, 1969; Ambassador to India, Nepal, Sri Lanka, and Minister to Afghanistan, 1972; Ambassador to Poland, E Germany and Bulgaria, 1976; Dir-Gen. of Political Dept, 1977; Under-Sec. of State (Permanent Sec.) for For. Affairs, 1979; Ambassador to France and Perm. Representative to UNESCO, 1980; Ambassador to Switzerland and to Holy See, 1983. Commander: Order of Phoenix, Greece, 1963; Order of Orange-Nassau, Netherlands, 1963; Bintang Djasa (1st Cl.), Indonesia, 1970; Order of Merit, Poland,

1979; Grand Officier, L'Ordre Nat. du Mérite, France, 1983. *Publication:* The Evolution of Thailand's Foreign Relations since 1855: from extraterritoriality to equality, 1955. *Recreations:* reading, music. *Clubs:* Athenæum, Travellers', Hurlingham.

SUTTIE, Sir (George) Philip Grant-, 8th Bt, *cr* 1702; *b* 20 Dec. 1938; *o s* of late Maj. George Donald Grant-Suttie and Marjorie Neville, *d* of Capt. C. E. Carter, RN, of Newfoundland; *S* cousin, 1947; *m* 1962, Elspeth Mary (marr. diss. 1969), *e d* of Maj.-Gen. R. E. Urquhart, *qv*; one *s*. *Educ:* Sussex Composite High School, NB, Canada; Macdonald College, McGill University, Montreal. *Recreations:* flying, fishing, farming, forestry. *Heir: s* James Edward Grant-Suttie, *b* 29 May 1965. *Address:* (seat) Balgone, North Berwick; Sheriff Hall, North Berwick, East Lothian. *T:* 2569. *Club:* Puffin's (Edinburgh).

SUTTILL, Dr Margaret Joan, (Mrs G. A. Rink); *d* of Ernest Montrose and Caroline Hyde; *m* 1st, 1935, F. A. Suttill, DSO, LLB (*d* 1945); two *s*; 2nd, 1949, G. A. Rink, QC (*d* 1983). *Educ:* Royal Free Hospital Medical School. MB, BS 1935; MRCP 1972. Director, Medical Dept, and Chief Medical Advr, British Council, retired. *Recreations:* music (especially opera), reading, walking, bird watching, consumer problems. *Address:* 173 Oakwood Court, W14 8JE. *T:* 01–602 2143.

SUTTON, Alan John; Senior Vice-President, WINvest, USA West Coast Division, Welsh Development Agency, since 1985; *b* 16 March 1936; *s* of William Clifford Sutton and Emily Sutton (*née* Batten); *m* 1957, Glenis (*née* Henry); one *s* one *d*. *Educ:* Bristol Univ. BSc (Hons) Elec. Engrg; MIEE. Design, Production and Trials Evaluation of Guided Missiles, English Electric Aviation Ltd, 1957–63; Design, Production, Sales and General Management of Scientific Digital, Analogue and Hybrid Computers, Solartron Electronic Group Ltd, 1963–69; International Sales Manager, Sales Director, of A. B. Electronic Components Ltd, 1969–73; Managing Director, A. B. Connectors, 1973–76; Industrial Dir, Welsh Office, 1976–79; Welsh Development Agency: Exec. Dir (Industry and Investment), 1979–83; Exec. Dir (Marketing), 1983–85. *Recreations:* squash, golf. *Address:* (home) #267 San Marino Apartments, 2175 Aborn Road, San Jose, Calif. 95121, USA. *T:* 408 238 2140; (office) 410 Cambridge Avenue, Palo Alto, Calif. 94306, USA. *T:* 415 321 4226. 56 Heol-y-Delyn, Lisvane, Cardiff CF4 5SR. *T:* (office) Cardiff 32955; (home) Cardiff 753194.

SUTTON, Colin Bertie John, QPM 1985; Assistant Commissioner, Management Support Department, Metropolitan Police, since 1984; *b* 6 Dec. 1938; *s* of Bertie Sidney Russell Sutton and Phyllis May; *m* 1960, Anne Margaret Davis. *Educ:* King Edward VI Grammar School, Stratford-upon-Avon; University College London (LLB 1970). Police Constable, 1957, Sergeant, 1964, Inspector, 1966, Warwicks County Police; Chief Inspector, 1970, Supt, 1972, Chief Supt, 1974, Warwicks and Coventry Constabulary; Chief Supt, W Midlands Police, 1974–77; Asst Chief Constable, Leics Constabulary, 1977; Dep. Asst Comr, Metropolitan Police, 1983–84. *Recreations:* golf, angling, squash, music, art, literature. *Address:* New Scotland Yard, Broadway, SW1H 0BG. *T:* 01–230 1212.

SUTTON, Denys Miller, CBE 1985; Editor of Apollo since 1962; *b* 10 Aug. 1917; *s* of Edmund Sutton and Dulcie Laura Wheeler; *m* 1940, Sonja Kilbansky (marr. diss.); 1952, Gertrud Kœbke-Knudson (marr. diss.); 1960, Cynthia Sassoon; one *s* one *d*. *Educ:* Uppingham School; Exeter Coll., Oxford (BA, BLitt). Foreign Office Research Dept, 1940–45; Sec., Internat. Commn for Restitution of Cultural Material, 1945; Fine Arts Specialist at UNESCO 1948; Visiting lectr at Yale Univ., 1949. Organiser of exhibitions: Bonnard Exhibition, RA, 1966; France in the 18th Century, RA, 1968; British Art, Columbus, Ohio, 1971; Venice Rediscovered, Wildenstein, London, 1972; Irish Art, Columbus, Ohio, 1974; Fragonard, Tokyo, 1980; Boucher, Tokyo, 1982; Phillips Collection, Tokyo, 1983; Fantin-Latour, Wildenstein, London, 1984; Constable, Tokyo, 1985. Formerly: Art Critic to Country Life and to Financial Times; Saleroom Correspondent of Daily Telegraph. Mem. Exec. Cttee, Nat. Art Collections Fund. Corresp. Membre de l'Institut. Chevalier, Légion d'Honneur. *Publications:* Watteau's Les Charmes de la Vie, 1946; Matisse, 1946; Picasso, Blue and Pink Periods, 1948; French Drawings of the 18th Century, 1949; American Painting, 1949; Flemish Painting, 1950; Bonnard, 1957; Christie's since the War, 1959; André Derain, 1959; Nicholas de Staël, 1960; Gaspard Dughet, 1962; Toulouse-Lautrec, 1962; Titian, 1963; Nocturne: The Art of Whistler, 1964; Sergio de Castro, 1965; Triumphant Satyr, 1966; Whistler: Paintings, Drawings, Etchings and Water-colours, 1966; Vélazquez, 1967; An Italian Sketchbook by Richard Wilson RA, 1968; Van Dongen, 1971; (ed and introd) Letters of Roger Fry, 1973; Manguin, 1974; Walter Sickert: a biography, 1976; Fads and Fancies, 1980; Delights of a Dilettante, 1980; R. L. Douglas, Connoisseur of Art and Life, 1980; The World of Sacheverell Sitwell, 1981; Early Italian Art and the English, 1985; Degas: man and work, 1986; *introductions:* Vlaminck, Dangerous Corner, 1961; R. A. M. Stevenson, Velasquez, 1962; *jointly:* Artists in 17th Century Rome (with Denis Mahon), 1955; Catalogue of French, Spanish and German schools in Fitzwilliam Museum, Cambridge (with J. W. Goodison), 1960; Painting in Florence and Siena (with St John Gore), 1965; Richard Ford in Spain (with Brinsley Ford), 1974; contribs to magazines, etc. *Recreation:* theatre. *Address:* 22 Chelsea Park Gardens, SW3. *T:* 01–352 5141. *Club:* Travellers'.

SUTTON, Sir Frederick (Walter), Kt 1974; OBE 1971; Founder and Chairman of Directors of the Sutton Group of Companies; *b* 1 Feb. 1915; *s* of late William W. Sutton and Daisy Sutton; *m* 1934; three *s*; *m* 1977, Morna Patricia Smyth. *Educ:* Sydney Technical College. Motor Engineer, founder and Chief Executive of the Sutton group of Companies; Mem. Bd of Directors, and life Governor, Royal New South Wales Inst. for Deaf and Blind Children. *Recreations:* flying, going fishing, boating. *Address:* (office) 114 Bourke Street, Potts Point, Sydney, NSW 2011, Australia. *T:* Sydney 357–1777. *Clubs:* Royal Aero of NSW (Life Member); Royal Automobile of Australia; Royal Automobile of Victoria; American (Sydney).

SUTTON, Prof. John, DSc, PhD, ARCS; FRS 1966; FGS; Senior Research Fellow, Centre for Environmental Technology, since 1983, Professor of Geology, 1958–83, now Emeritus, Imperial College of Science and Technology, London; *b* 8 July 1919; *e s* of Gerald John Sutton; *m* 1st, 1949, Janet Vida Watson, FRS (*d* 1985); 2nd, 1985, Betty Middleton-Sandford. *Educ:* King's School, Worcester; Royal College of Science, London. Service with RAOC and REME, 1941–46. Imperial College: Research, 1946–48; Lecturer in Geology, 1948; Reader in Geology, 1956; Head of Geol. Dept, 1964–74; Dean, Royal Sch. of Mines, 1965–68, 1974–77; Pro-Rector, External Develt, 1979–80, Pro-Rector, 1980–83; Fellow, 1985. A Trustee, BM (Nat. Hist.), 1976–81. Mem., NERC, 1977–79. Mem. Council, Univ. of Zimbabwe, 1980–83. President, Geologists' Association, 1966–68. A Vice-Pres., Royal Society, 1975–77; Pres., Remote Sensing Soc., 1977–84. For. Mem., Royal Netherlands Acad., 1978; Hon. For. Fellow, Geol Soc. of Amer. Bigsby Medal, Geological Society of London, 1965 (jointly with Janet Watson); Murchison Medal, 1975. *Publications:* papers dealing with the Geology of the Scottish Highlands. *Recreation:* gardening. *Address:* Imperial College of Science and Technology, SW7.

SUTTON, Air Marshal Sir John (Matthias Dobson), KCB 1986 (CB 1981); Commander-in-Chief, Royal Air Force Support Command, since 1986; *b* 9 July 1932; *s* of Harry Rowston Sutton and late Gertrude Sutton; *m* 1954 (marr. diss. 1968); one *s* one *d*; *m* 1969, Angela Faith Gray; two *s*. *Educ:* Queen Elizabeth's Grammar Sch., Alford, Lincs. Joined RAF, 1950; pilot trng, commnd, 1951; served on Fighter Sqdns, UK and Germany; Staff Coll., 1963; OC 249 Sqdn, 1964–66; Asst Sec., Chiefs of Staff Cttee, 1966–69; OC 14 Sqdn, 1970–71; Asst Chief of Staff (Policy and Plans), HQ 2 ATAF, 1971–73; Staff, Chief of Def. Staff, 1973–74; RCDS, 1975; Comdt Central Flying Sch., 1976–77; Asst Chief of Air Staff (Policy), 1977–79; Dep. Comdr, RAF Germany, 1980–82; ACDS (Commitments), 1982–84; ACDS (Overseas), 1985. *Recreations:* golf, ski-ing. *Address:* c/o Royal Bank of Scotland, Holt's Branch, Whitehall, SW1A 2EB. *Clubs:* Royal Air Force; Liphook Golf.

SUTTON, Rt. Rev. Keith Norman; *see* Lichfield, Bishop of.

SUTTON, Leslie Ernest, MA, DPhil Oxon; FRS 1950; Fellow and Lecturer in Chemistry, Magdalen College, Oxford, 1936–73, Fellow Emeritus, 1973; Reader in Physical Chemistry, 1962–73 (University Demonstrator and Lecturer in Chemistry, 1945–62); *b* 22 June 1906; *o c* of Edgar William Sutton; *m* 1st, 1932, Catharine Virginia Stock (*d* 1962), *er d* of Wallace Teall Stock, Maplewood, NY, USA; two *s* one *d*; 2nd, 1963, Rachel Ann Long, *er d* of Lt-Col J. F. Batten, Swyncombe, Henley-on-Thames; two *s*. *Educ:* Watford Gram. Sch.; Lincoln Coll., Oxford (Scholar). 1st Class Hon. School Chemistry, 1928; research at Leipzig Univ., 1928–29, and at Oxford University; Fellow by Examination, Magdalen College, 1932–36; Rockefeller Fellow, California Inst. of Technology, 1933–34; Tilden Lectr, Chemical Soc., 1940; Visiting Prof., Heidelberg Univ., 1960, 1964, 1967. Vice-Pres., Magdalen College, 1947–48. Hon. Sec., Chemical Soc., 1951–57, Vice-Pres., 1957–60. Chairman: Lawes Agricl Trust Cttee, Rothamsted Experimental Stn, 1982– (Treas., 1978–82); Dielectrics Soc., 1975–86. Hon. DSc Salford, 1973. Meldola Medal, RIC, 1932; Harrison Prize, Chemical Soc., 1935. *Publications:* papers in scientific jls; (as scientific Editor) Tables of Interatomic Distances and Configuration in Molecules and Ions, 1958, 1964; Chemische Bindung und Molekülstruktur, 1961. *Address:* 62 Osler Road, Headington, Oxford OX3 9BN. *T:* Oxford 66456.

SUTTON, Rt. Rev. Peter (Eves); *see* Nelson, NZ, Bishop of.

SUTTON, Dr Peter Morgan; Director, Public Health Laboratory Service Centre for Applied Microbiology and Research, Porton Down, since 1979; *b* 21 June 1932; *s* of Sir Graham Sutton, CBE, FRS and late Lady Sutton (*née* Doris Morgan); *m* 1959, Helen Ersy Economides; two *s* two *d*. *Educ:* Bishop Wordsworth Sch., Salisbury; Wrekin Coll., Wellington; University Coll. (Fellow, 1985) and University Coll. Hosp. Med. Sch., London. House Surgeon and House Physician, UCH, 1956–57; Graham Scholar in Pathology, Univ. of London, 1958–59; on academic staff of UCH Med. Sch., 1960–65; Vis. Asst Prof. of Pathology, Univ. of Pittsburg, USA, 1966–67; Hon. Consultant Pathologist, UCH, 1967–79; Reader in Pathology, Univ. of London, 1971–79; Vice-Dean, UCH Med. Sch., 1973–78. Vis. Prof., Dept of Biochemical Pathology, UCL, 1983–. Sometime Examr in Pathology, Univ. of London and RCS. *Publications:* The Nature of Cancer, 1962; various papers on fibrinolytic enzymes and tissue culture. *Recreations:* English literature, history of science. *Address:* Manderley, Shady Bower, Bower Gardens, Salisbury, Wilts SP1 2RL. *T:* Salisbury 23902.

SUTTON, Philip John, ARA 1977; *b* 20 Oct. 1928; *m* 1954; one *s* three *d*. *Educ:* Slade Sch. of Fine Art, UCL. One-man exhibitions: Roland Browse and Delbanco (now Browse and Darby) Gallery, London, 1953–; Geffrye Museum, London, 1959; Leeds City Art Gallery, 1960; Newcastle-on-Tyne, 1962; Bradford, 1962; Edinburgh, 1962; Sydney, 1963, 1966, 1970, 1973; Perth, 1963; Battersea, 1963, 1972; Detroit, 1967; Bristol, 1970; Folkestone, 1970, 1974; Cape Town, 1976; Johannesburg, 1976; Falmouth Sch. of Art, 1977; Royal Acad. (Diploma Gall.), London, 1977; Annexe Gall., London, 1979; Holsworthy Gall., London, 1980; David Jones Gall., Sydney, 1980; Annexe Art Gall., 1980; Minden Gall., CI, 1981; Bonython Art Gall., Adelaide, 1981; Norwich, Bath and New York, 1983; Lichfield Fest., 1985; Beaux Arts Gall., Bath, 1985. *Recreations:* swimming, running. *Address:* 10 Soudan Road, Battersea, SW11 4HH. *T:* 01–622 2647.

SUTTON, Dr Richard, MB, FRCP, FACC; Consultant Cardiologist: Westminster and St Stephen's Hospitals, London, since 1976; to British Airways, since 1976; *b* 1 Sept. 1940; *s* of late Dick Brasnett Sutton and of Greta Mary (*née* Leadbeter); *m* 1964, Anna Gunilla (*née* Cassö); one *s*. *Educ:* Gresham's Sch.; King's Coll., London; King's Coll. Hosp. (MB, BS 1964). FRCP 1983 (MRCP 1967); FACC 1975. Gen. medical trng followed graduation; career in cardiology began at St George's Hosp., London, 1967; Fellow in Cardiol., Univ. of NC, 1968–69; Registrar, Sen. Registrar, then Temp. Consultant, National Heart Hosp., London, 1970–76. Hon. Cons. Cardiologist: Italian Hosp., London, 1977–; SW Thames RHA, 1979–; St Luke's Hosp., London, 1980–. Member: British Medical Assoc.; British Cardiac Soc.; British Pacing and Electrophysiology Group (Co-Founder, Mem. Council and Past Hon. Sec.). Governors' Award, Amer. Coll. of Cardiol., 1979 (Scientific Exhibit, Physiol Cardiac Pacing), and 1982 (1st Prize; Scientific Exhibit, 5 yrs of Physiol Cardiac Pacing). *Publications:* articles on many aspects of cardiology incl. cardiac pacing, coronary artery disease, left ventricular function, and assessment of pharm. agents, in Circulation, Amer. Jl of Cardiol., Amer. Heart Jl, Brit. Heart Jl, Pace, Lancet, BMJ, and Oxford Textbook of Medicine, 1967–. *Recreations:* opera, foreign travel, swimming, tennis. *Address:* 149 Harley Street, W1N 1HG. *T:* 01–935 4444.

SUTTON, Richard Lewis; Regional Director, Northern Region, Department of Industry, 1974–81; *b* 3 Feb. 1923; *s* of William Richard Sutton and Marina Susan Sutton (*née* Chudleigh); *m* 1944, Jean Muriel (*née* Turner). *Educ:* Ealing County Grammar Sch. Board of Trade, 1939. Served War: HM Forces (Lieut RA), 1942–47. Asst Trade Comr, Port of Spain, 1950–52; BoT, 1953–62; Trade Comr, Kuala Lumpur, 1962–66; Monopolies Commn, 1966; BoT, 1967–68; Dir, British Industrial Develt Office, New York, 1968–71; Regional Dir, West Midland Region, Dept of Trade and Industry, 1971–74. *Recreations:* music, walking, bridge. *Address:* Barton Toft, Dowlish Wake, Ilminster, Somerset. *T:* Ilminster 5127.

SUTTON, Sir Richard (Lexington), 9th Bt *cr* 1772; farmer; *b* 27 April 1937; *s* of Sir Robert Lexington Sutton, 8th Bt, and of Gwynneth Gwladys, *o d* of Major Arnold Charles Gover, MC; *S* father, 1981; *m* 1959, Fiamma, *o d* of G. M. Ferrari, Rome; one *s* one *d*. *Educ:* Stowe. *Recreations:* skiing, sailing, swimming, tennis. *Heir: s* David Robert Sutton, *b* 26 Feb. 1960. *Address:* Moorhill, Langham, Gillingham, Dorset. *T:* Gillingham 2665.

SUTTON, Robert William, CB 1962; OBE 1946; retired as Superintendent and Chief Scientific Officer, Services Electronics Research Laboratories, Baldock, Herts, 1946–70; *b* 13 Nov. 1905; *s* of late William Sutton; *m* 1951, Elizabeth Mary, *d* of George Maurice Wright, CBE, Chelmsford; one *s* two *d*. *Educ:* Brighton College; Royal College of Science, London University. Formerly with Ferranti Ltd, and then with E. K. Cole Ltd until 1938. Admiralty, 1939–68. *Address:* 33 Hitchin Street, Baldock, Herts. *T:* Baldock 3373.

SUTTON, Shaun Alfred Graham, OBE 1979; television producer and writer; Head of Drama Group, BBC Television, 1969–81; *b* 14 Oct. 1919; *s* of Eric Graham Sutton and Beryl Astley-Marsden; *m* 1948, Barbara Leslie; one *s* three *d*. *Educ:* Latymer Upper Sch.;

Embassy Sch. of Acting, London. Actor and Stage Manager, Q, Embassy, Aldwych, Adelphi, Arts, Criterion Theatres, 1938–40. Royal Navy, 1940–46, Lieut RNVR. Stage Dir, Embassy and provincial theatres, 1946–48; Producer, Embassy, Buxton, Croydon Theatres, 1948–50; toured S Africa as Producer, 1950; Producer, Embassy, Ipswich, Buxton, 1951–52; entered BBC TV Service, 1952; produced and wrote many children's TV plays and serials; directed many series incl. Z Cars, Softly Softly, Sherlock Holmes, Kipling, etc.; Head of BBC Drama Serials Dept, 1966–69; dramatised Rogue Herries and Judith Paris for BBC Radio, 1971; Producer, BBC TV Shakespeare series, 1982–84. Fellow, Royal TV Soc.; Mem., BAFTA. *Publications:* A Christmas Carol (stage adaptation), 1949; Queen's Champion (children's novel), 1961; The Largest Theatre in the World, 1982. *Recreations:* gardening, walking. *Address:* 15 Corringham Court, Corringham Road, NW11 7BY. *T:* 01–455 5417; The Cottage, Brewery Road, Trunch, Norfolk. *Club:* Lord's Taverners.

SUTTON, Sir Stafford William Powell F.; *see* Foster-Sutton.

SUTTON, Thomas Francis; Director and Executive Vice-President, J. Walter Thompson Co., New York, 1965–86; Executive Vice-President, JWT Group Inc., New York, 1982–86; Chairman, E-A Advertising, New York, 1982–86; *b* 9 Feb. 1923; *m* 1st, 1950, Anne Fleming (marr. diss. 1974); one *s* two *d*; 2nd, 1982, Maki Watanabe. *Educ:* King's School, Worcester; St Peter's College, Oxford. Research Officer, British Market Research Bureau Ltd, 1949–51; Advertising Manager, Pasolds Ltd, 1951–52; Managing Director, J. Walter Thompson GmbH, Frankfurt, Germany, 1952–59; Dir, J. Walter Thompson Co. Ltd, 1960–73; Man. Dir, 1960–66; Dir, internat. operations, J. Walter Thompson, NY, 1966–72; Man. Dir, J. Walter Thompson Co. Japan, Tokyo, 1972–80; Exec. Vice-Pres./Dir, J. Walter Thompson Asia/Pacific, 1980–81. Chm., Lansdowneuro, 1983. FIPA; FIS; FSS. Internat. Advertising Man of the Year Award, 1970. *Recreations:* chess, riding. *Address:* Rushway House, Willington, near Shipston-on-Stour, Warwicks.

SUTTON CURTIS, John, CBE 1974; Chairman, Workington Saw Mills Ltd, 1966–76; *b* 2 July 1913; *s* of Harold Ernest Curtis; *m* 1936, Muriel Rose Hastwell; one *s*. *Educ:* Watford Grammar School. Served War of 1939–45, Royal Artillery. Thames Board Mills Ltd: Director, 1958; Vice-Chm., 1965; Dep. Chm. and Man. Dir, 1966–69; Chm., 1969–76. Chm., Assoc. of Board Makers, 1965–70; Pres., British Paper and Board Makers' Assoc., 1971–73 (Dep. Pres., 1973–75); Pres., Confederation of European Pulp, Paper and Board Industries (CEPAC), 1974–75 (Vice-Pres., 1973). Paper Industry Gold Medal, 1973. *Recreation:* motoring. *Address:* Covertside, 115a Langley Road, Watford, Herts WD1 3RP. *T:* Watford 26375.

SUVA, Archbishop of, (RC), since 1976; **Most Rev. Petero Mataca;** *b* 28 April 1933; *s* of Gaberiele Daunivucu and Akeneta Taina. *Educ:* Holy Name Seminary, Dunedin, NZ; Propaganda Fidei, Rome. Priest, Rome, 1959; Vicar-Gen. of Archdiocese of Suva, 1966; Rector of Pacific Regional Seminary, 1973; Auxiliary Bishop of Suva, 1974. Pres., Episcopal Conf. of South Pacific, 1981. *Address:* Archbishop's House, Box 393, Suva, Fiji. *T:* 22851.

SUYIN; *see* Han Suyin.

SUZMAN, Mrs Helen; MP (Progressive Federal Party), Houghton, Republic of South Africa; *b* 7 Nov. 1917; *d* of late Samuel Gavronsky; *m* Dr M. M. Suzman, FRCP; two *d*. *Educ:* Parktown Convent, Johannesburg; Univ. of Witwatersrand (BCom). Lectr in Economic History, Univ. of Witwatersrand, 1944–52. Elected MP 1953; United Party 1953–61; Progressive Party (later Progressive Reform Party and Progressive Federal Party), 1961–. Hon. Fellow: St Hugh's Coll., Oxford, 1973; London Sch. of Economics, 1975. Hon. DCL Oxford, 1973; Hon. LLD: Harvard, 1976; Witwatersrand, 1976; Columbia, 1977; Smith Coll., 1977; Brandeis, 1981; Jewish Theological Seminary, NY, 1986; Cape Town, 1986; Hon. DHL: Denison, 1982; New Sch. for Social Res., NY, 1984; Sacred Heart Univ., USA, 1984. Roger E. Joseph Award, Hebrew Union Coll., NY, 1986. *Recreations:* golf, swimming, fishing, bridge. *Address:* 49 Melville Road, Hyde Park, Sandton, 2196 Transvaal, South Africa. *T:* 788–2833. *Clubs:* Lansdowne; River, Wanderers, Wanderers Golf, Houghton Golf, Glendower (Johannesburg).

SUZMAN, Janet; actress; *b* 9 Feb. 1939; *d* of Saul Suzman; *m* 1969, Trevor Nunn, *qv* (marr. diss. 1986); one *s*. *Educ:* Kingsmead Coll., Johannesburg; Univ. of the Witwatersrand (BA); London Acad. of Music and Dramatic Art. Vis Prof of Drama Studies, Westfield Coll., London, 1983–84. Mem., LAMDA Council, 1978–. Roles played for Royal Shakespeare Co. incl.: Joan La Pucelle in The Wars of the Roses, 1963–64; Lulu in The Birthday Party, Rosaline, Portia, 1965; Ophelia, 1965–66; Katharina, Celia, and Berinthia in The Relapse, 1967; Beatrice, Rosalind, 1968–69; Cleopatra and Lavinia, 1972–73; Clytemnestra and Helen of Troy in The Greeks, 1980. Kate Hardcastle, and Carmen in The Balcony, Oxford Playhouse, 1966; Hester in Hello and Goodbye, King's Head Theatre, 1973; Masha in Three Sisters, Cambridge, 1976; Good Woman of Setzuan, Newcastle, 1976, Royal Court, 1977; Hedda Gabler, Duke of York's, 1977; Boo-hoo, Open Space, 1978; The Duchess of Malfi, Birmingham, 1979; Cowardice, Ambassadors, 1983; Boesman and Lena, Hampstead, 1984; Vassa, Greenwich, 1985. *Films:* A Day in the Death of Joe Egg, 1970; Nicholas and Alexandra, 1971; The Priest of Love, 1980; The Draughtsman's Contract, 1981; E la Nave Va, 1983; *television:* plays for BBC and ITV incl.: St Joan, 1968; Three Sisters, 1969; Macbeth, 1970; Hedda Gabler, 1972; Twelfth Night, 1973; Antony and Cleopatra, 1974; Miss Nightingale, 1974; Clayhanger, serial, 1975–76; Mountbatten—The Last Viceroy, 1986; The Singing Detective, 1986. Acad. Award Nomination, Best Actress, 1971; Evening Standard Drama Awards, Best Actress, 1973, 1976; Plays and Players Award, Best Actress, 1976. Hon. MA Open, 1984. *Address:* William Morris (UK) Ltd, 147/149 Wardour Street, W1V 3TB. *T:* 01–734 9361.

SVENSON, Mrs Sven G.; *see* Grey, Beryl.

SVOBODA, Prof. Josef; Chief Scenographer, National Theatre, Prague, CSSR, since 1948; Professor at Academy of Applied Arts, since 1968; *b* Čáslav, 10 May 1920; *m* 1948, Libuše Svobodová; one *d*. *Educ:* Gymnasium; special sch. for interior architecture; Academy of Applied Arts (architecture). EXPO 58, Brussels: success with Laterna Magica; EXPO 67, Montreal: polyvision, polydiaekran. He co-operates with many theatres all over the world (Metropolitan Opera, New York; Covent Garden; Geneva; Bayreuth; Frankfurt, etc); Chief of Laterna Magica, experimental scene of National Theatre, Prague, 1973–. Laureate of State Prize, 1954; Merited Artist of CSSR, 1966; National Artist of CSSR, 1968; Hon. RA, London, 1969. *Publications:* relevant monographs: Josef Svoboda (by Theatre Inst.) 1967 (Prague); Josef Svoboda (by Denis Bablet) 1970 (France); The Scenography of J. Svoboda (by Jarka Burian) 1971, 1974 (USA); Teatr Josefa Svobody (by V. Berjozkin) 1973 (USSR). *Recreations:* theatre, photography, creative arts, music, literature. *Address:* Filmařská 535/17, 15200 Prague 5, CSSR.

SWAFFIELD, Sir James (Chesebrough), Kt 1976; CBE 1971; RD 1967; DL; Chairman, British Rail Property Board, since 1984; solicitor; *b* 16 Feb. 1924; *s* of Frederick and Kate Elizabeth Swaffield, Cheltenham; *m* 1950, Elizabeth Margaret Ellen, 2nd *d* of A. V. and K. E. Maunder, Belfast; two *s* two *d*. *Educ:* Cheltenham Grammar Sch.; Haberdashers'

Aske's Hampstead Sch.; London Univ. (LLB); MA Oxon 1974. RNVR, 1942–46. Articled Town Clerk, Lincoln, 1946–49; Asst Solicitor: Norwich Corp., 1949–52; Cheltenham Corp., 1952–53; Southend-on-Sea Corp., 1953–56; Dep. Town Clerk, subseq. Town Clerk and Clerk of Peace, Blackpool, 1956–62; Sec., Assoc. of Municipal Corpns, 1962–72; Dir-Gen. and Clerk to GLC, Clerk to ILEA and Clerk of Lieutenancy for Greater London, 1973–84. Vice-Pres., Age Concern, Greater London. Chm., St Paul's Cathedral Ct of Advrs; Mem. Council, St Paul's Cathedral Trust; Trustee, Civic Trust; Chm., Governors, Dulwich Coll. Hon. Fellow, Inst. Local Govt Studies, Birmingham Univ. DL Greater London, 1978. OStJ. *Address:* 10 Kelsey Way, Beckenham, Kent. *Clubs:* Reform, Naval.

SWAIN, Air Commodore (Francis) Ronald Downs, CB 1954; CBE 1946 (OBE 1941); AFC 1937; psa; retired; *b* 31 Aug. 1903; *s* of late Major Charles Sanchez de Pina Swain, TD, Southsea, Hants; *m* 1938, Sarah Mitchell, *d* of Charles H. Le Fèvre, Washington, DC; three *d*. *Educ:* Stonyhurst Coll. Joined Royal Air Force, 1922; Wing Comdr, 1939; Air Commodore, 1949. Commanded Cairo-Rhodesia Flight, 1933; gained World High Altitude Record, 1936 (AFC); served War of 1939–45 (despatches, OBE, CBE); Air Officer Commanding No 28 Group, RAF, 1949–50; Senior Air Staff Officer and Deputy Head of Air Force Staff, British Joint Services Mission, Washington, 1950–54, retired 1954. *Address:* 1121 River Road, Johns Island, S Carolina 29455, USA. *T:* 803–559–3402. *Clubs:* Royal Air Force; Carolina Yacht (S Carolina).

SWAIN, Henry Thornhill, CBE 1971; RIBA; County Architect, Nottinghamshire County Council, since 1964; *b* 14 Feb. 1924; *s* of Thornhill Madge Swain and Bessie Marion Swain; *m*; three *d*. *Educ:* Bryanston Sch.; Architectural Assoc. (Hons Dipl.). Served with RN, 1943–46. Herts County Architect's Dept, 1949; worked in primary school group; Notts CC, 1955; Group Leader i/c initial develt of CLASP construction; Dep. County Architect, 1958. *Publications:* many articles in architectural jls. *Recreation:* sailing. *Address:* 50 Loughborough Road, West Bridgford, Nottingham. *T:* Nottingham 818059.

SWAINE, Edward Thomas William, CMG 1968; MBE 1952; Director, Exhibitions Division, Central Office of Information, 1961–71, retired; *b* 17 July 1907; *s* of Edward James Swaine; *m* 1942, Ruby Louise (*née* Ticehurst) (*d* 1974). Entered Govt Service, Min. of Information, 1940; Festival of Britain, 1948–52; Dir of Exhibns, British Pavilion, Montreal World Exhibn, 1967; UK Dep. Comr-Gen. and Dir of Exhbns, Japan World Exhbn, 1970. *Recreation:* photography. *Address:* 6/12 Northwood Hall, Highgate, N6 5PN. *T:* 01–340 4392.

SWAINSON, Eric, CBE 1981; Managing Director, IMI plc, 1974–86; *b* 5 Dec. 1926; *m* 1953, Betty Heywood; two *d*. *Educ:* Sheffield Univ. (BMet 1st cl. Hons; W. H. A. Robertson medal, 1959). Joined Imperial Chemical Industries Metals Div. (now IMI), 1946; Technical Officer, Res. Dept, 1946–53; Manager, Titanium Melting Plant, 1953–56; Asst Manager, Technical Dept, 1956–59; Gen. Manager and Man. Dir, Lightning Fasteners, 1961–69; Dir, IMI, 1969–; Asst Man. Dir, 1972–74; Dep. Chm., Pegler-Hattersley plc, 1986. Director: Birmingham Broadcasting, 1973–; Lloyds Bank plc, 1986–; Chm., Birmingham and West Midlands Reg. Bd, Lloyds Bank, 1985– (Reg. Dir, 1979–). Chm., W Midlands Industrial Develt Bd, 1985–; Member: Review Bd for Govt Contracts, 1978–; NEDC Cttee on Finance for Industry, 1978–86; Council, CBI, 1975–86; W Midlands Reg. Council, CBI, 1973–83 (Chm. 1976–78); Industrial Develt Adv. Bd, 1982–. Pro-Chancellor, Aston Univ., 1981–86. FRSA 1985. Hon. DSc Aston, 1986. *Address:* 268 Station Road, Knowle, Solihull, W Midlands B93 0ES.

SWALLOW, Comdt Daphne Patricia, CBE 1986; Director, Women's Royal Naval Service, 1982–86; Hon. ADC to the Queen, 1982–86; *b* 25 Sept. 1932; *d* of Captain Ralph Geoffrey Swallow, RN retd and Daphne Lucy Regina Swallow (*née* Parry). *Educ:* St George's Sch., Ascot; Portsmouth Polytechnic (Hon. Fellow, 1983). Joined WRNS as Signal Wren, 1950; qualified as WRNS Communications Officer, 1955; served in HMS Drake and Malta, 1956–58; Oslo, Portsmouth, HMS Mercury, Northwood and Gibraltar, 1958–67; HMS Pembroke and HMS Heron, 1968–71; passed Naval Staff Course, 1972; HMS Dauntless, 1973–74; Staff of C-in-C Naval Home Comd and MoD, 1974–76; National Defence College Latimer Course, 1976–77; Staff of Naval Secretary, 1977; Command Personnel Officer to C-in-C Naval Home Comd, 1977–79; Dep. Dir, WRNS, 1979–81; Staff Officer Training Coordination and Comd WRNS Officer to C-in-C Naval Home Comd, 1981–82. Mem. Nat. Exec. Cttee, Forces Help Soc. and Lord Roberts Workshops, 1986–. FBIM 1986. *Recreations:* tennis, dressmaking and needlework, reading, theatre, opera, music. *Address:* c/o Lloyds Bank plc, 15 The Village, Blackheath, SE3 9LH. *Club:* Naval.

SWALLOW, John Crossley, PhD; FRS 1968; physical oceanographer, Institute of Oceanographic Sciences (formerly National Institute of Oceanography), 1954–83; *b* 11 Oct. 1923; *s* of Alfred Swallow and Elizabeth (*née* Crossley); *m* 1958, Mary Morgan (*née* McKenzie); one step *d*. *Educ:* Holme Valley Gram. Sch.; St John's Coll., Cambridge. Admty Signal Estabt, 1943–47; research in marine geophysics, at Cambridge and in HMS Challenger, 1948–54; work on ocean circulation, in RRS Discovery II, and in RRS Discovery, and other vessels, 1954–83. Rossby Fellow, Woods Hole Oceanographic Inst., 1973–74. Murchison Grant of RGS, 1965. Foreign Hon. Mem., Amer. Acad. of Arts and Sciences, 1975. Holds American awards in oceanography. Commem. medal of Prince Albert I of Monaco, Inst Océanographique, Paris, 1982. *Publications:* papers on physical oceanography. *Address:* Heath Cottage, Station Road, Drakewalls, Gunnislake, Cornwall. *T:* Tavistock 832100.

SWALLOW, Sydney; Procurement Consultant; *b* 29 June 1919; *s* of William and Charlotte Lucy Swallow; *m* 1950, Monica Williams; one *s*. *Educ:* Woking County Sch.; St Catharine's Coll., Cambridge (MA). Mines Dept, Board of Trade, 1940–42. Served War: Royal Engineers (Survey), 1942–46. Nat. Coal Bd, 1946–59; Central Electricity Generating Bd, 1959–65; Associated Electrical Industries Ltd, 1965–68; General Electric Co. Ltd, 1968; Dir of Supplies, GLC, 1968–77; Senior Dir, Procurement, Post Office, 1977–81; Chief Procurement Officer, and Chief Exec., Consumer Products, British Telecom, 1981–83. Chm., Educn Cttee, Inst. of Purchasing and Supply, 1967–77; Visiting Prof., Univ. of Bradford Management Centre, 1972–75; Vis. Fellow, ASC, 1976–80. FInstPS. *Publications:* various articles on purchasing and supply in professional jls. *Recreations:* narrowboats, cricket. *Address:* 101 Muswell Hill Road, N10. *T:* 01–444 8775.

SWALLOW, Sir William, Kt 1967; FIMechE; *b* 2 Jan. 1905; *s* of William Turner Swallow, Gomersal, Yorks; *m* 1929, Kathleen Lucy Smith; no *c*. *Educ:* Batley and Huddersfield Technical Colleges. Draughtsman, Karrier Motors Ltd, 1923; senior draughtsman, chief body designer, Short Bros, 1926; Gilford Motors Ltd, 1930; development engineer, Pressed Steel Co., 1932; chief production engineer, Short Bros, 1943; development engineer, General Motors Overseas Operations, New York, 1947; i/c manufacturing staff, General Motors Ltd, 1948; gen. man., A. C. Sphinx Spark Plug Div. of Gen. Motors Ltd, 1950; Managing Director, General Motors Ltd, 1953, Chairman, 1958; Chm., Vauxhall Motors Ltd, Luton, Beds, 1961–66 (Man. Dir, 1961–65). Mem.,

Advisory Council on Technology, 1968–70; Chairman: NPL Adv. Bd, 1969–; Shipbuilding and Shiprepairing Council, 1967–71; EDC for Hotel and Catering Industry, 1966–72; Shipbuilding Industry Bd, 1966–71. Governor, Ashridge Coll., 1965–72. ARAeS; MSAE. President: SMMT, 1964–65 (Dep. Pres. 1966–67); Inst. Road Tspt Engrs, 1966–68. *Address:* Alderton Lodge, Ashridge Park, Berkhamsted, Herts. *T:* Little Gaddesden 2284.

SWAMINATHAN, Dr Monkombu Sambasivan, FRS 1973; Director-General, International Rice Research Institute, Manila, since 1982; *b* 7 Aug. 1925; *m* Mina Swaminathan; three *d. Educ:* Univs of Kerala, Madras and Cambridge. BSc Kerala, 1944; BSc (Agric.) Madras, 1947; Assoc. IARI 1949; PhD Cantab, 1952. Responsible for developing Nat. Demonstration Project, 1964, and for evolving Seed Village concept; actively involved in develt of High Yielding Varieties, Dryland Farming and Multiple Cropping Programmes. Vice-Pres., Internat. Congress of Genetics, The Hague, 1963; Gen. Pres., Indian Science Congress, 1976; Mem. (Agriculture), Planning Commn, 1980–82 (formerly Dir-Gen., Indian Council of Agricultural Research). First Zakir Hussain Meml .Lectr, 1970; UGC Nat. Lectr, 1971; lectures at many internat. scientific symposia. Foreign Associate, US Nat. Acad. of Scis; For. Mem., All Union Acad. of Agricl Scis, USSR; Hon. Mem., Swedish Seed Assoc.; Hon. Fellow, Indian Nat. Acad. of Sciences. FNA; Fellow, Italian Nat. Sci. Acad. Shanti Swarup Bhatnagar Award for contribs in Biological Scis, 1961; Mendel Centenary Award, Czechoslovak Acad. of Scis, 1965; Birbal Sahni Award, Indian Bot. Soc., 1965; Ramon Magsaysay Award for Community Leadership, 1971; Silver Jubilee Award, 1973, Meghnath Saha Medal, 1981, Indian Nat. Science Acad.; R. B. Bennett Commonwealth Prize, RSA, 1984. Padma Shri, 1967; Padma Bhushan, 1972. Hon. DSc from twenty-two universities. *Publications:* numerous scientific papers. *Address:* International Rice Research Institute, PO Box 933, Manila, The Philippines.

SWAN, Conrad Marshall John Fisher, CVO 1986 (LVO 1978); PhD; York Herald of Arms, since 1968; Registrar, College of Arms, since 1982; Genealogist: of Order of the Bath, since 1972; of Grand Priory, OStJ, since 1976; *b* 13 May 1924; *yr s* of late Dr Henry Peter Swan, Major RAMC and RCAMC, of BC, Canada and Colchester, Essex, and of Edna Hanson Magdalen (*née* Green), Cross of Honour Pro Ecclesia et Pontifice *m* 1957, Lady Hilda Susan Mary Northcote, Dame of Honour and Devotion, SMO Malta, 1979, and of Justice of SMO of Constantine St George, 1975, *yr d* of 3rd Earl of Iddesleigh; one *s* four *d. Educ:* St George's Coll., Weybridge; Sch. of Oriental and African Studies, Univ. of London; Univ. of Western Ontario; Peterhouse, Cambridge. BA 1949, MA 1951, Univ. of W Ont; PhD 1955, Cambridge. Served Europe and India (Capt. Madras Regt, IA), 1942–47. Assumption Univ. of Windsor, Ont.: Lectr in History, 1955–57; Asst Prof. of Hist., 1957–60; Univ. Beadle, 1957–60. Rouge Dragon Pursuivant of Arms, 1962–68. On Earl Marshal's staff for State Funeral of Sir Winston Churchill, 1965 and Investiture of HRH Prince of Wales, 1969. In attendance: upon HM The Queen at Installation of HRH Prince of Wales as Great Master of Order of the Bath, 1975; during Silver Jubilee Thanksgiving Service, 1977; on Australasian Tour, 1977; Gentleman Usher-in-Waiting to HH the Pope, GB visit, 1982. Woodward Lectr, Yale, 1964; Centennial Lectr, St Thomas More Coll., Univ. of Saskatchewan, 1967; Inaugural Sir William Scott Meml Lectr, Ulster-Scot Hist. Foundn, 1968; first Herald to execute duties in Tabard across Atlantic (Bermuda, 1969) and in S Hemisphere (Brisbane, Qld, 1977); to visit Australia, 1970, S America, 1972, Thailand, Japan, 1973, NZ, 1976. World lecture tours, 1970, 1973, 1976. Adviser to PM of Canada on establishment of Nat. Flag of Canada and Order of Canada, 1964–67. Co-founder (with Lady Hilda Swan), Heraldic Bird Garden, Boxford, Suffolk, 1983. Hon. Citizen, State of Texas; Freemanships in USA; Freeman: St George's, Bermuda, 1969; City of London, 1974. Fellow, 1976, Hon. Vice-Pres. and a Founder, Heraldry Soc. of Canada; Fellow, Geneal. Soc. of Victoria (Australia), 1970; FSA 1971. Liveryman and Freeman, 1974, and Mem., Ct of Assts, 1983, Gunmakers' Co. KStJ 1976. Kt of Honour and Devotion, SMO of Malta, 1979 (Kt of Grace and Devotion, 1964) (Genealogist Br. Assoc., 1974–); Cross of Comdr of Order of Merit, SMO of Malta, 1983. *Publications:* Heraldry: Ulster and North American Connections, 1972; Canada: Symbols of Sovereignty, 1977; many articles in learned jls on heraldic, sigillographic and related subjects. *Recreations:* hunting, driving (horse drawn vehicles), rearing ornamental pheasants and waterfowl, marine biology. *Address:* College of Arms, Queen Victoria Street, EC4V 4BT. *T:* 01–248 1850; Boxford House, Suffolk CO6 5JT. *T:* Boxford (Suffolk) 210208.

SWAN, Maj.-Gen. Dennis Charles Tarrant, CB 1953; CBE 1948; *b* 2 Sept. 1900; *s* of late Lt-Col C. T. Swan, IA; *m* 1930, Patricia Ethel Mary Thorne (*d* 1960); one *s* one *d. Educ:* Wellington Coll., Berks; Royal Military Academy, Woolwich. Commissioned as 2nd Lt RE, 1919; served War of 1939–45 (despatches twice): with BEF France, Feb.-May 1940; CRE 1 Burma Div., 1941; Comdt No 6 Mech. Eqpt Group, IE, 1944; Chief Engineer, 15 Ind. Corps, 1945; District Chief Engineer, BAOR, 1946, Chief Engineer, 1948; Director of Fortification and Works, War Office, 1952–55, retired. Captain 1930; Adjutant, 36 (Mx) AA Bn, 1935; Major, 1938; Lt-Col, 1945; Colonel 1947; Brig. 1948; Maj.-Gen., 1952. Pres., Instn of Royal Engineers, 1961–65. *Address:* 15 Lancastrian Grange, Tower Street, Chichester, West Sussex. *T:* Chichester 786899.

SWAN, Dermot Joseph, MVO 1972; HM Diplomatic Service, retired; HM Consul-General, Marseilles, 1971–77; *b* 24 Oct. 1917; *s* of Dr William Swan and Anne Cosgrave; *m* 1947, Jeanne Labat; one *d. Educ:* St George's, Weybridge; University Coll., London Univ. BA (Hons) French and German. Served War, HM Forces, 1939–46. HM Foreign (later Diplomatic) Service: Vice-Consul, Marseilles, 1947; Saigon, 1949; Foreign Office, 1951; Brazzaville, 1951; Budapest, 1953; FO 1955; First Sec., 1958; Head of Chancery, Phnom Penh, 1959, and Budapest, 1961; UK Mission, New York, 1963; FO (later FCO), 1967; Counsellor, Special Asst to Sec.-Gen. of CENTO, Ankara, 1969. *Recreations:* ice-skating, skiing, swimming. *Address:* Résidence du Golf, 66120 Font Romeu, France. *Club:* Roehampton.

SWAN, Hon. John (William David), JP; MP (United Bermuda Party) Paget East, since 1972; Premier of Bermuda, since 1982; *b* 3 July 1935; *s* of late John N. Swan and of Margaret E. Swan; *m* 1965, Jacqueline A. D. Roberts; one *s* two *d. Educ:* West Virginia Wesleyan Coll. (BA). Mem., Lloyd's of London. Salesman, Real Estate, Rego Ltd, 1960–62; Founder, Chairman and Chief Exec., John W. Swan Ltd, 1962–. Minister for: Marine and Air Services; Labour and Immigration, 1977–78; Home Affairs, 1978–82; formerly: Parly Sec. for Finance; Chairman: Bermuda Hosps Bd; Dept of Civil Aviation. Mem., Young Presidents Organization Inc. *Recreations:* sailing, tennis. *Address:* Grape Bay, Paget, Bermuda. *T:* 809–296–1303. *Clubs:* Hamilton Rotary, Royal Bermuda Yacht (Bermuda).

SWAN, Sheriton Clements; *b* 15 Jan. 1909; *s* of late Sir Charles Sheriton Swan, Stocksfield-on-Tyne; *m* 1936, Rosalind Maitland, *d* of late D. S. Waterlow; two *s* one *d. Educ:* Cambridge Univ. Went to Architectural Assoc. in London to complete architectural training; joined firm of Swan, Hunter and Wigham Richardson, Ltd, in 1935; retired 1971. *Address:* Milestone Cottage, Wall, Hexham, Northumberland NE46 4ED. *T:* Humshaugh 319.

SWAN, Lt-Col William Bertram, CBE 1968; TD 1955; JP; farmer since 1933; Lord-Lieutenant of Berwickshire since 1969; *b* 19 Sept. 1914; *er s* of late N. A. Swan, Duns, Berwickshire; *m* 1948, Ann Gilroy, *d* of late G. G. Hogarth, Ayton, Berwickshire; four *s. Educ:* St Mary's Sch., Melrose; Edinburgh Academy. Served 1939–42 with 4 Bn KOSB (UK and France) and 1942–45 with IA. President: Nat. Farmers Union of Scotland, 1961–62; Scottish Agric. Organisation Society Ltd, 1966–68; Mem., Development Commn, 1964–76; Chairman: Rural Forum Scotland, 1982–; Scottish Veterans' Garden City Assoc., 1983–. County Comdt, Roxburgh, Berwick and Selkirk Bn, ACF, 1955–73. President: Scottish Cricket Union, 1972–73; Lowlands TA&VRA, 1983–86. JP 1964. *Recreation:* sport. *Address:* Blackhouse, Reston, Eyemouth, Berwickshire TD14 5LR. *T:* Duns 82842.

SWANN, family name of **Baron Swann.**

SWANN, Baron *cr* 1981 (Life Peer); **Michael Meredith Swann;** Kt 1972; MA, PhD; FRS 1962; FRSE 1952; Principal and Vice-Chancellor, University of Edinburgh, 1965–73; Chairman, BBC, 1973–80; Chancellor, University of York, since 1979; *b* 1 March 1920; *er s* of late M. B. R. Swann, MD, Fellow of Gonville and Caius Coll., Cambridge, and late Marjorie (*née* Dykes) (she *m* 2nd, Sir Sydney Roberts, he *d* 1966); *m* 1942, Tess, ARCM, ARCO, *d* of late Prof. R. M. Y. Gleadowe, CVO, Winchester and late Cecil (*née* Rotton); two *s* two *d. Educ:* Winchester (Fellow, 1979); Gonville and Caius College, Cambridge (Hon. Fellow, 1977). Served War, 1940–46, in various capacities, mainly scientific (despatches, 1944). Fellow of Gonville and Caius College, Cambridge, 1946–52; University Demonstrator in Zoology, Cambridge, 1946–52; Professor of Natural History, University of Edinburgh, 1952–65 (Dean, Faculty of Science, 1963–65). Member: Adv. Council on Educn in Scotland, 1957–61; Fisheries Adv. Cttee, Develt Commn, 1957–65; Council St George's School for Girls, 1959–75; Edinburgh Univ. Court, 1959–62; MRC, 1962–65; Cttee on Manpower Resources, 1963–68; Council for Scientific Policy, 1965–69; SRC, 1969–73; Adv. Council, Civil Service Coll., 1970–76; Council, St George's House, Windsor, 1975–84; Scientific Foundn Bd, RCGP, 1978–83. Chairman: Nuffield Foundation Biology Project, 1962–65; Jt Cttee on Use of Antibiotics in Animal Husbandry and Veterinary Medicine, 1967–68; Scottish Health Services Scientific Council, 1971–72; Jt Cttee of Inquiry into the Veterinary Profession, 1971–75; Council for Science and Society, 1974–78; Council for Applied Science in Scotland, 1978–80; Technical Change Centre, 1980–; Cttee of Inquiry into Educn of Children from Ethnic Minority Gps, 1981–85; Co. Pensions Information Centre, 1984–. Author of Swann reports on Scientific Manpower, 300 GEV Accelerator, Antibiotics, Veterinary Profession, Educn of Ethnic Minority Children. Director: Inveresk Res. Internat., Midlothian, 1969–72; New Court Natural Resources Ltd, 1973–85; Roy. Acad. of Music, 1980– (Chm. Governors, 1983–); Charities Investment Managers Ltd, 1981–; M & G Group plc, 1981–. Chm., Cheltenham Fest., 1983–. Mem. Bd of Trustees, Wellcome Trust, 1973–; Trustee, BM (Nat. Hist.), 1982–. Pres., Aslib, 1982–84. Governor, Ditchley Foundn, 1975–; Chm., Cttee of Management, LSHTM, 1982–. Provost, Oriel Coll., Oxford, 1980–81. Crossbencher. FIBiol; Hon. FRCSE 1967; Hon. FRCPE 1972; Hon. ARCVS 1976; Hon. Associate, BVA, 1984. Hon. LLD Aberdeen, 1967; DUniv: York, 1968; Edinburgh, 1983; Hon. DSc Leicester, 1968; Hon. DLitt Heriot Watt, 1971. *Publications:* papers in scientific journals. *Recreations:* gardening, sailing. *Address:* Tallat Steps, Coln St Denys, near Cheltenham. *T:* Fossebridge 533; 23 Sheffield Terrace, W8. *Clubs:* Athenæum; New (Edinburgh).

See also Bishop of London.

SWANN, Sir Anthony (Charles Christopher), 3rd Bt *cr* 1906; CMG 1958; OBE 1950; Minister for Defence and Internal Security, Kenya, 1959–63; *b* 29 June 1913; *s* of Sir (Charles) Duncan Swann, 2nd Bt,; *m* 1940, Jean Margaret Niblock-Stuart; one *s. Educ:* Eton College; New College, Oxford. Joined Colonial Service, Kenya, 1936. Served, 1940–43, with King's African Rifles (Major). District Commissioner, Kenya, 1946–54; Provincial Commissioner, Kenya, 1955–59. Chairman East African Land Forces Organisation, 1959–60. *Recreations:* music, reading, fishing, shooting. *Heir: s* Michael Christopher Swann, TD [*b* 23 Sept. 1941; *m* 1965, Hon. Lydia Mary Hewitt, *e d* of Viscount Lifford, *qv*; two *s* one *d*]. *Address:* 23 Montpelier Square, SW7. *Clubs:* Army and Navy, Pratt's.

SWANN, Benjamin Colin Lewis; Controller, Finance, British Council, 1975–79, retired; *b* 9 May 1922; *s* of Henry Basil Swann and Olivia Ophelia Lewis; *m* 1946, Phyllis Julia Sybil Lewis; three *s* one *d. Educ:* Bridgend County School. CA. RAFVR, 1941; Transatlantic Ferry, 1942; Flt Lieut, Transport Command, 1944; Flt Supervisor, BOAC, 1946. Apprentice Chartered Accountant, 1950; Audit Asst, George A. Touche & Co., 1953; Treasury Acct, Malaya, 1954; Financial Adviser, Petaling Jaya, 1956; Partner, Milligan Swann & Co., Chartered Accountants, Exeter, 1957; British Council, 1960; Regional Acct, SE Asia, 1961; Dep. Dir Audit, 1965; Asst Representative, Delhi, 1970; Director, Budget, 1972; Dep. Controller, Finance, 1972. *Recreations:* cuisine, lepidoptery. *Address:* Les Malardeaux, St Sernin de Duras 47120, France.

SWANN, Donald Ibrahim, MA; composer and performer, free-lance since 1948; *b* 30 Sept. 1923; *s* of late Dr Herbert William Swann, Richmond, Surrey and Naguimé Sultan; *m* 1955, Janet Mary (*née* Oxborrow) (marr. diss. 1983), Ipswich, Suffolk; two *d. Educ:* Westminster School; Christ Church, Oxford. Hons Degree Mod. Lang. (Russian and Mod. Greek). Contributed music to London revues, including Airs on a Shoestring, 1953–54, as joint leader writer with Michael Flanders; Wild Thyme, musical play, with Philip Guard, 1955; in At the Drop of a Hat, 1957, appeared for first time (with Michael Flanders) as singer and accompanist of own songs (this show ran over 2 yrs in London, was part of Edinburgh Festival, 1959; Broadway, 1959–60; American and Canadian tour, 1960–61; tour of Great Britain and Ireland, 1962–63); At the Drop of Another Hat (with Michael Flanders), Haymarket, 1963–64, Globe, 1965; Aust. and NZ tour, 1964; US Tour, 1966–67. Arranged concerts of own settings: Set by Swann, An Evening in Crete; Soundings by Swann; Between the Bars: an autobiography in music; A Crack in Time, a concert in search of peace. Musician in Residence, Quaker Study Center, Pendle Hill, USA, Jan.-June 1983; has worked in song-writing and performing partnerships with Jeremy Taylor, Sydney Carter, Frank Topping, John Amis; solo entertainments in theatres and concert halls (Stand Clear for Wonders, with peace exploration songs). Founded Albert House Press for special publications, 1974. *Compositions and Publications include:* Lucy and the Hunter, musical play with Sydney Carter; satirical music to Third Programme series by Henry Reed, ghosting for Hilda Tablet. London Sketches with Sebastian Shaw, 1958; Festival Matins, 1962; Perelandra, music drama with David Marsh based on the novel of C. S. Lewis, 1961–62; Settings of John Betjeman Poems, 1964; Sing Round the Year (Book of New Carols for Children), 1965; The Road Goes Ever On, book of songs with J. R. R. Tolkien, 1968, rev. edn 1978; The Space Between the Bars: a book of reflections, 1968; Requiem for the Living, to words of C. Day Lewis, 1969; The Rope of Love: around the earth in song, 1973; Swann's Way Out: a posthumous adventure, 1974; (with Albert Friedlander) The Five Scrolls, 1975; Omnibus Flanders and Swann Songbook, 1977; Round the Piano with Donald Swann, 1979; (with Alec Davison) The Yeast Factory, music drama, 1979; Alphabetaphon: 26 essays A-Z (illus. by Natasha Etheridge); *songs and operas* with Arthur Scholey: The Song of Caedmon, 1971; Singalive, 1978; Wacky and his Fuddlejig (children's musical play), 1978; Candle Tree,

1980; Baboushka (a Christmas cantata), 1980; The Visitors (based on Tolstoy), 1984; Brendan A-hoy! (with Evelyn Kirkhart and Mary Morgan) Mamahuhu (musical play), 1986; Envy, 1986. *Recreation:* going to the launderette. *Address:* 13 Albert Bridge Road, SW11 4PX. *T:* 01-622 4281.

SWANN, Frederick Ralph Holland, CBE 1974 (OBE (mil.) 1944); Life Vice President, Royal National Lifeboat Institution (Chairman, 1972–75); *b* 4 Oct. 1904; *s* of F. Holland Swann, JP, Steeple, Dorset; *m* 1940, Philippa Jocelyn Braithwaite (*d* 1968); no *c. Educ:* Eton; Trinity Coll., Cambridge (MA). Mem. London Stock Exchange, 1932–64. Joined RNVSR, 1937; served in HMS Northern Gift, 1939–40 (despatches); comd HMS Sapphire, 1940–41; Senior Fighter Direction Officer, HMS Formidable, 1941–43; Comdr RNVR 1944, QO status, 1945; Exec. Officer, HMS Biter, 1944 and HMS Hunter, 1944–45 (in comd, 1945). Mem. Cttee of Management, RNLI, 1953, Dep. Chm. 1964–72. A Vice-Pres., Royal Humane Soc., 1973; Hon. Life Mem., Norwegian Soc. for Sea Rescue, 1975. A Comr of Income Tax, City of London, 1964–76. *Recreations:* fishing, gardening. *Address:* Stratford Mill, Stratford-sub-Castle, Salisbury, Wilts SP1 3LJ. *T:* Salisbury 336563. *Clubs:* United Oxford & Cambridge University, Royal Cruising (Cdre 1966–72), Cruising Association (Hon. Mem.); Royal Corinthian Yacht.

SWANN, Julian Dana Nimmo H.; *see* Hartland-Swann.

SWANN, Peter Geoffrey, CBE 1981 (OBE 1973); MD, FRCP, FFOM; FInstPet; Director of Medical Services, Esso Europe Inc., since 1975; Civil Consultant in Occupational Medicine to the Royal Air Force and the Royal Navy, since 1979; *b* 18 Feb. 1921; *s* of Arthur Swann and Annette (*née* Watkins); *m* 1954, Ruth Audrey Stapleton; one *s* one *d. Educ:* Chigwell Sch.; London Hosp. Med. Coll. (MB, BS 1943; MD 1949). LRCP 1942, MRCP 1949, FRCP 1969; MRCS 1942. FInstPet 1975. Served War, RAFVR Med. Br., 1943–46, Flt Lieut. House physician appts, London Hosp., 1942; jt appt in pathology, Univ. of Oxford and Emergency Public Health Lab. Service, Oxford, 1943; Med. Registrar, subseq. Sen. Registrar, London Hosp. and Oldchurch Hosp., 1946–54; SMO, Esso Petroleum Co., 1954–61, CMO, 1961–75; Dean, Faculty of Occupational Medicine, RCP, 1978–81 (Fellow of Faculty, 1978). FRSM (Pres., Occup. Med. Sect., 1975). Chairman: Working Party on Occup. Med., RCP, 1976; Standing Cttee on Occup. Med., RCP, 1971–78; Health Adv. Cttee, Oil Cos Internat. Study Gp for Conservation of Clean Air and Water, Europe, 1972–. Member: Specialist Adv. Cttee on Occup. Med., 1971–76 (Chm., 1973–76); Jt Cttee on Higher Med. Trng, 1973–76; Bd, Offshore Medical Support Ltd, Aberdeen, 1977–; Working Party of MOs in Chemical Industry, EEC, Luxembourg, 1976–; Standing Med. Adv. Cttee, DHSS, 1980–; BMA; Council, RCP; Soc. of Occup. Med. (Hon. Sec., 1966–70); Exec. Cttee and Advisory Bd, Inst. of Occupational Health, Univ. of Birmingham, 1980–. Mem., Conf. on Med. Royal Colls and their Faculties, UK, 1978–81. Dep. Pres., RoSPA, 1980–. Clinical Prof., Univ. of Miami, 1979. *Publications:* contrib. med. jls. *Recreations:* sailing, golf, squash. *Address:* 43 Upper Berkeley Street, W1H 7PL. *T:* 01–723 8333; Robinswood, Second Avenue, Frinton-on-Sea, Essex. *T:* Frinton-on-Sea 3678. *Clubs:* Royal Air Force; Royal Harwich Yacht; Frinton Golf.

SWANSEA, 4th Baron *cr* 1893; **John Hussey Hamilton Vivian,** Bt 1882; DL; *b* 1 Jan. 1925; *s* of 3rd Baron and Hon. Winifred Hamilton (*d* 1944), 4th *d* of 1st Baron Holm Patrick; *S* father, 1934; *m* 1st, 1956, Miriam Antoinette (marr. diss. 1973; she *d* 1975), 2nd *d* of A. W. F. Caccia-Birch, MC, of Guernsey Lodge, Marton, NZ; one *s* two *d*; 2nd, 1982, Mrs Lucy Temple-Richards (*née* Gough). *Educ:* Eton; Trinity Coll., Cambridge. DL Powys (formerly Brecknock), 1962. OStJ 1980. *Recreations:* shooting, fishing, rifle shooting. *Heir: s* Hon. Richard Anthony Hussey Vivian, *b* 24 Jan. 1957. *Address:* 16 Cheyne Gardens, SW3 5QT. *Club:* Carlton.

SWANSEA and BRECON, Bishop of, since 1976; **Rt. Rev. Benjamin Noel Young Vaughan;** *b* 25 Dec. 1917; *s* of late Alderman and Mrs J. O. Vaughan, Newport, Pembs; *m* 1945, Nesta Lewis (*d* 1980). *Educ:* St David's Coll., Lampeter (BA); St Edmund Hall, Oxford (MA); Westcott House, Cambridge. Deacon, 1943; Priest, 1944. Curate of: Llannon, 1943–45; St David's, Carmarthen, 1945–48; Tutor, Codrington Coll., Barbados, 1948–52; Lecturer in Theology, St David's Coll., Lampeter, and Public Preacher, Diocese of St David's, 1952–55; Rector, Holy Trinity Cathedral, Port of Spain, and Dean of Trinidad, 1955–61; Bishop Suffragan of Mandeville, 1961–67; Bishop of British Honduras, 1967–71; Assistant Bishop and Dean of Bangor, 1971–76. Examining Chaplain to Bishop of Barbados, 1951–52, to Bishop of Trinidad, 1955–61; Commissary for Barbados, 1952–55. Formerly Chairman: Nat. Council for Educn in British Honduras; Govt Junior Secondary Sch.; Provincial Commn on Theological Educn in WI; Provincial Cttee on Reunion of Churches, Christian Social Council of British Honduras; Ecumenical Commn of British Honduras; Agric. Commn of Churches of British Honduras. Chairman: Provincial Cttee on Missions, Church in Wales; Church and Society Dept, Council of Churches for Wales; Adv. Cttee on Church and Society, Church in Wales, 1977; Judge of Provincial Court, Church in Wales. Pres., Council of Churches for Wales, 1980–82. Member: Council, St David's Univ. Coll., Lampeter, 1976; Council and Ct, Swansea Univ. Coll., 1976; Ct, Univ. of Wales, 1986. Sub-Prelate, OStJ, 1977; Order of Druids, Gorsedd y Beirdd. *Publications:* Structures for Renewal, 1967; Wealth, Peace and Godliness, 1968; The Expectation of the Poor, 1972. *Address:* Ely Tower, Brecon, Powys.

SWANSON, Prof. Sydney Alan Vasey; Professor of Biomechanics, Imperial College, University of London, since 1974; *b* 31 Oct. 1931; *s* of Charles Henry William Swanson and Hannah Elizabeth Swanson (*née* Vasey); *m* 1956, Mary Howarth; one *s* one *d. Educ:* Scarborough Boys' High Sch.; Imperial Coll., London. DSc (Eng), PhD, DIC, FCGI, FIMechE. Engineering Laboratories, Bristol Aircraft Ltd, 1955–58; Imperial College, London: Lectr, Mechanical Engineering, 1958–69; Reader in Biomechanics, 1969–74; Dean, City and Guilds Coll., 1976–79; Head of Mechanical Engineering Dept, 1978–83; Pro Rector, 1983–86. FRSA. *Publications:* Engineering Dynamics, 1963; Engineering in Medicine (with B. M. Sayers and B. Watson), 1975; (with M. A. R. Freeman) The Scientific Basis of Joint Replacement, 1977; papers on bone, cartilage and joints in learned jls. *Recreations:* photography, fell-walking. *Address:* Mechanical Engineering Department, Imperial College, SW7 2BX. *T:* 01–589 5111. *Club:* Lyke Wake (Northallerton).

SWANSTON, Commander David, DSO 1945; DSC 1941, and Bar, 1942; RN; Deputy Serjeant at Arms, House of Commons, 1976–81; *b* 13 Feb. 1919; *s* of late Capt. D. S. Swanston, OBE RN; *m* 1st, 1942, Sheila Ann Lang (marr. diss.); one *s* (and one *s* decd); 2nd, 1953, Joan Margaret Nest Stockwood (*d* 1985), *d* of late I. H. Stockwood and Mrs Stockwood; one *s* one *d. Educ:* Royal Naval College, Dartmouth. Joined Royal Navy, 1932; served in submarines at Home, Mediterranean, and East Indies Stations, from 1939. Comd Shakespeare, 1944–45; Alaric, 1948; Tudor, 1949; Naval Liaison Officer, RMA Sandhurst, 1951–53; passed RN Staff course, 1953; Commander, 1953; invalided from Royal Navy, 1955. Asst Serjeant at Arms, House of Commons, 1957–76. Industrial employment, 1955–56. *Recreations:* golf, rifle shooting. *Address:* High Meadow, Linchmere, Haslemere, Surrey GU27 3NF.

SWANTON, Ernest William, OBE 1965; author; Cricket and Rugby football Correspondent to the Daily Telegraph, retired 1975; BBC Commentator, 1934–75; *b* 11 Feb. 1907; *s* of late William Swanton; *m* 1958, Ann, *d* of late R. H. de Montmorency and *widow* of G. H. Carbutt. *Educ:* Cranleigh. Evening Standard, 1927–39. Played Cricket for Middlesex, 1937–38. Served 1939–46; captured at Singapore, 1942; POW Siam, 1942–45; Actg Maj. Bedfordshire Yeomanry (RA). Joined Daily Telegraph staff, 1946. Covered 20 Test tours to Australia, W Indies, S Africa, New Zealand and India; managed own XI to West Indies, 1956 and 1961 and to Malaya and Far East, 1964. Editorial Director, The Cricketer. Mem. Cttee, MCC and Kent CCC (Pres. 1981–82); President: Cricket Soc., 1976–83; Forty Club, 1983–86. *Publications:* (with H. S. Altham) A History of Cricket, 1938, 4th edn 1962; Denis Compton, A Cricket Sketch, 1948; Elusive Victory, 1951; Cricket and The Clock, 1952; Best Cricket Stories, 1953; West Indian Adventure, 1954; Victory in Australia, 1954/5, 1955; Report from South Africa, 1957; West Indies Revisited, 1960; The Ashes in Suspense, 1963; Cricket from all Angles, 1968; Sort of a Cricket Person (memoirs), 1972; Swanton in Australia, 1975; Follow On (memoirs), 1977; As I Said at the Time: a lifetime of cricket, 1983; Gubby Allen: Man of Cricket, 1985; (with C. H. Taylor) Kent Cricket: a photographic history 1744–1984, 1985; General Editor, The World of Cricket, 1966, revised as Barclay's World of Cricket, 1980, 3rd edn 1986. *Recreations:* cricket, golf. *Address:* Delf House, Sandwich, Kent. *Clubs:* Naval and Military, MCC; Royal St George's (Edinburgh).

SWANWICK, Betty, RA 1979 (ARA 1972); RWS 1976; artist; book illustrator and mural painter; now painting in watercolours; *b* 22 May 1915; *d* of Henry Gerad Swanwick. *Educ:* Lewisham Prendergast Sch.; Goldsmiths' Coll. Sch. of Art; Royal Coll. of Art. Has designed posters and press advertisements for LPTB, Shell-Mex, etc; murals for various organizations. *Publications:* The Cross Purposes, 1945; Hoodwinked, 1957; Beauty and the Burglar, 1958. *Recreation:* gardening. *Address:* Caxton Cottage, Frog Lane, Tunbridge Wells, Kent.

SWANWICK, Sir Graham Russell, Kt 1966; MBE 1944; Judge of the High Court of Justice (Queen's Bench Division), 1966–80; Presiding Judge, Midland and Oxford Circuit, 1975–78; *b* 24 August 1906; *s* of Eric Drayton Swanwick and Margery Eleanor (*née* Norton), Whittington House, Chesterfield; *m* 1st, 1933, Helen Barbara Reid (marr. diss., 1945; she *d* 1970); two *s*; 2nd, 1952, Audrey Celia Parkinson. *Educ:* Winchester Coll.; University Coll., Oxford (BA). Called to Bar, Inner Temple, 1930, Master of the Bench, 1962; QC 1956; Leader Midland Circuit, 1961–65. Wing Comdr RAFVR, 1940–45 (MBE, despatches). Recorder: City of Lincoln, 1957–59; City of Leicester, 1959–66; Judge of Appeal, Channel Islands, 1964–66; Derbyshire QS: Chm., 1963–66; Dep. Chm., 1966–71. *Recreation:* shooting. *Address:* Burnett's Ashurst, Steyning, West Sussex. *T:* Partridge Green 710241. *Club:* Royal Air Force.

SWARBRICK, Prof. James, PhD, DSc; FRSC, CChem; Professor of Pharmaceutics and Chairman, Division of Pharmaceutics, University of North Carolina, since 1981; *b* 8 May 1934; *s* of George Winston Swarbrick and Edith M. C. Cooper; *m* 1960, Pamela Margaret Oliver. *Educ:* Sloane Grammar Sch.; Chelsea Coll., Univ. of London (BPharm Hons 1960; PhD 1964; DSc 1972). MPS 1961; FRIC 1970; FPS 1978. Asst Lectr, 1962, Lectr, 1964, Chelsea Coll.; Vis. Asst Prof., Purdue Univ., 1964; Associate Prof., 1966, Prof. and Chm. of Dept of Pharmaceutics, 1969, Asst Dean, 1970, Univ. of Conn; Dir of Product Develt, Sterling-Winthrop Res. Inst., NY, 1972; first Prof. of Pharmaceutics, Univ. of Sydney, 1975–76; Dean, Sch. of Pharmacy, Univ. of London, 1976–78; Prof. of Pharmacy and Chm., Res. Council, Univ. of S California, Los Angeles, 1978–81. Vis. Scientist, Astra Labs, Sweden, 1971; Indust. Cons., 1965–72, 1975–; Cons., Aust. Dept. of Health, 1975–76; Mem., Cttee on Specifications, National Formulary, 1970–75; Chm., Jt US Pharmacopoeia-Nat. Formulary Panel on Disintegration and Dissolution Testing, 1971–75. Member: Cttee on Grad. Programs, Amer. Assoc. of Colls of Pharmacy, 1969–71; Practice Trng Cttee, Pharm. Soc. of NSW, 1975–76; Academic Bd, Univ. of Sydney, 1975–76; Collegiate Council, 1976–78; Educn Cttee, Pharmaceutical Soc. of GB, 1976–78; Working Party on Pre-Registration Training, 1977–78. Pharmaceutical Manufacturers Assoc. Foundation: Mem., Basic Pharmacology Adv. Cttee, 1982–; Chm., Pharmaceutics Adv. Cttee, 1986–; Scientific Adv. Cttee, 1986–. FAAAS 1966; Fellow, Acad. of Pharm. Sciences, 1973. Mem. Editorial Board: Jl of Biopharmaceutics and Pharmacokinetics, 1973–79; Drug Development Communications, 1974–82; Pharmaceutical Technology, 1978–; Biopharmaceutics and Drug Disposition, 1979–; series Editor, Current Concepts in the Pharmaceutical Sciences, Drugs and the Pharmaceutical Sciences. *Publications:* (with A. N. Martin and A. Cammarata) Physical Pharmacy, 2nd edn 1969, 3rd edn 1983; (ed jtly) Encyclopedia of Pharmaceutical Technology; contributed: American Pharmacy, 6th edn 1966 and 7th edn 1974; Remington's Pharmaceutical Sciences, 14th edn 1970 to 17th edn 1985; contrib. Current Concepts in the Pharmaceutical Sciences: Biopharmaceutics, 1970; res. contribs to internat. sci. jls. *Recreation:* woodworking, listening to music, golf. *Address:* School of Pharmacy, University of North Carolina at Chapel Hill, Beard Hall 200H, Chapel Hill, NC 27514, USA. *T:* (919) 962–0092.

SWARTZ, Rt. Rev. George Alfred; *see* Kimberley and Kuruman, Bishop of.

SWARTZ, Col Hon. Sir Reginald (William Colin), KBE 1972 (MBE (mil.) 1948); ED; FAIM, FBIM; retired parliamentarian and company director (director of nine companies, 1973–83); *b* 14 April 1911; *s* of late J. Swartz, Toowoomba, Qld; *m* 1936, Hilda, *d* of late G. C. Robinson; two *s* one *d. Educ:* Toowoomba and Brisbane Grammar Schs. Commonwealth Military Forces, 1928–40, Lieut, 1934. Served War of 1939–45: Captain 2–26 Bn, 8 Div., AIF, 1940; Malaya (PoW): Singapore, Malaya, Thailand (Burma-Thailand Rly); CMF, in Darling Downs Regt, Lt-Col, AQMG, CMF, N Comd, Col (RL), 1961. Hon. Col Australian Army Aviation Corps, 1969–75. MHR (L) Darling Downs, Qld, 1949–72; Parly Under-Sec. for Commerce and Agric., 1952–56; Parly Sec. for Trade, 1956–61; Minister: (of State) for Repatriation, Dec. 1961–Dec. 1964; for Health, 1964–66; for Social Services, 1965; for Civil Aviation, 1966–69; for Nat. Develt, 1969–72; Leader, House of Representatives, Canberra, 1971–72. Leader of many delegns overseas incl. Aust. Delegn to India, 1967, and Trade Mission to SE Asia, 1958; Parly Delegn to S and SE Asia, 1966. Patron and/or Vice-Pres. or Mem. of numerous public organizations. Life Chm. of Trustees, Australian Army Aviation Corps. Past Chm., Inst. of Dirs (Queensland). Member, RSL. JP Queensland, 1947–81. *Recreations:* bowls, boating. *Address:* 32 Leawarra Crescent, Doncaster East, Melbourne, Victoria 3109, Australia. *Clubs:* United Service (Brisbane); Royal Automobile Club of Victoria; Australian (Melbourne); Twin Towns Services (Tweed Head); Darling Downs Aero; Probus (Doncaster) (Foundation Pres.); Templestowe Bowling (Melbourne).

SWASH, Stanley Victor, MC 1917 and Bar 1918; *b* 29 February 1896; British; *s* of A. W. Swash, JP and Sylvia Swash; *m* 1924; *m* 1955, Jane Henderson. *Educ:* Llandovery College; St John's College, Oxford; Lincoln's Inn. Served European War, 1915–19, RFA. MA (Mathematics); short period in Ministry of Pensions; served Royal Navy as Lieut Inst., 1921–24; worked in Woolworth Company, 1924–55; Director, 1939, Chairman, 1951–55; retired 1955. Called to Bar, Lincoln's Inn, 1938. OC 57 County of London Home Guard Battalion, Lieut-Colonel, 1940–45. Chairman, Horticultural Marketing Advisory Council, 1958; Member Milk Marketing Board, 1957–63; Chm. BOAC/MEA Cttee of Enquiry, 1963–64. *Recreations:* swimming, bridge. *Address:* Park Avenue, St Andrews, Malta. *Club:* United Oxford & Cambridge University.

SWAYNE, Sir Ronald (Oliver Carless), Kt 1979; MC 1945; Director: National Freight Co., 1973–85 (Consortium since 1982); Banque Nationale de Paris Ltd, since 1981; Member, Monopolies and Mergers Commission, since 1982; *b* 11 May 1918; *s* of Col O. R. Swayne, DSO, and Brenda (*née* Butler); *m* 1941, Charmian (*d* 1984), *d* of Major W. E. P. Cairnes, Bollingham, Herefordshire; one *s* one *d*. *Educ:* Bromsgrove Sch., Worcester; University Coll., Oxford, 1936–39 and 1945–46 (MA). Served with Herefordshire Regt, 1939–40, No 1 Commando, 1940–45 (MC). Joined Ocean Steam Ship Co., 1946; became partner of Alfred Holt & Co. and Man. Dir of Ocean Steam Ship Co., 1955. Dir, 1965, Dep. Chm., 1969, Chm., 1973–82, Man. Dir, 1978–82, Overseas Containers Ltd. Vice-Chm., British Shipping Fedn, 1967; President: Cttee des Assocs d'Armateurs of EEC, 1974–75; Gen. Council of British Shipping, 1978–79; Inst. of Freight Forwarders, 1980. Industrial Adviser, Churchill Coll., Cambridge, 1974–82; Member: Design Council, 1975–78; Careers Res. Adv. Council, 1975–82; New Philharmonia Trust, 1968–82; Vice-Pres., British Maritime League, 1982–84. *Recreations:* fishing, shooting, music. *Address:* Puddle House, Chicksgrove, Tisbury, Salisbury SP3 6NA. *T:* Teffont 454; 32 Edith Road, W14. *T:* 01–602 4103. *Clubs:* Flyfishers'; Houghton (Stockbridge).

SWAYTHLING, 3rd Baron, *cr* 1907; **Stuart Albert Samuel Montagu,** Bt, *cr* 1894; OBE 1947; late Grenadier Guards; Director, Messrs Samuel Montagu and Co. Ltd, 1951–54; *b* 19 Dec. 1898; *e s* of 2nd Baron and Gladys Helen Rachel, OBE, (*d* 1965), *d* of late Col A. E. Goldsmid; *S* father, 1927; *m* 1st, 1925, Mary Violet (from whom he obtained a divorce, 1942), *e d* of late Major Levy, DSO, and late Hon. Mrs Ionides; two *s* one *d*; 2nd, 1945, Mrs Jean Knox, Director ATS (*see* Lady Swaythling). *Educ:* Clifton; Westminster; Trinity College, Cambridge. JP: Co. Southampton, 1928–48; Surrey, 1948–80. Pres., English Guernsey Cattle Society, 1950–51, 1971–72; Dep. Pres., Royal Assoc. of British Dairy Farmers, 1970–72, 1973–74 (Pres., 1972–73); Mem. Council: Nat. Cattle Breeders Assoc., 1955–67; Royal Agricl Soc., 1961–. Master of The Company of Farmers, 1962–63. *Heir: s* Hon. David Charles Samuel Montagu, *qv*. *Address:* St Jacques House, St Jacques, St Peter Port, Guernsey, CI. *T:* Guernsey (0481) 22022.

SWAYTHLING, Lady, (Jean M.), CBE 1943; Chief Controller and Director, Auxilliary Territorial Service, 1941–43 (as Mrs Jean Knox); *b* 14 Aug. 1908; *m* Squadron Leader G. R. M. Knox; one *d*; *m* 1945, 3rd Baron Swaythling, *qv*. *Address:* St Jacques House, St Jacques, St Peter Port, Guernsey, CI. *T:* Guernsey 22022.

SWEANEY, William Douglas, CMG 1965; retired 1972, as Establishment Officer, Overseas Development Administration, Foreign and Commonwealth Office; *b* 12 Nov. 1912; *s* of late Lt-Comdr William Sweaney, MBE, RN, and late Elizabeth Bridson; *m* 1939, Dorothy Beatrice Parsons; one *s*. *Educ:* Gillingham County Sch.; London Sch. of Economics. BSc(Econ). Clerical Officer, Inland Revenue (Special Comrs of Income Tax), 1929; Officer of Customs and Excise, 1932; seconded to Colonial Office, 1943 (promoted Surveyor of Customs and Excise *in absentia*); transferred to Colonial Office, 1948; Principal, 1948; Private Sec. to Minister of State for Colonial Affairs, 1953; Asst Sec., 1955; Dept of Technical Co-operation, 1961; ODM, later ODA, FCO, 1964–72; Establishment Officer, 1965. Panel of Chairmen, Agricl Dwelling House Adv. Cttees, 1977–. *Recreations:* travel, ornithology. *Address:* 1 Beech Hurst Close, Haywards Heath, West Sussex. *T:* Haywards Heath 450341.

SWEENEY, Thomas Kevin; Senior Medical Officer, Department of Health and Social Security, since 1983; *b* 10 Aug. 1923; *s* of John Francis and Mildred Sweeney; *m* 1950, Eveleen Moira Ryan; two *s* two *d*. *Educ:* O'Connell Sch., Dublin; University Coll., Dublin (MB, BCh, BAO NUI; DTM&H London; TDD Wales). FFCM 1983. Principal Med. Officer, Colonial Medical Service, 1950–65, retd; Asst Sen. Med. Officer, Welsh Hosp. Bd, 1965–68; Department of Health and Social Security: Med. Officer, 1968–72; Sen. Med. Officer, 1972–79; SPMO, 1979–83. QHP 1984–. *Publication:* contrib. BMJ. *Recreations:* gardening, golf, cathedrals. *Address:* The White House, Sheerwater Avenue, Woodham, Weybridge, Surrey. *T:* Byfleet 43559.

SWEET, Prof. Peter Alan, MA, PhD; Regius Professor of Astronomy in the University of Glasgow, 1959–82; retired; *b* 15 May 1921; *s* of David Frank Sweet; *m* 1947, Myrtle Vera Parnell; two *s*. *Educ:* Kingsbury County Grammar School, London; Sidney Sussex College, Cambridge. Open Maj. Schol. in Maths, Sidney Sussex Coll., 1940–42, Wrangler, 1942, BA Cantab 1943. Junior Scientific Officer, Min. of Aircraft Prod., 1942–45; BA Scholar, at Sidney Sussex Coll., 1945–47; MA Cantab 1946; Mayhew Prizeman, 1946, PhD Cantab 1950. Lectr in Astronomy, Univ. of Glasgow, 1947–52; Lectr in Astronomy and Asst Director of the Observatory, Univ. of London, 1952–59; Dean, Faculty of Science, Univ. of Glasgow, 1973–75. Visiting Asst Professor of Astronomy, Univ. of California, Berkeley, 1957–58; Vis. Sen. Res. Fellow, NASA Inst. for Space Studies, NY, 1965–66. *Publications:* papers on Stellar Evolution, Cosmic Magnetism, and Solar Flares in Monthly Notices of Royal Astronomical Soc., etc. *Recreations:* music, gardening. *Address:* 17 Westbourne Crescent, Glasgow G61 4HB. *T:* 041–942 4425.

SWEETING, William Hart, CMG 1969; CBE 1961; Chairman, Board of Directors, Bank of London and Montreal, 1970–79; *b* 18 Dec. 1909; *s* of late Charles Cecil Sweeting, Nassau, Bahamas; *m* 1950, Isabel Jean (*née* Woodall). *Educ:* Queen's Coll., Nassau; London Univ. Entered Bahamas Public Service as Cadet, 1927; served in Colonial Secretary's Office, 1927–37; acted as Asst Colonial Sec. for short periods in 1928 and 1936; transferred to Treasury, 1937; Cashier, Public Treasury, 1941; Asst Treasurer and Receiver of Crown Dues, 1946; seconded as Financial Sec., Dominica, 1950–52; Receiver-Gen. and Treasurer, Bahamas, 1955; MLC, Bahamas, 1960–64; Chairman: Bahamas Currency Comrs, 1955–63; Bahamas Broadcasting and Television Commn, 1957–62; Bahamas Public Disclosure Commn, 1978–84. Acted as Governor various periods 1959, 1964, 1965, 1966, 1968, 1969; acted as Colonial Secretary various periods, 1962–63; Chief Secretary, Bahamas 1964; Dep. Governor, Bahamas, 1969, retired 1970. Mem., Bahamas Music Soc.; Elder, St Andrew's Presbyterian Church; Chairman: Trinity Coll. of Music Local Exams Cttee; Hon. Treasurer, United World Colleges Local Cttee. *Recreations:* swimming, painting, music, bird watching. *Address:* PO Box N 573, Nassau, Bahamas. *T:* 3–1518. *Club:* Corona.

SWEETMAN, Mrs Ronald Andrew; *see* Dickson, Jennifer J.

SWEETNAM, (David) Rodney, MA; FRCS; Orthopaedic Surgeon to the Queen, since 1982; Consultant Surgeon to: The Middlesex Hospital, since 1960; King Edward VII Hospital for Officers, London, since 1964; *b* 5 Feb. 1927; second *s* of late Dr William Sweetnam and Irene (*née* Black); *m* 1959, Patricia Ann, *er d* of A. Staveley Gough, OBE, FRCS; one *s* one *d*. *Educ:* Clayesmore; Peterhouse, Cambridge (Titular Scholar; BA 1947, MA 1951); Middlesex Hosp. Med. Sch. (MB, BChir 1950). FRCS 1955. Surg. Lieut RNVR, 1950–52. Jun. appts, Mddx Hosp., London Hosp. and Royal National Orthopaedic Hosp. Hon. Civil Consultant in Orth. Surgery to the Army, 1974–; Hon. Consultant Orthopaedic Surgeon, Royal Hosp., Chelsea, 1974–. Hon. Consultant, King Edward VII's Convalescent Home for Officers, IW, 1980–; Consultant Advisor in Orth. Surgery to DHSS, 1981–; Hon. Consultant Surgeon, Royal Nat. Orthopaedic Hosp., 1983–. Dir, Medical Sickness Annuity and Life Assce Soc. Ltd, 1982–. Chm., MRC's Working Party on Bone Sarcoma, 1980–85. Member: Council, RCS, 1985–; Exec. Cttee, Arthritis and Rheumatism Council, 1985–. Royal College of Surgeons: Jacksonian Prize, 1966; Hunterian Prof., 1967; Gordon Taylor Meml Lectr, 1982; Stanford Cade Meml Lectr, 1986. President: Combined Services Orthopaedic Soc., 1983–86; British Orthopaedic Assoc., 1984–85. Mem. Res. Adv. Cttee, Royal Hosp. for Incurables, Putney, 1985–. Trustee, Develt Trust, Queen Elizabeth Foundn for the Disabled, 1984–. Dir (Sec. and Treas.), British Editorial Soc. of Bone and Joint Surgery, 1975–. *Publications:* (ed jtly) The Basis and Practice of Orthopaedics, 1980; contrib. med. books and jls in field of gen. orth. surgery, trauma and bone tumours. *Recreation:* gardening. *Address:* 33 Harley Street, W1N 1DA. *T:* 01–580 5409.

SWEETT, Cyril, CEng, AIStructE; FRICS; FCIArb; Founder Partner, Cyril Sweett & Partners, Chartered Quantity Surveyors, 1928; *b* 7 April 1903; *s* of William Thomas Sweett; *m* 1931, Barbara Mary, *d* of late Henry Thomas Loft, Canterbury and London; one *d*. *Educ:* Whitgift Sch.; Coll. of Estate Management. Artists Rifles, TA, 1923–27. Army Service: RE, 1939–43, France, N Africa and Italy; demob. as Lt-Col. Member: Council, RICS, 1959–61, 1970–72; Cttee, London Library, 1973–86; Chm., Nat. Jt Consultative Cttee of Architects, Quantity Surveyors and Builders, 1962–63. Master, Worshipful Co. of Painter Stainers, 1964–65, 1966–67; Sheriff of City of London, 1965–66. Jordanian Star, 1966; Silver Star of Honour, Austria, 1966. *Address:* 5 Oak Lodge, 47/49 Palmeira Avenue, Hove, East Sussex BN3 3GE. *T:* Brighton 777292. *Clubs:* Garrick, MCC; Royal Thames Yacht, Royal Burnham Yacht (Cdre, 1963–65).

SWIFT, John Anthony; QC 1981; *b* 11 July 1940; *s* of late Jack Swift and of Mrs Clare Medcalf; *m* 1972, Jane Carol Sharples; one *s* one *d*. *Educ:* Birkenhead Sch.; University Coll., Oxford (MA); Johns Hopkins Univ.; Bologna. Called to the Bar, Inner Temple, 1965. *Address:* Wittenham House, Little Wittenham, Abingdon, Oxon. *Club:* Reform.

SWIFT, Lionel, QC 1975; JD; Barrister, since 1961; a Recorder of the Crown Court, since 1979; *b* Bristol, 3 Oct. 1931; *s* of late Harris and of Bessie Swift, Hampstead; *m* 1966, Elizabeth (*née* Herzig) (Liz E, London fashion writer); one *d*. *Educ:* Whittingehame Coll., Brighton; University Coll., London (LLB 1951); Brasenose Coll., Oxford (BCL 1959); Univ. of Chicago (Juris Doc, 1960). Solicitor, Natal, S Africa, 1954; called to the Bar, Inner Temple, 1959, Bencher, 1984. British Commonwealth Fellow, Univ. of Chicago Law Sch., 1960; Amer. Social Science Res. Council Grant for work on admin of criminal justice, 1960. Jun. Counsel to Treasury in Probate Matters, 1974. Chm., Inst. of Laryngology and Otology, 1985–. *Publication:* The South African Law of Criminal Procedure (Gen. Editor, A. B. Harcourt, QC), 1957. *Address:* (chambers) 4 Paper Buildings, Temple, EC4Y 7EX.

SWIFT, Michael Charles, MC 1943; Member, Economic and Social Committee of the European Communities, 1983–86; Secretary-General, British Bankers' Association, 1978–82; *b* 29 Aug. 1921; *s* of late Comdr C. C. Swift, OBE, RN; *m* 1957, Dorothy Jill, *d* of late R. G. Bundey; one *s* one *d*. *Educ:* Radley College. Served War, Royal Artillery (Captain), 1940–45. Bank of England, 1946–58; Committee of London Clearing Bankers, 1958–75; Dep. Sec., British Bankers' Assoc., 1975–78. UK Rep., European Communities Banking Fedn Central Cttee, 1978–82, Chm. 1980–82. Gen. Comr for City of London, 1982–. *Recreations:* golf, birdwatching. *Club:* Royal West Norfolk Golf.

SWIFT, Reginald Stanley, CB 1969; Under-Secretary, Department of Health and Social Security, 1968–76, retired; *b* 2 Nov. 1914; *e s* of Stanley John and Annie Swift; *m* 1940, Mildred Joan Easter; no *c*. *Educ:* Watford Grammar School; Christ's College, Cambridge. BA Cantab (1st Cl. Hons in Classics) 1936; MA Cantab 1940; BSc (Econ.) London 1944. Entered Civil Service as Asst Comr, National Savings Cttee, 1938; transferred to Min. of National Insurance as Principal, 1947; Principal Private Secretary to Minister, 1953–54; Assistant Secretary, 1954; Under-Secretary, 1962. *Recreations:* gardening, golf. *Address:* 16 Beechfield, Banstead, Surrey. *T:* Burgh Heath 61773. *Club:* Kingswood Golf.

SWINBURNE, Hon. Ivan Archie, CMG 1973; Member of Legislative Council of Victoria, Australia, 1946–76, retired; *b* 6 March 1908; *s* of George Arthur and Hilda Maud Swinburne; *m* 1950, Isabella Mary, *d* of James Alexander Moore; one *d*. *Educ:* Hurdle Creek West and Milawa State Schs; Wangaratta and Essendon High Schs. MLC, for NE Prov., 1946–76; Dep. Leader of Country Party, 1954–69; Leader of Country Party in Legislative Council, 1969–76; Minister of Housing and Materials, 1950–52; Mem., Subordinate Legislation Cttee, 1961–67 and 1973. Councillor, Shire of Bright, 1940–47 (Pres., 1943–44). Mem., Bush Nursing Council of Victoria, 1948–84; Chm. Cttee of Management, Mount Buffalo National Park, 1963–84. *Recreation:* football administration. *Address:* PO Box 340, Myrtle Street, Myrtleford, Victoria 3737, Australia. *T:* Myrtleford 521167. *Clubs:* RACV (Melbourne); Wangaratta (Wangaratta).

SWINBURNE, Nora; actress; retired from stage and films, 1975; *b* Bath, 24 July 1902; *d* of H. Swinburne Johnson; *m* 1st, Francis Lister (marr. diss.); one *s*; 2nd, Edward Ashley-Cooper (marr. diss.); 3rd, 1946, Esmond Knight, *qv*. *Educ:* Rossholme College, Weston-super-Mare; Royal Academy of Dramatic Art. First West End appearance, 1916; went to America, 1923; returned to London stage, 1924; New York, again, 1930; continuous successes in London, from 1931; went into management, 1938, in addition to acting. Played as Diana Wentworth in The Years Between (which ran for more than a year), Wyndhams, 1945; Red Letter Day, Garrick; A Woman of No Importance, Savoy, 1953; The Lost Generation, Garrick, 1955; Fool's Paradise, Apollo, 1959; Music at Midnight, Westminster, 1962; All Good Children, Hampstead, 1964; Family Reunion, 1973, The Cocktail Party, 1975, Royal Exchange, Manchester. *Films include:* Jassy, Good Time Girl, The Blind Goddess, Fanny by Gaslight, They Knew Mr Knight, Quartet, Christopher Columbus, My Daughter Joy, The River (made in India), Quo Vadis, also Helen of Troy (made in Italy), Third Man on the Mountain, Conspiracy of Hearts, Music at Midnight, Interlude, Anne of the Thousand Days. Has appeared on television (incl. Forsyte Saga, Post Mortem, Kate serial, Fall of Eagles). *Address:* 52 Cranmer Court, SW3.

SWINBURNE, Prof. Richard Granville; Nolloth Professor of Philosophy of Christian Religion, University of Oxford, since 1985; *b* 26 Dec. 1934; *s* of William Henry Swinburne and Glenys Edith Swinburne (*née* Parker); *m* 1960, Monica Holmstrom; two *d*. *Educ:* Exeter College, Oxford (Scholar). BPhil 1959, MA 1961, DipTheol 1960. Fereday Fellow, St John's Coll., Oxford, 1958–61; Leverhulme Res. Fellow in Hist. and Phil. of Science, Univ. of Leeds, 1961–63; Lectr in Philosophy, then Sen. Lectr, Univ. of Hull, 1963–72; Prof. of Philosophy, Univ. of Keele, 1972–84. Vis. Associate Prof. of Philosophy, Univ. of Maryland, 1969–70; Vis. Prof. of Philosophy, Syracuse Univ., 1987; Lectures: Wilde, Oxford Univ., 1975–78; Forwood, Liverpool Univ., 1977; Marrett Meml, Exeter Coll., Oxford, 1980; Gifford, Univ. of Aberdeen, 1982–84; Dist. Vis. Scholar, Univ. of Adelaide, 1982. *Publications:* Space and Time, 1968, 2nd edn 1981; The Concept of Miracle, 1971; An Introduction to Confirmation Theory, 1973; The Coherence of Theism, 1977; The Existence of God, 1979; Faith and Reason, 1981; (with S. Shoemaker) Personal Identity, 1984; The Evolution of the Soul, 1986; articles and reviews in learned jls. *Address:* Oriel College, Oxford OX1 4EW. *T:* Oxford 276589.

SWINBURNE, Dr Terence R.; Director, Institute of Horticultural Research, Agricultural and Food Research Council, since 1985; *b* 17 July 1936; *s* of Reginald and Gladys

Swinburne; *m* 1958, Valerie Parkes; two *s*. *Educ:* Imperial Coll., Univ. of London (DSc, ARCS, DIC, PhD); FIHort. Plant Pathology Res. Div., Min., later Dept, of Agriculture for NI, 1960–80; Scientific Officer, 1960–62; Sen. Scientific Officer, 1962–71; PSO, 1971–79; SPSO, 1979–80; Queen's University, Belfast: Asst Lectr, Faculty of Agriculture, 1961–64; Lectr, 1965–77; Reader, 1977–80; Head of Crop Protection Div., E Malling Res. Stn, 1980–85. Kellogg Fellow, Oregon State Univ., 1964–65; Vis. Prof., Dept of Pure and Applied Biology, Imperial Coll., London, 1986–. *Publication:* Iron Siderophores and Plant Diseases, 1986. *Recreation:* sailing. *Address:* Tan House, 15 Frog Lane, West Malling, Kent. *T:* West Malling 846090.

SWINDELLS, Maj.-Gen. George Michael Geoffrey, CB 1985; Head of Administration, Smith and Williamson, Chartered Accountants, since 1985; *b* 15 Jan. 1930; *s* of George Martyn Swindells and Marjorie Swindells; *m* 1955, Prudence Bridget Barbara Tully; one *s* two *d*. *Educ:* Rugby School. Nat. Service Commission, 5th Royal Inniskilling Dragoon Guards, 1949; served in Germany, Korea and Canal Zone; Regular Commission, 1953; Adjutant, Cheshire Yeomanry, 1955–56; Staff Coll., 1960; Brigade Major, 7th Armd Brigade, 1967–69; transfer to 9th/12th Royal Lancers, to command, 1969–71; GSO1 Directing Staff and Col GS, Staff Coll., 1972–74; Comdr 11th Armd Brigade, 1975–76; RCDS course, 1977; Dir of Op. Requirements (3), MoD, 1978–79; Chief of Jt Services Liaison Organisation, Bonn, 1980–83; ACDS (Intelligence), MoD, 1983–84; Dir of Management (Intelligence), MoD, 1985. *Recreations:* skiing and country life. *Club:* Army and Navy.

SWINDEN, (Thomas) Alan, CBE 1971; Executive Chairman, Institute of Manpower Studies, 1978–86; *b* 27 Aug. 1915; *s* of Thomas and Ethel Swinden; *m* 1941, Brenda Elise Roe; one *d*. *Educ:* Rydal Sch.; Sheffield Univ. (BEng). With Rolls-Royce, 1937–55; seconded to AFV Div., Min. of Supply, 1941–45; with Engrg Employers Fedn, 1955–65, Dir, 1964–65; Dir, Engrg Industry Trng Bd, 1965–70; Confederation of British Industry: Dep. Dir Gen. (Industrial Relations), 1970–74; Chief Advr, Social Affairs, 1974–78; Consultant, 1978–81; Chm., 1974–85, Dir, 1980–84, Kingston Regional Management Centre. Chm., Derby No 1 HMC, 1953–55. Council Member: British Employers Confedn, 1955–65; ACAS, 1974–84; British Assoc. for Commercial and Industrial Educn, 1982–; Inst. of Manpower Studies, 1986–; Mem., BBC Consultative Gp on Industrial and Business Affairs, 1977–83. *Address:* 85 College Road, Epsom, Surrey KT17 4HH. *T:* Epsom 20848. *Club:* Royal Automobile.

SWINDLEHURST, Rt. Rev. Owen Francis; Bishop Auxiliary of Hexham and Newcastle, (RC), since 1977; Titular Bishop of Chester-le-Street; *b* 10 May 1928; *s* of Francis and Ellen Swindlehurst. *Educ:* Ushaw College, Durham; English College, Rome. PhL, STL, LCL (Gregorian Univ., Rome). Assistant Priest: St Matthew's, Ponteland, 1959–67; St Bede's, Denton Burn, Newcastle, 1967–72; Parish Priest at Holy Name, Jesmond, Newcastle, 1967–77. *Recreations:* walking, geriatric squash, reading. *Address:* Oaklea, Tunstall Road, Sunderland SR2 7JR. *T:* Sunderland 41158.

SWINDON, Archdeacon of; *see* Clark, Ven. K. J.

SWINFEN, 3rd Baron *cr* 1919; **Roger Mynors Swinfen Eady;** *b* 14 Dec. 1938; *s* of 2nd Baron Swinfen and of Mary Aline, *d* of late Col H. Mynors Farmar, CMG, DSO; *S* father, 1977; *m* 1962, Patricia Anne, *o d* of late F. D. Blackmore, Dundrum, Dublin; one *s* three *d*. *Educ:* Westminster; RMA, Sandhurst. ARICS 1970. Mem., Direct Mail Services Standards Bd, 1983–. Chm., Parly Gp, Video Enquiry Working Party, 1983–85. Pres. SE Reg., British Sports Assoc. for the Disabled, 1986–. Fellow, Industry and Parlt Trust. *Heir:* *s* Hon. Charles Roger Peregrine Swinfen Eady, *b* 8 March 1971. *Address:* House of Lords, SW1.

SWINGLAND, Owen Merlin Webb, QC 1974; Barrister-at-Law; *b* 26 Sept. 1919; *er s* of Charles and Maggie Eveline Swingland; *m* 1941, Kathleen Joan Eason (*née* Parry), Newport, Mon; one *s* two *d*. *Educ:* Haberdashers' Aske's Hatcham Sch.; King's Coll., London. LLB 1941, AKC. Called to Bar, Gray's Inn, 1946, Bencher, 1985; practice at Chancery Bar, 1948–; Barrister of Lincoln's Inn, 1977. A Church Comr, 1982–. Past Pres., British Insurance Law Assoc. Mem., Court of Assts, Haberdashers' Co. (Warden, 1986); Freeman of the City of London. Chm. Governors, Haberdashers' Aske's Hatcham Schools. *Recreations:* music, theatre, fishing, reading; interested in competitive sports. *Address:* Ightham Warren, Kent. *T:* Borough Green 884157.

SWINGLER, Bryan Edwin, CBE 1979; British Council Representative in France, 1980–84, retired; *b* 20 Sept. 1924; *s* of late George Edwin Swingler, Birmingham, and Mary Eliza Frayne; *m* 1954, Herta, *er d* of late Edwin Jaeger, Schoenlinde; one *d*. *Educ:* King Edward's Sch., Birmingham; Peterhouse, Cambridge (Sen. Schol.); Charles Univ., Prague. BA 1948, MA 1953. Served War, Royal Navy (Leading Signalman), 1943–46. Apptd to British Council, 1949; Vienna, 1949–52; Lahore, 1952–55; Karachi, 1955–56; Oslo, 1956–59; Berlin, 1959–61; Cologne, 1961–63; Dir, Scholarships, 1963–67; Dep. Controller, Commonwealth Div., 1967–68; Rep. Indonesia, Djakarta, 1968–71; Controller Finance, 1972–73; Controller, Home, 1973–75; Asst Dir-Gen., 1975–77; Head of British Council Div., India, and Minister (Educn), British High Commn, New Delhi, 1977–80. Vice-Chm., British Council Staff Assoc., 1965–67; Member: British-Austrian Mixed Commn, 1973–77; British-French Mixed Commn, 1976–77, 1980–84. *Recreations:* music, painting, oriental ceramics, contemplating sailing. *Address:* 5 quai Commandant Mages, 34300 Agde, France. *T:* 67–94–46–21. *Club:* Travellers'.

SWINGLER, Raymond John Peter; Secretary, Press Council, and conciliator, since 1980; *b* 8 Oct. 1933; *s* of Raymond Joseph and Mary Swingler; *m* 1960, Shirley (*d* 1980), *e d* of Frederick and Dorothy Wilkinson, Plymouth; two *d*. *Educ:* St Bede's Coll., Christchurch, NZ; Canterbury Univ. Journalist, The Press, Christchurch, NZ, 1956–57; Marlborough Express, 1957–59; Nelson Mail, 1959–61; freelance Middle East, 1961–62; Cambridge Evening News, 1962–79. Member: Press Council, 1975–78, Press Council Complaints Cttee, 1976–78; Nat. Exec. Council, Nat. Union of Journalists, 1973–75, 1978–79; Provincial Newspapers Industrial Council, 1976–79; Chm., General Purposes Cttee (when journalists' Code of Professional Conduct (revised) introduced), 1974–75. *Recreations:* horses, and horsewomen. *Address:* Wicken Hall, Wicken, Cambs CB7 5XT. *T:* Ely 720745.

SWINLEY, Margaret Albinia Joanna, OBE 1980; Controller, Home Division, British Council, since 1986; *b* 30 Sept. 1935; *er* twin *d* of late Captain Casper Silas Balfour Swinley, DSO, DSC, RN and of Sylvia Jocosa Swinley, 4th *d* of late Canon W. H. Carnegie. *Educ:* Southover Manor Sch., Lewes; Edinburgh Univ. (MA Hons Hist.). English Teacher/Sec., United Paper Mills, Jämsänkoski, Finland, 1958–60; joined British Council, 1960; Birmingham Area Office, 1960–63; Tel Aviv, 1963; Lagos, 1963–66; seconded to London HQ of VSO, 1966–67; New Delhi, 1967–70; Dep. Rep., Lagos, 1970–73; Dir, Tech. Assistance Trng Dept, 1973–76; Rep., Israel, 1976–80; Asst, then Dep., Controller, Educn, Medicine and Science Div., 1980–82; Controller, Africa and Middle East Div., 1982–86. *Recreations:* theatre-going, country life, keeping dogs. *Address:* c/o British Council, 10 Spring Gardens, SW1A 2BN. *T:* 01–930 8466. *Clubs:* Royal Commonwealth Society, Soroptimist International of Greater London.

SWINNERTON-DYER, Prof. Sir (Henry) Peter (Francis), 16th Bt *cr* 1678; FRS 1967; Professor of Mathematics, University of Cambridge, since 1971 (on leave of absence); Chairman, University Grants Committee, since 1983; *b* 2 Aug. 1927; *s* of Sir Leonard Schroeder Swinnerton Dyer, 15th Bt, and of Barbara, *d* of Hereward Brackenbury, CBE; *S* father, 1975; *m* 1983, Dr Harriet Crawford. *Educ:* Eton; Trinity College, Cambridge (Hon. Fellow 1981). University of Cambridge: Research Fellow, 1950–54, Fellow, 1955–73, Dean, 1963–73, Trinity Coll.; Master, St Catharine's Coll., 1973–83 (Hon. Fellow, 1983); Univ. Lectr, 1960–71 (at Mathematical Lab., 1960–67); Vice-Chancellor, 1979–81. Commonwealth Fund Fellow, Univ. of Chicago, 1954–55. Vis. Prof., Harvard Univ., 1971. Hon. Fellow, Worcester Coll., Oxford, 1980. Chairman: Cttee on Academic Organisation, Univ. of London, 1980–82; Meteorological Cttee, 1983–. Hon. DSc Bath, 1981. *Publications:* numerous papers in mathematical journals. *Recreations:* tennis, squash. *Heir:* *kinsman* Richard Dyer-Bennet [*b* 6 Oct. 1913; *m* 1st, 1936, Elizabeth Hoar Pepper (marr. diss. 1941); two *d*; 2nd, 1942, Melvene Ipcar; one *s* one *d*]. *Address:* University Grants Committee, 14 Park Crescent, W1N 4DH. *T:* 01–636 7799; The Dower House, Thriplow, Royston, Herts. *T:* Fowlmere 220.

SWINSON, Sir John (Henry Alan), Kt 1984; OBE 1974; Commercial Director (Ireland), Trusthouse Forte plc, since 1965; Chairman, Northern Ireland Tourist Board, since 1979 (Member since 1970); *b* 12 July 1922; *s* of Edward Alexander Stanley Swinson and Mary Margaret McLeod; *m* 1944, Margaret Sturgeon Gallagher; two *s*. *Educ:* Royal Belfast Academical Institution. Founded J. H. A. Swinson and Co. Ltd, 1946; Man. Dir (also of associated cos), until 1959; merged with Lockhart Gp, 1959, which merged with Trust Houses (later Trusthouse Forte plc), 1965. Chairman: Catering Industry Training Board, 1966–75; NI Training Executive, 1975–83; Livestock Marketing Commn (NI), 1970–85; Member: Council, NIHCA, 1961– (Past Pres.); Catering Wages Council, 1965–82; NI Economic Council, 1977–81; Industrial Forum for NI, 1980–83. *Recreation:* sailing. *Address:* 10 Circular Road East, Cultra, Co. Down BT18 0HA. *T:* (office) Belfast 612101; (home) Holywood 2494.

SWINTON, 2nd Earl of, *cr* 1955; **David Yarburgh Cunliffe-Lister,** JP; DL; Viscount Swinton, 1935; Baron Masham, 1955; *b* 21 March 1937; *s* of Major Hon. John Yarburgh Cunliffe-Lister (*d* of wounds received in action, 1943) and Anne Irvine (*d* 1961), *yr d* of late Rev. Canon R. S. Medlicott (she *m* 2nd, 1944, Donald Chapple-Gill); *S* grandfather, 1972; *m* 1959, Susan Lilian Primrose Sinclair (*see* Baroness Masham of Ilton); one *s* one *d* (both adopted). *Educ:* Winchester; Royal Agricultural College. Member: N Riding Yorks CC, 1961–74; N Yorks CC, 1973–77. Captain of the Yeoman of the Guard (Dep. Govt Chief Whip), 1982–86. JP North (formerly NR) Yorks, 1971; DL North Yorks, 1978. *Heir:* *b* Hon. Nicholas John Cunliffe-Lister [*b* 4 Sept. 1939; *m* 1966, Hon. Elizabeth Susan, *e d* of Viscount Whitelaw, *qv*; two *s* one *d*]. *Address:* Dykes Hill House, Masham, N Yorks. *T:* Ripon 89241; 46 Westminster Gardens, SW1. *T:* 01–834 0700.

SWINTON, Countess of; *see* Masham of Ilton, Baroness.

SWINTON, Maj.-Gen. Sir John, KCVO 1979; OBE 1969; DL; *b* 21 April 1925; *s* of late Brig. A. H. C. Swinton, MC, Scots Guards; *m* 1954, Judith, *d* of late Harold Killen, Merribee, NSW; three *s* one *d*. *Educ:* Harrow. Enlisted, Scots Guards, 1943, commissioned, 1944; served NW Europe, 1945 (twice wounded); Malaya, 1948–51 (despatches); ADC to Field Marshal Sir William Slim, Governor-General of Australia, 1953–54; Staff College, 1957; DAA&QMG 1st Guards Brigade, 1958–59; Regimental Adjutant Scots Guards, 1960–62; Adjutant, RMA Sandhurst, 1962–64; comd 2nd Bn Scots Guards, 1966–68; AAG PS12 MoD, 1968–70; Lt Col Comdg Scots Guards, 1970–71; Comdr, 4th Guards Armoured Brigade, BAOR, 1972–73; RCDS 1974; Brigadier Lowlands and Comdr Edinburgh and Glasgow Garrisons, 1975–76; GOC London Dist and Maj.-Gen. Comdg Household Divn, 1976–79; retired 1979. Brigadier, Queen's Body Guard for Scotland (Royal Co. of Archers), 1977–; Hon. Col 2nd Bn 52nd Lowland Volunteers, 1983–. Nat. Chm., Royal British Legion, Scotland, 1986– (Nat. Vice-Chm., 1984–86); Mem. Council, Commonwealth Ex-Services League, 1984–. Mem., Central Adv. Cttee on War Pensions, 1986–. Trustee: Army Museums Ogilby Trust, 1978–; Scottish Nat. War Meml, 1984–; Chm., Thirlestane Castle Trust, 1984–. Borders Liaison Officer, Duke of Edinburgh's Award Scheme, 1982–84. Chairman: Berwicks Civic Soc., 1982–; Roxburgh and Berwickshire Cons. Assoc., 1983–85. DL Berwickshire, 1980. *Address:* Kimmerghame, Duns, Berwickshire. *T:* Duns 83277.

SWIRE, Sir Adrian (Christopher), Kt 1982; Deputy Chairman, John Swire and Sons Ltd, since 1966 (Director, 1961); Chairman, China Navigation Co. Ltd, since 1968; Deputy Chairman, Overseas Containers Pacific Ltd; Director: Swire Pacific Ltd, Cathay Pacific Airways; NAAFI (Deputy Chairman, 1982–85); *b* 15 Feb. 1932; *yr s* of late John Kidston Swire and Juliet Richenda, *d* of Theodore Barclay, Fanshaws, Hertford; *m* 1970, Lady Judith Compton, *e d* of 6th Marquess of Northampton, DSO; two *s* one *d*. *Educ:* Eton; University Coll., Oxford (MA). Coldstream Guards, 1950–52; RAFVR and Royal Hong Kong AAF (AE 1961). Joined Butterfield & Swire in Far East, 1956. Dir, Brooke Bond Gp, 1972–82. Mem., Gen. Cttee, Lloyd's Register. Pres., General Council of British Shipping, 1980–81; Chm., Internat. Chamber of Shipping, 1982–. Vis. Fellow, Nuffield Coll., Oxford, 1981–. Trustee, RAF Museum, 1983–. *Address:* Regis House, 43 King William Street, EC4. *Clubs:* White's, Brooks's, Pratt's, City of London.

SWIRE, John Anthony, CBE 1977; Chairman, John Swire & Sons Ltd, since 1966 (Director, 1955); Director, James Finlay plc, since 1976; *b* 28 Feb. 1927; *s* of late John Kidston Swire and Juliet Richenda, *d* of Theodore Barclay; *m* 1961, Moira Cecilia Ducharne; two *s* one *d*. *Educ:* Eton; University Coll., Oxford (MA). Served Irish Guards, UK and Palestine, 1945–48. Joined Butterfield & Swire, Hong Kong, 1950; Director: Swire Pacific Ltd, 1965–; Royal Insurance plc, 1975–80; British Bank of the Middle East, 1975–79; Ocean Transport & Trading plc, 1977–83. Chm., Hong Kong Assoc., 1975–. Member: London Adv. Cttee, Hongkong and Shanghai Banking Corp., 1969–; Euro-Asia Centre Adv. Bd, 1980–; Adv. Council, Sch. of Business, Stanford Univ., 1981–. Chm., Cook Soc., 1984. *Address:* Luton House, Selling, near Faversham, Kent ME13 9RQ. *T:* (0227) 752 234. *Clubs:* Brooks's, Pratt's, Cavalry and Guards, City, Flyfishers'; Union (Sydney).

See also Sir A. C. Swire.

SWISS, Sir Rodney (Geoffrey), Kt 1975; OBE 1964; JP; FDSRCS; President, General Dental Council, 1974–79 (Member, 1957–79); *b* 4 Aug. 1904; *e s* of Henry H. Swiss, Devonport, Devon, and Emma Jane Swiss (*née* Williams); *m* 1928, Muriel Alberta Gledhill (*d* 1985). *Educ:* Plymouth Coll.; Dean Close Sch., Cheltenham; Guy's Hosp. LDSRCS 1926, FDSRCS 1978. General dental practice, Harrow, Mddx, 1930–69 (Hon. dental surgeon, Harrow Hosp., 1935–67). NHS Mddx Exec. Council, 1947–74 (Chm., 1970–71); Chm., Visiting Cttee and Bd of Visitors, Wormwood Scrubs Prison, 1958–63; Mem., Central Health Services Council, 1964–74; Chairman: Standing Dental Advisory Cttee, 1964–74; Hendon Juvenile Court, 1959–64; Gore Petty Sessional Div., 1965–67 and 1970–74; Management Cttee, Sch. for Dental Auxiliaries, 1972–74. JP Mddx area, 1949. *Publications:* contribs to dental press. *Recreation:* philately. *Address:* Shrublands, 23 West Way, Pinner, Mddx HA5 3NX.

SWITZER, Barbara; Deputy General Secretary, TASS—The Manufacturing Union, since 1983; *b* 26 Nov. 1940; *d* of Albert and Edith McMinn; *m* 1973, John Michael Switzer. *Educ:* Chorlton Central Sch., Manchester; Stretford Technical Coll. City & Guilds Final Cert. for Electrical Technician. Engrg apprentice, Metropolitan Vickers, 1957–62; Draughtswoman: GEC, Trafford Park, 1962–70; Cableform, Romiley, 1970–71; Mather & Platt, 1972–76; Divisional Organiser 1976–79, National Organiser 1979–83, AUEW (TASS). Associate Mem., Women's Engineering Soc. TUC Women's Gold Badge for services to Trade Unionism, 1976. *Address:* 16 Follett Drive, Abbots Langley, Herts WD5 0LP. *T:* Garston 674662.

SWORD, John Howe; Director, Oral History Project, University of Toronto, since 1981; Director, Toronto District Heating Corp., since 1983; a Vice-President, Associated Medical Services Inc., since 1984; *b* Saskatoon, Saskatchewan, 22 Jan. 1915; *m* 1947, Constance A. Offen; one *s* one *d*. *Educ:* public and high schs, Winnipeg; Univ. of Manitoba (BA); Univ. of Toronto (MA). Served War, RCAF, Aircrew navigation trg and instr in Western Canada. Taught for six years, before War, in Roland, Teulon and Winnipeg, Manitoba. Secretary, Manitoba Royal Commn on Adult Educn, 1945–46. Univ. of Toronto: Asst Sec. and Sec., Sch. of Grad. Studies, 1947–60; Exec. Asst to the President, 1960–65; Vice-Provost, 1965–67; Actg Pres., 1967–68; Exec. Vice-Pres. (Academic), and Provost, 1968–71; Actg Pres., 1971–72; Vice-Pres., Institutional Relations and Planning, 1972–74; Special Asst to the President, Institutional Relations, 1974–80; Acting Dir, Sch. of Continuing Studies, 1980–81 and 1983–84. Chm., Art Cttee, 1980–83, Finance Cttee, 1983–, Hart House, Univ. of Toronto; Chm., Certificate Review Adv. Cttee, Min. of Educn, 1984–; Member: Bd, Addiction Res. Foundn of Ont, 1981–; Council, Royal Canadian Inst., Toronto, 1981–. Mem., United Church. Hon. LLD, Univ. of Manitoba, 1970. *Recreations:* tennis, swimming. *Address:* 8 Wychwood Park, Toronto, Ontario M6G 2V5, Canada. *T:* 6565876. *Clubs:* Faculty (Univ. of Toronto); Arts and Letters, Queen's.

SWYER, Dr Gerald Isaac Macdonald, FRCP; Consultant Endocrinologist, Department of Obstetrics and Gynæcology, University College Hospital, London, 1951–78, retired; Councillor, London Borough of Camden, 1982–86; *b* 17 Nov. 1917; *s* of Nathan Swyer; *m* 1945, Lynda Irene (*née* Nash); one *s* one *d*. *Educ:* St Paul's School; Magdalen College and St John's College, Oxford; University of California; Middlesex Hospital Medical School. Foundation Schol. and Leaving Exhib., St Paul's School, 1931–36; Open Exhib. and Casberd Schol., St John's Coll., Oxford, 1936–39; Welsh Memorial Prize, 1937; Theodore Williams Schol. in Anatomy, 1938; 1st Cl. Final Honour School of Animal Physiology, 1939; Senior Demy, Magdalen Coll., 1940; Rockefeller Medical Student, Univ. of Calif, 1941. MA, DPhil, BM Oxon 1943; MD Calif, 1943; DM Oxon 1948; MRCP 1945; FRCP 1964; FRCOG *ad eundem* 1975. Mem. of Scientific Staff, Nat. Inst. for Med. Res., 1946–47; Endocrinologist, UCH Med. Sch., 1947. 1st Sec., formerly Chm., Soc. for the Study of Fertility; formerly Mem. Council, Soc. for Endocrinology (Hon. Mem.); formerly Pres., Sect. of Endocrinology, Roy. Soc. Med.; formerly Sec.-Gen., Internat. Fedn of Fertility Societies and Mem. Exec. Sub-Cttee Internat. Endocrine Soc. *Publications:* Reproduction and Sex, 1954; papers in medical and scientific journals. *Recreations:* music, making things. *Address:* FLat 4, 71 Fitzjohn's Avenue, NW3 5LS. *T:* 01–435 4723.

SWYNNERTON, Sir Roger (John Massy), Kt 1976; CMG 1959; OBE 1951; MC 1941; consultant in tropical agriculture and development; Director, Booker Agriculture International Ltd; *b* S Rhodesia, 16 Jan. 1911; *s* of late C. F. M. Swynnerton, CMG, formerly Dir Tsetse Research, Tanganyika, and Mrs N. A. G. Swynnerton (*née* Watt Smyth); *m* Grizel Beryl Miller, *d* of late R. W. R. Miller, CMG, formerly Member for Agriculture and Natural Resources, Tanganyika; two *s*. *Educ:* Lancing Coll.; Gonville and Caius Coll., Cambridge (BA Hons 1932; DipAgric 1933); Imperial Coll. of Tropical Agriculture, Trinidad. AICTA 1934. O/c CUOTC Artillery Bty, 1932–33; TARO, 1933–60. Entered Colonial Agricultural Service as Agric. Officer and Sen. Agric. Officer, 1934–50, in Tanganyika Territory. Served War, 1939–42, with 1/6 Bn KAR (Temp. Capt.), Abyssinian Campaign. Seconded to Malta on Agric. duty, 1942–43. Transferred to Kenya on promotion, Asst Director of Agric., 1951, Dep. Dir, 1954, Director, 1956. Nominated Member of Kenya Legislative Council, 1956–61; Permanent Sec., Min. of Agriculture, 1960–62; Temp. Minister for Agriculture, Animal Husbandry and Water Resources, 1961, retd 1963. Mem. Advisory Cttee on Development of Economic Resources of S Rhodesia, 1961–62; Agric. Adviser and Mem. Exec. Management Bd, Commonwealth Develt Corp., 1962–76. Mem. Adv. Bd, Inst. of Irrigation Studies, Southampton Univ., 1980–. President: Swinnerton Family Soc., 1982–; Tropical Agriculture Assoc., 1983–. *Publications:* All About KNCU Coffee, 1948; A Plan to Intensify the Development of African Agriculture in Kenya, 1954; various agricultural and scientific papers. *Address:* 35 Lower Road, Fetcham, Leatherhead, Surrey KT22 9EL. *Clubs:* Royal Commonwealth Society, Royal Over-Seas League.

SYDNEY, Archbishop of, and Metropolitan of New South Wales, since 1982; **Most Rev. Donald William Bradley Robinson,** AO 1984; *b* 9 Nov. 1922; *s* of Rev. Richard Bradley Robinson and Gertrude Marston Robinson (*née* Ross); *m* 1949, Marie Elizabeth Taubman; three *s* one *d*. *Educ:* Sydney Church of England Gram. Sch.; Univ. of Sydney (BA); Queens' Coll., Cambridge (MA). Australian Army, 1941–45, Lieut Intell. Corps, 1944. Deacon 1950, Sydney; priest 1951; Curate, Manly, NSW, 1950–52; St Philip's, Sydney, 1952–53; Lecturer: Moore Coll., 1952–81 (Vice-Principal, 1959–72); Sydney Univ., 1964–81; Asst Bishop, Diocese of Sydney (Bishop in Parramatta), 1973–82. Hon. ThD Aust. Coll. of Theology, 1979. *Address:* St Andrew's House, Sydney Square, NSW 2000, Australia. *T:* (02) 265 1555.

SYDNEY, Archbishop of, (RC), since 1983; **Most Rev. Edward Bede Clancy,** AO 1984; DD; *b* 13 Dec. 1923; *s* of John Bede Clancy and Ellen Lucy Clancy (*née* Edwards). *Educ:* Marist Brothers Coll., Parramatta, NSW; St Patrick's Coll., Manly, NSW; Biblical Inst., Rome (LSS); Propaganda Fide Univ., Rome (DD). Ordained to priesthood, 1949; parish ministry, 1950–51; studies in Rome, 1952–54; parish ministry, 1955–57; seminary staff, 1958–61; studies in Rome, 1962–64; seminary staff, Manly, 1966–73; Auxiliary Bishop, Sydney, 1974–78; Archbishop of Canberra and Goulburn, 1979–82. *Publications:* The Bible—The Church's Book, 1974; contribs to Australian Catholic Record. *Recreation:* golf. *Address:* St Mary's Cathedral, Sydney, NSW 2000, Australia. *T:* 264–7211 (02).

SYDNEY, Assistant Bishops of; see Cameron, Rt Rev. E. D.; Reid, Rt Rev. J. R.; Short, Rt Rev. K. H.

SYER, William George, CVO 1961; CBE 1957; *b* 22 June 1913; *s* of late William Robert Syer and late Beatrice Alice Theresa Syer, Alton, Hants; *m* 1948, Marjorie Leila, *d* of late S. G. Pike, Essex; no *c*. *Educ:* Kent College, Canterbury. Joined Colonial Police Service, 1933; Gibraltar, 1933–35; Jamaica, 1935–40; Nigeria, 1940–51; Comr of Police, Sierra Leone, 1951; retired, 1962; Comr of Police, Swaziland, 1964–68. Sec., West Africa Cttee, 1970–78. Formerly Comr St John Ambulance Brigade, Sierra Leone. CStJ 1969. *Recreations:* travelling, birdwatching, walking. *Address:* Goldsborough Nursing Home, 9 Ripon Road, Harrogate HG1 2JA.

SYKES, Lt-Col Arthur Patrick, MBE 1945; JP; DL; *b* 1 Sept. 1906; *e s* of late Herbert R. Sykes, JP; *m* 1936, Prudence Margaret, *d* of late Maj.-Gen. D. E. Robertson, CB, DSO, Indian Army (marr. diss. 1966); one *s* one *d*; *m* 1968, Katharine Diana, *d* of Lt-Col. A. J. N. Bartlett, DSO, OBE. *Educ:* Eton; Magdalene College, Cambridge. 2nd Lt 60th Rifles, 1929; served India, Burma, Palestine; ADC to Governor of Bengal, 1933–35; War of 1939–45, Middle East (wounded); Lt-Col 1944. JP 1950, DL 1951, High Sheriff, 1961, Shropshire. *Address:* Lydham Manor, Bishop's Castle, Shropshire. *T:* Bishop's Castle 638486.

SYKES, Bonar Hugh Charles; farmer; formerly Counsellor in HM Diplomatic Service; *b* 20 Dec. 1922; *s* of late Sir Frederick Sykes and of Isabel, *d* of Andrew Bonar Law; *m* 1949, Mary, *d* of late Sir Eric Phipps and of Frances Phipps; four *s*. *Educ:* Eton; The Queen's Coll., Oxford. War service in Navy (Lieut RNVR), 1942–46. Trainee with Ford Motor Co. (Tractor Div.), 1948–49. Joined Foreign Service, 1949: served in Prague, Bonn, Tehran, Ottawa, FCO; retired 1970. Pres., Wiltshire Archaeological and Natural History Soc., 1975–85 (Trustee, 1947–). Chm., Bd of Visitors of Erlestoke Prison, 1983–85 (Mem., 1977–); Member: Area Museums Council (SW), 1976–; Council, Museums Assoc., 1981–84. FSA 1986. *Address:* Conock Manor, Devizes, Wiltshire. *T:* Chirton 227.

SYKES, Christopher Hugh, FRSL; author; Member, London Library Committee, 1965–74; *b* 17 Nov. 1907; 2nd *s* of late Sir Mark Sykes, Bt, Sledmere; *m* 1936, Camilla Georgiana (*d* 1983), *d* of El Lewa Sir Thomas Russell Pasha, CMG; one *s*. *Educ:* Downside; Christ Church, Oxford. Hon. Attaché to HM Embassy, Berlin, 1928–29, and to HM Legation, Tehran, 1930–31. Served War of 1939–45: 7 Battalion The Green Howards; GHQ, Cairo; HM Legation, Tehran; SAS Bde (despatches, Croix de Guerre). Special correspondent of the Daily Mail for the Persian Azerbaijan Campaign, 1946; Deputy Controller, Third Programme, BBC, 1948; Features Dept, BBC, 1949–68. *Publications:* Wassmuss, 1936; (with late R. Byron), Innocence and Design, 1936; Stranger Wonders, 1937; High Minded Murder, 1943; Four Studies in Loyalty, 1946; The Answer to Question 33, 1948; Character and Situation, 1949; Two Studies in Virtue, 1953; A Song of A Shirt, 1953; Dates and Parties, 1955; Orde Wingate, 1959; Cross Roads to Israel, 1965; Troubled Loyalty : a Biography of Adam von Trott, 1968; Nancy, the life of Lady Astor, 1972; Evelyn Waugh, 1975. *Recreation:* music.

SYKES, Dr Donald Armstrong; Principal of Mansfield College, Oxford, 1977–86 (Senior Research Fellow, since 1986); *b* 13 Feb. 1930; *s* of Rev. Leonard Sykes and late Edith Mary Sykes (*née* Armstrong); *m* 1962, Marta Sproul Whitehouse; two *s*. *Educ:* The High Sch. of Dundee; Univ. of St Andrews (MA 2nd cl. Classics 1952; Guthrie Scholar); Mansfield Coll., Oxford (BA 1st cl. Theol. 1958; MA 1961; DPhil 1967); Univ. of Glasgow (DipEd). Fellow in Theology, 1959–77, and Senior Tutor, 1970–77, Mansfield Coll., Oxford. Vis. Prof. in Religion, St Olaf Coll., Northfield, Minn, 1969–70 (Hon. DD 1979). *Publications:* (contrib.) Studies of the Church in History: essays honoring Robert S. Paul, ed Horton Davies, 1983; articles and reviews in Jl Theological Studies, Studia Patristica, Byzantinische Zeitschrift. *Recreations:* gramophone records, walking, gardening. *Address:* 23 Weyland Road, Headington, Oxford OX3 8PE. *T:* Oxford 61576. *Club:* United Oxford & Cambridge University.

SYKES, Edwin Leonard, CMG 1966; *b* 1 May 1914; *m* 1st, 1946, Margaret Elizabeth McCulloch (*d* 1973); 2nd, 1976, Dorothy Soderberg. *Educ:* Leys School, Cambridge (Schol.); Trinity Coll., Cambridge (Senior Schol.). Entered Dominions Office, 1937; Asst Priv. Sec. to Secretary of State, 1939. Served War, 1939–45 (despatches). Served in British High Commissions, Canada, 1945–47, India, 1952–54; idc 1955; Dep. UK High Commissioner in Federation of Rhodesia and Nyasaland, 1956–59; Asst Under-Sec. of State, CRO, 1964–65; Dep. UK High Commissioner in Pakistan, 1965–66; Sec., Office of the Parly Comr for Administration, 1967–74. *Address:* 7 Upper Rose Hill, Dorking, Surrey.

SYKES, Sir Francis (Godfrey), 9th Bt, *cr* 1781, of Basildon; *b* 27 Aug. 1907; *s* of Francis William Sykes (*d* 1945) (*g g s* of 2nd Bt) and Beatrice Agnes Sykes (*née* Webb) (*d* 1953); *S* cousin, Rev. Sir Frederic John Sykes, 8th Bt, 1956; *m* 1st, 1934, Eira Betty (*d* 1970), *d* of G. W. Badcock; one *s* one *d*; 2nd, 1972, Nesta Mabel (*d* 1982), *d* of late Col and Mrs Harold Platt Sykes; 3rd, 1985, Ethel Florence, *d* of late Lt-Col and Mrs J. S. Liddell, and *widow* of W. G. Ogden. *Educ:* Blundell's School, Devon; Nelson College, New Zealand. Tea planting, 1930; Air Ministry, 1939; fruit farming and estate management, 1945–57; Regional Sec., Country Landowners' Assoc., 1957–72. FCIS. *Heir: s* Francis John Badcock Sykes [*b* 7 June 1942; *m* 1966, Susan Alexandra, *er d* of Adm. of the Fleet Sir E. B. Ashmore, *qv*; three *s*]. *Address:* 7 Linney, Ludlow, Shropshire SY8 1EF. *T:* Ludlow 4336.

SYKES, (James) Richard, QC 1981; *b* 28 May 1934; *s* of late Philip James and Lucy Barbara Sykes; *m* 1959, Susan Ethne Patricia Allen, *d* of late Lt-Col J. M. and Mrs E. M. B. Allen, Morrinsville, NZ; one *s* three *d*. *Educ:* Charterhouse; Pembroke Coll., Cambridge. BA 1957, MA 1971. Nat. Service, 2nd Lieut RASC, 1952–54. Called to the Bar, Lincoln's Inn, 1958. Member: City Company Law Cttee, 1974–79; City Capital Markets Cttee, 1980–; Chm., Judging Panel, Accountant and Stock Exchange Annual Awards, 1982–. Mem. Management Cttee, Internat. Exhibn Co-operative Wine Soc. Ltd, 1986–. *Publications:* (Consultant Editor) Gore-Browne on Companies, 42nd edn 1972, 44th edn 1986; (ed jtly) The Conduct of Meetings, 20th edn 1966, 21st edn 1975. *Address:* Vassars, Langley, Hitchin, Herts SG4 7PH. *T:* Stevenage 352271.

SYKES, Dr John Bradbury; Head of German Dictionaries, Oxford University Press, since 1981; *b* Folkestone, Kent, 26 Jan. 1929; *s* of late Stanley William Sykes and late Eleanor Sykes Sykes (*née* Bradbury); *m* 1955, Avril Barbara Hart; one *s*. *Educ:* Wallasey Grammar Sch.; Rochdale High Sch.; St Lawrence Coll.; Wadham Coll., Oxford (BA Maths 1950); Balliol Coll., Oxford (Skynner Sen. Student); Merton Coll., Oxford (Harmsworth Sen. Schol., MA and DPhil Astrophysics 1953). AERE, Harwell, 1953–71 (Head of Translations Office 1958, Principal Scientific Officer 1960); Member, Internat. Astronomical Union, 1958 (Pres., Commn for Documentation, 1967–73). Editor, Concise and Pocket Oxford Dictionaries, 1971–81. Mem. Bd, Translators' Guild, 1980– (Chm., 1984–). Fellow, Inst. of Linguists, 1960–86 (Mem. Council, 1977–86; Editor, Incorporated Linguist, 1980–86); Chm. Interim Council, Inst. of Translation and Interpreting, 1986. Hon. DLitt City, 1984. *Publications:* (with B Davison) Neutron Transport Theory, 1957; (ed) Technical Translator's Manual, 1971; (ed) Concise Oxford Dictionary, 6th edn, 1976, 7th edn, 1982; (ed) Pocket Oxford Dictionary, 6th edn, 1978; translations of many Russian textbooks in physics and astronomy; contribs to Incorporated Linguist. *Recreation:* crossword-solving (National Champion 1958, 1972–75, 1977, 1980, 1983, 1985). *Address:* 19 Walton Manor Court, Adelaide Street, Oxford OX2 6EL. *T:* Oxford 57532. *Club:* PEN.

SYKES, Sir John (Charles Anthony le Gallais), 3rd Bt *cr* 1921; *b* 19 April 1928; *s* of Stanley Edgar Sykes (*d* 1963) (2nd *s* of 1st Bt) and Florence Anaise le Gallais (*d* 1955); *S* uncle, 1974; *m* (marr. diss.). *Educ:* Churchers College. Export merchant. Mem., British Epicure Soc. *Recreations:* golf, wine, food, travel. *Heir: nephew* David Michael Sykes [*b* 10 June 1954; *m* 1974, Susan Elizabeth, 3rd *d* of G. W. Hall; one *s*]. *Address:* 58 Alders View Drive, East Grinstead, Sussex RH19 2DN. *T:* East Grinstead 22027.

SYKES, Joseph Walter, CMG 1962; CVO 1953; Chairman, Fiji Public Service Commission, 1971–80, retired 1981; *b* 10 July 1915; *s* of Samuel Sykes and Lucy M. Womack; *m* 1940, Elima Petrie, *d* of late Sir Hugh Hall Ragg; three *s* two *d*. *Educ:* De La Salle Coll., Sheffield; Rotherham Gram. Sch.; Jesus Coll., Oxford. Colonial Administrative Service, Fiji; Cadet, 1938; Dist Officer, 1940; District Commissioner, 1950; Deputy Secretary for Fijian Affairs, 1952; Assistant Colonial Secretary, 1953; transferred to Cyprus as Dep. Colonial Sec., Nov. 1954; Admin. Sec., Cyprus. 1955–56; Colonial Sec., Bermuda, 1956–68; Chief Sec., Bermuda, 1968–71; retired. *Publication:* The Royal Visit to Fiji 1953, 1954. *Recreations:* photography, tennis. *Address:* 8 Dorking Road, City Beach, Perth, WA 6015, Australia. *Club:* United Oxford & Cambridge University.

SYKES, Prof. Keble Watson; Vice-Principal, 1978–86, Professor of Physical Chemistry, 1956–86, Queen Mary College, University of London; *b* 7 Jan. 1921; *s* of Watson and Victoria May Sykes; *m* 1950, Elizabeth Margaret Ewing Forsyth; three *d* (and one *s* decd). *Educ:* Seascale Preparatory Sch.; St Bees Sch.; The Queen's Coll., Oxford, MA, BSc, DPhil (Oxon.). ICI Research Fellow, Physical Chemistry Lab., Oxford, 1945–48; Lecturer, 1948–51, and Senior Lecturer in Chemistry, 1951–56, University Coll. of Swansea, Univ. of Wales; Head of Chemistry Dept, 1959–78, and Dean, Fac. of Science, 1970–73, QMC, London. Hon. Sec. Chemical Soc. of London, 1960–66, Vice-Pres., 1966–69, Mem. Council, 1977–80. Member Council, Westfield College, University of London, 1962–77. *Publications:* scientific papers in journals of Royal Society, Faraday Soc. and Chem. Soc. *Address:* 58 Wood Vale, Muswell Hill, N10 3DN. *T:* 01–883 1502.

SYKES, Prof. Malcolm Keith; Nuffield Professor of Anaesthetics, and Fellow of Pembroke College, University of Oxford, since 1980; *b* 13 Sept. 1925; *s* of Joseph and Phyllis Mary Sykes; *m* 1956, Michelle June (*née* Ratcliffe); one *s* three *d*. *Educ:* Magdalene Coll., Cambridge (MA, MB, BChir); University Coll. Hosp., London (DA; FFARCS). RAMC, 1950–52. House appointments, University Coll. and Norfolk and Norwich Hosps, 1949–50; Sen. House Officer, Registrar and Sen. Registrar in anaesthetics, UCH, 1952–54 and 1955–58; Rickman Godlee Travelling Scholar and Fellow in Anesthesia, Mass. General Hosp., Boston, USA, 1954–55; RPMS and Hammersmith Hosp., 1958–80: Lectr and Sen. Lectr, 1958–67; Reader, 1967–70; Prof. of Clinical Anaesthesia, 1970–80. Vis. Prof., univs in Canada, USA, Australia, NZ, Malaysia, Europe. Eponymous lectures: Holme, 1970; Clover, 1976; Weinbren, 1976; Rowbottom, 1978; Gillespie, 1979; Gillies, 1985; Wesley Bourne, 1986. Member: Council, Assoc. of Anaesthetists, 1967–70; Bd, Fac. of Anaesthetists, 1969–85; Senator and Vice Pres., European Acad. of Anaesthesiology, 1978–85. Hon. FFARACS 1979. Dudley Buxton Prize, Fac. of Anaesthetists, 1980. *Publications:* Respiratory Failure, 1969, 2nd edn 1976; Principles of Measurement for Anaesthetists, 1970; Principles of Clinical Measurement, 1980; chapters and papers on respiratory failure, intensive care, respiratory and cardiovascular physiology applied to anaesthesia, etc. *Recreations:* sailing, walking, birdwatching, gardening, music. *Address:* 10 Fitzherbert Close, Iffley, Oxford OX4 4EN. *T:* Oxford 771152.

SYKES, Richard; *see* Sykes, J. R.

SYKES, Rev. Prof. Stephen Whitefield, MA; Regius Professor of Divinity, and Fellow of St John's College, Cambridge University, since 1985; *b* 1939; *m* 1962; one *s* two *d*. *Educ:* St John's Coll., Cambridge. BA (Cantab) 1961; MA (Cantab) 1964. Univ. Asst Lectr in Divinity, Cambridge Univ., 1964–68, Lectr, 1968–74; Fellow and Dean, St John's Coll., Cambridge, 1964–74; Van Mildert Canon Prof. of Divinity, Durham Univ., 1974–85. Mem., Archbishop's Cttee on Religious Educn, 1967. Hon. Canon of Ely Cathedral, 1985–. Examining Chaplain to Bishop of Chelmsford, 1970–. Edward Cadbury Lectr, Univ. of Birmingham, 1978; Hensley Henson Lectr, Univ. of Oxford, 1982–83. Chm., North of England Inst. for Christian Educn, 1980–85. Pres., Council of St John's Coll., Durham, 1984–. *Publications:* Friedrich Schleiermacher, 1971; Christian Theology Today, 1971; (ed) Christ, Faith and History, 1972; The Integrity of Anglicanism, 1978; (ed) Karl Barth: studies in his theological method, 1980; (ed) New Studies in Theology, 1980; (ed) England and Germany, Studies in Theological Diplomacy, 1982; The Identity of Christianity, 1984. *Recreation:* walking. *Address:* St John's College, Cambridge.

SYKES, Sir Tatton (Christopher Mark), 8th Bt *cr* 1783; landowner; *b* 24 Dec. 1943; *s* of Sir (Mark Tatton) Richard Tatton-Sykes, 7th Bt and Virginia (*d* 1970), *d* of late John Francis Grey Gilliat; *S* father, 1978; granted use of additional arms of Tatton, 1980. *Educ:* Eton; Univ. d'Aix-Marseille; Royal Agric. Coll., Cirencester. *Heir:* *b* Jeremy John Sykes [*b* 8 March 1946; *m* 1982, Pamela June, *o d* of Thomas Wood]. *Address:* Sledmere, Driffield, East Yorkshire.

SYKES, Air Vice-Marshal William, OBE; CEng, FRAeS; FIIM; FBIM; RAF retired, 1975; General Manager, British Aerospace (Oman), 1976–85; *b* 14 March 1920; *s* of Edmund and Margaret Sykes, Appleby, Westmorland; *m* 1946, Jean Begg (*d* 1985), *d* of Alexander and Wilemena Harrold, Watten, Caithness; one *s* one *d*; *m* 1986, Suzanne Penelope Margaret Lane, *d* of Ronald Frederick and Sylvia Lane, Hempsted, Kent. *Educ:* Raley Sch. and Technical Coll., Barnsley, Yorks. HNC Mech. and Aero Eng. 1942; CEng, AFRAeS 1968, FRAeS 1974, FBIM (MBIM 1975), FIIM 1979. Joined RAF as Aircraft Apprentice, 1936. Served War: No 51 (Bomber) Sqdn, 1939–41; various engrg specialist courses; commissioned, 1942; Coastal Command: Invergordon, Pembroke Dock, Gibraltar, Hamworthy, Reykjavik (Iceland) and Tain. After 1945: appts at Marine Aircraft Exptl Estabt, Felixstowe; HQ No 23 Gp; Central Servicing Develt Estabt (CSDE); RAE; 2nd TAF, Germany; Dept of ACAS(OR); Electrical Specialist Course, 1948; Staff Coll., 1953–54; jssc 1959–60. During period 1960–72: served a further tour with CSDE as OC Projects Wing; was OC Engrg Wing, Wyton; Station Comdr, No 8 of TT, Weeton; Comd Engrg Officer, FEAF; Dir of Mechanical Engrg (RAF), MoD (AFD); Air Officer Engrg, NEAF; Vice-Pres., Ordnance Board, 1972–74, Pres., 1974–75. Attended IDC, 1967. *Recreation:* travel. *Address:* 5 Clifton Court, 297 Clifton Drive South, St Anne's-on-Sea, Lancs. *T:* St Anne's 727689. *Clubs:* Royal Air Force; St Anne's District (St Anne's).

SYKES, Willie, MBE 1975; CEng, FIMinE; former Member, West Yorkshire Metropolitan County Council (Chairman 1983–84); *b* 19 Dec. 1914; *s* of Albert and Teresa Sykes; *m* 1936, Ida Clamp; six *s* one *d*. *Educ:* Doncaster College (Mining). Colliery Managers Cert. Mining Engineer, 1948–75; Chm., Development Control, West Yorks Metropolitan CC. *Recreations:* music, horticulture, sports. *Address:* Haxby House, Westfield Lane, South Elmsall, West Yorks WF9 2JY. *T:* South Elmsall 42868.

SYLVESTER, Albert James, CBE 1920; JP; *b* Harlaston, Staffs, 24 Nov. 1889; *s* of late Albert and Edith Sylvester; *m* Evelyn (*d* 1962), *d* of late Rev. W. Welman, Reading; one *d*. *Educ:* Guild Street School, Burton-on-Trent; privately (champion typist). Private Secretary to Sec. of Cttee of Imperial Defence, 1914–21; Private Sec. to Sec. of War Cabinet and of Cabinet, 1916–21; Private Secretary to Secretary, Imperial War Cabinet, 1917; Private Secretary to British Secretary, Peace Conference, 1919; Private Secretary to successive Prime Ministers, 1921–23; Principal Secretary to Earl Lloyd George of Dwyfor, 1923–45. Film, The Very Private Secretary, BBC TV, 1974; portrayed in BBC TV Series The Life and Times of Lloyd George, 1981; life story, The Principal Private Secretary, BBC Radio Wales, 1982, repeated BBC Radio 4, 1983. JP Wilts, 1953. Commander of the Order of the Crown of Italy, and Sacred Treasure of Japan. Supreme Award (with Honours), Ballroom and Latin American Dancing, Imperial Soc. of Teachers of Dancing, 1977; Alex Moore Award, 1977; Guinness Book of Records states is the oldest competitive ballroom dancer. *Publications:* The Real Lloyd George, 1947; Life with Lloyd George (diaries, ed Colin Cross), 1975. *Recreations:* riding and golf. *Address:* Rudloe Cottage, Corsham, Wilts. *T:* Hawthorn 810375. *Club:* National Liberal.

See also A. Sylvester-Evans.

SYLVESTER, (Anthony) David (Bernard), CBE 1983; writer on art, etc; editing catalogue raisonné of René Magritte; *b* 21 Sept. 1924; *s* of Philip Silvester and Sybil Rosen; *m* Pamela Briddon; three *d*. *Educ:* University Coll. Sch. Arts Council of Great Britain: Mem., 1980–82; Mem., Art Panel, 1962–70, 1972–77, Chm., 1980–82. Mem., BFI Prodn Bd, 1966–69; Mem., Commn d'Acquisitions, Musée Nat. D'Art Moderne, Paris, 1984–; Trustee, Tate Gall., 1967–69. Vis. Lecturer: Slade Sch. of Fine Art, 1953–57; RCA, 1960–70; Swarthmore Coll., Pa, 1967–68. *Exhibitions:* Henry Moore, Tate, 1951; Alberto Giacometti, Arts Council, 1955; Chaim Soutine, Tate, 1963; Giacometti, Tate, 1965; Moore, Tate, 1968; René Magritte, Tate, 1969; (with M. Compton) Robert Morris, Tate, 1971; (with J. Drew) Henri Laurens, Hayward, 1971; Joan Miró bronzes, Hayward, 1972; Islamic carpets, Hayward, 1972; Willem de Kooning, Serpentine, 1977; Dada and Surrealism Reviewed (Chm. of Cttee), Hayward, 1978; Moore, Serpentine, 1978; Magritte, Palais des Beaux-Arts, Brussels, and Musée National d'Art Moderne, Paris, 1978–79; Giacometti, Serpentine, 1981; (with D. King) The Eastern Carpet in the Western World, Hayward, 1983, etc; *films and TV:* Ten Modern Artists (writer/presenter of series), 1964; Giacometti (writer/producer), 1967; Matisse and His Model (writer), 1968; Magritte: The False Mirror (dir), 1970, etc; *radio:* many interviews, talks and discussions for BBC. *Publications:* Henry Moore, 1968; Magritte, 1969; Interviews with Francis Bacon, 1975, enlarged edn 1980; exhibn catalogues; articles, incl. some on films or sport, 1942–, in Tribune, New Statesman, Burlington Mag., Listener, Encounter, The Times, Observer, Sunday Times Mag., etc. *Address:* 35 Walpole Street, SW3 4QS. *T:* 01–730 2284.

SYLVESTER, George Harold, CBE 1967; retired 1967 as Chief Education Officer for Bristol; *b* 26 May 1907; *s* of late George Henry and Martha Sylvester; *m* 1936, Elsie Emmett; one *s*. *Educ:* Stretford Grammar School; Manchester University. BA Manchester 1928; MA Bristol 1944. Teaching, Manchester, 1929–32; Administrative posts (Education) in Wolverhampton and Bradford, 1932–39; Assistant Education Officer, Bristol, 1939–42; Chief Education Officer, Bristol, 1942–67. Hon. MEd Bristol, 1967. *Recreations:* golf, music. *Address:* 43 Hill View, Henleaze, Bristol BS9 4QE. *T:* Bristol 629287.

SYLVESTER-EVANS, Alun, CB 1975; Deputy Chief Executive, Property Services Agency, Department of the Environment, 1973–78, retired; Member, Chairman's Panel of Assessors, Civil Service Selection Boards, since 1980; *b* 21 April 1918; *o c* of Daniel Elias Evans and Esther Evans, Rhymney, Mon.; *m* 1945, Joan Maureen, *o c* of A. J. Sylvester, *qv*; two *s*. *Educ:* Lewis' School, Pengam; University of Wales, Aberystwyth. Armed services, 1940–46. Asst Research Officer, Min. of Town and Country Planning, 1946–47; Asst Principal, 1947–48; Principal Private Sec. to Minister of Housing and Local Govt, 1954–57; Asst Secretary, 1957–66, Under-Sec., 1966–73, Min. of Housing and Local Govt, later DoE. *Recreation:* golf. *Address:* 2 Enmore Road, Putney, SW15. *T:* 01–788 3043. *Club:* Royal Commonwealth Society.

SYME, Dr James, FRCPE; FRCPGlas; Consultant Paediatrician, Edinburgh, since 1965; *b* 25 Aug. 1930; *s* of James Wilson Syme and Christina Kay Syme (*née* Marshall); *m* 1956, Pamela McCormick; one *s* one *d*. *Educ:* University of Edinburgh (MB ChB). House Officer posts, 1954–55; Captain, RAMC, 1955–57; Royal Infirmary, Edinburgh, 1957–62; Senior Registrar on Paediatrics, Glasgow, 1962–65. Royal College of Physicians of Edinburgh: Secretary, 1971–75; Mem. Council, 1976–85; Vice-Pres., 1985–. External examnr, London, Glasgow, Dundee, Nigeria, Hong Kong, Dublin, Singapore. *Publications:* contribs to Textbook of Paediatrics (Forfar & Arneil), 1st edn to 3rd edn; papers in med. jls on paediatric topics. *Recreations:* travel, visiting churches, gardening. *Address:* 13 Succoth Park, Edinburgh EH12 6BX. *T:* 031–337 6069. *Clubs:* Aesculapian, Harveian Society (Edinburgh).

SYME, Sir Ronald, OM 1976; Kt 1959; FBA 1944; retired as Camden Professor of Ancient History, Oxford, 1949–70; *b* 11 March 1903; *e s* of David and Florence Syme, Eltham, New Zealand. *Educ:* NZ; Oriel College, Oxford (Classical Prizes and First Class Hons, Lit Hum, 1927). Fellow of Trinity College, 1929–49; Conington Prize, 1939. Press Attaché with rank of First Secretary, HM Legation, Belgrade, 1940–41; HM Embassy, Ankara, 1941–42; Professor of Classical Philology, University of Istanbul, 1942–45; President, Society for the Promotion of Roman Studies, 1948–52; President, International Federation of Classical Societies, 1951–54; Secretary-General, Internat. Council for Philosophy and Humanistic Studies, 1952–71, Pres., 1971–75; Vice-President: Prize Cttee of Balzan Foundation, 1963; Assoc. Internat. pour l'Etude du Sud-Est Européen, 1967. Prof. of Ancient History, Royal Acad. of Arts, 1976–. Hon. Fellow: Oriel College, Oxford, 1958; Trinity College, Oxford, 1972; Emeritus Fellow, Brasenose College, 1970; Fellow, Wolfson Coll., 1970. Hon. LittD NZ, 1949; Hon. DLitt: Durham, 1952; Liège, 1952; Belfast, 1961; Graz, 1963; Emory, US, 1963; D ès L: Paris, 1963; Lyon, 1967; Ohio, 1970; Boston Coll., 1974; Tel-Aviv, 1975; Louvain, 1976; New York, 1984. Membre Associé de l'Institut de France (Académie des Inscriptions et Belles-Lettres), 1967; Corresp. Member, German Archæological Institute, 1931, Member, 1953; Member, Royal Danish Acad. of Letters and Sciences, 1951; For. Mem. Lund Society of Letters, 1948. Corresponding Member Bavarian Academy, 1955; For. Member: American Philosophical Soc., 1959; Amer. Acad. of Arts and Sciences, 1959; Massachusetts Historical Society, 1960; Istituto di Studi Romani, 1960; Amer. Historical Soc., 1963; Real Academia de la Historia, 1963; Istituto Lombardo, 1964; Acc. Torino, 1972; Corresponding Member Austrian Academy, 1960. Kenyon Medal, British Acad., 1975. Commandeur de l'Ordre des Arts et des Lettres, 1975; Member, Orden Pour le Mérite für Wissenschaften und Künste, 1975. Hon. LittD: Cambridge, 1984; Pavia, 1986. *Publications:* The Roman Revolution, 1939; Tacitus (2 vols), 1958; Colonial Elites, 1958; Sallust, 1964; Ammianus and the Historia Augusta, 1968; Ten Studies in Tacitus, 1970; Emperors and Biography, 1971; The Historia Augusta: a call for clarity, 1971; Danubian Papers, 1971; History in Ovid, 1978; Roman Papers, 2 vols, 1979; Some Arval Brethren, 1980; Historia Augusta Papers, 1983; Roman Papers, vol. 3, 1984; The Augustan Aristocracy, 1986. *Address:* Wolfson College, Oxford. *Clubs:* Athenæum; Odd Volumes (Boston).

SYMES, (Lilian) Mary; Clerk to Justices, 6 Divisions in Suffolk, 1943–74; Chairman, Norfolk and Suffolk Rent Tribunal, 1974–83; *b* 18 Oct. 1912; *d* of Walter Ernest and Lilian May Hollowell; *m* 1953, Thomas Alban Symes (*d* 1984); one *s*. *Educ:* St Mary's Convent, Lowestoft; Great Yarmouth High School. Articled in Solicitor's Office; qualified as Solicitor, 1936. Became first woman Clerk to Justices (Stowmarket), 1942; first woman Deputy Coroner, 1945; Clerk to the Justices, Woodbridge, 1946, Bosmere and Claydon, 1951; first woman Coroner, 1951; Deputy Coroner, Northern District, Suffolk, 1956–82.

Recreations: Worcester porcelain, gardening. *Address:* Gusford, California, Woodbridge, Suffolk. *T:* Woodbridge 3682.

SYMINGTON, Stuart; United States Senator from Missouri, 1952–76; Director and Vice-Chairman, First American Bankshares Inc., Washington DC; *b* Amherst, Massachusetts, 26 June 1901; *s* of William Stuart and Emily Harrison Symington; *m* 1924, Evelyn Wadsworth (decd); two *s*; *m* 1978, Ann Hemingway Watson. *Educ:* Yale University; International Correspondence School. Joined Symington Companies, Rochester, New York, 1923; President Colonial Radio Co., Rochester, 1930–35; President, Rustless Iron & Steel Co., Baltimore, 1935–37; President and Chairman, Emerson Electric Manufacturing Co., St Louis, 1938–45; Surplus Property Administrator, Washington, 1945–46; Assistant Secretary of War for Air, 1946–47; Secretary of Air Force, National Defense, 1947–50; Chairman, National Security Resources Board, 1950–51; Administrator, Reconstruction Finance Corporation, 1951–52. Is a Democrat. *Address:* Box 1087, New Canaan, Conn 06840, USA.

SYMINGTON, Prof. Sir Thomas, Kt 1978; MD; FRSE; Director, 1970–77, and Professor of Pathology, 1970–77, Institute of Cancer Research, Royal Cancer Hospital; *b* 1 April 1915; *m* 1943, Esther Margaret Forsyth, MB, ChB; two *s* one *d*. *Educ:* Cumnock Academy. BSc 1936; MB ChB, 1941; MD 1950. St Mungo (Notman) Prof. of Pathology, Univ. of Glasgow, 1954–70. Visiting Prof. of Pathology, Stanford Univ., Calif., 1965–66. Member, Medical Research Council, 1968–72. FRSE, 1956; FRIC, 1958 (ARIC, 1951); FRCP(G), 1963; FRFPS (G), 1958; FRCPath, 1964. Hon. MD Szeged Univ., Hungary, 1971; Hon. DSc McGill Univ., Canada, 1983. *Publications:* Functional Pathology of the Human Adrenal Gland, 1969; Scientific Foundations of Oncology, 1976; numerous papers on problems of adrenal glands in Journals of Endocrinology and Pathology. *Recreation:* golf. *Address:* Greenbriar, 2 Lady Margaret Drive, Troon KA10 7AL. *T:* Troon 315707.

SYMMERS, Prof. William St Clair, senior; MD; retired; Emeritus Professor of Histopathology, University of London, since 1986; *b* 16 Aug. 1917; *s* of William St Clair Symmers, Columbia, S Carolina (Musgrave Professor of Pathology and Bacteriology, QUB) and Marion Latimer (*née* Macredie), Sydney, NSW; *m* 1941, Jean Noble, *d* of Kenyon and Elizabeth Wright, Paisley, Renfrewshire; one *s*. *Educ:* Royal Belfast Academical Instn; Queen's Univ. of Belfast (MB, BCh, BAO 1939; Johnson Symington Medal in Anatomy, 1936; Sinclair Medal in Surgery, 1939; MD 1946); Univ. of Freiburg, Breisgau, Germany. PhD Birmingham, 1953; DSc London, 1979; FRCP, FRCPI, FRCPE; FRCS; FRCPA; FRCPath; FFPath, RCPI. Surg.-Lieut, RNVR, 1940–46. Demonstrator in Pathology and pupil of Prof. G. Payling Wright, Guy's Hosp. Med. Sch., 1946–47; Registrar in Clinical Pathology, Guy's Hosp., 1946–47; Deptl Demonstrator of Pathology, Univ. of Oxford, 1947; Sen. Asst Pathologist, 1947–48, Consultant, 1948, Radcliffe Infirmary, Oxford; Sen. Lectr in Pathology, Univ. of Birmingham, England, 1948–53; Hon. Consultant Pathologist: United Birmingham Hosps, 1948–53; Birmingham Regional Hosp. Bd, 1949–53; Prof. of Morbid Anatomy, later of Histopathology, Univ. of London at Charing Cross Hosp. Med. Sch., 1953–82; Hon. Consultant Pathologist, Charing Cross Hosp., 1953–82, Hon. Consulting Pathologist, 1983–. Pres., Section of Pathology, RSM, 1969–70. Hon. FRCPA 1980; Hon. FACP 1982. Dr Dhayagude Meml Prize, Seth GS Med. Sch., Univ. of Bombay, 1967; Yamagiwa Medal, Univ. of Tokyo, 1969; Scott-Heron Medal, Royal Victoria Hosp., Belfast, 1975; Morgagni Medal, Univ. of Padua, 1979. *Publications:* Systemic Pathology, 1966 (ed with late Prof. G. Payling Wright), (ed) 2nd edn, 6 vols, 1976–80, (gen. editor), 3rd edn, 15 vols, 1986–; Curiosa, 1974; Exotica, 1984. *Address:* 30 Sandy Lodge Way, Northwood, Middlesex HA6 2AS.

SYMMONDS, Algernon Washington, GCM 1980; Permanent Secretary, Prime Minister's Office, Barbados, 1983–86 and Head of the Civil Service, Barbados, 1986; *b* 19 Nov. 1926; *s* of late Algernon F. Symmonds and Olga Ianthe (*née* Harper); *m* 1954, Gladwyn Ward; one *s* one *d*. *Educ:* Combermere Sch.; Harrison Coll.; Codrington Coll., Barbados. Solicitor, Barbados, 1953, enrolled in UK, 1958; in practice as Solicitor, Barbados, 1953–55; Dep. Registrar, Barbados, 1955–59; Crown Solicitor, Barbados, 1959–66; Permanent Secretary: Min. of Home Affairs, 1966–72; Min. of Educn, 1972–76; Min. of External Affairs and Head of Foreign Service, 1976–79; appointed to rank of Ambassador, 1977; High Comr in UK, 1979–83 and non-resident Ambassador to Denmark, Finland, Iceland, Norway and Sweden, 1981–83, and to the Holy See, 1982–83. President: Barbados CS Assoc., 1958–65; Fedn of British CS Assocs in Caribbean, 1960–64; Dep. Mem. Exec., Public Services Internat., 1964–66. Dep. Chm., Caribbean Examinations Council, 1973–76. Past Pres., Barbados Lawn Tennis Assoc. *Recreations:* tennis, cricket broadcasting (represented Barbados in football, lawn tennis, basketball). *Clubs:* Bridgetown, Empire (Cricket and Football) (Life Mem. and Past Vice-Pres.), Summerhayes Tennis (Past Pres.) (Barbados).

SYMONDS, Ann Hazel S.; *see* Spokes Symonds.

SYMONDS, Jane Ursula; *see* Kellock, J. U.

SYMONDS, (John) Richard (Charters); Senior Research Officer (Honorary), Oxford University Institute of Commonwealth Studies, and Senior Associate Member, St Antony's College, Oxford, since 1979; *b* 2 Oct. 1918; *s* of Sir Charles Putnam Symonds, KBE, CB, DM, FRCP, and Janet (*née* Poulton); *m* 1980, Ann Hazel Spokes (*see* A. H. Spokes Symonds); two *s* by a previous marriage. *Educ:* Rugby Sch.; Corpus Christi Coll., Oxford (Scholar in Mod. History, MA); Secretary Elect, Oxford Union, 1939. Friends Amb. Unit, 1939–44; Dep. Dir Relief and Rehab., Govt of Bengal, 1944–45; UNRRA, Austria, 1946–47; Friends Service Unit, Punjab and Kashmir, 1947–48; UN Commn for India and Pakistan (Kashmir), 1948–49; UN Technical Assistance Board: New York, 1950–51; Liaison Officer in Europe, 1952–53; Resident Rep., Ceylon, 1953–55, Yugoslavia, 1955–58; Rep. in Europe, 1959–62; Reg. Rep., E Africa, 1961. Sen. Res. Officer, Oxford Univ. Inst. of Commonwealth Studies, 1962–65; Reg. Rep. in Southern Africa, UNTAB, 1964–65; Professorial Fellow, IDS, Univ. of Sussex, 1966–69, later Vis. Prof.; Consultant, UN Population Div., 1968–69; Rep. in Europe, UNITAR, 1969–71; UNDP Resident Rep. in Greece, 1972–75, and in Tunisia, 1975–78; Sen. Adviser, UNDP and UN Fund for Population Activities, NY, 1978–79; Consultant: Commonwealth Foundn, 1980; WHO, 1981. Mem. Council, Royal Commonwealth Soc., 1983–86. *Publications:* The Making of Pakistan, 1950; The British and their Successors, 1966; (ed) International Targets for Development, 1970; (with M. Carder) The United Nations and the Population Question, 1973; Oxford and Empire—the last lost cause?, 1986. *Recreations:* walking, travel. *Address:* 43 Davenant Road, Oxford OX2 8BU. *T:* Oxford 55661. *Club:* Royal Commonwealth Society.
See also R. C. Symonds.

SYMONDS, Richard; *see* Symonds, J. R. C.

SYMONDS, Ronald Charters, CB 1975; *b* 25 June 1916; *e s* of late Sir Charles Symonds, KBE, CB, and late Janet Palmer Poulton; *m* 1939, Pamela Painton; two *s* one *d*. *Educ:* Rugby Sch.; New Coll., Oxford. British Council, 1938–39 and 1946–51. Military Service, 1939–45. War Office, later MoD, 1951–76, retired. Advr, Royal Commn on Gambling, 1976–78. Consultant, ICI Ltd, 1978–81. United States Bronze Star, 1948. *Recreations:* walking, ornithology. *Address:* 10 Bisham Gardens, N6 6DD.
See also J. R. C. Symonds.

SYMONS, Ernest Vize, CB 1975; Director General, Board of Inland Revenue, 1975–77; *b* 19 June 1913; *s* of Ernest William Symons and Edith Florence Elphick; *m* 1938, Elizabeth Megan Jenkins; one *s* two *d*. *Educ:* Stationers' Company's Sch.; University Coll., London (Fellow, 1979). Asst Inspector, 1934; Admin. Staff Coll., Henley, 1956; Dep. Chief Inspector of Taxes, 1964–73; Chief Inspector of Taxes, 1973–75. Mem., Keith Cttee on Enforcement Powers of the Revenue Depts, 1980. Governor, E-SU, 1978, Dep. Chm., 1983–; Hon. Treas., Nat. Assoc. for Care of Offenders and Prevention of Crime, 1979. Mem. College Council, UCL, 1975; Vice-Chm., London Welsh Trust, 1981– (Mem. Council, 1978–). Hon. Treasurer, Hon. Soc. of Cymmrodorion, 1980–. *Recreations:* chess, bridge. *Address:* 1 Terrace House, 128 Richmond Hill, Richmond, Surrey. *T:* 01–940 4967. *Club:* Athenæum.

SYMONS, Julian Gustave, FRSL; author; *b* 30 May 1912; *y s* of M. A. Symons; *m* 1941, Kathleen Clark; one *s* (one *d* decd). Editor, Twentieth Century Verse, 1937–39. Chairman: Crime Writers Association, 1958–59; Cttee of Management, Soc. of Authors, 1970–71; Sunday Times Reviewer, 1958–. Pres., Detection Club, 1976–85. Mem. Council, Westfield Coll., Univ. of London, 1972–75. Grand Master: Swedish Acad. of Detection, 1977; Mystery Writers of America, 1982. FRSL 1975. *Publications:* Confusions About X, 1938; (ed) Anthology of War Poetry, 1942; The Second Man, 1944; A. J. A. Symons, 1950; Charles Dickens, 1951; Thomas Carlyle, 1952; Horatio Bottomley, 1955; The General Strike, 1957; A Reasonable Doubt, 1960; The Thirties, 1960; The Detective Story in Britain, 1962; Buller's Campaign, 1963; England's Pride, 1965; Critical Occasions, 1966; A Picture History of Crime and Detection, 1966; (ed) Essays and Biographies by A. J. A. Symons, 1969; Bloody Murder: from the detective story to the crime novel, a history, 1972 (MWA Edgar Allan Poe Award), rev. edn 1985; Notes from Another Country, 1972; Between the Wars, 1972; The Hungry Thirties, 1976; The Tell-Tale Heart, 1978; Conan Doyle, 1979; The Great Detectives, 1981; Critical Observations, 1981; The Tigers of Subtopia (short stories), 1982; (ed) New Poetry 9, 1983; Dashiell Hammett, 1985; (ed) Tchekov's The Shooting Party, 1986; author of 24 crime novels, including: The 31st of February, 1950; The Broken Penny, 1952; The Colour of Murder, 1957 (CWA Critics Award); The Progress of a Crime, 1960 (MWA Edgar Allan Poe Award); The End of Solomon Grundy, 1964; The Man Who Killed Himself, 1967; The Man Whose Dreams Came True, 1968; The Man Who Lost His Wife, 1970; The Players and the Game, 1972; A Three Pipe Problem, 1975; The Blackheath Poisonings, 1978; Sweet Adelaide, 1980; The Detling Murders, 1982; The Name of Annabel Lee, 1983; (ed) The Penguin Classic Crime Omnibus, 1984; The Criminal Comedy of the Contented Couple, 1985; several plays for television. *Recreations:* watching cricket and Association football, wandering in cities. *Address:* Groton House, 330 Dover Road, Walmer, Deal, Kent CT14 7NX. *T:* Deal 365209.

SYMONS, Prof. Martyn Christian Raymond, FRS 1985; Professor of Physical Chemistry, Leicester University, since 1960; *b* 12 Nov. 1925; *s* of Marjorie LeBrasseur and Stephen White Symons; *m* 1st, 1950, Joy Lendon (decd); one *s* one *d*; 3rd, 1970, Janice O'Connor. *Educ:* Battersea Polytechnic (BSc, PhD, DSc London); CChem, FRIC. Army, 1945–48. Lecturer: Battersea Polytechnic, 1948–53; Southampton Univ., 1953–60. FRSA. *Publications:* The Structure of Inorganic Radicals (with P. W. Atkins), 1967; Chemical and Biochemical Aspects of Electron Spin Resonance Spectroscopy, 1978; numerous scientific articles mainly in chem. jls. *Recreations:* watercolour landscape painting, piano playing. *Address:* 144 Victoria Park Road, Leicester LE2 1XD. *T:* Leicester 700314.

SYMONS, Vice-Adm. Sir Patrick (Jeremy), KBE 1986; Chief of Staff to Commander, Allied Naval Forces Southern Europe, since 1985; *b* 9 June 1933; *s* of Ronald and Joanne Symons; *m* 1961, Elizabeth Lawrence; one *s* one *d*. *Educ:* Dartmouth Royal Naval College. Commissioned 1951; in command, HMS Torquay, 1968–70, HMS Birmingham, 1976–77, HMS Bulwark, 1980–81; Naval Attaché, Washington, 1982–84. *Recreations:* sailing, skiing, swimming. *Address:* c/o Lloyds Bank, Cox's and King's Branch, 6 Pall Mall, SW1. *Clubs:* Royal Commonwealth Society; Royal Naval Sailing Association (Portsmouth).

SYMONS, Patrick Stewart, ARA 1983; Painter in oils; teacher, Chelsea School of Art, since 1959; *b* 24 Oct 1925; *s* of Norman H. Symons and Nora Westlake. *Educ:* Bryanston Sch.; Camberwell Sch. of Arts and Crafts. One-man exhibitions: New Art Centre, 1960; William Darby Gall., 1975–76; Browse and Darby, 1982. *Address:* 20 Grove Hill Road, Camberwell, SE5 8DG. *T:* 01–274 2373.

SYMS, John Grenville St George, OBE 1981; QC 1962; Barrister-at-Law; a Recorder of the Crown Court, 1972–80; *b* 6 Jan. 1913; *s* of late Harold St George Syms and Margaret (*née* Wordley); *m* 1951, Yvonne Yolande (*née* Rigby) (marr. diss. 1971); one *s*. *Educ:* Harrow; Magdalen College, Oxford (BA). Called to the Bar, 1936. Dep. Chm., Huntingdon and Peterborough QS, 1965–71. Chm., SE Agricultural Land Tribunal, 1972–83. Served in RAFVR, 1940–45 (despatches); Wing Commander, 1944. *Recreations:* shooting and fishing. *Address:* Brook Lodge, Brook, Albury, near Guildford, Surrey GU5 9DJ. *T:* Shere 2393.

SYNGE, Henry Millington; Chairman, Union International Co. Ltd, since 1969 (Director since 1955); Consultant, Tilney (Stockbrokers), Liverpool and Shrewsbury; *b* 3 April 1921; *s* of Richard Millington Synge, MC, Liverpool and Eileen Hall; *m* 1947, Joyce Helen, *d* of Alexander Ross Topping and Mrs Topping (*née* Stileman); two *s* one *d*. *Educ:* Shrewsbury School. Mercantile Marine: Radio Officer, 1941; Purser, Bibby Line, 1943; demobilised, 1946. Partner, Sing White & Co. (Stockbrokers), 1947. Manager, Liverpool Trustee Savings Bank, 1957, Chm. 1968–69; Regional Bd Mem., Trustee Savings Bank, England and Wales, 1970–85. *Recreations:* private flying, fishing, amateur radio. *Address:* Lake Cottage, Llynelys Hill, Oswestry, Shropshire SY10 8LL. *T:* Oswestry 830845.

SYNGE, John Lighton, FRS 1943; MA, ScD Dublin; MRIA, FRSC (Tory Medal, 1943); Senior Professor, School of Theoretical Physics, Dublin Institute for Advanced Studies, 1948–72, now Emeritus; *b* Dublin, 1897; *y s* of Edward Synge; *m* 1918, Elizabeth Allen; three *d*. *Educ:* St Andrew's Coll., Dublin; Trinity Coll., Dublin. Senior Moderator and Gold Medallist in Mathematics and Experimental Science, 1919; Lecturer in Mathematics, Trinity College, Dublin, 1920; Assistant Professor of Mathematics, University of Toronto, 1920–25; Secretary to the International Mathematical Congress, Toronto, 1924; Fellow of Trinity College, Dublin, and University Professor of Natural Philosophy, 1925–30; Treas., Royal Irish Academy, 1929–30. Sec., 1949–52. Pres., 1961–64; Professor of Applied Mathematics, Univ. of Toronto, 1930–43; Professor of Mathematics and Chm. of Dept, Ohio State Univ., 1943–46; Prof. of Mathematics and Head of Dept, Carnegie Inst. of Technology, 1946–48; Visiting Lecturer, Princeton Univ., 1939; Vis. Prof.: Brown Univ., 1941–42; Inst. for Fluid Dynamics and Applied Maths, University of Maryland, 1951. Ballistics Mathematician, United States Army Air Force, 1944–45. Hon. FTCD. Hon. LLD St Andrews, 1966; Hon. ScD: QUB, 1969; NUI, 1970. Boyle Medal,

RDS, 1972. *Publications:* Geometrical Optics, 1937; (with B. A. Griffith) Principles of Mechanics, 1942; (with A. E. Schild) Tensor Calculus, 1949; Science: Sense and Nonsense, 1951; Geometrical Mechanics and de Broglie Waves, 1954; Relativity: the Special Theory, 1956; The Hypercircle in Mathematical Physics, 1957; The Relativistic Gas, 1957; Kandelman's Krim, 1957; Relativity: the General Theory, 1960; Talking about Relativity, 1970; papers on geometry and applied mathematics; Ed. Sir W. R. Hamilton's Mathematical Papers, Vol. I. *Address:* Torfan, 8 Stillorgan Park, Blackrock, Co. Dublin. *T:* 881251.

SYNGE, Richard Laurence Millington, FRS 1950; Hon. Professor of Biology, University of East Anglia, Norwich, 1968–84; *b* 28 Oct. 1914; *s* of late Laurence M. Synge and Katharine C. Synge (*née* Swan), Great Barrow, Chester; *m* 1943, Ann, *d* of late Adrian L. Stephen and Karin Stephen (*née* Costelloe), both of London; three *s* four *d*. *Educ:* Winchester College; Trinity College, Cambridge (Hon. Fellow, 1972). International Wool Secretariat Research Student, University of Cambridge, 1938; Biochemist: Wool Industries Research Assoc., Leeds, 1941; Lister Institute of Preventive Medicine, London, 1943; Rowett Research Inst., Bucksburn, Aberdeen, 1948; Food Research Inst., Norwich, 1967–76. Editorial Board, Biochemical Journal, 1949–55. Hon. MRIA 1972; Hon. DSc East Anglia, 1977; Hon. PhD Uppsala, 1980. (Jtly) Nobel Prize for Chemistry, 1952. *Publications:* papers in biochemical and chemical journals, etc, 1937–. *Address:* 19 Meadow Rise Road, Norwich NR2 3QE. *T:* Norwich 53503.

SYNGE, Sir Robert Carson, 8th Bt, *cr* 1801; Manager and Owner, Rob's Furniture; *b* 4 May 1922; *s* of late Neale Hutchinson Synge (2nd *s* of 6th Bt) and Edith Elizabeth Thurlow (*d* 1933), Great Parndon, Essex; *m* 1944, Dorothy Jean Johnson, *d* of T. Johnson, Cloverdale; two *d*. S uncle, 1942. *Heir: cousin* Neale Francis Synge [*b* 28 Feb. 1917; *m* 1939, Kathleen Caroline Bowes; one *s* one *d*]. *Address:* 19364 Fraser Highway, RR4, Langley, British Columbia, Canada.

SYNNOT, Adm. Sir Anthony (Monckton), KBE 1979 (CBE 1972); AO 1976; Hon. JMN 1965; Hon. PSM 1982; *b* 5 Jan. 1922; *m* 1st, 1959, M. Virginia (*d* 1965), *d* of late Dr W. K. Davenport; two *d*; 2nd, 1968, E. Anne, *d* of late E. W. Manifold, MC. *Educ:* Geelong Grammar School. Joined RAN, 1939; served War of 1939–45 in HMA Ships Canberra, Stuart, Quiberon; HM Ships Barham, Punjabi; CO HMAS Warramunga, 1956–57; HMAS Vampire, 1961–62; OC Royal Malaysian Navy, 1964–65; CO HMAS Sydney, 1966, HMAS Melbourne, 1967; IDC 1968; Chief of Naval Personnel, 1970; Dep. Chief of Naval Staff, 1971–72; Commanding HM Australian Fleet, 1973; Director Joint Staff, 1974–76; Chief of Naval Staff, 1976–79; Chief of Defence Force Staff, 1979–82, retired. Chm., Australian War Meml Council, 1982–85. *Recreations:* tennis, golf, horse-driving. *Address:* Wanna Wanna, Box 33, Queanbeyan, NSW 2620, Australia. *T:* 062–971161. *Clubs:* Commonwealth (Canberra); Melbourne (Melbourne).

SYNNOTT, Hilary Nicholas Hugh; HM Diplomatic Service; Head of Chancery and Consul General, Amman, since 1985; *b* 20 March 1945; *s* of late Jasper Nicholas Netterville Synnott and Florence England Synnott (*née* Hillary); *m* 1973, Anne Penelope Clarke; one *s* decd. *Educ:* Beaumont College, Old Windsor; Britannia Royal Naval College, Dartmouth; Peterhouse, Cambridge (MA); RN Engineering College, Manadon. CEng, MIEE 1971. Joined RN, 1962; Midshipman, Far East Fleet, 1963–64; entered Submarine Service, 1968; retired as Lieut, 1973; joined HM Diplomatic Service, FCO, 1973; UK Delegn to OECD, Paris, 1975; Bonn, 1978; FCO, 1981–85. *Recreations:* sub-aqua diving, squash, photography. *Address:* c/o Foreign and Commonwealth Office, King Charles Street, SW1. *Club:* Royal Automobile (Amman).

SYSONBY, 3rd Baron, *cr* 1935, of Wonersh; **John Frederick Ponsonby;** *b* 5 Aug. 1945; *s* of 2nd Baron Sysonby, DSO and Sallie Monkland, *d* of Dr Leonard Sanford, New York; S father 1956. *Address:* c/o Friars, White Friars, Chester.

SYTHES, Percy Arthur, CB 1980; retired 1980; Comptroller and Auditor General for Northern Ireland, 1974–80; *b* 21 Dec. 1915; *s* of William Sythes and Alice Maud Grice; *m* 1941, Doreen Smyth Fitzsimmons; three *d*. *Educ:* Campbell Coll., Belfast; Trinity Coll., Dublin. Exhibr, Scholar; BA (Mod. Lit.), 1st cl. hons Gold Medal 1938; Vice-Chancellor's Prizeman 1939. Asst Master: Royal Sch., Dungannon, 1939; Portadown Coll., 1940. Royal Artillery, 1940–46 (Major); GSO2, 1946. Asst Principal, NI Civil Service, 1946; Asst Sec. 1963; Dep. Sec. 1971. Chm., Bd of Governors, Strathearn Sch., 1982– (Mem., 1966–). *Recreations:* gardens, family. *Address:* Malory, 37 Tweskard Park, Belfast BT4 2JZ. *T:* Belfast 63310.

SZEMERÉNYI, Prof. Oswald John Louis, DrPhil (Budapest); FBA 1982; Professor of Indo-European and General Linguistics, University of Freiburg-im-Breisgau, 1965–81, now Emeritus Professor; *b* London, 7 Sept. 1913; *m* 1940, Elizabeth Kövér; one *s*. *Educ:* Madách Imre Gimnázium; University of Budapest. Classics Master in Beregszász and Mátyásföld, 1939–41; Lecturer in Greek, 1942–45, Reader, 1946, Professor of Comparative Indo-European Philology in University of Budapest, 1947–48. Came to England, Oct. 1948; employed in industry, 1949–52; Research Fellow, Bedford Coll., London, 1952–53; Asst Lecturer, 1953–54, Lecturer, 1954–58, Reader, 1958–60, in Greek at Bedford College; Professor of Comparative Philology, University College, London, 1960–65. Collitz Prof., Linguistic Inst., USA, 1963; Vis. Prof., Seattle, 1964. *Publications:* The Indo-European liquid sonants in Latin, 1941; Studies in the Indo-European System of Numerals, 1960; Trends and Tasks in Comparative Philology, 1962; Syncope in Greek and Indo-European, 1964; Einführung in die vergleichende Sprachwissenschaft, 1970 (trans. Spanish, 1978, Russian, 1980, Italian, 1985), 3rd edn 1987; Richtungen der modernen Sprachwissenschaft, part I, 1971 (trans. Spanish, 1979), part II, 1982; Four Old Iranian Ethnic Names, 1980; (contrib.) Comparative Linguistics in: Current Trends in Linguistics 9, 1972; The Kinship Terminology of the Indo-European Languages, 1978; contribs to British and foreign learned jls; Studies in Diachronic, Synchronic and Typological Linguistics, Festschrift for Oswald Szemerényi (ed Bela Brogyanyi), I-II, 1979. *Recreation:* motoring. *Address:* Albert-Ludwigs-Universität, D-78 Freiburg-im-Breisgau, W Germany.

SZENT-GYÖRGYI, Albert, MD, PhD Cantab, Dhc; Scientific Director, National Foundation for Cancer Research, Massachusetts, USA, since 1975; *b* Budapest, 16 Sept. 1893; *s* of Nicholas Szent-Györgyi and Josephine, *d* of Joseph Lenhossék, Professor of Anatomy; *m* 1st, 1941; one *d*; 2nd, Marcia Houston. *Educ:* Budapest University; Cambridge University. Matriculated Medical Faculty, Budapest, 1911; war service, 1914–18 (wounded); Assistant, University Pozsony, 1918; working at Prague and Berlin, 1919; in Hamburg in scientific research, 1919–20; Assistant at Univ. Leiden, Holland, 1920–22; privaat dozent at Groningen, 1922–26; working at Cambridge, England, with the interrruption of one year spent in USA, 1926–30; Prof. of Medical Chemistry, Szeged Univ., 1931–45; Professor of Biochemistry Univ. of Budapest, Hungary, 1945–47; Dir of Research, Inst. of Muscle Research, Mass, 1947–75. Formerly: Pres. Acad. of Sciences, Budapest; Vice-Pres. Nat. Acad., Budapest. Prix Nobel of Medicine, 1937; Visiting Prof., Harvard Univ., 1936; Franchi Prof., Univ. of Liége, Belgium, 1938. Cameron Prize (Edinburgh), 1946. Lasker Award, 1954. Hon. ScD Cantab, 1963. Hon. Fellow, Fitzwilliam Coll., Cambridge, 1967. *Publications:* Oxidation, Fermentation, Vitamins, Health and Disease, 1939; Muscular Contraction, 1947; The Nature of Life, 1947; Contraction in Body and Heart Muscle, 1953; Bioenergetics, 1957; Submolecular Biology, 1960; Science, Ethics and Politics, 1962; Bioelectronics, 1968; The Living State, 1972; Electronic Biology and Cancer, 1976; many scientific papers. *Recreations:* sport of all kinds, chiefly sailing, swimming and fishing. *Address:* Marine Biological Laboratory, Woods Hole, Mass 02543, USA; Penzance, Woods Hole, Mass, USA.

SZERYNG, Henryk; Hon. Professor, Faculty of Music, Mexican National University, Mexico City; Concert Violinist, since 1933; *b* Warsaw, 22 Sept. 1918; Mexican Citizen since 1946; *m* 1984, Waltraud Von Neviges. *Educ:* Warsaw, Berlin, Paris. Graduated violin class of Carl Flesch, Berlin, 1933; 1st Prize special mention, Paris Conservatoire, 1937; Composition study with Nadia Boulanger, 1934–39. War of 1939–45: played over 300 concerts for Allied Armed Forces, Red Cross and other welfare institutions in Scotland, England, Canada, USA, Caribbean area, Middle East, North Africa, Brazil and Mexico. Has covered the five continents in recitals, also soloist with major orchestras, 1953–. Mexican Cultural Ambassador, 1960–; Cultural Adviser to Mexican delegn, UNESCO, Paris, and to Mexican Foreign Ministry, 1970–. Numerous recordings; Grand Prix du Disque, 1955, 1957, 1960, 1961, 1967, 1969. Hon. RAM, 1969. Hon. Pres., Musical Youth of Mexico, 1974. Hon. DHL Georgetown Univ., 1982. Officer of Cultural Merit, Roumania, 1935; Kt Comdr, Order of Polonia Restituta (Poland), 1956; Silver Medal of City of Paris, 1963; Officer, Order of Arts and Letters (France), 1964; Comdr, Order of the Lion (Finland), 1966; Ordre du Mérite en faveur de la culture polonaise, 1970; Alfonso el Sabio Cross (Spain), 1972; Chevalier, 1972, Officier, 1984, Légion d'Honneur (France); Mozart Medal, Salzburg, 1972; Comdr Al Merito (Italy), 1974; Comdr, Order of Flag with Golden Star (Yugoslavia), 1976; Order of the Crown (Belgium), 1976; Gran Premio Nacional, Mexico, 1979; Golden Medal, City of Paris, 1981; Hon. Citizen, Poznan, Poland, 1981; Golden Medal, City of Jerusalem, 1983; Commandeur, Ordre de St Charles (Monaco), 1985. *Publications:* several chamber music works, also for piano and violin. Revised violin concertos by Nardini, Vivaldi and others, sonatas and partitas by Bach; re-discovered Paganini Concerto No 3 (World Première, London, 1971). *Recreations:* golf, reading. *Address:* c/o Mexican Embassy, 9 rue Longchamp, 75116 Paris, France.

SZWARC, Michael M., FRS 1966; Distinguished Professor of Chemistry of the State University of New York, 1966–79, now Professor Emeritus; *b* 9 June 1909; Polish; *m* 1933, Marja Frenkel; one *s* two *d*. *Educ:* Warsaw Inst. of Technology (Chem. Eng. 1933); Hebrew Univ., Jerusalem (PhD 1942). University of Manchester (Lecturer), 1945–52; PhD (Phys. Chem.) 1947; DSc 1949; State University Coll. of Environmental Scis at Syracuse, NY, 1952 82: Prof. of Physical and Polymer Chemistry; Research Prof.; Distinguished Prof. of Chemistry; Dir, Polymer Research Inst. Baker Lectr, Cornell Univ., 1972. Nobel Guest Prof., Univ. of Uppsala, 1969; Visiting Professor: Univ. of Leuven, 1974; Univ. of Calif, San Diego, 1979–80. Hon. Dr: Leuven, Belgium, 1974; Uppsala, Sweden, 1975; Louis Pasteur Univ., France, 1978. Amer. Chem. Soc. Award for Outstanding Achievements in Polymer Chemistry, 1969; Gold Medal, Soc. of Plastic Engrs, 1972; Gold Medal, Benjamin Franklin Inst., 1978. *Publications:* Carbanions, Living Polymers and Electron Transfer Processes, 1968; Ions and Ion-pairs in Organic Chemistry, Vol. I, 1972, Vol. II, 1974; numerous contribs to Jl Chem. Soc., Trans Faraday Soc., Proc. Royal Soc., Jl Am. Chem. Soc., Jl Chem. Phys., Jl Phys. Chem., Jl Polymer Sci., Nature, Chem. Rev., Quarterly Reviews, etc. *Address:* 1176 Santa Luisa Drive, Solana Beach, Calif 92075, USA. *T:* (619) 481–1863.

T

TABACHNIK, Eldred, QC 1982; *b* 5 Nov. 1943; *s* of Solomon Joseph Tabachnik and Esther Tabachnik; *m* 1966, Jennifer Kay Lawson; two *s* one *d*. *Educ*: Univ. of Cape Town (BA, LLB); Univ. of London (LLM). Called to the Bar, Inner Temple, 1970. Lectr, UCL, 1969–72. *Recreation*: reading. *Address*: 3 Drax Avenue, SW20 0EG. *T*: 01–947 0699. *Club*: Reform.

TABBARA, Hani Bahjat; Hon. GCVO 1984; Ambassador of the Hashemite Kingdom of Jordan to Turkey, since 1985; *b* 10 Feb. 1939; *s* of Bahjat and Nimat Tabbara; *m* 1980, Wafa Tabbara; two *s*. *Educ*: University of Alexandria. Govt service, 1963; Jordan Embassy, London, 1971–73; Counsellor, Foreign Ministry, Amman, 1973; Minister Plenipotentiary, Jordan Embassy, London, 1973–76; Chief of Staff, Prime Minister's Office, Amman, 1976–77; Ambassador: Morocco, 1977–80; Romania, 1980–82; Saudi Arabia, 1982–84; UK, 1984–85. Al Kawkab decoration, 1st Class, 1976. *Address*: c/o Ministry of Foreign Affairs, Amman, Jordan.

TABOR, Prof. David, PhD, ScD; FRS 1963; Professor of Physics in the University of Cambridge, 1973–81, now Emeritus, and Head of Physics and Chemistry of Solids, Cavendish Laboratory, 1969–81; Fellow of Gonville and Caius College, Cambridge, since 1957; *b* 23 Oct. 1913; *s* of Charles Tabor and Rebecca Weinstein; *m* 1943, Hannalene Stillschweig; two *s*. *Educ*: Regent St Polytechnic; Universities of London and Cambridge. BSc London 1934; PhD Cambridge 1939; ScD Cambridge 1956. Reader in Physics, Cambridge Univ., 1964–73. Vis. Prof., Imperial Coll., London, 1981–. Hon. DSc Bath, 1985. Inaugural Gold Medal of Tribology, Inst. of Engrs, 1972; Guthrie Medal, Inst. Physics, 1975. *Publications*: The Hardness of Metals, 1951; Gases, Liquids and Solids, 1969, 2nd edn 1979; (with F. P. Bowden) Friction and Lubrication of Solids, Part I, 1950 (rev. edn, 1954); Part II, 1964; contributions to learned jls on friction, adhesion, lubrication and hardness. *Recreation*: Judaica. *Address*: Cavendish Laboratory, Madingley Road, Cambridge CB3 0HE; Gonville and Caius College, Cambridge; 8 Rutherford Road, Cambridge. *T*: Cambridge 841336.

TABOR, Maj.-Gen. David John St Maur, CB 1977; MC 1944; late Royal Horse Guards; GOC Eastern District, 1975–77, retired; *b* 5 Oct. 1922; *y s* of late Harry Tabor, Hitchin, Herts; *m* 1955, Hon. Pamela Roxane, 2nd *d* of 2nd Baron Glendyne; two *s*. *Educ*: Eton; RMA, Sandhurst. Served War: 2nd Lieut, RHG, 1942; NW Europe, 1944–45 (wounded, 1944); Major, 1946. Lt-Col Comdg RHG, 1960; Lt-Col Comdg Household Cavalry, and Silver Stick in Waiting, 1964; Col, 1964; Brig., 1966; Comdr Berlin Infty Bde, 1966; Comdr, British Army Staff and Mil. Attaché, Washington, 1968; RCDS, 1971; Maj.-Gen., 1972; Defence Attaché, Paris, 1972–74. Vice-Chm., ACFA, 1979. *Recreations*: shooting, fishing, sailing, golf, gardening. *Address*: Shipton Sollars Manor, Andoversford, Glos GL54 4HU. *T*: Cheltenham 820207. *Clubs*: Turf, Royal Automobile, MCC.

See also Baron Glendyne.

TACKABERRY, John Antony, QC 1982; FCIArb, FFB; *b* 13 Nov. 1939; *s* of late Thomas Raphael Tackaberry and Mary Catherine (*née* Geoghegan); *m* 196 Penelope Holt (separated); two *s*. *Educ*: Downside; Trinity Coll., Dublin; Downing Coll., Cambridge (MA, LLB). Called to the Bar, Gray's Inn, 1967. FFB 1979. Teacher in China, 1963–64 and in London, 1965–66. Pres., Soc. of Construction Law, 1983–. *Recreations*: good food, good wine, good company; and if there's any time left, wind-surfing and photography. *Address*: 22 Willes Road, NW5 3DS. *T*: 01–267 2137; 22 Old Buildings, Lincoln's Inn, WC2A 3UJ.

TACON, Air Cdre Ernest William, CBE 1958; DSO 1944; MVO 1950; DFC 1940 (Bar 1944); AFC 1942 (Bar 1953); *b* 6 Dec. 1917; *s* of Ernest Richard Tacon, Hastings, New Zealand; *m* 1st, 1949, Clare Keating (*d* 1956), *d* of late Michael Keating, Greymouth, NZ; one *s* two *d*; 2nd, 1960, Bernardine, *d* of Cecil Leamy, Wellington, NZ; three *s*. *Educ*: St Patrick's College, Silverstream, New Zealand. Joined RNZAF, 1938. Served with RAF, 1939–46. Transferred to RAF, 1946. CO, King's Flight, Benson, 1946–49. Overseas Services since War: Canal Zone, 1951–53; Cyprus, 1956–58; Persian Gulf, 1961–63; Commandant, Central Fighter Establishment, 1963–65; Air Cdre, Tactics, HQ Fighter Comd, 1966–67; AOC Military Air Traffic Ops, 1968–71, retired. MBIM. *Address*: 69 McLeans Road, Bucklands Beach, Auckland, NZ.

TAFTI, Rt. Rev. Hassan Barnaba D.; *see* Dehqani-Tafti.

TAHOURDIN, John Gabriel, CMG 1961; HM Diplomatic Service, retired; *b* 15 Nov. 1913; *s* of late John St Clair Tahourdin; *m* 1957, Margaret Michie; one *s* one *d*. *Educ*: Merchant Taylors' School; St John's College, Oxford. Served HM Embassy, Peking, 1936–37; Private Secretary to HM Ambassador at Shanghai, 1937–40; BoT, 1940–41; Vice-Consul, Baltimore, 1941; Foreign Office, 1942; Private Secretary to Parliamentary Under-Secretary of State, 1943, and to Minister of State, 1945; Athens, 1946; returned to Foreign Office, 1949; Counsellor, British Embassy, The Hague, 1955; Foreign Office, 1957; Minister, UK Delegn to 18 Nation Disarmament Conf., Geneva, 1963–66; HM Ambassador to: Senegal, 1966–71, and concurrently to Mauritania, 1968–71; to Mali, 1969–71, and to Guinea, 1970–71; Bolivia, 1971–73. Mem., Internat. Inst. for Strategic Studies. Price Commission, 1975–77; Kleinwort Benson, 1977–79. *Recreations*: music cinematography, foreign languages, travel. *Address*: Diana Lodge, Little Kineton, Warwick CV35 0DL. *T*: Warwick 640276. *Clubs*: Athenæum, Travellers', Beefsteak; Norfolk.

TAIT, Dr Alan Anderson; Deputy Director, Fiscal Affairs Department, International Monetary Fund, Washington, since 1982; *b* 1 July 1934; *s* of Stanley Tait and Margaret Ruth (*née* Anderson); *m* 1963, Susan Valerie Somers; one *s*. *Educ*: Heriot's Sch., Edinburgh; Univ. of Edinburgh (MA); Trinity Coll., Dublin (PhD). Lectr, Trinity Coll., Dublin, 1959–71 (Fellow, 1968, Sen. Tutor, 1970); Visiting Prof., Univ. of Illinois, 1965–66. Economic adviser to Irish Govt on industrial develt and taxation and chief economic adviser to Confedn of Irish Industry, 1967–71; economic consultant to Sec. of State for Scotland, 1972–77; International Monetary Fund: Visiting Scholar, 1972; Consultant, 1973 and 1974; Chief, Fiscal Analysis Div., 1976–79; Asst Dir, 1979–82. Prof. of Money and Finance, Univ. of Strathclyde, 1971–77. *Publications*: The Taxation of Personal Wealth, 1967; (with J. Bristow) Economic Policy in Ireland, 1968; (with J. Bristow) Ireland: some problems of a developing economy, 1971; The Value Added Tax, 1972; articles on public finance in Rev. of Economic Studies, Finanzarchiv, Public Finance, Staff Papers, etc. *Recreations*: sailing, painting. *Address*: 4284 Vacation Lane, Arlington, Va 22207, USA. *T*: 202–623–8725. *Clubs*: Cosmos (Washington DC); Royal Irish Yacht (Dun Laoghaire); Annapolis Yacht (Annapolis).

TAIT, Adm. Sir (Allan) Gordon, KCB 1977; DSC 1943; Chief of Naval Personnel and Second Sea Lord, 1977–79; Chairman, Regional Television Network News; *b* 30 Oct. 1921; *s* of Allan G. Tait and Ann Gordon, Timaru, NZ; *m* 1952, Philippa, *d* of Sir Bryan Todd, *qv*; two *s* two *d*. *Educ*: Timaru Boys' High Sch.; RNC Dartmouth; War Service, Atlantic and N Russia Convoys, 1939–42; Submarines, Mediterranean and Far East, 1942–45 (despatches); Commanded HM Submarines: Teredo, 1947; Solent, 1948; ADC to Governor-General of New Zealand, 1949–51; commanded HM Submarines: Ambush, 1951; Aurochs, 1951–53; Tally Ho, 1955; Sanguine, 1955–56; Asst Naval Adviser, UK High Commn, Canada, 1957–59; commanded HM Ships: Caprice, 1960–62; Ajax, 1965–66; Maidstone, 1967; commanded: 2nd Destroyer Squadron (Far East), 1965–66; 3rd Submarine Sqdn, 1967–69; Chief of Staff, Submarine Comd, 1969–70; commanded, Britannia RNC, 1970–72; Rear-Adm., 1972; Naval Secretary, MoD, 1972–74; Vice-Adm., 1974; Flag Officer, Plymouth, Port Admiral, Devonport, NATO Comdr, Central Sub Area, Eastern Atlantic, 1975–77; Adm., 1978. Naval ADC to the Queen, 1972. Chm., Lion Corp. Ltd (formerly Lion Breweries Ltd); Director: Todd Bros Ltd; Todd Motors Corp.; Westpac Merchant Finance; NZ Bd, Westpac Banking Corp; Owens Investments Ltd. Pres. and Chm. of Trustees, NZ Sports Foundn; Chm., NZ Family Trust; Mem., Spirit of Adventure Trust Board. *Address*: 22 Orakei Road, Auckland 5, New Zealand; Hiwiroa Farm, PO Box 2, Tokaanu, New Zealand. *Clubs*: White's; Royal Yacht Squadron; Northern (Auckland).

TAIT, Andrew Wilson, OBE 1967; Chairman, National House-Building Council, since 1984 (Director-General, 1967–84); *b* 25 Sept. 1922; *s* of late Dr Adam and Jenny Tait; *m* 1954, Elizabeth Isobel Maclennan; three *d*. *Educ*: George Watson's Coll., Edinburgh; Edinburgh Univ. (MA 1st Class Hons History). Served Army, 1942–45. Leader writer, The Scotsman, 1947–48; Scottish Information Office, 1948–59; Principal, SHHD, 1959; Jt Sec., Cohen Cttee on Health Educn in UK, 1962–63; Dir, NHBC, 1964. Dir, Housing Res. Foundn, 1969–. Consultant: Nat. Assoc. of Home Builders of US, 1973–74; Home Owners Warranty Corp. of US, 1974–76; New Home Warranty Prog., Ontario, 1976–80. Founder, Internat. Housing and Home Warranty Assoc., 1979; Chairman: Jt Land Requirements Cttee, 1981; Home Buyers Adv. Service, 1985–; Bridging the Gap, 1986–. *Recreations*: golf, tennis, chess. *Address*: Orchard Croft, Grimmshill, Great Missenden, Bucks. *T*: Great Missenden 2061. *Club*: Caledonian.

TAIT, Eric, MBE 1980; Secretary, Institute of Chartered Accountants of Scotland, since 1984; *b* 10 Jan. 1945; *s* of William Johnston Tait and Sarah Tait (*née* Jones); *m* 1967, Agnes Jean Boag (*née* Anderson); one *s* one *d*. *Educ*: George Heriot's Sch., Edinburgh; RMA Sandhurst; RMCS Shrivenham (BSc Eng); Churchill Coll., Cambridge (MPhil); 2nd Lieut, Royal Engineers, 1965; despatches 1976; student, RAF Staff Coll., Bracknell, 1977; OC 7 Field Sqn, RE, 1979–81; Lt-Col 1982; Directing Staff, Staff Coll., Camberley, 1982–83, retired, at own request, 1983. Mem. of Exec., Scottish Council (Develt and Industry), 1984–. Editor in Chief, The Accountant's Magazine. *Publications*: occasional contribs to RE Jl. *Recreations*: swimming, hill walking, reading. *Address*: Institute of Chartered Accountants of Scotland, 27 Queen Street, Edinburgh EH2 1LA. *T*: 031–225 5673.

TAIT, Prof. James Francis, PhD; FRS 1959; engaged in theoretical research on mathematical modelling of endocrine systems; Emeritus Professor, University of London, since 1982; *b* 1 December 1925; *s* of Herbert Tait and Constance Levinia Brotherton; *m* 1956, Sylvia Agnes Simpson (*née* Wardropper) (*see* S. A. Tait). *Educ*: Darlington Grammar Sch.; Leeds Univ. Lectr in Medical Physics, Middlesex Hospital Medical School, 1948–55; External Scientific Staff, Medical Research Council, Middlesex Hospital Medical School, 1955–58; Senior Scientist, Worcester Foundation for Experimental Biology, USA, 1958–70; Joel Prof. of Physics as Applied to Medicine, Univ. of London, 1970–82; Co-Dir, Biophysical Endocrinology Unit, Physics Dept, Middlesex Hosp. Med. Sch., 1970–85. Hon. DSc Hull, 1979. Society for Endocrinology: Medal, 1969 and Sir Henry Dale Medal, 1979; Tadens Reichstein Award, Internat. Soc. of Endocrinology, 1976; CIBA Award, Amer. Heart Assoc. for Hypertension Research, 1977. *Publications*: papers on medical physics, biophysics and endocrinology. *Recreation*: gardening. *Address*: Moorlands, Main Road, East Boldre, near Brockenhurst, Hants SO42 7WT. *T*: East End 312.

TAIT, Sir James (Sharp), Kt 1969; DSc, LLD, PhD, BSc(Eng), CEng, FIEE, FIMechE; Vice-Chancellor and Principal, The City University, 1966–74; retired (formerly Northampton College of Advanced Technology, London, of which he was Principal, 1957–66); *b* 13 June 1912; *s* of William Blyth Tait and Helen Sharp; *m* 1939, Mary C. Linton; two *s* one *d*. *Educ*: Royal Technical College, Glasgow; Glasgow Univ. (BSc (Eng.), PhD). Lecturer, Royal Technical Coll., Glasgow, 1935–46; Head of Electrical Engineering Department: Portsmouth Municipal Coll., 1946–47; Northampton Polytechnic, EC1,

1947–51; Principal, Woolwich Polytechnic, SE18, 1951–56. Member: Adv. Council on Scientific Policy, 1959–62; National Electronics Council, 1964–76, Hon. Mem., 1976. Pres., Inst. of Information Scientists, 1970–72. Hon. Fellow: Inst. of Measurement and Control, 1970; Inst. of Inf. Scientists, 1973. Hon. LLD Strathclyde, 1967; Hon. DSc City, 1974. *Recreation:* open-air pursuits. *Address:* 23 Trowlock Avenue, Teddington, Mddx. *T:* 01-977 6541.

TAIT, Michael Logan, LVO 1972; HM Diplomatic Service; Ambassador to United Arab Emirates, since 1986; *b* 27 Sept. 1936; *m* 1968, Margaret Kirsteen Stewart; two *s* one *d.* Foreign Office, 1961; Bahrain, 1963; Asst Political Agent, UAE, 1963; FO, 1966; Private Sec. to Minister of State, FO, later FCO, 1968; First Sec. and Hd of Chancery, Belgrade, 1970; First Sec. (Political), Hd of Chancery and Consul, Amman, 1972; FCO, 1975; Counsellor and Hd of Chancery, Baghdad, 1977; Counsellor, FCO, 1978; CSCE, Madrid, 1980; Counsellor (Econ. and Finance), UK Delegn, OECD, Paris, 1982; Hd of Economic Relns Dept, FCO, 1984. *Address:* c/o Foreign and Commonwealth Office, SW1A 2AH.

TAIT, Sir Peter, KBE 1975 (OBE 1967); JP; financial consultant, New Zealand; Chairman: Alexander Associates Ltd; Tait Associates Ltd, since 1972; *b* Wellington, NZ, 5 Sept. 1915; *s* of John Oliver Tait and Barbara Ann Isbister; *m* 1946, Lilian Jean Dunn; one *s* one *d. Educ:* Wellington Coll., NZ. MP, New Zealand National Party, 1951–54; Mayor, City of Napier, 1956–74; Pres., NZ Municipal Assoc., 1968–69. Chairman: Napier Fire Bd, 1956–75; Hawke's Bay Airport Authority, 1962–74; Napier Marineland Trust Bd, 1963–; Princess Alexandra Hosp. Bd, 1972–. Patron, Napier Develt Assoc.; Freeman, City of Napier. JP 1956–. *Recreations:* bowls, gardening. *Address:* 1 Avon Terrace, Taradale, Napier, New Zealand. *T:* (private) 445266, (business) 55555. *Clubs:* Royal Over-Seas League; Lions, (Hon.) Cosmopolitan (both Napier).

TAIT, Mrs Sylvia Agnes Sophia, (Mrs James F. Tait), FRS 1959; Honorary Research Associate and Co-Director, Biophysical Endocrinology Unit, Physics Department, Middlesex Hospital Medical School, since 1982; biochemist; distinguished for her work on the hormones controlling the distribution of salts in the body; *m* 1956, James Francis Tait, *qv.* Research Asst, Courtauld Inst. of Biochemistry, Middlesex Hosp. Med. Sch., 1944–45; External Scientific Staff, MRC, Middlesex Hosp. Med. Sch., 1955–58; Senior Scientist, Worcester Foundn for Experimental Biology, USA, 1958–70; Research Associate and Co-Director, Biophysical Endocrinology Unit, Dept of Physics as Applied to Medicine, Middlesex Hosp. Med. School, 1970–82. Hon. DSc Hull, 1979. Tadeus Reichstein Award, Internat. Endocrine Society, 1976; Gregory Pincus Meml Medal, 1977; CIBA Award, American Heart Assoc. for Hypertension Research, 1977; Sir Henry Dale Medal of Soc. for Endocrinology, 1979. *Address:* Biophysical Endocrinology Unit, Department of Physics as Applied to Medicine, Middlesex Hospital Medical School, Cleveland Street, W1P 6DB. *T:* 01–636 8333 (ext. 7162).

TAIT, Air Vice-Marshal Sir Victor Hubert, KBE 1944 (OBE 1938); CB 1943; *b* 8 July 1892; *s* of Samuel Tait, Winnipeg; *m* 1st, 1917; one *d*; 2nd, 1929; one *s*; 3rd, 1957, Nancy Margaret, *d* of late Andrew Muecke, Adelaide, Australia. *Educ:* University of Manitoba (BSc). Canadian Army, 1914–17; RFC and RAF, 1917–45. Director of Radar and Director-General of Signals, Air Ministry, 1942–45; Operations Director, BOAC, 1945–56. Chairman: International Aeradio Ltd, 1946–63; Lindley Thompson Transformer Co., 1959–66; Ultra Electronics (Holdings) Ltd, 1963–67 (Dir, 1955–72); Dir, Ultra Electronics Ltd, 1956–72. Air Transport Electronic Council, UK, 1958. Governor, Flight Safety Foundn of America, 1959–69. President, British Ice Hockey Assoc., 1958–71. Mem. Council, RGS, 1965–70. Order of the Nile (Egypt), 1936; Order of Merit (USA), 1945. *Address:* 81 Swan Court, SW3. *T:* 01–352 6864. *Clubs:* Hurlingham, Royal Air Force.

TALBOT, family name of **Baron Talbot of Malahide.**

TALBOT OF MALAHIDE, 9th Baron *cr* 1831 (Ire.); **Joseph Hubert George Talbot;** Baron Malahide of Malahide (Ire.), 1831; Hereditary Lord Admiral of Malahide and adjacent seas (15 Edward IV); retired; *b* 22 April 1899; *s* of John Reginald Charles Talbot (*d* 1909) and Maria Josephine (*d* 1939), *d* of 3rd Duc de Stacpoole; *S* brother, 1975; *m* 1st, 1924, Hélène (*d* 1961), *o d* of M. Gouley; 2nd, 1962, Beatrice Bros (marr. diss. 1970). *Educ:* Beaumont College. *Heir: cousin* Reginald John Richard Arundell [*b* 9 Jan. 1931; *m* 1955, Laura Duff, *yr d* of late Group Captain Edward John Tennant, DSO, MC; one *s* four *d*].

TALBOT, Vice-Adm. Sir (Arthur Allison) FitzRoy, KBE 1964; CB 1961; DSO 1940 and Bar 1942; DL; Commander-in-Chief, Plymouth, 1965–67; retired; *b* 22 October 1909; *s* of late Henry FitzRoy George Talbot, Captain Royal Navy, and of Susan Blair Athol Allison; *m* 1st, 1940, Joyce Gertrude Linley (*d* 1981); two *d*; 2nd, 1983, Lady (Elizabeth) Durlacher. *Educ:* RN College, Dartmouth. Served War of 1939–45: Comd 10th A/S Striking Force, North Sea, 1939, and 3rd MGB Flotilla, Channel, 1940–41 (DSO); Comd HMS Whitshed, East Coast, 1942 (Bar to DSO); Comd HMS Teazer, Mediterranean, 1943–44. Comdr 1945; Chief Staff Officer, Commodore Western Isles, 1945; Staff Officer Ops to C-in-C Brit. Pacific Fleet and Far East Station, 1947–48; Comd HMS Alert, 1949. Capt. 1950; Naval Attaché, Moscow and Helsinki, 1951–53. Imperial Defence College, 1954. Capt. (D) 3rd Destroyer Squadron, 1955–57; Commodore RN Barracks Portsmouth, 1957–59; Rear-Adm. 1960; Flag Officer: Arabian Seas and Persian Gulf, 1960–61; Middle East, 1961–62; Vice-Adm. 1962; Commander-in-Chief, S Atlantic and S America, 1963–65. DL Somerset, 1973. *Recreations:* riding, shooting. *Address:* Wootton Fitzpaine Manor, Bridport, Dorset. *T:* Charmouth 60455. *Club:* Naval and Military.

TALBOT, Maj.-Gen. Dennis Edmund Blaquière, CB 1960; CBE 1955; DSO 1945; MC 1944; DL; *b* 23 Sept. 1908; *s* of late Walter Blaquière Talbot, St John, Jersey and The White House, Hadlow, Kent; *m* 1939, Barbara Anne, *o d* of late Rev. R. B. Pyper, Rector of Pluckley, Kent; three *s* two *d. Educ:* Tonbridge; RMC Sandhurst. 2nd Lieut Roy. West Kent Regt, 1928; served India, 1928–37. Served War of 1939–45 (despatches, DSO, MC); Brigade Major: 30th Infantry Bde, BEF; 141 Inf. Bde; GSO 2, HQ 1st Corps; GSO 2 and 1, Combined Ops; 2nd i/c 5th Bn Dorset Regt; in command, 7th Bn Hampshire Regt, NW Europe, 1944–45. I/c 2nd Bn Royal W Kent Regt, 1945–46; GSO 1, HQ, Far ELF, 1947–48; Senior UK Army Liaison Officer, NZ, 1948–51; Lt-Col 1949; AAG (Col), War Office, 1951–53; Col 1952; i/c 18th Inf. Bde and 99th Gurkha Inf. Bde, Malaya, 1953–55; Brig. 1956; BGS, HQ, BAOR, 1957–58; Maj.-Gen. 1958; GOC, E Anglian Dist and 54th Inf. Div. (TA), 1958–61; Dep. Comdr, BAOR, and Comdr British Army Group Troops, 1961–63; Chief of Staff, BAOR, and GOC Rhine Army Troops, 1963–64, retired; Civil Service, 1964–73. Chm., Kent Cttee, Army Benev. Fund, 1964–84. Graduate of: Staff Coll., Camberley; RN Staff Coll., Greenwich; Joint Services Staff Coll., Latimer; Imperial Defence College, London; Civil Defence Staff Coll., Sunningdale. Col, The Queen's Own Royal West Kent Regt, 1959–61; Dep. Colonel, The Queen's Own Buffs, The Royal Kent Regt, 1961–65; Hon. Col, 8 Queen's Cadre (formerly 8 Bn The Queen's Regt (West Kent)), 1968–71. Pres., local horticultural soc.; Vice Pres., local br., Royal British Legion. DL Kent, 1964. Knight Commander 1962, Grand Cross 1965, Order of the Dannebrog (Denmark). *Recreation:* gardening. *Address:* Oast Court, Barham, near Canterbury, Kent CT4 6PG.

TALBOT, Vice-Adm. Sir FitzRoy, *see* Talbot, Vice-Adm. Sir A. A. F.

TALBOT, Frank Heyworth, QC 1949; *b* 4 June 1895; *s* of Edward John Talbot and Susan (*née* Heyworth); *m* 1st, 1922, Mabel Jane (*d* 1956), *d* of John Williams, Brecon; two *s*; 2nd, 1969, Heather, *d* of J. F. Williams, Great Missenden. *Educ:* Tottenham Grammar School; London Univ. (LLB). Civil Service, 1912–31. Inns of Court Regt, 1918. Called to the Bar, Middle Temple, 1931 (Bencher, 1958); *aeg* Lincoln's Inn, 1951. Practice at the Bar, 1931–84. *Recreation:* music. *Address:* 9 West Field, Little Abington, Cambridge CB1 6BE. *T:* Cambridge 891330.

TALBOT, Godfrey Walker, LVO 1960; OBE 1946; author, broadcaster, lecturer, journalist; Senior News Reporter and Commentator on staff of British Broadcasting Corporation, 1946–69; official BBC observer accredited to Buckingham Palace, 1948–69; *b* 8 Oct. 1908; *s* of Frank Talbot and Kate Bertha Talbot (*née* Walker); *m* 1933, Bess, *d* of Robert and Clara Owen, Bradford House, Wigan; one *s* (and one *s* decd). *Educ:* Leeds Grammar School. Joined editorial staff on The Yorkshire Post, 1928; Editor of The Manchester City News, 1932–34; Editorial Staff, Daily Dispatch, 1934–37. Joined BBC, 1937; War of 1939–45: BBC war correspondent overseas, 1941–45 (despatches, OBE); organised BBC Home Reporting Unit, as Chief Reporter, after the war. BBC Commentator, Royal Commonwealth Tour, 1953–54, and other overseas visits by HM the Queen. Pres., Queen's English Soc., 1982–. *Publications:* Speaking from the Desert, 1944; Ten Seconds from Now, 1973; Queen Elizabeth the Queen Mother, 1973; Permission to Speak, 1976; Royal Heritage, 1977; Royalty Annual, 1952, 1953, 1954, 1955, 1956; The Country Life Book of Queen Elizabeth The Queen Mother, 1978, new edn 1983; The Country Life Book of the Royal Family, 1980, new edn 1983. *Recreation:* keeping quiet. *Address:* Holmwell, Hook Hill, Sanderstead, Surrey. *T:* 01–657 3476. *Club:* Royal Over-Seas League (Dep. Chm., 1986; Vice-Chm., 1985–86).

TALBOT, Sir Hilary Gwynne, Kt 1968; a Judge of the High Court of Justice, Queen's Bench Division, 1968–83; Judge of the Employment Appeals Tribunal, 1978–81; *b* 22 Jan. 1912; *s* of late Rev. Prebendary A. T. S. Talbot, RD, and Mrs Talbot; *m* 1963, Jean Whitworth (JP Wilts), *o d* of late Mr and Mrs Kenneth Fisher. *Educ:* Haileybury Coll.; Worcester Coll., Oxford. MA Oxon. Served War of 1939–45; Captain, RA. Called to Bar by Middle Temple Jan. 1935, Bencher, 1968. Dep. Chm., Northants QS, 1948–62; Chm., Derbyshire QS, 1958–63; Dep. Chm. Hants QS, 1964–71; Judge of County Courts, 1962–68; a Presiding Judge, Wales and Chester Circuit, 1970–74. Mem., Parole Bd, 1980–82. Dep. Chm., Boundary Commn for Wales, 1980–83. Formerly Dep. Chm., Agricultural Land Tribunals. *Recreations:* fishing, walking, bird-watching. *Address:* Old Chapel House, Little Ashley, Bradford on Avon, Wilts BA15 2PN.

TALBOT, Commandant Mary (Irene), CB; Director, Women's Royal Naval Service, 1973–76; *b* 17 Feb. 1922. *Educ:* Bristol Univ. BA Hons, Philosophy and Economics. Joined WRNS as a Naval recruiting asst, Nov. 1943; Officer training course, 1944, and apptd to HMS Eaglet, in Liverpool, as an Educn and Resettlement Officer; served on staffs of C-in-Cs: Mediterranean; the Nore; Portsmouth, 1945–61; First Officer, and apptd to staff of Dir Naval Educn Service, 1952; subseq. served HMS Condor, Dauntless and Raleigh; Chief Officer, and apptd Sen. WRNS Officer, the Nore, 1960; on staff of Dir Naval Manning, 1963–66, and then became Asst Dir, WRNS; Superintendent, and served on staff of C-in-C Naval Home Command, 1969; Supt in charge, WRNS training estabt, HMS Dauntless, near Reading, 1972–73. Hon. ADC, 1973–76. *Recreations:* usual spinster ones: bridge, gardening, racing. *Address:* Sonning Cottage, Pound Lane, Sonning-on-Thames. *T:* Sonning 3323; Flat 2, 35 Buckingham Gate, SW1. *T:* 01–834 2579.

TALBOT, Very Rev. Maurice John; Dean Emeritus of Limerick; *b* 29 March 1912; 2nd *s* of late Very Rev. Joseph Talbot, sometime Dean of Cashel; *m* 1942, Elisabeth Enid Westropp (*d* 1975); four *s*; 2nd, 1980, Reta Soames. *Educ:* St Columba's College; Trinity College, Dublin (MA). Curate of Nantenan, 1935; Rector of Rathkeale, 1942; Rector of Killarney, 1952; Dean of Limerick, 1954–71; Prebendary of Taney, St Patrick's Nat. Cathedral, Dublin; Bishop's Curate, Kilmallock Union of Parishes, 1971–73; Rector of Drumcliffe, 1980–84. *Publications:* Pictorial Guide to St Mary's Cathedral, Limerick, 1969; contrib. to North Munster Studies, 1967; The Monuments of St Mary's Cathedral, 1976. *Recreations:* tennis, shooting, fishing. *Address:* 4 Meadow Close, Caherdavin, Limerick, Ireland; The Rectory, Banagher, Co Offaly.

TALBOT, His Honour Richard Michael Arthur Chetwynd; a Circuit Judge, 1972–83; *b* 28 Sept. 1911; 3rd *s* of late Reverend Prebendary A. H. Talbot and late Mrs E. M. Talbot; unmarried. *Educ:* Harrow; Magdalene College, Cambridge (MA). Called to Bar by Middle Temple, 1936, Bencher, 1962. Mem. Bar Council, 1957–61. Dep. Chm., 1950–67, Chm., 1967–71, Shropshire QS; Recorder of Banbury, 1955–71, Hon. Recorder, 1972–. Served War of 1939–45, in Army; Major, King's Shropshire Light Infantry. *Address:* 7 St Leonard's Close, Bridgnorth, Salop WV16 4EJ. *T:* Bridgnorth 3619.

TALBOT, Thomas George, CB 1960; QC 1954; Counsel to the Chairman of Committees, House of Lords, 1953–77; *b* 21 Dec. 1904; *s* of late Rt Hon. Sir George John Talbot and late Gertrude Harriet, *d* of late Albemarle Cator, Woodbastwick Hall, Norfolk; *m* 1933, Hon. Cynthia Edith Guest; one *s* three *d. Educ:* Winchester; New Coll., Oxford. Called to Bar, Inner Temple, 1929; Bencher, 1960. RE (TA), 1938; Scots Guards, 1940–44 (Hon. Captain). Assistant, subsequently Deputy, Parliamentary Counsel to Treasury, 1944–53; Asst Counsel to Chm. of Cttees, H of L, 1977–82. *Address:* Falconhurst, Edenbridge, Kent. *T:* Cowden 641. *Club:* Brooks's.

TALBOYS, Rt. Hon. Brian Edward, Hon. AC 1982; CH 1981; PC 1977; Chairman: Board, Indosuez New Zealand Ltd, since 1982; Genestock New Zealand, since 1983; Ericsson Communications, since 1983; *b* Wanganui, 1921; *m*; two *s. Educ:* Wanganui Collegiate Sch.; Univ. of Manitoba; Victoria Univ., Wellington (BA). Served war of 1939–45, RNZAF. MP for Wallace, NZ, 1957–81; Dep. Leader, National Party, 1974–81; Parly Under-Sec. to Minister of Trade and Industry, 1960; Minister of Agriculture, 1962–69; Minister of Science, 1964–72; Minister of Education, 1969–72; Minister of Overseas Trade and Trade and Industry, 1972; Minister of Nat. Develt, 1975–77; Dep. Prime Minister and Minister of For. Affairs and Overseas Trade, 1975–81. Leader of a number of NZ delegns to overseas confs. Owns 500 acre sheep farm, Heddon Bush. Grand Cross 1st Class, Order of Merit (FRG), 1978. Hon. DSc Massey Univ., 1981; Hon. DLitt Chung-Ang Univ., Seoul, 1981. *Address:* 1 Hamilton Avenue, Winton, New Zealand.

TALINTYRE, Douglas George; Director of Finance and Resource Management and Principal Finance Officer, Department of Employment, since 1986; *b* 26 July 1932; *o s* of late Henry Matthew Talintyre and of Gladys Talintyre; *m* 1956, Maureen Diana Lyons; one *s* one *d. Educ:* Harrow County Grammar School; London School of Economics. BSc (Econ.) 1956; MSc (Industrial Relns and Personnel Management) 1983. Joined National Coal Board, 1956: Administrative Assistant, 1956–59; Marketing Officer, Durham Div., 1959–61; Head of Manpower Planning and Intelligence, HQ, 1961–62; Dep. Head of

Manpower, HQ, 1962–64; Head of Wages and Control, NW Div., 1964–66. Entered Civil Service, 1966: Principal, Naval Personnel (Pay) Div., MoD, 1966–69; Senior Industrial Relations Officer, CIR, 1969–71; Director of Industrial Relations, CIR, 1971–74; Asst Secretary, Training Services Agency, 1974–75; Counsellor (Labour), HM Embassy, Washington DC, 1975–77; Head of Policy and Planning, Manpower Services Commn, 1977–80; Department of Employment: Hd of Health and Safety Liaison, 1980–83; Asst Sec., Industrial Relations Div., 1983–86; Under Sec., 1986. Freeman, Co. of Cordwainers, Newcastle upon Tyne, 1952. *Address:* Woodwards, School Lane, Cookham Dean, Berks SL6 9PQ.

TALLACK, Sir Hugh M.; *see* Mackay-Tallack.

TALLBOYS, Richard Gilbert, CMG 1981; OBE 1974; FCA; FCIS; FASA (CPA); HM Diplomatic Service; Ambassador to Vietnam, since 1985; *b* 25 April 1931; *s* of late Harry Tallboys; *m* 1954, Margaret Evelyn, *d* of late Brig. H. W. Strutt, DSO, ED, Hobart; two *s* two *d*. *Educ:* Palmer's School. LLB (London), BCom (Tasmania). Lt-Comdr RANR. Merchant Navy apprentice, 1947–51; Third/Second Mate, Australian coast, 1952–55; accounting profession in Australia, 1955–62; Alderman, Hobart City Council, 1958–62; Australian Govt Trade Commissioner, Johannesburg, Singapore, Jakarta, 1962–68. HM Diplomatic Service, 1968; First Secretary i/c Brasilia, 1969; Head of Chancery, Phnom Penh, 1972 (Chargé d'Affaires *ai* 1972, 1973); FO, 1973; Counsellor Commercial, Seoul, 1976–80 (Chargé d'Affaires *ai* 1977, 1978, 1979); Consul-General, Houston, 1980–85. *Recreations:* squash, skiing, cautious adventuring. *Address:* c/o Foreign and Commonwealth Office, SW1. *Clubs:* Travellers', Naval; Tasmanian (Hobart).

TALLING, John Francis, DSc; FRS 1978; Senior Principal Scientific Officer, Freshwater Biological Association, since 1958; *b* 23 March 1929; *s* of Frank and Miriam Talling; *m* 1959, Ida Björnsson; one *s* one *d*. *Educ:* Sir William Turner's Sch., Coatham; Univ. of Leeds. BSc, PhD, DSc. Lecturer in Botany, Univ. of Khartoum, 1953–56; Visiting Research Fellow, Univ. of California, 1957; Plant Physiologist, Freshwater Biological Assoc., 1958–; Hon. Reader, Univ. of Lancaster, 1979–84. *Publications:* co-author, Water Analysis: some revised methods for limnologists, 1978; papers in various learned jls. *Recreation:* country walking. *Address:* Buhuka, Brow Crescent, Windermere, Cumbria LA23 2EZ. *T:* Windermere 2836.

TAMBLIN, Air Cdre Pamela Joy, CB 1980; retired; Director, Women's Royal Air Force, 1976–80; *b* 11 Jan. 1926; *d* of late Albert Laing and Olga Victoria Laing; *m* 1970, Douglas Victor Tamblin; one step *s* one step *d*. *Educ:* James Gillespie's High Sch., Edinburgh; Heaton High Sch., Newcastle upon Tyne; Durham Univ. (BA Hons). ATS, 1943–45. Essex County Council Planning Officer, 1949–51. Joined Royal Air Force, 1951; served Education Branch, 1951–55: RAF Locking; RAF Stanmore Park; RAF Wahn, Germany; Secretarial (now Administrative) Branch, 1955–76; Schools Liaison Recruiting, 1955–59; Accountant Officer, RAF St Mawgan and RAF Steamer Point, Aden, 1959–61; Staff College, 1962–63; MoD, Air Secretary's Dept, 1963–66; Sen. Trng Officer, RAF Spitalgate, 1966–68; Admin. Plans Officer, HQ Maintenance Comd, 1968–69; Command WRAF Admin. Officer, HQ Strike Comd, 1969–71; Station Comdr, RAF Spitalgate, 1971–74; Command Accountant, HQ Strike Comd, 1974–76. Chm., Cttee on Women in Nato Forces, 1977–79. Pres., E Cornwall Branch, RAFA, 1984–; Mem., S Western Area Council, RAFA, 1986–. FBIM 1977, CBIM 1979; FRSA 1979. *Recreations:* various charitable works, tapestry work, beachcombing. *Address:* Trecairne, 3 Plaidy Park Road, Looe, Cornwall. *Club:* Royal Air Force.

TAME, William Charles, CB 1963; Deputy Secretary, Ministry of Agriculture, Fisheries and Food, 1967–71; *b* 25 June 1909; *s* of late Charles Henry Tame, Wimbledon, Surrey; *m* 1935, Alice Margaret, *o d* of late G. B. Forrest, Witherslack, Cumbria; one *s* one *d*. *Educ:* King's College School, Wimbledon; Hertford College, Oxford. Entered Ministry of Agriculture as Assistant Principal, 1933. Chairman: International Whaling Commission, 1966–68; Fisheries R&D Bd, 1972–78. Member: Council, Royal Veterinary Coll., Univ. of London, 1972–80 (Vice-Chm., 1973–80); Governing Body, Animal Virus Res. Inst., 1972–76. *Recreation:* music. *Address:* Windrush, Walton Lane, Bosham, Chichester. *T:* Bosham 573217.

TAMMADGE, Alan Richard; Headmaster, Sevenoaks School, 1971–81; *b* 9 July 1921; *m* 1950, Rosemary Anne Broadribb; two *s* one *d*. *Educ:* Bromley County Sch.; Dulwich Coll.; Emmanuel Coll., Cambridge. BA (Maths) 1950; MA 1957. Royal Navy Special Entry, 1940; resigned, 1947 (Lt); Cambridge, 1947–50; Lectr, RMA Sandhurst, 1950–55; Asst Master, Dulwich College, 1956–58; Head of Mathematics Dept, Abingdon School, 1958–67; Master, Magdalen College School, Oxford, 1967–71. Pres., Mathematical Assoc., 1978–79. Chm, Battle Fest., 1984–. FIMA 1965. *Publications:* Complex Numbers, 1965; (jtly) School Mathematics Project Books 1–5, 1965–69; (jtly) General Education, 1969; Parents' Guide to School Mathematics, 1976; articles in Mathemat. Gazette, Mathematics Teacher (USA), Aspects of Education (Hull Univ.). *Recreations:* music, gardens. *Address:* 20 Claverham Way, Battle, East Sussex.

TAMUNO, Prof. Tekena Nitonye, PhD; Research Professor in History, Institute of African Studies, University of Ibadan, since 1979; Pro-Chancellor and Chairman of Council, Rivers State University of Science and Technology, Port-Harcourt, since 1981; *b* 28 Jan. 1932; *s* of late Chief Mark Tamuno Igbiri and Mrs Ransoline I. Tamuno; *m* 1963, Olu Grace Tamuno (*née* Esho); two *s* two *d*. *Educ:* University Col Ibadan; Birkbeck Coll., Univ. of London; Columbia Univ., New York City. BA (Hons) History, PhD History (London). Univ. of Ibadan: Professor of History, 1971; Head, Dept of History, 1972–75; Dean of Arts, 1973–75; Chairman, Cttee of Deans, 1974–75; Vice-Chancellor, 1975–79. Principal, University Coll., Ilorin, Oct-Nov. 1975. Chm., Bd of Dirs, New Nigerian Newspapers Ltd, 1984. Nat. Vice-Pres., Historical Soc. of Nigeria, 1974–78. JP Ibadan, 1976. *Publications:* Nigeria and Elective Representation, 1923–1947, 1966; The Police in Modern Nigeria, 1961–1965, 1970; The Evolution of the Nigerian State: The Southern Phase, 1898–1914, 1972; (ed, with Prof. J. F. A. Ajayi) The University of Ibadan, 1948–1973: A History of the First Twenty-Five Years, 1973; History and History-makers in Modern Nigeria, 1973; Herbert Macaulay, Nigerian Patriot, 1975; (ed with E. J. Alagoa) Eminent Nigerians of the Rivers State, 1980; (ed) Ibadan Voices: Ibadan University in Transition, 1981; Songs of an Egg-Head (poems), 1982; (ed) National Conference on Nigeria since Independence: addresses at the formal opening, 1983; (ed) Proceedings of the National Conference on Nigeria since Independence, Zaria, March 1983, Vol. III: The Civil War Years, 1984. *Recreations:* music, photography, swimming, horse-riding, gardening, domestic pets. *Address:* Institute of African Studies, University of Ibadan, Ibadan, Nigeria. *T:* (office) 400550, (home) 410540. *Club:* (Hon.) Senior Staff (University of Ibadan).

TAMWORTH, Viscount; Robert William Saswalo Shirley, FCA; Financial Controller and Company Secretary, Viking Property Group Ltd; *b* 29 Dec. 1952; *s* and *heir* of 13th Earl Ferrers, *qv*; *m* 1980, Susannah, *y d* of C. E. W. Sheepshanks, Arthington Hall, Yorks; one *s* one *d*. *Educ:* Ampleforth. Teaching in Kenya, under CMS's Youth Service Abroad Scheme, 1971–72. Articled to Whinney Murray & Co, CA, 1972–76; employed at Ernst & Whinney, 1976–82; BICC plc, 1982–86. Admitted to Inst. of Chartered Accountants of England and Wales, 1976. *Recreations:* the countryside and related activities. *Heir:* *s* Hon. William Robert Charles Shirley, *b* 10 Dec. 1984. *Address:* The Old Vicarage, Shirley, Derby DE6 3AZ. *T:* Ashbourne 60815. *Club:* Boodle's.

TANBURN, Jennifer Jephcott; research consultant, since 1984; *b* 6 Oct. 1929; *d* of late Harold Jephcott Tanburn and Elise Noel Tanburn (*née* Armour). *Educ:* St Joseph's Priory, Dorking; Settrington Sch., Hampstead; University Coll. of the South West, Exeter (BSc (Econ)). Market Research Dept, Unilever Ltd, 1951–52; Research and Information, Lintas Ltd, 1952–66, Head of Div., 1962–66, Head of Special Projects, 1966–74; British Airways Board, 1974–76; Head of Res. and Consumer Affairs, Booker McConnell Food Distbn Div., 1975–76 (a Dir, 1976–83). Member: Marketing Policy Cttee, 1977–80, and Potato Product Gp, 1980–82, Central Council for Agricl and Hortl Co-operation; Market Research Soc.; Marketing Gp of GB; Packaging Council, 1978–82; Chm., Consumers' Cttees for GB and England and Wales under Agricl Marketing Act of 1958, 1982–. *Publications:* Food, Women and Shops, 1968; People, Shops and the '70s, 1970; Superstores in the '70s, 1972; Retailing and the Competitive Challenge: a study of retail trends in the Common Market, Sweden and the USA, 1974; Food Distribution: its impact on marketing in the '80s, 1981; articles on retailing and marketing subjects. *Recreations:* travel, golf, gardening, dressmaking, television viewing, reading. *Address:* 8 Ellwood Rise, Vache Lane, Chalfont St Giles, Bucks HP8 4SU. *T:* Chalfont St Giles 5205. *Club:* Beaconsfield Golf.

TANCRED, Sir H. L.; *see* Lawson-Tancred.

TANDY, Jessica; actress, stage and screen; *b* London, 7 June 1909; *d* of Harry Tandy and Jessie Helen (*née* Horspool); *m* 1st, 1932, Jack Hawkins (marr. diss.); one *d*; 2nd, 1942, Hume Cronyn; one *s* one *d*. *Educ:* Dame Owen's Girls' Sch.; Ben Greet Acad. of Acting. Birmingham Repertory Theatre, 1928; first London appearance, 1929; first New York appearance, 1930; subsequently alternated between London and New York. *New York plays include:* The Matriarch, 1930; The Last Enemy, 1930; Time and the Conways, 1938; The White Steed, 1939; Geneva, 1940; Jupiter Laughs, 1940; Anne of England, 1941; Yesterday's Magic, 1942; A Streetcar Named Desire, 1947–49 (Antoinette Perry Award, 1948); Hilda Crane, 1950; The Fourposter, 1951–53 (Comœdia Matinee Club Bronze Medallion, 1952); Madame Will You Walk?, 1953; Face to Face, 1954; the Honeys, 1955; A Day by the Sea, 1955; The Man in the Dog Suit, 1957–58; Triple Play, 1959; Five Finger Exercise, 1959 (New York League's Delia Austria Medal, 1960); The Physicists, 1964; A Delicate Balance, 1966–67; Camino Real, 1970; Home, 1971; All Over, 1971; Promenade All (tour), 1972; Happy Days, Not I (Samuel Beckett Festival), 1972 (Drama Desk Award, 1973); Foxfire, 1982 (Antoinette Perry, Drama Desk, Outer Critics Circle awards, 1983); Tours: Not I, 1973; Many Faces of Love, 1974, 1975 and 1976; Noel Coward in Two Keys, 1974, 1975; The Gin Game, 1977 (US and USSR Tour, 1978–79; Sarah Siddons Award, Chicago and Los Angeles Critics' Award); The Glass Menagerie, 1983; Salonika, 1985; Foxfire, LA, 1985; The Petition, 1986. *London plays include:* The Rumour, 1929; Autumn Crocus, Lyric, 1931; Children in Uniform, Duchess, 1932; Hamlet, New, 1934; French without Tears, Criterion, 1936; Anthony and Anna, Whitehall, 1935; The Gin Game, Lyric, 1979. Open-Air Theatre, London, 1933 and 1939; Old Vic, 1937 and 1940, leading Shakespearian rôles, etc. Toured Canada, 1939; tour of US with husband, (poetry and prose readings), 1954; they also toured Summer Theatres (in plays), 1957. Opening Season of the Tyrone Guthrie Theatre Minneapolis, USA: Hamlet, Three Sisters, Death of A Salesman, 1963; The Way of the World, The Cherry Orchard, The Caucasian Chalk Circle, 1965; Foxfire, 1981. The Miser, Los Angeles, 1968; Heartbreak House, Shaw Festival, Niagara-on-the-Lake, Ontario, 1968; Tchin-Tchin, Chicago, 1969; Eve, The Way of the World and A Midsummer Night's Dream, Stratford, Ontario Festival, 1976; Long Day's Journey Into Night, London, Ontario, 1977; The Gin Game, Long Wharf Theatre, New Haven, Conn, 1977 (Drama Desk Award, 1977–78; Antoinette Perry Award, 1978); Long Day's Journey, Foxfire, Stratford, Ont., 1980; Rose, NYC, 1981. *Films include:* The Indiscretions of Eve, The Seventh Cross, The Valley of Decision, Dragonwyck, The Green Years, A Woman's Vengeance, Forever Amber, September Affair, Rommel-Desert Fox, A Light in the Forest, Adventures of a Young Man, The Birds, Butley; Honky Tonk Freeway, 1980; Still of the Night, 1981; Garp, 1981; Best Friends, 1982; The Bostonians, 1983; Cocoon, 1984. *Television:* all major American dramatic programs. Obie Award, 1972–73; Brandeis Theatre Arts Medal, 1978; Elected to Theatre Hall of Fame, 1979; Commonwealth Award for distinguished service in dramatic arts, 1983. Hon. LLD Univ. of Western Ontario, 1974; Hon. DHL Fordham Univ., 1985.

TANG, Sir Shiu-kin, Kt 1964; CBE 1957 (OBE 1949; MBE 1934); JP; Chairman and Managing Director of Kowloon Motor Bus Co. (1933) Ltd since its inception; *b* 21 Mar. 1901; *s* of late Tang Chi-Ngong, JP; *m* May Fung. *Educ:* Queen's Coll., Hong Kong; St Stephen's Coll., Hong Kong. Dir, Tung Wah Hosp., 1924 (Chm. Bd of Dirs, 1928); Life Mem., Court of Univ. of Hong Kong; Member: Urban Coun., 1938–41; St John Coun. for Hong Kong, St John Ambulance Assoc. and Bde; Grantham Scholarships Fund Cttee; Cttee of Aberdeen Tech. Sch.; Chinese Temples Cttee, 1934–64; Bd of Chinese Perm. Cemetery; Tung Wah Gp of Hosps Adv. Bd; Po Leung Kuk Perm. Bd of Dirs (Chm. 1932); Exec. Cttee, Nethersole, Alice and Ho Miu Ling Hosp.; Trustee, Street Sleepers' Shelter Soc.; Vice-Pres. and Trustee of Hong Kong Br., Brit. Red Cross Soc.; Vice-President: The Boy Scouts' Assoc.; S China Athletic Assoc.; Adviser: Hongkong Juvenile Care Centre; Chinese Chamber of Commerce. Hon. LLD, Hong Kong, 1961. JP Hong Kong, 1929. Certificate of Honour Class I, and Life Mem., British Red Cross Soc., 1967. KStJ 1962. *Address:* 5 Broom Road, Hong Kong.

TANGE, Sir Arthur (Harold), AC 1977; Kt 1959; CBE 1955 (OBE 1953); retired civil servant; *b* 18 August 1914; 2nd *s* of late Charles L. Tange, Solicitor, Gosford, New South Wales; *m* 1940, Marjorie Florence, 2nd *d* of late Professor Edward O. G. Shann; one *s* one *d*. *Educ:* Gosford High School; Western Australia University (BA; 1st Cl. Hons Economics). Joined Bank of NSW, 1931; Economist, Bank of NSW, 1938; Economic Research in Commonwealth Depts, Canberra, 1942–46. Entered Australian Diplomatic Service, 1946; First Secretary, Australian Mission to United Nations, 1946–48; Counsellor, United Nations Division, Canberra, 1948–50; Assistant Secretary, Department of External Affairs, Canberra, 1950–53; Minister at Australian Embassy, Washington, 1953–54; Secretary of Dept of External Affairs, Canberra, 1954–65; High Comr in India and Ambassador to Nepal, 1965–70; Sec., Dept of Defence, 1970–79. Represented Australia at many international diplomatic, economic and trade conferences, 1944–63. *Publication:* (jointly) Australia Foots the Bill, 1942. *Recreation:* stream fishing. *Address:* 32 La Perouse Street, Canberra, ACT 2603, Australia. *T:* 95–8879. *Club:* Commonwealth (Canberra).

TANKERVILLE, 10th Earl of, *cr* 1714; **Peter Grey Bennet;** Baron Ossulston, 1682; *b* 18 Oct. 1956; *s* of 9th Earl of Tankerville, and of Georgiana Lilian Maude, *d* of late Gilbert Wilson, MA, DD, PhD; *S* father, 1980. *Educ:* Oberlin Conservatory, Ohio (Bachelor of Music). Working as musician, San Francisco. *Heir:* *uncle* Rev. the Hon. George Arthur Grey Bennet [*b* 12 March 1925; *m* 1957, Hazel Glyddon, *d* of late E. W. G. Judson; two *s* one *d*]. *Address:* 139 Olympia Way, San Francisco, California 94131, USA. *T:* 415–826–6639.

TANLAW, Baron *cr* 1971 (Life Peer), of Tanlawhill, Dumfries; **Simon Brooke Mackay;** Chairman and Managing Director, Fandstan Ltd, since 1973; *b* 30 March 1934; *s* of 2nd Earl of Inchcape; *m* 1st, 1959, Joanna Susan, *d* of Major J. S. Hirsch; one *s* two *d* (and one *s* decd); 2nd, 1976, Rina Siew Yong Tan, *d* of late Tiong Cha Tan and Mrs Tan; one *s* one *d*. *Educ:* Eton College; Trinity College, Cambridge (MA 1966). Served as 2nd Lt XII Royal Lancers, Malaya. Inchcape Group of Companies, India and Far East, 1960–66; Managing Director, Inchcape & Co., 1967–71, Dir 1971–; Chm., Thwaites & Reed Ltd, 1971–74; Chm. and Man. Dir, Fandstan Group of private cos, 1973–. Chm., Building Cttee, Univ. of Buckingham (formerly UC at Buckingham), 1973–78, Mem. Council of Management 1973–. Hon. Fellow, 1981, DUniv 1983; Mem. Ct of Governors and External Relations Cttee, LSE, 1980–. Mem., Lord Chancellor's Inner London Adv. Cttee on Justices of the Peace, 1972–83. Contested (L) Galloway, by-election and gen. election, 1959, and gen. election, 1964. Mem., EC Cttee Sub-Cttee F (Energy, Transport Technology and Research), 1980–83; Chm., Parly Liaison Gp for Alternative Energy Strategies, 1981–83. Joint Treasurer, 1971–72, Dep. Chm., 1972, Scottish Liberal Party. Pres., Sarawak Assoc., 1973–75. Chm., Nat. Appeal, Elizabeth FitzRoy Homes for the mentally handicapped, 1985–. Inventor, Chronolog system of time measurement; Mem. Consultative Panel, Horological Inst. *Publication:* article, The Case for a British Astrophysical Master Clock. *Recreations:* normal. *Address:* Tanlawhill, Eskdalemuir, By Langholm, Dumfriesshire. *T:* Eskdalemuir 273; 31 Brompton Square, SW3. *Clubs:* White's, Oriental, Buck's.

TANNER, Dr Bernice Alture; FRCGP; General Practitioner in London W11 area, since 1948; *b* 23 Sept. 1917; *m* 1942, Prof. James M. Tanner, MD, FRCP, FRCPsych; one *d* (one *s* decd). *Educ:* Cornell Univ., USA; New York Univ.; McGill Univ., Canada; Medical Coll. of Pennsylvania, USA. BA 1939; MD 1943 (Med. Coll., Pa); FRCGP 1980. Convenor, Educational Cttee, London NW Faculty RCGP; Course organizer, St Charles Hosp. Vocational Trng Scheme for Gen. Practice; Mem., AHA Cttee paediatric care, London NW Area. Mem., Supplementary Benefits Commn, 1976–79. *Publication:* (ed) Language and Communication in General Practice, 1976. *Recreations:* music, postgraduate medical education. *Address:* 127 Oakwood Court, W14. *T:* 01–603 7881.

TANNER, David Williamson, DPhil; Under Secretary, Head of Science Branch, Department of Education and Science, since 1981; *b* 28 Dec. 1930; *s* of late Arthur Bertram Tanner, MBE and of Susan (*née* Williamson); *m* 1960, Glenis Mary (*née* Stringer); one *s* two *d*. *Educ:* Raynes Park County Grammar Sch.; University Coll., Oxford. MA, DPhil (Oxon). Univ. of Minnesota (post-doctoral research), USA, 1954–56; Dept of Scientific and Industrial Research (Fuel Research Station and Warren Spring Lab.), 1957–64; Dept of Educn and Science, 1964–. *Publications:* papers on physical chem. in Trans. Faraday Soc., Jl Applied Chem., Jl Heat and Mass Transfer, etc. *Recreations:* family, yoga. *Address:* 31 Clarence Road, Teddington, Middx TW11 0BN. *T:* 01–977 1762.

TANNER, Dr John Ian, CBE 1979; Founding Director: Royal Air Force Museum, since 1963; Battle of Britain Museum, since 1978; Cosford Aero-Space Museum, since 1978; Bomber Command Museum, since 1982; Hon. Archivist, since 1980, Senior Research Fellow, since 1982, Pembroke College, Oxford; *b* London, 2 Jan. 1927; *o s* of R. A. and I. D. M. Tanner; *m* 1953, April Rothery; one *d*. *Educ:* City of London Library Sch.; Universities of London, Nottingham (MA, PhD) and Oxford (MA). Reading Public Library, 1950; Archivist-Librarian, Kensington Library, 1950–51; Leighton House Art Gall. and Museum, 1951–53; Curator, Librarian and Tutor, RAF Coll., 1953–63; Hon. Sec., Old Cranwellian Assoc., 1956–64; Extra-mural Lectr in History of Art, Univ. of Nottingham, 1959–63. Walmsley Lectr, City Univ., 1980. Vis. Fellow, Wolfson Coll., Cambridge, 1983–. Mem., Adv. Council, Inst. of Heraldic and Genealogical Studies. Chm., Internat. Air Museum Cttee; Vice-President: Guild of Aviation Artists; Croydon Airport Museum Soc.; Trustee, Manchester Air and Space Museum; Mem. Founding Cttee, All England Lawn Tennis Museum; President: Anglo-American Ecumenical Assoc; USAF European Meml Foundn. FLA, FMA, FRHistS, FRAeS, FSA. Hon. DLitt City, 1982. Freeman, City of London, 1966; Liveryman: Worshipful Co. of Gold and Silver Wyre Drawers, 1966; Scriveners' Co., 1978. Freeman, Guild of Air Pilots and Air Navigators, 1979. Hon. Mem. Collegio Araldico of Rome, 1963; Tissandier Award, Fedn Aeronautique Internat., 1977. KStJ 1978 (OStJ 1964; St John Service Medal, 1985); KCSG 1977; KCSG, with Star, 1985; Cross of Merit, Order of Malta, 1978. Grand Comdr, OM Holy Sepulchre (Vatican), etc. *Publications:* (ed) List of Cranwell Graduates, 2nd edn, 1963; (jtly) Encyclopedic Dictionary of Heraldry, 1968; How to trace your Ancestors, 1971; Man in Flight (limited edn), 1973; The Royal Air Force Museum: one hundred years of aviation history, 1973; (with W. E. May and W. Y. Carman) Badges and Insignia of the British Armed Services, 1974; Charles I, 1974; Who's Famous in Your Family: a Reader's Digest guide to genealogy, 1975, 2nd edn 1979; Wings of the Eagle (exhibition catalogue), 1976; (ed) They Fell in the Battle, 1980 (limited edn, to commemorate 40th anniv. of Battle of Britain); Sir William Rothenstein: an RAF Museum exhibition catalogue, 1985; Editor, RAF Museum Air Publication series, 10 vols; General Editor: Museums and Libraries (Internat. Series); Studies in Air History; reviews and articles in professional and other jls. *Recreations:* cricket, opera, reading. *Address:* Flat One, 57 Drayton Gardens, SW10 9RU. *Clubs:* Athenæum, Beefsteak, Buck's, Reform, MCC, Royal Air Force.

TANNER, John W., CBE 1983; FRIBA, FRTPI; Director, United Nations Relief and Works Agency for Palestine Refugees, Jordan, 1971–83 (accorded rank of Ambassador to Hashemite Kingdom of Jordan, 1973); *b* 15 Nov. 1923; *s* of Walter George Tanner and Elizabeth Wilkes Tanner (*née* Humphreys); *m* 1948, Hazel Harford Harford-Jones; one *s* two *d*. *Educ:* Clifton Coll.; Liverpool Univ. Sch. of Architecture and Dept of Civic Design. MCD, BArch (Hons). Sen. Planning Officer, Nairobi, 1951; Architect, Nairobi, 1953; Hon. Sec., Kenya Chapter of Architects, 1954; UN Relief and Works Agency: Architect and Planning Officer, Beirut, 1955; Chief Techn. Div., 1957. Past Mem. Cttee, Fedn of Internat. Civil Servants Assoc., 1968–70. *Buildings:* vocational and teacher training centres, schools; low cost housing and health centres; E African Rugby Union HQ, Nairobi; training centres: Damascus, Syria; Siblin, Lebanon; Ramallah; Wadi Seer; Amman, Jordan. *Publications:* The Colour Problem in Liverpool: accommodation or assimilation, 1951; Building for the UNRWA/UNESCO Education and Training Programme, 1968. *Recreations:* formerly: Rugby football (Waterloo, Lancs, 1950; Kenya Harlequins, Kenya and E Africa); skiing, board sailing. *Address:* 70 Scenic Drive, Titirangi, Auckland, New Zealand. *Clubs:* Royal Automobile; Kandahar Ski.

TANNER, Meg; *see* Beresford, M.

TANSLEY, Sir Eric (Crawford), Kt 1953; CMG 1946; Chairman, Pacol, 1962–72; formerly Director: Bank of West Africa; Standard Bank Ltd; Standard & Chartered Banking Group Ltd; Gill & Duffus Ltd; *b* 25 May 1901; *o s* of William and Margaret Tansley; *m* 1931, Iris, *yr d* of Thomas Richards; one *s* one *d*. *Educ:* Mercers' Sch. Formerly: Mem., Colonial, now Commonwealth, Development Corporation, 1948–51, 1961–68; Chairman: London Cocoa Terminal Market Assoc., 1932; Cocoa Assoc. of London, 1936–37; Marketing Director, West African Produce Control Board (Colonial Office), 1940–47. Retired, 1961 as Managing Director, Ghana Cocoa Marketing Co. and Adviser, Nigerian Produce Marketing Co. *Address:* 11 Cadogan Square, SW1. *T:* 01–235 2752.

TANZANIA, Archbishop of, since 1984; **Most Rev. John Acland Ramadhani;** Bishop of Zanzibar and Tanga, since 1980; *b* 1932. *Educ:* Univ. of Birmingham (DipTh 1975); Univ. of Dar-es-Salaam (BA 1967); Queen's Coll., Birmingham. Deacon 1975, Birmingham; priest 1976, Dar-es-Salaam; Asst Chaplain, Queen's Coll., Birmingham, 1975–76; Warden, St Mark's Theol Coll., Dar-es-Salaam, 1976–80. *Address:* PO Box 35, Korogwe, Tanzania.

TAPP, Maj.-Gen. Sir Nigel (Prior Hanson), KBE 1960 (CBE 1954); CB 1956; DSO 1945; DL; *b* 11 June 1904; *y s* of late Lt-Col J. Hanson Tapp, DSO, and of late Mrs Hanson Tapp (*née* Molesworth), Duns, Berwickshire; *m* 1948, Dorothy (*d* 1978), *y d* of late Alexander Harvey. *Educ:* Cheltenham College; Royal Military Academy, Woolwich. 2nd Lieutenant RA, 1924; Sudan Defence Force, 1932–38; ADC to Governor-General, Sudan, 1935–36; Staff College, Camberley, 1939; GSO 3, 1 Corps BEF, 1940; GSO 2, War Office, 1940–41; GSO 1 Staff College, Camberley, 1941–42; CO, 7 Field Regt, RA, UK, Normandy, Belgium, and Holland, 1942–45; Comd RA 25 Div., SEAC, 1945; District Commander, Eritrea, 1946–47; Dep. Dir Land/Air Warfare, 1948; Dep. Dir RA, 1949; idc, 1950; Commander 1 Corps Royal Artillery, BAOR, 1951–53; General Officer Commanding 2 AA Group, 1954; Director of Military Training, War Office, 1955–57; GOC East Africa Command, 1957–60; retd 1961; Lieut-Governor and Sec., Royal Hosp., Chelsea, 1967–73. Pres., Assoc. of Service Newspapers, 1974–86. Col Comdt, Royal Regt of Artillery, 1963–68. Hon. Freeman, City of London, 1978. DL Greater London, 1973–82. *Recreations:* reading, fishing. *Address:* 9 Cadogan Square, SW1. *Club:* Army and Navy.

TAPPER-JONES, Sydney, LLB (London); Town Clerk and Clerk of the Peace, Cardiff, 1942–70; *b* 12 March 1904; *s* of David and Frances Caroline Mary Jones; *m* 1947, Florence Mary (Joan) Hellyer; one *d*. *Educ:* Pentre (Rhondda) Secondary School. Articled Cousins, Botsford & Co., Solicitors, Cardiff. LLB Lond. (External) (Hons), 1924. Solicitors' Final Exam. (Hons), 1925; Admitted Solicitor, 1925. Managing Clerk with Allen Pratt & Geldard (with whom were amalgamated Vachell & Co.), Solicitors, Cardiff, 1925–27; Cardiff Corporation: Conveyancing Solicitor, 1927–29, Prosecuting Solicitor, 1929–33; Deputy Town Clerk and Deputy Clerk of the Peace, 1933–42; Commissioner for Oaths. Member of Convocation, 1925. Member: S Wales Cancer Res. Council; Exec. Cttee, Cancer Inf. Centre, Cardiff; Rep. on Bd of Governors, Howell's Sch., Llandaff, 1960–85. Member, Order of St John, 1966. *Address:* Maes-y-Coed, 59 Heath Park Avenue, Cardiff. *T:* Cardiff 751306.

TAPSELL, Sir Peter (Hannay Bailey), Kt 1985; MP (C) East Lindsey (Lincs), since 1983 (Nottingham West, 1959–64; Horncastle, Lincs, 1966–83); *b* 1 Feb. 1930; *s* of late Eustace Tapsell; *m* 1st, 1963, Hon. Cecilia Hawke (marr. diss. 1971), 3rd *d* of 9th Baron Hawke; one *s* decd; 2nd, 1974, Mlle Gabrielle Jocelyne Mahieu, *e d* of late Jean Mahieu, Normandy, France. *Educ:* Tonbridge Sch.; Merton Coll., Oxford (1st Cl. Hons Mod. Hist., 1953; Hon. Postmaster, 1953; MA 1957). Nat. Service, Subaltern, Royal Sussex Regt, 1948–50 (Middle East). Librarian of Oxford Union, 1953; Rep. Oxford Union on debating tour of United States, 1954 (Trustee, Oxford Union, 1985–). Personal Asst to Prime Minister (Anthony Eden) during 1955 General Election Campaign. Conservative Research Department, 1954–57 (Social Services and Agriculture). Contested (C) Wednesbury, bye-election, Feb. 1957. Opposition front bench spokesman on Foreign and Commonwealth affairs, 1976–77, on Treasury and economic affairs, 1977–78. Member of London Stock Exchange, 1960–86; Partner, James Capel & Co. (Stockbrokers), 1960–. Member: Trilateral Commn; Council, Inst. for Fiscal Studies; Court Mem., Univ. of Hull. Chm., Coningsby Club, 1957–58. Jt Chm., British-Caribbean Assoc., 1963–64; Treas., Anglo-Chinese Parly Gp, 1970–74; Hon. Mem., Brunei Investment Adv. Bd, 1976–83; internat. investment advr to several Third World central banks and monetary authorities. Mem. Organising Cttee, Zaire River Expedn, 1974–75. Vice Pres., Tennyson Soc. Hon. Life Mem., 6th Sqdn RAF, 1971. Brunei Dato, 1971. *Recreations:* overseas travel, lawn tennis, walking, reading, opera. *Address:* Albany, Piccadilly, W1. *T:* 01–734 6641; Roughton Hall, near Woodhall Spa, Lincolnshire. *T:* Horncastle 2572. *Clubs:* Carlton, Hurlingham; Skegness Working Men's; Louth Conservative Working Men's.

TARBAT, Viscount; John Ruaridh Grant MacKenzie; MIExpE; explosives engineer; *b* 12 June 1948; *s* and *heir* of 4th Earl of Cromartie, *qv*; *m* 1973, Helen, *d* of John Murray; (one *s* decd). *Educ:* Rannoch School, Perthshire; Strathclyde University. Mem. Council, IExpE. *Publications:* Selected Climbs in Skye, 1982; articles in Classic Rock Climbs and Cold Climbs. *Recreations:* mountaineering, art, astronomy, geology. *Address:* Castle Leod, Strathpeffer, Ross-shire. *Clubs:* Army and Navy; Scottish Mountaineering.

TARN, Prof. John Nelson; Roscoe Professor of Architecture, University of Liverpool, since 1974; *b* 23 Nov. 1934; *s* of Percival Nelson Tarn and Mary I. Tarn (*née* Purvis); unmarried. *Educ:* Royal Grammar Sch., Newcastle upon Tyne; Univ. of Durham (BArch); Univ. of Cambridge (PhD). 1st cl. hons Dunelm; FRIBA, FRSA, FRHistS, FSA. Lectr in Architecture, Univ. of Sheffield, 1963–70; Prof. of Architecture, Univ. of Nottingham, 1970–73. Member: Professional Literature Cttee, RIBA, 1968–77; RIBA Educn Cttee, 1978– (Vice-Chm., 1983–; Chm., Moderators and Examiners Cttee, 1975–); Council, ARCUK, 1980– (Vice-Chm., 1986–; Vice-Chm., Bd of Educn, 1981–83, Chm., 1983–86); Technology Sub-Cttee, UGC, 1974–84; Ministerial nominee, Peak Park Jt Planning Bd, 1973–82, a rep. of Greater Manchester Council, PPJPB, 1982–86 (Vice-Chm. of Bd, 1981–86); Chm., Planning Control Cttee, 1979–; Mem., Design and Planning Cttee, Central Council for Care of Churches, 1981–; Mem., Diocesan Adv. Cttee for Derby, 1979–. *Publications:* Working Class Housing in Nineteenth Century Britain, 1971; The Peak District National Park: its architecture, 1971; Five Per Cent Philanthropy, 1974. *Recreation:* music. *Address:* 2 Ashmore Close, Barton Hey Drive, Caldy, Wirral, Merseyside L48 2JX. *T:* 051–625 9557. *Club:* Athenæum.

TARUA, Ilinome Frank, OBE 1980; Papua New Guinea High Commissioner in London, since 1983; concurrently Ambassador to German Federal Republic, Greece, Israel and Italy; *b* 22 Sept. 1942; *s* of Peni Frank Tarua and Anaiele Tarua; *m* 1970, Susan Christine (*née* Reeves); two *d*. *Educ:* Sydney University; University of Papua New Guinea (BL 1971). Legal Officer, Dept of Law, 1971–72; Legal Constitutional Advisor to Prime Minister, 1972–76; Dep. Perm. Head, Prime Minister's Dept, 1977–78; Secretary to Cabinet, 1978–79; High Commissioner to NZ, 1980; Ambassador to UN, 1980–81; Perm. Head, Dept of Public Service, 1982; Perm. Head, Prime Minister's Dept, 1982–83. *Recreations:* cricket, squash, golf. *Address:* Papua New Guinea High Commission, 14 Waterloo Place, SW1R 4AR. *T:* 01–930 0922. *Club:* Australia House Cricket.

TASKER, Antony Greaves, CBE 1966 (OBE 1945; MBE 1943); Assistant Secretary-General and Managing Director Commonwealth Fund for Technical Co-operation, Commonwealth Secretariat, 1974–78; *b* 27 March 1916; *o s* of late Captain R. G. Tasker, Worcestershire Regt, and Vera, OBE, *d* of Rev. T. M. Everett (she *m* 2nd, Harold Raymond, OBE, MC, who *d* 1975); *m* 1940, Elizabeth Gilmor, *e d* of late Maj. Harold Carter, TD. *Educ:* Bradfield Coll.; Christ Church, Oxford. Served War of 1939–45 (despatches twice); Western Desert, Sicily, Italy, NW Europe, SE Asia; Col GS(I). Org. Dir, Internat. Tea Market Expansion Bd, 1948–52; Dir Public Rel., Booker Gp of Cos in Guyana, 1954–62 (Chm., 1962–67); Dir, Overseas Develt Inst., 1968–74. Member, Br. Guiana Senate, 1961–64 (MLC, 1957–61); Governor: Inst. of Develt Studies, Sussex, 1968–78; Oversea Service Coll., 1968–78; Mem. Council, Overseas Develt Inst., 1975–78. Member: Econ. and Social Cttee, EEC, 1973–74; Exec. Cttee, British Council, 1970–74; Voluntary Cttee on Overseas Aid and Develt, 1968–74; British Volunteer Programme, 1968–74. US Bronze Star, 1944; Officer, US Legion of Merit, 1945. *Address:* 1A North Pallant, Chichester, W Sussex PO19 1TJ. *T:* Chichester 787513.

TASMANIA, Bishop of, since 1982; **Rt. Rev. Phillip Keith Newell;** *b* 30 Jan. 1930; *s* of Frank James and Ada Miriam Newell; *m* 1959, Merle Edith Callaghan; three *s. Educ:* Univ. of Melbourne; Trinity Coll., Melbourne. BSc 1953; DiplEd(Hons) 1954; ThL(Hons) 1959; BEd 1960; MEd 1969; MACE. Mathematics Master: Melbourne High School, 1954–56; University High School, 1957–58; Tutor in Physics, Secondary Teachers' Coll., 1957; Assistant Curate: All Saints, East St Kilda, Melbourne, 1960–61; S Andrew's, Brighton, Melbourne, 1962–63; Asst Priest, S James, King Street, Sydney, 1963–67; Chaplain, Sydney Hosp., 1963–67; Rector, Christ Church, St Lucia, Brisbane, 1967–82; Residentiary Canon, S John's Cathedral, Brisbane, 1973–82; Archdeacon of Lilley, Brisbane, 1976–82. KStJ 1981. *Recreations:* education; music (classical and light opera); singing; choral conducting; wine making; travel; cricket (spectator); tennis (occasional game). *Address:* GPO Box 748H, Hobart, Tasmania 7001. *T:* 236128. *Club:* Tasmanian (Hobart).

TATA, Dr Jamshed Rustom, FRS 1973; Head, Laboratory of Developmental Biochemistry, National Institute for Medical Research, since 1973; *b* 13 April 1930; *s* of Rustom and Gool Tata; *m* 1954, Renée Suzanne Zanetto; two *s* one *d. Educ:* Univ. of Bombay (BSc); Univ. of Paris, Sorbonne (D-ès-Sc). Post-doctoral Fellow, Sloan-Kettering Inst., New York, 1954–56; Beit Memorial Fellow, Nat. Inst. for Med. Research, 1956–60; Vis. Scientist, Wenner-Gren Inst., Stockholm, 1960–62; Mem., Scientific Staff, MRC, Nat. Inst. for Med. Research, 1962–. Visiting Prof.: King's Coll., London, 1968–69, and 1970–77; Univ. of California, Berkeley, 1969–70; Vis. Senior Scientist, Nat. Institutes of Health, USA, 1977; Fogarty Scholar, NIH, USA, 1983, 1986; Fellow, Indian Nat. Science Acad., 1978. Van Meter Award, 1954; Colworth Medal, 1966; Medal of Soc. for Endocrinology, 1973; Jubilee Medal, Indian Inst. of Sci., 1985. *Publications:* (jtly): The Thyroid Hormones, 1959; The Chemistry of Thyroid Diseases, 1960; papers in jls of: Biochemistry; Developmental Biology. *Address:* 15 Bittacy Park Avenue, Mill Hill, NW7 2HA. *T:* 01-346 6291.

TATE, Ellalice; *see* Hibbert, Eleanor.

TATE, Francis Herbert; Vice-Chairman, Tate & Lyle Ltd, 1962–78; *b* 3 April 1913; 2nd *s* of late Alfred Herbert Tate and late Elsie Tate (*née* Jelf Petit); *g g s* of Sir Henry Tate, Bt, founder of Henry Tate & Sons (now Tate & Lyle, Ltd) and donor of the Tate Gallery; *m* 1937, Esther, *d* of late Sir John Bromhead-Matthews, KC, JP, and late Lady Matthews, JP; one *s* two *d. Educ:* Private Tutor; Christ Church Oxford (BA 1934, MA 1963). Called to the Bar, Inner Temple, 1937. War Service, 1940–46, Royal Corps of Military Police (Lt-Col). Joined Tate & Lyle Ltd, 1946; Man. Dir, 1949. Chairman: British Sugar Bureau, 1966–78; Council, London Chamber of Commerce, 1962–64 (Vice-Pres., 1964–); Federation of Commonwealth Chambers of Commerce, 1964–69. Dir, Lloyds Bank, Southern Region, 1977–83; a Managing Trustee, Bustamente Foundn, 1979–. General Comr for Income Tax, Woking Div., 1980–. Dep. Chm., Royal Commonwealth Soc. for the Blind, 1984–; Chm. Central Council, Royal Commonwealth Soc., 1969–72; Mem. Council, Australia Soc., 1974–78. Governor, Commonwealth Inst., 1975–. Master of Mercers' Company, 1967–68. *Recreations:* golf (played for Oxford, 1934–35); motoring. *Address:* Little Wissett, Hook Heath, Woking, Surrey. *T:* Woking 60532. *Club:* Woking Golf (Pres., 1986–).

TATE, Lt-Col Sir Henry, 4th Bt, *cr* 1898; TD; DL; late Royal Welch Fusiliers TA; *b* 29 June 1902; *s* of Sir Ernest Tate, 3rd Bt and Mildred Mary, 2nd *d* of F. H. Gossage of Camp Hill, Woolton, Liverpool; *S* father, 1939; *m* 1927, Nairne (*d* 1984), *d* of late Saxon Gregson-Ellis, JP; two *s*. Sometime Lt Grenadier Guards. Joint Master Cottesmore Hounds, 1946–58. Councillor Rutland CC, 1958–69, 1970–74; High Sheriff of Rutland, 1949–50. Commanding 1st Bn Rutland Home Guard, 1954–57. DL, Co. of Rutland, 1964. *Heir: s* Henry Saxon Tate, *qv. Address:* Preston Lodge, Withcote, Oakham, Rutland, Leics LE15 8DP. *Club:* Buck's.

TATE, (Henry) Saxon; Chairman, London Commodity Exchange Co. Ltd, since 1985; Director, Tate & Lyle Ltd, since 1956; *b* 28 Nov. 1931; *s* and *heir* of Lt-Col Sir Henry Tate, Bt, *qv*; *m* 1st, 1953, Sheila Ann (marr. diss. 1975), *e d* of Duncan Robertson; four *s* (incl. twin *s*); 2nd, 1975, Virginia Sturm. *Educ:* Eton; Christ Church, Oxford. FBIM 1975. National Service, Life Guards (Lieut), 1949–50. Joined Tate & Lyle Ltd, 1952, Director, 1956; Pres. and Chief Executive Officer, Redpath Industries Ltd, Canada, 1965–72; Tate & Lyle Ltd: Chm., Executive Cttee, 1973–78; Man. Dir, 1978–80; Vice Chm., 1980–82. Chief Executive, Industrial Development Bd of NI, 1982–85. Fellow, Amer. Management Assoc., 1972. *Recreations:* various. *Address:* London Commodity Exchange (1986) Ltd, Commodity Quay, St Katherine's Dock, EC1. *Club:* Buck's.

TATE, Dr Jeffrey Philip; Principal Conductor: English Chamber Orchestra, since 1985; Royal Opera House, Covent Garden, since 1986; Chief Guest Conductor, Geneva Opera, since 1983; *b* 28 April 1943; *s* of Cyril Henry Tate and Ivy Ellen Naylor (*née* Evans). *Educ:* Farnham Grammar Sch.; Christ's Coll., Cambridge (MA; MB, BChir); St Thomas' Hosp., London. Trained as doctor of medicine, 1961–67; left medicine for London Opera Centre, 1969; joined Covent Garden Staff, 1970; assisted conductors who included Kempe, Krips, Solti, Davies, Kleiber, for performances and recordings; records made as harpsichordist, 1973–77; Assistant to Boulez for Bayreuth Ring, 1976–81; joined Cologne Opera as assistant to Sir John Pritchard, 1977; conducted Gothenberg Opera, Sweden, 1978–80; Metropolitan Opera début, USA, 1979; Covent Garden début, 1982; Salzburg Fest. début (world première Henze/Monteverdi), 1985. Appearances with major symph. orchs in Europe and Amer.; numerous recordings with English Chamber Orch. *Recreation:* church-crawling, with gastronomic interludes. *Address:* c/o Royal Opera House, Covent Garden, WC2E 7QA. *T:* 01–240 1200.

TATE, Phyllis (Margaret Duncan), (Mrs Alan Frank); composer (free-lance); *b* 6 April 1911; *d* of Duncan Tate, FRIBA, and Annie S. Holl; *m* 1935, Alan Frank; one *s* one *d. Educ:* Royal Academy of Music, London. FRAM 1964. *Works:* (some commissioned by the BBC, and for festivals, etc, and several commercially recorded): Saxophone Concerto, 1944; Nocturne for four voices, 1945; Sonata for clarinet and cello, 1947; Choral Scene from The Bacchae, 1953; The Lady of Shalott, for tenor and instruments, 1956; Air and Variations for violin, clarinet and piano, 1958; London Fields, 1958; Opera: The Lodger, 1960; Television Opera: Dark Pilgrimage, 1963; A Victorian Garland, for two voices and instruments, 1965; Gravestones, for Cleo Laine, 1966; Seven Lincolnshire Folk Songs, for chorus and instruments, 1966; A Secular Requiem, for chorus and orchestra, 1967; Christmas Ale, for soloist, chorus and orchestra, 1967; Apparitions, for tenor and instruments, 1968; Coastal Ballads, for baritone and instruments, 1969; Illustrations, for brass band, 1969; To Words by Joseph Beaumont, for women's chorus, 1970; Variegations, for solo viola, 1970; Serenade to Christmas, for mezzo-soprano, chorus and orchestra, 1972; Lyric Suite, for piano duet, Explorations around a Troubadour Song, for piano solo, 1973; The Rainbow and the Cuckoo, for oboe, violin, viola and cello, 1974; Sonatina Pastorale for harmonica and harpsichord, 1974; Songs of Sundrie Kindes, for tenor and lute, 1975; St Martha and the Dragon, for narrator, soloists, chorus and orchestra, 1976; Scenes from Kipling, for baritone and piano, 1976; A Seasonal Sequence, for viola and piano, 1977; Panorama, for strings, 1977; All the World's a Stage, 1977, Compassion, 1978, for chorus and organ (or orchestra); Three Pieces for Solo Clarinet, 1979; The Ballad of Reading Gaol, for baritone, organ and cello, 1980; Movements, for string quartet, 1980; Prelude Aria Interlude Finale, for clarinet and piano, 1981; and many small choral pieces, songs and works for young people, including: Street Sounds, The Story of Lieutenant Cockatoo; Twice in a Blue Moon; A Pride of Lions; Scarecrow; Solar. *Address:* 12 Heath Hurst Road, NW3. *T:* 01–435 0607.

TATE, Prof. Robert Brian, FBA 1980; Professor and Head of Department of Hispanic Studies, Nottingham University, 1958–83, retired; *b* 27 Dec. 1921; *s* of Robert and Jane Grantie Tate; *m* 1951, Beth Ida Lewis; one *s* one *d. Educ:* Royal Belfast Academical Instn; Queen's Univ. Belfast (MA, PhD). Asst Lectr, Manchester Univ., 1949–52; Lectr, QUB, 1952–56; Reader in Hispanic Studies, Nottingham Univ., 1956–58. Corresponding Fellow: Institut d'Estudis Catalans, Barcelona, 1964; Real Academia de Historia, Madrid, 1974; Real Academia de Buenas Letras de Barcelona, 1980. *Publications:* Joan Margarit i Pau, Cardinal Bishop of Gerona: a biographical study, 1954; Ensayos sobre la historiografia peninsular del siglo XV, 1970; The Medieval Kingdoms of the Iberian Peninsula, in P. E. Russell, Spain: a companion to Spanish studies, 1973; El Cardenal Joan Margarit, vida i obra, 1976; (ed with A. Yates) Actes del Colloqui internacional de llengua i literatura catalanes, 1976; (ed) Essays on Narrative Fiction in the Iberian Peninsula, 1982; *edited with introduction and notes:* Fernán Pérez de Guzmán, Generaciones y Semblanzas, 1965; Fernando del Pulgar, Claros varones de Castilla, 1971, rev. edn 1985; (with I. R. Macpherson) Don Juan Manuel, Libro de los estados, 1974, rev. edn 1987; Anon, Directorio de prïncipes, 1977; Alfonso de Palencia, Epistolario, 1983; contrib. articles in numerous learned jls. *Recreations:* architecture and the history of art, jazz. *Address:* 42 Main Street, Sutton Bonington, Loughborough, Leics. *T:* Kegworth 2559.

TATE, Saxon; *see* Tate, H. S.

TATHAM, David Everard; HM Diplomatic Service; Ambassador to Yemen Arab Republic, also accredited to Republic of Djibouti, since 1984; *b* 28 June 1939; *s* of Lt-Col Francis Everard Tatham and Eileen Mary Wilson; *m* 1963, Valerie Ann Mylechreest; three *s. Educ:* St Lawrence Coll., Ramsgate; Wadham Coll., Oxford (BA History). Entered HM Diplomatic Service, 1960; 3rd Sec., UK Mission to the UN, New York, 1962–63; Vice-Consul (Commercial), Milan, 1963–67; ME Centre for Arabic Studies, 1967–69; Jeddah, 1969–70; FCO, 1971–74; Muscat, 1974–77; Asst Head of ME Dept, FCO, 1977–80; Counsellor, Dublin, 1981–84. *Recreation:* walking uphill. *Address:* c/o Foreign and Commonwealth Office, SW1. *Club:* Athenæum.

TATHAM, Francis Hugh Currer; Editor of Whitaker's Almanack, 1950–81; *b* 29 May 1916; *s* of late Harold Lewis Tatham, Gravesend, Kent, and late Frances Eva (*née* Crook); *m* 1945, Nancy Margaret, *d* of John Robins, Newton Abbot; two *s. Educ:* Charterhouse; Christ Church, Oxford. Missioner, Shrewsbury School Mission, Liverpool, 1939–42; Sub-Warden, Mary Ward Settlement, 1942–45; Army Cadet Force, 1943–45; Editor, Church of England Newspaper, 1945–47. Vice-Pres., Harrow RFC. *Recreations:* watching cricket (formerly playing and umpiring); travel. *Address:* 27 Montacute Road, Lewes, East Sussex. *T:* Lewes 473585. *Clubs:* Lansdowne, MCC.

TATLOW, John Colin, PhD, DSc (Birmingham); CChem; FRSC; consultant; Professor of Organic Chemistry, University of Birmingham, 1959–82, now Emeritus; *b* 19 Jan. 1923; *s* of Thomas George and Florence Annie Tatlow, Cannock, Staffs; *m* 1946, Clarice Evelyn Mabel, *d* of Eric Millward and Mabel Evelyn Joiner, Sutton Coldfield; two *d. Educ:* Rugeley Grammar School, Staffs; University of Birmingham. Scientific Officer, Min. of Supply, 1946–48; University of Birmingham: Lectr in Chemistry, 1948–56; Sen. Lectr, 1956–57; Reader in Organic Chemistry, 1957–59; Head of Dept of Chemistry, 1974–81. Council of Chemical Society, 1957–60. Examiner, Royal Inst. of Chemistry, 1963–67. *Publications:* over 300 scientific papers on fluorine chemistry, mainly in Jl of Chem. Soc., Tetrahedron, Nature, and Jl of Fluorine Chem.; Editor, Jl of Fluorine Chemistry. *Address:* 30 Grassmoor Road, King's Norton, Birmingham B38 8BP. *T:* 021–458 1260.

TATTON BROWN, William Eden, CB 1965; ARIBA; retired architect; *b* 13 Oct. 1910; *m* 1936, Aileen Hope Johnston Sparrow; two *s* one *d* (and one *d* decd). *Educ:* Wellington Coll.; King's Coll., Cambridge (MA); Architectural Association School, London; School of Planning, London. Special Final Examination of Town Planning Institute. Chief Design Asst, Messrs Tecton, Architects, 1934–38; private practice, 1938–40; Finsbury Borough Council, 1940–41. Served in HM Forces, Major, Royal Engineers, 1941–46. Asst Regional Planning Officer, Min. of Town and Country Planning, 1946–48; Dep. County Architect, Herts CC, 1948–59; Chief Architect, Min. of Health, later Dept of Health and Social Security, 1959–71. Steuben-Corning Research Fellowship, Travelling Scholarship to USA, 1957. Guest Lectr, Internat. Hosp. Confs: Finland, 1966; Holland, 1967; Australia, 1967; Düsseldorf, 1969; Tunisia, 1969; Sweden, 1970; Canada, 1970; S Africa, 1971; WHO Commn to Madrid, 1968. Lecturer and broadcaster. *Publications:* (with Paul James) Hospitals: design and development, 1986; contributor to technical and national press. *Recreations:* building, water-skiing, oil painting. *Address:* 47 Lansdowne Road, W11 2LG. *T:* 01–727 4529.

TAUBE, Prof. Henry, PhD; Professor, Department of Chemistry, Stanford University, since 1962; *b* 30 Nov. 1915; *s* of Samuel and Albertina (Tiledetski) Taube; *m* 1952, Mary Alice Wesche; two *s* two *d. Educ:* Univ. of Saskatchewan (BS 1935, MS 1937); Univ. of California, Berkeley (PhD 1940). Instructor, Univ. of California, Berkeley, 1940–41; Instructor and Asst Prof., Cornell Univ., 1941–46; Asst Prof., Associate Prof., Prof., Univ. of Chicago, 1946–61; Chm., Dept. of Chemistry, Univ. of Chicago, 1956–59; Chm., Stanford Univ., 1972–74 and 1978–79. Hon. Mem., Canadian Soc. for Chemistry, 1986. Hon. LLD Saskatchewan, 1973; Hon. PhD Hebrew Univ. of Jerusalem, 1979; Hon. DSc: Chicago, 1983; Polytechnic Inst., NY, 1984; State Univ. of NY, 1985. Guggenheim Fellow, 1949, 1955. ACS Award for Nuclear Applications in Chemistry, 1955; ACS Award for Distinguished Service in the Advancement of Inorganic Chemistry, 1967; Willard Gibbs Medal, Chicago Section, ACS, 1971; Nat. Medal of Science, Washington DC, 1977; T. W. Richards Medal of the Northwestern Section, ACS, 1980; ACS Award in Inorganic Chemistry of the Monsanto Co., 1981; Nat. Acad. of Sciences Award in Chemical Sciences, 1983; Robert A. Welch Foundn Award in Chemistry, 1983; Nobel Prize for Chemistry, 1983; Priestly Medal, ACS, 1985; Dist. Achievement Award, Internat. Precious Metals Inst., 1986. *Publications:* numerous papers in scientific jls on the reactivity of coordination compounds. *Recreations:* gardening, collecting classical vocal records. *Address:* 441 Gerona Road, Stanford, Calif 94305, USA. *T:* (415) 328–2759.

TAUKALO, Sir (David) Dawea, Kt 1985; MBE 1970; Independence Medal, Solomon Islands, 1984; Doctor, retired 1975; *b* 24 Feb. 1920; *s* of J. Paiyom and H. Tevio; *m* 1951, Anne Kamamara; three *s* five *d* (and one *s* decd). *Educ:* Church School, The Solomons; Govt School, Fiji (Dip. in Medicine and Surgery; Cert. in Public Health). General practitioner, Central Hosp. sanitary and mosquito control inspection, Honiara Town, 1947; MO i/c Eastern District Hosp. and clinics, 1951; postgrad. course, Fiji, 1960; returned to Central Hosp., i/c medical patients; rural hosp., eastern Solomons, 1969, to advise Council and field med. workers that good health could not be achieved by building huge hosp. and employing numerous doctors, but by telling people to develop their lands and seas. Premier in Provincial Assembly until 1984. *Publication:* booklet on health of Solomon Islands. *Recreations:* soccer fan; farming, sailing. *Address:* Rocky Hill, Lata, Santa Cruz Temotu Province, Solomon Islands.

TAUNTON, Bishop Suffragan of, since 1986; **Rt. Rev. Nigel Simeon McCulloch;** *b* 17 Jan. 1942; *s* of late Pilot Officer Kenneth McCulloch, RAFVR, and of Audrey Muriel McCulloch; *m* 1974, Celia Hume Townshend, *d* of Canon H. L. H. Townshend; two *d*. *Educ:* Liverpool College; Selwyn Coll., Cambridge (Kitchener Schol., BA 1964, MA 1969); Cuddesdon Coll., Oxford. Ordained, 1966; Curate of Ellesmere Port, 1966–70; Chaplain of Christ's Coll., Cambridge, 1970–73; Director of Theological Studies, Christ's Coll., Cambridge, 1970–75; Diocesan Missioner for Norwich Diocese, 1973–78; Rector of St Thomas' and St Edmund's, Salisbury, 1978–86; Archdeacon of Sarum, 1979–86. *Recreations:* music, walking in the Lake District. *Address:* Sherford Farm House, Sherford, Taunton TA1 3RF. *T:* Taunton 88759.

TAUNTON, Archdeacon of; *see* Olyott, Ven. L. E.

TAUNTON, Doidge Estcourt, CB 1951; DSO and bar 1945; DL; Secretary, Northamptonshire TA and AFA, 1952–68; *b* 9 Nov. 1902; *s* of late J. G. C. Taunton, Launceston, Cornwall; *m* 1930, Rhona Caroline Wetherall (*d* 1951); one *s* and one *s* decd). *Educ:* Cheltenham College; RMC Sandhurst; 2nd Lt Northamptonshire Regt, 1923; Lt 1925; Capt. 1935, and Adjt TA, 1932–36; Major 1940; Lt-Col 1941; Col 1948; Temp. Brig. 1945–47 and 1948–52. Served NWF India, 1936–38 (Medal and 2 clasps); War of 1939–45, India and Burma, 1936–45; French Indo-China and Netherlands East Indies, 1945–46 (Medal and clasp); Comd Somaliland Area, 1948–50; Comd 2nd Inf. Brigade, 1950–51; retired pay, 1951. DL Northants, 1969. *Address:* Great Hayne, Duston, Northampton.

TAUSKY, Vilem, CBE 1981; FGSM 1968; Director of Opera, Guildhall School of Music, since 1966; Artistic Director, Phoenix Opera Co., since 1967; BBC Conductor since 1950; *b* 20 July 1910; *s* of Emil Tausky, MD, Prerov, Czechoslovakia, and Josefine Ascher, opera singer; *m* 1948, Margaret Helen Powell (*d* 1982). *Educ:* Univ. of Brno; Janáček Conservatoire, Brno; Meisterschule, Prague. Military Service in France and England, 1939–45. National Opera House, Brno, Czechoslovakia, 1929–39; Musical Director, Carl Rosa Opera, 1945–49. Guest Conductor: Royal Opera House, Covent Garden, 1951–; Sadler's Wells Opera, 1953–. Freeman, City of London, 1979. Czechoslovak Military Cross, 1944; Czechoslovak Order of Merit, 1945. *Publications:* Czechoslovak Christmas Carols, 1942; Oboe Concerto, 1957; Concertino for harmonica and orchestra, 1963; Divertimento for strings, 1966; Soho: Scherzo for orchestra, 1966; Concert Overture for Brass Band, 1969; Cakes and Ale: Overture for Brass Band, 1971; Ballad for Cello and Piano; From Our Village: orchestral suite, 1972; Sonata for Cello and Piano, 1976; Suite for Violin and Piano, 1979; String Quartet, 1981; (book) Vilem Tausky Tells his Story, 1979; Leoš Janáček, Leaves from his Life, 1982; contribs to: Tension in the Performance of Music, 1979; The Spectator, 1979. *Recreation:* country life. *Address:* 44 Haven Green Court, W5. *T:* 01–997 6512; Rose Cottage, Towersey, near Thame, Oxon. *T:* Thame 2192.

TAVAIQIA, Ratu Sir Josaia (Nasorowale), KBE 1986; JP; Minister of State for Forests, Fiji, since 1977; *b* 25 Dec. 1930; *s* of Ratu Josaia Tavaiqia and Adi Lusiana Ratu; *m* 1955, Adi Lady Merewalesi Naqei; three *d*. *Educ:* Queen Victoria Sch.; Natabua Indian Secondary Sch., Fiji (Sen. Cambridge Examination). Custom Officer, Custom Dept, Fiji, 1949–59; Hotel Manager, 1961–75. Pres., Rural Youth Council of Fiji. Traditional role as Tui (Chief) of Vuda, with tradit. title of Tui Vuda (Chief of Vuda). *Recreation:* Rugby management. *Address:* (office) Ministry of Forests, Box 2218, Suva, Fiji. *T:* 313439; (home) Viseisei, Vuda, Fiji. *T:* 61273. *Clubs:* Royal Commonwealth Society, Union.

TAVARÉ, Andrew Kenneth; Special Commissioner of Income Tax, since 1976; *b* 10 Jan. 1918; *s* of late L. A. Tavaré, Bromley, Kent; *m* 1950, June Elinor Attwood, Beckenham, Kent; three *s*. *Educ:* Chatham House School, Ramsgate; King's College, London University. LLB (London). Solicitor of the Supreme Court. Served War with 79th HAA Regt (Hertfordshire Yeomanry), RA, 1940–45; N Africa and Italy, rank of Captain. Admitted Solicitor, 1948; Solicitor's Office, Inland Revenue, 1953–; Assistant Solicitor, 1965–75. Consultant Editor of Sergeant on Stamp Duties, 4th edition 1963, to 8th edition 1982. *Publications:* (contrib.) Simon's Taxes, 2nd edn, 1965, and 3rd edn, 1970.

TAVENER, John; composer; Professor of Music at Trinity College of Music since 1969; *b* 28 Jan. 1944; *m* 1974, Victoria Marangopoulou. *Educ:* Highgate Sch.; Royal Academy of Music (LRAM). Hon. ARAM, Hon. FTCL. Russian Orthodox religion. *Publications:* compositions: Piano Concerto; Three Holy Sonnets (Donne); Cain and Abel (1st Prize, Monaco); Chamber Concerto; The Cappe-makers; Three Songs of T. S. Eliot; Grandma's Footsteps; In Memoriam Igor Stravinsky; Responsorium in memory of Annon Lee; The Whale; Introit for March 27th; Three Surrealist Songs; In Alium; Celtic Requiem; Ultimos Ritos; Thérèse (opera); A Gentle Spirit (opera); Kyklike Kinesis; Palin; Palintropos: Canticle of the Mother of God; Divine Liturgy of St John Chrysostom; The Immurement of Antigone; Lamentation, Last Prayer and Exaltation; Six Abbasid Songs; Greek Interlude; Akhmatova: Rékviem; Sappho: Lyrical Fragments; Prayer for the World; The Great Canon of St Andrew of Crete; Trisāgion; Risen!; Mandelion; The Lamb (a Christmas carol); Mandoodles; Towards the Son; 16 Haiku of Seferis; Ikon of Light; All-Night Vigil Service of the Orthodox Church. *Address:* c/o Chester Music, 7 Eagle Court, EC1M 5QD.

TAVERNE, Dick, QC 1965; Chairman, Public Policy Centre (formerly Social Science Research Trust), since 1984; *b* 18 Oct. 1928; *s* of Dr N. J. M. and Mrs L. V. Taverne; *m* 1955, Janice Hennessey; two *d*. *Educ:* Charterhouse School; Balliol College, Oxford (First in Greats). Oxford Union Debating tour of USA, 1951. Called to Bar, 1954. MP (Lab) Lincoln, March 1962–Oct. 1972, resigned; MP (Democratic Lab) Lincoln, March 1973–Sept. 1974; Parliamentary Under-Secretary of State, Home Office, 1966–68; Minister of State, Treasury, 1968–69; Financial Secretary to the Treasury, 1969–70. Chm., Public Expenditure (General) Sub-Cttee, 1971–72. Institute for Fiscal Studies: First Dir, 1970; Dir-Gen., 1979–81; Chm., 1981–82. Director: Equity and Law Life Assurance Co.; BOC Group; Stork Pumps Ltd. Mem., Internat. Ind. Review Body to review workings of European Commn, 1979. Mem. Nat. Cttee, SDP, 1981–; contested (SDP): Southwark,

Peckham, Oct. 1982; Dulwich, 1983. *Publication:* The Future of the Left: Lincoln and after, 1973. *Recreations:* running, sailing. *Address:* 60 Cambridge Street, SW1V 4QQ.

TAVISTOCK, Marquess of; Henry Robin Ian Russell, DL; a Director, Trafalgar House Ltd, since 1977; *b* 21 Jan. 1940; *s* and *heir* of 13th Duke of Bedford, *qv*; *m* 1961, Henrietta Joan, *d* of Henry F. Tiarks, *qv*; three *s*. *Educ:* Le Rosey, Switzerland; Harvard University. Partner, De Zoete and Bevan, 1970–82; Chairman: Cedar Investment Trust, 1977–82; TR Property Investment Trust, 1982–; TR Berkeley Develt Capital Management Ltd; Director: Touche, Remnant Holdings, 1977–; United Racecourses, 1977–; Berkeley Technology plc, 1985–. Chm. Trustees, Kennedy Memorial Trust, 1985–. Pres., Woburn Golf and Country Club. DL Beds, 1985. *Heir: s* Lord Howland, *qv*. *Address:* Woburn Abbey, Woburn, Bedfordshire MK43 0TP. *T:* Woburn 666. *Clubs:* White's; Jockey Club Rooms; The Brook (New York).

TAYLER, Harold Clive, QC 1979; **His Honour Judge Tayler;** a circuit Judge, since 1984; *b* 4 Nov. 1932; *m* 1959, Catherine Jane (*née* Thomas); two *s* one *d*. *Educ:* Solihull Sch.; Balliol Coll., Oxford. BCL and BA (Jurisprudence). Called to the Bar, Inner Temple, 1956; in practice, Birmingham, 1958–84, and London, 1979–84; a Recorder of the Crown Court, 1974–84; Midland and Oxford Circuit. *Address:* c/o Midland and Oxford Circuit Administrators' Office, 2 Newton Street, Birmingham B4 7LU.

TAYLOR; *see* Suenson-Taylor, family name of Baron Grantchester.

TAYLOR, family name of **Barons Ingrow, Taylor, Taylor of Blackburn, Taylor of Gryfe, Taylor of Hadfield** and **Taylor of Mansfield.**

TAYLOR, Baron *cr* 1958 (Life Peer), of Harlow; **Stephen James Lake Taylor,** MD, BSc, FRCP; FRCGP; Visiting Professor of Medicine, Memorial University of Newfoundland, since 1973; *b* 30 Dec. 1910; *s* of John Reginald Taylor, MInstCE, and Beatrice Violet Lake Taylor; *m* 1939, Dr May Doris Charity Clifford (*see* Lady Taylor); two *s* one *d*. *Educ:* Stowe Sch.; St Thomas's Hosp. Med. Sch., Univ. of London. BSc 1st cl. Hons; MB, BS (Hons Hygiene and Forensic Medicine); MD. FRCP 1960; FFOM RCP, 1979. Served War of 1939–45: Surg. Lt-Comdr (Neuro-psychiatric Specialist), RNVR; Dir of Home Intelligence and Wartime Social Survey, MOI, 1941–45. Formerly: Casualty Officer and HP, St Thomas' Hosp.; Grocers' Co. Research Scholar, Med. Unit, St Thomas' Hosp.; Sen. Resident Med. Officer, Royal Free Hosp.; HP, Bethlem Royal Hosp.; Asst Med. Officer, Maudsley Hosp. MP (Lab) Barnet Div. of Herts, 1945–50; PPS to Dep. Prime Minister and Lord President of Council, 1947–50; Under-Sec. of State for Commonwealth Relations and Colonies, 1964–65; resigned from Labour Party, 1981, to sit as a cross-bencher. Consultant in Occupational Health, Richard Costain Ltd, 1951–64 and 1966–67; Med. Dir, Harlow Industrial Health Service, 1955–64 and 1965–67; Pres. and Vice-Chancellor, Meml Univ. of Newfoundland, 1967–73. Visiting Research Fellow, Nuffield Provincial Hospitals Trust, 1953–55; Mem., Harlow New Town Develt Corp., 1950–64 and 1966–67. Former Chm., Labour Party Study Group on Higher Educn; Vice-Chm., British Film Inst.; former Member: N-W Metropolitan Regional Hosp. Bd; Health Adv. Cttee of Labour Party; Cohen Cttee on Gen. Practice, Beveridge Cttee on BBC; Mem., Bd of Governors, UCH. Lectures: Chadwick, RSH, 1963; Clarke, Univ. of Surrey, 1975; Lloyd Hughes, Liverpool, 1981. Hon. FRCPsych 1986. Hon. LLD: St Thomas Univ., NB, 1972; Meml Univ. of Newfoundland, 1986. *Publications:* Scurvy and Carditis, 1937; The Suburban Neurosis, 1938; Mental Illness as a Clue to Normality, 1940; The Psychopathic Tenth, 1941; The Study of Public Opinion, 1943; Battle for Health, 1944; The Psychopath in our Midst, 1949; Shadows in the Sun, 1949; Good General Practice, 1954; The Health Centres of Harlow, 1955; The Survey of Sickness, 1958; First Aid in the Factory, 1960; Mental Health and Environment, 1964; articles in Lancet, BMJ, World Medicine, etc. *Address:* Plas y Garth, Glyn Ceiriog, near Llangollen, Clwyd. *T:* Glyn Ceiriog 216.

TAYLOR, Lady, (Charity), MB, BS, MRCS, LRCP; retired as Assistant Director and Inspector of Prisons (Women), (1959–66); Member, BBC General Advisory Council, 1964–67; President, Newfoundland and Labrador Social Welfare Council, 1968–71; *b* Sept. 1914; *d* of W. George and Emma Clifford; *m* 1939, Stephen J. L. Taylor (*see* Lord Taylor); two *s* one *d*. *Educ:* The Grammar School, Huntingdon; London (Royal Free Hospital) School of Medicine for Women. HS Royal Free Hospital; HS Elizabeth Garrett Anderson Hospital; Assistant Medical Officer HM Prison, Holloway; Medical Officer, HM Prison Holloway; Governor, HM Prison, Holloway, 1945–59. *Recreations:* reading, conversation. *Address:* Plas y Garth, Glyn Ceiriog, near Llangollen, Clwyd.

TAYLOR OF BLACKBURN, Baron *cr* 1978 (Life Peer), of Blackburn in the County of Lancashire; **Thomas Taylor,** CBE 1974 (OBE 1969); JP; Consultant, Shorrock Security Systems Ltd, and other companies, since 1976; *b* 10 June 1929; *s* of James and Edith Gladys Taylor; *m* 1950, Kathleen Nurton; one *s*. *Educ:* Mill Hill Primary Sch.; Blakey Moor Elementary Sch. Mem., Blackburn Town Council, 1954–76 (Leader, chm. of cttees and rep. on various bodies); Treas., Blackburn Labour Party, 1964–76; former Chm., Blackburn Br., USDAW. Chm., Electricity Cons. Council for NW and Mem. Norweb Bd, 1977–80; Member: NW Econ. Planning Council; NW AHA (Chm. Brockhall HMC, 1972–74, Vice-Chm. Blackburn HMC, 1964–74); Council for Educational Technology in UK; Nat. Foundn for Educn Research in Eng. and Wales; Schools Council; Regional Rent Tribunal. Chairman: Govt Cttee of Enquiry into Management and Govt of Schools; Nat. Foundn for Visual Aids. Former Mem., Public Schools Commn; past Pres., Assoc. of Educn Cttees. Dir, Councils and Education Press. Univ. of Lancaster: Founder Mem. and Mem. Council; Rep. on Lancs CC Educn Cttee; author of Taylor Report on problems; Dep. Pro-Chancellor. Former Dep. Dir, Central Lancs Family and Community Project. JP Blackburn, 1960; former Chm., Juvenile Bench. Elder, URC; Pres., Free Church Council, 1962–63. Chm., Mill Hill Operatic Soc., 1953–63. *Address:* 34 Tower Road, Feniscliffe, Blackburn BB2 5LE. *T:* Blackburn 22808.

TAYLOR OF GRYFE, Baron *cr* 1968 (Life Peer), of Bridge of Weir; **Thomas Johnston Taylor;** DL; FRSE 1977; Chairman, Morgan Grenfell (Scotland) Ltd, since 1973; *b* 27 April 1912; *m* 1943, Isobel Wands; two *d*. *Educ:* Bellahouston Acad., Glasgow. Member: British Railways Bd, 1968–80 (Chm., Scottish Railways Board, 1971–80); Board of Scottish Television Ltd, 1968–82; Forestry Commn, 1963–76 (Chm., 1970–76). President, Scottish CWS, 1965–70; Mem., Scottish Economic Council, 1971–74. Director: Whiteaway Laidlaw & Co. Ltd, 1971–; Friends' Provident Life Office, 1972–82; Scottish Metropolitan Property Co. Ltd, 1972–; BR Property Bd, 1972–82; Mem., Internat. Adv. Council, Morgan Grenfell. Chm., Economic Forestry Group, 1976–81. Trustee, Dulverton Trust, 1980–; Chm., Isaac and Edith Wolfson Trust, 1972–. DL Renfrewshire, 1970. Hon. LLD Strathclyde, 1974. *Recreations:* theatre, golf, walking. *Address:* The Cottage, Auchenames, Kilbarchan, Renfrewshire PA10 2PM. *T:* Kilbarchan 2648. *Clubs:* Caledonian; New (Edinburgh); Royal and Ancient (St Andrews).

TAYLOR OF HADFIELD, Baron *cr* 1982 (Life Peer), of Hadfield in the County of Derbyshire; **Francis Taylor;** Kt 1974; Founder, 1921, and Life President and Executive Director, since 1979, Taylor Woodrow Group (Managing Director, 1935–79; Chairman, 1937–74); Director, Taylor Woodrow of Canada Ltd since 1953; *b* 7 Jan. 1905; *s* of late

Francis Taylor and late Sarah Ann Earnshaw; *m* 1st, 1929 (marr. diss.); two *d*; 2nd, 1956, Christine Enid Hughes; one *d*. Founded, 1921, Taylor Woodrow, Building, Civil & Mechanical Engineering Contractors, which became Public Company, in 1935. Member of Advisory Council to Minister of State, 1954–55; Chm. Export Group for Constructional Industries, 1954–55; President Provident Institution of Builders' Foremen and Clerks of Works, 1950; Dir, Freedom Federal Savings and Loan Assoc., Worcester, Mass, 1972–82. Director: BOAC, 1958–60; Monarch Investments Ltd, Canada, 1954–84. Vice-Pres., Aims, 1978–. Governor, Queenswood School for Girls, 1948–77. Hon. DSc Salford, 1973. Fellow, Chartered Inst. of Building, Hon. Fellow 1979. *Recreations:* tennis, swimming, riding. *Address:* 10 Park Street, W1Y 4DD. *Clubs:* Royal Automobile, Queen's, Hurlingham, All England.

TAYLOR OF MANSFIELD, Baron *cr* 1966 (Life Peer), of Mansfield; **Harry Bernard Taylor**, CBE 1966; *b* 18 Sept. 1895; *s* of Henry Taylor, Mansfield Woodhouse; *m* 1921, Clara (*d* 1983), *d* of John Ashley; one *s*. *Educ:* Council Schools. A Coal Miner. MP (Lab.) Mansfield Div. of Nottinghamshire, 1941–66; Parliamentary Private Secretary to Parliamentary Secretary, Ministry of Aircraft Production, 1942; to Minister of National Insurance, 1945; Parliamentary Secretary, Ministry of National Insurance, 1950–51. *Publication:* Uphill all the Way (autobiog.), 1973. *Address:* 47 Shakespeare Avenue, Mansfield Woodhouse, Nottinghamshire.

TAYLOR, Alan Broughton; barrister-at-law; a Recorder of the Crown Court (Midland and Oxford Circuit), since 1979; *b* 23 Jan. 1939; *yr s* of Valentine James Broughton Taylor and Gladys Maud Taylor; *m* 1964, Diana Hindmarsh; two *s*. *Educ:* Malvern Coll.; Geneva Univ.; Birmingham Univ. (LLB); Brasenose Coll., Oxford (BLitt, re-designated MLitt 1979). Called to the Bar, Gray's Inn, 1961; barrister on Oxford Circuit, subseq. Midland and Oxford Circuit, 1963–. *Publication:* (contrib.) A Practical Guide to the Care of the Injured, ed P. S. London, 1967. *Recreations:* Christian youth work, philately, walking. *Address:* 94 Augustus Road, Edgbaston, Birmingham B15 3LT. *T:* 021–454 8600.

TAYLOR, Alan John Percivale; historian and journalist; Hon. Fellow of Magdalen College, Oxford, 1976 and of Oriel College, Oxford, 1980; *b* Birkdale, Lancs, 25 March 1906; *o s* of Percy Lees and Constance Sumner Taylor; four *s* two *d*. *Educ:* Bootham School, York; Oriel Coll., Oxford. Formerly Lectr in Modern History, University of Manchester. Lecturer in International History, Oxford University, 1953–63; Tutor in Modern History, Magdalen College, 1938–63, Fellow, 1938–76. Lectures: Ford's, in English History, Oxford Univ., 1955–56; Leslie Stephen, Cambridge Univ., 1960–61; Creighton, London Univ., 1973; Andrew Lang, St Andrews Univ., 1974; Romanes, Oxford, 1981; Benjamin Meaker Vis. Prof. of History, Bristol Univ., 1976–78. Pres., City Music Soc. (London). FBA 1956–80. For. Hon. Mem., Amer. Acad. of Arts and Scis, 1985; Hon. Member: Yugoslav Acad. of Scis, 1985; Hungarian Acad. of Scis, 1986. Hon. DCL, New Brunswick, 1961; DUniv York, 1970; Hon. DLitt: Bristol, 1978; Warwick, 1981; Manchester, 1982. *Publications:* (many of them translated into other languages): The Italian Problem in European Diplomacy 1847–49, 1934; Germany's First Bid for Colonies 1884–85, 1938; The Habsburg Monarchy 1815–1918, 1941, rewritten 1948; The Course of German History, 1945; From Napoleon to Stalin, 1950; Rumours of Wars, 1952; The Struggle for Mastery in Europe, 1848–1918, 1954; Bismarck, 1955; Englishmen and Others, 1956; The Trouble Makers: Dissent over Foreign Policy, 1792–1939, 1957; The Russian Revolution of 1917, 1958 (script of first lectures ever given on television); The Origins of the Second World War, 1961; The First World War: an Illustrated History, 1963; Politics in Wartime and Other Essays, 1964; English History, 1914–1945, 1965; From Sarajevo to Potsdam, 1966; Europe: Grandeur and Decline, 1967; War by Timetable, 1969; Beaverbrook, 1972; The Second World War: an illustrated history, 1975; Essays in English History, 1976; The Last of Old Europe, 1976; The War Lords, 1977; The Russian War, 1978; How Wars Begin, 1979; Revolutions and Revolutionaries, 1980; Politicians, Socialism and Historians, 1980; A Personal History (autobiog.), 1983; An Old Man's Diary, 1984; How Wars End, 1985; (ed) Lloyd George: twelve essays, 1971; (ed) Lloyd George, a Diary by Frances Stevenson, 1971; (ed) Off the Record: political interviews 1933–43 by W. P. Crozier, 1973; (ed) My Darling Pussy: the letters of Lloyd George and Frances Stevenson, 1975. *Address:* 32 Twisden Road, NW5 1DN. *T:* 01–485 1507.

TAYLOR, Lt-Gen. Sir Allan (Macnab), KBE 1972; MC 1944; Deputy Commander-in-Chief, United Kingdom Land Forces, 1973–76, retired; *b* 26 March 1919; *s* of Alexander Lawrence Taylor and Winifred Ethel (*née* Nisbet); *m* 1945, Madeleine Turpin (marr. diss. 1963); two *d*. *Educ:* Fyling Hall School, Robin Hood's Bay. Joined TA, 1938; Troop Leader, 10th R Tank Regt, 1940; Squadron Leader, 7th R Tank Regt, 1942; 6th R Tank Regt, 1946; Staff College, 1948; GSO, 2, 56 London Armoured Div., 1949; Bde Major 20 Armoured Bde, 1952; Instructor, Staff College, 1954; Squadron Leader, 1st R Tank Regt, 1957; Second in Comd 5th RTR, 1959; Comdg Officer: 5th RTR, 1960 and 3rd, 1961; AA & QMG, 1st Div., 1962; Commandant, RAC Gunnery School, 1963; Comd Berlin Brigade, 1964; Imperial Defence College, 1967; Comdr, 1st Div., 1968; Commandant, Staff College, Camberley, 1969–72; GOC South East District, April-Dec. 1972. Chm., Cttee on Regular Officer Training, 1972–. Col Comdt, RTR, 1973–. *Recreation:* golf. *Address:* 4 Mill Close, Middle Assendon, Henley-on-Thames, Oxon.

TAYLOR, Sir Alvin B.; see Burton-Taylor.

TAYLOR, Andrew James, CBE 1965; Chairman, British Manufacturing and Research Co., Grantham, Lincs, 1968–73; *b* 1902; *s* of late Alfred George Ralph Meston Taylor, Broughty Ferry, Dundee; *m* 1925, Mary Ann Symmers, *d* of George Cowie, Aberdeen; one *s* one *d* (and two *s* decd). *Educ:* Robert Gordon's Coll., Aberdeen. Dir of Manufacture and Exec. Dir, Ford Motor Co. Ltd, 1962–65; Deputy Managing Director, 1965–67. *Recreations:* photography, fishing. *Address:* Flat 107, Queen's Court, Queen's Promenade, Ramsey, Isle of Man. *Club:* Royal Automobile.

TAYLOR, Mrs Ann; see Taylor, Mrs W. A.

TAYLOR, Arnold Joseph, CBE 1971; DLitt, MA; Docteur *hc* Caen; FBA 1972; FSA; Hon. Vice-President, Society of Antiquaries, since 1978 (Vice-President, 1963–64; Secretary, 1964–70; Director, 1970–75; President, 1975–78); *b* 24 July 1911; *y s* of late John George Taylor, Headmaster of Sir Walter St John's School, Battersea; *m* 1940, Patricia Katharine, *d* of late S. A. Guilbride, Victoria, BC; one *s* one *d*. *Educ:* Merchant Taylors' School; St John's College, Oxford (MA). Assistant master, Chard School, Somerset, 1934; Assistant Inspector of Ancient Monuments, HM Office of Works, 1935. Served War of 1939–45, Intelligence Officer, RAF, 1942–46. Inspector of Ancient Monuments for Wales, Min. of Works, 1946–54; Asst Chief Inspector, 1954–61; Chief Inspector of Ancient Monuments and Historic Buildings, MPBW, later DoE, 1961–72. Commissioner: Royal Commissions on Ancient and Historical Monuments (Wales and Monmouthshire), 1956–83; Historical Monuments (England), 1963–78; Mem., Ancient Monuments Board: for England, 1973–82; for Scotland, 1974–79; for Wales, 1974–82. Member: Cathedrals Advisory Cttee, 1964–80; Adv. Bd for Redundant Churches, 1973–82 (Chm., 1975–77); Westminster Abbey Architectural Adv. Panel, 1979; Vice-

Pres., English Place-Name Soc., 1986; Hon. Vice-President: Flintshire Hist. Soc., 1953; Royal Archaeol. Inst., 1968; Surrey Archaeol. Soc., 1979; President: Cambrian Archaeolog. Assoc., 1969; London and Mddx Archaeolog. Soc., 1971–74; Soc. for Medieval Archaeology, 1972–75; Friends of Lydiard Tregoze, 1983–86; Sir Walter St John's Old Boys' Assoc., 1969–70; Old Merchant Taylor's Soc., 1985–86. Mem., Sir Walter St John's Schools Trust, 1970. Reckitt Lectr, British Acad., 1977. Hon. Corres. Mem., Société Jersiaise, 1983. Hon. DLitt Wales, 1970. Docteur *hc* Caen, 1980. Silver Jubilee Medal, 1977. *Publications:* Records of the Barony and Honour of the Rape of Lewes, 1940; official guides to various historical monuments in care Ministry of Works (now DoE), 1939–80; chapter on Military Architecture, in vol. Medieval England, 1958; (part author) History of the King's Works, 1963; Four Great Castles, 1983; Studies in Castles and Castle-Building, 1986; contribs on medieval architectural history in Eng. Hist. Rev., Antiquaries Jl, Archaeologia Cambrensis, etc. *Recreations:* reading and using records, resisting iconoclasts. *Address:* Rose Cottage, Lincoln's Hill, Chiddingfold, Surrey. *T:* Wormley 2069. *Club:* Athenæum.

TAYLOR, Sir (Arthur) Godfrey, Kt 1980; Chairman, London Residuary Body, since 1985; *b* 3 Aug. 1925; *s* of Fred and Lucy Taylor; *m* 1945, Eileen Dorothy Daniel; one *s* three *d*. *Educ:* Stockport Secondary Sch. Sutton and Cheam Borough Council: Councillor, 1951–62; Alderman, 1962–65; London Bor. of Sutton: Alderman, 1964–78; Councillor, 1978–82; Hon. Freeman, 1978. Managing Trustee, Municipal Mutual Insurance Ltd, 1979–86; Chm., Southern Water Authority, 1981–85. Chm., Assoc. of Metropolitan Authorities, 1978–80. Chm., London Bor. Assoc., 1968–71. High Sheriff, Greater London, 1984. *Recreation:* golf. *Address:* 23 Somerhill Lodge, Somerhill Road, Hove, E Sussex BN3 1RU. *T:* Brighton 776161.

TAYLOR, Prof. Arthur John; Professor of Modern History, Leeds University, 1961–84, now Emeritus; University Archivist, Leeds, since 1984; *b* 29 Aug. 1919; *s* of Victor Henry and Mary Lydia Taylor, Manchester; *m* 1955, Elizabeth Ann Jeffries; one *s* two *d*. *Educ:* Manchester Grammar School; Manchester University. Assistant Lecturer in History, University Coll. London, 1948; Lecturer, 1950. Pro-Vice Chancellor, Leeds Univ., 1971–73. Chm., Jt Matriculation Bd, 1970–73. *Publications:* Laissez-faire and State Intervention in Nineteenth Century Britain, 1973; The Standard of Living in Britain in the Industrial Revolution, 1975; (with P. H. J. H. Gosden) Studies in the History of a University: Leeds 1874–1974, 1975; contrib. to books and learned journals. *Address:* Redgarth, Leeds Road, Collingham, Wetherby, West Yorks. *T:* Collingham Bridge 72930.

TAYLOR, Arthur Robert; Chairman, Arthur Taylor & Co., Inc., since 1977; Dean, Graduate School of Business, Fordham University, since 1985; Chairman, American Assembly at Columbia University, since 1978; *b* 6 July 1935; *s* of Arthur Earl Taylor and Marian Hilda Scott; three *d*. *Educ:* Brown Univ., USA (AB, MA). Asst Dir, Admissions, Brown Univ., June 1957–Dec. 1960; Vice-Pres./Dir, The First Boston Co., Jan. 1961–May 1970; Exec. Vice-Pres./Director, Internat. Paper Co., 1970–72; Pres., CBS Inc., 1972–76. Director: Travelers Corp.; Louisiana Land & Exploration Co.; Pitney Bowes; First Boston Corp.; Eastern Air Lines; Korn/Ferry Internat.; Diebold Computer Leasing Inc.; The Joffrey Ballet; Nomura Pacific Basin Fund, Inc. Hon. degrees: Dr Humane Letters: Simmons Coll., 1975; Rensselaer Polytechnic Inst., 1975; Dr of Humanities, Bucknell Univ., 1975. *Publication:* contrib. chapter to The Other Side of Profit, 1975. *Recreations:* sailing, tennis. *Address:* (office) 113 West 60th Street, New York, NY 10023, USA. *Clubs:* The Brook, Century (New York); Metropolitan (Washington); California (Los Angeles).

TAYLOR, Arthur Ronald, MBE (mil.) 1945; Chairman, Willis Faber plc, 1978–81; Vice-Chairman, Legal and General Group plc, 1984–86 (Director, 1982–86); *b* 13 June 1921; *yr s* of late Arthur Taylor and Kathleen Frances (*née* Constable Curtis); *m* 1949, Elizabeth Josephine Kiek; three *s*. *Educ:* Winchester Coll.; Trinity Coll., Oxford. Served Grenadier Guards, 1940–53 (despatches); sc; Bde Major 32nd Guards Bde. Laurence Philipps & Co. (Insurance) Ltd, 1953–58; Member of Lloyd's, 1955; Director, Willis, Faber and Dumas Ltd, 1959; Dep. Chm., Willis Faber Ltd, 1974. Vice-President: Corporation of Insurance Brokers, 1967–78; British Insurance Brokers Assoc., 1978–81. *Recreations:* golf, shooting. *Address:* Coutts & Co., 15 Lombard Street, EC3V 9AU.

TAYLOR, Arthur William Charles, CBE 1981; PhD; CChem, FRSC; Chairman, Heavy Organics (Petrochemical Division), Imperial Chemical Industries Ltd, 1972–75; *b* 4 Jan. 1913; *s* of Edward Charles Taylor and Alice (*née* Lucas); *m* 1936, Rosina Peggy (*née* Gardner); one *s* one *d*. *Educ:* Brighton Hove and Sussex Grammar Sch.; University Coll. London (BSc, PhD). FInstPet. Imperial Chemical Industries Ltd: Billingham Division: Research Chemist, 1935–45; Jt Research Manager, 1945–57; Plastics Division: Technical and Research Director, 1958–64; Heavy Organics (Petrochemical Division): Technical Dir, 1964–66; Dep. Chm., 1966–72. Chairman: British Ports Assoc., 1978–80; Tees and Hartlepool Port Authority, 1976–82 (Mem., 1974–83); Tees Pilotage Authority, 1978–83; Mem., Nat. Ports Council, 1978–80; Chm., NE Industrial Develt Bd, 1979–81. Chm. of Governors, Teesside Polytechnic, 1975–78. Fellow, University Coll. London, 1977; FRSA 1976. *Publications:* papers in Chemistry and Industry, particularly the Holroyd Meml Lecture, 1976. *Address:* 35 The Grove, Marton, Middlesbrough, Cleveland TS7 8AF. *T:* Middlesbrough 315639.

TAYLOR, Arthur Wood, CB 1953; *b* 23 June 1909; *s* of late Richard Wood and Ann Taylor; *m* 1936, Mary Beatrice Forster (*d* 1982); one *d*. *Educ:* Royal School, Wolverhampton; Wolverhampton Grammar School; Sidney Sussex College, Cambridge. Wrangler (Tyson Medal), 1930; joined HM Customs and Excise, 1931; Principal, 1936; Asst Secretary, 1943. Comr of Customs and Excise, 1949; Under-Secretary, HM Treasury, 1957–63; Comr of Customs and Excise, 1964–65, Dep. Chm., 1965–70. Chm., Horserace Totalisator Bd, 1970–72 (Dep. Chm., 1972–73). *Publications:* Amusements with Prizes: social implications, 1974 (report for Churches Council on Gambling); History of Beaconsfield, 1976. *Address:* 72 Wattleton Road, Beaconsfield, Bucks. *T:* Beaconsfield 2285. *Club:* Reform.

TAYLOR, Bernard David; Chief Executive, Glaxo Holdings plc, since 1986; *b* 17 Oct. 1935; *s* of Thomas Taylor and Winifred (*née* Smith); *m* 1959, Nadine Barbara; two *s* two *d*. *Educ:* Univ. of Wales, Bangor (BSc Zoology). Science Teacher, Coventry Educn Authority, 1958; Sales and Marketing, SK&F, 1960; Sales and Marketing Manager, Glaxo NZ, 1964; New Products Manager, Glaxo UK, 1967; Man. Dir, Glaxo Australia, 1972; Dir, Glaxo Holdings plc, and Man. Dir, Glaxo Pharmaceuticals UK, 1984. Councillor and Vice-Pres., Aust. Pharm. Manufrs' Assoc., 1974–79; Councillor, Victorian Coll. of Pharmacy, 1976–82; Chm., Wexham Hosp. Appeal Cttee, 1986–. *Address:* Clarges House, 6–12 Clarges Street, W1Y 8DH. *T:* 01–493 4060.

TAYLOR, Brian Hyde; Secretary General, Committee of Vice-Chancellors and Principals, since 1983; *b* 18 Aug. 1931; *s* of late Robert E. Taylor and late Ivy Taylor (*née* Wash), Woodford, Essex; *m* 1960, Audrey Anne Barnes; two *s*. *Educ:* Buckhurst Hill County High Sch.; SW Essex Technical Coll.; LSE (BSc (Econ)). Nat. Service, commnd RASC, 1954–56. Clerk, Corp. of Lloyd's, 1947–48; Personal Asst to Principal, Univ. of London, 1956–59; administrative posts, Univ. of London, 1959–66; Asst Sec., ACU (and Vice-

Chancellors Cttee), 1966; Exec. Sec., Cttee of Vice-Chancellors and Principals, 1973; Sec., Univ. Authorities Panel, 1980. *Recreations:* walking, travel, browsing in bookshops. *Address:* 29 Tavistock Square, WC1H 9EZ. *T:* 01–387 9231. *Club:* Athenæum.

TAYLOR, Brian William; Under Secretary, Department of Health and Social Security, since 1982; *b* 29 April 1933; *s* of late Alan Taylor and Betty Taylor; *m* 1959, Mary Evelyn Buckley; two *s* two *d*. *Educ:* Emanuel School. Entered Ministry of Nat. Insurance (later DHSS) as Exec. Officer, 1952; Higher Exec. Officer, 1963; Principal, 1968; Asst Sec., 1976. *Recreations:* music, theatre, literature, tennis. *Address:* 3 Box Ridge Avenue, Purley, Surrey. *T:* 01–668 1184. *Club:* Royal Commonwealth Society.

TAYLOR, Dr Charity; *see* Taylor, Lady.

TAYLOR, Prof. Charles Margrave, DPhil; FBA 1979; Professor of Political Science, McGill University, since 1982; *b* 5 Nov. 1931; *s* of Walter Margrave Taylor and Simone Beaubien; *m* 1956, Alba Romer; five *d*. *Educ:* McGill Univ. (BA History); Oxford Univ. (BA PPE, MA, DPhil). Fellow, All Souls Coll., Oxford, 1956–61; McGill University: Asst Prof., later Associate Prof., later Prof. of Polit. Science, Dept of Polit. Science, 1961–76; Prof. of Philosophy, Dept. of Philos., 1973–76; Chichele Prof. of Social and Political Theory, and Fellow of All Souls Coll., Oxford Univ., 1976–81; Mem., Sch. of Social Science, Inst. for Advanced Study, Princeton, 1981–82. Prof. asst, later Prof. agrégé, later Prof. titulaire, Ecole Normale Supérieure, 1962–64, Dept de Philos., 1963–71, Univ. de Montréal. Vis. Prof. in Philos., Princeton Univ., 1965; Mills Vis. Prof. in Philos., Univ. of Calif, Berkeley, 1974. For. Hon. Mem., Amer. Acad. of Arts and Scis, 1986. *Publications:* The Explanation of Behavior, 1964; Pattern of Politics, 1970; Hegel, 1975; Erklarung und Interpretation in den Wissenschaften vom Menschen, 1975; Social Theory as Practice, 1983; Philosophical Papers, 1985. *Recreations:* skiing, swimming. *Address:* 344 Metcalfe Avenue, Montréal, Canada.

TAYLOR, Sir Charles (Stuart), Kt 1954; TD; MA Cantab; DL; *b* 10 April 1910; *s* of Alfred George and Mary Taylor; *m* 1936, Constance Ada Shotter; three *s* one *d*. *Educ:* Epsom College; Trinity College, Cambridge (BA 1932); Hons Degree Law Tripos. Chm., Onyx Country Estates Co. Ltd, and other cos; formerly: Man. Dir, Unigate & Cow & Gate Ltd; Dir, Trust Houses Ltd; Chm., later Pres., Grosvenor House (Park Lane) Ltd. President, Residential Hotels Association of Great Britain, until 1948 and Vice-Chairman of Council of British Hotels and Restaurants Association until 1951; Mem. of Honour, Internat. Hotels Assoc. MP (C) Eastbourne, March 1935–Feb. 1974; Leader of Parly Delegns to Germany, Ethiopia, Mauritius; Mem., Parly Delegn to Romania. Joined TA 1937 (Royal Artillery), Capt., August 1939; DAAG and Temp. Major, Jan. 1941; attended Staff College, June 1941 (war course), graduated sc. Hon. Colonel. DL Sussex, 1948. Serving Brother, Order of St John. Master, Worshipful Co. of Bakers, 1980–81. Hon. Freeman, Co. Borough of Eastbourne, 1971. Hon. FHCIMA. Paduka Seri Laila Jasa (Dato), Brunei, 1971. *Recreations:* yachting (rep. Gt Britain *v* USA and Old World *v* New World in six-metre yacht races, 1955), shooting, fishing. *Address:* 4 Reeves House, Reeves Mews, W1. *T:* 01–499 3730. *Clubs:* 1900, Buck's, MCC; Royal Thames Yacht (Hon. Life Mem.); Ski Club of Great Britain (Hon. Life Mem.).

TAYLOR, Dr Daniel Brumhall Cochrane; JP; Vice-Chancellor, Victoria University of Wellington, New Zealand, 1968–82; Referee of the Small Claims Tribunal, Wellington, since 1985; *b* 13 May 1921; *s* of Daniel Brumhall Taylor, Coleraine, NI and Anna Martha Taylor (*née* Rice); *m* 1955, Elizabeth Page, Christchurch, NZ; one *s* one *d*. *Educ:* Coleraine Academical Instn, NI; Queen's Univ., Belfast. BSc (Mech. Engrg) 1942, BSc (Elec. Engrg) 1943, MSc 1946, PhD 1948, QUB; MA Cantab 1956; FIMechE 1968. Lecturer in Engineering: Liverpool Univ., 1948–50; Nottingham Univ., 1950–53; ICI Fellow, Cambridge Univ., 1953–56; Lectr in Mechanical Sciences, Cambridge Univ., 1956–68; Fellow of Peterhouse, 1958–68, Fellow Emeritus, 1968; Tutor of Peterhouse, 1958–65, Senior Tutor, 1965–68. Member: NZ/USA Educnl Foundn, 1970–; Council, Assoc. of Commonwealth Univs, 1974–77 (Chm., 1975–76); Chm., NZ Vice-Chancellors' Cttee, 1975–77. JP New Zealand, 1985. Hon. LLD Victoria Univ. of Wellington, 1983. *Publications:* numerous engrg and metallurgical papers. *Recreation:* golf. *Address:* PO Box 40895, Upper Hutt, New Zealand. *T:* Wellington 267904. *Clubs:* Athenæum; Leander (Henley-on-Thames); Wellington (NZ).

TAYLOR, David George Pendleton; Chief Executive, Falkland Islands Government and Executive Vice Chairman, FI Development Corporation, 1983–April 1987; *b* 5 July 1933; *s* of George James Pendleton Taylor and Dorothy May Taylor (*née* Williams). *Educ:* Clifton College; Clare College, Cambridge (MA). Nat. Service as Sub-Lieut (Special) RNVR, 1952–54; Admin. Officer, HMOCS Tanganyika, 1958–63; joined Booker McConnell, 1964; Chm. and Chief Exec., Bookers (Malaŵi) Ltd, 1976–77; Director: Consumer Buying Corp. of Zambia, 1978; National Drug Co., Zambia, 1978; Bookers (Zambia), 1978; Minvielle & Chastanet Ltd, St Lucia, 1979; United Rum Merchants Ltd, 1981; Estate Industries Ltd, Jamaica, 1981; seconded full time to Falkland Is Govt, Dec. 1983. *Recreations:* water colour painting, travel, rural France, pandas. *Address:* (until April 1987) The Secretariat, Stanley, Falkland Islands, South Atlantic. *T:* (office) Stanley 110; (home) Stanley 36; 53 Lillian Road, Barnes, SW13 9JF. *Clubs:* United Oxford & Cambridge Universities, Royal Commonwealth Society, MCC.

TAYLOR, Desmond S.; *see* Shawe-Taylor.

TAYLOR, Douglas Hugh Charles, PhD; Managing Director, Ricardo Consulting Engineers plc, since 1984; *b* 4 April 1938; *s* of Richard Hugh Taylor and Alice Mary Davies; *m* 1970, Janet Elizabeth Scott; two *d*. *Educ:* King Edward VI Grammar Sch., Lichfield; Loughborough University of Technology. PhD, BTech; CEng, FIMechE. Ruston & Hornsby/GEC Ruston Diesels, 1962–72, Chief Research Engineer, 1968; Ricardo Consulting Engineers, 1972–: Head of Large Engines, 1973; Dir, 1977. *Recreation:* campanology. *Address:* Ellington House, 20 Coombe Drove, Bramber, Steyning, Sussex BN4 3PW. *T:* Steyning 813566.

TAYLOR, Edward Macmillan, (Teddy); MP (C) Southend East, since March 1980; journalist, consultant and company director; *b* 18 April 1937; *s* of late Edward Taylor and of Minnie Hamilton Taylor; *m* 1970, Sheila Duncan; two *s* one *d*. *Educ:* Glasgow High School and University (MA (Hons) Econ. and Politics). Commercial Editorial Staff of Glasgow Herald, 1958–59; Industrial Relations Officer on Staff of Clyde Shipbuilders' Assoc., 1959–64. Director: Ansvar (Temperance) Insurance; Shepherds Foods; Adviser: Port of London Police Fedn; Joan Lawrence (Glasgow) Ltd. MP (C) Glasgow, Cathcart, 1964–79; Parly Under-Sec. of State, Scottish Office, 1970–71, resigned; Parly Under-Sec. of State, Scottish Office, 1974; Opposition spokesman on Trade, 1977, on Scotland affairs, 1977–79. Sec., Cons. Parly Party Home Affairs Cttee. *Publications:* (novel) Hearts of Stone, 1968; contributions to the press. *Address:* 12 Lynton Road, Thorpe Bay, Southend-on-Sea, Essex.

TAYLOR, Edward Plunket, CMG 1946; President: Lyford Cay Co. Ltd; Windfields Farm Ltd; Chairman: New Providence Development Co., Nassau; International Housing Ltd, Bermuda; Director, several companies; *b* Ottawa, Ontario, 29 January 1901; *s* of late Lieut-Colonel Plunket Bourchier Taylor and Florence Gertrude Magee; *m* 1927, Winifred Thornton, *d* of late Charles F. M. Duguid, Ottawa, Ontario; one *s* two *d*. *Educ:* Ashbury College; Ottawa Collegiate Institute, Ottawa; McGill University, Montreal (BSc in Mechanical Engineering, 1922). Director Brading Breweries Limited, 1923, also entered the investment house of McLeod, Young, Weir & Co., Limited, Ottawa, 1923, a Director 1929, resigned to become Pres. Canadian Breweries Ltd, 1930 (Chm. of Board, 1944). Mem. Bd of Governors: Trinity Coll. Sch.; Ashbury College. Wartime appointments held: Member, Executive Committee, Dept of Munitions and Supply, Ottawa, April 1940; Joint Director-General of Munitions Production, Nov. 1940; Executive Assistant to the Minister of Munitions and Supply, Feb. 1941; President War Supplies Limited, Washington, DC, April 1941; by Prime Minister Churchill appointed President and Vice-Chairman, British Supply Council in North America, Sept. 1941; Director-General British Ministry of Supply Mission, Feb. 1942; Canadian Deputy Member on the Combined Production and Resources Board, Nov. 1942; also Canadian Chairman, Joint War Aid Committee, US-Canada, Sept. 1943. Hon. Chairman: Jockey Club of Canada; Ontario Jockey Club; Mem., Jockey Club, NY. Member, Delta Upsilon Fraternity. Anglican. Hon. LLD McGill, 1977. *Recreation:* riding. *Address:* Lyford Cay, New Providence, Bahamas. *Clubs:* Buck's, Turf; Royal Yacht Squadron (Cowes); Toronto, York (Toronto); Rideau (Ottawa); Metropolitan (New York); Lyford Cay, East Hill (Nassau).

TAYLOR, Prof. Edwin William, FRS 1978; Professor of Molecular Genetics and Cell Biology, University of Chicago, since 1984 (Professor, Department of Biophysics, since 1975; Professor and Chairman, Department of Biology, 1979); *b* Toronto, 8 June 1929; *s* of William Taylor and Jean Taylor (*née* Christie); *m* 1956, Jean Heather Logan; two *s* one *d*. *Educ:* Univ. of Toronto (BA 1952); McMaster Univ. (MSc 1955); Univ. of Chicago (PhD 1957). Asst Prof., 1959–63, Associate Prof., 1963–67, Prof., 1967–72, Univ. of Chicago; Prof. of Biology, King's College and MRC Unit, London, 1972–74; Associate Dean, Div. of Biol Sci and Medicine, Chicago Univ., 1977–79. Rockefeller Foundn Fellow, 1957–58; Nat. Insts of Health Fellow, 1958–59, cons. to NIH, 1970–72, 1976–80. Member: Amer. Biochem. Soc.; Biophysical Soc. *Address:* Cummings Life Sciences Center, University of Chicago, 920 East 58th Street, Chicago, Ill 60637, USA. *T:* (312) 962–1660; 5634 South Harper Avenue, Chicago, Ill 60637, USA. *T:* (312) 955–2441.

TAYLOR, Elizabeth; film actress; *b* London, 27 Feb. 1932; *d* of Francis Taylor and Sara (*née* Sothern); *m* 1st, 1950, Conrad Nicholas Hilton, Jr (marr. diss.; he *d* 1969); 2nd, 1952, Michael Wilding, *qv* (marr. diss.); two *s*; 3rd, 1957, Mike Todd (*d* 1958); one *d*; 4th, 1959, Eddie Fisher (marr. diss.); 5th, 1964, Richard Burton, CBE (*d* 1984) (marr. diss.; remarried 1975; marr. diss. 1976); 7th, 1976, Senator John Warner (marr. diss. 1982). *Educ:* Byron House, Hampstead; Hawthorne School, Beverly Hills; Metro-Goldwyn-Mayer School; University High School, Hollywood. *Films include:* Lassie Come Home, 1942; National Velvet, 1944; Courage of Lassie, 1946; Little Women, 1948; The Conspirator, 1949; Father of the Bride, 1950; A Place in the Sun, 1950; Ivanhoe, 1951; Beau Brummel, 1954; Giant, 1956; Raintree County, 1957; Suddenly Last Summer, 1959; Butterfield 8 (Academy Award for Best Actress), 1960; Cleopatra, 1963; the VIPs, 1963; The Sandpiper, 1965; Who's Afraid of Virginia Woolf?, 1966; The Taming of the Shrew, 1967; Boom, 1968; The Comedians, 1968; Reflections in a Golden Eye, 1968; Secret Ceremony, 1968; The Only Game in Town, 1970; Under Milk Wood, 1972; Zee and Co., 1972; Hammersmith is Out, 1972; Night Watch, 1973; Blue Bird, 1975; A Little Night Music, 1976; The Mirror Cracked, 1980; Winter Kills, 1985. Stage debut as Regina in The Little Foxes, NY, 1981, London stage debut, Victoria Palace, 1982; Private Lives, NY, 1983. *Publication:* Elizabeth Taylor, 1966. *Address:* c/o Major D. Neville-Willing, 85 Kinnerton Street, Belgravia, SW1. *T:* 01–235 4640.

TAYLOR, Eric; a Recorder of the Crown Court, since 1978; *b* 22 Jan. 1931; *s* of Sydney Taylor and Sarah Helen (*née* Lea); *m* 1958, Margaret Jessie Taylor, *qv*. *Educ:* Wigan Grammar Sch.; Manchester Univ. (LLB 1952; Dauntesey Sen. Legal Scholar; LLM 1954). Admitted solicitor, 1955. Partner, Temperley Taylor & Wilkinson, Middleton, Manchester, 1957–. Part-time Lectr in Law, Manchester Univ., 1958–80, Hon. Special Lectr in Law, 1980–. Examr (Old) Law Soc. Final Exams, 1968–81, Chief Examr (New) Law Soc. Final Exams, 1978–83. Pres., Oldham Law Assoc., 1970–72. Chairman: Manchester Young Solicitors' Gp, 1963; Manchester Nat. Insurance Appeal Tribunal, 1967–73. Member: Council, Law Soc., 1972– (Chm., Educn and Trng Cttee, 1980–83; Chm., Criminal Law Council, 1984–); CNAA Legal Studies Bd, 1975–84; Lord Chancellor's Adv. Cttee on Trng of Magistrates, 1974–79. Governor, Coll. of Law, 1984–. *Publications:* Modern Conveyancing Precedents, 1964, 2nd edn, 1986; Modern Wills Precedents, 1969, 2nd edn, 1986; contrib. legal jls. *Recreations:* riding, squash, chess. *Address:* 10 Mercers Road, Heywood, Lancs OL10 2NP. *T:* Heywood 66630. *Club:* Farmers'.

TAYLOR, Eric Scollick, PhD; Presiding Bishop, Liberal Catholic Church, since 1984; Clerk of Committee Records, House of Commons, 1975–83; *b* 16 April 1918; *s* of late Percy Scollick Taylor and Jessie Devlin. *Educ:* Durham Univ. (MA); Edinburgh Univ. (PhD 1942). Asst Clerk, House of Commons, 1942; Dep. Principal Clerk, 1962; Principal Clerk, 1972. Clerk to: Cttee of Privileges, 1949–57; Estimates Cttee, 1957–64; Cttee of Public Accounts, 1964–68; Clerk of the Journals, 1972–75. Ordained priest, Liberal Catholic Church, 1943; consecrated Bishop, 1977; Regionary Bishop, Great Britain and Ireland, 1985. *Publications:* The House of Commons at Work, 1951, 9th rev. edn 1979; The Liberal Catholic Church—what is it?, 1966, 2nd edn 1979 (also foreign trans); The Houses of Parliament, 1976; contribs to Times Lit. Supp., etc. *Recreations:* walking, listening to music, preaching to the converted, worship. *Address:* 113 Beaufort Street, SW3 6BA. *T:* 01–351 1765; 71 Woodbine Road, Gosforth, Newcastle upon Tyne NE3 1DE. *T:* Newcastle upon Tyne 857040.

TAYLOR, Eric W., RE 1948 (ARE 1935); ARCA 1934; ASIA (Ed) 1965; printmaker, painter and sculptor; *b* 6 Aug. 1909; *s* of Thomas John and Ethel Annie Taylor; *m* 1939, Alfreda Marjorie Hurren; one *s* one *d*. *Educ:* William Ellis School, Hampstead; Royal College of Art, South Kensington. Worked for 3 years in London Studio; then as a free-lance illustrator; won British Inst. Scholarship, 1932; runner-up in Prix de Rome, 1934, while at Royal College of Art. Exhibited: Royal Academy; Royal Scottish Academy; Doncaster Art Gallery; New York; Brooklyn; Chicago; London Group; New English Art Club. Pictures in permanent Collections of Stockholm Art Gallery, Art Inst. of Chicago, Washington Art Gallery, War Museum, London, V&A and British Museum Print Rooms. Logan Prize for best Etching in International Exhibition of Etching and Engraving at Art Institute of Chicago, 1937. Selected by British Council to exhibit in Scandinavian Exhibition, 1940, S America, 1942–44, Spain and Portugal, 1942–44, Turkey, 1943–45, Iceland, 1943, Mexico, 1943–45, China, 1945, Czechoslovakia, 1948, and Rotterdam, 1948. Associate Chicago Society of Etchers, 1937. War pictures bought by National Gallery Advisory Committee for Imperial War Museum, 1945. Volunteered for RA, Nov. 1939. Instructor at Northern Command Camouflage School, 1941–43; Royal Engineers, France and Germany, 1943–45; Normandy Landing, Battle of Caen, crossings of Rhine and Maas. instructing for Educational Corps Germany, 1946; Art Instructor Camberwell School of Art, 1936–39; Willesden School of Art, 1936–49;

Central School of Art, 1948–49; Examiner: Bristol Univ., 1948–51; Durham Univ., 1971–74; Min. of Education NDD Pictorial Subjects, 1957–59. Designer and Supervisor of Lubeck School of Art for the Services, 1946. Head of the Design School, Leeds Coll. of Art, 1949–56, Principal, 1956–69, Organiser and Administrator of revolutionary Leeds Basic Course which played considerable part in changing whole direction of British art education; Asst Dir, Leeds Polytechnic, 1969–71. Leverhulme Research Awards, 1958–59, visiting Colleges of Art in Austria, Germany, Holland, Denmark and Italy. Study of Mosaics, Italy, 1965. Representative Exhibitions: Wakefield Art Gall., 1960; Goosewell Gall., Menston, 1972, 1973, 1976; Middlesbrough Art Gall., 1972; Northern Artists Gall., Harrogate, 1977; Linton Ct Gall., Settle, 1983. British Representative Speaker, International Design Conference, Karachi, 1962. Print selected by Royal Soc. of Painter Etchers for Presentation to Print Collections Club, 1947. Mem. of Senefelder Club, 1947. Picture purchased by British Council, 1948. *Publications:* etching published in Fine Prints of the Year, 1935, 1936, 1937, and in 1939 and 1940 issues of Print Collectors Quarterly. *Address:* Gordale, 13 Tredgold Avenue, Bramhope, near Leeds, W Yorks.

TAYLOR, Ernest Richard; Headmaster of Wolverhampton Grammar School, 1956–April 1973; *b* Oldham, 9 Aug. 1910; *e s* of late Louis Whitfield Taylor and Annie Taylor; *m* 1936, Muriel Hardill; twin *s. Educ:* Hulme Grammar School, Oldham; Trinity College, Cambridge. Hist. Tripos, Class I, 1931; Sen. Schol. and Earl of Derby Research Student (Trinity), 1931–32; Thirlwall and Gladstone Prizes, 1933; MA 1935. Asst Master, Culford School, 1932–36; Moseley Gram. Sch., Birmingham, 1936–39; Manchester Gram. Sch., 1939–47. War Service in RA and AEC, 1940–46. Headmaster of Quarry Bank High School, Liverpool, 1947–56; Member, Schools Council for Curriculum and Examinations (formerly Secondary Schools Examinations Council), 1962–84. Walter Hines Page Scholar, HMC, 1964. Pres. Incorporated Assoc. of Head Masters, 1965; Chm. Central Exec., Jt Four Secondary Assocs, 1970–72. Member: President's Council of Methodist Church, 1976–79; Churches' Council for Covenanting, 1978–82. Hon. Life Mem., Secondary Heads Assoc., 1979. *Publications:* Methodism and Politics, (1791–1851), 1935; Padre Brown of Gibraltar, 1955; Religious Education of pupils from 16 to 19 years, 1962. *Recreation:* golf. *Address:* Highcliff, Whitcliffe, Ludlow, Shropshire. *T:* Ludlow 2093.

TAYLOR, Frank, CBE 1969; QFSM 1965; fire consultant; Chief Fire Officer, Merseyside County Fire Brigade, 1974–76, retired (Liverpool Fire Brigade, 1962–74); *b* 6 April 1915; *s* of Percy and Beatrice Taylor; *m* 1940, Nancy (*née* Hefford); two *s* two *d; m* 1976, Florence Mary Latham. *Educ:* Council Sch., Sheffield. Fireman, Sheffield Fire Bde, 1935–41; Instr, NFS West Riding, 1941–42; Company Officer up to Station Officer (ops), NFS in Yorkshire, 1942–49; Chief Officer, Western Fire Authority, NI, 1949–51; Divl Officer NI Fire Authority, 1951–57; Belfast: Dep. Chief Officer, 1958–60; Chief Officer, 1960–62. *Recreations:* football, gardening. *Address:* Onchan, Hall Lane, Wrightington, near Wigan, Lancs.

TAYLOR, Dr Frank; Deputy Director and Principal Keeper, The John Rylands University Library of Manchester, 1972–77; Hon. Lecturer in Manuscript Studies, University of Manchester, since 1967. *Educ:* Univ. of Manchester (MA, PhD). FSA. Served with RN, 1942–46: Lieut, RNVR, 1943–46. Research for Cttee on History of Parlt, 1934–35; Keeper of Western Manuscripts, 1935–49, Keeper of Manuscripts, 1949–72, Librarian, 1970–72, John Rylands Library. Jt. Hon. Sec., Lancs Parish Record Soc., 1937–56, Hon. Sec., 1956–82; Registrar of Research, Soc. of Architectural Historians, 1978–82. Member: British Acad. Oriental Documents Cttee, 1974–80; British Acad. Medieval Latin Dictionary Cttee, 1973–83. Editor, Bulletin of the John Rylands Univ. Lib. of Manchester, 1948–87. *Publications:* various Calendars of Western Manuscripts and Charter Room collections in the Rylands Library, 1937–77; The Chronicle of John Strecche for the Reign of Henry 5, 1932; An Early Seventeenth Century Calendar of Records Preserved in Westminster Palace Treasury, 1939; The Parish Registers of Aughton, 1541–1764, 1942; contrib. to Some Twentieth Century Interpretations of Boswell's Life of Johnson (ed J. L. Clifford), 1970; The Oriental Manuscript Collections in the John Rylands Library, 1972; (ed with J. S. Roskell) Gesta Henrici Quinti, 1975; (with G. A. Matheson) Hand-List of Personal Papers from the Muniments of the Earl of Crawford and Balcarres, 1976; revised edn of M. R. James's Descriptive Catalogue of Latin Manuscripts in the John Rylands Library (1921), 1980; (ed) Society of Architectural Historians, Research Register No 5, 1981; The John Rylands University Library of Manchester, 1982; articles in Bulletin of John Rylands Library, Indian Archives. *Recreations:* cricket, walking. *Address:* The John Rylands University Library of Manchester, Deansgate, Manchester M3 3EH. *T:* 061–834 5343.

TAYLOR, Frank Henry, Principal, Frank H. Taylor & Co., City of London, Chartered Accountants; *b* 10 Oct. 1907; 2nd *s* of George Henry Taylor, Cambridgeshire; *m* 1936, Margaret Dora Mackay (*d* 1944), Invernesshire; one *d; m* 1948, Mabel Hills (*d* 1974), Hertfordshire; two *s; m* 1978, Glenys Mary Edwards, MBE, Bethesda, N Wales. *Educ:* Rutlish School, Merton, Surrey, FCIS 1929; FCA 1930. Commenced in practice as Chartered Accountant, 1930; Ministry of Food Finance Director of Tea, Coffee, Cocoa and Yeast, 1942; Min. of War Transport Finance Rep. overseas, 1944; visited over 40 countries on financial and political missions. Lt-Colonel comdg 1st Caernarvonshire Bn Home Guard, 1943. Contested (C) Newcastle under Lyme, 1955, Chorley, 1959; MP (C) Manchester, Moss Side, Nov. 1961–Feb. 1974. Governor of Rutlish School, 1946–. Liveryman, City of London. Master, Bakers' Co., 1981–82; Mem., Guild of Air Pilots. *Recreations:* numerous including Rugby (for Surrey County), sculling (Thames Championship), punting (several Thames championships), golf (Captain RAC 1962). *Address:* 4 Barrie House, Lancaster Gate, W2. *T:* 01–262 5684; Tinker Taylor, Sennen Cove, Cornwall. *T:* Sennen 220. *Clubs:* City Livery, Arts, Royal Automobile, British Sportsman's.

TAYLOR, Prof. Frederick William, MA Cantab, LLM Wales; Professor of Law, University of Hull, 1956–74, now Emeritus (Dean of Faculty of Arts, 1954–57); *b* 8 March 1909; *o s* of late James Edward Taylor, Solicitor, and of Emily Price; *m* 1938, Muriel Vera Markreed, *d* of Onek Vosguerchian; two *d. Educ:* Twynyrodyn Elementary and Cyfarthfa Secondary Schools, Merthyr Tydfil; University College of Wales, Aberystwyth; St John's College, Cambridge. Solicitor, 1931; LLB Wales, Sir Samuel Evans Prize 1933, BA Cantab, Scholar of St John's Coll., 1935; Asst Lectr in Law, University Coll., Hull, 1935; Acting Head, Dept of Law: University Coll., Southampton, 1940; Hull, 1941; called to Bar, Cert. of Honour, Middle Temple Prize, 1943; Head of Dept of Law, University Coll., Hull, 1949; LLM Wales 1954. Formerly Mem. of Bd of Studies in Laws of Univ. of London. Equity draftsman and conveyancer, 1944–, formerly at Leeds and later at Hull. *Publications:* articles in Law Journal, The Conveyancer, Jl of Soc. of Public Teachers of Law, Solicitors' Journal, The Solicitor, Secretaries Chronicle. *Recreations:* natural history, etc. *Address:* 40 Porthill Road, Shrewsbury, Shropshire.

TAYLOR, Geoffrey H.; *see* Handley-Taylor.

TAYLOR, Geoffrey William, FIB; Group Chief Executive, 1982–86, Vice-Chairman, 1986–87, and Director, since 1982, Midland Bank plc; *b* 4 Feb. 1927; *s* of late Joseph William and Doris Taylor; *m* 1951, Joyce (*née* Walker); three *s* one *d. Educ:* Heckmondwike Grammar School; Univ. of London. BComm. Joined Midland Bank Ltd, 1943; Gen. Man. and Man. Dir, Midland Bank Finance Corp. Ltd, 1967–76; Asst Chief General Manager, 1974–80, Dep. Group Chief Exec., 1980–82, Midland Bank Ltd. Gilbart Banking Lectr, 1973. *Recreations:* golf, reading, music. *Address:* Midland Bank plc, 27–32 Poultry, EC2P 2BX. *T:* 01–606 9911. *Clubs:* Buck's, Overseas Bankers'.

TAYLOR, Sir George, Kt 1962; DSc; FRS 1968, FRSE, FLS; Director, Stanley Smith Horticultural Trust, since 1970; Visiting Professor, Reading University, since 1969; *b* 15 February 1904; *o s* of George William Taylor and Jane Sloan; *m* 1st, 1929, Alice Helen Pendrich (*d* 1977); two *s;* 2nd, Norah English (*d* 1967); 3rd, Beryl, Lady Colwyn. *Educ:* George Heriot's Sch., Edinburgh; Edinburgh Univ. BSc (1st class hons Botany), 1926; Vans Dunlop Scholar. Member of Botanical Expedition to South Africa and Rhodesia, 1927–28; Joint Leader of British Museum Expedition to Ruwenzori and mountains of East Africa, 1934–35; Expedition to SE Tibet and Bhutan, 1938. Principal in Air Ministry, 1940–45. Deputy Keeper of Botany, British Museum (Natural History), 1945–50; Keeper of Botany, 1950–56; Dir, Royal Botanic Gardens, Kew, 1956–71. Botanical Sec. Linnean Soc., 1950–56; Vice-Pres. 1956. Percy Sladen Trustee, 1951–81. Royal Horticultural Soc.: Mem. Council, 1951–73, Vice-Pres., and Prof. of Botany, 1974–; Council Member: National Trust (Chm. Gardens Cttee), 1961–72; RGS 1957–61 (Vice-Pres. 1964); Mem. Min. of Transport Adv. Cttee on Landscaping Treatment of Trunk Roads, 1956–81 (Chm. 1969–81). Editor, Curtis's Botanical Magazine, 1962–71. Gen. Sec., Brit. Assoc. for the Advancement of Science, 1951–58. Hon. Botanical Adviser, Commonwealth War Graves Commn, 1956–77. President: Botanical Society of British Isles, 1955; Division of Botany, Internat. Union Biol Sci., 1964–69; Internat. Assoc. for Plant Taxonomy, 1969–72. Member Royal Society Science, Uppsala, 1956; Corr. Member Royal Botanical Soc. Netherlands; Hon. Mem., Botanical Soc. of S Africa; Hon. Mem., American Orchid Soc. Hon. FRHS 1948. Hon. Freeman, Worshipful Co. of Gardeners, 1967. Hon. LLD Dundee, 1972. VMH 1956; Veitch Gold Medal, Royal Horticultural Soc., 1963; Bradford Washburn Award, Museum of Science, Boston, USA, 1969; Scottish Horticultural Medal, Royal Caledonian Horticultural Soc., 1984. Hon. DrPhil Gothenburg, 1958. *Publications:* An Account of the Genus Meconopsis, 1934; contributions on flowering plants to various periodicals. *Recreations:* angling, gardening, music. *Address:* Belhaven House, Dunbar, East Lothian EH42 1NS. *T:* Dunbar 62392, 63546. *Clubs:* Athenæum; New (Edinburgh).

TAYLOR, Prof. Gerard William, MS, FRCS; Hon. FACS; Professor of Surgery, University of London, 1960–84; Surgeon and Director Surgical Professorial Unit, St Bartholomew's Hospital, London; Honorary Consultant in Vascular Surgery to the Army since 1962; *b* 23 September 1920; *s* of William Ivan Taylor; *m* 1951, Olivia Gay; one *s* one *d. Educ:* Bemrose School, Derby; St Bartholomew's Hospital Medical College. Served War of 1939–45, Capt. RAMC, 1944–47. Fellow in Surgery, Asst Resident, Fulbright Schol., Stanford Univ. Hosp., San Francisco, Calif., 1950–51; Surgeon, St Bartholomew's Hosp., London, Reader in Surgery, Univ. of London, 1955; Hunterian Prof., RCS, 1962; Vis. Prof. of Surgery: Univ. of Calif., Los Angeles, 1965; Univ. of Melbourne, 1969; Sir James Wattie Prof., NZ, 1972. Examiner in Surgery: Univ. of London, 1960; NUI, 1966; Univ. of Cambridge, 1966; Trinity Coll., Dublin, 1969; Univ. of Liverpool, 1974; Univ. of Birmingham, 1978. Governor, St Bartholomew's Hosp., 1971; Mem. Council, Epsom Coll., 1972. President: Vascular Surgical Soc. of GB and Ireland, 1975; Surgical Res. Soc., 1976; Assoc. of Surgeons of GB and Ireland, 1979. *Publications:* articles on general and arterial surgery in scientific journals. *Recreation:* motoring. *Address:* Maple Farm, Shantock Lane, Bovingdon, Herts. *T:* Hemel Hempstead 833170.

TAYLOR, Sir Godfrey; *see* Taylor, Sir A. G.

TAYLOR, Dr Gordon William; Managing Director, Robson Refractories Ltd, 1970; *b* 26 June 1928; *s* of William and Elizabeth Taylor; *m* 1954, Audrey Catherine Bull; three *s* two *d. Educ:* J. H. Burrows Sch., Grays, Essex; Army Apprentice Sch.; London Univ. (BScEng Hons, PhDEng). MICE, MIMechE, AMIEE. Kellogg Internat. Corp., 1954–59; W. R. Grace, 1960–62; Gen. Man., Nalco Ltd, 1962–66; BTR Industries, 1966–68; Managing Director: Kestrel Chemicals, 1968–69; Astral Marketing, 1969–70. Greater London Council: Alderman, 1972–77; Mem. for Croydon Central, 1977–80; Chairman: Public Services Cttee, 1977–78; London Transp. Cttee, 1978–79. *Recreations:* theatre, reading, tennis. *Address:* 33 Royal Avenue, Chelsea, SW3 4QE. *Club:* Holland Park Lawn Tennis.

TAYLOR, Greville Laughton; company director; *b* 23 Oct. 1902; *s* of Rowland Henry and Edith Louise Taylor; *m* 1947, Mary Eileen Reece Mahon; one *s* one *d. Educ:* Lodge School, Barbados; St John's College, Oxford. Called to the Bar, Lincoln's Inn, 1927. Clerk to the House of Assembly, Barbados, 1930–36. Police Magistrate, Barbados, 1936–44; Army 1940–44 (UK, N Africa, Italy); Registrar, Barbados, 1944–46; Judge of the Assistant Court of Appeal, Barbados, 1947–57; Puisne Judge, Windward Islands and Leeward Islands, 1957–64. *Recreations:* reading, shooting, fishing. *Address:* Cole's House, Cole's, St Philip, Barbados, West Indies. *T:* 207. *Clubs:* Royal Barbados Yacht; Bridgetown (Bridgetown).

TAYLOR, Harold Joseph, CBE 1966; Chief Director, Prison Department, Home Office, 1965–68, retired; *b* 7 May 1904; *s* of Herbert Taylor and Gertrude Mary Taylor; *m* 1940, Olive Alice Slade, *d* of Harry Slade, Honor Oak Park, SE; one *s* (adopted). *Educ:* Blandford Sec. Gram. Sch.; Southampton University. Teacher, Brighton Education Authority, 1924–28; Asst Housemaster, Prison Commission, HM Borstal, Portland, 1928; Housemaster, Portland Borstal, 1930; Superintendent, Borstal Training School, Thayetmyo, Burma, 1933–37; Governor, HM Borstal: Feltham, Middx, 1938–41; Lowdham Grange, 1941–46; Governor, HM Prison: Camp Hill, IoW, 1946–49; Sudbury, Derby, 1949–51; Asst Comr, HM Prison Commission, 1951–57; Comr and Director of Borstal Administration, 1958–65. *Recreations:* fishing, country lore, tinkering. *Address:* 45 Church Way, Pagham, Bognor Regis, West Sussex. *T:* Pagham 263750.

TAYLOR, Harold McCarter, CBE 1955; TD 1945; retired, 1967; *b* Dunedin, New Zealand, 13 May 1907; *s* of late James Taylor, and late Louisa Urquhart Taylor; *m* 1st, 1933, Joan (*d* 1965), *d* of late George Reginald Sills, Lincoln; two *s* two *d;* 2nd, 1966, Dorothy Judith, *d* of late Charles Samuel, Liverpool. *Educ:* Otago Boys' High School and Univ. of Otago, NZ; Clare Coll., Cambridge. MSc New Zealand, 1928; MA, PhD Cambridge, 1933. Allen Scholar and Smith's Prizeman, 1932. Fellow of Clare College, Cambridge, 1933–61; Hon. Fellow, 1961–; Lecturer in Mathematics, University of Cambridge, 1934–45; Treasurer of the University, 1945–53; Secretary General of the Faculties, 1953–61; Vice-Chancellor, University of Keele, 1962–67 (Principal, University College of North Staffordshire, 1961–62); Rede Lecturer, Cambridge University, 1966. Mem., Royal Commn on Historical Monuments (England), 1972–78. Pres., Royal Archaeol Inst., 1972–75; Vice-Pres., Soc. of Antiquaries of London, 1974–77. Hon. LLD Cambridge, 1967; Hon. DLitt: Keele, 1968; Birmingham, 1983. Commissioned in TA, NZ, 1925; served War of 1939–45 as Major and Lieut-Col RA; Instructor and Senior Instructor in Gunnery at School of Artillery, Larkhill. *Publications:* Anglo-Saxon Architecture, vols I and II (with Joan Taylor), 1965, vol. III, 1978; many articles in nat.

and county archaeological jls. *Recreations:* mountaineering and ski-ing; Anglo-Saxon art and architecture; photography. *Address:* 192 Huntingdon Road, Cambridge CB3 0LB. *T:* Cambridge 276324.

TAYLOR, Henry George, DSc(Eng); Director of Electrical Research Association, 1957–69, retired; *b* 4 Nov. 1904; *m* 1931, Gwendolyn Hilda Adams; one *s* two *d. Educ:* Taunton School; Battersea Polytechnic Inst., City and Guilds Engineering College. Metropolitan Vickers, 1929–30; Electrical Research Assoc., 1930–38; Copper Development Assoc., 1938–42; Philips Lamps Ltd, 1942–47; British Welding Research Assoc., 1947–57. *Publications:* contribs to: Instn of Electrical Engineers Jl, Jl of Inst. of Physics, etc. *Recreation:* walking. *Address:* The Island, Ford Street, Wellington TA21 9PE.

TAYLOR, Sir Henry Milton, Kt 1980; JP; Editor of Hansard, Bahamas House of Assembly, since 1979; *b* 4 Nov. 1903; adopted *s* of Joseph and Evelyn Taylor; *m* 1962, Eula Mae Sisco; three step *c*; four *d* by previous marriage. *Educ:* Govt Grade Sch.; privately. Teacher; Headmaster, Public Sch. at Pompey Bay, Acklins Island, 1925–26. Elected Mem., House of Assembly, 1949; Co-founded and organized estabt of Progressive Liberal Party of Bahamas (first political party of Bahamas), 1953–64; Nat. Party Chm., 1953–64, Hon. Chm. for life, 1963; MP for 10 yrs; Leader of delegns to Westminster: to upgrade antiquated Acts of Parliament, 1956; in interest of Women's Suffrage, 1960. Temp. Dep. Governor-General of The Bahamas, July-Aug. and Nov. 1981, Aug.-Nov. 1982 and June 1984. Mem., Develt Bd (Tourist), 1960–62; successfully toured Britain, Eire, W Germany and Sweden in interests of tourism and financial investments; officially visited Nassau/Lahn. (First) Dir, Princess Margaret Hosp. Blood Bank, 1954–55. Organised Bahamas Soc. of Arms and Awards, 1984. Letters Patent for Armorial Bearing approved by Duke of Norfolk, 1981. JP Bahama Isles, 1984. *Publications:* (compiled and ed) United Bahamian Party Annual Handbook, 1967, 1968; My Political Memoirs. *Address:* PO Box N10846, Nassau, Bahamas; Lucaya at Brentwood, 221 NE 44 Street, Miami, Fla 33137, USA. *Club:* British Floridian (Miami).

TAYLOR, Hermon, MA, MD, MChir, FRCS; retired; formerly Consulting Surgeon: London Hospital, E1; King George Hospital, Ilford; *b* 11 May 1905; *s* of Enoch Oliver Taylor and L. M. Taylor (*née* Harrison); *m* 1st, 1932, Méarie Amélie Pearson (*d* 1981); three *s* two *d*; 2nd, 1983, Mrs Noreen Cooke. *Educ:* Latymer School, Edmonton; St John's Coll., Cambridge (scholar); St Bartholomew's Hospital (Entrance Scholar). BA 1926; MRCS, LRCP 1929; MB, ChB Cantab. 1930; FRCS Eng. 1930. House Surgeon, Demonstr of Pathology, St Bart's Hosp.; Res. Surgical Officer: Hertford Co. Hosp., Lincoln Co. Hosp.; Surgical Registrar, Prince of Wales' Hosp., Tottenham. MChir Cantab 1932; MD Cantab 1934; Horton Smith Prize, Univ. Cantab; Luther Holden Research Scholar, St Bartholomew's Hospital; BMA Research Scholar, Surgical First Assistant London Hospital. Moynihan Fellow, Assoc. of Surgeons of GB and Ireland; Hunterian Professor, RCS. Past President, British Society of Gastro-enterology; Hon. Member Amer. Gastro-enterological Assoc. *Publications:* Carcinoma of the Stomach, in Modern Trends in Gastro-Enterology, 1952; contrib. to BMJ, Lancet, etc, 1942–. *Address:* Coppice Field, Bosham Hoe, Chichester, West Sussex PO18 8ET. *T:* Chichester 573385. *Club:* Athenæum.

TAYLOR, Rev. Canon Humphrey Vincent; Secretary, United Society for the Propagation of the Gospel, since 1984; *b* 5 March 1938; *s* of Maurice Humphrey Taylor and Mary Patricia Stuart Taylor (*née* Wood), now Pearson; *m* 1965, Anne Katharine Dart; two *d. Educ:* Harrow School; Pembroke College, Cambridge (MA); London University (MA). Nat. Service Officer, RAF, 1956–58; Cambridge 1958–61; College of the Resurrection, Mirfield, 1961–63; Curate in London, 1963–66; Rector of Lilongwe, Malaŵi, 1967–71; Chaplain, Bishop Grosseteste Coll., Lincoln, 1971–74; Sec. for Chaplaincies in Higher Education, Gen. Synod Bd of Education, 1974–80; Mission Programmes Sec., USPG, 1980–84. Hon. Canon of Bristol Cathedral, 1986–. *Recreations:* music, squash, gardening. *Address:* 15 Tufton Street, SW1P 3QQ. *T:* 01–222 4222.

TAYLOR, Prof. Ian Galbraith; Ellis Llwyd Jones Professor of Audiology and Education of the Deaf, University of Manchester, since 1964; *b* 24 Apr. 1924; *s* of David Oswald Taylor, MD, and Margaret Ballantine Taylor; *m* 1954, Audrey Wolstenholme; two *d. Educ:* Manchester Grammar Sch.; Univ. of Manchester. MB, ChB, DPH Manchester; MD (Gold Medal) Manchester 1963; MRCP 1973; FRCP 1977. Ho. Surg., Manchester Royal Infirm., 1948; DAD, Army Health of N Regional Canal Zone, and OC Army Sch. of Hygiene, ME, 1949–51; Asst MO, City of Manchester, 1951–54. Univ. of Manchester: Hon. Special Lectr and Ewing Foundn Fellow, Dept of Education of the Deaf, 1956–60; Lectr in Clinical Audiology, 1963–64. Consultant in Audiological Medicine, United Manchester Hosps, 1968. *Publication:* Neurological Mechanisms of Hearing and Speech in Children, 1964. *Recreations:* gardening, fishing. *Address:* 7 Hall Moss Lane, Bramhall, Cheshire SK7 1RB. *T:* 061–440 8410.

TAYLOR, Ivor Ralph, QC 1973; **His Honour Judge Taylor;** a Circuit Judge, since 1976; *b* 26 Oct. 1927; *s* of Abraham Taylor and late Ruth Taylor; *m* 1st, 1954, Ruth Cassel (marr. diss. 1974); one *s* one *d* (and one *d* decd); 3rd, 1984, (Audrey) Joyce Goldman (*née* Wayne). *Educ:* Stand Grammar Sch., Whitefield; Manchester Univ. Served War of 1939–45, AC2 in RAF, 1945. Called to Bar, Gray's Inn, 1951. Standing Counsel to Inland Revenue, N Circuit, 1969–73; a Recorder of the Crown Court, 1972–76. Former Chm., PTA, Dept of Audiology, Manchester Univ. Pres., Manchester and District Medico Legal Soc., 1974, 1975. Sometime Gov., Royal Manchester Children's Hosp.; Mem. Management Cttee, Salford Hosp. *Recreations:* walking, indifferent golfing. *Address:* 5 Eagle Lodge, 19 Harrop Road, Hale, Altrincham, Cheshire WA15 9DA. *T:* 061–941 5591.

TAYLOR, Sir James, Kt 1966; MBE 1945; DSc, FRSC, Hon. FInstP, Hon. MIMinE; Director, Surrey Independent Hospital plc, since 1981; Deputy Chairman: Royal Ordnance Factories Board, 1959–72 (Member, 1952–72); Chairman, Chloride Silent Power Ltd, 1974–81; *b* 16 Aug. 1902; *s* of James and Alice Taylor; *m* 1929, Margaret Lennox Stewart; two *s* one *d. Educ:* Bede College, Sunderland; Rutherford College, Newcastle upon Tyne; Universities of Durham, Sorbonne, Utrecht, Cambridge. BSc (1st cl. Hons Physics) 1923; PhD 1925; Dr of Physics and Maths (*cum laude*) Utrecht, 1927; DSc Dunelm, 1931. ICI Ltd: joined Nobel Div. 1928; Research Dir, 1946; Jt Man. Dir, 1951; Director, 1952–64. Chairman: Yorkshire Imperial Metals Ltd, 1958–64; Imperial Aluminium Co. Ltd, 1959–64; Imperial Metal Industries Ltd, 1962–64; Fulmer Res. Institute, 1976–78. Director: Nuclear Developments Ltd, 1961–64; European Plumbing Materials Ltd, 1962–64; BDH Group Ltd, 1965–67; Oldham & Son Ltd, 1965–69; Oldham (International) Ltd, 1969–72. Member: Adv. Coun. on Scientific Research and Tech. Develt, MoD, 1965–68; NPL Steering Committee, 1966; Adv. Coun. on Calibration and Measurement, 1966; Chm., Glazebrook Cttee, NPL, 1966. Member: Court, Brunel Univ., 1967–82; Council, British Non-Ferrous Metals Research Assoc., 1954–67 (Vice-Chm. 1961–67); Council, City and Guilds of London, 1969–71; Court, RCA, 1969–71; Pres. Section B British Assoc. 1960, Council 1965; Pres. Inst. of Physics and Physical Society, 1966–68 (Hon. Treas. 1957–66); FRIC 1945; MIMinE 1947 (Hon. Member, 1960); FInstP 1948 (Hon. FInstP 1972); MInstD. FRSA 1962 (Member Council 1964–86, Vice-Pres., 1969, Chm., 1969–71, Silver Medal, 1969); Hon. Pres., Research

and Development Soc., 1970; Hon. Mem., Newcomen Soc. in N America, 1970. Mem., Inst. of Dirs, 1964–. Hon. DSc Bradford, 1968; Hon. DCL Newcastle, 1969. Medal, Society Chemical Industry, 1965; Silver Medal, Chem. Soc., 1972. *Publications:* On the Sparking Potentials of Electric Discharge Tubes, 1927; Detonation in Condensed Explosives, 1952; British Coal Mining Explosives, 1958; Solid Propellent and Exothermic Compositions, 1959; The Modern Chemical Industry in Great Britain (Cantor Lectures, Jl of Roy. Soc. Arts), 1961; Restrictive Practices (Soc. of Chem. Ind. Lecture), 1965; Monopolies and Restrictive Practices (RSA), 1967; The Scientist and The Technologist in Britain today (Pres. Address, IPPS), 1967; Britain's Technological Future (IOP Jubilee Address), 1968; Arts, Crafts and Technology (RSA), 1969; Cobalt, Madder and Computers (RSA), 1969; The Seventies and the Society (RSA), 1970; The American Dream and the RSA, 1971; New Horizons in Research and Development (RSA), 1971; The Scientific Community, 1973; numerous contribs to Proc. Roy. Soc., Phil. Mag., Trans Inst. Min. Eng., Advancement of Science, ICI Magazine. *Recreations:* gardening, cooking and writing. *Address:* Culvers, Seale, near Farnham, Surrey GU10 1JN. *T:* Runfold 2210. *Club:* RNVR Carrick (Hon.) (Glasgow).

TAYLOR, Dame Jean (Elizabeth); DCVO 1978 (CVO 1976; MVO 4th Cl. 1971, 5th Cl. 1964); retired; *b* 7 Nov. 1916; *d* of late Captain William Taylor (killed in action, 1917). *Educ:* Tunbridge Wells High School (GPDST). Entered Office of Private Secretary to the Queen, 1958; Chief Clerk, 1961–78. *Recreations:* music, walking, looking at old buildings. *Address:* Balcombe Farm, Frittenden, Cranbrook, Kent TN17 2EL.

TAYLOR, Jessie; *see* Taylor, M. J.

TAYLOR, Dr Joe; JP; Councillor, Greater Manchester County Council, 1973–86 (Chairman, 1981–82); *b* 6 Sept. 1906; *s* of Sam Taylor and Anne Taylor; *m* 1935, Edith Dante; two *s. Educ:* Leeds Central High School; Leeds University and Leeds Med. Sch. MB ChB 1932. Medical Practitioner in Manchester, 1935–; Mem., Crossley Hosp. Board, 1955–. Councillor, Manchester City, 1954–70, Alderman, 1970–73. Appeals Advisory Cttees, BBC and ITA: Chm., N Regional, 1961–67; Chm., Northern, 1967–76; Central, 1961–79. Member: Salvation Army Adv. Council, Manchester Region, 1965–; Gtr Manchester Police Authority, 1973–86; NW Water Authority, 1977–86; Court, Univ. of Manchester, 1981–; Court, Univ. of Salford, 1981–86; Royal Exchange Theatre Trust, 1981–; Palace Theatre Trust, 1981–86; NW Arts Executive, 1981–82; Gtr Manchester County Disaster Relief Trust, 1980–; Hallé Concerts Soc., 1973–86; President: Gtr Manchester Council for Voluntary Service, 1981–82; Gtr Manchester Schools Football Assoc., 1981–82; Gtr Manchester Council Olympic Wrestling Team, 1981–82; Vice-Pres., Gtr Manchester Youth Assoc., 1981–82; Dep. Chm., British-American Assoc. for Gtr Manchester, 1985. Mem., Manchester Lit. and Phil Soc. JP Manchester City, 1961. *Recreations:* fishing, gardening, reading. *Address:* 32 Old Hall Road, Broughton Park, Salford M7 0JH. *T:* 061–740 4433. *Club:* Manchester Luncheon.

TAYLOR, John Barrington, MBE 1945; TD 1957; JP; **His Honour Judge John Taylor;** a Circuit Judge, since 1977; *b* 3 Aug. 1914; *y s* of Robert Edward Taylor, Bath; *m* 1941, Constance Aleen, *y d* of J. Barkly Macadam, Edinburgh and Suffolk; two *s* three *d* (and one *s* decd). *Educ:* King Edward's Sch., Bath. LLB (London). Admitted a Solicitor, 1936, and practised at Bath until 1960. Enlisted Somerset LI, 1939; overseas service 1942–46: DAAG, HQ 5 Corps, 1943; AAG, Allied Commn for Austria, 1945; AAG, No 1 Dist. (Milan), 1946. HM Coroner, City of Bath, 1958–72; Registrar, Bath Gp of County Courts, 1960–77; a Recorder of the Crown Court, 1972–77. Mem., County Court Rule Cttee, 1980–85. JP Somerset, 1962, Essex, 1978. *Recreation:* gardening. *Address:* c/o Crown Court, Chelmsford, Essex.

TAYLOR, Rt. Rev. John Bernard; *see* St Albans, Bishop of.

TAYLOR, Dr John Bryan, FRS 1970; Chief Physicist, Culham Laboratory, since 1981; *b* 26 Dec. 1928; *s* of Frank and Ada Taylor, Birmingham; *m* 1951, Joan M. Hargest; one *s* one *d. Educ:* Oldbury Grammar Sch.; Birmingham Univ., 1947–50 and 1952–55. RAF, 1950–52. Atomic Weapons Research Establishment, Aldermaston, 1955–59 and 1960–62; Harkness Fellow, Commonwealth Fund, Univ. of California (Berkeley), 1959–60; Culham Laboratory (UKAEA), 1962–69 and 1970– (Head of Theoretical Physics Div., 1963–81); Inst. for Advanced Study, Princeton, 1969. FInstP 1969. Fellow, Amer. Phys. Soc., 1984. Maxwell Medal, IPPS, 1971; Max Born Medal, German Phys. Soc., 1979. *Publications:* contribs to scientific learned jls. *Recreation:* gliding. *Address:* Culham Laboratory, Abingdon, Oxon. *T:* Abingdon 463344, Abingdon 21840 ext. 3344.

TAYLOR, John Charles; QC 1983; *b* 22 April 1931; *s* of late Sidney Herbert and Gertrude Florence Taylor, St Ives, Cambs; *m* 1964, Jean Aimée Monteith; one *d. Educ:* Palmers Sch., Grays, Essex; Queens' Coll., Cambridge (MA, LLB); Harvard Law School (LLM). Called to the Bar, Middle Temple, 1958. Mem., Stephens Cttee on Minerals Planning Control, 1972–74. Contested (C) Kettering, 1970. *Recreations:* country pursuits, art, boardsailing, motorcycling. *Address:* Clifton Grange, Clifton, Shefford, Beds SG17 5EW. *Clubs:* Athenæum, Travellers'.

TAYLOR, Prof. John Clayton, PhD; FRS 1981; Professor of Mathematical Physics, Cambridge University, and Fellow of Robinson College, since 1980; *b* 4 Aug. 1930; *s* of Leonard Taylor and Edith (*née* Tytherleigh); *m* 1959, Gillian Mary (*née* Schofield); two *s. Educ:* Selhurst Grammar Sch., Croydon; Cambridge Univ. (MA). Lectr, Imperial Coll., London, 1956–60; Lectr, Cambridge Univ., and Fellow of Peterhouse, 1960–64; Reader in Theoretical Physics, Oxford Univ., and Fellow of University Coll., Oxford, 1964–80. *Publication:* Gauge Theories of Weak Interactions, 1976. *Recreation:* pottering about. *Address:* 9 Bowers Croft, Cambridge CB1 4RP.

TAYLOR, Rt. Hon. John David, PC (N Ire.) 1970; MP (UU) Strangford, since 1983 (resigned seat Dec. 1985 in protest against Anglo-Irish Agreement; re-elected Jan. 1986); Member (UU) Northern Ireland, European Parliament, since 1979; *b* 24 Dec. 1937; *er s* of George D. Taylor and Georgina Baird; *m* 1970, Mary Frances Todd; one *s* four *d. Educ:* Royal Sch., Armagh; Queen's Univ. of Belfast (BSc). CEng; AMInstHE, AMICEI. MP (UU) S Tyrone, NI Parlt, 1965–73; Mem. (UU), Fermanagh and S Tyrone, NI Assembly, 1973–75; Mem. (UU), North Down, NI Constitutional Convention, 1975–76; Parly Sec. to Min. of Home Affairs, 1969–70; Minister of State, Min. of Home Affairs, 1970–72; Mem. (UU), North Down, NI Assembly, 1982–86. Partner, G. D. Taylor and Associates, Architects and Civil Engineers, 1966–74; Director: Bramley Apple Restaurant Ltd, 1974–; West Ulster Estates Ltd, 1968–; West Ulster Hotels Co. Ltd, 1976–; Gosford Housing Assoc. Ltd, 1977–; Tontine Rooms Ltd, 1978–; Ulster Gazette (Armagh) Ltd, 1983–; Ardac (Belfast) Ltd, 1986–; Tyrone Printing Co. Ltd, 1986–. *Publication:* (jtly) Ulster—the facts, 1982. *Recreation:* foreign travel. *Address:* Mullinure, Portadown Road, Armagh, Northern Ireland BT61 9EL. *T:* Armagh 522409. *Clubs:* Farmers'; Armagh County (Armagh).

TAYLOR, John D.; *see* Debenham Taylor.

TAYLOR, Prof. John Gerald; Professor of Mathematics, King's College, University of London, since 1971; *b* 18 Aug. 1931; *s* of William and Elsie Taylor; *m* Pamela Nancy (*née*

Cutmore); two *s* three *d*. *Educ:* King Edward VI Grammar Sch., Chelmsford; Mid-Essex Polytechnic, Chelmsford; Christ's Coll., Cambridge. Fellow, Inst. for Advanced Study, Princeton, NJ, USA, 1956–58 (Mem., 1961–63); Fellow, Christ's Coll., Cambridge, 1958–60; Asst Lectr, Faculty of Mathematics, Univ. of Cambridge, 1959–60. Member: Inst. des Hautes Etudes Scient., Paris, 1960; Res. Inst. Advanced Study, Baltimore, Md, USA, 1960. Sen. Res. Fellow, Churchill Coll., Cambridge, 1963–64; Prof. of Physics, Rutgers Univ., New Brunswick, NJ, 1964–66; Fellow, Hertford Coll., Oxford, and Lectr, Math. Inst., Oxford, 1966–67; Reader in Particles and Fields, Queen Mary Coll., London, 1967–69; Prof. of Physics, Univ. of Southampton, 1969–71. Chm., Mathematical Physics Gp, Inst. of Physics, 1982–. *Publications:* Quantum Mechanics, an Introduction, 1969; The Shape of Minds to Come, 1970; The New Physics, 1972; Black Holes: the end of the Universe?, 1973; Superminds, 1975; Special Relativity, 1975; Science and the Supernatural, 1980; The Horizons of Knowledge, 1982; edited: Supergravity, 1981; Supersymmetry and Supergravity, 1982; also scientific papers in Proc. Royal Soc., Phys. Rev., Proc. Camb. Phil. Soc., Jl Math. Phys. etc. *Recreations:* listening to music, walking. *Address:* 42 Fairmead Road, N19. *T:* 01–272 1558.

TAYLOR, Sir John Lang, (Sir Jock Taylor), KCMG 1979 (CMG 1974); HM Diplomatic Service, retired; Chairman: Klöckner INA Industrial Plants Ltd, since 1985; Siemens Ltd, since 1986; Director, Schering Holdings Ltd, since 1986; *b* 3 Aug. 1924; *y s* of Sir John William Taylor, KBE, CMG; *m* 1952, Molly, *o d* of James Rushworth; five *s* three *d*. *Educ:* Prague; Vienna; Imperial Services Coll., Windsor; Baltimore Polytechnic Inst., Md; Cornell Univ.; Trinity Coll., Cambridge. RAFVR, 1944–47 (Flt-Lt 1946). Joined HM Foreign (now Diplomatic) Service, 1949; served in: FO, 1949–50 and 1957–60; Saigon, 1950–52; Hanoi, 1951; Beirut, 1952–55; Prague, 1955–57; Montevideo, 1960–64; Bonn, 1964–69; Minister (Commercial), Buenos Aires, 1969–71; RCDS, 1972; Head of Industry, Science and Energy Dept, FCO, 1972–73; Asst Under-Sec. of State, FCO, 1973–74; Under-Sec., Dept of Energy, 1974–75; Ambassador to: Venezuela, 1975–79; the Netherlands, 1979–81; FRG, 1981–84. Chm., Latin Amer. Trade Adv. Gp, BOTB, 1986. *Address:* The Old Flint, Boxgrove, near Chichester, W Sussex. *Club:* Travellers'.

TAYLOR, John Mark; MP (C) Solihull, since 1983; *b* 19 Aug. 1941; *s* of Wilfred and Eileen Martha Taylor; *m* 1979, Catherine Ann Hall. *Educ:* Eversfield Prep. School; Bromsgrove School and College of Law. Admitted Solicitor, 1966; Senior Partner, John Taylor & Co. Member: Solihull County Borough Council, 1971–74; W Midlands Metropolitan County Council, 1973–86 (Opposition (Conservative) Leader, 1975–77; Leader, 1977–79). Mem., Select Cttee on the Environment, 1983–; Sec., Cons. Backbench Cttee on Eur. Affairs, 1983–. Vice-Pres., AMA, 1979– (Dep. Chm., 1978–79). Mem., W Midlands Economic Planning Council, 1978–79; Governor, Univ. of Birmingham, 1977–81. Contested (C) Dudley East, Feb. and Oct. 1974. Mem. (C) Midlands E, European Parlt, 1979–84; European Democratic Group spokesman on Community Budget, 1979–81, Group Dep. Chm., 1981–82. *Recreations:* fellowship, cricket, reading. *Address:* 211 St Bernards Road, Solihull, West Midlands B92 7DL. *T:* 021–707 1076; (office) 021–704 3071. *Clubs:* Carlton, MCC; Birmingham (Birmingham).

TAYLOR, John Ralph Carlisle, CIE 1943; Past Director, Davy-Ashmore International Co. Ltd; *b* Sydney, NSW, Australia, 18 Aug. 1902; *o s* of Charles Carlisle Taylor and Jean Sawers; *m* 1933, Nancy (Ann) Marguerite Sorel-Cameron (*d* 1972); one *s* decd. *Educ:* Winchester. Shaw Wallace & Co., London, Calcutta, Karachi, 1921–28; Burmah-Shell, 1928–39 and 1945–54; General Manager in India, 1951–54. Service in RIASC (Lt-Col) 1941–42, GHQ India (Lt-Col) 1942; Petroleum Officer; *ex-officio* Dep. Sec., Defence Dept, Govt of India, 1942–45. Chairman, Shell Group of Companies in Australia, 1955–60; retired from Shell, 1960. *Recreations:* walking, reading, racing. *Address:* 166 Oakwood Court, W14. *Clubs:* Hurlingham, Oriental.

TAYLOR, John Russell; Art Critic, The Times, since 1978; *b* 19 June 1935; *s* of Arthur Russell and Kathleen Mary Taylor (*née* Picker). *Educ:* Dover Grammar Sch.; Jesus Coll., Cambridge (MA); Courtauld Inst. of Art, London. Sub-Editor, Times Educational Supplement, 1959; Editorial Asst, Times Literary Supplement, 1960; Film Critic, The Times, 1962–73. Lectr on Film, Tufts Univ. in London, 1970–71; Prof., Div. of Cinema, Univ. of Southern California, 1972–78. Editor, Films and Filming, 1983–. *Publications:* Anger and After, 1962; Anatomy of a Television Play, 1962; Cinema Eye, Cinema Ear, 1964; Penguin Dictionary of the Theatre, 1966; The Art Nouveau Book in Britain, 1966; The Rise and Fall of the Well-Made Play, 1967; The Art Dealers, 1969; Harold Pinter, 1969; The Hollywood Musical, 1971; The Second Wave, 1971; David Storey, 1974; Directors and Directions, 1975; Peter Shaffer, 1975; The Revels History of Drama in English, vol. VII, 1978; Hitch, 1978; Impressionism, 1981; Strangers in Paradise, 1983; Ingrid Bergman, 1983; Alec Guinness, 1984; Vivien Leigh, 1984; Portraits of the British Cinema, 1985; Hollywood 1940s, 1985; Orson Welles, 1986; Edward Wolfe, 1986. *Address:* c/o The Times, 1 Pennington Street, E1.

TAYLOR, Rt. Rev. John Vernon; *b* 11 Sept. 1914; *s* of late Bishop J. R. S. Taylor and Margaret Irene Taylor (*née* Garrett); *m* 1940, Margaret Wright; one *s* two *d*. *Educ:* St Lawrence Coll., Ramsgate; Trinity Coll., Cambridge; St Catherine's Soc., Oxford; Wycliffe Hall, Oxford; Institute of Education, London. Curate, All Souls, Langham Place, W1, 1938–40; Curate in Charge, St Andrew's Church, St Helens, Lancs, 1940–43; Warden, Bishop Tucker College, Mukono, Uganda, 1945–54; Research Worker, Internat. Missionary Council, 1955–59; Africa Sec., CMS, 1959–63; Gen. Sec., CMS, 1963–74; Bishop of Winchester, 1975–85. Chm., Doctrine Commn of C of E, 1978–85. Examng Chap. to Bishop of Truro, 1974–75. Hon. Canon of Namirembe Cathedral, 1963–74. Hon. Fellow New Coll., Oxford, 1985. Hon. DD (Wycliffe Coll., Toronto), 1964. *Publications:* Man in the Midst, 1955; Christianity and Politics in Africa, 1957; The Growth of the Church in Buganda, 1958; African Passion, 1958; Christians of the Copperbelt, 1961; The Primal Vision, 1963; For All the World, 1966; Change of Address, 1968; The Go-Between God, 1972; Enough is Enough, 1975; Weep not for Me, 1986; A Matter of Life and Death, 1986. *Recreations:* theatre, music. *Address:* 65 Aston Street, Oxford OX4 1EW. *T:* Oxford 248502.

TAYLOR, John William Ransom; Editor-in-Chief (formerly Editor and Compiler), Jane's All the World's Aircraft, since 1959; *b* 8 June 1922; *s* of late Victor Charles Taylor and late Florence Hilda Taylor (*née* Ransom); *m* 1946, Doris Alice Haddrick; one *s* one *d*. *Educ:* Ely Cathedral Choir Sch., Soham Grammar Sch., Cambs. FRAeS, FRHistS, FSLAET, AFAIAA. Design Dept, Hawker Aircraft Ltd, 1941–47; Editorial Publicity Officer, Fairey Aviation Gp, 1947–55; Author/Editor, 1955–; Air Corresp., Meccano Magazine, 1943–72; Editor, Air BP Magazine, British Petroleum, 1956–72; Jt Editor, Guinness Book of Air Facts and Feats, 1974–83; Contributing Editor: Air Force Magazine (USA), 1971–; Jane's Defence Weekly (formerly Jane's Defence Review), 1980–; Asian Aviation (Singapore), 1983–84. Mem., Académie Nat. de l'Air et de l'Espace, 1985–. Pres., Chiltern Aviation Soc.; Vice-President: Horse Rangers Assoc.; Guild of Aviation Artists; Croydon Airport Soc., Surbiton Scout Assoc. Warden, Christ Church, Surbiton Hill, 1976–80. Freeman, Guild of Air Pilots and Air Navigators, 1983. C. P. Robertson Memorial

Trophy, 1959; Cert. of Honour, Commn of Bibliography, History and Arts, Aero Club de France, 1971; Order of Merit, World Aerospace Educn Organization, 1981. *Publications:* Spitfire, 1946; Aircraft Annual, 1949–75; Civil Aircraft Markings, 1950–78; Wings for Tomorrow, 1951; Military Aircraft Recognition, 1952–79; Civil Airliner Recognition, 1953–79; Picture History of Flight, 1955; Science in the Atomic Age, 1956; Rockets and Space Travel, 1956; Best Flying Stories, 1956; Jane's All the World's Aircraft, 1956–; Helicopters Work Like This, 1957; Royal Air Force, 1957; Fleet Air Arm, 1957; Jet Planes Work Like This, 1957; Russian Aircraft, 1957; Rockets and Missiles, 1958; CFS, Birthplace of Air Power, 1958; Rockets and Spacecraft Work Like This; British Airports, 1959; US Military Aircraft, 1959; Warplanes of the World, 1959, rev. as Military Aircraft of the World; BP Book of Flight Today, 1960; Combat Aircraft of the World, 1969; Westland 50, 1965; Pictorial History of the Royal Air Force, 3 vols 1968–71, rev. 1980; Aircraft Aircraft, 1967, 4th edn 1974; Encyclopaedia of World Aircraft, 1966; The Lore of Flight, 1971; Rockets and Missiles, 1971; Light Plane Recognition, 1970; Civil Aircraft of the World, 1970–79; British Civil Aircraft Register, 1971; (with M. J. H. Taylor) Missiles of the World, 1972–79; (with D. Mondey) Spies in the Sky, 1972; (with K. Munson) History of Aviation, 1973, 2nd edn, 1978; Jane's Aircraft Pocket Books, 1973–; History of Aerial Warfare, 1974; (with S. H. H. Young) Passenger Aircraft and Airlines, 1975; Jets, 1976; (with M. J. H. Taylor) Helicopters of the World, 1976–79; (with Air Vice-Marshal R. A. Mason) Aircraft, Strategy and Operations of the Soviet Air Force, 1986. *Recreations:* historical studies, travel. *Address:* 36 Alexandra Drive, Surbiton, Surrey KT5 9AF. *T:* 01–399 5435. *Clubs:* Royal Aero, Royal Air Force (Hon.); Fenland Motor.

TAYLOR, Judy, (Julia Marie), (Judy Hough), MBE 1971; writer; *b* 12 Aug. 1932; adopted *d* of Gladys Spicer Taylor; *m* 1980, Richard Hough, *qv*. *Educ:* St Paul's Girls' Sch. Joined The Bodley Head, 1951, specialising in children's books; Director: The Bodley Head Ltd, 1967–84 (Dep. Man. Dir, 1971–80); Chatto, Bodley Head & Jonathan Cape Ltd, 1973–80; Chatto, Bodley Head & Jonathan Cape Australia Pty Ltd, 1977–80. Publishers Association: Chm., Children's Book Gp, 1969–72; Mem. Council, 1972–78; Member: Book Develt Council, 1973–76; Unicef Internat. Art Cttee, 1968–70, 1976, 1982–83; UK Unicef Greeting Card Cttee, 1982–85. Consultant to Penguin (formerly to Frederick Warne) on Beatrix Potter, 1981–; Associate Dir, Weston Woods Inst., USA, 1984–. *Publications:* Sophie and Jack, 1982; Sophie and Jack Help Out, 1983; My First Year: a Beatrix Potter baby book, 1983; Sophie and Jack in the Snow, 1984; Beatrix Potter: artist, storyteller and countrywoman, 1986; Dudley and the Monster, 1986; Dudley Goes Flying, 1986; Dudley in a Jam, 1986; Dudley and the Strawberry Shake, 1986; numerous professional articles. *Recreations:* collecting early children's books, gardening. *Address:* Denfurlong, Lower Chedworth, near Cheltenham, Glos GL54 4AP. *T:* Fossebridge 422; Flat 7, 217 Sussex Gardens, W2 2RJ. *T:* 01–723 7327. *Club:* Groucho.

TAYLOR, Keith Breden, MA, DM; FRCP; George de Forest Barnett Professor of Medicine, Stanford University, 1966–81 and since 1982; *b* 16 April 1924; *yr s* of Francis Henry Taylor and Florence (*née* Latham); *m* 1st, 1949, Ann Gaynor Hughes Jones (*d* 1971); three *s* one *d* (and one *s* decd); 2nd, 1972, Kym Williams, Adelaide, Aust. *Educ:* King's College Sch., Wimbledon; Magdalen Coll., Oxford (Exhibnr; BA Hons Physiology 1946, BM BCh 1949). Member, SHAEF Nutrition Survey Team, 1945; RAMC (Major), 1951–53; Dir Gen., Health Educn Council, 1981–82. Late Hon. Consultant, Central Middlesex Hosp.; Mem., MRC Gastroenterology Research Unit; Asst in Nuffield Dept Clin. Med., Oxford. Radcliffe Travelling Fellow, 1953; Rockefeller Foundn Fellow, 1959; Guggenheim Fellow, 1971; Fogarty Sen. Fellow, USPHS, 1978–79. Cons., US National Insts of Health; Mem., USPHS Trng Grants Cttee in Gastroenterology and Nutrition, 1965–70; Chm., Stanford Univ. Cttee on Human Nutrition, 1974–81; Vis. Professorships include: Rochester, NY, 1966; Columbia-Presbyterian, NY, 1969; Univ. of Adelaide, 1971; Academic Medical Unit, Royal Free Hosp., 1978–79. *Publications:* contribs to scientific jls, also texts, espec. in biochemistry and physiology of vitamin B12, immunological and other aspects of gastrointestinal disease and nutrition. *Recreations:* theatre, tennis, walking, sailing, gardening. *Address:* School of Medicine, Stanford University, Stanford, Calif 94305, USA. *Club:* Athenæum.

TAYLOR, Kenneth, CB 1975; Secretary, Export Credits Guarantee Department, 1975–83; *b* 10 Oct. 1923; *s* of William and May Taylor; *m* 1952, Mary Matilda Jacobs; one *s* one *d*. *Educ:* Merchant Taylors' Sch., Crosby; University Coll., Oxford (MA). Commnd RAF, 1943; Flt-Lt 212 Sqdn, 1944–45. Entered Min. of Civil Aviation as Asst Principal, 1947; BoT, later DTI, 1948–56, 1959–74; Treasury, 1957–59; Asst Sec. 1963; idc 1967; Under-Sec., 1969–73; Dep. Sec., 1973; Sec., Price Commn, 1973–74. Member: BOTB, 1975–83; Bd, Crown Agents for Oversea Govts and Admins, 1985–; Crown Agents Holding and Realisation Bd, 1985–. *Recreations:* tennis, chess. *Address:* High Trees, West Hill Way, Totteridge, N20 8QX. *T:* 01–445 7173.

TAYLOR, Kenneth, OBE 1981; FEng, FIMechE, FIEE; FCIT; consultant on railway mechanical and electrical engineering; Director of Mechanical and Electrical Engineering, British Railways Board, 1977–82; *b* 29 Sept. 1921; *s* of Charles Taylor and Amy (*née* Booth); *m* 1945, Elsie Armitt; one *d*. *Educ:* Manchester Coll. of Technol. FIMechE, FIEE 1971; FCIT 1977; FEng 1981. Principal appts with British Railways: Electric Traction Engr, Manchester, 1956; Electrical Engr, LMR, 1963; Chief Mech. and Elec. Engr, LMR, 1970; Traction Engr, BR Bd HQ, 1971. *Recreations:* golf, gardening. *Address:* 137 Burley Lane, Quarndon, Derby DE6 4JS. *T:* Derby 550123.

TAYLOR, Kenneth John; His Honour Judge Kenneth Taylor; a Circuit Judge, since 1977; *b* 29 March 1929; *s* of Hereford Phillips Taylor and Florence Gertrude Taylor; *m* 1953, Joan Cattermole; one *s* one *d*. *Educ:* William Hulme's Grammar Sch., Manchester; Manchester Univ. (LLB). Called to Bar, Middle Temple, 1951. A Recorder of the Crown Court, 1972–77. *Recreations:* reading, music. *Address:* 25 Mill Lane, off The Bank, Scholar Green, Stoke-on-Trent. *T:* Stoke-on-Trent 512102.

TAYLOR, Prof. Kenneth MacDonald, MD; FRCSE, FRCSGlas; FSAScot; British Heart Foundation Professor of Cardiac Surgery, University of London, since 1983, and Professor and Chief of Cardiac Surgery, Royal Postgraduate Medical School, Hammersmith Hospital, since 1983; *b* 20 Oct. 1947; *s* of Hugh Baird Tayor and late Mary Taylor (*née* MacDonald); *m* 1971, Christine Elizabeth (*née* Buchanan); one *s* one *d*. *Educ:* Jordanhill College School; Univ. of Glasgow (MB ChB, MD; Cullen Medal, 1968; Gardner Medal, 1969; Allan Hird Prize, 1969). Univ. of Glasgow: Hall Fellow in Surgery, 1971–72, Lectr and Sen. Lectr in Cardiac Surgery, 1975–83; Consultant Cardiac Surgeon, Royal Infirmary and Western Infirmaries, Glasgow, 1979–83. Member: British Cardiac Soc., 1983–; Amer. Soc. of Thoracic Surgeons, 1984. Editor, Perfusion, 1986–. Peter Allen Prize, Soc. of Thoracic and Cardiovascular Surgeons, 1975; Patey Prize, Surgical Res. Soc., 1977; Fletcher Prize, RCSG, 1977; Watson Prize, RCSG, 1982. *Publications:* Pulsatile Perfusion, 1979, 2nd edn 1982; Handbook of Intensive Care, 1984; Cardiopulmonary Bypass, 1986; numerous articles on cardiac surgery. *Recreations:* music, sport. *Address:* 129 Argyle Road, Ealing, W13 0DB. *T:* 01–997 2322.

TAYLOR, Kenneth Roy E.; *see* Eldin-Taylor.

TAYLOR, Kim; *see* Taylor, L. C.

TAYLOR, Prof. Laurie, (Laurence John); Professor of Sociology, University of York, since 1974; *s* of Stanley Douglas Taylor and Winifred Agnes (*née* Cooper); marr. diss.; one *s*. *Educ:* St Mary's Coll., Liverpool; Rose Bruford College of Drama, Kent; Birkbeck Coll., Univ. of London (BA); Univ. of Leicester (MA). Librarian, 1952–54; Sales Asst, 1954–56; Professional Actor, 1960–61; English Teacher, 1961–64; Lectr in Sociology, 1965–73, Reader in Sociology, 1973–74, Univ. of York. *Publications:* Deviance and Society, 1971; (jtly) Psychological Survival, 1972; (jtly) Crime, Deviance and Socio-Legal Control, 1972; (ed jtly) Politics and Deviance, 1973; Man's Experience of the World, 1976; (jtly) Escape Attempts, 1976; (jtly) Prison Secrets, 1978; (jtly) In Whose Best Interests?, 1980; In the Underworld, 1984; (jtly) Uninvited Guests, 1986; articles, reviews, broadcasts, TV series. *Address:* c/o Department of Sociology, University of York, Heslington, York YO1 5DD. *T:* York 59861.

TAYLOR, Len Clive, (Kim); Director, Calouste Gulbenkian Foundation (UK Branch), since 1982; *b* 4 Aug. 1922; *s* of late S. R. Taylor, Calcutta, India; *m* 1951, Suzanne Dufault, Spencer, Massachusetts, USA; one *s* two *d*. *Educ:* Sevenoaks School; New College, Oxford; Chicago University. New College, Oxford; 1st Cl. Hons Mod. Hist.; Commonwealth Fund Fellowship. Assistant Master, St Paul's School, Darjeeling, India, 1940–42 and 1945–46; Indian Army Intelligence Corps, 1942–45; New College, Oxford, 1946–49; Chicago University, 1949–50; Senior History Master, Repton School, 1950–54; Headmaster, Sevenoaks School, 1954–68; Dir, Nuffield Foundn 'Resources for Learning' Project, 1966–72; Principal Administrator, Centre for Educnl Res. and Innovation, OECD, Paris, 1972–77; Head of Educnl Prog. Services, IBA, 1977–82. *Publications:* Experiments in Education at Sevenoaks, 1965; Resources for Learning, 1971. *Address:* 43 The Drive, Sevenoaks, Kent. *T:* Sevenoaks 451448.

TAYLOR, Leon Eric Manners; Research Analyst; *b* 28 Oct. 1917; *s* of late Leon Eric Taylor and Veronica Dalmahoy (*née* Rogers); *m* 1963, Margaret Betty Thompson; no *c*. *Educ:* Fettes Coll., Edinburgh; Oriel Coll., Oxford. Captain RA (Service, 1939–46). Asst Principal, 1945, Principal, 1948, in Bd of Trade until 1963. First Sec., UK Delegn to the European Communities, 1963–66; Econ. Counsellor, British High Commn, Kuala Lumpur, 1966–70. Called to Bar, Inner Temple, 1951. Attended Joint Services Staff College, 1952. Hon. Visiting Fellow, Centre for Contemporary European Studies, University of Sussex, 1970–71; Counsellor (Commercial), The Hague, 1971–72; Research Fellow, Univ. of Sussex, 1973–75. *Recreations:* walking, amateur theatre, golf. *Address:* Sam's Hill Cottage, 47 North Street, Middle Barton, Oxford OX5 4BH. *T:* Steeple Aston 47256.

TAYLOR, (Margaret) Jessie; Headmistress, Whalley Range High School for Girls, since 1976; *b* 30 Nov. 1924; *d* of Thomas Brown Gowland and Ann Goldie Gowland; *m* 1958, Eric Taylor, *qv*. *Educ:* Queen Elizabeth's Grammar Sch., Middleton; Manchester Univ. (BA Hons, DipEd). Jun. Classics Teacher, Cheadle Hulme Sch., 1946–49; North Manchester Grammar School for Girls: Sen. Classics Teacher, 1950; Sen. Mistress, 1963; Actg Headmistress, Jan.-July 1967; Dep. Head Teacher, Wright Robinson Comprehensive High Sch., 1967–75. Member: Council and Exams Cttee, Associated Lancs Schs Examining Bd, 1976– (Mem. Classics Panel, 1968–72); Nursing Educn Cttee, S Manchester Area, 1976–; Home Office Cttee on Obscenity and Film Censorship, 1977–79; Consultant Course Tutor, NW Educnl Management Centre, Padgate, 1980–82. Mem. Court, Salford Univ., 1982–. FRSA 1980. *Recreations:* music, drama, riding. *Address:* 10 Mercers Road, Hopwood, Heywood, Lancs OL10 2NP. *T:* Heywood 66630.

TAYLOR, Rt. Rev. Maurice; *see* Galloway, Bishop of, (RC).

TAYLOR, General Maxwell Davenport, DSC (US) 1944; DSM (US) 1945 (3 Oak Leaf Clusters, 1954, 1959, 1964); Silver Star 1943 (Oak Leaf Cluster, 1944); Legion of Merit; Bronze Star; Purple Heart; Consultant to President of US; President, Institute of Defense Analyses; Member, Foreign Intelligence Advisory Board, since 1965; *b* 26 Aug. 1901; *s* of John Earle Maxwell Taylor and Pearle Davenport; *m* 1925, Lydia Gardner (*née* Happer); two *s*. *Educ:* US Milit. Academy (BS). Became artillery commander of 82nd Airborne Division by Dec. 1942; served in Sicilian and Italian Campaigns; in 1944 became Commanding Gen. of 101st Airborne Div., which he led in the airborne invasion of Normandy, the airborne invasion of Holland, and in the Ardennes and Central Europe Campaigns; supt US Mil. Acad., 1945; Chief of Staff, European Comd HQ, Heidelberg, Jan. 1949; first US Comdr, Berlin, Sept. 1949; Asst Chief of Staff for Ops, G3, Dept of Army, Feb. 1951; Dep. Chief of Staff for Ops and Admin. of Army, Aug. 1951; Comdg Gen., 8th US Army in Korea, 1953; Comdr of all ground forces in Japan, Okinawa and Korea, at Camp Zama, Japan, Nov. 1954; C-in-C of Far East Comd and UN Comd, 1955; Chief of Staff, US Army, 1955–59; Mil. Representative of the President of the USA, 1961–62; Chairman, Joint Chiefs of Staff, US, Oct. 1962–June 1964; American Ambassador to South Vietnam, 1964–65; Special Consultant to President, 1965–69. Formerly Director of companies (including Chairman Board, Mexican Light & Power Co.); was also President, Lincoln Center for the Performing Arts. Holds fifteen Honorary doctorates. Many foreign decorations. *Publications:* The Uncertain Trumpet, 1960; Responsibility and Response, 1967; Swords and Plowshares, 1972; Precarious Security, 1976. *Recreations:* tennis, handball and squash. *Address:* 2500 Massachusetts Avenue NW, Washington, DC 20008, USA. *Clubs:* University (NYC); Army and Navy, International, Chevy Chase, Alibi (Washington).

TAYLOR, Rev. Michael Hugh; JP; Director, Christian Aid, since 1985; *b* 8 Sept. 1936; *s* of Albert Ernest and Gwendoline Louisa Taylor; *m* 1960, Adèle May Dixon; two *s* one *d*. *Educ:* Northampton Grammar School; Univ. of Manchester (BA, BD, MA); Union Theological Seminary, NY (STM). Baptist Minister, N Shields, 1961–66, Birmingham Hall Green, 1966–69; Principal, Northern Baptist Coll., Manchester, 1970–85; Lectr, Univ. of Manchester, 1970–85. JP Manchester, 1980. *Publications:* Variations on a Theme, 1973; Sermon on the Mount, 1982; (ed) Christians and the Future of Social Democracy, 1982; Learning to Care, 1983; contribs to books and jls. *Recreations:* walking, cooking, theatre. *Address:* c/o Christian Aid, PO Box No 1, SW9 8BH.

TAYLOR, Neville; Director-General, Central Office of Information, since 1985; *b* 17 Nov. 1930; *y s* of late Frederick Taylor and of Lottie Taylor; *m* 1954, Margaret Ann, *y d* of late Thomas Bainbridge Vickers and Gladys Vickers; two *s*. *Educ:* Sir Joseph Williamson's Mathematical Sch., Rochester; Coll. of Commerce, Gillingham, Kent. Junior Reporter, Chatham News Group, 1947; Royal Signals, 1948–50; Journalism, 1950–58; Asst Information Officer, Admiralty, 1958; Information Officer (Press), Admiralty, 1960; Fleet Information Officer, Singapore, 1963; Chief Press Officer, MoD, 1966; Information Adviser to Nat. Economic Develt Office, 1968; Dep. Dir, Public Relns (Royal Navy), 1970; Head of Information, Min. of Agriculture, Fisheries and Food, 1971; Dep. Dir of Information, DoE, 1973–74, Dir of Information, 1974–79; Dir of Information, DHSS, 1979–82; Chief of Public Relations, MOD, 1982–85. *Recreation:* fishing. *Address:* Crow Lane House, Crow Lane, Rochester, Kent ME1 1RF. *T:* Medway 42990.

TAYLOR, Nicholas George Frederick, CMG 1970; FIPR 1973; Development Director, East Caribbean; Higgs & Hill (UK) Ltd, 1973–80; Chairman: Higgs & Hill (St Kitts) Ltd, 1973–80; West Indies General Insurance Co., since 1979; Caribbean (East) Currency Authority, 1983 (Director, since 1981); Director, Cariblue Hotels Ltd, St Lucia, since 1968; Local Adviser, Barclays Bank International, St Lucia, since 1974; *b* 14 Feb. 1917; 3rd *s* of Louis Joseph Taylor and Philipsie (*née* Phillip); *m* 1952, Morella Agnes, *e d* of George Duncan Pitcairn and Florence (*née* La Guerre); two *s* two *d*. *Educ:* St Mary's Coll., St Lucia; LSE, London; Gonville and Caius Coll., Cambridge. Clerk, various Depts, St Lucia, 1937–46; Asst Social Welfare Officer, 1948–49; Public Relations and Social Welfare Officer, 1949–54; District Officer, and Authorised Officer, Ordnance Area, St Lucia, 1954–57; Dep. Dir St Lucia Br., Red Cross Soc., 1956–57; Perm. Sec., Min. of Trade and Production, 1957–58 (acted Harbour Master in conjunction with substantive duties); Commn for W Indies in UK: Administrative Asst, 1959; Asst Sec.-Chief Community Development Officer, Migrants Services Div., 1961; Commn in UK for Eastern Caribbean Govts: Officer-in-Charge, 1962–63; Actg Comr, 1964–66; Comr for E Caribbean Govts in UK, 1967–73. Dir, St Lucia (Co-operative) Bank Ltd, 1973–74. Mem., Civil Service Appeals Bd, 1973–77. Vice-Chm. Commonwealth Assoc., Bexley, Crayford and Erith, 1965–67; a Patron, British-Caribbean Assoc., 1962–73. Member: West India Committee Executive, 1968–; Bd of Governors, Commonwealth Inst., 1968–73. Assoc. Mem. 1951, Mem. 1962, Fellow, 1973, (British) Inst. of Public Relations. Chairman: Central Library Bd, 1973–81, Nat. Insurance Scheme, 1979–81, St Lucia; Central Housing Authority, St Lucia, 1975–77; Income Tax Comrs Appeals Bd, 1980–; St Lucia Boy Scouts Assoc., 1977–79. Vice-Chm., Nat. Develt Corp., 1979–. Founder Life Mem., Cambridge Soc., 1976. JP 1948. Coronation Medal, 1953; British Red Cross Medal, 1949–59. *Recreations:* cricket, lawn tennis, reading. *Address:* PO Box 816, Castries, St Lucia, West Indies. *T:* 8513. *Clubs:* Royal Commonwealth Society (West Indian), Travellers'.

TAYLOR, Sir Nicholas Richard S.; *see* Stuart Taylor.

TAYLOR, Peter, BScEcon, FCIS; Clerk of the Senate, University of London, since 1977; *b* 5 Jan. 1924; *s* of late Frederick and Doris Taylor; *m* 1948, Jeannette (*née* Evans); two *d*. *Educ:* Salt Boys' High Sch., Saltaire, Yorks; Bradford Technical Coll. (BScEcon London, 1949). FCIS 1959. Served War, FAA, 1942–46. WR Treasurer's Dept, 1940–50; Registrar, Lincoln Technical Coll., 1950–58; Secretary: Wolverhampton and Staffs Coll. of Technol., 1959–60; Chelsea Coll., Univ. of London, 1961–77. Pres., Assoc. of Coll. Registrars, 1970–72. *Recreations:* walking, painting, sailing. *Address:* April Cottage, 52 Wattleton Road, Beaconsfield, Bucks.

TAYLOR, Dr Peter John; International Medical Adviser, Unilever PLC, since 1981; Chief Examiner, Faculty of Occupational Medicine, Royal College of Physicians, since 1984; Hon. Consultant in Occupational Medicine: Guy's Hospital, since 1968; King's College Hospital Medical School, since 1975; Civil Consultant in Occupational Medicine, Royal Air Force, since 1984; *b* 24 Sept. 1929; *s* of late Comdr Sam Taylor and Alice (*née* Storm); *m* 1959, Josephine Marian Hetherington; one *s* one *d*. *Educ:* Clifton Coll.; St Thomas's Hosp. Med. Sch. (BSc (Hons) 1951; MB (Hons) 1954); DIH (Soc. of Apothecaries) 1962; MD 1966; FRCP 1971; FFCM 1976; FFOM 1978. RAF Medical Br., 1956–58, Sqn Ldr. St Thomas's Hospital: House Physician appts, 1955–56; Medical Registrar, 1959–60; MO PT, Shell Indonesia, 1960–63; Sen. MO, Shell Haven Refinery, Essex, 1963–68; Dep. Dir, TUC Centenary Inst. of Occupational Health, LSHTM, 1968–71; CMO, Post Office, 1971–81. Visiting Professor: McMaster Univ., Ontario, 1979–80; in Occupational Medicine, LSHTM, 1982–; Examiner: MSc Occupational Med., Univ. of London, 1978–81; DIH, Conjoint Bd, 1973–77; Dundee Univ., 1977–79; Soc. of Apothecaries, 1978–. Member: Med. Adv. Cttee, Health and Safety Commn, 1977–83; Standing Med. Adv. Cttee, DHSS, 1982–; Vice Dean, 1978–81, and Dean, 1981–84, Faculty of Occupational Medicine, RCP. Royal Society of Medicine: Fellow, 1960; Hon. Sec., then Vice-Pres., Occupational Medicine Sect., 1966–72; Pres., Soc. of Occupational Medicine, 1974–75. Vice Pres., E Anglian Donkey Show, 1984–. OStJ 1982. *Publications:* Absenteeism, 1969, 4th edn 1982; Health at Work, 1975; chapters in Occupational Health Practice, 1973, 2nd edn 1981; papers on occupational medicine, sickness absence, shift work, employment of disabled, etc. *Recreations:* music, gardening, donkeys. *Address:* Pudingswell, Monks Eleigh, Ipswich, Suffolk IP7 7AD. *T:* Bildeston 740695. *Club:* Royal Air Force.

TAYLOR, Hon. Sir Peter (Murray), Kt 1980; **Hon. Mr Justice Taylor**; a Judge of the High Court of Justice, Queen's Bench Division, since 1980; Presiding Judge, North-Eastern Circuit, since 1984; *b* 1 May 1930; *s* of Herman Louis Taylor, medical practitioner and Raie Helena Taylor (*née* Shockett); *m* 1956, Irene Shirley, *d* of Lionel and Mary Harris; one *s* three *d*. *Educ:* Newcastle upon Tyne Royal Gram. Sch.; Pembroke Coll., Cambridge (Exhibr). Called to Bar, Inner Temple, 1954, Bencher, 1975; QC 1967; Vice-Chm. of the Bar, 1978–79, Chm., 1979–80. Recorder of: Huddersfield, 1969–70; Teesside, 1970–71; Dep. Chm., Northumberland QS, 1970–71; a Recorder of the Crown Court, 1972–80. Leader of NE Circuit, 1975–80. Hon. Member: Amer. Bar Assoc., 1980–; Canadian Bar Assoc., 1980–. *Recreation:* music. *Address:* Royal Courts of Justice, Strand, WC2A 2LL. *Club:* Garrick.

TAYLOR, Peter William Edward, QC 1981; *b* 27 July 1917; *s* of late Peter and Julia A. Taylor; *m* 1948, Julia Mary Brown, *d* of Air Cdre Sir Vernon Brown, *qv*; two *s*. *Educ:* Peter Symonds' Sch., Winchester; Christ's Coll., Cambridge (MA; Wrangler, Math. Tripos, Part II; 1st Class, Law Tripos, Part II). Served RA, 1939–46: France and Belgium, 1939–40; N Africa, 1942–43; NW Europe, 1944–45 (mentioned in dispatches); Actg Lt-Col 1945; transferred to TARO as Hon. Major, 1946. Called to the Bar, Inner Temple, 1946; Lincoln's Inn, *ad eundem*, 1953 (Bencher, 1976); practice at the Bar, 1947–; Occasional Lectr, LSE, 1946–56; Lectr in Construction of Documents, Council of Legal Educn, 1952–70; Conveyancing Counsel of the Court, 1974–81. Member: General Council of the Bar, 1971–74; Senate of Inns of Court and the Bar, 1974–75; Inter-Professional Cttee on Retirement Provision, 1974–; Land Registration Rule Cttee, 1976–81; Standing Cttee on Conveyancing, 1985–; Incorporated Council of Law Reporting, 1977–; Council, Selden Soc., 1977–. *Recreations:* sailing, shooting, music. *Address:* 46 Onslow Square, SW7 3NX. *T:* 01–589 1301; Carey Sconce, Yarmouth, Isle of Wight.

TAYLOR, Philippe Arthur; Chief Executive, Birmingham Convention and Visitor Bureau Ltd, since 1981; *b* 9 Feb. 1937; *s* of Arthur Peach Taylor and Simone Vacquin; *m* 1973, Margaret Nancy Wilkins; two *s*. *Educ:* Trinity College, Glenalmond; St Andrews University. Procter & Gamble, 1963; Masius International, 1967; British Tourist Authority, 1970; Chief Executive, Scottish Tourist Board, 1975–80. *Publications:* childrens' books; various papers and articles on tourism. *Recreations:* sailing, making things, tourism, reading. *Address:* Cadogan House, Beauchamp Avenue, Leamington Spa, Warwickshire. *Clubs:* Royal Yachting Association; Royal Northumberland Yacht (Blyth).

TAYLOR, Phyllis Mary Constance, MA; Honorary Associate, Institute of Education, London, since 1983; *b* 29 Sept. 1926; *d* of Cecil and Constance Tedder; *m* 1949, Peter

Royston Taylor; one *s*. *Educ:* Woodford High Sch.; Sudbury High Sch., Suffolk; Girton Coll., Cambridge (State Scholar; BA Hons History, 1948; MA 1951). Asst Hist. Mistress, Loughton High Sch., 1948–51, Head of Hist., 1951–58; Teacher of Hist. and Religious Educn, Lancaster Royal Grammar Sch. for Boys, 1959; Head of Hist., Casterton Sch. (private boarding), Kirby Lonsdale, 1960; Teacher of Gen. Subjects, Lancaster Girls' Grammar Sch., 1960–61, Head of Hist., 1961–62; Dep. Headmistress, Carlisle Sch., Chelsea, 1962–64; Headmistress: Walthamstow High Sch. for Girls, 1964–68; Walthamstow Sen. High Sch., 1968–75; Wanstead High Sch., London Borough of Redbridge, 1976–82. Consultant Head to NE London Polytechnic (Counselling/Careers sect.), 1974–78; Moderator, Part-time Diploma, Pastoral Care and Counselling, 1979–85. Pres., Essex Sector, Secondary Heads' Assoc., 1978–79. Member: UGC, 1978–83 (Mem., Educn Sub-Cttee, 1978–, and Wkg Party on Continuing Educn, 1983); Teacher Trng Sub-Cttee, Adv. Cttee on Supply and Educn of Teachers, 1980–85; former Mem., Nat. Exec., Assoc. of Head Mistresses. Mem., RAM Foundn Appeals Cttee, 1985–. Chm., Dunmow Liberals, 1986–. *Recreations:* music, theatre, horse riding, driving, country life, ecology. *Address:* White Horses, High Roding, Great Dunmow, Essex CM6 1NS. *T:* Great Dunmow 3161.

TAYLOR, Robert Carruthers; His Honour Judge Robert Taylor; a Circuit Judge, since 1984; *b* 6 Jan. 1939; *o s* of late John Taylor, CBE, TD, MA, DL and of Barbara Mary Taylor; *m* 1968, Jacqueline Marjorie, *er d* of Nigel and Marjorie Chambers; one *s* one *d*. *Educ:* Moorlands School; Wycliffe Coll.; St John's Coll., Oxford (Exhibnr). MA 1967. Called to Bar, Middle Temple, 1961; Member, NE Circuit, 1962–84 (Junior, 1964); a Recorder, 1976–84; Prosecuting Counsel to Inland Revenue, NE Circuit, 1978–84. Chm., Agricl Land Tribunal, Yorks and Lancs Area, 1979–82, Yorks and Humberside Area, 1982–; Asst Parly Boundary Comr, Rotherham, Sheffield, Bolton, 1981–82. *Recreations:* reading, music, spectating, gardening, domestic life. *Address:* The Courthouse, 1 Oxford Row, Leeds LS1 3BE. *T:* Leeds 451616.

TAYLOR, Robert Martin, OBE 1976; Editorial Director, The Croydon Advertiser Ltd, 1967–76; *b* 25 Nov. 1914; *s* of Ernest H. and Charlotte Taylor; *m* 1947, Ray Turney; one *s* one *d*. *Educ:* Simon Langton, Canterbury. Croydon Advertiser: Editor, 1950–58; Managing Editor, 1958–74; Dir, 1967–76. Mem., Nat. Council for the Training of Journalists, 1967–71; Pres., Guild of British Newspaper Editors, 1971–72, Hon. Vice-Pres., 1976; Mem., Press Council, 1974–76. Sec., Glenurquhart Community Council, 1982–; Hon. Treasurer, Glenurquart Rural Community Assoc., 1984–. *Publications:* Editor and co-author, Essential Law for Journalists, 1954, 6th edn 1975; Glenurquhart Official Guide, 1980. *Address:* Glengarry, Milton, Drumnadrochit, Inverness-shire. *T:* Drumnadrochit 291.

TAYLOR, Robert Richardson, QC (Scotland) 1959; MA, LLB, PhD; Sheriff-Principal of Tayside Central and Fife, since 1975; *b* 16 Sept. 1919; *m* 1949, Märtha Birgitta Björkling; two *s* one *d*. *Educ:* Glasgow High School; Glasgow University. Called to Bar, Scotland, 1944; called to Bar, Middle Temple, 1948. Lectr in Internat. Private Law, Edinburgh Univ., 1947–69; Sheriff-Principal, Stirling, Dunbarton and Clackmannan, 1971–75. Contested (U and NL): Dundee East, 1955; Dundee West, 1959 and Nov. 1963. Chm., Central and Southern Region, Scottish Cons. Assoc., 1969–71. Chm., Northern Lighthouse Bd, 1985–86. *Recreations:* fishing, ski-ing. *Address:* 51 Northumberland Street, Edinburgh. *T:* 031–556 1722.

TAYLOR, (Robert) Ronald, CBE 1971; Chairman: Robert Taylor Ironfounders (Holdings) Ltd; Tayforth Foundry Ltd; *b* 25 Aug. 1916; *e s* of late Robert Taylor, ironfounder, Larbert; *m* 1941, Margaret, *d* of late William Purdie, Coatbridge; two *s* two *d*. *Educ:* High Sch., Stirling. Chm., Glenrothes Develt Corp., 1964–78. *Recreations:* fishing, shooting, golf. *Address:* Beoraid, Caledonian Crescent, Auchterarder, Perthshire. *Club:* Army and Navy.

TAYLOR, Rt. Rev. Robert Selby, CBE 1983; *b* 1 March 1909; *s* of late Robert Taylor, Eden Bank, Wetheral, Cumberland; unmarried. *Educ:* Harrow; St Catharine's Coll., Cambridge; Cuddesdon Coll. Ordained deacon, 1932; priest, 1933; served as a curate at St Olave's, York; went out to Diocese of Northern Rhodesia in 1935 as a Mission priest; Principal of Diocesan Theological Coll., 1939; Bishop of Northern Rhodesia, 1941–51; Bishop of Pretoria, 1951–59; Bishop of Grahamstown, 1959–64; Archbishop of Cape Town, 1964–74; Bishop of Central Zambia, 1979–84. Hon. Fellow, St Catharine's Coll., Cambridge, 1964. DD (Hon.) Rhodes Univ., 1966. *Address:* 36 Alexandra Road, Wynberg 7700, South Africa. *T:* 77 1440. *Clubs:* Royal Commonwealth Society; City and Civil Service (Cape Town).

TAYLOR, Dr Robert Thomas; Representative, British Council, Greece, since 1986; *b* 21 March 1933; *s* of George Taylor and Marie Louise Fidler; *m* 1965, Rosemary Janet Boileau; three *s* one *d*. *Educ:* Boteler Grammar Sch., Warrington; University Coll., Oxford (Open Exhbnr; BA 1954, MA 1957; DPhil 1957). Fulbright Scholar. Research Associate, Randall Lab. of Physics, Univ. of Michigan, USA, 1957–58; ICI Research Fellow, 1958–59, Lectr, Physics Dept, 1959–61, Univ. of Liverpool; Chief Examr for NUJMB, GCE Physics (Scholarship Level), 1961; British Council: Asst Regional Rep., Madras, 1961–64; Science Officer, Madrid, 1964–69; Dir, Staff Recruitment Dept, 1969–73; Regional Educn Advr, Bombay, 1973–77; Rep., Mexico, 1977–81; Controller, Personnel, 1981–86. *Publications:* contrib. to Chambers Encyclopaedia, 1967 edn; papers in scientific jls. *Recreations:* making harpsichords, computers, music, theatre. *Address:* Mark Haven, High Street, Cranbrook, Kent TN17 3EW. *T:* Cranbrook 714212.

TAYLOR, Roger Miles Whitworth; Town Clerk and Chief Executive, City of Manchester, since 1985; *b* 18 May 1944; *s* of Richard and Joan Taylor; *m* 1969, Georgina Lucy Tonks; two *s* two *d*. *Educ:* Repton School; Birmingham University (LLB). Solicitor, admitted 1968; Asst Sol., Cheshire CC, 1969–71; Asst County Clerk, Lincs parts of Lindsey, 1971–73; Dep. County Secretary, Northants CC, 1973–79; Dep. Town Clerk, City of Manchester, 1979–85. Mem., Farrand Cttee on Conveyancing, 1983–84; Company Secretary, Manchester Airport plc, 1986–; Clerk, Greater Manchester Passenger Transport Authy, 1986–. *Publications:* contribs to Local Govt Chronicle, Municipal Review, Municipal Jl. *Recreations:* sailing, walking. *Address:* 98 Wythenshawe Road, Northenden, Manchester M23 0PA.

TAYLOR, Ronald; *see* Taylor, R. R.

TAYLOR, Ronald George; Director-General, Association of British Chambers of Commerce, since 1984; *b* 12 Dec. 1935; *s* of Ernest and May Taylor; *m* 1960, Patricia Stoker; one *s* two *d*. *Educ:* Jesus College, Oxford (BA Modern Langs). Commnd Royal Signals, 1957–59. Leeds Chamber of Commerce and Industry: joined, 1959; Asst Sec., 1964–74; Director, 1974–84. Reg. Sec., Assoc. of Yorks and Humberside Chambers of Commerce, 1974–84. *Recreations:* Rugby Union, bridge. *Address:* 2 Holly Bush Lane, Harpenden, Herts. *T:* Harpenden 2139.

TAYLOR, Selwyn Francis, DM, MCh, FRCS; Dean Emeritus and Fellow, Royal Postgraduate Medical School, London; Senior Lecturer in Surgery, and Surgeon, Hammersmith Hospital; Emeritus Consultant to Royal Navy; Member, Armed Forces Medical Advisory Board; Examiner in Surgery, Universities of Oxford, London, Manchester, Leeds, National University of Ireland, West Indies, Makerere and Society of Apothecaries; *b* Sale, Cheshire, 16 Sept. 1913; *s* of late Alfred Petre Taylor and Emily Taylor, Salcombe, Devon; *m* 1939, Ruth Margaret, 2nd *d* of late Sir Alfred Howitt, CVO; one *s* one *d*. *Educ:* Peter Symonds, Winchester; Keble College, Oxford; King's College Hospital. BA (Hons) Oxford, 1936; Burney Yeo Schol., King's Coll. Hosp., 1936; MA Oxon; MRCS, LRCP, 1939; FRCS 1940; MCh, 1946; DM 1959. Surgical Registrar, King's Coll. Hosp., 1946–47; Oxford Univ. George Herbert Hunt Travelling Schol., Stockholm, 1947; Rockefeller Travelling Fellow in Surgery, 1948–49; Research Fellow, Harvard Univ., and Fellow in Clin. Surgery, Massachusetts Gen. Hosp., Boston, Mass, USA, 1948–49. RNVR, 1940–46; Surgeon Lt-Comdr; Surgeon Specialist, Kintyre, East Indies, Australia; Surgeon: Belgrave Hosp. for Children, 1946–65; Hammersmith Hosp., 1947–78; King's Coll. Hospital, 1951–65. Bradshaw Lectr, RCS, 1977; Legg Meml Lectr, KCH, 1979. President: Harveian Soc., 1969; Internat. Assoc. Endocrine Surgeons, 1979–81; Member: Council, RCS, 1966– (Senior Vice-Pres., 1976–77 and 1977–78; Joll Prize, 1976); GMC, 1974–83; Surgical Research Soc.; Internat. Soc. for Surgery; Fellow Assoc. Surgeons of GB; FRSM; Hon. FRCSE 1976; Hon. FCS (S Africa) 1978; Corresp. Fellow Amer. Thyroid Assoc.; Pres., London Thyroid Club and Sec., Fourth Internat. Goitre Conference. Mem., Senate of London Univ., 1970–75. Chm., Heinemann Medical Books, 1972–83. *Publications:* books and papers on surgical subjects and thyroid physiology. *Recreations:* sailing, tennis, wine. *Address:* Trippets, Bosham, West Sussex. *T:* Bosham 573387. *Clubs:* Garrick, Hurlingham; Bosham Sailing (Trustee).

TAYLOR, Maj.-Gen. Walter Reynell, CB 1981; Director, Middle East Centre for Management Studies, Nicosia, Cyprus, since 1984; *b* 5 April 1928; *s* of Col Richard Reynell Taylor and Margaret Catherine Taylor (*née* Holme); *m* 1st, 1954, Doreen Myrtle Dodge; *s* one *d*; 2nd, 1982, Mrs Rosemary Gardner (*née* Breed). *Educ:* Wellington; RMC, Sandhurst. Commissioned 4th/7th Royal Dragoon Guards, Dec. 1948; Directing Staff, Staff Coll., 1963–66; GSO1 Jt Planning Staff, Far East Comd, 1967–69; Commanded: 4th/7th Royal Dragoon Guards, 1969–71; 12 Mechanised Bde, 1972–74; rcds 1975; Brig., Mil. Operations, MoD, 1976–78; Administrator, Sovereign Base Areas of Cyprus, Comdr British Forces and Land Forces, Cyprus, 1978–80; COS, HQ BAOR, 1980–83. *Recreations:* sailing, riding, golf. *Address:* PO Box 2098, Nicosia, Cyprus. *Clubs:* Special Forces; Royal Automobile Yacht.

TAYLOR, Wendy Ann; sculptor; Specialist Adviser, Fine Art Board, Council of National Academic Awards, since 1985 (Member, 1980–85); Royal Fine Art Commission, since 1981; *b* 29 July 1945; *d* of Edward Philip Taylor and Lilian Maude Wright; *m* 1982, Bruce Robertson; one *s*. *Educ:* St Martin's School of Art. LDAD (Hons). One-man exhibitions: Axiom Gall., London, 1970; Angela Flowers Gall., London, 1972; 24th King's Lynn Fest., Norfolk, and World Trade Centre, London, 1974; Annely Juda Fine Art, London, 1975; Oxford Gall., Oxford, 1976; Oliver Dowling Gall., Dublin, 1976 and 1979; Building Art—the process, London. Shown in over 100 group exhibitions, 1964–82. Represented in collections in GB, USA, Eire, NZ, Germany, Sweden, Qatar, Switzerland, Seychelles. Major commissions: The Travellers 1969, London; Gazebo (edn of 4) 1970–72, London, New York, Suffolk, Oxford; Triad 1971, Oxford; Timepiece 1973, London; Calthae 1977, Leicestershire; Octo 1979, Milton Keynes; Counterpoise 1980, Birmingham; Compass Bowl 1980, Basildon; Sentinel 1981, Reigate; Bronze Relief 1981, Canterbury; Equatorial Sundial 1982, Bletchley; Essence 1982, Milton Keynes; Opus 1983, Morley Coll., London; Gazebo 1983, Golder's Hill Park, London; Network, London, 1984; Geo I & Geo II, Stratford-Upon-Avon, 1985; Landscape, and Tree of the Wood 1986, Fernhurst, Surrey; Pharos 1986, Peel Park, E Kilbride; Globe Sundial 1987, Swansea. Design Consultant, Basildon Develt Corp., 1985–. Examiner, Univ. of London, 1982; Mem. Court, RCA, 1982–; Mem. Council, Morley Coll., 1985. Awards: Walter Neurath, 1964; Pratt, 1965; Sainsbury, 1966; Arts Council, 1977; Duais Na Riochta (Kingdom Prize) Gold Medal, Eire, 1977; 1st Prize Silk Screen, Barcham Green Print Comp., 1978. *Recreation:* gardening. *Address:* 73 Bow Road, Bow E3 2AN. *T:* 01–981 2037.

TAYLOR, Prof. William, CBE 1982; Vice-Chancellor, University of Hull, since 1985; *b* 31 May 1930; *s* of Herbert and Maud E. Taylor, Crayford, Kent; *m* 1954, Rita, *d* of Ronald and Marjorie Hague, Sheffield; one *s* two *d*. *Educ:* Erith Grammar Sch.; London Sch. of Economics; Westminster Coll.; Univ. of London Inst. of Educn. BSc Econ 1952, PhD 1960. Teaching in Kent, 1953–56; Deputy Head, Slade Green Secondary Sch., 1956–59; Sen. Lectr, St Luke's Coll., Exeter, 1959–61; Head of Educn Dept, Bede Coll., Durham, 1961–64; Tutor and Lectr in Educn, Univ. of Oxford, 1964–66; Prof. of Educn and Dir of Sch. of Educn, Univ. of Bristol, 1966–73; Dir, Univ. of London Inst. of Educn, 1973–83; Principal, Univ. of London, 1983–85. Research Consultant, Dept of Educn and Science (part-time), 1968–73; Chairman: European Cttee for Educnl Research, 1969–71; Cttee on Training of Univ. Teachers, 1981–; NFER, 1983–; Council for the Accreditation of Teacher Educn, 1984–. UK Rep., Permanent Educn Steering Cttee, Council of Europe, 1971–73; Rapporteur, OECD Review of Educn in NZ, 1982–83; Chairman: UK Nat. Commn for UNESCO, 1975–85 (Mem., 1973–85); Educnl Adv. Council, IBA, 1974–82; UCET, 1976–79. Member: UGC Educn Cttee, 1971–80; British Library Res. and Develt Cttee, 1975–79; Open Univ. Academic Adv. Cttee, 1975–82; SSRC Educnl Research Board, 1976–80 (Vice-Chm., 1978–80); Adv. Cttee on Supply and Training of Teachers, 1976–79; Working Gp on Management of Higher Educn, 1977–78; Steering Cttee on Future of Examinations at 16+, 1977–78; Cttee of Vice-Chancellors and Principals, 1980–; Adv. Cttee on Supply and Educn of Teachers (Sec. of State's nominee), 1980–. Member: Senate, Univ. of London, 1977–85; Cttee of Management, Inst. of Advanced Legal Studies, 1980–83; Council, Open Univ., 1984–. Commonwealth Vis. Fellow, Australian States, 1975; NZ UGC Prestige Fellowship, 1977. President: Council for Educn in World Citizenship, 1979–; English New Educn Fellowship, 1979–; Comparative Educn Soc. of GB, 1981–; Pres., Assoc. of Colls of Further and Higher Educn, 1984–86; Vice President: Soc. for Research in Higher Educn, 1983–. British Educnl Admin, and Management Soc., 1985–. Chm., NFER/Nelson Publishing Co., 1985–86. Governor, Wye Coll., 1981–83. Freeman, City of London, 1985. Hon. DSc Aston (Birmingham), 1977; Hon. LittD Leeds, 1979; Hon. DCL Kent, 1981; DUniv Open, 1983; Hon. DLitt Loughborough, 1984. Hon. FCP 1977. Hon. FCCEA 1980. Yeoman, Worshipful Soc. of Apothecaries of London, 1983–. *Publications:* The Secondary Modern School, 1963; Society and the Education of Teachers, 1969; (ed with G. Baron) Educational Administration and the Social Sciences, 1969; Heading for Change, 1969; Planning and Policy in Post Secondary Education, 1972; Theory into Practice, 1972; Research Perspectives in Education, 1973; (ed with R. Farquhar and R. Thomas) Educational Administration in Australia and Abroad, 1975; Research and Reform in Teacher Education, 1978; (ed with B. Simon) Education in the Eighties: the central issues, 1981; (ed) Metaphors of Education, 1984; The Role and Functions of Universities, 1986; articles and papers in professional jls. *Recreations:* writing, walking. *Address:* University of Hull, Hull HU6 7RX.

TAYLOR, William Bernard; Public Sector Specialist Adviser to Arthur Young, MIM Ltd and Sedgwick UK Ltd, since 1986; *b* 13 Dec. 1930; *s* of Frank and Elizabeth Taylor;

m 1956, Rachel May Davies; one *s* two *d*. *Educ:* Dynevor Sch., Swansea; Univ. of Kent. MA; IPFA, FRSA, FBIM. Nat. Service, RN, 1949–51; commnd RNVR; served in coastal forces. District Audit Service, 1951–61; Llwchwr UDC, 1961–70; Asst Educn Officer, Manchester Corp., 1970–72; Asst County Treasurer, 1972–73, Dep. County Treasurer, 1973–80, County Treasurer, 1980–86, Kent. Financial Adviser: Social Servs, ACC, 1983–86; Standing Conf. of Planning Auths in SE England, 1983–86; Hon. Treas., SE England Tourist Bd, 1980–86; consultant to wkg party of Council of Europe on borrowing by municipalities of member states, 1982–. Mem., Rotary Club. *Publications:* The Management of Assets: terotechnology in the pursuit of economic life cycle costs, 1980; contribs to local govt and other learned journals. *Recreations:* cricket, rugby, public speaking. *Address:* Selby Shaw, Heath Road, Boughton Monchelsea, near Maidstone, Kent ME17 4JE. *T:* Maidstone 45022.

TAYLOR, Lt-Comdr William Horace, GC 1941; MBE 1973; Commissioner of the Scout Association, since 1946; *b* 23 Oct. 1908; *s* of William Arthur Taylor; *m* 1946, Joan Isabel Skaife d'Ingerthorpe; one *s* three *d*. *Educ:* Manchester Grammar Sch. Junior Partner, 1929; Managing Dir, 1937. Served War: Dept of Torpedoes and Mines, Admiralty, 1940 (despatches, 1941); Founder Mem., Naval Clearance Divers, HMS Vernon (D), 1944. Travelling Commissioner for Sea Scouts of UK, 1946; Field Commissioner for SW England, Scout Association, 1952–74, Estate Manager, 1975–84. *Recreations:* scouting, boating, music. *Address:* The Bungalow, Carbeth, Blanefield, near Glasgow. *T:* Blanefield 70847. *Clubs:* Naval; Manchester Cruising Association.

TAYLOR, William Leonard, CBE 1982; JP; DL; solicitor in private practice; *b* 21 Dec. 1916; *s* of Joseph and May Taylor; *m* 1943, Gladys Carling; one *s*. *Educ:* Whitehill School; Glasgow Univ. (BL). Chairman: Livingston Develt Corp., 1965–72; Scottish Water Adv. Cttee, 1969–72; Mem., Scottish Adv. Cttee on Civil Aviation, 1965–72; Chm., Panel of Assessors, River Clyde Planning Study, 1972–74. Chairman: Planning Exchange, 1972–; Scottish Adv. Council on Social Work, 1974–81; Vice-Chm., Commn for Local Authority Accounts in Scotland, 1974–83; Mem., Housing Corp., 1974–80; Chm. Scottish Special Housing Assoc., 1978–81; Member: Scottish Economic Council, 1975–81; Extra-Parly Panel under Private Legislation Procedure (Scotland) Act 1936, 1971–. Councillor, City of Glasgow, 1952–69; Magistrate, City of Glasgow, 1956–60; Sen. Magistrate, 1960–61; Leader, Labour Gp in Glasgow Corp., 1962–69; Leader of Council, 1962–68; Convener of Cttees: Planning, Glasgow Airport, Sports Centre, Parly Bills. Governor, Centre for Environmental Studies, 1966–79; Trustee, Scottish Civic Trust, 1967–; Chm., Glasgow Citizens' Theatre Ltd, 1970–; Mem., Nat. Executive (and Chm. Scottish Exec.), Town & Country Planning Assoc. Hon. Vice-Pres., Scotland-USSR Friendship Soc. Hon. FRTPI. JP 1953; DL Glasgow, 1971. Knight, Order of Polonia Restituta (Poland), 1969. *Recreations:* fishing, theatre, reading. *Address:* Cruachan, 18 Bruce Road, Glasgow G41 5EF. *T:* 041–429 1776. *Clubs:* Arts, Carrick (Glasgow).

TAYLOR, William McCaughey; Under Secretary, Northern Ireland Office, and Secretary, Police Authority, since 1979; *b* 10 May 1926; *s* of William and Georgina Lindsay Taylor; *m* 1955, June Louise Macartney; two *s* two *d*. *Educ:* Campbell College, Belfast; Trinity College, Oxford (MA 1950). Lieut, Royal Inniskilling Fusiliers, 1944–47. International Computers Ltd, 1950–58; Lobitos Oilfields Ltd, 1958–60; HM Vice Consul, New York, 1960–63, Consul, 1963–65; N Ireland Dept of Commerce, 1965–79. *Recreations:* golf, bridge, music. *Address:* River House, 48 High Street, Belfast BT1 2DR. *Clubs:* Ulster Reform (Belfast); Royal Belfast Golf.

TAYLOR, Mrs (Winifred) Ann; Monitoring Officer, Housing Corporation, since 1985; *b* Motherwell, 2 July 1947; *m* 1966, David Taylor; one *s* one *d*. *Educ:* Bolton Sch.; Bradford Univ.; Sheffield Univ. Formerly teaching. Past part-time Tutor, Open Univ.; interested in housing, regional policy, and education. Member: Association of Univ. Teachers; APEX; Holmfirth Urban District Council, 1972–74. MP (Lab) Bolton W, Oct. 1974–1983; PPS to Sec. of State for Educn and Science, 1975–76; PPS to Sec. of State for Defence, 1976–77; an Asst Govt Whip, 1977–79; Opposition spokesman on Education, 1979, on Housing, 1980–83. Contested (Lab): Bolton W, Feb. 1974; Bolton NE, 1983; prospective parly candidate (Lab) for Dewsbury, 1986–. Hon. Fellow, Birkbeck Coll. *Address:* Glyn Garth, Stoney Bank Road, Thongsbridge, Huddersfield, Yorks.

TAYLOR-SMITH, Prof. Ralph Emeric Kasope; Professor of Chemistry, Fourah Bay College, University of Sierra Leone, 1980–84, (formerly Associate Professor, on leave, as Ambassador of Sierra Leone to Peking, 1971–74, High Commissioner in London for Sierra Leone, and Ambassador to Norway, Sweden and Denmark, 1974–78); *b* 24 Sept. 1924; *m* 1953, Sarian Dorothea; five *s*. *Educ:* CMS Grammar Sch., Sierra Leone; Univ. of London (BSc (2nd Cl. Hons Upper Div.); PhD (Org. Chem.)). CChem, FRSC. Analytical chemist, 1954; Demonstrator, Woolwich Polytechnic, 1956–59; Lectr, Fourah Bay Coll., Sierra Leone, 1959–62 and 1963; post-doctoral Fellow, Weizmann Inst. of Sci., 1962–63; Research Associate, Princeton Univ., 1965–69; Fourah Bay College: Sen. Lectr, 1965; Dean, Faculty of Pure and Applied Sci., 1967; Associate Prof., 1968 and 1969; Visiting Prof., Kalamazoo Coll., Mich, 1969. Service in academic and public cttees, including: Mem. Council, Fourah Bay Coll., 1963–65 and 1967–69; Member: Senate, 1967–69, Court, 1967–69, Univ. of Sierra Leone; Mem., Student Welfare Cttee, 1967–69; Univ. Rep., Sierra Leone Govt Schol. Cttee, 1965–68; Mem., Bd of Educn, 1970. Pres., Teaching Staff Assoc., Fourah Bay Coll., 1971. Chm., Sierra Leone Petroleum Refining Co., 1970. Delegate or observer to academic confs, 1958–69, incl. those of W African Science Assoc., and Commonwealth Univ. Conf., Sydney, Aust., 1968. Fellow, Thames Polytechnic, 1975; FRSA 1979. *Publications:* papers to learned jls, especially on Investigations on Plants of West Africa. *Recreations:* tennis, swimming. *Address:* c/o Department of Chemistry, Fourah Bay College, University of Sierra Leone, Private Mail Bag, Freetown, Sierra Leone.

TAYLOR THOMPSON, John Derek, CB 1985; Commissioner of Inland Revenue, since 1973; *b* 6 Aug. 1927; *o s* of John Taylor Thompson and Marjorie (*née* Westcott); *m* 1954, Helen Laurie Walker; two *d*. *Educ:* St Peter's Sch., York; Balliol Coll., Oxford. MA. Asst Principal, Inland Revenue, 1951; Private Sec. to Chm., 1954; Private Sec. to Minister without Portfolio, 1962; Asst Sec., Inland Revenue, 1965. Chm., Fiscal Affairs Cttee, OECD, 1984–. *Recreations:* rural pursuits, reading. *Address:* Jessops, Nutley, Sussex. *Club:* United Oxford & Cambridge University.

TAYLORSON, John Brown; Head of Catering Services, British Airways, since 1981; *b* 5 March 1931; *s* of John Brown Taylorson and Edith Maria Taylorson; *m* 1st, 1960, Barbara June (*née* Hagg) (marr. diss.); one *s* one *d*; 2nd, 1985, Helen Anne (*née* Parkinson). *Educ:* Forest School, Snaresbrook; Hotel School, Westminster. Sales Director, Gardner Merchant Food Services Ltd, 1970–73; Managing Director: International Division, Gardner Merchant Food Services, 1973–77; Fedics Food Services, 1977–80; Chief Executive, Civil Service Catering Organisation, 1980–81. Pres., Internat. Flight Catering Assoc., 1983–85; Chm., Inflight Services Gp, Assoc. of European Airlines, 1983–85. *Recreations:* squash, tennis, theatre, crossword puzzles. *Address:* 10 Ruxley Ridge, Claygate, Surrey. *Clubs:* Old Foresters; Lingfield Park Squash; Wanderers (RSA).

TAYLOUR, family name of **Marquess of Headfort.**

TEAR, Robert, CBE 1984; concert and operatic tenor; *b* 8 March 1939; *s* of Thomas Arthur and Edith Tear; *m* 1961, Hilary Thomas; two *d*. *Educ:* Barry Grammar Sch.; King's Coll., Cambridge (MA). Hon. RCM, RAM. FRSA. Mem., King's Coll. Choir, 1957–60; subseq. St Paul's Cathedral and solo career; joined English Opera Group, 1964. By 1968 worked with world's leading conductors, notably Karajan, Giulini, Bernstein and Solti; during this period created many rôles in operas by Benjamin Britten. Has appeared in all major festivals; close association with Sir Michael Tippett, 1970–; Covent Garden: début, The Knot Garden, 1970, closely followed by Lensky in Eugène Onégin; Fledermaus, 1977; Peter Grimes, 1978; Rake's Progress, 1979; Thérèse, 1979; Loge in Rheingold, 1980; Admetus in Alceste, 1981; David in Die Meistersinger, 1982; Captain Vere in Billy Budd, 1982; appears regularly with Royal Opera. Started relationship with Scottish Opera (singing in La Traviata, Alceste, Don Giovanni), 1974. Paris Opera: début, 1976; Lulu 1979. Début as conductor with Thames Chamber Orchestra, QEH, 1980. Has worked with every major recording co. and made numerous recordings (incl. solo recital discs). *Publication:* Victorian Songs and Duets, 1980. *Recreations:* any sport; interested in 18th and 19th century English water colours. *Address:* 11 Ravenscourt Square, W6. *T:* 01–748 6130. *Club:* Garrick.

TEARE, Dr (Hugo) Douglas, CVO 1973; Physician Superintendent, King Edward VII Hospital, Midhurst, Sussex, 1971–77; *b* 20 April 1917; *s* of A. H. Teare, JP, and Margaret Green; *m* 1945, Evelyn Bertha Hider; three *s*. *Educ:* King William's Coll., Isle of Man; Gonville and Caius Coll., Cambridge; St George's Hospital, London. BA 1938; MRCS, LRCP 1941; MB, BChir 1942. House Physician and Casualty Officer, St George's Hospital, 1941; Resident Surgical Officer and Med. Registrar, Brompton Hospital, 1943; Dep. Med. Superintendent, King Edward VII Hospital (Sanatorium), Midhurst, 1946–70. MHK 1981–84. OStJ. *Recreation:* golf. *Address:* Lismore, 6 St Olave's Close, Ramsey, Isle of Man. *T:* Ramsey 812065.

TE ATAIRANGIKAAHU, Arikinui, DBE 1970; Arikinui and Head of Maori Kingship, since 1966; *b* 23 July 1931; *o d* of King Koroki V; *m* 1952, Whatumoana; two *s* five *d*. *Educ:* Waikato Diocesan School, Hamilton, NZ. Elected by the Maori people as Head of the Maori Kingship on the death of King Koroki, the fifth Maori King, with title of Arikinui (Queen), in 1966. Hon. Dr Waikato, 1979. OStJ 1986. *Recreation:* the fostering of all aspects of Maori culture and traditions. *Address:* Turongo House, Turangawaewae Marae, Ngaruawahia, New Zealand.

TEBALDI, Renata; Italian Soprano; *b* Pesaro, Italy, 1 Feb. 1922; *o c* of Teobaldo and Giuseppina (Barbieri) Tebaldi. Studied at Arrigo Boito Conservatory, Parma; Gioacchino Rossini Conservatory, Pesaro; subsequently a pupil of Carmen Melis and later of Giuseppe Pais. Made professional début as Elena in Mefistofele, Rovigo, 1944. First sang at La Scala, Milan, at post-war reopening concert (conductor Toscanini), 1946. Has sung at Covent Garden and in opera houses of Naples, Rome, Venice, Pompeii, Turin, Cesana, Modena, Bologna and Florence; toured England, France, Spain and South America. American début in title rôle Aïda, San Francisco, 1950; Metropolitan Opera House Season, New York, 1955. Recordings of complete operas include: Otello; Adriana Lecouvreur; Il Trittico; Don Carlo; La Gioconda; Un Ballo in Maschera; Madame Butterfly; Mefistofele; La Fanciulla Del West; La Forza Del Destino; Andrea Chenier; Manon Lescaut; La Tosca; Il Trovatore; Aida, La Bohème. *Address:* c/o S. A. Gorlinsky Ltd, 33 Dover Street, W1X 4NJ; 1 Piazza della Guastella, Milan, Italy.

TEBBIT, Sir Donald (Claude), GCMG 1980 (KCMG 1975; CMG 1965); HM Diplomatic Service, retired; Chairman, English-Speaking Union of the Commonwealth, since 1983; *b* 4 May 1920; *m* 1947, Barbara Margaret Olson Matheson; one *s* three *d*. *Educ:* Perse School; Trinity Hall, Cambridge (MA). Served War of 1939–45, RNVR. Joined Foreign (now Diplomatic) Service, 1946; Second Secretary, Washington, 1948; transferred to Foreign Office, 1951; First Secretary, 1952; transferred to Bonn, 1954; Private Secretary to Minister of State, Foreign Office, 1958; Counsellor, 1962; transferred to Copenhagen, 1964; Commonwealth Office, 1967; Asst Under-Sec. of State, FCO, 1968–70; Minister, British Embassy, Washington, 1970–72; Chief Clerk, FCO, 1972–76; High Comr in Australia, 1976–80. Chm., Diplomatic Service Appeals Bd, 1980–; Mem., Appeals Bd, Council of Europe, 1981–. Dir, Rio Tinto Zinc Corp., 1980–. Dir Gen., British Property Fedn, 1980–85. Pres. (UK), Australian-British Chamber of Commerce, 1980–; Chairman: Zimbabwe Tech. Management Training Trust, 1983–; Marshall Aid Commemoration Commn, 1985–; Governor, Nuffield Hospitals, 1980–; President: Old Persean Soc., 1981–82; Trinity Hall Assoc., 1984–85. *Address:* Priory Cottage, Toft, Cambridge CB3 7RH; 35 Buckingham Gate, SW1E 6PA.

TEBBIT, Rt. Hon. Norman (Beresford), PC 1981; MP (C) Chingford, since 1974 (Epping, 1970–74); Chancellor of the Duchy of Lancaster, since 1985; Chairman of the Conservative Party, since 1985; journalist; *b* 29 March 1931; 2nd *s* of Leonard and Edith Tebbit, Enfield; *m* 1956, Margaret Elizabeth Daines; two *s* one *d*. *Educ:* Edmonton County Grammar Sch. Embarked on career in journalism, 1947. Served RAF: commissioned GD Branch; qualif. Pilot, 1949–51; Reserve service RAuxAF, No 604 City of Mddx Sqdn, 1952–55. Entered and left publishing and advertising, 1951–53. Civil Airline Pilot, 1953–70 (Mem. BALPA; former holder various offices in that Assoc.). Active mem. and holder various offices, Conservative Party, 1946–. PPS to Minister of State, Dept of Employment, 1972–73; Parly Under Sec. of State, Dept of Trade, 1979–81; Minister of State, Dept of Industry, 1981; Secretary of State for: Employment, 1981–83; Trade and Industry, 1983–85. Former Chm., Cons. Members Aviation Cttee; former Vice-Chm. and Sec., Cons. Members Housing and Construction Cttee; Sec. House of Commons New Town Members Cttee. *Address:* House of Commons, SW1.

TEBBLE, Norman, DSc; FRSE; FIBiol; Director, Royal Scottish Museum, 1971–84; *b* 17 Aug. 1924; 3rd *s* of late Robert Soulsby Tebble and Jane Anne (*née* Graham); *m* 1954, Mary Olivia Archer, *o d* of H. B. and J. I. Archer, Kenilworth; two *s* one *d*. *Educ:* Bedlington Grammar School; St Andrews Univ.; BSc 1950, DSc 1968; MA, Merton Coll., Oxford, 1971; FIBiol 1971, FRSE 1976. St Andrews Univ. Air Squadron, 1942–43; Pilot, RAFVR, Canada, India and Burma, 1943–46. Scientific Officer, British Museum (Natural History), 1950, Curator of Annelida; John Murray Travelling Student in Oceanography, Royal Soc., 1958; Vis. Curator, Univ. of California, Scripps Inst. of Oceanography, 1959; Curator of Molluscs, British Museum, 1961; Univ. Lecturer in Zoology and Curator, zoological collection, Univ. of Oxford, 1968; Curator, Oxford Univ. Museum, 1969. Member Council: Marine Biological Assoc., UK, 1963–66; Scottish Marine Biological Assoc., 1973–78; Museums Assoc., 1972– (Vice-Pres., 1976–77; Pres., 1977–78). *Publications:* (ed jtly) Speciation in the Sea, 1963; British Bivalve Seashells, 1966, 2nd edn 1976; (ed jtly) Bibliography British Fauna and Flora, 1967; scientific papers in Systematics of Annelida and Distribution in the World Oceans. *Recreations:* Tebbel-Tebble genealogy, gardening, swimming, car-free travel, cricket-history. *Address:* 4 Bright's Crescent, Edinburgh EH9 2DB. *T:* 031–667 5260.

TEDDER, family name of **Baron Tedder.**

TEDDER, 2nd Baron, *cr* 1946, of Glenguin; **John Michael Tedder,** MA, ScD, PhD, DSc; Purdie Professor of Chemistry, St Salvator's College, University of St Andrews, since

1969; *b* 4 July 1926; 2nd and *er* surv. *s* of 1st Baron Tedder, GCB, and Rosalinde (*née* Maclardy); *S* father, 1967; *m* 1952, Peggy Eileen Growcott; two *s* one *d*. *Educ:* Dauntsey's School, Wilts; Magdalene College, Cambridge (MA 1951; ScD 1965); University of Birmingham (PhD 1951; DSc 1961). Roscoe Professor of Chemistry, University of Dundee, 1964–69. Mem., Ct of Univ. of St Andrews, 1971–76. Vice-Pres., Perkin Div., RSC, 1980–83. FRSE; FRSC. *Publications:* Valence Theory, 1966; Basic Organic Chemistry, 1966; The Chemical Bond, 1978; Radicals, 1979; papers in Jl of RSC and other scientific jls. *Heir: s* Hon. Robin John Tedder [*b* 6 April 1955; *m* 1st, 1977, Jennifer Peggy (*d* 1978), *d* of John Mangan, NZ; 2nd, 1980, Rita Aristeia, *yr d* of John Frangidis, Sydney, NSW]. *Address:* Little Rathmore, Kennedy Gardens, St Andrews, Fife. *T:* St Andrews 73546; Department of Chemistry, St Salvator's College, St Andrews, Fife, Scotland. *T:* St Andrews 76161.

TEESDALE, Edmund Brinsley, CMG 1964; MC 1945; *b* 30 Sept. 1915; *s* of late John Herman Teesdale and late Winifred Mary (*née* Gull); *m* 1947, Joyce, *d* of late Walter Mills and of Mrs J. T. Murray; three *d*. *Educ:* Lancing; Trinity College, Oxford. Entered Colonial Administrative Service, Hong Kong, 1938. Active Service in Hong Kong, China, India, 1941–45. Subsequently various administrative posts in Hong Kong; Colonial Secretary, Hong Kong, 1963–65. Dir, Assoc. of British Pharmaceutical Industry, 1965–76. *Publication:* The Queen's Gunstonemaker, 1984. *Recreations:* gardening, swimming, reading. *Address:* The Hogge House, Buxted, Sussex.

TE HEUHEU, Sir Hepi (Hoani), KBE 1979; New Zealand sheep and cattle farmer; Paramount Chief of Ngati-Tuwharetoa tribe of Maoris; *b* 1919; *m*; six *c*. Chairman: Tuwharetoa Maori Trust Board; Puketapu 3A Block (near Taupo); Rotoaira Lake Trust; Rotoaira Forest Trust; Tauranga-Taupo Trust; Motutere Point Trust; Turamakina Tribal Cttee; Lake Taupo Forest Trust; Oraukura 3 Block; Hauhungaroa 1C Block; Tuaropaki D2 Block; Waihi Pukawa Block; Member: Waitangi Trust Board; Maori Land Board; Tongariro National Park Board (great grandson of original donor). OStJ. *Address:* Taumarunui, New Zealand.

TEI ABAL, Sir, Kt 1976; CBE 1974; MHA, PNG; *b* 1932; *m*; six *c*. Became a tea-planter and trader in Papua New Guinea; a Leader of the Engi Clan in Western Highlands. Member for Wabag, open electorate, PNG; Former Member (Ministerial) in 1st, 2nd and 3rd Houses of Assembly; Leader of the Opposition, UP, and later Minister of Public Utilities, 1979–80, in Somare Govt. *Address:* c/o PO Box 3534, Port Moresby, Papua New Guinea; Wabag, Papua New Guinea.

TEJAN-SIE, Sir Banja, GCMG 1970 (CMG 1967); Governor-General of Sierra Leone, 1970–71 (Acting Governor-General, 1968–70); international business and legal consultant; *b* 7 Aug. 1917; *s* of late Alpha Ahmed Tejan-Sie; *m* 1946, Admira Stapleton; three *s* one *d*. *Educ:* Bo Sch., Freetown; Prince of Wales Sch., Freetown; LSE, London University. Called to Bar, Lincoln's Inn, 1951. Station Clerk, Sierra Leone Railway,1938–39; Nurse, Medical Dept, 1940–46; Ed., West African Students' Union, 1948–51; Nat. Vice-Pres., Sierra Leone People's Party, 1953–56; Police Magistrate: Eastern Province, 1955; Northern Province, 1958; Sen. Police Magistrate Provinces, 1961; Speaker, Sierra Leone House of Representatives, 1962–67; Chief Justice of Sierra Leone, 1967–70. Mem. Keith Lucas Commn on Electoral Reform, 1954. Hon. Sec. Sierra Leone Bar Assoc., 1957–58. Chm. Bd of Management, Cheshire Foundn, Sierra Leone, 1966. Has led delegations and paid official visits to many countries throughout the world. Hon. Treasurer, Internat. African Inst., London, 1978–. Pres., Freetown Golf Club, 1970–. GCON (Nigeria), 1970; Grand Band, Order of Star of Africa (Liberia), 1969; Special Grand Cordon, Order of propitious clouds (Taiwan), 1970; Grand Cordon, Order of Knighthood of Pioneers (Liberia), 1970; Order of Cedar (Lebanon), 1970. *Recreations:* music, reading. *Address:* 3 Tracy Avenue, NW2. *T:* 01–452 2324. *Club:* Royal Commonwealth Society.

TE KANAWA, Dame Kiri (Janette), DBE 1982 (OBE 1973); opera singer; *b* Gisborne, New Zealand, 6 March 1944; *m* 1967, Desmond Stephen Park; one *s* one *d*. *Educ:* St Mary's Coll., Auckland, NZ; London Opera Centre. Major rôles at Royal Opera House, Covent Garden, include: the Countess, in Marriage of Figaro; Elvira, in Don Giovanni; Mimi, in La Bohème; Desdemona, in Otello; Marguerite, in Faust; Amelia, in Simon Boccanegra; Fiordiligi, in Cosi Fan Tutti; Tatiana, in Eugene Onegin; title rôle in Arabella; Rosalinde, in Die Fledermaus; Violetta, in La Traviata; Manon, in Manon Lescaut. Has sung leading rôles at Metropolitan Opera, New York, notably, Desdemona, Elvira, and Countess; also at the Paris Opera, Elvira, Fiordiligi and Pamina in Magic Flute, title rôle in Tosca; at San Francisco Opera, Amelia and Pamina; at Sydney Opera House, Mimi, Amelia, and Violetta in La Traviata; Elvira, with Cologne Opera; Amelia at la Scala, Milan; Countess in Le Nozze di Figaro at Salzburg fest. Hon. Fellow, Somerville Coll., Oxford, 1983; Hon. DMus Oxford, 1983. *Recreations:* golf, swimming. *Address:* c/o Basil Horsfield, L'Estoril (B), Avenue Princesse Grace 31, Monte Carlo, Monaco.

TELFER, Robert Gilmour Jamieson, (Rab), CBE 1985; PhD; Director, Manchester Business School, since 1984; *b* 22 April 1928; *s* of James Telfer and Helen Lambie Jamieson; *m* 1953, Joan Audrey Gunning; three *s*. *Educ:* Bathgate Academy (Dawson Trust Bursary); Univ. of Edinburgh (Mackay-Smith Prize; Blandfield Prize; BSc (Hons 1st cl.) 1950, PhD 1953). Shift Chemist, AEA, 1953–54; Imperial Chemical Industries Ltd: Res. Chemist, Billingham Div., 1954–58; Heavy Organic Chemicals Div., 1958–71; Fibre Intermediates Dir and R & D Dir, 1971–75; Div. Dep. Chm., 1975–76, Div. Chm., 1976–81, Petrochemicals Div.; Chm. and Man. Dir, 1981–84, Dir, 1984, Mather & Platt Ltd. Mem. Bd, Philips-Imperial Petroleum Ltd, 1975–81; Director: Renold PLC, 1984–; Volex PLC, 1986–. Group Chm., Duke of Edinburgh's Study Conf., 1974; Mem., ACORD for Fuel and Power, 1981–; Chm., Adv. Council on Energy Conservation, 1982–84. Personal Adviser to Sec. of State for Energy, 1984–. Exec. Mem., Council of Univ. Management Schs, 1986–; Mem., Civil Service Coll. Adv. Council, 1986–. Mem., Oxford Energy Policy Club. CBIM. *Publications:* papers in Jl Chem. Soc. and Chemistry and Industry. *Recreations:* walking, swimming, poetry, decorative egg collecting. *Address:* 75 Porchfield Square, St John's Gardens, Manchester M3 4FG. *T:* 061–834 2835. *Club:* Caledonian.

TELFORD, Sir Robert, Kt 1978; CBE 1967; DL; FEng, FIEE, FIProdE, CBIM, FRSA; Life President, The Marconi Company Ltd, 1984 (Managing Director, 1965–81; Chairman, 1981–84, retired); Chairman: DRI Holdings Ltd, since 1984; Prelude Technology Investments Ltd, since 1985; Director, BAJ Holdings, since 1985; *b* 1 Oct. 1915; *s* of Robert and Sarah Annie Telford; *m* 1st, 1941 (marr. diss. 1950); one *s*; 2nd, 1958, Elizabeth Mary (*née* Shelley); three *d*. *Educ:* Quarry Bank Sch., Liverpool; Queen Elizabeth's Grammar Sch., Tamworth; Christ's Coll., Cambridge (MA). Manager, Hackbridge Works, The Marconi Co. Ltd, 1940–46; Man. Dir, Companhia Marconi Brasileira, 1946–50; The Marconi Company Ltd: Asst to Gen. Manager, 1950–53; Gen. Works Manager, 1953–61; Gen. Manager, 1961–65; Man. Dir, GEC-Marconi Electronics Ltd, 1968–84; Chm., GEC Avionics Ltd, 1982–86; Director: The General Electric Co., 1973–84; Canadian Marconi Co., Montreal, 1968–84; Ericsson Radio Systems AB (formerly SRA Communications, AB), Stockholm, 1969–85. Pres., IProdE, 1982–83; Chairman: Alvey Steering Cttee, 1983–; SERC Teaching Company Management Cttee, 1984–; Member: SERC Engrg Bd, 1985–; Engrg Council, 1985–; IT Adv. Gp, DTI. Mem., Council and Court, Univ. of Essex, 1981–. DL Essex, 1981. Hon. DSc: Salford, 1981; Cranfield, 1982; Bath, 1984; Aston, 1985; Hon. DEng: Bradford, 1986; Birmingham, 1986. Hon. FIMechE, 1983. *Address:* Rettendon House, Rettendon, Chelmsford, Essex CM3 8DW. *T:* Wickford 3131. *Club:* Royal Air Force.

TELFORD BEASLEY, John; Chairman and Managing Director, London Buses Ltd, and Director, London Regional Transport, since 1984; *b* 26 March 1929; *s* of James George and Florence Telford Beasley; *m* (marr. diss.); one *s* two *d*. *Educ:* Watford Grammar School. Dep. Chm., Cadbury Ltd, 1970–73; Chm., Cadbury Schweppes Food Ltd, 1973–75; Dir, Cadbury Schweppes, 1973–77; Chm., Schweppes Ltd, 1975–77; Regional Pres., Warner Lamber Co., 1977–84. *Recreations:* squash, flying, bus driving. *Address:* 3 Monmouth Square, Winchester, Hants SO22 4HY.

TELLER, Prof. Edward; Senior Research Fellow, Hoover Institution, since 1975; University Professor, University of California, Berkeley, 1971–75, now Emeritus (Professor of Physics, 1960–71); Chairman, Department of Applied Science, University of California, 1963–66; Associate Director, Lawrence Radiation Laboratory, University of California, 1954–75, now Emeritus; *b* Budapest, Hungary, 15 January 1908; *s* of a lawyer; became US citizen, 1941; *m* 1934, Augusta Harkanyi; one *s* one *d*. *Educ:* Karlsruhe Technical Inst., Germany; Univ. of Munich; Leipzig (PhD). Research Associate, Leipzig, 1929–31; Research Associate, Göttingen, 1931–33; Rockefeller Fellow, Copenhagen, 1934; Lectr, Univ. of London, 1934–35; Prof. of Physics, George Washington Univ., Washington, DC, 1935–41; Prof. of Physics, Columbia Univ., 1941–42; Physicist, Manhattan, Engineer District, 1942–46, Univ. of Chicago, 1942–43; Los Alamos Scientific Laboratory, 1943–46; Prof. of Physics, Univ. of Chicago, 1946–52; Asst Dir, Los Alamos (on leave, Chicago), 1949–52; Consultant, Livermore Br., Univ. of Calif, Radiation Laboratory, 1952–53; Prof. of Physics, Univ. of Calif, 1953–60; Dir, Livermore Br., Lawrence Livermore Lab., Univ. of Calif, 1958–60. Mem. Nat. Acad. of Sciences, etc. Holds several hon. degrees, 1954–. Has gained awards, 1957–, incl. Enrico Fermi Award, 1962; Harvey Prize, Israel, 1975; Gold Medal, Amer. Coll. of Nuclear Med., 1980; Man of the Year, Achievement Rewards for College Scientists, 1980; Nat. Medal of Science, 1983. *Publications:* The Structure of Matter, 1949; Our Nuclear Future, 1958; The Legacy of Hiroshima, 1962; The Reluctant Revolutionary, 1964; The Constructive Uses of Nuclear Explosives, 1968; Great Men of Physics, 1969; Nuclear Energy in a Developing World, 1977; Energy from Heaven and Earth, 1979; Pursuit of Simplicity, 1980. *Address:* Stanford, Calif 94305, USA.

TELLO, Manuel, CMG (Hon.) 1975; Permanent Representative of Mexico to International Organizations, Geneva, since 1982; *b* 15 March 1935; *s* of late Manuel Tello and Guadalupe M. de Tello; *m* 1983, Rhonda M. de Tello. *Educ:* schools in Mexico City; Georgetown Univ.; Sch. for Foreign Service, Washington, DC; Escuela Libre de Derecho; Institut de Hautes Etudes Internationales, Geneva. Equivalent of BA in Foreign Service Studies; post-grad. studies in Internat. Law. Joined Mexican Foreign Service, 1957; Asst Dir Gen. for Internat. Organizations, 1967–70, Dir Gen., 1970–72; Dir for Multilateral Affairs, 1972–74; Dir for Political Affairs, 1975–76; Ambassador to UK, 1977–79; Under Sec., Dept of Foreign Affairs, Mexico, 1979–82. Alternate Rep. of Mexico to: OAS, 1959–63; Internat. Orgs, Geneva, 1963–65; Conf. of Cttee on Disarmament, Geneva, 1963–66; Rep. of Mexico to: Org. for Proscription of Nuclear Weapons in Latin America, 1970–73; 3rd UN Conf. on Law of the Sea, 1971–76 and 1982. Has attended 13 Sessions of UN Gen. Assembly. Holds decorations from Chile, Ecuador, Egypt, France, Italy, Jordan, Panama, Senegal, Sweden, Venezuela, Yugoslavia. *Publications:* contribs to learned jls in the field of international relations. *Recreations:* tennis, theatre, music. *Address:* Permanent Mission of Mexico, 6 ch. de la Tourelle, 1209 Geneva, Switzerland.

TEMIN, Prof. Howard M(artin), PhD; Professor of Oncology, since 1969, Harry Steenbock Professor of Biological Science, since 1982, Harold P. Rusch Professor of Cancer Research, since 1980 and American Cancer Society Professor of Viral Oncology and Cell Biology, since 1974, University of Wisconsin-Madison; *b* 10 Dec. 1934; *s* of Henry Temin and Annette Lehman Temin; *m* 1962, Rayla Greenberg; two *d*. *Educ:* Swarthmore Coll., Swarthmore, Pa (BA 1955); Calif Inst. of Technol., Pasadena (PhD 1959). Postdoctoral Fellow, Calif Inst. of Technol., Pasadena, 1959–60; Asst Prof. of Oncology, Univ. of Wis-Madison, 1960–64, Associate Prof. of Oncol., 1964–69, Wisconsin Alumni Res. Foundn Prof. of Cancer Res, 1971–80. US Public Health Service Res. Career Develt Award, National Cancer Inst., 1964–74; (jtly) Nobel Prize for Physiology or Medicine, 1975. Hon. DSc: Swarthmore Coll., 1972; NY Med. Coll., 1972; Univ. of Pa, 1976; Hahnemann Med. Coll., 1976; Lawrence Univ., 1976; Temple Univ., 1979; Medical Coll., Wisconsin, 1981. *Publications:* articles on viruses and cancer, on RNA-directed DNA synthesis, on evolution of viruses from cellular movable genetic elements and on retrovirus vectors. *Address:* McArdle Laboratory, University of Wisconsin-Madison, Madison, Wis 53706, USA. *T:* 608–262–1209.

TEMPANY, Myles McDermott, OBE 1984; Vice-Principal (External Affairs), King's College London, since 1986; *b* 31 March 1924; *y s* of late Martin Tempany and Margaret (*née* McDermott); *m* 1951, Pamela Allan; one *s* one *d*. *Educ:* St Muredach's College, Ballina, Co. Mayo; Intermediate and University College, Dublin. Military service, 1944–47. King's College London: Asst Acct, 1948–70; Acct, 1970–73; Finance Officer and Acct, 1973–77; FKC 1975; Bursar, 1977–81; Head of Admin and Bursar, 1981–83; Secretary, 1983–85; Mem. Council, 1986–. Mem. Delegacy, King's Coll. Sch. of Medicine and Dentistry, 1986–; Founder Chm., St Raphael's Training Centre Develt Trust, 1978–; Mem., Governing Body, Hatfield Polytechnic, 1985–; Chm., Bd of Governors, Pope Paul Sch., Potters Bar, 1986–. KHS 1972, KCHS 1978; KSG 1983. President's Award, Develt Bd, Univ. of Texas Health Science Center, Houston, 1986. *Recreations:* golf, watching Association Football. *Address:* 18 Tiverton Road, Potters Bar, Herts EN6 5HY. *T:* Potters Bar 56860. *Clubs:* Institute of Directors; Brookman's Park Golf.

TEMPLE OF STOWE, 7th Earl, *cr* 1822; **Ronald Stephen Brydges Temple-Gore-Langton;** *b* 5 November 1910; *s* of Captain Hon. Chandos Graham Temple-Gore-Langton (*d* 1921); granted rank, title and precedence as an Earl's son, which would have been his had his father survived to succeed to the title; nephew of 5th Earl; *S* brother, 1966. Company representative. *Heir: cousin* Walter Grenville Algernon Temple Gore Langton [*b* 2 Oct. 1924; *m* 1st, 1954, Lillah Ray (*d* 1966), *d* of James Boxall; two *s* one *d*; 2nd, 1968, Margaret Elizabeth Graham, *o d* of late Col H. W. Scarth]. *Recreations:* sailing, swimming, bird watching, conservation, radio. Resident in Victoria, Australia.

TEMPLE, Anthony Dominic Afamado; QC 1986; *b* 21 Sept. 1945; *s* of Sir Rawden Temple, *qv*; *m* 1st, 1975 (marr. diss.); 2nd, 1983, Suzie Bodansky; one *d*. *Educ:* Haileybury and ISC; Worcester College, Oxford. Called to the Bar, Inner Temple, 1968; Crown Law Office, Western Australia, 1969; Assistant Recorder, 1984. *Recreations:* modern pentathlon, travel, history. *Address:* 4 Pump Court, EC4.

TEMPLE, Ernest Sanderson, MBE; MA; QC 1969; **His Honour Judge Temple;** a Circuit Judge, since 1977; Honorary Recorder of Kendal, since 1972, and of Liverpool, since 1978; *b* 23 May 1921; *o s* of Ernest Temple, Oxenholme House, Kendal; *m* 1946,

June Debonnaire, *o d* of W. M. Saunders, JP, Wennington Hall, Lancaster; one *s* two *d*. *Educ:* Kendal School; Queen's Coll., Oxford. Served in Border Regt in India and Burma, attaining temp. rank of Lt-Col (despatches, 1945). Barrister-at-Law, 1943. Joined Northern Circuit, 1946; Dep. Recorder of Salford, 1962–65; Dep. Chm., Agricultural Land Tribunal (Northern), 1966–69; Chm., Westmorland QS, 1969–71 (Dep. Chm., 1967); a Recorder of the Crown Court, 1972–77; Mem., Bar Council, 1965. Jt Master, Vale of Lune Hunt, 1963–85. Hon. FICW. *Recreations:* farming and horses. *Address:* Yealand Hall, Yealand Redmayne, near Carnforth, Lancs LA5 9TD. *T:* Burton (Cumbria) 781200. *Club:* Racquet (Liverpool).

TEMPLE, Rt. Rev. Frederick Stephen; Honorary Assistant Bishop, Diocese of Bristol, since 1983; *b* 24 Nov. 1916; *s* of Frederick Charles and Frances Temple; *m* 1947, Joan Catharine Webb; one *s* one *d* (and one *s* decd). *Educ:* Rugby; Balliol Coll., Oxford; Trinity Hall, Cambridge; Westcott House, Cambridge. Deacon, 1947, Priest, 1948; Curate, St Mary's, Arnold, Notts, 1947–49; Curate, Newark Parish Church, 1949–51; Rector, St Agnes, Birch, Manchester, 1951–53; Dean of Hong Kong, 1953–59; Senior Chaplain to the Archbishop of Canterbury, 1959–61; Vicar of St Mary's, Portsea, 1961–70; Archdeacon of Swindon, 1970–73; Bishop Suffragan of Malmesbury, 1973–83. Proctor, Canterbury Convocation, 1964; Hon. Canon, Portsmouth Cathedral, 1965. *Publication:* (ed) William Temple, Some Lambeth Letters, 1942–44, 1963. *Recreations:* gardening, reading. *Address:* 7 The Barton, Wood Street, Wootton Bassett, Wilts SN4 7BG. *T:* Wootton Bassett 851227.

TEMPLE, George, CBE 1955; PhD, DSc, MA; FRS 1943; Sedleian Professor of Natural Philosophy, University of Oxford, 1953–68, now Professor Emeritus; Honorary Fellow of Queen's College, Oxford; *b* 2 Sept. 1901; *o s* of late James Temple, London; *m* 1930, Dorothy Lydia (*d* 1979), *e d* of late Thomas Ellis Carson, Liverpool. *Educ:* Ealing County School; Birkbeck College, University of London; Trinity College, Cambridge. Research Assistant and Demonstrator, Physics Dept, Birkbeck College, 1922–24; Assistant Lecturer, Maths Dept, City and Guilds (Eng.) College, 1924–28; Keddey Fletcher Warr Studentship, 1928; 1851 Exhibition Research Student, 1928–30; Assistant Professor in Maths Dept, Royal College of Science, 1930–32; Professor of Mathematics, University of London, King's College, 1932–53. Seconded to Royal Aircraft Establishment, Farnborough, 1939–45. Chairman, Aeronautical Research Council, 1961–64. Professed as Benedictine monk, 1982. Leverhulme Emeritus Fellowship, 1971–73. Hon. DSc: Dublin, 1961; Louvain, 1966; Reading, 1980; Hon. LLD W Ontario, 1969. Sylvester Medal (Royal Soc.), 1970. *Publications:* An Introduction to Quantum Theory, 1931; Rayleigh's Principle, 1933; General Principles of Quantum Theory, 1934; An Introduction to Fluid Dynamics, 1958; Cartesian Tensors, 1960; The Structure of Lebesgue Integration Theory, 1971; papers on Mathematical Physics, Relativity, Quantum Theory, Aerodynamics, Distribution Theory, History of Mathematics. *Address:* Quarr Abbey, Ryde, Isle of Wight.

TEMPLE, Ven. George Frederick; Archdeacon of Bodmin, since 1981; Diocesan Director of Ordinands, since 1985; *b* 16 March 1933; *s* of George Frederick and Lilian Rose Temple; *m* 1961, Jacqueline Rose Urwin; one *s* one *d*. *Educ:* St Paul's, Jersey; Wells Theological College. Deacon 1968, priest 1969, Guildford; Curate: St Nicholas, Great Bookham, 1968–70; St Mary the Virgin, Penzance, 1970–72; Vicar of St Just in Penwith with Sancreed, 1972–74; Vicar of St Gluvias, Penryn, 1974–81; Vicar of Saltash, 1982–85. Mem., General Synod of C of E, 1981–85; Chm., House of Clergy, Truro Diocesan Synod, 1982–85. Hon. Canon of Truro, 1981–. *Recreations:* poetry, history, walking. *Address:* 28 Athelstan Park, Bodmin, Cornwall PL31 1DS.

TEMPLE, Sir John (Meredith), Kt 1983; JP; DL; *b* 1910; *m* 1942, Nancy Violet, *d* of late Brig.-Gen. Robert Wm Hare, CMG, DSO, DL, Cobh, Eire, and Norwich; one *s* one *d*. *Educ:* Charterhouse; Clare College, Cambridge (BA). Served War of 1939–45 (despatches). ADC to Governor of S Australia, 1941. MP (C) City of Chester, Nov. 1956–Feb. 1974. Pres., Ellesmere Port and Neston Cons. Assoc.; Vice-Pres., Chester Conservative Club; Vice-Pres., Army Benevolent Fund (Chester Branch); Vice-Chairman: British Group, IPU, 1973–74; Cons. Finance Cttee, 1966–68; Vice-President: Anglo-Colombian Society; Cerro Galan Expedn, Argentina, 1981; Salmon and Trout Assoc. JP Cheshire 1949, DL 1975; High Sheriff of Cheshire, 1980–81. Great Officer: Order of San Carlos, Colombia, 1973; Order of Boyacà, Colombia, 1974; Order of the Liberator, Venezuela, 1974. *Address:* Picton Gorse, Chester CH2 4JU. *T:* Mickle Trafford 300239. *Clubs:* Carlton, Army and Navy; Racquet (Liverpool); City (Chester).

TEMPLE, Sir Rawden (John Afamado), Kt 1980; CBE 1964; QC 1951; Chief Social Security (formerly National Insurance) Commissioner, 1975–81 (a National Insurance Commissioner, 1969); a Referee under Child Benefit Act, 1975, since 1976; *b* 1908; *m* 1936, Margaret Jessie Wiseman (*d* 1980), *d* of late Sir James Gunson, CMG, CBE; two *s*. *Educ:* King Edward's School, Birmingham; The Queen's College, Oxford. BA 1930; BCL, 1931; called to Bar, 1931; Master of the Bench, Inner Temple, 1960 (Reader, 1982; Treasurer, 1983); Vice-Chairman, General Council of the Bar, 1960–64. Mem., Industrial Injuries Adv. Council, 1981–84. War Service, 1941–45. Liveryman Worshipful Company of Pattenmakers, 1948. *Recreations:* fishing; collecting portraits and oriental rugs. *Address:* 3 North King's Bench Walk, Temple, EC4.
See also A. D. A. Temple.

TEMPLE, Reginald Robert, CMG 1979; HM Diplomatic Service, retired; Oman Government Service, since 1979; *b* 12 Feb. 1922; *s* of Lt-Gen. R. C. Temple, CB, OBE, RM, and Z. E. Temple (*née* Hunt); *m* 1st, 1952, Julia Jasmine Anthony (marr. diss. 1979); one *s* one *d*; 2nd, 1979, Susan McCorquodale (*née* Pick); one *d* (one step *s* one step *d*). *Educ:* Wellington College; Peterhouse, Cambridge. HM Forces, 1940–46, RE and Para Regt; Stockbroking, 1947–51; entered Foreign Service, 1951; Office of HM Comr Gen. for SE Asia, 1952–56; 2nd Sec., Beirut, 1958–62; 1st Sec., Algiers, 1964–66, Paris, 1967–69; FCO, 1969–79; Counsellor 1975. American Silver Star, 1944. *Recreation:* sailing. *Address:* c/o Lloyds Bank, 6 Pall Mall, SW1; PO Box 5272, Ruwi, Sultanate of Oman. *Clubs:* Army and Navy, Royal Cruising, Royal Ocean Racing, Hurlingham.

TEMPLE, Sir Richard Anthony Purbeck, 4th Bt, *cr* 1876; MC 1941; *b* 19 Jan. 1913; *s* of Sir Richard Durand Temple, 3rd Bt, DSO; *S* father, 1962; *m* 1st, 1936, Lucy Geils (marr. diss., 1946), 2nd *d* of late Alain Joly de Lotbinière, Montreal; two *s*; 2nd, 1950, Jean, *d* of late James T. Finnie, and *widow* of Oliver P. Croom-Johnson; one *d*. *Educ:* Stowe; Trinity Hall, Cambridge; Lausanne University. Served War of 1939–45 (wounded, MC). Sometime Major, KRRC. *Recreation:* sailing. *Heir:* *s* Richard Temple [*b* 17 Aug. 1937; *m* 1964, Emma Rose, 2nd *d* of late Maj.-Gen. Sir Robert Laycock, KCMG, CB, DSO; three *d*]. *Address:* c/o National Westminster Bank, 94 Kensington High Street, W8.

TEMPLE-BLACKWOOD; *see* Blackwood, Hamilton-Temple-.

TEMPLE-GORE-LANGTON, family name of **Earl Temple of Stowe.**

TEMPLE-MORRIS, Peter; MP (C) Leominster since Feb. 1974; *b* 12 Feb. 1938; *o s* of His Honour Sir Owen Temple-Morris, QC; *m* 1964, Taheré, *e d* of HE Senator Khozeimé Alam, Teheran; two *s* two *d*. *Educ:* Hillstone Sch., Malvern; Malvern Coll.; St Catharine's Coll., Cambridge (MA). Chm., Cambridge Univ. Conservative Assoc., 1961; Mem. Cambridge Afro-Asian Expedn, 1961. Called to Bar, Inner Temple, 1962. Judge's Marshal, Midland Circuit, 1958; Mem., Young Barristers' Cttee, Bar Council, 1962–63; in practice on Wales and Chester Circuit, 1963–66; London and SE Circuit, 1966–76; 2nd Prosecuting Counsel to Inland Revenue, SE Circuit, 1971–74. Contested (C): Newport (Mon), 1964 and 1966; Norwood (Lambeth), 1970. PPS to Minister of Transport, 1979. Mem. Exec. Cttee, Soc. of Conservative Lawyers, 1968–71; Chm., Hampstead Conservative Political Centre, 1971–73; Mem. Council, Iran Soc., 1968–80; Sec., Anglo-Iranian Parly Gp; Chm., Anglo-Lebanese Parly Gp; Mem. Royal Inst. Internat. Affairs; Chm., Bow Group Standing Cttee on Home Affairs, 1975–79; Vice-Chm., Soc. of Cons. Lawyers' Standing Cttee on Criminal Law, 1976–79; Secretary: Conservative Parly Transport Cttee, 1976–79; Cons. Parly Legal Cttee, 1977–78; Vice-Chm., Cons. Parly Foreign and Commonwealth Affairs Cttee, 1982– (Sec., 1979–82); Mem., Select Cttee on Agriculture, 1982–83; Mem. Exec. British Branch, IPU, 1977– (Chm., 1982–85); British delegate, IPU fact-finding mission on Namibia, 1977; Mem., 1980, Leader, 1984, Parly Delegation to UN Gen. Assembly. Chm., Afghanistan Support Cttee, 1981–82. Freeman, City of London; Liveryman, Basketmakers' Co. Governor, Malvern Coll., 1975– (Council Mem., 1978–). Hon. Associate, BVA, 1976. *Recreations:* shooting; wine and food; family relaxation. *Address:* House of Commons, SW1A 0AA; Huntington Court, Three Elms, Hereford HR4 7RA. *T:* Hereford 272684. *Club:* Carlton.

TEMPLEMAN, family name of **Baron Templeman.**

TEMPLEMAN, Baron *cr* 1982 (Life Peer), of White Lackington in the County of Somerset; **Sydney William Templeman;** Kt 1972; MBE 1946; PC 1978; a Lord of Appeal in Ordinary, since 1982; *b* 3 March 1920; *s* of late Herbert William and Lilian Templeman; *m* 1946, Margaret Joan (*née* Rowles); two *s*. *Educ:* Southall Grammar School; St John's College, Cambridge (Schol.; MA 1944; Hon. Fellow 1982). Served War of 1939–45: commnd 4/1st Gurkha Rifles, 1941; NW Frontier, 1942; Arakan, 1943; Imphal, 1944; Burma with 7 Ind. and 17 Ind. Divisions, 1945 (despatches; Hon. Major). Called to the Bar, 1947; Harmsworth and MacMahon schols; Mem., Middle Temple and Lincoln's Inn; Mem., Bar Council, 1961–65, 1970–72; QC 1964; Bencher, Middle Temple, 1969 (Dep. Treasurer, 1986). Attorney Gen. of the Duchy of Lancaster, 1970–72; a Judge of the High Court of Justice, Chancery Div., 1972–78; a Lord Justice of Appeal, 1978–82. Member: Tribunal to inquire into matters relating to the Vehicle and General Insurance Co., 1971; Adv. Cttee on Legal Education, 1972–74; Royal Commn on Legal Services, 1976–79. Treasurer, Senate of the Four Inns, 1972–74; Pres., Senate of the Inns of Court and the Bar, 1974–76. Pres., Bar Assoc. for Commerce, Finance and Industry, 1982–85. Pres., Holdsworth Club, 1983–84. Hon. Member: Canadian Bar Assoc., 1976; Amer. Bar Assoc., 1976; Newfoundland Law Soc., 1984. Hon. DLitt Reading, 1980; Hon. LLD Birmingham, 1986. *Address:* Manor Heath, Knowl Hill, Woking, Surrey. *T:* Woking 61930.

TEMPLEMAN, Geoffrey, CBE 1980; MA London; PhD Birmingham; FSA; DL; Vice-Chancellor, University of Kent at Canterbury, 1963–80; *b* 15 February 1914; *s* of R. C. Templeman; *m* 1939, Dorothy May Heathcote; two *s* one *d*. *Educ:* Handsworth Grammar School; Universities of Birmingham, London and Paris. University of Birmingham: teaching history from 1938, Registrar, 1955–62. Chairman: Northern Univs Jt Matric. Bd, 1961–64; Universities Central Council on Admissions, 1964–75; Schs Cttee, Bd of Educn, General Synod of C of E, 1971–76 (Mem., 1971–78); Univ. Authorities Panel, 1972–80; Christ Church Coll., Canterbury, 1966–; Inst. of Germanic Studies, Univ. of London, 1966–84. Mem., SE Metropolitan Reg. Hosp. Bd, 1972–74; Mem., SE Thames RHA, 1974–84. Mem. Review Body on Doctors' and Dentists' Remuneration, 1965–70. DL Kent 1979. Hon. DTech Brunel, 1974; Hon. DCL Kent, 1980. Hon. Fellow, Inst. of Germanic Studies, Univ. of London, 1982. *Publications:* Dugdale Soc. Pubs vol. XI together with articles in learned jls, incl. Trans Royal Hist. Soc. and Cambridge Hist. Jl. *Address:* 2a St Augustine's Road, Canterbury, Kent. *Club:* Athenæum.

TEMPLER, Maj.-Gen. James Robert, OBE 1978 (MBE 1973); Assistant Chief of Defence Staff (Concepts), since 1986; *b* 8 Jan. 1936; *s* of Brig. Cecil Robert Templer, DSO and Angela Mary Templer (*née* Henderson); *m* 1963 (marr. diss. 1979); two *s* one *d*; 2nd, 1981, Sarah Ann Evans (*née* Rogers). *Educ:* Charterhouse; RMA Sandhurst. RCDS, psc. Commissioned Royal Artillery, 1955; Instructor, Staff Coll., 1974–75; Comd 42nd Regt, 1975–77; Comd 5th Regt, 1977–78; CRA 2nd Armd Div., 1978–82; RCDS 1983; ACOS Training, HQ UKLF, 1983–86. Mem., British Cross Country Ski Team, 1958; European 3 Day Event Champion, 1962; Mem., British Olympic 3 Day Event Team, 1964. *Recreations:* sailing, ski-ing, riding, gardening, fishing, beekeeping, DIY. *Address:* c/o Lloyds Bank, Crediton, Devon.

TEMPLETON, Prof. (Alexander) Allan; Professor of Obstetrics and Gynaecology, University of Aberdeen, since 1985; *b* 28 June 1946; *s* of Richard and Minnie Templeton; *m* 1980, Gillian Constance Penney; two *s* one *d*. *Educ:* Aberdeen Grammar School; Univ. of Aberdeen (MB ChB 1969; MD Hons 1982); MRCOG 1974. Resident and Registrar, Aberdeen Hosps, 1969–75; Lectr and Sen. Lectr, Dept of Obst. and Gyn., Univ. of Edinburgh, 1976–85. *Publications:* clinical and sci. articles on human infertility and *in vitro* fertilisation. *Recreation:* mountaineering. *Address:* Aultmore, Maryculter, Aberdeenshire AB1 0BJ. *T:* Aberdeen 733947.

TEMPLETON, Darwin Herbert, CBE 1975; *b* 14 July 1922; *s* of Malcolm and Mary Templeton; *m* 1950; two *s* one *d*. *Educ:* Rocavan Sch.; Ballymena Academy. FICAI. Qualified as Chartered Accountant, 1945. Partner, Ashworth Rowan, 1947; Senior Partner, Price Waterhouse Northern Ireland (formerly Ashworth Rowan Craig Gardner), 1967–82. Chm., Ulster Soc. of Chartered Accountants, 1961–62; Pres., ICAI, 1970–71. Mem., Royal Commn on Legal Services, 1976–79. Chairman: Northern Publishing Office (UK) Ltd; Ballycassidy Sawmills Ltd; NI Local Govt Officers Superannuation Fund; Gilbert Logan & Sons Ltd; Ulster Develoment Capital; Director: Larne Harbour Ltd; Boxmore International Ltd; Nationwide Building Soc. (Chm., NI Region); Qubis Ltd; Ulster Orchestra Soc. Mem. Senate, Queen's Univ. of Belfast. *Recreations:* music, golf, motor racing. *Address:* 4 Cashel Road, Broughshane, Ballymena, Co. Antrim, Northern Ireland BT42 4PL. *T:* Broughshane 861017. *Club:* Royal Scottish Automobile.

TEMPLETON, Mrs Edith; author, since 1950; *b* 7 April 1916; *m* Edmund Ronald, MD; one *s*. *Educ:* Prague and Paris; Prague Medical University. During War of 1939–45 worked in American War Office, in office of Surgeon General. Conference (1945–46) and Conference Interpreter for British Forces in Germany, rank of Capt. *Publications:* Summer in the Country, 1950 (USA 1951), repr. 1985; Living on Yesterday, 1951; The Island of Desire, 1952, repr. 1985; The Surprise of Cremona, 1954 (USA 1957), repr. 1985; This Charming Pastime, 1955; Three (USA 1971). Contributor to The New Yorker, Holiday, Atlantic Monthly, Vogue, Harper's Magazine. *Recreation:* travel, with the greatest comfort possible. *Address:* 55 Compayne Gardens, NW6.

TEMPLETON, John Marks; President of Templeton World Fund Inc., since 1978; chartered financial analyst, since 1965; *b* 29 Nov. 1912; *s* of Harvey Maxwell Templeton and Vella Templeton (*née* Handly); *m* 1st, 1937, Judith Dudley Folk (*d* 1950); two *s* one *d*; 2nd, 1958, Irene Reynolds Butler; one step *s* one step *d*. *Educ:* Yale Univ. (BA *summa* *cum laude*); Balliol Coll., Oxford (MA; Rhodes Scholar). Vice Pres., Nat. Geophysical Co., 1937–40; President: Templeton Dobbrow and Vance Inc., 1940–60; Templeton Growth Fund Ltd, 1954–85; Templeton Investment Counsel Ltd of London, 1976–; Sec., Templeton Foundn, 1960–. Pres., Bd of Trustees, Princeton Theol Seminary, 1967–73 and 1979–85; Mem. Council, Templeton College (formerly Oxford Centre for Management Studies), 1983–. Hon. LLD: Beaver Coll., 1968; Marquette Univ., 1980; Jamestown Coll., 1983; Maryville Coll., 1984; Hon. LHD Wilson Coll., 1974; Hon. DD Buena Vista Coll., 1979; Hon. DCL Univ. of the South, 1984. *Publications:* The Humble Approach, 1982; articles in professional jls. *Recreations:* swimming, gardening. *Address:* Lyford Cay, Nassau, Bahamas. *T:* 809–326–4295. *Clubs:* Athenæum, United Oxford & Cambridge University; University (NY); Lyford Cay (Bahamas).

TEMPLETON-COTILL, Rear-Adm. John Atrill, CB 1972; retired; *b* 4 June 1920; *s* of late Captain Jack Lionel Cottle, Tank Corps. *Educ:* Canford Sch.; New Coll., Oxford. Joined RNVR, 1939; served war 1939–45; HMS Crocus, 1940–41; British Naval Liaison Officer, French warship Chevreuil, 1941–42; staff, GOC New Caledonia (US), 1942; US Embassy, London, 1943; Flag Lieutenant to Vice-Adm., Malta, 1943–44; 1st Lieut, MTB 421, 1944–45; ADC to Governor of Victoria, 1945–46; served in HMS London, Loch Quoich, Whirlwind, Jutland, Barrosa and Sparrow, 1946–55; Comdr 1955; comd HMS Sefton and 108th Minesweeping Sqdn, 1955–56; jssc 1956; Comdr-in-Charge, RN School of Work Study, 1957–59; HMS Tiger, 1959–61; Captain 1961; British Naval Attaché, Moscow, 1962–64; comd HMS Rhyl and Captain (D), 23rd Escort Sqdn, 1964–66; Senior Naval Mem., Defence Operational Analysis Estabt, 1966–68; comd HMS Bulwark, 1968–69; Rear-Adm. Jan. 1970; Chief of Staff to Comdr Far East Fleet, 1970–71; Flag Officer, Malta, and NATO Comdr, SE Area Mediterranean, 1971–73; Comdr, British Forces Malta, 1972–73. Director: Sotheby Parke Bernet (France), 1974–81; Sotheby Parke Bernet (Monaco), 1975–81. *Recreations:* gardening, riding, shooting, travel, skiing. *Address:* Moulin de Fontvive, Ribas, par 30290 Laudun, France. *T:* 66.79.47.37.

TENBY, 3rd Viscount *cr* 1957, of Bulford; **William Lloyd-George;** *b* 7 Nov. 1927; 2nd *s* of 1st Viscount Tenby, TD, PC, and Edna Gwenfron (*d* 1971), *d* of David Jones, Gwynfa, Denbigh; *S* brother, 1983; *m* 1955, Ursula Diana Ethel, *y d* of late Lt-Col Henry Edward Medlicott, DSO; one *s* two *d*. *Educ:* Eastbourne College; St Catharine's Coll., Cambridge (Exhibnr; BA 1949). Captain, Royal Welch Fusiliers, TA. JP Hants (Dep. Chm., Odiham Bench, 1984). *Heir: s* Hon. Timothy Henry Gwilym Lloyd-George, *b* 19 Oct. 1962. *Address:* Triggs, Crondall, near Farnham, Surrey.

TENCH, David Edward; Legal Adviser, Consumers' Association (publishers of Which?), since 1969; *b* 14 June 1929; *s* of late Henry George Tench and Emma Rose (*née* Orsborn); *m* 1957, Judith April Seaton Gurney (*d* 1986); two *s* one *d*. *Educ:* Merchant Taylors' Sch., Northwood, Mddx. Solicitor, 1952. Private practice, 1954–58; Office of Solicitor of Inland Revenue, 1958–69. Chm., Domestic Coal Consumers' Council, 1976–; Energy Comr, 1977–79. Broadcaster on consumer affairs, 1964–. *Publications:* The Law for Consumers, 1962; The Legal Side of Buying a House, 1965 (2nd edn 1974); Wills and Probate, 1967 (6th edn 1977); How to Sue in the County Court, 1973; Towards a Middle System of Law, 1981. *Recreations:* music, amateur re-upholstery, bland gardening. *Address:* Pleasant View, The Platt, Amersham, Bucks. *T:* Amersham 4974.

See also W. H. Tench.

TENCH, William Henry, CBE 1980; Consultant on aircraft accident investigation to the Ministry of Defence; Special Adviser on Air Safety to the EEC Commissioner for Transport; *b* 2 Aug. 1921; *s* of Henry George Tench and Emma Rose Tench (*née* Orsborn); *m* 1944, Margaret Ireland; one *d*. *Educ:* Portsmouth Grammar School. CEng, FRAeS. Learned to fly in Fleet Air Arm, 1940; pilot with oil co. in S America, 1947 and 1948; joined KLM Royal Dutch Airlines, W Indies Div., 1948; transf. to Holland, 1951, flying N and S Atlantic, S African, ME and European routes; joined Min. of Transport and Civil Aviation as Inspector of Accidents, 1955; Chief Inspector of Accidents, DoT, 1974–81. *Publication:* Safety is no Accident, 1985. *Recreations:* music, sailing. *Address:* Seaways, Restronguet Point, Feock, Cornwall TR3 6RB.

See also D. E. Tench.

TENISON; *see* Hanbury-Tenison.

TENISON; *see* King-Tenison.

TENNANT, family name of **Baron Glenconner.**

TENNANT, Emma Christina, FRSL 1982; writer; *b* 20 Oct. 1937; *d* of 2nd Baron Glenconner and Elizabeth Lady Glenconner; one *s* two *d*. *Educ:* St Paul's Girls' School. Freelance journalist to 1973; became full time novelist, 1973; founder Editor, Bananas, 1975–78; general editor: In Verse, 1982–; Lives of Modern Women, 1985–. *Publications:* The Colour of Rain (pseud. Catherine Aydy), 1963; The Time of the Crack, 1973; The Last of the Country House Murders, 1975; Hotel de Dream, 1976; (ed) Bananas Anthology, 1977; (ed) Saturday Night Reader, 1978; The Bad Sister, 1978; Wild Nights, 1979; Alice Fell, 1980; Queen of Stones, 1982; Woman Beware Woman, 1983; Black Marina, 1985; Adventures of Robina by Herself, ed Emma Tennant, 1986; (contrib.) Novelists in Interview (ed John Haffenden), 1985; (contrib.) Women's Writing: a challenge to theory (ed Maria Monteith), 1986; *for children:* The Boggart (with Mary Rayner), 1979; The Search for Treasure Island, 1981; The Ghost Child, 1984; contribs to Guardian. *Recreation:* walking in Dorset. *Address:* c/o Faber & Faber, 3 Queen Square, WC1. *T:* 01–278 6881.

TENNANT, Harry; Member, Civil Service Appeal Board; *b* 10 Dec. 1917; *s* of late Robert and Mary Tennant; *m* 1944, Bernice Baker; one *s*. *Educ:* Oldham High School. Appointed Officer of Customs and Excise, 1938; Inspector, 1960; Principal Inspector, 1970; Asst Sec., 1971; Dep. Chief Inspector, 1973; Commissioner of Customs and Excise, 1975–78. *Publications:* Back to the Bible, 1962, repr. 1984; Moses My Servant, 1966, repr. 1975; The Man David, 1968, repr. 1983. *Recreations:* walking, travel. *Address:* Strathtay, Alexandra Road, Watford, Herts WD1 3QY. *T:* Watford 22079.

TENNANT, Captain Iain Mark, JP; Lord-Lieutenant of Morayshire, since 1963; Crown Estate Commissioner, since 1970; *b* 11 March 1919; *e s* of late Col Edward Tennant, Innes, Elgin and Mrs Georgina Tennant; *m* 1946, Lady Margaret Helen Isla Marion Ogilvy, 2nd *d* of 12th Earl of Airlie, Kt, GCVO, MC; two *s* one *d*. *Educ:* Eton College; Magdalene College, Cambridge. Scots Guards, 1939–46. Caledonian Cinemas, 1947; Chm., Grampian Television Ltd, 1968–; Director: Times Publishing Co. Ltd, 1962–66; Clydesdale Bank Ltd, 1968–; The Seagram Co. Ltd, Montreal, 1978–81; Chairman: The Glenlivet Distillers Ltd, 1964–84; Seagram Distillers, 1979–84. Mem. Newspaper Panel, Monopolies and Mergers Commn, 1981–. Moray Enterprise Trust. Chm. Bd of Governors, Gordonstoun School, 1954–71. Ensign, Queen's Body Guard for Scotland (Royal Company of Archers), 1981–. FRSA 1971; CBIM 1983. DL Moray, 1954; JP Moray, 1961. *Recreations:* shooting, fishing; formerly rowing (rowed for Eton, 1937). *Address:* (home) Lochnabo, Lhanbryde, Moray. *T:* Lhanbryde 2228; (office) Innes House, Elgin, Moray. *T:* Lhanbryde 2410.

TENNANT, Sir Mark (Dalcour), KCMG 1964 (CMG 1951); CB 1961; Deputy Secretary, Department of the Environment, 1970–71; *b* 26 Dec. 1911; *o surv. s* of late N. R. D. Tennant, Haileybury, Hertford; *m* 1936, Clare Elisabeth Ross, *o d* of late Sir Ross Barker, KCIE, CB. *Educ:* Marlborough; New College, Oxford (Open Classical Schol.). Entered Min. of Labour as Asst Principal, 1935; Private Secretary to Parliamentary Secretary, Ministry of Labour, 1938–39; and to Parliamentary Secretary, Ministry of Food, 1939–40. Served War of 1939–45, Royal Artillery, 1942–44. Assistant Secretary, 1945; Member of UK Delegation to International Labour Conference, 1949–53; Student Imperial Defence College, 1956; Under-Secretary, 1957; Secretary-General Monckton Commission on the Review of the Constitution of the Federation of Rhodesia and Nyasaland, 1960; Dir Organisation and Establishments, Min. of Labour, 1960; Secretary, Central African Office, 1962–64. Third Secretary, HM Treasury, 1964–65; Dep. Sec., Min. of Public Building and Works, 1965–70. *Address:* c/o Barclays Bank, 1 Pall Mall East, SW1. *Club:* Travellers'.

TENNANT, Sir Peter (Frank Dalrymple), Kt 1972; CMG 1958; OBE 1945; Director-General, British National Export Council, 1965–71; Industrial Adviser, Barclays Bank International Ltd, 1972–81; Director: Prudential Assurance Company Ltd, 1973–81; Prudential Corporation plc, 1979–86; C. Tennant Sons & Company Ltd, 1972–80; Anglo-Romanian Bank, 1973–81; Northern Engineering Industries (International) Ltd, 1979–82; International Energy Bank, 1981–84; *b* 29 Nov. 1910; *s* of G. F. D. Tennant and Barbara Tennant (*née* Beck); *m* 1st, 1934 (marr. diss. 1952), Hellis, *d* of Professor Fellenius, Stockholm; one *s* two *d*; 2nd, 1953, Galina Bosley, *d* of K. Grunberg, Helsinki; one step *s*. *Educ:* Marlborough; Trinity College, Cambridge. Sen. Mod. Languages Scholar, Trinity College, Cambridge, 1929; Cholmondely Studentship, Lincoln's Inn; 1st Cl. Hons Mod. Langs Tripos, 1931; BA 1931, MA 1936, Cambridge. Cambridge Scandinavian Studentship, Oslo, Copenhagen, Stockholm, 1932–33; Fellow Queens' College, Cambridge, and University Lecturer, Scandinavian Languages, 1933; Press Attaché, British Legation, Stockholm, 1939–45; Information Counsellor, British Embassy, Paris, 1945–50; Deputy Commandant, British Sector, Berlin, 1950–52; resigned Foreign Service to become Overseas Director, FBI, 1952–63. Deputy Director-General, FBI, 1963–65. Special Advr, CBI, 1964–65. Former Mem., Council of Industrial Design; past acting Chm., Wilton Park Academic Council; former Mem. Bd, Centre for Internat. Briefing, Farnham Castle; past Chm., Gabbitas Thring Educational Trust; Pres., London Chamber of Commerce and Industry, 1978–79 (Chm., 1976–78); Chm., British Cttee, European Cultural Foundn. Vis. Fellow, St Cross Coll., Oxford, 1982. MA Oxford, 1982. *Publications:* Ibsen's Dramatic Technique, 1947; The Scandinavian Book, 1952. *Recreations:* writing, talking, painting, travel, languages, sailing, country life. *Address:* Blue Anchor House, Linchmere Road, Haslemere, Surrey GU27 3QF. *T:* Haslemere 3124. *Club:* Travellers'.

TENNEKOON, Victor; Chairman, Law Commission of Sri Lanka, since 1978; *b* 9 Sept. 1914; *s* of Loku Banda Tennekoon and Nandu Menike Tennekoon (*née* Rambukwella); *m* 1946, Semitha Murie Wijeyewardene; one *s* two *d*. *Educ:* St Anthony's Coll., Kandy; University Coll., Colombo. BA London Univ. (External) 1935. Called to Sri Lanka Bar, 1942. QC 1965. Practised at Kegalle, 1943–46; Crown Counsel, 1946; Solicitor-General, 1964; Attorney-General, 1970; Judge of Court of Appeal, Sri Lanka, 1973; Chief Justice of Sri Lanka, 1974–77. Chancellor, Univ. of Peradeniya, 1979–84. *Recreations:* tennis, golf, billiards, bridge, chess. *Address:* 40/1 Ananda Coomaraswamy Nawata, Green Path, Colombo 3, Sri Lanka. *T:* 20853. *Club:* Orient (Colombo).

TENNSTEDT, Klaus; Principal Conductor and Music Director, London Philharmonic Orchestra, since 1983; *b* 6 June 1926; *s* of Hermann and Agnes Tennstedt; *m* 1960, Ingeborg Fischer. *Educ:* Leipzig Conservatory (violin, piano). Conductor at: Landersoper, Dresden, 1958–62; Staatstheater, Schwerin, 1962–70; Operhaus, Kiel, 1972–76; guest conductor with Boston, Chicago, New York Philharmonic, Cleveland, Philadelphia, Berlin and Israel Philharmonic Orchestras. Hon. DMus Colgate Hamilton, NY State, 1984. *Recreations:* astronomy, hot air ballooning. *Address:* c/o London Philharmonic Orchestra, 35 Doughty Street, WC1. *T:* 01–833 2744.

TENNYSON, family name of **Baron Tennyson.**

TENNYSON, 4th Baron *cr* 1884; **Harold Christopher Tennyson;** *b* 25 March 1919; *e s* of 3rd Baron and Hon. Clarissa Tennant (*d* 1960), *o d* of 1st Baron Glenconner; *S* father 1951. *Educ:* Eton; Trinity Coll., Cambridge. BA 1940. Employed War Office, 1939–46. Co-founder, Tennyson Research Centre, Lincoln. Hon. Freeman, City of Lincoln, 1964. *Heir: b* Hon. Mark Aubrey Tennyson, DSC 1943; RN retd [*b* 28 March 1920; *m* 1964, Deline Celeste Budler. *Educ:* RN College, Dartmouth. Served War of 1939–45 (despatches, DSC); Comdr RN, 1954]. *Address:* 18 Rue Galilée, 75016 Paris, France. *Clubs:* White's, Royal Automobile; Royal and Ancient.

TENNYSON-d'EYNCOURT, Sir (John) Jeremy (Eustace), 3rd Bt *cr* 1930; *b* 8 July 1927; *s* of Sir Eustace Gervais Tennyson-d'Eyncourt, 2nd Bt, and Pamela (*d* 1962), *d* of late W. B. Gladstone; *S* father, 1971; *m* 1st, 1964, Mrs Sally Fyfe-Jamieson (marr. diss.; she *m* 1982, Baron Vernon), *e d* of Robin Stratford, KC; 2nd, 1972, Brenda Mary Veronica (marr. diss. 1976), *d* of Dr Austin Stafford; 3rd, 1977, Norah, *d* of late Thomas Gill. *Educ:* Eton; Glasgow University. Served as Sub Lieut, RNVR, 1945–48. *Recreations:* fishing and wild-life; cooking and gardening. *Address:* Bayons House, Gas Lane, Hinton St George, Somerset TA17 8RX.

TEŌ, Sir (Fiatau) Penitala, GCMG 1979; GCVO 1982; ISO 1970; MBE 1956; Governor-General of Tuvalu, 1978–86; *b* 23 July 1911; *s* of Teō Veli, Niutao, and Tilesa Samuelu, Funafuti; *m* 1st, 1931, Muniara Apelu, Vaitupu; one *d* (one *s* decd); 2nd, 1949, Uimai Tofiga, Nanumaga; eight *s* three *d* (and one *d* decd). *Educ:* Elisefou, Vaitupu, Tuvalu. Asst Sch. Master, Elisefou, 1930–32; Clerk and Ellice Interpreter: Dist Admin, Funafuti, 1932–37; Resident Comr's Office, Ocean Is., 1937–42; under Japanese Occupation (Ocean Is. and Tarawa), 1942–43 (1939–45 Star, Pacific Star and War Medal); re-joined Res. Comr's Office, 1943 (i/c Labour Force), Special Clerk 1944; Asst Admin. Officer and Mem., Gilbert and Ellice Is Defence Force (2nd Lieut), 1944; Asst and Actg Dist Officer for Ellice Is, 1944–50; transf. to Tarawa to re-organise Information Office, 1953; Dep. Comr for Western Pacific, 1960; Lands Officer for Gilbert and Ellice Is, 1960–62; Dist Commissioner: Ocean Is., 1963; Ellice Is, 1967–69; Asst and Actg Supt of Labour, British Phosphate Comrs, Ocean Is., 1971–78. ADC to High Comr of Western Pacific during tours, 1954 and 1957; Dist Officer for visit of Prince Philip to Vaitupu Is., Ellice Is, 1959. Represented Gilbert and Ellice Is at confs. Coronation Medal, 1953. *Recreations:* formerly fishing, cricket, football, Rugby, local games. *Address:* Alapi, Funafuti, Tuvalu.

TERESA, Mother, (Agnes Gonxha Bojaxhiu), MC; Hon. OM 1983; Hon. OBE 1978; Padma Shri, 1962; Bharat Ratna (Star of India), 1980; Roman Catholic nun; *b* Skopje, Yugoslavia, 27 Aug. 1910; *d* of Albanian parents. *Educ:* government school in Yugoslavia. Joined Sisters of Loretto, Rathfarnam, Ireland, 1928; trained at Loretto insts in Ireland and India; came to Calcutta, 1929; Principal, St Mary's High School, Calcutta. Founded the Missionaries of Charity (Sisters), 1950, Missionary Brothers of Charity, 1963, and the Internat. Co-Workers of Mother Teresa, 1969, to give free service to the poor and the unwanted, irrespective of caste, creed, nationality, race or place; she has set up: slum schools; orphanages; Nirmol Hridoy (Pure Heart) Homes for sick and dying street cases; Shishu Bhavan Homes for unwanted, crippled and mentally-retarded children; mobile gen. clinics and centres for malnourished; mobile clinics and rehabilitation centres for leprosy patients; homes for drug addicts and alcoholics; night shelters for the homeless. Hon. DD Cambridge, 1977; Hon. DrMed: Catholic Univ. of Sacred Heart, Rome, 1981; Catholic Univ. of Louvain, 1982. Ramón Magsaysay Internat. Award, 1962; Pope John XXIII Peace Prize, 1971; Kennedy Internat. Award, 1971; Jawaharlal Nehru Internat. Award, 1972; Templeton Foundation Prize, 1973; first Albert Schweitzer Internat. Prize, 1975; Nobel Peace Prize, 1979. Hon. Citizen, Assisi, 1982. *Publication:* Gift for God, 1975. *Address:* 54A Acharya Jagadish Chandra Bose Road, Calcutta 700016, India. *T:* 24–7115.

TERESHKOVA, Valentina N.; *see* Nikolayeva-Tereshkova.

TERLEZKI, Stefan; MP (C) Cardiff West, since 1983; hotel and catering consultant; *b* Ukraine, 29 Oct. 1927; *s* of late Oleksa Terlezki and Olena Terlezki; *m* 1955, Mary; two *d. Educ:* Cardiff Coll. of Food Technol. and Commerce. Member: Hotel and Catering Inst., 1965–80; Chamber of Trade, 1975–80. Member: Cardiff CC, 1968–83 (Press Officer, 1970–83; Chairman: Licensing Cttee, 1975–78; Environment Services Cttee, 1978–80; Housing Liaison Cttee, 1978–80); S Glam CC, 1973–85; S Wales Police Auth., 1975–80; Welsh Jt Educn Cttee, 1975–85; Chm., Jt Consultative Cttee, S Glam Health Auth., 1978–79; Member: Educn Authority for Cardiff CC and S Glam CC, 1969–85; Planning, Finance and Policy Cttee, 1965–83. Member: Welsh Tourist Council, 1965–80; Welsh Games Council, 1974–80. Contested (C): Cardiff South East, Feb. and Oct. 1974; South Wales, European Parlt elecn, 1979. Chm., Keep Britain in Europe Campaign, 1973. Pres., Cardiff N Young Conservatives, 1974–; Vice-Pres., Wales Area Young Conservatives, 1975–; Member: Central Council, CPC; Official Nat. Speaking Panels of Cons. Party, European Movement, and Eur. Parlt; Cons. Gp for Eur. Movement, 1973; Council of Europe; WEU; UN Organisation, Temple of Peace, Cardiff; Foreign Affairs Forum. Chairman: Cardiff City Football Club, 1975–77; Cardiff High Sch. Bd of Governors, 1975–83. Languages: Ukrainian, Polish, Russian, German (basic). Radio and television broadcasts; occasional journalism. *Address:* 16 Bryngwyn Road, Cyncoed, Cardiff. *T:* 01–219 3000.

TERRAINE, John Alfred; author; *b* 15 Jan. 1921; *s* of Charles William Terraine and Eveline Holmes; *m* 1945, Joyce Eileen Waite; one *d. Educ:* Stamford Sch.; Keble Coll., Oxford. Joined BBC, 1944; Pacific and S African Programme Organiser, 1953–63; resigned from BBC, 1964. Associate producer and chief scriptwriter of The Great War, BBC TV, 1963–64; part-scriptwriter The Lost Peace, BBC TV, 1965; scriptwriter, The Life and Times of Lord Mountbatten, Rediffusion/Thames TV, 1966–68; scriptwriter, The Mighty Continent, BBC TV, 1974–75. Founder Pres., Western Front Assoc., 1980–; Mem. Council, RUSI, 1976–84. Chesney Gold Medal, RUSI, 1982; Yorkshire Post Book of the Year Award, 1985; C. P. Robertson Meml Trophy, Air Public Relations Assoc., 1985. *Publications:* Mons: The Retreat to Victory, 1960; Douglas Haig: The Educated Soldier, 1963; The Western Front, 1964; General Jack's Diary, 1964; The Great War: An Illustrated History, 1965 (NY), unillustrated reprint, The First World War, 1983; The Life and Times of Lord Mountbatten, 1968; Impacts of War 1914 and 1918, 1970; The Mighty Continent, 1974; Trafalgar, 1976; The Road to Passchendaele, 1977; To Win a War: 1918 The Year of Victory, 1978; The Smoke and the Fire, 1980; White Heat: the new warfare 1914–1918, 1982; The Right of the Line: the Royal Air Force in the European War 1939–45, 1985. *Recreation:* convivial and congenial conversation. *Address:* 74 Kensington Park Road, W11. *T:* 01–229 8152; Vittoria, Church Street, Amberley, Arundel, West Sussex. *T:* Bury 638.

TERRELL, Colonel Stephen, OBE 1952; TD; QC 1965; DL. Called to the Bar, Gray's Inn, 1946; Bencher, Gray's Inn, 1970. South Eastern Circuit. Pres., Liberal Party, 1972. Contested (L) Eastbourne, Feb. 1974. DL Middlesex, 1961.

TERRINGTON, 4th Baron, *cr* 1918, of Huddersfield; **James Allen David Woodhouse;** former Member, Stock Exchange; Partner in Sheppards and Chase, 1952–80; *b* 30 December 1915; *er s* of 3rd Baron Terrington, KBE, and Valerie (*née* Phillips) (*d* 1958), Leyden's House, Edenbridge, Kent; *S* father, 1961; *m* 1942, Suzanne, *y d* of Colonel T. S. Irwin, DL, JP, late Royal Dragoons, Justicetown, Carlisle, and Mill House, Holton, Suffolk; three *d. Educ:* Winchester; Royal Military College, Sandhurst. Commnd Royal Norfolk Regiment, TA, 1936. Farming in Norfolk, 1936–39. Served War of 1939–45 in India, North Africa and Middle East (wounded); ADC to GOC Madras, 1940; Staff Coll., Haifa, 1944; psc 1944; GSOII, Allied Force HQ Algiers, Ninth Army, Middle East, and War Office, Military Operations; retired as Major, 1948; joined Queen's Westminster Rifles (KRRC), TA. Joined Messrs Chase Henderson and Tennant, 1949 (now Sheppards and Chase). Deputy Chairman of Cttees, House of Lords, 1961–63. Member: Ecclesiastical Cttee, 1979–; Exec. Cttee, Wider Shareownership Council, 1981– (former Dep. Chm. of Council); Dep. Chm., Nat. Listening Library, 1977–. Mem. Internat. Adv. Bd, American Univ., Washington DC, 1985–. *Recreations:* shooting, racing. *Heir:* *b* Hon. Christopher Montague Woodhouse, *qv. Address:* The Manor House, Barford St Martin, Salisbury, Wilts. *Clubs:* Boodle's, Pratt's.

See also Earl Alexander of Tunis.

TERRY, Sir George (Walter Roberts), Kt 1982; CBE 1976; QPM 1967; DL; Chief Constable of Sussex, 1973–83; *b* 29 May 1921; *s* of late Walter George Tygh Terry and Constance Elizabeth Terry; *m* 1942, Charlotte Elizabeth Kresina; one *s. Educ:* Peterborough, Northants. Served War, Northamptonshire Regt, in Italy, 1942–46 (Staff Captain). Chief Constable: Pembrokeshire, 1958–65; East Sussex, 1965–67; Dep. Chief Constable, Sussex, 1968–69; Chief Constable, Lincolnshire, 1970–73. Chm., Traffic Cttee, 1976–79, Pres., 1980–81, Assoc. of Chief Police Officers; Dir, Police Extended Interviews, 1977–83. CStJ. DL E Sussex, 1983. *Recreations:* horticulture, motoring. *Address:* c/o National Westminster Bank, 173 High Street, Lewes, Sussex BN7 1XD.

TERRY, Sir John Elliott, Kt 1976; Consultant with Denton Hall & Burgin; Managing Director, National Film Finance Corporation, 1958–78; *b* 11 June 1913; *s* of Ernest Fairchild Terry, OBE, FRICS, and Zabelle Terry (*née* Costikyan), Pulborough, Sussex; *m* 1940, Joan Christine, *d* of Frank Alfred Ernest Howard Fell and Ethel Christine Fell (*née* Nilson), Stoke D'Abernon, Surrey; one *s* one *d. Educ:* Mill Hill School; Univ. of London (LLB). Articled with Denton Hall & Burgin, London; admitted solicitor, 1938. London Fire Service, 1939–40; Friends' Ambulance Unit, 1941–44; Nat. Council of Social Service, 1944–46; Film Producers' Guild, 1946–47; The Rank Organisation's Legal Dept, 1947–49; joined Nat. Film Finance Corp. as Solicitor, 1949, also Sec., 1956. Governor: Nat. Film Sch., 1970–81; London Internat. Film Sch., 1982–; Royal Nat. Coll. for the Blind, 1980–; Pres., Copinger Soc., 1981–83. *Address:* Still Point, Branscombe, Devon.

TERRY, (John) Quinlan, FRIBA 1962; architect in private practice, since 1967; *b* 24 July 1937; *s* of Philip and Phyllis Terry; *m* 1961, Christine de Ruttié; one *s* four *d. Educ:* Bryanston School; Architectural Association; Rome Scholar. Assistant to Raymond Erith, RA, FRIBA, 1962, Partner 1967–, Erith & Terry; work includes: new country houses in classical style; Common Room Building, Gray's Inn; offices and flats, Dufours Place, Soho; Richmond Riverside Scheme; New Lecture Theatre, Downing Coll., Cambridge. *Recreation:* sketching classical buildings. *Address:* Higham Hall, Higham, Colchester, Essex. *T:* Higham 209.

TERRY, Michael, FRGS; FRGSA; explorer and author; *b* Newcastle upon Tyne, 3 May 1899; *s* of late Major A. M. and late Catherine Terry; *m* 1940, Ursula (marr. diss. 1945), *yr d* of Captain Noel Livingstone-Learmonth. *Educ:* Preston House School, East Grinstead; King Edward School, Birmingham; Durham University. Served in Russia; invalided out; went to Australia upon discharge; took first motor across Northern Australia from Winton, Queensland, to Broome on the North-West Coast, in 1923; Cuthbert-Peek Grant in support of expedition undertaken, 1925, from Darwin to Broome; authorised to name Dummer Range and Mount Rosamund; third expedition started Port Hedland, 1928; proceeded Broome, Halls Creek, Tanami, Alice Springs, Melbourne. Made gold and potassium nitrate discoveries. Explored extensively in N Territory, also in S and W Australia, 1929–33; found Hidden Basin, a 40x20 mile subsided area, covered 1200 miles on camels and collected data for Waite Research Inst., Met. Bureau, and Lands Dept; Sept.-Nov. 1933, Tennants Creek Goldfield; 1934–36, prospecting NE of Laverton, WA; farming, Terrigal, NSW, 1946–60. Received by Prince of Wales, 1926; presented to King George, 1939. Has completed 14 Australian inland expeditions. Life Member: Aust. Soc. Authors; Life Associate, Path Finders Assoc. of NSW; Mem., Nat. Geographic Soc., Washington, USA. *Publications:* Across Unknown Australia, 1925; Through a Land of Promise, 1927; Untold Miles, 1928; Hidden Wealth and Hiding People, 1931; Sand and Sun, 1937; Bulldozer, 1945; War of the Warramullas, 1974; My Historical Years, 1980; and in numerous journals. *Recreation:* riding.

TERRY, Sir Michael Edward Stanley I.; *see* Imbert-Terry.

TERRY, Air Chief Marshal Sir Peter (David George), GCB 1983 (KCB 1978; CB 1975); AFC 1968; QCVSA 1959 and 1962; Governor and Commander-in-Chief, Gibraltar, since 1985; *b* 18 Oct. 1926; *s* of James George Terry and Laura Chilton Terry (*née* Powell); *m* 1946, Betty Martha Louisa Thompson; one *s* one *d* (and one *s* decd). *Educ:* Chatham House Sch., Ramsgate. Joined RAF, 1945; commnd in RAF Regt, 1946; Pilot, 1953. Staff Coll., 1962; OC, No 51 Sqdn, 1966–68; OC, RAF El Adem, 1968–70; Dir, Air Staff Briefing, MoD, 1970–71; Dir of Forward Policy for RAF, 1971–74; ACOS (Policy and Plans), SHAPE, 1975–77; VCAS, 1977–79; C-in-C RAF Germany and Comdr Second Allied Tactical Air Force, 1979–81; Dep. C-in-C, Allied Forces Central Europe, Feb.-April 1981; Dep. Supreme Allied Commander, Europe, 1981–84. KStJ 1986. *Recreation:* golf. *Address:* The Convent, Gibraltar, BFPO 52. *Club:* Royal Air Force.

TERRY, Quinlan; *see* Terry, J. Q.

TERRY, Walter; Political Editor, The Sun, 1978–83 (Member of Political Staff, 1976–83); *b* 18 Aug. 1924; *s* of Fred Terry and Helen MacKenzie Bruce; *m* 1950, Mavis Landen; one *s* one *d* (and one *s* decd). *Educ:* at school and later by experience. Entered journalism, Glossop Chronicle, 1943; Derby Evening Telegraph, 1947; Nottingham Journal, 1948; Daily Mail, Manchester, 1949; Daily Mail: Parliamentary Staff, 1955; Political Correspondent, 1959; Political Editor, 1965; Washington Correspondent, 1969; Dep.-Editor, 1970–71; Political Editor, 1971–73; Political Editor, Daily Express, 1973–75. Journalist of the Year (first awards), 1963. *Address:* St Germans House, Eliot Place, SE3 0QL. *T:* 01–852 2526; 8 Fort Rise, Newhaven Harbour, Sussex BN9 9DW. *T:* Newhaven 514347. *Club:* Reform.

TERRY-THOMAS, (Thomas Terry Hoar Stevens); Actor; *b* 14 July 1911; *s* of Ernest Frederick Stevens and Ellen Elizabeth (*née* Hoar); *m* 1938, Ida Patlanskey; *m* 1963, Belinda Cunningham; two *s. Educ:* Ardingly Coll., Sussex. Served War of 1939–45: in army, Royal Corps of Signals, 1941–46. Piccadilly Hayride, Prince of Wales Theatre, 1946–47; Radio Series: To Town With Terry, 1948–49; Top Of The Town, 1951–52; TV Series: How Do You View, 1951–52. *Films:* Private's Progress, Green Man, 1956; Brothers-in-Law, Blue Murder at St Trinians, Lucky Jim, Naked Truth, 1957; Tom Thumb, Happy is the Bride, 1958; Carlton Browne of the FO, I'm All Right Jack, Too Many Crooks, 1959; Make Mine Mink, School for Scoundrels, His and Hers, 1960; A Matter of Who, Bachelor Flat, Operation Snatch, The Wonderful World of the Brothers Grimm, 1961; Kill or Cure, Its a Mad, Mad, Mad, Mad World, 1962; Wild Affair, 1963; How to Murder Your Wife, 1964; Those Magnificent Men in their Flying Machines, 1965; Jules Verne's Rocket to the Moon, 1967; Don't Look Now, 1968; Where Were You When the Lights Went Out?, 1968; Monte Carlo or Bust!, 1969; Thirteen, 1970; Seven Times Seven, 1970; Arthur, Arthur, 1970; Atlantic Wall, 1970; Dr Phibes, 1970; Lei, Lui, Loro, la Legge, 1971; Dr Phibes rises again, 1972; The Heros, 1972; Tom Jones, 1975; Side by Side, 1975; Spanish Fly, 1975; The Last Remake of Beau Geste, 1976; The Hound of the Baskervilles, 1978. *Publication:* (as Terry-Thomas) Filling the Gap, 1959. *Recreations:* horse-riding and water ski-ing. *Address:* Juan de Saridakis 83, Genova Palma, Mallorca. *Club:* Savage.

TESH, Robert Mathieson, CMG 1968; HM Diplomatic Service, retired; Ambassador to Ethiopia, 1979–82; *b* 15 Sept. 1922; *s* of late E. Tesh, Hurst Green, Surrey; *m* 1950, Jean Bowker; two *s* one *d. Educ:* Queen Elizabeth's, Wakefield; Queen's College, Oxford (MA). Oxford, 1940–42 and 1945–47; Rifle Brigade, 1942–45; HM Foreign Service, 1947: New Delhi, 1948–50; FO, 1950–53 and 1957–60; Delegation to NATO, Paris, 1953–55; Beirut, 1955–57; Bangkok, 1960–64; Dep. High Comr, Ghana, 1965–66; Lusaka, 1966; Consul-General British Interests Section, Canadian Embassy, Cairo, 1966–67; Counsellor, British Embassy, Cairo, 1968; IDC, 1969; Head of Defence Dept, FCO, 1970–72; Ambassador to Bahrain, 1972–75; Ambassador to: the Democratic Republic of Vietnam, 1976; the Socialist Republic of Vietnam, 1976–78; FCO, 1978–79. *Recreations:* singing, acting, golf. *Address:* Ashenden, 10 Albany Close, Esher, Surrey. *T:* Esher 64192. *Club:* Travellers'.

TESLER, Brian, CBE 1986; Managing Director, since 1976, Chairman, since 1984, London Weekend Television Ltd (Deputy Chairman, 1982–84); *b* 19 Feb. 1929; *s* of late David Tesler and of Stella Tesler; *m* 1959, Audrey Mary Maclean; one *s. Educ:* Chiswick County School for Boys; Exeter Coll., Oxford (State Schol.; MA). Theatre Editor, The Isis, 1950–51; Pres., Oxford Univ. Experimental Theatre Club, 1951–52. British Forces Broadcasting Service, 1947–49; Producer/Director: BBC Television, 1952; ATV, 1957; ABC Television: Head of Features and Light Entertainment, 1960; Programme Controller, 1961; Dir of Programmes, 1962; Dir of Programmes, Thames Television, 1968; Dep. Chief Exec., London Weekend Television, 1974; Chm., ITV Superchannel Ltd, 1986–; Director: ITN, 1979–; Channel Four Television Ltd, 1980–85; Oracle Teletext Ltd, 1980–; LWT International Ltd, 1982–; Services Kinema Corp., 1981–82; Services Sound and Vision Corp., 1982–. Member: Working Party on future of British film industry, 1975–77; Interim Action Cttee on film industry, 1977–85; British Screen Adv. Council, 1985–; Governor, Nat. Film and Television Sch. (formerly Nat. Film Sch.), 1977–; Pres., Television and Radio Industries Club, 1979–80; Vice-Pres., RTS, 1984–; Chairman: Indep. TV Cos Assoc., 1980–82; ITCA Cable and Satellite Television Working Party, 1981–. Daily Mail Nat. Television Award, 1954; Guild of Television Producers and Directors Award, 1957; Lord Willis Trophy for Outstanding Services to Television,

Pye Television Awards, 1986. *Recreations*: books, theatre, cinema, music. *Address*: London Weekend Television Ltd, South Bank Television Centre, Kent House, Upper Ground, SE1 9LT. *T*: 01–261 3434.

TESTAFERRATA, Marquis; *see* San Vincenzo Ferreri, Marquis of.

TETLEY, Glen; choreographer, since 1948; *b* 3 Feb. 1926; *s* of Glenford Andrew Tetley and Mary Eleanor (*née* Byrne). *Educ*: Franklyn and Marshal Coll., Lancaster, USA (pre-med); New York Univ. (BSc). Studied medicine, then dance with Hanya Holm, Antony Tudor, Martha Graham. Danced with Holm's Co., 1946–51; New York City Opera, 1952–54; John Butler Dance Theatre, 1955; Joffrey Ballet, 1956–57; Martha Graham Co., 1958; American Ballet Theatre, 1960; Robbins Ballets USA, 1961. Joined Netherlands Dance Theatre as dancer and choreographer, 1962, eventually becoming artistic co-director; directed own company, 1969; Dir, Stuttgart Ballet, 1974–76. *Choreography*: Pierrot Lunaire, own company, 1962, Ballet Rambert, 1985; The Anatomy Lesson, Netherlands Dance Theatre, 1964; Mythical Hunters, Batsheva Dance Co., 1965; Ricercare, American Ballet Theatre, 1966; Freefall, Ballet Rambert, 1967; Ziggurat, Ballet Rambert, 1967; Circles, NDT, 1968; Embrace Tiger and Return to Mountain, Ballet Rambert, 1968; Field Figures, Royal Ballet, 1970; Imaginary Film, NDT, 1970; Mutations, NDT, 1970; Rag Dances, Ballet Rambert, 1971; Laborintus, Royal Ballet, 1972; Voluntaries, Stuttgart Ballet, 1973; Le Sacre du Printemps, Munich State Opera Ballet, 1974; Tristan, Paris Opera, 1974; Daphnis and Chloe, Stuttgart Ballet, 1975; Greening, Stuttgart Ballet, 1975; Nocturne, ABT, 1977; Sphinx, ABT, 1977; Praeludium, Ballet Rambert, 1978; Contredances, ABT, 1979; The Tempest, first full-length work, Ballet Rambert, 1979; Summer's End, NDT, 1980; Dances of Albion, Royal Ballet, 1980; Firebird, Royal Danish Ballet, 1981; Murderer, Hope of Women, Ballet Rambert, 1983; Revelation and Fall, Australian Dance Theatre, 1984; Pulcinella, Festival Ballet, 1984; Dream Walk of the Shaman, Aterballetto, 1985; Alice, Nat. Ballet of Canada, 1986. Queen Elizabeth Coronation Award, Royal Acad. of Dancing, 1980; Prix Italia, 1982; Ohloana Career Medal, 1986. *Address*: 15 West Ninth Street, New York, NY 10011, USA. *T*: (212) 475 4604.

TETLEY, Sir Herbert, KBE 1965; CB 1958; Government Actuary, 1958–73; *b* 23 April 1908; *s* of Albert Tetley, Leeds; *m* 1941, Agnes Maclean Macfarlane Macphee; one *s*. *Educ*: Leeds Grammar School; The Queen's College, Oxford. Hastings Scholar, Queen's College, 1927–30; 1st Cl. Hons Mods (Mathematics), 1928; 1st Cl. Final Hons School of Mathematics, 1930. Fellow of Institute of Actuaries, 1934; Fellow of Royal Statistical Society; served with London Life Assoc., 1930–36; Scottish Provident Instn, 1936–38; National Provident Instn, 1938–51 (Joint Actuary). Joined Government Actuary's Dept as Principal Actuary, 1951; Deputy Government Actuary, 1953; Chairman: Civil Service Insurance Soc., 1961–73; Cttee on Economics Road Research Board, 1962–65; Cttee on Road Traffic Research, 1966–73. Pres., Inst. of Actuaries, 1964–66. *Publications*: Actuarial Statistics, Vol. I, 1946; (jtly) Statistics, An Intermediate Text Book, Vol. I, 1949, Vol. II, 1950. *Recreations*: gardening, music, fell-walking. *Address*: 37 Upper Brighton Road, Surbiton, Surrey KT6 6QX. *T*: 01–399 3001.

TETLEY, Air Vice-Marshal John Francis Humphrey, CVO 1978; Senior Directing Staff (Air), Royal College of Defence Studies, 1986–87; *b* 5 Feb. 1932; *s* of Humphrey and Evelyn Tetley; *m* 1960, Elizabeth, *d* of Wing Comdr Arthur Stevens; two *s*. *Educ*: Malvern College. RAF Coll., Cranwell, 1950–53; served No 249 Sqn, No 204 Sqn and HQ Coastal Command, 1955–64; RAF Staff Coll., 1964; HQ Middle East Command, 1965–67; OC No 24 Sqn, 1968–70; JSSC 1970; MoD (Air), 1971–72; RAF Germany, 1973–75; Dir Air Staff Briefing, MoD (Air), 1975–76; Silver Jubilee Project Officer, 1977; RCDS, 1978; SASO HQ 38 Group, 1979–82; Dir of Ops (Air Support), RAF, 1982–83; AO Scotland and NI, 1983–86. *Recreations*: fishing, gardening, photography. *Club*: Royal Air Force.

TETLEY, Kenneth James; a Recorder of the Crown Court, since 1972; *b* Ashton-under-Lyne, Lancs, 17 Oct. 1921; *o s* of William Tetley, Dukinfield, Cheshire, and Annie Lees, Oldham; *m* 1945, Edna Rita, *e d* of Peter Charles Spurrin Gray and Annie Gray, Audenshaw, Manchester; one *s* three *d*. *Educ*: Ashton-under-Lyne Grammar Sch.; Manchester Univ. Served War of 1939–45: joined RN, 1941; Lieut RNVR (attached Combined Ops); discharged, 1945. Admitted Solicitor, 1947; Councillor, Ashton-under-Lyne Borough Council, 1955; Alderman, 1967. *Recreations*: Rugby Union football, golf, photography. *Address*: Green Meadows, 156 Strines Road, Strines, Stockport, Cheshire SK12 3AA. *T*: 061–427 3755. *Clubs*: Rugby, Golf (Ashton-under-Lyne); Romiley Golf; Lancashire County RFU.

TETT, Sir Hugh (Charles), Kt 1966; ARCS, BSc, DIC; *b* Exeter, Devon, 28 Oct. 1906; *e s* of late James Charles Tett and late Florence Tett (*née* Lihou); *m* 1st, 1931, Katie Sargent (*d* 1948); one *d*; 2nd, 1949, Joyce Lilian (*née* Mansell) (*d* 1979); one *d*; 3rd, 1980, Barbara Mary (*née* Mackenzie). *Educ*: Hele's School, Exeter; University College, Exeter; Royal College of Science (Kitchener's Scholar). Joined Esso Petroleum Co. Ltd, 1928; Technical Advisory Committee, Petroleum Board, 1940–45; Lieut-Colonel, Combined Intelligence Objectives Sub-Cttee, 1944–45; Chairman of Council, Institute of Petroleum, 1947–48; Managing Director, Esso Research Ltd, 1947–49; Director, Esso Petroleum Co. Ltd, 1951, Chairman, 1959–67. Member: Council for Scientific and Industrial Research, 1961–64; Advisory Council, Ministry of Technology, 1964–67. Chairman, Economic Development Cttee for Motor Manufacturing Industry, 1967–69. Pro-Chancellor, Univ. of Southampton, 1967–79. Fellow, Imperial Coll. of Science and Technology, 1964. Hon. DSc: Southampton, 1965; Exeter, 1970. *Address*: Primrose Cottage, Bosham, Chichester, West Sussex PO18 8HZ. *T*: Bosham 572705. *Club*: Athenæum.

TEUSNER, Hon. Berthold Herbert, CMG 1972; JP; Solicitor since 1931; Speaker, South Australian Parliament, 1956–62; *b* 16 May 1907; *s* of Carl Theodor Teusner and Agnes Sophie Elisabeth Teusner (*née* Christian); *m* 1934, Viola Hilda Kleeman; two *s*. *Educ*: Immanuel Coll., Adelaide; Univ. of Adelaide (LLB). Legal Practice at Tanunda, SA, 1932–. MP for Angas, S Australian Parlt, 1944–70; Govt Whip, 1954–55; Dep. Speaker and Chm. of Cttees: 1955–56, 1962–65 and 1968–70. Councillor, Dist. Council of Tanunda, 1936–56 (Chm. for 17 years); JP, 1939–. Member: Bd of Governors, Adelaide Botanical Gdns, 1956–70; SA Nat. Fitness Council, 1953–70; Royal Adelaide Hosp. and Queen Elizabeth Hosp. Advisory Cttees (Chm., 1962–65); Immanuel Coll. Council, 1933–71; Hon. Assoc. Life Mem., SA Br. of Commonwealth Parly Assoc.; Mem., Transport Control Bd of SA, 1971–74. *Recreations*: bowls, gardening. *Address*: 18 Elizabeth Street, Tanunda, South Australia. *T*: 632422.

TEVIOT, 2nd Baron, *cr* 1940, of Burghclere; **Charles John Kerr**; genealogist; *b* 16 Dec. 1934; *s* of 1st Baron Teviot, DSO, MC, and Florence Angela (*d* 1979), *d* of late Lt-Col Charles Walter Villiers, CBE, DSO; *S* father, 1968; *m* 1965, Patricia Mary Harris; one *s* one *d*. *Educ*: Eton. Bus Conductor and Driver; genealogical and historical record agent. Director: Debrett's Peerage Ltd, 1977–; Burke's Peerage Research, 1983–; Burke's Peerage Ltd, 1984–. Mem., Adv. Council on Public Records, 1974–83. Fellow, Soc. of Genealogists, 1975. *Recreations*: reading, walking. *Heir*: *s* Hon. Charles Robert Kerr, *b* 19 Sept. 1971. *Address*: 12 Grand Avenue, Hassocks, West Sussex. *T*: Hassocks 4471.

TEW, Prof. John Hedley Brian, PhD; External Professor, Economics Department, University of Loughborough, since 1982; Midland Bank Professor of Money and Banking, University of Nottingham, 1967–82; *b* 1 Feb. 1917; *s* of Herbert and Catherine Mary Tew; *m* 1944, Marjorie Hoey Craigie; one *s* one *d*. *Educ*: Mill Hill School, Leicester; University College, Leicester; Peterhouse, Cambridge. BSc (Econ.) London; PhD Cantab. Iron and Steel Control, 1940–42; Ministry of Aircraft Production, 1942–45; Industrial and Commercial Finance Corp., 1946; Professor of Economics, Univ. of Adelaide (Australia), 1947–49; Professor of Economics, University of Nottingham, 1950–67. Part-time Member: Iron and Steel Board, 1964–67; East Midlands Electricity Board, 1965–76; Tubes Div., BSC, 1969–73; Mem., Cttee of Enquiry on Small Firms, Dept of Trade and Industry, 1969–71. *Publications*: Wealth and Income, 1950; International Monetary Co-operation 1952; (jt editor) Studies in Company Finance, 1959; Monetary Theory, 1969; The Evolution of the International Monetary System, 1977. *Address*: 121 Bramcote Lane, Wollaton, Notts.

TEWKESBURY, Bishop Suffragan of, since 1986; **Rt. Rev. Geoffrey David Jeremy Walsh**; *b* 7 Dec. 1929; *s* of late Howard Wilton Walsh, OBE and Helen Maud Walsh (*née* Lovell); *m* 1961, Cynthia Helen, *d* of late F. P. Knight, FLS, VMH, and H. I. C. Knight, OBE; two *s* one *d*. *Educ*: Felsted Sch., Essex; Pembroke Coll., Cambridge (MA Econ.); Lincoln Theological Coll. Curate, Christ Church, Southgate, London, 1955–58; Staff Sec., SCM, and Curate, St Mary the Great, Cambridge, 1958–61; Vicar, St Matthew, Moorfields, Bristol, 1961–66; Rector of Marlborough, Wilts, 1966–76; Rector of Elmsett with Aldham, 1976–80; Archdeacon of Ipswich, 1976–86. Hon. Canon, Salisbury Cathedral, 1973–76. *Recreations*: gardening, golf, bird-watching. *Address*: Green Acre, 166 Hempsted Lane, Gloucester GL2 6LG. *T*: Gloucester 21824.

TEYNHAM, 20th Baron *cr* 1616; **John Christopher Ingham Roper-Curzon**; *b* 25 Dec. 1928; *s* of 19th Baron Teynham, DSO, DSC, and Elspeth Grace (who *m* 2nd, 1958, 6th Marquess of Northampton, DSO, and *d* 1976), *e d* of late William Ingham Whitaker; *S* father, 1972; *m* 1964, Elizabeth, *yr d* of Lt-Col the Hon. David Scrymgeour-Wedderburn, DSO, Scots Guards (killed on active service 1944), and of Patricia, Countess of Dundee; five *s* five *d* (of whom one *s* one *d* are twins). *Educ*: Eton. A Land Agent. Late Captain, The Buffs (TA), formerly Coldstream Guards; active service in Palestine, 1948. ADC to Governor of Bermuda, 1953 and 1955; ADC to Governor of Leeward Islands, 1955; Private Secretary and ADC, 1956; ADC to Governor of Jamaica, 1962. Pres., Inst. of Commerce, 1972–. Member of Council, Sail Training Association, 1964–. OStJ. *Recreations*: shooting and fishing. *Heir*: *s* Hon. David John Henry Ingham Roper-Curzon [*b* 5 Oct. 1965; *m* 1985, Lydia Lucinda, *d* of Maj.-Gen. Christopher Airy, CBE; one *s*]. *Address*: The Walton Canonry, The Close, Salisbury, Wilts. *T*: Salisbury 336896. *Clubs*: Turf; House of Lords Yacht; Ocean Cruising; Puffins (Edinburgh).

THAIN, Eric Malcolm, PhD; FRSC; Director, Tropical Development and Research Institute, Overseas Development Administration, 1983–86; *b* 29 Nov. 1925; *s* of late Arthur Robert Thain and Olive Grace (*née* Parsons); *m* 1954, Nancy Garbutt Key *d* of late Mr and Mrs T. G. Key; one *s* one *d*. *Educ*: St Dunstan's Coll., Catford; Univ. of London (BSc, PhD). Lister Institute of Preventive Medicine, 1949; ICI Research Fellow, 1953–54; Royal Society/National Academy of Science Research Fellow, Univ. of California, Berkeley, 1954–55; ICI Research Fellow, University Coll. London, 1955–57; Tropical Products Institute: Member, Scientific Staff, 1957; Asst Director, 1963; Dep. Director, 1969; Director, 1981–83. Member: WHO and FAO Expert Committees on Pesticides, 1961–; Executive Cttee, Essex Bird Watching and Preservation Soc., 1950– (Chm. 1970–73); Queckett Microscopical Club (Pres., 1980–81). Hon. Res. Fellow, Chemistry Dept, UCL. *Publications*: research papers on organic chemistry and pesticides in jls of various learned societies. *Recreations*: natural history, visiting museums. *Address*: 30 Friars Quay, Norwich, Norfolk NR3 1ES. *T*: Norwich 625017. *Club*: Savage.

THALBEN-BALL, Sir George (Thomas), Kt 1982; CBE 1967; DMus Cantuar 1935; ARCM; FRCM 1951; FRCO; FRSCM 1956 (diploma 1963); FRSA; Bard Ylewyth Mur; Freeman of City of London; Civic and University Organist, Birmingham, 1949–82; Organist, the Temple Church, 1923–81, Organist Emeritus, since 1982; Curator-Organist, The Royal Albert Hall, London; Professor and Examiner, the Royal College of Music; Examiner to the Associated Board of the Royal Academy of Music and the Royal College of Music; Member of the Council and Examiner of Royal College of Organists; Examiner on behalf of the Cape University, 1925; Adviser and Consultant to BBC, 1941; *b* Sydney, NSW; *s* of George Charles Thalben-Ball and Mary Hannah Spear, Newquay, Cornwall; *m* Evelyn (*d* 1961), *d* of Francis Chapman, NZ; one *s* one *d*. *Educ*: private tuition. Exhbnr and Grove Scholar, RCM, Chappell and Hopkinson Gold Medallist; Lafontaine Prize, RCO; Organist: Whitefield's Tabernacle; Holy Trinity Church, Castlenau; Paddington Parish Church; acting Organist, the Hon. Socs of Temple, 1919, Organist, 1923–; studied pianoforte with Fritz Hartvigson, Franklin Taylor, and Fanny Davies; harmony and composition with Sir Frederick Bridge, Sir Charles Stanford, and Dr Charles Wood; musical history with Sir Hubert Parry; organ with Sir Walter Parratt and F. A. Sewell. President: London Soc. of Organists, 1936; RCO, 1948; Incorporated Assoc. of Organists, 1944–46; Mem. Bd of Governors, Royal Nat. Coll. of the Blind. FRSA 1971; Fellow, Royal Canadian Coll. of Organists. Hon. RAM 1973. Hon. Bencher, Inner Temple, 1959. Guest Organist, Les Amis de l'Orgue, Paris, 1937; Toured Australia as guest organist in connection with Jubilee of the formation of the Commonwealth, 1951, toured: South Africa, 1954, New Zealand, 1971; Guest of honour, Amer. Guild of Organists Convention, NY, 1956; Guest, Philadelphia, 1973; toured USA and Canada, 1975 (opening organ recital, Carnegie Hall, NY). Mem. Jury, Concours international d'orgue, Grand Prix de Chartres, 1973. EMI Gold Disc, 1963. Has played the organ on the Continent and in America and was a regular broadcaster and performer at the Sir Henry Wood Promenade Concerts. Composer of Organ and Choral music including Sursum Corda for chorus, orchestra and trumpet fanfares (commissioned by BBC). Hon. DMus and Gold Medal, Birmingham, 1972. *Recreations*: golf and riding. *Address*: 3 Paper Buildings, Inner Temple, EC4. *Club*: Athenæum.

THALMANN, Dr Ernesto; retired Swiss Ambassador; *b* 14 Jan. 1914; *s* of Friedrich Thalmann and Clara (*née* Good) *m* 1943, Paula Degen; two *s* one *d*. *Educ*: Gymnasien, Berne and Zürich; Univ. of Zürich (LLD). Entered Federal Dept of Public Economy, 1941; Federal Political Dept (Swiss Foreign Office), 1945; Minister/Counsellor and Dep. Head of Mission, Swiss Embassy, Washington, 1957–61; Permanent Observer to UN, New York (Ambassador Extraordinary and Plenipotentiary), 1961–66; Head of Internat. Organizations Div., Fed. Political Dept, Berne, 1966–71; Special Mission in Jerusalem, after 6–day war, as Personal Rep. of UN Secretary-General, U Thant, 1967; Secretary-General, Fed. Political Dept and Director of Political Affairs, 1971–75; Swiss Ambassador to the Court of St James's, 1976–79. Pres., Nat. Swiss Unesco Commn, 1981–85. *Address*: 8 Anshelmstrasse, 3005 Berne, Switzerland.

THAPAR, Prem Nath, CIE 1944; lately Vice-Chancellor, Punjab Agricultural University, Lydhiana, 1962–68; Indian Civil Service; *b* 13 April 1903; *s* of Diwan Bahadur Kunj Behari Thapar, CBE; *m* 1932, Leela Dutta; one *s* two *d*. *Educ*: Govt Coll., Lahore; New Coll., Oxford. Joined ICS 1926. Dep. Commissioner, Kangra, Attock; Deputy

Commissioner and Colonisation Officer, Montgomery, 1934–37; Settlement Officer, Jhelum, 1937–41; Joint Secretary, Information and Broadcasting Department, Government of India, 1941–46; Secretary, Food and Civil Supplies Department, Punjab, 1946–47; Commissioner, Lahore Division, 1947; Financial Commissioner, East Punjab, 1947–53; Chief Administrator, Chandigarh Capital Project, 1950–53; Adviser, Planning Commission, Government of India, 1953–54; Sec., Min. of Food and Agric., Govt of India, 1954–58; Member, Atomic Energy Commission and *ex officio* Secretary to Government of India, Dept of Atomic Energy, Bombay, 1958–62. Mem. Punjab Admin. Reforms Commn, 1964–65; Consultant, Review Team, FAO, UN, Rome, 1966–67. Trustee, Internat. Rice Research Inst., Manila, Philippines. *Publications:* Settlement Report, Jhelum District, 1945; Customary Law, Jhelum District, 1946. *Address:* Ashok Farm, PO Maidan Garhi, New Delhi-30, India. *T:* 72382.

THATCHER, Arthur Roger, CB 1974; Director, Office of Population Censuses and Surveys, and Registrar General for England and Wales, since 1978; *b* 22 Oct. 1926; *s* of Arthur Thatcher; *m* 1950, Mary Audrey Betty (*née* Street); two *d. Educ:* The Leys Sch.; St John's Coll., Cambridge (MA). Royal Navy, 1947–49. North Western Gas Board, 1949–52; Admiralty, 1952–61; Cabinet Office, 1961–63; Ministry of Labour, 1963–68; Director of Statistics, Dept of Employment, 1968–78, Dep. Sec., 1972–78. *Publications:* official publications; articles in jls. *Address:* Office of Population Censuses and Surveys, St Catherine's House, 10 Kingsway, WC2B 6JP. *Club:* Army and Navy.

THATCHER, Rt. Hon. Mrs Margaret (Hilda), PC 1970; FRS 1983; MP (C) Finchley, since 1959; Prime Minister and First Lord of the Treasury, since 1979; *b* 13 Oct. 1925; *d* of late Alfred Roberts, Grantham, Lincs; *m* 1951, Denis Thatcher; one *s* one *d* (twins). *Educ:* Kesteven and Grantham Girls' School; Somerville College, Oxford (MA, BSc). Research Chemist, 1947–51; called to the Bar, Lincoln's Inn, 1954, Hon. Bencher, 1975. Joint Parly Sec., Min. of Pensions and National Insurance, Oct. 1961–64; Sec. of State for Educn and Sci., 1970–74; Leader of the Opposition, 1975–79. Co-Chm., Women's Nat. Commn, 1970–74. Hon. Fellow, Somerville Coll., Oxford, 1970. Freedom of Borough of Barnet, 1980. Donovan Award, USA, 1981. *Recreations:* music, reading. *Address:* House of Commons, SW1. *Club:* Carlton.

THAW, Mrs John; *see* Hancock, Sheila.

THAYRE, Albert Jesse, CBE 1980 (MBE 1945); DL; Director, N. G. Bailey Organisation Ltd, since 1982; Chief General Manager and Director, Halifax Building Society, 1974–82; *b* 30 May 1917; *s* of Alfred and Louisa Thayre; *m* 1940, Margaret Elizabeth Wheeler; one *d. Educ:* Bromley County Sch. for Boys; City of London Coll. BCom (London) 1948. Stockbrokers' Clerk, 1933–39. Served War: Rifleman/NCO with 2/London Irish Rifles, 1939–41; Lieut to Captain 51 (H) Bn Reconnaissance Corps, 1941–42; Captain, then Major and Lt-Col 14 Highland LI, 1942–46 (incl. appts as DAQMG and AA&QMG). Investment Analyst, 1946–50. Halifax Building Soc.: Clerk, then Inspector and Br. Manager, 1951–55; Staff Manager, 1955–56; Asst Gen. Man., 1956–60; Gen. Man., 1960; Dir, 1968; Asst Chief Gen. Man., 1970. Bradford Univ.: Mem. Council, 1966–; Chm. Finance Cttee, 1966–; Pro-Chancellor, 1969–. Chm., Centre for Indust. and Educnl Liaison (W and N Yorks), 1983–; Hon. Treas., Standing Conf. on Schs Sci. and Tech., 1986–; Mem., Univs Authorities Panel, 1970–79; Dir and Dep. Chm., Univs Superannuation Scheme Ltd, 1974–79. FSS, FCBSI, CBIM. Hon. DLitt Bradford, 1982. DL West Yorks, 1982. *Address:* Stonedale, 42 Northowram Green, Halifax, West Yorkshire HX3 7SL. *T:* Halifax 202581.

THELLUSSON, family name of **Baron Rendlesham.**

THELWELL, Norman; freelance artist-cartoonist since 1957; *b* Birkenhead, 3 May 1923; *s* of Christopher Thelwell and Emily (*née* Vick); *m* 1949, Rhona Evelyn Ladbury; one *s* one *d. Educ:* Rock Ferry High Sch., Birkenhead; Liverpool Coll. of Art. Nat. Diploma of Art; ATD. Teacher of Art, Wolverhampton Coll. of Art, 1950–57. Regular contributor to Punch, 1952–; cartoonist for: News Chronicle, 1956–60; Sunday Dispatch, 1960–61; Sunday Express, 1962–. Drawings for general publications, advertising, book jackets, illustrations, etc. *Publications:* Angels on Horseback, 1957; Thelwell Country, 1959; A Place of Your Own, 1960; Thelwell in Orbit, 1961; A Leg at Each Corner, 1962; The Penguin Thelwell, 1963; Top Dog, 1964; Thelwell's Riding Academy, 1965; Drawing Ponies, 1966; Up the Garden Path, 1967; Thelwell's Compleat Tangler, 1967; Thelwell's Book of Leisure, 1968; This Desirable Plot, 1970; The Effluent Society, 1971; Penelope, 1972; Three Sheets in the Wind, 1973; Belt Up, 1974; Thelwell Goes West, 1975; Thelwell's Brat Race, 1977; A Plank Bridge by a Pool, 1978; Thelwell's Gymkhana, 1979; Thelwell Annual, 1980; A Millstone Round My Neck, 1981; Thelwell Annual, 1981; Pony Cavalcade, 1981; How to Draw Ponies, 1982; Some Damn Fool's Signed the Rubens Again, 1982; Thelwell's Magnificat, 1983; Thelwell's Sporting Prints, 1984; Wrestling with a Pencil: the life of a freelance artist, 1986. *Recreations:* trout and salmon angling, painting. *Address:* Herons Mead, Timsbury, Romsey, Hants SO5 0NE. *T:* Braishfield 68238.

THEOBALD, George Peter, JP; company director, since 1958; *b* 5 Aug. 1931; *s* of late George Oswald Theobald and Helen (*née* Moore); *m* 1955, Josephine Mary (*née* Boodle); two *s* three *d. Educ:* Betteshanger Sch.; Harrow. National Service commission, 5 Regt RHA, 1950–52; 290 (City of London) RA (TA), 1953–59. Robert Warner Ltd, 1953–74: Director, 1958; Man. Dir, Chm. Gp subsidiaries, 1965; Director: of four private companies, 1974–; Tea Clearing House, 1959–72 (Chm., 1970–72); Moran Tea Holdings plc, 1980–; Moran Tea (India) plc, 1981–. City of London (Queenhithe Ward): Chm., Ward Club, 1966–68; Common Councilman, 1968–74; Alderman, 1974–79. Member: Transport Users' Consultative Cttee for London, 1969–84 (Dep. Chm. 1978); London Regional Passengers Cttee, 1984–; Governor: Bridewell Royal Hosp., 1974–; King Edward's Sch., Witley, 1974– (Trustee, Educational Trust, 1977–); Donation Governor, Christ's Hosp., 1976–; Governor, St Leonards-Mayfield Sch., 1982–; Mem. Cttee, Langford Cross Children's Home, 1976–; Trustee: National Flood and Tempest Distress Fund, 1977–; Harrow Club W10, 1978–. Church Commissioner for England, 1978–79. Asst, Merchant Taylors' Co., 1983–. JP City of London, 1974. *Recreations:* skiing, gardening, swimming, tennis, walking. *Address:* Towerhill Manor, Gomshall, Guildford, Surrey GU5 9LP. *T:* Shere 2381. *Clubs:* Oriental, City Livery, Guildhall.

THEROUX, Paul Edward, FRSL; FRGS; writer; *b* 10 April 1941; *s* of Albert Eugene Theroux and Anne Dittami Theroux; *m* 1967, Anne Castle; two *s. Educ:* Univ. of Massachusetts (BA). Lecturer: Univ. of Urbino, 1963; Soche Hill Coll., Malawi, 1963–65; Makerere Univ., Kampala, Uganda, 1965–68; Univ. of Singapore, 1968–71; Writer-in-Residence, Univ. of Virginia, 1972. Mem., AAIL, 1984. Hon. DLitt: Trinity Coll., Washington DC, 1980; Tufts Univ., Mass, 1980. *Publications: novels:* Waldo, 1967; Fong and the Indians, 1968; Girls at Play, 1969; Murder in Mount Holly, 1969; Jungle Lovers, 1971; Sinning with Annie, 1972; Saint Jack, 1973 (filmed, 1979); The Black House, 1974; The Family Arsenal, 1976; The Consul's File, 1977; Picture Palace, 1978 (Whitbread Award, 1978); A Christmas Card, 1978; London Snow, 1980; World's End, 1980; The Mosquito Coast, 1981; The London Embassy, 1982; Doctor Slaughter, 1984; O-Zone, 1986; *criticism:* V. S. Naipaul, 1972; *travel:* The Great Railway Bazaar, 1975; The Old Patagonian Express, 1979; The Kingdom by the Sea, 1983; Sailing through China, illus. Patrick Procktor, 1983; Sunrise with Seamonsters: travels and discoveries 1964–84, 1985; The Imperial Way, 1985; *screenplay:* Saint Jack, 1979; reviews in The Sunday Times, New York Times, etc. *Recreation:* rowing. *Address:* c/o Hamish Hamilton Ltd, 59 Long Acre, WC2E 9JL.

THESIGER, family name of **Viscount Chelmsford.**

THESIGER, Roderic Miles Doughty; Director, P. & D. Colnaghi and Co. Ltd, 1955–71; *b* 8 Nov. 1915; *y s* of late Hon. Wilfred Thesiger, DSO, and Mrs Reginald Astley, CBE; *m* 1st, 1940, Mary Rose (marr. diss. 1946; she *d* 1962), *d* of Hon. Guy Charteris; 2nd, 1946, Ursula, *d* of A. W. Whitworth, Woollas Hall, Pershore; one *s* one *d. Educ:* Eton; Christ Church, Oxford; Courtauld Institute. Served War of 1939–45, Welsh Guards, 1939–41; 1st Parachute Bde, 1941–44 (twice wounded, POW). Assistant, Tate Gallery, 1945–46; afterwards worked with Messrs Sotheby and privately until 1954. *Recreations:* visiting Italy and France. *Address:* The Paddocks, Lucton, Leominster, Herefordshire. *T:* Yarpole 327.

See also W. P. Thesiger.

THESIGER, Wilfred Patrick, CBE 1968; DSO 1941; MA Oxon; *b* 3 June 1910; *e s* of late Hon. Wilfred Thesiger, DSO, and Mrs Reginald Astley, CBE. *Educ:* Eton; Magdalen College, Oxford (MA; Hon. Fellow, 1982). Repres. Oxford at boxing, 1930–33; Captain Oxford Boxing Team, 1933; Hon. Attaché Duke of Gloucester's Mission to Abyssinia, 1930; served Middle East, 1941 (DSO); explored Danakil country of Abyssinia and the Aussa Sultanate, 1933–34 (awarded Back Grant by RGS, 1935); Sudan Political Service, Darfur-Upper Nile, 1935–40; served in Ethiopian, Syrian and Western Desert campaigns with SDF and SAS regiment with rank of Major; explored in Southern Arabia, 1945–49; twice crossed the Empty Quarter. Founder's Medal, RGS, 1948; Lawrence of Arabia Medal, RCAS, 1955; Livingstone Medal, RSGS, 1962; W. H. Heinemann Award (for 1964), RSL, 1965; Burton Memorial Medal, Roy. Asiatic Soc., 1966. FRSL; Hon. FBA 1982; Hon. DLitt Leicester, 1967. 3rd Class Star of Ethiopia, 1930. *Publications:* Arabian Sands, 1959; The Marsh Arabs, 1964; Desert, Marsh and Mountain: the world of a nomad, 1979. *Recreations:* travelling, photography. *Address:* 15 Shelley Court, Tite Street, SW3. *T:* 01–352 7213. *Clubs:* Travellers', Beefsteak.

See also R. M. D. Thesiger.

THETFORD, Bishop Suffragan of, since 1981; **Rt. Rev. Timothy Dudley-Smith;** *b* 26 Dec. 1926; *o s* of Arthur and Phyllis Dudley Smith, Buxton, Derbyshire; *m* 1959, June Arlette MacDonald; one *s* two *d. Educ:* Tonbridge Sch.; Pembroke Coll., and Ridley Hall, Cambridge. BA 1947, MA 1951; Certif. in Educn 1948. Deacon, 1950; priest, 1951; Asst Curate, St Paul, Northumberland Heath, 1950–53; Head of Cambridge Univ. Mission in Bermondsey, 1953–55; Hon. Chaplain to Bp of Rochester, 1953–60; Editor, Crusade, and Editorial Sec. of Evangelical Alliance, 1955–59; Asst Sec. of Church Pastoral-Aid Soc., 1959–65, Sec., 1965–73; Archdeacon of Norwich, 1973–81; Commissary to Archbp of Sydney, 1971–; Exam. Chap. to Bp of Norwich, 1971–85. *Publications:* Christian Literature and the Church Bookstall, 1963; What Makes a Man a Christian?, 1966; A Man Named Jesus, 1971; Someone who Beckons, 1978; Lift Every Heart, 1984; contributor to various hymn books. *Recreations:* reading, verse, woodwork, family and friends. *Address:* Rectory Meadow, Bramerton, Norwich NR14 7DW. *T:* Surlingham 251. *Club:* Norfolk (Norwich).

THEUNISSEN, Most Rev. John Baptist Hubert, DD; Titular Archbishop of Skálholt, since 1968; *b* Schimmert, Holland, 3 Oct. 1905; *Educ:* Schimmert and Oirschot, Holland; Rome University. DD 1929. Professor, Major Seminary, Oirschot, Holland, 1930; Professor, Major Seminary, Portugal, 1935; Superior Regional of the Missions in Portuguese East Africa, 1937; Superior Provincial of Dutch Province of Montfort Fathers, 1947; consecrated Bishop of Blantyre, 1950; Archbishop of Blantyre, Malawi, 1959; Apostolic Administrator of Iceland, 1967; retd, 1968. Knight, Order of the Lion (Netherlands), 1960. *Recreation:* music. *Address:* Bishop's House, Langstraat 84, Schimmert (L.), The Netherlands.

THIESS, Sir Leslie Charles, Kt 1971; CBE 1968; Chairman of Directors: Daihatsu Distributors Pty Ltd, since 1975; Thiess Watkins Group of Companies, since 1982; Queensland Metals Corp., since 1983; Breakwater Island Ltd, since 1984; Governing Dir, Drayton Investments Pty Ltd; *b* 8 April 1909; *m* 1929, Christina Mary (*née* Erbacher); two *s* three *d. Educ:* Drayton, Queensland. Founded Thiess Bros as a private company, 1933; Managing Dir, Thiess Holdings Ltd when it was formed in 1950; also when firm became a public company, 1958; Chairman: Thiess Group of Cos, 1968–80; Thiess Consortium, 1981–82; Chm. of Dirs, 1971–86, Hon. Chm., 1986–, Thiess Toyota Pty Ltd. FCIT (London), 1971. Order of the Sacred Treasure (third class), Japan, 1972. *Publication:* Thiess Story. *Recreation:* deep sea fishing. *Address:* 121 King Arthur Terrace, Tennyson, Qld 4105, Australia. *T:* 848 3314. *Clubs:* Brisbane, Tattersalls, Royal Queensland Yacht (all of Brisbane); Huntington, NSW Sports (NSW).

THIMANN, Prof. Kenneth Vivian; Professor of Biology, 1965–72, and Provost of Crown College, 1966–72, Emeritus Professor, recalled to duty since 1972, University of California, Santa Cruz, Calif, USA; *b* 5 Aug. 1904; *s* of Phoebus Thimann and Muriel Kate Thimann (*née* Harding); *m* 1931, Ann Mary Bateman, Sutton Bridge, Lincs; three *d. Educ:* Caterham Sch., Surrey; Imperial Coll., London. BSc, ARCS 1924; DIC 1925; PhD 1928. Beit Memorial Res. Fellow, 1927–29; Demonstr in Bacteriology, King's Coll. for Women, 1926–28; Instr in Biochem., Calif Inst. of Techn., 1930–35; Harvard University: Lectr on Botany, 1935; (Biology): Asst Prof., 1936, Associate Prof., 1939, Prof., 1946, and Higgins Prof., 1962–65, now Prof. Emeritus. Vis. Professor: Sorbonne, 1954; Univ. of Massachusetts, 1974; Univ. of Texas, 1976. Scientific Consultant, US Navy, 1942–45. Dir, Amer. Assoc. for Adv. of Science, 1968–71. Pres., XIth Internat. Botanical Congress, Seattle, USA, 1969; 2nd Nat. Biol Congress, Miami, 1971. Hon. AM Harvard, 1940; PhD (Hon.) Univ. of Basle, 1959; Doctor (Hon.) Univ. of Clermont-Ferrand, 1961. Fellow: Nat. Acad. of Scis (Councillor, 1967–71); Amer. Acad. of Arts and Scis; Amer. Philosophical Soc. (Councillor, 1973–76); and professional biological socs in USA and England; Foreign Member: Royal Society (London); Institut de France (Acad. des Sciences, Paris); Académie d'Agriculture; Accademia Nazionale dei Lincei (Rome); Leopoldina Akademie (Halle); Roumanian Academy (Bucharest); Botanical Societies of Japan and Netherlands. Silver Medal, Internat. Plant Growth Substance Assoc.; Balzan Prize, 1983. *Publications:* (in USA) Phytohormones (with F. W. Went), 1937; The Action of Hormones in Plants and Invertebrates, 1948; The Life of Bacteria, 1955, 2nd edn 1963 (German edn 1964); L'Origine et les Fonctions des Auxines, 1956; The Natural Plant Hormones, 1972; Hormones in the Whole Life of Plants, 1977; (ed) Senescence in Plants, 1980; (with J. Langenheim) Botany: Plant Biology in relation to Human Affairs, 1981; about 280 papers in biological and biochemical jls. *Recreations:* music (piano), gardening. *Address:* Thimann Laboratories, University of California, Santa Cruz, Calif. 95064, USA. *Clubs:* Harvard Faculty (Cambridge, Mass); Harvard (San Francisco).

THIMONT, Bernard Maurice, CB 1979; Secretary, Churches' Main Committee, since 1981; *b* 1 July 1920; *s* of Georges André Thimont; *m* 1949, Joy Rowe; one *s* one *d. Educ:*

St Ignatius Coll., London. Served War of 1939–45, in Army (Major), 1939–48. Foreign Office, 1948–50; HM Treasury, 1950–65; IDC, 1966; Cabinet Office, 1967; HM Treasury, 1967–68; Civil Service Dept, 1968–77; Controller, HM Stationery Office and Queen's Printer of Acts of Parlt, 1977–80. *Recreations:* music, building. *Address:* 10 Oakhill Court, Edge Hill, Wimbledon, SW19. *T:* 01–946 0918.

THIRD, Rt. Rev. Richard Henry McPhail; *see* Dover, Bishop Suffragan of.

THIRKELL, Lancelot George, (Lance Thirkell); Secretary and Administrator, New Bridge Association for befriending ex-offenders, 1980–84; *b* 9 Jan. 1921; *s* of George Lancelot Thirkell, engineer, and Angela Margaret Mackail (Angela Thirkell, novelist); *m* 1946, Katherine Mary Lowinsky, *d* of Thomas Esmond Lowinsky, artist, and Ruth Jeanette Hirsch; two *s* two *d.* *Educ:* Saint Paul's School (Schol.); Magdalen Coll. Oxford (Demy). HM Forces, 1942–46; active service D-day to the Rhine with Essex Yeo. and in SE Asia with RA. HM Foreign Service, 1946–50; granted Civil Service Certificate, 1946; Third Sec., Western Dept, 1946; Third Sec., Budapest, 1947; Second Sec., Eastern Dept, 1948. Joined BBC as Report Writer, Monitoring Service, 1950; Assistant, Appointments Dept, 1953; Assistant Staff Administration, 1956; Head of Secretariat, 1961; Controller, Staff Trng and Appointments, 1964; Chief Asst to Man. Dir, External Broadcasting, 1972–75; Controller, Administration, External Broadcasting, 1975–80. Chm., Ascension Island London Users' Cttee, 1972–84; Dir Caribbean Relay Co., 1976–84. Governor, Thomson Foundn Television Coll., 1964–72. Councillor, Royal Borough of Kensington, 1959–62; Chm. Notting Hill Adventure Playground, 1964–76; Appeals Sec., Portobello Project for unattached youth; Mem., European Adv. Council, Salzburg Seminar in American Studies. Pres., Angela Thirkell Soc., 1980–. *Publications:* A Garden Full of Weeds, 1962; (with Ruth Lowinsky) Russian Food for Pleasure, 1953. *Recreations:* ski-ing, sailing. *Address:* 31 Lansdowne Road, W11. *T:* 01–727 6046; Oxbow, Harkstead, Suffolk. *Clubs:* Leander (Henley-on-Thames); Royal Harwich Yacht.

THIRKETTLE, (William) Ellis, CBE 1959; Principal, London College of Printing, 1939–67; *b* 26 July 1904; *s* of William Edward Thirkettle; *m* 1930, Alva, *d* of Thomas Tough Watson; two *s.* *Educ:* Tiffin School. Principal, Stow College of Printing, Glasgow, 1936–39. *Address:* 21 Astley Close, Hollybush Lane, Pewsey, Wilts.

THIRLWALL, Air Vice-Marshal George Edwin, CB 1976; Director, Sand and Gravel Association, since 1983; *b* 24 Dec. 1924; *s* of Albert and Clarice Editha Thirlwall; *m* 1st, 1949, Daphne Patricia Wynn Giles (*d* 1975); 2nd, 1977, Louisa Buck Russell (*née* Cranston). *Educ:* Sheffield Univ.; Cranfield Inst. of Technology. BEng, MSc, CEng, FRAeS, FBIM. Joined RAF, 1950; OC RAF Sealand, 1969; Dir Air Guided Weapons, MoD, 1972; AO Ground Trng, RAF Trng Comd, 1974–76; AO Engineering, Strike Command, 1976–79, retired. Dir, Ceramics, Glass and Mineral ITB, 1979–82. Liveryman, Glass-Sellers Co., 1983; Freeman, City of London, 1983. *Recreations:* gardening, golf. *Address:* Che Sara Sara, Gosmore Road, Hitchin, Herts. *T:* Hitchin 34182. *Club:* Royal Air Force.

THIRSK, Dr (Irene) Joan, FBA 1974; Reader in Economic History in the University of Oxford, and Fellow of St Hilda's College, Oxford, 1965–83 (Hon. Fellow, 1983); *b* 19 June 1922; *d* of William Henry Watkins and Daisy (*née* Frayer); *m* 1945, James Wood Thirsk; one *s* one *d.* *Educ:* Camden School for Girls, NW5; Westfield Coll., Univ. of London. BA, PhD London; MA Oxford. Subaltern, ATS, Intelligence Corps, 1942–45. Asst Lectr in Sociology, LSE, 1950–51; Sen. Res. Fellow in Agrarian History, Dept of English Local History, Leicester Univ., 1951–65. Ford Lectr in English History, Oxford, 1975. Member: Royal Commn on Historical Monuments (England), 1977–; Econ. and Social Hist. Cttee, SSRC, 1978–82. Mem. Council, Economic Hist. Soc., 1955–83; Vice-Chm., Standing Conf. for Local Hist., 1965–82; President: British Agricl Hist. Soc., 1983– (Mem. Exec. Cttee, 1953–83, Chm. Exec. Cttee, 1974–77); Edmonton Hundred Historical Soc., 1978–; Oxfordshire Local Hist. Assoc., 1981–86 (Vice-Pres., 1980–81); Conf. of Teachers of Regional and Local Hist. in Tertiary Educn, 1981–82; British Assoc. for Local Hist., 1986–; Vice-Pres., Soc. for Lincs Hist. and Archaeol., 1979–; Foreign Mem., Amer. Philos. Soc., 1982–; Corresp. Mem., Colonial Soc. of Massachusetts, 1983–. Editor, Agricultural History Review, 1964–72; Gen. Editor, The Agrarian History of England and Wales, 1974– (Dep. Gen. Ed., 1966–74); Mem. Editorial Bd, Past and Present, 1956–. Hon. DLitt Leicester, 1985. *Publications:* English Peasant Farming, 1957; Suffolk Farming in the Nineteenth Century, 1958; Tudor Enclosures, 1959; The Agrarian History of England and Wales: vol. IV, 1500–1640, 1967; vol. V 1640–1750, 1984; (with J. P. Cooper) Seventeenth-Century Economic Documents, 1972; The Restoration, 1976; Economic Policy and Projects, 1978; The Rural Economy of England (collected essays), 1985; articles in Economic History Rev., Agric. History Rev., Past and Present, History, Jl Modern History, etc. *Recreations:* gardening, sewing, machine-knitting. *Address:* 1 Hadlow Castle, Hadlow, Tonbridge, Kent.

THISELTON, Rev. Dr Anthony Charles; Principal of St John's College, Nottingham, and Special Lecturer in Theology, University of Nottingham, since 1986; *b* 13 July 1937; *s* of Eric Charles Thiselton and Hilda Winifred (*née* Kevan); *m* 1963, Rosemary Stella Harman; two *s* one *d.* *Educ:* City of London School; King's Coll., London. BD, MTh (London); PhD (Sheffield). Curate, Holy Trinity, Sydenham, 1960–63; Lectr and Chaplain, Tyndale Hall, Bristol, 1963–67, Sen. Tutor, 1967–70; Recognised Teacher in Theology, Univ. of Bristol, 1965–71; University of Sheffield: Sir Henry Stephenson Fellow, 1970–71; Lectr in Biblical Studies, 1971–79; Sen. Lectr, 1979–86. Visiting Professor: Calvin Coll., Grand Rapids, USA, 1982–83; Regent Coll., Vancouver, 1983; Fuller Theolog. Seminary, Pasadena, Calif, 1984; North Park Coll. and Seminary, Chicago, 1984. Exam. Chaplain to Bishop of Sheffield, 1977–80, to Bishop of Leicester 1979–. Member: C of E Faith and Order Adv. Group, 1971–81; Doctrine Commn, 1977–. Adv. Editor, Jl for Study of NT, 1981–; Vice-Chm., Bd of Theol and Religious Studies, CNAA, 1984–. *Publications:* The Two Horizons: New Testament Hermeneutics and Philosophical Description, 1980; (with C. Walhout and R. Lundin) The Responsibility of Hermeneutics, 1985; contribs to learned jls and other books on New Testament, doctrine, and philosophical hermeneutics. *Recreation:* choral and organ music. *Address:* St John's College, Bramcote, Nottingham NG9 3DS. *T:* Nottingham 251114.

THISTLETHWAITE, Prof. Frank, CBE 1979; Emeritus Professor, University of East Anglia; founding Vice-Chancellor, 1961–80; *b* 24 July 1915; *s* of late Lee and Florence Nightingale Thistlethwaite; *m* 1940, Jane, *d* of H. Lindley Hosford, Lyme, Connecticut, USA; one *s* three *d* (and one *s* decd). *Educ:* Bootham School; St John's College, Cambridge (Exhibitioner and Scholar). BA 1938, MA 1941. Editor, The Cambridge Review, 1937. Commonwealth Fund Fellow, University of Minnesota, 1938–40; British Press Service, New York, 1940–41. RAF, 1941–45; seconded to Office of War Cabinet, 1942–45. Fellow, St John's College, Cambridge, 1945–61; at various times, Tutor, Praelector, Steward; University Lecturer in Faculty of Economics and Politics, 1949–61; Visiting Prof. of American Civilization, Univ. of Pennsylvania, 1956; Vis. Fellow, Henry E. Huntington Library, Calif, 1973. Chairman: British Assoc. for Amer. Studies, 1955–59; Cttee of Management, Inst. of US Studies, Univ. of London, 1966–80; IUC, 1977–81 (Mem., 1962–81); Member: Inst. for Advanced Study, Princeton, 1954; Academic Adv. Committee: Chelsea Coll. of Science and Technology, 1964–66; Open Univ., 1969–74; Provisional Council, Univ. of Zambia, 1965–69; Univ. of Malaŵi, 1971–75; Univ. of Mauritius, 1974–84; Marshall Aid Commemoration Commn, 1964–80; US-UK Educnl Commn, 1964–79; European Adv. Council, Salzburg Seminar in Amer. Studies, 1969–74; Bd, British Council, 1971–82; British Cttee of Award, Harkness Fellowships, 1974–80; Adviser to Nat. Council of Higher Educn, Ceylon, 1967. Governor, Sedbergh Sch., 1958–73. Hon. Fellow, St John's Coll., Cambridge, 1974. Hon. Prof. of History, Univ. of Mauritius, 1981. Hon. LHD Colorado, 1972; Hon. DCL East Anglia, 1980. FRHistS; Hon. FRIBA 1985. *Publications:* The Great Experiment: An Introduction to the History of the American People, 1955 (trans. 14 languages); The Anglo-American Connection in the Early Nineteenth Century, 1958; contrib. New Cambridge Modern History and other historical works and journals; New Universities in the Modern World (ed M. G. Ross). *Recreation:* music. *Address:* 15 Park Parade, Cambridge CB5 8AL; Island Cottage, Winson, Glos. *Club:* Athenæum.

THISTLETON-SMITH, Vice-Admiral Sir Geoffrey, KBE 1959; CB 1956; GM 1941; DL; *b* 10 May 1905; *m* 1st, 1931, Mary Katherine Harvey (*d* 1976); one *s* one *d*; 2nd, 1982, Joyce, Lady Fairhaven. Captain, 1944; HMS Pembroke, Royal Naval Barracks, Chatham (in Command), 1952; Chief of Staff to C-in-C Home Fleet and Eastern Atlantic, Dec. 1953; Rear-Admiral, 1954; Admiral Commanding Reserves, 1956–58; Vice-Admiral, 1957; Admiral, British Joint Services Mission, Washington, 1958–60, retd. CC West Sussex, 1964–77. DL Sussex, 1972. *Address:* Down Place, Harting, Petersfield, Hants.

THODAY, Prof. John Marion, BSc Wales, PhD, ScD Cantab; FRS 1965; Arthur Balfour Professor of Genetics, Cambridge University, 1959–83, now Emeritus; Life Fellow of Emmanuel College, 1983 (Fellow, 1959); *b* 30 Aug. 1916; *s* of Professor D. Thoday, FRS; *m* 1950, Doris Joan Rich, PhD (Fellow, Lucy Cavendish College); one *s* one *d.* *Educ:* Bootham School, York; University Coll. of N Wales, Bangor; Trinity College, Cambridge. Photographic Intelligence, Royal Air Force, 1941–46; Cytologist, Mount Vernon Hospital, 1946–47; Asst Lectr, then Lectr for Cytogenetics, Departments of Botany and Zoology, University of Sheffield, 1947–54; Head of Department of Genetics: Sheffield, 1954–59; Cambridge, 1959–82. Leverhulme Emeritus Res. Fellow, 1984–86. Director, OECD Project for reform of secondary school Biology teaching 1962, 1963. Chm., UK Nat. Cttee for Biology, 1982–. Pres., Genetical Soc., 1975–78. *Publications:* (with J. N. Thompson) Quantitive Genetics, 1979; articles on radiation cytology, experimental evolution, the genetics of continuous variables, biological progress and on genetics and society. *Address:* 7 Clarkson Road, Cambridge CB3 0EH.

THODE, Dr Henry George, CC (Canada) 1967; MBE 1946; FRS 1954; FRSC 1943; FCIC 1948; Professor Emeritus, McMaster University, Canada, since 1979; *b* 10 September 1910; Canadian; *m* 1935, Sadie Alicia Patrick; three *s.* *Educ:* University of Saskatchewan (BSc 1930, MSc 1932); University of Chicago (PhD 1934). Research Asst, Columbia Univ., 1936–38; Research Chemist, US Rubber Co., 1938; McMaster University: Asst Prof. of Chem., 1939–42; Assoc. Prof. of Chem., 1942–44; Prof. of Chem., 1944–79; Head, Department of Chemistry, 1948–52; Dir of Res., 1947–61; Principal of Hamilton Coll., 1944–63; Vice-Pres., 1957–61; Pres. and Vice-Chancellor, 1961–72. California Inst. of Technology, Pasadena, Calif: Nat. Science Foundn Sen. Foreign Res. Fellow, 1970; Sherman Fairchild Distinguished Scholar, 1977. National Research Council, War Research-Atomic Energy, 1943–45. Member: Nat. Research Council, 1955–61; Defence Research Bd, 1955–61; Commn on Atomic Weights (SAIC), IUPAC, 1963–79; Board of Governors, Ontario Research Foundn, 1955–82; Director: Atomic Energy of Canada Ltd, 1966–81; Stelco Inc., 1969–85. Hon. Fellow, Chemical Inst. of Canada, 1972; Shell Canada Merit Fellowship, 1974. Hon. DSc: Universities: Toronto, 1955; BC, Acadia, 1960; Laval, 1963; RMC, 1964; McGill, 1966; Queen's, 1967; York, 1972; McMaster, 1973. Hon. LLD: Sask., 1958; Regina, 1983. Medal of Chemical Inst. of Canada, 1957; Tory Medal, Royal Soc. of Canada, 1959; Arthur L. Day Medal, Geological Soc. of America, 1980; Centenary Medal, Royal Soc. of Canada, 1982. *Publications:* numerous publications on nuclear chemistry, isotope chemistry, isotope abundances in terrestrial and extraterrestrial material, separation of isotopes, magnetic susceptibilities, electrical discharges in gases, sulphur concentrations and isotope ratios in lunar materials. *Recreations:* swimming, farming. *Address:* Department of Chemistry, Nuclear Research Building, McMaster University, 1280 Main Street West, Hamilton, Ontario L8S 4K1, Canada. *T:* (416) 525–9140. *Club:* Rotary (Hamilton, Ont.).

THODY, Prof. Philip Malcolm Waller; Professor of French Literature, University of Leeds, since 1965; *b* Lincoln, 21 March 1928; *s* of Thomas Edwin Thody and Florence Ethel (*née* Hart); *m* 1954, Joyce Elizabeth Woodin; two *s* two *d.* *Educ:* Lincoln Sch.; King's Coll., Univ. of London. FIL 1982. Temp. Asst Lectr, Univ. of Birmingham, 1954–55; Asst Lectr, subseq. Lectr, QUB, 1956–65; Chairman: Dept of French, Univ. of Leeds, 1968–72, 1975–79, 1982–85; Bd of Faculties of Arts, Social Studies and Law, Univ. of Leeds, 1972–74. Vis. Professor: Univ. of Western Ontario, Canada, 1963–64; Berkeley Summer Sch., 1964; Harvard Summer Sch., 1968; Centenary Vis. Prof., Adelaide Univ., 1974; Canterbury Vis. Fellow, Univ. of Canterbury, NZ, 1977, 1982. Pres., Modern Languages Assoc., 1980, 1981. Officer dans l'Ordre des Palmes Académiques, 1981. *Publications:* Albert Camus, a study of his work, 1957; Jean-Paul Sartre, a literary and political study, 1960; Albert Camus, 1913–1960, 1961; Jean Genet, a study of his novels and plays, 1968; Jean Anouilh, 1968; Choderlos de Laclos, 1970; Jean-Paul Sartre, a biographical introduction, 1971; Aldous Huxley, a biographical introduction, 1973; Roland Barthes: a conservative estimate, 1977; A True Life Reader for Children and Parents, 1977; Dog Days in Babel (novel), 1979; (jtly) Faux Amis and Key Words, 1985; Marcel Proust, novelist, 1987; contribs to French Studies, Times Literary Supplement, Times Higher Educational Supplement, Modern Languages Review, London Magazine, Twentieth Century, Encounter, Yorkshire Post. *Recreations:* talking, golf, Wodehouse inter-war first editions. *Address:* 6 The Nook, Primley Park, Alwoodley, Leeds LS17 7JU. *T:* Leeds 687350.

THOM, Kenneth Cadwallader; HM Diplomatic Service, retired; *b* 4 Dec. 1922; *m* 1948, Patience Myra (*née* Collingridge); three *s* one *d.* *Educ:* University College School, London; St Andrews Univ.; MA(Hons). Army Service, 1942–47; Assistant District Officer, then District Officer, Northern Nigerian Administration, 1950–59; 1st Secretary: FO, 1959; UK Mission to UN, NY, 1960–63; FO, 1963–66; Budapest, 1966–68; FCO, 1968–72; Counsellor, Dublin, 1972–74; Counsellor, FCO, 1974–78; Consul-General: Hanover, 1978–79; Hamburg, 1979–81; retired, and re-employed, FCO, 1981–85. FIL 1981. *Address:* Prospect House, Bruton, Somerset.

THOMAS, family name of **Baron Thomas of Swynnerton** and **Viscount Tonypandy.**

THOMAS OF SWYNNERTON, Baron *cr* 1981 (Life Peer), of Notting Hill in Greater London; **Hugh Swynnerton Thomas;** historian; Chairman, Centre for Policy Studies, since 1979; *b* 21 Oct. 1931; *s* of Hugh Whitelegge Thomas, CMG, Colonial Service, Gold Coast (Ghana) and Margery Swynnerton; *m* 1962, Vanessa Jebb, *d* of 1st Baron Gladwyn, *qv*; two *s* one *d.* *Educ:* Sherborne; Queens' Coll., Cambridge (Scholar); Sorbonne, Paris. Pres. Cambridge Union, 1953. Foreign Office, 1954–57; Sec. to UK delegn to UN

Disarmament Sub-Cttee, 1955–56; Lectr at RMA Sandhurst, 1957; Prof. of History, 1966–76, and Chm., Grad. Sch. of Contemp. European Studies, 1973–76, Univ. of Reading. Somerset Maugham Prize, 1962; Arts Council prize for History (1st Nat. Book Awards), 1980. Order of Isabel la Católica, Spain, 1986. *Publications:* (as Hugh Thomas) The World's Game, 1957; The Spanish Civil War, 1961, rev. edn 1977, rev. illustrated edn, Spain, 1979; The Story of Sandhurst, 1961; The Suez Affair, 1967; Cuba, or the Pursuit of Freedom, 1971; (ed) The selected writings of José Antonio Primo de Rivera, 1972; Goya and The Third of May 1808, 1972; Europe, the Radical Challenge, 1973; John Strachey, 1973; The Cuban Revolution, 1977; An Unfinished History of the World, 1979, rev. edn 1982 (US 1979, A History of the World); The Case for the Round Reading Room, 1983; Havannah (novel), 1984; Armed Truce, 1986. *Address:* 29 Ladbroke Grove, W11. *T:* 01–727 2288; Well House, Sudbourne, Suffolk. *Clubs:* Beefsteak, Garrick; Travellers' (Paris).

THOMAS, Alston Havard Rees; Diary Editor, Bristol Evening Post, since 1970; Member, Press Council, since 1979; *b* Dinas, Pembrokeshire, 8 July 1925. Trainee and reporter, West Wales Guardian, 1939–44; Dist Reporter, Wilts Times, 1944–46; Bristol Evening Post, 1946–: successively Industrial, Speedway, Municipal, Ecclesiastical, Crime and Med. correspondent. Inst. of Journalists: Mem., 1974–; Chm. Nat. Exec., 1981–84; Pres., 1985–86; Chm. SW Region, 1975–. Mem., St John Council (Avon Co., 1974–). *Recreations:* rugby union, music, travel, gardening. *Address:* Havene, Maysmead Lane, Langford, Avon BS18 7HX. *T:* Weston-super-Mare 862515. *Club:* Savages (Bristol).

THOMAS, Ambler Reginald, CMG 1951; Under-Secretary, Ministry of Overseas Development, retired 1975; *b* 12 Feb. 1913; *s* of late John Frederick Ivor Thomas, OBE, MICE, MIME and Elizabeth Thomas; *m* 1943, Diana Beresford Gresham; two *s* three *d. Educ:* Gresham's School, Holt; Corpus Christi College, Cambridge. Entered Home Civil Service as Asst Principal and apptd to Ministry of Agriculture and Fisheries, 1935; transferred to Colonial Office, 1936. Asst Private Sec. to Sec. of State for Colonies, 1938–39; Principal, Colonial Office, 1939; Asst Sec., 1946; Chief Sec. to Govt of Aden, 1947–49; Establishment and Organization Officer, Colonial Office, 1950–52; Assistant Under-Sec. of State, Colonial Office, 1952–64; Under-Sec., Min. of Overseas Develt, and Overseas Develt Administration, 1964–73. Member, Exec. Cttee, British Council, 1965–68. Chairman: Commn of Inquiry into Gilbert Is Develt Authority, 1976; Corona Club. *Address:* Champsland, North Chideock, Bridport, Dorset. *Club:* United Oxford & Cambridge University.

THOMAS, Aneurin Morgan; Director, Welsh Arts Council, 1967–84; *b* 3 April 1921; *s* of Philip Thomas and Olwen Amy Thomas (*née* Davies); *m* 1947, Mary Dineen; one *s* one *d. Educ:* Ystalyfera Intermediate Sch., Glamorgan; Swansea School of Art and Crafts. British and Indian Armies, 1941–46 (Major). Lecturer, later Vice-Principal, Somerset College of Art, 1947–60; Vice-Principal, Hornsey College of Art, 1960–67. Member, Board of Governors: Loughborough Coll. of Art and Design, 1980–; S Glamorgan Inst. of Higher Educn, 1985– (Chm., Faculty of Art and Design Adv. Cttee, 1985); Carmarthenshire Coll. of Tech. and Art, 1985– (Chm., Faculty of Art and Design Adv. Cttee, 1985); Vice-Pres., Nat. Soc. for Art Educn, 1967–68. Chm., Assoc. of Art Instns, 1977–78. *Publications:* periodic contribs to books and professional jls. *Recreation:* enjoying the arts. *Address:* Netherwood, 8 Lower Cwrt-y-vil Road, Penarth, South Glamorgan CF6 2HQ. *T:* Penarth 702239.

THOMAS, Prof. (Antony) Charles, DLitt; FSA; Professor of Cornish Studies, University of Exeter, and Director, Institute of Cornish Studies, since 1971; *b* 24 April 1928; *s* of late Donald Woodroffe Thomas and Viva Warrington Thomas; *m* 1959, Jessica Dorothea Esther, *d* of F. A. Mann, *qv*; two *s* two *d. Educ:* Winchester; Corpus Christi Coll., Oxon (BA Hons Jurisp.); Univ. of London (Dipl. Prehist. Archaeol.). DLitt Oxon, 1983. Lectr in Archaeology, Univ. of Edinburgh, 1957–67; Prof. of Archaeology, Univ. of Leicester, 1967–71. Leverhulme Fellowship, 1965–67; Sir John Rhys Fellow, Univ. of Oxford, and Vis. Sen. Res. Fellow, Jesus Coll., 1985–86. Lectures: Hunter Marshall, Univ. of Glasgow, 1968; O'Donnell, Univ. of Edinburgh, 1970; Jarrow, 1973; Willans, UC, Aberystwyth, 1975; Henry Lewis, UC, Swansea, 1977; O'Donnell, Univ. of Wales, 1978. President: Council for British Archaeology, 1970–73; Royal Instn of Cornwall, 1970–72; Cornwall Archaeol. Soc., 1984–; Sect. H, BAAS, Bath, 1978; Chairman: BBC SW Reg. Adv. Council, 1975–80; DoE Area Archaeol Cttee, Cornwall and Devon, 1975–79; Cornwall Cttee Rescue Archaeol., 1976–; Mem., Royal Commn on Historical Monuments (England), 1983–. Hon. Archaeol Consultant, National Trust, 1970–. Hon. Mem., Royal Irish Acad., 1973; Hon. Fellow, RSAI, 1975. William Frend Medal, Soc. of Antiquaries, 1982. *Publications:* Christian Antiquities of Camborne, 1967; The Early Christian Archaeology of North Britain, 1971; Britain and Ireland in Early Christian Times, 1971; (with A. Small and D. Wilson) St Ninian's Isle and its Treasure, 1973; (with D. Ivall) Military Insignia of Cornwall, 1974; Christianity in Roman Britain to AD 500, 1981; Exploration of a Drowned Landscape, 1985; Celtic Britain, 1986. *Recreations:* military history, archaeological fieldwork. *Address:* Lambessow, St Clement, Truro, Cornwall.

THOMAS, Brig. Arthur Frank Friend, CIE 1942; *b* 8 Aug. 1897; *s* of Arthur Ernest Thomas, Parkhurst, South Norwood; *m* 1928, Elizabeth Stephenson Walker (decd), MB, BCh, DPH, *d* of Rev. S. Walker, MA, Donaghadee, Co. Down; one *d* (one *s* decd). *Educ:* Melbourne College. ADC, EEF, 1920–21; DADOS Waziristan District, 1928–31; Staff Capt. AHQ 1931–33; DADOS, AHQ, 1933–36; AD of C, AHQ, 1936–39; DD of C 1939–40; D of C 1940; CCPM 1940–41; Deputy Controller-General of Inspection, GHQ, India, 1941–45; Director of Civil Personnel, 1945–47; retired, 1947. Served European War, 1914–21, Egypt, 1914–16, France, 1916–17, EEF 1918 (wounded, despatches); NW Frontier, India, 1930; War of 1939–45. *Recreations:* gardening, cine-photography. *Address:* Coughton Lodge Residential Home, Birmingham Road, Coughton, near Alcester, Warwicks B49 5HU.

THOMAS, Brian (Dick Lauder), OBE 1961; Mural Painter and Stained Glass Designer; *b* 19 Sept. 1912; *s* of Frank Leslie Thomas, MB, BS, and Margaret Mary (*née* Lauder). *Educ:* Bradfield College. Rome Scholarship in Mural Painting, 1934; Camouflage Directorate, Min. of Home Security, 1939–45; Principal, Byam Shaw Sch. of Art, 1946–54; Master, Art Workers Guild, 1957, Editor, Artifex, 1968–71; Fellow, Brit. Soc. of Master Glass Painters, 1958; Chm. of Governors, Hurstpierpoint Coll., 1958–67; Mem. Council, Artists' Gen. Benevolent Instn, 1964; Chm. Council, Fedn of British Craft Socs, 1971–73; Mem., Crafts Adv. Cttee, 1971–73. Vice-Pres., SPCK, 1976. Master, Glaziers Co., 1976. *Principal works:* St Paul's Cathedral (stained glass in American and OBE Chapels); Westminster Abbey (stained glass); Winchester Cathedral (shrine of St Swithun); Wellington Cathedral, NZ (War Memorial windows); St George's Chapel, Windsor (panels in altar rails); St George's Church, Stevenage New Town (stained glass); Livery Co. Windows: London Guildhall, Pewterers' Hall, Innholders' Hall, Watermen's Hall; Biographical Window in Harpur Trust Court-Room, Bedford; memorials to Dame Nellie Melba, John Ireland, Russell Colman, Sir Harold Graham-Hodgson, Lord Webb-Johnson and others; painted ceiling at Templewood, Norfolk; murals and mosaics in many religious and secular buildings of London and the provinces. *Publications:* Vision and Technique in European Painting, 1952; Geometry in Pictorial Composition, 1971;

(ed) Directory of Master Glass-Painters, 1972. *Address:* The Studio, 3 Hill Road, NW8. *T:* 01–286 0804. *Clubs:* Arts, Athenæum.

THOMAS, Brinley, CBE 1971 (OBE 1955); MA, PhD; FBA 1973; Professor of Economics, University College, Cardiff, 1946–73, Director, Manpower Research Unit, 1974–76; *b* 6 Jan. 1906; *e s* of late Thomas Thomas and Anne Walters; *m* 1943, Cynthia, *d* of late Dr Charles T. Loram, New Haven, Connecticut; one *d. Educ:* Port Talbot County School; University College of Wales, Aberystwyth; London School of Economics. MA (Wales) (with distinction), 1928; Fellow of the University of Wales, 1929–31; Social Science Research Training Scholar, 1929–31; PhD (London), 1931; Hutchinson Silver Medal, London School of Economics, 1931; Acland Travelling Scholar in Germany and Sweden, 1932–34; Lecturer in Economics, London School of Economics, 1931–39; War Trade Department, British Embassy, Washington, 1941–42; Dir, Northern Section, Political Intelligence Dept of Foreign Office, 1942–45. Member: National Assistance Bd, 1948–53; Anderson Cttee on Grants to Students, 1958–60; Dept of Employment Retail Prices Index Advisory Cttee; Prince of Wales Cttee, 1969–76. Chairman: Welsh Advisory Cttee of British Council, 1966–74; Welsh Council, 1968–71; Assoc. of Univ. Teachers of Econs, 1965–68; Mem. Exec. Cttee, British Council, 1966–74; Pres., Atlantic Economic Soc. Nat. Science Foundn Fellow, 1971. University of California, Berkeley: Ford Vis. Res. Prof., 1976–77; Vis. Prof., 1978–79 and 1979–83; Visiting Professor: Queen's Univ., Canada, 1977–78; Univ. of California, Davis, 1984–86. Governor, Centre for Environmental Studies, 1972–74. *Publications:* Monetary Policy and Crises, A Study of Swedish Experience, 1936; Migration and Economic Growth, A Study of Great Britain and the Atlantic Economy, 1954, 2nd edn 1973; International Migration and Economic Development: A Trend Report and Bibliography, 1961; Migration and Urban Development, 1972; (ed) Economics of International Migration, 1958; (ed) The Welsh Economy: Studies in Expansion, 1962; articles in various journals. *Address:* 44a Church Road, Whitchurch, Cardiff. *T:* Cardiff 693835. *Club:* Reform.

THOMAS, Charles; see Thomas, A. C.

THOMAS, Ven. Charles Edward; Archdeacon of Wells, since 1983; *b* 1927. *Educ:* St David's College, Lampeter (BA 1951); College of the Resurrection, Mirfield. Deacon 1953, priest 1954; Curate of Ilminster, 1953–56; Chaplain and Asst Master, St Michael's Coll., Tenbury, 1956–57; Curate of St Stephen's, St Albans, 1957–58; Vicar, St Michael and All Angels, Boreham Wood, 1958–66; Rector, Monksilver with Elworthy, 1966–74, with Brompton Ralph and Nettlecombe, 1969–74 (Curate-in-charge of Nettlecombe, 1968–69); Vicar of South Petherton with the Seavingtons, 1974–83. RD of Crewkerne, 1977–82. *Address:* 6 The Liberty, Wells, Som BA5 2SU. *T:* Wells 72224.

THOMAS, Dr Claudius Cornelius, CMG 1979; Commissioner for the Eastern Caribbean Governments in the United Kingdom, since 1975; High Commissioner, in the United Kingdom, for: St Lucia, and St Vincent and the Grenadines, since 1979; Antigua-Barbuda, 1981–84; Saint Christopher and Nevis, since 1983; *b* 1 Oct. 1928; *s* of Charles Malin Thomas and Ada Thomas (*née* Dyer). *Educ:* Castries Intermed. Sch., St Lucia; London Univ. (LLB); Univ. de Strasbourg (Dr en droit). Called to Bar, Gray's Inn, 1957. Cadet Officer, Commn for the West Indies in UK, 1961; Translator, EEC, Brussels, 1962; Attaché, L'Institut Internat. des Sciences Administratives, Brussels, 1962–63; Free University of (West) Berlin: Wissenschaftlicher Asst, 1963–72, Asst Prof., 1972–75. Ambassador of Saint Lucia to: Paris, 1983–; Bonn, 1983–; Stockholm, 1984–; Permanent Representative of Saint Lucia to: Stockholm, 1984–; UNESCO, 1984–; EEC, 1984–. Member: Hon. Soc. of Gray's Inn; British Inst. of Internat. and Comparative Law. *Publications:* contrib. to and assisted in, Multitudo Legum Ius Unum, 1973; contrib. to: Deutches Jahrbuch des Öffentlichen Rechts, 1966; Anglo-American Law Review, 1973; and other legal jls. *Recreations:* cricket, table tennis, sailing. *Address:* High Commission for Eastern Caribbean States, 10 Kensington Court, W8. *Clubs:* Royal Commonwealth Soc., Hurlingham.

THOMAS, Colin Agnew; chartered accountant; *b* 14 Feb. 1921; *s* of Harold Alfred Thomas and Nora (*née* Williams); *m* 1947, Jane Jardine Barnish, *d* of Leonard Barnish, FRIBA; one *s* one *d. Educ:* Oundle School. Lieut, RNVR, 1941–46. Finance Comptroller, Lloyd's, 1964–75, Sec.-Gen., 1976–79. *Recreations:* golf, sailing, gardening. *Address:* 33 Cobham Road, Leatherhead, Surrey KT22 9AY. *T:* Leatherhead 374335; 15 Ravenspoint, Trearddur Bay, Anglesey. *Clubs:* Effingham Golf, Holyhead Golf, Trearddur Bay Sailing.

THOMAS, Dafydd Elis; MP (Plaid Cymru) Meirionnydd Nant Conwy, since 1983 (Merioneth, Feb. 1974–1983); President, Plaid Cymru, since 1984; *b* 18 Oct. 1946; *m* 1970, Elen M. Williams; three *s. Educ:* Ysgol Dyffryn Conwy; UC North Wales. Research worker, Bd of Celtic Studies, 1970; Tutor in Welsh Studies, Coleg Harlech, 1970; Lectr, Dept of English, UC North Wales, 1974. Part-time freelance broadcaster, BBC Wales, HTV, 1970–73. *Recreations:* hill walking, camping. *Address:* Tanyfynwent, Dolgellau, Gwynedd LL40 1ET. *T:* (constituency office) Dolgellau 422661; (London) 01–219 4172/5021. *Club:* Sport and Social (Trawsfynydd).

THOMAS, Rev. David; Principal, St Stephen's House, Oxford, since 1982; *b* 22 July 1942; *s* of Rt Rev. John James Absalom Thomas, *qv*; *m* 1967, Rosemary Christine Calton; one *s* one *d. Educ:* Christ College, Brecon; Keble College, Oxford; St Stephen's House, Oxford. MA Oxon. Curate of Hawarden, 1967–69; Tutor, St Michael's College, Llandaff, Cardiff, 1969–70, Chaplain 1970–75; Secretary, Church in Wales Liturgical Commn, 1970–75; Vice-Principal, St Stephen's House, Oxford, 1975–79; Vicar of Chepstow, 1979–82. *Publication:* (contrib.) The Ministry of the Word (ed G. J. Cuming), 1979. *Recreations:* music, walking. *Address:* St Stephen's House, 16 Marston Street, Oxford OX4 1JX. *T:* Oxford 247874.

THOMAS, Prof. David; Head of Department of Geography, since 1978, and Pro Vice-Chancellor, since 1984, University of Birmingham; *b* 16 Feb. 1931; *s* of William and Florence Grace Thomas; *m* 1955, Daphne Elizabeth Berry; one *s* one *d. Educ:* Bridgend Grammar School; University College of Wales, Aberystwyth (BA, MA); PhD London. Asst Lectr, Lectr, Reader, University College London, 1957–70; Prof. and Head of Dept, St David's University College, Lampeter, 1970–78. *Publications:* Agriculture in Wales during the Napoleonic Wars, 1963; London's Green Belt, 1970; (ed) An Advanced Geography of the British Isles, 1974; (with J. A. Dawson) Man and his world, 1975; (ed) Wales: a new study, 1977; (with P. T. J. Morgan) Wales: the changing shape of a nation, 1984; articles in learned jls. *Recreations:* music, wine, dedicated spectator. *Address:* 6 Plymouth Drive, Barnt Green, Birmingham B45 8JB. *T:* 021–445 3295.

THOMAS, David Bowen, PhD; Keeper, Department of Physical Sciences, Science Museum, since 1984 (Keeper, Department of Physics, 1978–84); *b* 28 Dec. 1931; *s* of Evan Thomas and Florence Annie Bowen. *Educ:* Tredegar Grammar Sch.; Manchester Univ. (BSc). Research Fellow, Wayne Univ., Detroit, USA, 1955–57; Research Scientist, Min. of Agriculture, Fisheries and Food, Aberdeen, 1957–61; Asst Keeper, Science Museum, Dept of Chemistry, 1961–73; Keeper, Dept of Museum Services, 1973–78. *Publications:* The First Negatives, 1964; The Science Museum Photography Collection,

1969; The First Colour Motion Pictures, 1969. Hon. FRPS 1985. *Recreation:* country walking. *Address:* 81 Lambton Road, SW20.

THOMAS, David Churchill, CMG 1982; HM Diplomatic Service, retired; Assistant Under Secretary of State, Foreign and Commonwealth Office, 1984–86; *b* 21 Oct. 1933; *o s* of late David Bernard Thomas and Violet Churchill Thomas (*née* Quicke); *m* 1958, Susan Petronella Arrow; one *s* two *d*. *Educ:* Eton Coll.; New Coll., Oxford (Exhibnr). Mod. Hist. 1st Cl., 1957. Army, 2nd Lieut, Rifle Brigade, 1952–54. Foreign Office, 1958; 3rd Sec., Moscow, 1959–61; 2nd Sec., Lisbon, 1961–64; FCO, 1964–68; 1st Sec. (Commercial), Lima, 1968–70; FCO, 1970–73; Head of South West European Dept, 1974; Asst Sec., Cabinet Office, 1973–78; Counsellor (Internal Affairs), Washington, 1978–81; Ambassador to Cuba, 1981–84. *Recreations:* photography, listening to music. *Address:* 54 Tournay Road, SW6.

THOMAS, David Hamilton Pryce, CBE 1977; solicitor; Chairman, Land Authority for Wales, 1980–86 (Deputy Chairman, 1975–80); President, Rent Assessment Panel for Wales, since 1971 (Member, 1966); *b* 3 July 1922; *s* of Trevor John Thomas and Eleanor Maud Thomas; *m* 1948, Eluned Mair Morgan; two *s* one *d*. *Educ:* Barry County Sch.; University College, Cardiff. Served War of 1939–45; British and Indian Armies, terminal rank T/Captain (GSO III), 1941–46. Qualified as Solicitor, 1948, with hons; Partner in J. A. Hughes & Co., Solicitors, Barry, 1950–75; Notary Public, 1953. Director 1962–67, Vice-Chm. 1967–71, Chm. 1971–78, Barry Mutual Building Society; Vice Chm., 1978, Chm., 1982–84, Glam. Building Soc.; Chm., Wales Area Bd, Bradford and Bingley Bldg Soc., 1984–; Vice-Chm., Building Socs Assoc. for Wales, 1983; Mem., Adv. Cttee on Fair Rents, 1973; Chm., E Glam. Rent Tribunal, 1967–71; District Comr of Scouts, Barry and District, 1963–70; Chm., Barry District Scout Assoc. 1971–81; Vice-Chm., S Glam. Scout Council, 1975–81. *Recreations:* books, music. *Address:* 27 Romilly Park, Barry, South Glamorgan CF6 8RQ. *T:* Barry 732229.

See also R. L. Thomas.

THOMAS, David Monro; retired; *b* 31 July 1915; *s* of late Henry Monro and Winifred Thomas, East Hagbourne, Berks; *m* 1948, Ursula Mary, *d* of late H. W. Liversidge; two *s* one *d*. *Educ:* St Edward's School, Oxford; St Edmund Hall, Oxford. Oxford House, 1937; Army, 1939, Major, Royal Welch Fusiliers; Head of Oxford House, 1946–48; Secretary of Greek House, 1948–51; Legal & General Assurance Soc. Ltd, 1951–75; YWCA, 1975–80; Co. Sec., YWCA, 1977–80. *Address:* Watcombe Corner, Watlington, Oxford OX9 5QJ. *T:* Watlington 2403.

THOMAS, David Owen, QC 1972; a Recorder of the Crown Court, since 1972; *b* 22 Aug. 1926; *s* of late Emrys Aeron Thomas and Dorothy May Thomas; *m* 1967, Mary Susan Atkinson; four *d*. *Educ:* Queen Elizabeth's, Barnet; John Bright Sch., Llandudno; Queen's Univ., Belfast. Served War, HM Forces, 1943–45 and to 1948. Called to the Bar, Middle Temple, 1952, Bencher, 1980; Dep. Chairman, Devon QS, 1971. *Recreations:* acting, cricket, Rugby football. *Address:* 2 King's Bench Walk, Temple, EC4Y 7DE. *T:* 01–353 1746; Briar Cottage, Church Lane, Kings Worthy, Winchester, Hants SO23 7QS. *T:* Winchester 882141. *Clubs:* Garrick, MCC; Hampshire (Winchester).

THOMAS, Derek John, IPFA; County Treasurer, Surrey County Council, since 1979; *b* 3 Dec. 1934; *s* of late James Llewellyn Thomas and Winifred Mary Thomas; *m* 1st (marr. diss.); three *d*; 2nd, 1978, Christine (*née* Brewer); one *s*. *Educ:* Hele's Sch., Exeter. Formerly: Treasurer's Depts: Devon CC; Corby Development Corporation; Bath CC; Taunton Bor. Council; Sen. Asst Bor. Treasurer, Poole Bor. Council; Asst County Treasurer, Gloucestershire CC; Principal Asst County Treasurer, Avon CC. CIPFA: Mem. Council, 1977–78, 1985–; Chm., Higher Educn Finance Exec., 1980–85; Chm., SE Region, 1984–85. *Address:* County Hall, Penrhyn Road, Kingston upon Thames, Surrey. *T:* 01–541 9200.

THOMAS, Derek Morison David, CMG 1977; HM Diplomatic Service; Deputy Under Secretary of State for Europe and Political Director, Foreign and Commonwealth Office, since 1984; *b* 31 Oct. 1929; *s* of K. P. D. Thomas and Mali McL. Thomas; *m* 1956, Carolina Jacoba van der Mast; two *c*. *Educ:* Radley Coll., Abingdon; Trinity Hall, Cambridge (MA). Mod. Langs Tripos. Articled apprentice, Dolphin Industrial Developments Ltd, 1947. Entered HM Foreign Service, 1953; Midshipman 1953, Sub-Lt 1955, RNVR; FO, 1955; 3rd, later 2nd, Sec., Moscow, 1956–59; 2nd Sec., Manila, 1959–61; UK Delegn to Brussels Conf., 1961–62; 1st Sec., FO, 1962; Sofia, 1964–67; Ottawa, 1967–69; seconded to Treasury, 1969–70; Financial Counsellor, Paris, 1971–75; Head of N American Dept, FCO, 1975–76; Asst Under Sec. of State, FCO, 1976–79; Minister Commercial and later Minister, Washington, 1979–84. *Recreations:* listening to people and music; being by, in or on water. *Address:* c/o Foreign and Commonwealth Office, SW1. *Clubs:* United Oxford & Cambridge University; Leander.

THOMAS, Dewi Alun, MBE; **His Honour Judge Thomas;** a Circuit Judge since 1972; *b* 3 Dec. 1917; *e s* of late Joshua and Martha Ann Thomas; *m* 1952, Doris Maureen Smith, Barrister; one *s* one *d*. *Educ:* Christ Coll., Brecon; Jesus Coll., Oxford (MA). Served War of 1939–45 (MBE, despatches): mobilised with TA (RA), 1939; served Sicily, Italy, the Balkans; Major, 2nd in Comd, No 2 Commando; demobilised 1946. Called to Bar, Inner Temple, 1951, Bencher 1969. *Recreations:* golf, watching Rugby football. *Address:* 16 Westhall Park, Warlingham, Surrey. *T:* Upper Warlingham 4127. *Club:* Cardiff and County.

THOMAS, Donald Martin; *see* Thomas, Martin.

THOMAS, Donald Michael; poet and novelist; *b* Redruth, Cornwall, 27 Jan. 1935; *s* of Harold Redvers Thomas and Amy (*née* Moyle); two *s* one *d* *Educ:* Redruth Grammar Sch.; Univ. High Sch., Melbourne; New Coll., Oxford (BA 1st cl. Hons in English; MA). School teacher, Teignmouth Grammar Sch., 1959–63; Lectr, Hereford Coll. of Educn, 1964–78; full-time author, 1978–. *Publications: poetry:* Penguin Modern Poets 11, 1968; Two Voices, 1968; Logan Stone, 1971; Love and Other Deaths, 1975; The Honeymoon Voyage, 1978; Dreaming in Bronze, 1981; Selected Poems, 1983; *novels:* The Flute-Player, 1979; Birthstone, 1980; The White Hotel, 1981; Ararat, 1983; Swallow, 1984; Sphinx, 1986; *translations:* Requiem and Poem without a Hero, Akhmatova, 1976; Way of All the Earth, Akhmatova, 1979; Bronze Horseman, Pushkin, 1982. *Recreations:* travel, Russia and other myths, the culture and history of Cornwall, the life of the imagination. *Address:* 10 Greyfriars Avenue, Hereford HR4 0BE.

THOMAS, Elizabeth; *see* Thomas, M.E.

THOMAS, Elizabeth Marjorie; Secretary General, 1979–83, Literary Consultant, 1984–85, The Authors' Lending and Copyright Society; *b* 10 Aug. 1919; *d* of Frank Porter and Marjorie Porter (*née* Pascall); *m* 1941, George Thomas; one *s* one *d*. *Educ:* St George's Sch., Harpenden; Girton Coll., Cambridge (BA 1st Cl.). Journalist, 1951–59 and Literary Editor, 1959–71, Tribune; Asst Literary Editor, New Statesman, 1971–76; Political Adviser to Rt Hon. Michael Foot, MP, Lord Pres. of the Council and Leader of the House of Commons, 1976–79. Mem., Arts Council, 1974–77 (Mem., Literature Panel, 1971–77); Chm., Literature Panel, Eastern Arts Assoc., 1978–84; Member: Ethnic Minority Arts Cttee, Commission for Racial Equality, 1979–82; British Council Bd, 1982–. *Publication:* (ed) Tribune 21, 1959. *Address:* Anchor House, North Street, Winchcombe. Glos. *T:* Cheltenham 602788.

THOMAS, Emyr, CBE 1980; LLB, LMTPI; DL; General Manager, Telford New Town Development Corporation, 1969–80; Chairman, Telford Community Council, 1980–84; *b* 25 April 1920; *s* of late Brinley Thomas, MA, Aldershot; *m* 1947, Barbara J. May; one *d*. *Educ:* Aldershot County High School. Served War of 1939–45, RASC. Admitted Solicitor, 1947. Asst Solicitor, Exeter City Council, 1947–50; Sen. Asst Solicitor, Reading County Borough Council, 1950–53; Dep. Town Clerk, West Bromwich County Borough Council, 1953–64; Sec. and Solicitor, Dawley (later Telford) Development Corp., 1964–69. First Hon. Sec., Ironbridge Gorge Museum Trust, 1968–. DL Salop, 1979. *Recreation:* industrial archaeology. *Address:* 8 Kynnersley Lane, Leighton, near Shrewsbury, Shropshire.

THOMAS, Rt. Rev. Eryl Stephen; *b* 20 Oct. 1910; *s* of Edward Stephen and Margaret Susannah Thomas; *m* 1939, Jean Mary Alice Wilson; three *s* one *d*. *Educ:* Rossall Sch.; St John's Coll., Oxford; Wells Theological Coll. BA 2nd Class Hon. Theology, Oxford, 1932; MA 1935. Curate of Colwyn Bay, 1933–38, of Hawarden, 1938–43; Vicar of Risca, Mon, 1943–48; Warden of St Michael's Theological Coll., Llandaff, 1948–54; Dean of Llandaff, 1954–68; Bishop of Monmouth, 1968–71, of Llandaff, 1971–75. Chaplain and Sub-Prelate, Order of St John of Jerusalem, 1969. *Address:* 17 Orchard Close, Gilwern, Abergavenny, Gwent NP7 0EN. *T:* Gilwern 831050.

THOMAS, Rt. Rev. Francis Gerard; *see* Northampton, Bishop of, (RC).

THOMAS, Frank; *see* Thomas, J. F. P.

THOMAS, Franklin Augustine; President, Ford Foundation, since 1979; *b* 27 May 1934; *s* of James Thomas and Viola Thomas (*née* Atherley); *m* (mar diss.); two *s* two *d*. *Educ:* Columbia College, New York (BA 1956); Columbia Univ. (LLB 1963). Admitted to NY State Bar, 1964; Attorney, Fed. Housing and Home Finance Agency, NYC, 1963–64; Asst US Attorney for Southern District, NY, 1964–65; Dep. Police Comr, charge legal matters, NYC, 1965–67; Pres., Chief Exec. Officer, Bedford Stuyvesant Restoration Corp., Brooklyn, 1967–77. Hon. LLD: Yale, 1970; Fordham, 1972; Pratt Institute, 1974; Pace, 1977; Columbia, 1979. *Address:* The Ford Foundation, 320 East 43rd Street, New York, NY 10017, USA. *T:* (212) 573–5383.

THOMAS, Sir Frederick William, Kt 1959; Councillor, City of Melbourne, 1953–65 (Lord Mayor, 1957–59); *b* 27 June 1906; *s* of F. J. Thomas; *m* 1968, Dorothy Alexa Gordon; three *s* by former marr. *Educ:* Melbourne Grammar School. Served War of 1939–45, RAAF (Air Efficiency Award, two bars); Group Captain. Comdr Order of Orange Nassau with swords (Holland), 1943. *Recreation:* golf. *Address:* 35 Hitchcock Avenue, Barwon Heads, Victoria 3227, Australia. *Clubs:* Naval and Military, Royal Automobile of Victoria (Melbourne); Barwon Heads Golf, Melbourne Cricket, Victoria Racing.

THOMAS, Air Vice-Marshal Geoffrey Percy Sansom, CB 1970; OBE 1945; retired; *b* 24 April 1915; *s* of Reginald Ernest Sansom Thomas, New Malden; *m* 1940, Sally, *d* of Horace Biddle, Gainsborough; one *s* one *d*. *Educ:* King's College School, Wimbledon. Commissioned RAF, 1939; served India and Ceylon, 1942–45; on loan to Turkish Air Force, 1950–52; Group Captain, 1958; served with RAAF, 1960–62; Air Commodore, 1965; Director of Movements, 1965; Air Vice-Marshal, 1969; SASO, Maintenance Comd, 1969–71. *Address:* Elms Wood House, Elms Vale, Dover, Kent. *T:* Dover 206375.

THOMAS, Maj.-Gen. George Arthur, CB 1960; CBE 1957; retired; *b* 2 May 1906; *s* of Colonel F. H. S. Thomas, CB, and Diana Thomas; *m* 1936, Diana Zaidee Browne; one *s* one *d*. *Educ:* Cheltenham College; Royal Military Academy, Woolwich. Commissioned, Royal Artillery, 1926; served in UK and Egypt; Staff College, 1940; CO 17 Field Regt, 1st Army, 1942–43; GSO1, 4 Division, 1943–44; BGS 8th Army, 1944–45; CRA 16 Airborne Div., 1947–48; Imperial Defence Coll., 1952; BGS, MELF, 1955–57; Chief of Staff, HQ Northern Command, 1958–60; Chief of Staff, GHQ Far ELF, 1960–62. Retired, 1962. *Recreations:* games and sports of all kinds. *Address:* Fishing Cottage, Upper Clatford, Andover, Hants. *T:* Andover 52120. *Club:* Army and Navy.

THOMAS, Sir (Godfrey) Michael (David), 11th Bt, *cr* 1694; Member of Stock Exchange, London, since 1959; *b* 10 Oct. 1925; *o s* of Rt Hon. Sir Godfrey Thomas, PC, GCVO, KCB, CSI, 10th Bt, and Diana, *d* of late Ven. B. G. Hoskyns (*d* 1985); *S* father 1968; *m* 1956, Margaret Greta Cleland, *yr d* of John Cleland, Stormont Court, Godden Green, Kent; one *s* two *d*, of whom one *s* one *d* are twins. *Educ:* Harrow. The Rifle Brigade, 1944–56. *Heir: s* David John Godfrey Thomas, *b* 11 June 1961. *Address:* 2 Napier Avenue, SW6. *T:* 01–736 6896. *Clubs:* MCC, Hurlingham.

THOMAS, Graham Stuart, OBE 1975; VMH 1968; Gardens Consultant to National Trust, since 1974; *b* 3 April 1909; *s* of W. R. Thomas and L. Thomas. *Educ:* horticultural and botanical training, Cambridge Univ. Botanic Garden, 1926–29. Six Hills Nursery, Stevenage, 1930; Foreman, later Manager, T. Hilling & Co., Chobham, 1931–55; Manager, Sunningdale Nurseries, Windlesham, 1956, Associate Dir, 1968–71; Gardens Adviser, National Trust, 1955–74. Vice-President: Garden History Soc.; British Hosta and Hemerocallis Soc.; Royal Nat. Rose Soc. (Dean Hole Medal, 1976); Hon. Mem., Irish Garden Plant Soc. Veitch Meml Medal, RHS, 1966. *Publications:* The Old Shrub Roses, 1955, 5th edn 1978; Colour in the Winter Garden, 1957, 3rd edn 1984; Shrub Roses of Today, 1962, rev. edn 1980; Climbing Roses Old and New, 1965, new edn 1983; Plants for Ground Cover, 1970, rev. edn 1977; Perennial Garden Plants, 1976, rev. edn 1982; Gardens of the National Trust, 1979; Three Gardens, 1983; Trees in the Landscape, 1983; The Art of Planting, 1984. *Recreations:* horticulture, music, painting and drawing plants. *Address:* 21 Kettlewell Close, Horsell, Woking, Surrey.

THOMAS, Gwyn Edward Ward; *see* Ward Thomas.

THOMAS, Harvey; *see* Thomas, J. H. N.

THOMAS, Howard, CBE 1967; Chairman: Thames Television Ltd, 1974–79; Thames Television International Ltd, 1974–81; Independent Television News, 1974–76 (Director, since 1956); Managing Director of ABC Television, 1955–68, of Thames Television, 1968–74; *b* 5 March 1909; *s* of W. G. Thomas and A. M. Thomas; *m* 1934, Hilda, *d* of Harrison Fogg; two *d*. Trained in advertising, journalism and broadcasting. Started Commercial Radio Department, London Press Exchange Ltd, 1938. Writer and Producer for BBC Sound Radio and during 3 years directed and produced 500 programmes. Entered film industry as Producer-in-Chief, Associated British Pathé Ltd, 1944. Divnl Dir, EMI Ltd; Director: EMI Film and Theatre Corp. Ltd; EMI Film Distributors Ltd; Euston Films Ltd; Independent Television Companies Association; Literators Ltd; Argus Press Ltd, 1973–; Television International Enterprises Ltd, 1985–; BAFTA Management Ltd, 1975–80; Logospheres Ltd, 1979–; Thames Valley Broadcasting Ltd, 1975–80; Tempo Video Ltd, 1981–. Broadcasting Consultant to: EMI Ltd and Rediffusion Television Ltd, 1979–81; to Thames Television Internat. Ltd, 1982–84. A Governor, BFI, 1974–82

(Chm., BFI Funding and Develt Cttee). Member: Advertising Standards Authority, 1962–73; Govt Adv. Cttee on Advertising, 1973–. Vice-Chm., Advertising Assoc., 1973–77. Dir, Internat. Council, Nat. Acad. of TV Arts & Scis (USA), 1971–78. Mem., 'London Looks Forward' Silver Jubilee 1977 Conf. Hon. Fellow, British Kinematograph Sound & Television Soc., 1967; FRSA 1975 (Mem. Council, 1978–84); Vice-Pres., Royal Television Soc., 1976–84; Hon. Life Mem., Gtr London Arts Assoc., 1977–; Former President: Radio Industries Club; Cinema & Television Veterans. Radio Programmes: Showmen of England, Beauty Queen, The Brains Trust, Shipmates Ashore, Books that Changed the World (series), 1985, etc. Films: Elizabeth is Queen (Coronation) and many documentaries. *Publications:* The Brighter Blackout Book, 1939; How to Write for Broadcasting, 1940; Britain's Brains Trust, 1944, The Truth About Television, 1962; With an Independent Air, 1977. *Address:* Old Ship House, Wharfe Lane, Henley-on-Thames, Oxon.

THOMAS, Hugh; *see* Thomas of Swynnerton, Baron.

THOMAS, Ivor B.; *see* Bulmer-Thomas.

THOMAS, Jean Olwen, ScD; FRS 1986; University Lecturer in Biochemistry, Cambridge, since 1973; Fellow and College Lecturer, since 1969, Vice-President, since 1983, New Hall, Cambridge; *b* 1 Oct. 1942; *o c* of John Robert Thomas and Lorna Prunella Thomas (*née* Harris). *Educ:* Llwyn-y-Bryn High School for Girls, Swansea; University Coll., Swansea, Univ. of Wales (BSc and Ayling Prize, 1964; PhD and Hinkel Research Prize, 1967 (Chem.)); MA Cantab 1969; ScD Cantab 1985. CChem, MRSC. Beit Meml Fellow, MRC Lab. of Molecular Biology, Cambridge, 1967–69; Demonstrator in Biochemistry, Univ. of Cambridge, 1969–73; Tutor, New Hall, Cambridge, 1970–76. Mem., EMBO, 1982–. K. M. Stott Research Prize, Newnham Coll., Cambridge, 1976. *Publications:* Companion to Biochemistry: selected topics for further study, vol. 1, 1974, vol. 2, 1979 (ed jtly and contrib.); papers in sci. jls, esp. on histones and chromatin structure. *Recreations:* reading, music, walking. *Address:* Department of Biochemistry, Tennis Court Road, Cambridge CB2 1QW. *T:* Cambridge 333670; New Hall, Huntingdon Road, Cambridge. *T:* Cambridge 351721.

THOMAS, Jeffrey, QC 1974; a Recorder of the Crown Court, since 1975; *b* 12 Nov. 1933; *s* of John James Thomas and Phyllis Thomas (*née* Hile). *Educ:* Abertillery Grammar Sch.; King's Coll. London; Gray's Inn. Called to the Bar, Gray's Inn, 1957. Pres., Univ. of London Union, 1955–56. Served Army (National Service): commnd in Royal Corps of Transport, 1959 (Senior Under Officer); later served in Directorate of Army Legal Services: Major, Dep. Asst Dir, HQ BAOR, 1961. Contested: (Lab) Barry, 1966; (SDP) Cardiff W, 1983. MP (Lab 1970–81, SDP 1981–83) Abertillery, 1970–83; PPS to Sec. of State for Wales, 1977–79; opposition spokesman on legal affairs, 1979–81; SDP spokesman on legal affairs, 1981–83; rejoined Labour Party, 1986–. Chm., Brit. Caribbean Assoc.; Mem. Council, Justice; Vice Chm., British Gp, IPU, 1979–82. Mem. Court, Univ. of London, 1981–. *Recreations:* watching Rugby football, travelling. *Address:* (home) 26 Ellington Street, N7. *T:* 01–609 2440; (chambers) 3 Temple Gardens, Temple, EC4. *T:* 01–583 0010. *Clubs:* Reform; Abertillery Rugby Football.

THOMAS, Jenkin; HM Diplomatic Service; Counsellor (Economic and Commercial), Athens, since 1983; *b* 2 Jan. 1938; *s* of late William John Thomas and of Annie Muriel (*née* Thomas). *Educ:* Maesydderwen Sch.; University Coll. London (BA Hons); Univ. of Michigan, Ann Arbor (MA). Joined HM Foreign (subseq. Diplomatic) Service, 1960; Foreign Office, 1960–63; Pretoria/Cape Town, 1963–66; Saigon, 1966–68; FCO, 1968–73; Washington, 1973–77; FCO, 1977–79; Cabinet Office, 1979–80; Tokyo, 1980–82. *Recreations:* reading, music. *Address:* c/o Foreign and Commonwealth Office, SW1.

THOMAS, Jeremy Cashel, CMG 1980; HM Diplomatic Service; Ambassador to Greece, since 1985; *b* 1 June 1931; *s* of Rev. H. C. Thomas and Margaret Betty (*née* Humby); *m* 1957, Diana Mary Summerhayes; three *s*. *Educ:* Eton; Merton Coll., Oxford. HM Forces, 1949–51; entered FO, 1954; served Singapore, Rome and Belgrade; Dep. Head, Personnel Ops Dept, FCO, 1970–74; Counsellor and Head of Chancery, UK Mission to UN, NY, 1974–76; Head of Perm. Under-Sec.'s Dept, FCO, 1977–79; Ambassador to Luxembourg, 1979–82; Asst Under-Sec. of State, FCO, 1982–85. *Recreations:* sailing, fishing. *Address:* c/o Foreign and Commonwealth Office, SW1. *Clubs:* United Oxford & Cambridge University, Flyfishers'; Oxford and Cambridge Sailing Society, Itchenor Sailing, Royal Yacht Squadron.

THOMAS, (John) Frank (Phillips); Telecommunications Consultant to British Telecom, international industry and commerce; *b* 11 April 1920; *s* of late John and Catherine Myfanwy Phillips Thomas; *m* 1942, Edith V. Milne; one *s* one *d*. *Educ:* Christ's Coll., Finchley; Univ. of London (BSc). CEng, MIEE. Joined Post Office Research Dept, 1937; trans-oceanic telephone cable system develt, 1947–63; planning UK inland telephone network, 1963–69; Dep. Dir London Telephone Region, 1969–71; Dep. Dir Engrg, Network Planning Dept, 1971; Dir, Network Planning Dept, 1972–79; Dir, Overseas Liaison and Consultancy Dept, Post Office, 1979–81. *Publications:* contrib. scientific and technical jls on telecommunications subjects. *Recreations:* fly fishing, automated horticulture. *Address:* 24 Moneyhill Road, Rickmansworth, Herts. *T:* Rickmansworth 772992. *Club:* Rickmansworth Lawn Tennis (Vice-Pres.).

THOMAS, (John) Harvey (Noake); Public Relations Consultant, since 1976; Director of Presentation and Promotion, Conservative Party, since 1986; *b* 10 April 1939; *s* of John Humphrey Kenneth Thomas and Olga Rosina Thomas (*née* Noake); *m* 1978, Marlies (*née* Kram); two *d*. *Educ:* Westminster School; Northwestern Bible College, Minneapolis; Univs of Minnesota and Hawaii. Billy Graham Evangelistic Assoc., 1960–75; Internat. Public Relations and Project Consultant, 1976–; Dir of Press and Communications, Conservative Party, 1985–86. Mem., Bd of Dirs, London Cremation Co., 1984–. MIPR, MJI, ACE. *Publication:* In the Face of Fear, 1985. *Recreations:* travel, reading. *Address:* 105A High Road, N22 6BB. *T:* 01–889 6466. *Club:* Institute of Directors.

THOMAS, Rt. Rev. John James Absalom, DD Lambeth 1958; *b* 17 May 1908; *s* of William David and Martha Thomas; *m* 1941, Elizabeth Louise, *d* of Very Rev. H. L. James, DD, former Dean of Bangor; one *s*. *Educ:* University College of Wales, Aberystwyth; Keble College, Oxford. Curate of Llanguicke, 1931–34; Curate of Sketty, 1934–36; Bishop's Messenger and Examining Chaplain, 1936–40; Warden of Church Hostel, Bangor, and Lecturer in University Coll. of N Wales, 1940–44; Vicar of Swansea, 1945–58, also Chaplain to Bishop of Swansea and Brecon; Canon of Brecon Cathedral, 1946; Precentor, 1952; Rural Dean of Swansea, 1952–54; Archdeacon of Gower, 1954–58; Bishop of Swansea and Brecon, 1958–76. Chm. of Governors, Christ Coll., Brecon, 1961–. Chaplain and Sub-Prelate, Order of St John of Jerusalem, 1965. *Address:* Woodbine Cottage, St Mary Street, Tenby, Dyfed.

See also Rev. David Thomas.

THOMAS, Sir (John) Maldwyn, Kt 1984; President, Liberal Party of Wales, 1985–86; *b* 17 June 1918; *s* of Daniel and Gwladys Thomas; *m* 1975, Maureen Elizabeth. *Educ:* Porth Rhondda Grammar Sch. FCIS. Called to Bar, Gray's Inn, 1953; Solicitor, 1965. Lewis & Tylor Ltd, Cardiff, 1940–56; Signode Ltd, Swansea, 1956–59; Commercial Agreements Manager, UKAEA, 1959–63; Rank Xerox Ltd: Sec., 1964–70; Man. Dir, 1970–72; Chm., 1972–79; Dir, Westland PLC, 1985–. Contested (L) Aberavon, 1950; Prosp. Parly Cand (L) W Flints, 1962–64. Mem. Council, Internat Bd, and Appeals Cttee, Richmond Fellowship, 1984–; Trustee, Venture Trust, 1984–. Vice-Pres., London Welsh Rugby Football Club. *Address:* 9 Chester Terrace, Regent's Park, NW1 4ND. *Club:* Reform.

THOMAS, Prof. John Meurig, MA, PhD, DSc; FRS 1977; Director of the Royal Institution of Great Britain, and Resident Professor and Director of the Davy Faraday Research Laboratory, since 1986; *b* Llanelli, Wales, 15 Dec. 1932; *s* of David John and Edyth Thomas; *m* 1959, Margaret (*née* Edwards); two *d*. *Educ:* Gwendraeth Grammar Sch. (State Scholar); University College of Swansea (Hon. Fellow, 1985); Queen Mary Coll., London. Scientific Officer, UKAEA, 1957–58; Asst Lectr 1958–59, Lectr 1959–65, Reader 1965–69, in Chemistry, UCNW, Bangor; Prof. and Head of Dept of Chemistry, UCW, Aberystwyth, 1969–78; Prof. and Head of Dept of Physical Chemistry, and Fellow of King's Coll., Univ. of Cambridge, 1978–86. Visiting appointments: Tech. Univ. Eindhoven, Holland, 1962; Penna State Univ., USA, 1963, 1967; Tech. Univ. Karlsruhe, Germany, 1966; Weizmann Inst., Israel, 1969; Univ. of Florence, Italy, 1972; Amer. Univ. in Cairo, Egypt, 1973; IBM Res. Center, San José, 1977. Ind. Mem., Radioactive Waste Management Cttee, 1978–80; Member: Chem. Cttee, SRC, 1976–78; Main Cttee, SERC, 1986–; Adv. Cttee, Davy-Faraday Labs, Royal Instn, 1978–80; Scientific Adv. Cttee, Sci. Center, Alexandria, 1979–; ACARD (Cabinet Office), 1982–; Bd of Governors, Weizmann Inst., 1982–. Hon. Visiting Professor: in Physical Chem., QMC, 1986–; of Chem., Imperial Coll., London, 1986–; Academia Sinica, Beijing; Inst. of Ceramic Sci., Shanghai, 1986–. Corday Morgan Silver Medal, Chem. Soc., 1967; first Pettinos Prize, American Carbon Soc., 1969; Tilden Medal and Lectr, Chem. Soc., 1973; Chem. Soc. Prizewinner in Solid State Chem., 1978; Hugo Müller Medal, RSC, 1983. Winegard Vis. Prof., Guelph Univ., 1982; BBC Welsh Radio Annual Lectr, 1978; Gerhardt Schmidt Meml Lectr, Weizmann Inst., 1979; Distinguished Vis. Lectr, London Univ., 1980; Royal Soc.-British Assoc. Lectr, 1980; Baker Lectr, Cornell Univ., 1982–83; Dist. Lectr in Chem., Univ. of Western Ontario, 1983; Sloan Vis. Prof., Harvard, 1983; Dist. Vis. Lectr, Texas A & M, 1984; Salters Lectr, Royal Instn, 1985, 1986; Dist. Vis. Lectr, Univ. of Notre Dame, Indiana, 1986; SCHUIT Lectr, Inst. of Catalysis, Univ. of Delaware, 1986. Hon. Fellow: Indian Acad. of Science, 1980; UMIST, 1984; Foreign Fellow, INA, 1985. Hon. LLD Wales, 1984. *Publications:* (with W. J. Thomas) Introduction to the Principles of Heterogeneous Catalysis, 1967; Pan edrychwyf ar y nefoedd, 1978; numerous articles on solid state and surface chemistry, catalysis and influence of crystalline imperfections, in Proc. Royal Soc., Jl Chem. Soc., etc. *Recreations:* ancient civilizations, bird watching, hill walking, Welsh literature. *Address:* The Royal Institution, 21 Albemarle Street, W1X 4BS.

THOMAS, Sir John S.; *see* Stradling Thomas.

THOMAS, Keith Henry Westcott, CB 1982; OBE 1962; FEng, FRINA, FIIM; RCNC; Chief Executive, Royal Dockyards, 1979–83; *b* 20 May 1923; *s* of Henry and Norah Thomas; *m* 1946, Brenda Jeanette Crofton; two *s*. *Educ:* Portsmouth Southern Secondary Sch.; HM Dockyard Sch., Portsmouth; RNC, Greenwich. Asst Constructor, Admiralty Experiment Works, Haslar, 1947–49; Constructor: Admty, London, 1949–56; Large Carrier Design Section, Admty, Bath, 1956–60; Submarines and New Construction, HM Dockyard, Portsmouth, 1960–63; Project Leader, Special Refit HMS Hermes, Devonport, 1963–66; Dep. Planning Manager, HM Dockyard, Devonport, 1966–68; Project Man., Ikara Leanders, MoD(N), 1968–70; Dir-Gen. of Naval Design, Dept of Navy, Canberra, Aust. (on secondment), 1970–73; Planning Man., 1973–75, Gen. Man., 1975–77, HM Dockyard, Rosyth; Gen. Manager, HM Dockyard, Devonport, 1977–79. *Recreations:* music, lapidary. *Address:* 6 Wyborn Close, Hayling Island, Hants PO11 9HY. *T:* Hayling Island 463435.

THOMAS, Keith Vivian, FBA 1979; President of Corpus Christi College, Oxford, since Oct. 1986; *b* 2 Jan. 1933; *s* of Vivian Jones Thomas and late Hilda Janet Eirene (*née* Davies); *m* 1961, Valerie Little; one *s* one *d*. *Educ:* Barry County Grammar Sch.; Balliol Coll., Oxford (Brackenbury Schol.; 1st Cl. Hons Mod. History, 1955; Hon. Fellow 1984). Senior Scholar, St Antony's Coll., Oxford, 1955; Fellow of All Souls Coll., Oxford, 1955–57; Fellow of St John's Coll., Oxford, 1957–86 (Tutor, 1957–85); Reader in Modern Hist., 1978–85, Prof. in Modern Hist, Jan.–Sept. 1986, Univ. of Oxford. Vis. Professor, Louisiana State Univ., 1970; Vis. Fellow, Princeton Univ., 1978. Joint Literary Director, Royal Historical Soc., 1970–74, Mem. Council, 1975–78, Vice-Pres., 1980–84. Mem., ESRC, 1985–. Delegate, OUP, 1980–. Lectures: Stenton, Univ. of Reading, 1975; Raleigh, British Acad., 1976; Neale, University Coll. London, 1976; G. M. Trevelyan, Univ. of Cambridge, 1978–79; Sir D. Owen Evans, University Coll. of Wales, Aberystwyth, 1980; Kaplan, Univ. of Pennsylvania, 1983; Creighton, Univ. of London, 1983; Ena H. Thompson, Pomona Coll., 1986. For. Hon. Mem., Amer. Acad. of Arts and Scis, 1983. Hon. DLitt Kent, 1983. Gen. Editor, Past Masters Series, OUP, 1979–. *Publications:* Religion and the Decline of Magic, 1971 (Wolfson Lit. Award for History, 1972); Rule and Misrule in the Schools of Early Modern England, 1976; Age and Authority in Early Modern England, 1977; ed (with Donald Pennington), Puritans and Revolutionaries, 1978; Man and the Natural World, 1983; contribs to historical books and jls. *Recreation:* visiting secondhand bookshops. *Address:* Corpus Christi College, Oxford OX1 4JF. *T:* Oxford 249431.

THOMAS, Kenneth Rowland; General Secretary, Civil and Public Services Association, 1976–82; *b* 7 Feb. 1927; *s* of William Rowland Thomas and Anne Thomas; *m* 1955, Nora (*née* Hughes); four *s*. *Educ:* St Joseph's Elementary Sch., Penarth; Penarth Grammar Sch. Trainee Reporter, South Wales Echo and Western Mail, 1943–44; Civil Servant, 1944–54; Asst Sec., Civil and Public Services Assoc., 1955, Dep. Gen. Sec., 1967. Mem., TUC Gen. Council, 1977–82. Member: Occupational Pensions Bd, 1981–; Civil Service Appeal Bd, 1984–; Law Soc. Professional Purposes Cttee, 1984–; Trustee: London Develt Capital Fund, 1984–; British Telecommunications Fund, 1983–; Charity Aid Foundn, 1982–; Director: Postel, 1982–; West Midlands Enterprise Bd, 1982–; Univ. of Warwick Sci. Park, 1986–. *Recreations:* music, anything Welsh. *Address:* Penycoed Hall, Dolgellau, Gwynedd. *T:* Dolgellau 423403.

THOMAS, Leslie John; author; *b* 22 March 1931; *s* of late David James Thomas and late Dorothy Hilda Court Thomas, Newport (Mon); *m* 1st, 1956, Maureen Crane (marr. diss.); two *s* one *d*; 2nd, 1970, Diana Miles; one *s*. *Educ:* Dr Barnardo's, Kingston-upon-Thames; Kingston Technical Sch.; SW Essex Technical Coll., Walthamstow. Local Newspapers, London area, 1948–49 and 1951–53; Army, 1949–51 (rose to Lance-Corporal); Exchange Telegraph News Agency, 1953–55; Special Writer, London Evening News, 1955–66; subseq. author. *Publications: autobiography:* This Time Next Week, 1964; In My Wildest Dreams, 1984; *novels:* The Virgin Soldiers, 1966; Orange Wednesday, 1967; The Love Beach, 1968; Come to the War, 1969; His Lordship, 1970; Onward Virgin Soldiers, 1971; Arthur McCann and All His Women, 1972; The Man with Power, 1973; Tropic of Ruislip, 1974; Stand up Virgin Soldiers, 1975; Dangerous Davies,

1976; Bare Nell, 1977; Ormerod's Landing, 1978; That Old Gang of Mine, 1979; The Magic Army, 1981; The Dearest and the Best, 1984; *non-fiction:* Some Lovely Islands, 1968; The Hidden Places of Britain, 1981; A World of Islands, 1983; TV Plays and Documentaries, etc. *Recreations:* islands, antiques, cricket. *Address:* Greatbridge House, Greatbridge, Romsey, Hants. *Clubs:* Wig and Pen, Lord's Taverners; Press.

THOMAS, (Lewis John) Wynford V.; *see* Vaughan-Thomas.

THOMAS, Sir Maldwyn; *see* Thomas, Sir J. M.

THOMAS, Margaret, Women's International Art Club, 1940; RBA 1947; NEAC 1950; Contemporary Portrait Society, 1970; RWA 1971; Practising Artist (Painter); *b* 26 Sept. 1916; *d* of late Francis Stewart Thomas and of Grace Whetherly. *Educ:* privately; Slade Sch.; RA Schools. Slade Scholar, 1936. Hon. Sec. Artists International Assoc., 1944–45; FRSA 1971. Group exhibitions, Wildensteins, 1946, 1949 and 1962; First one-man show at Leicester Galls, 1949, and subsequently at same gallery, 1950; one-man shows in Edinburgh (Aitken Dotts), 1952, 1955, 1966, and at Outlook Tower, Edinburgh, during Internat. Fest., 1961; RBA Galleries, London, 1953; at Canaletto Gall. (a barge, at Little Venice), 1961; Exhibition of Women Artists, Wakefield Art Gall., 1961; Howard Roberts Gallery Cardiff, 1963, The Minories, Colchester, 1964, QUB, 1967, Mall Galls, London, 1972; Octagon Gall., Belfast, 1973; Court Lodge Gallery, Kent, 1974; Gallery Paton, Edinburgh, 1977; Scottish Gall., Edinburgh, 1982; Regular exhibitor Royal Academy and Royal Scottish Academy. Official purchases: Prince Philip, Duke of Edinburgh; Chantrey Bequest; Arts Council; Exeter College, Oxford; Min. of Education; Min. of Works; Wakefield, Hull, Paisley and Carlisle Art Galleries; Edinburgh City Corporation; Nuffield Foundation Trust; Steel Co. of Wales; Financial Times; Mitsukoshi Ltd, Tokyo; Scottish Nat. Orchestra; Robert Flemming collection; GLC and county education authorities in Yorks, Bucks, Monmouth, Derbyshire, Hampshire and Wales. Coronation painting purchased by Min. of Works for British Embassy in Santiago. Winner, Hunting Gp Award for best oil painting of the year, 1981. *Publications:* work reproduced in: Daily Telegraph, News Chronicle, Listener, Studio, Scottish Field, Music and Musicians, The Lady, Arts Review, Western Mail; Illustrated London News, The Artist. *Recreations:* antique collecting, gardening, vintage cars. *Address:* Ellingham Mill, near Bungay, Suffolk NR35 2EP. *T:* Kirby Cane 656; 8 North Bank Street, Edinburgh EH1 2LP. *T:* 031–225 3343.

THOMAS, Martin, OBE 1982; QC 1979; a Recorder of the Crown Court, since 1976; *b* 13 March 1937; *s* of Hywel and Olwen Thomas; *m* 1961, Nan Thomas (*née* Kerr); three *s* one *d*. *Educ:* Grove Park Grammar Sch., Wrexham; Peterhouse, Cambridge. MA, LLB (Cantab). Solicitor at Wrexham, 1961–66; Lectr in Law, 1966–68; called to the Bar, Gray's Inn, 1967; Barrister, Wales and Chester Circuit, 1968–; Dep. Circuit Judge, 1974–76. Contested (L): W Flints, 1964, 1966, 1970; Wrexham, Feb. and Oct. 1974, 1979, 1983; Vice Chm., Welsh Liberal Party, 1967–69, Chm. 1969–74; President: Wrexham Liberal Assoc., 1975–; Welsh Liberal Party, 1977, 1978, 1979. Vice Chm., Marcher Sound (ind. local radio for NE Wales and Cheshire), 1983–. *Recreations:* Rugby football, rowing, golf, music-making, amateur theatre, fishing. *Address:* Glasfryn, Gresford, Wrexham, Clwyd. *T:* Gresford 2205. *Clubs:* Reform; Western (Glasgow); Wrexham Rugby Football, Bristol Channel Yacht.

THOMAS, (Mary) Elizabeth; Member, Arts Council of Great Britain, since 1984, and Chairman, Planning and Development Board, 1986; *b* 22 March 1935; *d* of Kathleen Mary Thomas (*née* Dodd) and David John Thomas; *m* 1962, Brian Haydn Thomas; two *d*. *Educ:* Dr Williams' School, Dolgellau; Talbot Heath School, Bournemouth; Royal Acad. of Music. ARCM, GRSM. Head of Music, High Sch., Totnes, 1958–61; Music Lectr, Ingestre Hall, Stafford, 1962; Berkshire Music Schs, 1964–66; Adult Educn Lectr, Bridgnorth Coll. of Further Educn, 1966–69. Dir, W Midlands Bd, Central Television plc, 1982–; Chm., Pentabus Arts Ltd, 1983–. Chairman: W Midlands Arts, 1980–84; Council, Regional Arts Assocs, 1982–85; Nat. Assoc. of Local Arts Councils, 1980–82 (Vice-Pres., 1982); Regional Adv. Cttee, Arts Council of GB, 1984–86; Vice-Pres., Playboard, 1984. *Recreations:* collecting antique glass, gardening, string quartet playing. *Address:* Cutters House, 48 Shineton Street, Much Wenlock, Shropshire TF13 6HU. *Club:* Royal Over-Seas League.

THOMAS, Rt. Rev. Maxwell McNee, ThD; Warden of St Paul's College, Sydney, since 1985; Lecturer in History and Thought of Christianity, University of Sydney, since 1986; *b* 23 Aug. 1926; *s* of Rev. Charles Elliot Thomas, ThL, and Elsie Frances Thomas (*née* McNee); *m* 1952, Elaine Joy Walker; two *s* one *d*. *Educ:* St Paul's Coll., Univ. of Sydney (MA, BD); General Theological Seminary, New York (ThD). Lectr in Theology and Greek, St John's Coll, Morpeth, NSW, 1950; deacon, 1950; priest, 1952; Curate: St Peter's, E. Maitland, 1951–52; St Mary Magdalene, Richmond, Surrey, 1952–54; All Saints', Singleton, NSW, 1955. Priest-in-Charge and Rector, The Entrance, NSW, 1955–59; Fellow and Tutor, General Theol. Seminary, NY, 1959–63; Hon. Chaplain to Bishop of New York, 1959–63, Chaplain, 1963–64; Chaplain, Univ. of Melbourne and of Canterbury Fellowship, 1964–68; Consultant Theologian to Archbishop of Melbourne, Stewart Lectr in Divinity, Trinity Coll. and Chaplain of Canterbury Fellowship, 1968–75; Bishop of Wangaratta, 1975–85. Member: Gen. Synod's Commn on Doctrine, 1970– (Chm., 1976–); Faith and Order Commn, WCC, 1977–; Anglican-Orthodox Jt Doctrinal Discussion Gp, 1978. *Address:* St Paul's College, Sydney, NSW 2006, Australia. *Clubs:* Melbourne, Royal Automobile of Victoria; Australian (Sydney).

THOMAS, Melbourne, QPM 1953; Chairman, St John Council, Mid Glamorgan, 1972–80; *b* 1 May 1906; *s* of David and Charlotte Frances Thomas; *m* 1930, Marjorie Elizabeth Phillips; one *d*. *Educ:* Newport (St Julian's) High School. Metropolitan Police, 1928–29; Newport Borough Police, 1929–45 (Dep. Chief Constable, 1941–45); Chief Constable: Merthyr Borough Police, 1945–63; Glamorgan Constabulary, 1963–69; 1st Chief Constable, South Wales Police, 1969–71. Chm., Bd of Governors, Coleg-y-Fro, 1971; Almoner, St John Priory, Wales, 1978. KStJ 1974. *Recreations:* Rugby, cricket, athletics. *Address:* The Lower Flat, Stafford Coach House, Westgate, Cowbridge, South Glamorgan. *T:* Cowbridge 4245.

THOMAS, Sir Michael, 3rd Bt; *see* Thomas, Sir W. M. M.

THOMAS, Sir Michael, 11th Bt; *see* Thomas, Sir G. M. D.

THOMAS, Hon. Michael David, CMG 1985; QC 1973; Attorney-General of Hong Kong, since 1983; Member, Executive and Legislative Councils, Hong Kong, since 1983; *b* 8 Sept. 1933; *s* of late D. Cardigan Thomas and Kathleen Thomas; *m* 1st, 1958, Jane Lena Mary (marr. diss. 1978), *e d* of late Francis Neate; two *s* two *d*; 2nd, 1981, Mrs Gabrielle Blakemore (marr. diss. 1986). *Educ:* Chigwell Sch., Essex; London Sch. of Economics. LLB 1954. Called to Bar, Middle Temple, 1955 (Blackstone Entrance Schol., 1952; Harmsworth Schol., 1957); Bencher, 1981. Nat. Service with RN, Sub-Lt RNVR, 1955–57. In practice at Bar from 1958. Junior Counsel to Minister of Defence (RN) and to Treasury in Admty matters, 1966–73. Wreck Commissioner under Merchant Shipping Act 1970; one of Lloyd's salvage arbitrators. Governor, Chigwell Sch., 1971–83. *Publications:* (ed jtly) Temperley: Merchant Shipping Acts, 6th edn 1963 and 7th edn 1974. *Recreations:* music, travel. *Address:* Attorney-General's Chambers, Queensway Government Office, Hong Kong. *T:* Hong Kong 296061; 2 Essex Court, Temple, EC4Y 9AP. *T:* 01–353 4559. *Clubs:* Garrick; Hong Kong (Hong Kong).

THOMAS, Lt-Col Michael John Glyn, RAMC; Senior Specialist in Pathology, Cambridge Military Hospital, since 1984; *b* 14 Feb. 1938; *s* of Glyn Pritchard Thomas and Mary Thomas (*née* Moseley); *m* 1969, Sheelagh Thorpe; one *d*. *Educ:* Haileybury and ISC; Trinity College, Cambridge; St Bartholomew's Hosp. MA, MB, BChir, LMSSA, DTM&H. Qualified 1962; House Surgeon, Essex County Hosp. and House Physician, St James, Balham, 1963; Regtl MO, 2nd Bn The Parachute Regt, 1965; Trainee Pathologist, BMH Singapore, 1968; Specialist in Pathology, Colchester Mil. Hosp., 1971; Senior Specialist in Pathology, Army Blood Supply Depot, 1977; Exchange Pathologist, Walter Reed Army Inst. of Research, 1982–84. Mem. Council, BMA, 1974–82 (Chm., Junior Mems Forum, 1974–75; Chm., Central Ethical Cttee, 1978–82). *Publications:* contribs to ref. books and jls on Medical Ethics, Haematology and Blood Banking and Malariology. *Recreations:* sailing, travel, photography, philately. *Address:* 4 Christchurch Close, Church Crookham, Aldershot, Hants GU13 0PY. *Club:* Tanglin (Singapore).

THOMAS, Michael Stuart, (Mike Thomas); consultant, information, marketing, public affairs and public relations; *b* 24 May 1944; *s* of Arthur Edward Thomas. *Educ:* Latymer Upper Sch.; King's Sch., Macclesfield; Liverpool Univ. (BA). Pres., Liverpool Univ. Guild of Undergraduates, 1965–66; Past Mem. Nat. Exec., NUS. Head of Research Dept, Co-operative Party, 1966–68; Sen. Res. Officer, Political and Economic Planning (now PSI), 1968–73; Dir, Volunteer Centre, 1973–74. MP (Lab and Co-op 1974–81, SDP 1981–83) Newcastle upon Tyne E, Oct. 1974–1983. Mem., Select Cttee on Nationalised Industries, 1975–79; Chm., PLP Trade Gp, 1979–81; SDP spokesman on health and social services, 1981–83; Member: SDP Nat. Cttee, 1981–; SDP Policy Cttee, 1981–; Chairman: Organisation Cttee of SDP, 1981–; By-election Cttee, SDP, 1984–; Mem., Alliance Strategy Cttee, 1973–. Contested (SDP) Newcastle upon Tyne East, 1983; Prosp. Parly Cand. (SDP) Exeter, 1985–. Mem., USDAW; founder of parly jl The House Magazine. *Publications:* Participation and the Redcliffe Maud Report, 1970; (ed) The BBC Guide to Parliament, 1979, 1983; various PEP pamphlets, contribs, etc, 1971–; various articles, reviews, etc. *Recreations:* theatre, music, cooking, collecting political and historical objects (particularly pottery). *Address:* 3½ London Wall Buildings, EC2M 5SY. *T:* 01–638 9571.

THOMAS, Neville; *see* Thomas, R. N.

THOMAS, Norman, CBE 1980; HM Chief Inspector of Schools, 1973–81; Visiting Professor, North East London Polytechnic, since 1986; *b* 1 June 1921; *s* of Bowen Thomas and Ada Thomas (*née* Redding); *m* 1942, Rose Henshaw; one *s* one *d*. *Educ:* Latymer's Sch., Edmonton; Camden Coll. Qual. Teacher. Commerce and Industry, then primary schs in London and Herts, 1948–56; Head, Longmeadow Sch., Stevenage, 1956–61; HM Inspector of Schools, Lincs and SE England, 1962–68; HMI, Staff Inspector for Primary (Junior and Middle) Schs, 1969–73. Chm., Cttee of Enquiry on Primary Educn in ILEA, 1983–84. Adviser to Parly Cttee on Educn, Science and Art, 1984–. Hon. Prof., Univ. of Warwick, 1986–. *Publications:* articles in professional jls. *Recreations:* photography, reading. *Address:* 19 Langley Way, Watford, Herts WD1 3EJ.

THOMAS, Patricia Anne; Commissioner for Local Administration in England, since 1985; *b* 3 April 1940; *d* of Frederick S. Lofts and Ann Elizabeth Lofts; *m* 1968, Joseph Glyn Thomas; one *s* two *d*. *Educ:* King's College London. LLB, LLM. Lectr in Law, Univ. of Leeds, 1962–63, 1964–68; Teaching Fellow, Univ. of Illinois, 1963–64; Sen. Lectr, then Principal Lectr, Head of Sch. of Law and Prof., Lancashire Polytechnic, 1973–85. Mem., 1976–84, Vice-Pres., 1984, Pres., 1985, Greater Manchester and Lancashire Rent Assessment Panel; Chm., Blackpool Supplementary Benefit Appeal Tribunal, 1980–85. *Publication:* Law of Evidence, 1972. *Recreations:* walking, cooking, reading, travel. *Address:* Greenbank Farm, Over Kellet, Carnforth, Lancs LA6 1BS. *T:* Carnforth 733296.

THOMAS, Sir Patrick (Muirhead), Kt 1974; DSO 1945; TD 1945; DL; *b* 31 Jan. 1914; *s* of Herbert James Thomas, Barrister-at-Law and Charis Thomas (*née* Muirhead); *m* 1939, Ethel Mary Lawrence; one *s* three *d*. *Educ:* Clifton Coll.; Corpus Christi Coll., Cambridge (MA). FInstT. Served War of 1939–45, France, N Africa, Italy, Greece, Middle East, Austria; Lt-Col comdg 71st Field Regt RA, 1944–45. Steel Industry, United Steel Cos and Arthur Balfour & Co. Ltd, Sheffield, 1935–39; Wm Beardmore & Co. Ltd, Parkhead Steelworks, Glasgow, 1946: Man. Dir, 1954; Dir, 1967–76. Hon. Vice-Pres., Iron and Steel Inst., 1968. Col Comdt, City of Glasgow Army Cadet Force, 1956 (Hon. Col 1963–70, 1977–84). Pres., FBI Scottish Council, 1961–62; Pres., Scottish Engrg Employers' Assoc., 1967–68; Chm., Scottish Transport Gp, 1968–77; Part-time Mem., Scottish Gas Board, 1966–72; Director: Brightside Engrg Holdings Ltd, 1967–71; Midland Caledonian Investment Trust Ltd, 1972–75. Chm., Scottish Opera, 1976–81 (Dir, 1965–81); Member: Court, Univ. of Strathclyde, 1967– (Chm., 1970–75); Lloyd's Register of Shipping Scottish Cttee, 1967–81; Panel Mem., Industrial Tribunals, 1967–80; Deacon Convener, Trades of Glasgow, 1970–71; Member: Exec. Cttee, Officers Assoc. (Scotland), 1964–75, 1978–; Exec. Cttee, Earl Haig Fund (Scotland), 1964–75, 1978–84 (Chm., 1981–84; Vice-Pres., 1984–); Artillery Council for Scotland, 1978–84; Chairman: Lady Haig's Poppy Factory, 1967–72; Royal Artillery Assoc. (Scottish Region), 1978–83. Governor, Clifton Coll., 1979–. DL Renfrewshire, 1980. Hon. LLD Strathclyde, 1973. US Bronze Star, 1945. OStJ 1970. *Recreations:* golf, gardening. *Address:* Bemersyde, Kilmacolm, Renfrewshire PA13 4EA. *T:* Kilmacolm 2710.

THOMAS, Rt. Hon. Peter John Mitchell, PC 1964; QC 1965; MP (C) Hendon South, since 1970; a Recorder of the Crown Court, since 1974; *b* 31 July 1920; *o s* of late David Thomas, Solicitor, Llanrwst, Denbighshire, and Anne Gwendoline Mitchell; *m* 1947, Frances Elizabeth Tessa (*d* 1985), *o d* of late Basil Dean, CBE and Lady Mercy Greville; two *s* two *d*. *Educ:* Epworth College, Rhyl; Jesus College, Oxford (MA). Served War of 1939–45, in RAF; Prisoner of War (Germany), 1941–45. Called to Bar, 1947, Middle Temple, Bencher, 1971, Member of Wales and Chester Circuit. MP (C) Conway Div. of Caernarvonshire, 1951–66; PPS to the Solicitor-General, 1954–59; Parly Secretary, Min. of Labour, 1959–61; Parly Under-Sec. of State, Foreign Office, 1961–63; Minister of State for Foreign Affairs, 1963–64; Opp. Front Bench Spokesman on Foreign Affairs and Law, 1964–66; Sec. of State for Wales, 1970–74. Chm., Cons. Party Organisation, 1970–72. Pres., Nat. Union of Conservative and Unionist Assocs, 1974 and 1975. Dep. Chairman: Cheshire QS, 1966–70; Denbighshire QS, 1968–70. Member, Historic Buildings Council for Wales, 1965–67. *Address:* 37 Chester Way, SE11. *T:* 01–735 6047; Millicent Cottage, Elstead, Surrey. *Clubs:* Carlton; Cardiff and County (Cardiff).

THOMAS, Quentin Jeremy; Assistant Under Secretary of State, Broadcasting Department, Home Office, since 1984; *b* 1 Aug. 1944; *s* of late Arthur Albert Thomas and Edith Kathleen Thomas (*née* Bigg); *m* 1969, Anabel Jane, *d* of J. H. Humphreys, *qv*; one *s* two *d*. *Educ:* Perse School, Cambridge; Gonville and Caius College, Cambridge. Home Office, 1966; Private Sec. to Perm. Under-Sec. of State, 1970; Crime Policy Planning Unit, 1974–76; Sec. to Royal Commn on Gambling, 1976–78; Civil Service (Nuffield and Leverhulme) Travelling Fellowship, 1980–81. *Address:* Home Office, 50 Queen Anne's Gate, SW1. *T:* 01–213 3000.

THOMAS, Ralph Philip, MC 1942; Film Director; *b* Hull, Yorks, 10 Aug.; *m* 1944, Joy Spanjer; one *s* one *d. Educ:* Tellisford School, Clifton. Entered film industry, 1932, and worked in all production depts, particularly editing, until 1939. Served War of 1939–45, as Regimental Officer 9th Lancers until 1944; thereafter Instructor Royal Military College. Returned to Film Industry, in Rank Organisation Trailer Dept, 1946; Joined Gainsborough Pictures, 1948, and directed Once Upon a Dream, Traveller's Joy. Films directed at Pinewood Studios: The Clouded Yellow, Appointment with Venus, The Venetian Bird, A Day to Remember, Doctor in the House, Mad About Men, Above Us The Waves, Doctor at Sea, The Iron Petticoat, Checkpoint, Doctor at Large, Campbell's Kingdom, A Tale of Two Cities, The Wind Cannot Read, The 39 Steps, Upstairs and Downstairs, Conspiracy of Hearts, Doctor in Love, No My Darling Daughter, No Love for Johnnie, The Wild and the Willing, Doctor in Distress, Hot enough for June, The High Bright Sun, Doctor in Clover, Deadlier than the Male, Nobody Runs Forever, Some Girls Do, Doctor in Trouble, Quest, Percy, It's a 2 foot 6 inch Above the Ground World, Percy's Progress, A Nightingale Sang in Berkeley Square, Doctors' Daughters, Pop Pirates. *Address:* 20 Hyde Park Gardens Mews, W2. *Club:* Garrick.

THOMAS, Dr Reginald; Austrian Ambassador to the Court of St James's, since 1982; *b* 28 Feb. 1928; *s* of Dr Leopold Thomas and Irma Thomas (*née* von Smekal); *m* 1960, Ingrid Renate Leitner; three *s* one *d. Educ:* Univ. of Vienna (Dr jur 1950). Entered Austrian Foreign Service, 1951; Austrian Legation, Bern, 1952–56; Dep. Legal Adviser on Internat. Law, Min. of Foreign Affairs, Vienna, 1956–59; Austrian Embassy, Tokyo, 1959–62; Head of Office of Sec. Gen. for Foreign Affairs, Vienna, 1962–68; Ambassador to Pakistan and concurrently accredited to Union of Burma, 1968–71; Ambassador to Japan and concurrently accredited to Republic of Korea, 1971–75; Head of Dept of Administration, Min. of Foreign Affairs, Vienna, 1975–82; concurrently Dep. Sec. Gen. for Foreign Affairs, Vienna, 1978–82. Mem., Austrian Assoc. for Foreign Policy and Internat. Relations, Vienna, 1978–82. Foreign orders include: Grand Cross: Order of the Rising Sun (Japan); Order of Diplomatic Service (Korea); Independence Order (Jordan); Order of F. de Miranda (Venezuela); Hilal-i-Qaid-i-Azam (Pakistan). *Recreation:* sports. *Address:* 18 Belgrave Square, SW1. *T:* 01–235 3731. *Clubs:* Travellers', Hurlingham, Queen's.

THOMAS, Lt-Col Reginald Silvers W.; *see* Williams-Thomas.

THOMAS, Richard; HM Diplomatic Service; Overseas Inspector, since 1986; *b* 1938; *s* of Anthony Hugh Thomas and Molly Thomas, MBE; *m* 1966, Catherine Jane Hayes, Sydney, NSW; one *s* two *d. Educ:* Leighton Park; Merton Coll., Oxford (MA). Nat. Service, 2nd Lt, RASC, 1959–61. Asst Principal, CRO, 1961; Private Sec. to Parly Under Sec., 1962–63; Second Secretary: Accra, 1963–65; Lomé, 1965–66; (later First Sec.) UK Delegn NATO, Paris and Brussels, 1966–69; First Secretary: FCO, 1969–72; (Economic), New Delhi, 1972–75; and Asst Head of Dept, FCO, 1976–78; FCO Visiting Res. Fellow, RIIA, 1978–79; Counsellor, Prague, 1979–83; Ambassador, Iceland, 1983–86. *Publication:* India's Emergence as an Industrial Power: Middle Eastern Contracts, 1982. *Recreations:* music, mountains, gardening, skiing. *Address:* c/o Foreign and Commonwealth Office, SW1A 2AH. *Club:* Royal Commonwealth Society.

THOMAS, Sir Robert (Evan), Kt 1967; DL, JP; Leader, Greater Manchester Metropolitan County Council, 1973–77; Deputy Chairman, Manchester Ship Canal, 1971–74; *b* 8 Oct. 1901; *s* of Jesse and Anne Thomas; *m* 1924, Edna Isherwood; one *s* one *d. Educ:* St Peter's, Leigh, Lancs. Miner, 1914; served Army, 1919–21; Bus Driver, 1924–37; Trade Union Official, 1937–66; Member, Manchester City Council, 1944–74; Lord Mayor of Manchester, 1962–63. Chairman: Assoc. of Municipal Corps, 1973–74; Assoc. of Metropolitan Authorities, 1974–77; British Sector, Internat. Union of Local Authorities, 1974–77. JP Manchester, 1948; DL: County Palatine of Lancaster, 1967–73, County Palatine of Greater Manchester, 1974. Hon. MA Manchester, 1974. *Recreations:* dancing, gardening, golf. *Address:* 29 Milwain Road, Manchester M19 2PX. *T:* 061–224 5778.

THOMAS, (Robert) Neville, QC 1975; barrister-at-law; a Recorder of the Crown Court, 1975–82; *b* 31 March 1936; *s* of Robert Derfel Thomas and Enid Anne Thomas; *m* 1970, Jennifer Anne Brownrigg; one *s* one *d. Educ:* Ruthin Sch.; University Coll., Oxford (MA, BCL). Called to Bar, Inner Temple, 1962, Bencher, 1985. *Recreations:* fishing, walking, reading. *Address:* Glansevern, Berriew, Welshpool, Powys SY21 8AH. *Club:* Garrick.

THOMAS, Dr Roger Gareth; MP (Lab) Carmarthen, since 1979; Family Medical Practitioner, since 1952; *b* 14 Nov. 1925; *m* 1958, Indeg Thomas; one *s* one *d. Educ:* Amman Valley Grammar Sch.; London Hosp. Med. Coll. Captain, RAMC, 1949–52. *Recreation:* music. *Address:* Ffynnon Wên, Capel Hendre, Ammanford, Dyfed SA18 3SD. *T:* Cross Hands 843093.

THOMAS, Roger John Laugharne; QC 1984; *b* 22 Oct. 1947; *s* of Roger Edward Laugharne Thomas and Dinah Agnes Thomas; *m* 1973, Elizabeth Ann Buchanan; one *s* one *d. Educ:* Rugby School; Trinity Hall, Cambridge (BA); Univ. of Chicago (Commonwealth Fellow; JD). Called to Bar, Gray's Inn, 1969. Asst Teacher, Mayo College, Ajmer, India, 1965–66. *Publications:* papers and articles on maritime and insurance law. *Recreations:* gardens, opera, walking, travel. *Address:* 4 Essex Court, Temple, EC4. *T:* 01–583 9191.

THOMAS, Roger Lloyd; Senior Clerk (Acting), Committee Office, House of Commons, 1979–84 and Clerk, Select Committee on Welsh Affairs, 1982–84, retired; *b* 7 Feb. 1919; *er s* of Trevor John Thomas and Eleanor Maud (*née* Jones), Abercarn, Mon; *m* 1945, Stella Mary, *d* of Reginald Ernest Willmett, Newport, Mon; three *s* one *d. Educ:* Barry County Sch.; Magdalen Coll., Oxford (Doncaster Schol.; Heath Harrison Trav. Schol.). BA 2nd Mod. Langs, 1939; MA 1946. Served 1939–46, RA and Gen. Staff (Major GSO2) in India, Middle East, N Africa, Italy and Germany. Civil Servant, 1948–70: Min. of Fuel and Power, Home Office, Treasury, Welsh Office and Min. of Housing and Local Govt; Private Sec. to Perm. Under-Sec. of State, Home Office, 1950 and to successive Parly Under-Secs of State, 1951–53; Sec., Interdeptl Cttee on powers of Subpoena, 1960; Asst Sec., 1963; Sec., Aberfan Inquiry Tribunal, 1966–67; Chm., Working Party on Building by Direct Labour Organisations, 1968–69; Gen. Manager, The Housing Corporation, 1970–73; Asst Sec., DoE, 1974–79. *Publications:* sundry reports. *Recreation:* growing flowers. *Address:* 5 Park Avenue, Caterham, Surrey CR3 6AH. *T:* Caterham 42080. *Club:* Union (Oxford).

See also D. H. P. Thomas.

THOMAS, Ronald Richard; *b* March 1929. *Educ:* Ruskin Coll. and Balliol Coll., Oxford (MA). Sen. Lectr, Econ. and Indust. Studies, Univ. of Bristol. Contested (Lab) Bristol North-West, Feb. 1974; MP (Lab) Bristol NW, Oct. 1974–1979. Former Mem., Bristol DC. Mem. ASTMS. *Address:* 64 Morris Road, Lockleaze, Bristol BS7 9TA.

THOMAS, Rev. Ronald Stuart; poet; *b* 29 March 1913; *m* Mildred E. Eldridge; one *s. Educ:* University of Wales (BA); St Michael's College, Llandaff. Ordained deacon, 1936; priest, 1937. Curate of Chirk, 1936–40; Curate of Hanmer, in charge of Talarn Green, 1940–42; Rector of Manafon, 1942–54; Vicar of Eglwysfach, 1954–67; Vicar of St Hywyn, Aberdaron, with St Mary, Bodferin, 1967–78, and Rector of Rhiw with Llanfaelrhys, 1972–78. First record, reading his own poems, 1977. Queen's Gold Medal for Poetry, 1964; Cholmondeley Award, 1978. *Publications:* poems: Stones of the Field (privately printed), 1947; Song at the Year's Turning, 1955 (Heinemann Award of the Royal Society of Literature, 1956); Poetry for Supper, 1958; Tares, 1961; Bread of Truth, 1963; Pieta, 1966; Not That He Brought Flowers, 1968; H'm, 1972; Selected Poems 1946–1968, 1974; Laboratories of the Spirit, 1976; Frequencies, 1978; Between Here and Now, 1981; Later Poems 1972–1982, 1983; Experimenting with an Amen, 1986; edited A Book of Country Verse, 1961; George Herbert, A Choice of Verse, 1967; A Choice of Wordsworth's Verse, 1971. *Address:* Sarn-y-Plas, Y Rhiw, Pwllheli, Gwynedd.

THOMAS, Roydon Urquhart; QC 1985; a Recorder, since 1986; *b* 17 May 1936; *s* of Rowland Daniel Thomas and Jean Milne Thomas; *m* 1984, Caroline; one *s* one *d* (and one *s* decd). *Educ:* Fettes College; Sidney Sussex College, Cambridge (BA). Called to the Bar, Middle Temple, 1960; South Eastern Circuit. *Publication:* (Asst Editor) Tolstoy on Divorce, 1964. *Recreations:* golf, fishing. *Address:* 1 Essex Court, Temple, EC4Y 9AR. *T:* 01–353 5362. *Club:* Hurlingham.

THOMAS, Hon. Sir Swinton (Barclay), Kt 1985; **Hon. Mr Justice Swinton Thomas;** a Judge of the High Court of Justice, Family Division, since 1985; Presiding Judge, Western Circuit, since 1987; *b* 12 Jan. 1931; *s* of late Brig. William Bain Thomas, CBE, DSO, and Mary Georgina Thomas; *m* 1967, Angela, Lady Cope; one *s* one *d. Educ:* Ampleforth Coll.; Lincoln Coll., Oxford (Scholar) (MA). Served with Cameronians (Scottish Rifles), 1950–51, Lieut. Called to Bar, Inner Temple, 1955 (Bencher, 1983); QC 1975; a Recorder of the Crown Court, 1975–85. Member: General Council of the Bar, 1970–74; Criminal Injuries Compensation Bd, 1984–85. *Recreations:* reading, travel. *Address:* 36 Sheffield Terrace, W8. *T:* 01–727 2923. *Club:* Garrick.

THOMAS, Terry; *see* Terry-Thomas.

THOMAS, Trevor, BA; artist, author; retired; *b* 8 June 1907; 2nd *s* of William Thomas and Mary Richards; *m* 1947; two *s. Educ:* Sir Alfred Jones Scholar, University Coll. of Wales, Aberystwyth. Demonstrator, Dept of Geography and Anthropology, University Coll. of Wales, Aberystwyth, 1929–30; Secretary and Lecturer-Assistant, Department of Geography, Victoria University, Manchester, 1930–31; Cartographer to Geographical Association, Manchester, 1930–31; Keeper, Departments of Ethnology and Shipping, Liverpool Public Museums, 1931–40; Rockefeller Foundation Museums Fellow, USA, 1938–39; Director, Museum and Art Gallery, Leicester, 1940–46; Surveyor, Regional Guide to Works of Art, Arts Council of Great Britain, 1946–48; Designer of Exhibitions for the British Institute of Adult Education, 1946–48; Director, Crafts Centre of Great Britain, 1947–48; Programme Specialist for Education through the Arts, UNESCO, Paris, 1949–56; Visiting Prof. of Art Education, Teachers' Coll., Columbia Univ., NY, USA, 1956; Prof. of Art, State Univ. of New York, College for Teachers, Buffalo, 1957–58; Prof. of Art Hist., University of Buffalo, and Art Critic, Buffalo Evening News, 1959–60; Art Editor, Gordon Fraser Gall. Ltd, 1960–72. Mem. Exec. Cttee, Campaign for Homosexual Equality, 1976–78, 1979–82; Hon. Sec., Gaydaid, 1980–; Hon. Mem., United Soc. of Artists, 1980–. *Publications:* Penny Plain Twopence Coloured: the Aesthetics of Museum Display (Museums Jl, April 1939); Educations and Art: a Symposium (jt Editor with Edwin Ziegfeld), Unesco, 1953; Creating with Paper: basic forms and variations (Foreword and associate writer with Pauline Johnson), 1958; contribs to: Museums Journal, Dec. 1933, April 1935, April 1939, Oct. 1941; Parnassus, Jan. and April 1940; Unesco Educn Abstracts, Feb. 1953. *Recreations:* art, music, theatre, gardening. Research: Art. *Address:* 36 Pembroke Street, Bedford MK40 3RH. *T:* Bedford 58879.

THOMAS, Maj.-Gen. Walter Babington, CB 1971; DSO 1943; MC and Bar, 1942; Commander, HQ Far East Land Forces, Nov. 1970–Nov. 1971 (Chief of Staff, April–Oct. 1970); retired Jan. 1972; *b* Nelson, NZ, 29 June 1919; *s* of Walter Harington Thomas, Farmer; *m* 1947, Iredale Edith Lauchlan (*née* Trent); three *d. Educ:* Motueka Dist High Sch., Nelson, NZ. Clerk, Bank of New Zealand, 1936–39. Served War of 1939–45 (despatches, MC and Bar, DSO): 2nd NZEF, 1940–46, in Greece, Crete, Western Desert, Tunis and Italy; Comd 23 (NZ) Bn, 1944–45; Comd 22 (NZ) Bn, in Japan, 1946; transf. to Brit. Army, Royal Hampshire Regt, 1947; Bde Major, 39 Inf. Bde Gp, 1953–55 (despatches); GSO2, UK JSLS, Aust., 1958–60; AA&QMG, HQ 1 Div. BAOR, 1962–64; Comd 12 Inf. Bde Gp, 1964–66; IDC, 1967; GOC 5th Div., 1968–70. Silver Star, Medal, 1945 (USA). *Publications:* Dare to be Free, 1951; Touch of Pitch, 1956. *Recreation:* riding. *Address:* Kerry Road, M/S 413, Beaudesert, Qld 4285, Australia.

THOMAS, Sir William James Cooper, 2nd Bt, *cr* 1919; TD; JP; DL; Captain RA; *b* 7 May 1919; *er s* of Sir William James Thomas, 1st Bt, and Maud Mary Cooper, Bexhill-on-Sea; *S* father 1945; *m* 1947, Freida Dunbar, *yr d* of late F. A. Whyte; two *s* one *d. Educ:* Harrow; Downing Coll., Cambridge. Barrister, Inner Temple, 1948. Member TA, 1938. Served War of 1939–45. Monmouthshire: JP 1958; DL 1973; High Sheriff, 1973. *Heir: s* William Michael Thomas, *b* 5 Dec. 1948. *Address:* Tump House, Llanrothal, Monmouth, Gwent. *T:* Monmouth 2757. *Club:* Army and Navy.

THOMAS, Ven. William Jordison; Archdeacon of Northumberland, since 1983; *b* 16 Dec. 1927; *s* of Henry William and Dorothy Newton Thomas; *m* 1954, Kathleen Jeffrey Robson, *d* of William Robson, Reaveley, Powburn, Alnwick. *Educ:* Holmwood Prep. School, Middlesbrough; Acklam Hall Grammar School, Middlesbrough; Giggleswick School; King's Coll., Cambridge (BA 1951, MA 1955); Cuddesdon College. National Service, RN, 1946–48. Assistant Curate: St Anthony of Egypt, Newcastle upon Tyne, 1953–56; Berwick Parish Church, 1956–59; Vicar: Alwinton with Holystone and Alnham and the Lordship of Kidland, 1959–70; Alston with Garrigill, Nenthead and Kirkhaugh, 1970–80; i/c Knaresdale, 1973–80; Team Rector of Glendale, 1980–82; RD of Bamburgh and Glendale, 1980–82. *Recreations:* sailing own dinghy and other people's yachts, making pictures, travelling and making magic. *Address:* 80 Moorside North, Fenham, Newcastle upon Tyne NE4 9DU. *T:* Tyneside 2738245. *Club:* Victory Ex-Services.

THOMAS, Sir (William) Michael (Marsh), 3rd Bt *cr* 1918; *b* 4 Dec. 1930; *s* of Sir William Eustace Rhyddlad Thomas, 2nd Bt, and Enid Helena Marsh; *S* father 1957; *m* 1957, Geraldine Mary, *d* of Robert Drysdale, Anglesey; three *d. Educ:* Oundle School, Northants. Formerly Man. Dir, Gors Nurseries Ltd. *Address:* Belan, Rhosneigr, Gwynedd LL64 5JE.

THOMAS, Rear-Adm. William Richard Scott, OBE 1974; Deputy Supreme Allied Commander Atlantic, from April 1987, in the rank of Vice-Admiral; *b* 22 March 1932; *s* of late Comdr William Scott Thomas, DSC, RN and of Mary Hilda Bertha Hemelryk, Findon, Sussex; *m* 1959, Patricia (Paddy) Margaret, *d* of late Dr and Mrs J. H. Cullinan, Fressingfield, Suffolk; three *s* four *d* (and one *s* decd). *Educ:* Penryn Sch., Ross-on-Wye; Downside Sch., Bath. psc 1963, jssc 1966, rcds 1979. Midshipman, 1951–52; Sub-Lt and Lieut, 1953–62 (CO HM Ships Buttress, Wolverton and Greetham); CO HMS Troubridge, 1966–68; Staff Officer Ops to Flag Officer First Flotilla and Flag Officer Scotland and NI, 1970–74; Directorate of Naval Plans, MoD, 1974–77; CO HMS Fearless, 1977–78; Dir of Office Appts (Seamen), 1980–83; Naval Sec., 1983–85; Flag

Officer Second Flotilla, 1985–86. *Recreations:* family, gardening. *Address:* Holmwood House, King Street, Emsworth, Hants PO10 7AZ. *T:* Emsworth 372986.

THOMAS, Wyndham, CBE 1982; Chairman, Inner City Enterprises, since 1983; *b* 1 Feb. 1924; *s* of Robert John Thomas and Hannah Mary; *m* 1947, Elizabeth Terry Hopkin; one *s* three *d. Educ:* Maesteg Grammar School. Served Army (Lieut, Royal Welch Fusiliers), 1943–47. Schoolmaster, 1950–53; Director, Town and Country Planning Association, 1955–67; Gen. Manager, Peterborough New Town Develt Corp., 1968–83. Member: Land Commission, 1967–68; Commission for the New Towns, 1964–68; Property Adv. Gp, DoE, 1975–; London Docklands Develt Corp., 1981–. Mayor of Hemel Hempstead, 1958–59. Hon. MRTPI 1979. Officer of the Order of Orange-Nassau (Netherlands), 1982. *Publications:* many articles on town planning, housing, etc, in learned jls. *Recreations:* collecting old furniture, work, golf. *Address:* 8 Westwood Park Road, Peterborough. *T:* Peterborough 64399.

THOMAS, Wynford V.; *see* Vaughan-Thomas.

THOMASON, Prof. George Frederick, CBE 1983; Montague Burton Professor of Industrial Relations, University College, Cardiff, 1969–85, now Emeritus; *b* 27 Nov. 1927; *s* of George Frederick Thomason and Eva Elizabeth (*née* Walker); *m* 1953, Jean Elizabeth Horsley; one *s* one *d. Educ:* Kelsick Grammar Sch.; Univ. of Sheffield (BA); Univ. of Toronto (MA); PhD (Wales). CIPM, FBIM. University College, Cardiff: Research Asst, 1953; Asst Lectr, 1954; Research Associate, 1956; Lectr, 1959; Asst Man. Dir, Flex Fasteners Ltd, Rhondda, 1960; University College, Cardiff: Lectr, 1962; Sen. Lectr, 1963; Reader, 1969; Dean, Faculty of Economics, 1971–73; Dep. Principal (Humanities), 1974–77. Member: Doctors' and Dentists' Pay Review Body, 1979–; Pay Rev. Body for Nurses, Midwives, Health Service Visitors and Professions allied to Medicine, 1983–. *Publications:* Welsh Society in Transition, 1963; Personnel Manager's Guide to Job Evaluation, 1968; Professional Approach to Community Work, 1969; The Management of Research and Development, 1970; Improving the Quality of Organization, 1973; Textbook of Personnel Management, 1975, 4th edn 1981; Job Evaluation: Objectives and Methods, 1980; Textbook of Industrial Relations Management, 1984. *Recreation:* gardening. *Address:* Ty Gwyn, 149 Lake Road West, Cardiff CF2 5PJ. *T:* Cardiff 754236. *Clubs:* Athenæum; Cardiff and County (Cardiff).

THOMPSON, Alan, CB 1978; Chairman, Review Group on the Youth Service; *b* 16 July 1920; *s* of Herbert and Esther Thompson; *m* 1944, Joyce Nora Banks; two *s* one *d. Educ:* Carlisle Grammar Sch.; Queen's Coll., Oxford. Joined Min. of Education, 1946; Private Sec. to Minister of Education, 1954–56; Asst Sec., Further Education Br., 1956–64; Under Sec., UGC, 1964–71; Under Sec., Science Br., DES, 1971–75; Dep. Sec., DES, 1975–80. *Address:* 1 Drax Avenue, Wimbledon, SW20. *T:* 01–946 1837.

THOMPSON, Prof. Alan Eric; Professor of the Economics of Government, Heriot-Watt University, since 1972; *b* 16 Sept. 1924; *o c* of late Eric Joseph Thompson and of Florence Thompson; *m* 1960, Mary Heather Long; three *s* one *d. Educ:* University of Edinburgh (MA 1949, MA (Hons Class I, Economic Science), 1951, PhD 1953, Carnegie Research Scholar, 1951–52). Served army (including service with Central Mediterranean Forces), World War II. Asst in Political Economy, 1952–53, Lectr in Economics (formerly Political Economy), 1953–59, and 1964–71, Univ. of Edinburgh. Parly Adviser to Scottish Television, 1966–76; Scottish Governor, BBC, 1976–79. Visiting Professor, Graduate School of Business, Stanford Univ., USA, 1966, 1968. Contested (Lab) Galloway, 1950 and 1951; MP (Lab) Dunfermline, 1959–64. Mem., Speaker's Parly Delegn to USA, 1962. Chm., Adv. Bd on Economics Educn (Esmée Fairbairn Research Project), 1970–76; Jt Chm., Scottish-Soviet Co-ordinating Cttee for Trade and Industry, 1985–; Member: Scottish Cttee, Public Schools Commn, 1969–70; Cttee enquiring into conditions of service life for young servicemen, 1969; Scottish Council for Adult Educn in HM Forces, 1973–; Jt Mil. Educn Cttee, Edinburgh and Heriot-Watt Univs, 1975–; Local Govt Boundary Commn for Scotland, 1975–82; Royal Fine Art Commn for Scotland, 1975–80; Chm., Northern Offshore (Maritime) Resources Study, 1974–77; Chm., Edinburgh Cttee, Peace Through NATO, 1984–. Parly Adviser, Pharmaceutical Gen. Council (Scotland), 1984–. Hon. Vice-Pres., Assoc. of Nazi War Camp Survivors, 1960–; Pres., Edinburgh Amenity and Transport Assoc., 1970–75. Chm. of Governors, Newbattle Abbey Coll., 1980–82 (Governor, 1975–82); Governor, Leith Nautical Coll., 1981–; Trustee, Bell's Nautical Trust, 1981–. Has broadcast and appeared on TV (economic and political talks and discussions) in Britain and USA. FRSA 1972. *Publications:* Development of Economic Doctrine (jtly), 1980; contribs to learned journals. *Recreations:* writing children's stories and plays, bridge, croquet. *Address:* 11 Upper Gray Street, Edinburgh EH9 1SN. *T:* 031–667 2140; Ardtrostan Cottage, St Fillans, Perthshire. *T:* St Fillans 275. *Clubs:* New, Edinburgh University Staff (Edinburgh); Loch Earn Sailing.

THOMPSON, Anthony Arthur Richard; QC 1980; a Recorder, since 1985; *b* 4 July 1932; *s* of late William Frank McGregor Thompson and of Doris Louise Thompson (*née* Hill); *m* 1958, Françoise Alix Marie Reynier; two *s* one *d* (and one *s* decd). *Educ:* Latymer; University Coll., Oxford; La Sorbonne. Called to the Bar, Inner Temple, 1957, Bencher, 1986. Chm., Bar European Gp, 1984–86 (Vice-Chm., 1982–84); Mem., Internat. Relations Cttee, Bar Council, 1984–. QC, St Vincent and the Grenadines, 1986. Contested (Lab) Arundel and Shoreham, Oct. 1964. *Recreations:* food and wine, lawn tennis, squash. *Address:* 1 Essex Court, Temple, EC4. *T:* 01–353 5362. *Club:* Roehampton.

THOMPSON, Aubrey Gordon D.; *see* Denton-Thompson.

THOMPSON, Brenda, (Mrs Gordon Thompson); writer on education; *b* 27 Jan. 1935; *d* of Thomas Barnes Houghton and Marjorie Houghton; *m* 1956, Gordon Thompson; one *s. Educ:* Leeds Univ. BSc Hons in Biochemistry. Food chemist with J. Lyons & Co., 1957; Hosp. Biochemist, Chelsea Women's Hosp., 1958–60. Entered primary school teaching, 1964; Head Teacher, Northwold I (Primary) Sch., 1971–78, Stamford Hill Sch., 1978–81. Mem., Press Council, 1973–76. Indep. Councillor for London Borough of Islington, 1968–71. *Publications:* Learning to Read, 1970; Learning to Teach, 1973; The Pre-School Book, 1976; Reading Success, 1979; Editor various children's books. *Address:* Nantddu, Rhandirmwyn, Llandovery, Dyfed SA20 0NG. *T:* Llandovery 20159.

THOMPSON, Charles; HM Diplomatic Service; High Commissioner to Kiribati, since 1983; *b* 20 March 1930; *s* of Walter Thompson and Irene Thompson; *m* 1st, 1956, Claudia Hilpern; 2nd, 1977, Maria Anna Kalderimis. *Educ:* Harrison Jones School, Liverpool. GPO, 1944–55; entered Foreign (later Diplomatic) Service, 1955; served Rome, Washington, Tokyo, Leopoldvile (late Kinshasa), 1956–68; FCO, 1968–71; Second Sec., Rangoon, 1972–74; Second Sec. (Commercial), Wellington, 1974–79; Second (later First) Sec., FCO, 1980–83. *Recreations:* music, reading, travel, real ale. *Address:* c/o Foreign and Commonwealth Office, SW1. *Club:* Civil Service.

THOMPSON, Charles Allister; HM Diplomatic Service, retired; *b* 21 July 1922; *yr s* of late Herbert Ivie and Margaret (*née* Browne-Webber) Thompson, Managua, Nicaragua; *m* 1950, Jean Margaret, *er d* of late Alexander Bruce Dickson; two *s* two *d. Educ:* Haileybury; Hertford Coll., Oxford (MA, BLitt). War Service, 1942–46, 1st King's Dragoon Guards. Joined Foreign Service (now Diplomatic Service), 1947, and served in FO until 1949; 3rd Sec., Prague, 1949–50; 2nd Sec. (Commercial), Mexico City, 1950–53; FO 1953–56; 1st Sec., Karachi, 1956–59; Head of Chancery, Luxembourg, 1959–62; FO, 1962–65; Counsellor, 1965; Dep. Consul-Gen., New York, 1965–67; Dep. High Comr, Port of Spain, 1967–70; HM Consul-Gen., Philadelphia, 1970–74; Vis. Fellow, Centre for Internat. Studies, LSE, 1974–75; Head of Training Dept, FCO, and Dir, Diplomatic Service Language Centre, 1975–76. *Recreations:* gardening, golf, gerontology. *Address:* MGCA 212, Jávea, Alicante, Spain. *T:* (965) 792283.

THOMPSON, Charles Norman, CBE 1978; CChem; FRSC; Head of Research and Development Liaison, and Health, Safety and Environment Administration, Shell UK Ltd, 1978–82, retired; Consultant to Shell UK Ltd, since 1982; *b* 23 Oct. 1922; *s* of Robert Norman Thompson and Evelyn Tivendale Thompson (*née* Wood); *m* 1946, Pamela Margaret Wicks; one *d. Educ:* Birkenhead Institute; Liverpool Univ. (BSc). Research Chemist, Thornton Research Centre (Shell Refining & Marketing Co. Ltd), 1943; Lectr, Petroleum Chemistry and Technology, Liverpool Coll. of Technology, 1947–51; Personnel Supt and Dep. Associate Manager, Thornton Research Centre, Shell Research Ltd, 1959–61; Dir (Res. Admin), Shell Research Ltd, 1961–78. Mem. Council, 1976–82, Vice Pres., 1977–80, 1981–82, Inst. of Petroleum (Chm., Res. Adv. Cttee, 1973–82). Pres., RIC, 1976–78. Chairman: Professional Affairs Bd, RSC, 1980–84; Council of Science and Technology Insts, 1981–83 (Chm., Health Care Scientific Adv. Cttee, 1986–); Bd Mem., Thames Water Authority, 1980–; Member: Technician Educn Council, 1980–83; Ct, Univ. of Surrey, 1980–; Parly and Scientific Cttee, 1976–. *Publications:* Reviews of Petroleum Technology, vol. 13: insulating and hydraulic oils, 1953; numerous papers in Jl Inst. Petroleum, Chem. and Ind., Chem. in Brit., on hydrocarbon dielectrics, insulating oils, diffusion as rate-limiting factor in oxidation, antioxidants in the oil industry, mechanism of copper catalysis in insulating oil oxidation, scientific manpower, etc. *Recreation:* golf. *Address:* Delamere, Horsell Park, Woking, Surrey GU21 4LW. *T:* Woking 4939.

THOMPSON, Maj.-Gen. Christopher Noel; Director of Military Survey, Ministry of Defence, since 1984; *b* 25 Dec. 1932; *s* of late Brig. William Gordon Starkey Thompson and Kathleen Elizabeth (*née* Craven); *m* 1964, Margaret (*née* Longsworth); one *s* twin *d. Educ:* Wellington College; RMA Sandhurst; Sidney Sussex College, Cambridge (BA); University College London. Commissioned RE, 1953; served BAOR, 1957–59; Bomb Disposal, UK, 1959–62; Aden, 1963–66; Canada, 1966–68; OC 13 Field Survey Sqn, 1969–70; USA, 1971–75; CO 42 Survey Engr Regt, 1975–77; Dep. Dir, Planning and Develt, Ordnance Survey, 1978–79; Dir, Surveys and Production, Ordnance Survey, 1980–83. Pres., Commission D, European Organisation for Experimental Photogrammetric Research, 1980–. *Publications:* articles on surveying and mapping in Chartered Surveyor, Photogrammetric Record. *Recreations:* sailing, tennis, gardening, house restoration. *Address:* c/o Lloyds Bank, Sway Road, Brockenhurst, Hants.

THOMPSON, Lt-Col Sir Christopher (Peile), 6th Bt *cr* 1890; Commanding Officer, The Royal Hussars (Prince of Wales's Own), since 1985; *b* 21 Dec. 1944; *s* of Sir Peile Thompson, 5th Bt, OBE, and of Barbara Johnson, *d* of late H. J. Rampling; *S* father, 1985; *m* 1969, Anna Elizabeth, *d* of Major Arthur Callander; one *s* one *d. Educ:* Marlborough; RMA Sandhurst. Commnd 11th Hussars (PAO), 1965; Tank Troop Leader and Reconnaissance Troop Leader, 11th Hussars, 1965–69; Gunnery Instructor, RAC Gunnery Sch., 1970–72; Sqdn Second i/c, A Sqdn, Royal Hussars, 1972–75; GSO 3 Intelligence, Allied Staff, Berlin, 1975–76; RMCS Shrivenham, 1977; Staff Coll., Camberley, 1978; DAAG (a) M2 (A) (Officer Manning), MoD, 1978–81; C Sqdn Ldr, Royal Hussars, 1981–83; GSO 2 (Operational Requirements), HQ DRAC, 1983–85. *Recreations:* fishing, shooting, windsurfing, skiing, reading, gardening, sailing, fitness, holidays. *Heir: s* Peile Richard Thompson, *b* 3 March 1975. *Address:* The Royal Hussars (PWO), BFPO 38. *T:* 01049 5162 1633; Old Farm, Augres, Trinity, Jersey. *T:* Jersey 62289; Hill House, The Village, Appleshaw, Andover, Hants. *Club:* Cavalry and Guards.

THOMPSON, Christopher Ronald; Senior Partner, Aldenham Business Services Ltd, since 1984; *b* 14 Dec. 1927; *s* of Col S. J. Thompson, DSO, DL and Margaret Thompson (née Green); *m* 1949, Rachael Meynell; one *s* one *d* (and one *s* decd). *Educ:* Shrewsbury School; Trinity College, Cambridge. 1st Bn KSLI (Lieut), 1946–48. Dir, John Thompson Ltd, 1954–68, Chm., 1969; Dir, Rockwell-Thompson Ltd, 1973–74; Vice-Pres., Rockwell Europe, 1974–78. Chairman: NEI Internat., 1979–84; Wynn Electronics, 1983–; Hoccum Developments Ltd, 1985–; Director: Barclays Bank Birmingham Bd, 1974–; G. T. Japan Investment Trust, 1983–; Isotron plc, 1984–; Saraswati Syndicate pte India, 1954–. Member: Overseas Projects Bd, BOTB, 1981–84; Sino-British Trade Council, 1983–85. Pres., BEAMA, 1984–85. Chm., Anglo-Venezuelan Soc., 1981–85. Trustee, Hereford Cathedral Trust, 1984–. High Sheriff, Shropshire, 1984–85. *Recreations:* flyfishing, shooting, forestry. *Address:* Aldenham Park, near Bridgnorth, Shropshire. *T:* Morville 218. *Clubs:* Brooks's, Boodle's.

THOMPSON, Colin Edward, CBE 1983; FRSE 1978; Director, National Galleries of Scotland, 1977–84; *b* 2 Nov. 1919; *s* of late Edward Vincent Thompson, CB, and Jessie Forbes Cameron; *m* 1950, Jean Agnes Jardine O'Connell; one *s* one *d. Educ:* Sedbergh Sch.; King's College, Cambridge; Chelsea Polytechnic Sch. of Art. MA (Cantab). FMA. FS Wing CMP, 1940–41; Foreign Office, 1941–45. Lectr, Bath Acad. of Art, Corsham, 1948–54; Asst Keeper, 1954, Keeper, 1967, National Gall. of Scotland. Sen. Adviser, Res. Centre in Art Educn, Bath Acad. of Art, 1962–65; Chm., Scottish Museums Council, 1984–; Member: Scottish Arts Council, 1976–83; Edinburgh Fest. Council, 1979–82 (Chm., Art Adv. Panel, 1979–); Bd of Governors, Edinburgh Coll. of Art, 1985–. DUniv Edinburgh, 1985. *Publications:* (with Lorne Campbell) Hugo van der Goes and the Trinity Panels in Edinburgh, 1974; guide books, catalogues and a history of the National Gallery of Scotland; articles in Burlington Magazine, Museums Jl, etc. *Address:* Edenkerry, Lasswade, Midlothian. *T:* 031–663 7927. *Club:* New.

See also D. C. Thompson.

THOMPSON, David Richard, CB 1974; QC 1980; Master of the Crown Office and Queen's Coroner and Attorney, Registrar of Criminal Appeals and of the Courts Martial Appeal Court since 1965; *b* 11 Feb. 1916; *s* of William George Thompson; *m* 1952, Sally Jennifer Rowntree Thompson (*née* Stockton); two *s* four *d. Educ:* Alleyn's Sch., Dulwich; Jesus Coll., Oxford. BA Physics 1938. Royal Corps of Signals, 1939–46 (despatches). Called to Bar, Lincoln's Inn, 1946, Bencher, 1982; Office of Director of Public Prosecutions, 1948–54; Dep. Asst Registrar, then Asst Registrar, Court of Criminal Appeal, 1954–65. Mem., Judicial Studies Bd, 1979–. *Publications:* (with H. W. Wollaston) Court of Appeal Criminal Division, 1969; (with Morrish and McLean) Proceedings in the Criminal Division of the Court of Appeal, 1979. *Recreations:* family, work. *Address:* 54 Highbury Grove, N5. *T:* 01–226 6514.

THOMPSON, David Robin Bibby; Director, Bibby Line Ltd, since 1974; Member, Development Commission, since 1986; *b* 23 July 1946; *s* of Noel Denis Thompson and Cynthia Joan (*née* Bibby); *m* 1971, Caroline Ann Foster; one *s* one *d. Educ:* Uppingham Sch.; Mons Officer Cadet Sch. Short service commn, QRIH, 1965; comd Queen's Own Yeomanry (TA), 1984–86. Chm., NAC Housing Assoc., 1983–; Vice-Chm., NAC Rural

Trust, 1983–; Mem. Council, Royal Agricl Soc. of England, 1985–. *Recreations:* ski-ing, horses, conservation. *Address:* Sansaw Hall, Clive, Shrewsbury, Shropshire SY4 3JR. *Clubs:* Cavalry and Guards; Northern Counties (Newcastle upon Tyne).

THOMPSON, Dennis Cameron, FCIArb; Founder, 1967, and Editor since 1977, Journal of World Trade Law; Consulting Editor, Journal of International Arbitration, since 1985; *b* 25 Oct. 1914; *s* of late Edward Vincent Thompson, CB, and late Jessie Forbes; *m* 1959, Maria von Skramlik; one *d. Educ:* Oundle; King's Coll., Cambridge. Nat. Sci. Tripos Pt I, Law Pt II; MA 1949. RAF, 1940–45: Sqdn-Ldr, personnel staff, Desert Air Force, and Germany. Called to Bar, Inner Temple, 1939; practised London and Midland Circuit, 1946–63; Asst Dir (European Law), British Inst. of Internat. and Comparative Law, 1963–66; Legal Adviser, Secretariat of EFTA, Geneva, 1967–73; participated in negotiations for European Patent Convention, 1969–73; Dir, Restrictive Practices and Dominant Positions, EEC, 1973–76; Consultant to UNCTAD on Restrictive Business Practices and Transfer of Technol., 1977–82. Vis. Prof., Georgia Univ. Sch. of Law, Athens, GA, 1978. Trustee, Federal Trust, 1962–71. Member: Assoc. Suisse de L'Arbitrage; Panel of Arbitrators, Amer. Arbitration Assoc. *Publications:* (ed) Kennedy, CIF Contracts, 3rd edn 1959; (with Alan Campbell) Common Market Law, 1962; The Proposal for a European Company, 1969; articles in Internat. and Compar. Law Quarterly; (ed jtly) Common Market Law Review, 1963–67. *Recreations:* walking, ski-ing, sailing. *Address:* 8 rue des Belles Filles, 1299 Crans, Switzerland. *T:* (22) 76 16 87. *Club:* United Oxford & Cambridge University.

See also C. E. Thompson.

THOMPSON, Donald; MP (C) Calder Valley, since 1983 (Sowerby, 1979–83); Parliamentary Secretary, Ministry of Agriculture, Fisheries and Food, since 1986; *b* 13 Nov. 1931; *s* of Geoffrey and Rachel Thompson; *m* 1957, Patricia Ann Hopkins; two *s. Educ:* Hipperholme Grammar School. National Service, 1950–52. Farmer/butcher, 1952–74. Formerly Dir, Halifax Farmers' Trading Assoc.; Man. Dir, Armadillo Plastics (Glass Fibre Manufacturers), 1974–79, Dir, 1979–. Member: WR CC, 1967–74; W Yorks CC, 1974–75; Calderdale Dist Council, 1975–79 (Chm. Educn Cttee, 1975–76). Contested (C): Batley and Morley, 1970; Sowerby, Feb. and Oct. 1974. An Asst Govt Whip, 1981–83; a Lord Comr of HM Treasury, 1983–86. Chm., Cons. Candidates' Assoc., 1972–74. *Recreations:* Rugby football, poor golf, conversation. *Address:* Moravian House, Lightcliffe, near Halifax, West Yorks. *T:* Halifax 202920. *Clubs:* St Stephen's Constitutional; Brodleians (Hipperholme); Octave (Elland).

THOMPSON, Donald Henry, MA Oxon; Headmaster, Chigwell School, Essex, 1947–71; *b* 29 Aug. 1911; *s* of H. R. Thompson, solicitor, Swansea; *m* 1942, Helen Mary Wray; four *s. Educ:* Shrewsbury School; Merton College, Oxford. Postmaster in Classics, Merton Coll., Oxford, 1930; 1st Class Hon. Mod., 1932; 1st Class Literae Humaniores, 1934; Asst Master Haileybury Coll., Hertford, 1934–46. Served War of 1939–45, RA, 1940–45. Chm., Frome Area, Somerset Trust for Nature Conservation. JP Essex, 1955–81. *Recreations:* cricket, bird-watching, conservation. *Address:* Glasses Farm, Holcombe Bath, Somerset. *T:* Stratton-on-Fosse 232322.

THOMPSON, Prof. Edward Arthur, FBA 1964; Professor of Classics, University of Nottingham, 1948–79; *b* 22 May 1914; *s* of late Robert J. Thompson and late Margaret Thompson, Waterford. *Educ:* Trinity Coll., Dublin. Lecturer in Classics: Dublin, 1939–41; Swansea, 1942–45; King's College, London, 1945–48. Vis. Bentley Prof. of History, Univ. of Michigan, 1969–71; H. F. Johnson Res. Prof., Univ. of Wisconsin (Madison), 1979–80. *Publications:* The Historical Work of Ammianus Marcellinus, 1947; A History of Attila and The Huns, 1948; A Roman Reformer and Inventor, 1952; The Early Germans, 1965; The Visigoths in the Time of Ulfila, 1966; The Goths in Spain, 1969; Romans and Barbarians, 1982; St Germanus of Auxerre and the End of Roman Britain, 1984; Who was St Patrick?, 1985. *Address:* 4 Castle Grove, The Park, Nottingham.

THOMPSON, Sir Edward (Hugh Dudley), Kt 1967; MBE 1945; TD; DL; Director: Allied Breweries Ltd, 1961–78; P-E Consulting Group Ltd, 1968–73 (Chm., 1971–73); *b* 12 May 1907; *s* of Neale Dudley Thompson and Mary Gwendoline Scutt; *m* 1st, 1931, Ruth Monica, 3rd *d* of Charles Henry Wainwright, JP; two *s*; 2nd, 1947, Doreen Maud, *d* of George Tibbitt; one *s* one *d. Educ:* Uppingham; Lincoln Coll., Oxford. Served War of 1939–45 (despatches twice, MBE); 1st Derbyshire Yeomanry, 1939–43, in N Africa; General Staff, 1943–45, in Italy and Germany. Solicitor, 1931–36. Asst Man. Dir, Ind Coope & Allsopp Ltd, 1936–39, Managing Director, 1939; Chairman: Ind Coope Ltd, Burton on Trent, 1955–62; Allied Breweries Ltd (formerly Ind Coope Tetley Ansell Ltd), 1961–68. Director: Sun Insurance Ltd, 1946–59; Sun Alliance & London Insurance Ltd, 1959–77. Chm., Brewers' Soc., 1959–61; Trustee, Civic Trust; Mem. Northumberland Foot and Mouth Cttee. Mem. Council, Nottingham Univ., 1969–. Mem. Council, RASE, 1972–. High Sheriff of Derbyshire, 1964; DL Derbyshire, 1978. Hon. LLD Nottingham, 1984. *Recreations:* farming, sailing, ski-ing. *Address:* Culland Hall, Brailsford, Derby. *T:* Ashbourne 60247. *Club:* Boodle's.

THOMPSON, Sir Edward (Walter), Kt 1957; JP; Chairman, John Thompson Ltd, Wolverhampton, 1947–67; Director, Barclays Bank, 1958–73; Local Director, Barclays Bank (Birmingham), 1952–73; *b* 11 June 1902; *s* of late Albert E. Thompson and late Mary Thompson; *m* 1930, Ann E., *d* of Rev. George L. Amphlett, Four Ashes Hall, Stourbridge, Worcs; one *s* three *d. Educ:* Oundle; Trinity Hall, Cambridge. MA (Engineering) Cambridge. Joined family firm of John Thompson's, 1924; Dir John Thompson Watertube Boilers, 1930; Joint Man. Dir John Thompson Ltd, 1936–62. Chm. Watertube Boilermakers Assoc., 1951–54; Pres. Brit. Engineers Assoc., 1957–59 (Vice-Pres. 1956). Mem. Midland Chapter Woodard Schools. Chairman: Birmingham Regional Hosp. Bd, 1957–61; Redditch Development Corp., 1964–74; Leader SE Asia Trade Delegation, 1961. JP Co. Salop, 1953; Dep. Chm. Bridgnorth Bench, 1956–66; High Sheriff, Staffordshire, 1955–56. *Recreations:* shooting, fishing, gardening. *Address:* Gatacre Park, Bridgnorth, Salop. *T:* Bobbington 211.

See also Viscount Bledisloe.

THOMPSON, Eric John; Director of Statistics, Department of Transport, since 1980; *b* Beverley, E Yorks, 26 Sept. 1934; *o s* of Herbert William Thompson and late Florence Thompson (*née* Brewer). *Educ:* Beverley Grammar Sch.; London School of Economics (BScEcon). National Service: Pilot Officer in Dept of Scientific Adviser to Air Ministry, 1956–58. Operations Planning Dept, International Computers and Tabulators Ltd, 1958–60; Supply and Planning Dept, Shell International Petroleum Co. Ltd, 1960–65; Head of Regional Demography Unit, General Register Office, 1965–67; Head of Population Studies Section, 1967–72, Asst Dir of Intelligence, 1972–74, GLC Research and Intelligence Unit; Head of Social Monitoring Branch, Central Statistical Office, 1975–80. Royal Statistical Society: Fellow, 1956, Mem. Council 1981–85, Vice-Pres., 1982–83; ESRC (formerly SSRC): Assessor, Statistics Cttee, 1979–80; Mem., Research Resources and Methods Cttee, 1982–84; Mem., British Computer Soc., 1959–76 (MBCS 1968). Member: East Yorkshire Local History Soc., 1974–; Housman Soc., 1976–; Richard III Soc., 1979– (Mem. Cttee, 1984–); Friends of Nat. Libraries, 1981–; Trustee, Richard III and Yorkist Hist. Trust, 1985–. *Publications:* ed, Social Trends, Nos 6–10,

1975–80; contrib. chapters in three books on regional and urban planning; articles and reviews in GLC Intelligence Unit's quarterly bulletin and various statistical jls; article on historical bibliography in The Ricardian. *Recreations:* reading and collecting books, British mediæval history, English literature. *Address:* Department of Transport, Romney House, SW1P 3PY.

THOMPSON, Prof. Francis Michael Longstreth, FBA 1979; Director, Institute of Historical Research, and Professor of History in the University of London, since 1977; *b* 13 Aug. 1925; *s* of late Francis Longstreth-Thompson, OBE; *m* 1951, Anne Challoner; two *s* one *d. Educ:* Bootham Sch., York; Queen's Coll., Oxford (Hastings Schol.); MA, DPhil). ARICS 1968. War service, with Indian Artillery, 1943–47; James Bryce Sen. Schol., Oxford, 1949–50; Harmsworth Sen. Schol., Merton Coll., Oxford, 1949–51; Lectr in History, UCL, 1951–63; Reader in Economic History, UCL, 1963–68; Prof. of Modern Hist., Univ. of London, and Head of Dept of Hist., Bedford Coll., London, 1968–77. Joint Editor, Economic History Review, 1968–80. Sec., British Nat. Cttee of Historical Scis, 1978–; Pres., Economic History Soc., 1983–86; British Mem., Standing Cttee for Humanities, European Sci. Foundn, 1983–. Member: Senate and Academic Council, Univ. of London, 1970–78; Senate and Collegiate Council, 1981–. FRHistS 1964. *Publications:* English Landed Society in the Nineteenth Century, 1963; Chartered Surveyors: the growth of a profession, 1968; Victorian England: the horse-drawn society, 1970; Countrysides, in The Nineteenth Century, ed Asa Briggs, 1970; Hampstead: building a borough, 1650–1964, 1974; introd. to General Report on Gosford Estates in County Armagh 1821, by William Greig, 1976; Britain, in European Landed Elites in the Nineteenth Century, ed David Spring, 1977; Landowners and Farmers, in The Faces of Europe (ed Alan Bullock), 1980; 2 chapters in The Victorian Countryside (ed G. E. Mingay), 1981; (ed) The Rise of Suburbia, 1982; (ed) Horses in European Economic History, 1983; numerous articles in Economic History Review, History, English Historical Review, etc. *Recreations:* gardening, walking, carpentry, tennis. *Address:* Holly Cottage, Sheepcote Lane, Wheathampstead, Herts. *T:* Wheathampstead 3129.

THOMPSON, Air Commodore Frederick William, CBE 1957; DSO 1944; DFC 1942; AFC 1944; Director, Air Weapons, British Aerospace Dynamics Group, 1977–80; *b* 9 July 1914; *s* of William Edward Thompson, Winster, Poulton-le-Fylde, Lancs; *m* 1941, Marian, *d* of Wm Bootyman, Hessle, E Yorks; two *d. Educ:* Baines's Grammar School; Liverpool University. BSc 2nd Cl. Hons Maths; Advanced Diploma in General Hygiene (Hons). Joined RAF, 1935, invalided 1936. S Rhodesian Education Dept, 1936–39. Served War of 1939–45 (despatches, DFC, AFC, DSO): S Rhodesian Air Force, 1940, Pilot Officer; seconded to RAFVR, 4 Gp Bomber Command, 1940; Flight Comdr 10 Sqdn Bombers, 1941; 1658 HCU, 1942; CO 44 Bomber Sqdn, 1944; Bomber Command Instructor's School, 1944; Station Commander, RAF Heany, 1945; HQ Mid Med., 1946–47; Min. of Defence, 1947–50; HQ CC, 1950–53; OC Aswdu, 1953; Group Capt., CO Luqa, 1954; Deputy Director Operational Requirements (1), Air Ministry, 1957–60. Air Cdre Imperial Defence Coll., 1960; Director of Guided Weapons (Trials), Ministry of Aviation, 1961. Retired from RAF at own request to join de Havilland Aircraft Co. Ltd as Representative of the Company on the West Coast of America; Engrg Manager, Hawker Siddeley Dynamics Co. Ltd, 1964, Divisional Manager, Air Weapons Div., 1972–77. idc, jssc, psc, cfs. *Recreations:* tennis, swimming. *Address:* Westwick, Lye Green Road, Chesham, Bucks. *T:* Chesham 785413. *Club:* Royal Air Force.

THOMPSON, Rt. Rev. Geoffrey Hewlett; *see* Exeter, Bishop of.

THOMPSON, George H.; Principal Teacher of French, Annan Academy, Dumfriesshire, since 1979; *b* Sept. 1928. *Educ:* Dalry Sch.; Kirkcudbright Acad.; Edinburgh Univ. Teacher, modern languages, Kirkcudbright Academy. Contested (SNP) Galloway, Feb. 1974. Former SNP Asst Nat. Sec.; MP (SNP) Galloway, Oct. 1974–1979; SNP Spokesman: on health, Oct. 1974–79; on forestry, 1975. *Address:* 53 Kirkland Street, St John's Town of Dalry, Castle Douglas, Kircudbrightshire. *T:* Dalry 254.

THOMPSON, Gerald Francis Michael Perronet; Chairman, Kleinwort Benson Ltd, 1971–75, retired (Director 1961, Vice-Chairman 1970); Member, Accepting Houses Committee, 1971–75; *b* 10 Oct. 1910; *s* of late Sir John Perronet Thompson, KCSI, KCIE, and Ada Lucia Tyrrell; *m* 1944, Margaret Mary Bodenham Smith; two *s* one *d. Educ:* Repton; King's Coll., Cambridge (Scholar, MA); London Sch. of Economics (post graduate). Kleinwort Sons & Co., 1933. Served War, RAFVR, 1939–46 (despatches): in France, UK, and Middle East, Wing Comdr. Director: Kleinwort Sons & Co., 1960; Kleinwort Benson Lonsdale Ltd, 1970–82. Lectures and broadcasts on monetary and internat. affairs, 1957–; lecture on merchant banking, RSA, 1966 (FRSA). Received into RC Church, 1939; Hon. Treasurer, Westminster Cathedral Appeal Fund, 1978–84; Trustee, Tablet Trust, 1977–. Governor, New Hall Sch., 1977–83. *Publication:* contrib. Festschrift presented to Fernand Collin, 1972. *Recreations:* travel, garden. *Address:* Whitewebs, Margaretting, Essex CM4 9HX. *T:* Ingatestone 352002. *Club:* United Oxford & Cambridge University.

See also Rear-Adm. J. Y. Thompson, Sir E. H. T. Wakefield, Bt.

THOMPSON, Godfrey; *see* Thompson, W. G.

THOMPSON, Godfrey James M.; *see* Milton-Thompson.

THOMPSON, Mrs Gordon; *see* Thompson, B.

THOMPSON, Rt. Rev. Hewlett; *see* Thompson, Rt Rev. G. H.

THOMPSON, Vice-Adm. Hugh Leslie Owen, CEng, FIMechE; Deputy Controller Warships, Ministry of Defence, since 1986; Chief Naval Engineer Officer, since 1987; *b* 2 April 1931; *s* of Hugh Thompson and Elsie Standish (*née* Owen); *m* 1st, 1957, Sheila Jean Finch (*d* 1974); one *s* two *d*; 2nd, 1977, Rosemary Ann (*née* Oliver). *Educ:* Royal Belfast Academical Institution; RNC Dartmouth; RNEC Manadon. Asst Dir, Submarines Mechanical, 1976–79; RCDS, 1980; Dep. Dir, Systems 1, 1981–83; Dir Gen., Marine Engineering, 1983–84; Dir Gen. Surface Ships, MoD, 1984–86. *Recreations:* railways, woodwork. *Address:* Ministry of Defence (Navy), Whitehall, SW1. *Club:* Army and Navy.

THOMPSON, (Hugh) Patrick; MP (C) Norwich North, since 1983; *b* 21 Oct. 1935; *s* of Gerald Leopold Thompson and Kathleen Mary Landsdown Thompson; *m* 1962, Kathleen Howson. *Educ:* Felsted Sch., Essex; Emmanuel Coll., Cambridge (MA). MInstP 1964. Nat. Service, 2nd Lieut, KOYLI, 1957–59; TA, Manchester, 1960–65; Gresham's Sch., CCF, 1965–82 (CFM 1980); Major, retd. Engr, English Electric Valve Co., Chelmsford, 1959–60; Sixth Form Physics Master: Manchester Grammar Sch., 1960–65; Gresham's Sch., Holt, 1965–83. Mem., Parly and Scientific Cttee, 1983–; Founder Mem., All Party Gp for Engrg Develt, 1985–. *Publication:* Elementary Calculations in Physics, 1963. *Recreations:* travel, music, gardening. *Address:* The Cottage, Swanton Novers, Norfolk NR24 2RB. *T:* Melton Constable 860529. *Club:* Norfolk (Norwich).

THOMPSON, Sir (Humphrey) Simon M.; *see* Meysey-Thompson.

THOMPSON, Dr Ian McKim; Deputy Secretary, British Medical Association, since 1969; *b* 19 Aug. 1938; *s* of late J. W. Thompson and of Dr E. M. Thompson; *m* 1962, Dr Veronica Jane Richards; two *s* one *d*. *Educ:* Epsom Coll.; Birmingham Univ. (MB, ChB 1961). Lectr in Pathology, Univ. of Birmingham, 1964–67; Sen. Registrar, Birmingham RHB, 1967–69. Consulting Forensic Pathologist to HM Coroner, City of Birmingham, 1966–. Member: GMC, 1979–; Birmingham Med. Inst. Hon. Collegian, Med. Colls of Spain, 1975. *Publications:* (ed) The Hospital Gazeteer, 1972; (ed) BMA Handbook for Hospital Junior Doctors, 1977, 4th edn 1984; (ed) BMA Handbook for Trainee Doctors in General Practice, 1982, 3rd edn 1985; various medical scientific papers. *Recreations:* inland waterways, rambling. *Address:* 9 Old Rectory Green, Fladbury, Pershore, Worcs WR10 2QX. *T:* Evesham 860668.

THOMPSON, James Craig; Managing Director, since 1973, Chairman, since 1979, Adverkit International Ltd; *b* 27 Oct. 1933; *s* of Alfred Thompson and Eleanor (*née* Craig); *m* 1957, Catherine (*née* Warburton); one *s* one *d*. *Educ:* Heaton Grammar Sch., Newcastle upon Tyne; Rutherford Coll., Newcastle upon Tyne. Commercial Exec., Belfast Telegraph, Newcastle Chronicle and Journal, Scotsman Publications, Liverpool Post and Echo, 1960–76; Advertising and Marketing Manager, Kent Messenger Gp, 1976–79, Dir, 1972–79; Man. Dir, South Eastern Newspapers, 1975–79; Chm. and Man. Dir, Eadons Newspaper Services Ltd, 1982–; Chm., Harvest Publications Ltd, 1983–. Dir, Weekly Newspaper Advtg Bureau, 1977. Dir., Ad Builder Ltd, 1971–. Life Governor, Kent County Agricl Soc., 1976. Hon. Life Mem., Kent CCC, 1978; Member: MCC; Catenian Assoc. (Pres., Maidstone Circle, 1974–75); Dir, Weekly Newspaper Advtsg Bureau, 1977. Chairman: Southern Football League, 1977–79 (Life Mem., 1985); Alliance Premier Football League, 1979–; President: Eastern Professional Floodlight League, 1976–; Kent League, 1984–; Dir and Chm., Maidstone United FC Ltd, 1970–; Mem. Council, Football Assoc., 1982–. FInstD; MInstM; MBIM. Liveryman, Worshipful Co. of Stationers and Newspaper Makers; Freeman, City of London. Distinguished Service Award, Internat. Classified Advertising Assoc., Baltimore, 1968. *Publications:* numerous articles on commercial aspects of newspaper publishing and Association football. *Recreations:* squash, Northumbrian history. *Address:* Prescott House, Otham, Kent ME15 8RL. *T:* Maidstone 861606. *Clubs:* East India; Maidstone (Maidstone).

THOMPSON, Rt. Rev. James Lawton; *see* Stepney, Area Bishop of.

THOMPSON, Sir John, Kt 1961; Judge of the High Court of Justice, Queen's Bench Division, 1961–82; *b* Glasgow, 16 Dec. 1907; *e s* of Donald Cameron Thompson and Jeanie Dunn Thompson (*née* Nisbet); *m* 1934, Agnes Baird, (Nancy), *o d* of John and Jeanie Drummond, Glasgow; two *s*. *Educ:* Bellahouston Academy; Glasgow University; Oriel College, Oxford (Neale Schol.). Glasgow University: MA and Arthur Jones Memorial Prize, 1928; Ewing Gold Medal, 1929; Oxford University: BA, 1930; MA 1943. Barrister-at-Law, Powell Prize, Middle Temple, 1933. QC 1954; Bencher, Middle Temple, 1961; Lent Reader, 1977; Dep. Treasurer, 1977; Treasurer, 1978. Vice-Chm., Gen. Council of the Bar, 1960–61 (Mem. 1958–61). Commissioner of Assize (Birmingham) 1961. *Publications:* (edited with H. R. Rogers) Redgrave's Factories, Truck and Shops Acts. *Recreation:* golf. *Address:* 73 Sevenoaks Road, Orpington, Kent. *T:* Orpington 22339. *Clubs:* Royal & Ancient Golf, Sundridge Park Golf (Capt., 1958–59), Woking Golf.

THOMPSON, John; MP (Lab) Wansbeck, since 1983; *b* 27 Aug. 1928; *s* of Nicholas and Lilian Thompson; *m* 1952, Margaret Clarke; one *s* one *d*. *Educ:* Bothal Sch.; Ashington Mining Coll. Electrical Engr, 1966–83. Councillor: Wansbeck DC, 1974–79; Northumberland CC, 1974–85 (Leader, and Chm., Policy and Resources, and Employment Cttees, 1981–83). Mem., Select Cttee on Educn, Science and Arts, 1985–. *Address:* 20 Falstone Crescent, Ashington, Northumberland NE63 0TY. *T:* Ashington 817830.

THOMPSON, John Alan, CMG 1974; HM Diplomatic Service, retired; *b* 21 June 1926; *m* 1956, Maureen Sayers. *Educ:* Bromsgrove Sch.; Brasenose Coll., Oxford. Control Commission for Germany, 1952; Vice-Consul, Hanoi, 1954; Second Sec., Saigon, 1956; Warsaw, 1959; Foreign Office, 1961; First Sec. (Commercial), Havana, 1964; First Sec., FO (later FCO), 1966–75; Counsellor, 1973. *Recreations:* music, mountains. *Address:* Sun House, Hall Street, Long Melford, Suffolk CO10 9HZ. *T:* Sudbury 78252.

THOMPSON, John Brian, CBE 1980; Director of Radio, Independent Broadcasting Authority, since 1973; *b* 8 June 1928; *y s* of late John and Lilian Thompson; *m* 1957, Sylvia, *d* of late Thomas Waterhouse, CBE, and of Doris Waterhouse (*née* Gough); two *s* one *d*. *Educ:* St Paul's; Pembroke College, Oxford (BA; MA). Eileen Power Studentship, LSE, 1950; Glaxo Laboratories Ltd, 1950–54; Masius & Fergusson Ltd, 1955; Asst Editor, Truth, 1956–57; Daily Express, 1957–59 (New York Correspondent; Drama Critic); ITN, 1959–60 (Newscaster/Reporter); Editor, Time and Tide, 1960–62; News Editor, The Observer, 1962–66; Editor, Observer Colour Magazine, 1966–70; Publisher and Editorial Dir, BPC Publishing Ltd, 1971. Sen. Advr on Radio to Minister of Posts and Telecommunications, 1972; Mem., MoD Study Group on Censorship, 1983. Sony Radio special award, 1983. *Address:* 4 Edith Grove, SW10. *T:* 01–352 5414. *Club:* Garrick.
See also Hon. Sir R. G. Waterhouse.

THOMPSON, John Derek T.; *see* Taylor Thompson.

THOMPSON, Prof. John Griggs, PhD; FRS 1979; Rouse Ball Professor of Mathematics, University of Cambridge, since 1971; Fellow of Churchill College, since 1968; *b* Kansas, 13 Oct. 1932; *s* of John and Eleanor Thompson; *m* 1960, Diane Oenning; one *s* one *d*. *Educ:* Yale (BA 1955); Chicago (PhD 1959); MA Cantab 1972. Prof. of Mathematics, Chicago Univ., 1962–68; Vis. Prof. of Mathematics, Cambridge Univ., 1968–70. Cole Prize, 1966; Field Medal, 1970; Berwick Prize, London Math. Soc., 1982; Sylvester Medal, Royal Soc., 1985. *Address:* 16 Millington Road, Cambridge CB3 9HP.

THOMPSON, John Handby; Director of Establishments and Organisation, Department of Education and Science, since 1985; *b* 21 Feb. 1929; *s* of late Rev. John Thomas Thompson and Clara Handby; *m* 1957, Catherine Rose, *d* of Charles Bowman Heald; two *s* one *d*. *Educ:* Silcoates Sch., Wakefield; St John's Coll., Oxford (MA). Served Intell. Corps, 1947–49. HM Inspector of Taxes, 1953–63; Dept of Educn and Science, 1964–: Schs Council, 1971–73; Asst Sec., 1973; Mem., Prep. Cttee of European Univ. Inst., 1973–75; Dep. Accountant-Gen., 1976–78; Under Sec., 1978; Head of Schs Br. 1, 1978–80; Head of Further and Higher Educn Br. 1, 1980–84. *Recreations:* reading about Albania, Nonconformist history. *Address:* Department of Education and Science, Elizabeth House, York Road, SE1 7PH. *Clubs:* National Liberal, Reform.

THOMPSON, Prof. John Jeffrey, PhD; CChem, FRSC; Professor of Education, since 1979, and Pro-Vice-Chancellor, since 1986, University of Bath; *b* 13 July 1938; *s* of John Thompson and Elsie May Thompson (*née* Wright); *m* 1963, Kathleen Audrey Gough; three *d*. *Educ:* King George V Sch., Southport; St John's Coll., Cambridge (MA); Balliol Coll., Oxford (MA); PhD (CNAA); DipEd (Oxon). Asst Master, Blundell's Sch., 1961–65; Head of Chemistry, Watford Grammar Sch., 1965–69; Lectr in Educn, KCL, 1968–69; Shell Fellow, UCL, 1969–70; Lectr and Tutor, Dept of Educnl Studies, Oxford Univ., 1970–79; Lectr in Chemistry, Keble Coll., Oxford, 1970–76. Chief Examnr, Internat. Baccalaureate, 1970– (Chm., Bd of Chief Examnrs, 1985–). Chm., Assoc. for Science Educn, 1981; Pres., Educn Div., Royal Soc. of Chemistry, 1983–85; Vice-Pres. and Gen. Sec., BAAS, 1985–. Mem. Council, Wildfowl Trust, 1981–. FRSA 1983. *Publications:* Introduction to Chemical Energetics, 1967; European Curriculum Studies; Chemistry, 1972; (ed) Practical Work in Sixthform Science, 1976; Foundation Course in Chemistry, 1982; Modern Physical Chemistry, 1982; (ed) Dimensions of Science, 1986; The Chemistry Dimension, 1987. *Recreations:* music (brass bands and blue grass), North Country art, collecting sugar wrappers. *Address:* 9 Hensley Gardens, Bath BA2 2DS.

THOMPSON, John Keith Lumley, CMG 1982; MBE (mil.) 1965; TD 1961; President, Lumley Associates, since 1983; *b* 31 March 1923; *s* of late John V. V. and Gertrude Thompson; *m* 1950, Audrey Olley; one *s*. *Educ:* Wallsend Grammar Sch.; King's Coll., Durham Univ. (BSc). FBIM (MBIM 1975). Served War of 1939–45: Officer in REME, 1942–47, NW Europe; BEME 44 Para Bde (V), 1948–70. Dep. Inspector, REME (V) Southern Comd, 1970–72 (Lt-Col); Dep. Comdr, 44 Para Bde (V), 1972–75 (Col). Road Research Lab., DSIR, 1948–55; AWRE, Aldermaston, 1955–64; Staff of Chief Scientific Adviser, MoD, 1964–65; Head of E Midlands Regional Office, Min. Tech., 1965–70; Head, Internat. Affairs, Atomic Energy Div., Dept of Energy, 1972–74; Regional Dir, W Midlands and Northern Regional Offices, DoI, 1970–72 and 1974–78; Counseller (Sci. and Tech.), Washington, 1978–83. ADC to the Queen (TAVR), 1974–78. *Publications:* papers on vehicle behaviour, crash helmets and implosion systems; numerous articles on American science and technology. *Recreations:* outdoor activities, reading. *Address:* c/o Lumley Associates, 5905 Osceola Road, Bethesda, Md 20816, USA. *Club:* Cosmos (Washington).

THOMPSON, John Leonard C.; *see* Cloudsley-Thompson.

THOMPSON, Air Commodore John Marlow, CBE 1954; DSO 1943; DFC 1940 (and Bar 1942); AFC 1952; RAF retired; *b* 16 Aug. 1914; *s* of late John Thompson and Florence Thompson (*née* Marlow); *m* 1938, Margaret Sylvia Rowlands; one *s* one *d* (and one *s* decd). *Educ:* Bristol Grammar School. Joined RAF 1934; comd 111 Sqdn, Battle of Britain; Spitfire Wing, Malta, 1942–43; SASO 11 Group, 1952–54; comd RAF Leeming, 1956–57; Dir of Air Defence, Air Ministry, 1958–60; Graduate Imperial Defence Coll., 1961; AOC, Military Air Traffic Ops, 1962–65; Gen. Manager, Airwork Services, Saudi Arabia, 1966–68. Belgian MC 1st Class, 1942; Danish Order of Dannebrog, 1951. *Recreation:* golf. *Address:* Flat 3, 35 Adelaide Crescent, Hove, East Sussex BN3 2JJ. *T:* Brighton 722859. *Clubs:* Royal Air Force; Monte-Carlo; Moor Park Golf, Monte Carlo Golf (Dir, 1973–83).

THOMPSON, John Michael Anthony, FMA; Director, Art Galleries and Museums, Tyne and Wear County Museums, since 1975; *b* 3 Feb. 1941; *s* of George Thompson and Joan Smith; *m* 1965, Alison Sara Bowers; two *d*. *Educ:* William Hulme's Grammar Sch., Manchester; Univ. of Manchester. BA, MA; FMA 1980. Research Asst, Whitworth Art Gall., 1964–66; Keeper, Rutherston Collection, City Art Gall., Manchester, 1966–68; Director: North Western Museum and Art Gall. Service, 1968–70; Arts and Museums, Bradford City Council, 1970–74; Chief Arts and Museums Officer, Bradford Metropolitan Council, 1974–75. Councillor, Museums Assoc., 1977–80, 1984– (Chm., Accreditation Cttee, 1978–80); Advisor to Arts and Recreation Cttee, AMA, 1981–; Pres., Museums North, 1977; Chm., Soc. of County Museum Dirs, 1982–86; Founder Mem. and Hon. Sec., Gp of Dirs of Museums in the British Isles, 1985–. *Publications:* (ed) The Manual of Curatorship: a guide to museum practice, 1984; articles in Museums Jl, Penrose Annual, Connoisseur. *Recreations:* classical guitar, long distance running, walking. *Address:* 18 The Poplars, Gosforth, Newcastle upon Tyne. *T:* Newcastle upon Tyne 2842797. *Club:* Gosforth Harriers and Athletic.

THOMPSON, Prof. John Michael Tutill, FRS 1985; Professor of Structural Mechanics, Department of Civil Engineering, University College London, since 1977; *b* 7 June 1937; *s* of John Hornsey Thompson and Kathleen Rita Thompson (*née* Tutill); *m* 1959, Margaret Cecilia Chapman; one *s* one *d*. *Educ:* Hull Grammar Sch.; Clare Coll., Cambridge (MA, PhD, ScD). FIMA. Research Fellow, Peterhouse, 1961–64; Vis. Res. Associate, Stanford (Fulbright grant), 1962–63; Lectr, 1964–68, Reader, 1968–77, UCL; Chm., Bd of Studies in Civil and Mech. Eng., Univ. of London, 1984–86. Vis. Prof., Faculté des Sciences, Univ. Libre de Bruxelles, 1976–78; Vis. Mathematician, Brookhaven Nat. Lab., 1984. OMAE Award, ASME, 1985. Organizer and Editor, IUTAM Symp. on Collapse: the buckling of structures in theory and practice, 1982; sci. contribs to radio and TV, 1975–. *Publications:* (with G. W. Hunt) A general theory of elastic stability, 1973; Instabilities and catastrophes in science and engineering, 1982; (with G. W, Hunt) Elastic instability phenomena, 1984; (with H. B. Stewart) Nonlinear dynamics and chaos, 1986; articles in learned jls (and mem., editl bds). *Recreations:* walking, music, tennis, table tennis. *Address:* 31 Hillside Road, Bushey, Herts. *T:* Watford 29803.

THOMPSON, John William McWean, CBE 1986; Editor, Sunday Telegraph, 1976–86; *b* 12 June 1920; *s* of Charles and Charlotte Thompson; *m* 1947, Cynthia Ledsham; one *s* one *d*. *Educ:* Roundhay Sch., Leeds. Previously on staffs of Yorkshire Evening News, Evening Standard, London, and The Spectator (Dep. Editor); joined Sunday Telegraph, 1970; Asst Editor, 1975. *Publication:* (as Peter Quince) Country Life, 1975. *Address:* Corner Cottage, Burnham Norton, King's Lynn, Norfolk PE31 8DS. *T:* Fakenham 738396. *Club:* Travellers'.

THOMPSON, Rear-Adm. John Yelverton, CB 1960; DL; retired 1961; *b* 25 May 1909; *s* of late Sir John Perronet Thompson, KCSI, KCIE, and Ada Lucia, Lady Thompson (*née* Tyrrell); *m* 1934, Barbara Helen Mary Aston Key; two *s*. *Educ:* Mourne Grange, Kilkeel, Co. Down; RN College, Dartmouth. Midshipman: HMS Repulse and Berwick, 1926–29; Sub-Lieutenant: HMS Warspite, 1931; Lieutenant: HMS Queen Elizabeth, 1931–32, Restless 1933, Excellent 1933–34, Queen Elizabeth 1935, Glasgow 1936–39; Lieut-Commander: HMS Excellent 1939–41, Anson 1941–43; Commander: Admiralty, Naval Ordnance Dept, 1943–45; US Fifth Fleet, 1946; HMS Liverpool, 1947; HMS Newcastle, 1948; Captain: Ordnance Board, 1948–50; HMS Unicorn, 1951–52; Director, Gunnery Division, Naval Staff, 1952–54; Imperial Defence College, 1955; Commodore: Royal Naval Barracks, Portsmouth, 1956–57; Rear-Admiral: Admiralty Interview Boards, 1958; Adm. Superintendent, HM Dockyard, Chatham, 1958–61. ADC to the Queen, 1957. Governor, Aldenham Sch., 1967–73. DL: Hertfordshire, 1966–73; Cornwall, 1973. American Legion of Merit, 1953. *Address:* Flushing Meadow, Manaccan, near Helston, Cornwall TR12 6HQ.
See also G. F. M. P. Thompson.

THOMPSON, Julian; *see* Thompson, R. J. de la M.

THOMPSON, Maj.-Gen. Julian Howard Atherden, CB 1982; OBE 1978; Major General Commanding Training and Reserve Forces Royal Marines, 1983–86; *b* 7 Oct. 1934; *s* of late Major A. J. Thompson, DSO, MC and Mary Stearns Thompson (*née* Krause); *m* 1960, Janet Avery, *d* of late Richard Robinson Rodd; one *s* one *d*. *Educ:* Sherborne School. 2nd Lieut RM, 1952; served 40, 42, 43, 45 Commandos RM, 1954–69; Asst Sec., Chiefs of Staff Cttee, 1970–71; BM, 3 Cdo Brigade, 1972–73; Directing Staff,

Staff Coll., Camberley, 1974–75; CO 40 Cdo RM, 1975–78; Comdr 3 Cdo Brigade, 1981–83, incl. Falklands campaign (CB). *Publication:* No Picnic: 3 Commando Brigade in the South Atlantic 1982, 1985. *Recreations:* sailing, shooting, history. *Address:* c/o Lloyds Bank, Royal Parade, Plymouth, Devon. *Clubs:* Army and Navy; Royal Western Yacht, Royal Marines Sailing.

THOMPSON, Julian O.; *see* Ogilvie Thompson.

THOMPSON, Hon. Lindsay Hamilton Simpson, CMG 1975; Premier of Victoria, 1981–82; Leader of the Opposition, Victoria, 1982; *b* 15 Oct. 1923; *s* of Arthur K. Thompson and Ethel M. Thompson; *m* 1950, Joan Margaret Poynder; two *s* one *d*. *Educ:* Caulfield Grammar Sch., Victoria (Captain and Dux 1941); Melbourne Univ. (BA Hons, BEd). MACE. AIF, New Guinea, 1942–45. MP (Lib.) in Victorian Legislative Council: Higinbotham Prov., 1955–67; Monash Prov., 1967–70; MLA Malvern, 1970–82; Member of Cabinet, 1956–82; Parly Sec. of Cabinet, 1956–58; Asst Chief Sec. and Asst Attorney-Gen., 1958–61; Asst Minister of Transport, 1960–61; Minister of Housing and Forests, 1961–67; Dep. Leader of Govt in Legislative Council, 1962–70; Minister in charge of Aboriginal Welfare, 1965–67; Minister of Educn, 1967–79 (longest term ever in this portfolio); Leader of Legislative Assembly, 1972–79; Dep. Premier of Victoria, 1972–81; Minister for Police and Emergency Services, 1979–81; Treasurer, 1979–82; served longest period as Cabinet Minister in history of Victoria. Dep. Chm., Statewide Building Soc. State Govt Rep., Melbourne Univ. Council, 1955–59. Pres., Royal Life Saving Soc., 1970–. Bronze Medal, Royal Humane Soc., 1974. Trustee: Melb. Cricket Ground, 1967–; Nat. Tennis Centre Trust, 1986–; Patron: Victorian Cricket Assoc.; Prahran CC; Aust. Quadriplegic Assoc.; Richmond FC. *Publications:* Australian Housing Today and Tomorrow, 1965; Looking Ahead in Education, 1969; A Fair Deal for Victoria, 1981. *Recreations:* cricket, golf, tennis. *Address:* 19 Allenby Avenue, Glen Iris, Victoria 3146, Australia. *T:* 25 6191. *Clubs:* Melbourne (Melbourne), Kingston Heath Golf, Sorrento Golf.

THOMPSON, Sir Lionel; *see* Thompson, Sir T. L. T., Bt.

THOMPSON, Major Lloyd H.; *see* Hall-Thompson.

THOMPSON, Michael Jacques, OBE 1977; HM Diplomatic Service; Counsellor, Foreign and Commonwealth Office, since 1985; *b* 31 Jan. 1936; *s* of late Christopher Thompson and of Colette Jeanne-Marie Thompson; *m* 1967, Mary Susan (*née* Everard); one *s* one *d*. *Educ:* Uppingham; Christ's Coll., Cambridge (Law Tripos, 1956–60; MA). National Service, Kenya, Aden and Cyprus, 1954–56. HMOCS, Kenya, 1960–63; FCO, 1964; served Kuala Lumpur, Saigon, Lusaka and FCO, 1965–79; Counsellor, Kuala Lumpur, 1979–82; seconded to Comdr, British Land Forces, Hong Kong, 1982–85. *Recreations:* squash, tennis, golf, gardening. *Address:* c/o Foreign and Commonwealth Office, SW1. *Clubs:* United Oxford & Cambridge University; Selangor, Lake (Kuala Lumpur).

THOMPSON, Prof. Michael Warwick, DSc; FInstP; Vice-Chancellor, University of Birmingham, since 1987; *b* 1 June 1931; *s* of Kelvin Warwick Thompson and Madeleine Thompson; *m* 1954, Sybil (*née* Spooner); two *s*. *Educ:* Rydal Sch.; Univ. of Liverpool (BSc, DSc). Research scientist, AERE, Harwell, 1953–65; Sussex University: Prof. of Experimental Physics, 1965–80; Pro-Vice-Chancellor, 1973–77, actg Vice-Chancellor, 1976; Vis. Prof., 1980–; Vice-Chancellor, UEA, 1980–86. Member: E Sussex AHA, 1974–79; E Sussex Educn Cttee, 1973–78. Dir, Alliance & Leicester Building Soc., 1985– (Dir, Alliance Building Soc., 1979–85). Mem. Council, Eastbourne Coll., 1977–; Governor, St Bedes Sch., Eastbourne, 1978–. Oliver Lodge Prizewinner, Univ. of Liverpool, 1953; Prizewinner, Materials Science Club, 1970; C. V Boys Prizewinner, Inst. of Physics, 1972. *Publications:* Defects and Radiation Damage in Metals, 1969; (jtly) Channelling, 1973; over 90 papers in sci. jls, incl. Philosophical Magazine, Radiation Effects, Proc. Royal Society. *Recreations:* the arts, sailing. *Address:* University of Birmingham, Edgbaston, Birmingham B15 2TT.

THOMPSON, Nicolas de la Mare; Managing Director, Heinemann Group of Publishers, since 1985; Director, Octopus Publishing Group Plc, since 1985; *b* 4 June 1928; *s* of Rupert Spens Thompson and Florence Elizabeth Thompson (*née* de la Mare); *m* 1956, Erica Pennell; two *s* one *d*. *Educ:* Eton; Christ Church, Oxford (MA). Managing Director, George Weidenfeld and Nicolson, 1956–70; Publishing Dir, Pitman, 1970–85. Chm., Book Development Council, 1984–86; Treas., Publishers Assoc., 1986–. *Address:* 8 Ennismore Gardens, SW7.

THOMPSON, Dr Noel Brentnall Watson; Under Secretary, Department of Education and Science (Head of Higher and Further Education III Branch), since 1980; *b* 11 Dec. 1932; *s* of George Watson Thompson and Mary Henrietta Gibson; *m* 1957, Margaret Angela Elizabeth Baston; one *s*. *Educ:* Manchester Grammar School; Cambridge Univ. (MA); Imperial College, London (MSc Eng, PhD). National Service, RN (Sub-Lieut), 1951–53. Research, Imperial Coll., 1958–61; Lectr in Physical Metallurgy, Univ. of Birmingham, 1961–65; Dept of Education and Science, 1966–67, 1969–77 and 1979–; Secretary, National Libraries Cttee, 1967–69; Cabinet Office, 1977–79. *Publications:* papers in scientific journals. *Recreations:* railways of all sizes, mechanics, music, modern history, photography, walking. *Address:* c/o Department of Education and Science, Elizabeth House, York Road, SE1 7PH. *T:* 01-934 9928. *Clubs:* other people's.

THOMPSON, Norman Sinclair, CBE 1980; Chairman: C-Tin Ltd; EHG Project Management Co. Ltd; Vice-Chairman, New Hong Kong Tunnel Co. Ltd; *b* 7 July 1920; *s* of Norman Whitfield Thompson and Jane Thompson (*née* Robinson); *m* 1945, Peggy Sivil; two *s* (one *d* decd). *Educ:* Middlesbrough High Sch. Qual. Chartered Accountant, 1947 (FCA); Cost and Management Accountant (ACMA). Served War, Merchant Seaman, 1940–45. Asst Sec., Paton's and Baldwin's Ltd, 1947; Commercial Manager, Cowan's Sheldon & Co. Ltd, 1955; Group Secretary, Richardson's Westgarth & Co. Ltd, 1957; Financial Dir, David Brown & Sons (Huddersfield) Ltd, 1961; Gen. Manager, Malta Drydocks, Swan Hunter Group Ltd, 1963; apptd Swan Hunter Bd, 1964; Overseas Dir, 1967; Dep. Managing Dir, 1969; The Cunard Steam-Ship Co. Ltd: Man. Dir, Cargo Shipping, 1970; Man. Dir, 1971–74; Chairman: Mass Transit Railway Corp., Hong Kong, 1975–83; Poole Harbour Comrs, 1984–86; Director: Hong Kong and Shanghai Banking Corp., 1978–86; British Shipbuilders, 1983–86. *Recreations:* sailing, music. *Address:* 15 Mount Cameron Road, The Peak, Hong Kong. *T:* Hong Kong 5-8498315. *Clubs:* Oriental, Royal Ocean Racing; Hong Kong, Royal Hong Kong Yacht.

THOMPSON, Oliver Frederic, OBE 1945; Pro-Chancellor of The City University, 1966–72; *b* 26 Jan. 1905; 3rd *s* of late W. Graham Thompson and late Oliveria C. Prescott; *m* 1939, Frances Phyllida, *d* of late F. H. Bryant; one *s* three *d*. *Educ:* Tonbridge. Mem. Shell Gp of Cos, 1924–64: managerial posts in USA, Caribbean, London. Head of Oil Sect., Min. of Econ. Warfare, and Mem. War Cabinet Sub-Cttee on Oil, 1942–46; rep. UK, Suez Canal Users Assoc.; rep. UK on various UN and OECD Cttees; Mem. Parly and Sci. Cttee, 1955–65. Past Master and Mem. Ct, Worshipful Co. of Skinners. Chm. Governing Body, Northampton Coll. of Advanced Technology, 1956–66 (now City University); Governor, Tonbridge Sch. FInstP (Past Mem. Council); Chm. Qualifications Cttee, British Computer Society, 1968 (Hon. Fellow, 1972). County Councillor, Surrey, 1965–77 (Majority Leader, 1970–73). Hon. DSc, City Univ., 1967. *Publications:* various papers on economics of energy and petroleum. *Recreation:* country pursuits. *Address:* 32 Park Road, Aldeburgh, Suffolk IP15 5EU. *T:* Aldeburgh 2424.

THOMPSON, Patrick; *see* Thompson, H. P.

THOMPSON, Sir Paul (Anthony), 2nd Bt *cr* 1963; company director; *b* 6 Oct. 1939; *s* of Sir Kenneth Pugh Thompson, 1st Bt, and of Nanne, *yr d* of Charles Broome, Walton, Liverpool; *S* father, 1984; *m* 1971, Pauline Dorothy, *d* of Robert O. Spencer, Bolton, Lancs; two *s* two *d*. *Educ:* Aldenham School, Herts. *Heir:* *s* Richard Kenneth Spencer Thompson, *b* 27 Jan. 1976. *Address:* 28 Dowhills Road, Blundellsands, Liverpool.

THOMPSON, Paul Richard, DPhil; social historian; Reader in Sociology, University of Essex, since 1971; *b* 1935; *m* 1st, Thea Vigne; one *s* one *d*; 2nd, Natasha Burchardt; one *d*. *Educ:* Bishop's Stortford Coll., Corpus Christi Coll., Oxford; The Queen's Coll., Oxford (Junior Research Fellow, 1961–64). MA, DPhil 1964. Lectr in Sociology, Univ. of Essex, 1964–69, Sen. Lectr, 1969–71; Sen. Res. Fellow, Nuffield Coll., Oxford, 1968–69; Vis. Prof. of Art History, Johns Hopkins Univ., 1972; Hoffman Wood Prof. of Architecture, Univ. of Leeds, 1977–78. Editor: Victorian Soc. Conf. Reports, 1965–67; Oral History, 1970–; Life Stories, 1985–. *Publications:* History of English Architecture (with Peter Kidson and Peter Murray), 1965, 2nd edn 1979; The Work of William Morris, 1967, new edn 1977; Socialists, Liberals and Labour: the struggle for London 1880–1914, 1967; The Edwardians: the remaking of British Society, 1975; The Voice of the Past: Oral History, 1978; Living the Fishing, 1983. *Address:* Department of Sociology, University of Essex, Wivenhoe Park, Colchester CO4 3SQ.

THOMPSON, Sir Peter (Anthony), Kt 1984; FCIT; Chairman, National Freight Consortium, since 1982 (Chief Executive, 1982–84); *b* 14 April 1928; *s* of late Herbert Thompson and of Sarah Jane Thompson; *m* 1958, Patricia Anne Norcott (*d* 1983); one *s* two *d*. *Educ:* Royal Drapers Sch.; Bradford Grammar Sch.; Leeds Univ. BA. Unilever, 1952–62; GKN, 1962–64; Transport Controller, Rank Organisation, 1964–66; Head of Transport, BSC, 1968–72; Group Co-ordinator, BRS Ltd, 1972–75; Exec. Vice-Chm. (Operations), NFC, 1976–77; Dep. Chm. and Chief Exec., Nat. Freight Corp., later Nat. Freight Co., 1977–82. Chm., Community Hospitals Ltd. Pres., Inst. of Freight Forwarders, 1982–83; Vice-Pres., Inst. of Transport, 1982–. Chm., Inst. of Physical Distribution Management, 1984. CBIM. Hambros Businessman of the Year, 1983. *Recreations:* golf, music. *Address:* 37 Newlands Avenue, Radlett, Herts. *T:* Radlett 5996; (office) National Freight Consortium, Merton Centre, 45 St Peters Street, Bedford MK40 2UB. *T:* Bedford 67444. *Club:* Royal Automobile.

THOMPSON, Peter Kenneth James; Under Secretary, Department of Health and Social Security, since 1983; *b* 30 July 1937; *s* of Kenneth George Thompson and Doreen May Thompson; *m* 1970, Sandy Lynne Harper; two *d*. *Educ:* Worksop Coll.; Christ's Coll., Cambridge (MA, LLB). Called to the Bar, Lincoln's Inn, 1961; practised at Common Law Bar, 1961–73; Lawyer in Govt Service: Law Commission, 1973–78; Lord Chancellor's Dept, 1978–83. *Publications:* The Unfair Contract Terms Act 1977, 1978; The Recovery of Interest, 1985; *radio plays:* A Matter of Form, 1977; Dormer and Grand-Daughter, 1978. *Recreation:* writing. *Address:* 9 Hillfield Park, Muswell Hill, N10 3QT.

THOMPSON, Pratt; *see* Thompson, W. P.

THOMPSON, Sir Ralph (Patrick), Kt 1980; Barrister and Solicitor of the Supreme Court of New Zealand, since 1938; *b* 19 June 1916; *m* 1940, Dorothy Maud Simes; one *s* two *d*. *Educ:* Napier Boys High Sch.; Dannevirke High Sch.; Canterbury Univ. (LLB 1937). Admitted barrister and solicitor, 1938; in practice in Christchurch. Former Chairman: United Building Soc; Waitaki NZ Refrigerating Ltd; Director: New Zealand Refining Co. Ltd, 1967–; Waitaki International Ltd (formerly Waitiki NZ Ltd), 1975–; Former Director: Barclays Bank New Zealand Ltd (formerly New Zealand United Corp. Ltd); M. O'Brien & Co. Ltd. *Recreations:* reading, racing, walking. *Address:* 115 Heaton Street, Christchurch 5, New Zealand. *T:* 557.490. *Clubs:* Canterbury, Canterbury University (Hon. Life Mem.).

THOMPSON, Prof. Raymond, PhD; FRSC; FEng 1985, FIMM; Business Development Director, Borax Holdings Ltd since 1986 (Research Director, 1969–86); Deputy Chairman, Borax Research Ltd, since 1986 (Managing Director, 1980–86); Director, Borax Consolidated (Borides) Ltd, since 1986; *b* 4 April 1925; *s* of late William Edward Thompson and of Hilda Thompson (*née* Rowley). *Educ:* Longton High Sch.; Univ. of Nottingham (MSc 1950, PhD 1952); Imperial Coll., Univ. of London (DIC 1953). Research Manager, Borax Consolidated, 1961. Special Professor of Inorganic Chemistry, Univ. of Nottingham, 1975–; Hon. Prof., Molecular Sciences, Univ. of Warwick, 1975–. Member Council: Royal Inst. of Chemistry, 1969–72; Chemical Soc., 1977–80 (Chm., Inorganic Chemicals Gp, 1972–83); RSC, 1983– (Vice-Pres., Industrial Div., 1981–83, Pres., 1983–85). Governor, Kingston-upon-Thames Polytechnic, 1978–. Hon. Associate, RHC, London Univ., 1984–. Liveryman, Glass Sellers' Co.; Freeman, City of London. FRSA. Industrial Chemistry Award, Chem. Soc., 1976. *Publications:* (ed) The Modern Inorganic Chemicals Industry, 1977; (ed) Mellors Comprehensive Treatise, Boron Supplement, Part A, 1979, Part BI, 1981; (ed) Speciality Inorganic Chemicals, 1981; (ed) Energy and Chemistry, 1981; (ed) Trace Metal Removal From Aqueous Solution, 1986; various papers on inorganic boron and nitrogen chemistry. *Recreation:* gardening. *Address:* The Garth, Winchester Close, Esher, Surrey KT10 8QH. *T:* Esher 64428. *Club:* City Livery.

THOMPSON, Reginald Aubrey, CMG 1964; *b* 22 Nov. 1905; *s* of John Thompson, Mansfield; *m* 1932, Gwendoline Marian Jackson (*d* 1978); one *s*. *Educ:* Brunts Sch., Mansfield; University Coll., Nottingham. BSc London (1st Cl. Hons Chemistry), 1927. Research, Organic Chemistry, 1927–29; Science Master, various grammar schools, 1929–41; Scientific Civil Service, Min. of Supply, 1941–46; transf. to Admin. Class (Principal), 1946; Asst Sec., 1953; Assistant Secretary, Department of Education and Science (formerly Office of Minister of Science), 1956–64; Ministry of Technology, 1964; retd, 1966. Led UK Delegn at Confs on: liability of operators of nuclear ships, Brussels Convention, 1962; liability for nuclear damage, Vienna Convention, 1963. *Recreations:* golf, reading, music. *Address:* Qualicum, 81 Bentsbrook Park, North Holmwood, Dorking, Surrey RH5 4JL. *T:* Dorking 882289.

THOMPSON, Reginald Harry; Chairman, National Dock Labour Board, since 1983; *b* 26 Oct. 1925; *s* of late Ernest and Phyllis Thompson; *m* 1951, Winifred (*née* Hoyle); one *s* one *d*. *Educ:* Ecclesfield Grammar School, Sheffield. Thorncliffe Collieries, 1940; Yorkshire Mineworkers Assoc., 1941; RN, 1942; Admin. and Conciliation Officer, NUM (Yorks Area), 1946; National Coal Board: Labour Officer, S Barnsley Area, 1955; Area Ind. Relations Officer, N Barnsley Area, 1962, N Yorks Area, 1967; Dep. Area Dir, N Yorks Area, 1970; Dir of Wages, HQ, 1973; Dep. Dir Gen., 1974, Dir Gen., 1975–83, Ind. Relations. FBIM 1978. *Publications:* articles in technical jls. *Recreations:* local government affairs; golf. *Address:* Rowley Road, Priory Hill, St Neots, Huntingdon, Cambs. *T:* Huntingdon 73691.

THOMPSON, Reginald Stanley; Headmaster of Bloxham School, 1952–65, retired; *b* 23 Sept. 1899; *s* of late Reverend Canon C. H. Thompson, formerly Vicar of Eastleigh, Hants, and of Newport, Isle of Wight; *m* 1938, Phyllis Barbara, *y d* of Henry White, Solicitor, Winchester, Hants; one *s* two *d*. *Educ:* Hereford Cathedral School; Lancing College; Oriel College, Oxford. Assistant Master at Sherborne School, 1922–52 (Housemaster, 1936–52). *Recreations:* music, gardening, books, cricket. *Address:* Westcott Close, Clifton-upon-Teme, Worcestershire. *T:* Shelsley Beauchamp 234.

THOMPSON, Sir Richard (Hilton Marler), 1st Bt *cr* 1963; *b* Calcutta, India, 5 Oct. 1912; *m* 1939, Anne Christabel de Vere, *d* of late Philip de Vere Annesley, MA, and of Mrs Annesley, BEM; one *s*. *Educ:* Malvern College. In business in India, Burma and Ceylon, 1930–40; travelled in Tibet, Persia, Iraq, Turkey, etc. Served in RNVR, 1940–46, volunteering as ordinary seaman; commissioned, 1941 (despatches, 1942); Lieut-Comdr 1944. MP (C) Croydon West, 1950–55; Assistant-Government Whip, 1952; Lord Commissioner of the Treasury, 1954; MP (C) Croydon South, 1955–66 and 1970–Feb. 1974; Vice-Chamberlain of HM Household, 1956; Parly Sec., Ministry of Health, 1957–59; Under-Secretary of State, CRO, 1959–60; Parly Sec., Ministry of Works, Oct. 1960–July 1962. Mem., Public Accounts Cttee, 1973–74. A Cottonian family Trustee of the British Museum, 1951–63, a Prime Minister's Trustee, 1963–84; Trustees' representative on Council of Nat. Trust, 1978–84. Chm., Overseas Migration Bd, 1959; led UK delegation to ECAFE in Bangkok, 1960; signed Indus Waters Agreement with India, Pakistan and World Bank for UK, Sept. 1960; led UK Parly Delegn to Tanganyika, to present Speaker's chair, Jan. 1963. Chm., Capital and Counties Property Co., 1971–77, retired; Pres., British Property Fedn, 1976–77; Director, British Museum Publications Ltd. Chm., British Museum Society, 1970–74. *Recreations:* gardening, collecting, study of history. *Heir:* *s* Nicholas Annesley Marler Thompson [*b* 19 March 1947; *m* 1982, Venetia, *y d* of Mr and Mrs John Heathcote, Conington]. *Address:* Rhodes House, Sellindge, Kent. *Clubs:* Carlton, Army and Navy.

THOMPSON, Richard Paul Hepworth, DM; FRCP; Physician to the Royal Household, since 1982; Consultant Physician, St Thomas' Hospital, since 1972; Physician, King Edward VII Hospital for Officers, since 1982; *b* 14 April 1940; *s* of Stanley Henry and Winifred Lilian Thompson; *m* 1974, Eleanor Mary Hughes. *Educ:* Epsom Coll.; Worcester Coll., Oxford (MA, DM); St Thomas's Hosp. Med. Sch. MRC Clinical Res. Fellow, Liver Unit, KCH, 1967–69; Fellow, Gastroenterology Unit, Mayo Clinic, USA, 1969–71; Lectr, Liver Unit, KCH, 1971–72. Mem., Lambeth, Southwark and Lewisham AHA, 1979–82. Examiner in Medicine: Soc. of Apothecaries, 1976–80; Faculty of Dental Surgery, RCS, 1980–. Governor, Guy's Hosp. Med. Sch., 1980–82; Member Cttee of Management: Inst. of Psychiatry, 1981–; King Edward VII Hosp. Fund, 1985–. *Publications:* Physical Signs in Medicine, 1980; papers and reviews in med. jls. *Address:* 36 Dealtry Road, SW15. *T:* 01–789 3839.

THOMPSON, Sir Robert Grainger Ker, KBE 1965; CMG 1961; DSO 1945; MC 1943; *b* 12 April 1916; *s* of late Canon W. G. Thompson; *m* 1950, Merryn Newboult; one *s* one *d*. *Educ:* Marlborough; Sidney Sussex College, Cambridge (MA). Cadet, Malayan Civil Service, 1938. Served War of 1939–45 (MC, DSO), RAF, 1941–46. Asst Commissioner of Labour, Perak, 1946; jssc 1948–49; Staff Officer (Civil) to Director of Operations, 1950; Co-ordinating Officer, Security, 1955; Dep. Sec. for Def., Fedn of Malaya, 1957; Perm. Sec. for Def., 1959–61; Head, British Advisory Mission to Vietnam, 1961–65. Author and consultant. Johan Mangku Negara (JMN), Malaya, 1958. *Publications:* Defeating Communist Insurgency, 1966; The Royal Flying Corps, 1968; No Exit from Vietnam, 1969; Revolutionary War in World Strategy, 1945–1969, 1970; Peace Is Not At Hand, 1974; (ed) War in Peace: an analysis of warfare since 1945, 1981. *Recreations:* all country pursuits. *Address:* Pitcott House, Winsford, Minehead, Som.

THOMPSON, Robert Henry Stewart, CBE 1973; MA, DSc, DM, BCh; FRS 1974; FRCP; FRCPath; Courtauld Professor of Biochemistry, Middlesex Hospital Medical School, University of London, 1965–76; now Emeritus Professor; Trustee, Wellcome Trust, 1963–82; *b* 2 Feb. 1912; *s* of Dr Joseph Henry Thompson and Mary Eleanor Rutherford; *m* 1938, Inge Vilma Anita Gebert; one *s* two *d*. *Educ:* Epsom College; Trinity College, Oxford; Guy's Hospital Medical School. Millard Scholar, Trinity College, Oxford, 1930; Theodore Williams Scholar in Physiology, Oxford, 1932; 1st Class Animal Physiology, Oxford, 1933; Senior Demy, Magdalen College, Oxford, 1933; Univ. Scholar, Guy's Hosp. Med. School, 1933; Adrian Stokes Travelling Fellowship to Hosp. of Rockefeller Inst., New York, 1937–38; Gillson Research Scholar in Pathology, Soc. of Apothecaries of London, 1938; Fellow of University Coll., Oxford, 1938–47, Hon. Fellow, 1983; Demonstrator in Biochemistry, Oxford, 1938–47; Dean of Medical School, Oxford, 1946–47; Prof. of Chemical Pathology, Guy's Hosp. Medical School, Univ. of London, 1947–65; Secretary-General International Union of Biochemistry, 1955–64; Hon. Sec. Royal Society of Medicine, 1958–64; Mem. of Medical Research Council, 1958–62; Mem., Bd of Governors, Middlesex Hosp., 1972–74. Governor, Epsom Coll., 1982–. Hon. Mem., Biochemical Soc. Radcliffe Prize for Medical Research, Oxford, 1943. Served War of 1939–45, Major, RAMC, 1944–46. *Publications:* (with C. W. Carter) Biochemistry in relation to Medicine, 1949; Joint Editor (with E. J. King) Biochemical Disorders in Human Disease, 1957; numerous papers on biochemical and pathological subjects in various scientific journals. *Recreation:* gardening. *Address:* 1 Church Way, Hurst Green, Oxted, Surrey RH8 9EA. *T:* Oxted 3526; Orchard's Almshouses, Launcells, N Cornwall. *T:* Bude 3817. *Club:* Athenæum.

THOMPSON, Major Robert Lloyd H.; *see* Hall-Thompson.

THOMPSON, (Rupert) Julian (de la Mare); Chairman, Sotheby's International, 1982–85 and since 1986; Vice-Chairman, Sotheby's, since 1986 (Chairman, 1982–86); *b* 23 July 1941; *s* of Rupert Spens Thompson and Florence Elizabeth (*née* de la Mare); *m* 1965, Jacqueline Mary Ivimy; three *d*. *Educ:* Eton Coll.; King's Coll., Cambridge (MA). Joined Sotheby's, 1963; appointed a Director, 1969. *Address:* 43 Clarendon Road, W11 4JD. *T:* 01–727 6039.

THOMPSON, Sir (Thomas) Lionel (Tennyson), 5th Bt, *cr* 1806; Barrister-at-Law; *b* 19 June 1921; *s* of Lt-Col Sir Thomas Thompson, 4th Bt, MC, and of Milicent Ellen Jean, *d* of late Edmund Charles Tennyson-d'Eyncourt, Bayons Manor, Lincolnshire; *S* father, 1964; *m* 1955, Mrs Margaret van Beers (marr. diss. 1962), *d* of late Walter Herbert Browne; one *s* one *d*. *Educ:* Eton. Served War of 1939–45: Royal Air Force Volunteer Reserve, 1940; Flying Officer, 1942 (invalided, 1944); Able Seaman, Royal Fleet Auxiliary, 1944–46. Awarded 1939–45 Star, Aircrew (Europe) Star, Defence and Victory Medals. Called to the Bar, Lincoln's Inn, 1952. *Recreations:* shooting, sailing, flying and photography. *Heir:* *s* Thomas d'Eyncourt John Thompson, *b* 22 Dec. 1956. *Address:* 184/185 Temple Chambers, Temple Avenue, EC4Y 0BB. *T:* 01–353 8850; 16 Old Buildings, Lincoln's Inn, WC2. *T:* 01–405 7929.

THOMPSON, Vernon Cecil, MB, BS London; FRCS; retired 1970 as Surgeon to Department of Thoracic Surgery, The London Hospital; Surgeon, London Chest Hospital; Hon. Consulting Thoracic Surgeon to: West London Hospital, Hammersmith; King Edward VII Hospital, Windsor; Harefield Hospital, Middlesex; Broomfield and Black Notley Hospitals, Essex; *b* 17 Sept. 1905; 2nd *s* of Dr C. C. B. Thompson, Tidenham, Glos; *m* 1942, Jean, *d* of late H. J. Hilary; one *s* one *d*. *Educ:* Monmouth School; St Bartholomew's Hospital. Resident House appointments followed by First Assistant to a Surgical Unit, St Bartholomew's Hospital, 1929–37. Dorothy Temple Cross Travelling Fellowship, Vienna, and University Hosp., Ann Arbor, Michigan, USA, 1937. President, Soc. of Thoracic Surgeons of Great Britain and Ireland, 1966; Hon. Mem. Amer. Soc. for Thoracic Surgery, 1967. *Publications:* contrib. on surgical diseases of the chest to jls and text books. *Recreations:* fishing, shooting, gardening. *Address:* Vicarage House, Llowes, Hereford. *T:* Glasbury 323.

THOMPSON, William Bell, MA, PhD; Professor of Physics, University of California, since 1965; Chairman, Department of Physics, University of California at San Diego, 1969–72; *b* N Ireland, 27 Feb. 1922; *m* 1953, Gertrud Helene Goldschmidt, PhD (marr. diss. 1972); one *s* one *d*; *m* 1972, Johanna Elzelina Ladestein Korevaar. *Educ:* Universities of British Columbia and Toronto, Canada. BA 1945, MA 1947, Univ. of BC; PhD Toronto, 1950. AERE Harwell: Senior Research Fellow, 1950; Deputy Chief Scientist, 1959. Visiting Prof., Univ. of California, 1961; Head, Theoretical Physics Division, Culham Laboratory, UKAEA, 1961–63; Prof. of Theoretical Plasma Physics, Oxford Univ., 1963–65. *Publications:* Introduction to Plasma Physics, 1962; numerous papers in learned journals, on controlled thermonuclear research, plasma physics, kinetic theory, etc. *Recreations:* music, walking. *Address:* Physics Department, University of California at San Diego, La Jolla, California 92093, USA.

THOMPSON, (William) Godfrey, MA; FSA, FLA, FRSA; Cultural Consultant, United Arab Emirates, Abu Dhabi, 1983–86; *b* 28 June 1921; *s* of late A. and E. M. Thompson, Coventry; *m* 1946, Doreen Mary Cattell; one *s*. *Educ:* King Henry VIII Sch., Coventry. MA Loughborough, 1977. Served with Royal Signals, 1941–46. Entered Library Service, Coventry, 1937; Dep. Borough Librarian, Chatham, 1946; Dep. City Librarian: Kingston-upon-Hull, 1952; Manchester, 1958; City Librarian, Leeds, 1963; Guildhall Librarian, Director of Libraries and Art Galleries, City of London, 1966–83. Hon. Librarian to Clockmakers' Co., Gardeners' Co., Charles Lamb Soc.; Pres., Assoc. of Assistant Librarians, 1962. Member: Council, Library Assoc., 1968– (Hon. Treasurer, 1974–; Pres., 1978); Council, Aslib, 1968–71; Hon. Sec. Internat. Assoc. Metropolitan Libraries, 1968–70; Adv. Bd, New Library World. Member: Adv. Panel to Sec. of State on allocation of books received under Capital Transfer Tax; Adv. Panel to Sec. of State on Export of Works of Art. Mem. Exec. Cttee, Friends of the Nat. Libraries. Governor, St Bride Foundn. Consultant on libraries to several overseas governments, including the planning of five nat. libraries. *Publications:* London's Statues, 1971; Planning and Design of Libraries, 1972, 2nd edn 1977; (ed) London for Everyman, 1969; (ed) Encyclopædia of London, 1969. *Address:* 24 Morden Road, Blackheath, SE3 0AA.

THOMPSON, (William) Pratt; Chairman: AIDCOM International plc, since 1983 (Director since 1982); AIDCOM Technology, since 1982; Husky Computers Ltd; *b* 9 Feb. 1933; *s* of Philip Amos Thompson and Regina Beatrice (*née* Kirby); *m* 1963, Jenny Frances Styles; two *d*. *Educ:* Princeton Univ.; Columbia Univ. (BA Econ *magna cum laude*, Phi Beta Kappa); University of Geneva (MBA). AMF Incorporated, 1959–73: Research Analyst, New York, 1959–62; Executive Asst, Tobacco Machinery Gp, Geneva, 1962–63; Director, Marketing and Planning, AMF-C. Itoh Co. Ltd, Tokyo, 1963–66; Vice Pres. and Gen. Manager, AMF Overseas Corp., Hong Kong, 1966–67; Vice Pres., AMF Incorporated, London, 1968–73; Dep. Managing Director, Bowthorpe Holdings Ltd, 1973–78; BL Limited, 1978–81: Man. Dir, Jaguar Rover Triumph Ltd, 1978–79; Chm., BL Internat. Ltd, 1979–81; Vice-Chm., Colbert Gp (Geneva), 1981–84. Dir, Metalurgica de Santa Ana SA (Madrid), 1978–81. Member: Council, SMM&T, 1978–81; Council on Foreign Relations (USA), 1980–. Advisor, Internat. Centre for Child Studies, Bristol Univ., 1982–85. *Recreations:* various. *Address:* 24 Edge Street, W8 7PN. *Clubs:* Brooks's, Hurlingham; Knickerbocker (New York).

THOMPSON, Willoughby Harry, CMG 1974; CBE 1968 (MBE 1954); *b* 3 Dec. 1919; *m* 1963, Sheelah O'Grady; no *c*. Served War: RA, and E African Artillery, 1939–47. Kenya Govt Service, 1947–48; Colonial Administrative Service, Kenya, 1948–63; Colonial Sec., Falkland Islands, 1963–69 (Actg Governor, 1964 and 1967); Actg Judge, Falkland Islands and Dependencies Supreme Court, 1965–69; Actg Administrator, British Virgin Islands, May-July 1969; HM Commissioner in Anguilla, July 1969–71; Governor of Montserrat, 1971–74.

THOMPSON HANCOCK, P(ercy) E(llis); *see* Hancock.

THOMSON, family name of **Barons Thomson of Fleet** and **Thomson of Monifieth.**

THOMSON OF FLEET, 2nd Baron *cr* 1964; **Kenneth Roy Thomson;** newspaper proprietor; Chairman of the Board, President, Chief Executive Officer and Director, Thomson Newspapers Ltd (owners of 39 daily newspapers in Canada); Chairman of the Board and Director: International Thomson Holdings Inc.; International Thomson Organisation Ltd; Ontario Newspapers Ltd; TECL Holdings Ltd; The Standard St Lawrence Company Ltd; The Thomson Corporation Ltd; The Thomson Organisation PLC; The Woodbridge Company Ltd; Thomson Equitable Corporation Ltd; Thomson International Corporation Ltd; Thomson Investments Ltd; Thomson Newspapers Inc. (owners of 93 daily newspapers in the USA); *b* Toronto, Ont., 1 Sept. 1923; *s* of 1st Baron Thomson of Fleet, GBE, founder of Thomson Newspapers, and Edna Alice (*d* 1951), *d* of John Irvine, Drayton, Ont.; *S* father, 1976; *m* 1956, Nora Marilyn, *d* of A. V. Lavis; two *s* one *d*. *Educ:* Upper Canada Coll.; Univ. of Cambridge, England (MA). Served War of 1942–45 with RCAF. Began in editorial dept of Timmins Daily Press., Timmins, Ont., 1947; Advertising Dept, Galt Reporter, Galt, 1948–50, General Manager, 1950–53; returned to Toronto Head Office of Thomson Newspapers to take over direction of Company's Canadian and American operations. President and Director: Fleet Street Publishers Ltd; Kenthom Holdings Ltd; Thomfleet Holdings Ltd; Thomson Works of Art Ltd; Vice President and Director: Cablevue (Quinte) Ltd; Veribest Products Ltd; Director: Abitibi-Price Inc.; Caribbean Trust Ltd; Central Canada Insurance Service Ltd; Hudson's Bay Co.; IBM (Canada) Ltd; International Thomson Organisation PLC (Chm., 1975–86); Nipa Lodge Co. Ltd; Orchid Lodge Co. Ltd; Scottish & York Holdings Ltd; Scottish & York Insurance Co. Ltd; Thomson Scottish Associates Ltd; Thomson Television Ltd; The Toronto-Dominion Bank; Victoria Insurance Co. of Canada. Dep. Chm., 1966–67, Chm., 1968–70, Co-Pres., 1971–81, Times Newspapers Ltd. Member, Baptist Church. *Recreations:* collecting paintings and works of art, walking. *Heir:* *s* Hon. David Kenneth Roy Thomson, *b* 12 June 1957. *Address:* (home) 8 Castle Frank Road, Toronto, Ont M4W 2Z4, Canada; 8 Kensington Palace Gardens, W8; (office) Thomson Newspapers Ltd, 65 Queen Street West, Toronto, Ont. M5H 2M8, Canada; International Thomson Organisation PLC, The Quadrangle, PO Box 4YG, 180 Wardour Street, W1A 4YG. *Clubs:* York Downs, National, Toronto, Granite, York, Toronto Hunt (Toronto).

THOMSON OF MONIFIETH, Baron *cr* 1977 (Life Peer), of Monifieth, Dundee; **George Morgan Thomson,** KT 1981; PC 1966; Chairman, Independent Broadcasting Authority, since 1981 (Deputy Chairman, 1980); Chancellor, Heriot Watt University, since 1977; *b* 16 Jan. 1921; *s* of late James Thomson, Monifieth; *m* 1948, Grace Jenkins;

two *d. Educ:* Grove Academy, Dundee. Served War of 1939–45, in Royal Air Force, 1940–45. Assistant Editor, Forward, 1946, Editor, 1948–53. Contested (Lab) Glasgow, Hillhead, 1950; MP (Lab) Dundee East, July 1952–72. Joint Chm., Council for Education in the Commonwealth, 1959–64; Adviser to Educational Institute of Scotland, 1960–64. Minister of State, Foreign Office, 1964–66; Chancellor of the Duchy of Lancaster, 1966–67; Joint Minister of State, Foreign Office, 1967; Secretary of State for Commonwealth Affairs, Aug. 1967–Oct. 1968; Minister Without Portfolio, 1968–69; Chancellor of the Duchy of Lancaster, 1969–70; Shadow Defence Minister, 1970–72. Chm., Labour Cttee for Europe, 1972–73; Commissioner, EEC, 1973–Jan. 1977. Chairman: European Movement in Britain, 1977–80; Advertising Standards Authority, 1977–80; First Crown Estate Comr, 1978–80. Director: Royal Bank of Scotland Gp, 1982–; ICI plc; Woolwich Equitable Building Soc. Pres., Hist. of Advertising Trust, 1985–; Vice-Pres., RTS, 1982–. Dep. Chm., Ditchley Foundn, 1983–; Pilgrims Trustee, 1977–; Trustee, Leeds Castle Foundn, 1978–. FRSE 1985. Hon. LLD Dundee, 1967; Hon. DLitt: Heriot-Watt, 1973; New Univ. of Ulster, 1984; Hon. DSc Aston, 1976. *Address:* IBA, 70 Brompton Road, SW3 1EY. *T:* 01–584 7011. *Club:* Brooks's.

THOMSON, Sir Adam, Kt 1983; CBE 1976; Chairman and Chief Executive, British Caledonian Group (formerly The Caledonian Aviation Group plc), since 1970 (formerly Airways Interests (Thomson) Ltd, Chairman and Managing Director, 1964–70); Chairman and Chief Executive, British Caledonian Airways Ltd, since 1970; *b* 7 July 1926; *s* of Frank Thomson and Jemina Rodgers; *m* 1948, Dawn Elizabeth Burt; two *s*. *Educ:* Rutherglen Acad.; Coatbridge Coll.; Royal Technical Coll., Glasgow. Pilot; Fleet Air Arm, 1944–47; Flying Instructor/Commercial Pilot, 1947–50; BEA, West African Airways, Britavia, 1951–59. Caledonian Airways: Man Dir, 1961–64; Chm. and Man Dir, 1964–70; Chairman: Caledonian Airmotive Ltd; Caledonian Hotel Holdings. Dep. Chm., Martin Currie Pacific Trust PLC, 1985–; Director: Williams & Glyn's Bank Ltd, 1978–82; Royal Bank of Scotland Gp, 1982–; Otis Elevators Ltd, 1978–84; MEPC plc, 1982–. Chm., Assoc. of European Airlines, 1977–78. FRAeS; FCIT; FBIM. Hon. LLD: Glasgow, 1979; Sussex, 1984; Strathclyde, 1986. Businessman of the Year, Hambro Award, 1970; first Scottish Free Enterprise Award, Aims for Freedom and Enterprise, 1976. *Recreations:* golf, sailing. *Address:* 154 Buckswood Drive, Crawley, West Sussex. *Clubs:* Caledonian; Royal & Ancient Golf (St Andrews); Old Prestwick Golf; Walton Heath Golf.

THOMSON, Brian Harold, TD 1947; Chairman, since 1974, Joint Managing Director, since 1948, D. C. Thomson & Co. Ltd; *b* 21 Nov. 1918; *e s* of late William Harold Thomson of Kemback and Helen Irene, *d* of Sir Charles Ballance; *m* 1947, Agnes Jane Patricia Cunninghame; one *s* four *d*. *Educ:* Charterhouse. Served War of 1939–45: 1st Fife and Forfar Yeomanry, and on Staff, DAQMG 1st Armoured Div., N Africa and Italy, 1943–44, GS02 Instructor, Staff Coll., Haifa, 1944–46; Lt-Col Comdg Fife and Forfar Yeomanry TA, 1953–56. Entered D. C. Thomson & Co. Ltd, 1937. Director: John Leng & Co. Ltd, 1948–; Southern Television, 1959–; Alliance Trust and Second Alliance Trust, 1961–. *Recreations:* golf, shooting. *Club:* Royal and Ancient Golf (St Andrews).

THOMSON, Bryden; Orchestral Conductor; Artistic Director, since 1977, and Principal Conductor, 1977–85 (now Conductor Emeritus) Ulster Orchestra; Principal Conductor, RTE Symphony Orchestra, from 1984; *b* Ayr, Scotland. *Educ:* Ayr Academy; Royal Scottish Academy of Music; Staatliche Hochschule für Musik, Hamburg. BMus Dunelm; DipMusEd (Hons); RSAM; LRAM; ARCM; FRSAMD. Asst Conductor, BBC Scottish Orchestra, 1958; Conductor: Royal Ballet, 1962; Den Norske Opera, Oslo, 1964; Stora Teatern, Göteborg, Sweden, 1965; Royal Opera, Stockholm, 1966; NI Opera Trust, 1981 and 1982; Associate Conductor, Scottish National Orch., 1966; Principal Conductor: BBC Northern Symphony Orch., 1968–73; BBC Welsh Symphony Orch., 1978–83. Guest Conducting: Norway; Sweden; Denmark; Canada; Germany; S Africa; France; Italy; Principal Guest Conductor, Trondheim Symphony Orch., 1977. Recordings of works by Harty, Elgar and Bax. Hon. DLitt NUU, 1984. *Recreations:* golf, learning about music. *Address:* 2 Leeson Village, Dublin 4.

THOMSON, Sir David; *see* Thomson, Sir F. D. D.

THOMSON, David Kinnear, CBE 1972 (MBE 1945); TD; JP, DL; Former President, Peter Thomson (Perth) Ltd, whisky blenders and exporters; Chairman, Tayside Health Board, 1973–77; *b* Perth, 26 March 1910; *s* of Peter Thomson, whisky blender, and Jessie Kinnear; unmarried. *Educ:* Perth Academy; Strathallan School. Mem., Perth Local Authority, 1949–72; Chm. Bd of Management, Perth Technical Coll., 1972–75; Mem., ITA (Scottish Br.), 1968–73; Mem., Scottish Economic Council, 1968–75; Director: Scottish Transport Gp, 1972–76; Scottish Opera, 1973–81; Chm., Perth Festival of the Arts, 1973–. Mem. Court, Dundee Univ., 1975–79. Chm., Scottish Licensed Trade, 1981–82. Lord Provost of Perth, 1966–72, and Hon. Sheriff of Perth; DL 1966–72, 1980–, JP 1955, Perth and Kinross; Freeman, Perth and Kinross District, 1982. CStJ 1984. *Recreations:* golf, walking, listening to music. *Address:* Fairhill, Oakbank Road, Perth. *T:* Perth 26593. *Club:* Royal Perth Golfing Society.

THOMSON, David Paget, RD 1969; Director, Lazard Brothers & Co.; Member, Monopolies and Mergers Commission, since 1984; Chairman, Jufcrest, since 1984; *b* 19 March 1931; *s* of Sir George Paget Thomson, FRS and Kathleen Buchanan Smith; *m* 1959, Patience Mary, *d* of Sir William Lawrence Bragg, CH, OBE, MC, FRS; two *s* two *d*. *Educ:* Rugby Sch.; Grenoble Univ.; Trinity Coll., Cambridge (scholar; BA 1953, MA 1957). Nat. Service, RN (Sub-Lieut), 1953–55; subseq. Lieut-Comdr RNR. Senior Scholar, Trinity Coll., Cambridge, 1955; Lazard Bros & Co., 1956, Managing Dir, 1965, non-exec. Dir, 1984–; seconded to HM Diplomatic Service, 1971–73, as Counsellor (Economic), Bonn. Director: Finance Co. Viking, Zurich, 1969–71, 1973–; Richard Daus & Co., bankers, Frankfurt, 1974–81; Applied Photophysics, 1976–. Member: Editl Bd, Round Table; Internat. Maritime Industries Forum; Cttee of British and S Asia Trade Assoc.; Council, Brunel Univ., 1974–85; Court of Governors, Henley Admin. Staff Coll., 1979–; Dir, Henley Distance Learning Ltd, 1985. Hon. Treasurer, British Dyslexia Assoc. Trustee, Portsmouth Naval Base Property Trust, 1985–; Royal Institution: Manager, 1969–72, 1974–76; Treasurer, 1976–81; Vice Pres., 1970–71, 1976–81, 1985–; Chm. Council, 1985. CC Oxon 1985. Master, Plumbers' Co., 1980–81. *Recreations:* hill-walking, gardening, historical biography. *Address:* Little Stoke House, North Stoke, Oxon OX9 6AX. *T:* Wallingford 37161. *Clubs:* Athenaeum, City Livery.
See also S. L. Bragg, Sir J. A. Thomson.

THOMSON, Rt. Hon. David Spence, MC 1942; ED; PC 1981; MP (National) for Stratford/Taranaki, New Zealand, since 1963; *b* Stratford, 14 Nov. 1915; *s* of Percy Thomson, MBE; *m* 1942, June Grace Adams; one *s* three *d*. *Educ:* Stratford Primary and High Sch. Territorial Army, 1931–; served Middle East, 19th Inf. Bat. 1st Echelon, 1939–42; 2nd NZED, 1939–45; POW 1942; Hon. Col, 5 RNZIR, 1955–81; Brigadier (Reserve of Officers), 2nd Inf. Brig., 1959–60. Dairy farmer; Pres., NZ Federated Farmers Central Taranaki Exec., 1959–63. Minister of Defence, War Pensions and Rehabilitation, 1966–72, and 1980–84; Minister of Tourism, 1966–69; Minister of Police, 1969–72; Minister of Labour and Immigration, 1972; Minister of Justice, 1975–78; Minister of State Services and Leader, House of Reps, 1978–84. *Recreations:* golf, gardening, classical music. *Address:* Parliament Buildings, Wellington, New Zealand; (home) 22 Bird Road, Stratford, New Zealand.

THOMSON, Duncan, PhD; Keeper, Scottish National Portrait Gallery, since 1982; *b* 2 Oct. 1934; *s* of Duncan Murdoch Thomson and Jane McFarlane Wilson; *m* 1964, Julia Jane Macphail; one *d*. *Educ:* Airdrie Acad.; Univ. of Edinburgh (MA 1956, PhD 1970); Edinburgh Coll. of Art (Cert. of Coll.; Post-Dip. Scholarship); Moray House Coll. of Educn. Teacher of Art, 1959–67; Asst Keeper, Scottish National Portrait Gall., 1967–82. Scottish Arts Council: Mem., Art Cttee, 1983–; Chm., Exhibn Panel, 1985–. *Publications:* The Life and Art of George Jamesone, 1974; *exhibition catalogues:* A Virtuous and Noble Education, 1971; Painting in Scotland 1570–1650, 1975; Eye to Eye, 1980; (jtly) John Michael Wright, 1982. *Recreation:* reading poetry (and thinking about writing it). *Address:* 3 Eglinton Crescent, Edinburgh EH12 5DH. *T:* 031–225 6430.

THOMSON, Sir Evan (Rees Whitaker), Kt 1977; FRCS, FRACS, FACS; Hon. Consultant Surgeon, Princess Alexandra Hospital, Brisbane; *b* 14 July 1919; *s* of Frederick Thorpe Thomson and Ann Margaret Thomson (*née* Evans); *m* 1955, Mary Kennedy. *Educ:* Brisbane Boys' Coll.; Univ. of Queensland (MB BS). Full time staff, Brisbane General Hospital, 1942–48; RAAF Reserve, 1942–45; Visiting Surgeon: Brisbane General Hospital, 1950–56; Princess Alexandra Hospital, 1956–71; Clinical Lectr in Surgery, Univ. of Queensland, 1951–71. Qld Branch, Australian Medical Association: Councillor, 1966–78; Pres., 1967–68; a Vice-Pres., 1980–; Chm. of Council; Chm. of Ethics Cttee. Pres., 4th Aust. Med. Congress, 1971. Member: Med. Bd of Queensland; Wesley Hospital Bd, etc.; Pres., Qld Council of Professions, 1970–72; Vice-Patron, Medico-Legal Soc. of Qld; Governor, Univ. of Qld Foundn; Life Governor, Aust. Postgrad. Fedn in Medicine. Patron, Aust. Nat. Flag Assoc. (Qld). Silver Jubilee Medal, 1977. *Publications:* Future Needs for Medical Education in Queensland (ed), 1981; papers in medical and allied jls. *Recreations:* golf, swimming. *Address:* Alexandra, 201 Wickham Terrace, Brisbane, Queensland 4000, Australia. *T:* 221 4688. *Clubs:* Queensland, University of Queensland Staff and Graduates (Life Mem.); Mooloolaba Yacht.

THOMSON, Ewen Cameron, CMG 1964; nutrition consultant; *b* 12 April 1915; *s* of Francis Murphy Thomson, Woodhill, Forfar, Angus; *m* 1948, Betty, *d* of Lt-Col J. H. Preston, MBE, Far Horizons, Trearddur Bay, Anglesey; one *s* three *d*. *Educ:* Forfar Academy; St Andrews University. Cadet, Northern Rhodesia Provincial Admin., 1938. War Service, 1st Bn Northern Rhodesia Regt, 1939–46. District Commissioner, 1946; Dep. Prov. Comr, 1956; Prov. Comr, 1957; Senior Provincial Commissioner, 1961; Permanent Sec. for Native Affairs, 1962; Minister for Native Affairs, 1962; Permanent Secretary, Ministry of Transport and Works, Zambia, 1964; Director of Communications, Contingency Planning Organisation, Zambia, 1966; Exec. Sec., Nat. Food and Nutrition Commn, Zambia, 1967; Temp. Project Manager, UNDP/FAO, Nat. Food and Nutrition Programme, Zambia, 1970. Consultant: SIDA Nat. Food and Nutrition Programme, Tanzania, 1972; World Bank, 1974–86; Nat. Food and Nutrition Projects, Indonesia and Brazil, 1974–82; Urban Projects, Kenya, Botswana and Lesotho; Nutrition Component, Philippines, 1977–78; State Nutrition Project, Tamil Nadu, India, 1978–86; Food and Nutrition Project, Egypt, 1980–81; Food and Nutrition Sector Study, Bangladesh, 1983; Leader FFHC UK Reconnaissance Mission, Malaŵi, 1972; Co-Dir, Preparatory Team, Tanzania Food and Nutrition Centre, 1973. Leader, Planning Team, Nat. Food and Nutrition Programme, Malaŵi, 1973. Gave keynote address, Rockefeller Conf. on Nutrition and Govt Policy in Developing Countries, 1975. *Publication:* Symbiosis of Scientist, Planner and Administrator in Nutrition Programme Intervention, 1978. *Recreations:* walking, cooking, winemaking. *Address:* Manleys, Beacon Hill Park, Hindhead, Surrey. *T:* Hindhead 6972. *Club:* Royal Commonwealth Society.

THOMSON, Rt. Rev. Francis; Former Bishop of Motherwell (Bishop, 1964–83); Parish Priest of St Isidore's, Biggar, since 1983; Hon. Canon of St Andrews and Edinburgh, since 1961; *b* 15 May 1917; *s* of late Francis Thomson, MA and late Winifred Mary Clare (*née* Forsyth). *Educ:* George Watson's Coll., Edinburgh; Edinburgh Univ.; Christ's Coll., Cambridge; St Edmund's Coll., Ware; Angelicum Univ., Rome. MA Edinburgh 1938; BA Cambridge 1940; Priest, 1946; STL (Angelicum, Rome) 1949. Asst Priest: St Patrick's, Kilsyth, 1946–48; St James', St Andrews, 1949–52; St Cuthbert's, Edinburgh, 1952–53; Prof. of Dogmatic Theology, St Andrew's Coll. Drygrange, Melrose, 1953–60; Rector of St Mary's Coll., Blairs, Aberdeen, 1960–64. *Address:* 6 Coulter Road, Biggar, Lanarkshire ML12 6EP. *T:* Biggar 20189.

THOMSON, Francis Paul, OBE 1975; CEng, MIERE; Consultant on Post Office and Bank Giro Systems, since 1968; *b* Corstorphine, Edinburgh, 17 Dec. 1914; *y s* of late William George and Elizabeth Hannah Thomson, Goring-by-Sea; *m* 1954, E. Sylvia, *e d* of late Lokförare J. Erik Nilsson, Bollnäs, Sweden. *Educ:* Friends' Sch., Sibford Ferris; Sch. of Engrg, Polytechnic, London; in Denmark and Sweden. TV and radar research, 1935–42; Special Ops Exec., 1942–44; Sen. Planning Engr, Postwar research and reconstruction, communications industry; founded British Post Giro Campaign, 1946 and conducted Campaign to victory in Parlt, 1965; Lectr, Stockholm Univ. Extension, 1947–49; Founder, and Man. Editor, English Illustrated, 1950–61; techn. exports promotion with various firms, esp. electronic equipment, 1950–60; pioneered electronic language laboratory equipment and methods, 1930, subseq. joined consultancy-production groups; Bank Computerisation Consultant, 1967–. Governor, Watford Coll. of Technology, 1965–70 (Engrg Dept Adv. Cttee, 1972–); Mem., Communication of Technical Information Adv. Cttee, CGLI; Advr to PO Users' Nat. Council's Giro Sub Cttee, 1975; Founder and first Hon. Sec., SW Herts Post Office Adv. Cttee, 1976; Cttee Mem., Writers Guild of GB; First British Cttee Mem., Internat. Centre for Ancient and Modern Tapestry (CITAM), Lausanne, 1974–. Founder and Hon. Sec., St Andrews Residents' Assoc. (Watford). AMBIM; FIQA 1978. Hon. Fellow, Inst. of Scientific and Technical Communicators, 1975. Life Member: Corstorphine Trust; Anglo-Swedish Soc. *Publications:* Giro Credit Transfer Systems, 1964; Money in the Computer Age, 1968; (ed jtly) Banking Automation, 1971; (ed with E. S. Thomson) rev. repr. of A History of Tapestry (2nd edn), by W. G. Thomson, 1973; Tapestry: mirror of history, 1979; originated Household Directory, Personal Record books, Home and Car Emergency Card series; numerous papers in European and other learned jls. *Recreations:* gardening, archaeology, walking, campaigning to prohibit smoking in public places.

THOMSON, Sir (Frederick Douglas) David, 3rd Bt *cr* 1929; Deputy Chairman, Ben Line Steamers Ltd, since 1984 (Managing Director, 1964–84); *b* 14 Feb. 1940; *s* of Sir James Douglas Wishart Thomson, 2nd Bt, and of Evelyn Margaret Isabel, (Bettina), *d* of Lt-Comdr D. W. S. Douglas, RN; *S* father, 1972; *m* 1967, Caroline Anne, *d* of Major Timothy Stuart Lewis; two *s* one *d*. *Educ:* Eton; University College, Oxford (BA Agric). Joined family business, Ben Line, 1961; Partner, Wm Thomson & Co., 1963–64. Member: Queen's Body Guard for Scotland, Royal Company of Archers. *Recreation:* shooting. *Heir:* *s* Simon Douglas Charles Thomson, *b* 16 June 1969. *Address:* Glenbrook House, Balerno, Midlothian. *T:* 031–449 4116.

THOMSON, Garry, CBE 1983; Scientific Adviser to the Trustees and Head of the Scientific Department, National Gallery, London, 1960–85; *b* 13 Sept. 1925; *s* of Robert

Thomson and Mona Spence; *m* 1954, M. R. Saisvasdi Svasti; four *s. Educ:* Charterhouse; Magdalene College, Cambridge (MA). Editorial Staff of A History of Technology, 1951; Research Chemist, National Gallery, 1955; Hon. Editor, Studies in Conservation, 1959–67; Pres., Internat. Inst. for Conservation of Historic and Artistic Works, 1983–86. Vice-Pres., Buddhist Soc., London. Trustee, Nat. Museums and Galls on Merseyside, 1986. *Publications:* Recent Advances in Conservation (ed), 1963; Museum Climatology (ed), 1967; The Museum Environment, 1978; Reflections on the Life of the Buddha, 1982. *Address:* Squire's Hill, Tilford, Surrey. *T:* Runfold 2206.

THOMSON, Prof. George Derwent; Professor of Greek, University of Birmingham, 1937–70; *b* 19 Aug. 1903; *s* of William Henry and Minnie Thomson; *m* 1934, Katharine Fraser Stewart; two *d. Educ:* Dulwich College; King's College, Cambridge. Craven Student, University of Cambridge, 1926–27; Fellow of King's College, Cambridge, 1927–33 and 1934–36. Member, Czechoslovak Academy of Sciences, 1960–. Hon. Dr Univ. of Thessaloniki, 1979. Hon. Citizen of Eleusis, 1986. *Publications:* Greek Lyric Metre, 1929 (new edn, 1960); Aeschylus, Prometheus Bound, 1932; M. O'Sullivan, Twenty Years A-Growing (trans. from the Irish), 1933 (World's Classics edition, 1953); Aeschylus, Oresteia, 2 vols, 1938 (new edn, 1966); Aeschylus and Athens, 1941 (new edn 1973); Marxism and Poetry, 1946 (new edn, 1954); Studies in Ancient Greek Society, Vol. I, The Prehistoric Aegean, 1949 (new edn 1973); Vol. II, The First Philosophers, 1955 (new edn, 1973); The Greek Language, 1960 (new edn, 1966); Geras: Studies Presented to G. T. on his Sixtieth Birthday, 1963; A Manual of Modern Greek, 1966; Palamas, Twelve Lays of the Gipsy, 1969; From Marx to Mao Tse-tung, 1971; Capitalism and After, 1973; The Human Essence, 1975; The Blasket That Was, 1982; books in Irish and Greek and articles in learned and other journals; foreign editions of his books in 22 languages. *Address:* 58 Billesley Lane, Birmingham B13 9QS. *T:* 021–449 2656.

THOMSON, Rev. George Ian Falconer; Chaplain of All Souls College, Oxford, 1981–84; *b* 2 Sept. 1912; *s* of Rev. G. D. Thomson, DD; *m* 1st, 1938, Hon. Bridget de Courcy (marr. diss. 1951), *e d* of 34th Baron Kingsale, DSO; one *d*; 2nd, 1952, Mary Josephine Lambart Dixon, OBE, *d* of Archdeacon H. T. Dixon, DD, Hereford; one *s. Educ:* Shrewsbury Sch.; Balliol Coll., Oxford (MA); Westcott House, Cambridge. Ellerton Theol Essay Prize, Oxford, 1936. Pilot, RAFO, 1932–37; Chaplain, RAFVR, 1942–46. Curate, St Luke's, Chelsea, 1936–37; Chaplain, Hertford Coll., Oxford, 1937–46; Junior Dean and Dean of Degrees, 1939–42; Rector of Hilgay, Norfolk, 1946–51; Sec. of Gen. Ordination Examn, 1946–52; Master, Maidstone Grammar Sch., 1951–62; Chaplain and Sen. Lectr, St Paul's Coll., Cheltenham, 1962–66; Exam. Chaplain to Bp of Gloucester, 1964–76; Vis. Lectr, McMaster Univ., Ont, 1964; Dir, research project, Conf. of British Missionary Socs, 1966–68; re-visited China during Cultural Revolution, 1967. Director, Bible Reading Fellowship, 1968–77. Rowing Corresp., The Observer, 1938–65. NADFAS Lectr on James Tissot, 1980–. Press Officer, Oxford Diocese, 1979–83. Freeman, City of London. *Publications:* History of the Oxford Pastorate, 1946; Experiment in Worship, 1951; The Rise of Modern Asia, 1957; Changing Patterns in South Asia, 1961; Two Hundred School Assemblies, 1966; Mowbray's Mini-Commentary No 4, 1970. *Recreations:* rowing (Oxford Blue, 1934), travel, writing. *Address:* Jackson's Farm, Yarnton, Oxford OX5 1QD. *Clubs:* Royal Air Force; Leander.

THOMSON, George Malcolm; Author and Journalist; *b* Leith, Scotland, 2 Aug. 1899; *e s* of Charles Thomson, journalist, and Mary Arthur, *d* of John Eason; *m* 1926, Else (*d* 1957), *d* of Harald Ellefsen, Tœnsberg, Norway; one *s* one *d*; *m* 1963, Diana Van Cortland Robertson. *Educ:* Daniel Stewart's College, Edinburgh; Edinburgh University. Journalist. *Publications:* Caledonia, or the Future of the Scots, 1927; A Short History of Scotland, 1930; Crisis in Zanat, 1942; The Twelve Days, 1964; The Robbers Passing By, 1966; The Crime of Mary Stuart, 1967; Vote of Censure, 1968; A Kind of Justice, 1970; Sir Francis Drake, 1972; Lord Castlerosse, 1973; The North-West Passage, 1975; Warrior Prince: Prince Rupert of the Rhine, 1976; The First Churchill: the life of John, 1st Duke of Marlborough, 1979; The Prime Ministers, 1980; The Ball at Glenkerran, 1982; Kronstadt '21, 1985. *Address:* 5 The Mount Square, NW3. *T:* 01–435 8775. *Club:* Garrick.

THOMSON, Very Rev. Ian; *see* White-Thomson.

THOMSON, Sir Ivo Wilfrid Home, 2nd Bt, *cr* 1925; *b* 14 Oct. 1902; *s* of Sir Wilfrid Thomson, 1st Bt, and Ethel Henrietta, 2nd *d* of late Hon. Reginald Parker; *S* father 1939; *m* 1st, 1933, Sybil Marguerite (from whom he obt. a divorce), *yr d* of C. W. Thompson, The Red House, Escrick; one *s* (and one *d* decd); 2nd, 1954, Viola Mabel (who *m* 1937, Keith Home Thomson, from whom she obt. a divorce), *d* of Roland Dudley, Linkenholt Manor, Andover. *Educ:* Eton. *Heir:* *s* Mark Wilfrid Home Thomson [*b* 29 Dec. 1939; *m* 1976, Lady Jacqueline Rufus Isaacs, *d* of 3rd Marquess of Reading, MBE, MC; three *s* one *d*]. *Address:* Barfield, Chapel Row, Bucklebury, Reading, Berks RG7 6PB. *T:* Woolhampton 712172.

THOMSON, Prof. James Leonard, CBE 1955; Professor Emeritus in Civil Engineering, Royal Military College of Science, Shrivenham, since 1970; *b* 9 Aug. 1905; *s* of James Thomson, Liverpool. *Educ:* University of Manchester; St John's College, Cambridge. Mather & Platt, Ltd, Manchester, 1923–26; Univ. of Manchester, 1926–30 (BSc (Tech.) 1st Cl. Hons and Stoney Prizeman); Lecturer, Technical College, Horwich, 1930–32; Whitworth Senior Scholar, 1931; St John's Coll., Cambridge, 1932–34 (BA 1934, MA 1938); Research Engineer, ICI, Billingham-on-Tees, 1934–38; Lecturer, Dept of Civil and Mechanical Engineering, Univ. of London, King's College, 1938. Seconded for War-time Service: Managing Engineer, HM Royal Ordnance Factory, Pembrey, Carms, 1940–42; Principal Technical Officer, School of Tank Technology, 1942–46. Royal Military College of Science, Shrivenham: Prof. of Mechanical Engrg and Head of Dept of Civil and Mechanical Engrg, 1946–61; Prof. of Civil Engrg and Head of Dept of Civil Engrg, 1965–70; seconded to ME Technical Univ., Ankara, Turkey, 1961–65 : Consultant Dean and Mechanical Engrg Specialist; later Chief Technical Adviser for UNESCO project in Turkey. *Publications:* various scientific papers dealing with High Pressure Techniques. *Recreations:* mountaineering, sailing. *Address:* Astral House, Netherbury, Bridport, Dorset DT6 5LU.

THOMSON, Sir John, KBE 1972; TD 1944; MA; Chairman, Morland and Co. Ltd, 1979–83; Director: Barclays Bank Ltd, 1947–78 (Chairman, 1962–73); Union Discount Company of London Ltd, 1960–74; *b* 1908; *s* of late Guy Thomson, JP, Woodperry, Oxford; *m* 1st, 1935, Elizabeth, JP (*d* 1977), *d* of late Stanley Brotherhood, JP, Thornhaugh Hall, Peterborough; no *c*; 2nd, 1979, Eva Elizabeth, *d* of Marcus Ralph Russell, and *widow* of Tom Dreaper. *Educ:* Winchester; Magdalen College, Oxford. Commanded Oxfordshire Yeomanry Regt, RATA, 1942–44 and 1947–50. Deputy High Steward of Oxford University; a Curator of Oxford University Chest, 1949–74; Chairman: Nuffield Medical Benefaction, 1951–82 (Trustee, 1947–82); Nuffield Orthopædic Centre Trust, 1949–81. President, British Bankers' Association, 1964–66 (Vice-President, 1963–64); FIB. Mem. Royal Commn on Trade Unions and Employers' Assocs, 1965–68; Mem. BNEC, 1968–71. Hon. Fellow St Catherine's Coll., Oxford. Hon. Colonel: 299 Fd Regt RA (TA), 1964–67; Oxfordshire Territorials, 1967–75; Bt Col, 1950. DL Oxfordshire, 1947–57;

High Sheriff of Oxfordshire, 1957; Vice-Lieut, 1957–63; Lord-Lieut, 1963–79. A Steward, Jockey Club, 1974–77. Hon. DCL Oxford, 1957. KStJ 1973. *Address:* Manor Farm House, Spelsbury, Oxford OX7 3LG. *T:* Charlbury 810266. *Club:* Cavalry and Guards.

THOMSON, Sir John (Adam), GCMG 1985 (KCMG 1978; CMG 1972); MA; HM Diplomatic Service; United Kingdom Permanent Representative to the United Nations, since 1982; *b* 27 April 1927; *s* of late Sir George Thomson, FRS, Master of Corpus Christi Coll., Cambridge, 1952–62 (*s* of Sir J. J. Thomson, OM, FRS, Master of Trinity Coll., Cambridge, 1919–40), and late Kathleen, *d* of Very Rev. Sir George Adam Smith, DD, LLD, Principal of Aberdeen Univ., 1909–35; *m* 1953, Elizabeth Anne McClure, *d* of late Norman McClure, Pres. of Ursinus Coll., Penn, USA; three *s* one *d. Educ:* Phillips Exeter Acad., USA; Univ. of Aberdeen; Trinity Coll., Cambridge. Foreign Office, 1950; Third Sec., Jedda, 1951; Damascus, 1954; FO, 1955; Private Sec. to Permanent Under-Secretary, 1958–60; First Sec., Washington, 1960–64; FO, 1964; Acting Head of Planning Staff, 1966; Counsellor, 1967; Head of Planning Staff, FO, 1967; seconded to Cabinet Office as Chief of Assessments Staff, 1968–71; Minister and Dep. Permanent Rep. to N Atlantic Council, 1972–73; Head of UK Delegn to MBFR Exploratory Talks, Vienna, 1973; Asst Under-Sec. of State, FCO, 1973–76; High Comr to India, 1977–82. Hon. LLD: Ursinus Coll., Penn, 1984; Aberdeen, 1986; Hon. DHL Allegheny Coll., Penn, 1985. *Publication:* Crusader Castles (with R. Fedden), 1956. *Recreations:* carpets, castles, walking. *Address:* c/o Foreign and Commonwealth Office, SW1. *Club:* Athenæum.
  See also Janet Adam Smith (Mrs John Carleton), Baron Balerno, D. P. Thomson.

THOMSON, Sir John Sutherland, (Sir Ian), KBE 1985 (MBE (mil.) 1944); CMG 1968; Chairman: Economic Development Board, Fiji, since 1980; Sedgwick (Fiji) Ltd, since 1984; Air Pacific Ltd, since 1984; Fiji National Tourism Assoc., since 1984; *b* 8 Jan. 1920; *s* of late William Sutherland Thomson and of Jessie McCaig Malloch; *m* 1945, Nancy Marguerite Kearsley, Suva, Fiji; seven *s* one *d. Educ:* High Sch. of Glasgow; Univ. of Glasgow (MA Hons). Served War of 1939–45: Black Watch, 1940; Fiji Military Forces, 1941–45 (Captain). Appointed Cadet, Colonial Administrative Service, Fiji and Western Pacific, 1941; District Administration and Secretariat, Fiji, 1946–54; Seconded to Colonial Office, 1954–56; Dep. Comr, Native Lands and Fisheries, Fiji, 1957–58; Comr of Native Reserves and Chairman, Native Lands and Fisheries Commission, Fiji, 1958–62; Divisional Commissioner, Fiji, 1963–66; Administrator, British Virgin Islands, 1967–71; Acting Governor-Gen., Fiji, 1980–83 on occasions. Indep. Chm., Fiji Sugar Industry, 1971–84; Chairman: Fiji Coconut Bd, 1973–83; Fiji Liquor Laws Review Cttee. *Recreations:* golf, gardening. *Address:* GPO Box 13018, Suva, Fiji. *T:* 23142.

THOMSON, Nigel Ernest Drummond; Sheriff of Lothian and Borders, at Edinburgh, since 1976; *b* 19 June 1926; *y s* of late Rev. James Kyd Thomson, and late Joan Drummond; *m* 1964, Snjólaug Magnússon, *yr d* of late Consul-General Sigursteinn Magnússon; one *s* one *d. Educ:* George Watson's College, Edinburgh; Univs of St Andrews and Edinburgh. Served with Scots Guards and Indian Grenadiers, 1944–47. MA (St Andrews) 1950; LLB (Edin.) 1953. Called to Scottish Bar, 1953. Standing Counsel to Scottish Educn Dept, 1961–66; Sheriff of Lanarkshire, later S Strathclyde, Dumfries and Galloway, at Hamilton, 1966–76. Chm., Music Cttee, Scottish Arts Council, 1978–83. Pres., Speculative Soc., Edinburgh, 1960. Hon. Pres., Tenovus, Edinburgh. *Recreations:* music, woodwork, golf. *Address:* 50 Grange Road, Edinburgh. *T:* 031–667 2166. *Clubs:* Arts (Strathaven); Bruntsfield Golf (Edinburgh).

THOMSON, Peter; *b* 1914; *s* of John Thomson, SSC, and Martha Lindsay Miller; *m* 1939, Jean Laird Nicoll; two *s* one *d. Educ:* Royal High School, Edinburgh; Edinburgh University. Gordon Highlanders, 1941–46; Capt. 1944. Called to Scottish Bar, 1946. Founded Scottish Plebiscite Society, 1947. Sheriff Substitute of Caithness, Sutherland, Orkney and Zetland, 1955; Sheriff of South Strathclyde, Dumfries and Galloway (formerly Lanarkshire) at Hamilton, 1962–77. Dir, Inst. of Scotland, 1979–. *Recreations:* walking, golf. *Address:* Haughhead Farm House, Uddingston, Glasgow G71 7RR.

THOMSON, Peter Alexander Bremner; HM Diplomatic Service; Counsellor, Peking, since 1984; *b* 16 Jan. 1938; *s* of Alexander Thomson, financial journalist, and Dorothy (*née* Scurr); *m* 1965, Lucinda Sellar; three *s. Educ:* Canford School; RN College, Dartmouth; Sch. of African and Oriental Studies, London (BA, MPhil). Sub Lieut and Lieut RN in HM Ships Albion, Plover, Tiger, Ark Royal, Eagle; Lt Comdr ashore in Taiwan and Hong Kong; joined Diplomatic Service, 1975; First Sec., FCO, Lagos, Hong Kong. *Recreations:* sailing, walking. *Address:* c/o Foreign and Commonwealth Office, SW1; The Red House, Charlton Horethorne, near Sherborne. *T:* Corton Denham 301. *Clubs:* Travellers'; Hong Kong.

THOMSON, Robert Howard Garry; *see* Thomson, Garry.

THOMSON, Robert John Stewart, CMG 1969; MBE 1955; Ministry of Defence, 1969–81; *b* 5 May 1922; *s* of late John Stewart Thomson, FRIBA, and late Nellie Thomson (*née* Morris). *Educ:* Bromsgrove Sch.; Worcester Coll., Oxford. Service with Sudan Defence Force, 1943–45. Sudan Political Service, 1943–54 (District Commissioner, 1950–54). Attached Ministry of Defence, 1955–56; First Sec., British High Commission, Accra, 1956–60, 1962–64, Counsellor, 1966–69. *Recreations:* gardening, singing. *Address:* Ardgowan, 119 Lenthay Road, Sherborne, Dorset DT9 6AQ. *Clubs:* Royal Over-Seas League; Polo (Accra).

THOMSON, Robert Norman; Executive Director, Royal Society of Medicine, since 1982; Director, Royal Society of Medicine Foundation Inc., New York, since 1984; *b* 14 Nov. 1935. *Educ:* Wells Cathedral School; Clare College, Cambridge (MA). Royal Society of Medicine: Assistant Executive Director, 1973; Deputy Executive Director, 1977. *Recreations:* music, cooking. *Address:* 9 Downside Lodge, 29 Upper Park Road, NW3 2UY. *T:* 01–722 7176. *Club:* University (New York).

THOMSON, Thomas Davidson, CMG 1962; OBE 1959; *b* 1 April 1911; *s* of J. A. Thomson, FFA, FRSE, and Barbara M. Davidson, Edinburgh; *m* 1st, 1938, Jean (marr. diss. 1946), *d* of Dr J. L. Annan, Edinburgh; 2nd, 1947, Marjorie Constance (*d* 1980), *d* of T. R. Aldred, Limbe, Nyasaland; one *s*; 3rd, 1981, Kathleen Ramsay, *d* of D. Craig, Morebattle, Roxburghshire and *widow* of Nicholas Pestereff. *Educ:* George Watson's Coll., Edinburgh; Edinburgh Univ. (MA, LLB); Magdalene Coll., Cambridge. Editor, The Student, 1932; Travel Secretary, Scottish National Union of Students, 1932; Cadet, Nyasaland Administration, 1934; Civil Demobilisation Officer, 1945; Assistant Secretary, Nyasaland, 1947; Officer in charge, Domasi Community Development Scheme, 1949; Officer in charge, School of Local Government, 1955, Social Development, 1958; retired as Commissioner for Social Development, Nyasaland, 1963. Carried out survey of Adult Education in Nyasaland, 1956–57; organised Nyasaland Council of Social Service, 1959. Served War of 1939–45, E Africa (Major). Sec., Eastern Border Development Assoc., 1962–67. Chairman: Scottish Community Development Cttee, 1968–75; Berwicks Council of Social Service, 1971–75; Hon. Vice-Pres., Scottish Council of Social Service, 1976–. Pres., Berwickshire Naturalists' Club, 1969–70. Vice-Pres., Soc. of Antiquaries of Scotland, 1971–74. Brain of Britain, BBC Radio, 1969. FRPSL 1984. *Publications:* A

Practical Approach to Chinyanja, 1947; Coldingham Priory, 1973; sundry reports and papers on Nyasaland affairs; papers in Hist. Berwickshire Naturalists' Club; sundry papers in philatelic jls. *Recreations:* gardening, philately, contemplative archaeology, Scouting (Chief Commissioner, Nyasaland, 1958; County Commissioner, Berwickshire, 1966–75). *Address:* The Hill, Coldingham, Berwickshire. *T:* Coldingham 209.

THOMSON, Dr Thomas James, CBE 1984 (OBE 1978); FRCPGlas, FRCP, FRCPEd, FRCPI; Consultant Physician and Gastroenterologist, Stobhill General Hospital, Glasgow, since 1961; Hon. Lecturer, Department of Materia Medica, University of Glasgow, since 1961; *b* 8 April 1923; *s* of Thomas Thomson and Annie Jane Grant; *m* 1948, Jessie Smith Shotbolt; two *s* one *d.* *Educ:* Airdrie Acad.; Univ. of Glasgow (MB, ChB 1945). FRCPGlas 1964 (FRFPSG 1949); FRCP 1969 (MRCP 1950); FRCPEd 1982; FRCPI 1983. Lectr, Dept of Materia Medica, Univ. of Glasgow, 1953–61; Postgrad. Adviser to Glasgow Northern Hosps, 1961–80. Hon. Sec., RCPGlas, 1965–73; Sec., Specialist Adv. Cttee for Gen. Internal Medicine for UK, 1970–74; Chairman: Medico-Pharmaceutical Forum, 1978–80 (Chm., Educn Adv. Bd, 1979–); Conf. of Royal Colls and Faculties in Scotland, 1982–84; National Med. Consultative Cttee for Scotland, 1982–; Pres., RCP Glas., 1982–84; active participation in postgrad. med. educnl cttees, locally, nationally and in EEC. Hon. FACP 1983. *Publications:* (ed jtly) Dilling's Pharmacology, 1969; Gastroenterology—an integrated course, 1972, 3rd edn 1983; pubns related to gen. medicine, gastroent. and therapeutics. *Recreations:* swimming, golfing. *Address:* 1 Varna Road, Glasgow G14 9NE. *T:* 041–959 5930. *Club:* Royal Air Force.

THOMSON, William Oliver, MD, DPH, DIH; Chief Administrative Medical Officer, Lanarkshire Health Board, since 1973; *b* 23 March 1925; *s* of William Crosbie Thomson and Mary Jolie Johnston; *m* 1956, Isobel Lauder Glendinning Brady; two *s.* *Educ:* Allan Glen's Sch., Glasgow; Univ. of Glasgow (MB ChB, MD). DPA; FFCM; MRCPGlas 1986. Chronic student of Gray's Inn, London. Captain, RAMC, 1948–50. Hospital appointments, 1951–53; appointments in Public Health, Glasgow, 1953–60; Admin. MO, Western Regional Hospital Bd, 1960–70; Group Medical Superintendent, Glasgow Maternity and Women's Hospitals, 1970–73; Mem., Health Services Ind. Adv. Cttee, 1980–86. Visiting Lecturer: Univ. of Michigan, Ann Arbor; Ministry of Health, Ontario; Hon. Lectr, Univ. of Glasgow. Diploma of Scottish Council for Health Educn (for services to health educn), 1979. *Publications:* articles on clinical medicine, community medicine, general practice, occupational health and health education, in various medical jls; humorous pieces in The Lancet, BMJ, etc. *Recreations:* walking, talking, writing. *Address:* Flat 7, Silverwells Court, Silverwells Crescent, Bothwell, Glasgow G71 8LT. *T:* Bothwell 852586.

THONEMANN, Peter Clive, MSc, DPhil; Professor Emeritus, Department of Physics, University College, Swansea (Professor and Head of Department, 1968–84); *b* 3 June 1917. *Educ:* Melbourne Grammar Sch., Melbourne; Sydney and Oxford Univs. BSc Melbourne, 1940; MSc Sydney, 1945; DPhil Oxford, 1949. Munition Supply Laboratories, Victoria, Australia, 1940; Amalgamated Wireless, Australia, 1942; University of Sydney, Commonwealth Research Fellow, 1944; Clarendon Laboratory, Oxford, ICI Research Fellow, 1946; United Kingdom Atomic Energy Authority, 1949, Chief Scientist, 1964; Dep. Dir, Culham Laboratory, 1967–68. *Address:* Department of Physics, University College, Swansea, Singleton Park, Swansea, Wales.

THORBURN, Andrew, BSc; FRTPI; FTS; consultant in town planning and tourism development; management consultant, Grant Thornton, since 1986; Principal, Andrew Thorburn Associates, since 1985; *b* 20 March 1934; *s* of James Beresford Thorburn and Marjorie Clara Burford; *m* Margaret Anne Crack; one *s* two *d.* *Educ:* Bridport Grammar Sch.; Univ. of Southampton (BSc). MRTPI 1959, FRTPI 1969. National Service, RN, 1954–56. Planning Asst, Kent CC, 1957–59; Planning Officer, Devon CC, 1959–63; Asst County Planning Officer, Hampshire CC, 1963–68; Dir, Notts and Derbyshire Sub-Region Study, 1968–70; Dep. County Planning Dir, Cheshire CC, 1970–73; County Planning Officer, E Sussex CC, 1973–83; Chief Exec., English Tourist Bd, 1983–85. Pres., RTPI, 1982; Mem. Exec., Town and Country Planning Assoc., 1969–81; Founder Trustee, Sussex Heritage Trust, 1978–; Fellow, Tourism Soc., 1983–. *Publication:* Planning Villages, 1971. *Recreations:* sailing, countryside appreciation. *Address:* Hyde Manor, Kingston, Lewes, East Sussex BN7 3PB.

THORLEY, Charles Graham; *b* 4 Jan. 1914; *s* of Charles Lord Thorley; *m* 1958, Peggy Percival Ellis (*née* Boor); one step *s* one step *d.* *Educ:* Manchester Grammar Sch.; King's Coll., Cambridge (Mod. Lang. Scholar). Served War of 1939–45, Eritrea and Cyrenaica (Lt-Col). Entered Civil Service as Economist, Bd of Trade, 1936; attached to British Embassy, China, 1936–38; Mem. British Economic Mission to Belgian Congo, 1940–41; HM Treasury, 1940–57; served on UK financial delegns and missions in Japan, US, Egypt, France, Switzerland, W Germany, etc; Min. of Power, 1957; Under-Secretary and Head of Coal Div., 1965–69; Acct-Gen. and Dir of Finance, 1969. Chm., NATO Petroleum Planning Cttee, 1962–65; Under-Sec., Min. of Technology and DTI, 1969–74. Specialist Advr, House of Lords, 1975–79. *Recreation:* travel. *Address:* Preston House, Corton Denham, Sherborne, Dorset DT9 4LS. *T:* Corton Denham 269.

THORLEY, Sir Gerald (Bowers), Kt 1973; TD; Director, Fitch Lovell plc; *b* 26 Aug. 1913; *s* of Clement Thorley and Ethel May Davy; *m* 1947, Beryl Preston, *d* of G. Preston Rhodes; one *s* one *d.* *Educ:* Ratcliffe College. FRICS. FRSA. Served War of 1939–45, RA; BEF, 1939–40; Malaya, 1941; POW, 1942–45. Ind Coope & Allsopp Ltd, 1936. Underwriting Member of Lloyd's, 1952. Chairman: Allied Breweries Ltd, 1970–75; British Sugar plc, 1968–82; MEPC plc, 1976–84. *Recreations:* gardening, golf. *Address:* Church House, Bale, Fakenham, Norfolk NR21 0QR. *T:* Thursford 314. *Club:* Naval and Military.

THORN, E. Gaston; Politician, Luxembourg; President: Banque Internationale, Luxembourg, since 1985; Mouvement Européen International, since 1985; Vice President—Director General, RTL Luxembourg, since 1985; Member, Public Review Board, Arthur Andersen & Co.; *b* 3 Sept. 1928; *s* of Edouard Thorn and Suzanne Weber; *m* 1957, Liliane Petit; one *s.* *Educ:* Univs of Montpellier, Lausanne, and Paris. DenD. Admitted to Luxembourg Bar; Pres., Nat. Union of Students, Luxembourg, 1959; Member, European Parlt, 1959–69, Vice-Pres., Liberal Group; Pres., Democratic Party, Luxembourg, 1969; Minister of Foreign Affairs and of Foreign Trade, also Minister of Physical Educn and Sport, 1974–77; Prime Minister and Minister of State, 1974–79; Minister of Nat. Econ. and Middle Classes, 1977; of Justice, 1979; Dep. Prime Minister, and Minister of Foreign Affairs, July 1979–1980; Pres., EEC, 1981–84. Pres., 30th Session of UN Gen. Assembly, 1975–76. President: Liberal International, 1970–82; Fedn of Liberal and Democratic Parties of European Community, 1976–80. Decorations include Grand Cross of Orders of Adolphe de Nassau, Couronne de Chêne, and Mérite (Luxembourg), Grand Cross of Légion d'Honneur (France), GCVO and GCMG (GB) and other Grand Crosses. *Recreations:* tennis, reading. *Address:* 1 rue de la Forge, Luxembourg.

THORN, John Leonard, MA; writer and educational consultant; Director, Winchester Cathedral Trust, since 1986; Headmaster of Winchester College, 1968–85; *b* 28 April 1925; *s* of late Stanley and Winifred Thorn; *m* 1955, Veronica Laura, *d* of late Sir Robert Maconochie, OBE, QC; one *s* one *d.* *Educ:* St Paul's School; Corpus Christi College, Cambridge. Served War of 1939–45, Sub-Lieutenant, RNVR, 1943–46. 1st Class Historical Tripos, Parts I and II. Asst Master, Clifton Coll., 1949–61; Headmaster, Repton School, 1961–68. Dir, Royal Opera House, Covent Garden, 1971–76. Chm., Headmasters' Conference, 1981. Trustee: British Museum, 1980–85; Oakham Sch. Governor: King Edward VI Sch., Southampton; King Alfred's Coll., Winchester; Stowe Sch. *Publications:* (joint) A History of England, 1961, various articles. *Address:* 6 Chilbolton Avenue, Winchester SO22 5HD. *T:* 55990. *Club:* Garrick.

THORN, Sir John (Samuel), Kt 1984, OBE 1977; Member, since 1950, Mayor, since 1956, Port Chalmers Borough Council; *b* 19 March 1911; *s* of J. S. Thorn; *m* 1936, Constance Maud, *d* of W. T. Haines; one *s.* *Educ:* Port Chalmers School; King Edward Technical College. Served 1939–45 war, 3rd Div. Apprentice plumber, later plumbing contractor and land agent; Manager, Thorn's Bookshop, 1950–. Chairman: Municipal Insce Co.; Coastal N Otago United Council. Pres., Municipal Assoc., 1974–; Dep. Chm., Nat. Roads Board, 1974–83. *Address:* Dalkeith, Port Chalmers, New Zealand.

THORNE, Benjamin, CMG 1979; MBE 1966; consultant on Far East trade; *b* 19 June 1922; *m* 1949, Sylvia Una (*née* Graves); one *s* two *d.* *Educ:* St Marylebone Grammar Sch.; Regent Street Polytechnic. Served War, RAF, 1940–46. Joined Civil Service, 1946; British Trade Commission: India, 1950–54; Ghana, 1954–58; Nigeria, 1958–61; Hong Kong, 1964–68; Dir, British Week in Tokyo, 1968–69; Commercial Counsellor, Tokyo, 1973–79, retd. Japanese Order of the Sacred Treasure, 3rd cl., 1975. *Recreations:* cricket, travel, gardening, reading. *Address:* Hill Brow, 34 Quarry Hill Road, Borough Green, Sevenoaks, Kent. *T:* Borough Green 882547. *Clubs:* Civil Service; Hong Kong (Hong Kong); Foreign Correspondents' (Tokyo); Yokohama Country and Athletic.

THORNE, Prof. Christopher Guy, DLitt; FBA 1982; FRHistS; Professor of International Relations, University of Sussex, since 1977; *b* 17 May 1934; *s* of Reginald Harry Thorne and late Alice Thorne (*née* Pickard); *m* 1958, Beryl Lloyd Jones; two *d.* *Educ:* King Edward VI Royal Grammar Sch., Guildford; St Edmund Hall, Oxford. BA 1958; MA 1962; DLitt 1980. Nat. Service, RN, 1953–55. Teacher, St Paul's Sch., London, 1958–61; Sen. Hist. Master, Charterhouse, 1961–66; Head of Further Educn, BBC Radio, 1966–68; Lectr in Internat. Relations, 1968, Reader, 1972, Univ. of Sussex. Resident Fellow, Netherlands Inst. for Advanced Study, 1979–80. Lees-Knowles Lectr, Cambridge, 1977; Raleigh Lectr, British Acad., 1980; Phillips Lectr, British Acad., 1986. *Publications:* Ideology and Power, 1965; Chartism, 1966; The Approach of War 1938–39, 1967; The Limits of Foreign Policy: the West, the League, and the Far Eastern Crisis of 1931–33, 1972; Allies of a Kind: the United States, Britain, and the war against Japan 1941–1945, 1978 (Bancroft Prize, 1979); Racial Aspects of the Far Eastern War of 1941–45, 1982; The Issue of War: states, societies and the Far Eastern conflict of 1941–45, 1985. *Recreations:* music, Crete. *Address:* School of European Studies, University of Sussex, Brighton, Sussex BN1 9QN. *T:* Brighton 606755.

THORNE, Maj.-Gen. Sir David (Calthrop), KBE 1983 (CBE 1979; OBE 1975); Director of Infantry, since 1986; *b* 13 Dec. 1933; *s* of Richard Everard Thorne and Audrey Ursula (*née* Bone); *m* 1962, Susan Anne Goldsmith; one *s* two *d.* *Educ:* St Edward's Sch., Oxford; RMA, Sandhurst. Staff Coll., Camberley, 1963; jssc 1967; Defence Intelligence Staff, MoD, 1968–70; Instructor, RAF Staff Coll., 1970–72; CO 1 Royal Anglian, 1972–74; Col, General Staff, MoD, 1975–77; Comdr, 3rd Inf. Bde, 1978–79; RCDS 1980; VQMG, 1981–82; Comdr, British Forces Falkland Islands, July 1982–April 1983; Comdr, 1st Armoured Div., 1983–85. Dep. Col, Royal Anglian Regt, 1981–. *Recreations:* cricket, squash, butterfly collecting. *Address:* c/o Barclays Bank, 52 Abbeygate Street, Bury St Edmunds, Suffolk IP33 1LL. *Clubs:* Army and Navy, MCC, Jesters'; I Zingari; Free Foresters.

THORNE, Rear-Adm. (retd) Edward Courtney, CB 1975; CBE 1971; FNZIM; Chairman, New Zealand Fire Service Commission, since 1977; Chief of Naval Staff, New Zealand, 1972–75; *b* 29 Oct. 1923; *s* of Ernest Alexander Thorne and Ethel Violet Thorne; *m* 1949, Fay Bradburn (*née* Kerr); three *s.* *Educ:* Nelson Coll., NZ. Chm., Nat. Council, United World Colls, 1982–; Mem., Nat. Council, Duke of Edinburgh Award Scheme; Pres., NZ Navy League Council, 1982–. FNZIM 1980; Hon. FIFireE 1983. *Recreations:* golf, gardening. *Address:* 75 Hatton Street, Karori, Wellington 5, New Zealand. *Club:* Wellington (New Zealand).

THORNE, Neil Gordon, OBE 1980; TD 1969; MP (C) Ilford South, since 1979; *b* 8 Aug. 1932; *s* of late Henry Frederick Thorne and Ivy Gladys Thorne. *Educ:* City of London Sch.; London Univ. BSc. FRICS. Asst Adjt, 58 Med. Regt, RA, BAOR, 1957–59. Sen. Partner, Hull & Co., Chartered Surveyors, 1962–76. Councillor, London Borough of Redbridge, 1965–68, Alderman, 1975–78; mem., GLC and Chm., Central Area Bd, 1967–73. Chairman: Nat. Council for Civil Defence, 1982–; Ilford Age Concern, 1984–. Chairman: Unpaired Members Gp, 1982–85; Anglo Nepalese All Pty Parly Gp, 1983–; Mem., Defence Select Cttee, 1983–. Chm., H of C Motor Club, 1985–. Mem., TA, 1952–82; CO, London Univ. OTC, 1976–80. Fellow, Industry and Parliament Trust, 1980. Chm., St Edward's Housing Assoc., 1986–; President: Ilford S Carnival Assoc., 1982–; Redbridge Parkinson's Disease Soc., 1982–; Ilford Arthritis Care, 1986–; Patron, Jubilee Club for Visually Handicapped, 1986–. Silver Jubilee Medal, 1977. *Publication:* Pedestrianised Streets: a study of Europe and America, 1973. *Address:* House of Commons, SW1A 0AA. *T:* 01–219 4123. *Clubs:* Carlton; Ilford Conservative.

THORNE, Sir Peter (Francis), KCVO 1981; CBE 1966; Serjeant at Arms, House of Commons, 1976–82; *b* 1914; *y s* of late Gen. Sir Andrew Thorne, KCB, CMG, DSO; *m* 1959, Lady Anne Pery, MA, DPhil, Senior Lecturer, Imperial College of Science and Technology, *d* of 5th Earl of Limerick, GBE, CH, KCB, DSO, TD; one *s* three *d.* *Educ:* Eton; Trinity Coll., Oxford. Served War of 1939–45: with 3rd Bn Grenadier Guards (wounded), 1939–41; HQ 2nd Div., 1941–42; Staff College, Quetta, 1942; on staff of India Command and HQ, SACSEA, 1943–45; demobilised with rank of Hon. Lieut-Col, 1946. With Imperial Chemical Industries Ltd, 1946–48. Assistant Serjeant at Arms, House of Commons, 1948–57, Dep. Serjeant at Arms, 1957–76. *Address:* Chiddinglye Farmhouse, West Hoathly, East Grinstead, West Sussex RH19 4QS. *T:* Sharpthorne 810338. *Clubs:* Cavalry and Guards; Royal Yacht Squadron.

THORNE, Robin Horton John, CMG 1966; OBE 1963; HM Overseas Service, retired; *b* 13 July 1917; *s* of late Sir John Anderson Thorne; *m* 1946, Joan Helen Wadman; one *s.* *Educ:* Dragon Sch., Oxford; Rugby (open scholar); Exeter College, Oxford (open scholar). War Service, Devonshire Regiment and King's African Rifles, 1939–46. Colonial Administrative Service (now HM Overseas Civil Service), 1946–67; Tanganyika Administration, 1946–58; Aden, 1958–67; Asst Chief Sec. (Colony), MLC and Mem. of Governor's Exec. Coun., 1959–63; Ministerial Sec. to Chief Minister, 1963–65; Assistant High Commissioner, 1966–67. With Vice-Chancellors' Cttee, 1967–77; part-time admin. work, Univ. of Sussex, 1978–81. Trustee of Aden Port Trust, 1959–66; Chm., Staines Trust, 1979–85; Mem., Management Cttee, Sussex Housing Assoc. for the Aged, 1983–.

Recreations: various. *Address:* The Old Vicarage, Old Heathfield, East Sussex. *T:* Heathfield 3160. *Club:* Royal Commonwealth Society.

THORNE, Stanley George; MP (Lab) Preston, since 1983 (Preston South, Feb. 1974–1983); *b* 22 July 1918; *s* of postman and dressmaker; *m* Catherine Mary Rand; two *s* three *d*. *Educ:* Ruskin Coll., Oxford; Univ. of Liverpool. Dip. Social Studies Oxon 1968; BA Hons Liverpool 1970. 30 yrs in industry and commerce: coal-miner, semi-skilled fitter, chartered accountant's clerk, rly signalman, office manager, auditor, commercial manager, etc; lectr in govt and industrial sociology. *Recreations:* chess, bridge, golf. *Address:* 26 Station Road, Gateacre, Liverpool L25 3PZ. *T:* (office) 01–219 4183.

THORNELY, Gervase Michael Cobham; Headmaster of Sedbergh School, 1954–75; *b* 21 Oct. 1918; *er s* of late Major J. E. B. Thornely, OBE, and late Hon. Mrs M. H. Thornely; *m* 1954, Jennifer Margery, *d* of Sir Hilary Scott, *qv*, Knowle House, Addington, Surrey; two *s* two *d*. *Educ:* Rugby Sch.; Trinity Hall, Cambridge. Organ Scholar; 2nd Cl. Hons, Modern and Mediæval Languages Tripos; BA, 1940; MA, 1944. FRSA 1968. Assistant Master, Sedbergh School, 1940. *Recreations:* music, fly-fishing. *Address:* High Stangerthwaite, Killington, Cumbria. *T:* Sedbergh 20444.

THORNEYCROFT, family name of **Baron Thorneycroft.**

THORNEYCROFT, Baron *cr* 1967 (Life Peer), of Dunston; **(George Edward) Peter Thorneycroft,** CH 1980; PC 1951; Barrister-at-law; late RA; Chairman of the Conservative Party, 1975–81; Chairman: Pirelli General Cable Works Ltd; Pirelli Ltd; President, Trusthouse Forte Ltd, since 1982 (Chairman, 1969–81); *b* 26 July 1909; *s* of late Major George Edward Mervyn Thorneycroft, DSO, and Dorothy Hope, *d* of Sir W. Franklyn, KCB; *m* 1st, 1938, Sheila Wells Page (who obtained a divorce, 1949); one *s*; 2nd, 1949, Countess Carla Roberti; one *d*. *Educ:* Eton; Roy. Mil. Acad., Woolwich. Commissioned in Royal Artillery, 1930; resigned Commission, 1933; called to Bar, Inner Temple, 1935; practised Birmingham (Oxford Circuit); MP (C) Stafford, 1938–45, Monmouth, 1945–66. Parliamentary Secretary, Ministry of War Transport, 1945. President of the Board of Trade, October 1951–January 1957; Chancellor of the Exchequer, Jan. 1957–Jan. 1958, resigned; Minister of Aviation, July 1960–July 1962; Minister of Defence, 1962–64; Secretary of State for Defence, Apr.-Oct. 1964. Chairman: SITPRO, 1968–75; BOTB, 1972–75; Pye of Cambridge Ltd, 1967–79; British Reserve Insurance Co. Ltd, 1980–; Gil, Carvajal & Partners Ltd, 1981–; Cinzano UK Ltd, 1982–85; Director: Riunione Adriatica di Sicurta, 1981–; Banca Nazionale del Lavoro, 1984–. Exhibitions of paintings: Trafford Gallery, 1961, 1970; Café Royal, 1981; Mall Galls, 1984. Mem., Royal Soc. of British Artists, 1978. *Publication:* The Amateur: a companion to watercolour, 1985. *Address:* House of Lords, SW1. *T:* 01–219 4093. *Club:* Army and Navy.

THORNHILL, Andrew Robert; QC 1985; *b* 4 Aug. 1943; *s* of Edward Percy Thornhill and Amelia Joy Thornhill; *m* 1971, Helen Mary Livingston; two *s* two *d*. *Educ:* Clifton Coll. Prep. Sch.; Clifton Coll.; Corpus Christi Coll., Oxford. Called to the Bar, Middle Temple, 1969; entered chambers of H. H. Monroe, QC, 1969. *Publications:* (ed) Potter & Monroe: Tax Planning with Precedents, 7th edn 1974, to 9th edn 1982; (jtly) Tax Planning Through Wills, 1981, 1984; (jtly) Passing Down the Family Farm, 1982; (jtly) Passing Down the Family Business, 1984. *Recreations:* dinghy sailing, squash, walking. *Address:* 37 Canynge Road, Clifton, Bristol. *T:* Bristol 744015. *Clubs:* United Oxford & Cambridge University; Tamesis (Teddington).

THORNHILL, Lt-Col Edmund Basil, MC 1918; *b* 27 Feb. 1898; *e s* of late E. H. Thornhill, Manor House, Boxworth, Cambridge; *m* 1934, Diana Pearl Day (*d* 1983), *d* of late Hubert G. D. Beales, Hambleden and Cambridge; two *s* one *d*. *Educ:* St Bees School; Royal Military Academy. 2nd Lieut Royal Artillery, 1916; served European War, 1914–18, France and Belgium (wounded, MC); served War of 1939–45, France, Western Desert (Eighth Army) and Italy (despatches); psc 1934; Lt-Col 1945; retd 1948. Chm., Cambs and I of Ely TA & AFA, 1957–62. DL Cambs and Isle of Ely, 1956, Vice-Lieut, 1965–75. *Address:* Manor House, Boxworth, Cambridge. *T:* Elsworth 209. *Club:* Army and Navy.

THORNTON, Dr (Clara) Grace, CBE 1964 (OBE 1959); LVO 1957; *b* 27 June 1913; *d* of late Arthur Augustus Thornton and Clara Maud Hines; unmarried. *Educ:* Kettering High School; Newnham Coll., Cambridge (MA, PhD; Hon. Fellow, 1982). Research: Iceland, Cambridge, 1935–39. Min. of Information, 1940–45. Press Attaché, Copenhagen, 1945–48; Vice-Consul, Reykjavik, 1948–51 (Chargé d'Affaires during 1949 and 1950); Foreign Office, 1951–54; 1st Sec. and Consul, Copenhagen, 1954–60; 1st Sec. and Information Officer, Brussels, 1960–62; 1st Sec. and Consul, Djakarta, 1962–64 (Consul-General, 1963–64); Consul-General, Lisbon, 1965–70; Head of Consular Dept, FCO, 1970–73; Sec., Women's Nat. Commn, Cabinet Office, 1973–78. Alternate UK Deleg., UN Status of Women Commn, 1978. Associate Fellow, Newnham Coll., Cambridge, 1972–81. President: London Assoc. of University Women, 1974–78; Associates of Newnham Coll., 1975–78; Pres., Newnham Roll, 1982–84 (Vice-Pres., 1980–82). Governor, GB/E Europe Centre, 1981–. FRSA 1969. Danish Freedom Medal, 1945; Order of Dannebrog, 1957; Order of Icelandic Falcon, 1983. *Publications:* Conversation Piece (University Women's Club), 1979, 2nd edn 1985; Notes on No 2 Audley Square, 1980; (ed) Take Your Hare When it is Cased, 1980 (recipes); *translated and edited:* Hans Christian Andersen: A Visit to Portugal 1866, 1972; A Visit to Spain 1862, 1975; A Visit to Germany, Italy and Malta 1840–41, 1985. *Recreations:* music, embroidery, Scandinavica, cats. *Address:* 17 Onslow Court, Drayton Gardens, SW10 9RL. *T:* 01–373 2965. *Club:* University Women's (Chm. 1976–79).

THORNTON, Clive Edward Ian, CBE 1983; LLB (Lond); FInstLEx, FCBSI; Chairman: Financial Weekly, since 1985; Universe Publications, since 1986; Partner, Stoneham Langton and Passmore, Solicitors, since 1985; *b* 12 Dec. 1929; *s* of Albert and Margaret Thornton; *m* 1956, Maureen Carmine (*née* Crane); one *s* one *d*. *Educ:* St Anthony's Sch., Newcastle upon Tyne; Coll. of Commerce, Newcastle upon Tyne; College of Law, London; LLB London. Solicitor. FInstLEx 1958; FCBSI 1970. Associate, Pensions Management Inst. Articled to Kenneth Hudson, solicitor, London, 1959; admitted solicitor of Supreme Court, 1963. Asst Solicitor, Nationwide Building Soc., 1963; Solicitor, Cassel Arenz Ltd, Merchant Bankers, 1964–67; Abbey National Building Society: Chief Solicitor, 1967; Dep. Chief Gen. Man., 1978; Chief Gen. Manager, 1979–83; Dir, 1980–83. Chm., Metropolitan Assoc. of Building Socs, 1981–82. Chm., Mirror Group Newspapers, 1984. Member: Law Soc. (Chm., Commerce and Industry Gp, 1974); Council, Chartered Bldg Socs Inst., 1973–81; Council, Building Socs Assoc., 1979–83; Bd, Housing Corp., 1980–. Chairman: SHAC, 1983–86; Thamesmead Town Ltd, 1986–. Mem. Council, St Mary's Hosp. Med. Sch., 1984–. Freeman, City of London; Liveryman, Worshipful Co. of Bakers. *Publication:* Building Society Law, Cases and Materials, 1969 (2nd edn 1975). *Recreations:* antique collecting, music, reading, farming. *Address:* The Old Rectory, Creeton, Grantham, Lincs. *Club:* City Livery.

THORNTON, Ernest, MBE 1951; JP; DL; *b* Burnley, Lancs, 18 May 1905; *s* of Charles Thornton and Margaret (*née* Whittaker); *m* 1930, Evelyn, *d* of Fred Ingham, Blacko, Nelson; one *s* (and one *s* decd). *Educ:* Walverden Council Sch., Nelson, Lancs. Cotton weaver, 1918–26; costing clerk, 1926–29. Rochdale Weavers and Winders' Assoc.; Asst Secretary, 1929–40, Secretary, 1940–70. President, Amalgamated Weavers' Assoc., 1960–65. Secretary, United Textile Factory Workers' Assoc., 1943–53. Member: Lord President's Advisory Council for Scientific and Industrial Research, 1943–48; Council of British Cotton Industry Research Assoc., 1948–53. MP (Lab) Farnworth, 1952–70; Joint Parliamentary Secretary, Min. of Labour, 1964–66. Member: UK Trade Mission to China, 1946; Anglo-American Cotton Textile Mission to Japan, 1950; Cotton Board's Mission to India, 1950. Mayor of County Borough of Rochdale, 1942–43. Comp. TI 1966. JP 1944, DL Manchester Metropolitan County (formerly Lancaster), 1970. *Address:* 31 Lynnwood Drive, Rochdale, Lancs. *T:* Rochdale 31954.

THORNTON, (George) Malcolm; MP (C) Crosby, since 1983 (Liverpool, Garston, 1979–83); *b* 3 April 1939; *s* of George Edmund and Ethel Thornton; *m* 1st, 1962; 2nd, 1972, Shirley Ann, (Sue) (*née* Banton); one step *s* one step *d*. *Educ:* Wallasey Grammar Sch.; Liverpool Nautical Coll. Liverpool Pilot Service, 1955–79 (Sen. 1st cl. Licence holder). Member: Wallasey County Borough Council, 1965–74 (Chm., Transport Cttee, 1968–69); Wirral Metropolitan Council, 1973–79 (Council Leader, 1974–77); Chairman: Merseyside Metropolitan Districts Liaison Cttee, 1975–77; Educn Cttee, AMA, 1978–79 (Mem., 1974–79); Council of Local Educn Authorities, 1978. Mem., Burnham (Primary and Secondary) Cttee, 1975–79. PPS to Sec. of State for Industry, 1981–83, for the Environment, 1983–84. Mem., Select Cttee on Educn, Sci. and the Arts, 1985–. *Recreations:* fishing, sailing, cooking. *Address:* House of Commons, SW1A 0AA. *T:* 01–219 4489. *Clubs:* Carlton; Birkenhead Squash Raquets (Wirral).

THORNTON, Dr Grace; *see* Thornton, Dr C. G.

THORNTON, Jack Edward Clive, CB 1978; OBE 1964 (MBE 1945); *b* 22 Nov. 1915; *s* of late Stanley Henry Thornton and Elizabeth (*née* Baxter); *m* 1st, Margaret, JP, *d* of John David and Emily Copeland, Crewe, Cheshire; 2nd, Helen Ann Elizabeth, *d* of Henry Gerard and Valerie Meixner, Ravenshoe, N Qld, Australia. *Educ:* Solihull Sch.; Christ's Coll., Cambridge (Open Exhibnr 1936; BA 1938). Cert. Educn 1939; MA 1942. Served in RASC, 1939–46 (despatches, 1946); Lt-Col 1944. Teaching in UK, 1946–47; Asst, then Dep. Educn Officer, City of York, 1947–51; Asst Educn Officer, WR Yorks, 1951–54; Dep. Dir of Educn, Cumberland, 1954–62; Sec., Bureau for External Aid for Educn, Fed. Govt of Nigeria, 1962–64; Educn Consultant, IBRD, 1964–65; Adviser on Educn in W Africa and Controller Appts Div., British Council, 1965–68; Dep. Educn Adviser, 1968–70, Chief Educn Adviser and Under Sec., 1970–77, Ministry of Overseas Develt (now Overseas Develt Admin in FCO). Lectr, Dept of Educn in Developing Countries, Inst. of Educn, Univ. of London, 1978–79. Dep. Exec. Chm., Council for Educn in the Commonwealth; Chm., Council of Parents' Nat. Educational Union World-wide Educn Service; Member: Educational Panel, Independent Schs Tribunal; Lloyd Foundn; British Council Recognition Adv. Cttee. *Recreations:* books, conservation, mountains, music, railways, travel. *Address:* 131 Dalling Road, W6 0ET. *T:* 01–748 7692.

THORNTON, John Henry, QPM 1980; Deputy Assistant Commissioner, Metropolitan Police, 1981–86; *b* 24 Dec. 1930; *s* of late Sidney Thornton and Ethel Thornton (*née* Grinnell); *m* 1st, 1952, Norma Lucille, *d* of Alfred and Kate Scrivenor (marr. diss. 1972); two *s*; 2nd, 1972, Hazel Ann, *d* of William and Edna Butler; one *s* one *d* (and one *s* decd). *Educ:* Prince Henry's Grammar School. Evesham. RN 1949–50. Metropolitan Police, 1950; Head of Community Relations, 1977–80; RCDS, 1981; Dep. Asst Commissioner, 1981; Dir of Information, 1982–83; Hd of Training, 1983–85; NW Area, 1985–86. Vice-Pres., British Section, Internat. Police Assoc., 1969–79. Liveryman, Glaziers' Co., 1983. CStJ 1984. *Recreations:* music, gardening. *Address:* c/o Midland Bank, 1 High Street, Harpenden, Herts.

THORNTON, Lt-Gen. Sir Leonard (Whitmore), KCB 1967 (CB 1962); CBE 1957 (OBE 1944); *b* Christchurch, 15 Oct. 1916; *s* of late Cuthbert John Thornton and Frances Caverhill Thornton; *m* 1942, Gladys Janet Sloman, Wellington; three *s*; *m* 1971, Ruth Leicester, Wellington. *Educ:* Christchurch Boys' High Sch.; Royal Military Coll., Duntroon, Australia. Commissioned in New Zealand Army, 1937. Served War of 1939–45 (despatches twice, OBE), Middle East and Italy in 2nd New Zealand Expeditionary Force; Commander, Royal Artillery, 2 New Zealand Division. Commander, Tokyo Sub-area, 1946; Deputy Chief of General Staff, 1948; idc 1952; Head, New Zealand Joint Service Liaison Staff, 1953 and 1954; QMG, New Zealand, 1955; AG, 1956–58; Chief, SEATO Planning Office, Thailand, 1958–59; Chief of General Staff, NZ, 1960–65; Chief of Defence Staff, NZ, 1965–71; Ambassador for New Zealand in S Vietnam and Khmer Republic, 1972–74. Chm., Alcoholic Liquor Adv. Council, 1977–83. *Recreation:* fishing. *Address:* 67 Bedford Street, Wellington 5, New Zealand. *Club:* Wellington (Wellington).

THORNTON, Malcolm; *see* Thornton, G. M.

THORNTON, Michael James, CBE 1978; MC 1942; *b* 6 Dec. 1919; *s* of late Arthur Bruce Thornton and Dorothy Kidston Thornton (*née* Allsop); *m* 1949, Pauline Elizabeth Heppell; one *s* two *d*. *Educ:* Christ's Hospital; London Sch. of Economics (BSc(Econ)). Entered Bank of England, 1938; Deputy Chief Cashier, 1962–67; Chief of Economic Intelligence Dept, 1967–78. *Recreation:* sailing.

THORNTON, Sir Peter (Eustace), KCB 1974 (CB 1971); Director: Courtaulds, since 1977; Laird Group, since 1978; Permanent Secretary, Department of Trade, 1974–77; *b* 28 Aug. 1917; *s* of Douglas Oscar Thornton and Dorothy (*née* Shepherd); *m* 1946, Rosamond Hobart Myers, US Medal of Freedom, Sewanee, Tennessee; two *s* one *d*. *Educ:* Charterhouse; Gonville and Caius Coll., Cambridge. Served with RA, mainly in Middle East and Italy, 1940–46. Joined Board of Trade, 1946. Secretary, Company Law Cttee (Jenkins Cttee), 1959–62; Assistant Under-Secretary of State, Department of Economic Affairs, 1964–67; Under-Sec., 1967–70, Dep. Sec., 1970–72, Cabinet Office, with central co-ordinating role during British negotiations for membership of EEC; Dep. Sec., DTI, March-July 1972; Sec. (Aerospace and Shipping), DTI, 1972–74; Second Permanent Sec., Dept of Trade, 1974. Director: Hill Samuel Gp, 1977–83; Rolls Royce, 1977–85; Superior Oil, 1980–84. Mem., Megaw Cttee of Inquiry into Civil Service Pay, 1981–82. Pro-Chancellor, Open Univ., 1979–83 (D Univ 1984). Governor, Sutton's Hosp., Charterhouse, 1980–. *Address:* 22 East Street, Alresford, Hants SO24 9EE.

THORNTON, Peter Kai, FSA 1976; Curator of Sir John Soane's Museum, since 1984; *b* 8 April 1925; *s* of Sir Gerard Thornton, FRS, and of Gerda, *d* of Kai Nørregaard, Copenhagen; *m* 1950, Mary Ann Rosamund, *d* of E. A. P. Helps, Cregane, Rosscarbery, Co. Cork; three *d*. *Educ:* Bryanston Sch.; De Havilland Aeronautical Technical Sch.; Trinity Hall, Cambridge. Served with Army, Intelligence Corps, Austria, 1945–48; Cambridge, 1948–50; Voluntary Asst Keeper, Fitzwilliam Museum, Cambridge, 1950–52; Joint Secretary, National Art-Collections Fund, London, 1952–54; entered Victoria and Albert Museum as Asst Keeper, Dept of Textiles, 1954; transf. to Dept of Woodwork, 1962; Keeper, Dept of Furniture and Woodwork, 1966–84. Sen. Vis. Res. Fellow, St John's Coll., Oxford, 1985–86. Chm., Furniture History Soc., 1974–84;

Member: Council, Nat. Trust, 1983–85; London Adv. Cttee, English Heritage, 1986–. *Publications*: Baroque and Rococo Silks, 1965; Seventeenth Century Interior Decoration in England, France and Holland, 1978 (Alice Davis Hitchcock Medallion, Soc. of Architectural Historians of GB, 1982); (jtly) The Furnishing and Decoration of Ham House, 1981; Musical Instruments as Works of Art, 1982; Authentic Décor: the domestic interior 1620–1920, 1984 (Sir Bannister Fletcher Prize, RIBA, 1985); numerous articles on interior decoration, furniture and textiles. *Address*: 15 Cheniston Gardens, W8. *T*: 01–937 8868; Carrigillihy, Union Hall, Co. Cork; Phillips Farm Cottage, Eaton Hastings, Faringdon, Oxon. *Club*: Kilmacabea and Castlehaven Gun (Co. Cork).

THORNTON, Richard Eustace, OBE 1980; JP; HM Lord Lieutenant of Surrey, since 1986; *b* 10 Oct. 1922; *m* 1954, Gabrielle Elizabeth Sharpe; four *d*. *Educ*: Eton Coll.; Trinity Coll., Cambridge (MA). Member: Royal Commission on Environmental Pollution, 1977–84; Governing Body, Charterhouse Sch. (Chm., 1981–). Surrey: DL; High Sheriff 1978–79; JP. KStJ 1986. *Address*: Hampton, Seale, near Farnham, Surrey. *T*: Guildford 810208.

THORNTON, Robert John, CB 1980; Assistant Under Secretary of State and Director General of Supplies and Transport (Naval), Ministry of Defence, 1977–81; *b* 23 Dec. 1919; *s* of Herbert John Thornton and Ethel Mary Thornton (*née* Dunning); *m* 1944, Joan Elizabeth Roberts; three *s*. *Educ*: Queen Elizabeth Grammar School, Atherstone. MBIM 1970. Joined Naval Store Dept, Admiralty, as Asst Naval Store Officer, 1938; Singapore, 1941; Dep. Naval Store Officer, Colombo, 1942; Support Ship Hong Siang, 1943; Naval Store Officer, Admiralty, 1945; Gibraltar, 1951; Asst Dir of Stores, 1955; Superintending Naval Store Officer, Portsmouth, 1960; Dep. Dir of Stores, 1964; Dir of Victualling, 1971; Dir of Supplies and Transport (General Stores and Victualling), 1971. *Recreations*: squash, fly fishing, gardening.

THORNTON, Robert Ribblesdale, CBE 1973; DL; solicitor; Deputy Chairman, Local Government Boundary Commission for England, 1982 (Member, 1976–82); *b* 2 April 1913; *s* of Thomas Thornton and Florence Thornton (*née* Gatenby); *m* 1940, Ruth Eleonore Tuckson; one *s* one *d*. *Educ*: Leeds Grammar Sch.; St John's Coll., Cambridge (MA, LLM). Asst Solicitor, Leeds, 1938–40 and 1946–47; Served War, 1940–46. Asst Solicitor, Bristol, 1947–53; Dep. Town Clerk, Southampton, 1953–54; Town Clerk: Salford, 1954–66; Leicester, 1966–73; Chief Exec., Leicestershire CC, 1973–76. Pres., Soc. of Town Clerks, 1971. Treasurer, Leicester Univ., 1980–85. DL Leicestershire, 1974–85. French Croix de Guerre, 1946. *Recreations*: music, sport. *Address*: 16 St Mary's Close, Winterborne Whitechurch, Blandford Forum, Dorset DT11 0DJ. *T*: Milton Abbas 880980. *Club*: National Liberal.

THORNYCROFT, John Ward, CBE 1957; CEng; FIMechE; beef farmer; Hon. President, John I. Thornycroft & Co. Ltd, since 1966 (Chairman, 1960–66; Managing Director, 1942–66); Director, Southampton, Isle of Wight and South of England Royal Mail Steam Packet Co. Ltd, 1960–77, retired; *b* 14 Oct. 1899; *s* of late Sir John E. Thornycroft; *m* 1930, Esther Katherine (*d* 1985), *d* of J. E. Pritchard; one *s* one *d*. *Educ*: Royal Naval Colleges, Osborne, Dartmouth and Keyham; Trinity Coll., Cambridge. Served War, 1914–18, HMS Canada, HMS Opal, HM Submarine G10, HMS Spenser (1914–15 War Service Star). Hon. Vice-Pres., RINA; FRSA. *Recreations*: golf, sailing and gardening. *Address*: Steyne House, Bembridge, Isle of Wight. *T*: Bembridge 2502. *Clubs*: Naval and Military; Bembridge Sailing (IOW).
See also Baron Inverforth.

THOROGOOD, Alfreda, (Mrs D. R. Wall), ARAD (PDTC); teacher; Deputy Ballet Principal, Bush Davies School, since 1984 (Senior Teacher, 1982–84); *b* 17 Aug. 1942; *d* of Alfreda and Edward Thorogood; *m* 1967, David Wall, *qv*; one *s* one *d*. *Educ*: Lady Eden's Sch.; Royal Ballet Sch. Joined Royal Ballet Co., Feb. 1960; Soloist, Aug. 1965; Principal Dancer, 1968. *Recreations*: listening to music, cooking, interior design, art, painting. *Address*: 34 Croham Manor Road, S Croydon CR2 7BE.

THOROGOOD, Rev. Bernard George; General Secretary, United Reformed Church, since 1980; Moderator, Executive Committee, British Council of Churches, since 1984; *b* 21 July 1927; *s* of Frederick and Winifred Thorogood; *m* 1952, Jannett Lindsay Paton (*née* Cameron); two *s*. *Educ*: Glasgow Univ. (MA); Scottish Congregational College. Ordained in Congregational Church, 1952; missionary appointment under London Missionary Society in South Pacific Islands, 1953–70; Gen. Sec., Council for World Mission, 1971–80. Mem., Central Cttee, WCC, 1984–. *Publications*: Not Quite Paradise, 1960; Guide to the Book of Amos, 1971; Our Father's House, 1983. *Recreation*: sketching *Address*: Church House, 86 Tavistock Place, WC1H 9RT. *T*: 01–837 7661.

THOROGOOD, Kenneth Alfred Charles; Chairman, Ardil (Holdings) UK Ltd, since 1984; Director: Welbeck Finance plc, since 1984; Trade and Industry Acceptance Corporation (London) Ltd, since 1984; *b* 1924; *s* of Albert Jesse and Alice Lucy Thorogood; *m* 1st, 1947, José Patricia Smith; two *d*; 2nd, 1979, Mrs Gaye Lambourne. *Educ*: Highbury County Grammar School. Pres., Deepsoval Services Ltd; Chm., Tozer Kemsley & Millbourn (Holdings) plc, 1972–82; Director: Alexanders Discount Co. Ltd, to 1983; Royal Insurance Co. Ltd; Abelson Plant (Holdings) Ltd; Spicer-Firgos Ltd. Chairman, Brit. Export Houses Assoc., 1968–70; Mem., Cttee of Invisibles, 1968–70. *Recreations*: aviation, music. *Address*: 71 Chester Square, SW1W 9DU. *Clubs*: Travellers', City of London, Royal Air Force; Wanderers (Johannesburg).

THOROLD, Captain Sir Anthony (Henry), 15th Bt, *cr* 1642; OBE 1942; DSC 1942, and Bar 1945; DL; JP; RN Retired; *b* 7 Sept. 1903; *s* of Sir James (Ernest) Thorold, 14th Bt; *S* father, 1965; *m* 1939, Jocelyn Elaine Laura, *er d* of late Sir Clifford Heathcote-Smith, KBE, CMG; one *s* two *d*. *Educ*: Royal Naval Colleges Osborne and Dartmouth. Entered RN 1917; qualified as Navigating Officer, 1928; psc 1935; Commander, 1940; served in Mediterranean and Home Fleets, 1939–40; Staff Officer Operations to Flag Officer Commanding Force 'H', 1941–43; in command of Escort Groups in Western Approaches Comd, 1944–45; Captain, 1946; Naval Assistant Secretary in Cabinet Office and Ministry of Defence, 1945–48; Sen. Officer, Fishery Protection Flotilla, 1949–50; Captain of HMS Dryad (Navigation and Direction Sch.), 1951–52; Commodore in Charge, Hong Kong, 1953–55; ADC to the Queen, 1955–56; retired, 1956. DL Lincs, 1959; JP Lincolnshire (Parts of Kesteven), 1961; High Sheriff of Lincolnshire, 1968. Chairman: Grantham Hospital Management Cttee, 1963–74; Lincoln Diocesan Trust and Board of Finance, 1966 71; Community Council of Lincs, 1974–81; CC Kesteven, 1958–74; Leader, Lincs County Council, 1973–81. *Recreation*: shooting. *Heir*: *s* (Anthony) Oliver Thorold [*b* 15 April 1945; *m* 1977, Genevra M., *y d* of John Richardson, Midlothian; one *s* one *d*]. *Address*: Syston Old Hall, Grantham, Lincs NG32 2BX. *T*: Loveden 50270. *Club*: Army and Navy.

THORPE, Adrian Charles, MA; HM Diplomatic Service; Counsellor (Economic), Bonn, since 1985; *b* 29 July 1942; *o s* of late Prof. Lewis Thorpe and of Dr Barbara Reynolds, *qv*; *m* 1968, Miyoko Kosugi. *Educ*: The Leys Sch., Cambridge; Christ's Coll., Cambridge (MA). HM Diplomatic Service, 1965–: Tokyo, 1965–70; FCO, 1970–73; Beirut, 1973–76 (Head of Chancery, 1975–76); FCO, 1976; Tokyo, 1976–81; FCO,

1981–85, Hd of IT Dept, 1982–85. FRSA. *Publications*: articles in journals. *Recreations*: opera, travel, bookshops, comfort. *Address*: c/o Foreign and Commonwealth Office, SW1. *Club*: Tokyo (Japan).

THORPE, Bernard; Founder and Senior Partner, Bernard Thorpe & Partners, 1922–82; Land Agent, Surveyor, Farmer; *b* 27 June 1895; *m* 1st, 1916, Hilda Mary (*d* 1971), *d* of Edwin Wilkinson, Coventry; one *s* one *d* (and one *s* killed as Pilot Officer Royal Air Force); 2nd, 1972, Mary Philomena, *d* of George Cregan, Limerick, Eire. *Educ*: private tutor; Nottingham Univ. Member Godstone (Surrey) RDC and of its Board of Guardians, 1926–36; Past President, (1939) and Past Chairman, Surrey and Sussex Br. Incorp. Society of Auctioneers and Landed Property Agents; sometime Member Council, Home Grown Timber Marketing Assoc.; Director (Tile Section), Redland Holdings Ltd; Chairman, Park Investments Ltd, 1958–63; Chairman, Assoc. of Land and Property Owners, 1962–64. Past Master, Worshipful Company of Gold and Silver Wyre Drawers, 1966 (Member 1938, and Past Warden); Member Court of Assistants, Worshipful Company of Paviors 1938 (past Warden; Master, 1975); Freeman, City of London. Freemason. *Recreations*: hunting and shooting; formerly Rugby football. *Address*: c/o Mrs J. M. Winney, 12 Lamorna Gardens, Ferring, Worthing, Sussex. *Club*: City Livery.

THORPE, Rt. Hon. (John) Jeremy, PC 1967; Chairman, Jeremy Thorpe Associates (Development Consultants in the Third World), since 1984; *b* 29 April 1929; *s* of late J. H. Thorpe, OBE, KC, MP (C) Rusholme, and Ursula, *d* of late Sir John Norton-Griffiths, Bt, KCB, DSO, sometime MP (C); *m* 1st, 1968, Caroline (*d* 1970), *d* of Warwick Allpass, Kingswood, Surrey; one *s*; 2nd, 1973, Marion, *d* of late Erwin Stein. *Educ*: Rectory Sch., Connecticut, USA; Eton Coll.; Trinity Coll., Oxford, Hon. Fellow, 1972. President, Oxford Union Society, Hilary, 1951; Barrister, Inner Temple, 1954. Member Devon Sessions. Contested (L) N Devon, 1955; MP (L) Devon N, 1959–79. Hon. Treasurer, Liberal Party Organisation, 1965–67; Leader, Liberal Party, 1967–76. United Nations Association: Chm., Exec., 1976–80; Chm., Political Cttee, 1977–85. A Vice-Pres., Anti-Apartheid Movement, 1969–. FRSA. Hon. LLD Exeter, 1974. *Publications*: (jtly) To all who are interested in Democracy, 1951; Europe: the case for going in, 1971; contrib. to newspapers and periodicals. *Recreations*: music; collecting Chinese ceramics. *Address*: 2 Orme Square, W2. *Clubs*: National Liberal; N Devon Liberal.

THORPE, Mathew Alexander, QC 1980; a Recorder of the Crown Court, since 1982; *b* 1938; *s* of late Michael Alexander Thorpe and of Dorothea Margaret Lambert; *m* 1966, Lavinia Hermione Buxton; three *s*. *Educ*: Stowe; Balliol Coll., Oxford. Called to the Bar, Inner Temple, 1961, Bencher, 1985. *Address*: Seend Green House, Melksham, Wilts. *T*: Seend 493. *Club*: Turf.

THORPE, Sir Ronald Laurence G.; *see* Gardner-Thorpe.

THOULESS, Prof. David James, FRS 1979; Professor of Physics, University of Washington, since 1980; Royal Society Research Professor, and Fellow of Clare Hall, University of Cambridge, since 1983; *b* 21 Sept. 1934; *s* of late Robert Henry Thouless; *m* 1958, Margaret Elizabeth Scrase; two *s* one *d*. *Educ*: Winchester Coll.; Trinity Hall, Cambridge (BA); Cornell Univ. (PhD). Physicist, Lawrence Radiation Laboratory, Berkeley, Calif, 1958–59; ICI Research Fellow, Birmingham Univ., 1959–61; Lecturer, Cambridge Univ., and Fellow of Churchill Coll., 1961–65; Prof. of Mathematical Physics, Birmingham Univ., 1965–78; Prof. of Applied Science, Yale Univ., 1979–80. *Publication*: Quantum Mechanics of Many-Body Systems, 1961, 2nd edn 1972. *Address*: Department of Physics FM-15, University of Washington, Seattle, Wash 98195, USA.

THOURON, Sir John (Rupert Hunt), KBE 1976 (CBE 1967); *b* 10 May 1908; *m* 1st, 1930, Lorna Ellett (marr. diss. 1939); one *s*; 2nd, 1953, Esther duPont (*d* 1984). *Educ*: Sherborne School, Dorset. Served War of 1939–45; Major, Black Watch. With Lady Thouron, Founder of the Thouron University of Pennsylvania Fund for British-American Student Exchange, 1960. *Recreations*: shooting, fishing, golf, gardening. *Address*: Glencoe Farm, Unionville, Chester County, Pa 19375, USA. *T*: (215) 384–5542; (winter) 416 South Beach Road, Hobe Sound, Fla 33455, USA. *T*: 305–546–3577. *Clubs*: White's; Brook (NY); Sunningdale Golf; Royal St George Golf; Wilmington, Wilmington Country, Vicmead (all Delaware); Pine Valley, British Officers Club of Philadelphia (Pennsylvania); Seminole Golf, Island Club of Hobe Sound (Florida).

THOYTS, Robert Francis Newman; solicitor in private practice; *b* 13 March 1913; *o s* of late Lt-Comdr Robert Elmhirst Thoyts, RN, and late Kathleen Olive Thoyts (*née* Hobbs); *m* 1938, Joyce Eliza Gillingham, *er d* of late Rev. William Samuel Probert and late Evangeline Eliza Probert; one *s* four *d*. *Educ*: Bradfield Coll. Admitted Solicitor, 1936. Served War, RAF, 1941–45; Flt Lieut. Govt Legal Service, 1936–78, Under Sec., DHSS, 1971–78. Civil Service Legal Soc.: Gen. Sec. 1945–50; Chm. 1965–67. Mem. Salaried Solicitors' Cttee of Law Soc., 1948–78. *Recreations*: sailing (Civil Service Rep. Sailing Badge, 1966); amenity interests. *Address*: 37 Queen's Drive, Thames Ditton, Surrey KT7 0TJ. *T*: 01–398 0469. *Clubs*: Law Society; Civil Service Sailing Assoc. (Hon. Life Mem., Chm., 1959–74; Rear-Cdre, 1977–80; Trustee); River Thames Soc. (Vice-Chm. 1971; Hon. Gen. Sec., 1978–86; Vice-Pres., 1986–); Littleton Sailing (Cdre, 1961–65; Hon. Life Mem.); Frostbite Yacht Club of America (Hon. Cdre); Island Sailing, etc.

THRELFALL, Richard Ian, QC 1965; *b* 14 Jan. 1920; *s* of William Bernhard and Evelyn Alice Threlfall; *m* 1948, Annette, *d* of George C. H. Matthey; two *s* three *d* (and one *s* decd). *Educ*: Oundle; Gonville and Caius Coll., Cambridge. War service, 1940–45 (despatches twice); Indian Armoured Corps (Probyn's Horse) and Staff appointments. Barrister, Lincoln's Inn, 1947, Bencher 1973. FSA, 1949. Member: Court of Assistants, Worshipful Co. of Goldsmiths (Prime Warden, 1978–79); British Hallmarking Council; East Surrey HA; Surrey FPC. *Address*: Pebble Hill House, Limpsfield, Surrey. *T*: Oxted 2452.

THRING, Rear-Adm. George Arthur, CB 1958; DSO 1940 and Bar 1952; DL; *b* 13 Sept. 1903; *s* of late Sir Arthur Thring, KCB; *m* 1929, Betty Mary (*d* 1983), *er d* of Colonel Stewart William Ward Blacker, DSO; two *s* two *d*. *Educ*: Royal Naval Colleges, Osborne and Dartmouth. Commander, 1941; Captain, 1946; Rear-Admiral, 1956; retired, 1958. Commanded: HMS Deptford, 1940–41; 42nd and 20th Escort Groups, Atlantic, 1943–45; HMS Ceylon, 1951–52; Flag Officer, Malayan Area, 1956–58. Officer, Legion of Merit (USA), 1945. DL Somerset, 1968. *Recreations*: golf, shooting and fishing. *Address*: Alford House, Castle Cary, Somerset. *T*: Wheathill 329.

THRING, Prof. Meredith Wooldridge, ScD; FEng; Professor of Mechanical Engineering, Queen Mary College, London University, 1964–81; *b* 17 Dec. 1915; *s* of Captain W. H. C. S. Thring, CBE, RN, and Dorothy (*née* Wooldridge); *m* 1940, Alice Margaret Hooley (*d* 1986), two *s* one *d*. *Educ*: Malvern Coll., Worcs; Trinity Coll., Cambridge (Senior Scholar, 1937). Hons Degree Maths and Physics, 1937; ScD, 1964. Student's Medal, Inst. of Fuel, for work on producer gas mains, 1938; British Coal Utilisation Research Assoc.: Asst Scientific Officer, 1937; Senior Scientific Officer and Head of Combustion Research Laboratory, 1944; British Iron and Steel Research Assoc.: Head of Physics Dept, 1946; Superintendent, 1950; Assistant Director, 1953; Prof. of Fuel Technology and Chemical Engineering, Sheffield Univ., 1953–64. Sir Robert Hadfield medal of Iron and Steel Inst. for studies on open hearth furnaces, 1949; Parsons Memorial Lecture on Magnetohydrodynamics, 1961; General Superintendent International Flame Radiation Research Foundn, 1951–76. Visitor: Production Engineering Research Assoc., 1967; Machine Tool Industry Research Assoc., 1967. Member Clean Air Council, 1957–62; Fuel Research Board, 1957–58; Fire Research Board, 1961–64; BISRA Council, 1958–60; President, Inst. of Fuel, 1962–63 (Vice-President, 1959–62); Member: Adv. Council on Research and Development, Ministry of Power, 1960–66; Acad. Adv. Council, University of Strathclyde, 1962–67; Education Cttee, RAF, 1968–76; Unesco Commn to Bangladesh, 1979. FInstP 1944; FInstF 1951; FIChemE 1972 (MIChemE 1956); FIMechE 1968 (MIMechE 1964); FIEE 1968 (MIEE 1964); FEng 1976; FRSA 1964; MRI 1965; FRAeS 1969. Elected Mem., Royal Norwegian Scientific Soc., 1974; Corresp. Mem., Nat. Acad. of Engineering of Mexico, 1977. DUniv Open, 1982. *Publications:* The Science of Flames and Furnaces, 1952, 2nd edn, 1960; (with J. H. Chesters) The Influence of Port Design on Open Hearth Furnace Flames (Iron and Steel Institute Special Report 37), 1946; (with R. Edgeworth Johnstone) Pilot Plants, Models and Scale-up Methods in Chemical Engineering, 1957; (ed.) Air Pollution, 1957; Nuclear Propulsion, 1961; Man, Machines and Tomorrow, 1973; Machines—Masters or Slaves of Man?, 1973; (ed with R. J. Crookes) Energy and Humanity, 1974; (with E. R. Laithwaite) How to Invent, 1977; The Engineer's Conscience, 1980, Robots and Telechirs, 1983. *Recreations:* carpentry, wood-carving. *Address:* Bell Farm, Brundish, Suffolk IP13 8BL. *Club:* Athenæum.

THROCKMORTON, Sir Robert George Maxwell, 11th Bt, *cr* 1642; *b* 15 Feb. 1908; *s* of Lt-Col Courtenay Throckmorton (killed in action, 1916), and Lilian (*d* 1955), *o d* of Colonel Langford Brooke, Mere Hall, Cheshire; *S* grandfather, 1927; *m* 1st, 1942, Jean (marr. diss. 1948), (former wife of Arthur Smith-Bingham, *d* of late Charles Garland; she *m* 1959, 3rd Baron Ashcombe, and *d* 1973); 2nd, 1953, Lady Isabel Guinness, *d* of 9th Duke of Rutland. *Educ:* Downside; RMC, Sandhurst. 2nd Lieut, Grenadier Guards, 1928–30; Lieut (A) RNVR, 1940–44. *Heir: cousin* Anthony John Benedict Throckmorton [*b* 9 Feb. 1916; *m* 1972, Violet Virginia, *d* of late Anders William Anderson]. *Address:* Coughton Court, Alcester, Warwickshire. *T:* Alcester 763370; Molland Bottreaux, South Molton, N Devon. *T:* Bishops Nympton 325. *Clubs:* Army and Navy, White's.

THROWER, Frank, FSIAD 1975; glass and ceramic designer; Design Director, Dartington Glass and, since 1983, Design Director, Wedgwood Crystal; *b* 11 April 1932; *m* G. Inga-Lill (marr. diss.); one *s* two *d* and three adopted *s* (and one *s* decd). *Educ:* flunked out of Stationers' Company's Sch. due to enjoying both fine summer and Denis Compton's batting at Lord's Cricket Ground, 1947; no further trng or educn. Worked in shipbroker's office as general dogsbody, 1947–50; four other people in office: 1 Plymouth Brother, 1 Baptist, 1 Methodist, 1 Quaker; decided against organised religion—and shipbroking; various office jobs carried out with no interest or competence, 1950–51; bought a hat and tried to sell carbon paper, failed, 1951; sold hat and tried to sell pottery and glass, 1953–60; succeeded; saw where there was scope for new ideas and improved design; joined Portmeirion as Sales Director, 1960; sold year's prodn in four weeks; designed some glass to set up as importer under Portmeirion banner; glass sold successfully and ... first talks with Dartington about building glass factory in UK, 1963; Dartington Glass factory opened, 1967. Observer Award for design, 1969; Duke of Edinburgh Award for design, 1972; Design Council Award for design, 1972. *Recreation:* maintaining the level of essential bodily fluids whilst waiting for something to turn up. *Address:* 32–34 Wigmore Street, W1H 0HU. *Clubs:* MCC, Queen's.

THROWER, Percy John, MBE 1984; with garden centre and nursery business (Murrells of Shrewsbury, Portland Nurseries, Shrewsbury); Parks Superintendent, Shrewsbury, 1946–74; *b* 30 Jan. 1913; British; *m* 1939, Constance Margaret (*née* Cook); three *d*. *Educ:* Church of England Sch., Little Horwood. NDH 1945. Improver, Horwood House Gdns, Winslow, 1927–31; Journeyman Gardener, Royal Gdns, Windsor, 1931–35; Journeyman Gardener, City of Leeds Parks Dept, 1935–37; Asst Parks Supt, Borough of Derby Parks Dept, 1937–46. Frequent broadcaster, radio and TV, 1947–. RHS: Associate of Honour, 1963; VMH 1974. *Publications:* In Your Garden Week by Week, 1959, rev. edn 1973; Encyclopædia of Gardening, 1962; In Your Greenhouse, 1963, rev. edn 1972; Gardening is Fun; Colour in Your Garden, 1966, rev. 1976; Everyday Gardening, 1969; Vegetables and Fruit, 1977; My Lifetime of Gardening, 1977; Vegetables and Herbs; Month by Month in Your Garden; Picture Book of Gardening; contrib. Amateur Gardening. *Recreation:* shooting. *Address:* The Magnolias, Bomere Heath, Shrewsbury, Salop SY4 3QJ. *T:* Bomere Heath 290225.

THRUSH, Prof. Brian Arthur, FRS 1976; Professor of Physical Chemistry, University of Cambridge, since 1978; Fellow, since 1960, Vice-Master, since 1986, Emmanuel College, Cambridge; *b* Hampstead Garden Suburb, 23 July 1928; *s* of late Arthur Albert Thrush and late Dorothy Charlotte Thrush (*née* Money); *m* 1958, Rosemary Catherine Terry, *d* of late George and Gertrude Terry, Ottawa; one *s* one *d*. *Educ:* Haberdashers' Aske's Sch.; Emmanuel Coll., Cambridge (Schol. 1946–50). BA 1949, MA, PhD 1953, ScD 1965. University of Cambridge: Demonstrator in Physical Chemistry, 1953; Asst Dir of Research, 1959; Lectr in Physical Chemistry, 1964, Reader, 1969; Tutor, 1963–67, and Dir of Studies in Chemistry, 1963–78, Emmanuel Coll. Consultant Physicist, US Nat. Bureau of Standards, Washington, 1957–58; Sen. Vis. Scientist, Nat. Res. Council, Ottawa, 1961, 1971, 1980. Tilden Lectr, Chem. Soc., 1965; Vis. Prof., Chinese Acad. of Science, 1980–; Member: Faraday Council, Chem. Soc., 1976–79; US Nat. Acad. of Scis Panel on Atmospheric Chemistry, 1975–80; Lawes Agric. Trust Cttee, 1979–; NERC, 1985–. M. Polanyi Medal, RSC, 1980. *Publications:* papers on gas kinetics and spectroscopy in Proc. Royal Soc., Trans Faraday Soc., etc. *Recreations:* wine, fell-walking. *Address:* Brook Cottage, Pemberton Terrace, Cambridge CB2 1JA. *T:* Cambridge 357637. *Club:* Athenæum.

THUILLIER, Maj.-Gen. Leslie de Malapert, (Pete), CB 1958; CVO 1966; OBE 1944; *b* 26 Sept. 1905; *s* of late Lt-Col L. C. Thuillier, Indian Army; *m* 1936, Barbara Leonard Rawlins; one *s* two *d*. *Educ:* Berkhamsted Sch.; Royal Military Academy, Woolwich. Commissioned as 2nd Lieut, Royal Corps of Signals, 1926; Lieut, 1929; Captain, 1937; Staff Coll., Camberley, 1939; Temp. Major, 1940; Temp. Lt-Col, 1941; Temp. Colonel, 1945; Colonel, 1949, Brigadier, 1951; Maj.-Gen., 1955. War Office, 1940–41; Middle East and Italy, 1941–45; Chief Signal Officer, Northern Ireland District, 1945–46; British Troops in Egypt, 1951–53; Northern Command, 1954–55; Director of Telecommunications, War Office, 1955–58; Asst Sec., Cabinet Office, 1958–67. Leader, UK Govtl Mission to USA to discuss experimental civil mil. satellite communications systems, 1960; Mem., UK Delegn to Internat. Conf. in Paris, Rome and London to discuss estabt of internat. communication satellite systems, 1963–65. Consultant, Airwork Services Ltd, 1969–84. CEng; MIEE 1968 (AIMEE 1958). *Recreation:* gardening. *Address:* The Red Barn, Patney, Devizes, Wilts SN10 3RA. *T:* Chirton 669. *Club:* Naval and Military.

THURBURN, Gwynneth Loveday, OBE 1956; Hon. FCST; Principal, Central School of Speech and Drama, 1942–67; *b* 17 July 1899; *d* of Robert Augustus Thurburn and Bertha Loveday. *Educ:* Birklands, St Albans; Central School of Speech and Drama. Vice-Pres., Central Sch. of Speech and Drama. *Publication:* Voice and Speech. *Address:* Church Cottage, Darsham, Saxmundham, Suffolk.

THURBURN, Brigadier Roy Gilbert, CB 1950; CBE 1945 (OBE 1941); Secretary, Army Museums Ogilby Trust, 1957–72; *b* 6 July 1901; *y s* of late Reginald Phibbs Thurburn; *m* 1936, Rhona Moneen Hignett; one *s*. *Educ:* St Paul's Sch.; Royal Military Coll., Sandhurst. Commissioned in the Cameronians (Scottish Rifles), 1921; took part in operations in Southern Kurdistan, 1923; attended Staff Coll., Camberley, 1933–34. Served War of 1939–45, in Middle East, North Africa and Italy (despatches twice). ADC to the Queen, 1952–53; retired, 1953. Gold Medallist, United Services Institution of India, 1932. Legion of Merit (USA), 1947. *Publications:* (ed) Index to British Military Costume Prints, 1972; various in journals. *Recreations:* many. *Address:* 7 Elmhurst Court, Lower Edgeborough Road, Guildford, Surrey GU1 2DP.

THURLOW, 8th Baron *cr* 1792; **Francis Edward Hovell-Thurlow-Cumming-Bruce,** KCMG 1961 (CMG 1957); Governor and C-in-C of the Bahamas, 1968–72; *b* 9 March 1912; *s* of 6th Baron Thurlow and Grace Catherine, *d* of Rev. Henry Trotter; *S* brother, 1971; *m* 1949, Yvonne Diana Aubyn Wilson, CStJ 1969; one *s* two *d* (and one *s* decd). *Educ:* Shrewsbury Sch.; Trinity Coll., Cambridge. Asst Principal, Dept of Agriculture for Scotland, 1935; transferred to Dominions Office, 1937; Asst Private Sec. to Sec. of State, 1939; Asst Sec., Office of UK High Comr in NZ, 1939; Asst Sec., Office of UK High Comr in Canada, 1944; Secretariat, Meeting of Commonwealth Prime Ministers in London, 1946; served with UK Delegn at Paris Peace Conf., 1946, and at UN Gen. Assemblies, 1946 and 1948; Principal Private Sec. to Sec. of State, 1946; Asst Sec., CRO, 1948; Head of Political Div., Office of UK High Comr in New Delhi, 1949; Establishment Officer, CRO, 1952; Head of Commodities Dept, CRO, 1954; Adviser on External Affairs to Governor of Gold Coast, 1955; Deputy High Comr for the UK in Ghana, 1957; Asst Under-Sec. of State, CRO, April 1958; Deputy High Comr for the UK in Canada, 1958; High Comr for UK: in New Zealand, 1959–63; in Nigeria, 1964–67; Dep. Under-Sec. of State, FCO, 1964. Chairman: Inst. for Comparative Study of History, Philosophy and the Sciences, 1974–80; Alexandria Foundn, 1980–83. KStJ 1969. *Recreations:* fishing, golf. *Heir:* *s* Hon. Roualeyn Robert Hovell-Thurlow-Cumming-Bruce [*b* 13 April 1952; *m* 1980, Bridget Anne, *o d* of H. B. Ismay Cheape, Fossoway Lodge, Kinross; one *s*]. *Address:* Old Vicarage, Mapledurham, near Reading, Berks. *T:* Reading 723339; 17c Bristol Gardens, W9. *T:* 01–289 2639. *Club:* Travellers'.

See also Rt Hon. Sir J. R. H.-T.-Cumming-Bruce.

THURLOW, Very Rev. Alfred Gilbert Goddard, MA; Dean of Gloucester, 1972–82, now Dean Emeritus; *b* 6 April 1911; *s* of Rev. A. R. Thurlow; *m* 1955, Thelda Mary Hook; two *s*. *Educ:* Selwyn Coll., Cambridge; Cuddesdon Coll., Oxford. MA Cantab, 1936. Curate, All Saints, Wokingham, 1934–39; Precentor of Norwich Cathedral, 1939–55; Rector of St Clement, St George Colegate and St Edmund Norwich, 1943–52; Vicar of: St Andrew and St Michael at Plea, Norwich, 1952–55; St Nicholas, Great Yarmouth, 1955–64; Canon Residentiary of Norwich, 1964–72, Vice-Dean, 1969–72. FSA 1948; FRHistS 1962. *Publications:* Church Bells and Ringers of Norwich, 1947; St George Colegate Norwich, a Redundant Church, 1950; The Mediæval Painted Panels of Norwich Cathedral, 1959; Norwich Cathedral, 1962; Great Yarmouth Priory and Parish Church, 1963; Cathedrals at Work, 1966; City of Norwich, 1970; Cathedrals in Colour, 1971; Norwich Cathedral, 1972; Biblical Myths and Mysteries, 1974; Gloucester and Berkeley: Edward II, Martyr King, 1976; City of Gloucester, 1981; Cathedrals and Abbeys, 1986. *Recreations:* change ringing, travel, interpreting historic buildings. *Address:* 2 East Pallant, Chichester, West Sussex PO19 1TR. *T:* Chichester 783977. *Clubs:* Cambridge Union; Rotary.

THURNHAM, Peter Giles; MP (C) Bolton North-East, since 1983; Chairman, Wathes Holdings (formerly First and Third Ltd), since 1972; *b* 21 Aug. 1938; *s* of Giles Rymer Thurnham and Marjorie May (*née* Preston); *m* 1963, Sarah Janet Stroude; one *s* three *d* and one adopted *s*. *Educ:* Oundle Sch.; Peterhouse, Cambridge (MA 1967); Cranfield Inst. of Technol. (Dip. in Advanced Engrg, 1967); SRC/NATO Scholarship, Harvard Business Sch., Harvard Univ. (MBA 1969). CEng 1967; FIMechE 1985. Design Engr, NEI Parsons Ltd, 1957–66; Divl Dir, British Steam Specialties Ltd, 1967–72. Mem., Select Cttee on Employment, 1983–. Treas., All-Party Parly Gp, Chemical Industry, 1985–. Conservative Back Bench 1922 Committees: Vice-Chairman: Smaller Business Cttee, 1985–; Home Improvement Sub-Cttee, 1986–; Sec., Employment Cttee, 1986–. Mem. Council, PSI, 1985–. Founder Mem., 1985 and Mem. Cttee, 1985–, Progress, Campaign for Res. into Reproduction. *Publications:* contrib. technical jls. *Recreation:* Lake District family life. *Address:* Sidegarth, Staveley, Kendal, Cumbria LA8 9NN. *T:* Staveley 821382; 4 North Court, Great Peter Street, SW1P 3LL. *T:* 01–799 5859.

THURSO, 2nd Viscount *cr* 1952, of Ulbster; **Robin Macdonald Sinclair;** Bt 1786; Baron of Thurso; JP; Lord-Lieutenant of Caithness, since 1973; Founder and first Chairman, Caithness Glass Ltd; Chairman: Sinclair Family Trust Ltd; Lochdhu Hotels Ltd; Thurso Fisheries Ltd; Ulbster Estates (Sporting) Ltd; Director, Stephens (Plastics) Ltd; *b* 24 Dec. 1922; *s* of 1st Viscount Thurso, KT, PC, CMG, and Marigold (*d* 1975), *d* of late Col J. S. Forbes, DSO; *S* father, 1970; *m* 1952, Margaret Beaumont Brokensha, *widow* of Lieut G. W. Brokensha, DSC, RN, and *d* of Col J. J. Robertson, DSO, DL, TD; two *s* one *d*. *Educ:* Eton; New College, Oxford; Edinburgh Univ. Served RAF, 1941–46; Flight Lieut 684 Sqdn, 540 Sqdn, commanded Edinburgh Univ. Air Sqdn, 1946; Captain of Boats, Edinburgh Univ. Boat Club, 1946–47, Green 1946, Blue, 1947. Caithness CC, 1949, 1952, 1955, 1958; Thurso Town Council, 1957, 1960, resigned 1961, re-elected 1965, 1968, 1971, Dean of Guild 1968, Baillie 1960, 1969, Police Judge 1971. President: North Country Cheviot Sheep Soc., 1951–54; Assoc. of Scottish Dist Salmon Fishery Bds; Mem., Red Deer Commn, 1965–74. Chm. Caithness and Sutherland Youth Employment Cttee, 1957–75; Brigade Pres., Boys Brigade, 1985–. Pres., Highland Soc. of London, 1980–82. DL 1952, JP 1959, Vice-Lieutenant, 1964–73, Caithness. *Recreations:* fishing, shooting, amateur drama. *Heir:* *s* Hon. John Archibald Sinclair [*b* 10 Sept. 1953; *m* 1976, Marion Ticknor, *d* of Louis D. Sage, Connecticut, USA, and of Mrs A. R. Ward; one *s* one *d*]. *Address:* Thurso East Mains, Thurso, Caithness, Scotland. *T:* Thurso 62600. *Clubs:* Royal Air Force; New (Edinburgh).

See also A. M. Lyle.

THURSTON, Thea; *see* King, T.

THWAITE, Anthony Simon, FRSL 1978; poet; co-editor of Encounter, 1973–85; *b* 23 June 1930; *s* of late Hartley Thwaite, JP, FSA, and of Alice Evelyn Mallinson; *m* 1955, Ann Barbara Harrop; four *d*. *Educ:* Kingswood Sch.; Christ Church, Oxford (MA). Vis. Lectr in English, Tokyo Univ., 1955–57; Producer, BBC, 1957–62; Literary Editor, The Listener, 1962–65; Asst Prof. of English, Univ. of Libya, 1965–67; Literary Editor, New Statesman, 1968–72; Henfield Writing Fellow, Univ. of East Anglia, 1972; Vis. Prof., Kuwait Univ., 1974; Japan Foundn Fellow, Tokyo Univ., 1985–86. Chm. of Judges, Booker Prize, 1986. Cholmondeley Poetry Award, 1983. *Publications: poetry:* Home Truths, 1957; The Owl in the Tree, 1963; The Stones of Emptiness, 1967 (Richard Hillary Memorial Prize, 1968); Inscriptions, 1973; New Confessions, 1974; A Portion for Foxes, 1977; Victorian Voices, 1980; Poems 1953–1983, 1984; Letter from Tokyo, 1987; *criticism:* Contemporary English Poetry, 1959; Poetry Today, 1973, rev. and expanded, 1985; Twentieth Century English Poetry, 1978; Six Centuries of Verse, 1984 (companion to Thames TV/Channel 4 series); *travel:* (with Roloff Beny) Japan, 1968; The Deserts of Hesperides, 1969; (with Roloff Beny and Peter Porter) In Italy, 1974; (with Roloff Beny) Odyssey: Mirror of the Mediterranean, 1981; *editor:* (with Geoffrey Bownas) Penguin Book of Japanese Verse, 1964; (with Peter Porter) The English Poets, 1974; (with Fleur Adcock) New Poetry 4, 1978; Larkin at Sixty, 1982; (with John Mole) Poetry 1945 to 1980, 1983; *for children:* Beyond the Inhabited World, 1976. *Recreations:* archaeology, travel. *Address:* The Mill House, Low Tharston, Norfolk NR15 2YN. *T:* Fundenhall 569.

THWAITES, Brian St George, CMG 1958; *b* 22 April 1912; *s* of late Henry Thwaites and Ada B. Thwaites (*née* Macnutt); *m* 1938, Madeleine Elizabeth Abell; one *s* two *d*. *Educ:* Canford School; Clare Coll., Cambridge. Entered Colonial Service (later HM Overseas Civil Service), 1935; served as Administrative Officer in Eastern Nigeria, 1935–47 and 1948–57; Palestine, 1947–48; retired, 1957. Planning Inspector, DoE, 1966–76. *Recreations:* golf, walking. *Address:* Painshill, Donhead St Andrew, Shaftesbury, Dorset SP7 9EA. *T:* Donhead 248.

THWAITES, Sir Bryan, Kt 1986; MA, PhD; FIMA; Principal, 1966–83, Hon. Fellow, since 1983, Westfield College; Chairman, Wessex Regional Health Authority, since 1982; *b* London, 6 December 1923; *e s* of late Ernest James and Dorothy Marguerite Thwaites; *m* 1948, Katharine Mary, 4th *c* of late H. R. Harries and late Mrs L. Harries, Longhope, Glos; four *s* two *d*. *Educ:* Dulwich College; Winchester College; Clare College, Cambridge. Scientific Officer, National Physical Laboratory, 1944–47; Lecturer, Imperial College, London, 1947–51; Assistant Master, Winchester College, 1951–59; Professor of Theoretical Mechanics, Southampton Univ., 1959–66, Hon. Prof., 1983–; Co-founder and Co-Chm., Education 2000, 1982–. Chm. of Collegiate Council, London Univ., 1973–76. Chm. and Mem. ARC Cttees, 1948–69. Special Lecturer, Imperial College, 1951–58. Director of the School Mathematics Project, 1961–75, Chm. of Trustees, 1967–84, Pres., 1984–; Chm. of Internat. Mathematical Olympiad, first in UK, 1979; Chm. of Adv. Council, ICL/CES, 1968–84. Member: United States Educational Commn, 1966–76; Ct of London Univ., 1975–81; Chm. of Delegacy, Goldsmiths' Coll., 1975–80; Mem. Acad. Advisory Committee: Univ. of Bath, 1963–72; Open Univ., 1969–75. Chairman of: Council of C of E Colleges of Education, 1969–71; Church of England Higher Educn Cttee, 1974–76; Northwick Park Hosp. Management Cttee, 1970–74; Brent and Harrow AHA, 1973–82; King's Fund Enquiry into Sen. Management Trng in NHS, 1975–76; Nat. Staff Cttee for Admin. and Clerical Staff, NHS, 1983–86; Heythrop Coll., 1978–82. Trustee: Westfield Coll. Develt Trust, 1979–83; Southampton Med. Sch. Trust, 1982–. Gresham Prof. in Geometry, City Univ., 1969–72; Mercier Lectr, Whitelands Coll., 1973. Shadow Vice-Chancellor, Independent Univ., July-Nov. 1971; Hon. Sec. and Treasurer, Dulwich College Mission, 1946–57; Member of Approved School Committee, Hampshire CC, 1954–58, 1961–66; JP, Winchester City Bench, 1963–66; Governor of various schools; a Vice-Pres., Friends of Girls' Public Day School Trust. Mem. Council, 1964–, Pres., 1966–67, Institute of Mathematics and its Applications. Sponsor of The Responsible Society, 1979–. Dir, Associated Microprocessor Systems, 1981–. *Publications:* (ed) Incompressible Aerodynamics, 1960; (ed) On Teaching Mathematics, 1961; The SMP: the first ten years, 1973; (ed) Hypotheses for Education in AD 2000, 1983; numerous contributions to Proc. Royal Soc., Reports and Memoranda of Aeronautical Research Council, Quart. Jl of Applied Mech., Jl of Royal Aeronautical Soc., etc. *Recreations:* music, sailing. *Address:* Milnthorpe, Winchester, Hants SO22 4NF. *T:* Winchester 52394. *Club:* Institute of Directors.

THWAITES, Jacqueline Ann, JP; Principal of Inchbald Schools of Design and Fine Arts since 1960; *b* 16 Dec. 1931; *d* of Mrs Donald Whitaker; *m* 1st, 1955, Michael Inchbald, *qv* (marr. diss. 1964); one *s* one *d*; 2nd, 1974, Brig. Peter Trevenen Thwaites, *qv*. *Educ:* Convent of the Sacred Heart, Brighton; House of Citizenship, London. Founded: Inchbald Sch. of Design, 1960; Inchbald Sch. of Fine Arts, 1970; Inchbald Sch. of Garden Design, 1972. Member: Monopolies Commn, 1972–75; Whitford Cttee on Copyright and Design, 1974–76; London Electricity Cons. Council, 1973–76; Westminster City Council (Warwick Ward), 1974–78. JP South Westminster, 1976. *Publications:* Directory of Interior Designers, 1966; Bedrooms, 1968; Design and Decoration, 1971. *Recreations:* fishing, travel. *Address:* 24 Clarendon Street, SW1; The Manor, Ayot St Lawrence, Herts; (office) 32 Eccleston Square, SW1.

THWAITES, Brig. Peter Trevenen; Chairman: Individual School Direction Ltd, since 1981; Hurlingham Polo Association, since 1982; *b* 30 July 1926; *yr* surv. *s* of late Lt-Col Norman Graham Thwaites, CBE, MVO, MC, and Eleanor Lucia Thwaites, Barley End, Tring, Herts; *m* 1st, 1950, Ellen Theresa King (marr. diss.; she *d* 1976); one *s* two *d* (and one *s* decd); 2nd, 1974, Jacqueline Ann Inchbald (*see* Jacqueline Ann Thwaites). *Educ:* Rugby. Commnd Grenadier Guards, 1944; served 1st, 2nd and 4th Bns in Germany, Egypt, British Cameroons, British Guiana; Mem., Sir William Penney's Scientific Party to UK Atomic Trials in S Australia, 1956; Bde Mayor, 2 Fed. Inf. Bde, Malaya; Staff Coll., Malaya, JSSC, MoD, 1958–67; Aden, 1967; comd Muscat Regt, Sultan of Muscat's Armed Forces, 1967–70; AQMG London Dist, 1970–71; Comdr, British Army Staff, Singapore (Col), and Governor, Singapore Internat. Sch., 1971–73; Dep. Dir, Defence Operational Plans (Army), 1973–74; Brig. 1975; Head of MoD Logistics Survey Team to Saudi Arabia, 1976, retired 1977. Chm., Jt Staff, Sultan of Oman's Armed Forces, 1977–81. Sultan's Commendation, 1967; Sultan's Dist. Service Medal, 1969; Sultan's Bravery Medal, 1970. *Publications: plays:* (with Charles Ross) Love or Money, 1958; (with Charles Ross) Master of None, 1960; Roger's Last Stand, 1976; Caught in the Act, 1981; (with Charles Ross) Relative Strangers, 1984. *Recreations:* polo, shooting. *Address:* 24 Clarendon Street, SW1; The Manor House, Ayot St Lawrence, Herts. *Clubs:* White's, Beefsteak, Cavalry and Guards.

THWAITES, Roy; Leader of South Yorkshire County Council, 1979–86; *b* 13 Aug. 1931; *s* of Walter and Emily Alice Thwaites; *m* 1954, Margaret Anne (*née* Noble); one *s*. *Educ:* Southey Green Secondary Sch.; Sheffield Central Technical Sch. City Councillor, Sheffield, 1965, Chief Whip and Chm. of Transport Cttee, 1969–74; South Yorkshire County Council: Councillor, 1973–86; Chief Whip and Chm. Passenger Transport Authority, 1973–78; Dep. Leader, 1978–79; Leader, and Chm. of Policy Cttee, 1979–86. Mem., E Midlands Airport Consultative Gp, 1982–86. Chm., Yorks and Humberside County Councils Assoc., 1983–86; Vice-Chm., Assoc. of Metropolitan Authorities, 1984–86 (Dep. Chm., 1979–84); Mem., Local Authorities' Conditions of Service Adv. Bd, 1979–86; Vice-Chm., NJC Local Govt Manual Workers Employers, 1982. Mem., Special Employment Measures Adv. Gp, MSC, 1983–86. *Recreation:* reading. *Address:* 14 Foxhill Drive, Sheffield S6 1GD. *T:* Sheffield 311222.

THYATEIRA AND GREAT BRITAIN, Archbishop of; *see* Fouyas, Archbishop Methodios.

THYNE, Malcolm Tod, MA; Headmaster of St Bees School, since 1980; *b* 6 Nov. 1942; *s* of late Andrew Tod and Margaret Melrose Thyne; *m* 1969, Eleanor Christine Scott; two *s*. *Educ:* The Leys Sch., Cambridge; Clare Coll., Cambridge (MA Nat. Scis with Pt II in Chem.; Cert. of Educn). Asst Master, Edinburgh Acad., 1965–69; Asst Master, Oundle Sch., 1969–72, Housemaster, 1972–80. *Publications:* Periodicity, Atomic Structure and Bonding (Revised Nuffield Chemistry), 1976; (chapters in) Revised Nuffield Chemistry Handbook for Pupils, 1978; (contrib.) Revised Nuffield Chemistry Teachers' Guides, Vols II and III, 1978. *Recreation:* mountaineering. *Address:* The School House, St Bees, Cumbria CA27 0DU. *T:* Egremont 822263.

THYNN, Alexander; *see* Weymouth, Viscount.

THYNNE, family name of **Marquess of Bath.**

THYNNE, John Corelli James, PhD, DSc; Under Secretary, Electronics Applications Division, Department of Trade and Industry, since 1986; *b* 27 Nov. 1931; *s* of Corelli James Thynne and Isabel Ann (*née* Griffiths). *Educ:* Milford Haven Grammar Sch.; Nottingham Univ. (BSc, PhD); Edinburgh Univ. (DSc). Res. Chemist, English Electric Co. (Guided Missile Div.), 1956–58; Fellow: Nat. Res. Council, Ottawa, 1958–59; UCLA, 1959–60; Univ. of Leeds, 1960–63; Lectr in Chemistry and Dir of Studies, Univ. of Edinburgh, 1963–70; Principal, DTI, 1970–73; Counsellor (Scientific), British Embassy, Moscow, 1974–78; Asst Sec., Inf. Technol. Div., DoI, 1978–83; Regl Dir, NW Reg., DTI, 1983–86. Mem. Council, Salford Univ., 1984–. *Publications:* contribs on physical chemistry to scientific journals. *Recreation:* cricket. *Address:* 5 Eldon Grove, NW3. *T:* 01–794 1356. *Clubs:* Athenæum, MCC.

TIARKS, Rt. Rev. Geoffrey Lewis, MA Cantab; *b* 8 Oct 1909; *s* of Lewis Herman Tiarks, Clerk in Holy Orders, and Edith Margaret Tiarks; *m* 1934, Betty Lyne, *d* of Henry Stock; one *s* (one *d* decd). *Educ:* Marlborough; S John's College, Cambridge. Ordained at Southwark, 1932; Curate of St Saviour's with St Peter, Southwark, 1932–33; Chaplain, RN, 1934–47; Chaplain, Diocesan College, Rondebosch, CP, 1948–50; Rector of S Paul's, Rondebosch, 1950–54; Vicar of Lyme Regis, Dorset, 1954–61; Archdeacon of the Isle of Wight, 1961–65; Archdeacon of Portsmouth, 1965–69; Bishop Suffragan of Maidstone, 1969–76; Senior Chaplain to Archbishop of Canterbury, 1969–74. *Address:* Primrose Cottage, Netherbury, Bridport, Dorset. *T:* Netherbury 277.

TIARKS, Henry Frederic, FRAS; *b* 8 Sept. 1900; *e s* of late Frank Cyril Tiarks, OBE; *m* 1st, 1930, Lady Millicent Olivia Taylour (marr. diss. 1936), *d* of 4th Marquess of Headfort; (one *s* decd); 2nd, 1936, Joan, *d* of Francis Marshman-Bell; one *d* (one *s* decd). *Educ:* Eton College. Served European War 1914–19. Midshipman RNVR 1918; Sqdn Ldr AAF, 1940; Wing Commander, 1942–43, Retd (invalided). Former directorships: J. Henry Schroder & Co., Partner 1926–57, J. Henry Schroder & Co. Ltd, 1957–62, J. Henry Schroder Wagg & Co. Ltd, 1962 (May to Sept.), Schroders Ltd, 1962–65; J. Henry Schroder Banking Corpn, NY, 1945–62; Antofagasta (Chili) and Bolivia Railway Co. Ltd, 1926–67 (Chairman 1966–67); Securicor Ltd (founder) 1939–68; Pressed Steel Co. Ltd, 1936–66; Joseph Lucas Ltd, 1946–68; Bank of London & South America Ltd, 1958–68; Bank of London & Montreal Ltd, Nassau, 1959–69; Anglo-Scottish Amalgamated Corpn Ltd, 1935–68. Member: Dollar Exports Council, 1952–60; Western Hemisphere Exports Council, 1960–64; European League for Economic Co-operation (European Central Council); Internat. EFTA Action Cttee, 1967–75; Vice-Pres., European-Atlantic Gp. Mem., The Wildfowl Trust; Trustee, World Wildlife Fund (International), Morges, Switzerland, 1966–76. Mem. Cttee of Managers, Royal Institution, 1960–62. Gran Oficial, Order of Merit, Chile. *Recreations:* golf, observational astronomy, photography, travel. *Address:* Casa Ina, Marbella Club, Marbella (Málaga), Spain. *Clubs:* Overseas Member: White's, Royal Thames Yacht; Royal and Ancient Golf (St Andrews), Swinley Forest Golf (Ascot), Royal St George's Golf (Sandwich), Berkshire Golf (Bagshot); Valderrama Golf (Cadiz); The Brook (New York), Lyford Cay (Nassau, Bahamas); Royal Bermuda Yacht.

See also Marquess of Tavistock.

TIBBER, Anthony Harris; His Honour Judge Tibber; a Circuit Judge, since 1977; *b* 23 June 1926; *s* of Maurice and Priscilla Tibber; *m* 1954, Rhona Ann Salter; three *s*. *Educ:* University College School, London; Magdelen College School, Brackley. Served in Royal Signals, 1945–48; called to the Bar, Gray's Inn, 1950; a Recorder of the Crown Court, 1976. Member: Matrimonial Causes Rule Cttee, 1980–84; Matrimonial Causes Procedure Cttee (Booth Cttee), 1983–85. *Recreations:* cultivating, idling, pottering. *Address:* c/o Edmonton County Court, 59 Fore Street, N18 2TM. *T:* (home) 01–348 3605.

TIBBITS, Captain Sir David (Stanley), Kt 1976; DSC 1942; FNI; RN retired; Deputy Master and Chairman of Board, Trinity House, 1972–76; *b* 11 April 1911; *s* of late Hubert Tibbits, MB, BCh, Warwick, and Edith Lucy (*née* Harman) Tibbits; *m* 1938, Mary Florence Butterfield, Hamilton, Bermuda; two *d*. *Educ:* Wells House, Malvern Wells; RNC, Dartmouth. RN Cadet 1925; navigation specialist, 1934; served War, 1939–45, HMS York, Devonshire and Anson; Comdr 1946; Captain 1953; Dir, Radio Equipment Dept, Admty, 1953–56; in comd, HM Ships Manxman, Dryad and Hermes, 1956–61; retd. Trinity House: Elder Brother, 1961; Warden, 1969. Hon. Sec., King George's Fund for Sailors, 1974–80; Lay Vice-Pres., Missions to Seamen, 1972–. Engaged in various voluntary activities in Bermuda including: Mem., Marine Board and Port Authy, 1978–; Chm., Pilotage Commn, 1978–; Pres., Sea Cadet and Sail Trng Assoc., 1978–; Chm. and Jt Pres., Bermuda Soc. for Blind, 1982– (Mem. Cttee, 1977–). Mem. Court, Worshipful Co. of Shipwrights, 1976–. Trustee, National Maritime Museum, 1974–77. Governor, Pangbourne Coll., 1973–78. Founder Mem., 1972, Fellow 1979–, Nautical Inst. *Recreations:* sailing, colour photography, classical music. *Address:* Harting Hill, PO Box HM 1419, Hamilton, Bermuda HM FX; c/o Trinity House, Tower Hill, EC3N 4DH. *Clubs:* Army and Navy, Hurlingham; Royal Yacht Squadron (Naval Mem.); Royal Bermuda Yacht (Bermuda).

TIBBS, Craigie John; Head of Estates and Planning Department, BBC, since 1980; *b* 17 Feb. 1935; *s* of Arthur and Gladys Tibbs; *m* 1959, Carol Ann (*née* Linsell); two *d* *Educ:* King George V School, Southport; Heaton Grammar School, Newcastle upon Tyne; RMA Sandhurst; London University. BSc; FRICS. Trainee Estates Officer, London Transport, 1959–62; Valuer and Senior Valuer, Luton Corp., 1962–67; Chief Valuer and Surveyor, London Borough of Newham, 1967–71; Development Officer, City of Birmingham, 1971–73; County Estates Officer, Hants County Council, 1973–76; Under Sec. (Dir of Land Economy), Depts of Environment and Transport, 1976–80. *Recreations:* music, reading, writing, walking, swimming, golf, the Well Game. *Address:* Estates and Planning Department, BBC, Portland Place, W1A 1AA.

TIBBS, (Geoffrey) Michael (Graydon); Secretary of the Royal College of Physicians, 1968–86 (Secretary of Joint Faculty of Community Medicine, 1971–72 and of Faculty of Occupational Medicine, 1978–86); *b* 21 Nov. 1921; *s* of Rev. Geoffrey Wilberforce Tibbs, sometime Chaplain RN and Vicar of Lynchmere, Sussex, and Margaret Florence Tibbs (*née* Skinner); *m* 1951, Anne Rosemary Wortley; two *s*. *Educ:* Berkhamsted Sch.; St Peter's Hall, Oxford. BA Hons Geography, 1948; MA 1952. FInstAM; MIPM; FRGS. Served RNVR, Ordinary Seaman/Lieut, 1940–46 (despatches), HMS Cottesmore, HMS Sheffield, HM S/M Tantalus, HM S/M Varne. Sudan Political Service, 1949–55, retired on independence as Dist Comr, Dar Messeria District. Various appointments in personnel, organisation and overseas services depts, Automobile Assoc., 1955–68. Hon. Mem., Soc. of Occupational Medicine, 1983; Hon. FRCP 1986. Freeman, City of London, 1986. *Recreations:* producing pantomimes, parish affairs, making bonfires. *Address:* Welkin, Lynchmere Ridge, Haslemere, Surrey GU27 3PP. *T:* Haslemere 3120, 2176. *Club:* Naval.

TICKELL, Sir Crispin (Charles Cervantes), KCVO 1983 (MVO 1958); HM Diplomatic Service; Permanent Secretary, Overseas Development Administration, Foreign and Commonwealth Office, since 1984; *b* 25 Aug. 1930; *s* of late Jerrard Tickell and Renée (*née* Haynes); *m* 1st, 1954, Chloë (marr. diss. 1976), *d* of late Sir James Gunn, RA, PRP; two *s* one *d*; 2nd, 1977, Penelope, *d* of late Dr Vernon Thorne Thorne. *Educ:* Westminster (King's Schol.); Christ Church, Oxford (Hinchliffe and Hon. Schol.). 1st Cl. Hons Mod. Hist. 1952. Served with Coldstream Guards, 1952–54; entered HM Diplomatic Service, 1954. Served at: Foreign Office, 1954–55; The Hague, 1955–58; Mexico, 1958–61; FO (Planning Staff), 1961–64; Paris, 1964–70; Private Sec. to successive Chancellors of the Duchy of Lancaster responsible for negotiations for British entry into the European Communities, 1970–72; Head of Western Organisations Dept, FCO, 1972–75; Fellow, Center for Internat. Affairs, Harvard Univ., 1975–76; Chef de Cabinet to Rt Hon. Roy Jenkins, Pres. of Commn of European Communities, 1977–81; Vis. Fellow, All Souls Coll., Oxford, 1981; Ambassador to Mexico, 1981–83; Dep. Under-Sec. of State, FCO, 1983–84. FRGS; FZS. Mem. (Dr *hc*), Mexican Acad. of Internat. Law, 1983. Officer, Order of Orange Nassau (Holland), 1958. *Publications:* (contrib.) The Evacuees, 1968; (contrib.) Life After Death, 1976; Climatic Change and World Affairs, 1977, 1986. *Recreations:* climatology; palæohistory; art, especially pre-Columbiana; mountains. *Address:* c/o Foreign and Commonwealth Office, SW1. *Club:* Brooks's.

TICKELL, Maj.-Gen. Marston Eustace, CBE 1973 (MBE 1955); MC 1945; CEng, FICE; Commandant Royal Military College of Science, 1975–78, retired; *b* 18 Nov. 1923; *er s* of late Maj.-Gen. Sir Eustace Tickell, KBE, CB, MC; *m* 1961, Pamela Vere, *d* of Vice-Adm. A. D. Read, CB; no *c. Educ:* Wellington Coll.; Peterhouse, Cambridge (MA). Commnd in RE, 1944; NW Europe Campaign and Middle East, 1944–45; psc 1954; Mil. Ops, MoD, 1955–57; served in Libya, Cyprus and Jordan, 1958–59; US Armed Forces Staff Coll. and Instructor RMCS and Staff Coll., 1959–62; Defence Planning Staff, MoD, 1962–64; CRE 4th Div., 1964–66; comd 12 Engr Bde, 1967–69; Indian Nat. Defence Coll., 1970; COS Northern Ireland, 1971–72; E-in-C, MoD, 1972–75. Col Comdt, RE, 1978–83. Hon. Col, Engr and Transport Staff Corps, 1983–. Pres., Instn of Royal Engrs, 1979–82. FICE 1974. *Recreation:* sailing. *Address:* The Old Vicarage, Branscombe, Seaton, Devon EX12 3DW. *Clubs:* Army and Navy; Royal Ocean Racing.

TICKLE, Brian Percival, CB 1985; Senior Registrar of the Family Division, High Court of Justice, since 1982 (Registrar, since 1970); *b* 31 Oct. 1921; *m* 1945, Margaret Alice Pendrey; one *s* one *d. Educ:* The Judd Sch., Tonbridge. Entered Civil Service, 1938. Served War, Royal Signals, 1939–45. Civil Service, 1946–70. Mem., Matrimonial Causes Rules Cttee, 1982–. *Publications:* Rees Divorce Handbook, 1963; Atkins Court Forms and Precedents (Probate), 1974, 2nd edn 1984. *Recreation:* golf. *Address:* Principal Registry, Family Division, High Court of Justice, Somerset House, Strand, WC2R 1LP. *Club:* Royal Automobile.

TICKLE, Rt. Rev. Gerard William; Titular Bishop of Bela; *b* 2 Nov. 1909; 2nd *s* of William Joseph Tickle and Rosanna Kelly. *Educ:* Douai School; Venerable English College, Rome. Priest, 1934. Curate at St Joseph's Church, Sale, 1935–41; Army Chaplain, 1941–46; Vice-Rector, 1946, Rector, 1952, Venerable English College, Rome. Bishop-in-Ordinary to HM Forces, 1963–78; Apostolic Administrator, 1978–79. Privy Chamberlain to Pope Pius XII, 1949; Domestic Prelate to Pope Pius XII, 1953. *Address:* Ty Mair, 115 Mwrog Street, Ruthin, Clwyd LL15 1LE.

TIDBURY, Charles Henderson; Chairman, William and Mary Tercentenary Trust Ltd, since 1986; *b* 26 Jan. 1926; *s* of late Brig. O. H. Tidbury, MC, and Beryl (*née* Pearce); *m* Anne, *d* of late Brig. H. E. Russell, DSO, and of Lady O'Connor; two *s* three *d. Educ:* Eton Coll. Served KRRC, 1943–52: Palestine, 1946–48 (despatches); Queen's Westminsters TA, 1952–60. Joined Whitbread & Co. Ltd, 1952; a Man. Dir, 1959; Chief Exec., 1974; Dep. Chm., 1977; Chm., 1978–84. Chm., Brickwoods Brewery Ltd, 1966–71. Director: Whitbread & Co. PLC; Whitbread Investment Co. PLC; Barclays PLC; Barclays Bank PLC; Barclays Bank UK Ltd; Mercantile Credit Co. Ltd, 1985–; Nabisco Gp Ltd, 1985–; Vaux Gp plc, 1985–; ICL (UK), 1985–; Pearl Assurance PLC, 1986–. Pres., Inst. of Brewing, 1976–78; Chm., 1982–84, Vice-Pres., 1984–, Brewers' Soc.; President: Shire Horse Soc., 1985; British Inst. of Innkeeping, 1985–. Chairman: Mary Rose Development Trust, 1980–86; Brewing Res. Foundn, 1985–. Trustee, Nat. Maritime Museum, 1984–. Middle Warden, Brewers' Co., 1985–. *Recreations:* my family, sailing, shooting, countryside. *Address:* Crocker Hill Farm, Forest Lane, Wickham, Hants PO17 5DW; 22 Ursula Street, SW11 3DW; (office) 20 Queen Anne's Gate, SW1H 9AA. *T:* 01–222 7060. *Clubs:* Brooks's; Royal Yacht Squadron, Island Sailing, Bembridge Sailing.

TIDY, Morley David; Assistant Under Secretary (Ordnance), Ministry of Defence, since 1985; *b* 23 April 1933; *s* of James Morley and Winnie Tidy; *m* 1957, Wendy Ann Bennett; one *s* two *d. Educ:* Hove County Grammar School; Magdalene College, Cambridge (MA). National Service, RAF, 1951–53. Dept of Employment, 1956–57; HM Inspector of Taxes, Inland Revenue, 1957–66; MoD, 1966; Manchester Business School, 1967; First Sec. (Defence), UK Delegn to NATO, 1969–72; MoD, 1973; RCDS, 1977; Chief Officer, SBAA, Cyprus, 1980–83; Asst Under-Sec., Air Staff, MoD, 1984. *Recreations:* tennis, cricket, golf.

TIERNEY, Dom Francis Alphonsus, OSB; MA; Parish Priest since 1977; *b* 7 March 1910; *s* of James Francis Tierney and Alice Mary Claypoole. *Educ:* Douai; St Benet's Hall, Oxford. Headmaster of: Douai Junior School, Ditcham Park, 1948–52; Douai Sch., 1952–73. Prior of Douai Abbey, 1973–77. *Address:* Douai Abbey, Woolhampton, Berkshire. *T:* Woolhampton 3163.

TIERNEY, Sydney; JP; President, 1977–81, and since 1983, and National Officer, since 1979, Union of Shop, Distributive and Allied Workers; Member, Labour Party National Executive Committee; Vice-Chairman, Labour Party, 1985–86; *b* Sept. 1923. *Educ:* Secondary Modern Sch., Dearne; Plater Coll., Oxford. Mem., Co-operative Party; an Official and Member, USDAW. Vice-Chm., W Midlands Labour Gp of MPs, 1974–79. MP (Lab) Birmingham, Yardley, Feb. 1974–1979; PPS to Min. of State for Agriculture, 1976–79. JP Leicester, 1966. *Address:* 14 Low Meadow, Whaley Bridge, Stockport, Cheshire SK12 7AY.

TIGHE, Maj.-Gen. Patrick Anthony Macartan, CB 1977; MBE 1958; FBIM; *b* 26 Feb. 1923; *s* of late Macartan H. Tighe, BA, RUI, Barrister-at-Law, Dublin and Dorothy Isabel (*née* Vine); *m* 1st, 1950, Elizabeth Frazer Stewart (*d* 1971); two *s*; 2nd, 1972, Princine Merendino Calitri, authoress, W Virginia, USA. *Educ:* Christ's Hospital. Served RAF, 1940–41; commnd Royal Signals, 1943; served NW Europe, 1944–45, Palestine, 1945–47; psc 1955; DAAQMG Gurkha Bde Malaya, 1956 (MBE); Mil. Asst Comd British Forces Hong Kong, 1963; Force Signals Officer Borneo, 1964–66 (despatches); Asst Mil. Sec., 1966; Col Asst Adjt Gen., 1968; Brig. Comd Trng Bde Royal Signals, 1970; Inspector of Intell. Corps, 1973; Signal Officer-in-Chief (Army), 1974–77. Col Comdt, Royal Signals, 1977–84. With Hongkong Land Gp, 1977–84. Gen. Cttee, Ex-Services Mental Welfare Soc. *Publications:* radio plays (BBC), film and book reviews for press and radio in Far East. *Recreations:* cinema (Mem. British Film Inst. 1947), golf. *Address:* c/o Lloyds Bank, 6 Pall Mall, SW1Y 5NH. *Clubs:* Army and Navy; Worthing Golf.

TIKARAM, Sir Moti, KBE 1980; **Hon. Justice Sir Moti Tikaram;** Ombudsman, Fiji, since 1972; *b* 18 March 1925; *s* of Tikaram and Singari; *m* 1944, Satyawati (*d* 1981); two *s* one *d. Educ:* Marist Brothers High Sch., Suva; Victoria Univ., Wellington, NZ (LLB 1954). Started law practice, 1954; Stipendiary Magistrate, 1960; Puisne Judge, 1968; acted as Chief Justice, 1971. Patron, Fiji Lawn Tennis Assoc. Scouting Medal of Merit, 1986. *Publications:* articles in The Pacific Way and in Recent Law 131. *Recreation:* tennis. *Address:* (home) PO Box 514, 45 Domain Road, Suva, Fiji. *T:* 22135; (office) PO Box 982, Suva. *T:* 211652. *Clubs:* Fiji, Fiji Golf (Suva).

TILEY, Arthur, CBE 1972; JP; retired as Insurance Broker and Marine Underwriter; *b* 17 January 1910; *m* 1936, Mary, *d* of late Craven and Mary Tankard, Great Horton; one *s* one *d. Educ:* Grange High School, Bradford. Treasurer, Young Women's Christian Association, Bradford, 1934–50. Contested (C and Nat. L) Bradford Central, 1951. MP (C and Nat. L) Bradford West, 1955–66. Served War of 1939–45 as Senior Company Officer, National Fire Service. Mem. Council, Churchill Memorial Trust, 1965–76. Hon. MA Bradford, 1981. JP Bradford, 1967. *Address:* 40 The Majestic, North Promenade, St Annes-on-Sea, Lancs FY8 2LZ.

TILL, Barry Dorn; Principal of Morley College, London, 1965–86; Adviser, Baring Foundation, since 1973; *b* 1 June 1923; *s* of John Johnson and Hilda Lucy Till; *m* 1st, 1954, Shirley Philipson (marr. diss. 1965); two *s*; 2nd, 1966, Antonia, *d* of Sir Michael Clapham, *qv*; two *d. Educ:* Harrow; Jesus College and Westcott House, Cambridge. 1st Class Theology Pt III, 1949; Lightfoot Scholar, 1949. Served War, Coldstream Guards, 1942–46; Italian campaign. Deacon, 1950; Priest, 1951; Asst Curate, Bury Parish Church, Lancs, 1950–53; Fellow of Jesus Coll., Cambridge, 1953–60, Chaplain, 1953–56, Dean, 1956–60, Tutor, 1957–60; Univ. Preacher, Cambridge, 1955; Examining Chaplain to Bishop of Lichfield, 1957–60; Dean of Hong Kong, 1960–64. Chm., Asia Christian Colleges Assoc., 1968–76, Vice-Pres., 1976–. Governor, British Inst. of Recorded Sound, 1967–72; Mem. Board, Youth and Music, 1965–; Mem., Adv. Council, V&A Museum, 1977–83. Chm., Greater London AACE, 1976–82. Governor, St Olaf's Grammar Sch., 1973–82 (Chm., 1980–82); Mem., Cultural Cttee, European Culture Foundn, 1976–78. Trustee, Thomas Cubitt Trust, 1978–. *Publications:* contrib. to The Historic Episcopate, 1954; Change and Exchange, 1964; Changing Frontiers in the Mission of the Church, 1965; contrib. to A Holy Week Manual, 1967; The Churches Search for Unity, 1972. *Recreations:* travel, gardening, opera. *Address:* 44 Canonbury Square, N1 2AW. *T:* 01–359 0708.

TILL, Ven. Michael Stanley; Archdeacon of Canterbury, since 1986; *b* 19 Nov. 1935; *s* of Stanley Brierley Till and Mary Till; *m* 1965, Tessa, *d* of Capt. Stephen Roskill; one *s* one *d. Educ:* Brighton, Hove and Sussex Grammar School; Lincoln Coll., Oxford (BA, History 1960, Theology 1962; MA 1967); Westcott House, Cambridge. Curate, St John's, St John's Wood, NW8, 1964–67; Chaplain 1967–70, Dean and Fellow 1970–81, King's College, Cambridge; Vicar of All Saints', Fulham, 1981–86; Area Dean, Hammersmith and Fulham, 1984–86. *Address:* 29 The Precincts, Canterbury, Kent CT1 2EP. *T:* Canterbury 463036.

TILLARD, Maj.-Gen. Philip Blencowe, CBE 1973; (OBE 1966); with Borough of Brighton, 1977–Jan. 1988; *b* 2 Jan. 1923; *s* of late Brig. John Arthur Stuart Tillard, OBE, MC and of Margaret Penelope (*née* Blencowe); *m* 1953, Patricia Susan (*née* Robertson); three *s* one *d. Educ:* Winchester College. Commnd into 60th Rifles, 1942; served Syria, Italy and Greece, 1943–46; transf. to 13th/18th Royal Hussars (QMO), 1947; served in Libya, Malaya (despatches, 1950) and Germany, comd Regt, 1964–66; psc 1956; jssc 1962; Comdr RAC 3rd Div., 1967–69; BGS (Army Trng), MoD, 1970–73; ADC to the Queen, 1970–73; COS, BAOR, 1973–76. *Recreations:* normal family pursuits; shooting. *Address:* Church House, Chailey Green, Lewes, East Sussex BN8 4DA. *T:* Newick 2759. *Clubs:* Farmers'; Sussex.

TILLER, Rev. Canon John; Chancellor and Canon Residentiary of Hereford Cathedral, since 1984; *b* 22 June 1938; *s* of Harry Maurice Tiller and Lucille Maisie Tiller; *m* 1961, Ruth Alison (*née* Watson); two *s* one *d. Educ:* St Albans Sch.; Christ Church, Oxford (MA, 2nd Cl. Mod. Hist.); Bristol Univ. (MLitt). Ordained deacon 1962, priest 1963, St Albans. Asst Curate: St Cuthbert, Bedford, 1962–65; Widcombe, Bath, 1965–67; Chaplain and Tutor, Tyndale Hall, Bristol, 1967–71; Lectr in Church History and Worship, Trinity Coll., Bristol, 1971–73; Priest-in-Charge, Christ Church, Bedford, 1973–78; Chief Sec., ACCM, 1978–84. Hon. Canon of St Albans Cathedral, 1979–84. *Publications:* The Service of Holy Communion and its Revision (with R. T. Beckwith), 1972; A Modern Liturgical Bibliography, 1974; The Great Acquittal, 1980; Puritan, Pietist, Pentecostalist, 1982; A Strategy for the Church's Ministry, 1983; (contrib.) Anglican Worship Today, 1980; The Gospel Community, 1987. *Recreations:* walking, bird-watching, spuddling. *Address:* Canon's House, 3 St John Street, Hereford HR1 2NB. *T:* Hereford 265659.

TILLEY, John Vincent; Chief Economic Advisor, London Borough of Hackney; *b* June 1941; *m* Kathryn Riley; one *c*. Mem., Wandsworth Borough Council, 1971–78. Mem., Co-operative Party. MP (Lab) Lambeth Central, Apr. 1978–83. Contested (Lab): Kensington Div. of Kensington and Chelsea, Feb. and Oct. 1974; Southwark and Bermondsey, 1983.

TILLING, George Henry Garfield; Chairman, Scottish Postal Board, 1977–84, retired; *b* 24 Jan. 1924; *s* of late Thomas and Anne Tilling; *m* 1956, Margaret Meriel, *d* of late Rear-Adm. Sir Alexander McGlashan, KBE, CB, DSO; two *s* two *d. Educ:* Hardye's Sch., Dorchester; University Coll., Oxford (Open Exhibnr, Kitchener Schol., Farquharson Prizeman, MA). Served War of 1939–45, NW Europe: Captain, Dorset Regt, 1943–46. Post Office: Asst Principal, 1948; Principal, 1953; Private Sec. to Postmaster General, 1964; Dep. Dir of Finance, 1965; Dir, Eastern Postal Region, 1967; Sec. of the Post Office, 1973–75; Dir of Postal Ops, 1975–77. Mem. Council, Lord Kitchener Nat. Meml Fund, 1979–. Mem. Council, Order of St John for London, 1975–77, Mem. Cttee of the Order for Edinburgh, 1978–. Hon. Mem., St Andrew's Ambulance Assoc., 1980. CStJ. FSAScot; FCIT. *Recreations:* orders and medals, heraldry, uniforms. *Address:* Standpretty, Gorebridge, Midlothian EH23 4QG. *T:* Gorebridge 22409. *Club:* Royal Over-Seas League.

TILLINGHAST, Charles Carpenter, Jr; aviation and financial consultant; *b* 30 Jan. 1911; *s* of Charles Carpenter Tillinghast and Adelaide Barrows Shaw; *m* 1935, Elizabeth (Lisette) Judd Micoleau; one *s* three *d. Educ:* Horace Mann Sch.; Brown Univ. (PhB); Columbia Univ. (JD). Associate, Hughes, Schurman & Dwight, 1935–37; Dep. Asst Dist

Attorney, NY County, 1938–40; Associate, Hughes, Richards, Hubbard & Ewing, 1940–42; Partner, Hughes, Hubbard and Ewing (and successor firm, Hughes, Hubbard, Blair & Reed), 1942–57; Vice-Pres. and Dir, The Bendix Corp., 1957–61; Pres. and Chief Exec. Officer, Trans World Airlines Inc., 1961–69 (Director, 1961–81; Chm. and Chief Exec. Officer, 1969–76); Vice-Chm., White, Weld & Co. Inc., 1977–78; Man. Dir, Merrill Lynch White Weld Capital Markets Gp, 1978–83; Vice-Pres., Merrill Lynch Pierce Fenner & Smith Inc., 1978–84; Director: Amstar Corp., 1964–83; Merck & Co., 1962–83; Trustee: Mutual Life Ins. Co. of NY, 1966–84; Brown Univ., 1954–61, 1965–79 (Chancellor, 1968–79; Fellow, 1979–); Mem. IATA Executive Cttee, 1969–76. Hon. Degrees: LHD, South Dakota Sch. of Mines and Tech., 1959; LLD: Franklin Coll., 1963, Univ. of Redlands, 1964; Brown Univ., 1967; Drury Coll., 1967; William Jewell Coll., 1973. *Recreations:* golf, shooting, gardening, woodworking, reading, Philharmonic and opera. *Address:* 25 John Street, Providence, RI 02906, USA. *T:* 401–861–6676. *Clubs:* Agawam Hunt, Blind Brook, Brown Univ. (New York); Economic (NY); Hope (RI); Sky; Sakonnet Golf (all in USA).

TILLOTSON, Maj.-Gen. Henry Michael, CB 1983; CBE 1976 (OBE 1970, MBE 1956); *b* 12 May 1928; *er s* of Henry Tillotson, Keighley, Yorks; *m* 1956, Angela, *d* of Bertram Wadsworth Shaw, E Yorks; two *s* one *d. Educ:* Chesterfield Sch.; RMA Sandhurst. Commnd E Yorks Regt, 1948; served: Austria, 1948–50; Germany, 1951–52; Indo-China (attached French Union Forces), 1953; Malaya, 1953–55; Staff Coll., Camberley, 1958; JSSC, Latimer, 1963–64; Malaysia, 1964–65; S Arabia, 1965–67 (Queen's Commendation); CO 1st Bn Prince of Wales's Own Regt of Yorks, Cyprus, 1969–71; Col GS, Hong Kong, 1974–76; Chief of Staff UN Force, Cyprus, and Comdr British Contingent, 1976–78; Dep. Dir, Army Staff Duties, MoD, 1978–79; Chief of Staff to C-in-C UKLF, 1980–83. Regl Dir, SE Asia, Internat. Mil. Services Ltd, 1983–86. Col, Prince of Wales's Own Regt of Yorks, 1979–86. *Recreations:* travel, birds, listening to music. *Address:* c/o Lloyds Bank, 6 Pall Mall, SW1Y 5NH. *Club:* Army and Navy.

TILLOTSON, Prof. Kathleen Mary, OBE 1983; MA, BLitt; FRSL 1984; FBA 1965; Hildred Carlile Professor of English in the University of London, at Bedford College, 1958–71, now Emeritus; *b* 3 April 1906; *e d* of late Eric A. Constable, BLitt (Durham), journalist, and Catherine H. Constable, Berwick-on-Tweed and Birmingham; *m* 1933, Geoffrey Tillotson, FBA (*d* 1969); two adopted *s. Educ:* Ackworth School; Mount School, York; Somerville College, Oxford (Exhibitioner and Shaw Lefevre Scholar). Charles Oldham Shakespeare Scholarship, 1926; BA 1927; temporary tutor, Somerville College, 1928–29; BLitt 1929; teaching at Somerville and St Hilda's Colleges, 1929–39; part-time Assistant, later Junior Lecturer, 1929, Lecturer, 1939, Fellow, 1971, Bedford College; Reader in the University of London at Bedford College, 1947–58. Vice-Pres., Dickens Fellowship; Brontë Soc.; Trustee: Dove Cottage; Bosanquet Trust. Warton Lecture, British Academy, 1956; Annual Brontë Lecture, 1966, 1986; Dickens Meml Lecture, 1970; Annual Tennyson Lecture, 1974; Robert Spence Watson Lecture, 1978. James Bryce Memorial Lecturer, Somerville College, Oxford, 1963, Hon. Fellow, 1965. Hon. DLit Belfast, 1972; Hon. DLitt: Oxon, 1982; London, 1982. Rose Mary Crawshay prize, British Academy, 1943. *Publications:* (with J. W. Hebel and B. H. Newdigate) Works of Michael Drayton, vol. V, 1941; Novels of the Eighteen-Forties, 1954; Matthew Arnold and Carlyle (Warton Lecture), 1957; (with John Butt) Dickens at Work, 1957; Introductions to Trollope's Barsetshire novels, 1958–75; The Tale and the Teller (inaug. lect.), 1959; Vanity Fair (ed with G. Tillotson), 1963; Mid-Victorian Studies (with G. Tillotson), 1965; Letters of Charles Dickens, vol. 1, 1965, vol. 2, 1969, vol. 3, 1974 (Associate Editor); vol. 4, 1977 (Editor) (General Editor, 1978–); Oliver Twist, 1966 (General Editor, Clarendon Dickens, 1957–, seven novels published by 1986); (ed with A. Trodd) The Woman in White, 1969; (ed) Oliver Twist (World's Classics), 1982; contributions to periodicals. *Address:* 23 Tanza Road, NW3 2UA. *T:* 01–435 5639. *Club:* University Women's.

TILMOUTH, Prof. Michael; first Tovey Professor of Music, University of Edinburgh, since 1971; *b* 30 Nov. 1930; *s* of Herbert George Tilmouth and Amy Tilmouth (*née* Hall); *m* 1966, Mary Jelliman; two *s* one *d. Educ:* Wintringham Grammar Sch., Grimsby; Christ's Coll., Cambridge (MA, PhD). Lectr, Glasgow Univ., 1959–71; Dean, Faculty of Music, Edinburgh Univ., 1973–76, 1980–84, 1985–. Dir, Scottish Opera, 1975–. Mem., BBC Archives Adv. Cttee, 1975–. Mem. Council, Royal Musical Assoc., 1970–76 (Editor, Research Chronicle, 1968–77); Member, Editorial Committee: Musica Britannica, 1972– (Gen. Editor, 1984–); Purcell Soc., 1976– (Chm., 1984–). *Publications:* (ed) Matthew Locke: Chamber Music and Dramatic Music (Musica Britannica, vols xxxi, 1971, vol. xxxii, 1972, vol. li, 1986); (ed) Purcell: Collected Works, vol. v, 1976, vol. vii, 1981, vol. xxxi, 1986; contribs to: Galpin Soc. Jl, Music & Letters, Proc. of Royal Musical Assoc., Musical Times, Musical Quarterly, Royal Mus. Assoc. Res. Chronicle, Encyc. de la Pléiade, Die Musik in Geschichte und Gegenwart, Grove's Dictionary, Monthly Mus. Record, The Consort, Brio, Early Music. *Recreations:* gardening, hill walking. *Address:* 62 Northumberland Street, Edinburgh EH3 6JE. *T:* 031–556 3293.

TILNEY, Charles Edward, CMG 1956; Minister for Finance and Economics, Tanganyika, 1957–60; *b* 13 April 1909; *yr s* of late Lt-Col N. E. Tilney, CBE, DSO, and Mrs Tilney; *m* 1952, Rosalind Hull, *e d* of late Lt-Col E. C. de Renzy-Martin, CMG, DSO, MC, and Mrs de Renzy-Martin; two *s. Educ:* Rugby School; Oriel College, Oxford. Ceylon Civil Service, 1932; Tanganyika: Asst Chief Secretary (Finance), 1948; Dep. Financial Secretary, 1948; Secretary for Finance, 1950; Member for Finance and Economics, 1953. Retd from E Africa, 1960. *Address:* 8 Butts Close, Biddestone, Chippenham, Wilts. *T:* Corsham 714770.

TILNEY, Dame Guinevere, DBE 1984; Adviser to Rt Hon. Margaret Thatcher, MP, 1975–83; UK Representative on United Nations Commission on Status of Women, 1970–73; *b* 8 Sept. 1916; *y d* of late Sir Hamilton Grant, 12th Bt, KCSI, KCIE, and late Lady Grant; *m* 1st, 1944, Captain Lionel Hunter (*d* 1947), Princess Louise Dragoon Guards; one *s*; 2nd, 1954, Sir John Tilney, *qv. Educ:* Westonbirt. WRNS, 1941–45; Private Sec. to Earl of Selborne, 1949–54; Vice-Chm., SE Lancs Br., British Empire Cancer Campaign, 1957–64; Founder Mem., 1st Chm., 1st Pres., Merseyside Conservative Ladies Luncheon Club, 1957–75, now 1st Hon. Life Mem.; Nat. Council of Women of Great Britain: Vice-Pres., 1958–61, Pres., 1961–68, Liverpool and Birkenhead Br.; Sen. Nat. Vice-Pres., 1966–68; Nat. Pres., 1968–70; Co-Chm., Women's Nat. Commn, 1969–71; Mem., North Thames Gas Consultative Council, 1967–69; Mem., BBC Gen. Adv. Council, 1967–76. Co-Chm., Women Caring Trust, 1972–75. DL: Co. Palatine of Lancaster, 1971–74; Co. Merseyside, 1974–76. *Recreations:* reading, music, theatre. *Address:* 3 Victoria Square, SW1W 0QZ. *T:* 01–828 8674.

TILNEY, Sir John (Dudley Robert Tarleton), Kt 1973; TD; JP; *b* 19 Dec. 1907; *yr s* of late Col R. H. Tilney, DSO; *m* 1954, Dame Guinevere Tilney, *qv*; one step *s. Educ:* Eton; Magdalen College, Oxford. Served during War of 1939–45 (despatches), with 59th (4th West Lancs) Medium Regt, RA, and 11th Medium Regt, RA; commanded 47/49 359 (4th West Lancs), Medium Regt RATA; Hon. Col 470 (3 W Lancs), LAA Regt, 1957–61. MP (C) Wavertree, Liverpool, 1950–Feb. 1974; Parliamentary Private Sec. to: Sec. of State for War, 1951–55; Postmaster-General, 1957–59; Chm. Inter-Parly Union,

Brit. Gp, 1959–62; Chm. Conservative Commonwealth Council W Africa Cttee, 1954–62; PPS to Minister of Transport, 1959–62; Parly Under-Sec. of State for Commonwealth Relations, 1962–64 and for the Colonies, 1963–64; Member: Select Cttee on Expenditure; Exec. Cttee, Nat. Union of Conservative and Unionist Assocs, 1965–73; Chm. Merseyside Conservative MPs, 1964–74 (Vice-Chm., NW Area Cttee); Treasurer, UK Branch, Commonwealth Parly Assoc., 1968–70; Mem., Exec. Cttee, Cons. Political Centre, 1972–81. Chairman: Liverpool Luncheon Club, 1948–49; Liverpool Branch, Royal Commonwealth Soc., 1955–60 (Pres., 1965); Victoria Square Assoc., 1959–; Winston Churchill Meml Statue Cttee; Pres., Airey Neave Meml Trust, 1983– (Chm., 1979–83). Member: Liverpool Cathedral Gen Council; Exec. Cttee, Westminster Soc., 1975–; Council, Imperial Soc. of Knights Bachelor, 1978–. Pres., Assoc. of Lancastrians in London, 1980–81. Trustee, Bluecoat Sch.; Governor, Liverpool Coll. JP Liverpool, 1946. Croix de Guerre with Gilt Star, 1945; Legion of Honour, 1960. *Recreations:* gardening, travel. *Address:* 3 Victoria Square, SW1W 0QZ. *T:* 01–828 8674. *Clubs:* Pratt's; Jesters; Liverpool Racquet.

TILSON, Joseph Charles, (Joe), ARA 1985; painter, sculptor and printmaker; *b* 24 Aug. 1928; *s* of Frederick Albert Edward Tilson and Ethel Stapley Louise Saunders; *m* 1956, Joslyn Morton; one *s* two *d. Educ:* St Martin's School of Art; Royal Coll. of Art (ARCA); British School at Rome (Rome Scholar). RAF, 1946–49. Worked in Italy and Spain, 1955–59; Vis. Lectr, Slade Sch., Univ. of London and King's Coll., Univ. of Durham, 1962–63; taught at Sch. of Visual Arts, NY, 1966; Vis. Lectr, Staatliche Hochschule für Bildende Kunste, Hamburg, 1971–72. Mem., Arts Panel, Arts Council, 1966–71. Exhib. Venice Biennale, 1964; work at Marlborough Gall., 1961–77, later at Waddington Galls; retrospective exhibitions: Boymans Van Beuningen Mus., Rotterdam, 1973; Vancouver Art Gall., 1979; Volterra, 1983. Biennale Prizes: Krakow, 1974; Ljubljana, 1985. Subject of TV films, 1963, 1968, 1974. *Recreation:* planting trees. *Address:* The Old Rectory, Christian Malford, Wilts SN15 4BW. *T:* Seagry 720223; Woolley Dale, 44 Broomwood Road, SW11 6HT. *T:* 01–223 4078.

TILSTON, Col Frederick Albert, VC 1945; CD; *b* Toronto, Ontario, 11 June 1906; *s* of late Fred Tilston, English birth, and late Agnes Estelle Le May, Cdn birth; *m* 1946; one *s. Educ:* De La Salle Collegiate, Toronto; Ontario College of Pharmacy (graduated 1929). Salesman for Sterling Products Ltd, Windsor, Ont., manufacturers of nationally advertised drug products, 1930–36; Canadian Sales Manager for Sterling Products Ltd, 1937–40; Vice-Pres. in charge of sales, Sterling Products Ltd, Windsor, Ontario, 1946–57; Pres., Sterling Drug Ltd, 1957–70; retired 1971. Canadian Army, 1941–46. Hon. Col, Essex and Kent Scottish Regt. KStJ 1984. Hon. Dr Laws Windsor, 1977. *Recreations:* swimming, ice hockey, golf; amateur pianist. *Address:* RR No 1, Kettleby, Ont L0G 1J0, Canada. *T:* 416–727 5945. *Clubs:* New Windsor, Essex County Golf and Country (Windsor, Ont); Royal Canadian Military Institute (Toronto); Summitt Golf and Country (Oak Ridges).

TIMBERLAKE, Herman Leslie Patterson, (Tim); Director, Abbey National Building Society, since 1972 (Chief General Manager, 1971–79; Deputy Chairman, 1976–79); *b* 3 Feb. 1914; *s* of William Walter and Mabel Timberlake; *m* 1940, Betty (*née* Curtis); two *s. Educ:* Watford Grammar Sch. FCIS; FCBSI; CBIM. Served War of 1939–45. Joined Abbey Road Building Soc., 1930; Asst Branch Manager, Watford, 1936; became Abbey National Building Soc., 1944; Branch Manager appts, 1946–59; Manager: Branches Admin. Dept, 1959; Investments Admin. Dept, 1964; Branches and Agencies, 1966; Jt General Manager, 1968. Mem. Council, Building Societies Assoc.; Pres., Building Societies Institute, 1977–78. *Address:* 1 Rochester Drive, Pinner, Mddx HA5 1DA. *T:* 01–866 1554.

TIMMS, Dr Cecil, DEng, CEng, FIMechE, FIProdE; Engineering Consultant, Department of Trade and Industry, later Department of Industry, since 1974; *b* 13 Dec. 1911; *m*; no *c. Educ:* Liverpool Univ. Head of Metrology, Mechanisms and Noise Control Div., 1950–61, Supt of Machinery Group, 1961–65, National Engrg Laboratory; Head of Machine Tools Branch, Min. of Technology, later DTI, 1965–73. *Publications:* contribs to Proc. IMechE, Metalworking Prod. and Prod. Engr. *Address:* Broom House, Ballsdown, Chiddingfold, Surrey. *T:* Wormley 2014.

TIMMS, Ven. George Boorne; Archdeacon of Hackney, 1971–81, now Emeritus; Vicar of St Andrew, Holborn, 1965–81; *b* 4 Oct. 1910; *s* of late George Timms and Annie Elizabeth Timms (*née* Boorne); unmarried. *Educ:* Derby Sch.; St Edmund Hall, Oxford; Coll. of the Resurrection, Mirfield. MA Oxon. Deacon, 1935; Priest, 1936; Curate: St Mary Magdalen, Coventry, 1935–38; St Bartholomew, Reading, 1938–49; Oxford Diocesan Inspector of Schools, 1944–49; Sacrist of Southwark Cath., 1949–52; Vicar of St Mary, Primrose Hill, NW3, 1952–65; Rural Dean of Hampstead, 1959–65; Prebendary of St Paul's Cathedral, 1964–71. Proctor in Conv., 1955–59, 1965–70, 1974–80; Member: Standing Cttee Church Assembly, 1968–70; Anglican-Methodist Unity Commn, 1965–69. Dir of Ordination Trg, and Exam. Chap. to Bp of London, 1965–81; Chm., Alcuin Club, 1968–. Pres., Sion Coll., 1980–81. Papal Medallion for services to Christian Unity, 1976. *Publications:* Dixit Cranmer, 1946; The Liturgical Seasons, 1965; (jtly) The Cloud of Witnesses, 1982; contributor to A Manual for Holy Week, 1967; (ed) English Praise, 1975; (ed) The New English Hymnal, 1985. *Address:* Cleve Lodge, Minster-in-Thanet, Ramsgate, Kent CT12 4BA. *T:* Thanet 821777.

TIMMS, Prof. Noel Walter; Director, School of Social Work, University of Leicester, since 1984; *b* 25 Dec. 1927; *s* of Harold John Timms and Josephine Mary Cecilia Timms; *m* 1956, Rita Caldwell; three *s* three *d. Educ:* Cardinal Vaughan School; Univ. of London (BA Hons History; MA Sociology); Univ. of Oxford. Social Worker, Family Service Units, 1952–54; Psychiatric social worker, 1955–57; Lectr, Dept of Social Science, Cardiff University Coll., 1957–61; Lectr, LSE, 1963–69; Prof. of Applied Social Studies, Bradford Univ., 1969–75; Prof. of Social Studies, Newcastle upon Tyne Univ., 1975–84; Prof. of Social Work, Leicester Univ., 1984–. *Publications:* Social Casework, Principles and Practice, 1964; Language of Social Casework, 1968; (with John Meyer) The Client Speaks, 1970; (with Rita Timms) Dictionary of Social Welfare, 1982; Social Work Values: an enquiry, 1983. *Recreations:* Evensong; looking at old furniture and at performances of Don Giovanni. *Address:* Glen House, Dalby Avenue, Bushby, Leics LE7 9RE. *T:* Leicester 433311.

TIMMS, Vera Kate, (Mrs E. W. Gordon); Counsellor, Paris, on secondment to HM Diplomatic Service, since 1984; *b* 8 Oct. 1944; *d* of late Kenneth Timms and of Elsie Timms (*née* Cussans); *m* 1977, Ernest William Gordon; one step *d. Educ:* Queen Anne Grammar School, York; St Hilda's College, Oxford (PPE hons). Ministry of Agriculture, Fisheries and Food, 1970; Asst Private Sec. to Minister of Agric., 1974–75; seconded to European Secretariat of Cabinet Office, 1976–79; Principal Private Sec. to Minister of Agric. 1980–82; Asst Sec. responsible for marketing policy, MAFF, 1982–84. *Recreation:* growing things. *Address:* 2 rue de Miromesnil, 75008 Paris, France; 42 The Foreshore, SE8. *T:* 01–691 0823. *Club:* Cercle de l'Union Internalliée (Paris).

TIMPSON, John Harry Robert; BBC Staff Reporter and Correspondent, since 1959; Presenter of Today, BBC Radio 4, 1970–76 and since 1978; Chairman, Any Questions?, BBC Radio 4, since 1984; *b* 2 July 1928; *s* of late John Hubert Victor Timpson and

Caroline (*née* Willson); *m* 1951, (Muriel) Patricia Whale; two *s*. *Educ:* Merchant Taylors' Sch. National Service, RASC, 1946–49. Reporter: Wembley News, 1945–46 and 1949–51; Eastern Daily Press, 1951–59; BBC Dep. Court Correspondent, 1962–67 (reporting Australian, Ethiopian and other Royal tours); Presenter: Newsroom, BBC-2, 1968–70; Tonight, BBC-1, 1976–78. Sony Gold Award for outstanding services to radio, 1986. *Publications:* Today and Yesterday (autobiog.), 1976; The Lighter Side of Today, 1983; The Early Morning Book, 1986. *Recreations:* catching up on sleep, avoiding gardening. *Address:* Timbertoft, Shire Lane, Chorleywood, Herts WD3 5NT; The Cottage, Wellingham, Norfolk.

TIMSON, Penelope Anne Constance; *see* Keith, P. A. C.

TINBERGEN, Dr Jan; Officer, Order of The Lion; Commander, Order of Orange Nassau; Professor Emeritus, Erasmus University, Rotterdam; *b* 12 April 1903; *s* of Dirk Cornelis Tinbergen and Jeannette Van Eek; *m* 1929, Tine Johanna De Wit; three *d* (and one *d* decd). *Educ:* Leiden University. On Staff, Central Bureau of Statistics, 1929–45; Prof., Netherlands Sch. of Economics (now Erasmus Univ.), 1933–73; Staff, League of Nations, 1936–38; Director, Central Planning Bureau (Dutch Government), 1945–55; Advisor to various governments and international organisations, 1955–; Chm., UN Develt Planning Cttee, 1965–72. Hon. Degrees from 20 Universities, 1954–. (Jointly) Prize in Economics to the memory of Alfred Nobel, 1969. *Publications:* Economic Policy, Principles and Design, 1956; Selected Papers, 1959; Shaping the World Economy, 1962; Income Distribution, 1975; articles. *Recreations:* languages, drawing. *Address:* Haviklaan 31, 2566XD The Hague, Netherlands. *T:* 070–644630.

See also N. Tinbergen.

TINBERGEN, Prof. Nikolaas, DPhil, MA; FRS 1962; Professor in Animal Behaviour, Oxford University, 1966–74, Emeritus Professor, 1974 (Lecturer, 1949–60, Reader, 1960–66); Fellow of Wolfson College, 1966–74, now Emeritus; *b* 15 April 1907; *s* of Dirk C. Tinbergen and Jeannette Van Eek; *m* 1932, Elisabeth A. Rutten; two *s* three *d*. *Educ:* Leiden; Vienna; Yale. Lecturer, 1936, Prof. of Experimental Zoology, 1947, Leiden University; Fellow, Merton Coll., Oxford Univ., 1950–66. Hon. Mem. of many learned socs. Hon. DSc: Edinburgh, 1973; Leicester, 1974. Godman-Salvin Medal, British Ornithol. Union, 1969. Italia Prize (documentaries), 1969; Swammerdam Medal, 1973; Nobel Prize for Physiology or Medicine (jt), 1973. *Publications:* Eskimoland, 1935; The Study of Instinct, 1951; The Herring Gull's World, 1953; Social Behaviour in Animals, 1953; Curious Naturalists, 1959; Animal Behaviour, 1965; Signals for Survival, 1970; The Animal in its World, vol. 1, 1972, vol. 2, 1973; (with E. A. Tinbergen) 'Autistic' Children: new hope for a cure, 1983; contribs to German, Dutch, British and American journals. *Address:* 88 Lonsdale Road, Oxford OX2 7ER. *T:* Oxford 58662.

See also Dr J. Tinbergen.

TINDAL-CARILL-WORSLEY, Air Commodore Geoffrey Nicolas Ernest, CB 1954; CBE 1943; Royal Air Force, retired; *b* 8 June 1908; *s* of late Philip Tindal-Carill-Worsley; *m* 1st, 1937, Berys Elizabeth Gilmour (marr. diss., 1951; she *d* 1962); one *s*; 2nd, 1951, Dorothy Mabel Murray Stanley-Turner. *Educ:* Eton; RAF Coll., Cranwell. Commanding Officer, RAF Station, Halton, Bucks, 1954–56; Sen. Technical Staff Officer, Far East Air Force, 1956–59; Director of Technical Training, Air Ministry, 1959; retired 1960. *Recreation:* country life.

TINDALE, Lawrence Victor Dolman, CBE 1971; Deputy Chairman Investors in Industry Group plc (formerly FFI), since 1974; *b* 24 April 1921; *s* of late John Stephen and Alice Lilian Tindale; *m* 1946, Beatrice Mabel (Betty) Barton; one *s* one *d*. *Educ:* Latymer Upper Sch., Hammersmith; Inst. of Chartered Accountants of Scotland. Apprenticed McClelland Ker, 1938. Served War, Army, in E Africa and Burma, 1941–45. Returned to McClelland Ker, and qualified, 1946; Partner, 1951. Invited to join ICFC Ltd as Asst Gen. Manager, 1959; Dir and Gen. Manager, 1966–72. On secondment, DTI, as Dir of Industrial Development, 1972–74. Member: DTI Cttee of Inquiry on Small Firms, 1969–71; Adv. Council on Energy Conservation, 1977–80; British Technology Gp (NRDC, 1974–; NEB, 1981–); Chm., EDC for Mechanical Engrg Industry, 1968–72. Director: Commodore Shipping Co. Ltd, 1969–; Guernsey Gas Light Co. Ltd, 1970–; Investment Trust of Guernsey Ltd, 1970–; General Funds Investment Trust, 1974–; Edbro Holdings plc (Chm.), 1974–; Northern Engineering Industries plc, 1974– (Dep. Chm., 1986–); Flextech (Holdings) Ltd, 1975– (Chm., 1984–); London Atlantic Investment Trust plc (Chm.), 1977–; N British Canadian Investment Trust Ltd (Chm.), 1979–; Transpec Holdings Ltd, 1980–; Dewrance MacNeil Ltd, 1980–; British Caledonian Gp (formerly Caledonian Airways) plc, 1980–; BNOC, 1980–84; Britoil, 1984–; Penspen Ltd, 1985–; Polly Peck (International) plc, 1985–; C. & J. Clark, 1986– (Chm., 1986–). Mem. Council: Consumer Assoc., 1970– (Vice Chm., 1981–85); BIM, 1974– (Chm. 1982–84; Vice-Chm., 1984–); Soc. for Protection of Ancient Buildings (Hon. Treasurer), 1974–. CA; CBIM. *Recreation:* opera. *Address:* 3 Amyand Park Gardens, Twickenham, TW1 3HS. *T:* 01–892 9457; Le Bouillon House, St George's Esplanade, St Peter Port, Guernsey. *T:* Guernsey 21688. *Clubs:* Reform; St James's (Manchester).

TINDALE, Patricia Randall; architect; Chief Architect, Department of the Environment, 1982–86; *b* 11 March 1926; *d* of Thomas John Tindale and May Tindale (*née* Uttin). *Educ:* Blatchington Court, Seaford, Sussex; Architectural Assoc. Sch. of Architecture (AADip.). ARIBA. Architect, Welsh Dept, Min. of Educn, 1949–50; Min. of Educn Develt Gp, 1951–60; Min. of Housing and Local Govt R&D Gp, 1960–70; DoE Housing Develt Gp, 1970–72; Head, Building Regulations Professional Div., DoE, 1972–74; Dir, Housing Develt Directorate, DoE, 1974–81; Dir, Central Unit of Built Environment, DoE, 1981–82. Mem., AA Council, 1965–68. *Publication:* Housebuilding in the USA, 1966. *Recreations:* weaving, sailing. *Address:* 34 Crescent Grove, SW4 7AH. *T:* 01–622 1926. *Club:* Reform.

TINDALL, Rev. Canon Frederick Cryer, BD 1923; AKC 1922; Principal Emeritus of Salisbury Theological College since 1965; Canon and Prebendary Emeritus of Salisbury Cathedral since 1981; *b* 2 July 1900; *s* of late Frederick and Frances Tindall, Hove, Sussex; *m* 1942, Rosemary Phyllis, *d* of late Frank and Katharine Alice Newman, Woking; one *s* (one *d* decd). *Educ:* Brighton Grammar Sch.; King's Coll., London (Fellow, 1951–); Ely Theological College. Curate of S Cyprian, S Marylebone, 1924–28; Lecturer and Bursar, Chichester Theological College, 1928–30, Vice-Principal, 1930–36; Warden of Connaught Hall and Lecturer in Theology, Southampton Univ., 1936–39; Vicar of St Augustine, Brighton, 1939–50; Principal, Salisbury Theological Coll., 1950–65 (Sabbatical Year 1965–66). Proctor in Convocation for Diocese of Chichester, 1936–45, 1949–50; Examining Chaplain to Bishop of Chichester, 1941–50, Canon and Prebendary of Chichester Cathedral, 1948–50; Canon and Prebendary of Salisbury Cathedral, 1950–81; Proctor in Convocation for Diocese of Salisbury, 1950–75; Vice-Pres. and Chm. House of Clergy, Salisbury Diocesan Synod, 1970–76; Chm., Salisbury Diocesan Liturgical Cttee, 1973–81; Member: Commn for Revision of the Catechism, 1958; Church Assembly Standing Orders Cttee, 1963; Archbishop's Commn on London and SE England, 1965; Greater London Area Liaison Cttee, 1968; Pastoral Measure Appeal Tribunal, 1969–75; General Synod Standing Orders Cttee, 1970–75. Clerical Judge, Court of Arches, Canterbury, 1969–80. Pro-Prolocutor, Lower House of Convocation of Canterbury, 1959–75. Trustee, St John's Hosp., Heytesbury, 1968–83. *Publications:* England Expects, 1946; a History of S Augustine's Brighton, 1946; Christian Initiation, Anglican Principles and Practice, 1951; contributor to: History of Christian Thought, 1937; Encyclopædia Britannica Year Book, 1939; Baptism To-Day, 1949; Theology, Church Quarterly Review, Guardian, etc. *Recreations:* music, travelling, golf, gardening. *Address:* 16 The Close, Salisbury, Wilts SP1 2EB. *T:* Salisbury 22373. *Clubs:* Athenæum, Royal Commonwealth Society, Ski Club of Great Britain.

TINDALL, Gillian Elizabeth; novelist, biographer, historian; *b* 4 May 1938; *d* of D. H. Tindall and U. M. D. Orange; *m* 1963, Richard G. Lansdown; one *s*. *Educ:* Univ. of Oxford (BA 1st cl., MA). Freelance journalism: for Observer; subseq. Guardian and New Statesman, 1960–; for Evening Standard, 1973–; for The Times, 1983–. Occasional broadcasts, BBC. *Publications: novels:* No Name in the Street, 1959; The Water and the Sound, 1961; The Edge of the Paper, 1963; The Youngest, 1967; Someone Else, 1969, 2nd edn 1975; Fly Away Home, 1971 (Somerset Maugham Award, 1972); The Traveller and His Child, 1975; The Intruder, 1979; Looking Forward, 1983; To the City, 1987; *short stories:* Dances of Death, 1973; The China Egg and Other Stories, 1981; *biography:* The Born Exile (George Gissing), 1974; *other non-fiction:* A Handbook on Witchcraft, 1965; The Fields Beneath, 1977; City of Gold: the biography of Bombay, 1981; Rosamond Lehmann: an Appreciation, 1985; (contrib.) Architecture of the British Empire, 1986; contribs to Encounter. *Recreations:* keeping house, foreign travel. *Address:* c/o Curtis Brown Ltd, 162–168 Regent Street, W1.

TINDEMANS, Leo; Minister of Foreign Relations, Belgium, since 1981; Visiting Professor in the Faculty of Social Sciences, Catholic University, Louvain; *b* Zwijndrecht, 16 April 1922; *m* 1960, Rosa Naesens; two *s* two *d*. *Educ:* State Univ., Ghent; Catholic Univ., Louvain. Mem. (Christian Democratic Party), House of Representatives, 1961–; Minister: for Community Relations, 1968–71; of Agriculture and Middle Class Affairs, 1972–73; Dep. Prime Minister and Minister for the Budget, 1973–74; Prime Minister of Belgium, 1974–78. Mem., Eur. Parlt, 1979–81. Mayor of Edegem, 1965–76. Nat. Sec., 1958–65, Pres., 1979–81, Christian Democratic Party; Pres., European People's Party, 1976–85. Charlemagne Prize, 1976; St Liborius Medaille für Einheit und Frieden, 1977; Stresemann Medaille, 1979; Schuman Prize, 1980. Hon. DLitt: City Univ., 1976; Heriot-Watt Univ., 1978; Georgetown Univ., Washington, 1984. *Publications:* Ontwikkeling van de Benelux, 1958; L'autonomie culturelle, 1971; Regionalized Belgium, Transition from the Nation State to the Multinational State, 1972; Een handvest voor woelig België, 1972; Dagboek van de werkgroep Eyskens, 1973; European Union, 1975; Europe, Ideal of our Generation, 1976; Atlantisch Europa, 1980. *Recreations:* reading, writing, walking. *Address:* (office) rue Quatre Bras 2, 1000 Brussels, Belgium.

TINDLE, David, RA 1979 (ARA 1973); painter; Ruskin Master of Drawing, Oxford University, and Professorial Fellow, St Edmund Hall, Oxford, since 1985; Dealer and Agent, Fischer Fine Art Ltd, since 1985; *b* 29 April 1932; *m* 1969, Janet Trollope; one *s* two *d*. *Educ:* Coventry Sch. of Art. MA Oxon 1985. Worked as scene painter and commercial artist, 1946–51; subseq. taught at Hornsey Coll. of Art; Vis. Tutor, Royal Coll. of Art, 1972–83, Fellow, 1981, Hon. FRCA, 1984. First showed work, Archer Gall., 1952 and 1953; regular one-man exhibns, Piccadilly Gall., from 1954; one-man exhibns at many public and private galleries in Gt Britain incl. Fischer Fine Art, 1985; Galerie du Tours, San Francisco and Los Angeles, 1964; Gallerie Vinciana, Milan, 1968; Galleria Carbonesi, Bologna, 1968; Gallery XX, Hamburg, 1974, 1977, 1980; rep. in exhibns at: Piccadilly Gall., 1954–; Royal Acad.; Internat. Biennale of Realist Art, Bruges, 1958 and Bologna, 1967; British Exhibn Art, Basel, 1958; John Moores, 1959 and 1961; Arts Council Shows: British Self-Portraits; Painters in East Anglia; Thames in Art; The British Art Show, 1979–80; Salon de la Jeune Peinture, Paris, 1967; Mostra Mercato d'Arte Contemporanea, Florence, 1967; British Painting 1974, Hayward Gall.; British Painting 1952–77, RA. Set of 3 Mural decorations for Open Univ., Milton Keynes, 1977–78. Work rep. in numerous public and private collections, incl. Nat. Portrait Gall.; Chantrey Bequest purchases, 1974 and 1975, now in Tate Gall. Critic Prize, 1962; Europe Prize for Painting, 1969; Critics' Choice, Tooths, 1974; Waddington Prize, Chichester Nat. Art Exhibn, 1975; Johnson Wax Award, RA, 1983. *Address:* The Grange, East Street, Long Buckby, Northants NN6 7RB; St Edmund Hall, Oxford.

TING, Prof. Samuel Chao Chung; Thomas D. Cabot Institute Professor, Massachusetts Institute of Technology, since 1977; *b* 27 Jan. 1936; *s* of K. H. Ting and late T. S. Wang; *m*; two *d*; *m* 1985, Susan Carol Marks. *Educ:* Univ. of Michigan (PhD). Ford Fellow, CERN, Geneva, 1963; Asst Prof. of Physics, Columbia Univ., 1965; Prof. of Physics, MIT, 1969. Assoc. Editor, Nuclear Physics B, 1970; Mem. Editorial Board: Nuclear Instruments and Methods, 1977; Mathematical Modeling, 1980. Member: US Nat. Acad. of Science, 1976; European Physical Soc.; Italian Physical Soc.; Foreign Member: Pakistan Acad. of Science, 1984; Academia Sinica (Republic of China), 1975; Fellow, Amer. Acad. of Arts and Science, 1975. Nobel Prize for Physics (jt), 1976; Ernest Orlando Lawrence Award, US Govt, 1976; A. E. Eringen Medal, Soc. of Engineering Science, USA, 1977. Hon. ScD Michigan, 1978. *Publications:* articles in Physical Review and Physical Review Letters. *Address:* 51 Vassar Street, Cambridge, Mass 02139, USA. *Club:* Explorers' (NY).

TINKER, Prof. Hugh Russell; Professor of Politics, University of Lancaster, 1977–82, now Emeritus; *b* 20 July 1921; *s* of late Clement Hugh Tinker and Gertrude Marian Tinker; *m* 1947, Elisabeth McKenzie (*née* Willis); two *s* (and one *s* killed in action). *Educ:* Taunton Sch.; Sidney Sussex Coll., Cambridge (BA Scholar). Indian Army, 1941–45; Indian civil admin, 1945–46. Lectr, Reader and Prof., SOAS, 1948–69; Dir, Inst. of Race Relations, 1970–72; Sen. Fellow, Inst. of Commonwealth Studies, Univ. of London, 1972–77. Prof., Univ. of Rangoon, 1954–55; Prof., Cornell Univ., USA, 1959. Vice-Pres., Ex-Services Campaign for Nuclear Disarmament. Trustee, Noel Buxton Trust. Contested (L): Barnet, gen. elecs 1964 and 1966; Morecambe and Lonsdale, 1979. *Publications:* The Foundations of Local Self-Government in India, Pakistan and Burma, 1954; The Union of Burma, a Study of the First Years of Independence, 1957 (4th edn 1967); India and Pakistan, a Political Analysis, 1962; Ballot Box and Bayonet, People and Government in Emergent Asian Countries, 1964; Reorientations, Studies on Asia in Transition, 1965; South Asia, a Short History, 1966; Experiment with Freedom, India and Pakistan 1947, 1967; (ed and wrote introduction) Henry Yule: Narrative of the Mission to the Court of Ava in 1855, 1969; A New System of Slavery: the export of Indian labour overseas 1830–1920, 1974; Separate and Unequal: India and the Indians in the British Commonwealth 1920–1950, 1976; The Banyan Tree: overseas emigrants from India, Pakistan and Bangladesh, 1977; Race, Conflict and the International Order: from Empire to United Nations, 1977; The Ordeal of Love: C. F. Andrews and India, 1979; A Message from the Falklands: the life and gallant death of David Tinker, 1982; (ed) Burma: the struggle for independence, vol. I 1944–1946, 1983, vol. II 1946–1948, 1984. *Recreations:* writing, walking. *Address:* Montbegon, Hornby, near Lancaster; Aspen Lea, Little Hampden, Bucks.

TINN, James; MP (Lab) Redcar, since 1974 (Cleveland, 1964–74); *b* 23 Aug. 1922; *s* of James Tinn and Nora (*née* Davie). *Educ:* Consett Elementary School; Ruskin College;

Jesus College, Oxford. Cokeworker until 1953; Branch official, Nat. Union of Blastfurnacemen. Full-time study for BA (PPE Oxon). Teacher, secondary modern school, 1958–64. PPS to Sec. of State for Commonwealth (formerly for Commonwealth Relations), 1965–66, to Minister for Overseas Development, 1966–67; an Asst Govt Whip, 1976–79; an Opposition Whip, 1979–82. Mem. Exec. Cttee, CPA. *Address:* 1 Norfolk Road, Moorside, Consett, Co. Durham. *T:* Consett 509313; 05 Raleigh House, Dolphin Square, SW1V 3NP. *Club:* United Oxford & Cambridge University.

TINNISWOOD, Maurice Owen; *b* 26 March 1919; *y s* of late Robert Tinniswood, OBE; *m* 1946, Anne Katharine, *yr d* of late Rev. J. Trevor Matchett; one *s* one *d. Educ:* Merchant Taylors' School. Served with Royal Hampshire Regt, 1939 46 (Major). Joined PO, 1938 as Executive Officer, Principal, 1949; Asst Secretary, 1958; Imperial Defence College, 1963; Director of Establishments and Organisation, 1965; Director of Reorganization, 1966; Secretary to the Post Office, 1969–70; Dir of Personnel, BBC, 1970–77. Chm., Kingston, Richmond and Esher Community Health Council, 1980–81; Mem., Kingston and Esher HA, 1982–85. CBIM. *Address:* Little Croft, Weston Green Road, Thames Ditton, Surrey KT7 0HY. *T:* 01–398 4561. *Club:* Chichester Yacht.

TINSLEY, Charles Henry, FRICS; Deputy Chief Valuer, Inland Revenue Valuation Office, 1974–78; *b* 3 March 1914; *s* of Arthur William and Teresa Tinsley; *m* 1938, Solway Lees; two *s* one *d. Educ:* Ratcliffe Coll., Leicester. Served War: joined TA, 1939; commn in Royal Artillery, 1941; with Lanarkshire Yeomanry, RA, in ME, Sicily and Italy; GSOII, in ME Supply Centre, Tehran, 1945–46. Nottinghamshire and W Riding of Yorkshire County Valuation Depts, 1929–39; Co. Valuer, N Riding of Yorkshire, 1948. Re-joined TA, 1948, and retd as Lt-Col, 1955. Joined Valuation Office, 1949; Suptg Valuer (Rating) Northern Region, 1949–68; Asst Chief Valuer, 1968. *Recreations:* the violin, travel, reading. *Address:* 44 Belgrave Manor, Brooklyn Road, Woking, Surrey GU22 7TW. *T:* Woking 67444.

TINSLEY, Rt. Rev. Ernest John; *b* 22 March 1919; *s* of Ernest William and Esther Tinsley; *m* 1947, Marjorie Dixon (*d* 1977); two *d. Educ:* St John's Coll., Univ. of Durham (BA, MA, BD); Westcott House, Cambridge. Priest, 1942; Curate: S Mary-le-Bow, Durham, 1942–44; South Westoe, 1944–46. Lectr in Theology, University Coll. of Hull, 1946–61; Sen. Lectr and Head of Dept of Theology, Univ. of Hull, 1961–62; Lectr of St Mary, Lowgate, Hull, 1955–62; Prof. of Theology, 1962–75, and Dean of Faculty of Arts, 1965–67, Univ. of Leeds; Bishop of Bristol, 1976–85; Special Lectr in Theology, Univ. of Bristol, 1976–84. Hulsean Preacher, Cambridge Univ., 1982; Bishop John Prideaux Lectr, Exeter Univ., 1982. Examining Chaplain: to Archbp of York, 1957–63; to Bp of Sheffield, 1963–75. Hon. Canon of Ripon Cath., 1966–75. Jt Chm., Gen. Synod's Bd of Educn and of Nat. Soc. for Promoting Religious Educn, 1979–82; Member: Doctrine Commn, 1967–69; Home Office Cttee on obscenity and film censorship, 1977–79. *Publications:* The Imitation of God in Christ, 1960; The Gospel according to Luke, 1965; (ed) Modern Theology, 1979; Tragedy, Irony and Faith, 1985; contributor to: The Church and the Arts, 1960; Vindications, 1966; A Dictionary of Christian Ethics, 1967; A Dictionary of Christian Theology, 1969; Art and Religion as Communication, 1974; Dictionary of Christian Spirituality, 1983; In Search of Christianity, 1986. *Recreations:* France, Romanesque art, gardening. *Address:* 100 Acre End Street, Eynsham, Oxford OX8 1PD. *T:* Oxford 880822.

TIPPET, Vice-Adm. Sir Anthony (Sanders), KCB 1984; CBIM; Chief of Fleet Support, 1983–86; General Manager, Hospitals for Sick Children, since 1987; *b* 2 Oct. 1928; *s* of W. K. R. Tippet and H. W. P. Kitley (*née* Sanders); *m* 1950, Lola Bassett; two *s* one *d* (and one *s* decd). *Educ:* West Buckland Sch., Devon. Called to the Bar, Gray's Inn, 1959. Entered RN, 1946; Lieut 1950; HM Ships Ceres, Superb, Staff C-in-C Mediterranean; Lt Comdr 1958; HMS Trafalgar, Britannia RNC; Comdr 1963; Secretary: to Director of Naval Intelligence; to Flag Officer Middle East; CO HMS Jufair, Supply Officer, HMS Eagle; Captain 1970: Asst Director Naval Plans (Warfare), 1970–72; CSO (Administration) to Flag Officer Plymouth, 1972–74; Director of Naval Officers' Appointments (Supply and WRNS Officers), 1974–76; Captain HMS Pembroke and Flag Captain to Flag Officer Medway, 1976–79; Rear-Adm. 1979; Asst Chief of Fleet Support, MoD, 1979–81; Flag Officer and Port Admiral, Portsmouth, and Chief Naval Supply and Secretariat Officer, 1981–83. *Recreations:* sailing, hill walking. *Club:* Royal Naval Sailing Association (Portsmouth).

TIPPETT, Sir Michael (Kemp), OM 1983; CH 1979; Kt 1966; CBE 1959; Composer; *b* 2 Jan. 1905; *s* of Henry William Tippett and Isabel Kemp. *Educ:* Stamford Grammar Sch.; Royal College of Music (Foley Scholar; FRCM 1961). Ran Choral and Orchestral Society, Oxted, Surrey, and taught French at Hazelwood School, till 1931. Entered Adult Education work in music (LCC and Royal Arsenal Co-operative Soc. Educn Depts), 1932. Director of Music at Morley College, London, 1940–51. Sent to prison for 3 months as a conscientious objector, June 1943. A Child of Our Time first performed March 1944, broadcast Jan. 1945. 1st Symphony performed Nov. 1945 by Liverpool Philharmonic Society. Artistic Dir, Bath Festival, 1969–74. President: Kent Opera Company, 1979–; London Coll. of Music, 1983–. Hon. Mem., Amer. Acad. of Arts and Letters, 1976; Extraordinary Mem., Akad. der Künste, Berlin, 1976. Cobbett Medal for Chamber Music, 1948; Gold Medal, Royal Philharmonic Society, 1976; Prix de Composition Musicale, Fondation Prince Pierre de Monaco, 1984. Honorary degrees include: MusD Cambridge, 1964; DMus: Trinity Coll., Dublin, 1964; Leeds, 1965; Oxford, 1967; London, 1975; Keele, 1986; DUniv York, 1966; DLitt Warwick, 1974. *Works include:* String Quartet No 1, 1935; Piano Sonata, 1937; Concerto for Double String Orchestra, 1939; A Child of Our Time, Oratorio, 1941; Fantasia on a theme of Handel for Piano and Orchestra, 1942; String Quartet, No 2, 1943; Symphony No 1, 1945; String Quartet No 3, 1946; Little Music for Strings, 1946; Suite in D, 1948; Song Cycle, The Heart's Assurance, 1951; Opera, The Midsummer Marriage, 1952 (first performed 1955); Ritual Dances, excerpts from the Opera for Orchestra, 1952; Fantasia Concertante on a Theme of Corelli for String Orchestra, 1953 (commnd for Edinburgh Festival); Divertimento, 1955; Concerto for piano and orchestra, 1956 (commnd by City of Birmingham Symphony Orch.); Symphony No 2, 1957 (commnd by BBC); Crown of the Year (commnd by Badminton School), 1958; Opera, King Priam (commnd by Koussevitsky Foundation of America), 1961; Magnificat and Nunc Dimittis (commnd by St John's Coll., Cambridge), 1961; Piano Sonata No 2, 1962; Incidental music to The Tempest, 1962; Praeludium for Brass etc (commnd by BBC), 1962; Cantata, The Vision of St Augustine, 1966; The Shires Suite, 1970; Opera, The Knot Garden, 1970; Songs for Dov, 1970; Symphony No 3, 1972; Piano Sonata no 3, 1973; Opera, The Ice Break, 1977; Symphony No 4, 1977 (commnd by Chicago SO); String Quartet No 4, 1979; Triple Concerto, 1979 (commnd by LSO with Ralph Vaughan Williams Trust); The Mask of Time, 1983 (commnd by Boston SO); The Blue Guitar, 1983 (commnd by Ambassador Internat. Cultural Foundn); Festal Brass with Blues, 1983 (commnd by Hong Kong Fest.); Piano Sonata No 4, 1984 (commnd by LA Philharmonic Assoc.). *Publications:* Moving into Aquarius, 1959, rev. edn 1974; Music of the Angels, 1980. *Recreation:* walking. *Address:* c/o Schott & Co., 48 Great Marlborough Street, W1Y 2BN. *TA:* Shotanco, London. *T:* 01 437 1246; 01–439 2640.

TIPPETTS, Rutherford Berriman; *b* 8 Feb. 1913; *s* of late Percy William Berriman Tippetts and Katherine Brown Rutherford; *m* 1948, Audrey Helen Wilson Cameron; one *s* one *d. Educ:* Rugby; Trinity Coll., Oxford (MA). Asst Principal, BoT, 1936; Principal Private Sec. to Ministers of Supply and Presidents of BoT, 1941–45; idc 1954; Chief Exec., Dollar Exports Council, 1959–61; served in Commercial Relations and Exports, Industry and Tourism Divs of BoT; Under-Sec., Export Services Div., DTI, 1970–73. Mem., Exec. Cttee and Council, CGLI. Master, Worshipful Co. of Armourers and Brasiers, 1975–76. *Address:* 74 Ebury Mews East, SW1W 9QA. *T:* 01–730 6464. *Clubs:* Carlton, Royal Wimbledon, Roehampton.

TIPPLER, John; Director, Network, British Telecom, Inland Communications Division, since 1986; *b* 9 Aug. 1929; *s* of George Herbert and Sarah Tippler, Spalding, Lincs; *m* 1952, Pauline Taylor (marr. diss. 1983); two *s. Educ:* Spalding Grammar School. Architect's Dept, Spalding RDC, 1945; Post Office Telephone Service, 1947; Royal Signals, 1949–50; Staff Mem., PO Central Engineering Sch., 1954–59; PO Engineering Develt, 1960–80; Dir, Exchange and Data Systems Op. and Develt, 1980; Dir of Engrg, BT, 1982–86. Dir, IT Inst., 1986. *Recreations:* music, country walking, motor-cycling, cinema, theatre. *Address:* 213 Bunyan Court, Barbican, EC2. *T:* 01–628 5829.

TITCHENER, Alan Ronald; Under Secretary, Overseas Trade Division, Department of Trade and Industry, since 1982; *b* 18 June 1934; *s* of Edmund Hickman Ronald Titchener and Minnie Ellen Titchener; *m* 1959, Joyce Blakesley; two *s. Educ:* Harrow County Grammar Sch.; London School of Economics. BSc(Econ) 1962. RAF, 1952–54. Colonial Office, 1954–62; Min. of Transport, 1962–64; Board of Trade, 1964–68; HM Diplomatic Service, New York, 1969–73; Dept of Trade, 1973–78; HM Consul-Gen., Johannesburg, 1978–82. *Address:* c/o Department of Trade and Industry, 1 Victoria Street, SW1. *Club:* Royal Air Force.

TITCHENER, John Lanham Bradbury, CMG 1955; OBE 1947; *b* 28 Nov. 1912; *s* of late Alfred Titchener and late Alicia Marion Leonora Bradbury; *m* 1937, Catherine Law Clark (*decd*) (marr. diss. 1958); no *c; m* 1958, Rikke Marian Lehmann (*née* Bendixsen), *e d* of late Frederik Carl Bendixsen and Kammerherreinde Nina Grandjean of Vennerslund, Falster, Denmark; two step *s. Educ:* City of London Sch.; Royal College of Music. Nat. Council of Education of Canada, 1934; BBC 1938–43; War of 1939–45: served HM Forces, Jan.-Aug. 1943; Psychological Warfare Branch, Allied Force HQ, Algiers, 1943; 15th Army Group HQ, Italy, 1944–45; Asst Dep. Director, Political Warfare Div., SACSEA, 1945; Political Warfare Adviser to C-in-C, Netherlands East Indies, 1945–46; First Secretary, HM Foreign Service, 1947; served in FO until 1950, when transferred to HM Embassy, Moscow; then at HM Embassy, Ankara, 1953–54; Economic Counsellor, HM Embassy, Tehran, 1954–56, Chargé d'Affaires, 1955. Resigned HM Foreign Service, 1957. *Recreations:* music, gardening, fishing. *Address:* 3 Impasse du Château, 06190 Roquebrune Village, France. *T:* 93 350785. *Club:* Travellers'.

TITCHENER-BARRETT, Sir Dennis (Charles), Kt 1981; TD 1953, 2 bars; Chairman, Woodstock (London) Ltd (industrial minerals), since 1962; *m* 1940, Joan Wilson; one *s* three *d.* Served War, RA, 1939–46; commanded 415 Coast Regt RA (TA), 1950–56; Mem., Kent T&AFA, 1950–56. An Underwriting Member of Lloyd's, 1977–. ILEA School Governor, 1956–73; Member: Gtr London Central Valuation Panel, 1964–75; Cons. Bd of Finance, 1968–75; Cons. Policy Gp for Gtr London, 1975–78; National Union of Conservative Associations: Mem., Central Council and Exec. Cttee, 1968–81; Treasurer, 1968–75, Chm., 1975–78, Gtr London Area; Vice-Pres., Nat. Soc. of Cons. Agents, Gtr London Area, 1975–; Chm., S Kensington Cons. Assoc., 1954–57; Pres., Kensington Cons. Assoc., 1975–. Mem., RUSI, 1947–. Fellow, Inst. of Dirs, 1952. High Sheriff of Greater London, 1977–78. *Address:* 8 Launceston Place, W8 5RL. *T:* 01–937 0613. *Club:* Carlton.

TITE, Dr Michael Stanley, FSA; Keeper, Department of Scientific Research (formerly Research Laboratory), British Museum, since 1975; *b* 9 Nov. 1938; *s* of late Arthur Robert Tite and Evelyn Frances Violet Tite (*née* Endersby); *m* 1967, Virginia Byng Noel; two *d. Educ:* Trinity Sch. of John Whitgift, Croydon; Christ Church, Oxford (MA, DPhil). FSA 1977. Research Fellow in Ceramics, Univ. of Leeds, 1964–67; Lectr in Physics, Univ. of Essex, 1967–75. *Publications:* Methods of Physical Examination in Archaeology, 1972; papers on scientific methods applied to archaeology in various jls. *Recreations:* travelling with "The Buildings of England", gardening. *Address:* Crossing Cottage, Boley Road, White Colne, Colchester, Essex. *T:* Earls Colne 2161.

TITFORD, Rear-Adm. Donald George, CEng, FRAeS; retired 1978; Deputy Controller of Aircraft, Ministry of Defence, 1976–78; *b* 15 June 1925; *s* of late Percy Maurice Titford and Emily Hannah Titford (*née* McLaren). *Educ:* Highgate Sch Royal Naval Engineering Coll.; Coll. of Aeronautics, Cranfield. MSc. Entered RN as Cadet, 1943; Comdr 1959; Air Engr Officer, HMS Victorious, 1965; Captain 1967; comd, RN Air Station, Lee-on-Solent, 1972–74; Comd Engr Officer, Naval Air Comd, 1974–76. *Recreations:* modern pentathlon, old English watercolours. *Address:* Merry Hill, North Road, Bath BA2 6HD. *T:* Bath 62132. *Club:* Army and Navy.

TITHERIDGE, Roger Noel, QC 1973; a Recorder of the Crown Court since 1972; Barrister-at-Law; *b* 21 Dec. 1928; *s* of Jack George Ralph Titheridge and Mabel Titheridge (*née* Steains); *m* 1963, Annabel Maureen (*née* Scott-Fisher); two *d. Educ:* Midhurst Grammar Sch.; Merton Coll., Oxford (Exhibnr). MA (History and Jurisprudence). Called to the Bar, Gray's Inn, 1954; Holker Sen. Scholar, Gray's Inn, 1954; Bencher, Gray's Inn, 1985. *Recreations:* tennis, sailing. *Address:* 1 Paper Buildings, Temple, EC4. *T:* 01–353 3728; 13 The Moat, Traps Lane, New Malden, Surrey. *T:* 01–942 2747.

TITTERTON, Major David Maitland M.; *see* Maitland-Titterton.

TITTERTON, Prof. Sir Ernest (William), Kt 1970; CMG 1957; FRSA; FAA; Professor of Nuclear Physics, Australian National University, since 1950; Dean of the Research School of Physical Sciences, Australian National University, 1966–68, Director of Research School of Physical Sciences, 1968–73; *b* 4 March 1916; *e s* of W. A. Titterton, Tamworth, Staffs; *m* 1942, Peggy Eileen, *o d* of Captain A. Johnson, Hagley, Worcs; one *s* two *d. Educ:* Queen Elizabeth's Grammar Sch., Tamworth; University of Birmingham (BSc, MSc, PhD). Research Officer, Admiralty, 1939–43; Member British Scientific Mission to USA on Atomic Bomb development, 1943–47; Sen. Member of Timing Group at 1st Atomic Bomb Test, Alamagordo, 1945; Adviser on Instrumentation, Bikini Atomic Weapon Tests, 1946; Head of Electronics Div., Los Alamos Lab., USA, 1946–47; Group Leader in charge of Research team at AERE, Harwell, 1947–50. Member Australian Atomic Energy Commn Scientific Advisory Cttee, 1955–64; Dep. Chairman Australian Atomic Weapons Safety Cttee, 1954–56; Chm., Atomic Weapons Safety Cttee, 1957–73 (in this capacity attended all British Atom Bomb tests in Australia, 1952–57); Member, Defence Research and Development Policy Cttee, 1958–75; Member National Radiation Advisory Cttee, 1957–73. Vice-Pres., Aust. Inst. of Nuclear Science and Engineering, 1968–72, Pres., 1973–75. *Publications:* Progress in Nuclear Physics, 4, 1955; Facing the Atomic Future (London, New York, Melbourne), 1955; Selected Lectures in Modern Physics for School Science Teachers, 1958; Uranium: energy source of the future?, 1979;

some 212 papers mainly on nuclear physics, atomic energy and electronics in technical journals. *Recreations:* music and tennis. *Address:* 21 Gilmore Crescent, Garran, Canberra, ACT 2605, Australia. *T:* Canberra 812164.

TIVERTON, Viscount; *see* Giffard, A. E.

TIZARD, Prof. Barbara, PhD, FBPsS; Director, Thomas Coram Research Unit, Institute of Education, University of London, since 1980; Professor of Education, Institute of Education, since 1982; *b* 16 April 1926; *d* of late Herbert Parker and Elsie Parker (*née* Kirk); *m* 1947, Jack Tizard (*d* 1979); one *s* two *d* (and two *s* decd). *Educ:* St Paul's Girls' School; Somerville College, Oxford. BA Oxon, PhD London. Lectr, Dept of Experimental Neurology, Inst. of Psychiatry, 1963–67; Res. Officer then Senior Res. Fellow, Inst. of Education, 1967–77, Reader in Education, 1978–80. Chm., Assoc. of Child Psychology and Psychiatry, 1976–77. Co-editor, British Jl of Psychology, 1975–79; Mem., Editorial Bd, Jl of Child Psychology and Psychiatry, 1979–. *Publications:* Early Childhood Education, 1975; Adoption: a second chance, 1977; (with J. Mortimore and B. Burchell) Involving Parents in Nursery and Infant Schools, 1981; (with M. Hughes) Young Children Learning, 1984; articles on epilepsy, children in care, child development and early education. *Recreation:* working for the peace movement. *Address:* 4 The Gables, Vale of Health, NW3. *T:* 01–435 4475.

See also M.C. Parker.

TIZARD, Dame Catherine (Anne), DBE 1985; Mayor of Auckland, New Zealand, since 1983; *b* 4 April 1931; *d* of Neil Maclean and Helen Montgomery Maclean; *m* 1951, Hon. Robert James Tizard, *qv* (marr. diss. 1983); one *s* three *d. Educ:* Matamata College; Auckland University (BA). Tutor in Zoology, Univ. of Auckland, 1967–84. Member: Auckland City Council, 1971–83; Auckland Regional Authy, 1980–83. *Recreations:* music, reading, drama, skin diving. *Address:* 84A Beresford Street, Freeman's Bay, Auckland 1, New Zealand. *T:* 760239.

TIZARD, Sir (John) Peter (Mills), Kt 1982; Professor of Pædiatrics, University of Oxford, and Fellow of Jesus College, Oxford, 1972–83, Hon. Fellow 1983; Hon. Consultant Children's Physician, Oxfordshire Health Authority, 1972–83; *b* London, 1 April 1916; *e s* of late Sir Henry Thomas Tizard, GCB, AFC, FRS, and late Lady (Kathleen Eleanor) Tizard; *m* 1945, Elisabeth Joy, *yr d* of late Clifford John Taylor, FRCSE; two *s* one *d. Educ:* Rugby Sch.; Oriel Coll., Oxford; Middlesex Hospital. BA Oxon 1938 (3rd cl. Hons Honour Sch. of Natural Science); Oxford and Cambridge Schol. (Biochemistry and Physiology), Middlesex Hospital, 1938; MA, BM, BCh Oxon 1941; MRCP 1944; FRCP 1958; DCH England 1947. Served War of 1939–45 with RAMC, 1942–46 (Temp. Major). Med. Registrar and Pathologist, Hospital for Sick Children, Great Ormond Street, 1947; Asst Director, Pædiatric Unit, St Mary's Hospital Medical Sch., 1949; Physician, Paddington Green Children's Hospital, 1949; Nuffield Foundation Medical Fellow, 1951; Research Fellow in Pediatrics, Harvard Univ., 1951; Reader in Child Health, 1954–64, Prof. of Pædiatrics, Inst. of Child Health, Royal Postgraduate Med. Sch., Univ. of London, 1964–72; Hon. Cons. Children's Physician, Hammersmith Hosp., 1954–72; Chm., Med. Cttee, Hammersmith Hosp., 1970–71; Mem., Oxford AHA, 1979–82. Lectures: Blackfan Meml, Harvard Univ., 1963; Samuel Gee, RCP, 1972; Carl Fridericksen, Danish Paediatric Soc., 1972; Perlstein, Louisville Univ., 1973; Clausen Meml, Rochester Univ., NY, 1975; Choremis Meml, Hellenic Paediatric Soc., 1975; Croonian, RCP 1978; Orator, Reading Pathological Soc., 1973. Mem. Ct of Assistants, 1971–, Master, 1983–84, Soc. of Apothecaries of London. FRSocMed 1941 (Pres., Sect. of Paediatrics, 1980–81, Hon. Fellow, 1984); Second Vice-Pres., RCP, 1977–78; Member: British Pædiatric Assoc., 1953 (Pres. 1982–85); European Pædiatric Research Soc., 1959 (Pres., 1970–71); Neonatal Society, 1959–83 (Hon. Sec. 1964–66; Pres., 1975–78; Hon. Mem., 1983); Assoc. Physicians of Great Britain and Ireland, 1965; Assoc. British Neurologists, 1969; German Acad. of Scientists, Leopoldina, 1972; Harveian Soc., 1974– (Pres., 1977); British Pædiatric Neurol. Assoc., 1975– (Chm. 1979–82); Corresp. Member: Société française de Pédiatrie, 1969; Pædiatric Soc. of Chile, 1968; Austrian Paediatric Soc., 1972; Swiss Paediatric Soc., 1973; Hon. Member: Pædiatric Soc. of Concepcion, 1968; Czechoslovak Med. Assoc. J. E. Purkyněi, 1971; Dutch Pædiatric Soc., 1971; Amer. Pediatric Soc., 1976; Hellenic Soc. Perinatal Medicine, 1979. Dawson Williams Meml Prize, BMA, 1982. *Publications:* Medical Care of Newborn Babies (jtly), 1972; papers in scientific and medical journals. *Address:* Ickenham Manor, Ickenham, Uxbridge, Mddx UB10 8QT. *T:* Ruislip 32262; Jesus College, Oxford OX1 3DW. *Club:* Athenæum.

TIZARD, Hon. Robert James, PC (Canada) 1985; MP for Otahuhu, Pakuranga, and now Panmure, New Zealand, since 1957; Minister of Energy, Science and Technology, Statistics, and Minister in Charge of the Audit Department, since 1984; *b* 7 June 1924; *s* of Henry James and Jessie May Tizard; *m* 1951, Catherine Anne Maclean (*see* Dame Catherine Tizard) (marr. diss. 1983); one *s* three *d*; *m* 1983, Mary Christina Nacey; one *s. Educ:* Auckland Grammar Sch.; Auckland Univ. MA, Hons Hist., 1949. Served War: RNZAF, 1943–46, incl. service in Canada and Britain; (commnd as a Navigator, 1944). Pres., Students' Assoc., Auckland Univ., 1948; Lectr in History, Auckland Univ., 1949–53; teaching, 1954–57 and 1961–62. MP 1957–60 and 1963–; Minister of Health and State Services, 1972–74; Dep. Prime Minister and Minister of Finance, 1974–75; Dep. Leader of the Opposition, 1975–84. *Recreation:* golf. *Address:* 38 Clutha Avenue, Khandallah, Wellington, New Zealand.

TOBIN, Prof. James, PhD; Sterling Professor of Economics, Yale University, since 1957; *b* 5 March 1918; *s* of Louis Michael and Margaret Edgerton Tobin; *m* 1946, Elizabeth Fay Ringo; three *s* one *d. Educ:* Harvard Univ. AB 1939 (*summa cum laude*); MA 1940; PhD 1947. Economist, Office of Price Admin, and Civilian Supply and War Production Bd, Washington, 1941–42; line officer, destroyer, USN, 1942–46. Teaching Fellow in Econs, 1946–47, Jun. Fellow, Soc. of Fellows, 1947–50, Harvard Univ.; Yale University: Associate Prof. of Econs, 1950–55; Prof. of Econs, 1955–; Dir, Cowles Foundn for Res. in Econs, 1955–61; Chm., Dept of Econs, 1968–69, 1974–78. Vis. Prof., Univ. of Nairobi, 1972–73; Ford Vis. Res. Prof. of Econs, Univ. of Calif, Berkeley, 1983. Mem., Pres.'s Council of Econ. Advrs, 1961–62. Corresp. FBA 1984. LLD *hc:* Syracuse Univ., 1967; Univ. of Illinois, 1969; Dartmouth Coll., 1970; Swarthmore Coll., 1980; New Sch. for Social Res., and New York Univ., 1982; Univ. of Hartford, 1984; Colgate Univ., 1984; Univ. of New Haven, 1986; DEcon *hc* New Univ. of Lisbon, 1980; Hon. DHL: Bates Coll., 1982; Hofstra Univ., 1983; DSocSc *hc* Helsinki, 1986. Foreign Associate, Acad. of Sciences, Portugal, 1980. Nobel Prize in Economics, 1981. *Publications:* (jtly) The American Business Creed, 1956; National Economic Policy, 1966; Essays in Economics: vol. 1, Macroeconomics, 1971; vol. 2, Consumption and Econometrics, 1975; vol. 3, Theory and Policy, 1982; The New Economics One Decade Older, 1974; Asset Accumulation and Economic Activity, Reflections on Contemporary Macroeconomic Theory, 1980; contribs to professional jls. *Recreations:* tennis, ski-ing, sailing, canoeing, fishing, chess. *Address:* Yale University, Box 2125 Yale Station, New Haven, Conn 06520, USA. *T:* 203–436–2330. *Clubs:* Yale (New York); Mory's Association, The Club (New Haven).

TOD, Sir John Hunter H.; *see* Hunter-Tod.

TODD, family name of **Baron Todd.**

TODD, Baron, *cr* 1962, of Trumpington (Life Peer); **Alexander Robertus Todd,** OM 1977; Kt 1954; FRS 1942; DSc Glasgow; Dr Phil nat Frankfurt; DPhil Oxon; MA Cantab; FRSC; Master of Christ's College, Cambridge, 1963–78 (Fellow, 1944); Professor of Organic Chemistry, University of Cambridge, 1944–71; (first) Chancellor, University of Strathclyde, Glasgow; Visitor, Hatfield Polytechnic, since 1978; Director, Fisons Ltd, 1963–78; *b* Glasgow, 2 Oct. 1907; *e s* of Alexander Todd, JP, Glasgow; *m* 1937, Alison Sarah, *e d* of Sir H. H. Dale, OM, GBE, FRS; one *s* two *d. Educ:* Allan Glen's Sch.; University of Glasgow. Carnegie Research Scholar, University of Glasgow, 1928–29; Univ. of Frankfurt a M, 1929–31; 1851 Exhibition Senior Student, Univ. of Oxford, 1931–34; Assistant in Medical Chemistry, 1934–35, and Beit Memorial Research Fellow, 1935–36, University of Edinburgh; Member of Staff, Lister Institute of Preventive Medicine, London, 1936–38; Reader in Biochemistry, University of London, 1937–38; Visiting Lecturer, California Institute of Technology, USA, 1938; Sir Samuel Hall Professor of Chemistry and Director of Chemical Laboratories, University of Manchester, 1938–44. Chairman, Advisory Council on Scientific Policy, 1952–64. Visiting Professor: University of Chicago, 1948; University of Sydney, 1950; Mass. Inst. Tech., 1954. Chemical Society, Tilden Lecturer, 1941, Pedler Lecturer, 1946; Meldola Medal, 1936; Leverhulme Lecturer, Society of Chemical Industry, 1948; President: Chemical Soc., 1960–62; Internat. Union of Pure and Applied Chemistry, 1963–65; BAAS, 1969–70; Royal Soc., 1975–80; Soc. of Chem. Industry, 1981–82. Chairman: Royal Commn on Medical Education, 1965–68; Board of Governors, United Cambridge Hospitals, 1969–74. Member Council, Royal Society, 1967–70; Mem., NRDC, 1968–76. Hon. Member French, German, Spanish, Belgian, Swiss, Japanese Chemical Societies; Foreign Member: Nat. Acad. Sciences, USA; American Acad. of Arts and Sciences; Akad. Naturf. Halle; American Phil. Soc.; Australian, Austrian, Indian, Iranian, Japanese, New York, Soviet and Polish Academies of Science. Hon. Fellow: Australian Chem. Institute; Manchester College Technology; Royal Society Edinburgh. Chairman, Managing Trustees, Nuffield Foundation, 1973–79 (Trustee, 1950–79); Chm., Trustees, Croucher Foundn (Hong Kong), 1980– (Trustee, 1979–); Pres., Parly and Scientific Cttee, 1983–86. Lavoisier Medallist, French Chemical Society, 1948; Davy Medal of Royal Society, 1949; Bakerian Lecturer, 1954; Royal Medal of Royal Society, 1955; Nobel Prize for Chemistry, 1957; Cannizzaro Medal, Italian Chemical Society, 1958; Paul Karrer Medal, Univ. Zürich, 1962; Stas Medal, Belgian Chemical Society, 1962; Longstaff Medal, Chemical Society, 1963; Copley Medal, Royal Society, 1970; Lomonosov Medal, USSR Acad. Sci., 1979; Copernicus Medal, Polish Acad. Sci., 1979; Hanbury Medal, Pharmaceutical Soc., 1986. Hon. FRCP 1975; Hon. FRCPS(Glas) 1980; Hon. FIMechE. Hon. Fellow: Oriel Coll., Oxford, 1955; Churchill Coll., Cambridge, 1971; Darwin Coll., Cambridge, 1981. Hon. LLD: Glasgow, Melbourne, Edinburgh, Manchester, California, Hokkaido, Chinese Univ. of Hong Kong; Hon. Dr rer nat Kiel; Hon. DSc: London, Madrid, Exeter, Leicester, Aligarh, Sheffield, Wales, Yale, Strasbourg, Harvard, Liverpool, Adelaide, Strathclyde, Oxford, ANU, Paris, Warwick, Durham, Michigan, Cambridge, Widener, Philippines, Tufts, Hong Kong; Hon. DLitt Sydney. Pour le Mérite, German Federal Republic, 1966; Order of Rising Sun (Japan), 1978. Master, Salters' Company, 1961. *Publications:* A Time to Remember (autobiog.), 1983; numerous scientific papers in chemical and biochemical journals. *Recreations:* fishing, golf. *Address:* 9 Parker Street, Cambridge. *T:* Cambridge 356688. *Club:* Athenæum.

TODD, Rev. Alastair, CMG 1971; *b* 21 Dec. 1920; *s* of late Prof. James Eadie Todd, MA, FRHistS (formerly Prof. of History, Queen's University, Belfast) and Margaret Simpson Johnstone Maybin; *m* 1952, Nancy Hazel Buyers; two *s* two *d. Educ:* Royal Belfast Academical Institution; Fettes Coll., Edinburgh; Corpus Christi Coll., Oxford; London Univ. (External); Salisbury and Wells Theological Coll. BA (Oxon), DipTheol (London). Served War, Army, 1940–46, Capt. RHA. Apptd Colonial Administrative Service, Hong Kong, 1946; Joint Services Staff Coll., 1950; Defence Sec., Hong Kong, 1957–60; Dep. Colonial Sec., Hong Kong, 1963–64; Dir of Social Welfare, also MLC, 1966–68; and, again, Defence Sec., 1968–71, retd. Ordained Deacon by Bishop of Chichester, 1973 and Priest, 1974; Asst Curate, Willingdon, 1973–77; Vicar, St Augustine's, Brighton, 1978–86. *Recreations:* reading, walking, embroidery, gardening. *Address:* 50 Wish Hill, Eastbourne. *T:* Eastbourne 505843.

TODD, (Alfred) Norman, FCA; CompIEE; Chairman, National Bus Company, 1969–71; retired; *b* 18 Oct. 1904; *s* of late Alfred and Rachel Todd; *m* 1935, Mary Watson; one *s* one *d. Educ:* Bishops Stortford College. With Deloitte Plender Griffiths & Co., 1929–48; Assistant, then Deputy Chief Accountant, Merseyside and North Wales Electricity Board, 1948–51; Assistant Chief Accountant, British Electricity Authority, 1951–54; Chief Accountant, London Electricity Board, 1954–56; Dep. Chairman, London Electricity Board, 1956–61; Chairman, East Midlands Electricity Board, 1962–64. Member, Central Electricity Generating Board, 1965–68. Hon. Treasurer, IEE, 1972–75. *Recreation:* golf. *Address:* Allendale, 139 Cooden Drive, Bexhill-on-Sea, East Sussex. *T:* Cooden 4147.

TODD, Ann; Actress; *m* 1933, Victor Malcolm; one *s*; *m* 1939, Nigel Tangye; one *d*; *m* 1949, Sir David Lean, *qv* (marr. diss.). Stage plays and films include: *Plays:* Peter, in Peter Pan, Winter Garden, 1942–43; Lottie, in Lottie Dundass, Vaudeville, 1943; Madeleine Smith, in The Rest is Silence, Prince of Wales, 1944; Francesca Cunningham in The Seventh Veil, Princes, 1951; Foreign Field, 1953; Old Vic Season, 1954–55; Macbeth; Love's Labour's Lost; Taming of the Shrew; Henry IV, Parts I and II; Jennifer Dubedat in The Doctor's Dilemma, Saville, 1956; Four Winds, New York, 1957; Duel of Angels, London, 1958. *Films:* The Seventh Veil, 1945; Daybreak, 1948; The Paradine Case, 1948; So Evil My Love, 1948; The Passionate Friends, 1949; Madeleine, 1950; The Sound Barrier, 1952; The Green Scarf, 1954; Time Without Pity, 1956; Taste of Fear, 1960; Son of Captain Blood, 1961; 90 Degrees in the Shade, 1964; The Vortex, 1965; Beware my Brethren, 1970; The Fiend, 1971; The Human Factor, 1980; Persian Fairy Tale; produced, wrote and appeared in Diary Documentaries, 1964–76: Thunder in Heaven (Kathmandu); Thunder of the Gods (Delphi); Thunder of the Kings (Egypt); Free in the Sun (Australia); Thunder of Silence (Jordan); Thunder of Light (Scotland); Hebrides (Scotland). TV appearances include: The Last Target, BBC, 1972; Maelstrom (series) Norway, 1983; The McGuffin, 1985; frequent radio and television appearances both in USA and GB. *Publications:* two novels; The Eighth Veil (autobiog.), 1980. *Address:* 3 Sutherland House, Marloes Road, W8. *T:* 01–938 3281; Sea Green Cottage, Walberswick, Suffolk.

TODD, Sir Bryan (James), Kt 1976; Chairman: Todd Petroleum Mining Co. Ltd, since 1955; Viking Mining Co. Ltd, since 1970; Director: Todd Motors Ltd, since 1924; Shell, BP & Todd Oil Services Ltd, since 1955; Waipipi Iron Sands Ltd, since 1970; Maui Development Ltd, since 1973; *b* 8 Sept. 1902; *s* of Charles Todd and Mary (*née* Hegarty); *m* 1928, Helen Ann Buddo; three *d. Educ:* Christian Bros, Dunedin, NZ; Riverview Coll., Sydney, NSW, Australia. Automotive industry, 1922–; prominent in petroleum industry of NZ, 1930–; Founder and formerly Managing Director: Europa Oil (NZ) Ltd (marketing and refining); Todd Petroleum Mining Co. Ltd (exploration and production of oil and gas in NZ); Viking Mining Co. Ltd (ironsand prodn, refining and export). Chairman: Ruapehu Alpine Lifts Ltd, 1953–; Todd Foundn, 1972–. *Recreations:* skiing, sailing, golf, shooting. *Address:* 38 Wesley Road, Wellington, New Zealand. *T:* (home) 727 040, (office) 722 970. *Clubs:* Wellington, Wellesley (Wellington, NZ); Wellington Golf (Heretaunga, NZ); Ruapehu Ski (NZ).

See also Adm. Sir Gordon Tait.

TODD, Hon. Sir Garfield; *see* Todd, Hon. Sir R. S. G.

TODD, Sir Geoffrey Sydney, KCVO 1951 (CVO 1947); OBE 1946; DL; MB, ChM, FRCP; FRACP; Medical Superintendent, King Edward VII Hospital, Midhurst, 1934–70; *b* 2 Nov. 1900; *s* of late George William Todd, and Amy Louisa Webb; *m* 1955, Margaret Alan Sheen, *o d* of late F. A. Sheen, MC, and of Mrs Sheen, Tudor Cottage, Midhurst. *Educ:* King's Sch., Parramatta, Australia; Sydney Univ., Australia. Resident MO, 1925–26, Medical Superintendent, 1926–27, Wagga District Hospital; House Physician 1929, House Surgeon 1930, Resident MO 1930–34, Brompton Hospital for Chest Diseases, London. DL Sussex, 1968, West Sussex, 1974. Guthrie Meml Medal, 1971. CStJ. *Publications:* various, in medical journals, 1936–56. *Recreations:* sailing, golf, photography. *Address:* c/o West Heath Cottage, King Edward VII Hospital, Midhurst, W Sussex. *Club:* Naval and Military.

TODD, Ian Pelham, FRCS; Consultant Surgeon, King Edward VII Hospital for Officers, since 1972; Consulting Surgeon: St Bartholomew's Hospital, since 1958; St Mark's Hospital, since 1954; President, Royal College of Surgeons, since 1986; *b* 23 March 1921; *s* of Alan Herepath and Constance Todd; *m* 1946, Jean Audrey Ann Noble; two *s* three *d.* *Educ:* Sherborne Sch.; St Bartholomew's Hosp. Med. Coll. (MD, DCH); Toronto Univ. (MS). MRCS, LRCP 1944; FRCS 1949. Served RAMC, Captain (AER Major). Rockefeller studentship, 1940–43; Hunterian Prof., RCS, 1953; Wellcome Res. Fellow, 1955–56. Arris and Gale Lectr, RCS, 1957–58; Gordon Watson Lectr, St Bart's Hosp., 1982; Zachary Cope Meml Lectr, RCS, 1985. Examiner in Surgery, Univ. of London, 1958–64; Ex-civilian Cons. (Proctology), RN, 1970–1986. Mem. Council, RCS, 1975–87; President: Sect. Colo-proctology, RSM, 1970–71; Med. Soc. of London, 1984–85. Fellow, Assoc. of Surgeons of GB and Ire., 1960; Hon. Member: Amer. Soc. of Colon and Rectal Surgs, 1974; RACS, 1974; Soc. Gastroent. Belge, 1964, and S Amer. socs. Lister Prize in Surgery, Toronto, 1956. FRGS 1986. Star of Jordan, 1973. *Publications:* Intestinal Stomas, 1978; (ed) Rob and Smith, Operative Surgery, vol. 3, 1982; many articles on surgery of colon and rectum in Brit. and Amer. jls. *Recreations:* ski-ing, travel, philately, music. *Address:* 149 Harley Street, W1N 2DE. *T:* 01–935 4444; 34 Chester Close North, NW1 4JE. *T:* 01–486 7776; Pumphill Cottage, Brent Pelham, Buntingford, Herts. *T:* Brent Pelham 316.

TODD, James Maclean, MA; Secretary to the Oxford University Delegacy for the Inspection and Examination of Schools and Oxford Secretary to the Oxford and Cambridge Schools Examination Board, 1964–74; Founder Fellow of St Cross College, Oxford; *b* 1907; *s* of late John Todd, Oxford, and Mary, *d* of late Robert Spottiswoode, Gattonside; *m* 1944, Janet, *d* of late Andrew Holmes, Glasgow; one *s* one *d.* *Educ:* City of Oxford School; The Queen's Coll., Oxford (Open Mathematical Scholar). First Class Mathematical Mods, 1928; 2nd Class Lit. Hum., 1930; 2nd Class Hon. School of Theology, 1931. Awarded Holwell Studentship in Theology. Assistant Master, Radley, Bryanston, Bromsgrove and Stowe. Headmaster, The High School, Newcastle, Staffs, 1948–63. *Publications:* The Ancient World, 1938; Hymns and Psalms for use in Newcastle High School (New Edn), 1951; Voices from the Past: a Classical Anthology (with Janet Maclean Todd), 1955 (Grey Arrow edn, 1960); Peoples of the Past (with Janet Maclean Todd), 1963. *Address:* Foxton Lodge, Foxton Close, Oxford OX2 8LB. *T:* Oxford 58840.

TODD, John Arthur, FRS 1948; PhD; Emeritus Reader in Geometry in the University of Cambridge; Fellow of Downing College, 1958–73, Hon. Fellow 1973; *b* 23 Aug. 1908; *s* of John Arthur and Agnes Todd. *Educ:* Liverpool Collegiate School; Trinity Coll., Cambridge. Assistant Lecturer in Mathematics, University of Manchester, 1931–37; Lecturer in Mathematics in the University of Cambridge, 1937–60, Reader in Geometry 1960–73. *Publications:* Projective and Analytical Geometry, 1947; various mathematical papers. *Address:* 10 Reddington Close, Sanderstead, South Croydon, Surrey CR2 0QZ. *T:* 01–657 4994.

TODD, John Francis James, PhD, CChem, FRSC; Senior Lecturer in Chemistry, Faculty of Natural Sciences, University of Kent at Canterbury, since 1973; *b* 20 May 1937; *o s* of late Eric Todd and Annie Lewin Todd (*née* Tinkler); *m* 1963, Mavis Georgina Lee; three *s.* *Educ:* Leeds Grammar Sch.; Leeds Univ. (BSc, Cl. I Hons Chem.). FInstMC; MIEnvSci. Research Fellow: Leeds Univ., 1962–63; Yale Univ., USA, 1963–65; University of Kent at Canterbury: Asst Lectr in Chemistry, 1965–66; Lectr in Chemistry, 1966–73; Master of Rutherford Coll., 1975–85. J. B. Cohen Prizeman, Leeds Univ., 1963; Fulbright Research Scholar, 1963–65. Chm., Canterbury and Thanet HA, 1982–86. Chairman: Kent Section of Chem. Soc., 1975; British Mass Spectroscopy Soc., 1980–81; Titular Mem., IUPAC Commn on Molecular Structures and Spectroscopy, 1979–. Mem., Kent Educn Cttee, 1983–. Member: Clergy Orphan Corp., 1985–; Council, Strode Park Foundn for the Disabled, 1986–. Governor, S Kent Coll. of Technology, 1977–. Mem., Amer. Soc. of Sigma Xi, Yale Chapter. Jt Editor, Internat. Jl of Mass Spectrometry and Ion Processes, 1985–. *Publications:* Dynamic Mass Spectrometry, vol. 4, 1975, vol. 5, 1978, vol. 6, 1981; Advances in Mass Spectrometry 1985, 1986; reviews and papers, mainly on mass spectrometry, in Jl of Chem. Soc. and Jl of Physics, etc. *Recreations:* music, travel. *Address:* University Chemical Laboratory, University of Kent at Canterbury, CT2 7NH. *T:* Canterbury 66822 (ext. 518); West Bank, 122 Whitstable Road, Canterbury, Kent CT2 8EG. *T:* Canterbury 69552.

TODD, Prof. Malcolm, FSA 1970; Professor of Archaeology, University of Exeter, since 1979; *b* 27 Nov. 1939; *s* of Wilfrid and Rose Evelyn Todd; *m* 1964, Molly Tanner; one *s* one *d.* *Educ:* Univ. of Wales (BA, DLitt); Brasenose Coll., Oxford (Dip. Class. Archaeol (Dist.)). Res. Assistant, Rheinisches Landesmus., Bonn, 1963–65; Lectr 1965–74, Sen. Lectr 1974–77, Reader in Archaeology 1977–79, Univ. of Nottingham. Vis. Prof., New York Univ., 1979; Vis. Fellow, All Souls Coll., Oxford, 1984. Vice-Pres., Roman Soc., 1985–; Mem., RCHM, 1986–; Corr. Mem., German Arch. Inst., 1977–. Editor, Britannia, 1984–. *Publications:* The Northern Barbarians, 1975, 2nd edn 1986; The Walls of Rome, 1978; Roman Britain, 1981, 2nd edn 1985; The South-West to AD 1000, 1987; papers in Germania, Britannia, Antiquaries Jl, Antiquity, Amer. Jl of Arch. *Recreations:* reading, writing, travel on foot. *Address:* The University, Exeter, Devon EX4 4QH. *T:* Exeter 264351.

TODD, Mary Williamson Spottiswoode, MA; Headmistress of Harrogate College, 1952–73; *b* 11 June 1909; *d* of John and Mary Todd, Oxford. *Educ:* Oxford High School; Lady Margaret Hall, Oxford. MA Hons Oxon. Final Hon. Sch.: Mathematics, 1932, Nat. Science, 1933; London Diploma in Theology, 1941. Various teaching posts: St Felix School, Southwold, 1933–37; Clifton High School, Bristol, 1937–39; Westonbirt School, Glos, 1939–46; Headmistress of Durham, 1946–52. *Address:* 93 Oakdale, Harrogate, North Yorks. *T:* Harrogate 66411.

TODD, Norman; *see* Todd, A. N.

TODD, Hon. Sir (Reginald Stephen) Garfield, Kt 1986; *b* 13 July 1908; *s* of late Thomas and Edith C. Todd; *m* 1932, Jean Grace Wilson; three *d.* *Educ:* Otago Univ.; Glen Leith Theol Coll., NZ; University of Witwatersrand. Superintendent Dadaya Mission, 1934–53, Chm. Governing Bd 1963–85. MP for Shabani, 1946–58; Prime Minister of S Rhodesia, 1953–58; Mem. Senate, Parlt of Zimbabwe, 1980–85. First Vice-President, World Convention of Churches of Christ, 1955–60; awarded Citation for Christian Leadership in Politics and Race Relations; former Member Executive: United Coll. of Educn, Bulawayo; Rhodesian Christian Council. Arrested by Smith regime in 1965 and confined to Hokonui Ranch for one year; arrested by Smith regime in 1972 and imprisoned, then detained, Jan 1972–June 1976. Received medal acknowledging efforts for peace and justice in Rhodesia, from Pope Paul, 1973. Holds hon. doctorates, NZ and USA. Knighted for services to NZ and Africa. *Address:* PO Dadaya, Zimbabwe. *Club:* Bulawayo.

See also Baron Acton.

TODD, Richard, (Richard Andrew Palethorpe-Todd); actor; *b* 11 June 1919; *s* of Major A. W. Palethorpe-Todd, Castlederg, Co. Tyrone, and Marvil Agar-Daly, Ballymalis Castle, Kerry; *m* 1st, 1949, Catherine Stewart Crawford Grant-Bogle (marr. diss. 1970); one *s* one *d*; 2nd, 1970, Virginia Anne Rollo Mailer; two *s.* *Educ:* Shrewsbury; privately. Entered the theatre in 1937. Served in King's Own Yorkshire Light Infantry and The Parachute Regt, 1940–46; GSO iii (Ops), 6 Airborne Div., 1944–45. Films since War of 1939–45 include: The Hasty Heart, 1949; Stage Fright, 1950; Robin Hood, 1952; Rob Roy, 1953; A Man Called Peter, 1954; The Dambusters, 1954; The Virgin Queen, 1955; Yangtse Incident, 1957; Chase a Crooked Shadow, 1957; The Long and the Short and the Tall, 1960; The Hellions, 1961; The Longest Day, 1962; Operation Crossbow, 1964; Coast of Skeletons, 1964; The Love-Ins (USA), 1967; Subterfuge, 1968; Dorian Grey, 1969; Asylum, 1972; Secret Agent 008, 1976; The House of the Long Shadows, 1982. Stage appearances include: An Ideal Husband, Strand, 1965–66; Dear Octopus, Haymarket, 1967; USA tour, The Marquise, 1972; Australia tour, Sleuth, 1973; led RSC N American tour, 1974; Equus, Australian Nat. Theatre Co., 1975; On Approval (S Africa), 1976; nat. tour of Quadrille, and The Heat of the Moment, 1977; Nightfall (S Africa), 1979; This Happy Breed (nat. tour), 1980; The Business of Murder, Duchess, 1981, Mayfair, 1982–85. Formed Triumph Theatre Productions, 1970. Past Grand Steward, Past Master, Lodge of Emulation No 21. *Publication:* Caught in the Act (autobiog.), 1986. *Recreations:* shooting and farming. *Address:* Chinham Farm, Faringdon, Oxon; Little Ponton House, near Grantham, Lincs. *Club:* Army and Navy.

TODD, Ronald; General Secretary, Transport and General Workers' Union, since 1985; *b* 11 March 1927; *s* of George Thomas Todd and Emily Todd; *m* 1945, Josephine Tarrant; one *s* two *d.* *Educ:* St Patrick's Sch., Walthamstow, E17. Served with Royal Marine Commandos; spent considerable time in China. Joined TGWU; worked at Ford Motor Co., 1954–62, latterly Dep. Convener; full-time officer of TGWU, 1962; Regional Officer, 1969; Reg. Sec., 1976; Nat. Organiser, 1978. Mem., TUC Gen. Council, 1984–. Chm. (TU side), Ford Nat. Jt Council; Jt Sec., Nat. Jt Council for Stable Staff (Workpeople's side). Mem., NEDC, 1985–. Hon. Vice-Pres., CND. *Recreations:* collecting Victorian music covers, archaeology. *Address:* Transport and General Workers' Union, Transport House, Smith Square, SW1P 3JB. *T:* 01–828 7788.

TOGANIVALU, Ratu Josua Brown, CBE 1980; JP; High Commissioner for Fiji in London, 1981–85; *b* Fiji, 2 May 1930; *m*; two *s* one *d.* *Educ:* Levuka Public Sch.; Marist Brothers Sch., Suva; Queensland Agricultural Coll.; Royal Agricultural Coll., Cirencester. With Native Lands Trust Board, 1953–71; MP Fiji, 1966–77: Minister for Lands, Mines and Mineral Resources, 1972–73; Minister for Agriculture, Fisheries and Forests, 1974–77; High Commissioner for Fiji to New Zealand, 1978–81. Represented Fiji at ACP Meeting, Guyana, 1975, ACP Meeting, Malawi, 1976, ACP/EEC Sugar Meetings, Brussels, 1976. JP (Fiji) 1968. *Recreations:* cricket, Rugby, boxing. *Address:* Box 13326, Suva, Fiji. *Clubs:* United, Defence (Fiji).

TOH CHIN CHYE, BSc, PhD, DipSc; Member of Parliament, Singapore, since 1959; *b* 10 Dec. 1921; *m.* *Educ:* Raffles Coll., Singapore; University College, London; Nat. Inst. for Medical Research, London. Reader in Physiology, 1958–64, Research Associate 1964, Vice-Chancellor, 1968–75, Univ. of Singapore. Chm., People's Action Party, 1954–81 (a Founder Mem.); Dep. Prime Minister of Singapore, 1959–68; Minister for Science and Technology, 1968–75; Minister for Health, 1975–81. Chm. Board of Governors: Singapore Polytechnic, 1959–75; Regional Inst. of Higher Educn and Develt, 1970–74; Mem. Admin. Bd, Assoc. of SE Asian Insts of Higher Learning, 1968–75. DLitt (*hc*) Singapore, 1976. *Publications:* papers in Jl of Physiology and other relevant jls. *Address:* 23 Greenview Crescent, Singapore 1128.

TOKATY, Prof. Grigori Alexandrovich; Professor Emeritus, City University; *b* North Caucasus, Russia; Ossetian by mother tongue. *Educ:* Leningrad Rabfak, 1929–30; Rykov Rabfak, Moscow Higher Technical Coll. MVTU, 1930–32; Zhukovsky Air Force Academy of Aeronautics, Moscow, 1932–37. DEng, PhD, DAeSc, CEng, CanTechSc. Lt Col, Air Force. Zhukovsky Academy: Aeronautical Research Engineer, 1937–38; Head of Aeronautics Laboratory, 1938–41; Dep. Head of Res. Dept, 1941; Lectr in Aerodynamics and Aircraft Design, 1941–45; Acting Prof. of Aviation, Moscow Engrg Inst, 1939–45; Rocket research and development, 1944–45; Rocket scientist, Berlin, 1945–47. Varied work for HM Govt, London, 1948–52; Imperial Coll., and Coll. of Aeronautics, Cranfield, 1953–56; work on theoretical rocket dynamics and orbital flight mechanics associated with Apollo programme, 1956–68; Reader in Aeronautics and Astronautics, Northampton Coll. of Advanced Technology, 1960–61; Head, 1961–75, and Prof., 1967–75, Dept of Aeronautics and Space Technology, Northampton Coll. of Advanced Technology and City Univ. Chief Scientific Adviser, WTI, 1976–78. Visiting Professor: Univs of the US, Jordan, Nigeria, Iran, Turkey, Holland. FRAeS, FAIAA, FIMA. *Publications:* numerous, including seven books: Rocketdynamics, 1961; The History of Rocket Technology (jt), 1964; A History and Philosophy of Fluid Mechanics, 1971; Cosmonautics-Astronautics, 1976; The Anatomy and Inculcation of Higher Education, 1982; articles and booklets (alone or jointly) in the fields of fluid mechanics, gasdynamics, rocketdynamics, theory and philosophy of educn, and non-scientific subjects. *Recreations:* writing, broadcasting, travelling. *Address:* Department of Aeronautics, The City University, St John Street, EC1V 4PB. *Club:* National Liberal.

TOLER; *see* Graham-Toler, family name of Earl of Norbury.

TOLER, Maj.-Gen. David Arthur Hodges, OBE 1963; MC 1945; DL; *b* 13 Sept. 1920; *s* of Major Thomas Clayton Toler, DL, JP, Swettenham Hall, Congleton; *m* 1951, Judith Mary, *d* of James William Garden, DSO, Aberdeen; one *s* one *d.* *Educ:* Stowe; Christ Church, Oxford (MA). 2nd Lieut Coldstream Guards, 1940; served War of 1939–45, N Africa and Italy; Regimental Adjt, Coldstream Guards, 1952–54; Bde Major, 4th Gds Bde, 1956–57; Adjt, RMA Sandhurst, 1958–60; Bt Lt-Col 1959; comd 2nd Bn Coldstream Guards, 1962–64; comd Coldstream Guards, 1964–65; comd 4th Guards Bde, 1965–68; Dep. Comdt, Staff Coll., Camberley, 1968–69; Dep. Comdr, Army, N

Ireland, 1969–70; GOC E Midland Dist, 1970–73; retired 1973. Dep. Hon. Col, Royal Anglian Regt (Lincolnshire) TAVR, 1979–84. Emergency Planning Officer, Lincolnshire CC, 1974–77. Chm., Lincoln Dio. Adv. Cttee, 1981–86. Pres., SSAFA, Lincs, 1978–. DL Lincs, 1982. *Recreations:* shooting, fishing, gardening. *Address:* Grove House, Fulbeck, Lincs. *Club:* Army and Navy.

TOLLEMACHE, family name of **Baron Tollemache.**

TOLLEMACHE, 5th Baron *cr* 1876; **Timothy John Edward Tollemache;** DL; Director: Tollemache & Cobbold Breweries Ltd, since 1973; NRG London Re-insurance Co. Ltd, since 1976; AMEV (UK) Ltd, since 1980, and other companies; Kanga Collections Ltd, since 1982; farmer and landowner; *b* 13 Dec. 1939; *s* of 4th Baron Tollemache, MC, DL, and of Dinah Susan, *d* of late Sir Archibald Auldjo Jamieson, KBE, MC; *S* father, 1975; *m* 1970, Alexandra Dorothy Jean, *d* of late Col Hugo Meynell, MC; two *s* one *d*. *Educ:* Eton. Commissioned into Coldstream Guards, 1959; served Kenya, Persian Gulf and Zanzibar, 1960–62; Course of Estate Management at Sandringham, Norfolk, 1962–64; Trainee, Barings Bank Ltd, 1964–65; joined Tollemache & Cobbold Breweries Ltd, 1965. Mem., BTA Marketing Cttee, 1976–79; President: Suffolk Assoc. of Local Councils, 1978–; Cheshire Cereal Soc., 1983–; E Anglian Productivity Assoc., 1984–; Chm., Historic Houses Assoc. (East Anglia Region), 1979–83. Vice Pres., Cheshire Red Cross, 1980–; Chm., St John's Council for Suffolk, 1982–. Pres., Friends of Ipswich Museums, 1980–. Chm., Bury St Edmunds Cathedral Appeal, 1986–. Patron, Suffolk Accident Rescue Service, 1983–. DL Suffolk, 1984. *Recreations:* shooting, fishing, natural history. *Heir: s* Hon. Edward John Hugo Tollemache, *b* 12 May 1976. *Address:* Helmingham Hall, Stowmarket, Suffolk IP14 6EF. *T:* Helmingham 217. *Clubs:* White's, Pratt's, Special Forces.

TOLLEMACHE, Maj.-Gen. Sir Humphry (Thomas), 6th Bt *cr* 1793; CB 1952; CBE 1950; DL; *b* 10 Aug. 1897; *s* of Sir Lyonel Tollemache, 4th Bt (*d* 1952), and Hersilia Henrietta Diana (*d* 1953), *d* of late H. R. Oliphant; *S* brother, 1969; *m* 1926, Nora Priscilla, *d* of John Taylor, Broomhill, Eastbourne; two *s* two *d*. *Educ:* Eastbourne Coll. 2nd Lieut, Royal Marines, 1915; served European War, Grand Fleet, 1916–18; War of 1939–45 in Middle East and Far East; Bt Major, 1934; Bt Lt-Col, 1942; Actg Colonel Comdt, temp. Brigadier, 1943; Colonel, 1946; Maj.-Gen., 1949; comd 3rd Mobile Naval Base Bde, 1943–44; comd Small Ops Gp, 1944–45; comd Depot, 1946–47; Director of Pay and Records, 1947–49; commanded Portsmouth Group, Royal Marines, 1949–52, Hon. Colonel Comdt, 1958–60; Colonel Comdt, Royal Marines, 1961–62; Rep. Colonel Comdt, 1961. Member Hampshire CC, 1957–74; Alderman, 1969–74. Chm., C of E Soldiers, Sailors and Airmen Clubs, 1955–65, Pres., 1974. DL Hampshire, 1965. *Heir: s* Lyonel Humphry John Tollemache JP, DL, FRICS [*b* 10 July 1931; *m* 1960, Mary Joscelyne, *e d* of William Henry Whitbread, *qv*; two *s* two *d*]. *Address:* Sheet House, Petersfield, Hants. *Club:* Army and Navy.

TOLLEY, Rev. Canon George; Curate, St Andrew's, Sharrow; Hon. Canon of Sheffield Cathedral, since 1976; *b* 24 May 1925; *s* of George and Elsie Tolley, Old Hill, Staffordshire; *m* 1947, Joan Amelia Grosvenor; two *s* one *d*. *Educ:* Halesowen Grammar Sch.; Birmingham Central Tech. Coll. (part-time); Princeton Univ., USA. BSc, MSc, PhD (London); FRSC; CBIM. Rotary Foundation Fellow, Princeton Univ., 1949–50. Head, Department of Chemistry, College of Advanced Technology, Birmingham, 1954–58; Head of Research and Experimental Dept, Allied Ironfounders Ltd, 1958–61; Principal, Worcester Tech. College, 1961–65; Senior Director of Studies, Royal Air Force Coll., Cranwell, 1965–66; Principal, Sheffield Coll. of Technology, 1966–69, Sheffield City Polytechnic, 1969–82; Manpower Services Commission: Dir, Open Tech Unit, 1983–84; Head, Quality Branch, 1984–85; Chief Officer, Review of Vocational Qualifications, 1985–86. Chairman: Council, Plastics Inst., 1959–61; Further Educn Adv. Cttee, Food, Drink and Tobacco Ind. Trng Bd, 1974–78; Bd, Further Educn Curriculum Unit, 1978–82; BTec Continuing Educn Cttee, 1983–85; Council of the Selly Oak Colls, Birmingham, 1984–; Hon. Sec., Assoc. of Colleges of Further and Higher Educn, 1975–82; Member: CNAA (Chm., Cttee for Business and Management Studies, 1972–83); Yorks and Humberside Economic Planning Council, 1976–79; RAF Trng and Educn Cttee, 1975–80; Bd of Management, Further Educn Unit, 1984–; Governing Body, Derbyshire Coll. of Higher Educn, 1984–. Member Council: PSI; RSA. Dep. Chm., S Yorks Foundn, 1986–. Sheffield Church Burgess. Hon. FCP; Hon. Fellow: Sheffield City Polytechnic, 1982; Columbia - Pacific Univ., 1983; CGLI, 1984. Hon. DSc Sheffield, 1984; DUniv Open, 1984. *Publications:* Meaning and Purpose in Higher Education, 1976; many papers relating to plastics and education in British and foreign journals. *Recreations:* music, hill walking, bird watching. *Address:* 74 Furniss Avenue, Dore, Sheffield S17 3QP. *Club:* Athenæum.

TOLLEY, Leslie John, CBE 1973; FEng 1977; Chairman, Excelsior Industrial Holdings Ltd (formerly Wheatfield Engineering Holdings), since 1983; *b* Oxford, 11 Nov. 1913; *s* of late Henry Edward Charles and Gertrude Eleanor Tolley; *m* 1939, Margaret Butterfield, *d* of late Walter Bishop and Nellie May Butterfield; one *s* one *d*. *Educ:* Oxford Sch. of Technology. FIProdE; CBIM. Gen. Manager, Nuffield Metal Products, 1941–52; Gen. Works Manager, 1952, Works Dir, 1954, Renold Chains Ltd; Gp Man. Dir, 1962, Chm., 1972–82, Renold Ltd; Chairman: Fodens Ltd, 1975–80; Francis Shaw & Co. Ltd, 1977–81; Dir, NW Regional Bd, Lloyds Bank Ltd, 1975–84. A Vice-Chm., 1973–78, Chm., 1978–80, BIM. *Recreation:* golf. *Address:* Silver Birches, Dale Brow, Prestbury, Macclesfield SK10 4BN. *T:* Prestbury 829073.

TOLOLO, Sir Alkan, KBE 1985 (CBE); High Commissioner for Papua New Guinea in Malaysia, since 1986; *m* Nerrie Tololo, MBE; two *s* two *d*. Teaching, 1957–61; supervisory teacher, 1963–65; Superintendent of Schools, 1967–69; Mem., Public Service Board, 1969–70; First Comr, PNG Teaching Service, 1971–73; Dir of Education, 1973–79; Chm., Public Services Commn, 1979–80; Consul-General Sydney, 1981; High Comr in Australia, 1983–86. Former Mem. or Chm. of numerous Boards and Cttees on education, culture and employment, PNG. Hon. LLD 1982, Hon. DTech 1982, Univ. of Papua New Guinea. *Address:* Papua New Guinea High Commission, 1 Lorong Ru Kedua, off Jalan Ru, Ampang, Kuala Lumpur, Malaysia.

TOLSTOY, Dimitry, (Dimitry Tolstoy-Miloslavsky), QC 1959; Barrister-at-Law; *b* 8 Nov. 1912; *s* of late Michael Tolstoy-Miloslavsky and Eileen May Hamshaw; *m* 1st, 1934, Frieda Mary Wicksteed (marr. diss.); one *s* one *d*; 2nd, 1943, Natalie Deytrikh; one *s* one *d*. *Educ:* Wellington; Trinity Coll., Cambridge. President of Cambridge Union, 1935. Called to Bar, Gray's Inn, 1937. Lecturer in Divorce to Inns of Court, 1952–68. *Publications:* Tolstoy on Divorce, 1946–7th edn 1971; articles in legal periodicals. *Address:* c/o Barclays Bank, High Street, Guernsey, CI.

TOMALIN, Claire; writer; *b* 20 June 1933; *d* of Emile Delavenay and Muriel Herbert; *m* 1955, Nicholas Osborne Tomalin (*d* 1973); one *s* two *d* (and one *d* decd). *Educ:* Hitchin Girls' Grammar Sch.; Dartington Hall Sch.; Newnham Coll., Cambridge (MA). Publishers' reader and editor, Messrs Heinemann, Hutchinson, Cape, 1955–67; Evening Standard, 1967–68; New Statesman: Asst Literary Editor, 1968–70; Literary Editor, 1974–77; Literary Editor, Sunday Times, 1979–. FRSL. *Publications:* The Life and Death of Mary Wollstonecraft, 1974, paperback 1977; Shelley and his World, 1980; Parents and Children, 1981; Literary journalism. *Address:* 57 Gloucester Crescent, NW1 7EG. *T:* 01-485 6481.

TOMBS, Sir Francis (Leonard), Kt 1978; FEng 1977; Chairman: Turner & Newall, since 1982; Rolls-Royce, since 1985 (Director, since 1982); Director: N. M. Rothschild & Sons, since 1981; Shell-UK, since 1983; *b* 17 May 1924; *s* of Joseph and Jane Tombs; *m* 1949, Marjorie Evans; three *d*. *Educ:* Elmore Green Sch., Walsall; Birmingham Coll. of Technology. BSc (Econ); FIMechE; FIEE; FInstE. GEC, 1939–45; Birmingham Corp., 1946–47; British Electricity Authority, Midlands, then Central Electricity Authority, Merseyside and N Wales, 1947–57; GEC, Erith, 1957–65; C. A. Parsons, Erith, 1965–68; James Howden & Godfrey Ltd, 1968–69; successively Dir of Engrg, Dep. Chm., Chm., South of Scotland Electricity Bd, 1969–77; Chm., Electricity Council, 1977–80. Chm., Weir Group, 1981–83. Member: Nature Conservancy Council, 1978–; Standing Commn on Energy and the Environment, 1978–; SERC, 1982–85; ACARD, 1984– (Chm., 1985–); Chm., Engrg Council, 1985–. Pres., IEE, 1981–82. Chm., Assoc. of British Orchestras, 1982–86. Hon. FIChemE 1985; Hon. FICE 1986. Hon. LLD Strathclyde, 1976; Hon. D(Tech) Loughborough, 1979; Hon. DSc: Aston, 1979; Lodz, Poland, 1980; Cranfield, 1985; DSc(Eng) QUB, 1986; Hon. DLitt Bradford, 1986. *Recreations:* music, golf, sailing. *Address:* Honington Lodge, Honington, Shipston-upon-Stour, Warwickshire CV36 5AA.

TOMKINS, Sir Edward Emile, GCMG 1975 (KCMG 1969; CMG 1960); CVO 1957; Grand Officiér, Légion d'Honneur, 1984; HM Diplomatic Service, retired; HM Ambassador to France, 1972–75; *b* 16 Nov. 1915; *s* of late Lt-Col E. L. Tomkins; *m* 1955, Gillian Benson; one *s* two *d*. *Educ:* Ampleforth Coll.; Trinity Coll., Cambridge. Foreign Office, 1939. Military service, 1940–43. HM Embassy, Moscow, 1944–46; Foreign Office, 1946–51; HM Embassy, Washington, 1951–54; HM Embassy, Paris, 1954–59; Foreign Office, 1959–63; HM Embassy, Bonn, 1963–67; HM Embassy, Washington, 1967–69; Ambassador to the Netherlands, 1970–72. Mem., Bucks CC, 1977–85. *Address:* Winslow Hall, Winslow, Bucks. *T:* Winslow 2323. *Club:* Garrick.

TOMKINS, Rt. Rev. Oliver Stratford, MA, DD, LLD; *b* 9 June 1908; *s* of Rev. Leopold Charles Fellows Tomkins and Mary Katie (*née* Stratford); *m* 1939, Ursula Mary Dunn; one *s* three *d*. *Educ:* Trent Coll; Christ's Coll, Cambridge; Westcott House, Cambridge. Asst Gen. Sec., Student Christian Movement, 1933–40, and Editor, Student Movement Magazine, 1937–40. Deacon, 1935; Priest, 1936; Vicar of Holy Trinity, Millhouses, Sheffield, 1940–45; an Associate Gen. Sec. World Council of Churches and Sec. of its Commission on Faith and Order, 1945–52; Warden of Lincoln Theological College (Scholae Cancellarii) and Canon and Prebend, Lincoln Cathedral, 1953–59; Bishop of Bristol, 1959–75. Mem. Central Cttee, World Council of Churches, 1968–75. DD (*hon. causa*) Edinburgh University, 1953; Hon. LLD Bristol, 1975. *Publications:* The Wholeness of the Church, 1949; The Church in the Purpose of God, 1950. Editor and contributor The Universal Church in God's Design, 1948; Intercommunion, 1951; (ed) Faith and Order (Lund Conference Report), 1953; Life of E. S. Woods, Bishop of Lichfield, 1957; A Time for Unity, 1964; Guarded by Faith, 1971. *Recreation:* gardening. *Address:* 14 St George's Square, Worcester WR1 1HX. *T:* Worcester 25330.

See also Very Rev. T. W. I. Cleasby.

TOMKINSON, John Stanley, CBE 1981; FRCS; Hon. Secretary General, International Federation of Gynaecology and Obstetrics (Secretary General, 1976–85); Obstetric Surgeon, Queen Charlotte's Maternity Hospital, 1953–79; Obstetric and Gynæcological Surgeon, Guy's Hospital, 1953–79; Gynæcological Surgeon, Chelsea Hospital for Women, 1971–79; *b* 8 March 1916; *o s* of Harry Stanley and Katie Mills Tomkinson, Stafford; *m* 1954, Barbara Marie Pilkington; one *s* one *d* (and one *s* decd). *Educ:* Rydal Sch.; Birmingham University Medical Sch.; St Thomas' Hospital. MRCS, LRCP 1941; MB, ChB Birmingham 1941; FRCS 1949; MRCOG 1952; FRCOG 1967. Medal in Surgery and Priestley-Smith Prize, Birmingham. Demonstrator of Anatomy, Birmingham Medical School, 1946; appointments in General Surgery, Obst. and Gynæcol., at Birmingham and Midland Hosp. for Women, Birmingham Maternity Hospital, and Queen Elizabeth Hospital, Birmingham, 1941–42 and 1947–52; Registrar, Professorial Unit in General Surgery and Professorial Unit in Obst. and Gynæcol., Birmingham; Chief Asst, Chelsea Hospital for Women, 1952–53; Resident Obstetrician and Tutor in Obstetrics (Postgrad. Inst. of Obst. and Gynæcol. of University of London), Queen Charlotte's Maternity Hospital, 1952–53. Travelling Fellow (Guy's Hospital), USA and Canada, 1954. Vis. Prof., Spanish Hospital, Mexico City, 1972. Consultant Advr in Obstetrics and Gynæcol., Min. of Health, later DHSS, 1966–81; Consultant, WHO, 1981–. William Hawksworth Meml Lectr, 1969; Sir Winston Churchill Meml Lectr, Canterbury, 1970; Edward Sharp Meml Lectr, 1977; Foundn Lectr, Amer. Assoc. of Gynaecol. and Obstetrics, 1978; Charter Day Lectr, Nat. Maternity Hosp. Dublin, 1979. Examiner for: Univs of Oxford, Cambridge, London, Birmingham, QUB; Univs of Haile Selassie I in Ethiopia, East Africa in Uganda, El Fateh in Tripoli, Singapore; RCOG; Conjoint Examining Bd, Central Midwives Bd. FRSM. Member: Gynæcological Club of Great Britain; Birmingham and Midland Obst. and Gynæcol. Society; Central Midwives Board; Member Council: RCOG; RCS; section of Obstetrics and Gynæcology, RSM; Mem. Exec. Council, Internat. Fedn of Obstetrics and Gynaecology; Past Chm., Jt Study Working Gp of Internat. Confedn of Midwives and Internat. Fedn of Gynaecology and Obstetrics. Jt Editor, Report on Confidential Enquiries into Maternal Deaths in England and Wales, 1964–66, 1967–69, 1970–72, 1973–75, 1976–78. Foreign Member, Continental Gynæcol. Society (of America). Hon. Fellow: Soc. of Gynaecologists and Obstetricians of Colombia, 1972; Nigerian Soc. Obst. and Gynaecol., 1977; Italian Soc. Obst. and Gynaecol., 1978; Romanian Soc. Obst. and Gynaecol., 1978; South African Soc. Obst. and Gynaecol., 1980; Spanish Soc. Obst. and Gynaecol., 1981.; Polish Soc. Obst. and Gynaecol., 1984 (Hon. Mem. 1985); Canadian Soc. Obst. and Gynaecol., 1984; Brazilian Soc. Obst. and Gynaecol., 1985; Jordanian Soc. Obst. and Gynaecol., 1985; Korean Soc. Obst. and Gynaecol., 1986. Surgeon Lieut, RNVR, 1942–46. Copernicus Medal, Copernicus Acad. of Medicine, Cracow, 1985; Medal of Polish Nation for Aid and Co-operation in Medicine, 1985. *Publications:* (ed) Queen Charlotte's Textbook of Midwifery; papers of general surgical, obstetric and gynæcological interest. *Recreations:* fly-fishing, painting, and the arts generally. *Address:* Keats House, Guy's Hospital, SE1. *T:* 01-407 7600, ext. 3090; 140 Priory Lane, SW15. *T:* 01-876 2006; Rose Cottage, Up Somborne, Hants SO20 6QY. *Clubs:* Athenæum, Flyfishers', MCC.

TOMKYS, (William) Roger, CMG 1984; HM Diplomatic Service; Ambassador to Syria, since 1984; *b* 15 March 1937; *s* of late William Arthur and Edith Tomkys; *m* 1963, Margaret Jean Abbey; one *s* one *d*. *Educ:* Bradford Grammar Sch.; Balliol Coll., Oxford (Domus Scholar; 1st cl. Hons Lit. Hum.). Entered Foreign Service, 1960; MECAS, 1960; 3rd Sec., Amman, 1962; 2nd Sec., FCO, 1964; 1st Sec., Head of Chancery, Benghazi, 1967; Planning Staff, FCO, 1969; Head of Chancery, Athens, 1972; Counsellor, seconded to Cabinet Office, 1975; Head of Near East and North Africa Dept, FCO, 1977–80; Counsellor, Rome, 1980–81; Ambassador to Bahrain, 1981–84. Commendatore dell'Ordine al Merito, 1980; Order of Bahrain, 1st cl., 1984. *Address:* c/o Foreign and

Commonwealth Office, SW1A 2AH. *Clubs:* United Oxford & Cambridge University; Royal Blackheath Golf.

TOMLIN, Eric Walter Frederick, CBE 1965 (OBE 1959); FRSL; author; *b* 30 Jan. 1913; *s* of Edgar Herbert Tomlin and Mary (*née* Dexter); *m* 1st, 1945, Margaret Stuart (marr. diss. 1952); one *s*; 2nd, 1974, Judith, *yr d* of late Lt-Gen. Sir Euan Miller, KCB, KBE, DSO, MC. *Educ:* Whitgift; Brasenose Coll., Oxford (BA degrees in PPE and Mod. Hist.); MA (Oxon), 1958; MA (Cantab), 1972. Asst Master: Sloane Sch., Chelsea, 1936–38; Marlborough, 1939; Resident Tutor, Wilts, Bristol Univ. Bd of Extra-Mural Studies, 1939–40; joined Local Defence Volunteers, 1940; British Council Lecturer, Staff Coll. Baghdad and RMC, 1940–41; worked in Information Dept, British Embassy, Baghdad, 1941; British Council: Ankara, 1941–42; Regional Dir, S Turkey, 1942–45; Headquarters London, 1945–47 and 1952–56; Paris, 1947–51; Rep. in Turkey and Cultural Attaché British Embassy, Ankara, 1956–61; Rep. in Japan and Cultural Counsellor British Embassy, Tokyo, 1961–67; Leverhulme Foundn Fellow, 1967–69; British Council Rep. in France, and Cultural Attaché, British Embassy, Paris, 1969–71. Bollingen Foundn Fellow and Vis. Prof., Univ. of Southern California, 1961; Vis. Fellow, Univ. Coll., Cambridge, 1971–72; Vis. Prof., Nice, 1972–74. Fellow: Royal Asiatic Soc.; Inst. of Cultural Research; Life Mem., Royal Inst. of Cornwall; Associate Mem., Magic Circle; Hon. Mem., British Council; Pres., Royal Soc. of St George, Tokyo, 1965; Vice-Pres., The Dickens Fellowship, 1985–. Member: Exec. Cttee, English Centre, Internat. PEN, 1985–; Council, Philosophical Soc., 1986–. *Publications:* Turkey, the Modern Miracle, 1939; Life in Modern Turkey, 1946; The Approach to Metaphysics, 1947; The Western Philosophers, 1950; The Eastern Philosophers, 1952; Simone Weil, 1954; R. G. Collingwood, 1954; Wyndham Lewis, 1955; Living and Knowing, 1955; La Vie et l'Oeuvre de Bertrand Russell, 1963; (ed) T. S. Eliot: a Tribute from Japan, 1965; Tokyo Essays, 1967; Wyndham Lewis: an Anthology of his Prose, 1969; (ed) Charles Dickens, a Centenary Volume, 1969; Japan, 1973; Man, Time and the New Science, 1973; The Last Country, 1974; (ed) Arnold Toynbee: a selection from his works, 1978; The World of St Boniface, 1980; In Search of St Piran, 1982; The Church of St Morwenna and St John the Baptist, Morwenstow: a guide and history, 1982; Psyche, Culture and the New Science, 1985; Philosophers of East and West, 1986; The Tall Trees of Marshland: reflections on life and time, 1986; T. S. Eliot: a friendship, 1987; contribs to Criterion, Scrutiny, Times Literary Supplement, Economist, Arts Review, PN Review, Agenda, Temenos, and many foreign reviews, etc. *Recreations:* travel, reading, music. *Address:* 31 Redan Street, W14. *T:* 01–602 6414. *Clubs:* Athenæum; Union Society (Oxford).

TOMLINSON, Prof. (Alfred) Charles, FRSL; Professor of English, University of Bristol, since 1982; *b* 8 Jan. 1927; *s* of Alfred Tomlinson and May Lucas; *m* 1948, Brenda Raybould; two *d. Educ:* Longton High School; Queens' Coll., Cambridge (MA); Royal Holloway and Bedford Colls, Univ. of London (MA). Lecturer, 1957–68, Reader in English poetry, 1968–82, Bristol Univ. Visiting Prof., Univ. of New Mexico, 1962–63; O'Connor Prof., Colgate Univ., NY, 1967–68; Vis. Fellow, Princeton Univ., 1981. Arts Council Poetry Panel, 1964–66; Witter Bynner Lectr, Univ. of New Mexico, 1976; Clark Lectr, Cambridge, 1982. Exhibition of Graphics: Ely House, OUP, London, 1972; Clare Coll., Cambridge, 1975; Arts Council touring exhibn, 1978–80. Hon. Fellow, Queens' Coll., Cambridge, 1975. FRSL 1975. Hon. DLitt: Keele, 1981; Colgate, 1981; New Mexico, 1986. Cholmondeley Award, 1979. *Publications: poetry:* Relations and Contraries, 1951; The Necklace, 1955, repr. 1966; Seeing is Believing, 1960 (US 1958); A Peopled Landscape, 1963; Poems, 1964; American Scenes, 1966; The Poem as Initiation, (US) 1968; The Way of a World, 1969; Poems, in Penguin Modern Poets, 1969; Renga (France) 1970, (US) 1972, (England) 1979; Written on Water, 1972; The Way In, 1974; Selected Poems, 1978; The Shaft, 1978; (with Octavio Paz) Air Born, 1981 (Mexico 1979); The Flood, 1981; Notes from New York and other Poems, 1984; Collected Poems, 1985; *prose:* Some Americans: a personal record, 1980 (US); Poetry and Metamorphosis, 1983; *graphics:* Words and Images, 1972; In Black and White, 1975; Eden, 1985; *translations:* (with Henry Gifford): Versions from Fyodor Tyutchev, 1960; Castilian Ilexes: Versions from Antonio Machado, 1963; Ten Versions from Trilce by César Vallejo, (US) 1970; Translations, 1983; *edited:* Marianne Moore: A Collection of Critical Essays, (US) 1969; William Carlos Williams: A Collection of Critical Essays, 1972; William Carlos Williams: Selected Poems, 1976, rev. edn (US) 1985; Octavio Paz: Selected Poems, 1979; The Oxford Book of Verse in English Translation, 1980; contribs to: Essays in Criticism, Hudson Review, Poetry (Chicago), Poetry Nation Review, Sewanee Review, Times Lit. Supp. *Recreations:* music, walking. *Address:* c/o English Department, University of Bristol, Bristol BS8 1TB.

TOMLINSON, Prof. Bernard Evans, CBE 1981; MD, FRCP, FRCPath; Chairman, Northern Regional Health Authority, since 1982; Emeritus Professor of Pathology, University of Newcastle upon Tyne, since 1985; Consultant Neuropathologist, Newcastle Health Authority (formerly Area Health Authority), since 1976; *b* 13 July 1920; *s* of James Arthur Tomlinson and Doris Mary (*née* Evans); *m* 1944, Betty Oxley; one *s* one *d. Educ:* Brunts Sch., Mansfield; University Coll. and University Coll. Hosp., London (BS 1943, MD 1962). FRCP 1965; FRCPath 1964. Trainee Pathologist, EMS, 1943–47; served RAMC as Specialist Pathologist, 1947–49 (Major). Newcastle upon Tyne General Hospital: Sen. Registrar, Pathology, 1949–50; Consultant Pathologist, 1950–53; Sen. Consultant Pathologist, 1953–82; Hon. Lectr in Path., Univ. of Newcastle upon Tyne, 1960–71, Hon. Prof., 1973–85. *Publications:* articles and book chapters on neuropath., partic. on path. of brain injury, brain changes in old age and on dementia. *Recreations:* gardening, golf, music, walking. *Address:* Greyholme, Wynbury Road, Low Fell, Gateshead, Tyne and Wear NE9 6TS.

TOMLINSON, David (Cecil MacAlister); Actor; *b* 7 May 1917; *s* of C. S. Tomlinson, Solicitor, Folkestone, Kent, and F. E. Tomlinson (*née* Sinclair-Thomson); *m* Audrey Freeman, actress; four *s. Educ:* Tonbridge Sch. Guardsman, Grenadier Guards, 1935–36; served War of 1939–45, Flight Lieut, Pilot, RAF; demobilised, 1946. Chief roles include: Henry, in The Little Hut, Lyric, Aug. 1950–Sept. 1953; Clive, in All for Mary, Duke of York's, June 1954–May 1955; David, in Dear Delinquent, Westminster and Aldwych, June 1957–July 1958; Tom, in The Ring of Truth, Savoy, July 1959; Robert in Boeing Boeing, Apollo, 1962; acted and directed: Mother's Boy (Nero), Globe, 1964; A Friend Indeed, Cambridge, 1966; The Impossible Years, Cambridge, 1966; On the Rocks (Prime Minister), Dublin Festival, 1969; A Friend Indeed, and A Song at Twilight, South Africa, 1973–74; The Turning Point, Duke of York's, 1974. First appeared in films, 1939; since then has appeared, in leading roles, in over 50 films. *Recreation:* antique collecting. *Address:* Brook Cottage, Mursley, Bucks. *T:* Mursley 213. *Club:* Travellers'.

TOMLINSON, Sir (Frank) Stanley, KCMG 1966 (CMG 1954); HM Diplomatic Service, retired; *b* 21 March 1912; *m* 1959, Nancy, *d* of late E. Gleeson-White and Mrs Gleeson-White, Sydney, Australia. *Educ:* High Pavement Sch., Nottingham; University College, Nottingham. Served in various consular posts in Japan, 1935–41; Saigon, 1941–42; United States, 1943; Washington, 1945; Acting Consul-General, Manila, 1945, Chargé d'Affaires, 1946; Foreign Office, 1947; Washington, 1951; Imperial Defence Coll., 1954; Counsellor and Head, SE Asia Dept, 1955; Dep. Commandant, Berlin, 1958;

Minister, UK Permanent Delegation to NATO, 1961–64; Consul General, New York, 1964–66; British High Comr, Ceylon, 1966–69; Dep. Under-Sec. of State, FCO, 1969–72. Hon. LLD Nottingham, 1970. *Recreations:* trout fishing, oenophily, reading. *Address:* 32 Long Street, Devizes, Wilts. *Club:* Oriental.

TOMLINSON, John; operatic bass; *b* 22 Sept. 1946; *s* of Rowland and Ellen Tomlinson; *m* 1969, Moya (*née* Joel); one *s* two *d. Educ:* Manchester Univ. (BSc Civil Engrg); Royal Manchester Coll. of Music. Since beginning career with Glyndebourne in 1970, has sung over 100 operatic bass roles with ENO and Royal Opera House, Covent Garden, and in Geneva, Lisbon, Milan, Copenhagen, Amsterdam, Stuttgart, Paris, Bordeaux, Avignon, Aix-en-Provence, Orange, San Diego, San Francisco, Pittsburgh and Vancouver. *Address:* c/o Music International, 13 Ardilaun Road, Highbury, N5 2QR. *T:* 01–359 5183.

TOMLINSON, John Edward; Member (Lab) Birmingham West, since 1984, and Chief Whip, Socialist Group, since 1985, European Parliament; *b* 1 Aug. 1939; *s* of Frederick Edwin Tomlinson, headmaster, and Doris Mary Tomlinson; *m* 1963, Marianne Solveig Sommar, Stockholm; three *s* one *d. Educ:* Westminster City Sch.; Co-operative Coll., Loughborough; Nottingham Univ. (Dip. Polit. Econ. Social Studies); MA (Industrial Relations) Warwick, 1982. Sec., Sheffield Co-operative Party, 1961–68; Head of Research Dept, AUEW, 1968–70; Lectr in Industrial Relations, 1970–74. MP (Lab) Meriden, Feb. 1974–1979; PPS to Prime Minister, 1975–76; Parly Under-Sec. of State, FCO, 1976–79, and ODM, 1977–79. Sen. Lectr in Industrial Relations and Management, later Hd of Social Studies, Solihull Coll. of Tech., 1979–84. Contested (Lab) Warwicks N, 1983. *Publication:* Left, Right: the march of political extremism in Britain, 1981. *Address:* 23 Meriden Road, Hampton-in-Arden, near Solihull, W Midlands. *Club:* West Bromwich Labour.

TOMLINSON, Prof. John Race Godfrey, CBE 1983; MA; Professor of Education and Director, Institute of Education, University of Warwick, since Jan. 1985; *b* 24 April 1932; *s* of John Angell Tomlinson and Beatrice Elizabeth Race Godfrey; *m* 1954, Audrey Mavis Barrett; two *s* two *d. Educ:* Stretford Grammar Sch.; Manchester Univ. (MA); London Inst. of Historical Research. Flt Lt, RAF, 1955–58. Teaching, 1958–60; Admin. Asst, Salop LEA, 1960–63; Asst Educn Officer, Lancs LEA, 1963–67; Dep. Dir of Educn, Cheshire LEA, 1967–72; Dir of Educn, Cheshire CC, 1972–84. Chairman: Schools Council, 1978–81; NICEC, 1985–; Arts in Education Project, SCDC, 1985–. Member: Court Cttee on Child Health Services, 1973–76; Gulbenkian enquiries into Drama, Music and Dance, 1974–78; Founder Chm., Further Educn Curriculum Review and Develt Unit, 1976; Member: Special Programmes Bd, MSC, 1977–82; Delegacy for Continuing Educn, Open Univ., 1978–81; Study Commn on the Family, 1978–83; Adv. Cttee on Supply and Trng of Teachers, 1979–82; Educn Advr, RNCM, 1972–85. Chm., Exec. Cttee and Trustees, Nat. Schs Curriculum Award, 1982–; Mem., Educn Cttee, Goldsmiths' Co., 1982–. Pres., Soc. of Educn Officers, 1982; Trustee, Community Service Volunteers, 1981–; Governor, Chetham's Sch., Manchester, 1984–. Hon. Prof., Dept of Educn, Keele Univ., 1981–84. Lectures: Wilfred Fish Meml, GDC, 1978; Charles Gittens Meml, Univ. of Wales, 1980; Lockyer, RCP, 1980; Schools Council, BAAS, 1981. FRSA 1976 (Mem. Council, 1982–; Vice-Pres., 1986); FBIM (MBIM 1976); FCP 1980. Hon. RNCM 1980. *Publications:* Additional Grenville Papers 1763–65, 1962; (ed) The Changing Government of Education, 1986; articles in various jls. *Recreations:* family and garden, music and walking, a relentless search for good bitter. *Address:* Institute of Education, University of Warwick, Coventry CV4 7AL; Barn House, 76 Birmingham Road, Allesley, Coventry CV5 9GX. *Clubs:* Army and Navy, Royal Over-Seas League.

TOMLINSON, Maj.-Gen. Michael John, CB 1981; OBE 1973 (MBE 1964); Secretary, The Dulverton Trust, since 1984; Director Royal Artillery, 1981–84, retired; *b* 20 May 1929; *s* of Sidney Tomlinson and Rose Hodges; *m* 1955, Patricia, *d* of late Lt-Col A. Rowland; one *s* one *d. Educ:* Skinners' Sch.; Royal Military Academy. Commissioned, RA, 1949; served in Brunei (despatches, 1962); GSO2 to Dir of Ops Borneo, 1962–64; DAMS, MoD, 1966–68; GSO1, Staff Coll. Camberley, 1968–70; CO, 2 Field Regt RA, 1970–72; Col GS, Staff Coll. Camberley, 1972–73; CRA 3rd Div., 1973–75; Student, RCDS, 1976; Dep. Mil. Sec. (B), MoD, 1976–78; Dir of Manning, Army, 1978–79; Vice-Adjt Gen., 1979–81. Col Comdt, RA, 1982–; Hon. Colonel: 2 Field Regt, RA; 104 Regt RA (Volunteers), 1985–. FBIM 1984; FRSA 1985. *Recreations:* music, gardening, wine-making. *Address:* The Dulverton Trust, 30A St James's Square, SW1Y 4JH. *Club:* Army and Navy.

TOMLINSON, Sir Stanley; *see* Tomlinson, Sir F. S.

TOMPKINS, Prof. Frederick Clifford, FRS 1955; Professor in Physical Chemistry, Imperial College of Science and Technology, SW7, 1959–77, now Emeritus; Editor and Secretary of Faraday Division of The Chemical Society (formerly The Faraday Society), 1950–77, President, 1978; *b* 29 Aug. 1910; *m* 1936, Catherine Livingstone Macdougal; one *d. Educ:* Yeovil Sch.; Bristol Univ. Asst Lectr, King's Coll., Strand, 1934–37; Lectr and Senior Lectr, Natal Univ., Natal, S Africa, 1937–46; ICI Fellow, King's College, Strand, 1946–47; Reader in Physical Chemistry, Imperial College of Science and Technology, 1947; Hon. ARCS 1964. Hon. DSc Bradford, 1975. *Publications:* Chemisorption of Gases on Metals, 1978; contributions to Proc. Royal Society, Journal Chem. Soc., Trans Faraday Soc., Jl Chem. Physics, Zeitung Elektrochem. *Address:* 9 St Helens Close, Southsea, Portsmouth, Hants. *T:* Portsmouth 731901.

TOMPKINS, (Granville) Richard (Francis); Founder, Chairman and Managing Director: Green Shield Trading Stamp Co. Ltd, since 1958; Argos Distributors Ltd, 1973–79; *b* 15 May 1918; *s* of late Richard and Ethel May Tompkins; *m* 1970, Elizabeth Nancy Duke (Cross of Merit with Crown Order, Order Pro Merito Melitensi SMO Malta; Comdr, Order of Holy Cross of Jerusalem, Bailiwick of St Louis); one *d* (and two *d* of a former marriage). *Educ:* Pakeman St LCC Sch., London, N7. Engineering Draughtsman, Home Forces, 1939–46; founded several companies in printing and advertising, 1945. Patron: The Tompkins Foundn, 1980; Regimental Museum of the Buffs—the East Kent Regt, 1985; Floral Lunch, Forces Help Soc. and Lord Roberts Workshops, 1985; SSAFA Centenary Dinner, London, 1985; Friend, Duke of Edinburgh's Award, 1986. Vice-Pres., City of London Lifeboat and RNLI Selsey, 1985. Liveryman, Glaziers' and Painters of Glass Co., 1986; Hon. Freeman, Painter–Stainers' Co., 1984. Hon. DH Lewis Univ., Chicago, 1985. Hon. FRCP, 1985. OStJ 1984; Knight Grand Cross of Merit, Order Pro Merito Melitensi SMO Malta, 1984; Grand Cross, Order of Holy Cross of Jerusalem, Bailiwick of Saint Louis, 1985; Grand Comdr, Noble Companions of the Swan, 1985. *Recreations:* travel, theatre, golf. *Address:* 7 Belgrave Square, SW1.

TOMS, Carl, OBE 1969; First Head of Design, and Associate Director, for the Young Vic at the National Theatre, since 1970; *b* 29 May 1927. *Educ:* High Oakham Sch., Mansfield, Nottingham; Mansfield College of Art; Royal Coll. of Art; Old Vic Sch. Designing for theatre, films, opera, ballet, etc, on the London stage, 1957–; also for productions at Glyndebourne, Edinburgh Festival, Chichester Festival, and Aldeburgh (world première of Midsummer Night's Dream, 1960). Theatre designs include: Vivat! Vivat Regina!, Chichester and London, 1970, NY 1972; Sherlock Holmes, London, 1974, NY 1974 (Tony Award and Drama Desk Award for Theatre Design); Travesties, London, 1974,

NY 1975, Vienna Burgtheater, 1976; Long Day's Journey into Night, LA 1977; Man and Superman, Malvern Festival and London, 1977; The Devil's Disciple, LA 1977, NY 1978; Look After Lulu, Chichester, 1978, Haymarket, 1978; Night and Day, Phoenix, 1978, NY, 1979; Stage Struck, Vaudeville, 1979; Windy City, Victoria Palace, 1982; The Real Thing, Strand, 1982; The Winslow Boy, Lyric, 1983; A Patriot for Me, Chichester and Haymarket, 1983, LA, 1984 (Hollywood Dramalogue Critics Award); The Hothouse, Vienna Burgtheater, 1983; Jeeves Takes Charge, NY, 1983; Hay Fever, Queen's, 1983; The Aspern Papers, 1984; Jumpers, Aldwych, 1985; The Dragon's Tail, Apollo, 1985; Blithe Spirit, Vaudeville, 1986. Designs for the Royal Opera House, Covent Garden, include: Gala perf. for State Visit of King and Queen of Nepal, 1960; Iphigénie en Tauride, 1961; Ballet Imperial, 1963; Die Frau ohne Schatten (costumes), 1967; Fanfare for Europe, 1973; Queen's Silver Jubilee Gala, 1977; Fanfare for Elizabeth, 1986; for London Festival Ballet: Swan Lake, 1982; for Sadler's Wells: Cenerentola, 1959; The Barber of Seville, 1960; Our Man in Havana, 1963; for Nat. Theatre: Edward II, Love's Labour's Lost, 1968; Cyrano de Bergerac, 1970; For Services Rendered, 1979; Playbill, The Provok'd Wife, 1980 (SWET Designer of the Year award); The Second Mrs Tanqueray, On the Razzle, 1981; Rough Crossing, 1984; Brighton Beach Memoirs, Dalliance, The Magistrate, 1986; for RSC: The Happiest Days of Your Life, 1984; for Vienna Nat. Theatre: Travesties, 1977; She Stoops to Conquer, 1978; Betrayal, 1978; The Guardsman, 1979; Night and Day, 1980; for Vienna State Opera: Macbeth, 1982; Faust, 1985; for NY City Opera: Die Meistersinger von Nürnberg, 1975; The Marriage of Figaro, 1977; The Voice of Ariadne, 1977; Der Freischutz, 1981; for NY Metropolitan Opera: Thais, 1978; for San Diego Opera Co.: Norma, 1976; La Traviata, 1976; The Merry Widow, 1977; Hamlet, 1978; Romeo and Juliet, 1982; for San Francisco Opera: Peter Grimes, 1973; Thais, 1976; The Italian Girl in Algiers (costumes), Geneva, 1984; Lucia di Lammermoor (costumes), Cologne Opera, 1985; Oberon, Edinburgh Fest. and Frankfurt, 1986. Other companies and theatres designed for include Old Vic, Young Vic, Welsh Nat. Opera, NY State Opera. Completed re-designing of Theatre Royal, Windsor, 1965; re-designing of Theatre Royal, Bath, 1982; design consultant for Investiture of Prince of Wales, Caernarvon Castle, 1969. Has designed sets and costumes for numerous films; work has incl. decoration of restaurants, hotels, houses, etc; has also designed exhibns, programmes, cards, etc. *Publications:* Winter's Tale (designs for stage prod.), 1975; Scapino (designs for stage prod.), 1975. *Recreations:* gardening, travel. *Address:* The White House, Beaumont, near Wormley, Broxbourne, Herts EN10 7QJ. *T:* Hoddesdon 63961.

TOMS, Edward Ernest; Director, Porcelain & Pictures Ltd (Picture Framers), since 1983; *b* 10 Dec. 1920; *s* of Alfred William and Julia Harrington Toms; *m* 1946, Veronica Rose, Dovercourt, Essex; three *s* one *d. Educ:* St Boniface's Coll.; Staff Coll., Camberley (psc), Nat. Defence Coll. (jssc). War service 1939–45; Captain Seaforth Highlanders; Special Forces, W Desert, Italy, Balkans, NW Europe; Regular Army, 1946, Seaforth Highlanders and QO Highlanders; Brigade Major, Berlin, 1959–61; Col GS, 1967–69. Principal, Home Civil Service, 1969; Asst Sec., Dept of Employment, 1973; seconded to Diplomatic Service as Counsellor, Bonn and Vienna, 1977–81; Internat. Labour Advr, FCO, 1981–83. *Publications:* infrequent contribs to Punch and Pick of Punch. *Recreation:* hill-walking (founder Mem., Aberdeen Mountain Rescue Assoc., 1964). *Address:* c/o Clydesdale Bank, 5 Castle Street, Aberdeen. *Clubs:* Army and Navy, Special Forces.

TOMSETT, Alan Jeffrey, OBE 1974; Finance Director, Associated British Ports Holdings PLC, since 1983; chartered accountant; *b* 3 May 1922; *s* of Maurice Jeffrey Tomsett and Edith Sarah (*née* Mackelworth); *m* 1948, Joyce May Hill; one *s* one *d. Educ:* Trinity School of John Whitgift, Croydon; Univ. of London (BCom). JDipMA. Hodgson Harris & Co., Chartered Accountants, London, 1938. Served War, with RAF, 1941–46 (Middle East, 1942–45). Smallfield Rawlins & Co., Chartered Accountants, London, 1951; Accountant and Asst Sec. (later Sec.), Northern Mercantile & Investment Corp. Ltd, 1955; William Baird & Co. Ltd, 1962–63. British Transport Docks Board, later Associated British Ports: Dep. Chief Accountant, 1963; Chief Accountant, 1964; Financial Controller, 1970; Bd Mem., 1974–; Finance Dir, 1974–85. FCA, FCMA, IPFA, FCIS, FCIT (Hon. Treasurer, 1982–). *Address:* 102 Ballards Way, Croydon, Surrey CR0 5RG. *T:* 01–657 5069.

TONBRIDGE, Bishop Suffragan of, since 1982; **Rt. Rev. David Henry Bartleet;** *b* 11 April 1929; *s* of Edmund Arthur Bartleet and Helen Bartleet (*née* Holford); *m* 1956, Jean Mary (*née* Rees); one *s* two *d. Educ:* St Edward's School, Oxford; AA School of Architecture, London; St Peter's Hall, Oxford; Westcott House, Cambridge. Curate: St Mary-le-Tower, Ipswich, 1957–60; St George's, Doncaster (in charge of St Edmund's), 1960–64; Vicar: Edenbridge, Kent, 1964–73; Bromley, Kent, 1973–82. *Recreations:* music, woodturning, beekeeping; architecture; icons. *Address:* Bishop's Lodge, 48 St Botolph's Road, Sevenoaks, Kent. *T:* Sevenoaks 456070.

TONBRIDGE, Archdeacon of; *see* Mason, Ven. R. J.

TONČIĆ-SORINJ, Dr Lujo; Secretary-General, Council of Europe, 1969–74; *b* Vienna, 12 April 1915; *s* of Dušan Tončić-Sorinj (formerly Consul-Gen. in service of Imperial Ministry for Foreign Affairs), and Mabel (*née* Plason de la Woesthyne); *m* 1956, Renate Trenker; one *s* four *d. Educ:* Secondary sch. (Gymnasium), Salzburg. Studied law and philosophy at Univs of Vienna and Agram (Zagreb), 1934–41, also medicine and psychology (LLD Vienna); political science, Institut d'Etudes Politiques, Paris. Head of Polit. Dept of Austrian Research Inst. for Economics and Politics in Salzburg and Editor of Berichte und Informationen (political periodical published by Austrian Research Inst. for Economics and Politics), 1946–49. MP for Land Salzburg, 1949–66; Chairman: Legal Cttee of Austrian Parl., 1953–56; For. Affairs Cttee, 1956–59; in charge of For. Affairs questions, Austrian People's Party, 1959–66. Austrian Parly Observer to Consultative Assembly of Council of Europe, 1953–56; Austrian Mem., Consultative Assembly, 1956–66; Vice-Pres., Council of Europe; Vice-Pres., Political Commn, 1961–62; Minister for Foreign Affairs, Austria, 1966–68. Permanent Rep. of Austrian People's Party to Christian-Democratic Gp, European Parlt, 1980–. Chm., Austrian Assoc. of UN, 1978–. Grand Cross of several orders including Order of St Michael and St George, Great Britain (Hon. GCMG). *Publications:* Erfüllte Träume (autobiog.), 1982; over 350 articles and essays on politics, economics, internat. law and history. *Recreations:* swimming, diving, history, geography. *Address:* 5020 Salzburg, Schloss Fürberg, Pausingerstrasse 11, Austria. *T:* 0662–73437.

TONGA, HM the King of; **King Taufa'ahau Tupou IV,** Hon. GCMG 1977 (Hon. KCMG 1968); Hon. GCVO 1970; Hon. KBE 1958 (Hon. CBE 1951); *b* 4 July 1918; *s* of Prince Uiliami Tupoulahi Tungi and Queen Salote Tupou of Tonga; *S* mother, 1966; *m* 1947, Halaevalu Mata'aho 'Ahome'e; three *s* one *d. Educ:* Tupou College, Tonga; Newington College, Sydney; Wesley College, Sydney University. Minister for Health and Education, Tonga, 1943–50; Prime Minister, 1950–65. *Heir:* *s* HRH Prince Tupouto'a, *b* 4 May 1948. *Address:* The Palace, Nukualofa, Tonga. *T:* Nukualofa 1.

See also HRH Prince Fatafehi Tu'ipelehake.

TONGE, Brian Lawrence, PhD; FRSC; Director, Oxford Polytechnic, 1981–85; *b* 19 April 1933; *s* of Lawrence and Louisa Tonge; *m* 1955, Anne Billcliff; one *d. Educ:* Bury High Sch.; London Univ. (BSc 1st Cl. Chemistry); Manchester Univ. (PhD). FRIC 1964. Scientific Officer, Hirst Research Centre, GEC Ltd, 1956–59; Chemist, Medical Research Council Carcinogenic Substances Research Unit, Exeter Univ., 1959; Lectr in Chemistry, Plymouth Coll. of Technology, 1960–63; Research Manager, Pure Chemicals Ltd, 1963–65; Principal Lectr in Chemistry, West Ham Coll. of Technology, 1965–67; Head of Dept of Applied Science and Dean of Faculty of Science, Wolverhampton Polytechnic, 1967–71; Dep. Director, Oxford Polytechnic, 1971–81. Member, Wolfson Coll., Oxford, 1975–85. *Publications:* numerous contribs to learned jls and articles in scientific and educnl press. *Recreations:* gardening, reading, music. *Address:* 2 Pullens Field, Oxford OX3 0BU. *T:* Oxford 69666.

TONGE, Prof. Cecil Howard, TD; DDSc; FDSRCS; Professor of Oral Anatomy, 1964–81, Professor Emeritus 1981, and Dental Postgraduate Sub-Dean, 1968–82, University of Newcastle upon Tyne; *b* 16 Dec. 1915; *s* of Norman Cecil Tonge and Gladys Marian (*née* Avison); *m* 1946, Helen Wilson Currie. *Educ:* Univ. of Durham. DDSc, MB, BS, BDS (Dunelm); FDSRCS. House Surg., later Asst Resident MO, Royal Victoria Inf., 1939; Demonstrator in Anatomy, Medical Sch., Newcastle upon Tyne, 1940; Lectr in Anatomy, 1944, Sen. Lectr, 1952, Reader in Oral Anatomy, 1956, Univ. of Durham. Lieut RAMC (TA), 1941; Lt-Col RAMC (TA) Comdg 151 (N) Field Ambulance, 1954–58; Hon. Col, Northumbrian Univ. OTC, 1974–82. Chairman, Council of Military Educn Cttees of Univs of UK, 1968–82; Pres., British Div. Internat. Assoc. for Dental Research, 1968–71; Northern Regional Adviser in Postgrad. Dental Educn of RCS, 1970–83; Chm., Dental Cttee, Council for Postgrad. Medical Educn, 1978–84; British Dental Association: Pres., 1981–82; (Life) Vice-Pres., 1983–; Member: Representative Bd, 1970–; Council, 1970–82; Chm., Central Cttee for Univ. Teachers and Res. Workers, 1976–81. Member, Sunderland AHA, 1973–82; Vice-Chm., Sunderland DHA, 1982–. *Publications:* chapter in Scientific Foundations of Dentistry, 1976; papers in Dental Anatomy and Embryology; contribs to Brit. Jl of Nutrition, Jl of Anatomy, Jl of Dental Res., Jl of RCSE, Brit. Dental Jl, Dental Update, Nature, Internat. Dental Jl. *Recreation:* history.

TONGE, Rev. David Theophilus; Chaplain to the Queen, since 1984; Vicar of St Godwald's, Finstall, Bromsgrove, since 1976; *b* 15 Sept. 1930; *s* of Magdalene Tonge and Robert Tonge; *m* 1952, Christobelle Augusta Richards; three *d. Educ:* Johnson's Point Public School, Antigua; Teacher's Certificate (Leeward); General Ordination Certificate. Pupil teacher, 1944; uncertificated teacher, 1952; postman, 1956; postal and telegraph officer, 1960. Wells Theol. Coll., 1968; deacon 1970, priest 1971; Curate of Kidderminster, 1970–75; Asst C of E Chaplain, Brockhill Remand Centre, Redditch, 1983. *Recreations:* gardening, music. *Address:* The Vicarage, 15 Finstall Road, Bromsgrove, Worcs. *T:* Bromsgrove 72459.

TONGUE, Carole; Member (Lab) London East, European Parliament, since 1984; *b* 14 Oct. 1955; *d* of Muriel Esther Lambert and Walter Archer Tongue. *Educ:* Brentwood County High School; Loughborough University of Technology (BA Govt (Hons) and French). Asst Editor, Laboratory Practice, 1977–78; courier/guide in France with Sunsites Ltd, 1978–79; Robert Schuman scholarship for research in social affairs with European Parlt, Dec. 1979–March 1980; sec./admin. asst., Socialist Group of European Parlt, 1980–84. Member: CND; World Disarmament Campaign; Socialist Envt and Resources Assoc.; Quaker Council for European Affairs; Co-operative Party; Fabian Soc.; World Women Parliamentarians for Peace. *Recreations:* piano, cello, tennis, squash, horse riding, cinema, theatre, opera. *Address:* 84 Endsleigh Gardens, Ilford, Essex IG1 3EG. *T:* 01–554 0930.

TONKIN, Hon. David Oliver, FRACO; Secretary-General, Commonwealth Parliamentary Association, since 1986; in private ophthalmic practice, since 1958; *b* 20 July 1929; *s* of Oliver Athelstone Prisk Tonkin and Bertha Ida Louise (*née* Kennett); *m* 1954, Prudence Anne Juttner; three *s* three *d. Educ:* St Peter's Coll., Adelaide; Univ. of Adelaide (MB, BS 1953); Inst. of Ophthalmology, London (DO 1958). FRACO 1974. Vis. staff, Royal Adelaide Hosp., 1958–68. Mem., Social Adv. Council, SA Govt, 1968–70; MLA (L) for Bragg, SA, 1970–83; Leader, Liberal Party of SA, 1975–82; Leader of the Opposition, 1975–79; Premier, Treasurer, Minister of State Development and of Ethnic Affairs, SA, 1979–82. Chm., Patient Care Review Cttee, Adelaide Children's Hosp., 1984–86. Chm., State Opera of SA, 1985. Hon. Consul of Belgium for SA and NT, 1984–85. *Publication:* Patient Care Review: quality assurance in health care, 1985. *Recreations:* the family, music and theatre. *Address:* 7 Old Palace Yard, Westminster, SW1P 3JY. *Club:* Adelaide.

TONKIN, Derek, CMG 1982; HM Diplomatic Service; Ambassador to Thailand, since 1986, and concurrently Ambassador to Laos, since 1986; *b* 30 Dec. 1929; *s* of Henry James Tonkin and Norah Wearing; *m* 1953, Doreen Rooke; one *s* two *d* (and one *s* decd). *Educ:* High Pavement Grammar Sch., Nottingham; St Catherine's Society, Oxford (MA). HM Forces, 1948–49; FO, 1952; Warsaw, 1955; Bangkok, 1957; Phnom Penh, 1961; FO, 1963; Warsaw, 1966; Wellington, 1968; FCO, 1972; East Berlin, 1976; Ambassador to Vietnam, 1980–82; Minister, Pretoria, 1983–86. *Publication:* Modern Cambodian Writing, 1962. *Recreations:* tennis, music. *Address:* c/o Foreign and Commonwealth Office, SW1. *Club:* United Oxford & Cambridge University.

TONYPANDY, 1st Viscount *cr* 1983, of Rhondda in the County of Mid Glamorgan; **Thomas George Thomas;** PC 1968; *b* 29 Jan. 1909; *s* of Zacharia and Emma Jane Thomas. *Educ:* University Coll., Southampton. Schoolmaster. MP (Lab): Cardiff Central, 1945–50; Cardiff West, 1950–76 (when elected Speaker); MP Cardiff W and Speaker of the House of Commons, 1976–83; PPS, Min. of Civil Aviation, 1951; Mem., Chairman's Panel, H of C, 1951–64; Jt Parly Under-Sec. of State, Home Office, 1964–66; Minister of State: Welsh Office, 1966–67; Commonwealth Office, 1967–68; Secretary of State for Wales, 1968–70; Dep. Speaker and Chm. of Ways and Means, House of Commons, 1974–76. First Chm., Welsh Parly Grand Cttee, 1951; Chairman: Welsh PLP, 1950–51; Jt Commonwealth Societies' Council, 1984–. Chm., Commercial Bank of Wales, 1985–. Vice-Pres., Methodist Conf., 1960–61; President: Nat. Brotherhood Movement, 1955; Luton Methodist Industrial Coll., 1982; College of Preceptors, 1984–; Chm. and Treasurer, National Children's Home, 1983–. Hon. Mem., Ct of Assts, Blacksmiths' Co., 1980. Freeman: Borough of Rhondda, 1970; City of Cardiff, 1975; City of London, 1980. Hon. Master Bencher, Gray's Inn, 1982; Hon. Fellow: UC Cardiff, 1972; College of Preceptors, 1977; Polytechnic of Wales, 1982; St Hugh's Coll., Oxford, 1983; Hertford Coll., Oxford, 1983; Hon. DCL Oxford, 1983; Hon. LLD: Asbury Coll., Kentucky, 1976; Southampton, 1977; Wales, 1977; Birmingham, 1978; Oklahoma, 1981; Liverpool, 1982; Leeds, 1983; Keele, 1984; Warwick, 1984; DUniv Open, 1984; Hon. DD Centenary Univ., Louisiana, 1982. Dato Setia Negara, Brunei, 1971; Grand Cross of the Peruvian Congress, 1982; Gold Medal for Democratic Services, State of Carinthia, Austria, 1982; William Hopkins Bronze Medal, St David's Soc., New York, 1982. *Publications:* The Christian Heritage in Politics, 1960; George Thomas, Mr Speaker, 1985; My Wales, 1986. *Heir:* none. *Address:* House of Lords, SW1. *Clubs:* Athenæum, Travellers', Reform, English-Speaking Union; County (Cardiff).

TOOHEY, Mrs Joyce, CB 1977; Under-Secretary, Department of the Environment, 1970–76; *b* 20 Sept. 1917; *o d* of Louis Zinkin and Lena Zinkin (*née* Daiches); *m* 1947, Monty I. Toohey, MD, MRCP, DCH (*d* 1960); two *d*. *Educ:* Brondesbury and Kilburn High Sch.; Girton Coll., Cambridge; London Sch. of Economics. BA 1938, MA 1945, Cambridge. Asst Principal, Min. of Supply, 1941; transferred to Min. of Works (later Min. of Public Building and Works, now Dept of the Environment), 1946; Principal, 1948; Asst Secretary, 1956; Under-Secretary, 1964. Harvard Business Sch., 1970. *Recreations:* reading, walking. *Address:* 11 Kensington Court Gardens, W8 5QE. *T:* 01–937 1559. *Club:* Hurlingham.

TOOK, John Michael Exton, MBE 1964; Controller, Europe and North Asia Division, British Council, 1983–86; *b* 15 Sept. 1926; *s* of George Took, Dover, and Ailsa Clowes (*née* Turner); *m* 1964, Judith Margaret, *d* of Brig. and Mrs W. J. Birkle; two *d*. *Educ:* Dover Coll.; Jesus Coll., Cambridge (MA, Mod. and Med. Langs Tripos). Served Indian Army, 1944–47, Captain. HM Colonial Admin. Service (later HMOCS), N Rhodesia, 1950–57; Min. of External Affairs, Fedn of Rhodesia & Nyasaland, 1957–63; Min. of External Affairs, Republic of Zambia, 1964–65; joined British Council, 1965; Asst Reg. Dir, Frankfurt, 1965–67; Reg. Dir, Cape Coast, 1967–69; Rep., Cyprus, 1971–74; Cultural Attaché, British Embassy, Budapest, 1974–77; Dep. Controller, European Div., 1977–80; Rep., Greece, 1980–83. *Publications:* Common Birds of Cyprus, 1973, 3rd edn 1983; contribs to ornithological jls. *Recreations:* ornithology, fishing, natural history. *Address:* Pilgrims, Appledore, near Ashford, Kent. *T:* Appledore 215. *Club:* United Oxford & Cambridge University.

TOOKER, H. C. W.; *see* Whalley-Tooker.

TOOKEY, Richard William, CBE 1984; Director, since 1984 and Group Public Affairs Co-ordinator, since 1984, Shell International Petroleum Co. Ltd; part-time Member, British Railways Board, since 1985; *b* 11 July 1934; *s* of Geoffrey William Tookey, QC and Rosemary Sherwell Tookey (*née* Clogg); *m* 1956, Jill (*née* Ransford); one *s* one *d* (and one *s* decd). *Educ:* Charterhouse. National Service, 2nd Lieut, 1st King's Dragoon Guards, 1952–54; Lanarkshire Yeomanry (TA), 1954–56; Inns of Court Regt/Inns of Court and City Yeomanry (TA), 1957–64. Joined Royal Dutch/Shell Group, 1954; posts in internat. oil supply and trading, 1954–73; Head of Supply Operations, 1973–75; Vice-Pres., Shell Internat. Trading Co., 1975–77; Man. Dir, Shell Tankers (UK) Ltd, 1978–79, Chm., 1980–84; Man. Dir, Shell Internat. Marine Ltd, 1980–84; Marine Co-ordinator, Shell Internat. Petroleum Co. Ltd, 1980–84. Mem., Gen. Cttee, Lloyd's Register of Shipping, 1978–85; Pres., Gen. Council of British Shipping, 1983–84. Liveryman, Shipwrights' Co., 1983–. *Recreations:* sailing, home, garden. *Address:* Shell Centre, SE1 7NA. *T:* 01–934 5522.

TOOLEY, Sir John, Kt 1979; General Director, Royal Opera House, Covent Garden, since 1980; *b* 1 June 1924; *yr s* of late H. R. Tooley; *m* 1st, 1951, Judith Craig Morris (marr. diss., 1965); three *d*; 2nd, 1968, Patricia Janet Norah Bagshawe, 2nd *d* of late G. W. S. Bagshawe; one *s*. *Educ:* Repton; Magdalene Coll., Cambridge. Served The Rifle Brigade, 1943–47. Sec., Guildhall School of Music and Drama, 1952–55; Royal Opera House, Covent Garden: Asst to Gen. Administrator, 1955–60; Asst Gen. Administrator, 1960–70; Gen. Administrator, 1970–80. Chm., Nat. Music Council Executive, 1970–72. Director: Royal Opera House Trust; English Music Theatre Co. Ltd; Nat. Opera Studio; Covent Garden Video Productions Ltd; National Video Corp. Ltd. Governor: Royal Ballet; Royal Ballet Sch.; Repton Sch. Hon. FRAM; Hon. GSM; Hon. RNCM. Commendatore, Italian Republic, 1976. *Recreations:* walking, theatre. *Address:* 2 Mart Street, WC2; Avon Farm House, Stratford-sub-Castle, Salisbury, Wilts. *Clubs:* Garrick, Arts.

TOOMEY, Ralph; Under-Secretary, Department of Education and Science, 1969–78; *b* 26 Dec. 1918; *s* of late James and Theresa Toomey; *m* 1951, Patricia Tizard; two *d*. *Educ:* Cyfarthfa Grammar Sch., Merthyr Tydfil; University Coll., London; Univ. of Caen. Served British and Indian Army, 1940–46. Teacher, Enfield Grammar Sch., 1947; Lecturer, Univ. of London, at Sch. of Oriental and African Studies, 1948. Min. of Education, 1948–60 and 1963–78 (seconded to Govt of Mauritius, 1960–63, Principal Asst Sec. in Colonial Secretary's Office and Min. of Local Govt and Co-operative Develt). A UK Rep., High Council, European Univ. Inst., Florence, 1974–78. DUniv Open, 1979. *Address:* 8 The Close, Montreal Park, Sevenoaks, Kent. *T:* Sevenoaks 452553. *Clubs:* Chelsea Arts; Knole Park Golf (Sevenoaks).

TOOTH, Hon. Sir Douglas; *see* Tooth, Hon. Sir S. D.

TOOTH, Geoffrey Cuthbert, MD, MRCP, DPM; Visiting Scientist, National Institute of Mental Health, USA, 1968–71; *b* 1 Sept. 1908; *s* of late Howard Henry Tooth, CB, CMG, MD, FRCP, and late Helen Katherine Tooth, OBE (*née* Chilver); *m* 1st, 1934, Princess Olga Galitzine (*d* 1955), *d* of Prince Alexander Galitzine, MD; 2nd, 1958, HSH Princess Xenia of Russia, *d* of Prince Andrew of Russia. *Educ:* Rugby Sch.; St John's Coll., Cambridge; St Bartholomew's Hosp.; Johns Hopkins Hosp., Baltimore, Md, USA. MRCS, LRCP 1934, MA Cantab 1935, MD Cantab 1946, DPM 1944; MRCP 1965. Asst Psychiatrist, Maudsley Hosp., 1937–39. Surg. Lt-Comdr, RNVR, Neuropsychiatric Specialist, 1939–45. Colonial Social Science Research Fellow, 1946–53; Comr, Bd of Control, 1954–60; transf. to Min. of Health, and retd as Sen. PMO, Head of Mental Health Section, Med. Div., 1960. Mem. Expert Advisory Panel (Mental Health), WHO. *Publications:* Studies in Mental Illness in the Gold Coast, 1950; various reports to learned societies; articles and papers in med. jls. *Recreations:* sailing, gardening, metal work, photography. *Address:* Grand Prouillac, Plazac, 24580 Rouffignac, France.

TOOTH, Sir (Hugh) John L.; *see* Lucas-Tooth.

TOOTH, Hon. Sir (Seymour) Douglas, Kt 1975; retired from Government of Queensland; *b* 28 Jan. 1904; *s* of Percy Nash Tooth and Laura Tooth; *m* 1937, Eileen Mary O'Connor; one *d*. *Educ:* Univ. of Queensland (Teacher's Trng). Cl. 1 Teacher's Certif. Certificated Teacher, Qld Dept of Educn, 1922. Entered Qld Parlt as MP: Kelvin Grove, 1957; Ashgrove, 1960–74; apptd Minister for Health in Govt of Qld, 1964; retd from Parlt and Cabinet, 1974. Chairman: Duke of Edinburgh Award Cttee, Qld, 1977–; Brisbane Forest Park Adv. Bd.

TOPE, Graham Norman; Deputy General Secretary, Voluntary Action Camden, since 1975; *b* 30 Nov. 1943; *s* of late Leslie Tope, Plymouth and Winifred Tope (*née* Merrick), Bermuda; *m* 1972, Margaret East; two *s*. *Educ:* Whitgift Sch., S Croydon. Company Sec., 1965–72; Insce Manager, 1970–72. Pres., Nat. League of Young Liberals, 1973– (Vice-Chm., 1971–73); Mem., Liberal Party Nat. Council, 1970–; Exec. Cttee, London Liberal Party, 1981–84. Sutton Council: Councillor and Leader, Liberal SDP Alliance Group, 1974–; Leader of Opposition, 1984–86; Leader of Council, 1986–. MP (L) Sutton and Cheam, 1972–Feb. 1974; Liberal Party spokesman on environment, Dec. 1972–1974; contested (L) Sutton and Cheam, Oct. 1974. *Publication:* (jtly) Liberals and the Community, 1974. *Address:* 88 The Gallop, Sutton, Surrey SM2 5SA. *T:* 01–642 1459.

TOPHAM, Surgeon Captain Lawrence Garth, RN (Retd); Consultant Physician in Geriatric Medicine, Central Hampshire District Winchester and Andover Hospitals, 1974–83; *b* 14 Nov. 1914; *s* of late J. Topham and late Mrs Topham; *m* 1943, Olive Barbara Marshall (VAD), *yr d* of late J. Marshall and late Mrs Marshall; one *s* one *d*. *Educ:* Bradford Grammar Sch.; Univ. of Leeds. MB, ChB 1937; MD 1946; MRCPE 1957; FRCPE 1967; MRCP 1969. Joined RN 1938. Served War: HMS Newcastle and HMS Milford, 1939–41; USN Flight Surgeon's Wings, 1943; RN Fleet Air Arm Pilot's Wings, 1944. Pres., Central Air Med. Bd, 1949; HMS Sheffield, 1951; Med. Specialist and Consultant in Medicine, at RN Hosps, Trincomalee, Haslar and Plymouth, 1952–66; Prof. of Med., RN, and RCP, 1966–71; QHP 1970; retd at own request, from RN, 1971. House Governor and Medical Superintendent, King Edward VII Convalescent Home for Officers, Osborne, IoW, 1971–74. Member: British Nat. Cttee, Internat. Soc. of Internal Medicine; British Geriatric Soc.; Wessex Physicians Club. OStJ (Officer Brother) 1970. *Publications:* several articles in med. jls, especially on subject of diseases of the chest. *Recreations:* Rugby football refereeing, rowing, photography, Oriental cookery. *Address:* Tilings, Holt Close, Wickham, Hants PO17 5EY. *T:* Wickham 832072.

TOPLEY, Kenneth Wallis Joseph, CMG 1976; Secretary, University of East Asia, Macau, since 1984; *b* 22 Oct. 1922; *s* of William Frederick Topley and Daisy Elizabeth (*née* Wellings); *m* 1949, Marjorie Doreen Wills; two *s* two *d*. *Educ:* Dulwich Coll.; Aberdeen Univ.; London Sch. of Econs and Pol. Science (BScEcon 1949). Served War, RAFVR, 1941–46 (Flt Lieut). Westminster Bank, 1939–41; Mass-Observation, 1941; Malayan Civil Service, 1950–55: Econ. Affairs Secretariat, Comr Gen.'s Office, and Labour Dept; Hong Kong Civil Service, 1955–83: various appts, 1955–62; Comr for Co-operative Develt and Fisheries, 1962–64; Sec., UGC, 1965–67; Comr for Census and Statistics, 1970–73; Dir of Social Welfare, 1973–74; Dir of Educn, 1974–80; Chm., Cttee to Review Post-Secondary and Technical Educn, 1980–81; Sec. for Educn and Manpower, Hong Kong, 1981–83, retired. *Recreations:* walking, study of society. *Address:* University of East Asia, PO Box 3001, Macau. *T:* Macau 27322. *Clubs:* Royal Commonwealth Society; Ladies Recreation, Royal Hong Kong Jockey (Hong Kong).

TOPLEY, William Keith, MA; Master of Supreme Court (Queen's Bench Division), since 1980; Admiralty Registrar of the Supreme Court, since 1986; *b* 19 Jan. 1936; *s* of late Bryan Topley and Grizel Hester (*née* Stirling); *m* 1980, Clare Mary Pennington; one *s* by former marriage. *Educ:* Bryanston School; Trinity Coll., Oxford (MA). Called to Bar, Inner Temple, 1959. Mem., Bar Council, 1967–68. *Recreations:* golf, sailing. *Address:* Basset Shaw, Checkendon, near Reading, Berks RG8 0TD. *T:* Checkendon 680244. *Clubs:* Garrick; Royal Yacht Squadron, Royal London Yacht (Cowes); Huntercombe Golf.

TOPOLSKI, Feliks; Painter; *b* 14 Aug. 1907; *s* of Edward Topolski (actor) and Stanislawa Drutowska; *m* 1st, 1944, Marion Everall (marr. diss. 1975; she *d* 1985); one *s* one *d*; 2nd, 1975, Caryl J. Stanley. *Educ:* Mikolaj Rey Sch.; Acad. of Art, Warsaw; Officers' Sch. of Artillery Reserve, Wlodzimierz Wolynski; self-tutoring in Italy, Paris. Settled in England, 1935. Exhibited in London and provincial galleries, in Poland, USA, Canada, Eire, France, India, Australia, Italy, Argentine, Switzerland, Denmark, Norway, Israel, Germany, Brazil and Portugal; has contributed to numerous publications; to BBC television programmes; and designed theatrical settings and costumes; as War Artist (1940–45) pictured Battle of Britain, sea and air war, Russia, Middle East, India, Burma, China, Africa, Italy, Germany. British subject since 1947. Painted the Cavalcade of Commonwealth (60′ × 20′) for Festival of Britain, 1951 (later in Victoria Memorial Hall, Singapore, removed on Independence and returned to artist); four murals for Finsbury Borough Council, 1952 (since erased); Coronation of Elizabeth II (100′ × 4′) for Buckingham Palace, 1958–60; murals for Carlton Tower Hotel, London, 1960 (removed); St Regis Hotel, New York, 1965; twenty portraits of English writers for University of Texas, 1961–62. At present engaged on mural-environment, Memoir of the Century (600′ × 12′ to 20′), London S Bank Art Centre, Hungerford Viaduct Arches 150–152, 1975–. Films: Topolski's Moscow (for CBS TV), 1969; Topolski (Polish TV), 1976; Paris Lost, 1980; (with Daniel Topolski) South American Sketchbook (BBC TV), 1982. Works at British Museum, Victoria and Albert Museum, Imperial War Museum, Theatre Museum; Galleries: the Tate, Edinburgh, Glasgow, Aberdeen, Nottingham, Brooklyn, Toronto, Tel Aviv, New Delhi, Melbourne, Lisbon, Warsaw. Dr *hc*, Jagiellonian Univ. of Cracow, 1974. *Publications:* The London Spectacle, 1935; Illustrator of Bernard Shaw's Geneva, 1939, In Good King Charles's Golden Days, 1939, and Pygmalion, 1941; Penguin Prints, 1941; Britain in Peace and War, 1941; Russia in War, 1942; Three Continents, 1944–45; Portrait of GBS, 1946; Confessions of a Congress Delegate, 1949; 88 Pictures, 1951; Coronation, 1953; Sketches of Gandhi, 1954; The Blue Conventions, 1956; Topolski's Chronicle for Students of World Affairs, 1958; Topolski's Legal London, 1961; Face to Face, 1964; Holy China, 1968; (with Conor Cruise O'Brien) The United Nations: Sacred Drama, 1968; Shem Ham & Japheth Inc., 1971; Paris Lost, 1973 (trans. as Paris Disparu, 1974); Topolski's Buckingham Palace Panoramas, 1977; Sua Sanctitas Johannes Paulus Papa II, 1979; The London Symphony Orchestra 75th Anniversary Prints, 1979; Topolski's Panoramas, 1981; prints for Christie's Contemporary Art, 1974–85; (with Daniel Topolski) Travels with my Father: a journey through South America, 1983; Topolski's Chronicle, 1953–79, 1982; Fourteen Letters (autobiog.), 1987. *Address:* Bridge Arch 158, opposite Artists' Entrance, Royal Festival Hall, SE1. *T:* 01–928 3405.

TOPP, Air Commodore Roger Leslie, AFC 1950 (Bar 1955, 2nd Bar 1957); Consultant to Ferranti Defence Systems Ltd, Scotland (Aviation and Defence, Federal Republic of Germany), since 1978; *b* 14 May 1923; *s* of William Horace Topp and Kathleen (*née* Peters); *m* 1945, Audrey Jane Jeffery; one *s* one *d*. *Educ:* North Mundham Sch.; RAF, Cranwell. Served War: Pilot trg, Canada, 1943–44, commissioned 1944; 'E' Sqdn Glider Pilot Regt, Rhine Crossing, 1945. Nos 107 and 98 Mosquito Sqdns, Germany, 1947–50; Empire Test Pilots' Sch. and RAE Farnborough, 1951–54; Commanded No 111 Fighter Sqdn (Black Arrows) Aerobatic Team, 1955–58; Allied Air Forces Central Europe, Fontainbleau, 1959; Sector Operational Centre, Brockzetel, Germany, 1959–61; jssc, Latimer, 1961–62; commanded Fighter Test Sqdn, Boscombe Down, 1962–64; Station Cmdr, RAF Coltishall, 1964–66; Nat. Def. Coll., Canada, 1966–67; Opl Requirements, MoD (Air), London, 1967–69; Multi-role Combat Aircraft Project, Munich, 1969–70; HQ No 38 Gp, Odiham, 1970; Commandant, Aeroplane and Armament Experimental Estabt, Boscombe Down, 1970–72; Dep. Gen. Man., Multi-role Combat Aircraft Develt and Production Agency, Munich, 1972–78; retd from RAF, 1978. *Recreations:* golf, sailing. *Address:* c/o Midland Bank, 22 Market Place, North Walsham, Norfolk. *Club:* Royal Air Force.

TOPPING, Rev. Frank; author and broadcaster; Hon. National Chaplain of Toc H, since 1986 (National Chaplain, 1984–86); *b* 30 March 1937; *s* of late Frank and Dorothy Topping; *m* 1958, June Berry; two *s* one *d*. *Educ:* St Anne's Convent Sch., Birkenhead; St Anselm's Christian Brother Coll., Birkenhead; North West School of Speech and Drama; Didsbury Coll., Bristol. Served RAF, in Cyprus during EOKA and Suez crisis, 1955–57. Stage manager, electrician, asst carpenter and actor, Leatherhead Rep. Th., 1957–59; played Krishna in Dear Augustine, Royal Court, Chelsea, 1959; tour of Doctor in the House, 1959; stage manager/actor, Wolverhampton Rep. Th., 1959; stage-hand with zoological film unit, Granada TV, 1960; TV Studio Floor Man., 1960; 1st Asst Film Dir,

1962; read Theology at Didsbury Coll., Bristol, 1964–67; asst minister at Dome Methodist Mission, Brighton, and methodist univ. chaplain at Sussex, 1967–70; also freelance broadcaster, BBC Radio Brighton, 1967–70; ordained 1970. Producer, BBC Radio Bristol, responsible for religious and farming progs, a music magazine, a comedy record prog., and was short-story editor, 1970–72; asst religious progs organizer for network progs, BBC N Region, 1972–73; network series editor and producer, London, 1973–80; many progs, incl. Pause for Thought and Thought for the Day; has written and presented a Pause for Thought prog. almost every week, 1973–. Began making progs and writing songs with Donald Swann, 1973; became freelance, 1980; in partnership with Donald Swann wrote two man show, Swann with Topping, played in London fringe theatre, then at Ambassadors; presented three one-man plays, Frank Topping 1 Man–3 Shows, Edinburgh Fest. Fringe, 1986. Many TV appearances; own series, Sunday Best, 1981, and Topping on Sunday, 1982–84; has written radio plays: On the Hill, 1974 (Grace Wyndham Goldie UNDA Dove award, 1975); A Particular Star, 1977. *Publications*: Lord of the Morning, 1977; Lord of the Evening, 1979; Lord of my Days, 1980; Working at Prayer, 1981; Pause for Thought with Frank Topping, 1981; Lord of Life, 1982; The Words of Christ: forty meditations, 1983; God Bless You—Spoonbill, 1984; Lord of Time, 1985; An Impossible God, 1985; Wings of the Morning, 1986. *Recreations*: sailing, painting (watercolours), photography, conversation into the small hours. *Address*: Wildcat Cottage, 25 Keyhaven Road, Milford-on-Sea, Lymington, Hants SO41 0QW. *T*: Lymington 45074. *Clubs*: Naval; Hurst Castle Sailing (Keyhaven, Hants).

TOPPING, Prof. James, CBE 1977; MSc, PhD, DIC, FInstP; FIMA; Vice-Chancellor, Brunel University, 1966–71; Emeritus Professor, 1971; *b* 9 Dec. 1904; 3rd *s* of James and Mary A. Topping, Ince, Lancashire; *m* 1934, Muriel Phyllis Hall (*d* 1963); one *s*; *m* 1965, Phyllis Iles. *Educ*: Univ. of Manchester; Imperial Coll. of Science and Technology. BSc (Manchester), 1924; PhD (London), 1926; Beit Scientific Research Fellow, 1926–28. Asst Lectr, Imperial Coll., 1928–30; Lectr Chelsea Polytechnic, 1930–32; Lectr, Coll. of Technology, Manchester, 1932–37; Head, Dept of Maths and Physics, Polytechnic, Regent St, 1937–53; Principal, Technical Coll., Guildford, 1953–54; Principal, Brunel College, W3, 1955–66. Vice-Pres., Inst. of Physics, 1951–54, 1960–63; Chairman: Nuffield Secondary Science Consultative Cttee, 1965–71; Hillingdon Gp Hosp. Management Cttee, 1971–74; London Conf. on Overseas Students, 1971–81; Council, Roehampton Inst. of Higher Educn, 1975–78; Council, Polytechnic of the S Bank, 1975–81; Vis. Cttee, Cranfield Inst. of Technol., 1970–78; Member: Anderson Cttee on Student Grants, 1958–60; Nat. Council for Technological Awards, 1955–64; CNAA, 1964–70. Hon. DTech Brunel, 1967; Hon. DSc CNAA, 1969. *Publications*: Shorter Intermediate Mechanics (with D. Humphrey), 1949; Errors of Observation, 1955; The Beginnings of Brunel University, 1981; papers in scientific jls. *Address*: Forge Cottage, Forest Green, near Dorking, Surrey. *T*: Forest Green 358. *Club*: Athenæum.

TORDOFF, family name of **Baron Tordoff.**

TORDOFF, Baron *cr* 1981 (Life Peer), of Knutsford in the County of Cheshire; **Geoffrey Johnson Tordoff;** President of the Liberal Party, 1983–84; Liberal Chief Whip, House of Lords, since 1984 (Deputy Chief Whip, 1983–84); *b* 11 Oct. 1928; *s* of Stanley Acomb Tordoff and Annie Tordoff (*née* Johnson); *m* 1953, Mary Patricia (*née* Swarbrick); two *s* three *d*. *Educ*: North Manchester Grammar School; Manchester Grammar School; Univ. of Manchester. Contested (L), Northwich 1964, Knutsford 1966, 1970. Chairman: Liberal Party Assembly Cttee, 1974–76; Liberal Party, 1976–79 (and its Campaigns and Elections Cttee, 1980, 1981); Member, Liberal Party Nat. Executive, 1975–84. *Address*: House of Lords, SW1.

TORLESSE, Rear-Adm. Arthur David, CB 1953; DSO 1946; retired; Regional Director of Civil Defence, North Midlands Region, 1955–Jan. 1967; *b* 24 Jan. 1902; *e s* of Captain A. W. Torlesse, Royal Navy, and H. M. Torlesse (*née* Jeans); *m* 1933, Sheila Mary Susan, *d* of Lt-Col Duncan Darroch of Gourock; two *s* one *d*. *Educ*: Stanmore Park; Royal Naval Colleges, Osborne and Dartmouth. Served as midshipman, Grand Fleet, 1918; specialised as observer, Fleet Air Arm, 1926; Commander, 1935; staff appointments in HMS Hood and at Singapore and Bangkok (Naval Attaché), 1936–39; Executive officer, HMS Suffolk, 1939–40; aviation staff appointments at Lee on Solent and Admiralty, 1940–44; Captain, 1942; commanded HMS Hunter, 1944–45; Director of Air Equipment, Admiralty, 1946–48; Imperial Defence College, 1949; commanded HMS Triumph, Far East, 1950, taking part in first 3 months of Korean War (despatches); Rear-Admiral, 1951; Flag Officer, Special Squadron and in command of Monte Bello atomic trial expedition, 1952; Flag Officer, Ground Training, 1953–54, retired Dec. 1954. Officer, US Legion of Merit, 1954. *Recreations*: fishing, entomology. *Address*: 1 Sway Lodge, Sway, near Lymington, Hants. *T*: Lymington 682550. *Club*: Naval and Military.

TORNARITIS, Criton George, QC (Cyprus); LLB (Hons, Athens); Attorney-General of the Republic of Cyprus, 1960–84 (Attorney-General, Cyprus, 1952); seconded as Commissioner for Consolidation of the Cyprus Legislation, 1956; Special Legal Adviser of the President of the Republic of Cyprus; *b* 27 May 1902; *m* 1934, Mary (*née* Pitta) (*d* 1973); one *s*. *Educ*: Gymnasium of Limassol; Athens University; Gray's Inn. Advocate of the Supreme Court of Cyprus, 1924; District Judge, Cyprus, 1940; President District Court, Cyprus, 1942; Solicitor-General, Cyprus, 1944; Attorney-General, Cyprus, 1952. Attached to Legal Div. of the Colonial Office, 1955. Legal Adviser to Greek-Cypriot Delegation on the Mixed Constitutional Commission, 1959; Greek-Cypriot delegate to Ankara for initialling of Constitution of Republic of Cyprus, 1960. Prize of Academy of Athens, 1984. *Publications*: The individual as a subject of international law, 1972; The Turkish invasion of Cyprus and legal problems arising therefrom, 1975; The European Convention of Human Rights in the Legal Order of the Republic of Cyprus, 1975; The Ecclesiastical Courts especially in Cyprus, 1976; Cyprus and its Constitutional and other Legal Problems, 1977, 2nd edn 1980; Federalism and Regionalism in the Contemporary World, 1979; The State Law of the Republic of Cyprus, 1982; Constitutional Review of the Laws in the Republic of Cyprus, 1983; The Legal System in the Republic of Cyprus, 1984; contributions to legal journals and periodicals; The Laws of Cyprus, rev. edn, 1959. *Recreations*: walking, reading. *Address*: Penelope Delta Street, Nicosia, Cyprus. *T*: 77242.

TORNEY, Thomas William; JP; MP (Lab) Bradford South since 1970; *b* London, 2 July 1915; *m*; one *d*. *Educ*: elementary school. Joined Labour Party, 1930; Election Agent: Wembley North, 1945; Derbyshire West, 1964. Derby and Dist Area Organizer, USDAW, 1946–70. Member: (Past Chm.) North Midland Regional Joint Apprenticeship Council for catering industry, 1946–68; Local Appeals Tribunal, Min. of Social Security, 1946–68; Parly Select Cttee on Race Relations and Immigration, 1970–; Parly Select Cttee on Agriculture, 1979–; Chm., PLP Gp on Agriculture, Fish and Food, 1981–. Especially interested in education, social security, industrial relations, agriculture and food. JP Derby, 1969. Chevalier, Commanderie of GB, Confrérie des Chevaliers du Sacavan d'Anjou, 1976. *Address*: House of Commons, SW1; 76 The Hollow, Littleover, Derby. *T*: Derby 760705.

ToROBERT, Sir Henry Thomas, KBE 1981; Governor and Chairman of the Board of the Bank of Papua New Guinea since its formation in 1973; Chairman, Management Board, PNG Bankers' College, since 1973; President, PNG Amateur Sports Federation, and PNG Olympic and Commonwealth Games Committees, since 1980; *b* Kokopo, 1942. *Educ*: primary educn in East New Britain; secondary educn in Qld, Australia; Univ. of Sydney, Aust. (BA Econ. 1965). Asst Research Officer, Reserve Bank of Australia, Port Moresby, 1965 (one of first local officers to join the bank); Dep. Manager, Port Moresby Branch, 1971; Manager of the Reserve Bank, 1972 (the first Papua New Guinean to hold such a position at a time when all banks were branches of the Aust. commercial banks). Member of the cttee responsible for working out a PNG banking system which came into effect by an act of parliament in 1973; Chairman: PNG Currency Working Group advising the Govt on arrangements leading to the introduction of PNG currency, the Kina; ToRobert Cttee to look into problems of administration in PNG Public Service, 1979 (ToRobert Report, 1979); Council, PNG Inst. of Applied Social and Econ. Res., 1975–82. *Address*: PO Box 898, Port Moresby, Papua New Guinea.

TORONTO, Archbishop of, since 1979; **Most Rev. Lewis Samuel Garnsworthy,** DD; *b* 18 July 1922; *m* 1954, Jean Valance Allen; one *s* one *d*. *Educ*: Univ. of Alberta (BA); Wycliffe Coll., Toronto (LTh). Asst Curate: St Paul's, Halifax, 1945; St John, Norway, Toronto, 1945–48; Rector: St Nicholas, Birchcliff, Toronto, 1948–56; Transfiguration, Toronto, 1956–59; St John's Church, York Mills, Toronto, 1960–68; Suffragan Bishop, Diocese of Toronto, 1968–72; Bishop of Toronto, 1972; Metropolitan of Ontario, 1979–85. Fellow, Coll. of Preachers, Washington, DC. DD *hc*: Wycliffe Coll., Toronto, 1969; Trinity Coll., Toronto, 1973; Huron Coll., 1976. *Address*: 135 Adelaide Street E, Toronto M5C 1L8, Canada. *T*: 363–6021. *Clubs*: Albany, York (Toronto).

TORONTO, Archbishop of, (RC), since 1978; **His Eminence Cardinal (Gerald) Emmett Carter,** CC 1983; *b* Montreal, Quebec, 1 March 1912; *s* of Thomas Carter and Mary Kelty. *Educ*: Univ. of Montreal (BA, MA, PhD); Grand Seminary of Montreal (STL). Founder, Director and Teacher at St Joseph's Teachers' Coll., Montreal, 1939–61; Auxiliary Bishop of London, Ont., 1961; Bishop of London, 1964. Cardinal, 1979. Chairman, Internat. Cttee for English in the Liturgy, 1971; President, Canadian Catholic Conf. of Bishops, 1975–77. Elected Member, Permanent Council of the Synod of Bishops in Rome, 1977. Hon. LLD: Univ. of W Ontario, 1964; Concordia Univ., 1976; Univ. of Windsor, 1977; McGill Univ., Montreal, 1980; Notre Dame Univ., 1981; Hon. DD, Huron Coll., Univ. of W Ont., 1978; Hon. DHL, Duquesne Univ., Pittsburg, 1965; Hon. DLitt, St Mary's Univ., Halifax, 1980. *Publications*: The Catholic Public Schools of Quebec, 1957; Psychology and the Cross, 1959; The Modern Challenge, 1961. *Recreations*: tennis, skiing. *Address*: Chancery Office, 355 Church Street, Toronto, Ontario M5B 1Z8, Canada. *T*: 416/977–1500.

TORONTO, Bishops Suffragan of; see Brown, Rt Rev. A. D.; Hunt, Rt Rev. D. C.; Pryce, Rt Rev. J. T.

TORPHICHEN, 15th Lord *cr* 1564; **James Andrew Douglas Sandilands;** *b* 27 Aug. 1946; *s* of 14th Lord Torphichen, and Mary Thurstan, *d* of late Randle Henry Neville Vaudrey; *S* father, 1975; *m* 1976, Margaret Elizabeth, *o d* of late William A. Beale and of Mrs Margaret Patten Beale, Peterborough, New Hampshire, USA; three *d*. Heir: cousin Douglas Robert Alexander Sandilands [*b* 31 Aug. 1926; *m* 1949, Ethel Louise Burkitt; one *s*; *m* Suzette Véva (*née* Pernet); two *s*]. *Address*: Calder House, Mid-Calder, West Lothian EH53 0HN.

TORRANCE, Rev. Professor James Bruce; Professor of Systematic Theology, King's College, University of Aberdeen, and Christ's College, Aberdeen, since 1977 (Dean of the Faculty of Divinity, 1978–81); *b* 3 Feb. 1923; *s* of late Rev. Thomas Torrance and Annie Elizabeth Sharp; *m* 1955, Mary Heather Aitken, medical practitioner; one *s* two *d*. *Educ*: Royal High School, Edinburgh; Edinburgh Univ. (MA Hons Philosophy, 1st Cl.); New Coll., Edinburgh (BD Systematic Theol., Distinction); Univs of Marburg, Basle and Oxford. Licensed Minister of Church of Scotland, 1950; parish of Invergowrie, Dundee, 1954; Lectr in Divinity and Dogmatics in History of Christian Thought, New Coll., Univ. of Edinburgh, 1961; Sen. Lectr in Christian Dogmatics, New Coll., 1972. Visiting Prof.: of New Testament, Union Theol. Seminary, Richmond, Va, 1960; of Theology, Columbia Theol. Seminary, Decatur, Ga., 1965, and Vancouver Sch. of Theology, BC, 1974–75. *Publications*: (trans. jtly) Oscar Cullmann's Early Christian Worship, 1953; contribs: Essays in Christology for Karl Barth (Karl Barth's Festschrift), 1956; Where Faith and Science Meet, 1954; Calvinus Ecclesiae Doctor, 1978; Incarnation (on Nicene-Constantinopolitan Creed, 381 AD), 1981; The Westminster Confession in the Church Today, 1982; Calvinus Reformator, 1982; articles to Biblical and Biographical Dictionaries, Scottish Jl of Theology, Interpretation, Church Service Society Annual, and other symposia. *Recreations*: beekeeping, fishing, gardening, swimming. *Address*: Don House, 46 Don Street, Old Aberdeen AB2 1UU. *T*: Aberdeen 41526.

See also Very Rev. Prof. T. F. Torrance.

TORRANCE, Very Rev. Prof. Thomas Forsyth, MBE 1945; DLitt, DTh, DThéol, Dr Teol, DD, DSc; FRSE 1979; FBA 1983; Professor of Christian Dogmatics, University of Edinburgh, and New College, Edinburgh, 1952–79; Moderator of General Assembly of Church of Scotland, May 1976–77; *b* 30 Aug. 1913; *e s* of late Rev. T. Torrance, then of Chengtu, Szechwan, China; *m* 1946, Margaret Edith, *y d* of late Mr and Mrs G. F. Spear, The Brow, Combe Down, Bath; two *s* one *d*. *Educ*: Chengtu Canadian School; Bellshill Academy; Univs of Edinburgh, Oxford, Basel. MA Edinburgh 1934; studies in Jerusalem and Athens, 1936; BD Edinburgh 1937; post-grad. studies, Basel, 1937–38; DLitt Edinburgh 1971. Prof. of Theology, Auburn, NY, USA, 1938–39; post-grad. studies, Oriel Coll., Oxford, 1939–40; ordained minister of Alyth Barony Parish, 1940; Church of Scotland chaplain (with Huts and Canteens) in MEF and CMF, 1943–45; returned to Alyth; DTh Univ. of Basel, 1946; minister of Beechgrove Church, Aberdeen, 1947; Professor of Church History, Univ. of Edinburgh, and New Coll., Edinburgh, 1950–52. Participant, World Conf. on Faith and Order, Lund, 1952; Evanston Assembly of WCC, 1954; Faith and Order Commn of WCC, 1952–62; Participant in Conversations between: Church of Scotland and Church of England, 1950–58; World Alliance of Reformed Churches and Greek Orthodox Church, 1979–. Lectures: Hewett, 1959 (NY, Newton Center and Cambridge, Mass); Harris, Dundee, 1970; Anderson, Presbyterian Coll., Montreal, 1971; Taylor, Yale, 1971; Keese, Univ. of Mississippi, Chattanooga, 1971; Cummings, McGill Univ., Montreal, 1978; Richards, Univ. of Virginia at Charlottesville, 1978; Staley, Davidson Coll., NC, 1978; Cosgrove, Glasgow, 1981; Warfield, Princeton, 1981; Payton, Pasadena, 1981; Didsbury, Manchester, 1982; Staley, Regent Coll., Vancouver, 1982. Mem., Académie Internationale des Sciences Religieuses, 1965 (Pres., 1972–81); For. Mem., Société de l'Histoire du Protestantisme Français, 1968; Mem. Soc. Internat. pour l'Etude de la Philosophie Médiévale, 1969; Hon. President: Soc. for Study of Theology, 1966–68; Church Service Soc. of the Church of Scotland, 1970–71; New Coll. Union, 1972–73. Vice-Pres., Inst. of Religion and Theology of GB and Ireland, 1973–76 (Pres., 1976–78); Protopresbyter of Greek Orthodox Church (Patriarchate of Alexandria), 1973. Curator, Deutsches Institut für Bildung und Wissen, 1982–. Membre d'honneur, Acad. Internat. de Philosophie des Scis, 1976. DD (*hc*) Presbyterian Coll., Montreal, 1950; DThéol (*hc*) Geneva, 1959; DThéol (*hc*) Paris, 1959; DD (*hc*) St Andrews, 1960; Dr Teol (*hc*) Oslo, 1961; Hon. DSc Heriot-Watt, 1983. Templeton Foundn Prize,

1978. Cross of St Mark (first class), 1970. *Publications:* The Modern Theological Debate, 1942; The Doctrine of Grace in the Apostolic Fathers, 1949; Calvin's Doctrine of Man, 1949; Royal Priesthood, 1955; Kingdom and Church, 1956; When Christ Comes and Comes Again, 1957; The Mystery of the Lord's Supper (Sermons on the Sacrament by Robert Bruce), 1958; ed Calvin's Tracts and Treatises, Vols I-III, 1959; The School of Faith, 1959; Conflict and Agreement in the Church, Vol. I, Order and Disorder, 1959; The Apocalypse Today, 1959; Conflict and Agreement in the Church, Vol. II, The Ministry and the Sacraments of the Gospel, 1960; Karl Barth: an Introduction to his Early Theology, 1910–1930, 1962; ed (with D. W. Torrance) Calvin's NT Commentaries, 1959–73; Theology in Reconstruction, 1965; Theological Science, 1969 (Collins Religious Book Award); Space, Time and Incarnation, 1969; God and Rationality, 1971; Theology in Reconciliation: Essays towards Evangelical and Catholic Unity in East and West, 1975; The Centrality of Christ, 1976; Space, Time and Resurrection, 1976; The Ground and Grammar of Theology, 1980; Christian Theology and Scientific Culture, 1980; (ed) Belief in Science and in Christian Life, 1980; (ed) The Incarnation: ecumenical studies in the Nicene. Constantinopolitan Creed, 1981; Divine and Contingent Order, 1981; Reality and Evangelical Theology, 1982; Juridical Law and Physical Law, 1982; (ed) James Clerk Maxwell: A Dynamical Theory of the Electromagnetic Field, 1982; The Meditation of Christ, 1983; Transformation and Convergence in the Frame of Knowledge, 1984; The Christian Frame of Mind, 1985; Reality and Scientific Theology, 1985; (ed) Theological Dialogue between Orthodox and Reformed Churches, 1985; Editor, Theology and Science at the Frontiers of Knowledge, series, 1985–; Jt Editor, Church Dogmatics, Vols 1, 2, 3 and 4, by Karl Barth, 1956–69; Jt Editor: Scottish Jl Theology; SJT Monographs. *Recreations:* golf, fishing. *Address:* 37 Braid Farm Road, Edinburgh EH10 6LE. *Clubs:* New, University (Edinburgh).

See also Rev. Prof. J. B. Torrance.

TORRENS-SPENCE, Captain (Frederick) Michael (Alexander), DSO 1941; DSC 1941; AFC 1944; Royal Navy retired; Lord Lieutenant of County Armagh, since 1981; *b* 10 March 1914; *s* of Lt-Col Herbert Frederick Torrens-Spence and Mrs Eileen Torrens-Spence; *m* 1944, Rachel Nora Clarke; three *s* one *d*. *Educ:* RNC, Dartmouth. Commnd Sub Lieut, 1934; specialised as pilot, 1936; Battle of Taranto, 1940; commanded 815 Naval Air Sqdn, 1941; Battle of Matapan, 1941; Chief Instructor, Empire Test Pilots Sch., 1947–48; Dep. Dir, Air Warfare Div., Naval Staff, 1952–54; commanded HMS Delight, 1955–56, HMS Albion, 1959–61; ADC to the Queen, 1961. Comdr 1946, Captain 1952. Co. Comdt, Ulster Special Constabulary, 1961–70; commanded 2nd (Co. Armagh) Bn, Ulster Defence Regt, 1970–71. High Sheriff, Co. Armagh, 1979. DFC, Greece, 1941. *Club:* MCC.

TORRINGTON, 11th Viscount, *cr* 1721; **Timothy Howard St George Byng;** Bt 1715; Baron Byng of Southill, 1721; Director, Berkeley Exploration and Production plc, since 1985; *b* 13 July 1943; *o s* of Hon. George Byng, RN (*d* on active service, 1944; *o s* of 10th Viscount) and Anne Yvonne Wood (she *m* 2nd, 1951, Howard Henry Masterton Carpenter); *S* grandfather, 1961; *m* 1973, Susan, *d* of M. G. T. Webster, *qv*; three *d*. *Educ:* Harrow; St Edmund Hall, Oxford. Mem., Select Cttee on EEC, H of L; Chm., Sub-Cttee F (Energy, Transport and Broadcasting). *Recreation:* travel. *Heir: kinsman,* John Launcelot Byng, MC [*b* 18 March 1919; *m* 1955, Margaret Ellen Hardy; one *s* two *d*]. *Address:* Great Hunts Place, Owslebury, Winchester, Hants. *Clubs:* White's, Pratt's; Muthaiga (Nairobi).

TORTELIER, Paul; cellist, composer, conductor; *b* 21 March 1914; *s* of Joseph Tortelier, cabinet maker; *m* 1946, Maud Martin; one *s* three *d*. *Educ:* Conservatoire National de Musique, Paris; gen. educn privately. Leading Cellist, Monte Carlo, 1935–37; Cellist, Boston Symphony Orch., 1937–40; Leading Cellist, Société des Concerts du Conservatoire de Paris, 1945–47; Internat. solo career began in Concertgebouw, Amsterdam, 1946, and London, 1947 (under Sir Thomas Beecham's baton). Concert tours: Europe, N America, North Africa, Israel, S America, USSR, Japan, etc. As a conductor: debut with Israel Philharmonic, 1956; Prof. of Violoncello: Conservatoire Nat. Supérieur de Musique, Paris, 1956–69; Folkwang Hochschule, Essen; conducts in Paris and in England. Master classes, for BBC TV, 1970. Hon. Prof., Central Conservatory, Peking, 1980–. Hon. Mem., Royal Acad. of Music (England). Hon. DMus: Leicester, 1972; Oxford, 1975; Birmingham (Aston), 1980. Comdr, Order of the Lion (Finland), 1981. *Publications:* Cello Sonata, Trois P'tits Tours, Spirales, Elegie, Toccata, Sonata Breve, Pishnetto, Cello Books, for cello and piano; edns of Sammartini Sonata and Bach Suites; Cadenzas for Classical Concertos; Double Concerto for 2 cellos (also for violin and cello); Suite for unaccompanied cello; Offrande for string orchestra; (arr.) Paganini: Variazione di Bravura; (books) How I Play, How I Teach, 1973; (with David Blum) Paul Tortelier: a self portrait, 1984. *Recreations:* no time for these! *Address:* Ibbs & Tillett, 450–452 Edgware Road, W2 1EG.

TORY, Sir Geofroy (William), KCMG 1958 (CMG 1956); HM Diplomatic Service, retired; *b* 31 July 1912; *s* of William Frank Tory and Edith Wreghitt; *m* 1st, 1938, Emilia Strickland; two *s* one *d*; 2nd, 1950, Hazel Winfield (*d* 1985). *Educ:* King Edward VII Sch., Sheffield; Queens' Coll., Cambridge. Apptd Dominions Office, 1935; Private Sec. to Perm. Under-Sec. of State, 1938–39; served War, 1939–43, in Royal Artillery; Prin. Private Sec. to Sec. of State, 1945–46; Senior Sec., Office of UK High Comr, Ottawa, 1946–49; Prin. Sec., Office of UK Rep. to Republic of Ireland, 1949–50; Counsellor, UK Embassy, Dublin, 1950–51; idc 1952; Dep. High Comr for UK in Pakistan (Peshawar), 1953–54, in Australia, 1954–57; Asst Under-Sec. of State, CRO, 1957; High Comr for UK in Fedn of Malaya, 1957–63; Ambassador to Ireland, 1964–66; High Commissioner to Malta, 1967–70. PMN (Malaysia) 1963. *Recreation:* painting. *Address:* 2 Burlington Gardens, W4 4LT.

TOTNES, Archdeacon of; *see* Hawkins, Ven. R. S.

TOTTENHAM, family name of **Marquess of Ely.**

TÖTTERMAN, Richard Evert Björnson, Kt Comdr, Order of the White Rose of Finland; Hon. GCVO 1976 (Hon. KCVO 1969); Hon. OBE 1961; DPhil; Finnish Ambassador to Switzerland, since 1983; *b* 10 Oct. 1926; *s* of Björn B. Tötterman and Katharine C. (*née* Wimpenny); *m* 1953, Camilla Susanna Veronica Huber; one *s* one *d*. *Educ:* Univ. of Helsinki (LLM); Brasenose Coll., Oxford (DPhil; Hon. Fellow, 1982). Entered Finnish Foreign Service, 1952: served Stockholm, 1954–56; Moscow, 1956–58; Ministry for Foreign Affairs, Finland, 1958–62; Berne, 1962–63; Paris, 1963–66; Dep. Dir, Min. for For. Affairs, Helsinki, 1966; Sec.-Gen., Office of the President of Finland, 1966–70; Sec. of State, Min. for For. Aff., 1970–75; Ambassador, UK, 1975–83. Chm. or Mem. of a number of Finnish Govt Cttees, 1959–75, and participated as Finnish rep. in various internat. negotiations; Chm., Multilateral Consultations preparing Conf. on Security and Co-operation in Europe, 1972–73. Holds numerous foreign orders (Grand Cross, Kt Comdr, etc). *Recreations:* music, out-door life. *Address:* Weltpoststrasse 4, Case Postale 11, 3000 Berne 15, Switzerland.

TOTTLE, Prof. Charles Ronald; Professor of Medical Engineering, University of Bath, 1975–78, now Emeritus, a Pro Vice-Chancellor, 1973–77; Director, Bath Institute of Medical Engineering, 1975–78; Editor, Materials Science, Research Studies Press, since

1977; *b* 2 Sept. 1920; *m* 1944, Eileen P. Geoghegan; one *s* one *d*. *Educ:* Nether Edge Grammar School; University of Sheffield (MMet). English Electric Co. Ltd, 1941–45; Lecturer in Metallurgy, University of Durham, King's College, 1945–50; Ministry of Supply, Atomic Energy Division, Springfields Works, 1950–51; Culcheth Laboratories, 1951–56 (UKAEA); Head of Laboratories, Dounreay, 1956–57; Deputy Director, Dounreay, 1958–59; Prof. of Metallurgy, 1959–67, Dean of Science, 1966, Univ. of Manchester; Prof. and Head of School of Materials Science, Univ. of Bath, 1967–75; Man. Dir, South Western Industrial Research Ltd, 1970–75. Resident Research Associate, Argonne Nat. Laboratory, Illinois, USA, 1964–65. Vice-Pres., Instn of Metallurgists, 1968–70; Jt Editor, Institution of Metallurgists Series of Textbooks, 1962–70. Governor, Dauntsey's Sch., 1979–. CEng 1978; FIM; FInstP 1958, CPhys 1985. Hon. MSc Manchester. *Publications:* The Science of Engineering Materials, 1965; An Encyclopaedia of Metallurgy and Materials, 1984; various contribs to metallurgical and engineering jls. *Recreations:* music, model making, gardening. *Address:* Thirdacre, Hilperton, Trowbridge, Wilts BA14 7RL.

TOUCH, Dr Arthur Gerald, CMG 1967; Chief Scientist, Government Communications Headquarters, 1961–71; *b* 5 July 1911; *s* of A. H. Touch, Northampton; *m* 1938, Phyllis Wallbank, Birmingham; one *s*. *Educ:* Oundle; Jesus College, Oxford. MA, DPhil 1937. Bawdsey Research Station, Air Ministry, 1936; Radio Dept, RAE, Farnborough, 1940; British Air Commn, Washington, DC, 1941; Supt, Blind Landing Experimental Unit, RAE, 1947; Director: Electronic R and D (Air), Min. of Supply, 1953; Electronic R and D (Ground), Min. of Supply, 1956–59; Imperial Defence College, 1957; Head, Radio Dept, RAE, 1959; Min. of Defence, 1960. *Recreations:* fly fishing, horticulture (orchids). *Address:* Yonder, Ideford, Newton Abbot, Devon TQ13 0BG. *T:* Chudleigh 852258.

TOUCHE, Sir Anthony (George), 3rd Bt *cr* 1920; Director, Touche, Remnant & Co., since 1965 (Chairman, 1971–81); Deputy Chairman, National Westminster Bank PLC, since 1977; *b* 31 Jan. 1927; *s* of Donovan Meredith Touche (*d* 1952) (2nd *s* of 1st Bt) and of Muriel Amy Frances (*d* 1983), *e d* of Rev. Charles R. Thorold Winckley; *S* uncle, 1977; *m* 1961, Hester Christina, *er d* of Dr Werner Pleuger; two *s* one *d* (and one *s* decd). *Educ:* Eton College. FCA. Partner in George A. Touche & Co. (now Touche Ross & Co.), 1951; Director of investment trust companies, 1952–; retired from Touche Ross & Co., 1968; Director: Westminster Bank Ltd, 1968; Yorkshire Bank, 1979; International Westminster Bank Ltd, 1980; Chairman, Assoc. of Investment Trust Companies, 1971–73. *Recreations:* music, reading, walking. *Heir: s* William George Touche, *b* 26 June 1962. *Address:* Stane House, Ockley, Dorking, Surrey RH5 5TQ. *T:* Oakwood Hill 397.

TOUCHE, Sir Rodney (Gordon), 2nd Bt *cr* 1962; *b* 5 Dec. 1928; *s* of Rt Hon. Sir Gordon Touche, 1st Bt, and of Ruby, Lady Touche (formerly Ruby Ann Macpherson); *S* father 1972; *m* 1955, Ouida Ann, *d* of F. G. MacLellan, Moncton, NB, Canada; one *s* three *d*. *Educ:* Marlborough; University Coll., Oxford. *Heir: s* Eric MacLellan Touche, *b* 22 Feb. 1960. *Address:* 2403 1100 8th Avenue NW, Calgary, Alberta, Canada. *T:* 403–233–8800.

TOULMIN, John Kelvin, QC 1980; barrister-at-law; a Recorder, since 1984; *b* 14 Feb. 1941; *s* of Arthur Heaton Toulmin and B. Toulmin (*née* Fraser); *m* 1967, Carolyn Merton (*née* Gullick), barrister-at-law; one *s* two *d*. *Educ:* Winchester Coll.; Trinity Hall, Cambridge (Patterson Law Scholar, 1959; BA 1963, MA 1966); Univ. of Michigan (Ford Foundn Fellow and Fulbright Scholar, 1964; LLM 1965). Middle Temple: Harmsworth Exhibnr, 1960; Astbury Scholar, 1965; called to the Bar, 1965; Bencher, 1986; Western Circuit. Cambridge Univ. Debating Tour, USA, 1963. Chm., Young Barristers, 1973–75; Member: Bar Council, 1971–77, 1978–81; Supreme Court Rules Cttee, 1976–80; Council of Legal Educn, 1981–83; UK delegation to Consultative Cttee of Bars of Europe, 1983–; DHSS Enquiry into Unnecessary Dental Treatment in NHS (Report, 1986). Member: SHA, 1982–; Bd of Governors, Maudsley and Bethlem Royal Hosps, 1979–82; Cttee of Management, Inst. of Psychiatry, 1982–. *Publication:* (contrib.) The Influence of Litigation in Medical Practice, 1977. *Recreations:* cricket, theatre. *Address:* 4 Paper Buildings, Temple, EC4Y 7EX. *T:* 01–353 3366. *Clubs:* Pilgrims, MCC; Surrey County Cricket.

TOULMIN, Stephen Edelston, MA, PhD; Avalon Professor of the Humanities, Northwestern University, since 1986; *b* 25 March 1922; *s* of late G. E. Toulmin and Mrs E. D. Toulmin. *Educ:* Oundle School; King's College, Cambridge. BA 1943; MA 1946; PhD 1948; MA (Oxon) 1948. Junior Scientific Officer, Ministry of Aircraft Production, 1942–45; Fellow of King's College, Cambridge, 1947–51; University Lecturer in the Philosophy of Science, Oxford, 1949–55; Acting Head of Department of History and Methods of Science, University of Melbourne, Australia, 1954–55; Professor of Philosophy, University of Leeds, 1955–59; Visiting Prof. of Philosophy, NY Univ. and Stanford Univ. (California) and Columbia Univ. (NY), 1959–60; Director, Nuffield Foundation Unit for History of Ideas, 1960–64; Prof. of Philosophy, Brandeis Univ., 1965–69, Michigan State Univ., 1969–72; Provost, Crown College, Univ. of California, Santa Cruz, 1972–73; Prof. in Cttee on Social Thought, Chicago Univ., 1973–86. Counsellor, Smithsonian Institution, 1966–75. *Publications:* The Place of Reason in Ethics, 1950; The Philosophy of Science: an Introduction, 1953; Metaphysical Beliefs (3 essays: author of one of them), 1957; The Uses of Argument, 1958; Foresight and Understanding, 1961; The Ancestry of Science, Vol. I (The Fabric of the Heavens) 1961, Vol. II (The Architecture of Matter), 1962, Vol. III (The Discovery of Time), 1965; Night Sky at Rhodes, 1963; Human Understanding, vol. 1, 1972; Wittgenstein's Vienna, 1973; Knowing and Acting, 1976; An Introduction to Reasoning, 1979; The Return to Cosmology, 1982; The Abuse of Casnistry, 1987; also films, broadcast talks and contribs to learned jls and weeklies. *Address:* Northwestern University, Department of Philosophy, 1818 Hinman, Evanston, Ill 60201, USA.

TOULSON, Roger Grenfell, QC 1986; *b* 23 Sept. 1946; *s* of Stanley Kilsha Toulson and late Lilian Mary Toulson; *m* 1973, Elizabeth, *d* of Henry Bertram Chrimes, *qv*; two *s* two *d*. *Educ:* Mill Hill School; Jesus College, Cambridge (MA, LLB). Called to the Bar, Inner Temple, 1969. *Recreations:* ski-ing, tennis, gardening. *Address:* Billhurst Farm, Wood Street Village, near Guildford, Surrey GU3 3DZ. *T:* Worplesdon 235246. *Club:* Old Millhillians.

TOURS, Kenneth Cecil, CMG 1955; MA; *b* 16 Feb. 1908; *y s* of late Berthold George Tours, CMG, HM Consul-General in China; *m* 1934, Ruth Grace, *y d* of late Hugh Lewis; two *s*. *Educ:* Aldenham School; Corpus Christi College, Cambridge. RARO. Administrative Service, Gold Coast, 1931; Gambia, 1935; Palestine, 1938; Malaya, 1945; Col (Food Control and Supplies), Brit. Mil. Administration, Malaya, 1945–46; Chm., Jt Supply Board, 1946; Establishment Office, Singapore, 1947; Permanent Sec., Min. of Finance, Gold Coast, 1950; Financial Sec. and Minister of Finance, 1954; Economic Adviser, Ghana, 1954; retd from Colonial Service, 1957. *Recreation:* reading.

TOUT, Herbert, CMG 1946; MA; Reader in Political Economy, University College, London, 1947–68, retired; *b* Manchester, 20 April 1904; *e s* of Professor T. F. Tout, Manchester University, and Mary Johnstone; unmarried. *Educ:* Sherborne School; Hertford College, Oxford. Instructor in Economics, University of Minnesota, USA, 1929–35; Assistant Lecturer, University College, London, 1936; Colston Research Fellow and Director of University of Bristol Social Survey, 1936–38; Lecturer, University of Bristol, 1938–47; Temp. Principal, Board of Trade, 1940–41; Assistant Secretary, 1941–45. *Recreations:* walking, farming, gardening. *Address:* Little Greeting, West Hoathly, East Grinstead, West Sussex RH19 4PW. *T:* Sharpthorne 810400.

TOVELL, Laurence, FCA, IPFA; Chief Inspector of Audit, Department of the Environment, 1977–79; *b* 6 March 1919; *s* of William Henry Tovell and Margaret Tovell (*née* Mahoney); *m* 1945, Iris Joan (*née* Lee); two *s* one *d. Educ:* Devonport High School. Entered Civil Service as Audit Assistant, District Audit Service, 1938. Served War, 1940–46; Lieut RNVR, 1942–46. District Auditor, No 4 Audit District, Birmingham, 1962. *Recreation:* do-it-yourself. *Address:* White Lions, Links Road, Bramley, Guildford, Surrey. *T:* Guildford 892702.

TOVEY, Sir Brian (John Maynard), KCMG 1980; Defence and Political Adviser, Plessey Electronic Systems Ltd, since 1985; *b* 15 April 1926; *s* of Rev. Collett John Tovey (Canon, Bermuda Cathedral, 1935–38) and Kathleen Edith Maud Tovey (*née* Maynard). *Educ:* St Edward's Sch., Oxford; St Edmund Hall, Oxford, 1944–45; School of Oriental and African Studies, London, 1948–50. BA Hons London. Service with Royal Navy and subseq. Army (Intelligence Corps and RAEC), 1945–48. Joined Government Communications Headquarters as Jun. Asst, 1950; Principal, 1957; Asst Sec., 1967; Under Sec., 1975; Dep. Sec., 1978; Dir, 1978–83, retired. Defence Systems Consultant, Plessey Electronic Systems Ltd, and Dir, Plessey Defence Systems Ltd, 1983–85. *Recreations:* music, walking, history of art (espec. 16th Century Italian). *Club:* Naval and Military.

TOWER, Maj.-Gen. Philip Thomas, CB 1968; DSO 1944; MBE 1942; National Trust Administrator, Blickling Hall, 1973–82; *b* 1 March 1917; *s* of late Vice-Admiral Sir Thomas Tower, KBE, CB and late Mrs E. H. Tower; *m* 1943, Elizabeth, *y d* of late Thomas Ralph Sneyd-Kynnersley, OBE, MC and late Alice Sneyd-Kynnersley. *Educ:* Harrow; Royal Military Acad., Woolwich. 2nd Lt Royal Artillery, 1937; served in India, 1937–40; served War of 1939–45 (despatches); Middle East, 1940–42; POW Italy, 1942–43; escaped, 1943; Arnhem, 1944; Norway, 1945; Staff Coll., 1948; Instructor at RMA Sandhurst, 1951–53; comd J (Sidi Rezegh) Bty RHA in Middle East, 1954–55; Joint Services Staff Coll., 1955–56; GSO1 Plans, BJSM Washington, DC, 1956–57; comd 3rd Regt RHA, 1957–60; Imperial Defence Coll., 1961; Comd 51 Inf. Bde Gp, 1961–62; Comd 12 Inf. Bde Gp, BAOR, 1962–64; Director of Public Relations (Army), 1965–67; GOC Middle East Land Forces, 1967 (despatches); Comdt, RMA Sandhurst, 1968–72, retd 1972. Col Comdt, Royal Regt of Artillery, 1970–80. County Comr (Norfolk), SJAB, 1975–78. OStJ 1977. *Recreations:* shooting, gardening. *Address:* Hall Farm, East Raynham, Fakenham, Norfolk NR21 7EE. *T:* Fakenham 4904; Studio A, 414 Fulham Road, SW6 1EB. *T:* 01–385 8538. *Club:* Army and Navy.

TOWLER, Eric William, CBE 1971; farmer; farms 2,000 acres; *b* 28 April 1900; *s* of William Towler and Laura Mary (*née* Trew); *m* 1st, 1921, Isabel Edith Ina Hemsworth; two *s* (one *d* decd), 2nd, 1964, Stella Prideaux-Brune; two *s. Educ:* Morley Grammar Sch. Founder, Cawoods Holdings Ltd and Cawood Wharton & Co. Ltd, 1931; Managing Dir, Cawood Wharton & Co. Ltd, 1931–42, Chm., 1942–71; Chm., Cawoods Holdings Ltd, 1961–72, Dir, 1972–82, Hon. Pres., 1977–82; Mining Director: Dorman Long & Co. Ltd, 1937–65; Pearson Dorman Long Ltd, 1937–65; Richard Thomas & Co. Ltd, 1929–31. MFH: Badsworth Hunt, 1938–43; South Shropshire Hunt, 1951–56. Chm., Nuffield Orthopaedic Centre, 1960–66; Chm., Bd of Governors, Oxford United Hosp., 1964–72. Hon. MA (Oxon) 1964. *Recreations:* hunting, gardening. *Address:* Glympton Park, near Woodstock, Oxon. *T:* Woodstock 811300; Willett House, Lydeard St Lawrence, Somerset. *T:* Lydeard St Lawrence 234. *Club:* Carlton.

TOWNDROW, Ven. Frank Noel; Archdeacon of Oakham, 1967–77, now Archdeacon Emeritus; Residentiary Canon of Peterborough, 1966–77, now Canon Emeritus; a Chaplain to the Queen, 1975–81; *b* 25 Dec. 1911; *e s* of F. R. and H. A. Towndrow, London; *m* 1947, Olive Helen Weinberger (*d* 1978); one *d* (one *s* decd). *Educ:* St Olave's Grammar Sch.; King's Coll., Cambridge; Coll. of Resurrection, Mirfield. Curate, Chingford, E4, 1937–40; Chaplain, RAFVR, 1940–47; Rector of Grangemouth, Stirlingshire, 1947–51; Vicar of Kirton Lindsey, Lincs, 1951–53; Rector of Greenford, Middx, 1953–62; Vicar of Ravensthorpe, E Haddon and Rector of Holdenby, 1962–66. *Recreation:* modern history. *Address:* 2 Bourne Road, Swinstead, Grantham, Lincs. *T:* Corby Glen 422.

TOWNELEY, Simon Peter Edmund Cosmo William; Lord-Lieutenant and Custos Rotulorum of Lancashire, since 1976; *b* 14 Dec. 1921; *e s* of late Col A. Koch de Gooreynd, OBE and of Baroness Norman, *qv*; assumed surname and arms of Towneley by royal licence, 1955, by reason of descent from *e d* and senior co-heiress of Col Charles Towneley of Towneley; *m* 1955, Mary, 2nd *d* of Cuthbert Fitzherbert; one *s* six *d. Educ:* Stowe; Worcester Coll., Oxford (MA, DPhil). Served War of 1939–45, KRRC. Lectr in History of Music, Worcester Coll., Oxford, 1949–55. Mem., Agricultural Lands Tribunal, 1960–. Dir, Granada Television, 1981–. CC Lancs, 1961–64; JP 1956; DL 1970; High Sheriff of Lancashire, 1971. Mem. Council, Duchy of Lancaster, 1986–. Patron, Nat. Assoc. for Mental Health (North-West). President: Community Council of Lancashire; Mid-Pennine Assoc. for the Arts; Lancashire Playing Field Assoc.; NW of England and IoM TA&VRA; Chm., Northern Ballet Theatre, 1969–86; Member: Court and Council, Univ. of Manchester; Court and Council, Royal Northern Coll. of Music; Vice-Pres., NW Arts; Trustee, Historic Churches Preservation Trust, 1984–. Hon. Col, Duke of Lancaster's Own Yeomanry, 1979–. Hon. FRNCM. KStJ; KCSG. *Publications:* Venetian Opera in the Seventeenth Century, 1954 (repr. 1968); contribs to New Oxford History of Music. *Recreation:* playing chamber music. *Address:* Dyneley, Burnley, Lancs. *T:* Burnley 23322. *Clubs:* Boodle's, Pratt's, Beefsteak.

See also P. G. Worsthorne.

TOWNEND, James Barrie Stanley; QC 1978; a Recorder of the Crown Court, since 1979; *b* 21 Feb. 1938; *s* of late Frederick Stanley Townend and Marjorie Elizabeth Townend (*née* Arnold); *m* 1970, Airelle Claire (*née* Nies); one step *d. Educ:* Tonbridge Sch.; Lincoln Coll., Oxford (MA). National Service in BAOR and UK, 1955–57: 2nd Lieut, 18th Medium Regt, RA. Called to Bar, Middle Temple, 1962. Chm., Sussex Crown Court Liaison Cttee, 1978–; Member: Kingston and Esher DHA, 1983–; Bar Council, 1984–. *Recreations:* sailing, fishing. *Address:* 1 King's Bench Walk, Temple, EC4Y 2DB. *T:* 01–583 6266. *Clubs:* Bar Yacht, Thames Sailing.

TOWNEND, John Ernest; MP (C) Bridlington, since 1979; *b* 12 June 1934; *s* of Charles Hope Townend and Dorothy Townend; *m* 1963, Jennifer Ann; two *s* two *d. Educ:* Hymers Coll., Hull. FCA (Plender Prize). Articled Clerk, Chartered Accountants, 1951–56; National Service: Pilot Officer, RAF, 1957–59; J. Townend & Sons Ltd (Hull) Ltd: Co. Sec./Dir, 1959–67; Man. Dir, 1967–77; Chm.,—1977–. Mem., Hull City Council, 1966–74 (Chm., Finance Cttee, 1968–70); Chm., Humber Bridge Bd, 1969–71; Member, Humberside County Council, 1973–79: Cons. Leader of Opposition, 1973–77; Leader, 1977–79; Chm., Policy Cttee, 1977–79. Mem., Policy Cttee, Assoc. of County Councils, 1977–79. PPS to Minister of State for Social Security, 1981–83. Mem., Treasury and Civil Service Select Cttee, 1983–; Vice-Chairman: Cons. backbench Finance Cttee, 1983–;

Cons. Small Business Cttee, 1983–. *Recreations:* swimming, tennis. *Address:* Sigglesthorne Hall, Sigglesthorne, Hull, North Humberside. *Club:* Carlton.

TOWNES, Charles Hard; University Professor, University of California, USA; *b* Greenville, South Carolina, 28 July 1915; *s* of Henry Keith Townes and Ellen Sumter (*née* Hard); *m* 1941, Frances H. Brown; four *d. Educ:* Furman Univ. (BA, BS); Duke Univ. (MA); California Institute of Technology (PhD). Assistant in Physics, California Inst. of Technology, 1937–39; Member Techn Staff, Bell Telephone Labs, 1939–47; Associate Prof. of Physics, Columbia Univ., 1948–50; Prof. of Physics, Columbia Univ., 1950–61; Exec. Director, Columbia Radiation Lab., 1950–52; Chairman, Dept of Physics, Columbia Univ., 1952–55; Vice-President and Director of Research, Inst. for Defense Analyses, 1959–61; Provost and Professor of Physics, MIT, 1961–66; Institute Professor, MIT, 1966–67. Guggenheim Fellow, 1955–56; Fulbright Lecturer, University of Paris, 1955–56, University of Tokyo, 1956; Lecturer, 1955, 1960, Dir, 1963, Enrico Fermi Internat. Sch. of Physics; Scott Lecturer, University of Cambridge, 1963. Centennial Lecturer, University of Toronto, 1967. Director: Perkin-Elmer Corp.; Bulletin of Atomic Scientists, 1964–69. Board of Editors: Review of Scientific Instruments, 1950–52; Physical Review, 1951–53; Journal of Molecular Spectroscopy, 1957–60; Columbia University Forum, 1957–59. Fellow: American Phys. Society (Richtmyer Lecturer, 1959; Member Council, 1959–62, 1965–71; President, 1967); Inst. of Electrical and Electronics Engrs; Chairman, Sci. and Technology Adv. Commn for Manned Space Flight, NASA, 1964–69; Member: President's Science Adv. Cttee, 1966–69 (Vice-Chm., 1967–69); Scientific Adv. Bd, US Air Force, 1958–61; Soc. Française de Physique (Member Council, 1956–58); Nat. Acad. Scis (Mem. Council, 1969–72); American Acad. Arts and Sciences; American Philos. Society; American Astron. Society; American Assoc. of Physics Teachers; Société Royale des Sciences de Liège; Pontifical Acad., 1983; Foreign Mem., Royal Society, 1976; Hon. Mem., Optical Soc. of America. Trustee: Salk Inst. for Biological Studies, 1963–68; Rand Corp., 1965–70; Carnegie Instn of Washington, 1965–; Calif Inst. of Technol., 1979–. Chairman: Space Science Bd, Nat. Acad. of Sciences, 1970–73; Science Adv. Cttee, General Motors Corp., 1971–73; Bd of Dirs, General Motors, 1973–; Perkin-Elmer Corp., 1966–. Trustee: Pacific Sch. of Religion, 1983–; Enshrinee, Engrg and Sci. Hall of Fame, Ohio, 1983–. Holds numerous honorary degrees. Nobel Prize for Physics (jointly), 1964. Research Corp. Annual Award, 1958; Comstock Prize, Nat. Acad. of Sciences, 1959; Stuart Ballantine Medal, Franklin Inst., 1959, 1962; Rumford Premium, Amer. Acad. of Arts and Sciences, 1961; Thomas Young Medal and Prize, Inst. of Physics and Physical Soc., England, 1963; Medal of Honor, Inst. of Electrical and Electronics Engineers, 1967; C. E. K. Mees Medal, Optical Soc. of America, 1968; Churchman of the Year Award, Southern Baptist Theological Seminary, 1967; Distinguished Public Service Medal, NASA, 1969; Michelson-Morley Award, 1970; Wilhelm-Exner Award (Austria), 1970; Medal of Honor, Univ. of Liège, 1971; Earle K. Plyler Prize, 1977; Niels Bohr Internat. Gold Medal, 1979; Nat. Medal of Sci., 1983. National Inventors Hall of Fame, 1976; S Carolina Hall of Fame, 1977. *Publications:* (with A. L. Schawlow) Microwave Spectroscopy, 1955; (ed) Quantum Electronics, 1960; (ed with P. A. Miles) Quantum Electronics and Coherent Light, 1964; many scientific articles on microwave spectroscopy, molecular and nuclear structure, quantum electronics, radio and infra-red astrophysics; fundamental patents on masers and (with A. L. Schawlow) lasers. *Address:* Department of Physics, University of California, Berkeley, California 94720, USA. *T:* 642–1128. *Clubs:* Cosmos (Washington, DC); University (New York); Bohemian (San Francisco).

TOWNLEY, Sir John (Barton), Kt 1960; *b* 14 June 1914; *s* of Barton Townley and Margaret Alice, *d* of Richard Gorst; *m* 1939, Gwendoline May Ann, *d* of Arthur Simmonds; one *s* three *d. Educ:* Rydal Sch.; Downing Coll., Cambridge (Hon. Fellow); Sorbonne. MA Cambridge, 1939; PhD Cantab; DLit Sorbonne. Man. Dir and Vice-Chm., Northern Commercial Vehicles and associated cos, 1936–72. President: Preston Conservative Assoc., N and S Divisions, 1954–72 (Chairman: Preston S Conserv. Assoc., 1949–54; Preston N Cons. Assoc., 1958, first Life Pres., 1961); Preston Sea Cadet Corps, 1954–72; Preston Circle King George's Fund for Sailors, 1949–72; Preston Charities Assoc., 1949–; Life Vice-Pres., Preston, Chorley, Leyland Conservative Clubs Council (Pres. 1949–; Cons. Clubs Council of GB Medal, 1959). Life Mem., North Western Industrial Assoc. Adv. Bd. Vice-Pres., RNLI. Chairman: Preston YMCA Special Appeals Cttee; British Police Athletic Assoc., 1949–60; Pres., Lancs Police Clubs, 1959–63; Founder, and Pres., Police Hathersall Hall Youth Camp (now Lancs Boys Club), 1949–70; Founder Mem., Nat. Playing Fields Assoc.; Chm., Spastics Appeal, 1950–53; Founder Mem. 1948, and former Pres., OAP's Assoc. Founder many youth clubs (known as Rydal Clubs), inc. Liverpool, Manchester and Bermondsey, from 1934. Chm., Preston Arts Cttee, 1951–59. Hon. Plenipotentiary: Antigua, 1966; Barbados, 1967; Malta, 1968, 1969; Cyprus, 1972–74. *Recreations:* talking about rugby, cricket, boxing, golf. *Address:* The Lodge, Bilsborrow Hall, Preston, Lancs. *Clubs:* Hawks, Union, Pitt (Cambridge); Royal & Ancient Golf (St Andrews).

TOWNSEND, Albert Alan, FRS 1960; PhD; Reader (Experimental Fluid Mechanics), Cavendish Laboratory, University of Cambridge, since 1961 (Assistant Director of Research, 1950–61); Fellow of Emmanuel College, Cambridge, since 1947; *b* 22 Jan. 1917; *s* of A. R. Townsend and D. Gay; *m* 1950, V. Dees; one *s* two *d. Educ:* Telopea Park IHS; Melbourne and Cambridge Universities. PhD 1947. *Publications:* The Structure of Turbulent Shear Flow, 1956; papers in technical journals. *Address:* Emmanuel College, Cambridge.

TOWNSEND, Bryan Sydney; Chairman, Midlands Electricity Board, since 1986; *b* 2 Feb. 1930; *s* of Sydney and Gladys Townsend; *m* 1951, Betty Eileen Underwood; one *s* two *d. Educ:* Wolverton Technical Coll. CEng, FIEE; FBIM. Trainee, Northampton Electric Light & Power Co., 1946–50; successive appts, E Midlands, Eastern and Southern Electricity Bds, 1952–66; Southern Electricity Board: Swindon Dist Manager, 1966–68; Newbury Area Manager, 1968–70; Asst Chief Engr, 1970–73; Dep. Chief Engr, SE Electricity Bd, 1973–76; Chief Engr, S Wales Electricity Bd, 1976–78; Dep. Chm., SW Electricity Bd, 1978–86. *Recreation:* golf. *Address:* Midlands Electricity Board, Mucklow Hill, Halesowen, West Midlands B62 8BP. *T:* 021-422 4000.

TOWNSEND, Cyril David; MP (C) Bexleyheath since Feb. 1974; *b* 21 Dec. 1937; *s* of Lt-Col Cyril M. Townsend and Lois (*née* Henderson); *m* 1976, Anita, MA, *d* of late Lt-Col F. G. W. Walshe and of Mrs Walshe; two *s. Educ:* Bradfield Coll.; RMA Sandhurst. Commnd into Durham LI; served in Berlin and Hong Kong; active service in Cyprus, 1958 and Borneo, 1966; ADC to Governor and C-in-C Hong Kong 1964–66; Adjt 1DLI, 1966–68. A Personal Asst to Edward Heath, 1968–70; Mem. Conservative Research Dept, 1970–74. PPS to Minister of State, DHSS, 1979; Member: Select Cttee on Violence in the Family, 1975; Select Cttee on Foreign Affairs, 1982–83; Vice-Chm., Cons. Parly Defence Cttee, 1985– (Jt Sec., 1982–85); Chairman: Select Cttee on Armed Forces Bill, 1981; British-Cyprus Parly Gp; All-Party Freedom for Rudolf Hess Campaign; South Atlantic Council. Jt Chm., Council for Advancement of Arab-British Understanding, 1982–; Vice-Chairman: Friends of Cyprus, 1980–; Political Cttee, UNA, 1980–. Introduced Protection of Children Act, 1979. *Recreations:* books, music, exercise. *Address:* House of Commons, SW1A 0AA.

TOWNSEND, Mrs Joan, MA, MSc; Headmistress, Oxford High School, GPDST, since 1981; *b* 7 Dec. 1936; *d* of Emlyn Davies and Amelia Mary Davies (*née* Tyrer); *m* 1960, Prof. William Godfrey Townsend, RMCS, Shrivenham; two *d. Educ:* Somerville Coll., Oxford (Beilby Schol.; BA (Cl.I), MA); University College of Swansea, Univ. of Wales (MSc). School teaching and lecturing of various kinds, including: Tutor, Open University, 1971–75; Lectr, Oxford Polytechnic, 1975–76; Head of Mathematics, School of S Helen and S Katharine, Abingdon, 1976–81. *Publication:* paper in Qly Jl Maths and Applied Mech., 1965. *Address:* Silver Howe, 62 Iffley Turn, Oxford OX4 4HN. *T:* Oxford 715807.

TOWNSEND, Mrs Lena Moncrieff, CBE 1974; Member, Race Relations Board, 1967–72; *b* 3 Nov. 1911; twin *d* of late Captain R. G. Westropp, Cairo, Egypt; *m* (twice); two *s* one *d. Educ:* Downe House, Newbury; Somerville Coll., Oxford; Heidelberg Univ., Germany. During War of 1939–45 was an Organiser in WVS and in Women's Land Army, and then taught at Downe House. Mem. for Hampstead, LCC, 1955–65; Alderman, London Borough of Camden, 1964–65; Mem. for Camden, GLC, 1967–70; Alderman, GLC, 1970–77, and Dep. Chm., 1976–77; Inner London Education Authority: Dep. Leader, later Leader, 1969–70; Leader of the Opposition, 1970–71; Chm., Management Panel, Burnham Cttee, 1967–70; Mem., Women's European Cttee, 1972–75. Pres., Anglo-Egyptian Assoc., 1961–; Exec. Member: British Section, European Union of Women, 1970–81; British Council, European Movement, 1970– (Mem., Speaker's Panel); Cons. Gp for Europe, 1967– (Founder Mem.); British Section, Internat. Union of Local Authorities and Council of European Municipalities, 1975– (rep. on Jt Twinning Cttee, to 1983); London Europe Soc., 1977– (Vice-Pres. 1981–); Arkwright Arts Trust, 1971–84 (Chm., 1971–73); Chm., Students' Accommodation Cttee, Univ. of London, 1977–86 (and Mem., Intercollegiate Halls Management Cttee); Member: Council, Westfield Coll., London Univ., 1965–; Cons Nat. Adv. Cttee on Education, 1976–82; Governor: Barrett Street Coll., later London Coll. of Fashion, 1958–86 (Chm., 1967–86); Old Vic Trust, 1976–; Hampstead Parochial Primary Sch., 1979–. Former Patron, Lewis Carroll Soc. Hon. Fellow, Westfield Coll., 1983. *Recreations:* foreign languages, travel, the arts, gardening. *Address:* 16 Holly Mount, NW3 6SG. *T:* 01–435 8555.

TOWNSEND, Rear-Adm. Sir Leslie (William), KCVO 1981; CBE 1973; Member, Lord Chancellor's Panel of Independent Inspectors, since 1982; *b* 22 Feb. 1924; *s* of Ellen (*née* Alford) and William Bligh Townsend; *m* 1947, Marjorie Bennett; one *s* three *d. Educ:* Regent's Park School, Southampton. Joined RN, 1942; served in HMS Durban, 1942–43; Commissioned, 1943; HM Ships Spurwing, Astraea, Liverpool, Duke of York, Ceres, 1944–53; HMS Ceylon, 1956–58; Secretary to ACNS, 1959, to VCNS, 1967, to First Sea Lord, 1970; MA to CDS, 1971–73, to Chm. NATO Mil. Cttee, 1974; Dir, Naval and WRNS Officers' Appointments, 1977; Rear-Adm. 1979; Defence Services Sec., 1979–82. *Recreations:* fishing, cooking. *Address:* 21 Osborne View Road, Hill Head, near Fareham, Hants. *T:* Stubbington 663446. *Clubs:* Army and Navy; Hill Head Sailing.

TOWNSEND, Prof. Peter Brereton; Professor of Social Policy, University of Bristol, since 1982; *b* 6 April 1928; *s* of Philip Brereton Townsend and Alice Mary Townsend (*née* Southcote); *m* 1st, 1949, Ruth (*née* Pearce); four *s*; 2nd, 1977, Joy (*née* Skegg); one *d*; 3rd, 1985, Jean (formerly Corston); one step *s* one step *d. Educ:* Fleet Road Elementary Sch., London; University Coll. Sch., London; St John's Coll., Cambridge Univ.; Free Univ., Berlin. Research Sec., Political and Economic Planning, 1952–54; Research Officer, Inst. of Community Studies, 1954–57; Research Fellow and then Lectr in Social Administration, London Sch. of Economics, 1957–63; Prof. of Sociology, 1963–81, Pro-Vice-Chancellor (Social Policy), 1975–78, Univ. of Essex; Dir, Sch. of Applied Social Studies, Bristol Univ., 1983–85. Vis. Prof. of Sociology, Essex Univ., 1982–. Chm., the Fabian Society, 1965–66 (Chairman: Social Policy Cttee, 1970–82; Res. and Pubns Cttee, 1983–); Pres., Psychiatric Rehabilitation Assoc., 1968–; Chairman: Child Poverty Action Gp, 1969–; Disability Alliance, 1974–; Member: Chief Scientist's Cttee, DHSS, 1976–78; Govt Working Gp on Inequalities and Health, 1977–80; MSC Working Gp on Quota Scheme for Disabled, 1983–85. UNESCO consultant on poverty and development, 1978–80; Consultant: to GLC on poverty and the labour market in London, 1985–86; to Northern RHA on Inequalities of Health, 1985–86. *Publications:* The Family Life of Old People, 1957; National Superannuation (co-author), 1957; Nursing Homes in England and Wales (co-author), 1961; The Last Refuge: a survey of residential institutions and homes for the aged in England and Wales, 1962; The Aged in the Welfare State (co-author), 1965; The Poor and the Poorest (co-author), 1965; Old People in Three Industrial Societies (co-author), 1968; (ed) The Concept of Poverty, 1970; (ed) Labour and Inequality, 1972; The Social Minority, 1973; Sociology and Social Policy, 1975; Poverty in the United Kingdom: a survey of household resources and standards of living, 1979; (ed) Labour and Equality, 1980; Inequalities in Health (co-author), 1980; Manifesto (co-author), 1981; (ed jtly) Disability in Britain, 1981; The Family and Later Life, 1981; (ed jtly) Responses to Poverty: lessons from Europe, 1984; (jtly) Inequalities of Health in the Northern Region, 1986; Poverty and the London Labour Market: interim report, 1986. *Recreation:* athletics. *Address:* 149 Leander Road, SW2 2LP.

TOWNSEND, Group Captain Peter Wooldridge, CVO 1947; DSO 1941; DFC and Bar, 1940; *b* 22 Nov. 1914; *s* of late Lt-Col E. C. Townsend; *m* 1959, Marie Luce, *d* of Franz Jamagne, Brussels, Belgium; one *s* two *d* (two *s* by former marriage). *Educ:* Haileybury; Royal Air Force Coll., Cranwell. Royal Air Force, 1933; served War of 1939–45, Wing Commander, 1941 (despatches, DFC and Bar, DSO). Equerry to King George VI, 1944–52; Deputy Master of HM Household, 1950; Equerry to the Queen, 1952–53; Air Attaché, Brussels, 1953–56. *Publications:* Earth, My Friend, 1959; Duel of Eagles, 1970; The Last Emperor, 1975; Time and Chance (autobiog.), 1978; The Smallest Pawns in the Game, 1979; The Girl in the White Ship, 1981; The Postman of Nagasaki, 1984; Duel in the Dark, 1986. *Address:* La Mare aux Oiseaux, 78116 Saint-Leger-en-Yvelines, France.

TOWNSEND, Air Vice-Marshal William Edwin, CB 1971; CBE 1965 (OBE 1957); RAAF retired; *b* 25 April 1916; *s* of William Edwin Townsend (Senior) and Jessie May Lewry; *m* 1939, Linda Ruth Deakins; two *s* two *d. Educ:* Longerenong Coll., Vic, Australia. Grad. Pt Cook, 1937; Chief Flying Instr and 2nd i/c No 8 EFTS, 1940; Sen. Trg Staff Officer, 1941; Comdg Officer 67 and 22 Sqdns, 1942–43; shot down over enemy territory, escaped and returned to Aust., 1944; Comdg Officer, 5 Operational Trg Unit, 1944; SASO, NE Area, 1946; OC, Port Moresby, 1947–48; Sec., Australian Jt Staff, Washington, 1949–50; OC, East Sale, 1951–52; CO and Sen. Officer i/c Admin, Home Command, 1953–54; OC 78 Fighter Wing, 1955–56; Dir of Ops, 1957–60; OC, RAAF Williamtown, 1960–62; Dir Gen. Personnel, 1962–64; OC, RAAF, Butterworth, Malaysia, incl. service in Vietnam, 1964–67 (Vietnam Service Medal); Dep. CAS, 1967–69; AOC Operational Comd, RAAF, 1969–72; Dir, State Emergency Services and Civil Defence, and Chm., Bush Fire Council of NSW, 1973–80. Dir-Gen., Australia-Britain Soc., 1981–84. Pres., Aust. Branch, RAF Escaping Soc.; Vice-Pres., St John Ambulance Assoc., NSW Centre. Councillor, Royal Humane Soc. of NSW. FAIM; Mem., Aust. Inst. of Emergency Services. *Address:* 8 Tutus Street, Balgowlah Heights, NSW 2093, Australia. *Clubs:* Royal Automobile; Imperial Service (Sydney); Manly Golf.

TOWNSHEND, family name of **Marquess Townshend.**

TOWNSHEND, 7th Marquess *cr* 1787; **George John Patrick Dominic Townshend;** Bt 1617; Baron Townshend, 1661; Viscount Townshend, 1682; *b* 13 May 1916; *s* of 6th Marquess and Gladys Ethel Gwendolen Eugenie (*d* 1959), *e d* of late Thomas Sutherst, barrister; *S* father, 1921; *m* 1st, 1939, Elizabeth (marr. diss. 1960; she *m* 1960, Brig. Sir James Gault, KCMG, MVO, OBE), *o d* of Thomas Luby, Indian CS; one *s* two *d*; 2nd, 1960, Ann Frances, *d* of Arthur Pellew Darlow; one *s* one *d*. Norfolk Yeomanry TA, 1936–40; Scots Guards, 1940–45. Chairman: Anglia Television Gp plc, 1971–86; Anglia Television Ltd, 1958–86; Survival Anglia, 1971–86; Anchor Enterprises Ltd, 1967–; AP Bank Ltd, 1975–; East Coast Grain Ltd, 1982–; D. E. Longe & Co. Ltd, 1982–; Norfolk Agricultural Station, 1973–; Raynham Farm Co. Ltd, 1957–; Vice-Chairman: Norwich Union Life Insurance Society Ltd, 1973–86; Norwich Union Fire Insurance Society Ltd, 1975–86; Director: Scottish Union & National Insurance Co., 1968–86; Maritime Insurance Co. Ltd, 1968–86; London Merchant Securities plc, 1964–; Norwich Union (Holdings) plc, 1981–86; Napak Ltd, 1982–. Chairman, Royal Norfolk Agricultural Association. DL Norfolk, 1951–61. *Heir: s* Viscount Raynham, *qv. Address:* Raynham Hall, Fakenham, Norfolk. *T:* Fakenham 2133. *Clubs:* White's, Pratt's, MCC; Norfolk (Norwich); Royal Yacht Squadron; House of Lords Yacht.

TOWNSING, Sir Kenneth (Joseph), Kt 1982; CMG 1971; ISO 1966; Director: Western Mining Corporation Ltd, since 1975; Central Norseman Gold Corporation, since 1982; *b* 25 July 1914; *s* of J. W. and L. A. Townsing; *m* 1942, Frances Olive Daniel; two *s* one *d. Educ:* Perth Boys' Sch.; Univ. of Western Australia. Treasury Officer, 1933–39. Served War, AIF (Middle East), 1940–46, Major. Public Service Inspector, 1946–49; Sec., Public Service Commissioner's Office, 1949–52; Dep. Under Treasurer, 1952–57; Public Service Comr, 1958–59; Under Treasurer (Permanent Head), 1959–75. Chm., Salaries and Allowances Tribunal, 1975–84. Mem. Senate, Univ. of Western Australia, 1954–70 (Chm. Finance Cttee, 1956–70; Pro-Chancellor, 1968–70); Comr, Rural and Industries Bank, 1959–65; Member: Jackson Cttee on Tertiary Educn, 1967; Tertiary Educn Commn, 1971–74; Past Mem. numerous other Bds and Cttees. Fellow, W Australian Museum, 1975; Hon. Zoo Associate, 1979. FASA. Hon. LLD Univ. of W Australia, 1971; DUniv Murdoch, 1982. *Recreation:* gardening. *Address:* 22 Robin Street, Mount Lawley, WA 6050, Australia. *T:* 272 1393. *Club:* University House (Perth).

TOWRY, Peter; *see* Piper, Sir D. T.

TOY, Francis Carter, CBE 1947; DSc, FInstP; *b* 5 May 1892; 2nd *s* of late Sir Henry Toy, CA, JP, Helston, Cornwall; *m* 1921, Gladys Marguerite, *d* of late James Thomas, CA, JP, Tregays, Lostwithiel, Cornwall; one *d. Educ:* Launceston Coll., Cornwall; University College, London. Fellow of University College, London. Served European War, 1914–18; Lieut, Cornwall Fortress Engineers, 1914–16; Lieut, First Army Field Survey Co. (Sound Ranging, Y section), BEF France, 1917–18. Physicist, British Photographic Research Association, 1919–29; Deputy Director of the Shirley Institute, Research Station of British Cotton Industry Research Association, 1930–43, Director, 1944–55. President: Manchester Fedn of Scientific Societies, 1953–55; Inst of Physics, 1948–50; Manchester Statistical Society, 1951–53; Manchester Literary and Philosophical Society, 1956–58; Past Chairman Cttee of Directors of Research Associations; Fellow of the Textile Institute; Past Member Court and Council, UMIST. *Publications:* numerous scientific. *Recreations:* travel, music and sport (cricket and golf). *Address:* 8 Fulshaw Court, Wilmslow, Cheshire. *T:* Wilmslow 525141. *Club:* Athenæum.

TOY, Rev. Canon John, PhD; Chancellor of York Minster, since 1983 (also Librarian and Guestmaster); Prebendary of Tockerington, since 1983; *b* 25 Nov. 1930; *e s* of late Sidney Toy, FSA and late Violet Mary (*née* Doudney); *m* 1963, Mollie *d* of Eric and Elsie Tilbury; one *s* one *d. Educ:* Epsom County Grammar Sch.; Hatfield Coll., Durham (BA 1st cl. Hons. Theol. 1953, MA 1962). PhD Leeds, 1982. Ordained deacon, 1955, priest, 1956; Curate, St Paul's, Lorrimore Sq., Southwark, 1955–58; Student Christian Movement Sec. for S of England, 1958–60; Chaplain: Ely Theol Coll., 1960–64; St Andrew's Church, Gothenburg, Sweden, 1965–69; St John's College, York: Lectr in Theology, 1969; Sen. Lectr, 1972; Principal Lectr, 1979–83. *Publications:* contrib. to learned jls and cathedral booklets. *Recreations:* music, history, architecture. *Address:* 10 Precentor's Court, York YO1 2EJ. *T:* York 20877. *Club:* Yorkshire (York).

TOY, Sam; Chairman and Managing Director, Ford Motor Co. Ltd, 1980–86; *b* 21 Aug. 1923; *s* of Edward and Lillian Toy; *m* 1st, 1944, Jean Balls; one *s*; 2nd, 1950, Joan Franklin Rook; two *s* one *d*; 3rd, 1984, Janetta McMorrow. *Educ:* Falmouth Grammar Sch.; Fitzwilliam Coll., Cambridge (MA; Hon. Fellow, 1984). Pilot (Flt Lieut), RAF, 1942–48. Graduate trainee, Ford Motor Co. Ltd, 1948; thereafter, all business career with Ford Motor Co. Ltd. Pres., SMMT, 1986– (Vice-Pres., 1982–86). *Recreations:* trout and salmon fishing, golf. *Address:* c/o Society of Motor Manufacturers and Traders, Forbes House, Halkin Street, SW1. *Clubs:* Lord's Taverners', Eccentric.

TOYE, Wendy; theatrical producer; film director; choreographer, actress, dancer; *b* 1 May 1917. First professional appearance as Mustard-seed in A Midsummer Night's Dream, Old Vic, 1929; principal dancer in Hiawatha, Royal Albert Hall, 1931; Marigold, Phœbe in Toad of Toad Hall and produced dances, Royalty, Christmas, 1931–32; in early 1930s performed and choreographed for the very distinguished Carmargo Society of Ballet; guest artist with Sadler's Wells Ballet and Mme Rambert's Ballet Club; went to Denmark as principal dancer with British Ballet, organized by Adeline Genée, 1932; danced in C. B. Cochran's The Miracle, Lyceum, 1932; masked dancer in Ballerina, Gaiety, 1933; member of Ninette de Valois' original Vic Wells Ballet, principal dancer for Ninette de Valois in The Golden Toy, Coliseum, 1934; toured with Anton Dolin's ballet (choreog. for divertissements and short ballets), 1934–35; in Tulip Time, Alhambra, then Markova-Dolin Ballet as principal dancer and choreog., 1935; in Love and How to Cure It, Globe, 1937. Arranged dances and ballets for many shows and films including most of George Black's productions for next 7 years, notably Black Velvet in which also principal dancer, 1939. Shakespearean season, Open Air Theatre, 1939. *Theatre productions:* Big Ben, Bless the Bride, Tough at the Top (for C. B. Cochran), Adelphi; The Shepherd Show, Prince's; Co-Director and Choreographer, Peter Pan, New York; And So To Bed, New Theatre; Co-Director and Choreographer, Feu d'Artifice, Paris; Night of Masquerade, Q; Second Threshold, Vaudeville; Choreography for Three's Company in Joyce Grenfell Requests the Pleasure, Fortune; Wild Thyme, Duke of York's; Lady at the Wheel, Lyric, Hammersmith; Majority of One, Phœnix; Magic Lantern, Saville; As You Like It, Old Vic; Virtue in Danger, Mermaid and Strand; Robert and Elizabeth, Lyric; On the Level, Saville; Midsummer Night's Dream, Shakespeare quatercentenary Latin American tour, 1964; Soldier's Tale, Edinburgh Festival, 1967; Boots and Strawberry Jam, Nottingham Playhouse, 1968; The Great Waltz, Drury Lane, 1970; Showboat, Adelphi, 1971; She Stoops to Conquer, Young Vic, 1972; Cowardy Custard, Mermaid, 1972; Stand and Deliver, Roundhouse, 1972; R loves J, Chichester, 1973; The Confederacy, Chichester, 1974; The Englishman Amused, Young Vic, 1974; Follow The Star, Chichester, 1974, Westminster Theatre, 1976; Made in Heaven, Chichester, 1975; Make Me a World, Chichester, 1976; Once More with Music (with Cicely Courtneidge and Jack Hulbert),

1976; Oh, Mr Porter, Mermaid, 1977; Dance for Gods, Conversations, 1979; Colette, Comedy, 1980; Gingerbread Man, Water Mill, 1981; This Thing Called Love, Ambassadors, 1983; (Associate Prod.) Singin' in the Rain, Palladium, 1983; (dir and narr.) Noel and Gertie, Monte Carlo and Canada; (Associate Prod.) Barnham, Manchester, 1984, Victoria Palace, 1985; Birds of a Feather, 1984, and Mad Woman of Chaillot, 1985, Niagara-on-the-Lake; Gala for Joyce Grenfell Tribute, 1985; (Associate Prod.) Torvill and Dean World Tour, 1985; Once Upon a Mattress, Watermill Theatre, 1985; Kiss Me Kate, Aarhus and Copenhagen, 1986. *Opera Productions:* Bluebeard's Castle (Bartok), Sadler's Wells and Brussels; The Telephone (Menotti), Sadler's Wells; Russalka (Dvořák), Sadler's Wells; Fledermaus, Coliseum and Sadler's Wells; Orpheus in the Underworld, Sadler's Wells and Australia; La Vie Parisienne, Sadler's Wells; Seraglio, Bath Festival, 1967; The Impresario, Don Pasquale (for Phoenix Opera Group), 1968; The Italian Girl in Algiers, Coliseum, 1968; La Cenerentola; Merry Widow, 1979, Orpheus in the Underworld, 1981, ENO North; The Mikado, Nat. Opera Co., Ankara, 1982; Italian Girl in Algiers, ENO, 1982. *Films directed:* The Stranger Left No Card; The Teckman Mystery; Raising a Riot; The Twelfth Day of Christmas; Three Cases of Murder; All for Mary; True as a Turtle; We Joined the Navy; The King's Breakfast; Cliff in Scotland; A Goodly Manor for a Song; Girls Wanted—Istanbul; Trial by Jury (TV). Productions for TV, etc, inc. Golden Gala, ATV, 1978; Follow the Star, BBC2, 1979; Stranger in Town, Anglia, 1981. Trained with Euphen MacLaren, Karsavina, Dolin, Morosoff, Legat, Rambert. Silver Jubilee Medal, 1977. *Address:* c/o David Watson, Simpson Fox, 57 Filmer Road, SW6 7JF.

TOYN, Richard John; His Honour Judge Toyn; a Circuit Judge since 1972; *b* 24 Jan. 1927; *s* of Richard Thomas Millington Toyn and Ethel Toyn; *m* 1955, Joyce Evelyn Goodwin; two *s* two *d*. *Educ:* Solihull Sch.; Bristol Grammar Sch.; Bristol Univ. (LLB). Royal Army Service Corps, 1948–50. Called to the Bar, Gray's Inn, 1950. Mem., Parole Bd, 1978–80. *Recreations:* music, drama, photography. *Address:* c/o Victoria Law Courts, Birmingham.

TOYNBEE, Polly; Columnist, The Guardian, since 1977; writer; *b* 27 Dec. 1946; *d* of late Philip Toynbee, and of Anne Powell; *m* 1970, Peter Jenkins, *qv*; one *s* two *d* and one step-*d*. *Educ:* Badminton Sch.; Holland Park Comprehensive; St Anne's Coll., Oxford. Reporter, The Observer, 1968–71; Editor, The Washington Monthly, USA, 1972–73; Feature Writer, The Observer, 1974–76. Contested (SDP) Lewisham E, 1983. Mem., Nat. Cttee, 1981–, Policy Cttee, 1981–, SDP. Catherine Pakenham Award for Journalism, 1975; British Press Award, 1977, 1982. *Publications:* Leftovers, 1966; A Working Life, 1970 (paperback 1972); Hospital, 1977 (paperback 1979); The Way We Live Now, 1981; Lost Children, 1985. *Address:* 1 Crescent Grove, SW4. *T:* 01–622 6492.

TRACEY, Richard Patrick, JP; MP (C) Surbiton, since 1983; Parliamentary Under Secretary of State, Department of the Environment (with special responsibility for sport), since 1985; *b* 8 Feb. 1943; *o s* of late P. H. (Dick) Tracey and of Hilda Tracey; *m* 1974, Katharine Gardner; one *s* three *d*. *Educ:* King Edward VI Sch., Stratford-upon-Avon; Birmingham Univ. (LLB Hons). Leader Writer, Daily Express, 1964–66; Presenter/Reporter, BBC Television and Radio, 1966–78: internat. news and current affairs (The World at One, PM, Today, Newsdesk, 24 Hours, The Money Prog.); feature programmes (Wheelbase, Waterline, Motoring and the Motorist, You and Yours, Checkpoint); also documentaries; Public Affairs Consultant/Advisor, 1978–83. Member: Econ. Res. Council, 1981–; ISIS Assoc., 1981–. Various Conservative Party Offices, 1974–81; Dep. Chm., Greater London Cons. Party, 1981–83; Mem., Cons. National Union Exec. Cttee, 1981–83. PPS to Min. of State for Trade and Industry (IT), 1984–85. Sec., Cons. Parly Media Cttee, 1983–84; Jt Sec., Cons. Parly Greater London MP's Cttee, 1983–84. Contested (C) Northampton N, Oct. 1974. JP SW London (Wimbledon PSD), 1977. Freeman, City of London, 1984. *Publications:* (with Richard Hudson-Evans) The World of Motor Sport, 1971; (with Michael Clayton) Hickstead—the first twelve years, 1972; articles, pamphlets. *Recreations:* riding, boating, debating. *Address:* House of Commons, SW1A 0AA. *T:* 01–219 5196. *Club:* Wig and Pen.

TRACY; *see* Hanbury-Tracy, family name of Baron Sudeley.

TRACY, Rear-Adm. Hugh Gordon Henry, CB 1965; DSC 1945; *b* 15 Nov. 1912; *e s* of Comdr A. F. G. Tracy, RN; *m* 1938, Muriel, *d* of Maj.-Gen. Sir R. B. Ainsworth, CB, DSO, OBE; two *s* one *d*. *Educ:* Nautical Coll., Pangbourne. Joined RN, 1929; Lieut, 1934; served in HMS Shropshire, Hawkins and Furious, in Admiralty and attended Advanced Engineering course before promotion to Lt-Comdr, 1942; Sen. Engineer, HMS Illustrious, 1942–44; Asst to Manager, Engineering Dept, HM Dockyard Chatham, 1944–46; Comdr 1946; served in HMS Manxman, Admiralty, RN Engineering Coll. and HM Dockyard Malta; Captain, 1955; Asst Director of Marine Engineering, Admiralty, 1956–58; CO HMS Sultan, 1959–60; Imperial Defence Coll., 1961; CSO (Tech.) to Flag Officer, Sea Training, 1962–63; Rear-Admiral, 1963; Director of Marine Engineering, Ministry of Defence (Navy), 1963–66; retired, 1966. Chm., Wilts Gardens Trust. *Recreations:* gardening, plant ecology. *Address:* Orchard House, Claverton, Bath BA2 7BG. *T:* Bath 65650. *Club:* Army and Navy.

TRACY, Walter Valentine, RDI; *b* 14 Feb. 1914; *s* of Walter and Anne Tracy; *m* 1942, Muriel Frances Campbell. *Educ:* Central Sch. of Arts and Crafts. Apprentice compositor, Wm Clowes Ltd, 1930–35; typographic studio, Baynard Press, 1935–38; Notley Advertising, 1938–46; freelance, 1946–47; on staff of (British) Linotype Co., editor Linotype Matrix, i/c typographic design, 1947–73; Linotype-Paul, 1973–78. In 1965, assisted Editor of The Times in re-designing the paper for news on front page, May 1966; designed newspaper types: Jubilee, 1953; Adsans, 1959; Maximus, 1967; Telegraph Modern, 1969; Times-Europa, 1972; also designed: Hebrew types Gold, Silver, 1975 (under pseudonym David Silver) for Linotype-Paul; Arabic types Kufic Light, Med., Bold, 1979 for Letraset; Qadi, 1983 for Linotype-Paul; Oasis, 1985 for Kroy. RDI 1973. *Publications:* Letters of Credit: a view of type design, 1986; contribs to Penrose Annual, Alphabet, Motif, Typographica, Bulletin of British Society for Middle Eastern Studies. *Address:* 2 Cedar Court, The Drive, Finchley Way, N3 1AE. *T:* 01–349 3785. *Club:* Double Crown (Hon. Mem.).

TRAFFORD; *see* de Trafford.

TRAFFORD, Sir Anthony; *see* Trafford, Sir J. A. P.

TRAFFORD, Ian Colton, OBE 1967; Publisher, The Times Supplements, since 1981; Deputy Chairman, Times Books Ltd, since 1981; *b* 8 July 1928; *s* of Dr Harold Trafford and late Laura Dorothy Trafford; *m* 1st, 1949, Nella Georgara (marr. diss. 1964); one *d*; 2nd, 1972, Jacqueline Carole Trenque. *Educ:* Charterhouse; St John's Coll., Oxford. Feature writer and industrial correspondent, The Financial Times, 1951–58; UK Correspondent, Barrons Weekly, New York, 1954–60; Director, Industrial and Trade Fairs Holdings Ltd, 1958–71, Managing Director, 1966–71; Director-General British Trade Fairs in: Peking, 1964; Moscow, 1966; Bucharest, 1968; Sao Paulo, 1969; Buenos Aires, 1970; Man. Dir, Economist Newspaper, 1971–81; Chm., Economist Intelligence Unit, 1971–79. Local Dir, W London Board, Commercial Union Assce, 1974–83. OBE awarded for services to exports. *Address:* Grafton House, Westhall Road, Warlingham, Surrey CR3 9NA. *T:* Upper Warlingham 2048.

See also Sir J. A. P. Trafford.

TRAFFORD, Sir (Joseph) Anthony (Porteous), Kt 1985; Consultant Physician, Brighton Health Authority, since 1965; Director of Renal and Artificial Kidney Unit, Brighton, since 1966; *b* 20 July 1932; *s* of Dr Harold Trafford, Warlingham, Surrey, and late Laura Trafford; *m* 1960, Helen Chalk; one *s* one *d*. *Educ:* St Edmund's, Hindhead; Charterhouse; Guy's Hosp., Univ. of London. MB, BS Hons 1957; MRCP 1961, FRCP 1974. Sen. Registrar, Guy's Hosp., 1963–66; Fulbright Scholar, Johns Hopkins Univ., 1963; MP (C) The Wrekin, 1970–Feb. 1974. Chm. of Council and Senior Pro-Chancellor, Univ. of Sussex, 1985–. *Publications:* contribs to med. jls and textbooks. *Recreations:* golf, tennis, bridge, military history. *Address:* 103 The Drive, Hove, East Sussex. *T:* Brighton 731567.

See also I. C. Trafford.

TRAHAIR, John Rosewarne; Chairman, Plymouth District Health Authority, since 1981; *b* 29 March 1921; *s* of late Percy Edward Trahair and Edith Irene Trahair; *m* 1948, Patricia Elizabeth (*née* Godrich); one *s* one *d*. *Educ:* Leys Sch.; Christ's Coll., Cambridge (MA). FCIS. Served with Royal Artillery, 1941–46 (Captain). Finance Dir, Farleys Infant Food Ltd, 1948–73; Dir 1950–74, Dep. Chm. 1956–74, Western Credit Holdings Ltd. Chairman: Moorhaven HMC, 1959–66; Plymouth and District HMC, 1966–74; Member: SW Regional Hosp. Bd, 1965–74 (Vice-Chm. 1971–73, Chm. 1973–74); South Western RHA, 1974–81. Mem., Devon CC, 1977–81. *Recreations:* sailing, walking. *Address:* West Park, Ivybridge, South Devon. *T:* Plymouth 892466. *Club:* Royal Western Yacht.

TRAHERNE, Sir Cennydd (George), KG 1970; Kt 1964; TD 1950; MA; HM Lord-Lieutenant of Mid, South and West Glamorgan, 1974–85 (HM Lieutenant for Glamorgan, 1952–74); *b* 14 Dec. 1910; *er s* of late Comdr L. E. Traherne, RN, of Coedarhydyglyn, near Cardiff, and Dorothy, *d* of G. F. S. Sinclair; *m* 1934, Olivera Rowena, OBE, BA, JP, DStJ, *d* of late James Binney, and late Lady Marjory Binney, Pampisford Hall, Cambridgeshire. *Educ:* Wellington; Brasenose Coll., Oxford. Barrister, Inner Temple, 1938 (Hon. Bencher, 1983). 81st Field Regt RA (TA), 1934–43; 102 Provost Coy, Corps of Military Police, 1943–45 (despatches); Dep. Asst Provost Marshal, Second British Army, 1945; 53rd Div. Provost Company, Royal Military Police, 1947–49, TA; Hon. Colonel: 53 Div. Signal Regt, 1953–58; 282 (Glamorgan Yeomanry) Field Regt RA (TA), 1958–61; 282 (Glam and Mon) Regt RA (TA), 1962–67; 37 (Wessex and Welsh) Signal Regt, T&AVR, 1971–75; Glamorgan ACF, 1982. DL 1946, JP 1946, Glamorgan. Deputy Chairman Glamorgan Quarter Sessions, 1949–52; President, Welsh College of Advanced Technology, 1957–65. Chairman, Rep. Body of the Church in Wales, 1965–77; Pres., Welsh Nat. Sch. of Medicine, 1970. Director: Cardiff Building Society, 1953–85 (Chm., 1964–85); Wales Gas Board, 1958–71; Commercial Bank of Wales, 1972–; Chm., Wales Gas Consultative Council, 1958–71. Member, Gorsedd of the Bards of Wales. Honorary Freeman: Borough of Cowbridge, 1971; Borough of Vale of Glamorgan, 1984; City of Cardiff, 1985. Hon. LLD University of Wales. KStJ (Sub Prior, Priory of Wales, 1978). *Address:* Coedarhydyglyn, near Cardiff, S Wales CF5 6SF. *T:* Peterston-super-Ely 760321. *Clubs:* Athenæum; Cardiff and County (Cardiff).

TRAILL, Sir Alan Towers, GBE 1984; Director, PWS International, since 1986; Underwriting Member of Lloyd's, since 1963; *b* 7 May 1935; *s* of George Traill and Margaret Eleanor (*née* Matthews); *m* 1964, Sarah Jane (*née* Hutt); one *s*. *Educ:* St Andrew's Sch., Eastbourne; Charterhouse; Jesus Coll., Cambridge (MA). Dir, Lyon Jago Webb, 1983–. Mem., London Ct of Internat. Arbitration, 1981–. Mem. Council, British Insurance Brokers Assoc., 1978–79; Chm., Reinsurance Brokers Cttee of the Assoc., 1978–. Member, Court of Common Council, City of London, 1970; Alderman for Langbourn Ward, 1975–; Sheriff, 1982–83; Lord Mayor of London, 1984–85. Master, Worshipful Co. of Cutlers, 1979–80; Dir, City Arts Trust, 1980–; Governor: Royal Shakespeare Co., 1982–; King Edward's Sch., Witley, 1980–; Almoner, Christ's Hosp. Foundn, 1980–. KStJ 1985. *Recreations:* shooting, skiing, DIY, travel, opera, assisting education. *Address:* 52 Minories, EC3N 1JJ. *T:* 01–480 6622. *Clubs:* City Livery, Royal Automobile.

TRAIN, Christopher John, CB 1986; Deputy Under Secretary of State, Home Office, and Director-General, Prison Service, since 1983; *b* 12 March 1932; *s* of late Keith Sydney Sayer Train and of Edna Ashby Train; *m* 1957, Sheila Mary Watson; one *s* one *d*. *Educ:* Nottingham High Sch.; Christ Church Oxford (BA Lit. Hum., MA). Served Royal Navy, 1955–57; Assistant Master, St Paul's Sch., W Kensington, 1957–67; Principal, Home Office, 1968; Asst Sec., Home Office, 1972; Secretary, Royal Commn on Criminal Procedure, 1978–80; Asst Under Sec. of State, Home Office, 1980–83. *Recreations:* playing cricket, collecting cricket books, jogging, gardening. *Address:* c/o Home Office, 50 Queen Anne's Gate, SW1. *Clubs:* Reform; Vincent's (Oxford).

TRAIN, David, MC 1945; PhD; FCGI, FPS, FRSC; FEng, FIChemE; Senior Consultant, Cremer and Warner, Consulting Engineers and Scientists, since 1982 (Senior Partner, 1980–82); *b* 27 Feb. 1919; *s* of Charles and Elsie Louisa Train; *m* 1943, Jeanne Catherine, *d* of late William R. and M. M. Edmunds; two *s*. *Educ:* Lady Hawkins' Grammar Sch., Kington; School of Pharmacy, Univ. of London; Northampton Coll. of Advanced Technology; Imperial Coll., Univ. of London. Fairchild Schol. 1940, MPS 1941, Hewlett Exhibn 1941; BPharm 1942, PhC 1942; BScChemEng 1949, PhD 1956, DIC 1956. ARIC 1949; FRSH 1972; FCGI 1982 (ACGI 1949); FEng 1983. Apprenticed to F. T. Roper and Daughter, Kington, 1935–38. War service: St John's Hosp. Reserve, 1939; RAMC (non-med.), NW Europe, 1942–45; 212 Fd Amb. 53rd Welsh (Lieut). Lectr in Pharmaceutical Engrg Science, 1949–59, Reader, 1959–61, Sch. of Pharmacy, London; Vis. Prof., Univ. of Wisconsin, 1959. Partner, Cremer and Warner, 1961–82. Examiner: for Pharm. Soc. of Gt Brit., 1949–56; IChemE, 1956–66; Mem. Bd of Studies in Chem. Engrg, Univ. of London, 1958–; External Examr, PhD Theses, 1956–75; Jt Hon. Secretary: Brit. Pharm. Conf., 1958–64; IChemE, 1972–77. Mem. Council: Science and Technology Insts, 1972–; Engrg Instns Technical Cttee, 1980–; Member: Adv. Cttee on Oil Pollution of the Sea, 1973–84; Air Pollution Control Assoc., USA, 1971–84; Fédn Internat. Pharmaceutique, 1970–82. Liveryman: Worshipful Soc. of Apothecaries, 1975–; Worshipful Co. of Engineers, 1983–. *Publications:* various, on compression of powders, protection of the environment, acidic emissions, hazards in medicaments, preventative toxicology. *Recreations:* gardening, travelling. *Address:* 3 Grayland Close, Bromley, Kent BR1 2PA. *T:* 01–464 4701. *Club:* Athenæum.

TRAINOR, James P.; a Judge of the High Court of Kenya, 1980–85, retired; *b* Belfast, 14 Oct. 1914; *s* of Owen Trainor and Mary Rose (*née* McArdle); *m* 1954, Angela (*née* O'Connor); one *s* two *d*. *Educ:* Mount St Joseph's, Monaghan, Ireland; University Coll., Dublin (BA). Admitted solicitor, Dublin, 1936; called to Irish Bar, King's Inn, 1950. Colonial Service: Magistrate, Singapore, 1954–55; Justice, Special Court, Cyprus, 1955–60; Called to English Bar, Gray's Inn, 1957; Comdr, High Commissioner's Court, W Pacific High Commn, 1960–61; Co-Pres., Jt Court, Anglo-French Condominium of the New Hebrides, 1960–72; Judge, Fiji Court of Appeal, 1960–70; Judge, High Court of the Western Pacific, 1961–72; Judge of Supreme Court, Hong Kong, 1972–79, retired from HM Overseas Judiciary, 1980. Commandeur de l'Ordre Nationale du Mérite (France), 1967. *Recreations:* golf, reading, music. *Address:* 4 Mount Rule House, Braddan, Isle of Man. *Clubs:* Hong Kong, Royal Hong Kong Golf, Royal Hong Kong Jockey (Hong Kong); United Services, Milltown Golf (Dublin); Castletown Golf (IoM).

TRANMIRE, Baron *cr* 1974 (Life Peer), of Upsall, North Yorkshire; **Robert Hugh Turton,** PC 1955; KBE 1971; MC 1942; JP; DL; *b* 8 Aug. 1903; *s* of late Major R. B. Turton, Kildale Hall, Kildale, York; *m* 1928, Ruby Christian, *d* of late Robert T. Scott, Beechmont, Sevenoaks; three *s* one *d*. *Educ:* Eton; Balliol Coll., Oxford. Called to Bar, Inner Temple, 1926; joined 4th Bn of Green Howards at outbreak of war, 1939; served as DAAG 50th (N) Division, AAG GHQ MEF. MP (C) Thirsk and Malton, 1929–Feb. 1974. Parly Sec., Min. of Nat. Insurance, 1951–53. Min. of Pensions and Nat. Insce, 1953–54; Joint Parly Under-Sec. of State for Foreign Affairs, Oct. 1954–Dec. 1955; Minister of Health, Dec. 1955–Jan. 1957; Chm., Select Cttee on Procedure, 1970–74. Chm., Commonwealth Industries Assoc., 1963–74. JP 1936, DL 1962, N Riding, Co. York. Hon. Colonel, 4/5th Bn The Green Howards (TA), 1963–67. *Address:* Upsall Castle, Thirsk, N Yorks YO7 2QJ. *T:* Thirsk 537202; 15 Grey Coat Gardens, SW1P 2QA. *T:* 01–834 1535.

TRANT, Gen. Sir Richard (Brooking), KCB 1982 (CB 1979); Quarter Master General, 1983–86; *b* 30 March 1928; *s* of Richard Brooking Trant and Dora Rodney Trant (*née* Lancaster); *m* 1957, Diana Clare, 2nd *d* of Rev. Stephen Zachary and Ruth Beatrice Edwards, Llystanwg, Harlech, N Wales; one *s* two *d*. Commissioned RA 1947; Defence Services Staff Coll., India, 1962–63; Jt Services Staff Coll., 1965; commanded 3rd Regt RHA, 1968–71, 5th Airportable Brigade, 1972–74; Dep. Mil. Sec., MoD (Army), 1975–76; Comdr Land Forces, NI, 1977–79; Dir, Army Staff Duties, 1979–82; GOC South East District, 1982–83, Land Dep. C-in-C Fleet during S Atlantic Campaign, 1982. Col Comdt: RAEC, 1979–86; RA, 1982–; RAOC, 1984–; HAC (TA), 1984–. Pres., RA Hunt Club and RA Saddle Club, 1984–; Admiral, Army Sailing Assoc., 1984–87. CBIM 1985. Order of South Arabia, 3rd Class, 1965. *Recreations:* golf, field sports, natural history, sailing. *Address:* c/o Lloyds Bank, Newquay, Cornwall. *Clubs:* Army and Navy; Royal Fowey Yacht.

TRANTER, Professor Clement John, CBE 1967 (OBE 1953); Bashforth Professor of Mathematical Physics, Royal Military College of Science, Shrivenham, 1953–74, now Emeritus; *b* 16 Aug. 1909; *s* of late Archibald Tranter, and Mrs Tranter, Cirencester, Glos.; *m* 1937, Joan Louise Hatton, *d* of late J. Hatton, MBE, and Mrs Hatton, Plumstead, SE18. *Educ:* Cirencester Grammar Sch.; Queen's Coll., Oxford (Open Math. Scholar; 1st Class Hons Mathematical Mods, 1929; 1st Class Hons Final Sch. of Maths, 1931; MA (Oxon) 1940; DSc (Oxon) 1953). Commissioned RA, TA, 1932; Captain, 1938. Junior Assistant Research Dept, Woolwich, 1931–34; Senior Lecturer, Gunnery and Mathematics Branch, Military College of Science, Woolwich, 1935–40; Asst Professor 1940–46; Assoc. Professor of Mathematics, Royal Military College of Science, Shrivenham, 1946–53. *Publications:* Integral Transforms in Mathematical Physics, 1951; Advanced Level Pure Mathematics, 1953; Techniques of Mathematical Analysis, 1957; (with C. G. Lambe) Differential Equations for Engineers and Scientists, 1961; Mathematics for Sixth Form Scientists, 1964; (with C. G. Lambe) Advanced Level Mathematics, 1966; Bessel Functions with some Physical Applications, 1968; mathematical papers in various journals. *Recreations:* painting, golf, fly-fishing. *Address:* Flagstones, Stanton Fitzwarren, near Swindon, Wilts SN6 7RZ. *T:* Swindon 762913.

TRANTER, Nigel Godwin, OBE 1983; novelist and author since 1936; *b* Glasgow, 23 Nov. 1909; *yr s* of Gilbert T. Tranter and Eleanor A. Cass; *m* 1933, May Jean Campbell Grieve (*d* 1979); one *d* (one *s* decd). *Educ:* St James Episcopal Sch., Edinburgh; George Heriot's Sch., Edinburgh. Served War of 1939–45, RASC and RA. Accountancy trng, then in small family insce co., until could live on writing, after war service; much and actively interested in Scottish public affairs; Chm., Scottish Convention, Edinburgh Br., 1948–51; Vice-Convener, Scottish Covenant Assoc., 1951–55; Pres., E Lothian Liberal Assoc., 1960–76; Chm., Nat. Forth Road Bridge Cttee, 1953–57; Pres., Scottish PEN, 1962–66, Hon. Pres., 1973–; Chm., Soc. of Authors, Scotland, 1966–72; Pres., E Lothian Wildfowlers' Assoc., 1952–73; Chm., St Andrew Soc. of E Lothian, 1966–; Chm., Nat. Book League, Scotland, 1972–77; Mem., Cttee of Aberlady Bay Nature Reserve, 1953–76, etc. Hon. Mem., Mark Twain Soc. of Amer., 1976. Hon. Freeman, Blackstone, Va, 1980. Hon. MA Edinburgh, 1971. Chevalier, Order of St Lazarus of Jerusalem, 1961 (Vice-Chancellor of the Order, Scotland, 1980, Chancellor, 1986). *Publications: fiction:* 64 novels, from Trespass, 1937, including: Bridal Path, 1952; Macgregor's Gathering, 1957; the Master of Gray trilogy: The Master of Gray, 1961; The Courtesan, 1963; Past Master, 1965; Chain of Destiny, 1964; the Robert the Bruce trilogy: The Steps to the Empty Throne, 1969; The Path of the Hero King, 1970; The Price of the King's Peace, 1971; The Young Montrose, 1972; Montrose: the Captain General, 1973; The Wisest Fool, 1974; The Wallace, 1975; Lords of Misrule, 1976; A Folly of Princes, 1977; The Captive Crown, 1977; Macbeth the King, 1978; Margaret the Queen, 1979; David the Prince, 1980; True Thomas, 1981; The Patriot, 1982; Lord of the Isles, 1983; Unicorn Rampant, 1984; The Riven Realm, 1984; James, By the Grace of God, 1985; Rough Wooing, 1986; 12 children's novels; *non-fiction:* The Fortalices and Early Mansions of Southern Scotland, 1935; The Fortified House in Scotland (5 vols), 1962–71; Pegasus Book of Scotland, 1964; Outlaw of the Highlands: Rob Roy, 1965; Land of the Scots, 1968; Portrait of the Border Country, 1972; Portrait of the Lothians, 1979; The Queen's Scotland Series: The Heartland: Clackmannan, Perth and Stirlingshire, 1971; The Eastern Counties: Aberdeen, Angus and Kincardineshire, 1972; The North East: Banff, Moray, Nairn, East Inverness and Easter Ross, 1974; Argyll and Bute, 1977; Nigel Tranter's Scotland, 1981; Scottish Castles: tales and traditions, 1982; Scotland of Robert the Bruce, 1986; contribs to many jls, on Scots history, genealogy, topography, castellated architecture, knighthood, etc. *Recreations:* walking, wildfowling, historical research. *Address:* Quarry House, Aberlady, East Lothian. *T:* Aberlady 258. *Club:* PEN.

TRAPNELL, Barry Maurice Waller, CBE 1982; DL; MA, PhD Cantab; Headmaster of Oundle School, 1968–84; Chairman, Cambridge Occupational Analysts, since 1986; Director, Thomas Wall Trust, since 1984; *b* 18 May 1924; *s* of Waller Bertram and late Rachel Trapnell; *m* 1951, Dorothy Joan, *d* of late P. J. Kerr, ICS; two *d*. *Educ:* University College Sch., Hampstead; St John's Coll., Cambridge (Scholar). Research in physical chemistry in Department of Colloid Science, Cambridge, 1945–46, and Royal Institution, London, 1946–50; Commonwealth Fund Fellow, Northwestern Univ., Ill., 1950–51; Lecturer in chemistry: Worcester Coll., Oxford, 1951–54; Liverpool Univ., 1954–57; Headmaster, Denstone Coll., 1957–68. Visiting Lecturer, American Association for Advancement of Science, 1961. Pres., Independent Schools Assoc. Inc., 1984–; Member: Adv. Cttee on Supply and Training of Teachers; C of E Commn on Religious Education. E Anglian Regl Dir, Index, 1985–. Mem. Governing Body, UCS. FRSA. DL: Staffs, 1967; Northants, 1974–84. Hon. Liveryman, Worshipful Co. of Grocers, 1984. *Publications:* Chemisorption, 1955 (Russian edition, 1958; 2nd English edition, 1964); Learning and Discerning, 1966; papers in British and American scientific journals. *Recreations:* several games (represented Cambridge *v* Oxford at cricket and squash rackets, and Gentlemen *v* Players at cricket; won Amateur Championships at Rugby Fives); English furniture and silver. *Address:* 6 Corfe Close, Cambridge CB2 2QA. *T:* Cambridge 249278. *Club:* East India, Devonshire, Sports and Public Schools.

TRAPNELL, John Arthur; Under-Secretary, Departments of Trade and Industry, 1973–77; *b* 7 Sept. 1913; *s* of Arthur Westicote Trapnell and Helen Trapnell (*née* Alles); *m* 1939, Winifred Chadwick Rushton; two *d*. *Educ:* privately; Law Soc.'s Sch. of Law. Admitted Solicitor 1938; private practice until 1940; served HM Army, 1940–46: commnd Som. LI, 1943; served with 82nd W African Div. (Major). Civil Service from 1946; Board of Trade, Solicitors Dept. Mem. Law Soc. *Recreations:* golf, bridge. *Address:* 29 Connaught Road, New Malden, Surrey. *T:* 01–942 3183.

TRAPP, Rt. Rev. Eric Joseph; *b* 17 July 1910; *s* of late Archibald Edward Trapp and Agnes Trapp, Leicester and Coventry; *m* 1937, Edna Noreen Thornton, SRN; two *d*. *Educ:* Alderman Newton's Sch., Leicester; Leeds Univ.; College of the Resurrection, Mirfield. BA 1st Class, philosophy. Asst Curate, St Olave's, Mitcham, Surrey, 1934–37; Director, Masite Mission, Basutoland, 1937–40; Rector, St Augustine's Bethlehem, Orange Free State, 1940–43; Rector, St John's, Maseru and Director of Maseru Mission, Basutoland, 1943–47; Canon of Bloemfontein Cathedral, 1944–47; Bishop of Zululand, 1947–57; Sec., Soc. for the Propagation of the Gospel, 1957–64, United Soc. for the Propagation of the Gospel, 1965–70; Bishop of Bermuda, 1970–75; Hon. Asst Bishop, Dio. St Albans, 1976–final retirement in 1980. Hon. DD Trinity College, Toronto, 1967. *Address:* 18 Sorrel Garth, Hitchin, Herts SG4 9PS. *T:* Hitchin 34097.

TRAPP, Prof. Joseph Burney, FSA; FBA 1980; Director, Warburg Institute (University of London) and Professor of the History of the Classical Tradition, since 1976; *b* 16 July 1925; *s* of H. M. B. and Frances M. Trapp; *m* 1953, Elayne M. Falla; two *s*. *Educ:* Dannevirke High Sch. and Victoria University Coll., Wellington, NZ (MA). FSA 1978. Alexander Turnbull Library, Wellington, 1946–50; Jun. Lectr, Victoria University Coll., 1950–51; Asst Lectr, Reading Univ., 1951–53; Asst Librarian, Warburg Inst., 1953–66, Librarian, 1966–76. Visiting Professor: Univ. of Toronto, 1969; Univ. of Melbourne, 1980. Member: Advisory Council: V&A Museum, 1977–83; British Library, 1980–; Exec. Cttee, British Sch. at Rome, 1983–; Vice-Pres., British Academy, 1983–85. *Publications:* (ed) The Apology of Sir Thomas More, 1979; articles in learned jls. *Address:* Warburg Institute, Woburn Square, WC1H 0AB. *T:* 01–580 9663.

TRASENSTER, Michael Augustus Tulk, CVO 1954; Photographer, ARPS 1979; *b* 26 Jan. 1923; *er s* of late Major William Augustus Trasenster, MC, and Brenda de Courcy Trasenster; *m* 1950, Fay Norrie Darley, *d* of late Thomas Bladworth Darley, Cantley Hall, Yorkshire; two *d*. *Educ:* Winchester. Served with 4th/7th Royal Dragoon Guards, 1942–; NW Europe, 1944; Middle East, 1946; ADC to Governor of South Australia, 1947–49; School of Tank Technology, 1951; Military Secretary and Comptroller to the Governor General of New Zealand, 1952–55. Chevalier of Order of Leopold II of Belgium, with palm, 1944; Belgian Croix de Guerre, with palm, 1944. *Recreations:* painting, tennis. *Address:* c/o Royal Bank of Scotland, High Street, Winchester, Hants.

TRASLER, Prof. Gordon Blair, PhD; FBPsS; JP; first Professor of Psychology, University of Southampton, since 1964; *b* 7 March 1929; *s* of Frank Ferrier Trasler and Marian (*née* Blair); *m* 1953, Kathleen Patricia Fegan. *Educ:* Isleworth Grammar Sch.; Bryanston Sch.; University Coll., Exeter (MA); London Univ. (BSc, PhD). FBPsS 1963. Tutorial Asst, UC, Exeter, 1952–53; Psychologist, HM Prisons, Wandsworth and Winchester, 1955–57; Lectr, Southampton Univ., 1957–64. Visiting Lecturer: LSE, 1962–63; Inst. of Criminology, Cambridge Univ., 1968–; Vis. Prof., Univ. of Alberta at Edmonton, 1977. Mem., Winchester Health Authority, 1981–. Chairman: Inst. for Study and Treatment of Delinquency, 1981–; Div. of Criminolog. and Legal Psychol., BPsS, 1980–83. Chief Scientist's Advr, DHSS, 1977–80 and 1983–; Member: Adv. Council on Penal System, 1968–74; Wootton Cttee on Non-custodial penalties, 1968–70; Younger Cttee on Young Adult Offenders, 1970–74. Editor-in-chief, British Jl of Criminology, 1980–85. JP Hants, 1978. *Publications:* In Place of Parents, 1960; The Explanation of Criminality, 1962; The Shaping of Social Behaviour, 1967; (jtly) The Formative Years, 1968; (with D. P. Farrington) Behaviour Modification with Offenders, 1980; many papers in jls and chapters on psychology and criminology. *Recreations:* reading, photography, writing. *Address:* Fox Croft, Old Kennels Lane, Oliver's Battery, Winchester SO22 4JT. *T:* Winchester 52345.

TRAVANCORE, Rajpramukh of; Maj.-Gen. HH Sri Padmanabha Dasa Bala Rama Varma; GCSI 1946; GCIE 1935; *b* 1912. Founder of Travancore University and sometime Chancellor. Formerly: Colonel-in-Chief of Travancore State Forces; Hon. Major-General in British Army. Has introduced many reforms. Holds Hon. Doctorates. *Address:* Kaudiar Palace, Trivandrum 3, Kerala State, S India.

TRAVERS, Basil Holmes, AM 1983; OBE 1943; BA (Sydney); MA (Oxon); BLitt (Oxon); FACE; FRSA; FAIM; Headmaster of Sydney Church of England Grammar School, North Sydney, NSW, 1959–84; *b* 7 July 1919; *m* 1942, Margaret Emily Marr; three *d*. *Educ:* Sydney Church of England Grammar Sch.; Sydney Univ.; New Coll., Oxford Univ. Rhodes Scholar for NSW, 1940. Served War of 1939–45 (despatches, OBE); AIF, 2/2 Australian Infantry Battalion; ADC to Maj.-Gen. Sir I. G. Mackay, 1940; Brigade Major, 15 Aust. Inf. Bde, 1943–44; psc 1944; GSO 2, HQ, 2 Aust. Corps, 1944–45. Assistant Master, Wellington Coll., Berks, England, 1948–49; Assistant Master, Cranbrook Sch., Sydney, 1950–52; Headmaster, Launceston Church Grammar Sch., Launceston, Tasmania, 1953–58. Chm., Headmasters' Conf. of Australia, 1971–73. Lt-Col commanding 12 Inf. Bn (CMF), 1955–58. Member: Soldiers' Children Education Board, 1959–; NSW Cttee, Duke of Edinburgh's Award Scheme in Australia, 1959– (Chm., 1979–84). Col Comdt, Royal Australian Army Educn Corps, 1984–. *Publications:* Let's Talk Rugger, 1949; The Captain General, 1952. *Recreations:* cricket (Oxford Blue, 1946, 1948), swimming, rugby (Oxford Blue, 1946, 1947), athletics (Half Blue, 1947); also Sydney Blue, football, cricket; Rugby Union International for England, 1947, 1948, 1949; represented NSW, 1950. *Address:* 17 Malo Road, Whale Beach, NSW 2107, Australia. *T:* 919 4196. *Clubs:* Union, Rugby Union (Sydney); Elanora Country.

TRAVERS, Rt. Rev. Mgr. Brendan; *b* 21 March 1931; *s* of Dr Charles Travers and Eileen Travers (*née* Gordon). *Educ:* Belmont Abbey Sch.; Venerable English College, Rome; Gregorian Univ., Rome. (STL, JCL, PhL). Ordained priest, 1955; Curate, Salford diocese, 1957–72; Bishop's Secretary, 1961–64; Chm., Manchester Catholic Marriage Adv. Council, 1966–71; Rector, Pontifical Beda College, Rome, 1972–78; Parish Priest, All Souls, Salford, 1978–. *Recreation:* golf. *Address:* All Souls Presbytery, Liverpool Street, Weaste, Salford M5 2HQ. *Club:* Worsley Golf (Manchester).

TRAVERS, Sir Thomas (à Beckett), Kt 1972; Consulting Ophthalmologist, Royal Melbourne Hospital, since 1962; *b* 16 Aug. 1902; *s* of late Walter Travers, Warragul, Vic and late Isabelle Travers; *m* Tone, *widow* of late R. S. Burnard; no *c*. *Educ:* Melbourne Grammar School. MB, BS 1925, DSc 1941, Melbourne; MRCP 1928; DOMS London

1928; FRACS. *Publications:* various on strabismus. *Recreation:* gardening. *Address:* 55 Victoria Parade, Fitzroy, Vic 3065, Australia. *T:* 417 1722. *Club:* Melbourne (Melbourne).

TRAVERSE-HEALY, Tim, FIPR, FPA; Chairman, Traverse-Healy & Regester Ltd, Corporate Affairs Counsel, since 1985; *b* 25 March 1923; *s* of John Healy, MBE, and Gladys Traverse; *m* 1946, Joan Thompson; two *s* three *d. Educ:* Stonyhurst Coll.; St Mary's Hosp., London Univ. DipCAM. Served War, Royal Marines Commandos and Special Forces, 1941–46. Sen. Partner, Traverse-Healy Ltd, 1947–85; Public Affairs Adviser to: *inter alia,* National Westminster Bank plc, Hong Kong Bank Group, Royal Bank of Canada, Esso PLC, Guardian Royal Exchange. Pres., Internat. PR Res. and Educn Foundn, 1983–. Inst. of Public Relations: Mem. 1948, Fellow 1956; Pres. 1967–68; Tallents Gold Medal, 1985; European PR Federation: Vice-Pres. 1965–69; Internat. PR Assoc.: Sec. 1950–61, Pres. 1968–73, Mem. Emeritus, 1982; Presidential Gold Medal, 1985. FRSA 1953; FIPA 1957. Member, US Public Affairs Council, 1975; Board Mem., Centre for Public Affairs Studies, 1969; Pres., World PR Congress: Tel Aviv, 1970; Geneva, 1973. Congress Foundn Lecture: Boston, 1976; Bombay, 1982. *Publications:* numerous published lectures and articles in professional jls. *Recreations:* French politics, Irish Society. *Address:* 57 Britton Street, EC1M 5NA. *T:* 01–251 6414. *Clubs:* Athenæum, Norwegian.

TREACHER, Adm. Sir John (Devereux), KCB 1975; Director, since 1978, Group Marketing Director, since 1982, Vice Chairman, since 1984, Westland plc; Chairman, Westland Inc., since 1983; *b* Chile, 23 Sept. 1924; *s* of late Frank Charles Treacher, Bentley, Suffolk; *m* 1st, 1953, Patcie Jane (marr. diss. 1968), *d* of late Dr F. L. McGrath, Evanston, Ill; one *s* one *d*; 2nd, 1969, Kirsteen Forbes, *d* of late D. F. Landale; one *s* one *d. Educ:* St Paul's School. Served in HM Ships Nelson, Glasgow, Keppel and Mermaid in Mediterranean, Russian convoys; qual. Fleet Air Arm pilot, 1947; CO: 778 Sqdn 1951, 849 Sqdn 1952–53; CO, HMS Lowestoft, 1964–66; CO, HMS Eagle, 1968–70; Flag Officer Carriers and Amphibious Ships and Comdr Carrier Striking Gp 2, 1970–72; Flag Officer, Naval Air Comd, 1972–73; Vice-Chief of Naval Staff, 1973–75; C-in-C Fleet, and Allied C-in-C Channel and Eastern Atlantic, 1975–77. Chief Exec., 1977–81, and Dir, 1977–85, Nat. Car Parks. Non-press Mem., Press Council, 1978–81; Mem. Council, SBAC, 1983–. FRAeS 1973. *Recreations:* shooting, photography. *Address:* 4 Carlton Gardens, SW1. *Clubs:* Boodle's, Institute of Directors.

TREADGOLD, Hazel Rhona; Central President of the Mothers' Union, since 1983; *b* 29 May 1936; *m* 1959, John David Treadgold, *qv;* two *s* one *d.* Mothers' Union: has held office, Dioceses of Southwell and Durham, and at HQ; Chm., Central Young Families Cttee, 1971–76; a Central Vice-Pres., 1978–83. JP. *Recreations:* tennis, travel, reading, cookery. *Address:* Chaplain's Lodge, Windsor Great Park, Windsor, Berks SL4 2HP. *T:* Egham 32434; 8 The Cloisters, Windsor Castle, Berks.

TREADGOLD, Rev. Canon John David; Canon of Windsor and Chaplain to Windsor Great Park, since 1981; Chaplain to the Queen, since 1983; *b* 30 Dec. 1931; *s* of Oscar and Sybil Treadgold; *m* 1959, Hazel Rhona Bailey (*see* H. R. Treadgold); two *s* one *d. Educ:* Nottingham Univ. (BA); Wells Theological College. Deacon 1959, priest 1960; Vicar Choral, Southwell Minster, 1959–64; Rector of Wollaton, Nottingham, 1964–74; Vicar of Darlington, 1974–81. Chaplain, TA, 1962–67; TAVR, 1974–78; Chaplain to High Sheriff: of Nottinghamshire, 1963–64 and 1975–76; of Durham, 1978–79. *Recreations:* musical appreciation; church architecture. *Address:* Chaplain's Lodge, Windsor Great Park, Windsor, Berks SL4 2HP. *T:* Egham 32434; 8 The Cloisters, Windsor Castle, Berks.

TREADGOLD, Sydney William, FCA; Under Secretary, General Policy Division, Department of Trade and Industry, since 1985; *b* 10 May 1933; *s* of Harold Bryan Treadgold and Violet Gladys (*née* Watson); *m* 1961, Elizabeth Ann White; two *s. Educ:* Larkmead Sch., Abingdon. Chartered accountant (ACA 1960, FCA 1970). Served RAF, 1951–53 (Navigator). Wenn Townsend & Co., Chartered Accountants, 1954–62; Asst Finance Officer, Univ. of Liverpool, 1963–65; Principal: Min. of Aviation, 1965–67; Min. of Technol., 1967–71; Asst Sec., DTI, 1972–78; Under Secretary: Price Commn, 1978–79; Depts of Industry and Trade, 1979–83; DTI, 1983–. *Address:* 23 Sturges Road, Wokingham, Berks RG11 2HG.

TREADWELL, Charles James, CMG 1972; CVO 1979; HM Diplomatic Service, retired; Adviser on Middle East affairs to: Hill Samuel & Co. Ltd, since 1979; Hill Samuel Investment Management Ltd, since 1981; Adviser, Abu Dhabi Investment Authority, since 1983; *b* 10 Feb. 1920; *s* of late C. A. L. Treadwell, OBE, Barrister and Solicitor, Wellington, NZ. *Educ:* Wellington Coll., NZ; University of New Zealand (LLB). Served with HM Forces, 1939–45. Sudan Political Service and Sudan Judiciary, 1945–55; FO, 1955–57; British High Commn, Lahore, 1957–60; HM Embassy, Ankara, 1960–62; HM Embassy, Jedda, 1963–64; British Dep. High Comr for Eastern Nigeria, 1965–66; Head of Joint Information Services Department, Foreign Office/Commonwealth Office, 1966–68; British Political Agent, Abu Dhabi, 1968–71; Ambassador, United Arab Emirates, 1971–73; High Comr to Bahamas, 1973–75; Ambassador to Oman, 1975–79. *Address:* Cherry Orchard Cottage, Buddington Lane, Midhurst, W Sussex GU29 0QP. *Club:* Army and Navy.

TREASE, Geoffrey; *see* Trease, R. G.

TREASE, Prof. George Edward, BPharm, Dr *hc* Strasbourg; Dr *hc* Clermont; FPS, FRSC; Professor of Pharmacognosy, Nottingham University, 1957–67, now Emeritus Professor; Head of Department of Pharmacy, University of Nottingham, 1944–67; *b* 8 July 1902; *e s* of George and Florence Trease; *m* 1928, Phyllis Thornton Wilkinson; two *d* (one *s* decd). *Educ:* Nottingham High Sch.; London College of Pharmacy. Lecturer in Pharmacognosy, University College, Nottingham, 1926. Served in Min. of Economic Warfare, 1939–40. Reader in Pharmacognosy, 1945; Examiner in Pharmacognosy to: Pharmaceutical Society, 1934–; University of London, 1937–; QUB, 1949, 1963–65; University of Glasgow, 1950–; University of Wales, 1945–; University of Nottingham, 1950–; University of Singapore, 1962; University of Bradford, 1966–; Pharmaceutical Society of Eire, 1959–. Vice-Pres., British Soc. for History of Pharmacy, 1967–70; Worshipful Society of Apothecaries of London, 1959. Dr *hc* Strasbourg University, 1954; Dr *hc* Clermont University, 1962. *Publications:* Chemistry of Crude Drugs, 1928 (with Prof. J. E. Driver); Textbook of Pharmacognosy, 1934, 12th edn 1983; Pharmacy in History, 1964; many papers and articles on pharmacognosy, pharmaceutical history and pharmaceutical education. *Recreation:* local history. *Address:* George Hill, Crediton, Devon. *T:* Crediton 2983.
See also R. G. Trease.

TREASE, (Robert) Geoffrey, FRSL 1979; *b* 11 Aug. 1909; *s* of George Albert Trease and Florence (*née* Dale); *m* 1933, Marian Haselden Granger Boyer; one *d. Educ:* Nottingham High Sch.; Queen's Coll., Oxford (schol.). Chm., 1972–73, Mem. Council 1974–, Society of Authors. *Publications:* Walking in England, 1935; Such Divinity, 1939; Only Natural, 1940; Tales Out of School, 1949; Snared Nightingale, 1957; So Wild the Heart, 1959; The Italian Story, 1963; The Grand Tour, 1967; (ed) Matthew Todd's Journal, 1968;

Nottingham, a biography, 1970; The Condottieri, 1970; A Whiff of Burnt Boats, an early autobiography, 1971; Samuel Pepys and his World, 1972; Laughter at the Door, a continued autobiography, 1974; London, a concise history, 1975; Portrait of a Cavalier: William Cavendish, first Duke of Newcastle, 1979; *for young readers:* Bows Against the Barons, 1934; Cue for Treason, 1940; The Hills of Varna, 1948; No Boats on Bannermere, 1949; The Seven Queens of England, 1953; This Is Your Century, 1965; The Red Towers of Granada, 1966; Byron, A Poet Dangerous to Know, 1969; A Masque for the Queen, 1970; Horsemen on the Hills, 1971; D. H. Lawrence: the Phoenix and the Flame, 1973; Popinjay Stairs, 1973; Days to Remember, 1973; The Iron Tsar, 1975; The Chocolate Boy, 1975; When the Drums Beat, 1976; Violet for Bonaparte, 1976; The Field of the Forty Footsteps, 1977; Mandeville, 1980; A Wood by Moonlight and Other Stories, 1981; Saraband for Shadows, 1982; The Cormorant Venture, 1984; The Edwardian Era, 1986, and many others; *plays:* After the Tempest, 1938 (Welwyn Fest. award); Colony, 1939. *Recreations:* walking, the theatre. *Address:* 1 Yomede Park, Newbridge Road, Bath BA1 3LS.
See also Prof. G. E. Trease.

TREASURE, Prof. John Albert Penberthy, PhD; Vice Chairman, Saatchi & Saatchi Compton Ltd, since 1983; *b* 20 June 1924; *s* of Harold Paul Treasure and Constance Frances Treasure; *m* 1954, Valerie Ellen Bell; three *s. Educ:* Cardiff High Sch.; University Coll., Cardiff (BA 1946); Univ. of Cambridge (PhD 1956). Joined British Market Research Bureau Ltd, 1952, Man. Dir 1957; Marketing Dir, J. Walter Thompson Co. Ltd, 1960, Chm. 1967; Dir, J. Walter Thompson Co. USA, 1967, Vice Chm. 1974. Director: Rowntree Mackintosh plc, 1976–; Dolan Packaging, 1984–; Household Mortgage Corp. plc, 1986–. Dean and Prof. of Marketing, City Univ. Business Sch., 1978–82. President: Inst. of Practitioners in Advertising, 1975–77; Market Res. Soc., 1975–78; Nat. Advertising Benevolent Soc., 1977–78; Chm., History of Advertising Trust, 1985–. *Publications:* articles on marketing, market research and economics in Financial Times, Times, New Soc., Econ. Jl, Commentary, and Advertising Qly. *Recreations:* golf, tennis. *Address:* Cholmondeley Lodge, Friars Lane, Richmond, Surrey TW9 1NS. *T:* (office) 01–636 5060. *Clubs:* Beefsteak, Queen's, Hurlingham; Royal Mid-Surrey Golf (Richmond).

TREDGOLD, Joan Alison, MA Cantab; Principal, Cheltenham Ladies' College, 1953–64; *b* 6 Sept. 1903; *d* of Alfred Frank Tredgold, MD, FRCP, and Zoë B. T. Tredgold. *Educ:* Cheltenham Ladies' College; Newnham College, Cambridge. Mathematical Tripos part II, Class I, 1924; Fourth Year Scholarship, Newnham, 1924–25. Assistant Mistress, Sherborne School for Girls, 1925–29; Assistant Mistress, Cheltenham Ladies' College, 1929–35. Senior Mathematical Mistress, 1935–53, Assistant House Mistress, 1938–39, Second Mistress, 1939–53, Roedean School. *Address:* 12 Newcourt Park, Charlton Kings, Cheltenham, Glos. *T:* Cheltenham 519242. *Club:* University Women's.

TREFGARNE; family name of **Baron Trefgarne.**

TREFGARNE, 2nd Baron, *cr* 1947, of Cleddau; **David Garro Trefgarne;** Minister of State for Defence Procurement, since 1986; *b* 31 March 1941; *s* of 1st Baron Trefgarne and of Elizabeth (who *m* 1962, Comdr A. T. Courtney (from whom she obt. a divorce, 1966); *m* 1971, H. C. H. Ker, Dundee), *d* of C. E. Churchill; *S* father, 1960; *m* 1968, Rosalie, *d* of Sir Peter Lane, *qv;* two *s* one *d. Educ:* Haileybury; Princeton University, USA. Opposition Whip, House of Lords, 1977–79; a Lord in Waiting (Govt Whip), 1979–81; Parly Under Sec. of State, DoT, 1981, FCO, 1981–82, DHSS, 1982–83, (Armed Forces) MoD, 1983–85; Minister of State for Defence Support, 1985–86. Awarded Royal Aero Club Bronze Medal (jointly) for flight from England to Australia and back in light aircraft, 1963. *Recreation:* photography. *Heir: s* Hon. George Garro Trefgarne, *b* 4 Jan. 1970. *Address:* House of Lords, SW1.

TREFUSIS; *see* Fane Trefusis, family name of Baron Clinton.

TREGEAR, Mary, FBA 1985; Senior Assistant Keeper, Chinese, Ashmolean Museum, Oxford, since 1961; *b* 11th Feb. 1924; *d* of Thomas R. and Norah Tregear. *Educ:* Sidcot Sch.; West of England Coll. of Art (ATD 1946); London Univ. (BA); MA Oxon. Taught Art, Wuhan, China, 1947–50; Curator/Lectr, Hong Kong Univ., 1956–61. *Publications:* Arts of China, vol. 1 (co-ordinating ed.), 1968; Catalogue of Chinese Greenwares in the Ashmolean Museum, 1976; Chinese Art, 1980; Song Ceramics, 1982; contribs to Oriental Art, Connoisseur, Burlington Magazine.

TREGLOWN, Jeremy Dickinson; Editor, Times Literary Supplement, since 1982; *b* 24 May 1946; *s* of Rev. Geoffrey and of Beryl Treglown; *m* 1st, 1970, Rona Bower (marr. diss. 1982); one *s* two *d*; 2nd, 1984, Holly Eley (*née* Urquhart). *Educ:* Bristol Grammar Sch.; St Peter's Coll., Oxford. MA, BLitt Oxon; PhD London. Lecturer: Lincoln Coll., Oxford, 1974–77; University College London, 1977–80; Asst Editor, Times Literary Supplement, 1980–82. Contributor to Plays and Players, The Guardian, Sunday Times, etc. General Editor, the Plays in Performance series, 1981–85. *Publications:* (ed) The Letters of John Wilmot, Earl of Rochester, 1980; Spirit of Wit, 1982; articles on poetry, drama and literary history in various learned jls. *Address:* 102 Savernake Road, NW3.

TREHANE, Sir (Walter) Richard, Kt 1967; Chairman of the Milk Marketing Board, 1958–77; *b* 14 July 1913; *s* of James Trehane and Muriel Yeoman Cowl; *m* 1948, Elizabeth Mitchell; two *s. Educ:* Monkton Combe School, Somerset; University of Reading (BSc (Agric.)). On staff of School of Agriculture, Cambridge, 1933–36; Manager of Hampreston Manor Farm, Dorset, 1936–. Member Dorset War Agric. Exec. Cttee, 1942–47; Mem. Milk Marketing Board, 1947–77 (Vice-Chm., 1952–58); Dep. Chm. Dorset Agric. Exec. Cttee, 1947–52; Mem. (later Vice-Chm.) Avon and Stour Catchment Bd, subseq. Avon & Dorset Rivers Bd, 1944–53; Mem. Dorset County Council and Chm. Secondary Education Cttee, 1946–49; Chm. Dorset National Farmers' Union, 1947–48; Member, Nat. Milk Publicity Council, 1954–77 (1st Pres. 1954–56); Chm. English Country Cheese Council, 1955–77; Pres. British Farm Produce Council, 1963–78 (Chm. 1960–63). Chm. Govg Body, Grassland Research Institute, Hurley, Berks, 1959–78 (Hon. Fellow, 1981); Chm. and Pres. European Cttee on Milk/Butterfat Recording, 1957–60; Director of British Semen Exports Ltd, 1960–77; Vice-President: World Assoc. Animal Production, 1965–68; President: European Assoc. Animal Prodn, 1961–67; British Soc. Animal Prodn, 1954, 1961; British Friesian Cattle Soc., 1969–70; Royal Assoc. British Dairy Farmers, 1968, 1977; Internat. Dairy Fedn, 1968–72, Hon. Pres., 1972–76. Chm., UK Dairy Assoc., 1963–69. Chm., Alfa-Laval Co. Ltd, 1982–84 (Dir, 1977–84); Director: Southern Television, 1969–81; The Rank Organisation Ltd, 1970–84; Beaumont UK, 1980–. Trustee, UK Farming Scholarship Trust, 1970. Governor: Monkton Combe School, 1957–; British Nutrition Foundn, 1975–77. FRAgSs 1970. Hon. DSc Reading, 1976. Justus-von-Liebig Prize, Kiel Univ., 1968; Gold Medal, Soc. of Dairy Technology, 1969; Massey-Fergusson Award, 1971. Comdr du Mérite Agricole, 1964. *Address:* Hampreston Manor Farm, Wimborne, Dorset. *Clubs:* Farmers'; Royal Motor Yacht (Poole).

TREHARNE, Prof. Kenneth John, FIBiol; Professor of Agricultural Sciences, University of Bristol, and Director, Long Ashton Research Station, since 1984; *b* 17 Aug. 1939; *s* of

Captain W. J. Treharne and M. A. Treharne; *m* 1974, Carys Wyn Evans; two *s* two *d*. *Educ*: University College of Wales, Aberystwyth (BSc, PhD Biochemistry). Post-doctoral Fellow, UCW Aberystwyth, 1964–66; Biochemist, Welsh Plant Breeding Station, 1966–74; study leave: Cornell Univ., NY, 1972; Royal Soc. Fellow, Univ. of Göttingen, 1973; Cereal Physiologist, Internat. Inst. of Tropical Agric., Ibadan, Nigeria, 1974–77; Head: Plant Physiol. Div., East Malling Res. Stn, Kent, 1977–81; Plant Scis Div., Long Ashton, 1982–84. FRSA. *Publications*: various chapters; numerous research papers. *Recreations*: golf, Rugby football—ex!, violin. *Address*: The Grey House, Yatton, Bristol BS19 4JA. *T*: Yatton 833199. *Club*: Farmers'.

TREHERNE, John Edwin, ScD, PhD; writer; President of Downing College, Cambridge, since 1985 (Fellow since 1966), Hon. Director of AFRC Unit of Insect Neurophysiology and Pharmacology (formerly of Invertebrate Chemistry and Physiology), Department of Zoology, University of Cambridge, since 1969; University Reader in Invertebrate Physiology, since 1971; *b* 15 May 1929; *s* of Arnold Edwin Wilson Treherne and Marion Grace Spiller; *m* 1955, June Vivienne Freeman; one *s* one *d*. *Educ*: Headlands Sch., Swindon, Wilts; Univ. of Bristol (BSc, PhD); Univ. of Cambridge (MA, ScD). Nat. Service, Lieut RAMC, 1953–55. Principal Sci. Officer, ARC Unit of Insect Physiology, Cambridge, 1955–67; Univ. Lectr in Zoology, Cambridge, 1968–71. Visiting Prof., Univ. of Virginia, 1963–64. Vice-Pres., Royal Entomological Soc., 1967–68. Scientific Medal of Zoological Soc., 1968. Dir, Company of Biologists Ltd, 1969–74; Editor: Advances in Insect Physiology, 1964–85; Jl of Experimental Biology, 1974–; Key Environments series, 1980–; Chm. of Editl Boards of Insect Biochemistry and Jl of Insect Physiology, 1977–. *Publications*: Neurochemistry of Arthropods, 1966; Insect Neurobiology, 1974; The Galapagos Affair, 1983; The Strange History of Bonnie and Clyde, 1984; The Trap, 1985; Mangrove Chronicle, 1986; research papers in: Jl of Experimental Biology; Tissue and Cell; Nature; Animal Behaviour. *Recreations*: domestic; military and naval Staffordshire figures; postcards of Edwardian actresses; marine insects; writing. *Address*: The Manor House, Soham, Cambs CB7 5HA. *T*: Ely 720688; Downing College, Cambridge CB2 1DQ.

TREITEL, Prof. Guenter Heinz, DCL; FBA 1977; QC 1983; Vinerian Professor of English Law, Oxford University, since 1979; Fellow of All Souls College, Oxford, since 1979; *b* 26 Oct. 1928; *s* of Theodor Treitel and Hanna Lilly Treitel (*née* Levy); *m* 1957, Phyllis Margaret Cook; two *s*. *Educ*: Kilburn Grammar School; Magdalen College, Oxford. BA 1949, BCL 1951, MA 1953, DCL 1976. Called to the Bar, Gray's Inn, 1952, Hon. Bencher, 1982. Asst Lectr, LSE, 1951–53; Lectr, University Coll., Oxford, 1953–54; Fellow, Magdalen Coll., Oxford, 1954–79, Fellow Emeritus, 1979; All Souls Reader in English Law, Univ. of Oxford, 1964–79. Vis. Lectr, Univ. of Chicago, 1963–64; Visiting Professor: Chicago, 1968–69 and 1971–72; W Australia, 1976; Houston, 1977; Southern Methodist, 1978; Virginia, 1978–79 and 1983–84; Santa Clara, 1981. Trustee, British Museum, 1983–; Mem. Council, National Trust, 1984–. *Publications*: The Law of Contract, 1962, 6th edn 1983; An Outline of the Law of Contract, 1975, 3rd edn 1984; International Encyclopedia of Comparative Law, Vol. VII Ch. 16, on Remedies for Breach of Contract, 1976; edited jointly: Dicey's Conflict of Laws, 7th edn 1958; Dicey and Morris, Conflict of Laws, 8th edn 1967; Chitty on Contracts, 23rd edn 1968 to 25th edn 1983; Benjamin's Sale of Goods, 1974, 3rd edn 1986. *Recreations*: music, reading. *Address*: All Souls College, Oxford OX1 4AL. *T*: Oxford 722251.

TRELAWNY, Sir John Barry Salusbury-, 13th Bt *cr* 1628; Director, Goddard Kay Rogers and Associates Ltd, since 1984; *b* 4 Sept. 1934; *s* of Sir John William Robin Maurice Salusbury-Trelawny, 12th Bt and of his 1st wife, Glenys Mary (*d* 1985), *d* of John Cameron Kynoch; *S* father, 1956; *m* 1958, Carol Knox, *yr d* of late C. F. K. Watson, The Field, Saltwood, Kent; one *s* three *d*. *Educ*: HMS Worcester. Subseq. Sub-Lt RNVR (National Service). Dir, The Martin Walter Group Ltd, 1971–74; various directorships, 1974–; Dir, 1978–83, Jt Dep. Man. Dir 1981–83, Korn/Ferry Internat. Inc. FInstM 1974. JP 1973–78. *Heir*: *s* John William Richard Salusbury-Trelawny [*b* 30 March 1960; *m* 1980, Anita, *d* of Kenneth Snelgrove; one *s* one *d*]. *Address*: Beavers Hill, Rectory Lane, Saltwood, Kent. *T*: Hythe 66476. *Clubs*: Army and Navy, Buck's.

TRELFORD, Donald Gilchrist; Editor of The Observer, since 1975; Director, The Observer Ltd, since 1975; *b* 9 Nov. 1937; *s* of Thomas Trelford and Doris Trelford (*née* Gilchrist) *m* 1st, 1963, Janice Ingram; two *s* one *d*; 2nd, 1978, Katherine Louise, *d* of Mr and Mrs John Mark, Guernsey, and *g d* of late John Mark and Louisa (*née* Hobson) one *d*. *Educ*: Bablake Sch., Coventry; Selwyn Coll., Cambridge; MA; University rugby and cricket. Pilot Officer, RAF, 1956–58. Reporter and Sub-Editor, Coventry Standard and Sheffield Telegraph, 1960–63; Editor, Nyasaland Times, 1963–66; Correspondent in Africa for The Observer, The Times, and BBC, 1963–66; Dep. News Editor, The Observer, 1966, Asst Man. Editor, 1968, Dep. Editor, 1969. Member: British Executive Cttee, IPI, 1976–; British Cttee, Journalists in Europe, 1980–; Assoc. of British Editors, 1984–; Guild of British Newspaper Editors, 1985–; Patron: Milton Keynes Civic Forum, 1977–; Internat. Centre for Child Studies, 1984–; Sponsor: Educn for Capability, 1983–; Educnl Trust for Southern Africa, 1986–; Member: Council, Media Soc., 1981–; judging panel, British Press Awards, 1981–; judging panel, Scottish Press Awards, 1985; Olivier Awards Cttee, SWET, 1984–; Communications Cttee, Inter Action Council, 1985–; Defence, Press and Broadcasting Cttee, 1986. Liveryman, Worshipful Co. of Stationers and Newspaper Makers, 1986; Freeman, City of London, 1986. Granada Newspaper of the Year Award, 1983; commended, Internat. Editor of the Year, World Press Rev., NY, 1984. Frequent broadcasts (writer, presenter and panellist) on TV and radio; speaker at internat. media confs in Spain, Egypt, W Germany, USA and India. *Publications*: Siege, 1980; (ed) Sunday Best, 1981, 1982, 1983; (contrib.) County Champions, 1982; Snookered, 1986; The Queen Observed, 1986. *Recreations*: golf, snooker. *Address*: c/o The Observer, 8 St Andrew's Hill, EC4V 5JA. *T*: 01–236 0202. *Clubs*: Garrick, Royal Air Force, MCC (Mem., Arts and Library Cttee, 1985–).
See also J. Mark, Sir R. Mark.

TREMBLAY, Dr Marc-Adélard, OC 1981; Professor of Anthropology, Université Laval, Québec, since 1956; *b* Les Eboulements, Qué., 24 April 1922; *s* of Willie Tremblay and Lauretta (*née* Tremblay); *m* 1949, Jacqueline Cyr; one *s* five *d*. *Educ*: Montréal Univ. (AB, LSA (Agricl Engrg)); Laval (MA Sociol.); Cornell Univ. (PhD Anthropol.). Research Associate, Cornell Univ., 1953–56; Université Laval: Vice-Dean, Faculty Social Scis, 1969–71; Head, Anthropology Dept, 1970; Dean, Graduate Sch., 1971–79. Pres., RSC, 1982–85. Hon. LLD: Ottawa, 1982; Guelph, 1984. *Publications*: The Acadians of Portsmouth, 1954; (jtly) People of Cove and Woodlot, 1960; (jtly) Les Comportements économiques de la famille salariée, 1964; Les Fondements Sociaux de la Maturation chez l'enfant, 1965; (jtly) Rural Canada in Transition, 1966; (jtly) A Survey of Contemporary Indians of Canada, 1967; Initiation à la recherche dans les sciences humaines, 1968; (jtly) Etude sur les Indiens contemporains du Canada, 1969; (jtly) Les Changements socio-culturels à Saint-Augustin, 1969; (jtly) Famille et parenté en Acadie, 1971; (jtly) Communautés et Culture, 1973 (Eng. trans. 1973); (jtly) Patterns of Amerindian Identity, 1976; (jtly) The Individual, Language and Society in Canada, 1977; L'Identité Québécoise en péril, 1983; (jtly) Conscience et Enquête, 1983; over one hundred scientific articles.

Recreations: gardening, cross-country skiing. *Address*: 835 Nouvelle-Orléans, Sainte Foy, Québec G1X 3J4, Canada. *T*: (418) 653–5411.

TREMLETT, Rt. Rev. Anthony Paul; *b* 14 May 1914; *s* of late Laurence and Nyda Tremlett; unmarried. *Educ*: King's Sch., Bruton; King's Coll., Cambridge; Cuddesdon Theological Coll. Ordained, 1938; Curate of St Barnabas, Northolt Park, Middx. Chaplain to the Forces (Emergency Commission), 1941–46 (despatches). Domestic Chaplain to the Bishop of Trinidad, BWI, 1946–49; Chaplain of Trinity Hall, Cambridge, 1949–58; Vicar of St Stephen with St John, Westminster, 1958–64; Bishop Suffragan of Dover, 1964–80. *Address*: Doctors Commons, The Square, Northleach, Gloucestershire. *T*: Northleach 426.

TREMLETT, George William, OBE 1981; author, journalist and bookseller; Director, Corran Books Ltd, since 1981; Founder Chairman: One London Group Ltd, since 1985; Home Comforts (Charity Furnishings) Ltd, since 1983; *b* 5 Sept. 1939; *s* of late Wilfred George and of Elizabeth Tremlett; *m* 1971, Jane, *o c* of late Benjamin James Mitchell and Mrs P. A. Mitchell; three *s*. *Educ*: Taunton School; King Edward VI School, Stratford upon Avon. Member of Richmond upon Thames Borough Council, 1963–74; Chairman: Further Education Cttee, 1966–68; Barnes School Governors, 1967–73; Schools Cttee, 1972–73; Shene VIth Form Coll. Governors, 1973–74; Housing Cttee, 1972–74; Thames Water Authority, 1973–74. Greater London Council: Mem. for Hillingdon, 1970–73, for Twickenham, 1973–86; Opposition Housing Spokesman, 1974–77; Leader of Housing Policy Cttee, 1977–81. Consultant: Nat. Assoc. of Voluntary Hostels, 1980–84; Local Govt Inf. Unit, 1985–; Appeal Dir, SHAC and Help the Homeless National Appeal, 1985–. Member: Housing Minister's Adv. Cttee on Co-operatives, 1977–79; Housing Consultative Council for England, 1977–81; Northampton Develt Corp., 1979–83; Stonham Housing Assoc., 1978–; Chiswick Family Rescue Appeal Fund, 1979–; Bd, Empty Property Unit, 1985–; Adv. Panel, BBC Community Prog. Unit, 1985–. Governor, Kingston Polytechnic and Twickenham Coll. of Technology, 1967–70; Court of City Univ., 1968–74. *Publications*: 17 biographies of rock musicians, 1974–77—on John Lennon, David Bowie, 10cc, Paul McCartney, The Osmonds, Alvin Stardust, Cat Stevens, Cliff Richard, Slade, The Who, David Essex, Slik, Gary Glitter, Marc Bolan, Rod Stewart, Queen and the Rolling Stones (published in many different countries); Living Cities, 1979. *Recreations*: ornithology, exploring old churches, local history, rock 'n' roll music. *Address*: 32 Fitzwilliam House, The Little Green, Richmond, Surrey. *T*: 01–940 4655; Corran House, Laugharne, Carmarthen, Dyfed. *T*: Laugharne 444. *Clubs*: Carlton, Wig and Pen, United and Cecil; Laugharne RFC.

TRENAMAN, Nancy Kathleen, (Mrs M. S. Trenaman); Principal of St Anne's College, Oxford, 1966–84; *b* 1919; *d* of Frederick Broughton Fisher and Edith Fisher; *m* 1967, M. S. Trenaman. *Educ*: Bradford Girls' Grammar School; Somerville College, Oxford (Hon. Fellow, 1977). Board of Trade, 1941–51; Assistant Secretary, Ministry of Materials, 1951–54; Counsellor, British Embassy, Washington, 1951–53; Board of Trade, 1954–66, Under-Sec. 1962–66. Mem., Commn on the Constitution, 1969–73. *Address*: 4 Fairlawn End, Oxford OX2 8AR. *T*: Oxford 57723. *Club*: United Oxford & Cambridge University.

TRENCH, family name of **Baron Ashtown**.

TRENCH, *see* Le Poer Trench, family name of Earl of Clancarty.

TRENCH, Sir David (Clive Crosbie), GCMG 1969 (KCMG 1962; CMG 1960); MC 1944; DL; Vice-Chairman, Advisory Committee on Distinction Awards, Department of Health and Social Security, 1972–79; Chairman, Dorset Area Health Authority, 1973–82; *b* 2 June 1915; *s* of late William Launcelot Crosbie Trench, CIE, and Margaret Zephanie (*née* Huddleston); *m* 1944, Margaret Gould; one *d*. *Educ*: Tonbridge School; Jesus College, Cambridge (MA). Cadet, British Solomon Islands Protectorate, 1938; seconded to W Pacific High Commission, 1941. Served War of 1939–45 (MC, US Legion of Merit); British Solomon Islands Defence Force, 1942–46, Lt-Col. Secretary to the Government, British Solomon Islands Protectorate, 1947; attended Joint Services Staff Coll., 1949; Asst Sec., Deputy Defence Sec., Hong Kong, 1950; Deputy Financial Sec., 1956; Commissioner of Labour and Mines, 1957; attended Imperial Defence College, 1958; Deputy Colonial Secretary, Hong Kong, 1959; High Commissioner for The Western Pacific, 1961–63; Governor and C-in-C, Hong Kong, 1964–71. Mem., new Dorset CC, 1973–81. Pres. for Dorset, St John Ambulance Brigade and Assoc., 1972–. DL Dorset, 1977. Hon. LLD: Univ. of Hong Kong, 1968; Chinese Univ. of Hong Kong, 1968. Legion of Merit (US), 1944. KStJ 1964. *Address*: Church House, Church Road, Shillingstone, Blandford, Dorset DT11 0SL. *Clubs*: United Oxford & Cambridge University; Royal & Ancient (St Andrews).

TRENCH, Sir Nigel (Clive Cosby), KCMG 1976 (CMG 1966); HM Diplomatic Service, retired; *b* 27 Oct. 1916; *s* of Clive Newcome Trench and Kathleen, 2nd *d* of Major Ivar MacIvor, CSI; *heir-pres.* to cousin, 6th Baron Ashtown, *qv*; *m* 1939, Marcelle Catherine Clotterbooke Patyn; one *s*. *Educ*: Eton; Univ. of Cambridge. Served in KRRC, 1940–46 (despatches). Appointed a Member of the Foreign (subseq. Diplomatic) Service, 1946; Lisbon, 1946; First Secretary, 1948; returned Foreign Office, 1949; First Secretary (Commercial) Lima, 1952; transf. Foreign Office, 1955; Counsellor, Tokyo, 1961; Counsellor, Washington, 1963; Cabinet Office, 1967; HM Ambassador to Korea, 1969–71; CS Selection Board, 1971–73; Ambassador to Portugal, 1974–76. Mem., Police, Prison and Fire Service Selection Bds, 1977–86. *Address*: 4 Kensington Court Gardens, Kensington Court Place, W8 5QE. *Clubs*: Naval and Military, MCC.

TRENCH, Sir Peter (Edward), Kt 1979; CBE 1964 (OBE 1945); TD 1949; *b* 16 June 1918; *s* of James Knights Trench and Grace Sim; *m* 1940, Mary St Clair Morford; one *s* one *d*. *Educ*: privately; London Sch. of Economics, London Univ.; St John's Coll., Cambridge Univ. BSc (Econ.) Hons. Served in The Queen's Royal Regt, 1939–46: Staff Coll., 1942; AAG, HQ 21 Army Gp, 1944–45 (OBE). Man. Dir, Bovis Ltd, 1954–59; Dir, Nat. Fedn of Bldg Trades Employers, 1959–64; Dir, Nat. Bldg Agency, 1964–66; Part-time Mem., Nat. Bd for Prices and Incomes, 1965–68; Chm., Y. J. Lovell (Holdings) plc, 1972–83. Vis. Prof. in Construction Management, Reading Univ., 1981–. Chm., Construction and Housing Res. Adv. Council, 1973–79; Pres., Construction Health Safety Gp, 1974–80; Vice-President: NHBC, 1984– (Chm., 1978–84); Building Centre; Member: Review of Housing Finance Adv. Gp, 1975–76; Council, CBI, 1981–83; Council, RSA, 1981–83; Hon. Mem., Architectural Assoc. Mem. Court of Governors, LSE; Hon. Treasurer, St Mary's Hosp. Med. Sch. JP Inner London, 1963–71. Hon. FCIOB; Hon. FFB; FCIArb; FRSA; CBIM; Hon. FRIBA; Hon. DSc. *Recreations*: ski-ing, swimming, travelling. *Address*: 4 Napier Close, Napier Road, W14 8LG. *T*: 01–602 3936. *Club*: MCC.

TRENCHARD, family name of **Viscount Trenchard**.

TRENCHARD, 2nd Viscount, *cr* 1936, of Wolfeton; **Thomas Trenchard**, MC 1944; Baron, *cr* 1930; Bt, *cr* 1919; *b* 15 Dec. 1923; *o surv. s* of 1st Viscount Trenchard, GCB, OM, GCVO, DSO, first Marshal of the RAF, and of Katherine Viscountess Trenchard (*d* 1960); *S father* 1956; *m* 1948, Patricia, *d* of late Admiral Sir Sidney Bailey, KBE, CB,

DSO and of Lady Bailey; three *s. Educ:* Eton. Served War of 1939–45, Captain, King's Royal Rifle Corps (MC). Director: T. Wall & Sons Ltd, 1953–56; Unilever Ltd and Unilever NV, 1967–77; Carpets International Ltd, 1977–79; Abbey Panels Investments Plc, 1983–; Chairman: Wall's Meat Co. Ltd, 1960–66; Schlumberger Measurement and Control (UK), 1985–. Chm., Sausage and Meat Pie Manufrs Assoc., 1959–70. Minister of State: DoI, 1979–81; for Defence Procurement, MoD, 1981–83. President: RIPH&H, 1970–79; Inst. of Grocery Distribution, 1974–77; Bacon and Meat Manufrs Assoc., 1974–79; Royal Warrant Holders' Assoc., 1968; Mem., ARC, 1970–79. Vice Pres., RAF Benevolent Assoc., 1970–; Trustee, RAF Museum, 1984–. *Heir: s* Hon. Hugh Trenchard [*b* 12 March 1951; *m* 1975, Fiona, *d* of Hon. James Morrison, *qv*; two *s* one *d*]. *Address:* House of Lords, SW1. *Club:* Brooks's.

TREND, family name of **Baron Trend.**

TREND, Baron *cr* 1974 (Life Peer), of Greenwich; **Burke St John Trend,** PC 1972; GCB 1968 (KCB 1962; CB 1955); CVO 1953; *b* 2 Jan. 1914; *o s* of late Walter St John Trend and Marion Tyers; *m* 1949, Patricia Charlotte, *o d* of Rev. Gilbert Shaw; two *s* one *d. Educ:* Whitgift; Merton College, Oxford (Postmaster). 1st Cl. Honour Mods, 1934; 1st Cl. Lit. Hum., 1936; Hon. Fellow, Merton College, 1964. Home Civil Service Administrative Class, 1936; Min. of Education, 1936; transferred to HM Treasury, 1937; Asst Private Sec. to Chancellor of Exchequer, 1939–41; Principal Private Sec. to Chancellor of Exchequer, 1945–49; Under Secretary, HM Treasury, 1949–55; Office of the Lord Privy Seal, 1955–56; Deputy Secretary of the Cabinet, 1956–59; Third Secretary, HM Treasury, 1959–60, Second Secretary, 1960–62; Secretary of the Cabinet, 1963–73. Rector, Lincoln Coll., Oxford, 1973–83 (Hon. Fellow, 1983); Pro-Vice-Chancellor, Oxford Univ., 1975–83. Chm. Trustees, British Museum, 1979–86 (Trustee, 1973–86); Chm., Managing Trustees, Nuffield Foundn, 1980– (Trustee, 1973–); Mem., Adv. Council on Public Records, 1974–82. Pres., Royal Commonwealth Soc., 1982–. High Bailiff of Westminster and Searcher of the Sanctuary, 1983–; Mem. Governing Body, Westminster Sch. Hon. DCL Oxford, 1969; Hon. LLD St Andrews, 1974; Hon. DLitt Loughborough, 1984. *Address:* Flat 10, 102 Rochester Row, SW1P 1JP. *Club:* Athenæum.

TRENDALL, Prof. Arthur Dale, AC 1976; CMG 1961; MA, LittD; FSA; FBA; FAHA; Resident Fellow, Menzies College, La Trobe University; Emeritus Professor, University of Sydney, 1954; *b* Auckland, NZ, 28 March 1909; *s* of late Arthur D. Trendall and late Iza W. Uttley-Todd; unmarried. *Educ:* King's College, Auckland; Univs of Otago (MA 1929, LittD 1936) and Cambridge (MA 1937, LittD 1968). NZ Post-Graduate Scholar in Arts, 1931; Rome Scholar in Archæology, 1934–35; Fellow of Trinity Coll., Cambridge, 1936–40; Librarian British School at Rome, 1936–38; FSA 1939; Professor of Greek, Univ. of Sydney, 1939–54; Dean, Faculty of Arts, 1947–50; Chairman Professorial Board, 1949–50, 1952; Acting Vice-Chancellor, 1953; Master of Univ. House, ANU, 1954–69, retd; Hon. Fellow, 1969. Hon. Curator, Greek and Roman Section, Nicholson Museum, 1954, and Hon. Consultant, National Gallery of Victoria, 1957; Deputy Vice-Chancellor, ANU, 1958–64; Mem. Royal Commn on Univ. of Tas., 1955. Geddes-Harrower Professor of Greek Art and Archæology, Aberdeen Univ., 1966–67; Guest Scholar, J. Paul Getty Mus., 1985. Chm. Aust. Humanities Research Council, 1957–59. Mem., Nat. Capital Planning Cttee, 1958–67; Mem. Australian Universities Commission, 1959–70. Member: Accademia dei Lincei, Rome, 1971; Athens Acad., 1973; Corresp. Mem., Pontifical Acad. of Archaeology, Rome, 1973; Life Mem., Nat. Gall. of Victoria, 1976; For. Mem., Royal Netherlands Acad., 1977. Hon. Fellow: Athens Archaeological Soc., 1975; British School at Rome, 1983; Hon. Mem., Hellenic Soc., 1982. FBA 1968. Hon. LittD: Melbourne, 1956; ANU 1970; Hon. DLitt: Adelaide, 1960; Sydney, 1972; Tasmania, 1979; Hon. Dott. in Lettere Lecce, 1981. For. Galileo Galilei Prize for Archaeology, 1971; Cassano Gold Medal for Magna Graecia Studies, 1971; Britannica Award (Australia), 1973; Kenyon Medal, British Acad., 1983. KCSG, 1956; Commendatore, Ordine al Merito, Republic of Italy, 1965 (Cav. Uff. 1961). *Publications:* Paestan Pottery, 1936; Frühitaliotische Vasen, 1938; Guide to the Cast Collection of the Nicholson Museum, Sydney, 1941; The Shellal Mosaic, 1942, 4th edn 1973; Handbook to the Nicholson Museum (editor), 2nd edn 1948; Paestan Pottery, Supplement, 1952; Vasi Italioti del Vaticano, vol. i, 1953; vol. ii, 1955; The Felton Greek Vases, 1958; Phlyax Vases, 1959, 2nd edn 1967; Paestan Addenda, 1960; Apulian Vase Painters of the Plain Style (with A. Cambitoglou), 1962; South Italian Vase Painting (British Museum Guide), 1966, 2nd edn 1976; The Red-figured Vases of Lucania, Campania and Sicily, 1967, Supplement I, 1970, Supplement II, 1973, Supplement III, 1983; Greek Vases in the Felton Collection, 1968, 2nd edn 1978; Greek Vases in the Logie Collection, Christchurch, NZ, 1971; Illustrations of Greek Drama (with T. B. L. Webster), 1971; Early South Italian Vase-painting, 1974; Eine Gruppe Apulischer Grabvasen in Basel (with M. Schmidt and A. Cambitoglou), 1976; Vasi antichi dipinti del Vaticano—Collezione Astarita: (iii) Vasi italiòti, 1976; (with A. Cambitoglou) The Red-figured Vases of Apulia, 2 vols, 1978, 1982, Supplement I, 1983; several articles in learned periodicals. *Address:* Menzies College, La Trobe University, Bundoora, Vic 3083, Australia.

TRENTHAM, Dr David Rostron, FRS 1982; Head of Physical Biochemistry Division, National Institute for Medical Research, Mill Hill, since 1984; *b* 22 Sept. 1938; *s* of John Austin and Julia Agnes Mary Trentham; *m* 1966, Kamalini; two *s. Educ:* Univ. of Cambridge (BA Chemistry, PhD Organic Chemistry). Biochemistry Dept, University of Bristol: Jun. Research Fellow (Medical Research Council), 1966–69; Research Associate, 1969–72; Lectr in Biochemistry, 1972–75; Reader in Biochemistry, 1975–77; Edwin M. Chance Prof., Biochemistry and Biophysics Dept, Univ. of Pennsylvania, 1977–84. Colworth Medal (an annual award), Biochemical Soc., UK, 1974. *Publications:* numerous research papers in scientific jls. *Address:* Physical Biochemistry Division, National Institute for Medical Research, The Ridgeway, Mill Hill, NW7 1AA. *T:* 01–959 3666.

TRESCOWTHICK, Sir Donald (Henry), KBE 1979; Chairman: Charles Davis Ltd and subsidiaries, since 1971; Investment & Merchant Finance Corporation Ltd and subsidiaries, since 1976; Perpetual Insurance and Securities (Aust.) Ltd, since 1979; Swann Insurance Ltd and subsidiaries, since 1959; Signet Group Pty Ltd, since 1968; *b* 4 Dec. 1930; *s* of Thomas Patrick Trescowthick; *m* 1952, Norma Margaret Callaghan; two *s* two *d.* FASA. Member, Lloyd's of London. Director: DOXA Youth Welfare Foundn; Minus Children's Fund; Aust. Ballet Develt Fund Appeal; Melbourne to Hobart Yacht Race Cttee; Tasmanian Fiesta; Chm., Sir Donald and Lady Trescowthick Foundn. CLJ, 1982; Knight of Magistral Grace, SMO, Malta, 1984. *Recreations:* tennis, swimming, reading. *Address:* 22–32 William Street, Melbourne, Vic. 3000, Australia. *T:* (03) 614 1233; 38A Lansell Road, Toorak, Vic. 3142, Australia. *T:* (03) 62 7658. *Clubs:* Les Ambassadeurs; Athenæum, Victoria Racing, Victorian Amateur Turf (Melbourne); Moonee Valley Racing, Tasmanian Turf, Tasmanian Racing (Hobart); Geelong Football.

TRESIDDER, Gerald Charles, FRCS; Lecturer, Department of Anatomy, University of Leicester; *b* Rawalpindi, 5 Dec. 1912; *s* of late Lt-Col A. G. Tresidder, CIE, MD, MS, FRCS; *m* 1940, Marguerite Bell; one *s* two *d. Educ:* Haileybury College; Queen Mary College and The London Hospital Medical College, Univ. of London. LRCP, MRCS 1937; MB, BS London 1938; FRCS 1946. Surgical Specialist, Major, Indian Medical Service, 1940–46. Surgeon, 1951–64, Urologist, 1964–76, at The London Hospital; Lectr in Surgery and part-time Sen. Lectr in Anatomy, The London Hosp. Med. Sch., 1951–76; Senior Lectr, Human Morphology, Univ. of Southampton, 1976–80. Past Pres., Section of Urology, RSocMed; FRSM; Senior Mem., British Assoc. of Urological Surgeons; Sen. Fellow, British Assoc. of Clinical Anatomists; formerly Examr in Anatomy for Primary FRCSEng and Ed. *Publications:* contributions to: Rob and Smith's Operative Surgery; Smith and Aitkenhead's Textbook of Anaesthesia, 1985; British Jl of Surgery; British Jl of Urology; Lancet; BMJ. *Recreations:* walking and talking. *Address:* Woodspring, Penny Long Lane, Derby DE3 1AW. *T:* Derby 558026.

TRESS, Ronald Charles, CBE 1968; BSc (Econ.) London, DSc Bristol; Director, The Leverhulme Trust, 1977–84; *b* Upchurch, Sittingbourne, Kent, 11 Jan. 1915; *er s* of S. C. Tress; *m* 1942, Josephine Kelly, *d* of H. J. Medland; one *s* two *d. Educ:* Gillingham (Kent) County School; Univ. College, Southampton. Gladstone Student, St Deiniol's Library, Hawarden, 1936–37; Drummond Fraser Research Fellow, Univ. of Manchester, 1937–38; Asst Lecturer in Economics, Univ. Coll. of the S West, Exeter, 1938–41; Economic Asst, War Cabinet Offices, 1941–45; Economic Adviser, Cabinet Secretariat, 1945–47; Reader in Public Finance, Univ. of London, 1947–51; Prof. of Political Economy, Univ. of Bristol, 1951–68; Master of Birkbeck Coll., 1968–77, Fellow, 1977–; Mem., Univ. of London Senate, 1968–77, and Court, 1976–77. Managing Editor, London and Cambridge Economic Service, 1949–51; Member: Reorganisation Commn for Pigs and Bacon, 1955–56; Nigeria Fiscal Commn, 1957–58; Departmental Cttee on Rating of Charities, 1958; Develt Commn, 1959–81; Financial Enquiry, Aden Colony, 1959; East Africa Economic and Fiscal Commn, 1960, Uganda Fiscal Commn, 1962; Kenya Fiscal Commn (Chm.), 1962–63; National Incomes Commn, 1963–65; Chm., SW Economic Planning Council, 1965–68; Mem., Cttee of Inquiry into Teachers' Pay, 1974; Chm., Cttee for Univ. Assistance to Adult Educn in HM Forces, 1974–79; Lay Mem., Solicitors' Disciplinary Tribunal, 1975–79; Chm., Lord Chancellor's Adv. Cttee on Legal Aid, 1979–84. Trustee, City Parochial Foundn, 1974–77, 1979–. Governor, Christ Church Coll., Canterbury, 1975–; Mem. Council, Kent Univ., 1977–. Royal Economic Society: Council, 1960–70, Sec.-Gen., 1975–79, Vice-Pres., 1979–. Hon. LLD: Furman Univ., S Carolina, 1973; Exeter, 1976; DUniv Open Univ., 1974; Hon. DSc (SocSc) Southampton, 1978; Hon. DCL Kent, 1984. *Publications:* articles and reviews in Economic Journal, Economica, LCES Bulletin, etc. *Address:* 22 The Beach, Walmer, Deal, Kent CT14 7HJ. *T:* Deal 373254. *Club:* Athenæum.

TRETHOWAN, Sir (James) Ian (Raley), Kt 1980; Chairman, Horserace Betting Levy Board, since 1982; Director, Barclays Bank (UK), since 1982; Consultant, Thorn EMI, since 1982 (Director, since 1986); an Independent Director, Times Newspapers Holdings Ltd, since 1982; Director, Thames Television Ltd, since 1986; *b* 20 Oct. 1922; *s* of late Major J. J. R. Trethowan, MBE and Mrs R. Trethowan; *m* 1st, 1951, Patricia Nelson (marr. diss.); 2nd, 1963, Carolyn Reynolds; three *d. Educ:* Christ's Hospital. Entered Journalism, 1939. Fleet Air Arm, 1941–46. Political Corresp., Yorkshire Post, 1947–55; News Chronicle, 1955–57; Dep. Editor/Political Editor, Independent Television News, 1958–63; joined BBC, 1963, as Commentator on Politics and Current Affairs; Man. Dir, Radio, BBC, 1969–75; Man. Dir, Television, BBC, 1976–77; Dir-Gen. of the BBC, 1977–82. Political Commentator: The Economist, 1953–58, 1965–67; The Times, 1967–68. Member: Cttee on Official Secrets Act, 1971; Board, British Council, 1980–. Chm., BM Soc., 1982–; Trustee: Glyndebourne Arts Trust, 1982–; BM, 1984–; Governor, Ditchley Foundn, 1985–. Hon. DCL East Anglia, 1979. *Publication:* Split Screen (memoirs), 1984. *Recreations:* racing, opera, sailing. *Address:* Horserace Betting Levy Board, 17/23 Southampton Row, WC1B 5HH. *T:* 01–405 5346. *Clubs:* Travellers', Beefsteak, MCC.

TRETHOWAN, Prof. Sir William (Henry), Kt 1980; CBE 1975; FRCP, FRACP; Professor of Psychiatry, University of Birmingham, 1962–82, Emeritus since 1983; Hon. Consultant Psychiatrist: Hollymoor Hospital, 1964–82; Midland Centre for Neurosurgery, 1975–82; Central Birmingham Health District, since 1983; *b* 3 June 1917; *s* of William Henry Trethowan and Joan Durham Trethowan (*née* Hickson); *m* 1941, Pamela Waters (*d* 1985); one *s* two *d. Educ:* Oundle Sch.; Clare Coll., Cambridge; Guy's Hosp. Med. Sch. MA, MB, BChir (Cantab) 1943; MRCP 1948; FRACP 1961; FRCP 1963; FRCPsych 1971 (Hon. Fellow 1983). Served War, RAMC: Major, Med. Specialist, 1944–47. Psychiatric Registrar, Maudsley Hosp., 1948–50; Psychiatric Resident, Mass Gen. Hosp., and Hon. Teaching Fellow, Harvard, 1951; Lectr and Sen. Lectr in Psychiatry, Univ. of Manchester, 1951–56; Prof. of Psychiatry, Univ. of Sydney, and Hon. Consultant Psychiatrist, Royal Prince Alfred and Royal North Shore Hosps, Sydney, 1956–62. Mem. GMC, 1969–81 (Treasurer, 1978–81); Cons. Adviser in Psychiatry, DHSS, 1964–78; Dean, Univ. of Birmingham Med. Sch., 1968–74; Chm., Standing Mental Health Adv. Cttee, 1968–74; Mem., UGC Med. Subcttee, 1974–81. Member: Birmingham Reg. Hosp. Bd, 1964–74; Standing Med. Adv. Cttee, 1966–82 (Chm., 1976); Central Health Services Council, 1966–80 (Vice-Chm., 1976–80); W Midlands Regional Health Authority, 1974–76. Chm., Med. Acad. Adv. Cttee, Chinese Univ. of Hong Kong, 1976–. FRSocMed; Hon. Fellow, Royal Aust. and NZ Coll. of Psychiatry (FRANZCP 1962); Corresp. Fellow, Amer. Psychiatric Assoc. Hon. DSc Chinese Univ. of Hong Kong, 1979. Hon. FRCPsych. *Publications:* Psychiatry, 2nd edn (with Prof. E. W. Anderson), 1967, 5th edn (with Prof. A. C. P. Sims), 1983; Uncommon Psychiatric Syndromes, 1967, 2nd edn (with M. D. Enoch), 1979; numerous scientific and other articles in various jls; book reviews, etc. *Recreations:* music, cooking, natural history. *Address:* 99 Bristol Road, Edgbaston, Birmingham B5 7TX.

TREVASKIS, Sir (Gerald) Kennedy (Nicholas), KCMG 1963 (CMG 1959); OBE 1948; *b* 1 Jan. 1915; *s* of late Rev. Hugh Kennedy Trevaskis; *m* 1945, Sheila James Harrington, *d* of Col F. T. Harrington; two *s* one *d. Educ:* Summer Fields; Marlborough; King's College, Cambridge. Entered Colonial Service, 1938, as Administrative Cadet, N Rhodesia. Enlisted N Rhodesia Regt 1939; captured by Italian Forces Tug Aqan, Br. Somaliland, 1940 and POW until 1941. Seconded British Military Administration, Eritrea, 1941–48 (Lt-Col) and British Administration, 1948–50; Senior Divisional Officer, Assab, 1943; Serae, 1944; Western Province, 1946; Political Secretary, 1950. Member British delegation four Power Commission ex-Italian Colonies, 1947–48 and Liaison Officer, United Nations Commission, Eritrea, 1950. N Rhodesia, 1950–51; District Commissioner, Ndola. Political Officer, Western Aden Protectorate, 1951, Deputy British Agent, 1952, Adviser and British Agent, 1954; High Commissioner for Aden and the Protectorate of South Arabia, 1963–65 (Deputy High Commissioner, Jan.-Aug. 1963). Member British Delegation, Anglo-Yemeni meeting in London, 1957. *Publications:* A Colony in transition: the British occupation of Eritrea, 1941–52, 1960; Shades of Amber: A South Arabian Episode, 1968. *Recreations:* travel, writing. *Address:* 9th Floor, Berkeley Square House, Berkeley Square, W1. *Clubs:* Carlton, MCC, RAC.

TREVELYAN, Dennis John, CB 1981; MA; FIPM; First Civil Service Commissioner and Deputy Secretary, Cabinet Office (Management and Personnel Office), since 1983; *b* 21 July 1929; *s* of John Henry Trevelyan; *m* 1959, Carol Coombes; one *s* one *d. Educ:* Enfield Grammar Sch.; University Coll., Oxford (Scholar). Entered Home Office, 1950;

Treasury, 1953–54; Sec. to Parly Under-Sec. of State, Home Office, 1954–55; Principal Private Sec. to Lord President of Council and Leader of House, 1964–67; Asst Sec., 1966; Asst Under-Sec. of State, NI Office, 1972–76; Home Office: Asst Under-Sec. of State, Broadcasting Dept, 1976–77; Dep. Under-Sec. of State and Dir-Gen., Prison Service, 1978–83. Secretary: Lord Radcliffe's Cttee of Privy Counsellors to inquire into D Notice Matters, 1967; Peppiatt Cttee on a Levy on Betting on Horse Races. Vice-Chm., CS Sports Council, 1981–; Mem. Bd of Management, Eur. Inst. of Public Admin, Maastricht, 1984–; Governor: Ashridge Management Coll., 1985–; Contemporary Dance Trust, 1986–. FRSA 1986. *Recreations:* sailing, music. *Address:* c/o Cabinet Office (MPO), SW1P 3AL. *Clubs:* Athenæum; MCC.

TREVELYAN, Sir George (Lowthian), 4th Bt, *cr* 1874; retired; Hon. President, Wrekin Trust, since 1985 (Founder, 1971; Director, 1971–86); *b* 5 Nov. 1906; *e s* of Rt Hon. Sir C. P. Trevelyan, 3rd Bt; *S* father 1958; *m* 1940, Editha Helen, *d* of Col John Lindsay-Smith; one adopted *d*. *Educ:* Sidcot School; Trinity College, Cambridge. Worked as artist-craftsman with Peter Waals workshops, fine furniture, 1930–31. Trained and worked in F. M. Alexander re-education method, 1932–36. Taught at Gordonstoun School and Abinger Hill School, 1936–41. Served War, 1941–45, Home Guard Training (Captain). Taught No 1 Army Coll., Newbattle Abbey, 1945–47. Warden, Shropshire Adult College, Attingham Park, Shrewsbury, 1947–71. *Publications:* A Vision of the Aquarian Age, 1977; The Active Eye in Architecture, 1977; Magic Casements, 1980; Operation Redemption, 1981; Summons to a High Crusade, 1986. *Heir:* *b* Geoffrey Washington Trevelyan [*b* 4 July 1920; *m* 1947, Gillian Isabel, *d* of late Alexander Wood; one *s* one *d*]. *Address:* The Old Vicarage, Hawkesbury, near Badminton, Avon GL9 1BW. *T:* Didmarton 359.

TREVELYAN, Julian Otto; Hon. Senior RA, 1986; painter and etcher; *b* 20 Feb. 1910; *s* of late R. C. Trevelyan; *m* 1934, Ursula Darwin (divorced, 1950); one *s*; *m* 1951, Mary Fedden. *Educ:* Bedales; Trinity College, Cambridge. Studied art in Paris, Atelier 17, 1930–33; has since lived and worked in Hammersmith. One man exhibitions: Lefèvre Gall., 1935, 1938, 1942, 1943, 1944, 1946, 1948; Gimpel Fils, 1950; Redfern Gall., 1952; Zwemmer Gall., 1955, 1958, 1960, 1963, 1966, 1967; Galerie de France, Paris, 1947; St George's Gall., 1959; Alex Postan Gall., 1974; New Grafton Gall., 1977, 1983, 1985; Tate Gall., 1977; Holsworthy Gall., 1981; Retrospective of Prints, Bohun Gall., Henley, 1983; Retrospective, Watermans Art Centre, Brentford, 1986; Royal W of England Acad., 1986. Pictures in public and private collections in England, America, Sweden, France, Eire and the USSR. Served War of 1939–45, as Camouflage Officer in Roy. Engineers, 1940–43. Engraving tutor at the Royal College of Art, 1955–63 (Sen. Fellow 1986). *Publications:* Indigo Days, 1957; The Artist and His World, 1960; Etching (Studio Books), 1963; A Place, a State, 1975. *Recreation:* listening to music. *Address:* Durham Wharf, Hammersmith Terrace, W6. *T:* 01–748 2749.

TREVELYAN, Sir Norman Irving, 10th Bt *cr* 1662; *b* 29 Jan. 1915; *s* of Edward Walter Trevelyan (*d* 1947), and of Kathleen E. H., *d* of William Irving; *S* kinsman, Sir Willoughby John Trevelyan, 9th Bt, 1976; *m* 1951, Jennifer Mary, *d* of Arthur E. Riddett, Burgh Heath, Surrey; two *s* one *d*. *Educ:* The Cate School, Carpinteria, California (grad. 1932); Harvard Univ., Cambridge, Mass (grad. 1936). *Heir:* *s* Edward Norman Trevelyan, *b* 14 Aug. 1955. *Address:* 1041 Adella Avenue, Coronado, California 92118, USA.

[*But his name does not, at the time of going to press, appear on the Roll of the Baronetage.*

TREVELYAN OMAN, Julia; *see* Oman.

TREVETHIN, 4th Baron **AND OAKSEY**, 2nd Baron; *see under* Oaksey, 2nd Baron.

TREVOR, 4th Baron *cr* 1880; **Charles Edwin Hill-Trevor**, JP; *b* 13 Aug. 1928; *e s* of 3rd Baron and Phyllis May, 2nd *d* of J. A. Sims, Ings House, Kirton-in-Lindsey, Lincolnshire; *S* father, 1950; *m* 1967, Susan Janet Elizabeth, *o d* of Dr Ronald Bence; two *s*. *Educ:* Shrewsbury. Royal Forestry Society: Mem. Council and Trustee; Chm., N Wales Div. Trustee, Robert Jones and Agnes Hunt Orthopaedic Hosp. Inst. Cttee. JP Clwyd (formerly Denbighshire) 1959; Chm., Berwyn PSD. CStJ. *Recreations:* shooting, fishing. *Heir:* *s* Hon. Marke Charles Hill-Trevor, *b* 8 Jan. 1970. *Address:* Brynkinalt, Chirk, Wrexham, Clwyd. *T:* Chirk 3425; Auch, Bridge of Orchy, Argyllshire. *T:* Tyndrum 282. *Clubs:* East India, Flyfishers'.

TREVOR, David; Hon. Consulting Orthopædic Surgeon: Charing Cross Hospital; St Bartholomew's Hospital; Hon. Consulting Surgeon Royal National Orthopædic Hospital; *b* 24 July 1906; *m* 1935, Kathleen Fairfax Blyth (*d* 1984); two *d*. *Educ:* Tregaron County School; St Bartholomew's Hospital Medical College; Charing Cross Hospital (Post Graduate). MRCS, LRCP 1931; MB, BS London 1931; FRCS 1932; MS London, University Medal, 1934. Past Mem., Internat. Soc. Orthop. and Traumatology, 1951. Past Pres., Orthopædic Section, RSocMed (Hon. Mem. 1982); late Examr in Surgery, Univ. of London; late Mem. Council, RCS (Hunterian Prof., 1968; late Mem. Court of Examrs); Past Vice-Pres., British Orthopædic Assoc. Robert Jones Lectr, RCS, 1971. *Publications:* contributor to BMJ, Journal of Bone and Joint Surgery, Proc. RSM, Annals RCS. *Recreations:* golf, gardening. *Address:* 19 Garden Court, Wheathampstead, Herts AL4 8RE. *T:* Wheathampstead 2611.

TREVOR, Elleston; author; *b* Bromley, Kent, 17 Feb.; *m* Jonquil Burgess; one *s*. *Educ:* Sevenoaks. Apprenticed as a racing driver upon leaving school, 1938. Served in Royal Air Force, War of 1939–45. Began writing professionally in 1945. Member: Writers' Guild of GB; Authors' Guild of America. Amer. Mystery Writers' award, 1965; French Grand Prix de Littérature Policière, 1965. *Plays:* Touch of Purple, Globe, London, 1972; Just Before Dawn, Murder by All Means, 1972. *Publications:* Chorus of Echoes, 1950 (filmed); Tiger Street, 1951; Redfern's Miracle, 1951; A Blaze of Roses, 1952; The Passion and the Pity, 1953; The Big Pick-up, 1955 (filmed); Squadron Airborne, 1955; The Killing-Ground, 1956; Gale Force, 1956 (filmed); The Pillars of Midnight, 1957 (filmed); The VIP, 1959 (filmed); The Billboard Madonna, 1961; The Burning Shore (The Pasang Run, USA), 1962; Flight of the Phœnix, 1964 (filmed); The Shoot, 1966; The Freebooters, 1967 (filmed); A Place for the Wicked, 1968; Bury Him Among Kings, 1970; The Theta Syndrome, 1977 (filmed); Blue Jay Summer, 1977; Deathwatch, 1985. Under pseudonym Warwick Scott: Image in the Dust, 1951; The Domesday Story, 1951; Naked Canvas, 1952. Under pseudonym Simon Rattray: Knight Sinister, Queen in Danger, Bishop in Check, Dead Silence, Dead Circuit (all 1951–53). Under pseudonym Adam Hall: Volcanoes of San Domingo, 1964; The Berlin Memorandum, 1964 (filmed as The Quiller Memorandum); The 9th Directive, 1966; The Striker Portfolio, 1969; The Warsaw Document, 1971; The Tango Briefing, 1973; The Mandarin Cypher, 1975; The Kobra Manifesto, 1976; The Sinkiang Executive, 1978; The Scorpion Signal, 1979; The Pekin Target, 1981; Northlight, 1985. Under pseudonym Caesar Smith: Heatwave, 1957 (filmed). Under pseudonym Roger Fitzalan: A Blaze of Arms, 1967. Under pseudonym Howard North: Expressway, 1973; The Paragon (Night Stop, USA), 1974; The Sibling, 1979; The Damocles Sword, 1981; The Penthouse, 1982. Under pseudonym Lesley Stone: Siren Song, 1985. *Recreations:* chess, reading, travelling, astronomy. *Address:* 16122 Ocotillo Drive, Fountain Hills, Arizona 85268, USA. *T:* (602)837–1484.

TREVOR, Brig. Kenneth Rowland Swetenham, CBE 1964 (OBE 1952); DSO 1945; Brigadier (retired 1966); *b* 15 April 1914; 2nd *s* of late Mr and Mrs E. S. R. Trevor, formerly of The Acres, Upton Heath, Chester; *m* 1941, Margaret Baynham, *er d* of late Reverend J. H. Baynham, ACG; two *s*. *Educ:* Rossall; RMC, Camberley. Joined 22nd (Cheshire) Regt, 1934; served in India and with RWAFF in Nigeria. War of 1939–45 (despatches and DSO): No. 1 Commando, N Africa and Burma, 1941–45, as CO, 1943–45; Staff College, Camberley, 1945–46; Bde Major, 29 Infantry Brigade Group, 1949–51; served Korea, 1950–51 (despatches, OBE); GSO1 and Chief Instructor, RMA, Sandhurst, 1954–56; Commanded 1st Bn Cheshire Regt, 1956–58; Malaya, 1957–58 (despatches); Deputy Commander, 50 Infantry Brigade Group/Central Area, Cyprus, 1959, Brigade Col Mercian Brigade, 1960–61; Commander, 2 Infantry Brigade Group and Devon/Cornwall Sub District, 1961–64; Commander, British Guiana Garrison, 1963; Inspector of Boys' Training (Army), 1964–66. With Runcorn Develt Corp., 1966–78. Vice-Pres., The Commando Assoc. *Recreation:* golf. *Address:* Barrelwell Hill, Chester. *Club:* Army and Navy.

TREVOR, Meriol; Author; *b* 15 April 1919; *d* of Lt-Col Arthur Prescott Trevor and Lucy M. E. Trevor (*née* Dimmock). *Educ:* Perse Girls' Sch., Cambridge; St Hugh's Coll., Oxford. FRSL. *Publications:* *novels:* The Last of Britain, 1956; The New People, 1957; A Narrow Place, 1958; Shadows and Images, 1960; The City and the World, 1970; The Holy Images, 1971; The Fugitives, 1973; The Two Kingdoms, 1973; The Marked Man, 1974; The Enemy at Home, 1974; The Forgotten Country, 1975; The Fortunate Marriage, 1976; The Treacherous Paths, 1976; The Civil Prisoners, 1977; The Fortunes of Peace, 1978; The Wanton Fires, 1979; The Sun with a Face, 1984; The Golden Palaces, 1986; *poems:* Midsummer, Midwinter, 1957; *biography:* Newman: The Pillar of the Cloud, 1962; Newman: Light in Winter, 1962 (James Tait Black Meml Prize); Apostle of Rome, 1966; Pope John, 1967; Prophets and Guardians, 1969; The Arnolds, 1973; also books for children. *Address:* 70 Pulteney Street, Bath, Avon BA2 4DL.

TREVOR, William, (William Trevor Cox), CBE (Hon.) 1977; writer; *b* 24 May 1928; *er s* of J. W. Cox; *m* 1952, Jane, *yr d* of C. N. Ryan; two *s*. *Educ:* St Columba's College, Co. Dublin; Trinity College, Dublin. Mem., Irish Acad. Letters. Television plays include: The Mark-2 Wife; O Fat White Woman; The Grass Widows; The General's Day; Love Affair; Last Wishes; Matilda's England; Secret Orchards; Autumn Sunshine. Radio plays include: The Penthouse Apartment; Beyond the Pale (Giles Cooper award, 1980); Travellers; Autumn Sunshine (Giles Cooper award, 1982). Allied Irish Banks Award for Literature, 1976. Hon. DLitt: Exeter, 1984; TCD, 1986. *Publications:* A Standard of Behaviour, 1956; The Old Boys, 1964 (Hawthornden Prize; as play, produced Mermaid, 1971); The Boarding-House, 1965; The Love Department, 1966; The Day We Got Drunk on Cake, 1967; Mrs Eckdorf in O'Neill's Hotel, 1969; Miss Gomez and the Brethren, 1971; The Ballroom of Romance, 1972 (adapted for BBC TV, 1982); Going Home (play), 1972; A Night with Mrs da Tanka (play), 1972; Marriages (play), 1973; Elizabeth Alone, 1973; Angels at the Ritz, 1975 (RSL award); The Children of Dynmouth, 1976 (Whitbread Award); Lovers of Their Time, 1978; Other People's Worlds, 1980; Beyond the Pale, 1981; Scenes from an Album (play), 1981; Fools of Fortune, 1983; (Whitbread Award) A Writer's Ireland, 1984; The News from Ireland and other stories, 1986. *Address:* c/o The Bodley Head, 30 Bedford Square, WC1.

TREVOR COX, Major Horace Brimson; *o s* of late C. Horace Cox, Roche Old Court, Winterslow, Wilts and formerly of Whitby Hall, nr Chester; *m* 1957, Gwenda Mary, *d* of Alfred Ellis, Woodford, Essex; one *d*. *Educ:* Eton (played football for Eton Field and Wall game, 1926 and 1927, boxed for Eton, 1925, 1926, 1927); Germany and USA. Major late Welsh Guards (SR); served in France with BEF, 1939–40, and on General Staff, 1940–44; Major AA Comd. HQ, 1944–46, RARO, 1946–61. Studied commercial and political conditions in Germany, 1927–29, in America and Canada, 1929–30, and in Near East (Egypt and Palestine), 1934; contested (C) NE Derbyshire, 1935, Stalybridge and Hyde, 1937; MP (C) County of Chester, Stalybridge and Hyde, 1937–45; Parliamentary Private Secretary to: Rt Hon. Sir Ronald Cross when Under-Secretary Board of Trade, 1938–39, and when Minister of Economic Warfare, 1939–40; Minister of Health Rt Hon. H. U. Willink, 1945. Hon. Treasr, Russian Relief Assoc., 1945–47. Contested (C) Stalybridge and Hyde, 1945, Birkenhead, 1950; Parly Candidate (C) for Romford and Brentwood, Essex, 1953–55; contested (Ind) Salisbury by-election, 1965; later joined Labour Party; contested (Lab): RDC, Wilts, 1970; Wilts CC, 1973. Mem. Fabian Soc. Member of Exec. County Committee, British Legion, Wilts, 1946–62; Chairman: Salisbury and S Wilts Branch, English-Speaking Union, 1957–63; Salisbury Road Safety Cttee, 1985 (Mem., 1977–85); Mem. Exec. Cttee, CLA, for Wilts, Hants, IoW and Berks. Farmer and landowner. Lord of Manor of East Winterslow. *Address:* Roche Old Court, Winterslow, Wilts. *Club:* Brooks's.

TREVOR-ROPER, family name of **Baron Dacre of Glanton.**

TREVOR-ROPER, Patrick Dacre, MA, MD, BChir Cantab; FRCS, DOMS England; FZS; FRGS; Consultant Ophthalmic Surgeon: Westminster Hospital, 1947–82; Moorfields Eye Hospital, 1961–81; King Edward VII Hospital for Officers, since 1964; Teacher of Ophthalmology, University of London, 1953–82; *b* 1916; *yr s* of Dr B. W. E. Trevor-Roper, Alnwick, Northumberland; unmarried. *Educ:* Charterhouse (senior classical schol.); Clare Coll., Cambridge (exhibitioner); Westminster Hospital Medical Sch. (scholar). Served as Captain, NZ Medical Corps, 1943–46, in Central Mediterranean Forces. Held resident appointments, Westminster Hospital and Moorfields Eye Hospital. Vice-Pres., Ophthalmol Soc. of UK; Chm., Ophth. Qualifications Cttee, 1974–; Founder Mem., Internat. Acad. of Ophthalmology, 1976; FRSocMed (Pres., Ophthalmol Sect., June 1978–80). Formerly: Examnr for Diploma of Ophthalmology, RCS; Mem., Ophth. Group Cttee, BMA; Mem., London Med. Cttee. Hon. Member: Brazilian Society of Ophthalmology, 1958; Ophthalmological Soc. of NZ, 1975; Hon. dipl., Peruvian and Columbian Societies of Otolaryngology and Ophthalmology, 1958; President, etc., of various clubs in connection with sports, music and drama, both hospital and county. Freeman, City of London; Liveryman, Soc. of Spectaclemakers. Doyne medal, 1980; (first) de Lancey medal, RSocMed. *Publications:* (ed) Music at Court (Four 18th century studies by A. Yorke-Long), 1954; Ophthalmology, a Textbook for Diploma Students, 1955, new edn 1962; Lecture-notes in Ophthalmology, 1959, 7th edn 1986 (trans. French, Spanish, Portuguese, Malay); (ed) International Ophthalmology Clinics VIII, 1962; The World Through Blunted Sight: an inquiry into the effects of disordered vision on character and art, 1971, new edn 1972; The Eye and Its Disorders, 1973, new edn 1984; (ed) Recent Advances in Ophthalmology, 1975; (ed) The Bowman Lectures, 1980; (ed) Procs 6th Congress of European Ophth. Soc., 1980; Ophthalmology (pocket consultant series), 1981, 2nd edn 1984; miscellaneous articles in medical and other journals; Editor, Trans Ophthalmological Society UK, 1949–; Mem. Editorial Board, Modern Medicine, Annals of Ophth., The Broadway. *Recreations:* music, travel. *Address:* 3 Park Square West, Regent's Park, NW1. *T:* 01–935 5052; Long Crichel House, near Wimborne, Dorset. *Clubs:* Athenæum, Beefsteak.

See also Baron Dacre of Glanton.

TREW, Francis Sidney Edward, CMG 1984; HM Diplomatic Service; Ambassador to Bahrain, since 1984; *b* 22 Feb. 1931; *s* of Harry Francis and Alice Mary Trew; *m* 1958,

Marlene Laurette Regnery; three *d. Educ:* Taunton's Sch., Southampton. Served Army, 1949–51; 2nd Lieut, Royal Hampshire Regt. FO, 1951; Lebanon, 1952; Amman, 1953; Bahrain, 1953–54; Jedda, 1954–56; Vice-Consul, Philadelphia, 1956–59; Second Sec., Kuwait, 1959–62; FO, 1962; seconded as Sec., European Conf. on Satellite Communications, 1963–65; Consul, Guatemala City, 1965–70; First Sec., Mexico City, 1971–74; FCO, 1974–77; Consul, Algeciras, 1977–79; FCO, 1980–81; High Comr at Belmopan, Belize, 1981–84. Order of Aztec Eagle (Mexico), 1975. *Recreations:* carpentry, fishing. *Address:* c/o Lloyds Bank, 6 Pall Mall, SW1.

TREW, Peter John Edward, FCIS, MICE; Director, Rush & Tompkins Group plc, since 1973 (Chairman of Executive Committee, since 1986); *b* 30 April 1932; *s* of Antony Trew, DSC; *m* 1955, Angela (marr. diss. 1985), *d* of Kenneth Rush, CBE; two *s* one *d*; *m* 1985, Joan, *d* of Allan Haworth. *Educ:* Diocesan Coll., Rondebosch, Cape. Royal Navy, 1950–54; served HMS Devonshire, Unicorn and Charity. Awarded Chartered Inst. of Secretaries Sir Ernest Clarke Prize, 1955. Contested (C) Dartford, 1966; MP (C) Dartford, 1970–Feb. 1974; Jt Sec., Cons. Parly Finance Cttee, 1972–74; Mem., Select Cttee on Tax Credits, 1972–73. Chm., Kent West Cons. European Constituency Council, 1978–80. Mem. Council, CBI, 1975–83 (Mem., Econ. and Fin. Policy Cttee, 1980–86). Foundn Fellow, Assoc. of Corporate Treasurers, 1979. *Address:* 1 Painshill House, Cobham, Surrey. *T:* Cobham 63315.

TREWBY, Vice-Adm. Sir (George Francis) Allan, KCB 1974; FEng 1978; retired; *b* Simonstown, S Africa, 8 July 1917; *s* of late Vice-Admiral G. Trewby, CMG, DSO, and Dorothea Trewby (*née* Allan); *m* 1942, Sandra Coleridge Stedham; two *s. Educ:* RNC, Dartmouth; RNEC, Keyham; RNC, Greenwich. Naval Cadet, Dartmouth, 1931 (King's Dirk, 1934). Served in HMS: Frobisher, Barham, Nelson, Duke of York, Dido, Cadiz, Albion. Comdg Officer, HMS Sultan, 1963–64; IDC, 1965; Captain of Naval Base, Portland, 1966–68; Asst Controller (Polaris), MoD, 1968–71; Chief of Fleet Support and Member of Board of Admiralty, 1971–74. Commander, 1950; Captain, 1959; Rear-Adm., 1968; Vice-Adm., 1971. Naval ADC to HM the Queen, 1968. FIMechE; FIMarE; CBIM. Akroyd Stuart Award of InstMarE for 1954–55. *Publications:* papers on naval marine engineering, in UK, USA, Sweden and Italy. *Recreations:* swimming; Past Captain Navy Athletics Team. *Address:* 2 Radnor Close, Henley-on-Thames RG9 2DA. *T:* Henley 577260. *Clubs:* MCC, Ebury Court; Phyllis Court (Henley).

TREWIN, John Courtenay, OBE 1981; FRSL; dramatic critic and author; *b* 4 Dec. 1908; *o s* of Captain John Trewin, The Lizard, Cornwall, and Annie (*née* James); *m* 1938, Wendy Monk; two *s. Educ:* Plymouth Coll. Editorial Staff: Western Independent, 1926–32; The Morning Post, London, 1932–37; second dramatic critic, 1934–37. Contributor to The Observer, 1937–; editorial staff, 1942–53; Literary Editor, 1943–48; second dramatic critic, 1943–53. Dramatic critic: Punch, 1944–45; John o' London's, 1945–54; The Illustrated London News, 1946–; The Sketch, 1947–59; The Lady, 1949–; The Birmingham Post, 1955–; Radio-drama critic of The Listener, 1951–57; Editor: The West Country Magazine, 1946–52; Plays of the Year series (50 vols), 1948–; The Year's Work in the Theatre (for the British Council), 1949–51. President, The Critics' Circle, 1964–65; Chairman, W Country Writers' Assoc., 1964–73. Hon. MA Birmingham, 1978. Devised (with David Toguri) Farjeon Reviewed, Mermaid Theatre, 1975. *Publications:* Shakespeare Memorial Theatre, 1932; The English Theatre, 1948; Up From The Lizard, 1948; We'll Hear a Play, 1949; (with H. J. Willmott) London-Bodmin, 1950; Stratford-upon-Avon, 1950; The Theatre Since 1900, 1951; The Story of Bath, 1951; Drama 1945–50, 1951; Down To The Lion, 1952; (with E. M. King) Printer to the House, 1952; A Play To-night, 1952; (with T. C. Kemp) The Stratford Festival, 1953; Dramatists of Today, 1953; Edith Evans, 1954; (ed) Theatre Programme, 1954; Mr Macready, 1955; Sybil Thorndike, 1955; Verse Drama Since 1800, 1956; Paul Scofield, 1956; The Night Has Been Unruly, 1957; Alec Clunes, 1958; The Gay Twenties: A Decade of the Theatre, 1958; Benson and the Bensonians, 1960; The Turbulent Thirties, 1960; A Sword for A Prince, 1960; John Neville, 1961; The Birmingham Repertory Theatre, 1963; Shakespeare on the English Stage, 1900–1964, 1964; completion of Lamb's Tales, 1964; Drama in Britain, 1951–64, 1965; (with H. F. Rubinstein) The Drama Bedside Book, 1966; (ed) Macready's Journals, 1967; Robert Donat, 1968; The Pomping Folk, 1968; Shakespeare Country, 1970; (with Arthur Colby Sprague) Shakespeare's Plays Today, 1970; Peter Brook, 1971; (ed) Sean: memoirs of Mrs Eileen O'Casey, 1971; I Call My Name (verse pamphlet), 1971; Portrait of Plymouth, 1973; Long Ago (verse pamphlet), 1973; Theatre Bedside Book, 1974; Tutor to the Tsarevich, 1975; (ed) Eileen, 1976; The Edwardian Theatre, 1976; Going to Shakespeare, 1978; (ed and revd) Nicoll, British Drama, 1978; The West Country Book, 1981; Companion to Shakespeare, 1981; (ed with Lord Miles) Curtain Calls, 1981; (with Wendy Trewin) The Arts Theatre, London, 1927–81, 1986; ed several other books. *Recreation:* all things Cornish: a Bard of the Cornish Gorsedd (Den an Lesard). *Address:* 15 Eldon Grove, Hampstead, NW3. *T:* 01–435 0207. *Club:* Garrick.

TRIBE, Geoffrey Reuben, OBE 1968; Controller, Higher Education Division, British Council, 1981–83, retired; *b* 20 Feb. 1924; *s* of late Harry and Olive Tribe; *m* 1st, 1946, Sheila Mackenzie (marr. diss. 1977); 2nd, 1978, Malvina Anne Butt. *Educ:* Southern Grammar Sch., Portsmouth; University Coll. London (BA). Served War, Royal Hampshire Regt (Lieut), 1942–45. Teaching, 1948–58. Appointed to British Council, 1958; Asst Regional Rep., Madras, 1958–63; Regional Dir, Mwanza, 1963–65; Regional Rep., E Nigeria, 1965–67; Asst Controller, Personnel and Staff Recruitment, 1968–73; Controller, Arts Div., 1973–79; Representative, Nigeria, 1979–81. *Recreation:* sailing. *Address:* Tilhayes, Iwerne Minster, Blandford Forum, Dorset DT11 8LU. *T:* Fontmell Magna 811258.

TRIBE, Rear-Admiral Raymond Haydn, CB 1964; MBE 1944; DL; *b* 9 April 1908; *s* of Thomas and Gillian Ada Tribe; *m* 1938, Alice Mary (*née* Golby); no *c*. Served War of 1939–45 (MBE, despatches twice). Commander, 1947; Captain, 1955; Rear-Admiral, 1962. Inspector-General, Fleet Maintenance, and Chief Staff Officer (Technical) to C-in-C Home Fleet, 1962–65; retired from Royal Navy, Sept. 1965. Distinguished Battle Service Medal of Soviet Union, 1943. CC Berks, 1970–77. DL Berks, 1975. *Recreations:* gardening, painting. *Address:* Oak Cottage, Compton, near Newbury, Berks. *T:* Compton, Berks, 253.

TRICKER, Prof. Robert Ian, DLitt; FCA; FCMA; Professor of Finance and Accounting, University of Hong Kong, since 1986; Director, Corporate Policy Group, Oxford, since 1979; *b* 14 Dec. 1933; *s* of Ralph Edward Tricker, Coventry; *m* 1st, 1958, Doreen Murray (marr. diss. 1982); two *d*; 2nd, 1982, Gretchen Elizabeth Bigelow. *Educ:* King Henry VIII Sch., Coventry; Harvard Business Sch., USA. MA, JDipMA; DLitt CNAA, 1983. Articled Clerk, Daffern & Co., 1950–55; Sub-Lt, RNVR, 1956–58; Controller, Unbrako Ltd, 1959–64; Directing Staff, Iron & Steel Fedn Management Coll., 1965; Barclays Bank Prof. of Management Information Systems, Univ. of Warwick, 1968–70. Director, Oxford Centre for Management Studies, 1970–79, Professorial Fellow, 1979–84 (P. D. Leake Res. Fellow, 1966–67); Res. Fellow, Nuffield Coll., Oxford, 1979–84 (Vis. Fellow, 1971–79); Dir, Management Develt Centre of Hong Kong, 1984–86. Institute of Chartered Accountants in England and Wales: Mem. Council, 1979–84; Mem. Educn and Trng Directorate, 1979–82; Chairman: Examination Cttee, 1980–82; Tech. and Res. Cttee, 1982–84. Member: Council, ICMA, 1969–72; Management and Industrial Relations Cttee, SSRC, 1973–75; Chm., Independent Inquiry into Prescription Pricing Authority for Minister for Health, 1976. Member: Nuffield Hosp. Management Cttee, 1972–74; Adv. Panel on Company Law, Dept of Trade, 1980–83; Company Affairs Cttee, Inst. of Directors, 1980–84. *Publications:* The Accountant in Management, 1967; Strategy for Accounting Research, 1975; Management Information and Control Systems, 1976, 2nd edn 1982; The Independent Director, 1978; Effective Information Management, 1982; Governing the Institute, 1983; Corporate Governance, 1984; The Effective Director, 1986. *Address:* Department of Management Studies, University of Hong Kong, Hong Kong.

TRICKETT, (Mabel) Rachel; Principal, St Hugh's College, Oxford, since Aug. 1973; *b* 20 Dec. 1923. *Educ:* Lady Margaret Hall, Oxford, 1942–45. BA Hons 1st Cl. in English; MA 1947; Hon. Fellow, 1978. Asst to Curator, Manchester City Art Galleries, 1945–46; Asst Lectr in English, Univ. of Hull, 1946–49; Commonwealth Fund Fellow, Yale Univ., 1949–50; Lectr in English, Hull Univ., 1950–54; Fellow and Tutor in English, St Hugh's Coll., Oxford, 1954–73. *Publications:* The Honest Muse (a study in Augustan verse), 1967; *novels:* The Return Home, 1952; The Course of Love, 1954; Point of Honour, 1958; A Changing Place, 1962; The Elders, 1966; A Visit to Timon, 1970. *Address:* St Hugh's College, Oxford OX2 6LE. *T:* Oxford 57341.

TRICKEY, Edward Lorden, FRCS; Dean, Institute of Orthopaedics, London University, since 1981; Consultant Orthopaedic Surgeon, Royal National Orthopaedic Hospital, London, and Edgware General Hospital, since 1960; *b* 22 July 1920; *s* of E. G. W. Trickey and M. C. Trickey; *m* 1944, Ivy Doreen Harold; two *s* one *d. Educ:* Dulwich College; King's College, London Univ. (MB BS). Consultant Orthopaedic Surgeon, Ashton under Lyne, 1957–60. *Publications:* various articles on orthopaedic trauma and knee joint surgery. *Recreations:* cricket, bridge. *Address:* 5 Hive Road, Bushey Heath, Herts. *T:* 01–950 3137. *Clubs:* MCC, Middlesex CC.

TRIER, Peter Eugene, CBE 1980; MA; FEng, FIEE; FInstP, FIMA; Pro-Chancellor, Brunel University, since 1980; Director of Research and Development, Philips Electronics UK, 1969–81, retired; *b* 12 Sept. 1919; *s* of Ernst and Nellie Trier; *m* 1946, Margaret Nora Holloway; three *s. Educ:* Mill Hill Sch.; Trinity Hall, Cambridge (Wrangler 1941). Royal Naval Scientific Service, 1941–50; Mullard Research Labs, 1950–69, Dir, 1953–69. Dir, Mullard Ltd and other Philips subsidiaries, 1957–85; Main Bd Dir, Philips Electronics, 1969–85. Specialist Advr, House of Lords Select Cttee on Sci and Technol., 1982–84; Member: Electronics Res. Council, MoD, 1963–80 (Chm., 1976–80); Defence Scientific Adv. Council, 1975–85 (Chm., 1981–85); ACARD Working Party on IT, 1980; ACARD sub-group on Annual Review of Govt-funded R&D, 1985–86. IEE: Vice-Pres., 1974–77; Faraday Lectr, 1968–69; Chm., Electronics Div. Bd, 1971–72; Pres., IMA, 1982–83. FEng 1978 (Hon. Sec. for Electrical Engrg Disciplines, 1985–; Mem. Council, 1980–83 and 1985–); Pres., Electronic Engrg Assoc., 1980–81; Member: Management Cttee, Royal Instn, 1978–81; Adv. Bd, RCDS, 1980–. Brunel University: Mem. Council, 1968– (Chm., 1973–78); Chm., Supervisory Bd, Brunel Inst. of Bio-Engineering, 1983–; Chm., Bute Engrg Adv. Cttee, UWIST, 1983–86; External Examr in Maths: Polytechnic of Central London, 1983–86; Coventry Lanchester Polytechnic, 1986–. Mem. Editorial Bd, Interdisciplinary Science Reviews, 1975–. Mem., Management Cttee, Wine Soc., 1977–. Liveryman, Co. of Scientific Instrument Makers, 1967–. Hon. DTech Brunel, 1975. Glazebrook Medal and Prize, Inst. of Physics, 1984. *Publications:* Strategic Implications of Micro-electronics, 1982; Mathematics and Information, 1983; papers in scientific and technical jls. *Recreations:* travel, sailing, railway history. *Address:* Yew Tree House, Bredon, Tewkesbury, Glos GL20 7HF. *T:* Bredon 72200. *Club:* Savile.

TRILLO, Rt. Rev. Albert John, MTh; *b* 4 July 1915; *s* of late Albert Chowns and late Margaret Trillo; *m* 1942, Patricia Eva Williams; two *s* one *d. Educ:* The Quintin Sch.; King's Coll., University of London. Business career, 1931–36; University, 1936–38, BD (1st Class Hons) and AKC (1st Class Hons), 1938; MTh 1943. Asst Curate, Christ Church, Fulham, 1938–41; Asst Curate, St Gabriel's, Cricklewood (in charge of St Michael's), 1941–45; Secretary, SCM in Schools, 1945–50; Rector of Friern Barnet and Lecturer in New Testament Greek, King's Coll., London, 1950–55; Principal, Bishops' Coll., Cheshunt, 1955–63; Bishop Suffragan of Bedford, 1963–68; Bishop Suffragan of Hertford, 1968–71; Bishop of Chelmsford, 1971–85. Examining Chaplain to Bishop of St Edmundsbury and Ipswich, 1955–63, to Bishop of St Albans, 1963–71. Hon. Canon, Cathedral and Abbey Church at St Albans, 1958–63; Canon Residentiary, 1963–65. Fellow of King's Coll., London, 1959. Proctor in Convocation for Dean and Chapter of St Albans, 1963–64; Proctor-in-Convocation for the Clergy, 1965. Governor: Aldenham Sch., 1963–71; Harper Trust Schs, Bedford, 1963–68; Queenswood Sch., 1969–71; Forest Sch., 1976–. Chairman: Church of England Youth Council, 1970–74; Exec. Cttee, British Council of Churches, 1974–77 (Chm., Fund for Ireland, 1978–); Church of England's Cttee on Roman Catholic Relations, 1975–85; Jt Chm., English Anglican/Roman Catholic Commn. *Recreations:* reading and walking. *Address:* Copperfield, Back Road, Wenhaston, Halesworth, Suffolk.

TRIMLESTOWN, 19th Baron *cr* 1461; **Charles Aloysius Barnewall;** *b* 2 June 1899; *o* surv. *s* of 18th Baron and Margaret (*d* 1901), *d* of R. J. Stephens, Brisbane, Queensland; *S* father, 1937; *m* 1st, 1926, Muriel (*d* 1937), *o c* of Edward Oskar Schneider, Mansfield Lodge, Whalley Range, Manchester; two *s* one *d*; 2nd, 1952, Freda Kathleen Watkins, *d* of late Alfred Watkins, Ross-on-Wye. *Educ:* Ampleforth. Lieut, Irish Guards, 1918; served European War. *Heir:* *s* Hon. Anthony Edward Barnewall [*b* 2 Feb. 1928; *m* 1977, Mary W., *er d* of late Judge Thomas F. McAllister]. *Address:* Tigley, Dartington, Totnes, Devon.

TRINDER, Sir (Arnold) Charles, GBE 1969; Kt 1966; *b* 12 May 1906; *s* of Arnold Anderson Trinder, Oxshott; *m* 1st, 1929, Elizabeth Cairns; one *d*; 2nd, 1937, Elaine Chaytor; two *d. Educ:* Wellington Coll.; Clare Coll., Cambridge (MA (Hons)). Entered Trinder Anderson & Co., 1927; Sen. Partner, 1940–53; Chm., 1953–72; Consultant, 1972–76. Member, Baltic Exchange, 1928, Hon. Member, 1973. Common Councilman, 1951; Alderman of Aldgate, 1959–76; Sheriff, City of London, 1964; Lord Mayor of London for 1968–69. Chm., London Broadcasting Co. Ltd, 1972–74. Chairman: Family Welfare Assoc., 1967–73; Missions to Seamen (London Reg.), 1972–76. Chm., City of London Archaeol Trust, 1978–79. Chancellor, City University, 1968–69; Trustee, Morden Coll., Blackheath, 1970. Prime Warden, Worshipful Company of Shipwrights, 1973; Master, Worshipful Company of Fletchers, 1966. FICS 1963. Hon. DSc, City Univ., 1968. KStJ 1969. Order of Merit, Chile, 1965; Nat. Order of Niger, 1969; Order of Merit, Italy, 1969; Order of Lion of Finland, 1969. *Publication:* O Men of Athens, 1946. *Recreations:* gardening, astronomy, ancient history, logodaedaly. *Address:* Hoo End Farm, Whitwell, Herts. *Clubs:* Royal Automobile, City Livery, Guildhall.

TRINDER, Air Vice-Marshal Frank Noel, CB 1949; CBE 1944; psa; *b* 24 Dec. 1895; *s* of Alfred Probus Trinder, MRCS, LRCP, Parkstone, Dorset; *m* 1925, Marjorie Agnes Scott, *d* of Archie Scott Blake, Melrose, Scotland; one *s. Educ:* Epsom College. Served European War, 1914–18, with North Staffordshire Regt, 1915–17; France, 1915 (wounded); Lieut, 1916; transferred to RFC, 1917. Egypt, 1917–20; Iraq, 1920; Air Ministry, 1921–28; Staff College, 1929; Headquarters, India, 1930–35; Wing Commander, 1937; War of 1939–45 (despatches, CBE); Group Captain, 1940; Headquarters, Far East, 1938–40; USA, 1940–43; Air Commodore, 1943; Cossac Staff, 1943–44; SHAEF, 1944–45; Air Div. CCG, 1945–46; Senior Air Staff Officer, Headquarters Maintenance Command, 1947–49; Director-General of Equipment, Air Ministry, 1949–52; retired, 1952. *Address:* Broom Lodge, Teddington, Mddx. *Club:* Royal Air Force Yacht.

TRINDER, Frederick William; Charity Commissioner, 1984–85; *b* 18 Nov. 1930; *s* of Charles Elliott Trinder and Grace Johanna Trinder (*née* Hoadly); *m* 1964, Christiane Friederike Brigitte Dorothea (*née* Hase); one *s*. *Educ:* LSE, Univ. of London (BSc). Admitted Solicitor, 1966; Legal Asst/Sen. Legal Asst, Charity Commn, 1966–74; Dep. Charity Comr, 1974–84. *Recreations:* travel, gardening, music. *Address:* 37 The Common, West Wratting, Cambridge CB1 5LR. *T:* West Wratting 469. *Club:* Royal Over-Seas League.

TRINDER, Thomas Edward, (Tommy Trinder), CBE 1975; comedian; Chairman, Fulham Football Club Ltd, 1955–76, Life President, since 1976; *b* 24 March 1909; *s* of Thomas Henry Trinder and Jean Mills. *Educ:* St Andrew's, Holborn. First London appearance, Collins's Music-hall, 1922; continued in variety, pantomimes and revues, including Band Waggon, Top of the World, Gangway, Best Bib and Tucker, Happy and Glorious, Here, There and Everywhere, Fancy Free; tours in Canada, NZ, South Africa, USA; numerous Royal Variety and Command performances; radio and TV shows. Films include: The Foreman Went to France; The Bells Go Down; Champagne Charlie. *Recreation:* Fulham Football Club.

TRING, A. Stephen; *see* Meynell, L. W.

TRIPP, Rt. Rev. Howard George; an Auxiliary Bishop in Southwark, (RC), since 1980; Titular Bishop of Newport, since 1980; *b* 3 July 1927; *s* of late Basil Howard Tripp and Alice Emily Tripp (*née* Haslett). *Educ:* John Fisher School, Purley; St John's Seminary, Wonersh. Priest, 1953; Assistant Priest: Blackheath SE3, 1953–56; East Sheen, 1956–62; Asst Diocesan Financial Sec., 1962–68; Parish Priest, East Sheen, 1965–71; Director, Southwark Catholic Children's Soc., 1971–80. *Recreation:* vegetable gardening. *Address:* 8 Arterberry Road, SW20 8AJ. *T:* 01–946 4609.

TRIPP, (John) Peter, CMG 1971; Director, Al-Tajir Bank, since 1986; *b* 27 March 1921; *s* of Charles Howard and Constance Tripp; *m* 1948, Rosemary Rees Jones; one *s* one *d*. *Educ:* Bedford Sch.; Sutton Valence Sch.; L'Institut de Touraine. Served War of 1939–45: Royal Marines, 1941–46. Sudan Political Service, 1946–54. Foreign (subsequently Diplomatic) Service, 1954–81; Political Agent, Trucial States, 1955–58; Head of Chancery, Vienna, 1958–61; Economic Secretary, Residency Bahrain, 1961–63; Counsellor 1963; Political Agent, Bahrain, 1963–65; sabbatical year at Durham Univ., 1965; Amman, 1966–68; Head of Near Eastern Dept, FCO, 1969–70; Ambassador to Libya, 1970–74; High Comr in Singapore, 1974–78; Ambassador to Thailand, 1978–81. Political Adviser, Inchcape Gp, 1981–86; Chm., Private Investment Co. for Asia (UK), 1981–84. Chm., Anglo-Thai Soc., 1983–. County Councillor, Powys, 1985–. *Recreations:* theatre, gardening. *Address:* 30 Ormonde Gate, SW3.

TRIPPIER, David Austin; RD 1983; JP; MP (C) Rossendale and Darwen, since 1983 (Rossendale, 1979–83); Parliamentary Under-Secretary of State, Department of Employment, since 1985; *b* 15 May 1946; *s* of Austin Wilkinson Trippier, MC and late Mary Trippier; *m* 1975, Ruth Worthington, Barrister; two *s*. *Educ:* Bury Grammar School. Commnd Officer, Royal Marines Reserve, 1968. Member of Stock Exchange, 1968–. Mem., Rochdale Council, 1969–78, Leader Cons. Gp, 1974–76. Secretary: All Party Parly Footwear Cttee, 1979–83; Cons. Parly Defence Cttee, 1980–82; PPS to Minister for Health, 1982–83; Parly Under-Sec. of State, DTI, 1983–85. Nat. Vice Chm., Assoc. of Cons. Clubs, 1980–84. JP Rochdale, 1975. *Publication:* Defending the Peace, 1982. *Recreation:* gardening. *Address:* House of Commons, SW1A 0AA. *Club:* Army and Navy.

TRISTRAM, William John, CBE 1965; JP; Pharmaceutical Chemist; Liverpool City Council, 1934–55 (Alderman, 1944–55); appointed Hon. Alderman, 1964; *b* 6 Oct. 1896; *s* of late Rev. W. J. Tristram and Elizabeth Critchlow; *m* 1966, Philomena Mary Moylan (*d* 1986), Drogheda. *Educ:* Scarborough High Sch.; Leeds Central High Sch.; Liverpool College of Pharmacy. Member Council Pharmaceutical Society of Great Britain, 1944–67 (President, 1952–53, FPS, 1966, Gold Medal, 1968); Hon. Treasurer and Member Executive National Pharmaceutical Union, 1936–68 (Chairman, 1943–44); Chairman, Joint Cttee for the Pharmaceutical Service, 1946–52; Member Central Health Services Council (Min. of Health), 1948–64. Vice-Chairman, Standing Pharmaceutical Advisory Cttee (Min. of Health), 1946–48 (Chairman, 1948–59); Chairman, Liverpool Licensing Cttee, 1965–70; Dep. Chairman, South Liverpool Hospitals Management Cttee, 1965–70; Liverpool Exec. Council (Min. of Health), 1948–70 (Chairman, 1960–64); Chairman, Liverpool Homœopathic Hospital, 1960–70. JP, Liverpool, 1938–; Lord Mayor of Liverpool, 1953–54; Dep. Lord Mayor, 1954–55. *Recreations:* cricket-watching, walking. *Address:* Childwall, 6 Westway, Heswall, Wirral, Merseyside L60 8PL. *T:* 051–342 1678. *Clubs:* National Liberal; Lyceum (Liverpool).

TRITTON, Alan George; Director: Barclays Bank Ltd, since 1974; Mercantile Credit Co. Ltd, since 1973; a Vice-President, Equitable Life Assurance Society, since 1983 (Director, since 1976); *b* 2 Oct. 1931; *s* of George Henton Tritton, Lyons Hall, Essex, and Iris Mary Baillie, Lochloy; *m* 1st, 1958, Elizabeth Clare d'Abreu (marr. diss.); two *s* one *d*; 2nd, 1972, Diana Marion Spencer. *Educ:* Eton. Member of British Schools Exploring Soc. Expedn, N Norway, 1949. Served with 1st Batt. Seaforth Highlanders, Malaya, 1950–52 (wounded in action, Pahang). Falkland Islands Dependencies Survey, 1952–54; entered Barclays Bank Ltd, 1954; local Dir, 54 Lombard Street, 1964; Dir, Barclays Bank UK Management Ltd, 1972. A Vice-Pres., Royal Geographical Soc., 1983– (Mem. Council, 1975–, Hon. Treas., 1984–). Member: Cttee, British Trans-Arctic Expedn, 1966–69; Cttee, British Everest SW Face Expedn, 1974–75; Cttee of Management, Mount Everest Foundn, 1976–; Friends' Cttee, Scott Polar Research Inst., 1976–. Commissioner, Public Works Loan Bd, 1970–74; Chm., Westminster Abbey Investment Cttee; Member: Governing Body, British Nat. Cttee, Internat. Chamber of Commerce, 1975 (Hon. Treas. 1985); Council, Essex Agricl Soc., 1973–76. *Recreations:* travelling, shooting. *Address:* 54 Lombard Street, EC3. *T:* 01–283 2161. *Clubs:* Boodle's, Pratt's, Antarctic, Geographical, Essex.

TRITTON, Major Sir Anthony (John Ernest), 4th Bt *cr* 1905; *b* 4 March 1927; *s* of Sir Geoffrey Ernest Tritton, 3rd Bt, CBE, and Mary Patience Winifred (*d* 1960), *d* of John Kenneth Foster; *S* father, 1976; *m* 1957, Diana, *d* of Rear-Adm. St J. A. Micklethwait, CB, DSO, and of Clemence Penelope Olga Welby-Everard; one *s* one *d*. *Educ:* Eton. Commissioned 3rd Hussars, Oct. 1945; retired as Major, 1962, The Queen's Own Hussars. *Recreations:* shooting, fishing. *Heir:* *s* Jeremy Ernest Tritton, *b* 6 Oct. 1961. *Address:* Riverside House, Heytesbury, Wilts. *Club:* Cavalry and Guards.

TROLLOPE, Sir Anthony Owen Clavering, 16th Bt, *cr* 1642; *b* 15 Jan. 1917; *s* of Sir Gordon Clavering Trollope, 15th Bt; *S* father, 1958; *m* 1942, Joan Mary Alexis, *d* of Alexis Robert Gibbs, Manly, New South Wales; two *s*. Served War of 1939–45: 2nd/5th Australian Field Regt, Royal Australian Artillery, Middle East and New Guinea. Director, Thomas C. Denton and Co. Pty Ltd. JP for State of NSW. *Heir:* *s* Anthony Simon Trollope, *b* 1945. *Address:* Clavering, 77 Roseville Avenue, Roseville, NSW 2069, Australia.

TROTMAN-DICKENSON, Dr Aubrey Fiennes; Principal, University of Wales Institute of Science and Technology, Cardiff, since 1968; Vice-Chancellor, University of Wales, 1975–77 and 1983–85; *b* 12 Feb. 1926; *s* of Edward Newton Trotman-Dickenson and Violet Murray Nicoll; *m* 1953, Danusia Irena Hewell; two *s* one *d*. *Educ:* Winchester Coll.; Balliol Coll., Oxford. MA Oxon, BSc Oxon; PhD Manchester; DSc Edinburgh. Fellow, National Research Council, Ottawa, 1948–50; Asst Lecturer, ICI Fellow, Manchester Univ., 1950–53; E. I. du Pont de Nemours, Wilmington, USA, 1953–54; Lecturer, Edinburgh Univ., 1954–60; Professor, University College of Wales, Aberystwyth, 1960–68. Chm., Job Creation Programme, Wales, 1975–78. Member: Welsh Council, 1971–79; Planning and Transport Res. Adv. Council, DoE, 1975–79. Tilden Lectr, Chem. Soc., 1963. *Publications:* Gas Kinetics, 1955; Free Radicals, 1959; Tables of Bimolecular Gas Reactions, 1967; (ed) Comprehensive Inorganic Chemistry, 1973; contrib. to learned journals. *Address:* Radyr Chain, Llantrisant Road, Cardiff CF5 2PW. *T:* Cardiff 563263.

TROTTER, Neville Guthrie, FCA; JP; MP (C) Tynemouth, since Feb. 1974; *b* 27 Jan. 1932; *s* of Captain Alexander Trotter and Elizabeth Winifred Trotter (*née* Guthrie); *m* 1983, Caroline, *d* of Captain John Farrow, RN retd and Oona Farrow (*née* Hall); one *d*. *Educ:* Shrewsbury; King's Coll., Durham (BCom). Short service commn in RAF, 1955–58. Partner, Thornton Baker & Co., Chartered Accountants, 1962–74, now Consultant; Dir, William Baird; Consultant: Bowring; British Marine Equipment Council. Mem., Newcastle City Council, 1963–74 (Alderman, 1970–74; Chm., Finance Cttee, Traffic Highways and Transport Cttee, Theatre Cttee). Mem., CAA Airline Users Cttee, 1973–79. Mem., Tyne and Wear Metropolitan Council, 1973–74; Vice-Chm., Northumberland Police Authority, 1970–74. Chm., Cons. Party Shipping and Shipbuilding Cttee, 1979– (Vice-Chm., 1976–79); Secretary: Cons. Party Industry Cttee, 1981–83; Cons. Party Transport Cttee, 1983–84; Mil. Sec., Cons. Party Aviation Cttee, 1976–79; Member: Industry Sub-Cttee, Select Cttee on Expenditure, 1976–79; Select Cttee on Transport, 1983–. Private Member's Bills: Consumer Safety, 1978; Licensing Amendment, 1980; Intoxicating Substances Supply (Glue Sniffing), 1985. Former Member: Northern Economic Planning Council; Tyne Improvement Commn; Tyneside Passenger Transport Authority; Industrial Relations Tribunal; Council, RUSI. Member: Council British Maritime League; US Naval Inst. JP Newcastle upon Tyne, 1973. *Recreations:* aviation, gardening, fell-walking, study of foreign affairs, defence and industry. *Address:* (office) Higham House, Higham Place, Newcastle upon Tyne NE1 8EE. *T:* Newcastle upon Tyne 612631. *Clubs:* Royal Air Force; Northern Counties (Newcastle upon Tyne); Tynemouth and Whitley Bay Conservative.

TROTTER, Sir Ronald (Ramsay), Kt 1985; Chairman and Chief Executive, Fletcher Challenge Ltd, since 1981; *b* 9 Oct. 1927; *s* of Clement George Trotter, CBE and Annie Euphemia Trotter (*née* Young); *m* 1955, Margaret Patricia, *d* of James Rainey; three *s* one *d*. *Educ:* Collegiate School, Wanganui; Victoria Univ. of Wellington; Lincoln Coll., Canterbury (BCom, Cert in Agric.). FCA. Wright Stephenson & Co., 1958: Dir, 1962; Man. Dir, 1968–70; Chm. and Man. Dir, 1970–72; Chm. and Man. Dir, Challenge Corp., 1972–81. Trustee, NZ Inst. of Economic Research, 1973–; Chm., NZ Business Roundtable, 1985–; Internat. Pres., Pacific Basin Economic Council, 1986–; Past President: NZ Stock and Station Agents' Assoc.; NZ Woolbrokers' Assoc.; Past Chm., Overseas Investment Commn. Hon. LLD Wellington 1984. Silver Jubilee Medal, 1977. *Address:* 16 Wesley Road, Wellington 1, New Zealand. *T:* (4) 726–628. *Club:* Wellington (NZ).

TROUBRIDGE, Sir Peter, 6th Bt, *cr* 1799; RN retired; *b* 6 June 1927; *s* of late Vice-Admiral Sir T. H. Troubridge, KCB, DSO, and Lily Emily Kleinwort; *S* cousin, 1963; *m* 1954, Hon. Venetia Daphne Weeks; one *s* two *d*. *Educ:* Eton; Cambridge. Served Korean War, 1952–53, HMS Ocean; retired from RN (Lt-Comdr), 1967. Chm., Standing Council of the Baronetage, 1981–83 (Vice-Chm., 1979–81). CStJ 1983. *Recreations:* shooting, gardening, birdwatching. *Heir:* *s* Thomas Richard Troubridge [*b* 23 Jan. 1955; *m* 1984, Hon. Rosemary Douglas-Pennant, *yr d* of Baron Penrhyn, *qv*]. *Address:* The Manor House, Elsted, Midhurst, West Sussex. *T:* Harting 286. *Clubs:* White's, City of London, MCC.

TROUGHTON, Sir Charles (Hugh Willis), Kt 1977; CBE 1966; MC 1940; TD 1959; Director: Electric & General Investment Co., since 1967 (Chairman, 1977–80); Wm Collins and Sons, since 1977 (a Vice Chairman, 1984–85, Deputy Chairman, since 1985); Whitbread Investment Co. Ltd, since 1981; Times Newspapers Holdings Ltd, since 1983; *b* 27 Aug. 1916; *o s* of late Charles Vivian and Constance Scylla Troughton; *m* 1947, Constance Gillean Mitford, DL, *d* of Colonel Philip Mitford, Berryfield House, Lentran, Inverness-shire; three *s* one *d*. *Educ:* Haileybury Coll.; Trinity Coll., Cambridge. BA 1938. Joined TA, 1938; served War of 1939–45, Oxford and Bucks Light Infantry; Prisoner of War, 1940–45. Called to the Bar, 1945. Dir, 1949–77 and Chm., 1972–77, W. H. Smith & Son (Holdings) Ltd; former Dir, Equity & Law Life Assce Soc. Ltd; Director: Thomas Tilling Ltd, 1973–79; Barclays Bank UK Management Ltd, 1973–81; Barclays Bank Internat., 1977–82; Whitbread & Co. Ltd, 1978–85. President: British Council, 1985– (Chm., 1977–84); National Book League, 1985–. Member: Board of Management of NAAFI, 1953–73; Design Council, 1975–78; Council, RCA, 1977–79; Governor, LSE, 1975–. Chm., Brit. Kidney Patient Assoc. Investment Trust, 1982–. *Address:* Woolleys, Hambleden, Henley-on-Thames, Oxon. *Clubs:* MCC, Boodles.

TROUGHTON, Henry Lionel, BSc(Eng), CEng, FIMechE, MIEE; Deputy Director, Projects and Research, Military Vehicles and Engineering Establishment, Ministry of Defence, 1970–74; *b* 30 March 1914; *o s* of late Henry James Troughton; *m* 1940, Dorothy Janet Louie (*née* Webb); one *d*. *Educ:* Mill Hill Sch.; University Coll., London. War of 1939–45: commissioned REME (Major), 1940–47; Fighting Vehicles Research and Development Estabt, 1947 (now Mil. Vehicles and Engineering Estabt); Asst Dir (Electrical), later Asst Dir (Power Plant), and Dep. Dir (Vehicles), 1960, retired 1974. *Recreations:* gardening, travel. *Address:* 10 Brookside Close, Feltham, Mddx TW13 7HR.

TROUGHTON, Peter, PhD; Director and Partner, Alan Patricof Associates, since 1986; *b* 26 Aug. 1943; *s* of Frank Sidney Troughton and Joan Vera Troughton (*née* Root); *m* 1967, Joyce Uncles; two *s*. *Educ:* City Univ. (BSc Eng); University College London (PhD). Technical apprentice, Plessey Co., then Post Office apprentice, 1959; PO scholarship, 1964; research for PhD, 1967; develt of microprocessor techniques for control of telephone switching systems, 1970; Dep. Gen. Manager, South Central Telephone Area, 1977; Head of Ops, Prestel, with special responsibility for establishing Prestel network, 1979; Gen. Manager, City Telephone Area, 1980; Regional Dir, British Telecom London, 1983; Man. Dir, British Telecom Enterprises, 1984–86. *Publications:* articles and papers on microwave systems, computers and communications. *Recreations:* travel, archaeology, bridge. *Address:* 39 Dukes Wood, Crowthorne, Berks.

TROUNSON, Rev. Ronald Charles, MA; Principal of S Chad's College, and Lecturer in Classics, University of Durham, since 1978; *b* 7 Dec. 1926; *s* of Edwin Trounson and Elsie Mary Trounson (*née* Bolitho); *m* 1952, Leonora Anne Keate; two *s* three *d*. *Educ:* Plymouth Coll.; Emmanuel Coll., Cambridge (Schol.); Ripon Hall, Oxford (MA). Deacon, 1956; Priest, 1957. National Service, RAF, 1948–50. Asst Master, Scaitcliffe Sch., Englefield Green, Surrey, 1950–52; Sixth Form Classics Master, Plymouth Coll., 1953–58; Asst Curate, St Gabriel's, Plymouth, 1956–58; Chaplain, Denstone Coll., 1958–76; Second Master, 1968–76, Bursar, 1976–78. Fellow, Woodard Corporation, 1983. FRSA 1984. *Address:* 25 North Bailey, Durham DH1 3EW. *T:* Durham 47852.

TROUP, Alistair Mewburn; His Honour Judge Troup; a Circuit Judge, since 1980; *b* 23 Nov. 1927; *y s* of late William Annandale Troup, MC, MD, and Margaret Loïs Troup (*née* Mewburn); *m* 1969, Marjorie Cynthia (*née* Hutchinson); one *s* three *d* by previous marriages. *Educ:* Merchant Taylor's School; New College, Oxford (BA). Served Army, 1946–48. Called to the Bar, Lincoln's Inn, 1952; Crown Counsel, Tanganyika, 1955–62, Sen. Crown Counsel, 1962–64; returned to practice at English bar, 1964; Dep. Circuit Judge, 1975–77; a Recorder of the Crown Court, 1977–80. Member Panel of Counsel: for Courts Martial Appeals Court, 1970–80; for Comrs of Customs and Excise at VAT Tribunals, 1973–80; Inspector for Dept of Trade, Hartley-Baird Ltd Inquiry, 1974–76. *Recreations:* golf, gardening. *Address:* 2 Woodfield Avenue, Hildenborough, Kent TN11 9ES. *T:* Hildenborough 833406. *Clubs:* Sloane; Wildernesse (Sevenoaks).

TROUP, Sir Anthony; *see* Troup, Sir J. A. R.

TROUP, Vice-Adm. Sir (John) Anthony (Rose), KCB 1975; DSC and Bar; Defence Adviser, Scicon (UK), since 1979; *b* 18 July 1921; *s* of late Captain H. R. Troup, RN and N. M. Troup (*née* Milne-Thompson); *m* 1st, 1943, B. M. J. Gordon-Smith (marr. diss. 1952); two *s* one *d*; 2nd, 1953, C. M. Hope; two *s* one *d*. *Educ:* Naut. Trng Coll., HMS Worcester, 1934; RNC Dartmouth, 1936; service includes: Submarines Turbulent and Strongbow, 1941–45; HMS Victorious, 1956–59; Comd 3rd Submarine Sqdn, 1961–63; HMS Intrepid, 1966–68; Flag Officer Sea Training, 1969–71; Comdr Far East Fleet, 1971; Flag Officer Submarines and NATO Comdr Submarines, Eastern Atlantic, 1972–74; Flag Officer, Scotland and NI, and NATO Comdr Norlant, 1974–77. *Recreations:* sailing, shooting, gardening. *Address:* Bridge Gardens, Hungerford, Berks. *T:* Hungerford 82742. *Clubs:* Army and Navy; Royal Yacht Squadron.

TROWBRIDGE, George William Job, CBE 1969; CEng; Deputy Managing Director, Wickman Ltd, Coventry, since 1966; *b* 21 July 1911; *s* of George Clarke Trowbridge and Thirza Lampier Trowbridge (*née* Dingle); *m* 1938, Doris Isobel Morrison (decd); one *s*. *Educ:* Southall Technical Coll. Works Manager, Gays (Hampton) Ltd, 1938–45; Works Dir, Kingston Instrument Co. Ltd, 1945–52; Wickman Ltd, Coventry, 1952–: London Area Manager, 1952–57; General Sales Manager, 1957–62; General Sales Dir, 1962–64; Man. Dir, Machine Tool Sales Ltd, 1964–79; Dep. Chm., Wickman Machine Tools (Overseas) Ltd, 1966–; Director: Wickman Machine Tool Mfg Co. Ltd, 1962–; Wickman Lang Ltd, Johnstone, 1964–; John Brown & Co. Ltd, 1969–79; Machine Tools (India) Ltd, Calcutta, 1976–; W. Billinton & Co. Ltd, Calcutta, 1976–; Drury Wickman Ltd, Johannesburg, 1976–; Wickman (Australia) Ltd, Melbourne, 1976–; Chairman: Wickman Scrivener Ltd, Birmingham, 1966–; John Stirk & Sons Ltd, Halifax, 1966–; Kitchen & Walker Ltd, Halifax, 1966–; Coventry Machine Tool Works Ltd, Halifax, 1966–; Taylor & Challen Ltd, Birmingham, 1967–; Webster & Bennett Ltd, Coventry; Addison Tool Co., 1982–; Wickman Machine Tools Inc., USA; Wickman Machine Tools SA, France. President: Machine Tool Trades Assoc., 1975–77; Comité Européen de Coopération des Industries de la Machine-Outil, 1975–77; Mem., Economic Develt Cttee for Machine Tools, 1968–. MIProdE. *Publications:* A Handbook for Marketing Machinery, 1970; A Financial Study of British Machine Tool Companies, 1974. *Recreations:* walking, fishing. *Address:* 100 Kenilworth Road, Coventry CV4 7AH. *T:* Coventry 62775. *Club:* Institute of Directors.

TROWBRIDGE, Martin Edward O'Keeffe, CEng; FIChemE; FRSA; Director General, Chemical Industries Association, 1973–May 1987; *b* 9 May 1925; *s* of late Edward Stanley Trowbridge and Ida Trowbridge (*née* O'Keeffe); *m* 1946, Valerie Ann Glazebrook; one *s*. *Educ:* Royal College of Science: Imperial Coll. of Science and Technology, London Univ. (BSc Eng (Chem. Eng); ACGI); Amer. Management Assoc. Coll., NYC (Dip. Bus. Studies). Hinchley Medallist, IChemE, 1946. Technical Officer, ICI (Billingham Div.) Ltd, 1946–48; Division Manager, HWP/Fluor, 1948–53; Technical Dir, Sharples Co., 1953–57; Man. Dir, Sharples Co., 1957–59; Group Managing Director: Sharples International Corp., 1959–63; Pennwalt International Corp., 1963–72; Pegler-Hattersley Ltd, 1972–73. Member: Process Plant Working Party, NEDO, 1970–77; Chemicals EDC, NEDO, 1973–; Process Plant EDC, NEDO, 1977–80; CBI Council; CBI Heads of Sector Group; CBI Europe Cttee; Nat. Cttee of Eur. Acad.; Eur. Chem. Ind. PR Cttee, Brussels; CEFIC R&D Cttee, Brussels; Anglo-German Gp for Chem. Ind.; Anglo-French Gp for Chem. Ind.; ESRC Govt Industry Relns Cttee. Chairman: NEDO Task-Group on Tech., Research and Develt; Conseil d'Administration/CEFIC, Brussels, 1984– (Mem., 1973–84). *Publications:* Purification of Oils for Marine Service, 1960; Scaling Up Centrifugal Separation Equipment, 1962; Collected Poems, 1963; Centrifugation, 1966; Exhibiting for Profit, 1969; Market Research and Forecasting, 1969; The Financial Performance of Process and Plant Companies, 1970; contribs to Chemical Engineer, Chemistry in Britain, Gems, Engineering and Process Economics, etc. *Recreations:* writing, shooting, mineralogy, print making, wooden containers. *Address:* 51A Moreton Terrace, SW1.

TROWBRIDGE, Rear-Adm. Sir Richard (John), KCVO 1975; Governor of Western Australia, 1980–83; *b* 21 Jan. 1920; *s* of A. G. Trowbridge, Andover, Hants; *m* 1955, Anne Mildred Perceval; two *s*. *Educ:* Andover Grammar Sch.; Royal Navy. Joined RN as Boy Seaman, 1935. War of 1939–45: commissioned as Sub Lieut, Dec. 1940 (despatches Aug. 1945). Comdr, 1953; commanded Destroyer Carysfort, 1956–58; Exec. Officer, HMS Bermuda, 1958–59, and HMS Excellent, 1959–60; Captain, 1960; commanded Fishery Protection Sqdn, 1962–64; completed course IDC, 1966; commanded HMS Hampshire, 1967–69; Rear-Adm., 1970; Flag Officer Royal Yachts, 1970–75. An Extra Equerry to the Queen, 1970–. Younger Brother of Trinity Hse, 1972. KStJ 1980. *Recreations:* fishing, sailing, golf; most outdoor pursuits. *Address:* Old Idsworth Garden, Finchdean, Portsmouth. *T:* Rowlands Castle 412714. *Club:* Army and Navy.

TROWELL, Prof. Brian Lewis, PhD; King Edward Professor of Music, University of London at King's College, since 1974; *b* 21 Feb. 1931; *s* of Richard Lewis and Edith J. R. Trowell; *m* 1958, Rhianon James; two *d*. *Educ:* Christ's Hospital; Gonville and Caius Coll., Cambridge. MA 1959; PhD 1960. Asst Lectr, later Lectr, in Music, Birmingham Univ., 1957–62; freelance scholar, conductor, opera producer, lecturer and editor, 1962–67; Head of BBC Radio opera, 1967–70; Reader in Music, 1970, Professor of Music, 1973, KCL. Regents' Prof., Univ. of California at Berkeley, 1970; Vis. Gresham Prof. of Music, City Univ., 1971–74. Pres., Royal Musical Assoc., 1983–. Hon. RAM,

1972; Hon. FGSM, 1972; FRCM 1977; FTCL 1978. Chm., Editorial Cttee, Musica Britannica, 1983–. *Publications:* The Early Renaissance, Pelican History of Music vol. ii, 1963; Four Motets by John Plummer, 1968; (ed jtly) John Dunstable: Complete Works, ed M. F. Bukofzer, 2nd edn, 1970; (ed) Invitation to Medieval Music, vol. 3 1976, vol. 4 1978; opera translations; contrib. dictionaries of music and articles in learned journals. *Recreations:* theatre, reading, gardening. *Address:* 15 Crescent East, Hadley Wood, near Barnet, Herts EN4 0EY.

TROYAT, Henri; Légion d'Honneur; writer; Member of the French Academy, 1959; *b* Moscow, 1 Nov. 1911; *m* 1948, Marguerite Saintagne; one *s* one *d*. *Educ:* Paris. *Publications:* novels: l'Araigne (Prix Goncourt, 1938) (The Web, 1984); Les Semailles et les Moissons (5 vols), 1957; Tant que la Terre durera (3 vols), 1960; La Lumière des Justes (5 vols), 1963; Viou, 1980; Le Pain de l'Etranger, 1982 (The Children, 1983); Le Bruit solitaire du Coeur, 1985; biographies: Pushkin, Dostoievsky, Tolstoi, Gogol, Catherine la Grande, Pierre le Grand, Alexandre 1er, Ivan le Terrible, Tchekhov. *Address:* Académie Française, Quai de Conti, Paris.

TRUBSHAW, (Ernest) Brian, CBE 1970 (OBE 1964); MVO 1948; FRAeS; consultant; *b* 29 Jan. 1924; *s* of late Major H. E. Trubshaw, DL, and Lumly Victoria (*née* Carter); *m* 1973, Mrs Yvonne Edmondson, *widow* of Richard Edmondson, and *d* of late J. A. Clapham, Harrogate, Yorks. *Educ:* Winchester College. Royal Air Force, 1942–50: Bomber Command, 1944; Transport Command, 1945–46; The King's Flight, 1946–48; Empire Flying School, 1949; RAF Flying Coll., 1949–50. Joined Vickers-Armstrongs (Aircraft) Ltd as Experimental Test Pilot, 1950; Dep. Chief Test Pilot, 1953; Chief Test Pilot, 1960; Dir of Flight Test, 1966–80; Divl Dir and Gen. Man. (Filton), Civil Aircraft Div., BAe plc, 1980–86. Mem. Bd (part-time), CAA, 1986–. Warden, Guild of Air Pilots, 1958–61; Fellow, Society Experimental Test Pilots, USA. Hon. DTech Loughborough, 1986. Derry and Richards Memorial Medal, 1961 and 1964; Richard Hansford Burroughs Memorial Trophy (USA), 1964; R. P. Alston Memorial Medal, 1964; Segrave Trophy, 1970; Air League Founders' Medal, 1971; Iven C. Kinchloe Award, USA, 1971; Harmon Aviation Trophy, 1971; Bluebird Trophy, 1973; French Aeronautical Medal, 1976. *Recreations:* cricket, golf. *Address:* Northland Cottage, Tetbury, Glos GL8 8HH. *T:* Tetbury 52410. *Club:* Royal Air Force.

TRUDEAU, Rt. Hon. Pierre Elliott, CH 1984; PC (Can.); QC (Can.) 1969; FRSC; MP (L) Mount Royal, Montreal, since 1965; Prime Minister of Canada, 1968–79 and 1980–84; Leader of Liberal Party of Canada, 1968–84; *b* Montreal, 18 Oct. 1919; *s* of Charles-Emile Trudeau and late Grace Elliott; *m* 1971, Margaret (marr. diss. 1984), *d* of late James Sinclair and of Kathleen Bernard; three *s*. *Educ:* Jean-de-Brébeuf College, Montreal; University of Montreal; Harvard University; Ecole des Sciences Politiques, Paris; London School of Economics. Called to Bar, Quebec, 1943; practised law, Quebec; co-founder of review Cité Libre; Associate Professor of Law, University of Montreal, 1961–65. Parliamentary Secretary to Prime Minister, Jan. 1966–April 1967; Minister of Justice and Attorney General, April 1967–July 1968; Leader of the Opposition, 1979. Mem., Bars of Provinces of Quebec and Ontario. Founding Member, Montreal Civil Liberties Union. Hon. LLD, Univ. of Alberta, 1968; Dr *hc* Duke Univ., 1974. Hon. Fellow, LSE, 1969; Freeman of City of London, 1975. *Publications:* La Grève de l'Amiante, 1956; (with Jacques Hébert) Deux Innocents en Chine Rouge, 1961 (Two Innocents in Red China, 1969); Le Fédéralisme et la Société canadienne-française, 1968 (Federalism and the French Canadians, 1968); Réponses, 1968. *Recreations:* swimming, ski-ing, flying, scuba diving, canoeing. *Address:* House of Commons, Ottawa, Ontario K1A 0A2, Canada.

TRUDGILL, Dr Peter John; Reader in Sociolinguistics, Department of Language and Linguistics, University of Essex, since 1986; *b* 7 Nov. 1943; *s* of John Trudgill and Hettie Jean Trudgill (*née* Gooch), *m* 1980, Jean Marie Hannah. *Educ:* City of Norwich Sch.; King's Coll., Cambridge (BA; MA 1966); Edinburgh Univ. (Dip Gen Linguistics 1967; PhD 1971). Asst Lectr, Lectr, Reader, Prof., Dept of Linguistic Sci., Univ. of Reading, 1970–86. Vis. Prof. at Univs of Hong Kong, Bergen, Aarhus, Illinois, Stanford, Osmania, Tokyo International Christian, ANU, Texas Austin, Toronto. *Publications:* The Social Differentiation of English in Norwich, 1974; Sociolinguistics: an introduction, 1974, 2nd edn 1983; Accent, Dialect and the School, 1975; Sociolinguistic Patterns in British English, 1978; (with A. Hughes) English Accents and Dialects, 1979; (with J. K. Chambers) Dialectology, 1980; (with J. M. Hannah) International English, 1982, 2nd edn 1985; On Dialect, 1983; Coping with America, 1983, 2nd edn 1985; Language in the British Isles, 1984; Applied Sociolinguistics, 1984; Dialects in Contact, 1986. *Recreations:* Norwich City FC, reading, playing the 'cello. *Address:* Department of Language and Linguistics, University of Essex, Wivenhoe Park, Colchester CO4 3SQ. *T:* Colchester 862286.

TRUEMAN, Prof. Edwin Royden; Beyer Professor of Zoology, University of Manchester, 1974–82, now Emeritus; *b* 7 Jan. 1922; *s* of late Sir Arthur Trueman, KBE, FRS, and late Lady (Florence Kate) Trueman (*née* Offler); *m* 1945, Doreen Burt; two *d*. *Educ:* Bristol Grammar Sch.; Univ. of Glasgow. DSc Glasgow, MSc Manchester. Technical Officer (Radar), RAF, 1942–46. Asst Lectr and Lectr, Univ. of Hull, 1946–58, Sen. Lectr and Reader, 1958–68; Dean, Faculty of Science, Univ. of Hull, 1954–57; Prof. of Zoology, Univ. of Manchester, 1969–74. R. T. French Vis. Prof., Univ. of Rochester, NY, 1960–61; Nuffield Travelling Fellowship in Tropical Marine Biology, Univ. of West Indies, Jamaica, 1968–69; Leverhulme Emeritus Fellowship, 1983–85. *Publications:* Locomotion of Soft-bodied Animals, 1975; (ed) Aspects of Animal Movement, 1980; (ed) Evolution, vol. 10 of series The Mollusca, 1985; articles on animal locomotion, littoral physiology and Mollusca. *Address:* Heron's Creek, Yealm View Road, Newton Ferrers, Plymouth, Devon. *T:* Plymouth 872775.

TRUEMAN, Frederick Sewards; writer and broadcaster; *b* Stainton, Yorks, 6 Feb. 1931; *s* of late Alan Thomas Trueman; *m* 1st, 1955, Enid (marr. diss.); one *s* two *d* (incl. twin *s* and *d*); 2nd, Veronica. *Educ:* Maltby Secondary Sch. Apprentice bricklayer, 1946; worked in tally office of Maltby Main pit, 1948–51; Nat. service, RAF, 1951–53. Played club cricket, 1945–48; Yorks Fedn cricket tour, 1948; played for Yorks CCC, 1949–68 (took 2304 wickets in first class games, incl. 100 wickets in a season twelve times; also made 3 centuries); county cap, 1951; captained Yorkshire 31 times, 1962–68; played 6 one day matches for Derby CCC, 1972; first Test series, against India, 1952; MCC tours to WI, 1953–54, 1959–60, and to Australia, 1958–59, 1962–63 (took a total of 307 Test wickets, 1952–65, incl. 10 in a match and 7 in an innings three times, and was first bowler to take 300 Test wickets, 1963). Journalist, Sunday People, 1957–; anchorman, Indoor League series, Yorks TV; cricket commentator for BBC. *Publications:* Fast Fury, 1961; Cricket, 1963; Book of Cricket, 1964; The Freddie Trueman Story, 1966; Ball of Fire (autobiog.), 1976; (with John Arlott) On Cricket, 1977; Thoughts of Trueman Now, 1978; (with Frank Hardy) You Nearly Had Him That Time, 1978; My Most Memorable Matches, 1982; (with Don Mosey) Fred Trueman's Yorkshire, 1984. *Recreations:* ornithology, working for children's charities. *Address:* c/o BBC, Broadcasting House, W1A 1AA. *Clubs:* Yorkshire County Cricket (Hon. Life Mem.), MCC (Hon. Life Mem.), Lord's Taverners, Variety of GB, Forty, Saint Cricket; Ilkley Golf.

TRUMPINGTON, Baroness *cr* 1980 (Life Peer), of Sandwich in the County of Kent; **Jean Alys Barker;** Parliamentary Under-Secretary of State, Department of Health and

Social Security, since 1985; *d* of late Arthur Edward Campbell-Harris, MC and late Doris Marie Robson; *m* 1954, William Alan Barker, *qv*; one *s*. *Educ:* privately in England and France. Land Girl to Rt Hon. David Lloyd George, MP, 1940–41; Foreign Office, Bletchley Park, 1941–45; European Central Inland Transport Orgn, 1945–49; Sec. to Viscount Hinchingbrooke, MP, 1950–52. Conservative Councillor, Cambridge City Council, Trumpington Ward, 1963–73; Mayor of Cambridge, 1971–72; Deputy Mayor, 1972–73; Conservative County Councillor, Cambridgeshire, Trumpington Ward, 1973–75; Hon. Councillor of the City of Cambridge, 1975–. Baroness in Waiting (Government Whip), 1983–85. UK Delegate to UN Status of Women Commn, 1979–82. Member: Air Transport Users' Cttee, 1972–80 (Dep. Chairman 1978–79, Chm. 1979–80); Bd of Visitors to HM Prison, Pentonville, 1975–81, Mental Health Review Tribunal, 1975–81. Gen. Commissioner of Taxes, 1976–83. Pres., Assoc. of Heads of Independent Schs, 1980–. Steward, Folkestone Racecourse, 1980–. Hon. Fellow, Lucy Cavendish Coll., Cambridge, 1980. JP Cambridge, 1972–75, South Westminster, 1976–82. *Recreations:* bridge, racing, collecting antiques, needlepoint. *Address:* Luckboat House, King Street, Sandwich, Kent. *T:* Sandwich 613007; 25 Laxford House, Cundy Street, SW1. *T:* 01-730 4016.

TRURO, Bishop of, since 1981; **Rt. Rev. Peter Mumford;** *b* 14 Oct. 1922; *s* of late Peter Walter Mumford, miller, and of Kathleen Eva Mumford (*née* Walshe); *m* 1950, Lilian Jane, *d* of Captain George Henry Glover; two *s* one *d*. *Educ:* Sherborne School, Dorset; University Coll., Oxford; Cuddesdon Theological Coll. BA 1950, MA 1954 (Hons Theology). War Service, 1942–47, Captain, RA. Deacon, 1951; priest, 1952; Assistant Curate: St Mark, Salisbury, 1951–55; St Alban's Abbey, 1955–57; Vicar: Leagrave, Luton, 1957–63; St Andrew, Bedford, 1963–69; Rector of Crawley, Sussex, 1969–73; Canon and Prebendary of Ferring in Chichester Cathedral, 1972–73; Archdeacon of St Albans, 1973–74; Bishop Suffragan of Hertford, 1974–81. Vice Chm., Central Bd of Finance, 1984–; Chm., Consultative Cttee, Foundation for Christian Communication, 1981–. Pres., Royal Cornwall Agricl Assoc., 1985–86. *Address:* Lis Escop, Truro, Cornwall TR3 6QQ. *T:* Truro 862657. *Club:* United Oxford & Cambridge University.

TRURO, Dean of; *see* Shearlock, Very Rev. D. J.

TRUSCOTT, Sir Denis (Henry), GBE 1958; Kt 1953; TD 1950; President of Brown Knight and Truscott Ltd; *b* 9 July 1908; *s* of Henry Dexter Truscott, JP, and Evelyn Metcalf Truscott (*née* Gibbes); *m* 1932, Ethel Margaret, *d* of late Alexander Lyell, of Gardyne Castle, Guthrie, Angus, and Mrs Lyell; four *d*. *Educ:* Bilton Grange; Rugby Sch.; Magdalene Coll., Cambridge. Joined family firm of Jas. Truscott & Son Ltd, printers, 1929; Director, 1935; Chairman, 1951–66, of Brown, Knight & Truscott Ltd (amalgamation of Jas. Truscott & Son Ltd with Wm Brown & Chas. Knight Ltd, 1936). Director: Bedford General Insurance Co. Ltd (Chm., 1974–78); Zurich Life Assurance Society Ltd (Chm., 1974–78). Elected to Court of Common Council, City of London, 1938, for Ward of Dowgate; Deputy, 1943; Alderman: Dowgate Ward, 1947–73; Bridge Without Ward, 1973–78; Sheriff of City of London, 1951–52; Lord Mayor of London, 1957–58; one of HM Lieutenants, City of London, 1943–78. Master Worshipful Company of Vintners, 1955–56; Master Worshipful Company of Musicians, 1956–57, 1970–71; Master, Guild of Freemen of the City of London, 1957; Master of Worshipful Company of Stationers and Newspaper Makers, 1959–60. Treasurer, St Bartholomew's Hospital Voluntary Bd; Vice-Pres., Royal Hospital and Home for Incurables, Putney; Chairman Trustees Rowland Hill Benevolent Fund, 1954–82; Member Exec. Cttee, Automobile Assoc., 1952–78; President: Printing and Allied Trades Research Assoc., 1956–64; Inst. of Printing, 1961–63; London Cornish Assoc., 1977–; Vice-Pres., Soc. for Protection of Animals in N Africa; Chairman, Squash Racquets Assoc. of England, 1961–74. FGSM 1978. Grand Officer of Order of Merit, Italian Republic; Grand Cross of Merit of Order of Merit, Republic of Germany. *Recreations:* lawn tennis, golf. *Address:* Invermark, 30 Drax Avenue, Wimbledon, SW20. *T:* 01-946 6111. *Clubs:* United Oxford & Cambridge University, Royal Automobile, City Livery, All England Lawn Tennis, MCC.

TRUSCOTT, Sir George (James Irving), 3rd Bt *cr* 1909; *b* 24 Oct. 1929; *s* of Sir Eric Homewood Stanham Truscott, 2nd Bt, and Lady (Mary Dorcas) Truscott (*née* Irving) (*d* 1948); *S* father, 1973; *m* 1962, Yvonne Dora (*née* Nicholson); one *s* one *d*. *Educ:* Sherborne School. *Heir:* *s* Ralph Eric Nicholson Truscott, *b* 21 Feb. 1966. *Address:* BM QUILL, London WC1N 3XX.

TRUSS, Leslie S.; *see* Seldon-Truss.

TRUSTRAM EVE; *see* Eve, family name of Baron Silsoe.

TRUSWELL, Prof. (Arthur) Stewart, MD, FRCP, FFCM, FRACP; Boden Professor of Human Nutrition, University of Sydney, since 1978; *b* 18 Aug. 1928; *s* of George Truswell and Molly Truswell (*née* Stewart-Hess); *m* 1st, 1956, Sheila McGregor (marr. diss. 1983); four *s*; 2nd, 1986, Catherine Hull. *Educ:* Ruthin Sch., Clwyd; Liverpool and Cape Town Univs. MB, ChB 1952, MD 1959; FRCP 1975; FFCM 1979; FRACP 1980. Registrar in Pathology, Cape Town Univ., 1954; Registrar in Med., Groote Schuur Hosp., 1955–57; Research Bursar, Clin. Nutrition Unit, Dept. of Med., Cape Town Univ., 1958 and 1959; Adams Meml Trav. Fellowship to London, 1960; Sen. Fellow, Clin. Nutrition, Tulane Univ., USA, 1961; Res. Officer, Clin. Nutrition Unit, Cape Town Univ., 1962; Sen. Mem., Scientific Staff, MRC Atheroma Research Unit, Western Infirmary, Glasgow, 1963 and 1964; full-time Lectr, then Sen. Lectr in Med. and Consultant Gen. Physician, Cape Town Univ. and Groote Schuur Hosp., 1965–71; Warden of Med. Students' Residence, Cape Town Univ., 1967–69; Prof. of Nutrition and Dietetics, Queen Elizabeth Coll., London Univ., 1971–78. Vice-Pres., Internat. Union of Nutritional Sciences, 1985–; Member, numerous cttees, working parties, editorial bds and socs related to nutrition. *Publications:* Human Nutrition and Dietetics, 7th edn (with S. Davidson, R. Passmore, J. F. Brock), 1979; ABC of Nutrition, 1986; numerous research papers in sci. jls on various topics in human nutrition and medicine. *Recreations:* gardening, walking (esp. on mountains), running. *Address:* 6A Harbour Street, Mosman, NSW 2088, Australia; Human Nutrition Unit, Department of Biochemistry, Sydney University, Sydney, NSW 2006, Australia. *T:* 692–3726.

TRYON, family name of **Baron Tryon.**

TRYON, 3rd Baron *cr* 1940, of Durnford; **Anthony George Merrik Tryon;** *b* 26 May 1940; *s* of 2nd Baron Tryon, PC, GCVO, KCB, DSO, and of Etheldreda Josephine, *d* of Sir Merrik Burrell, 7th Bt, CBE; *S* father, 1976; *m* 1973, Dale Elizabeth, *d* of Barry Harper; two *s* two *d* (of whom one *s* one *d* are twins). *Educ:* Eton. Page of Honour to the Queen, 1954–56. Captain Wessex Yeomanry, 1972. Dir, Lazard Bros & Co. Ltd, 1976–83; Chairman, English & Scottish Investors Ltd, 1977. *Recreations:* fishing and shooting. *Heir:* *s* Hon. Charles George Barrington Tryon, *b* 15 May 1976. *Address:* Ogbury House, Great Durnford, near Salisbury, Wilts. *T:* Middle Woodford 225. *Clubs:* White's, Pratt's.

TRYON-WILSON, Brig. Charles Edward, CBE 1945 (MBE 1943); DSO 1944; Vice Lord-Lieutenant of Cumbria, 1980–83; *b* 20 Sept. 1909; 2nd *s* of late Charles Robert Tryon; *m* 1st, 1937, Cicely Joan (*d* 1969), *y d* of Captain Henry Whitworth; one *d* (and one *d* decd); 2nd, 1975, Rosemary Lucas. *Educ:* Shawnigan Lake School, BC; Trinity Coll., Glenalmond. Served 60th Rifles, 1927–30, Royal Fusiliers, 1930–36 and 1938–45 (N Africa, Italy, Austria; despatches twice). DL Westmorland (later Cumbria), 1971–85. *Recreations:* shooting, fishing. *Address:* Dallam Tower, Milnthorpe, Cumbria LA7 7AG. *T:* Milnthorpe 3368. *Clubs:* Army and Navy, Lansdowne; Flyfishers' (Buck's).

TRYPANIS, Constantine Athanasius, MA (Oxon); DLitt (Oxon) 1970; DPhil (Athens); FRSL; President, Academy of Athens, 1986 (Secretary-General, 1981–85); Minister of Culture and Science, Government of Greece, 1974–77; *b* Chios, 22 Jan. 1909; *s* of Athanasius G. Trypanis and Maria Zolota; *m* 1942, Alice Macri; one *d*. *Educ:* Chios Gymnasium; Universities of Athens, Berlin and Munich. Classical Lecturer, Athens Univ., 1939–47; Bywater and Sotheby Professor of Byzantine and Modern Greek Language and Literature, and Fellow of Exeter Coll., Oxford, 1947–68; Emeritus Fellow, 1968–; Univ. Prof. of Classics, Chicago Univ., 1968–74, Emeritus Prof., 1974–. Gray Lectr, Cambridge Univ., 1947. Mem. Poetry Panel, Arts Council of GB, 1962–65. FRSL, 1958; Hon. FBA 1978; Life Fellow, International Institute of Arts and Letters, 1958; Member Institute for Advanced Study, Princeton, USA, 1959–60; Visiting Professor: Hunter Coll., New York, 1963; Harvard Univ., 1963, 1964; Univ. of Chicago, 1965–66; Univ. of Cape Town, 1969; Univ. of Vienna, 1971. Corresp. Mem., Inst. for Balkan Studies (Greece); Member: Athens Academy, 1974 (Corres. Mem., 1971); Medieval Acad. of America; Accademia Tiburina, Rome, 1982. Hon. Fellow, Internat. Poetry Soc., 1977; Fellow: Greek Archaeol Soc., 1985; Soc. for Promotion of Greek Letters, 1985; Hon. Mem., Soc. for Promotion of Hellenic Studies, 1979. Dr of Humane Letters *hc*: MacMurray Coll., USA, 1974; Assumption Coll., 1977. Gottfried von Herder Prize, Vienna Univ., 1983. Ordre des Arts et des Lettres; Ordre National du Mérite. Archon Megas Hieromnemon of the Oekumenical Patriarchate. *Publications:* Influence of Hesiod upon Homeric Hymn of Hermes, 1939; Influence of Hesiod upon Homeric Hymn on Apollo, 1940; Alexandrian Poetry, 1943; Tartessos, 1945; Medieval and Modern Greek Poetry, 1951; Pedasus, 1955; Callimachus, 1956; The Stones of Troy, 1956; The Cocks of Hades, 1958; (with P. Maas) Sancti Romani Melodi Cantica, 1963, vol. II, 1970; Pompeian Dog, 1964; The Elegies of a Glass Adonis, 1967; Fourteen Early Byzantine Cantica, 1968; (ed) The Penguin Book of Greek Verse, 1971; The Glass Adonis, 1973; The Homeric Epics, 1975; Greek Poetry: from Homer to Seferis, 1981; Atticism and the Greek Language Question, 1984; articles in classical and literary periodicals. *Recreations:* walking, tennis, painting. *Address:* 3 Georgiou Nikolaou Kefisia, Athens, Greece. *Clubs:* Athenæum; Athens.

TRYTHALL, Maj.-Gen. Anthony John, CB 1983; Director of Army Education, 1980–84; Managing Director, Brassey's Defence Publishers Ltd, since 1984; *b* 30 March 1927; *s* of Eric Stewart Trythall and Irene (*née* Hollingham); *m* 1952, Celia Haddon; two *s* one *d*. *Educ:* Lawrence Sheriff Sch., Rugby; St Edmund Hall, Oxford (BA Hons Mod. Hist., 1947, DipEd 1951); Institute of Education, London Univ. (Academic DipEd 1962); King's College, London (MA in War Studies, 1969). National Service as RAEC Officer, UK, Egypt and Akaba, 1947–49; teaching, 1951–53; Regular RAEC Officer, 1953; seconded to Malay Regt for service at Fedn Mil. Coll., Port Dickson, 1953–56; WO, 1957–62; BAOR, 1962–66; Inspector, 1967–68; Educn Adviser, Regular Commns Bd, 1969–71; Head of Officer Educn Br., 1971–73; Chief Inspector of Army Educn, and Col Res., 1973–74; MoD, 1974–76; Chief Educn Officer, UKLF, 1976–80. Col Comdt, RAEC, 1986–. Member: Council, Royal United Services Instn for Def. Studies, 1978–84; London Univ. Bd of War Studies, 1983–; Chm., Gallipoli Meml Lecture Trust, 1986–. 1st Prize, Trench-Gascoigne Essay Competition, 1969. *Publications:* Boney Fuller: the intellectual general, 1977 (USA, as Boney Fuller: soldier, strategist and writer); (contrib.) The Downfall of Leslie Hore-Belisha in the Second World War, 1982; Fuller and the Tanks in Home Fires and Foreign Fields, 1985; articles in Army Qly, Jl of RUSI, British Army Rev., and Jl of Contemp. Hist. *Address:* c/o Royal Bank of Scotland, Holt's Farnborough Branch, 31–37 Victoria Road, Farnborough, Hants GU14 7PA. *Club:* Naval and Military.

TRYTHALL, Rear-Adm. John Douglas, CB 1970; OBE 1953; *b* 21 June 1914; *er s* of Alfonso Charles Trythall, Camborne, and Hilda Elizabeth (*née* Monson); *m* 1943, Elizabeth Loveday (*née* Donald); two *s* two *d*. *Educ:* Stretford Grammar Sch. Cadet, 1931; appointments in Home Fleet, America and West Indies, East Indies. Lent to RNZN, 1939; Battle of River Plate; Western Approaches; BJSM, Washington; Pacific; Hong Kong; Mediterranean. Secretary to: Second Sea Lord, C-in-C The Nore, and C-in-C Plymouth; Asst Director of Plans, 1960–62; Captain of the Fleet, Medit., 1964–65; Head of Personnel Panel, MoD, 1966–67; subseq. on MoD Cttee; Asst Chief, Personnel and Logistics, MoD, 1969–72. JSSC, 1953; IDC, 1963. Commander, 1949; Captain, 1959; Rear-Admiral, 1968; retired 1972. FCIS 1956. Commander and Commissioner, St John Ambulance in Somerset, 1975–82. KStJ 1982 (OStJ 1973, CStJ 1977). *Address:* The Old Vicarage, Corfe, Taunton, Som. *T:* Blagdon Hill 463. *Club:* MCC.

TS'ONG, Fou; *see* Fou Ts'ong.

TUAM, Archbishop of, (RC), since 1969; **Most Rev. Joseph Cunnane;** *b* 5 Oct. 1913; *s* of William and Margaret Cunnane, Knock, Co. Mayo. *Educ:* St Jarlath's Coll., Tuam; St Patrick's Coll., Maynooth. BA 1st Hons, Ancient Classics, 1935; DD 1941; Higher Dip. Educn 1941. Priest, 1939. Prof. of Irish, St Jarlath's Coll., 1941–57; Curate, Balla, Co. Mayo, 1957–67; Curate, Clifden, Co. Galway, 1967–69. Cross of Chaplain Conventual, SMO Malta, 1970. *Publications:* Vatican II on Priests, 1967; contribs to Irish Ecclesiastical Record, Furrow, Doctrine and Life, Studies in Pastoral Liturgy, etc. *Address:* Archbishop's House, Tuam, Co. Galway, Ireland. *T:* Tuam 24166.

TUAM, KILLALA AND ACHONRY, Bishop of, since 1986; **Rt. Rev. John Robert Winder Neill;** *b* 17 Dec. 1945; *s* of Eberto Mahon Neill and Rhoda Anne Georgina Neill; *m* 1968, Betty Anne (*née* Cox); three *s*. *Educ:* Sandford Park School, Dublin; Trinity Coll., Dublin (Foundation Schol., BA 1st Cl., MA); Jesus Coll., Cambridge (MA, Gardiner Memorial Schol., Univ. of Cambridge); Ridley Hall, Cambridge (GOE). Curate Asst, St Paul's, Glenageary, Dublin, 1969–71; Lectr (Old Testament) in Divinity Hostel, 1970–71; Bishop's Vicar and Dio. Registrar, Kilkenny, 1971–74; Rector of Abbeystrewry, Skibbereen, Co. Cork, 1974–78; Rector of St Bartholomew's, and Leeson Park, Dublin, 1978–84; Lectr (Liturgy) in Theological Coll., 1982–84; Exam. Chaplain to Archbishop of Dublin, 1982–84; Dean of Christ Church Cathedral, Waterford, 1984–86; Archdeacon of Waterford, 1984–86. *Publications:* contribs to Theology, New Divinity and Search. *Recreations:* photography, travel. *Address:* Bishop's House, Knockglass, Crossmolina, Co. Mayo, Ireland. *T:* Ballina 31317.

TUBBS, Oswald Sydney, FRCS; Consulting Surgeon: in Cardiothoracic Surgery, St Bartholomew's Hospital; to Brompton Hospital; *b* 21 March 1908; *s* of late Sydney Walter Tubbs, The Glebe, Hadley Common, Hertfordshire; *m* 1934, Marjorie Betty Wilkins (*d* 1976); one *s* one *d*. *Educ:* Shrewsbury School; Caius College, Cambridge; St Bartholomew's Hospital. MA, MB, BCh, FRCS. Surgical training at St Bartholomew's Hosp. and Brompton Hosp. Dorothy Temple Cross Fellowship, spent as Surgical Fellow at Lahey Clinic, Boston, USA. Served War of 1939–45, in EMS. Consulting Chest

Surgeon to Royal Navy, Papworth Village Settlement and to various Local Authorities. President: Soc. of Thoracic and Cardiovascular Surgeons of GB and Ireland, 1971–72; Thoracic Soc., 1973. *Publications:* papers on surgical subjects. *Recreations:* fishing and gardening. *Address:* The White Cottage, 136 Coast Road, West Mersea, Colchester, Essex CO5 8PA. *T:* Colchester 382355.

TUBBS, Ralph, OBE 1952; FRIBA; architect; *b* 9 Jan. 1912; *s* of late Sydney W. Tubbs and Mabel Frost; *m* 1946, Mary Taberner; two *s* one *d. Educ:* Mill Hill School; Architectural Assoc. School (Hons Dip.). Sec. MARS Group (Modern Architectural Research), 1939; Member: Council and Executive Committee of RIBA, 1944–50, re-elected Council, 1951; Vice-Pres. Architectural Assoc., 1945–47; Associate Institute of Landscape Architects, 1942–. Member Presentation Panel and Design Group for 1951 Festival of Britain, and architect of Dome of Discovery in London Exhibn (then the largest dome in world, 365 ft diam.). Other works include: Baden-Powell House for Boy Scouts' Assoc., London; Indian Students' Union building, Fitzroy Sq., London; Granada TV Centre and Studios, Manchester; Cambridge Inst. Educn; Halls of residence for University Coll., London, Residential Areas at Harlow and Basildon New Towns; Industrial Buildings. Architect for new Charing Cross Hospital and Med. Sch., London; Consultant for Hospital Develt, Jersey, CI. Pres., British Entomological and Natural Hist. Soc., 1977; Vice-Pres., Royal Entomol Soc. of London, 1982–84. *Publications:* Living in Cities, 1942; The Englishman Builds (Penguin), 1945. *Recreation:* study of the natural world. *Address:* 43 Portland Place, W1. *T:* 01–637 2558.

TUCK, Anthony; *see* Tuck, J. A.

TUCK, Sir Bruce (Adolph Reginald), 3rd Bt, *cr* 1910; *b* 29 June 1926; *o s* of Major Sir (William) Reginald Tuck, 2nd Bt, and Gladys Emily Kettle (*d* 1966), *d* of late N. Alfred Nathan, Wickford, Auckland, New Zealand, and *widow* of Desmond Fosberry Kettle, Auckland Mounted Rifles; *S* father 1954; *m* 1st, 1949, Luise (marr. diss., in Jamaica, 1964), *d* of John C. Renfro, San Angelo, Texas, USA; two *s*; 2nd, 1968, Pamela Dorothy Nicholson, *d* of Alfred Nicholson, London; one *d. Educ:* Canford School, Dorset. Lieutenant, Scots Guards, 1945–47. *Heir: s* Richard Bruce Tuck, *b* 7 Oct. 1952.

TUCK, Clarence Edward Henry; Civil Service Commissioner, 1977–83; *b* 18 April 1925; *s* of Frederick and May Tuck; *m* 1950, Daphne Robinson; one *s* one *d. Educ:* Rendcomb Coll., Cirencester; Merton Coll., Oxford. BA 1949. Served in Royal Signals, 1943–47. Inland Revenue, 1950; Min. of Supply, 1950–55; seconded to Nigerian Federal Govt, Lagos, 1955–57; Ministry of: Supply, 1957–59; Aviation, 1959–60; Defence, 1960–62; Aviation, 1962–66; IDC, 1967; Min. of Technology, 1968–70; Trade and Industry, 1970; CSD, 1971; Trade and Industry, 1973; Dept of Energy, 1974; Civil Service Dept, 1976; Management and Personnel Office, 1981; Dir, Civil Service Selection Board, 1977–81. Asst Principal, 1950; Principal, 1953; Asst Sec., 1962; Under-Sec., 1970.

TUCK, (John) Anthony, MA, PhD; Master of Collingwood College and Honorary Lecturer in History, University of Durham, since 1978; *b* 14 Nov. 1940; *s* of Prof. John Philip Tuck, *qv*; *m* 1976, Amanda, *d* of Dr L. J. Cawley, Carlton Husthwaite, near Thirsk, Yorks; two *s. Educ:* Newcastle upon Tyne Royal Grammar Sch.; Jesus Coll., Cambridge (BA, MA, PhD). Lecturer in History, 1965–75, Sen. Lectr, 1975–78, Univ. of Lancaster. *Publications:* Richard II and the English Nobility, 1973; Crown and Nobility 1272–1461, 1985; contribs to English Historical Rev., Northern History, etc. *Recreations:* walking, gardening, amateur dramatics. *Address:* The Master's House, Collingwood College, Durham DH1 3LT. *T:* Durham 66465.

TUCK, Prof. John Philip; Professor of Education, University of Newcastle upon Tyne (formerly King's College, University of Durham) 1948–76, now Emeritus; *b* 16 April 1911; *s* of late William John and Annie Tuck, Uplyme, Lyme Regis; *m* 1936, Jane Adelaide (*née* Wall); two *s. Educ:* Strand School; Jesus College, Cambridge. BA Hons English and History, Class I, 1933; Cambridge certificate in Education, 1934; Adelaide Stoll Bachelor Research Scholar, Christ's College, 1935; MA 1937. English Master: Gateshead Grammar School, 1936; Manchester Central High School, 1938; Wilson's Grammar School, 1939 and 1946. Served War of 1939–45, East Surrey Regt, and Army Education Corps, N Africa, Sicily, Italy, Austria. Lecturer in Education, King's College, Newcastle upon Tyne, 1946–48. Mem. Council, GPDST, 1976–84. FRSA 1970. Hon. Fellow, Coll. of Speech Therapists, 1966. *Address:* Chillingham House, Church Street, Great Gransden, Sandy, Beds. *T:* Great Gransden 512.

See also J. A. Tuck.

TUCK, Wing Comdr Robert Roland S.; *see* Stanford-Tuck.

TUCK, Prof. Ronald Humphrey; Professor of Agricultural Economics, University of Reading, 1965–86 (part-time, 1982–86), now Emeritus; *b* 28 June 1921; *s* of Francis Tuck and Edith Ann Tuck (*née* Bridgewater); *m* Margaret Sylvia Everley; one *s* two *d. Educ:* Harrow County Sch.; Corpus Christi Coll., Oxford. War Service, RAOC and REME, mainly N Africa and Italy, 1941–45 (despatches). Univ. of Reading, Dept of Agric. Economics: Research Economist, 1947–49; Lecturer, 1949–62; Reader, 1962–65; Head of Dept of Agricultural Economics and Management, Univ. of Reading, and Provincial Agricultural Economist (Reading Province), 1965–81; Dean, Faculty of Agriculture and Food, Univ. of Reading, 1971–74. *Publications:* An Essay on the Economic Theory of Rank, 1954; An Introduction to the Principles of Agricultural Economics, 1961 (Italian trans., 1970); reviews etc in Jl of Agric. Economics and Economic Jl. *Recreations:* reading, music, drawing, walking. *Address:* 211 Kidmore Road, Caversham, Reading, Berks. *T:* Reading 473426.

TUCKER, Brian George, CB 1976; OBE 1963; Deputy Secretary, Department of Energy, 1974–81; Member, UKAEA, 1976–81; *b* 6 May 1922; *s* of late Frank Ernest Tucker and May Tucker; *m* 1948, Marion Pollitt; three *d. Educ:* Christ's Hospital. Entered Home Civil Service, 1939, as Clerical Officer, Admty; successive postings at home, in Africa, the Middle East, Ceylon and Hong Kong till 1953; promoted Executive Officer, 1945; Higher Executive Officer, 1949. Min. of Power, Asst Principal, 1954, Principal, 1957; seconded to HMOCS, 1957–62, Asst Sec., Govt of Northern Rhodesia; returned to MOP, 1962, Principal Private Sec. to Minister, 1965–66, Asst Sec., 1966, Under-Sec., Ministry of Technology, 1969–70, Cabinet Office, 1970–72, DTI, 1972–73; Dep. Sec., 1973. *Recreations:* gardening, music. *Address:* 1 Sondes Place Drive, Dorking, Surrey. *T:* Dorking 884720.

TUCKER, Rt. Rev. Cyril James, CBE 1975; *b* 17 Nov. 1911; British; *s* of Henry Castledine and Lilian Beatrice Tucker; *m* 1936, Kathleen Mabel, *d* of Major Merry; one *s* two *d. Educ:* Highgate Sch.; St Catharine's Coll., Cambridge (MA); Ridley Hall, Cambridge. MA Oxford (by Incorporation), 1951. Deacon, 1935; Priest, 1936; Curate, St Mark's, Dalston (in charge Highgate Sch. Mission), 1935; Curate, St Barnabas, Cambridge, 1937; Youth Sec., British and Foreign Bible Soc., 1938. Chaplain, RAFVR, 1939–46. Warden of Monmouth Sch., 1946; Chaplain, Wadham Coll., Oxford, and Chaplain of the Oxford Pastorate, 1949; Vicar of Holy Trinity, Cambridge, 1957–63; Rural Dean of Cambridge, 1959–63; Chaplain of the Cambridge Pastorate, 1957–63; Bishop in Argentina and Eastern S America, 1963–75; Bishop of the Falkland Islands, 1963–76. Hon. Exec. Dir, Argentine Dio. Assoc., 1976–83. *Recreations:* walking, fishing. *Address:* 202 Gilbert Road, Cambridge CB4 3PB. *T:* Cambridge 358345. *Clubs:* Hawks (Cambridge); Hurlingham (Buenos Aires).

TUCKER, Prof. David Gordon; Hon. Senior Research Fellow, Department of Economic History, since 1981, and Professor Emeritus, University of Birmingham; *b* 17 June 1914; *s* of John Ferry and Frances Tucker; *m* 1945, Florence Mary Barton; three *s* one *d. Educ:* Sir George Monoux Grammar School, London; University of London. BSc 1936; PhD 1943; DSc 1948. On research staff of GPO, at the PO Research Station, Dollis Hill, 1934–50; Royal Naval Scientific Service (Senior Principal Scientific Officer), 1950–55; Birmingham University: Prof. and Head of Dept of Electronic and Electrical Engrg, 1955–73; Sen. Fellow in Hist. of Technology, 1974–81. Member: Gen. Council of IERE, 1958–62 and 1965–66, Educn Cttee, 1958–65, Research Cttee, 1962–; Council of British Acoustical Soc. 1965–73 (Vice-Pres., 1967–70; Pres., 1970–73); Council, Soc. for Underwater Technology, 1967–70; National Electronics Research Council, 1963–66; Treasury Cttee on Scientific Civil Service, 1964–65; Oceanography and Fisheries Cttee, NERC, 1965–70; Cttee on History of Technology, IEE, 1970–76, 1978–84 (Chm., 1973–75); Adv. Cttee for Nat. Archive in Electrical Sci. and Technol. (Chm., 1973–79); Council, Newcomen Soc., 1977–84 (Vice-Pres., 1981–84); Royal Commn on Ancient and Historical Monuments in Wales, 1979–84; and of various other Univ., Government, professional and educational committees. FIERE, 1953; FIEE, 1954; FSA 1984. Clerk Maxwell Premium of IERE, 1961. *Publications:* Modulators and Frequency-Changers, 1953; Electrical Network Theory, 1964; Circuits with Periodically-Varying Parameters, 1964; Applied Underwater Acoustics (with B. K. Gazey) 1966; Underwater Observation Using Sonar, 1966; Sonar in Fisheries: A Forward Look, 1967; papers in professional, scientific and historical journals. *Recreations:* history of technology, industrial archaeology. *Address:* 26 Twatling Road, Barnt Green, Birmingham B45 8HT. *T:* 021–445 1820.

TUCKER, Edward William, CB 1969; Head of Royal Naval Engineering Service, 1966–70; Director of Dockyards, Ministry of Defence, at Bath, 1967–70, retired; *b* 3 Nov. 1908; *s* of Henry Tucker, Plymouth; *m* 1935, Eva (*d* 1986), *d* of Arthur Banks, Plymouth. *Educ:* Imperial Coll. of Science and Technology, London Univ.; Royal Naval Coll., Greenwich. BSc (Eng). Electrical Engineer in Admiralty service, at Plymouth, London, Hong Kong and Bath, 1935–64; General Manager of HM Dockyard, Chatham, 1964–66. *Recreations:* gardening, golf. *Address:* Gulls Cry, Thurlestone, Kingsbridge, Devon. *T:* Thurlestone 265.

TUCKER, Elizabeth Mary; Head Mistress, Headington School, Oxford, since 1982; *b* 20 July 1936; *d* of Harold and Doris Tucker. *Educ:* Cheltenham Ladies' College; Newnham College, Cambridge (MA Classical Tripos); King's College London (PGCE). Assistant Mistress, Queen Anne's School, Caversham, 1959–64; Head of Classics, Notting Hill and Ealing High School, GPDST, 1964–72; Head Mistress, Christ's Hospital, Hertford, 1972–82. Member: Cttee, Boarding Schs Assoc., 1983–86; Church of England Synod Bd of Educn Schs Cttee, 1982–85; Council, Classical Assoc., 1983–86; Council, St Hugh's Sch., Faringdon. Trustee, Bloxham Project, 1982–; Joint Educnl Trust GSA Rep., 1983–. *Recreations:* music (piano, spinet, singing), art and architecture (sketching), literature and poetry, fell walking, travel (especially in Greece). *Address:* Headington School, Oxford OX3 7TD. *T:* Oxford 62711. *Club:* University Women's.

TUCKER, (Henry John) Martin, QC 1975; **His Honour Judge Tucker;** a Circuit Judge, since 1981; *b* 8 April 1930; *s* of late P. A. Tucker, LDS, RCS and Mrs Dorothy Tucker (*née* Hobbs); *m* 1957, Sheila Helen Wateridge, LRAM; one *s* four *d. Educ:* St Peter's Sch., Southbourne; Downside Sch.; Christ Church, Oxford (MA). Called to Bar, Inner Temple, 1954; Dep. Chm., Somerset QS, 1971; a Recorder of the Crown Court, 1972–81. *Recreations:* walking occasionally; gardening gently; listening to music. *Address:* Chingri Khal, Sleepers Hill, Winchester, Hants. *T:* Winchester 53927. *Club:* Hampshire (Winchester).

TUCKER, Herbert Harold, OBE 1965; HM Diplomatic Service, retired; Director, Roberts Centre, since 1984; Consultant, Centre for Security and Conflict Studies, 1986; *b* 4 Dec. 1925; *o s* of late Francis Tucker and late Mary Ann Tucker; *m* 1948, Mary Stewart Dunlop; three *s. Educ:* Queen Elizabeth's, Lincs; Rossington Main, Yorks. Western Morning News, Sheffield Telegraph, Nottingham Journal, Daily Telegraph, 1944–51; Economic Information Unit, Treasury, 1948–49; FO, later FCO, 1951; Counsellor (Information) and Dir, British Information Services, Canberra, 1974–78; Consul-General, Vancouver, 1979–83; Disarmament Information Coordinator, FCO, 1983–84. *Recreations:* gardening, reading, watercolouring. *Address:* Wootton House, Fairmile Lane, Cobham, Surrey KT11 2DJ. *T:* Cobham 65930. *Clubs:* Travellers', Royal Commonwealth Society.

TUCKER, Martin; *see* Tucker, H. J. M.

TUCKER, Peter Louis; practising barrister, Sierra Leone; Commissioner/Chairman, Sierra Leone Population Census, since 1984; *b* 11 Dec. 1927; *s* of Peter Louis Tucker and Marion Tucker; *m* 1st, 1955, Clarissa Mary Harleston; three *s* one *d* (and one *d* decd); 2nd, 1972, Teresa Josephine Ganda; one *s. Educ:* Fourah Bay Coll., Sierra Leone (MA Latin, Dunelm); Jesus Coll., Oxford (MA Jurisp.); DipEd. Called to Bar, Gray's Inn, 1970. Teacher, 1952–57; Education Officer, 1957–61; Secretary, Training and Recruitment, Sierra Leone Civil Service, 1961–63; Establishment Sec., 1963–66; Sec. to the Prime Minister and Head of Sierra Leone Civil Service, 1966–67; Asst Director, UK Immigrants Advisory Service, 1970–72; Principal Admin. Officer, Community Relations Commn, 1972–74, Dir of Fieldwork and Admin., 1974–77; Dir of Legal and Gen. Services, and Sec., 1977, Chief Exec., 1977–82, CRE; Special Envoy on Foreign Aid to Sierra Leone and Chm., Nat. Aid Co-ordinating Cttee, 1986. Dep. Chm., Court of Sierra Leone Univ. Papal Medal Pro Ecclesia et Pontifice, 1966. *Publications:* miscellaneous booklets and articles for Community Relations Commission. *Recreations:* photography, listening to music. *Address:* 24 Carlton Carew Road, Free Town, Sierra Leone. *T:* Sierra Leone 24868; (home) 30728.

TUCKER, Hon. Sir Richard (Howard), Kt 1985; **Hon. Mr Justice Tucker;** a Judge of the High Court of Justice, Queen's Bench Division, since 1985; a Presiding Judge, Midland and Oxford Circuit, since 1986; *b* 9 July 1930; *s* of Howard Archibald Tucker, later His Honour Judge Tucker, and Margaret Minton Tucker; *m* 1st, 1958, Paula Mary Bennett Frost (marr. diss. 1974); one *s* two *d*; 2nd, 1975, Wendy Kate Standbrook. *Educ:* Shrewsbury Sch.; The Queen's Coll., Oxford (MA). Called to Bar, Lincoln's Inn, 1954; Bencher, 1979. QC 1972; a Recorder, 1972–85; Mem. Senate, Inns of Court and the Bar, 1984–86; Dep. Leader, Midland and Oxford Circuit, 1984–85. Mem., Employment Appeal Tribunal, 1986–. *Recreations:* sailing, shooting, gardening. *Address:* Royal Courts of Justice, Strand, WC2. *Clubs:* Garrick; Bar Yacht.

TUCKER, Robert St John P.; *see* Pitts-Tucker.

TUCKER, William Eldon, CVO 1954; MBE 1944; TD 1951; FRCS; formerly Honorary Orthopædic Surgeon, Royal London Homœopathic Hospital; Director and Surgeon, The Clinic, Park Street, 1936–80; *b* 6 Aug. 1903; *s* of late Dr W. E. Tucker,

Hamilton, Bermuda; *m* 1931, Jean Stella (marr. diss. 1953), *d* of James Ferguson, Rudgwick, Sussex; two *s*; *m* 1956, Mary Beatrice Castle. *Educ:* Sherborne; Gonville and Caius Coll., Cambridge. MA 1931; FRCS 1930; MB, BCh 1946. St George's Hospital, 1925–34; Lt RAMC, TA, 1930–34; Major RAMC, Orthopædic Specialist, 1939–45; Lt-Col, RAMC, TA, 1946–51; Col and Hon. Col 17th General Hospital, TA, 1951–63. Surgeon, St John's Hosp., Lewisham, 1931–37; Registrar, Royal Nat. Orthop. Hosp. 1933–34; Orthopædic Consultant, Horsham Hosp., 1945, Dorking Hosp., 1956. Hunterian Prof., RCS, Oct. 1958. Fellow, British Orthopædic Assoc. Corresp. Mem., Amer. Orthopædic Assoc.; Emeritus Mem., Société Internationale de Chirugie Orthopaedique et Traumatologie. Vice-Pres., Amateur Dancing Assoc.; Pres. and Patron, Blackheath Football Club. Past Master, Co. of Makers of Playing Cards. *Publications:* Active Alerted Posture, 1960; Home Treatment in Injury and Osteoarthritis, 1961, new edn, Home Treatment and Posture in Injury, Rheumatism and Osteoarthritis, 1969; (with J. R. Armstrong) Injury in Sport, 1964; (with Molly Castle) Sportsmen and their Injuries, 1978. *Recreations:* tennis, Rugby football exec. (formerly Cambridge XV, Captain 1925; England XV, 1926–30, 3 caps); ball-room dancing. *Address:* West Dunes, 44 South Road, Paget 6–04, Bermuda. *T:* Bermuda 6–4637. *Clubs:* Pilgrims, MCC (Hon. Life Mem.); Middlesex CCC (Life Vice-Pres.), Surrey CCC (Life Vice-Pres.); Royal Bermuda Yacht, Royal Hamilton Amateur Dinghy.

TUCKEY, Simon Lane, QC 1981; a Recorder, since 1984; *b* 17 Oct. 1941; *s* of late Henry Lane Tuckey and of Aileen Rosemary Newsom Tuckey; *m* 1964, Jennifer Rosemary (*née* Hardie); one *s* two *d*. *Educ:* Plumtree School, Zimbabwe. Called to Bar, Lincoln's Inn, 1964. *Recreations:* sailing, tennis. *Address:* 6 Regent's Park Terrace, NW1. *T:* 01–485 8952.

TUCKMAN, Fred, FCIS, FIPM; Member (C) Leicester, European Parliament, since 1979; *b* 9 June 1922; *s* of Otto and Amy Tina Tuchmann (*née* Adler); *m* 1966, Patricia Caroline Myers; two *s* one *d*. *Educ:* English and German schools; London School of Economics, 1946–49 (BScEcon). Served RAF, 1942–46. Commercial posts, 1950–65; Management Consultant and Partner, Hay Gp, 1965–85; Managing Director, HAY GmbH, Frankfurt, 1970–80; Partner, Hay Associates, 1975–85; Chm., Suomen HAY, OY, Helsinki, 1973–81; consultant assignments in Europe, Africa and N America. Hon. Sec., Bow Gp, 1958–59; Councillor, London Borough of Camden, 1965–71 (Chm., Library and Arts, 1968–71). Mem. Council, Inst. of Personnel Management, 1963–70. Chm., Greater London Area, CPC, 1968–70. European Parliament: Budget Cttee, 1979–81; Social and Employment Cttee, 1981– (Cons. spokesman, 1984–); substitute Mem., Economic and Monetary Cttee, 1979–; substitute Mem., Budgetary Control Cttee, 1984–; First Vice Pres., Latin American Delegn, 1982; Chm., Inter Gp on Small Business, 1985–86. UK Chm., European Year of Small Business, 1983; Vice Chm., Small Business Bureau, London; Vice Pres., Eur. Medium and Small Units, 1985. *Recreations:* reading, arguing, travel, swimming; priority—family. *Address:* 6 Cumberland Road, Barnes, SW13 9LY. *T:* 01–748 2392. *Club:* Carlton.

TUCKWELL, Barry Emmanuel, OBE 1965; horn soloist; conductor; Conductor and Music Director, Maryland Symphony Orchestra, since 1982; *b* 5 March 1931; *s* of Charles Tuckwell, Australia; *m* Hilary Jane, *d* of James Warburton, Australia; two *s* one *d*. *Educ:* various schs, Australia; Sydney Conservatorium. Melbourne Symph. Orch., 1947; Sydney Symph. Orch., 1947–50; Hallé Orch., 1951–53; Scottish Nat. Orch., 1953–54; Bournemouth Symphony Orch., 1954–55; London Symph. Orch., 1955–68; founded Tuckwell Wind Quintet, 1968; Conductor, Tasmanian Symphony Orch., 1979–83. Mem. Chamber Music Soc. of Lincoln Center, 1974–81; Horn Prof., Royal Academy of Music, 1963–74; Pres., Internat. Horn Soc., 1969–77. Plays and conducts annually throughout Europe, Gt Britain, USA and Canada; has appeared at many internat. festivals, incl. Salzburg and Edinburgh; took part in 1st Anglo-Soviet Music Exchange, Leningrad and Moscow, 1963; toured: Far East, 1964 and 1975; Australia, 1970–; S America, 1976; USSR, 1977; People's Republic of China, 1984. Many works dedicated to him; has made numerous recordings. Editor, complete horn literature for G. Schirmer Inc. Hon. RAM, 1966; Hon. GSM, 1967. Harriet Cohen Internat. Award for Solo Instruments, 1968; Grammy Award Nominations. *Publications:* Playing the Horn, 1978; The Horn, 1981. *Recreations:* photography, sailing. *Club:* Athenæum.

TUCKWELL, Sir Edward (George), KCVO 1975; MCh, FRCS; Serjeant-Surgeon to the Queen, 1973–75 (Surgeon to the Queen, 1969–73, to HM Household, 1964–69); Surgeon, St Bartholomew's Hospital, London, 1947–75; Surgeon, Royal Masonic Hospital, 1958–75; Consultant Surgeon, King Edward VII Convalescent Home, Osborne, 1965–78; *b* 12 May 1910; *e s* of Edward Henry Tuckwell and Annie Clarice (*née* Sansom); *m* 1st, 1934, Phyllis Courthope Regester (*d* 1970); two *s* one *d*; 2nd, 1971, Barbara Gordon, *widow* of Major A. J. Gordon. *Educ:* Charterhouse; Magdalen College, Oxford; St Bartholomew's Hospital. BM, BCh Oxon 1936; MCh 1948; FRCS 1939. War Service in EMS and RAMC, Surgical Specialist, North-West Europe and South-East Asia, Lt-Col. Examiner in Surgery to Univs of London, Manchester, Oxford, and in Pathology to Conjoint Board and Royal College of Surgeons; Dean of Medical School, St Bartholomew's Hospital, 1952–57; Surgeon, King Edward VII Hospital for Officers, 1961–75. Member: Medical Appeal Tribunal, 1975–82; Vaccine Damage Appeal Tribunal, 1978–82. Pres., Phyllis Tuckwell Meml Hospice, Farnham; Member: Council, Metrop. Hosp. Sunday Fund, 1981–; Governing Body of Charterhouse School, 1966–82 (Chm., 1973–81) (London University representative); Council, Epsom Coll., 1981–83; Governor: St Bartholomew's Hosp., 1954–74; Sutton's Hosp. in Charterhouse, 1980–. Mem. Ct of Assts, 1973–, Warden 1978, Master 1981–82, and Freeman, Barbers' Co. FRSA 1982. *Publications:* articles in medical journals. *Recreations:* gardening, shooting, travelling. *Address:* Berthorpe, Puttenham Heath Road, Guildford, Surrey GU3 1DU. *T:* Guildford 810217.

TUDHOPE, David Hamilton, CMG 1984; DFC 1944, and Bar 1944; Chairman: National Bank of New Zealand, since 1983; National Mutual Life Association, since 1983; Deputy Chairman, Crown Corporation, since 1984; Director: Emco Group, since 1981; Commercial Union Insurance, since 1982; Steel & Tube Ltd, since 1986; Shell Holdings Ltd, since 1981; *b* 9 Nov. 1921; *s* of William and Sybil Tudhope; *m* 1946, Georgina Charity Lee; two *s* two *d*. *Educ:* Wanganui Collegiate Sch., NZ; King's Coll., Cambridge (MA, LLB). Served War, 1941–45: Pilot RNZAF, UK (Flt Lieut) (DFC and Bar, Pathfinder Force, Bomber Comd). Barrister and Solicitor, NZ, 1947–49; Shell Oil, NZ, 1949–60; Gen. Manager, Shell Oil Rhodesia, N Rhodesia and Nyasaland, 1960–62; Area Co-ordinator, Shell London, 1962–67; Chm. and Chief Exec., Shell Interests in NZ, 1967–81; Chm., Shell BP & Todd Oil Services, 1967–81; Chm. (in rotation), NZ Oil Refinery, 1969, 1974, 1980, and Maui Development, 1975, 1980. Chm., Pukeiti Rhododendron Trust, 1981–. *Recreations:* gardening, golf. *Address:* 7 Cluny Avenue, Kelburn, Wellington, New Zealand. *T:* Wellington 759–358. *Club:* Wellington.

TUDHOPE, James Mackenzie; Regional Procurator Fiscal for Glasgow and Strathkelvin, since 1980; *b* 11 Feb. 1927; *m* Margaret Willock Kirkwood; two *s*. *Educ:* Dunoon Grammar School; Univ. of Glasgow (BL 1951). Private legal practice, 1951–55; Procurator Fiscal Depute, 1955, Senior PF Depute, 1962, Asst PF, 1968–70, Glasgow; PF, Kilmarnock, 1970–73, Dumbarton, 1973–76; Regional PF, S Strathclyde, Dumfries and Galloway at Hamilton, 1976–80. Mem. Council, Law Soc. of Scotland, 1982–. *Recreation:* serendipity.

TUDOR, James Cameron, CMG 1970; Permanent Representative of Barbados to the United Nations, 1976–79; *b* St Michael, Barbados, 18 Oct. 1919; *e s* of James A. Tudor, JP, St Michael, Barbados; unmarried. *Educ:* Roebuck Boys' Sch.; Combermere Sch.; Harrison Coll., Barbados; Lodge Sch.; (again) Harrison Coll.; Keble Coll., Oxford, 1939–43. BA Hons (Mod. Greats), 1943, MA 1948; Pres., Oxford Union, 1942. Broadcaster, BBC: Lobby Correspondent (Parliament); Overseas Service, 1942–44; Lectr, Extra Mural Dept, Reading Univ., 1944–45; History Master, Combermere Sch., Barbados, 1946–48; Civics and History Master, Queen's Coll., British Guiana, 1948–51; Sixth Form Master, Modern High Sch., Barbados, 1952–61, also free-lance Journalist, Lectr, Broadcaster, over the same period. Mem., Barbados Lab. Party, 1951–52; MLC, Barbados, 1954–72; Foundn Mem., Democratic Lab. Party, 1955 (Gen. Sec., 1955–63; Third Vice-Chm., 1964–65 and 1965–66). Minister: of Educn, 1961–67; of State for Caribbean and Latin American Affairs, 1967–71 (Leader of the House, 1965–71); of External Affairs, 1971–72 (Leader of the Senate, 1971–72); High Comr for Barbados in UK, 1972–75. Mem. Council, Univ. of the West Indies, 1962–65; awarded US State Dept Foreign Leader Grant, to study US Educn Instns, 1962. Silver Star, Order of Christopher Columbus (Dominican Republic), 1969. *Recreations:* reading, lecturing; keen on Masonic and other fraternities. *Address:* Lemon Grove, Westbury New Road, St Michael, Barbados.

TUDOR, Rev. Dr (Richard) John, BA; Superintendent Minister, Westminster Central Hall, London, since 1981; *b* 8 Feb. 1930; *s* of Charles Leonard and Ellen Tudor; *m* 1956, Cynthia Campbell Anderson; one *s* one *d*. *Educ:* Clee Grammar Sch., Grimsby; Queen Elizabeth's, Barnet; Univ. of Manchester, 1951–54 (BA Theology). Served RAF, 1948–51. Junior Methodist Minister, East Ham, London, 1954–57; Ordained, Newark, 1957; Minister, Thornton Cleveleys, Blackpool, 1957–60; Superintendent Minister: Derby Methodist Mission, 1960–71: Chaplain to Mayor of Derby, Factories and Association with Derby Football Club; Coventry Methodist Mission, 1971–75; Chaplain to Lord Mayor; Brighton Dome Mission, 1975–81; Free Church Chaplain, Westminster Hosp., 1982–. Hon. DD, Texas Wesleyan Coll., Fort Worth, USA, 1981; Hon. Texan, 1965; Freeman of Fort Worth, 1970. *Recreations:* motoring, cooking, photography, the delights of family life. *Address:* The Methodist Church, Central Hall, Westminster, SW1. *T:* 01–222 8010.

TUDOR EVANS, Hon. Sir Haydn, Kt 1974; **Hon. Mr Justice Tudor Evans;** a Judge of the High Court of Justice, Queen's Bench Division, since 1978 (Family Division, 1974–78); a Judge of the Employment Appeal Tribunal, since 1982; *b* 20 June 1920; 4th *s* of John Edgar Evans and Ellen Stringer; *m* 1947, Sheilagh Isabella Pilkington; one *s*. *Educ:* West Monmouth School; Lincoln College, Oxford. RNVR, 1940–41. Open Scholar, Lincoln Coll., Oxford (Mod. History), 1940; Stewart Exhibitioner, 1942; Final Hons Sch., Mod. History, 1944; Final Hons Sch., Jurisprudence, 1945. Cholmeley Scholar, Lincoln's Inn, 1946; called to the Bar, Lincoln's Inn, 1947, Bencher 1970. QC 1962; Recorder of Crown Court, 1972–74. *Recreation:* watching Rugby, racing and cricket. *Address:* c/o Royal Courts of Justice, Strand, WC2A 2LL. *Clubs:* Garrick, MCC.

TUDWAY QUILTER, David C.; *see* Quilter.

TUFFIN, Alan David; General Secretary, Union of Communication Workers, since 1982; *b* 2 Aug. 1933; *s* of Oliver Francis and Gertrude Elizabeth Tuffin; *m* 1957, Jean Elizabeth Tuffin; one *s* one *d*. *Educ:* Eltham Secondary Sch., SE9. Post Office employment, London, 1949–69; London Union Regional Official for UCW, 1957–69; National Official, 1969; Deputy General Secretary, 1979. Member: TUC Gen. Council, 1982–; Council, NIESR, 1985–. Director: Unity Trust, 1984–; Trade Union Unit Trust, 1985–. *Recreations:* reading, squash, West Ham United FC. *Address:* UCW House, Crescent Lane, SW4 9RN.

TUFTON, family name of **Baron Hothfield.**

TUGENDHAT, Christopher Samuel; Chairman, Civil Aviation Authority, since 1986; Director: National Westminster Bank, since 1985; The BOC Group, since 1985; *b* 23 Feb. 1937; *er s* of late Dr Georg Tugendhat; *m* 1967, Julia Lissant Dobson; two *s*. *Educ:* Ampleforth Coll.; Gonville and Caius Coll., Cambridge (Pres. of Union). Financial Times leader and feature writer, 1960–70. MP (C) City of London and Westminster South, 1974–76 (Cities of London and Westminster, 1970–74); Mem., 1977–84, a Vice-Pres., 1981–84, EEC. Director: Sunningdale Oils, 1971–76; Phillips Petroleum International (UK) Ltd, 1972–76. Chm., RIIA (Chatham House), 1986–; Member: Council, Centre for Eur. Policy Studies, Brussels, 1985–; Council, Hughenden Foundn, 1986–; Governor, Council of Ditchley Foundn, 1986–; Vice-Pres., Council of British Lung Foundn, 1986–. *Publications:* Oil: the biggest business, 1968; The Multinationals, 1971 (McKinsey Foundn Book Award, 1971); Making Sense of Europe, 1986; various pamphlets and numerous articles. *Recreations:* being with my family, reading, conversation. *Address:* 35 Westbourne Park Road, W2. *Clubs:* Carlton, Anglo-Belgian.

See also M. G. Tugendhat.

TUGENDHAT, Michael George; QC 1986; *b* 21 Oct. 1944; *s* of Georg Tugendhat and Maire Littledale; *m* 1970, Blandine Menche de Loisne; three *s*. *Educ:* Ampleforth Coll.; Gonville and Caius Coll., Cambridge (MA); Yale Univ. Henry Fellowship. Called to the Bar, Inner Temple, 1969. *Address:* 10 South Square, Gray's Inn, WC1R 5EU. *T:* 01–242 2902. *Club:* Brooks's.

See also C. S. Tugendhat.

TU'IPELEHAKE, HRH Prince Fatafehi, Hon. KBE 1977 (Hon. CBE); Prime Minister of Tonga, since 1965; also Minister for Agriculture and Marine Affairs; *b* 7 Jan 1922; *s* of HRH Prince Viliami Tupoulahi Tungi and HM Queen Salote of Tonga; *m* 1947, Princess Melenaite Topou Moheofo; two *s* four *d*. *Educ:* Newington College, Sydney; Gatton Agricultural College, Queensland. Governor of Vava'u, 1949–51. Chm., Commodities Board. 'Uluafi Medal, 1982. *Address:* Office of the Prime Minister, Nuku'alofa, Tonga.

See also HM King of Tonga.

TUITE, Sir Christopher (Hugh), 14th Bt *cr* 1622; President, Spirutec Inc., Arizona, since 1982; *b* 3 Nov. 1949; *s* of Sir Dennis George Harmsworth Tuite, 13th Bt, MBE, and of Margaret Essie, *d* of late Col Walter Leslie Dundas, DSO; *S* father, 1981; *m* 1976, Deborah Anne, *d* of A. E. Martz, Pittsburgh, Pa; two *s*. *Educ:* Univ. of Liverpool (BSc Hons); Univ. of Bristol (PhD). Research Officer, The Wildfowl Trust, 1978–81. *Publications:* contribs to Jl of Animal Ecology, Jl of Applied Ecology, Freshwater Biology, Wildfowl. *Heir:* *s* Thomas Livingstone Tuite, *b* 24 July 1977. *Address:* c/o The Midland Bank, 33 The Borough, Farnham, Surrey.

TUIVAGA, Hon. Sir Timoci (Uluiburotu), Kt 1981; **Hon. Mr Justice Tuivaga;** Chief Justice of Fiji, since 1980; *b* 21 Oct. 1931; *s* of Isimeli Siga Tuivaga and Jessie Hill; *m* 1958, Vilimaina Leba Parrott Tuivaga; three *s* one *d*. *Educ:* Univ. of Auckland (BA).

Called to Bar, Gray's Inn, 1964, and NSW, 1968. Native Magistrate, 1958–61; Crown Counsel, 1965–68; Principal Legal Officer, 1968–70; Acting Director of Public Prosecutions, 1970; Crown Solicitor, 1971; Puisne Judge, 1972; Acting Chief Justice, 1974; sometime Acting Gov.-Gen., 1983–. *Recreations:* golf, gardening. *Address:* 228 Ratu Sukuna Road, Suva, Fiji. *T:* 313–782. *Club:* Fiji Golf (Suva).

TUKE, Sir Anthony (Favill), Kt 1979; Chairman, Savoy Hotel, since 1984 (Director, since 1982); Director: Barclays Bank, since 1965 (Vice-Chairman, 1972–73; Chairman, 1973–81); Barclays Bank International, since 1966 (Chairman, 1972–79; Vice-Chairman, 1968–72); *b* 22 Aug. 1920; *s* of late Anthony William Tuke; *m* 1946, Emilia Mila; one *s* one *d. Educ:* Winchester; Magdalene Coll., Cambridge. Scots Guards, 1940–46. Barclays Bank Ltd, 1946–; Dir, Barclays Bank UK, 1971–81. Dep. Chm., Royal Insurance, 1985– (Dir, 1978–); Director: Merchants Trust, 1969–; RTZ Corp., 1980– (Chm., 1981–85); Whitbread Investment Company PLC, 1984–. Vice-President: Inst. of Bankers, 1973–81; British Bankers' Assoc., 1977–81; Chm., Cttee of London Clearing Bankers, 1976–78 (Dep. Chm., 1974–76); Pres., Internat. Monetary Conference, 1977–78. Mem., Trilateral Commn, 1973–. Chm., 1980 British Olympic Appeal; Pres., MCC, 1982–83. Mem., Stevenage Develt Corp., 1959–64. Governor, Motability, 1978–85. Mem. Council, Warwick Univ., 1966–73; Treas., English-Speaking Union, 1969–73. *Recreation:* gardening. *Address:* Freelands, Wherwell, near Andover, Hants. *Club:* MCC.

TUKE, Comdr Seymour Charles, DSO 1940; Royal Navy; *b* 20 May 1903; 3rd *s* of late Rear-Adm. J. A. Tuke; *m* 1928, Marjorie Alice Moller (*d* 1985); one *s* one *d. Educ:* Stonyhurst; RNC, Osborne and Dartmouth. Midshipman, 1921; Lieutenant, 1926; Acting Commander, 1945; FAA, 1927–29; Local Fishery Naval Officer, English Channel, 1935–37; served War of 1939–45 (DSO, 1939–45 Medal, Atlantic Star, Italy Star, War Medal); in command of SS Hannah Boge (first prize of the war), 1939; Senior Officer Res. Fleet, Harwich, 1946; Maintenance Comdr to Senior Officer Res. Fleet, 1947–48; retired, 1948. *Address:* c/o National Westminster Bank, 32 Market Place, Cirencester, Glos GL7 2NW.

TULLIS, Major Ramsey; Vice Lord-Lieutenant of Clackmannanshire, since 1974; farmer; *b* 16 June 1916; *s* of late Major J. Kennedy Tullis, Tullibody, Clackmannanshire; *m* 1943, Daphne Mabon, *d* of late Lt-Col H. L. Warden, CBE, DSO, Edinburgh; three *s. Educ:* Trinity Coll., Glenalmond; Worcester Coll., Oxford (BA). 2nd Lieut, Cameronians, 1936. Served War, 1939–45: Cameronians, Parachute Regt; Major 1943; psc 1949; retired, 1958. Income Tax Comr, 1964–. County Comr for Scouts, Clackmannanshire, 1958–73; Mem. Cttee, Council of Scout Assoc., 1967–72; Activities Comr, Scottish HQ, Scout Assoc., 1974. Chm. Visiting Cttee, Glenochil Young Offenders Instn and Detention Centre, 1974–83. Clackmannanshire: JP 1960, DL 1962. *Recreations:* golf and gardening. *Address:* Woodacre, Pool of Muckhart, by Dollar, Clackmannanshire FK14 7JW.

TULLY, (William) Mark, OBE 1985; Chief of Bureau, British Broadcasting Corporation, Delhi, since 1972; *b* 24 Oct. 1935; *s* of William Scarth Carlisle Tully, CBE and Patience Treby Tully; *m* 1960, Frances Margaret (*née* Butler) two *s* two *d. Educ:* Twyford School, Winchester; Marlborough College; Trinity Hall, Cambridge (MA). Regional Dir, Abbeyfield Soc., 1960–64; BBC, 1964–: Asst, Appointments Dept, 1964–65; Asst, then Actg Rep., New Delhi, 1965–69; Prog. Organiser and Talks Writer, Eastern Service, 1969–71. *Publication:* Amritsar: Mrs Gandhi's last battle, 1985. *Recreations:* fishing, bird watching, reading. *Address:* 1 Nizamuddin (East), New Delhi 110 013, India. *T:* Delhi 616108/616102. *Clubs:* Oriental; Press, India International (Delhi).

TUMIM, Stephen; His Honour Judge Tumim; a Circuit Judge, since 1978; a Judge of the Willesden County Court, since 1980; *b* 15 Aug. 1930; *yr s* of late Joseph Tumim, CBE (late Clerk of Assize, Oxford Circuit) and late Renée Tumim; *m* 1962, Winifred, *er d* of late Col A. M. Borthwick; three *d. Educ:* St Edward's Sch., Oxford; Worcester Coll., Oxford (Scholar). Called to Bar, Middle Temple, 1955. A Recorder of the Crown Court, 1977–78. Chm., Nat. Deaf Children's Soc., 1974–79 (Vice-Chm., 1966–74). Member of Committee: Royal Lit. Fund; Contemp. Art Soc.; Museum of Modern Art, Oxford; Chm., Friends of Tate Gall., 1983–. *Publications:* Great Legal Disasters, 1983; Great Legal Fiascos, 1985; occasional reviews. *Recreations:* books and pictures. *Address:* River House, Upper Mall, Hammersmith W6 9TA. *T:* 01–748 5238. *Clubs:* Garrick, Beefsteak.

TUNC, Prof. André Robert; Croix de Guerre 1940; Officier de la Légion d'Honneur 1984; Professor, University of Paris, since 1958; *b* 3 May 1917; *s* of Gaston Tunc and Gervaise Letourneur; *m* 1941, Suzanne Fortin. *Educ:* Law Sch., Paris. LLB 1937, LLM 1941. Agrégé des Facultés de Droit, 1943. Prof., Univ. of Grenoble, 1943–47; Counsellor, Internat. Monetary Fund, 1947–50; Prof., Univ. of Grenoble, 1950–58; Legal Adviser, UN Economic Commn for Europe, 1957–58. Hon. Doctorates: Free Univ. of Brussels, 1958; Cath. Univ. of Louvain, 1968; Cambridge, 1986; DCL: Oxford, 1970; Stockholm, 1978; Geneva, 1984; Gent, 1986; MA Cantab, 1972; Corr. FBA (London), 1974; Corresp. Fellow, Royal Acad. of Belgium, 1978; Foreign Member: Royal Acad. of the Netherlands, 1980; Amer. Acad. of Arts and Scis. Officier de l'Ordre d'Orange-Nassau, 1965. *Publications:* Le contrat de garde, 1941; Le particulier au service de l'ordre public, 1942; (with Suzanne Tunc) Le Système constitutionnel des Etats-Unis d'Amérique, 2 vols, 1953, 1954; (with Suzanne Tunc) Le droit des Etats-Unis d'Amérique, 1955; (with François Givord) (tome 8) Le louage: Contrats civils, du Traité pratique de droit civil français de Planiol et Ripert, 2nd edn 1956; Traité théorique et pratique de la responsabilité civile de Henri et Léon Mazeaud, vols, 1957, 1958, 1960, 5th edn, and 6th edn (Vol. I) 1965; Les Etats-Unis—comment ils sont gouvernés, 1958, 3rd edn 1974; Dans un monde qui souffre, 1962, 4th edn 1968; Le droit des Etats-Unis (Que sais-je?), 1964, 4th edn 1982; La sécurité routière, 1965; Le droit anglais des sociétés anonymes, 1971, 2nd edn 1979; Traffic Accident Compensation: Law and Proposals (Internat. Encycl. of Comparative Law, Vol. XI: Torts, chap. 14), 1971; Introd. to Vol. XI: Torts (Internat. Encycl. of Comparative Law), 1974; La cour judiciaire suprême: une enquête comparative, 1978; La responsabilité civile, 1981; Pour une loi sur les accidents de la circulation, 1981; Le droit américain des sociétés anonymes, 1985; articles in various legal periodicals. *Address:* 112 rue de Vaugirard, 75006 Paris, France.

TUNNELL, Hugh James Oliver Redvers; HM Diplomatic Service; Consul General, Brisbane, since 1983; *b* 31 Dec. 1935; *s* of Heather and Oliver Tunnell; *m* 1st, 1958, Helen Miller (marr. diss.); three *d*; 2nd, 1979, Margaret, *d* of Sir Richard John Randall; one *d. Educ:* Chatham House Grammar School, Ramsgate. Royal Artillery, 1954–56. FO, 1956–59; Amman, 1959–62; Middle East Centre for Arab Studies, 1962–63; served FO, Aden, CRO, Damascus and FO, 1964–67; UK Delegn to European Communities, 1968–70; FCO, 1970–72; Kuwait, 1972–76; FCO, 1976–79; Head of Chancery, Muscat, 1979. *Recreations:* water sports, tennis. *Address:* c/o Foreign and Commonwealth Office, SW1; 12 Gladesville Street, Kenmore, Brisbane, Qld 4069, Australia. *T:* Brisbane 378 6881. *Clubs:* Royal Commonwealth Society; Queensland, United Services, Brisbane, Tattersalls, Cricketers (Brisbane).

TUOHY, John Francis, (Frank Tuohy); FRSL 1965; novelist; short story writer; *b* 2 May 1925; *s* of late Patrick Gerald Tuohy and Dorothy Marion (*née* Annandale). *Educ:* Stowe Sch.; King's College, Cambridge. Prof. of English Language and Literature, Univ. of São Paulo, 1950–56; Contract Prof., Jagiellonian Univ., Cracow, Poland, 1958–60; Visiting Professor: Waseda Univ., Tokyo, 1964–67; Rikkyo Univ., Tokyo, 1983–; Writer-in-Residence, Purdue Univ., Indiana, 1970–71, 1976, 1980. *Publications:* The Animal Game, 1957; The Warm Nights of January, 1960; The Admiral and the Nuns, short stories (Katherine Mansfield Memorial Prize), 1962; The Ice Saints (James Tait Black and Geoffrey Faber Memorial Prizes), 1964; Portugal, 1970; Fingers in the Door, short stories (E. M. Forster Meml Award, 1972), 1970; Yeats: a biographical study, 1976; Live Bait, short stories (Heinemann Award, 1979), 1978.; Collected Stories, 1984. *Recreation:* travel. *Address:* 5/3 Sussex Square, Brighton BN2 1FJ.

TUOHY, Thomas, CBE 1969; Managing Director, British Nuclear Fuels Ltd, 1971–73; *b* 7 Nov. 1917; *s* of late Michael Tuohy and Isabella Tuohy, Cobh, Eire; *m* 1949, Lilian May Barnes (*d* 1971); one *s* one *d. Educ:* St Cuthberts Grammar Sch., Newcastle; Reading Univ. (BSc). Chemist in various Royal Ordnance Factories, 1939–46. Manager: Health Physics, Springfields Nuclear Fuel Plant, Dept Atomic Energy, 1946; Health Physics, Windscale Plutonium Plant, 1949; Plutonium Piles and Metal Plant, Windscale, 1950; Works Manager: Springfields, 1952; Windscale, UKAEA, 1954; Windscale and Calder Hall: Dep. Gen. Manager, 1957; Gen. Manager, 1958; Man. Dir, Production Gp, UKAEA, 1964–71. Managing Director: Urenco, 1973–74; Vorsitzender der Geschäftsführung Centec GmbH, 1973–74; Dep. Chm., Centec, 1973–74; former Dir, Centec-Algermann Co. Mem. Council, Internat. Inst. for Management of Technology, 1971–73. *Publications:* various technical papers on reactor operation and plutonium manufacture. *Recreations:* golf, gardening, travel. *Address:* Ingleberg, Beckermet, Cumbria. *T:* Beckermet 226.

TUPMAN, William Ivan, DPhil; Director General of Internal Audit, Ministry of Defence, 1974–81; *b* 22 July 1921; *s* of Leonard and Elsie Tupman; *m* 1945, Barbara (*née* Capel); two *s* one *d. Educ:* Queen Elizabeth's Hosp., Bristol; New Coll., Oxford (Exhibnr; MA, DPhil). Served War, 1942–45, RN (Lieut RNVR). Entered Admiralty as Asst Principal, 1948; Private Sec. to Parly Sec., 1950–52; Principal, 1952; Civil Affairs Adviser to C-in-C, Far East Station, 1958–61; Private Sec. to First Lord of the Admiralty, 1963; Asst Sec., 1964; IDC, 1967.

TUPPER, Sir Charles Hibbert, 5th Bt *cr* 1888, of Armdale, Halifax, Nova Scotia; *b* 4 July 1930; *o s* of Sir James Macdonald Tupper, 4th Bt, formerly Assistant Commissioner, Royal Canadian Mounted Police, and of Mary Agnes Jean Collins; *S* father, 1967; *m* (marr. diss. 1976); one *s. Heir: s* Charles Hibbert Tupper, *b* 10 July 1964. *Address:* 955 Marine Drive, Apt 1101, West Vancouver, BC V7T 1A9, Canada.

TURBERVILLE, Geoffrey, MA; Principal, Leulumoega High School, Samoa, 1959–62, (retired); *b* 31 Mar. 1899; *o s* of A. E. Turberville, FCA, Stroud Green, London; *m* Jane Campbell Lawson. *Educ:* Westminster Sch. (King's Scholar); Trinity College, Cambridge (Exhibitioner). 2nd Lieut, Queen's Royal West Surrey Regt, 1917–19; Senior Classical Master, Liverpool Collegiate School, 1921–25; Senior Classical Master, Epsom College, 1925–30; Headmaster of Eltham College, 1930–59. Chm. Dorset Congregational Assoc., 1970–71. *Publications:* Cicero and Antony; Arva Latina II; Translation into Latin. *Address:* 4 Spiller's House, Shaftesbury, Dorset.

TURBOTT, Sir Ian (Graham), Kt 1968; CMG 1962; CVO 1966; *b* Whangarei, New Zealand, 9 March 1922; *s* of late Thomas Turbott and late E. A. Turbott, both of New Zealand; *m* 1952, Nancy Hall Lantz, California, USA; three *d. Educ:* Takapuna Grammar School, Auckland, NZ; Auckland University; Jesus College, Cambridge; London University. NZ Forces (Army), 1940–46: Solomon Is area and 2 NZEF, Italy. Colonial Service (Overseas Civil Service): Western Pacific, Gilbert and Ellice Is, 1948–56; Colonial Office, 1956–58; Administrator of Antigua, The West Indies, 1958–64; also Queen's Representative under new constitution, 1960–64; Administrator of Grenada and Queen's Representative, 1964–67; Governor of Associated State of Grenada, 1968–84. Partner, Spencer Stuart and Associates Worldwide, 1973–84; Chairman: Spencer Stuart and Associates Pty Ltd; Chloride Batteries Australia Ltd, 1978–85; TNT Group 4 Pty Ltd; Stuart Brooke Consultants Pty Ltd, Sydney, 1974–82; 2MMM Broadcasting Co. Pty Ltd; Melbourne F/M Radio Pty Ltd; Three CV Radio Pty Ltd; Penrith Lakes Develt Corp.; Adv. Bd, Amer. Internat. Underwriting (Aust.) Ltd; Essington Ltd, 1984–; Director: Suncoast Group of Cos; City Mutual Life Assurance Soc. Ltd; Standard Chartered Finance Ltd; Standard Chartered Bank Australia Ltd. Chairman: Internat. Piano Competition Ltd, Sydney, 1977–84; Duke of Edinburgh's Award Scheme, NSW. Governor, NSW Conservatorium of Music, 1974–. FRSA, JP. Silver Jubilee Medal, 1977. Holds 1939–45 Star, Pacific Star, Italy Star, Defence Medal, War Medal, New Zealand Service Medal. CStJ 1964. *Publications:* various technical and scientific, 1948–51, in Jl of Polynesian Society (on Pacific area). *Recreations:* boating, farming, golf, fishing. *Address:* 27 Amiens Road, Clontarf, NSW 2093, Australia; Lazy B Ranch, Mangrove Creek Road, NSW 2250, Australia. *Clubs:* Australian (Sydney); Royal Sydney Yacht.

TURCAN, Henry Watson; a Recorder of the Crown Court, since 1985; *b* 22 Aug. 1941; *s* of late Henry Hutchison Turcan and Lilias Cheyne; *m* 1969, Jane Fairrie Blair; one *s* one *d. Educ:* Rugby School; Trinity College, Oxford (BA, MA). Called to the Bar, Inner Temple, 1965. Legal Assessor to General Optical Council, 1983. *Recreations:* hunting, shooting, golf. *Address:* 4 Paper Buildings, Temple, EC4. *T:* 01–353 3420. *Clubs:* Royal and Ancient Golf (St Andrews); Hon. Company of Edinburgh Golfers (Muirfield).

TURECK, Rosalyn; concert artist (Bach specialist); conductor; writer; *b* Chicago, 14 Dec. 1914; *d* of Samuel Tureck and Monya (*née* Lipson); *m* 1964, George Wallingford Downs (*d* 1964). *Educ:* Juilliard Sch. of Music, NY. Member Faculty: Philadelphia Conservatory of Music, 1935–42; Mannes School, NYC, 1940–44; Juilliard School of Music, 1943–53; Lecturer in Music: Columbia University, NY, 1953–55; London Univ., 1955–56. Visiting Professor, Washington University, St Louis, 1963–64; Regents Professorship, University of California, San Diego, 1966; Professor of Music: 4th Step, Univ. of California, San Diego, 1966–72; Univ. of Maryland, 1982–; Vis. Fellow, St Hilda's Coll., Oxford, 1974 and 1976–, Hon. Life Fellow, 1974; Vis. Fellow, Wolfson Coll., Oxford, 1975. Has appeared as soloist and conductor of leading orchestras in US, Europe and Israel, and toured US, Canada, South Africa, South America; since 1947 has toured extensively in Europe, and played at festivals in Edinburgh, Venice, Holland, Wexford, Schaffhausen, Bath, Brussels World Fair, Glyndebourne, Barcelona, etc, and in major Amer. festivals including Mostly Mozart Festival, NY, Caramoor, Detroit, etc; extensive tours: India, Australia and Far East, 1971. Formed: Composers of Today, 1951–55; Tureck Bach Players, 1959; Internat. Bach Soc., Inc., 1966; Inst. for Bach Studies, 1968; Tureck Bach Inst. Inc., 1982. Hon. Member, Guildhall School of Music and Drama, London, 1961; Member: Royal Musical Assoc., London; Inc. Soc. of Musicians, London; Amer. Musicological Soc; Amer. Br., New Bach Soc. Editor, Tureck/Bach Urtext series, 1979–. Numerous recordings. Hon. Dr of Music, Colby Coll., USA, 1964; Hon. DMus: Roosevelt Univ., 1968; Wilson Coll., 1968; Oxon, 1977. Has won several awards. Officer's Cross, Order of Merit, Fed. Republic of Germany, 1979. *Films:* Fantasy and Fugue: Rosalyn Tureck plays Bach, 1972; Rosalyn Tureck plays on Organ and Harpsichord, 1977; Joy of Bach, 1978. *Publications:* An Introduction to the

Performance of Bach, 1960; (ed) Bach: Sarabande, C minor, 1950; (transcribed) Paganini: Moto Perpetuo, 1950; (Urtext and performance edns) Bach: Italian Concerto, 1983; J. S. Bach, Lute Suite in E minor, set for classical guitar, 1984, Lute Suite in C minor, 1985; many articles. *Address:* c/o Ibbs and Tillett Ltd, 450–452 Edgware Road, W2 1EG.

TURING, Sir John Leslie, 11th Bt *cr* 1638; MC; *b* 13 Sept. 1895; *s* of Sir James Walter Turing, 9th Bt and Mabel Rose, *d* of Andrew Caldecott; *S* twin brother, 1970; *m* 1975, Irene Nina, *d* of Trevor John Tatham and *widow* of Captain W. W. P. Shirley-Rollison, RN. *Educ:* Wellington College. Formerly Lieut, Seaforth Highlanders; served European War, 1914–18 (wounded, MC). *Heir: kinsman* John Dermot Turing [*b* 26 Feb. 1961; *m* 1986, Nicola J., *er d* of M. D. Simmonds]. *Address:* Hillcrest, Heatherwood, Midhurst GU29 9LH.

TURMEAU, Dr William Arthur, PhD; CEng, FIMechE; Principal, Napier College, Edinburgh, since 1982; *b* 19 Sept. 1929; *s* of Frank Richard Turmeau and Catherine Lyon Linklater; *m* 1957, Margaret Moar Burnett, MA, BCom; one *d*. *Educ:* Stromness Acad., Orkney; Univ. of Edinburgh (BSc); Moray House Coll. of Educn; Heriot-Watt Univ. (PhD). FIMechE, CEng, 1971. Royal Signals, 1947–49. Research Engr, Northern Electric Co. Ltd, Montreal, 1952–54; Mechanical Engr, USAF, Goose Bay, Labrador, 1954–56; Contracts Manager, Godfrey Engrg Co. Ltd, Montreal, 1956–61; Lectr, Bristo Technical Inst., 1962–64; Napier College: Lectr and Sen. Lectr, 1964–68; Head, Dept of Mechanical Engrg, 1968–75; Asst Principal and Dean, Faculty of Technology, 1975–82. Member Council: CNAA, 1982– (Member: Engrg Bd, 1979–; Scotland Cttee, 1983–); IMechE, 1983–; Soc. Européenne de Formation des Ingènieurs, 1983–; Mem., CICHE, British Council, 1982–. *Publications:* various papers relating to engrg educn. *Recreations:* modern jazz, Leonardo da Vinci. *Address:* 71 Morningside Park, Edinburgh EH10 5EZ. *T:* 031–447 4639. *Club:* Caledonian.

TURNBULL, Prof. Alexander Cuthbert, CBE 1982; MD, FRCOG; Nuffield Professor of Obstetrics and Gynaecology, University of Oxford, since 1973; Fellow of Oriel College, Oxford, since 1973; Hon. Consultant Obstetrician and Gynaecologist, Oxfordshire Health Authority, since 1973; *b* 18 Jan. 1925; *s* of George Harley and Anne White Turnbull, Aberdeen, Scotland; *m* 1953, Elizabeth Paterson Nicol Bell; one *s* one *d*. *Educ:* Merchant Taylors' Sch., Crosby; Aberdeen Grammar Sch. (Modern Dux, 1942); Aberdeen Univ. MB, ChB 1947; MD (with Hons and Thursfield Prize) 1966; MRCOG 1954; FRCOG 1966. (Jun. Vice-Pres., 1982–83; Sen. Vice-Pres., 1984–). Sen. Lectr and Hon. Cons. Obstetrician and Gynaecologist (with Prof. J. Walker), Univ. of Dundee, 1957–61; Sen. Lectr and Hon. Cons. Obstetrician and Gynaecologist (with Sir Dugald Baird), Univ. of Aberdeen, 1961–66; Prof. of Obst. and Gynaecol., Welsh Nat. Sch. of Med., Cardiff, and Hon. Cons. Gynaecologist, also Adviser in Obst. and Gynaecol., Welsh Hosp. Bd, 1966–73; Adviser in Obst. and Gynaecol. to CMO, DHSS, 1975–. Member: Med. Educn Sub-cttee of UGC, 1973–; Lane Commn, 1971–; Clinical Research Bd of MRC, 1969–72. Hon. MA Oxford, 1973. Blair-Bell Medal, RSocMed (Sect. of Obst. and Gynaecol.), 1984. *Publications:* (co-ed) The Oxygen Supply to the Human Fetus, 1960; (chap. in) The Scientific Basis of Obstetrics and Gynaecology (ed R. R. Macdonald), 1969; (jtly) Confidential Enquiries into Maternal Mortality in England and Wales (HMSO), 1973–75, 1976–78 and 1979–81; contribs to: Brit. Jl Obstetrics and Gynaecol., Lancet, BMJ, Jl of Endocrinology and various others. *Recreations:* reading, travelling, occasionally playing golf. *Address:* Nuffield Department of Obstetrics and Gynaecology, University of Oxford, Oxford OX3 9DU; John Radcliffe Hospital, Headington, Oxford.

TURNBULL, Ven. (Anthony) Michael (Arnold); Archdeacon of Rochester, also Canon Residentiary of Rochester Cathedral and Chairman, Diocesan Board for Mission and Unity, since 1984; *b* 27 Dec. 1935; *s* of George Ernest Turnbull and Adeline Turnbull (*née* Awty); *m* 1963, Brenda Susan Merchant; one *s* two *d*. *Educ:* Ilkley Grammar Sch.; Keble Coll., Oxford (MA); St John's Coll., Durham (DipTh). Deacon, 1960; priest, 1961; Curate: Middleton, 1960–61; Luton, 1961–65; Domestic Chaplain to Archbishop of York, 1965–69; Rector of Heslington and Chaplain, York Univ., 1969–76; Chief Secretary, Church Army, 1976–84. Mem., General Synod, 1970–75. Examining Chaplain to Bishop of Norwich, 1982–84. *Publications:* (contrib.) Unity: the next step?, 1972; God's Front Line, 1979; Parish Evangelism, 1980; Learning to Pray, 1981. *Recreations:* cricket, family life. *Address:* The Archdeaconry, Rochester, Kent ME1 1SX. *T:* Medway 42527. *Clubs:* Athenæum, MCC.

TURNBULL, Sir Frank (Fearon), KBE 1964; CB 1954; CIE 1946; HM Civil Service, retired; *b* 30 April 1905; *m* 1947, Gwynnedd Celia Marian Lewis; three *s*. *Educ:* Marlborough Coll.; Trinity Hall, Cambridge. Entered India Office, 1930; Principal Private Secretary to Secretary of State, 1941–46; Secretary to Cabinet Mission to India, 1946; Under-Secretary, HM Treasury, 1949–59; Secretary, Office of the Minister for Science, 1959–64; Deputy Under-Secretary of State, Dept of Education and Science, 1964–66. Member, Board of Governors, Imperial College, 1967–73. Hon. DSc Edinburgh, 1967. *Address:* 26 Green Lane, Amersham, Bucks HP6 6AS. *T:* Amersham 7647.

TURNBULL, George Henry, BSc (Hons), CEng, FIMechE, FIProdE; Chairman and Chief Executive, Inchcape PLC, since 1986 (Group Managing Director, 1984–86; Group Chief Executive, 1985–86); *b* 17 Oct. 1926; *m* 1950, Marion Wing; one *s* two *d*. *Educ:* King Henry VIII Sch., Coventry; Birmingham Univ. (BSc (Hons)). PA to Techn. Dir, Standard Motors, 1950–51; Liaison Officer between Standard Motors and Rolls Royce, 1951–53; Exec., i/c Experimental, 1954–55; Works Manager, Petters Ltd, 1955–56; Standard Motors: Divl Manager Cars, 1956–59; Gen. Man., 1959–62; Standard Triumph International: Dir and Gen. Man., 1962; Dep. Chm., 1969; British Leyland Motor Corporation Ltd: Dir, 1967; Dep. Man. Dir, 1968–73; Man. Dir, 1973; Man. Dir, BL Austin Morris Ltd, 1968–73; Chm., Truck & Bus Div., BL, 1972–73; Vice-Pres. and Dir, Hyundai Motors, Seoul, South Korea, 1974–77; Consultant Advr to Chm. and Man. Dir, Iran Nat. Motor Co., Tehran, 1977–78, Dep. Man. Dir, 1978–79; Chm., Talbot UK, 1979–84. Pres., SMMT, 1982–84 (Dep. Pres., 1984–). Mem. Council, Birmingham Chamber of Commerce and Industry, 1972 (Vice-Pres., 1973); past Member: Careers Adv. Bd, Univ. of Warwick; Management Bd, Engineering Employers' Assoc.; Engineering Employers' Fedn; Engrg Industry Trng Bd. Governor, Bablake Sch., Coventry. FIMI; Fellow, Inst. of Directors. *Recreations:* golf, tennis, fishing. *Address:* Inchcape plc, 40 St Mary Axe, EC2.

TURNBULL, Ven. Michael; *see* Turnbull, Ven. A. M. A.

TURNBULL, Reginald March; *b* 10 Jan. 1907; *s* of late Sir March and Lady (Gertrude) Turnbull; *m* twice; one *s*. *Educ:* Horton Sch.; Eton; Cambridge Univ. (MA). Family shipping firm, Turnbull, Scott & Co., 1928–77. *Recreations:* teaching golf, motoring, water mills. *Address:* Sarum, Church Lane, Worplesdon, Surrey.

TURNBULL, Sir Richard (Gordon), GCMG 1962 (KCMG 1958, CMG 1953); *b* 7 July 1909; *s* of Richard Francis Turnbull; *m* 1939, Beatrice (*d* 1986), *d* of John Wilson, Glasgow; two *s* one *d*. *Educ:* University College School, London; University College, London; Magdalene Coll., Cambridge. Colonial Administrative Service, Kenya: District Officer, 1931–48; Provincial Comr, 1948–53; Minister for Internal Security and Defence, 1954; Chief Secretary, Kenya, 1955–58; Governor and C-in-C, Tanganyika, 1958–61; Governor-General and Commander-in-Chief, 1961–62; Chairman, Central Land Board, Kenya, 1963–64; High Commissioner for Aden and the Protectorate of South Arabia, 1965–67. Fellow of University College, London; Hon. Fellow, Magdalene College, Cambridge, 1970–. KStJ 1958. *Address:* Bergamot House, Jedburgh, Roxburghshire. *T:* Jedburgh 62430.

TURNER, family name of **Baron Netherthorpe** and **Baroness Turner of Camden.**

TURNER OF CAMDEN, Baroness *cr* 1985 (Life Peer), of Camden in Greater London; **Muriel Winifred Turner;** Assistant General Secretary, Association of Scientific, Technical and Managerial Staffs, since 1970; *b* 1927; *m* Reginald T. F. Turner. Member: TUC General Council; Equal Opportunities Commission; Occupational Pensions Board; Central Arbitration Committee. *Address:* House of Lords, SW1.

TURNER, Alan B.; *see* Brooke Turner.

TURNER, Rt. Hon. Sir Alexander (Kingcome), PC 1968; KBE 1973; Kt 1963; *b* Auckland, New Zealand, 18 Nov. 1901; *s* of J. H. Turner; *m* 1934, Dorothea F., *d* of Alan Mulgan; two *s* one *d*. *Educ:* Auckland Grammar Sch.; Auckland Univ. (Scholar). BA 1921; MA 1922; LLB 1923. Served War of 1939–45, National Military Reserve, New Zealand. Barrister and Solicitor, 1923; QC (NZ) 1952. Carnegie Travelling Fellowship, 1949. Judge of the Supreme Court of New Zealand, 1953–62; Senior Resident Judge at Auckland, 1958–62; Judge of Court of Appeal, 1962–71, Pres., 1972–73. President, Auckland University Students' Assoc., 1928; President, Auckland District Court of Convocation, 1933; Member, Auckland Univ. Council, 1935–51; Vice-President, Auckland Univ., 1950–51; a Governor, Massey Agricultural Coll., 1944–53. Hon. LLD Auckland, 1965. *Publications:* (with George Spencer Bower) The Law of Estoppel by Representation, 1966; Res Judicata, 1969; The Law of Actionable Misrepresentation, 1974. *Recreations:* gardening, golf, Bush conservation, agriculture. *Address:* 14 St Michael's Crescent, Kelburn, Wellington 5, New Zealand. *T:* 757768. *Clubs:* Wellington; Auckland.

TURNER, Amédée Edward, QC 1976; Member (C) Suffolk, European Parliament, since 1979; *b* 26 March 1929; *s* of Frederick William Turner and Ruth Hempson; *m* 1960, Deborah Dudley Owen; one *s* one *d*. *Educ:* Temple Grove, Heron's Ghyll, Sussex; Dauntsey Sch., Wilts; Christ Church, Oxford (MA). Called to Bar, Inner Temple, 1954; practised patent bar, 1954–57; Associate, Kenyon & Kenyon, patent attorneys, NY, 1957–60; London practice, 1960–. Contested (C) Norwich N, gen. elections, 1964, 1966, 1970. European Parliament: EDG spokesman on energy res. and technol., 1984–; Vice Chm., Legal Cttee, 1979–84; Member: Economic and Monetary Cttee, 1979–84; ACP Jt Cttee, 1980–; Transport Cttee, 1981–84; Energy Cttee, 1984–; Legal Affairs Cttee, 1984–. *Publications:* The Law of Trade Secrets, 1962, supplement, 1968; The Law of the New European Patent, 1979; many Conservative Party study papers on defence, oil and Middle East. *Recreations:* garden design, art deco collection, fish keeping, oil painting, Annexe 3A Royal Festival Hall. *Address:* 3 Montrose Place, SW1. *T:* 01–235 2894, 01–235 3191; 1 Essex Court, Temple, EC4. *T:* 01–353 8507; Widenmayerstrasse 46, D8000 Munich 22, Germany. *T:* 29 51 25; The Barn, Westleton, Saxmundham, Suffolk. *T:* Westleton 235; La Combe de la Boissière, St Maximin, Uzès 30700, France. *Clubs:* Carlton, Coningsby, United & Cecil.

TURNER, Ven. Antony Hubert Michael; Archdeacon of the Isle of Wight, since 1986; *b* 17 June 1930; *s* of Frederick George and Winifred Frances Turner; *m* 1956, Margaret Kathleen (*née* Philips); one *s* two *d*. *Educ:* Royal Liberty Grammar School, Romford, Essex; Tyndale Hall, Bristol. FCA 1963 (ACA 1952); DipTh (Univ. of London), 1956. Deacon, 1956; Curate, St Ann's, Nottingham, 1956–59; Curate in Charge, St Cuthbert's, Cheadle, Dio. Chester, 1959–62; Vicar, Christ Church, Macclesfield, 1962–68; Home Sec., Bible Churchmen's Missionary Soc., 1968–74; Vicar of St Jude's, Southsea, 1974–86; RD of Portsmouth, 1979–84. Church Commissioner, 1983–. *Recreations:* photography, caravanning. *Address:* 3 Beech Grove, Ryde, Isle of Wight PO34 3AM. *T:* Isle of Wight 65522.

TURNER, Adm. Sir (Arthur) Francis, KCB 1970 (CB 1966); DSC 1945; Chief of Fleet Support, Ministry of Defence, 1967–71; *b* 23 June 1912; *s* of Rear-Admiral A. W. J. Turner and Mrs A. M. Turner (*née* Lochrane); *m* 1963, Elizabeth Clare de Trafford; two *s*. *Educ:* Stonyhurst Coll. Entered RN, 1931; Commander, 1947; Captain, 1956; Rear-Admiral, 1964; Vice-Admiral, 1968; Admiral, 1970. Dir.-Gen. Aircraft (Navy), MoD, 1966–67. *Recreations:* cricket, golf. *Address:* Plantation House, East Horsley, Surrey. *Clubs:* Army and Navy; Union (Malta).

TURNER, Comdr Bradwell Talbot, CVO 1955; DSO 1940; OBE 1951; JP; RN, retired April 1957; *b* 7 April 1907; *s* of late A. F. and A. I. Turner; *m* 1937, Mary G. B., *d* of Professor W. Nixon; three *d*. *Educ:* Christ's Hospital; RN Colleges Osborne and Dartmouth. Joined Royal Navy, 1921; Barrister-at-Law, 1956; Naval Attaché, Oslo, Norway, 1954–57. With The Marconi Co., 1957–72. MIEE 1946. JP Chelmsford 1962 (Chm. Bench, 1974–77). Officer, Legion of Merit (USA), 1945. *Address:* 44 St Johns Road, Writtle, Essex CM1 3EB.

TURNER, Air Vice-Marshal Cameron Archer, CB 1968; CBE 1960 (OBE 1947); Royal New Zealand Air Force, retired; *b* Wanganui, NZ, 29 Aug. 1915; *s* of James Oswald Turner and Vida Cathrine Turner; *m* 1941, Josephine Mary, *d* of George Richardson; two *s*. *Educ:* New Plymouth Boys' High Sch.; Victoria University of Wellington. CEng, FIEE, FRAeS. Commn RAF, 1936–39; commn RNZ Air Force, 1940; served War of 1939–45, UK, NZ, and Pacific; comd RNZAF Station Nausori, Fiji, 1944; comd RNZAF Station, Guadalcanal, Solomon Islands, 1944; Director of Signals, 1945–47; psa 1947; RNZAF Liaison Officer, Melbourne, Australia, 1948–50; comd RNZAF Station, Taieri, NZ, 1950–52; Director of Organization, HQ, RNZAF, 1953–56; comd RNZAF Station Ohakea, NZ, 1956–58; Asst Chief of Air Staff, HQ, RNZAF, 1958; Air Member for Personnel, HQ, RNZAF, 1959; idc 1960; AOC HQ, RNZAF, London, 1961–63; Air Member for Supply, HQ, RNZAF, 1964–65; Chief of Air Staff, HQ RNZAF, 1966–69. Dir, NZ Inventions Develt Authority, 1969–76. Pres., RNZAF Assoc., 1972–81. *Recreations:* fishing, golf. *Address:* 37a Parkvale Road, Wellington 5, New Zealand. *T:* 766063. *Clubs:* Wellington, United Services Officers' (Wellington); Taranaki (New Plymouth).

TURNER, Brig. Charles Edward Francis, CBE 1944 (OBE 1941); DSO 1943; late RE; *b* 23 April 1899; *s* of late Lieut A. E. Turner, RE, and E. B., *d* of Maj.-Gen. Sir C. H. Scott, KCB; *m* 1930, Mary Victoria (*d* 1985), *d* of H. Leeds Swift, York; one *s* two *d*. *Educ:* Twyford Sch., Winchester; Wellington Coll., Berks; Royal Military Academy, Woolwich. Regular Officer, Royal Engineers, Sept. 1917; BEF France, June-Nov. 1918; NREF Russia, July-Sept. 1919; India, 1920–23, including two years on North-West Frontier on service (despatches); Christ's Coll., Cambridge, 1923–24; Ordnance Survey, York and Edinburgh, 1925–30; Staff Coll., Camberley, 1931–32; Singapore, Egypt, Palestine, 1934–37, including service in Palestine (Bt Major, despatches); War Office, 1937–39; MEF 1940–43 (OBE, DSO, CBE, despatches twice); Malaya, 1948–50; retired pay, 1950. National

Council of Social Service, 1950–58; Secretary, Iona Appeal Trust, 1958–61. *Address:* The Colleens, Cousley Wood, Wadhurst, East Sussex TN5 6HE. *T:* Wadhurst 2387.

TURNER, Christopher Gilbert; Headmaster, Stowe School, since 1979; *b* 23 Dec. 1929; *s* of late Theodore F. Turner, QC; *m* 1961, Lucia, *d* of late Prof. S. R. K. Glanville (Provost of King's Coll., Cambridge); one *s* two *d*. *Educ:* Winchester Coll. (Schol.); New Coll., Oxford (Exhibnr), MA. Asst Master, Radley Coll., 1952–61; Senior Classics Master, Charterhouse, 1961–68; Headmaster, Dean Close Sch., 1968–79. Schoolmaster Student at Christ Church, Oxford, 1967. Foundation Member of Council, Cheltenham Colleges of Educn, 1968. Mem., HMC Cttee, 1974–75; Chm., Common Entrance Cttee, 1976–80; Governor: Oakdene Sch., Elstree; Lambrook Sch.; Bilton Grange Sch.; Aldro Sch.; Monkton Combe Sch.; Chm. of Governors, Beachborough Sch. Lay Reader. FRSA. Rotarian. *Publication:* chapter on History, in Comparative Study of Greek and Latin Literature, 1969. *Recreations:* music (violin-playing), reading, walking, different forms of manual labour; OUBC 1951. *Address:* Stowe School, Buckingham. *T:* Buckingham 813164. *Club:* Vincent's (Oxford).

See also W. H. Hughes, Hon. Sir M. J. Turner.

TURNER, Christopher John, OBE 1977; Governor, Turks and Caicos Islands, since 1982; *b* 17 Aug. 1933; *s* of Arthur Basil Turner and Joan Meddows (*née* Taylor); *m* 1961, Irene Philomena de Souza; two *d* (one *s* decd). *Educ:* Truro Cathedral Sch.; Jesus Coll., Cambridge (MA). Served RAF, Pilot Officer (Navigator), 1951–53. Tanganyika/Tanzania: Dist Officer, 1958–61; Dist Comr, 1961–62; Magistrate and Regional Local Courts Officer, 1962–64; Sec., Sch. Admin, 1964–69; Anglo-French Condominium of New Hebrides: Dist Agent, 1970–73; Develt Sec., 1973; Financial Sec., 1975; Chief Sec., 1977–80; Admin. Officer (Staff Planning), Hong Kong, 1980–82. Vanuatu Independence Medal, 1981. *Recreations:* ornithology, photography, diving, tropical gardening. *Address:* Government House, Grand Turk, Turks and Caicos Islands; 98 Christchurch Road, Winchester SO23 9TE. *T:* Winchester 61318.

TURNER, Air Cdre Clifford John, CB 1973; MBE 1953; *b* 21 Dec. 1918; *s* of J. E. Turner; *m* 1942, Isabel Emily Cormack; two *s*. *Educ:* Parkstone Grammar Sch.; RAF Techn. College. Engrg Apprentice, 1935–38; various RAF engrg appts, 1938–64; Group Dir, RAF Staff Coll., 1965–67; Stn Comdr, RAF Colerne, 1968–69; AO Engineering, Training Comd, 1969–73. *Address:* Garnet Drive, Vernon, RR4, BC V1T 6L7, Canada.

TURNER, Colin Francis; Registrar, Family Division of High Court, since 1971; *b* 11 April 1930; *s* of Sidney F. and Charlotte C. Turner; *m* 1951, Josephine Alma Jones; two *s* one *d*. *Educ:* Beckenham Grammar Sch.; King's Coll., London. LLB 1955. Entered Principal Probate Registry, 1949; District Probate Registrar, York, 1965–68. *Publications:* (ed jtly) Rayden on Divorce, 9th, 11th, 12th and 13th edns, consulting editor to 14th edn; an editor of Supreme Court Practice, 1972–; (jtly) Precedents in Matrimonial Causes and Ancillary Matters, 1985. *Recreations:* birding, fishing. *Address:* 18 South Eden Park Road, Beckenham, Kent BR3 3BG. *T:* 01–777 0344.

TURNER, Colin William; Rector, Glasgow Academy, since 1983; *b* 10 Dec. 1933; *s* of William and Joyce Turner; *m* 1958, Priscilla Mary Trickett; two *s* two *d*. *Educ:* Torquay Grammar Sch.; King's Coll., London (BSc; AKC). Edinburgh Academy: Asst Master, 1958–82; OC CCF, 1960–74; Head, Maths Dept, 1973–75; Housemaster, 1975–82. *Recreations:* mountaineering, caravanning. *Address:* 11 Kirklee Terrace, Glasgow G12 0TH. *T:* 041–357 1776.

TURNER, Colin William Carstairs, CBE 1985; DFC 1944; Chairman, The Colin Turner Group, International Media Representatives and Marketing Consultants, since 1985; *b* 4 Jan. 1922; *s* of late Colin C. W. Turner, Enfield; *m* 1949, Evelyn Mary, *d* of late Claude H. Buckard, Enfield; three *s* one *d*. *Educ:* Highgate Sch. Served War of 1939–45 with RAF, 1940–45, Air observer; S. Africa and E Africa, 223 Squadron; Desert Air Force, N. Africa, 1942–44; commissioned, 1943; invalided out as Flying Officer, 1945, after air crash; Chm., 223 Squadron Assoc., 1975–. Mem., Enfield Borough Council, 1956–58. Pres., Overseas Press and Media Association, 1965–67, Life Pres., 1982 (Hon. Secretary, 1967; Hon. Treasurer, 1974–82; Editor, Overseas Media Guide, 1968, 1969, 1970, 1971, 1972, 1973, 1974); Chm., PR Cttee, Commonwealth Press Union, 1970–; Chm., Cons. Commonwealth and Overseas Council, 1976–82 (Dep. Chm. 1975); Vice-Pres., Cons. Foreign and Commonwealth Council (formerly Cons. Commonwealth and Overseas Council), 1985; Mem., Nat. Exec., Cons. Party, 1946–53, 1968–73, 1976–82; Pres., Enfield North Cons. Assoc., 1984– (Chm., 1979–84); Chm., Cons. Europ. Constituency Council, London N, 1984–. Contested (C) Enfield (East), 1950 and 1951; MP (C) Woolwich West, 1959–64. Editor, The Cholmeleian, 1982– (Pres., Old Cholmeleian Soc., 1985–86). *Recreations:* gardening, do-it-yourself, sailing, fishing. *Address:* 55 Rowantree Road, Enfield, Mddx. *T:* 01–363 2403.

TURNER, Prof. David Warren, FRS 1973; Fellow of Balliol College, Oxford, since 1967; Professor of Electron Spectroscopy, Oxford, since 1985; *b* 16 July 1927; *s* of Robert Cecil Turner and Constance Margaret (*née* Bonner); *m* 1954, Barbara Marion Fisher; one *s* one *d*. *Educ:* Westcliff High Sch.; Univ. of Exeter. MA, BSc, PhD, DIC. Lectr, Imperial Coll., 1958; Reader in Organic Chemistry, Imperial Coll., 1965; Oxford University: Lectr in Physical Chem., 1968; Reader in Physical Chemistry, 1978; Reader in Electron Spectroscopy, 1984. Lectures: Kahlbaum, Univ. of Basle, 1971; Van Geuns, Univ. of Amsterdam, 1974; Harkins, Chicago Univ., 1974; Kistiakowski, Harvard, 1979; Liversidge, RSC, 1981–82. Tilden Medal, Chemical Soc., 1967; Harrison Howe Award, Amer. Chem. Soc., 1973. Hon. DTech, Royal Inst., Stockholm, 1971; Hon. DPhil Basle, 1980. *Publications:* Molecular Photoelectron Spectroscopy, 1970; contrib. Phil. Trans Royal Soc., Proc. Royal Soc., Jl Chem. Soc., etc. *Recreations:* music, gardening, tinkering with gadgets. *Address:* Balliol College, Oxford.

TURNER, Donald William, CEng, FICE; Chairman, British Airports International, since 1984; *b* 17 Aug. 1925; *s* of William John Turner and Agnes Elizabeth Jane (*née* Bristow); *m* 1947, Patricia (*née* Stuteley); one *s* one *d*. *Educ:* Wanstead County High Sch.; Birmingham Univ. Served War, Army, 1943–45. Subseq. completed engrg trng in Britain; then took up post in Australia with Qld Railways, 1949. Left Qld, 1954; joined firm of UK consulting engrs and then worked in W Africa on rly and highway construction until 1960. Returned to UK, but remained with consultants until 1966; Chief Engr, Heathrow Airport, 1970; joined British Airports Authority, 1973; Dir of Planning, 1973; Dir of Privatisation, 1985. Dir, London Underground, 1985–. *Address:* 13 Ditchling Road, Brighton, Sussex.

TURNER, Dudley Russell Flower, CB 1977; Secretary, Advisory, Conciliation and Arbitration Service, 1974–77; *b* 15 Nov. 1916; *s* of Gerald Flower Turner and Dorothy May Turner (*née* Gillard), Penang; *m* 1941, Sheila Isobel Stewart; one *s* one *d*. *Educ:* Whitgift Sch.; London Univ. (BA Hons). Served RA (Captain), 1940–46. Entered Ministry of Labour, 1935; HM Treasury, 1953–56; Principal Private Secretary to Minister of Labour, 1956–59; Assistant Secretary: Cabinet Office, 1959–62; Ministry of Labour, 1962–64, 1966; Under-Sec., Ministry of Labour, 1967; Asst Under-Sec. of State, Dept of Employment and Productivity, 1968–70; Under-Sec., Trng Div., 1970–72, Manpower Gen. Div., 1972–73, Dept of Employment; Sec., Commn on Industrial Relations, 1973–74. Imperial Defence Coll., 1965. Pres., East Surrey Decorative and Fine Arts Soc., 1986– (Chm., 1980–86). *Recreations:* music, gardening. *Address:* 9 Witherby Close, Croydon, Surrey CR0 5SU. *Club:* Civil Service.

TURNER, Dame Eva, DBE 1962; FRAM; prima donna; *b* Oldham, Lancashire, 10 March 1892; unmarried. Began to sing at an early age and, whilst in her teens, spent some years at the Royal Academy of Music; joined Royal Carl Rosa Opera Company in 1915, and became the Prima donna of the Company, remaining with it until 1924, when Toscanini engaged her for La Scala, Milan. Appeared all over Europe and USA with Chicago Civic Opera, and in S America; appeared in London, at Covent Garden in 1928 in internat. season, when she sang in Puccini's opera Turandot, Aida, and various other operas; for the Celebrations in connection with the commemoration of the Centenary of Bolivar, was specially chosen by President Gomez to be the Prima Donna; in London at Covent Garden in 1937 internat. season, sang Turandot to the first Calaf of Giovanni Martinelli, also chosen to sing National Anthem from stage of Royal Opera House following Coronation of King George VI and Queen Elizabeth; Professor of Voice to Music Faculty of University of Oklahoma, USA, 1949–59 (resigned); Professor of Voice Royal Academy of Music, London, 1959–66 (resigned). Pres., Wagner Soc., 1971–85. Hon. Internat. Member Sigma Alpha Iota, 1951–; Hon. Internat. Soroptomist, 1955–. Member National Assoc. of Teachers of Singing (USA). Hon. GSM 1968; FRCM 1974; FRNCM 1978; Hon. FTCL, 1982. Hon. Citizen, State of Oklahoma, USA, 1982; First Freeman, Metropolitan Borough of Oldham, 1982. Hon. DMus: Manchester, 1979; Oxford, 1984. Hon. Fellow, St Hilda's Coll., Oxford, 1984. *Recreations:* swimming, riding, motoring. *Address:* 26 Palace Court, W2; Junesca, Brusino-Arsizio, Lake of Lugano, Switzerland. *Club:* Royal Over-Seas League.

TURNER, Brig. Dame Evelyn Marguerite; *see* Turner, Brig. Dame Margot.

TURNER, Sir Francis; *see* Turner, Sir Arthur Francis.

TURNER, Prof. Grenville, FRS 1980; Professor of Physics, Sheffield University, since 1980; *b* 1 Nov. 1936; *o s* of Arnold and Florence Turner, Todmorden, Yorks; *m* 1961, Kathleen, *d* of William and Joan Morris, Rochdale, Lancs; one *s* one *d*. *Educ:* Todmorden Grammar Sch.; St John's Coll., Cambridge (MA); Balliol Coll., Oxford (DPhil). Asst Prof., Univ. of Calif at Berkeley, 1962–64; Lectr, Sheffield Univ., 1964–74, Sen. Lectr, 1974–79, Reader, 1979–80. Vis. Associate in Nuclear Geophysics, Calif Inst. of Technol., 1970–71. *Publications:* scientific papers. *Recreation:* photography. *Address:* 9 Canterbury Crescent, Sheffield S10 3RW. *T:* Sheffield 305904.

TURNER, Harry Edward; Managing Director, Television South West PLC, since 1985; *b* 28 Feb. 1935; *s* of Harry Turner and Bessie Elizabeth Jay; *m* 1956, Carolyn Bird; one *s* one *d*. *Educ:* Sloane Grammar Sch., Chelsea. Served Middlesex Regt, Austria, 2nd Lieut, 1953–55. Sales Representative, Crosse & Blackwell Foods, 1955–56; Advertising Executive: Daily Herald, 1956–58; Kemsley Newspapers, 1958–60; Feature Writer and Advtsg Manager, TV International Magazine, 1960–62; Sales Dir, Westward Television, 1962–80; Dir of Marketing, Television South West, 1980–85. FRSA 1986. *Publications:* The Man Who Could Hear Fishes Scream (short stories), 1978; The Gentle Art of Salesmanship, 1985. *Recreations:* tennis, riding, ski-ing, literature, travel. *Address:* Four Acres, Lake Road, Deepcut, Surrey GU16 6RB. *T:* Deepcut 835527; 10 Ocean Court, Plymouth, Devon. *Club:* Mannheim (New York).

TURNER, Rev. Professor Henry Ernest William, DD; Canon Residentiary, Durham Cathedral, 1950–73; Treasurer, 1956–73; Sub-Dean, 1959–73; Acting Dean, 1973; Van Mildert Professor of Divinity, Durham University, 1958–73, now Emeritus; *b* 14 Jan. 1907; *o s* of Henry Frederick Richard and Ethel Turner, Sheffield; *m* 1936, Constance Parker, *d* of Dr E. P. Haythornthwaite, Rowrah, Cumberland; two *s*. *Educ:* King Edward VII Sch., Sheffield; St John's Coll., Oxford; Wycliffe Hall, Oxford. MA 1933; BD 1940; DD 1955. Curate, Christ Church, Cockermouth, 1931–34; Curate, Holy Trinity, Wavertree, 1934–35; Fellow, Chaplain and Tutor, Lincoln Coll., Oxford, 1935–50; Chaplain, RAFVR, 1940–45; Librarian, Lincoln Coll., 1945–48; Senior Tutor, Lincoln Coll., 1948–50; Lightfoot Prof. of Divinity, Durham Univ., 1950–58. Select Preacher, Oxford Univ., 1950–51; Bampton Lectr, Oxford, 1954. Member: Anglican delegation to Third Conference of World Council of Churches, Lund, 1952; Doctrine Commn of the Church of England, 1967–76; formerly Mem., Anglican-Presbyterian Conversations; Theological Consultant to Anglican Roman Catholic Conversations, 1970. *Publications:* The Life and Person of Jesus Christ, 1951; The Patristic Doctrine of Redemption, 1952; Jesus Master and Lord, 1953; The Pattern of Christian Truth (Bampton Lectures), 1955; Why Bishops?, 1955; The Meaning of the Cross, 1959; (jt author with H. Montefiore) Thomas and the Evangelists, 1962; Historicity and the Gospels, 1963; Jesus the Christ, 1976; contributions to the Guardian, Theology and Church Quarterly Review. *Address:* Realands, Eskdale, near Holmrook, Cumbria CA19 1TW. *T:* Eskdale 321.

TURNER, Prof. Herbert Arthur (Frederick), BSc Econ London, PhD Manchester, MA Cantab; Montague Burton Professor of Industrial Relations, University of Cambridge, 1963–83, now Professor Emeritus; Fellow of Churchill College, Cambridge, since 1963; Leverhulme Senior Research Fellow, since 1985; *b* 11 Dec. 1919; *s* of Frederick and May Turner. *Educ:* Henry Thornton Sch., Clapham; LSE (Leverhulme Schol., then Leverhulme Res. Student, 1936–40; BSc (Econ) 1939); PhD Manchester, 1960. Army, then naval staff, 1940–44. Member, Trades Union Congress Research and Economic Department, 1944; Assistant Education Secretary, TUC, 1947; Lecturer, 1950, Senior Lecturer, 1959, University of Manchester; Council of Europe Res. Fellow, 1957–58; Montague Burton Professor of Industrial Relations, University of Leeds, 1961–63. Mem., NBPI, 1967–71. Visiting Professor: Harvard and MIT, 1971–72; Sydney Univ., 1976–77; Hong Kong Univ., 1978–79 and 1985; Monash Univ., 1982. Sometime Adviser to Govts of Congo, Zaïre, Egypt, Tanzania, Fiji, Papua New Guinea, Zambia and other developing countries; Chm., Incomes Policies Commn of E African Community, 1973; ILO Adviser: Malawi, 1967; Iran, 1975; Labour Adviser, UNECA, 1980. *Publications:* Arbitration, 1951; Wage Policy Abroad, 1956; Trade Union Growth, Structure and Policy, 1962; Wages: the Problems for Underdeveloped Countries, 1965, 2nd edn 1968; Prices, Wages and Incomes Policies, 1966; Labour Relations in the Motor Industry, 1967; Is Britain Really Strike-Prone?, 1969; Do Trade Unions Cause Inflation?, 1972, 3rd edn 1978; Management Characteristics and Labour Conflict, 1978; The Last Colony: labour in Hong Kong, 1980; various reports of ILO, monographs, papers and articles on labour economics and statistics, industrial relations, developing countries. *Recreations:* minimal but mostly excusable. *Address:* Churchill College, Cambridge. *Clubs:* United Oxford & Cambridge University; Melbourne (Hon.).

TURNER, Hugh Wason, CMG 1980; Director, National Gas Turbine Establishment, 1980–83, retired; *b* 2 April 1923; *s* of Thomas W. Turner and Elizabeth P. Turner (*née* Pooley); *m* 1950, Rosemary Borley; two *s* two *d*. *Educ:* Dollar Academy; Glasgow University. BSc Hons (Mech. Eng); CEng; FRAeS. Aeroplane and Armament Experimental Establishment, 1943–52; Chief Tech. Instructor, Empire Test Pilots School, 1953; A&AEE (Prin. Scientific Officer), 1954–64; Asst Director, RAF Aircraft, Min. of

Technology, 1965–68; Superintendent, Trials Management, A&AEE, 1968–69; Division Leader, Systems Engineering, NATO MRCA Management Agency (NAMMA), Munich, 1969–74; Chief Superintendent, A&AEE, 1974–75; DGA1 (Dir Gen., Tornado), MoD (PE), 1976–80. *Recreations:* ski-ing, model building, photography, DIY. *Address:* Lavender Cottage, 1 Highcliff Road, Lyme Regis, Dorset DT7 3EW. *T:* Lyme Regis 2310.

TURNER, Prof. James Johnson; Professor of Inorganic Chemistry, since 1979, and Pro-Vice-Chancellor since 1986, University of Nottingham; *b* 24 Dec. 1935; *s* of Harry Turner and Evelyn Turner (*née* Johnson); *m* 1961, Joanna Margaret Gargett; two *d*. *Educ:* Darwen Grammar Sch.; King's Coll., Cambridge (MA, PhD 1960; ScD 1985). CChem; FRSC. Research Fellow, King's Coll., Cambridge, 1960, Harkness Fellow, Univ. of Calif, Berkeley, 1961–63; University of Cambridge: Univ. Demonstrator, 1963–68; Univ. Lectr, 1968–71; College Lectr, 1963–71, Admissions Tutor, 1967–71, King's Coll.; Prof. and Head of Dept of Inorganic Chemistry, Univ. of Newcastle upon Tyne, 1972–78. Visiting Professor: Univ. of Western Ontario, 1975; Texas, 1977; MIT, 1984; Chicago, 1986. Science and Engineering Research Council (formerly SRC): Mem., 1974–77, Chm., 1979–82, Chemistry Cttee; Mem., Science Bd, 1979–86; Mem. Council, 1982–86. Royal Society of Chemistry: Mem., 1974–77, Vice-Pres., 1982–84, Dalton Council; Tilden Lectr, 1978. *Publications:* papers mainly in jls of Chem. Soc. and Amer. Chem. Soc. *Recreation:* walking. *Address:* Department of Chemistry, University of Nottingham, University Park, Nottingham NG7 2RD. *T:* Nottingham 506101.

TURNER, Hon. Joanna Elizabeth, (Hon. Mrs Turner), MA; Classics Teacher, Ellesmere College, Salop, 1975–80; *b* 10 Jan. 1923; 2nd *d* of 1st Baron Piercy, CBE, and Mary Louisa, *d* of Hon. Thomas Pelham; *m* 1968, James Francis Turner (*d* 1983), *er s* of late Rev. P. R. Turner. *Educ:* St Paul's Girls' Sch.; Somerville Coll., Oxford (Sen. Classics Schol.). Asst Classics Mistress: Downe House, Newbury, 1944–46; Gordonstoun Sch., 1947–48; Badminton Sch., Bristol, 1948–65, Headmistress, Badminton Sch., Bristol, 1966–69. JP Inner London (Juvenile Courts), 1970–75. *Recreations:* painting, foreign travel, reading. *Address:* The Old Coach House, Burford, Oxon. *T:* Burford 2368.

TURNER, Prof. John Derfel; Sarah Fielden Professor of Education, since 1985, and Dean of Faculty of Education, 1972–74 and since 1986, University of Manchester; *b* 27 Feb. 1928; *s* of Joseph Turner and Dorothy Winifred Turner; *m* 1951, Susan Broady Hovey; two *s*. *Educ:* Manchester Grammar Sch.; Univ. of Manchester. BA 1948, MA 1951, Teacher's Diploma 1951. Education Officer, RAF, 1948–50; teacher, Prince Henry's Grammar Sch., Evesham, 1951–53; Lectr in English, 1953–56, Sen. Lectr in Educn, 1956–61, Nigerian Coll. of Arts, Science and Technology; Lectr in Educn, Univ. of Exeter Inst. of Education, 1961–64; Prof. of Educn and Dir, Sch. of Educn, 1964–70, and Pro-Vice-Chancellor, 1966–70, Univ. of Botswana, Lesotho and Swaziland, Emeritus Prof., 1970; University of Manchester: Prof. of Educn and Dir of Sch. of Educn, 1970–76; Prof. of Adult and Higher Educn, 1976–85. Rector, University Coll. of Botswana, Univ. of Botswana and Swaziland, 1981–82 and Vice-Chancellor, Univ. of Botswana, 1982–84. Vice-Chm., 1976–79 and Chm., 1979–81, Univs Council for Educn of Teachers; Member: UK Nat. Commn for UNESCO, 1975–81; IUC Working Parties on East and Central Africa and on Rural Development, 1975–81; Educn Sub-Cttee, UGC, 1980–81; Educn Cttee and Further Educn Bd, CNAA, 1979–81; Chm., European Develt Fund/IUC Working Party on Academic Develt of Univ. of Juba, 1977–78; Chm. and Mem. Council, Social Studies Adv. Cttee, Selly Oak Colleges, 1975–81. Chm., Bd of Governors, Abbotsholme Sch., 1980–. Chm., Editl Bd, Internat. Jl of Educn and Develt, 1978–81. Hon. FCP 1985. Hon. LLD Ohio Univ., 1982. *Publications:* Introducing the Language Laboratory, 1963; (ed with A. P. Hunter) Educational Development in Predominantly Rural Countries, 1968; (ed with J. Rushton) The Teacher in a Changing Society, 1974; (ed with J. Rushton) Education and Deprivation, 1975; (ed with J. Rushton) Education and Professions, 1976; school text books and contribs to edited works and to jls. *Recreations:* reading, music, theatre, walking; Methodist local preacher. *Address:* 13 Firswood Mount, Gatley, Cheadle, Cheshire SK8 4JY. *T:* 061–428 2734. *Clubs:* Royal Commonwealth Society, Royal Over-Seas League.

TURNER, Rt. Hon. John Napier, PC (Can.) 1965; QC (Can.); MP; Leader of the Liberal Party of Canada, and Leader of the Opposition, since 1984; *b* 7 June 1929; *s* of Leonard Turner and Phyllis Turner (*née* Gregory); *m* 1963, Geills McCrae Kilgour; three *s* one *d*. *Educ:* Norman Model Public Sch., Ottawa, Ont.; Ashbury Coll., 1939–42; St Patrick's Coll., 1942–45; Univ. of BC; Oxford Univ. BA (PolSci, Hons) BC, 1949; Rhodes Scholar, Oxford Univ., BA (Juris.) 1951; BCL 1952; MA 1957. Joined Stikeman, Elliott, Tamaki, Mercier & Turner, Montreal, Quebec; practised with them after being called to English Bar, 1953, Bar of Quebec, 1954 and Bar of Ont., 1968; QC (Can.) 1968; with McMillan Binch, Toronto, 1976–84. MP for St Lawrence-St George, Montreal, 1962–68, Ottawa-Carleton, 1968–75; Parly Sec. to Minister of Northern Affairs and Nat. Resources, 1963–65; Minister without Portfolio, Dec. 1965–April 1967; Registrar-Gen. of Canada April 1967–Jan. 1968; Minister of Consumer and Corporate Affairs, Jan.-July 1968; Solicitor-Gen., April-July 1968; Minister of Justice and Attorney-Gen. of Canada, July 1968–Jan. 1972; Minister of Finance, 1972–75; Prime Minister of Canada, June–Sept. 1984. Barbados Bar, 1969; Yukon and Northwest Territories, 1969; Trinidad Bar, 1969; British Columbia, 1969. Hon. Dr of Laws: Univ. of New Brunswick, 1968; York Univ., Toronto, 1969; Hon. Dr of Civil Law, Mt Allison Univ., NB, 1980. *Publications:* Senate of Canada, 1961; Politics of Purpose, 1968. *Recreations:* tennis, canoeing, ski-ing; Canadian Track Field Champion 1950–51, Mem. English Track and Field Team. *Address:* (office) House of Commons, Ottawa, Ont K1A 0A6, Canada; (home) 541 Acacia Street, Ottawa, Ont K1M 0M5, Canada.

TURNER, Prof. John Stewart, FAA 1979; FRS 1982; Professor of Geophysical Fluid Dynamics, Australian National University, since 1975; *b* Sydney, Aust., 11 Jan. 1930; *s* of Ivan Stewart Turner and Enid Florence (*née* Payne); *m* 1959, Sheila Lloyd Jones; two *s* one *d*. *Educ:* North Sydney Boys' High Sch.; Wesley Coll., Univ. of Sydney (BSc, MSc); Trinity Coll., Univ. of Cambridge (PhD). FInstP 1969. Research Officer, CSIRO cloud physics group, 1953–54 and 1960–61; 1851 Exhibition Overseas Schol., 1954–57; postdoctoral research post, Univ. of Manchester, 1958–59; Rossby Fellow, then Associate Scientist, Woods Hole Oceanographic Instn, 1962–66; Asst Director of Research, then Reader, Dept of Applied Mathematics and Theoretical Physics, Univ. of Cambridge, 1966–75; Fellow of Darwin Coll., Cambridge, 1974; Foundation Prof. of Geophysical Fluid Dynamics in the Research Sch. of Earth Sciences, ANU, 1975–; Overseas Fellow, Churchill Coll., Cambridge, 1985. Member, Australian Marine Sciences and Technologies Adv. Cttee (AMSTAC), 1979–84. Associate Editor, Journal of Fluid Mechanics, 1975–; Mem. Editorial Adv. Board, Deep-Sea Research, 1974–84. *Publications:* Buoyancy Effects in Fluids, 1973, paperback 1979; papers in various scientific jls. *Recreations:* bushwalking, photography, home handyman. *Address:* (home) 16 Juwin Street, Aranda, ACT 2614, Australia; (office) Research School of Earth Sciences, Australian National University, GPO Box 4, Canberra, ACT 2601. *T:* (062) 49 4530.

TURNER, John Turnage; His Honour Judge Turner; a Circuit Judge, since 1976; Resident Judge at Ipswich, since 1984; *b* 12 Nov. 1929; *s* of Wilfrid Edward and May Martha Turner; *m* 1956, Gillian Mary Rayner; two *d*. *Educ:* Earls Colne Grammar School. Called to the Bar, Inner Temple, 1952. *Recreations:* tennis, music appreciation, gardening, watching cricket. *Address:* Bolberry House, Bures, Suffolk CO8 5JG. *T:* Bures 227207. *Clubs:* MCC; Colchester Garrison Officers'.

TURNER, Lloyd Charles; Editor, The Daily Star, since 1980; Director: Express Newspapers plc, since 1982; Daily Star plc, since 1982; *b* 2 Oct. 1938; *s* of Charles Thomas and Lily Turner; *m* 1st, 1961, Rosemary Munday (marr. diss. 1966); 2nd, 1967, Jennifer Anne Cox (marr. diss. 1972); 3rd, 1973, Jill Marguerite King. *Educ:* Giants Creek Primary Sch., Australia; The Armidale Sch., Armidale, Australia. Newcastle Morning Herald, Australia: Cadet journalist, 1956; Chief Crime Reporter, 1960; Features Editor, 1961; Picture Editor, 1962; Asst Editor, 1964, Industrial Correspondent, Manchester Evening News, 1968; Daily Express: Sub-Editor, 1968; Asst Chief Sub-Editor, 1974; Dep. Chief Sub-Editor, 1975; Asst Night Editor, 1976; Dep. Night Editor, 1977; Night Editor, 1979. CPU Scholar, 1966. Pres., Australian Journalists Assoc. (Provincial), 1962–65; Chm., (Father), Daily Express/Sunday Express NUJ Chapel, 1969–74. *Recreations:* golf, gardening, horse-racing. *Address:* 121 Fleet Street, EC4P 4JT. *T:* 01–353 8000; Great Ancoats Street, Manchester M60 4HB. *T:* 061–236 9575. *Clubs:* St James's; Journalists' (Sydney).

TURNER, Brig. Dame Margot, (E. M. Turner), DBE 1965 (MBE 1946); RRC 1956; Matron-in-Chief and Director Army Nursing Service, 1964–68; *b* 10 May 1910; *d* of late Thomas Frederick Turner and late Molly Cecilia (*née* Bryan). *Educ:* Finchley County Sch., Middlesex. Trained at St Bartholomew's Hospital, London, 1931–35. Joined QAIMNS, 1937 (became QARANC, 1949). Served in UK, India, Malaya, Hong Kong, Bermuda, Germany and Near East. POW Sumatra, Feb. 1942–Aug. 1945. Col Comdt, QARANC, 1969–74. CStJ 1966. *Relevant Publication:* Sir John Smyth, Will to Live: the story of Dame Margot Turner, 1970. *Recreations:* reading, photography, golf, tennis. *Address:* 2 Chantry Court, Frimley, Surrey. *T:* Camberley 22030.

TURNER, Hon. Sir Michael John; Hon. Mr Justice Turner; Kt 1985; a Judge of the High Court of Justice, Queen's Bench Division, since 1985; *b* 31 May 1931; *s* of late Theodore F. Turner, QC; *m* 1st, 1956, Hon. Susan Money-Coutts (marr. diss. 1965); one *s* one *d*; 2nd, 1965, Frances Deborah Croom-Johnson; two *s*. *Educ:* Winchester; Magdalene Coll., Cambridge (BA). Called to Bar, Inner Temple, 1954 (Bencher 1981); a Recorder, 1972–85; QC 1973–85. Chm., E Mids Agricultural Tribunal, 1979–82. *Recreations:* horses, listening to music. *Address:* Orchard House, Maidford, Towcester, Northants. *T:* Blakesley 860391; 30 Shrewsbury House, Cheyne Walk, SW3. *T:* 01–352 2832.

See also W. H. Hughes, C. G. Turner.

TURNER, Michael Ralph, FRSA; Group Managing Director since 1976, and Chief Executive since 1982, Associated Book Publishers PLC; Chairman, Associated Book Publishers (UK) Ltd, since 1977; *b* 26 Jan. 1929; *s* of Ralph Victor Turner and May Turner; *m* 1955, Ruth Baylis; two *s* two *d*. *Educ:* Newport Sch., Essex; Trinity Coll., Cambridge (BA Hons). Served RAF, Transport Comd, 1947–49. Jun. Editor, J. M. Dent & Sons, 1949–50; Methuen & Co.: Jun. Editor, 1953; subseq. Publicity and Promotion Manager, and Dir; Associated Publishers Ltd: Marketing Dir, 1973; Asst Gp Man. Dir, 1975; Gp Man. Dir, 1976. Chm., Methuen Inc., New York, 1981–; Pres., Carswell Co. Ltd, Toronto, 1982–84; Dir, ABP Investments (Aust.) Pty Ltd, 1976–. Chm., Book Marketing Council, 1981–84; Member: Book Trade Working Party, 1973–74; Council, Publishers Assoc., 1981– (Vice-Pres., 1985–); National Council and Exec., NBL, 1980–. FRSA 1984. *Publications:* The Bluffer's Guide to the Theatre, 1967; Parlour Poetry, 1967; (with Antony Miall) The Parlour Song Book, 1972; (with Antony Miall) Just a Song at Twilight, 1975; (with Antony Miall) The Edwardian Song Book, 1982; (with Michael Geare) Gluttony, Pride and Lust and Other Sins from the World of Books, 1984; (with Leslie Lonsdale-Cooper) translations of Hergé's Tintin books, 1958–83. *Recreations:* reading, music, theatre — the more frivolous arts generally. *Address:* Cobdens, Binsted, Alton, Hants GU34 4PF. *T:* Bentley (Hants) 22273. *Club:* Garrick.

TURNER, Norman Henry, CBE 1977; Official Solicitor to the Supreme Court of Judicature, 1970–80; *b* 11 May 1916; *s* of late Henry James Turner, MA and Hilda Gertrude Turner; *m* 1939, Dora Ardella (*née* Cooper); three *s* two *d*. *Educ:* Nottingham High School. Articled, Nottingham, 1933; admitted Solicitor (Hons), 1938; joined Official Solicitor's Dept, 1948; Asst Official Solicitor, 1958. *Recreation:* caravanning. *Address:* 48 Rushington Avenue, Maidenhead, Berks. *T:* Maidenhead 22918.

TURNER, Patricia, OBE 1981; Head of National Equal Rights Department, and National Industrial Officer, General, Municipal, Boilermakers and Allied Trades Union (formerly General and Municipal Workers' Union), since 1971; Member, General Council, TUC, since 1981; *b* 14 May 1927; *d* of John Richard and Maire Collins; *m* 1954, Donald Turner, BSc (Econ). *Educ:* London School of Economics (BSc (Econ), MSc (Econ)). Industrial Sociology Lectr, 1965–69; Consultant, Manpower and Productivity Service (Dept of Employment and Productivity), 1969–70; Sen. Industrial Relations Officer, Commn on Industrial Relations, 1970–71. Member: Confedn of Shipbuilding and Engineering Unions Exec. Council, 1971– (Pres., 1982–83); Engineering Industry Training Bd, 1971–; Women's Nat. Commn, 1973–; Dept of Employment Adv. Cttee on Women's Employment, 1980–. *Recreations:* reading, theatre. *Address:* (office) GMBATU, Thorne House, Ruxley Ridge, Claygate, Esher, Surrey KT10 0TL. *T:* Esher 62081.

TURNER, Peter; *see* Turner, T. P.

TURNER, Air Vice-Marshal Peter, CB 1979; MA; Bursar and Steward, Wolfson College, Cambridge, since 1979; *b* 29 Dec. 1924; *s* of late George Allen and of Emma Turner; *m* 1949, Doreen Newbon; one *s*. *Educ:* Tapton House Sch., Chesterfield. Served War of 1939–45; 640 Sqdn, 1943–45; Nos 51, 242 and 246 Sqdns, 1945–48; psa 1961; NATO staff, 1963–67; jssc 1967; Chief Equipment and Secretarial Instructor, RAF Coll., Cranwell, 1967–68; Comd Accountant, HQ Air Support Comd, 1968–69; Station Comdr, RAF Uxbridge, 1969–71; RCDS, 1972; Dir of Personnel (Ground) (RAF), MoD, 1973–75; AOA, HQ RAF Support Command, 1975–79, and Head of RAF Admin. Branch, 1976–79. MA Cantab 1979. *Recreation:* retrospective contemplation. *Address:* Hedge End, Potton Road, Hilton, Cambs PE18 9NG. *Club:* Royal Air Force.

TURNER, Peter William; District Secretary, Transport and General Workers' Union; *m* Maureen Ann Turner (*née* Hill), Councillor, JP. *Educ:* Bordesley Green Infant and Junior Sch.; Saltley Grammar Sch. (until 1940); various Trade Union weekend courses. Appointed District Officer, TGWU, 1969; District Sec., CSEU, 1974–76; seconded as Industrial Advr to DoI, 1976–78. Member of various cttees including: Chemical Industry Area Productivity Cttee, 1969–76 (Vice-Chm., 1970–72, Chm., 1972–74); TUC Regional Educn Adv. Cttee, 1970–76; Birmingham Crime Prevention Panel, 1973–76; W Midlands Consultative Cttee on Race Relations, 1974–76; DoE Working Party on Race Relations, 1974–76; Teaching Co. Management Cttee, 1977–82. Member: Birmingham Trades Council, 1956–76; Local Appeals Tribunal, 1969–74. *Recreations:* motoring, motor cycling, caravanning, do-it-yourself, reading, electronics. *Address:* Transport and General Workers' Union, 8 Severn Street, Worcester WR1 2ND. *T:* Worcester 24894.

TURNER, Phil; Deputy Director of Staff Pay and Conditions, British Coal (formerly National Coal Board), since 1980; *b* 7 June 1939; *s* of William Morris Turner and Eileen Lascelles Turner; *m* 1963, Gillian Sharp; one *s* two *d* (and one *s* decd). *Educ:* Beckenham and Penge Grammar School for Boys; University Coll. London (BScEcon). Joined Labour Party, 1963; Chairman, Hampstead Labour Party, 1968–70; Councillor, Camden Bor. Council, 1971–: Chm., Building Works and Services Cttee, 1978–80 and 1986–; Leader of Council, 1982–86. Member: Assoc. of London Authorities, 1983–86; Policy Cttee, AMA, 1984–86. Contested (Lab) Cities of London and Westminster South, Feb. and Oct. 1974; prospective parly cand. (Lab) Hampstead and Highgate, 1985–. *Recreations:* family, conversation at the Blenheim Arms, collecting books. *Address:* 33 Minster Road, NW2 3SH. *T:* 01–794 8805. *Club:* National Coal Board Sports and Social.

TURNER, Philip, CBE 1975; LLB (London); in private practice with Infields, Hampton Wick, Surrey; *b* 1 June 1913; *er s* of late George Francis and late Daisy Louise Turner (*née* Frayn), Alverstoke, Hants; *m* 1938, Hazel Edith, *d* of late Douglas Anton and late Edith Ada Benda; one *d* (one *d* decd). *Educ:* Peter Symonds, Winchester. Admitted Solicitor, 1935. Entered General Post Office Solicitor's Dept, 1935. Served in Royal Navy, 1940–46 (Lt-Comdr). Asst Solicitor to General Post Office, 1953; Principal Asst Solicitor, 1962–72, Solicitor to the Post Office, 1972–75; temp. mem. of legal staff, DoE, 1976–77. Chm., Civil Service Legal Soc., 1957–58; Chm., Internat. Bar Assoc.'s Cttee on Public Utility Law, 1972–77. FRSA 1955. *Recreations:* piano, golf. *Address:* 8 Walters Mead, Ashtead, Surrey. *T:* Ashtead 73656. *Clubs:* Naval, Royal Automobile, Law Society; Hampshire County Cricket, Surrey County Cricket.

TURNER, Surgeon Rear-Admiral (D) Philip Stanley, CB 1963; QHDS 1960–64; Director of Dental Services, RN, Admiralty, Nov. 1961–64; *b* 31 Oct. 1905; *s* of Frank Overy Turner and Ellen Mary Turner, Langton Green, Tunbridge Wells; *m* 1934, Marguerite Donnelly; one *d* (and one *s* decd). *Educ:* Cranbrook Coll.; Guy's Hospital. LDS, RCS 1927. Surgeon Lieut (D) Royal Navy, 1928; Surgeon Captain (D) 1955; Surgeon Rear-Admiral (D), 1961; Senior Specialist in Dental Surgery, 1946–61. Served in: HMS Ramillies, Vanguard, Implacable, Indomitable; HMHS Maine, Tjitjalengka; RN Hospitals Haslar, Plymouth; RN Barracks Portsmouth, etc; Naval HQ, Malta. Foundation Fellow, British Assoc. of Oral Surgeons, 1962. *Address:* Woodhurst, Warren Lane, Cross-in-Hand, Heathfield, East Sussex. *T:* Heathfield 3532.

TURNER, Raymond C.; *see* Clifford-Turner.

TURNER, Richard, CMG 1956; LRIBA; consultant architect, retired 1983; *b* 2 May 1909; *m* 1933, Annie Elizabeth, *d* of late Rev. R. W. Gair; one *d*. *Educ:* Dame Alice Owen's School. Entered Office of Works, 1929; in charge of ME Office, 1938–47, centred in Istanbul and, later, Cairo; Asst Chief Architect, Min. of Works, 1951; Dir of Works (Overseas), 1960–65; Dir, Overseas Svcs, MPBW, 1965–69, retired. Mem., Esher UDC, 1969–72. *Address:* Flat 3, Western Field, Manor Road, Sidmouth, Devon EX10 8RR. *T:* Sidmouth 3805. *Club:* Travellers'.

TURNER, Dr Richard Wainwright Duke, OBE 1945; Senior Research Fellow in Preventive Cardiology, University of Edinburgh, since 1974 (Reader in Medicine, 1960–74); Senior Physician and Physician in Charge of the Cardiac Department, Western General Hospital, Edinburgh, 1946–74; *b* Purley, Surrey, 30 May 1909; *s* of Sydney Duke Turner, MD (General Practitioner), and Lilian Maude, *d* of Sir James Wainwright; *m* Paula, *d* of Henry Meulen, Wimbledon; three *s* one *d*. *Educ:* Epsom Coll.; Clare Coll., Cambridge; St Thomas' Hosp., London. 1st Class Hons Nat. Sci. Tripos, Cambridge, 1934. MA, MB, BChir Cantab 1934; MRCS, LRCP 1935; MRCP 1936; MD Cantab 1940; FRCP 1950; FRCPE 1952. Served in RAMC, 1939–45: UK, Egypt and Italy (Lt-Col); officer i/c Med. Div. 31st and 92nd British General Hospitals. Examiner in Medicine: Univs of Edinburgh and Leeds; RCP; RCPE. Chm., Coronary Prevention Group, 1978–. Member: Assoc. Physicians of GB; British Cardiac Soc.; Hon. Member, Cardiol Socs of India and Pakistan. *Publications:* Diseases of Cardiovascular System in Davidson's Principles and Practice of Medicine, vols 1–11, 1952–65; Electrocardiography, 1963; Auscultation of the Heart, 1st edn 1963 to 6th edn 1984; contribs to British Heart Jl, Lancet, BMJ, Quarterly Jl of Med., American Heart Jl, etc. *Recreations:* travel, climbing, gardening, photography. *Address:* Cotterlings, Ditchling, Sussex BN6 8TS. *T:* Hassocks 3392; Cardiac Department, Western General Hospital, Edinburgh EH4 2XU. *T:* 031–332 2525. *Clubs:* Royal Over-Seas League; University Staff (Edinburgh).

TURNER, Robert Lockley; Master of the Supreme Court, Queen's Bench Division, since 1984; *b* 2 Sept. 1935; *s* of James Lockley Turner and Maud Beatrice Turner; *m* 1963, Jennifer Mary Leather; one *s* one *d*. *Educ:* Clifton Coll.; St Catharine's Coll., Cambridge (BA 1957, MA 1973). Called to the Bar, Gray's Inn, 1958. Commnd Gloucestershire Regt (28th/61st), 1959 (2nd Lieut); transf. to Army Legal Services, 1960 (Captain); Major 1962; retd from Army, 1966 (GSM with clasp South Arabia, 1966). Practised at Common Law Bar in London and on Midland and Oxford Circuit, 1967–84; a Recorder of the Crown Court, 1981–84. Hon. Steward, Westminster Abbey, 1985–. *Recreations:* parish churches, music, messing about in boats. *Address:* Royal Courts of Justice, WC2; Polruan by Fowey, Cornwall. *Clubs:* Hurlingham; Royal Fowey Yacht (Fowey).

TURNER, Robert Noel, CMG 1955; retired; *b* 28 Dec. 1912; *s* of late Engr Rear-Adm. A. Turner and late Mrs V. E. Turner; *m* 1946, Evelyn Heynes Dupree (*d* 1976); two *s*. *Educ:* Dover Coll.; Wadham Coll., Oxford (MA). First Class Hons Modern History. Cadet, Malayan Civil Service, 1935; Third Asst Sec. to Govt, FMS, 1936; Asst District Officer, Lower Perak, FMS, 1938; Supernumerary Duty (Lower Perak), 1939; Asst Resident, Brunei, 1940 (interned by Japanese, Borneo, Dec. 1941–Sept. 1945); Asst Sec. to Governor-General, Malaya, May 1946; Prin. Asst Sec., Sarawak, Aug. 1946; First Asst Malayan Establishment Officer, 1948; Acting Dep. Malayan Establishment Officer, April 1950; Chief Sec., Barbados, 1950–56 (title changed from Colonial Sec., 1954); Acting Governor, Barbados, Nov. 1952–May 1953 and 1955, North Borneo, 1957–62 (commended by Sec. of State 'Hurricane Janet', 1955); Chief Sec., North Borneo, 1956–63 (Mem. Exec. Council and Legislative Council, 1950–63); State Sec., Sabah, Fedn of Malaysia, 1963–64 (Mem. State Cabinet, 1963–64). Hon. Mem., First Grade, Order of Kinabalu, Sabah (title: Datuk; lettering: SPDK), 1963. *Recreations:* reading history, watching cricket. *Address:* Kinabalu, The Rise, Brockenhurst, Hants SO42 7SJ. *T:* Lymington 23197.

TURNER, Theodora, OBE 1961; ARRC 1944; retired as Matron of St Thomas' Hospital and Superintendent Nightingale Training School (1955–65); *b* 5 Aug. 1907; *er d* of H. E. M. Turner. *Educ:* Godolphin School, Salisbury; Edinburgh School of Domestic Economy. Ward Sister, St Thomas' Hosp., 1935–38; Administrative Course, Florence Nightingale Internat. Foundn, 1938–39. QAIMNS Reserve, 1939–45. Administrative Sister, St Thomas' Hosp., 1946–47; Matron Royal Infirmary, Liverpool, 1948–53; Education Officer, Educn Centre, Royal College of Nursing, Birmingham, 1953–55. President: Florence Nightingale Internat. Nurses Assoc., 1971–74; Royal Coll. of Nursing and Nat. Council of Nurses of UK, 1966–68. Mem., Argyll and Clyde Health Bd, 1974–75. *Recreations:* gardening and painting.

TURNER, (Thomas) Peter; Evaluation Consultant, Metropolitan Police, since 1985; *b* 8 May 1928; *s* of Thomas Turner and Laura Crawley; *m* 1952, Jean Rosalie Weston; one *s* one *d*. *Educ:* Ilford County High Sch.; London University. BSc (1st Class Hons), Maths and Physics. GEC, North Wembley, 1947–50; Armament Design Establishment, 1950–54; Air Ministry (Science 3), 1954–58 and 1962–63; Chief Research Officer, RAF Maintenance Command, 1958–62; Police Research and Development Branch, Home Office, 1963–68; Civil Service Dept (OR), 1968–73; Head of Treasury/CSD Joint Operational Research Unit, 1973–76; Head of Operational Res., CSD, 1977–81, HM Treasury, 1981–84. *Address:* 8 Waring Drive, Green St Green, Orpington, Kent BR6 6DW. *T:* Farnborough (Kent) 51189.

TURNER, Wilfred, CMG 1977; CVO 1979; HM Diplomatic Service, retired; Director, Southern Africa Association, since 1983; *b* 10 Oct. 1921; *s* of late Allen Turner and Eliza (*née* Leach); *m* 1947, June Gladys Tite; two *s* one *d*. *Educ:* Heywood Grammar Sch., Lancs; London Univ. BSc 1942. Min. of Labour, 1938–42. Served War, REME, 1942–47. Min. of Labour, 1947–55; Brit. High Commn, New Delhi (Asst Lab. Adviser), 1955–59; Senior Wages Inspector, Min. of Labour, 1959–60; Min. of Health (Sec., Cttee on Safety of Drugs, 1963–66), 1960–66. Joined HM Diplomatic Service, 1966; Commonwealth Office, 1966; First Sec.: Kaduna, Nigeria, 1966–69; Kuala Lumpur, 1969–73; Dep. High Comr, and Commercial/Economic Counsellor, Accra, 1973–77; High Comr to Botswana, 1977–81. *Recreation:* hill walking. *Address:* 44 Tower Road, Twickenham TW1 4PE. *T:* 01–892 1593. *Club:* Royal Commonwealth Society.

TURNER, Dr William; Regional Medical Officer, Yorkshire Regional Health Authority, 1976–86, retired; *b* 23 Feb. 1927; *s* of Clarence and Mabel Turner; *m* 1950, Patricia Bramham Wilkinson; one *s* two *d*. *Educ:* Prince Henry's Grammar Sch., Otley, Yorks; Leeds Univ. MB, ChB; DPH, FFCM; LLB. House Officer, Leeds Gen. Infirmary, 1950–51; RAMC, 1951–53; Gen. Practitioner, 1953–55; Public Health Trng, 1955–60; Medical Officer of Health: Hyde, 1960–63; Huddersfield, 1963–67; Bradford, 1967–74; Area MO, Bradford, 1974–76. Member: Standing Med. Adv. Cttee, 1978–82; NHS Steering Gp on Health Services Inf., 1979–84. *Publications:* contrib. BMJ, Medical Officer. *Address:* Bentcliffe, 1 Premiere Park, Ilkley, West Yorks LS29 9RQ. *T:* Ilkley 600114.

TURNER, Lt-Gen. Sir William (Francis Robert), KBE 1962; CB 1959; DSO 1945; Lord-Lieutenant of Dumfries, 1972–82; *b* 12 Dec. 1907; *er s* of late Mr and Mrs F. R. Turner, Kelso, Roxburghshire; *m* 1938, Nancy Maude Stilwell, *er d* of late Lt-Col and Mrs J. B. L. Stilwell, Yateley, Hants; one *s*. *Educ:* Winchester College; RMC Sandhurst. 2nd Lieut, KOSB, 1928; served in Great Britain and India, 1928–39; Capt. 1938; BEF, 1939–40; Staff College, 1941; OC, 5 KOSB, 1942–45 (despatches), NW Europe; OC, 1 KOSB, 1945–46, NW Europe and Middle East; GSO1, Middle East and Great Britain, 1947–50. Colonel Brit. Military Mission to Greece, 1950–52; Comd 128 Inf. Bde (TA), 1952–54; BGS HQ Western Comd, 1954–56; GOC 44 (Home Counties) Infantry Div. (TA) and Home Counties District, and Deputy Constable of Dover Castle, 1956–59; President, Regular Commissions Board, 1959–61; GOC-in-C, Scottish Comd, and Governor of Edinburgh Castle, 1961–64; retd 1964; Colonel, King's Own Scottish Borderers, 1961–70; Brigadier, 1965–82, Ensign, 1982–85, Queen's Body Guard for Scotland (Royal Company of Archers), retd. HM Comr, Queen Victoria School, Dunblane, 1965–85. DL, Dumfriesshire, 1970–72. Comdr with Star, Order of Saint Olav, Class II (Norway), 1962; Order of the Two Niles, Class II (Republic of the Sudan), 1963. *Address:* Milnhead, Kirkton, Dumfries. *T:* Dumfries 710319. *Clubs:* Naval and Military; New (Edinburgh).

TURNER CAIN, Maj.-Gen. George Robert, CB 1967; CBE 1963; DSO 1945; President, Anglia Maltings (Holdings) Ltd, since 1982 (Chairman, 1976–82); Chairman: Anglia Maltings Ltd, 1976–82; F. & G. Smith Ltd, 1962–82; Walpole & Wright Ltd, 1968–82; Director: Crisp Maltings Ltd, 1967–82; Crisp Malt Products Ltd, 1968–82; Edme Ltd, 1972–82; *b* 16 Feb. 1912; *s* of late Wing Comdr G. Turner Cain; *m* 1938, Lamorna Maturin, *d* of late Col G. B. Hingston; one *s* one *d*. *Educ:* Norwich Sch.; RMC Sandhurst. 2nd Lt Norfolk Regt, 1932; 1st Bn Royal Norfolk Regt, India, 1933–38; Waziristan Campaign, 1937. Served War of 1939–45 with 1st Royal Norfolk and 1st Hereford Regt, BLA, 1944–45. Comd 1st Royal Norfolk Regt, Berlin, 1947–48; Hong Kong and UK, 1953–55; Comd Tactical Wing, School of Infantry, 1955–57; Comd 1st Fed. Inf. Bde, Malaya, in operations in Malaya, 1957–59; BGS, HQ, BAOR, 1961; Maj.-Gen. Administration, GHQ FARELF, 1964–67, retired; ADC, 1961–64. Dep. Col, Royal Anglian Regt, 1971–74. Croix de Guerre avec Palm, 1945; Star of Kedah (Malaya), 1959. *Recreation:* shooting. *Address:* Holbreck, Hollow Lane, Stiffkey, near Wells-next-the-Sea, Norfolk.

TURNER-SAMUELS, David Jessel, QC 1972; Barrister-at-Law; *b* 5 April 1918; *s* of late Moss Turner-Samuels, QC, MP, and Gladys Deborah Turner-Samuels (*née* Belcher); *m* 1939, Norma Turner-Samuels (*née* Verstone) (marr. diss. 1975); one *s* one *d*; *m* 1976, Norma Florence Negus, *qv*. *Educ:* Westminster Sch. Called to Bar, Middle Temple, 1939 (Bencher 1980); admitted to Trinidad bar, 1976. Served War of 1939–45, in Army, 1939–46. *Publication:* (jointly) Industrial Negotiation and Arbitration, 1951. *Recreation:* getting away from it all. *Address:* Cherry Tree Cottage, Petworth Road, Anstead Brook, Haslemere, Surrey GU27 3BG. *T:* Haslemere 51970; New Court, Temple, EC4Y 9BE. *T:* 01–353 7613.

TURNER-SAMUELS, Norma Florence, (Mrs D. J. Turner-Samuels); *see* Negus, N. F.

TURNER-WARWICK, Prof. Margaret Elizabeth Harvey, MA, DM, PhD; FRCP; FRACP; FFOM; Professor of Medicine (Thoracic Medicine), since 1972, Dean, since 1984, Cardiothoracic Institute, Brompton Hospital; *b* 19 Nov. 1924; *d* of William Harvey Moore, QC, and Maud Baden-Powell; *m* 1950, Richard Trevor Turner-Warwick, *qv*; two *d*. *Educ:* St Paul's Sch.; Lady Margaret Hall (Open Schol. 1943), Oxford. University Coll. Hosp., 1947–50: Tuke silver medal, Filliter exhibn in Pathology, Magrath Schol. in Medicine, Atchison Schol.; Postgrad. trng at UCH and Brompton Hosp., 1950–61; Cons. Physician: (Gen. Med.), Elizabeth Garrett Anderson Hosp., 1961–67; Brompton and London Chest Hosps, 1967–72. Sen. Lectr, Inst. of Diseases of the Chest, 1961–72. Lectures: Marc Daniels, 1974, Phillip Ellman, 1980, Tudor Edwards, 1985, RCP; Lettsomian, Med. Soc. of London, 1982. Pres., British Thoracic Soc., 1982–85; Chairman: Central Academic Council, BPMF, 1982–85; Med. Res. Cttee, Asthma Res. Council, 1982–; Member: MRC Systems Bd (DHSS nomination), 1982–85; Council, British Lung Foundn, 1984–. University of London: Mem. Senate, 1983–; Mem., Academic Council, 1983–; Mem., Scholarships Cttee, 1984–; Mem., Cttee of Extramural Studies, 1984–. Hon. DSc City Hosp., New York, 1985. *Publications:* Immunology of the Lung, 1978; (jtly) Occupational Lung Diseases: research approaches and methods, 1981; chapters in various textbooks on immunology and thoracic medicine, particularly fibrosing lung disorders and asthma; contrib. original articles: Lancet, BMJ, Quarterly Jl Med., Thorax, Tubercle, Jl Clin. Experimental Immunology, etc. *Recreations:* her family and their hobbies, gardening, country life, music. *Address:* 55 Fitzroy Park, Highgate, N6 6JA. *T:* 01–340 6339.

TURNER-WARWICK, Richard Trevor, MA, BSc, DM Oxon, MCh; Hon. DSc; FRCP, FRCS, FACS; Hon. FRACS; specialist in reconstruction and functional restoration of the urinary tract; Surgeon and Senior Urologist to the Middlesex Hospital, W1, since 1961; Senior Urologist to: King Edward VII Hospital for Officers; St Peter's Hospital Group and Royal National Orthopædic Hospital; Senior Lecturer, London University Institute of Urology, since 1962; Hon. Consultant Urologist, Royal Prince Alfred Hospital, Sydney, since 1980; *b* 21 Feb. 1925; *s* of W. Turner Warwick, FRCS; *m* 1950, Prof. Margaret Elizabeth Turner-Warwick, *qv*; two *d*. *Educ:* Bedales School; Oriel Coll., Oxford; Middlesex Hosp. Medical School. Pres. OUBC, 1946; Mem. Univ. Boat Race Crew, Isis Head of River crew and Univ. Fours, 1946; Winner OU Silver Sculls, 1946; BSc thesis in neuroanatomy, 1946. Sen. Broderip Schol., Lyell Gold Medallist and Freeman Schol., Middx Hosp., 1949; surgical trng at Middx Hosp. and St Paul's Hosp., London, and Columbia Presbyterian Med. Centre, NY, 1959. Hunterian Prof. of RCS, 1957, 1976; Moynihan Prize of Assoc. of Surgeons, 1957; Comyns Berkeley Travelling Fellowship to USA, 1959. British Assoc. of Urological Surgeons: Mem. Council, 1975–78 and 1982–; Pres.-elect, 1986; Fellow, 1961; St Peter's Medal, 1978. Fellow, Assoc. of Surgeons of GB and Ireland, 1960; Member: Council, Royal Coll. of Surgeons, 1980–; Internat. Soc. of Urology, 1966–; European Soc. of Urology; Soc. of Pelvic Surgeons, 1963; Founder Mem., 1969, Pres., 1985, Internat. Continence Soc.; Corresp. Member: Amer. Assoc. of Genito Urinary Surgeons, 1972; American, Australasian and Belgian Urological Assocs. Hon. FRACS, 1981. Hon. DSc New York, 1985. *Publications:* various articles in scientific jls, contributing to surgery, to develt of operative procedures for the reconstruction and restoration of function of the urinary tract, and to design of surgical instruments. *Recreation:* water. *Address:* 61 Harley House, NW1. *T:* 01–935 2550; Tirnanog, 55 Fitzroy Park, Highgate, N6. *T:* 01–340 6339. *Clubs:* Flyfishers'; Vincent's (Oxford); The Houghton (Stockbridge); Leander (Henley); Ottery St Mary Fly Fishers; Royal Motor Yacht (Poole).

TURNOUR, family name of **Earl Winterton.**

TURPIN, James Alexander, CMG 1966; HM Diplomatic Service, retired; business consultant, since 1977; *b* 7 Jan. 1917; *s* of late Samuel Alexander Turpin; *m* 1942, Kathleen Iris Eadie; one *d*. *Educ:* King's Hosp., Dublin; Trinity Coll., Dublin (schol., 1st cl. Hons, Gold Medal, MA). Asst Lectr, Trinity College, Dublin, 1940. Served Army (Royal Irish Fusiliers), 1942–46. Joined Foreign Service, 1947; Mem., UK Delegn to OEEC, Paris, 1948; 1st Sec., 1949; FO, 1950; Warsaw, 1953; Tokyo, 1955; Counsellor, 1960; seconded to BoT, 1960–63; Counsellor (Commercial), The Hague, 1963–67; Minister (Economic and Commercial), New Delhi, 1967–70; Asst Under-Sec. of State, FCO, 1971–72; Ambassador to the Philippines, 1972–76; retired, 1977. Chm., British-Philippine Soc., 1986. *Publications:* New Society's Challenge in the Philippines, 1980; The Philippines: problems of the ageing New Society, 1984. *Recreations:* tennis, music, swimming, wine, cookery. *Address:* 12 Grimwood Road, Twickenham, Middlesex.

TURPIN, Kenneth Charlton; Provost of Oriel College, Oxford, 1957–80, and Hon. Fellow since 1980; Vice-Chancellor, Oxford University, 1966–69 (Pro-Vice Chancellor, 1964–66, 1969–79); Member, Hebdomadal Council, 1959–77; *b* 13 Jan. 1915; *e s* of late Henry John Turpin, Ludlow. *Educ:* Manchester Grammar Sch.; Oriel College, Oxford. Treasury, 1940–43; Asst Private Sec. to C. R. Attlee, Lord President and Dep. Prime Minister, 1943–45; 2nd Asst Registrar, University Registry, Oxford, 1945–47; Sec. of Faculties, Univ. of Oxford, 1947–57; professorial fellow, Oriel Coll., 1948; Hon. Fellow Trinity Coll., Dublin, 1968. A Church Commissioner, 1984–. *Recreations:* gardening, walking. *Address:* 13 Apsley Road, Oxford. *Clubs:* Athenæum; Vincent's (Oxford).

TURPIN, Maj.-Gen. Patrick George, CB 1962; OBE 1943; FCIT; *b* 27 April 1911; 3rd *s* of late Rev. J. J. Turpin, MA, BD, late Vicar of Misterton, Somerset; *m* 1947, Cherry Leslie Joy, *d* of late Major K. S. Grove, York and Lancaster Regiment; one *s* one *d*. *Educ:* Haileybury Coll., Hertford; Exeter College, Oxford (Sen. Classical Schol.). BA (Hons) Oxford (Lit. Hum.), 1933; MA 1963. Commd RASC, 2nd Lt, 1933; Lt 1936; Capt. 1941; Major 1946; Lt-Col 1949; Col 1953; Brig. 1959; Maj.-Gen. 1960. Served War of 1939–45 (despatches twice, OBE): Adjt, 1939–40; AQMG, 30 Corps, W Desert, 1943; AA&QMG, 5th Div., Italy, 1943–44; DA&QMG (Brig.), 1 Corps, BLA, 1945; Brig. A, 21 Army Gp, 1945–46; Comd 6 Training Bn, RASC, 1947; ADS&T, WO, 1948; AA&QMG (Plans), HQ, BTE (Egypt), 1950; GSO1 (instructor), Jt Services Staff Coll., 1951–53; ADS&T (Col), WO, 1953–54; DAG, HQ, BAOR, 1956–59; Brig. i/c Adm., 17 Gurkha Div., Malaya, 1959–60; DST, 1960–63; Dir of Movements, MoD (Army), 1963–66; psc 1941; jssc 1949; idc 1955; Col Comdt, Royal Corps of Transport, 1965–71; Col Gurkha Army Service Corps, 1960–65; Col Gurkha Transport Regt, 1965–73. Sec.-Gen., Assoc. of British Travel Agents, 1966–69. Pres., Army Lawn Tennis Assoc., 1968–73. Governor, Royal Sch. for Daughters of Officers of the Army, Bath, 1963–83. FCIT (MInstT 1961). *Recreations:* lawn tennis (Somerset County Champion, 1948, Army Colours, 1952); squash rackets (Bucks County Colours, 1952); golf. *Address:* c/o National Westminster Bank, 121 High Street, Oxford OX1 4DD. *Clubs:* Oxford Union Society; All England Lawn Tennis; International Lawn Tennis; Escorts Squash Rackets.

TURTON, family name of **Baron Tranmire.**

TURTON, Victor Ernest; Managing Director: V. E. Turton (Tools) Ltd; V. E. Turton (Motor Spares) Ltd; V. E. Turton (Wholesalers) Ltd; *b* 29 June 1924; *s* of H. E. Turton; *m* 1951, Jean Edith Murray; two *d*. *Educ:* Paget Secondary Modern Sch.; Aston Techn. Coll.; Birmingham Central Techn. Coll. Birmingham City Councillor (Lab) Duddeston Ward, 1945–63; Saltley Ward, 1970–71; Alderman, Birmingham, 1963–70 and 1971–74, Hon. Alderman, 1974–; Lord Mayor of Birmingham, 1971–72, Dep. Lord Mayor, 1972–73; West Midlands County Council: Mem., 1974–77, 1981–86; Vice-Chm., 1983–84, Chm., 1984–85; Chm., Airport Cttee, 1974–77; Member: Airport and Fire Bde Cttee; Transportation Cttee. Chm., Birmingham Airport, 1959–66; Dir, Birmingham Exec. Airways. Chairman: Smallholdings and Agric. Cttee, 1954–58; West Midlands Regional Adv. Cttee for Civil Aviation, 1966–72; Jt Airports Cttee of Local Authorities, 1975–77. Vice Pres., Heart of England Tourist Bd, 1977– (Chm., 1975–77). Chm., Hall Green Div. Labour Party, 1957–59. Former Governor, Coll. of Technology (now Univ. of Aston in Birmingham). *Recreations:* football, cricket, table tennis, philately. *Address:* 32 Tenbury Road, King's Heath, Birmingham B14 6AD. *Club:* Rotary (Birmingham).

TURTON-HART, Sir Francis (Edmund), KBE 1963 (MBE 1942); *b* 29 May 1908; *s* of David Edwin Hart and Zoe Evelyn Turton; *m* 1947, Margaret Greaves; one *d*. *Educ:* Uppingham. Served with Royal Engineers, 1939–46 (Hon. Major, 1946). East Africa, 1924–38; Portugal, 1939; West Africa, 1946–65; Federal House of Representatives, Nigeria, 1956–60; President, Lagos Chamber of Commerce, 1960–63. *Recreations:* shooting, fishing, golf. *Address:* 39 Hunters Moon, Dartington, Totnes, South Devon TQ9 6JT. *T:* Totnes 863126. *Club:* Thurlestone Golf.

TURVEY, Garry; Director-General, Freight Transport Association, since 1984; *b* 11 Oct. 1934; *s* of Henry Oxley Turvey and Annie Maud Braley; *m* 1960, Hilary Margaret Saines; three *s*. *Educ:* Morecambe Grammar School. FCIS; FCIT. Metropolitan Vickers Ltd, Manchester, 1956–58; AEI Manchester Ltd, 1958–60; Asst Sec., 1960–67, Sec., 1967–69, Traders' Road Transport Assoc.; Sec., 1969–84 and Dep. Dir-Gen., 1974–84, Freight Transport Assoc. *Recreations:* cricket, gardening. *Address:* 139 Imberhorne Lane, East Grinstead, West Sussex. *T:* East Grinstead 25829. *Clubs:* Royal Automobile; Sussex County Cricket.

TURVEY, Ralph, DSc (Econ); economist; Chief, Department of Labour Information and Statistics, International Labour Office; *b* 1 May 1927; *s* of John and Margaret Turvey; *m* 1957, Sheila Bucher; one *s* one *d*. *Educ:* Sidcot School; London School of Economics; Uppsala University. Lectr, then Reader, in Economics, at London School of Economics, 1948–64, with interruptions. Vis. Lectr, Johns Hopkins Univ., 1953; Ford Foundation Vis. Res. Prof., Univ. of Chicago, 1958–59; Economic Section, HM Treasury, 1960–62; Center of Economic Research, Athens, 1963. Chief Economist, The Electricity Council, 1964–67. Member, NBPI, 1967–71, Jt Dep. Chm. 1968–71; Economic Advr, Scientific Control Systems Ltd, 1971–75; Economic Advr, then Chief Statistician, ILO, 1975–. Mem., Nat. Water Council, 1974–75. Vis. Prof. of Econs, LSE, 1973–75. Governor, Kingston Polytechnic, 1972–75. Mem., Inflation Accounting Cttee, 1974–75. *Publications:* The Economics of Real Property, 1957; Interest Rates and Asset Prices, 1960; Studies in Greek Taxation (joint author), 1964; Optimal Pricing and Investment in Electricity Supply, 1968; Economic Analysis and Public Enterprises, 1971; Demand and Supply, 1971; (jtly) Electricity Economics, 1977; papers on applied welfare economics in Economic Jl, Amer. Economic Review, etc. *Recreations:* computing, piano, alpine walking. *Address:* Case Postale 500, 1211 Geneva 22, Switzerland. *Club:* Reform.

TUSA, John; Managing Director, External Broadcasting, BBC, since 1986; *b* 2 March 1936; *s* of John Tusa and Lydia Sklenarova; *m* 1960, Ann Hilary Dowson; two *s*. *Educ:* Trinity Coll., Cambridge (BA 1st Cl. Hons History). BBC general trainee, 1960; Producer, BBC External Services, 1962; freelance radio journalist, 1965; Presenter: BBC Radio 4 The World Tonight, 1968; BBC2 Newsnight, 1979–86. Mem. Council, RIIA, 1984–. TV Journalist of the Year, RTS 1983; Richard Dimbleby Award, BAFTA, 1984. Mem., Editorial Board, Political Quarterly, 1978–. *Publication:* (with Ann Tusa) The Nuremberg Trial, 1983. *Recreations:* squash, opera, talking. *Address:* 21 Christchurch Hill, NW3 1JY. *T:* 01–435 9495. *Club:* United Oxford & Cambridge University.

TUSHINGHAM, Rita; actress; *b* 14 March 1942; *d* of John Tushingham; *m* 1962, Terence William Bicknell (marr. diss. 1976); two *d*; *m* 1981, Ousama Rawi. *Educ:* La Sagesse Convent, Liverpool. Student, Liverpool Playhouse, 1958–60. *Stage appearances:* Royal Court Theatre: The Changeling, 1960; The Kitchen, 1961; A Midsummer Night's Dream, 1962; Twelfth Night, 1962; The Knack, 1962; other London theatres: The Giveaway, 1969; Lorna and Ted, 1970; Mistress of Novices, 1973; My Fat Friend, 1981; Children, Children, 1984. *Films:* A Taste of Honey, 1961 (Brit. Film Acad. and Variety Club awards for Most Promising Newcomer, 1961; NY Critics, Cannes Film Festival and Hollywood Foreign Press Assoc. awards); The Leather Boys, 1962; A Place to Go, 1963; Girl with Green Eyes, 1963 (Variety Club award); The Knack, 1964 (Silver Goddess award, Mexican Assoc. of Film Corresps); Dr Zhivago, 1965; The Trap, 1966; Smashing Time, 1967; Diamonds For Breakfast, 1967; The Guru, 1968; The Bed-Sitting Room, 1970; Straight on till Morning, 1972; Situation, 1972; Instant Coffee, 1973; Rachel's Man, 1974; The Human Factor, 1976; Pot Luck, 1977; State of Shock, 1977; Mysteries, 1978; Incredible Mrs Chadwick, 1979; The Spaghetti House Siege, 1982; Flying, 1984; A Judgement in Stone, 1986; Single Room, 1986. *TV appearances include:* Red Riding Hood (play), 1973; No Strings (own series), 1974; Don't Let Them Kill Me on Wednesday, 1980; Confessions of Felix Krull, 1980; Seeing Red, 1983; Pippi Longstocking, 1984. *Recreations:* interior decorating, cooking. *Address:* c/o Jean Diamond, London Management, 235 Regent Street, W1.

TUSTIN, Arnold; Professor Emeritus, MSc, FIEE, retired; *b* 1899; *m* 1948; no *c*. *Educ:* King's Coll., Univ. of Durham. Subsequently Chief Asst Engineer, Metropolitan-Vickers Electrical Co., until 1945. Visiting Webster Prof., Massachusetts Inst. of Technology, 1953–54; Prof. of Electrical Engineering, Univ. of Birmingham, 1947–55; Prof. of Heavy Electrical Engineering, Imperial Coll., Univ. of London, 1955–64. Chm. Measurement and Control Section, IEE, 1959–60; Chm. Research Adv. Council, Transport Commn, 1960. Hon. DTech Bradford, 1968. *Publications:* Direct Current Machines for Control Systems, 1952; The Mechanism of Economic Systems, 1953; (ed) Automatic and Manual Control, 1951. *Address:* 17 Orchard Lane, Amersham-on-the-Hill, Bucks HP6 5AA.

TUSTIN, Rt. Rev. David; *see* Grimsby, Bishop Suffragan of.

TUTE, Warren Stanley; author; *b* 22 Feb. 1914; *s* of Stanley Harries Tute and Laura Edith Thompson; *m* 1st, 1944, Annette Elizabeth Neil (marr. diss. 1955); 2nd, 1958, Evelyn Mary Dalley; two *d*. *Educ:* Dragon Sch., Wrekin Coll. Entered RN 1932, served in HM Ships Nelson and Ajax; took part in N African, Sicilian and Normandy landings (despatches 1944), retired as Lt Comdr, 1946. Wrote for BBC, 1946–47; Dir, Random Film Productions Ltd, 1947–52; made films and trained scriptwriters for US Govt, 1952–54; Argentina, 1955; Dir, Theatrework (London) Ltd, 1960–81; produced (jtly) Little Mary Sunshine, Comedy, 1962; Head of Scripts, London Weekend TV, 1968–69; Liaison Officer, Capital Radio—Operation Drake, 1978–81; Trustee, The Venture Trust, 1983– (Dir, 1982–83). Archivist, Worshipful Co. of Cordwainers, 1976–84. *Publications: novels:* The Felthams, 1950; Lady in Thin Armour, 1951; Gentleman in Pink Uniform, 1952; The Younger Felthams, 1953; Girl in the Limelight, 1954; The Cruiser, 1955; The Rock, 1957; Leviathan, 1959; The Golden Greek, 1960; The Admiral, 1963; A Matter of Diplomacy, 1969; The Powder Train, 1970; The Tarnham Connection, 1971; The Resident, 1973; Next Saturday in Milan, 1975; Honours of War and Peace, 1976; The Cairo Sleeper, 1977; *history:* The Grey Top Hat, 1961; Atlantic Conquest, 1962; Cochrane, 1965; Escape Route Green, 1971; The Deadly Stroke, 1973; Hitler—The Last Ten Days, 1973; D Day, 1974; The North African War, 1976; The True Glory: the story of the Royal Navy over a thousand years, 1983; *plays:* Jessica, 1956; A Time to be Born, 1956; Frost at Midnight (trans.), 1957; Quartet for Five, 1958; A Few Days in Greece, 1959; *other works:* Chico, 1950; Life of a Circus Bear, 1952; Cockney Cats, 1953; Le Petomane (trans.), 1967; (contrib.) The Commanding Sea, 1981 (originator of BBC TV series). *Recreations:* people, cats, wine, France. *Address:* c/o Finaccounting Services SA, 40 Rue du Rhône, 1204 Geneva, Switzerland; Bardigues, 82340 Auvillar, France. *T:* 63.39.60.30. *Clubs:* Garrick, Whitefriars (Past Chm.).

TUTIN, Dorothy, CBE 1967; actress (stage and films); *b* 8 April 1931; *d* of late John Tutin, DSc, and of Adie Evelyn Tutin; *m* 1963, Derek Barton-Chapple (stage name Derek Waring); one *s* one *d*. *Educ:* St Catherine's, Bramley, Surrey; RADA. Began career, 1950; Stratford Festival, 1958, 1960. *Parts include:* Rose, in The Living Room; Katherine, in Henry V; Sally Bowles, in I am a Camera; St Joan, in The Lark; Catherine, in The Gates of Summer; Hedwig, in The Wild Duck; Viola, in Twelfth Night; Juliet, in Romeo and Juliet; Ophelia, in Hamlet; during Shakespeare Memorial Theatre tour of Russia, 1958, played parts of Ophelia, Viola and Juliet; Dolly, in Once More, With Feeling (New), 1959; Portia, Viola, Cressida (S-on-A), 1960; Sister Jeanne, in The Devils (Aldwych), 1961, 1962; Juliet, Desdemona (S-on-A), 1961; Varya, in The Cherry Orchard (S-on-A, and Aldwych), 1961; Cressida, Prioress, in The Devils (Edinburgh), 1962; Polly Peachum, in The Beggar's Opera (Aldwych), 1963; The Hollow Crown (New York), 1963; Queen Victoria, in Portrait of a Queen, Vaudeville, 1965; Rosalind, As You Like It, Stratford, 1967, Los Angeles, 1968; Portrait of a Queen, NY, 1968; Play on Love, St Martin's, 1970; Old Times, Aldwych, 1971; Peter Pan, Coliseum, 1971, 1972; What Every Woman Knows, 1973, Albery, 1974; Natalya Petrovna, in A Month in the Country, Chichester, 1974, Albery, 1975; Cleopatra, in Antony and Cleopatra, Edinburgh, 1977; Madame Ranevsky, The Cherry Orchard, Lady Macbeth, in Macbeth, Lady Plyant, in The Double Dealer (Soc. of W End Theatre Award, 1978), Nat. Theatre, 1978; Undiscovered Country, Nat. Theatre, 1979; Reflections, Theatre Royal, Haymarket, 1980; The Provok'd Wife, Nat. Theatre, 1980; Hester, in The Deep Blue Sea, Greenwich, 1981; After the Lions, Royal Exchange, Manchester, 1982; Ballerina, Churchill Theatre, Bromley, 1984; A Kind of Alaska, Duchess Theatre, 1985; The Chalk Garden, Chichester, 1986. *Films:* Polly Peachum, in The Beggar's Opera; Cecily, in The Importance of Being Earnest; Lucie Manette, in A Tale of Two Cities; Henrietta Maria in Cromwell; Sophie Breska in Savage Messiah (Variety Club of GB Film Actress Award, 1972); The Shooting Party. Has appeared on television. *Recreations:* music; Isle of Arran. *Address:* c/o Barry Burnett, Suite 42–43, Grafton House, 2–3 Golden Square, W1.

TUTIN, Prof. Thomas Gaskell, FRS 1982; Professor of Taxonomy, University of Leicester, 1967–73, now Emeritus; University Fellow, University of Leicester, 1974; *b* 21 April 1908; *o s* of Frank and Jane Tutin; *m* 1942, Winifred Anne Pennington (*see* W. A. Tutin); one *s* three *d*. *Educ:* Cotham Sch., Bristol; Downing Coll., Cambridge (schol.). Expedition to British Guiana, 1933; Marine Laboratory, Plymouth, 1934–37; expedition to Lake Titicaca, 1937; part-time Demonstrator, KCL, 1938–39; Asst Lectr, Univ. of Manchester, 1939–42; Geographer, Naval Intelligence Div., 1942–44; Lectr, Univ. College of Leicester, 1944–47; Prof. of Botany, Univ. of Leicester, 1947–67. Pres., Botanical Soc. of British Isles, 1957–61. Foreign Member, Societas Scientiarum Fennica (Section for Natural Science), 1960. Linnean Medal, Linnean Soc., 1977. Hon. ScD Dublin, 1979. *Publications:* (with Clapham and Warburg) Flora of the British Isles, 1952, 3rd edn 1987; (with Clapham and Warburg) Excursion Flora of the British Isles, 1959, 3rd edn 1980; (with V. H. Heywood *et al*) Flora Europaea, Vol. I 1964, Vol. II 1968, Vol. III 1972, Vol. IV 1976, Vol. V 1979; (with A. C. Jermy) British Sedges, 1968; Umbellifers of the British Isles, 1980; papers in Annals of Botany, New Phytologist, Jl of Ecology, Watsonia, etc. *Recreations:* botany, music. *Address:* Home Farm, Knighton, Leicester LE2 3WG. *T:* Leicester 707356.

TUTIN, Mrs Winifred Anne, (Winifred Pennington), PhD; FRS 1979; Principal Scientific Officer, Freshwater Biological Association, 1967–81, retired; *b* 8 Oct. 1915; *d* of Albert R. Pennington and Margaret S. Pennington; *m* 1942, Thomas Gaskell Tutin, *qv*; one *s* three *d*. *Educ:* Barrow-in-Furness Grammar Sch.; Reading Univ. (BSc, PhD). Research posts with Freshwater Biological Assoc., 1940–45; Demonstrator and Special Lectr, Univ. of Leicester, 1947–67; Hon. Reader in Botany, Univ. of Leicester, 1971–79, Hon. Professor, 1980–. Foreign Member, Royal Danish Academy, 1974. *Publications:* (as Winifred Pennington): The History of British Vegetation, 1969, 2nd edn 1974; (with W. H. Pearsall) The Lake District, 1973; papers in New Phytologist, Jl of Ecology, Phil. Trans of Royal Society, and others. *Recreations:* gardening, plain cooking. *Address:* Home Farm, Knighton, Leicester LE2 3WG. *T:* Leicester 707356.

TUTTLE, Sir Geoffrey (William), KBE 1957 (OBE 1940); CB 1945; DFC 1937; FRAeS 1960; Air Marshal retired; *b* 2 Oct. 1906; *s* of late Maj. E. W. Tuttle, Lowestoft. *Educ:* St Paul's School. Joined RAF, 1925; served war, 1939–45: France, Photo Reconnaissance Units, UK, Tunisia, Corsica, Sardinia, Italy, Greece; AOC RAF, Greece, 1944–46; Air Cdre 1948; Dir of Operational Requirements, Air Min., 1948–49; AOA, HQ Coastal Comd, 1950–51; Air Vice-Marshal 1952; ACAS (Operational Requirements), 1951–54; AOC No 19 Gp, RAF, 1954–56; Air Marshal 1957; DCAS, 1956–59, retd. British Aircraft Corp. Ltd, 1960–77; Aerospace Consultant, 1977–81. Order of Patriotic War, 2nd Class (Soviet), 1944; Grand Officer Royal Order of the Phœnix (Greece), 1945; Commandeur Légion d'Honneur (France); Croix de Guerre (France). *Recreation:* sailing. *Address:* 73 Numa Court, Justin Close, Brentford TW8 8QF. *T:* 01–568 1084. *Club:* Royal Air Force.

TUTU, Most Rev. Desmond Mpilo; *see* Cape Town, Archbishop of.

TUZO, Gen. Sir Harry (Craufurd), GCB 1973 (KCB 1971); OBE 1961; MC 1945; DL; *b* 26 Aug. 1917; *s* of John Atkinson Tuzo and Annie Katherine (*née* Craufurd); *m* 1943, Monica Patience Salter; one *d*. *Educ:* Wellington Coll.; Oriel Coll., Oxford (Hon. Fellow 1977). BA Oxon 1939, MA 1970. Regimental Service, Royal Artillery, 1939–45; Staff appts, Far East, 1946–49; Royal Horse Artillery, 1950–51 and 1954–58; Staff at Sch. of Infantry, 1951–53; GSO1, War Office, 1958–60; CO, 3rd Regt, RHA, 1960–62; Asst Comdt, Sandhurst, 1962–63; Comdr, 51 Gurkha Infantry Bde, 1963–65; Imp. Def. Coll., 1966; Maj.-Gen. 1966; Chief of Staff, BAOR, 1967–69; Director, RA, 1969–71; Lt-Gen. 1971; GOC and Dir of Operations, NI, 1971–73; Gen. 1973; Comdr Northern Army Gp and C-in-C BAOR, 1973–76; Dep. Supreme Allied Comdr, Europe, 1976–78. ADC (Gen.) to the Queen, 1974–77. Colonel Commandant: RA, 1971–; RHA, 1976–83; Master Gunner, St James's Park, 1977–83. Chairman: Marconi Space and Defence Systems, 1979–83; RUSI, 1980–83; Member: Council, IISS, 1978–87; Council, Inst. for Study of Conflict, 1979–. Chairman: Fermoy Centre Foundn, Kings Lynn, 1982–; Imperial War Mus. Redevelt Appeal, 1984–. Governor, Wellington Coll. DL Norfolk, 1983. Dato Setia Negeri Brunei, 1965. *Recreations:* shooting, gardening, music, theatre. *Address:* Heath Farmhouse, Fakenham, Norfolk NR21 8LZ. *Club:* Army and Navy.

See also Sir William Garthwaite, Bt.

TWEEDDALE, 13th Marquis of, *cr* 1694; **Edward Douglas John Hay;** Lord Hay of Yester, 1488; Earl of Tweeddale, 1646; Viscount Walden, Earl of Gifford, 1694; Baron Tweeddale (UK), 1881; Hereditary Chamberlain of Dunfermline; insurance intermediary; *b* 6 Aug. 1947; *s* of 12th Marquis of Tweeddale, GC, and of Sonia Mary, *d* of 1st Viscount Ingleby; *S* father, 1979. *Educ:* Milton Abbey, Blandford, Dorset; Trinity Coll., Oxford (BA Hons PPE). *Heir:* *yr* twin *b* Lord Charles David Montagu Hay, *b* 6 Aug. 1947. *Address:* House of Lords, SW1.

TWEEDIE, Jill Sheila; author, journalist, scriptwriter; *b* 1936; *d* of Patrick Graeme Tweedie, CBE and Sheila (*née* Whittall); *m* 1954, Count Bela Cziraky; one *s* one *d*; 1963, Robert d'Ancona; one *s*; *m* 1973, Alan Brien, *qv*. *Educ:* eight girls' schools, ranging from PNEU to GPDST and Switzerland. Columnist with the Guardian newspaper, 1969–; freelance writer for Press, radio and television. Woman Journalist of the Year, IPC Nat. Press Awards, 1971; Granada TV Award, 1972. *Publications:* In The Name Of Love, 1979; It's Only Me, 1980; Letters from a Faint-hearted Feminist, 1982; More from Martha, 1983; Bliss (novel), 1984; Internal Affairs (novel), 1986; contribs to various European and American anthologies. *Recreations:* getting out of London, getting back to London. *Address:* 14 Falkland Road, NW5.

TWEEDIE, Brig. John William, CBE 1958; DSO 1944; *b* 5 June 1907; *e s* of late Col William Tweedie, CMG, CBE; *m* 1937, Sheila Mary, (*d* 1984), *d* of Brig.-Gen. Thomas Hudson, CB; one *s* one *d*. *Educ:* Ampleforth; Royal Military College, Sandhurst. 2/Lt Argyll and Sutherland Highldrs, 1926; Adjutant, 1935–39; OC 2nd Bn, 1942–44; Brigade Commander, 39 Inf. Bde, 1951–54; ADC to the Queen, 1959–61; retired 1961. DL Dumfries, 1975. Croix de Guerre, 1944. *Club:* Army and Navy.

TWEEDSMUIR, 2nd Baron, *cr* 1935, of Elsfield; **John Norman Stuart Buchan,** CBE 1964 (OBE (mil.) 1945); CD 1964; FRSE; Lt-Col Canadian Infantry Corps, retired; LLD (Hon.), Aberdeen, 1949, Queen's (Canada), 1955; *b* 25 November 1911; *e s* of 1st Baron and Susan Charlotte (*d* 1977), *d* of Hon. Norman Grosvenor; *S* father, 1940; *m* 1st, 1948, Priscilla Jean Fortescue, later Baroness Tweedsmuir of Belhelvie, PC (*d* 1978); one *d*; 2nd, 1980, Jean Margherita, *widow* of Sir Francis Grant, 12th Bt. *Educ:* Eton; Brasenose Coll., Oxford (BA). Asst District Comr, Uganda Protectorate, 1934–36; joined Hudson's Bay Company, 1937; wintered in their service at Cape Dorset, Baffin Land, Canadian Arctic, 1938–39; served War of 1939–45 in Canadian Army (wounded, despatches twice, OBE (mil.) 1945, Order of Orange-Nassau, with swords); comd Hastings and Prince Edward Regt in Sicily and Italy, 1943; Hon. Col, 1955–60. Rector of Aberdeen Univ., 1948–51; Chm., Joint East and Central African Board, 1950–52; UK Delegate: UN Assembly, 1951–52; Council of Europe, 1952; Pres., Commonwealth and British Empire Chambers of Commerce, 1955–57; a Governor: Commonwealth Inst., 1958–77, Trustee, 1977–; Ditchley Foundn; Pres., Inst. of Export, 1964–67; Mem. Board, BOAC, 1955–64; Chairman: Advertising Standards Authority, 1971–74; Council on Tribunals, 1973–80. Mem., Scottish Cttee, Nature Conservancy, 1971–73. President: Institute of Rural Life at Home and Overseas, 1951–85; British Schools Exploring Society, 1964–85; Chm., British Rheumatism and Arthritis Assoc., 1971–78, Pres., 1978–86. Chancellor, Primrose League, 1969–75. FRSA. *Publications:* (part author) St Kilda papers, 1931; Hudson's Bay Trader, 1951; Always a Countryman, 1953; One Man's Happiness, 1968. *Recreations:* fishing, shooting, falconry. *Heir:* *b* Hon. William de l'Aigle Buchan, RAFVR [*b* 10 Jan. 1916; *m* 1st, Nesta (marr. diss. 1946), *o d* of Lt-Col C. D. Crozier; one *d*; 2nd, 1946, Barbara (marr. diss. 1960), 2nd *d* of E. N. Ensor, late of Hong Kong; three *s* three *d*; 3rd, 1960, Sauré Cynthia Mary, *y d* of late Major G. E. Tatchell, Royal Lincolnshire Regt; one *s*. *Educ:* Eton; New College, Oxford]. *Address:* Kingston House, Kingston Bagpuize, Oxon OX13 5AX. *T:* Longworth 820259. *Clubs:* Carlton, Travellers', Pratt's, Flyfishers'.

See also Lord James Douglas-Hamilton

TWELVETREE, Eric Alan; County Treasurer, Essex County Council, since 1974; *b* 26 Dec. 1928; *m* 1953, Patricia Mary Starkings; two *d*. *Educ:* Stamford Sch., Lincs; qualif. IPFA and ACCA. Served with Borough Councils: Gt Yarmouth, Ipswich, Stockport, Southampton; County Councils: Gloucestershire, Kent. *Address:* County Hall, Chelmsford, Essex CM1 1JZ. *T:* Chelmsford 267222.

TWIGG, Patrick Alan; QC 1986; *b* 19 May 1943; *s* of Alan Oswald Twigg and Gwendoline Mary Twigg; *m* 1974, Gabrielle Madeline Bay Green; one *s* one *d*. *Educ:* Repton Sch., Derbyshire; Universities of: The Sorbonne, Paris; Perugia, Italy; Bristol (LLB); Virginia, USA (LLM). Called to the Bar, Inner Temple, 1967; Mem., Western Circuit. Member of Lloyd's, 1984–. *Recreations:* music (particularly piano and chamber music), amateur dramatics (Mem. Old Stagers 1969–), travel, tropical climate sports. *Address:* 2 Temple Gardens, Temple, EC4Y 9AY. *T:* 01–583 6041. *Club:* Delta Theta Phi Fraternity (Charlottesville, Virginia).

TWIGGY, (Lesley Hornby); actress and singer; *b* 19 Sept. 1949; *y d* of (William) Norman Hornby and Nell (Helen) Hornby (*née* Reeman); *m* 1977, Michael Whitney Armstrong (*d* 1983); one *d*. Started modelling in London, 1966; toured USA and Canada, 1967; world's most famous model, 1966–71. *Films:* The Boy Friend, 1971; W, 1973; There Goes the Bride, 1979; Blues Brothers, 1981; The Doctor and the Devils, 1986; Club Paradise, 1986; *stage:* Cinderella, 1976; Captain Beaky, 1982; My One and Only, 1983, 1984; *television:* numerous appearances and series, UK and USA; numerous recordings. Many awards and honours including Hon. Col, Tennessee Army, 1977. *Publications:* Twiggy, 1975; An Open Look, 1985. *Recreations:* daughter Carly, music, design. *Address:* c/o Neville Shulman, Manager, 43 Welbeck Street, W1. *T:* 01–486 6363.

TWINING, Prof. William Lawrence; Quain Professor of Jurisprudence, University College London, since 1983; *b* 22 Sept. 1934; *s* of Edward Francis Twining and Helen Mary Twining (*née* Dubuisson); *m* 1957, Penelope Elizabeth Wall Morris; one *s* one *d*. *Educ:* Charterhouse School; Brasenose College, Oxford (BA 1955, MA 1960); Univ. of Chicago (JD 1958). Lectr in Private Law, Univ. of Khartoum, 1958–61; Sen. Lectr in Law, University Coll., Dar-es-Salaam, 1961–65; Prof. of Jurisprudence, The Queen's Univ., Belfast, 1965–72; Prof. of Law, Univ. of Warwick, 1972–82. Mem., Cttee on Legal Educn in N Ireland, 1972–74; President: Soc. of Public Law Teachers of Law, 1978–79; UK Assoc. for Legal and Social Philosophy, 1980–83; Chairman: Bentham Cttee, 1982–; Commonwealth Legal Educn Assoc., 1983–; vis. appts in several Univs. Hon. LLD Univ. of Victoria, BC, 1980. General Editor: Law in Context series, 1966–; Jurists series, 1979–. *Publications:* The Karl Llewellyn Papers, 1968; Karl Llewellyn and the Realist Movement, 1973; (with David Miers) How to Do Things with Rules, 1976, 2nd edn 1982; (with J. Uglow) Law Publishing and Legal Information, 1981; (ed) Facts in Law, 1983; Theories of Evidence, 1985; (ed) Legal Theory and Common Law, 1986. *Address:* 10 Mill Lane, Iffley, Oxford OX4 4EJ.

TWINN, Ian David, PhD; MP (C) Edmonton, since 1983; *b* 26 April 1950; *s* of David Twinn and Gwynneth Irene Twinn; *m* 1973, Frances Elizabeth Holtby; two *s*. *Educ:* Netherhall Secondary Modern School, Cambridge; Cambridge Grammar School; University College of Wales, Aberystwyth (BA hons); University of Reading (PhD). Senior Lecturer in Planning, Polytechnic of the South Bank, 1975–83. PPS to Minister of State for Industry, 1985–. *Publications:* papers on planning matters. *Recreations:* collecting secondhand books, renovating antique furniture. *Address:* House of Commons, SW1. *T:* 01–219 3000.

TWINN, John Ernest; consulting engineer; company director; Director General Guided Weapons and Electronics, Ministry of Defence, 1978–81, retired; *b* 11 July 1921; *s* of late Col Frank Charles George Twinn, CMG and Lilian May Twinn (*née* Tomlinson); *m* 1950, Mary Constance Smallwood; three *d*. *Educ:* Manchester Grammar Sch.; Christ's Coll., Cambridge (MA). FIEE 1981. Air Min., 1941; Telecommunications Research Estabt (later Royal Radar Estabt), 1943; Head of Guided Weapons Gp, RRE, 1965; Head of Space Dept, RAE, 1968; Head of Weapons Dept, RAE, 1972; Asst Chief Scientific Advr (Projects), MoD, 1973; Dir Underwater Weapons Projects (Naval), 1976. *Recreations:* sailing, music, genealogy. *Address:* Timbers, 9 Woodway, Merrow, Guildford, Surrey. *T:* Guildford 68993.

TWISK, Russell Godfrey; Editor, The Listener, since 1981; *b* 24 Aug. 1941; *s* of K. Y. Twisk of Twisk, Holland, and Joyce Brunning; *m* 1965, Ellen Elizabeth Banbury; two *d*. *Educ:* Salesian Coll., Farnborough. Harmsworth Press, Dep. Editor, Golf Illustrated, 1960; Sub Editor, Sphere; freelance journalist, 1962; joined BBC, editorial staff Radio Times, 1966; Deputy Editor, Radio Times, 1971; Development Manager, BBC, 1975. Has edited numerous BBC publications; Publisher, BBC Adult Literacy Project; devised Radio Times Drama Awards. Governor, London College of Printing, 1967– (Chm., 1974,

1978). *Recreations:* marathon running, map reading. *Address:* 20 Elm Grove Road, W5 3JJ. *T:* 01–567 5125.

TWISLETON-WYKEHAM-FIENNES; *see* Fiennes.

TWISLETON-WYKEHAM-FIENNES, Sir John (Saye Wingfield), KCB 1970 (CB 1953); QC 1972; First Parliamentary Counsel, 1968–72, retired; *b* 14 April 1911; *s* of Gerard Yorke Twisleton-Wykeham-Fiennes and Gwendolen (*née* Gisborne); *m* 1937, Sylvia Beatrice, *d* of Rev. C. R. L. McDowall; two *s* one *d. Educ:* Winchester; Balliol College, Oxford. Called to Bar, Middle Temple, 1936; Bencher, 1969. Joined parliamentary counsel office, 1939; Second Parly Coun., Treasury, 1956–68. Parliamentary Counsel, Malaya, 1962–63 (Colombo Plan). With Law Commission, 1965–66. Hon. JMN (Malaysia). *Address:* Mill House, Preston, Sudbury, Suffolk.

TWISS, Adm. Sir Frank (Roddam), KCB 1965 (CB 1962); KCVO 1978; DSC 1945; Gentleman Usher of the Black Rod, House of Lords, 1970–78; Serjeant-at-Arms, House of Lords, and Secretary to the Lord Great Chamberlain, 1971–78; *b* 7 July 1910; *s* of Col E. K. Twiss, DSO; *m* 1st, 1936, Prudence Dorothy Hutchison (*d* 1974); two *s* one *d*; 2nd, 1978, Rosemary Maitland (*née* Howe), *widow* of Captain Denis Chilton, RN. *Educ:* RNC Dartmouth. Cadet 1924; Midshipman 1928; Lieut 1931; Comdr 1945; Captain 1950; Rear-Adm. 1960; Vice-Adm. 1963; Adm. 1967. Naval Sec., Admty, 1960–62; Flag Officer, Flotillas, Home Fleet, 1962–64; Comdr Far East Fleet, 1965–67; Second Sea Lord and Chief of Naval Personnel, 1967–70. Mem., Commonwealth War Graves Commn, 1970–79. *Recreations:* fishing, walking. *Address:* East Marsh Farm, Bratton, near Westbury, Wilts. *Club:* Army and Navy.

TWISS, (Lionel) Peter; OBE 1957; DSC 1942 and Bar 1943; Director and General Manager, Hamble Point Marina Ltd, since 1978; formerly Chief Test Pilot of Fairey Aviation Ltd; *b* 23 July 1921; *m* 1950, Mrs Vera Maguire (marr. diss.); one *d* (and one *d* decd), one step *s* one step *d*; *m* 1960, Cherry (marr. diss.), *d* of late Sir John Huggins, GCMG, MC; one *d*; *m* 1964, Mrs Heather Danby, Titchfield; one step *s* one step *d. Educ:* Sherborne Sch. Joined Fleet Air Arm, 1939; served on catapult ships, aircraft-carriers, 1941–43; night fighter development, 1943–44; served in British Air Commn, America, 1944. Empire Test Pilots School, Boscombe Down, 1945; Test Pilot, Fairey Aviation Co. Ltd, 1946, Chief Test Pilot, 1957–60. Dir, Fairey Marine Ltd, 1968–78. Holder of World's Absolute Speed Record, 10 March 1956. *Publication:* Faster than the Sun, 1963. *Address:* Nettleworth, 33 South Street, Titchfield, Hants. *T:* 43146. *Clubs:* Royal Southern Yacht, Royal London Yacht, Island Sailing.

TWIST, Henry Aloysius, CMG 1966; OBE 1947; company director; *b* 18 June 1914; *s* of John Twist, Preston; *m* 1941, Mary Monica, *yr d* of Nicholas Mulhall, Manchester; one *s* one *d. Educ:* Liverpool Univ. (BA). Senior Classics Master, St Chad's Coll., Wolverhampton, 1936–40; Lecturer in English, South Staffordshire High School of Commerce, 1939–40. Served War of 1939–45 with RASC and RAEC, 1940–46; released with rank of Lt-Col, 1946. Principal, Dominions Office, 1946; Official Secretary, Office of the British High Commissioner in Ceylon, 1948–49; Office of the British High Commissioner in Australia, 1949–52; Commonwealth Relations Office, 1952–54; Secretariat, Commonwealth Economic Conference, London, 1952; Deputy High Commissioner for the United Kingdom in Bombay, 1954–57; Assistant Secretary, Commonwealth Relations Office, 1957–60; British Deputy High Commissioner, Kaduna, Northern Region, Federation of Nigeria, 1960–62; Commonwealth Service representative on the 1963 Course at Imperial Defence College; Commonwealth Office, 1964; Asst Under-Sec., 1966; Dep High Comr, 1966–70, Minister (Commercial), 1968–70, Rawalpindi; retired 1970. Dir of Studies, RIPA, 1973–82. *Recreation:* gardening. *Address:* Pine Lodge, Woodham Lane, Woking, Surrey. *Club:* Royal Commonwealth Society.

TWITCHETT, Prof. Denis Crispin, FBA 1967; Gordon Wu Professor of Chinese Studies, Princeton University, since 1980; *b* 23 Sept. 1925; *m* 1956, Umeko (*née* Ichikawa); two *s. Educ:* St Catharine's Coll., Cambridge. Lectr in Far-Eastern History, Univ. of London, 1954–56; Univ. Lectr in Classical Chinese, Univ. of Cambridge, 1956–60; Prof. of Chinese, SOAS, London Univ., 1960–68; Prof. of Chinese, Univ. of Cambridge, 1968–80. Vis. Prof., Princeton Univ., 1973–74, 1978–79. Principal Editor, Cambridge History of China, 1977–. *Publications:* (ed with A. F. Wright) Confucian Personalities, 1962; The Financial Administration under the T'ang dynasty, 1963, 2nd edn 1971; (ed with A. F. Wright) Perspectives on the T'ang, 1973; (ed with P. J. M. Geelan) The Times Atlas of China, 1975; (ed) Cambridge History of China, Vol. 10 1978, Vol. 3 1979, Vol. 11 1980, Vol. 12 1983, Vol. 1 1986; Vol. 13 1986; Vol. 7 1987; Printing and Publishing in Medieval China, 1983; Reader in T'ang History, 1986. *Address:* 24 Arbury Road, Cambridge; 14 College Road, Princeton, NJ 08540, USA.

TWITE, Robin, OBE 1982; Controller, Books, Libraries and Information Division, British Council, since 1984; *b* 2 May 1932; *s* of Reginald John Twite and May Elizabeth Walker; *m* 1st, 1958, Sally Randall (marr. diss.); 2nd, 1980, Sonia Yaari; one *s* three step *d. Educ:* Lawrence Sheriff School, Rugby; Balliol College, Oxford (BA History 1955). Asst Editor, Schoolmaster, weekly jl of NUT, 1956–58; British Council, 1958–73: served in Israel and London as Sec., Overseas Students Fees Awards Scheme; Sec., Open Univ. of Israel, 1973–76; British Council, 1976–: adviser on adult and further educn, 1977–79; regional rep., Calcutta, 1980–84. *Recreations:* travel, local history. *Address:* c/o Personnel Records Department, British Council, 10 Spring Gardens, SW1A 2BN.

TWYFORD, Donald Henry; Under Secretary, Export Credits Guarantee Department, since 1981, Director and Chairman of Project Group Board, since 1986; *b* 4 Feb. 1931; *s* of Henry John Twyford and Lily Hilda (*née* Ridler). *Educ:* Wembley County School. Joined Export Credits Guarantee Dept, 1949; Principal, 1965; seconded to Dept of Trade: Principal (Commercial Relations with East Europe), 1972–75; Asst Secretary (Country Policy), 1976; Establishment Officer, 1979–81; Under Secretary, Head of Services Group (internat. and country policy), ECGD, 1981–85; Hd of Project Underwriting Gp, 1985–. Chairman, European Policy Coordination Group, 1981. *Recreations:* gardening (especially growing exhibition daffodils), music, travel. *Address:* 2 Beehive Close, Ferring, Worthing, Sussex; 7 Andrewes House, Barbican, EC2Y 8AX.

TYACKE, Maj.-Gen. David Noel Hugh, CB 1970; OBE 1957; Controller, Army Benevolent Fund, 1971–80; *b* 18 Nov. 1915; *s* of Capt. Charles Noel Walker Tyacke (killed in action, March 1918) and late Phoebe Mary Cicely (*née* Coulthard), Cornwall; *m* 1940, Diana, *d* of Aubrey Hare Duke; one *s. Educ:* Malvern Coll.; RMC Sandhurst. Commissioned DCLI, 1935; India, 1936–39; France and Belgium, 1939–40; India and Burma, 1943–46; Instructor, Staff Coll., Camberley, 1950–52; CO 1st Bn DCLI, 1957–59; Comdr 130 Inf. Bde (TA), 1961–63; Dir of Administrative Planning (Army), 1963–64; Brig. Gen. Staff (Ops), Min. of Defence, 1965–66; GOC Singapore Dist., 1966–70, retired. Col, The Light Infantry, 1972–77. Mem., Malvern Coll. Council, 1978–. *Recreations:* walking, motoring, bird-watching. *Address:* c/o Lloyds Bank, Cox's & King's Branch, 6 Pall Mall, SW1.

TYDEMAN, Col Frank William Edward, CMG 1966; CIE 1945; Port Consultant; *b* 20 January 1901; *s* of Harvey James and Kate Mary Anne Tydeman; *m* 1924, Jessie Sarah Mann (*d* 1947); two *s. Educ:* London University. BSc (Eng) London 1920. Chartered Civil Engineer. FICE, FIMechE, FIStructE, FIEAust, FCIT. Served Palestine; Haifa Harbour, 1930; Jaffa Port, 1934; Singapore Harbour Board, 1937; Colonel, Deputy Director Transportation, India, Burma and Malaya, 1947; Port Consultant, Australia, to Commonwealth and WA govts and port authorities, on develt of ports of Fremantle, Bunbury, Townsville, Davenport, Mackay, Lae, Tjilatjap; retired 1965. *Recreation:* golf. *Address:* c/o ANZ Banking Group Ltd, Perth, WA 6000, Australia. *Clubs:* Naval and Military, West Australian Golf (Perth).

TYE, James; Director-General, British Safety Council, since 1968; *b* 21 Dec. 1921; *s* of late Benjamin Tye and Rose Tye, *m* 1950, Mrs Rosalie Hooker; one *s* one *d. Educ:* Upper Hornsey LCC Sch. Served War of 1939–45; RAF, 1940–46. Advertising Agent and Contractor, 1946–50; Managing Dir, 1950–62: Sky Press Ltd; Safety Publications Ltd. Joined British Safety Council as Exec. Dir, 1962. Chm., Bd of Governors, Internat. Inst. of Safety Management, 1975–. FBIM; Associate, Inst. of Occupational Safety and Health; Member: Amer. Soc. of Safety Engineers; Amer. Safety Management Soc.; Vice-Pres., Jamaica Safety Council; Fellow, Inst. of Accident Prevention, Zambia. FRSA. Freeman, City of London, 1976; Liveryman, Worshipful Co. of Basketmakers; Mem., Guild of Freemen of City of London. *Publications:* Communicating the Safety Message, 1968; Management Introduction to Total Loss Control, 1971; Safety-Uncensored (with K. Ullyett, JP), 1971; (with Bowes Egan) The Management Guide to Product Liability, 1979; *handbooks:* Industrial Safety Digest, 1953; Skilful Driving, 1952; Advanced Driving, 1954; International Nautical Safety Code (with Uffa Fox), 1961; Why Imprison Untrained Drivers?, 1980; Papers and Reports to Parly Groups and British Safety Council Members on: product liability, training safety officers, vehicle seat belts, anti-jack knife devices for articulated vehicles, lifejackets and buoyancy aids, motorway safety barriers, Britain's filthy beaches, dangers of: mini fire extinguishers, safety in fairgrounds, drip feed oil heaters, children's flammable nightwear, vehicle recall procedures, need for a nat. vehicle defects hotline, brain injuries caused by boxing and recommendations to improve the rules, pollution caused by diesel engines, safe toys, introduction of defensive driving techniques, risk management — stress at work, incr. risk of accidents thereof, use of colour in envt to promote safety and productivity, dangers of smoke masks, fire prevention — recommendations to industry. *Recreations:* squash, badminton, ski-ing, golf, sailing. *Address:* 55 Hartington Road, Chiswick, W4 3TS. *T:* 01–995 3206. *Clubs:* London Press, City Livery, Royal Automobile.

TYE, Dr Walter, CBE 1966; CEng; *b* 12 Dec. 1912; *s* of Walter and Alice Tye; *m* 1939, Eileen Mary Whitmore; one *s* one *d. Educ:* Woodbridge Sch.; London Univ. (BScEng). Fairey Aviation Co., 1934; RAE, 1935–38; Air Registration Bd, 1938–39; RAE, 1939–44; Air Registration Bd, 1944–72 (Chief Techn. Officer, 1946, Chief Exec., 1969); Mem., CAA (Controller Safety), 1972–74. Hon. FRAeS; Hon. DSc Cranfield Inst. of Technology, 1972. *Publications:* articles, lectures and contrib. Jl RAeS. *Address:* 12 Bramble Rise, Cobham, Surrey. *T:* Cobham 63692.

TYLECOTE, Dame Mabel, DBE 1966; Hon. Life Member of National Federation of Community Associations since 1979 (President, 1958–61; Vice-President, 1961–79); *b* 4 Feb. 1896; *d* of late John Ernest Phythian and Ada Prichard Phythian (*née* Crompton); *m* 1932, Frank Edward Tylecote (*d* 1965); one *s* (and one step *s* one step *d*). *Educ:* Univ. of Manchester; Univ. of Wisconsin (USA). BA, PhD (Manchester). Lectr in History, Huddersfield Techn. Coll., 1920–24; Asst Lectr in History, Univ. of Manchester, 1926–30; Warden of Elvington Settlement, 1930–32; part-time Lectr, Univ. of Manchester Joint Cttee for Adult Educn, 1935–51; Vice-Pres., WEA, 1960–68. Member: Pensions Appeal Tribunal, 1944–50; Manchester City Council, 1940–51; (co-opted) Manchester Educn Cttee, 1951–77; Stockport Borough Council, 1956–63; Chm. of Council, Assoc. of Art Instns, 1960–61. Mem. Court, 1945–80, Mem. Council, 1960–75, Univ. of Manchester; Mem. Court, UMIST, 1960–77; Governor, Manchester Polytechnic, 1969–77 (Hon. Fellow, 1973); Vice-President: Manchester and Salford Council of Social Service, 1968–; Union of Lancashire and Cheshire Institutes, 1969–75; Hon. Life Mem., Nat. Inst. of Adult Educn, 1974– (Chm., 1960–63). Contested (Lab): Fylde, 1938; Middleton and Prestwich, 1945; Norwich South, 1950, 1951, 1955. Hon. LLD Manchester, 1978. *Publications:* The Education of Women at Manchester University 1883–1933, 1941; The Mechanics' Institutes of Lancashire and Yorkshire before 1851, 1957; The Future of Adult Education (Fabian pamphlet), 1960; contrib., Artisan to Graduate, ed D. S. L. Cardwell, 1974; The Work of Lady Simon of Wythenshawe for Education in Manchester (address), 1974; articles in various social and educnl jls. *Address:* Alexandra House, 359 Wilbraham Road, Manchester M16 8NP. *T:* 061–860 5400.

TYLER, Brig. Arthur Catchmay, CBE 1960; MC 1945; DL; a Military Knight of Windsor, since 1978; *b* 20 Aug. 1913; 4th *s* of Hugh Griffin Tyler and Muriel Tyler (*née* Barnes); *m* 1938, Sheila, *d* of James Kinloch, Meigle, Perthshire; three *s* one *d. Educ:* Allhallows Sch.; RMC, Sandhurst. Commissioned, The Welch Regt, 1933. Served War of 1939–45: Africa, India and Burma (despatches). Staff Coll., 1946; JSSC, 1951; Sec., BJSM, Washington, 1952–54; Bt Lt-Col, 1953; Comd 4th (Carms) Bn The Welch Regt, 1954–57; Col, 1957; AAG, War Office, 1957–60; Brig. 1960; Senior UK Liaison Officer and Military Adviser to High Commissioner, Canada, 1960–63; Asst Chief of Staff (Ops and Plans), Allied Forces Central Europe, 1963–65. Sec., Council, TA&VR Assocs, 1967–72. Hon. Col., 7th(V) Bn, The Queen's Regt, T&AVR, 1971–75. Governor, Allhallows Sch., 1968, Chm., 1977–80. DL Surrey, 1968. *Address:* 19 Lower Ward, Windsor Castle, Berks.

TYLER, Cyril, DSc, PhD, FRSC; Professor of Physiology and Biochemistry, University of Reading, 1958–76, now Emeritus; Deputy Vice-Chancellor, 1968–76; *b* 26 Jan. 1911; *er s* of John and Annie Tyler; *m* 1st, 1939, Myra Eileen (*d* 1971), *d* of George and Rosa Batten; two *s* one *d*; 2nd, 1971, Rita Patricia, *d* of Sidney and Lilian Jones. *Educ:* Ossett Grammar Sch.; Univ. of Leeds. BSc 1st Class Hons 1933, PhD 1935, DSc 1959, Leeds. Lectr in Agricultural Chemistry. RAC, Cirencester, 1935–39; Univ. of Reading: Lecturer in Agricultural Chemistry, 1939–47; Professor, 1947–58; Dean of the Faculty of Agriculture, 1959–62. Playing Mem., Glos CCC, 1936–39. *Publications:* Organic Chemistry for Students of Agriculture, 1946; Animal Nutrition (2nd edn), 1964; Wilhelm von Nathusius 1821–1899 on Avian Eggshells, 1964; numerous papers on poultry metabolism and egg shells in scientific journals. *Recreations:* gardening, history of animal nutrition. *Address:* 22 Belle Avenue, Reading, Berks RG6 2BL.

TYLER, Ven. Leonard George; Rector of Easthampstead, 1973–85; *b* 15 April 1920; *s* of Hugh Horstead Tyler and Mabel Adam Stewart Tyler; *m* 1946, Sylvia May Wilson; one *s* two *d. Educ:* Darwen Grammar School; Liverpool University; Christ's College, Cambridge; Westcott House. Chaplain, Trinity College, Kandy, Ceylon, 1946–48; Principal, Diocesan Divinity School, Colombo, Ceylon, 1948–50; Rector, Christ Church, Bradford, Manchester, 1950–55; Vicar of Leigh, Lancs, 1955–66 (Rural Dean, 1955–62); Chaplain, Leigh Infirmary, 1955–66; Archdeacon of Rochdale, 1962–66; Principal, William Temple College, Manchester, 1966–73. Anglican Adviser to ABC Television, 1958–68. *Publications:* contributor to Theology. *Address:* 11 Ashton Place, Kintbury, Newbury, Berks RG15 0XS. *T:* Kintbury 58510.

TYLER, Maj.-Gen. Sir Leslie (Norman), KBE 1961 (OBE 1942); CB 1955; BScEng; CEng; FIMechE; *b* 26 April 1904; *s* of late Major Norman Tyler, Addiscombe, Surrey; *m* 1st, 1930, Louie Teresa Franklin (*d* 1950); one *s* one *d*; 2nd, 1953, Sheila, *widow* of Maj.-Gen. L. H. Cox, CB, CBE, MC; two *s* two step *d*. *Educ:* Diocesan Coll., Rondebosch, SA; RN Colleges Osborne and Dartmouth; King's College, Univ. of London. Commissioned Lieut, RAOC, 1927; served War of 1939–45, Malta and NW Europe; transferred to REME, 1942; DDME, Second Army, 1945; Comdt REME Training Centre, 1945–47; AAG, War Office, 1948–49; DME, MELF, 1949–50; DDME, War Office, 1950–53; DME, MELF, 1953–55; Commandant, Headquarters Base Workshop Group, REME, 1956–57; Director of Electrical and Mechanical Engineering, War Office, 1957–60; retd 1960. Regional Dir, MPBW, Central Mediterranean Region, 1963–69. Chm., Royal Hosp. and Home for Incurables, Putney, 1971–76. Colonel Commandant, REME, 1962–67. Freeman, City of London; Liveryman, 1961, Master, 1982–83, Worshipful Company of Turners. FKC 1969. FRSA 1984. *Address:* 51 Chiltley Way, Liphook, Hants GU30 7HE. *T:* Liphook 722335. *Club:* Army and Navy.

TYLER, Paul Archer, CBE 1985; politician and public affairs consultant; Chairman, GR Public Affairs Ltd, since 1986 (Chief Executive, 1984–86); Director, Good Relations Group plc, since 1985; Chairman, National Executive Committee, Liberal Party, since 1983; *b* 29 Oct. 1941; *s* of Oliver Walter Tyler and Ursula Grace Gibbons Tyler (*née* May); *m* 1970, Nicola Mary Ingram; one *s* one *d*. *Educ:* Mount House Sch., Tavistock; Sherborne Sch.; Exeter Coll., Oxford (MA). Pres., Oxford Univ. Liberal Club, 1962. Royal Inst. of British Architects: Admin. Asst, 1966; Asst Sec., 1967; Dep. Dir Public Affairs, 1971; Dir Public Affairs, 1972. Man. Dir, Cornwall Courier newspaper gp, 1976–81; Exec. Dir, Public Affairs Div., Good Relations plc, 1982–84. County Councillor, Devon, 1964–70; Mem., Devon and Cornwall Police Authority, 1965–70; Vice-Chm., Dartmoor Nat. Park Cttee, 1965–70; Chm., CPRE Working Party on the Future of the Village, 1974–81; Mem. Bd of Shelter (Nat. Campaign for the Homeless), and rep. in Devon and Cornwall, 1975–76. Sec., L/SDP Jt Commn on Employment and Industrial Recovery, 1981–82. Chm., Devon and Cornwall Region Liberal Party, 1981–82. Contested (L): Totnes, 1966; Bodmin, 1970, 1979; Beaconsfield, 1982; MP (L) Bodmin, Feb.-Sept. 1974; Parly Liberal Spokesman on Housing and Transport, 1974; Parly Adviser to RIBA, 1974. *Publication:* A New Deal for Rural Britain (jtly), 1978. *Recreations:* sailing, gardening, walking. *Address:* Tregrove House, Rilla Mill, Callington, Cornwall. *Clubs:* National Liberal; Liskeard Liberal (Cornwall); Saltash Sailing.

TYMMS, Sir Frederick, KCIE 1947 (CIE 1935); Kt 1941; MC; FRAeS; *b* 4 Aug. 1889; *s* of William Henry Tymms. *Educ:* Tenby; King's College, London. War Service: 4th Bn South Lancs Regt and Royal Flying Corps, France; British Aviation Mission to the USA, 1915–18 (MC, Chevalier de l'Ordre de la Couronne, Croix de Guerre, Belgium). Civil Aviation Dept, Air Min., 1920–27; Oxford Univ. Arctic Expedition to Spitsbergen, 1924; Air Min. Supt of Egypt-India air route, 1927; seconded to Govts of the Sudan, Kenya, Uganda and Tanganyika, 1928; Chief Technical Asst to Dir of Civil Aviation, Air Min., 1928–31; Air Min. Representative on the Commn to Africa, to organise the Cape to Cairo air route, 1929–30; Dir of Civil Aviation in India, 1931–42 and 1943–45; Man. Dir, Tata Aircraft Ltd, Bombay, 1942–43; Dir-Gen. of Civil Aviation in India, Sept. 1945–March 1947; UK Representative on Council of Internat. Civil Aviation Organisation, Montreal, 1947–54; retd from Civil Service, 1955. Govt of India delegate to Internat. Civil Aviation Conf., Chicago, 1944; Leader of UK Civil Aviation Mission to New Zealand, 1948. Master of Guild of Air Pilots and Air Navigators, 1957–58. Chm., Commn of Enquiry on Civil Aviation in West Indies, 1960. *Address:* Clare Park, Crondall, near Farnham, Surrey; c/o Lloyds Bank, Pall Mall, SW1. *Club:* Naval and Military.

TYMMS, Prof. Ralph Vincent, MA; Professor of German Language and Literature in the University of London (Royal Holloway College), 1956–80, now Emeritus; Head of German Department 1948–80, Vice-Principal 1969–75, Royal Holloway College; *b* 9 Jan. 1913; *s* of Arthur Hugh Tymms and Janet Scott Coventon; *m* 1980, Dr Marion Gibbs. *Educ:* Bradford Grammar Sch., Yorkshire; Magdalen Coll., Oxford; Univs of Vienna and Giessen. John Doncaster Scholar in German, Magdalen Coll., Oxford, 1931–34; 1st Class Hons, Oxford, 1934. Asst Lectr in German, Univ. of Manchester, 1936. Intelligence Corps, 1941–45; Major, 1945. Lecturer in German, Manchester Univ., 1945; Reader in German Language and Literature in Univ. of London, 1948. *Publications:* Doubles in Literary Psychology, 1949; German Romantic Literature, 1955. *Address:* Merrow Down, Northcroft Road, Englefield Green, Egham, Surrey TW20 0DU. *T:* Egham 32125.

TYNAN, Prof. Michael John, MD, FRCP; Professor of Paediatric Cardiology, Guy's Hospital, since 1982; *b* 18 April 1934; *s* of Jerry Joseph Tynan and Florence Ann Tynan; *m* 1958, Eirlys Pugh Williams. *Educ:* Bedford Modern School; London Hospital. MD, BS. Senior Asst Resident, Children's Hosp., Boston, Mass, 1962; Registrar, Westminster Hosp., 1964; Registrar, later Lectr, Hosp. for Sick Children, Great Ormond St, 1966; consultant paediatric cardiologist, Newcastle Univ. Hospitals, 1971, Guy's Hosp., 1977. *Publications:* (jtly) Paediatric Cardiology, vol. 5, 1983; articles on nomenclature and classification of congenital heart disease and on heart disease in children. *Recreations:* singing, watching cricket, playing snooker. *Address:* 5 Ravensdon Street, SE11 4AQ. *T:* 01–735 7119.

TYNDALE-BISCOE, Rear-Adm. Alec Julian, CB 1959; OBE 1946; lately Chairman of Blaw Knox Ltd; *b* 10 Aug. 1906; *s* of late Lt-Col A. A. T. Tyndale-Biscoe, Aubrey House, Keyhaven, Lymington, Hants; *m* 1st, 1939, Emma Winifred Haselden (*d* 1974); four *d*; 2nd, 1974, Hugolyne Cotton Cooke, *widow* of Captain Geoffrey Cotton Cooke. *Educ:* RN Colleges Osborne and Dartmouth. Entered RN, 1920. Served War, 1939–46; HMS Vanguard, 1947–49; Captain, 1949; Asst Engineer-in-Chief, Fleet, 1950–53; Comdg RN Air Station, Anthorn, 1953–55; Fleet Engr Officer, Mediterranean, 1955–57; Rear-Adm. 1957; Flag-Officer Reserve Aircraft, 1957–59, retired. *Address:* Bunces Farm Gardens, Birch Grove, Haywards Heath, West Sussex.

TYNDALL, Nicholas John; Chief Officer, National Marriage Guidance Council, 1968–86; *b* 15 Aug. 1928; *s* of Rev. Edward Denis Tyndall and Nora Mildred Tyndall; *m* 1953, Elizabeth Mary (*née* Ballard); two *s* two *d*. *Educ:* Marlborough College; Jesus College, Cambridge. BA. HM Prison and Borstal Service, 1952–68; Dir, Council of Europe Co-ordinated Research Fellowship on Marriage Guidance and Family Counselling, 1973–75; Mem., Home Office/DHSS Working Party on Marriage Guidance, 1976–78; Chairman: British Assoc. for Counselling, 1976–78; Marriage and Marriage Guidance Commn of Internat. Union of Family Organisations, 1971–. Mem., Gen. Synod of Church of England, 1981–. *Publication:* Prison People, 1968. *Recreations:* folk dancing, children. *Address:* 22 Hillmorton Road, Rugby, Warwicks. *T:* Rugby 71942.

See also Rev. T. Tyndall.

TYNDALL, Rev. Canon Timothy; Chief Secretary, Advisory Council for the Church's Ministry, since 1985; *b* 24 April 1925; *s* of Rev. Denis Tyndall and Nora Tyndall; *m* 1953, Dr Ruth Mary Turner; two *s* twin *d*. *Educ:* Jesus Coll., Cambridge (BA). Parish Incumbent: Newark, 1955; Nottingham, 1960; Sunderland, 1975. *Address:* ACCM, Church House, Dean's Yard, Westminster, SW1P 3NZ. *T:* 01–222 9011.

See also N. J. Tyndall.

TYREE, Sir (Alfred) William, Kt 1975; OBE 1971; engineer and pastoralist; Chairman and Founder A. W. Tyree Foundation (incorporating Medicheck Referral Centre, Tyree Chair of Electrical Engineering, University of New South Wales, Chair of Otolaryngology (ENT), University of Sydney); *b* 4 Nov. 1921; *m* 1946, Joyce, *d* of F. Lyndon; two *s* one *d*. *Educ:* Auckland Grammar Sch.; Sydney Technical Coll. FIE(Aust). Founder: Tyree Industries Ltd; Westralian Transformers and subsids; Chairman: Tycan Australia Pty Ltd; Tyree Hldgs Pty Ltd; C. P. R. Constructions Pty Ltd; Tyronsea Plastics Pty Ltd; A. W. Tyree Transformers Pty Ltd; Technical Components Pty Ltd. Hon. Fellow, Univ. of Sydney, 1985. Hon. Life Governor, Aust. Postgrad. Fedn in Medicine, 1985. *Recreations:* ski-ing, private flying, water ski-ing, yachting, tennis, music, golf, sail board riding. *Address:* 60 Martin Place, Sydney, NSW 2000, Australia. *Clubs:* Royal Aero, American National, Royal Automobile (NSW); Royal Prince Alfred Yacht, Royal Motor Yacht, Cruising Yacht, Kosciusko Alpine, Australian Alpine, RAC, Australian Golf.

TYRELL-KENYON; *see* Kenyon.

TYRER, Christopher John Meese; a Recorder of the Crown Court, since 1983; *b* 22 May 1944; *s* of Jack Meese Tyrer and Margaret Joan Tyrer (*née* Wyatt); *m* 1974, Jane Beckett, JP, LLB, barrister; one *s* one *d*. *Educ:* Wellington College; Bristol University. LLB hons. Called to the Bar, Inner Temple, 1968. Governor, St John's Sch., Lacey Green, 1984–. *Recreations:* music, growing fuchsias, photography. *Address:* Randalls Cottage, Loosley Row, Princes Risborough, Bucks. *T:* Princes Risborough 4650; (chambers) Devereux Chambers, Devereux Court, WC2R 3JJ. *T:* 01–353 7534.

TYRONE, Earl of; Henry Nicholas de la Poer Beresford; *b* 23 March 1958; *s* and *heir* of 8th Marquess of Waterford, *qv*. *Educ:* Harrow School.

TYRRELL, Alan Rupert, QC 1976; a Recorder of the Crown Court, since 1972; Barrister-at-Law; *b* 27 June 1933; *s* of Rev. T. G. R. Tyrrell, and Mrs W. A. Tyrrell, MSc; *m* 1960, Elaine Eleanor Ware, LLB; one *s* one *d*. *Educ:* Bridport Grammar Sch.; London Univ. (LLB). Called to the Bar, Gray's Inn, 1956; Chm. of the Bar Eur. Gp, 1986–. Chm. London Reg., and Mem. Nat. Exec., Nat. Fedn of Self-Employed, 1978–79. Mem. (C) London E, European Parlt, 1979–84; contested same seat, 1984. *Publications:* (ed) Moore's Practical Agreements, 10th edn 1965; Students' Guide to Europe, 1984. *Recreations:* bridge, budgerigars. *Address:* 15 Willifield Way, Hampstead Garden Suburb, NW11. *T:* 01–455 5798; Francis Taylor Building, Temple, EC4. *T:* 01–353 2182; 42 rue du Taciturne, 1040 Brussels, Belgium. *T:* Brussels 2305059. *Clubs:* Hampshire (Winchester); Exeter and County (Exeter).

TYRRELL, Dr David Arthur John, CBE 1980; FRCP; FRS 1970; Director, MRC Common Cold Unit, since 1983; *b* 19 June 1925; *s* of Sidney Charles Tyrrell and Agnes Kate (*née* Blewett); *m* 1950, Betty Moyra Wylie; two *d* (one *s* decd). *Educ:* Sheffield University. Junior hosp. appts, Sheffield, 1948–51; Asst, Rockefeller Inst., New York, 1951–54; Virus Research Lab., Sheffield, 1954–57; MRC Common Cold Unit, Salisbury, 1957–; Dep. Dir of Clin. Res. Centre, Northwick Park, Harrow, and Head of Div. of Communicable Diseases, 1970–84. First Chm., Adv. Cttee on Dangerous Pathogens, 1981–. Managing Trustee, Nuffield Foundn, 1977–. Sir Arthur Sims Commonwealth Travelling Prof., 1985. Hon. DSc Sheffield, 1979. Stewart Prize, BMA, 1977; Ambuj Nath Bose Prize, RCP, 1983. *Publications:* Common Colds and Related Diseases, 1965; Interferon and its Clinical Potential, 1976; (jtly) Microbial Diseases, 1979; The Abolition of Infection: hope or illusion?, 1982; numerous papers on infectious diseases and viruses. *Recreations:* music-making, gardening, sailing, walking; various Christian organizations. *Address:* MRC Common Cold Unit, Coombe Road, Salisbury, Wilts SP2 8BW; Ash Lodge, Dean Lane, Whiteparish, Salisbury, Wilts SP5 2RN.

TYRRELL, Gerald Fraser; former Buyer, Stewart Dry Goods Co., Louisville, USA, and London; retired 1974; *b* London, 7 March 1907; *s* of late Lt-Col G. E. Tyrrell, DSO, RA, and C. R. Tyrrell (*née* Fraser); *m* 1937, Virginia Lee Gettys, Louisville, Kentucky; three *s* one *d*. *Educ:* Eton; Magdalene Coll., Cambridge. Student Interpreter, China Consular Service, 1930; served in Tientsin, Chungking, Shanghai, Foochow, Canton; Vice-Consul at San Francisco, 1941; Vice-Consul, Boston, 1942, Acting Consul-General, 1944; 1st Secretary, Washington, 1945; Consul at Cincinnati, 1946; Acting Consul-General, New Orleans, 1947; Consul-General, Canton, 1948; Foreign Office, 1949, resigned, 1950. *Address:* 2333 Glenmary Avenue, Louisville, Kentucky 40204, USA.

TYRRELL, Prof. (Henry John) Valentine, FRSC; Vice-Principal, King's College London (KQC), 1985–Sept. 1987; *b* 14 Feb. 1920; *s* of John Rice Tyrrell and Josephine (*née* McGuinness); *m* 1st, 1947, Sheila Mabel (*née* Straw) (*d* 1985); three *s* three *d*; 2nd, 1986, Dr Bethan Davies. *Educ:* state schools; Jesus Coll., Oxford. DSc. Chemical Industry, 1942–47; Sheffield Univ., 1947–65; Chelsea College: Professor of Physical and Inorganic Chemistry, 1965–84; Head of Dept, 1972–82; Vice-Principal, 1976–84; Principal, 1984–85. Sec. and Vice-Pres., Royal Instn of GB, 1978–84. *Publications:* Diffusion and Heat Flow in Liquids, 1961; Thermometric Titrimetry, 1968; Diffusion in Liquids, 1984; papers in chemical and physical jls. *Recreations:* foreign travel, gardening. *Address:* Fair Oaks, Coombe Hill Road, Kingston-on-Thames KT2 7DU. *Clubs:* Athenæum, Royal Institution.

TYRRELL, Sir Murray (Louis), KCVO 1968 (CVO 1954); CBE 1959; JP; Official Secretary to Governor-General of Australia, 1947–73; *b* 1 Dec. 1913; *s* of late Thomas Michael and Florence Evelyn Tyrrell; *m* 1939, Ellen St Clair, *d* of late E. W. St Clair Greig; one *s* two *d*. *Educ:* Orbost and Melbourne Boys' High Schools, Victoria. Central Office, Postmaster General's Department, Melbourne, 1929–39; Asst Private Secretary to Minister for Air and Civil Aviation, 1940; Private Secretary to Minister for Air, 1940, to Minister for Munitions, 1940; Personal Asst to Secretary, Min. of Munitions, 1942; Private Secretary: Commonwealth Treas. and Min. for Post-War Reconstruction, 1943, to Prime Minister and Treasurer, 1945; Official Secretary and Comptroller to Governor-General, 1947; resigned Comptrollership, 1953. Attached Royal Household, Buckingham Palace, May-Aug. 1962. Director: Nat. Heart Foundn of Australia, 1970–; Canberra C of E Girls' Grammar Sch., 1952–65; Canberra Grammar Sch., 1954–65; Registrar, Order of St John of Jerusalem in Australia, 1976–; Mem., Buildings and Grounds Cttee, ANU, 1974–. Alderman, Queanbeyan CC, 1974; Mem., Southern Tablelands CC, 1974. CStJ 1969. Australian of the Year, 1977. *Recreation:* fishing. *Address:* 11 Blundell Street, Queanbeyan, NSW 2620, Australia.

TYRRELL, Valentine; *see* Tyrrell, H. J. V.

TYRWHITT, Brig. Dame Mary (Joan Caroline), DBE 1949 (OBE 1946); TD; *b* 27 Dec. 1903; *d* of Admiral of the Fleet Sir Reginald Tyrwhitt, 1st Bt, GCB, DSO; unmarried. Senior Controller, 1946 (rank altered to Brigadier, 1950); Director, ATS, 1946–49, Women's Royal Army Corps, 1949–50, retired Dec. 1950; Hon. ADC to the King, 1949–50. *Address:* 14 Manor Court, Pewsey, Wilts.

TYRWHITT, Sir Reginald (Thomas Newman), 3rd Bt, *cr* 1919; company director; *b* 21 Feb. 1947; *er s* of Admiral Sir St John Tyrwhitt, 2nd Bt, KCB, DSO, DSC and Bar (*d* 1961), and of Nancy (Veronica) Gilbey (who *m* 1965, Sir Godfrey Agnew, *qv*); *S* father, 1961; *m* 1972, Sheila Gail (marr. diss. 1980), *d* of William Alistair Crawford Nicoll, Liphook, Hants; *m* 1984, Charlotte, *o d* of Captain and Hon. Mrs Angus Hildyard, The White Hall, Winestead, Kingston-upon-Hull. *Educ:* Downside. 2nd Lieut, RA, 1966, Lieut 1969; RARO 1969. *Recreations:* shooting, fishing, drawing. *Heir: b* John (Edward Charles) Tyrwhitt [*b* 27 July 1953; *m* 1978, Melinda Ngaire, *o d* of Anthony Philip Towell, MC, Long Island, NY, USA; three *s*]. *Address:* c/o Lloyds Bank, Ascot, Berks SL5 7JE.
    See also Dame Mary Tyrwhitt.

TYSON, Dr Alan Walker, FBA 1978; musicologist and psychoanalyst; Fellow of All Souls College, Oxford, since 1952, Senior Research Fellow, since 1971; *b* 27 Oct. 1926; *e s* of Henry Alan Maurice Tyson and Dorothy (*née* Walker). *Educ:* Rugby School; Magdalen College, Oxford; University College Hospital Medical School, London. BA 1951, MA 1952; MB, BS 1965; MRCPsych 1972. Vis. Lectr in Psychiatry, Montefiore Hosp., NY, 1967–68; Lectr in Psychopathology and Developmental Psychology, Oxford Univ., 1968–70. Vis. Prof. of Music, Columbia Univ., 1969; James P. R. Lyell Reader in Bibliography, Oxford Univ., 1973–74; Ernest Bloch Prof. of Music, Univ. of California at Berkeley, 1977–78; Mem., Inst. for Advanced Study, Princeton, 1983–84; Vis. Prof. of Music, Graduate Center, City Univ. of New York, 1985. Assoc. Mem., British Psychoanalytical Soc., 1957–. On editorial staff, Standard Edition of Freud's Works, 1952–74. *Publications:* The Authentic English Editions of Beethoven, 1963; (with O. W. Neighbour) English Music Publishers' Plate Numbers, 1965; (ed) Selected letters of Beethoven, 1967; Thematic Catalogue of the Works of Muzio Clementi, 1967; (ed) Beethoven Studies, Vol. 1, 1973, Vol. 2, 1977, Vol. 3, 1982; (with D. Johnson and R. Winter) The Beethoven Sketchbooks, 1985. *Address:* 7 Southcote Road, N19 5BJ. *T:* 01–609 2981.

TYSON, Monica Elizabeth; Editor, A La Carte, since 1986; *b* 7 June 1927; *d* of F. S. Hill and E. Hill; *m* R. E. D. Tyson; one *d*. *Educ:* George Watson's Ladies Coll.; Edinburgh Coll. of Domestic Science (Dip. in Dom. Sci.). Asst Home Editor, Modern Woman, 1958–60; Ideal Home: Domestic Planning Editor, 1960–64; Asst Editor, 1964–68; Editor, 1968–77; Editor: Woman's Realm, 1977–82; Special Assignments, IPC Magazines, 1982–84; Mother, 1984–86. *Recreations:* walking, reading, cooking. *Address:* 12 Warwick Square, SW1V 2AA.

TYTLER, Christian Helen F.; *see* Fraser-Tytler.

TYTLER, Rt. Rev. Donald Alexander; *see* Middleton, Bishop Suffragan of.

TYZACK, Margaret Maud, OBE 1970; *b* 9 Sept. 1931; *d* of Thomas Edward Tyzack and Doris Moseley; *m* 1958, Alan Stephenson; one *s*. *Educ:* St Angela's Ursuline Convent; Royal Academy of Dramatic Art. Trained at RADA (Gilbert Prize for Comedy). First engagement, Civic Theatre, Chesterfield. Vassilissa in The Lower Depths, Royal Shakespeare Co., Arts Theatre, 1962; Lady MacBeth, Nottingham, 1962; Miss Frost in The Ginger Man, Royal Court Theatre, London, 1964; Madame Ranevsky in The Cherry Orchard, Exeter and Tour, 1969; Jacqui in Find Your Way Home, Open Space Theatre, London, 1970; Queen Elizabeth in Vivat! Vivat Regina!, Piccadilly, 1971; Tamora in Titus Andronicus, Portia in Julius Caesar and Volumnia in Coriolanus, Royal Shakespeare Co., Stratford-on-Avon, 1972; Portia in Julius Caesar, and Volumnia in Coriolanus, RSC, Aldwych, 1973; Maria Lvovna in Summerfolk, RSC, Aldwych, and NY, 1974–75; Richard III, All's Well That Ends Well, Ghosts, Stratford, Ont., 1977; People Are Living There, Manchester Royal Exchange, 1979; Martha, in Who's Afraid of Virginia Woolf?, Nat. Theatre, 1981 (SWET Best Actress in a Revival Award); Countess of Rossilion, in All's Well That Ends Well, RSC Barbican and NY (Tony Nomination), 1983; An Inspector Calls, Greenwich Theatre, 1983; Tom and Viv, Royal Court, 1984, also New York; Mornings at Seven, Westminster, 1984. *Films:* Ring of Spies, 2001: A Space Odyssey, The Whisperers, A Clockwork Orange, The Legacy. *Television series include:* The Forsyte Saga; The First Churchills; Cousin Bette, 1970–71; I, Claudius, 1976; Quatermass, 1979; A Winter's Tale. Actress of the Year Award (BAFTA) for Queen Anne in The First Churchills, 1969. *Address:* c/o Representation Joyce Edwards, 275 Kennington Road, SE11 6BY. *T:* 01–735 5736.

U

UATIOA, Dame Mere, DBE 1978; *b* 19 Jan. 1924; *d* of Aberam Takenibeia and Bereti Bamatang; *m* 1950, Reuben K. Uatioa, MBE (*d* 1977); three *s* one *d*. *Educ:* Hiram Bingham High School, Beru Island. Widow of Reuben K. Uatioa, MBE, a leading Gilbertese nationalist and former Speaker, House of Assembly, Gilbert Islands; supported her husband throughout his long public service, demonstrating those qualities of wife and mother which are most admired in the Pacific. After his death, she devoted herself to her family. *Recreations:* social and voluntary work for Churches. *Address:* Erik House, Antebuka, Tarawa, Gilbert Islands.

UBBELOHDE, Prof. Alfred R. J. P., CBE 1963; MA, DSc Oxon; FRS 1951; FRSC; FInstP; FEng; FIChemE; Hon. Laureate, Padua University, 1963; Senior Research Fellow, since 1975, Fellow, since 1981, Imperial College of Science and Technology; Professor of Thermodynamics, University of London (Imperial College), 1954–75, now Emeritus, and Head of Department of Chemical Engineering and Chemical Technology, 1961–75; *b* 14 Dec. 1907; 3rd *s* of F. C. Ubbelohde and Angele Verspreeuwen; unmarried. *Educ:* St Paul's Sch.; Christ Church, Oxford (Hon. Student, 1979). Dewar Fellow of Royal Instn, 1935–40; research on explosives; Min. of Supply, 1940–45; Prof. of Chemistry, Queen's Univ., Belfast, 1945–54, Dean of the Faculty of Science, 1947–51. Chairman Fire Research Board, 1956–61; President of Council Institut Solvay, 1957–64, 1965–; Director of Salters' Institute, 1959–75; Past President, Faraday Society, 1963–; Past Vice-President, Society of Chemical Industry; Chairman, Science and Engineering Panel, British Council, 1964; Member: Agricl Research Council, 1966–76; Pontifical Academy of Sciences, 1968–. Hon. FCGI. Dr *hc* Faculty of Science, Univ. Libre, Brussels, 1962; Hon. DSc: QUB, 1972; Nancy Univ., 1982. Alfred Egerton Medal, 1970; Messel Medal, 1972; George Skakel Award, 1975; Paul Lebeau Medal, 1975. *Publications:* Modern Thermodynamical Principles, 1937 (2nd edn 1952); Time and Thermodynamics, 1947; Man and Energy, 1954, 2nd edn 1963; Graphite and its crystal compounds, 1960; Melting and Crystal Structure, 1965; The Molten State of Matter, 1978; papers in Proceedings and Journals of scientific societies. *Address:* Imperial College, South Kensington, SW7; Platts Farm, Burwash, Sussex. *Clubs:* Athenæum, Royal Automobile.

UBEE, Air Vice-Marshal Sydney Richard, CB 1952; AFC 1939; Royal Air Force; retired as Air Officer Commanding, No 2 Group, 2nd Tactical Air Force, Germany (1955–58); *b* 5 March 1903; *s* of late Edward Joseph Ubee, London; *m* 1942, Marjorie Doris (*d* 1954), *d* of George Clement-Parker, Newport, Mon; two step *s*. *Educ:* Beaufoy Technical Institute. Joined RAF, 1927, with short service commission; permanent commission, 1932; test pilot, Royal Aircraft Establishment, Farnborough, 1933–37; served in India, Iraq, Iran, Burma, and Ceylon, 1937–43; Airborne Forces Experimental Establishment, 1943–45; Comdg Officer, Experimental Flying, RAE Farnborough, 1946–47; Commandant Empire Test Pilots' Sch., Cranfield, Bucks, and Farnborough, 1947–48; Deputy Director Operational Requirements, Air Min., 1948–51; Commandant RAF Flying Coll., Manby, 1951–54; Director-General of Personnel (II), Air Ministry, 1954–55. *Address:* Harwood Lodge, 100 Lodge Hill Road, Lower Bourne, Farnham, Surrey GU10 3RD. *Club:* Royal Air Force.

UDOMA, Hon. Sir (Egbert) Udo, CFR 1978; Kt 1964; Justice, Supreme Court of Nigeria, Lagos, 1969–82, retired; Commissioner for Law Reform, Cross River State, Nigeria, since 1985; *b* 21 June 1917; *s* of Chief Udoma Inam of Ibekwe Ntanaran Akama of Opobo, Nigeria; *m* 1950, Grace Bassey; six *s* one *d*. *Educ:* Methodist Coll., Uzuakoli, Nigeria; Trinity Coll., Dublin; St Catherine's Coll., Oxford. BA 1942; LLB 1942; PhD 1944; MA 1945. President, Dublin Univ. Philosophical Society, 1942–43. Called to Bar, Gray's Inn, 1945; practised as Barrister-at-Law in Nigeria, 1946–61; Member, House of Representatives, Nigeria, 1952–59; Judge of High Court of Federal Territory of Lagos, Nigeria, 1961–63. Member Nigeria Marketing Board and Director Nigeria Marketing Co. Board, 1952–54; Member Managing Cttee, West African Inst. for Oil Palm Research, 1953–63; Nat. President, Ibibio State Union, 1947–61; Vice-President, Nigeria Bar Assoc., 1957–61; Member: Internat. Commn of Jurists; World Assoc. of Judges; Chief Justice, High Court, Uganda, 1963–69; Acting Gov.-Gen., Uganda, 1963; Vice-President, Uganda Sports Union, 1964; Chairman, Board of Trustees, King George V Memorial Fund, 1964–69; Chancellor, Ahmadu Bello Univ., Zaria, 1972–75. Chm., Constituent Assembly for Nigerian Constitution, 1977–78; Dir, Seminar for Judges, 1980–82. Patron, Nigerian Soc. of Internat. Law, 1968–82; Mem., Nigerian Inst. of Internat. Affairs, 1979–. LLD (*hc*): Ibadan, 1967; Zaria, 1972; TCD, 1973. Awarded title of Obong Ikpa Isong Ibibio, 1961. *Publications:* The Lion and the Oil Palm and other essays, 1943; (jtly) The Human Right to Individual Freedom—a Symposium on World Habeas Corpus, ed by Luis Kutner, 1970. *Recreations:* billiards, tennis, gardening. *Address:* Mfut Itiat Enin, 8 Dr Udoma Street, PO Box 47, Ikot Abasi, Cross River State, Nigeria, West Africa. *Clubs:* Island, Metropolitan (Lagos); Yoruba Tennis (Vice-Patron, 1982–) (Lagos).

UFF, John Francis, QC; PhD, CEng, FICE, FCIArb; arbitrator, consulting engineer and advocate; Visiting Professor, Civil Engineering Department, King's College London, since 1985; *b* 30 Jan. 1942; *s* of Frederick and Eva Uff; *m* 1967, Diana Muriel Graveson; two *s* one *d*. *Educ:* Stratton Sch.; King's College London. BSc (Eng), PhD. Asst engineer, Rendel Palmer & Tritton, 1966–70; Vis. Lectr in civil engineering, 1963–68; called to the Bar, Gray's Inn, 1970; practice at Bar in construction cases, 1970–; arbitrator in construction disputes; Lectr to professional bodies in engineering law and arbitration. Mem. Council, ICE, 1982–85. *Publications:* Construction Law, 1974, 4th edn 1985; Commentary on ICE Conditions of Contract, 1978; (jtly) ICE Arbitration Practice, 1986; (jtly) Methods of Procurement in the Ground Investigation Industry, 1986; technical papers in civil engineering; papers and articles in engineering law and procedure. *Recreations:* playing

and making violins. *Address:* 6 Southwood Lane, Highgate, N6. *T:* 01–340 5127. *Club:* Ronnie Scott's.

UFFEN, Kenneth James, CMG 1977; HM Diplomatic Service, retired; Ambassador and UK Permanent Representative to OECD, Paris, 1982–85; *b* 29 Sept. 1925; *s* of late Percival James Uffen, MBE, former Civil Servant, and late Gladys Ethel James; *m* 1954, Nancy Elizabeth Winbolt; one *s* two *d*. *Educ:* Latymer Upper Sch.; St Catharine's Coll., Cambridge. HM Forces (Flt-Lt, RAFVR), 1943–48; St Catharine's Coll., 1948–50; 3rd Sec., FO, 1950–52; Paris, 1952–55; 2nd Sec., Buenos Aires, 1955–58; 1st Sec., FO, 1958–61; 1st Sec. (Commercial), Moscow, 1961–63; seconded to HM Treasury, 1963–65; FCO, 1965–68; Counsellor, Mexico City, 1968–70; Economic Counsellor, Washington, 1970–72; Commercial Counsellor, Moscow, 1972–76; Res. Associate, IISS, 1976–77; Ambassador to Colombia, 1977–82. *Recreation:* music. *Address:* 40 Winchester Road, Walton-on-Thames, Surrey KT12 2RH.

UGANDA, Archbishop of, since 1984; **Most Rev. Yona Okoth;** Bishop of Kampala, since 1984; *b* 15 April 1927; *s* of Nasanairi Owora and Tezira Akech; *m* Jessica Naome Okoth; four *s* five *d*. Bishop's clerk, 1947; Ordination Class, 1953–54 (certificate); deacon 1954, priest 1955; Parish Priest, Nagongera, 1956–60; St Augustine's Coll., Canterbury, 1963 (Diploma); Diocesan Treasurer, Mbale Diocese, 1961–65; Provincial Sec., Kampala, 1965–66; studies, Wycliffe Coll., Toronto Univ., 1966–68 (Dip. and LTh); Provincial Sec., Kampala, 1968–72; Diocesan Bishop of Bukedi, 1972–83. Hon. DD Wycliffe Coll., Toronto, 1978. *Recreation:* interest in farming. *Address:* PO Box 14123, Kampala, Uganda. *T:* 70218.

ULANOVA, Galina Sergeyevna; Order of Lenin, 1953, 1970; Hero of Socialist Labour, 1974, 1980; People's Artist of the USSR, 1951; Order of Red Banner of Labour, 1939, 1951; Badge of Honour, 1940; Prima Ballerina, Bolshoi Theatre, Moscow, 1944–60, retired; ballet-mistress at the Bolshoi Theatre since 1963; *b* 8 Jan. 1910; *d* of Sergei Nikolaevich Ulanov and Maria Feodorovna Romanova (dancers at Mariinsky Theatre, Petersburg). *Educ:* State School of Choreography, Leningrad. Début Kirov Theatre of Opera and Ballet, Leningrad, 1928; danced Odette-Odile in Swan Lake, 1929; Raimonda, 1931; Solweig in The Ice Maiden, 1931; danced Diane Mirelle in first performance of Flames of Paris, 1932; Giselle, 1933; Masha in The Nutcracker Suite, 1933; The Fountain of Bakhchisarai, as Maria, 1934; Lost Illusions, as Coralie, 1936; Romeo and Juliet, as Juliet, 1940; with Bolshoi: Cinderella, as Cinderella, 1945; Parasha in The Bronze Horseman, 1949; Tao Hua in The Red Poppy, 1950; Katerina in The Stone Flower, 1954. Visited London with the Bolshoi Theatre Ballet, 1956. Awarded State Prize, 1941; for Cinderella, 1945; for Romeo and Juliet, 1947; for Red Poppy, 1950. Awarded Lenin prize for outstanding achievement in ballet, 1957. FRAD, 1963. *Address:* Bolshoi Theatre, Moscow. *Clubs:* All-Russian Theatrical Society, Central House of Workers in the Arts.

ULLENDORFF, Prof. Edward, MA Jerusalem, DPhil Oxford; FBA 1965; Professor of Semitic Languages, School of Oriental and African Studies, University of London, 1979–82, now Professor Emeritus (Professor of Ethiopian Studies, 1964–79; Head of Africa Department, 1972–77); *b* 25 Jan. 1920; *s* of late Frederic and Cilli Ullendorff; *m* 1943, Dina Noack. *Educ:* Gymnasium Graues Kloster; Universities of Jerusalem and Oxford. Chief Examiner, British Censorship, Eritrea, 1942–43; Editor, African Publ., British Ministry of Information, Eritrea-Ethiopia, 1943–45; Assistant Political Secretary, British Military Admin., Eritrea, 1945–46; Asst Secretary, Palestine Government, 1947–48; Research Officer and Librarian, Oxford Univ. Inst. of Colonial Studies, 1948–49; Scarbrough Senior Research Studentship in Oriental Languages, 1949–50; Reader (Lectr, 1950–56) in Semitic Languages, St Andrews Univ., 1956–59; Professor of Semitic Languages and Literatures, University of Manchester, 1959–64. Carnegie Travelling Fellow to Ethiopia, 1958; Research Journeys to Ethiopia, 1964, 1966, 1969. Catalogued Ethiopian Manuscripts in Royal Library, Windsor Castle. Chairman: Assoc. of British Orientalists, 1963–64; Anglo-Ethiopian Soc., 1965–68 (Vice-Pres. 1969–77); Pres., Soc. for Old Testament Study, 1971; Vice-Pres., RAS, 1975–79, 1981–85. Joint Organizer, 2nd Internat. Congress of Ethiopian Studies, Manchester, 1963. Chm., Editorial Bd, Bulletin of SOAS, 1968–78; Mem., Adv. Bd, British Library, 1975–83. Vice-Pres., British Acad., 1980–82; Schweich Lectr, British Acad., 1967. FRAS. Imperial Ethiopian Gold Medallion, 1960; Haile Sellassie Internat. Prize for Ethiopian studies, 1972. MA Manchester, 1962; Hon. DLitt St Andrews, 1972. *Publications:* The definite article in the Semitic languages, 1941; Exploration and Study of Abyssinia, 1945; Catalogue of Ethiopian Manuscripts in the Bodleian Library, Oxford, 1951; The Semitic Languages of Ethiopia, 1955; The Ethiopians, 1959, 3rd edn 1973; (with Stephen Wright) Catalogue of Ethiopian MSS in Cambridge University Library, 1961; Comparative Semitics in Linguistica Semitica, 1961; (with S. Moscati and others) Introduction to Comparative Grammar of Semitic Languages, 1964; An Amharic Chrestomathy, 1965, 2nd edn 1978; The Challenge of Amharic, 1965; Ethiopia and the Bible, 1968; (with J. B. Pritchard and others) Solomon and Sheba, 1974; annotated and trans., Emperor Haile Sellassie, My Life and Ethiopia's Progress (autobiog.), 1976; Studies in Semitic Languages and Civilizations, 1977; (with M. A. Knibb) Book of Enoch, 1978; The Bawdy Bible, 1979; (jtly) The Amharic Letters of Emperor Theodore of Ethiopia to Queen Victoria, 1979; (with C. F. Beckingham) The Hebrew Letters of Prester John, 1982; A Tigrinya Chrestomathy, 1985; Joint Editor of Studies in honour of G. R. Driver, 1962; Joint Editor of Ethiopian Studies, 1964; articles and reviews in journals of learned societies; contribs to Encyclopaedia Britannica, Encyclopaedia of Islam, etc; Joint Editor, Journal of Semitic Studies, 1961–64. *Recreations:* music, motoring in Scotland. *Address:* 4 Bladon Close, Oxford OX2 8AD.

ULLMANN, Liv (Johanne); actress; *b* Tokyo, 16 Dec. 1938; *d* of late Viggo Ullmann and of Janna (*née* Lund), Norway; *m* 1960, Dr Gappe Stang (marr. diss. 1965). *Educ:* Norway; London (dramatic trng). Stage début, The Diary of Anne Frank (title role),

Stavanger, 1956; major roles, National Theatre and Norwegian State Theatre, Oslo; Amer. stage début, A Doll's House, New York Shakespeare Festival, 1974–75; Anna Christie, USA, 1977; The Bear, La Voix humaine, Australia, 1978; I Remember Mama, USA, and Ghosts (Ibsen), Broadway, 1979; British theatre début, Old Times, Guildford, 1985. Wrote and dir. short film, Parting, 1981. *Films:* Pan, 1965; The Night Visitor, 1971; Pope Joan, 1972; The Emigrants, 1972 (Golden Globe Award); The New Land, 1973 (Best Actress, Nat. Soc. of Film Critics, USA); Lost Horizon, 1973; 40 Carats, 1973; Zandy's Bride, 1973; The Abdication, 1974; The Wild Duck, 1983; The Bay Boy, 1985; *(dir. by Ingmar Bergman):* Persona, 1966; The Hour of the Wolf, 1968 (Best Actress, Nat. Soc. of Film Critics, USA); Shame, 1968 (Best Actress, Nat. Soc. of Film Critics, USA); The Passion of Anna, 1969; Cries and Whispers, 1972; Scenes from a Marriage, 1974; Face to Face, 1976; The Serpent's Egg, 1977; The Autumn Sonata, 1978. Peer Gynt Award, Norway (1st female recipient). Order of St Olav (Norway), 1979. *Publications:* (autobiog.) Changing, 1977; Choices, 1985. *Address:* Drammensviens 91, Oslo, Norway; c/o London Management, 235 Regent Street, W1.

ULLSWATER, 2nd Viscount *cr* 1921, of Campsea Ashe, Suffolk; **Nicholas James Christopher Lowther;** *b* 9 Jan. 1942; *s* of Lieut John Arthur Lowther, MVO, RNVR (*d* 1942), and Priscilla Violet (*d* 1945), *yr d* of Reginald Everitt Lambert; *S* great-grandfather, 1949; *m* 1967, Susan, *d* of James Howard Weatherby; two *s* two *d. Educ:* Eton; Trinity Coll., Cambridge. Captain, Royal Wessex Yeomanry, T&AVR, 1973–78. *Heir: s* Hon. Benjamin James Lowther, *b* 26 Nov. 1975. *Address:* Barrow Street House, near Mere, Warminster, Wilts. *T:* Mere 860621.

ULRICH, Walter Otto; Deputy Secretary, Department of Education and Science, since 1977; *b* 1 April 1927. Ministry of Works: Asst Principal, 1951; Principal, 1955; Treasury 1958–60; Principal Private Sec. to Minister of Public Building and Works, 1963–65; Asst Sec., 1965; Min. of Housing and Local Govt, 1966; DoE, 1970; Under-Sec., 1972; Cabinet Office, 1974–76. *Address:* 41 Beechwood Avenue, St Albans, Herts AL1 4XR. *T:* St Albans 34024.

ULSTER, Earl of; Alexander Patrick Gregers Richard Windsor; *b* 24 Oct. 1974; *s* of HRH the Duke of Gloucester and HRH the Duchess of Gloucester.
See under Royal Family.

UNDERHILL, family name of **Baron Underhill.**

UNDERHILL, Baron *cr* 1979 (Life Peer), of Leyton in Greater London; **Henry Reginall Underhill,** CBE 1976; Deputy Leader of the Opposition, House of Lords, since 1982; *b* 8 May 1914; *s* of Henry James and Alice Maud Underhill; *m* 1937, Flora Janet Philbrick; two *s* one *d. Educ:* Norlington Road Elementary School; Tom Hood Central School, Leyton. Junior Clerk, C. A. Hardman & Sons Ltd, Lloyd's Underwriters, 1929; joined Labour Party Head Office as Junior Accounts Clerk, 1933. National Fire Service, 1939–45. Assistant to Mr Morgan Phillips, Labour Party Gen. Sec., 1945; Admin. Assistant to National Agent, 1945; Propaganda Officer, 1947; Regional Organiser, W Midlands, 1948; Assistant National Agent, 1960; National Agent, 1972–79. Pres., AMA, 1982–. Joined Labour Party, 1930; Vice-Chm. 1933, Hon. Sec. 1937–48, Leyton West Constituency Labour Party. Opposition front bench spokesman on electoral affairs, 1983–, and on transport, 1980–, H o L. Member: APEX, 1931– (Life Mem. and Gold Badge); Nat. Union of Labour Organisers, 1945– (Hon. Mem.); Fire Bdes Union, 1939–45 (Br. Sec. and Chm., Dist, Div. and Area Cttees). Member: HO Electoral Adv. Cttee, 1970–79; Houghton Cttee on Financial Aid to Political Parties, 1975–76; Parly delegn to Zimbabwe, 1980 and to USSR, 1986; Kilbrandon Ind. Inquiry into New Ireland Forum, 1984. Hon. Sec., British Workers' Sports Assoc., 1935–37. *Recreations:* golf, life-long support of Leyton Orient FC, countryside rambling. *Address:* 94 Loughton Way, Buckhurst Hill, Essex IG9 6AH. *T:* 01–504 1910.

UNDERHILL, Herbert Stuart; President, Victoria (BC) Press, 1978–79; Publisher, Victoria Times, 1971–78, retired; *b* 20 May 1914; *s* of Canon H. J. Underhill and Helena (*née* Ross); *m* 1937, Emma Gwendolyn MacGregor; one *s* one *d. Educ:* University Sch., Victoria, BC. Correspondent and Editor, The Canadian Press, Vancouver, BC, Toronto, New York and London, 1936–50; Reuters North American Editor, 1950; Asst General Manager, Reuters, 1958; Managing Editor, 1965–68; Dep. Gen. Manager, with special responsibility for North and South America and Caribbean, 1963–70. Director: Canadian Daily Newspaper Publishers' Assoc., 1972–76; The Canadian Press, 1972–78. *Publication:* The Iron Church, 1984. *Recreations:* travel, reading. *Address:* 308 Beach Drive, Victoria, BC, Canada.

UNDERHILL, Michael Thomas Ben, QC 1972; **His Honour Judge Underhill;** a Circuit Judge, since 1978; *b* 10 Feb. 1918; *s* of late Rev. P. C. Underhill and Viola Underhill; *m* 1950, Rosalie Jean Kinloch; three *s. Educ:* Radley Coll.; Brasenose Coll., Oxford (MA). Served Glos Regt, 1939–42; 2nd KEO Goorkha Rifles, 1942–46 (Major). Called to the Bar, Gray's Inn, 1947; Master of the Bench, Gray's Inn, 1978; Oxford Circuit; Dep. Chm., Salop QS, 1967–71; Recorder of Reading, later a Recorder of the Crown Court, 1970–78. *Address:* 6 Ormond Road, Richmond, Surrey TW10 6TH. *Club:* Leander (Henley-on-Thames).

UNDERWOOD, Michael; *see* Evelyn, J. M.

UNGER, Michael Ronald; Editor, Manchester Evening News, since 1983; Director, The Guardian and Manchester Evening News plc, since 1983; Trustee, Scott Trust, since 1986; *b* 8 Dec. 1943; *s* of Ronald and Joan Maureen Unger; *m* 1966, Eunice Dickens; one *s* one *d. Educ:* Wirral Grammar School. Trainee journalist, Thomson Regional Newspapers, 1963; Reading Evening Post, 1965–67; Perth Daily News, W Australia, 1967–71; Daily Post, Liverpool, 1971, Editor, 1979–82; Editor, Liverpool Echo, 1982–83. *Publication:* ed, The Memoirs of Bridget Hitler, 1979. *Recreation:* reading. *Address:* The Moorings, Lees Lane, Little Neston, South Wirral, Cheshire L64 4DB. *T:* 051–336 5186. *Club:* Press (Manchester).

UNSTEAD, Robert John; author; *b* 21 Nov. 1915; *s* of Charles and Elizabeth Unstead; *m* 1939, Florence Margaret Thomas; three *d. Educ:* Dover Grammar Sch.; Goldsmiths' Coll., London. Schoolmaster, 1936–40. Served in RAF, 1940–46; Sector Controller, Comb. Ops, Normandy, Greece, Italy. Headmaster, Norton Road CP Sch., Letchworth, 1947–51, Grange Sch., Letchworth, 1951–57. Member, Herts Education Cttee, 1951–57; Chairman, Letchworth Primary Schools' Cttee of Management, 1960–64; Governor, Leiston Middle School, 1973–85. Chm., Educational Writers' Group, Soc. of Authors, 1965–68; Mem. Council, East Anglian Writers, 1976–. *Publications:* Looking at History, 1953; People in History, 1955; Teaching History, 1956; Travel by Road, 1958; Houses, 1958; Looking at Ancient History, 1959; Monasteries, 1961; Black's Children's Encyclopædia (co-author), 1961; Some Kings and Queens, 1962; A History of Britain, 1963; Royal Adventurers, 1964; Early Times, 1964; Men and Women in History, 1965; Britain in the Twentieth Century, 1966; The Story of Britain, 1969; Homes in Australia, 1969; Castles, 1970; Transport in Australia, 1970; Pioneer Homelife in Australia, 1971; History of the English-speaking World, 1972; Look and Find Out, 1972; The Twenties, 1973; The Thirties, 1974; Living in Aztec Times, 1974; Living in Samuel Pepys' London, 1975; A Dictionary of History, 1976; Living in Ancient Egypt, 1977; Living in Pompeii, 1977; See Inside a Castle, 1977; See Inside an Egyptian Town, 1977; R. J. Unstead's Book of Kings and Queens, 1978; Greece and Rome, 1978; Egypt and Mesopotamia, 1978; The Assyrians, 1980; The Egyptians, 1980; How They Lived in Cities Long Ago, 1980; A History of the World, 1983; general editor, Black's Junior Reference series, Looking at Geography, See Inside series; (contrib.) Encyclopedia Americana. *Recreations:* golf, gardening, watching cricket. *Address:* Reedlands, Thorpeness, Suffolk. *T:* Aldeburgh 2665. *Clubs:* MCC; Aldeburgh Golf, Thorpeness Golf.

UNSWORTH, Sir Edgar (Ignatius Godfrey), Kt 1963; CMG 1954; QC (N Rhodesia) 1951; *b* 18 April 1906; *yr s* of John William and Minnie Unsworth; *m* 1964, Eileen, *widow* of Raymond Ritzema. *Educ:* Stonyhurst Coll.; Manchester Univ. (LLB Hons). Barrister-at-Law, Gray's Inn, 1930; private practice, 1930–37. Parly Cand. (C) for Farnworth, General Election, 1935. Crown Counsel: Nigeria, 1937; N Rhodesia, 1942; Solicitor-General: N Rhodesia, 1946; Fedn of Malaya, 1949; Chm. of Cttees, N Rhodesia, 1950; Attorney-General, N Rhodesia, 1951–56. Acting Chief Sec. and Dep. to Governor of N Rhodesia for periods during 1953, 1954 and 1955; Attorney-General, Fedn of Nigeria, 1956–60; Federal Justice of Federal Supreme Court of Nigeria, 1960–62; Chief Justice, Nyasaland, 1962–64; Director of a Course for Government Officers from Overseas, 1964–65; Chief Justice of Gibraltar, 1965–76; Justice of Appeal, Gibraltar, 1976–81. Member Rhodesia Railways Arbitration Tribunal, 1946; Chm., Commn of Enquiry into Central African Airways Corp., 1947; Mem., British Observers' Group, Independence Elections, Rhodesia, 1980 (submitted independent report). *Publication:* Laws of Northern Rhodesia (rev. edn), 1949. *Recreations:* gardening, bridge. *Address:* Pedro El Grande 9, Sotogrande, Provincia de Cadiz, Spain. *Club:* Royal Gibraltar Yacht.

UNWIN, Brian; *see* Unwin, J. B.

UNWIN, Rev. Canon Christopher Philip, TD 1963; MA; Archdeacon of Northumberland, 1963–82; *b* 27 Sept. 1917; *e s* of Rev. Philip Henry and Decima Unwin. *Educ:* Repton Sch.; Magdalene Coll., Cambridge; Queen's Theological Coll., Birmingham. Deacon, 1940, Priest, 1941. Asst Curate of: Benwell, 1940–43; Sugley, 1944–47; Vicar of: Horton, Northumberland, 1947–55; Benwell, 1955–63. *Recreations:* reading, walking. *Address:* 60 Sandringham Avenue, Benton, Newcastle upon Tyne NE12 8JX. *T:* Newcastle upon Tyne 2700418.

UNWIN, David Storr; author; *b* 3 Dec. 1918; *e s* of late Sir Stanley Unwin, KCMG; *m* 1945, Periwinkle, *yr d* of late Captain Sidney Herbert, RN; twin *s* and *d. Educ:* Abbotsholme. League of Nations Secretariat, Geneva, 1938–39; George Allen & Unwin Ltd, Publishers, 1940–44. *Publications:* The Governor's Wife, 1954 (Authors' Club First Novel Award, 1955); A View of the Heath, 1956; Fifty Years with Father: a Relationship (autobiog.), 1982; *for children:* (under pen name David Severn) Rick Afire!, 1942; A Cabin for Crusoe, 1943; Waggon for Five, 1944; Hermit in the Hills, 1945; Forest Holiday, 1946; Ponies and Poachers, 1947; Dream Gold, 1948; The Cruise of the Maiden Castle, 1948; Treasure for Three, 1949; My Foreign Correspondent through Africa, 1950; Crazy Castle, 1951; Burglars and Bandicoots, 1952; Drumbeats!, 1953; The Future Took Us, 1958; The Green-eyed Gryphon, 1958; Foxy-boy, 1959; Three at the Sea, 1959; Clouds over the Alberhorn, 1963; Jeff Dickson, Cowhand, 1963; The Girl in the Grove, 1974; The Wishing Bone, 1977. *Recreations:* travel, gardening. *Address:* Garden Flat, 31 Belsize Park, NW3. *Club:* PEN.
See also R. S. Unwin.

UNWIN, (James) Brian, CB 1986; Deputy Secretary, Cabinet Office, since 1985; *b* 21 Sept. 1935; *s* of Reginald Unwin and Winifred Annie Walthall; *m* 1964, Diana Susan, *d* of Sir D. A. Scott, *qv*; three *s. Educ:* Chesterfield School; New College, Oxford (1st class Mods; 2nd class Greats; MA); Yale University (MA). Asst Principal, CRO, 1960; Private Sec. to British High Commissioner, Salisbury, 1961–64; 1st Secretary, British High Commission, Accra, 1964–65; FCO, 1965–68; transferred to HM Treasury, 1968; Private Sec. to Chief Secretary to Treasury, 1970–72; Asst Secretary, 1972; Under Sec., 1976; seconded to Cabinet Office, 1981–83; Dep. Sec., HM Treasury, 1983–85; Dir, Eur. Investment Bank, 1983–85. *Recreations:* bird watching, Wellingtoniana, cricket. *Address:* 25 Links Road, Epsom, Surrey. *T:* Epsom 24148. *Clubs:* Reform; Kingswood Village (Surrey).

UNWIN, Sir Keith, KBE 1964 (OBE 1937); CMG 1954; MA; *b* 3 Aug. 1909; *er s* of late Edwin Ernest Unwin and Jessie Magdalen Black; *m* 1935, Linda Giersé; one *s* two *d. Educ:* Merchant Taylors' Sch.; Lycée Condorcet, Paris; St John's Coll., Oxford; BA 1931. Department of Overseas Trade, 1932; Mem., Commercial Diplomatic Service, later HM Diplomatic Service, 1934–69; Madrid, 1934; Istanbul, 1937; San Sebastian (later Madrid), 1939; Mexico City, 1944; Paris, 1946; Prague, 1949; Buenos Aires, 1950; Rome, 1955–59; Foreign Service Inspector, 1959–62; UK Representative on Economic and Social Council of the United Nations, 1962–66; HM Ambassador to Uruguay, 1966–69. UK Mem., UN Commn on Human Rights, 1970–78. *Recreations:* gardening, reading. *Address:* Great Kingley, Dodington Lane, Chipping Sodbury, Bristol. *T:* Chipping Sodbury 310913. *Club:* Canning.

UNWIN, Ven. Kenneth; Archdeacon of Pontefract, since 1981; *b* 16 Sept. 1926; *s* of Percy and Elsie Unwin; *m* 1958, Beryl Riley; one *s* four *d. Educ:* Chesterfield Grammar School; St Edmund Hall, Oxford (MA Hons); Ely Theological Coll. Assistant Curate: All Saints, Leeds, 1951–55; St Margaret, Durham City (in charge, St John's, Neville's Cross), 1955–59; Vicar: St John Baptist, Dodworth, Barnsley, 1959–69; St John Baptist, Royston, Barnsley, 1969–73; St John's, Wakefield, 1973–82. Hon. Canon, Wakefield Cathedral, 1980–; RD of Wakefield, 1980–81. Proctor in Convocation, 1972–82. *Address:* Pontefract House, 19a Tithe Barn Street, Horbury, Wakefield WF4 6LJ. *T:* Wakefield 263777.

UNWIN, Dr (Peter) Nigel (Tripp), FRS 1983; Professor of Cell Biology, Stanford University School of Medicine, Stanford, Calif, since 1980; *b* 1 Nov. 1942; *s* of Peter Unwin and Cara Unwin (*née* Pinckney); *m* 1968, Janet Patricia Ladd; one *s* one *d. Educ:* Univ. of Otago, NZ (BE); Univ. of Cambridge (PhD 1968). Scientist, MRC Lab. of Molecular Biology, Cambridge, 1968–80. *Recreation:* mountaineering. *Address:* 972 Wing Place, Stanford, Calif 94305, USA. *T:* 415 424 0370.

UNWIN, Peter William, CMG 1981; HM Diplomatic Service; Ambassador to Denmark, since 1986; *b* 20 May 1932; *s* of Arnold and Norah Unwin; *m* 1955, Monica Steven; two *s* two *d. Educ:* Ampleforth; Christ Church, Oxford (MA). Army, 1954–56; FO, 1956–58; British Legation, Budapest, 1958–61; British Embassy, Tokyo, 1961–63; FCO, 1963–67; British Information Services, NY, 1967–70; FCO, 1970–72; Bank of England, 1973; British Embassy, Bonn, 1973–76; Head of Personnel Policy Dept, FCO, 1976–79; Fellow, Center for Internat. Affairs, Harvard, 1979–80; Minister (Economic), Bonn, 1980–83; Ambassador to Hungary, 1983–86. *Address:* c/o Foreign and Commonwealth Office, SW1; 2 Coleherne Road, SW10. *T:* 01–373 5250.

UNWIN, Rayner Stephens, CBE 1977; Chairman, Unwin Hyman, since 1986; *b* 23 Dec. 1925; *s* of late Sir Stanley Unwin and Mary Storr; *m* 1952, Carol Margaret, *d* of Harold Curwen; one *s* three *d. Educ:* Abbotsholme Sch.; Trinity Coll., Oxford (MA); Harvard,

USA (MA). Sub-Lt, RNVR, 1944–47. Entered George Allen & Unwin Ltd, 1951; Chm., 1968–86. Mem. Council, Publishers' Assoc., 1965–85 (Treasurer, 1969; Pres., 1971; Vice-Pres., 1973); Chm., British Council Publishers' Adv. Cttee, 1981–. Chm., Little Missenden Festival, 1981–. *Publications:* The Rural Muse, 1954; The Defeat of John Hawkins, 1960. *Recreations:* skiing downhill, walking up-hill, birds and gardens. *Address:* Limes Cottage, Little Missenden, near Amersham, Bucks. *T:* Great Missenden 2900. *Club:* Garrick.
See also D. S. Unwin.

UPDIKE, John Hoyer; freelance writer; *b* 18 March 1932; *s* of Wesley R. and Linda G. Updike; *m* 1st, 1953, Mary E. Pennington (marr. diss.); two *s* two *d*; 2nd, 1977, Martha Bernhard. *Educ:* Harvard Coll. Worked as journalist for The New Yorker magazine, 1955–57. *Publications: poems:* Hoping for a Hoopoe (in America, The Carpentered Hen), 1958; Telephone Poles, 1968; Midpoint and other poems, 1969; Tossing and Turning, 1977; Facing Nature, 1985; *novels:* The Poorhouse Fair, 1959; Rabbit, Run, 1960; The Centaur, 1963; Of the Farm, 1966; Couples, 1968; Rabbit Redux, 1972; A Month of Sundays, 1975; Marry Me, 1976; The Coup, 1979; Rabbit is Rich (Pulitzer Prize), 1982; The Witches of Eastwick, 1984; *short stories:* The Same Door, 1959; Pigeon Feathers, 1962; The Music School, 1966; Bech: A Book, 1970; Museums and Women, 1973; Problems, 1980; Bech is Back, 1982; (ed) The Year's Best American Short Stories, 1985; *miscellanies:* Assorted Prose, 1965; Picked-Up Pieces, 1976; Hugging the Shore, 1983; *play:* Buchanan Dying, 1974. *Address:* Beverly Farms, Mass 01915, USA.

UPHAM, Captain Charles Hazlitt, VC 1941 and Bar, 1943; JP; sheep-farmer; *b* Christchurch, New Zealand, 21 Sept. 1908; *s* of John Hazlitt Upham, barrister, and Agatha Mary Upham, Christchurch, NZ; *m* 1945, Mary Eileen, *d* of James and Mary McTamney, Dunedin, New Zealand; three *d* (incl. twins). *Educ:* Waihi Prep. School, Winchester; Christ's Coll., Christchurch, NZ; Canterbury Agric. Coll., Lincoln, NZ (Diploma). Post-grad. course in valuation and farm management. Farm manager and musterer, 1930–36; govt valuer, 1937–39; farmer, 1945–. Served War of 1939–45 (VC and Bar, despatches): volunteered, Sept. 1939; 2nd NZEF (Sgt 1st echelon advance party); 2nd Lt; served Greece, Crete, W Desert (VC, Crete; Bar, Ruweisat); Captain; POW, released 1945. *Relevant Publication:* Mark of the Lion: The Story of Captain Charles Upham, VC and Bar (by Kenneth Sandford), 1962. *Recreations:* rowing, Rugby (1st XV Lincoln Coll., NZ). *Address:* Lansdowne, Hundalee, North Canterbury, NZ. *Clubs:* Canterbury, Christchurch, RSA (all NZ).

UPJOHN, Maj.-Gen. Gordon Farleigh, CB 1966; CBE 1959 (OBE 1955); *b* 9 May 1912; *e s* of late Dudley Francis Upjohn; *m* 1946, Rita Joan, *d* of late Major Clarence Walters; three *d*. *Educ:* Felsted School; RMC Sandhurst. 2nd Lieut, The Duke of Wellington's Regt; RWAFF, 1937; Adjt 3rd Bn The Nigeria Regt, 1940; Staff Coll., 1941; GSO2 Ops GHQ Middle East, 1941; Bde Maj. 3 WA Inf. Bde, 1942 (despatches); Lt-Col Comd 6 Bn The Nigeria Regt, 1944 (despatches); DAA&QMG Southern Comd India, 1946; GSO2 Mil. Ops Directorate WO, 1948; Lt-Col Chief Instructor RMA Sandhurst, 1951; Lt-Col Comd WA Inf. Bn, 1954; Bde Comdr 2 Inf. Bde Malaya, 1957 (despatches; Meritorious Medal (Perak Malaya)); Provost Marshal WO, 1960; GOC Yorkshire District, 1962–65. Automobile Assoc., 1965–76. *Recreations:* golf, cricket, field sports. *Address:* c/o Lloyds Bank, 62 Brook Street, W1. *Clubs:* Army and Navy, MCC.

UPWARD, Mrs Janet; Secretary, South Birmingham Community Health Council, since 1983. *Educ:* Newnham College, Cambridge. BA (Geog. Hons) 1961, MA 1966. Sec., National Fedn of Consumer Gps, 1972–82; Mem., 1978–84, Dep. Chm., 1978–83, Domestic Coal Consumers' Council; Chm., National Consumer Congress, 1981–83. *Address:* 61 Valentine Road, Birmingham B14 7AJ. *T:* 021–444 2837.

URE, James Mathie, OBE 1969; British Council Representative, India, and Minister (Education), British High Commission, New Delhi, 1980–84; *b* 5 May 1925; *s* of late William Alexander Ure, and of Helen Jones; *m* 1950, Martha Walker Paterson; one *s* one *d*. *Educ:* Shawlands Acad., Glasgow; Glasgow Univ. (MA); Trinity Coll., Oxford (BLitt). Army Service, 1944–47. Lectr, Edinburgh Univ., 1953–59; British Council: Istanbul, 1956–57; India, 1959–68; Dep. Controller, Arts Div., 1968–71; Rep., Indonesia, 1971–75; Controller, Home Div., 1975–80. *Publications:* Old English Benedictine Office, 1952; (with L. A. Hill) English Sounds and Spellings, 1962; (with L. A. Hill) English Sounds and Spellings—Tests, 1963; (with J. S. Bhandari and C. S. Bhandari) Read and Act, 1965; (with C. S. Bhandari) Short Stories, 1966. *Address:* Southlands, Downs Side, Belmont, Surrey. *T:* 01–642 7241.

URE, John Burns, CMG 1980; LVO 1968; HM Diplomatic Service; Ambassador to Brazil, since 1984; *b* 5 July 1931; *s* of late Tam Ure; *m* 1972, Caroline, *d* of Charles Allan, Roxburghshire; one *s* one *d*. *Educ:* Uppingham Sch.; Magdalene Coll., Cambridge (MA); Harvard Business Sch. (AMP). Active Service as 2nd Lieut with Cameronians (Scottish Rifles), Malaya, 1950–51; Lieut, London Scottish (Gordon Highlanders) TA, 1952–55. Book publishing with Ernest Benn Ltd, 1951–53; joined Foreign (subseq. Diplomatic) Service, 1956; 3rd Sec. and Private Sec. to Ambassador, Moscow, 1957–59; Resident Clerk, FO, 1960–61; 2nd Sec., Leopoldville, 1962–63; FO, 1964–66; 1st Sec. (Commercial), Santiago, 1967–70; FCO, 1971–72; Counsellor, and intermittently Chargé d'Affaires, Lisbon, 1972–77; Head of South America Dept, FCO, 1977–79; Ambassador to Cuba, 1979–81; Asst Under-Sec. of State, FCO, 1981–84. Life Fellow and Mem. Council, RGS, 1982–84. Comdr, Mil. Order of Christ, Portugal, 1973. *Publications:* Cucumber Sandwiches in the Andes, 1973 (Travel Book Club Choice); Prince Henry the Navigator, 1977 (History Guild Choice); The Trail of Tamerlane, 1980 (Ancient History Club Choice); The Quest for Captain Morgan, 1983; Trespassers on the Amazon, 1986; book reviews in TLS. *Recreation:* travelling uncomfortably in remote places and writing about it comfortably afterwards. *Address:* c/o Foreign and Commonwealth Office, SW1. *Clubs:* White's, Beefsteak.

UREN, Reginald Harold, FRIBA; private practice of architecture, 1933–68; *b* New Zealand, 5 March 1906; *s* of Richard Ellis and Christina Uren; *m* 1930, Dorothy Marion Morgan; one *d*. *Educ:* Hutt Valley High School, New Zealand; London University. Qualified as Architect in New Zealand, 1929; ARIBA, London, 1931; won open architectural competition for Hornsey Town Hall (281 entries), 1933; joined in partnership with J. Alan Slater and A. H. Moberly, 1936; architectural practice includes public buildings, department stores, domestic, commercial and school buildings. Works include: John Lewis Store, Oxford Street; Arthur Sanderson & Sons Building, Berners Street; Norfolk County Hall. Freeman of City of London, 1938; Master, Tylers and Bricklayers Company, 1966. War service, 1942–46, Capt. Royal Engineers. Council, RIBA, 1946–65; London Architecture Bronze Medal, 1935; Tylers and Bricklayers Company Gold Medal, 1936; Min. of Housing and Local Govt Medal for London Region, 1954; New Zealand Inst. of Architects Award of Merit, 1965. *Recreation:* debate. *Address:* PO Box 9039, Newmarket, Auckland, New Zealand. *Club:* Reform.

URIE, Wing Comdr John Dunlop, AE 1942; bar 1945; *b* 12 Oct. 1915; *s* of late John Urie, OBE, Glasgow; *m* 1939, Mary Taylor, *d* of Peter Bonnar, Dunfermline; one *s* two *d*. *Educ:* Sedbergh; Glasgow Univ. Served War of 1939–45: with RAuxAF, in Fighter Command and Middle East Command; Wing Comdr, 1942. DL Co. of Glasgow, 1963. OStJ. *Address:* 50 Westbrook Avenue, Wahroonga, NSW 2076, Australia. *Club:* Royal Northern and Clyde Yacht.

URMSON, James Opie, MC 1943; Emeritus Professor of Philosophy, Stanford University; Emeritus Fellow of Corpus Christi College, Oxford; *b* 4 March 1915; *s* of Rev. J. O. Urmson; *m* 1940, Marion Joyce Drage; one *d*. *Educ:* Kingswood School, Bath; Corpus Christi College, Oxford. Senior Demy, Magdalen College, 1938; Fellow by examination, Magdalen College, 1939–45. Served Army (Duke of Wellington's Regt), 1939–45. Lecturer of Christ Church, 1945–46; Student of Christ Church, 1946–55; Professor of Philosophy, Queen's College, Dundee, University of St Andrews, 1955–59; Fellow and Tutor in Philosophy, CCC, Oxford, 1959–78. Visiting Associate Prof., Princeton Univ., 1950–51. Visiting Lectr, Univ. of Michigan, 1961–62, 1965–66, and 1969; Stuart Prof. of Philosophy, Stanford, 1975–80. *Publications:* Philosophical Analysis, 1956; The Emotive Theory of Ethics, 1968; Berkeley, 1982; edited: Encyclopedia of Western Philosophy, 1960; J. L. Austin: How to Do Things with Words, 1962; (with G. J. Warnock) J. L. Austin: Philosophical Papers, 2nd edn, 1970; articles in philosophical jls. *Recreations:* gardening, music. *Address:* Standfast, Tumbledown Dick, Cumnor, Oxford OX2 9QE. *T:* Oxford 862769.

URQUHART, Sir Andrew, KCMG 1963 (CMG 1960); MBE 1950; Principal, St Godric's College, 1975–85 (Vice-Principal, 1970–75); *b* 6 Jan. 1918; *s* of late Rev. Andrew Urquhart and of J. B. Urquhart; *m* 1956, Jessie Stanley Allison; two *s*. *Educ:* Greenock Academy; Glasgow University. Served War of 1939–45, Royal Marines, 1940–46. Cadet, Colonial Administrative Service, 1946; Senior District Officer, 1954; Admin. Officer, Class I, 1957; Permanent Sec., 1958; Deputy Governor, Eastern Region, Nigeria, 1958–63; Gen. Manager, The Housing Corp., 1964–70. *Address:* BM/JNTC, WC1N 3XX.

URQUHART, Sir Brian (Edward), KCMG 1986; MBE 1945; Scholar-in-Residence, Ford Foundation; an Under-Secretary-General, United Nations, 1974–86; *b* 28 Feb. 1919; *s* of Murray and Bertha Urquhart; *m* 1st, 1944, Alfreda Huntington (marr. diss. 1963); two *s* one *d*; 2nd, 1963, Sidney Damrosch Howard; one *s* one *d*. *Educ:* Westminster; Christ Church, Oxford (Hon. Student, 1985). British Army: Dorset Regt and Airborne Forces, N Africa, Sicily and Europe, 1939–45; Personal Asst to Gladwyn Jebb, Exec. Sec. of Preparatory Commn of UN, London, 1945–46; Personal Asst to Trygve Lie, 1st Sec.-Gen. of UN, 1946–49; Sec., Collective Measures Cttee, 1951–53; Mem., Office of Under-Sec.-Gen. for Special Political Affairs, 1954–71; Asst Sec.-Gen., UN, 1972–74; Exec. Sec., 1st and 2nd UN Conf. on Peaceful Uses of Atomic Energy, 1955 and 1958; active in organization and direction of UN Emergency Force in Middle East, 1956; Dep. Exec. Sec., Preparatory Commn of Internat. Atomic Energy Agency, 1957; Asst to Sec.-Gen.'s Special Rep. in Congo, July-Oct. 1960; UN Rep. in Katanga, Congo, 1961–62; responsible for organization and direction of UN peace-keeping ops and special political assignments. Hon. LLD: Yale, 1981; Tufts, 1985; DUniv: Essex, 1981; City Univ. NY, 1986; Grinnell, 1986; State Univ. NY, 1986; Oxford, 1986. *Publications:* Hammarskjold, 1972; various articles and reviews on internat. affairs. *Address:* 131 East 66th Street, New York, NY 10021, USA; Howard Farm, Tyringham, Mass 01264. *T:* LE 5–0805. *Club:* Century (New York).

URQUHART, Donald John, CBE 1970; Director General, British Library Lending Services, 1973–74; *b* 27 Nov. 1909; *s* of late Roderick and Rose Catherine Urquhart, Whitley Bay; *m* 1939, Beatrice Winefride, *d* of late W. G. Parker, Sheffield; two *s*. *Educ:* Barnard Castle School; Sheffield University (BSc, PhD). Research Dept, English Steel Corp., 1934–37; Science Museum Library, 1938–39; Admiralty, 1939–40; Min. of Supply, 1940–45; Science Museum Library, 1945–48; DSIR Headquarters, 1948–61; Dir, Nat. Lending Library for Science and Technology, 1961–73. Hon. Lectr, Postgrad. Sch. of Librarianship and Information Science, Sheffield Univ., 1970–; Vis. Prof., Loughborough Univ. Dept of Library and Information Studies, 1973–80. Chm., Standing Conf. of Nat. and Univ. Libraries, 1969–71. FLA, Pres., Library Assoc., 1972. Hon. DSc: Heriot-Watt, 1974; Sheffield, 1974; Salford, 1974. Hon. Citation, Amer. Library Assoc., 1978. *Publications:* The Principles of Librarianship, 1981; papers on library and scientific information questions. *Recreation:* gardening. *Address:* Wood Garth, First Avenue, Bardsey, near Leeds. *T:* Collingham Bridge 73228. *Club:* Athenæum.

URQUHART, James Graham, CVO 1983; FCIT, FIMH; Chairman: British Transport Police, since 1977; BRE-Metro, since 1978; Transmark, since 1983; *b* 23 April 1925; *s* of James Graham Urquhart and Mary Clark; *m* 1949, Margaret Hutchinson; two *d*. *Educ:* Berwickshire High Sch. Served War, RAF, 1941–44. Management Trainee, Eastern Region, BR, 1949–52; Chief Controller, Fenchurch Street, 1956–59; Dist Traffic Supt, Perth, 1960–62; Divl Operating Supt, Glasgow, 1962–64; Divl Manager, Glasgow and SW Scotland, 1964–67; Asst Gen. Man., Eastern Reg., 1967–69; BR Bd HQ: Chief Ops Man., 1969–72; Exec. Dir, Personnel, 1972–75; Gen. Manager, London Midland Reg., BR, 1975–76; BR Bd: Exec. Mem., Operations and Productivity, 1977–83; Mem., Exports, 1983–85; Chairman: BR Engrg Ltd, 1979–85; Freightliners, 1983–85. MIPM, MInstM, CBIM, MBMHB. *Recreations:* golf, travel, gardening. *Address:* Wychcotes, Caversham, Reading. *T:* Reading 479071.

URQUHART, Lawrence McAllister, CA; Group Managing Director, Burmah Oil PLC, since 1985; *b* 24 Sept. 1935; *s* of Robert and Josephine Urquhart; *m* 1961, Elizabeth Catherine Burns; three *s* one *d*. *Educ:* Strathallan; King's Coll., London (LLB). Price Waterhouse & Co., 1957–62; Shell International Petroleum, 1962–64; P. A. Management Consultants, 1964–68; Charterhouse Gp, 1968–74; TKM Gp, 1974–77; Burmah Oil PLC, 1977–. *Recreations:* golf, music. *Address:* Beechwood, Ashley Road, Battledown, Cheltenham GL52 6PG. *T:* Cheltenham 510683. *Clubs:* Frilford Heath Golf; Lilley Brook Golf (Cheltenham).

URQUHART, Maj.-Gen. Robert Elliott, CB 1944; DSO and Bar 1943; *b* 28 Nov. 1901; *e s* of Alexander Urquhart, MD; *m* 1939, Pamela Condon; one *s* three *d*. *Educ:* St Paul's, West Kensington; RMC Sandhurst. 2nd Lt HLI 1920; Staff Coll., Camberley, 1936–37; Staff Capt., India, 1938; DAQMG, AHQ, India, 1939–40; DAAG, 3 Div., 1940; AA&QMG, 3 Div., 1940–41; commanded 2nd DCLI, 1941–42; GSO1, 51st Highland Div. N Africa, 1942–43; commanded 231 Malta Brigade, Sicily, 1943, and in landings Italy, 1943 (DSO and Bar); BGS 12 Corps, 1943; GOC 1st Airborne Div., 1944–45 (CB); Col 1945; Maj.-Gen. 1946; Director Territorial Army and Army Cadet Force, War Office, 1945–46; GOC 16th Airborne Division, TA, 1947–48; Commander, Lowland District, 1948–50; Commander Malaya District and 17th Gurkha Division, Mar.-Aug. 1950; GOC Malaya, 1950–52; GOC-in-C British Troops in Austria, 1952–55; retired, Dec. 1955. Col Highland Light Infantry, 1954–58. Dir, Davy and United Engineering Co. Ltd, 1957–70. Netherlands Bronze Lion, 1944; Norwegian Order of St Olaf, 1945. *Publication:* Arnhem, 1958. *Recreation:* golf. *Address:* Bigram, Port of Menteith, Stirling. *T:* Port of Menteith 267. *Club:* Naval and Military.
See also W. M. Campbell, Sir G. P. Grant-Suttie, Bt, Sir John Kinloch, Bt.

URSELL, Prof. Fritz Joseph, FRS 1972; Beyer Professor of Applied Mathematics, Manchester University, since 1961; *b* 28 April 1923; *m* 1959, Katharina Renate (*née* Zander); two *d*. *Educ:* Clifton; Marlborough; Trinity College, Cambridge. BA 1943,

MA 1947, ScD 1957, Cambridge. Admiralty Service, 1943–47; ICI Fellow in Applied Mathematics, Manchester Univ., 1947–50. Fellow (Title A), Trinity Coll., Cambridge, 1947–51; Univ. Lecturer in Mathematics, Cambridge, 1950–61; Stringer Fellow in Natural Sciences, King's Coll., Cambridge, 1954–60. Georg Weinblum Lectr in Ship Hydrodynamics, Hamburg and Washington, 1986. FIMA 1964. MSc (Manchester), 1965. *Address:* 28 Old Broadway, Withington, Manchester M20 9DF. *T:* 061–445 5791.

URSELL, Rev. Philip Elliott; Principal of Pusey House, Oxford, since 1982; *b* 3 Dec. 1942; *o s* of Clifford Edwin Ursell and Hilda Jane Ursell (*née* Tucker). *Educ:* Cathays High Sch.; University Coll. Cardiff (Craddock Wells Exhibnr; BA); St Stephen's House, Oxford. MA Oxon. Curate of Newton Nottage, Porthcawl, 1968–71; Asst Chaplain of University Coll. Cardiff, 1971–77; Chaplain of Polytechnic of Wales, 1974–77; Chaplain, Fellow and Dir of Studies in Music, Emmanuel Coll., Cambridge, 1977–82; Fellow, St Cross Coll., Oxford, 1982–. Select Preacher, Harvard Univ., 1982, 1983; Univ. Preacher, Harvard Summer Sch., 1985. Warden, Soc. of Most Holy Trinity, Ascot Priory, 1985–. Mem. Governing Body, Church in Wales, 1971–77. *Publications:* contribs to theological, musical and other journals. *Recreations:* gardening, painting, sailing. *Address:* Pusey House, Oxford OX1 3LZ. *T:* Oxford 59519.

URWICK, Sir Alan (Bedford), KCVO 1984; CMG 1978; HM Diplomatic Service; Ambassador to Egypt, since 1985; *b* 2 May 1930; *s* of late Col Lyndall Fownes Urwick, OBE, MC and Joan Wilhelmina Saunders (*née* Bedford); *m* 1960, Marta, *o d* of Adhemar Montagne; three *s*. *Educ:* Dragon Sch.; Rugby (Schol.); New Coll., Oxford (Exhibr). 1st cl. hons Mod. History 1952. Joined HM Foreign (subseq. Diplomatic) Service, 1952; served in: Brussels, 1954–56; Moscow, 1958–59; Baghdad, 1960–61; Amman, 1965–67; Washington, 1967–70; Cairo, 1971–73; seconded to Cabinet Office as Asst Sec., Central Policy Review Staff, 1973–75; Head of Near East and N Africa Dept, FCO, 1975–76; Minister, Madrid, 1977–79; Ambassador to Jordan, 1979–84. KStJ 1982. Grand Cordon, first class, Order of Independence (Jordan), 1984. *Address:* c/o Foreign and Commonwealth Office, SW1. *Club:* Garrick.

URWIN, Harry, (Charles Henry); Associate Fellow, Industrial Relations Research Unit, Warwick University, since 1981; Member, TUC General Council, 1969–80; Deputy General-Secretary, Transport and General Workers Union, 1969–80; Chairman, TUC Employment Policy and Organisation Committee, 1973–80; *b* 24 Feb. 1915; *s* of Thomas and Lydia Urwin; *m* 1941, Hilda Pinfold; one *d*. *Educ:* Durham County Council Sch. Convenor, Machine Tool Industry, until 1947; Coventry Dist Officer, TGWU, 1947–59; Coventry Dist Sec., Confedn of Shipbuilding and Engineering Unions, 1954–59; Regional Officer, TGWU, 1959–69; Member: Industrial Develt Adv. Bd, Industry Act, 1972–79; Sir Don Ryder Inquiry, British Leyland Motor Corp., 1974–75; Manpower Services Commn, 1974–79; Nat. Enterprise Bd, 1975–79; Energy Commn, 1977–79; Council, ACAS, 1978–80; Standing Cttee on Pay Comparability, 1979–80. *Recreation:* swimming. *Address:* 4 Leacliffe Way, Aldridge, Walsall WS9 0PW.

USBORNE, Henry Charles, MA; Chairman, UA Engineering Ltd, Sheffield; President, Parliamentary Group for World Government; *b* 16 Jan. 1909; *s* of Charles Frederick Usborne and Janet Lefroy; *m* 1936; two *s* two *d*. *Educ:* Bradfield; Corpus Christi, Cambridge. MP (Lab) Yardley Div. of Birmingham, 1950–59 (Acock's Green Div. of Birmingham, 1945–50). JP Worcs, 1964–79. *Address:* Totterdown, Evesham, Worcs WR11 5JP.

See also R. A. Usborne.

USBORNE, Richard Alexander; writer; *b* 16 May 1910; *s* of Charles Frederick Usborne, ICS, and Janet Muriel (*née* Lefroy); *m* 1938, Monica (*d* 1986), *d* of Archibald Stuart MacArthur, Wagon Mound, New Mexico, USA; one *s* one *d*. *Educ:* Summer Fields Preparatory Sch.; Charterhouse; Balliol Coll., Oxford. BA Mods and Greats; MA 1981. Served War, 1941–45: Army, SOE and PWE, Middle East, Major, Gen. List. Advertising agencies, 1933–36; part-owner and Editor of What's On, 1936–37; London Press Exchange, 1937–39; BBC Monitoring Service, 1939–41; Asst Editor, Strand Magazine, 1946–50; Dir, Graham & Gillies Ltd, Advertising, retd, 1970; Custodian, National Trust, 1974–81. *Publications:* Clubland Heroes, 1953 (rev. 1975, 1983); (ed) A Century of Summer Fields, 1964; Wodehouse at Work, 1961, rev. edn, as Wodehouse at Work to the End, 1977; (ed) Sunset at Blandings, 1977; (ed) Vintage Wodehouse, 1977; A Wodehouse Companion, 1981; (ed) Wodehouse 'Nuggets', 1983; adaptations of Wodehouse novels and stories for BBC radio serials. *Recreations:* reading, writing light verse. *Address:* Flat 8, Crofton House, 1 New Cavendish Street, W1. *T:* 01–486 9869.

See also H. C. Usborne.

USHER, Sir Leonard (Gray), KBE 1986 (CBE 1971); JP; Secretary, Fiji Press Council, since 1985; Chairman, Suva Stock Exchange, since 1978; *b* 29 May 1907; *s* of Robert Usher and Mary Elizabeth (*née* Johnston); *m* 1st, 1940, Mary Gertrude Lockie; one *s* one *d*; 2nd, 1962, Jane Hammond Derné (*d* 1984). *Educ:* Auckland Grammar Sch., NZ; Auckland Training Coll. (Trained Teachers Cert. B); Auckland Univ. (BA). Headmaster, Levuka Public Sch., Provincial Schs, Queen Victoria Sch., 1930–43; Fiji Govt PRO, 1943–56; Exec. Dir, Fiji Times and Herald Ltd, 1957–73; Editor, Fiji Times, 1958–73; Org. Dir, Pacific Is News Assoc., 1974–85 (Councillor and Life Mem., 1985–). Chm., Fiji Develt Bank, 1978–82; Dep. Chm., Nat. Bank of Fiji, 1974–83. Mem., Suva CC, 1962–71, 1975–77; Mayor of Suva, 1966–70, 1975–76. *Publications:* Satellite Over The Pacific, 1975; 50 Years in Fiji, 1978; (jtly) Suva—a history and guide, 1978; Levuka School Century, 1979; (jtly) This is Radio Fiji, 1979; (ed) Pacific News Media, 1986. *Recreations:* reading, computer programmes, conversation. *Address:* 24 Des Voeux Road, Suva, Fiji. *T:* 312–025; PO Box 1478, Suva, Fiji. *Clubs:* Defence, Fiji, United, Ex-Servicemen's (Fiji); Royal Automobile (Sydney); Grammar (Auckland).

USHER, Sir Peter Lionel, 5th Bt *cr* 1899, of Norton, Midlothian, and of Wells, Co. Roxburgh; *b* 31 Oct. 1931; *er s* of Sir (Robert) Stuart Usher, 4th Bt, and Gertrude Martha (*d* 1984), 2nd *d* of Lionel Barnard Sampson, Tresmontes, Villa Valeria, Prov. Cordoba, Argentina; *S* father, 1962. *Educ:* privately. *Heir:* *b* Robert Edward Usher, *b* 18 April 1934. *Address:* (Seat) Hallrule, Hawick, Roxburghshire. *T:* Bonchester Bridge 216.

USHERWOOD, Kenneth Ascough, CBE 1964; President, Prudential Assurance Co. Ltd, 1979–82; *b* 19 Aug. 1904; *s* of late H. T. Usherwood and late Lettie Ascough; *m* 1st, Molly Tidbeck (marr. diss. 1945), Johannesburg; one *d*; 2nd, 1946, Mary Louise, *d* of T. L. Reepmaker d'Orville; one *s*. *Educ:* City of London School; St John's College, Cambridge (MA). Prudential Assurance Co. Ltd, 1925–82: South Africa, 1932–34, Near East, 1934–37; Dep. Gen. Man. 1947–60; Chief Gen. Man., 1961–67; Dir, 1968–79; Chm., 1970–75; Dir, Prudential Corp., 1978–79. Director of Statistics, Ministry of Supply, 1941–45. Chm., Industrial Life Offices Assoc., 1966–67. Institute of Actuaries: Fellow (FIA) 1925; Pres. 1962–64. Mem. Gaming Board, 1968–72; Treasurer, Field Studies Council, 1969–77. *Address:* 24 Litchfield Way, NW11. *T:* 01–455 7915; Laurel Cottage, Walberswick, Suffolk. *T:* Southwold 723265. *Club:* Oriental.

USTINOV, Peter Alexander, CBE 1975; FRSA, FRSL; actor, dramatist, film director; Rector of the University of Dundee, 1968–74; Goodwill Ambassador for UNICEF, 1969; *b* London, 16 April 1921; *s* of late Iona Ustinov and Nadia Benois, painter; *m* 1st, 1940, Isolde Denham (marr. diss. 1950); one *d*; 2nd, 1954, Suzanne Cloutier (marr. diss. 1971); one *s* two *d*; 3rd, 1972, Hélène du Lau d'Allemans. *Educ:* Westminster School. Served in Army, Royal Sussex Regt and RAOC, 1942–46. Author of plays: House of Regrets, 1940 (prod Arts Theatre 1942); Blow Your Own Trumpet, 1941 (prod Playhouse [Old Vic] 1943); Beyond, 1942 (prod Arts Theatre, 1943); The Banbury Nose, 1943 (prod Wyndham's 1944); The Tragedy of Good Intentions, 1944 (prod Old Vic, Liverpool, 1945); The Indifferent Shepherd (prod Criterion, 1948); Frenzy (adapted from Swedish of Ingmar Bergman, prod and acted in St Martin's, 1948); The Man in the Raincoat (Edinburgh Festival, 1949); The Love of Four Colonels (and acted in, Wyndham's, 1951), The Moment of Truth (Adelphi, 1951); High Balcony, 1952 (written 1946); No Sign of the Dove (Savoy, 1953); The Empty Chair (Bristol Old Vic, 1956); Romanoff and Juliet (Piccadilly, 1956, film, 1961; musical, R loves J, Chichester, 1973); Photo Finish (prod and acted in it, Saville, 1962); The Life in My Hands, 1963; The Unknown Soldier and his Wife, 1967 (prod and acted in it, Chichester, 1968, New London, 1973); Halfway up the Tree (Queen's), 1967; compiled, prod and acted in The Marriage, Edinburgh, 1982; wrote and acted in Beethoven's Tenth (Vaudeville, 1983). Co-Author of film: The Way Ahead, 1943–44. Author and Director of films: School for Secrets, 1946; Vice-Versa, 1947. Author, director, producer and main actor in film Private Angelo, 1949; acted in films: Odette, Quo Vadis, Hotel Sahara, 1950; Beau Brummell, The Egyptian, We're No Angels, 1954; An Angel Flew Over Brooklyn, 1957; Spartacus, 1960 (Academy Award, Best Supporting Actor, 1961); The Sundowners, 1961; Topkapi (Academy Award, Best Supporting Actor), 1964; John Goldfarb, Please Come Home, 1964; Blackbeard's Ghost, 1967; The Comedians, 1968; Hot Millions, 1968; Viva Max, 1969; Treasure of Matecumbe, 1977; Un Taxi Mauve, 1977; The Last Remake of Beau Geste, 1977; Death on the Nile, 1978 (Best Film Actor, Variety Club of GB); Ashanti, The Thief of Baghdad, 1979; Charlie Chan and the Curse of the Dragon Queen, 1981; Evil under the Sun, 1981; director, producer and actor in film Billy Budd, 1961; director and actor in films: Hammersmith is Out, 1971; Memed My Hawk, 1984. Directed operas at: Covent Garden, 1962; Hamburg Opera, 1968; Paris Opera, 1973; Edinburgh Fest., 1973, 1981; Berlin Opera, 1978; Piccola Scala, Milan, 1981, 1982; Hamburg Opera, 1985; Master's Course, Salzburg, 1986. Acted in: revues: Swinging the Gate, 1940, Diversion, 1941; plays: Crime and Punishment, New Theatre, 1946; Love in Albania, St James's, 1949; King Lear, Stratford, Ont, 1979; directed Lady L, 1965; *television:* Omnibus: the life of Samuel Johnson (Emmy Award); Barefoot in Athens (Emmy Award), 1966; Storm in Summer (Emmy Award), 1970; The Mighty Continent (series), 1974; Einstein's Universe, 1979; 13 at Dinner, 1985; Dead Man's Folly, 1985; Peter Ustinov's Russia, 1985; World Challenge, 1985. Member, British Film Academy. Mem., British USA Bicentennial Liaison Cttee, 1973–. Benjamin Franklin Medal, Royal Society of Arts, 1957; Grammy Award. Order of the Smile (for dedication to idea of internat. assistance to children), Warsaw, 1974; Commandeur des Arts et des Lettres, France, 1985. *Publications:* House of Regrets, 1943; Beyond, 1944; The Banbury Nose, 1945; Plays About People, 1950; The Love of Four Colonels, 1951; The Moment of Truth, 1953; Romanoff and Juliet (Stage and Film); Add a Dash of Pity (short stories), 1959; Ustinov's Diplomats (a book of photographs), 1960; The Loser (novel), 1961; The Frontiers of the Sea, 1966; Krumnagel, 1971; Dear Me (autobiog.), 1977; Overheard (play), 1981; My Russia, 1983; contributor short stories to Atlantic Monthly. *Recreations:* lawn tennis, squash, collecting old masters' drawings, music. *Address:* 11 rue de Silly, 92100 Boulogne, France. *Clubs:* Garrick, Savage, Royal Automobile, Arts Theatre, Queen's.

UTIGER, Ronald Ernest, CBE 1977; Chairman, TI Group (formerly Tube Investments Ltd), since 1984 (Managing Director, 1984–86; Deputy Chairman and Group Managing Director, 1982–84; Director, since 1979); Director: British Alcan Aluminium, since 1982; Ultramar, since 1983; *b* 5 May 1926; *s* of Ernest Frederick Utiger and Kathleen Utiger (*née* Cram); *m* 1953, Barbara Anna von Mohl; one *s* one *d*. *Educ:* Shrewsbury Sch.; Worcester Coll., Oxford (2nd cl. Hons PPE 1950; MA). Economist, Courtaulds Ltd, 1950–61; British Aluminium Ltd: Financial Controller, 1961–64; Commercial Dir, 1965–68; Man. Dir, 1968–79; Chm., 1979–82. BNOC: Dir, 1976–80, Chm., 1979–80. Member: NEDC, 1981–84; BBC Consultative Gp on Industrial and Business Affairs, 1985–. Chm., Internat. Primary Aluminium Inst., 1976–78; Pres., European Primary Aluminium Assoc., 1976–77. Chm., CBI Economic and Financial Policy Cttee, 1980–83; Governor, NIESR, 1983–. FRSA; CBIM 1975. *Recreations:* music, gardening. *Address:* 9 Ailsa Road, St Margaret's-on-Thames, Twickenham, Mddx. *T:* 01–892 5810.

UTLEY, (Clifton) Garrick; journalist and broadcaster, since 1964; *b* 19 Nov. 1939; *s* of late Clifton Maxwell Utley and of Frayn Garrick Utley; *m* 1973, Gertje Rommeswinkel. *Educ:* Carleton Coll., Northfield, Minn, USA (BA 1961); Free Univ., Berlin. Correspondent, NBC News: Saigon, Vietnam, 1964–65; Berlin, Germany, 1966–68; Paris, France, 1969–71; NY, 1971–72; London (Senior European Correspondent), 1973–79; New York, 1980– (Chief Foreign Correspondent). Numerous documentary films on foreign affairs. Hon. LLD, Carleton Coll., 1979. *Recreations:* music, conversation. *Address:* c/o NBC News, 30 Rockefeller Plaza, New York, NY 10020, USA. *T:* 664–4444.

UTLEY, Peter; *see* Utley, T. E.

UTLEY, Thomas Edwin, (Peter), CBE 1980; Assistant Editor, The Daily Telegraph, since 1980; *b* 1 Feb. 1921; adopted *s* of late Miss Anne Utley; *m* 1951, Brigid Viola Mary, *yr d* of late D. M. M. Morrah, and of Ruth Morrah, *qv*; two *s* two *d*. *Educ:* privately; Corpus Christi Coll., Cambridge (1st cl. Hons Hist. Tripos; Foundn Schol.; MA). Sec., Anglo-French Relations post-War Reconstruction Gp, RIIA, 1942–44; temp. Foreign Leader writer, The Times, 1944–45; Leader writer, Sunday Times, 1945–47; Editorial staff, The Observer, 1947–48; Leader writer, The Times, 1948–54; Associate Editor, Spectator, 1954–55; freelance journalist and broadcasting, 1955–64; Leader writer, The Daily Telegraph, 1964–80. Contested (U) North Antrim, Feb. 1974. Pres., Paddington Cons. Assoc., 1979–80 (Chm., 1977–79); a Consultant Dir, Cons. Res. Dept, 1980–. *Publications:* Essays in Conservatism, 1949; Modern Political Thought, 1952; The Conservatives and the Critics, 1956; (ed jtly) Documents of Modern Political Thought, 1957; Not Guilty, 1957; Edmund Burke, 1957; Occasion for Ombudsmen, 1963; Your Money and Your Life, 1964; Enoch Powell: the Man and his Thinking, 1968; What Laws May Cure, 1968; Lessons of Ulster, 1975. *Address:* 60 St Mary's Mansions, St Mary's Terrace, W2. *T:* 01–723 1149.

UTTING, William Benjamin, CB 1985; Chief Inspector, Social Services Inspectorate, Department of Health and Social Security, since 1985; *b* 13 May 1931; *s* of John William Utting and Florence Ada Utting; *m* 1954, Mildred Jackson; two *s* one *d*. *Educ:* Great Yarmouth Grammar Sch.; New Coll., Oxford; Barnett House, Oxford. MA Oxon. Probation Officer: Co. Durham, 1956–58; Norfolk, 1958–61; Sen. Probation Officer, Co. Durham, 1961–64; Principal Probation Officer, Newcastle upon Tyne, 1964–68; Lectr in Social Studies, Univ. of Newcastle upon Tyne, 1968–70; Dir of Social Services, Kensington and Chelsea, 1970–76; Chief Social Work Officer, DHSS, 1976–85. Member: Chief Scientist's Res. Cttee, DHSS, 1973–76; SSRC, 1979–83; ESRC, 1984. *Publications:*

contribs to professional jls. *Recreations:* literature, music, art. *Address:* 76 Great Brownings, College Road, SE21 7HR. *T:* 01–670 1201.

UVAROV, Dame Olga (Nikolaevna), DBE 1983 (CBE 1978); DSc, FRCVS; President, Laboratory Animals Association, since 1984 (Vice-President, 1983–84); *d* of Nikolas and Elena Uvarov. *Educ:* Royal Vet. Coll. (Bronze Medals for Physiol. and Histol.). MRCVS 1934; FRCVS 1973. Asst in gen. mixed practice, 1934–43; own small animal practice, 1944–53; licence to practice and work at greyhound stadium, 1945–68; clinical res., Pharmaceutical industry, 1953–70; Head of Vet. Adv. Dept, Glaxo Laboratories, 1967–70; BVA Technical Inf. Service, 1970–76; Advr on Tech. Inf., BVA, 1976–78; Mem. MAFF Cttees under Medicines Act (1968), 1971–78. RCVS: Mem. Council, 1968–; Chm. Parly Cttee, 1971–74; Jun. Vice-Pres., 1975; Pres., 1976–77; President: Soc. Women Vet. Surgeons, 1947–49 (Sec., 1946); Central Vet. Soc., 1951–52; Assoc. Vet. Teachers and Res. Workers, 1967–68 (Pres. S Reg., 1967–68); Section of Comparative Medicine, RSocMed, 1967–68 (Sec., 1965–67; Sec. for Internat. Affairs, 1971–78, 1983–); Vice-Pres., Inst. of Animal Technicians, 1983–; Member Council: BVA, 1944–67; RSocMed, 1968–70 (Hon. Fellow, 1982); Res. Defence Soc., 1968–82 (Hon. Sec., 1978–82; Vice-Pres., 1982–); Member: Medicines Commn, 1978–82; Vet. Res. Club, 1967–; British Small Animal Vet. Assoc.; British Codex Sub-Cttee, Pharmaceutical Soc., 1970–71;

Senior Vice-Pres., RCVS, 1977–. FRVC 1979; Hon. FIBiol, 1983; Hon. DSc Guelph, 1976. Victory Gold Medal, Central Vet. Soc., 1965. *Publications:* contribs to: The Veterinary Annual; International Encyclopaedia of Veterinary Medicine, 1966; also papers in many learned jls. *Recreations:* work, travel, literature, flowers. *Address:* c/o The Royal College of Veterinary Surgeons, 32 Belgrave Square, SW1X 8QP. *Club:* Royal Society of Medicine.

UXBRIDGE, Earl of; Charles Alexander Vaughan Paget; *b* 13 Nov 1950; *s* and *heir* of 7th Marquess of Anglesey, *qv. Educ:* Dragon School, Oxford; Eton; Exeter Coll., Oxford. *Address:* Plâs-Newydd, Llanfairpwll, Gwynedd.

UZIELL-HAMILTON, Adrianne Pauline; a Recorder of the Crown Court, since 1985; *b* 14 May 1932; *e d* of late Dr Marcus and Ella Grantham; *m* 1952, Mario Reginald Uziell-Hamilton; one *s* one *d. Educ:* Maria Gray's Academy for Girls and privately. Called to the Bar, Middle Temple, 1965; *ad eundem* Mem., Inner Temple, 1976–; Head of Chambers, 1976–. Member: Legal Aid Panel, 1969–; General Council of the Bar, 1970–74 (Exec. Cttee, 1973–74). FRSA. *Publications:* articles on marriage contracts. *Recreations:* collecting ballet and theatre costume design, cooking for friends, conversation. *Address:* 3 Dr Johnson's Buildings, Temple, EC4. *T:* 01–353 8778. *Club:* Lloyds.

V

VACHON, His Eminence Cardinal Louis-Albert; *see* Quebec, Archbishop of, (RC).

VAEA, Baron of Houma; Minister for Labour, Commerce and Industries, Tonga, since 1973; *b* 15 May 1921; *s* of Viliami Vilai Tupou and Tupou Seini Vaea; *m* 1952, Tuputupu Ma'afu; three *s* three *d*. *Educ:* Wesley College, Auckland, NZ. RNZAF, 1942–45; Tonga Civil Service, 1945–53; ADC to HM Queen Salote, 1954–59; Governor of Haapai, 1959–68; Commissioner and Consul in UK, 1969; High Comr in UK, 1970–72. Given the title Baron Vaea of Houma by HM The King of Tonga, 1970. *Recreations:* Rugby, cricket, fishing. *Heir: e s* Albert Tuivanuavou Vaea, *b* 19 Sept. 1957. *Address:* PO Box 262, Nuku'alofa, Tonga.

VAES, Baron Robert, Hon. KCMG 1966; LLD; Grand Officer, Order of Leopold, Belgium; Director of Sotheby's, since 1984; *b* Antwerp, 9 Jan. 1919; created Baron, 1985; *m* 1947, Anne Albers; one *d*. *Educ:* Brussels Univ. (LLD; special degree in Commercial and Maritime Law). Joined Diplomatic Service, 1946: postings to Washington, Paris, Hong Kong, London, Rome and Madrid; Personal Private Sec. to Minister of Foreign Trade, 1958–60; Dir-Gen. of Polit. Affairs, 1964–66; Permanent Under-Sec., Min. of For. Affairs, For. Trade and Develt Cooperation, 1966–72; Ambassador: to Spain, 1972–76; to UK, 1976–84. Numerous foreign decorations including: Grand Officer, Legion of Honour (France); Grand Cross, Order of Isabela la Católica (Spain). *Recreation:* bridge. *Address:* 45 Gloucester Square, W2. *Clubs:* White's, Beefsteak, Anglo-Belgian; Royal Yacht of Belgium.

VAISEY, David George, FSA; FRHistS; Bodley's Librarian, Oxford, since 1986; Professorial Fellow, Exeter College, Oxford, since 1975; *b* 15 March 1935; *s* of William Thomas Vaisey and Minnie Vaisey (*née* Payne); *m* 1965, Maureen Anne (*née* Mansell); two *d*. *Educ:* Rendcomb Coll., Glos (schol.); Exeter Coll., Oxford (Exhibnr; BA Mod. Hist., MA). 2nd Lieut, Glos Regt and KAR, 1955–56. Archivist, Staffordshire CC, 1960–63; Asst then Sen. Asst Librarian, Bodleian Liby, 1963–75; Dep. Keeper, Oxford Univ. Archives, 1966–75; Keeper of Western Manuscripts, Bodleian Liby, 1975–86. Vis. Prof., Liby Studies, UCLA, 1985. FRHistS 1973; FSA 1974. *Publications:* Staffordshire and The Great Rebellion (jtly), 1964; Probate Inventories of Lichfield and District 1568–1680, 1969; (jtly) Victorian and Edwardian Oxford from old photographs, 1971; (jtly) Oxford Shops and Shopping, 1972; (jtly) Art for Commerce, 1973; Oxfordshire: a handbook for students of local history, 1973, 2nd edn 1974; The Diary of Thomas Turner 1754–65, 1984; articles in learned jls and collections. *Address:* 12 Hernes Road, Oxford OX2 7PU. *T:* Oxford 59258; Bodleian Library, Oxford OX1 3BG. *T:* Oxford 244675.

VAIZEY, Lady; Marina Vaizey; Art Critic of the Sunday Times, since 1974; *b* 16 Jan. 1938; *o d* of Lyman Stansky and late Ruth Stansky; *m* 1961, Lord Vaizey (*d* 1984); two *s* one *d*. *Educ:* Brearley Sch., New York; Putney Sch., Putney, Vermont; Radcliffe Coll., Harvard Univ. (BA Medieval History and Lit.); Girton Coll., Cambridge (BA, MA). Art Critic, Financial Times, 1970–74; Dance Critic, Now!, 1979–81; Mem. Arts Council, 1976–78 (Mem. Art Panel, 1973–78, Dep. Chm., 1976–78); Member: Advisory Cttee, DoE, 1975–81; Paintings for Hospitals, 1974–; Cttee, Contemporary Art Soc., 1975–79, 1980–; Hist. of Art and Complementary Studies Bd, CNAA, 1978–82; Photography Bd, CNAA, 1979–81; Fine Art Bd, CNAA, 1980–83; Passenger Services Sub-Cttee, Heathrow Airport, 1979–83; Adv. Cttee, Dulwich Picture Gall., 1986–; Trustee, Nat. Museums and Galleries on Merseyside, 1986–; Exec. Dir, Mitchell Prize for the Hist. of Art, 1976–. Governor: Camberwell Coll. of Arts and Crafts, 1971–82; Bath Acad. of Art, Corsham, 1978–81. Broadcaster, occasional exhibition organiser and lecturer; organised Critic's Choice, Tooth's, 1974; Painter as Photographer, touring exhibn, UK, 1982–85. Co-Sec., Radcliffe Club of London, 1968–74. *Publications:* 100 Masterpieces of Art, 1979; Andrew Wyeth, 1980; The Artist as Photographer, 1982; Peter Blake, 1985; articles in various periodicals, anthologies, exhibition catalogues. *Recreations:* arts, cats, travel. *Address:* 24 Heathfield Terrace, W4 4JE. *T:* 01–994 7994.

VAJPAYEE, Atal Bihari; Member, Rajya Sabha, 1962–67 and since 1986; Leader, Bharatiya Janata Party Parliamentary Party, 1980–84 and since 1986; *b* Gwalior, Madhya Pradesh, 25 Dec. 1926; *s* of Shri Krishna Bihari; unmarried. *Educ:* Victoria Coll., Gwalior; D.A.V. Coll., Kanpur (MA). Journalist and social worker. Arrested in freedom movement, 1942; Founder Mem., Jana Sangh, 1951–77; Leader, Jana Sangh Parly Party, 1957–77; Pres., Bharatiaya Jana Sangh, 1968–73; detained 26 June 1975, during Emergency; Founder Member: Janata Party, 1977–80; Bharatiya Janata Party, 1980– (Pres., 1980–86). Mem., Lok Sabha, 1957–62 and 1967–84; Minister of External Affairs, 1977–79; Chairman: Cttee on Govt Assurances, 1966–67; Public Accounts Cttee, 1969–70. Member: Parly Goodwill Mission to E Africa, 1965; Parly Delegns to Australia, 1967, Eur. Parlt, 1983; Indian Delegn to CPA meetings in Canada, 1966, Zambia, 1980, IOM, 1984; Indian Delegn to IPU Confs in Japan, 1974, Sri Lanka, 1975, Switzerland, 1984. Mem., Nat. Integration Council, 1958–62, 1967–73, 1986. President: All India Station Masters and Asst Station Masters Assoc., 1965–70; Pandit Deen Dayal Upadhyay Smarak Samiti, 1968–84; Pandit Deen Dayal Upadhyaya Janma Bhumi Smarak Samiti, 1979–. Formerly Editor: Rashtra-dharma; Panchajanya; Veer Arjun. *Publications:* Lok Sabha Men Atalji (collection of speeches); Qaidi Kavirai ki Kundaliyan; New Dimensions of India's Foreign Policy. *Address:* Shinde ki Chhawni, Gwalior, MP, India; 6 Raisina Road, New Delhi 110001, India. *T:* 385166.

VALDAR, Colin Gordon; Consultant Editor; *b* 18 Dec. 1918; 3rd *s* of Lionel and Mary Valdar; *m* 1st, 1940, Evelyn Margaret Barriff (marr. diss.); two *s*; 2nd, Jill, (*née* Davis). *Educ:* Haberdashers' Aske's Hampstead School. Free-lance journalist, 1936–39. Served

War of 1939–45, Royal Engineers, 1939–42. Successively Production Editor, Features Editor, Asst Editor, Sunday Pictorial, 1942–46; Features Editor, Daily Express, 1946–51; Asst Editor, Daily Express, 1951–53; Editor, Sunday Pictorial, 1953–59; Editor, Daily Sketch, 1959–62. Director, Sunday Pictorial Newspapers Ltd, 1957–59; Director, Daily Sketch and Daily Graphic Ltd, 1959–62; Chm., Bouverie Publishing Co., 1964–83. Founded UK Press Gazette, 1965. *Address:* 2A Ratcliffe Wharf, 18–22 Narrow Street, E14 8DQ. *T:* 01–791 2155.

VALE, Brian, OBE 1977; British Council Representative in Egypt and Cultural Counsellor, British Embassy, Cairo, since 1983; *b* 26 May 1938; *s* of Leslie Vale and May (*née* Knowles); *m* 1966, Margaret Mary Cookson; two *s*. *Educ:* Sir Joseph Williamson's Mathematical Sch., Rochester; Keele Univ. (BA, DipEd); King's Coll., London (MPhil). HMOCS, N Rhodesia, 1960–63; Assistant to Comr for N Rhodesia, London, 1963–64; Educn Attaché, Zambia High Commn, London, 1964–65; British Council: Rio de Janeiro, 1965–68; Appts Div., 1968–72; Educn and Sci. Div., 1972–75; Rep., Saudi Arabia, 1975–78; Dep. Controller, Educn and Sci. Div., 1978–80; Dir Tech. Educn and Trng Orgn for Overseas Countries, 1980–81; Controller, Sci., Technol. and Educn Div., 1981–83. *Publications:* contribs to specialist jls on educnl subjects and naval hist. *Recreations:* reading, talking, naval history. *Address:* c/o 10 Spring Gardens, SW1A 2BN. *T:* 01–930 8466. *Club:* Travellers'.

VALENTIA, 15th Viscount *cr* 1622 (Ireland); **Richard John Dighton Annesley;** Bt 1620; Baron Mountnorris 1628; farmer in Zimbabwe, since 1957; *b* 15 Aug. 1929; *s* of 14th Viscount Valentia, MC, MRCS, LRCP, and Joan Elizabeth (*d* 1986), *d* of late John Joseph Curtis; *S* father, 1983; *m* 1957, Anita Phyllis, *o d* of William Arthur Joy, Bristol; three *s* one *d*. *Educ:* Marlborough; RMA Sandhurst. BA Univ. of S Africa. Commnd RA, 1950; retd, rank of Captain, 1957. Schoolmaster, Ruzawi Prep. Sch., Marondera, Zimbabwe, 1977–83. *Recreations:* sport, shooting, fishing, leisure riding. *Heir: s* Hon. Francis William Dighton Annesley [*b* 29 Dec. 1959; *m* 1982, Shaneen Hobbs]. *Address:* East Range Farm, PO Chinhoyi, Zimbabwe.

VALENTINE, Rt. Rev. Barry, MA, BD, LTh, DD; Assistant Bishop of Maryland, since 1986; *b* 26 Sept. 1927; *s* of Harry John Valentine and Ethel Margaret Purkiss; *m* 1st, 1952, Mary Currell Hayes; three *s* one *d*; 2nd, 1984, Shirley Carolyn Shean Evans. *Educ:* Brentwood Sch.; St John's Coll., Cambridge; McGill Univ., Montreal. Curate, Christ Church Cath., Montreal, 1952; Incumbent, Chateauguay-Beauharnois, 1954; Dir, Religious Educn, Dio. Montreal, 1957; Rector of St Lambert, PQ, 1961; Exec. Officer, Dio. Montreal, 1965; Dean of Montreal, 1968; Bishop Coadjutor of Rupert's Land, 1969; Bishop of Rupert's Land, 1970–82; Chaplain, Univ. of British Columbia, 1984–85. Chancellor, 1970, Res. Fellow, 1983, St John's Coll., Winnipeg. Hon. DD: St John's Coll., Winnipeg, 1969; Montreal Dio. Theol Coll., 1970. *Publication:* The Gift that is in you, 1984. *Recreations:* music, theatre, walking, reading; over-aged and bibulous cricket. *Address:* Diocese of Maryland, 105 W Monument Street, Baltimore, Maryland 21201, USA. *Club:* Taverners Cricket.

VALENTINE, Prof. David Henriques; George Harrison Professor of Botany, University of Manchester, 1966–79, now Emeritus; *b* 16 Feb. 1912; *s* of Emmanuel and Dora Valentine; *m* 1938, Joan Winifred Todd; two *s* three *d*. *Educ:* Manchester Grammar Sch.; St John's Coll., Cambridge. MA 1936, PhD 1937. Curator of the Herbarium and Demonstrator in Botany, Cambridge, 1936; Research Fellow of St John's Coll., Cambridge, 1938; Ministry of Food (Dehydration Division), 1941; Reader in Botany, Durham, 1945, Prof., 1950–66. Trustee, BM (Natural History), 1975–83. Foreign Mem., Societas Scientiarum Fennica (Section for Natural Sciences), 1964. *Publications:* Flora Europaea, Vol. 1, 1964, Vol. 2, 1968, Vol. 3, 1972, Vol. 4, 1976, Vol. 5, 1980; Taxonomy, Phytogeography and Evolution, 1972; papers on experimental taxonomy in botanical journals. *Recreation:* reading novels. *Address:* 4 Pine Road, Didsbury, Manchester M20 0UY. *T:* 061–445 7224.

VALIN, Reginald Pierre; Chairman, Valin Pollen International plc, since 1984; *b* 8 March 1938; *s* of Pierre Louis Valin and Molly Doreen Valin; *m* 1960, Brigitte Karin Leister; one *d*. *Educ:* Emanuel School. National Service, RAF, 1957–59. Trainee Exec., Bank of America, 1959–60; Charles Barker & Sons Ltd, later Charles Barker City: Account Exec., 1960–64; Account Supervisor, 1964–68; Account Dir, 1968–70; Associate Dir, 1970–71; Dir, 1971–73; Man. Dir, 1973–76; Chief Exec., 1976–79; Founder Dir, Valin Pollen, 1979. *Address:* 86 Winchester Court, W8. *T:* 01–937 0825.

VALLANCE, Iain David Thomas; Chief Executive, British Telecom, since 1986 (a Corporate Director, since 1984); *b* 20 May 1943; *s* of Edmund Thomas Vallance and Janet Wright Bell Ross Davidson; *m* 1967, Elizabeth Mary McGonnigill; one *s* one *d*. *Educ:* Edinburgh Acad.; Dulwich Coll.; Glasgow Acad.; Brasenose Coll., Oxford; London Graduate School of Business Studies (MSc). Assistant Postal Controller, Post Office, 1966; Personal Asst to Chairman, 1973–75; Head of Finance Planning Division, 1975–76; Director: Central Finance, 1976–78; Telecommunications Finance, 1978–79; Materials Dept, 1979–81; Board Mem. for Orgn and Business Systems, BT, 1981–83; Man. Dir, Local Communications Services Div., BT, 1983–85; Chief of Operations, BT, 1985–86. Dir, Postel Investment Management Ltd, 1983–85; Trustee, British Telecom Staff Superannuation Fund, 1983–85. *Address:* 22 Dulwich Wood Avenue, SE19 1HD.

VALLANCE, Michael Wilson; Headmaster of Bloxham School since 1982; *b* 9 Sept. 1933; *er s* of late Vivian Victor Wilson Vallance and Kate Vallance, Wandsworth and Helston; *m* 1970, Mary Winifred Ann, *d* of John Steele Garnett; one *s* two *d*. *Educ:* Brighton Coll.; St John's Coll., Cambridge (MA). On staff of United Steel Companies Ltd, 1952–53; awarded United Steel Companies Scholarship (held at Cambridge), 1953; Asst Master, Abingdon School, 1957–61; Asst Master, Harrow School, 1961–72;

Headmaster, Durham Sch., 1972–82. Chairman: Cttee of Northern Isis, 1976–77; NE Div., HMC, 1981–82. *Recreations:* reading, cricket, gardening, the sea. *Address:* Bloxham School, Banbury, Oxon OX15 4PE. *T:* Banbury 720206. *Clubs:* MCC, Jesters.

VALLANCE-OWEN, Prof. John, MA, MD, FRCP, FRCPI, FRCPath; Foundation Professor and Chairman, Department of Medicine, since 1983, and Associate Dean, Faculty of Medicine, since 1984, Chinese University of Hong Kong; *b* 31 Oct. 1920; *s* of late Prof. E. A. Owen; *m* 1950, Renee Thornton; two *s* two *d. Educ:* Friar's Sch., Bangor; Epsom Coll.; St John's Coll., Cambridge (de Havilland Schol. from Epsom); London Hosp. (Schol.). BA 1943; MA, MB, BChir Cantab, 1946; MD Cantab 1951; FRCP 1962; Hon. FRCPI 1970; FRCPath 1971; FRCPI 1973. Various appts incl. Pathology Asst and Med. 1st Asst, London Hosp., 1946–51; Med. Tutor, Royal Postgrad. Med. Sch., Hammersmith Hosp., 1952–55 and 1956–58; Rockefeller Trav. Fellowship, at George S. Cox Med. Research Inst., Univ. of Pennsylvania, 1955–56; Cons. Phys. and Lectr in Medicine, Univ. of Durham, 1958–64; Cons. Phys., Royal Victoria Infirmary and Reader in Medicine, Univ. of Newcastle upon Tyne, 1964–66; Prof. of Medicine, QUB, 1966–82; Consultant Physician: Royal Victoria Hosp., Belfast, 1966–82 (Chm., Med. Div., 1979–81); Belfast City Hosp., 1966–82; Forster Green Hosp., Belfast, 1975–82 (Chm., Med. Staff Cttee, 1979–82). Hon. Consultant Physician to Hong Kong Govt, 1983–; Hon. Consultant to Army in Hong Kong, 1985–. Member: Standing Med. Adv. Cttee, Min. of Health and Social Services, NI, 1970–73; Specialist Adv. Cttee (General Internal Medicine) to the Govt; Northern Health and Social Services Bd, Dept of Health and Soc. Services, NI; Mem., Exec. Cttee, Assoc. of Physicians of GB and Ireland, 1976–79; Regional Adviser for N Ire, to RCP, 1970–75 and Councillor, RCP, 1976–79 (Oliver-Sharpey Prize, RCP, 1976); Councillor, RCPI, 1978–82; Mem. Research Cttee, Brit. Diabetic Assoc.; Brit. Council Lectr, Dept Medicine, Zürich Univ., 1963; 1st Helen Martin Lectr, Diabetic Assoc. of S Calif, Wm H. Mulberg Lectr, Cincinnati Diabetes Assoc., and Lectr, Brookhaven Nat. Labs, NY, 1965; Brit. Council Lectr, Haile Selassie Univ., Makerere UC and S African Univs, 1966; Guest Lectr: Japan Endocrinological Soc., 1968; Madrid Univ., 1969; Endocrine Soc. of Australia, 1970, Bologna Univ., 1976. *Publications:* Essentials of Cardiology, 1961 (2nd edn 1968); Diabetes: its physiological and biochemical basis, 1976; papers in biochem., med., and scientific jls on carbohydrate and fat metabolism and aetiology of diabetes mellitus and related conditions, with special reference to insulin antagonism. *Recreations:* tennis, golf, music. *Address:* Department of Medicine, The Chinese University of Hong Kong, Prince of Wales Hospital, Shatin, New Territories, Hong Kong. *T:* Hong Kong 0–6363127. *Clubs:* East India; Beas River Country (Royal Hong Kong Jockey); United Services Recreation (Hong Kong).

VALLANCE WHITE, James Ashton; Principal Clerk, Judicial Office and Fourth Clerk at the Table, House of Lords, since 1983; *b* 25 Feb. 1938; *s* of Frank Ashton White and Dieudonnée Vallance. *Educ:* Allhallows School; Albert Schweitzer College, Switzerland; St Peter's College, Oxford (MA). Clerk, House of Lords, 1961; Clerk of Committees, 1971–78; Chief Clerk, Public Bill Office, 1978–83. *Address:* 14 Gerald Road, SW1. *T:* 01–730 7658; Biniparrell, San Luis, Menorca. *T:* 366369. *Club:* Brooks's.

VALLAT, Prof. Sir Francis Aimé, GBE 1982; KCMG 1962 (CMG 1955); QC 1961; Barrister-at-Law; Emeritus Professor of International Law, University of London; *b* 25 May 1912; *s* of Col Frederick W. Vallat, OBE; *m* 1939, Mary Alison Cockell (marr. diss. 1973); one *s* one *d. Educ:* University College, Toronto (BA Hons); Gonville and Caius Coll., Cambridge (LLB). Called to Bar, Gray's Inn, 1935, Bencher, 1971; Assistant Lecturer, Bristol Univ., 1935–36; practice at Bar, London, 1936–39; RAFVR (Flt Lieut), 1941–45; Asst Legal Adviser, Foreign Office, 1945–50; Legal Adviser, UK Permanent Deleg. to UN, 1950–54; Deputy Legal Adviser, FO, 1954–60, Legal Adviser, 1960–68. (On leave of absence) Actg Director, Inst. of Air and Space Law, and Vis. Prof. of Law, McGill Univ., 1965–66. Dir of International Law Studies, King's Coll. London, 1968–76 (Reader, 1969–70, Prof., 1970–76). Dir of Studies, Internat. Law Assoc., 1969–73. UK Mem., UN Fact Finding Panel, 1969–. Associate Mem., Institut de Droit International, 1965, elected Mem. 1977; Member: Internat. Law Commn, 1973–81 (Chm. 1977–78); Permanent Court of Arbitration, 1980–; Curatorium, Hague Acad., 1982–. Expert Consultant, UN Conf. on Succession of States in respect of Treaties, 1977–78. Dr en dr. *hc*, Lausanne Univ., 1979. *Publications:* International Law and the Practitioner, 1966; Introduction to the Study of Human Rights, 1972; articles in British Year Book of International Law and other journals. *Recreation:* restoration of antiques. *Address:* 17 Ranelagh Grove, SW1W 8PA. *T:* 01–730 6656; 3 Essex Court, Temple, EC4. *T:* 01–583 9294. *Club:* Hurlingham.

VALLINGS, Vice-Adm. Sir George (Montague Francis), KCB 1986; Flag Officer, Scotland and Northern Ireland, since 1985; *b* 31 May 1932; *s* of Robert Archibald Vallings and Alice Mary Joan Vallings (*née* Bramsden); *m* 1964, Tessa Julia Cousins; three *s. Educ:* Belhaven Hill, Dunbar; Royal Naval College, Dartmouth. Midshipman, HMS Theseus, 1950–51; HMS Scarborough, 1961–65; HMS Defender, 1967–68; HMS Bristol, 1970–73; Naval Adviser and RNLO Australia, 1974–76; Captain F2, HMS Apollo, 1977–78; Dir, Naval Ops and Trade, 1978–80; Commodore, Clyde, 1980–82; Flag Officer, Gibraltar, 1983–85. *Recreations:* family and sport. *Address:* Meadowcroft, 25 St Mary's Road, Long Ditton, Surrey. *T:* 01–398 6932. *Club:* Royal Ocean Racing.

VALLIS, Rear-Adm. Michael Anthony, CB 1986; Director General, Marine Engineering, Ministry of Defence, 1984–86; *b* 30 June 1929; *s* of R. W. H. Vallis and S. J. Dewsnup; *m* 1959, Pauline Dorothy Abbott, Wymondham, Leics; three *s* one *d. Educ:* RN College, Dartmouth; RN Engineering College, Plymouth; RN College, Greenwich. CEng, MIMechE, FIMarE. HMS Vanguard, 1951–52; HMS Triumph, 1954–56; Ship Dept, MoD, 1956–59; Liaison Officer with French Navy, 1959–61; HMS Scorpion, 1961–63; Staff of RNEC Manadon, 1963–66; Ship Dept, MoD, 1966–69; HMS Fearless, 1969–71; JSSC, 1971; Naval Staff, 1971–73; Ship Dept, MoD, 1973–77; HMS Cochrane, 1977–79; Director of Naval Recruiting, 1979–82; Dir Gen., Surface Ships, MoD, 1983–84. *Recreations:* fishing, gardening, walking, food and wine, theatre. *Address:* Holly Lodge, 54 Bloomfield Park, Bath, Avon BA2 2BX. *Club:* Royal Commonwealth Society.

VALOIS, Dame Ninette de; *see* de Valois.

VAN ALLAN, Richard; principal bass; Director, National Opera Studio, since 1986; *b* 28 May 1935; *s* of Joseph Arthur and Irene Hannah Van Allan; *m*; two *s* one *d. Educ:* Worcester College of Education (DipEd Science); Birmingham School of Music. Glyndebourne, 1964; Welsh National Opera, 1968; English National Opera, 1969; Royal Opera House, Covent Garden, 1971; performances also: l'Opéra de Paris, Bordeaux, Nice, Toulouse; USA: Boston, San Diego, Phoenix, Houston, Austin, San Antonio, New Orleans, NY; Argentina: Buenos Aires; Spain: Madrid and Barcelona; Hong Kong. Recordings incl. Don Giovanni (Grammy nomination), Così fan tutte (Grammy Award), Luisa Miller, L'Oracolo. *Recreations:* shooting, tennis, golf. *Address:* 3 Baytree Court, Baytree Road, SW2 5RR.

VAN ALLEN, Prof. James Alfred; Professor of Physics and Head of Department of Physics (of Physics and Astronomy since 1959), since 1951, Carver Professor of Physics, since 1972, University of Iowa, USA; *b* Iowa, 7 Sept. 1914; *s* of Alfred Morris and Alma Olney Van Allen; *m* 1945, Abigail Fithian Halsey II; two *s* three *d. Educ:* Public High School, and Iowa Wesleyan Coll., Mount Pleasant, Iowa (BSc); University of Iowa, Iowa City (MSc, PhD). Research Fellow, then Physicist, Carnegie Instn of Washington, 1939–42; Physicist, Applied Physics Lab., Johns Hopkins Univ., Md, 1942. Ordnance and Gunnery Officer and Combat Observer, USN, 1942–46, Lt-Comdr 1946. Supervisor of High-Altitude Research Group and of Proximity Fuze Unit, Johns Hopkins Univ., 1946–50. Leader, various scientific expeditions to Central and S Pacific, Arctic and Antarctic, for study of cosmic rays and earth's magnetic field, using Aerobee and balloon-launched rockets, 1949–57. Took part in promotion and planning of International Geophysical Year, 1957–58; developed radiation measuring equipment on first American satellite, Explorer I, and subseq. satellites (discoverer of Van Allen Radiation Belts of the earth, 1958); has continued study of earth's radiation belts, aurorae, cosmic rays, energetic particles in interplanetary space, planetary magnetospheres. Research Fellow, Guggenheim Memorial Foundation, 1951; Research Associate (controlled thermonuclear reactions), Princeton Univ., Project Matterhorn, 1953–54; Regents' Fellow, Smithsonian Inst., 1981. Mem., Space Science Bd of Nat. Acad. of Sciences, 1958–70, 1980–83; Fellow: American Phys. Society; Amer. Geophysical Union (Pres., 1982–84), etc; Member: Nat. Acad. of Sciences; RAS; Royal Swedish Acad. of Sciences; Founder Member, International Acad. of Astronautics, etc. Holds many awards and hon. doctorates; Gold Medal, RAS, 1978. *Publications:* numerous articles in learned journals and contribs to scientific works. *Address:* Department of Physics and Astronomy, University of Iowa, Iowa City, Iowa 52242, USA; 5 Woodland Mounds Road, RFD 6, Iowa City, Iowa 52240, USA.

van BELLINGHEN, Jean-Paul; Grand Officer, Order of Leopold II; Knight, Order of the Crown; Belgian Ambassador to the Court of St James's, since 1984; *b* 21 Oct. 1925; *s* of Albert and Fernande van Bellinghen; *m* Martine Vander Elst; one *s* one *d* (and one *s* decd). *Educ:* Catholic University of Leuven. Fellow, Centre for Internat. Affairs, Harvard Univ.; Lectr, Univ. of Grenoble. Joined Diplomatic Service, 1953; served Cairo, Washington, New York (UN), Min. of Foreign Affairs, Geneva, 1968–74; Chef de Cabinet to Minister of Foreign Affairs, 1974–77, to Minister of Foreign Trade, 1977–79; Ambassador in Kinshasa, 1980–83. Holds numerous foreign decorations. *Publication:* Servitude in the Sky (Harvard Centre for Internat. Affairs), 1967. *Recreations:* golf, sailing, skiing, filming. *Address:* 36 Belgrave Square, SW1X 8QB. *T:* 01–235 1752. *Club:* Anglo-Belgian.

VAN CAENEGEM, Prof. Raoul Charles Joseph; Ordinary Professor of Medieval History and of Legal History, University of Ghent, Belgium, since 1964; *b* 14 July 1927; *s* of Joseph Van Caenegem and Irma Barbaix; *m* 1954, Patricia Mary Carson; two *s* one *d. Educ:* Univ. of Ghent (LLD 1951; PhD 1953); Univ. of Paris; London Univ. Ghent University: Assistant to Prof. of Mediaeval Hist., 1954; Lectr, 1960. Vis. Fellow, UC, Cambridge, 1968; Arthur L. Goodhart Prof. in Legal Science, and Vis. Fellow of Peterhouse, Cambridge Univ., 1984–85. Corresp. Fellow, Medieval Acad. of Amer., 1971; Corresp. FBA 1982. Mem. Acad. of Scis, Brussels, 1974; For. Mem., Acad. of Scis, Amsterdam, 1977. Hon. Dr: Tübingen, 1977; Catholic Univ., Louvain, 1984. Francqui Prize, Brussels, 1974. *Publications:* Royal Writs in England from the Conquest to Glanvill: studies in the early history of the common law, 1959; The Birth of the English Common Law, 1973; Geschiedenis van Engeland: van Stonehenge tot het tijdperk der vakbonden (History of England: from Stonehenge to the era of the trade unions), 1982; (contrib.) International Encyclopaedia of Comparative Law, 1973. *Recreations:* wine (Bordeaux, Alsace), swimming, classical music, bridge. *Address:* Veurestraat 47, 9821 Gent-Afsnee, Belgium. *T:* 091–226211. *Club:* Universitaire Stichting (Brussels).

VANCE, Charles Ivan; actor, director and theatrical producer; *b* 6 Dec. 1929; *s* of Eric Goldblatt and Sarah (*née* Freeman); *m* 1959, Hon. Imogen Moynihan; one *d. Educ:* Royal Sch., Dungannon; Queen's Univ., Belfast. FInstD 1972; FRSA 1975. Early career as broadcaster; acting debut with Anew MacMaster Co., Gaiety, Dublin, 1949; dir, first prodn, The Glass Menagerie, Arts, Cambridge, 1960; founded Civic Theatre, Chelmsford, 1962; i/c rep. cos, Tunbridge Wells, Torquay, Whitby and Hastings, 1962–; as Dir of Charles Vance Prodns, created Eastbourne Theatre Co., 1969; dir. own adaptation of Wuthering Heights, 1972; wrote and staged four pantomimes, 1972–75; devised and dir. The Jolson Revue, 1974 (staged revival, Australia, 1978; world tour, 1981); played Sir Thomas More in A Man for All Seasons, and dir, Oh! What a Lovely War, Greenwood, 1975; prod and dir. world tour of Paddington Bear, 1978; produced: Cinderella, Stafford, 1981; Aladdin, Bognor, 1981. Purchased Leas Pavilion Theatre, Folkestone, 1976 (HQ of own theatre organisation until 1985). Produced (London and national tours): Stop the World—I Want to Get Off (revival), 1976; Salad Days (revival), 1977; (also dir.) In Praise of Love, 1977; Witness for the Prosecution, (revival), 1979; Hallo Paris, 1980; This Happy Breed (revival), 1980; Starlite Spectacular, 1981; The Kingfisher (revival), 1981; The Hollow (revival), 1982 (also dir.); The Little Hut, Australia (also dir.), 1982; Cinderella, Aladdin, 1982 (also wrote); Lady Chatterley's Lover, 1983; The Mating Game, 1983; Cinderella, The Sleeping Beauty, The Gingerbread Man, The Wizard of Oz, 1983; Dick Whittington, Jack and the Beanstalk, Cinderella, Pinocchio, Jesus Christ Superstar (revival), 1984; Mr Cinders (revival), 1985; Policy for Murder, 1984 (also dir.); Jane Eyre, 1985 (also wrote and dir.); Oh Calcutta! (revival), 1985–86; directed: Verdict (revival), 1984; Alice in Wonderland, 1985 (also wrote); Dick Whittington, Aladdin, Jack and the Beanstalk, Cinderella, 1986–87 (also wrote). Controls: Floral Hall Th., Scarborough; Beck Th., Hillingdon. Theatrical Management Association: Mem. Council, 1969; Pres., 1971–73 and 1973–76; Exec. Vice-Pres., 1976– (also of Council of Reg. Theatre). Advisor to Govt of Ghana on bldg Nat. Theatre, 1969. Director: Theatres Investment Fund, 1975–83; Entertainment Investments Ltd, 1980–82; International Holiday Investments, 1980–; Southern Counties Television, 1980–; Channel Radio, 1981–; Gateway Broadcasting Ltd, 1982; Trustee Dir, Folkestone Theatre Co., 1979–. Chairman: Provincial Theatre Council, 1971–; Standing Adv. Cttee on Local Authority and the Theatre, 1977– (Vice-Chm., 1975–77). Vice-Chairman: Theatres Adv. Council, resp. for theatres threatened by develt, 1974–; (also Dir) Festival of Brit. Theatre, 1975–. Member: Theatres Nat. Cttee, 1971–; Drama Adv. Panel, SE Arts Assoc., 1974–; Prince of Wales' Jubilee Entertainments Cttee, 1977; Entertainment Exec. Cttee, Artists' Benev. Fund, 1980–; Variety Club of GB, 1984–; Rotary Internat., 1971–; Vice-Pres., E Sussex Br., RSPCA, 1975–; Rotary Club of London, 1986. Founded Vance Offord (Publications) Ltd, publishers of British Theatre Directory, British Theatre Review, and Municipal Entertainment, 1971. Launched theatre jl, Post (in assoc. with Pearl and Dean), 1986. *Publication:* British Theatre Directory, 1972, 1973, 1974, 1975. *Recreations:* sailing (crossed Atlantic single-handed, 1956), cooking (Cordon Bleu, 1957), travelling, animals. *Address:* Quince Cottage, Bilsington, near Ashford, Kent. *T:* Aldington 311. *Clubs:* Hurlingham, Royal Automobile, Directors', Kennel.

VANCE, Cyrus Roberts; Secretary of State, USA, 1977–80; barrister-at-law; *b* Clarksburg, W Va, 27 March 1917; *m* 1947, Grace Elsie Sloane; one *s* four *d. Educ:* Kent Sch.; Yale Univ. (BA 1939); Yale Univ. Law Sch. (LLB 1942). Served War, USNR, to Lieut (s.g.), 1942–46. Asst to Pres., The Mead Corp., 1946–47; admitted to New York Bar, 1947; Associate and Partner of Simpson Thacher & Bartlett, New York, 1947–60, Partner, Jan. 1956–60, 1967–77 and 1980–. Special Counsel, Preparedness Investigation Sub-cttee of

Senate Armed Services Cttee, 1957–60; Consulting Counsel, Special Cttee on Space and Astronautics, US Senate, 1958; Gen. Counsel, Dept of Defense, 1961–62; Sec. of the Army, 1962–64; Dep. Sec. of Defense, 1964–67; Special Rep. of the President: in Civil Disturbances in Detroit, July-Aug. 1967 and in Washington, DC, April 1968; in Cyprus, Nov.-Dec. 1967; in Korea, Feb. 1968; one of two US Negotiators, Paris Peace Conf. on Vietnam, May 1968–Feb. 1969; Mem., Commn to Investigate Alleged Police Corruption in NYC, 1970–72; Pres., Assoc. of Bar of City of New York, 1974–76. Mem. Bd of Trustees: Rockefeller Foundn, 1970–77, 1980–82 (Chm., 1975–77); Yale Univ., 1968–78, 1980–; Amer. Ditchley Foundn, 1980– (Chm., 1981–); Mayo Foundn, 1980–. Hon. degrees: Marshall, 1963; Trinity Coll., 1966; Yale, 1968; West Virginia, Bowling Green, 1969; Salem Coll., 1970; Brandeis, 1971; Amherst, W Virginia Wesleyan, 1974; Harvard, Colgate, Gen. Theol Seminary, Williams Coll., 1981. Medal of Freedom (US), 1969. *Publications:* The Choice is Ours, 1983; Hard Choices, 1983. *Address:* Simpson Thacher & Bartlett, One Battery Park Plaza, New York, NY 10004, USA. *T:* 212/483–9000.

VANCOUVER, Archbishop of, (RC), since 1969; **Most Rev. James F. Carney,** DD; *b* Vancouver, BC, 28 June 1915. *Educ:* Vancouver College; St Joseph's Seminary, Edmonton, Alta. Ordained, 1942; Vicar-General and Domestic Prelate, 1964; Auxiliary Bishop of Vancouver, 1966. *Address:* 150 Robson Street, Vancouver, BC V6B 2A7, Canada. *T:* 683–0281.

VAN CULIN, Rev. Canon Samuel; Secretary General, Anglican Consultative Council, since 1983; *b* 20 Sept. 1930; *s* of Samuel Van Culin and Susie (*née* Mossman). *Educ:* High School, Honolulu; Princeton University (AB); Virginia Theological Seminary (BD). Ordained 1955; Curate, St Andrew's Cathedral, Honolulu, 1955–56; Canon Precentor and Rector, Hawaiian Congregation, 1956–58; Asst Rector, St John, Washington DC, 1958–60; Gen. Sec., Laymen International, Washington, 1960–61; Asst Sec., Overseas Dept, Episcopal Church, USA, 1962–68; Sec. for Africa and Middle East, Episcopal Church, USA, 1968–76; Executive, World Mission, 1976–83. Hon. Canon: Canterbury Cathedral, 1983; Ibadan, Nigeria, 1983; Jerusalem, 1984. Hon. DD: Virginia Seminary, 1977; Gen. Theol Seminary, 1983. *Recreations:* music, swimming. *Address:* Anglican Consultative Council, 14 Great Peter Street, SW1P 3NQ. *T:* 01–222 2851. *Clubs:* Athenæum; Princeton, Huguenot Society (New York).

VANDEN-BEMPDE-JOHNSTONE; *see* Johnstone.

VAN DEN BERGH, James Philip, CBE 1946; Director of Unilever Ltd, 1937–65, retired; Vice-Chairman of Lindustries, 1965–75; Deputy Chairman, William Baird & Co., 1965–75; Chairman, National Cold Stores (Management Ltd), 1965–70; *b* 26 April 1905; *s* of Albert Van den Bergh; *m* 1929, Betty D'Arcy Hart; one *s* one *d*. *Educ:* Harrow; Trinity Coll., Cambridge. Entered Van den Berghs Ltd, 1927; subseq. Man. Dir; Chm., 1942. Min. of Food: Dir of Margarine and Cooking Fats, 1939; Dir of Dehydration, 1940; Dir of Fish Supplies, 1945. Government Director, British Sugar Corp., 1956–58, retired. Member Exec. Council, Food Manufacturers' Federation, 1957 (President, 1958–61); Member Food Research Advisory Cttee, 1960–65 (Chairman, 1963); Member Council, Queen Elizabeth Coll., London Univ., 1961–73; Hon. Fellow, 1968. *Address:* Field House, Cranleigh, Surrey. *Club:* Leander (Henley).

VAN DEN BOGAERDE, Derek Niven, (Dirk Bogarde); actor; *b* 28 March 1921. *Educ:* University College School; Allan Glen's (Scotland). Served War of 1939–45: Queen's Royal Regt, 1940–46, Europe and Far East, and Air Photographic Intelligence. Hon. DLitt St Andrews, 1985. Chevalier de l'Ordre des Arts et des Lettres, 1982. Films include (since 1947): Hunted, Appointment in London, They Who Dare, The Sleeping Tiger, Doctor in the House, Doctor at Sea, Doctor at Large, Simba, The Spanish Gardener, Cast a Dark Shadow, Ill Met by Moonlight, The Blue Lamp, So Long at the Fair, Quartet, A Tale of Two Cities (Sidney Carton), The Wind Cannot Read, The Doctor's Dilemma, Libel, Song Without End, The Angel Wore Red, The Singer Not The Song, Victim, HMS Defiant, The Password is Courage, The Lonely Stage, The Mindbenders, The Servant, Doctor in Distress, Hot Enough for June, The High Bright Sun, King and Country, Darling . . ., Modesty Blaise, Accident, Our Mother's House, Mister Sebastian, The Fixer, Oh What A Lovely War, Götterdämmerung, Justine, Death in Venice, Upon This Rock, Le Serpent, The Night Porter, Permission To Kill, Providence, A Bridge Too Far, Despair; *TV:* The Patricia Neal Story (USA), 1981 (film); May We Borrow Your Husband? (also adapted), 1986 (play). *Theatre:* Cliff, in Power Without Glory, 1947; Orpheus, in Point of Departure, 1950; Nicky, in The Vortex, 1953; Alberto, in Summertime, 1955–56; Jezebel, Oxford Playhouse, 1958, etc. *Publications:* A Postillion Struck by Lightning (autobiog.), 1977; Snakes and Ladders (autobiog.), 1978; A Gentle Occupation (novel), 1980; Voices in the Garden (novel), 1981; An Orderly Man (autobiog.), 1983; West of Sunset (novel), 1984; Backcloth (autobiog.), 1986. *Recreations:* gardening, painting, motoring. *Address:* London Management, 235–241 Regent Street, W1.

VAN DEN HOVEN, Helmert Frans; *see* Hoven.

VANDERFELT, Sir Robin (Victor), KBE 1973 (OBE 1954); Secretary-General, Commonwealth Parliamentary Association, 1961–86; *b* 24 July 1921; *y s* of late Sydney Gorton Vanderfelt, OBE, and Ethel Maude Vanderfelt (*née* Tremayne); *m* 1962, Jean Margaret Becker, *d* of John and Eve Steward; two *s* (and one step *s* one step *d*). *Educ:* Haileybury; Peterhouse, Cambridge. Served War in India and Burma, 1941–45. Asst Secretary, UK Branch, CPA, 1949–59; Secretary, 1960–61. Secretary, UK Delegn, Commonwealth Parly Conf., India, 1957; as Sec.-Gen., CPA, has served as Secretary to Parliamentary Conferences throughout Commonwealth, 1961–85, also attended many area and regional confs, including Conf. of Commonwealth Speakers and Clerks. Mem. Council, RIPA, 1986–; Governor: Queen Elizabeth House, Oxford, 1980–; E-SU, 1984–. *Recreation:* gardening. *Address:* No 6 Saddler's Mead, Wilton, Salisbury, Wilts SP2 0DE. *T:* Salisbury 742637.

VAN DER KISTE, Wing Commander Robert Edgar Guy, DSO 1941; OBE 1957; Royal Auxiliary Air Force, retired; Director, Plymouth Incorporated Chamber of Trade and Commerce, 1974–80 (Secretary, 1964–74); *b* 20 July 1912; *y s* of late Lt-Col F. W. Van der Kiste, DSO; *m* 1939, Nancy Kathleen, *er d* of Alec George Holman, MRCS, LRCP, and Grace Kathleen Brown; one *s* two *d* (and one *s* decd). *Educ:* Cheltenham College. Commissioned Royal Air Force, Nov. 1936. Served War of 1939–45 (despatches, DSO); retired, 1959. Commanded No 3 MHQ Unit, Royal Auxiliary Air Force. *Recreation:* caravanning. *Address:* Lavandou, Moorland Park, South Brent, Devon TQ10 9AR.

van der LOON, Prof. Piet; Professor of Chinese, University of Oxford, and Fellow of University College, Oxford, 1972–Oct. 1987; *b* 7 April 1920; *m* 1947, Minnie C. Snellen; two *d*. *Educ:* Univ. of Leiden. Litt. Drs Leiden, MA Cantab. Univ. Asst Lectr, Cambridge, 1948; Univ. Lectr, Cambridge, 1949. *Publications:* Taoist Books in the Libraries of the Sung Period, 1984; articles in Asia Major, T'oung Pao, Jl Asiatique. *Recreation:* travel. *Address:* University College, Oxford.

VANDERMEER, (Arnold) Roy; QC 1978; a Recorder of the Crown Court, since 1972; *b* London, 26 June 1931; *o s* of late William Arnold Vandermeer and Katherine Nora Vandermeer; *m* 1964, Caroline Veronica (*née* Christopher); one *s* two *d*. *Educ:* Dame Alice Owen's Sch., Islington; King's Coll., London (LLB). Called to Bar, Gray's Inn, 1955. Flt-Lt, RAF, 1955–58. Chairman: Greater Manchester Structure Plan Examination in Public, 1978; County of Avon Structure Plan Examination in Public, 1983. *Recreations:* reading, cricket. *Address:* The Field House, Barnet Lane, Elstree, Herts. *T:* 01–953 2244. *Club:* MCC.

van der MEER, Dr Simon; Ridder Nederlandse Leeuw, 1985; Senior Engineer, CERN, Geneva (European Organisation for Nuclear Research), since 1956; *b* 24 Nov. 1925; *s* of Pieter van der Meer and Jetske Groeneveld; *m* 1966, Catharina M. Koopman; one *s* one *d*. *Educ:* Technical University, Delft, Netherlands; physical engineer. Philips Research Laboratories, Eindhoven, 1952–56. Hon. degrees: Univ. of Geneva, 1983; Amsterdam, 1984; Genoa, 1985. Nobel Prize for Physics (jtly), 1984. *Recreation:* literature. *Address:* CERN, 1211 Genève 23, Switzerland. *T:* 832915.

van der MEULEN, Daniel; Netherlands Indies civil servant and diplomat; Arabist author and traveller; *b* 4 Sept. 1894; *m* 1st, 1917, A. C. E. Kelling; three *s* (and one *s* murdered in Germany) two *d*; 2nd, 1959, Dr H. M. Duhm; one *s*. *Educ:* Leyden Univ. Netherlands Indies Civil Service, North of Sumatra in Toba-lake district of Toba Batak country, 1915–23; studied Arabic and Islam under Prof. Dr C. Snouck Hurgronje, Leyden Univ.; consular and diplomatic service, Jeddah, Sa'oudi-Arabia, 1926–31; first exploration in South Arabia, 1931; Netherlands Indies Civil Service, Pajakumbuh, Central Sumatra, Palembang, South Sumatra, 1932–38; second exploration in South Arabia, 1939; Netherlands Indies Civil Service, Makassar, South Celebes, 1939–41; Minister in Jeddah, Sa'oudi-Arabia, 1941–45; Resident Adviser to Netherlands East India Government at Batavia, 1945–48; Chief of the Arabic Section of Radio Netherland World-broadcast at Hilversum, 1949–51. Hon. Mem., Royal Netherlands Geographical Soc., 1956. Officer, Oranje Nassau; Patron's Medal, Royal Geographical Society, London, 1947. *Publications:* Hadhramaut, some of its mysteries unveiled (with map by Prof. Dr H. von Wissmann), 1932; Aden to the Hadhramaut, 1947 (numerous trans.); Onbekend Arabië, 1947; Ontwakend Arabië, 1954; Mÿn weg naar Arabië en de Islaam, 1954; The Wells of Ibn Sa'ud, 1954; Verdwijnend Arabië, 1959; Faces in Shem, 1961; Ik Stond Erbÿ, het einde van ons koloniale rÿk, 1965; Hoort Ge de donder niet? (autobiog.), 1977, trans. as Don't You Hear the Thunder?: a Dutchman's story, 1981. *Address:* 9 Flierder Weg, 7213LT Gorssel, Holland. *T:* 05759–1684.

van der POST, Sir Laurens (Jan), Kt 1981; CBE 1947; writer, farmer, soldier, explorer, conservationist; Trustee, World Wilderness Foundation, since 1974; *b* Philippolis, S Africa, 13 Dec. 1906; *s* of late C. W. H. Van Der Post, Chairman of Orange Free State Republic Volksraad, and late M. M. Lubbe, Boesmansfontein, Wolwekop, and Stilton; *m* 1928, Marjorie Wendt; one *d* (one *s* decd); *m* 1949, Ingaret Giffard. Served War of 1939–45: Ethiopia; North Africa; Syria; Dutch East Indies; Java; commanded 43 Special Military Mission, Prisoner of War 1943–45, thereafter Lord Mountbatten's Military-Political Officer, attached to 15 Indian Army Corps, Java, and subseq. to British Minister, Batavia, until 1947. Since then has undertaken several missions for British Government and Colonial Development Corp. in Africa, including Government Mission to Kalahari, 1952. FRSL. Hon. DLitt: Univ. of Natal, 1964; Univ. of Liverpool, 1976; Rhodes Univ., 1978; St Andrews, 1980; DUniv Surrey, 1971. *Films:* Lost World of Kalahari, 1956; A Region of Shadow, 1971; The Story of Carl Gustav Jung, 1971; All Africa Within Us, 1975; Zulu Wilderness: Black Umfolozi Re-discovered, 1979. *Publications:* In a Province, 1934; Venture to the Interior, 1952 (Book Society choice and Amy Woolf Memorial Prize); A Bar of Shadow, 1952 (repr., 1972); The Face Beside the Fire, 1953; Flamingo Feather, 1955 (German Book Society choice); The Dark Eye in Africa, 1955; Creative Pattern in Primitive Man, 1956; The Lost World of the Kalahari, 1958 (American Literary Guild Choice); The Heart of the Hunter, 1961; The Seed and the Sower, 1963 (South African CNA Award for best work published in 1963; filmed, 1983, as Merry Christmas, Mr Lawrence); Journey into Russia, 1964; A Portrait of all The Russias, 1967; The Hunter and the Whale, 1967 (CNA and Yorkshire Post Fiction Awards); A Portrait of Japan, 1968; The Night of the New Moon, 1970; A Story like the Wind, 1972; A Far Off Place, 1974; A Mantis Carol, 1975; Jung and the Story of Our Time, 1976; First Catch Your Eland: a taste of Africa, 1977; Yet Being Someone Other, 1982; (with Jane Taylor) Testament to the Bushmen, 1984. *Recreations:* walking, climbing, ski-ing, tennis, studying grasses and cooking in winter. *Address:* lives, London, Aldeburgh, Suffolk, and Wolwekop, Philippolis, South Africa.

VANDORE, Peter Kerr; QC (Scot.) 1982; *b* 7 June 1943; *s* of James Vandore and Janet Kerr Fife; *m* 1970, Hilary Ann Davies; two *d*. *Educ:* Berwickshire High Sch., Duns; Edinburgh Univ. (MA Hons Hist.; LLB). Called to the Scottish Bar, 1968; Standing Counsel to Sec. of State for Scotland, for private legislation procedure, 1975–86. Mem., Legal Aid Central Cttee, 1972–85. *Publications:* contribs to Juridical Rev. *Address:* 26 India Street, Edinburgh. *T:* 031–225 1980.

VANDYK, Neville David, PhD; Editor, Solicitors' Journal, since 1968; *b* 6 Sept. 1923; *yr s* of late Arthur Vandyk, solicitor, and Constance Vandyk (*née* Berton); *m* 1956, Paula (*née* Borchert); one *d*. *Educ:* St Paul's Sch.; London School of Economics, Univ. of London (BCom 1947, PhD 1950). Admitted Solicitor, 1957. HM Forces, incl. service in India, Burma and Japan, 1942–46; research asst, LSE, 1951–52; with Herbert Oppenheimer, Nathan & Vandyk, Solicitors, 1953–58; Asst Editor, 1958, Managing Editor, 1963, Solicitors' Journal; Member for its duration, Law Society's Constitution Cttee prior to the adoption in 1969 of their revised Bye-Laws, 1966–68. Founder Mem., W London Law Soc. (Pres., 1970–71); Mem. Council, Medico-Legal Soc., 1963–66, Vice-Pres. 1966–67, and 1985–, Hon. Treas. 1967–85; Founder Mem., Assoc. of Disabled Professionals, Vice-Chm. 1972–80; Mem. for its duration, Royal Bor. of Kensington and Chelsea's Working Gp on the Disabled and their Families, 1980–81. Governor (nominated by Univ. of London) William Blake County Secondary Sch., 1957–70. Freeman 1962, Liveryman 1963, Worshipful Co. of Solicitors of City of London. Founder's Meml Lecture, Brit. Council for Rehabilitation of the Disabled, 1971; Hon. Prof. of Legal Ethics, Univ. of Birmingham, 1981–83. *Publications:* Tribunals and Inquiries, 1965; Accidents and the Law, 1975, 2nd edn 1979; (title) National Health Service, in Halsbury's Laws of England, 3rd edn 1959, 4th edn 1982. *Address:* 21 Lamb's Conduit Street, WC1N 3NJ.

VANE; *see* Fletcher-Vane, family name of Baron Inglewood.

VANE, family name of **Baron Barnard.**

VANE, Sir John (Robert), Kt 1984; FRS 1974; Group Research and Development Director, The Wellcome Foundation, 1973–85; *b* 29 March 1927; *s* of Maurice Vane and Frances Florence Vane (*née* Fisher); *m* 1948, Elizabeth Daphne Page; two *d*. *Educ:* Birmingham Univ. (BSc Chemistry, 1946); St Catherine's Coll., Oxford (BSc Pharmacology, 1949; DPhil 1953; DSc 1970; Hon. Fellow, 1983). Stothert Research Fellow of Royal Soc., 1951–53; Asst Prof. of Pharmacology, Yale Univ., 1953–55; Sen. Lectr in Pharmacology, Inst. of Basic Medical Sciences, RCS, 1955–61; Reader in

Pharmacology, RCS, Univ. of London, 1961–65; Prof. of Experimental Pharmacology, RCS, Univ. of London, 1966–73. Visiting Professor: King's Coll., London, 1976; Charing Cross Hosp. Med. Sch., 1979; Harvard Univ., 1979. British Pharmacological Soc.: Meetings Sec., 1967–70; Gen. Sec., 1970–73; For. Sec., 1979–85; Hon. Mem., 1985. Mem., Royal Acad. of Medicine, Belgium, 1978 (Hon. Foreign Mem., 1983). Foreign Member: Royal Netherlands Acad. of Arts and Scis, 1979; Polish Acad. of Scis, 1980; For. Associate, US Nat. Acad. of Scis, 1983; For. Hon. Mem., Amer. Acad. of Arts and Scis, 1982; Hon. Mem., Polish Pharmacological Soc., 1973; Hon. FACP, 1978; Hon. FRCP, 1983; Hon. Fellow, Swedish Soc. of Medical Scis, 1982. Hon. DM Krakow, 1977; Hon. Dr René Descartes Univ., Paris, 1978; Hon. DSc: Mount Sinai Med. Sch., NY, 1980; Aberdeen, 1983; NY Med. Coll., 1984; Birmingham, 1984. (Jtly) Albert Lasker Basic Med. Res. Award, 1977; Baly Medal, RCP, 1977; (jtly) Peter Debye Prize, Univ. of Maastricht, 1980; Feldberg Foundn Prize, 1980; Ciba Geigy Drew Award, Drew Univ., 1980; Dale Medal, Soc. for Endocrinol., 1981; Nobel Prize for Medicine (jtly), 1982; Galen Medal, Apothecaries' Soc., 1983; Biol Council Medal, 1983; Louis Pasteur Foundn Prize, Calif, 1984. *Publications:* (ed jtly) Adrenergic Mechanisms, 1960; (ed jtly) Prostaglandin Synthetase Inhibitors, 1974; (ed jtly) Metabolic Functions of the Lung, Vol. 4, 1977; (ed jtly) Handbook of Experimental Pharmacology, 1978; (ed jtly) Prostacyclin, 1979; (ed jtly) Interactions Between Platelets and Vessel Walls, 1981; numerous papers in learned jls. *Recreations:* photography, travel, underwater swimming. *Clubs:* Athenæum, Garrick.

VANE-TEMPEST-STEWART, family name of **Marquess of Londonderry.**

VANGEKE, Most Rev. Sir Louis, MSC; KBE 1980 (OBE 1974); Member, Legion of Honour of French Republic, 1980; Bishop of Bereina, Papua New Guinea, 1976–80, and Auxiliary to Archbishop V. P. Copas (RC), 1974; Member, Society of Missionaries of the Sacred Heart of Jesus, French Province, 1941; *b* 25 June 1904; *s* of Vagu'u Kaoka, Veifa'a; *Educ:* CM Yule Island, 1909–19; Minor and Major Jesuit Seminary of Madagascar; Little Brother Oblate of St Joseph, 1922–28; in training for 12 years for his ordination as first Papuan Priest in the Roman Catholic Church, in Madagascar, 1928–37, and worked for many years among Kuni people in Papua, 1941–70; Auxiliary Bishop of Port Moresby, 1970–73 (RC Bp of Culusi); ordained first indigenous Papuan Bishop of RC Church by Pope Paul VI, in Sydney, 1970, and acclaimed Chief (*hc*) of Mekeo Village of Veifa'a, Papua, 1970. Hon. LLD Univ. of Papua New Guinea, 1974. *Publications:* Liturgical Texts in the Kuni language, 1968–70; composed music for jubilee mass, 1962; hymns; songs. *Address:* Catholic Parish, Kubana CP, PO Box 177, Port Moresby, Papua New Guinea.

van HASSELT, Marc; Headmaster, Cranleigh School, 1970–84; *b* 24 April 1924; *s* of Marc and Helen van Hasselt; *m* 1949, Geraldine Frances Sinclair; three *s* one *d*. *Educ:* Sherborne; Selwyn Coll., Cambridge (MA). Served War of 1939–45 (despatches): commissioned in Essex Yeomanry, RHA, 1944; served North-West Europe. Lecturer in Commonwealth Studies, RMA, Sandhurst, 1950–58; Asst Master, Oundle School, 1959–70 (Housemaster, Sanderson House, 1963–70). *Publications:* occasional articles in Yachting World. *Recreation:* cruising under sail. *Address:* 2 Winton Close, Lymington, Hants. *Clubs:* East India, Devonshire, Sports and Public Schools, Royal Cruising; Royal Lymington Yacht.

van HEYNINGEN, William Edward, MA Oxon, ScD Cantab; Founding Master of St Cross College, Oxford, 1965–79, Hon. Fellow, 1979; Reader in Bacterial Chemistry, University of Oxford, 1966–79, now Emeritus; *b* 24 Dec. 1911; *s* of late George Philipus Stephanus van Heyningen and late Mabel Constance (*née* Higgs); *m* 1940, Ruth Eleanor Treverton; one *s* one *d*. *Educ:* village schools in S Africa; Univs of Stellenbosch and Cambridge. Commonwealth Fund Fellow, Harvard Univ., and College of Physicians and Surgeons, Columbia Univ., 1936–38; Senior Student of Royal Commn for Exhibn of 1851, 1938–40. Staff Member, Wellcome Physiological Research Laboratories, 1943–46; Sen. Res. Officer, Sir William Dunn School of Pathology, Oxford Univ., 1947–66; Sec., Soc. for Gen. Microbiology, 1946–52; Curator of the Bodleian Library, 1962–85; Mem. Hebdomadal Council, Oxford Univ., 1963–69. Vis. Prof., State Univ. of New York, 1967. Visitor of the Ashmolean Museum, 1969–. Trustee, Ruskin Sch. of Drawing, 1975–77. Consultant, Cholera Adv. Cttee, Nat. Insts of Health, USA, 1968–73. Chevalier de l'Ordre National du Mérite, 1980. *Publications:* Bacterial Toxins, 1950; Cholera: the American scientific experience 1947–1980, 1983; The Key to Lockjaw: an autobiography, 1986; papers mainly concerned with bacterial toxins in various books and journals. *Address:* College Farm, North Hinksey Village, Oxford OX2 0NA. *Club:* Reform.

van LENNEP, Jonkheer Emile; Commander, Order of the Netherlands Lion; Commander, Order of Orange Nassau; Minister of State; Secretary-General, OECD, 1969–84; *b* 20 Jan. 1915; *s* of Louis Henri van Lennep and Catharina Hillegonda Enschede; *m* 1941, Alexa Alison Labberton; two *s* two *d*. *Educ:* Univ. of Amsterdam. Foreign Exchange Inst., 1940–45; Netherlands Bank, 1945–48; Financial Counsellor, High Representative of the Crown, Indonesia, 1948–50; Netherlands Bank, 1950–51. Treasurer-General, Ministry of Finance, The Netherlands, 1951–69. Chairman: Monetary Cttee, EEC, 1958; Working Party No 3, OECD, 1962; Mem., Board Directors, KLM (Airline), 1951. KStJ. Grand Cross or Grand Officer in various foreign orders. *Address:* Ruychrocklaan 444, The Hague, Netherlands. *Club:* Haagsche (The Hague).

van MAURIK, Ernest Henry, OBE 1944; HM Diplomatic Service, retired; *b* 24 Aug. 1916; *s* of late Justus van Maurik and Sybil van Maurik (*née* Ebert), BEM; *m* 1945, Winifred Emery Ritchie Hay (*d* 1984); one *s* one *d*. *Educ:* Lancing Coll.; Ecole Sup. de Commerce, Neuchatel, Switzerland. Worked in Tea Export, Mincing Lane, 1936–39. Commnd as 2nd Lt, in Wiltshire Regt, 1939; seconded to Special Ops Exec., 1941–46; demob. with hon. rank of Lt-Col (subst. Major), 1946. Joined Foreign Office, 1946; Moscow, 1948–50; West Germany and West Berlin, 1952–56; Buenos Aires, 1958–62; Copenhagen, 1965–67; Rio de Janeiro, 1968–71; FCO, 1971–75. Officier de la Couronne (Belgium), 1944. *Recreations:* golf, gardening, languages. *Address:* Parkside, The Common, Sevenoaks, Kent. *T:* Sevenoaks 452173. *Club:* Special Forces.

VANN, (William) Stanley, DMus(Cantuar); *b* 15 Feb. 1910; *s* of Frederick and Bertha Vann; *m* 1934, Frances Wilson; one *s* one *d*. *Educ:* privately. BMus London; FRCO; ARCM. Asst Organist, Leicester Cath., 1931–33; Chorus Master, Leicester Phil. Soc., 1931–36; Organist and Choirmaster, Gainsborough Parish Ch., Dir of Music, Queen Elizabeth Grammar Sch. and High Sch., Gainsborough, Conductor, Gainsborough Mus. and Orch. Socs, also Breckin Choir, Doncaster, 1933–39; Organist and Choirmaster, Holy Trinity PC, Leamington Spa, Founder-Conductor, Leamington Bach Choir and Warwicks Symph. Orch., and Dir of Music, Emscote Lawn Sch., Warwick, 1939–49. Served War of 1939–45, RA, final rank Captain. Master of Music, Chelmsford Cath., Conductor, Chelmsford Singers and Essex Symph Orch., Prof., Trinity Coll. of Music, London, 1949–53; Master of Music, Peterborough Cath., Conductor, Peterborough Phil. Choir and Orch., 1953–77; retired. Examiner, TCL, 1953–77; Mem. Council and Examr RCO, 1972–; Mem., ISM; Adjudicator, Brit. Fed. of Festivals, Canadian Fed. Fest. and Hong Kong Fest., 1950–84; Chairman: Peterborough Music Fest., 1953–; Eastern Area Council, British Fedn of Music Festivals, 1982–. Hon. DMus Cantuar 1971 (for eminent services

to church music); Hon. FTCL 1953. *Publications:* three settings of Missa Brevis; Evening Services in E minor, C major and in D; anthems, motets, carols and choral arrangements of folk-songs and of Handel; four sets of Preces and Responses and a Collection of Anglican Chants. *Recreations:* railway modelling, painting, gardening. *Address:* Holly Tree Cottage, Wansford, Peterborough PE8 6PL. *T:* Stamford 782192.

VANNECK, family name of **Baron Huntingfield.**

VANNECK, Air Commodore Hon. Sir Peter Beckford Rutgers, GBE 1977 (OBE (mil.) 1963); CB 1973; AFC 1955; AE 1954; MA, DSc; JP; DL; Member (C) Cleveland, and Yorkshire North, European Parliament, since 1984 (Cleveland, 1979–84); *b* 7 Jan. 1922; *y s* of 5th Baron Huntingfield, KCMG and Margaret Eleanor, *d* of Judge Ernest Crosby, NY; *m* 1st, 1943, Cordelia (marr. diss. 1984), *y d* of Captain R. H. Errington, RN (retd); one *d* (and one *d* decd); 2nd, 1984, Mrs Elizabeth Forbes. *Educ:* Geelong Grammar Sch.; Stowe Sch. (Scholar); Trinity Coll., Cambridge (MA); Harvard. MIAgrE; TEng (CEI). Cadet, RN, 1939; served in Nelson, King George V, Eskimo, 55th LCA Flot., Wren, MTB 696 (in comd), 771 Sqdn and 807 Sqdn FAA, resigned 1949; Cambridge Univ. Air Sqdn, 1949; 601 (Co. of London) Sqdn RAuxAF, 1950–57 (101 Sqdn Mass. Air Nat. Guard, 1953); 3619 (Co. of Suffolk) Fighter Control Unit, 1958–61 (in comd 1959–61); No 1 Maritime HQ Unit, 1961–63; Group Captain, 1963; Inspector RAuxAF, 1963–73, Hon. Inspector-General 1974–83; ADC to the Queen, 1963–73; Hon. Air Cdre, No 1 (Co. Hertford) Maritime HQ Unit, RAuxAF, 1973–87. Gentleman Usher to the Queen, 1967–79. Mem., Stock Exchange Council, 1968–79 (Dep. Chm., 1973–75). Prime Warden, Fishmongers' Co., 1981–82; Past Master: Gunmakers' Co., 1977; Guild of Air Pilots and Air Navigators, 1976–77; Freeman, Watermen's and Lightermen's Co.; Alderman of Cordwainer Ward, City of London, 1969–79; Sheriff, City of London, 1974–75; Lord Mayor of London, 1977–78. Member: Ipswich Gp Hosps Bd, 1956–62; City and E London AHA, 1973–77; Gov. Body, Brit. Post Graduate Medical Fedn, Univ. of London, 1963–71; St Bartholomew's Hosp. Bd of Governors, 1971–73; Special Trustee, St Bartholomew's Hosp., 1974–82; Trustee: RAF Museum, 1976–87; Royal Academy Trust, 1981–87; Governor, Royal Shakespeare Theatre, 1974–87. President: Gun Trades Assoc., 1976–87; Stock Exchange Ski Club, 1977–87. KStJ (Mem. Chapter General). Hon. DSc City Univ. DL Greater London, 1970; High Sheriff, Suffolk, 1979. Churchwarden of St Mary-le-Bow, 1969–84. Supernumerary JP, City of London. Commander, Legion of Honour (France), 1981; Grand Officer, Order of the Crown (Belgium), 1983. *Recreations:* sailing, shooting, ski-ing, bad bridge. *Address:* 2/10 Brompton Square, SW3 2AA. *Clubs:* White's, Pratt's; Royal Yacht Squadron, Royal London Yacht (Commodore, 1977–78); Seawanhaka Corinthian Yacht (US).

See also Baron Huntingfield, H. D. Stevenson.

VAN OSS, (Adam) Oliver, MA; FSA; Master of the London Charterhouse, 1973–84; *b* 28 March 1909; *s* of S. F. Van Oss, The Hague, newspaper proprietor; *m* 1945, Audrey (*d* 1960), *widow* of Capt. J. R. Allsopp; two *d*. *Educ:* Dragon Sch., Oxford; Clifton; Magdalen Coll., Oxford. Housemaster and Head of Modern Language Dept, Eton Coll.; Lower Master, Eton Coll., 1959–64, Acting Headmaster, 1964; Headmaster of Charterhouse, 1965–73. Mem. Council, City Univ. Chevalier de la Légion d'Honneur. *Publications:* Eton Days, 1976; (ed jtly) Cassell's French Dictionary, 8th edn; articles on ceramics, travel and education. *Recreations:* all forms of art and sport. *Address:* 7 Park Lane, Woodstock OX7 1UD. *Clubs:* Pratt's, Beefsteak.

VAN PRAAGH, Dame Peggy, DBE 1970 (OBE 1966); Member of Council and Guest Teacher, Australian Ballet School, 1975–82; director and producer of ballet in UK and many other countries; *b* London, 1 Sept. 1910; *d* of Harold John Van Praagh, MD, and Ethel Louise Shanks. *Educ:* King Alfred Sch., Hampstead. Studied and trained in the Cecchetti Method of classical ballet with Margaret Craske; passed Advanced Cecchetti Exam., 1932; danced in Tudor's Adam and Eve, Camargo Society, 1932. Joined Ballet Rambert and danced at Ballet Club, 1933–38; created rôles in Tudor's Ballets: Jardin aux Lilas, Dark Elegies, Gala Performance, Soirée Musicale, etc; joined Tudor's Co., the London Ballet, as a Principal Dancer, 1938. Examiner and Cttee member, Cecchetti Society, 1937–. Joined Sadler's Wells Ballet as dancer and teacher, 1941; danced Swanhilda in Coppelia, Blue Girl in Patineurs, etc. Producer and Asst Director to Ninette De Valois, Sadler's Wells Theatre Ballet, and worked with that company, 1946–56. Produced many TV ballets for BBC. Guest Teacher and Producer for National Ballet of Canada, 1956; Guest Producer: Munich, Bavarian Opera House, 1956; Theatre Royal, Stockholm, 1957; Director: Norsk Ballet, 1957–58; Edinburgh International Festival Ballet, 1958; Borovansky Ballet in Australia, 1960; Guest Teacher: Jacob's Pillow, USA, 1959; Ballet of Marquis de Cuevas, 1961; Artistic Dir, Australian Ballet, 1962–74 and 1978. Brought Australian Ballet to Commonwealth Festival, London, 1965; to Expo '67 Montreal, followed by tour of S America, 1967. Hon. DLitt, Univ. of New England, NSW, 1974; Hon. LLD Melbourne, 1981. Queen Elizabeth II Coronation Award, Royal Academy of Dancing, 1965; Distinguished Artist Award, Australia Council, 1975. *Publications:* How I Became a Ballet Dancer, 1954; The Choreographic Art (with Peter Brinson), 1963. *Recreations:* motoring, swimming. *Address:* 5/248 The Avenue, Parkville, Victoria 3052, Australia.

van RIEMSDIJK, John Theodore, CIMechE; Keeper of Mechanical and Civil Engineering, Science Museum, 1976–84; author and broadcaster; *b* 13 Nov. 1924; *s* of late Adrianus K. van Riemsdijk and Nora P. van Riemsdijk (*née* James); *m* 1957, Jocelyn Kilma Arfon-Price. *Educ:* University College Sch.; Birkbeck Coll. (BA). Served SOE, 1943–46. Manufacturer of gearing, 1946–54; Science Museum: Asst, 1954; Lectr, 1961; Educn Officer, 1969. Engaged in setting up Nat. Railway Mus., York, 1973–75. *Publications:* Pregrouping Railways, 1972; Pictorial History of Steam Power, 1980; Compound Locomotives, 1982; Science Museum Books; contribs to: BBC Publications; Newcomen Soc. Trans, Procs of IMechE. *Recreations:* oil painting, making models. *Address:* 2 Farquhar Street, Hertford. *T:* Hertford 52750.

VANSITTART, Guy Nicholas; formerly Chairman, Vauxhall Motors and General Motors Ltd; *b* 8 Sept. 1893; *y s* of late Capt. Robert Arnold Vansittart and late Alice (*née* Blane). *Educ:* Eton; Trinity Coll., Oxford. BA (Oxon), Honour School of History. Captain, Indian Army, Central India Horse, 1913–22. *Address:* Flat 7, 20 Charles Street, W1X 7HD.

van STRAUBENZEE, Sir William (Radcliffe), Kt 1981; MBE 1954; MP (C) Wokingham since 1959; Second Church Estates Commissioner, since 1979; *b* 27 Jan. 1924; *o s* of late Brig. A. B. van Straubenzee, DSO, MC and late Margaret Joan, 3rd *d* of A. N. Radcliffe, Kensington Square, W8, and Bag Park, Widecombe-in-the-Moor, Newton Abbot, S Devon. *Educ:* Westminster. Served War of 1939–45: five years with Royal Artillery (Major); Regimental and Staff Appointments, including two years in Far East. Admitted a Solicitor, 1952. Chairman, Young Conservative Nat. Advisory Cttee, 1951–53; contested Wandsworth (Clapham), 1955; PPS to Minister of Educn (Sir David Eccles), 1960–62; Jt Parly Under-Sec. of State, Dept of Educn and Science, 1970–72; Minister of State, NI Office, 1972–74. Chairman: Select Cttee on Assistance to Private Members, 1975–77; Select Cttee on Educn and the Arts, 1984–; Cons. Parly Educn Cttee,

1979–83. Mem. Exec. Cttee, 1922 Cttee, 1979–. Member of Richmond (Surrey) Borough Council, 1955–58. Chairman: United and Cecil Club, 1965–68 (Hon. Sec., 1952–59); Westminster House Boys' Club, Camberwell, 1965–68 (Hon. Sec., 1952–65); Nat. Council for Drama Training, 1976–81; Mem., Court of Reading Univ. Hon. Sec., Fedn of Conservative Students, 1965–71, Vice-Pres., 1974. A Church Comr; Mem. House of Laity, Church Assembly, 1965–70, Mem. General Synod, 1975–85; Chm., Dioceses Commn, 1978–86. Patron of Living of Rockbourne, Hants. Trustee, Lambeth Palace Library. Hon. Vice-Pres., National Union of Students. *Recreations:* walking, reading. *Address:* 199 Westminster Bridge Road, SE1. *T:* 01–928 6855; 30 Rose Street, Wokingham, Berkshire. *T:* Wokingham 784464. *Clubs:* Carlton, Garrick.

van WACHEM, Lodewijk Christiaan; Knight in the Order of the Netherlands Lion, 1981; CBE (Hon.) 1977; mechanical engineer, Netherlands; President, Royal Dutch Petroleum Co., The Hague, since 1982 (Managing Director, 1976–82); Member, Presidium of Board of Directors of Shell Petroleum NV; Managing Director, The Shell Petroleum Co. Ltd; Director, Shell Canada Ltd, since 1982; Chairman: Shell Oil Co., USA, since 1982; Committee of Managing Directors of Royal Dutch/Shell Group of Companies, since 1985; *b* Pangkalan Brandan, Indonesia, 31 July 1931; *m* 1958, Elisabeth G. Cristofoli; two *s* one *d*. *Educ:* Technological Univ., Delft (mech. engr). Joined BPM, The Hague, 1953; Mech. Engr, Compania Shell de Venezuela, 1954–63; Shell-BP Petr. Develt Co. of Nigeria: Chief Engr, 1963–66; Engrg Manager, 1966–67; Brunei Shell Petr. Co. Ltd: Head of Techn. Admin., 1967–69; Techn. Dir, 1969–71; Head of Prod. Div., SIPM, The Hague, 1971–72; Chm. and Managing Dir, Shell-BP Petr. Develt Co. of Nigeria, 1972–76; Co-ordinator, Exploration and Prod., SIPM, The Hague, 1976–79. *Address:* Carel van Bylandtlaan 30, The Hague, Holland. *T:* 070–77.21.18.

VARAH, (Doris) Susan, OBE 1976; *b* 29 Oct. 1916; *d* of Harry W. and Matilda H. Whanslaw; *m* 1940, Rev. (Edward) Chad Varah, *qv*; four *s* (three of them triplets) one *d*. *Educ:* Trinity Coll. of Music. Mothers' Union: Diocesan Pres., Southwark, 1956–64; Vice-Chm., Central Young Members' Cttee, 1962–64; Central Vice-Pres., 1962–70; Vice-Chm., Central Social Problems Cttee, 1965–67, Chm., 1970–76; Chm., Central Overseas Cttee, 1968–70, 1977–82; Central Pres., 1970–76. *Recreations:* music, gardening, motoring. *Address:* 42 Hillersdon Avenue, SW13 0EF. *T:* 01–876 5720.

VARAH, Rev. Dr (Edward) Chad, OBE 1969; Founder, The Samaritans (to befriend the suicidal and despairing), 1953, President of London Branch, 1974–86 (Director, 1953–74); President, Befrienders International (Samaritans Worldwide), 1983–86 (Chairman 1974–83); Rector, Lord Mayor's Parish Church of St Stephen Walbrook, in the City of London, since 1953; a Prebendary of St Paul's Cathedral, since 1975; *b* 12 Nov. 1911; *e s* of Canon William Edward Varah, Vicar of Barton-on-Humber, and Mary (*née* Atkinson); *m* 1940, Doris Susan Whanslaw (*see* D. S. Varah); four *s* (three of them triplets) one *d*. *Educ:* Worksop Coll., Notts; Keble Coll., Oxford (Hon. Fellow 1981); Lincoln Theol. Coll.; Exhibnr in Nat. Sci. (Keble); BA Oxon (Hons in PPE), 1933, MA 1943. Secretary: OU Russian Club, 1931; OU Slavonic Club, 1932; Founder Pres., OU Scandinavian Club, 1931–33. Deacon, 1935, Priest, 1936. Curate of: St Giles, Lincoln, 1935–38; Putney, 1938–40; Barrow-in-Furness, 1940–42; Vicar of: Holy Trinity, Blackburn, 1942–49; St Paul, Clapham Junction, 1949–53. Staff Scriptwriter-Visualiser for Eagle and Girl, 1950–61; Sec., Orthodox Churches Aid Fund, 1952–69; Pres., Cttee for Publishing Russian Orthodox Church Music, 1960–76; Chm., The Samaritans (Inc.), 1963–66; Pres., Internat. Fedn for Services of Emergency Telephonic Help, 1964–67. Hon. Liveryman, Worshipful Co. of Carmen, 1977. Hon. LLD Leicester, 1979. Roumanian Patriarchal Cross, 1968. Albert Schweitzer Gold Medal, 1972; Louis Dublin Award, Amer. Assoc. Suicidology, 1974; with Befrienders International, Prix de l'Institut de la Vie, 1978; Honra ao Mérito Medal, São Paulo TV, Brazil, 1982. *Publications:* Notny Sbornik Russkogo Pravoslavnogo Tserkovnogo Peniya, vol. 1 Bozhestveniya Liturgia, 1962, vol. 2 Pt 1 Vsenoshchnaya, 1975; (ed) The Samaritans, 1965; Samariter: Hilfe durchs Telefon, 1966; Vänskap som hjälp, 1971; (TV play) Nobody Understands Miranda, 1972; (ed) The Samaritans in the 70s, 1973, rev. edn 1977; Telephone Masturbators, 1976; (ed) The Samaritans in the 80s, 1980, rev. edn as The Samaritans: befriending the suicidal, 1984, rev. edn 1987; Some Day I'll find you (play), 1984. *Recreations:* reading, writing autobiography, watching videos of nature programmes on television. *Address:* St Stephen's Church, Walbrook, EC4N 8BN. *T:* 01–283 4444. *Clubs:* Sion College (EC4); Oxford Union.

VARAH, Susan; *see* Varah, Doris S.

VARCOE, (Christopher) Stephen; baritone; *b* 19 May 1949; *s* of Philip William and Mary Northwood Varcoe; *m* 1972, Melinda Davies; two *s* one *d* (and one *s* decd). *Educ:* King's School, Canterbury; King's College, Cambridge (MA). Freelance concert and opera singer, 1970–; Calouste Gulbenkian Foundation Fellowship, 1977. *Recreations:* painting, gardening, building. *Address:* Ansells Farm, Alphamstone, Bures, Suffolk. *T:* Twinstead 570.

VARCOE, Jeremy Richard Lovering Grosvenor; HM Diplomatic Service; on special leave with Standard Chartered Bank, Istanbul, since 1985; *b* 20 Sept. 1937; *s* of Ronald Arthur Grosvenor Varcoe and late Zoe Elizabeth Varcoe (*née* Lovering); *m* 1961, Wendy Anne Moss; two *d*. *Educ:* Charterhouse; Lincoln Coll., Oxford (MA). National Service, Royal Tank Regt, 2nd Lieut, 1956–58. HMOCS: District Officer, Swaziland, 1962–65. Called to the Bar, Gray's Inn, 1966; Lectr in Law, Univ. of Birmingham, 1967–70; resigned to enter HM Diplomatic Service, 1970; FCO, 1970–72; Dep. Secretary General, Pearce Commn on Rhodesian Opinion, 1972; First Sec. (Information), Ankara, 1972–74; First Sec. and Head of Chancery, Lusaka, 1974–78; FCO, 1978–79; Commercial Counsellor, Kuala Lumpur, 1979–82; Head of Southern African Dept, FCO, 1982–84; Counsellor, Ankara, 1984–85. *Publication:* Legal Aid in Criminal Proceedings—a Regional Survey (Birmingham Univ.), 1970. *Recreations:* sailing, golf. *Club:* Royal Commonwealth Society.

VARCOE, Stephen; *see* Varcoe, C. S.

VAREY, Prof. John Earl, PhD, LittD; FBA 1985; Principal, Westfield College, since Jan. 1984, and Professor of Spanish, since 1963, London University; *b* 26 Aug. 1922; *s* of Harold Varey and Dorothy Halstead Varey; *m* 1948, Cicely Rainford Virgo; two *s* one *d* (and one *s* decd). *Educ:* Blackburn Grammar Sch.; Emmanuel Coll., Cambridge. MA 1948; PhD 1951; LittD 1981. Served Bomber and Transport Commands, RAF, 1942–45. Westfield College: Lectr in Spanish, 1952; Reader, 1957; Actg Principal, 1983. Leverhulme Trust Fellow, 1970–71 and 1976; Visiting Professor: Univ. of Indiana, 1970, 1971; Purdue Univ., 1977. Pres., Assoc. of Hispanists of GB and Ireland, 1979–81. Corresp. Mem., Spanish Royal Acad., 1981. Hijo ilustre de Madrid, 1980. *Publications:* Historia de los títeres en España, 1957; (with N. D. Shergold) Los autos sacramentales en Madrid en la época de Calderón: 1637–1681, 1961; (ed) Galdós Studies, 1970; (ed with N. D. Shergold and Jack Sage) Juan Vélez de Guevara: Los celos hacen estrellas, 1970; Pérez Galdós: Doña Perfecta, 1971; (with N. D. Shergold) Fuentes para la historia del teatro en España, 8 vols, 1971–; (with D. W. Cruickshank) The Comedias of Calderón, 19 vols, 1973; (ed with J. M. Ruano) Lope de Vega: Peribáñez y el Comendador de Ocaña, 1980; contrib. Bull. of Hispanic Studies, etc. *Recreation:* publishing. *Address:* 38 Platt's Lane, NW3 7NT. *T:* 01–435 1764.

VARFIS, Grigoris; Greek Commissioner to the European Communities, since 1985; responsible for structural funds and consumer protection, since 1986; Member, European Parliament, since 1984; *b* 1927. *Educ:* Univ. of Athens; Univ. of Paris. Journalist, Paris, 1953–58; OECD, 1958–62; Econ. Adviser to permt Greek delegn to EEC, 1963–74; Dir-Gen., Econ. Min. of Co-ordination, 1974–77; Man. Dir in chemical industry, 1977–81; Vice-Minister of Foreign Affairs, 1981–84. *Address:* Commission of the European Communities, 200 rue de la Loi, 1049 Brussels, Belgium; Spefsipou 35, 10676 Athens, Greece.

VARLEY, Rt. Hon. Eric Graham, PC 1974; Chairman and Chief Executive, Coalite Group, since 1984; *b* 11 Aug. 1932; *s* of Frank Varley, retired miner, and Eva Varley; *m* 1955, Marjorie Turner; one *s*. *Educ:* Secondary Modern and Technical Schools; Ruskin Coll., Oxford. Apprentice Engineer's Turner, 1947–52; Engineer's Turner, 1952–55; Mining Industry (Coal) Craftsman, 1955–64. National Union of Mineworkers: Branch Sec., 1955–64; Mem. Area Exec. Cttee, Derbyshire, 1956–64. MP (Lab) Chesterfield, 1964–84; Asst Govt Whip, 1967–68; PPS to the Prime Minister, 1968–69; Minister of State, Min. of Technology, 1969–70; Chm., Trade Union Gp of Labour MPs, 1971–74; Secretary of State: for Energy, 1974–75; for Industry, 1975–79; Principal Opposition Spokesman on employment, 1979–83; Treasurer, Labour Party, 1981–83. Vis. Fellow, Nuffield Coll., 1977–81. *Recreations:* reading, gardening, music, sport. *Address:* Coalite Group, Buttermilk Lane, Bolsover, Derbyshire S44 6AB.

VARLEY, Dame Joan (Fleetwood), DBE 1985 (CBE 1974); *b* 22 Feb. 1920; *d* of late F. Ireton and Elizabeth Varley. *Educ:* Cheltenham Ladies' College; London School of Economics (BSc Econ). Section Officer, WAAF, 1944–46. Conservative Agent, Shrewsbury, 1952–56; Dep. Central Office Agent, NW Area, 1957–65; Dep. Dir Organisation, 1966–74, Dir, Central Admin, 1975–76, Cons Central Office; Dir, Local Govt Organisation, 1976–84. *Recreations:* gardening, walking. *Address:* 9 Queensdale Walk, W11 4QQ. *T:* 01–727 1292. *Club:* St Stephen's Constitutional.

VARNAM, Ivor; Deputy Director, Royal Armament Research and Development Establishment, 1974–82, retired; *b* 12 Aug. 1922; *s* of Walter Varnam and Gertrude Susan Varnam (*née* Vincent); *m* 1942, Doris May Thomas; two *s* *Educ:* Alleyn's Coll., Dulwich; University Coll., Cardiff; Birkbeck Coll., London. BSc Wales 1944; BSc (Hons) London 1952. Served War, RAF, 1940–46 (commnd 1944). Joined Tannoy Products, 1946; Atomic Energy Research Estabt, 1947; Siemens Bros., 1948; Royal Armament Research and Development Estabt, 1953–60 and 1962–82 (Defence Research Staff, Washington, USA, 1960–62), as: Supt Mil. ADP Br., 1964; Supt GW Br., 1967; Prin. Supt Systems Div., 1969; Head, Applied Physics Dept, 1972. *Publications:* official reports. *Recreations:* gardening, photography, bridge, music.

VARVILL, Michael Hugh, CMG 1959; *b* 29 Sept. 1909; *s* of Dr Bernard and Maud Varvill; unmarried. *Educ:* Marlborough; New Coll., Oxford (Scholar; BA). Appointed to Colonial Service, Nigeria, 1932; seconded to Colonial Office, 1943–47; Senior District Officer, 1951; Nigeria, Permanent Secretary: Ministry of Transport, 1952; Ministry of Works, 1953–54; and again (Federal) Ministry of Transport, 1955, retired 1960. With G. Bell & Sons, publishers, 1960–73 (Dir, 1963–73). *Recreations:* tennis, hockey, chess. *Address:* 125 Marsham Court, Marsham Street, SW1. *Club:* Travellers'.

VASARY, Tamàs; pianist and conductor; Joint Musical Director, Northern Sinfonia Orchestra, since 1979; *b* 8 Nov. 1933; *s* of Jozsef Vâsàry and Elizabeth (*née* Baltazàr); *m* 1967, Ildiko (*née* Kovàcs). *Educ:* Franz Liszt Music Academ Budapest. First concert at age of 8 in Debrecen, Hungary; First Prize, Franz Liszt Competition, Budapest, 1947; prizes at internat. competitions in Warsaw, Paris, Brussels, Rio de Janeiro; Bach and Paderewski medals, London, 1961; début in London, 1961, in Carnegie Hall, NY, 1961; plays with major orchestras and at festivals in Europe, USA, Australasia and Far East; 3 world tours. Conducting debut, 1970; conducts in Europe and USA. Records Chopin, Debussy, Liszt, Rachmaninov (in Germany). *Recreations:* yoga, writing, sports. *Address:* 9 Village Road, N3. *T:* 01–346 2381.

VASCONCELLOS, Josephina de, MBE 1985; Hon. DLitt; FRBS; Founder Member, Society of Portrait Sculptors; Founder, Outpost Emmaus; current projects: Adventure Base for Deprived Youngsters; The Harriet Trust, Beached Trawler adapted for Nature-observation Base for Young Disabled; *d* of late H. H. de Vasconcellos, Brazilian Consul-General in England, and Freda Coleman; *m* 1930, Delmar Banner, (*d* 1983), painter. *Educ:* sculpture: London, Paris, Florence; Royal Academy Schools. Works: High Altar and Statue, Varengeville, Normandy, 1925; Bronze St Hubert, Nat. Gall. of Brazil, 1926; Music in Trees, in stone, Southampton Gall., 1933; Ducks, in marble, Glasgow Art Gall., 1946; Refugees, in stone, Sheffield Art Gall., 1949; Episcopal Crozier, in perspex, for Bristol Cathedral, 1948. Exhibits RA, Leicester Galls. Exhibn with husband, of 46 sculptures in 20 materials at RWS Gall., 1947; Last Chimera, Canongate Kirk, Edinburgh; 8ft Christ (in Portland Stone), Nat. War Meml to Battle of Britain, Aldershot, 1950. Two works, Festival of Britain, Lambeth Palace, 1951; Sculpture Exhibn, with husband, RWS Galls, 1955; War Memorial, St Bees School, 1955; two figures, St Bees Priory, 1955; life-size Mary and Child and design group of 11 sculptures by 11 collaborators, for Nativity, St Paul's Cathedral, Christmas 1955; Mary and Child bought for St Paul's, 1956; life-size Resurrection for St Mary, Westfield, Workington, 1956–57; Madonna and Child, St James's, Piccadilly, (now in Burrswood, Dorothy Kerin Trust), 1957; Rising Christ in St Bartholomew the Great, Smithfield; Winter, carving in Perspex, Oldham Gallery, 1958; Nativity (for ruins of Coventry Cathedral), 1958; Flight into Egypt, for St Martin-in-the-Fields, 1958 (now in Cartmel Priory); War Memorial, Reredos of carved oak, Rossall School Chapel, 1959; Nativity Set, life-size figures, St Martin-in-the-Fields, annually in Trafalgar Sq.; Winged Victory Crucifix, Clewer Church, 1964, and Canongate Kirk, Edinburgh; life-size Holy Family, Liverpool Cathedral and Gloucester Cathedral, 1965; life-size Virgin and Child, Blackburn Cathedral, 1974; Reunion, Bradford Univ., 1977; Return of the Carpenter, group of 10 life-size children, Samlesbury Hall, 1978; life-size Holy Family, for St Martin-in-the-Fields, 1983; life-size Holy Family, in cold cast stone, Norwich Cathedral, 1985; 'and God shall wipe the tears from their eyes', life-size two figure group, in plaster, for Lake Artists Exhibn, Grasmere, 1986; sculptures at Dallas, Tulsa, Chicago, USA; Portraits: bronze of Lord Denning, 1969; Bishop Fleming; Rev. Austen Williams and Mario Borelli. Documentary film Out of Nature (on her work), 1949; BBC programme, Viewpoint TV, 1968. Pres., Guild of Lakeland Craftsmen, 1971–73. Mem., Inst. of Patentees and Inventors; Hon. Member, Glider Pilots Regimental Assoc. Hon. DLitt Bradford, 1977. *Publications:* Woodcut illustrations for The Cup (Poems by F. Johnson), 1938; contrib. to They Became Christians (ed Dewi Morgan), 1966. *Recreations:* musical composition, dance. *Address:* 4 Fairview Road, Ambleside, Cumbria LA22 9EH. *T:* Ambleside 32418. *Club:* The Reynolds.

VASSAR-SMITH, Major Sir Richard Rathborne, 3rd Bt, *cr* 1917; TD; RA; Partner at St Ronan's Preparatory School, since 1957; *b* 24 Nov. 1909; *s* of late Major Charles Martin Vassar-Smith (2nd *s* of 1st Bt); *S* uncle, 1942; *m* 1932, Mary Dawn, *d* of late Sir

Raymond Woods, CBE; one *s* one *d*. *Educ:* Lancing; Pembroke College, Cambridge. Employed by Lloyds Bank Ltd, 1932–37; Schoolmaster, 1938–39. War of 1939–45, Major, RA. *Recreation:* Association football (Cambridge, 1928–31). *Heir:* *s* John Rathborne Vassar-Smith [*b* 23 July 1936; *m* 1971, Roberta Elaine, *y d* of Wing Comdr N. Williamson; two *s*]. *Address:* Orchard House, Hawkhurst, Kent. *T:* Hawkhurst 2300. *Clubs:* Hawks (Cambridge); Rye Golf.

VAUGHAN, family name of **Earl of Lisburne.**

VAUGHAN, Viscount; David John Francis Malet Vaughan; artist; *b* 15 June 1945; *e s* of 8th Earl of Lisburne, *qv*; *m* 1973, Jennifer Jane Sheila Fraser Campbell, artist, *d* of James and Dorothy Campbell, Invergarry; one *s* one *d*. *Educ:* Ampleforth Coll.

VAUGHAN, Rt. Rev. Benjamin Noel Young; *see* Swansea and Brecon, Bishop of.

VAUGHAN, David Arthur John; QC 1981; QC (NI) 1981; *b* 24 Aug. 1938; *s* of late Captain F. H. M. Vaughan, OBE, RN and J. M. Vaughan; *m* 1st, 1967, Philippa Mary Maclure (marr. diss.); 2nd, 1985, Leslie Ann Fenwick Irwin. *Educ:* Eton Coll.; Trinity Coll., Cambridge (MA). 2nd Lieut, 14th/20th King's Hussars, 1958–59. Called to the Bar, Inner Temple, 1962; Member: Bar Council, 1968–72, 1984–86; International Relations Committee of Bar Council, 1968–86 (Chm., 1984–86); UK Delegation to Consultative Committee of the Bars and Law Societies of the European Communities, 1978–81 (Chm., Special Cttee on EEC Competition Law, 1978–); Chm., Bar/Law Soc. Working Party on EEC Competition Law, 1977–. Law Adv. Cttee, British Council, 1982–85. *Publications:* co-ordinating editor, vols on European community law, Halsbury's Laws of England, 1986; (ed) Vaughan on Law of the European Communities, 1986. *Recreation:* fishing. *Address:* 50 Oxford Gardens, W10. *T:* 01–960 5865; 01–969 0707; 1 Brick Court, Temple, EC4. *T:* 01–583 0777. *Clubs:* Brooks's, Flyfishers'.

VAUGHAN, Sir Edgar; *see* Vaughan, Sir G. E.

VAUGHAN, Elizabeth, (Mrs Ray Brown), FRAM; international operatic soprano; *b* Llanfyllin, Montgomeryshire; *m* 1968, Ray Brown (Manager, Scottish Opera Orch.); one *s* one *d*. *Educ:* Llanfyllin Grammar Sch.; RAM (ARAM, LRAM); Kathleen Ferrier Prize. Has sung leading roles in: Benvenuto Cellini; La Bohème; Midsummer Night's Dream; Madame Butterfly; Otello; Rigoletto; Simon Boccanegra; La Traviata; Il Trovatore; Turandot; Don Giovanni; Un Ballo in Maschera; Ernani; Nabucco; Aida; Cassandra; La Forza del Destino; Tosca; Idomeneo; Macbeth; Gloriana. Has appeared with: Royal Opera; ENO; WNO; Opera North; Scottish Opera; Vienna State Opera; Deutsche Oper, Berlin; Hamburg State Opera; Metropolitan Opera, NY; Paris Opera. Has toured in: Europe; USA; Australia; Canada; Japan; S America. *Recreations:* tennis, driving, cookery. *Address:* c/o Music International, 13 Ardilaun Road, Highbury, N5.

VAUGHAN, Ernest James, CBE 1961; retired as Director of Materials Research, Royal Naval Scientific Service; *b* 19 Oct. 1901; 3rd *s* of late James and Helena Vaughan; *m* 1927, Marjorie Solly; one *s* decd. *Educ:* Brockley; London University. BSc, MSc London; ARCS; DIC. Jun. Chemist, War Dept; Chemist, 1925–27; Chemist, Chemical Dept, Portsmouth Dockyard, 1927–36; Dep. Supt, then Supt, Bragg Laboratory, 1936–49; Dep. Dir, then Dir of Materials Research, Royal Naval Scientific Service, 1949–66. Hon. Treas., Royal Inst. of Chemistry, 1963–72. *Publications:* Protective Coatings for Metals, 1946; (monograph) Metallurgical Analysis; papers in learned jls. *Address:* Flat 2, Ashmede, 56 West Cliff Road, Bournemouth, Dorset BH4 8BE. *T:* Bournemouth 764232.

VAUGHAN, Sir (George) Edgar, KBE 1963 (CBE 1956; OBE 1937); *b* 24 Feb. 1907; *s* of late William John Vaughan, BSc, of Cardiff, and Emma Kate Caudle; *m* 1933, Elsie Winifred Deubert (*d* 1982); one *s* two *d*. *Educ:* Cheltenham Grammar Sch.; Jesus Coll., Oxford (Exhibitioner and later Hon. Scholar; Hon. Fellow, 1966). 1st Cl. Honour School of Mod. Hist., 1928; 1st Cl. Honour School of Philosophy, Politics and Economics, 1929; Laming Travelling Fellow of the Queen's College, Oxford, 1929–31. Entered Consular Service, 1930; Vice-Consul at: Hamburg, 1931; La Paz, 1932–35; Barcelona, 1935–38; Buenos Aires, 1938–44; Chargé d'Affaires, Monrovia, 1945–46; Consul at Seattle, Washington, 1946–49; Consul-General at Lourenço Marques, 1949–53, Amsterdam, 1953–56; Minister and Consul-General at Buenos Aires, 1956–60; Ambassador, 1960–63 and Consul-General, 1963, at Panama; Ambassador to Colombia, 1964–66. Retired from Diplomatic Service, 1966. Univ. of Saskatchewan, Regina Campus: Special Lectr, 1966–67; Prof. of History, 1967–74; Dean of Arts and Science, 1969–73. FRHistS 1965. *Recreation:* golf. *Address:* 27 Birch Grove, W3 9SP. *Club:* Travellers'.

VAUGHAN, Sir Gerard (Folliott), Kt 1984; FRCP; MP (C) Reading East, since 1983 (Reading, 1970–74; Reading South, 1974–83); *b* Xinavane, Portuguese E Africa, 11 June 1923; *s* of late Leonard Vaughan, DSO, DFC, and Joan Vaughan (*née* Folliott); *m* 1955, Joyce Thurle (*née* Laver); one *s* one *d*. *Educ:* privately in E Africa; London Univ.; Guy's Hosp. MB, BS 1947; MRCP 1949; Academic DPM London 1952; FRCP 1966; FRCPsych 1972. Consultant Staff, Guy's Hosp., 1958–79, now Consultant Emeritus. Minister for Health, DHSS, 1979–82; Minister of State (Consumer Affairs), Dept of Trade, 1982–83. Parly Mem., MRC, 1973–76; Alderman: LCC, 1955–61; LCC Streatham, 1961–64; GLC Lambeth, 1966–70; Alderman, GLC, 1970–72; Chm., Strategic Planning Cttee GLC, 1968–71; Mem., SE Economic Planning Council, 1968–71. Governor, UCL, 1959–68. Liveryman, Worshipful Co. of Barbers. Contested (C) Poplar, 1955. Hon. FFAS, 1978. *Publications:* various professional and general literary publications. *Recreations:* painting, fishing. *Address:* House of Commons, SW1. *Club:* Carlton.

VAUGHAN, Henry William Campbell, JP; DL; Lord Provost and Lord Lieutenant of the City of Dundee, 1977–80; *b* 15 March 1919; *s* of Harry Skene Vaughan and Flora Lamont Campbell Blair; *m* 1947, Margaret Cowie Flett; one *s* one *d*. *Educ:* Dundee Training Coll.; Logie and Stobswell Secondary Schools. Apprentice Stationer, Burns & Harris, 1934–39; RAF (Volunteer Reserve), 1939–46; Chief Buyer, Messrs Valentine & Son, Fine Art Publishers, Dundee, 1946–64; Group Purchasing Officer, Scott & Robertson (Tay Textiles Ltd), 1964–75; Stationery Manager, Burns & Harris Ltd, Dundee, 1975–78; Paper Sales Rep., James McNaughton Paper Gp Ltd, London, 1978–79. Mem., Inst. of Purchasing and Supply. JP Dundee, 1969; DL Dundee, 1980. Silver Jubilee Medal, 1977. *Recreations:* cine photography, fishing, water colour painting, sketching. *Address:* 15 Fraser Street, Dundee. *T:* Dundee 826175.

VAUGHAN, Dame Janet (Maria), DBE 1957 (OBE 1944); DM, FRCP; FRS 1979; Principal of Somerville College, Oxford, 1945–67, Hon. Fellow since 1967; *b* 18 October 1899; *d* of William Wyamar Vaughan and Margaret Symonds; *m* 1930, David Gourlay (*d* 1963); two *d*. *Educ:* North Foreland Lodge; Somerville College, Oxford; University College Hospital (Goldsmith Entrance Scholar). Asst Clinical Pathologist, Univ. Coll. Hosp.; Rockefeller Fellowship, 1929–30; Beit Memorial Fellowship, 1930–33; Leverhulme Fellow, RCP, 1933–34; Asst in Clinical Pathology, British Post-Graduate Medical School, 1934–39; Mem. Inter-Departmental Cttee on Medical Schools, 1942; Nuffield Trustee, 1943; late Medical Officer in charge North-West London Blood Supply Depot for Medical Research Council. Mem., Royal Commn on Equal Pay, 1944; Chm., Oxford Regional Hosp. Board, 1950–51 (Vice-Chm. 1948); Member: Cttee on Economic and Financial Problems of Provision for Old Age, 1953–54; Medical Adv. Cttee of University Grants Cttee; University Grants Cttee on Libraries; Commonwealth Scholarship Commn in the UK. Fogarty Scholar, NIH, 1973. Hon. FRSM, 1980. Osler Meml Medal, Univ. of Oxford. Hon. Fellow: Wolfson Coll., Oxford, 1981; Girton Coll., Cambridge, 1986. Hon. DSc: Wales, 1960; Leeds, 1973; Hon. DCL: Oxford, 1967; London, 1968; Bristol, 1971. *Publications:* The Anæmias, 1st edn 1934, 2nd edn 1936; The Physiology of Bone, 1969, 3rd edn 1981; The Effects of Irradiation on the Skeleton, 1973; numerous papers in scientific jls on blood diseases, blood transfusion and metabolism of strontium and plutonium isotopes; section on leukæmias, Brit. Ency. Med. Pract.; section on blood transfusion in British Surgical Practice, 1945. *Recreations:* travel, gardening. *Address:* 5 Fairlawn Flats, First Turn, Wolvercote, Oxford. *T:* Oxford 514069.

VAUGHAN, Prof. Leslie Clifford, FRCVS; Professor of Veterinary Surgery, since 1974, and Vice-Principal, since 1982, Royal Veterinary College; *b* 9 Jan. 1927; *s* of Edwin Clifford and Elizabeth Louise Vaughan; *m* 1951, Margaret Joyce Lawson; one *s* one *d*. *Educ:* Bishop Gore Grammar School, Swansea; Royal Veterinary College, Univ. of London (DVR 1967, DSc 1970). FRCVS 1957. Lectr in Veterinary Surgery, RVC, 1951; Reader, London Univ., 1968; Prof. of Vet. Orthopaedics, 1972. Junior Vice-Pres., RCVS, 1986. Francis Hogg Prize for contribs to small animal medicine and surgery, 1962; Simon Award for small animal surgery, 1966; Victory Medal, Central Vet. Soc., 1982. *Publications:* papers in sci jls. *Recreations:* gardening, watching rugby football. *Address:* Royal Veterinary College, Hawkshead Lane, North Mymms, near Hatfield, Herts. *T:* Potters Bar 55486.

VAUGHAN, Ven. Peter St George; Archdeacon of Westmorland and Furness since 1983; *b* 27 Nov. 1930; *s* of Dr Victor St George Vaughan and Dorothy Marguerite Vaughan; *m* 1961, Elisabeth Fielding Parker; one *s* two *d*. *Educ:* Charterhouse; Selwyn Coll., Cambridge (MA Theology); Ridley Hall, Cambridge. Deacon 1957, priest 1958; Asst Curate, Birmingham Parish Church, 1957–62; Chaplain to Oxford Pastorate, 1963–67; Asst Chaplain, Brasenose Coll., Oxford, 1963–67; Vicar of Christ Church, Galle Face, Colombo, 1967–72; Precentor of Holy Trinity Cathedral, Auckland, NZ, 1972–75; Principal of Crowther Hall, CMS Training Coll., Selly Oak Colleges, Birmingham, 1975–83. Commisary for Bishop of Colombo. MA Oxon (By Incorporation). *Recreations:* gardening, reading, people. *Address:* Helsfell House, 235 Windermere Road, Kendal, Cumbria LA9 5EY. *T:* Kendal 23553.

VAUGHAN, Roger Davison, OBE 1986; FEng 1981; General Manager, Fast Reactor Projects, National Nuclear Corporation Ltd, since 1977; Director, Fast Reactor Technology Ltd, since 1984; *b* 2 Oct. 1923; *s* of David William and late Olive Marion Vaughan; *m* 1951, Doreen Stewart; four *s*. *Educ:* University High Sch., Melbourne; Univ. of Melbourne, Aust. BMechE; FIMechE. Engineer Officer, RAAF, 1945–46. Chemical Engr, Commonwealth Serum Laboratories, 1946–47; Works apprenticeship, C. A. Parsons & Co., 1948–49; Chief Engr, C. A. Parsons Calcutta, 1950–53; AERE, Harwell, 1954; Chief Engineer: Nuclear Power Plant Co., 1955–59 (Director, 1958); The Nuclear Power Group, 1960–75; Manager, Technology Div., Nuclear Power Co., 1976–77. Chairman: Gas-cooled Breeder Reactor Assoc., Brussels, 1970–; BSI Nuclear Standards Cttee, 1976–82; BSI Engineering Council, 1983–; Mem. Council, IMechE, 1977–81, 1985– (Chm., Power Industries Div., 1985–). *Publications:* papers in jls of IMechE, Brit. Nuc. Energy Soc., World Energy Conf. *Recreations:* skiing, mountain walking; questionable performer on piano and clarinet. *Address:* Otterburn House, Manor Park South, Knutsford, Cheshire WA16 8AG. *T:* Knutsford 2514. *Clubs:* Ski of Great Britain; Himalayan (Bombay).

VAUGHAN, William Randal; Founder and Proprietor, W. R. Vaughan Associates Ltd (formerly W. R. Vaughan Ltd), since 1945; *b* 11 March 1912; *m* 1945, K. A. Headland; three *s* one *d*. *Educ:* Centaur Trade School, Coventry. FIProdE. Apprenticed, Alfred Herbert Ltd, 1926; Coventry Gauge & Tool Co. Ltd, 1933; A. C. Wickman Ltd, 1934; A. Pattison Ltd, 1942; C. G. Wade Ltd, London, 1943. Chairman, Machine Tool Industry Research Assoc., 1974–83 (Vice-Pres., 1983–); President, Machine Tool Trades Assoc., 1977–79. Member of Lloyd's. *Recreations:* squash, skiing, sailing, flying. *Address:* Rowley Bank, Rowley Lane, Arkley, Barnet, Herts EN5 3HS. *T:* 01–441 4800. *Clubs:* Lansdowne, Royal Automobile.

VAUGHAN-JACKSON, Oliver James, VRD 1951; FRCS; Consulting Orthopaedic Surgeon to London Hospital, since 1971; *b* 6 July 1907; *e s* of Surgeon Captain P. Vaughan-Jackson, RN, Carramore, Ballina, County Mayo; *m* 1939, Joan Madeline, *er d* of E. A. Bowring, CBE, St Johns, Newfoundland; two *s*. *Educ:* Berkhamsted School; Balliol Coll., Oxford; The London Hospital. Kitchener Scholar; BA, BM, BCh Oxon, 1932; MRCS, LRCP, 1932; FRCS 1936. House Physician, Demonstrator of Pathology, House Surgeon, Resident Accoucheur, and Surgical Registrar at The London Hosp. Surgeon Lieut-Comdr RNVR, Retd, Surgical specialist, Roy. Naval Hosp., Sydney, Australia. Sen. Registrar (Orthopædic), The London Hosp.; Orthopaedic Surgeon to: The London Hosp., 1946–71; St Bartholomew's Hosp., Rochester, 1947–70; Medway Hosp., 1970–71; Claybury Mental Hosp., 1946–64; Halliwick Cripples Sch., 1946–71; Cons. In Orthopaedics to Royal Navy, 1956–71; Vis. Prof. of Orthopaedics, Memorial Univ. of Newfoundland, 1971–73; Senior Consultant in Orthopaedics at St John's Gen. Hosp., St Clare Mercy Hosp. and Janeway Child Health Centre, St John's, Newfoundland, 1971–73. Fellow: British Orthopædic Assoc.; RSM (Pres., Section of Orthopædics, 1968–69); Med. Soc. London; Member: Soc. Internat. de Chirurgie Orthopédique et de Traumatologie; British Soc. for Surgery of the Hand. Former Mem., Editorial Board of Jl of Bone and Joint Surgery. Hon. DSc Memorial Univ. of Newfoundland, 1973. *Publications:* Sections on: Arthrodesis (Maingot's Techniques in British Surgery), 1950; Arthrodesis of the Hip, and Osteotomy of the Upper End of Femur (Operative Surgery, ed Rob and Smith), 1958; Surgery of the Hand; Orthopædic Surgery in Spastic conditions; Peripheral Nerve Injuries (Textbook of British Surgery, ed Sir Henry Souttar and Prof. J. C. Goligher), 1959; The Rheumatoid Hand; Carpal Tunnel Compression of the Median Nerve (Clinical Surgery, ed Rob and Smith), 1966; Surgery in Arthritis of the Hand, in Textbook of Rheumatic Diseases, 1968; The Rheumatoid Hand, in Operative Surgery, 2nd edn, 1971; contribs to Jl of Bone and Joint Surgery, etc. *Recreations:* gardening, photography. *Address:* The White Cottage, Bowesden Lane, Shorne, near Gravesend, Kent DA12 3LA. *T:* Shorne 2321. *Club:* Naval and Military.

VAUGHAN-MORGAN, family name of **Baron Reigate.**

VAUGHAN-THOMAS, (Lewis John) Wynford, CBE 1986 (OBE 1974); MA Oxon; radio and television commentator since 1937; author, journalist; Director, Harlech Television Ltd; *b* 15 Aug. 1908; *s* of Dr David Vaughan-Thomas and Morfydd Vaughan-Thomas; *m* 1946, Charlotte Rowlands, MBE; one *s*. *Educ:* Swansea Grammar Sch.; Exeter College, Oxford. Keeper of MSS and Records, National Library of Wales, 1933; Area Officer, S Wales Council of Social Service, 1934–37; joined BBC, 1937. Dir of Programmes, Harlech Television Ltd, 1968–71. Commentator, Royal Commonwealth Tours, BBC War Correspondent, 1942–45; Governor, BFI, 1977–80. FRSA 1980. Hon. MA Open Univ., 1982. Croix de Guerre, 1945. *Publications:* Royal Tour, 1953–54, 1954;

Anzio, 1961; Madly in all Directions, 1967; (with Alun Llewellyn) The Shell Guide to Wales, 1969; The Splendour Falls, 1973; Gower, 1975; The Countryside Companion, 1979; Trust to Talk (autobiog.), 1980; Wynford Vaughan-Thomas's Wales, 1981; The Princes of Wales, 1982; Wales, a History, 1985; How I Liberated Burgundy, 1985. *Recreations:* mountaineering, sailing. *Address:* Pentower, Tower Hill, Fishguard, Dyfed. *T:* Fishguard 873424. *Clubs:* Climbers', Savile; Cardiff and County (Cardiff).

VAUX OF HARROWDEN, 10th Baron *cr* 1523; **John Hugh Philip Gilbey;** *b* 4 Aug. 1915; 2nd *s* of William Gordon Gilbey (*d* 1965) and Grace Mary Eleanor, 8th Baroness Vaux of Harrowden (*d* 1958); *S* brother, 1977; *m* 1939, Maureen Pamela, *e d* of Hugh Gilbey; three *s* one *d. Educ:* Ampleforth College; Christ Church, Oxford (BA 1937). Formerly Major, Duke of Wellington's Regt; served War of 1939–45. *Heir: s* Hon. Anthony William Gilbey [*b* 25 May 1940; *m* 1964, Beverley Anne, *o d* of Charles Alexander Walton; two *s* one *d*]. *Address:* Cholmondeley Cottage, 2 Cholmondeley Walk, Richmond, Surrey.

VAVASOUR, Comdr Sir Geoffrey William, 5th Bt *cr* 1828; DSC 1943; RN (retired); a Director of W. M. Still & Sons, 1962–80; *b* 5 Sept. 1914; *s* of Captain Sir Leonard Vavasour, 4th Bt, RN, and Ellice Margaret Nelson; *S* father, 1961; *m* 1st, 1940, Joan Robb (marr. diss. 1947); two *d*; 2nd, 1971, Marcia Christine, *d* of late Marshall Lodge, Batley, Yorks. *Educ:* RNC Dartmouth. *Heir: kinsman* Hugh Bernard Moore Vavasour [*b* 4 July 1918; *m* 1950, Monique Pauline Marie Madeleine (*d* 1982), *d* of Maurice Erick Beck; one *s* one *d*]. *Address:* 8 Bede House, Manor Fields, Putney, SW15. *Clubs:* MCC, All England Lawn Tennis.

VEAL, Group Captain John Bartholomew, CBE 1956; AFC 1940; Civil Aviation Safety Adviser, Department of Trade and Industry, 1972–74, retired; *b* 28 September 1909; *er s* of John Henry and Sarah Grace Veal; *m* 1933, Enid Marjorie Hill; two *s. Educ:* Christ's Hosp. Special trainee, Metropolitan-Vickers, 1926–27; commissioned in RAF as pilot officer, 1927; served in Nos 4 and 501 Squadrons and as flying Instructor at Central Flying School, transferring to RAFO, 1932; Flying-Instructor, Chief Flying Instructor, and Test Pilot, Air Service Training Ltd, 1932–39; recalled to regular RAF service, 1939; commanded navigation and flying training schools, 1939–43; Air Staff No. 46 Transport Group, 1944 and Transport Command, 1945–46 (despatches); released from RAF, 1946, to become Deputy Director of Training, Ministry of Civil Aviation; Director of Air Safety and Training, 1947; Director of Operations, Safety and Licensing, 1952; Deputy Director-General of Navigational Services, Ministry of Transport and Civil Aviation, 1958; Director-General of Navigational Services, Ministry of Aviation, 1959–62; Chief Inspector of Accidents, Civil Aviation Department, Board of Trade (formerly Min. of Aviation), 1963–68; Dir Gen. of Safety and Operations, DTI (formerly BOT), 1968–72. FRAeS 1967 (AFRAeS 1958). *Recreation:* trout fishing. *Address:* Woodacre, Horsham Road, Cranleigh, Surrey GU6 8DZ. *T:* Cranleigh 274490. *Club:* Royal Air Force.

VEALE, Sir Alan (John Ralph), Kt 1984; FEng 1980; Director, General Electric Co. plc, 1973–85; *b* 2 Feb. 1920; *s* of Leslie H. Veale and Eleanor Veale; *m* 1946, Muriel Veale; two *s* (and one *s* decd). *Educ:* Exeter School; Manchester College of Technology. AMCT, FIMechE, FIProdE. Manufacturing Dir, AEI Turbine Generators Ltd, 1963; Director and General Manager: Heavy Plant Div., AEI, 1966; Motor Control Group, AEI, 1967; Managing Director: GEC Diesels Ltd, 1969; GEC Power Engineering Ltd, 1970–85. Pres., IProdE, 1985–86. CBIM. Hon. DSc Salford, 1984. *Recreations:* sailing, walking. *Address:* 41 Northumberland Road, Leamington Spa CV32 6HF. *T:* Leamington Spa 24349.

VEASEY, Josephine, CBE 1970; opera singer (mezzo soprano), retired; teaching privately, since 1982; vocal consultant to English National Opera, since 1985; *b* London, 10 July 1930; *m* (marr. diss.); one *s* one *d. Educ:* coached by Audrey Langford, ARCM. Joined chorus of Royal Opera House, Covent Garden, 1949; a Principal there, 1955– (interval on tour, in opera, for Arts Council). Teacher of voice production, RAM, 1983–84. Has sung at Royal Opera House, Glyndebourne, Metropolitan (NY), La Scala, and in France, Germany, Spain, Switzerland, South America; operatic Roles include: Octavian in Der Rosenkavalier; Cherubino in Figaro; name role in Iphigenie; Dorabella in Cosi fan Tutte; Amneris in Aida, Fricka in Die Walküre; Fricka in Das Rheingold; name role in Carmen; Dido and Cassandra in the Trojans; Marguerite in The Damnation of Faust; Charlotte in The Sorrows of Werther; Eboli, Don Carlos; name role, Orfeo; Adalgesa in Norma; Rosina in The Barber of Seville; Kundry in Parsifal; Gertrude in Hamlet, 1980. Concerts, 1960–70 (Conductors included Giulini, Bernstein, Solti, Mehta, Sargent). Verdi's Requiem; Monteverdi's Combattimento di Tancredi e Clorinda, Aix Festival, 1967; various works of Mahler; two tours of Israel (Solti); subseq. sang in Los Angeles (Mehta); then Berlioz: Death of Cleopatra, Royal Festival Hall, and L'enfance du Christ, London and Paris; Rossini's Petite Messe Solennelle, London and Huddersfield (with late Sir Malcolm Sargent); Handel's Messiah, England, Munich, Oporto, Lisbon; Berlioz' Romeo and Juliette, London, and Bergen Festival; Rossini's Stabat Mater, Festival d'Angers and London, 1971; Berlioz' Beatrice and Benedict, NY, and London; Emperor in 1st perf. Henze's We Come to the River, Covent Garden, 1976. Has sung Elgar's Dream of Gerontius all over England. Frequently makes recordings. Hon. RAM, 1972. *Recreations:* reading, gardening. *Address:* 2 Pound Cottage, St Mary Bourne, Andover, Hants. *T:* St Mary Bourne 282.

VEEDER, Van Vechten; QC 1986; *b* 14 Dec. 1948; *s* of John Van Vechten Veeder and Helen Letham Townley; *m* 1970, Hazel Burbidge; one *s* one *d. Educ:* Ecole Rue de la Ferme, Neuilly, Paris; Clifton College, Bristol; Jesus College, Cambridge. Called to the Bar, Inner Temple, 1971. *Recreations:* travelling, reading. *Address:* 4 Essex Court, Temple, EC4Y 9AJ. *T:* 01-583 9191.

VEGA TREJOS, Guillermo; Ambassador of Panama to the Court of St James's, since 1984; *b* 14 Aug. 1927; *s* of late Simon Vega and Onofre Trejos de Vega; *m* Lesley Ann de Vega; three *s* two *d. Educ:* National Institute, Panama; British College, Buenos Aires; Univ. of La Plata, Argentina. Licenciado. Editor: La Hora, 1952–55; La Nación, 1955–58; Pres., Sindicate of Journalists, 1958–60; Sec. Gen., Housing Inst., Panama, 1960–64; Pres., Municipal Council, Panama, 1964–68; Pres., Nat. Municipalities Assoc., 1964–68; Editor, Panama America, 1969–73; Ambassador to France and Switzerland, 1973–84. *Publications:* Muchos son los Llamados; Cuentos para una Esquina Redonda. *Recreations:* theatre, music. *Address:* Embassy of Panama, 109 Jermyn Street, SW1. *T:* 01-930 1591/2.

VEIL, Simone Annie, Chevalier de l'Ordre national du Mérite; Magistrate; Member, European Parliament, since 1979 (President, 1979–82); Chairman, Liberal and Democratic Reformist Group, European Parliament, since 1984; *b* Nice, 13 July 1927; *d* of André Jacob and Yvonne (*née* Steinmetz); *m* 1946, Antoine Veil, Inspecteur des Finances, President of International Aeroplane Co. and Chief Exec. Officer, La Compagnie Internationale des Wagons Lits et des Tourisme; three *s. Educ:* Lycée de Nice; Lic. en droit, dipl. de l'Institut d'Etudes Politiques, Paris; qualified as Magistrate, 1956. Deported to Auschwitz and Bergen-Belsen, March 1944–May 1945. Ministry of Justice, 1957–69; Technical Advr to Office of Minister of Justice, 1969; Gen.-Sec., Conseil Supérieur de la magistrature, 1970–74; Minister of Health, France, 1974–79. Monismanie Prize, 1978; Athens Prize, 1980; Charlemagne Prize, Prix Louise Weiss, 1981; Louise Michel Prize, 1983; European Merit Prize, 1983; Jabotinsky Prize, 1983; Prize for Everyday Courage, 1984; Special Freedom Prize, Eleanor and Franklin Roosevelt Foundn, 1984; Fiera di Messina Prize, 1984. *Dhc:* Princeton, 1975; Institut Weizmann, 1976; Yale, Cambridge, 1980; Edinburgh, Jerusalem, Georgetown, Urbino, 1981; Yeschiva, Sussex, 1982; Free Univ., Brussels, 1984. *Publication:* (with Prof. Launay and Dr Soulé) L'Adoption, données médicales, psychologiques et sociales, 1969. *Address:* 11 place Vauban, 75007 Paris, France.

VENABLES, Harold David Spenser; Official Solicitor to the Supreme Court, since 1980; *b* 14 Oct. 1932; *s* of late Cedric Venables and Gladys Venables (*née* Hall); *m* 1964, Teresa Grace, *d* of late J. C. Watts; one *d* one *s. Educ:* Denstone College. Admitted Solicitor, 1956. Pilot Officer, Royal Air Force, 1957–58. Legal Assistant, Official Solicitor's Office, 1960; Secretary, Lord Chancellor's Cttee on the Age of Majority, 1965–67; Asst Official Solicitor, 1977–80. *Publications:* A Guide to the Law Affecting Mental Patients, 1975; The Racing Fifteen-Hundreds: a history of voiturette racing 1931–40, 1984; contributor, Halsbury's Laws of England, 4th edn. *Recreations:* vintage cars, motoring and military history. *Address:* Penderel House, 287 High Holborn, WC1. *T:* 01–936 7116.

VENABLES, Richard William Ogilvie; Member of Council and Board, Direct Mail Services Standards Board, since 1983; *b* 23 Feb. 1928; *s* of late Canon and Mrs E. M. Venables; *m* 1952, Ann Richards; three *s* two *d. Educ:* Marlborough Coll.; Christ Church, Oxford (BA, MA). Joined former Mather and Crowther Ltd, as trainee, 1952; Account Group Director, 1965; Board Member, 1966; Mem. Executive Cttee, 1972; Managing Director, 1974; joined Board of Ogilvy and Mather International, 1975; Chm., Ogilvy Benson and Mather Ltd, 1978–81; retired early, 1981, to pursue new career in the making of violins, violas, lutes, harpsichords. Chm., Apple and Pear Develt Council, 1980–83; Council and Bd Mem., Direct Mail Services Standards Bd, 1983–. *Recreation:* fly fishing. *Address:* First Field, Combe Hay, Bath, Avon BA2 8RD. *T:* Bath 833694.

VENABLES-LLEWELYN, Sir John (Michael) Dillwyn-, 4th Bt *cr* 1890; farmer, since 1975; *b* 12 Aug. 1938; *s* of Sir Charles Michael Dillwyn-Venables-Llewelyn, 3rd Bt, MVO, and of Lady Delia Mary Dillwyn-Venables-Llewelyn, *g d* of 1st Earl St Aldwyn; *S* father, 1976; *m* 1st, 1963, Nina (marr. diss. 1972), *d* of late Lt J. S. Hallam; two *d*; 2nd, 1975, Nina Gay Richardson Oliver; one *d* decd. *Recreation:* racing vintage cars. *Address:* Llysdinam, Newbridge-on-Wye, Llandrindod Wells, Powys LD1 6NB.

VENKATARAMAN, Ramaswamy; Vice-President of India, since 1984; *b* 4 Dec. 1910; *s* of Ramaswami Iyer; *m* Janata; three *d. Educ:* Madras Univ. (MA, LLB). Formerly in practice as a lawyer, Madras High Court and Supreme Court; prominent trade union leader, also political and social worker. Mem., Provisional Parlt, 1950; Mem., Lok Sabha, 1952–57 and (for Madras S), 1977–84; Leader of the House, Madras Legislative Council, and Minister of Industries, 1957–67; Mem., Planning Commn, Madras, 1967–71. Minister of: Finance and Industry, 1980–82; Defence, 1982–84. Chm., Nat. Research and Develt Corp. Leader, Indian delegation to Internat. Labour Organisation, 1958, and delegate, UN Gen. Assembly, 1953–61. Managing Editor, Labour Law Jl, 1971–. *Address:* Vice-President's House, 6 Maulana Azad Road, New Delhi-110011, India.

VENN, Edward James (Alfred), OBE 1985; Director-General, Royal National Institute for the Blind, 1980–83; *b* 25 Nov. 1919; *s* of Sidney and Jennie Venn; *m* 1944, Anne Minter; one *s* one *d*. Qualified as Chartered Secretary and Administrator, 1949. Local Government Officer, 1937–51; General Secretary, Royal Leicester, Leicestershire and Rutland Instn for the Blind, 1952–58; Head, Services to the Blind Dept, RNIB, 1959–71; Dep. Director-General, RNIB, 1972–79. World Council for the Welfare of the Blind: Chm., Rehabilitation Commn, European Regl Cttee, 1977–83; Mem., Cttee on Cultural Affairs, 1980–83; Mem., British Delegn, 1980–83; Member: British Council for Prevention of Blindness, 1980–; Council, Royal Commonwealth Soc. for the Blind, 1980–; British Wireless for the Blind Fund, 1982–. Trustee: The Gift of Thomas Pocklington 1982–; Cecilia Charity for the Blind, 1983–. Governor, Royal Sch. for the Blind, Leatherhead, 1983–. *Publications:* various articles on blind welfare. *Recreations:* gardening, reading. *Address:* Lyndwood, 3 Silverdale Avenue, Oxshott, Surrey. *T:* Oxshott 3130. *Club:* Rugby.

VENNING, Philip Duncombe Riley; Secretary, Society for the Protection of Ancient Buildings, since 1984; *b* 24 March 1947; *s* of late Roger Venning and of Rosemary (*née* Mann). *Educ:* Sherborne Sch., Dorset; Trinity Hall, Cambridge (MA). Times Educational Supplement: Reporter, 1970–76; News Editor, 1976–78; Asst Editor, 1978–81; freelance journalist and writer, 1981–84. *Publications:* contribs to books and other pubns on educn and on historic buildings. *Recreations:* archaeology, book collecting. *Address:* 25 Southwood Lane, N6 5ED. *T:* 01–340 8971.

VENTRY, 7th Baron, *cr* 1800; **Arthur Frederick Daubeney Olav Eveleigh-de-Moleyns;** *b* Norton Malreward, Som, 28 July 1898; *er s* of 6th Baron and Evelyn Muriel Stuart (*d* 1966), *y d* of Lansdowne Daubeney, Norton Malreward, Somerset; *S* father, 1936. *Educ:* Old Malthouse, Swanage; Wellington Coll., Berks. Served Irish Guards, 1917–18 (wounded); afterwards in RAF; served RAF, 1939–45. Certificated Aeronaut. King Häkon of Norway Freedom Medal, 1945. *Publications:* on aerostation and scouting. *Recreations:* music, travelling, airship piloting. *Heir: nephew* Andrew (Harold) Wesley Daubeny de Moleyns [*b* 28 May 1943; *m* 1963, Nelly Edouard Renée (marr. diss. 1979), *d* of Abel Chaumillon, Torremolinos, Spain; one *s* two *d*; *m* 1983, Jill Rosemary, *d* of C. W. Oramon]. *Address:* Lindsay Hall, Lindsay Road, Branksome Park, Poole, Dorset. *Clubs:* Naval and Military, Norwegian, Balloon and Airship.

VENTURI, Robert; architect; Principal, Venturi, Rauch and Scott Brown, since 1980; *b* 25 June 1925; *s* of Robert Charles Venturi and Vanna Venturi (*née* Lanzetta); *m* 1967, Denise Scott Brown; one *s. Educ:* Princeton Univ. (AB 1947, MFA 1950). Designer, Oskar Stonorov, 1950, Eero Saarinen & Assoc., 1950–53; Rome Prize Fellow, Amer. Acad. in Rome, 1954–56; designer, Louis I Kahn, 1957; Principal: Venturi, Cope and Lippincott, 1958–61; Venturi and Short, 1961–64; Venturi and Rauch, 1964–80. Associate Prof., Univ. of Pennsylvania, 1957–65; Charlotte Shepherd Davenport Prof. of Architecture, Yale, 1966–70. Works include: Vanna Venturi House, 1964, Guild House, 1965, Franklin Court, 1976, Inst. for Sci. Inf. Corp. HQ, 1979 (all Philadelphia); Allen Meml Art Museum Addition (Oberlin, Ohio), 1976; Gordon Wu Hall (Princeton), 1983. Fellow: Amer. Inst. of Architects; Amer. Acad. in Rome; Accad. Nazionale di San Luca; Amer. Acad. of Arts and Scis; Hon. FFRIAS. Hon. DFA: Oberlin Coll., 1977; Yale, 1979; Univ. of Pennsylvania, 1980; Princeton Univ., 1983; Philadelphia Coll. of Art, 1985; Hon. LHD NJ Inst. of Technology, 1984. James Madison Medal, Princeton Univ., 1985; Thomas Jefferson Meml Foundn Medal, Univ. of Virginia, 1983. *Publications:* A View from the Campidoglio: selected essays, 1953–84 (with Denise Scott Brown), 1984; Complexity and Contradiction in Architecture, 1966, 2nd edn 1977; Learning from Las Vegas (with Denise Scott Brown and Steven Izenour), 1972, 2nd edn 1977; articles in periodicals. *Recreation:* travel. *Address:* Venturi, Rauch and Scott Brown, 4236 Main Street, Philadelphia, Pa 19127, USA. *T:* (215) 487–0400.

VENUGOPAL, Dr Sriramashetty; Principal in General Practice, Aston, Birmingham, since 1967; *b* 14 May 1933; *s* of Satyanarayan and Manikyamma Sriramashetty; *m* 1960, Subhadra Venugopal; one *s* one *d*. *Educ:* Osmania Univ., Hyderabad, India (BSc, MB BS); Madras Univ. (DMRD). Medical posts, Osmania Hosp., State Med. Services, Hyderabad, Singareni Collieries, 1959–65; Registrar, Radiology, Selly Oak Hosp., Birmingham, 1965–66; Registrar, Chest Medicine, Springfield Hosp., Grimsby, 1966–67; Hosp. Practitioner, Psychiatry, All Saints Hosp., Birmingham, 1972–. Member: Working Group, DHSS, 1984–; Local Med. Cttee, 1975–; Dist. Med. Cttee, 1978–; GMC, 1984–; Vice-Chm., Birmingham Div., BMA, 1986– (Chm., 1985–86). Founder Mem., Overseas Doctors' Assoc., 1975 (Dep. Treasurer, 1975–81; Nat. Vice-Chm., 1981–; Inf. and Adv. Service, 1981–); Founder Mem. and Chm., Link House Council, 1975–. FRSocMed 1986. *Publications:* contribs to learned jls on medico-political topics. *Recreations:* medical politics, music, gardening. *Address:* Aston Health Centre, 175 Trinity Road, Aston, Birmingham B6 6JA. *T:* 021–328 3597; 24 Melville Road, Edgbaston, Birmingham B16 9JT. *T:* 021–454 1725. *Club:* Aston Rotary.

VERCO, Sir Walter (John George), KCVO 1981 (CVO 1970; MVO 1952); OStJ 1954; Secretary of the Order of the Garter, since 1974; Secretary to the Earl Marshal, since 1961; Surrey Herald of Arms Extraordinary, since 1980; *b* 18 January 1907; *s* of late John Walter Verco, Chelsea; *m* 1929, Ada Rose, *d* of late Bertram Leonard Bennett, Lymington, Hants; one *s* one *d*. Served War, 1940–45, with RAFVR, Flight Lt. Secretary to Garter King of Arms, 1949–60; Rouge Croix Pursuivant of Arms, 1954–60; Chester Herald, 1960–71; Norroy and Ulster King of Arms, 1971–80. Hon. Genealogist to Order of the British Empire, 1959–, to Royal Victorian Order, 1968–; Inspector, RAF Badges, 1970–, RAAF Badges, 1971–; Adviser on Naval Heraldry, 1970–. *Address:* College of Arms, Queen Victoria Street, EC4. *T:* 01–248 6185; 8 Park Court, Linkfield Lane, Redhill, Surrey. *T:* Redhill 71794.

VERCOE, Rt. Rev. Whakahuihui; *see* Aotearoa, Bishop of.

VERCORS; (pen-name of Jean Bruller); writer; designer-engraver (as Jean Bruller); Légion d'honneur; médaille de la Résistance; Commandeur des Arts et des Lettres; *b* Paris, 26 February 1902; *s* of Louis Bruller and E. Bourbon; *m* 1931, Jeanne Barusseaud (marr. diss.); three *s*; *m* Rita Barisse. *Educ:* Ecole Alsacienne, Paris. Dessinateur-graveur, 1926–; retrospective exhibitions: Vienna, 1970; Budapest, Cologne, 1971. Designed set and costumes for Voltaire's L'Orphelin de la Chine, Comédie Française, 1965. *Plays produced include:* Zoo, Carcassonne, 1963, Paris, 1964, and other European countries and USA; Oedipe-Roi (adaptation), La Rochelle, 1967, Paris, 1970; Le Fer et le Velours, Nîmes, 1969; Hamlet (adaptation), Lyons, 1977; Macbeth (adaptation), Anjou, Paris and Martinique, 1977. Founded Editions de Minuit clandestines, 1941, and began to publish under the name of Vercors. *Publications: as Jean Bruller:* albums: 21 Recettes de Mort Violente, 1926, repr. 1977; Hypothèses sur les Amateurs de Peinture, 1927; Un Homme Coupé en tranches, 1929; Nouvelle Clé des Songes, 1934; L'enfer, 1935; Visions intimes et rassurantes de la guerre, 1936; Silences, 1937; Les Relevés Trimestriels, planches dont l'ensemble (160 planches) forme La Danse des Vivants, 1932–38; nombreuses illustrations pour livres de luxe; *as Vercors:* Le Silence de la Mer, 1942; La Marche à l'Etoile, 1943; Le Songe, 1944; Le Sable du Temps, 1945; Les Armes de la Nuit, 1946; Les Yeux et la Lumière, 1948; Plus ou Moins Homme, 1950; La Puissance du jour, 1951; Les Animaux dénaturés (Borderline), 1952; Les Pas dans le Sable, 1954; Portrait d'une Amitié, 1954; Divagations d'un Français en Chine, 1956; Colères, 1956 (The Insurgents); PPC, 1957; Sur ce rivage (I Le Périple, 1958, II Monsieur Prousthe, 1958, III Liberté de Décembre, 1959); Sylva, 1961; Hamlet (trans. and illus.), 1965; (with P. Misraki) Les Chemins de L'Etre, 1965; (with M. Coronel) Quota ou les Pléthoriens, 1966; La Bataille du Silence, 1967; Le Radeau de la Méduse, 1969; Oedipe et Hamlet, 1970; Contes des Cataplasmes, 1971; Sillages, 1972; Sept Sentiers du Désert (short stories), 1972; Questions sur la vie à Messieurs les Biologistes (essay), 1973; Comme un Frère, 1973; Tendre Naufrage, 1974; Ce que je crois (essay), 1976; Je cuisine comme un chef (cook book), 1976; Les Chevaux du Temps, 1977; Collected Plays, vol. 1 (Zoo, Le Fer et le Velours, Le Silence de la Mer), 1978, Vol. 2, Pour Shakespeare (Hamlet, Macbeth), 1978; Sens et Non-sens de l'Histoire (essay), 1978; Camille ou l'Enfant double (children's story), 1978; Le Piège à Loup (novel), 1979; Assez Mentir! (essay, collab. O. Wormser-Migot), 1980; Cent ans d'histoire de France 1862–1962: vol. I, Moi Aristide Briand, 1981; vol. II, Les Occasions Perdues, 1982; vol. III, Les nouveaux jours, 1984; Anne Boleyn, 1985; Le Tigre d'Anvers, 1986; numerous articles in periodicals. *Address:* Moulin des Iles, 77120 St Augustin, France. *Clubs:* PEN, section française; Comité National des Ecrivains (Hon. Pres.).

VERDON-SMITH, Sir (William) Reginald, Kt 1953; Pro-Chancellor, Bristol University, since 1965; Vice Lord-Lieutenant, Avon, since 1980; *b* 5 Nov. 1912; *s* of late Sir William G. Verdon Smith, CBE, JP; *m* 1946, Jane Margaret, *d* of late V. W. J. Hobbs; one *s* one *d*. *Educ:* Repton School; Brasenose College, Oxford (Scholar), 1st class School of Jurisprudence, 1935; BCL 1936 and Vinerian Law Scholar; Barrister-at-law, Inner Temple. Bristol Aeroplane Co., 1938–68: Dir., 1942; Jt Asst Man. Dir., 1947; Jt Man. Dir., 1952; Chm. 1955. Vice-Chm., Rolls Royce Ltd, 1966–68; Chm., British Aircraft Corp. (Hldgs) Ltd, 1969–72; Dir, Lloyds Bank Ltd, 1951–83; Chairman: Lloyds Bank Internat., 1973–79; Lloyds Bank Bristol Region, 1976–83. Pres. SBAC, 1946–48; Chm., Fatstock and Meat Marketing Committee of Enquiry, 1962–64; Mem. of Council, Univ. of Bristol (Chm., 1949–56). Mem. Cttee on the Working of the Monetary System (Radcliffe Cttee), 1957–59. Mem., Review Body on Remuneration of Doctors and Dentists, 1964–68. Master, Worshipful Co. of Coachmakers and Coach Harness Makers, 1960–61; Master, Soc. of Merchant Venturers, 1968–69. FRSA. DL Avon, 1974. Hon. LLD Bristol, 1959; Hon. DSc, Cranfield Inst. of Technology, 1971; Hon. Fellow: Brasenose Coll., Oxford, 1965; Bristol Univ., 1986. *Recreations:* golf and sailing. *Address:* Flat 3, Spring Leigh, Church Road, Leigh Woods, Bristol BS8 3PG; The Pheasantry, Boldre, Lymington, Hants SO4 8PP. *Clubs:* United Oxford & Cambridge University, Royal Cruising; Royal Yacht Squadron, Royal Lymington Yacht.
See also Sir G. S. J. White, Bt.

VERE OF HANWORTH, Lord; Charles Francis Topham de Vere Beauclerk; *b* 22 Feb. 1965; *s* and *heir* of Earl of Burford, *qv*.

VEREKER, family name of **Viscount Gort.**

VEREKER, John Michael Medlicott; Under Secretary, since 1983, and Principal Finance Officer, since 1986, Overseas Development Administration, Foreign and Commonwealth Office; *b* 9 Aug. 1944; *s* of Comdr C. W. M. Vereker and late M. H. Vereker (*née* Whatley); *m* 1971, Judith Diane, *d* of Hobart and Alice Rowen, Washington, DC; one *s* one *d*. *Educ:* Marlborough Coll.; Keele Univ. (BA Hons 1967). Asst Principal, ODM, 1967–69; World Bank, Washington, 1970–72; Principal, ODM, 1972; Private Sec. to successive Ministers of Overseas Develt, 1977–78; Asst Sec., 1978; Prime Minister's Office, 1980–83. *Address:* c/o Overseas Development Administration, Eland House, Stag Place, SW1E 5DH. *T:* 01–213 3000.
See also P. W. M. Vereker.

VEREKER, Peter William Medlicott; HM Diplomatic Service; Counsellor and Consul-General, Bangkok, since 1983 (acted as Chargé d'Affaires, 1984, 1986); *b* 13 Oct. 1939; *s* of Comdr Charles William Medlicott Vereker and late Marjorie Hughes Whatley; *m* 1967, Susan Elizabeth, *d* of Maj.-Gen. A. J. Dyball, CBE, MC, TD and of E. M. Dyball; three *s*. *Educ:* Elstree Sch.; Marlborough Coll.; Trinity Coll., Cambridge (MA); Harvard Univ. (Henry Fellow, 1962). CUAS (RAFVR), 1958–61. Assistant d'Anglais, Paris, 1963; joined FO, 1963; Bangkok, 1964; Chiang Mai, 1967; FCO, 1968; Canberra, 1971; Head of Chancery, Athens, 1975; Asst Head, W European Dept, FCO, 1978; RCDS, 1982. *Recreations:* tennis, sailing, ski-ing. *Address:* c/o Foreign and Commonwealth Office, SW1A 2AH. *Clubs:* Royal Bangkok Sports, Royal Varuna Yacht (Thailand).
See also J. M. M. Vereker.

VEREY, Michael John, TD 1945; *b* 12 Oct. 1912; *yr s* of late Henry Edward and late Lucy Alice Verey; *m* 1947, Sylvia Mary, *widow* of Charles Bartlet and *d* of late Lt-Col Denis Wilson and late Mrs Mary Henrietta Wilson; two *s* one *d*. *Educ:* Eton; Trinity College, Cambridge (MA). Joined Helbert, Wagg & Co. Ltd, 1934. Served War of 1939–45, Middle East, Italy, Warwickshire Yeomanry (Lt-Col). Chairman: J. Henry Schroder Wagg & Co. Ltd, 1972–73 (Dep. Chm., 1966–72); Schroders Ltd, 1973–77; Accepting Houses Cttee, 1974–77; Broadstone Investment Trust Ltd, 1962–83; Brixton Estate Ltd 1971–83; Trustees, Charities Official Investment Fund, 1974–83; American Energy Investments Ltd, 1981–83; Director: British Petroleum Co. Ltd, 1974–82; The Boots Co. (Vice-Chm., 1978–83); Commercial Union Assurance Co. Ltd (Vice-Chm., 1975–78; Dep. Chm., 1978–82); BI International, and other cos; Mem., Covent Garden Market Authority, 1961–66. High Sheriff of Berkshire, 1968. Pres., Royal Worcestershire and Warwickshire Yeomanry Regtl Assoc., 1976. *Recreations:* gardening, travel. *Address:* Little Bowden, Pangbourne, Berks. *T:* Pangbourne 2210. *Club:* Boodle's.

VERITY, Anthony Courtenay Froude, MA; Master of Dulwich College, since 1986; *b* 25 Feb. 1939; *s* of Arthur and Alice Kathleen Verity; *m* 1962, Patricia Ann Siddall; one *s* one *d*. *Educ:* Queen Elizabeth's Hosp., Bristol; Pembroke Coll., Cambridge (MA). Assistant Master: Dulwich Coll., 1962–65; Manchester Grammar Sch., 1965–69; Head of Classics, Bristol Grammar Sch., 1969–76; Headmaster, Leeds Grammar Sch., 1976–86. Editor, Greece and Rome, 1971–76. *Publications:* Latin as Literature, 1971; contribs to Jl of Arabic Lit. *Recreations:* music, fell-walking, squash, cricket. *Address:* Elm Lawn, Dulwich Common, SE21 7EW.

VERMES, Dr Geza, FBA 1985; Reader in Jewish Studies and Fellow of Wolfson College, Oxford University, since 1965; *b* 22 June 1924; *s* of late Ernö Vermes and Terézia Riesz; *m* 1958, Mrs Pamela Curle (*née* Hobson). *Educ:* Univ. of Budapest; Coll. St Albert de Louvain, Louvain Univ. Licencié en Histoire et Philologie Orientales (avec la plus grande distinction), 1952; DTheol 1953; MA Oxon 1965. Asst Editor, Cahiers Sioniens, Paris, 1953–55; research worker, CNRS, Paris, 1955–57; Lectr, later Sen. Lectr in Divinity, Newcastle Univ., 1957–65; Chm. of Curators of Oriental Inst., Oxford, 1971–74; Chm. Bd of Faculty of Oriental Studies, Oxford, 1978–80; Governor, Oxford Centre for Postgrad. Hebrew Studies, 1972–. Vis. Prof. in Religious Studies, Brown Univ., 1971; Rosenstiel Res. Fellow, Univ. of Notre Dame, 1972; Margaret Harris Lectr in Religion, Dundee Univ., 1977; Riddell Meml Lectr, Newcastle Univ., 1981; Dist. Vis. Prof. in Judeo-Christian Studies, Tulane Univ., 1982; Igor Kaplan Vis. Lectr, Toronto Sch. of Theology, 1985. Pres., British Assoc. for Jewish Studies, 1975; Pres., European Assoc. for Jewish Studies, 1981–84. Editor, Jl of Jewish Studies, 1971–. *Publications:* Les manuscrits du désert de Juda, 1953; Discovery in the Judean Desert, 1956; Scripture and Tradition in Judaism, 1961; The Dead Sea Scrolls in English, 1962; Jesus the Jew, 1973 (trans. Spanish, French, Japanese, Italian); Post-Biblical Jewish Studies, 1975; (with Pamela Vermes) The Dead Sea Scrolls: Qumran in perspective, 1977 (trans. Spanish); The Gospel of Jesus the Jew, 1981; (ed jtly) Essays in Honour of Y. Yadin, 1982; Jesus and the World of Judaism, 1983; (ed and rev., with F. G. B. Millar and M. D. Goodman)) E. Schürer, The History of the Jewish People in the Age of Jesus Christ I–III, 1973–86. *Recreations:* watching wild life, correcting proofs. *Address:* Oriental Institute, Pusey Lane, Oxford OX1 2LE. *T:* Oxford 59272; West Wood Cottage, Foxcombe Lane, Boars Hill, Oxford OX1 5DH. *T:* Oxford 735384.

VERMEULE, Prof. Emily Dickinson Townsend, FSA; Zemurray-Stone-Radcliffe Professor, Harvard University, since 1970; Fellow for Research, Museum of Fine Arts, Boston, since 1963; *b* 11 Aug. 1928; *d* of Clinton Blake Townsend and Eleanor Mary Meneely; *m* 1957, Cornelius Clarkson Vermeule III; one *s* one *d*. *Educ:* The Brearley Sch.; Bryn Mawr Coll. (BA, PhD); Radcliffe Coll. (MA). Instructor in Greek: Bryn Mawr, 1956–57; Wellesley Coll., 1957–58; Asst Prof. of Classics, 1958–61, Associate Prof. of Classics, 1961–64, Boston Univ.; Prof. of Greek and Fine Arts, Wellesley, 1965–70. James Loeb Vis. Prof. of Classical Philology, Harvard Univ., 1969; Sather Prof. of Classical Literature, Univ. of California, Berkeley, 1975; Geddes-Harrower Prof. of Greek Art and Archaeology, Univ. of Aberdeen, 1980–81; Bernhard Vis. Prof., Williams Coll., 1986. Corresp. Member: British Academy; German Archaeological Inst. Member: Bd of Scholars, Library of Congress, 1982–; Smithsonian Council, 1983–; Amer. Philosophical Soc.; Amer. Acad. of Arts and Scis; Archaeological Inst. of America; Soc. for Preservation of Hellenic Studies. National Endowment for the Humanities Jefferson Lectr, 1981. Hon. degrees: DLitt: Douglass Coll., Rutgers, 1968; Smith Coll., 1971; Wheaton Coll., 1973; Tufts, 1980; Univ. of Pittsburgh, 1983; Bates Coll., 1983; DFA, Univ. of Massachusetts at Amherst, 1970; LLD: Regis Coll., 1970; LHD: Trinity Coll., Hartford, Conn., 1974; Emmanuel Coll., Boston, 1980. Gold Medal, Radcliffe Coll., 1968; Charles Goodwin Award of Merit, American Philological Assoc., 1980. *Publications:* Euripides' Electra, 1959; Greece in the Bronze Age, 1964, 7th edn 1980; The Trojan War in Greek Art, 1964; Götterkult, Archaeologia Homerica V, 1974; The Mound of Darkness, 1974; The Art of the Shaft Graves, 1975; Death in Early Greek Art and Poetry, 1979; (with V. Karageorghis) Mycenaean Pictorial Vase-Painting, 1982; contribs to Jl of Hellenic Studies, American Jl of Archaeology, Jahrbuch des d.Arch. Insts, Classical Philology, etc. *Recreations:* dogs, gardening. *Address:* 47 Coolidge Hill Road, Cambridge, Mass 02138, USA. *T:* (617) UN 4–1879. *Club:* Cosmopolitan (New York City).

VERNEY, family name of **Baron Willoughby de Broke.**

VERNEY, Sir John, 2nd Bt, *cr* 1946; MC 1944; TD 1970; painter, illustrator, author; *b* 30 Sept. 1913; *s* of Sir Ralph Verney, 1st Bt (Speaker's Secretary, 1921–55); *S* father, 1959; *m* 1939, Lucinda, *d* of late Major Herbert Musgrave, DSO; one *s* five *d* (and one *s* decd). *Educ:* Eton; Christ Church, Oxford. Served War of 1939–45 with N. Somerset Yeomanry, RAC and SAS Regt in Palestine, Syria, Egypt, Italy, France and Germany (despatches twice, MC). Exhibitor: RBA; London Group; Leicester, Redfern, New Grafton Gall., etc. Légion d'Honneur, 1945. *Publications:* Verney Abroad, 1954; Going to the Wars, 1955; Friday's Tunnel, 1959; Look at Houses, 1959; February's Road, 1961; Every Advantage, 1961; The Mad King of Chichiboo, 1963; ismo, 1964; A Dinner of Herbs, 1966; Fine Day for a Picnic, 1968; Seven Sunflower Seeds, 1968; Samson's Hoard, 1973; periodic contributor to Cornhill etc; annually, The Dodo Pad (the amusing telephone diary). *Heir:* *s* John Sebastian Verney, *b* 30 Aug. 1945. *Address:* The White House, Clare, Suffolk. *T:* Clare 277494.

VERNEY, Lawrence John, TD 1955; DL; **His Honour Judge Verney;** a Circuit Judge (formerly Deputy Chairman, Middlesex Sessions) since 1971; *b* 19 July 1924; *y s* of Sir Harry Verney, 4th Bt, DSO; *m* 1972, Zoë Auriel, *d* of Lt-Col P. G. Goodeve-Docker. *Educ:* Harrow; Oriel Coll., Oxford. Called to Bar, Inner Temple, 1952. Dep. Chm., Bucks QS, 1962–71. Editor, Harrow School Register, 1948–; Governor, Harrow Sch., 1972–. DL Bucks 1967. *Address:* Windmill House, Oving, Aylesbury, Bucks HP22 4HL.
See also Sir R. B. Verney, Bt, Rt Rev. S. E. Verney.

VERNEY, Sir Ralph (Bruce), 5th Bt *cr* 1818; KBE 1974; JP; Landowner; Vice-Lord-Lieutenant (formerly Vice-Lieutenant) of Buckinghamshire, 1965–84; *b* 18 Jan. 1915; *e s* of Sir Harry Calvert Williams Verney, 4th Bt, DSO, and Lady Rachel Bruce (*d* 1964), *d* of 9th Earl of Elgin; *S* father, 1974; *m* 1948, Mary Vestey; one *s* three *d*. *Educ:* Canford; Balliol Coll., Oxford. 2nd Lieut Bucks Yeomanry, 1940; Major, Berks Yeomanry, 1945 and Bucks Yeomanry, 1946. Pres., Country Landowners' Assoc., 1961–63; Vice-President for Great Britain, Confédération Européenne de L'Agriculture, 1965–71, Counsellor, 1971–; Chairman, Forestry Commn Cttee for England, 1967–80; Member: Forestry Commn, 1968–80; Milton Keynes New Town Corporation, 1967–74; BBC Adv. Cttee on Agriculture, 1970–78; Royal Commn on Environmental Pollution, 1973–79; Chm., Nature Conservancy Council, 1980–83 (Mem., 1966–71); Chm., Sec. of State for the Environment's Adv. Cttee on Aggregates for Construction Industry, 1972–77. Trustee: Radcliffe Trust; Ernest Cook Trust; Chequers Trust; Sch. of Water Sciences, Cranfield, 1982–. Member, Council: Buckingham Univ., 1983–; Royal Soc. of Arts, 1983– (FRSA 1972). Buckinghamshire County Council: Member, 1951; Chairman, Finance Cttee, 1957; Planning Cttee, 1967; CA 1961; JP Bucks, 1954; High Sheriff of Buckinghamshire, 1957–58; DL Bucks, 1960; High Steward of Buckingham, 1966. Prime Warden, Worshipful Co. of Dyers, 1969–70. Hon. Fellow: RIBA, 1977; Green Coll., Oxford, 1980. Chevalier de Tastevin, Clos Vougeot, 1978. *Recreation:* shooting. *Heir:* *s* Edmund Ralph Verney [*b* 28 June 1950; *m* 1982, Daphne Fausset-Farquhar; one *s* one *d*]. *Address:* Claydon House, Middle Claydon, Buckingham MK18 2EX. *T:* Steeple Claydon 297; Plas Rhôscolyn, Holyhead LL65 2NZ. *T:* Trearddur Bay 860288. *Club:* Cavalry and Guards.
See also L. J. Verney, Rt Rev. S. E. Verney.

VERNEY, Rt. Rev. Stephen Edmund, MBE 1945; *b* 17 April 1919; 2nd *s* of late Sir Harry Verney, 4th Bt, DSO and Lady Rachel Verney (*née* Bruce); *m* 1st, 1947, Priscilla Avice Sophie Schwerdt (*d* 1974); one *s* three *d*; 2nd, 1981, Sandra Ann Bailey; (one *s* decd). *Educ:* Harrow School; Balliol College, Oxford (MA). Curate of Gedling, Nottingham, 1950; Priest-in-charge and then first Vicar, St Francis, Clifton, Nottingham, 1952; Vicar of Leamington Hastings and Diocesan Missioner, Dio. Coventry, 1958; Canon Residentiary, Coventry Cathedral, 1964; Canon of Windsor, 1970; Bishop Suffragan of Repton, 1977–85. *Publications:* Fire in Coventry, 1964; People and Cities, 1969; Into the New Age, 1976; Water into Wine, 1985. *Recreations:* conversation and aloneness; music, gardening, travel. *Address:* Charity School House, Church Road, Blewbury, Oxon OX11 9PY. *Club:* English-Speaking Union.
See also L. J. Verney, Sir R. B. Verney, Bt.

VERNIER-PALLIEZ, Bernard Maurice Alexandre; Commandeur de la Légion d'Honneur; Croix de Guerre; Médaille de la Résistance; Ambassadeur de France, 1984; *b* 2 March 1918; *s* of Maurice Vernier and Marie-Thérèse Palliez; *m* 1952, Denise Silet-Pathe; one *s* three *d*. *Educ:* Ecole des Hautes Etudes Commerciales; Ecole Libre des Sciences Politiques. Licencié en Droit. Joined Régie Nationale des Usines, Renault, 1945 (dealing with personnel and trade unions); Sécretaire Général, RNUR, 1948–67; Directeur Général Adjoint, RNUR, 1967–71; Président Directeur Général, SAVIEM, 1967–74; Délégué Général aux Vehicules Industriels, Cars et Bus à la RNUR, Président du Directoire de Berliet, and Vice-Président du Conseil de Surveillance de SAVIEM, Jan.-Dec. 1975; Président Directeur Général, RNUR, Dec. 1975–1981; Ambassador to Washington, 1982–84. Pres., Adv. Bd, Poclain SA; Member: AIG Internat. Adv. Bd; Tenneco European Adv. Council; Byrnes Internat. Center Adv. Bd. *Address:* 25 Grande Rue, 78170 La Celle St-Cloud, France. *T:* (1) 39 69 30 11.

VERNON, family name of **Barons Lyveden** and **Vernon.**

VERNON, 10th Baron, *cr* 1762; **John Lawrance Vernon;** *b* 1 Feb. 1923; *s* of 9th Baron, and Violet (*d* 1978), *d* of Colonel Clay; *S* father, 1963; *m* 1st, 1955, Sheila Jean (marr. diss. 1982), *d* of W. Marshall Clark, Johannesburg; two *d*; 2nd, 1982, Sally, *d* of Robin Stratford, QC. *Educ:* Eton; Magdalen Coll., Oxford. Served in Scots Guards, 1942–46, retiring with rank of Captain. Called to Bar, Lincoln's Inn, 1949. Served in various Government Departments, 1950–61; attached to Colonial Office (for service in Kenya), 1957–58. JP Derbyshire, 1965–77. *Heir: kinsman* Robert Vernon-Harcourt [*b* 26 Dec. 1918; *m* 1948, Sylvia Jeanette, *d* of late Lt-Col Charles Henry Kitching, DSO]. *Address:* Sudbury House, Sudbury, Derbyshire DE6 5HT.

VERNON, David Bowater; Under Secretary, Inland Revenue, 1975–84; *b* 14 Nov. 1926; *s* of Lt-Col Herbert Bowater Vernon, MC, and Ivy Margaret Vernon; *m* 1954, Anne de Montmorency Fleming; three *s* three *d*. *Educ:* Marlborough Coll.; Oriel Coll., Oxford (MA). RA, 1945–48 (Lieut). Inland Revenue, 1951–84. *Recreation:* gardening. *Address:* The Oast, Gedges Farm, Matfield, Tonbridge, Kent. *T:* Brenchley 2400.

VERNON, Sir James, AC 1980; Kt 1965; CBE 1962 (OBE 1960); Director, Westham Dredging Co. Pty Ltd; Chairman: Volvo Australia Pty Ltd; C.I.B.C. Australia Ltd; *b* 1910; *s* of Donald Vernon, Tamworth, New South Wales; *m* 1935, Mavis, *d* of C. Lonsdale Smith; two *d*. *Educ:* Sydney Univ. (BSc); University College, London (PhD). CSR Ltd: Chief Chemist, 1938–51; Senior Exec. Officer, 1951–56; Asst General Manager, 1956–57; Gen. Manager, 1958–72; Dir, 1958–82; Chm., 1978–80. Chairman: Commonwealth Cttee of Economic Enquiry, 1963–65; Australian Post Office Commn of Inquiry, 1973; Internat. Pres., Pacific Basin Econ. Council, 1980–82. FRACI; FAIM; FTS. Hon. DSc: Sydney, 1965; Newcastle, 1969. Leighton Medal, Royal Australian Chemical Inst., 1965; John Storey Medal, Aust. Inst. of Management, 1971. Order of Sacred Treasure, 1st cl. (Japan), 1983. *Address:* 27 Manning Road, Double Bay, NSW 2028, Australia. *Clubs:* Australian, Union, Royal Sydney Golf (Sydney).

VERNON, James William, CMG 1964; barrister-at-law; *b* 1915; *s* of late John Alfred Vernon; *m* 1941, Betty Désirée, *d* of Gordon E. Nathan; one *s* one *d*. *Educ:* Wallasey Grammar Sch.; Emmanuel Coll., Cambridge (Scholar). BA 1937, MA 1940. Entered Civil Service, Ministry of Food, 1939; Flt Lieut, RAF, 1943; Wing Comdr (despatches), 1945; Principal Scientific Officer, Ministry of Works, 1945; Assistant Secretary, Colonial Office, 1954–64; Economic Adviser, British High Commission, Lusaka, 1966; Asst Under-Sec. of State, DEA, 1966–69; Under-Sec., Min. of Housing and Local Govt, later DoE, 1969–72. Called to Bar, Inner Temple, 1975. Queen's Commendation for Brave Conduct, 1955. *Recreations:* gardening, computer science. *Address:* 20 Grove Hill, Topsham, Devon.

VERNON, Kenneth Robert, CBE 1978; Deputy Chairman and Chief Executive, North of Scotland Hydro-Electric Board, since 1973; *b* 15 March 1923; *s* of late Cecil W. Vernon and Jessie McGaw, Dumfries; *m* 1946, Pamela Hands, Harrow; one *s* three *d* (and one *d* decd). *Educ:* Dumfries Academy; Glasgow University. BSc, FEng, FIEE, FIMechE. BTH Co., Edinburgh Corp., British Electricity Authority, 1948–55; South of Scotland Electricity Bd, 1955–56; North of Scotland Hydro-Electric Bd, 1956: Chief Electrical and Mech. Engr, 1964; Gen. Man., 1966; Bd Mem., 1970. Dir, British Electricity International Ltd, 1976–; Mem. Bd, Northern Ireland Electricity Service, 1979–85. *Publications:* various papers to technical instns. *Recreation:* fishing. *Address:* 10 Keith Crescent, Edinburgh EH4 3NH. *T:* 031–332 4610. *Club:* Royal Commonwealth Society.

VERNON, Prof. Magdalen Dorothea, MA (Cantab) 1926; ScD (Cantab) 1953; Professor of Psychology in the University of Reading, 1956–67; *b* 25 June 1901; *d* of Dr Horace Middleton Vernon and Katharine Dorothea Ewart. *Educ:* Oxford High Sch.; Newnham Coll., Cambridge. Asst Investigator to the Industrial Health Research Board, 1924–27; Research Investigator to the Medical Research Council, in the Psychological Laboratory, Cambridge, 1927–46; Lecturer in Psychology, 1946–51, Senior Lecturer in Psychology, 1951–55, Reader in Psychology, 1955–66, University of Reading. President, British Psychological Society, 1958 (Hon. Fellow, 1970); President, Psychology Section, British Assoc., 1959. *Publications:* The Experimental Study of Reading, 1931; Visual Perception, 1937; A Further Study of Visual Perception, 1952; Backwardness in Reading, 1957; The Psychology of Perception, 1962; Experiments in Visual Perception, 1966; Human Motivation, 1969; Perception through Experience, 1970; Reading and its Difficulties, 1971; numerous papers on Perception, etc. in British Journal of Psychology and British Journal of Educational Psychology. *Recreations:* walking, gardening. *Address:* 50 Cressingham Road, Reading, Berks. *T:* Reading 871088. *Club:* University Women's.

VERNON, Michael; *see* Vernon, William M.

VERNON, Sir Nigel (John Douglas), 4th Bt, *cr* 1914; Director, Travel Finance Ltd, since 1971; Consultant, Hogg Robinson Ltd, since 1984; *b* 2 May 1924; *s* of Sir (William) Norman Vernon, 3rd Bt, and Janet Lady Vernon (*d* 1973); *S* father, 1967; *m* 1947, Margaret Ellen (*née* Dobell); two *s* one *d*. *Educ:* Charterhouse. Royal Naval Volunteer Reserve (Lieutenant), 1942–45. Spillers Ltd, 1945–65; Director: Castle Brick Co Ltd, 1965–71; Deeside Merchants Ltd, 1971–74. *Recreations:* golf, shooting, gardening. *Heir:* *s* James William Vernon, FCA [*b* 2 April 1949; *m* 1981, Davinia, *er d* of Christopher David Howard, Ryton, Shrewsbury; one *d*]. *Address:* Top-y-Fron Hall, Kelsterton, near Flint, N Wales. *T:* Deeside 812129. *Club:* Naval.

VERNON, Prof. Philip Ewart, MA, PhD, DSc; Professor Emeritus, University of Calgary, 1979; Emeritus Professor, University of London; *b* 6 June 1905; *e s* of late Horace Middleton Vernon; *m* 1st, 1938, Annie C. Gray; 2nd, 1947, Dorothy Anne Fairley Lawson, MA, MEd; one *s*. *Educ:* Oundle Sch.; St John's Coll., Cambridge; Yale and Harvard Universities. First Class Hons in Nat. Sci. Tripos, Part I, 1926, and Moral Sci. Tripos, Part II, 1927; John Stewart of Rannoch Scholarship in Sacred Music, 1925; Strathcona Research Studentship, 1927–29; Laura Spelman Rockefeller Fellowship in Social Sciences, 1929–31; Fellowship of St John's Coll., Cambridge, 1930–33; Pinsent-Darwin Studentship in Mental Pathology, 1933–35. Psychologist to LCC at Maudsley Hospital Child Guidance Clinic, 1933–35; Head of Psychology Dept, Jordanhill Training Centre, Glasgow, 1935–38; Head of Psychology Dept, University of Glasgow, 1938–47; Psychological Research Adviser to Admiralty and War Office, 1942–45; Prof. of Educational Psychology, Inst. of Education, University of London, 1949–64; Prof. of Psychology, 1964–68; Prof. of Educational Psychology, Univ. of Calgary, 1968–78. Fellow, Centre for Advanced Studies in Behavioural Scis, Stanford, Calif, 1961–62, Vis. Canada Council Fellow, 1975. Visiting Professor: Princeton Univ. and Educnl Testing Service, 1957; Teachers' Coll., Sydney, 1977; numerous internat. educnl consultancies and lect. tours for British Council, 1953–68. President: Psych. Sect., British Assoc. Advancement of Science, 1952; BPsS, 1954–55. Govt of Alberta Achievement Award, 1972. Hon. LLD Univ. of Calgary, 1980. *Publications:* (with G. W. Allport) Studies in Expressive Movement, 1933; The Measurement of Abilities, 1940, 2nd edn, 1956; (with J. B. Parry) Personnel Selection in the British Forces, 1949; The Structure of Human Abilities, 1950, 2nd edn, 1961; Personality Tests and Assessments, 1953; Secondary School Selection, 1957; Intelligence and Attainment Tests, 1960; Personality Assessment: A Critical Survey, 1963; Intelligence and Cultural Environment, 1969; Readings in Creativity, 1971; (with G. Adamson and Dorothy F. Vernon) Psychology and Education of Gifted Children, 1977; Intelligence: Heredity and Environment, 1979; Abilities and Achievements of Orientals in North America, 1982; numerous papers in British and American psychological journals. *Recreations:* music, snowshoeing, cross-country ski-ing. *Address:* No 402B, 3719 49th Street NW, Calgary, Alberta, Canada.

VERNON, (William) Michael; Chairman, Granville Meat Co. Ltd, since 1981; Director, Strong & Fisher (Holdings) plc, since 1980; *b* 17 April 1926; *o* surv. *s* of late Sir Wilfred Vernon; *m* 1st, 1952, Rosheen O'Meara; one *s*; 2nd, 1977, Mrs Jane Colston (*née* Kilham-Roberts). *Educ:* Marlborough Coll.; Trinity Coll., Cambridge. MA 1948. Lieut, Royal Marines, 1944–46. Joined Spillers Ltd, 1948: Dir 1960; Jt Man. Dir 1962; Chm. and Chief Exec., 1968–80; Dir, EMI Ltd, 1973–80; Chm., Famous Names Ltd, 1981–85. Pres., Nat. Assoc. of British and Irish Millers, 1965; Vice-Chm., Millers' Mutual Assoc., 1968–80; Pres., British Food Export Council, 1977–80; Vice-Pres. and Dep. Chm., RNLI, 1980–. CBIM. *Recreations:* sailing, shooting, ski-ing. *Address:* Fyfield Manor, Andover, Hants. *Clubs:* Hurlingham; Royal Ocean Racing (Cdre 1964–68); Royal Yacht Squadron.

VERNON-HUNT, Ralph Holmes, DFC; Deputy Chairman, Pan Books Ltd, 1980–82, retired (Managing Director, 1970); *b* 23 May 1923; *m* 1946, Elizabeth Mary Harris; four *s* two *d* (and one *s* decd). *Educ:* Malvern College. Flt-Lt RAF, 1941–46; Bookseller, 1946–47; Sales Dir, Pan Books Ltd, 1947–62; Sales Dir, Paul Hamlyn Ltd, 1963–69. *Recreation:* hydroponics. *Address:* 45 Rosemont Road, Richmond, Surrey TW10 6QN.

VERONESE, Dr Vittorino; Cavaliere di Gran Croce della Repubblica Italiana; Gold Medal Awarded for Culture (Italian Republic); Doctor of Law (Padua, 1930); lawyer, banker, administrator; Chairman, Board of Directors, Banco di Roma, 1961–76 (Auditor, 1945–53; Director, 1953–57); *b* Vicenza, 1 March 1910; *m* 1939, Maria Petrarca; four *s* three *d*. General Secretary: Catholic Movement Graduates, 1939; Italian Catholic Action, 1944–46 (President, 1946–52); Vice-President, Internat. Movement of Catholic Intellectuals of Pax Romana, 1947–55. Vice-President, Banca Cattolica del Veneto, 1952–57; President, Consorzio di Credito per le Opere Pubbliche and Istituto di Credito per le Imprese di Pubblica Utilitá, 1957–58; Italian Deleg. to General Conf. of UNESCO, Beirut, 1950, Paris, 1952–53; Member Italian Nat. Commn, 1953–58; Vice-President, Exec. Board, 1954–56; President, 1956–58. Director-General of UNESCO, 1958–61, resigned; Member, Comité Consultatif International pour l'Alphabétisation, UNESCO, 1967; Vice-President: Comité Consultatif International pour Venise, UNESCO; Societa Italiano per l'Organizzazione Internationale (SIOI); Pres., Italian Consultative Cttee for Human Rights, 1965. Pres., Circolo di Roma, 1968. Lay Observer in Concilio Ecumenico Vaticano II; Member, Pontificia Commissione Justitia et Pax, 1967. Cav. di Gran Croce dell' Ordine di S Silvestro Papa; Commendatore dell' Ordine Piano. Holds several foreign orders. *Address:* c/o Banco di Roma, Via del Corso 307, Rome, Italy; 21 Via Cadlolo, Rome, Italy.

VERSEY, Henry Cherry; Emeritus Professor of Geology, University of Leeds, since 1959; *b* 22 Jan. 1894; *s* of Charles Versey, Welton, East Yorkshire; *m* 1923, Hypatia Ingersoll, *d* of Greevz Fysher, Leeds; two *s* two *d*. *Educ:* Hymers Coll., Hull; University of Leeds. Service with RAOC, European War, 1916–19. Lecturer in Geology, University of Leeds, 1919–49; Reader in Applied Geology, 1949–56, Professor of Geology, 1956–59, University of Leeds. Hon. LLD (Leeds), 1967. Phillips Medal, Yorkshire Geological Society, 1964. *Publications:* Geology of the Appleby District, 1941; Geology and Scenery of the Countryside round Leeds and Bradford, 1948. Many papers on Yorkshire geology. *Recreation:* philately. *Address:* 1 Stainburn Terrace, Leeds LS17 6NJ. *T:* Leeds 682244.

VERULAM, 7th Earl of, *cr* 1815; **John Duncan Grimston;** Bt 1629; Baron Forrester (Scot.), 1633; Baron Dunboyne and Viscount Grimston (Ire.), 1719; Baron Verulam (Gt. Brit.), 1790; Viscount Grimston (UK), 1815; *b* 21 April 1951; *s* of 6th Earl of Verulam, and of Marjorie Ray, *d* of late Walter Atholl Duncan; *S* father, 1973; *m* 1976, Dione Angela, *e d* of Jeremy Smith, Balcombe House, Sussex; three *s* one *d*. *Educ:* Eton; Christ Church, Oxford (MA 1976). *Heir: s* Viscount Grimston, *qv*. *Address:* Gorhambury, St Albans, Herts AL3 6AH. *T:* St Albans 55000. *Clubs:* White's, Beefsteak, Turf.

VERYKIOS, Dr Panaghiotis Andrew; Kt Commander of Order of George I, of Greece, and of Order of the Phoenix; MM (Greece); Greek Ambassador, retired; *b* Athens, 1910; *m* 1939, Mary (*née* Dracoulis); three *s*. *Educ:* Athens and Paris. Law (Dr) and Political Sciences. Greek Diplomatic Service, 1935. Served in the Army, 1939–40. Various diplomatic posts until 1946; Secretary of Embassy, London, 1947–51; Counsellor, Dep. Representative of NATO, Paris, 1952–54; Counsellor of Embassy, Paris, 1954–56; Head of NATO Div., Min. of Foreign Affairs, Athens, 1956–60; Ambassador to: The Netherlands, 1960–64; Norway, 1961–67; Denmark, 1964–67; Iceland, 1967; Court of St James's, 1967–69; Spain, 1969–70. Holds foreign decorations. *Publication:* La Prescription en Droit International, 1934 (Paris). *Recreation:* music. *Address:* 6 Iras Street, Ekali, Athens. *T:* 8131216; 23 Avenue Juste Olivier, 1006 Lausanne, Switzerland. *T:* (021) 224697. *Club:* Athenian (Athens).

VESEY, family name of **Viscount de Vesci.**

VESEY, Sir Henry; *see* Vesey, Sir N. H. P.

VESEY, Sir (Nathaniel) Henry (Peniston), Kt 1965; CBE 1953; Chairman, H. A. & E. Smith Ltd, since 1939; Chairman, Bank of N. T. Butterfield & Son Ltd, since 1970; Member of House of Assembly, Bermuda, 1938–72; *b* 1 June 1901; *s* of late Hon. Nathaniel Vesey, Devonshire, Bermuda; *m* 1920, Louise Marie, *d* of late Captain J. A. Stubbs, Shelly Bay, Bermuda; two *s*. *Educ:* Saltus Grammar Sch. Chairman: Food and Supplies Control Board, 1941–42; Board of Trade, 1943; Finance Cttee of House of Assembly, 1943–44; Bermuda Trade Development Board, 1945–56, 1960–69; Board of Civil Aviation, 1957–59; Board of Agriculture, 1957–59. MEC, 1948–57, Mem. Executive Council for Tourism and Trade, 1968–69. *Recreations:* fishing, golf. *Address:* Windward, Shelly Bay, 2–15, Bermuda. *T:* 3–0186. *Clubs:* Naval and Military; Royal Bermuda Yacht, Mid Ocean (Bermuda).

VESSEY, Prof. Martin Paterson; Professor of Social and Community Medicine, University of Oxford, since 1974; Fellow of St Cross College, Oxford, since 1973; *b* 22 July 1936; *s* of Sidney J. Vessey and Catherine P. Vessey (*née* Thomson); *m* 1959, Anne Platt; two *s* one *d*. *Educ:* University College Sch., Hampstead; University Coll. London; University Coll. Hosp. Med. Sch., London. MB, BS London 1959; MD London 1971; FFCM RCP 1972; MA Oxon 1974; MRCPE 1978; FRCPE 1979; FRCGP 1983. Scientific Officer, Dept of Statistics, Rothamsted Exper. Stn, 1960–65; House Surg. and House Phys., Barnet Gen. Hosp., 1965–66; Mem. Sci. Staff, MRC Statistical Research Unit, 1966–69; Lectr in Epidemiology, Univ. of Oxford, 1969–74. Member: Cttee on Safety of Medicines, 1980–; Royal Commn on Environmental Pollution, 1984–. *Publications:* many sci. articles in learned jls, notably on med. aspects of fertility control, safety of drugs, and epidemiology of cancer. *Recreations:* motoring, singing, conservation. *Address:* 8 Warnborough Road, Oxford OX2 6HZ. *T:* Oxford 52698.

VESTEY, family name of **Baron Vestey.**

VESTEY, 3rd Baron, *cr* 1922, of Kingswood; **Samuel George Armstrong Vestey;** Bt, *cr* 1913; DL; *b* 19 March 1941; *s* of late Captain the Hon. William Howarth Vestey (killed in action in Italy, 1944; *o s* of 2nd Baron Vestey and Frances Sarah Howarth) and of Pamela Helen Fullerton, *d* of George Nesbitt Armstrong; *S* grandfather, 1954; *m* 1st, 1970, Kathryn Mary (marr. diss. 1981), *er d* of John Eccles, Moor Park, Herts; two *d*; 2nd, 1981, Celia Elizabeth, *d* of Major Guy Knight, MC, Lockinge Manor, Wantage, Oxon; two *s*. *Educ:* Eton. Lieut, Scots Guards. Director, Union International plc and associated companies. President: London Meat Trade and Drovers Benevolent Assoc., 1973; Three Counties Agricl Soc., 1978; Inst. of Meat, 1978–83. Pres., Glos Assoc. of Boys' Clubs; County Pres., St John Ambulance Brigade (Glos). Liveryman, Butchers' Co. DL Glos, 1982. OStJ. *Recreations:* racing, shooting. *Heir: s* Hon. William Guy Vestey, *b* 27 Aug. 1983. *Address:* Stowell Park, Northleach, Glos. *Clubs:* White's; Jockey (Newmarket); Melbourne (Melbourne).

VESTEY, Edmund Hoyle, DL; Chairman: Blue Star Line; Lamport & Holt Line; Albion Insurance Co.; Associated Container Transportation (Australia); Director, Union International Co. and associated companies; *b* 1932; *o s* of Ronald Arthur Vestey, *qv*; *m* 1960, Anne Moubray, *yr d* of Gen. Sir Geoffry Scoones, KCB, KBE, CSI, DSO, MC; four *s*. *Educ:* Eton. 2nd Lieut Queen's Bays, 1951; Lieut, City of London Yeomanry. Pres., Gen. Council of British Shipping, 1981–82. FRSA; FCIT, 1982. Joint Master, Puckeridge and Thurlow Foxhounds; Pres., Essex County Scout Council, 1979–. High Sheriff, Essex, 1977; DL Essex, 1978. *Address:* Waltons, Ashdon, Saffron Walden, Essex; Glencanisp Lodge, Lochinver, Sutherland; Sunnyside Farmhouse, Hawick, Roxburghshire. *Clubs:* Cavalry and Guards, Carlton.

VESTEY, Sir (John) Derek, 2nd Bt, *cr* 1921; *b* 4 June 1914; *s* of John Joseph Vestey (*d* 1932) and Dorothy Mary (*d* 1918), *d* of John Henry Beaver, Gawthorpe Hall, Bingley, Yorkshire; *g s* of Sir Edmund Vestey, 1st Bt; *S* grandfather 1953; *m* 1938, Phyllis Irene, *o d* of H. Brewer, Banstead, Surrey; one *s* one *d*. *Educ:* Leys Sch., Cambridge. Served War of 1939–45: Flt-Lieut, RAFVR, 1940–45. *Heir: s* Paul Edmund Vestey [*b* 15 Feb. 1944; *m* 1971, Victoria Anne Scudamore, *d* of John Salter, Tiverton, Devon; three *d*. *Educ:* Radley]. *Address:* 5 Carlton Gardens, SW1. *T:* 01–930 1610. *Clubs:* MCC, Royal Automobile.
See also R. A. Vestey.

VESTEY, Ronald Arthur; DL; Director, Union International Co.; *b* 10 May 1898; 4th but *e* surv. *s* of Sir Edmund Hoyle Vestey, 1st Bt; *m* 1923, Florence Ellen McLean (*d* 1966), *e d* of Colonel T. G. Luis, VD, Broughty Ferry, Angus; one *s* three *d*. *Educ:* Malvern Coll. Travelled extensively throughout world, with interests in many countries. High Sheriff of Suffolk, 1961; DL Suffolk, 1970. *Recreations:* shooting, fishing. *Address:* Great Thurlow Hall, Suffolk. *T:* Thurlow 240. *Clubs:* Carlton, MCC.
See also E. H. Vestey.

VIAL, Sir Kenneth Harold, Kt 1978; CBE 1969; chartered accountant; retired; *b* 11 Aug. 1912; *s* of G. O. Vial, Melbourne; *m* 1937, Adele, *d* of R. G. R. Ball; one *s* two *d*. *Educ:* Scotch Coll., Melbourne. Served RAAF, 1941–46 (Flight Lieut). Partner, Arthur Andersen & Co. (formerly Fuller King & Co.), 1946–69; Chairman: Yarra Falls Ltd, 1969–74; Rocke Tompsitt & Co. Ltd, 1975–79; Director: Michaelis Bayley Ltd, 1969–81 (Chm., 1975–81); Mono Pumps (Aust.) Pty Ltd, 1969–81; F. H. Faulding & Co. Ltd, 1978–84; Hortico Ltd, 1981–84 (Chm., 1981–84). Member: Aust. Nat. Airlines Commn, 1956–79 (Chm., 1975–79); Aviation Industry Adv. Council, 1978–79; Council, Aust. Services Canteens Organisation, 1959–76 (Chm., Bd of Management, 1971–76); Council, La Trobe Univ., 1966–74 (Dep. Chancellor, 1970–72); Melbourne Underground Rail Loop Authority, 1971–81. *Address:* 6–393 Barkers Road, Kew, Vic 3101, Australia. *Clubs:* Athenæum, Naval and Military (Melbourne).

VICARS-HARRIS, Noël Hedley, CMG 1953; *b* 22 Nov. 1901; *o s* of late C. F. Harris and Evelyn C. Vicars, The Gate House, Rugby; *m* 1st, 1926, Maria Guimarães of Sao Paulo, Brazil (marr. dissolved, 1939); two *s*; 2nd, 1940, Joan Marguerite Francis; one *s*. *Educ:* Charterhouse; St John's Coll., Cambridge. BA Agric., 1924. Employed in Brazil by Brazil Plantations Syndicate Ltd, 1924–27; HM Colonial Service, Tanganyika, 1927–55; Official Member of Legislative and Executive Councils, Tanganyika, 1950–Nov. 1953; Member for Lands and Mines, Tanganyika, 1950–55. *Recreation:* gardening. *Address:* Bampfylde Cottage, Sparkford, Somerset. *T:* North Cadbury 40454.

VICARY, Rev. Canon Douglas Reginald; Canon Residentiary and Precentor of Wells Cathedral, since 1975; *b* 24 Sept. 1916; *e s* of R. W. Vicary, Walthamstow; *m* 1947, Ruth, *y d* of late F. J. L. Hickinbotham, JP, and of Mrs Hickinbotham, Edgbaston; two *s* two *d*. *Educ:* Sir George Monoux Grammar Sch., Walthamstow; Trinity Coll., Oxford (Open Scholar), Wycliffe Hall, Oxford. 1st Class Nat. Sci. 1939; BSc 1939, MA 1942; Diploma in Theology with distinction, 1940; deacon, 1940; priest, 1941. Curate of St Peter and St Paul, Courteenhall, and Asst Chaplain and House Master, St Lawrence Coll., Ramsgate, while evacuated at Courteenhall, Northampton, 1940–44; Chaplain, Hertford Coll., Oxford, 1945–48; Tutor at Wycliffe Hall, 1945–47, Chaplain 1947–48; Dir of Religious Education, Rochester Diocese, 1948–57; Sec., CACTM Exams Cttee and GOE, 1952–57; Dir, Post-Ordination Training, 1952–57, Headmaster of King's School, Rochester, 1957–75; Chaplain to HM the Queen, 1977–86. Minor Canon, Rochester Cathedral, 1949–52; Canon Residentiary and Precentor, 1952–57; Hon. Canon, 1957–75. Exam. Chaplain to Bishop of Rochester, 1950–, to Bishop of Bath and Wells, 1975–. Mem. Court, Kent Univ., 1965–75. FRSA 1970. *Publication:* contrib. Canterbury Chapters, 1976. *Recreations:* music, architecture, hill-walking, reading. *Address:* 4 The Liberty, Wells, Somerset BA5 2SU. *T:* Wells 73188.

VICK, Arnold Oughtred Russell; QC 1980; **His Honour Judge Russell Vick;** a Circuit Judge, since 1982; *b* 14 Sept. 1933; *yr s* of late His Honour Judge Sir Godfrey Russell Vick, QC and late Lady Russell Vick, JP, *d* of J. A. Compston, KC; *m* 1959, Zinnia Mary, *e d* of Thomas Brown Yates, Godalming; two *s* one *d*. *Educ:* The Leys Sch., Cambridge; Jesus Coll., Cambridge (MA). Pilot, RAF, 1952–54. Called to Bar, Inner Temple, 1958; Mem. Gen. Council of the Bar, 1964–68; Prosecuting Counsel to the Post Office, 1964–69; Dep. Recorder, Rochester City QS, 1971; a Recorder of the Crown Court, 1972–82. Mem., Lord Chancellor's County Court Rules Cttee, 1972–80; Recorder, SE Circuit Bar Mess, 1978–80. Gov., New Beacon Sch., Sevenoaks, 1982–. Master, Curriers' Co., 1976–77. *Recreations:* golf, cricket. *Address:* The Law Courts, Barker Road, Maidstone. *T:* Maidstone 54966. *Clubs:* MCC; Hawks (Cambridge); Wildernesse (Captain 1978) (Sevenoaks); Royal Worlington and Newmarket Golf.

VICK, Sir (Francis) Arthur, Kt 1973; OBE 1945; PhD; FIEE, FInstP; MRIA; President and Vice-Chancellor, Queen's University of Belfast, 1966–76; Pro-Chancellor and Chairman of Council, University of Warwick, since 1977; *b* 5 June 1911; *s* of late Wallace Devenport Vick and late Clara (*née* Taylor); *m* 1943, Elizabeth Dorothy Story; one *d*. *Educ:* Waverley Grammar School, Birmingham; Birmingham Univ. Asst Lectr in Physics, University Coll., London, 1936–39, Lectr, 1939–44; Asst Dir of Scientific Research, Min. of Supply, 1939–44; Lectr in Physics, Manchester Univ., 1944–47, Sen. Lectr, 1947–50; Prof. of Physics, University Coll. of N Staffs, 1950–59 (Vice-Principal, 1950–54, Actg Principal, 1952–53); Dep. Dir, AERE, Harwell, 1959–60, Dir, 1960–64; Dir of Research Group, UKAEA, 1961–64; Mem. for Research, 1964–66. Institute of Physics: Mem. Bd, 1946–51; Chm., Manchester and District Branch, 1948–51; Vice-Pres., 1953–56; Hon. Sec., 1956–60. Chairman: Manchester Fedn of Scientific Societies, 1949–51; Naval Educn Adv. Cttee, 1964–70; Academic Adv. Council, MoD, 1969–76; Standing Conf. on Univ. Entrance, 1968–75. Pres., Assoc. of Teachers in Colls and Depts of Educn, 1964–72, Hon. Mem., 1972; Vice-Pres., Arts Council of NI, 1966–76. Member: Adv. Council on Bldg Research, Min. of Works, 1955–59; Scientific Adv. Council, Min. of Supply, 1956–59; UGC, 1959–66; Colonial Univ. Grants Adv. Cttee, 1960–65; Adv. Council on Research and Develt, Min. of Power, 1960–63; Nuclear Safety Adv. Cttee, Min. of Power, 1960–66; Governing Body, Nat. Inst. for Research in Nuclear Science, 1964–65. MRIA 1973. Hon. DSc: Keele, 1972; NUI, 1976; Hon. LLD: Dublin, 1973; Belfast, 1977; Hon. DCL Kent, 1977. Kt Comdr, Liberian Humane Order of African Redemption, 1962. *Publications:* various scientific papers and contributions to books. *Recreations:* music, gardening, using tools. *Address:* Fieldhead Cottage, Fieldhead Lane, Myton Road, Warwick CV34 6QF. *T:* Warwick 491822. *Clubs:* Athenæum, Savile.

VICK, Richard (William); His Honour Judge Vick; a Circuit Judge (formerly County Court Judge, since 1969, and Deputy Chairman of Quarter Sessions for Middlesex Area of Greater London, since 1965); Resident Judge, Kingston Group of Courts, since 1978; Honorary Recorder of Guildford, since 1973; *b* 9 Dec. 1917; *s* of late Richard William Vick, JP, and Hilda Josephine (*née* Carlton), Windsor, Berks; *m* 1st, 1947, Judith Jean (*d* 1974), *d* of Denis Franklin Warren; one *s* two *d*; 2nd, 1975, Mrs Joan Chesney Frost, BA, *d* of Arthur Blaney Powe, MA, Sydney, Australia. *Educ:* Stowe; Jesus Coll., Cambridge (BA). Served in RNVR, 1939–46. Called to Bar, Inner Temple, 1940. Dep. Chairman, W Kent QS, 1960–62; Dep. Chairman, Kent QS, 1962–65. Vice-Chm., Surrey Magistrates Soc., 1972; Member: Magistrates' Courts Cttee; Probation Cttee; Circuit Adviser, Judicial Studies Bd, 1981–. Mem. Court, Surrey Univ. *Publication:* The Administration of Civil Justice in England and Wales, 1967. *Recreations:* sailing, shooting, swimming, bridge. *Address:* The Town House, Godalming, Surrey. *Clubs:* United Oxford & Cambridge University; Hawks (Cambridge).

VICKERMAN, Prof. Keith, FRS 1984; FRSE 1971; Regius Professor of Zoology, University of Glasgow, since 1984; *b* 21 March 1933; *s* of Jack Vickerman and Mabel Vickerman (*née* Dyson); *m* 1961, Moira Dutton, LLB; one *d*. *Educ:* King James' Grammar School, Almondbury; University College London (Fellow, 1985). BSc 1955; PhD 1960; DSc 1970. Wellcome Trust Lectr, Zoology Dept, UCL, 1958–63; Royal Soc. Tropical Res. Fellow, UCL, 1963–68; Glasgow University: Reader in Zoology, 1968–74; Prof., 1974–; Head of Dept of Zoology, 1979–85. Mem., WHO Panel of Consultant Experts on Parasitic Diseases, 1973–. *Publications:* The Protozoa (with F. E. G. Cox), 1967; numerous papers on protozoa (esp. trypanosomes) in scientific and med. jls. *Recreations:* sketching, gardening. *Address:* Department of Zoology, University of Glasgow, Glasgow G12 8QQ. *T:* 041–339 8855; 16 Mirrlees Drive, Glasgow G12 0SH. *T:* 041–334 2794.

VICKERS, family name of **Baroness Vickers.**

VICKERS, Baroness *cr* 1974 (Life Peer), of Devonport; **Joan Helen Vickers,** DBE 1964 (MBE 1946); *e d* of late Horace Cecil Vickers and late Lilian Monro Lambert Grose. *Educ:* St Monica's Coll., Burgh Heath, Surrey. Member, LCC, Norwood Division of Lambeth, 1937–45. Contested (C) South Poplar, 1945. Served with British Red Cross in SE Asia (MBE); Colonial Service in Malaya, 1946–50. MP (C) Plymouth, Devonport, 1955–Feb. 1974; UK Delegate (C), Council of Europe and WEU, 1967–74. Chairman: Anglo-Indonesian Society; UK Delegate, UK Status of Women Commn, 1960–64; President: Status of Women Cttee; Internat. Friendship League; Inst. of Qualified Private Secretaries; Europe China Assoc. Chm., National Centre for Cued Speech. Netherlands Red Cross Medal. *Address:* The Manor House, East Chisenbury, Pewsey, Wilts.

VICKERS, Eric, CB 1979; Director of Defence Services, Department of the Environment, 1972–81; *b* 25 April 1921; *s* of late Charles Vickers and late Ida Vickers; *m* 1945, Barbara Mary Jones; one *s* one *d*. *Educ:* King's School, Grantham. Joined India Office, 1938; RAF (Fl/Lt Coastal Command), 1941–46; Ministry of Works, 1948; Principal, 1950; Assistant Secretary, 1962; Imperial Defence College, 1969; Dir of Home Estate Management, DoE, 1970–72. *Recreation:* photography, caravanning. *Address:* 46 Stamford Road, Oakham, Rutland, Leicestershire LE15 6JA. *T:* Oakham 4166.

VICKERS, James Oswald Noel, OBE 1977; General Secretary, Civil Service Union, 1963–77 (Deputy General Secretary, 1960–62); *b* 6 April 1916; *s* of Noel Muschamp and Linda Vickers; *m* 1940, Winifred Mary Lambert; one *s* one *d*. *Educ:* Stowe Sch.; Queens' Coll., Cambridge. Exhibnr, BA Hons Hist., MA. Served War, HM Forces, 1939–45. Warden, Wedgwood Memorial Coll., 1946–49; Educn Officer, ETU, and Head of Esher Coll., 1949–56. Member: Civil Service Nat. Whitley Council, 1962–77 (Chm. Staff Side, 1975–77); TUC Inter-Union Disputes Panel, 1970–77; TUC Non-Manual Workers Adv. Cttee, 1973–75; Fabian Soc. Trade Union and Industrial Relations Cttee, 1964–81 (Chm. 1973–78; Vice-Chm., 1978–79); UCL Coll. Cttee, 1974–79; Council, Tavistock Inst., 1976–80; Employment Appeal Tribunal, 1978–86; CS Appeal Bd, 1978–86. *Publications:* contrib. to Fabian pamphlets. *Recreations:* bird-watching, gardening, travel. *Address:* 5 The Butts, Brentford, Mddx TW8 8BJ. *T:* 01–560 3482; Heber Vale Cottage, Timberscombe, near Minehead, Som.

VICKERS, Jon, CC (Canada) 1968; dramatic tenor; *b* Prince Albert, Saskatchewan, 1926; *m* 1953, Henrietta Outerbridge; three *s* two *d*. Studied under George Lambert, Royal Conservatory of Music, Toronto. Made debut with Toronto Opera Company, 1952; Stratford (Ontario) Festival, 1956. Joined Royal Opera House, Covent Garden, 1957. First sang at: Bayreuth Festival, 1958; Vienna State Opera, San Francisco Opera, and Chicago Lyric, 1959; Metropolitan, New York, and La Scala, Milan, 1960; Buenos Aires, 1962; Salzburg Festival, 1966; appears in other opera houses of Argentina, Austria, Brazil, France, Germany, Greece, Mexico and USA. *Films:* Carmen; Pagliacci; Otello; Norma; Peter Grimes; Fidelio. Has made many recordings. Presbyterian. Hon. Dr: University of Saskatchewan, 1963; Bishop's Univ., 1965; Univ. West Ontario, 1970; Brandon Univ., 1976; Laval Univ., 1977; Univ. of Guelph, 1978; Illinois, 1983; Queens, 1984. RAM 1977. Canada Centennial Medal, 1967; Critics' Award, London, 1978; Grammy Award, 1979. *Address:* c/o John Coast, 1 Park Close, SW1.

VICKERS, Prof. Michael Douglas Allen; Professor of Anaesthetics, University of Wales College of Medicine (formerly Welsh National School of Medicine), since 1976; *b* 11 May 1929; *s* of George and Freda Vickers; *m* 1959, Ann Hazel Courtney; two *s* one *d*. *Educ:* Abingdon Sch.; Guy's Hosp. Med. Sch. MB, BS; FFARCS; FRSM. Lectr, RPMS, 1965–68; Consultant Anaesthetist, Birmingham AHA, 1968–76. Mem. Bd, Faculty of Anaesthetists, 1971–85; Sec., European Acad. of Anaesthesiology, 1982–84; Pres., Assoc. of Anaesthetists of GB and Ireland, 1982–84 (Hon. Sec., 1974–76; John Snow Lectr, 1982). Hon. FFARACS. Editor, European Journal of Anaesthesiology, 1983–. *Publications:* (jtly) Principles of Measurement for Anaesthetists, 1970 (2nd edn, as Principles of Measurement, 1981); (jtly) Drugs in Anaesthetic Practice, 6th edn 1984; Medicine for Anaesthetists, 1977, 3rd edn 1987. *Recreations:* music, theatre. *Address:* Department of Anaesthetics, University of Wales, College of Medicine, Heath Park, Cardiff CF4 4XN. *T:* Cardiff 755944.

VICKERS, Ven. Michael Edwin; Archdeacon of the East Riding, since 1981; *b* 13 Jan. 1929; *s* of William Edwin and Florence Alice Vickers; *m* 1960, Janet Cynthia Croasdale; three *d*. *Educ:* St Lawrence Coll., Ramsgate; Worcester Coll., Oxford (BA Mod. History, 1952, MA 1956); Cranmer Hall, Durham (DipTheol with distinction, 1959). Company Secretary, Hoares (Ceylon) Ltd, 1952–56; Refugee Administrator for British Council for Aid to Refugees, 1956–57; Lay Worker, Diocese of Oklahoma, 1959; Curate of Christ Church, Bexleyheath, 1959–62; Sen. Chaplain, Lee Abbey Community, 1962–67; Vicar of St John's, Newland, Hull, 1967–81; Area Dean, Central and North Hull, 1972–81. Chm., York Diocesan House of Clergy, 1975–85; Canon and Prebendary of York, 1981–. Mem., Gen. Synod, 1975– (Proctor in Convocation, 1975–85). *Recreations:* gardening, fell-walking, travel, drama. *Address:* Brimley Lodge, 27 Molescroft Road, Beverley, North Humberside HU17 7DX. *T:* Hull 881659.

VICKERS, Lt-Gen. Sir Richard (Maurice Hilton), KCB 1983; LVO 1959; OBE 1970 (MBE 1964); Director General Winston Churchill Memorial Trust, since 1983; a Gentleman Usher to the Queen, since 1986; *b* 21 Aug. 1928; *s* of Lt-Gen. W. G. H. Vickers, *qv*; *m* 1957, Gaie, *d* of Maj.-Gen. G. P. B. Roberts, *qv*; three *d*. *Educ:* Haileybury and Imperial Service Coll.; RMA. Commissioned Royal Tank Regt, 1948; 1st RTR, BAOR, Korea, Middle East, 1948–54; Equerry to HM The Queen, 1956–59; Brigade Major, 7 Armd Bde, 1962–64; 4th RTR, Borneo and Malaysia, 1964–66; CO The Royal Dragoons, 1967–68, The Blues and Royals, 1968–69; Comdr, 11th Armd Brigade, 1972–74; Dep. Dir of Army Training, 1975–77; GOC 4th Armoured Div., 1977–79; Comdt, RMA, 1979–82; Dir-Gen. of Army Training, 1982–83. *Recreations:* squash, flyfishing. *Address:* Little Minterne, Dorchester, Dorset DT2 7AP. *Club:* Cavalry and Guards.

VICKERS, Thomas Douglas, CMG 1956; *b* 25 Sept. 1916; 2nd *s* of late Ronald Vickers, Scaitcliffe, Englefield Green, Surrey; *m* 1951, Margaret Awdry, *o c* of late E. A. Headley, Wagga, NSW; one *s* one *d*. *Educ:* Eton; King's Coll., Cambridge (MA Hons). Cadet, Colonial Administrative Service, 1938. Served War of 1939–45: Coldstream Guards, 1940–45. Colonial Office, 1938–40 and 1945–50; Gold Coast, 1950–53; Colonial Secretary, British Honduras, 1953–60; Chief Secretary, Mauritius, 1960–67, Dep. Governor, 1967–68; retired from HMOCS, Oct. 1968. Head of Personnel Services, Imperial Cancer Research Fund, 1969–81. *Address:* Wood End, Worplesdon, Surrey GU3 3RJ. *T:* Worplesdon 233468. *Club:* Army and Navy.

VICKERS, Dr Tony; UK Administrator, Ludwig Institute for Cancer Research, since 1985; *b* 6 July 1932; *s* of Harry and Frances Vickers; *m* 1964, Anne Dorothy Wallis (marr. diss. 1986); two *d*. *Educ:* Manchester Grammar Sch.; Sidney Sussex Coll., Cambridge (MA, PhD). University of Cambridge: Demonstrator, 1956; Lectr in Physiology, 1961–72; Fellow, Sidney Sussex Coll., 1956–70; Headquarters Office, MRC, 1972–84 (Head of Medical Div., 1980–84). Member of Council: BAAS, 1969–72, 1982–85 (Pres., Biomed. Scis Sect., 1977); Cancer Res. Campaign, 1980–85 (Mem., Scientific Cttee, 1979–85); Paterson Labs, Manchester, 1984–85. Governor, Beatson Inst., Glasgow, 1983–85. *Address:* 42 Bengeo Street, Hertford, Herts SG14 3ET. *T:* Hertford 56758.

VICKERS, Lt-Gen. Wilmot Gordon Hilton, CB 1942; OBE 1919; DL; *b* 8 June 1890; *s* of late Lt-Col Hilton Vickers, IA; *m* Mary Catherine (*decd*), *d* of Dr A. E. Nuttall; two *s*. *Educ:* United Services Coll., Westward Ho!, and Windsor (now Haileybury and Imperial Service Coll.). Commissioned Indian Army (Unattached List), 1910; 2nd Lieut, Indian Army, 1911; Captain, 1915; Major, 1926; Bt Lt-Col, 1931; Col, 1935; Maj.-Gen., 1940; Lt-Gen., 1943; Comdt and Chief Instructor, Equitation Sch., India, 1934–35; Dep. Dir of Staff Duties, India, 1935–37; Brigade Comdr, India, 1939–40; Dir of Supplies and Transport, India, 1940–41; Maj.-Gen. i/c Administration, Iraq-Persia, 1941–42; Quartermaster-General, India, 1942–44; retired, 1944. DL County of Gloucestershire, 1946. County Cadet Commandant, Gloucestershire, Army Cadet Force, 1946–55. County Chief Warden, Civil Defence, Gloucestershire, 1949–60. *Address:* 4 Oakhurst Court, Parabola Road, Cheltenham, Glos. *Clubs:* Cavalry and Guards; New (Cheltenham).

See also Sir R. M. H. Vickers.

VICKERY, Prof. Brian Campbell, FLA, FIInfSc; Professor of Library Studies and Director, School of Library Archive and Information Studies, University College London, 1973–83, now Professor Emeritus; *b* 11 Sept. 1918; *s* of Adam Cairns McCay and Violet Mary Watson; *m* 1st, 1945, Manuletta McMenamin; one *s* one *d*; 2nd, 1970, Alina Gralewska. *Educ:* King's Sch., Canterbury; Brasenose Coll., Oxford. MA. Chemist, Royal Ordnance Factory, Somerset, 1941–45; Librarian, ICI Ltd, Welwyn, 1946–60; Principal Scientific Officer, Nat. Lending Library for Sci. and Technology, 1960–64; Librarian, UMIST, 1964–66; Head of R&D, Aslib, 1966–73. *Publications:* Classification and Indexing in Science, 1958, 3rd edn 1975; On Retrieval System Theory, 1961, 2nd edn 1965; Techniques of Information Retrieval, 1970; Information Systems, 1973; articles in professional jls. *Recreations:* reading history, poetry, philosophy; music and theatre; personal computing. *Address:* 138 Midhurst Road, W13 9TP. *T:* 01–567 6544.

VICKERY, Sir Philip Crawford, Kt 1948; CIE 1939; OBE 1923; *b* 23 Feb. 1890; *s* of late John Evans Vickery and Alice Maud Mary Vickery; *m* 1920, Phyllis Field Fairweather (*d* 1982); one *s* (*yr s*, Coldstream Guards, died of wounds in Italy, April 1945). *Educ:* Portora Royal Sch., Enniskillen; Dean Close Sch., Cheltenham; Trinity Coll., Dublin. Joined Indian Police, 1909; Coronation Durbar, Delhi, 1911; served European War, 1915–21 and War of 1939–45; Lieut-Colonel, Sept. 1939, and Acting Colonel, 1942. Commonwealth Relations Office, 1952–65. *Club:* East India and Sports.

VICTOR, Ed; Chairman and Managing Director, Ed Victor Ltd, since 1977; *b* 9 Sept. 1939; *s* of Jack Victor and Lydia Victor; *m* 1st, 1963, Michelene Dinah Samuels (marr. diss.); two *s*; 2nd, 1980, Carol Lois Ryan; one *s*. *Educ:* Dartmouth Coll. USA (BA *summa cum laude* 1961); Pembroke Coll., Cambridge (MLitt 1963). Began as art books editor, later editorial Dir, Weidenfeld & Nicolson, 1964–67; editorial Dir, Jonathan Cape Ltd, 1967–71; Senior Editor, Alfred A. Knopf Inc., NY, 1972–73; literary agent and Dir, John Farquharson Ltd (lit. agents), 1974–76; founded Ed Victor Ltd (lit. agency), 1977. *Recreations:* running, tennis, travel, opera. *Address:* 4 Cambridge Gate, Regent's Park, NW1. *T:* 01–935 3096. *Club:* Groucho.

VICUÑA, Francisco O.; *see* Orrego-Vicuña.

VIDAL, Gore; author; *b* 3 Oct. 1925; *s* of Eugene and Nina Gore Vidal. *Educ:* Phillips Exeter Academy, New Hampshire, USA (grad. 1943). Army of the US, 1943–46: Private to Warrant Officer (jg) and First Mate, Army FS-35, Pacific Theatre Ops. Democratic-Liberal candidate for US Congress, 1960; candidate for Democratic nomination for election to US Senate from California, 1982. Apptd to President Kennedy's Adv. Council of the Arts, 1961–63. *Publications: novels:* Williwaw, 1946; In a Yellow Wood, 1947; The City and the Pillar, 1948; The Season of Comfort, 1949; A Search for the King, 1950; Dark Green, Bright Red, 1950; The Judgment of Paris, 1952; Messiah, 1954; Julian, 1964; Washington, DC, 1967; Myra Breckinridge, 1968 (filmed 1969); Two Sisters, 1970; Burr, 1973; Myron, 1975; 1876, 1976; Kalki, 1978; Creation, 1981; Duluth, 1983; Lincoln, 1984; *essays:* Rocking the Boat, 1962; Reflections upon a Sinking Ship, 1969; Homage to Daniel Shays (collected essays 1952–72), 1972; Matters of Fact and of Fiction, 1977; The Second American Revolution (UK title, Pink Triangle and Yellow Star and other essays (1976–1982)), 1982; *short stories:* A Thirsty Evil, 1956; *plays:* Visit to a Small Planet (NY prod.), 1957; The Best Man (NY prod.), 1960; Romulus (adapted from F. Dürrenmatt) (NY prod.), 1962; Weekend (NY prod.), 1968; On the March to the Sea (German prod.), 1962; An Evening with Richard Nixon (NY prod.), 1972; *screenplays,* from 1955: Wedding Breakfast, 1957; Suddenly Last Summer, 1958; The Best Man, 1964, etc; *television plays:* 1954–56: The Death of Billy the Kid (translated to screen as The Lefthanded Gun, 1959), etc; *literary and political criticism for:* NY Review of Books, Esquire, Partisan Review, TLS, etc. *Recreations:* as noted above. *Address:* La Rondinaia, Ravello, (Salerno), Italy. *Club:* Athenæum.

VIDIC, Dobrivoje, Order of Yugoslav Flag 1st class; Order of Service to the People; Order of Brotherhood and Unity 1st class; Order for Bravery; Partisan Remembrance Medal 1941; Member of Presidium, Central Committee of League of Communists of Yugoslavia, since 1982; *b* 24 Dec. 1918; *m* 1941, Mrs Vukica; one *s*. *Educ:* Skoplje University. Diplomatic Service, 1951–86: served as: Minister Counsellor, London; Ambassador to Burma; Ambassador to USSR; Under-Sec. of State for Foreign Affairs; Perm. Rep. to UN, New York; Chm., Commn for Internat. Relations of Socialist Alliance of Yugoslavia; Ambassador to USSR; Ambassador of Yugoslavia to the Court of St James's, 1970–73. Mem. Exec. Cttee of Presidium, Central Cttee of League of Communists of Yugoslavia, 1974–79; Pres. of Presidium, Socialist Republic of Serbia, 1978–82; Chm., Commn for Internat. Relations, League of Communists of Yugoslavia, 1986–. *Address:* Central Committee of League of Communists of Yugoslavia, Bulaver Lengina 6, Belgrade, Yugoslavia.

VIDLER, Rev. Alexander Roper, LittD; Dean of King's College, Cambridge, 1956–66; Fellow of King's College, 1956–67, Hon. Fellow since 1972; *b* 1899; *s* of late Leopold Amon Vidler, JP, Rye, Sussex; unmarried. *Educ:* Sutton Valence Sch.; Selwyn Coll., Cambridge. BA 2nd Class Theol. Tripos, 1921; MA 1925; Norrisian Prize, 1933; BD 1938; LittD 1957; University of Edinburgh, DD, 1946; Hon. DD: University of Toronto, 1961; College of Emmanuel and St Chad, Saskatoon, 1966. Wells Theological Coll.; Deacon, 1922; Priest, 1923; Curate of St Philip's, Newcastle upon Tyne, 1922–24; of St Aidan's, Birmingham, 1925–31; on staff of the Oratory House, Cambridge, 1931–38; Warden of St Deiniol's Library, Hawarden, 1939–48; Hon. Canon of Derby Cathedral,

1946–48; Canon of St George's Chapel, Windsor, 1948–56; licensed by Cambridge Univ. to preach throughout England, 1957; University Lecturer in Divinity, 1959–67; Commissary for Bishop of New Guinea, 1936–62; Hale Lecturer (USA), 1947; Birkbeck Lecturer (Trinity Coll., Cambridge), 1953; Firth Lecturer (Nottingham Univ.), 1955; Robertson Lecturer (Glasgow Univ.), 1964; Sarum Lecturer (Oxford Univ.), 1968–69. Sec., Christian Frontier Council, 1949–56. Mayor of Rye, 1972–74. Acting Principal, Chichester Theological Coll., 1981. Editor, Theology, 1939–64; Co-editor of The Frontier, 1950–52. *Publications:* Magic and Religion, 1930; Sex, Marriage and Religion, 1932; The Modernist Movement in the Roman Church, 1934; A Plain Man's Guide to Christianity, 1936; God's Demand and Man's Response, 1938; God's Judgement on Europe, 1940; Secular Despair and Christian Faith, 1941; Christ's Strange Work, 1944; The Orb and the Cross, 1945; Good News for Mankind, 1947; The Theology of F. D. Maurice, 1949; Christian Belief, 1950; Prophecy and Papacy, 1954; Christian Belief and This World, 1956; Essays in Liberality, 1957; Windsor Sermons, 1958; The Church in an Age of Revolution, 1961; A Century of Social Catholicism, 1964; 20th Century Defenders of the Faith, 1965; F. D. Maurice and Company, 1966; A Variety of Catholic Modernists, 1970; Scenes from a Clerical Life, 1977; Read, Mark, Learn, 1980; (jointly): The Development of Modern Catholicism, 1933; The Gospel of God and the Authority of the Church, 1937; Natural Law, 1946; Editor, Soundings: Essays concerning Christian Understanding, 1962; Objections to Christian Belief, 1963; (with Malcolm Muggeridge) Paul: envoy extraordinary, 1972. *Recreations:* gardening, golf, beekeeping. *Address:* Friars of the Sack, Rye, East Sussex TN31 7HE.

VIELER, Geoffrey Herbert, FCA; Member of Board, Post Office Corporation, 1969–71; *b* 21 Aug. 1910; *s* of late Herbert Charles Stuart Vieler, Huddersfield, and Emily Mary; *m* 1934, Phyllis Violet; one *d*. *Educ:* Fairway Sch., Bexhill-on-Sea. With Vale & West, Chartered Accountants, Reading, 1927–41 (qual. 1932); War Service, 1941–46: commnd RAOC, 1943, Major 1945; joined Binder Hamlyn, Chartered Accountants, 1946, Partner 1959–69; Managing Dir, Posts and National Giro, 1969–71. Mem. Techn. Adv. Cttee, Inst. of Chartered Accountants in England and Wales, 1967–74. Chm., London Chartered Accountants, 1976–77; Chm., Taxation Cttee, ABCC, 1985–. *Address:* Robins Wood, Monks Drive, South Ascot, Berks SL5 9BB; Riversmeet, Mill Lane, Lower Shiplake RG9 3LY.

VIERTEL, Deborah Kerr; *see* Kerr, D. J.

VIGARS, Robert Lewis; *b* 26 May 1923; *s* of late Francis Henry Vigars and Susan Laurina May Vigars (*née* Lewis); *m* 1962, Margaret Ann Christine, *y d* of late Sir John Walton, KCIE, CB, MC, and Lady Walton; two *d*. *Educ:* Truro Cathedral Sch.; London Univ. (LLB (Hons)). Served War of 1939–45: RA and Royal Corps of Signals, 1942–47; attached Indian Army (Captain), 1944–47; Captain, Princess Louise's Kensington Regt, TA, 1951–54. Qualified as solicitor (Hons), 1948. Partner, Simmons & Simmons, London, EC2, 1951–75. Member: Kensington Borough Council, 1953–59; London and Home Counties Traffic Adv. Cttee, 1956–58; London Roads (Nugent) Cttee, 1958–59; LCC and GLC Kensington (formerly South Kensington), 1955–86; Environmental Planning Cttee, GLC, 1967–71 (Chm.); Strategic Planning Cttee, GLC, 1971–73 (Chm.); Leader of Opposition, ILEA, 1974–79; Chm. of the GLC, 1979–80; Mem., Standing Conf. on London and SE Regional Planning and SE Economic Planning Council, 1968–75. Mem., Historic Buildings and Monuments Commn for England, 1986– (Chm., London Adv. Cttee). Mem. Court, London Univ., 1977–82. FRSA. *Publication:* Let Our Cities Live (Bow Gp, jointly). *Recreation:* mountain walking. *Address:* 24 Cope Place, Kensington, W8 6AA. *Club:* Hurlingham.

VIGGERS, Peter John; MP (C) Gosport, since Feb. 1974; Parliamentary Under-Secretary of State, Northern Ireland Office, since 1986; *b* 13 March 1938; *s* of late J. S. Viggers and of E. F. Viggers (later Mrs V. E. J. Neal), Gosport; *m* 1968, Jennifer Mary McMillan, MB, BS, LRCP, MRCS, DA, *d* of late Dr R. B. McMillan, MD, FRCP, Guildford, and late Mrs J. T. C. McMillan, MA, MIB; two *s* one *d*. *Educ:* Portsmouth Grammar Sch.; Trinity Hall, Cambridge (MA). Solicitor 1967. Trained as RAF Pilot with Royal Canadian Air Force, awarded Wings 1958. Cambridge, 1958–61; Chm. Cambridge Univ. Conservative Assoc., 1960. Commnd in 457 (Wessex) Regt Royal Artillery (TA), 1963. PPS to Solicitor-General, 1979–83, to Chief Sec. of HM Treasury, 1983–85. Select Cttee on Armed Forces Bill, 1986. Deleg. to North Atlantic Assembly, 1981–; Vice-Chm., Cons. Energy Cttee, 1977–79 (a Sec., 1975–76). Dir, Premier Consolidated Oilfields Ltd, 1973–, and others cos. Underwriting Member of Lloyd's. Chairman: Campaign for Defence and Multilateral Disarmament, 1984–; Cttee for Peace with Freedom, 1984–; UK Deleg., Jt IPU and UN Conf. on Conventional Disarmament, Mexico City, 1985. Mem., Management Cttee, RNLI, 1979–. *Recreations:* walking, reading, country pursuits. *Address:* House of Commons, SW1.

VIGNOLES, Roger Hutton, ARCM; pianoforte accompanist; *b* 12 July 1945; *s* of Keith Hutton Vignoles and Phyllis Mary (*née* Pearson); *m* 1st, 1972, Teresa Ann Elizabeth Henderson (marr. diss. 1982); 2nd, 1982, Jessica Virginia, *d* of Prof. Boris Ford, *qv*. *Educ:* Canterbury Cathedral Choir Sch.; Sedbergh Sch.; Magdalene Coll., Cambridge (BA, BMus); Royal College of Music, London (ARCM). Accompanist of national and internat. reputation, regularly appearing with the most distinguished internat. singers and instrumentalists, both in London and provinces and at major music festivals (*eg* Aldeburgh, Cheltenham, Edinburgh, Brighton, Bath, Salzburg, etc) and broadcasting for BBC Radio 3 and television. International tours incl. USA, Canada, Australia-New Zealand, Hong Kong, Scandinavia, and recitals at Opera Houses of Cologne, 1982, Brussels, 1983, Frankfurt, 1984, Lincoln Center, NY, 1985, Tokyo, 1985. Repetiteur: Royal Opera House, Covent Garden, 1969–71; English Opera Group, 1968–74; Australian Opera Company, 1976. Professor of Accompaniment, RCM, 1974–81. Gramophone records include English songs and works by Schumann, Brahms, Dvorak, Britten, Gershwin, Dankworth, Franck, Grieg, and Parry and the première recording of Nicholas Maw's The Voice of Love. Hon. RAM 1984. *Recreations:* drawing, painting, looking at pictures, swimming, sailing. *Address:* 30 Leverton Street, Kentish Town, NW5 2PJ. *T:* 01–267 3187.

VILE, Prof. Maurice John Crawley; Professor of Political Science, 1968–84, now Emeritus, and Director of International Programmes, University of Kent at Canterbury; *b* 23 July 1927; *s* of Edward M. and Elsie M. Vile; two *s*. *Educ:* London Sch. of Economics. BSc (Econ) 1951; PhD London, 1954; MA Oxford, 1962. Lectr in Politics, Univ. of Exeter, 1954–62; Fellow of Nuffield Coll., Oxford, 1962–65; University of Kent: Reader in Politics and Govt, 1965–68; Dean of Faculty of Social Scis, 1969–75; Pro-Vice-Chancellor, 1975–81; Dep. Vice-Chancellor, 1981–84. Visiting Professor: Univ. of Massachusetts, 1960; Smith College, Mass., 1961. Royer Lectr, Univ. of Calif., Berkeley, 1974. *Publications:* The Structure of American Federalism, 1961; Constitutionalism and the Separation of Powers, 1967; Politics in the USA, 1970, 3rd edn, 1983; Federalism in the United States, Canada and Australia (Res. Paper No 2, Commn on the Constitution), 1973; The Presidency (Amer. Hist. Documents Vol. IV), 1974. *Address:* The Registry, The University, Canterbury, Kent. *T:* Canterbury 66822.

VILJOEN, Marais, DMS 1976; State President of the Republic of South Africa, 1979–84; *b* 2 Dec. 1915; *s* of Gabriel François Viljoen and Magdalena Debora (*née* de Villiers); *m* 1940, Dorothea Maria Brink; one *d*. *Educ:* Jan van Riebeeck High Sch., Cape Town; Univ. of Cape Town. After leaving school, employed in Dept of Posts and Telegraphs, 1932–37; on editorial staff, Die Transvaler newspaper, 1937–40; manager, Transvaler book trade business, Potchefstroom, 1940; co-founder and provincial leader of Nat. Youth League, 1940–45; organiser of Transvaal National Party, 1945–49; Member, Provincial Council, Transvaal, 1949–53; Information Officer, Transvaal National Party, several years from 1951; Chairman, Inf. Service of Federal Council, National Party of S Africa, 1969–74; Dep. Chm., Nat. Party, Transvaal, 1966–75. MP Alberton, 1953–76; Dep. Minister of Labour and of Mines, 1958–61; various other ministerial offices, incl. Interior and Immigration, until 1966; Cabinet appointments, 1966–: Minister of Labour and of Coloured Affairs, 1966–69, also of Rehoboth Affairs, 1969–70; Minister of Labour and of Posts and Telecommunications, 1970–76. President of the Senate, 1976–79. Special Cl., Grand Collar, Order of Good Hope, Republic of S Africa, 1981. *Recreations:* golf, bowls, reading. *Address:* PO Box 5555, Pretoria, 0001, Republic of South Africa. *Clubs:* (Hon. Member) various South African, including: Pretoria, City and Civil Service, Cape Town.

VILLIERS; *see* Child-Villiers, family name of Earl of Jersey.

VILLIERS; *see* de Villiers.

VILLIERS, family name of **Earl of Clarendon.**

VILLIERS, Viscount; George Henry Child Villiers; *b* 29 Aug. 1948; *s* and *heir* of 9th Earl of Jersey, *qv*; *m* 1st, 1969, Verna (marr. diss. 1973), 2nd *d* of K. A. Stott, St Mary, Jersey; one *d*; 2nd, 1974, Sandra, step *d* of H. Briginshaw, Feremina, St Martin, Guernsey; one *s* two *d*. *Educ:* Eton; Millfield. Late The Royal Hussars (PWO). Managing Dir, Villiers Trading Ltd. *Heir:* *s* Hon. George Francis William Child Villiers, *b* 5 Feb. 1976. *Address:* Bel Respiro, Mont au Prêtre, St Helier, Jersey, CI.

VILLIERS, Sir Charles (Hyde), Kt 1975; MC 1945; Chairman: BSC (Industry), since 1977 (Chairman, British Steel Corporation, 1976–80); Small Business Research Trust; 13th International Small Business Congress; Theatre Royal, Windsor; *b* 14 Aug. 1912; *s* of Algernon Hyde Villiers (killed in action, 1917) and Beatrix Paul (later Lady Aldenham) (*d* 1978); *m* 1st, 1938, Pamela Constance Flower (*d* 1943); one *s*; 2nd, 1946, Marie José, *d* of Count Henri de la Barre d'Erquelinnes, Jurbise, Belgium; two *d*. *Educ:* Eton; New Coll., Oxford. Asst to Rev. P. B. Clayton, of Toc H, 1931; Glyn Mills, Bankers, 1932. Grenadier Guards (SRO), 1936; served at Dunkirk, 1940 (wounded, 1942); Special Ops Exec., London and Italy, 1943–45; parachuted into Yugoslavia and Austria, 1944; Lt-Col and Comd 6 Special Force Staff Section, 1945 (MC). A Man. Dir, Helbert Wagg, 1948, and J. Henry Schroder Wagg, 1960–68; Managing Director, Industrial Reorganisation Corporation, 1968–71; Chm., Guinness Mahon & Co. Ltd, 1971–76; Exec. Dep. Chm., Guinness Peat Gp, 1973–76. Director: Bass Charrington; Courtaulds; Sun Life Assurance; Banque Belge; Financor SA; Darling & Co. (Pty); Formerly Chm., Ashdown Trans-Europe and Trans-Australian Investment Trusts. Chairman: Federal Trust Gp on European Monetary Integration, 1972; Northern Ireland Finance Corp., 1972–73. Co-Chm., Europalia Festival, 1973. Member: Inst. Internat. d'Etudes Bancaires, 1959–76 (Pres. 1964); Minister of Labour's Resettlement Cttee for London and SE, 1958 (Chm. 1961–68); Review Body for N Ireland Economic Develt, 1971; NEDC, 1976–80. Lubbock Meml Lectr, Oxford, 1971. Mem., Chelsea Borough Council, 1950–53. Order of the People, Yugoslavia, 1970; Grand Officier de l'Ordre de Léopold II (Belgium), 1974; Gold Medal of IRI, Italy, 1975. *Publication:* Start again, Britain, 1984. *Recreation:* gardening. *Address:* 65 Eaton Square, SW1. *T:* 01–235 7634; Blacknest House, Sunninghill, Berks. *T:* Ascot 22137.

VILLIERS, Charles Nigel, FCA; Director, National Westminster Bank PLC, since 1985; Chairman, County Group Ltd, since 1986; Chief Executive, NatWest Investment Bank Ltd, since 1986; *b* 25 Jan. 1941; *s* of Robert Alexander and Elizabeth Mary Villiers; *m* 1970, Sally Priscilla Magnay; one *s* one *d*. *Educ:* Winchester Coll.; New Coll., Oxford (BA German and Russian). Arthur Andersen & Co., 1963–67; ICFC, 1967–72; County Bank Ltd, 1972–86; Dir, 1974; Dep. Chief Exec., 1977; Chm. and Chief Exec., 1984; Exec. Chm., 1985; Exec. Dir, National Westminster Bank, 1985; Chief Exec., NatWest Investment Bank Ltd (estab. June 1986 incorporating the business of County Bank Ltd), 1986. *Recreations:* opera, squash, skiing, tennis. *Address:* 8 Sutherland Street, SW1. *T:* 01–834 7351. *Clubs:* Hurlingham, Overseas Bankers', Institute of Directors.

VILLIERS, Vice-Adm. Sir (John) Michael, KCB 1962 (CB 1960); OBE 1943; *b* 22 June 1907; 3rd *s* of late Rear-Adm. E. C. Villiers, CMG and of Mrs Villiers; *m* 1936, Rosemary, CStJ, 2nd *d* of late Lt-Col B. S. Grissell, DSO, and late Lady Astley-Cubitt; two *d*. *Educ:* Oundle School; Royal Navy. Served War of 1939–45 (despatches, OBE). Comd HMS Ursa, 1945, and HMS Snipe, 1946–47; directing staff of Joint Services Staff College, 1948–49; Assistant Director of Plans Admiralty, 1950–51; Queen's Harbour Master, Malta, 1952–54; comd HMS Bulwark, 1954–57; Chief of Naval Staff, New Zealand, 1958–60; a Lord Commissioner of the Admiralty, Fourth Sea Lord and Vice-Controller, 1960–63; Lt-Governor and C-in-C Jersey, 1964–69. KStJ 1964. *Address:* Decoy House, Melton, Woodbridge, Suffolk IP13 6DH. *Club:* Army and Navy.

VINCENT, Anthony Lionel; Deputy High Commissioner for Australia in London, since 1984; *b* 18 Oct. 1933; *s* of Harold Francis Vincent and Lesley Allison Vincent; *m* 1958, Helen Frances Beasley; one *s* one *d*. *Educ:* Univ. of Western Australia, Perth (LLB); Univ. of Oxford (BCL). Joined Dept of Foreign Affairs, Aust., 1958; served: Karachi, 1959–61; Hong Kong, 1963–66; Singapore, 1966–69; Belgrade, 1972–74; Paris, 1977–80; Australian Ambassador to: Iraq, 1981–83; GDR, 1984. *Recreations:* walking, cycling, reading. *Address:* c/o Australian High Commission, The Strand, WC2B 4LA. *T:* 01–438 8213. *Club:* Canberra Yacht.

VINCENT, Maj.-Gen. Douglas, CB 1969; OBE 1954; Director, Standard Telephones & Cables Pty Ltd, since 1973; *b* Australia, 10 March 1916; *s* of William Frederick Vincent, civil engineer, and Sarah Jane Vincent; *m* 1947, Margaret Ector, *d* of N. W. Persse, Melbourne; two *s* one *d*. *Educ:* Brisbane State High School; Royal Military Coll., Duntroon. Commissioned, Dec. 1938; Middle East (7 Div.), 1940–42; BLA, 1944; NW Europe (30 Corps); Borneo Campaign, 1945; Brit. Commonwealth Forces, Korea, 1954; Dir of Signals, 1954–58; Dir of Staff Duties, 1958–60; Chief of Staff, Eastern Command, 1960–62; Commander, Aust. Army Force, 1962–63 (Singapore, Malaya); idc 1964; Commander: 1 Task Force, 1965; 1st Div., 1966; Aust. Force, Vietnam, 1967–68; Head, Aust. Jt Services Staff, Washington, DC, USA, 1968–70; Adjutant General, Australian Army, 1970–73. Mem. Nat. Exec., RSL (Defence Adviser, 1975–). SMIREE(Aust). *Recreations:* golf, swimming. *Address:* 41 Hampton Circuit, Yarralumla, Canberra, ACT 2600, Australia.

VINCENT, Prof. Ewart Albert; Professor of Geology, and Fellow of University College, Oxford, 1967–86, now Emeritus; *b* 23 Aug. 1919; *o s* of Albert and Winifred Vincent, Aylesbury; *m* 1944, Myrtle Ablett; two *d*. *Educ:* Reading Sch.; Univ. of Reading. BSc (Reading) 1940; PhD 1951; MA (Oxon) 1952; MSc (Manch.) 1966. FGS. Chemist, Min.

of Supply, 1940–45; Geologist, Anglo-Iranian Oil Co., 1945–46; Lectr in Mineralogy and Crystallography, Univ. of Durham, 1946–51; Lectr in Geology, Oxford Univ., 1951–56; Reader in Mineralogy, Oxford Univ., 1956–62; Prof. of Geology, Manchester Univ., 1962–66. Mem. NERC, 1975–78. Vice-Pres., Internat. Assoc. of Volcanology, 1968–71; Pres., Mineralogical Soc. of GB, 1974–76; Mem. Council, Geol Soc., 1973–76. Fellow, Mineralogical Soc. of Amer. Hon. Corresp. Mem., Soc. Géol. de Belgique. Awarded Wollaston Fund, Geol Soc. London, 1961. *Publications:* scientific papers in learned jls. *Recreations:* music, photography. *Address:* 2 Linch Farm, Wytham, Oxford. *T:* Oxford 723170; Department of Earth Sciences, Parks Road, Oxford. *T:* Oxford 54511.

VINCENT, Rev. Irvin James; Minister, Temple Methodist Church, Taunton, since 1986; *b* 22 July 1932; *s* of Amy Mary Catharine Vincent (*née* Nye) and Vince Thomas Vincent; *m* 1959, Stella Margaret (*née* Chaplin); one *s* two *d. Educ:* Mitcham Grammar School; Didsbury College (Methodist), Bristol. BA Open Univ. Accountancy, 1948; National Service, RAF, 1950–52; Local Govt, 1952–55; theological training, 1955–59; Methodist Circuit, Stonehouse and Dursley, 1959–61; entered RN as Chaplain, 1961; Malta, 1968–72; exchange with USN, 1976–78; Principal Chaplain, Church of Scotland and Free Churches (Navy), 1984–86; QHC, 1984–86. *Recreations:* soccer, cricket, drama, music, gardening. *Address:* Temple Methodist Church, Upper High Street, Taunton, Somerset. *T:* Taunton 88662.

VINCENT, Ivor Francis Sutherland, CMG 1966; MBE 1945; HM Diplomatic Service, retired; Hon. Secretary, The Andean Project, since 1983; *b* 14 Oct. 1916; *s* of late Lt-Col Frank Lloyd Vincent and Gladys Clarke; *m* 1949, Patricia Mayne; three *d* (and one *d* decd). *Educ:* St Peter's Coll., Radley; Christ Church, Oxford. Served Indian Army, Royal Garhwal Rifles, 1941–46. Entered HM Foreign Service, 1946; Second Secretary, Foreign Office, 1946–48; First Sec., Buenos Aires, 1948–51; UK Delegn, NATO, Paris, 1951–53; FO, 1954–57; Rabat, 1957–59; Geneva (Disarmt Delegn), 1960; Paris (UK Delegn to OECD), 1960–62; Counsellor, FO, 1962–66; Baghdad, Jan.–June, 1967; Caracas, Oct. 1967–70; Ambassador to Nicaragua, 1970–73; Consul-Gen., Melbourne, 1973–76, retired. Dir, Fairbridge Soc. (Inc.), 1978–83. *Recreations:* music, walking. *Address:* 101 Barkston Gardens, SW5. *T:* 01–373 5273. *Club:* Lansdowne.

VINCENT, Prof. John Joseph, MSc, MSc Tech., CText, FTI; Professor of Textile Technology, University of Manchester Institute of Science and Technology, 1957–74, now Emeritus; *b* 29 June 1907; 2nd *s* of J. H. Vincent, MA, DSc; *m* 1935, M. Monica Watson, MSc, PhD, of Sheffield; one *s* one *d. Educ:* County Grammar Sch., Harrow; University Coll., London. Mathematics Dept, University Coll., London, 1927–29; Shirley Inst., Manchester, 1929–42 and 1945–57. Ministry of Aircraft Production, 1942–45. Hon. Life Mem., Textile Institute, 1976 (Mem. Council, 1959–74; Vice-Pres., 1971–74); Pres., British Assoc. of Managers of Textile Works, 1963–64; Mem., Cotton and Allied Textiles Industry Training Bd, 1966–74. Textile Inst. Medal, 1968; Leverhulme Emeritus Fellowship, 1976. *Publications:* Shuttleless Looms, 1980; papers on textile technology. *Recreations:* gardening, reading, listening to music. *Address:* The White House, Perranarworthal, Truro, Cornwall TR3 7QE. *T:* Truro 863504.

See also J. R. Vincent.

VINCENT, Prof. John Russell; Professor of Modern History, University of Bristol, since 1970; *b* 20 Dec. 1937; *s* of Prof. J. J. Vincent, *qv*; *m* 1972, Nicolette Elizabeth Kenworthy; one *s* (and one *s* decd). *Educ:* Bedales Sch.; Christ's Coll., Cambridge. Lectr in Modern British History, Cambridge Univ., 1967–70. Chm., Bristol Br., NCCL, 1972–74. *Publications:* The Formation of the Liberal Party, 1966 (2nd edn as The Formation of the British Liberal Party 1857–68, 1980); Poll Books: How Victorians voted, 1967; (ed with A. B. Cooke) Lord Carlingford's Journal, 1971; (ed with M. Stenton) McCalmont's Parliamentary Poll Book 1832–1918, 1971; (with A. B. Cooke) The Governing Passion: Cabinet Government and party politics in Britain 1885–86, 1974; (ed) Disraeli, Derby and the Conservative Party: the political journals of Lord Stanley 1849–69, 1978; Gladstone and Ireland (Raleigh Lecture), 1979; (ed) The Crawford Papers: the journals of David Lindsay, Twenty-Seventh Earl of Crawford and Tenth Earl of Balcarres during the years 1892 to 1940, 1984. *Recreation:* journalism. *Address:* History Department, The University, Bristol BS8 1TB.

VINCENT, Leonard Grange, CBE 1960; FRIBA, FRTPI, Distinction Town Planning (RIBA); formerly architect and town planner, and Principal Partner, Vincent and Gorbing, Architects and Planning Consultants; *b* 13 April 1916; *s* of late Godfrey Grange Vincent; *m* 1942, Evelyn (*née* Gretton); twin *s* one *d. Educ:* Forest House School. Trained as architect in London, 1933, and subsequently as a town planner; experience in private practice and local government. Served War of 1939–45: Royal Engineers (Major); mostly overseas, in Western Desert, and Italian campaigns with 8th Army, 1940–45. Formerly Chief Architect and Planner, Stevenage Development Corporation. *Publications:* various technical and planning articles in technical press. *Recreations:* archaeology, painting. *Address:* Medbury, Rectory Lane, Stevenage, Hertfordshire. *T:* Stevenage 351175.

VINCENT, Gen. Sir Richard (Frederick), KCB 1984; DSO 1972; Master-General of the Ordnance, since 1983; *b* 23 Aug. 1931; *s* of Frederick Vincent and late Frances Elizabeth (*née* Coleshill); *m* 1955, Jean Paterson, *d* of Kenneth Stewart and Jane (*née* Banks); one *s* one *d* (and one *s* decd). *Educ:* Aldenham Sch. Commnd RA, National Service, 1951; Germany, 1951–55; Gunnery Staff, 1959; Technical Staff, 1964; Staff Coll., 1965; Commonwealth Bde, Malaysia, 1966–68; MoD, 1968–70; Comd 12th Light Air Def. Regt, Germany, UK and NI, 1970–72; Instr, Staff Coll., 1972–73; Mil. Dir of Studies, RMCS, 1974–75; Comd 19 Airportable Bde, 1975–77; RCDS, 1978; Dep. Mil. Sec., 1979–80; Comdt, Royal Military College of Science, 1980–83. Col Commandant: REME, 1981–; RA, 1983–; Hon. Col, 100 (Yeomanry) Field Regt RA, TA, 1982–. President: Combined Services Winter Sports Assoc., 1983–; Army Ski-ing Assoc., 1983–. Mem. Court, Cranfield Inst. of Technol., 1981–83. Hon. DSc Cranfield, 1985. *Publications:* contrib. mil. jls and pubns. *Recreations:* travel, reading, film making, pottering around the family cottage. *Address:* c/o Midland Bank, Shaftesbury, Dorset SP7 8JX. *Club:* Army and Navy.

VINCENT, Sir William (Percy Maxwell), 3rd Bt, *cr* 1936; Head of Investment Division, Touche, Remnant & Co.; *b* 1 February 1945; *o s* of Sir Lacey Vincent, 2nd Bt, and of Helen Millicent, *d* of Field Marshal Sir William Robert Robertson, 1st Bt, GCB, GCMG, GCVO, DSO; *S* father, 1963; *m* 1976, Christine Margaret, *d* of Rev. E. G. Walton; three *s. Educ:* Eton College. 2nd Lieutenant, Irish Guards, 1964–67. *Recreations:* water ski-ing, sailing. *Heir: s* Edward Mark William Vincent, *b* 6 March 1978. *Address:* Whistlers, Buriton, Petersfield, Hampshire. *T:* Petersfield 63532.

VINCENT BROWN, Kenneth; *see* Brown.

VINCENT-JONES, Captain Desmond, DSC; Royal Navy; retired 1964; *b* 13 Feb. 1912; *s* of late Sir Vincent Jones, KBE; *m* 1944, Jacqueline, *e d* of Col Sloggett, DSO; two *d. Educ:* Beacon School, Crowborough; Royal Naval College, Dartmouth. Served in Royal Navy, 1929–64; War of 1939–45, in aircraft carrier operations in Atlantic and Mediterranean (DSC and Bar); Served in Air Staff appointments and in Command of HM Ships, 1946–64. Graduate of US Armed Forces and British Services Staff Colleges. Naval and Military Attaché to Buenos Aires and Montevideo, 1958–60. On retirement from RN joined Marine Consortiums as consultant. *Recreations:* golf, tennis, fishing, cruising. *Address:* 8 High Street, Chobham, Surrey. *T:* Chobham 7274. *Clubs:* Free Foresters; Sunningdale Golf.

VINCZE, Paul, FRBS, FRNS; *b* Hungary, 15 August 1907; *s* of Lajos Vincze; British subject, 1948; *m* 1958, Emilienne Chauzeix. *Educ:* High School of Arts and Crafts, Budapest, later under E. Telcs. Won a travelling scholarship to Rome, 1935–37; came to England, 1938. *Exhibited:* Royal Academy, Rome, Budapest, Paris, etc; *works represented in:* British Museum, London; Museum of Fine Arts, Budapest; Ashmolean Museum, Oxford; Swedish Historical Museum; Danish Nat. Museum; Museum of Amer. Numismatic Soc.; Smithsonian Instn, Washington; Cabinet des Medailles, Paris, etc. *Works include:* Aga Khan Platinum Jubilee Portrait; Sir Bernard Pares Memorial Tablet, Senate House, London Univ.; President Truman, portrait medallion; Pope Paul VI, portrait medallion; official medal to commemorate 400th Anniversary of birth of William Shakespeare; medal to commemorate Independence of Ghana; official seal of Ghana Govt; (designed) Smithsonian Instn Award Medal (1965); Nat. Commemorative Society (USA) Winston Churchill Medal; Florence Nightingale Medal for Société Commemorative de Femmes Célèbres; E. and J. De Rothschild Medal for inauguration of Knesset, 1966; Yehudi Menuhin 50th Birthday Medal, 1966; Prince Karim Aga Khan 10th Anniversary Medal, 1968; Cassandra Memorial Tablet for Internat. Publishing Corp. Bldg, 1968; Shakespeare-Garrick Medal, 1969; Medal to commemorate 100th Anniversary of birth of Sir Henry J. Wood, 1969; Dickens 100th Anniversary Medal for Dickens Fellowship, 1970; Medal to commemorate J. B. Priestley's 80th birthday, 1974; Internat. Shakespeare Assoc. Congress Medal, USA, 1976; Self-portrait Medal to commemorate 70th birthday, 1978; Wall Panel illustrating all Shakespeare's plays for new Shakespeare Centre, Stratford-upon-Avon, 1981; Archie F. Carr award medal for Conservation for Florida State Museum, USA; (designed) Amer. Numismatic Assoc. 90th Anniversary Medal, 1981; Karim Aga Khan Silver Jubilee Medal, 1983; portrait-tablets: Harry Guy Bartholomew, Cecil H. King, Lord Cudlipp, for the Mirror's headquarters, 1985. *Coin designs:* obverse and reverses, Libya, 1951; obverses, Guatemala, 1954; reverses, threepence, sixpence and shilling, Cen. African Fedn, 1955; obverses, Ghana, 1958; reverses, Guernsey, 1957; threepence and florin, Nigeria, 1960; Guinea, obverse and reverses, Malawi, 1964; reverse, Uganda crown, 1968; Bustamante Portrait for obverse of Jamaican Dollar, 1969; reverses for decimal coins, Guernsey, 1970, etc. Awarded Premio Especial, Internat. Exhib., Madrid, 1951; Silver Medal, Paris Salon, 1964; first gold Medal of Amer. Numismatic Assoc., 1966. *Address:* 8A Yeomans Row, Brompton Road, Knightsbridge, SW3. *T:* 01–589 6037; Villa La Méridienne, Domaine Bastide, avenue La Bastide, 06520 Magagnosc, France. *T:* 36.47.54.

VINE, Prof. Frederick John, FRS 1974; Professor of Environmental Sciences, University of East Anglia, since 1974; *b* 17 June 1939; *s* of Frederick Royston Vine and Ivy Grace Vine (*née* Bryant); *m* 1964, Susan Alice McCall; one *s* one *d. Educ:* Latymer Upper Sch., Hammersmith; St John's Coll., Cambridge (BA, PhD). Instructor, 1965–67, and Asst Professor, 1967–70, Dept of Geological and Geophysical Sciences, Princeton Univ., NJ, USA; Reader, School of Environmental Sciences, Univ. of E Anglia, 1970–74. *Publications:* articles in Nature, Science, Phil. Trans Roy. Soc. London, etc. *Recreations:* walking, camping. *Address:* 144 Christchurch Road, Norwich NR2 3PG. *T:* Norwich 53875.

VINE, Philip Mesban, CBE 1981; DL; Chairman, New Towns Staff Commission, since 1977 (Member, since 1976); Member, New Towns Commission, since 1978; *b* 26 Oct. 1919; *s* of late Major George H. M. Vine and Elsie Mary (*née* Shephard), London; *m* 1944, Paulina, JP, *d* of late Arthur Oyler, Great Hormead Hall, Herts; one *s* one *d. Educ:* Sherborne Sch.; Taft Sch., USA; Sidney Sussex Coll., Cambridge (MA, LLM); Nottingham Univ. (MPhil 1981). Served in Royal Artillery, 1939–45; Adjutant 90th Field Regt, RA. Articled to W. H. Bentley, Town Clerk of Paddington; admitted Solicitor, 1948; Asst Solicitor, Paddington, 1948–50; Chief Asst Solicitor, Birkenhead, 1950–53; Deputy Town Clerk: Wallasey, 1953–59; Southend-on-Sea, 1959–62; Town Clerk, Cambridge, 1963–66; Town Clerk and Chief Exec. Officer, Nottingham, 1966–74. Chairman: Notts Local Valuation Panel, 1974–85; London Housing Staff Commn, 1979–86; Mem., Local Radio Council for BBC Radio Nottingham, 1970–76; Indep. Chm., Home Sec.'s Adv. Cttee, Wireless and Telegraphy Act 1949, 1975–; Member: Panel of Asst Comrs of Local Govt Boundary Commn, 1974–; Panel of Indep. Inspectors, DoE, 1974–; Bd Telford (New Town) Develt Corp., 1975–; Police Complaints Bd, 1977–80; Ind. Review of the Radio Spectrum (30–960 MHz), 1982–83. Gen. Comr of Income Tax, 1975–. Gov., Derbyshire Coll. of Higher Educn, 1985–; Mem. Court, Nottingham Univ., 1966–74. Liveryman, Clockmakers' Co. (Mem. Court, 1981; Senior Warden, 1987). DL Notts, 1974. *Publication:* The Neolithic and Bronze Age Cultures of the Middle and Upper Trent Basin (British Archaeological Reports, British Series 105), 1982. *Recreations:* fishing, archaeology, enjoyment of music. *Address:* 42 Magdala Road, Mapperley Park, Nottingham NG3 5DF. *T:* Nottingham 621269. *Clubs:* Army and Navy; United Services (Nottingham).

VINE, Col (Roland) Stephen, FRCPath, FZS; Chief Inspector, Cruelty to Animals Act (1876), Home Office, 1962–75; *b* 26 Dec. 1910; *s* of late Joseph Soutter Vine and of Josephine Vine (*née* Moylan); *m* 1935, Flora Betty, *d* of Charles Strutton Brookes, MBE, Dovercourt; three *d. Educ:* Southend-on-Sea High Sch.; Guy's Hosp. BSc; MRCS, LRCP, FRCPath, FZS(Scientific). Royal Army Medical Corps, 1934–60 (incl. War of 1939–45). Home Office, 1960–75. Member: Council, Res. Defence Soc., 1977–; Mem. Editorial Bd, Fund for Replacement of Animals in Med. Experiments, 1979–. *Publications:* chapter in: Biomedical Technology in Hospital Diagnosis, 1972; Animals in Scientific Research, 1983; articles in RAMC Jl. *Recreations:* gardening, swimming. *Address:* Shola, Fielden Road, Crowborough, Sussex TN6 1TR. *T:* Crowborough 61381. *Club:* Civil Service.

VINE, Roy; Vice-Chairman, Barclays Bank UK Ltd, 1982–84; Director, Barclays Bank PLC, 1979–84 (General Manager, 1972; Senior General Manager, 1979–81); *b* 1923; *m*; one *s* one *d. Educ:* Taunton's Sch., Southampton. Served RAF, 1942–46 and 1951–53 (Flt Lieut). Director: First National Finance Corp. PLC, 1984–; First National Securities Ltd, 1985–. *Recreations:* golf, football, music.

VINELOTT, Hon. Sir John (Evelyn), Kt 1978; **Hon. Mr Justice Vinelott;** Judge of the High Court of Justice, Chancery Division, since 1978; *b* 15 Oct. 1923; *s* of George Frederick Vine-Lott and Vera Lilian Vine-Lott (*née* Mockford); *m* 1956, Sally Elizabeth, *d* of His Honour Sir Walker Kelly Carter, QC; two *s* one *d. Educ:* Queen Elizabeth's Gram. Sch., Faversham, Kent; Queens' Coll., Cambridge (MA). War Service, Sub-Lieut RNVR, 1942–46. Called to Bar, Gray's Inn, 1953 (Atkin Scholar); QC 1968; Bencher, 1974; practised at the Chancery Bar. Chm., Insolvency Rules Adv. Cttee, 1984–. *Publications:* essays and articles on Revenue and Administration Law, in specialist periodicals. *Address:* 22 Portland Road, W11. *T:* 01–727 4778; Dolphin House, Orford, Suffolk. *T:* Orford 357.

VINEN, William Frank, FRS 1973; Poynting Professor of Physics, University of Birmingham, since 1974 (Professor of Physics, 1962–74); *b* 15 Feb. 1930; *o s* of Gilbert

Vinen and Olive Maud Vinen (*née* Roach); *m* 1960, Susan-Mary Audrey Master; one *s* one *d*. *Educ:* Watford Grammar Sch.; Clare College, Cambridge. Research Fellow, Clare College, 1955–58. Royal Air Force, 1948–49. Demonstrator in Physics, Univ. of Cambridge and Fellow of Pembroke Coll., 1958–62. Simon Meml Prize, Inst. of Physics, 1963; Holweck Medal and Prize, Inst. of Physics and French Physical Soc., 1978; Rumford Medal, Royal Soc., 1980. *Recreation:* good food. *Address:* 52 Middle Park Road, Birmingham B29 4BJ.

VINER, Monique Sylvaine, (Mrs M. S. Gray), QC 1979; MA; barrister-at-law; a Recorder, since 1986; *b* 3 Oct. 1926; *d* of Hugh Viner and Eliane Viner; *m* 1958, Dr Pieter Francis Gray; one *s* three *d*. *Educ:* Convent of the Sacred Heart, Roehampton; St Hugh's Coll., Oxford (MA). Called to the Bar, Gray's Inn, 1950. In teaching, publishing, factory and shop work, 1947–50. Chm. or Ind. Mem. of Wages Councils (various), 1952–; Mem., Industrial Court, 1976. *Recreations:* talking, reading, tennis, golf, sailing, walking, gardening, cooking, bird watching, history, sketching, painting. *Address:* Old Glebe, Waldron, Heathfield, East Sussex. *T:* Heathfield 3865; 2 Mitre Court Buildings, Temple, EC4Y 7BX. *T:* 01–353 2246.

VINES, Eric Victor, CMG 1984; OBE 1971; HM Diplomatic Service; Ambassador to Uruguay, since 1986; *b* 28 May 1929; *s* of late Henry E. Vines; *m* 1953, Ellen-Grethe Ella Küppers; one *s*. *Educ:* St Dunstan's Coll., London; St Catharine's Coll., Cambridge (MA). Army service, 1947–49. Joined Commonwealth Relations Office, 1952; Colombo, 1954–55; 1st Sec., Singapore, 1958–61; Canberra, 1961–65; Diplomatic Service Administration Office, 1965–68; 1st Sec., Information, Mexico City, 1968–70; Counsellor, Exec. Sec.-Gen., SEATO Conf., London, 1971; Head, Cultural Exchange Dept, FCO, 1971–74; Counsellor (Commercial), Tel Aviv, 1974–77, Stockholm, 1977–80; Consul-Gen., Barcelona, 1980–83; Ambassador to Mozambique, 1984–85. *Recreations:* opera, archaeology, walking. *Address:* c/o Foreign and Commonwealth Office, King Charles Street, SW1. *Club:* Royal Commonwealth Society.

VINES, Sir William (Joshua), Kt 1977; CMG 1969; FASA, ACIS; psc; Chairman, ANZ Banking Group, since 1982 (Director, since 1976); Director: Port Phillip Mills Pty Ltd, since 1969; Dalgety Australia Ltd, since 1980 (Chairman, 1970–80); ANZ UK Holdings plc (formerly Grindlays Holdings), since 1985; grazier at Tara, Queensland, 1965–82 and Cliffdale, Currabubula, NSW, since 1982; *b* 27 May 1916; *s* of P. V. Vines, Canterbury, Victoria, Australia; *m* 1939, Thelma J., *d* of late F. J. Ogden; one *s* two *d*. *Educ:* Haileybury College, Brighton Beach, Victoria. Managing Director: Internat. Wool Secretariat, 1961–69 (Board Mem., 1969–79); Berger, Jenson & Nicholson Ltd, 1960 (Dir, 1961–69); Dalgety Australia Ltd, 1971–76 (Chm., 1970–80); Group Managing Director, Lewis Berger & Sons Ltd, 1955; Director: Lewis Berger & Sons (Aust.) Pty Ltd & Sherwin Williams Co. (Aust.) Pty Ltd, 1952–55; Goodlass Wall & Co. Pty Ltd, 1947–49; Dalgety Ltd; Dalgety New Zealand Ltd, 1969–80; Wiggins Teape Ltd (UK), 1970–79; Tubemakers of Australia Ltd, 1970–86 (Dep. Chm., 1973–86); Associated Pulp & Paper Mills Ltd, 1971–83 (Dep. Chm. 1977, Chm. 1979–83); Conzinc Rio Tinto of Australia, 1977–84; Chm., Thorn Holdings Pty Ltd, 1969–74. Vice-President Melbourne Legacy, 1949–51; Pres. Building Industry Congress, Vic., 1954–55. Chm., Aust. Wool Commn, 1970–72; Mem. Exec., CSIRO, 1973–78; Chm. Council, Hawkesbury Agric. Coll., 1975–85. Mem., Australia New Zealand Foundn, 1979–84. Chm., The Sir Robert Menzies Meml Trust. Served War of 1939–45 (despatches, C-in-C's commendation for gallantry, El Alamein), 2nd AIF, 2/23 Aust. Inf. Bn, Middle East, New Guinea and Borneo, Capt. *Address:* Cliffdale, Currabubula, NSW 2342, Australia. *T:* (067) 689109. *Clubs:* Union, Royal Sydney Golf (Sydney); Australian, Melbourne (Melbourne).

VINEY, Hon. Anne Margaret, (Hon. Mrs Viney), JP; barrister; *b* 14 June 1926; *d* of late Baron Morton of Henryton, PC, MC, and of Lady Morton of Henryton; *m* 1947, Peter Andrew Hopwood Viney; one *s* two *d*. *Educ:* Priorsfield, Godalming, Surrey. Left school after matriculation, 1943; worked in publicity dept of Internat. Wool Secretariat, 1945–47. Called to the Bar, Lincoln's Inn, 1979. Councillor, Kensington and Chelsea BC, 1960–62. JP, 1961; apptd to Inner London Juvenile Court panel, 1961 (Chm. 1970); currently Jt Co-Chm., Hackney Juvenile Court. Helped to found London Adventure Playground Assoc., 1962 (Sec. 1962–69); Chm., Consumer Protection Adv. Cttee, 1973–82. *Recreations:* conversation, playing poetry game. *Address:* 4 Lansdowne Road, W11 3LW. *T:* 01–727 4884; Worth House, Worth Matravers, near Swanage, Dorset.

VINEY, Elliott (Merriam), DSO 1945; MBE 1946; TD; JP; DL; FSA; Director: British Printing Corporation Ltd, 1964–75; Hazell, Watson & Viney Ltd, 1947–78; *b* 21 Aug. 1913; *s* of late Col. Oscar Viney, TD, DL, and Edith Merriam; *m* 1950, Rosamund Ann Pelly; two *d*. *Educ:* Oundle; Univ. Coll., Oxford. Bucks Bn, Oxford and Bucks Light Infantry (TA), 1932–46. Governor and Trustee, Museum of London, 1972–. Pres., British Fedn of Master Printers, 1972–73. Master, Grocers' Company, 1970–71. County Dir, Bucks St John Amb. Assoc., 1953–55; Pres., Bucks Archaeol. Soc., 1979 (Hon. Sec., 1954–79). JP 1950, DL 1952, High Sheriff, 1964, Buckinghamshire. OStJ 1953. Editor: Oxford Mountaineering, 1935; Climbers' Club Jl, 1936–39; (jt) Records of Bucks, 1947–74. *Publications:* The Sheriffs of Buckinghamshire, 1965; (jtly) Old Aylesbury, 1976. *Recreations:* conservation, music, walking. *Address:* Cross Farmhouse, Quainton, Aylesbury, Bucks HP22 4AR. *Clubs:* Alpine; County Hall (Aylesbury).

VINING, Rowena Adelaide, OBE 1979 (MBE 1964); HM Diplomatic Service, retired; *b* 25 Sept. 1921; *er d* of late Col Percival Llewellyn Vining and Phyllis Servante Vining. *Educ:* privately, and at Chiddingstone Castle, Edenbridge, Kent. Foreign Office, 1941–52 (war service in Italy, Indonesia, 1943–45). Commonwealth Relations Office, 1952–55; Second Secretary: Karachi, 1955–58; Sydney, 1958–62; First Sec.: CRO, 1962–65; Canberra, 1965–67; Commonwealth Office (later Foreign and Commonwealth Office), 1967–71; Vienna, 1972–74; Consul, Florence and Consul-General, San Marino, 1974–78; Dep. UK Permanent Rep. to the Council of Europe, 1978–81; Consul-General, Strasbourg, 1979–80. Staff Assessor, FCO, 1983–86. *Recreations:* gardening, music. *Address:* Dorchester Cottage, Greywell, near Basingstoke RG25 1BT. *Club:* Royal Commonwealth Society.

VINSON, family name of **Baron Vinson.**

VINSON, Baron *cr* 1985 (Life Peer), of Roddam Dene in the County of Northumberland; **Nigel Vinson,** LVO 1979; Inventor; Chairman, Development Commission, since 1980 (Member, since 1978); President, Industrial Participation Association, since 1979 (Chairman, 1971–78); *b* Nettlestead Place, Kent, 27 Jan. 1931; *s* of late Ronald Vinson and Bettina Vinson (*née* Southwell-Sander); *m* 1972, Yvonne Ann Collin; three *d*. *Educ:* Pangbourne Naval Coll. Lieut, Queen's Royal Regt, 1949–51. Chm., 1952–72, and Founder, Plastic Coatings Ltd (started in a Nissen hut, 1952, flotation, 1969; Queen's Award to Industry, 1971). Member: Crafts Adv. Cttee, 1971–77; Design Council, 1973–80 (Chm., Finance and Gen. Purposes Cttee); Dep. Chm., CBI Smaller Firms Council, 1979–; Chairman: CoSIRA, 1980–82; Newcastle Technol. Centre, 1985–; Industry Year Steering Cttee, RSA, 1985–. Director: British Airports Authority, 1973–80; Centre for Policy Studies, 1974–80; Mem. Council, King George V Jubilee Trust, 1974–78; Hon. Dir, Queen's Silver Jubilee Appeal, 1976–78; Director: Sugar Bd, 1968–75; Techn. Investment Trust, 1972–; Electra Investment Trust, 1975–; Barclays Bank UK, 1982–. Member: Northumbrian Nat. Parks Countryside Cttee, 1977–; Regional Cttee, Nat. Trust, 1977–84. Trustee, Inst. of Economic Affairs, 1972–. FRSA, CBIM. *Publications:* Personal and Portable Pensions for All, 1984; (jtly) Owners All, 1985; financial contribs to periodicals. *Recreations:* fine art and craftmanship, horses, conservation (foundation donor Martin Mere Wildfowl Trust), farming. *Address:* 34 Kynance Mews, SW7. *T:* Wooperton 230. *Club:* Boodle's.

VINTER, (Frederick Robert) Peter, CB 1965; *b* 27 March 1914; *e s* of P. J. Vinter (Headmaster, Archbishop Holgate's Grammar Sch., York, 1915–37) and Harriet Mary (*née* Cammack); *m* 1938, Margaret, *d* of S. I. Rake, Pembroke; two *s*. *Educ:* Haileybury Coll.; King's Coll., Cambridge (2nd cl. hons English Tripos Pt I, 1st cl. hons Hist. Tripos Pt II); MA. Min. of Economic Warfare, 1939; Cabinet Office, 1943; HM Treasury, 1945–69, Third Sec., 1965–69; Dep. Sec., Min. of Technology and DTI, 1969–73. Overseas Adviser to CEGB, 1973–79; Dir (non-Exec.), Vickers Ltd, 1974–80. Nuffield Travelling Fellowship (in India), 1950–51. *Address:* 3 Sunnyside, Wimbledon, SW19 4SL. *T:* 01–946 4137. *Club:* United Oxford & Cambridge University.

VINTER, Peter; *see* Vinter, F. R. P.

VIOT, Jacques Edmond; Officier de la Légion d'Honneur; Commandeur de l'Ordre National du Mérite; French Ambassador to the Court of St James's, 1984–86; *b* 25 Aug. 1921; *m* 1950, Jeanne de Martimprey de Romécourt. *Educ:* Bordeaux and Paris Lycées; Ecole Normale Supérieure; Ecole Nationale d'Administration. Foreign Office (European Dept), 1951–53; Second Sec., London, 1953–57; First Sec., Rabat, 1957–61; Tech. Advisor to Foreign Minister, 1961–62; Head of Technical Co-operation, FO, 1962–68; Dir for Personnel and Gen. Admin, 1968–72; Ambassador to Canada, 1972–77; Gen. Inspector for Foreign Affairs, 1977–78; Directeur de Cabinet to Foreign Minister, 1978–81; Gen. Inspector for Foreign Affairs, 1981–84. Fellow, St Antony's College, Oxford. *Address:* 19 rue de Civry, 75016 Paris, France. *Clubs:* Athenæum, White's, Travellers'; Le Siècle (Paris).

VIRTUE, Hon. Sir John (Evenden), KBE 1975; Judge of Supreme Court of Western Australia, 1951–75 (retd); Senior Puisne Judge, 1969–75; *b* 25 April 1905; *s* of Ernest Evenden Virtue and Mary Hamilton Virtue; *m* 1938, Mary Joan, *d* of Reginald and Mary Lloyd. *Educ:* Hale Sch., Perth, WA; Univs of Melbourne and Western Australia. LLM (Melb), BA (WA). Barrister and solicitor, admitted to practise in Supreme Courts of Western Australia and Victoria; in practice as barrister and solicitor, Supreme Court of W Australia, 1928–50. Lectured (part-time) in Torts and Criminal Law, Univ. of WA, 1930–49. Served War, AIF (Major), 1940–43. Pres., Law Soc. of WA, 1950. *Recreations:* lawn bowls, contract bridge. *Address:* 74 Kingsway, Nedlands, WA 6009, Australia. *T:* 86–1856. *Clubs:* Weld, Royal Perth Yacht (Perth, WA).

VISHNEVSKAYA, Galina; soprano; *b* 25 Oct. 1926; *m* 1955, Mstislav Rostropovich, *qv*; two *d*. *Educ:* studied with Vera Garina. Toured with Leningrad Light Opera Co., 1944–48, with Leningrad Philharmonic Soc., 1948–52; joined Bolshoi Theatre, 1952. Concert appearances in Europe and USA, 1950–; first appeared at Metropolitan Opera, NY, 1961. Rôles include: Leonora in Fidelio, Tatiana in Eugene Onegin, Iolanta. Has sung in Britain at Festival Hall, Aldeburgh Festival, Edinburgh Festival, Covent Garden, Rostropovich Festival, Snape. Makes concert tours with her husband. Has made many recordings. *Publication:* Galina (autobiog.), 1984. *Address:* c/o Victor Hochhauser, 4 Holland Park Avenue, W11 3QU.

VISSER, John Bancroft; Director of Administration, Science and Engineering Research Council (formerly Science Research Council), since 1974; *b* 29 Jan. 1928; *o s* of late Gilbert and Ethel Visser; *m* 1955, Astrid Margareta Olson; two *s* one *d*. *Educ:* Mill Hill Sch.; New Coll., Oxford (Exhibnr). Entered Civil Service, Asst Principal, Min. of Supply, 1951; Principal, 1956; Min. of Aviation, 1959; Admin. Staff Coll., 1965; Asst Sec., 1965; Min. of Technology, 1967; Royal Coll. of Defence Studies, 1970; Civil Service Dept, 1971; Procurement Exec., MoD, 1971; Under-Sec., 1974; Sec. of Nat. Defence Industries Council, 1971–74. *Recreations:* sport, music, gardening, walking. *Address:* Rosslyn, 3 Berkeley Road, Cirencester, Glos GL7 1TY. *T:* Cirencester 2626. *Club:* Old Millhillians.

VIVENOT, Baroness de, (Hermine Hallam Hipwell), OBE 1967; free lance writer; *b* Buenos Aires, 23 April 1907; *d* of late Humphrey Hallam Hipwell and Gertrude Hermine Isebrée-Moens tot Bloois; *m* 1931, Baron Raoul de Vivenot (*d* 1973), *e s* of Baron de Vivenot and Countess Kuenburg, Vienna; one *s*. *Educ:* Northlands, Buenos Aires. Staff of Buenos Aires Herald, 1928–31. Joined Min. of Information, 1941; transferred Foreign Office, 1946; appointed to Foreign (subseq. Diplomatic) Service, Jan. 1947; Vice-Consul, Bordeaux, 1949–52, Nantes, 1952–53; Foreign Office, 1953–55; First Secretary (Information), HM Embassy, Brussels, 1955–59; Foreign Office, 1959–62; First Secretary (Information), HM Embassy, The Hague, 1962–66; retired 1967. External Examiner in Spanish, Univ. of London. *Publications:* The Niñas of Balcarce, a novel, 1935; Younger Argentine Painters; Argentine Art Notes; Buenos Aires Vignettes; contribs to La Nación and Buenos Aires Herald. *Recreations:* Whippet racing and coursing, gardening, grandchildren. *Address:* The Flat, Aughton House, Collingbourne Kingston, Marlborough, Wilts SN8 3SA. *T:* Collingbourne Ducis 682.

VIVIAN, family name of **Barons Swansea** and **Vivian.**

VIVIAN, 5th Baron, *cr* 1841; **Anthony Crespigny Claude Vivian;** Bt *cr* 1828; *b* 4 March 1906; *e s* of 4th Baron and Barbara, *d* of William A. Fanning; *S* father 1940; *m* 1930, Victoria (*d* 1985), *er d* of late Captain H. G. L. Oliphant, DSO, MVO; two *s* one *d*. *Educ:* Eton. Served RA. *Heir:* *s* Lt-Col Nicholas Crespigny Laurence Vivian, 16/5 Lancers [*b* 11 Dec. 1935; *m* 1st, 1960, Catherine Joyce (marr. diss. 1972), *y d* of late James Kenneth Hope, CBE; one *s* one *d*; 2nd, 1972, Carol, *d* of F. Alan Martineau; two *d*]. *Address:* 154 Coleherne Court, SW5; Boskenna Ros, St Buryan, near Penzance, Cornwall.
See also Marquess of Bath, Earl Haig.

VIVIAN, Michael Hugh; Full-time Board Member, 1974–80, and Deputy Chairman, 1978–80, Civil Aviation Authority; *b* 15 Dec. 1919; *s* of Hugh Vivian and Mary (*née* Gilbertson); *m* 1st, 1951, June Stiven; one *s* one *d*; 2nd, Joy D. Maude. *Educ:* Uppingham; Oxford. Served War: RAF (139 Sqdn), Flying Instructor, Test Pilot, 1940–44. Min. of Civil Aviation, 1945; Private Sec. to Parly Sec. for Civil Aviation, 1945–46; various operational appts, 1947–61; Dep. Dir of Flight Safety, 1961–66; Dir of Flight Safety, 1966–67; Dir of Advanced Aircraft Ops, 1967–71; Civil Aviation Authority, 1972: Dir-Gen. Safety Ops, 1972–74; Gp Dir, Safety Services, 1974–78; Dir, CSE Aviation Ltd, 1980–82. *Recreations:* golf, vintage cars. *Address:* Willow Cottage, The Dickredge, Steeple Aston, Oxfordshire. *T:* Steeple Aston 47171. *Club:* Royal Air Force.

VOCKLER, Rt. Rev. John Charles, (Rt. Rev. Brother John Charles, SSF); engaged in writing and research; Acting Bishop Protector, Poor Clares of Reparation, Mt Sinai, NY, since 1985 (Warden, 1982–83; Acting Warden, 1981–82); *b* 22 July 1924; *e s* of John Thomas Vockler and Mary Catherine Vockler (*née* Widerberg), Dee Why, New South Wales. *Educ:* Sydney Boys' High Sch.; after studying accountancy, matriculated by private study and correspondence (Metropolitan Business Coll. and Internat.

Correspondence Schs, Sydney) to the University of Sydney; University of Queensland; Moore Theological Coll.; St John's Theological College, Morpeth, NSW; General Theological Seminary, New York. LTheol, Australian College of Theology, 1948; received Hey Sharp Prize for NT Greek. Junior Clerk, W. R. Carpenter & Co. Ltd, Sydney, NSW, 1939–43. Deacon, 1948; priest, 1948; Asst Deacon, Christ Church Cathedral, Newcastle, 1948; Asst Priest, 1948–50; Vice-Warden of S John's Coll., within University of Queensland, 1950–53; Acting Chaplain, C of E Grammar School for Boys, Brisbane, 1953. BA (1st Class Hons History) University of Queensland, 1953; University Gold Medal for outstanding achievement, 1953; BA University of Adelaide, aegr, 1961; Walter and Eliza Hall Foundation Travelling Scholarship, University of Queensland, 1953; Fulbright Scholar, 1953. Acting Vice-Warden, S John's Coll., Morpeth and Lecturer in Old Testament, 1953; Graduate Student, General Theological Seminary, New York, 1954. MDiv (General Seminary), 1954. Asst Priest, Cathedral of S John the Divine, NY and Chaplain, St Luke's Home for Aged Women and the Home for Old Men and Aged Couples, 1954; Australian Delegate to Anglican Congress, 1954; Fellow and Tutor Gen. Theol. Seminary, 1954–56; STM Gen. Theol. Seminary, 1956. Asst Priest, St Stephen's Church, West 69th Street, NY, 1955; Priest-in-charge, St Stephen's, New York, 1956; Asst Priest, parish of Singleton, NSW, 1956–59; Lecturer in Theology, St John's Theological College, Morpeth, NSW, 1956–59; Secretary, Newcastle Diocesan Board of Education, 1958–59. Titular Bishop of Mount Gambier and Assistant Bishop of Adelaide (Coadjutor, 1959; title changed to Assistant, 1961), until 1962; also Archdeacon of Eyre Peninsula, 1959–62; Vicar-General, Examining Chaplain to Bishop of Adelaide, 1960–62; Bishop of Polynesia, 1962–68. Warden: Community of St Clare, Newcastle, NSW, 1975–80; Soc. of Sacred Advent, 1976–80. Collegial Mem., House of Bishops, Episcopal Church, USA, 1983–; Mem., House of Bishops' Cttee on Religious Life, 1986–. President, Harry Charman's All Races Sports and Social Club, Suva, Fiji, 1962–68, Hon. Life Vice-Pres., 1968; Chairman: S Pacific Anglican Council, 1963–68; Council of Pacific Theological Coll., 1963–68; President: Fiji Council of Social Services, 1964–68; Fiji Branch, Royal Commonwealth Soc., 1966–68. Writing Grant, Literature Bd of Australia Council, 1979, 1981. Member: Soc. of Authors; Australian Soc. of Authors; PEN (International), Sydney Br. and New York Br.; Guild of Writers Inc., NY; Christian Writers' Fellowship (USA); Aust. Professional Writers' Services; Penman Club (UK); National Writers' Club (USA); Federated Clerks Union of Aust., 1978–81; Internat. Center for Integrative Studies, NY 1983–; Internat. Ecumenical Fellowship; Guild of All Souls; Confraternity of the Blessed Sacrament; Soc. of Mary; Catholic and Evangelical Mission; Anglican Pacifist Fellowship; Fellowship of Reconciliation; Integrity USA; Gay Christian Movement; Fellowship of S Alban and S Sergius; Anglican Fellowship of Prayer, USA; Fellowship of Three Kings, Haddington, Scotland; Amnesty Internat., USA (Mem., Urgent Action Gp). Priest Associate, Shrine of Our Lady, Walsingham and Priory of Our Lady of Pew, Westminster Abbey; Priest Member, Oratory of the Good Shepherd, 1952–75. Entered Soc. of St Francis, 1969, to test vocation to religious life; professed, 1972; Chaplain to Third Order, Soc. of St Francis (European Province), 1972–74; made life profession in Soc. of St Francis, 1975; Guardian, Friary of St Francis, Brisbane, 1975–77, Islington, NSW, 1978–79; Minister Provincial, Pacific Province, Soc. of St Francis, 1976–81; Sec., Adv. Council for Religious Communities in Aust. and Pacific, 1976–80. Permission to officiate: dio. Salisbury, 1969–70; dio. Fulham and Gibraltar, with Episcopal Commn, 1971–73; dio. Newcastle, NSW, 1975–81; dio. Auckland, NZ, 1976–81; dio. Long Island, 1981–; dio. of NY, 1981–. Vice-Pres. and Mem. Council, USPG, 1973–74; Vice-Pres., Missions to Seamen, 1963–69; Hon. Asst Bp of Worcester, 1972–73; Assistant Bishop: Chelmsford, 1973–74; Southwark, 1974–75; Hon. Canon of Southwark, 1975, Canon Emeritus 1975; Hon. Mission Chaplain, dio. Brisbane, 1975–79, permission to officiate, 1979–81. Examnr for Aust. Coll. of Theology, 1975–76 and 1979. ThD (*jure dig.*) ACT, 1961; STD (*hc*) Gen. Theological Seminary, NY, 1961; BD (*ad eund.*) Melbourne College of Divinity, 1960. *Publications:* Can Anglicans Believe Anything—The Nature and Spirit of Anglicanism, 1961 (NSW); Forward Day by Day, 1962; (ed) Believing in God (by M. L. Yates), 1962 (Australian edn), revd edn 1983 (US). One Man's Journey, 1972; St Francis: Franciscanism and the Society of St Francis, 1980; contributions to: Preparatory Volume for Anglican Congress, Toronto, 1963; Mutual Responsibility: Questions and Answers, 1964; All One Body (ed T. Wilson), 1968; Australian Dictionary of Biography (4 articles); St Mark's Review, Australian Church Quarterly, The Anglican, The Young Anglican, Pacific Journal of Theology, New Zealand Theological Review, weekly feature, Newcastle Morning Herald, NSW; book reviews in Amer. theol jls; Aust. corresp. to New Fire, 1980–81. *Recreations:* classical music, detective stories, theatre, films, prints and engravings. *Address:* St Elizabeth's Friary, 1474 Bushwick Avenue, Brooklyn, NY 11206, USA. *T:* 718–455–5963. *Clubs:* Tonga (Nukualofa); St John's Coll. (Brisbane) (Hon Mem., 1976–).

VOELCKER, Christopher David, TD 1967; Metropolitan Stipendiary Magistrate, since 1982; *b* 10 May 1933; *s* of Eric Voelcker and Carmen Muriel Lyon Voelcker (*née* Henstock); *m* 1964, Sybil Russell Stoneham (marr. diss. 1985); two *d.* *Educ:* Wellington Coll., Berks. Called to Bar, Middle Temple, 1955. National Service, 8th King's Royal Irish Hussars, 1952–53. 3/4 County of London Yeomanry (Sharpshooters) TA, 1953–60; Kent and County of London Yeomanry (Sharpshooters) TA, 1960–67. *Recreations:* military history, gardening. *Address:* 6 Pump Court, Temple, EC4Y 7AR. *T:* 01–353 7242. *Club:* Cavalry and Guards.

VOGEL, Hans-Jochen, Hon. CBE; Dr jur; Member, Bundestag, since 1972 (Social Democratic Party); Leader of the Opposition, since 1983; *b* 3 Feb. 1926; *s* of Dr Hermann Vogel and Caroline (*née* Brinz); *m* 1st, 1951, Ilse Leisnering (marr. diss. 1970); one *s* two *d*; 2nd, 1972, Liselotte Sonnenholzer. *Educ:* Göttingen and Giessen; Univs of Marburg and Munich (Dr jur 1950). Army service, 1943–45 (PoW). Admitted Bavarian Bar, 1951; Legal Asst, Bavarian Min. of Justice, 1952–54; District Court Counsel, Traunstein, 1954–58; staff of Bavarian State Chancellery, 1955–58; Munich City Council, 1958, Oberbürgermeister (Chief Executive), Munich, 1960–72 (re-elected, 1966); Vice-Pres., Org. Cttee, Olympic Games, 1972. Chm., Bavarian SDP, 1972–77; Minister of regional planning, housing and urban devclt, 1972–74; Minister of Justice, 1974–81; Mayor of West Berlin, Jan.–June 1981, leader of opposition, 1981–83. Bundesverdienstkreuz; Bavarian Verdienstorden. *Publications:* Städte im Wandel, 1971; Die Amtskette: Meine 12 Münchner Jahre, 1972; Reale Reformen, 1973. *Recreations:* mountaineering, swimming, reading history. *Address:* c/o Bundeshaus, 5300 Bonn 1, Federal Republic of Germany.

VOGELPOEL, Pauline, MBE 1962; Vice-President, Contemporary Art Society; *d* of late Pieter Vogelpoel and Yvonne Vogelpoel, Mozambique; *m* 1975, Richard David Mann, *s* of F. F. A. Mann, *qv*. *Educ:* Herschel School, Cape Town; University of Cape Town (BA). Joined Contemporary Art Society, 1954, as Organising Secretary; Director 1976–82. Mem., Adv. Council, Victoria and Albert Museum, 1977–82. *Publications:* occasional journalism. *Recreations:* cooking, music, junkshops, pugs. *Address:* Oberer Rheinweg 31, CH-4058 Basle, Switzerland.

VOGT, Dr Marthe Louise, FRS 1952; Dr med Berlin, Dr phil Berlin; PhD Cantab; *b* 1903; *d* of Oskar Vogt and Cécile Vogt (*née* Mugnier). *Educ:* Auguste Viktoria-Schule, Berlin; University of Berlin. Research Assistant, Department of Pharmacology, Berlin Univ., 1930; Research Assistant and head of chemical division, Kaiser Wilhelm Institut für Hirnforschung, Berlin, 1931–35; Rockefeller Travelling Fellow, 1935–36; Research Worker, Dept of Pharmacology, Cambridge Univ., 1935–40; Alfred Yarrow Research Fellow of Girton Coll., 1937–40; Member Staff of College of Pharmaceutical Society, London, 1941–46; Lecturer, later Reader, in Pharmacology, University of Edinburgh, 1947–60; Head of Pharmacology Unit, Agricultural Research Council Institute of Animal Physiology, 1960–68. Vis. Associate Prof. in Pharmacology, Columbia Univ., New York, 1949; Vis. Prof., Sydney 1965, Montreal 1968. Life Fellow, Girton Coll., Cambridge, 1970. For. Hon. Mem., Amer. Acad. of Arts and Scis, 1977. Hon. Fellow RSM 1980. Corresp. Mem., Deutsche Physiologische Gesellschaft, 1976; Hon. Member: Physiological Soc., 1974; British Pharmacological Soc., 1971; Hungarian Acad. of Scis, 1981; British Assoc. for Psychopharmacol., 1983. Hon. DSc: Edinburgh, 1974; Cambridge, 1983. Royal Medal, Royal Soc., 1981. *Publications:* papers in neurological, physiological and pharmacological journals. *Address:* Agricultural and Food Research Council Institute of Animal Physiology, Babraham, Cambridge CB2 4AT.

VOLCKER, Paul A.; Chairman, American Federal Reserve Board, since 1979; *b* Cape May, New Jersey, 5 Sept. 1927; *s* of Paul A. Volcker and Alma Louise Klippel; *m* 1954, Barbara Marie Bahnson; one *s* one *d.* *Educ:* Princeton Univ. (AB *summa cum laude*); Harvard Univ. (MA); LSE. Special Asst, Securities Dept, Fed. Reserve Bank, NY, 1953–57; Financial Economist, Chase Manhattan Bank, NYC, 1957–62; Vice-Pres. and Dir of Forward Planning, 1965–69; Dir, Office of Financial Analysis, US Treasury Dept, 1962–63; Dep. Under-Sec. for Monetary Affairs, 1963–65; Under-Sec. for Monetary Affairs, 1969–74; Senior Fellow, Woodrow Wilson Sch. of Public and Internat. Affairs, Princeton Univ., 1974–75; Pres. NY Federal Reserve Bank, 1975–79. *Address:* Federal Reserve, Washington, DC 20551, USA.

VOLLRATH, Prof. Lutz Ernst Wolf; Professor of Histology and Embryology, University of Mainz, Germany, since 1974; *b* 2 Sept. 1936; *s* of Pastor Richard Hermann Vollrath and Rita (*née* Brügmann); *m* 1963, Gisela (*née* Dialer); three *d.* *Educ:* Ulrich von Hutten-Schule, Berlin; Univs of Berlin, Kiel and Tübingen. Dr med Kiel, 1961. Wissenschaftlicher Assistent, Dept of Anatomy, Würzburg, Germany, 1963; Res. Fellow, Dept of Anatomy, Birmingham, 1964; Wissenschaftlicher Assistent, Dept of Anatomy, Würzburg, 1965–71 (Privatdozent, 1968; Oberassistent, 1969; Universitätsdozent, 1970); King's College London: Reader in Anatomy, 1971; Prof. of Anatomy, 1973–74. *Publications:* (co-editor) Neurosecretion: the final neuroendocrine pathway, 1974; The Pineal Organ, 1981; (editor): Cell & Tissue Research; Handbuch der mikr. Anat. des Menschen; research publications on histochemistry and ultrastructure of organogenesis and various aspects of neuroendocrinology, in Z Zellforsch., Histochemie, Phil. Trans Royal Society B, Erg. Anat. Entw.gesch. *Recreations:* gardening, tennis. *Address:* c/o Anatomisches Institut, 65 Mainz, Saarstr. 19/21, Germany.

von BITTENFELD; *see* Herwarth von Bittenfeld.

von CLEMM, Michael; Chairman, Merrill Lynch Capital Markets, since 1986; *b* 18 March 1935; *s* of Werner Conrad Clemm von Hohenberg and Veronica Rudge Green; *m* 1956, Louisa Bronson Hunnewell; two *d.* *Educ:* Harvard College (AB cum laude 1956); Harvard Graduate School of Arts and Sciences; Corpus Christi College, Oxford (MLitt 1959, DPhil 1962). Staff journalist, Boston Globe, 1959–60; First National City Bank, 1962–67; Faculty, Harvard Graduate Sch. of Business Administration, 1967–71; Chm., Roux Restaurants, 1971–; White Weld & Co.: Exec. Dir, 1971–75; Man. Dir, 1975–78; Dep. Chm., 1976; Chm., Credit Suisse First Boston Ltd, 1978–86. Member: Management Cttee, City of London Archaeol Trust, 1979–; Court of The Mary Rose, 1982–; Trustee and Hon. Treasurer, British Museum Develt Trust, 1985. *Publications:* Agriculture & Sentiment on Kilimanjaro; Economic Botany, 1963; The Rise of Consortium Banking. *Recreations:* collecting Michelin Guide stars (with Albert and Michel Roux), collecting airline boarding passes. *Address:* 97–99 Park Street, W1Y 3HA. *T:* 01–499 7812. *Clubs:* Buck's, Boodle's; Porcellian (Cambridge, Mass); Brook (NY).

von HASE, Karl-Günther, Hon. GCVO 1972; Hon. KCMG 1965; Chairman, Deutsch-Englische Gesellschaft, Düsseldorf, since 1982; *b* 15 Dec. 1917; *m* 1945, Renate Stumpff; five *d.* *Educ:* German schools. Professional Soldier, 1936–45; War Academy, 1943–44; Training College for Diplomats, 1950–51; Georgetown Univ., Washington DC, 1952. German Foreign Service: German Embassy, Ottawa, 1953–56; Spokesman, Foreign Office Bonn, 1958–61; Head, West European Dept, 1961–62; Spokesman of German Federal Government, 1962–67; State Secretary, Min. of Defence, German Federal Govt, 1968–69; German Ambassador to the Court of St James's, 1970–77; Dir-Gen., Zweites Deutsches Fernsehen, 1977–82. Holds German and other foreign decorations. *Recreations:* shooting, music. *Address:* Am Stadtwald 60, 5300 Bonn 2, West Germany.

von KARAJAN, Herbert; Conductor; Director: Salzburg Festival, since 1964; Vienna State Opera, since 1976 (Artistic Manager, 1956–64); Life Director Gesellschaft der Musikfreunde, Vienna; Conductor, Berlin Philharmonic Orchestra; *b* Salzburg, 5 April 1908; *s* of Ernest von Karajan and Martha v. Karajan Cosmâc. *Educ:* Salzburg Hochschule and Mozarteum; Vienna Univ. Conductor: Ulm Opernhaus, 1927–33; Aachen Opernhaus, 1933–40; Berlin Staatsoper, 1938–42; Festivals: Salzburg; Bayreuth; Edinburgh, 1953–54; Lucerne, 1947–56; Conductor and régisseur, La Scala, Milan, 1948–55; Musical Director, Berlin Philharmonic Orchestra, 1955–56. First European Tour with Philharmonia Orchestra, 1952; Director, Salzburg Festival, 1957. Films directed and conducted include: Bajazzo, Carmen, Beethoven's 9th Symphony. Hon. DMus Oxon, 1978. Gold Medal, Royal Phil. Soc., 1984. *Recreations:* ski-ing, mountaineering, flying, yachting, motoring, theatre, acoustical research. *Address:* Festspielhaus, Salzburg, Austria.

von KLITZING, Prof. Klaus, PhD; Director, Max-Planck-Institut für Festkörperforschung, Stuttgart, since 1985; *b* 28 June 1943; *s* of Bogislav and Anny von Klitzing; *m* 1971, Renate Falkenberg; two *s* one *d.* *Educ:* Technische Univ., Braunschweig (DipPhys); Univ. of Würzburg (PhD; Habilitation (univ. teaching qual.). Prof., Technische Univ., München, 1980–84; Hon. Prof., Univ. of Stuttgart, 1985. Nobel Prize for Physics, 1985. *Address:* Max-Planck-Institut für Festkörperforschung, Heisenbergstrasse 1, D-7000 Stuttgart 80, Federal Republic of Germany. *T:* (0711) 6860–570.

von MALLINCKRODT, Georg Wilhelm; Chairman and Chief Executive Officer, Schroders Incorporated, New York, since 1986; Chairman, J. Henry Schroder Bank AG, Zurich, since 1984; Executive Chairman, Schroders plc, since 1984 (Director, since 1977); *b* 19 Aug. 1930; *s* of Arnold Wilhelm von Mallinckrodt and Valentine von Mallinckrodt (*née* von Joest); *m* 1958, Charmaine Brenda Schroder; two *s* two *d.* *Educ:* Salem, West Germany. Agfa AG Munich, 1948–51; Münchmeyer & Co., Hamburg, 1951–53; Kleinwort Sons & Co., London, 1953–54; J. Henry Schroder Banking Corp., New York, 1954–59; Union Bank of Switzerland, Geneva 1956; J. Henry Schroder Bank & Trust Co., NY, 1957–60; J. Henry Schroder & Co., subseq. J. Henry Schroder Wagg & Co., London, 1960–85, Director, 1967–; Chm. and Chief Exec. Officer, J. Henry Schroder Bank & Trust Co., NY, 1984–86; Pres. and Chief Exec. Officer, Schroders Inc., NY, 1984–86. Director: Schroders Australia Hldgs Ltd, Sydney, 1984–; Wertheim, Schroder

Hldgs Inc., NY, 1986–; Wertheim Schroder & Co. Inc., NY, 1986–. Vice-Pres., German Chamber of Industry and Commerce in UK, 1971–. Verdienstkreuz am Bande des Verdienstordens (GFR), 1986. *Recreations:* shooting, ski-ing. *Address:* 120 Cheapside, EC2V 6DS. *T:* 01–382 6000. *Club:* River (New York).

VONNEGUT, Kurt, Jr; writer; *b* Indianapolis, 11 Nov. 1922; *m* 1st, 1945, Jane Marie Cox (marr. diss. 1979); one *s* two *d*; 2nd, 1979, Jill Krementz. *Educ:* Cornell Univ.; Carnegie Inst. of Technol.; Univ. of Chicago. Served War, US Army, 1942–45 (POW). Reporter, Chicago City News Bureau, 1945–47; PRO, GEC, Schenectady, 1947–50; freelance writer, 1950–65; Lectr, Writers' Workshop, Univ. of Iowa, 1965–67; Guggenheim Fellow, 1967–68; Lectr in English, Harvard, 1970; Dist. Prof., City Coll., New York, 1973–74. Mem., National Inst. of Arts and Letters. *Publications:* Player Piano, 1951; The Sirens of Titan, 1959; Mother Night, 1961; Cat's Cradle, 1963; God Bless You, Mr Rosewater, 1964; Welcome to the Monkey House (short stories), 1968; Slaughterhouse-Five, 1969; Happy Birthday, Wanda June (play), 1970; Between Time and Timbuktu or Prometheus-5 (TV script), 1972; Breakfast of Champions, 1973; Wampeters, Foma and Granfalloons (essays), 1974; Slapstick, or Lonesome No More, 1976; Jailbird, 1979; (with Ivan Chermayeff) Sun Moon Star, 1980; Palm Sunday (autobiog.), 1981; Deadeye Dick, 1982; Galapagos, 1985. *Address:* c/o Donald C. Farber Esq., Tanner Gilbert Propp & Sterner, 99 Park Avenue, 25th Floor, New York, NY 10016, USA.

von REITZENSTEIN, Hans-Joachim Freiherr; *see* Leech, John.

von SCHRAMEK, Sir Eric (Emil), Kt 1982; FRIBA; Chairman, von Schramek and Dawes Pty Ltd, Architects and Planners, since 1963; *b* 4 April 1921; *s* of Emil and Annie von Schramek; *m* 1948, Edith, *d* of Dipl. Ing. W. Popper; one *s* two *d*. *Educ:* Stefans Gymnasium, Prague; Technical Univ., Prague. DiplIngArch; Life Fellow RAIA, FIArbA, Affiliate RAPI. Town Planner, Bavaria, 1946–48; Sen. Supervising Architect, Dept of Works and Housing, Darwin, NT, 1948–51; Evans, Bruer & Partners (now von Schramek and Dawes), 1951–; work includes multi-storey office buildings in Adelaide (Nat. Mutual Centre; State Govt Insce Bldg; Wales House; TAA Bldg; Qld Insce Bldg, etc); Wesley House, Melbourne; Westpac House, Hobart; AMP Bldg and TAA Bldg, Darwin; numerous churches throughout Australia and New Guinea. National Pres., Building Science Forum of Aust., 1970–72; President: RAIA (SA Chapter), 1974–76; Inst. of Arbitrators, Aust. (SA Chapter), 1977–80. Past Vis. Lectr, Univ. of Adelaide; Vis. Lectr, S Australian Inst. of Technol. Past National Dep. Chm., Austcare; past Councillor, Council of Professions; past Chm., Commn on Worship and other Depts, Lutheran Church of Australia. *Publications:* contribs and articles in architectural pubns. *Recreations:* music, reading, golf. *Address:* 4/118 Brougham Place, North Adelaide, SA 5006, Australia. *T:* (08) 267 4352; The Olives, Yankalilla, South Australia 5203. *T:* (085) 58 2205.

von WECHMAR, Baron Rüdiger; Ambassador of Federal Republic of Germany to the Court of St James's, since 1983; *b* 15 Nov. 1923; *s* of Irnfried von Wechmar and Ilse (*née* von Binzer); *m* 1961, Dina-Susanne (Susie) (*née* Woldenga); one *d* (one *s* one *d* of previous marr.). *Educ:* Oberrealschule, Berlin; Univ. of Minnesota, USA (as prisoner of war). MA Journalism. Army, 3rd Reconnaissance Battalion, Western Desert and PoW Camp, 1941–46. Journalist, 1946–58; joined German Foreign Service as Consul, New York, 1958; Dir, German Inf. Centre, NY; Dep. Head, Govt Press and Inf. Office, Bonn, 1969; State Sec. and Chief Govt Spokesman, 1972; Perm. Rep. to UN, 1974–81; Pres., UN Security Council, 1977–78; Pres., 35th Gen. Assembly, UN, 1980–81; Ambassador to Italy, 1981–83. Trustee, UNITAR, NY, 1981–; Sen. Fellow, Aspen Inst. for Humanistic Studies, Aspen Co., 1971–; Trustee, Aspen-Italy; Member: North-South Round Table, Deutsche Ges. für Auswärtige Politik; Council, Friedrich Naumann Foundn; Dir, World Affairs Council, NY; UNA Presidium. Commander's Cross, Order of Merit (FRG), 1980; decorations from Sweden, Norway, Japan, Netherlands, Egypt, Mexico, Italy, Romania. Paul Klinger Award, DAG, 1973; UN Peace Gold Medal, 1980. *Recreations:* stamp collecting, ski-ing. *Address:* Embassy of Federal Republic of Germany, 23 Belgrave Square, SW1X 8PZ. *T:* 01–235 5033. *Clubs:* Athenæum, Travellers', Royal Automobile; Bathing Corporation (Southampton, NY).

von WEIZSÄCKER, Freiherr Carl-Friedrich, Dr Phil; University Professor Emeritus; *b* Kiel, 28 June 1912; *m* 1937, Gundalena (*née* Wille); three *s* one *d*. *Educ:* Universities of Leipzig, Göttingen, Copenhagen, 1929–33. Dr.phil 1933, Dr.phil.habil, 1936, Univ. Leipzig; Asst., Inst. of Theor. Physik, Univ. of Leipzig, 1934–36; Wissenschaftl. Mitarb., Kaiser Wilhelm Inst., Berlin, 1936–42; Dozent, Univ. of Berlin, 1937–42; pl. ao. Prof. Theor. Physik, Univ. of Strassburg, 1942–44; Kaiser-Wilhelm-Inst., Berlin and Hechingen, 1944–45; Hon. Prof., Univ. Göttingen and Abt. Leiter, Max Planck Inst. für Physik, Göttingen, 1946–57; Hon. Prof. of Theor. Physik, Univ. of Göttingen, 1946–57; Ord. Prof. of Philosophy, Univ. of Hamburg, 1957–69. Hon. Prof., Univ. of Munich, and Dir, Max-Planck-Institut on the preconditions of human life in the modern world, 1970–80. Gifford Lecturer, Glasgow Univ., 1959–61. Member: Deutsche Akademie der Naturforscher Leopoldina, Halle (DDR); Akademie der Wissenschaften, Göttingen; Joachim-Jungius-Gesellschaft der Wissenschaften, Hamburg; Bayerische Akademie der Wissenschaften, München; sterreichische Akademie der Wissenschaften, Wien; Sächsische Akademie der Wissenschaften zu Leipzig. Verdienstorden der Bundesrepublik Deutschland, 1959–73; Orden Pour le Mérite für Wissenschaften und Künste, 1961; Wiss. Mitglied der Max-Planck-Gesellschaft, Göttingen. Max Planck Medal, 1957; Goethe Prize (Frankfurt) 1958; Friedenspreis des deutschen Buchhandels, 1963; Erasmus Prize (with Gabriel Marcel), 1969. Hon. Dr theol, Univ. Tübingen, 1977; Hon. Dr iur, Free Univ., Amsterdam, 1977. *Publications:* Die Atomkerne, 1937; Zum Weltbild der Physik, 11th edn, 1970 (English, London, 1952); Die Geschichte der Natur, 7th edn, 1970 (English, Chicago, 1949); Physik der Gegenwart (with J. Juilfs), 2nd edn, 1958 (Engl., 1957); Die Verantwortung der Wissenschaft im Atomzeitalter, 5th edn, 1969; Atomenergie und Atomzeitalter, 3rd edn, 1958; Bedingungen des Friedens, 1963, 5th edn, 1970; Die Tragweite der Wissenschaft, 1964; Der ungesicherte Friede, 1969; Die Einheit der Natur, 1971, 3rd edn, 1972; (ed) Kriegsfolgen und Kriegsverhütung, 1970, 3rd edn, 1971; Voraussetzungen der naturwissenschaftlichen Denkens, 1972, 2nd edn, 1972; Fragen zur Weltpolitik, 1975; Wege in der Gefahr, 1976; Der Garten des Menschlichen, Beiträge zur geschichtlichen Anthropologie, 1977; Deutlichkeit, Beiträge zu politischen und religiösen Gegenwartsfragen, 1978; Der bedrohte Friede, 1981; Wahrnehmung der Neuzeit, 1983; *relevant Publication:* bibliography in Einheit und Vielheit, Festschrift...ed Scheibe and Süssmann, 1973. *Recreations:* hiking, chess. *Address:* D-813(0) Starnberg, Bahnhofplatz 4, Germany.

See also R. von Weizsäcker.

von WEIZSÄCKER, Richard, Dr jur; President of the Federal Republic of Germany, since 1984; *b* 15 April 1920; *s* of late Baron Ernst von Weizsäcker; *m* 1953, Marianne von Kretschman; three *s* one *d*. *Educ:* Berlin and Bern; Univs of Oxford, Grenoble and Göttingen (Dr jur). Army service, 1938–45 (Captain, wounded). Formerly with Allianz Lebensversicherung, Stuttgart and Robeco-Gruppe, Amsterdam. Member: Robert Bosch Foundn, Stuttgart; Synod and Council, German Evangelical Church, 1969– (Pres., Congress). Joined Christian Democratic Union, 1954: Mem., Fed. Board; Chm., Gen. Policy Commn, 1971–74; Chm., Basic Prog. Commn, 1974–77; Dep. Chm., CDU/CSU Parlt Gp, 1972–79; Presidential candidate, 1974; First Chm., Berlin CDU, 1981–83. Mem., Bundestag, 1969–81, Vice-Pres., 1979–81; Governing Mayor of West Berlin, 1981–84. *Address:* Villa Hammerschmidt, 5300 Bonn, Adenauer-Allee 135, Federal Republic of Germany.

See also Carl-Friedrich von Weizsäcker.

von WINTERFELDT, (Hans) Dominik; Executive Chairman, Hoechst UK Ltd, since 1984; *b* 3 July 1937; *s* of late Curt von Winterfeldt and Anna Franziska Margaretha Luise (*née* Petersen); *m* 1966, Cornelia Waldthausen; one *s* one *d*. *Educ:* German schools; Stanford-INSEAD, Fontainebleau (Industriekaufmann). DipICC. Joined Hoechst AG, Frankfurt/Main, 1957; Asst Manager, Hoechst Colombiana Ltda, 1960; Commercial Manager, Pharmaceuticals, Hoechst Peruana SA, 1963; General Manager, Hoechst Dyechemie W. L. L., Iraq, 1965; Man. Dir, Hoechst Pakistan Ltd and Hoechst Pharmaceuticals Ltd, 1967; Dep. Man. Dir, 1972, Man. Dir and Chief Exec., 1975, Hoechst UK Ltd. Director: Messer Griesheim Ltd, 1975–; Hoechst Finance plc, 1975–; Berger, Jenson & Nicholson Ltd, 1979–; Rochas Perfumes Ltd, 1979–; Balenciaga Ltd, 1980–; Hoechst Investments Ltd, 1984–. Member: British Inst. of Directors, 1975–; Deutsches Industriegespraech/German Chamber of Industry & Commerce in London, 1976–; European-Atlantic Gp, 1983–; Chemical Industries Assoc., 1984–. Member: Anglo-German Assoc.; British Deer Soc.; British Assoc. for Shooting and Conservation. *Recreations:* music, deer stalking, golf. *Address:* Hoechst UK Ltd, Hoechst House, Salisbury Road, Hounslow, Mddx TW4 6JH. *T:* 01–570 7712. *Clubs:* Royal Automobile, Les Ambassadeurs; Sind (Karachi).

VOS, Geoffrey Michael; His Honour Judge Vos; a Circuit Judge, since 1978; *b* 18 Feb. 1927; *s* of Louis and Rachel Eva Vos; *m* 1955, Marcia Joan Goldstone (marr. diss. 1977); two *s* two *d*; *m* 1981, Mrs Anne Wilson. *Educ:* St Joseph's College, Blackpool; Gonville and Caius College, Cambridge. MA, LLB. Called to the Bar, Gray's Inn, 1950. A Recorder of the Crown Court, 1976–78. *Recreations:* swimming, walking. *Address:* c/o The Crown Court, Kenton Bar, Ponteland Road, Newcastle-upon-Tyne. *T:* Newcastle-upon-Tyne 864023.

VOUEL, Raymond; Member, Commission of the European Communities, responsible for Competition Policy, 1977–84; *b* 1923; *m*; three *c*. Journalist on Socialist daily newspaper, Tageblatt; Admin. Dir, Esch Hosp., 1954–64; Mem. Town Council, Esch (Chm. Bldgs Cttee), 1973. Member, Chamber of Deputies, Luxembourg, 1964–76; Sec. of State: for Public Health; for Employment; for Social Security; for Mining Industry, 1964–69. Chm., Parly Socialist Group, 1970–74; Gen. Sec., Parti Ouvrier Socialiste Luxembourgeois (Socialists), 1970; Dep. Prime Minister, Minister for Finance and Land Develt, 1974–76; Mem., Commission of European Communities with responsibility for Competition, July-Dec. 1976. *Address:* c/o Ministry of Foreign Affairs, Luxembourg-Ville, Luxembourg.

VOWDEN, His Honour Desmond Harvey Weight; QC 1969; a Circuit Judge, 1975–86; *b* 6 Jan. 1921; *s* of late Rev. A. W. J. Vowden, MBE, TD; *m* 1964, Iris, *d* of L. A. Stafford-Northcote. *Educ:* Clifton Coll. Served in RN and RM, 1938–50; Captain RM, retired 1950. Called to the Bar, 1950; Dep. Chm., Wiltshire Quarter Sessions, 1968–71; Recorder of Devizes, later a Recorder of Crown Court, 1971–75. Comr, CCC, 1969–72. Steward of Appeal, BBB of C, 1967–81. *Recreations:* music, gardening. *Address:* Orchard Cottage, Worton, Devizes, Wilts. *T:* Devizes 2877. *Club:* Garrick.

VOWLES, Paul Foster; Academic Registrar, University of London, 1973–82; *b* 12 June 1919; *s* of late E. F. Vowles and G. M. Vowles, Bristol; *m* 1948, Valerie Eleanor Hickman; one *s* two *d*. *Educ:* Bristol Grammar Sch.; Corpus Christi Coll., Oxford (schol.; MA). Served Gloucestershire Regt and King's African Rifles, 1939–46 (despatches, Major). Asst Secretary: Appts Bd, Univ. of Birmingham, 1947–48; Inter-University Council for Higher Educn Overseas, 1948–51; Registrar, Makerere University Coll., E Africa, 1951–63; Sen. Asst to Principal, Univ. of London, 1964–68; Warden, Lillian Penson Hall, 1965–69; External Registrar, 1968–73. *Address:* 13 Dale Close, Oxford OX1 1TU. *T:* Oxford 244042. *Club:* Athenæum.

VOYSEY, Reginald George, FIMechE; Consultant; Deputy Director, National Physical Laboratory, 1970–77; *s* of Richard Voysey and Anne Paul; *m* 1943, Laidley Mary Elizabeth Barley; one *s* three *d* (and one *s* decd). *Educ:* Royal Dockyard Sch., Portsmouth; Imperial Coll. of Science. ACGI, DIC, WhSch. Dep. Develt Manager, Power Jets Ltd, 1940–45; Gas Turbine Dept Manager, C. A. Parsons & Co., 1945–48; Engineering Asst to Chief Scientist, Min. of Fuel and Power, 1948–66; IDC 1963; Scientific Counsellor, British Embassy, and Dir, UK Sci. Mission to Washington, 1966–69. *Publications:* patents and articles in jls. *Recreations:* swimming, sailing, painting. *Address:* 16 Beauchamp Road, East Molesey, Surrey. *T:* 01–979 3762.

VREDELING, Hendrikus, (Henk); Member of the Dutch Emancipation Council, 1981–85; *b* 20 Nov. 1924. *Educ:* Agricultural Univ., Wageningen. Member: Second Chamber of States-General, Netherlands, 1956–73; European Parliament, 1958–73; Socio-Economic Adviser to Agricultural Workers' Union, Netherlands, 1950–73; Minister of Defence, 1973–76; Mem. and Vice-Pres. of Commn of European Communities (for Employment and Social Affairs), 1977–80. *Address:* Rembrandtlaan 13A, 3712 AJ Huis ter Heide, Netherlands.

VULLIAMY, Shirley, (Mrs J. S. P. Vulliamy); *see* Hughes, S.

VYNER, Clare George; *b* 1894; 2nd *s* of late Lord Alwyne Frederick Compton and Mary Evelyn, *e d* of Robert Charles de Grey Vyner, of Newby Hall, Yorks, and Gautby, Lincs; *m* 1923, Lady Doris Gordon-Lennox (*d* 1980), 2nd *d* of 8th Duke of Richmond and Gordon; one *s* (and one *s* one *d* decd). Formerly Lieut, RN, serving war of 1939–45, Commander. Assumed surname of Vyner, 1912. Formerly DL, W Riding of Yorkshire and City and Co. of York. *Address:* Keanchulish, Ullapool, Ross-shire. *T:* Ullapool 2100.

See also Marquess of Northampton.

VYSE, Lt-Gen. Sir Edward D. H.; *see* Howard-Vyse.

VYVYAN, Sir John (Stanley), 12th Bt *cr* 1645; Owner and Manager of Trelowarren Estate, since 1950 (property acquired by marriage in 1427); *b* 20 Jan. 1916; *s* of Major-General Ralph Ernest Vyvyan, CBE, MC (*d* 1971) and Vera Grace (*d* 1956), *d* of Robert Arthur Alexander; *S* cousin, 1978; *m* 1958, Jonet Noël, *d* of Lt-Col Alexander Hubert Barclay, DSO, MC; one *s* one *d* (and one *d* (decd) of former marriage). *Educ:* Charterhouse; and British-American Tobacco Co. Ltd, who sent him to London School of Oriental Studies. With British-American Tobacco Co. Ltd in England and China until War. Commissioned RCS in India, 1940 and served, 1940–46, in Arakan, Bangalore, etc; Temp. Major; GSO II Signals, Southern Army, 1944. *Recreations:* gardening, photography and books; travel when possible. *Heir:* *s* Ralph Ferrers Alexander Vyvyan, *b* 21 Aug. 1960. *Address:* Trelowarren, Mawgan, Helston, Cornwall. *T:* Mawgan 224. *Clubs:* Army and Navy; Royal Cornwall Yacht (Falmouth).

W

WACHER, David Mure; Metropolitan Stipendiary Magistrate, 1962–74, retired; *b* 9 Oct. 1909; *s* of late Dr Harold Wacher, FSA, and Violet Amy Wacher (*née* Peebles); *m* 1935, Kathleen Margaret Roche, *yr d* of late Rev. George Ralph Melvyrn Roche; one *s* one *d*. *Educ:* Charterhouse. Called to Bar, Middle Temple, 1935. Served in Royal Artillery, 1939–43. Acting Attorney-General, Gibraltar, 1943; Stipendiary Magistrate, Gibraltar, 1943–49; Acting Chief Justice, Gibraltar, 1948. Vice-Chairman, Mental Health Review Tribunal for SW Metropolitan RHB Area, 1960–62. *Recreations:* music and the theatre. *Address:* Strapp Farm House, Chiselborough, Stoke-Sub-Hamdon, Somerset TA14 6TW. *T:* Chiselborough 689.

WADDELL, Sir Alexander (Nicol Anton), KCMG 1959 (CMG 1955); DSC 1944; HM Overseas Civil Service, retired; *b* 8 Nov. 1913; *yr s* of late Rev. Alexander Waddell, Eassie, Angus, Scotland, and late Effie Thompson Anton Waddell; *m* 1949, Jean Margot Lesbia, *d* of late W. E. Masters. *Educ:* Fettes Coll., Edinburgh; Edinburgh Univ. (MA); Gonville and Caius Coll., Cambridge. Colonial Administrative Service, 1937; British Solomon Islands Protectorate: Cadet, 1937; District Officer, 1938; District Commissioner, 1945; Acting Resident Commissioner, 1945; Malayan Civil Service, 1946; Principal Asst Secretary, North Borneo, 1947–52 (Acting Dep. Chief Secretary, periods, 1947–51). Colonial Secretary, Gambia, 1952–56; Colonial Secretary, Sierra Leone, 1956–58; Dep. Governor, Sierra Leone, 1958–60; Governor and Commander-in-Chief of Sarawak, 1960–63; UK Comr, British Phosphate Commissioners, 1965–77. Mem., Panel of Independent Inspectors, Dept of the Environment, 1979–85. On Naval Service, 1942–44. Lieut, RANVR; on Military Service, 1945–47, Lt-Col, Gen. List (British Mil. Administration). *Recreations:* golf, gardening. *Address:* Pilgrim Cottage, Ashton Keynes, Wilts. *Clubs:* Naval, Royal Commonwealth Society, East India, Devonshire, Sports and Public Schools.

WADDELL, Gordon Herbert; Director, E. Oppenheimer & Son Ltd, since 1965; Chairman: Johannesburg Consolidated Investment Co. Ltd, since 1981; Rustenburg Platinum Mines Ltd, since 1981; South African Breweries Ltd, since 1984; Executive Director, Anglo American Corporation of South Africa Ltd, since 1971; *b* Glasgow, 12 April 1937; *s* of Herbert Waddell; *m* 1st, 1965, Mary (marr. diss. 1971), *d* of H. F. Oppenheimer, *qv*; 2nd, 1973, Kathy May, *d* of W. S. Gallagher. *Educ:* St Mary's Sch., Melrose; Fettes Coll., Edinburgh; Cambridge Univ. (BA); Stanford Univ. (MBA). Rugby Blue, Cambridge Univ., 1958, 1960, 1961; Member, British Isles Rugby Touring Team: to Australia and NZ, 1955; to South Africa, 1962; fourteen rugby caps for Scotland. MP (Progressive Party) for Johannesburg North, April 1974–Nov. 1977. *Recreation:* golf. *Address:* Cloud End, West Road South, Morningside, Sandton, Transvaal, SA. *Clubs:* Rand, Hawks, Muirfield, Kimberley, River, Royal and Ancient (St Andrews).

WADDELL, Sir James (Henderson), Kt 1974; CB 1960; Deputy Chairman, Police Complaints Board, 1977–81; *b* 5 Oct. 1914; *s* of D. M. Waddell and J. C. Fleming; *m* 1940, Dorothy Abbie Wright; one *s* one *d*. *Educ:* George Heriot's Sch.; Edinburgh Univ. Assistance Board, 1936; Ministry of Information, 1940; Reconnaissance Corps, 1942; Ministry of Housing and Local Government, 1946; Under-Secretary, 1955; Under-Secretary, Cabinet Office, 1961–63; Dep.-Secretary, Min. of Housing and Local Government, 1963–66; Dep. Under-Sec., Home Office, 1966–75. *Recreation:* sailing. *Address:* Oakwood, East Lavant, Chichester, Sussex. *T:* Chichester 527129.

WADDELL, Rear-Adm. William Angus, CB 1981; OBE 1966; Secretary and Chief Executive, Royal Institute of Public Health and Hygiene, since 1982; *b* 5 Nov. 1924; *s* of late James Whitefield Waddell and late Christina Maclean; *m* 1950, Thelma Evelyn Tomlins; one *s* one *d*. *Educ:* Glasgow University. BSc (Hons) Maths and Nat. Phil.; CEng; FIEE. Midshipman, Sub Lieut RNVR (Special Branch), HMS Ranee, HMS Collingwood, 1945–47; Instr Lieut, HMS Collingwood, HMS Glasgow, HMS Siskin, HMS Gambia, 1947–59 (RMCS 1956–57); Instr Comdr, HMS Albion, 1959–61; Staff of Dir, Naval Educn Service, 1961–63; Sen. British Naval Officer, Dam Neck, Virginia, 1963–66; Officer i/c RN Polaris Sch., 1966–68; Instr Captain, Staff of SACLANT (Dir, Inf. Systems Gp), 1969–72; Dean, RN Coll., Greenwich, 1973–75; Dir Naval Officer Appointments (Instr), 1975–78; Rear-Adm. 1979; Chief Naval Instructor Officer, 1978–81 and Flag Officer, Admiralty Interview Bd, 1979–81. ADC to the Queen, 1976–79. Assoc. Teacher, City Univ., 1973–75. *Publication:* An Introduction to Servomechanisms (with F. L. Westwater), 1961, repr. 1968. *Address:* c/o National Westminster Bank, 1 Lee Road, Blackheath, SE3 9RM.

WADDILOVE, Lewis Edgar, CBE 1978 (OBE 1965); JP; Deputy Chairman, Housing Corporation, 1978–83 (Member since 1968); Director, Joseph Rowntree Memorial Trust, 1961–79 (Executive Officer of the Trust, 1946–61); *b* 5 Sept. 1914; *s* of Alfred and Edith Waddilove; *m* 1st, 1940, Louise Power (*d* 1967); one *s* one *d*; 2nd, 1969, Maureen Piper. *Educ:* Westcliff High Sch.; Univ. of London (DPA). Admin. Officer, LCC Educn Dept, 1936–38; Govt Evacuation Scheme, Min. of Health, 1938–43; Friends Ambulance Unit, Middle East, 1943–45 (Exec. Chm., 1946); Chairman, Friends Service Council, 1961–67. Chm., Nat. Fedn of Housing Assocs (formerly Socs), 1965–73 and 1977–79 (Vice-Pres. 1982–); Member: Cttee on Housing in Greater London (Milner Holland), 1963–65; Nat. Cttee for Commonwealth Immigrants, 1966–68; Social Science Research Council, 1967–71; Public Schools Commn, 1968–70; Central Housing Advisory Cttee, 1960–75; Standing Cttee, Centre for Socio-Legal Studies at Oxford, 1972–75; Legal Aid Advisory Cttee, 1972–78; Adv. Cttee on Rent Rebates and Rent Allowances, 1975–81; Cttee on Voluntary Organisations, 1974–78; Working Party on Housing Cooperatives, 1974–76; Central Appeals Adv. Cttee (BBC and IBA), 1974–84 (Chm., 1978–84); Chairman:

Advisory Cttee on Fair Rents, 1973–74; Advisory Cttee on Housing Cooperatives, 1976–79; York City Charities, 1957–65 and 1972–; York Univ. Council, 1977–87; Personal Social Services Council, 1977–80; Coal Mining Subsidence Compensation Review Cttee, 1983–84; Trustee, Shelter, 1966–74 (Chm. 1970–72). Presiding Clerk, 4th World Conf. of Friends, in N Carolina, 1967. Governor, Co. of Merchant Adventurers, City of York, 1978–79. Governor: Leighton Park Sch., 1951–71; Bootham and The Mount Schs., 1972–81 (Chm. 1974–81). JP York, 1968. DUniv Brunel, 1978. *Publications:* One Man's Vision, 1954; Housing Associations (PEP), 1962; Private Philanthropy and Public Welfare, 1983; various articles in technical jls. *Address:* Red Oaks, Hawthorn Terrace, New Earswick, York YO3 8AJ. *T:* York 768696.

WADDINGTON, David Charles, QC 1971; MP (C) Ribble Valley, since 1983 (Clitheroe, March 1979–1983); Minister of State, Home Office, since 1983; a Recorder of the Crown Court, since 1972; *b* 2 Aug. 1929; *o s* of late Charles Waddington and of Mrs Minnie Hughan Waddington; *m* 1958, Gillian Rosemary, *d* of Alan Green, *qv*; three *s* two *d*. *Educ:* Sedbergh; Hertford Coll., Oxford. President, Oxford Univ. Conservative Assoc., 1950. 2nd Lieut, XII Royal Lancers, 1951–53. Called to Bar, Gray's Inn, 1951, Bencher, 1985. Contested (C): Farnworth Div., 1955; Nelson and Colne Div., 1964; Heywood and Royton Div., 1966; MP (C) Nelson and Colne, 1968–Sept. 1974; a Lord Comr, HM Treasury, 1979–81; Parly Under-Sec. of State, Dept of Employment, 1981–83. *Address:* Whins House, Sabden, near Blackburn, Lancs. *T:* Padiham 71070; 9 Denny Street, SE11.

WADDINGTON, Prof. David James; Head of Department of Chemistry, since 1984, and Pro-Vice-Chancellor, since 1985, University of York; *b* 27 May 1932; *s* of Eric James and Marjorie Edith Waddington; *m* 1957, Isobel Hesketh; two *s* one *d*. *Educ:* Marlborough College; Imperial College, Univ. of London (BSc, ARCS, DIC, PhD). Head of Chemistry Dept, 1959, Head of Science Dept, 1961, Wellington College; Sen. Lectr, 1965, Prof. of Chemical Educn, 1978, Univ. of York. Pres., Educn Div., Royal Soc. of Chem., 1981–83; Sec., 1977, Chm., 1981–86, Cttee on Teaching of Chemistry, IUPAC; Sec., Cttee on Teaching of Science, ICSU. Nyholm Medal, RSC, 1985. *Publications:* Organic Chemistry, 1962; (with H. S. Finlay) Organic Chemistry Through Experiment, 1965; (with R. O. C. Norman) Modern Organic Chemistry, 1972; (with A. Kornhauser and C. N. R. Rao) Chemical Education in the 70s, 1980; (ed) Teaching School Chemistry, 1985. *Recreations:* golf, gardening. *Address:* Murton Hall, York YO1 3UQ. *Club:* Tang Hall Horticultural Society (York).

WADDINGTON, Gerald Eugene, CBE 1975; QC (Cayman Islands) 1971; Attorney General of the Cayman Islands, 1970–April 1977; *b* 31 Jan. 1909; *o s* of Walter George Waddington and Una Blanche Waddington (*née* Hammond); *m* 1935, Hylda Kathleen (*née* Allen); one *s* one *d*. *Educ:* Jamaica Coll.; Wolmer's Schl., Jamaica. Solicitor, Supreme Court, Jamaica, 1932; LLB (London) 1949; Solicitor, Supreme Court, England, 1950; called to the Bar, Gray's Inn, 1957. Deputy Clerk of Courts, Jamaica, 1939; Asst Crown Solicitor, Jamaica, 1943–48; Resident Magistrate, 1948–58; Puisne Judge, 1959–64; Judge of the Court of Appeal, Jamaica, 1964–70, retired. Joint ed. West Indian Law Reports. Vice-Pres. Nat. Rifle Assoc. Chm. St John Council for Jamaica. CStJ 1962, KStJ 1970. *Recreation:* shooting (Member of Jamaica Rifle Team to Bisley, 1937, 1950, 1953, 1956, 1957, 1960, 1963, 1965, 1967, 1968; Captain, 1950, 1953, 1957, 1967; Captain, WI Rifle Team, 1960). *Address:* PO Box 864, Stittsville, Ontario K0A 3G0, Canada.

WADDINGTON, Very Rev. John Albert Henry, MBE 1945; TD 1951; MA (Lambeth) 1959; Provost of Bury St Edmunds, 1958–76, now Provost Emeritus; a Church Commissioner, 1972–76; *b* 10 Feb. 1910; *s* of H. Waddington, Tooting Graveney, Surrey; *m* 1938, Marguerite Elisabeth, *d* of F. Day, Wallington, Surrey; two *d*. *Educ:* Wandsworth Sch.; London Univ.; London College of Divinity. BCom London Univ., 1929. Deacon, 1933; priest, 1934; Curate of St Andrew's, Streatham, 1933–35; Curate of St Paul's, Furzedown, 1935–38; Rector of Great Bircham, 1938–45; Vicar of St Peter Mancroft, Norwich, 1945; Chaplain to High Sheriff of Norfolk, 1950; Proctor in Convocation of Canterbury, 1950; Hon. Canon of Norwich, 1951. Chaplain to Forces (TA) 1935–58; Staff Chaplain, Eighth Army, 1943 (despatches twice); DACG XIII Corps, 1945, Eastern Command TA, 1951. *Recreations:* travel, theatre and cinema, religious journalism. *Address:* The Chantry, 67 Churchgate Street, Bury St Edmunds, Suffolk IP33 1RL. *T:* Bury St Edmunds 4494.

WADDINGTON, Leslie; Managing Director, Waddington Galleries, since 1966; *b* Dublin, 9 Feb. 1934; *s* of late Victor and Zelda Waddington; *m* 1967, Ferriel Lyle (marr. diss. 1983); two *d*; *m* 1985, Clodagh Frances Fanshawe. *Educ:* Portora Royal School; Sorbonne; Ecole du Louvre (Diplômé). Formed Waddington Galleries with father, 1957. *Recreations:* chess, backgammon, ping pong, reading. *Address:* 11 Cork Street, W1. *T:* 01–437 8611.

WADDINGTON, Very Rev. Robert Murray; Dean of Manchester, since 1984; *b* 24 Oct. 1927; *s* of Percy Nevill and Dorothy Waddington. *Educ:* Dulwich Coll.; Selwyn Coll., Cambridge; Ely Theological Coll. MA (2nd cl. Theol.). Asst Curate St John's, Bethnal Green, 1953–55; Chaplain, Slade Sch., Warwick, Qld, Aust., 1955–59; Curate, St Luke's, Cambridge, 1959–61; Headmaster, St Barnabas Sch., Ravenshoe, N Qld, Aust., 1961–70; Oxford Univ. Dept of Education, 1971–72; Residentiary Canon, Carlisle Cathedral, and Bishop's Adviser for Education, 1972–77; Gen. Sec., C of E Bd of Education and Nat. Soc. for Promoting Religious Education, 1977–84. *Recreations:* cooking, films, sociology. *Address:* The Cathedral, Manchester M3 1SX. *T:* 061–834 7503; The Deanery, 44 Shrewsbury Road, Prestwich, Manchester M25 8GQ. *T:* 061–773 2959. *Club:* St James's (Manchester).

WADDS, Mrs Jean Casselman, OC 1982; Member, Royal Commission on Economic Union and Development Prospects for Canada, since 1983; *b* 16 Sept. 1920; *d* of Hon. Earl Rowe and Treva Lennox Rowe; *m* 1st, 1946, Clair Casselman; one *s* one *d*; 2nd, 1964, Robert Wadds (marr. diss. 1977). *Educ:* Univ. of Toronto (BA); Weller Business Coll. First elected to Canadian House of Commons (Riding Grenville-Dundas), 1958; re-elected: 1962, 1963, 1965; defeated (Riding Grenville-Carlton), 1968. Member, Canada's Delegn to United Nations, 1961; Parliamentary Sec. to Minister of Health and Welfare, 1962. National Sec., Progressive Conservative Party, 1971–75; Member, Ontario Municipal Bd, 1975–79. Canadian High Comr to UK, 1980–83. Freeman, City of London, 1981. Hon. DCL Acadia Univ., NS, 1981. Hon. Fellowship Award, Bretton Hall Coll., W Yorks, 1982. *Recreations:* golf, skiing, swimming. *Address:* 151 Sparks Street, Suite 1204, Ottawa, Ont K1P 5R3, Canada.

WADDY, Rev. Lawrence Heber; retired; Lecturer, University of California, San Diego, 1970–80; Hon. Assistant, St James', La Jolla, since 1974; *b* 5 Oct. 1914; *s* of late Archdeacon Stacy Waddy, Secretary of SPG, and Etheldred (*née* Spittal). *Educ:* Marlborough Coll.; Balliol Coll., Oxford. Domus Exhibitioner in Classics, Balliol, 1933; 1st Class Hon. Mods., Oxford, 1935; de Paravicini Scholar, 1935; Craven Scholar, 1935; 2nd Class Lit. Hum., 1937; BA 1937; MA 1945; Asst Master: Marlborough Coll., 1937–38; Winchester Coll., 1938–42 and 1946–49 (Chaplain, 1946). Headmaster, Tonbridge Sch., 1949–62. Select Preacher, Cambridge Univ., 1951; Oxford Univ., 1954–56. Examining Chaplain to the Bishop of Rochester, 1959–63; Hon. Canon of Rochester, 1961–63; Hon. Chaplain to the Bishop of Rochester, 1963. Deacon, 1940; Priest, 1941; Chaplain, RNVR, 1942–46. Lecturer in Classics, University of California, 1961. Education Officer, School Broadcasting Council, 1962–63; Chaplain to The Bishop's School, La Jolla, California, 1963–67; Headmaster, Santa Maria Internat. Acad., Chula Vista, Calif, 1967–70; Vicar, Church of the Good Samaritan, University City, 1970–74. *Publications:* Pax Romana and World Peace, 1950; The Prodigal Son (musical play), 1963; The Bible as Drama, 1974; Faith of Our Fathers, 1975; Symphony, 1977; Drama in Worship, 1978; Mayor's Race, 1980. *Recreations:* cricket and other games. *Address:* 5910 Camino de la Costa, La Jolla, California 92037, USA.

WADE, family name of **Baron Wade.**

WADE, Baron, *cr* 1964 (Life Peer); **Donald William Wade,** DL; MA, LLB; *b* 16 June 1904; *s* of William Mercer and Beatrice Hemington Wade; *m* 1932, Ellenora Beatrice (*née* Bentham); two *s* two *d. Educ:* Mill Hill; Trinity Hall, Cambridge. Admitted Solicitor, 1929. MP (L) Huddersfield West, 1950–64; Liberal Whip, 1956–62; Deputy Leader, Liberal Parliamentary Party, 1962–64; Deputy Liberal Whip, House of Lords, 1965–67; President, Liberal Party, 1967–68. DL, W Riding, Yorks, 1967, N Yorks, 1974. *Publications:* Democracy, 1944; Way of the West, 1945; Our Aim and Purpose, 1961; Yorkshire Survey: a report on community relations in Yorkshire, 1972; Europe and the British Health Service, 1974; (with Lord Banks) The Political Insight of Elliott Dodds, 1977; Behind the Speaker's Chair, 1978. *Address:* Meadowbank, Wath Road, Pately Bridge, Harrogate, N Yorks HG3 5PG. *Club:* National Liberal.

WADE, Maj.-Gen. (Douglas) Ashton (Lofft), CB 1946; OBE 1941; MC 1918; BA; CEng; MIEE; *b* 13 March 1898; 2nd *s* of C. S. D. Wade, Solicitor, Saffron Walden, Essex; *m* 1st, 1926, Heather Mary Patricia Bulmer (*d* 1968), Sowerby, Thirsk, Yorkshire; one *d*; 2nd, 1972, Cynthia Halliday (*née* Allen). *Educ:* St Lawrence Coll., Ramsgate; Royal Military Acad., Woolwich; Clare Coll., Cambridge. Commnd into Royal Artillery, 1916; served European War, France, Italy and S Russia; seconded RE 1918–21; transferred to Royal Signals, 1921; Staff Coll., Camberley, 1933–34; DAQMG India, 1937–40; GSO 1, GHQ, BEF and GHQ Home Forces, 1940–41; AA and QMG 2nd Division, 1941–42; Dep. Ajt.-General, India, 1942–44; Comdr, Madras Area, India, 1944–47; GOC Malaya District, 1947–48; Mem., Indian Armed Forces Nationalisation Cttee, 1947; Special Appointment War Office, 1948–49; retired, 1950; Telecommunications Attaché, British Embassy, Washington, 1951–54; Sen. Planning Engineer, Independent Television Authority, 1954–60; Regional Officer, East Anglia, Independent Television Authority, 1960–64. Technical Consultant: Inter-University Research Unit, Cambridge, 1965–69; WRVS Headquarters, 1970–75. Chm., South East Forum for closed circuit TV in educn, 1967–73. Chm., Royal Signals Institute, 1957–63; National Vice-Chairman Dunkirk Veterans' Association, 1962–67, National Chairman, 1967–74. *Publications:* contributed to various Services publications, including RUSI Journal, United Services Journal (India), and Brassey's Annual. *Recreation:* gardening. *Address:* Phoenix Cottage, 6 Church Street, Old Catton, Norwich NR6 7DS. *T:* Norwich 45755.

WADE, Prof. Sir (Henry) William (Rawson), Kt 1985; QC 1968; FBA 1969; MA; LLD (Cantab); DCL (Oxon); Master of Gonville and Caius College, Cambridge, since 1976; Barrister-at-Law; *b* 16 Jan. 1918; *s* of late Colonel H. O. Wade and of E. L. Rawson-Ackroyd; *m* 1st, 1943, Marie (*d* 1980), *d* of late G. E. Osland-Hill; two *s*; 2nd, 1982, Marjorie, *d* of late Surgeon-Capt. H. Hope-Gill, RN, and *widow* of B. C. Browne. *Educ:* Shrewsbury Sch. (Governor, 1977–85); Gonville and Caius Coll., Cambridge. Henry Fellow, Harvard Univ., 1939; temp. officer, Treasury, 1940–46. Called to the Bar, Lincoln's Inn, 1946; Hon. Bencher, 1964. Fellow of Trinity Coll., Cambridge, 1946–61; University Lecturer, 1947; Reader, 1959; Prof. of English Law, Oxford Univ., 1961–76; Fellow, St John's College, Oxford, 1961–76, Hon. Fellow, 1976; Rouse Ball Prof. of English Law, Cambridge Univ., 1978–82. Lectr, Council of Legal Education, 1957; British Council Lectr in Scandinavia, 1958, and Turkey, 1959; Cooley Lectr, Michigan Univ., 1961; Vithalbai Patel Lectr, New Delhi, 1971; Chettyar Lectr, Madras, 1974; Chitaley Lectr, New Delhi, 1982. Vice-Pres., British Acad., 1981–83. Member: Council on Tribunals, 1958–71; Relationships Commn, Uganda, 1961; Royal Commn on Tribunals of Inquiry, 1966. *Publications:* The Law of Real Property, 1957 (with Rt Hon. Sir Robert Megarry) 5th edn, 1984; Administrative Law, 1961, 5th edn, 1982; Towards Administrative Justice, 1963; (with Prof. B. Schwartz) Legal Control of Government, 1972; Constitutional Fundamentals (Hamlyn Lectures), 1980; articles in legal journals; broadcast talks. *Recreations:* climbing, gardening. *Address:* Master's Lodge, Caius College, Cambridge. *T:* Cambridge 332404. *Clubs:* Alpine, United Oxford & Cambridge University.

WADE, Joseph Frederick; General Secretary, National Graphical Association, 1976–84; Visiting Professor, University of Strathclyde, since 1985; *b* 18 Dec. 1919; *s* of James and Ellen Wade; *m* Joan Ann; two *s. Educ:* elementary sch., Blackburn, Lancs. Trained as compositor, The Blackburn Times, 1934–40; served UK and overseas, East Lancs Regt and RAOC, 1940–46; newspaper compositor, 1946–56. Full-time Trade Union official, Typographical Assoc., 1956; Nat. Officer, NGA, 1964; Asst Gen. Sec., NGA, 1968; Gen. Sec., NGA, 1976, NGA '82 (after amalgamation) 1982. Member: Exec. Cttee, Printing and Kindred Trades Fedn, 1971–74; Exec. Cttee, Internat. Graphical Fedn, 1976–85 (Vice-Pres.); TUC Printing Industries Cttee, 1976–84; TUC Gen. Council, 1983–84; Printing and Publishing Industry Training Bd, 1977–82; Printing Industries EDC, 1979–84. Mem., Blackburn County Borough Council, 1952–56. *Recreations:* walking, Scrabble, gardening. *Address:* 13 Wilden Road, Renhold, Bedfordshire MK41 0JR.

WADE, Sir Oulton; see Wade, Sir W. O.

WADE, Prof. Owen Lyndon, CBE 1983; MD, FRCP; Professor of Therapeutics and Clinical Pharmacology, 1971–86, Pro-Vice-Chancellor and Vice-Principal, 1985–86, University of Birmingham; *b* 17 May 1921; *s* of J. O. D. Wade, MS, FRCS, and Kate Wade, Cardiff; *m* 1948, Margaret Burton, LDS; three *d. Educ:* Repton; Cambridge; University College Hospital, London. Senior Scholar, Emmanuel Coll., Cambridge, 1941; Achison and Atkinson Morley Schol., UCH, 1945; Resident Medical Officer, UCH, 1946; Clinical Assistant, Pneumoconiosis Research Unit of the Medical Research Council, 1948–51; Lecturer and Sen. Lecturer in Medicine, Dept of Medicine, University of Birmingham, 1951–57; Whitla Prof. of Therapeutics and Pharmacology, Queen's Univ., Belfast, 1957–71; Dean, Faculty of Medicine and Dentistry, Univ. of Birmingham, 1978–84. Rockefeller Travelling Fellowship in Medicine, 1954–55; Research Fellow, Columbia Univ. at Department of Medicine, Presbyterian Hospital, New York, 1954–55; Consultant, WHO. Chm., Cttee on the Review of Medicines, 1978–84; Chm., Jt Formulary Cttee for British Nat. Formulary, 1978–86. Mem. GMC, 1981–84. *Publications:* (with J. M. Bishop) The Cardiac Output and Regional Blood Flow, 1962; Adverse Reactions to Drugs, 1970, 2nd edn with L. Beeley, 1976; papers on cardiorespiratory research, adverse reactions to drugs and drug use in the community, in Jl Physiology, Clinical Science, Brit. Med. Bull., Jl Clin. Invest. *Recreations:* books, travel and sailing. *Address:* c/o The Medical School, Birmingham University. *Club:* Athenæum.

WADE, R(obert) Hunter; New Zealand diplomat, retired; *b* 14 June 1916; *s* of R. H. Wade, Balclutha, NZ; *m* 1941, Avelda Grace Petersen; two *s* two *d. Educ:* Waitaki; Otago Univ. NZ Treasury and Marketing Depts, 1939; NZ Govt diplomatic appts, Delhi, Simla, Sydney, Canberra, 1941–49; Head of Eastern Political Div., Dept of External Affairs, Wellington, NZ, 1949; NZ Embassy, Washington, 1951; NZ High Commn, Ottawa, 1956; Director of Colombo Plan Bureau, Colombo, 1957; Dir, External Aid, Wellington, 1959; Comr for NZ in Singapore and British Borneo, 1962; High Comr in Malaya/Malaysia, 1963–67; Dep. High Comr in London, 1967–69; NZ Ambassador to Japan and Korea, 1969–71; Dep. Sec.-Gen. of the Commonwealth, 1972–75; NZ Ambassador to Federal Republic of Germany and to Switzerland, 1975–78. Represented New Zealand at Independence of: Uganda, 1962; Botswana, 1966; Lesotho, 1966. Pres., Asiatic Soc. of Japan, 1971. *Address:* 12 Pleasant Place, Howick, Auckland, New Zealand.

WADE, Major-General Ronald Eustace, CB 1961; CBE 1956; retired; *b* 28 Oct. 1905; *s* of late Rev. E. V. Wade and Marcia Wade; *m* 1933, Doris, *d* of late C. K. Ross, Kojonup, WA; one *s* one *d. Educ:* Melbourne Church of England Grammar Sch.; RMC, Duntroon. ACT. Commissioned, 1927; attached 4/7 DG (India), 1928–29; Adjutant 10 LH and 9 LH, 1930–38; Captain, 1935; Major, 1940; served War of 1939–45, Lieut-Colonel (CO 2/10 Aust. Armd Regt), 1942; Colonel (Colonel A, Adv. LHQ, Morotai), 1945; Colonel Q, AHQ, Melbourne, 1946; idc 1948; Director of Cadets, 1949; Director of Quartering, 1950–51; Director of Personal Services, 1951–52; Military Secretary, 1952–53; Comd 11 Inf. Bde (Brig.), 1953–55; Maj.-General (Head Aust. Joint Service Staff, Washington), 1956–57; Adjutant-General, 1957–60; GOC Northern Command, 1961–62, retired, 1962. *Address:* Windsor, 8/20 Comer Street, Como, WA 6152, Australia.

WADE, Rosalind (Herschel), (Mrs R. H. Seymour), OBE 1985; novelist; Editor, Contemporary Review, since 1970; *d* of Lieut-Colonel H. A. L. H. Wade and Kathleen Adelaide Wade; *m* William Kean Seymour, FRSL (*d* 1975); two *s. Educ:* Glendower Sch., London; privately, abroad and Bedford Coll., London. Member: Society of Women Writers and Journalists (Chairman, 1962–64, Vice President, 1965–); Committee West Country Writers Assoc., 1953–65 (Vice-Pres., 1975–); General and Exec. Councils, The Poetry Society Inc., 1962–64, 1965–66; Guildford Centre of Poetry Soc. (Chm. 1969–71); Alresford Historical and Literary Soc. (Chm. 1968–70, 1972–73); Literature Panel, Southern Arts Assoc., 1973–75; conducting Writing and Literary Courses at Moor Park College, Farnham (jointly with William Kean Seymour, 1962–74), Writers' Workshop, 1976–81. Editor, PEN Broadsheet, 1975–77. *Publications:* novels: As the Narcissus, 1946; The Widows, 1948; The Raft, 1950; The Falling Leaves, 1951; Alys at Endon, 1953; The Silly Dove, 1953; Cassandra Calls, 1954; Come Fill The Cup, 1955; Morning Break, 1956; Mrs Jamison's Daughter, 1957; The Grain Will Grow, 1959; The Will of Heaven, 1960; A Small Shower, 1961; The Ramerson Case, 1962; New Pasture, 1964; The Vanished Days, 1966; Ladders, 1968; The Umbrella, 1970; The Golden Bowl, 1970; Mrs Medlend's Private World, 1973; Red Letter Day: Twelve Stories of Cornwall, 1980; *contributor to:* The Fourth Ghost Book, 1965; The Unlikely Ghosts, 1967; Happy Christmas, 1968; Haunted Cornwall, 1973; People Within, 1974; Cornish Harvest, 1974; Tales from the Macabre, 1976; My Favourite Story, 1977; More Tales from the Macabre, 1979; Women Writing, 1979; Stories of Haunted Inns, 1983; Ghosts in Country Villages, 1983; Phantom Lovers, 1984; After Midnight Stories, I, 1985, II, 1986; Contemporary Review, Poetry Review, Books and Bookmen, Cornish Review, etc. *Recreations:* walking, theatre and historical research. *Address:* 4 Dollis Drive, Guildford Road, Farnham, Surrey GU9 9QD. *T:* Farnham 713883. *Club:* Royal Commonwealth Society.

WADE, Air Chief Marshal Sir Ruthven (Lowry), KCB 1974 (CB 1970); DFC 1944; Chief of Personnel and Logistics, Ministry of Defence, 1976–78, retired 1978; Director, Acatos and Hutcheson, since 1979; *b* 1920. *Educ:* Cheltenham Coll.; RAF Coll., Cranwell. RAF, 1939; served War of 1939–45, UK and Mediterranean (DFC), psa, 1953; HQ 2nd Tactical Air Force, Germany; RAF Flying Coll.; Gp Captain 1960; Staff Officer, Air HQ, Malta; Comdr, Bomber Comd station, RAF Gaydon, 1962–65; Air Cdre, 1964; idc 1965; Air Exec. to Deputy for Nuclear Affairs, SHAPE, 1967–68; AOC No 1 (Bomber) Gp, Strike Comd, 1968–71; Air Vice-Marshal, 1968; Dep. Comdr, RAF Germany, 1971–72; ACAS (Ops), 1973; Vice Chief of Air Staff, 1973–76; Air Marshal, 1974; Air Chief Marshal, 1976. *Address:* White Gables, Westlington, Dinton, Aylesbury, Bucks HP17 8UR. *T:* Stone 8884.

WADE, (Sarah) Virginia, OBE 1986 (MBE 1969); tennis player and commentator; *b* 10 July 1945; *d* of Eustace Holland Wade and Joan Barbara Wade. *Educ:* Sussex Univ. (BSc). Won tennis championships: US Open, 1968; Italian, 1971; Australian, 1972; Wimbledon, 1977; played for GB in Wightman Cup and Federation Cup 20 times (record); Captain, GB team. Mem. Cttee, All England Lawn Tennis Club, 1983–. Hon. LLD Sussex, 1985. *Publications:* Courting Triumph, 1978; Ladies of the Court, 1984. *Address:* Sharsted Court, near Sittingbourne, Kent. *T:* Sittingbourne 89223.

WADE, Sir William; see Wade, Sir H. W. R.

WADE, Sir (William) Oulton, Kt 1982; JP; farmer and company director; Chairman and Managing Director: William Wild & Son (Mollington) Ltd; Wilds Farm (Cheese Exports) Ltd; Mollington Farmhouse Cheese Co.; Cheshire Hybrids. Chairman and President, British Royal Foods Ltd, New York; Chairman: Marlow Wade and Partners Ltd, Consultants; Kendal Stuart Ltd (Grain Merchants); Joint Treasurer, Conservative Party, since 1982; *b* 24 Dec. 1932; *s* of Samuel Norman Wade and Joan Ferris Wade (*née* Wild); *m* 1959 Gillian Margaret Leete, Buxton, Derbys; one *s* one *d. Educ:* Birkenhead Sch.; Queen's Univ., Belfast. Mem., Food from Britain Export Cttee. JP Cheshire 1967.

Freeman, City of London, 1980; Liveryman, Farmers' Co., 1980–. *Publications:* contribs to Dairy Industries Internat., Jl of Soc. of Dairy Technol. *Recreations:* politics, reading, shooting, food, travel. *Address:* Chorlton Lodge, Chorlton-by-Backford, Chester CH2 4DB. *T:* Chester 381451. *Clubs:* Carlton, Farmers'; Chester City, Grosvenor (Chester); St James's (Manchester).

WADE-GERY, Sir Robert (Lucian), KCMG 1983 (CMG 1979); KCVO 1983; HM Diplomatic Service; High Commissioner to India, since 1982; *b* 22 April 1929; *o s* of late Prof. H. T. Wade-Gery; *m* 1962, Sarah, *er d* of A. D. Marris, CMG; one *s* one *d*. *Educ:* Winchester; New Coll., Oxford. 1st cl. Hon. Mods 1949 and Lit. Hum. 1951; Hon. Fellow, 1985. Fellow, All Souls Coll., Oxford, 1951–73. Joined HM Foreign (now Diplomatic) Service, 1951; FO (Economic Relations Dept), 1951–54; Bonn, 1954–57; FO (Private Sec. to Perm. Under-Sec., later Southern Dept), 1957–60; Tel Aviv, 1961–64; FO (Planning Staff), 1964–67; Saigon, 1967–68; Cabinet Office (Sec. to Duncan Cttee), 1968–69; Counsellor 1969; on loan to Bank of England, 1969; Head of Financial Policy and Aid Dept, FCO, 1969–70; Under-Sec., Central Policy Review Staff, Cabinet Office, 1971–73; Minister, Madrid, 1973–77; Minister, Moscow, 1977–79; Dep. Sec. of the Cabinet, 1979–82. *Recreations:* walking, sailing, travel. *Address:* c/o Foreign and Commonwealth Office, SW1; Church Cottage, Cold Aston, Cheltenham. *T:* Cotswold 21115. *Club:* Athenæum.

WADSWORTH, James Patrick, QC 1981; barrister; a Recorder of the Crown Court, since 1980; *b* 7 Sept. 1940; *s* of Francis Thomas Bernard Wadsworth, Newcastle, and Geraldine Rosa (*née* Brannan); *m* 1963, Judith Stuart Morrison, *e d* of Morrison Scott, Newport-on-Tay; one *s* one *d*. *Educ:* Stonyhurst; University Coll., Oxford (MA). Called to the Bar, Inner Temple, 1963. *Recreations:* eating, idling. *Address:* 4 Paper Buildings, Temple, EC4. *T:* 01–353 3366.

WADSWORTH, Vivian Michael, DSc; former Chairman of several public and private companies, retired 1986; *b* 12 April 1921; *s* of Frank Wadsworth and Tillie Wadsworth (*née* Widdop); *m* 1943, Ethel Mary Rigby; three *s* four *d*. *Educ:* Univs of Reading (BScAgric), Bristol, Leeds, and Natal, S Africa (MA, DSc). Economics Lectr, Bristol, Leeds and Natal Univs, 1942–49; Economic Adviser to Govt of S Rhodesia, 1949–55; Under Secretary for Agriculture, Fedn of Rhodesia and Nyasaland, 1955–61; Asst Sec. to Industrial Division, and Principal Economic Adviser, Distillers Co., 1961–63; Man. Dir, Fabrica Nacional de Margerina (SARL), Lisbon, Portugal (food company and former Distillers subsidiary), 1963–68; Tanganyika Concessions: Dir, Chief Exec. and Chm. of all UK subsidiaries, of which Elbar Group Industrial Holding Co. was the principal, 1968–83; Dir, Benguela Railway, Angola, 1974–83; Chm., Harland and Wolff Ltd, Belfast, 1981–83. CBIM. *Recreations:* gardening, travel, walking. *Address:* High Walls, Houndscroft, near Stroud, Glos GL5 5DG. *T:* Amberley 2434. *Club:* Buck's.

WAECHTER, Sir (Harry Leonard) d'Arcy, 2nd Bt, *cr* 1911; Lieut, RASC; *b* 22 May 1912; *s* of 1st Bt and Josephine (*d* 1955), *o d* of late John d'Arcy, of Corbetstown, Westmeath; *S* father, 1929; *m* 1939, Philippa Margaret (marr. diss. 1957), *y d* of late James Frederick Twinberrow, Suckley, Worcestershire. *Educ:* Pangbourne Nautical School. Lieut, East Yorkshire Regt (SR), 1931–35; Lieut, RASC, 1942–47; Captain, Worcestershire Regt, GSO 3 159 Inf. Bde (TA), 1947–48; Captain, TARO, 1949. Joint MFH North Ledbury. *Heir:* none. *Recreation:* hunting.

WAGNER, Sir Anthony (Richard), KCB 1978; KCVO 1961 (CVO 1953); DLitt, MA, Oxon; FSA; Clarenceux King of Arms, since 1978; Director, Heralds' Museum, Tower of London, 1978–83; Kt Principal, Imperial Society of Knights Bachelor, 1962–83; Secretary of Order of the Garter, 1952–61; Joint Register of Court of Chivalry, since 1954; Editor, Society of Antiquaries' Dictionary of British Arms, since 1940; *b* 6 Sept. 1908; *o s* of late Orlando Henry Wagner, 90 Queen's Gate, SW7, and late Monica, *d* of late Rev. G. E. Bell, Henley in Arden; *m* 1953, Gillian Mary Millicent (*see* G. M. M. Wagner); two *s* one *d*. *Educ:* Eton (King's Scholar); Balliol Coll., Oxford (Robin Hollway Scholar; Hon. Fellow, 1979). Portcullis Pursuivant, 1931–43. Richmond Herald, 1943–61; Garter King of Arms, 1961–78; served in WO, 1939–43; Ministry of Town and Country Planning, 1943–46; Private Secretary to Minister, 1944–45; Secretary (1945–46), member, 1947–66, Advisory Cttee on Buildings of special architectural or historic interest. Registrar of College of Arms, 1953–60; Genealogist: the Order of the Bath, 1961–72; the Order of St John, 1961–75. Inspector of Regtl Colours, 1961–77. President: Chelsea Soc., 1967–73; Aldeburgh Soc., 1970–83. Mem. Council, Nat. Trust, 1953–74; Trustee, Nat. Portrait Gallery, 1973–80; Chm. of Trustees, Marc Fitch Fund, 1971–77. Master, Vintners' Co., 1973–74. Hon. Fellow, Heraldry Soc. of Canada, 1976. KStJ. *Publications:* Catalogue of the Heralds' Commemorative Exhibition, 1934 (compiler); Historic Heraldry of Britain, 1939, repr. 1972; Heralds and Heraldry in the Middle Ages, 1939; Heraldry in England, 1946; Catalogue of English Mediæval Rolls of Arms, 1950; The Records and Collections of the College of Arms, 1952; English Genealogy, 1960, 1983; English Ancestry, 1961; Heralds of England, 1967; Pedigree and Progress, 1975; Heralds and Ancestors, 1978; Stephen Martin Leake's Heraldo-Memoriale (Roxburghe Club), 1982; The Wagners of Brighton, 1983 (jt author); How Lord Birkenhead Saved the Heralds, 1987; genealogical and heraldic articles, incl. in Chambers's Encyclopædia. *Address:* College of Arms, Queen Victoria Street, EC4. *T:* 01–248 4300; 68 A Chelsea Square, SW3. *T:* 01–352 0934; Wyndham Cottage, Aldeburgh, Suffolk. *T:* Aldeburgh 2596. *Clubs:* Athenæum, Garrick, Beefsteak.

WAGNER, Gerrit Abram, KBE (Hon.) 1977 (CBE (Hon.) 1964); Kt, Order of Netherlands Lion, 1969; Grand Officer, Order of Oranje Nassau, 1983 (Commander 1977); Chairman Supervisory Board, Royal Dutch Petroleum Co., since 1977 (President, 1971–77); *b* 21 Oct. 1916; *m* 1946, M. van der Heul; one *s* three *d*. *Educ:* Leyden Univ. LLM 1939. After a period in a bank in Rotterdam and in Civil Service in Rotterdam and The Hague, joined Royal Dutch Shell Group, 1946; assignments in The Hague, Curaçao, Venezuela, London and Indonesia; apptd Man. Dir, Royal Dutch Petroleum Co. and Shell Petroleum Co. Ltd; Mem. Presidium of Bd of Directors of Shell Petroleum NV, 1964; Dir, Shell Canada Ltd, 1971–77; Chm., Cttee of Man. Dirs, Royal Dutch/Shell Group, 1972–77; Chm., Shell Oil USA, 1972–77. Chairman: De Nederlandsche Bank NV; Gist-Brocades NV; Supervisory Bd, KLM; Vice-Chm., Supervisory Bd, Hoogovens Gp BV, Beverwijk; Member, International Advisory Committee: Chase Manhattan Bank, NY; Robert Bosch, Stuttgart. Order of Francisco de Miranda, Grand Officer (Venezuela), 1965; Officier Légion d'Honneur (France), 1974. *Address:* c/o Royal Dutch Petroleum Company, 30 Carel van Bylandtlaan, The Hague, The Netherlands.

WAGNER, Gillian Mary Millicent, (Lady Wagner), OBE 1977; Chairman, Volunteer Centre, since 1984; *b* 25 Oct. 1927; *e d* of late Major Henry Archibald Roger Graham, and of Hon. Margaret Beatrix, *d* of 1st Baron Roborough; *m* 1953, Sir Anthony Wagner, *qv*; two *s* one *d*. *Educ:* Cheltenham Ladies' Coll.; Geneva Univ. (Licence ès Sciences Morales); London Sch. of Economics (Dip. Social Admin). PhD London 1977. Mem. Council, Dr Barnado's, 1969– (Chm., Exec./Finance Cttee, 1973–78; Chm. Council, 1978–84); Chm., Review of Residential Care, 1986–. Governor, Thomas Coram Foundation for Children; Mem. Exec. Cttee, Georgian Group, 1970–78; President: Nat. Bureau Handicapped Students, 1978–; IAPS, 1985–. Chm. of Governors, Felixstowe Coll., 1980–. Trustee, Carnegie UK Trust, 1980–. *Publications:* Barnardo, 1979; Children of the Empire, 1982; The Chocolate Conscience, 1987. *Recreations:* sailing, gardening, travelling. *Address:* 68 A Chelsea Square, SW3. *T:* 01–352 0934; Wyndham Cottage, Crespigny Road, Aldeburgh, Suffolk. *T:* Aldeburgh 2596. *Club:* Aldeburgh Yacht.

WAGNER, Jean; Luxembourg Ambassador to the Court of St James's, since 1986; *b* 31 May 1924; *m* 1957, Laura Wissiak; one *s* two *d*. *Educ:* Univs of Bâle, Lausanne and Paris; Collège d'Europe, Bruges (LLD). Luxembourg Bar, 1951–55; Foreign Ministry, 1954; Delegate to 11th session, UN Gen. Assembly, 1956–57; Counsellor, Paris, 1959–64; Perm. Rep. to Council of Europe, 1964–69; Dir, Political Affairs, Foreign Ministry, 1965–69; Ambassador: to USA (also accredited to Mexico and Canada), 1969–74; to Italy, 1974–81; to Vatican, 1981; Sec. Gen., Foreign Affairs, 1981–84; Ambassador to Belgium (and NATO), 1984–86. Commandeur de l'Ordre National de la Couronne de Chêne; Commandeur avec Couronne de l'Ordre de Mérite civil et militaire d'Adolphe de Nassau (Cour grand-ducale); Grand Officier de l'Ordre national du Mérite; numerous foreign orders and decorations. *Address:* Luxembourg Embassy, 27 Wilton Crescent, SW1X 8SD. *T:* 01–235 6961.

WAGSTAFF, Ven. Christopher John Harold; Archdeacon of Gloucester, since 1982; *b* 25 June 1936; *s* of Harold Maurice Wagstaff and Kathleen Mary Wagstaff (*née* Bean); *m* 1964, Margaret Louise (*née* Macdonald); two *s* one *d*. *Educ:* Bishop's Stortford College, Herts; Essex Inst. of Agriculture, Chelmsford (Dipl. in Horticulture 1959); St David's Coll., Lampeter (BA 1962, Dipl. in Theol. 1963). Deacon 1963, priest 1964; Curate, All Saints, Queensbury, 1963–68; Vicar, St Michael's, Tokyngton, Wembley, 1968–73; Vicar of Coleford with Staunton, 1973–83; RD, South Forest, 1975–82. Chairman: House of Clergy; Gloucester Dio. Bd of Social Responsibility. Freeman, City of London; Liveryman, Worshipful Co. of Armourers and Brasiers. *Recreations:* gardening, walking, travel. *Address:* Christchurch Vicarage, Montpellier, Gloucester GL1 1LB. *T:* Gloucester 28500.

WAGSTAFF, David St John Rivers; a Recorder of the Crown Court, since 1974; barrister; *b* 22 June 1930; *s* of late Prof. John Edward Pretty Wagstaff and Dorothy Margaret (*née* McRobie); *m* 1970, Dorothy Elizabeth Starkie; two *d*. *Educ:* Winchester Coll. (Schol.); Trinity Coll., Cambridge (Schol., MA, LLB). Called to Bar, Lincoln's Inn, 1954. *Recreations:* mountaineering, fencing. *Address:* 8 Breary Lane East, Bramhope, Leeds. *Clubs:* Alpine; Fell and Rock Climbing (Lake District), Leeds (Leeds).

WAGSTAFF, Edward Malise Wynter; HM Diplomatic Service; Counsellor, Foreign and Commonwealth Office, since 1982; *b* 27 June 1930; *s* of Col Henry Wynter Wagstaff, *qv* and Jean Mathieson, MB, BS; *m* 1957, Eva Margot, *d* of Erik Hedelius; one *s* two *d*. *Educ:* Wellington Coll.; RMA Sandhurst; Pembroke Coll., Cambridge (MA; Mech Scis Tripos); Staff Coll., Camberley; psc. Commissioned RE, 1949; served in UK, Germany and Gibraltar, 1950–62; seconded to Federal Regular Army, Fedn of S Arabia, 1963–65; Asst Mil. Attaché, Amman, 1967–69 (Major, 1962; GSM; South Arabia Radfan bar). Joined FCO, 1969; served Saigon, 1973, FCO, 1975, Oslo, 1976, Copenhagen, 1978, FCO, 1981. Kt, First Degree, Order of Dannebrog, 1979. *Recreations:* God, concern for the bewildered, plumbing. *Address:* St Andrews, Ashwood Road, Woking, Surrey. *T:* Woking 61110. *Club:* Travellers'.

WAGSTAFF, Colonel Henry Wynter, CSI 1945; MC 1917; FCIT; RE (retired); *b* 19 July 1890; *s* of Edward Wynter Wagstaff and Flora de Smidt; *m* 1st, 1918, Jean, MB, BS, *d* of George Frederick Mathieson; two *s*; 2nd, 1967, Margaret, *o d* of late Sir John Hubert Marshall, CIE. *Educ:* Woodbridge; RMA, Woolwich. Commissioned RE 1910; served in India and Mesopotamia in European War, 1914–18 (despatches, MC); Captain, 1916; seconded Indian State Railways, 1921; Major, 1927; Lieut-Colonel, 1934; Colonel, 1940. 1929–46, employed on problems connected with Labour in general and Railway Labour in particular. Member, Railway Board, Government of India, New Delhi, 1942–46; retired, 1948. *Publication:* Operation of Indian Railways in Recent Years, 1931. *Recreations:* reading and writing. *Address:* c/o Lloyds Bank, 6 Pall Mall, SW1.
See also E. M. W. Wagstaff.

WAHLSTRÖM, General Jarl Holger; International Leader of The Salvation Army, 1981–July 1986; *b* 9 July 1918; *s* of Rafael Alexander Wahlström and Aina Maria Wahlström (*née* Dahlberg); *m* 1944, Maire Helfrid Nyberg; two *s* one *d*. *Educ:* Salvation Army International Training Coll. Salvation Army, Finland: Corps Officer, 1939–45; Scout Organizer, 1945–52; Private Sec. to Territorial Commander, 1952–54; Youth Sec., 1954–60; Divisional Comdr, 1960–63; Principal, Training Coll., 1963–68; Chief Secretary, 1968–72; Territorial Comdr, 1976–80; Salvation Army, Canada and Bermuda: Chief Secretary, 1972–76; Salvation Army, Sweden: Territorial Comdr, 1981. Hon. DHL Western Illinois, 1985. Cross of Liberty, IV cl., Finland, 1941; Knight, Order of Lion of Finland, 1964; Order of Civil Merit, Mugunghwa Medal, Republic of Korea, 1983. *Publications:* contribs to Salvation Army papers and magazines, English, Finnish, Swedish. *Recreation:* music. *Address:* 101 Queen Victoria Street, EC4P 4EP. *T:* 01–236 5222; 5/53 Wickham Road, Beckenham, Kent; (from July 1986) Borgströminkuja 1 A 10, 00840 Helsinki, Finland.

WAIAPU, Bishop of, since 1983; **Rt. Rev. Peter Geoffrey Atkins;** *b* 29 April 1936; *s* of late Lt-Col Owen Ivan Atkins and of Mrs Mary Atkins; *m* 1968, Rosemary Elizabeth (*née* Allen); one *d*. *Educ:* Merchant Taylors' School, Crosby, Liverpool; Sidney Sussex Coll., Cambridge; St John's Coll., Auckland, NZ. MA (Cantab), BD (Otago), LTh (NZ). Deacon 1962, priest 1963; Curate, Karori Parish, Wellington, 1962–66; Priest-Tutor, St Peter's Theological Coll., Siota, Solomon Is, 1966–67; Curate, Dannevirke Parish, dio. Waiapu, 1968–70; Vicar of Waipukurau Parish, 1970–73; Diocesan Sec. and Registrar, Diocese of Waiapu, 1973–79; Canon of St John's Cathedral, Napier, 1974–79; Vicar of Havelock North, 1979–83; Archdeacon of Hawkes Bay, 1979–83; Vicar-Gen., Diocese of Waiapu, 1980–83; Commissary to Archbishop of NZ, 1983. *Recreations:* gardening, tennis, music. *Address:* Bishop's House, 8 Cameron Terrace, Napier, NZ. *T:* (64–70) 57846; (office) Box 227, Napier, NZ. *T:* (64–70) 58230.

WAIN, John Barrington, CBE 1984; author; Professor of Poetry, University of Oxford, 1973–78; *b* 14 March 1925; *e surv. s* of Arnold A. Wain and Anne Wain, Stoke-on-Trent; *m* 1960, Eirian, *o d* of late T. E. James; three *s*. *Educ:* The High Sch., Newcastle-under-Lyme; St John's Coll., Oxford (Hon. Fellow, 1985). Fereday Fellow, St John's Coll., Oxford, 1946–49; Lecturer in English Literature, University of Reading, 1947–55; resigned to become freelance author and critic. Churchill Visiting Prof., University of Bristol, 1967; Vis. Prof., Centre Universitaire Expérimentale de Vincennes, Paris, 1969. First Fellow in creative arts, Brasenose College, Oxford, 1971–72, Supernumerary Fellow, 1973–. Pres., Johnson Soc. of Lichfield, 1976–77. FRSL 1960, resigned 1961. Hon. DLitt: Keele, 1985; Loughborough, 1985. *Publications include: fiction:* Hurry On Down, 1953, repr. 1978; Living in the Present, 1955; The Contenders, 1958; A Travelling Woman, 1959; Nuncle and other stories, 1960; Strike the Father Dead, 1962; The Young Visitors, 1965; Death of the Hind Legs and other stories, 1966; The Smaller Sky, 1967; A Winter in the Hills, 1970; The Life Guard and Other Stories, 1971; The Pardoner's Tale, 1978; Lizzie's Floating Shop, 1981; Young Shoulders, 1982 (Whitbread Prize) (televised, BBC,

1984); *plays*: stage: Harry in the Night, 1975; radio: You Wouldn't Remember, 1978; Frank, 1983; Good Morning Blues, 1986; *poetry*: A Word Carved on a Sill, 1956; Weep Before God, 1961; Wildtrack, 1965; Letters to Five Artists, 1969; Feng, 1975; Poems 1949–79, 1981; *criticism*: Preliminary Essays, 1957; Essays on Literature and Ideas, 1963; The Living World of Shakespeare, 1964, new edn 1979; A House for the Truth, 1972; Professing Poetry, 1977; *biography*: Samuel Johnson, 1974, new edn 1980 (James Tait Black Meml Prize; Heinemann Award, 1975); *autobiography*: Sprightly Running, 1962; Dear Shadows: portraits from memory, 1986; much work as editor, anthologist, reviewer, broadcaster, etc. *Recreations*: wet country walks; travelling by train, especially in France. *Address*: c/o Century Hutchinson Ltd, 62–65 Chandos Place, WC2.

WAIN, Prof. Ralph Louis, CBE 1968; DSc, PhD; FRS 1960, FRSC; Hon. Professor of Chemistry, University of Kent, since 1977 and Emeritus Professor, University of London, since 1978; Professor of Agricultural Chemistry, University of London, 1950–78, and Head of Department of Physical Sciences at Wye College (University of London), 1945–78; Hon. Director, Agricultural Research Council Unit on Plant Growth Substances and Systemic Fungicides, 1953–78; Fellow of Wye College, since 1981; *b* 29 May 1911; 2nd *s* of late G. Wain, Hyde, Cheshire; *m* 1940, Joan Bowker; one *s* one *d*. *Educ*: County Grammar Sch., Hyde, Cheshire; University of Sheffield (First Class Hons Chemistry, 1932; MSc 1933; PhD 1935; Hon. DSc 1977); DSc London, 1949; Town Trustees Fellow, University of Sheffield, 1934; Research Assistant, University of Manchester, 1935–37; Lecturer in Chemistry, Wye Coll., 1937–39; Research Chemist, Long Ashton Research Station (University of Bristol), 1939–45; Rockefeller Fellow, 1950 and 1962. Vice-President, Royal Institute of Chemistry, 1961–64, 1975–78; Member: Governing Body, Glasshouse Crops Res. Inst., 1953–71; E African Natural Resources Res. Council, 1963–; Manager, Royal Instn, 1971–74. Chm., AFRC Wain Fellowships Cttee, 1976–. Nuffield Vis. Prof., Ibadan Univ., 1959; Vis. Prof., Cornell Univ., 1966; NZ Prestige Fellowship, 1973; Leverhulme Emeritus Fellowship, 1978–. Elected to Académie Internationale de Lutèce, 1980. Lectures: Sir Thomas Middleton Meml, London, 1955; Frankland Meml, Birmingham, 1965; Benjamin Minge Duggar Meml, Alabama, 1966; Amos Meml, E Malling, 1969; Masters Meml, London, 1973; Sir Jesse Boot Foundn, Nottingham, 1974; Ronald Slack Meml, London, 1975; Extramural Centenary, London Univ., 1976; Vis. Lectr, Pontifical Acad. Scis, 1976; Douglas Wills, Bristol, 1977; Gooding Meml, London, 1978; Drummond Meml, London, 1979; John Dalton, Manchester, 1979; Holden, Nottingham, 1984; Hannaford Meml, Adelaide, 1985. Royal Soc. Vis. Prof. to Czechoslovakia, 1968, Mexico, 1971, China, 1973 and 1982, Romania, 1974, Poland, 1976, Israel, 1979, Hungary, 1980, West Indies and Philippines, 1981; Hong Kong, 1984. Pruthivi Gold Medal, 1957; RASE Research Medal, 1960; John Scott Award, 1963; Flintoff Medal, Chem. Soc., 1969; Internat. Award, Amer. Chem. Soc., 1972; Internat. Medal for Research on Plant Growth Substances, 1973; John Jeyes Gold Medal and Award, Chem. Soc., 1976; Royal Instn Actonian Award, 1977. Hon. DAgricSci, Ghent, 1963; Hon. DSc: Kent, 1976; Lausanne, 1977. *Publications*: numerous research publications in Annals of Applied Biology, Journal of Agric. Science, Journal of Chemical Society, Berichte der Deutschen Chemischen Gesellschaft, Proc. Royal Society, etc. *Recreations*: painting, travel. *Address*: Crown Point, Scotton Street, Wye, Ashford, Kent TN25 5BZ. *T*: Wye 812157.

WAINE, Rt. Rev. John; *see* Chelmsford, Bishop of.

WAINWRIGHT, Edwin, BEM 1957; *b* 12 Aug. 1908; *s* of John Wainwright and Ellen (*née* Hodgson); *m* 1938, Dorothy Metcalfe; two *s* two *d*. *Educ*: Darfield Council School; Wombwell and Barnsley Technical Colleges. WEA student for 20 years. Started work at 14, at Darfield Main Colliery; Nat. Union of Mineworkers: Member Branch Cttee, 1933–39; Delegate, 1939–48; Branch Sec., 1948–59; Member, Nat. Exec. Cttee, 1952–59. Member, Wombwell UDC, 1939–59. Sec./Agent, Dearne Valley Labour Party, 1951–59. MP (Lab) Dearne Valley, S Yorks, Oct. 1959–1983; Mem., Select Cttee on Energy, 1979–83. Secretary: PLP Trade Union Gp, 1966–83; Yorkshire Gp of PLP, 1966–83. *Recreations*: gardening, reading. *Address*: 20 Dovecliffe Road, Wombwell, near Barnsley, South Yorks. *T*: Barnsley 752153.

WAINWRIGHT, Geoffrey John, PhD; FSA; Principal Inspector, English Heritage (formerly Department of the Environment), since 1963; Director, Society of Antiquaries, since 1984; *b* 19 Sept. 1937; *s* of Frederick and Dorothy Wainwright; *m* 1977, Judith; one *s* two *d*. *Educ*: Pembroke Docks Sch.; Univ. of Wales (BA); Univ. of London (PhD). Prof. of Archaeology, Univ. of Baroda, India, 1961–63; Inspectorate of Ancient Monuments, HBMC, 1963–. President: Cornwall Archaeological Soc., 1980–84; Prehistoric Soc., 1982–86. Fellow, University Coll., Cardiff, 1985. *Publications*: Stone Age in North India, 1964; Coygan Camp, Carms, 1967; Durrington Walls, Wilts, 1971; Mount Pleasant, Dorset, 1979; Gussage All Saints, Dorset, 1979; numerous articles in learned jls. *Recreations*: Rugby football, flat racing, food and drink. *Address*: 81 St Margaret's Road, Twickenham, TW1 2LJ. *T*: 01–891 2429.

WAINWRIGHT, Richard Scurrah; MP (L) Colne Valley, 1966–70 and since Feb. 1974; *b* 11 April 1918; *o s* of late Henry Scurrah and Emily Wainwright; *m* 1948, Joyce Mary Hollis; one *s* two *d* (and one *s* decd). *Educ*: Shrewsbury Sch.; Clare Coll., Cambridge (Open Scholar). BA Hons (History), 1939. Friends Ambulance Unit, NW Europe, 1939–46. Retired Partner, Peat Marwick Mitchell & Co., Chartered Accountants. Pres., Leeds/Bradford Society of Chartered Accountants, 1965–66. Chm., Liberal Party Research Dept, 1968–70; Chm., Liberal Party, 1970–72; Mem., Select Cttee on Treasury, 1979–; Liberal spokesman on the economy, 1979–85, on employment, 1985–. *Recreations*: gardening, swimming. *Address*: The Heath, Adel, Leeds LS16 8EG. *T*: Leeds 673938. *Clubs*: Golcar Liberal, Honley Liberal, Linthwaite Liberal, Marsden Liberal.

WAINWRIGHT, Robert Everard, CMG 1959; *b* 24 June 1913; *s* of Dr G. B. Wainwright, OBE, MB; *m* 1939, Bridget Alan-Williams; two *s*. *Educ*: Marlborough; Trinity College, Cambridge (BA). District Officer, Kenya, 1935; Provincial Commissioner, Rift Valley Province, 1953–59. Imperial Defence College, 1959. Chief Commissioner, Kenya, 1960–63; Administrator, Turks and Caicos Is, WI, 1967–71. Member: Gp of British observers, Zimbabwe elections, 1980; Gp of Commonwealth observers, Ugandan elections, 1980. *Recreations*: sailing, cabinet-making. *Address*: Wagoners Cottage, Cann Common, Shaftesbury, Dorset. *T*: Shaftesbury 2877. *Club*: Mombasa (Mombasa).

WAINWRIGHT, Rear-Adm. Rupert Charles Purchas, CB 1966; DSC 1943; Vice Naval Deputy to Supreme Allied Commander Europe, 1965–67; retired 1967; with Redditch Development Corporation, 1968–77; *b* 16 Oct. 1913; *s* of late Lieut Comdr O. J. Wainwright and late Mrs S. Wainwright; *m* 1937, Patricia Mary Helen, *d* of late Col F. H. Blackwood, DSO and late Mrs Blackwood; two *s* two *d*. *Educ*: Royal Naval College, Dartmouth. Commanded HM Ships Actaeon, Tintagel Castle, Zephyr, 1952–54; Captain HMS Cambridge, 1955–57; Chief of Staff, S Atlantic and S America Station, 1958–60; Director Naval Recruiting, 1960–62; Commodore Naval Drafting, 1962–64. Comdr 1949; Capt. 1955; Rear-Adm. 1965. ADC to the Queen, 1964. Mem. Council, Missions to Seamen. Member: Stratford-on-Avon DC, 1973–86 (Vice-Chm., 1983–84; Chm.,

1984–85); Assoc. District Councils, 1976–83. Vice-President: Stratford-upon-Avon Soc.; Keep Britain Tidy Group. Mem., Waste Management Adv. Council, 1978–81. *Publications*: two Prize Essays, RUSI Jl. *Recreations*: hockey (Combined Services; a Vice-Pres., England Hockey Assoc.), swimming (Royal Navy), tennis. *Address*: Regency Cottage, Maidenhead Road, Stratford-upon-Avon, Warwicks CV37 6XS. *Club*: Royal Navy.

WAINWRIGHT, Sam, CBE 1982; Member, Monopolies and Mergers Commission, since 1985; Chairman, Manders (Holdings), since 1986 (Deputy Chairman, 1985–86; Director, since 1972); Director, BICC, since 1985; *b* 2 Oct. 1924; *m* Ruth Strom; three *s* one *d*. *Educ*: Regent Street Polytechnic; LSE (MSc Econ). Financial journalist, Glasgow Herald, 1950; Deputy City Editor, 1952–55; Director: Rea Brothers Ltd (Merchant Bankers), 1960–77 (Managing Dir, 1965–77); Furness Withy & Co. Ltd, 1971–77; Stothert & Pitt Ltd, 1970–77 (Chm., 1975–77); Aeronautical & General Instruments Ltd, 1968–77; Lancashire & London Investment Trust Ltd, 1963–77; Scottish Cities Investment Trust Ltd, 1961–77; Scottish & Mercantile Investment Co. Ltd, 1964–77; Post Office Corporation: Mem. Bd, 1977–85; Man. Dir, Nat. Girobank, 1977–85; Dep. Chm., 1981–85; Dir Postel Investment Ltd, 1982–85. Mem. Council, Soc. of Investment Analysts, 1961–75, Fellow, 1980. Hon. Editor, The Investment Analyst, 1961–74. *Publications*: articles in various Bank Reviews. *Recreations*: reading, bridge. *Address*: 6 Heath Close, NW11 7DX. *T*: 01–455 4448. *Club*: Reform.

WAITE, Hon. Sir John (Douglas), Kt 1982; **Hon. Mr Justice Waite;** a Judge of the High Court of Justice, Family Division, since 1982; *b* 3 July 1932; *s* of late Archibald Harvey Waite, Coleshill, Bucks, and Betty, *d* of late Ernest Bates; *m* 1966, Julia Mary, *er d* of late Joseph Tangye, Bellington, Kidderminster, Worcs; three *s* two step *s*. *Educ*: Sherborne Sch.; Corpus Christi Coll., Cambridge (MA). President of Cambridge Union, 1955. Nat. Service, 2nd Lieut, RA, 1951–52. Called to Bar, Gray's Inn, 1956, Bencher, 1981; QC 1975. Mem., General Council of the Bar, 1968–69; Junior Counsel to Registrar of Trade Unions, 1972–74. Pres., Employment Appeal Tribunal, 1983–85. *Recreations*: keeping weeds down, boats afloat, and children happy. *Address*: Royal Courts of Justice, Strand, WC2A 2LL.

See also Maj.-Gen. Sir (E.) J. (H.) Bates.

WAITE, Terence Hardy, MBE 1982; Adviser to Archbishop of Canterbury on Anglican Communion Affairs, since 1980; *b* 31 May 1939; *s* of Thomas William Waite and Lena (*née* Hardy); *m* 1964, Helen Frances Watters; one *s* three *d*. *Educ*: Wilmslow and Stockton Heath, Cheshire; Church Army Coll., London; privately in USA and Europe. Lay training adviser to Bishop and Diocese of Bristol, 1964–68; Adviser to Archbishop of Uganda, Rwanda and Burundi, 1968–71; Internat. Consultant working with Roman Catholic Church, 1972–79. Member, National Assembly, Church of England, 1966–68 (resigned on moving to Africa); Co-ordinator, Southern Sudan Relief Project, 1969–71. Founder-Chm., Y Care International, 1985–. Mem., Royal Inst. of International Affairs, 1980–. Paul Harris Fellow, Internat. Rotarian Organisation, 1983–. Member: World Wildlife Council, 1985–; Council, Internat. Year of Shelter for the Homeless, 1987; Council, Uganda Soc. for Disabled Children. Trustee, Butler Trust. Patron: Strode Park Foundn for the Disabled, Herne, Kent, 1985; Friends of the Commonwealth Inst. Templeton UK Project Award, 1985. Hon. DCL: City, 1986; Kent at Canterbury, 1986; Hon. LLD Liverpool, 1986. *Recreations*: music, walking, travel (esp. in remote parts of the world), Jungian studies, international affairs and politics, Left-Handed Society, preservation of old Blackheath. *Address*: Lambeth Palace, SE1 7JU. *T*: 01–928 8282. *Club*: Travellers'.

WAKE, Sir Hereward, 14th Bt *cr* 1621; MC 1942; Vice Lord-Lieutenant of Northamptonshire, since 1984; Major (retired) King's Royal Rifle Corps; *b* 7 Oct. 1916; *e s* of Sir Hereward Wake, 13th Bt, CB, CMG, DSO, and Margaret W. (*d* 1976), *er d* of R. H. Benson; *S* father, 1963; *m* 1952, Julia Rosemary, JP, *yr d* of late Capt. G. W. M. Lees, Falcutt House, Nr Brackley, Northants; one *s* three *d*. *Educ*: Eton; RMC, Sandhurst. Served War of 1939–45 (wounded, MC). Retired from 60th Rifles, 1947, and studied Estate Management and Agriculture. High Sheriff, 1955, DL 1969, Northants. *Heir*: *s* Hereward Charles Wake [*b* 22 Nov. 1952; *m* 1977, Lady Doune Ogilvy, *e d* of Earl of Airlie, *qv*; two *s* (and one *s* decd)]. *Address*: Courteenhall, Northampton. *Club*: Brooks's.

WAKEFIELD, Bishop of, since 1985; **Rt. Rev. David Michael Hope,** DPhil; Warden, Community of St Mary the Virgin, Wantage, since 1980; *b* 14 April 1940. *Educ*: Nottingham Univ. (BA Hons Theol.); Linacre Coll., Oxford (DPhil). Curate of St John, Tuebrook, Liverpool, 1965–70; Chaplain, Church of Resurrection, Bucharest, 1967–68; Vicar, St Andrew, Warrington, 1970–74; Principal, St Stephen's House, Oxford, 1974–82; Vicar of All Saints', Margaret Street, 1982–85. Examining Chaplain to: Bp of Bath and Wells, 1976–85; Bp of Wakefield, 1979–85; Bp of Norwich, 1981–85; Bp of London, 1984–85. *Publication*: The Leonine Sacramentary, 1971. *Address*: Bishop's Lodge, Woodthorpe Lane, Wakefield, W Yorks WF2 6JJ. *T*: Wakefield 255349.

WAKEFIELD, Provost of; *see* Allen, Very Rev. J. E.

WAKEFIELD, Derek John, CB 1982; Under Secretary, Government Communications Headquarters, 1978–82; *b* 21 Jan. 1922; *s* of Archibald John Thomas and Evelyn Bessie Wakefield; *m* 1951, Audrey Ellen Smith, FRHS; one *d*. *Educ*: The Commonweal School. Air Ministry, 1939–42 and 1947–52. Served War, Lieut, Royal Pioneer Corps, 1942–47. Government Communications Headquarters, 1952–82. Mem., Airship Assoc. Governor, Barnwood House Trust, Gloucester, 1973–. *Recreation*: airships. *Club*: Naval and Military.

WAKEFIELD, Sir (Edward) Humphry (Tyrrell), 2nd Bt *cr* 1962; *b* 11 July 1936; *s* of Sir Edward Birkbeck Wakefield, 1st Bt, CIE, and of Constance Lalage, *e d* of late Sir John Perronet Thompson, KCSI, KCIE; *S* father, 1969; *m* 1st, 1960, Priscilla (marr. diss. 1964), *e d* of O. R. Bagot; 2nd, 1966, Hon. Elizabeth Sophia (from whom he obt. a divorce, 1971), *e d* of Viscount De L'Isle, VC, KG, PC, GCMG, GCVO, and former wife of G. S. O. A. Colthurst; one *s*; 3rd, 1974, Hon. Katharine Mary Alice Baring, *d* of 1st Baron Howick of Glendale, KG, GCMG, KCVO, and of Lady Mary Howick; one *s* one *d* (and one *s* decd). *Educ*: Gordonstoun; Trinity Coll., Cambridge (MA Hons). Formerly Captain, 10th Royal Hussars. Exec. Vice-Pres., Mallett, America Ltd, 1970–75; Chairman: Tyrrell & Moore Ltd, 1978–; Nicolai Patricia Co. Ltd, 1978–; Director: Mallett & Son (Antiques) Ltd, 1971–78; Tree of Life Foundn; Save Piccadilly Foundn. Dir, Spoleto Fest. of Two Worlds, USA and Italy. Appeals Consultant, London Br., British Red Cross Soc. Mem., Standing Council of Baronetage. Fellow, Pierrepont Morgan Library. *Recreations*: riding, writing, music, shooting. *Heir*: *s* Maximilian Edward Vereker Wakefield, *b* 22 Feb. 1967. *Address*: Chillingham Castle, Alnwick, Northumberland; c/o Barclays Bank, St James' Street, Derby DE1 1QU. *Clubs*: Cavalry and Guards, Turf.

WAKEFIELD, Rev. Gordon Stevens; Principal of the Queen's College, Birmingham, since 1979; *b* 15 Jan. 1921; *s* of Ernest and Lucy Wakefield; *m* 1949, Beryl Dimes; one *s* three *d*. *Educ*: Crewe County Sec. School; Univ. of Manchester; Fitzwilliam Coll. and Wesley House, Cambridge; St Catherine's Coll., Oxford. MA (Cantab); MLitt (Oxon). Methodist Circuit Minister in Edgware, Woodstock, Stockport, Newcastle upon Tyne, Bristol, 1944–63; Methodist Connexional Editor, 1963–72; Chairman, Manchester and Stockport Methodist District, 1971–79. Fernley-Hartley Lectr, 1957; Select Preacher,

Univ. of Oxford, 1971 and 1982. Recognized Lectr, Univ. of Birmingham, 1979. Member, Joint Liturgical Group (Chairman, 1978–84). DD Lambeth, 1986. *Publications:* Puritan Devotion, 1957; (with Hetley Price) Unity at the Local Level, 1965; Methodist Devotion, 1966; The Life of the Spirit in the World of Today, 1969; On the Edge of the Mystery, 1969; Robert Newton Flew, 1971; Fire of Love, 1976; (ed, with biographical introdns of E. C. Hoskyns and F. N. Davey) Crucifixion—Resurrection, 1981; (ed) Dictionary of Christian Spirituality, 1983; Kindly Light, 1984; The Liturgy of St John, 1985; contribs to theological jls. *Recreations:* watching and talking cricket; churches and cathedrals. *Address:* The Queen's College, Birmingham B15 2QH. *T:* 021–454 1527.

WAKEFIELD, Sir Humphry; *see* Wakefield, Sir E. H. T.

WAKEFIELD, Sir Peter (George Arthur), KBE 1977; CMG 1973; HM Diplomatic Service, retired; Director, National Art-Collections Fund, since 1982; *b* 13 May 1922; *s* of John Bunting Wakefield and Dorothy Ina Stace; *m* 1951, Felicity Maurice-Jones; four *s* one *d. Educ:* Cranleigh Sch.; Corpus Christi Coll., Oxford. Army Service, 1942–47; Military Govt, Eritrea, 1946–47; Hulton Press, 1947–49; entered Diplomatic Service, 1949; Middle East Centre for Arab Studies, 1950; 2nd Sec., Amman, 1950–52; Foreign Office, 1953–55; 1st Sec., British Middle East Office, Nicosia, 1955–56; 1st Sec. (Commercial), Cairo, 1956; Administrative Staff Coll., Henley, 1957; 1st Sec. (Commercial), Vienna, 1957–60; 1st Sec. (Commercial), Tokyo, 1960–63; Foreign Office, 1964–66; Consul-General and Counsellor, Benghazi, 1966–69; Econ. and Commercial Counsellor, Tokyo, 1970–72; Econ. and Commercial Minister, Tokyo, 1973; seconded as Special Adviser on the Japanese Market, BOTB, 1973–75; Ambassador to the Lebanon, 1975–78, to Belgium, 1979–82. *Recreations:* ceramics and restoring ruins; swimming. *Address:* 28 Lincoln House, Montpelier Row, Twickenham, Mddx. *T:* 01–892 6390; La Molineta, Frigiliana, near Malaga, Spain. *Club:* Travellers'.

WAKEFIELD, William Barry; Director of Statistics, Department of Education and Science, since 1979; *b* 6 June 1930; *s* of Stanley Arthur and Evelyn Grace Wakefield; *m* 1953, Elizabeth Violet (*née* Alexander); three *s* one *d. Educ:* Harrow County Grammar Sch.; University Coll., London. BSc; FSS. Statistician, NCB, 1953–62; DES, 1962–67; Chief Statistician, MoD, 1967–72, CSO, 1972–75; Asst Dir, CSO, Cabinet Office, 1975–79. Member, United Reformed Church. *Recreations:* horse racing, gardening. *Address:* 7 The Spinneys, Hockley, Essex. *T:* Southend 203514.

WAKEFORD, Geoffrey Michael Montgomery; Clerk to the Worshipful Company of Mercers, since 1974; Barrister-at-Law; *b* 10 Dec. 1937; *o s* of Geoffrey and late Helen Wakeford; *m* 1966, Diana Margaret Loy Cooper; two *s* two *d. Educ:* Downside; Clare Coll., Cambridge (Classical Schol., MA, LLB). Called to Bar, Gray's Inn and South Eastern Circuit, 1961; practised at Common Law Bar until 1971. Apptd Dep. Clerk to the Mercers Co., 1971. Clerk to: Governors St Paul's Schs; Joint Grand Gresham Cttee; City & Metropolitan Welfare Trustees; Collyers Foundn Trustees; Council of Gresham Coll., 1980–84. Chm., Islington Soc. for the Mentally Handicapped. Governor: London Internat. Film Sch., 1981–85; Molecule Theatre. *Address:* Mercers' Hall, Ironmonger Lane, EC2V 8HE. *T:* 01–726 4991. *Club:* Travellers'.

WAKEFORD, John Chrysostom Barnabas, CMG 1948; *b* 23 Aug. 1898; *o s* of Rev. John Wakeford, Anfield, Liverpool; *m* 1st, 1921, Grace (*d* 1965), *d* of Charles Cooke, Church Coppenhall; one *d*; 2nd, 1970, Dorothy May, *d* of Frederick Ward, Aldeburgh, Suffolk. *Educ:* Malvern College; RMA, Woolwich; Clare College, Cambridge. Commissioned Royal Engineers, 1917; served European War, France and Belgium, 1917–18; N Russia Campaign (despatches). Dep. Dir Transportn, W Africa, 1941–43; Ceylon, 1943–44 (Col); Dir of Transportn, SE Asia, 1944–45 (Brig.). Chief Railway Commissioner, Burma; General Manager, Burma Railways and Technical Adviser to Government of Burma, 1945–48; Chief Engineer, Cameroons Development Corporation, W Africa, 1948–50; with Rendel Palmer & Tritton, 1950–63; FICE, FIMechE, FCIT, FRSA. *Address:* 41 South Road, Saffron Walden, Essex. *T:* Saffron Walden 22010.

WAKEFORD, Air Marshal Sir Richard (Gordon), KCB 1976; LVO 1961; OBE 1958; AFC 1952; Secretary, RAF Benevolent Fund, Scotland, since 1978; *b* 20 April 1922; *s* of Charles Edward Augustus Wakeford; *m* 1948, Anne Butler; two *s* one *d* (and one *d* decd). *Educ:* Montpelier Sch., Paignton; Kelly Coll., Tavistock. Joined RAF, 1941; flying Catalina flying boats, Coastal Comd, operating out of India, Scotland, N Ireland, 1942–45; flying Liberator and York transport aircraft on overseas routes, 1945–47; CFS 1947; Flying Instructor, RAF Coll. Cranwell; CFS Examining Wing; ground appts, incl. 2½ years on staff of Dir of Emergency Ops in Malaya, 1952–58; comdg Queen's Flight, 1958–61; Directing Staff, RAF Staff Coll., 1961–64; subseq.: comdg RAF Scampton; SASO, HQ 3 Group Bomber Comd; Asst Comdt (Cadets), RAF Coll. Cranwell; idc 1969; Comdr N Maritime Air Region, and Air Officer Scotland and N Ireland, 1970–72; Dir of Service Intelligence, MoD, 1972–73; ANZUK Force Comdr, Singapore, 1974–75; Dep. Chief of Defence Staff (Intell.), 1975–78; HM Comr, Queen Victoria Sch., Dunblane; Vice-Chm. (Air), Lowland T&AVR. Trustee, McRobert Trusts (Chm., 1982–); Director: Thistle Foundn; Cromar Nominees. CStJ 1986. *Recreations:* golf, fishing. *Address:* Earlston House, Forgandenny, Perth. *T:* Bridge of Earn 812392. *Clubs:* Flyfishers', Royal Air Force.

WAKEHAM, Rt. Hon. John, PC 1983; JP; FCA; MP (C) Colchester South and Maldon, since 1983 (Maldon, Feb. 1974–1983); Parliamentary Secretary to HM Treasury and Government Chief Whip, since 1983; *b* 22 June 1932; *s* of late Major W. J. Wakeham and late Mrs E. R. Wakeham; *m* 1st, 1965, Anne Roberta Bailey (*d* 1984); two *s*; 2nd, 1985, Alison Bridget Ward, MBE, *d* of Ven. E. J. G. Ward, *qv. Educ:* Charterhouse. Chartered Accountant. Asst Govt Whip, 1979–81; a Lord Comr of HM Treasury (Govt Whip), 1981; Parly Under-Sec. of State, DoI, 1981–82; Minister of State, HM Treasury, 1982–83. JP Inner London 1972. *Publications:* The Case against Wealth Tax, 1968; A Personal View, 1969. *Recreations:* farming, sailing, racing, reading. *Address:* House of Commons, SW1. *Clubs:* Carlton, St Stephen's Constitutional.

WAKEHURST, 3rd Baron *cr* 1934, of Ardingly; **(John) Christopher Loder;** Chairman: Anglo-American Securities Corporation PLC, since 1980 (Director, since 1968); North Atlantic Securities Corporation PLC, since 1980; Philadelphia National Ltd, since 1985; Deputy Chairman, London and Manchester Group PLC (Director, since 1966); *b* 23 Sept. 1925; *s* of 2nd Baron Wakehurst, KG, KCMG, and of Dowager Lady Wakehurst, *qv*; *S* father, 1970; *m* 1956, Ingeborg Krumbholz-Hess (*d* 1977); one *s* one *d*; *m* 1983, Brigid, *yr d* of William Noble, Cirencester. *Educ:* Eton; King's School, nr Sydney, NSW; Trinity College, Cambridge (BA 1948, LLB 1949, MA 1953). Served War as Sub Lieut RANVR and RNVR; West Pacific, 1943–45. Barrister, Inner Temple, 1950. Director: Mayfair & City Properties plc, 1984–; The Nineteen Twenty-Eight Investment Trust plc, 1984–; Hampton Gold Mining Areas (Chm., 1981–86); Chm., Continental Illinois Ltd, 1973–84. Trustee, The Photographers' Gallery Ltd, 1979–. CStJ. *Heir: s* Hon. Timothy Walter Loder, *b* 28 March 1958. *Address:* 26 Wakehurst Road, SW11 6BY. *Clubs:* City of London, Chelsea Arts.

WAKEHURST, Dowager Lady; Dame Margaret Wakehurst, DBE 1965; *b* 4 Nov. 1899; *d* of Sir Charles Tennant, Bt and of Marguerite (*née* Miles); *m* 1920, John de Vere Loder (later 2nd Baron Wakehurst, KG, KCMG) (*d* 1970); three *s* one *d.* Founder, Northern Ireland Assoc. for Mental Health; Founder Mem., National Schizophrenia Fellowship (Pres., 1984–86); Vice-Pres., Royal College of Nursing, 1958–78. Hon. LLD Queen's Univ., Belfast; Hon. DLitt New Univ. of Ulster, 1973. DStJ 1959; GCStJ 1970. *Address:* 31 Lennox Gardens, SW1. *T:* 01–589 0956.

WAKELEY, Sir John (Cecil Nicholson), 2nd Bt *cr* 1952; FRCS; Consultant Surgeon, West Cheshire Group of Hospitals, since 1961; *b* 27 Aug. 1926; *s* of Sir Cecil Pembrey Grey Wakeley, 1st Bt, KBE, CB, MCh, FRCS, and Elizabeth Muriel (*d* 1985), *d* of James Nicholson-Smith; *S* father, 1979; *m* 1954, June Leney; two *s* one *d. Educ:* Canford School. MB, BS London 1950; LRCP 1950, FRCS 1955 (MRCS 1950), FACS 1973. Lectr in Anatomy, Univ. of London, 1951–52. Sqdn Ldr, RAF, 1953–54. Councillor, RCS, 1971–83; Member: Mersey Regional Health Authority, 1974–78; Editorial Bd, Health Trends, DHSS, 1968–71; Examiner for Gen. Nursing Council for England and Wales, 1954–59; Consultant Adviser in Surgery to RAF, 1981–. Liveryman: Worshipful Soc. of Apothecaries; Worshipful Co. of Barbers; Freeman of City of London. FACS 1973. CStJ 1959. *Publications:* papers on leading med. jls, incl. British Empire Cancer Campaign Scientific Report, Vol. II: Zinc 65 and the prostate, 1958; report on distribution and radiation dosimetry of Zinc 65 in the rat, 1959. *Recreations:* music, photography, bird-watching. *Heir: s* Nicholas Jeremy Wakeley, *b* 17 Oct. 1957. *Address:* Mickle Lodge, Mickle Trafford, Chester CH2 4EB. *T:* Mickle Trafford 300316. *Club:* Council Club of Royal College of Surgeons.

WAKELING, Rt. Rev. John Denis, MC 1945; *b* 12 Dec. 1918; *s* of Rev. John Lucas Wakeling and Mary Louise (*née* Glover); *m* 1941, Josephine Margaret, *d* of Dr Benjamin Charles Broomhall and Marion (*née* Aldwinckle); two *s. Educ:* Dean Close Sch., Cheltenham; St Catharine's Coll., Cambridge. MA Cantab 1944. Commnd Officer in Royal Marines, 1939–45 (Actg Maj.). Ridley Hall, Cambridge, 1946–47. Deacon, 1947; Priest, 1948. Asst Curate, Barwell, Leics, 1947; Chaplain of Clare Coll., Cambridge, and Chaplain to the Cambridge Pastorate, 1950–52; Vicar of Emmanuel, Plymouth, 1952–59; Prebendary of Exeter Cathedral, 1957, Prebendary Emeritus, 1959; Vicar of Barking, Essex, 1959–65; Archdeacon of West Ham, 1965–70; Bishop of Southwell, 1970–85. Entered House of Lords, June 1974. Chairman: Archbishops' Council on Evangelism, 1976–79; Lee Abbey Council, 1976–84. *Recreations:* formerly cricket and hockey (Cambridge Univ. Hockey Club, 1938, 1939, 1945, 1946, English Trials Caps, 1939, 1946–49), gardening, water colours, fly fishing. *Address:* The Maples, The Avenue, Porton, Salisbury, Wilts. *Clubs:* National; Hawks (Cambridge).

WAKELY, Leonard John Dean, CMG 1965; OBE 1945; *b* 18 June 1909; *s* of Sir Leonard Wakely, KCIE, CB; *m* 1938, Margaret Houssemayne Tinson; two *s. Educ:* Westminster School; Christ Church, Oxford; School of Oriental Studies, London. Indian Civil Service, 1932–47. Served in the Punjab and in the Defence Co-ordination, Defence and Legislative Departments of the Government of India. Appointed to Commonwealth Relations Office, 1947; Office of UK High Commissioner in the Union of South Africa, 1950–52; Dep. UK High Comr in India (Madras), 1953–57; Asst Sec., 1955; Dep. UK High Comr in Ghana, 1957–60; Dep. British High Comr in Canada, 1962–65; British Ambassador in Burma, 1965–67. *Address:* Long Meadow, Forest Road, East Horsley, Surrey.

WAKEMAN, Sir (Offley) David, 5th Bt *cr* 1828; *b* 6 March 1922; *s* of Sir Offley Wakeman, 4th Bt, CBE, and Winifred (*d* 1924), 2nd *d* of late Col C. R. Prideaux-Brune; *S* father, 1975; *m* 1946, Pamela Rose Arabella, *d* of late Lt-Col C. Hunter Little, DSO, MBE. *Educ:* Canford School. *Heir: half-brother* Edward Offley Bertram Wakeman, *b* 31 July 1934. *Address:* Peverey House, Bomere Heath, Shrewsbury, Salop. *T:* Shrewsbury 850561. *Club:* Lansdowne.

WAKERLEY, Richard MacLennon; QC 1982; a Recorder of the Crown Court, since 1982; *b* 7 June 1942; *s* of late Charles William Wakerley and Gladys MacLennon Wakerley; *m* Marian Heather Dawson; two *s* two *d. Educ:* De Aston Sch., Market Rasen; Emmanuel Coll., Cambridge (MA), Called to the Bar, Gray's Inn, 1965. *Recreations:* theatre, bridge, gardening. *Address:* Croft House, Grendon, Atherstone, Warwicks CV9 3DP. *T:* Atherstone 2329.

WAKLEY, Bertram Joseph, MBE 1945; **His Honour Judge Wakley;** a Circuit Judge, since 1973; *b* 7 July 1917; *s* of Major Bertram Joseph Wakley and Hon. Mrs Dorothy Wakley (*née* Hamilton); *m* 1953, Alice Margaret Lorimer. *Educ:* Wellington Coll.; Christ Church, Oxford. BA 1939, MA 1943. Commnd S Lancs Regt, 1940; Captain 1941; Major 1943; served N Africa, Italy, Greece (despatches). Called to Bar, Gray's Inn, 1948. A Recorder of the Crown Court, 1972–73. *Publications:* History of the Wimbledon Cricket Club, 1954; Bradman the Great, 1959; Classic Centuries, 1964. *Recreations:* cricket, golf. *Address:* Hamilton House, Kingston Hill, Surrey. *T:* 01–546 9961. *Clubs:* Carlton, MCC, Roehampton.

WALBANK, Frank William, FBA 1953; MA; Rathbone Professor of Ancient History and Classical Archæology in the University of Liverpool, 1951–77, now Professor Emeritus; Dean, Faculty of Arts, 1974–77; Joint Editor, Cambridge Ancient History, since 1977; *b* 10 Dec. 1909; *s* of A. J. D. Walbank, Bingley, Yorks; *m* 1935, Mary Woodward, *e d* of O. C. A. Fox, Shipley, Yorks; one *s* two *d. Educ:* Bradford Grammar School; Peterhouse, Cambridge (Hon. Fellow, 1984). Scholar of Peterhouse, 1928–31; First Class, Parts I and II Classical Tripos, 1930–31; Hugo de Balsham Research Student, Peterhouse, 1931–32; Senior Classics Master at North Manchester High School, 1932–33; Thirlwall Prize, 1933; Asst Lecturer, 1934–36, Lecturer, 1936–46, in Latin, Professor of Latin, 1946–51, University of Liverpool; Public Orator, 1956–60; Hare Prize, 1939. J. H. Gray Lectr, Univ. of Cambridge, 1957; Andrew Mellon Vis. Prof., Univ. Pittsburgh, 1964; Myres Memorial Lectr, Univ. of Oxford, 1964–65; Sather Prof., Univ. of Calif (Berkeley), 1971. Pres., Cambridge Phil Soc., 1982–84; Member Council: Classical Assoc., 1944–48, 1958–61 (Pres. 1969–70); Roman Soc., 1948–51 (Vice-Pres., 1953–; Pres., 1961–64); Hellenic Soc., 1951–54, 1955–56; Classical Journals Bd, 1948–66; British Acad., 1960–63; British Sch. at Rome, 1979–. Mem., Inst. for Advanced Study, Princeton, 1970–71; Foreign Mem., Royal Netherlands Acad. of Arts and Sciences, 1981–. *Publications:* Aratos of Sicyon, 1933; Philip V of Macedon, 1940; Latin Prose Versions contributed to Key to Bradley's Arnold, Latin Prose Composition, ed J. F. Mountford, 1940; The Decline of the Roman Empire in the West, 1946; A Historical Commentary on Polybius, Vol. i, 1957, Vol. ii, 1967, Vol. iii, 1979; The Awful Revolution, 1969; Polybius, 1972; The Hellenistic World, 1981; Selected Papers: Studies in Greek and Roman history and historiography, 1985; chapters in: The Cambridge Economic History of Europe, Vol. II, 1952; A Scientific Survey of Merseyside, 1953; contribs to: the Oxford Classical Dictionary, 1949; Chambers' Encyclopædia, 1950; Encyclopædia Britannica, 1960 and 1974; English and foreign classical books and periodicals. *Address:* 64 Grantchester Meadows, Cambridge CB3 9JL. *T:* Cambridge 64350.

WALD, Prof. George; Higgins Professor of Biology, Harvard University, 1968–77, now Emeritus Professor; *b* 18 Nov. 1906; *s* of Isaac Wald and Ernestine (*née* Rosenmann); *m* 1st, 1931, Frances Kingsley (marr. diss.); two *s*; 2nd, 1958, Ruth Hubbard; one *s* one *d*. *Educ:* Washington Square Coll. of New York Univ. (BS); Columbia Univ. (PhD). Nat. Research Coun. Fellowship, 1932–34. Harvard University: Instr and Tutor in Biology, 1934–39; Faculty Instr, 1939–44; Associate Prof., 1944–48; Prof. of Biology, 1948–77, Emeritus Prof., 1977–. Nobel Prize in Physiology and Medicine (jointly), 1967. Vice-Pres., People's Permanent Tribunal, Rome (Pres., internat. tribunals on El Salvador, Philippines, Afghanistan, Zaire, Guatemala). Writes and lectures on cold war, arms race, human rights, nuclear power and weapons; developed World-Third World relations. Has many hon. doctorates from univs in USA and abroad; Guest, China Assoc. for Friendship with Foreign Peoples, Jan.-Feb. 1972; US/Japan Distinguished Scientist Exchange, 1973. *Publications:* (co-author) General Education in a Free Society; (co-author) Twenty-six Afternoons of Biology. Many sci. papers (on the biochemistry and physiology of vision and on biochem. evolution) in: Jl of Gen. Physiology, Nature, Science, Jl of Opt. Soc. of Amer., etc. *Recreations:* art, archæology. *Address:* 21 Lakeview Avenue, Cambridge, Mass 02138, USA. *T:* (617) 868–7748.

WALDEGRAVE, family name of **Earl Waldegrave.**

WALDEGRAVE, 12th Earl, *cr* 1729, **Geoffrey Noel Waldegrave,** KG 1971; GCVO 1976; TD; DL; Bt 1643; Baron Waldegrave, 1685; Viscount Chewton, 1729; Member of the Prince's Council of the Duchy of Cornwall, 1951–58 and 1965–76, Lord Warden of the Stannaries, 1965–76; *b* 21 Nov. 1905; *o s* of 11th Earl and Anne Katharine (*d* 1962), *d* of late Rev. W. P. Bastard, Ashburton and Kitley, Devon; *S* father, 1936; *m* 1930, Mary Hermione, *d* of Lt-Col A. M. Grenfell, DSO; two *s* five *d*. *Educ:* Winchester; Trinity Coll., Cambridge (BA). Served War of 1939–45, Major RA (TA). Chm., Som AEC, 1948–51; Liaison Officer to Min. of Agriculture, Fisheries and Food (formerly Min. of Agriculture and Fisheries), for Som, Wilts and Glos, 1952–57; Jt Parly Sec., Min. of Agriculture, Fisheries and Food, 1958–62; Chairman: Forestry Commn, 1963–65; Adv. Cttee on Meat Research, 1969–73. Director: Lloyds Bank Ltd, 1964–76 (Chm., Bristol Regional Bd, 1966–76); Bristol Waterworks Co., 1938–58 and 1963–78. Pres., Somerset Trust for Nature Conservation, 1964–80. Mem., BBC Gen. Adv. Council, 1963–66. Mem. Council and Trustee, Royal Bath and W Southern Counties Soc. (Pres., 1974); Trustee, Partis Coll., Bath; formerly Mem. Court and Council, and Chm. Agricl Cttee, Bristol Univ. Chm., Friends of Wells Cathedral, 1970–84. Hon. LLD Bristol, 1976. Former Governor: Wells Cathedral Sch.; Nat. Fruit and Cider Inst., Long Ashton. Mem. Som CC, 1937–58; CA, 1949–58; DL Somerset, 1951; Vice-Lieutenant Somerset, 1955–60. Officer, Legion of Merit, USA. *Heir: s* Viscount Chewton, *qv. Address:* Chewton House, Chewton Mendip, Bath BA3 4LQ. *T:* Chewton Mendip 264. *Club:* Travellers'.
See also Sir J. D. Boles, Baron Forteviot, M. J. Hussey, Lady Susan Hussey, Baron Strathcona and Mount Royal, Hon. William Waldegrave.

WALDEGRAVE, Hon. William Arthur; MP (C) Bristol West, since 1979; Minister of State for the Environment and Countryside, since 1985, and for Planning, since 1986, Department of the Environment; Fellow of All Souls College, Oxford, since 1979 (also from 1971–78); *b* 15 Aug. 1946; *yr s* of Earl Waldegrave, *qv; m* 1977, Caroline, *y d* of Major and Mrs Richard Burrows, Kemsing, Kent; one *s* two *d*. *Educ:* Eton (Newcastle Schol.); Corpus Christi Coll., Oxford (Open Schol.; 1st Cl. Lit. Hum. 1969) (President, Oxford Union and Oxford Univ. Conservative Assoc.); Harvard Univ. (Kennedy Fellow). Central Policy Review Staff, Cabinet Office, 1971–73; Political Staff, 10 Downing Street, 1973–74; Head of Leader of Opposition's Office, 1974–75. Parly Under-Sec. of State, DES, 1981–83, DoE, 1983–85. Vice Chm., Conservative Backbench Finance Cttee, 1980–81. GEC Ltd (Group HQ and GEC Gas Turbines Ltd, Leicester), 1975–81. JP Inner London Juvenile Court, 1975–79. Mem., IBA Adv. Council, 1980–81. *Publication:* The Binding of Leviathan, 1977. *Address:* 18 Wellington Terrace, Bristol BS8 4LE. *T:* Bristol 734817. *Clubs:* Brooks's, Beefsteak, Pratt's.

WALDEN, (Alastair) Brian; Presenter, Weekend World, London Weekend Television, 1977–86; *b* 8 July 1932; *s* of W. F. Walden; *m* Hazel Downes, *d* of William A. Downes; three *s* of former marriages. *Educ:* West Bromwich Grammar School; Queen's College and Nuffield College, Oxford; Pres., Oxford Union, 1957. University Lecturer. MP (Lab): Birmingham, All Saints, 1964–74; Birmingham, Ladywood, 1974–77. Mem., W Midland Bd, Central TV, 1981–84. TV presenter and journalist; Columnist: London Standard, 1983–; Thomson Regional Newspapers, 1983–. Shell International Award, 1982. *Recreations:* chess, gardening. *Address:* 29 Warwick Avenue, W9.

WALDEN, George Gordon Harvey, CMG 1981; MP (C) Buckingham, since 1983; Parliamentary Under-Secretary of State, Department of Education and Science, since 1985; *b* 15 Sept. 1939; *s* of G. G. Walden; *m* 1970, Sarah Nicolette Hunt; two *s* one *d*. *Educ:* Latymer Upper Sch.; Jesus Coll., Cambridge; Moscow Univ. (post-graduate). Research Dept, Foreign Office, 1962–65; Chinese Language Student, Hong Kong Univ., 1965–67; Second Secretary, Office of HM Chargé d'Affaires, Peking, 1967–70; First Sec., FCO (Soviet Desk), 1970–73; Ecole Nationale d'Administration, Paris, 1973–74; First Sec., HM Embassy, Paris, 1974–78; Principal Private Sec. to Foreign and Commonwealth Sec., 1978–81; sabbatical year, Harvard, 1981; Head of Planning Staff, FCO, 1982–83; retired from HM Diplomatic Service, 1983. PPS to Sec. of State for Educn and Science, 1984–85. *Address:* House of Commons, SW1.

WALDEN, Herbert Richard Charles, CBE 1986; Director and General Manager, Heart of England Building Society, 1974–86; *b* 6 Oct. 1926; *s* of Reginald George Walden and Matilda Ethel Walden; *m* 1950, Margaret Walker; two *d*. *Educ:* Westgate Sch., Warwick. FCIS; FCBSI. War service, 1944–47, Royal Warwickshire Regt and Royal Leicestershire Regt (UK and Gold Coast) (Captain). Asst Sec., Warwick Building Soc., 1955, Gen. Manager 1962; Gen. Manager, Rugby and Warwick Building Soc. (on merger), 1967; Gen. Manager, Heart of England Building Soc. (on merger), 1974. Chm., Midland Assoc. of Building Socs, 1972–73, Vice-Pres., 1985–86; Mem. Council, Building Societies Assoc., 1974–86, Dep. Chm. 1981–83, Chm., 1983–85. Mem. Bd, Housing Corp., 1985–; pt-time Mem., Building Societies Commn, 1986–. Mem., Warwick BC, 1955–63; Chm., S Warwickshire HMC, 1964–72; Vice Chm., Warwick Schs Foundn; Trustee, various Warwick Charities; Founder Pres., Rotary Club of Warwick, 1965; Vice Pres., Warwickshire Scout Assoc. (former County Treasurer). Commissioner of Taxes. *Recreation:* watching cricket and soccer. *Address:* Fieldgate House, 24 Hill Wootton Road, Leek Wootton, Warwick CV35 7QL. *T:* Kenilworth 54291. *Club:* Naval and Military.

WALDER, Edwin James, CMG 1971; management consultant and company director, since 1981; *b* 5 Aug. 1921; *s* of Edwin James Walder and Dulcie Muriel Walder (*née* Griffiths); *m* 1944, Norma Cheslin; two *d*. *Educ:* North Newtown High Sch.; Univ. of Sydney (BEc). Apptd NSW Civil Service, 1938; NSW State Treasury: 1945; Asst Under-Sec. (Finance), 1959–61; Dep. Under-Sec., 1961–63; Under-Sec. and Comptroller of Accounts, 1963–65; Pres., Metrop. Water, Sewerage and Drainage Bd, Sydney, 1965–81. Member: State Pollution Control Commn, 1971–81; Metropolitan Waste Disposal Authority (Sydney), 1971–81. *Recreations:* lawn bowls, fishing, swimming. *Address:* PO Box 208, Padstow, NSW 2211, Australia. *Clubs:* City Tattersall's, Roselands Bowling, St George Leagues (all in Sydney).

WALDER, Ruth Christabel, (Mrs Wesierska), OBE 1956; *b* 15 Jan. 1906; *d* of Rev. Ernest Walder; *m* 1955, Maj.-Gen. George Wesierski (*d* 1967), formerly Judge Advocate General of the Polish Forces. *Educ:* Cheltenham Ladies' College. General Organiser, National Federation of Women's Institutes, 1934–40; Admiralty, 1940–41; Relief Department, Foreign Office, 1942–44; UNRRA, Sec. Food Cttee of Council for Europe, 1944–47; Secretary United Nations Appeal for Children (in the UK), 1948; National General Secretary, YWCA of Great Britain, 1949–67. Lectr for the European Community, 1970–. Defence Medal, 1946. Polish Gold Cross of Merit, 1969. *Address:* Westhope, Langton Herring, Weymouth, Dorset. *T:* Abbotsbury 871233. *Clubs:* Naval and Military; Royal Dorset Yacht.

WALDHEIM, Dr Kurt; President of the Republic of Austria, since 1986; *b* 21 Dec. 1918; *m* 1944, Elisabeth Ritschel Waldheim; one *s* two *d*. *Educ:* Consular Academy, Vienna; Univ. of Vienna (Dr Jr 1944). Entered Austrian foreign service, 1945; served in Min. for Foreign Affairs; Mem., Austrian Delegn to Paris, London and Moscow for negotiations on Austrian State Treaty, 1945–47; 1st Sec., Embassy, Paris, 1948–51; apptd Counsellor and Head of Personnel Div., Min. of Foreign Affairs, 1951–55; Permanent Austrian Observer to UN, 1955–56; Minister Plenipotentiary to Canada, 1956–58; Ambassador to Canada, 1958–60; Dir-Gen. for Political Affairs, Min. of Foreign Affairs, 1960–64; Permanent Rep. of Austria to UN, 1964–68 (Chm., Outer Space Cttee of UN 1965–68 and 1970–71); Federal Minister for Foreign Affairs, 1968–70; Candidate for the Presidency of Republic of Austria, 1971; Permanent Rep. of Austria to UN, 1970–Dec. 1971; Sec.-Gen. of UN, 1972–81. Guest Prof. of Diplomacy, Georgetown Univ., Washington DC, 1982–84. Chm., InterAction Council for Internat. Co-operation, 1983–85. Hon. LLD: Chile, Carleton, Rutgers, Fordham, 1972; Jawaharlal Nehru, Bucharest, 1973; Wagner Coll., NY, Catholic Univ. of America, Wilfrid Laurier, 1974; Catholic Univ. of Leuven, Charles Univ., Hamilton Coll., Clinton, NY, 1975; Denver, Philippines, Nice, 1976; American Univ., Kent State, Warsaw, Moscow State Univ., Mongolian State Univ., 1977; Atlanta Univ., Humboldt Univ., Univ. of S Carolina, 1979; Keele, Notre Dame, USA, 1980. George Marshall Peace Award, USA, 1977; Dr Karl Renner Prize, City of Vienna, 1978. *Publications:* The Austrian Example, 1971, English edn 1973; The Challenge of Peace, 1977, English edn 1980; Building the Future Order, 1980; In the Eye of the Storm, 1985. *Recreations:* sailing, swimming, skiing, horseback riding. *Address:* Argentinierstrasse 20, A–1040 Vienna, Austria.

WALDMAN, Stanley John; Master of the Supreme Court, Queen's Bench Division, since 1971; *b* 18 Sept. 1923; *s* of late Michael Ernest Waldman, OBE, JP; *m* 1951, Naomi Sorsky; one *s* two *d*. *Educ:* Owen's School, London; Pembroke College, Oxford. BA; MA 1948. RAF, 1942–46; called to the Bar, Gray's Inn, 1949; practised in London and on SE Circuit. *Address:* 80 South Hill Park, NW3.

WALDRON, Brig. John Graham Claverhouse, CBE 1958 (OBE 1944); DSO 1945; *b* 15 Nov. 1909; *s* of William Slade Olver (*d* 1909), Falmouth; *m* 1933, Marjorie, *d* of Arthur Waldron (*d* 1953), Newbury; one *s* one *d*. *Educ:* Marlborough; RMC, Sandhurst. jssc, psc. 2nd Lieut, Gloucestershire Regt, 1929. Served War of 1939–45 (OBE, DSO): 5 British Division and 1st Bn Green Howards, in India, Middle East, Italy, NW Europe. Lt-Col, 10th Gurkha Rifles, 1951; Brigadier, 1958; ADC to the Queen, 1960–61; retired, 1961. *Address:* c/o Banco Hispano Americano, Avenida Ramón y Cajal 12, Marbella, Spain. *Clubs:* Army and Navy, Royal Cruising.

WALDRON-RAMSEY, Waldo Emerson; Barrister and Attorney-at-Law; Senator, Parliament of Barbados, since 1983; Editor, The Beacon Newspaper, Barbados, since 1982; *b* 1 Jan. 1930; *s* of Wyatt and Delcina Waldron-Ramsey; *m* 1954, Shiela Pamella Beresford, Georgetown, Guyana; one *s* two *d*. *Educ:* Barbados; Hague Academy; London Sch. of Economics; Yugoslavia. LLB Hons; BSc (Econ) Hons; PhD. Called to Bar, Middle Temple; practised London Bar and SW Circuit, 1957–60; Marketing Economist, Shell International, 1960–61; Tanzanian Foreign Service, 1961–70; High Comr for Barbados in UK, and Ambassador to France, Netherlands and Germany, 1970–71; Ambassador and Perm. Rep. for Barbados to UN, 1971–76. UN Legal Expert: in field of human rights, 1967–71; on Israel, 1968–71. Mem., National Exec., Barbados Labour Party, 1980–. Member: Amer. Acad. of Political and Social Sciences; Amer. Soc. of Internat. Law; Amer. Inst. of Petroleum (Marketing Div.). Hon. Fellow, Hebrew Univ. of Jerusalem, 1972. DSc (Pol. Econ.) Univ. of Phnom-Penh, 1973; Hon. LLD Chung-Ang Univ., Republic of Korea, 1975. Grand Officer (1st Class), Nat. Order of Honneur et Mérite, Republic of Haiti, 1968; Grand Officier, Ordre Nat. de l'Amitié et Mérite, Khymèr, 1973; Order of Distinguished Diplomatic Service Merit, Gwangwha (1st Class), Republic of Korea, 1974. *Recreations:* cricket, tennis, bridge, travel. *Address:* (chambers) 50 Swan Street, Bridgetown, Barbados; (chambers) 26 Court Street, Brooklyn, New York 11225, USA; The Monticello, 30 Park Avenue, Mount Vernon, New York 10550. *Clubs:* Royal Automobile; Lincoln Lodge (Connecticut).

WALES, Archbishop of; *no new appointment at time of going to press.*

WALES, Geoffrey, RE 1961 (ARE 1948); ARCA 1936; wood engraver; Lecturer, Norwich School of Art, 1953–77; *b* 26 May 1912; *s* of Ernest and Kathleen Wales; *m* 1940, Marjorie Skeeles, painter; two *d*. *Educ:* Chatham House School, Ramsgate; Thanet School of Art; Royal College of Art. Served War of 1939–45, in Royal Air Force, 1940–46. Prints and drawings in Victoria and Albert Museum; Whitworth Gallery, Manchester; Kunsthaus, Graz; and private collections. Exhibits with Royal Society of Painter Etchers and Engravers. Illustrated books for Golden Cockerel Press, Kynoch Press, Folio Soc. and general graphic work. Engravings included in publications and articles on wood-engraving. *Address:* 15 Heigham Grove, Norwich, Norfolk NR2 3DQ. *T:* Norwich 629066.

WAŁESA, Lech; Polish labour leader; *b* Popowo, 29 Sept. 1943; *s* of late Bolesław Wałesa and Feliksa Wałesa; *m* 1969, Mirosława; four *s* four *d*. *Educ:* Lipno primary and tech. schools; trained as electrician. Lenin Shipyard, Gdańsk, 1966–76, 1980– (Chm., Strike Cttees, 1970, 1980); founder Chm., Nat. Co-ordinating Commn of Indep. Autonomous Trade Union Solidarity (NSZZ Solidarność), 1980–82; in custody, 1981–82. Dr *hc:* Alliance Coll., Cambridge, Mass, 1981; Harvard, 1983. Nobel Peace Prize, 1983. *Address:* ul. Pilotow 17D/3, Gdańsk-Zaspa, Poland.

WALEY, (Andrew) Felix, VRD 1960 and Clasp 1970; QC 1973; **His Honour Judge Waley;** a Circuit Judge, since 1982; Resident Judge, County of Kent, since 1985; Judge Advocate of the Fleet, since 1986; *b* 14 April 1926; *s* of Guy Felix Waley and Anne Elizabeth (*née* Dickson); *m* 1955, Petica Mary, *d* of Sir Philip Rose, 3rd Bt; one *s* three *d* (and one *d* decd). *Educ:* Charterhouse; Worcester Coll., Oxford (MA). RN, 1944–48; RNR, 1951–71, retd as Comdr. Oxford, 1948–51; called to the Bar, Middle Temple, 1953, Bencher, 1981; a Recorder of the Crown Court, 1974–82. Conservative Councillor, Paddington, 1956–59. Contested (C) Dagenham, 1959. *Recreations:* gardens, boats, birds.

Address: Pleasure House, East Sutton, Kent ME17 3NW. *T:* Maidstone 842282. *Clubs:* Garrick; Royal Naval Sailing Association.

WALEY, Daniel Philip, PhD; Keeper of Manuscripts, British Library, 1973–86 (Keeper of Manuscripts, British Museum, 1972–73); *b* 20 March 1921; *er s* of late Hubert David Waley and of Margaret Hendelah Waley; *m* 1945, Pamela Joan Griffiths; one *s* two *d. Educ:* Dauntsey's Sch.; King's Coll., Cambridge (MA, PhD). Historical Tripos, Cambridge, 1939–40 and 1945–46 (cl. 1). Served War, 1940–45. Fellow of King's Coll., Cambridge, 1950–54. Asst Lectr in Medieval History, London School of Economics and Political Science, Univ. of London, 1949–51, Lectr, 1951–61, Reader in History, 1961–70, Prof. of History, 1970–72. Hon. Res. Fellow, Westfield Coll., London; Emer. Fellow, Leverhulme Trust, 1986–87. British Acad. Italian Lectr, 1975. *Publications:* Mediaeval Orvieto, 1952; The Papal State in the 13th Century, 1961; Later Medieval Europe, 1964 (2nd edn 1985); The Italian City Republics, 1969 (2nd edn 1978); British Public Opinion and the Abyssinian War, 1935–36, 1975; (ed) George Eliot's Blotter: A Commonplace-Book, 1980; contributor to: Dizionario Biografico degli Italiani, English Hist. Review, Trans Royal Hist. Soc., Papers of British Sch. at Rome, Jl of Ecclesiastical Hist., Jl of the History of Ideas, Rivista Storica Italiana, Rivista di Storia della Chiesa in Italia, Procs Brit. Acad., British Library Jl, etc. *Recreation:* walking. *Address:* The Croft, 43 Southover High Street, Lewes, E Sussex BN7 1HX.

WALEY, Felix; *see* Waley, A. F.

WALEY-COHEN, Sir Bernard (Nathaniel), 1st Bt *cr* 1961; Kt 1957; Director: Lloyds Bank Ltd Central London Region, 1962–84; Matthews Wrightson Pulbrook Ltd, 1971–84; Kleeman Industrial Holdings Ltd, since 1957 and other companies; *b* 29 May 1914; *er s* of late Sir Robert Waley Cohen, KBE and Alice Violet, *d* of Henry Edward Beddington, London and Newmarket; *m* 1943, Hon. Joyce Constance Ina Nathan (*see* Lady Waley-Cohen); two *s* two *d. Educ:* HMS Britannia (RNC Dartmouth); Clifton College; Magdalene Coll., Cambridge (MA). Mem. of staff, Duke of York's Camp, Southwold, 1932–36; Mem. of Public School Empire Tour, New Zealand, 1932–33; Liveryman, Clothworkers' Company, 1936, Court 1966, Chm., Finance Cttee, 1971–79, Master, 1975. Gunner, HAC, 1937–38; Underwriting Member of Lloyd's 1939; Principal Ministry of Fuel and Power 1940–47. Alderman, City of London Portsoken Ward, 1949–84; Sheriff, City of London, 1955–56; Lord Mayor of London, 1960–61; one of HM Lieutenants, City of London, 1949–. Mem. Council and Board of Governors, Clifton Coll., 1952–81; Mem., College Cttee, University College London, 1953–80, Treasurer 1962–70; Vice-Chm. 1970; Chm., 1971–80; Mem. Senate, 1962–78; Court, 1966–78, London Univ.; Governor, Wellesley House Prep. Sch., 1965, Chm., 1965–77. Hon. Sec. and Treasurer, Devon and Somerset Staghounds, 1940, Chm. 1953–85, Pres, 1985–; Mem. Finance and General Purposes Cttee, British Field Sports Soc., 1957, Treasurer 1965–78, Trustee, 1979, Dep. Pres., 1980; President: Bath and West and Southern Counties Show, 1963; Devon Cattle Breeders' Soc., 1963; W of England Hound Show, Honiton, 1974. Mem., Marshall Aid Commemoration Commn, 1957–60; Member: Jewish Cttee, HM Forces, 1947, Vice-Pres., 1980; Jewish Meml Council, 1947; Treasurer, Jewish Welfare Board, 1948–53; Vice-President: United Synagogue, 1952–61; Anglo-Jewish Assoc., 1962; Trades Adv. Council, 1963, Pres., 1981–84; Pres., Jewish Museum, 1964; Vice-Chairman: Palestine Corp., 1947–53; Union Bank of Israel Ltd, 1950–53; Chm., Simo Securities Trust Ltd, 1955–70; Mem., Nat. Corporation for Care of Old People, 1965–78; Mem., Executive Cttee and Central Council, Probation and After Care Cttees, 1965–69; Mem., Club Facilities Cttee, MCC, 1965–77; Trustee, Coll. of Arms Trust, 1970; Mem., Exec. Cttee, St Paul's Cathedral Appeal, 1970–72. Comr and Dep. Chm., Public Works Loan Board, 1971–72, Chm. 1972–79. Governor, Hon. Irish Soc., 1973–76. Mem. Foundn Cttee, Cambridge Soc., 1975, Exec. Cttee and Council 1976, Vice-Pres., 1980. Hon. Liveryman of Farmers' Company, 1961. Assoc. KStJ 1961. Hon. LLD London, 1961. *Recreations:* hunting, racing, shooting. *Heir: s* Stephen Harry Waley-Cohen [*b* 22 June 1946; *m* 1st, 1972, Pamela Elizabeth Doniger (marr. diss.); two *s* one *d*; 2nd, 1986, Josephine Burnett Spencer, *yr d* of late Duncan M. Spencer and Josephine Spencer; one *d. Educ:* Eton (Oppidan Scholar); Magdalene Coll., Cambridge (BA 1968). Financial Journalist, Daily Mail, 1968–73; Exec. Dir/Publisher, Euromoney, 1973–83; Chief Executive, Maybox PLC, 1984–]. *Address:* Honeymead, Simonsbath, Minehead, Somerset TA24 7JX. *T:* Exford 242. *Clubs:* Boodle's, Pratts, MCC, Harlequins RFC, City Livery; Jockey Club Rooms (Newmarket); University Pitt (Cambridge).

WALEY-COHEN, Hon. Joyce Constance Ina, JP; MA; **(Hon. Lady Waley-Cohen);** President, Independent Schools Information Service Council, 1981–85 (Member, 1972–80); *b* 20 Jan. 1920; *o d* of 1st Baron Nathan, PC, TD, and Eleanor Joan Clara, *d* of C. Stettauer; *m* 1943, Sir Bernard Nathaniel Waley-Cohen, Bt, *qv*; two *s* two *d. Educ:* St Felix Sch., Southwold; Girton Coll., Cambridge (MA). Member: Governing Body, St Felix Sch., 1945–83 (Chm., 1970–83); Westminster Hosp. Bd of Governors, 1952–68; Chairman: Westminster Children's Hosp., 1952–68; Gordon Hosp., 1961–68; Governing Bodies of Girls' Schools' Assoc., 1974–79 (Mem., 1963); Ind. Schs Jt Council, 1977–80. Governor: Taunton Sch., 1978–; Wellington Coll., 1979–. JP Mddx 1949–59, Somerset 1959–. *Recreations:* hunting, spinning, family life. *Address:* Honeymead, Simonsbath, Minehead, Somerset TA24 7JX. *T:* Exford 242.

WALFORD, Major-General Alfred Ernest, CB 1946; CBE 1944; MM 1916; ED; Legion of Merit (USA); CA; FCIS; *b* Montreal, 20 Aug. 1896; *s* of Alfred G. S. and Phoebe Anne Walford, Montreal; *m* 1922, Olive Marjorie, *d* of James A. Dyke, Westmount Province of Quebec; one *s. Educ:* Westmount Acad. Served European War, 1914–19, with Royal Canadian Artillery, and War of 1939–45, HQ 1st Canadian Div., 1st Canadian Corps and as DA&QMG 1st Canadian Army in NW Europe; Adjutant-General Canadian Forces, and mem., Army Council, Nat. Defence Headquarters, Ottawa, 1944–46. Partner, Alfred Walford & Sons, Chartered Accountants, 1923–29; Dir, Sec. and Treasurer, of James A. Ogilvy Ltd, 1929–39, of Henry Morgan & Co. Ltd, 1946–61; Pres., Morgan Trust Co., 1946–65; Chairman: E. G. M. Cape & Co. Ltd, 1965–68; Canadian Vickers Ltd, 1959–67; Dir and Chm., Montreal Adv. Bd of Canada Trust Co., 1961–72; Dir, Excelsior Life Insurance Co., 1951–70; Dir and Vice-Pres., Mercantile Bank of Canada, 1961–70; Hon. Dir, Canada Trust, 1972–. Member: Metropolitan Adv. Bd, YMCA; Nat Adv. Bd, Salvation Army; Past President: Fedn Commonwealth Chambers of Commerce; National Cttee, English-Speaking Union; Montreal Board of Trade; Past Chairman, Exec. Development Institute. Fellow, Royal Commonwealth Society; FCIS; Life Mem., Order of Chartered Accountants of Quebec. *Address:* (office) Suite 1400, 635 Dorchester Boulevard West, Montreal PQ H3B 1S3, Canada; (home) E90, The Chateau Apartments, 1321 Sherbrooke West, Montreal, PQ H3G 1J4. *Clubs:* St James's, Forest and Stream (Montreal).

WALFORD, Dr Diana Marion; Senior Principal Medical Officer (Under Secretary), Department of Health and Social Security, since 1983; Hon. Consultant Haematologist, Central Middlesex Hospital, since 1977; *b* 26 Feb. 1944; *d* of Lt-Col Joseph Norton, LLM, and Thelma Norton (*née* Nurick); *m* 1970, Arthur David Walford; one *s* one *d. Educ:* Calder High Sch. for Girls, Liverpool; Liverpool Univ. (George Holt Medal, Physiol.; J. H. Abram Prize, Pharmacol.; BSc (1st Cl. Hons Physiol.) 1965; MB ChB 1968; MD 1976). MRCP 1972; FRCPath (MRCPath 1974). Ho. Officer posts, Liverpool Royal Inf., 1968–69; Sen. Ho. Officer posts and Sen. Registrar, St Mary's Hosp., Paddington, and Northwick Park Hosp., Harrow, 1969–75; MRC Research (Training) Fellow, Clin. Res. Centre, 1975–76; Sen. MO 1976–79, PMO 1979–83, DHSS. Mem., British Soc. for Haematology, 1978–; Founder Mem., British Blood Transfusion Soc., 1983–; FRSM. *Publications:* chapters on haematological side effects of drugs in: Meyler's Side Effects of Drugs, 9th edn 1980; Side Effects of Drugs Annual, 1980; Drug-Induced Emergencies, 1980; articles on alpha-thalassaemia. *Recreations:* theatre, painting, travel. *Address:* 94 London Road, Stanmore, Middlesex HA7 4NS. *T:* 01–954 3640.

WALFORD, John Howard; President, Solicitors' Disciplinary Tribunal, since 1979; *b* 16 May 1927; *s* of Henry Howard Walford and Marjorie Josephine Solomon; *m* 1953, Peggy Ann Jessel; two *s* two *d. Educ:* Cheltenham College; Gonville and Caius College, Cambridge; MA (Hons). Solicitor, 1950; Senior Partner, Bischoff & Co., 1979–. Mem. Council, Law Society, 1961–69; Governor, College of Law, 1967–; Senior Warden, City of London Solicitors' Co., 1980–81, Master, 1981–82. Governor, St John's Hosp. for Diseases of the Skin, 1960–82; Chm., Appeal Cttee, Skin Disease Research Fund. Commander, Order of Bernardo O'Higgins, Chile, 1972. *Address:* Pheasant Court, Northchapel, near Petworth, W Sussex; 9 Palliser Court, Palliser Road, W14. *Clubs:* Garrick, City Law.

WALKER, Rev. Sir Alan, Kt 1981; OBE 1955; Director of World Evangelism, World Methodist Council, since 1978; *b* 1911; *s* of Rev. Alfred Edgar Walker, former Pres., NSW Methodist Conf., and Violet Louise Walker; *m* 1938, Winifred Garrard Walker (*née* Channon); three *s* one *d. Educ:* Leigh Theological Coll., Sydney; Univ. of Sydney (BA, MA); Bethany Biblical Seminary, Chicago. Minister, Cessnock, NSW, 1939–44; Supt, Waverley Methodist Mission, 1944–54; Dir, Australian Mission to the Nation, 1953–56; Vis. Professor: of Evangelism, Boston Sch. of Theology, 1957; of Evangelism and Preaching, Claremont Sch. of Theol., USA, 1973; Supt, Central Methodist Mission, Sydney, 1958–78. Deleg. to First Assembly of WCC, Amsterdam, 1948; Adviser to: Aust. Delegn at UN, 1949; Third Ass. of WCC, New Delhi, 1962; Fourth Ass., WCC, Uppsala, 1968; Missions to: Fiji, S Africa, S America, Singapore and Malaysia, Sri Lanka, 1962–75; Founder, Sydney Life Line Tel. Counselling Centre, 1963 (Pres., Life Line Internat., 1966–); Sec., NSW Methodist Conf., 1970, Pres., 1971; lectures, various times, USA. Hon. DD Bethany Biblical Sem., 1954; Inst. de la Vie award, Paris, for services to humanity, 1978. *Publications include:* There is Always God, 1938; Everybody's Calvary, 1943; Coal Town, 1944; Heritage Without End, 1953; The Whole Gospel for the Whole World, 1957; The Many Sided Cross of Jesus, 1962; How Jesus Helped People, 1964; A Ringing Call to Mission, 1966; The Life Line Story, 1967 (USA, As Close as the Telephone); Breakthrough, 1969; God, the Disturber, 1973 (USA); Jesus, the Liberator, 1973 (USA); The New Evangelism, 1974 (USA); Love in Action, 1977; Life Grows with Christ, 1981. *Recreations:* swimming, tennis. *Address:* 14 Owen Stanley Avenue, Beacon Hill, NSW 2100, Australia. *T:* 451 3923.

WALKER, Alexander; Film Critic, The Standard (formerly London Evening Standard), since 1960; *b* Portadown, N Ireland, 22 March 1930; *s* of Alfred and Ethel Walker. *Educ:* Portadown Grammar Sch.; The Queen's Univ., Belfast (BA); Collège d'Europe, Bruges; Univ. of Michigan, Ann Arbor. Lecturer in political philosophy and comparative govt, Univ. of Michigan, 1952–54. Features editor, Birmingham Gazette, 1954–56; leader writer and film critic, The Birmingham Post, 1956–59; columnist, Vogue magazine, 1974–. Frequent broadcaster on the arts on radio and television; author of TV series Moviemen; author and co-producer of TV programmes on History of Hollywood, Garbo and Chaplin. Member: British Screen Adv. Council (formerly Wilson Interim Action Cttee on the Film Industry), 1977–; British Screen Adv. Council, 1985–. Chevalier de l'Ordre des Arts et des Lettres, 1981. Twice named Critic of the Year, in annual British Press awards, 1970, 1974, commended, 1985; Award of Golden Eagle, Philippines, for services to internat. cinema, 1982. *Publications:* The Celluloid Sacrifice: aspects of sex in the movies, 1966; Stardom: the Hollywood phenomenon, 1970; Stanley Kubrick Directs, 1971; Hollywood, England: the British film industry in the sixties, 1974; Rudolph Valentino, 1976; Double Takes: notes and afterthoughts on the movies 1956–76, 1977; Superstars, 1978; The Shattered Silents: how the talkies came to stay, 1978; Garbo, 1980; Peter Sellers: the authorized biography, 1981; Joan Crawford, 1983; Dietrich, 1984; (ed) No Bells on Sunday: journals of Rachel Roberts, 1984; National Heroes: British cinema industry in the seventies and eighties, 1985; Bette Davis, 1986; trans., Benayoun, Woody Allen: beyond words, 1986; contributor to Encounter and other British and for. publications. *Recreations:* ski-ing, persecuting smokers. *Address:* 1 Marlborough, 38–40 Maida Vale, W9 1RW. *T:* 01–289 0985.

WALKER, (Alfred) Cecil, JP; MP (OUP) Belfast North, since 1983 (resigned seat Dec. 1985 in protest against Anglo-Irish Agreement; re-elected Jan. 1986); *b* 17 Dec. 1924; *s* of Alfred George Walker and Margaret Lucinda Walker; *m* 1953, Ann May Joan Verrant; two *s. Educ:* Methodist College. Senior Certificate. In timber business with James P. Corry & Co. Ltd, Belfast, 1941–, Departmental Manager, 1952. JP Belfast, 1966. *Recreations:* sailing, sea angling. *Address:* 1 Wynnland Road, Newtownabbey, Northern Ireland. *T:* Glengormley 3463. *Club:* Down Cruising.

WALKER, Sir Allan (Grierson), Kt 1968; QC (Scotland); Sheriff Principal of Lanarkshire, 1963–74; *b* 1 May 1907; *er s* of late Joseph Walker, merchant, London, and Mary Grierson; *m* 1935, Audrey Margaret, *o d* of late Dr T. A. Glover, Doncaster; one *s. Educ:* Whitgift Sch., Croydon; Edinburgh Univ. Practised at Scottish Bar, 1931–39; Sheriff-Substitute of Roxburgh, Berwick, and Selkirk at Selkirk and of the County of Peebles, 1942–45; Sheriff-Substitute of Stirling, Dumbarton and Clackmannan at Dumbarton, 1945–50; Sheriff-Substitute of Lanarkshire at Glasgow, 1950–63; Member, Law Reform Cttee for Scotland, 1964–70; Chm., Sheriff Court Rules Council, 1972–74. Hon. LLD Glasgow, 1967. *Publications:* The Law of Evidence in Scotland (joint author); Purves' Scottish Licensing Laws (7th, 8th edns). *Recreations:* walking, gardening. *Address:* 24 Moffat Road, Dumfries. *T:* Dumfries 53583.

WALKER, Angus Henry; Director, Strategic Business Planning, British Telecom PLC, since 1984; *b* 30 Aug. 1935; *s* of late Frederick William Walker and of Esther Victoria Nicholas; *m* 1st, 1968, Beverly Phillpotts (marr. diss. 1976); 2nd, 1979, Ann Snow (*née* Griffiths; one *d* and two step *d. Educ:* Erith Grammar Sch., Kent; Balliol Coll., Oxford (Domus Scholar; BA Mod. Hist.; Stanhope Prize, 1958; MA). Nat. Service, 1954–56 (2nd Lieut RA). Senior Scholar, St Antony's Coll., Oxford, 1959–63; HM Diplomatic Service, 1963–68: FO, 1963–65; First Sec., Washington, 1965–68. Lectr, SSEES, London Univ., 1968–70; Univ. Lectr in Russian Social and Political Thought, Oxford, and Lectr, Balliol Coll., 1971–76; Fellow, Wolfson Coll., Oxford, 1972–76; Dir, SSEES, London Univ., 1976–79; British Petroleum Co. Plc, 1979–84. *Publications:* trans. from Polish: Political Economy, by Oskar Lange, vol. 1, 1963; Marx: his theory in its context, 1978. *Address:* 5 North Square, NW11 7AA. *T:* 01–455 2726. *Club:* Reform.

WALKER, Lt-Gen. Antony Kenneth Frederick; Deputy Chief of the Defence Staff (Commitments), Ministry of Defence, since April 1987; *b* 16 May 1934; *o s* of late

Kenneth Walker and Iris Walker; *m* 1st, 1961, Diana Merran Steward (marr. diss. 1983); one *s* one *d*; 2nd, 1985, Mrs S. C. Lawson-Baker. *Educ:* Merchant Taylors' School; RMA Sandhurst. Commissioned into Royal Tank Regt, 1954; served BAOR, Libya, Ghana, Northern Ireland, Hong Kong, Cyprus; Instructor, Staff Coll., 1971–73; CO 1st Royal Tank Regt, 1974–76 (despatches); Col GS HQ UK Land Forces, 1976–78; Comd Task Force Golf (11 Armd Bde), 1978–80; Dep. Mil. Sec. (A), 1980–82; Comdr, 3rd Armoured Div., 1982–84; Chief of Staff, HQ UKLF, 1985–87. Col Comdt, Royal Tank Regt, 1983– (Rep., 1985–). *Recreations:* bird watching, country sports, music, practical study of wine. *Address:* c/o National Westminster Bank plc, 151 The Parade, High Street, Watford, Herts WD1 1NQ. *Club:* Army and Navy.

WALKER, Arthur Geoffrey, FRS 1955; Professor of Pure Mathematics, Liverpool University, 1952–74, now Emeritus; *b* 17 July 1909; 2nd *s* of late A. J. Walker, Watford, Herts; *m* 1939, Phyllis Ashcroft, *d* of late Sterry B. Freeman, CBE. *Educ:* Watford Grammar Sch.; Balliol Coll., Oxford. MA (Oxon); PhD, DSc (Edinburgh); FRSE; Lectr at Imperial Coll. Science and Technology, 1935–36; at Liverpool Univ., 1936–47; Prof. of Mathematics in the Univ. of Sheffield, 1947–52. Mem. of Council, Royal Soc., 1962–63. Pres., London Mathematical Soc., 1963–65. Junior Berwick Prize of London Mathematical Soc., 1947; Keith Medal of Royal Society of Edinburgh, 1950. *Publication:* Harmonic Spaces (with H. S. Ruse and T. J. Willmore), 1962. *Address:* Beechcroft, Roundabout Lane, West Chiltington, Pulborough, W Sussex RH20 2RL. *T:* West Chiltington 2412.

WALKER, Air Chief Marshal Sir Augustus; *see* Walker, Air Chief Marshal Sir G. A.

WALKER, Sir Baldwin Patrick, 4th Bt, *cr* 1856; *b* 10 Sept. 1924; *s* of late Comdr Baldwin Charles Walker, *o s* of 3rd Bt and Mary, *d* of F. P. Barnett of Whalton, Northumberland; *S* grandfather, 1928; *m* 1948, Joy Yvonne (marr. diss., 1954); *m* 1954, Sandra Stewart; *m* 1966, Rosemary Ann, *d* of late Henry Hollingdrake; one *s* one *d*; *m* 1980, Vanessa Hilton. *Educ:* Gordonstoun. Served Royal Navy, Fleet Air Arm, 1943–58. Lieut, RN, retired. Mem. Cttee, S African Solar Energy Soc. *Heir: s* Christopher Robert Baldwin Walker, *b* 25 Oct. 1969. *Address:* 27 Rose Avenue, Tokai, 7945, South Africa.

WALKER, Bill; *see* Walker, W. C.

WALKER, Bobby; *see* Walker, W. B. S.

WALKER, Brian Wilson; President, International Institute for Environment and Development, since 1985; *b* 31 Oct. 1930; *s* of Arthur Walker and Eleanor (*née* Wilson); *m* 1954, Nancy Margaret Gawith; one *s* five *d*. *Educ:* Heversham Sch., Westmorland; Leicester Coll. of Technology; Faculty Technology, Manchester Univ. Management Trainee, Sommerville Bros, Kendal, 1952–55; Personnel Man., Pye Radio, Larne, 1956–61; Bridgeport Brass Ltd, Lisburn: Personnel Man., 1961–66; Gen. Man. (Develt), 1966–69; Gen. Man. (Manufrg), 1969–74; Dir Gen., Oxfam, 1974–83; Dir, Independent Commn on Internat. Humanitarian Issues, 1983–85. Chm., Band Aid—Live Aid Projects Cttee, 1985–86. Founder Chm., New Ulster Movt, 1969–74; Founder Pres., New Ulster Movt Ltd, 1974. Mem., Standing Adv. Commn on Human Rights for NI, 1975–77. Hon. MA Oxon, 1983. Kt, Sov. Order of St Thomas of Acre; Kentucky Colonel, 1966. *Publications:* Authentic Development—Africa, 1986; various political/religious papers on Northern Ireland problem and Third World subjects. *Recreations:* gardening, Irish politics, classical music, active Quaker. *Address:* 14 Upland Park Road, Oxford OX2 7RU; (office) 3 Endsleigh Street, WC1 0DD.

WALKER, Carl, GC 1972; Police Inspector, 1976–82; *b* 31 March 1934; English; *m* 1955, Kathleen Barker; one *s*. *Educ:* Kendal Grammar Sch., Westmorland. RAF Police, 1952–54 (Corporal). Lancashire Police, Oct. 1954–March 1956, resigned; Blackpool Police, 1959–82 (amalgamated with Lancashire Constabulary, April 1968); Sergeant, 1971. Retired 1982, as a result of the injuries sustained from gunshot wounds on 23 Aug. 1971 during an armed raid by thieves on a jeweller's shop in Blackpool (GC). *Recreations:* Rugby; Cumberland and Westmorland wrestling.

WALKER, Cecil; *see* Walker, A. C.

WALKER, Sir (Charles) Michael, GCMG 1976 (KCMG 1963; CMG 1960); HM Diplomatic Service, retired; Chairman, Commonwealth Scholarship Commission in the UK, since 1977; *b* 22 Nov. 1916; *s* of late Col C. W. G. Walker, CMG, DSO; *m* 1945, Enid Dorothy, *d* of late W. A. McAdam, CMG; one *s* one *d*. *Educ:* Charterhouse; New Coll., Oxford. Clerk of House of Lords, June 1939. Enlisted in Army, Oct. 1939, and served in RA until 1946 when released with rank of Lt-Col. Dominions Office, 1947; First Sec., British Embasssy, Washington, 1949–51; Office of United Kingdom High Comr in Calcutta and New Delhi, 1952–55; Establishment Officer, Commonwealth Relations Office, 1955–58. Imperial Defence Coll., 1958; Asst Under-Sec. of State and Dir of Establishment and Organisation, CRO, 1959–62; British High Commissioner in: Ceylon, 1962–65 (concurrently Ambassador to Maldive Islands, July-Nov. 1965), Malaysia, 1966–71; Sec., ODA, FCO, 1971–73; High Comr, India, 1974–76. Chm., Festival of India Trust, 1980–83. Hon. DCL City, 1980. *Recreations:* fishing, gardening, golf. *Address:* Herongate House, West Chiltington Common, Pulborough, Sussex. *T:* West Chiltington 3473. *Club:* Oriental.

WALKER, Vice-Adm. Sir (Charles) Peter (Graham), KBE 1967; CB 1964; DSC 1944; *b* 23 Feb. 1911; *s* of Charles Graham Walker and Lilla Geraldine (*née* Gandy); *m* 1938, Pamela Marcia Hawley, *d* of late George W. Hawley, Cape, SA; one *s* one *d*. *Educ:* Worksop College. Entered Royal Navy, 1929; Royal Naval Engineering Coll., 1930–34; Advanced Engineering Course at RN Coll., Greenwich, 1935–37. War service in HM Ships Cornwall, Georgetown, Duke of York and Berwick and at the Admiralty; Vice-Admiral, 1965; Dir-Gen., Dockyards and Maintenance, MoD (Navy), 1962–67; Chief Naval Engr Officer, 1963–67; retired 1967. *Address:* Brookfield Coach House, Weston Lane, Bath BA1 4AG. *T:* Bath 23863.

See also T. A. P. Walker.

WALKER, Charls E., PhD; Consultant, Washington, DC, since 1973; *b* Graham, Texas, 24 Dec. 1923; *s* of Pinkney Clay and Sammye McCombs Walker; *m* 1949, Harmolyn Hart, Laurens, S Carolina; one *s* one *d*. *Educ:* Univ. of Texas (MBA); Wharton Sch. of Finance, Univ. of Pennsylvania (PhD). Instructor in Finance, 1947–48, and later Asst and Associate Prof., 1950–54, at Univ. of Texas, in the interim teaching at Wharton Sch. of Finance, Univ. of Pennsylvania; Associate Economist, Fed. Reserve Bank: of Philadelphia, 1953, of Dallas, 1954 (Vice-Pres. and Economic Advr, 1958–61); Economist and Special Asst to Pres. of Republic Nat. Bank of Dallas, 1955–56 (took leave to serve as Asst to Treasury Sec., Robert B. Anderson, April 1959–Jan. 1961); Exec. Vice-Pres., Amer. Bankers Assoc., 1961–69. Under-Sec. of the Treasury, 1969–72, Dep. Sec., 1972–73. Chm., American Council for Capital Formation; Mem. Council on Foreign Relations; Chm. Exec. Cttee and Treasurer, Cttee on the Present Danger; Co-Chm., Bretton Woods Cttee. Adjunct Prof. of Finance and Public Affairs, Univ. of Texas at Austin. Hon. LLD Ashland Coll., 1970. *Publications:* Co-editor of The Banker's Handbook, 1978–; New Directions in Federal Tax Policy, 1983; contribs to learned jls, periodicals. *Recreations:* golf, fishing, music. *Address:* 10120 Chapel Road, Potomac, Md 20854, USA. *T:* 301/299–5414. *Club:* Burning Tree Golf (Bethesda, Md).

WALKER, (Christopher) Roy; Under Secretary, Manpower Divison I, Department of Employment, since 1986; *b* 5 Dec. 1934; *s* of Christopher Harry Walker and late Dorothy Jessica Walker; *m* 1961, Hilary Mary Biddiscombe; two *s*. *Educ:* Sir George Monoux Grammar Sch., E17; Sidney Sussex Coll., Cambridge (BA); Université Libre de Bruxelles. National Service, Essex Regt, 1952–54. BoT, 1958; CSD, 1968; Private Sec. to Lord Privy Seal, 1968–71; Treasury, 1973; DTI, 1973; Dept of Energy, 1974; Cabinet Office, 1974; Dept of Energy, 1975; DES, 1977. *Recreations:* hill walking, sailing. *Address:* 54 The Drive, Sevenoaks, Kent. *T:* Sevenoaks 455168. *Club:* Medway Yacht (Rochester).

WALKER, David Alan, PhD, DSc; FRS 1979; FIBiol; Director of Research Institute for Photosynthesis, University of Sheffield, since 1984; *b* 18 Aug. 1928; *s* of Cyril Walker and Dorothy Walker (*née* Dobson); *m* 1956, Shirley Wynne Walker (*née* Mason); one *s* one *d*. *Educ:* King's Coll., Univ. of Durham (BSc, PhD, DSc). Royal Naval Air Service, 1946–48. Lecturer, 1958–63, Reader, 1963–65, Queen Mary Coll., Univ. of London; Reader, Imperial Coll., Univ. of London, 1965–70; Prof. of Biology, Univ. of Sheffield, 1970–86. FIBiol 1971; Corres. Mem., Amer. Soc. Plant Physiol., 1979. *Publications:* Energy Plants and Man, 1979; (with G. E. Edwards) C3, C4—Mechanisms, Cellular and Environmental Regulation of Photosynthesis, 1983; papers, mostly in field of photosynthesis. *Recreation:* singing the Sheffield Carols. *Address:* Research Institute for Photosynthesis, The University, Sheffield S10 2TN. *T:* Sheffield 78555.

WALKER, David Alan; Executive Director, Bank of England, since 1982; *b* 31 Dec. 1939; *s* of Harold and Marian Walker; *m* 1963, Isobel Cooper; one *s* two *d*. *Educ:* Chesterfield Sch.; Queens' Coll., Cambridge (MA). Joined HM Treasury, 1961; Private Sec. to Joint Permanent Secretary, 1964–66; seconded to Staff of International Monetary Fund, Washington, 1970–73; Asst Secretary, HM Treasury, 1973–77; joined Bank as Chief Adviser, then Chief of Economic Intelligence Dept, 1977; Asst Director, 1980. *Recreations:* music, long-distance walking. *Address:* Bank of England, Threadneedle Street, EC2R 8AH. *Club:* Reform.

WALKER, David Bruce; Chief Executive, Britoil plc, since 1985; *b* 30 Aug. 1934; *s* of Noel B. Walker and June R. Walker (*née* Sutherland); *m* 1961, Leonora C. Freeman; two *s*. *Educ:* Knox Grammar Sch., Wahroonga, NSW; Univ. of Sydney (BSc (Hons), MSc, Geology). Demonstrator in Geology: Univ. of Sydney, 1956–58; Bristol Univ., 1958–59; British Petroleum Co., 1959–85: worked as geologist in UK, Gambia, Algeria, Libya, Colombia, Kuwait, Iran and US; Vice-Pres., Production Planning, USA, 1974–77; Regional Coordinator, Western Hemisphere, 1977–79; Controller, BP Exploration, 1979–80; Chief Executive, BP Petroleum Development (UK), 1980–82; Dir, Resources Development, BP Australia, 1982–85. Distinguished Lectr, Soc. of Petroleum Engineers, 1976. President, UK Offshore Operators Assoc., 1982. *Recreations:* cricket, music, gardening. *Address:* Whippletrees, Chetnole, Sherborne, Dorset DT9 6PD. *T:* Sherborne 872604.

WALKER, David Critchlow, MVO 1976; HM Diplomatic Service; Minister, Madrid, since 1986; *b* 9 Jan. 1940; *s* of John Walker and Mary Walker (*née* Cross); *m* 1965, Tineke van der Leek; three *s*. *Educ:* Manchester Grammar Sch.; St Catharine's Coll., Cambridge (BA,MA,DipEd). Assistant Lecturer, Dept of Geography, Manchester Univ., 1962; Commonwealth Relations Office, 1963; Third Secretary, British Embassy, Mexico City, 1965; Second Secretary, Brussels, 1968; First Secretary: FCO, 1970; Washington, 1973; First Sec., later Counsellor, FCO, 1978–83; Consul General, São Paulo, 1983–86. *Address:* c/o Foreign and Commonwealth Office, SW1.

WALKER, Major David Harry, MBE 1946; Author; *b* 9 Feb. 1911; *s* of Harry Giles Walker and Elizabeth Bewley (*née* Newsom); *m* 1939, Willa Magee, Montreal; four *s*. *Educ:* Shrewsbury; Sandhurst. The Black Watch, 1931–47 (retired); ADC to Gov.-Gen. of Canada, 1938–39; Comptroller to Viceroy of India, 1946–47. Member: Royal Company of Archers; Canada Council, 1957–61; Chm., Roosevelt-Campobello Internat. Park Commn, 1970–72 (Canadian Comr, 1965). Hon. DLitt, Univ. of New Brunswick, 1955. FRSL. *Publications: novels:* The Storm and the Silence, 1950 (USA 1949); Geordie, 1950 (filmed 1955); The Pillar, 1952; Digby, 1953; Harry Black, 1956 (filmed, 1957); Sandy was a Soldier's Boy, 1957; Where the High Winds Blow, 1960; Storms of Our Journey and Other Stories, 1962; Dragon Hill (for children), 1962; Winter of Madness, 1964; Mallabec, 1965; Come Back, Geordie, 1966; Devil's Plunge (USA, Cab-Intersec), 1968; Pirate Rock, 1969; Big Ben (for children), 1970; The Lord's Pink Ocean, 1972; Black Dougal, 1973 (USA 1974); Ash, 1976; Pot of Gold, 1977; *non-fiction:* Lean, Wind, Lean: a few times remembered (memoirs), 1984. *Address:* Strathcroix, St Andrews, New Brunswick, Canada. *Club:* Royal and Ancient.

WALKER, Prof. David Maxwell, CBE 1986; QC (Scot.) 1958; FBA 1976; FRSE 1980; Regius Professor of Law, Glasgow University, since 1958; Dean of the Faculty of Law, 1956–59; Senate Assessor on University Court, 1962–66; *b* 9 April 1920; *o s* of James Mitchell Walker, Branch Manager, Union Bank of Scotland, and Mary Paton Colquhoun Irvine; *m* 1954, Margaret Knox, MA, *yr d* of Robert Knox, yarn merchant, Brookfield, Renfrewshire. *Educ:* High School of Glasgow (Mackindlay Prizeman in Classics); Glasgow, Edinburgh and London Universities. MA (Glasgow) 1946; LLB (Distinction), Robertson Schol., 1948; Faulds Fellow in Law, 1949–52; PhD (Edinburgh), 1952; Blackwell Prize, Aberdeen Univ., 1955; LLB (London), 1957; LLD (Edinburgh), 1960; LLD (London), 1968; LLD (Glasgow), 1985. Served War of 1939–45, NCO Cameronians; commissioned HLI, 1940; seconded to RIASC, 1941; served with Indian Forces in India, 1942, Middle East, 1942–43, and Italy, 1943–46, in MT companies and as Brigade Supply and Transport Officer (Captain). HQ 21 Ind. Inf. Bde, 8 Ind. Div. Advocate of Scottish Bar, 1948; Barrister, Middle Temple, 1957; QC (Scotland) 1958; practised at Scottish Bar, 1948–53; studied at Inst. of Advanced Legal Studies, Univ. of London, 1953–54; Prof. of Jurisprudence, Glasgow Univ., 1954–58. Dir, Scottish Univs' Law Inst., 1974–80. Trustee, Hamlyn Trust, 1954–. Governor: Scottish College of Commerce, 1957–64; High School of Glasgow (and Chm., Educational Trust), 1974–. Hon. Sheriff of Lanarkshire at Glasgow, 1966–82. FSA Scotland. Hon. LLD Edinburgh, 1974. *Publications:* (ed) Faculty Digest of Decisions, 1940–50, Supplements, 1951 and 1952; Law of Damages in Scotland, 1955; The Scottish Legal System, 1959, 5th edn 1981; Law of Delict in Scotland, 1966, 2nd edn 1981; Scottish Courts and Tribunals, 1969, 5th edn 1985; Principles of Scottish Private Law (2 vols), 1970, 3rd edn (4 vols), 1982–83; Law of Prescription and Limitation in Scotland, 1973, 3rd edn 1981 and Supp. 1985; Law of Civil Remedies in Scotland, 1974; Law of Contracts in Scotland, 1979, 2nd edn 1985; Oxford Companion to Law, 1980; (ed) Stair's Institutions (6th edn), 1981; (ed) Stair Tercentenary Studies, 1981; The Scottish Jurists, 1985; Scottish Part of Topham and Ivamy's Company Law, 12th edn 1955, to 16th edn 1978; contribs to collaborative works; articles in legal periodicals. *Recreations:* motoring, book collecting, Scottish history. *Address:* 1 Beaumont Gate, Glasgow G12 9EE. *T:* 041–339 2802. *Club:* Royal Scottish Automobile (Glasgow).

WALKER, Maj.-Gen. Derek William Rothwell, CEng, FIMechE, FIEE; Manager, CBI Overseas Scholarships, since 1980; *b* 12 Dec. 1924; *s* of Frederick and Eileen Walker; *m* 1950, Florence Margaret Panting; two *s* (and one *s* decd). *Educ:* Mitcham County Grammar Sch.; Battersea Polytechnic. Commissioned REME, 1946; served: Middle East, 1947–50 (despatches 1949); BAOR, 1951–53; Far East, 1954–56 (despatches 1957); Near East, 1960–62; Far East, 1964–67; psc 1957. Lt-Col 1964, Col 1970, Brig. 1973. Appts include: Comdr, REME Support Group, 1976–77; Dir, Equipment Engineering, 1977–79. Mem. Council, IEE, 1975–79; Pres., SEE, 1979–81. *Recreations:* fishing, sailing, wine-making. *Address:* 26 Cranford Drive, Holybourne, Alton, Hants GU34 4HJ. *T:* Alton 84737.

WALKER, Prof. Donald, FRS 1985; Professor of Biogeography, Institute of Advanced Studies, Australian National University, Canberra, since 1969; *b* 14 May 1928; *s* of Arthur Walker and Eva (*née* Risdon); *m* 1959, Patricia Mary Smith; two *d*. *Educ:* Morecambe Grammar School; Sheffield Univ. (BSc); MA, PhD Cantab. Commission, RAF (Nat. Service), 1953–55. Research Scholar and Asst in Res., later Sen. Asst, Sub-Dept of Quaternary Res., Cambridge Univ., 1949–60; Fellow of Clare College, 1952–60 (Asst Tutor, 1955–60); Reader in Biogeography, ANU, 1960–68; Head of Dept of Biogeography and Geomorphology, ANU, 1969–. *Publications:* articles on plant ecology, palaeoecology and related topics in sci. jls. *Recreations:* pottery, architecture, prehistory. *Address:* 8 Galali Place, Aranda, ACT 2614, Australia. *T:* 062–513136.

WALKER, Sir E(dward) Ronald, Kt 1963; CBE 1956; Australian economist and diplomat; *b* 26 Jan. 1907; *s* of Rev. Frederick Thomas Walker; *m* 1933, Louise Donckers; one *s* one *d*. *Educ:* Sydney Univ. (MA, DSc Econ); Cambridge Univ. (PhD, LittD). Lecturer in Economics, Sydney Univ., 1927–30, 1933–39; Fellow of Rockefeller Foundation, 1931–33; Economic Adviser: NSW Treasury, 1938–39; Govt of Tasmania, 1939–41; Prof. of Economics, Univ. of Tasmania, 1939–46; Chief Economic Adviser and Dep. Dir-Gen., Australian Dept of War Organisation of Industry, 1941–45; UNRRA HQ, Washington, 1945; Counsellor, Australian Embassy, Paris, 1945–50; Exec. Member, Nat. Security Resources Board, Prime Minister's Dept, Canberra, 1950–52; Australian Ambassador to Japan, 1952–55; Ambassador and Permanent Representative of Australia at United Nations, 1956–59 (Aust. Rep., Security Council, 1956–57); Ambassador: to France, 1959–68; to the Federal Republic of Germany, 1968–71; to OECD, Paris, 1971–73. Delegate to many confs and cttees connected with UN, ILO, Unesco, etc; Pres., UN Economic and Social Council, 1964. *Publications:* An Outline of Australian Economics, 1931; Australia in the World Depression, 1933; Money, 1935; Unemployment Policy, 1936; Wartime Economics, 1939; From Economic Theory to Policy, 1943; The Australian Economy in War and Reconstruction, 1947. *Address:* 1 rue de Longchamp, 75116 Paris, France. *T:* 4553.0300.

WALKER, Mrs Esme, CBE 1985; WS; Vice-Chairman, National Consumer Council, since 1984; Chairman, Scottish Association of Citizens' Advice Bureaux, since 1986; *b* 7 Jan. 1932; *d* of David Burnett, SSC and Jane Burnett (*née* Thornton); *m* 1956, Ian Macfarlane Walker, WS; one *s*. *Educ:* St George's School for Girls, Edinburgh; Univ. of Edinburgh (MA, LLB). NP; Mem., Law Soc. of Scotland. Lectr in Legal Studies, Queen Margaret College, Edinburgh, 1977–83. Voluntary worker, Citizens' Advice Bureau, 1960–85. Comr, Equal Opportunities Commn, 1986–. Member: Expert Cttee, Multiple Surveys and Valuations (Scotland), 1982–84; Working Party on Procedure for Judicial Review of Admin. Action, 1983–84; Cttee on Conveyancing, 1984; Scottish Cttee, Council on Tribunals, 1986–. FRSA. *Recreation:* crosswords. *Address:* Clinton House, Whitehouse Loan, Edinburgh. *T:* 031–447 5191. *Clubs:* New (Edinburgh), University of Edinburgh Staff.

WALKER, Frank Stockdale, MC 1919; Chairman, Lever Brothers, Port Sunlight Limited, 1954–60, retired; Director, Thames Board Mills Limited (until 1960); Director, Glycerine Limited; *b* 24 June 1895; *s* of Frank and Mary Elizabeth Walker; *m* 1921, Elsie May Nicholas (*d* 1974); one *s*. *Address:* Glenside Nursing Home, Manor Road, Sidmouth, Devon EX10 8RP. *T:* Sidmouth 78298.

WALKER, Prof. Frederick, MD; FRCPath; Regius Professor of Pathology, University of Aberdeen, since 1984; Consultant Pathologist, Grampian Health Board, since 1984; *b* 21 Dec. 1934; *s* of Frederick James Walker and Helen Stitt Halliday; *m* 1963, Cathleen Anne Gordon, BSc; two *d*. *Educ:* Kirkcudbright Academy; Univ. of Glasgow. MB ChB 1958; PhD 1964; MD 1971; MRCPath 1966, FRCPath 1978. Lectr in Pathology, Univ. of Glasgow, 1962–67; Vis. Asst Prof., Univ. of Minnesota, 1964–65; Sen. Lectr in Pathology, Univ. of Aberdeen, 1968–73; Foundation Prof. of Pathology, Univ. of Leicester, 1973–84. Gen. Editor, Biopsy Pathology Series, 1978–; Editor, Jl of Pathology, 1983–. *Publications:* papers in scientific and med. jls, esp. on connective tissues. *Recreations:* writing, walking, landscape gardening. *Address:* Department of Pathology, University Medical Buildings, Foresterhill, Aberdeen AB9 2ZD. *T:* Aberdeen 681818.

WALKER, Geoffrey Basil W.; *see* Woodd Walker.

WALKER, Air Chief Marshal Sir (George) Augustus, GCB 1969 (KCB 1962; CB 1959); CBE 1945; DSO 1941; DFC 1941; AFC 1956; *b* 24 Aug. 1912; *s* of G. H. Walker, Garforth, Leeds; *m* 1942, Brenda Brewis; one *s* one *d*. *Educ:* St Bees' Sch.; St Catharine's, Cambridge. Entered RAF Univ. Commission, 1934; Air Min. (R&D), 1938–39; commanded Bomber Sqdn, Stations and Base, 1940–45; SASO No 4 Group, 1945–46; Air Min., Dep. Dir, Operational Training, 1946–48; SASO Rhodesian Air Training Group, 1948–50; JSSC 1950; IDC 1953; Commandant, Royal Air Force Flying Coll., 1954–56; AOC No 1 Group, 1956–59; Chief Information Officer, Air Min., 1959–61; AOC-in-C, Flying Training Command, 1961–64; Inspector-General, RAF, 1964–67; Dep. C-in-C Allied Forces, Central Europe, 1967–70; retd 1970. ADC to the Queen, 1952–56, to King George VI, 1943–52; Air ADC to the Queen, 1968–70. Dir, Philips Electronics, 1970–82. Hon. Col, 33rd (Lancashire and Cheshire) Signal Regt, Royal Corps of Signals, T&AVR, 1970–75. Pres., RFU, 1965–66; Chm., Royal Air Forces Assoc., 1973–78, Pres., 1978–81; Chm., Nat. Sporting Club, 1973–83; Chm., Exec. Cttee, Lord Kitchener Nat. Meml Fund, 1977–82 (Chm., Scholarship Cttee, 1974–77). Governor and Commandant, Church Lads Brigade, 1970–78, Church Lads and Church Girls Brigade, 1978–79. *Recreations:* Rugby (played for England, 1939, Barbarians, RAF, Blackheath, Yorkshire; Captained RAF, 1936–39), golf, sailing. *Address:* The Hoe, Brancaster Staithe, Kings Lynn, Norfolk. *Club:* Royal Air Force.

WALKER, Dr George Patrick Leonard, FRS 1975; G. A. Macdonald Professor of Volcanology, University of Hawaii, since 1981; *b* 2 March 1926; *s* of Leonard Richard Thomas Walker and Evelyn Frances Walker; *m* 1958, Hazel Rosemary (*née* Smith); one *s* one *d*. *Educ:* Wallace High Sch., Lisburn, N Ire.; Queen's Univ., Belfast (BSc, MSc); Univ. of Leeds (PhD); Univ. of London (DSc 1982). Research, Univ. of Leeds, 1948–51; Asst Lectr and Lectr, Imperial Coll., 1951–64; Reader in Geology, Imperial Coll., 1964–79; Captain J. Cook Res. Fellow, Royal Soc. of NZ, 1978–80. Awarded moiety of Lyell Fund of Geological Soc. of London, 1963, Lyell Medal, 1982. Hon. Mem., Vísindafjelag Íslendiga, (Iceland), 1968. McKay Hammer Award, Geol Soc. of NZ, 1982. Icelandic Order of the Falcon, Knight's Class, 1980. *Publications:* scientific papers on mineralogy, the geology of Iceland, and volcanology. *Recreation:* visiting volcanoes. *Address:* Department of Geology and Geophysics, University of Hawaii at Manoa, 2525 Correa Road, Honolulu, Hawaii 96822, USA. *T:* (808) 948–7826.

WALKER, Sir Gervas (George), Kt 1979; JP; DL; Chairman and Leader, Avon County Council, 1973–81; *b* 12 Sept. 1920; *yr s* of late Harry James Walker and Susanna Mary Walker; *m* 1944, Jessie Eileen (*née* Maxwell); two *s*. *Educ:* Monmouth Sch. Bristol City Council: Councillor, 1956–74; Alderman, 1970–74; Leader of Council, 1966–72; Leader of Opposition Party, 1972–74; Chm., Planning and Transportation Cttee, 1960–63 and 1966–72; Chm., Bristol Avon River Authority, 1963–66. Member: SW Regional Economic Planning Council, 1972–79; Local Authorities' Conditions of Service Adv. Bd, 1974–81; Severn Barrage Cttee, 1978–81; British Rail (Western) Bd, 1979–85. Chm., Assoc. of County Councils, 1979–81 (Vice-Chm., 1978–79). Chairman, Bristol Conservative Assoc., 1975–79. JP Bristol, 1969; DL Avon, 1982. *Recreation:* fly-fishing. *Address:* The Lodge, Cobblestone Mews, Clifton Park, Bristol BS8 3DQ. *T:* Bristol 737063; Bulverton Well Farm, Sidmouth, Devon EX10 9DW. *T:* Sidmouth 6902.

WALKER, Rt. Hon. Harold, PC 1979; MP (Lab) Doncaster Central, since 1983 (Doncaster, 1964–83); Chairman of Ways and Means and Deputy Speaker, House of Commons, since 1983; *b* 12 July 1927; *s* of Harold and Phyllis Walker; *m* 1984, Mary Griffin; one *d* by former marriage. *Educ:* Manchester College of Technology. An Assistant Government Whip, 1967–68; Jt Parly Under-Sec. of State, Dept of Employment and Productivity, 1968–70; Opposition Front-Bench spokesman on Industrial Relations, 1970–74, on Employment, 1980–; Parly Under-Sec. of State, Dept of Employment, 1974–76; Minister of State, Dept of Employment, 1976–79. *Recreations:* reading, gardening. *Address:* House of Commons, SW1. *Clubs:* Westminster, Clay Lane, Doncaster Trades, RN, Catholic (all Doncaster).

WALKER, Harold Berners, CMG 1979; HM Diplomatic Service; Ambassador to Ethiopia, since 1986; *b* 19 Oct. 1932; *s* of late Admiral Sir Harold Walker, KCB, RN, and of Lady Walker (*née* Berners); *m* 1960, Jane Bittleston; one *s* two *d*. *Educ:* Winchester (Exhibition 1946); Worcester Coll., Oxford (Exhibition 1952). BA 1955. 2nd Lieut RE, 1951–52. Foreign Office, 1955; MECAS, 1957; Asst Political Agent, Dubai, 1958; Foreign Office, 1960; Principal Instructor, MECAS, 1963; First Sec., Cairo, 1964; Head of Chancery and Consul, Damascus, 1966; Foreign Office (later FCO), 1967; First Sec. (Commercial), Washington, 1970; Counsellor, Jedda, 1973; Dep. Head, Personnel Operations Dept, FCO, 1975–76, Head of Dept, 1976–78; Corpus Christi Coll., Cambridge, 1978; Ambassador to Bahrein, 1979–81, to United Arab Emirates, 1981–86. *Recreation:* tennis. *Address:* c/o Foreign and Commonwealth Office, SW1. *Club:* United Oxford & Cambridge University.

WALKER, His Honour Judge Harry; *see* Walker, P. H. C.

WALKER, Major Sir Hugh (Ronald), 4th Bt, *cr* 1906; *b* 13 Dec. 1925; *s* of Major Sir Cecil Edward Walker, 3rd Bt, DSO, MC, and Violet (*née* McMaster); *S* father, 1964; *m* 1971, Norna, *er d* of Lt-Cdr R. D. Baird, RNR; two *s*. *Educ:* Wellington Coll., Berks. Joined Royal Artillery, 1943; commissioned Sept. 1945; 2 iC, RA Range, Benbecula, Outer Hebrides, 1964–66; Commanding No 1 Army Information Team, in Aden and Hong Kong, 1966–68; Larkhill, 1969–73, retired. Mem., Assoc. of Supervisory and Executive Engineers. *Recreation:* horses. *Heir:* *s* Robert Cecil Walker, *b* 26 Sept. 1974. *Address:* Ballinamona, Hospital, Kilmallock, Co. Limerick, Ireland.

WALKER, Prof. James, CBE 1971; BSc, MD, FRCPGlas, FRCOG; Professor of Obstetrics and Gynæcology, University of Dundee, 1967–81 (University of St Andrews, 1956–67); *b* 8 March 1916; *s* of James Walker, FEIS; *m* 1940, Catherine Clark Johnston, *d* of George R. A. Johnston; one *s* two *d*. *Educ:* High Schs of Falkirk and Stirling; Univ. of Glasgow. BSc 1935; MB, ChB (Hons) 1938; Brunton Memorial Prize; MRCOG 1947; MD (Hons) 1954; FRCOG 1957; MRCPGlas 1963, FRCPGlas 1968. Blair Bell Memorial Lectr, Royal Coll. Obstetrics and Gynæcology, 1953. Served War of 1939–45, RAFVR, UK and India, 1941–46. Hon. Surgeon to Out Patients, Royal Infirmary, Glasgow, Hall Tutor in Midwifery, Univ. Glasgow, 1946; Sen. Lectr in Midwifery and Gynæcology, Univ. of Aberdeen, Consultant NE Regional Hospital Board (Scotland), 1948; Reader in Obst. and Gynæcology, Univ. of London, Consultant, Hammersmith Hospital, 1955. Consultant, Eastern Regional Hosp. Bd, Scotland, 1956–81; Chm., Nat. Medical Consultative Cttee, Scotland, 1979–81; Chm., Cttee on Annual Reports Records and Definition of Terms in Human Reproduction of the Internat. Fedn of Gynæcology and Obstetrics, 1976–. Visiting Professor: New York State, 1957, 1970; Florida, 1965, 1970; McGill, 1967; Alexandria, 1979; Malaysia, 1981, 1984; Duke (USA), 1981; Stellenbosch, 1986; Prof. of Obst. and Gyn., Univ. Kebangsaan Malaysia, 1982–83. *Publications:* senior editor, Combined Textbook of Obstetrics and Gynæcology, 9th edn, 1976; contrib. on Obstetrics and Gynæcology to textbooks and learned jls. *Address:* 31 Ravenscraig Gardens, West Ferry, Dundee DD5 1LT. *T:* Dundee 79238. *Club:* Royal Air Force.

WALKER, James Findlay, QPM 1964; Commandant, National Police College, 1973–76; *b* 20 May 1916; *m* 1941, Gertrude Eleanor Bell; one *s*. *Educ:* Arbroath High Sch., Angus, Scotland. Joined Metropolitan Police, 1936. Served War, 1943–46: commissioned Black Watch; demobilised rank Captain. Served in Metropolitan Police through ranks to Chief Supt, 1963; Staff of Police Coll., 1963–65; Asst Chief Constable: W Riding Constabulary, 1965–68; W Yorks Constabulary, 1968–70; Dep. Chief Constable, W Yorks Constabulary, 1970–73. *Recreations:* gardening, golf. *Address:* Mayfield, Quarry Hill, Horbury, Wakefield, W Yorks.

WALKER, Sir James (Graham), Kt 1972; MBE 1963; Part Owner of Cumberland Santa Gertrudis Stud and Camden Park, Greenwoods and Wakefield sheep properties; *b* Bellingen, NSW, 7 May 1913; *s* of late Albert Edward Walker and Adelaide Walker, Sydney, NSW; *m* 1939, Mary Vivienne Maude Poole; two *s* three *d*. *Educ:* New England Grammar Sch., Glen Innes, NSW. Councillor, Longreach Shire Council, 1953– (Chm., 1957–85); Vice-Pres., Local Authorities of Qld, 1966, Sen. Vice-Chm., 1972. Dep. Chm., Longreach Pastoral Coll., since inception, 1966–78, Chm. 1978–85. Exec. Mem., Central Western Queensland Local Authorities' Assoc. and Queensland Local Authorities' Assoc., 1964–79. Chm., Central Western Electricity Bd, 1966–76; Dep. Chm., Capricornia Electricity Bd, 1968–76, Chm., 1976–85; Dep. Chm., Longreach Printing Co. Chm., Santa Gertrudis Assoc., Australia, 1976–77. Past Asst Grand Master, United Grand Lodge of Qld, 1970. Session Clerk, St Andrews Church, Longreach, 1948–78. Fellow, Internat. Inst. of Community Service, 1975; Paul Harris Fellow, 1985. Hon. LLD Queensland Univ., 1985. *Recreations:* bowls, golf, surfing, painting. *Address:* Camden Park, Longreach, Queensland 4730, Australia. *T:* Longreach 074581–331. *Clubs:* Queensland, Tattersall's (Brisbane); Longreach, Longreach Rotary, Diggers (Longreach).

WALKER, Sir James Heron, 5th Bt, *cr* 1868; *b* 7 April 1914; *s* of 4th Bt and Synolda, *y d* of late James Thursby-Pelham; *S* father, 1930; *m* 1st, 1939, Angela Margaret, *o d* of Victor Alexandre Beaufort; one *s* (one *d* decd); 2nd, 1972, Sharrone, *er d* of David Read; one *s*. *Educ:* Eton Coll.; Magdalene Coll., Cambridge. *Recreations:* long haired Dachshunds and music. *Heir:* *s* Victor Stewart Heron Walker [*b* 8 Oct. 1942; *m* 1st, 1969, Caroline

Louise (marr. diss. 1982), *d* of late Lt-Col F. E. B. Wignall; two *s* one *d*; 2nd, 1982, Svea, *o d* of late Captain Ernst Hugo Gothard Knutson Borg and of Mary Hilary Borg]. *Address:* Oakhill, Port Soderick, Isle of Man.

See also Baron Cornwallis.

WALKER, John; Director, National Gallery of Art, Washington, DC, 1956–69, now Director Emeritus; *b* 24 Dec. 1906; *s* of Hay Walker and Rebekah Jane Friend; *m* 1937, Lady Margaret Gwendolen Mary Drummond; one *s* one *d*. *Educ:* Harvard Univ. (AB). Associate in charge Dept Fine Arts American Acad., Rome, 1935–39 (now Trustee); Chief Curator, National Gall., Washington DC, 1939–56. Connected with protection and preservation of artistic and historic monuments; John Harvard Fellow, Harvard Univ., 1930–31; American Federation of Arts; Board of Advisers, Dumbarton Oaks; Trustee: Andrew W. Mellon Educational and Charitable Trust; American Federation of Arts; Wallace Foundation, NY; National Trust for Historic Preservation; Mem., Art Adv. Panel, National Trust (UK); Member Advisory Council: Univ. of Notre Dame; New York Univ.; Hon. Dr Fine Arts: Tufts Univ., 1958; Brown Univ., 1959; La Salle Coll., 1962; LittD: Notre Dame, 1959, Washington and Jefferson Univs, 1960; LHD: Catholic Univ. of America, 1964; Univ. of New York, 1965; Maryland Inst.; Georgetown Univ., 1966; William and Mary Univ., 1967. Holds foreign decorations. *Publications:* (with Macgill James) Great American Paintings from Smibert to Bellows, 1943; (with Huntington Cairns) Masterpieces of Painting from National Gallery of Art, 1944; Paintings from America, 1951; (with Huntington Cairns) Great Paintings from the National Gallery of Art, 1952; National Gallery of Art, Washington, 1956; Bellini and Titian at Ferrara, 1957; Treasures from the National Gallery of Art, 1963; The National Gallery of Art, Washington, DC, 1964; (with H. Cairns) Pageant of Painting, 1966; Self-Portrait with Donors, 1974; National Gallery of Art, 1976; Turner, 1976; Constable, 1978. *Address:* 1729 H Street, NW, Washington, DC 20006, USA. *Clubs:* Turf, Dilettanti, Pilgrims'; Century Association (New York City); Chevy Chase, Metropolitan (Washington, DC).

WALKER, John; Under Secretary, Scottish Development Department, 1985, retired; *b* 16 Dec. 1929; *s* of John Walker and Elizabeth Whyte Fish; *m* 1952, Rena Robertson McEwan; two *d*. *Educ:* Falkirk High School. Entered Civil Service, Min. of Labour, as clerical officer, 1946. National Service, RAF, 1948–50. Asst Principal, Dept of Health for Scotland, 1958; Scottish Home and Health Dept: Principal, 1960; Secretary, Cttee on General Medical Services in the Highlands and Islands, 1964–67; Asst Sec., 1969; Scottish Development Dept, 1975–78; Under Sec., Scottish Home and Health Dept, 1978–85. *Recreations:* grandparenthood, viticulture, being looked after by Rena. *Address:* Rosyth House, Grahamsdyke Road, Bo'ness, West Lothian EH51 9ED. *T:* Bo'ness 822426.

WALKER, John David, DL; **His Honour Judge Walker;** a Circuit Judge, since 1972; *b* 13 March 1924; *y s* of late L. C. Walker, MA, MB (Cantab), BCh, and late Mrs J. Walker, Malton; *m* 1953, Elizabeth Mary Emma (*née* Owbridge); one *s* two *d*. *Educ:* Oundle (1937–42); Christ's Coll., Cambridge (1947–50); BA 1950, MA 1953. War of 1939–45: commissioned Frontier Force Rifles, Indian Army, 1943; demob., Captain, 1947. Called to the Bar, Middle Temple, 1951; a Recorder, 1972. A Pres., Mental Health Review Tribunals, 1986. DL Humberside, 1985. *Recreations:* shooting, fishing. *Address:* Arden House, North Bar Without, Beverley, North Humberside HU17 7AG. *T:* Beverley 881359. *Club:* Lansdowne.

WALKER, John Malcolm; Principal Assistant Director of Public Prosecutions (Grade 3), since 1985; *b* 25 Feb. 1930; *s* of James and Mary Walker; *m* 1955, Barbara Anne Fawcett; two *d*. *Educ:* St Edward's Sch., Oxford; Leeds Univ. (LLB). Served Royal Artillery, 1948–50 . Called to Bar, Gray's Inn, 1955; joined Director of Public Prosecutions as Temp. Legal Asst, 1956; Legal Asst, 1958; Sen. Legal Asst, 1964; Asst Solicitor, 1974; Asst Director, 1977. *Recreations:* music, painting. *Address:* 12 Queen Anne's Gate, SW1H 9AZ. *T:* 01-222 7944.

WALKER, Julian Fortay, CMG 1981; MBE 1960; HM Diplomatic Service; Ambassador to Qatar, since 1984; *b* 7 May 1929; *s* of Kenneth Macfarlane Walker, FRCS, and Eileen Marjorie Walker (*née* Wilson); *m* 1983, Virginia Anne Austin (*née* Stevens); three step *d*. *Educ:* Harvey Sch., Hawthorne, New York; Stowe; Bryanston; Cambridge Univ. (MA). National Service, RN, 1947–49; Cambridge, 1949–52; London Univ. Sch. of African and Oriental Studies, 1952. Foreign Service: MECAS, 1953; Asst Political Agent, Trucial States, 1953–55; 3rd and 2nd Sec., Bahrain Residency, 1955–57; FCO and Frontier Settlement, Oman, 1957–60; 2nd and 1st Sec., Oslo, 1960–63; FCO News Dept Spokesman, 1963–67; 1st Sec., Baghdad, 1967; 1st Sec., Morocco (Rabat), 1967–69; FCO, 1969–71; Political Agent, Dubai, Trucial States, 1971, Consul-Gen. and Counsellor, British Embassy, Dubai, United Arab Emirates, 1971–72; Cambridge Univ. on sabbatical leave, 1972–73; Political Advr and Head of Chancery, British Mil. Govt, Berlin, 1973–76; NI Office, Stormont Castle, 1976–77; Dir, MECAS, 1977–78; Ambassador to Yemen Arab Republic and Republic of Jibuti, 1979–84. *Recreations:* skiing, sailing, tennis, music, cooking. *Address:* c/o Foreign and Commonwealth Office, SW1. *Club:* Royal Automobile.

WALKER, Prof. Kenneth Richard, DPhil; Professor of Economics with Reference to Asia, University of London, School of Oriental and African Studies, since Oct. 1978 (Professor of Economics with Special Reference to China, 1972–78); *b* 17 Oct. 1931; *s* of Arthur Bedford Walker and Olive Walker; *m* 1959, June Abercrombie Collie; one *s* one *d*. *Educ:* Prince Henry's Grammar Sch., Otley, Yorks; Univ. of Leeds (BA); Lincoln Coll., Oxford. DPhil Oxon. Asst in Political Economy, Univ. of Aberdeen, 1956–59; Research Fellow, 1959–61, Lectr, 1961–66, Reader, 1966–72, in Economics, Hd of Dept of Economic and Political Studies, 1972–85, SOAS, Univ. of London. *Publications:* Planning in Chinese Agriculture, Socialisation and the Private Sector 1956–1962, 1965; Food Grain Procurement and Consumption in China, 1984; contribs to Scottish Jl of Political Economy, Economic Development and Cultural Change, China Qly. *Recreations:* golf, hill-walking, bird-watching, choral singing. *Address:* 4 Harpenden Road, St Albans, Herts AL3 5AB.

WALKER, Sir Michael; *see* Walker, Sir C. M.

WALKER, Michael; His Honour Judge Michael Walker; a Circuit Judge, since 1978; *b* 13 April 1931; *m* 1959, Elizabeth Mary Currie; two *s*. *Educ:* Chadderton Grammar Sch.; Sheffield Univ. (LLM). Called to the Bar, Gray's Inn, 1956. Joined North Eastern Circuit, 1958. A Recorder of the Crown Court, 1972–78.

WALKER, Sir Michael Leolin F.; *see* Forestier-Walker.

WALKER, Prof. Nigel David, CBE 1979; MA Oxon, PhD Edinburgh, DLitt Oxon; Wolfson Professor of Criminology and Fellow of King's College, Cambridge, 1973–84 (Director, Institute of Criminology, 1973–80); *b* 6 Aug. 1917; *s* of David B. Walker and Violet Walker (*née* Johnson); *m* 1939, Sheila Margaret Johnston; one *d*. *Educ:* Tientsin Grammar Sch.; Edinburgh Academy; Christ Church, Oxford (Hon. Scholar). Served War, Infantry officer (Camerons and Lovat Scouts), 1940–46. Scottish Office, 1946–61; Gwilym Gibbon Fellow, Nuffield Coll., 1958–59; University Reader in Criminology and Fellow of Nuffield Coll., Oxford, 1961–73. Visiting Professor: Berkeley, 1965; Yale, 1973; Stockholm, 1978; Cape Town, 1984. Chairman: Home Secretary's Adv. Council on Probation and After-care, 1972–76; Study Gp on Legal Training of Social Workers, 1972–73; President: Nat. Assoc. of Probation Officers, 1980–84; British Soc. of Criminology, 1984–87; Member: Home Sec.'s TV Research Cttee, 1963–69; Adv. Council on Penal System, 1969–; Cttee on Mentally Abnormal Offenders, 1972–75; Working Party on Judicial Training and Information, 1975–78; Floud Cttee on Dangerous Offenders; Hodgson Cttee on Profits of Crime. Hon. LLD: Leicester, 1976, Edinburgh 1985. *Publications:* Delphi, 1936 (Chancellor's Prize Latin Poem); A Short History of Psychotherapy, 1957 (various trans); Morale in the Civil Service, 1961; Crime and Punishment in Britain, 1965; Crime and Insanity in England, 2 vols, 1968 and 1972; Sentencing in a Rational Society, 1969 (various trans.); Crimes, Courts and Figures, 1971; Explaining Misbehaviour (inaug. lecture), 1974; Treatment and Justice (Sandoz lecture), 1976; Behaviour and Misbehaviour, 1977; Punishment, Danger and Stigma, 1980; Sentencing Theory Law and Practice, 1985; Crime and Criminology, 1987; reports, articles, etc. *Recreations:* chess, hill-climbing. *Address:* King's College, Cambridge. *Club:* Royal Society of Medicine.

WALKER, Patricia Kathleen Randall; *see* Mann, P. K. R.

WALKER, Dr Paul Crawford, JP; District General Manager, Frenchay Health Authority, since 1985; *b* 9 Dec. 1940; *s* of Joseph Viccars Walker and Mary Tilley (*née* Crawford); *m* 1962, Barbara Georgina Bliss; three *d*. *Educ:* Queen Elizabeth Grammar Sch., Darlington; Downing Coll., Cambridge (BA); University College Hospital (MB, BChir); Edinburgh Univ. (DipSocMed). FFCM; FRSM 1981; LHA 1985. Assistant Senior Medical Officer, Birmingham Regional Hosp. Bd, 1969–72; Dep. Medical Officer of Health and Dep. Principal Sch. MO, 1974, Wolverhampton County Borough Council; District Community Physician, N Staffs Health District, Staffordshire AHA, 1974–76; Area MO, Wakefield AHA, 1976–77; Regional MO, NE Thames RHA, 1978–85. Hon. Sen. Lectr, Dept of Community Medicine, LSHTM, 1983–; Vis. Prof., QMC, London Univ., 1985–. Governor, Moorfields Eye Hosp., 1981–82; Member: Bd of Management, London Sch. of Hygiene and Trop. Med., 1983–85; Adv. Cttee on Drug Misuse, 1983–; Exec. Cttee, Greater London Alcohol Adv. Service, 1978–85; Editorial Bd, Jl of Med. Management; NHS Computer Policy Cttee, 1984–85; Program for Health Systems Management, Harvard Business Sch., 1980; Health Care Management Program, Yale Sch. of Organisation and Management, 1984; Essex Commn for the Peace, 1980–85; Avon Commn for the Peace, 1985–. JP Epping and Ongar, 1980–. Captain, RAMC (V). *Publications:* contribs to medical and health service jls. *Recreations:* music, railway history. *Address:* Chagford, 8 Church Avenue, Sneyd Park, Bristol BS9 1LD. *T:* Bristol 682209.

WALKER, Sir Peter; *see* Walker, Sir C. P. G.

WALKER, Rt. Hon. Peter Edward, PC 1970; MBE 1960; MP (C) Worcester since March 1961; Secretary of State for Energy, since 1983; *b* 25 March 1932; *s* of Sydney and Rose Walker; *m* 1969, Tessa, *d* of G. I. Pout; three *s* two *d*. *Educ:* Latymer Upper Sch. Member, National Executive of Conservative Party, 1956–; Nat. Chairman, Young Conservatives, 1958–60; Parliamentary Candidate (C) for Dartford, 1955 and 1959. PPS to Leader of House of Commons, 1963–64; Opposition Front Bench Spokesman: on Finance and Economics, 1964–66; on Transport, 1966–68; on Local Government, Housing, and Land, 1968–70; Minister of Housing and Local Govt, June-Oct. 1970; Secretary of State for: the Environment, 1970–72; Trade and Industry, 1972–74; Opposition Spokesman on Trade, Industry and Consumer Affairs, Feb.-June 1974, on Defence, June 1974–Feb. 1975; Minister of Agric., Fisheries and Food, 1979–83. *Publication:* The Ascent of Britain, 1977. *Address:* Abbots Morton Manor, Gooms Hill, Abbots Morton, Worcester WR7 4LT. *Clubs:* Buck's, Pratt's; Worcestershire County Cricket, Union and County (Worcester).

WALKER, Rt. Rev. Peter Knight; *see* Ely, Bishop of.

WALKER, Prof. Peter Martin Brabazon, CBE 1976; FRSE; Honorary Professor and Director, MRC Mammalian Genome Unit, 1973–80; *b* 1 May 1922; *e s* of Major Ernest Walker and Mildred Walker (*née* Heaton-Ellis), Kenya; *m* 1943, Violet Norah Wright (*d* 1985); one *s* three *d*. *Educ:* Haileybury Coll.; Trinity Coll., Cambridge, 1945. BA, PhD. Tool and instrument maker, 1939 (during War); Scientific Staff, MRC Biophysics Research Unit, King's Coll., London, 1948; Royal Society Research Fellow, Edinburgh, 1958; Univ. of Edinburgh: Lectr in Zoology, 1962; Reader in Zoology, 1963; Professor of Natural History, 1966–73. Member: Biological Research Bd, MRC, 1967 (Chm., 1970–72); MRC, 1970–72; Ext. Scientific Staff, MRC; Chief Scientist Cttee, Scottish Home and Health Dept, 1973–85; Chm., Equipment Res. Cttee, Scottish Home and Health Dept, 1973–79; Mem. Council, Imp. Cancer Res. Fund, 1971–; Chm., Imp. Cancer Res. Fund Scientific Adv. Cttee, 1975–85; Mem., Scientific Adv. Cttee of European Molecular Biology Lab., 1976–81. *Publications:* contribs to the molecular biology of the genetic material of mammals in: Nature; Jl of Molecular Biology, etc. *Recreations:* gardening, design of scientific instruments, railway history. *Address:* Drumlaggan, The Ross, Comrie, Perthshire. *T:* Comrie 70303.

WALKER, Philip Gordon, FCA; Chairman: Chapman Industries PLC, 1968–83; *b* 9 June 1912; *s* of late William and Kate Blanche Walker; *m* 1st, 1938, Anne May (marr. diss.); one *s* two *d*; 2nd, 1962, Elizabeth Oliver. *Educ:* Epworth Coll., Rhyl, North Wales. Bourner, Bullock & Co., Chartered Accountants, 1929–35; Walkers (Century Oils) Ltd, 1935–40; Layton Bennett, Billingham & Co., Chartered Accountants, 1940, Partner, 1944–51 (now Arthur Young McLelland Moore); Albert E. Reed & Co Ltd (now Reed International), Man. Dir, 1951–63; Chm. and Man. Dir, Philblack Ltd, 1963–71; Chm., Sun Life Assurance Soc. Ltd, 1971–82 (Exec. Chm. 1976–82). Part-time Mem. Monopolies Commn, 1963–65; Member: Performing Right Tribunal, 1971–83; Restrictive Practices Court, 1973–83. *Recreation:* golf. *Address:* The Garden Flat, Scotswood, Devenish Road, Sunningdale, Berks SL5 9QP. *Clubs:* Brooks's; Wildernesse (Sevenoaks); Rye; Berkshire.

WALKER, Philip Henry Conyers; His Honour Judge Harry Walker; a Circuit Judge, since 1979; *b* 22 Dec. 1926; *o c* of Philip Howard and Kathleen Walker; *m* 1953, Mary Elizabeth Ross; two *s* two *d*. *Educ:* Marlborough; Oriel Coll., Oxford. MA, BCL (Oxon); DipTh (London). Army (6 AB Sigs), 1944–48 (despatches, 1948). Solicitor in private practice, 1954–79; a Recorder of the Crown Court, 1972–79. Mem., Church Assembly, Nat. Synod of C of E, 1960–80. Chm., Agricultural Land Tribunal (Yorks & Lancs), 1977–79; Mem., Criminal Law Revision Cttee, 1981–. *Recreations:* fishing, shooting, sailing, walking. *Address:* Pond House, Askwith, Otley, West Yorks. *T:* Otley 463196.

WALKER, Raymond James; Chief Executive, Simplification of International Trade Procedures Board, since 1983; *b* 13 April 1943; *s* of Cyril James Walker and Louie Walker; *m* 1969, Mary Eastwood Whittaker; one *d*. *Educ:* St Audreys', Hatfield; University of Lancaster. BA (Hons). Personnel Director, Saracen Ltd, 1971–73; Jt Man. Dir, Carrington Viyella Exports Ltd, 1973–78; Export Dir, Carrington Viyella Home Furnishings (DORMA), 1978–83. *Recreations:* collecting wine labels, sailing. *Address:*

Fairview, Church Road, Goudhurst, Cranbrook, Kent TN17 1BH. *Clubs:* Royal Automobile; Belle Toute (Lancaster).

WALKER, Richard Alwyne F.; *see* Fyjis-Walker.

WALKER, Richard John Boileau, MA; FSA; picture cataloguer; *b* 4 June 1916; *s* of Comdr Kenneth Walker and Caroline Livingstone-Learmonth; *m* 1946, Margaret, *d* of Brig. Roy Firebrace, CBE; one *s* two *d*. *Educ:* Harrow; Magdalene Coll., Cambridge (MA); Courtauld Institute of Art. Active service, RNVR, 1939–45. British Council, 1946; Tate Gallery, 1947–48; Min. of Works Picture Adviser, 1949–76; Curator of the Palace of Westminster, 1950–76; Nat. Portrait Gallery Cataloguer, 1976–85; Royal Collection Cataloguer, 1985–. Trustee: Nat. Maritime Museum, 1977–84; Army Museums Ogilby Trust, 1979–. *Publications:* Catalogue of Pictures at Audley End, 1950 and 1973; Old Westminster Bridge, 1979; Regency Portraits, 1985. *Recreations:* looking at pictures and finding quotations. *Address:* 31 Cadogan Place, SW1X 9RX. *T:* 01–235 1801. *Clubs:* Athenæum, United Oxford & Cambridge University.

WALKER, Robert; HM Diplomatic Service, retired; *b* 1 May 1924; *s* of Young and Gladys Walker, Luddendenfoot, Yorks; *m* 1949, Rita Thomas; one *s* one *d*. *Educ:* Sowerby Bridge Grammar Sch.; Peterhouse, Cambridge. Commissioned RNVR 1944; served in minesweepers in home waters. Cambridge, 1942–43 and 1946–48; BA Hons History, 1948; MA 1963. Joined CRO, 1948; served Peshawar and Karachi, 1949–51; New Delhi, 1955–59; Sen. First Sec., Accra, 1962–64; Dep. British High Comr, in Ghana, 1964–65; FCO, 1965–68. IDC, 1969; Commercial Counsellor, Ankara, 1970–71; Dep. High Comr, Nairobi, 1971–72. Dep. Registrar, Hull Univ., 1972–79. Mem., Craven DC, 1984–. Contested (L): Haltemprice, Feb. and Oct. 1974, 1979; Humberside, European election, 1979; South Ribble, 1983. Mem., Liberal Party Council; Chm., Yorkshire Liberal Fedn, 1977–81. Mem. Council, Lancaster Univ., 1986–. *Recreations:* coarse golf, country wine making, interior decorating. *Address:* Manor Farm, Langcliffe, North Yorks BD24 9NQ. *T:* Settle 3205.

WALKER, Robert, QC 1982; *b* 17 March 1938; *s* of Ronald Robert Anthony Walker and Mary Helen Walker (*née* Welsh); *m* 1962, Suzanne Diana Leggi; one *s* three *d*. *Educ:* Downside Sch.; Trinity Coll., Cambridge (BA). Called to Bar, Lincoln's Inn, 1960; in practice at Chancery Bar, 1961–. *Recreations:* riding, running, skiing. *Address:* Freeman's Farm, Thaxted, Essex CM6 3PY. *T:* Thaxted 830577.

WALKER, Robert Scott, FRICS; City Surveyor, City of London Corporation, 1955–75; *b* 13 June 1913; *s* of Harold and Mary Walker; *m* 1946, Anne Armstrong; no *c*. *Educ:* West Buckland Sch., North Devon. War Service, 1939–45, Major RA. Assistant City Surveyor, Manchester, 1946–55. *Address:* 10 Woodcote Close, Epsom, Surrey. *T:* Epsom 21220.

WALKER, Sir Ronald; *see* Walker, Sir E. R.

WALKER, Ronald Jack; QC 1983; a Recorder, since 1986; *b* 24 June 1940; *s* of Jack Harris Walker and Ann Frances Walker; *m* 1964, Caroline Fox; two *s*. *Educ:* Owen's School, London; University College London. LLB (Hons). Called to the Bar, Gray's Inn, 1962. *Publication:* English Legal System (with M. G. Walker), 1967, 6th edn 1985. *Recreations:* golf, wine, horse racing. *Address:* 12 King's Bench Walk, Temple, EC4. *T:* 01–583 0811; 45 Nassau Road, Barnes, SW13.

WALKER, Roy; *see* Walker, C. R.

WALKER, Samuel Richard, CBE 1955; DL; Founder, 1920, and Hon. President, Walker & Rice (Walric Fabrics Ltd); *b* 6 Jan. 1892; *s* of Samuel Reuben and Elizabeth Louise Walker; *m* 1923, Marjorie Jackson Clark (*d* 1977), *d* of A. J. Clark, Hove, Sussex; one *s* two *d*; *m* 1986, Mrs Kathleen Mary Fawcett. *Educ:* William Ellis's. Queen Victoria Rifles, 1909–14; served European War, 1914–19, in France: 1st King Edward's Horse and RFA; Home Guard, 1939–45. City of London: DL 1951; Member Common Council (Bread Street Ward, 1937–76; Deputy, 1951–76), Chief Commoner, 1953–54; Chairman: Officers and Clerks Cttee, 1952; Privileges Cttee, 1957–73; Comr of Income Tax, 1960–66. Sheriff of City of London, 1957–58; one of HM Lieutenants, City of London. Master, Worshipful Company of Farriers, 1954–55; Master, Worshipful Company of Founders, 1962–63, Liveryman of Worshipful Company of Weavers, 1964–; Chairman: Cattle Markets Cttee, 1945–46; Central Criminal Court Extension Cttee, 1964–75; Benevolent Assoc. of Corporation of London, 1970–76; Reconstruction of Guildhall Cttee, 1953–76; various Cttees, City of London, 1950–54. Pres., Assoc. of Chief Commoners, 1984–; Vice-Pres., Mid Sussex Assoc. for Mentally Handicapped Children, 1970–. Governor, Bridewell Royal Hosp., 1942–; Life Governor and Vice-Chm., City of London Sheriffs' and Recorders' Fund Soc., 1957–; Chm., Thomas Carpenter and John Lane Trust, 1951–; Governor and Almoner, Christ's Hosp., 1966–; Trustee, Seaforth Hall, Warninglid. Commendatore of Order Al Merito della Repubblica (Italy), 1957. *Recreations:* golf, riding. *Address:* Salters Court, Bow Lane, EC4; Copyhold Rise, Copyhold Lane, Cuckfield, Sussex. *Clubs:* City Livery (President, 1955–56), Guildhall, Oriental; West Hove Golf (Life Pres.), West Sussex Golf, Haywards Heath Golf.

WALKER, Sarah Elizabeth Royle, (Mrs R. G. Allum); mezzo-soprano; *d* of Elizabeth Brownrigg and Alan Royle Walker; *m* 1972, Graham Allum. *Educ:* Pate's Grammar School for Girls, Cheltenham; Royal College of Music. ARCM, LRAM. Pres., Cheltenham Bach Choir, 1986–. Major appearances at concerts and in recital in Britain, America, Australia, New Zealand, Europe; operatic débuts include: Coronation of Poppea, Kent Opera, 1969, San Francisco Opera, 1981; La Calisto, Glyndebourne, 1970; Les Troyens, Scottish Opera, 1972, Wien Staatsoper, 1980; Principal Mezzo Soprano, ENO, 1972–77; Die Meistersinger, Chicago Lyric Opera, 1977; Werther, Covent Garden, 1979; Giulio Caesare, Le Grand Théâtre, Genêve, 1983; Capriccio, Brussels, 1983; Teseo, Sienna, 1985; Samson, NY Metropolitan Opera, 1986; numerous recordings and video recordings, incl. title rôle in Britten's Gloriana. *Recreations:* interior design, encouraging my husband with the gardening. *Address:* 152 Inchmery Road, SE6 1DF. *T:* 01–697 6152.

WALKER, Sheila Mosley, (Mrs Owen Walker), CBE 1981; JP; Chief Commissioner, Girl Guides Association, 1975–80; *b* 11 Dec. 1917; *yr d* of late Charles Eric Mosley Mayne, Indian Cavalry, and Evelyn Mary, *d* of Sir Thomas Skewes-Cox, MP; *m* 1st, 1940, Major Bruce Dawson, MC, Royal Berkshire Regt (killed, Arnhem, 1944); one *s* one *d*; 2nd, 1955, Henry William Owen, *s* of late Sir Henry Walker, CBE; one step *s* one step *d*. *Educ:* St Mary's Hall, Brighton; St James' Secretarial Coll., London. Midlands Regional Chief Comr, Girl Guides Assoc., 1970–75. JP Nottingham City, 1970. *Recreations:* children, animals, all country and nature preservation. *Address:* Dingley Hall, near Market Harborough, Leics. *T:* Dingley 388. *Club:* New Cavendish (Chm. Bd, 1983–).

WALKER, Stanley Kenneth; Director and Chief General Manager, Leeds Permanent Building Society, 1978–82; *b* 18 Feb. 1916; *s* of Robert and Gertrude Walker; *m* 1956, Diana, *d* of Fred Broadhead; one *s*. *Educ:* Cockburn Sch., Leeds. FCIS, FCBSI. Served War of 1939–45, Middle East (despatches, 1944). Leeds Permanent Building Society: Branch Manager, Newcastle upon Tyne, 1960–62; Asst Sec., 1962–66; Asst Gen. Manager, 1967–77; Gen. Manager, 1977–78. Member: Council, Building Societies Assoc., 1978–81; Vice-Pres., Leeds Centre, Chartered Building Socs Inst., 1983. *Recreations:* tennis, walking, theatre. *Club:* Royal Automobile.

WALKER, Dame Susan (Armour), DBE 1972 (CBE 1963); Vice-Chairman, Women's Royal Voluntary Service, 1969–75; *d* of James Walker, Bowmont, Dunbar; unmarried. *Educ:* Grammar School, Dunbar. Conservative Central Office Agent, Yorkshire, 1950–56; Deputy Chief Organisation Officer, Conservative Central Office, 1956–64; Vice-Chm., Cons. Party Organisation, 1964–68, retired 1968. *Recreations:* golf, walking. *Address:* The Glebe House, Hownam, Kelso, Roxburghshire. *T:* Morebattle 277.

WALKER, Terence William, (Terry Walker); *b* 26 Oct. 1935; *s* of William Edwin and Lilian Grace Walker; *m* 1959, Priscilla Dart; two *s* one *d*. *Educ:* Grammar Sch. and Coll. of Further Educn, Bristol. Employed by Courage (Western) Ltd at Bristol for 23 yrs, Mem. Chief Accountant's Dept. MP (Lab) Kingswood, Feb. 1974–1979; Second Church Estates Comr, 1974–79. Contested (Lab) Kingswood, 1983. Mem., Avon CC, 1981–; Chm., Avon Public Protection Cttee, 1981–. *Recreations:* cricket, football. *Address:* 19 Forest Edge, Hanham, Bristol BS15 3PP. *T:* Bristol 672301.

WALKER, Prof. Thomas William, ARCS; DSc; DIC; Professor of Soil Science, Lincoln College, New Zealand, 1961–79, now Emeritus; *b* 22 July 1916; *m* 1940, Edith Edna Bott; four *d*. *Educ:* Loughborough Grammar School; Royal College of Science. Royal Scholar and Kitchener Scholar, 1935–39; Salter's Fellow, 1939–41; Lecturer and Adviser in Agricultural Chemistry, Univ. of Manchester, 1941–46. Provincial Advisory Soil Chemist, NAAS, 1946–51; Prof. of Soil Science, Canterbury Agric. Coll., New Zealand, 1952–58; Prof. of Agric., King's Coll., Newcastle upon Tyne, 1958–61. *Publications:* numerous research. *Recreations:* fishing, gardening. *Address:* 843 Cashmere Road, Christchurch 3, New Zealand.

WALKER, Timothy Ashley Peter; Director: Henderson Administration Group Plc, since 1983; Henderson Administration Ltd, since 1980; Deputy Chairman, Henderson Unit Trust Management Ltd, since 1984 (Director since 1979); Chairman: Greenwood Oil Ltd, since 1981; Credit and Commerce Life, since 1983; New London Oil plc, since 1985; Director, HTV Ltd, since 1985; *b* 2 Feb. 1942; *s* of Vice-Adm. Sir C. Peter G. Walker, *qv*; *m* 1st, 1963, Carola Ashton (marr. diss.); one *s*; 2nd, 1972, Rosemary Vere Keep Thompson (*née* Edwards); two step *s* two step *d*. *Educ:* Charterhouse School. Lieut, Queen's Royal Irish Hussars, 1960–63. Imperial Life Assurance Co. of Canada, 1963–66; Dir, Abbey Life Assurance, 1966–70; Founder Dir, Hambro Life Assurance, 1970–78. Chairman: WWF UK, 1984–; of Trustees, Marwell Zool Soc., 1979–; Vice-Pres., FFPS, 1983–; Mem. Animal Welfare and Husbandry Cttee, 1982–85, Council Mem., 1985–, Zoological Soc. of London; Cttee Mem., King Mahendra Trust—UK, 1984–; Trustee: Game Conservancy, 1983–; WWF Internat., 1986–; Patron: Farming and Wildlife Adv. Group, 1983–; Rhino Rescue, 1985–. *Publications:* articles in Financial Times etc. *Recreations:* shooting, farming, breeding endangered species. *Address:* Midway Manor, near Bradford-on-Avon, Wilts. *T:* Bradford-on-Avon 2225. *Club:* Boodle's.

WALKER, Timothy Edward; QC 1985; a Recorder of the Crown Court, since 1986; *b* 13 May 1946; *s* of George Edward Walker, solicitor, and Muriel Edith Walker; *m* 1968, Mary (*née* Tyndall); two *d*. *Educ:* Harrow Sch. (Entrance Schol., Leaving Schol.); University Coll., Oxford (MA); Plumptre Schol., 1965; 1st Cl. Hons Jurisprudence, 1967; Asst Lectr in Law, King's Coll., London, 1967–68; Profumo scholarship, Inner Temple, 1968; called to the Bar, Inner Temple, 1968; Eldon Law schol., 1969. *Address:* Fountain Court, Temple EC4 9DH. *T:* 01–353 7356; (home) 58 Lamont Road, SW10 0HX. *T:* 01–352 6440; Well House, Ham Road, Shalbourne, Marlborough, Wilts SNQ 3QN. *T:* Marlborough 870572.

WALKER, Walter Basil Scarlett, (Bobby Walker), MA; FCA; Deputy UK Senior Partner, Peat, Marwick, Mitchell & Co., 1979–82; *b* 19 Dec. 1915; *s* of James and Hilda Walker, Southport; *m* 1945, Teresa Mary Louise John; one *d* (and one *s* decd). *Educ:* Rugby Sch.; Clare Coll., Cambridge (MA). Joined Peat, Marwick, Mitchell & Co., 1937, leaving temporarily, 1939, to join RNVR; service in Home Fleet, incl. convoys to Russia and Malta, 1940–42; finally, Asst Sec. to British Naval C-in-C in Germany; Lt-Comdr. Returned to Peat, Marwick, Mitchell & Co., 1946, becoming a partner, 1956. Mem. (part-time), UKAEA, 1972–81. Governor, Royal Ballet, Covent Garden, 1980–. *Recreations:* ballet, gardening, golf. *Address:* 11 Sloane Avenue, SW3 3JD. *T:* 01–589 4133; Coles, Privett, near Alton, Hants GU34 3PH. *T:* Privett 223. *Club:* Royal Automobile.

WALKER, Gen. Sir Walter (Colyear), KCB 1968 (CB 1964); CBE 1959 (OBE 1949); DSO 1946 and Bars, 1953 and 1965; Commander-in-Chief, Allied Forces Northern Europe, 1969–72, retired; *b* 11 Nov. 1912; *s* of late Arthur Colyear Walker; *m* 1938, Beryl, *d* of late E.N.W. Johnston; two *s* one *d*. *Educ:* Blundell's; RMC, Sandhurst. Waziristan, 1939–41 (despatches twice); Burma, 1942, 1944–46 (despatches, DSO); Malaya, 1949–59 (despatches twice, OBE, Bar to DSO, CBE); Atomic Trials, Maralinga, SA, 1956; Dir of Operations, Borneo, 1962–65 (CB, Bar to DSO); Deputy Chief of Staff, HQ ALFCE, 1965; Acting Chief of Staff, 1966–67; GOC-in-C, Northern Command, 1967–69. pscWSD 1942; jssc 1950; idc 1960. Col, 7th Duke of Edinburgh's Own Gurkha Rifles, 1964–75. Dato Seri Setia, Order of Paduka Stia Negara, Brunei, 1964; Hon. Panglima Mangku Negara, Malaysia, 1965. *Publications:* The Bear at the Back Door, 1978; The Next Domino, 1980. *Recreations:* normal. *Address:* Haydon Farmhouse, Sherborne, Dorset DT9 5JB. *Club:* Army and Navy.

WALKER, Prof. William; FRCP, FRCPE; Regius Professor of Materia Medica, University of Aberdeen, 1973–82, retired; re-employed as Professor of Clinical Medicine, since 1982; *b* 1 Jan. 1920; *s* of William Sharp Walker and Joan Strachan Gloak; *m* 1948, Mary Cathleen Kenny; one adopted *s* one adopted *d*. *Educ:* Harris Academy, Dundee; Univ. of St Andrews. MA, MB, ChB; FRCP, FRCPE. Served War: commissioned Royal Scots, 1939; wounded, 1940; invalided, 1941. Lecturer in Pathology, Univ. of St Andrews, 1947; Medical Registrar, Newcastle, 1948. Research Fellow, Haematology, Boston Univ. Mass, 1954–55; Lectr in Therapeutics, St Andrews, 1952, Sen. Lectr, 1955; Consultant Physician, Aberdeen, 1964; Clinical Reader in Medicine, 1971. Pres., Anglo-German Medical Soc., 1976–81; Vice Chm., Cttee on the Review of Medicines, 1981–83 (Mem., 1975–83). *Publications:* various medical, chiefly in thrombotic and haemorrhagic disease, and drug therapy. *Recreations:* gardening, philosophy, social and political controversy. *Address:* Woodhill, Kinellar, Aberdeenshire AB5 0RZ. *T:* Aberdeen 79314.

WALKER, William Connoll, (Bill Walker), FIPM; MP (C) Tayside North, since 1983 (Perth and East Perthshire, 1979–83); Chairman, British Emerald Airways, since 1984; *b* 20 Feb. 1929; *s* of Charles and Williamina Walker; *m* 1956, Mavis Evelyn Lambert; three *d*. *Educ:* Logie Sch., Dundee; Trades Coll., Dundee; College for Distributive Trades. FIPM 1968; FBIM. Message boy, 1943–44; office boy, 1944–46. Commissioned RAF, 1946–49; Flt Lieut RAFVR, 1949–. Salesman, public service vehicle driver, general manager, 1949–59; civil servant, 1959–65; training and education officer, furnishing industry, 1965–67; company director, 1967–79; pt-time presenter, TV progs, 1969–75. FRSA 1970. *Recreations:* RAFVR, gliding, caravanning, walking, youth work. *Address:*

Candletrees, Golf Course Road, Rosemount, Blairgowrie, Perthshire PH10 6LQ. *T:* Blairgowrie 2660. *Clubs:* Naval, Royal Air Force.

WALKER, Sir William (Giles Newsom), Kt 1959; TD 1942; DL; *b* 20 Nov. 1905; *e s* of late H. Giles Walker, Over Rankeillour, Cupar, Fife and of late Mrs Elizabeth Bewley Newsom (Walker), Cork, Eire; *m* 1930, Mildred Brenda (*d* 1983), 3rd *d* of Sir Michael Nairn, 2nd Bt, Elie House, Fife, and Pitcarmick, Blairgowrie; one *s* two *d. Educ:* Shrewsbury Sch.; Jesus Coll., Cambridge (BA). War of 1939–45: Lt-Col comdg 1st Fife and Forfar Yeomanry, 1943–45 (mobilised Aug. 1939; despatches, TD). Jute Industries Ltd, Dundee: entered 1927; rejoined after War, 1945; Director, 1946–71; Managing Director, 1947–69; Chairman, 1948–70; Hon. Pres., 1971. Director: Nairn & Williamson (Holdings) Ltd, 1954–75; Clydesdale Bank Ltd, 1961–82; Scottish Television Ltd, 1964–74; Alliance Trust Co. Ltd, 1963–76; Second Alliance Trust Co. Ltd, 1963–76. Formerly: Jute Working Party (Employer Mem.); Dundee Chamber of Commerce (Dir); Scottish Industrial Estates Ltd. (Dir); Member, Scottish Railway Bd. Hon. Colonel: Fife and Forfar Yeomanry/Scottish Horse, 1967–69; Highland Yeomanry, 1969–71. DL Fife, 1958. USA Bronze Star, 1945. *Recreations:* shooting and golf. *Address:* Pitlair, Cupar, Fife. *T:* Ladybank 30413. *Clubs:* Royal and Ancient Golf (Capt. 1962–63) (St Andrews); The Honourable Company of Edinburgh Golfers (Muirfield).

WALKER, William MacLelland, QC (Scot.) 1971; *b* 19 May 1933; *s* of late Hon. Lord Walker; *m* 1957, Joan Margaret, *d* of late Charles Hutchison Wood, headmaster, Dundee; one *d. Educ:* Edinburgh Academy; Edinburgh Univ. (MA, LLB). Advocate, 1957; Flying Officer, RAF, 1957–59; Standing Junior Counsel: Min. of Aviation, 1963–68; BoT (Aviation), 1968–71; Min. of Technology, 1968–70; Dept of Trade and Industry (Power), 1971; Min. of Aviation Supply, 1971. Chairman: Industrial Tribunals in Scotland, 1972–; VAT Tribunals, 1985–. *Recreations:* shooting, travel, photography. *Address:* 17 India Street, Edinburgh EH3 6HE. *T:* 031–225 3846; Edenside, Gordon, Berwickshire TD3 6LB. *T:* Gordon 271. *Clubs:* Royal Air Force; New (Edinburgh).

WALKER-HAWORTH, John Liegh; Director-General, City Panel on Take-overs and Mergers, since 1985; *b* 25 Oct. 1944; *s* of William and Julia Walker-Haworth; *m* 1977, Caroline Mary Blair Purves; two *s. Educ:* Charterhouse; Pembroke College, Oxford. Called to the Bar, Inner Temple, 1967. Director, S. G. Warburg & Co., 1981–. *Address:* 23 Eldon Road, W8. *T:* 01–937 3883.

WALKER-OKEOVER, Sir Peter (Ralph Leopold), 4th Bt *cr* 1886; *b* 22 July 1947; *s* of Colonel Sir Ian Peter Andrew Monro Walker-Okeover, 3rd Bt, DSO, TD, and of Dorothy Elizabeth, *yr d* of Captain Josceline Heber-Percy; *S* father, 1982; *m* 1972, Catherine Mary Maule, *d* of Colonel George Maule Ramsay; two *s* one *d. Educ:* Eton; RMA Sandhurst. Captain, Blues and Royals, retired. *Heir: s* Andrew Peter Monro Walker-Okeover, *b* 22 May 1978. *Address:* Okeover Hall, Osmaston, Ashbourne, Derbyshire; House of Glenmuick, Ballater, Aberdeenshire.

WALKER-SMITH, family name of **Baron Broxbourne.**

WALKER-SMITH, John Jonah; a Recorder of the Crown Court, since 1980; *b* 6 Sept. 1939; *s* of Baron Broxbourne, *qv*; *m* 1974, Aileen Marie Smith; one *s* one *d. Educ:* Westminster School; Christ Church, Oxford. Called to Bar, Middle Temple, 1963. *Address:* 1 Dr Johnson's Buildings, Temple, EC4.

WALKEY, Maj.-Gen. John Christopher, CB 1953; CBE 1943; *b* 18 Oct. 1903; *s* of late S. Walkey, Dawlish, Devon; *m* 1947, Beatrice Record Brown; one *d* decd. *Educ:* Newton College, Devon. Commissioned into Royal Engineers from RMA Woolwich, 1923; Chief Engineer, 13 Corps, 1943–47; Asst Comdt, RMA Sandhurst, 1949–51; Chief Engineer, Middle East Land Forces, 1951–54; Engineer-in-Chief, War Office, 1954–57; retired, 1957. Col Comdt RE, 1958–68. Hon. Col RE Resources Units (AER), 1959–64. Officer Legion of Merit (USA), 1945. *Recreations:* usual country pursuits. *Address:* Holcombe House, Moretonhampstead, Devon TQ13 8PW. *Club:* Naval and Military.

WALKLING, Maj.-Gen. Alec Ernest, CB 1973; OBE 1954; *b* 12 April 1918; *s* of late Ernest George Walkling; *m* 1940, Marian Harris; one *s* one *d. Educ:* Weymouth Grammar School; Keble College, Oxford. MA (Oxon); BA Mod. Langs, 1939; BA Hons Nat. Science, 1949. Commissioned 2nd Lieut RA, 1940; served War of 1939–45, N Africa and Burma (despatches); Staff Coll., Quetta, 1944; Min. of Supply, 1949–53; British Joint Services Mission, Washington, 1956–58; Comd Regt in BAOR, 1961–63; Comd Brigade (TA), 1963–64; Imperial Defence Coll., 1965; Dep. Commandant, RMCS, 1966–68; Dir-Gen. of Artillery, 1969–70; Dep. Master-Gen. of the Ordnance, 1970–73, retired; Col Comdt, RA, 1974–83. Marks & Spencer PLC, 1973–80. *Recreations:* golf, oil and water colour painting. *Address:* Brackenhurst, Brackendale Road, Camberley, Surrey. *T:* Camberley 21016. *Club:* Army and Navy.

WALL, Alfreda, (Mrs D. R. Wall); *see* Thorogood, A.

WALL, (Alice) Anne, (Mrs Michael Wall), DCVO 1982 (CVO 1972; MVO 1964); Extra Woman of the Bedchamber to HM the Queen, since 1981; *b* 1928; *d* of late Admiral Sir Geoffrey Hawkins, KBE, CB, MVO, DSC and late Lady Margaret, *d* of 7th Duke of Buccleuch; *m* 1975, Commander Michael E. St Q. Wall, Royal Navy. *Educ:* Miss Faunce's PNEU School. Asst Press Sec. to the Queen, 1958–81. *Address:* Ivy House, Lambourn, Berks RG16 7PB. *T:* Lambourn 72348; 6 Chester Way, Kennington, SE11 4UT. *T:* 01-582 0692.

WALL, Prof. Charles Terence Clegg, FRS 1969; Professor of Pure Mathematics, Liverpool University, since 1965; *b* 14 Dec. 1936; *s* of Charles Wall, schoolteacher, Woodfield, Dursley, Glos; *m* 1959, Alexandra Joy, *d* of Prof. Leslie Spencer Hearnshaw, *qv*; two *s* two *d. Educ:* Marlborough Coll.; Trinity Coll., Cambridge. PhD Cantab 1960. Fellow, Trinity Coll., 1959–64; Harkness Fellow, Princeton, 1960–61; Univ. Lectr, Cambridge, 1961–64; Reader in Mathematics, and Fellow of St Catherine's Coll., Oxford, 1964–65. SERC Sen. Fellowship, 1983–. Royal Soc. Leverhulme Vis. Prof., CIEA, Mexico, 1967. Pres., London Mathematical Soc., 1978–80 (Mem. Council, 1973–80). *Publications:* Surgery on Compact Manifolds, 1970; A Geometric Introduction to Topology, 1972; papers on various problems in geometric topology, and related algebra. *Recreations:* gardening, home winemaking. *Address:* 5 Kirby Park, West Kirby, Wirral, Merseyside L48 2HA. *T:* 051–625 5063.

WALL, David (Richard), CBE 1985; Associate Director, Royal Academy of Dancing, since 1984; formerly Senior Principal, Royal Ballet Co.; *b* 15 March 1946; *s* of Charles and Dorothy Wall; *m* 1967, Alfreda Thorogood, *qv*; one *s* one *d. Educ:* Royal Ballet Sch. Joined Royal Ballet Co., Aug. 1964. Promotion to: Soloist, Aug. 1966; Junior Principal Dancer, Aug. 1967; Senior Principal Dancer, Aug. 1968; during period of employment danced all major roles and had many ballets created for him; retired from dancing, 1984. Evening Standard Award for Ballet, 1977. *Recreations:* music, theatre. *Address:* 34 Croham Manor Road, South Croydon, Surrey CR2 7BE.

WALL, Rt. Rev. Eric St Quintin; *b* 19 April 1915; *s* of Rev. Sydney Herbert Wall, MA, and Ethel Marion Wall (*née* Wilkins); *m* 1942, Doreen Clare (*née* Loveley); one *s* one *d. Educ:* Clifton; Brasenose Coll., Oxford (MA); Wells Theol. College. Deacon, 1938; Priest, 1939; Curate of Boston, 1938–41; Chaplain, RAFVR, 1941–45; Vicar of Sherston Magna, 1944–53; Rural Dean of Malmesbury, 1951–53; Vicar of Cricklade with Latton, 1953–60; Hon. Chaplain to Bp of Bristol, 1960–66; Hon. Canon, Bristol, 1960–72; Diocesan Adviser on Christian Stewardship, Dio. Bristol, 1960–66; Proc. Conv., 1964–69; Vicar, St Alban's, Westbury Park, Bristol, 1966–72; Rural Dean of Clifton, 1967–72; Canon Residentiary of Ely, 1972–80; Bishop Suffragan of Huntingdon, 1972–80. *Recreation:* golf. *Address:* 7 Peregrine Close, Diss, Norfolk. *T:* Diss 4331.

WALL, Gerard Aloysius; MP (Lab) Porirua, since 1969; Speaker, House of Representatives, New Zealand, since 1984; *b* 24 Jan. 1920; *m* 1951, Uru Raupo (Cameron); two *s* three *d. Educ:* St Bede's College, Christchurch; Canterbury Univ.; Otago Univ. MB ChB; FRCSE. House Surgeon, Christchurch Public Hosp., 1948–49; GP, Denniston, 1949–53; Mem., Buller Hosp. Bd, 1949–50; House Surgeon, Postgraduate Hosp., London, 1953; Royal Nat. Orthopaedic Hosp., London, 1955; Res. Surgical Officer, Hitchin Hosp., 1954–55; Sen. Plastic Surgical Registrar: Birmingham Accident Hosp., 1956–57; Norwich Hosp., 1957–59; Surgeon Dep. Supt, Wairau Hosp., 1960–69; Mem., Marlborough Hosp. Bd, 1965–68; Porirua Hosp., 1968–69. Mem., Blenheim Borough Council, 1962–68; Mem. Govt Select Committees: Maori Affairs, Health and Social Services, Local Govt, Statutes Revision, Foreign Affairs; Chm., Parly Service Comm, 1985. *Recreations:* woodworking, building. *Address:* 39 Tangare Drive, Elsdon, Porirua, New Zealand. *T:* (04) 375 015.

WALL, John William, CMG 1953; HM Diplomatic Service, retired 1966; *b* 6 Nov. 1910; *m* 1950, Eleanor Rosemary Riesle (*d* 1978); one *d. Educ:* Grammar Sch., Mexborough; Jesus Coll., Cambridge. Probationer Vice-Consul, Levant Consular Service, 1933; Vice-Consul, Cairo, 1936; in charge of Vice-Consulate, Suez, 1937; transferred to Jedda as 2nd Sec. in Diplomatic Service, 1939; acting Consul, Jedda, 1942, 1943; transferred to Tabriz, 1944, Isfahan, 1946, Casablanca, 1947; Brit. Middle East Office, Cairo: Head of Polit. Div., 1948, in charge 1949, 1950; Oriental Counsellor, Cairo, 1951; Political Agent, Bahrein, 1952–54; Consul-General at Salonika, 1955–57; HM Ambassador and Consul-General to Paraguay, 1957–59; Counsellor, Foreign Office, 1959–63; Consul-General at Alexandria, 1963–66. *Address:* Beech Cottage, Pen-y-Fan, Monmouth, Gwent. *Club:* United Oxford & Cambridge University.

WALL, Mrs Michael; *see* Wall, A. A.

WALL, Prof. Patrick David, MA, DM; FRCP; Professor of Anatomy and Director, Cerebral Functions Research Group, University College, London, since 1967; *b* 5 April 1925; *s* of T. Wall, MC, and R. Wall (*née* Cresswell). *Educ:* St Paul's; Christ Church, Oxford. MA 1947; BM, BCh 1948; DM 1960. Instructor, Yale School of Medicine, 1948–50; Asst Prof., Univ. of Chicago, 1950–53; Instructor, Harvard Univ., 1953–55; Assoc. Prof., 1957–60, Professor 1960–67, MIT. Vis. Prof., Hebrew Univ., Jerusalem, 1973–. Founding Chm., Brain Research Assoc. First Editor in Chief, Pain. *Publications:* Trio, The Revolting Intellectuals' Organizations (novel), 1966 (US 1965); (with R. Melzack) The Challenge of Pain, 1982; The Textbook of Pain, 1983; many papers on anat. and physiol. of nervous system. *Recreation:* kibbitzing. *Address:* Cerebral Functions Research Group, Department of Anatomy, University College, Gower Street, WC1.

WALL, Major Sir Patrick (Henry Bligh), Kt 1981; MC 1945; VRD 1957; RM (retd); MP (C) (Haltemprice Division of Hull, Feb. 1954–55; Haltemprice Division of East Yorkshire, 1955–83); Beverley, since 1983; *b* 19 Oct. 1916; *s* of Henry Benedict Wall and Gladys Eleanor Finney; *m* 1953, Sheila Elizabeth Putnam (*d* 1983); one *d. Educ:* Downside. Commissioned in RM 1935 (specialised in naval gunnery). Served in HM Ships, support craft, with RM Commandos and US Navy. Actg Major, 1943; RN Staff Coll., 1945; Joint Services Staff Coll., 1947; Major, 1949. Contested Cleveland Division (Yorks), 1951 and 1952. Parliamentary Private Secretary to: Minister of Agriculture, Fisheries and Food, 1955–57; Chancellor of the Exchequer, 1958–59. Westminster City Council, 1953–62; CO 47 Commando RMFVR, 1951–57; Comr for Sea Scouts for London, 1950–66; Pres. Yorks Area Young Conservatives, 1955–60; Chm. Mediterranean Group of Conservative Commonwealth Council, 1954–67; Chm. Cons. Parly East and Central Africa Cttee, 1956–59; Vice-Chairman: Conservative Commonwealth Affairs Cttee, 1960–68; Cons. Overseas Bureau, 1963–73; Cons. Defence Cttee, 1965–77; Vice-Chm. or Treasurer, IPU, 1974–82 (Chairman: British-Maltese, Anglo-Bahrain, Anglo-South African, Anglo-Taiwan Groups; Vice-Chm., Anglo-Portuguese, Treasurer, Anglo-Korean Groups). Pres., N Atlantic Assembly, 1983–85 (Chm., Mil. Cttee, 1978–81; Chm., Cons./Christian Democrat Gp); Chm., Pro Fide Movement, 1970–; Mem. Defence Cttee, WEU and Council of Europe, 1972–75. Chairman: Cons. Fisheries Sub-Cttee, 1962–; Africa Centre, 1961–65; Joint East and Central Africa Board, 1965–75; Cons. Southern Africa Group, 1970–78; Cons. Africa Sub-Cttee, 1979–; RM Parly Group, 1956–; British Rep. at 17th General Assembly of UN, 1962. Mem., Select Cttee on Defence, 1980–83. Vice-Pres., British Sub-Aqua Club. Kt, SMO Malta; USA Legion of Merit, 1945. *Publications:* Royal Marine Pocket Book, 1944; Student Power, 1968; Defence Policy, 1969; Overseas Aid, 1969; The Soviet Maritime Threat, 1973; The Indian Ocean and the Threat to the West, 1975; Prelude to Detente, 1975; Southern Oceans and the Security of the Free World, 1977; co-author of a number of political pamphlets. *Recreation:* ship and aircraft models. *Address:* 8 Westminster Gardens, Marsham Street, SW1. *T:* 01–828 1803; Brantinghamthorp, Brantingham, near Brough, North Humberside. *T:* Brough 667248. *Clubs:* Royal Yacht Squadron; Royal Naval Sailing Association.

WALL, Maj.-Gen. Robert Percival Walter, CB 1978; JP; Director, Land Decade Educational Council, since 1982; Chairman, Essex Family Practitioner Committee, since 1985; *b* 23 Aug. 1927; *s* of Frank Ernest and Ethel Elizabeth Wall; *m* 1st, 1953 (marr. diss. 1985); two *s* one *d*; 2nd, 1986, Jennifer Hilary Anning. Joined Royal Marines, 1945; regimental soldiering in Commandos, followed by service at sea and on staff of HQ 3 Commando Bde RM, 1945–58; psc(M) 1959; jssc 1961; Asst Sec., Chiefs of Staff Secretariat, 1962–65; 43 Commando RM, 1965–66; Naval Staff, 1966–68; Directing Staff, JSS Coll., 1969–71; Col GS Commando Forces and Dept of Commandant General RM, 1971–74; course at RCDS, 1975; Chief of Staff to Commandant General, RM, 1976–79. Vice-Pres., River Thames Soc., 1983– (Chm., 1978–83); Mem. Council, Thames Heritage Trust, 1980–83; Pres., Blackheath Football Club (RFU), 1983–85; Council, Officers' Pension Soc., 1980–. Freeman of City of London, 1977; Freeman, Co. of Watermen and Lightermen of River Thames, 1979. FBIM; FRSA 1985. JP City of London, 1982. *Recreations:* cricket, rugby, walking, reading. *Address:* c/o Barclays Bank, 116 Goodmayes Road, Goodmayes, Ilford, Essex. *Clubs:* Army and Navy, MCC.

WALL, Ronald George Robert, CB 1961; *b* 25 Jan. 1910; *s* of George Thomas and Sophia Jane Wall; *m* 1st, 1936, Winifred Evans (marr. diss., 1950); one *s*; 2nd, 1960, Mrs Muriel Sorrell (*née* Page). *Educ:* Alleyn's School, Dulwich; St John's College, Oxford (MA). Administrative Civil Service; entered Ministry of Agriculture and Fisheries, 1933; Fisheries Sec., 1952–59. Gwilym Gibbon Research Fellow, Nuffield College, Oxford, 1951–52. President of Permanent Commission under Internat. Fisheries Convention of

1946, 1953–56; Chairman of the International Whaling Commission, 1958–60; Dep. Sec., Min. of Agriculture, Fisheries and Food, 1961–70. Chm., Sugar Bd, 1970–77. *Recreations:* theatre, music, gardening. *Address:* 201 London Road, Twickenham, Mddx. *T:* 01–892 7086. *Clubs:* United Oxford & Cambridge University, Arts Theatre.

WALL, Prof. William Douglas, PhD, DLit; Professor of Educational Psychology, Institute of Education, University of London, 1972–78, now Professor Emeritus; *b* 22 Aug. 1913; *s* of late John Henry Wall and Ann McCulloch Wall, Wallington, Surrey; *m* 1st, 1936, Doris Margaret (*née* Satchel) (marr. diss. 1960); two *s* one *d*; 2nd, 1960, Ursula Maria (*née* Gallusser); one *s*. *Educ:* Univ. Coll. London, 1931–34 (BA Hons); Univ. Coll. London/Univ. of Birmingham, 1944–48 (PhD (Psychol.)); DLit (London) 1979. FBPsS. Mem., Social Psych. Sect., Child and Educnl Psych. Sect., Univ. of Birmingham Educn Dept, 1945–53; Reader, 1948–53; Head, Educn and Child Develt Unit, UNESCO, Paris, 1951–56; Dir, Nat. Foundn for Educnl Res. in England and Wales, 1956–68; Dean, Inst. of Educn, Univ. of London, 1968–73; Scientific Advr, Bernard van Leer Foundn, 1978–82. Visiting Professor: Univ. of Michigan, 1957; Univ. of Jerusalem, 1962; Univ. of Tel Aviv, 1967. Chm., Internat. Project Evaluation of Educnl Attainment, 1958–62; Mem., Police Trng Council, 1970–78; Co-Dir, 1958–75, and Chm., Nat. Child Develt Study, 1958–78; Mem. Council, Internat. Children's Centre, Paris, 1970–78. *Publications:* (many trans. various langs): Adolescent Child, 1948 (2nd edn, 1952); Education and Mental Health, 1955; Psychological Services for Schools, 1956; Child of our Times, 1959; Failure in School, 1962; Adolescents in School and Society, 1968; Longitudinal Studies and the Social Sciences, 1970; Constructive Education for Children, 1975; Constructive Education for Adolescents, 1977; Constructive Education for Handicapped, 1979; contrib: British Jl Educnl Psych.; British Jl Psych., Educnl Res. (Editor, 1958–68), Educnl Rev., Enfance, Human Develt, Internat. Rev. Educn. *Recreations:* painting, gardening. *Address:* La Geneste, Rose Hill, Burnham, Bucks SL1 8LW.

WALLACE, family name of **Barons Wallace of Campsie** and **Wallace of Coslany.**

WALLACE OF CAMPSIE, Baron *cr* 1974 (Life Peer), of Newlands, Glasgow; **George Wallace,** JP; DL; Life President, Wallace, Cameron (Holdings) Ltd, since 1981 (President, 1977–81); Director, Smith & Nephew Associated Companies Ltd, 1973–77; *b* 13 Feb. 1915; *s* of John Wallace and Mary Pollock; *m* 1977, Irene Alice Langdon Phipps, *er d* of Ernest Phipps, Glasgow. *Educ:* Queen's Park Secondary Sch., Glasgow; Glasgow Univ. Estd Wallace, Cameron & Co. Ltd, 1948, Chm., 1950–77. Solicitor before the Supreme Courts, 1950–; Hon. Sheriff at Hamilton, 1971–. Chm., E Kilbride and Stonehouse Develt Corp., 1969–75; Mem. Bd, S of Scotland Electricity Bd, 1966–68; founder Mem. Bd, Scottish Develt Agency, 1975–78; Chm., E Kilbride Business Centre, 1984–. Pres., Glasgow Chamber of Commerce, 1974–76; Vice-Pres., Scottish Assoc. of Youth Clubs, 1971–; Chm., Adv. Bd (Strathclyde) Salvation Army, 1972–; Mem. Court, Univ. of Strathclyde, 1973–74; Hon. Pres., Town and Country Planning Assoc. (Scottish Sect.), 1969–; Chm., Scottish Exec. Cttee, Brit. Heart Foundn, 1973–76; Chm., Britannia Cttee, British Sailors' Soc., 1967–77; Vice-Chm., Scottish Retirement Council, 1975–; Hon. Pres., Lanarkshire Samaritans, 1984–. FRSA 1970; FInstM 1968; MBIM 1969. JP 1968, DL 1971, Glasgow. KStJ 1976. *Recreation:* reading. *Address:* 14 Fernleigh Road, Newlands, Glasgow G43 2UE. *T:* 041–637 3337. *Clubs:* Caledonian; Royal Scottish Automobile (Glasgow).

WALLACE OF COSLANY, Baron *cr* 1974 (Life Peer), of Coslany in the City of Norwich; **George Douglas Wallace;** *b* 18 April 1906; *e s* of late George Wallace, Cheltenham Spa, Gloucestershire; *m* 1932, Vera Randall, Guildford, Surrey; one *s* one *d*. *Educ:* Central School, Cheltenham Spa. Mem. of Management Cttee, in early years, of YMCA at East Bristol and Guildford; Mem. Chislehurst-Sidcup UDC, 1937–46; has been Divisional Sec. and also Chm., Chislehurst Labour Party; also Chm. of Parks and Cemeteries Cttee of UDC, Schools Manager and Member of Chislehurst, Sidcup and Orpington Divisional Education Executive; Mem., Cray Valley and Sevenoaks Hosp. Management Cttee; Chm., House Cttee, Queen Mary's Hosp.; Vice-Chm., Greenwich and Bexley AHA, 1974–77. Joined Royal Air Force, reaching rank of Sergeant. Served in No 11 Group Fighter Command, 1941–45. MP (Lab) Chislehurst Div. of Kent, 1945–50; Junior Govt Whip, 1947–50; MP (Lab) Norwich North, Oct. 1964–Feb. 1974; PPS: to Lord President of the Council, Nov. 1964–65; to Sec. of State for Commonwealth Affairs, 1965; to Minister of State, Min. of Housing and Local Govt, 1967–68; Mem. Speaker's Panel of Chairmen, 1970–74; a Lord in Waiting (Govt Whip), 1977–79; opposition spokesman and Whip, H of L, 1979–84. Delegate to Council of Europe and WEU, 1975–77. Member: Commonwealth Parly Assoc.; Commonwealth War Graves Commn, 1970–86; Kent CC, 1952–57. Pres., London Soc. of Recreational Gardeners, 1977–. *Recreations:* interested in Youth Movements and social welfare schemes. *Address:* 44 Shuttle Close, Sidcup, Kent. *T:* 01–300 3634.

WALLACE, Albert Frederick, CBE 1963 (OBE 1955); DFC 1943; Controller of Manpower, Greater London Council, 1978–82; *b* 22 Aug. 1921; *s* of Major Frederick Wallace and Ada Wallace; *m* 1940, Evelyn M. White; one *s* one *d*. *Educ:* Roan School, Blackheath, SE3. MIPM, MBIM, MILGA. Regular Officer, Royal Air Force, 1939–69; retired in rank of Group Captain. Regional Advisory Officer, Local Authorities Management Services and Computer Cttee, 1969–71; Asst Clerk of the Council, Warwickshire CC, 1971–73; County Personnel Officer, W Midlands CC, 1973–78. *Recreations:* golf, bridge. *Address:* Earleydene, Chesterfield Road, Eastbourne BN20 7NT. *Club:* Royal Air Force.

WALLACE, Charles William, CMG 1983; CVO 1975; HM Diplomatic Service; Ambassador to Uruguay, 1983–86; *b* 19 Jan. 1926; *s* of Percival Francis and Julia Wallace; *m* 1957, Gloria Regina de Ros Ribas (*née* Sanz-Agero); two step *s*. *Educ:* privately and abroad. HM Foreign (later Diplomatic) Service, 1949; served: Asuncion; Barcelona; Bari; Bahrain; Tegucigalpa; Guatemala; Panama; Foreign Office; Baghdad; Buenos Aires; Montevideo; FO, later FCO, Asst Head of American Dept; Counsellor 1969; Rome and Milan; Mexico City; Ambassador: Paraguay, 1976–79; Peru, 1979–83. Freeman, City of London, 1981. Order of Aztec Eagle, 1975. *Recreations:* sailing, fishing. *Address:* c/o Foreign and Commonwealth Office, SW1A 2AH. *Club:* Travellers'.

WALLACE, Prof. David James, FRS 1986; FRSE; Tait Professor of Mathematical Physics, University of Edinburgh, since 1979; *b* 7 Oct. 1945; *s* of Robert Elder Wallace and Jane McConnell Wallace (*née* Elliot); *m* 1970, Elizabeth Anne Yeats; one *d*. *Educ:* Hawick High Sch.; Univ. of Edinburgh (BSc, PhD). FRSE 1982. Harkness Fellow, Princeton Univ., 1970–72; Lecturer in Physics, 1972–78, Reader in Physics, 1978–79, Southampton Univ. Frequent visiting scientist abroad, incl. Europe, Israel, North and South America. Maxwell Medal of Inst. of Physics, 1980. *Publications:* in research and review jls, in a number of areas of theoretical physics. *Recreations:* running, eating at La Potinière. *Address:* Physics Department, The University, Mayfield Road, Edinburgh EH9 3JZ. *T:* 031–667 1081 ext. 2850.

WALLACE, David Mitchell, CBE 1978 (OBE 1942); MS, FRCS; retired, 1978; Professor of Urology, Riyadh Medical College, Saudi Arabia, 1974–78; *b* 8 May 1913; *s* of F. David Wallace and M. I. F. Wallace; *m* 1940, Noel Wilson; one *s* three *d*. *Educ:* Mill Hill; University Coll., London, BSc 1934; MB, BS 1938; FRCS 1939; MS 1948. Served War of 1939–45, Wing Comdr, RAF (despatches). Hunterian Prof., Royal Coll. of Surgeons, London, 1956, 1978. Formerly: Surgeon, St Peter's Hospital; Urologist, Royal Marsden Hospital, Chelsea Hospital for Women, and Manor House Hospitals; Lecturer, Institute of Urology; Adviser on Cancer to WHO. Mem., Amer. Radium Soc., 1968. *Publications:* Tumours of the Bladder, 1957; contrib. to Cancer, British Jl of Urology, Proc. Royal Soc. Med. *Recreations:* cine photography, pistol shooting. *Address:* 45 Fort Picklecombe, Tor Point, Cornwall PL10 1JB.

WALLACE, Doreen, (Mrs D. E. A. Rash), MA; novelist; *b* 18 June 1897; *d* of R. B. Agnew Wallace and Mary Elizabeth Peebles; *m* 1922, Rowland H. Rash (*d* 1977), Wortham, Suffolk; one *s* two *d*. *Educ:* Malvern Girls' College; Somerville College, Oxford. Honours in English 1919; taught English in a grammar school for three years, then married; first novel published, 1931. *Publications:* -Esques (with E. F. A. Geach), 1918; A Little Learning; The Gentle Heart; The Portion of the Levites; Creatures of an Hour; Even Such is Time; Barnham Rectory, 1934; Latter Howe, 1935; So Long to Learn 1936; Going to the Sea, 1936; Old Father Antic, 1937; The Faithful Compass, 1937; The Time of Wild Roses, 1938; A Handful of Silver, 1939; East Anglia, 1939; The Spring Returns, 1940; English Lakeland, 1941; Green Acres, 1941; Land from the Waters, 1944; Carlotta Green, 1944; The Noble Savage, 1945; Billy Potter, 1946; Willow Farm, 1948; How Little We Know, 1949; Only One Life, 1950; (non-fiction) In a Green Shade, 1950; Norfolk (with R. Bagnall-Oakeley), 1951; Root of Evil, 1952; Sons of Gentlemen, 1953; The Younger Son, 1954; Daughters, 1955; The Interloper, 1956; The Money Field, 1957; Forty Years on, 1958; Richard and Lucy, 1959; Mayland Hall, 1960; Lindsay Langton and Wives, 1961; Woman with a Mirror, 1963; The Mill Pond, 1966; Ashbury People, 1968; The Turtle, 1969; Elegy, 1970; An Earthly Paradise, 1971; A Thinking Reed, 1973; Changes and Chances, 1975; Landscape with Figures, 1976. *Recreations:* painting, gardening. *Address:* 2 Manor Gardens, Diss, Norfolk.

WALLACE, (Dorothy) Jacqueline H.; *see* Hope-Wallace.

WALLACE, Fleming; *see* Wallace, J. F.

WALLACE, Sir Gordon, Kt 1968; President, Court of Appeal, New South Wales, 1966–70; Acting Chief Justice of New South Wales, Oct. 1968–Feb. 1969; *b* 22 Jan. 1900; *s* of A. C. Isaacs, Sydney; *m* 1927, Marjorie (*d* 1980), *d* of A. E. Mullins, Chepstow, Mon.; one *s* one *d*. *Educ:* Sydney High School; RMC Duntroon; Sydney University. Lt, Australian Staff Corps; AMF and AIF, 1939–44 (Col). KC 1940. Judge of Supreme Court, NSW, 1960–70. Pres., NSW Bar Assoc., 1957–58; Vice-Pres., Australian Law Council, 1957; Pres., Internat. Law Assoc., Aust. Br., 1959–65. Mem., Commonwealth Commn of Enquiry into Income Tax, 1952–53. Chm., Royal Commn on Great Barrier Reef Petroleum Drilling, 1970–74. *Publications:* (jtly with Sir Percy Spender) Company Law, 1937; (jtly with J. McI. Young, QC) Australian Company Law, 1965. *Recreations:* bowls, music. *Address:* 6 Lynwood Avenue, Killara, NSW 2071, Australia. *T:* 498 1818. *Clubs:* University, Pioneers (Sydney); Elanora Country.

WALLACE, Ian Alexander; JP; Headmaster, Canford School, 1961–76; *b* 5 Oct. 1917; *s* of late Very Rev. A. R. Wallace and Winifred, *d* of late Rev. H. C. Sturges; *m* 1947, Janet Glossop; two *s* two *d*. *Educ:* Clifton; Corpus Christi College, Cambridge (open scholar). Classical Tripos, Part I, 1st Cl.; Theological Tripos Part I, 2nd Cl. Div. One. Served War of 1939–45, Mountain Artillery, NW Frontier, India, 1941; School of Artillery, India, 1942–43; Arakan, 1944; Mandalay, 1945 (despatches). Rossall School: Assistant Master, 1946; Housemaster, 1951–61. SW Regional Sec., Independent Schools Careers Organisation, 1976–84; Project Manager for India, GAP Activity Projects, 1984–. Governor: Portsmouth Grammar Sch., 1977–; King's Sch., Bruton, 1977–. JP Poole Borough, 1966. *Address:* Steeple Close, Hindon, Salisbury, Wilts.

WALLACE, Ian Bryce, OBE 1983; Hon. RAM; Hon. RCM; singer, actor and broadcaster; *b* London, 10 July 1919; *o s* of late Sir John Wallace, Kirkcaldy, Fife (one-time MP for Dunfermline), and Mary Bryce Wallace (*née* Temple), Glasgow; *m* 1948, Patricia Gordon Black, Edenwood, Cupar, Fife; one *s* one *d*. *Educ:* Charterhouse; Trinity Hall, Cambridge (MA). Served War of 1939–45, (invalided from) RA, 1944. London stage debut in The Forrigan Reel, Sadler's Wells, 1945. Opera debut, as Schaunard, in La Bohème, with New London Opera Co., Cambridge Theatre, London, 1946. Sang principal roles for NLOC, 1946–49, incl. Dr Bartolo in Il Barbiere di Siviglia. Glyndebourne debut, Masetto, Don Giovanni, Edin. Fest., 1948. Regular appearances as principal *buffo* for Glyndebourne, both in Sussex and at Edin. Fest., 1948–61, incl. perfs as Don Magnifico in La Cenerentola, at Berlin Festwoche, 1954. Italian debut: Masetto, Don Giovanni, at Parma, 1950; also Don Magnifico, La Cenerentola, Rome, 1955, Dr Bartolo, Il Barbiere di Siviglia, Venice, 1956, and Bregenz Fest., 1964–65. Regular appearances for Scottish Opera, 1965–, incl. Leporello in Don Giovanni, Pistola in Falstaff, Duke of Plaza Toro in The Gondoliers. Don Pasquale, Welsh Nat. Opera, 1967, Dr Dulcamara, L'Elisir d'Amore, Glyndebourne Touring Opera, 1968. Devised, wrote and presented three series of adult education programmes on opera, entitled Singing For Your Supper, for Scottish Television (ITV), 1967–70. Recordings include: Gilbert and Sullivan Operas with Sir Malcolm Sargent, and humorous songs by Flanders and Swann. Theatrical career includes: a Royal Command Variety Perf., London Palladium, 1952; Cesar in Fanny, Theatre Royal, Drury Lane, 1956; 4 to the Bar, Criterion, 1960; Toad in Toad of Toad Hall, Queen's, 1964. Regular broadcaster, 1944–: radio and TV, as singer, actor and compere; a regular panellist on radio musical quiz game, My Music; Robert Forsyth in Take the High Road, STV. Pres., ISM, 1979–80. Sir Charles Santley Meml Award, Musicians' Co., 1984. *Publications:* Promise Me You'll Sing Mud (autobiog.), 1975; Nothing Quite Like It (autobiog.), 1982. *Recreations:* walking, reading, sport watching, photography; singing a song about a hippopotamus to children of all ages. *Address:* 18 Denewood Road, Highgate, N6 4AJ. *T:* 01–340 5802. *Clubs:* Garrick, MCC; Stage Golfing Society.

WALLACE, Sir Ian (James), Kt 1982; CBE 1971 (OBE 1942); Director, CMS Group Ltd, since 1986; Chairman, SNR Bearings (UK) Ltd, 1975–85; *b* 25 Feb. 1916; *s* of John Madder Wallace, CBE; *m* 1942, Catherine Frost Mitchell, *e d* of Cleveland S. Mitchell; one *s* one *d*. *Educ:* Uppingham Sch.; Jesus Coll., Cambridge (BA). Underwriting at Lloyd's, 1935–39. War Service, Fleet Air Arm: Cmdr (A) RNVR, 1939–46. Harry Ferguson Ltd from 1947: Dir 1950; later Massey Ferguson Ltd, Dir Holdings Board until 1970. Chm., Coventry Cons. Assoc., 1968– (Treas., 1956–68); Chm., W Midlands Cons. Council, 1967–70 (Treas., 1962–67); Pres., W Midlands Area Cons. Council. Member: Severn-Trent Water Authority, 1974–82; W Midlands Econ. Planning Council, 1965–75; Vice-Chm., Midland Regional Council, CBI, 1964, Chm., 1967–69; Pres., Coventry Chamber of Commerce, 1972–74. Pres., Worcs County Rifle Assoc., 1983–. *Recreation:* shooting (rifle and game). *Address:* Little House, 156 High Street, Broadway, Worcs WR12 7AJ. *T:* Broadway 852414. *Clubs:* Carlton, Naval and Military, North London Rifle.

WALLACE, Ian Norman Duncan, QC 1973; *b* 21 April 1922; *s* of late Duncan Gardner Wallace, HBM Crown Advocate in Egypt, Paymaster-Comdr RNR and Eileen Agnes Wallace. *Educ:* Loretto; Oriel Coll., Oxford (MA). Served War of 1939–45: Ordinary

Seaman RN, 1940; Lieut RNVR, 1941–46. Called to Bar, Middle Temple, 1948; Western Circuit, 1949. Vis. Scholar, Berkeley Univ., Calif, 1977–86. *Publications:* (ed) Hudson on Building and Civil Engineering Contracts, 8th edn 1959, 9th edn 1965 and 10th edn 1970, supplement 1979; Building and Civil Engineering Standard Forms, 1969; Further Building and Engineering Standard Forms, 1973; The International Civil Engineering Contract, 1974, supplement 1980; The ICE Conditions (5th edn), 1978; Construction Law: problems in Tort and Contract, 1986; contrib. Law Qly Review, Jl of Internat. Law and Commerce, Lloyd's Jl of Internat. Construction Law, Internat. Construction Law Rev. *Recreations:* keeping fit, foreign travel. *Address:* 53 Holland Park, W11 3RS. *T:* 01–727 7640. *Clubs:* Lansdowne, Hurlingham.

WALLACE, Irving; free-lance author; *b* 19 March 1916; *s* of Alexander Wallace and Bessie (*née* Liss); *m* 1941, Sylvia Kahn Wallace; one *s* one *d*. *Educ:* Kenosha (Wisc.) Central High Sch.; Williams Inst., Berkeley, Calif.; Los Angeles City College. Served USAAF and US Army Signal Corps, 1942–46. Magazine writer, Saturday Evening Post, Reader's Digest, Collier's, etc., 1931–54; film scenarist, 1955–58, Exploration: Honduras jungles, Wisconsin Collegiate Expedn, 1934–35. Member: PEN; Soc. of Authors; Authors League of America. Supreme Award of Merit, George Washington Carver Memorial Inst., Washington, DC, 1964; Commonwealth Club of Calif. Lit. Award for 1964; Nat. Bestsellers Inst. Paperback of the Year Award, 1965; Popular Culture Assoc. Award, 1974. *Publications:* The Fabulous Originals, 1955; The Square Pegs, 1957; The Fabulous Showman, 1959; The Sins of Philip Fleming, 1959; The Chapman Report, 1960; The Twenty-Seventh Wife, 1961; The Prize, 1962; The Three Sirens, 1963; The Man, 1964; The Sunday Gentleman, 1965; The Plot, 1967; The Writing of One Novel, 1968; The Seven Minutes, 1969; The Nympho and Other Maniacs, 1971; The Word, 1972; The Fan Club, 1974; The People's Almanac, 1975; The R Document, 1976; The Book of Lists, 1977; The Two, 1978; The People's Almanac 2, 1978; The Pigeon Project, 1979; The Book of Lists 2, 1980; The Second Lady, 1980; The Book of Predictions, 1981; The Intimate Sex Lives of Famous People, 1981; The People's Almanac 3, 1981; The Almighty, 1983; The Book of Lists 3, 1983; Significa, 1983; The Miracle, 1984; Contemporary Authors Autobiography Series, Vol. 1, 1984; The Seventh Secret, 1986; The Celestial Bed, 1987; contribs to Collier's Encyclopædia, American Oxford Encyclopædia, Encyclopædia Britannica. *Relevant publication:* Irving Wallace: a writer's profile, by John Leverance, 1974. *Recreations:* tennis and table tennis, hiking, billiards, travel abroad, collecting autographs, French Impressionist art, canes. *Address:* PO Box 49328, Los Angeles, Calif 90049, USA.

WALLACE, (James) Fleming; QC (Scot) 1985; Counsel to Scottish Law Commission, since 1979; *b* 19 March 1931; *s* of James F. B. Wallace, SSC and Margaret B. Gray, MA; *m* 1964, Valerie Mary (*d* 1986), *d* of Leslie Lawrence, Solicitor, and Madge Lawrence, Ramsbury, Wilts; two *d*. *Educ:* Edinburgh Academy; Edinburgh University (MA 1951; LLB 1954). Served RA, 1954–56 (2nd Lieut); TA 1956–60. Admitted Faculty of Advocates, 1957; practice at Scottish Bar until 1960; Parly Draftsman and Legal Secretary, Lord Advocate's Dept, London, 1960–79. *Publication:* The Businessman's Lawyer (Scottish Section), 1965, 2nd edn 1973. *Recreations:* hill walking, choral singing, golf, badminton. *Address:* 24 Corrennie Gardens, Edinburgh EH10 6DB. *Club:* Royal Mid-Surrey Golf.

WALLACE, James Robert; MP (L) Orkney and Shetland, since 1983; *b* 25 Aug. 1954; *s* of John F. T. Wallace and Grace Hannah Wallace (*née* Maxwell); *m* 1983, Rosemary Janet Fraser; one *d*. *Educ:* Annan Academy; Downing College, Cambridge (BA 1975, MA 1979); Edinburgh University (LLB 1977). Chm., Edinburgh Univ. Liberal Club, 1976–77. Called to the Scots Bar, 1979; practised as Advocate, 1979–83. Contested Dumfriesshire (L), 1979; contested South of Scotland (L), European Parlt election, 1979. Mem., Scottish Liberal Exec., 1976–85; Vice-Chm. (Policy), Scottish Liberal Party, 1982–85; Hon. Pres., Scottish Young Liberals, 1984–85; Liberal spokesman on defence and Deputy Whip, 1985–. *Recreations:* golf, music, travel. *Address:* Northwood House, Tankerness, Orkney KW17 2QS. *T:* Tankerness 383. *Clubs:* National Liberal; Scottish Liberal (Edinburgh).

WALLACE, Lawrence James, OC 1972; CVO 1983; Deputy Minister to the Premier of British Columbia, since 1980; *b* Victoria, BC, Canada, 24 April 1913; *s* of John Wallace and Mary Wallace (*née* Parker); *m* 1942, Lois Leeming; three *d*. *Educ:* Univ. of British Columbia (BA); Univ. of Washington, USA (MEd). Served War, Lt-Comdr, Royal Canadian Navy Voluntary Reserve, 1941–45. Joined British Columbia Govt, as Dir of Community Programmes and Adult Educn, 1953; Dep. Provincial Sec., 1959–77, Dep. to Premier, 1969–72; Agent-General for British Columbia in UK and Europe, 1977–80. General Chairman: four centennial celebrations, marking founding of Crown Colony of British Columbia in 1858, union of Crown Colonies of Vancouver Is. and British Columbia, 1866, Canadian Confedn, 1867, and joining into confedn by British Columbia in 1871. Past Chm., Inter-Provincial Lottery Corp., Queen Elizabeth II Schol. Cttee, and Nancy Green Schol. Cttee; Hon. Trustee, British Columbia Sports Hall of Fame. Director: Duke of Edinburgh Awards Cttee; BC Forest Museum; Adv. Bd, Salvation Army; Canadian Council of Christians and Jews. Named British Columbia Man of the Year, 1958, and Greater Vancouver Man of the Year, 1967; Canadian Centennial Medal, 1967; Comdr Brother, OStJ, 1969; City of Victoria Citizenship Award, 1971; Queen's Jubilee Medal, 1977. Freeman of City of London, 1978. Hon. LLD, Univ. of British Columbia, 1978. Hon. Member: BC High Sch. Basketball Assoc.; BC Recreation Assoc. Hon. Chief: Alberni, Gilford and Southern Vancouver Is Indian Bands. *Recreations:* gardening, community activities. *Address:* Parliament Buildings, Victoria, British Columbia V8V 4R3, Canada.

WALLACE, Reginald James, CMG 1979; OBE 1961; fiscal adviser; Chairman, Norwich Union Fire Insurance Society (Gibraltar) Ltd; Board Member, Gibraltar Broadcasting Corporation, since 1985; *b* 16 Aug. 1919; *s* of James Wallace and Doris (*née* Welch); *m* 1st, 1943, Doris Barbara Brown, MD, FRCS, MRCOG (decd); one *d*; 2nd, 1973, Maureen Coady (*d* 1983); 3rd, 1984, Marilyn Ryan (*née* Gareze); one *d*. *Educ:* John Gulson Sch., Coventry; Tatterford Sch., Norfolk; Leeds Univ. (BA); Queen's Coll., Oxford. Served War, 1939–46, 7th Rajput Regt, Indian Army (Major). Gold Coast/Ghana Admin. Service, 1947–58; Sen. District Comr, 1955; Asst Chief Regional Officer, Northern Region, 1957; Regional Sec., 1958; British Somaliland, 1958–60; Financial Sec., War Office, 1961–66; HM Treasury, 1966–78; seconded to Solomon Is, as Financial Sec. (later Financial Adviser), 1973–76; seconded, as British Mem., Anglo/French Mission on Admin. Reform in the Condominium of the New Hebrides, 1977; Governor of Gilbert Is, 1978 to Independence, July 1979; Financial and Develt Sec., Gibraltar, 1979–83. *Recreations:* walking, music. *Address:* 24 Marina Court, Glacis Road, Gibraltar. *Club:* Royal Commonwealth Society.

WALLACE, Robert, CBE 1970; BL; JP; Chairman, Highland Health Board, 1973–81; *b* 20 May 1911; *s* of late John Wallace, Glespin, Lanarkshire, and late Elizabeth Brydson; *m* 1940, Jane Maxwell (decd), *d* of late John Smith Rankin, Waulkmill, Thornhill, Dumfriesshire and late Jane Maxwell; no *c*. *Educ:* Sanquhar Sch.; Glasgow University. Solicitor 1932; BL (Dist.) 1933. Private legal practice, 1932–40; Depute Town Clerk, Ayr Burgh, 1940–44; Civil Defence Controller, Ayr Burgh, 1941–44; Depute County Clerk and Treas., Co. Inverness, 1944–48; County Clerk, Treasurer and Collector of the County of Inverness, 1948–73; Temp. Sheriff, Grampian, Highland and Islands, 1976–84. Hon. Sheriff at Inverness, 1967–. JP Co. Inverness, 1951–. *Recreations:* bowling, fishing, gardening. *Address:* Eildon, School Road, Conon Bridge, Ross-shire IV7 8AE. *T:* Dingwall 63592.

WALLACE, Walter Ian James, CMG 1957; OBE 1943; retired; *b* 18 Dec. 1905; *e s* of late David Wallace, Sandgate, Kent; *m* 1940, Olive Mary (*d* 1973), 4th *d* of late Col Charles William Spriggs, Southsea; no *c*. *Educ:* Bedford Modern School; St Catharine's College, Cambridge. Entered ICS 1928, posted to Burma; Dep. Commissioner, 1933; Settlement Officer, 1934–38; Dep. Commissioner, 1939–42; Defence Secretary, 1942–44; Military Administration of Burma (Col and Dep. Director Civil Affairs), 1944–45 (despatches); Commissioner, 1946; Chief Secretary, 1946–47. Joined Colonial Office, 1947, Asst Sec., 1949–62; Asst Under-Sec. of State, 1962–66, retired. *Publication:* Revision Settlement Operations in the Minbu District of Upper Burma, 1939. *Recreation:* local history. *Address:* c/o Grindlays Bank plc, 13 St James's Square, SW1Y 4LF. *Club:* East India, Devonshire, Sports and Public Schools.

WALLACE, Walter Wilkinson, CVO 1977; CBE 1973 (OBE 1964); DSC 1944; Foreign and Commonwealth Office; *b* 23 Sept. 1923; *s* of late Walter Wallace and of Helen Wallace (*née* Douglas); *m* 1955, Susan Blanche, *d* of Brig. F. W. B. Parry, CBE; one *s* one *d*. *Educ:* George Heriot's, Edinburgh. Served War, Royal Marines, 1942–46 (Captain). Joined Colonial Service, 1946; Asst Dist Comr, Sierra Leone, 1948; Dist Comr, 1954; seconded to Colonial Office, 1955–57; Sen. Dist Comr, 1961; Provincial Comr, 1961; Develt Sec., 1962–64; Estabt Sec., Bahamas, 1964–67; Sec. to Cabinet, Bermuda, 1968–73; HM Commissioner, Anguilla, 1973; Governor, British Virgin Islands, 1974–78. *Recreation:* golf. *Address:* Becketts, Itchenor, Sussex. *T:* Birdham 512438. *Club:* Army and Navy.

WALLACE, William, CMG 1961; Assistant Comptroller of Patent Office and Industrial Property and Copyright Department, Department of Trade and Industry (formerly Board of Trade (Patent Office)), 1954–73, retired; *b* 8 July 1911; *s* of A. S. Wallace, Wemyss Bay, Renfrewshire; *m* 1940, Sheila, *d* of Sydney Hopper, Wallington, Surrey; one *s* two *d*. *Educ:* Mill Hill School; St Edmund Hall, Oxford. Barrister, Inner Temple, 1936–39. Served War of 1939–45, Royal Artillery with final rank of Major. Board of Trade legal staff, 1945–54. UK Delegate, Internat. Confs on Copyright and Patents; Chm. Intergovernmental Cttee on Rights of Performers, Record Makers and Broadcasting Orgns, 1967–69; Actg Chairman: Intergovernmental Copyright Cttee, 1970; Exec. Cttee, Berne Copyright Union, 1970; Vice-Chm., Whitford Cttee on Copyright and Designs, 1974. Jean Geiringer Meml Lectr, USA, 1971. *Address:* Weavers, Capel, Surrey. *T:* Dorking 711205.

WALLEN, Ella Kathleen, MA (Oxon); Headmistress, St Mary's School, Wantage, 1977–80; *b* 15 Feb. 1914. *Educ:* Camden School for Girls; St Hugh's College, Oxford. History Mistress, Queen Victoria High School, Stockton-on-Tees, 1937–41; Senior History Mistress, High School for Girls, Gloucester, 1942–59; Headmistress: Queen Victoria High School, Stockton-on Tees, 1959–65; Bedford High Sch., 1965–76. *Address:* 15 Lynn Close, Marston Road, Oxford OX3 0JH.

WALLER, Gary Peter Anthony; MP (C) Keighley, since 1983 (Brighouse and Spenborough, 1979–83); *b* 24 June 1945; *s* of late John Waller and of Elizabeth Waller. *Educ:* Rugby Sch.; Univ. of Lancaster (BA Hons). Chairman: Lancaster Univ. Conservative Assoc., 1965; Spen Valley Civic Soc., 1978–80; Vice-Chm., Nat. Assoc. of Cons. Graduates, 1970–73 and 1976–77. Member: Exec. Cttee, Cons. Nat. Union, 1976–77; Management Cttee, Bradford and Dist Housing Assoc., 1976–. Exec. Sec., Wider Share Ownership Council, 1973–76. Contested (C): Bor. Council elecns, Kensington, 1971, 1974; Leyton, GLC elecn, 1973; Rother Valley, parly elecn, Feb. and Oct. 1974. PPS to Sec. of State for Transport, 1982–83. Member: H of C Select Cttee on Transport, 1979–82; Jt Cttee on Consolidation Bills, 1982–; Chm., All Party Wool Textile Gp, 1984– (Sec., 1979–83); Dep. Chm., Parly Food and Health Forum, 1985–; Secretary: Cons. Parly Sport and Recreation Cttee, 1979–81; Cons. Parly Transport Cttee, 1985–; Treasurer: Parly Information Technology Cttee, 1981–; Cons. Yorkshire Members, 1983– (Sec., 1979–83). Pres., Brighouse Citizens Advice Bureau, 1979–83; Vice-President: Newham S Cons. Assoc., 1979– (Chm., 1971–74); Bethnal Green and Bow Cons. Assoc., 1982–83. Vice-Pres., Keighley Sea Cadets, 1984–. Governor: George Green's Sch., Tower Hamlets, 1968–70; Isaac Newton Sch., N Kensington, 1971–73; Manager, Moorend C of E Primary Sch., Cleckheaton, 1977–80. *Recreations:* music, poetry, squash, football. *Address:* House of Commons, SW1A 0AA. *T:* 01–219 4010. *Clubs:* Keighley Conservative, Haworth Conservative, Silsden Conservative.

WALLER, George Mark; QC 1979; a Recorder, since 1986; *b* 13 Oct. 1940; *s* of Rt Hon. Sir George Waller, *qv*; *m* 1967, Rachel Elizabeth, *d* of His Honour Judge Beaumont, *qv*; three *s*. *Educ:* Oundle Sch.; Durham Univ. (LLB). Called to the Bar, Gray's Inn, 1964. *Recreations:* tennis, golf. *Address:* Mead House, Bradfield, Reading RG7 6HU. *T:* Bradfield 744218; 2 Verulam Buildings, Gray's Inn, WC1. *T:* 01–242 9393. *Clubs:* Garrick, MCC.

WALLER, Rt. Hon. Sir George (Stanley), Kt 1965; OBE 1945; PC 1976; a Lord Justice of Appeal, 1976–84; *b* 3 Aug. 1911; *s* of late James Stanley and late Ann Waller; *m* 1936, Elizabeth Margery, *d* of 1st Baron Hacking; two *s* one *d*. *Educ:* Oundle; Queens' Coll., Cambridge (Hon. Fellow 1974). Called to the Bar, Gray's Inn, 1934, Bencher, 1961, Treasurer, 1978. RAFO, 1931–36; served War of 1939–45, in RAFVR, Coastal Command; 502 Sqdn, 1940–41; Wing Comdr, 1943 (despatches). Chm., Northern Dist Valuation Bd, 1948–55; QC 1954; Recorder of Doncaster, 1953–54, of Sunderland, 1954–55, of Bradford, 1955–57, of Sheffield, 1957–61, and of Leeds, 1961–65; a Judge of the High Court, Queen's Bench Div., 1965–76; Presiding Judge, NE Circuit, 1973–76. Solicitor-General of the County Palatine of Durham, 1957–61; Attorney-General of the County Palatine of Durham, 1961–65; Member: Criminal Injuries Compensation Board, 1964–65; General Council of the Bar, 1958–62 and 1963–65; Parole Bd, 1969–72 (Vice-Chm., 1971–72); Adv. Council on the Penal System, 1970–73 and 1974–78; Criminal Law Revision Cttee, 1977–85; Chm., Policy Adv. Cttee on Sexual Offences, 1977–85. President: Inns of Court and Bar, 1979–80; British Acad. of Forensic Sciences, 1983–84. *Address:* Hatchway, Hatch Lane, Kingsley Green, Haslemere, Surrey GU27 3LJ. *T:* Haslemere 4629. *Clubs:* Army and Navy; Hawks (Cambridge).

See also G. M. Waller.

WALLER, Sir (John) Keith, Kt 1968; CBE 1961 (OBE 1957); Secretary, Department of Foreign Affairs, Canberra, 1970–74, retired; *b* 19 Feb. 1914; *s* of late A. J. Waller, Melbourne; *m* 1943, Alison Irwin Dent; two *d*. *Educ:* Scotch Coll., Melbourne; Melbourne Univ. Entered Dept of External Affairs, Australia, 1936; Private Sec. to Rt Hon. W. M. Hughes, 1937–40; Second Sec., Australian Legation, Chungking, 1941; Sec.-Gen., Australian Delegn, San Francisco Conf., 1945; First Sec., Australian Legation, Rio de Janeiro, 1945; Chargé d'Affaires, 1946; First Sec., Washington, 1947; Consul-Gen., Manila, 1948; Officer-in-Charge, Political Intelligence Div., Canberra, 1950; External Affairs Officer, London, 1951; Asst Sec., Dept of External Affairs, Canberra, 1953–57;

Ambassador to Thailand, 1957–60; Ambassador to USSR, 1960–62; First Asst Sec., Dept of External Affairs, 1963–64; Ambassador to US, 1964–70. Member: Australian Council for the Arts, 1973; Interim Film Board, 1974. Chm., Radio Australia Inquiry, 1975. *Address:* 17 Canterbury Crescent, Deakin, ACT 2600, Australia. *Club:* Commonwealth (Canberra).

WALLER, Sir John Stanier, 7th Bt, *cr* 1815; author, poet, and journalist; *b* 27 July 1917; *s* of Capt. Stanier Edmund William Waller (*d* 1923), and of Alice Amy (who *m* 2nd, 1940, Gerald H. Holiday), *d* of J. W. Harris, Oxford; *S kinsman* Sir Edmund Waller, 6th Bt, 1954; *m* 1974, Anne Eileen Mileham. *Educ:* Weymouth Coll.; Worcester Coll., Oxford (Exhibnr in History, 1936, BA in Eng. Lang. and Lit., 1939, OU DipEd (Teaching), 1940). Founder-Editor of Quarterly, Kingdom Come, first new literary magazine of war, 1939–41. Served 1940–46 with RASC (in Middle East, 1941–46); Adjt RASC, HQ, Cairo Area; Capt. 1942; Features Editor, Brit. Min. of Inf., Middle East, 1943–45; Chief Press Officer, Brit. Embassy, Bagdad, 1945; News and Features Editor, MIME, Cairo, 1945–46. Dramatic Critic Cairo Weekly, The Sphinx, 1943–46; Founder-Mem. Salamander Soc. of Poets, Cairo, 1942; lectured in Pantheon Theatre, Athens, 1945; Greenwood Award for Poetry, 1947; Keats Prize, 1974; FRSL 1948; Lectr and Tutor in English and Eng. Lit. at Carlisle and Gregson (Jimmy's), Ltd, 1953–54; Asst Master, London Nautical Sch., May-June 1954; Information Officer, Overseas Press Services Div., Central Office of Information, 1954–59. Director: Literature Ltd, 1940–42; Richard Congreve Ltd, 1948–50; Export Trade Ships Ltd, 1956; Bristol Stone and Concrete Ltd, 1974; Mercantile Land and Marine Ltd, 1979. *Publications:* The Confessions of Peter Pan, 1941; Fortunate Hamlet, 1941; Spring Legend, 1942; The Merry Ghosts, 1946; Middle East Anthology (Editor), 1946; Crusade, 1946; The Kiss of Stars, 1948; The Collected Poems of Keith Douglas (Editor), 1951 and 1966; Shaggy Dog, 1953; Alamein to Zem Zem by Keith Douglas (Editor), 1966; Goldenhair and the Two Black Hawks, 1971; Return to Oasis (co-editor), 1980; contrib. to numerous anthologies and periodicals at home and abroad. *Recreations:* portrait photography, teaching. *Heir:* none. *Address:* 21 Lyndhurst Road, Hove, Sussex BN3 6FA. *T:* Brighton 734836. *Club:* Press.

WALLER, Rt. Rev. John Stevens; *see* Stafford, Bishop Suffragan of.

WALLER, Sir Keith; *see* Waller, Sir J. K.

WALLER, Sir Robert William, 9th Bt, *cr* 1780, of Newport, Co. Tipperary; employed by the General Electric Co. of America as an Industrial Engineer, since 1957; *b* 16 June 1934; *s* of Sir Roland Edgar Waller, 8th Bt, and Helen Madeline, *d* of Joseph Radl, Matawan, New Jersey, USA; *S* father 1958; is a citizen of the United States; *m* 1960 (marr. diss.); two *s* two *d* (and one *s* decd). *Educ:* St Peter's Prep. Sch.; Newark Coll. of Engrg; Fairleigh Dickinson University. *Heir: s* John Michael Waller, *b* 14 May 1962. *Address:* 5 Lookout Terrace, Lynnfield, Mass 01940, USA.

WALLER, Prof. Ross Douglas, CBE 1958 (MBE 1945); Director of Extra-Mural Studies, 1937–60, and Professor of Adult Education, 1949–66 (Professor Emeritus, 1966), Manchester University; *b* 21 Jan. 1899; *m* 1928, Isobel May Brown; three *s* one *d*. *Educ:* Manchester Central High School for Boys; Manchester University. Served European War, KOYLI, and NF, 1917–19. BA, 1920; MA 1921; post-graduate studies in Florence, 1921–22; Schoolmaster, 1922–24; Lecturer in English Literature, Manchester Univ., 1924–37. Chm. North-Western Dist, WEA, 1943–57; Pres., Educational Centres Association, 1948–65; OECD Consultant on Adult Educn in Sardinia, 1961–62. Cavaliere Ufficiale, Order of Merit, Italy, 1956. *Publications:* The Monks and the Giants, 1926; The Rossetti Family, 1932; Marlowe, Edward II (with H. B. Charlton), 1933; Learning to Live, 1947; Harold Pilkington Turner, 1953; Residential College, 1954; Design for Democracy (Introductory Essay), 1956. Articles in Adult Education, Highway, Times Educational Supplement, etc. *Address:* 61 Porchfield Square, St John's Gardens, Manchester M3 4FG. *T:* 061–832 7107.

WALLEY, Francis, CB 1978; FEng 1985; consulting engineer; Consultant to the Ove Arup Partnership; Member, Standing Committee on Structural Safety, since 1977; *b* 30 Dec. 1918; *s* of late Reginald M. Walley and Maria M. Walley; *m* 1946, Margaret, *yr d* of late Rev. Thomas and Margaret J. Probert; two *d*. *Educ:* Cheltenham Grammar Sch.; Bristol Univ. MSc, PhD; FICE (Mem. Council, 1978–81); FIStructE (Vice-Pres., 1982–83; Hon. Treasurer, 1981; Hon. Sec., 1979–81); Lewis Kent Award, 1985. Entered Min. of Home Security as Engr, 1941; Min. of Works, 1945; Suptg Civil Engr, 1963; Dep. Dir of Building Develt, 1965; Dir of Estate Management Overseas, 1969; Dir of Post Office Services, 1971; Under-Sec., Dir of Civil Engineering Services, DoE, 1973–78. *Publications:* Prestressed Concrete Design and Construction, 1954; (with Dr S. C. C. Bate) A Guide to the Code of Practice CP 115, 1960; several papers to ICE and techn. jls. *Recreations:* gardening, furniture-making. *Address:* 13 Julien Road, Coulsdon, Surrey CR3 2DN. *T:* 01–660 3290.

See also Sir John Walley.

WALLEY, Sir John, KBE 1965; CB 1950; retired as Deputy Secretary, Ministry of Social Security, 1966 (Ministry of Pensions and National Insurance, 1958–66); *b* Barnstaple, Devon, 3 April 1906; *e s* of late R. M. Walley; *m* 1934, Elisabeth Mary, *e d* of late R. H. Pinhorn, OBE; two *s* two *d*. *Educ:* Hereford High Sch.; Hereford Cathedral Sch.; Merton Coll., Oxford; Postmaster, 1924–28; Hons Maths and Dip., Pol. and Econ. Sci. Ministry of Labour: Asst Principal, 1929; Sec., Cabinet Cttee on Unemployment, 1932; Principal, 1934; Asst Sec., Min. of National Service, 1941; promoted Under-Sec. to take charge of legislation and other preparations for Beveridge Nat. Insce Scheme, in new Min. of National Insurance, 1945; Chm., Dental Benefit Council, 1945–48. Chm., Hampstead Centre, National Trust, 1969–79, Pres., 1980–. *Publications:* Social Security-Another British Failure?, 1972; contribs: to The Future of the Social Services, ed Robson and Crick, 1970; on Children's Allowances, in Family Poverty, ed David Bull, 1971; vol. in British Oral Archive of Political and Administrative History, 1980; articles in journals and the press on Social Security matters. *Address:* 46 Rotherwick Road, NW11. *T:* 01–455 6528.

See also F. Walley.

WALLEY, Keith Henry, FEng 1981; FIChemE; Chairman, International Military Services Ltd, since 1985 (Director, since 1984); Deputy Chairman, Johnson Matthey plc, since 1986 (Director, since 1985); *b* 26 June 1928; *s* of Eric Henry James Walley and Rose Walley; *m* 1950, Betty Warner; one *s* one *d*. *Educ:* Hinckley Grammar School; Loughborough College (Dip. Chem. 1949, Dip. Chem. Eng. 1952); FIChemE 1972. Commissioned RAOC 1949–51. Joined Royal Dutch/Shell Group, 1952; served in Holland, 1952–69; Works Manager, Shell Chemicals, Carrington, 1970–71; Head, Manufacturing Economic and Ops, The Hague, 1972–73; Gen. Man., Base Chemicals Shell International Chemicals, 1974–77; Jt Man. Dir, Shell UK Ltd, 1978–84; Man. Dir, Shell Chemicals UK Ltd, 1978–84. Non-executive Director: John Brown plc, 1984–86; Reckitt & Colman, 1986–. Hon. Lectr, UCL, 1984–. Pres., Soc. of Chemical Industry, 1984–86 (Vice-Pres., 1981–84); Member Council: Chem. Ind. Assoc., 1978–84 (Chm., Educn and Sci. Policy Cttee, 1980–84); IChemE, 1983– (Vice-Pres., 1985); Fellowship of Engineering, 1984–. CBIM 1982. *Publications:* papers in chem. jls and planning jls. *Recreations:* the Pyrenees, opera, tennis, ski-ing. *Address:* International Military Services Ltd, 4 Abbey Orchard Street, SW1P 2JJ. *Club:* Athenæum.

WALLINGTON, Jeremy Francis; television producer; Chief Executive, Limehouse Productions Ltd, 1982–86; Director of Programmes, Southern Television Ltd, 1977–81; *b* 7 July 1935; *s* of Ernest Francis Wallington and Nell (*née* Howe); *m* 1955, Margaret Ivy Willment; three *s* one *d*. *Educ:* Royal Grammar Sch., High Wycombe, Bucks. Reporter on several Fleet Street newspapers, 1956–62; Managing Editor, Topic Magazine, 1962; Co-Founder of Insight, Sunday Times, 1963; Assistant Editor: Sunday Times, 1963–65; Daily Mail, 1965–67; Editor, Investigations Bureau, World in Action, Granada Television, 1967–68; Jt Editor, then Editor, World in Action, 1968–72, Head of Documentaries, Granada Television, 1972–77. *Publication:* (jtly) Scandal '63, 1963. *Recreation:* canal barges. *Address:* 6B Newell Street, E14. *T:* 01–987 8484. *Club:* British Academy of Film and Television Arts.

WALLIS, Captain Arthur Hammond, CBE 1952; RN (retired); *b* 16 Sept. 1903; *s* of late Harold T. Wallis; *m* 1940, Lucy Joyce (*d* 1974), *er d* of late Lt-Col L. E. Becher, DSO; one *s* one *d*. *Educ:* Wixenford; Osborne and Dartmouth. Entered Royal Navy as Cadet, 1917; specialised as Torpedo Officer, 1930; staff of Rear-Adm. Destroyers, 1936–38; Torpedo Officer, HMS Nelson, 1938–41; Comdr, 1941; i/c Torpedo Experimental Dept, HMS Vernon, 1941–43; Exec. Officer, HMS Illustrious, 1943–45; Captain, 1947; in command HM Underwater Detection Establishment at Portland, 1948–50; Sen. Naval Officer, Persian Gulf and in command HMS Wild Goose, 1950–51; Cdre, HMS Mauritius, 1951; UK Naval Delegate, Military Agency for Standardisation, NATO, 1952–53; Director of Under-water Weapons, Admiralty, 1953–56. Naval ADC to the Queen, 1956. Chief of Naval Information, Admiralty, 1957–64. *Recreations:* watching and listening. *Address:* Compton's Barn, Woodstreet, near Guildford, Surrey. *T:* Worplesdon 235143. *Club:* Naval and Military.

WALLIS, Frederick Alfred John E.; *see* Emery-Wallis.

WALLIS, Col Hugh Macdonell, OC 1969; DSO 1919; OBE 1945; MC, VD, CD, KCLJ; *b* 7 Dec. 1893; *s* of John McCall Wallis, Peterborough, Ont, and Gertrude Thornton, *d* of Lt-Col Samuel Smith Macdonell, QC, LLD, DCL, Windsor, Ont; *m* 1st, 1935, Leslie (marr. diss., 1953), *d* of late Mr and Mrs K. K. Carson, London; 2nd 1969, Corinne de Boucherville (*d* 1981), *widow* of Hon. Jean Desy. *Educ:* Lakefield Preparatory Sch.; Toronto Univ. Enlisted 1st CEF, Sept. 1914; served France, Belgium, Germany, 1915–19; Bde Major 4th Can. Inf. Bde, 1918 (DSO, MC, despatches twice); Colonel Comdg The Black Watch, Royal Highlanders of Canada, then Permanent Active Militia, 1930; VD 1930; CD 1967; R of O, 1931; Hon. ADC to Earl of Bessborough, Gov.-Gen. of Canada, 1931–35; Active Service, Canadian Forces, 1940–45; Colonel Asst DAG Nat. Defence HQ (OBE); Hon. Lt-Col 3rd Bn The Black Watch of Canada, 1961–68. Chartered Accountant, with McDonald, Currie & Co., 1923. Past President: Canadian Citizenship Council, St Andrews Soc. of Montreal, Canadian Club of Montreal, Montreal Museum of Fine Arts. Man. Dir and Pres., Mount Royal Rice Mills Ltd, Montreal, 1924–53. Governor: Council for Canadian Unity; Lakefield College Sch.; Montreal General Hosp.; Montreal Children's Hosp. (Past Chm. of Exec.); l'Hôpital Marie Enfant; Chm., Adv. Bd, Canadian Centenary (1967) Council (past Chm. Org. and Exec. Cttees). Hon. Sponsor, Trent Univ., Ont., 1963; Associate, McGill Univ. and l'Univ. de Montréal. FRSA 1959. Kt Companion, Order of St Lazarus of Jerusalem. Outstanding Citizen Award, Montreal Citizenship Council, 1967. Canada Centennial Medal, 1967; Jubilee Medal, 1977. *Recreations:* travel, fine arts, Canadiana books and history. *Address:* 131 Avenue de Breslay, Pointe Claire, PQ H9S 4M8, Canada. *Clubs:* Canadian, United Services (Montreal); Braeside Golf (Senneville).

WALLIS, Jeffrey Joseph; Managing Director, Eastoken, since 1981; *b* 25 Nov. 1923; *s* of Nathaniel and Rebecca Wallis; *m* 1948, Barbara Brickman; one *s* one *d*. *Educ:* Owen's; Coll. Aeronautical Engrg. Man. Dir, Wallis Fashion Group, 1948–80. Mem., Monopolies and Mergers Commn, 1981–85. Formerly Member: CNAA; Clothing Export Council; NEDC (Textiles). Involved in art educn throughout career; various governorships. *Recreations:* motor racing, motor boating, industrial design. *Address:* 37 Avenue Close, NW8 6DA. *T:* 01–722 8665.

WALLIS, Peter Gordon; HM Diplomatic Service; Head, Permanent Under-Secretary's Department, Foreign and Commonwealth Office, since 1983; *b* 2 Aug. 1935; *s* of Arthur Gordon Wallis, DFC, BScEcon, and Winifred Florence Maud (*née* Dingle); *m* 1965, Delysia Elizabeth (*née* Leonard); three *s* one *d*. *Educ:* Taunton and Whitgift Schools; Pembroke Coll., Oxford (MA). Ministry of Labour and National Service, 1958–59; HM Customs and Excise, 1959–68 (Private Sec., 1961–64); HM Diplomatic Service, 1968; Tel Aviv, 1970; Nairobi, 1974; Counsellor (Econ. and Comm.), Ankara, 1977–81; RCDS, 1981; Cabinet Office, 1982–83. *Recreations:* reading, writing, music, children. *Address:* c/o Foreign and Commonwealth Office, SW1A 2AH.

WALLIS, Peter Ralph; Deputy Controller, Aircraft Weapons and Electronics, Ministry of Defence, 1980–84; *b* 17 Aug. 1924; *s* of Leonard Francis Wallis and Molly McCulloch Wallis (*née* Jones); *m* 1949, Frances Jean Patricia Cowie; three *s* one *d*. *Educ:* University College Sch., Hampstead; Imperial Coll. of Science and Technology, London (BSc(Eng)). Henrici and Siemens Medals of the College, 1944. Joined Royal Naval Scientific Service 1944; work at Admty Signal and Radar Estab. till 1959, Admty Underwater Weapons Estab. till 1968; Asst Chief Scientific Advr (Research), MoD, 1968–71, Dir Gen. Research Weapons, 1971–75, Dir Gen. Guided Weapons and Electronics, 1975–78, Dir Gen. Research A (Electronics) and Dep. Chief Scientist (Navy), 1978–80. Marconi Award, IERE, 1964; FCGI, CEng, FIEE, FIMA. *Publications:* articles in Jl of IEE, IERE and Op. Res. Quarterly. *Recreations:* skiing, mountain walking, swimming, sailing, cycling, Gen. Sec., Hampstead Scientific Soc. *Address:* 22 Flask Walk, Hampstead, NW3 1HE. *Club:* Eagle Ski.

WALLIS, Victor Harry; Assistant Under Secretary of State, Police and Fire Department, Home Office, 1980–82; *b* 21 Dec. 1922; *s* of Harry Stewart Wallis, MBE, and Ada Elizabeth (*née* Jarratt); *m* 1948, Margaret Teresa (*née* Meadowcroft); one *s* three *d*. *Educ:* Wilson's Grammar School. Served Royal Scots and Indian Army (Major), 1941–47 (War, Burma and Defence medals); RARO; Territorial Army and TARO (Int. Corps), 1948–77. Entered Home Office, Immigration Service, 1947; Regional Officer, 1952; Policy Div., 1958; Chief Trng Officer, 1967; Establishments, 1972. Chm., various cttees, Fire Brigades Adv. Council, 1980–82. *Recreations:* philately, military history, painting. *Address:* 26 Lumley Road, Horley, Surrey RH6 7JL. *Clubs:* Civil Service, St Stephen's Constitutional, Royal British Legion.

WALLIS-JONES, His Honour Ewan Perrins; a Circuit Judge (formerly County Court Judge), 1964–84; *b* 22 June 1913; *s* of late William James Wallis-Jones, MBE, and late Ethel Perrins Wallis-Jones; *m* 1940, Veronica Mary (*née* Fowler); one *s* two *d*. *Educ:* Mill Hill Sch.; University Coll. of Wales, Aberystwyth; Balliol Coll., Oxford. LLB Hons Wales, 1934; BA Oxon 1936; MA Oxon 1941. Qualified Solicitor, 1935; called to Bar, Gray's Inn, 1938. Chm., Carmarthenshire QS, 1966–71 (Dep. Chm., 1965–66); Jt Pres.,

Council of Circuit Judges, 1982. ARPS. *Recreations:* music, reading and photography. *Address:* 25 Cotham Grove, Bristol BS6 6AN. *T:* Bristol 48908. *Club:* Royal Photographic Society.

WALLIS-KING, Maj.-Gen. Colin Sainthill, CBE 1975 (OBE 1971); retired; Director, Kongsberg Ltd, since 1982; *b* 13 Sept. 1926; *s* of late Lt-Col Frank King, DSO, OBE, 4th Hussars, and Colline Ammabel, *d* of late Lt-Col C. G. H. St Hill; *m* 1962, Lisabeth, *d* of late Swan Swanstrøm, Oslo, Norway; two *d. Educ:* Stowe. Commissioned Coldstream Guards, 1945; Liaison Officer with Fleet Air Arm, 1954; Staff Coll., 1960; Regtl Adjutant, Coldstream Guards, 1961; seconded to Para. Regt, 1963; ACOS HQ Land Norway, 1965; Comdr 2nd Bn Coldstream Guards, 1969; Dep. Comdr 8 Inf. Brigade, 1972; Comdr 3 Inf. Brigade, 1973; BGS Intell., MoD, 1975; Dir of Service Intelligence, 1977–80. *Recreations:* equitation, sailing, music, cross-country skiing. *Address:* c/o Royal Bank of Scotland, 19 Grosvenor Gardens, SW1. *Club:* Cavalry and Guards.

WALLOP, family name of **Earl of Portsmouth.**

WALLROCK, John; Chairman, Conocean International Consultants Group, Hong Kong, since 1984; *b* 14 Nov. 1922; *s* of Samuel and Marie Kate Wallrock; *m* 1967, Audrey Louise Ariow; one *s* two *d. Educ:* Bradfield Coll., Berks. Cadet, Merchant Navy, 1939; Lieut RNR, 1943; Master Mariner, 1949; J. H. Minet & Co. Ltd, 1950, Dir, 1955–79, Chm., 1972–79; Chm., Minet Holdings, 1972–82. Dir, Tugu Insce Co. Ltd, Hong Kong, 1976–84. Underwriting Mem. of Lloyd's, 1951–86. Mem., Council of Management, White Ensign Assoc. Ltd, 1974–83. Liveryman, Master Mariners' Co., 1954–; Freeman, City of London, 1965. FCIB, MNI. *Recreations:* yachting, shooting. *Address:* (office) 804A Admiralty Centre (Tower I), 18 Harcourt Road, Hong Kong. *T:* (5) 294686. *Clubs:* Boodle's, East India; Royal London Yacht, Royal Southern Yacht.

WALLS, Prof. Eldred Wright; Emeritus Professor of Anatomy in the University of London at Middlesex Hospital Medical School (Dean, Medical School, 1967–74); Hon. Consultant Anatomist, St Mark's Hospital; *b* 17 Aug. 1912; 2nd *s* of late J. T. Walls, Glasgow; *m* 1939, Jessie Vivien Mary Robb, MB, ChB, DPH, *o d* of late R. F. Robb and late M. T. Robb; one *s* one *d. Educ:* Hillhead High Sch.; Glasgow Univ. BSc, 1931; MB, ChB (Hons), 1934; MD (Hons), 1947, FRSE, FRCS, FRCSE; Struthers Medal and Prize, 1942. Demonstrator and Lectr in Anatomy, Glasgow Univ., 1935–41; Senior Lectr in Anatomy, University Coll. of S Wales and Monmouthshire, 1941–47; Reader in Anatomy, Middlesex Hospital Medical Sch. 1947–49, S. A. Courtauld Prof. of Anatomy, 1949–74; Lectr in Anatomy, Edinburgh Univ., 1975–82. Past President: Anatomical Soc. of GB and Ireland; Chartered Soc. of Physiotherapy. Lectures: West., UC Cardiff, 1965; Osler, Soc. of Apothecaries, 1967; Astor, Mddx Hosp., 1975; Gordon Taylor, RCS, 1976; Struthers, RCSE, 1983. *Publications:* (co-editor) Rest and Pain (by John Hilton) (6th edn), 1950; (co-author) Sir Charles Bell, His Life and Times, 1958; contrib. Blood-vascular and Lymphatic Systems, to Cunningham's Textbook Anat., 1981; contrib. to Journal of Anatomy, Lancet, etc. *Recreations:* golf and gardening. *Address:* 19 Dean Park Crescent, Edinburgh EH4 1PH. *T:* 031–332 7164. *Clubs:* MCC; New (Edinburgh); Royal Scottish Automobile (Glasgow).

WALLS, Henry James, BSc, PhD; Director, Metropolitan Police Laboratory, New Scotland Yard, 1964–68; *b* 1907; *s* of late William Walls, RSA, and late Elizabeth Maclellan Walls; *m* 1940, Constance Mary Butler; one *s* one *d. Educ:* George Watson's Boys' Coll., Edinburgh; Melville Coll., Edinburgh; Edinburgh Univ. BSc 1930; PhD 1933. Postgrad. research in physical chemistry, Munich, Edinburgh and Bristol, 1930–35; ICI (Explosives), 1935–36; Staff of Metropolitan Police Lab., 1936–46; Staff Chemist, Home Office Forensic Science Lab., Bristol, 1946–58; Director of Home Office Forensic Science Lab., Newcastle upon Tyne, 1958–64. Pres., British Acad. of Forensic Scis, 1935. *Publications:* Forensic Science, 1968, rev. edn 1974; (with Alistair Brownlie) Drink, Drugs and Driving, 1969, rev. edn 1985; Expert Witness, 1972; two books on photography; papers in journals dealing with forensic science. *Recreations:* reading, plays and films, talking, people, pottery. *Address:* 65 Marmora Road, SE22 0RY.

WALLS, Rev. Brother Roland Charles; Member, Community of the Transfiguration, since 1965; *b* 7 June 1917; *s* of late Roland William Walls and late Tina Josephine Hayward. *Educ:* Sandown Grammar Sch.; Corpus Christi Coll., Cambridge; Kelham Theological Coll. Curate of St James', Crossgates, Leeds, 1940–42; Curate of St Cecilia's, Parson Cross, Sheffield, 1942–45; Licensed preacher, Diocese of Ely, 1945–48; Fellow of Corpus Christi Coll., Cambridge, 1948–62; Lecturer in Theology, Kelham Theological Coll., 1948–51; Chaplain and Dean of Chapel, Corpus Christi Coll., Cambridge, 1952–58; Canon Residentiary, Sheffield Cathedral, 1958–62; Chaplain of Rosslyn Chapel, Midlothian, 1962–68. Examining Chaplain to Bishop of Edinburgh. Lecturer at Coates Hall Theological Coll.; Lecturer in Dogmatics Dept, New Coll., Edinburgh, 1963–74. Received into RC Church, ordained priest, 1983. *Publications:* (contrib.) Theological Word Book (ed A. Richardson), 1950; Law and Gospel, 1980; (contrib.) Dictionary of Christian Spirituality, 1983; (contrib.) Dictionary of Pastoral Counsel, 1984. *Recreations:* walking, music, etc. *Address:* Community House, 23 Manse Road, Roslin, Midlothian.

WALLWORK, John Sackfield, CBE 1982; Director, Daily Mail and General Trust PLC, since 1982; Managing Director, Northcliffe Newspapers Group Ltd, 1972–82 (General Manager, 1967–71); *b* 2 Nov. 1918; *s* of Peter Wallwork and Clara Cawthorne Wallwork; *m* 1945, Bessie Bray; one *s* one *d. Educ:* Leigh Grammar Sch., Leigh, Lancs. FCIS. General Manager, Scottish Daily Mail, Edinburgh, 1959–62; Asst Gen. Man., Associated Newspapers Gp Ltd, London, 1962–66, Dir, 1973–82. Chm., Press Association Ltd, 1973–74 (Dir, 1969–76); Director: Reuters Ltd, 1973–76; Reuters Founders Share Co. Ltd, 1984–; Reuters Trustee, 1978–; Member Press Council, 1974–75; Newspaper Society: Mem. Council, 1967–85; Jun. Vice-Pres. 1975; Sen. Vice-Pres., 1976, Pres., 1977–78. Commander, Order of Merit, Republic of Italy, 1973. *Recreations:* golf, motoring. *Address:* Greenfield, Manor Road, Sidmouth, Devon EX10 8RR. *T:* Sidmouth 3489.

WALLWORTH, Cyril; Assistant Under-Secretary of State, Ministry of Defence, 1964–76; Gwilym Gibbon Fellow, Nuffield College, Oxford, 1975–76; *b* 6 June 1916; *s* of Albert A. Wallworth and Eva (*née* Taylor); unmarried. *Educ:* Oldham High Sch.; Manchester Univ. BA (Hons) History, 1937. Asst Principal, Admiralty, 1939; Asst Private Secretary to First Lord, 1941–45, Principal, 1943; Asst Secretary, 1951; Under-Secretary, 1964. *Recreations:* music, wine, cooking, photography. *Address:* 5 Leinster Mews, W2. *Club:* Hurlingham.

WALMSLEY, Arnold Robert, CMG 1963; MBE 1946; HM Diplomatic Service, retired; *b* 29 Aug. 1912; *s* of late Rev. Canon A. M. Walmsley; *m* 1944, Frances Councell de Mouilpied. *Educ:* Rossall Sch.; Hertford Coll., Oxford. 1st Class Maths Mods, 1st Class Modern Greats. Private Sec. to Julius Meinl, Vienna, 1935–38; Foreign Office, 1939–45; established in Foreign Service, 1946; Foreign Office, 1946–50; British Consul in Jerusalem, 1950–54; Foreign Office, 1954–63; Head of Arabian Dept, 1961; Counsellor, Khartoum, 1963–65; Dir, Middle East Centre of Arab Studies, Lebanon, 1965–69. Order of the Two Niles (Sudan), 1965. *Publications:* (as Nicholas Roland) The Great One, 1967; Natural Causes, 1969; Who Came by Night, 1971. *Address:* Manor Farm, Dunmow Road, Bishop's Stortford, Herts. *Club:* Travellers'.

WALMSLEY, Brian; Under Secretary, Department of Health and Social Security, Supplementary Benefits Division, since 1985; *b* 22 April 1936; *s* of late Albert Edward Walmsley and Ivy Doreen Walmsley (*née* Black); *m* 1956, Sheila Maybury; two *d. Educ:* Lily Lane School, Moston, Manchester; Page Moss Primary School, Huyton; Prescot Grammar School. National Service, RAF, 1955–57. Joined Min. of Pensions and Nat. Insurance, 1957, later Min. of Social Security and DHSS; served in local offices to 1970; North West (Merseyside) Regional Office, DHSS, Bootle, 1970; DHSS HQ, London, 1973; Sec. to Industrial Injuries Adv. Council, 1978–79; Asst Sec., 1979. *Recreations:* following cricket, playing golf, reading, gardening, walking. *Address:* 28 Lime Tree Grove, Shirley, Croydon, Surrey CR0 8AU. *T:* 01–777 4205. *Club:* MCC.

WALMSLEY, Rt. Rev. Francis Joseph, CBE 1979; Bishop-in-Ordinary to HM Forces, since 1979; Titular Bishop of Tamalluma; *b* 9 Nov. 1926; *s* of Edwin Walmsley and Mary Walmsley (*née* Hall). *Educ:* St Joseph's Coll., Mark Cross, Tunbridge Wells; St John's Seminary, Wonersh, Guildford. Ordained, 1953; Asst Priest, Woolwich, 1953; Shoreham-by-Sea, Sussex, 1958; Chaplain, Royal Navy, 1960; Principal RC Chaplain, RN, 1975; retired from RN, 1979. Prelate of Honour to HH Pope Paul VI, 1975; ordained Bishop, 1979. *Recreations:* golf, photography, gardening.

WALMSLEY, Nigel Norman; Managing Director, Capital Radio, since 1982; Board Member: Independent Radio News, since 1983; South Bank Centre, since 1985; *b* 26 Jan. 1942; *s* of Norman and Ida Walmsley; *m* 1969, Jane Walmsley, broadcaster and author; one *d. Educ:* William Hulme's Sch.; Brasenose Coll., Oxford (BA English). Joined the Post Office, 1964; Asst Private Secretary to Postmaster General, 1967; Asst Director of Marketing, Post Office, 1973–75; Asst Sec., Industrial Planning Division of Dept of Industry, 1975–76; Director of Marketing, Post Office, 1977–81, Board Mem. for Marketing 1981–82; Dir, The Builder Gp, 1986–. Chm., GLAA, 1985–86. *Recreation:* intensive inactivity. *Address:* 26 Belsize Road, NW6 4RD. *T:* 01–586 1950.

WALMSLEY, Peter James, MBE 1975; Director of Petroleum Engineering Division, Department of Energy, since 1981; *b* 29 April 1929; *s* of George Stanley and Elizabeth Martin Walmsley; *m* 1970, Edna Fisher; three *s* one *d. Educ:* Caterham Sch., Surrey; Imperial Coll., London (BSc; ARSM). Geologist: Iraq Petroleum Co., 1951–59; BP Trinidad, 1959–65; BP London, 1965–72; Exploration Manager, BP Aberdeen, 1972–78; Dep. Chief Geologist, BP London, 1978–79; Regional Exploration Manager, BP London, 1979–81. Chairman, Petroleum Exploration Soc. of Gt Britain, 1971–72. *Publications:* contribs to various learned jls on North Sea geology. *Recreations:* home and garden. *Address:* Department of Energy, Thames House South, Millbank, SW1P 4QJ. *T:* 01–211 3000.

WALMSLEY, Prof. Robert, TD 1984; MD; DSc; FRCPE, FRCSE, FRSE; formerly Bute Professor of Anatomy, University of St Andrews, 1946–73; *b* 24 Aug. 1906; *s* of late Thomas Walmsley, Supt Marine Engr; *m* 1939, Isabel Mary, *e d* of James Mathieson, Aberdeen; two *s. Educ:* Greenock Acad.; Univ. of Edinburgh; Carnegie Inst. of Embryology, Baltimore, USA. MB, ChB (Edinburgh); MD (Edinburgh) with Gold Medal, 1937. Demonstrator, Lectr and Senior Lectr on Anatomy, Univ. of Edinburgh, 1931–46; Goodsir Fellowship in Anatomy, 1933; Rockefeller Fellowship, 1935–36; served as Pathologist in RAMC in UK and MEF, 1939–44. Struthers Lectr, Royal Coll. of Surgeons, Edinburgh, 1952; Fulbright Advanced Scholarship, 1960; Pres., Edinburgh Harveian Soc., 1963–64. Vis. Prof. of Anatomy: George Washington Univ., USA, 1960; Auckland, NZ, 1967. Formerly: Master, St Salvator's Coll.; Chm., Council St Leonards and St Katherines Schs; Hon. Pres., British Medical Students Assoc.; External Examiner in Anatomy, Cambridge, Edinburgh, Durham, Glasgow, Aberdeen, Liverpool, Singapore, Kingston (WI), Accra, etc. Life Mem. Anatomical Soc. Hon. Fellow, British Assoc. of Clinical Anatomists, 1980. Hon. DSc St Andrews, 1972. First Farquharson Award, RCSEd, 1974. *Publications:* Co-author Manual of Surgical Anatomy, 1964; (jtly) Clinical Anatomy of the Heart, 1978; co-reviser, Jamieson's Illustrations Regional Anatomy, 1981; contribs to various jls, on Heart, Bone and Joints, and on Whales. *Recreation:* gardening. *Address:* 45 Kilrymont Road, St Andrews, Fife. *T:* St Andrews 72879.

WALPOLE, family name of **Baron Walpole.**

WALPOLE, 9th Baron, of Walpole, *cr* 1723; 7th Baron Walpole of Wolterton, *cr* 1756; **Robert Henry Montgomerie Walpole,** TD; Captain, RA; *b* 25 April 1913; *s* of late Horatio Spencer Walpole and Dorothea Frances, *o d* of Frederick Butler Molyneux Montgomerie; *S* to baronies at the death of his cousin, 5th Earl of Orford, 1931; *m* 1937, Nancy Louisa, OBE, *y d* of late Frank Harding Jones, Housham Tye, Harlow, Essex; one *s* one *d* (and one *s* one *d* decd). *Educ:* Eton; South Eastern Agricultural Coll., Wye; Royal Agricultural Coll., Cirencester. *Recreations:* curling, shooting, golf. *Heir: s* Hon. Robert Horatio Walpole [*b* 8 Dec. 1938; *m* 1st, 1962, Judith (marr. diss. 1979), *yr d* of T. T. Schofield, Stockingwood House, Harpenden; two *s* two *d*; 2nd, 1980, Laurel Celia, *o d* of S. T. Ball, Swindon; two *s. Educ:* Eton; King's Coll., Cambridge]. *Address:* Wolterton Hall, Norwich NR11 7LY. *T:* Cromer 761210, Matlaske 274. *Club:* Norfolk (Norwich).

WALPOLE, Kathleen Annette, MA; Head Mistress of Wycombe Abbey School, Bucks, 1948–61; *b* Ootacamund, S India, 1899; *e d* of Major A. Walpole, RE. *Educ:* Southlands Sch., Exmouth; Westfield Coll., University of London. BA Hons London, 1921; History Mistress, The Church High Sch., Newcastle upon Tyne, 1922–27; Research Student, Westfield Coll., 1927–28; MA London, 1929; Alexander Prize of RHistSoc, 1931; History Mistress, The Royal Sch., Bath, 1928–34; Head Mistress, The Red Maids Sch., Bristol, 1934–47. *Publications:* articles in the Trans. of Historic Society of Lancashire and Cheshire, and of the RHistSoc, 1929 and 1931, on Emigration to British North America. *Recreations:* gardening, walking, study of antiques. *Club:* Royal Commonwealth Society.

WALSER, Ven. David; Archdeacon of Ely, and Hon. Canon, since 1981; Rector of St Botolph's, Cambridge, since 1981 and Priest-in-Charge of St Clement's, Cambridge, since 1985; *b* 12 March 1923; *s* of William and Nora Walser; *m* 1975, Dr Elizabeth Enid Shillito. *Educ:* Clayesmore School; St Edmund Hall, Oxford (MA, DipTh); St Stephen's House, Oxford. Served RA and Royal Indian Mountain Artillery, 1942–46. Deacon 1950, priest 1951; Asst Curate, St Gregory the Great, Horfield, 1950–54; Vice-Principal, St Stephen's House, 1954–60; Asst Chaplain, Exeter Coll., Oxford, 1956–57; Junior Chaplain, Merton Coll., Oxford, 1957–60; Minor Canon, Ely Cathedral and Chaplain of King's School, 1961–71; Vicar of Linton, dio. Ely, 1971–81; Rector of Bartlow, 1973–81; RD of Linton, 1976–81. *Recreations:* hill walking, music, reading, camping, crosswords, hymn writing for local use. *Address:* St Botolph's Rectory, Summerfield, Cambridge CB3 9HE. *T:* Cambridge 350684.

WALSH, Sir Alan, Kt 1977; DSc; FRS 1969; Consultant Spectroscopist; *b* 19 Dec. 1916; *s* of late Thomas Haworth and Betsy Alice Walsh, Hoddlesden, Lancs; *m* 1949, Audrey Dale Hutchinson; two *s. Educ:* Darwen Grammar Sch.; Manchester Univ. BSc 1938; MSc (Tech.) 1946; DSc 1960. FAA 1958. British Non-Ferrous Metals Research Assoc., 1939–42 and 1944–46; Min. of Aircraft Production, 1943; Div. of Chemical Physics,

CSIRO, Melbourne, 1946–77 (Asst Chief of Div., 1961–77). Einstein Memorial Lectr, Australian Inst. of Physics, 1967; Pres., Australian Inst. of Physics, 1967–69. Hon. Member: Soc. of Analytical Chemistry, 1969; Royal Soc. NZ, 1975. Foreign Mem., Royal Acad. of Sciences, Stockholm, 1969. FTS 1982. Hon. FCS, 1973; Hon. FAIP, 1981; Hon. Mem., Japan Soc. of Analytical Chemistry, 1981. Hon. DSc: Monash, 1970; Manchester, 1984, Britannica Australia Science Award, 1966; Research Medal, Royal Soc. of Victoria, 1968; Talanta Gold Medal, 1969; Maurice Hasler Award, Soc. of Applied Spectroscopy, USA, 1972; James Cook Medal, Royal Soc. of NSW, 1975; Torbern Bergman Medal, Swedish Chem. Soc., 1976; Royal Medal, Royal Soc., 1976; John Scott Award, City of Philadelphia, 1977; Matthew Flinders Medal, Aust. Acad. of Science, 1980; Robert Boyle Medal, RSC, 1982; K. L. Sutherland Medal, Aust. Acad. of Technol Sciences, 1982. *Publications:* papers in learned jls. *Address:* 11 Dendy Street, Brighton, Victoria 3168, Australia. *T:* 03–592 4897. *Club:* Metropolitan Golf (Melbourne).

WALSH, Brian, QC 1977; a Recorder of the Crown Court, since 1972. Called to the Bar, Middle Temple, 1961, Bencher, 1986. Prosecuting Counsel, DHSS. *Address:* 2 Park Square, Leeds LS1 2NE.

WALSH, Sir David (Philip), KBE 1962; CB 1946; retired as Deputy Secretary, Ministry of Housing and Local Goverment (1960–63); *b* 1902; *s* of late David Walsh and Margaret Walsh; *m* 1930, Edith Airey (*d* 1979), *d* of Frederick Airey and Henrietta Carline; two *s* one *d*. *Educ:* Quentin Sch.; UCL. Formerly: Principal Asst Secretary (Director of Establishments), Admiralty; Under Secretary, Ministry of Town and Country Planning; Under-Secretary, Ministry of Housing and Local Goverment (formerly Min. of Local Goverment and Planning), 1951–60; seconded to: Govt of Iraq as Personnel Advr, 1956; UN Orgn as Personnel Advr to Govt of Venezuela, 1959–60. *Address:* 26 Cottington Court, Cotmaton Road, Sidmouth, Devon EX10 8HD. *T:* Sidmouth 77274.

WALSH, Surgeon Rear-Adm. (retired) Dermot Francis, CB 1960; OBE 1952; FRCSE; *b* 21 Jan. 1901; *s* of Dr J. A. Walsh. *Educ:* Belvedere Coll., Dublin; Trinity Coll., Dublin. BA 1927; MB, BCh, BAO, 1928; FRCSE 1943, QHS 1958. CStJ 1958. *Recreations:* golf, gardening, music. *Address:* Latona, Torquay Road, Foxrock, Dublin 18. *T:* Dublin 893164.

WALSH, Maj.-Gen. Francis James, CB 1948; CBE 1945; psc†; *b* 12 Jan. 1900; *s* of F. J. Walsh, Wexford, Eire; *m* 1931, Marjorie Olive Watney; two *s*. *Educ:* Clongowes Coll., Eire. RMC, Sandhurst, 1918; Royal Irish Regt, 1918–22; King's African Rifles, 1922–28; South Lancashire Regt, 1928–31; Indian Army, 1931–48; Staff Coll., Camberley, 1933–34; staff employment, India, Burma, Malaya, 1935–48; DA&QMG 33 Corps, 1943; DQMG 11 Army Group, 1943–44; DA&QMG 4 Corps and 14 Army, 1944–45; MGA N Comd, India, 1945–47. Maj.-Gen. (Temp.) 1945; Subst., 1947; retired, 1948. *Recreation:* sailing. *Address:* Northlands, 25 Laurel Close, North Warnborough, Hants. *T:* Odiham 3051. *Club:* Naval and Military.

WALSH, Lt-Gen. Geoffrey, CBE 1944; DSO 1943; CD; *b* 1909; *s* of late H. L. Walsh; *m* 1935, Gwynn Abigail Currie; one *s*. *Educ:* Royal Military Coll., Kingston; McGill Univ. (BEngEE). DSc(Mil) RMC, Kingston, 1971. Chief Engineer, 1st Canadian Army, 1944–45; DQMG, 1945–46; Comdr Northwest Highway System, 1946–48; Comdr Eastern Ontario Area, 1948–51; Comdr 27 Bde (Europe), 1951–52; DGMT 1953–55; QMG 1955–58; GOC, Western Command, 1958–61; Chief of the General Staff, Canada, 1961–64; Vice Chief of the Defence Staff, Canada, 1964–65. Col Comdt, Royal Canadian Army Cadets and Cadet Services of Canada, 1970–73. Legion of Merit (US); Comdr of Orange Order of Nassau (Netherlands). *Recreations:* golf, fishing, philately. *Address:* 201 Northcote Place, Rockcliffe Park, Ottawa, Canada. *Clubs:* RMC, Royal Ottawa Golf (Ottawa); USI (Ottawa and Edmonton).

WALSH, Rt. Rev. Geoffrey David Jeremy; *see* Tewkesbury, Bishop Suffragan of.

WALSH, Graham Robert, FCA; Head of Corporate Finance Division, and Member, Management Committee, Morgan Grenfell & Co. Ltd, since 1981 (Director, since 1973); *b* 30 July 1939; *s* of Robert Arthur Walsh and Ella Marian (*née* Jacks); *m* 1967, Margaret Ann Alexander; one *s* one *d*. *Educ:* Hurstpierpoint Coll., Sussex. Qualified as chartered accountant, 1962; joined Philip Hill Higginson Erlangers (now Hill Samuel & Co. Ltd), 1964; Director, Hill Samuel, 1970, resigned 1973; Director: Armitage Shanks Group Ltd, 1973–80; Phoenix Opera Ltd, 1970–; Ward White Group plc, 1981–; Morgan Grenfell Group plc (formerly Morgan Grenfell Holdings), 1985–. Dir Gen., Panel on Takeovers and Mergers, 1979–81; Chm., Issuing Houses Assoc., 1985– (Dep. Chm., 1979 and 1983–85). *Recreations:* opera, theatre, music, gardening, tennis. *Address:* 19 Alleyn Park, Dulwich, SE21 8AU. *T:* 01–670 0676.

WALSH, Henry George; Head of Monetary Policy Division, HM Treasury, since 1985; *b* 28 Sept. 1939; *s* of James Isidore Walsh and Sybil Bertha Bazeley; *m* 1968, Janet Ann Grainger; two *d*. *Educ:* West Hill High Sch., Montreal; McGill Univ.; Churchill Coll., Cambridge. HM Treasury, 1966–74; Private Secretary to Chancellor of the Duchy of Lancaster, 1974–76; HM Treasury, 1976–78; Cabinet Office Secretariat, 1978–80; Counsellor (Economic), Washington, 1980–85. *Recreations:* golf, reading philosophical works, being taken for walks by Labrador retrievers. *Address:* c/o Foreign and Commonwealth Office, SW1.

WALSH, James Mark, CMG 1956; OBE 1948; HM Diplomatic Service; Consul-General, Zürich, 1962–68; *b* 18 Aug. 1909; *s* of Mark Walsh and Emily (*née* Porter); *m* 1st, 1937, Mireille Loir (*d* 1966); one *s*; 2nd, 1967, Bertha Hoch. *Educ:* Mayfield Coll., Sussex; King's Coll., London; Lincoln's Inn, London. BA (Hons), 1929; LLB, 1932; Barrister, 1932; passed an examination and appointed to Foreign Service, 1932; Vice-Consul: Paris, 1932–33, Rotterdam, 1933–34; Judge of HBM Provincial Court, Alexandria, Egypt, 1934–38; Acting Consul-General, Barcelona, 1939; Vice-Consul, Philadelphia, 1939–44; Consul, Antwerp, 1944–45. First Secretary, British Legation: Helsinki, 1945–46, Budapest, 1946–48; Dep. Consul-General, New York, 1948–50; Counsellor (Commercial), Ankara, 1950–54, and Berne, 1954–59; Consul-General, Jerusalem, 1959–62. *Recreations:* painting, golf. *Address:* Fairfield, The Paddock, Haslemere, Surrey. *T:* Haslemere 52089.

WALSH, Dr John James; Consultant to Paddocks Private Clinic, Aylesbury Road, Princes Risborough; *b* 4 July 1917; *s* of Dr Thomas Walsh and Margaret (*née* O'Sullivan); *m* 1946, Joan Mary, *d* of Henry Teasdale and Nita Birks; three *s* one *d*. *Educ:* Mungret Coll.; University Coll., Cork. MB, BCh 1940; MD 1963; MRCP 1968, FRCP 1975; FRCS 1969. Various hospital appointments, including Medical Officer, Spinal Injuries Centre, Stoke Mandeville Hospital, Aylesbury, 1947; Deputy Director, National Spinal Injuries Centre, Stoke Mandeville Hospital, 1957–66, Dir, 1966–77. *Publications:* Understanding Paraplegia, 1964; a number of publications on subjects pertaining to paraplegia in medical journals. *Recreation:* shooting. *Address:* Alena, Bridge Street, Great Kimble, Aylesbury, Bucks HP17 9TN. *T:* Princes Risborough 3347.

WALSH, John P.; *see* Pakenham-Walsh.

WALSH, Sir John (Patrick), KBE 1960; Professor of Dentistry and Dean and Director, University of Otago Dental School, 1946–72; *b* 5 July 1911; *s* of John Patrick Walsh and Lillian Jane (*née* Burbidge), Vic, Australia; *m* 1934, Enid Morris; one *s* three *d*. *Educ:* Ormond Coll.; Melbourne Univ. BDSc 1st Cl. Hons Melbourne; LDS Victoria, 1936; MB, BS Melbourne, 1943; DDSc Melbourne, 1950; FDSRCS 1950; FDSRCS Edinburgh, 1951; MDS NUI, 1952; FRSNZ 1961; FACD 1962; Hon. FACDS, 1967; Hon. DSc Otago, 1975. Hosp. and teaching appointments in Melbourne till 1946. MO, RAAF, 1945–46. Consultant, WHO Dental Health Seminars: Wellington, 1954; Adelaide, 1959. Speaker: 11th and 12th Internat. Dental Congresses, London and Rome; Centennial Congress of Amer. Dental Assoc., New York, 1959; 12th, 14th and 15th Australian Dental Congresses. Chairman: Dental Council of NZ, 1956–72; Mental Health Assoc. of Otago, 1960. Dominion Pres., UNA, 1960–64. Member: MRC of NZ, 1950–72 (Chm. Dental Cttee, 1947–60); Scientific Commn; Fedn Dentaire Internat., 1954–61; Council, Univ. of Otago, 1958–63; Nat. Commn for UNESCO, 1961–69; Educn Commn, 1961–; Expert Panel on Dental Health, WHO, 1962; Nat. Council, Duke of Edinburgh's Award, 1963–68. CC, Dunedin, 1968–73. Pres., Dunedin Rotary Club, 1960, Governor Dist 298, 1966–67. Paul Harris Fellow, 1981. Hon. Mem., American Dental Assoc., 1969–; List of Honour, FDI, 1969–. Holds hon. degrees. *Publications:* A Manual of Stomatology, 1957; Living with Uncertainty, 1968; Psychiatry and Dentistry, 1976; numerous articles in scientific literature. *Recreation:* retirement. *Address:* Unit 29, Hillsborough Heights Village, Dominion Road, Auckland 4, New Zealand. *T:* Auckland 676583.

WALSH, Maj.-Gen. Michael John Hatley, CB 1980; DSO 1968; DL; Chief Scout, since 1982; *b* 10 June 1927; *s* of Captain Victor Michael Walsh, late Royal Sussex, and Audrey Walsh; *m* 1952, Angela, *d* of Col Leonard Beswick; two *d*. *Educ:* Sedbergh Sch. Commnd, KRRC, 1946; served in Malaya, Germany, Cyprus, Suez, Aden, Australia and Singapore; Bde Maj. 44 Parachute Bde, 1960–61; GSO1 Defence Planning Staff, 1966; CO 1 Para Bn, 1967–69; Col AQ 1 Div., 1969–71; Comdr, 28 Commonwealth Bde, 1971–73; BGS HQ BAOR, 1973–76; GOC 3rd Armoured Div., 1976–79; Dir of Army Training, MoD, 1979–81. Hon. Col, 1st Bn Wessex Regt, TA, 1981–. Council Mem., Operation Raleigh, 1984. DL Greater London, 1986. A Knight of the Round Table; OStJ 1986. *Recreations:* athletics, boxing (Life Pres., Army Boxing Assoc., 1986), parachuting (Pres., Army Parachute Assoc., 1979–81), sailing, Australian Rules football. *Address:* c/o Barclays Bank, James Street, Harrogate.

WALSH, Michael Thomas; Secretary, International Department, Trades Union Congress, since 1980; *b* 22 Oct. 1943; *s* of Michael Walsh and Bridget (*née* O'Sullivan); *m* 1972, Margaret Patricia Blaxhall; two *s* two *d*. *Educ:* Gunnersbury Grammar Sch.; Exeter Coll., Oxford (Hons degree PPE). International Dept, TUC, 1966; Deputy Overseas Labour Adviser, FCO, 1977–79. Member, Economic and Social Committee of the European Community, 1976–77 and 1979–80. *Recreations:* cricket, Tudor history. *Address:* 77 Uvedale Road, Enfield EN2 6HD.

WALSH, Lt-Col Noel Perrings; Under Secretary, and Director of Home Regional Services, Department of the Environment, 1976–79; *b* 25 Dec. 1919; *s* of late John and Nancy Walsh; *m* 1945, Olive Mary, *y d* of late Thomas Walsh, Waterford; three *s* one *d*. *Educ:* Purbrook Park Grammar Sch.; Open Univ. Served Army, 1939–66; India, 1941–44; Arakan Campaign, 1944–45; DAQMG, 52 (L) Div., 1951–53; GSO2 RA, HQ BAOR, 1955–57; GSO1 PR, MoD Army, 1964–66; retired Lt-Col, RA, 1966. Entered Home Civil Service as Principal, MPBW, 1966; Regional Director: Far East, 1969–70; Midland Region, 1970–75. Vice-Chm., Midland Study Centre for Building Team, 1982–. *Recreations:* gardening, squash, gauge O railway modelling. *Address:* 25 Oakfield Road, Selly Park, Birmingham B29 7HH. *T:* 021–472 2031. *Clubs:* Naval and Military; Edgbaston Priory (Birmingham).

WALSH, Prof. William; Professor of Commonwealth Literature, 1972–84, now Emeritus, and Acting Vice-Chancellor, 1981–83, University of Leeds; Douglas Grant Fellow in Commonwealth Literature in the School of English, since 1969; Chairman, School of English, 1973–78; *b* 23 Feb. 1916; *e s* of William and Elizabeth Walsh; *m* 1945, May Watson; one *s* one *d*. *Educ:* Downing Coll., Cambridge; University of London. Schoolmaster, 1943–51; Senior English Master, Raynes Park County Grammar Sch., 1945–51; Lecturer in Education, University Coll. of N Staffordshire, 1951–53; Lecturer in Education, Univ. of Edinburgh, 1953–57; Prof. of Education, and Head of Dept. of Education, Univ. of Leeds, 1957–72; Chm., Sch. of Education, 1969–72; Chm., Bd of combined Faculties of Arts, Economics, Social Studies and Law, Univ. of Leeds, 1964–66; Pro-Vice-Chancellor, Univ. of Leeds, 1965–67; Chm. Bd of Adult Educn, 1969–77; Member: IBA Adult Educn Cttee, 1974–76; IBA Educn Adv. Cttee, 1976–81; Bd of Foundn for Canadian Studies in UK, 1981–. Dir, Yorkshire TV, 1967–86; Trustee, Edward Boyle Meml Trust, 1981–. Vis. Prof., ANU, 1968; Australian Commonwealth Vis. Fellow, 1970; Vis. Prof., Canadian Univs, 1973. Hon. LLD Leeds, 1984. *Publications:* Use of Imagination, 1959; A Human Idiom, 1964; Coleridge: The Work and the Relevance, 1967; A Manifold Voice, 1970; R. K. Narayan, 1972; V. S. Naipaul, 1972; Commonwealth Literature, 1973; Readings in Commonwealth Literature, 1973; D. J. Enright: poet of humanism, 1974; Patrick White: Voss, 1976; Patrick White's Fiction, 1977; F. R. Leavis, 1981; Introduction to Keats, 1981; R. K. Narayan, 1982; contributions to: From Blake to Byron, 1957; Young Writers, Young Readers, 1960; Speaking of the Famous, 1962; F. R. Leavis-Some Aspects of his Work, 1963; The Teaching of English Literature Overseas, 1963; Higher Education: patterns of change in the 1970s, 1972; Literatures of the World in English, 1974; Considerations, 1977; Indo-English Literature, 1977; Perspectives on Mulk Raj Anand, 1978; Awakened Conscience, 1978; The Study of Education, vol. 1, 1980; The Twofold Voice: essays in honour of Ramesh Mohan, 1982; papers and essays on literary and educational topics in British and American journals. *Address:* 27 Moor Drive, Headingley, Leeds LS6 4BY. *T:* Leeds 755705.

WALSH ATKINS, Leonard Brian, CMG 1962; CVO 1961; Vice Chairman, The Abbeyfield Society, since 1984; *b* 15 March 1915; *o c* of late Leonard and Gladys Atkins; step *s* of late Geoffrey Walsh, CMG, CBE; *m* 1st, 1940, Marguerite Black (marr. diss. 1968); three *s*; 2nd, 1969, Margaret Lady Runcorn. *Educ:* Charterhouse (Scholar); Hertford Coll., Oxford (Scholar; BA 1937). Asst Principal, India Office, 1937. Fleet Air Arm, 1940–45; Lieut-Comdr (A), RNVR (despatches). Burma Office, 1945–47; Commonwealth Relations Office, 1947; Counsellor, British Embassy, Dublin, 1953–56; Student, Imperial Defence Coll., 1957; Dep. High Comr, Pakistan, 1959–61; Asst Under-Sec. of State, 1962; retired 1970. *Recreation:* sailing. *Address:* Berkeley Cottage, Mayfield, E Sussex TN20 6AU.

WALSHAM, Rear-Adm. Sir John Scarlett Warren, 4th Bt, *cr* 1831; CB 1963; OBE 1944; RN, retired; Admiral Superintendent HM Dockyard, Portsmouth, 1961–64; *b* 29 Nov. 1910; *s* of Sir John S. Walsham, 3rd Bt, and Bessie Geraldine Gundreda (*d* 1941), *e d* of late Vice-Admiral John B. Warren; *S* father, 1940; *m* 1936, Sheila Christina, *o d* of Comdr B. Bannerman, DSO; one *s* two *d*. Rear-Admiral, 1961. *Heir: s* Timothy John Walsham [*b* 26 April 1939. *Educ:* Sherborne]. *Address:* Priory Cottage, Middle Coombe, Shaftesbury, Dorset.

WALSINGHAM, 9th Baron, *cr* 1780; **John de Grey,** MC 1952; Lieut-Colonel, Royal Artillery, retired, 1968; *b* 21 Feb. 1925; *s* of 8th Baron Walsingham, DSO, OBE, and Hyacinth (*d* 1968), *o d* of late Lt-Col Lambart Henry Bouwens, RA; *S* father, 1965; *m* 1963, Wendy, *er d* of E. Hoare, Southwick, Sussex; one *s* two *d*. *Educ:* Wellington Coll.; Aberdeen Univ.; Magdalen Coll., Oxford; RMCS. BA Oxon, 1950; MA 1959. Army in India, 1945–47; Palestine, 1947; Oxford Univ., 1947–50; Foreign Office, 1950; Army in Korea, 1951–52; Hong Kong, 1952–54; Malaya, 1954–56; Cyprus, Suez, 1956; Aden, 1957–58; Royal Military Coll. of Science, 1958–60; Aden, 1961–63; Malaysia, 1963–65. *Heir:* *s* Hon. Robert de Grey, *b* 21 June 1969. *Address:* Merton Hall, Thetford, Norfolk IP25 6QJ. *T:* Watton (Norfolk) 881226. *Clubs:* Army and Navy, Special Forces, Farmers'; Norfolk County (Norwich).

WALSTON, family name of **Baron Walston.**

WALSTON, Baron *cr* 1961 (Life Peer), of Newton; **Henry David Leonard George Walston,** CVO 1976; JP; farmer; *b* 16 June 1912; *o s* of late Sir Charles Walston, LittD, LHD, PhD, and Florence, *d* of David Einstein; *m* 1st, Catherine Macdonald (*d* 1978), *d* of late D. H. Crompton and late Mrs Charles Tobey; three *s* two *d* (and one *s* decd); 2nd, 1979, Mrs Elizabeth Scott. *Educ:* Eton; King's Coll., Cambridge (MA). Research Fellow in Bacteriology, Harvard, USA, 1934–35; Mem., Hunts War Agricultural Cttee, 1939–45; Dir of Agriculture, British Zone of Germany, 1946–47; Agricultural Adviser for Germany to FO, 1947–48; Counsellor, Duchy of Lancaster, 1948–54. Contested: (L) Hunts, 1945; (Lab) Cambridgeshire, 1951 and 1955; (Lab) Gainsborough, 1957 (by-election), and 1959. Parly Under-Sec. of State, FO, 1964–67; Parly Sec., BoT, Jan.-Aug. 1967; Member: UK Delegn to Council of Europe and WEU, 1970–75; European Parlt, 1975–77; joined SDP, 1981. HM Special Ambassador to inauguration of Presidents of Mexico, 1964, of Columbia, 1966, and of Liberia, 1968. Crown Estate Comr, 1968–76; Chm., Inst. of Race Relations, 1968–71; Mem., Commonwealth Development Corp., 1975–83 (Dep. Chm., 1981–83). Minister of Agriculture's Liaison Officer, 1969–70; Chairman: East Anglia Regional Planning Council, 1969–79; GB/East Europe Centre, 1974–86; Centre of E Anglian Studies, 1975–79; Harwich Harbour Conservancy Bd, 1975–79; Member: Cambs Agricultural Cttee, 1948–50; Home Office Cttee on Experiments on Animals, 1961–62. Chm., Harlow Group Hosp. Management Cttee, 1962–64; Dep. Chm., Council, Royal Commonwealth Soc., 1963–64 (Vice-Pres., 1970–); Vice-Pres., VSO, 1981–; Trustee, Rural Industries Bureau, 1959–64; Governor, Guy's Hosp., 1944–47. Hon. DCL East Anglia. JP Cambridge, 1944. *Publications:* From Forces to Farming, 1944; Our Daily Bread, 1952; No More Bread, 1954; Life on the Land, 1954; (with John Mackie) Land Nationalisation, for and against, 1958; Agriculture under Communism, 1961; The Farmer and Europe, 1962; The Farm Gate to Europe, 1970; Dealing with Hunger, 1976; contribs to Proc. of Experimental Biology and Medicine, Jl of Hygiene, Observer, Economist, New Statesman, Spectator. *Recreations:* shooting, sailing. *Address:* Town's End Springs, Thriplow, near Royston, Herts. *Clubs:* Brooks's, MCC; County (Cambridge); House of Lords Yacht.

WALTER, Hon. Sir Harold (Edward), Kt 1972; QC (Mauritius) 1985; Barrister-at-Law; MLA 1959–82, Minister of External Affairs, Tourism and Emigration, 1976–82, Mauritius; *b* 17 April 1920; *e s* of Rev. Edward Walter and Marie Augusta Donat; *m* 1942, Yvette Nidza, MBE, *d* of James Toolsy; no *c*. *Educ:* Royal Coll., Mauritius. Served in HM Forces, 1940–48, Mauritius Sub-Area; E Africa Comd, GHQ MELF. Called to Bar, Lincoln's Inn, 1951. Village Councillor, 1952; Municipal Councillor, Port Louis, 1956. Minister: of Works and Internal Communications, 1959–65; of Health, 1965–67 and 1971–76; of Labour, 1967–71; mem. numerous ministerial delegns. Chm., Commonwealth Med. Conf., 1972–74; Dep. Leader, UN General Assembly, NY, 1973, 1974, 1975; Pres., Security Council, UN, 1979; Mem. Exec. Bd, WHO, 1973–75, Pres., 1976–77. Chm., Council of Ministers, Organisation of African Unity, 1976–77; Vice Pres., Internat. Cttee for the Communities of Democracy (Washington), 1985. Trustee, Child Alive Program (Geneva), 1984–. Commandeur de l'Ordre National Français des Palmes Académiques, 1974; Comdr de la Légion d'Honneur (France), 1980; Diplomatic Order of Merit (Korea), 1981. *Recreations:* shooting, fishing, swimming, gardening. *Address:* La Rocca, Eau Coulée, Mauritius. *T:* 860300. *Clubs:* Wings, Racing (Mauritius).

WALTER, Kenneth Burwood, CVO 1978; Full-time Member, British Airports Authority, 1975–77; *b* 16 Oct. 1918; *s* of late Leonard James Walter and Jesse Florence Walter; *m* 1940, Elsie Marjorie Collett; two *s*. *Educ:* St Dunstan's Coll., SE6. Dept of Civil Aviation, Air Ministry, 1936. Served War, Royal Artillery (Anti Aircraft and Field), home and Far East, 1940–46. Ministries of: Civil Aviation; Transport and Civil Aviation; Aviation, 1946–66; British Airports Authority: Dep. Dir Planning, 1966; Dir Planning, 1972; Airport Dir, Heathrow, 1973–77. MCIT, ARAeS. *Publications:* various papers on airports. *Recreations:* music, swimming, fishing, gardening. *Address:* 7 Willersley Avenue, Orpington, Kent BR6 9RT.

WALTER, Neil Douglas; Deputy High Commissioner for New Zealand in London, since 1985; *b* 11 Dec. 1942; *s* of Ernest Edward Walter and Anita Walter (*née* Frethey); *m* 1966; one *s* two *d*. *Educ:* New Plymouth Boys' High School; Auckland University (MA). Second Sec., Bangkok, 1966–70; First Sec., NZ Mission to UN, NY, 1972–76; Official Sec., Tokelau Public Service, Apia, 1976–78; Minister, Paris and NZ Permt Deleg. to Unesco, 1981–85. *Recreations:* sport, reading. *Address:* 21 Tregunter Road, SW10 9LS.

WALTERS, Sir Alan (Arthur), Kt 1983; Professor of Political Economy, Johns Hopkins University, Maryland, since 1976; part-time Personal Economic Adviser to the Prime Minister, since 1983 (full-time, on secondment, 1981–83); *b* 17 June 1926; *s* of James Arthur Walters and Claribel Walters (*née* Heywood); *m* 1975, Margaret Patricia (Paddie) Wilson; one *d* of former marr. *Educ:* Alderman Newton's Sch., Leicester; University Coll., Leicester (BSc (Econ) London); Nuffield Coll., Oxford (MA). Lectr in Econometrics, Univ. of Birmingham, 1951; Visiting Prof. of Economics, Northwestern Univ., Evanston, Ill, USA, 1958–59; Prof. of Econometrics and Social Statistics, Univ. of Birmingham, 1961; Cassel Prof. of Economics, LSE, 1968–76. Vis. Prof. of Econs, MIT, 1966–67; Vis. Fellow, Nuffield Coll., Oxford, 1982–84; Sen. Fellow, Amer. Enterprise Inst., 1983–. Boyer Lectr, AE1, 1983. Mem. Commission on Third London Airport (the Roskill Commission), 1968–70. Fellow, Econometric Soc., 1971. Hon. DLitt Leicester, 1981; Hon. DSocSc Birmingham, 1984. *Publications:* Growth Without Development (with R. Clower and G. Dalton), 1966 (USA); Economics of Road User Charges, 1968; An Introduction to Econometrics, 1969 (2nd edn 1971); Economics of Ocean Freight Rates (with E. Bennathan), 1969 (USA); Money in Boom and Slump, 1970 (3rd edn 1971); Noise and Prices, 1974; (with R. G. Layard) Microeconomic Theory, 1977; (with Esra Bennathan) Port Pricing and Investment Policy for Developing Countries, 1979; Britain's Economic Renaissance, 1986. *Recreations:* music, Thai porcelain, tennis. *Address:* 2820 P Street NW, Washington, DC 2007, USA. *Clubs:* Athenæum, Political Economy.

WALTERS, Dennis, MBE 1960; MP (C) Westbury Division of Wiltshire since 1964; *b* Nov. 1928; *s* of late Douglas L. Walters; *m* 1st, 1955, Vanora McIndoe (marr. diss. 1969); one *s* one *d*; 2nd, 1970, Hon. Celia (*née* Sandys) (mar diss. 1979); one *s*; 3rd, 1981, Bridgett, *d* of J. Francis Shearer; one *s* one *d*. *Educ:* Downside; St Catharine's College (Exhibitioner), Cambridge (MA). War of 1939–45: interned in Italy; served with Italian Resistance Movement behind German lines after Armistice; repatriated and continued normal educn, 1944. Chm., Fedn of Univ. Conservative and Unionist Assocs, 1950; Personal Asst to Lord Hailsham throughout his Chairmanship of Conservative Party; Chm., Coningsby Club, 1959. Contested (C) Blyth, 1959 and Nov. 1960. Jt Hon. Sec., Conservative Parly Foreign Affairs Cttee, 1965–71, Jt Vice-Chm., 1974–78; Jt Chm., Euro-Arab Parly Assoc., 1978–81. Chm., Cons. ME Council, 1980–. Director: Cluff Oil Inc.; The Spectator, 1983–84. Chm., Asthma Research Council, 1969–; Jt Chm., Council for Advancement of Arab British Understanding, 1970–82 (jt Vice-Chm., 1967–70). Governor, British Inst. of Florence, 1965–. Comdr, Order of Cedar of Lebanon, 1969. *Address:* 43 Royal Avenue, SW3. *T:* 01–730 9431; Orchardleigh, Corton, Warminster, Wilts. *T:* Warminster 50369. *Club:* Boodle's.

WALTERS, Very Rev. Derrick; *see* Walters, Very Rev. R. D. C.

WALTERS, Sir (Frederick) Donald, Kt 1983; Deputy Managing Director, Chartered Trust plc, 1975–85; *b* 5 Oct. 1925; *s* of Percival Donald and Irene Walters; *m* 1950, Adelaide Jean McQuistin; one *s*. *Educ:* Howardian High Sch., Cardiff; London School of Economics and Political Science (LLB). Called to Bar, Inner Temple, 1946; practised at Bar, Wales and Chester circuit, 1948–59. Mem. Bd, 1980–, Dep. Chm., 1984–, Welsh Develt Agency; Member: Develt Bd for Rural Wales, 1984–; Exec. Cttee, WNO, 1985–. *Recreations:* politics, gardening, walking. *Address:* 120 Cyncoed Road, Cardiff CF2 6BL. *T:* Cardiff 753166. *Clubs:* Carlton; Pentwyn Conservative (Cardiff).

WALTERS, Geraint Gwynn, CBE 1958; Director for Wales, Ministry of Public Building and Works and Department of the Environment, 1966–72, retired; *b* in the Welsh Colony in Patagonia, 6 June 1910; *s* of Rev. D. D. Walters; *m* 1st, 1942, Doreena Owen (*d* 1959); 2nd, 1968, Sarah Ann Ruth Price; no *c*. *Educ:* various schools in Argentina and Wales; University Coll., Bangor (BA). Gladstone Prizeman, Foyle Prizeman. Schoolmaster, 1933–35; political organizer on staff of Rt Hon. David Lloyd George, 1935–40; Min. of Information, 1940–45; Dep. Regional Dir of Inf., Bristol and Plymouth, 1942–45; Principal, Min. of Works HQ, 1945–48; Dir for Wales, Min. of Works, 1948–63; Dir, Far East Region, Min. of Public Building and Works, 1963–66. Chm., Royal Inst. of Public Admin (S Wales Br.), 1960–61; Hon. Mem. of Gorsedd, 1961; Pres., St David's Soc. of Singapore, 1965; Leader of Welsh Overseas, at Nat. Eisteddfod of Wales, 1965; Chm., Argentine Welsh Soc., 1976–78, Pres., 1979–82. Chm., Civil Service Sports Council for Wales, 1970–72. Member: Welsh Bd for Industry, 1948–62; Housing Production Bd for Wales; Cttee of Inquiry on Welsh Television, 1963; Mem. Council, Univ. of Wales Inst. of Science and Technology, 1970– (Vice-Chm., 1980–83); Mem. Court, Univ. of Wales, 1982–; Govt Housing Comr for Merthyr Tydfil, 1972–73. *Recreations:* Rugby football, broadcasting, travel. *Address:* 29 The Rise, Llanishen, Cardiff. *T:* Cardiff 752070. *Clubs:* Civil Service; Cardiff and County (Cardiff).

WALTERS, Rear-Adm. John William Townshend, CB 1984; Chairman, Industrial Tribunals (Central London), since 1984; Deputy Chairman, Data Protection Tribunal, since 1985; *b* 23 April 1926; *s* of William Bernard Walters and Lilian Martha Walters (*née* Hartridge); *m* 1949, Margaret Sarah Patricia Jeffkins; two *s* one *d*. *Educ:* John Fisher Sch., Purley, Surrey. Called to Bar, Middle Temple, 1956. Special Entry to RN, 1944; HMS King George V, 1944–46; HMS London, 1946–49; RN Air Station, Arbroath, 1949–51; Staff of C-in-C Mediterranean, 1951–53; Office of Vice Chief of Naval Staff, 1954–56; Sqdn Supply Officer, 8th Destroyer Sqdn, 1957–59; Staff of C-in-C Mediterranean, 1959–62; Secretary: to Flag Officer Middle East, 1962–64; to Naval Secretary, 1964–66; jssc 1967; Supply Officer, HMS Albion, 1967–69; Secretary to Chief of Fleet Support, 1969–72; Chief Naval Judge Advocate, 1972–75; Captain Naval Drafting, 1975–78; Director Naval Administrative Planning, 1978–80; ACDS (Personnel and Logistics), 1981–84, retired. *Recreations:* sailing, gardening. *Address:* Good Holding, 5 Hollycombe Close, Liphook, Hants GU30 7HR. *T:* Liphook 723222. *Clubs:* Army and Navy, Royal Naval Sailing Association.

WALTERS, Joyce Dora; Headmistress, Clifton High School, Bristol, since 1985; *m* 1979, Lt-Col Howard C. Walters (*d* 1983); one *s*. *Educ:* St Anne's College, Oxford. Headmistress, St Mary's, Calne, 1972–85. *Recreations:* travelling, reading, cooking. *Address:* 4 Longwood House, Failand, Bristol. *T:* Bristol 392092.

WALTERS, Michael Quentin; Senior Partner, Theodore Goddard & Co., Solicitors, since 1983; *b* 14 Oct. 1927; *s* of Leslie Walters and Helen Marie Walters; *m* 1954, Lysbeth Ann Falconer. *Educ:* Merchant Taylors' School; Worcester College, Oxford. MA. Served Army, 1946–48, 2nd Lieut. Joined Theodore Goddard & Co., 1951; admitted Solicitor, 1954; Chm., EIS Group plc, 1977–; Dep. Chm., Martonair International plc, 1980–86; Dir, Delta Group plc, 1980–. *Recreations:* fishing, gardening, reading. *Address:* Derryfield Cottage, Ashton Keynes, Swindon, Wilts. *T:* Cirencester 861362.

WALTERS, Peter Ernest, CMG 1965; Group Staff Manager, Courage Ltd, 1967–78; Member, London (South) Industrial Tribunal, 1978–82; *b* 9 Oct. 1913; *s* of Ernest Helm Walters and Kathleen Walters (*née* Farrer-Baynes); *m* 1943, Ayesha Margaret, *d* of Alfred and Winifred Bunker; three *d*. *Educ:* Windlesham House Sch. Emigrated to Kenya, 1931. Army Service, 1939–45; commissioned KAR, 1940; Major 1944. Cadet, Colonial Admin. Service, Kenya, 1945; Dist Comr, 1948; Provincial Comr, Northern Prov., 1959; Civil Sec., Eastern Region, Kenya, 1963–65; retd from Colonial Service, 1965. Principal, Min. of Aviation (London), 1965–67. Staff Manager, Courage, Barclay and Simonds Ltd, 1967. Mem., Management Cttee, Coastal Counties Housing Assoc., 1983–. *Address:* Cherry Orchard, Ockley, near Dorking, Surrey RH5 5NS. *T:* Dorking 711119. *Club:* Nairobi (Kenya).

WALTERS, Peter (Hugh Bennetts) Ensor, OBE 1957; Public Relations and Fund Raising Consultant since 1959; *b* 18 July 1912; *yr s* of late Rev. C. Ensor Walters, a President of the Methodist Conference, and late Muriel Havergal, *d* of late Alderman J. H. Bennetts, JP, Penzance; *m* 1936, Marcia, *er d* of Percival Burdle Hayter; no *c*. *Educ:* Manor House Sch.; St Peter's Coll., Oxford. On staff of late Rt Hon. David Lloyd George, 1935–39; enlisted as volunteer in Army, 1940; commissioned in Royal Army Pay Corps, 1942; National Organizer, National Liberal Organization, 1944–51. General Sec., National Liberal Organization, Hon. Sec. and Treas., National Liberal Party Council, and Dir, National Liberal Forum, 1951–58. Vice-Chm., Nat. Liberal Club, 1972–74. Pres., Worthing Central Cons. Assoc., 1984–. *Recreation:* travel. *Address:* 2 Hopedene Court, Wordsworth Road, Worthing, W Sussex BN11 1TB. *T:* Worthing 205678. *Club:* Union Society (Oxford).

WALTERS, Sir Peter (Ingram), Kt 1984; Chairman, since 1981 and a Managing Director since 1973, British Petroleum Co. plc; *b* 11 March 1931; *s* of Stephen Walters and Edna Walters (*née* Redgate); *m* 1960, Patricia Anne (*née* Tulloch); two *s* one *d*. *Educ:* King Edward's Sch., Birmingham; Birmingham Univ. (BCom). RASC, 1952–54; British Petroleum Co., 1954–: Vice-Pres., BP North America, 1965–67; Chairman: BP Chemicals, 1976–81; BP Chemicals Internat., 1981; Dir, National Westminster Bank, 1981–; Member: Indust. Soc. Council, 1975–; Post Office Bd, 1978–79; Coal Industry

Adv. Bd, 1981–85; Inst. of Manpower Studies, 1986– (Vice-Pres., 1977–80; Pres., 1980–86); Gen. Cttee, Lloyds Register of Shipping, 1976–; President's Cttee, CBI, 1982–; IPSG, 1985–. President: Soc. of Chem. Industry, 1978–80; Gen. Council of British Shipping, 1977–78; Inst. of Directors, 1986–. Governor: London Business Sch., 1981– (Dep. Chm., 1981–); Nat. Inst. of Economic and Social Affairs, 1981–; Mem. Foundn Bd, 1982–83, Chm., 1984–, Internat. Management Inst. Trustee: Nat. Maritime Museum, 1983–; E Malling Res. Station, 1983–; Police Foundn, 1985–; Inst. of Economic Affairs, 1986–. Hon. DSocSc Birmingham, 1986. Comdr. Order of Leopold (Belgium), 1984. *Recreations:* golf, gardening, sailing. *Address:* Britannic House, Moor Lane, EC2Y 9BU.

WALTERS, Very Rev. (Rhys) Derrick (Chamberlain); Dean of Liverpool, since 1983; *b* 10 March 1932; *s* of Ivor Chamberlain Walters and Rosamund Grace Walters (*née* Jackson); 1959, Joan Trollope (*née* Fisher); two *s*. *Educ:* Gowerto Boys' Grammar School; London School of Economics; Ripon Hall, Oxford. BSc(Soc) Lond, 1955. Curate, Manselton, Swansea, 1957–58; Anglican Chaplain, University College, Swansea and Curate, St Mary's, 1958–62; Vicar of All Saints, Totley, 1962–67; Vicar of St Mary's, Boulton by Derby, 1967–74; Diocesan Missioner, Diocese of Salisbury, 1974–82; Vicar of Burcombe, 1974–79; Non-residentiary Canon of Salisbury, 1978; Residentiary Canon and Treasurer of Salisbury Cathedral, 1979–82. *Recreations:* escapist literature, croquet, classical music. *Address:* Liverpool Cathedral, L1 7AZ. *T:* 051–709 6271.

WALTERS, Sir Roger (Talbot), KBE 1971 (CBE 1965); FRIBA, FIStructE; architect in private practice, since 1984; *b* 31 March 1917; 3rd *s* of Alfred Bernard Walters, Sudbury, Suffolk; *m* 1976, Claire Myfanwy Chappell. *Educ:* Oundle; Architectural Association School of Architecture; Liverpool University. Diploma in Architecture, 1939. Served in Royal Engineers, 1943–46. Office of Sir E. Owen Williams, KBE, 1936; Directorate of Constructional Design, Min. of Works, 1941–43; Architect to Timber Development Assoc., 1946–49; Principal Asst Architect, Eastern Region, British Railways, 1949–59; Chief Architect (Development), Directorate of Works, War Office, 1959–62; Dep. Dir-Gen., R&D, MPBW, 1962–67; Dir-Gen., Production, 1967–69; Controller General, 1969–71; Architect and Controller of Construction Services, GLC, 1971–78; Birkbeck Coll., 1978–80 (BA 1980); Principal, The Self-Employed Agency, 1981–83. Hon. FAIA. *Address:* 46 Princess Road, NW1 8JL. *T:* 01–722 3740. *Club:* Reform.

WALTERS, Stuart Max, ScD; VMH; Director, University Botanic Garden, Cambridge, 1973–83, retired; *b* 23 May 1920; *s* of Bernard Walters and Ivy Dane; *m* 1948, Lorna Mary Strutt; two *s* one *d*. *Educ:* Penistone Grammar Sch.; St John's Coll., Cambridge. 1st cl. hons Pt I Nat. Scis Tripos 1940 and Pt II Botany 1946; PhD 1949. Research Fellow, St John's Coll., 1947–50; Curator of Herbarium, Botany Sch., Cambridge, 1948–73; Lectr in Botany 1962–73; Fellow of King's Coll., Cambridge, 1964–84. VMH 1984. *Publications:* (with J. S. L. Gilmour) Wild Flowers, 1954; (with J. Raven) Mountain Flowers, 1956; (ed, with F. H. Perring) Atlas of the British Flora, 1962; (with F. H. Perring, P. D. Sell and H. L. K. Whitehouse) A Flora of Cambridgeshire, 1964; (with D. Briggs) Plant Variation and Evolution, 1969, 2nd edn 1984; The Shaping of Cambridge Botany, 1981. *Address:* Inland Close, 46 Mill Way, Grantchester, Cambridge. *T:* Cambridge 841295.

WALTON, Anthony Michael, QC 1970; *b* 4 May 1925; *y s* of Henry Herbert Walton and Clara Martha Walton, Dulwich; *m* 1955, Jean Frederica, *o d* of William Montague Hey, Bedford; one *s*. *Educ:* Dulwich College (sometime Scholar); Hertford College, Oxford (sometime Scholar); pupil to W. L. Ferrar (maths) and C. H. S. Fifoot (law). BA 1946; BCL 1950; MA 1950. Pres., Oxford Union Society, Trinity Term 1945. Nat. Service as physicist. Called to the Bar, Middle Temple, 1950; Bencher, 1978; pupil to Lord Justice Winn. Interested in education. Liveryman, Worshipful Co. of Gunmakers. Freeman, City of London, 1968. *Publications:* (ed) (Asst to Hon. H. Fletcher-Moulton) Digest of the Patent, Design, Trade Mark and Other Cases, 1959; (ed) Russell on Arbitration, 17th edn, 1963–20th edn, 1982; (with Hugh Laddie) Patent Law of Europe and the United Kingdom, 1978. *Address:* 62 Kingsmead Road, SW2.

See also Hon. Sir Raymond Walton.

WALTON, Arthur Halsall, FCA; Partner in Lysons, Haworth & Sankey, 1949–85; *b* 13 July 1916; *s* of Arthur Walton and Elizabeth Leeming (*née* Halsall); *m* 1958, Kathleen Elsie Abram; three *s*. *Educ:* The Leys School. Articled in Lysons & Talbot, 1934; ACA 1940. Military Service, 1939–48: commnd Lancs Fusiliers, 1940. Inst. of Chartered Accountants: Mem. Council 1959; Vice-Pres., 1969; Dep. Pres. 1970; Pres. 1971. *Recreation:* reading. *Address:* Aldersyde, Prestbury Road, Wilmslow SK9 2LJ. *Club:* St James's (Manchester).

WALTON, Ernest Thomas Sinton, MA, MSc, PhD; Fellow of Trinity College, Dublin, 1934–74, Fellow emeritus 1974; Erasmus Smith's Professor of Natural and Experimental Philosophy 1947–74; *b* 6 October 1903; *s* of Rev. J. A. Walton, MA; *m* 1934, Winifred Isabel Wilson; two *s* two *d*. *Educ:* Methodist College, Belfast; Trinity College, Dublin; Cambridge University. 1851 Overseas Research Scholarship, 1927–30; Senior Research Award of Dept of Scientific and Industrial Research, 1930–34; Clerk Maxwell Scholar, 1932–34. Hon. DSc: Queen's Univ. of Belfast, 1959; Gustavus Adolphus Coll., Minn, USA, 1975. Awarded Hughes Medal by Royal Society, 1938; (with Sir John Cockcroft) Nobel prize for physics, 1951. Hon. Life Mem., RDS, 1981. Hon. FIEI 1985. *Publications:* papers on hydrodynamics, nuclear physics and micro-waves. *Address:* Trinity College, Dublin; 26 St Kevin's Park, Dartry Road, Dublin 6. *T:* 971328.

WALTON, Ven. Geoffrey Elmer; Archdeacon of Dorset, since 1982; *b* 19 Feb. 1934; *s* of Harold and Edith Margaret Walton; *m* 1961, Edith Mollie O'Connor; one *s*. *Educ:* St John's Coll., Univ. of Durham (BA); Queen's Coll., Birmingham (DipTh). Asst Curate, Warsop with Sookholme, 1961–65; Vicar of Norwell, Notts, 1965–69; Recruitment and Selection Sec., ACCM, 1969–75; Vicar of Holy Trinity, Weymouth, 1975–82; RD of Weymouth, 1980–82; Non-Residentiary Canon of Salisbury, 1981–. *Recreations:* conjuring, religious drama. *Address:* The Vicarage, Witchampton, Wimborne, Dorset BH21 5AP. *T:* Witchampton 840422.

WALTON, Sir John (Nicholas), Kt 1979; TD 1962; FRCP; Warden, Green College, University of Oxford, since 1983; *b* 16 Sept. 1922; *s* of Herbert Walton and Eleanor Watson Walton; *m* 1946, Mary Elizabeth Harrison; one *s* two *d*. *Educ:* Alderman Wraith Grammar Sch., Spennymoor, Co. Durham; Med. Sch., King's Coll., Univ. of Durham. MB, BS (1st Cl. Hons) 1945; MD (Durham) 1952; DSc (Newcastle) 1972; MA(Oxon) 1983; FRCP 1963 (MRCP 1950). Ho. Phys., Royal Victoria Inf., Newcastle, 1946–47; service in RAMC, 1947–49; Med. Registrar, Royal Vic. Inf., 1949–51; Research Asst, Univ. of Durham, 1951–56; Nuffield Foundn Fellow, Mass. Gen. Hosp. and Harvard Univ., 1953–54; King's Coll. Fellow, Neurological Res. Unit, Nat. Hosp., Queen Square, 1954–55; First Asst in Neurology, Newcastle upon Tyne, 1956–58; Cons. Neurologist, Newcastle Univ. Hosps, 1958–83; Prof. of Neurology, 1968–83, and Dean of Medicine, 1971–81, Univ. of Newcastle upon Tyne. Member: MRC, 1974–78; GMC, 1971– (Chm. Educn Cttee, 1975–82; Pres., 1982–); President: BMA, 1980–82; Royal Soc. of Medicine, 1984–86; UK Rep., EEC Adv. Cttee, Med. Educn, 1975–83; Editor-in-Chief, Jl of Neurological Sciences, 1966–77; First Vice-Pres., World Fedn Neurol. (Chm., Res. Cttee), 1981–; Chm., Muscular Dystrophy Gp of GB, 1970–, etc. Col (late RAMC) and OC 1 (N) Gen. Hosp. (TA), 1963–66; Hon. Col 201(N) Gen. Hosp. (T&AVR), 1971–77. Dr de l'Univ. (Hon.) Aix-Marseille, 1975; Hon. DSc: Leeds, 1979; Leicester, 1980. Hon. FACP 1980; Hon. FRCPE 1981; Hon. FRCP (Can) 1984. Hon. Foreign Member: Amer. Neurological Assoc., Amer. Acad. of Neurology, Amer. Soc. Phys., and of Canadian, French, German, Australian, Spanish, Polish, Venezuelan, Thai, Japanese and Brazilian Neurological Assocs. Numerous named lectureships and overseas visiting professorships. Hon. Freeman, Newcastle upon Tyne, 1980. *Publications:* Subarachnoid Haemorrhage, 1956; (with R. D. Adams) Polymyositis, 1958; Essentials of Neurology, 1961, 5th edn 1982; Disorders of Voluntary Muscle, 1964, 5th edn 1987; Brain's Diseases of the Nervous System, 7th edn 1969, 9th edn 1985; (with F. L. Mastaglia) Skeletal Muscle Pathology, 1982, etc; (ed jtly) The Oxford Companion to Medicine, 1986; numerous chapters in books and papers in sci. jls. *Recreations:* cricket, golf and other sports, reading, music. *Address:* 1A Observatory Street, Oxford; Green College, Oxford OX2 6HG. *Clubs:* Athenæum, United Oxford & Cambridge University.

WALTON, Sir John Robert, Kt 1971; retired; Director, Waltons Ltd Group, Australia (Managing Director, 1951–72, Chairman, 1961–72); Chairman, FNCB-Waltons Corp. Ltd, Australia, 1966–75; *b* 7 Feb. 1904; *s* of John Thomas Walton; *m* 1938, Peggy Everley Gamble; one *s* one *d*. *Educ:* Scots Coll., Sydney. National Cash Register Co. Pty Ltd, 1930: NSW Manager, 1934, Managing Director in Australia, 1946–51. *Recreations:* gardening, swimming, golf, reading. *Address:* 9A Longwood, 5 Thornton Street, Darling Point, NSW 2027, Australia. *Clubs:* Rotary, Royal Sydney Golf, American National, Tattersall's (all in Sydney).

WALTON, John William Scott; Director of Statistics, Board of Inland Revenue, 1977–85; *b* 25 Sept. 1925; *s* of late Sir John Charles Walton, KCIE, CB, MC, and late Nelly Margaret, Lady Walton, *d* of late Prof. W. R. Scott. *Educ:* Marlborough; Brasenose Coll., Oxford. Army (RA), 1943–47. Mutual Security Agency, Paris, 1952; Inland Revenue, 1954; Central Statistical Office, 1958, Chief Statistician, 1967, Asst Dir, 1972. *Publications:* (contrib. jtly) M. Perlman, The Organization and Retrieval of Economic Knowledge, 1977; articles in The Review of Income and Wealth, Economic Trends, Business Economist, Statistical News. *Club:* United Oxford & Cambridge University.

WALTON, Hon. Sir Raymond (Henry), Kt 1973; **Hon. Mr Justice Walton;** a Judge of the High Court of Justice, Chancery Division, since 1973; *b* 9 Sept. 1915; *e s* of Henry Herbert Walton and Clara Martha Walton, Dulwich; *m* 1940, Helen Alexandra, *e d* of Alexander Dingwall, Jedburgh; one *s* one *d* (and one *d* decd). *Educ:* Dulwich College; Balliol College, Oxford. Open Math. Schol., Balliol, 1933; BA 1937; MA 1942. Pres., Oxford Union Soc., Feb. 1938; BCL 1938. Called to Bar, Lincoln's Inn, 1939; Bencher, 1970. War service in Anti-Aircraft Artillery (including Instructor in Gunnery and Experimental Officer), 1940–46. Contested (L) North Lambeth, 1945. Returned to practice at Bar, 1946; QC 1963. Legal corresp., Financial Times, 1953–72. Mem., Lord Chancellor's Law Reform Cttee, 1959–83; Chm., Insolvency Rules Adv. Cttee, 1977–83. Church Comr for England, 1969–73; Dep. Chm., Boundaries Commn for England, 1973–86. Hon. Fellow, Coll. of Estate Management, 1977. Editor-in-Chief, Encyclopaedia of Forms and Precedents, 5th edn, 1985–. *Publications:* An introduction to the law of Sales of Land, 1949, 3rd edn 1969; (edited) Kerr on Receivers, 12th edn (with A. W. Sarson), 13th to 16th edns; Adkin's Law of Landlord and Tenant, 13th, 14th and (with Michael Essayan) 15th to 18th edns. *Recreation:* philately. *Address:* Royal Courts of Justice, WC2.

See also A. M. Walton.

WALTON, William Stephen; Chief Education Officer, Sheffield, since 1985; *b* 28 March 1933; *s* of Thomas Leslie Walton and Ena Walton (*née* Naylor); *m* 1964, Lois Elicia Petts; three *d* (incl. twins). *Educ:* King's School, Pontefract; Univ. of Birmingham (BA). RAF, gen. duties (flying), 1951–55. Production Management, Dunlop Rubber Co., 1958–61; Derbyshire Local Educn Authy School Teacher, 1961–67; Educational Administration: Hull, 1967–70; Newcastle upon Tyne, 1970–79; Sheffield 1979–. *Recreations:* golf, France. *Address:* 3 Bentham Road, Chesterfield, Derbyshire. *T:* Chesterfield 203769. *Club:* Royal Air Force.

WALWYN, Fulke Thomas Tyndall, CVO 1983; racehorse trainer; *b* 8 Nov. 1910; *s* of Col Fulke Walwyn, DSO and Norah Walwyn; *m* 1st, 1937, Diana Carlos Clarke; 2nd, 1952, Catherine de Trafford; one *d*. *Educ:* Malvern; RMA Sandhurst. 9th Lancers, 1930–36; leading amateur rider 3 times; turned professional jockey, 1936; rode Reynoldstown to Grand National win, 1936; started to train, 1939, to train for HM the Queen Mother, 1973; has trained over 2,000 winners; Leading Trainer 5 times. *Address:* Saxon House Stables, Lambourn, Berks. *T:* Lambourn 71555.

WALWYN, Peter Tyndall; racehorse trainer, since 1960; *b* 1 July 1933; *s* of late Lt-Col Charles Lawrence Tyndall Walwyn, DSO, OBE, MC, Moreton in Marsh, Glos; *m* 1960, Virginia Gaselee, *d* of A. S. Gaselee, MFH; one *s* one *d*. *Educ:* Amesbury Sch., Hindhead, Surrey; Charterhouse. Leading trainer on the flat, 1974, 1975; leading trainer, Ireland, 1974, 1975; a new record in earnings (£373,563), 1975. Major races won include: One Thousand Guineas, 1970, Humble Duty; Oaks Stakes, 1974, Polygamy; Irish Derby, 1974, English Prince, and 1975, Grundy; King George VI and Queen Elizabeth Stakes, Ascot, 1975, Grundy; Epsom Derby, 1975, Grundy. *Recreations:* foxhunting, shooting. *Address:* Seven Barrows, Lambourn, Berks RG16 7UJ. *T:* Lambourn 71347. *Clubs:* Turf; Jockey Club Rooms (Newmarket).

WANAMAKER, Sam; Actor; Director, Producer; *b* Chicago, 14 June 1919; *s* of Morris Wanamaker and Molly (*née* Bobele); *m* 1940, Charlotte Holland; three *d*. *Educ:* Drake University, Iowa, USA. Studied for the stage at Goodman Theatre, Chicago. Appeared in summer theatres, Chicago (acting and directing), 1936–39; joined Globe Shakespearian Theatre Group; first New York Appearance, Café Crown, 1941; Counter Attack, 1942. Served in United States Armed Forces, 1943–46. In several parts on New York stage, 1946–49; appeared in This, Too, Shall Pass, 1946; directed and played in: Joan of Lorraine, 1946–47; Goodbye My Fancy, 1948–49; directed: Caeser and Cleopatra, 1950; The Soldier and the Lady, 1954; created Festival Repertory Theatre, New York, 1950. First performance (also producer) on London stage as Bernie Dodd, in Winter Journey, St James's, 1952; presented and appeared in The Shrike, Prince's, 1953; produced: Purple Dust, Glasgow, 1953; Foreign Field, Birmingham, 1954; directed and appeared in One More River, Cat on a Hot Tin Roof, and The Potting Shed, 1957. In Liverpool, 1957, created New Shakespeare Theatre Cultural Center, where produced (appearing in some): Tea and Sympathy, A View from the Bridge, 1957; The Rose Tattoo, Finian's Rainbow, Bus Stop, The Rainmaker, and Reclining Figure (all in 1958). *Presented, prod and appeared in:* The Big Knife, Duke of York's, 1954; The Lovers, Winter Garden, 1955; The Rainmaker, St Martin's 1956; A Hatful of Rain, Prince's, 1957; The Rose Tattoo, New, 1959; Iago, Stratford-on-Avon, 1959; Dr Breuer, in A Far Country, New York, 1961; The Watergate Tapes, Royal Court, 1974; *produced:* The World of Sholom Aleichem, Embassy, 1955; King Priam, Coventry Theatre and Royal Opera House, Covent Garden, 1962, 1967, and 1972; Verdi's La Forza del Destino, Royal Opera House, Covent Garden, 1962; John Player season, Globe, 1972–73; Southwark Summer Festival, 1974; Shakespeare

Birthday Celebrations, 1974; *directed:* Children from their Games, New York, 1963; A Case of Libel, New York, 1963; A Murder Among Us, New York, 1964; Defenders, 1964; War and Peace (première), Sydney Opera House, 1973; The Ice Break, Royal Opera House, Covent Garden, 1977; Chicago Lyric Opera Gala, 1979; Stravinsky's Oedipus, Boston Symphony Orch., Tanglewood, 1982; *acted and directed* Macbeth, Goodman Theater, Chicago, 1964; *directed and wrote* This Wooden O, Carnegie Hall, Pittsburgh, 1983; *acted (films):* Give Us This Day; Taras Bulba; Those Magnificent Men in Their Flying Machines, 1964; The Winston Affair, 1964; The Spy Who Came in from the Cold, 1964; Warning Shot; The Law, 1974; Spiral Staircase, 1974; The Sell-Out, 1975; The Voyage, 1975; Billy Jack goes to Washington, 1976; From Hell to Victory, 1978; Private Benjamin, 1980; The Competition, 1980; Irreconcilable Differences, 1983; The Aviator, 1983; (film for TV) Embassy, 1985; *films directed:* Hawk, 1965; Lancer, 1966; Custer, 1967; File of the Golden Goose, 1968; The Executioner, 1969; Catlow, 1970; Sinbad and the Eye of the Tiger, 1975; The Killing of Randy Webster, 1981; *directed (opera):* Aida, San Francisco, 1981; *directed (television):* Colombo, 1977; Hawaii 5–0, 1978; Dark Side of Love, Man Undercover, Mrs Columbo, Hart to Hart, 1979; *acted and directed (TV):* The Holocaust, 1977; The Return of the Saint, 1978; *acted (TV):* Blind Love, 1976; Charlie Muffin, 1979; The Family Business, 1981; The Ghost Writer, 1982; The Berrengers, 1984; Heartsounds, 1984; The Ferret, 1984. Founder and Executive Director: Globe Playhouse Trust Ltd, 1971; Internat. Shakespeare Globe Centre (formerly World Centre for Shakespeare Studies Ltd). Directs and acts in TV productions and feature films in UK and USA. *Address:* Bear Gardens, SE1.

WANDSWORTH, Archdeacon of; *see* Coombs, Ven. P. B.

WANGARATTA, Bishop of, since 1985; **Rt. Rev. Robert George Beal;** *b* 17 Aug. 1929; *s* of Samuel and Phyllis Beal; *m* 1956, Valerie Francis Illich; two *s* four *d. Educ:* Sydney Grammar School; St Francis' College, Brisbane, Qld; Newcastle Univ., NSW (BA, ThL). Ordained, 1953; Priest, Asst Curate, St Francis', Nundah, Brisbane, 1953–55; Rector: South Townsville, 1955–59; Auchenflower, Brisbane, 1959–65; Dean of Wangaratta, 1965–72; Rector of Ipswich, Brisbane, and Residentiary Canon of St John's Cathedral, 1974–75; Dean of Newcastle, NSW, 1975–83; Archdeacon of Albury, 1983–85. *Recreations:* tennis, gardening. *Address:* Bishop's Lodge, Ovens Street, Wangaratta, Victoria 3677, Australia. *T:* (057) 21 3643.

WANI, Most Rev. Silvanus; *b* July 1916; *s* of late Mana Ada Wani and late Daa Miriam; *m* 1936, Penina Yopa Wani; six *s* two *d* (and two *s* decd). *Educ:* Kampala Normal School, Makerere (Teacher's Cert.). Teaching, Arua Primary School, 1936–39; student, Buwalasi Theol. Coll., 1940–42; ordained as one of first two priests in West Nile District, 1943; Chaplain, King's African Rifles, 1944–46; Parish Priest: Arua, 1947–50; Koboko, 1951–60; Canon and Rural Dean, Koboko, 1953–60; attended Oak Hill Theological Coll., 1955–56; Diocesan Secretary/Treasurer, N Uganda Diocese, 1961–64; Asst Bishop, later full Bishop, N Uganda, 1964; Bishop of Madi/West Nile Diocese, 1969; Dean, Province of Church of Uganda, Rwanda, Burundi and Boga Zaire, 1974–77; Archbishop of Uganda and Bishop of Kampala, 1977–83. Chaplain General to Uganda Armed Forces, 1964. *Recreations:* reading, walking, gardening. *Address:* c/o Provincial Secretariat, Church of Uganda, PO Box 14123, Kampala, Uganda.

WANNAMETHEE, Phan; Secretary General, Association of South East Asian Nations, 1984–86; *b* 30 Jan. 1924; *s* of Mr and Mrs Puhn Wannamethee; *m* 1958, M. L. Hiranyika Ladawan; three *s* one *d. Educ:* Oberlin Coll., Ohio, USA (BA); Univ. of Calif at Berkeley (MA). Entered Foreign Min., Bangkok, 1942; attached Royal Thai Embassy, Washington, 1945; Third Sec., Cairo, 1956; Private Sec. to Prime Minister, 1957; First Secretary: Karachi, 1958; Saigon, 1959; (later Counsellor), London, 1964; Foreign Min., Bangkok: Dep. Under-Sec. of State, 1972; Dir-Gen., Polit. Dept, 1973; Under-Sec. of State for Foreign Affairs, 1973; Ambassador to: Fed. Republic of Germany, 1976; UK, 1977–84. *Recreation:* swimming. *Address:* 66 Soi 10, Pibulwattana, Rama 6 Road, Bangkok, Thailand. *Clubs:* Athenæum, Travellers', Naval and Military, Special Forces, Hurlingham.

WANSTALL, Hon. Sir Charles Gray, Kt 1974; Chief Justice of Queensland, Australia, 1977–82; *b* 17 Feb. 1912; *m* 1938, Olwyn Mabel, *d* of C. O. John; one *d. Educ:* Roma and Gympie State Schs; Gympie High Sch., Queensland, Australia. Called to Queensland Bar, 1933. High Court, 1942. MLA (Liberal) for Toowong, 1944–50; Pres., Liberal Party of Australia (Qld Div.), 1950–53. QC 1956; Judge, Supreme Court, Qld, 1958; Sen. Puisne Judge, 1971. *Recreations:* reading, photography. *Address:* 26/36 Jerdanefield Road, St Lucia, Brisbane, Queensland 4067, Australia. *Clubs:* Queensland (Brisbane); St Lucia Bowling.

WARBURTON, Col Alfred Arthur, CBE 1961; DSO 1945; DL; JP; Chairman, SHEF Engineering Ltd, 1970–75; Company Director since 1953; *b* 12 April 1913; *s* of late A. V. Warburton. *Educ:* Sedbergh. Served War of 1939–45, with Essex Yeomanry; Lt-Col comdg South Notts Hussars Yeomanry, 1953–58; Hon. Col 1966–76; Col DCRA 49th Inf. Div. TA, 1958–60; ADC to the Queen, 1961–66; Chm., Notts Cttee TA&VR Assoc. for E Midlands, 1970–78. Director, John Shaw Ltd, Worksop, 1953–66. President: East Midlands Area, Royal British Legion, 1976–77, 1981–82, 1986–87; Notts County Royal British Legion, 1979–. DL 1966, High Sheriff 1968, JP 1968, Notts. *Recreations:* shooting, fishing. *Address:* Wigthorpe House, Wigthorpe, Worksop, Notts. *T:* Worksop 730357. *Club:* Cavalry and Guards.

WARBURTON, Dame Anne (Marion), DCVO 1979 (CVO 1965); CMG 1977; HM Diplomatic Service, 1957–85; President, Lucy Cavendish College, Cambridge, since 1985; *b* 8 June 1927; *d* of Captain Eliot Warburton, MC and Mary Louise (*née* Thompson), US. *Educ:* Barnard Coll., Columbia Univ. (BA); Somerville Coll., Oxford (BA, MA); Hon. Fellow, 1977. Economic Cooperation Administration, London, 1949–52; NATO Secretariat, Paris, 1952–54; Lazard Bros, London, 1955–57; entered Diplomatic Service, Nov. 1957; 2nd Sec., FO, 1957–59; 2nd, then 1st Sec., UK Mission to UN, NY, 1959–62; 1st Sec., Bonn, 1962–65; 1st Sec., DSAO, London, 1965–67; 1st Sec., FO, then FCO, 1967–70; Counsellor, UK Mission to UN, Geneva, 1970–75; Head of Guidance and Information Policy Dept, FCO, 1975–76; Ambassador to Denmark, 1976–83; Ambassador and UK Permanent Rep. to UN and other internat. organisations, Geneva, 1983–85. Dep. Leader, UK Delegn to UN Women's Conf., Nairobi, 1985. Mem., Equal Opportunities Commn, 1986–. FRSA 1986. Verdienstkreuz, 1st Class (West Germany), 1965; Grand Cross, Order of Dannebrog, 1979. *Recreations:* travel, walking, ski-ing, the arts. *Address:* Lucy Cavendish College, Cambridge. *Clubs:* United Oxford & Cambridge University, English-Speaking Union.

WARBURTON, David; Principal National Officer, General, Municipal, Boilermakers and Allied Trades Union, since 1985; *b* 10 Jan. 1942; *s* of Harold and Ada Warburton; *m* 1966, Carole Anne Susan Tomney; two *d. Educ:* Cottingley Manor Sch., Bingley, Yorks; Coleg Harlech, Merioneth, N Wales. Campaign Officer, Labour Party, 1964; Educn Officer, G&MWU, 1965–66, Reg. Officer, 1966–73; Nat. Industrial Officer, G&MWU, 1973–82, GMBATU, 1982–85. Secretary: Chemical Unions Council; Rubber Industry Jt Unions, 1980–86. Mem., Europ. Co-ord. Cttee, Chem., Rubber and Glass Unions, 1975–86. Chm., Chem. and Allied Industries Jt Indust. Council, 1973–86; Vice-Pres., Internat. Fedn of Chemical, Energy and Gen. Workers, 1986–. Member: EDC, 1973–86; Commonwealth Develt Corp., 1979–; Chm., TUC Gen. Purposes Cttee, 1984–. *Publications:* Pharmaceuticals for the People, 1973; Drug Industry: which way to control, 1975; The Way Forward, 1977; Economic Detente, 1980; The Case for Voters Tax Credits, 1983; Forward Labour, 1985. *Recreations:* music, American politics, flicking through reference books, films of the thirties and forties. *Address:* 47 Hill Rise, Chorleywood, Rickmansworth, Herts. *T:* Rickmansworth 778726.

WARBURTON, Eric John Newnham, CBE 1966; a Vice-Chairman, Lloyds Bank Ltd, 1967–75; *b* 22 Nov. 1904; *o s* of late E. and H. R. Warburton, Bexhill-on-Sea, Sussex; *m* 1933, Louise, *er d* of late C. J. and L. R. Martin, Crowborough, Sussex; one *s* one *d. Educ:* Eastbourne Grammar School. Entered Lloyds Bank Ltd, 1922; Jt General Man., 1953; Dep. Chief Gen. Man., 1958; Chief Gen. Man., 1959–66; Dir, 1965–75; Dep. Chm., Lloyds Bank International Ltd, 1971–75; Director: Lloyds Bank Unit Trust Managers Ltd, 1966–75; First Western Bank Trust Co., Calif., 1974–75; Lewis's Bank Ltd, 1967–75; Intercontinental Banking Services Ltd, 1968–75. Chairman: Exec. Cttee, Banking Information Service, 1965–71; Bank Education Service, 1966–71; Dep. Chairman: City of London Savings Cttee, 1962–74; Exports Credit Guarantee Dept Adv. Council, 1968–71 (Member, 1966–71); Member: Decimal Currency Bd, 1967–71; Nat. Savings Cttee, 1963–74; Council, CBI, 1971–75. Member Board: Trinity Coll. of Music, 1968–74; Management Cttee, Sussex Housing Assoc. for the Aged, 1970–; American Bankers Assoc. Internat. Monetary Conf., 1970–72. FRSA 1970; Hon. FTCL 1969. *Recreations:* golf, gardening, music. *Address:* 9 Denmans Close, Lindfield, Haywards Heath, West Sussex RH16 2JX. *T:* Lindfield 2351. *Club:* Oriental.

WARBURTON, Prof. Geoffrey Barratt, FEng 1985; Hives Professor of Mechanical Engineering, since 1982, a Pro Vice-Chancellor, since 1984, University of Nottingham; *b* 9 June 1924; *s* of Ernest McPherson and Beatrice Warburton; *m* 1952, Margaret Coan; three *d. Educ:* William Hulme's Grammar School, Manchester; Peterhouse, Cambridge (Open Exhibition in Mathematics, 1942; 1st cl. Hons in Mechanical Sciences Tripos, 1944; BA 1945; MA 1949); PhD Edinburgh, 1949. Junior Demonstrator, Cambridge Univ., 1944–46; Asst Lecturer in Engineering, Univ. Coll. of Swansea, 1946–47; Dept of Engineering, Univ. of Edinburgh: Assistant, 1947–48, Lecturer, 1948–50 and 1953–56; ICI Research Fellow, 1950–53; Head of Post-graduate School of Applied Dynamics, 1956–61; Prof. of Applied Mechanics, Nottingham Univ., 1961–82. FRSE 1960; FIMechE 1968. Rayleigh Medal, Inst. of Acoustics, 1982. Associate Editor, Earthquake Engineering and Structural Dynamics; Member, Editorial Boards: Internat. Jl of Mechanical Sciences; Internat. Jl for Numerical Methods in Engineering; Jl of Sound and Vibration; Communications in Applied Numerical Methods. *Publications:* The Dynamical Behaviour of Structures, 1964, 2nd edn 1976; research on mechanical vibrations, in several scientific journals. *Address:* University of Nottingham, Nottingham NG7 2RD.

WARBURTON, John Kenneth, CBE 1983; Director, Birmingham Chamber of Industry and Commerce, since 1978; Regional Secretary, West Midlands Regional Group of Chambers of Commerce, since 1978; *b* 7 May 1932; *s* of Frederick and Eva Warburton; *m* 1960, Patricia Gordon; one *d. Educ:* Newcastle-under-Lyme High Sch.; Keble Coll., Oxford (MA Jurisprudence). Called to Bar, Gray's Inn, 1977. London Chamber of Commerce, 1956–59; Birmingham Chamber of Industry and Commerce, 1959–. President, British Chambers of Commerce Executives, 1979–81; Member: European Trade Cttee, Business Link Gp and E European Trade Council, BOTB; Review Body on Doctors' and Dentists' Remuneration, 1982–; Exec. Council, Business in the Community, 1981–; National Council, Assoc. of British Chambers of Commerce, 1978–; Steering Cttee, Internat. Bureau of Chambers of Commerce, 1976–; Chm., Adv. Council, W Midlands Industrial Develt Assoc., 1983–. Governor, Univ. of Birmingham, 1982–. Director: National Garden Festival 1986 Ltd, 1983–; Birmingham Venture, 1980–. *Address:* 35 Hampshire Drive, Edgbaston, Birmingham B15 3NY. *T:* 021–454 6764.

WARBURTON, Richard Maurice; Director General, Royal Society for the Prevention of Accidents, since 1979; *b* 14 June 1928; *s* of Richard and Phylis Agnes Warburton; *m* 1952, Lois May Green; two *s. Educ:* Wigan Grammar Sch.; Birmingham Univ. (BA 1st Cl. Hons). Flying Officer, RAF, 1950–52. HM Inspector of Factories, 1952–79; Head of Accident Prevention Advisory Unit, Health and Safety Executive, 1972–79. *Recreations:* golf, gardening, fell walking. *Address:* Cornaa, Wyfordby Avenue, Blackburn, Lancs. *T:* Blackburn 56824.

WARD, family name of **Earl of Dudley** and of **Viscounts Bangor** and **Ward of Witley.**

WARD OF WITLEY, 1st Viscount, *cr* 1960; **George Reginald Ward,** PC 1957; *b* 20 Nov. 1907; 4th *s* (twin) of 2nd Earl of Dudley; *m* 1st, 1940, Anne Capel (marr. diss., 1951); one *d* (one *s* decd); 2nd, 1962, Hon. Mrs Barbara Astor (who *m* 1st, 1942, Hon. Michael Langhorne Astor; she *d* 1980). *Educ:* Eton; Christ Church, Oxford. AAF, 1929; RAF, 1932–37 and 1939–45. MP (C) for Worcester City, 1945–60. Parly Under-Sec. of State, Air Min., 1952–55; Parly and Financial Sec., Admiralty, Dec. 1955–Jan. 1957; Secretary of State for Air, 1957–60. *Heir:* none. *Address:* 23 Queens Gate Gardens, SW7 5LZ. *Clubs:* White's, Pratt's.

WARD, Prof. Alan Gordon, CBE 1972 (OBE 1959); Procter Professor of Food and Leather Science, Leeds University, 1961–77, now Emeritus; *b* 18 April 1914; *s* of Lionel Howell Ward and Lily Maud Ward (*née* Morgan); *m* 1938, Cicely Jean Chapman; one *s* two *d. Educ:* Queen Elizabeth's Grammar Sch., Wimborne; Trinity Coll., Cambridge (schol.). BA (Cantab) 1935; MA (Cantab) 1940; FInstP 1946; FIFST 1966. Lectr in Physics and Mathematics, N Staffs Technical Coll., 1937–40; Experimental Officer, Min. of Supply, 1940–46; Sen. Scientific Officer, Building Research Station, 1946–48; Principal Scientific Officer, 1948–49; Dir of Research, The British Gelatine and Glue Research Assoc., 1949–59; Prof. of Leather Industries, Leeds Univ., 1959–61. Chm., Food Standards Cttee set up by Minister of Agriculture, 1965–79. Hon. FIFST 1979; Hon. FAIFST 1979. *Publications:* Nature of Crystals, 1938; Colloids, Their Properties and Applications, 1945; The Science and Technology of Gelatin, 1977; papers in Trans. Far. Soc., Jl Sci. Instr, Biochem. Jl, etc. *Recreation:* music. *Address:* 35 Templar Gardens, Wetherby, West Yorkshire LS22 4TG. *T:* Wetherby 64177.

WARD, Alan Hylton; QC 1984; a Recorder, since 1985; *b* 15 Feb. 1938; *s* of late Stanley Victor Ward and of Mary Ward; *m* 1st, 1963, Joy (*née* Zeederburg) (marr. diss. 1982); one *s* two *d*; 2nd, 1983, Helen (*née* Gilbert); twin *d. Educ:* Christian Brothers Coll., Pretoria; Univ. of Pretoria (BA, LLB); Pembroke Coll., Cambridge (MA, LLB). Called to the Bar, Gray's Inn, 1964. Formerly an Attorney of Supreme Court of South Africa. Mem., Matrimonial Causes Procedure Cttee, 1982–85. *Recreations:* hitting or attempting to hit some ball or other. *Address:* 2 Dr Johnson's Buildings, Temple, EC4. *T:* 01–353 7291. *Club:* MCC.

WARD, (Albert Joseph) Reginald; Chief Executive, London Docklands Development Corporation, since 1981; *b* 5 Oct. 1927; *s* of Albert E. and Gwendolene M. E. Ward, Lydbook, Glos; *m* 1954, Betty Anne Tooze; one *s* one *d. Educ:* East Dean Grammar Sch., Cinderford, Glos; Univ. of Manchester (BA Hons History). HM Inspector of Taxes,

1952–65; Chief Administrator, County Architects Dept, Lancashire CC, 1965–68; Business Manager, Shankland Cox & Associates, 1968–69; Corporation Secretary, Irvine New Town Development Corporation, 1969–72; Chief Executive: Coatbridge Borough Council, 1972–74; London Borough of Hammersmith, 1974–76; Hereford and Worcester CC, 1976–80. *Recreations:* walking, tennis, music, architecture and urban design. *Address:* Abbott's Court, Deerhurst, Gloucester GL19 4BX. *T:* (0684) 292663; 18 Vinegar Street, Wapping, E1.

WARD, Mrs Ann Sarita; Chairman, Inner London Education Authority, 1981–82; Councillor, London Borough of Southwark, since 1971 (Deputy Leader, 1978–83); *b* 4 Aug. 1923; *d* of Denis Godfrey and Marion Phyllis Godfrey; *m* Frank Ward; one *s. Educ:* St Paul's Girls' Sch., Hammersmith. Professional photographer; photo journalist, Daily Mail, 1962–67; Daily Mirror, 1967–70; award winner, British Press Photographs of Year, 1967. Contested (Lab) Streatham, Gen. Election, 1970. Mem., Camberwell HA, 1982–. Special Trustee, KCH, 1983–. *Recreations:* politics, community self-help printing, gardening. *Address:* 204 Peckham Rye, SE22 0LU. *T:* 01–693 4251.

WARD, Ven. Arthur Frederick, BA; Archdeacon of Exeter, 1970–81, Archdeacon Emeritus since 1981; Canon Residentiary of Exeter Cathedral, 1970–81, Precentor, 1972–81; *b* 23 April 1912; *s* of William Thomas and Annie Florence Ward, Corbridge, Northumberland; *m* 1937, Margaret Melrose, Tynemouth, Northumberland; two *d. Educ:* Durham Choir School; Newcastle upon Tyne Royal Grammar School; Durham University; Ridley Hall, Cambridge. Curate, Byker Parish Church, Newcastle, 1935–40; Rector of Harpurhey, North Manchester, 1940–44; Vicar of Nelson, 1944–55; Vicar of Christ Church, Paignton, 1955–62; Archdeacon of Barnstaple and Rector of Shirwell with Loxhore, Devon, 1962–70. *Recreations:* gardening, cricket, touring. *Address:* Melrose, Christow, Devon EX6 7LY. *T:* Christow 52498.

WARD, Sir Arthur (Hugh), KBE 1979 (OBE 1962); ACA; FNZIAS; Chancellor, Massey University, 1975–81 (Pro-Chancellor, 1970–75); *b* 25 March 1906; *s* of Arthur Ward and Ada Elizabeth Ward; *m* 1936, Jean Bannatyne Mueller; one *s* three *d. Educ:* Middlesbrough High Sch., Yorks. ACA (NZ); FNZIAS 1969. Sec., NZ Co-op. Herd Testing Assoc., 1929–36; Dir, Herd Improvement, NZ Dairy Bd, 1945–54; Gen. Man., Dairy Bd, 1954–70. Chm., W. M. Angus & Co., 1970–75; Dep. Chm., Ivon Watkins Dow, 1971–76. Member: NZ Monetary and Econ. Council, 1970–79; Remuneration Authority, 1971–72; National Res. Adv. Council, 1970–72 (Chm., 1971–72); Council, Massey Univ., 1967–81. Marsden Medal for services to science, 1975; Queen's Silver Jubilee Medal, 1977. *Publications:* A Command of Co-operatives, 1975; articles on dairy cattle husbandry and dairy cattle breeding. *Recreations:* writing, reading, gardening, golf. *Address:* 17 Tui Crescent, Waikanae, New Zealand. *T:* Paraparaumu 36466; PO Box 56, Waikanae.

WARD, (Arthur) Neville, RDI 1971; BArch; RIBA, FSIAD; architect and designer; *b* 5 June 1922; *s* of Arthur Edward Ward and Winifred Alice Ward; *m* 1948, Mary Winstanley; one *s. Educ:* Wade Deacon Grammar Sch., Widnes; Sch. of Architecture, Univ. of Liverpool (BArch 1944); Edinburgh Coll. of Art. RIBA 1944; FSIA 1948. Mem., BoT Furniture Design Panel, 1946–48. Private practice, Ward and Austin, 1948–71, Ward Associates, 1972–; special concern in interiors, exhibns, ships accommodation, furniture; contrib. Britain Can Make It, 1946, and Festival of Britain, 1951. Pres., SIAD, 1967. Member: Nat. Adv. Cttee on Art Exams, 1952–57; Nat. Adv. Council on Art Educn, 1959–71; Council, RSA, 1965–70, and 1977–78; Council, RCA, 1968–72; Nat. Council for Diplomas in Art and Design, 1968–74. Master, Faculty of Royal Designers for Industry, 1977–78. *Publications:* (with Mary Ward) Living Rooms, 1967; (with Mary Ward) Home in the 20s and 30s, 1978; articles and essays in Arch. Rev., and Naval Arch. *Recreation:* jobbing. *Address:* Ward Associates, 68 Grafton Way, W1P 5LE. *T:* 01–387 0491.

WARD, Sir Aubrey (Ernest), Kt 1967; JP; DL; *b* 17 April 1899; *s* of Edward Alfred Ward; *m* 1919, Mary Jane Davidson Rutherford, MB, ChB (*d* 1979); one *d. Educ:* Royal Veterinary College, London. Served War of 1914–18; Night FO, RFC (now RAF). Veterinary Practice, 1923–66. Vice-Chm., Thames Conservancy Bd, 1964–74. Mayor of Slough, 1940–45, Hon. Freeman, 1961. JP 1957, DL 1963, Chm., CC, 1963–74, Buckinghamshire. *Address:* 54 Pound Lane, Marlow, Bucks. *T:* Marlow 5250.

WARD, Cecil; Town Clerk, Belfast City Council, since 1979; *b* 26 Oct. 1929; *s* of William and Mary Caroline Ward. *Educ:* Technical High Sch., Belfast; College of Technology, Belfast. Employed by Belfast City Council (formerly Belfast County Borough Council), 1947–; Asst Town Clerk (Administration), 1977–79. Mem., Local Govt Staff Commn, 1983–. Mem., NI Cttee, IBA, 1983–. Director: Ulster Orchestra Soc., 1980–; Opera Northern Ireland, 1985–. *Recreations:* music, reading, hill walking. *Address:* 24 Thornhill, Malone, Belfast, Northern Ireland BT9 6SS. *T:* Belfast 668950.

WARD, Rev. Canon Charles Leslie; Canon Treasurer of Wells and Prebendary of Warminster in Wells Cathedral, 1978–85, now Canon Emeritus; *b* 11 June 1916; *s* of Amos Ward and Maude Hazeldine Ballard; *m* 1943, Barbara, *d* of George and Alice Stoneman; two *s. Educ:* Mexborough Grammar Sch.; Lichfield Theological Coll. (Potter-Selwyn Exhibnr). Underground Surveyor, Cadeby Colliery, S Yorks, 1933–36. Assistant Curate: Parkgate, 1939; Rossington, 1940; Taunton, 1942; Bishop of Blackburn's Youth Chaplain and Succentor of Blackburn Cathedral, 1945; Vicar: St Michael, Ashton on Ribble, 1948; St Peter, Cheltenham, 1951; Northleach, Stowell, Hampnett, Yanworth and Eastington, 1960; Holy Trinity, Yeovil, 1964; Minehead, 1967. Fellow, St Paul's and St Mary's Colls, Cheltenham, 1954–. *Recreations:* church spotting, driving motor cars, listening to music. *Address:* 24 Colesbourne Road, Cheltenham, Glos GL51 6DL. *T:* Cheltenham 527311.

WARD, Christopher John; Editorial Director and Joint Managing Director, Redwood Publishing, since 1983; Director, Acorn Computer plc, since 1983; *b* 25 Aug. 1942; *s* of John Stanley Ward and Jacqueline Law-Hume Costin; *m* 1971, Fanny Brown; one *s* two *d. Educ:* King's Coll. Sch., Wimbledon. Successively on staff of Driffield Times, 1959, and Newcastle Evening Chronicle, 1960–63; Daily Mirror: reporter, 1963–65; sub-editor, 1965–66; feature writer and columnist, 1966–76; Assistant Editor: Sunday Mirror, 1976–79; Daily Mirror, 1979–81; Editor, Daily Express, 1981–83. *Publications:* How to Complain, 1974; Our Cheque is in the Post, 1980. *Recreations:* competition pistol shooting, fell walking. *Address:* 43 St Maur Road, SW6 4DR.

WARD, Christopher John Ferguson; solicitor; with Clark & Son, Reading, since 1965; *b* 26 Dec. 1942; *m* Janet Ward; one *s* one *d* and two *s* one *d* by former marr. *Educ:* Magdalen College Sch.; Law Society Sch. of Law. MP (C) Swindon, Oct. 1969–June 1970; contested (C) Eton and Slough, 1979. Mem., Berks CC, 1965–81 (Leader of the Council and Chm., Policy Cttee, 1979–81). Hon. Sec., United & Cecil Club, 1982–. *Address:* Ramblings, Maidenhead Thicket, Berks SL6 3QE. *T:* Littlewick Green 2577; (office) Reading 585320.

WARD, (Christopher) John (William); General Secretary, Association of First Division Civil Servants, since 1980; *b* 21 June 1942; *s* of Thomas Maxfield and Peggy Ward; *m*

1970, Diane Lelliott (separated 1982). *Educ:* Oundle Sch.; Corpus Christi Coll., Oxford (BA LitHum); Univ. of East Anglia (Graduate DipEcon). Overseas and Economic Intelligence Depts, Bank of England, 1965; General Secretary, Bank of England Staff Organisation, 1973. *Recreations:* opera, theatre, football. *Address:* Association of First Division Civil Servants, 2 Caxton Street, SW1H 0QH. *Club:* Swindon Town Supporters.

WARD, Rev. David Conisbee; Priest-in-Charge, Immanuel Church, Streatham Common, since 1984; *b* 7 Jan. 1933; *s* of late Sydney L. Ward and Ivy A. Ward; *m* 1958, Patricia Jeanette (*née* Nobes); one *s* one *d. Educ:* Kingston Grammar Sch.; St John's Coll., Cambridge (Scholar, MA). Asst Principal, Nat. Assistance Bd, 1956; Asst Private Sec. to Lord President of the Council and Minister for Science, 1960–61; Principal, Nat. Assistance Bd, 1961, Min. of Social Security, 1966, DHSS, 1968; Asst Sec., DHSS, 1970, Under Sec., 1976–83. Southwark Ordination Course, 1977–80; Deacon, 1980; Priest, 1981; Non-Stipendiary Curate, St Matthew, Surbiton, 1980–83; Curate, Immanuel Church, Streatham Common, 1983–84. *Recreations:* philately, Chelsea FC. *Address:* Immanuel House, 19 Streatham Common South, SW16. *T:* 01–764 5103. *Club:* Sion College.

WARD, Denzil Anthony Seaver, CMG 1967; retired Barrister, New Zealand; *b* Nelson, NZ, 26 March 1909; 3rd *s* of late Louis Ernest Ward, Civil Servant NZ Government and Secretary Geographic Board, and Theresa Ward (*née* Kilgour); *m* 1938, Mary Iredale Garland, *d* of late John Edwin Garland, Christchurch, NZ; three *d. Educ:* Christ's College and Cathedral Grammar Sch., Christchurch, NZ; Victoria Univ. of Wellington, NZ. BA 1928; LLB 1938; practised law as barrister and solicitor, 1938–42; Asst Law Draftsman, Law Drafting Office, 1942; First Asst, 1947; Law Draftsman, 1958–66; Counsel to Law Drafting Office and Compiler of Statutes, 1966–74. Lecturer in law subjects, Victoria Univ. of Wellington, NZ, 1944–45, 1949–55. Member: NZ Law Revision Commn, 1958–74; Public and Administrative Law Reform Cttee, 1966–80; Criminal Law Reform Cttee, 1971–83; Vice-Patron, Legal Research Foundation, 1965–68. Mem. Otaki and Porirua Trusts Bd, 1952–71, Chm., 1965–71; Mem. Papawai and Kaikokirikiri Trusts Bd, 1965–81, Chm., 1972–81. Foundation mem. and mem. Council, NZ Founders Soc., 1939–42; elected hon. life mem., 1941. Chm., Royal Wellington Choral Union, 1949–50; mem. Schola Cantorum, 1951–55. *Publications:* (jointly) Ward and Wild's Mercantile Law in New Zealand, 1947; (ed) NZ Statutes Reprint, 1908–57, vols 3–16; articles in legal periodicals. *Recreations:* music, reading, gardening, watching rugby and cricket. *Address:* 15 Plymouth Street, Karori, Wellington 5, New Zealand. *T:* 768–096.

WARD, Donald Albert; Secretary General, International Union of Credit and Investment Insurers (Berne Union), 1974–86; *b* 30 March 1920; *s* of Albert and Rosie Ward; *m* 1948, Maureen Molloy; five *s. Educ:* Brewery Road Elementary Sch.; Southend-on-Sea High Sch.; The Queen's Coll., Oxford. BA(Hons)(Maths). Served War, Indian Army (RIASC), 10th Indian Div., Middle East and Italy, 1940–45 (despatches). Min. of Food, 1946–53; Export Credits Guarantee Dept, 1953–74 (Under-Sec., 1971–74). *Address:* Lindisfarne, St Nicholas Hill, Leatherhead, Surrey. *Club:* United Oxford & Cambridge University.

WARD, General Sir Dudley, GCB 1959 (KCB 1957; CB 1945); KBE 1953 (CBE 1945); DSO 1944; *b* 27 Jan. 1905; *s* of L. H. Ward, Wimborne, Dorset; *m* 1st, 1933, Beatrice Constance (*d* 1962), *d* of Rev. T. F. Griffith, The Bourne, Farnham, Surrey; one *d*; 2nd, 1963, Joan Elspeth de Pechell, *d* of late Colonel D. C. Scott, CBE, Netherbury, Dorset. *Educ:* Wimborne Grammar Sch.; Royal Military Coll., Sandhurst. 2nd Lieut, Dorset Regt, 1929; Captain, The King's Regt, 1937. Served War of 1939–45 (DSO, CBE, CB); Director of Military Operations, War Office, 1947–48; Commandant, Staff Coll., Camberley, 1948–51; Commander of the 1st Corps, 1951–52; Deputy Chief of Imperial General Staff, 1953–56; Commander, Northern Army Group and Commander-in-Chief, British Army of the Rhine, 1957–Dec. 1959; Comdr in Chief, British Forces, Near East, 1960–62; Governor and Commander in Chief of Gibraltar, 1962–65. Colonel, King's Regt, 1947–57; Colonel Commandant, REME, 1958–63; ADC General to the Queen, 1959–61. DL Suffolk, 1968–84. *Recreation:* golf. *Address:* Wynney's Farmhouse, Dennington, Woodbridge, Suffolk. *T:* Badingham 663. *Club:* Army and Navy.

WARD, Edmund Fisher, CBE 1972; Architect; Member, Royal Fine Art Commission, 1974–83; Consultant (formerly Partner), Gollins Melvin Ward Partnership. *Address:* White Cottage, The Street, Chipperfield, near King's Langley, Hertfordshire WD4 9BH.

WARD, Edward; see Bangor, 7th Viscount.

WARD, Ven. Edwin James Greenfield, LVO 1963; Archdeacon of Sherborne, 1968–84; Archdeacon Emeritus and Canon Emeritus of Salisbury Cathedral, since 1985; Chaplain to the Queen, since 1955; *b* 26 Oct. 1919; *er s* of Canon F. G. Ward, MC, lately of Canberra, Australia; *m* 1946, Grizell Evelyn Buxton (*d* 1985); one *s* two *d. Educ:* St John's, Leatherhead; Christ's Coll., Cambridge (MA). Served King's Dragoon Guards, 1940; Reserve, 1946. Ordained 1948; Vicar of North Elmham, Norfolk, 1950–55; Chaplain, Royal Chapel, Windsor Great Park, 1955–67; Rector of West Stafford, 1967–84. Mem. of Council, Marlborough Coll., 1969–; Mem., Bd of Governors, Milton Abbey School, 1983–. *Recreation:* fishing. *Address:* Manor Cottage, Poxwell, Dorchester, Dorset. *T:* Warmwell 852062.

See also Rt Hon. J. Wakeham.

WARD, Air Cdre Ellacott Lyne Stephens, CB 1954; DFC 1939; RAF, retired; *b* 22 Aug. 1905; *s* of late Lt-Col E. L. Ward, CBE, IMS; *m* 1929, Sylvia Winifred Constance Etheridge (*d* 1974), *d* of late Lt-Col F. Etheridge, DSO, IA, and late Mrs Etheridge; one *s* one *d. Educ:* Bradfield; Cranwell. No 20 Sqdn, India, 1926–30; Engineering Course, and Engineering duties, UK, 1930–34; student, Army Staff Coll., Quetta, 1936–37; comd No 28 Sqdn, RAF, 1938–39; MAP, 1940–42; Instructor, RAF Staff Coll., 1942–43; Bomber Comd, 1943–44; Dep. Head, RAF Mission to Chinese Air Force Staff Coll., Chengtu, China, 1945–46; SASO, Burma, 1946–47; Air Ministry, 1947–49; Flying Training Comd, 1949–52; Head of British Services Mission to Burma, 1952–54; AOC No 64 (N) Group, Royal Air Force, 1954–57. Chinese Cloud and Banner, 1946; Chinese Chenyuan, 1946. *Recreation:* bookbinding. *Address:* Carousel, 37 Brownsea Road, Sandbanks, Poole, Dorset BH13 7QW. *T:* Canford Cliffs 709455.

WARD, Francis Alan Burnett, CBE 1964; PhD; Keeper, Department of Physics, Science Museum, London, SW7, 1945–70; *b* 5 March 1905; *o s* of late Herbert Ward, CBE, and late Eva Caroline (*née* Burnett); *m* 1953, E. Marianne Brown, Ilkley. *Educ:* Highgate Sch.; Sidney Sussex Coll., Cambridge. MA, PhD (Cantab), 1931. Research on nuclear physics at Cavendish Laboratory, Cambridge, 1927–31; Asst Keeper, The Science Museum, 1931; seconded to Air Ministry (Meteorological Office), 1939. Flt-Lieut, RAFVR (Meteorological Branch), 1943–45. In charge of Atomic Physics and Time Measurement sections, Science Museum, 1931–70. FBHI; FInstP; FMA. *Publications:* official Science Museum Handbooks on Time Measurement, 1936 and 1937, and later edns; Catalogue of European Scientific Instruments, British Museum, 1981. Various papers on atomic physics in Proc. Royal Society and Proc. Physical Soc. *Recreations:* bird-watching, gardening, photography, music. *Address:* Wendover, 8 Parkgate Avenue, Hadley Wood, Barnet, Herts EN4 0NR. *T:* 01–449 6880.

WARD, Frank D.; see Dixon Ward.

WARD, Hubert, MA; JP; Headmaster of the King's School, Ely, since 1970; b 26 Sept. 1931; s of Allan Miles Ward and Joan Mary Ward; m 1958, Elizabeth Cynthia Fearn Bechervaise; one s two d. Educ: Westminster Sch.; Trinity Coll., Cambridge. Asst Master (Maths), Geelong C of E Grammar Sch., Victoria, 1955–66; Asst Master (Maths), Westminster Sch., London, 1966–69. Mem. (L.) Cambs CC, 1985–. JP Cambs, 1976. Publication: (with K. Lewis) Starting Statistics, 1969. Recreations: rowing, sailing, bird-watching. Address: The King's School, Ely, Cambridgeshire. T: Ely 2824.

WARD, Prof. Ian Macmillan, FRS 1983; FInstP; Professor of Physics, University of Leeds, since 1970; b 9 April 1928; s of Harry Ward and Joan Moodie (née Burt); m 1960, Margaret (née Linley); two s one d. Educ: Royal Grammar Sch., Newcastle upon Tyne; Magdalen Coll., Oxford (MA, DPhil). FInstP 1965; FPRI 1974. Technical Officer, ICI Fibres, 1954–61; seconded to Division of Applied Mathematics, Brown Univ., USA, 1961–62; Head of Basic Physics Section, ICI Fibres, 1962–65, ICI Research Associate, 1964; Sen. Lectr in Physics of Materials, Univ. of Bristol, 1965–69; Prof. of Physics, Univ. of Leeds, 1970–, Chm. of Dept, 1975–78. Secretary, Polymer Physics Gp, Inst. of Physics, 1964–71, Chm. 1971–75; Chairman, Macromolecular Physics Gp, European Physical Soc., 1976–81; Pres., British Soc. of Rheology, 1984–. A. A. Griffith Medal, 1982; S. G. Smith Meml Medal, Textile Inst., 1984. Publications: Mechanical Properties of Solid Polymers, 1971, 2nd edn 1983; (ed) Structure and Properties of Oriented Polymers, 1975; (ed jtly) Ultra High Modulus Polymers, 1979; contribs to Polymer, Jl of Polymer Science, Jl of Materials Science, Proc. Royal Soc., etc. Recreations: music, walking. Address: Kirskill, 2 Creskeld Drive, Bramhope, Leeds LS16 9EL. T: Leeds 673637.

WARD, Ivor William, (Bill), OBE 1968; independent televison producer and director, since 1982; Deputy Managing Director, Associated Television (Network) Ltd, 1974–77; b 19 Jan. 1916; s of Stanley James Ward and Emily Ward; m 1st, 1940, Patricia Aston; two s one d; 2nd, 1970, Betty Nichols; one step s. Educ: Hoe Grammar Sch., Plymouth. Asst Engr, BBC Radio Plymouth, 1932; Technical Asst, BBC Experimental TV Service, Alexandra Palace, 1936; Maintenance Engr, BBC TV London, 1937. Instructor Radar, REME and Military Coll. of Science, 1939–45. Studio Manager, BBC TV, 1946; Producer, BBC TV, 1947–55; Head of Light Entertainment, ATV (Network) ITV, 1955–61; Production Controller, ATV, 1961–63; Executive Controller and Production Controller, ATV, 1963–67; Director of Programmes, ATV, 1968–76. Chm., ITV Network Sports Cttee, 1972–77; Head of Ops Gp, EBU: World Cup 1978, 1977–78; Moscow Olympics 1980, 1978–82; Exec. producer, Highway series, ITV, 1983. FRSA. Recreations: sport, golf, fishing, motor sport and motor cars, photography, music. Address: 50 Frith Street, W1.

WARD, John; see Ward, C. J. W.

WARD, Most Rev. John Aloysius; see Cardiff, Archbishop of, (RC).

WARD, Prof. John Clive, FRS 1965; Professor, Macquarie University, Sydney, NSW, 1967–84, now Emeritus; b 1 Aug. 1924; s of Joseph William Ward and Winifred Palmer. Educ: Bishops Stortford Coll.; Merton Coll., Oxford. Member, Inst. for Advanced Study, Princeton, 1951–52, 1955–56, 1960–61; Professor of Physics, Carnegie Inst. of Technology, Pittsburgh, 1959–60; The Johns Hopkins University, Baltimore, 1961–66. Hughes Medal, Royal Soc., 1983. Publications: various articles on particle theory and statistical mechanics. Recreations: ski-ing, music. Address: 16 Fern Street, Pymble, NSW 2073, Australia.

WARD, John Devereux, CBE 1973; BSc; CEng, FICE, FIStructE; MP (C) Poole, since 1979; b 8 March 1925; s of late Thomas Edward and Evelyn Victoria Ward; m 1955, Jean Miller Aitken; one s one d. Educ: Romford County Technical Sch.; Univ. of St Andrews (BSc). Navigator, RAF, 1943–47; student, 1949–53. Employed, Consulting Engineers, 1953–58, Taylor Woodrow Ltd, 1958–79; Man. Dir, Taylor Woodrow Arcon, Arcon Building Exports, 1976–78. PPS to Financial Sec. to Treasury, 1984–86. UK Rep. to Council of Europe, 1983–. Chm., Wessex Area Conservatives, 1966–69; Conservative Party: Mem., Nat. Union Exec., 1965–78 (Mem., Gen. Purposes Cttee, 1966–72, 1975–78); Mem., Central Bd of Finance, 1969–78; Vice-Chm., Cons. Trade and Industry Cttee, 1983–84. Address: 54 Parkstone Road, Poole, Dorset BH15 2PX. T: Poole 674771.

WARD, Sir John (Guthrie), GCMG 1967 (KCMG 1956; CMG 1947); b 3 March 1909; o s of late Herbert John Ward and Alice Ward (née Guthrie); m 1st, 1933, Bettine (d 1941), d of late Col Sydney Hankey; one s one d; 2nd, 1942, Daphne (d 1983), d of late Captain Hon. A. S. E. Mulholland and late Joan, Countess of Cavan; two d. Educ: Wellington Coll.; Pembroke Coll., Cambridge (History Schol.). BA 1929, Hon. Fellow 1976; Member of University Air Squadron. Entered Diplomatic Service, 1931; served Foreign Office and British Embassies, Baghdad (1932–34) and Cairo (1938–40); British Representative on League of Nations Cttee for settlement of Assyrians, 1935–37. Second Sec., 1936; First Sec., 1941; Mem. of UK Delegns to Moscow confs, 1943–44–45 and Potsdam conf., 1945; Counsellor and Head of UN Dept, Foreign Office, 1946; Counsellor, British Embassy, Rome, 1946–49; Civilian Member of Directing Staff of Imperial Defence Coll., London, 1950; Dep. UK High Comr in Germany, 1951–54; Dep. Under-Sec. of State, Foreign Office, 1954–56; British Ambassador to Argentina, 1957–61; British Ambassador to Italy, 1962–66; retired from HM Diplomatic Service, 1967. Chairman, British-Italian Soc., 1967–74. Mem. Council, RSPCA, 1970–75; Pres., ISPA. Recreations: history, gardening. Address: Lenox, St Margarets Bay, near Dover. Club: Royal Automobile.

WARD, Prof. John Manning, AO 1983; FASSA; FAHA; FRAHS; Vice-Chancellor and Principal, University of Sydney, since 1981; b 6 July 1919; s of Alexander Thomson Ward and Mildred Boughay Davis; m 1951, Patricia Bruce Webb; two d. Educ: Fort Street Boys' High Sch.; Univ. of Sydney (MA, LLB). FASSA 1954; FAHA 1969; FRAHS 1979. Challis Prof. of History, Sydney Univ., 1949–82; Dean, Faculty of Arts, 1962; Pro Dean, 1970–71; Chairman: Professorial Bd, 1974–75; Academic Bd, 1975–77; Dominion Fellow, St John's Coll., Cambridge, 1951; Vis. Prof., Yale Univ., 1963; Vis. Fellow, All Souls Coll., Oxford, 1968; Smuts Vis. Fellow, Cambridge, 1972. Trustee, NSW Public Library, 1968–69; Mem., CL Libr., NSW, 1970–82; Chm., Archives Authority, NSW, 1979–82 (Mem. 1961–82); Chm., NSW State Cancer Council, 1981–82; Member: Parramatta Hosps Bd, 1982–86; Bd, Royal Alexandra Hosp. for Children, 1982–; Bd, Royal Prince Alfred Hosp., 1986–; Menzie's Sch. of Health Res., 1986–. Publications: British Policy in the South Pacific, 1948, 3rd edn 1976; (jtly) Trusteeship in the Pacific, 1949; contrib. Australia (UN Series, Calif), 1947; Earl Grey and the Australian Colonies 1846–57, 1958; contrib. The Pattern of Australian Culture, 1963; Empire in the Antipodes, c 1840–1860, 1966; Changes in Britain 1919–1957, 1968; contrib. Historians at Work, 1973; Colonial Self-Government, The British Experience 1759–1856, 1976; James Macarthur: Colonial Conservative 1798–1867, 1981. Recreations: music, railways. Address: The University of Sydney, New South Wales 2006, Australia. T: (02) 692 2222. Club: Australian (Sydney).

WARD, John Stanton, CBE 1985; RA 1965 (ARA 1956); VPRP; b 10 Oct. 1917; s of Russell Stanton and Jessie Elizabeth Ward; m 1950, Alison Christine Mary Williams; four s twin d. Educ: St Owen's School, Hereford; Royal College of Art. Royal Engineers, 1939–46. Vogue Magazine, 1948–52. Has held exhibitions at Agnews Gallery and Maas Gallery. Hon. DLitt. Recreation: book illustration. Address: Bilting Court, Bilting, Ashford, Kent. T: Wye 812478. Clubs: Athenæum, Buck's, Harry's Bar.

WARD, Prof. (John Stephen) Keith; Professor of History and Philosophy of Religion, King's College London, since 1985; b 22 Aug. 1938; s of John George Ward and Evelyn (née Simpson); m 1963, Marian Trotman; one s one d. Educ: Universities of Wales and Oxford. BA Wales, BLitt Oxon; MA Cantab. Ordained priest of Church of England, 1972. Lecturer in Logic, Univ. of Glasgow, 1964–69; Lectr in Philosophy, Univ. of St Andrews, 1969–71; Lectr in Philosophy of Religion, Univ. of London, 1971–75; Dean of Trinity Hall, Cambridge, 1975–82. F. D. Maurice Prof. of Moral and Social Theology, Univ. of London, 1982–85. Publications: Ethics and Christianity, 1970; Kant's View of Ethics, 1972; The Divine Image, 1976; The Concept of God, 1977; The Promise, 1981; Rational Theology and the Creativity of God, 1982; Holding Fast to God, 1982. Recreations: music, walking. Address: 18 Leyborne Park, Kew, Richmond, Surrey TW9 3HA. T: 01–940 6667.

WARD, Joseph Haggitt; b 7 July 1926; s of Joseph G. and Gladys Ward; m 1961, Anthea Clemo; one s one d. Educ: St Olave's Grammar School; Sidney Sussex College, Cambridge. Asst Principal, Min. of National Insurance, 1951; Private Sec. to Minister of Social Security, 1966–68; Asst Sec., 1968; Min. of Housing, later DoE, 1969–72; DHSS, 1972; Under-Sec. (pensions and nat. insce contributions), DHSS, 1976–86. Recreations: Eton fives, music. Address: 34 Uffington Road, SE27 0ND. T: 01–670 1732.

WARD, Sir Joseph James Laffey, 4th Bt cr 1911; b 11 Nov. 1946; s of Sir Joseph George Davidson Ward, 3rd Bt, and of Joan Mary Haden, d of Major Thomas J. Laffey, NZSC; S father, 1970; m 1968, Robyn Allison, d of William Maitland Martin, Rotorua, NZ; one s one d. Heir: s Joseph James Martin Ward, b 20 Feb. 1971. Address: Westcoast Rd, RD2, Kankapakapa, Westport, NZ.

WARD, Keith; see Ward, J. S. K.

WARD, Malcolm Beverley; His Honour Judge Malcolm Ward; a Circuit Judge, Midland and Oxford Circuit, since 1979; b 3 May 1931; s of Edgar and Dora Mary Ward; m 1958, Muriel Winifred, d of Dr E. D. M. Wallace, Perth; two s two d. Educ: Wolverhampton Grammar Sch.; St John's Coll., Cambridge (Open Mathematical Schol.; MA, LLM). Called to the Bar, Inner Temple, 1956; practised Oxford (later Midland and Oxford) Circuit; a Recorder of the Crown Court, 1974–79. Governor, Wolverhampton Grammar Sch., 1972– (Chm., 1981–). Recreations: golf, music, (in theory) horticulture. Address: 1 Fountain Court, Birmingham B4 6DR.

WARD, Martyn Eric; His Honour Judge Ward; a Circuit Judge since 1972; b 10 Oct. 1927; 3rd s of Arthur George Ward, DSM and Dorothy Ward (née Perkins); m 1st, 1957, Rosaleen Iona Soloman; one d; 2nd, 1966, Rosanna Maria; two s. Royal Navy, 1945–48. Called to Bar, Lincoln's Inn, 1955. Recreations: ski-ing, tennis, swimming. Address: c/o County Court, Falkland House, 25 Southway, Colchester, Essex; The House on the Heath, Fordham Heath, Colchester, Essex CO3 5TL. T: Colchester 240624.

WARD, Michael Jackson, CBE 1980; Assistant Director-General, British Council, since 1985; b 16 Sept. 1931; s of Harry Ward, CBE, and of late Dorothy Julia Ward (née Clutterbuck); m 1955, Eileen Patricia Foster; one s one d. Educ: Drayton Manor Grammar Sch.; University Coll. London (BA); Univ. of Freiburg; Corpus Christi Coll., Oxford. HM Forces, 1953–55; 2nd Lieut Royal Signals. Admin. Officer, HMOCS, serving as Dist Comr and Asst Sec. to Govt, Gilbert and Ellice Is; British Council, 1961–: Schs Recruitment Dept, 1961–64; Regional Rep., Sarawak, 1964–68; Dep. Rep., Pakistan, 1968–70; Dir, Appointments Services Dept, 1970–72; Dir, Personnel Dept, 1972–75; Controller, Personnel and Appts Div., 1975–77; Representative, Italy, 1977–81; Controller, Home Div., 1981–85. Recreations: music, golf. Address: The British Council, 10 Spring Gardens, SW1A 2BN. T: 01–930 8466. Club: National Liberal.

WARD, Michael John; Public Affairs Officer, Gas Consumers' Council, since 1986; b 7 April 1931; s of Stanley William Ward and Margaret Annie Ward; m 1953, Lilian Lomas; two d. Educ: Mawney Road Jun. Mixed Sch., Romford; Royal Liberty Sch., Romford; Bungay Grammar Sch.; Univ. of Manchester. BA (Admin). MIPR. Education Officer, RAF, 1953–57; Registrar, Chartered Inst. of Secretaries, 1958–60; S. J. Noel-Brown & Co. Ltd: O&M consultant to local authorities, 1960–61; Local Govt Officer to Labour Party, 1961–65; Public Relns consultant to local authorities, 1965–70; Press Officer, ILEA, 1970–74 and 1979–80; Public Relns Officer, London Borough of Lewisham, 1980–84; Dir of Information, ILEA, 1984–86. Contested (Lab) Peterborough, 1966, 1970, Feb. 1974; MP (Lab) Peterborough, Oct. 1974–1979; PPS to Sec. of State for Educn and Science, 1975–76, to Minister for Overseas Develt, 1976, to Minister of State, FCO, 1976–79. Sponsored Unfair Contract Terms Act, 1977. Prospective parly cand. (SDP), Tonbridge and Malling, 1986–. Councillor, Borough of Romford, 1958–65; London Borough of Havering: Councillor, 1964–78; Alderman, 1971–78; Leader of Council, 1971–74. Labour Chief Whip, London Boroughs Assoc., 1968–71; Member: Essex River Authority, 1964–71; Greenwich DHA, 1982–85; Greenwich and Bexley FPC, 1982–85; Hon. Treas., GLAA, 1969–71; Pres., London Govt Public Relations Assoc., 1977–79. Recreations: gardens, music, reading, travel. Address: The Gateways, Brenchley Road, Horsmonden, Tonbridge, Kent TN12 8DN; (office) 162 Regent Street, W1R 5TB.

WARD, Michael Phelps, CBE 1983; FRCS; FRGS; Consultant Surgeon: City and East London Area Health Authority (Teaching), since 1964; St Andrew's Hospital, Bow, since 1964; Newham Hospital, since 1983; Lecturer in Clinical Surgery, London Hospital Medical College, since 1975; b 26 March 1925; s of late Wilfrid Arthur Ward, CMG, MC and Norah Anne Phelps; m 1957, Felicity Jane Ewbank; one s. Educ: Marlborough Coll., Wilts; Peterhouse, Cambridge (Ironmongers' Co. Exhibn); London Hosp. Med. Coll. BA Hons Cantab 1945, MA 1961; MB BChir 1949, MD 1968. FRCS 1955. Ho. Surg., Surgical Registrar, Sen. Surgical Registrar, London Hosp.; Asst Resident, Royal Victoria Hosp., Montreal, Canada; Consultant Surg., Poplar Hosp., E14, 1964–75; Hunterian Prof., RCS, 1954. Served RAMC, Captain, 1950–52. Fellow, Assoc. of Surgs of Gt Britain; FRSM. Court of Assts, Soc. of Apothecaries, 1986. Mount Everest Reconnaissance Expedn, 1951; Mount Everest Expedn, 1953 (1st Ascent); Scientific Expedn to Everest Region, 1960–61 (Leader, 1st Winter Ascents of Amadablam and other peaks); Scientific Expedns to Bhutan Himal, 1964 and 1965; scientific and mountaineering expedn to Southern Xinjian, China, 1980–81; Royal Soc./Chinese Acad. of Sciences Tibet Geotraverse, 1985. FRGS 1964. Dickson Asia Lectr, RGS, 1966, 1985; Cuthbert Peek Award, RGS, 1973; Founder's (Royal) Medal, RGS, 1982; Cullum Medal, Amer. Geog. Soc., 1954. Chm., Mount Everest Foundn, 1978–80. Publications: Mountaineers' Companion, 1966; In this Short Span, 1972; Mountain Medicine, 1975; many scientific and medical papers on the effects of great altitude, exposure to cold, and on exercise; also on exploratory journeys to Nepal, Bhutan, Chinese Central Asia and Tibet. *Recreations:* mountaineering, ski-ing. *Clubs:* Athenæum, Alpine (Vice-Pres., 1968–69).

WARD, Neville; *see* Ward, A. N.

WARD, Air Vice-Marshal Peter Alexander; General Manager, Bromley Health Authority, since 1985; *b* 26 Jan. 1930; *s* of Arthur Charles Ward and Laura Mary (*née* Squires); *m* 1963, Patricia Louise (*née* Robertson); two *s*. *Educ:* Woking Grammar School. Joined RAF, 1947; Flying and Staff appointments; OC 511 Sqdn, 1968–70; jssc 1970; ndc 1971; Station Comdr, RAF Brize Norton, 1974–75; Senior Air Staff Officer, HQ 38 Group, 1976–79; rcds 1979; Dir Gen., RAF Training, 1980–82; Dep. COS (Ops), HQ Allied Air Forces Central Europe, 1982–84. *Address:* Whiteladies, 49 Marlings Park Avenue, Chislehurst, Kent. *Club:* Royal Air Force.

WARD, Maj.-Gen. Sir Philip (John Newling), KCVO 1976; CBE 1972; DL; *b* 10 July 1924; *s* of George William Newling Ward and Mary Florence Ward; *m* 1948, Pamela Ann Glennie; two *s* two *d*. Commnd Welsh Guards, 1943; Adjt, RMA Sandhurst, 1960–62; Bde Major, Household Bde, 1962–65; Comdg 1st Bn Welsh Guards, 1965–67; Comdr Land Forces, Gulf, 1969–71; GOC London Dist and Maj.-Gen. comdg Household Div., 1973–76; Comdt, RMA, 1976–79. Communar of Chichester Cathedral, 1980–83. Dir, Public Affairs, Internat. Distillers and Vintners (UK), 1980–; Director: W & A Gilbey, 1983–; Morgan Furze, 1983–; Southern Reg., Lloyds Bank, 1983–. Chairman: Queen Alexandra Hosp. Home; Royal Soldiers Daughters School, 1980–83; Governor and Comdt, Church Lads and Church Girls Bde., 1980–86. Freeman, City of London, 1976. DL West Sussex, 1981, High Sheriff, 1985–86. *Recreation:* gardening. *Address:* The Old Rectory, Patching, near Worthing, West Sussex. *Clubs:* Cavalry and Guards, Buck's.

WARD, Reginald; *see* Ward, A. J. R.

WARD, Reginald George; Director, Business Statistics Office, Department of Trade and Industry, since 1986; *b* 6 July 1942; *s* of Thomas George and Ada May Ward; *m* 1964, Chandan Mistry; two *s* one *d*. *Educ:* Leicester, Aberdeen and Oxford Universities. Lectr in Economics, St Andrews Univ., 1965; Analyst, National Cash Register, 1969; Economist, ICL, 1970; DTI, 1971; Chief Statistician: HM Treasury, 1978; Cabinet Office, 1982. *Recreation:* sailing. *Address:* 2 Llandaff Chase, Llandaff, Cardiff. *T:* Cardiff 553957.

WARD, Gen. Sir Richard (Erskine), GBE 1976; KCB 1971 (CB 1969); DSO 1943 and Bar, 1943; MC 1942; Chief of Personnel and Logistics, Ministry of Defence, 1974–76, retired; *b* 15 Oct. 1917; *o s* of late John Petty Ward and Gladys Rose Ward (*née* Marsh-Dunn); *m* 1947, Stella Elizabeth, 2nd *d* of late Brig. P. N. Ellis, RA, and Mrs Rachel Ellis; two *s* two *d*. *Educ:* Marlborough Coll.; RMC, Sandhurst. Commissioned Royal Tank Corps, 1937; served War of 1939–45 (despatches thrice); 5th Royal Tank Regt, 1939–43; Staff Coll., Camberley, 1944; Bde Major, 4th Armoured Bde, 1944; CO Westminster Dragoons, 1945; Korea with 1st Royal Tank Regt, 1952 (despatches); Lt-Col Chiefs of Staff Secretariat, 1955; CO 3 Royal Tank Regt, 1957; idc 1961; on staff of Chief of Defence Staff, 1962; comd 20 Armoured Bde, 1963; GOC 1st Division 1965–67; Vice-Adjutant-General, 1968–70; Cmdr British Forces, Hong Kong, 1970–73. Maj.-Gen., 1965; Lt-Gen., 1970; Gen., 1974. Col Comdt RTR, 1970–75. Dep. Commonwealth Pres., Royal Life Saving Soc., 1976–82. Croix de Guerre, with palm, 1940; Chevalier, Order of Leopold II, with palm, 1945. *Address:* Bellsburn, 18 Lower Street, Rode, Somerset BA3 6PU. *Club:* Army and Navy.

WARD, Maj.-Gen. Robert William, MBE 1972; GOC Western District, since 1986; *b* 17 Oct. 1935; *s* of late Lt-Col William Denby Ward and Monica Thérèse Ward (*née* Collett-White); *m* 1966, Lavinia Dorothy Cramsie; two *s* one *d*. *Educ:* Rugby School; RMA Sandhurst. Commissioned Queen's Bays (later 1st Queen's Dragoon Guards), 1955; served Jordan, Libya, BAOR, Borneo and Persian Gulf; MA to C-in-C BAOR, 1973–75; CO 1st Queen's Dragoon Guards, 1975–77; Col GS Staff Coll., 1977–79; Comdr 22 Armd Brigade, 1979–82; RCDS Canada, 1982–83; Asst Chief of Staff, Northern Army Group, 1983–86. *Recreations:* gardening, outdoor sports, country pursuits. *Address:* Wrockwardine Hall, Wrockwardine, Telford, Shropshire TF6 5DG. *T:* Telford 42878. *Clubs:* MCC, I Zingari.

WARD, Robin William; Director-General, West Yorkshire Passenger Transport Executive, 1976–82; *b* 14 Jan. 1931; *s* of William Frederick and Elsie Gertrude Ward; *m* 1974, Jean Catherine Laird; three *s*. *Educ:* Colston's Sch., Bristol; University Coll. London. BScEcon, 1st Cl. Hons. Pilot Officer/Flying Officer, RAF Educn Br., 1954–55. Various posts, London Transport Exec., 1955–67; seconded to Brit. Transport Staff Coll. as mem. staff and latterly Asst Principal (incl. course at Harvard Business Sch.), 1967–70; Industrial Relations Officer, London Transport Exec., 1970–74; Dir of Personnel, W Yorks Passenger Transport Exec., 1974–76. *Recreations:* Scottish country dancing; trying to learn the piano. *Address:* 29 Stanley Street, Palmwoods, Qld 4555, Australia.

WARD, Roy Livingstone, QC 1972; **His Honour Judge Roy Ward;** a Circuit Judge, since 1979; *b* 31 Aug. 1925; *m* 1972, Barbara Anne (*née* Brockbank); one *s* one *d*. *Educ:* Taunton Sch.; Pembroke Coll., Cambridge. BA(Hons). Served RAF, 1943–47. Called to Bar, Middle Temple, 1950. A Recorder of the Crown Court, 1972–79. *Address:* Tethers End, Shelsley Drive, Colwall, Worcs. *Club:* United Oxford & Cambridge University.

WARD, Rt. Rev. Simon B.; *see* Barrington-Ward.

WARD, Sir Terence George, Kt 1971; CBE 1961 (MBE 1945); Dean of the Faculty of Dental Surgery, Royal College of Surgeons, 1965–68; *b* 16 Jan. 1906; *m* 1931, Elizabeth Ambrose Wilson (*d* 1981); one *s* one *d*. *Educ:* Edinburgh. Mem., SE Metropolitan Regional Hosp. Bd; Exmr, DSRCSEd, FDRCSIre. Pres., Internat. Assoc. Oral Surgeons; Past Pres., British Association of Oral Surgeons; Consulting Oral Surgeon to the Royal Navy; Consulting Dental Surgeon: to the British Army, 1954–71, Emeritus 1971; to the Royal Air Force; to Dept of Health and Social Security; to the Queen Victoria Hospital, East Grinstead. LRCP, LRCSEd 1928; LRFPS, 1930; LDS (Edinburgh) 1928; FDSRCS 1948; FACD (USA) 1959; FACDSurgeons; FFDRCS Ire., 1964; Hon. FDSRCSE, 1966; Hon. FRCCD, 1966. DDSc, Melbourne, 1963. Mem., SA Dental Assoc.; Hon. Member: Amer. Soc. Oral Surgeons; Dutch Soc. Oral Surgeons; Hon. Fellow: Scandinavian Assoc. Oral Surgeons; Spanish Assoc. Oral Surgeons. *Publication:* The Dental Treatment of Maxillo-facial Injuries, 1956. *Recreation:* golf. *Address:* 22 Marina Court Avenue, Bexhill-on-Sea, East Sussex. *T:* Bexhill-on-Sea 4760.

WARD, Thomas William, ARCA 1949; RE 1955; RWS 1957; sometime Course Director, Illustration, Harrow College of Technology and Art; painter in water colour and oil colour, draughtsman, engraver, illustrator; *b* 8 Nov. 1918; *s* of John B. Ward, Master Stationer, and Lilly B. Ward (*née* Hunt), Sheffield; *m* Joan Palmer, ARCA, *d* of F. N. Palmer, Blackheath; one *s* one *d*. *Educ:* Nether Edge Grammar Sch., Sheffield; Sheffield Coll. of Art (part-time); Royal Coll. of Art, 1946–49, Silver Medal, 1949, Postgrad. Scholarship, 1949–50. Cadet, Merchant Service, 1935–36; stationer, 1936–39; Military service, 1939–46: commissioned N Staffs Regt, 1942; GSO3 1944–46. *One Man Exhibitions include:* Walker Gall., 1957, 1960; Wakefield City Art Gall., 1962; Shipley Art Gall., 1962; Middlesbrough Art Gall., 1963; St John's Coll., York, 1965; Bohun Gall., Henley, 1974; Digby Gall., Colchester, 1981. *Group Exhibitions include:* Leicester Gall.; Kensington Gall.; Zwemmer Gall.; Bohun Gall. *Open Exhibitions include:* RA, RSA, NEAC, London Group, RSMA, and in Japan, USA, S Africa, NZ. *Important purchases include:* S London Art Gall.; V&A; Nat. Gall. of NZ; Leicester, Oxford and Durham Univs; Arts Council; Contemp. Art Soc.; Bowes Mus.; Graves Art Gall.; Rochdale Art Gall.; Lord Clark. *Illustrations include:* Colman Prentis Varley; Shell Mex; Editions Lausanne. Designer of theatre properties, Tom Arnold Ice Show. *Recreation:* sailing. *Address:* Hollydene, Ipswich Road, Holbrook, Ipswich IP9 2QT.

WARD, William Alan H.; *see* Heaton-Ward.

WARD, William Alec; HM Diplomatic Service, retired; *b* 27 Nov. 1928; *s* of William Leslie Ward and Gladys Ward; *m* 1955, Sheila Joan Hawking; two *s* two *d*. *Educ:* King's Coll. Sch., Wimbledon; Christ Church, Oxford. HM Forces, 1947–49. Colonial Office, 1952; Private Sec. to Permanent Under-Sec., 1955–57; Singapore, 1960–64; seconded to CRO, 1963; Karachi, 1964–66; Islamabad, 1966–68; joined HM Diplomatic Service, 1968; FCO, 1968–71; Salisbury, 1971–72; Dep. High Comr, Colombo, 1973–76; High Comr, Mauritius, 1977–81. *Recreations:* music, walking. *Address:* Nyewoods, Elm Road, Horsell, Woking, Surrey.

WARD, William Ernest Frank, CMG 1945; *b* 24 Dec. 1900; *s* of W. H. Ward, Borough Treasurer, Battersea; *m* 1926, Sylvia Grace, *d* of Arthur Clayton Vallance, Mansfield, Notts; no *c*. *Educ:* LCC elementary school; Mercers' Sch.; Dulwich Coll.; Lincoln Coll., Oxford (BLitt, MA); Ridley Hall, Cambridge (Diploma in Education). Master, Achimota Coll., Gold Coast, 1924; Director of Education, Mauritius, 1940; Deputy Educational Adviser, Colonial Office, 1945–56. Editor, Oversea Education, 1946–63. Member of UK delegation to seven general conferences of UNESCO and many other international meetings on education. *Publications:* History of Ghana, 1967 (originally published as History of the Gold Coast, 1948); Educating Young Nations, 1959; Fraser of Trinity and Achimota, 1965; The Royal Navy and the Slavers, 1969; various historical works and educational textbooks. *Recreations:* music, walking. *Address:* Flat 19, Ormsby, Stanley Road, Sutton, Surrey SM2 6TJ. *T:* 01–661 2878.

WARD, William Kenneth, CMG 1977; Under-Secretary, Department of Trade, 1974–78, retired; *b* 20 Jan. 1918; *e s* of late Harold and Emily Ward; *m* 1949, Victoria Emily, *d* of late Ralph Perkins, Carcavelos, Portugal; three *s* one *d*. *Educ:* Queen Elizabeth's Grammar Sch., Ashbourne; Trinity Coll., Cambridge. 1st class Hons Modern and Medieval Langs Tripos. Entered Ministry of Supply, 1939; Board of Trade, 1955; HM Principal Trade Commissioner, Vancouver, BC, 1959–63; Under-Sec., BoT, 1966–69, Min. of Technology, later DTI and Dept of Trade, 1969–; Sec., BOTB, 1973. *Recreation:* gardening. *Address:* 31 Plough Lane, Purley, Surrey. *T:* 01–660 2462.

WARD-BOOTH, Maj.-Gen. John Antony, OBE 1971; Secretary, Eastern Wessex Territorial and Auxiliary Volunteer Reserve Association, since 1982; *b* 18 July 1927; *s* of Rev. J. Ward-Booth and Mrs E. M. Ward-Booth; *m* 1952, Margaret Joan Hooper; two *s* two *d*. *Educ:* Worksop College, Notts. Joined Army, 1945; commnd into Worcestershire Regt in India, 1946; served India and Middle East, 1946–48; regular commn Bedfordshire and Hertfordshire Regt, 1948; served BAOR, Far East, Nigeria and Congo, 1950–63, trans. to Parachute Regt, 1963; commanded 3rd Bn, Parachute Regt, 1967–69; Hong Kong, 1969–70; Comdr, 16 Parachute Bde, 1970–73; Nat. Defence Coll., Canada, 1973–74; DAG, HQ BAOR, 1974–75; Dir, Army Air Corps, 1976–79; GOC Western District, 1979–82. Dep. Col, Royal Anglian Regt, 1982–. Governor: Enham Village Centre, 1982–; Clayesmore Sch., Dorset, 1985–. *Recreations:* sailing, golf, squash, cricket. *Address:* 22 Winchester Gardens, Andover, Hants SP10 2EH. *T:* Andover 54317. *Club:* Army and Navy.

WARD-JACKSON, Mrs (Audrey) Muriel; *b* 30 Oct. 1914; *d* of late William James Jenkins and Alice Jenkins (*née* Glyde); *m* 1946, George Ralph Norman Ward-Jackson (*d* 1982); no *c*. *Educ:* Queenswood, Hatfield, Herts; Lady Margaret Hall, Oxford (MA). Home Civil Service (Ministries of Works, Town and Country Planning, Housing and Local Government, and HM Treasury): Asst Principal, 1937; Principal, 1942; Asst Sec., 1946–55. A Director (concerned mainly with Finance), John Lewis Partnership, 1955–74; John Lewis Partnership Ltd: Dir, 1957–74; Dir, John Lewis Properties Ltd, 1969–74; Chm., John Lewis Partnership Pensions Trust, 1964–74. On Civil Service Arbitration Tribunal, 1959–64; Chm., Consumers Cttees (Agric. Marketing), 1971–75; Member: Nat. Savings Review Cttee, 1971–73; Royal Commn on Standards of Conduct in Public Life, 1974–76. A Governor, British Film Inst., 1962–65; Mem. Council, Bedford Coll., London Univ., 1967–72. *Recreation:* swimming. *Address:* 195 Cranmer Court, Whiteheads Grove, Chelsea SW3 3HG. *T:* 01–581 1926. *Clubs:* Lansdowne, Naval and Military.

WARD THOMAS, Gwyn Edward, CBE 1973; DFC; Chairman: Ward Thomas Associates; British Cable Services Ltd; Worldwide Television Associates; Director, Tyne Tees Television; Robert Vince Advertising; *b* 1 Aug. 1923; *o s* of William J. and Constance Thomas; *m* 1945, Patricia Cornelius; one *d*. *Educ:* Bloxham Sch.; The Lycée, Rouen. Served RAF, 1 Group Bomber Command and 229 Group Transport Command, 1941–46. Granada Television, 1955–61; Man. Dir, Grampian Television, 1961–67; Man. Dir, 1967–73, Dep. Chm., 1973–81, Yorkshire Television; Man. Dir, 1970–84, Chm., 1976–84, Trident Television. Chairman: Castlewood Investments Ltd, 1969–83; Don Robinson Holdings Ltd, 1969–83; Watts & Corry Ltd, 1969–83; Trident Casinos, 1982–84; Pres., Trident Independent Television Enterprises SA, 1969–. British Bureau of Television Advertising: Dir, 1966; Chm., 1968–70; Mem. Council, Independent Television Companies Assoc., 1961–76 (Chairman: Labour Relations Cttee, 1967; Network Programme Cttee, 1971); Mem., British Screen Adv. Council, 1985–. *Recreations:* ski-ing, boats, photography. *Address:* 23 Brook's Mews, W1.

WARDALE, Sir Geoffrey (Charles), KCB 1979 (CB 1974); Second Permanent Secretary, Department of the Environment, 1978–80; *b* 29 Nov. 1919; *m* 1944, Rosemary Octavia Dyer; one *s* one *d*. *Educ:* Altrincham Grammar Sch.; Queens' Coll., Cambridge (Schol.). Army Service, 1940–41. Joined Ministry of War Transport as Temp. Asst Princ., 1942; Private Sec. to Perm. Sec., 1946; Princ., 1948; Asst Sec., 1957; Under-Sec., Min. of Transport, later DoE, 1966; Dep. Sec., 1972. Led inquiry: into the Open Structure in the Civil Service (The Wardale Report), 1981; into cases of fraud and corruption in PSA, 1982–83. Mem. Council, Univ. of Sussex, 1986–; Chm., Brighton Coll. Council, 1985–. *Recreations:* transport history, painting, listening to music. *Address:* 89 Paddock Lane, Lewes, East Sussex BN7 1TW. *T:* Lewes 473468. *Club:* United Oxford & Cambridge University.

WARDE, John Robins; His Honour Judge John Warde; a Circuit Judge, since 1977; *b* 25 April 1920; (Guardian) A. W. Ormond, CBE, FRCS; *m* 1941, Edna Holliday Gipson; three *s*. *Educ:* Radley Coll., Abingdon, Berks; Corpus Christi Coll., Oxford (MA). Served War, 1940–45: Lieut, RA; awarded C-inC's certif. for outstanding good service in the campaign in NW Europe. Member: Devon CC, 1946–49; Devon Agricl Exec. Cttee, 1948–53, West Regional Advisory Council of BBC, 1950–53. Admitted a solicitor,

1950; Partner in Waugh and Co., Solicitors, Haywards Heath and East Grinstead, Sussex, 1960–70. A Recorder of the Crown Court, 1972–77. Registrar of Clerkenwell County Court, 1970–77. Liveryman, Gardeners' Co., 1983–. *Recreations:* mountaineering, watching cricket, listening to music. *Address:* 20 Clifton Terrace, Brighton, East Sussex BN1 3HA. *T:* Brighton 26642. *Clubs:* Law Society, MCC, Forty.

WARDELL, Gareth Lodwig; MP (Lab) Gower, since Sept. 1982; *b* 29 Nov. 1944; *s* of John Thomas Wardell and Jenny Ceridwen Wardell; *m* 1967, Jennifer Dawn Evans; one *s*. *Educ:* London Sch. of Econs and Pol. Science (BScEcon, MSc). Geography Master, Chislehurst and Sidcup Technical High Sch., 1967–68; Head of Econs Dept, St Clement Danes Grammar Sch., 1968–70; Sixth Form Econs Master, Haberdashers' Aske's Sch., Elstree, 1970–72; Educn Lectr, Bedford Coll. of Physical Educn, 1972–73; Sen. Lectr in Geography, Trinity Coll., Carmarthen, 1973–82. *Publications:* articles on regional issues in British Econ. Survey. *Recreations:* cycling, cross-country running. *Address:* 67 Elder Grove, Carmarthen, Dyfed SA31 2LH.

WARDEN, Andrée, (Mrs Roy Warden); *see* Grenfell, A.

WARDER, John Arthur, CBE 1957; General Managing Director, Oil Operating Companies in Iran, 1963–67, retired; *b* 13 Nov. 1909; *s* of John William Warder and Blanche Longstaffe, Bournemouth; *m* 1936, Sylvia Mary Hughes; two *s* one *d*. *Educ:* Kent Coll., Canterbury. Joined Asiatic Petroleum Co., 1927; was with Shell in Argentina and Cuba. Pres. and Gen. Man., Cia. Mexicana de Petroleo El Aguila, 1950; Gen. Man., Shell Cos in Colombia, 1953; Vice-Pres., Cia. Shell de Venezuela, 1957, Pres., 1959; Shell's Regional Co-ordinator (Oil), Middle East, 1961–63; Dir, Shell Internat. Petroleum Co. Ltd, and Mem. of Bds, Iranian Oil Participants Ltd and Iraq Petroleum Co. Ltd, 1961–63. Officer, Order of Arts and Culture (France), 1966; Order of Taj, 3rd degree (Iran), 1966. *Recreations:* yachting, golf. *Address:* Orchard Cottage, Howe Hill, Watlington, Oxon OX9 5EZ. *T:* Watlington 2737. *Clubs:* East India; Phyllis Court (Henley-on-Thames); Chapultepec Golf (Mexico); Royal Channel Islands Yacht; Royal Guernsey Golf.
See also W. J. M. Shelton.

WARDINGTON, 2nd Baron, *cr* 1936, of Alnmouth in the County of Northumberland; **Christopher Henry Beaumont Pease;** *b* 22 Jan. 1924; *s* of 1st Baron and Hon. Dorothy Charlotte (*d* 1983), *er d* of 1st Baron Forster; *S* father, 1950; *m* 1964, Margaret Audrey Dunfee, *d* of John and Eva White; one *s* two *d* (adopted). *Educ:* Eton. Served War of 1939–45, in Scots Guards, 1942–47, Captain. Partner in Stockbroking firm of Hoare Govett Ltd. Alderman of Broad Street Ward, City of London, 1960–63. Mem., Council of Foreign Bondholders, 1967–. Comr, Public Works Loan Bd, 1969–73. Trustee, Royal Jubilee Trusts; Chm., Athlone Trust, 1983–. *Recreations:* cricket, golf, book collecting. *Heir:* *b* Hon. William Simon Pease [*b* 15 Oct. 1925; *m* 1962, Hon. Elizabeth Jane Ormsby-Gore, *d* of 4th Baron Harlech, KG, PC, GCMG]. *Address:* Wardington Manor, Banbury, Oxon. *T:* Cropredy 202; 29 Moore Street, SW3. *T:* 01–584 5245. *Clubs:* Royal Automobile, Garrick; All England Lawn Tennis.

WARDLAW, Sir Henry (John), 21st Bt *cr* 1631, of Pitreavie; *b* 30 Nov. 1930; *s* of Sir Henry Wardlaw, 20th Bt, and of Ellen, *d* of John Francis Brady; *S* father, 1983; *m* 1962, Julie-Ann, *d* of late Edward Patrick Kirwan; five *s* two *d*. *Educ:* Melbourne Univ. (MB, BS). *Heir:* *s* (Henry) Justin Wardlaw, *b* 10 Aug. 1963. *Address:* 82 Vincent Street, Sandringham, Vic 3191, Australia.

WARDLE, Air Cdre Alfred Randles, CBE 1945; AFC 1929; MRAeS; RAF, retired; *b* 29 Oct. 1898; *s* of William Wardle, Stafford; *m* 1926, Sarah, *d* of David Brindley, Cotes Heath; one *s* one *d*. Joined Hon. Artillery Co., 1916; RFC 1917; RAF 1918; Director of Operational Requirements, Air Ministry, 1943–46; AOC Ceylon, 1947–49; AOC No. 66 (Scottish) Group, 1950–52. Air Commodore, 1943; retired 1952. Secretary: Corby Develt Corp., 1954–67; Milton Keynes Develt Corp., 1967–68; Peterborough Develt Corp., 1968–69; Northampton Develt Corp., 1969; Central Lancs Develt Corp., 1971–72. *Address:* 88 Gipsy Lane, Kettering, Northants. *T:* Kettering 85780. *Club:* Royal Air Force.

WARDLE, Charles Frederick; MP (C) Bexhill and Battle, since 1983; *b* 23 Aug. 1939; *s* of late Frederick Maclean Wardle; *m* 1964, Lesley Ann, *d* of Sidney Wells; one *d*. *Educ:* Tonbridge Sch.; Lincoln Coll., Oxford; Harvard Business Sch. MA Oxon 1968; MBA Harvard. Asst to Pres., American Express Co., NY, 1966–69; Merchant Banking, London, 1969–72; Chairman: Benjamin Priest Gp plc, 1977–84 (Dir, 1972–74, Man. Dir, 1974–77); Warne, Wright and Rowland, 1978–84; Dir, Asset Special Situations Trust plc, 1982–. CBI: Mem. Council, 1980–84; Mem., W Midlands Regional Council, 1980–84. PPS: to Minister of State (Health), 1984; to Sec. of State for Social Services, 1984–. Mem., Select Cttee on Trade and Industry, 1983–84. Member: Commercial and Econ. Cttee, EEF, 1981–83; Midlands Cttee, InstD, 1981–83. FRGS 1977. *Recreations:* books, sport, travel. *Address:* House of Commons, SW1A 0AA. *T:* 01–219 3000; The Dodo House, Caldbec Hill, Battle, East Sussex. *Club:* Carlton.

WARDLE, (John) Irving; Drama Critic, The Times, since 1963; *b* 20 July 1929; *s* of John Wardle and Nellie Partington; *m* 1958, Joan Notkin (marr. diss.); *m* 1963, Fay Crowder (marr. diss.); two *s*; *m* 1975, Elizabeth Grist; one *s* one *d*. *Educ:* Bolton Sch.; Wadham Coll., Oxford (BA); Royal Coll. of Music (ARCM). Joined Times Educational Supplement as sub-editor, 1956; Dep. Theatre Critic, The Observer, 1960. Editor, Gambit, 1973–75. Play: The Houseboy, prod Open Space Theatre, 1974, ITV, 1982. *Publication: biography:* The Theatres of George Devine, 1978. *Recreation:* piano playing. *Address:* 51 Richmond Road, New Barnet, Herts. *T:* 01–440 3671.

WARDLE, Sir Thomas (Edward Jewell), Kt 1970; Lord Mayor of Perth, Western Australia, 1967–72; *b* 18 Aug. 1912; *s* of Walter Wardle and Lily Wardle (*née* Jewell); *m* 1940, Hulda May Olson; one *s* one *d*. *Educ:* Perth Boys' Sch., Western Australia. Member: King's Park Bd, 1970–81; Bd, Churchland Teachers Coll., 1973–78; Chairman: Trustees, WA Museum, 1973–82; Aboriginal Loans Commn, 1974–80; Pres., Nat. Trust of WA, 1971–82. Hon. LLD Univ. of WA, 1973. Commendatore, Order of Merit (Italy), 1970. *Recreations:* boating, fishing. *Address:* 3 Kent Street, Bicton, WA 6157, Australia. *Club:* Returned Services League (Western Australia).

WARDS, Brig. George Thexton, CMG 1943; OBE 1935; late IA; Historian, Cabinet Office, 1951–69. *Educ:* Heversham Sch., Westmorland. Served European War, 1914–18, with 7 London Regt, France and Belgium, 1917–18; 2nd Lieut, Indian Army, 1918; attached to HM Embassy, Tokyo, 1923–28; NW Frontier of India, 1930; Bt Major, 1933; Staff Officer to British Troops in North China, 1932–36; Lt-Col and Asst Military Attaché, Tokyo, 1937–41; Brig., Military Attaché, Tokyo, 1941; GSO1, GHQ India, 1942; Commandant Intelligence Sch., India, 1943–45; Commandant Intelligence Corps, Training Centre, India, 1945–47. Lt-Col, 1944; Col, 1945. Official Interpreter in Japanese to Govt of India, 1928–32, 1936, and 1944–47. Information Officer, Min. of Food, 1949; Chief Enforcement Officer, Min. of Food, 1950. Chm., Nat. Anti-Vivisection Soc., 1954–57; Mem. Council, RSPCA, 1956–67; Official visit to Japan, 1966. *Publications:* Joint author, Official History, The War against Japan, Vol. I 1955, Vol. II 1958, Vol. III 1962, Vol. IV 1965, Vol. V 1969. *Club:* Army and Navy.

WARE, Cyril George, CB 1981; Under-Secretary, Inland Revenue, 1974–82; *b* 25 May 1922; *s* of Frederick George Ware and Elizabeth Mary Ware; *m* 1946, Gwennie (*née* Wooding); two *s* one *d*. *Educ:* Leyton County High Sch. Entered Inland Revenue as Tax Officer, 1939; Inspector of Taxes, 1949; Sen. Principal Inspector, 1969. *Recreations:* music, woodwork, gardening, swimming. *Address:* 86 Tycehurst Hill, Loughton, Essex. *T:* 01–508 3588.

WARE, Sir Henry (Gabriel), KCB 1972 (CB 1971); HM Procurator-General and Treasury Solicitor, 1971–75; *b* 23 July 1912; *o s* of late Charles Martin Ware and Dorothy Anne Ware (*née* Gwyn Jeffreys); *m* 1939, Gloria Harriet Platt (*d* 1986); three *s* (and one *s* decd). *Educ:* Marlborough; St John's Coll., Oxford. Admitted solicitor, 1938; entered Treasury Solicitor's Dept, 1939; Dep. Treasury Solicitor, 1969–71. Served War of 1939–45 with Royal Artillery. *Recreations:* fly fishing, gardening. *Address:* The Little House, Tilford, Farnham, Surrey. *T:* Frensham 2151. *Club:* Athenæum.

WARE, Martin, MB, MSc, FRCP; Editor, British Medical Journal, 1966–75; *b* 1 Aug. 1915; *o s* of late Canon Martin Stewart Ware and late Margaret Isabel (*née* Baker, later Baker Wilbraham); *m* 1938, Winifred Elsie Boyce; two *s* three *d*. *Educ:* Eton; St Bartholomew's Hospital. MB, BS (London) 1939; MRCP 1945; FRCP 1967; MSc (Wales) 1978. Editor, St Bartholomew's Hosp. Jl, 1937–38. House-surgeon, St Bartholomew's Hosp., 1939; served with RAMC, attached to Royal W African Frontier Force (Captain, graded physician), 1940–45; Publications Officer, Medical Research Council, 1946–50; Asst Editor, British Medical Jl, 1950; research in micropalaeontology, UCW, Aberystwyth, 1975–84. Vice-President: BMA; Internat. Union of Med. Press, 1966–75; Member: Council of Res. Defence Soc., 1960–65; Med. Panel of British Council, 1966–75. *Recreations:* bird watching, reading, music. *Address:* 35 Rhos Hendre, Waun Fawr, Aberystwyth, Dyfed SY23 3PT. *T:* Aberystwyth 4059.

WARE, Michael John, CB 1985; barrister-at-law; Solicitor and Legal Adviser, Department of the Environment, since 1982; *b* 7 May 1932; *s* of Kenneth George Ware and Phyllis Matilda (*née* Joynes); *m* 1966, Susan Ann Maitland three *d*. *Educ:* Cheltenham Grammar Sch.; Trinity Hall, Cambridge (BA(Law), LLB). Called to Bar, Middle Temple. Nat. Service, 2/Lieut RASC, 1954–56. Board of Trade (later Dept of Trade and Industry): Legal Asst, 1957–64; Sen. Legal Asst, 1964–72; Asst Solicitor, 1972–73; Dir, Legal Dept, Office of Fair Trading, 1973–77; Under Secretary: Dept of Trade, 1977–81; DoE, 1982. *Recreation:* gardening. *Address:* 2 Marsham Street, SW1P 3EB.

WAREHAM, Arthur George; *b* 24 April 1908; *y s* of late George Wareham and of Elizabeth Wareham; *m* 1936, Kathleen Mary, *d* of H. E. and Mabel Tapley; one *s* one *d*. *Educ:* Queen's Coll., Taunton. Joined Western Morning News, 1926; Daily Mail, 1935; Editor, Daily Mail, 1954–59. Chm., Arthur Wareham Associates Ltd, 1961–77. *Address:* Three Corners, Forest Ridge, Keston, Kent. *T:* Farnborough (Kent) 53606.

WAREING, Prof. Philip Frank, OBE 1986; PhD, DSc London; FRS 1969; FLS; Professor of Botany, University College of Wales, Aberystwyth, 1958–81, now Emeritus; *b* 27 April 1914; *e s* of late Frank Wareing; *m* 1939, Helen Clark; one *s* one *d* (and one *d* decd). *Educ:* Watford Grammar School; Birkbeck Coll., Univ. of London. Exec. Officer, Inland Revenue, 1931–41. Captain, REME, 1942–46. Lectr, Bedford Coll., Univ. of London, 1947–50; Lectr, then Sen. Lectr, Univ. of Manchester, 1950–58. Member: Nature Conservancy, 1965–68; Water Resources Board, 1968–71; Chm. Res. Adv. Cttee, Forestry Commn, 1972–86. President: Sect. K, British Assoc., 1970; Internat. Plant Growth Substances Assoc., 1982–85; Mem. Council, Royal Soc., 1972. Mem., Leopoldina Acad. of Science, 1971. *Publications:* Control of Plant Growth and Differentiation, 1970; various papers on plant physiology in scientific journals. *Recreations:* gardening, hill walking. *Address:* Bryn Rhedyn, Caemelyn, Aberystwyth, Dyfed SY23 3DA. *T:* Aberystwyth 3910.

WAREING, Robert Nelson; MP (Lab) Liverpool, West Derby, since 1983; *b* 20 Aug. 1930; *s* of late Robert Wareing and late Florence Wareing (*née* Mallon); *m* 1962, Betty Coward. *Educ:* Ranworth Square Sch., Liverpool; Alsop High Sch., Liverpool; Bolton Coll. of Educn. BSc (Econ) London Univ., 1956. RAF, 1948–50. Administrative Asst, Liverpool City Bldg Surveyor's Dept, 1946–56; Lecturer: Brooklyn Technical Coll., Birmingham, 1957–59; Wigan and Dist Mining and Technical Coll., 1959–63; Liverpool Coll. of Commerce, 1963–64; Liverpool City Inst. of Further Educn, 1964–72; Central Liverpool Coll. of Further Educn, 1972–83. Merseyside County Council: Mem., 1981–86; Chief Whip, Labour Gp, 1981–83; Chm., Economic Develt Cttee, 1981–83; Chm., Merseyside Economic Develt Co. Ltd, 1981–86. A Vice-Pres., AMA, 1984–. Joined Labour Party, 1947: Pres., Liverpool Dist Labour Party, 1974–81; Mem., ASTMS. Introduced Chronically Sick and Disabled Persons Bill, 1983; Vice-Chm., British–Yugoslav Parly Gp, 1985–. *Recreations:* watching soccer (especially Everton FC), concert-going and ballet, motoring and travel. *Address:* House of Commons, SW1A 0AA. *Club:* Pirrie Ward Labour (Liverpool).

WARHURST, Alan; Director, Manchester Museum, since 1977; *b* 6 Feb. 1927; *s* of W. Warhurst; *m* 1953, Sheila Lilian Bradbury; one *s* two *d*. *Educ:* Canon Slade Grammar Sch., Bolton; Manchester Univ. BA Hons History 1950. Commnd Lancashire Fusiliers, 1947. Asst, Grosvenor Museum, Chester, 1950–51; Asst Curator, Maidstone Museum and Art Gallery, 1951–55; Curator, Northampton Museum and Art Gallery, 1955–60; Director, City Museum, Bristol, 1960–70; Director, Ulster Museum, 1970–77. FSA 1958; FMA 1958. Pres., S Western Fedn Museums and Galleries, 1966–68; Chm., Irish Nat. Cttee, ICOM, 1973–75; President: Museums Assoc., 1975–76; N Western Fedn of Museums and Art Galls, 1979–80. Hon. MA Belfast, 1982. *Publications:* various archaeological and museum contribs to learned jls. *Address:* The Manchester Museum, The University, Manchester M13 9PL. *T:* 061–273 3333.

WARING, Sir (Alfred) Holburt, 3rd Bt *cr* 1935; *b* 2 Aug. 1933; *s* of Sir Alfred Harold Waring, 2nd Bt, and of Winifred, *d* of late Albert Boston, Stockton-on-Tees; *S* father, 1981; *m* 1958, Anita, *d* of late Valentin Medinilla, Madrid; one *s* two *d*. *Educ:* Rossall School; Leeds College of Commerce. Director: SRM Plastics Ltd; Waring Investments Ltd; Rotaprint Ltd; Property Realisation Co. Ltd; Moor Park Golf Club Ltd; Moor Park (1958) Ltd. Governor, Med. Coll. of St Bartholomew's Hosp. Chm., Moor Park Lawn Tennis Club. *Recreations:* tennis, golf, squash, swimming. *Heir:* *s* Michael Holburt Waring, *b* 3 Jan. 1964. *Address:* Earls Croft, 30 Russell Road, Moor Park, Northwood, Middlesex. *T:* Northwood 24570. *Clubs:* Moor Park Golf (Rickmansworth); Northwood Squash Centre (Northwood).

WARMAN, Ven. Francis Frederic Guy; Archdeacon of Aston, 1965–77, Emeritus since 1977; Canon Residentiary of Birmingham, 1965–77, Emeritus since 1977; *b* 1 Dec. 1904; *er s* of Frederic Sumpter Guy Warman, one time Bishop of Manchester, and Gertrude Warman (*née* Earle); *m* 1932, Kathleen Olive, *d* of O. C. Phillips; one *s* one *d*. *Educ:* Weymouth Coll.; Worcester Coll., Oxford; Ridley Hall, Cambridge. Ordained as Curate of Radford, Coventry, 1927; Curate of Chilvers Coton, Nuneaton, 1930; Vicar of: St James, Selby, 1932; Beeston, Leeds, 1936; Ward End, Birmingham, 1943; Aston-juxta-Birmingham, 1946. Rural Dean of East Birmingham, 1944–46; Proctor in Convocation,

1945–75; Hon. Canon of Birmingham, 1948–65. *Recreations:* music, golf. *Address:* 76 Winterbourne Close, Lewes, Sussex BN7 1JZ. *T:* Lewes 472440.

WARMAN, Oliver Byrne, RBA 1984; Chief Executive, Federation of British Artists, since 1984; *b* 10 June 1932; *s* of F. B. Warman and Jane Warman. *Educ:* Stowe; Exeter Univ.; Balliol Coll., Oxford. Commissioned Welsh Guards, 1952; GSO3 Cabinet Office; Instructor, Intelligence Centre; Staff College; RMCS; retired 1970. Dir, Public Relations, Ship and Boat Builders Fedn, 1970; Director: Ashlyns, 1978; Tulsemead, 1983. First exhibited RA, 1980; exhib. at RBA, RWA, NEAC, RSMA, ROI; work in public collections, incl. US Embassy and Crown Commn. *Publications:* Arnhem 1944, 1970; articles on wine and military history, 1968–. *Recreations:* France, food, wine, sailing, painting, mongrel dogs. *Address:* c/o National Westminster Bank, Hungerford, Berks. *Clubs:* Cavalry and Guards, Chelsea Arts; Royal Cornwall Yacht.

WARMINGTON, Eric Herbert, MA; FRHistS; Professor Emeritus of Classics, University of London; Fellow of Birkbeck College; Vice-Master, Birkbeck College, 1954–65, Vice-President, since 1966; Acting Master, 1950–51, 1965–66; *b* 15 March 1898; *s* of John Herbert Warmington, MA, and Maud Lockhart; *m* 1922, Marian Eveline Robertson, Kinsale, Co. Cork; one *s* two *d*. *Educ:* Perse School, Cambridge; Peterhouse, Cambridge (Scholar). Served in Garrison Artillery and King's Own Yorkshire Light Infantry, 1917–19; Cambridge University, 1919–22; First Class, Classical Tripos, Part I, 1921; First Class, Part II, 1922; BA 1922; Assistant master at Charterhouse, 1922–23; Classical Sixth Form master, Mill Hill School, 1923–25; Reader in Ancient History, University of London, 1925–35; Le Bas Prize, Cambridge University, 1925; MA 1925; FRHistS, 1928; Editor, Loeb Classical Library, 1937–74. Dean of Faculty of Arts, University of London, 1951–56; Member of Senate, University of London, 1956–66; Acting Director Univ. of London Inst. of Education, 1957–58; Chairman, Goldsmiths' College Delegacy, 1958–75; President London Branch Classical Assoc. 1963–66. *Publications:* The Commerce between the Roman Empire and India, 1928; Athens, 1928; The Ancient Explorers (with M. Cary), 1929; Greek Geography, 1934; Africa in Ancient and Medieval Times, in the Cambridge History of the British Empire, 1936; Remains of Old Latin, Vol. I, 1935; Vol. II, 1936; Vol. III, 1938, Vol. IV, 1940; articles in The Oxford Classical Dictionary, 1949; A History of Birkbeck College, University of London, during the second World War, 1939–1945, 1954; (ed) Great Dialogues of Plato (trans. by W. H. D. Rouse), 1956; various articles and reviews. *Recreations:* music, gardening and natural history. *Address:* 48 Flower Lane, Mill Hill, NW7. *T:* 01–959 1905.

WARMINGTON, Lt-Comdr Sir Marshall George Clitheroe, 3rd Bt, *cr* 1908; Royal Navy, retired; *b* 26 May 1910; *o s* of Sir Marshall Denham Warmington, 2nd Bt, and Alice Daisy Ing; *S* father, 1935; *m* 1st, 1933, Mollie (from whom he obtained a divorce, 1941), *er d* of late Capt. M. A. Kennard, RN (retired); one *s* one *d*; 2nd, 1942, Eileen Mary (*d* 1969), *o d* of late P. J. Howes; two *s*. *Educ:* Charterhouse. *Heir:* *s* Marshall Denham Malcolm Warmington, *b* 5 Jan. 1934. *Address:* Swallowfield Park, near Reading, Berks RG7 1TG. *T:* Reading 882210. *Club:* MCC.

See also Sir H. H. Trusted.

WARNE, (Ernest) John (David), CB 1982; Secretary, Institute of Chartered Accountants in England and Wales, since 1982; *b* 4 Dec. 1926; *m* 1953, Rena Wolfe; three *s*. *Educ:* Univ. of London (BA(Hons)). Civil Service Commission, 1953; Asst Comr and Principal, Civil Service Commn, 1958; BoT, later DTI and Dept of Industry: Principal, 1962; Asst Sec., 1967; Under-Sec., 1972; Dir for Scotland, 1972–75; Under-Secretary: Personnel Div., 1975–77; Industrial and Commercial Policy Div., 1977–79; Dep. Sec., Dep. Dir-Gen., OFT, 1979–82. *Recreations:* reading, collecting prints, languages. *Address:* 3 Woodville Road, Ealing, W5. *T:* 01–998 0215. *Club:* Reform.

WARNE, Rear-Adm. Robert Spencer, CB 1953; CBE 1945; retired; *b* 26 June 1903; *s* of E. S. Warne, London; *m* 1925, Dorothy Hadwen Wheelwright (*d* 1976); three *s*. *Educ:* RN Colleges, Osborne and Dartmouth. Joined Submarine Branch, 1925; Commander, 1936; Captain, 1941; Rear-Admiral 1951; Deputy Chief of Naval Personnel, Admiralty, 1951–53; Flag Officer, Germany and Chief British Naval Representative in the Allied Control Commission, 1953–55; retired 1955. *Recreation:* sailing. *Address:* Meath Cottage, Lion Lane, Turners Hill, Crawley, West Sussex RH10 4NU. *T:* Copthorne 715508. *Club:* Royal Naval and Royal Albert Yacht (Portsmouth).

WARNER, Prof. Anne Elizabeth, FRS 1985; Royal Society Foulerton Research Professor, University College, London, since 1986; *b* 25 Aug. 1940; *d* of James Frederick Crompton Brooks and Elizabeth Marshall; *m* 1963, Michael Henry Warner. *Educ:* Pate's Grammar School for Girls, Cheltenham; University College London (BSc); Nat. Inst. for Med. Res. (PhD). Lectr in Physiology 1971–75, Sen. Lectr 1975–76, Royal Free Hosp Sch. of Medicine; Sen. Lectr in Anatomy, 1976–80, Reader in Anatomy, 1980–86, UCL. *Publications:* papers in Jl of Physiology and other learned jls. *Address:* University College London, Gower Street, WC1E 6BT.

WARNER, Sir (Edward Courtenay) Henry, 3rd Bt, *cr* 1910; *m*; three *s*. *Heir:* *s* Philip Courtenay Thomas Warner, *b* 3 April 1951.

WARNER, Sir Edward (Redston), KCMG 1965 (CMG 1955); OBE 1948; HM Diplomatic Service, retired; *b* 23 March 1911; *s* of late Sir George Redston Warner, KCVO, CMG, and Margery Catherine (*née* Nicol); *m* 1943, Grizel Margaret Clerk Rattray; three *s* one *d*. *Educ:* Oundle; King's College, Cambridge. Entered Foreign Office and Diplomatic Service, 1935; UK Delegation to OEEC, Paris, 1956–59; Minister at HM Embassy, Tokyo, 1959–62; Ambassador to Cameroon, 1963–66; UK Rep., Econ. and Social Council of UN, 1966–67; Ambassador to Tunisia, 1968–70. *Address:* The Old Royal Oak, High Street, Blockley, Glos GL56 9EX. *Clubs:* United Oxford & Cambridge University, Royal Commonwealth Society.

WARNER, Francis (Robert Le Plastrier); poet and dramatist; Sir Gordon White Fellow in English Literature and Senior English Tutor, St Peter's College, Oxford; Dean of Degrees, since 1984; *b* Bishopthorpe, Yorks, 21 Oct. 1937; *s* of Rev. Hugh Compton Warner and Nancy Le Plastrier (*née* Owen); *m* 1st, 1958, Mary Hall (marr. diss. 1972); two *d*; 2nd, 1983, Penelope Anne Davis; one *d*. *Educ:* Christ's Hosp.; London Coll. of Music; St Catharine's Coll., Cambridge (BA, MA). Supervisor, St Catharine's Coll., Cambridge, 1959–63; Staff Tutor in English, Cambridge Univ. Bd of Extra-Mural Studies, 1963–65; Fellow and Tutor, St Peter's Coll., Oxford, and University Lectr (CUF), 1965–. Messing Internat. Award for distinguished contribns to Literature, 1972. *Publications: poetry:* Perennia, 1962; Early Poems, 1964; Experimental Sonnets, 1965; Madrigals, 1967; The Poetry of Francis Warner, USA 1970; Lucca Quartet, 1975; Morning Vespers, 1980; Spring Harvest, 1981; Epithalamium, 1983; Collected Poems 1960–84, 1985; *plays:* Maquettes, a trilogy of one-act plays, 1972; Requiem: Pt 1, Lying Figures, 1972, Pt 2, Killing Time, 1976, Pt 3, Meeting Ends, 1974; A Conception of Love, 1978; Light Shadows, 1980; Moving Reflections, 1983; Living Creation, 1985; *edited:* Eleven Poems by Edmund Blunden, 1965; Garland, 1968; Studies in the Arts, 1968; contrib. Antios, TLS, etc; *relevant publications:* Francis Warner—Poet and Dramatist, ed Tim Prentki, 1977; Chess in the Mirror: a study of theatrical cubism in Francis Warner's Requiem and its Maquettes, by R. Jeffrey, 1980; Francis Warner and Tradition, by G. Pursglove, 1981. *Recreations:* children, cathedral music, travel. *Address:* St Peter's College, Oxford OX1 2DL. *T:* Oxford 248436. *Club:* Athenæum.

WARNER, Sir Frederick Archibald, (Sir Fred Warner), GCVO 1975; KCMG 1972 (CMG 1963); HM Diplomatic Service, retired; Director: Guinness Peat Group; Job Creation Ltd; Loral International Inc.; *b* 2 May 1918; *s* of Frederick A. Warner, Chaguanas, Trinidad, and Marjorie Miller Winants, New Jersey, USA; *m* 1971, Mrs Simone Georgina de Ferranti, *d* of late Col. Hubert Jocelyn Nangle; two *s* and one step *d*. *Educ:* Wixenford; RNC Dartmouth; Magdalen Coll., Oxford; Sheffield Univ. Served War of 1939–45. Asst Principal, Foreign Office, Feb. 1946; Member of Foreign Service, April 1946; promoted 2nd Sec., May 1946; promoted 1st Sec., and transferred to Moscow, 1950; Foreign Office, Dec. 1951; Rangoon, 1956 (acted as Chargé d'Affaires, 1956); transferred to Athens, 1958; Head of South-East Asia Dept, Foreign Office, 1960; Imperial Defence College, 1964; Ambassador to Laos, 1965–67; Minister, NATO, 1968; Under-Secretary of State, FCO, 1969; Ambassador and Dep. Permanent UK Rep. to UN, 1969–72; Ambassador to Japan, 1972–75. Mem. (C) Somerset, European Parlt, 1979–84. Formerly Director: Mercantile and General Reinsurance Co. Ltd; Chloride Gp Ltd. Chairman: Overseas Cttee, CBI, 1985–; Wessex Region of National Trust, 1976–78. Order of the Rising Sun, 1st class (Japan). *Address:* Inkpen House, Newbury, Berks. *T:* Inkpen 266; 4 The Porticos, King's Road, SW3. *Clubs:* Beefsteak, Turf.

WARNER, Prof. Sir Frederick (Edward), Kt 1968; FRS 1976; FEng 1977; Emeritus Partner, Cremer and Warner; Visiting Professor: Bartlett School of Architecture, University College London, since 1970; Essex University, since 1983; *b* 31 March 1910; *s* of Frederick Warner; *m* 1st, Margaret Anderson McCrea; two *s* two *d*; 2nd, Barbara Ivy Reynolds. *Educ:* Bancrofts Sch.; University Coll., London. Pres., Univ. of London Union, 1933. Chemical Engr with various cos, 1934–56; self-employed, 1956–. Joined Cremer and Warner, 1956, Senior Partner 1963–80. Inst. of Chemical Engrs: Hon. Sec., 1953; Pres., 1966; Mem. Council, Engrg Instns, 1962; President: Fedn Européenne d'Assocs nationales d'Ingénieurs, 1968–71; Brit. Assoc. for Commercial and Industrial Educn, 1977–; Vice-Pres., BSI, 1976–80 and 1983– (Chm., Exec. Bd, 1973–76; Pres., 1980–83). Missions and Consultations in India, Russia, Iran, Egypt, Greece, France. Assessor, Windscale Inquiry, 1977. Chairman: Cttee on Detergents, 1970–74; Process Plant Working Party, 1971–77; Sch. of Pharmacy, Univ. of London, 1971–79; Member: Royal Commn on Environmental Pollution, 1973–76; Adv. Council for Energy Conservation, 1974–79; Treasurer, SCOPE (Scientific Cttee on Problems of Environment), 1982– (Chm., Environmental Consequences of Nuclear Warfare, 1983–). Vis. Prof., Imperial Coll., 1970–78; Pro-Chancellor, Open Univ., 1974–79; Member Court: Cranfield Inst. of Technology; Essex Univ. Fellow UCL, 1967. Hon. Fellow, Sch. of Pharmacy, 1979. Ordinario, Accademia Tiberina, 1969. Hon. DTech, Bradford, 1969; Hon. DSc: Aston, 1970; Cranfield, 1978; Heriot-Watt, 1978; Newcastle, 1979; DUniv. Open, 1980. Gold Medal, Czecho-Slovak Soc. for Internat. Relations, 1969; Medal, Insinöö-riliitto, Finland, 1969; Leverhulme Medal, Royal Soc., 1978; Buchanan Medal, 1982; Rheinland Medal, Technical Inspectorate and Inf. Service of the Rheinland, 1984. Hon. Mem., Koninklijk Instituut van Ingenieurs, 1972; Academico Correspondiente, AI Mexico, 1972. *Publications:* Problem in Chemical Engineering Design (with J. M. Coulson), 1949; Technology Today (ed de Bono), 1971; Standards in the Engineering Industries, NEDO, 1977; Risk Assessment, Royal Soc., 1982; papers on nitric acid, heat transfer, underground gasification of coal, air and water pollution, contracts, planning, safety, professional and continuous education. *Recreations:* monumental brasses, ceramics, gardens. *Address:* 140 Buckingham Palace Road, SW1W 9SQ. *T:* 01–730 0777. *Club:* Athenæum.

WARNER, Frederick Sydney, LDS RCS, 1926; LRCP, MRCS, 1928; FDS RCS, 1947; Dental Surgeon, Guy's Hospital, 1949–68, Emeritus since 1968; Sub-Dean, 1946–65; Lecturer in Oral Surgery, 1954–61, Guy's Hospital Dental School, SE1; Dean of Dental Studies, 1965–68; Member of Board of Examiners in Dental Surgery, Royal College of Surgeons of England, 1947–64, and University of London, 1953–57. *b* 14 April 1903; *s* of Frederick Watkin Warner; *m* 1937, Cicely Florence Michelson. *Educ:* Guy's Hospital Medical School. Asst Dental Surgeon, Guy's Hospital, 1936–49. Member of Board of Faculty of Dental Surgery, Royal College of Surgeons of England, 1946–65; Vice-Dean, 1954–55. *Recreations:* philately, photography. *Address:* Flat 11, 115A Ridgway, SW19.

WARNER, Gerald Chierici, CMG 1984; HM Diplomatic Service; Counsellor, Foreign and Commonwealth Office, since 1976; *b* 27 Sept. 1931; *s* of Howard Warner and Elizabeth (*née* Chierici-Kendall); *m* 1956, Mary Wynne Davies, DMath, Reader, City Univ.; one *s* two *d*. *Educ:* Univ. of Oxford (BA). 3rd Sec., Peking, 1956–58; 2nd Sec., Rangoon, 1960–61; 1st Sec., Warsaw, 1964–66, Geneva, 1966–68; Counsellor, Kuala Lumpur, 1974–76. *Address:* c/o Foreign and Commonwealth Office, SW1A 2AH.

WARNER, Sir Henry; *see* Warner, Sir E. C. H.

WARNER, Hon. Sir Jean-Pierre Frank Eugene, Kt 1981; **Hon. Mr Justice Warner;** Judge of the High Court of Justice, Chancery Division, since 1981; a Judge of the Restrictive Practices Court, since 1982; *b* 24 Sept. 1924; *s* of late Frank Cloudesley ffolliot Warner and of Louise Marie Blanche Warner (*née* Gouet); *m* 1950, Sylvia Frances, *d* of Sir Ernest Goodale, CBE, MC; two *d*. *Educ:* Sainte Croix de Neuilly; Ecole des Roches; Harrow; Trinity Coll., Cambridge (MA). Served in Rifle Bde, 1943–47, Actg Major, GSO2 (Ops) GHQ Far East. Called to Bar, Lincoln's Inn, 1950 (Cassel Schol.), Bencher 1966, Treasurer 1985; Mem. Gen. Council of Bar, 1969–72. Junior Counsel: to Registrar of Restrictive Trading Agreements, 1961–64; to Treasury (Chancery), 1964–72; QC 1972; Advocate-Gen., Ct of Justice of European Communities, 1973–81. Councillor: Royal Borough of Kensington, 1959–65 (Chm., Gen. Purposes Cttee, 1963–65); Royal Borough of Kensington and Chelsea, 1964–68. Dir, Warner & Sons Ltd and subsids, 1952–70. Pres., UK Assoc. for European Law, 1983– (Vice-Pres., 1975–83). Mem., Confrérie St Etienne d'Alsace, 1981; Hon. Mem., Soc. of Public Teachers of Law, 1982. Hon. LLD: Exeter, 1983; Leicester, 1984. Liveryman, Worshipful Co. of Weavers, 1957. Chevalier du Tastevin, 1952, Commandeur 1960. *Recreation:* sitting in the sun with a cool drink. *Address:* Royal Courts of Justice, WC2A 2LL. *T:* 01–936 6768; 32 Abingdon Villas, W8 6BX. *T:* 01–937 7023.

WARNER, Dr Michael Henry Charles; Head of ER3 Division, Ministry of Defence, 1981–84; *b* 21 May 1927; *s* of Captain Herbert H. M. Warner, MA, RGA, and Mrs Jessie R. H. Warner; *m* 1971, Gillian Margaret (*née* Easby); one *s* (by previous *m*). *Educ:* Monkton Combe Sch., Bath; Queens' Coll., Cambridge (BA 1951, MA 1955); King's Coll., London (PhD 1973). Served RAF, 1945–48. Govt Communications HQ: Exec. Officer, 1952; Higher Exec. Officer, 1956; Deptl Specialist Officer, 1957; Min. of Defence: Principal, 1965; Asst Sec., 1974; Counsellor, FCO, 1979; Dep. Leader, UK Delegn to Comprehensive Test Ban Treaty Negotiations, Geneva, 1979–80. Leverhulme Fellow, 1971–72. *Publications:* contrib. Thomas Hardy Yearbook, Anglo-Welsh Rev., Envoi, and BBC 2. *Recreations:* tennis, bridge. *Address:* 62 Poulett Gardens, Twickenham, Mddx TW1 4QR. *T:* 01–892 1456. *Club:* Royal Victoria League.

WARNER, Norman Reginald; Director of Social Services, Kent County Council, since 1985; *b* 8 Sept. 1940; *s* of Albert Henry Edwin Warner and Laura Warner; *m* 1961, Anne Lesley Lawrence; one *s* one *d* (marr. diss. 1981); one *s. Educ:* Dulwich College; University of California, Berkeley (MPH). Min. of Health, 1959; Asst Private Sec. to Minister of Health, 1967–68, to Sec. of State for Social Services, 1968–69; Executive Councils Div., DHSS, 1969–71; Harkness Fellowship, USA, 1971–73; NHS Reorganisation, DHSS, 1973–74; Principal Private Sec. to Sec. of State for Social Services, 1974–76; Supplementary Benefits Div., 1976–78; Management Services, DHSS, 1979–81; Regional Controller, Wales and S Western Region, DHSS, 1981–83; Gwilym Gibbon Fellow, Nuffield Coll., Oxford, 1983–84; Under Sec., Supplementary Benefits Div., DHSS, 1984–85. *Publications:* articles in Jl of Public Admin. *Recreations:* reading, cinema, theatre, exercise. *Address:* 8 College Gardens, Dulwich SE21 7BE. *T:* 01–693 7663.

WARNOCK, family name of **Baroness Warnock.**

WARNOCK, Baroness *cr* 1985 (Life Peer), of Weeke in the City of Winchester; **Helen Mary Warnock,** DBE 1984; Mistress of Girton College, Cambridge, since 1985; *b* 14 April 1924; *d* of late Archibald Edward Wilson, Winchester; *m* 1949, Sir Geoffrey Warnock, *qv*; two *s* three *d. Educ:* St Swithun's, Winchester; Lady Margaret Hall, Oxford (Hon. Fellow 1984). Fellow and Tutor in Philosophy, St Hugh's Coll., Oxford, 1949–66; Headmistress, Oxford High Sch., GPDST, 1966–72; Talbot Res. Fellow, Lady Margaret Hall, Oxford, 1972–76; Sen. Res. Fellow, St Hugh's Coll., Oxford, 1976–84 (Hon. Fellow, 1985). Member: IBA, 1973–81; Cttee of Inquiry into Special Educn, 1974–78 (Chm.); Royal Commn on Environmental Pollution, 1979–84; Adv. Cttee on Animal Experiments, 1979–85 (Chm.); SSRC, 1981–85; UK Nat. Commn for Unesco, 1981–84; Cttee of Inquiry into Human Fertilization, 1982–84 (Chm.); Cttee of Inquiry into Validation of Public Sector Higher Educn, 1984. FCP 1979. DUniv Open 1980; DU Essex, 1985; Hon. DLitt Melbourne, 1986. *Publications:* Ethics since 1900, 1960, 3rd edn 1978; J.-P. Sartre, 1963; Existentialist Ethics, 1966; Existentialism, 1970; Imagination, 1976; Schools of Thought, 1977; (with T. Devlin) What Must We Teach?, 1977; Education: a way forward, 1979; A Question of Life, 1985; Teacher Teach Thyself (Dimbleby Lect.), 1985. *Recreations:* music, gardening. *Address:* Hertford College, Oxford; Girton College, Cambridge; Brick House, Axford. *T:* Marlborough 54686.

WARNOCK, Sir Geoffrey (James), Kt 1986; Principal, Hertford College, Oxford, since 1971; Vice-Chancellor, University of Oxford, 1981–85; *b* 16 Aug. 1923; *s* of James Warnock, OBE, MD; *m* 1949, Helen Mary Wilson (*see* Baroness Warnock); two *s* three *d. Educ:* Winchester Coll.; New Coll., Oxford, Hon. Fellow, 1973. Served War of 1939–45: Irish Guards, 1942–45 (Captain). Fellow by Examination, Magdalen Coll., 1949; Fellow and Tutor, Brasenose Coll., 1950–53; Fellow and Tutor in Philosophy, Magdalen Coll., 1953–71, Emeritus Fellow, 1972, Hon. Fellow, 1980. Visiting Lectr, Univ. of Illinois, 1957; Visiting Professor: Princeton Univ., 1962; Univ. of Wisconsin, 1966. Hon. DH Univ. of Hartford, 1986. *Publications:* Berkeley, 1953; English Philosophy since 1900, 1958, 2nd edn 1969; Contemporary Moral Philosophy, 1967; (ed with J. O. Urmson) J. L. Austin: Philosophical Papers, 2nd edn, 1970; The Object of Morality, 1971; Morality and Language, 1983; articles in: Mind, Proc. Aristotelian Soc., etc. *Recreation:* golf. *Address:* Hertford College, Oxford. *T:* Oxford 242947.

WARR, George Michael, CBE 1966; HM Diplomatic Service, retired; *b* 22 Jan. 1915; *s* of late Sir Godfrey Warr, and of Lady Warr; *m* 1950, Gillian Addis (*née* Dearmer); one *s* two *d* (and one step *s). Educ:* Winchester; Christ Church, Oxford. Entered Foreign Service, 1938; served in Chile, Germany, Soviet Union, Uruguay; Counsellor, British Embassy, Brussels, 1959–62; British Consul-General, Istanbul, Turkey, 1962–67; Ambassador to Nicaragua, 1967–70. *Recreations:* gardening, beekeeping. *Address:* Woodside, Frant, Tunbridge Wells TN3 9HW. *T:* Frant 496.

WARRELL, Ernest Herbert; Organist, King's College, London, since 1980 (Lecturer in Music, KCL, 1953–80); *b* 23 June 1915; *er s* of Herbert Henry Warrell and Edith Peacock; *m* 1952, Jean Denton Denton; two *s* one *d. Educ:* Loughborough School. Articled pupil (Dr E. T. Cook), Southwark Cath., 1938; Asst Organist, Southwark Cath., 1946–54; Organist, St Mary's, Primrose Hill, 1954–57; Lectr in Plainsong, RSCM, 1954–59; Organist, St John the Divine, Kennington, SW9, 1961–68; Organist and Dir of Music, Southwark Cathedral, 1968–76; Musical Dir, Gregorian Assoc., 1969–82. Hon. FCTL 1977; FKC 1979. *Publications:* Accompaniments to the Psalm Tones, 1942; Plainsong and the Anglican Organist, 1943. *Recreation:* sailing. *Address:* 41 Beechhill Road, Eltham, SE9 1HJ. *T:* 01–850 7800. *Clubs:* Special Forces, Little Ship; Royal Scots (Edinburgh).

WARREN, Very Rev. Alan Christopher; Provost of Leicester, since 1978; *b* 1932; *s* of Arthur Henry and Gwendoline Catherine Warren; *m* 1957, Sylvia Mary (*née* Matthews); three *d. Educ:* Dulwich College; Corpus Christi Coll., Cambridge (Exhibnr, MA); Ridley Hall, Cambridge. Curate, St Paul's, Margate, 1957–59; Curate St Andrew, Plymouth, 1959–62; Chaplain of Kelly College, Tavistock, 1962–64; Vicar of Holy Apostles, Leicester, 1964–72; Coventry Diocesan Missioner, 1972–78; Hon. Canon, Coventry Cathedral, 1972–78; Proctor in Convocation, 1977–78, 1980–85; Mem., Cathedral Statutes Commn, 1981–. Chm., Council of Christians and Jews; President: Leicester Council of Churches; Leicester Civic Soc. *Publications:* Putting it Across, 1975; articles on church music, evangelism and sport in Church Times and other journals. *Recreations:* music, golf, steam trains. *Address:* Provost's House, St Martin's East, Leicester. *T:* Leicester 25294/5. *Clubs:* Free Foresters; Leicestershire; Hunstanton Golf.

WARREN, Alastair Kennedy, TD 1953; Regional Editor, Scottish and Universal Newspapers Ltd, since 1974; *b* 17 July 1922; *s* of John Russell Warren, MC, and Jean Cousin Warren; *m* 1952, Ann Lindsay Maclean; two *s. Educ:* Glasgow Acad.; Loretto; Glasgow Univ. (MA Hons). Served War of 1939–45; HLI, 1940–46; Major, 1946. Served 5/6th Bn HLI (TA) 1947–63. Sales Clerk, Stewarts & Lloyds Ltd, 1950–53; joined editorial staff of The Glasgow Herald as Sub-Editor, 1954; Leader Writer, 1955–58; Features Editor, 1958–59; Commercial Editor, 1960–64; City Editor, 1964–65; Editor, 1965–74; Editor, Dumfries and Galloway Standard, 1976–86. Provost of New Galloway and Kells Community Council, 1978–81. *Publications:* contribs to various periodicals. *Recreations:* swimming, hill walking, marathon running. *Address:* Rathan, New Galloway, Kirkcudbrightshire. *T:* New Galloway 257.

WARREN, Sir Alfred Henry, (Sir Freddie Warren), Kt 1976; CBE 1970 (MBE 1957); Secretary to the Government Chief Whip, 1958–79; *b* 19 Dec. 1915; *s* of William Warren and Clara Wooff; *m* 1940, Margaret Ann; one *s* one *d. Educ:* Sir Walter St John's Grammar Sch., SW11. Asst Private Secretary to the Secretary to the Cabinet, 1951–58. *Address:* 93 South Eden Park Road, Beckenham, Kent. *T:* 01–658 6951.

WARREN, Dame (Alice) Josephine (Mary Taylor); *see* Barnes, Dame A. J. M. T.

WARREN, Rt. Rev. Alwyn Keith, CMG 1967; MC 1945; *b* 23 Sept. 1900; 2nd *s* of Major T. J. C. Warren, JP, Penlee House, Te Aute, Hawkes Bay, NZ, and Lucy, *d* of Ven. Samuel Williams, Archdeacon of Hawkes Bay, NZ; *m* 1928, Doreen Eda (*d* 1983), *d* of Capt. C. F. Laws; one *s* two *d. Educ:* Marlborough College; Magdalen College, Oxford (BA 1922, Hons Nat. Sci.; MA 1926); Cuddesdon Theological College. Ordained, Canterbury, 1925; Curate of Ashford, Kent, 1925–29; Vicar of Ross and South Westland, NZ, 1929–32; Vicar of Waimate, South Canterbury, NZ, 1932–34; Vicar of St Mary's, Merivale, Christchurch, NZ, 1934–40; Archdeacon of Christchurch, 1937–44; Dean of Christchurch, 1940–51; Vicar-General, 1940–44 and 1946–51; Bishop of Christchurch, 1951–66. Delegate to Internat. Round Table of Christian Leaders, on a Just and Durable Peace, Princeton, USA, 1943; Chaplain to 2nd NZ Exped. Force (NZ Divisional Cavalry), Italy, 1944–45 (wounded, MC). Member Council, University Canterbury, 1946–73, Pro-Chancellor, 1961, Chancellor, 1965–69; Member Senate, University of New Zealand, 1948–61; Warden or Chm. Bds various colleges, schools and social service organisations. Chairman National Council of Churches of NZ, 1949–51; World Council of Churches: Mem. Central Cttee, 1954–67; Mem. Assembly, Evanston, USA, 1954 and New Delhi, 1961. Chaplain and Sub-Prelate, Order of St John; Chaplain, Priory of St John in NZ, 1966–72; formerly Pres., Canterbury and West Coast Centre, St John Ambulance Assoc.; Pres., Christchurch Rotary Club; Vice-President: Christchurch Civic Music Council; Christchurch Harmonic Soc.; Pres., Royal Christchurch Musical Soc.; Trustee, NZ National Library. *Publications:* Prayers in Time of War, 1940; Christianity Today: section on Churches in NZ, 1947. Contrib. to Stimmen aus der ökumene, 1963 (Berlin). *Recreations:* formerly rowing, tennis, now people, reading biographies, music, gardening. *Address:* Littlecourt, 193 Memorial Avenue, Christchurch 5, New Zealand. *Clubs:* Leander; Christchurch, University of Canterbury, University Staff (Christchurch).

WARREN, Sir Brian; *see* Warren, Sir H. B. S.

WARREN, Sir Brian Charles Pennefather, 9th Bt *cr* 1784; *b* 4 June 1923; *o s* of Sir Thomas Richard Pennefather Warren, 8th Bt, CBE; *S* father, 1961; *m* 1976, Cola, *d* of Captain E. L. Cazenove, Great Dalby, Leics. *Educ:* Wellington College. Served War of 1939–45; Lt, 1943–45, 2nd Bn Irish Guards. *Recreations:* hunting, squash. *Heir: cousin* Patrick Vaughton Warren, Major RA, *b* 11 Jan. 1917. *Address:* The Wilderness, Castle Oliver, Kilmallock, Co. Limerick. *T:* Kilfinane 89. *Club:* Cavalry and Guards.

WARREN, Rt. Rev. Cecil Allan; Rector, Old Brampton and Loundsley Green, since 1983; Assistant Bishop, Diocese of Derby, since 1983; *b* 25 Feb. 1924; *s* of Charles Henry and Eliza Warren; *m* 1947, Doreen Muriel Burrows. *Educ:* Sydney Univ. (BA 1950); Queen's Coll., Oxford (MA 1959). Deacon 1950, Priest 1951, Dio. of Canberra and Goulburn; appointments in Diocese of Oxford, 1953–57; Canberra, 1957–63; Organising Sec. Church Society, and Director of Forward in Faith Movement, Dio. of Canberra and Goulburn, 1963–65; Asst Bishop of Canberra and Goulburn, 1965–72; Bishop of Canberra and Goulburn, 1972–83. *Address:* 25 Oldridge Close, Holme Hall, Chesterfield, Derbyshire S40 4UF.

WARREN, Douglas Ernest, CMG 1973; *b* 8 June 1918; *s* of late Samuel Henry Warren; *m* 1945, Constance Vera (*née* Nix); two *d. Educ:* High Storrs Grammar Sch., Sheffield; Sheffield Univ. (BSc). FRICS. Royal Corps of Signals, 1940–46 (Captain): POW Thailand, 1942–45. Joined Colonial Service (later HMOCS), Tanganyika, as Surveyor, 1946: Supt of Surveys, 1955; transf. to Kenya as Asst Dir of Surveys, 1957; Dir of Survey of Kenya, 1961–65; retd from HMOCS, 1965; joined UK Civil Service as Dep. to Dir of Overseas Surveys, Min. of Overseas Develt, 1965, Dir of Overseas Surveys and Survey Adviser, 1968–80. Member: Land Surveyors Council, RICS, 1965–72; Council, RGS, 1968–71; various Royal Society cttees; Pres., Photogrammetric Soc., 1969–71. Patron's Medal, RGS. *Recreations:* travel, golf. *Address:* Flat 2, 19 St John's Road, Eastbourne, East Sussex. *Club:* Royal Eastbourne Golf.

WARREN, Frederick Lloyd, MA, BSc (Oxon), PhD, DSc (London); Professor of Biochemistry, London Hospital Medical College, 1952–78, now Emeritus; *b* 2 Oct. 1911; *s* of Frederick James and Edith Agnes Warren; *m* 1st, 1949, Natalia Vera Peierls (*née* Ladan) (marr. diss., 1958); two *s* one *d*; 2nd, 1961, Ruth Natallé Jacobs. *Educ:* Bristol Grammar Sch.; Exeter Coll., Oxford. Demonstrator, Biochem. Dept, Oxford, 1932–34; Sir Halley Stewart Res. Fellow, Chester Beatty Research Institute, Royal Cancer Hospital, 1934–46; Laura de Saliceto Student, University of London, 1937–42; Anna Fuller Research Student, 1942–46; Senior Lecturer in Biochemistry, St Mary's Hospital Medical School, 1946–48; Reader in Biochemistry, University College, London, 1948–52. *Publications:* papers and articles in scientific journals. *Address:* 5 River View, Enfield, Mddx EN2 6PX. *T:* 01–366 0674.

WARREN, Sir Frederick Miles, KBE 1985 (CBE 1974); FNZIA; ARIBA; Senior Partner, Warren & Mahoney, Architects; *b* Christchurch, 10 May 1929. *Educ:* Christ's Coll., Christchurch; Auckland Univ. DipArch; ARIBA 1952; FNZIA 1965. Founded Warren & Mahoney, 1958. Award-winning designs include: Christchurch Town Hall and Civic Centre; NZ Chancery, Washington; Canterbury Public Library; Michael Fowler Centre, Wellington. Pres., Canterbury Soc. of Arts, 1972–76. Gold Medal, NZIA, 1960, 1964, 1969, 1973; Nat. Awards, NZIA, 1980, 1981, 1983, 1984, 1985. *Recreation:* making a garden. *Address:* 65 Cambridge Terrace, Christchurch 1, New Zealand.

WARREN, Sir (Harold) Brian (Seymour), Kt 1974; physician; *b* 19 Dec. 1914; *er s* of late Harold Warren, St Ives, Hunts and Marian Jessie Emlyn; *m* 1st, 1942, Dame Alice Josephine Mary Taylor Barnes, *qv* (marr. diss. 1964); one *s* two *d*; 2nd, 1964, Elizabeth Anne (*d* 1983), *y d* of late Walter William Marsh, Wordsley, Staffs; two *s. Educ:* Bishop's Stortford Coll.; University Coll. London; University Coll. Hosp. MRCS, LRCP. Pres., Univ. of London Union, 1937–38. House Phys. and House Surg., UCH, 1942. War service with RAMC, RMO 1st Bn Gren. Gds and DADMS Gds Div., 1942–46 (despatches). Mem., Westminster City Council, 1955–64 and 1968–78; rep. West Woolwich on LCC, 1955–58, County Alderman 1961–62. Contested (C) Brixton Div. of Lambeth, 1959. Personal Phys. to Prime Minister, 1970–74. Mem., Westminster, Chelsea and Kensington AHA, 1975–77. Visitor and Mem. Emergency Bed Service Cttee, King Edward's Hosp. Fund for London, 1966–72; Mem. Governing Body, Westminster Hosp., 1970–74; Mem. Council, King Edward VII's Hosp. for Officers (Surg.-Apothecary, 1952–80). Pres., Chelsea Clinical Soc., 1955–56. Mem., Develt Cttee, BTA. Liveryman, Apothecaries' Soc., 1950; Freeman, City of London. *Publications:* contrib. Encycl. Gen. Practice. *Recreations:* shooting, gardening, travel, listening to music. *Address:* 94 Oakley Street, SW3 5NR. *T:* 01–351 6462. *Clubs:* Boodle's, Pratt's.

See also M. G. J. Neary.

WARREN, Ian Scott; Master of the Supreme Court (Queen's Bench Division) since 1970; *b* 30 March 1917; *er s* of Arthur Owen Warren and Margaret Cromarty Warren (*née* Macnaughton); *m* 1st, 1943, Barbara (marr. diss.), *er d* of Walter Myrick, Tillsonburg, Ont.; four *s* one *d*; 2nd, Jeanne Hicklin, *d* of late Frederick and Lydia Shaw, Crosland Moor. *Educ:* Charterhouse (Exhbnr); Magdalene Coll., Cambridge (Exhbnr); BA 1938, MA 1950. Colonial Administrative Service, 1938–41, serving Gold Coast (Asst DC, 1940); RAF, 1942–46; Flying Badge and commissioned, 1943; Flt Lieut, 1944. Called to Bar, Lincoln's Inn, 1947, Bencher 1967; practised at Common Law Bar, London, 1947–70. *Publications:* Verses from Lincoln's Inn (jtly), 1975; Aesop's Fables: a selection, 1982. *Recreations:* ski-ing, walking, poetry. *Clubs:* Garrick, MCC.

WARREN, Jack Hamilton, OC 1982; banker; Vice-Chairman, Bank of Montreal, since 1979; *b* 10 April 1921; *s* of Tom Hamilton Warren and Olive Sykes (*née* Horsfall); *m* 1953, Hilary Joan Titterington; two *s* two *d*. *Educ:* Queen's Univ., Kingston, Ont, Canada (BA). Served War, with Royal Canadian Navy (VR) as Lieut (Exec.), 1941–45. Joined Dept of Extl Affairs, 1945; served at Canadian High Commn, London, 1948–51; transf. to Dept of Finance, 1954; Financial Counsellor, Canadian Embassy, Washington, 1954–57, and as alternate Canadian Dir of Internat. Bank for Reconstruction and Develt, and of Internat. Monetary Fund; returned to Extl Affairs and joined Canadian Delegn to Council of NATO and OEEC, 1957; apptd Asst Dep. Minister of Dept of Trade and Commerce, 1958; elected Chm. of GATT Contracting Parties, 1962–65; apptd Dep. Minister of Trade and Commerce, 1964; Dep. Minister of Dept of Industry, Trade and Commerce, 1968; High Comr for Canada in London, 1971–74; Ambassador to USA, 1975–77; Canadian Co-ordinator for the Multilateral Trade Negotiations, 1977–79. Hon. LLD Queen's, Ont, 1974. Outstanding Achievement Award, Public Service of Canada, 1975. *Recreations:* fishing, gardening, golf, ski-ing. *Address:* Vice-Chairman, Bank of Montreal, 3rd Floor, Head Office, 129 St James Street, Montreal, PQ H2Y 1L6, Canada. *Clubs:* Mount Royal, St Denis (Montreal); Rideau (Ottawa); White Pine Fishing, Larrimac Golf (Canada); Chevy Chase (Washington).

WARREN, Dame Josephine; *see* Barnes, Dame A. J. M. T.

WARREN, Kenneth Robin, CEng, FRAeS; FCIT; FRSA; MP (C) Hastings and Rye, since 1983 (Hastings, 1970–83); Consultant in Engineering, Warren Woodfield Associates Ltd, since 1970; Director: Datapoint UK Ltd (formerly Ventek Ltd), since 1972; Loral International, since 1980; *b* 15 Aug. 1926; *s* of Edward Charles Warren and Ella Mary Warren (*née* Adams); *m* 1962, Elizabeth Anne Chamberlain, MA Cantab; one *s* two *d*. *Educ:* Midsomer Norton; Aldenham; London Univ.; De Havilland Aeronautical Technical Sch. Research Engineer, BOAC, 1951–57; Personal Asst to Gen. Manager, Smiths Aircraft Instruments Ltd, 1957–60; Elliott Automation Ltd, 1960–69; Military Flight Systems: Manager, 1960–63; Divisional Manager, 1963–66; Marketing Manager, 1966–69. Former branch officer, G&MWU. Mem., Select Cttee on Science and Technology, 1970–79 (Chm., Offshore Engrg Sub-Cttee, 1975–76); Mem., Council of Europe, 1973–80; Chm., WEU, Science, Technology and Aerospace Cttee, 1976–79; Chm., Cons. Parly Aviation Cttee, 1975–77; PPS to Sec. of State for Industry, 1979–81, to Sec. of State for Educn and Sci., 1981–83; Chairman: Select Cttee on Trade and Industry, 1983–; British Soviet Parly Gp, 1986–. Liveryman, Coachmakers' Co., Freeman, City of London. *Publications:* various papers to technical confs on on aeronautical engineering and operations, in USA, UK, Netherlands and Japan. *Recreations:* mountaineering, flying, gardening. *Address:* Woodfield House, Goudhurst, Kent. *T:* Goudhurst 211590.

WARREN, Prof. Michael Donald, MD, FRCP, FFCM; Emeritus Professor of Social Medicine, University of Kent, since 1983; *b* 19 Dec. 1923; *s* of late Charles Warren and Dorothy Gladys Thornton Reeks; *m* 1946, Joan Lavina Peacock; one *s* two *d*. *Educ:* Bedford Sch.; Guy's Hosp.; London Sch. of Hygiene and Tropical Medicine. MB 1946, MD 1952; DPH 1952, DIH 1952; MRCP 1969, FRCP 1975; FFCM 1972. Sqdn Ldr RAF, Med. Branch, 1947–51; Dep. MOH, Metropolitan Borough of Hampstead, 1952–54; Asst Principal MO, LCC, 1954–58; Sen. Lectr and Hon. Consultant in Social Medicine, Royal Free Hosp. Sch., Royal Free Hosp. and London Sch. of Hygiene and Tropical Medicine, 1958–64; Sen. Lectr in Social Medicine, LSHTM, 1964–67; Reader in Public Health, Univ. of London, 1967–71; Prof. of Community Health, Univ. of London, 1978–80; Dir, Health Services Res. Unit, and Prof. of Social Medicine, Univ. of Kent, 1971–83, jtly with Specialist in Community Medicine (Epidemiology and Health Services Res.), SE Thames RHA, 1980–83. Chm., Soc. of Social Medicine, 1982–83. Academic Registrar, Faculty of Community Medicine, Royal Colls of Physicians, 1972–77. Jt Editor, British Jl of Preventive and Social Medicine, 1969–72. *Publications:* (jt) Public Health and Social Services, 4th edn 1957, 6th edn 1965; (Jt Editor) Management and the Health Services, 1971; (jt) Physiotherapy in the Community, 1977; (jt) Physically Disabled People Living at Home, 1978; contribs to BMJ, Lancet, Internat. Jl of Epidemiology. *Recreations:* light gardening (crocuses, primroses, narcissi, irises and shrubs), genealogy, reading, listening to music. *Address:* 2 Bridge Down, Bridge, Canterbury, Kent CT4 5AZ. *T:* Bridge 830233. *Clubs:* Royal Society of Medicine; Kent County Cricket.

WARREN, Peter Francis; Chairman, Ogilvy & Mather (Holdings) Ltd, since 1981; Director, The Ogilvy Group, Inc., since 1985; *b* 2 Dec. 1940; *s* of Francis Joseph Warren and Freda Ruth Hunter; *m* 1962, Susan Poole; two *s* one *d*. *Educ:* Finchley Grammar School. Deputy Managing Director, Ogilvy Benson & Mather Ltd, 1977; Director, Ogilvy & Mather International Inc., 1978; Man. Dir, Ogilvy Benson & Mather Ltd, 1978. *Address:* Ogilvy & Mather Ltd, Brettenham House, Lancaster Place, WC2E 7EZ. *T:* 01-836 2466.

WARREN, Prof. Peter Michael, PhD; FSA; Professor of Ancient History and Classical Archaeology, University of Bristol, since 1977; *b* 23 June 1938; *s* of Arthur George Warren and Alison Joan Warren (*née* White); *m* 1966, Elizabeth Margaret Halliday; one *s* one *d*. *Educ:* Sandbach Sch.; Llandovery Coll.; University College of N Wales, Bangor (Ellen Thomas Stanford Schol.; BA 1st Cl. Hons Greek and Latin); Corpus Christi Coll., Cambridge (Exhibnr; BA Classical Tripos Pt II 1962; MA 1966; PhD 1966; Fellow, 1965–68); student, British Sch. at Athens, 1963–65. FSA 1973. Research Fellow in Arts, Univ. of Durham, 1968–70; Asst Director, British Sch. at Athens, 1970–72; University of Birmingham: Lectr in Aegean Archaeol., 1972–74; Sen. Lectr, 1974–76; Reader, 1976. Vis. Prof., Univ. of Minnesota, 1981; Geddes-Harrower Prof. of Greek Art and Archaeol., Univ. of Aberdeen, 1986–87. Dir of excavations, Myrtos, Crete, 1967–68; Debla, Crete, 1971; Knossos, 1971–73, 1978–82. Member: Managing Cttee, British Sch. at Athens, 1973–77, 1978–79, 1986– (Chm., 1979–83); Council, Soc. for Promotion of Hellenic Studies, 1978–81; Vice-Chm. Council, Bristol and Glos Archaeol Soc., 1980–81, Chm., 1981–84. *Publications:* Minoan Stone Vases, 1969; Myrtos, an Early Bronze Age Settlement in Crete, 1972; The Aegean Civilizations, 1975; articles on Aegean Bronze Age, particularly Minoan archaeology, in archaeol and classical jls. *Recreations:* South Balkan travel and Greek village life. *Address:* Claremont House, Merlin Haven, Wotton-under-Edge, Glos GL12 7BA. *T:* Dursley 842290.

WARREN, Peter Tolman, PhD; Executive Secretary, The Royal Society, since 1985; *b* 20 Dec. 1937; *s* of Hugh Alan Warren and Florence Christine Warren (*née* Tolman); *m* 1961, Angela Mary (*née* Curtis); two *s* one *d*. *Educ:* Whitgift Sch., Croydon; Queens' Coll., Cambridge (MA, PhD); FIGeol. Geological Survey of GB, 1962; Chief Scientific Adviser's Staff, Cabinet Office, 1972; Private Sec. to Lord Zuckerman, 1973–76; Science and Technology Secretariat, Cabinet Office, 1974–76; Safety Adviser, NERC, 1976–77; Dep. Exec. Sec., Royal Soc., 1977–85. Editor, Monographs of Palaeontographical Soc., 1968–77. *Publications:* (ed) Geological Aspects of Development and Planning in Northern England, 1970; (co-author) Geology of the Country around Rhyl and Denbigh, 1984; papers on geology in learned jls. *Recreations:* geology, gardening. *Address:* Flat One, 6 Carlton House Terrace, SW1Y 5AG. *T:* 01-839 5260. *Club:* Athenæum.

WARREN, Prof. Raymond Henry Charles, MusD; Stanley Hugh Badock Professor of Music, University of Bristol, since 1972; *b* 7 Nov. 1928; *m* 1953, Roberta Lydia Alice Smith; three *s* one *d*. *Educ:* Bancroft's Sch.; Corpus Christi Coll., Cambridge (MA, MusD). Music Master, Wolverstone Hall Sch., 1952–55; Queen's University Belfast: Lectr in Music, 1955–66; Prof. of Composition, 1966–72; Resident Composer, Ulster Orchestra, 1967–72. Compositions incl. 2 symphonies, 3 string quartets and 6 operas. *Publications: compositions:* The Passion, 1963; String Quartet No 1, 1967; Violin Concerto, 1967; Songs of Old Age, 1971. *Recreation:* walking. *Address:* 7 Redland Terrace, Redland, Bristol BS6 6TD. *T:* Bristol 737689.

WARREN, Robert Penn; writer; US Poet Laureate, 1986–Sept. 1987; Member of: American Academy and Institute of Arts and Letters; American Philosophical Society; American Academy of Arts and Sciences; Professor of English, Yale University, 1962–73, now Emeritus; *b* 24 April 1905; *s* of Robert Franklin Warren and Anna Ruth Penn; *m* 1930, Emma Brescia (*d* 1951); *m* 1952, Eleanor Clark; one *s* one *d*. *Educ:* Vanderbilt University, Univ. of California; Yale University; Oxford University. Asst Professor: Southwestern Coll., Tennessee, 1930–31; Vanderbilt Univ., 1931–34; Assoc. Prof., Univ. of Louisiana, 1934–42; Founder and an editor Southern Review, 1935–42; Prof., Univ. of Minnesota, 1942–50; Prof. of Drama, Yale University, 1951–56. Houghton Mifflin Fellow (fiction), 1936; Guggenheim Fellow 1939, 1947; Shelley Memorial Award (poetry), 1942; Chair of Poetry, Library of Congress, 1944–45; Pulitzer Prize (fiction), 1947; Meltzer Award for screen play, 1949; Sidney Hillman Award for Journalism, 1957; Millay Prize (Amer. Poetry Society), 1958; National Book Award (Poetry), 1958; Pulitzer Prize (poetry), 1958, 1979; Irita Van Doren Award (Herald Tribune), 1965; Bollingen Prize for Poetry, 1967; Nat. Arts Foundn Award, 1968; Van Wyck Brooks Award for Poetry, 1969; Nat. Medal for Literature, 1970; Emerson-Thoreau Medal (Amer. Acad. of Arts and Sciences), 1975; Copernicus Award for Poetry, 1976; Harriet Monroe Poetry Award, 1977; Common Wealth Award, poetry, 1976; Pulitzer Prize, poetry, 1979; Connecticut Council for the Arts Award, 1980; Gold Medal for Poetry, AAIL, 1985. Chancellor, Acad. of American Poets, 1972; Jefferson Lectr, Nat. Endowment for Humanities, 1974. Hon. DLitt: University of Louisville, 1949; Kenyon College, 1952; Colby College, 1956; University of Kentucky, 1957; Swarthmore College, 1959; Yale University, 1960; Fairfield Univ., 1969; Wesleyan Univ., 1970; Harvard Univ., 1973; New Haven, 1973; Southwestern Coll., 1974; Univ. of the South, 1974; Johns Hopkins Univ., 1977; Monmouth Coll., 1979; New York Univ., Oxford Univ., 1983; Hon. LLD, Univ. of Bridgeport, 1965. MacArthur Prize Fellowship, 1981. Presidential Medal of Freedom, 1980. *Publications:* John Brown: Making of a Martyr, 1929; XXXVI Poems, 1936; Night Rider (novel), 1939; At Heaven's Gate (novel), 1943; Eleven Poems on Same Theme, 1942; Selected Poems, 1944; All the King's Men (novel), 1946, several editions (film, 1949); Coleridge's Ancient Mariner, 1947; Blackberry Winter (Novelette), 1947; Circus in the Attic (stories), 1947; World Enough and Time (novel), 1950, 2nd edn, 1974; Brother to Dragons (poem), 1953, rewritten version, 1979; Band of Angels (novel), 1955, (film, 1957); Segregation: The Inner Conflict of the South, 1956; Promises: Poems 1954–56, 1957; Selected Essays, 1958; The Cave (novel), 1959; You, Emperors, and Others: Poems 1957–60, 1960; Legacy of the Civil War: A meditation on the centennial, 1961; Wilderness (novel), 1961; Flood: a romance of our time (novel), 1964; Who Speaks for the Negro?, 1965; Selected Poems, Old and New, 1923–1966, 1966; Incarnations: Poems 1966–68, 1968; Audubon: a Vision (poems), 1969; Homage to Theodore Dreiser, 1971; Meet Me in the Green Glen (novel), 1971; Or Else—Poem/Poems, 1968–74, 1974; Democracy and Poetry, 1975; Selected Poems 1923–75, 1977; A Place to Come To (novel), 1977; Now and Then: Poems 1976–78, 1978; Being Here: Poetry 1977–79, 1980; Rumor Verified: Poems 1977–81, 1981; Chief Joseph of the Nez Perce (poem), 1983; New and Selected Poems 1914–1984, 1985; various collections and anthologies. *Recreations:* swimming, walking. *Address:* 2495 Redding Road, Fairfield, Conn, USA. *Club:* Century (New York).

WARREN, Stanley Anthony Treleaven, CB 1984; CEng, FRINA, FIMechE; RCNC; Director General Submarines, Ministry of Defence (Procurement Executive), 1979–85, retired; *b* 26 Sept. 1925; *s* of Stanley Howard Warren and Mabel Harriett (*née* Ham); *m* 1950, Sheila Glo May (*née* Rowe); two *s* one *d*. *Educ:* King's Coll., Univ. of London (BSc 1st Cl. Hons Engrg); RNC, Greenwich (1st Cl. Naval Architecture). FRINA 1967; FIMechE 1970. Sub-Lieut, RN, 1945–47; Constructor Lieut, RCNC, 1947–51; Royal Yacht Britannia design, 1951–54; frigate modernisations, 1954–57; Constructor, HM Dockyard, Malta, 1957–60; Admiralty Constructor Overseer, John Brown and Yarrow, 1960–64; Polaris Submarine design, 1964–67; Chief Constructor and Principal Naval Overseer, Birkenhead, 1967–72; Asst Dir and Through Deck Cruiser Proj. Manager, 1972–76; Dep. Dir of Submarines (Polaris), MoD (PE), 1976–79. *Publications:* contribs to learned societies. *Recreations:* golf, motoring, gardening.

WARREN, Dr Wilfrid, FRCP, FRCPsych; Physician, Bethlem Royal Hospital and the Maudsley Hospital, 1948–75, now Emeritus; *b* 11 Oct. 1910; *s* of Frank Warren, FSA, JP, and Maud Warren; *m* 1938, Elizabeth Margaret Park; one *s* one *d*. *Educ:* Sherborne Sch.; Sidney Sussex Coll., Cambridge (MA; MD 1948); St Bartholomew's Hosp., London. DPM 1946. FRCP 1972; FRCPsych 1971. Served War, 1939–45: Surgeon Lt Comdr, RNVR. Consultant Adviser, Child and Adolescent Psychiatry, DHSS (formerly Min. of Health), 1961–76; Hon. Consultant in Child Psych. to Army, 1969–75. President: Sect. of Mental Health, Soc. of Med. Officers of Health, 1962–63; Sect. of Psych., RSM, 1970–71. Treasurer, Royal Coll. of Psychiatrists (formerly Royal Medico-Psychol Soc.), 1962–79 (Vice-Pres., 1974–76). Distinguished Hon. Fellow, Amer. Psychiatric Assoc., 1968; Hon. FRCPsych, 1979. *Publications:* articles in learned jls on child and adolescent psychiatry. *Recreations:* gardening, literature, music. *Address:* 54 Vincent Drive, Westminster Park, Chester CH4 7RL.

WARREN, William Phillip, CEng, FIEE, FInstPet; Senior Partner, Warren Associates, since 1985; Director, W. S. Atkins & Partners (Wales), since 1985; *b* 7 Oct. 1924; *yr s* of Herbert U. Warren and Rebecca Warren (*née* Thomas); *m* 1956, Janice Mary, *er d* of James and Lilian Holloway; one *s* one *d*. *Educ:* Quakers Yard Grammar Sch.; Univ. of Wales, Cardiff (BSc). Post graduate trng and early appts, General Electric Co. Ltd, 1943–48; Asst Chief Commercial Engr, S Wales Electricity Board, 1948–54; Chief Executive, subsidiary co., Metal Industries Ltd, 1954–56; First Commercial Manager, UKAEA, 1956–59; Dir, several subsid. companies, Powell Duffryn Ltd, 1959–68; Director, Chief Executive of subsid. companies, Tube Investments Ltd, 1968–74; Man. Dir, Davy Water Engineering Ltd, Davy International Ltd, 1974–76, Exec. Dir, Welsh Develt Agency, 1976–85. Governor: University of Wales, 1971–; University Coll. Cardiff, 1985–; Life Governor and Mem. Council, UWIST, 1968–; formerly Mem. Council: Industrial Assoc. of Wales and Mon. (now CBI, Wales); Brit. Manufrs of Petroleum Equipment. *Publications:* articles in learned jls include: UK Nuclear Power Programme; High Frequency Communications over EHT Circuits; Electronics in Industry. *Recreations:* gardening, occasional golf, charity fund raising. *Address:* Eastfield House, Cowbridge, S Glamorgan CF7 7EP. *T:* Cowbridge 2392. *Club:* Cardiff and County.

WARREN EVANS, (John) Roger, FCIOB; Managing Director, Demos Ltd, since 1985; *b* 11 Dec. 1935; *s* of Thomas and Mary Warren Evans; *m* 1966, Elizabeth M. James; one *s* one *d.* *Educ:* Leighton Park Sch., Reading; Trinity Coll., Cambridge (BA History, 1st Cl.); London Sch. of Economics. Called to Bar, Gray's Inn, 1962. Television Interviewer, Anglia Television, 1960–61; Research Officer, Centre for Urban Studies, London, 1961; practice at Bar, 1962–69; Legal Correspondent, New Society, 1964–68; general management functions with Bovis Gp, in construction and develt, 1969–74, incl. Man. Dir, Bovis Homes Southern Ltd, 1971–74; Under-Secretary, DoE, 1975; Industrial Advr on Construction, DoE, 1975–76; Man. Dir, Barratt Develts (London), Ltd, 1977–79; Dir, Swansea Centre for Trade and Industry, 1979–85. London Borough Councillor (Hackney), 1971–73. FCIOB 1976. *Recreations:* tennis, talking, playing the guitar. *Address:* 23 St Peter's Road, Newton, Swansea. *T:* Swansea 68003.

WARRENDER, family name of **Baron Bruntisfield.**

WARRENDER, Col the Hon. John Robert, OBE 1963; MC 1943; TD 1967; DL; *b* 7 Feb. 1921; *s* and *heir* of Baron Bruntisfield, *qv*; *m* 1st, 1948, (Anne) Moireen Campbell (*d* 1976), 2nd *d* of Sir Walter Campbell, KCIE; two *s* two *d*; 2nd, 1977, Mrs Shirley Crawley (*d* 1981), *o d* of E. J. L. Ross; 3rd, 1985, Mrs (Kathleen) Joanna Graham, *o d* of David Chancellor. *Educ:* Eton; RMC, Sandhurst. Royal Scots Greys (2nd Dragoons), 1939–48; ADC to Governor of Madras, 1946–48; comd N Somerset Yeomanry/44th Royal Tank Regt, 1957–62; Dep. Brigadier RAC (TA), Southern and Eastern Commands, 1962–67. Mem., Queen's Body Guard for Scotland (Royal Co. of Archers), 1973 (Brigadier, 1973–85). DL Somerset 1965. *Recreations:* shooting, fishing. *Address:* 4 Carlton Street, Edinburgh EH4 1NJ. *T:* 031–343 3122. *Clubs:* Pratt's; New (Edinburgh).
See also Hon. R. H. Warrender.

WARRENDER, Hon. Robin Hugh; Chairman and Chief Executive, London Wall Holdings PLC, since 1986; *b* 24 Dec. 1927; 3rd *s* of Baron Bruntisfield, *qv*; *m* 1951, Gillian, *d* of Leonard Rossiter; one *s* two *d.* *Educ:* Eton; Trinity Coll., Oxford. Underwriting Member of Lloyd's, 1953; Tudor & Co. (Insurance) Ltd, 1958–62; Managing Director, Fenchurch Insurance Holdings Ltd, 1963–69; Dep. Chm., A. W. Bain & Sons Ltd, 1970; Chm., Bain Dawes PLC and other group companies, 1973–85. Director: Comindus S. A. (France), 1980–; Worms & Co., 1981–; Varity Corporation (Canada), 1982–; Varity Holdings Ltd, 1982–; Heritable Group Holdings Ltd, 1983–. Mem. Council and Cttee of Lloyd's, 1983–. Mem. Council, Bath Univ., 1979–; Hon. Treas., Governing Cttee, Royal Choral Soc., 1979–. *Recreations:* shooting, gardening, bridge. *Address:* Widcombe Manor, Bath, Avon. *T:* Bath 317116. *Clubs:* City of London, Portland, White's.
See also Baron Colgrain, Col the Hon. J. R. Warrender.

WARRINGTON, Bishop Suffragan of, since 1976; **Rt. Rev. Michael Henshall;** *b* 29 Feb. 1928; *m* Ann Elizabeth (*née* Stephenson); two *s* one *d.* *Educ:* Manchester Grammar Sch.; St Chad's Coll., Durham (BA 1954, DipTh 1956). Deacon 1956, priest 1957, dio. York; Curate of Holy Trinity, Bridlington and of Sewerby, 1956–59; Priest-in-charge, All Saints, Conventional District of Micklehurst, 1959–62; Vicar, 1962–63; Vicar of Altrincham, 1963–75; Proctor in Convocation, 1964–75; Mem., Terms of Ministry Cttee, General Synod, 1970–75; Hon. Canon of Chester, 1972–75; Secretary, Chester Diocesan Advisory Board for Ministry, 1968–75; Canon Emeritus of Chester Cathedral, 1979. Chm., Northern Ordination Course Council, 1985. Editor for 12 years of local newspaper, Spearhead. *Recreations:* military history, old battlefields, etc. *Address:* Martinsfield, Elm Avenue, Great Crosby, Liverpool, Merseyside L23 2SX. *T:* 051–924 7004; (office) 051–709 9722.

WARRINGTON, Archdeacon of; *see* Woodhouse, Ven. C. D. S.

WARRINGTON, Anthony; Company Secretary and Director, Policy Co-ordination, Rolls-Royce plc, initially on secondment from Department of Industry, since 1978; *b* 15 Aug. 1929; *s* of Stanley Warrington and Gladys (*née* Sutcliffe); *m* 1955, Lavinia Lord; three *s.* *Educ:* Welwyn Garden City Grammar Sch.; London School of Economics. Asst Statistician: Admiralty, 1953; British Electricity Authority, 1954–55; Economist, British Transport Commn, 1956–58; Statistician, Min. of Power, 1958–66; Asst Secretary: Petroleum Div., Min. of Power (later Min. of Technology), 1966–72; Atomic Energy Div., DTI, 1972–73; Under-Sec., DoI, 1973; Air Div., 1973–78; Dir-Gen., Concorde Div. DoI, 1976–77. Mem. Council, SBAC, 1985–. *Recreations:* theatre, hockey, golf. *Address:* 9 Fern Grove, Welwyn Garden City, Herts AL8 7ND. *T:* Welwyn Garden 326110.

WARRINGTON, Prof. Elizabeth Kerr, FRS 1986; Professor of Clinical Neuropsychology, National Hospital, since 1982; *d* of late Prof. John Alfred Valentine Butler, FRS and Margaret Lois Butler; one *d.* *Educ:* University College London (BSc 1954; PhD 1960; DSc 1975). Research Fellow, Inst. of Neurology, 1956; National Hospital: Senior Clinical Psychologist, 1960; Principal Psychologist, 1962; Top Grade Clinical Psychologist, 1972–82. *Publications:* numerous papers in neurological and psychological jls. *Recreation:* gardening. *Address:* National Hospital, Queen Square, WC1N 3BG. *T:* 01–837 3611.

WARSOP, Rear-Adm. John Charles, CB 1984; Flag Officer Portsmouth and Naval Base Commander Portsmouth, 1983–85; RN retired, 1986; *b* 9 May 1927; *s* of John Charles Warsop and Elsie Lily Warsop; *m* 1958, Josephine Franklin Cotterell; two *d.* *Educ:* Gateway Sch., Leicester; RN Coll., Eaton Hall, Chester; RN Engineering Coll., Keyham, Plymouth, 1945–48. FIMechE 1983. HM Ships Theseus and Gambia, 1949–50; RNC Greenwich, 1950–52; HMS Superb, 1952–54; Staff, RNEC, 1954–56; Min. of Defence, 1956–59; Sen. Engr, HMS Ark Royal, 1959–61; MoD, 1961–65; British Defence Staff, Washington, USA, 1965–68; MoD, 1968–70; Engr Officer, HMS Blake, 1970–72; MoD, 1972–75; CO, HMS Fisgard, 1975–78; MoD, 1979–81; Rear-Adm. 1981; Port Adm., Rosyth, 1981–83. *Publications:* papers for Instn of Marine Engineers. *Recreations:* offshore cruising, Rugby. *Club:* Royal Naval Sailing Association.

WARTIOVAARA, Otso Uolevi, Hon. GCVO; Ambassador of Finland to the Court of St James's, 1968–74; *b* Helsinki, 16 Nov. 1908; *s* of J. V. Wartiovaara, Dir-Gen. of Finnish Govt Accounting Office, and Siiri Nystén; *m* 1936, Maine Alanen, three *s.* *Educ:* Helsinki Univ. Master of Law, 1932; Asst Judge, 1934. Entered Foreign Service, 1934; Attaché, Paris, 1936–39; Sec. and Head of Section, Min. for For. Affairs, 1939–42; Counsellor, Stockholm, 1942–44; Consul, Haaparanta, Sweden, 1944–45; Head of Section, Min. for For. Affairs, 1945–49; Counsellor, Washington, 1949–52; Head of Admin. Dept, Min. for For. Affairs, 1952–54; Envoy and Minister, 1954; Head of Legal Dept, Min. for For. Affairs, 1954–56; Minister, Belgrade and Athens, 1956–58; Ambassador, Belgrade, and Minister to Athens, 1958–61; Ambassador to Vienna, 1961–68, and to Holy See, 1966–68, also Perm. Rep. to Internat. Atomic Energy Organization, 1961–68. Grand Cross, Order of Lion of Finland; Kt Comdr, Order of White Rose of Finland; Cross of Freedom; Silver Cross of Sport, Finland. Grand Gold Cross of Austria; Grand Cross, Orders of Phœnix (Greece), Pius IX, Flag (Yugoslavia); Comdr, Orders of Northern Star (Sweden), St Olav (Norway) and Vasa (Sweden). *Recreations:* golf, shooting. *Address:* Lutherinkatn 6. A, 00100 Helsinki 10, Finland. *Club:* Travellers'.

WARTNABY, Dr John; Keeper, Department of Earth and Space Sciences, Science Museum, South Kensington, 1969–82; *b* 6 Jan. 1926; *o s* of Ernest John and Beatrice Hilda Wartnaby; *m* 1962, Kathleen Mary Barber, MD, MRCP, DPM; one *s* one *d.* *Educ:* Chiswick Grammar Sch.; Chelsea Coll. (BSc 1946); Imperial Coll. of Science and Technology (DIC 1950); University Coll., London (MSc 1967; PhD 1972). FInstP 1971. Asst Keeper, Dept of Astronomy and Geophysics, Science Museum, 1951; Deputy Keeper, 1960. *Publications:* Seismology, 1957; The International Geophysical Year, 1957; Surveying, 1968; papers in learned jls. *Recreations:* country walking, Zen, distance running. *Address:* 11 Greenhurst Lane, Oxted, Surrey RH8 0LD. *T:* Oxted 4461.

WARWICK; *see* Turner-Warwick.

WARWICK, 8th Earl of, *cr* 1759; **David Robin Francis Guy Greville;** Baron Brooke 1621; Earl Brooke 1746; *b* 15 May 1934; *s* of 7th Earl of Warwick, and Rose, *d* of late D. C. Bingham; *S* father, 1984; *m* 1956, Sarah Anne (marr. diss. 1967), *d* of late Alfred Chester Beatty and Mrs Pamela Neilson; one *s* one *d.* *Educ:* Eton. Life Guards, 1952; Warwicks Yeo. (TA), 1954. *Heir:* *s* Lord Brooke, *qv.* *Address:* Leeward Marina, Providenciales, Turks and Caicos Islands, BWI. *Clubs:* White's; The Brook (NY); Travellers' (Paris); Eagle Ski (Gstaad).

WARWICK, Bishop Suffragan of, since 1980; **Rt. Rev. Keith Appleby Arnold;** *b* 1 Oct. 1926; *s* of Dr Frederick Arnold, Hale, Cheshire, and Alice Mary Appleby Arnold (*née* Holt); *m* 1955, Deborah Noreen Glenwright; one *s* one *d.* *Educ:* Winchester; Trinity Coll., Cambridge (MA); Westcott House, Cambridge. Served as Lieut, Coldstream Guards, 1944–48. Curate: Haltwhistle, Northumberland, 1952–55; St John's, Princes St, Edinburgh, 1955–61; Chaplain, TA, 1956–61; Rector of St John's, Edinburgh, 1961–69; Vicar of Kirkby Lonsdale, Cumbria, 1969–73; Team Rector of Hemel Hempstead, 1973–80. Vice-Pres., Abbeyfield Soc., 1981–; Chm., Housing Assoc.'s Charitable Trust, 1981–. *Recreations:* skiing, gardening. *Address:* Warwick House, 139 Kenilworth Road, Coventry CV4 7AF. *T:* Coventry 416200.

WARWICK, Archdeacon of; *see* Bridges, Ven. P. S. G.

WARWICK, Diana; General Secretary, Association of University Teachers, since 1983; *b* 16 July 1945; *d* of Jack and Olive Warwick; *m* 1969. *Educ:* St Joseph's Coll., Bradford; Bedford Coll., Univ. of London (BA Hons). Technical Asst to the Gen. Sec., NUT, 1969–72; Asst Sec., CPSA, 1972–83. Mem. Bd, British Council, 1985–. *Recreations:* reading, riding, looking at pictures. *Address:* AUT, United House, 1 Pembridge Road, Notting Hill Gate, W11 3HJ. *T:* 01–221 4370.

WARWICK, Hannah Cambell Grant; *see* Gordon, H. C. G.

WARWICK, Prof. Roger; retired; Professor Emeritus, University of London. *Educ:* Altrincham Grammar Sch. (Victor Ludorum, 1930, 1931 and 1932; prizes in Greek, Latin and English); Victoria University of Manchester. BSc 1935; MB, ChB, Manchester, 1937 (Sydney Renshaw Prize in Physiology, 1937); MD (Gold Medal), 1952; PhD, 1955. House Physician and House Surgeon, Professorial Unit, Manchester Royal Infirmary, 1938–39; Surgeon Lieut, RNVR, 1939–45; Demonstrator and Lectr in Anatomy, Univ. of Manchester, 1945–55; Prof. of Anatomy and Dir of Dept of Anatomy, Guy's Hosp. Med. Sch., London Univ., 1955–80. Arris and Gale Lectr, RCS, 1960; Fison Lectr, Guy's Hosp., 1986. Member: Anatomical Society of Great Britain (Symington Memorial Prize, 1953); Anatomical Socs of Brazil, India and SA; Scientific Fellow of Zoological Society; Fellow, Linnean Soc.; Hon. Sec., Internat. Anat. Nomenclature Cttee. *Publications:* Gray's Anatomy (co-ed), 35th edn, 1973, 36th edn, 1980; (ed) Wolff's Anatomy of the Eye and Orbit, 7th edn, 1977; (ed) Nomina Anatomica, 4th edn, 1977, 5th edn, 1983, and other books; contributions to Brain, Journal Anat., Journal Comp. Neurol., etc. *Recreations:* Natural history, especially Lepidoptera, radio communication, archæology. *Address:* c/o Department of Anatomy, Guy's Hospital Medical School, SE1 9RT.

WARWICK, Captain William Eldon, CBE 1971; RD, RNR retired; Commodore, Cunard Line Ltd, 1970–75; First Master, RMS Queen Elizabeth 2, 1966–72; *b* 12 Nov. 1912; *e s* of Eldon Warwick, architect and Gertrude Florence Gent; *m* 1939, Evelyn King (*née* Williams); three *s.* *Educ:* Birkenhead Sch.; HMTS Conway. Joined Merchant Service, 1928, serving in Indian Ocean and Red Sea; awarded Master Mariner's Certificate, 1936; joined Cunard White Star as Jun. Officer (Lancastria), 1937; commissioned in RNR, 1937. Mobilized in RN War Service, 1939, in Coastal Forces and Corvettes in North Atlantic, Russian Convoys and Normandy Landings, 1939–46 (despatches, 1946). First cargo command, Alsatia, 1954; first passenger command, Carinthia, 1958; followed by command of almost all the passenger liners in Cunard fleet. Promoted Captain RNR, 1960; retd RNR, 1965. Younger Brother of Trinity House; Liveryman, Hon. Co. of Master Mariners (Master, 1976–77); Freeman of City of London. *Recreations:* reading, music, walking. *Address:* Greywell Cottage, Callow Hill, Virginia Water, Surrey. *T:* Wentworth 3361. *Club:* Naval.

WASHBOURN, Rear-Admiral Richard Everley, CB 1961; DSO 1940; OBE 1950; Chief of Naval Staff, RNZN, 1963–65, retired; *b* 14 Feb. 1910; *s* of H. E. A. Washbourn, Nelson, NZ; *m* 1943, June, *d* of L. M. Herapath, Auckland, NZ; one *s* one *d.* *Educ:* Nelson Coll., New Zealand. Entered Royal Navy by Special Entry from New Zealand, 1927; HMS Erebus, 1928; HMS London, 1929–31; Courses, 1932; HMS Warspite, 1933; HMS Diomede, 1934–35; Specialised in Gunnery, 1936–37; HMS Excellent, 1938; HMS Achilles, 1939–42; Battle of the Plate, 13 Dec. 1939 (DSO); HMS Excellent, 1942; HMS Anson, 1943. Admiralty Gunnery Establishment, 1944–45; Exec. Officer, HMNZS, Bellona, 1946–48; Comdr Supt HMNZ Dockyard, Devonport, 1950; Dep. Director of Naval Ordnance, 1950–53; HMS Manxman, 1953; Chief Staff Officer to Flag Officer (Flotillas), Mediterranean, 1954–55; Director of Naval Ordnance, Admiralty, 1956–58; HMS Tiger, 1959; Director-General, Weapons, 1960–62; retired Royal Navy, 1962; entered RNZN, 1963; retired RNZN, 1965. *Recreation:* beachcombing. *Address:* Onekaka, RD2, Takaka, Golden Bay, Nelson, New Zealand.

WASS, Dr Charles Alfred Alan; Director of Safety in Mines Research Establishment, Sheffield, 1970–74; *b* 20 July 1911; *s* of William and Louise Wass, Sutton-in-Ashfield, Nottinghamshire; *m* 1936, Alice Elizabeth Carpenter; two *d.* *Educ:* Brunt's Sch., Mansfield; Nottingham Univ. Post Office Radio Research Station, 1934–46; Royal Aircraft Establishment, 1946–55; Safety in Mines Research Establishment, 1955–74. *Publications:* Introduction to Electronic Analogue Computers, 1955 (2nd edn, with K. C. Garner, 1965); papers on electrical communication subjects and mine safety. *Recreations:* music making, reed instruments. *Address:* The Old School House, Swine, Hull, North Humberside HU11 4JE. *T:* Hull 811227.

WASS, Sir Douglas (William Gretton), GCB 1980 (KCB 1975; CB 1971); Chairman: Equity & Law Life Assurance Society plc, since 1986 (Director, since 1984); Nomura International, since 1986; Permanent Secretary to HM Treasury, 1974–83, and Joint Head of the Home Civil Service, 1981–83; *b* 15 April 1923; *s* of late Arthur W. and late Elsie W. Wass; *m* 1954, Dr Milica Pavičić; one *s* one *d.* *Educ:* Nottingham High Sch.; St John's Coll., Cambridge (MA; Hon. Fellow, 1982). Served War, 1943–46: Scientific Research with Admiralty, at home and in Far East. Entered HM Treasury as Asst Principal, 1946; Principal, 1951; Commonwealth Fund Fellow in USA, 1958–59; Vis. Fellow, Brookings Instn, Washington, DC, 1959; Private Sec.: to Chancellor of the Exchequer, 1959–61; to Chief Sec. to Treasury, 1961–62; Asst Sec., 1962; Alternate Exec. Dir, Internat. Monetary Fund, and Financial Counsellor, British Embassy, Washington, DC, 1965–67; HM Treasury: Under-Sec., 1968; Dep. Sec., 1970–73; Second Permanent Sec., 1973–74. Director: Barclays Bank, 1984–; De La Rue Company plc, 1984–; Consultant to Coopers & Lybrand, 1984–86. Chm., British Selection Cttee of Harkness Fellowships, 1981–84; Dep. Chm., Council of Policy Studies Inst, 1981–85; Vice-Pres., Constitutional Reform Centre, 1984–; Governor, Ditchley Foundn, 1981–; Member, Council: Centre for Econ. Policy Res., 1983–; Employment Inst., 1985–. Reith Lectr, BBC, 1983; Shell Lectr, St Andrews Univ., 1985. Hon. DLitt Bath, 1985. *Publications:* Government and the Governed,1984; articles in newspapers and jls. *Address:* 6 Dora Road, SW19 7HH. *T:* 01–946 5556. *Club:* Reform.

WASSERMAN, Gordon Joshua; Assistant Under Secretary of State, Home Office, since 1983; *b* Montreal, 26 July 1938; *s* of late John J. Wasserman, QC, and Prof. Rachel Chait Wasserman, Montreal; *m* 1964, Cressida Frances, *yr d* of late Rt Hon. Hugh Gaitskell, PC, CBE, MP, and of Baroness Gaitskell, *qv*; two *d.* *Educ:* Westmount High Sch., Montreal; McGill Univ. (BA); New Coll., Oxford (MA). Rhodes Scholar (Quebec and New Coll.), 1959; Sen. Research Scholar, St Antony's Coll., Oxford, 1961–64; Lectr in Economics, Merton Coll., Oxford, 1963–64; Research Fellow, New Coll., Oxford, 1964–67; joined Home Office as Economic Adviser, 1967, Sen. Econ. Adviser, 1972, Asst Sec., 1977–81; Head, Urban Deprivation Unit, 1973–77; Civil Service Travelling Fellowship in USA, 1977–78; Under Sec., Central Policy Review Staff, Cabinet Office, 1981–83. Vice-Pres., English Basket Ball Assoc., 1983–86. *Recreations:* gardening, walking, theatre, music. *Address:* c/o Home Office, SW1. *Clubs:* Reform, Beefsteak.

WASSERSTEIN, Prof. Abraham; Professor of Greek, Hebrew University of Jerusalem, since 1969; *b* Frankfurt/Main, Germany, 5 Oct. 1921; *s* of late Berl Bernhard Wasserstein and late Czarna Cilla (*née* Laub); *m* 1942, Margaret Eva (*née* Ecker); two *s* one *d.* *Educ:* Schools in Berlin and Rome; privately in Palestine; Birkbeck Coll., London Univ. BA 1949, PhD 1951. Assistant in Greek, 1951–52, Lecturer in Greek, 1952–60, Glasgow Univ.; Prof. of Classics, Leicester Univ., 1960–69, and Dean of Faculty of Arts, 1966–69. Visiting Fellow: Centre for Postgraduate Hebrew Studies, Oriental Inst., Univ. of Oxford, 1973–74; Wolfson Coll., Oxford, 1986; Vis. Professor: Hochschule für Jüdische Studien, Heidelberg, 1980–81; Univ. of Heidelberg, 1983. Mem. Inst. for Advanced Study, Princeton, 1975–76 and 1985–86. FRAS 1961; Pres., Classical Assoc. of Israel, 1971–74. *Publications:* Flavius Josephus, 1974; Galen, On Airs, Waters, Places (critical edn, with trans. and notes), 1982; contrib. to learned journals. *Recreations:* theatre, travel. *Address:* Department of Classics, The Hebrew University, Jerusalem, Israel.

WASTELL, Cyril Gordon, CBE 1975; Secretary General of Lloyd's, 1967–76, retired; *b* 10 Jan. 1916; *s* of Arthur Edward Wastell and Lilian Wastell; *m* 1947, Margaret Lilian (*née* Moore); one *d.* *Educ:* Brentwood Sch., Essex. Joined Staff of Corporation of Lloyd's, 1932; apart from war service (Lieut Royal Corps of Signals), 1939–46, progressed through various depts and positions at Lloyd's, until retirement. *Recreations:* sailing, reading, gardening under duress. *Address:* Candys, Burgmann's Hill, Lympstone, Devon EX8 5HP.

WASTIE, Winston Victor, CB 1962; OBE 1946 (MBE 1937); Under-Secretary, Ministry of Public Building and Works, Scotland, 1959–62, retired; *b* 5 March 1900; *s* of H. Wastie; *m* 1924, Charmbury Billows; one *d.* *Educ:* Greenwich Secondary Sch. Civil Service, New Scotland Yard, 1915–42; Chief Licensing Officer, Civil Building Control, Ministry of Works, 1942–46; Assistant Secretary, Scottish HQ, Ministry of Works, 1946–59; Under-Secretary, 1959. *Recreations:* bridge, gardening and sport. *Address:* Dirleton, Hazelbank Close, Petersfield, Hants.

WATERFIELD, Giles Adrian; Director, Dulwich Picture Gallery, since 1979; *b* 1949; *s* of Anthony and Honor Waterfield. *Educ:* Eton College; Magdalen College, Oxford (BA); Courtauld Institute (MA). Education Officer, Royal Pavilion, Art Gallery and Museums, Brighton, 1976–79. *Publications:* Faces, 1983; Collection for a King (catalogue), 1985; articles in Apollo, Connoisseur, Country Life. *Recreation:* sightseeing. *Address:* c/o Dulwich Picture Gallery, College Road, SE21 7AD. *Club:* Travellers'.

WATERFIELD, John Percival; *b* Dublin, 5 Oct. 1921; *er s* of late Sir Percival Waterfield, KBE, CB; *m* 1950, Margaret Lee Thomas; two *s* one *d.* *Educ:* Dragon Sch.; Charterhouse (schol.); Christ Church, Oxford (schol.). Served War of 1939–45: 1st Bn, The King's Royal Rifle Corps (60th Rifles), Western Desert, Tunisia, Italy and Austria (despatches). Entered HM Foreign (subseq. Diplomatic) Service, 1946; Third Secretary, Moscow, 1947; Second Secretary, Tokyo, 1950; Foreign Office, 1952; First Secretary, Santiago, Chile, 1954; HM Consul (Commercial), New York, 1957; FO, 1960; Ambassador to Mali Republic, 1964–65, concurrently to Guinea, 1965; duties connected with NATO, 1966; Counsellor and Head of Chancery, New Delhi, 1966–68; Head of Western Organizations Dept, FCO, 1969; Man. Dir, BEAMA, 1971; Principal Estabs and Finance Officer, NI Office, 1973–79; on secondment to Internat. Military Services Ltd, 1979–80; retired from public service, 1980; company dir and consultant, 1980–84. *Address:* 5 North Street, Somerton, Somerset. *T:* Somerton 72389. *Club:* Boodle's.

WATERFORD, 8th Marquess of, *cr* 1789; **John Hubert de la Poer Beresford;** Baron La Poer, 1375; Baronet, 1668; Viscount Tyrone, Baron Beresford, 1720; Earl of Tyrone, 1746; Baron Tyrone (Great Britain), 1786; *b* 14 July 1933; *er s* of 7th Marquess and Juliet Mary (who *m* 2nd, 1946, Lieut-Colonel John Silcock), 2nd *d* of late David Lindsay; *S* father, 1934; *m* 1957, Lady Caroline Wyndham-Quin, *yr d* of 6th Earl of Dunraven and Mount-Earl, CB, CBE, MC; three *s* one *d.* *Educ:* Eton. Lieut, RHG Reserve. *Heir:* *s* Earl of Tyrone, *qv.* *Address:* Curraghmore, Portlaw, Co. Waterford. *T:* Waterford 87102. *Club:* White's.

WATERHOUSE, Dr Douglas Frew, AO 1980; CMG 1970; FRS 1967; FAA 1954; FRACI 1948; Chief of Division of Entomology, Commonwealth Scientific and Industrial Research Organization, 1960–81, Honorary Research Fellow, since 1981; *b* 3 June 1916; *s* of late Prof. E. G. Waterhouse, CMG, OBE, and Janet Frew Kellie, MA; *m* 1944, Allison D., *d* of J. H. Calthorpe; three *s* one *d.* *Educ:* Sydney C of E Grammar Sch.; Universities of Sydney and Cambridge. BSc Hons, University Medal, MSc, DSc, Sydney. Served War of 1939–45, Captain, AAMC Medical Entomology. Joined Research Staff, CSIRO, 1938; Asst Chief, Div. of Entomology, 1953–60. Biological Secretary, Australian Acad. of Science, 1961–66; Chairman: Council, Canberra Coll. of Advanced Educn, 1969–84; Council for Internat. Congresses of Entomology, 1980–84; AIDC Nat. Sci. Summer Sch., 1985–; Pres. Nat. Trust of Australia, 1984–. Corresp. Mem., Brazilian Acad. of Sciences, 1974. Hon. For. Mem., All-Union Entomological Soc. of USSR, 1979; For. Mem., USSR Acad. of Science, 1982; Foreign Assoc., US Nat. Acad. of Scis, 1983. Hon. FRES 1972. David Syme Research Prize, 1953; Mueller Medal, ANZAAS, 1972; Farrer Medal, Farrer Meml Trust, 1973; Medal, 10th Internat. Congress of Plant Protection, 1983. Hon. DSc ANU, 1978. *Publications:* numerous articles on insect physiology, biochemistry, ecology and control of insects. *Recreations:* gardening, fishing, gyotaku. *Address:* 60 National Circuit, Deakin, ACT 2600, Australia. *T:* 731772. *Club:* Commonwealth (Canberra).

WATERHOUSE, Frederick Harry; tax and investment consultant; Partner, Bognor Antiques, Bognor Regis, since 1984; *b* 3 June 1932; *m* 1954, Olive Carter; two *d.* *Educ:* King Edward's, Aston, Birmingham; London Univ. (BScEcon). Associate Mem. Inst. of Cost and Management Accountants. Chief Accountant, Copper Div., Imperial Metal Industries, 1967–70; Asst Chief Accountant, Agricl Div., ICI, 1970–72; Chief Accountant, Plant Protection Div., ICI, 1972–78; Dir, Société pour la Protection d'Agriculture (SOPRA), France, 1976–78; Dir, Solplant SA, Italy, 1976–78; Bd Member, Finance and Corporate Planning, The Post Office, 1978–79; Treasurer's Dept, ICI Ltd, Millbank, 1979–82. *Recreations:* golf, gardening, sailing. *Address:* 47 Grosvenor Road, Chichester PO19 2RT. *T:* Chichester 783745.

WATERHOUSE, Keith Spencer; writer; *b* 6 Feb. 1929; 4th *s* of Ernest and Elsie Edith Waterhouse; *m* 1984, Stella Bingham; one *s* two *d* by previous *m.* *Educ:* Leeds. Journalist in Leeds and London, 1950–; Columnist with: Daily Mirror, 1970–86; Daily Mail, 1986–; Contributor to Punch, 1966–, Mem. Punch Table, 1979. Granada Columnist of the Year Award, 1970; IPC Descriptive Writer of the Year Award, 1970; IPC Columnist of the Year Award, 1973; British Press Awards Columnist of the Year, 1978; Granada Special Quarter Century Award, 1982. Films (with Willis Hall) include: Billy Liar; Whistle Down the Wind; A Kind of Loving; Lock Up Your Daughters. Plays: Mr and Mrs Nobody, 1986; plays with Willis Hall include: Billy Liar, 1960 (from which musical Billy was adapted, 1974); Celebration, 1961; All Things Bright and Beautiful, 1963; Say Who You Are, 1965; Whoops-a-Daisy, 1968; Children's Day, 1969; Who's Who, 1972; The Card (musical), 1973; Saturday, Sunday, Monday (adaptation from de Filippo), 1973; Filumena (adaptation from de Filippo), 1977; Worzel Gummidge, 1981. TV series: Budgie, Queenie's Castle, The Upper Crusts, Billy Liar, The Upchat Line, The Upchat Connection, Worzel Gummidge, West End Tales, The Happy Apple, Charters and Caldicott; TV films: Charlie Muffin, 1983; This Office Life, 1985; Slip-Up, 1986. *Publications:* *novels:* There is a Happy Land, 1957; Billy Liar, 1959; Jubb, 1963; The Bucket Shop, 1968; Billy Liar on the Moon, 1975; Office Life, 1978; Maggie Muggins, 1981; In the Mood, 1983; Thinks, 1984; *plays:* (all with Willis Hall) include: Billy Liar, 1960; Celebration, 1961; All Things Bright and Beautiful, 1963; Say Who You Are, 1965; Who's Who, 1974; Saturday, Sunday, Monday (adaptation from de Filippo), 1974; Filumena (adaptation from de Filippo), 1977; *general:* (with Guy Deghy) Café Royal, 1956; (ed) Writers' Theatre, 1967; The Passing of The Third-floor Buck, 1974; Mondays, Thursdays, 1976; Rhubarb, Rhubarb, 1979; Daily Mirror Style, 1980; Fanny Peculiar, 1983; Mrs Pooter's Diary, 1983; Waterhouse At Large, 1985; Collected Letters of a Nobody, 1986; The Theory and Practice of Lunch, 1986. *Recreation:* lunch. *Address:* 29 Kenway Road, SW5. *Clubs:* Garrick, Savile, PEN.

WATERHOUSE, Mrs Rachel Elizabeth, CBE 1980; PhD; Chairman, Consumers' Association, since 1982 (Member Council, since 1966, Deputy Chairman, 1979–82); *b* 2 Jan. 1923; *d* of Percival John Franklin and Ruby Susanna Franklin; *m* 1947, John A. H. Waterhouse; two *s* two *d.* *Educ:* King Edward's High Sch., Birmingham; St Hugh's Coll., Oxford (BA 1944, MA 1948); Univ. of Birmingham (PhD 1950). WEA and Extra-mural tutor, 1944–47. Birmingham Consumer Group: Sec., 1964–65, Chm. 1966–68, Mem. Cttee, 1968–; Member: Nat. Consumer Council, 1975–86; Consumers' Consultative Cttee of EEC Commn, 1977–84; Price Commn, 1977–79; Council, Advertising Standards Authority, 1980–85; NEDC, 1981–; BBC Consultative Gp on Industrial and Business Affairs, 1984–. Ministerial nominee to Potato Marketing Bd, 1969–81; Chm., Council for Licensed Conveyancers, 1986–; Member: Home Office Working Party on Internal Shop Security, 1971–73; Adv. Cttee on Asbestos, 1976–79; Council for the Securities Industry, 1983–85; Securities and Investments Board, 1985–; Organising Cttee, Marketing of Investments Bd, 1985–86; Council, Office of the Banking Ombudsman, 1985–; Duke of Edinburgh's Inquiry into British Housing, 1984–85. Pres., Inst. of Consumer Ergonomics, Univ. of Loughborough, 1980– (Chm., 1970–80). Chm., Birmingham Gp, Victorian Soc., 1966–67, 1972–74. Hon. DLitt, Univ. of Technology, Loughborough, 1978. *Publications:* The Birmingham and Midland Institute 1854–1954, 1954; A Hundred Years of Engineering Craftsmanship, 1957; Children in Hospital: a hundred years of child care in Birmingham, 1962; (with John Whybrow) How Birmingham became a Great City, 1976; King Edward VI High School for Girls 1883–1983, 1983. *Recreations:* conversation and sewing. *Address:* 252 Bristol Road, Birmingham B5 7SL. *T:* 021–472 0427. *Club:* Royal Commonwealth Society.

WATERHOUSE, Hon. Sir Ronald (Gough), Kt 1978; **Hon. Mr Justice Waterhouse;** Judge of the High Court of Justice, Family Division, since 1978; Judge, Employment Appeal Tribunal, since 1979; *b* Holywell, Flintshire, 8 May 1926; *s* of late Thomas Waterhouse, CBE, and of Doris Helena Waterhouse (*née* Gough); *m* 1960, Sarah Selina, *d* of late Captain E. A. Ingram; one *s* two *d.* *Educ:* Holywell Grammar Sch.; St John's Coll., Cambridge. RAFVR, 1944–48. McMahon Schol., St John's Coll., 1949; Pres., Cambridge Union Soc., 1950; MA, LLM; called to Bar, Middle Temple, 1952 (Harmsworth Schol.); Wales and Chester Circuit; QC 1969; Bencher 1977. A Recorder of the Crown Court, 1972–77; Presiding Judge, Wales and Chester Circuit, 1980–84. Mem. Bar Council, 1961–65. Deputy Chairman: Cheshire QS, 1964–71; Flintshire QS, 1966–71. Contested (Lab) West Flintshire, 1959. Chairman: Inter-departmental Cttee of Inquiry on Rabies, 1970; Cttees of Investigation for GB and England and Wales, under Agricultural Mkting Act, 1971–78; Local Govt Boundary Commn for Wales, 1974–78. Mem. Council, Zoological Soc. of London, 1972–, a Vice-Pres., 1981–84. Hon. LLD Wales, 1986. *Recreations:* music, golf. *Address:* Royal Courts of Justice, Strand, WC2. *Clubs:* Garrick, MCC; Cardiff and County (Cardiff).

See also J. B. Thompson.

WATERLOW, Sir Christopher Rupert, 5th Bt *cr* 1873; *b* 12 Aug. 1959; *s* of (Peter) Rupert Waterlow (*d* 1969) and Jill Elizabeth (*d* 1961), *e d* of E. T. Gourlay; *S* grandfather 1973; *m* 1986, Sally-Ann, *o d* of Maurice Bitten. *Educ:* Stonyhurst Coll., Lancs. With Metropolitan Police. *Recreations:* music, shooting, American football. *Heir:* *great-uncle* Derek Vaudrey Waterlow, *b* 19 Feb. 1902. *Address:* 26 Barfield Road, Bickley, Kent. *Clubs:* Metropolitan Police Motor, Federation of British Police Motor Clubs, National Football League Supporters UK, Stonyhurst Association.

WATERLOW, Sir (James) Gerard, 4th Bt *cr* 1930; *b* 3 Sept. 1939; *s* of Sir Thomas Gordon Waterlow, 3rd Bt, CBE and Helen Elizabeth (*d* 1970), *yr d* of Gerard A. H. Robinson; *S* father, 1982; *m* 1965, Diana Suzanne, *yr d* of Sir Thomas Skyrme, *qv*; one *s* one *d.* *Educ:* Marlborough; Trinity College, Cambridge. Coordinator for Science Research Council Manufacturing Systems, 1980–; consultant to SERC; previously employed in the computer industry. *Recreations:* tennis, bridge. *Heir:* *s* (Thomas) James Waterlow, *b* 20 March 1970. *Address:* Windmills House, Hurstbourne Tarrant, Hants. *T:* Hurstbourne Tarrant 547. *Club:* Lansdowne.

WATERLOW, Prof. John Conrad, CMG 1970; MD, ScD; FRCP; FRS 1982; FRGS; Professor of Human Nutrition, London School of Hygiene and Tropical Medicine,

1970–82, now Emeritus; *b* 13 June 1916; *o s* of Sir Sydney Waterlow, KCMG, CBE, HM Diplomatic Service; *m* 1939, Angela Pauline Cecil Gray; two *s* one *d*. *Educ:* Eton Coll.; Trinity Coll., Cambridge (MD, ScD); London Hosp. Med. College. Mem., Scientific Staff, MRC, 1942; Dir, MRC Tropical Metabolism Research Unit, Univ. of the West Indies, 1954–70. *Publications:* numerous papers on protein malnutrition and protein metabolism. *Recreation:* mountain walking. *Address:* 15 Hillgate Street, W8 7SP; Oare, Marlborough, Wilts. *Club:* Savile.

WATERMAN, Fanny, OBE 1971; FRCM; Chairman, Harveys Leeds International Pianoforte Competition, since 1963, also Chairman of Jury, since 1981; *b* 22 March 1920; *d* of Myer Waterman and Mary Waterman (*née* Behrmann); *m* 1944, Dr Geoffrey de Keyser; two *s*. *Educ:* Allerton High Sch., Leeds; Tobias Matthay, Cyril Smith, Royal College of Music, London (FRCM 1972). Concert pianist, teacher of international reputation. Vice-Pres., European Piano-Teachers Assoc., 1975–; Trustee, Edward Boyle Meml Trust, 1981–. Governor, Harrogate Fest., 1983. Founded (with Marion Harewood) Leeds International Pianoforte Competition, 1961. Member of International Juries: Beethoven, Vienna, 1977; Casagrande, Terni, 1978; Munich, 1979, 1986; Bach, Leipzig, 1980, 1984; Leeds (Chm.), 1981, 1984; Calgary, 1982; Gina Bachauer, Salt Lake City, 1982, 1984; Viña del Mar (Chm.), 1982; Maryland, 1983; Cologne, 1983, 1986; Pretoria, 1984; Santander, 1984; Rubinstein, Israel (Vice-Pres.), 1986; Tchaikowsky, Moscow, 1986; Vladigerov, Bulgaria, 1986. Piano Progress series on ITV Channel 4. Hon. MA Leeds, 1966. *Publications:* (with Marion Harewood): series of Piano Tutors (8 vols), 1967–: 1st Year Piano lessons: 1st Year Repertoire; 2nd Year Piano lessons: 2nd Year Repertoire; 3rd Year Piano lessons: 3rd Year Repertoire; Duets and Piano Playtime, 1978; Recital Book for pianists, Book 1, 1981; Sonatina and Sonata Book, 1982; Three Study Books for Piano, 1986; Merry Christmas Carols; Christmas Carol Time; (with Paul de Keyser) Young Violinists Repertoire books, 1–4; Fanny Waterman on Piano Playing and Performing, 1983; Music Lovers Diary, 1984–86. *Recreations:* travel, reading, voluntary work, cooking. *Address:* Woodgarth, Oakwood Grove, Leeds LS8 2PA. *T:* Leeds 655771.

WATERPARK, 7th Baron *cr* 1792; **Frederick Caryll Philip Cavendish,** Bt 1755; Deputy Chairman, CSE Aviation Ltd, since 1984; Managing Director, CSE International Ltd, since 1985; *b* 6 Oct. 1926; *s* of Brig.-General Frederick William Laurence Sheppard Hart Cavendish, CMG, DSO (*d* 1931) and Enid, Countess of Kenmare (she *m* 3rd, 1933, as his 3rd wife, 1st Viscount Furness, who *d* 1940; 4th, as his 2nd wife, 6th Earl of Kenmare), *d* of Charles Lindeman, Sydney, New South Wales, and *widow* of Roderick Cameron, New York; *S* uncle 1948; *m* 1951, Daniele, *e d* of Roger Guirche, Paris; one *s* two *d*. *Educ:* Eton. Lieut, 4th and 1st Bn Grenadier Guards, 1944–46. Served as Assistant District Commandant Kenya Police Reserve, 1952–55, during Mau Mau Rebellion. *Heir:* *s* Hon. Roderick Alexander Cavendish, *b* 10 Oct. 1959. *Address:* (office) CSE Aviation, Oxford Airport, Kidlington, Oxford; (home) 74 Elm Park Road, SW3. *Club:* Cavalry and Guards.

WATERS, Alwyn Brunow, CBE 1971 (MBE (mil.) 1943); GM 1944; Senior Partner, A. B. Waters, Consulting Architects, since 1983; *b* 18 Sept. 1906; *s* of Samuel Gilbert Waters and Gertrude Madeleine Brunow; *m* 1933, Ruby Alice Bindon (*d* 1983); one *s* one *d*. *Educ:* Regent Street Polytechnic; Central Sch. of Arts and Crafts; Royal Academy Schs; Imperial College. ARIBA 1933; FRIBA 1945; FCIArb. War service, RE (bomb disposal), 1940–46 (Major). Asst in various London offices, 1927–32; teaching at LCC Hammersmith Sch. of Bldg and private practice, 1932–46; founded Llewellyn Smith & Waters, 1937, Senior Partner 1946–70; Senior Partner: A. B. Waters and Partners, 1970–76; Waters Jamieson Partnership, 1977–82. Consultant, A. B. Waters and Partners, 1983. Member: various cttees, RIBA, 1945–; Council, Inst. of Arbitrators, 1958–70 (Pres. 1965); Nat. Jt Consultative Cttee for Building, 1965–74 (Chm. 1972). Governor, Willesden Coll. of Technology, 1946–71; Chm., Jt Contracts Tribunal, 1960–73. Bossom Lectr, RSA, 1970. Master, Masons' Co., 1982–83; Asst, Arbitrators' Co., 1981–; Mem., Soc. of Construction Arbitrators, 1984–. *Publications:* Story of a House, 1948; contrib. Building, Architects Jl, etc, primarily on warehousing and distribution. *Recreations:* architecture, fly fishing. *Address:* 16 Marsham Lodge, Marsham Lane, Gerrards Cross, Bucks. *T:* Gerrards Cross 882116. *Club:* Royal Automobile.

WATERS, Maj.-Gen. Charles John, CBE 1981 (OBE 1977); Commandant, Staff College, Camberley, since 1986; *b* 2 Sept. 1935; *s* of Patrick George Waters and Margaret Ronaldson Waters (*née* Clark); *m* 1962, Hilary Doyle Nettleton; three *s*. *Educ:* Oundle; Royal Military Academy, Sandhurst. Commissioned, The Gloucestershire Regt, 1955; GSO2, MO1 (MoD), 1970–72; Instructor, GSO1 (DS), Staff Coll., Camberley, 1973–74; Commanding Officer, 1st Bn, Gloucestershire Regt, 1975–77; Colonel General Staff, 1st Armoured Div., 1977–79; Comdr 3 Infantry Bde, 1979–81; RCDS 1982; Dep. Comdr, Land Forces, Falkland Islands, May-July 1982; Comdr 4th Armoured Div., 1983–85. Col, The Gloucestershire Regt, 1985–. *Recreations:* sailing, skiing, painting. *Address:* c/o National Westminster Bank, 13 Market Place, Reading, Berks. *Clubs:* Army and Navy, Ski Club of Great Britain, Eagle Ski (c/o Alpine Club).

WATERS, David Watkin, Lt-Comdr RN; *b* 2 Aug. 1911; *s* of Eng. Lt William Waters, RN, and Jessie Rhena (*née* Whitemore); *m* 1946, Hope Waters (*née* Pritchard); one step *s* one step *d*. *Educ:* RN Coll., Dartmouth. Joined RN, 1925; Cadet and Midshipman, HMS Barham, 1929; specialised in Aviation (Pilot), 1935. Served War of 1939–45: Fleet Air Arm, Malta (PoW, Italy, Germany, 1940–45). Admlty, 1946–50; retd, 1950. Admlty Historian (Defence of Shipping), 1946–60; Head of Dept of Navigation and Astronomy, Nat. Maritime Museum, 1960–76, and Sec. of Museum, 1968–71; Dep. Dir, 1971–78. Pres., British Soc. for Hist. of Sci., 1976–78 (Vice-Pres., 1972–74, 1978–81). Vis. Prof. of History, Simon Fraser Univ., Burnaby, BC, 1978; Regents' Prof., UCLA, 1979; Caird Res. Fellow, Nat. Maritime Museum, 1979–83. Chm., Japan Animal Welfare Soc., 1972–80. Gold Medal, Admiralty Naval History, 1936, and Special Award, 1946; FRHistS 1951; FRInstNav 1959; Fellow, Inst. Internac. da Cultura Portuguesa, 1966; FSA 1970. *Publications:* The True and Perfect Newes of Syr Francis Drake, 1955; (with F. Barley) Naval Staff History, Second World War, Defeat of the Enemy attack on Shipping, 1939–1945, 1957; The Art of Navigation in England in Elizabethan and Early Stuart Times, 1958, 2nd edn 1978; The Sea—or Mariner's Astrolabe, 1966; The Rutter of the Sea, 1967; (with Hope Waters) The Saluki in History, Art, and Sport, 1969, 2nd edn 1984; (with G. P. B. Naish) The Elizabethan Navy and the Armada of Spain, 1975; Science and the Techniques of Navigation in the Renaissance, 1976; contrib.: Jl RIN; RUSI; Mariners' Mirror; American Neptune; Jl RN Scientific Service; Jl British Soc. of History of Science; Navy International. *Recreations:* living with and judging Salukis; growing apples; history of technology (especially in the Renaissance and Scientific Revolution, and Chinese sailing craft). *Address:* Robin Hill, Bury, near Pulborough, West Sussex. *T:* Bury (Sussex) 687. *Club:* English-Speaking Union.

WATERS, Mrs Frank; *see* Brown, D. L.

WATERS, Montague, QC 1968; *b* 28 Feb. 1917; *s* of Elias Wasserman, BSc, and Rose Waters; *m* 1940, Jessica Freedman; three *s*. *Educ:* Central Foundation Sch., City of London; London University. LLB (Hons) London, 1938. Solicitor of the Supreme Court, 1939. Military Service, KRRC, Intelligence Corps and Dept of HM Judge Advocate General, 1940–46 (Defence and Victory Medals, 1939–45 Star). Called to the Bar, Inner Temple, 1946; released from HM Forces with rank of Major (Legal Staff), 1946. Governor, Central Foundation Schools, 1968. Freeman, City of London, 1962. *Recreations:* theatre, sport. *Address:* 37 Middleway, NW11. *T:* 01–458 7510.

WATERSTON, Dr Charles Dewar, FRSE, FGS; formerly Keeper of Geology, Royal Scottish Museum; *b* 15 Feb. 1925; *s* of Allan Waterston and Martha Dewar (*née* Robertson); *m* 1965, Marjory Home Douglas. *Educ:* Highgate Sch., London; Univ. of Edinburgh (BSc 1st Cl. Hons 1947; Vans Dunlop Scholar, PhD 1949; DSc 1980). FRSE 1958; FGS 1949. Asst Keeper, Royal Scottish Museum, 1950–63, Keeper, 1963–85. Member: Scottish Cttee, Nature Conservancy, 1969–73; Adv. Cttee for Scotland, Nature Conservancy Council, 1974–82; Chairman's Cttee, 1978–80, Exec. Cttee, 1980–82, Council for Museums and Galleries in Scotland; Sec., RSE, 1985– (Mem. Council, 1967–70; Vice-Pres., 1980–83); Hon. Sec., Edinburgh Geol Soc., 1953–58 (Pres., 1969–71). Keith Prize, RSE, 1969–71; Clough Medal, Edinburgh Geol Soc., 1984–85. *Publications:* (with G. Y. Craig and D. B. McIntyre) James Hutton's Theory of the Earth: the lost drawings, 1978; technical papers in scientific jls, chiefly relating to extinct arthropods and the history of geology. *Address:* 30 Boswall Road, Edinburgh EH5 3RN.

WATERSTONE, David George Stuart; Chief Executive, Welsh Development Agency, since 1983; *b* 9 Aug. 1935; *s* of Malcolm Waterstone and Sylvia Sawday; *m* 1960, Dominique Viriot; one *s* two *d*. *Educ:* Tonbridge; St Catharine's Coll., Cambridge (MA). HM Diplomatic Service, 1959–70; Sen. Exec., IRC, 1970–71; BSC, 1971–81: Board Mem., 1976–81; Man. Dir, Commercial, 1972–77; subseq. Executive Chairman, BSC Chemicals, 1977–81, and Redpath Dorman Long, 1977–81. *Recreations:* sailing, walking. *Address:* Welsh Development Agency, Pearl House, Greyfriars Road, Cardiff CF1 3XX. *T:* Cardiff 32955; 63 Cathedral Road, Cardiff CF1 9HE. *T:* Cardiff 382100. *Club:* Reform.

WATERTON, Sqdn Leader William Arthur, GM 1952; AFC 1942, Bar 1946; *b* Edmonton, Canada, 18 March 1916. *Educ:* Royal Military College of Canada; University of Alberta. Cadet Royal Military College of Canada, 1934–37; Subaltern and Lieut, 19th Alberta Dragoons, Canadian Cavalry, 1937–39; served RAF, 1939–46: Fighter Squadrons; Training Command; Transatlantic Ferrying Command; Fighter Command; Meteorological Flight; Fighter Experimental Unit; CFE High Speed Flight World Speed Record. Joined Gloster Aircraft Co. Ltd, 1946. 100 km closed circuit record, 1947; Paris/London record (618.5 mph), 1947; "Hare and Tortoise" Helicopter and jet aircraft Centre of London to Centre of Paris (47 mins), 1948. Chief Test Pilot Gloster Aircraft Co. Ltd, 1946–54. Prototype trials on first Canadian jet fighter, Canuck and British first operational delta wing fighter, the Javelin. *Publications:* The Comet Riddle, 1956; The Quick and The Dead, 1956; aeronautical and meteorological articles. *Recreations:* sailing, riding, photography, motoring, shooting. *Address:* c/o Royal Bank of Scotland, Kirkland House, Whitehall, SW1. *Club:* Royal Military College of Canada (Kingston, Ont.).

WATES, Christopher Stephen, FCA; Chief Executive, Wates Holdings, since 1976; Chairman: Criterion Holdings; English Industrial Estates Corp., since 1983 (Member, since 1980); Keymer Brick & Tile Co. Ltd; Wates Building Group Ltd; *b* 25 Dec. 1939; *s* of Norman Edward Wates and Margot Irene Sidwell; *m* 1965, Sandra Mouroutsos (marr. diss. 1975); three *d*. *Educ:* Stowe School; Brasenose College, Oxford. BA 1962; FCA 1965. Financial Director, Wates Ltd, 1970–76. Director: Chatham Historic Dockyard Trust; Electra Investment Trust; Equitable Life Assurance Society; North British Canadian Ivestment Co.; Wates City of London Properties PLC. *Address:* Tufton Place, Northiam, near Rye, East Sussex. *T:* Northiam 2125.

WATES, Michael Edward, Chairman, Wates Ltd, since 1975; Chairman, British Bloodstock Agency plc, since 1986; *b* 19 June 1935; 2nd *s* of Sir Ronald Wallace Wates and of Phyllis Mary Wates (*née* Trace); *m* 1959, Caroline Josephine Connolly; four *s* one *d*. *Educ:* Oundle School; Emmanuel College, Cambridge (MA). Joined Wates 1959; Director: Wates Construction, 1963; Wates Built Homes, 1966. Hon. FRIBA. *Address:* Manor House, Langton Long, Blandford Forum, Dorset DT11 9HS. *T:* Blandford 55241.

WATHEN, Julian Philip Gerard; Director, Barclays Bank PLC, since 1974 (Vice Chairman 1979–84); *b* 21 May 1923; *s* of late Gerard Anstruther Wathen, CIE, and Melicent Louis (*née* Buxton); *m* 1948 Priscilla Florence Wilson; one *s* two *d*. *Educ:* Harrow. Served War, 60th Rifles, 1942–46. Third Secretary, HBM Embassy, Athens, 1946–47. Barclays Bank DCO, 1948; Ghana Director, 1961–65; General Manager, 1966; Sen. Gen. Manager, Barclays Bank International, 1974; Vice Chm., 1976. Dep. Chm., Allied Arab Bank, 1977–84; Vice-Chm., Banque du Caire, Barclays International, 1976–83; Director: Barclays Australia International, 1973–84; Barclays Bank of Kenya, 1975–84; Mercantile & General Reinsurance Co., 1977–. Pres., Royal African Soc., 1984– (Chm., 1978–84); Chm., Hall Sch. Trust, 1972–; Vice Chm., London House for Overseas Graduates, 1984–; Governor: St Paul's Schs, 1981–; SOAS, 1983–; Dauntsey's Sch., 1985–; Abingdon Sch., 1985–. Master, Mercers' Co., 1984–85. *Address:* Woodcock House, Owlpen, Dursley, Glos GL11 5BY. *T:* Dursley 860214; 1 Montagu Place, Marylebone, W1H 1RG. *T:* 01–935 8569. *Club:* Travellers'.

WATKIN, Rt. Rev. Abbot (Christopher) Aelred (Paul); titular Abbot of Glastonbury; Headmaster of Downside School, 1962–75; *b* 23 Feb. 1918; *s* of late Edward Ingram Watkin and Helena Watkin (*née* Shepheard). *Educ:* Blackfriars Sch., Laxton; Christ's Coll., Cambridge (1st class Parts I and II, historical Tripos). Housemaster at Downside Sch., 1948–62. Mayor of Beccles, 1979. FRHistS, 1946; FSA, 1950; FRSA, 1969. *Publications:* Wells Cathedral Miscellany, 1943; (ed) Great Chartulary of Glastonbury, 3 vols, 1946–58; (ed) Registrum Archidiaconatus Norwyci, 2 vols, 1946–48; Heart of the World, 1954; The Enemies of Love, 1958; Resurrection is Now, 1975; articles in Eng. Hist. Rev., Cambridge Hist. Journal, Victoria County History of Wilts, etc. *Address:* St Benet's, Grange Road, Beccles, Suffolk. *T:* Beccles 713179.

WATKIN, David John, MA, PhD; FSA; Fellow of Peterhouse, Cambridge, since 1970; University Lecturer in History of Art, Cambridge, since 1972; Member, Historic Buildings Advisory Committee, Historic Buildings and Monuments Commission for England, since 1984 (Member, Historic Buildings Council for England, 1980–84); *b* 7 April 1941; *o s* of Thomas Charles and Vera Mary Watkin. *Educ:* Farnham Grammar Sch.; Trinity Hall, Cambridge (Exhibnr; BA (1st Cl. Hons Fine Arts Tripos); PhD). Librarian, Fine Arts Faculty, Cambridge, 1967–72. *Publications:* Thomas Hope (1769–1831) and the Neo-Classical Idea, 1968; (ed) Sale Catalogues of Libraries of Eminent Persons, vol. 4, Architects, 1970; The Life and Work of C. R. Cockerell, RA, 1974 (Alice Davis Hitchcock medallion, 1975); The Triumph of the Classical, Cambridge Architecture 1804–34, 1977; Morality and Architecture, 1977; The Rise of Architectural History, 1980; English Architecture, a Concise History, 1980; (with Hugh Montgomery-Massingberd) The London Ritz, a Social and Architectural History, 1980; (with Robin Middleton) Neo-Classical and Nineteenth-century Architecture, 1980; (jtly) Burke's and Savills Guide to Country Houses, vol. 3, East Anglia, 1981; The Buildings of Britain,

Regency: a Guide and Gazetteer, 1982; Athenian Stuart, Pioneer of the Greek Revival, 1982; The English Vision: The Picturesque in Architecture, Landscape and Garden Design, 1982; (contrib.) John Soane, 1983; The Royal Interiors of Regency England, 1984; Peterhouse: an architectural record 1284–1984, 1984; (contrib.) Grand Hotel: the golden age of palace hotels, an architectural and social history, 1984; (contrib.) A House in Town: 22 Arlington Street, its owners and builders, 1984; A History of Western Architecture, 1986; (with Tilman Mellinghoff) German Architecture and the Classical Ideal: 1740–1840, 1986. *Address:* Peterhouse, Cambridge; 67 Charlwood Street, SW1. *Clubs:* Travellers', Beefsteak; University Pitt (Cambridge).

WATKIN WILLIAMS, Sir Peter, Kt 1963; *b* 8 July 1911; *s* of late Robert Thesiger Watkin Williams, late Master of the Supreme Court, and Mary Watkin Williams; *m* 1938, Jane Dickinson (*née* Wilkin); two *d. Educ:* Sherborne; Pembroke Coll., Cambridge. Partner in Hansons, legal practitioners, Shanghai, 1937–40; served War of 1939–45, Rhodesia and Middle East, 1940–46. Resident Magistrate, Uganda, 1946–55; Puisne Judge, Trinidad and Tobago, 1955–58; Puisne Judge, Sierra Leone, 1958–61; Plebiscite Judge, Cameroons, 1961; Chief Justice of Basutoland, Bechuanaland and Swaziland, and President of the Court of Appeal, 1961–65; High Court Judge, Malawi, 1967–69; Chief Justice of Malawi, 1969–70. *Recreation:* fishing. *Address:* Lower East Horner, Stockland, Honiton, Devon.

WATKINS, family name of **Baron Watkins.**

WATKINS, Baron *cr* 1972 (Life Peer), of Glyntawe, Brecknock; **Tudor Elwyn Watkins;** Lieutenant of Powys, 1975–78; *b* 9 May 1903; *e s* of late County Councillor Howell Watkins, JP, Abercrave, Swansea Valley; *m* 1936, Bronwen R., 3rd *d* of late T. Stather, Talgarth; no *c. Educ:* local elementary schools; evening continuation classes; University Tutorial, WEA and NCLC classes; Coleg Harlech, N Wales (Bursary). Began working at local collieries at age of 13½; miner for 8 years; political agent for Brecon and Radnor, 1928–33; MP (Lab) Brecon and Radnor, 1945–70; PPS to Sec. of State for Wales, 1964–68. Alderman, Breconshire CC, 1940–74; Chm., Powys CC, 1974–77. General Secretary Breconshire Assoc. of Friendly Societies, 1937–48. Hon. Freeman, Brecon Borough; Chm., Brecon Beacons Nat. Park Cttee, 1974–78. *Recreations:* served as Secretary of Abercrave Athletic Club, Cricket Club, Ystalyfera Football League, Horticultural Society and Show. *Address:* Bronafon, Penyfan Road, Brecon, Powys. *T:* 2961.

WATKINS, Alan (Rhun); journalist; Political Columnist, Observer, since 1976; *b* 3 April 1933; *o c* of late D. J. Watkins, schoolmaster, Tycroes, Dyfed, and Violet Harris; *m* 1955, Ruth Howard (*d* 1982); one *s* one *d* (and one *d* decd). *Educ:* Amman Valley Grammar Sch., Ammanford; Queens' Coll., Cambridge. Chm., Cambridge Univ. Labour Club, 1954. National Service, FO, Educn Br., RAF, 1955–57. Called to Bar, Lincoln's Inn, 1957. Research Asst, Dept of Govt, LSE, 1958–59; Editorial Staff, Sunday Express, 1959–64 (New York Corresp., 1961; Actg Political Corresp., 1963; Cross-Bencher Columnist, 1963–64); Political Correspondent: Spectator, 1964–67; New Statesman, 1967–76; Political Columnist, Sunday Mirror, 1968–69; Columnist, Evening Standard, 1974–75; Rugby Corresp., Field, 1984–. Mem. (Lab) Fulham Bor. Council, 1959–62. Dir, The Statesman and Nation Publishing Co. Ltd, 1973–76. Chm., Political Adv. Gp, British Youth Council, 1978–81. Awards: Granada, Political Columnist, 1973; British Press, Columnist, 1982, commended 1984. *Publications:* The Liberal Dilemma, 1966; (contrib.) The Left, 1966; (with A. Alexander) The Making of the Prime Minister 1970, 1970; Brief Lives, 1982; (contrib.) The Queen Observed, 1986. *Recreations:* reading, walking. *Address:* 54 Barnsbury Street, N1 1ER. *T:* 01–607 0812. *Clubs:* Garrick, Beefsteak.

WATKINS, Prof. Arthur Goronwy, CBE 1967; Professor of Child Health, Welsh National School of Medicine, 1950–68, Emeritus Professor, since 1968; Dean of Clinical and Post-Graduate Studies, 1947–68; *b* 19 March 1903; *s* of Sir Percy Watkins; *m* 1933, Aileen Llewellyn; one *s* three *d. Educ:* Sidcot Sch.; University Coll., Cardiff; University Coll. Hospital, London. BSc (Wales) 1925; MD (London) 1930; FRCP 1943. Res. Hosp. appts, University Coll. Hosp., 1927–29, West London Hosp., 1929, Hosp. for Sick Children, Gt Ormond Street, 1930; First Asst, Dept of Pædiatrics, University Coll. Hosp., 1930–32; Lectr In Pædiatrics, Welsh Nat. Sch. of Medicine, 1932–50; Cons. Pædiatrician, Royal Infirmary and Llandough Hosp., Cardiff, 1932. Former Mem. Bd of Govs, United Cardiff Hosps; Consultant and Adviser in Pædiatrics, Welsh Hosp. Bd; Hon. Treas. Brit. Pædiatric Assoc., 1958–63, Pres., 1966–67; Pres. Children's Sect., Roy. Soc. Med., 1953, Hon. Mem. 1970; Pres. Cardiff Div., BMA, 1953; Corr. Mem. Soc. de Pédiatrie, Paris; Hon. Fellow, Amer. Academy of Pediatrics, 1967; Mem. Albemarle Cttee on Youth Service; Mem. Central Coun. of Educ. (Wales), 1954–56; External Examr, Univs of Bristol, Birmingham, Manchester, Leeds; Colonial Office Visitor to W Indies, 1956 and Far East, 1959. President Cardiff Medical Soc., 1963–64. Hon. LLD Wales, 1981. *Publications:* (with W. J. Pearson) The Infant, 1932; Pædiatrics for Nurses, 1947; articles in BMJ, Lancet, Archives of Disease in Childhood, etc. *Recreation:* golf. *Address:* Maldwyn, 71 Danycoed Road, Cyncoed, Cardiff CF2 6NE. *T:* Cardiff 751262.

WATKINS, Brian; HM Diplomatic Service; Consul General, Vancouver, since 1986; *b* 26 July 1933; *s* of late James Edward Watkins and late Gladys Anne Watkins (*née* Fletcher); *m* 1st, 1957 (marr. diss. 1978); one *s*; 2nd, 1982, Elisabeth, *d* of A. and M. Arfon-Jones, Littleton Hall, Chester; one *d. Educ:* London School of Economics (BSc Econ); Worcester College, Oxford. Solicitor. Flying Officer, RAF, 1955–58. HMOCS, Sierra Leone, 1959–63; Local Govt, 1963–66; Administrator, Tristan da Cunha, 1966–69; Lectr, Univ. of Manchester, 1969–71; HM Diplomatic Service, 1971; FCO, 1971–73; New York, 1973–75; seconded to N Ireland Office, 1976–78; FCO, 1978–81; Counsellor, 1981; Dep. Governor, Bermuda, 1981–83; Consul General and Counsellor (Economic, Commercial, Aid), Islamabad, 1983–86. *Recreations:* reading history and spy stories, watching theatre, watching TV, dancing. *Address:* c/o Foreign and Commonwealth Office, SW1; c/o Royal Bank of Scotland, Holts Branch, Whitehall, SW1. *Club:* Royal Bermuda Yacht.

WATKINS, David John; Director, Council for the Advancement of Arab-British Understanding, since 1983 (Joint Chairman, 1979–83); company director and consultant; *b* 27 Aug. 1925; *s* of Thomas George Watkins and Alice Elizabeth (*née* Allen); unmarried. *Educ:* Bristol. Member: Bristol City Council, 1954–57; Bristol Educn Cttee, 1958–66; Labour Party, 1950–; Amalgamated Engineering Union, 1942–; Sec., AEU Gp of MPs, 1968–77. Contested Bristol NW, 1964. MP (Lab) Consett, 1966–83; Mem., House of Commons Chairmen's Panel, 1978–83. Sponsored Employers Liability (Compulsory Insurance) Act, 1969, and Industrial Common Ownership Act, 1976 as Private Member's Bills; introd Drained Weight Bill, 1973, and Consett Steel Works Common Ownership Bill, 1980. Chm., Labour Middle East Council, 1974–83; Treas., Internat. Co-ord Cttee, UN Meeting of Non-Governmental Organisations on Question of Palestine, 1985–. *Publications:* Labour and Palestine, 1975; Industrial Common Ownership, 1978; The World and Palestine, 1980; The Exceptional Conflict, 1984. *Recreations:* reading, listening to music, swimming. *Address:* 1 Carisbrooke House, Courtlands, Sheen Road, Richmond, Surrey TW10 5AZ. *Club:* Royal Commonwealth Society.

WATKINS, Rev. Gordon Derek; Vicar of St Martin-within-Ludgate, City and Diocese of London, since 1984; *b* 16 July 1929; *s* of Clifford and Margaret Watkins; *m* 1957, Beryl Evelyn Whitaker. *Educ:* St Brendan's College, Clifton. Nat. Service, RAOC, 1947–49. Staff of W. D. & H. O. Wills, 1944–51; deacon 1953, priest 1954; Curate, Grafton Cathedral, NSW, 1953–56; Vicar of Texas, Qld, 1957–61; Curate, St Wilfrid's, Harrogate, 1961–63; Vicar of Upton Park, 1963–67; Rector: Great and Little Bentley, 1967–73; Great Canfield, 1973–78; Pastoral Sec., Dio. London, 1978–84. Sec., London Dio. Adv. Cttee, 1984–; Priest Vicar, Westminster Abbey, 1984–; Priest in Ordinary to the Queen, 1984–. Freeman, City of London, 1984. Kt Chaplain, Knights of the Round Table, 1984–. *Recreations:* reading, music, country life. *Address:* St Martin's Vestry, Ludgate Hill, EC4M 7DE. *T:* 01–248 6054. *Club:* Athenæum.

WATKINS, Maj.-Gen. Guy Hansard, CB 1986; OBE 1974; Chief Executive, Royal Hong Kong Jockey Club, since 1986; Director General, Army Manning and Recruiting, 1985–86; *b* 30 Nov. 1933; *s* of Col A. N. M. Watkins and Mrs S. C. Watkins; *m* 1958, Sylvia Margaret Grant; two *s* two *d. Educ:* The King's Sch., Canterbury; Royal Military Academy, Sandhurst. Commissioned into Royal Artillery, 1953; CO 39 Medium Regt RA, 1973; Comd Task Force 'B'/Dep. Comd 1 Armd Div., 1977; Director, Public Relations (Army), 1980; Maj. Gen. RA and GOC Artillery Div., 1982. Col Comdt, RA, 1986. *Recreations:* riding, fly fishing, skiing. *Address:* c/o National Westminster Bank PLC, 60 High Street, Bognor Regis, West Sussex. *Club:* Army and Navy.

WATKINS, Rt. Hon. Sir Tasker, Kt 1971; VC 1944; PC 1980; DL; **Rt. Hon. Lord Justice Watkins;** a Lord Justice of Appeal, since 1980; Senior Presiding Judge for England and Wales, since 1983; *b* 18 Nov. 1918; *s* of late Bertram and Jane Watkins, Nelson, Glam; *m* 1941, Eirwen Evans; one *d* (one *s* decd). *Educ:* Pontypridd Grammar Sch. Served War, 1939–45 (Major, the Welch Regiment). Called to Bar, Middle Temple, 1948, Bencher 1970; QC 1965; Deputy Chairman: Radnor QS, 1962–71; Carmarthenshire QS, 1966–71. Recorder: Merthyr Tydfil, 1968–70, Swansea, 1970–71; Leader, Wales and Chester Circuit, 1970–71; Judge of the High Court of Justice, Family Div., 1971–74, QBD, 1974–80; Presiding Judge, Wales and Chester Circuit, 1975–80. Counsel (as Deputy to Attorney-General) to Inquiry into Aberfan Disaster, 1966. Chairman: Mental Health Review Tribunal, Wales Region, 1960–71; Judicial Studies Bd, 1979–80. Hon. LLD Wales, 1979. DL Glamorgan, 1956–. *Address:* Royal Courts of Justice, Strand, WC2A 2LL; Fairwater Lodge, Fairwater Road, Llandaff, Glamorgan. *T:* Cardiff 563558; 5 Pump Court, Middle Temple, EC4. *T:* 01–353 1993. *Clubs:* Army and Navy; Cardiff and County (Cardiff).

See also J. G. Williams.

WATKINS, Thomas Frederick; Director, Chemical Defence Establishment, Porton, 1972–74; *b* 19 Feb. 1914; *s* of late Edward and late Louisa Watkins; *m* 1939, Jeannie Blodwen Roberts; two *d. Educ:* Cowbridge Grammar Sch.; Univ. of Wales, Cardiff. BSc Hons Wales 1935; MSc Wales 1936; FRIC 1947. Joined Scientific Staff of War Dept, 1936; seconded to Govt of India, 1939–44; seconded to Dept of Nat. Defence, Canada, 1947–49; Head of Research Section, CDRE, Sutton Oak and Min. of Supply CDE, Nancekuke, 1949–56; Supt Chemistry Research Div., CDE, Porton, 1956; Asst Dir Chemical Research, CDE, Porton, 1963; Dep. Dir, CDE, Porton, 1966. *Publications:* various papers on organic chemistry. *Recreation:* gardening. *Address:* 34 Harnwood Road, Salisbury, Wilts. *T:* Salisbury 5135.

WATKINS, Dr Winifred May, FRS 1969; Head of Division of Immunochemical Genetics, Clinical Research Centre, Medical Research Council, since 1976; *b* 6 Aug. 1924; *d* of Albert E. and Annie B. Watkins. *Educ:* Godolphin and Latymer Sch., London; Univ. of London. PhD 1950; DSc 1963. Research Asst in Biochemistry, St Bartholomew's Hosp. Med. Sch., 1948–50; Beit Memorial Research Fellow, 1952–55; Mem. of Staff of Lister Inst. of Preventive Medicine, 1955–76; Wellcome Travelling Research Fellow, Univ. of California, 1960–61; Reader in Biochemistry, 1965; Prof. of Biochemistry, Univ. of London, 1968–76; William Julius Mickle Fellow, London Univ., 1971. Mem. Council, Royal Soc., 1984–86. Hon. Mem., Internat. Soc. of Blood Transfusion, 1982. FRCPath 1983. Landsteiner Memorial Award (jtly), 1967; Paul Ehrlich-Ludwig Darmstädter Prize (jtly), 1969; Kenneth Goldsmith Award, British Blood Transfusion Soc., 1986. *Publications:* various papers in biochemical and immunological jls. *Address:* MRC Clinical Research Centre, Watford Road, Harrow, Middlesex HA1 3UJ.

WATKINS-PITCHFORD, Denys James, FRSA; ARCA; author and artist; *b* 25 July 1905; *s* of Rev. Walter Watkins-Pitchford, BA, and Edith Elizabeth (*née* Wilson); *m* 1939, Cecily Mary Adnitt (*d* 1974); one *d* (one *s* decd). *Educ:* privately; studied art in Paris, 1924, and at Royal Coll. of Art, London (Painting Schs), 1926–28. Asst Art Master, Rugby Sch., 1930–47. Served City of London Yeomanry RHA, 1926–29. Captain, Home Guard, 1940–46. Hon. MA Leicester Univ., 1986. Carnegie Medal, 1942. Broadcaster on natural history subjects. *Publications:* (under pseudonym 'BB'): Sportsman's Bedside Book, 1937; Wild Lone, 1939; Manka, 1939; Countryman's Bedside Book, 1941; Little Grey Men, 1941 (TV Serial, 1975); The Idle Countryman, 1943; Brendon Chase, 1944 (Radio Serial; TV Serial, Southern TV, 1981, shown in 14 countries); Fisherman's Bedside Book, 1945; The Wayfaring Tree, 1945; Down the Bright Stream, 1948; Shooting Man's Bedside Book, 1948; Meeting Hill, 1948; Confessions of a Carp Fisher, 1950; Letters from Compton Deverell, 1950; Tides Ending, 1950; Dark Estuary, 1952; The Forest of Boland Light Railway, 1955; Mr Bumstead, 1958; The Wizard of Boland, 1958; Autumn Road to the Isles, 1959; The Badgers of Bearshanks, 1961; The White Road Westwards, 1961; September Road to Caithness, 1962; Lepus the Brown Hare, 1962; The Summer Road to Wales, 1964; Pegasus Book of the Countryside, 1964; The Whopper, 1967; A Summer on the Nene, 1967; At the Back o' Ben Dee, 1968; The Tyger Tray, 1971; Pool of the Black Witch, 1974; Lord of the Forest, 1975; Recollections of a Longshore Gunner, 1976; A Child Alone (autobiog.), 1978; Ramblings of a Sportsman Naturalist, 1979; The Naturalist's Bedside Book, 1980; The Quiet Fields, 1981; Indian Summer, 1984; Best of 'BB' (anthology), 1985; contribs to Field, Country Life, Shooting Times. *Recreations:* natural history, fishing, shooting. *Address:* The Round House, Sudborough, Kettering, Northants. *T:* Thrapston 3215.

WATKINS-PITCHFORD, Dr John, CB 1968; Chief Medical Adviser, Department of Health and Social Security (formerly Ministry of Social Security and Ministry of Pensions and National Insurance), 1965–73; retired 1973; *b* 20 April 1912; *s* of Wilfred Watkins Pitchford, FRCS, first Director of South African Institute of Medical Research, and Olive Mary (*née* Nichol); *m* 1945, Elizabeth Patricia Wright; one *s. Educ:* Shrewsbury School; St Thomas's Hospital. MRCS, LRCP 1937; MB, BS 1939 (London); MD 1946 (London); DPH 1946; DIH 1949. Various hosp. appts War of 1939–45: served RAFVR, Sqdn Ldr. Med. Inspector of Factories, 1947–50; Sen. Med. Off., Min. of Nat. Insce, 1950. Mem., Industrial Injuries Adv. Council, 1975–84. QHP 1971–74. *Publications:* articles on occupational medicine. *Recreation:* gardening. *Address:* Hill House, Farley Lane, Westerham, Kent. *T:* Westerham 64448. *Club:* Athenæum.

WATKINSON, family name of **Viscount Watkinson.**

WATKINSON, 1st Viscount *cr* 1964, of Woking; **Harold Arthur Watkinson,** PC 1955; CH 1962; President, Confederation of British Industry, 1976–77; Chairman of Cadbury Schweppes Ltd, 1969–74 (Group Managing Director, Schweppes Ltd, 1963–68); Director: British Insulated Callender's Cables, 1968–77; Midland Bank Ltd, 1970–83; *b* 25 Jan. 1910; *e s* of A. G. Watkinson, Walton-on-Thames; *m* 1939, Vera, *y d* of John Langmead, West Sussex; two *d*. *Educ:* Queen's College, Taunton; King's College, London. Family business, 1929–35; technical and engineering journalism, 1935–39. Served War of 1939–45, active service, Lieut-Comdr RNVR. Chairman Production Efficiency Panel for S England, Machine Tool Trades Association, 1948; Chairman (first) Dorking Div. Conservative Assoc., 1948–49. MP (C) Woking Division of Surrey, 1950–64; Parliamentary Private Secretary to the Minister of Transport and Civil Aviation, 1951–52; Parliamentary Secretary to Ministry of Labour and National Service, 1952–55; Minister of Transport and Civil Aviation, Dec. 1955–59; Minister of Defence, 1959–62; Cabinet Minister, 1957–62. Mem., Brit. Nat. Export Council 1964–70; Chairman: Cttee for Exports to the United States, 1964–67; Nat. Advisory Cttee on the Employment of Older Men and Women, 1952–55; Companies Cttee, CBI, 1972–; a Vice-Pres., Council, BIM, 1970–73, Pres., 1973–78 (Chm., 1968–70). President: Grocers' Inst., 1970–71; Inst. of Grocery Distribution, 1972–73; Member: Council, RSA, 1972–77; NEDC, 1976–77; Falkland Islands Review Cttee, 1982–83. President: RNVR Officers' Assoc., 1973–76; Weald and Downland Museum, 1982–. Chairman: Council, Cranleigh and Bramley Schools, 1973–; Recruitment Working Party, Duke of Edinburgh's 1974 Study Conf., 1972–74. *Publications:* Blueprint for Industrial Survival, 1976; Turning Points, 1986. *Recreations:* mountaineering, walking, sailing. *Heir:* none. *Address:* Tyma House, Bosham, near Chichester, Sussex. *Clubs:* Naval; Royal Southern Yacht (Southampton).

WATKINSON, John Taylor; barrister; *b* 25 Jan. 1941; *s* of William Forshaw Watkinson; *m* 1969, Jane Elizabeth Miller; two *s* two *d*. *Educ:* Bristol Grammar Sch.; Worcester Coll., Oxford. Schoolmaster, Rugby Sch., Warwicks, 1964–71. Called to the Bar, Middle Temple, 1971; practised, Midland Circuit, 1972–74, South East Circuit, 1978–79. MP (Lab) Gloucestershire West, Oct. 1974–1979; PPS to Sec. of State, Home Office, 1975–79; Member: Public Accounts Cttee, 1976–79; Expenditure Cttee, 1978–79; Speakers' Conf. on Northern Ireland, 1979; Hon. Sec., Anglo-Swiss Parly Gp, 1977–79; Mem. and Rapporteur, Council of Europe and WEU, 1976–79; Rapporteur, first Europ. Declaration on the Police. Contested: (Lab) Warwick and Leamington, 1970; (SDP) Glos West, 1983; Mem., Council for Social Democracy, 1982. Financial Reporter, BBC TV, 1979–82; company dir, 1982–. Member: TGWU; NUJ. Amateur Rugby Fives Champion (Singles 3 times, Doubles 4 times), 1964–70. *Recreations:* sport, conversation. *Address:* Clanna Lodge, Alvington, Lydney, Glos.

WATKISS, Ronald Frederick, CBE 1981; company director, since 1950; Leader, Conservative Party, Cardiff City Council, since 1973; Lord Mayor of Cardiff, 1981–82; *b* 21 May 1920; *o s* of Bertie Miles Watkiss and Isabella Watkiss; *m* 1941, Marion Preston; one *d* (one *s* decd). *Educ:* Howard Gardens High Sch., Cardiff. Served War, TA, 1939, Royal Corps of Signals, 1939–46; Burma, 1944–46 (1939–45 star, Burma star, Territorial medal). Elected to Cardiff City Council, 1960; Alderman, 1967–74; re-elected Councillor, 1973; Leader, 1976–79, 1983–; Chairman: Planning Cttee, 1969–74, 1976–79; Policy Cttee, 1976–79, 1983–. Member, Assoc. District Councils, 1976–79, 1983–; Chm., 1978–81, Pres., 1983–, Cardiff North (formerly NW) Conservative Constituency Assoc. Pres., Cardiff Credit Traders Assoc., 1953–54 and 1963–64; Pres., S Wales Dist Council Credit Traders, 1957–58. Hon. Fellow, University Coll. Cardiff, 1985. Queen's Silver Jubilee Medal, 1977. *Recreations:* Rugby and cricket (regret only as spectator now); relaxing at caravan whenever possible. *Address:* 69 King George V Drive, Heath, Cardiff CF4 4EF. *T:* Cardiff 752716. *Club:* Victory Services.

WATLING, (David) Brian, QC 1979; **His Honour Judge Watling;** a Circuit Judge, since 1981; *b* 18 June 1935; *o s* of late Vernon Russell Watling and late Edith Stella (*née* Ridley); *m* 1964, Second Officer Noelle Louise Bugden, WRNS. *Educ:* Charterhouse; King's Coll., London (LLB). Called to Bar, Middle Temple, 1957. Nat. Service, Sub-Lieut RNR, 1957. Jun. Prosecuting Counsel to the Crown, Central Criminal Court, 1972, Sen. Prosecuting Counsel, 1975; Sen. Treasury Counsel, 1975–79; a Recorder of the Crown Court, 1979–81. Vis. Lectr in Law, Univ. Coll. at Buckingham, 1978–80, Vis. Prof. in Criminal Law, 1980–84. Reader, Dio. of St Edmundsbury, 1985–. Barrister and Advocate, Gibraltar. *Recreations:* sailing, fly fishing, cross country ski-ing, hill walking, theatre and ballet, fireside reading, the company of old friends. *Address:* Chelmsford Crown Court, PO Box 9, Chelmsford CM1 1EL. *Club:* Garrick.

WATSON, family name of **Baron Manton.**

WATSON, Adam; *see* Watson, John Hugh A.

WATSON, Alan; *see* Watson, W. A. J.

WATSON, Rear-Adm. Alan George, CB 1975. Served Royal Navy, 1941–77; Asst Chief of Naval Staff, 1974–77, retired. Chairman: Church of England Soldiers', Sailors' and Airmen's Clubs, 1979–; Church of England Soldiers', Sailors' and Airmen's Housing Assoc., 1979–.

WATSON, Alan John, CBE 1985; Chief Executive, Alan Watson Communications Ltd, since 1985; Director: Wadlow Grosvenor International Ltd, since 1985; ReedVision, since 1983; *b* 3 Feb. 1941; *s* of Rev. John William Watson and Edna Mary (*née* Peters); *m* 1965, Karen Lederer; two *s*. *Educ:* Diocesan Coll., Cape Town, SA; Kingswood Sch., Bath, Somerset; Jesus Coll., Cambridge (Open Schol. in History 1959, State Schol. 1959) (MA Hons). Vice-Pres., Cambridge Union; Pres., Cambridge Univ. Liberal Club. Research Asst to Cambridge Prof. of Modern History on post-war history of Unilever, 1962–64. General trainee, BBC, 1965–66; Reporter, BBC TV, The Money Programme, 1966–68; Chief Public Affairs Commentator, London Weekend Television, 1969–70; Reporter, Panorama, BBC TV, 1971–74; Presenter, The Money Programme, 1974–75; Head of TV, Radio, Audio-Visual Div., EEC, and Editor, European Community Newsreel Service to Lomé Convention Countries, 1975–79; Dir, Charles Barker City Ltd, 1980–85 (Chief Exec., 1980–83). Contested: (L) Richmond, Oct. 1974 and 1979; (Alliance) Richmond and Barnes, 1983. Pres., Liberal Party, 1984–85 (Mem., Party Council and Nat. Exec., 1983–). Mem. Cttee, National Children's Home, 1986–; Charities Mem., UK Bd of UNICEF, 1986–. Governor, Kingswood Sch., 1983–. MIPR 1986. Grand Prix Eurodiaporama of European Community for Common Market Coverage, 1974. *Publication:* Europe at Risk, 1972. *Recreation:* historical biography. *Address:* 2 Retreat Road, Richmond, Surrey TW9 1NN. *Clubs:* Brook's, United Oxford & Cambridge University, Royal Automobile, Kennel.

WATSON, Sir Andrew; *see* Watson, Sir J. A.

WATSON, Maj.-Gen. Andrew Linton, CB 1981; Lieutenant Governor and Secretary, Royal Hospital, Chelsea, since 1984; Colonel, The Black Watch, since 1981; *b* 9 April 1927; *s* of Col W. L. Watson, OBE, and Mrs D. E. Watson (*née* Lea); *m* 1952, Mary Elizabeth, *d* of Mr and Mrs A. S. Rigby, Warrenpoint, Co. Down; two *s* one *d*. *Educ:* Wellington Coll., Berks. psc, jssc, rcds. Commnd The Black Watch, 1946; served, 1946–66: with 1st and 2nd Bns, Black Watch, in UK, Germany, Cyprus and British Guiana; with UN Force, Cyprus; as GSO 2 and 3 on Staff, UK and Germany; GSO 1 HQ 17 Div./Malaya Dist, 1966–68; CO 1st Bn The Black Watch, UK, Gibraltar and NI, 1969–71; Comdr 19 Airportable Bde, Colchester, 1972–73; RCDS, 1974; Comdr British Army Staff, and Military Attaché, Washington, DC, 1975–77; GOC Eastern District, 1977–80; COS, Allied Forces, Northern Europe, 1980–82. *Recreations:* tennis, shooting, walking, classical music. *Address:* Lieutenant Governor's House, Royal Hospital, Chelsea, SW3 4SL; c/o Royal Bank of Scotland, 18 South Methven Street, Perth, Scotland. *T:* Perth 31441. *Clubs:* Army and Navy; Puffins (Edinburgh); Highland Brigade (Edinburgh).

WATSON, Anthony Heriot, CBE 1965; *b* 13 April 1912; *s* of William Watson and Dora Isabel Watson (*née* Fisher); *m* 1946, Hilary Margaret Fyfe. *Educ:* St Paul's Sch.; Christ Church, Oxford; University Coll., London. Statistical Officer, British Cotton Industry Research Assoc., 1936. Min. of Supply, 1940: Statistician; Asst Dir of Statistics; Min. of Aircraft Production, 1942; Statistician, Dept of Civil Aviation, Air Ministry, 1945; Chief Statistician: Min. of Civil Aviation, 1951; Min. of Transport and Civil Aviation, 1954; Min. of Aviation, 1959; Min. of Transport, 1964, Dir of Statistics, 1966; DoE, 1970; retired 1973. *Recreations:* music, garden. *Address:* 9 Kirk Park, Edinburgh EH16 6HZ. *T:* 031–664 7428.

WATSON, Antony Edward Douglas; QC 1986; *b* 6 March 1945; *s* of William Edward Watson and Margaret Watson (*née* Douglas); *m* 1972, Gillian Mary Bevan-Arthur; two *d*. *Educ:* Sedbergh School; Sidney Sussex College, Cambridge (MA). Called to the Bar, Inner Temple, 1968. *Publication:* (jtly) Terrell on Patents (1884), 13th edn. *Recreations:* wine, opera, country pursuits. *Address:* The Old Rectory, Milden, Suffolk IP7 7AF. *T:* Bildeston 740227.

WATSON, Arthur Christopher, CMG 1977; HM Diplomatic Service; Governor of Montserrat, West Indies, since 1985; *b* 2 Jan. 1927; *s* of late Dr A. J. Watson and Dr Mary Watson, Kunming, China, and Chinnor; *m* 1956, Mary Cecil Candler (*née* Earl); one *d*; and one step *s* one step *d*. *Educ:* Norwich Sch.; St Catharine's Coll., Cambridge. Naval Service, 1945–48 (commissioned RNVR, 1946). Colonial Administrative Service, Uganda, 1951; District Commissioner, 1959; Principal Asst Sec., 1960; Principal, Commonwealth Relations Office, 1963; HM Diplomatic Service, 1965; Karachi, 1964–67; Lahore, 1967; FCO, 1967–71; HM Comr in Anguilla, 1971–74; Governor, Turks and Caicos Islands, 1975–78; High Comr in Brunei, 1978–83; FCO, 1983–84. *Recreations:* boats, birds. *Address:* c/o Foreign and Commonwealth Office, SW1. *Club:* Royal Commonwealth Society.

WATSON, Sir Bruce (Dunstan), Kt 1985; Chairman and Chief Executive Officer, M.I.M. Holdings Limited, since 1983; *b* 1 Aug. 1928; *s* of James Harvey and Edith Mary (Crawford); *m* 1952, June Kilgour; one *s* two *d*. *Educ:* University of Queensland (BE (Elec) 1949, BCom 1957). Engineer, Tasmanian Hydro Elecricity Commn, 1950–54, Townsville Regional Electricity Board, 1954–56; MIM Group of Companies: Engineer, Copper Refineries Pty Ltd, Townsville, 1956–69; Mount Isa Mines Ltd, 1970–73; Group Industrial Relations Manager, MIM Group, Brisbane, 1973–75; First Gen. Man., Agnew Mining Co., WA, 1975–77; M.I.M. Holdings Ltd, Brisbane: Director, 1977; Man. Dir. 1980; Man. Dir and Chief Exec. Officer, 1981. Director: Asarco Inc., 1985–; National Australia Bank. Pres., Australia Mining Industry Council; Bd Mem., Australian Administrative Staff Coll. *Recreation:* golf. *Address:* M.I.M. Holdings Limited, 160 Ann Street, Brisbane, Qld 4000, Australia. *T:* 2281122.

WATSON, (Daniel) Stewart, CB 1967; OBE 1958; *b* 30 Dec. 1911; *s* of Reverend Dr William Watson, DD, DLitt, and Mary Mackintosh Watson; *m* 1939, Isabel (*née* Gibson); one *s*. *Educ:* Robert Gordon's Coll.; Aberdeen University. Student Apprentice, British Thomson Houston, Rugby, 1933, Research Engr, 1936. Scientific Officer, Admiralty, 1938–; Dir, Admiralty Surface Weapons Establishment, 1961–68; Dep. Chief Scientist (Naval), MoD, 1968–72; Dir Gen. Establishments, Resources Programme A, MoD, 1972–73. *Publications:* contribs to IEEJ. *Recreations:* thoroughbred cars; caravanning. *Address:* The Cedars, Jumps Road, Churt, Surrey GU10 2LD.

WATSON, Captain Sir Derrick William Inglefield Inglefield-, 4th Bt, *cr* 1895; TD 1945; 4th Battalion Queen's Own Royal West Kent Regimental Reserve of Officers (TA); Active List 3 Sept. 1939; now retired; *b* 7 Oct. 1901; *s* of Sir John Watson, 2nd Bt, and Edith Jane, *e d* of W. H. Nott, Liverpool; *S* brother, 1918; changed name by Deed Poll to Inglefield-Watson, Jan. 1946; *m* 1925, Margrett Georgina (who obtained a divorce, 1939), *o d* of late Col T. S. G. H. Robertson-Aikman, CB; one *s* one *d*; *m* 1946, Terezia (Terry), *d* of late Prof. Charles Bodon, Budapest. *Educ:* Eton; Christ Church, Oxford. County Councillor, Kent (No 4 Tonbridge Division), 1931–37. *Heir:* *s* John Forbes Watson, Lt-Col Royal Engineers (retd), *b* 16 May 1926. *Address:* Ringshill House, Wouldham, near Rochester, Kent. *T:* Medway 61514.

WATSON, Sir Duncan; *see* Watson, Sir N. D.

WATSON, Duncan Amos, CBE 1986; Principal Assistant Treasury Solicitor, Common Law, 1978–86; Chairman, Executive Council, Royal National Institute for the Blind, since 1975; *b* 10 May 1926; *m* 1954, Mercia Casey, Auckland, NZ. *Educ:* Worcester College for the Blind; St Edmund Hall, Oxford (BA). Solicitor. *Address:* 19 Great Russell Mansions, WC1B 3BE. *Clubs:* Reform, MCC.

WATSON, Vice-Adm. Sir Dymock; *see* Watson, Vice-Adm. Sir R. D.

WATSON, Sir Francis (John Bagott), KCVO 1973 (CVO 1965; MVO 1959); BA Cantab; Hon. MA Oxon 1969; FBA 1969; FSA; Director, Wallace Collection, 1963–74; Surveyor of The Queen's Works of Art, 1963–72, retired; Advisor for Works of Art, since 1972; *b* 24 Aug. 1907; *s* of Hugh Watson, Blakedown, and Helen Marian Bagott, Dudley; *m* 1941, Mary Rosalie Gray (*d* 1969), *d* of George Strong, Bognor; one adopted *s*. *Educ:* Shrewsbury School; St John's College, Cambridge. Registrar, Courtauld Inst. of Art, 1934–38; Asst Keeper (later Dep. Dir), Wallace Collection, 1938–63; Deputy Surveyor of The Queen's (until 1952 The King's) Works of Art, 1947–63; Trustee, Whitechapel Art Gallery, 1949–74; Chairman: Furniture History Society, 1966–74; Walpole Society, 1970–76; Slade Prof. of Fine Art, Oxford, 1969–70; Wrightsman Prof., NY Univ., 1970–71; Vis. Lectr, Univ. of California, 1970; Kress Prof., National Gallery, Washington DC, 1975–76; Regent Fellow, Smithsonian Instn, 1982–84. Uff. del Ord. al Merito della Repubblica Italiana, 1961. New York University Gold Medal, 1966. *Publications:* Canaletto, 1949 (rev. 2nd edn, 1954); (jtly) Southill, A Regency House, 1951; Wallace Collection: Catalogue of Furniture, 1956; Louis XVI Furniture, 1959 (rev. French edn, 1963); The Choiseul Gold Box (Charlton Lecture), 1963; (jtly) Great Family Collections, 1965; The Guardi Family of Painters (Fred Cook Memorial Lecture), 1966; (jtly) Eighteenth Century Gold Boxes, 1966; The Wrightsman Collection Catalogue, Vols 1 and 2: Furniture, 1966, Vols 3 and 4: Furniture, Goldsmith's Work and Ceramics, 1970, Vol. 5: Paintings and Sculpture; Giambattista Tiepolo, 1966; Fragonard, 1967; Chinese Porcelains in European Mounts, 1980; (jtly) Catalogue of the Mounted Oriental Porcelains in the J. Paul Getty Museum, 1983; (contrib.) Vergoldete Bronzen-Die Bronzearbeiten des Spätbarok zu Klassizmus: Einfurung, 1985; Oriental Porcelains in

European Mounts, 1986; Systematic Catalogue of Seventeenth and Eighteenth Century French Furniture, National Gallery, Washington, 1986; numerous contribs to learned journals, in Europe, America and Asia. *Recreations:* sinology, Western Americana. *Address:* West Farm House, Corton, Wilts BA12 0SY. *Club:* Beefsteak.

WATSON, Gerald Walter; Deputy Chairman, Building Societies Commission, since 1986; *b* 13 Dec. 1934; *s* of Reginald Harold Watson and Gertrude Hilda Watson (*née* Ruffell); *m* 1961, Janet Rosemary (*née* Hovey); one *s* two *d*. *Educ:* King Edward VI, Norwich School; Corpus Christi Coll., Cambridge (MA). National Service, RAF Regt, 1953–55. War Office, 1958–64; MoD, 1964–69; Civil Service Dept, 1969–73; Northern Ireland Office, 1973–75; CSD, 1975–81; HM Treasury, 1981–86; Dir, Central Computer and Telecommunications Agency, 1978–82. *Recreations:* opera and theatre going, gardening. *Address:* Topcroft Lodge, Bungay, Suffolk NR35 2BB. *T:* Woodton 435.

WATSON, Gilbert, CBE 1947; HM Senior Chief Inspector of Schools in Scotland, retired; *b* 28 Oct. 1882; *er s* of John Watson, Edinburgh; *m* 1st, 1911, Annie Macdonald (decd); 2nd, 1974, Christian M. Kennedy (*d* 1983). *Educ:* Royal High School, Edinburgh; Edinburgh and Oxford Universities. Rector, Inverness Royal Academy, 1909; entered inspectorate of Scottish Education Department, 1910; HM Senior Chief Inspector, 1944. *Publications:* Theriac and Mithridatium: a study in Therapeutics (Wellcome Historical Medical Library), 1966; A Short History of Craigmillar Park Golf Club, Edinburgh, 1974; co-author of books on Latin Grammar and Latin prose composition. *Recreation:* golf. *Address:* 1 Chamberlain Road, Edinburgh EH10 4DL.

WATSON, Henry, CBE 1969; QPM 1963; Chief Constable of Cheshire, 1963–74; *b* 16 Oct. 1910; *s* of John and Ann Watson, Preston, Lancs; *m* 1933, Nellie Greenhalgh; two *d*. *Educ:* Preston Victoria Junior Technical Coll. Admitted to Inst. of Chartered Accountants, 1934; joined Ashton-under-Lyne Borough Police, 1934; King's Lynn Borough Police, 1942; Norfolk County Constabulary, 1947; Asst Chief Constable, Cumberland and Westmorland, 1955, Chief Constable, 1959. CStJ 1973. *Recreation:* golf. *Address:* Gorgate Road, Hoe, Dereham, Norfolk.

WATSON, Maj.-Gen. (Henry) Stuart (Ramsay), CBE 1973 (MBE 1954); Deputy Director General, Institute of Directors, since 1985 (Executive Director, 1977–85); *b* 9 July 1922; *yr s* of Major H. A. Watson, CBE, MVO and Mrs Dorothy Bannerman Watson, OBE; *m* 1965, Susan, *o d* of Col W. H. Jackson, CBE, DL; two *s* one *d*. *Educ:* Winchester College. Commnd 2nd Lieut 13th/18th Royal Hussars, 1942; Lieut 1943; Captain 1945; Adjt 13/18 H, 1945–46 and 1948–50; psc 1951; GSO2, HQ 1st Corps, 1952–53; Instr RMA Sandhurst, 1955–57; Instr Staff Coll. Camberley, 1960–62; CO 13/18 H, 1962–64; GSO1, MoD, 1964–65; Col GS, SHAPE, 1965–68; Col, Defence Policy Staff, MoD, 1968; idc 1969; BGS HQ BAOR, 1970–73; Dir Defence Policy, MoD, 1973–74; Sen. Army Directing Staff, RCDS, 1974–76. Col, 13th/18th Royal Hussars, 1979–. *Recreation:* golf. *Address:* The Glebe House, Little Kimble, Aylesbury, Bucks HP17 0UE. *T:* Stoke Mandeville 2200. *Club:* Cavalry and Guards.

WATSON, Herbert James, CB 1954; *b* 9 Aug. 1895; *s* of Thomas Francis Watson, Inverness; *m* 1929, Elsie May Carter; two *s* one *d*. *Educ:* Royal Naval College, Greenwich. Entered Royal Corps of Naval Constructors, 1918; Chief Constructor: Admiralty, 1940–43; Chatham, 1943–45; Manager: Malta, 1945–46; Devonport, 1946–47; Asst Director of Dockyards, 1947–49; Deputy Director of Dockyards, 1949–56. *Recreation:* sailing. *Address:* Craigwood, Gardner Street, Como, WA 6152, Australia.

WATSON, Rev. Hubert Luing; retired as General Superintendent of the Baptist Union, North Western Area (1949–60); President of the Baptist Union of Great Britain and Ireland, 1963 (Vice-President, 1962); Chairman, Baptist Minister Fellowship, 1960–63; *b* 30 Nov. 1892; *s* of Austin and Margaret M. Watson; *m* 1914, Mercy (*née* Harwood); one *d*. *Educ:* Winslow School. Baptist Union Exams, External student, Manchester Coll. Pastor of: Milton and Little Leigh, 1918–23; Enon, Burnley, 1923–29; Ansdell, Lytham, 1929–35; Richmond, Liverpool, 1935–49. *Recreations:* gardening and motoring. *Address:* Cartref, Spurlands End Road, Great Kingshill, High Wycombe, Bucks. *T:* High Wycombe 712062.

WATSON, Hugh Gordon; Barrister-at-Law; one of the Special Commissioners of Income Tax, 1952–76; *b* 3 Feb. 1912; *o s* of late Andrew Gordon Watson, Physician, 21 The Circus, Bath, and late Clementina (*née* Macdonald); *m* 1940, Winefride Frances (*d* 1973), *d* of late Clement Brand, Westfield, Reigate, and late Winefride Denise (*née* Casella); three *s*. *Educ:* Ampleforth College; Pembroke College, Oxford. Insurance Broker, 1935–39. Served War of 1939–45 in RNVR. Called to the Bar, Lincoln's Inn, 1947. *Address:* 24 Evesham Close, Reigate, Surrey.

WATSON, Sir (James) Andrew, 5th Bt, *cr* 1866; *b* 30 Dec. 1937; *s* of 4th Bt and Ella Marguerite, *y d* of late Sir George Farrar, 1st Bt; *S* father, 1941; *m* 1965, Christabel Mary, *e d* of K. R. M. Carlisle and Hon. Mrs Carlisle; two *s* one *d*. *Educ:* Eton. Barrister-at-law. Contested (L) Sutton Coldfield, Feb. and Oct. 1974. *Heir:* *s* Roland Victor Watson, *b* 4 March 1966. *Address:* Talton House, Newbold on Stour, Stratford-upon-Avon, Warwickshire. *T:* Alderminster 212.

WATSON, Prof. James Dewey; Director, Cold Spring Harbor Laboratory, since 1969; *b* 6 April 1928; *s* of James D. and Jean Mitchell Watson; *m* 1968, Elizabeth Lewis; two *s*. *Educ:* Univ. of Chicago (BS); Indiana Univ. (PhD); Clare Coll., Cambridge. Senior Res. Fellow in Biology, California Inst. of Technology, 1953–55; Harvard University: Asst Prof. of Biology, 1955–57; Associate Prof., 1958–61; Prof. of Molecular Biology, 1961–76. Member: US National Acad. Sciences, 1962–; Amer Acad. of Arts and Sciences, 1957; Royal Danish Acad. 1962; Amer. Philosophical Soc., 1976; Foreign Mem., Royal Soc., 1981. Hon. DSc: Chicago, 1961; Indiana, 1963; Long Island, 1970; Adelphi, 1972; Brandeis, 1973; Albert Einstein Coll. of Medicine, 1974; Hofstra, 1976; Harvard, 1978; Rockefeller, 1980; Clarkson Coll., 1981; SUNY, 1983; Hon. MD Buenos Aires, 1986; Hon. LLD Notre Dame, 1965. Hon. Fellow, Clare Coll., Camb., 1967. Nobel Award in Medicine and Physiology (jointly), 1962. Carty Medal, US National Acad. of Sciences, 1971; Presidential Medal of Freedom, 1977. *Publications:* Molecular Biology of the Gene, 1965, 4th edn 1986; The Double Helix, 1968; (with John Tooze) The DNA Story, 1981; (with others) The Molecular Biology of the Cell, 1983; (with John Tooze and David T. Kuntz) Recombinant DNA, a short course, 1984; scientific papers on the mechanism of heredity. *Recreation:* mountain walking. *Address:* Bungtown Road, Cold Spring Harbor, New York 11724, USA. *Clubs:* Athenæum; Piping Rock (New York).

WATSON, James Kenneth, FCA; Deputy Chairman (Finance), National Freight Consortium, since 1985 (Finance Director, 1982–84); *b* 16 Jan. 1935; *s* of James and Helen Watson; *m* 1959, Eileen Fay Waller; two *s* one *d*. *Educ:* Watford Grammar Sch.; Stanford Univ., California, USA. Baker Sutton & Co., Chartered Accountants, 1964; Financial Controller, Times Group, 1968; Finance Director: British Road Services Ltd, 1970–76; Nat. Freight Corp., later Nat. Freight Co., 1977–82. *Publications:* contribs to transport and financial press. *Recreations:* cricket, hockey, theatre, history. *Address:* Inglands, Lower Icknield Way, Buckland, Aylesbury, Bucks HP22 5LR. *Clubs:* Royal Automobile, MCC.

WATSON, Prof. James Patrick; Professor of Psychiatry, Guy's Hospital Medical School, since 1974; *b* 14 May 1936; *e s* of Hubert Timothy Watson and Grace Emily (*née* Mizen); *m* 1962, Dr Christine Mary Colley; four *s*. *Educ:* Roan Sch. for Boys, Greenwich; Trinity Coll., Cambridge; King's Coll. Hosp. Med. Sch., London. MA, MD; FRCP, FRCPsych, DPM, DCH. Qualified, 1960. Hosp. appts in Medicine, Paediatrics, Pathology, Neurosurgery, at King's Coll. Hosp. and elsewhere, 1960–64; Registrar and Sen. Registrar, Bethlem Royal and Maudsley Hosps, 1964–71; Sen. Lectr in Psychiatry, St George's Hosp. Med. Sch., and Hon. Consultant Psychiatrist, St George's Hosp., 1971–74. Member: British Assoc. for Behavioural Psychotherapy; British Psychological Soc.; Soc. for Psychotherapy Res.; Assoc. of Sexual and Marital Therapists. Mem., various bodies concerned with interfaces between counselling and psychotherapy, religion and medicine. *Publications:* (ed jtly) Personal Meanings, 1982; papers on gp, family, marital and behavioural psychotherapy, treatment of phobias, hospital ward environmental effects on patients, postnatal depression, community psychiatry, in BMJ, Lancet, British Jl of Psychiatry, British Jl of Med. Psychology, British Jl of Clin. Psychology, Behaviour Research and Therapy. *Recreations:* mountains; music, especially opera, especially Mozart. *Address:* 36 Alleyn Road, SE21 8AL. *T:* 01–670 0444.

WATSON, Prof. James Wreford; Professor of Geography, 1954–82, and Convenor, Centre of Canadian Studies, 1972–82, Edinburgh University; *b* 8 Feb. 1915; *s* of Rev. James Watson; *m* 1939, Jessie W. Black; one *s* one *d*. *Educ:* George Watson's College, Edinburgh; Edinburgh Univ. (MA); Toronto Univ. (PhD). Asst Lecturer in Geography, Sheffield Eng., 1937–39; Prof. of Geography, and founder of Geog. Dept, McMaster University, Canada, 1945–49; Chief Geographer, Canada, and Director of the Geographical Branch, Department of Mines and Technical Surveys, Canada, 1949–54; Prof. and founder of Geog. Dept, Carleton Univ., Ottawa, 1952–54; Edinburgh University: Head of Dept of Geography, 1954, Convenor, Sch. of Scottish Studies, 1956–59, Dean, Faculty of Social Science, 1964–68. Visiting Professor: Queen's Univ., Kingston, Ont, 1959–60; Univ. of Manitoba, 1968–69; British Columbia Univ., 1971; Simon Fraser Univ., BC, 1976–77; Calgary Univ., 1980–81, 1983. Editor: Scottish Studies, 1957–64; Atlas of Canada, 1949–54; Hon. Ed., Scot. Geog. Magazine, 1975–78. Member: Brit. Nat. Cttee for Geog., 1960–82; Geog. Cttee, SSRC, 1965–68; Council SSRC, and Chm., Geog. Planning Jt Cttee, 1972–75; President: Geog. Section, Brit. Assoc. for Advancement of Science, 1971; British Assoc. for Canadian Studies, 1975–77; RSGS, 1977–83; Senior Vice-Pres., 1981, Pres., 1983–84, IBG. Hon. DLitt York Univ., Ont, 1985; Hon. LLD: McMaster Univ., 1977; Carleton Univ., Ottawa, 1979; Calgary Univ., 1981; Queen's Univ., Ont, 1985. Award of Merit, Amer. Assoc. of Geogrs, 1949; Murchison Award, RGS, 1956; Research Medal, RSGS, 1965; Special Award, Canadian Assoc. of Geographers, 1978; Gold Medal, RSGS, 1984; Gold Medal, Internat. Council of Canadian Studies, 1984. Governor General's Medal, Canada (literary), 1953. FRSC; FRSE. *Publications: geographical:* General Geography, 1957 (Toronto); North America: Its Countries and Regions, 1963 (London), 2nd edn 1968; A Geography of Bermuda, 1965 (London); Canada: Problems and Prospects, 1968 (Toronto); Geographical Essays (co-editor with Prof. R. Miller); (ed) The British Isles, A Systematic Geography, 1964 (London); (ed) Collins-Longmans Advanced Atlas, 1968; (ed with T. O'Riordan) The American Environment: perceptions and policies, 1975; (jtly with Jessie Watson) The Canadians: how they live and work, 1977; A Social Geography of the United States, 1978; The USA: habitation of hope, 1983; articles on historical and social geography in Geography, Scottish Geographical Magazine, Geographical Review, Jl of Geography, Canadian Jl of Economics and Political Science, etc; *literary:* Unit of Five, 1947; Of Time and the Lover, 1953; Scotland, the Great Upheaval, 1972; Cross-country Canada, 1979; verse in Canadian and British literary jls. *Address:* Broomhill, Kippford, Galloway DG5 4LG.

WATSON, John, FRCS, FRCSE; Consultant Plastic Surgeon to: King Edward VII Hospital for Officers; London Hospital, 1963–82; Hon. Consultant Plastic Surgeon, Queen Victoria Hospital, East Grinstead; *b* 10 Sept. 1914; *s* of late John Watson; *m* 1941, June Christine Stiles; one *s* three *d*. *Educ:* Leighton Park, Reading; Jesus Coll., Cambridge; Guy's Hospital. MRCS, LRCP 1938; MA, MB, BChir (Cantab) 1939; FRCS(Ed.) 1946; FRCS 1963. Served as Sqdn Ldr (temp.) RAF, 1940–46 (despatches twice). Marks Fellow in Plastic Surgery, Queen Victoria Hosp., E Grinstead, 1947–50; Consultant Plastic Surgeon, Queen Victoria Hospital, East Grinstead, and Tunbridge Wells Gp of Hospitals, 1950–77. Trustee, E Grinstead Research Trust for Blond-McIndoe Research Centre; Gen. Sec., Internat. Confedn for Plastic and Reconstructive Surgery, 1971–75; Mem. Brit. Assoc. of Plastic Surgeons (Hon. Sec., 1960–62, Pres., 1969); Hon. FRSM. *Publications:* numerous articles on plastic surgery in techn. jls and scientific periodicals. Chapters in: Textbook of Surgery, Plastic Surgery for Nurses, Modern Trends in Plastic Surgery, Clinical Surgery. *Recreations:* fishing, astronomy. *Address:* Iddons, Henley's Down, Catsfield, Battle, East Sussex TN33 9BN. *T:* Crowhurst 226.

WATSON, Rear-Adm. John Garth, CB 1965; BSc(Eng); CEng, FICE, FIEE; Secretary, Institution of Civil Engineers, 1967–79; *b* 20 February 1914; *er s* of Alexander Henry St Croix Watson and Gladys Margaret Watson (*née* Payne); *m* 1943, Barbara Elizabeth Falloon; two *s* one *d*. *Educ:* Univ. Coll. School, Hampstead; Northampton Engineering Coll., Univ. of London. BSc (Eng.). 1st Bn Herts Regt (TA), 1932; resigned on joining Admiralty, 1939; HMS Vernon, 1939; Development of Magnetic Minesweepers, Dec. 1939; Warship Electrical Supt, London and SE Area, 1943; BJSM, Washington, DC, 1945; Admlty, 1948; transf. to Naval Elec. Branch, 1949; served in Destroyers and on Staff of Flag Officer, Flot., Home Fleet, 1950; Admlty, 1952; HM Dockyard Devonport, 1953; promoted Capt. 1955; Staff of C-in-C Home Fleet, Fleet Elec. Officer, 1955; Suptg Elec. Engr, HM Dockyard Gibraltar, 1957; Sen. Officers' War Course, 1960; Asst Dir of Elec. Engineering, Admlty, Nov. 1961; promoted Rear Adm. 1963; Adm. Superintendent, Rosyth, 1963–66. ADC to the Queen, 1962. Mem., Smeatonian Soc. of Civil Engineers, 1978 (Pres., 1987). Hon. Mem., Soc. of Civil Engrg Technicians, 1979. Chm., Queen's Jubilee Scholarship Trust, ICE, 1980–86; Vice-Chm., Civil Engineers' Club, 1980–86. Liveryman: Engineers' Co., 1986; Guild of Freemen, 1986. Hon DSc City Univ., 1984. *Publications:* A Short History: Institution of Civil Engineers, 1982; The Civils, 1986; contrib. 15th edn Encyc. Britannica, 1974. *Recreations:* sailing and light gardening. *Address:* Little Hall Court, Shedfield, near Southampton SO3 2HL. *T:* Wickham 833216. *Clubs:* Athenæum, Royal Thames Yacht; Royal Naval and Royal Albert Yacht (Portsmouth).

See also Vice-Adm. Sir P. A. Watson.

WATSON, John Grenville Bernard; MP (C) Skipton and Ripon, since 1983 (Skipton, 1979–83); Director, John Waddington PLC, since 1979; *b* 21 Feb. 1943; *s* of Norman V. Watson and Ruby E. Watson; *m* 1965, Deanna Wood; one *s* two *d*. *Educ:* Moorlands Sch., Leeds; Bootham Sch., York; College of Law, Guildford. Articled, 1962, qualified as solicitor, 1967; joined John Waddington Ltd as managerial trainee, 1968; Export Director, Plastona John Waddington Ltd, 1972; Marketing Dir, 1975, Man. Dir, 1977, Waddington Games Ltd, responsible for Security Printing Div., 1984–. Joined Young Conservatives, 1965; Chairman, Yorkshire YC, 1969; Personal Asst to Rt Hon. Edward Heath, 1970; Chm., Nat. YC, 1971; contested (C) York, general elections, Feb. and Oct. 1974; Chm.,

Conservative Candidates Assoc., 1975–79. Mem., Parly Select Cttee on Energy, 1980–82; PPS, NI Office, 1982–83; PPS, Dept of Energy, 1983–85. Chm., British Atlantic Gp of Young Political Leaders, 1982–84; Nat. Vice Pres., Young Conservative Orgn, 1984–. Pres., British Youth Council, 1980–83. *Recreations:* walking, running, standing still. *Address:* Bay Horse Corner, Ling Lane, Scarcroft, Leeds LS14 3HY. *T:* Leeds 892209.

See also V. H. Watson.

WATSON, (John Hugh) Adam, CMG 1958; Professor, Center for Advanced Studies, University of Virginia, since 1980; *b* 10 Aug. 1914; *er s* of Joseph Charlton Watson and Alice (*née* Tate); *m* 1950, Katharine Anne Campbell; two *s* one *d*. *Educ:* Rugby; King's Coll., Camb. Entered the Diplomatic Service, 1937; Brit. Legation, Bucharest, 1939; Brit. Embassy, Cairo, 1940; Brit. Embassy, Moscow, 1944; FO, 1947; Brit. Embassy, Washington, 1950; Head of African Dept, Foreign Office, 1956–59; appointed British Consul-General at Dakar, 1959; British Ambassador: to the Federation of Mali, 1960–61; to Senegal, Mauritania and Togo, 1960–62; to Cuba, 1963–66; Under-Secretary, Foreign Office, 1966–68; Diplomatic Adviser, British Leyland Motor Corp., 1968–73. Gwilym Gibbon Fellow, Nuffield Coll., Oxford, Oct. 1962–Oct. 1963. Vis. Fellow, ANU, 1973; Vis. Prof., Univ. of Virginia, 1978. Dir Gen., Internat. Assoc. for Cultural Freedom, 1974. *Publications:* The War of the Goldsmith's Daughter, 1964; Nature and Problems of Third World, 1968; (ed) The Origins of History, 1981; Diplomacy: the dialogue between States, 1982; (with Hedley Bull) The Expansion of International Society, 1984; various plays broadcast by BBC. *Address:* Sharnden Old Manor, Mayfield, East Sussex. *T:* Mayfield 872441; 1871 Field Road, Charlottesville, Virginia 22903, USA. *Club:* Brooks's.

WATSON, John Parker, CBE 1972; TD 1945; Partner, Lindsays, WS (formerly Lindsay Howe & Co., WS), 1935–79; *b* 22 Aug. 1909; *s* of John Parker Watson, WS, and Rachel Watson (*née* Henderson); *m* 1936, Barbara Parkin Wimperis; two *s* one *d*. *Educ:* Merchiston Castle Sch., Edinburgh; Corpus Christi Coll., Oxford (scholar); Edinburgh Univ. MA Oxon; LLB Edin. Served War, 1939–45, RA; Adjt, 94th (City of Edinburgh) HAA Regt; Staff Capt., JAG'S Dept; Bde Major, 12th AA Bde (8th Army); Staff Coll., Haifa; GSO2 HQ 9th Army. Admitted Mem., WS Soc., 1934. Lectr in Public Internat. Law, Edinburgh Univ., 1937–39. Chairman: Edinburgh Marriage Guidance Council, 1951–54; Scottish Marriage Guidance Council, 1962–65; Scottish Solicitors' Discipline Tribunal, 1974–78; Mem., SE Scotland Regional Hosp. Bd, 1952–55. Mem. Council, Law Soc. of Scotland, 1950–75 (Vice-Pres., 1957–58, Pres., 1970–72). *Recreations:* travel, hill walking, listening to music, golf. *Address:* 66 Murrayfield Gardens, Edinburgh EH12 6DQ. *T:* 031–337 3405. *Clubs:* Travellers'; New (Edinburgh).

WATSON, Rev. John T., BA (London); LTCL; General Secretary, British and Foreign Bible Society, 1960–69, retired; *b* 13 Jan. 1904; *s* of late F. Watson, Sutton Bridge, Lincs; *m* 1933, Gertrude Emily Crossley (*d* 1982), Farsley, Leeds; two *s* one *d*. *Educ:* Moulton Grammar School; Westminster Training College, London; Didsbury Training College, Manchester. School-master, 1924–26. Missionary (under Methodist Missionary Soc.) in Dahomey, W Africa, 1929–34; Methodist Minister: Plymouth, 1935–38; Golders Green, 1938–46; Bible Society: Secretary for Schools and Colleges, 1946–49; Asst Home Sec., 1949–54; Asst Gen. Sec., 1954–60. Hon. DD, West Virginia Wesleyan Coll., 1966. *Publications:* Seen and Heard in Dahomey, 1934; Daily Prayers for the Methodist Church, 1951. *Recreation:* music. *Address:* 16 Beverington Road, Eastbourne, East Sussex. *T:* Eastbourne 29838.

WATSON, Joseph Stanley, MBE 1946; QC 1955; Social Security (formerly National Insurance) Commissioner, 1965–85, retired; *b* 13 Sept. 1910; *er s* of late Joseph Watson and late Gertrude Ethel (*née* Catton); *m* 1951, Elizabeth Elliston, *d* of late Col G. Elliston Allen, TD; four *d*. *Educ:* Rossall Sch.; Jesus Coll., Cambridge (MA). Barrister, Inner Temple, 1933. Served War of 1939–45 (MBE): RA (Field), UK, MEF, Force 281, Dodecanese in Unit and on G Staff (Greek Military Cross), rank of Major. No 7 (NW) Legal Aid Area Cttee, 1949–55. Mem. Gen. Council of the Bar, 1959–64; Master of the Bench, Inner Temple, 1961; Recorder of Blackpool, 1961–65. *Address:* The Old Dairy, Mickleham, Surrey. *T:* Leatherhead 374387.

WATSON, (Leslie) Michael (Macdonald) S.; *see* Saunders Watson.

WATSON, Air Cdre (retired) Michael, CB 1952; CBE 1945 (OBE 1942); *b* 12 Aug. 1909; *s* of late William Watson, Kew. *Educ:* St Paul's Prep. School; Saffron Walden School. Joined RAF 1929, and qualified as Pilot; trained as Signals Officer, 1933. Served War of 1939–45 (despatches twice); Air Min. Combined Ops Signals Plans 1942; HQ, AEAF, 1943; SHAEF 1944; HQ Middle East, 1946; Air Ministry, 1947; Comdg RAF Welford, 1949; HQ, Fighter Comd, 1950–53; Director of Signals, Air Ministry, 1953–54; retired from RAF at own request, 1954. Rolls Royce Representative with N American Aviation Inc., Calif., 1956–60; Asst Gen. Man., Sales and Service, Rolls Royce, Ltd, 1961–62; Space Div., N American Rockwell Inc., Calif, 1964–71, retired. Chevalier de la Légion d'Honneur, 1944; Officer US Legion of Merit, 1945. *Recreations:* fishing, sailing. *Address:* Box 5321, Big Bear Lake, Calif 92315, USA.

WATSON, Sir Michael M.; *see* Milne-Watson.

WATSON, Sir (Noel) Duncan, KCMG 1967 (CMG 1960); HM Diplomatic Service, retired; *b* 16 Dec. 1915; *s* of late Harry and Mary Noel Watson, Bradford, Yorks; *m* 1951, Aileen Bryans (*d* 1980), *d* of late Charles Bell, Dublin. *Educ:* Bradford Grammar School; New College, Oxford. Colonial Administrative Service: Admin. Officer, Cyprus, 1938–43; Assistant Colonial Secretary, Trinidad, 1943–45; Principal, Colonial Office (secondment), 1946; transferred to Home Civil Service, 1947; Principal Private Sec. to Sec. of State for the Colonies, 1947–50; Asst Sec.: CO, 1950–62, Cent. Af. Office, 1962–63; Under-Secretary, 1963; Asst Under-Sec. of State, CO and CRO, 1964–67; Political Adviser to C-in-C Far East, 1967–70; High Comr in Malta, 1970–72; Dep. Under-Sec. of State, FCO, 1972–74. Mem., Central Council, Royal Commonwealth Soc., 1975– (Dep. Chm., 1983–). *Address:* Sconce, Steels Lane, Oxshott, Surrey. *Clubs:* Travellers', Royal Commonwealth Society; Leander.

WATSON, Vice-Adm. Sir Philip (Alexander), KBE 1976; LVO 1960; Consultant to The Marconi Company Ltd, since 1977; *b* 7 Oct. 1919; *yr s* of A. H. St C. Watson; *m* 1948, Jennifer Beatrice Tanner; one *s* two *d*. *Educ:* St Albans School. FIEE 1963; FIERE 1965; CBIM 1973. Sub-Lt RNVR, 1940; qual. Torpedo Specialist, 1943; transf. to RN, 1946; Comdr 1955; HM Yacht Britannia, 1957–59; Captain 1963; MoD (Ship Dept), 1963; Senior Officers' War Course, 1966; comd HMS Collingwood, 1967; Dep. Dir of Engrg (Ship Dept), MoD, 1969; Dir Gen. Weapons (Naval), MoD, 1970–77; Chief Naval Engineer Officer, 1974–77. Rear-Adm. 1970; Vice-Adm. 1974. Director: Marconi International Marine Co. Ltd, 1977–86; Marconi Radar Systems Ltd, 1981–86 (Chm., 1981–85). Mem. Council, IEE, 1975–78, 1982–, Chm. South East Centre, 1982–83. Adm. Pres., Midland Naval Officers Assoc., 1979–85, Vice Pres., 1985–. *Address:* The Hermitage, Bodicote, Banbury, Oxon OX15 4BZ. *T:* Banbury 3300. *Club:* Army and Navy.

See also Rear-Adm. J. G. Watson.

WATSON, Reginald Frank William, AO 1985; CMG 1977; Chairman: State Bank of New South Wales, since 1986; Samuelson Group Pty Ltd (Australia); Director, Oakbridge Ltd (Australia); *b* 11 Nov. 1921; *s* of late F. H. Watson; *m* 1948, Helen Patricia Helmore; two *s*. *Educ:* various schools and colleges in China. Major, Fifth Royal Gurkha Rifles, India, Burma and China (despatches twice), and Adviser to Brit. Mil. Mission to China, 1941–46. Own retail co., Sydney, 1946–48; Gilbert Lodge & Co., Sydney, 1948–52; Admin. Officer, Aust. Defence Dept, Melbourne, 1952–54; Godfrey Phillips Ltd, Sydney, 1954–56; Rothmans of Pall Mall, Australia, 1956–76 (Man. Dir, 1968; Chief Exec., 1975); Man. Dir, Dri-Clad Industries, Aust., 1977–78; marketing and indust. relations consultant, 1978–82. Part-time appts to state govt and fed. govt bds and authorities, 1972–83 (Chm., NSW Overseas Trade Authority, 1978–83); Agent-Gen. for NSW in London, 1983–86. Mem., State Rail Authority of NSW, 1986–. Co-Founder, Variety Club of Australia, 1974. Freeman, City of London, 1983. *Recreations:* tennis, walking, Chinese studies, travel. *Address:* c/o State Bank of New South Wales, 52 Martin Place, Sydney, NSW 2000, Australia. *Clubs:* East India, Royal Automobile; Union, Elanora Country, American National (Sydney).

WATSON, Dr Reginald Gordon Harry, (Rex), CChem, FRSC; Director, Building Research Establishment, Department of the Environment, since 1983; *b* 3 Nov. 1928; *s* of Gordon Henry and Winifred Catherine Watson; *m* 1951, Molly Joyce Groom; one *s* two *d*. *Educ:* Chislehurst and Sidcup Grammar Sch.; Imperial Coll., London (Royal Schol.). BSc (1st cl. Hons Chem.), PhD; DIC; ARCS. Res. Worker (Fuel Cells), Dept of Chemical Engrg, Univ. of Cambridge, 1951–56; joined Royal Naval Scientific Service, 1956, as Sen. Scientific Officer, Admty Materials Lab.; Head of Chemical Engrg Div., 1958–66; Naval Staff Course, 1962; Individual Merit Sen. Principal Scientific Officer, 1965; Director: Naval R&D Admin, 1967–69; Admty Materials Lab., 1969–74; Chemical Defence Estab., Porton Down, 1974–83. *Publications:* papers on electrochemistry, chemical engineering and materials science. *Recreations:* photography, natural history, sailing. *Address:* 9 Chapel Cottages, Chapel Street, Hemel Hempstead, Herts HP2 5DJ. *T:* Hemel Hempstead 66523; 20 Merriefield Drive, Broadstone, Dorset BH18 8BP. *T:* Broadstone 692128. *Club:* Cambridge University Cruising.

WATSON, Rt. Rev. Richard Charles Challinor; *see* Burnley, Suffragan Bishop of.

WATSON, Richard (Eagleson Gordon) Burges, CMG 1985; HM Diplomatic Service; Minister (Commercial) and Consul-General, Milan, since 1983; *b* 23 Sept. 1930; *er s* of late Harold Burges Watson and Marjorie Eleanor (*née* Gordon); *m* 1966, Ann Rosamund Clarke; two *s* three *d*. *Educ:* King Edward VI Sch., Bury St Edmunds; St John's Coll., Cambridge. RA, 1948–50. Joined HM Foreign (subseq. Diplomatic) Service, 1954; Tokyo, 1954–60; FO, 1960–63; Bamako (Mali), 1963–66; British Delegn to OECD, 1966–69; FCO, 1969–71; Vis. Student, Woodrow Wilson Sch., Princeton, 1971–72; Tokyo, 1972–76; Brussels, 1976–78; FCO, 1978–81; Foundn for Internat. Research and Studies, Florence, 1981–82; FCO, 1982–83. *Recreations:* ski-ing, swimming, walking. *Address:* c/o Foreign and Commonwealth Office, SW1A 2AH. *Club:* Travellers'.

WATSON, Vice-Adm. Sir (Robert) Dymock, KCB 1959 (CB 1956); CBE 1948; DL; *b* 5 April 1904; *e s* of Robert Watson, FRIBA, Farnham, Surrey; *m* 1st, 1939, Margaret Lois (*d* 1968), *d* of late Rev. F. R. Gillespy; one *s* three *d*; 2nd, 1977, Elizabeth Evelyn Petronella, *widow* of Amyas Chichester, MC. *Educ:* Royal Naval Colls Osborne and Dartmouth. Captain; Asst Dir of Plans, Joint Planning Staff, Min. of Defence, 1944–46; Capt. (D) 1st Destroyer Flotilla Medit., 1947–48; idc, 1949; Dir of Plans, Admty, 1950–52; CO, HMS Illustrious, 1953; Rear-Adm., 1954; Flag Officer Flotillas, Medit., 1954–55, Vice-Adm. 1957; a Lord Commissioner of the Admiralty, Fourth Sea Lord, Chief of Supplies and Transport, 1955–58; Commander-in-Chief, South Atlantic and South America, 1958–60; retired, 1961. DL County of Brecknock, 1965, Powys 1974. *Address:* Manascin, Pencelli, near Brecon, Powys, Wales.

WATSON, Roderick Anthony, QC 1967; *b* 1920; *o s* of late O. C. Watson, CBE and Peggy (*née* Donnelly); *m* Ann, *o d* of late W. L. Wilson; three *s* one *d*. *Educ:* Christian Brothers, Beulah Hill; King's Coll., Univ. of London. Served War of 1939–45, Captain RASC. Called to the Bar, Lincoln's Inn, 1949, Bencher, 1975. *Address:* Merton House, 11 The Promenade, Castletown, Isle of Man. *Clubs:* Army and Navy, Garrick; Isle of Man Yacht.

WATSON, Roy William, CBE 1983; Director General, National Farmers' Union, 1979–85, retired; *b* 7 Feb. 1926; *s* of William and Eleanor Maud Watson; *m* 1st, 1947, Margaret Peasey; two *s*; 2nd, 1977, Phyllis Frances Brotherwood (*née* Farrer). *Educ:* Alleyn's Sch., Dulwich. National Farmers' Union, 1948–85: Asst Dir General, 1973–78; Dep. Dir General, 1978. *Recreations:* music, military history, golf, gardening. *Address:* Pinebrook, Offwell, Honiton, Devon EX14 9SR. *T:* Wilmington 454.

WATSON, Stewart; *see* Watson, D. S.

WATSON, Maj.-Gen. Stuart; *see* Watson, Maj.-Gen. H. S. R.

WATSON, Sydney, OBE 1970; MA; DMus; FRCO; FRCM; Student, Organist and Lecturer in Music, Christ Church, Oxford, 1955–70; Professor, Royal College of Music, 1946–71; Examiner, Royal Schools of Music, 1943–83; *b* Denton, Lancashire, 3 Sept. 1903; *s* of W. T. Watson; unmarried. *Educ:* Warwick Sch.; Royal College of Music; Keble Coll., Oxford (Organ Scholar). Assistant music master, Stowe School, 1925–28; Precentor of Radley Coll., 1929–33; Conductor of Abingdon Madrigal Society, 1931–36; Organist of New Coll., Oxford, 1933–38; Organist of Sheldonian Theatre, Conductor of Oxford Harmonic Society, 1933–38; Oxford Orchestral Society, 1936–38; Director of Concerts, Balliol Coll., 1933–38, 1962–69; Choragus to Oxford Univ., 1963–68; Master of Music, Winchester Coll., and Conductor Winchester Music Club, 1938–45; Precentor and Director of Music, Eton Coll., 1946–55; Conductor Petersfield Festival, 1946–64, Slough Philharmonic Society, 1946–55; Windsor and Eton Choral Society, 1949–55; Conductor, Oxford Bach Choir, 1955–70; Oxford Orchestral Society, 1956–70. *Publications:* Church Music. *Address:* Aynhoe Park, Aynho, Banbury, Oxon. *Club:* Athenæum.

WATSON, Thomas Frederick, FCA, FCIS; Governor, National Society for Epilepsy, 1971–81 (Chairman, 1974–78); Chairman, Finance Committee, 1975–78, Vice Chairman, 1978; retired; *b* 18 April 1906; *s* of late Frederick Watson and Jane Lucy (*née* Britton); *m* 1932, Eveline Dorothy Strang; one *d*. *Educ:* Tiffins Sch., Kingston-on-Thames. FCIS 1957; FCA 1960. With Deloitte Co., Chartered Accountants, 1925–45; qual. as Chartered Sec., 1930; Incorporated Accountant, 1945. Chm. and Chief Exec., Exchange Telegraph Co. Ltd, 1961–68, retired. Mem. Council, Commonwealth Press Union, 1959–68. *Recreations:* gardening, bridge, theatre, charity work. *Address:* Byeways Bungalow, Barrack Lane, Aldwick, Bognor Regis, W. Sussex. *T:* Pagham 263896.

WATSON, Thomas Yirrell, CMG 1955; MBE 1943; *b* 27 May 1906; *s* of William Scott Watson and Edith Rose Watson (*née* Yirrell); *m* 1st, 1935, Margaret Alice (*d* 1978), *d* of late J. J. Watson; one *d*; 2nd, 1984, Katharine Margaret, *widow* of W. J. Mill Irving, OBE and *d* of late James Kay. *Educ:* Aberdeen Grammar Sch.; Aberdeen Univ. (BSc); Cambridge Univ. (Diploma in Agricultural Science); Pretoria Univ., South Africa. Colonial Agricultural Scholar, 1929–31; Agricultural Officer, Kenya, 1931–43; Senior

Agricultural Officer, Kenya, 1943–48; Dep. Director of Agriculture, Uganda, 1948–51; Director of Agriculture, Uganda, 1951–53; Secretary for Agriculture and Natural Resources, Uganda, 1954–55; Minister of Natural Resources, 1955–56. General Manager, Uganda Lint Cotton Marketing Board, 1951–53; MEC and MLC, Uganda, 1951–56. Member: Commission of Inquiry into Land and Population Problems, Fiji, 1959–60; Economic Development Commn, Zanzibar, 1961; Commission of Inquiry into Cotton Ginning Industry, Uganda, 1962; Commissioner, Burley Tobacco Industry Inquiry, Malawi, 1964. Coronation Medal, 1953. *Address:* 2 Lennox Milne Court, Haddington, East Lothian EH41 4DF.

WATSON, Victor Hugo; Chairman: John Waddington PLC, since 1977; John Foster & Son PLC, since 1985; *b* 26 Sept. 1928; *s* of Norman Victor and Ruby Ernestine Watson; *m* 1952, Sheila May Bryan; two *d. Educ:* Clare Coll., Cambridge (MA). Served Royal Engineers (2nd Lieut), 1946–48. Joined John Waddington Ltd, 1951. Dir, Leeds and Holbeck Building Soc., 1985–. Pres., Inst. of Packaging, 1984–. *Recreations:* music, golf, sailing. *Address:* Moat Field, Moor Lane, East Keswick, Leeds LS17 9ET. *Club:* Eccentric.

WATSON, Prof. William, CBE 1982; MA; FBA 1972; FSA; Professor of Chinese Art and Archaeology in University of London, at the School of Oriental and African Studies, 1966–83, now Emeritus, and Head of the Percival David Foundation of Chinese Art, 1966–83; Trustee, British Museum, since 1980; *b* 9 Dec. 1917; *s* of Robert Scoular Watson and Lily Waterfield; *m* 1940, Katherine Sylvia Mary, *d* of Mr and Mrs J. H. Armfield, Ringwood, Hants; four *s. Educ:* Glasgow High Sch.; Herbert Strutt Sch.; Gonville and Caius Coll., Cantab (Scholar; tripos in Modern and Medieval Langs). Served Intelligence Corps, 1940–46, Egypt, N Africa, Italy, India, ending as Major. Asst Keeper, British Museum, first in Dept of British and Medieval Antiquities, then in Dept of Oriental Antiquities, 1947–66. Slade Prof. of Fine Art, Cambridge University, 1975–76. Pres., Oriental Ceramic Soc., 1981–84. Hon. DLitt Chinese Univ. of Hong Kong, 1984. Sir Percy Sykes Meml Medal, 1973. *Publications:* The Sculpture of Japan, 1959; Archaeology in China, 1960; China before the Han Dynasty, 1961; Ancient Chinese Bronzes, 1961; Jade Books in the Chester Beatty Library, 1963; Cultural Frontiers in Ancient East Asia, 1971; The Genius of China (catalogue of Burlington House exhibn), 1973; Style in the Arts of China, 1974; L'Art de l'Ancienne Chine, 1980; (ed) Catalogue of the Great Japan Exhibition (at Burlington House 1981–82); Tang and Liao Ceramics, 1984. *Recreation:* exploring N Wales, Romanesque France and Spain. *Address:* Cefnymaes, Parc, Bala, Gwynedd. *T:* Bala 4302; 54 St Augustine's Road, NW1. *T:* 01–485 4755.

WATSON, William Albert, PhD; FRCVS; Director, Veterinary Laboratories, Ministry of Agriculture, Fisheries and Food, since 1986; *b* 8 March 1930; *s* of Henry Watson and Mary Emily Watson; *m* 1956, Wilma, *d* of Rev. Theodorus Johannas Henricus Steenbeck; one *s* one *d. Educ:* Preston Grammar School; University of Bristol (PhD, BVSc). Private practice, Garstang, Lancs, 1954–55; Asst Vet. Investigation Officer, Weybridge, 1954–56, Leeds, 1956–66; Animal Health Expert, FAO, Turkey, 1966–67; Vet. Investigation Officer, Penrith, 1967–71; Dep. Regional Vet. Officer, Nottingham, 1971–75; Regional Vet. Officer, Edinburgh, 1975–77; Asst Chief Vet. Officer, Tolworth, 1977–84; Dep. Dir, Vet. Labs, Weybridge, 1984–86. External Examr, London, Liverpool, Dublin and Edinburgh Univs. *Publications:* contribs to vet. jls and textbooks. *Recreations:* fishing, gardening, restoration of listed property. *Address:* 57 Warren Farm, Warren Lane, Pyrford, Surrey.

WATSON, Prof. William Alexander Jardine; University Professor of Law, since 1986 and Director of Center for Advanced Studies in Legal History, since 1980, University of Pennsylvania; *b* 27 Oct. 1933; *s* of James W. and Janet J. Watson; *m* 1958, Cynthia Betty Balls, MA, MLitt (marr. diss.); one *s* one *d*; *m* 1986, Harriett Camilla Emanuel, BA, MS, JD, LLM. *Educ:* Univ. of Glasgow (MA 1954, LLB 1957); Univ. of Oxford (BA (by decree) 1957, MA 1958, DPhil 1960, DCL 1973). Lectr, Wadham Coll., Oxford, 1957–59; Lectr, 1959–60, Fellow, 1960–65, Oriel Coll., Oxford; Pro-Proctor, Oxford Univ., 1962–63; Douglas Prof. of Civil Law, Univ. of Glasgow, 1965–68; Prof. of Civil Law, Univ. of Edinburgh, 1968–79; University of Pennsylvania: Prof. of Law and Classical Studies, 1979–84; Nicholas F. Gallichio Prof. of Law, 1984–86. Visiting Professor of Law: Tulane Univ., 1967; Univ. of Virginia, 1970 and 1974; Univ. of Cape Town, 1974 and 1975; Univ. of Michigan, 1977. Mem. Council, Stair Soc., 1970–; Hon. Mem., Speculative Soc., 1975. *Publications:* (as Alan Watson): Contract of Mandate in Roman Law, 1961; Law of Obligations in Later Roman Republic, 1965; Law of Persons in Later Roman Republic, 1967; Law of Property in Later Roman Republic, 1968; Law of the Ancient Romans, 1970; Roman Private Law Around 200 BC, 1971; Law of Succession in Later Roman Republic, 1971; Law Making in Later Roman Republic, 1974; Legal Transplants, An Approach to Comparative Law, 1974; (ed) Daube Noster, 1974; Rome of the Twelve Tables, 1975; Society and Legal Change, 1977; The Nature of Law, 1977; The Making of the Civil Law, 1981; Sources of Law, Legal Change, and Ambiguity, 1984; The Evolution of Law, 1985; (ed) The Digest of Justinian, 1986; various articles. *Recreations:* Roman numismatics, shooting. *Address:* Law School, University of Pennsylvania, 3400 Chestnut Street, Philadelphia, Pa 19104, USA.

WATSON-ARMSTRONG, family name of **Baron Armstrong.**

WATT; *see* Gibson-Watt.

WATT; *see* Harvie-Watt.

WATT, Sir Alan (Stewart), Kt 1954; CBE 1952; Director, The Canberra Times, 1964–72; *b* 13 April 1901; *s* of George Watt and Susan Stewart Robb Gray; *m* 1927, Mildred Mary Wait; three *s* one *d. Educ:* Sydney Boys' High Sch.; Sydney and Oxford Universities. Rhodes Scholar for NSW, 1921; practised as Barrister-at-Law, Sydney; appointed to Dept of External Affairs, Canberra, 1937; First Secretary, Australian Legation, Washington, 1940–45; Adviser, Australian Deleg. to San Francisco, UN Conf., 1945; Alternate Deleg., UN General Assembly, London, 1946; Asst Secretary (Political), Dept of External Affairs, 1946; Del. to UN Gen. Assemblies, New York, 1946 and 1947, Paris, 1948; Leader, Australian Deleg. to Conf. on Freedom of Information, Geneva, 1948. Australian Minister to USSR, 1947–48; Australian Ambassador to USSR, 1949–50; Secretary, Department of External Affairs, Canberra, ACT, 1950–53; Australian Commissioner in SE Asia, 1954–56; Australian Ambassador: to Japan, 1956–60; to Federal Republic of Germany, 1960–62. Australian Delegate, Colombo Plan Cons. Cttee Meeting, Sydney, 1950; Member Deleg. accompanying Prime Minister to Prime Ministers' Conf., London, 1951 and 1953; Member Australian Delegation to ANZUS Council Meeting, Honolulu, 1952, and Geneva, 1954; alternate Leader, Australian Deleg. to Conf. on Indo-China and Korea, Geneva, 1954, Manila Treaty Conf., Manila 1954. Bangkok 1955. Retired from Commonwealth Public Service, July 1962. Visiting Fellow, Australian National Univ., 1963–83; Dir, Australian Inst. of Internat. Affairs, 1963–69. *Publications:* Evolution of Australian Foreign Policy 1938–1965, 1967; Vietnam, 1968; Memoirs, 1972; United Nations, 1974. *Recreation:* lawn tennis. *Address:* 1 Mermaid Street, Red Hill, Canberra, ACT 2603, Australia. *Club:* National Press (Canberra).

WATT, Rev. Canon Alfred Ian; Convenor, Mission Board of the General Synod, since 1982; Rector of St Paul's, Kinross, since 1982; *b* 1934. *Educ:* Edinburgh Theological College. Deacon, 1960, priest 1961, Diocese of Brechin; Curate, St Paul's Cathedral, Dundee, 1960–63; Precentor, 1963–66; Rector of Arbroath, 1966–69; Provost of St Ninian's Cathedral, Perth, 1969–82; Canon, 1982–. *Address:* The Rectory, Kinross.

WATT, Andrew, CBE 1963; Forestry Commissioner, 1965–69; *b* 10 Nov. 1909; 2nd surv. *s* of late James Watt, LLD, WS, and late Menie Watt; *m* 1943, Helen McGuffog (*d* 1969); two *s* one *d. Educ:* Winchester; Magdalen Coll., Oxford. BA 1931. District Officer, Forestry Commn, 1934; Divisional Officer, 1940; Conservator, 1946; Director of Forestry for Scotland, 1957–63; Director of Forest Research, 1963–65. *Address:* 7A Ravelston Park, Edinburgh EH4 3DX. *T:* 031–332 1084.

WATT, Charlotte Joanne, (Mrs G. L. Watt); *see* Erickson, Prof. C. J.

WATT, David; writer and consultant; *b* Edinburgh, 9 Jan. 1932; *s* of Rev. John Hunter Watt and Helen Garioch Bryce; *m* 1968, Susanne, *d* of Dr Frank Burchardt; four *s. Educ:* Marlborough; Hertford Coll., Oxford. Dramatic Critic, Spectator, 1956–57; Diplomatic Corresp., Scotsman, 1958–60; Common Market Corresp., Daily Herald, 1960–61; Polit. Corresp., Spectator, 1962–63; Washington Corresp., Financial Times, 1964–67, Polit. Editor, 1968–77; Dir, RIIA, 1978–83. Jt Editor, Political Qly, 1979–85; regular contributor to The Times, 1981–. Vis. Fellow, 1972–73, Fellow, 1981–83, All Souls Coll., Oxford. Member: Fisher Cttee on Self-regulation at Lloyd's, 1979–80; Bd of Visitors, Wandsworth Prison, 1977–81. *Recreations:* music, chess, golf. *Address:* 18 Groveway, SW9 0AR. *T:* 01–735 5195. *Clubs:* Travellers', Beefsteak.

WATT, Prof. Donald Cameron; *see* Cameron Watt.

WATT, Hamish, JP; Rector of Aberdeen University, since 1985; *b* 27 Dec. 1925; *s* of Wm Watt and Caroline C. Allan; *m* 1948, Mary Helen Grant; one *s* two *d. Educ:* Keith Grammar Sch.; St Andrews Univ. Engaged in farming (dairy and sheep). Subseq. company director, quarries. Contested (C), Caithness, 1966; contested (SNP): Banff, 1970; Moray, 1983. MP (SNP) Banff, Feb. 1974–1979. Regional and Dist Councillor. *Address:* Mill of Buckie, Buckie, Banffshire. *T:* Buckie 32591. *Clubs:* Farmers', Whitehall Court.

WATT, Ian Buchanan, CMG 1967; HM Diplomatic Service, retired; with Grindlays Bank, 1977–83; *b* 3 Aug. 1916; *s* of John Watt and Margaret Gibson Watt, Perth; *m* 1963, Diana Susan, *d* of Captain R. A. Villiers, Royal Navy (retired) and late Mrs R. A. Villiers; two *s* one *d. Educ:* Perth Academy; St Andrews Univ. MA 1939. Asst Principal, Government of N. Ireland, 1939. Naval Service, 1942–46; Lieut, RNVR. Principal, Colonial Office, 1946; Asst Secretary, 1956; Dep. UK Commissioner, Malta, 1962; Dep. High Commissioner, Malta, 1964; transf. to Diplomatic Service, 1964; Counsellor, CRO, 1965; High Comr, Lesotho, 1966–70; Counsellor, FCO, 1970–72; High Comr, Sierra Leone, 1972–76. *Recreations:* gardening, ornithology. *Address:* Kingswood House, 8 Lower Green Road, Esher, Surrey. *T:* 01–398 5728. *Club:* Travellers'.

WATT, Surgeon Vice-Adm. Sir James, KBE 1975; MS, FRCS; Medical Director-General (Navy), 1972–77; *b* 19 Aug. 1914; *s* of Thomas Watt and Sarah Alice Clarkson. *Educ:* King Edward VI Sch., Morpeth; Univ. of Durham. MB, BS 1938; MS 1949; FRCS 1955; MD 1972; FRCP 1975. Surgical Registrar, Royal Vic. Infirm., Newcastle upon Tyne, 1947; Surgical Specialist: N Ire., 1949; RN Hosp., Hong Kong, 1954; Consultant in Surgery, RN Hospitals: Plymouth, 1956; Haslar, 1959; Malta, 1961; Haslar, 1963; Jt Prof. of Naval Surgery, RCS and RN Hosp., Haslar, 1965–69; Dean of Naval Medicine and MO i/c, Inst. of Naval Medicine, 1969–72. Chm., RN Clin. Research Working Party, 1969–77; Chm. Bd of Trustees, Naval Christian Fellowship, 1968–75; Pres., Royal Naval Lay Readers Soc., 1973–83. QHS 1969–77. Surg. Comdr 1956; Surg. Captain 1965; Surg. Rear-Adm. 1969; Surg. Vice-Adm. 1972. Mem., Environmental Medicine Res. Policy Cttee, MRC, 1974–77. Thomas Vicary Lectr, RCS, 1974; University House Vis. Fellow, ANU, 1986. FICS 1964; Fellow: Assoc. of Surgeons of GB and Ire.; Med. Soc. of London (Mem. Council, 1976; Lettsomian Lectr, 1979; Pres., 1980–81; Vice-Pres., 1981–83); FRSM (Pres., 1982–84); Hon. FRCSE; Member: Brit. Soc. for Surgery of the Hand; Internat. Soc. for Burns Injuries; Corr. Mem., Surgical Research Soc., 1966–77; Mem. Editorial Bd, Brit. Jl of Surgery, 1966–77. FRGS 1982; Mem. Council, RGS, 1985–. Hon. Mem., Smeatonian Soc. of Civil Engineers, 1978–. Hon. Freeman, Co. of Barbers, 1978. Hon. DCh Newcastle, 1978. Errol-Eldridge Prize, 1968; Gilbert Blane Medal, 1971. CStJ 1972. *Publications:* papers on: burns, cancer chemotherapy, peptic ulceration, hyberbaric oxygen therapy, naval medical history. *Recreations:* mountain walking, music. *Address:* 7 Cambisgate, Church Road, Wimbledon, SW19 5AL. *Club:* Royal Over-Seas League.

WATT, Richard Lorimer, CA; FBIM; Director, First Leisure Corporation plc (formerly Trusthouses Forte Leisure Ltd), since 1981; *b* 20 June 1921; *s* of George Lorimer Watt and Sophia Fordyce Watt; *m* 1952, Elizabeth (*née* Hancock); one *s. Educ:* George Watson's Boys' Coll., Edinburgh; Edinburgh Univ. Brush Group (now part of Hawker Siddeley Group): various finance responsibilities, 1948–55; Planning Dir, 1955–57, Dir and Gen. Man., 1957–60, Mirrlees, Bickerton & Day Ltd; Dir and Gen. Man., National Gas Oil Engines Ltd, 1958–60; Booker Group: Exec. Dir, latterly Chm., Booker Industrial Holdings Ltd, 1960–70; Exec. Dir, latterly Dep. Chm., Booker Engineering Holdings Ltd, 1964–70; EMI Group: Gp Financial Controller, 1970–71; Gp Finance Dir, 1971–75; Asst Man. Dir, 1975–77; Gp Man. Dir, 1977–78; Vice-Chm., 1978–81. Director: Capitol Industries-EMI Inc., 1971–81; South Bank Theatre Bd, 1977–82. *Recreations:* music, ballet, swimming. *Address:* Flat 12, 32 Bryanston Square, W1H 7FL. *T:* 01–723 8355. *Club:* Caledonian.

WATT, Robert; His Honour Judge Watt; County Court Judge since 1971; *b* 10 March 1923; *s* of John Watt, schoolmaster, Ballymena, Co. Antrim; *m* 1951, Edna Rea; one *d. Educ:* Ballymena Academy; Queen's Univ., Belfast (LLB). Called to Bar, Gray's Inn, 1946; called to Bar of Northern Ireland, 1946; QC (NI) 1964; subseq. Sen. Crown Prosecutor Counties Fermanagh and Tyrone. *Recreation:* sailing. *Address:* 12 Deramore Drive, Belfast BT9 5JQ. *Club:* Royal North of Ireland Yacht.

WATT, Prof. W(illiam) Montgomery; Professor of Arabic and Islamic Studies, University of Edinburgh, 1964–79; *b* Ceres, Fife, 14 March 1909; *o c* of late Rev. Andrew Watt; *m* 1943, Jean Macdonald, *er d* of late Prof. Robert Donaldson; one *s* four *d. Educ:* George Watson's Coll., Edinburgh; University of Edinburgh; Balliol Coll., Oxford; University of Jena; Cuddesdon Coll. Warner Exhibition (Balliol), 1930; Ferguson Schol. in Classics, 1931; MA, PhD (Edinburgh); MA, BLitt (Oxon). Asst Lecturer, Moral Philosophy, University of Edinburgh, 1934–38; Curate, St Mary Boltons, London, 1939–41; Curate, Old St Paul's, Edinburgh, 1941–43; Arabic specialist to Bishop in Jerusalem, 1943–46; Lecturer, Ancient Philosophy, University of Edinburgh, 1946–47; Lectr, Sen. Lectr and Reader in Arabic, Univ. of Edinburgh, 1947–64. Visiting Professor: of Islamic Studies, University of Toronto, 1963; Collège de France, Paris, 1970; of Religious Studies, Univ. of Toronto, 1978; of Arab Studies, Georgetown Univ., 1978–79. Chairman, Assoc. of British Orientalists, 1964–65. Hon. DD Aberdeen, 1966. Levi Della Vida Medal, Los Angeles, 1981. *Publications:* Free Will and Predestination in Early Islam, 1949; The Faith and Practice of al-Ghazali, 1953; Muhammad at Mecca, 1953;

Muhammad at Medina, 1956; The Reality of God, 1958; The Cure for Human Troubles, 1959; Islam and the Integration of Society, 1961; Muhammad Prophet and Statesman, 1961; Islamic Philosophy and Theology, 1962, new enlarged edn, 1986; Muslim Intellectual, 1963; Truth in the Religions, 1963; Islamic Spain, 1965; Islam (in Propyläen Weltgeschichte, XI), 1965; A Companion to the Qur'an, 1967; What is Islam?, 1968; Islamic Political Thought, 1968; Islamic Revelation and the Modern World, 1970; Bell's Introduction to the Qur'an, 1970; The Influence of Islam on Medieval Europe, 1972; The Formative Period of Islamic Thought, 1973; The Majesty that was Islam, 1974; Der Islam, i, 1980, ii, 1985; Islam and Christianity Today, 1984; (ed) Islamic Surveys; contribs learned journals. *Address:* The Neuk, Dalkeith, Midlothian EH22 1JT. *T:* 031–663 3197.

WATT, Emeritus Prof. William Smith, MA (Glasgow and Oxon); Regius Professor of Humanity in the University of Aberdeen, 1952–79, Vice-Principal, 1969–72; *b* 20 June 1913; *s* of John Watt and Agnes Smith; *m* 1944, Dorothea, *e d* of R. J. Codrington Smith; one *s. Educ:* University of Glasgow; Balliol Coll., Oxford (Snell Exhibitioner and Hon. Scholar). First Class Hons in Classics, Glasgow Univ., 1933; Ferguson Schol., 1934; Craven Schol., 1934; First Class, Classical Moderations, 1935; Hertford Schol., 1935; Ireland Schol., 1935; First Class, Lit. Hum., 1937. Lecturer in Greek and Greek History, University of Glasgow, 1937–38; Fellow and Tutor in Classics, Balliol Coll., Oxford, 1938–52. Civilian Officer, Admiralty (Naval Intelligence Div.), 1941–45. Convener, Scottish Univs Council on Entrance, 1973–77. Governor, Aberdeen Coll. of Educn, 1958–75 (Chm. of Governors 1971–75). Pres., Classical Assoc. of Scotland, 1983–. *Publications:* (ed) Ciceronis Epistulae ad Quintum fratrem, etc, 1958, 1965; (ed) Ciceronis Epistularum ad Atticum Libri I-VIII, 1965; (ed) Ciceronis Epistulae ad familiares, 1982; (ed with P. J. Ford) George Buchanan's Miscellaneorum Liber, 1982; articles and reviews in classical periodicals. *Address:* 38 Woodburn Gardens, Aberdeen AB1 8JA. *T:* Aberdeen 314369. *Club:* Business and Professional (Aberdeen).

WATTON, Rt. Rev. James Augustus, BA, DD; *b* 23 Oct. 1915; *s* of Geo. A. Watton and Ada Wynn; *m* 1941, Irene A. Foster; one *s* two *d. Educ:* Univ. of Western Ontario (BA); Huron Coll. (STh); Post graduate Univ. of Michigan. Deacon 1938; Priest 1939. Bishop of Moosonee, 1963–80; Archbishop of Moosonee and Metropolitan of Ontario, 1974–79; retired 1980. DD (*jure dig.*), 1955. *Address:* Box 803, Southampton, Ontario N0H 2LO, Canada.

WATTS, Arthur Desmond, CMG 1977; Deputy Legal Adviser, Foreign and Commonwealth Office, since 1982; *b* 14 Nov. 1931; *o s* of Col A. E. Watts, MA (Cantab); *m* 1957, Iris Ann Collier, MA (Cantab); one *s* one *d. Educ:* Haileybury and Imperial Service College; Royal Military Academy, Sandhurst; Downing Coll., Cambridge (Schol.). BA 1954; LLB (First Cl.) 1955; Whewell Schol. in Internat. Law, 1955; called to Bar, Gray's Inn, 1957; MA. Legal Asst, Foreign Office, 1956–59; Legal Adviser, British Property Commn (later British Embassy), Cairo, 1959–62; Asst Legal Adviser, FO, 1962–67; Legal Adviser, British Embassy, Bonn, 1967–69; Asst Solicitor, Law Officers Dept, 1969–70; Legal Counsellor, FCO, 1970–73; Counsellor (Legal Advr), Office of UK Permanent Rep. to EEC, 1973–77; Legal Counsellor, FCO, 1977–82. *Publications:* Legal Effects of War, 4th edn (with Lord McNair), 1966; (with Parry and Grant) Encyclopaedic Dictionary of International Law, 1986; (contrib.) The Antarctic Treaty System—An Assessment, 1986; contribs to: British Year Book of Internat. Law; Internat. and Comparative Law Quarterly; Egyptian Review of Internat. Law. *Recreation:* cricket (County Cap, Shropshire, 1955; in Antarctica, 1985). *Address:* 61 Meriden Court, Chelsea Manor Street, SW3.

WATTS, Donald Walter, PhD; FRACI; FACE; Director, Western Australian Institute of Technology, since 1980; *b* 1 April 1934; *s* of late Horace Frederick Watts and of Esme Anne Watts; *m* 1960, Michelle Rose Yeomans; two *s. Educ:* Hale Sch., Perth; University of Western Australia (BSc Hons, PhD); University College London. FRACI 1967. Post-Doctoral Fellow, UCL, 1959–61; University of Western Australia: Sen. Lectr, 1962; Reader, 1969; Associate Prof., 1971; Personal Chair in Physical and Inorganic Chemistry, 1977–79. Vis. Scientist, Univ. of S California, 1967; Visiting Professor: Australian National Univ., 1973; Univ. of Toronto, 1974; Japan Foundn Vis. Fellow, 1984. Chm., Aust. Cttee of Dirs and Principals in Advanced Education Ltd, 1986–; Member: Aust. Science and Technol. Council, 1984–; Technology Develt Authority of WA, 1984–. *Publications:* Chemical Properties and Reactions (jtly) (Univ. of W Aust.), 1978; (jtly) Chemistry for Australian Secondary School Students (Aust. Acad. of Sci.), 1979; numerous papers on phys. and inorganic chemistry in internat. jls; several papers presented at nat. and internat. confs. *Recreations:* tennis (Mem. Interstate Tennis Team, 1952–53), squash (Mem. Interstate Squash Team, 1957–66), golf. *Address:* Western Australian Institute of Technology, Kent Street, Bentley, WA 6102, Australia. *T:* (09) 350 7001; (private) 2 Minora Road, Dalkeith, WA 6009, Australia. *T:* (09) 386 3855. *Clubs:* Royal Kings Park Tennis (Perth); Nedlands Tennis (Nedlands); Lake Karrinyup Golf (Karrinyup).

WATTS, Helen Josephine, (Mrs Michael Mitchell), CBE 1978; Hon. FRAM; concert, lieder and opera singer (contralto), retired 1985; *b* 7 Dec. 1927; *d* of Thomas Watts and Winifred (*née* Morgan); *m* 1980, Michael Mitchell. *Educ:* St Mary and St Anne's Sch., Abbots Bromley; Royal Academy of Music (LRAM). Hon. FRAM 1961 (Hon. ARAM 1955); FRSA 1982. *Recreation:* gardening.

WATTS, John Arthur, FCA; MP (C) Slough, since 1983; *b* 19 April 1947; *s* of late Arthur and Ivy Watts; *m* 1974, Susan Jennifer Swan; one *s* three *d. Educ:* Bishopshalt Grammar Sch., Hillingdon; Gonville and Caius Coll., Cambridge (MA). Qual. as chartered accountant, 1972; FCA 1979. Chairman: Cambridge Univ. Cons. Assoc., 1968; Uxbridge Cons. Assoc., 1973–76; Mem., Hillingdon Bor. Council, 1973–84 (Leader, 1978–84). PPS: to Minister for Housing and Construction, 1984–85; to Minister of State, Treasury, 1985–. Mem., Treasury and CS Select Cttee, 1986–. *Recreation:* reading. *Address:* House of Commons, SW1A 0AA. *T:* 01–219 3589.

WATTS, Colonel John Cadman, OBE 1959; MC 1946; FRCS 1949; Chairman, Armed Forces Committee, British Medical Association, 1978–82 (Chairman, North Bedfordshire Division, 1971; Member Council, 1972–74); *b* 13 April 1913; *s* of John Nixon Watts, solicitor, and Amy Bettina (*née* Cadman); *m* 1938, Joan Lillian (*née* Inwood); three *s* one *d. Educ:* Merchant Taylors' Sch.; St Thomas's Hospital. MRCS, LRCP, 1936; MB, BS, 1938. Casualty Officer, Resident Anæsthetist, House Surgeon, St Thomas's Hospital, 1937; Surgical Specialist, RAMC, 1938–60, serving in Palestine, Egypt, Libya, Syria, Tunisia, Italy, France, Holland, Germany, Malaya, Java, Japan, and Cyprus. Hunterian Professor, RCS, 1960; Professor of Military Surgery, RCS, 1960–64; Conslt Surgeon, Bedford Gen. Hosp., 1966–76. Co. Comr, St John Ambulance Brigade, 1970. Pres., Ipswich Div., BMA, 1982–83. OStJ 1970. *Publications:* Surgeon at War, 1955; Clinical Surgery, 1964; Exploration Medicine, 1964. *Recreations:* sailing, ski-ing, shooting. *Address:* Lowood Lodge, Hasketon, near Woodbridge, Suffolk. *T:* Grundisburgh 326. *Clubs:* Deben Yacht (Woodbridge); United Hospitals Sailing (Burnham-on-Crouch).

WATTS, John Francis, BA; educational writer; Principal, Countesthorpe College, Leicestershire, 1972–81; *b* 18 Oct. 1926; *s* of John Weldon Watts and Norah K. Watts; *m* 1950, Elizabeth Hamilton (marr. diss.); four *s* one *d*; *m* 1985, Madeleine Marshall. *Educ:*

West Buckland Sch.; Univ. of Bristol (BA). First Headmaster, Les Quennevais Sch., Jersey, CI, 1964–69; Lectr, Univ. of London, 1969–72. Chm., Nat. Assoc. for Teaching of English (NATE), 1974–76. *Publications:* Encounters, 1965, 2nd edn 1983; Contact, 1970 (Australia); Interplay, 1972; Teaching, 1974; The Countesthorpe Experience, 1977; Towards an Open School, 1980; contrib. to various publications. *Address:* 106 Kineton Green Road, Olton, Solihull, West Midlands.

WATTS, Lt-Gen. John Peter Barry Condliffe, CB 1985; CBE 1979 (OBE 1972); MC 1960; Chief of Defence Staff, Sultan of Oman's Armed Forces, since 1984; *b* 27 Aug. 1930; *m*; seven *c. Educ:* Westminster Sch.; Andover Acad., USA; RMA Sandhurst. Commissioned, RUR, 1951 (Royal Irish Rangers, 1968); served Hong Kong, Malaya (despatches), Cyprus, Oman (MC), BAOR, Borneo and Saudi Arabia; 48 Gurkha Inf. Bde, 1967–69; CO 22 SAS Regt, 1970–72; Directing Staff, Staff Coll., 1972–74; MoD, 1974; Comdr, Sultan of Oman's Land Forces, 1979–84. *Address:* HQ Sultan's Armed Forces, Baît al Falaj, PO Box 602, Muscat, Oman.

WATTS, Ronald George, CBE 1962; *b* 15 May 1914; *m* 1940, Ruth Hansen (*d* 1970); one *s* two *d*; *m* 1972, Margit Tester. *Educ:* Latymer Sch., Edmonton; St John's Coll., Cambridge. Entered Foreign Service, 1937; appointed Counsellor, Foreign Office, 1958; Consul-Gen., Osaka-Kobe, 1958–63; Head of Consular Dept, FO, 1963–65; Consul-Gen., Paris, 1966–67; FCO 1967–69, retired. *Recreation:* church organist.

WATTS, Roy, CBE 1978; Chairman: Thames Water Authority, since 1983; Cabletime Installations Ltd, since 1984; WaterAid, since 1984; Deputy Chairman, Brymon Airways, since 1983; *b* 17 Aug. 1925; *m* 1951, Jean Rosaline; one *s* two *d. Educ:* Doncaster Grammar Sch.; Edinburgh Univ. (MA). FIMTA, FRAeS, FCIT. Army, 1943–47: commnd Sandhurst; 8th RTR. Accountant in local govt until 1955; joined BEA, 1955: Head of Systems Study Section (O&M Br.); Chief Internal Auditor; Area Man., Sweden and Finland; Fleet Planning Man.; Regional Gen. Man., North and East Europe; Dir, S1–11 Div; Chief Exec. BEA British Airways, 1972–74 (Chm., Jan.-March 1974); Chief Exec., European Div., British Airways, 1974–77; Dir, Commercial Operations, British Airways, 1977, Dir, Finance and Planning, 1978–79, Chief Exec., 1979–82; Group Man. Dir, 1982–83; Jt Dep. Chm., BA Bd, 1980–83 (Mem., 1974–83). Chm., Assoc. of European Airlines, 1982. *Recreations:* squash, cricket. *Address:* Baywell House, Fawler Road, Charlbury, Oxford. *T:* Charlbury 810385.

WATTS, Thomas Rowland, CBE 1978; Chartered Accountant; Director, Jarrold & Sons Ltd, Norwich, since 1982; *b* 1 Jan. 1917; *s* of late Thomas William Watts and late Daisy Maud Watts (*née* Bultitude); *m* 1955, Hester Zoë Armitstead; one *s* two *d. Educ:* Gresham's Sch., Holt. Articled to Price Waterhouse & Co., 1934–39, Partner, 1963–82. Served War, TA, 1939–41, Royal Marines (Captain), 1941–46. Chm., Accounting Standards Cttee (UK and Ireland), 1978–82; Mem. Council, Inst. of Chartered Accountants in England and Wales, 1974–82; Mem. City EEC Cttee, 1974–82; Adviser to Dept of Trade on EEC company law, 1974–83; Vice-Pres. d'honneur, Groupe d'Etudes des experts comptables de la CEE, 1979– (Vice-Pres., 1975–79); Chm., Dental Rates Study Gp, 1982–85. A Gen. Comr of Income Tax, 1986–. Hon. Vis. Prof., City of London Polytech., 1983–86. Chartered Accountants Founding Socs' Centenary Award, 1982. *Publications:* editor, various professional books; papers in professional jls. *Recreations:* travel, music, opera costume designs. *Address:* 13 Fitzwalter Road, Colchester, Essex CO3 3SY. *T:* Colchester 573520; 29 Capstan Square, Isle of Dogs, E14.

WATTS, Victor Brian; His Honour Judge Watts; a Circuit Judge, since 1980; *b* 7 Jan. 1927; *o s* of Percy William King Watts and Doris Millicent Watts; *m* 1965, Patricia Eileen (*née* Steer); one *s* one *d. Educ:* Colfe's Grammar Sch.; University Coll., Oxford. MA(Oxon): BCL. Called to the Bar, Middle Temple, 1950; subseq. Western Circuit; a Recorder of the Crown Court, 1972–80. Flying Officer, Royal Air Force, 1950–52. *Publications:* Landlord and Tenant Act, 1954; Leading Cases on the Law of Contract, 1955; occasional articles of a legal nature. *Recreations:* the arts, walking, tennis. *Address:* 28 Abinger Road, W4. *T:* 01–994 4435. *Club:* Hurlingham.

WATTS, William Arthur, MA, DSc; Provost, Trinity College, Dublin, since 1981; *b* 26 May 1930; *s* of William Low Watts and Bessie (*née* Dickinson); *m* 1954, Geraldine Mary Magrath; two *s* one *d. Educ:* Trinity Coll., Dublin (MA, ScD). Lecturer in Botany, Univ. of Hull, 1953–55; Trinity College, Dublin: Lectr in Botany, 1955–65; Fellow, 1970; Professor of Botany, 1965–80; Prof. of Quaternary Ecology, 1980–81. Adjunct Prof. of Geology, Univ. of Minnesota, 1975–. Pres., RIA, 1982–85; Governor: National Gallery of Ireland, 1982–85; Marsh's Library, 1981–; Member: Dublin Inst. for Advanced Studies, 1981–; Scholarship Exchange Bd, Ireland, 1982–. Chairman: Federated Dublin Voluntary Hosps, 1983–; Mercer's Hosp., 1975–. *Publications:* numerous articles on aspects of quaternary ecology. *Recreations:* walking, conservation studies, music. *Address:* Provost's House, Trinity College, Dublin 2. *T:* 772941, ext. 1558. *Club:* Kildare Street and University (Dublin).

WAUCHOPE, Sir Patrick (George) Don-, 10th Bt, *cr* 1667; Horticulturist; *b* 7 May 1898; *o s* of late Patrick Hamilton Don-Wauchope (3rd *s* of 8th Bt) and late Georgiana Renira; *S* uncle 1951; *m* 1936, Ismay Lilian Ursula (marr. diss.), *d* of late Sidney Hodges, Edendale, Natal, South Africa; two *s. Educ:* The Edinburgh Academy. Served European War, 1914–18, with RFA, France and Belgium (wounded); War of 1939–46, Egypt and Italy. *Recreations:* cricket, golf. *Heir: s* Roger (Hamilton) Don-Wauchope [Chartered Accountant, S Africa; *b* 16 Oct. 1938; *m* 1963, Sallee, *yr d* of Lt-Col H. Mill Colman, OBE, AMICE, Durban; two *s* one *d*]. *Address:* c/o Hibiscus House, Village of Happiness, Margate 4280, Natal South Coast, S Africa.

WAUD, Christopher Denis George Pierre; barrister-at-law; a Recorder of the Crown Court, since Dec. 1974; full-time Chairman of Industrial Tribunals, since 1982 (part-time, 1977–82); *b* 5 Dec. 1928; *s* of late Christopher William Henry Pierre Waud and Vera Constance Maria Waud; *m* 1954, Rosemary Paynter Bradshaw Moorhead; one *s* four *d* (and one *s* decd). *Educ:* Charterhouse; Christ Church, Oxford. Called to Bar, Middle Temple, 1956. *Publications:* Redundancy and Unfair Dismissal, annually 1981–84; Guide to Employment Law, 1985. *Recreations:* sailing, walking. *Address:* 93 Ebury Bridge Road, SW1W 8RE. *Clubs:* Royal Lymington Yacht (Lymington), Bar Yacht.

WAUGH, Auberon Alexander; Editor, The Literary Review, since 1986; Columnist: The Spectator, since 1976; The Sunday Telegraph, since 1981; Chief Book Reviewer, Daily Mail, since 1981; *b* 17 Nov. 1939; *e s* of late Evelyn Waugh, writer, and late Laura Waugh, Combe Florey House, Somerset; *m* 1961, Teresa, *o d* of 6th Earl of Onslow, KBE, MC, and *sister* of 7th Earl of Onslow, *qv*; two *s* two *d. Educ:* Downside (schol. in Classics); Christ Church, Oxford (exhibn in English, read PPE). Editorial staff, Daily Telgraph, 1960–63. Commissioned Royal Horse Guards, 1957; served Cyprus; retd with wounds, 1958. Weekly Columnist, Catholic Herald, 1963–64; special writer, Mirror group, 1964–67; Political Correspondent: Spectator, 1967–70; Private Eye, 1970–86; Weekly Columnist, The Times, 1970–71; Chief Fiction Reviewer: Spectator, 1970–73; Evening Standard, 1973–80; Weekly Columnist, New Statesman, 1973–76; monthly contributor, Books and Bookmen, 1973–80. Contested (Dog Lovers' Party) Devon North, 1979. Pres.,

British Croatian Soc., 1973–. Nat. Press 'Critic of the Year' commendations, 1976, 1978; 'What the Papers Say' Columnist of the Year, Granada TV, 1979. *Publications: novels:* The Foxglove Saga, 1960; Path of Dalliance, 1963; Who are the Violets Now?, 1966; Consider the Lilies, 1968; A Bed of Flowers, 1971; *non-fiction:* (with S. Cronje) Biafra: Britain's Shame, 1969; Four Crowded Years: the Diaries of Auberon Waugh, 1976; The Last Word: an Eyewitness Account of the Thorpe Trial, 1980; Auberon Waugh's Yearbook, 1981; The Diaries of Auberon Waugh: a turbulent decade 1976–85, 1985; Waugh on Wine, 1986; *essays:* Country Topics, 1974; In The Lion's Den, 1978; Another Voice, 1986. *Recreation:* gossip. *Address:* Combe Florey House, near Taunton, Somerset; 7 Phoenix Lodge Mansions, Brook Green, W6; La Pesegado, 11320 Montmaur, France. *Club:* Beefsteak.

WAVERLEY, 2nd Viscount, *cr* 1952, of Westdean; **David Alastair Pearson Anderson;** Consultant Physician, Reading Group of Hospitals, since 1951; *b* 18 Feb. 1911; *s* of 1st Viscount Waverley, PC, GCB, OM, GCSI, GCIE, FRS, and Christina Anderson; *S father*, 1958; *m* 1948, Myrtle Ledgerwood; one *s* one *d* (and one *d* decd). *Educ:* Malvern Coll.; Universities of Frankfurt A/Main and Cambridge (Pembroke Coll.); St Thomas's Hospital, London. MB, BChir (Cantab), 1937; MRCP (London), 1946; FRCP (London), 1957. Appointments at St Thomas's Hospital, 1938–39. Served War of 1939–45, RAF Med. Br. Med. Registrar, Res. Asst Physician and Registrar Dept Clin. Pathology, St Thomas's Hospital, 1946–50. *Publications:* various communications to medical journals. *Recreations:* golf and fishing; formerly athletics and Association football (rep. Cambridge *v* Oxford, in Inter-Varsity Relays, etc). *Heir: s* Hon. John Desmond Forbes Anderson, *b* 31 Oct. 1949. *Address:* Chanders, Aldworth, Berks. *T:* Compton 377. *Clubs:* Travellers'; Hawks (Cambridge).

See also Brig. Hon. Dame Mary Pihl.

WAY, Sir Richard (George Kitchener), KCB 1961 (CB 1957); CBE 1952; Principal, King's College London, 1975–80; *b* 15 Sept. 1914; *s* of Frederick and Clara Way; *m* 1947, Ursula Joan Starr; one *s* two *d*. *Educ:* Polytechnic Secondary Sch., London. Joined Civil Service as Exec. Officer, 1933; Higher Executive Officer, 1940; Principal, 1942; Asst Secretary, 1946; Asst Under-Secretary of State, 1954; Deputy Under-Secretary of State, War Office, 1955–57; Dep. Secretary, Ministry of Defence, 1957–58; Dep. Secretary, Ministry of Supply, 1958–59; Permanent Under-Secretary of State, War Office, 1960–63; Permanent Secretary, Ministry of Aviation, 1963–66. Dep. Chm., Lansing Bagnall Ltd, 1966–67, Chm. 1967–69; Chm., LTE, 1970–74. Chairman, EDC Machine Tool Industry, 1967–70; Member (part-time) Board of: BOAC, 1967–73; Dobson Park Industries Ltd, 1975–85. Chm., Council of Roedean Sch., 1969–74; Chm., Royal Commn for the Exhibn of 1851, 1978–. London Zoological Society: Mem. Council 1977–82 and 1984–; Vice-Pres., 1979–82 and 1984–; Treasurer, 1983–84. FKC 1975. Coronation Medal, 1953. American Medal of Freedom (with bronze palm), 1946. CStJ 1974. *Address:* Manor Farm, Shalden, Alton, Hants. *T:* Alton 82383. *Clubs:* Brooks's, MCC.

WAYMOUTH, Charity, BSc (London), PhD (Aberdeen); Senior Staff Scientist, The Jackson Laboratory, Bar Harbor, Maine, 1963–81, now Emeritus; *b* 29 April 1915; *o d* of Charles Sydney Herbert Waymouth, Major, The Dorsetshire Regt, and Ada Curror Scott Dalgleish; unmarried. *Educ:* Royal School for Daughters of Officers of the Army, Bath; University of London; University of Aberdeen. Biochemist, City of Manchester General Hospitals, 1938–41; Research Fellow, University of Aberdeen, 1944; Beit Memorial Fellow for Medical Research, 1944–46; Member of scientific staff and head of tissue culture dept, Chester Beatty Research Institute for Cancer Research (University of London), 1947–52; British Empire Cancer Campaign-American Cancer Society Exchange Fellow, 1952–53; The Jackson Laboratory: Staff Scientist, 1952–63; Asst Dir (Training), 1969–72; Asst Dir (Research), 1976–77; Associate Dir (Scientific Affairs), 1977–80; Dir *ad interim*, 1980–81. Mem. Bd of Dirs, W. Alton Jones Cell Sci. Center, 1979–82. Rose Morgan Vis. Prof., Univ. of Kansas, 1971. Member: Tissue Culture Association (President, 1960–62, Editor-in-Chief 1968–75; Mem. Council, 1980–84); various British and American professional and learned societies. Hon. Life member and Hon. Director, Psora Society (Canada); Episcopal Church of the USA: Vice-Chm., Clergy Deployment Bd, 1971–79, and Exec. Council, 1967–70; Deputy, Gen. Convention, 1970, 1973, 1976, 1979, 1982, 1985; Member, Diocesan Council, 1962–70, 1971–76, and Standing Cttee, 1984–, Dio. of Maine; Chm., Cttee on the State of the Church, 1976–79. DD *hc* Gen. Theol Seminary, NY, 1979; Hon. ScD Bowdoin College, 1982. *Publications:* numerous papers in scientific journals, on nucleic acids and on tissue culture and cell nutrition. *Recreations:* reading, gardening. *Address:* 16 Atlantic Avenue, Bar Harbor, Maine 04609, USA. *T:* (207) 288–4008.

WAYNE, Sir Edward (Johnson), Kt 1964; MD, MSc, PhD, FRCP (London and Edinburgh); FRCP (Glasgow); Regius Professor of Practice of Medicine, Glasgow University, 1954–67; Physician to Western Infirmary, Glasgow; Hon. Physician to the Queen in Scotland, 1954–67; *b* 3 June 1902; *s* of late William Wayne, Leeds, Yorks, and late Ellen Rawding, Leadenham, Lincs; *m* 1932, Honora Nancy Halloran; one *s* one *d*. *Educ:* Leeds Univ. and Medical School (Akroyd Scholar and Sir Swire Smith Fellow); Manchester Univ. BSc Leeds (1st Class Hons Chemistry) 1923; MB, ChB (Leeds), 1st Class Hons, 1929; MD 1938; Hey Gold Medallist; Demonstrator in Physiology, University of Leeds, 1930–31; Assistant in Dept Clinical Research, University College Hospital, London, 1931–34; Professor of Pharmacology and Therapeutics, University of Sheffield, 1934–53 (formerly Physician to Royal Infirmary and Children's Hospital, Sheffield). Member Scottish Secretary of State's Advisory Cttee on Medical Research, 1958–67; Member of the Medical Research Council, 1958–62; Chairman, Clinical Research Board, 1960–64; Chairman, British Pharmacopœia Commn, 1958–63; Chairman, Advisory Cttee on Drug Dependence, 1967–69. Sims Commonwealth Travelling Professor, 1959. Bradshaw Lecturer, 1953; Lumleian Lecturer, RCP, 1959; Crookshank Lecturer and Medallist, Faculty of Radiol., 1966. Hon. DSc Sheffield, 1967. *Publications:* Papers in scientific and medical journals. *Address:* Lingwood Lodge, Lingwood, Norfolk NR13 4ES. *T:* Great Yarmouth 751370. *Club:* Athenæum.

WEARE, Trevor John, PhD; Managing Director, Hydraulics Research Ltd, since 1982; *b* 31 Dec. 1943; *s* of Trevor Leslie Weare and Edna Margaret (*née* Roberts); *m* 1964, Margaret Ann Wright; two *s*. *Educ:* Aston Technical Coll.; Imperial College of Science and Technology (BSc Physics, PhD). Post-doctoral Research Fellow: Dept of Mathematical Physics, McGill Univ., Montreal, 1968–70; Dept of Theoretical Physics, Univ. of Oxford, 1970–72; Sen. Scientific Officer, Hydraulics Res. Station, 1972; Principal Scientific Officer, 1975; Sen. Principal Scientific Officer, Head of Estuaries Div., 1978; Chief Scientific Officer, DoE, 1981. *Publications:* numerous contribs to scientific jls on theoretical High Energy Nuclear Physics, and on computational modelling in Civil Engineering Hydraulics; archaeological paper in Oxoniensia. *Recreations:* music, walking, archaeology. *Address:* Rose Cottage, Dunsomer Hill, North Moreton, Oxon. *T:* Didcot 818544.

WEATHERALL, Prof. David John, MD, FRCP; FRCPE 1983; FRS 1977; Nuffield Professor of Clinical Medicine, University of Oxford, since 1974; Fellow, Magdalen College, Oxford, since 1974; Hon. Director, Molecular Haematology Unit, Medical Research Council, since 1980; *b* 9 March 1933; *s* of late Harry and Gwendoline

Weatherall; *m* 1962, Stella Mayorga Nestler; one *s*. *Educ:* Calday Grange Grammar Sch.; Univ. of Liverpool. MB, ChB 1956; MD 1962; FRCP 1967; FRCPath 1969; MA Oxon 1974. Ho. Officer in Med. and Surg., United Liverpool Hosps, 1956–58; Captain, RAMC, Jun. Med. Specialist, BMH, Singapore, and BMH, Kamunting, Malaya, 1958–60; Research Fellow in Genetics, Johns Hopkins Hosp., Baltimore, USA, 1960–62; Sen. Med. Registrar, Liverpool Royal Infirmary, 1962–63; Research Fellow in Haematology, Johns Hopkins Hosp., 1963–65; Consultant, WHO, 1966–70; Univ. of Liverpool: Lectr in Med., 1965–66; Sen. Lectr in Med., 1966–69; Reader in Med., 1969–71; Prof. of Haematology, 1971–74; Consultant Physician, United Liverpool Hosps, 1966–74. Mem. Soc. of Scholars, and Centennial Schol., Johns Hopkins Univ., 1976; Physician-in-Chief *pro tem.*, Peter Bent Brigham Hosp., Harvard Med. Sch., 1980. RSocMed Foundn Vis. Prof., 1981; Sims Commonwealth Vis. Prof., 1982; Phillip K. Bondy Prof., Yale, 1982. K. Diamond Prof., UCSF, 1986; HM Queen Elizabeth the Queen Mother Fellow, Nuffield Prov. Hosps Trust, 1982. Lectures: Watson Smith, RCP, 1974; Foundn, RCPath, 1979; Darwin, Eugenics Soc., 1979; Croonian, RCP, 1984; Fink Meml, Yale, 1984; Sir Francis Frazer, Univ. of London, 1985; Roy Cameron, RCPath, 1986. Pres., British Soc. for Haematology, 1980–; Chm., Med. and Scientific Adv. Panel, Leukaemia Res. Fund, 1985–. Hon. Member: Assoc. of Physicians of GB and Ireland, 1968; Assoc. of Amer. Physicians, 1976; Amer. Soc. of Haematology, 1982; Eur. Molecular Biology Orgn, 1983; Hon. FACP 1986. Ambuj Nath Bose Prize, RCP, 1980; Ballantyne Prize, RCPE, 1982; Stratton Prize, Internat. Soc. Haematology, 1982; Feldberg Prize, 1984. *Publications:* (with J. B. Clegg) The Thalassaemia Syndromes, 1965, 3rd edn 1981; (with R. M. Hardisty) Blood and its Disorders, 1973, 2nd edn 1981; The New Genetics and Clinical Practice, 1982, 2nd edn 1985; (ed, with J. G. G. Ledingham and D. A. Warrell) Oxford Textbook of Medicine, 1983, 2nd edn 1987; many papers on Abnormal Haemoglobin Synthesis and related disorders. *Recreations:* music, oriental food. *Address:* 8 Cumnor Rise Road, Cumnor Hill, Oxford. *T:* Oxford 862467.

WEATHERALL, Miles, MA, DM, DSc; FIBiol; *b* 14 Oct. 1920; *s* of Rev. J. H. and Mary Weatherall; *m* 1944, Josephine A. C. Ogston; three *d*. *Educ:* Dragon School and St Edward's School, Oxford; Oriel College, Oxford. BA, BSc 1941; BM 1943; MA 1945; DM 1951; DSc 1966. Open Schol. in Nat. Sci., Oriel Coll., 1938. Lecturer in Pharmacology, Edinburgh University, 1945; Head of Dept of Pharmacology, London Hosp. Med. Coll., 1949–66; Prof. of Pharmacology, Univ. of London, 1958–66; Wellcome Research Laboratories: Head, Therapeutic Res. Div., 1967–75; Dep. Dir, 1969–74; Dir of Estblt, 1974–79. Member: Adv. Cttee on Pesticides and other Toxic Chemicals, 1964–66; Council, Pharmaceutical Soc., 1966–70; Council, Roy. Soc. Med., 1972–82 (Hon. Sec. 1974–82); Comr, Medicines Commn, 1979–81. Chm., Sci. Co-ord. Cttee, Arthritis and Rheumatism Council, 1983–. Chm., Council, Chelsea Coll., Univ. of London, 1970–83. Hon. Lecturer: UCL, 1968–; KCL, 1979–82; Hon. Fellow: Chelsea Coll., London, 1984; KCL (KQC), 1985. Mem. Cttee, Wine Soc., 1964–72. *Publications:* Statistics for Medical Students (jointly with L. Bernstein), 1952; Scientific Method, 1968; (ed jtly) Safety Testing of New Drugs, 1984; papers in scientific and medical journals. *Recreations:* writing, gardening, cooking. *Address:* Willows, Charlbury, Oxford OX7 3PX. *Club:* Royal Society of Medicine.

WEATHERHEAD, Alexander Stewart, OBE 1985; TD; solicitor; Partner in Tindal Oatts Buchanan and McIlwraith (formerly Tindal Oatts & Rodger), Solicitors, Glasgow, since 1960; *b* Edinburgh, 3 Aug. 1931; *er s* of Kenneth Kilpatrick Weatherhead and Katharine Weatherhead (*née* Stewart); *m* 1972, Harriet Foye, *d* of Rev. Dr Arthur Organ, Toronto, Canada; two *d*. *Educ:* Glasgow Acad.; Glasgow Univ. MA 1955, LLB 1958. Served in RA, 1950–52, 2nd Lieut, 1950. Solicitor, 1958; Temp. Sheriff, 1985–. Hon. Vice-Pres., Law Society of Scotland, 1983–84 (Mem. Council, 1971–84); Mem. Council, Soc. for Computers and Law, 1973–86 (Vice-Chm., 1973–82; Chm., 1982–84; Hon. Mem., 1986); Mem., Royal Commn on Legal Services in Scotland, 1976–80. Trustee, Nat. Technol. and Law Trust (formerly Nat. Law Library Trust), 1979–; Mem., Internat. Bar Assoc.; Examr in Conveyancing, Univ. of Aberdeen, 1984–86. Joined TA, 1952; Lt-Col Comdg 277 (A&SH) Field Regt, RA (TA), 1965–67; The Lowland Regt (RA(T)), 1967 and Glasgow & Strathclyde Univs OTC, 1970–73; Col 1974; TAVR Col Lowlands (West), 1974–76; ADC (TAVR) to the Queen, 1977–81; Member: TAVR Assoc. Lowlands, 1967–; RA Council for Scotland, 1972–. Hon. Col, Glasgow and Strathclyde Univs OTC, 1982–. Hon. Sec., Royal Western Yacht Club, 1981–84. *Recreations:* sailing, reading, music. *Address:* 52 Partickhill Road, Glasgow G11 5AB. *T:* 041–334 6277. *Clubs:* New (Edinburgh); Royal Highland Yacht (Oban); Royal Western Yacht, Clyde Cruising (Glasgow).

WEATHERHEAD, Rev. James Leslie; Principal Clerk, General Assembly of Church of Scotland, since 1985; *b* 29 March 1931; *s* of Leslie Binnie Weatherhead, MBE, MM and Janet Hood Arnot Smith or Weatherhead; *m* 1962, Dr Anne Elizabeth Shepherd; two *s*. *Educ:* High Sch., Dundee; Univ. of Edinburgh (MA, LLB); Senior Pres., Students' Repr. Council, 1953–54); New Coll., Univ. of Edinburgh (Pres., Univ. Union, 1959–60). Temp. Acting Sub-Lieut RNVR (Nat. Service), 1955–56. Licensed by Presb. of Dundee, 1960; ordained by Presb. of Ayr, 1960; Asst Minister, Auld Kirk of Ayr, 1960–62; Minister, Trinity Church, Rothesay, 1962–69; Minister, Old Church, Montrose, 1969–85. Convener, Business Cttee of Gen. Assembly, 1981–84. Mem., Broadcasting Council for Scotland, BBC, 1978–82. *Recreations:* sailing, music. *Address:* (home) 28 Castle Terrace, Edinburgh EH1 2EL. *T:* 031–228 6460; (office) Church of Scotland Offices, 121 George Street, Edinburgh EH2 4YN. *T:* 031–225 5722. *Club:* RNVR Yacht.

WEATHERILL, Rt. Hon. (Bruce) Bernard, PC 1980; MP Croydon North-East; Speaker of the House of Commons, since 1983; *b* 25 Nov. 1920; *s* of late Bernard Weatherill, Spring Hill, Guildford, and Annie Gertrude (*née* Creak); *m* 1949, Lyn, *d* of late H. T. Eatwell; two *s* one *d*. *Educ:* Malvern College. Served War of 1939–45; commissioned 4/7th Royal Dragoon Guards, 1940; transferred to Indian Army, 1941 and served with 19th King George V's Own Lancers, 1941–45 (Captain). Man. Dir, Bernard Weatherill Ltd, 1957–70. First Chm., Guildford Young Conservatives, 1946–49; Chm., Guildford Cons. Assoc., 1959–63; Vice-Chm., SE Area Prov. Council, 1962–64; Member National Union of Cons. Party, 1963–64. MP (C) Croydon NE, 1964–83 (when elected Speaker); an Opposition Whip, 1967; a Lord Comr of HM Treasury, 1970–71; Vice-Chamberlain, HM Household, 1971–72; Comptroller of HM Household, 1972–73; Treasurer of HM Household and Dep. Chief Govt Whip, 1973–74; Opposition Dep. Chief Whip, 1974–79; Chm. of Ways and Means and Dep. Speaker, 1979–83. Chm., Commonwealth Speakers and Presiding Officers, 1986–. Pres., CPA, 1986. Freeman of City of London, 1949; Freeman of Borough of Croydon, 1983. *Recreation:* playing with grandchildren. *Address:* Speaker's House, Westminster, SW1A 0AA. *T:* 01–219 4188.

WEATHERLEY, Prof. Paul Egerton, FRS 1973; Regius Professor of Botany in the University of Aberdeen, 1959–81, now Emeritus; *b* 6 May 1917; *o s* of late Leonard Roger Weatherley and late Ethel Maude (*née* Collin), Leicester; *m* 1942, Margaret Logan, *o d* of late John Pirie, JP, Castle of Auchry, Aberdeenshire; one *s* three *d*. *Educ:* Wyggeston School; Keble College (Open Schol.), Oxford. Final Sch. of Nat. Sci. (Hons Botany) 1939; Keble Research Schol., 1939–40, elected to Colonial Agric. Schol., 1940. Trained in RE, then Colonial Office cadet at Imperial Coll. of Tropical Agric. Trinidad, 1940–42. Govt Botanist in Dept of Agriculture, Uganda Protectorate, 1942–47; Asst Lectr, Univ. of Manchester, 1947–49; Lecturer in Botany, 1949–59 (Sen. Lectr 1956), Univ. of Nottingham. *Publications:* papers in (mainly) botanical journals. *Recreations:* music, sketching. *Address:* Greystones, Torphins, Aberdeenshire AB3 4HP.

WEATHERSTON, William Alastair Paterson; Fisheries Secretary, Department of Agriculture and Fisheries for Scotland, since 1986; *b* 20 Nov. 1935; *s* of William Robert Weatherston and Isabella (*née* Paterson); *m* 1961, Margaret Jardine; two *s* one *d. Educ:* Peebles High Sch.; Edinburgh Univ. (MA Hons History). Asst Principal, Dept of Health for Scotland and Scottish Educn Dept, 1959–63; Private Sec. to Permanent Under Sec. of State, Scottish Office, 1963–64; Principal, Scottish Educn Dept, 1964–72, Cabinet Office, 1972–74; Assistant Secretary: SHHD, 1974–77; Scottish Educn Dept, 1977–79; Central Services, Scottish Office, 1979–82; Dir, Scottish Courts Admin, 1982–86. *Recreations:* reading, music. *Address:* 1 Coltbridge Terrace, Edinburgh EH12 6AB. *T:* 031–337 3339.

WEAVER, Oliver; QC 1985; *b* 27 March 1942; *s* of Denis Weaver and Kathleen (*née* Lynch); *m* 1964, Julia (*née* MacClymont); one *s* two *d. Educ:* Friends' Sch., Saffron Walden; Trinity Coll., Cambridge (MA, LLM). President, Cambridge Union Society, 1963. Called to the Bar, Middle Temple, 1965; joined Lincoln's Inn, 1969. Mem. Bar Council, 1981–84. *Recreations:* fishing, racing, gun dogs. *Address:* Kennel Farm, Albury End, Ware, Herts SG11 2HS. *T:* Albury 331.

WEAVER, Sir Tobias Rushton, (Sir Toby Weaver), Kt 1973; CB 1962; *b* 19 July 1911; *s* of late Sir Lawrence Weaver, KBE, and late Lady Weaver (*née* Kathleen Purcell); *m* 1941, Marjorie, *d* of Rt Hon. Sir Charles Trevelyan, 3rd Bt, PC; one *s* three *d. Educ:* Clifton College; Corpus Christi College, Cambridge. Bank clerk, Toronto, 1932; teaching at Barking, 1935, Eton, 1936; Asst Director of Education: Wilts CC 1936, Essex CC 1939. Admiralty, 1941; War Office, 1942; Dept of Education and Science, 1946–73; Under-Secretary, 1956; Deputy Secretary, 1962. Visiting Professor of Education: Univ. of Southampton, 1973; Univ. of London Inst. of Educn, 1974; Open Univ., 1976–78. FIC 1986; Hon. Fellow: Manchester Poly., 1970; Huddersfield Poly., 1972; NE London Poly., 1985. LLD CNAA, 1972. *Address:* 14 Marston Close, NW6. *T:* 01–624 4263.

WEBB, Anthony Michael Francis, CMG 1963; QC (Kenya) 1961; JP; a Chairman of Industrial Tribunals, since 1978; *b* 27 Dec. 1914; *s* of late Sir (Ambrose) Henry Webb; *m* 1948, Diana Mary, *e d* of late Capt. Graham Farley, Indian Army, and Mrs Herbert Browne (*née* Pyper); one *s* one *d. Educ:* Ampleforth; Magdalen Coll., Oxford (MA). Barrister-at-Law, Gray's Inn, 1939. Served War, 1939–46, Maj. GSO2, The Queen's Bays. Colonial Legal Service (HMOCS), 1947–64 (Malaya; Kenya; MLC 1958–63; Attorney-General and Minister for Legal Affairs, 1961–63); Sec., Nat. Adv. Council on Trng of Magistrates, and Trng Officer, 1964–73, Dep. Sec. of Commns, 1969–75, Head of Court Business, 1975–77, Lord Chancellor's Office; retd 1977. Member of Council of Kenya Lawn Tennis Association, 1957–63. JP, Kent, 1966. *Publication:* The Natzweiler Trial (ed). *Address:* Yew Tree Cottage, Speldhurst Road, Langton Green, Tunbridge Wells, Kent TN3 0JH. *T:* Langton 2779. *Club:* Special Forces.

WEBB, Rear-Adm. Arthur Brooke, CB 1975; retired; *b* 13 June 1918; *m* 1949, Rachel Marian Gerrish; three *d.* Joined Royal Navy, 1936. Comdr 1954, Captain 1963, Rear-Adm. 1973. *Recreations:* gardening, walking. *Address:* c/o National Westminster Bank, 68 Palmerston Road, Southsea, Hants PO5 2DS.

WEBB, Colin Thomas; Editor-in-Chief, Press Association, since 1986; *b* 26 March 1939; *e s* of William Thomas and Ada Alexandra Webb; *m* 1970, Margaret Frances, *y d* of Maurice George and Joan Rowden Cheshire; two *s* one *d. Educ:* Portsmouth Grammar School. Reporter, Portsmouth Evening News, Surrey Mirror, Press Assoc., Daily Telegraph, The Times; Royal Army Pay Corps Short Service Commission (to Captain), 1960–64; Home News Editor, The Times, 1969–74; Editor, Cambridge Evening News, 1974–82; Dep. Editor, The Times, 1982–86; Journalist Dir, Times Newspaper Holdings, 1983–86. Member: Core Cttee, British Executive Internat. Press Inst., 1984–; Council, Commonwealth Press Union, 1985–. *Publication:* (co-author with The Times News Team) Black Man in Search of Power, 1968. *Recreations:* family, walking, history books, ballet. *Address:* 49 Winterbrook Road, SE24. *T:* 01–274 4533.

WEBB, Douglas Edward, CVO 1961; OBE 1947; Deputy Commissioner of Police of the Metropolis, 1961–66; retired; *b* 8 Oct. 1909; *yr s* of late Supt O. C. Webb, KPM, Metropolitan Police; *m* 1935, Mary McMillan, *yr d* of late Capt. J. S. Learmont, Trinity House; one *s* (one *d* decd). *Educ:* Bordon Grammar School; Devonport High School. Joined Metropolitan Police, 1929; Metropolitan Police Coll., Hendon, 1935–36 (Baton of Honour). Allied Commission, Italy and Austria, 1945–47. Chief Supt, Bow Street, 1952–53, West End Central, 1953–54; Dep. Commander, New Scotland Yard, 1954–55; Commander, No 3 District (E London), 1955–57; Asst Commissioner (Traffic), 1957–58; Assistant Commissioner, Administration and Operations (originated Special Patrol Gp), New Scotland Yard, Dec. 1958–61. Officer, Legion of Honour, 1961; Order of Merit, Chile, 1965. *Address:* Tanglewood, 5 Deer Park Close, Tavistock, Devon PL19 9HE. *T:* Tavistock 2377.

WEBB, Prof. Edwin Clifford; Vice-Chancellor, Macquarie University, 1976–86; *b* 21 May 1921; *s* of William Webb and Nellie Webb; *m* 1942, Violet Sheila Joan (*née* Tucker); one *s* four *d* (and one *s* decd). *Educ:* Poole Grammar Sch.; Cambridge Univ. (BA, MA, PhD). FRACI 1968. Cambridge University: Beit Meml Res. Fellow, 1944–46; Univ. Demonstrator in Biochem., 1946–50; Univ. Lectr in Biochem., 1950–62; University of Queensland: Foundn Prof. of Biochem. and Head of Dept, 1962–70, now Emeritus Prof.; Dep. Vice-Chancellor (Academic), 1970–76. Hon. DSc Queensland, 1978. *Publications:* Enzymes, 1959, 3rd edn 1979; 56 scientific papers. *Recreations:* photography, music, motoring, coin collecting.

WEBB, George Hannam, CMG 1984; OBE 1974; Director (Management Development), City University, London, since 1985; *b* 24 Dec. 1929; *s* of late George Ernest Webb, HM Colonial Service, Kenya, and Mary Hannam Webb (*née* Stephens); *m* 1956, Josephine (later MA Cantab; JP Surrey), *d* of R. Chatterton, Horncastle; two *s* two *d. Educ:* Malvern Coll.; King's Coll., Cambridge (MA). Served 14/20th King's Hussars, 1948–49; Parachute Regt (TA), 1950–53. Joined Colonial Administration, Kenya, 1953: District Officer, Central Nyanza, 1954–56; N Nyanza, 1956–57; District Commissioner, Moyale, 1958–60; MoD, Nairobi, 1960–62; retired 1963 and joined HM Diplomatic Service; First Sec., Bangkok, 1964–67; Accra, 1969–73; Counsellor, Tehran, 1977–79, Washington, 1980–82; retd 1985. Mem. Council, Royal Soc. for Asian Affairs, 1984–; Trustee, Hakluyt Soc. *Recreations:* books, travel; Editor, Kipling Journal, 1980–. *Address:* Weavers, Danes Hill, Woking GU22 7HQ. *T:* Woking 61989. *Clubs:* Travellers', Beefsteak, Royal Commonwealth Society.

WEBB, Prof. John Stuart, FEng; Professor of Applied Geochemistry in the University of London, 1961–79, now Emeritus, and Senior Research Fellow, since 1979, Imperial College of Science and Technology; *b* 28 Aug. 1920; *s* of Stuart George Webb and Caroline Rabjohns Webb (*née* Pengelly); *m* 1946, Jean Millicent Dyer; one *s. Educ:* Westminster City School; Royal School of Mines, Imperial College of Science and Technology, BSc, ARSM, 1941. Served War of 1939–45, Royal Engineers, 1941–43. Geological Survey of Nigeria, 1943–44; Royal School of Mines, Imperial Coll., 1945–; Beit Scientific Research Fellow, 1945–47; PhD, DIC, in Mining Geology, 1947; Lecturer in Mining Geology, 1947–55; Reader in Applied Geochemistry, 1955–61. DSc, 1967. Mem., Home Office Forensic Science Cttee, 1969–75. Mem. Council, Instn of Mining and Metallurgy, 1964–71, and 1974–83, Vice Pres., 1971–73, Pres., 1973–74; Mem. Bd, Council Engineering Instns, 1973–74; Reg. Vice-Pres. (Europe), Soc. of Econ. Geologists, USA, 1979–81. Mem., Royal Soc. Wkg Pty on Environmental Geochem. and Health, 1979–83. Hon. Mem., Assoc. Exploration Geochemists, USA, 1977; Hon. FIMM 1980. Consolidated Goldfields of SA Gold Medal, IMM, 1953; William Smith Medal, Geol Soc. of London, 1981. *Publications:* (with H. E. Hawkes) Geochemistry in Mineral Exploration, 1962, 2nd edn (with A. W. Rose) 1979; (jtly) Geochemical Atlas of Northern Ireland, 1973; (jtly) Wolfson Geochemical Atlas of England and Wales, 1978; contrib. to scientific and technical jls. *Recreations:* wild life photography, amateur radio. *Address:* Stone Cottage, Lyons Road, Slinfold, Horsham, Sussex RH13 7QT. *T:* Slinfold 790243.

WEBB, Prof. Joseph Ernest, PhD (London) 1944, DSc (London) 1949; FIBiol; Professor of Zoology, 1960–80, and Vice-Principal, 1976–80, Westfield College, University of London, now Emeritus Professor (Hon. Fellow, 1986); *b* 22 March 1915; *s* of Joseph Webb and Constance Inman Webb (*née* Hickox); *m* 1940, Gwenlilian Clara Coldwell; three *s. Educ:* Rutlish School; Birkbeck College, London. Research Entomologist and Parasitologist at The Cooper Technical Bureau, Berkhampsted, Herts, 1940–46; Lecturer, Univ. of Aberdeen, 1946–48; Senior Lecturer, 1948–50, Professor of Zoology, 1950–60, University Coll., Ibadan, Nigeria. FIBiol. *Publications:* (jointly) Guide to Invertebrate Animals, 1975, 2nd edn 1978; Guide to Living Mammals, 1977, 2nd edn 1979; Guide to Living Reptiles, 1978; Guide to Living Birds, 1979; Guide to Living Fishes, 1981; Guide to Living Amphibians, 1981; various on insect physiology, insecticides, systematics, populations, tropical ecology and marine biology. *Recreations:* art, music, photography. *Address:* 43 Hill Top, NW11. *T:* 01–458 2571. *Club:* Athenæum.

WEBB, Kaye, MBE 1974; Chairman and Founder of Puffin Club (for children), since 1967; Director, Unicorn Children's Theatre, since 1972; Managing Director, Kaye Webb Ltd, since 1973; *d* of Arthur Webb and Kathleen Stevens, journalists; *m* 1st, Christopher Brierley; 2nd, Andrew Hunter; 3rd, 1946, Ronald Searle, *qv*; one *s* one *d.* Entered journalism via Picturegoer, 1931; joined Picture Post, 1938; Asst Editor, Lilliput, 1941–47; Theatre Corresp., The Leader, 1947–49; Feature Writer, News Chronicle, 1949–55; Editor of children's magazine Elizabethan, 1955–58; Theatre Critic to National Review, 1957–58; Children's Editor, Puffin Books, and Publishing Dir, Children's Div., Penguin Books Ltd, 1961–79; Editor, Puffin Post, 1967–. Children's Advisor, Goldcrest TV, 1978–84; Mem. UK Branch, UNICEF. Mem., BAFTA. Eleanor Farjeon Award for services to Children's Literature, 1969. *Publications:* (ed) C. Fry: Experience of Critics; (ed) Penguin Patrick Campbell; (ed) The Friday Miracle; (ed) The St Trinian's Story; (with Ronald Searle): Looking at London; Paris Sketchbook; Refugees 1960; (with Treld Bicknell) 1st and 2nd Puffin Annuals; Puffins Pleasure; (ed) I Like This Poem, 1979; (ed) Lilliput Goes to War, 1985; (ed) I Like This Story, 1986. *Recreations:* children and their interests, theatre. *Address:* 8 Lampard House, Maida Avenue, W2. *T:* 01–262 4695. *Club:* Puffin.

WEBB, Margaret Elizabeth; *see* Barbieri, M. E.

WEBB, Maysie (Florence), CBE 1979; BSc; Deputy Director, British Museum, 1971–83 (Assistant Director 1968–71); *b* 1 May 1923; *d* of Charles and Florence Webb. *Educ:* Kingsbury County School; Northern Polytechnic. Southwark Public Libraries, 1940–45; A. C. Cossor Ltd, 1945–50; British Non-Ferrous Metals Research Assoc., 1950–52; Mullard Equipment Ltd, 1952–55; Morgan Crucible Co. Ltd, 1955–60; Patent Office Library, 1960–66; Keeper, National Reference Library of Science and Invention, 1966–68. General Comr in England and Wales, 1976–. Mem. Council, RSA, 1971–76, 1978–84 (Chm., Membership Cttee, 1974–76, 1980–84); Manager, Royal Instn, 1975–78; Trustee of the Royal Armouries, 1984–. *Recreations:* family and friends, gardens, houses.

WEBB, Pauline Mary, AKC; Organiser, Religious Broadcasting, BBC World Service, since 1979; author; *b* 28 June 1927; *d* of Rev. Leonard F. Webb. *Educ:* King's Coll., London Univ. (BA, AKC, FKC 1985); Union Theological Seminary, New York (STM). BA English Hons (King's), 1948; Teacher's Diploma, London Inst. of Educn, 1949. Asst Mistress, Thames Valley Grammar Sch., 1949–52; Editor, Methodist Missionary Soc., 1955–66; Vice-Pres., Methodist Conf., 1965–66; Dir, Lay Training, Methodist Church, 1967–73; Area Sec., Methodist Missionary Soc., 1973–79; Chm., Community and Race Relns Unit, BCC, 1976–79. Vice-Chm., Central Cttee, WCC, 1968–75. Hon. Dr: in Protestant Theology, Univ. of Brussels, 1984; of Sacred Letters, Victoria Univ., Toronto, Canada, 1985. *Publications:* Women of Our Company, 1958; Women of Our Time, 1960; Operation-Healing, 1964; All God's Children, 1964; Are We Yet Alive?, 1966; Agenda for the Churches, 1968; Salvation Today, 1974; Eventful Worship, 1975; Where are the Women?, 1979; Faith and Faithfulness, 1985. *Address:* Bush House, PO Box 76, Aldwych, WC2. *T:* 01–240 3456. *Club:* University Women's.

WEBB, Lt-Gen. Sir Richard (James Holden), KBE 1974 (CBE 1970, MBE 1952); CB 1972; *b* 21 Dec. 1919; *s* of late George Robert Holden Webb and Jessie Muriel Hair; *m* 1950, Barbara, *d* of Richard Griffin; one *s* one *d. Educ:* Nelson Coll., NZ; Royal Military Coll., Duntroon (Aust.); Staff Coll., Haifa; US Artillery School, Oklahoma; Joint Services Staff Coll., Latimer; Imperial Defence Coll. Commissioned NZ Army 1941. Served War, with Divisional Artillery, 2nd NZ Expeditionary Force, in Middle East and Italy, 1942–45, and Korea, 1950–51 (despatches twice). Quartermaster-Gen., NZ Army, 1967; Dep. Chief of Gen. Staff, NZ Army, 1969–70; Chief of Gen. Staff, NZ Army, 1970–71; Chief of Defence Staff, NZ, 1971–76. Chm., Local Govt Commn, 1978–85. Comdr, Legion of Merit (US), 1971. *Address:* Pahangahanga, Waimate North, RD1 Ohaeawai, Bay of Islands, New Zealand. *Club:* Wellington (Wellington, NZ).

WEBB, Stella Dorothea; *see* Gibbons, S. D.

WEBB, Sir Thomas (Langley), Kt 1975; *b* 25 April 1908; *s* of Robert Langley Webb and Alice Mary Webb; *m* 1942, Jeannette Alison Lang; one *s* one *d. Educ:* Melbourne Church of England Grammar Sch. Joined Huddart Parker Ltd, 1926 (Man. Dir, 1955–61). Served War, AIF, 1940–45. Dir, Commercial Bank of Aust., 1960–78 (Chm., 1970–78); Director: Bulkships Pty Ltd; McIlwraith McEacharn Ltd (Vice-Chm.). *Recreations:* golf, tennis. *Address:* 6 Yarradale Road, Toorak, Victoria 3142, Australia. *T:* Melbourne 2415259. *Clubs:* MCC; Australian, Melbourne, Royal Melbourne Golf, Royal South Yarra Tennis (all Melbourne).

WEBBER; *see* Lloyd Webber.

WEBBER, Fernley Douglas, CMG 1959; MC 1942; TD 1954; HM Diplomatic Service, retired; Secretary, Committee for Environmental Conservation, 1975–77; *b* 12 March 1918; *s* of Herbert Webber; *m* 1947, Veronica Elizabeth Ann, *d* of Major F. B. Hitchcock, MC; two *s* two *d. Educ:* Cotham School, Bristol; Jesus College, Cambridge. Entered

Colonial Office after open competition, 1939; Diplomatic Service, 1965. Served War of 1939–45, Burma, 1940–45; Comd 624 LAA Regt RA (RF) TA, 1952–54, Bt-Col, 1954. Principal, CO, 1946; Asst Sec. 1950; Establishment Officer, 1952–58; Head of E Af. Dept, 1958–63; idc 1964; Deputy High Commissioner in Eastern Malaysia during part of 1965; High Commissioner in Brunei, 1965–67; Asst Under-Sec. of State, FCO, 1967; Minister, British High Commn in Canberra, 1967–68; FCO, 1969–70. *Address:* 6 Mills Lane, Rodbridge Corner, Long Melford, Suffolk.

WEBBER, Roy Seymour, IPFA, FCCA; Town Clerk and Chief Executive, Royal Borough of Kensington and Chelsea, since 1979; *b* 8 April 1933; *s* of A. E. and A. M. Webber; *m* 1960, Barbara Ann (*née* Harries); one *s* three *d*. *Educ:* Ipswich School. Ipswich CBC, 1949–55; Coventry CBC, 1955–58; St Pancras BC, 1958–61, IBM (UK) Ltd, 1961–62; Woolwich BC, 1962–65; Greenwich LBC, 1965–68; Royal Borough of Kensington and Chelsea: Dep. Borough Treasurer, 1968–73; Director of Finance, 1973–79. *Recreations:* tennis, walking. *Address:* Woodland Cottage, Chelsfield Lane, Orpington, Kent BR6 7RP. *T:* Orpington 20935.

WEBER, (Edmund) Derek (Craig); Editor, The Geographical Magazine, 1967–81; *b* 29 April 1921; 3rd *s* of late R. J. C. and B. M. Weber; *m* 1953, Molly Patricia, *d* of the late R. O. and Ellen Podger; one *s* four *d*. *Educ:* Bristol Grammar School. Journalist on newspapers in Swindon, Bristol and Bath, and on magazines in London from 1937 until 1953, except for War Service in RAF, 1940–46. The Geographical Magazine: Art Editor, 1953; Assoc. Editor, 1965. Hon. FRGS 1980. Hon. Life Member: IBG, 1981; NUJ, 1981. Hon. MA Open, 1982. *Address:* 32 London Road, Maldon, Essex CM9 6HD. *T:* Maldon 52871. *Clubs:* Savage, Geographical.

WEBSTER, Very Rev. Alan Brunskill; Dean of St Paul's, since 1978; *b* 1918; *s* of Reverend J. Webster; *m* 1951, M. C. F. Falconer; two *s* two *d*. *Educ:* Shrewsbury School; Queen's College, Oxford. MA, BD. Ordained, 1942; Curate of Attercliffe Parishes, Sheffield, 1942; Curate of St Paul's, Arbourthorne, Sheffield, 1944; Westcott House, 1946; Vicar of Barnard Castle, 1953; Warden, Lincoln Theol Coll., 1959–70; Dean of Norwich, 1970–78. Hon. DD City Univ., 1983. *Publications:* Joshua Watson, 1954; Broken Bones May Joy, 1968; Julian of Norwich, 1974 (rev. edn 1980). Contributor to The Historic Episcopate, 1954; Living the Faith, 1980; Strategist for the Spirit, 1985. *Recreation:* writing. *Address:* The Deanery, 9 Amen Court, EC4M 7BU. *T:* 01–236 2827.

WEBSTER, Maj.-Gen. Bryan Courtney, CB 1986; CBE 1981; Director of Army Quartering, 1982–86; *b* 2 Feb. 1931; *s* of Captain H. J. Webster, Royal Fusiliers (killed in action, 1940) and late M. J. Webster; *m* 1957, Elizabeth Rowland Waldron Smithers, *d* of Prof. Sir David Smithers, *qv*; two *s* one *d*. *Educ:* Haileybury College; RMA Sandhurst. Commissioned Royal Fusiliers, 1951; ADC to GOC, 16 Airborne Div., 1953–55; served Korea, Egypt, Malta, Gibraltar, Hong Kong; Directing Staff, Staff Coll., 1969–70; Comd 1st Bn Royal Regt of Fusiliers, 1971–73; Comd 8th Inf. Brigade, 1975–77 (Despatches); Dep. Col, Royal Regt of Fusiliers (City of London), 1976; Nat. Defence Coll., India, 1979; Staff appts, Far East, MoD, incl. Dir of Admin Planning (Army), 1980–82. FBIM. Freeman, City of London, 1984. *Recreations:* ornithology, shooting. *Address:* Ewshot Lodge, Ewshot, Surrey GU10 5BS. *Club:* Army and Navy.

WEBSTER, Charles, DSc; FBA 1982; University Reader in the History of Medicine, University of Oxford, since 1972; Director, Wellcome Unit for the History of Medicine, since 1972; Fellow of Corpus Christi College, Oxford, since 1972. *Publications:* The Great Instauration, 1975; From Paracelsus to Newton, 1982. *Address:* Wellcome Unit for the History of Medicine, 45–47 Banbury Road, Oxford OX2 6PE. *T:* Oxford 274600.

WEBSTER, Dr Cyril Charles, CMG 1966; Chief Scientific Officer, Agricultural Research Council, 1971–75 (Scientific Adviser, 1965–71); *b* 28 Dec. 1909; *s* of Ernest Webster; *m* 1947, Mary, *d* of H. R. Wimhurst; one *s* one *d*. *Educ:* Beckenham County Sch.; Wye Coll.; Selwyn Coll., Cambridge; Imperial Coll. of Tropical Agriculture, Trinidad. Colonial Agricultural Service, 1936–57: Nigeria, 1936–38; Nyasaland, 1938–50; Kenya (Chief Research Officer), 1950–55; Malaya (Dep. Dir of Agriculture), 1956–57; Prof. of Agriculture, Imperial Coll. of Tropical Agriculture, Univ. of W Indies, 1957–60; Dir, Rubber Research Inst. of Malaya, 1961–65; Dir-Gen., Palm Oil Research Inst. of Malaya, 1978–80. JMN, 1965. *Publications:* (with P. N. Wilson) Agriculture in the Tropics, 1966; scientific papers in agricultural jls. *Address:* 5 Shenden Way, Sevenoaks, Kent. *T:* Sevenoaks 453984.

WEBSTER, David; Resident Associate, Carnegie Endowment, since 1985; consultant to international companies and institutions; *b* 11 Jan. 1931; *s* of Alec Webster and Clare Webster; *m* 1st, 1955, Lucy Law (marr. diss.), Princeton, NJ; two *s*; 2nd, 1981, Elizabeth Drew, author, Washington, DC. *Educ:* Taunton Sch.; Ruskin Coll., Oxford. British Broadcasting Corporation: Sub-Editor, External Services News Dept, 1953–59; Producer, Panorama, 1959–64; Exec. Producer, Enquiry, and Encounter, BBC-2, 1964–66; Dep. Editor, Panorama, 1966, Editor, 1967–69; Exec. Editor, Current Affairs Group, 1969, Asst Head, 1970; BBC Rep. in USA, 1971–76; Controller, Information Services, 1976–77; Dir, Public Affairs, 1977–80; Dir, US, BBC, 1981–85. Mem., Bd of Management, BBC, 1977–85. Mem., Twentieth Century Fund Task Force on the Flow of the News, 1978. Mem. Adv. Council, Ditchley Foundn of US, 1981–; Mem., Nat. Adv. Cttee for the William Benton Fellowship Prog., Univ. of Chicago, 1983–. Fellow, Internat. Council, National Acad. of Television Arts and Sciences, USA, 1980– (Chm., Internat. Council, 1974 and 1975). *Recreation:* coarse tennis. *Address:* Carnegie Endowment, 11 Dupont Circle, NW, Washington, DC 20036, USA. *T:* 202–797–6436. *Club:* Century Association (NY).

See also S. H. E. Kitzinger.

WEBSTER, David MacLaren, QC 1980; a Recorder of the Crown Court, since 1979; *b* 21 Dec. 1937; *s* of John MacLaren Webster and Winning McGregor Webster (*née* Rough); *m* 1964, Frances Sally McLaren, RE, *o d* of late Lt-Col J. A. McLaren and Mrs H. S. Scammell; three *s*. *Educ:* Hutchesons', Glasgow; Christ Church, Oxford (MA (Eng Lang. and Lit.)); Conservatoire d'Art Dramatique and Sorbonne (French Govt Schol. 1960–61). Radio and television work in drama and current affairs, Scotland, 1949–64; called to the Bar, Gray's Inn, 1964; joined Western Circuit; a Dep. Circuit Judge, 1976–79. Member: Bar Council, 1972–74; Senate of Inns of Court and Bar, 1974–79, 1982–85 (Senate Representative, Commonwealth Law Conf., Edinburgh, 1977); Matrimonial Causes Rules Cttee, 1976–79; Crown Court Rules Cttee, 1983–; Western Circuit Univs Liaison Cttee, 1978–84. Gold Medal, LAMDA, 1954; LRAM 1955. President, Oxford Univ. Experimental Theatre Club, 1958–59; Secretary, Mermaid's, 1958; Chm., Bar Theatrical Soc., 1976–. Governor, Port Regis Sch., 1983–. *Recreations:* theatre, sailing, cricket, Scottish literature. *Address:* 3 Pump Court, Temple, EC4. *T:* 01–353 0711. *Clubs:* Garrick, MCC, Bar Yacht; Hampshire.

WEBSTER, Derek Adrian, CBE 1979; Chairman and Editorial Director, Scottish Daily Record and Sunday Mail Ltd, since 1974; *b* 24 March 1927; *s* of James Tulloch Webster and Isobel Webster; *m* 1966, Dorothy Frances Johnson; two *s* one *d*. *Educ:* St Peter's, Bournemouth. Served RN, 1944–48. Reporter, Western Morning News, 1943; Staff Journalist, Daily Mail, 1949–51; joined Mirror Group, 1952; Northern Editor, Daily Mirror, 1964–67; Editor, Daily Record, 1967–72; Director: Mirror Gp Newspapers, 1974–; Clyde Cable Vision, 1983–. Mem., Press Council, 1981–84 (Jt Vice-Chm., 1982–83). Vice-Chm., Age Concern (Scotland), 1977–83; Hon. Vice-Pres., Newspaper Press Fund, 1983–; Mem. Council, CPU, 1984–. *Recreation:* boating. *Address:* Gateside, Blanefield, by Glasgow. *T:* Blanefield 70252.

WEBSTER, Henry George, CBE 1974; FSAE; Chairman, SKF Steel UK, since 1982; *b* Coventry, 27 May 1917; *s* of William George Webster; *m* 1943, Margaret, *d* of H. C. Sharp; one *d*. *Educ:* Welshpool County Sch.; Coventry Technical Coll. Standard Motor Co. Ltd: apprenticed, 1932; Asst Technl Engr, 1938–40; Dep. Chief Inspector, 1940–46; Asst Technl Engr, 1946–48; Chief Chassis Engr, 1948–55; Chief Engr, 1955–57; Dir and Chief Engr, Standard-Triumph Internat., 1957–68; Technical Dir, Austin Morris Div., British Leyland UK Ltd, 1968–74; Group Engineering Dir, Automotive Products, 1974–83. Joined original Instn of Automobile Engrs, as a grad., 1937 (Sec. of Grad. Section, Coventry Br. of Instn, 1941–45); transf. to Associate Mem., 1946, Mem., 1964. MSAE, 1958; FSAE, 1976; FRSA. Freeman, City of Coventry. *Recreation:* golf. *Address:* The Old School House, Barrowfield Lane, Kenilworth, Warwickshire CV8 1EP. *T:* Kenilworth 53363.

WEBSTER, Ian Stevenson; His Honour Judge Webster; a Circuit Judge, since 1981; *b* 20 March 1925; *s* of late Harvey Webster and late Annabella Stevenson Webster (*née* McBain); *m* 1951, Margaret (*née* Sharples); two *s*. *Educ:* Rochdale Grammar Sch.; Manchester Univ. Sub. Lieut (A), RNVR, 1944. Called to the Bar, Middle Temple, 1948. Asst Recorder: of Oldham, 1970; of Salford, 1971; a Recorder of the Crown Court, 1972–76, 1981; Chm., Industrial Tribunals for Manchester, 1976–81. *Recreations:* golf, sailing. *Address:* Moorside Cottage, 154 Syke Road, Rochdale, Lancs.

WEBSTER, John Alexander R.; *see* Riddell-Webster.

WEBSTER, John Lawrence Harvey, CMG 1963; *b* 10 March 1913; *s* of late Sydney Webster, Hindhead, and Elsie Gwendoline Webster (*née* Harvey); *m* 1st, 1940, Elizabeth Marshall Gilbertson (marr. diss., 1959); two *d*; 2nd, 1960, Jessie Lillian Royston-Smith. *Educ:* Rugby Sch.; Balliol College, Oxford (MA). District Officer, Colonial Administrative Service, Kenya, 1935–49; Secretary for Development, 1949–54; Administrative Sec., 1954–56; Sec. to Cabinet, 1956–58; Permanent Sec., Kenya, 1958–63; on retirement from HMOCS, with the British Council, 1964–80, in Thailand, Sri Lanka, Hong Kong, Istanbul and London. *Recreations:* travel, reading, swimming, golf. *Address:* Timbercroft, 11 Pevensey Road, West Worthing, Sussex. *Clubs:* Royal Commonwealth Society; Leander; Nairobi (Kenya).

WEBSTER, Vice-Adm. Sir John (Morrison), KCB 1986; Flag Officer Plymouth, Port Admiral Devonport, Commander Central Sub Area Eastern Atlantic, and Commander Plymouth Sub Area Channel, from March 1987; *b* 3 Nov. 1932; *s* of late Frank Martin Webster and of Kathleen Mary (*née* Morrison) *m* 1962, Valerie Anne Villiers; one *s* two *d*. *Educ:* Pangbourne College. Joined RN, 1951; specialised navigation, 1959; Royal Australian Navy, 1959–61; HMS Lowestoft, 1961–63; BRNC, Dartmouth, 1963–65; HMS Dido, 1965–67; RN Tactical Sch., 1967–69; in command HMS Argonaut, 1969–71; MoD Navy, 1971–73; RNLO Ottawa, 1974–76; in command HMS Cleopatra and 4th Frigate Sqdn, 1976–78; MoD, Director Naval Warfare, 1980–82; Flag Officer Sea Trng, 1982–84; C of S to C-in-C Fleet, 1984–86. Lt-Comdr 1963, Comdr 1967, Captain 1973, Rear-Adm. 1982, Vice-Adm. 1985. Younger Brother of Trinity House, 1970–. Member: Soc. for Nautical Res., 1985–; Armed Forces Art Soc., 1967–. Gov., Canford Sch., 1984–. *Recreations:* painting, sailing. *Address:* c/o Royal Bank of Scotland, 24 Lombard Street, EC3. *Clubs:* Royal Naval Sailing Association, Royal Naval of 1765 & 1785.

WEBSTER, Prof. John Roger, MA, PhD; DipEd; Professor of Education, and Dean of Faculty of Education, University College of Wales, Aberystwyth, since 1978; *b* 24 June 1926; *s* of Samuel and Jessie Webster; *m* 1963, Ivy Mary Garlick; one *s* one *d*. *Educ:* Llangefni Secondary Sch.; University College of Wales, Aberystwyth. Lectr, Trinity Coll., Carmarthen, 1948; Lectr in Educn, University Coll., Swansea, 1951; Director for Wales, Arts Council of GB, 1961–66; Prof. of Educn, University Coll. of North Wales, Bangor, 1966–78. Member: Lloyd Cttee on Nat. Film Sch., 1965–66; James Cttee on Teacher Educn and Trng, 1971; Venables Cttee on Continuing Educn, 1974–76; Council, Open Univ. (Chm., Educ. Studies Adv. Cttee), 1969–78; Chm., Standing Conf. on Studies in Educn, 1972–76; Member: CNAA, 1976–79; British Council Welsh Adv. Cttee, 1982–; Post Office Users Nat. Council, 1981– (Chm., Wales, 1981–); Chm., Wales Telecommunications Adv. Cttee, 1984–. Governor, Commonwealth Inst., 1985–. *Publications:* Ceri Richards, 1961; Joseph Herman, 1962; contribs on educn and the arts to collective works and learned jls. *Address:* Bron y Glyn, Rhydyfelin, Aberystwyth, Dyfed SY23 4QD.

WEBSTER, Prof. Keith Edward, PhD; Professor of Anatomy and Human Biology (formerly Professor of Anatomy), King's College, University of London, since 1975; *b* 18 June 1935; *e s* of Thomas Brotherwick Webster and Edna Pyzer; 1st marr. diss. 1983; two *s*; *m* 2nd, 1984, Felicity Grainger. *Educ:* UCL (BSc 1957, PhD 1960); UCH Med. Sch. (MB, BS 1962). University Coll. London: Lectr in Anatomy, 1962–66; Sen. Lectr in Anat., 1966–74; Reader in Anat., 1974–75. Symington Prize, British Anatomical Soc., 1966. *Publications:* A Manual of Human Anatomy, Vol. 5: The Central Nervous System (with J. T. Aitken and J. Z. Young), 1967; papers on the nervous system in Brain Res., Jl of Comp. Neurol., Neuroscience and Neurocytology. *Recreations:* Richard Wagner and myself. *Address:* Department of Anatomy and Human Biology, King's College London, Strand, WC2R 2LS. *T:* 01–836 5454.

WEBSTER, Michael George Thomas, DL; Chairman, DRG plc (formerly Dickinson Robinson Group), since 1985 (Director, since 1976; Deputy Chairman, 1983–85); *b* 27 May 1920; *s* of late J. A. Webster, CB, DSO, and late Constance A. Webster, 2nd *d* of late Richard and Lady Constance Combe; *m* 1947, Mrs Isabel Margaret Bucknill, *d* of late Major J. L. Dent, DSO, MC; three *d*. *Educ:* Stowe; Magdalen Coll., Oxford (MA). Commnd Grenadier Guards, 1940–46: NW Europe Campaign, 1944–45 (despatches); DAAG Guards Div., 1946. Joined Watney Combe Reid & Co. Ltd, 1946; Chm., Watney Combe Reid, 1963–68; Watney Mann Ltd: Vice-Chm., 1965–70; Chm., 1970–72; Deputy Chm., 1972–74; Chm., Watney Mann & Truman Holdings, 1974; Director: Grand Metropolitan Ltd, 1972–74; National Provident Instn, 1973–85; Chm., Fitch Lovell PLC, 1977–83 (Vice-Chm., 1976). Master of Brewers' Co., 1964–65; a Vice-Pres., The Brewers' Soc., 1975–. Chairman: Aldenham Sch. Governing Body, 1977–84; Truman and Knightley Educnl Trust, 1985–. High Sheriff, Berks, 1971; DL Berks, 1975. *Recreations:* fishing, shooting, golf. *Address:* The Vale, Windsor Forest, Berks. *Clubs:* White's, Cavalry and Guards, MCC.

See also Viscount Torrington.

WEBSTER, Patrick; Barrister-at-Law; a Recorder of the Crown Court, since 1972; Chairman, Industrial Tribunals, Cardiff Region, since 1976 (a part-time Chairman,

1965–75); *b* 6 January 1928; *s* of Francis Glyn Webster and late Ann Webster; *m* 1955, Elizabeth Knight; two *s* four *d*. *Educ:* Swansea Grammar Sch.; Rockwell Coll., Eire; St Edmund's Coll., Ware; Downing Coll., Cambridge (BA). Called to Bar, Gray's Inn, 1950. Practised at bar, in Swansea, 1950–75; Chm., Medical Appeals Tribunal (part-time), 1971–75. *Recreations:* listening to music, watching rowing and sailing. *Address:* 103 Plymouth Road, Penarth, South Glam CF6 2DE. *T:* Penarth 704758. *Clubs:* Penarth Yacht; Beechwood (Swansea).

WEBSTER, Hon. Sir Peter (Edlin), Kt 1980; **Hon. Mr Justice Webster;** a Judge of the High Court of Justice, Queen's Bench Division, since 1980; *b* 16 Feb. 1924; *s* of Herbert Edlin Webster and Florence Helen Webster; *m* 1955, Susan Elizabeth Richards (marr. diss.); one *s* two *d*; *m* 1968, Avril Carolyn Simpson, *d* of Dr John Ernest McCrae Harrisson. *Educ:* Haileybury; Merton Coll., Oxford (MA). RNVR, 1943–46 and 1950, Lieut (A). Imperial Tobacco Co., 1949; Lectr in Law, Lincoln Coll., Oxford, 1950–52; called to Bar, Middle Temple, 1952; Bencher, 1972; Standing Jun. Counsel to Min. of Labour, 1964–67; QC 1967; a Recorder of the Crown Court, 1972–80. Mem., Council of Justice, 1955–60, 1965–70; Mem., General Council of the Bar, 1967–74, and of Senate of the Inns of Court and the Bar, 1974–81 (Vice-Chm. 1975–76; Chm., 1976–77), Chm., London Common Law Bar Assoc., 1975–79; Mem., Judicial Studies Bd, 1979–83, Chm., 1981–83. Dir, Booker McConnell, 1978–79. *Address:* Royal Courts of Justice, Strand, WC2.

WEDD, George Morton; South-West Regional Director, Departments of the Environment and Transport, Bristol, since 1983; *b* 30 March 1930; *s* of Albert Wedd and Dora Wedd; *m* 1953, Kate Pullin; two *s* one *d*. *Educ:* various schs in Derbyshire; St John's Coll., Cambridge (BA 1951). Joined Min. of Housing and Local Govt (later DoE), 1951; Principal, 1957; Asst Sec., 1966; Under Sec., 1976. *Address:* The Lodge, High Littleton, Avon; 1 Horsebrook Cottages, Avonwick, Devon.

WEDDELL, Prof. (Alexander) Graham (McDonnell), MA (Oxon), MD, DSc (London); Professor of Anatomy, University of Oxford, 1973–1975; *b* 18 Feb. 1908; *s* of Alexander George Weddell and Maud Eileen McDonnell; *m* 1937, Barbara Monica Mills (*d* 1984); two *d*. *Educ:* Cheltenham Coll.; St Bartholomew's Hosp. Med. Sch., London. Demonstrator in Anatomy, St Bart's, London, 1933–34; Commonwealth Fund Fellow in Neuroanatomy and Neurological Surgery, USA, 1935–37; Demonstrator in Anatomy, University Coll. London, 1937–39. Served War: Neurosurgery, RAMC, until 1943; then Anatomical Research for Royal Naval Personnel Cttee of MRC, 1943–45. Apptd Demonstrator in Human Anatomy, Univ. of Oxford, with leave of absence, 1945. Reader in Human Anatomy, Univ. of Oxford, 1947–73; Fellow and Med. Tutor, Oriel Coll., Oxford, 1947; Sen. Proctor, Univ. of Oxford, 1951; elected Mem., Hebdomadal Council, 1952. WHO study team investigating neurological rehabilitation in leprosy, 1960; Harold Chaffer Lectureship, Dunedin Univ., NZ, 1961; Mem., MRC Leprosy Sub-Cttee, 1967; Designated WHO Leprosy Ref. Lab. (under dir of Dr R. J. W. Rees), 1967. Pres., Anatomical Soc. of GB and Ire., 1973–75. *Publications:* papers in learned jls on cutaneous sensibility and leprosy. *Recreations:* photography, swimming. *Address:* 7 Mill Street, Islip, Oxford OX5 2SZ. *T:* Kidlington 6326.

WEDDERBURN, family name of **Baron Wedderburn of Charlton.**

WEDDERBURN OF CHARLTON, Baron *cr* 1977 (Life Peer), of Highgate; **Kenneth William Wedderburn,** FBA 1981; Cassel Professor of Commercial Law, London School of Economics, University of London, since 1964; *b* 13 April 1927; *o s* of Herbert J. and Mabel Wedderburn, Deptford; *m* 1st, 1951, Nina Salaman; one *s* two *d*; 2nd 1962, Dorothy E. Cole; 3rd, 1969, Frances Ann Knight; one *s*. *Educ:* Aske's Hatcham School; Whitgift School; Queens' College, Cambridge. BA 1948; LLB 1949 (Chancellor's Medallist); MA 1951. Royal Air Force, 1949–51. Called to the Bar, Middle Temple, 1953. Fellow, 1952–64, Tutor, 1957–60, Clare College, Cambridge; Asst Lectr, 1953–55, Lectr 1955–64, Faculty of Law, Cambridge University. Visiting Professor: UCLA Law Sch., 1967; Harvard Law Sch., 1969–70. Staff Panel Mem., Civil Service Arbitration Tribunal; Chm., Independent Review Cttee, 1976–; Mem., Cttee on Industrial Democracy, 1976–77; Independent Chm., London and Provincial Theatre Councils. Gen. Editor, Modern Law Review. *Publications:* The Worker and the Law, 1965, 3rd edn 1986; Cases and Materials on Labour Law, 1967; (with P. Davies) Employment Grievances and Disputes Procedures in Britain, 1969; (ed) Contracts, Sutton and Shannon, 1956, 1963; Asst Editor: Torts, Clerk and Lindsell, 1969, 1975, 1982; Modern Company Law, Gower, 1969 (ed jtly 1979 edn); (ed with B. Aaron) Industrial Conflict, 1972; (with S. Sciarra *et al*) Democrazia Politica e Democrazia Industriale, 1978; (ed with Folke Schmidt) Discrimination in Employment, 1978; (with R. Lewis and J. Clark) Labour Law and Industrial Relations, 1983; (ed with W. T. Murphy) Labour Law and the Community, 1983; articles in legal and other jls. *Recreation:* Charlton Athletic Football Club. *Address:* London School of Economics, Aldwych, WC2. *T:* 01–405 7686.

WEDDERBURN, Sir Andrew John Alexander O.; *see* Ogilvy-Wedderburn.

WEDDERBURN, Prof. Dorothy Enid Cole; Principal, Royal Holloway and Bedford New College, since 1985, and a Pro-Vice-Chancellor, since 1986, University of London; *b* 18 Sept. 1925; *d* of Frederick C. Barnard and Ethel C. Barnard. *Educ:* Walthamstow High Sch. for Girls; Girton Coll., Cambridge (MA). Research Officer, subseq. Sen. Res. Officer, Dept of Applied Economics, Cambridge, 1950–65; Imperial College of Science and Technology: Lectr in Industrial Sociology, 1965–70, Reader, 1970–77, Prof., 1977–81; Dir, Industrial Sociol. Unit, 1973–81; Head, Dept of Social and Economic Studies, 1978–81, Senior Res. Fellow, 1981–; Principal, Bedford Coll., 1981–85. Mem. Court, Univ. of London, 1981–. Vis. Prof., Sloan Sch. of Management, MIT, 1969–70. Mem. SSRC, 1976–82; Chm., SERC/SSRC Jt Cttee, 1980–82. Mem., Govt Cttee on the Pay and Condition of Nurses, 1974–75; part-time Mem., Royal Commn on the Distribution of Income and Wealth, 1974–78; Mem. Council, Advisory Conciliation and Arbitration Service, 1976–82. Hon. Pres., Fawcett Soc., 1986–. Hon. Fellow Ealing Coll. of Higher Educn, 1985; Hon. FIC 1986; Hon. DLitt Warwick, 1984. *Publications:* White Collar Redundancy, 1964; Redundancy and the Railwayman, 1964; Enterprise Planning for Change, 1968; (with J. E. G. Utting) The Economic Circumstances of Old People, 1962; (with Peter Townsend) The Aged in the Welfare State, 1965; (jtly) Old Age in Three Industrial Societies, 1968; (with Rosemary Crompton) Workers' Attitudes and Technology, 1972; (ed) Poverty, Inequality and Class Structure, 1974; contrib. Jl of Royal Statistical Soc.; Sociological Review; New Society, etc. *Recreations:* politics, walking, cooking. *Address:* Royal Holloway and Bedford New College, Egham, Surrey TW20 0EX.

See also Professor G. A. Barnard.

WEDDERSPOON, Sir Thomas (Adam), Kt 1955; JP; *b* 4 August 1904; *s* of late Thomas and Margaret Wedderspoon; *m* 1936, Helen Catherine Margaret MacKenzie; one *s* two *d*. *Educ:* Seafield House, Broughty Ferry, Angus; Trinity College, Glenalmond, Perthshire; Trinity Hall, Cambridge. JP Angus, 1928. *Address:* Northfield, Keay Street, Blairgowrie, Perthshire PH10 6JD. *T:* Blairgowrie 2827.

WEDEGA, Dame Alice, DBE 1982 (MBE 1962); retired; *b* 20 Aug. 1905; *d* of Wedega Gamahari and Emma; *Educ:* Kwato Mission School, Milne Bay, PNG; trained in domestic arts, bookbinding, teaching and nursing. Missionary and teacher among head-hunting tribes of SE Papua during 1930s; first Papuan woman to attend internat. conf., Unesco/Pan Pacific, NZ, 1952; first Papuan Girl Guide Comr, 1956; welfare worker with Agric. Dept, helping village women upgrade land and crops, 1958; developed Ahioma Trng Centre, Milne Bay, for village women to learn domestic arts and child care, 1960–68; Mem., Legislative Council, 1961 (first Papuan woman); sent by Govt to assist women in Bougainville during copper mining dispute, 1969–70; as worker with Moral Re-Armament visited and lectured in Asia and Europe, incl. N Ireland, Sweden, Lapland; attended MRA internat. confs in Ceylon, India, Switzerland, Australia and PNG. *Publication:* Listen My Country (autobiog.), 1981. *Recreation:* swimming. *Address:* K.B. Mission, Box 32, Alotau, Milne Bay Province, Papua New Guinea.

WEDELL, Prof. (Eberhard Arthur Otto) George; Professor of Communications Policy, University of Manchester and Director, European Institute for the Media, since 1983; *b* 4 April 1927; *er s* of late Rev. Dr H. Wedell and Gertrude (*née* Bonhoeffer); *m* 1948, Rosemarie (*née* Winckler); three *s* one *d*. *Educ:* Cranbrook; London School of Economics (BSc Econ., 1947). Ministry of Education, 1950–58; Sec., Bd for Social Responsibility, Nat. Assembly of Church of England, 1958–60; Dep. Sec., ITA, 1960–61, Secretary, 1961–64; Prof. of Adult Educn and Dir of Extra-Mural Studies, Manchester Univ., 1964–75; Vis. Prof. of Employment Policy, 1975–83; Senior Official, European Commn, 1973–82. Contested (L) Greater Manchester West, 1979, (L-SDP Alliance) Greater Manchester Central, 1984, European Parly elections; Chm., British Liberals in EEC, 1980–82. Chairman: Wyndham Place Trust, 1983–; Beatrice Hankey Foundn, 1984–. Director, Royal Exchange Theatre Company, 1968–. FRSA; FRTS. Hon. MEd Manchester, 1968. *Publications:* The Use of Television in Education, 1963; Broadcasting and Public Policy, 1968; (with H. D. Perraton) Teaching at a Distance, 1968; (ed) Structures of Broadcasting, 1970; (with R. Glatter) Study by Correspondence, 1971; Correspondence Education in Europe, 1971; (ed) Education and the Development of Malawi, 1973; (with E. Katz) Broadcasting in the Third World, 1977 (Nat. Assoc. of Educational Broadcasters of USA Book Award, 1978); (with G. M. Luyken and R. Leonard) Mass Communications in Western Europe, 1985; (ed) Making Broadcasting Useful, 1986. *Recreations:* gardening, theatre, reading. *Address:* 18 Cranmer Road, Manchester M20 0AW. *T:* 061–445 5106; Vigneau, Lachapelle, 47350 Seyches, France. *T:* 53–838817. *Clubs:* Athenæum; Fondation Universitaire (Brussels).

See also Ven. H. Lockley.

WEDGWOOD, family name of **Baron Wedgwood.**

WEDGWOOD, 4th Baron *cr* 1942, of Barlaston; **Piers Anthony Weymouth Wedgwood;** *b* 20 Sept. 1954; *s* of 3rd Baron Wedgwood and of Lady Wedgwood (Jane Weymouth, *d* of W. J. Poulton, Kenjockety, Molo, Kenya); *S* father, 1970. *Educ:* Marlborough College; RMA Sandhurst. Royal Scots, 1973–80. GSM for N Ireland, 1976. *Heir: cousin* John Wedgwood, MD, FRCP [*b* 28 Sept. 1919; *m* 1st, 1943, Margaret (marr. diss. 1971), *d* of A. S. Mason; three *s* two *d*; 2nd, 1972, Joan, *d* of J. Ripsher]. *Address:* Harewood Cottage, Chicksgrove, Tisbury, Wilts. *T:* Fovant 325.

WEDGWOOD, Dame (Cicely) Veronica, OM 1969; DBE 1968 (CBE 1956); FRHistS; FBA 1975; Hon. LLD Glasgow; Hon. LittD Sheffield; Hon. DLitt: Smith College; Harvard; Oxford; Keele; Sussex; Liverpool; Historian; *b* 20 July 1910; *d* of Sir Ralph Wedgwood, 1st Bt, CB, CMG. *Educ:* privately; Lady Margaret Hall, Oxford. 1st Class Mod. Hist. 1931. Mem., Royal Commn on Historical MSS, 1953–78. President: English Assoc., 1955–56; English Centre of Internat. Pen Club, 1951–57; Society of Authors, 1972–77; Member: Arts Council, 1958–61; Arts Council Literature Panel, 1965–67; Institute for Advanced Study, Princeton, USA, 1953–68; Adv. Council, V&A Museum, 1960–69; Trustee, Nat. Gall., 1962–68, 1969–76; Hon. Member: American Academy of Arts and Letters, 1966; American Acad. of Arts and Scis, 1973; Amer. Philosophical Soc., 1973. Special Lecturer, UCL, 1962–85. Hon. Fellow: Lady Margaret Hall, Oxford, 1962; UCL, 1965. Hon. Bencher, Middle Temple, 1978. Officer, Order of Orange-Nassau, 1946; Goethe Medal, 1958. *Publications:* Strafford, 1935 (revd edn, as Thomas Wentworth, 1961); The Thirty Years' War, 1938; Oliver Cromwell 1939, rev. edn 1973; Charles V by Carl Brandi (trans.), 1939; William the Silent, 1944 (James Tait Black Prize for 1944); Auto da Fé by Elias Canetti (translation), 1946; Velvet Studies, 1946; Richelieu and the French Monarchy, 1949; Seventeenth Century Literature, 1950; Montrose, 1952; The King's Peace, 1955; The King's War, 1958; Truth and Opinion, 1960; Poetry and Politics, 1960; The Trial of Charles I, 1964 (in USA as A Coffin for King Charles, 1964); Milton and his World, 1969; The Political Career of Rubens, 1975; The Spoils of Time, vol. 1, 1984. *Address:* c/o Messrs Collins, 8 Grafton Street, W1.

See also Sir John Wedgwood, Bt.

WEDGWOOD, John Alleyne, CBE 1984; MA, FCIS; Chairman, Southern Electricity Board, 1977–84; *b* 26 Jan. 1920; *s* of Rev. Charles Henry Wedgwood and Myrtle Winifred Perry; *m* 1st, 1942, Freda Mary Lambert (*d* 1963); 2nd, 1974, Lilian Nora Forey; one *s*. *Educ:* Monkton Combe Sch.; Queens' Coll., Cambridge (MA Hons Hist. Tripos). FCIS, CompIEE, CBIM. Served War, Lincs Regt and Durham LI, 1940–46 (Actg Major). Asst Principal, Min. of Fuel and Power, 1946–48; Admin. Officer, British Electricity Authority, 1948–55; Dep. Sec., London Electricity Bd, 1955–58; Dep. Sec., Electricity Council, 1958–65, Sec., 1965–74; Dep. Chm., S Eastern Elec. Bd, 1974–77. President: Inst. of Chartered Secs and Administrators, 1976; Electric Vehicle Assoc., 1983–86; Chm. Bd of Management, Electrical and Electronics Industries Benevolent Assoc., 1977–83. Member: Worshipful Co. of Scriveners, 1973–; SE Econ. Planning Council, 1975–79. Founder Master, Worshipful Co. of Chartered Secs and Administrators, 1978. Freeman, City of London, 1973. *Recreations:* gardening, music, railways, ornithology. *Address:* Pengethley, 16 Rotherfield Road, Henley-on-Thames, Oxon RG9 1NN. *T:* Henley-on-Thames 576804. *Club:* Phyllis Court (Henley).

WEDGWOOD, Sir John Hamilton, 2nd Bt, *cr* 1942; TD 1948; Deputy-Chairman of Josiah Wedgwood and Sons Ltd, until 1966; Member, British National Export Council, 1964–66; *b* 16 Nov. 1907; *s* of Sir Ralph L. Wedgwood, 1st Bt, CB, CMG, TD, and Iris, Lady Wedgwood (*née* Pawson) (*d* 1982); *S* father 1956; *m* 1st, 1933 Diana Mildred (*d* 1976), *d* of late Col Oliver Hawkshaw, TD; three *s* one *d* (and one *s* decd); 2nd, 1982, Dr Pamela Tudor-Craig, FSA, *widow* (*née* Wynn Reeves); one step *d*. *Educ:* Winchester College; Trinity College, Cambridge; and abroad. Served War of 1939–45, Major GSO2 (1b). Chm., Anglo-American Community Relations, Lakenheath Base, 1972–76. Mem., adv. body, Harlaxton Coll. (Univ. of Evansville, Indiana), Lincs, 1975–. President: Utd Commercial Travellers' Assoc., 1959; Samuel Johnson Soc. (Lichfield), 1959. FRSA 1968; FRGS 1973. Liveryman, Worshipful Co. of Painter-Stainers, 1971. Hon. LLD Birmingham, 1966; Hon. DLitt Wm Jewell Coll., Kansas, 1983. *Recreations:* mountaineering, caving, foreign travel (Mem. Travelers' Century Club of California for those who have visited a hundred countries). *Heir: s* (Hugo) Martin Wedgwood [*b* 27 Dec. 1933; *m* 1963, Alexandra Mary Gordon Clark, *er d* of late Judge Alfred Gordon Clark, and Mrs Gordon Clark; one *s* two *d*. *Educ:* Eton; Trinity College, Oxford]. *Address:*

c/o English-Speaking Union, 37 Charles Street, W1. *Clubs:* Arts, Alpine; British Pottery Manufacturers' Federation (Stoke-on-Trent).
See also Dame C. V. Wedgwood.

WEDGWOOD, Dame Veronica; *see* Wedgwood, Dame C. V.

WEE CHONG JIN, Hon. Mr Justice; Chief Justice of the Supreme Court, Singapore; *b* 28 Sept. 1917; *s* of late Wee Gim Puay and Lim Paik Yew; *m* 1955, Cecilia Mary Henderson; three *s* one *d. Educ:* Penang Free Sch.; St John's Coll., Cambridge. Called to Bar, Middle Temple, 1938; admitted Advocate and Solicitor of Straits Settlement, 1940; practised in Penang and Singapore, 1940–57; Puisne Judge, Singapore, 1957, Chief Justice, 1963. *Recreation:* golf. *Address:* c/o Chief Justice's Chambers, Supreme Court, Singapore.

WEE KIM WEE; President of Singapore, since 1985; *b* 4 Nov. 1915; *m* 1936, Koh Sok Hiong; one *s* six *d. Educ:* Pearl's Hill School; Raffles Instn. Joined Straits Times, 1930; United Press Assoc., 1941 and 1945–59; Straits Times, 1959–73 (Dep. Editor, Singapore); High Comr to Malaysia, 1973–80; Ambassador to Japan, 1980–84 and to Republic of Korea, 1981–84; Chm., Singapore Broadcasting Corp., 1984–85. Formerly Member: Rent Control Bd, Film Appeal Cttee; Land Acquisition Bd; Bd of Visiting Justices; Nat. Theatre Trust; former Chm., Singapore Anti-Tuberculosis Assoc.; former Pres., Singapore Badminton Assoc. and Vice-Pres., Badminton Assoc. of Malaya. JP 1966. Public Service Star, 1963; Meritorious Service Medal, 1979. *Address:* Office of the President, Istana, Singapore.

WEEDON, Dr Basil Charles Leicester, CBE 1974; DSc; PhD; FRS 1971; FRSC; Vice-Chancellor, Nottingham University, since 1976; *b* 18 July 1923; *s* of late Charles William Weedon; *m* 1959, Barbara Mary Dawe; one *s* one *d. Educ:* Wandsworth Sch.; Imperial Coll. of Science and Technology (ARCS; DIC). Research Chemist, ICI Ltd (Dyestuffs Div.), 1943–47; Lecturer in Organic Chemistry, Imperial Coll., 1947–55, Reader, 1955–60; Prof. of Organic Chemistry, QMC, 1960–76, Fellow, 1984. Chm., Food Additives and Contaminants Cttee, 1968–83; Mem., EEC Scientific Cttee for Food, 1974–81; Scientific Editor, Pure and Applied Chemistry, 1960–75. Mem., UGC, 1974–76; Chm. Council, National Stone Centre, 1985–. Tilden Lecturer, Chemical Society, 1966. Hon. DTech Brunel Univ., 1975. Meldola Medal, Roy. Inst. of Chemistry, 1952. *Publications:* A Guide to Qualitative Organic Chemical Analysis (with Sir Patrick Linstead), 1956; scientific papers, mainly in Jl Chem. Soc. *Address:* c/o Nottingham University, University Park, Nottingham NG7 2RD. *T:* Nottingham 506101.

WEEDON, Dudley William, BSc(Eng), CEng, FIEE; Director, Hogg Robinson Space & Telecommunications (Consultants) Ltd, since 1983; *b* 25 June 1920; *s* of Reginald Percy and Ada Kate Weedon; *m* 1951, Monica Rose Smith; two *s* one *d. Educ:* Colchester Royal Grammar Sch.; Northampton Polytechnic. Marconi's Wireless Telegraph Co., 1937–48; Cable & Wireless Ltd, 1949–82 (Dir, 1979–82); Chm., Energy Communications Ltd, 1980–82. *Recreation:* sailing. *Address:* 103 Lexden Road, Colchester, Essex.

WEEKES, Rt. Rev. Ambrose Walter Marcus, CB 1970; FKC; Hon. Assistant Bishop of Rochester, since 1986; Hon. Canon of Rochester Cathedral, since 1986; *b* 25 April 1919; *s* of Lt-Comdr William Charles Tinnoth Weekes, DSO, RNVR, and Ethel Sarah Weekes, JP. *Educ:* Cathedral Choir Sch., Rochester; Sir Joseph Williamson's Sch., Rochester; King's Coll., London; AKC 1941, FKC 1972; Scholae Cancellarii, Lincoln. Asst Curate, St Luke's, Gillingham, Kent, 1942–44; Chaplain, RNVR, 1944–46, RN 1946–72; HMS: Ganges, 1946–48; Ulster, 1948–49; Triumph, 1949–51; Royal Marines, Deal, 1951–53; 3 Commando Bde, RM, 1953–55; HMS: Ganges, 1955–56; St Vincent, 1956–58; Tyne, 1958–60; Ganges, 1960–62; 40 Commando, RM, 1962–63; MoD, 1963–65; HMS: Eagle, 1965–66; Vernon, 1966–67; Terror, and Staff of Comdr Far East Fleet, 1967–68; HMS Mercury, 1968–69; Chaplain of the Fleet and Archdeacon for the Royal Navy, 1969–72; QHC, 1969–72; Chaplain of St Andrew, Tangier, 1972–73; Dean of Gibraltar, 1973–77; Assistant Bishop, Diocese of Gibraltar, 1977, until creation of new diocese, 1980; Suffragan Bishop of Gibraltar in Europe, 1980–86; Dean, Pro-Cathedral of the Holy Trinity, Brussels, 1980–86. *Recreations:* yachting, music. *Address:* Deanery Lodge, King's Orchard, Rochester, Kent ME1 1TG. *Clubs:* Naval and Military, Royal Automobile.

WEEKES, Philip Gordon, OBE 1977; CEng, FIMinE; Area Director, South Wales Coalfield, 1973–85, retired; *b* 12 June 1920; *s* of Albert Edwin and Gwladys Magdaline Weekes; *m* 1944, Branwen Mair Jones; two *s* two *d. Educ:* Tredegar Sch.; University Coll., Cardiff (BSc Hons; Fellow, 1982). Jun. official, Tredegar Iron & Coal Co., 1939. Served War, RAF, 1942–44. Manager: Wyllie Colliery, Tredegar (Southern) Colliery Co., 1946; Oakdale Colliery, 1948; seconded to Colonial Office, 1950; Colliery Agent, S Wales, 1951; HQ Work Study Engr, 1952; Gp Manager, Dep. Prod. Manager, Area Prod. Manager, in various areas in S Wales, 1954; Dir of Studies, NCB Staff Coll., 1964; Dep. Dir (Mining), S Midlands Area, 1967; Chief Mining Engr, Nat. HQ, 1970; Dir-Gen. of Mining, Nat. HQ, 1971; part-time Mem., NCB, 1977–84. Director: B.W. Aviation Ltd, 1986–; Flectalon Ltd, 1986–; Barracudaverken (GB) Ltd, 1986–. Member: St John's Priory for Wales, 1978–; Prince of Wales' Cttee, 1978–; IBA Wales Adv. Cttee, 1983–. Gov., United World Coll. of the Atlantic, 1981–. OStJ 1977. *Publications:* articles in professional and techn. jls and transactions. *Address:* Hillbrow, Llantwit Major, South Glamorgan CF6 9RE. *T:* Llantwit Major 2125. *Club:* Cardiff and County; Cambrian Flying (Rhoose).

WEEKS, Alan Frederick; Governor, Sports Aid Foundation, since 1983; *b* 8 Sept. 1923; *s* of late Captain Frederick Charles Weeks, MN, and Ada Frances Weeks; *m* 1947, Barbara Jane (*née* Huckle); one *s* one *d* (and one *s* decd). *Educ:* Brighton, Hove and Sussex Grammar School. Served: MN, Cadet, 1939–41; RNR, Midshipman to Lieut, 1941–46. PRO, Sports Stadium, Brighton, 1946–65; Sec., Brighton Tigers Ice Hockey Club, 1946–65; Dir, London Lions Ice Hockey Club, 1973–74; first Director, Sports Aid Foundn, 1976–83. BBC Commentator: Ice Hockey, Ice Skating, 1951–; Football, 1956–78; Gymnastics, 1962–; Swimming, 1971–; Presenter: Summer Grandstand, 1959–62; Olympics, 1960, 1964; BBC Commentator: Winter Olympics: 1964, 1968, 1972, 1976, 1980, 1984; Olympics: 1968, 1972, 1976, 1980, 1984; World Cup: 1966, 1970, 1974, 1978; Commonwealth Games: 1970, 1974, 1978, 1982, 1986; Presenter, Pot Black, 1970–84. Life Mem., Nat. Skating Assoc. of GB, 1984; Mem. Council, British Ice Hockey Assoc., 1983–; Hon. Life Vice Pres., Brighton and Hove Entertainment Managers' Assoc., 1985. *Recreation:* swimming. *Address:* c/o The Bagenal Harvey Organisation, 1a Cavendish Square, W1M 9HA.

WEEKS, Edward A.; Senior Editor and Consultant, Atlantic Monthly Press; American Field Service (Croix de Guerre, 1918); Fellow American Academy Arts and Sciences; *b* 19 Feb. 1898; *s* of Edward Augustus Weeks and Frederika Suydam; *m* 1925, Frederica Watriss (decd); one *s* one *d*; *m* 1971, Phœbe Adams. *Educ:* Pingry and Battin High School, Elizabeth, NJ; Cornell Univ.; BS Harvard, 1922; Camb. Univ. (Fiske Schol.). Hon. LittD: Northeastern Univ., Boston, 1938; Lake Forest Coll. (Illinois), 1939; Williams Coll., Mass., 1942; Middlebury College, Vt, 1944; University of Alabama, 1945; Dartmouth Coll., 1950; Bucknell Univ., 1952; Boston Univ., 1953; Hobart Coll., 1956;

Univ. of Richmond, 1957; New York Univ., 1958; further hon. degrees from: Clark Univ., Massachusetts, 1958 (Humane Letters); Pomona Coll., Calif., 1958 (LittD); Univ. of Pittsburgh, 1959 (Humane Letters); Univ. of Akron, 1961 (LittD); Northwestern Univ., 1961 (Humane Letters); Rutgers, 1962 (Dr Letters); Union College, 1962 (DCL); Washington and Jefferson, 1962 (Dr Laws). Began as manuscript reader and book salesman with Horace Liveright, Inc., New York City, 1923; Associate Editor, Atlantic Monthly, 1924–28; Editor: Atlantic Monthly Press, 1928–37; Atlantic Monthly, 1938–66. Overseer, Harvard Coll., 1945–51. Henry Johnson Fisher Award, 1968; Irita Van Doren Award, 1970. *Publications:* This Trade of Writing, 1935; The Open Heart, 1955; In Friendly Candour, 1959; Breaking into Print, 1962; Boston, Cradle of Liberty, 1965; The Lowells and their Institute, 1966; Fresh Waters, 1968; The Moisie Salmon Club, a chronicle, 1971; My Green Age: a memoir, 1974; Myopia: 1875–1975, 1975; Writers and Friends, 1982; Editor: Great Short Novels (Anthology), 1941; Jubilee, One Hundred Years of the Atlantic (with Emily Flint), 1957; The Miramichi Fish and Game Club, a history, 1984; contrib. essays, articles, and book reviews to magazines. *Recreations:* fishing, preferably with a light rod; golf; poker. *Address:* 59 Chestnut Street, Boston, Mass 02108, USA; 8 Arlington Street, Boston, Mass 02116, USA. *Cable address:* Lanticmon. *Clubs:* Tavern (Boston); Century (New York).

WEEKS, Major-Gen. Ernest Geoffrey, CB 1946; CBE 1944; MC (and bar); MM (and bar); CD; retired; *b* Charlottetown, PEI, 30 May 1896; *s* of William Arthur and Fanny Weeks; *m* 1930, Vivian Rose Scott, Toronto, Canada; one *s. Educ:* Prince of Wales Coll., Charlottetown, PEI. Canadian Militia, 1910–14; European War, Belgium and France, 1915–19; Canadian Permanent Force from 1920; War of 1939–45, Italy; Maj.-Gen. i/c Administration Canadian Military, HQ, London, England, 1944–45; Adjutant-General Canadian Army, 1946–49; retired, 1949. *Recreations:* gardening, fishing. *Address:* 46 Prince Charles Drive, Charlottetown, PEI C1A 3C2, Canada.

WEEKS, Sir Hugh (Thomas), Kt 1966; CMG 1946; Chairman: Leopold Joseph Holdings Ltd, 1966–78; London American Finance Corporation Ltd, 1970–78; Electrical Industrial Securities, 1971–77; *b* 27 April 1904; *m* 1929; one *d* (and one *s* decd); *m* 1949, Constance Tomkinson; one *d. Educ:* Hendon Secondary and Kilburn Grammar Schools; Emmanuel College, Cambridge (MA). Research and Statistical Manager, Cadbury Bros, till 1939; Director of Statistics, Min. of Supply, 1939–42; Director-General of Statistics and Programmes and Member of Supply Council, 1942–43; Head of Programmes and Planning Division, Ministry of Production, 1943–45. Represented Ministries of Supply and Production on various Missions to N America, 1941–45; Managing Director J. S. Fry & Sons, 1945–47; Mem. Economic Planning Bd, 1947–48, 1959–61; Joint Controller of Colonial Development Corporation, 1948–51; Chm., NIESR, 1970–74. Director: Finance Corp. for Industry, 1956–74; Industrial and Commercial Finance Corp., 1960–74. UK Representative, UN Cttee for Industrial Development, 1961–63. Dep. Chm., Richard Thomas & Baldwins, 1965–68; Dir, S Wales and Strip Mill Bds, BSC, 1968–72. Chairman: EDC for Distributive Trades, 1964–70; Econ. Cttees, FBI and CBI, 1957–72. Pres., British Export Houses Assoc., 1972–74. Medal of Freedom with Silver Palm (US). *Publications:* Market Research (with Paul Redmayne); various articles. *Address:* 14 St John's Street, Chichester, W Sussex PO19 1UU. *T:* Chichester 788631.

WEEKS, John Henry, QC 1983; *b* 11 May 1938; *s* of Henry James and Ada Weeks; *m* 1970, Caroline Mary Ross; one *s* two *d. Educ:* Cheltenham Coll.; Worcester Coll., Oxford (MA). Called to Bar, Inner Temple, 1963; in practice in Chancery, 1963–. *Recreation:* walking the dog. *Address:* 11 New Square, Lincoln's Inn, WC2. *T:* 01–831 0081.

WEETCH, Kenneth Thomas; MP (Lab) Ipswich, since Oct. 1974; *b* 17 Sept. 1933; *s* of Kenneth George and Charlotte Irene Weetch; *m* 1961, Audrey Wilson; two *d. Educ:* Newbridge Grammar Sch., Mon; London School of Economics. MSc(Econ), DipEd (London Inst. of Educn). National Service: Sgt, RAEC, Hong Kong, 1955–57; Walthamstow and Ilford Educn Authorities and Research at LSE, 1957–64; Head of History Dept, Hockerill Coll. of Educn, Bishop's Stortford, 1964–74. Contested (Lab) Saffron Walden, 1970. PPS to Sec. of State for Transport, 1976–79. Member: Lab Select Cttee on Home Affairs, 1981–83; Select Cttee on Parly Comr for Administration, 1983–. *Recreations:* walking, reading, watching Association football, playing the piano in pubs, eating junk food. *Address:* 4 Appleby Close, Ipswich, Suffolk. *Club:* Silent Street Labour (Ipswich).

WEEVERS, Theodoor, LitD (Leyden); Officier in de Orde van Oranje-Nassau; Professor of Dutch Language and Literature, University of London, 1945–71; *b* Amersfoort, 3 June 1904; *e s* of Prof. Theodorus Weevers and Cornelia Jeannette, *d* of J. de Graaff; *m* 1933, Sybil Doreen, 2nd *d* of Alfred Jervis; two *s. Educ:* Gymnasia at Amersfoort and Groningen; Universities of Groningen and Leyden. Lecturer in Dutch at University College and Bedford College, London, 1931–36; Reader in Dutch Language and Literature in University of London, 1937–45; Lecturer in Dutch at Birkbeck College (Univ. of London), 1942–45. During War of 1939–45 Language Supervisor and Announcer-Translator in European News Service of BBC (Dutch Section), 1940–44. Corr. mem. Koninklijke Nederlandse Akademie van Wetenschappen te Amsterdam; hon. mem. Koninklijke Academie voor Nederlandse Taal en Letterkunde, Gent; mem. Maatschappij der Nederlandse Letterkunde. *Publications:* Coornhert's Dolinghe van Ulysse, 1934; De Dolinge van Ulysse door Dierick Volckertsz Coornhert, 1939; The Idea of Holland in Dutch Poetry, 1948; Poetry of the Netherlands in its European Context, 1170–1930, 1960; Mythe en Vorm in de gedichten van Albert Verwey, 1965; Albert Verwey's Portrayal of the Growth of the Poetic Imagination, in Essays in German and Dutch Literature, 1973; Droom en Beeld: De Poëzie van Albert Verwey, 1978; Vision and Form in the Poetry of Albert Verwey, 1986; articles and reviews in Modern Language Review, Mededelingen Kon. Nederlandse Akademie van Wetenschappen, Tijdschrift v. Nederl. Taal en Letterkunde, De Nieuwe Taalgids, Neophilologus, Journal of English and Germanic Philology, German Life and Letters, Spiegel der Letteren, Publications of the English Goethe Society, English Studies. *Recreations:* music, walking. *Address:* Stratton Cottage, 67 Caswell Lane, Clapton-in-Gordano, Bristol BS20 9RT.

WEIDENBAUM, Murray Lew, PhD; Director, Center for the Study of American Business, Washington University, 1975–81 and since 1983; Mallinckrodt Distinguished University Professor, Washington University, 1971–81 and since 1982; *b* 10 Feb. 1927; *m* 1954, Phyllis Green; one *s* two *d. Educ:* City Coll., NY; Columbia Univ. (MA); Princeton Univ. (PhD 1958). Fiscal Economist, Budget Bureau, Washington, 1949–57; Corp. Economist, Boeing Co., Seattle, 1958–63; Sen. Economist, Stanford Res. Inst., 1963–64; Washington Univ., St Louis, 1964–81, 1982–, Prof. and Chm. of Dept of Econs, 1966–69; Asst Sec., Treasury Dept, Washington, 1969–71 (on secondment); Chairman, Council of Economic Advisers, USA, 1981–82. Hon. LLD: Baruch Coll., 1981; Evansville, 1983. Mem., Free Market Hall of Fame, 1983. Nat. Order of Merit, Republic of France, 1985. *Publications:* Federal Budgeting, 1964; Economic Impact of the Vietnam War, 1967; Modern Public Sector, 1969; Economics of Peacetime Defense, 1974; Government-Mandated Price Increases, 1975; Business, Government, and the Public, 1977, 3rd edn 1986; The Future of Business Regulation, 1980. *Address:* Center for the Study of American Business, Washington University, Campus Box 1208, St Louis, Missouri 63130, USA.

WEIDENFELD, family name of **Baron Weidenfeld.**

WEIDENFELD, Baron *cr* 1976 (Life Peer), of Chelsea; **Arthur George Weidenfeld,** Kt 1969; Chairman: Weidenfeld & Nicolson Ltd since 1948, and associated companies; Wheatland Corporation, New York, since 1985; Grove Press, New York, since 1985; Wheatland Foundation, San Francisco and New York, since 1985; *b* 13 Sept. 1919; *o s* of late Max and Rosa Weidenfeld; *m* 1st, 1952, Jane Sieff; one *d*; 2nd, 1956, Barbara Connolly (*née* Skelton) (marr. diss. 1961); 3rd, 1966, Sandra Payson Meyer (marr. diss. 1976). *Educ:* Piaristen Gymnasium, Vienna; University of Vienna (Law); Konsular Akademie (Diplomatic College). BBC Monitoring Service, 1939–42; BBC News Commentator on European Affairs on BBC Empire & North American service, 1942–46. Wrote weekly foreign affairs column, News Chronicle, 1943–44; Founder: Contact Magazine and Books, 1945; Weidenfeld & Nicolson Ltd, 1948. One year's leave as Political Adviser and Chief of Cabinet of President Weizmann of Israel. Vice-Chm., Bd of Governors, Ben Gurion Univ. of the Negev, Beer-Sheva; Governor: Univ. of Tel Aviv; Weizmann Inst. of Science; Bezalel Acad. of Arts, Jerusalem; Mem., Royal Opera House Trust, 1974–; Trustee: Aspen Inst., Colorado, 1985–; Wolfson History Prize; Chm., Mitchell Prize for History of Art. Hon. PhD Ben Gurion Univ. of the Negev, 1984. *Publication:* The Goebbels Experiment, 1943 (also publ. USA). *Recreations:* travel, opera. *Address:* 9 Chelsea Embankment, SW3. *Club:* Garrick.

WEIGALL, Peter Raymond; Managing Director, P. R. Weigall & Co. Ltd, 1976–84; *b* 24 Feb. 1922; *s* of Henry Stuart Brome Weigall and Madeleine Bezard; *m* 1950, Nancy, *d* of Alexander Webster, CIE, and Margaret Webster; one *s* one *d. Educ:* Lycée Janson, Paris; Edinburgh Univ. (BSc). Served War, Captain, RE, 1942–46. Henry Wiggin & Co. Ltd, Birmingham, 1949–51; Petrochemicals Ltd, London, 1951–54; Chemical Industry Admin, Shell Petroleum Co., London, 1954–58; Chemicals Manager, Shell Sekiyu, Tokyo, 1958–63; Shell Internat. Chemical Co., London, 1964–69; Managing Dir, Monteshell, Milan, 1970–73; Industrial Advr to HM Govt, DTI, 1973–75. Member: Movement of Exports EDC, 1974–75; Chemicals EDC, 1974–75; Motor Vehicle Distribution and Repair EDC, 1974–75; Mergers Panel, Office of Fair Trading, 1974–75. *Recreations:* sailing, skiing. *Address:* 16 Fairfield Road, Old Bosham, Chichester, West Sussex PO18 8JH. *T:* Chichester 572500.

WEIGH, Brian, CBE 1982; QPM 1976; HM Inspector of Constabulary for South-West England and part of East Anglia, since 1983; *b* 22 Sept. 1926; *s* of late Edwin Walter Weigh and Ellen Weigh; *m* 1952, Audrey; one *d. Educ:* St Joseph's Coll., Blackpool, Lancs; Queen's Univ., Belfast. All ranks to Supt, Metrop. Police, 1948–67; Asst Chief Constable, 1967–69, Dep. Chief Constable, 1969–74; Somerset and Bath Constab.; Chief Constable: Gloucestershire Constab., 1975–79; Avon and Somerset Constab., 1979–83 (Dep. Chief Constable, 1974–75). Mem., Royal Life Saving Soc. (Dep. Pres., UK Br.). *Recreations:* walking, gardening, golf, badminton. *Address:* Bridge House, Sion Place, Clifton Down, Bristol BS8 4XA.

WEIGHELL, Sidney; General Secretary, National Union of Railwaymen, 1975–Jan. 1983; Member, Trades Union General Council, 1975–83; *b* 31 March 1922; *s* of John Thomas and Rose Lena Weighell; *m* 1st, 1949, Margaret Alison Hunter (killed, 1956); one *s* (one *d*, killed, 1956); 2nd, 1959, Joan Sheila Willetts. *Educ:* Church of England Sch., Northallerton, Yorks. Joined LNER, Motive Power Dept, 1938. Elected to: NUR Exec., 1953; full-time NUR Official, 1954; Asst Gen. Sec., 1965. Labour Party Agent, 1947–52; Mem., Labour Party Exec., 1972–75. Pt-time Bd Mem., BAA plc (formerly BAA), 1983–; Mem., Programme Consultative Panel, Tyne Tees TV Ltd, 1984–. Mem. and Governor, Ditchley Foundn, 1983–. *Publications:* On the Rails, 1983; A Hundred Years of Railway Weighells (autobiog.), 1984. *Recreations:* trout fishing, swimming, gardening; professional footballer, Sunderland FC, 1945–47. *Address:* Blenheim, 2 Moor Park Close, Beckwithshaw, near Harrogate, North Yorkshire HG3 1TR.

WEIGHILL, Air Cdre Robert Harold George, CBE 1973; DFC 1944; Secretary, Rugby Football Union, 1973–86; *b* 9 Sept. 1920; *s* of late Harold James and Elsie Weighill, Heswall, Cheshire; *m* 1946, Beryl (*d* 1981), *d* of late W. Y. Hodgson, Bromborough, Cheshire; two *s* (one *d* decd). *Educ:* Wirral Grammar Sch., Bebington, Cheshire. Served War: RAF, 1941; No 2 F R Sqdn, 1942–44; No 19 F Sqdn, 1944–45. Sqdn Comdr, RAF Coll., Cranwell, 1948–52; Student, RAF Staff Coll., 1952; CO, No 2 FR Sqdn and 138 F Wing, 1953–57; Student, JSSC, 1959; Directing Staff, Imperial Defence Coll., 1959–61; CO, RAF, Cottesmore, 1961–64; Gp Captain Ops, RAF Germany, 1964–67; Asst Comdt, RAF Coll. of Air Warfare, 1967–68; Comdt, RAF Halton, 1968–73. ADC to the Queen, 1968–73. Hon. Sec., Internat. Rugby Football Bd, 1986–. *Recreations:* Rugby (Harlequins, Barbarians, Cheshire, RAF, Combined Services, England), squash, swimming. *Address:* South View, Whitton Road, Twickenham, Mddx. *Clubs:* Royal Air Force, East India, Devonshire, Sports and Public Schools.

WEIGHT, Prof. Carel Victor Morlais, CBE 1961; RA 1965 (ARA 1955); Hon. RBA 1972 (RBA 1934); Hon. RWS 1985; practising artist (painter); Professor Emeritus, since 1973, Senior Fellow, since 1984, Royal College of Art; *b* London, 10 Sept. 1908; *s* of Sidney Louis and Blanche H. C. Weight; British. *Educ:* Sloane School; Goldsmiths' Coll., Univ. of London (Sen. County Scholarship, 1933). First exhibited at Royal Acad., 1931; first one-man show, Cooling Galls, 1934; 2nd and 3rd exhibns, Picture Hire Ltd, 1936 and 1938. Official War Artist, 1945. Royal College of Art: Teacher of Painting, 1947; Fellow, 1956; Prof. of Painting, 1957–73. One-man Shows: Leicester Galls, 1946, 1952, 1968; Zwemmer Gall., 1956, 1959, 1961, 1965; Agnew's, 1959; Russell Cotes Gall., Bournemouth, 1962; Fieldbourne Galleries, 1972; New Grafton Gall., 1974, 1976; exhibited in: 60 Paintings for 1951; (by invitation) exhibns of Contemporary British Art in provinces and overseas, incl. USSR, 1957; Retrospective Exhibns: Reading Museum and Art Gallery, 1970; RCA, 1973; Royal Acad., 1982. Work purchased by: Chantry Bequest for Tate Gall., 1955, 1956, 1957, 1963, 1968; Walker Art Gall., Liverpool; Southampton, Hastings and Oldham Art Galls, etc; Art Gall., Melbourne; Nat. Gall., Adelaide; Arts Council; New Coll., Oxford; Contemporary Art Soc.; V & A Museum. Mural for: Festival of Britain, 1951; Manchester Cathedral, 1963. Picture, Transfiguration, presented by Roman Catholics to the Pope. Member: London Group, 1950; West of England Acad.; Fine Arts Panel, Arts Council, 1951–57; Rome Faculty of Art, 1960. Mem., Cttee of Enquiry into the Economic Situation of the Visual Artist (Gulbenkian Foundn), 1978. Vice-Pres., Artists' Gen. Benevolent Inst., 1980. Trustee, RA, 1975–84. Hon. DUniv. Heriot-Watt, 1983. *Recreations:* music, reading. *Address:* 33 Spencer Road, SW18. *T:* 01–228 6928. *Club:* Chelsea Arts.

WEILER, Terence Gerard; *b* 12 Oct. 1919; *s* of Charles and Clare Weiler; *m* 1952, Truda, *d* of Wilfrid and Mary Woollen; two *s* two *d. Educ:* Wimbledon College; University College, London. Army (RA and Queen's Royal Regiment), 1940–45; UCL, 1937–39 and 1946–47; Home Office: Asst Principal, 1947; Principal, 1948; Asst Sec., 1958; Asst Under-Sec. of State, 1967–80; Mem., Prisons Board, 1962–66, 1971–80; Chm., Working Party: on Habitual Drunken Offenders, 1967–70; on Adjudication Procedures in Prisons, 1975. *Recreations:* cinema, crime fiction. *Address:* 4 Vincent Road, Isleworth, Mddx. *T:* 01–560 7822.

WEINBERG, Prof. Felix Jiri, FRS 1983; CEng, FInstP, FInstE; Professor of Combustion Physics, Imperial College, University of London, since 1967; *b* 2 April 1928; *s* of Victor Weinberg and Nelly Marie (*née* Altschul); *m* 1954, Jill Nesta (*née* Piggott); three *s. Educ:* Univ. of London (BSc, PhD, DIC, DSc). Lecturer 1956–60, Sen. Lectr 1960–64, Reader in Combustion, 1964–67, Dept of Chemical Engrg and Chem. Technology, Imperial Coll. Director, Combustion Inst., 1978– (Chm. British Sect., 1975–80); Founder and first Chm., Combustion Physics Gp, Inst. of Physics, 1974–77, and Rep. on Watt Cttee on Energy, 1979–; Mem. Council, Inst. of Energy, 1976–79; Mem., Royal Institution. Combustion Inst. Silver Combustion Medal 1972, Bernard Lewis Gold Medal 1980. *Publications:* Optics of Flames, 1963; Electrical Aspects of Combustion, 1969; (ed) Combustion Institute European Symposium, 1973; Advanced Combustion Methods, 1986; over 140 papers in Proc., jls and symposia of learned socs. *Recreations:* Eastern philosophies, motor cycling, travel. *Address:* Imperial College, SW7 2BY. *T:* 01–589 5111, ext. 4360; 59 Vicarage Road, SW14 8RY. *T:* 01–876 1540.

WEINBERG, Mark Aubrey; Chairman, Allied Dunbar Assurance (formerly Hambro Life Assurance), since 1984 (Managing Director, 1971–83); *b* 9 Aug. 1931; *s* of Philip and Eva Weinberg; *m* 1st, 1961, Sandra Le Roith (*d* 1978); three *d*; 2nd, 1980, Anouska Hempel; one *s. Educ:* King Edward VII Sch., Johannesburg; Univ. of the Witwatersrand (BCom, LLB); London Sch. of Econs (LLM). Called to the Bar, South Africa, 1955. Barrister, S Africa, 1955–61; Man. Dir, Abbey Life Assurance Co., 1961–70. Chm., Organizing Cttee, Marketing of Investments Bd, 1985–86; Dep. Chm., Securities and Investment Bd, 1986– (Mem., 1985–); Trustee, Tate Gall., 1985–. *Publication:* Take-overs and Mergers, 1962, 4th edn 1980. *Recreations:* ski-ing, tennis. *Address:* 9/15 Sackville Street, W1X 1DE. *T:* 01–434 3211.

WEINBERG, Prof. Steven, PhD; Josey Regental Professor of Science, University of Texas, since 1982; *b* 3 May 1933; *s* of Fred and Eva Weinberg; *m* 1954, Louise Goldwasser; one *d. Educ:* Cornell Univ. (AB); Copenhagen Institute for Theoretical Physics; Princeton Univ. (PhD). Instructor, Columbia Univ., 1957–59; Research Associate, Lawrence Berkeley Laboratory, 1959–60; Faculty, Univ. of California at Berkeley, 1960–69; full prof., 1964; on leave: Imperial Coll., London, 1961–62; Loeb Lectr, Harvard, 1966–67; Vis. Prof., MIT, 1967–69; Prof., MIT, 1969–73; Higgins Prof. of Physics, Harvard Univ., and concurrently Senior Scientist, Smithsonian Astrophysical Observatory, 1973–83 (Sen. Consultant, 1983–). Morris Loeb Vis. Prof., Harvard Univ., 1983–; Dir, Jerusalem Winter Sch. of Theoretical Physics. Lectures: Richtmeyer, Amer. Assoc. of Physics Teachers, 1974; Scott, Cavendish Lab., 1975; Silliman, Yale Univ., 1977; Lauritsen, Calif. Inst. of Technol., 1979; Bethe, Cornell, 1979; Schild, Texas, 1979; de Shalit, Weizmann Inst., 1979; Henry, Princeton, 1981; Harris, Northwestern, 1981; Cherwell-Simon, Oxford, 1983; Bampton, Columbia, 1983; Einstein, Israel Acad. of Arts and Sciences, 1984; Hilldale, Wisconsin, 1985; Dirac, Cambridge, 1986. Fellow, Amer. Acad. of Arts and Scis; Member: US Nat. Acad. of Scis; Amer. Philosophical Soc.; IAU; Amer. Medieval Acad.; Amer. Historical Assoc.; Bd of Overseers, SSC Accelerator. For. Mem., Royal Soc.; Hon. ScD: Knox Coll. 1978; Chicago, 1978; Rochester, 1979; Yale, 1979; City Univ. of New York, 1980; Clark, 1982; Dartmouth Coll., 1984; Hon. PhD Weizmann Inst., 1985; Hon. DLitt, Washington Coll., 1985. J. R. Oppenheimer Prize, 1973; Heinemann Prize in Mathematical Physics, 1977; Amer. Inst. of Physics—US Steel Foundn Science Writing Award, 1977; Elliott Cresson Medal of Franklin Inst., 1979; (jtly) Nobel Prize in Physics, 1979. Co-editor, CUP Monographs on Mathematical Physics. *Publications:* Gravitation and Cosmology: principles and applications of the general theory of relativity, 1972; The First Three Minutes: a modern view of the origin of the universe, 1977; The Discovery of the Subatomic Particles, 1982; numerous articles in learned jls. *Recreation:* reading history. *Address:* Physics Department, University of Texas, Austin, Texas 78712, USA. *T:* (512) 471 4394. *Clubs:* Saturday (Boston, Mass); Cambridge Scientific (Cambridge, Mass); Headliners, Tuesday (Austin, Texas).

WEINBERGER, Caspar Willard; Secretary of Defense, United States of America, since 1981; *b* San Francisco, Calif, 18 Aug. 1917; *s* of Herman and Cerise Carpenter (Hampson) Weinberger; *m* 1942, Jane Dalton; one *s* one *d. Educ:* Harvard Coll. (AB *magna cum laude*); Harvard Law Sch. (LLB). Member: Phi Beta Kappa; Amer. Bar Assoc.; State Bar of Calif. Served in Infantry, Private to Captain, AUS, 1941–45 (Bronze Star). Law Clerk to US Ct of Appeals Judge William E. Orr, 1945–47; with law firm Heller, Ehrman, White & McAuliffe, 1947–69, partner, 1959–69. Member, Calif Legislature from 21st Dist, 1952–58; Vice-Chm., Calif Republican Central Cttee, 1960–62, Chm. 1962–64; Chm., Commn on Calif State Govt Organization and Economy, 1967–68; Dir of Finance, Calif, 1968–69; Chm., Fed. Trade Commn, 1970; Dep. Dir, 1970–72, Dir 1972–73, Office of Management and Budget; Counsellor to the President, 1973; Sec., HEW, 1973–75. Gen. Counsel, Vice-Pres., Dir, Bechtel gp of companies, 1975–81; former Dir, Pepsi Co. Inc., Quaker Oats Co. Formerly staff book reviewer, San Francisco Chronicle; moderator weekly TV prog., Profile, Bay area, station KQED, San Francisco, 1959–68. Frank Nelson Doubleday (Smithsonian) Lectr, 1974; Chm., Pres.'s Commn on Mental Retardation, 1973–75; former Member: Trilateral Commn; Adv. Council, Amer. Ditchley Foundn; Bd of Trustees, St Luke's Hosp., San Francisco; former Nat. Trustee, Nat. Symphony, Washington, DC. *Publications:* contributed a semi-weekly column for a number of Calif newspapers. *Address:* The Pentagon, Washington, DC 20301, USA. *T:* 202/695–5261. *Clubs:* Century (NY); Bohemian and Pacific-Union (San Francisco); Harvard (San Francisco/Washington DC); Burlingame Country.

WEINSTOCK, family name of **Baron Weinstock.**

WEINSTOCK, Baron *cr* 1980 (Life Peer), of Bowden in the County of Wiltshire; **Arnold Weinstock;** Kt 1970; BSc (Econ), FSS; Managing Director, General Electric Co. Ltd, since 1963; *b* 29 July 1924; *s* of Simon and Golda Weinstock; *m* 1949, Netta, *d* of Sir Michael Sobell, *qv*; one *s* one *d. Educ:* University of London. Degree in Statistics. Junior administrative officer, Admiralty, 1944–47; engaged in finance and property development, group of private companies, 1947–54; Radio & Allied Industries Ltd (later Radio & Allied Holdings Ltd), 1954–63 (Managing Director); General Electric Co. Ltd, Director 1961. Dir, Rolls-Royce (1971) Ltd, 1971–73. Trustee: British Museum, 1985–; Royal Philharmonic Soc. Foundn Fund. Mem., Jockey Club. Hon. FRCR 1975. Hon. Fellow: Peterhouse, Cambridge, 1982; LSE, 1985. Hon. Bencher, Gray's Inn, 1982. Hon. DSc: Salford, 1975; Aston, 1976; Bath, 1978; Reading, 1978; Hon. LLD: Leeds, 1978; Wales, 1985; Hon. DTech Loughborough, 1981. *Recreations:* racing and music. *Address:* 7 Grosvenor Square, W1.

WEIPERS, Prof. Sir William (Lee), Kt 1966; Director of Veterinary Education, 1949–68, Dean of the Faculty of Veterinary Medicine, 1968–74, University of Glasgow Veterinary School, retired 1974; *b* 21 Jan. 1904; *s* of Rev. John Weipers, MA, BD and Evelyn Bovelle Lee; *m* 1939, Mary MacLean (*d* 1984); one *d. Educ:* Whitehill Higher Grade School, Dennistoun, Glasgow; Glasgow Veterinary College (MRCVS). General practice, 1925–27; on staff of Royal (Dick) Veterinary College, 1927–29. DVSM 1927; general practice, 1927–49. Dean of Faculties, Glasgow Univ., 1981–84. Member Council of Royal College of Veterinary Surgeons, 1949–74, President, 1963–64. BSc (Glasgow), 1951; FRSE 1953; FRCVS 1958. DUniv Stirling, 1978; Hon. DVMS Glasgow, 1982.

Centennial Medal, Univ. of Pennsylvania Vet. Faculty, 1984. *Publications:* in professional papers. *Recreation:* tree culture. *Address:* Snab Cottage, Duntocher, Dunbartonshire. *T:* Duntocher 73216. *Club:* Royal Scottish Automobile.

WEIR, family name of **Baron Inverforth** and **Viscount Weir.**

WEIR, 3rd Viscount *cr* 1938; **William Kenneth James Weir;** Chairman, The Weir Group PLC, since 1983 (Vice-Chairman, 1981–83, Chairman and Chief Executive, 1972–81); Deputy Chairman, Charterhouse J. Rothschild plc, since 1984; a Vice Chairman, J. Rothschild Holdings plc, since 1985; Director: BICC Ltd, since 1977; Transcontinental Services Group NV; *b* Nov 1933; *e s* of 2nd Viscount Weir CBE, and Lucy (*d* 1972), *d* of late James F. Crowdy, MVO; *S* father, 1975; *m* 1st, 1964, Diana (marr. diss.), *o d* of Peter L. MacDougall; one *s* one *d*; 2nd, 1976, Mrs Jacqueline Mary Marr, *er d* of late Baron Louis de Chollet. *Educ:* Eton; Trinity Coll., Cambridge (BA). Dir, BSC, 1972–76. Dir, 1970, Chm., 1975–82, Great Northern Investment Trust Ltd; Co-Chm., RIT and Northern plc, 1982–83. Member: London Adv. Cttee, Hongkong & Shanghai Banking Corp., 1980–; Court, Bank of England, 1972–84. Mem., Scottish Econ. Council, 1972–. *Recreations:* shooting, golf, fishing. *Heir: s* Hon. James William Hartland Weir, *b* 6 June 1965. *Address:* Rodinghead, Mauchline, Ayrshire. *T:* Fiveways 233. *Club:* White's.

WEIR, Hon. Lord; David Bruce Weir; a Senator of the College of Justice in Scotland, since 1985; *b* 19 Dec. 1931; *yr s* of late James Douglas Weir and Kathleen Maxwell Weir (*née* Auld); *m* 1964, Katharine Lindsay, *yr d* of Hon. Lord Cameron, *qv*; three *s*. *Educ:* Kelvinside Academy; Glasgow Academy; The Leys Sch., Cambridge; Glasgow Univ. (MA, LLB). Royal Naval Reserve, 1955–64, Lieut RNR. Admitted to Faculty of Advocates, 1959; Advocate Depute for Sheriff Court, 1964; Standing Junior Counsel: to MPBW, 1969; to DoE, 1970; QC (Scot.) 1971; Advocate Depute, 1979–82. Chairman: Medical Appeal Tribunal, 1972–77; Pensions Appeal Tribunal for Scotland, 1978–84 (Pres., 1984–85); NHS Tribunal, Scotland, 1983–85; Member: Criminal Injuries Compensation Bd, 1974–79 and 1984–85; Transport Tribunal, 1979–85. *Recreations:* sailing, music. *Address:* Parliament House, Edinburgh EH1 1RQ. *T:* 031–225 2595. *Clubs:* New (Edinburgh); Royal Highland Yacht.

WEIR, Rear-Adm. Alexander Fortune Rose, CB 1981; JP; self-employed marine consultant; *b* 17 June 1928; *s* of late Comdr Patrick Wylie Rose Weir and Minna Ranken Forrester Weir (*née* Fortune); *m* 1953, Ann Ross Hamilton Crawford, Ardmore, Co. Londonderry; four *d*. *Educ:* Royal Naval Coll., Dartmouth. FBIM 1979; AVCM 1982. Cadet, 1945–46; Midshipman, 1946–47; Actg Sub-Lieut under trng, HMS Zephyr, Portland, 1947; Sub-Lieut professional courses, 1947–48; Sub-Lieut and Lieut, HMS Loch Arkaig, Londonderry Sqdn, 1949–51; ADC to Governor of Victoria, Aust., 1951–53; HMS Mariner, Fishery Protection Sqdn, Home waters and Arctic, 1953–54; qual. as Navigating Officer, 1954; HMS St Austell Bay, WI, Navigating Officer, 1955–56; HMS Wave, Fishery Protection Sqdn, Home, Arctic and Iceland, 1956–58; Lt-Comdr, advanced navigation course, 1958; Staff ND Officer, Flag Officer Sea Trng at Portland, Dorset, 1958–61; HMS Plymouth, Staff Officer Ops, 4th Frigate Sqdn, Far East Station, 1961–62; Comdr 1962; Trng Comdr, BRNC Dartmouth, 1962–64; Comd, HMS Rothesay, WI Station, 1965–66; Staff of C-in-C Portsmouth, Staff Officer Ops, 1966–68; 2nd in Comd and Exec. Officer, HMS Eagle, 1968–69; Captain 1969; jssc 1969–70; Pres., Far East Comd Midshipman's Bd, 1970; Asst Dir Naval Operational Requirements, MoD(N), 1970–72; Captain (F) 6th Frigate Sqdn (8 ships) and HMS Andromeda, 1972–74; NATO Def. Coll., Rome, 1974–75; ACOS Strategic Policy Requirements and Long Range Objectives, SACLANT, 1975–77; Captain HMS Bristol, 1977–78; Rear-Adm. 1978; Dep. Asst Chief of Staff (Ops) to SACEUR, 1978–81. FBIM. Associate, Victoria Coll. of Music. Member: Nautical Inst.; Royal Inst. of Navigation. Licenced Royal Naval Lay Reader, 1981; Licensed Lay Reader, St Kew Parish, Dio. Truro, 1984–. JP: Chichester, 1982–84; Bodmin, 1985–. *Recreations:* sailing, shooting, golf. *Address:* Tipton, St Kew, Bodmin, Cornwall PL30 3ET. *T:* St Mabyn 289. *Clubs:* Royal Navy 1765 and 1785, Institute of Directors; Royal Yacht Squadron, Royal Yachting Association, Royal Naval Sailing Association; Caravan (Sussex); United Retriever (Hants).

WEIR, Very Rev. Andrew John, MSc, DD; Clerk of Assembly and General Secretary, The Presbyterian Church in Ireland, 1964–85, Emeritus since 1985; *b* 24 March 1919; *s* of Rev. Andrew Weir and Margaret Weir, Missionaries to Manchuria of the Presbyterian Church in Ireland. *Educ:* Campbell Coll., Belfast; Queen's Univ., Belfast; New Coll., Edinburgh; Presbyterian Coll., Belfast. Ordained, 1944; Missionary to China, 1945–51; Minister, Trinity Presbyterian Church, Letterkenny, Co. Donegal, 1952–62; Asst Clerk of Assembly and Home Mission Convener, The Presbyterian Church in Ireland, 1962–64. Moderator of the General Assembly, The Presbyterian Church in Ireland, 1976–77. *Address:* 18 Cyprus Park, Belfast BT5 6EA. *T:* Belfast 651276.

WEIR, Rev. Cecil James Mullo, MA, DD, DPhil; Professor of Hebrew and Semitic Languages, University of Glasgow, 1937–68; *b* Edinburgh, 4 Dec. 1897; *e s* of late James Mullo Weir, SSC, FSAScot, Solicitor, Edinburgh; unmarried. *Educ:* Royal High School, Edinburgh; Universities of Edinburgh, Marburg, Paris and Leipzig; Jesus College, Oxford. Served European War, 1917–19, with Expeditionary Force in France, Belgium and Germany; Tutor in Hebrew, University of Edinburgh, 1921–22; MA Edinburgh with 1st Class Honours in Classics, 1923; 1st Class Honours in Semitic Languages, 1925; BD Edinburgh, 1926; DPhil Oxford, 1930; Minister of Orwell, Kinross-shire, 1932–34; Rankin Lecturer and Head of Department of Hebrew and Ancient Semitic Languages, University of Liverpool, 1934–37; Lecturer in the Institute of Archæology, Liverpool, 1934–37. President, Glasgow Archæological Soc., 1945–48; Dean of Faculty of Divinity, Univ. of Glasgow, 1951–54; Hon. DD (Edinburgh), 1959; FRAS, FSAScot. *Publications:* A Lexicon of Accadian Prayers in the Rituals of Expiation, 1934; contributed to A Companion to the Bible (ed Manson), 1939; Fortuna Domus, 1952; Documents from Old Testament Times (ed Thomas), 1958; Hastings's Dictionary of the Bible, 1963; A Companion to the Bible (ed Rowley), 1963; Archæology and Old Testament Study (ed Thomas), 1967; edited Transactions of Glasgow University Oriental Soc., Studia Semitica et Orientalia, Transactions of Glasgow Archæological Soc.; articles and reviews of books. *Recreations:* golf, travel. *Address:* 4/17 Gillsland Road, Edinburgh EH10 5BW. *T:* 031–228 6965.

WEIR, David Bruce; *see* Weir, Hon. Lord.

WEIR, Gillian; concert organist; *b* 17 Jan. 1941; *d* of Cecil Alexander Weir and Clarice M. Foy Weir. *Educ:* Royal College of Music, London. LRSM, LRAM, LTCL; Hon. FRCO. Winner of St Albans Internat. Organ Competition, 1964; Début, 1965: Royal Festival Hall, solo recital; Royal Albert Hall, concerto soloist, opening night of Promenade Concerts; since then, worldwide career solely as touring concert organist; concerto appearances with all major British orchestras, also with Boston Symphony, Seattle Symphony, Württemberg Chamber Orch., and others; solo appearances at leading internat. Festivals, incl. Bath, Aldeburgh, Edinburgh, English Bach, Europalia, Europe and USA (AGO Nat. Conventions, RCCO Diamond Jubilee Nat. Convention, etc). Frequent radio and television appearances: BBC Third Prog., USA, Australasia, Europe; TV film, Toccata: two weeks in the life of Gillian Weir, 1981 (shown NZ TV 1982); many first performances, incl. major works by Fricker, Connolly, Camilleri, Messiaen. Master-classes, adjudicator internat. competitions, UK, France, N America. Hon. FRCO and Mem. Council, RCO, 1977– (first woman Mem.); Pres., Incorp. Assoc. of Organists, 1981–83 (first woman Pres.). Internat. Performer of the Year Award, NY Amer. Guild of Organists, 1981; Internat. Music Guide's Musician of the Year Award, 1982; Turnovsky Prize for outstanding achievement in the arts, Turnovsky Foundn for the Arts, NZ, 1985. Hon. Fellow, Royal Canadian Coll. of Organists, 1983; Hon. DMus, Victoria Univ. of Wellington, NZ, 1983. *Publications:* contributor to: Grove's Internat. Dictionary of Music and Musicians, 1980; musical jls and periodicals. *Recreation:* theatre. *Address:* c/o Prima Artists Management, 23 Pepys Road, SE14. *T:* 01–639 1052. *Club:* University Women's.
See also Sir R. B. Weir.

WEIR, Sir Michael (Scott), KCMG 1980 (CMG 1974); HM Diplomatic Service, retired; Ambassador, Cairo, 1979–85; *b* 28 Jan. 1925; *s* of Archibald and Agnes Weir; *m* 1953, Alison Walker; two *s* two *d*; *m* 1976, Hilary Reid; two *s*. *Educ:* Dunfermline High School; Balliol College, Oxford. Served RAF (Flt Lt), 1944–47; subseq. HM Diplomatic Service; Foreign Office, 1950; Political Agent, Trucial States, 1952–54; FO, 1954–56; Consul, San Francisco, 1956–58; 1st Secretary: Washington, 1958–61; Cairo, 1961–63; FO, 1963–68; Counsellor, Head of Arabian Dept, 1966; Dep. Political Resident, Persian Gulf, Bahrain, 1968–71; Head of Chancery, UK Mission to UN, NY, 1971–73; Asst Under-Sec. of State, FCO, 1974–79. *Recreations:* golf, music. *Address:* 37 Lansdowne Gardens, SW8.

WEIR, Peter Lindsay, AM 1982; film director, since 1969; *b* 21 Aug. 1944; *s* of Lindsay Weir and Peggy Barnsley Weir; *m* 1966, Wendy Stites; one *s* one *d*. *Educ:* Scots Coll., Sydney; Vaucluse High Sch.; Sydney Univ. Short Film: Homesdale, 1971; Feature Films: The Cars That Ate Paris, 1973; Picnic at Hanging Rock, 1975; Last Wave, 1977; The Plumber (for TV), 1979; Gallipoli, 1980; The Year of Living Dangerously, 1982; Witness, 1985. *Address:* c/o Palm Beach, NSW 2108, Australia.

WEIR, Richard Stanton; Secretary General (Chief Executive), Building Societies Association, 1981–86; *b* 5 Jan. 1933; *o s* of Brig. R. A. Weir, OBE and Dr M. L. Cowan; *m* 1961, Helen Eugenie Guthrie; one *d*. *Educ:* Repton Sch., Derbys; Christ Church, Oxford (MA). Called to the Bar, Inner Temple, 1957. Commnd 3rd Carabiniers (Prince of Wales' Dragoon Guards), 1952. Head of Legal Dept, Soc. of Motor Mfrs and Traders Ltd, 1958–61; Exec., British Motor Corp. Ltd, 1961–64; Dep. Co. Sec., Rank Organisation Ltd, 1964–67; Head of Admin, Rank Leisure Services, 1967–69; Sec., CWS Ltd, 1969–74; Dir, The Retail Consortium, 1975–81. Mem., Consumer Protection Adv. Cttee set up under Fair Trading Act, 1973, 1973–76. *Recreations:* reading, walking, shooting. *Address:* 2 Lamont Road, SW10. *T:* 01–352 4809. *Club:* United Oxford & Cambridge University.

WEIR, Sir Roderick (Bignell), Kt 1984; Chairman, Crown Corp. Ltd, and all its major subsidiaries, since 1983; *b* 14 July 1927; *s* of Cecil Alexander Weir and Clarice Mildred Foy; *m* 1952, Loys Agnes Wilson (*d* 1984); one *d*; *m* 1986, Anna Jane Mcfarlane. *Educ:* Wanganui Boys' Coll., NZ. Various positions to regional manager, Dalgety NZ Ltd, Wanganui, 1943–63; formed stock and station co., Rod Weir & Co. Ltd, 1963; formed Crown Consolidated Ltd, 1976; Chm., McKechnie Brothers NZ; Director: James Smith; Rangatira; Sun Alliance Insurance Ltd; Provident Life Assurance Co.; Fluid Control. Board Mem., NZ Apple and Pear Marketing Board; Past Pres., NZ Stock and Station Agents' Assoc. Hon. Consul-Gen. for Austria, 1982–. *Recreations:* fishing, shooting, boxing. *Address:* 11a Salamanca Road, Kelburn, Wellington, New Zealand. *T:* Wellington 724–033; The Grove, Main Road, Waikanae, New Zealand. *Clubs:* Wellington (Wellington); Heretaunga (Lower Hutt); Levin (Levin).
See also Gillian Weir.

WEISKRANTZ, Lawrence, FRS 1980; Professor of Psychology, Oxford University, since 1967; Fellow, Magdalen College, Oxford; *b* 28 March 1926; *s* of Dr Benjamin Weiskrantz and Rose (*née* Rifkin); *m* 1954, Barbara Collins; one *s* one *d*. *Educ:* Girard College; Swarthmore; Univs of Oxford and Harvard. Part-time Lectr, Tufts University, 1952; Research Assoc., Inst. of Living, 1952–55; Sen. Postdoctoral Fellow, US Nat. Res. Coun., 1955–56; Research Assoc., Cambridge Univ., 1956–61; Asst Dir of Research, Cambridge Univ., 1961–66; Reader in Physiological Psychology, Cambridge Univ., 1966–67. Kenneth Craik Research Award, St John's Coll., Cambridge, 1975–76. Dep. Editor, Brain, 1981–; Co-Editor, Oxford Psychology Series, 1979–. *Publications:* (jtly) Analysis of Behavioural Change, 1967; The Neuropsychology of Cognitive Function, 1982; Animal Intelligence, 1985; articles in Science, Nature, Quarterly Jl of Experimental Psychology, Jl of Comparative and Physiological Psychology, Animal Behaviour. *Recreations:* music, walking. *Address:* Department of Experimental Psychology, South Parks Road, Oxford OX1 3UD.

WEISMAN, Malcolm; Barrister-at-law; a Recorder of the Crown Court, since 1980; *s* of David and Jeanie Pearl Weisman; *m* 1958, Rosalie, *d* of Dr and Mrs A. Spiro; two *s*. *Educ:* Harrogate Grammar Sch.; Parmiter's Sch.; London School of Economics; St Catherine's Coll., Oxford (MA). Blackstone Pupillage Prize. Chaplain (Sqdn Ldr), Royal Air Force, 1956; called to Bar, Middle Temple, 1961; Senior Jewish Chaplain, HM Forces, 1972. Religious advisor to small congregations, and Hon. Chaplain, Oxford, Cambridge and new universities, 1963–; Chm. and Sec.-Gen., Allied Air Forces in Europe Chief of Chaplains Cttee, 1981–; Mem., Cabinet of the Chief Rabbi. Asst Comr of Parly Boundaries, 1976–85. Mem., Senior Common Room, Essex, Kent and Lancaster Univs, 1964–; Member of Court: Univ. of Lancaster, 1970–; Warwick Univ., 1983–; Univ. of East Anglia, 1985–. Governor, Parmiter's Sch., 1980–. *Recreations:* travelling, reading, doing nothing. *Address:* 1 Gray's Inn Square, WC1R 5AA. *T:* 01–405 8946.

WEISS, Mrs Althea McNish; *see* McNish, A. M.

WEISS, Sir Eric, Kt 1980; President, Foseco Minsep plc, since 1979 (Chairman, 1969–78); *b* 30 Dec. 1908; *s* of late Solomon Weiss and Ada Weiss; *m* 1934, Greta Kobaltzky; two *s* two *d*. *Educ:* Augustinus Gymnasium, Weiden, Germany; Neues Gym., Nurnberg, Germany. Founder, Foundry Services Ltd (original co. of Foseco Group), 1932; Chm., Minerals Separation Ltd, 1964; Chm., Foseco Minsep Ltd, 1969, when co. formed by merger of Foseco Ltd with Minerals Separation Ltd. Underwriting Mem., Lloyd's, 1976–79. United World Colleges: Dep. Pres., 1973–76; Mem., UK Commn of United World Colls Project, 1968–74; Mem., Internat. Council, 1969–76; Mem., Bd of Dirs, 1970–76; Mem. Bd Governors, United World Coll. of Atlantic, 1976–85. Mem., Inst. of British Foundrymen. Trustee: Inst. for Archaeo-Metallurgical Studies, 1976–82; Oakham Sch., 1963–84. *Recreations:* golf, travel. *Address:* The Manor House, Little Marlow, Bucks SL7 3RZ. *T:* Marlow 2824. *Club:* Garrick.

WEISS, Prof. Robert Anthony, (Robin), PhD; FRCPath; Director, Institute of Cancer Research, since 1980; *b* 20 Feb. 1940; *s* of Hans Weiss and Stefanie Löwensohn; *m* 1964, Margaret Rose D'Costa; two *d*. *Educ:* University College London (BSc, PhD). Lecturer in Embryology, University Coll. London, 1963–70; Eleanor Roosevelt Internat. Cancer Research Fellow, Univ. of Washington, Seattle, 1970–71; Visiting Associate Prof., Microbiology, Univ. of Southern California, 1971–72; Staff Scientist, Imperial Cancer

Research Fund Laboratories, 1972–80, Gustav Stern Award in Virology, 1973. *Publications:* RNA Tumour Viruses, 1982, 2nd edn (2 vols) 1985; various articles on cell biology, virology and genetics. *Recreations:* music, natural history. *Address:* Institute of Cancer Research, Chester Beatty Laboratories, Fulham Road, SW3 6JB.

WEISSKOPF, Prof. Victor Frederick; Professor of Physics at Massachusetts Institute of Technology, Cambridge, Mass, USA, since 1946 (on leave, 1961–65); Chairman, Department of Physics, MIT, 1967–73; *b* 19 Sept. 1908; *m* 1934, Ellen Margrete Tvede; one *s* one *d*. *Educ:* Göttingen, Germany. PhD 1931. Research Associate: Berlin Univ., 1932; Eidgenossiche Technische Hochschule (Swiss Federal Institute of Technology), Zürich, 1933–35; Inst. for Theoretical Physics, Copenhagen, 1936; Asst Professor of Physics, Univ. of Rochester, NY, USA, 1937–43; Dep. Division Leader, Manhattan Project, Los Alamos, USA, 1943–45; Director-Gen., CERN, Geneva, 1961–65. Chm., High Energy Physics Adv. Panel, AEC, 1967–75. Mem., Nat. Acad. of Sciences, Washington, 1954; Pres., Amer. Acad. of Arts and Sciences, 1976–79; Corresp. Member: French Acad. of Sciences, 1957; Scottish Acad. of Scis, 1959; Royal Danish Scientific Soc., 1961; Bavarian Acad. of Scis, 1962; Austrian Acad. of Scis, 1963; Spanish Acad. of Scis, 1964; Soviet Acad. of Scis, 1976; Pontifical Acad. of Scis, 1976. Hon. Fellow: Weizmann Inst., Rehovot, Israel, 1962; Inst. of Physics, France, 1980. Hon. PhD: Manchester, 1961; Uppsala, 1964; Yale, 1964; Chicago, 1967; Hon. DSc: Montreal, 1959; Sussex, 1961; Lyon, 1962; Basle, 1962; Bonn, 1963; Genève, 1964; Oxford, 1965; Vienna, 1965; Paris, 1966; Copenhagen, 1966; Torino, 1968; Yale, 1968; Upsala, 1969; Harvard, 1984; Graz, 1985. Cherwell-Simon Memorial Lecturer, Oxford, 1963–64. Planck Medal, 1956; Gamov Award, 1969; Prix Mondial Del Duca, 1972; Killian Award, 1973; Smoluchovski Medal, Polish Physical Soc., 1979; Nat. Medal of Science, 1979; Wolf Prize (Israel), 1981. Légion d'Honneur (France), 1959; Pour le Mérite Order, Germany, 1978. *Publications:* Theoretical Nuclear Physics, 1952; Knowledge and Wonder, 1962; Physics in the XX Century, 1972; Concepts of Particle Physics, 1984; papers on theoretical physics in various journals. *Address:* 36 Arlington Street, Cambridge, Mass 02140, USA.

WEISSMÜLLER, Alberto Augusto, FIB; Representative of Banca Commerciale Italiana in Washington, DC, since 1983; Director, North American Bancorp Inc. (a subsidiary of Banca Commerciale Italiana), since 1982; *b* 2 March 1927; *s* of late Carlos Weissmüller and Michela Cottura; *m* 1976, Joan Ann Freifrau von Süsskind-Schwendi (*née* Smithson); one *s* one *d* by previous *m*. *Educ:* Univ. of Buenos Aires, Argentina; Illinois Inst. of Technol., Chicago, USA. Civil Engr, 1952; FIB 1977. The Lummus Co., New York, 1958–59; Office of Graham Parker, NY, 1960–62; Bankers Trust Co., NY, 1962–71: Edge Act subsid., 1962–64; Asst Treasurer, and mem., Bd of Corporation Financiera Nacional, Colombia, 1964–65; Asst Vice-Pres., 1965–67; Vice-Pres., 1967–71; Rome Rep., 1968–71; Crocker National Bank, San Francisco, seconded to United Internat. Bank (now Privatbanken Ltd), London, as Chief Exec., 1971–79; Chief Adviser, Bank of England, 1979–81; Chief Exec. (UK), Banca Commerciale Italiana, 1981–82; Chm., BCI Ltd, London, 1981–83; Dir, Long Island Trust Co., 1982–. *Publication:* Castles from the Heart of Spain, 1977. *Recreations:* medieval fortified architecture, photography (architectural). *Address:* Banca Commerciale Italiana, 801 Eighteenth Street, NW, Washington, DC 20006, USA. *Club:* Board Room (New York).

WEITZ, Dr Bernard George Felix, OBE 1965; DSc; MRCVS; FIBiol; Chief Scientist, Ministry of Agriculture, Fisheries and Food, 1977–81; *b* London, 14 Aug. 1919; *m* 1945, Elizabeth Shine; one *s* one *d*. *Educ:* St Andrew, Bruges, Belgium; Royal Veterinary College, London. MRCVS 1942; DSc London 1961. Temp. Research Worker, ARC Field Station, Compton, Berks, 1942; Research Officer, Veterinary Laboratory, Min. of Agric. and Fisheries, 1942–47; Asst Bacteriologist, Lister Inst. of Preventive Medicine, Elstree, Herts, 1947; Head of Serum Dept, 1952; Dir, Nat. Inst. for Res. in Dairying, Univ. of Reading, Shinfield, Berks, 1967–77. Vis. Prof., Dept of Agriculture and Horticulture, Univ. of Reading, 1980–. Member: ARC, 1978–81; NERC, 1978–81. Hon. FRASE, 1977. *Publications:* many contribs to scientific journals on Immunology and Tropical Medicine. *Recreations:* music, croquet. *Address:* Grazebrook, Brockhampton, Glos GL54 5XL.

WEITZMAN, David, QC 1951; Barrister-at-Law; *b* 18 June 1898; *s* of Percy Weitzman; *m* 1st, 1925 (wife *d* 1950); one *s* one *d*; 2nd, 1955, Lena (*d* 1969), *widow* of Dr S. H. Dundon, Liverpool; 3rd, 1972, Vivienne Hammond. *Educ:* Hutchesons' Grammar School, Glasgow; Manchester Central School; Manchester University. Private, 3rd Battalion Manchester Regiment, 1916; BA (History Honours), 1921; called to Bar (Gray's Inn), 1922; member of Northern Circuit. Member of Labour Party since 1923. Contested (Lab) Stoke Newington, 1935; MP (Lab) Stoke Newington, 1945–50, Hackney North and Stoke Newington, 1950–79. *Recreation:* golf. *Address:* Devereux Chambers, Devereux Court, Temple, WC2R 3JJ. *T:* 01–353 7534.

See also P. Weitzman.

WEITZMAN, Peter, QC 1973; a Recorder of the Crown Court, since 1974; Deputy Leader, Midland and Oxford Circuit, since 1985; *b* 20 June 1926; *s* of David Weitzman, *qv*, and late Fanny Weitzman; *m* 1954, Anne Mary Larkam; two *s* two *d*. *Educ:* Cheltenham Coll.; Christ Church, Oxford (MA). Royal Artillery, 1945–48. Called to Bar, Gray's Inn, 1952; Bencher, 1981. Mem., Senate of Inns of Court, 1980–81, 1984–. *Recreations:* hedging and ditching. *Address:* 21 St James's Gardens, W11; Little Leigh, Kingsbridge, Devon.

WELANDER, Rev. Canon David Charles St Vincent; Canon Residentiary, Gloucester Cathedral, since 1975; *b* 22 Jan. 1925; *s* of late Ernest Sven Alexis Welander, Orebro and Uppsala, Sweden, and Louisa Georgina Downes Welander (*née* Panter) *m* 1952, Nancy O'Rorke Stanley; two *s* three *d*. *Educ:* Unthank Coll., Norwich: London Univ. (BD 1947, Rubie Hebrew Prize 1947); ALCD (1st Cl.) 1947; Toronto Univ., 1947–48 (Hon. Mem. Alumni, Wycliffe Coll., 1948). FSA 1981. Deacon 1948, Priest 1949; Asst Curate, Holy Trinity, Norwich, 1948–51; Chaplain and Tutor, London Coll. of Divinity, 1952–56; Vicar: of Iver, Bucks, 1956–62; of Christ Church, Cheltenham, 1963–75; Rural Dean of Cheltenham, 1973–75. Member: Council, St Paul's and St Mary's Colls of Educn, Cheltenham, 1963–78; Council, Malvern Girls' Coll., 1982–; Bishops' Cttee on Inspections of Theol Colls, 1967–81; Sen. Inspector of Theol Colls, 1970–84; Mem., Gen. Synod of C of E, 1970–85; Trustee, Church Patronage Trust, 1969–78. Canon-Librarian of Gloucester, 1975–. *Publications:* History of Iver, 1954; Gloucester Cathedral, 1979; The Stained Glass of Gloucester Cathedral, 1984; contrib. Expository Times, etc. *Recreations:* walking, sailing, church architecture, music. *Address:* 6 College Green, Gloucester GL1 2LX. *T:* Gloucester 21954. *Club:* Royal Commonwealth Society.

WELBORE KER, Keith R.; *see* Ker.

WELBOURN, Prof. Richard Burkewood, MA, MD, FRCS; Professor of Surgical Endocrinology, Royal Postgraduate Medical School, University of London, 1979–82, now Emeritus Professor; *b* 1919; *y s* of late Burkewood Welbourn, MEng, MIEE, and Edith Welbourn, Rainhill, Lancs; *m* 1944, Rachel Mary Haighton, BDS, Nantwich, Cheshire; one *s* four *d*. *Educ:* Rugby School; Emmanuel College, Cambridge; Liverpool University. MB, BChir 1942; FRCS 1948; MA, MD Cambridge, 1953. War of 1939–45: RAMC. Senior Registrar, Liverpool Royal Infirmary, 1948; Research Asst, Dept of Surgery, Liverpool Univ., 1949. Fellow in Surgical Research, Mayo Foundation, Rochester, Minn., 1951. Professor of Surgical Science, Queen's University of Belfast, 1958–63; Surgeon, Royal Victoria Hospital, Belfast, 1951–63 and Belfast City Hosp., 1962–63; Prof. of Surgery, Univ. of London and Dir, Dept of Surgery, RPMS and Hammersmith Hosp., 1963–79; Hon. Consultant Surgeon, Hammersmith Hosp., 1979–84. Consultant Adviser in Surgery to Dept of Health and Social Security, 1971–79; Consultant (Vis. Schol.), Dept of Surgery, Univ. of California, LA, 1983–. Member: Council, MRC, 1971–75; Council, Royal Postgraduate Med. Sch, 1963–82. Hunterian Professor, RCS of England, 1958 (James Berry Prize, 1970). Member: Society of Sigma XI; British Medical Association; Internat. Assoc. of Endocrine Surgery, 1979– (Co-ordinator, Exec. Council, 1985–); Exec. Cttee, Internat. Surgical Soc., 1983–. Formerly Mem. Council, British Soc. of Gastro-enterology and Assoc. of Surgeons; 58th Member King James IV Surgical Association Inc.; Fellow, West African Coll. of Surgeons; FRSM (Former Mem. Council, Section of Endocrinology, former Vice-Pres., Section of Surgery); Hon. Fellow Amer. Surgical Assoc.; Hon. Mem., Soc. for Surgery of the Alimentary Tract; formerly: Pres., Surgical Res. Soc.; British Assoc. of Endocrine Surgeons (Hon. Mem.); Chm., Assoc. of Profs of Surgery; Mem., Jt Cttee for Higher Surgical Training; formerly Examr in Surgery, Univs of Manchester, Glasgow, Oxford, Sheffield, Edinburgh, QUB, and Liverpool; formerly Examr in Applied Physiology, RCS. Chm., Editorial Cttee, Journal of Medical Ethics; former Member: Editorial Cttee, Gut; Exec. Cttee, British Jl of Surgery. Formerly: Pres., Internat. Surgical Gp; Chm. Governing Body, Inst. of Medical Ethics; Pres., Prout Club. Hon. MD Karolinska Inst., Stockholm, 1974; Hon. Mem., Roy. Coll. of Surgeons of Univs of Denmark, 1978; Hon. FACS 1984. Hon. DSc QUB, 1985. *Publications:* (with D. A. D. Montgomery): Clinical Endocrinology for Surgeons, 1963, rev. edn, Medical and Surgical Endocrinology, 1975; (with A. S. Duncan and G. R. Dunstan) Dictionary of Medical Ethics, 1977, 2nd edn 1980, American edn 1981; contrib. chaps to Textbook of British Surgery, ed Souttar & Goligher; Surgery of Peptic Ulcer, ed Wells & Kyle; Progress in Clinical Surgery, ed Rodney Smith; British Surgical Practice, ed Rock-Carling & Ross; Scientific Foundations of Surgery, ed Wells & Kyle; Scientific Foundations of Oncology, ed Symington and Carter; Scientific Foundations of Family Medicine, ed Fry, Gambrill & Smith; Surgical Management, ed Taylor, Chisholm, O'Higgins & Shields; Recent Advances in Surgery, etc; papers, mainly on gastro-intestinal and endocrine surgery and physiology, in med. and surg. jls. *Recreations:* reading, writing, gardening, music. *Address:* 102 Gloucester Court, Kew Road, Kew, Richmond, Surrey TW9 3DZ; 2 The Beeches, Elsley Road, Tilehurst, Berks RG3 6RQ.

WELBY, Sir Bruno; *see* Welby, Sir R. B. G.

WELBY, Euphemia Violet, CBE 1944; JP; late Superintendent Women's Royal Naval Service; *b* 28 Sept. 1891; *d* of Admiral H. Lyon, CB; *m* 1917, Lt-Comdr R. M. Welby; two *s* one *d* (and one *d* decd). *Educ:* Private. Hon. Sec. SS&AFA Devonport, 1914–16; Red Cross Cook, Malta, 1916–19; later Hon. Sec. SS&AFA; served in WRNS, 1939–45; social work on committees in Plymouth and Chairman Astor Institute. JP Somerset, 1947. *Recreation:* riding. *Address:* College Farm, Tintinhull, near Yeovil BA22 8PQ. *T:* Martock 823536; Milton Lodge, Freshwater Bay, Isle of Wight. *T:* Isle of Wight 753139.

WELBY, Sir (Richard) Bruno (Gregory), 7th Bt *cr* 1801; *b* 11 March 1928; *s* of Sir Oliver Charles Earle Welby, 6th Bt, TD, and Barbara Angela Mary Lind (*d* 1983), *d* of late John Duncan Gregory, CB, CMG; *S* father, 1977; *m* 1952, Jane Biddulph, *y d* of late Ralph Wilfred Hodder-Williams, MC; three *s* one *d*. *Educ:* Eton; Christ Church, Oxford (BA 1950). *Heir:* *s* Charles William Hodder Welby [*b* 6 May 1953; *m* 1978, Suzanna, *o d* of Major Ian Stuart-Routledge, Harston Hall, Grantham; two *d*]. *Address:* Denton Manor, Grantham, Lincs.

WELBY-EVERARD, Maj.-Gen. Sir Christopher Earle, KBE 1965 (OBE 1945); CB 1961; DL; *b* 9 Aug. 1909; *s* of late E. E. E. Welby-Everard, Gosberton House, near Spalding, Lincolnshire; *m* 1938, Sybil Juliet Wake Shorrock; two *s*. *Educ:* Charterhouse; CCC, Oxford. Gazetted The Lincolnshire Regt, 1930; OC 2 Lincolns, 1944; GSO1, 49 (WR) Inf. Div., 1944–46; GSO1 GHQ, MELF, 1946–48; OC 1 Royal Lincolnshire Regt, 1949–51; Comd 264 Scottish Beach Bde and 157 (L) Inf. Bde, 1954–57. BGS (Ops), HQ, BAOR, and HQ Northern Army Group, 1957–59; Chief of Staff, HQ Allied Forces, Northern Europe, 1959–61; GOC Nigerian Army, 1962–65; retd. DL Lincolnshire, 1966; High Sheriff of Lincolnshire, 1974. *Recreations:* shooting, cricket. *Address:* The Manor House, Sapperton, Sleaford, Lincolnshire NG34 0TB. *T:* Ingoldsby 273. *Clubs:* Army and Navy; Free Foresters.

WELCH, Anthony Edward, CB 1957; CMG 1949; formerly Under-Secretary, Board of Trade, 1946–66 (Ministry of Materials, 1951–54); *b* 17 July 1906; *s* of late Francis Bertram Welch; *m* 1946, Margaret Eileen Strudwick (*d* 1978); no *c*. *Educ:* Cheltenham College; New College, Oxford. *Address:* Brandon Lodge, Walberswick, Suffolk. *T:* Southwold 722582.

WELCH, Colin; *see* Welch, J. C. R.

WELCH, Air Vice-Marshal Edward Lawrence C.; *see* Colbeck-Welch.

WELCH, (James) Colin (Ross); Columnist, The Spectator, since 1982; parliamentary sketch writer, Daily Mail, since 1984; *b* 23 April 1924; *s* of James William Welch and Irene Margherita (*née* Paton), Ickleton Abbey, Cambridgeshire; *m* 1950, Sybil Russell; one *s* one *d*. *Educ:* Stowe Sch. (schol.); Peterhouse, Cambridge (major schol., BA Hons). Commissioned Royal Warwickshire Regt, 1942; served NW Europe, twice wounded. Glasgow Herald, 1948; Colonial Office, 1949; Daily Telegraph: leader writer, columnist (Peter Simple, with Michael Wharton), Parliamentary sketch-writer, 1950–80; Dep. Editor, 1964–80; regular column, 1981–83; Editor-in-Chief, Chief Executive magazine, 1980–82. Knight's Cross, Order of Polonia Restituta, 1972. *Publications:* (ed) Sir Frederick Ponsonby: Recollections of Three Reigns, 1951; (trans. with Sybil Welch) Nestroy: Liberty Comes to Krähwinkel, 1954 (BBC); articles in Encounter, Spectator, New Statesman, etc; contribs to symposia, incl. The Future that Doesn't Work, 1977 (New York). *Address:* 15 Lottage Road, Aldbourne, Wilts. *T:* Marlborough 40010.

WELCH, John K.; *see* Kemp-Welch.

WELCH, Sir John (Reader), 2nd Bt *cr* 1957; *b* 26 July 1933; *s* of Sir (George James) Cullum Welch, 1st Bt, OBE, MC, and Gertrude Evelyn Sladin Welch (*d* 1966); *S* father, 1980; *m* 1962, Margaret Kerry, *o d* of K. Douglass, Killara, NSW; one *s* twin *d*. *Educ:* Marlborough College; Hertford Coll., Oxford (MA). National service in RCS, 1952–54. Admitted a solicitor, 1960. Partner: Bell Brodrick & Gray, 1961–71; Wedlake Bell, 1972–; Chm., John Fairfax (UK) Ltd, 1985–. Ward Clerk of Walbrook Ward, City of London, 1961–74, Common Councilman, 1975–86 (Chm., Planning and Communications Cttee, 1981, 1982); Registrar of Archdeaconry of London. Liveryman, Haberdashers' Co., 1955 (Court of Assistants, 1973); Freeman, Parish Clerks' Co. (Master, 1967). Chm., Cttee of Management, London Homes for the Elderly. CStJ 1981. *Recreation:* piano. *Heir:* *s* James Douglass Cullum Welch, *b* 10 Nov. 1973. *Address:* 28 Rivermead

Court, Ranelagh Gardens, SW6 3RU; 16 Bedford Street, Covent Garden, WC2E 9HF. *T:* 01–379 7266. *Clubs:* City Livery (Pres., 1986–87), MCC, Surrey County Cricket.

WELCH, Robert Radford, MBE 1979; RDI 1965; FSIAD 1962; designer and silversmith, since 1955; *b* 21 May 1929; *m* 1959, Patricia Marguerite Hinksman; two *s* one *d. Educ:* Hanley Castle Grammar Sch.; Malvern Sch. of Art; Birmingham Coll. of Art; Royal Coll. of Art (DesRCA). FRSA 1967. Hon. Fellow RCA, 1972. Started own workshop in Chipping Campden, 1955; Design Consultant to Old Hall Tableware, 1955–. Vis. Lecturer: Central Sch. of Art and Design, 1957–63; RCA, 1963–71; visited India by invitation of All India Handicraft Bd, 1975. Silver commns for various clients, incl. civic plate, university colls, Goldsmiths' Hall, Canterbury Cathedral, V&A Museum, and British Govt Gift to St Lucia; tableware for British Ambassador's residence, Manila; British Museum; design commns in Denmark, Germany, USA and Japan. Liveryman, Goldsmiths' Co., 1982. *Publications:* Design in a Cotswold Workshop (with Alan Crawford), 1973; Hand and Machine, 1986. *Recreations:* drawing, painting. *Address:* The White House, Alveston Leys, Alveston, Stratford-on-Avon, Warwicks. *T:* Stratford-on-Avon 4191.

WELCH, Rt. Rev. William Neville, MA; *b* 30 April 1906; *s* of Thomas William and Agnes Maud Welch; *m* 1935, Kathleen Margaret Beattie; two *s* two *d. Educ:* Dean Close Sch., Cheltenham; Keble Coll., Oxford; Wycliffe Hall, Oxford. Asst Curate: Kidderminster, 1929–32; St Michael's, St Albans, 1932–34; Organising Sec., Missions to Seamen, 1934–39; Vicar of Grays, 1939–43; Officiating Chaplain, Training Ship Exmouth, 1939–40; Vicar of Ilford, 1943–53; Rural Dean of Barking, 1948–53; Vicar of Great Burstead, 1953–56; Archdeacon of Southend, 1953–72; Bishop Suffragan of Bradwell, 1968–73. Proctor in Convocation, 1945 and 1950; Hon. Canon of Chelmsford, 1951–53. *Address:* 112 Earlham Road, Norwich. *T:* Norwich 618192.

WELD, Col Sir Joseph William, Kt 1973; OBE 1946; TD 1947 (two Bars); JP; DL; Lord-Lieutenant of Dorset, 1964–84; Chairman, Wessex Regional Health Authority (formerly Wessex Regional Hospital Board), 1972–75; *b* 22 Sept. 1909; *s* of Wilfrid Joseph Weld, Avon Dassett, Warwickshire; *m* 1933, Elizabeth, *d* of E. J. Bellord; one *s* six *d. Educ:* Stonyhurst; Balliol College, Oxford. Served with Dorset Regt, TA, 1932–41; Staff College, Camberley, 1941; GSO2, General Headquarters Home Forces, 1942; Instructor, Staff College, Camberley, 1942–43; GSO1, Headquarters SEAC, 1943–46; commanded 4th Battalion Dorset Regt, 1947–51; Colonel, 1951. Hon. Colonel, 4th Battalion Dorset Regiment (TA). Chairman of Dorset Branch, County Landowners' Assoc., 1949–60; Chm. S Dorset Conservative Assoc., 1952–55 (Pres., 1955–59); Privy Chamberlain of Sword and Cape to Pope Pius XII. JP 1938, High Sheriff 1951, DL 1952, CC 1961, Dorset. KStJ 1967. *Address:* Lulworth Manor, East Lulworth, Dorset. *T:* West Lulworth 2352. *Club:* Royal Dorset Yacht.

WELD FORESTER, family name of **Baron Forester.**

WELDON, Sir Anthony (William), 9th Bt *cr* 1723; *b* 11 May 1947; *s* of Sir Thomas Brian Weldon, 8th Bt, and of Marie Isobel (now Countess Cathcart), *d* of Hon. William Joseph French; *S* father, 1979; *m* 1980, Mrs Amanda Wigan, *d* of Major Geoffrey and Hon. Mrs North, Colleton Hall, Rackenford, Tiverton, Devon; two *d. Educ:* Sherborne. Formerly Lieutenant, Irish Guards. *Recreations:* stalking, fishing, antiquarian books, champagne. *Heir: cousin* Kevin Nicholas Weldon [*b* 19 April 1951; *m* 1973, Catherine Main; one *s*]. *Clubs:* White's, Stranded Whales.

WELDON, Duncan Clark; theatrical producer; Chairman and Managing Director, Triumph Theatre Productions Ltd; *b* 19 March 1941; *s* of Clarence Weldon and Margaret Mary Andrew; *m* 1974, Janet Mahoney; one *d. Educ:* King George V School, Southport. Formerly a photographer; first stage production, A Funny Kind of Evening, Theatre Royal, Bath, 1965; co-founder, Triumph Theatre Productions, 1970; Director: Theatre Royal Haymarket; Strand Theatre; Proscenium Productions Ltd; Compass Theatre Ltd. First London production, When We Are Married, Strand Theatre, 1970; over one hundred productions in the West End include, at the Theatre Royal Haymarket: Waters of the Moon, 1978; Virginia, 1981; Heartbreak House, A Patriot for Me, 1983; The Aspern Papers, Aren't We All?, The Way of the World, 1984; Sweet Bird of Youth, 1985; The Apple Cart, Long Day's Journey into Night, 1986; other notable productions include: The Last of Mrs Cheyney, Cambridge, 1980; Beethoven's Tenth, Vaudeville, 1983; Strange Interlude, and American Buffalo, Duke of York's, 1984; The Caine Mutiny Court-Martial, Queen's, 1985; he has also presented in Australia, Canada, USA. *Address:* Brackenhill, Munstead Park, near Godalming, Surrey. *T:* Godalming 5508.

WELDON, Fay; writer; *b* 22 Sept. 1931; *d* of Frank Birkinshaw and Margaret Jepson; *m* Ron Weldon; four *s. Educ:* Hampstead Girls' High Sch.; St Andrews Univ. Has written or adapted numerous television and radio plays, dramatizations, and series, and nine stage plays. Chm. of Judges, Booker McConnell Prize, 1983. *Publications:* The Fat Woman's Joke, 1967; Down Among the Women, 1971; Female Friends, 1975; Remember Me, 1976; Little Sisters, 1978 (as Words of Advice, NY, 1977); Praxis, 1978 (Booker Prize Nomination); Puffball, 1980; Watching Me, Watching You (short stories), 1981; The President's Child, 1982; The Life and Loves of a She-Devil, 1984; Letters to Alice—on First Reading Jane Austen, 1984; Polaris and other Stories, 1985; Rebecca West, 1985; The Shrapnel Academy, 1986. *Address:* c/o Giles Gordon, Anthony Sheil Associates, 43 Doughty Street, WC1N 2LF; c/o Phil Kelvin, Goodwin Associates, 12 Rabbit Row, Kensington Church Street, W8 4DX.

WELENSKY, Rt. Hon. Sir Roy, (Roland), PC 1960; KCMG 1959 (CMG 1946); Kt 1953; *b* Salisbury, Southern Rhodesia, 20 January 1907; *s* of Michael and Leah Welensky; *m* 1st, 1928, Elizabeth Henderson (*d* 1969); one *s* one *d*; 2nd, 1972, Valerie Scott; two *d. Educ:* Salisbury, S Rhodesia. Joined Railway service, 1924; Member National Council of the Railway Workers Union; Director of Manpower, Northern Rhodesia, 1941–46; formed N Rhodesia Labour Party, 1941; Member of Sir John Forster's commission to investigate the 1940 riots in Copperbelt; Chairman of various conciliation Boards and member of the Strauss (1943) and Grant (1946) Railway Arbitration Tribunals. Member of delegn to London to discuss Mineral Royalties (1949) and Constitution (1950 and 1951); Member of Northern Rhodesia delegation to Closer Association Conference at Victoria Falls, 1951. MLC, N Rhodesia, 1938, MEC 1940–53. Chm. Unofficial Members Assoc. 1946–53. Federation of Rhodesia and Nyasaland: Minister of Transport, Communications and Posts, 1953–56; Leader of the House and Deputy Prime Minister, 1955–56; Prime Minister and Minister of External Affairs, 1956–63 (also Minister of Defence, 1956–59). Heavy-weight boxing champion of the Rhodesias, 1926–28. *Publication:* Welensky's 4000 Days, The Life and Death of the Federation of Rhodesia and Nyasaland, 1964; *relevant publications:* The Rhodesian, by Don Taylor; Welensky's Story, by Garry Allighan; The Welensky Papers, by Dr J. R. T. Wood. *Recreation:* gardening. *Address:* Shaftesbury House, Milldown Road, Blandford Forum, Dorset DT11 7DE. *Club:* Farmers'.

WELFORD, Prof. Walter Thompson, PhD, DSc; FRS 1980; Emeritus Professor of Physics, University of London, and Senior Research Fellow, Imperial College, University of London, since 1983; *b* 31 Aug. 1916; *s* of Abraham and Sonia Weinstein; *m* 1948, Jacqueline Joan Thompson (marr. diss. 1978); two *s. Educ:* LCC primary and technical schools; Univ. of London (BSc, PhD, DSc). Laboratory asst, 1933–42; R&D physicist in industry, 1943–48; Imperial College, 1948–; successively research asst, lectr, sen. lectr, reader; Professor, 1973–83. Director, IC Optical Systems Ltd, 1970–. Thomas Young Medal, Inst. of Physics, 1973. *Publications:* Geometrical Optics, 1963; (with L. C. Martin) Technical Optics, Vol. 1, 1966; Aberrations of the Symmetrical Optical System, 1974 (trans. Chinese 1982); Optics (Oxford Phys. Series No 14), 1976, 2nd edn 1981 (Japanese edn 1976); (with R. Winston) The Optics of Non-Imaging Concentrators, 1978; Aberrations of Optical Systems, 1986; numerous contribs dealing with all aspects of applied optics to learned jls. *Recreation:* surviving. *Address:* 8 Chiswick Road, W4 5RB. *T:* 01–995 2340.

WELLAND, Colin, (Colin Williams); actor, playwright; *b* 4 July 1934; *s* of John Arthur Williams and Norah Williams; *m* 1962, Patricia Sweeney; one *s* three *d. Educ:* Newton-le-Willows Grammar Sch.; Bretton Hall Coll.; Goldsmiths' Coll., London (Teacher's Dip. in Art and Drama). Art teacher, 1958–62; entered theatre, 1962; Library Theatre, Manchester, 1962–64; television, films, theatre, 1962–. Films (actor): Kes; Villain; Straw Dogs; Sweeney; (original screenplay): Yanks, 1978; Chariots of Fire, 1980 (won Oscar, Evening Standard and Broadcasting Press Guild Awards, 1982); Twice in a Lifetime, 1986. Plays (author): Say Goodnight to Grandma, St Martin's, 1973; Roll on Four O'clock, Palace, 1981. Award winning TV plays include: Roll on Four O'clock, Kisses at 50, Leeds United, Jack Point, Your Man from Six Counties. Best TV Playwright, Writers Guild, 1970, 1973 and 1974; Best TV Writer, and Best Supporting Film Actor, BAFTA Awards, 1970; Broadcasting Press Guild Award (for writing), 1973. *Publications:* Northern Humour, 1982; plays: Roomful of Holes, 1972; Say Goodnight to Grandma, 1973. *Recreations:* sport, theatre, cinema, politics, dining out. *Address:* c/o Anthony Jones, A. D. Peters Ltd, 10 Buckingham Street, WC2N 6BU.

WELLBELOVED, James; Commercial Consultant; writer and broadcaster on foreign and domestic affairs; Director General, National Kidney Research Fund, since 1985; *b* 29 July 1926; *s* of Wilfred Henry Wellbeloved, Sydenham and Brockley (London), and Paddock Wood, Kent; *m* 1948, Mavis Beryl Ratcliff; two *s* one *d. Educ:* South East London Technical College. Boy seaman, 1942–46. MP (Lab 1965–81, SDP 1981–83) Erith and Crayford, Nov. 1965–1983; Parly Private Secretary: Minister of Defence (Admin), 1967–69; Sec. of State for Foreign and Commonwealth Affairs, 1969–70; an Opposition Whip, 1972–74; Parly Under-Sec. of State for Defence (RAF), MoD, 1976–79. UK Rep., North Atlantic Assembly, 1972–76, 1979–82. Dep. Chm., London MPs Parly Gp, 1970–81; Chairman: River Thames Gp; All Party Parly Camping and Caravanning Gp, 1967–74; Nat. Whitley Council, MoD, 1976–79; Mem., Ecclesiastical Cttee, 1971–76. Member: RACS Political Purposes Cttee, 1973–83; PLP Liaison Cttee, 1974–78; Defence Council, 1976–79; Vice Chm., Labour Party Defence Gp, 1970–81. Contested, 1983, Prospective Parly Cand., 1985 (SDP) Erith and Crayford. Dir, Assoc. of Former MPs, 1983–. Nat. Vice-Pres., Camping and Caravanning Club, 1974–. Former Governor, Greenwich Hosp. Sch. *Publication:* Local Government, 1971. *Recreations:* camping, travel. *Address:* Craigdon House, Lesney Park, Erith, Kent DA8 3DS. *T:* Dartford 347777.

WELLBY, Rear-Adm. Roger Stanley, CB 1958; DSO 1940; DL; Retired; lately Head of UK Services Liaison Staff in Australia and Senior Naval Adviser to UK High Commissioner, 1956–59; *b* 28 Apr. 1906; *o s* of Dr Stanley Wellby and Marian Schwann; *m* 1936, Elaine, *d* of late Sir Clifford Heathcote-Smith; three *s. Educ:* RNC, Dartmouth. Qualified as Torpedo Officer, 1931; Commander, 1939; Special Service in France, 1940 (DSO, Croix de Guerre); Captain, 1947; Imperial Defence College; Rear-Adm. 1956. Dep. Comr-in-Chief, St John Ambulance Brigade, 1963–71; Comr, St John Ambulance Brigade, Bucks, 1971–75. DL Bucks 1972. KStJ 1966. *Recreation:* hockey, for Navy. *Address:* Oakengrove, Hastoe, Tring, Herts. *T:* Tring 3233.

WELLER, Dr Thomas Huckle; Richard Pearson Strong Professor of Tropical Public Health, Harvard University, 1954–85, Emeritus 1985 (Head, Department of Tropical Public Health, 1954–81); Director Center for Prevention of Infectious Diseases, Harvard School of Public Health, 1966–81; *b* 15 June 1915; *s* of Carl V. and Elsie H. Weller; *m* 1945, Kathleen R. Fahey; two *s* two *d. Educ:* University of Michigan (AB, MS); Harvard (MD). Fellow, Departments of Comparative Pathology and Tropical Medicine and Bacteriology, Harvard Medical School, 1940–41; Intern, Children's Hosp., Boston, 1941–42. Served War, 1942–45: 1st Lieut to Major, Medical Corps, US Army. Asst Resident in Medicine, Children's Hosp., 1946; Fellow, Pediatrics, Harvard Medical School, 1947; Instructor, Dept Tropical Public Health, Harvard School of Public Health, 1948; Assistant Professor, 1949; Associate Professor, 1950. Asst Director, Research Div. of Infectious Diseases, Children's Medical Center, Boston, 1949–55; Dir, Commission on Parasitic Diseases, Armed Forces Epidemiological Bd, 1953–59, Mem. 1959–72; Mem. Trop. Med. and parasitology study sect., US Public Health Service, 1953–56. Diplomate, American Board of Pediatrics, 1948; Amer. Acad. of Arts and Sciences, 1955; National Academy of Sciences, USA. Consultant on tropical medicine and infectious diseases to foundations and industries, 1985–. Mead Johnson Award of Amer. Acad. of Pediatrics (jointly), 1954; Kimble Methodology Award (jointly), 1954; Nobel Prize Physiology or Medicine (jointly), 1954; Ledlie Prize, 1963; United Cerebral Palsy Weinstein-Goldenson Award, 1974; Bristol Award, Infectious Diseases Soc. of America, 1980. Hon. LLD Michigan, 1956; Hon. DSc: Gustavus Adolphus Coll., 1975; Univ. of Mass Med. Sch., 1986; Hon. LHD Lowell, 1977. *Publications:* numerous scientific papers on *in vitro* cultivation of viruses and on helminth infections of man. *Recreations:* gardening, photography. *Address:* 56 Winding River Road, Needham, Mass 02192, USA. *Club:* Harvard (Boston).

WELLER, Walter; Principal Conductor, Royal Philharmonic Orchestra, since 1980; *b* 30 Nov. 1939; *s* of Walter and Anna Weller; *m* 1966, Elisabeth Samohyl; one *s. Educ:* Realgymnasium, Vienna; Akademie für Musik, Vienna (degree for violin and piano). Founder of Weller Quartet, 1958–69; Member, Vienna Philharmonic, 1958–60. First Leader, 1960–69; Conductor, Vienna State Opera, 1969–75; Guest Conductor with all main European and American Orchestras, also in Japan and Israel, 1973–; Chief Conductor, Tonkünstler Orch., Vienna, 1974–77; Principal Conductor and Artistic Adviser, Royal Liverpool Philharmonic Orch., 1977–80, Guest Conductor Laureate, 1980–. Medal of Arts and Sciences, Austria, 1968. *Recreations:* magic, model railway, sailing, swimming, stamp-collecting, ski-ing. *Address:* Döblinger Hauptstrasse 40, 1190 Vienna, Austria. *T:* 34 01 64.

WELLESLEY, family name of **Earl Cowley** and of **Duke of Wellington.**

WELLESLEY, Julian Valerian; Director: Horizon Travel PLC; Chatsworth Food Ltd; *b* 9 Aug. 1933; *s* of late Gerald Valerian Wellesley, MC, and Elizabeth Thornton Harvey; *m* 1965, Elizabeth Joan Hall; one *s* one *d*; three step *d. Educ:* Royal Naval Colleges, Dartmouth (schol.) and Greenwich. Royal Navy, 1947–61: America and West Indies, 1955–56; Far East, 1957–58; Navigation Specialist, 1959. Joined Charles Barker, 1961: a Dir, 1963; Dep. Chm., 1975; Chm., Charles Barker Group, 1978–83. Consultant, TSB

Gp, 1984. Cttee Mem., Assoc. of Lloyd's Mems, 1985–. *Recreations:* family, music, reading, playing tennis, watching cricket. *Address:* Tidebrook Manor, Wadhurst, Sussex TN5 6PD; 2 Sheridan Court, 55 Barkston Gardens, SW5 0ET. *Clubs:* Brooks's; Sussex.

WELLINGS, Sir Jack (Alfred), Kt 1975; CBE 1970; Chairman, The 600 Group Ltd, since 1968 (Managing Director, 1963–84); *b* 16 Aug. 1917; *s* of Edward Josiah and Selina Wellings; *m* 1946, Greta, *d* of late George Tidey; one *s* two *d*. *Educ:* Selhurst Grammar Sch.; London Polytechnic. Vice-Pres., Hawker Siddeley (Canada) Ltd, 1954–62; Dep. Man. Dir, 600 Group Ltd, 1962. Member: NCB, 1971–77; NEB, 1977–79; part-time Mem., British Aerospace, 1980–; non-exec. Dir, Clausing Corp., USA, 1982–84. *Address:* Boundary Meadow, Collum Green Road, Stoke Poges, Bucks. *T:* Fulmer 2978.

WELLINGS, Victor Gordon, QC 1973; Member of the Lands Tribunal, since 1973; Deputy Judge of the High Court, since 1975; *b* 19 July 1919; *e s* of late Gordon Arthur Wellings, solicitor, and Alice Adelaide Wellings (now Mrs Alice Adelaide Poole); *m* 1948, Helen Margaret Jill Lovell; three *s*. *Educ:* Reading Sch.; Exeter Coll., Oxford (MA). Called to Bar, Gray's Inn, 1949; practised 1949–73. War service, 1940–46; Captain Indian Army, 17th Dogra Regt; Intell. Corps, India; Captain, TARO, 1949–. *Publications:* Editor, Woodfall, The Law of Landlord and Tenant, 28th edn, 1978 (Jt Editor 26th and 27th edns, 1963 and 1968), and other works on same subject. *Recreations:* golf, fishing. *Address:* Cherry Tree Cottage, Whitchurch Hill, Pangbourne, Berks RG8 7PT. *T:* Pangbourne 2918. *Club:* United Oxford & Cambridge University.

WELLINGTON, 8th Duke of, *cr* 1814; **Arthur Valerian Wellesley,** MVO 1952; OBE 1957; MC; DL; Baron Mornington, 1746; Earl of Mornington, Viscount Wellesley, 1760; Viscount Wellington of Talavera and Wellington, Somersetshire, Baron Douro, 1809; Earl of Wellington, Feb. 1812; Marquess of Wellington, Oct. 1812; Marquess Douro, 1814; Prince of Waterloo, 1815, Netherlands; Count of Vimeiro, Marquess of Torres Vedras and Duke of Victoria in Portugal; Duke of Ciudad Rodrigo and a Grandee of Spain, 1st class; *b* 2 July 1915; *s* of 7th Duke of Wellington, KG, and Dorothy Violet (*d* 1956), *d* of Robert Ashton, Croughton, Cheshire; *S* father, 1972; *m* 1944, Diana Ruth, *o d* of Maj.-Gen. D. F. McConnel; four *s* one *d*. *Educ:* Eton; New Coll., Oxford. Served War of 1939–45 in Middle East (MC), CMF and BLA. Lt-Col Comdg Royal Horse Guards, 1954–58; Silver Stick-in-Waiting and Lt-Col Comdg the Household Cavalry, 1959–60; Comdr 22nd Armoured Bde, 1960–61; Comdr RAC 1st (Br.) Corps, 1962–64; Defence Attaché, Madrid, 1964–67, retired; Col-in-Chief, The Duke of Wellington's Regt, 1974–; Hon. Col 2nd Bn, The Wessex Regt, 1974–80. Director: Massey Ferguson Holdings Ltd, 1967; Massey Ferguson Ltd, 1973. President: Game Conservancy, 1976–81 (Dep. Pres., 1981–); SE Branch, Royal British Legion, 1978–; BSJA, 1980–82; Rare Breeds Survival Trust, 1982–; Council for Environmental Conservation, 1983–; Atlantic Salmon Trust, 1983–. Vice-Pres., Zool Soc. of London; Member Council: RASE, 1976–; TAVR Wessex; St John of Jerusalem, Hampshire. Hampshire CC 1967–74; DL Hants, 1975. Governor of Wellington Coll., 1964–; Chm., Pitt Club. OStJ. Officier, Légion d'Honneur (France). *Heir: s* Marquess of Douro, *qv*. *Address:* Stratfield Saye House, Reading; Apsley House, 149 Piccadilly, W1V 9FA. *Clubs:* Turf, Buck's.

WELLINGTON (NZ), Archbishop of, (RC), since 1979; **His Eminence Cardinal Thomas Stafford Williams,** DD; Metropolitan of New Zealand; *b* 20 March 1930; *s* of Thomas Stafford Williams and Lillian Maude Kelly. *Educ:* Holy Cross Primary School, Miramar; SS Peter and Paul Primary School, Lower Hutt; St Patrick's Coll., Wellington; Victoria University Coll., Wellington; St Kevin's Coll., Oamaru; Holy Cross Coll., Mosgiel; Collegio Urbano de Propaganda Fide, Rome (STL); University Coll., Dublin (BSocSc); Hon. DD. Assistant Priest, St Patrick's Parish, Palmerston North, 1963–64; Director of Studies, Catholic Enquiry Centre, Wellington, 1965–70; Parish Priest: St Anne's Parish, Leulumoega, W Samoa, 1971–75; Holy Family Parish, Porirua, NZ, 1976–79. Cardinal, 1983. *Recreations:* table tennis, tennis. *Address:* Viard, 21 Eccleston Hill, (PO Box 198), Wellington 1, New Zealand. *T:* 728–576.

WELLINGTON (NZ), Bishop of; *see* New Zealand, Primate and Archbishop of.

WELLINGTON, Peter Scott, CBE 1981; DSC; PhD; ARCS; FLS; FIBiol; FRAgS; Director, National Institute of Agricultural Botany, 1970–81; Member, Governing Body, National Seed Development Organisation Ltd, since 1982; *b* 20 March 1919; *er s* of late Robert Wellington, MBE, MC; *m* 1947, Kathleen Joyce, *widow* of E. H. Coombe; one *s* one *d*. *Educ:* Kelly Coll.; Imperial Coll. of Science. BSc 1946. Observer, Fleet Air Arm, 1940–45 (Lt-Comdr (A) RNVR). Research Asst 1948–52, Chief Officer 1953–61, Official Seed Testing Stn for England and Wales; Asst Dir 1961–68, Dep. Dir 1968–69, Nat. Inst. of Agricultural Botany. Vice-Pres., Internat. Seed Testing Assoc., 1953–56 (Chm. Germination Cttee, 1956–70); Chief Officer, UK Variety Classification Unit, 1965–70; Chm., Technical Working Group, Internat. Convention for Protection of Plant Varieties, 1966–68. *Publications:* papers on germination of cereals and weeds, seed-testing and seed legislation. *Recreations:* gardening, walking, reading. *Address:* Colescus, Gorran Haven, St Austell, Cornwall. *T:* Mevagissey 842065. *Club:* Farmers'.

WELLS, Dean of; *see* Mitchell, Very Rev. P. R.

WELLS, Archdeacon of; *see* Thomas, Ven. C. E.

WELLS, Dr Alan Arthur, OBE 1982; FRS 1977; FEng 1978; Director-General, The Welding Institute, since 1977; *s* of Arthur John Wells and Lydia Wells; *m* 1950, Rosemary Edith Alice Mitchell; four *s* one *d*. *Educ:* City of London Sch.; Univ. of Nottingham (BScEng); Clare Coll., Cambridge (PhD). MIMechE, Hon. FWeldI. British Welding Res. Association: Asst Dir, 1956; Dep. Dir (Scientific), 1963; Queen's Univ. of Belfast: Prof. of Struct. Science, 1964; Head of Civil Engrg Dept, 1970–77; Dean, Faculty of Applied Science and Technol., 1973–76. MRIA 1976. Hon. Dr, Faculty of Engrg, Univ. of Gent, 1972; Hon. DSc: Glasgow, 1982; QUB, 1986. *Publications:* Brittle Fracture of Welded Plate (jtly), 1967; res. papers on welding technol. and fracture mechanics. *Recreation:* handyman about the house and garden. *Address:* The Welding Institute, Abington Hall, Abington, Cambs CB1 6AL. *T:* Cambridge 891162. *Club:* Athenæum.

WELLS, Bowen; MP (C) Hertford and Stortford, since 1983 (Hertford and Stevenage, 1979–83); *b* 4 Aug. 1935; *s* of Reginald Laird Wells and Agnes Mary Wells (*née* Hunter); 1975, Rennie Heyde; two *s*. *Educ:* St Paul's School; Univ. of Exeter (BA Hons); Regent St Polytechnic School of Management (Dip. Business Management). National Service, RN (promoted to Sub Lt), 1954–56. Schoolmaster, Colet Court, 1956–57; sales trainee, British Aluminium, 1957–58; Univ. of Exeter, 1958–61; Commonwealth Development Corporation, 1961–73: Personal Asst to Regional Controller and Ind. Relations Manager, 1962–65; Company Sec. and Ind. Relations Manager, Guyana Timbers, 1965–67; Manager, Guyana Housing and Develt Co., Guyana Mortgage Finance Co. and Cane Farming Develt Corp., 1967–71; Sen. Exec. for Subsidiary and Associated Develt Finance Co., 1971–73; Owner Manager, Substation Group Services Ltd, 1973–79. PPS to Min. of State for Employment, 1982–83. Member: For. Affairs Select Cttee, 1983–; European Legislation Select Cttee, 1983–; Chairman: UN Parly Gp, 1983–; British-Caribbean Gp; Jt Hon. Sec., Parly Cons. Trade and Industry Gp, 1984– (Vice-Chm., 1983–84); Sec., All Party Overseas Develt Gp., 1984–; Mem., British-American Gp, 1985. Mem., UK Br. Exec., CPA, 1984–. Trustee, Industry and Parlt Trust, 1985–. Governor: Outward Bound Wales, 1979–; Inst. of Development Studies, 1980–. *Recreations:* music, walking, gardening cooking, sailing. *Address:* House of Commons, SW1A 0AA. *T:* 01-219 5154.

WELLS, Charles Alexander, CBE 1963; SPk (Sitara-i-Pakistan) 1961; FRCS; Emeritus Professor of Surgery, University of Liverpool; Hon. Surgeon Royal Liverpool United Hospital and Consultant to Royal Prince Alfred, Sydney, NSW, and other hospitals; FRSocMed (President, Section of Surgery and Past President Section of Urology); Corresponding member Société Franc. d'Urologie; *b* 9 Jan, 1898; *o s* of late Percy M. and late Frances L. Wells, Liverpool; *m* 1928, Joyce Mary Rivett Harrington (*d* 1980); two *s*. *Educ:* Merchant Taylors', Crosby; Liverpool University (MB, ChB, 1st Hons). Active service, RFA, 1916–18. Lately surgeon and urologist to various hospitals; Resident Surgical Officer Ancoats Hospital, Manchester; Demonstrator in Anatomy McGill University, Montreal; Clinical Assistant St Peter's Hospital, London. Mem. Council RCS (Vice-Pres., 1965–66, Bradshaw Lectr, 1966); Mem. Med. Adv. Council, ODM, and Chm. Recruitment Panel; Chairman: Merseyside Conf. for Overseas Students; Cttee on Surgical Educn, Internat. Fedn Surgical Colls. Ex-Council of British Association of Urological Surgeons (Home and Overseas); Past President Liverpool Medical Institution; Pakistan Health Reforms Commn, 1960; Adrian Committee (Ministry of Health) on Radiation Hazards, 1958–; Medical Research Council's Committee, Pressure Steam Sterilisation. Litchfield Lectr, Oxford, 1953; Luis Guerrero Meml Lectr, Santo Tomas Univ., Manila, 1957; McIlraith Guest Prof., Univ. of Sydney, 1957; Murat Willis Orator, Richmond, Va, 1963. Hon. FACS 1968. Hon. LLD (Panjab), 1960. *Publications:* Surgery for Nurses, 1938; Text Book of Urology (ed Winsbury-White); Treatment of Cancer in Clinical Practice, 1960; contrib. to textbooks and symposia, various chapters, Prostatectomy (monograph), 1952; (with J. Kyle) Peptic Ulceration, 1960; (ed with J. Kyle) Scientific Foundations of Surgery, 1967, 2nd edn, 1974; numerous articles in scientific jls. *Recreations:* shooting, painting in oils. *Address:* 11 Curzon Road, Hoylake, Wirral, Merseyside L47 1HB. *T:* Hoylake 4326. *Club:* Carlton.

WELLS, Sir Charles Maltby, 2nd Bt *cr* 1944; TD 1960; *b* 24 July 1908; *e s* of 1st Bt, and Mary Dorothy Maltby (*d* 1956); *S* father, 1956; *m* 1935, Katharine Boulton, *d* of Frank Boteler Kenrick, Toronto; two *s*. *Educ:* Bedford School; Pembroke College, Cambridge. Joined RE (TA), 1933; Capt. 1939; served War of 1939–45: 54th (EA) Div., 1939–41; Lt-Col 1941; 76th Div., 1941–43; British Army Staff, Washington, 1943–45. *Heir: s* Christopher Charles Wells [*b* 12 Aug. 1936; *m* 1st, 1960, Elizabeth Florence Vaughan (marr. diss. 1983), *d* of I. F. Griffiths, Outremont, Quebec; two *s* two *d*; 2nd, 1985, Lynda; one *s*]. *Address:* Apt 507, 350 Lonsdale Road, Toronto, Ont, Canada.

WELLS, Prof. David Arthur; Professor of German, The Queen's University of Belfast, since 1974; *b* 26 April 1941; *s* of Arthur William Wells and Rosina Elizabeth (*née* Jones). *Educ:* Christ's Hosp., Horsham; Gonville and Caius Coll., Cambridge; Univs of Strasbourg, Vienna and Münster. Mod. and Med. Langs Tripos, BA 1963, Tiarks Studentship 1963–64, MA, PhD Cantab 1967. Asst Lectr 1966–67, Lectr 1967–69, in German, Univ. of Southampton; Lectr in German, Bedford Coll., Univ. of London, 1969–74; Sec., London Univ. Bd of Staff Examiners in German, 1973–74; Tutor, Nat. Extension Coll., Cambridge, 1966–74. Lecture tour of NZ univs, 1975. Mem., Managing Body, Oakington Manor Jun. Mixed and Infant Sch., London Bor. of Brent, 1972–74; Hon. Sec., Mod. Humanities Res. Assoc., 1969–; Hon. Treas., Assoc. for Literary and Linguistic Computing, 1973–78; Sec.-Gen., Internat. Fedn for Modern Langs and Lits, 1981–. Editor, MHRA Ann. Bull. of Modern Humanities Research Assoc., 1969–; Jt Editor, The Year's Work in Modern Language Studies, 1976– (Editor, 1982). FRSA 1983. *Publications:* The Vorau Moses and Balaam: a study of their relationship to exegetical tradition, 1970; The Wild Man from the Epic of Gilgamesh to Hartmann von Aue's Iwein, 1975; A Complete Concordance to the Vorauer Bücher Moses (Concordances to the Early Middle High German Biblical Epic), 1976; contribs to MHRA Style Book: Notes for Authors and Editors, 1971, 3rd edn 1981; articles, monographs and reviews in learned jls. *Recreations:* travel, theatre, music. *Address:* The Queen's University, Belfast BT7 1NN. *T:* Belfast 245133; 95 Cambridge Street, SW1. *T:* 01–834 6558.

WELLS, Doreen Patricia, (Marchioness of Londonderry); Ballerina of the Royal Ballet, 1955–74; *b* 25 June 1937; *m* 1972, 9th Marquess of Londonderry, *qv*; two *s*. *Educ:* Walthamstow; Bush Davies School; Royal Ballet School. Engaged in Pantomime, 1952 and 1953. Joined Royal Ballet, 1955; became Principal Dancer, 1960; has danced leading roles in Noctambules, Harlequin in April, Dance Concertante, Sleeping Beauty, Coppelia, Swan Lake, Sylvia, La Fille mal Gardée, Two Pigeons, Giselle, Invitation, Rendezvous, Blood Wedding, Raymonda, Concerto, Nutcracker, Romeo and Juliet, Concerto No 2 (Ballet Imperial); has created leading roles in Toccata, La Création du Monde, Sinfonietta, Prometheus, Grand Tour. Adeline Genée Gold Medal, 1954. *Recreations:* classical music, reading, theatre-going. *Address:* Wynyard Park, Billingham, Cleveland TS22 5NF. *T:* Wolviston 310.

See also Viscount Castlereagh.

WELLS, Prof. George Albert, MA, BSc, PhD; Professor of German, Birkbeck College, University of London, since 1968; *b* 22 May 1926; *s* of George John and Lilian Maud Wells; *m* 1969, Elisabeth Delhey. *Educ:* University College London (BA, MA German; PhD Philosophy; BSc Geology). Lecturer in German, 1949–64, Reader in German, 1964–68, University Coll. London. Director, Rationalist Press Assoc., 1974–. *Publications:* Herder and After, 1959; The Plays of Grillparzer, 1969; The Jesus of the Early Christians, 1971; Did Jesus Exist?, 1975, 2nd edn 1986; Goethe and the Development of Science 1750–1900, 1978; The Historical Evidence for Jesus, 1982; articles in Jl of History of Ideas, Jl of English and Germanic Philology, German Life and Letters, Question, Trivium, Wirkendes Wort. *Recreation:* walking. *Address:* 35 St Stephen's Avenue, St Albans, Herts AL3 4AA. *T:* St Albans 51347.

WELLS, Lt-Col Herbert James, CBE 1958; MC 1918; FCA 1934; JP; DL; *b* 27 March 1897; *s* of late James J. Wells, NSW; *m* 1926, Rose Hamilton, *d* of late H. D. Brown, Bournemouth; no *c*. *Educ:* NSW. Chartered Accountant; Consultant (formerly Sen. Partner), Amsdon Cossart & Wells. Surrey CC: Alderman, 1960; Vice-Chm., 1959–62; Chm., 1962–65. JP Surrey 1952 (Chm., Magistrates' Ct, Wallington, 1960–70); DL 1962, High Sheriff 1965, Surrey. A General Comr for Income Tax. Freeman, City of London. Former Pres. Brit. Red Cross, Carshalton and Sutton Division; former Member, Surrey T&AFA, retired 1968; Chairman, Queen Mary's Hospital for Children, Carshalton, 1958–60; Member, Carshalton UDC, 1945–62 (Chm. 1950–52 and 1955–56). Served European War, 1914–18 with Aust. Inf. and Aust. Flying Corps in Egypt and France (MC); served War of 1939–45. DUniv Surrey, 1975. *Recreations:* football, hockey, tennis, squash, now golf. *Address:* 17 Oakhurst Rise, Carshalton Beeches, Surrey. *T:* 01–643 4125. *Club:* Royal Automobile.

WELLS, Jack Dennis; Assistant Director, Central Statistical Office, since 1979; *b* 8 April 1928; *s* of late C. W. Wells and of H. M. Wells (*née* Clark); *m* 1953, Jean Allison; one *s* one *d*. *Educ:* Hampton Grammar Sch.; Polytechnic of Central London. AIS 1955. Ministry of Fuel and Power, 1947; Royal Air Force, 1947–49; Min. of (Fuel and) Power, 1949–69;

Private Secretary to Paymaster General, 1957–59; Chief Statistician, Dept of Economic Affairs, 1969; Min. of Technology, 1969; HM Treasury, 1970; Dept of (Trade and) Industry, 1971–79. Past Chairman, Old Hamptonians Assoc. *Publications:* contribs to Long Range Planning, Economic Trends, Statistical News, Review of Income and Wealth. *Recreations:* flying, cricket. *Clubs:* Civil Service, MCC.

WELLS, Sir John (Julius), Kt 1984; MP (C) Maidstone since October 1959; *b* 30 March 1925; *s* of A. Reginald K. Wells, Marlands, Sampford Arundel, Som; *m* 1948, Lucinda Meath-Baker; two *s* two *d*. *Educ:* Eton; Corpus Christi College, Oxford (MA). War of 1939–45: joined RN as ordinary seaman, 1942; commissioned, 1943, served in submarines until 1946. Contested (C) Smethwick Division, General Election, 1955. Chairman: Cons. Party Horticulture Cttee, 1965–71; Horticultural sub-Cttee, Select Cttee on Agriculture, 1968; Parly Waterways Group, 1974–; Vice-Chm., Cons. Party Agriculture Cttee, 1970; Mem., Mr Speaker's Panel of Chairmen, 1974. Hon. Freeman, Borough of Maidstone, 1979. Kt Comdr, Order of Civil Merit (Spain), 1972; Comdr, Order of Lion of Finland, 1984. *Recreations:* country pursuits. *Address:* Mere House, Mereworth, Kent.

WELLS, Malcolm Henry Weston, FCA; Joint Managing Director, Liechtenstein (UK) Ltd, since 1985; *b* 26 July 1927; *s* of Lt-Comdr Geoffrey Weston Wells; *m* 1952, Elizabeth A. Harland, *d* of late Rt Rev. M. H. Harland, DD; one *s* one *d*. *Educ:* Eton Coll. ACA 1951, FCA 1961. Served RNVR, 1945–48. Peat, Marwick Mitchell Ltd, 1948–58; Siebe Gorman and Co. Ltd, 1958–63; Charterhouse Japhet, 1963–80 (Chm., 1973–80); Dir, Charterhouse Gp, 1971–80; Chm., Charterhouse Petroleum, 1977–82; London rep., Bank in Liechtenstein, 1981–85; Dir, Carclo Engineering Gp plc, 1982–. Mem., CAA, 1974–77. Mem. Solicitors' Disciplinary Tribunal, 1975–81. *Recreation:* sailing. *Address:* Holmbush House, Findon, West Sussex BN14 0SY. *T:* Findon 3630. *Clubs:* City of London, Overseas Bankers; West Wittering Sailing.

WELLS, Petrie Bowen; *see* Wells, B.

WELLS, Ronald Alfred, OBE 1965; BSc, FRSC, FIMM; industrial consultant; *b* 11 February 1920; *s* of Alfred John Wells and Winifred Jessie (*née* Lambert); *m* 1953, Anne Brebner Lanshe; two *s*. *Educ:* Birkbeck College, London; Newport Technical College. Service with Government Chemist, 1939–40; Royal Naval Scientific Service, 1940–47; Joined Nat. Chemical Laboratory, 1947; Mem. UK Scientific Mission, Washington, 1951–52; Head of Radio-chemical Group, 1956; Head of Div. of Inorganic and Mineral Chemistry, 1963; Deputy Director, Nov. 1963; Director of National Chemical Laboratory, 1964; Dir of Research, TBA Industrial Products Ltd, 1965–70, Jt Man. Dir, 1970–77; Man. Dir, AMFU Ltd (Turner & Newall), 1977–81; Gp Scientist, Turner & Newall, 1981–83. Director: Salford Univ. Industrial Centre Ltd, 1981–82; Rochdale Private Surgical Unit, 1975–81; non-exec. Dir, Eversave (UK) Ltd, 1984–85. Mem. Council, Royal Inst. Chemistry, 1965–68. *Publications:* numerous contribs to Inorganic Chromatography and Extractive Metallurgy. *Recreations:* gardening, golf, mineralogy. *Address:* Westbury, 19 First Avenue, Charmandean, Worthing, Sussex BN14 9NJ. *T:* Worthing 33844.

WELLS, Mrs Stanley; *see* Hill, S. E.

WELLS, Dr Stanley William; General Editor of the Oxford Shakespeare and Head of the Shakespeare Department, Oxford University Press, since 1978; Senior Research Fellow, Balliol College, Oxford, since 1980; *b* 21 May 1930; *s* of Stanley Cecil Wells and Doris Wells; *m* 1975, Susan Elizabeth Hill, *qv*; two *d* (and one *d* decd). *Educ:* Kingston High Sch., Hull; University Coll., London (BA); Shakespeare Inst., Univ. of Birmingham (PhD). Fellow, Shakespeare Inst., 1962–77: Lectr, 1962; Sen. Lectr, 1971; Reader, 1973–77; Hon. Fellow, 1979–. Consultant in English, Wroxton Coll., 1964–80. Dir, Royal Shakespeare Theatre Summer Sch., 1971–; Pres., Shakespeare Club of Stratford-upon-Avon, 1972–73. Member: Council, Malone Soc., 1967–; Exec. Council, Royal Shakespeare Theatre, 1976– (Governor, 1974–); Exec. Cttee, Shakespeare's Birthplace, 1976–78 (Trustee, 1975–81, 1984–). Governor, King Edward VI Grammar Sch. for Boys, Stratford-upon-Avon, 1973–77. Guest lectr, British and overseas univs. Hon. DLitt Furman Univ., SC, 1978. Associate Editor, New Penguin Shakespeare, 1967–77; Editor, Shakespeare Survey, 1980–. *Publications:* (ed) Thomas Nashe, Selected Writings, 1964; (ed, New Penguin Shakespeare): A Midsummer Night's Dream, 1967, Richard II, 1969, The Comedy of Errors, 1972; Shakespeare, A Reading Guide, 1969 (2nd edn 1970); Literature and Drama, 1970; (ed, Select Bibliographical Guides): Shakespeare, 1973, English Drama excluding Shakespeare, 1975; Royal Shakespeare, 1977, 2nd edn 1978; (compiled) Nineteenth-Century Shakespeare Burlesques (5 vols), 1977; Shakespeare: an illustrated dictionary, 1978, 2nd edn 1985; Shakespeare: the writer and his work, 1978; (ed with R. L. Smallwood) Thomas Dekker, The Shoemaker's Holiday, 1979; (with Gary Taylor) Modernizing Shakespeare's Spelling, with three studies in the text of Henry V, 1979; Re-Editing Shakespeare for the Modern Reader, 1984; (ed) Shakespeare's Sonnets, 1985; (ed with Gary Taylor *et al*) The Complete Oxford Shakespeare, 1986; (ed) The Cambridge Companion to Shakespeare Studies, 1986; (with Gary Taylor *et al*) William Shakespeare: a textual companion, 1987; contrib. Shak. Survey, Shak. Qly, Shak. Jahrbuch, Theatre Notebook, Stratford-upon-Avon Studies, TLS, etc. *Recreations:* music, the countryside. *Address:* Midsummer Cottage, Church Lane, Beckley, Oxford. *T:* Stanton St John 252.

WELLS, Thomas Leonard; Agent General for Ontario in the United Kingdom, since 1985; *b* 2 May 1930; *s* of Leonard Wells and Lilian May Butler; *m* 1954, Audrey Alice Richardson; one *s* two *d*. *Educ:* University of Toronto. Advertising Manager: Canadian Hosp. Jl, 1951–61; Canadian Med. Assoc. Jl, 1961–67; Chm., Scarborough, Ont Bd of Educn, 1961, 1962; MLA (Progressive C) for Scarborough N, Ontario, 1963–85; Minister: without Portfolio (responsible for Youth Affairs), 1966–69; of Health, 1969–71; of Social and Family Services, 1971–72; of Education, 1972–78; of Intergovtl Affairs, 1978–85; Govt House Leader, Ont, 1980–85. Hon. Fellow, Ont Teachers' Fedn, 1976. Hon. DLitt Univ. of Windsor, Ont, 1985. Freeman, City of London, 1985. CLJ 1984. Confederation Medal, Canada, 1967; Silver Jubilee Medal, 1977. *Recreations:* photography, walking, theatre, cinema. *Address:* Ontario House, 21 Knightsbridge, SW1X 7LY; 6/12 Reeves Mews, W1Y 3PB. *T:* 01–629 6983. *Clubs:* Royal Automobile, Royal Over-Seas League, Royal Commonwealth Society; Albany, Empire (Toronto).

WELLS, Thomas Umfrey, MA; Headmaster, Wanganui Collegiate School, New Zealand, 1960–80; *b* 6 Feb. 1927; *s* of Athol Umfrey and Gladys Colebrook Wells; *m* 1953, Valerie Esther Brewis; two *s* one *d*. *Educ:* King's College, Auckland, New Zealand; Auckland University (BA); (Orford Studentship to) King's College, Cambridge. BA 1951; MA 1954. Assistant Master, Clifton College, 1952–60 (Senior English Master, 1957–60). Pres., NZ Assoc. of Heads of Independent Secondary Schs, 1972–75. Member: Univs Entrance Bd, 1972–80; HMC; Tongariro Forest Park Promotion Cttee, 1984–; Taumarunui and Dist Promotion and Develt Council, 1985–; Trustee, Outdoor Pursuits Centre, Tawhitikuri, 1985–; Pres., Taumarunui Cricket Club Assoc., 1984–; Mem., Rotary Club of Wanganui, 1961–80 (Pres., 1979–80); Chm., Dist 993 Rotaract Cttee, 1983–85. *Recreations:* reading, theatre, cricket (Cambridge Blue, 1950), tennis, fishing; formerly Rugby football (Cambridge Blue, 1951). *Address:* PO Box 48, Owhango, King Country, New Zealand. *Clubs:* MCC; Hawks (Cambridge); Wanganui, Rotary of Taumarunui (NZ).

WELLS, William Henry Weston, FRICS; Senior Partner, Chestertons, London, since 1984 (Partner, since 1965); Chairman, Frincon Holdings Ltd, since 1977; Chairman, Hampstead Health Authority, since 1982; *b* 3 May 1940; *s* of Sir Henry Wells, CBE, and Lady Wells; *m* 1966, Penelope Jean Broadbent; two *s* (and one *s* decd). *Educ:* Radley Coll.; Magdalene Coll., Cambridge (BA). Joined Chestertons, 1959; Chm., Land and House Property Corporation, 1977. Dir, London Life Assoc., 1984–. Member: Board of Governors, Royal Free Hosp., 1968–74; Camden and Islington AHA, 1974–82; Chm., Special Trustees of Royal Free Hosp., 1979–; Mem. Council, Royal Free Hosp. Sch. of Medicine, 1977–. *Recreations:* family, philately, gardening. *Club:* Boodle's.

WELLS, William Thomas; QC 1955; *b* 10 Aug. 1908; *s* of late William Collins Wells (formerly of Clare Coll., Cambridge, and Bexhill-on-Sea) and Gertrude Wells; *m* 1936, Angela, 2nd *d* of late Robert Noble, formerly of HM Colonial Legal Service; two *s* two *d*. *Educ:* Lancing Coll.; Balliol Coll., Oxford (BA 1930). Joined Fabian Society, 1930; called to Bar, Middle Temple, 1932, Bencher 1963 (Emeritus 1986). QC Hong Kong, 1968. Dep. Chm., Hertfordshire QS, 1961–71; Recorder of King's Lynn, 1965–71; a Recorder of the Crown Court, 1972–80. Formerly Mem., Internat. Adv. Committee of Labour Party and of Political Committee and Local Government Committee of the Fabian Society. Army, 1940–45: a General Staff Officer, 2nd grade, Directorate of Military Training, War Office, with temp. rank of Major, 1942–45. MP (Lab) Walsall, 1945–55, Walsall North, 1955–Feb. 1974; Member: Lord Chancellor's Cttee on Practice and Procedure of Supreme Court, 1947–53; Magistrates Courts Rules Cttee, 1954–83; Chm.'s Panel, House of Commons, 1948–50; Departmental Cttee on Homosexual Offences and Prostitution, 1954–57; Chm., Legal and Judicial Gp (Parly Labour Party), 1964–70; a Chm. (part-time) of Industrial Tribunals, 1975–79. Governor: Bedford Coll., 1963–85; Polytechnic of North London, 1971–74 (formerly Northern Polytechnic, 1938–71). Hon. Freeman, Borough of Walsall, 1974. *Publications:* How English Law Works, 1947; contributor to journals, incl. the Tablet, and former contributor to The Fortnightly, Spectator, Times Literary Supplement, etc, mainly on legal, political and military subjects. *Address:* 1 Garden Court, Temple, EC4Y 9BJ. *T:* 01–353 5984; 1 Gray's Inn Square, Gray's Inn, WC1R 5AA. *T:* 01–405 8946. *Club:* Athenæum.

WELLS-PESTELL, family name of **Baron Wells-Pestell.**

WELLS-PESTELL, Baron *cr* 1965 (Life Peer), of Combs in the County of Suffolk; **Reginald Alfred Wells-Pestell,** MA, LLD, FPhS; sociologist; Deputy Speaker, House of Lords and Deputy Chairman of Committees, since 1981; *b* 27 Jan. 1910; *o s* of Robert Pestell and Mary (*née* Manning); *m* 1935, Irene, *y d* of late Arthur Wells; two *s*. *Educ:* elementary and grammar schs; Univ. of London (Dip. in Econ. and Social Sciences). Formerly London Probation Service; Vice-Pres., Nat. Assoc. of Probation Officers, 1974–79. A Founder, Nat. Marriage Guidance Coun. (now a Vice-Pres.). Magistrate for London, 1946–; a Chm., Chelsea and E London Matrimonial Courts. Mem. LCC, 1946–52; Stoke Newington Borough, 1945–49 (Leader of Council, 1946; Mayor 1947–49); Mem. E Suffolk County Council, 1964–67. Contested (Lab) Taunton, 1955 and 1956, Hornsey, 1950 and 1951. Lord in Waiting (a Govt Whip), 1974–79; Spokesman in House of Lords for DHSS, 1974–79; Parly Under-Sec. of State, DHSS, 1979; Dep. Chief Opposition Whip, 1979–81. Member: Church of England Council for Social Aid (Vice-Chm.); Bridgehead Cttee (appointed by Home Office); Cttee and Council of Outcasts (providing help for the socially inadequate), and Chm. of Trustees; Wireless for the Bedridden (former Chm.); Pres., Handcrafts Adv. Assoc. for the Disabled; Pres. or Patron, other voluntary organisations; delegations to Far East, Africa and Israel, and to 5th Commonwealth Med. Conf., NZ, 1977. Captain KRRC, 9th Bn City of London HG, 1940–45. Freeman, City of London, 1952. *Publications:* articles and pamphlets on marriage and family life, delinquency and social problems for press and jls. *Recreations:* music, opera. *Address:* 22 Vicarage Close, Oxford OX4 4PL. *T:* Oxford 771142.

WELMAN, Douglas Pole, CBE 1966; *b* 22 June 1902; *s* of late Col Arthur Pole Welman and late Lady Scott; *m* 1st, 1929, Denise, *d* of Charles Steers Peel; one *d*; 2nd, 1946, Betty Marjorie, *d* of late Henry Huth. *Educ:* Tonbridge Sch.; Faraday House Engineering Coll. DFH, CEng, FIMechE, FIEE, CIGasE. Electrical and Mechanical Engineering career at home and abroad, West Indies, 1928–32; Consulting Practice, 1932–37; Man. Dir of Foster, Yates and Thom Limited, Heavy Precision Engineers, 1937–50; Chairman or Member of number of wartime committees in Lancashire including Armaments Production, Emergency Services Organisation, and Ministry of Production; went to Ministry of Aircraft Production at request of Minister as Director of Engine Production, 1942; Deputy Director-General, 1943; Control of Directorate-Gen. including Propeller and Accessory Production, 1944; Part Time Member North Western Gas Board, 1949, Chairman, 1950–64; Chairman, Southern Gas Board, 1964–67; Member, Gas Council, 1950–67; Chm. and Man. Dir, Allspeeds Holdings Ltd, 1967–72. Member, Ct of Govs, Univ. of Manchester Inst. of Sci. and Techn., 1956–64, 1968–72 (Mem. Coun., 1960–64, 1968–72). FRSA. CStJ 1968 (OStJ 1964). *Publications:* articles and papers on company management. *Recreations:* sailing, fishing. *Address:* 11 St Michael's Gardens, St Cross, Winchester SO23 9JD. *T:* Winchester 68091. *Club:* Royal Thames Yacht.

WELSBY, Rev. Canon Paul Antony; Canon Residentiary and Vice-Dean of Rochester Cathedral, since 1966; Chaplain to the Queen, since 1980; *b* 18 Aug. 1920; *m* 1948, Cynthia Mary Hosmer; one *d*. *Educ:* Alcester Grammar Sch.; University Coll., Durham (MA); Lincoln Theological Coll.; Univ. of Sheffield (PhD). Curate at Boxley, Kent, 1944–47; Curate, St Mary-le-Tower, Ipswich, 1947–52; Rector of Copdock with Washbrook, 1952–66; Rural Dean of Samford, 1964–66. Director of Post-Ordination Training for Dio. of Rochester, 1966–; Examining Chaplain to Bp of Rochester, 1966–. Member, Church Assembly, 1964–70, General Synod, 1970–80; Chm., House of Clergy at Gen. Synod and Prolocutor of Convocation of Canterbury, 1974–80. *Publications:* A Modern Catechism, 1956; Lancelot Andrewes, 1958; How the Church of England Works, 1960, new edn, 1985; The Unwanted Archbishop, 1962; The Bond of Church and State, 1962; Sermons and Society, 1970; A History of the Church of England 1945–80, 1984; contrib. Theology. *Recreations:* grandchildren, reading detective fiction, genealogy. *Address:* Southgate, The Precinct, Rochester, Kent ME1 1TH. *T:* Medway 45722.

WELSH, Andrew Paton; Senior Lecturer in Business and Administrative Studies, Angus Technical College, since 1983; *b* 19 April 1944; *s* of William and Agnes Welsh; *m* 1971, Sheena Margaret Cannon; one *d*. *Educ:* Univ. of Glasgow. MA (Hons) History and Politics; DipEd, 1980. Teacher of History, 1972–74; Lectr in Public Admin and Economics, Dundee Coll. of Commerce, 1979–83. MP (SNP) South Angus, Oct. 1974–1979; SNP Parly Chief Whip, 1978–79; SNP Spokesman on: Housing, 1974–78; Self Employed Affairs and Small Businesses, 1975–79; Agriculture, 1976–79; SNP Exec. Vice Chm. for Admin, 1979–. Contested (SNP) Angus E, 1983; prospective parly cand. (SNP) Angus E, 1986–. Mem., Angus District Council, 1984–; Provost of Angus, 1984.

Recreations: music, horse riding, languages. *Address:* Olympia Buildings, Market Place, Arbroath, Angus DD11 1HR. *T:* Arbroath 74522. *Club:* Glasgow University Union.

WELSH, Brig. David, CBE 1959; DSO 1944; late Royal Artillery; Retired; *b* 10 April 1908; *s* of late Capt. Tom Welsh, Earlshaugh, Peebleshire; *m* 1947, Maud Elinor Mitchell (*d* 1977), *d* of late Major M. I. M. Campbell, MC, of Auchmannoch; one *s. Educ:* Winchester; RMA. Commissioned 2nd Lieut, RA, 1928. Served War of 1939–45 (DSO): with Royal Horse Artillery and Royal Artillery in France, N Africa and Italy. Lt-Col, 1950; Brigadier, 1958; Brigadier, RA, FarELF, 1957–60; retd, 1961. *Address:* 27 Manor House Lane, Walkington, Beverley, North Humberside HU17 8SU. *Club:* Army and Navy.

WELSH, Frank Reeson; Chairman, London Industrial Association, since 1984; *b* 16 Aug. 1931; *s* of F. C. Welsh and D. M. Welsh; *m* 1954, Agnes Cowley; two *s* two *d. Educ:* Gateshead and Blaydon Grammar Schools; Magdalene Coll., Cambridge (schol.; MA). With John Lewis Partnership, 1954–1958; CAS Group, 1958–64; Man. Dir, William Brandt's Sons & Co. Ltd, 1965–72; Chairman: Hadfields Ltd, 1967–79; Jensen Motors Ltd, 1968–72; Cox & Kings, 1972–76; Director: Henry Ansbacher & Co., 1976–82; Grindlays Bank, 1971–85. Member: British Waterways Board, 1975–81; Gen. Adv. Council, IBA, 1976–80; Royal Commn on Nat. Health Service, 1976–79; Health Educn Council, 1978–80; N British Indust. Assoc., 1980–. Dir, Trireme Trust, 1983–. Vis. Lectr and Alcoa Schol., Graduate Sch. of Business Studies, Univ. of Tennessee, Knoxville, 1979–. CBIM. *Publications:* The Profit of the State, 1982; (contrib.) Judging People, 1982; The Afflicted State, 1983; First Blood, 1985; (with George Ridley) Bend'Or, Duke of Westminster, 1985; Uneasy City, 1986. *Recreation:* sailing. *Address:* Bridge House, Bungay, Suffolk. *Clubs:* Savile, United Oxford & Cambridge University.

WELSH, Michael Collins; MP (Lab) Doncaster North, since 1983 (Don Valley, 1979–83); *b* 23 Nov. 1926; *s* of Danny and Winnie Welsh; *m* 1950, Brenda Nicholson; two *s. Educ:* Sheffield Univ. (Dept of Extramural Studies, Day Release Course, three years); Ruskin Coll., Oxford. Miner from age of 14 years. Member, Doncaster Local Authority, 1962–. *Address:* House of Commons, SW1A 0AA. *Club:* Carcroft Village Workingmen's (Carcroft, near Doncaster).

WELSH, Michael John; Member (C) Lancashire Central, European Parliament, since 1979; *b* 22 May 1942; *s* of Comdr David Welsh, RN, and Una Mary (*née* Willmore); *m* 1963, Jennifer Caroline Pollitt; one *s* one *d. Educ:* Dover Coll.; Lincoln Coll., Oxford (BA (Hons) Jurisprudence). Proprietors of Hays Wharf Ltd, 1963–69; Levi Strauss & Co. Europe Ltd, 1969–79 (Dir of Market Development, 1976). *Publication:* The Case for a Common Trade Policy, 1981. *Recreations:* amateur drama, sailing, rough walking. *Address:* Watercrook, 181 Town Lane, Whittle le Woods, Chorley, Lancs PR6 8AG. *T:* Chorley 76992. *Club:* Carlton.

WELSH, Maj.-Gen. Peter Miles, OBE 1983; MC 1967; President, Regular Commissions Board, 1983–85; *b* 23 Dec. 1930; *s* of William Miles Moss O'Donnel Welsh and Mary Edith Margaret Gertrude Louise Welsh (*née* Hearn); *m* 1974, June Patricia McCausland (*née* Macadam); two step *s* one step *d. Educ:* Winchester College; RMA Sandhurst. Commissioned, KRRC, 1951; Kenya Regt, 1958–60; student, Staff Coll., 1961; Malaya and Borneo, 1965–66; Royal Green Jackets, 1966; JSSC, 1967; Instructor, Staff Coll., 1968–71; CO 2 RGJ, 1971–73; Comd 5 Inf. Bde, 1974–76; RCDS, 1977; HQ BAOR, 1978–80; Brig., Light Div., 1980–83. *Recreations:* shooting, fishing, vegetable gardening, cooking, golf. *Address:* c/o Lloyds Bank, Maidenhead, Berks. *Clubs:* MCC, Free Foresters, I Zingari, Jesters; Berks Golf.

WELTY, Eudora; Gold Medal for the Novel, Amer. Acad. and Inst. of Arts and Letters, 1972; National Medal for Literature, 1980; Presidential Medal of Freedom, 1980. *Publications:* A Curtain of Green, 1943; The Robber Bridegroom, 1944; The Wide Net, 1945; Delta Wedding, 1947; Golden Apples, 1950; The Ponder Heart, 1954; The Bride of Innisfallen, 1955; The Shoe Bird, 1964; Losing Battles, US 1970, UK 1982; One Time, One Place, 1971; The Optimist's Daughter, 1972 (Pulitzer Prize, 1973); The Eye of the Story, 1979; The Collected Stories of Eudora Welty, 1980; One Writer's Beginnings, 1984. *Address:* 1119 Pinehurst Street, Jackson, Miss 39202, USA.

WEMYSS, 12th Earl of *cr* 1633, **AND MARCH,** 8th Earl of *cr* 1697; **Francis David Charteris,** KT 1966; Lord Wemyss of Elcho, 1628; Lord Elcho and Methil, 1633; Viscount Peebles, Baron Douglas of Neidpath, Lyne and Munard, 1697; Baron Wemyss of Wemyss (UK), 1821; Lord-Lieutenant of East Lothian since 1967; President, The National Trust for Scotland (Chairman of Council, 1947–69); Lord Clerk Register of Scotland and Keeper of the Signet, since 1974; *b* 19 Jan. 1912; *s* of late Lord Elcho (killed in action, 1916) and Lady Violet Manners (she *m* 2nd, 1921, Guy Holford Benson (decd), and *d* 1971), 2nd *d* of 8th Duke of Rutland; *S* grandfather, 1937; *m* 1940, Mavis Lynette Gordon, BA, *er d* of late E. E. Murray, Hermanus, Cape Province; one *s* one *d* (and one *s* and one *d* decd). *Educ:* Eton; Balliol College, Oxford. Assistant District Commissioner, Basutoland, 1937–44. Served with Basuto Troops in Middle East, 1941–44. Lieut, Queen's Body Guard for Scotland, Royal Company of Archers; Lord High Comr to Gen. Assembly of Church of Scotland, 1959, 1960, 1977; Chairman: Scottish Cttee, Marie Curie Meml Foundn, 1952–86; Royal Commn on Ancient and Historical Monuments, Scotland, 1949–84; Scottish Churches Council, 1964–71; Hon. Pres., The Thistle Foundn; Former Mem., Central Cttee, WCC; Mem., Royal Commn on Historical Manuscripts, 1975–85. Director, Wemyss and March Estates Management Co. Ltd; formerly Director: Standard Life Assurance Co. Ltd; Scottish Television Ltd. Hon. LLD St Andrews, 1953; DUniv Edinburgh, 1983. *Heir: s* Lord Neidpath, *qv. Address:* Gosford House, Longniddry, East Lothian. *Club:* New (Edinburgh).

See also Baron Charteris of Amisfield.

WEMYSS, Rear-Adm. Martin La Touche, CB 1981; Clerk to the Brewers' Company, since 1981; *b* 5 Dec. 1927; *s* of Comdr David Edward Gillespie Wemyss, DSO, DSC, RN, and late Edith Mary Digges La Touche; *m* 1st, 1951, Ann Hall (marr. diss. 1973); one *s* one *d*; 2nd, 1973, Elizabeth Loveday Alexander; one *s* one *d. Educ:* Shrewsbury School. CO HMS Sentinel, 1956–57; Naval Intell. Div., 1957–59; CO HMS Alliance, 1959–60; CO Commanding Officers' Qualifying Course, 1961–63; Naval Staff, 1963–65; CO HMS Cleopatra, 1965–67; Naval Asst to First Sea Lord, 1967–70; CO 3rd Submarine Sqdn, 1970–73; CO HMS Norfolk, 1973–74; Dir of Naval Warfare, 1974–76; Rear-Adm., 1977; Flag Officer, Second Flotilla, 1977–78; Asst Chief of Naval Staff (Ops), 1979–81. *Recreations:* sailing, shooting. *Address:* The Old Post House, Emberton, near Olney, Bucks. *T:* Bedford 713838. *Clubs:* White's, Army and Navy.

WENBAN-SMITH, Charlotte Susanna; *see* Rycroft, C. S.

WENBAN-SMITH, Nigel; *see* Wenban-Smith, W. N.

WENBAN-SMITH, William, CMG 1960; CBE 1957; *b* 8 June 1908; *o s* of late Frederick Wenban-Smith, Worthing; *m* 1935, Ruth Orme, *e d* of late S. B. B. McElderry, CMG; three *s* two *d. Educ:* Bradfield; King's Coll., Cambridge (MA). Colonial Administrative Service, 1931–61: Cadet, Zanzibar, 1931; Administrative Officer, Grade II, 1933; Asst DO, Tanganyika, 1935; DO, 1943; Sen. DO, 1951 (acted on various occasions as Resident Magistrate, Comr for Co-op. Development, Provincial Comr, and Sec. for Finance); Dir of Establishments, 1953; Minister for Social Services, 1958; Minister for Education and Labour, 1959–61. Chairman, Public Service Commission and Speaker, Legislative Council, Nyasaland, 1961–63. HM Diplomatic Service, Kuala Lumpur, 1964–69. *Publication:* Walks in the New Forest, 1975. *Recreations:* music, gardening. *Address:* Crossways, 2 Kivernell Road, Milford on Sea, Lymington, Hants. *T:* Lymington 43207. *Club:* Royal Commonwealth Society.

See also W. N. Wenban-Smith.

WENBAN-SMITH, (William) Nigel; HM Diplomatic Service; Deputy High Commissioner in Ottawa, since 1986; *b* 1 Sept. 1936; *s* of William Wenban-Smith, *qv*; *m* 1st, 1961, Charlotte Chapman-Andrews; two *s* two *d*; 2nd, 1976, Charlotte Susanna Rycroft, *qv*; two *s. Educ:* King's Sch., Canterbury; King's Coll., Cambridge (BA). National Service, RN. Plebiscite Supervisory Officer, Southern Cameroons, 1960–61; Asst Principal, CRO, 1961–65 (Private Sec. to Parly Under Sec., 1963–64); Second Sec., Leopoldville, 1965–67; First Sec. and (1968) Head of Chancery, Kampala, 1967–70; FCO, 1970–74; Dublin, 1975; Commercial Sec., Brussels, 1976–78; Commercial Counsellor, Brussels, 1978–80; on loan to Cabinet Office, 1980–82; Hd of E Africa Dept and Comr, British Indian Ocean Territory, FCO, 1982–85; National Defence Coll. of Canada, 1985–86. *Recreations:* walking, gardening. *Address:* c/o Foreign and Commonwealth Office, King Charles Street, SW1A 2AF.

WENDT, Robin Glover; Chief Executive, Cheshire County Council and Clerk of Lieutenancy, since 1979; *b* 7 Jan. 1941; *er s* of William Romilly Wendt and late Doris May (*née* Glover), Preston, Lancs; *m* 1965, Prudence Ann Dalby; two *d. Educ:* Hutton Grammar Sch., Preston; Wadham Coll., Oxford Univ. (BA 1962). Asst Principal 1962, Principal 1966, Min. of Pensions and Nat. Insurance; Principal Private Sec. to Sec. of State for Social Services, 1970; Asst Sec., DHSS, 1972; Dep. Sec., Cheshire CC, 1975. Mem., Social Security Adv. Cttee, 1982–. *Publications:* various articles and reviews on public service issues. *Recreations:* music, swimming, following sport. *Address:* 28 Church Lane, Upton, Chester CH2 1DJ.

WENHAM, Brian George; Managing Director, BBC Radio, since 1986; *b* 9 Feb. 1937; *s* of late George Frederick Wenham and of Harriet Wenham, London; *m* 1966, Elisabeth Downing, *d* of Keith and Margery Woolley; two *d. Educ:* Royal Masonic Sch., Bushey; St John's Coll., Oxon. Television journalist, Independent Television News, 1962–69; Editor, Panorama, BBC, 1969–71; Head of Current Affairs Gp, 1971–78; Controller, BBC 2, 1978–82; Dir of Programmes, BBC TV, 1983–86. FRTS 1986. *Publication:* (ed) The Third Age of Broadcasting, 1982. *Address:* Red Cottage, Wey Road, Weybridge, Surrey; BBC Television Centre, W12 7RJ. *T:* 01–743 8000.

WENNER, Michael Alfred; HM Diplomatic Service, retired; Commercial Adviser, Consulate-General of Switzerland in Houston; President, Wenner Trading Co., since 1982; *b* 17 March 1921; *s* of Alfred E. Wenner and of Simone Roussel; *m* 1950, Gunilla Cecilia Ståhle, *d* of Envoyé Nils K. Ståhle, CBE, and of Birgit Olsson; four *s. Educ:* Stonyhurst; Oriel College, Oxford (Scholar). Served E Yorks Regt, 1940; Lancs Fusiliers and 151 Parachute Bn, India, 1941–42; 156 Bn, N Africa, 1943; No 9 Commando, Italy and Greece, 1944–45. Entered HM Foreign Service, 1947; 3rd Sec., Stockholm, 1948–51; 2nd Sec., Washington, 1951–53; Foreign Office, 1953–55; 1st Sec., Tel Aviv, 1956–59; Head of Chancery, La Paz, 1959–61, and at Vienna, 1961–63; Inspector of Diplomatic Establishments, 1964–67; Ambassador to El Salvador, 1967–70. *Publication:* Advances in Controlled Droplet Application, Agrichemical Age, 1979. *Recreations:* fly-fishing, old maps. *Address:* 8277 Kingsbrook No 255, Houston, Texas 77024, USA; Laythams Farm, Slaidburn, Clitheroe, Lancs.

WENTWORTH, Maurice Frank Gerard, CMG 1957; OBE 1946; *b* 5 Nov. 1908; *s* of F. B. Wentworth, Finchley, N3; *m* 1962, Belinda Margaret, *d* of late B. S. Tatham and Mrs Tatham, Mickleham, Surrey; one *s* one *d. Educ:* Haileybury; University Coll., London (BA). Military Service, 1939–46, Lieutenant-Colonel. Gold Coast: Inspector of Schools, 1930; Sen. Education Officer, 1945; Principal, Teacher Training Coll., Tamale, 1946; Administrative Officer Class I, 1951; Permanent Secretary, 1953; Establishment Secretary, 1954–57 (Ghana Civil Service); Chairman: Public Service Commission: Sierra Leone, 1958–61; E African High Commn, 1961–64; Appointments Officer, ODM, 1964–73. *Address:* Quarry Hill, Todber, Sturminster Newton, Dorset.

WENTWORTH, Stephen; Under Secretary and Head of Meat Group, Ministry of Agriculture, Fisheries and Food, since 1986; *b* 23 Aug. 1943; *s* of Ronald Wentworth, OBE and Elizabeth Mary Wentworth (*née* Collins); *m* 1970, Katharine Laura Hopkinson; three *d. Educ:* King's College Sch., Wimbledon; Merton Coll., Oxford (BA, MA, MSc). Ministry of Agriculture, Fisheries and Food, 1967–; seconded: to CSSB, 1974; to FCO, as First Sec., UK Perm. Repn to EEC, Brussels, 1976; to Cabinet Office, 1980; Head of: Beef Div., 1978; Milk Div., 1982; European Communities Div., 1985. *Address:* Ministry of Agriculture, Fisheries and Food, Whitehall Place, SW1A 2HH.

WERNER, Alfred Emil Anthony; Chairman, Pacific Regional Conservation Center, 1975–82, retired; *b* 18 June 1911; *o s* of late Professor Emil Alphonse Werner, Dublin; *m* 1939, Marion Jane Davies; two *d. Educ:* St Gerard's School, Bray; Trinity College, Dublin. MSc (Dublin Univ.) and ARIC 1936; MA (Dublin) and DPhil (Univ. of Freiburg im Breisgau) 1937; Hon. ScD (Dublin) 1971. Lecturer in Chemistry, TCD, 1937; Reader in Organic Chemistry, TCD, 1946; Research Chemist, National Gallery, 1948; Principal Scientific Officer, British Museum Research Laboratory, 1954, Keeper, 1959–75. Prof. of Chemistry, Royal Acad., 1962–75. FSA 1958; FMA 1959 (President, 1967); MRIA 1963. Pres., International Institute for the Conservation of Artistic and Historic Works, 1971 (Hon. Treasurer, 1962). *Publications:* The Scientific Examination of Paintings, 1952; (with H. Roosen-Runge) Codex Lindisfarnensis, Part V, 1961; (with H. J. Plenderleith) The Conservation of Antiquities and Works of Art, 1972; articles in scientific and museum journals. *Recreations:* chess, travelling. *Address:* Smalls Farm, Groton, Colchester, Essex. *T:* Boxford 210231; 11/73 South Street, Bellerive, Tas 7018, Australia. *Club:* Athenæum.

WERNER, Louis Ronald, AM 1980; MSc, PhD; President, New South Wales Institute of Technology, 1974–86; *b* 12 Sept. 1924; *s* of Frank Werner and Olive Maude Werner; *m* 1948, Valerie Irene (*née* Bean); two *s* one *d. Educ:* Univ. of New South Wales (BSc (1st Cl. Hons; Univ. Medal); MSc, PhD). FRACI. Sen. Lectr, 1954–60, Associate Prof., 1961–67, Head of Dept of Phys. Chemistry, 1964–67, Univ. of New South Wales; Dep. Dir, 1967–68, Director, 1968–73, NSW Inst. of Technology. Chm., NSW Advanced Educn Bd, 1969–71; Trustee, Mus. of Applied Arts and Scis, 1973–86 (Pres., Bd of Trustees, 1976–84); Chairman: Conf. of Dirs of Central Insts of Technology, 1975–; ACDP, 1982–83; Member: Science and Industry Forum, Aust. Acad. of Science, 1971–76; Council for Tech. and Further Educn, 1970–85; Hong Kong UPGC, 1972–; NSW Bicentennial Exhibition Cttee, 1985–; Adv. Council, Univ. of Western Sydney, 1986–; Governor, College of Law, 1972–76. Director: NRMA Life Ltd; NRMA Finance Ltd. Councillor, Nat. Roads and Motorists Assoc., 1977–. *Publications:* numerous papers in scientific jls. *Recreations:* yachting, golf. *Address:* 1 Crete Place, East Lindfield, NSW 2070, Australia. *T:* (02) 46–1081.

WERNHAM, Prof. Archibald Garden, MA Aberdeen, BA Oxford; Regius Professor of Moral Philosophy in the University of Aberdeen, 1960–81; *b* 4 March 1916; *e s* of Archibald Garden Wernham and Christina Noble; *m* 1944, Hilda Frances Clayton; two *s. Educ:* Robert Gordon's College, Aberdeen; Aberdeen University; Balliol College, Oxford. 1st Class Hons Classics, Aberdeen, 1938, Croom Robertson Fellow, Aberdeen, 1939; 1st Cl. Hons Classical Mods, Oxford, 1939, 1st Cl. Lit. Hum., Oxford, 1943. Served in RA, 1940–42. Lecturer in Moral and Political Philosophy, St Andrews Univ., 1945–53; Sen. Lecturer, 1953–59; Reader, 1959–60. *Publications:* Benedict de Spinoza-The Political Works, 1958; reviews and articles. *Recreations:* music, swimming, walking. *Address:* Ardil, Gladstone Place, Dyce, Aberdeen. *T:* Aberdeen 722489.

WERNHAM, Prof. Richard Bruce, MA Oxon; Professor of Modern History, Oxford University, 1951–72; Fellow of Worcester College, Oxford, 1951–72; now Professor and Fellow Emeritus; *b* 11 Oct. 1906; *o s* of Richard George and Eleanor Mary Wernham; *m* 1939, Isobel Hendry Macmillan, Vancouver BC; one *d. Educ:* Newbury Grammar School; Exeter College, Oxford. Research Asst, Inst. of Historical Research, London Univ., 1929–30; Temp. Asst, Public Record Office, 1930–32; Editor, PRO, State Papers, Foreign Series. 1933–; Lecturer in Modern History, University Coll., London, 1933–34; Fellow of Trinity College, Oxford, 1934–51, Senior Tutor, 1940–41 and 1948–51; University Lecturer in Modern History, Oxford, 1941–51; Examiner in Final Honour School of Modern History, Oxford, 1946–48. Vis. Professor: Univ. of S Carolina, 1958; Univ. of California, Berkeley, 1965–66; Una's Lectr, Berkeley, 1978. Served in RAF, 1941–45. *Publications:* Before the Armada: the Growth of English Foreign Policy 1485–1558, 1966; The Making of Elizabethan Policy, 1980; After the Armada: Elizabethan England and the Struggle for Western Europe 1588–95, 1984; Calendars of State Papers, Foreign Series, Elizabeth; (ed) Vol III, New Cambridge Modern History: The Counter-Reformation and Price Revolution, 1559–1610, 1968. Articles in English Hist. Review, History, Trans Royal Hist. Soc., Encyclopædia Britannica. *Address:* 63 Hill Head Road, Hill Head, Fareham, Hants PO14 3JL.

WESIERSKA, Mrs George; *see* Walder, Ruth C.

WESIL, Dennis; *b* 18 Feb. 1915; *e s* of Jack and Polly Wesil, London; *m* 1941, Kathleen, *d* of H. S. McAlpine; two *d. Educ:* Central Foundation Sch.; University Coll., London. Entered London telephone service as Asst Supt of Traffic, 1937; PO Investigation Branch, 1941; Asst Postal Controller, 1947; Principal, PO Headqrtrs, 1953; Dep. Chief Inspector of Postal Services, 1961; Asst Sec. in charge of Postal Mechanisation Branch, 1963; Dep. Dir, NE Region (GPO), 1966; Director: NE Postal Region, 1967; London Postal Region, 1970–71; Sen. Dir, Posts, PO, 1971–75. Mem., PO Management Bd, 1975. *Recreations:* music, theatre, reading, open air. *Address:* 2 Stoneleigh, Martello Road South, Poole, Dorset BH13 7HQ. *T:* Canford Cliffs 707304.

WESKER, Arnold; playwright; director: Founder Director of Centre 42, 1961 (dissolved 1970); Chairman, British Centre of International Theatre Institute, 1978–83; President, International Playwrights' Committee, 1981–83; *b* 24 May 1932; *s* of Joseph Wesker and Leah Perlmutter; *m* 1958, Dusty Bicker; two *s* two *d. Educ:* Upton House School, Hackney. Furniture Maker's Apprentice, Carpenter's Mate, 1948; Bookseller's Asst, 1949 and 1952; Royal Air Force, 1950–52; Plumber's Mate, 1952; Farm Labourer, Seed Sorter, 1953; Kitchen Porter, 1953–54; Pastry Cook, 1954–58. Former Mem., Youth Service Council. Author of plays: The Kitchen, produced at Royal Court Theatre, 1959, 1961 (filmed, 1961); Trilogy of plays (Chicken Soup with Barley, Roots, I'm Talking about Jerusalem) produced Belgrade Theatre (Coventry), 1958–60, Royal Court Theatre, 1960; Chips with Everything, Royal Court, 1962, Vaudeville, 1962 and Plymouth Theatre, Broadway, 1963; The Four Seasons, Belgrade Theatre (Coventry) and Saville, 1965; Their Very Own and Golden City, Brussels and Royal Court, 1966 (Marzotto Drama Prize, 1964); The Friends, Stockholm and London, 1970 (also dir); The Old Ones, Royal Court, 1972; The Wedding Feast, Stockholm, 1974, Leeds 1977; The Journalists, Coventry (amateur), 1977, Yugoslav TV, 1978, Germany, 1981; The Merchant, Stockholm and Aarhus, 1976, Broadway, 1977, Birmingham, 1978; Love Letters on Blue Paper, Nat. Theatre, 1978 (also dir); Fatlips (for young people), 1978; Caritas (Scandinavian Project commission), 1980, Nat. Theatre, 1981; Sullied Hand, 1981, Edinburgh Festival and Finnish TV, 1984; Four Portraits (Japanese commn), Tokyo, 1982, Edinburgh Festival, 1984; Annie Wobbler, Suddeutscher Rundfunk, Germany, Birmingham and New End Theatre, 1983, Fortune Theatre, 1984, New York, 1986; One More Ride on the Merry Go-Round, Leicester, 1985; Yardsale, Edinburgh Fest. and Stratford-on-Avon (RSC Actors' Fest.), 1985 (also dir); Lady Othello (film script), 1980. *Television:* (first play) Menace, 1963; Breakfast, 1981; (adapted) Thieves in the Night, by A. Koestler, 1984. *Radio:* Yardsale, 1984; Bluey (Eur. Radio Commn), Cologne Radio 1984, BBC Radio 3, 1985. *Publications:* Chicken Soup with Barley, 1959; Roots, 1959; I'm Talking about Jerusalem, 1960; The Wesker Trilogy, 1960; The Kitchen, 1961; Chips with Everything, 1962; The Four Seasons, 1966; Their Very Own and Golden City, 1966; Fears of Fragmentation, 1970; The Friends, 1970; Six Sundays in January, 1971; The Old Ones, 1972; The Journalists, 1974 (in Dialog; repr. 1975); Love Letters on Blue Paper, 1974; (with John Allin) Say Goodbye! You May Never See Them Again, 1974; Words—as definitions of experience, 1976; The Wedding Feast, 1977; Journey Into Journalism, 1977; Said the Old Man to the Young Man, 1978; The Merchant, 1978; The Journalists, a triptych (with Journey into Journalism and A Diary of the Writing of The Journalists), 1979; Collected Plays, vols 1–4, 1980; Distinctions, 1985. *Address:* 37 Ashley Road, N19 3AG.

WESSEL, Robert Leslie, OBE 1969; *b* 21 Oct. 1912; *s* of late H. L. Wessel, Copenhagen, Denmark; *m* 1936, Dora Elizabeth, *d* of G. C. G. Gee, Rothley, Leics; two *s* two *d. Educ:* Malvern College. Entered N. Corah & Sons Ltd, 1932, Chm., 1957–69, retired. Served War of 1939–45, 44th Searchlight Regt RATA, 1939–41. Chairman: Nat. Youth Bureau, 1972–76; Youth Service Information Centre, 1968–72; Nat. Coll. for training Youth Leaders, 1960–70. Member: Council of Industrial Soc. (Chm., 1969–72); Cttee of Management, RNLI, 1974–82; Pro-Chancellor, Loughborough University of Technology, 1969–78; Group Chairman, Duke of Edinburgh's Conference, 1956. Mem., N and E Midlands Regional Bd, Lloyds Bank Ltd, 1962–78; Dir, Loughborough Consultants Ltd, 1970–78. FBIM; FIWM. Hon. DTech Loughborough, 1978. Mem., Worshipful Co. of Framework Knitters (Master, 1969–70). *Recreations:* painting, photography, music, travel. *Address:* Moult End, De Courcy Road, Salcombe, South Devon TQ8 8LQ. *T:* Salcombe 2641.

WEST; *see* Sackville-West, family name of Baron Sackville.

WEST, Anthony Panther; author; *b* Hunstanton, Norfolk, 4 Aug. 1914; *m* 1936, Katharine Church; one *s* one *d*; *m* 1952, Lily Dulany Emmet; one *s* one *d. Educ:* in England. Became a breeder of registered Guernsey cattle and a dairy farmer, 1937. During war was with BBC's Far Eastern Desk, Home News Div., 1943–45, and then with their Japanese Service, 1945–47. Went to USA and joined staff of the New Yorker Magazine,

1950. Houghton Mifflin Fellow, 1947. *Publications:* Another Kind, (USA) 1949, (UK) 1951; One Dark Night, (UK) 1949, (as Vintage, USA, 1950); D. H. Lawrence (a critical biography), (UK) 1951, 2nd edn 1966; Gloucestershire, (UK) 1952; The Crusades, (USA) 1954 (as All About the Crusades, UK, 1967); Heritage, (USA) 1955 (repr. with new introduction, 1984); Principals and Persuasions, (USA) 1957, (UK) 1958, new edn 1970; The Trend Is Up, (USA) 1960; Elizabethan England, (USA) 1966, (UK) 1966; David Rees Among Others, (USA) 1970, (UK) 1970; Mortal Wounds, (USA) 1973, (UK) 1975; H. G. Wells: aspects of a life, 1984. *Address:* Box 122, Fisher's Island, NY 06390, USA.

WEST, David Arthur James; Assistant Under Secretary of State (Naval Personnel), Ministry of Defence, 1981–84, retired; *b* 10 Dec. 1927; *s* of Wilfred West and Edith West (*née* Jones). *Educ:* Cotham Grammar Sch., Bristol. Executive Officer, Air Ministry, 1946; Higher Executive Officer, 1955; Principal, 1961; Assistant Secretary, 1972; Asst Under Sec. of State, 1979. *Address:* 66 Denton Road, East Twickenham TW1 2HQ. *T:* 01–892 6890.

WEST, David Thomson, CBE 1982; *b* 10 March 1923; *m* 1958, Marie Sellar; one *s* one *d. Educ:* Malvern Coll.; St John's Coll., Oxford. Served in RNVR, 1942–45; HM Diplomatic Service, 1946–76; served in Foreign Office, Office of Comr General for UK in SE Asia, HM Embassies, Paris, Lima, and Tunis; Counsellor, 1964; Commercial Inspector, 1965–68; Counsellor (Commercial) Berne, 1968–71; Head of Export Promotion Dept, FCO, 1971–72; seconded to Civil Service Dept as Head of Manpower Div., 1972–76; transf. to Home Civil Service, 1976, retired 1983. *Address:* 7 St Paul's Place, N1. *T:* 01–226 7505. *Club:* Garrick.

WEST, Prof. Donald James; Professor of Clinical Criminology 1979–84, now Emeritus, and Director 1981–84, University of Cambridge Institute of Criminology; Fellow of Darwin College, Cambridge, since 1967; Hon. Consultant Psychiatrist, National Health Service, since 1961; *b* 9 June 1924; *s* of John Charles and Jessie Mercedes West. *Educ:* Merchant Taylors' Sch., Crosby; Liverpool Univ. (MD). LittD Cambridge. FRCPsych. Research Officer, Soc. for Psychical Research, London, and pt-time graduate student in psychiatry, 1947–50; in hospital practice in psychiatry, 1951–59; Sen. Registrar, Forensic Psychiatry Unit, Maudsley Hosp., 1957–59; Inst. of Criminology, Cambridge, 1960–. Vice Pres., 1981–, and former Pres., British Soc. of Criminology; Pres., Soc. for Psychical Research, 1963–65, 1984–86; Chm., Forensic Section, World Psychiatric Assoc., 1983–. *Publications:* Psychical Research Today, 1954 (revd edn 1962); Eleven Lourdes Miracles (med. inquiry under Parapsych. Foundn Grant), 1957; The Habitual Prisoner (for Inst. of Criminology), 1963; Murder followed by Suicide (for Inst. of Criminology), 1965; The Young Offender, 1967; Homosexuality, 1968; Present Conduct and Future Delinquency, 1969; (ed) The Future of Parole, 1972; (jtly) Who Becomes Delinquent?, 1973; (jtly) The Delinquent Way of Life, 1977; Homosexuality Re-examined, 1977; (ed, jtly) Daniel McNaughton: his trial and the aftermath, 1977; (jtly) Understanding Sexual Attacks, 1978; Delinquency: its roots, careers and prospects, 1982; Sexual Victimisation, 1985; Sexual Misconduct, 1987; various contribs to British Jl of Criminology, Jl of Adolescence. *Recreations:* travel, parapsychology. *Address:* 32 Fen Road, Milton, Cambridge CB4 4AD. *T:* Cambridge 860308; 11 Queen's Gate Gardens, SW7. *T:* 01–581 2875.

WEST, Edward Mark; Deputy Director-General, Food and Agriculture Organization of the United Nations, 1982–86; *b* 11 March 1923; *m* 1948, Lydia Hollander; three *s. Educ:* Hendon County Sch.; University Coll., Oxford (MA). Served RA (W/Lieut), 1943; ICU BAOR (A/Captain), 1945. Asst Principal, Colonial Office, 1947; Private Sec., PUS, Colonial Office, 1950–51, Principal, 1951–58; Head of Chancery, UK Commn, Singapore, 1958–61; Private Secretary to Secretary of State, Colonial Affairs, 1961–62; Private Secretary to Secretary of State for Commonwealth and Colonial Affairs, 1963; Asst Sec., ODM, 1964–70; Food and Agriculture Organization: Director, Programme and Budget Formulation, 1970; Asst Dir-Gen., Administration and Finance Dept, 1974; Asst Dir-Gen., Programme and Budget Formulation, 1976. *Address:* 10 Warwick Mansions, Cromwell Crescent, SW5 9QR.

WEST, Air Commodore Ferdinand, VC 1918; CBE 1945; MC; *b* London, 29 Jan. 1896; *s* of late Francis West and late Countess De la Garde de Saignes; *m* 1922, Winifred, *d* of John Leslie; one *s. Educ:* Xaverian Coll., Brighton; Lycée Berchet; Univ. of Genoa. 2nd Lieutenant, Lieutenant, and Acting Captain in the Royal Munster Fusiliers, 1914–17; attached to the Flying Corps, 1917–18; transferred to the Royal Air Force as a Captain, 1919 (wounded three times, MC, VC, despatches twice, Cavaliere Crown of Italy); Commanded 4 Squadron, RAF, Farnborough, 1933–36; Air Attaché, British Legations, Helsingfors, Riga, Tallin, Kovno, 1936–38; Commanded: RAF Station, Odiham, 1938–39; No 50 Wing in France, 1939; Air Attaché, British Embassy, Rome, 1940; Air Attaché, British Legation, Berne, 1940; retired from RAF, 1946. Man. Dir, J. Arthur Rank Overseas Film Distributors, 1947–58. Retired as Chairman: Hurst Park Syndicate, 1963–71; Continental Shipyard Agencies Ltd; Technical Equipment Supplies Ltd; Dir, Tokalon Ltd, 1963–73; Terravia Trading Services. Comdr Order of Orange Nassau, 1949; Chevalier Legion of Honour, 1958. First Class Army Interpreter (Italian) Second Class (French). *Address:* Zoar, Devenish Road, Sunningdale, Berks. *T:* Ascot 20579. *Club:* Royal Air Force.

WEST, Rt. Rev. Francis Horner, MA; *b* 9 Jan. 1909; *o s* of Sydney Hague and Mary West, St Albans, Herts; *m* 1947, Beryl Elaine, 2nd *d* of late Rev. W. A. Renwick, Smallbridge, Rochdale; one *s* one *d. Educ:* Berkhamsted School; Magdalene Coll. and Ridley Hall, Cambridge. Exhibitioner, Magdalene, Cambridge; MA 1934; Curate St Agnes, Leeds, 1933–36; Chaplain, Ridley Hall, Cambridge, 1936–38; Vicar of Starbeck, Yorks, 1938–42. Served War of 1939–45, as CF with BEF, MEF, CMF and SEAC, 1939–46 (despatches, 1945); Director of Service Ordination Candidates, 1946–47; Vicar of Upton, Notts, 1947–51; Archdeacon of Newark, 1947–62; Vicar of East Retford, 1951–55; Bishop Suffragan of Taunton, 1962–77; Prebendary of Wells, 1962–77; Rector of Dinder, Somerset, 1962–71. Select Preacher, Cambridge Univ., 1962. Visitor, Croft House School, 1968–79. *Publications:* Rude Forefathers, The Story of an English Village, 1600–1666, 1949; The Great North Road in Nottinghamshire, 1956; Sparrows of the Spirit, 1957; The Country Parish Today and Tomorrow, 1960; F. R. B.: a portrait of Bishop F. R. Barry, 1980. *Recreations:* writing, gardening. *Address:* 11 Castle Street, Aldbourne, Marlborough, Wilts. *T:* Marlborough 40630.

WEST, Lt-Col George Arthur Alston-Roberts-; Assistant Comptroller, Lord Chamberlain's Office, since 1981; an Extra Equerry to the Queen, since 1982; *b* 1937; *s* of Major W. R. J. Alston-Roberts-West, Grenadier Guards (killed in action 1940) and of Mrs W. R. J. Alston-Roberts-West; *m* 1970, Hazel, *d* of late Sir Thomas Cook and of Lady Cook. *Educ:* Eton Coll.; RMA, Sandhurst. Commissioned into Grenadier Guards, Dec. 1957; served in England, Northern Ireland, Germany and Cyprus; retired, 1980. *Address:* Stable House, St James's Palace, SW1. *Clubs:* Boodle's, Pratt's.

WEST, Rt. Hon. Henry William, PC (N Ire) 1960; Leader, Ulster Unionist Party, 1974–79; *b* 27 March 1917; *s* of late W. H. West, JP; *m* 1956, Maureen Elizabeth Hall; four *s* three *d. Educ:* Enniskillen Model School; Portora Royal School. Farmer. MP for

Enniskillen, NI Parlt, 1954–72; Mem. (U), Fermanagh and S Tyrone, NI Assembly, 1973–75; Parly Sec. to Minister of Agriculture, 1958; Minister of Agriculture, 1960–67, and 1971–72; MP (UUUC) Fermanagh and South Tyrone, Feb.-Sept. 1974; Mem. (UUUC), for Fermanagh and South Tyrone, NI Constitutional Convention, 1975–76. N Ireland representative on British Wool Marketing Board, 1950–58; President, Ulster Farmers' Union, 1955–56. High Sheriff, Co. Fermanagh, 1954. *Address:* Rossahilly House, Enniskillen, Northern Ireland. *T:* Enniskillen 3060.

WEST, Mrs James; *see* McCarthy, Mary.

WEST, Prof. John Clifford, CBE 1977; PhD, DSc; FEng; FIEE; Vice-Chancellor and Principal, University of Bradford, since 1979; *b* 4 June 1922; *s* of J. H. West and Mrs West (*née* Ascroft); *m* 1946, Winefride Mary Turner; three *d. Educ:* Hindley and Abram Grammar School; Victoria Univ., Manchester. PhD 1953, DSc 1957. Matthew Kirtley Entrance Schol., Manchester Univ., 1940. Electrical Lieutenant, RNVR, 1943–46. Lecturer, University of Manchester, 1946–57; Professor of Electrical Engineering, The Queen's University of Belfast, 1958–65; University of Sussex: Prof. of Electrical and Control Engineering, 1965–78; Founder Dean, Sch. of Applied Scis, 1965–73, Pro-Vice-Chancellor, 1967–71; Dir, Phillips' Philatelic Unit, 1970–78. Director, A. C. E. Machinery Ltd, 1966–79. Member: UGC, 1973–78 (Chm., Technology Sub-Cttee, 1973–78); Science Res. Council Cttee on Systems and Electrical Engineering, 1963–67; Science Res. Council Engrg Bd, 1976–79; Vis. Cttee, Dept of Educn and Science, Cranfield; Civil Service Commn Special Merit Promotions Panel, 1966–72; Naval Educn Adv. Cttee, 1965–72; Crawford Cttee on Broadcasting Coverage, 1973–74; Inter-Univ. Inst. of Engrg Control, 1967–83 (Dir, 1967–70); Chm., Council for Educnl Technology, 1980–85. Pres., IEE, 1984–85 (Dep. Pres. 1982–84); Chm., Automation and Control Div., IEE, 1970–71 (Vice-Chm., 1967–70). Member: Royal Philatelic Soc., 1960–; Sociedad Filatélica de Chile, 1970–; Chm., British Philatelic Council, 1980–81; FRPSL, 1970–; Hon. FInstMC 1984. Hartley Medal, Inst. Measurement and Control, 1979. *Publications:* Textbook of Servomechanisms, 1953; Analytical Techniques for Non-Linear Control Systems, 1960; papers in Proc. IEE, Trans Amer. IEE, Brit. Jl of Applied Physics, Jl of Scientific Instruments, Proc. Inst. Measurement and Control. *Recreation:* philately. *Address:* 6 Park Crescent, Guiseley, Leeds LS20 8EL. *T:* Guiseley 72605. *Club:* Athenæum.

WEST, Kenneth, CChem, FRSC; Managing Director, Thames Water Authority, 1984–85; Director, Water Research Council, 1984–85; *b* 1 Sept. 1930; *s* of Albert West and Ethel Kirby (*née* Kendall); *m* 1980, Elizabeth Ann Borland (*née* Campbell); one step *s*, and three *d* by a previous marriage. *Educ:* Archbishop Holgate's Grammar Sch., York; University Coll., Oxford (BA). Customer Service Manager, ICI Fibres, 1960; Res. and Engrg Manager, FII, 1967; Director: South African Nylon Spinners, Cape Town, 1970; Fibre Industries Inc., N Carolina, 1974; Tech. Dir, 1977, Dep. Chm., 1980, ICI Fibres Div. FRSA. *Recreations:* sailing, flying, music, whisky. *Address:* Sonning Mead, Thames Street, Sonning, near Reading, Berks HG4 0UR. *T:* Reading 690657. *Clubs:* Yorkshire Aeroplane; Lymington Town Sailing.

WEST, Martin Litchfield, DPhil; FBA 1973; Professor of Greek, Royal Holloway and Bedford New College (formerly at Bedford College), University of London, since 1974; *b* 23 Sept. 1937; *s* of Maurice Charles West and Catherine Baker West (*née* Stainthorpe); *m* 1960, Stephanie Roberta Pickard; one *s* one *d. Educ:* St Paul's Sch.; Balliol Coll., Oxford. Chancellor's Prizes for Latin Prose and Verse, 1957; Hertford and de Paravicini Schols, 1957; Ireland Schol., 1957; Woodhouse Jun. Research Fellow, St John's Coll., Oxford, 1960–63; Fellow and Praelector in Classics, University Coll., Oxford, 1963–74; MA (Oxon) 1962, DPhil (Oxon) 1963; Conington Prize, 1965. Editor of Liddell and Scott's Greek-English Lexicon, 1965–81. *Publications:* Hesiod, Theogony (ed), 1966; Fragmenta Hesiodea (ed with R. Merkelbach), 1967; Early Greek Philosophy and the Orient, 1971; Sing Me, Goddess, 1971; Iambi et Elegi Graeci (ed), 1971–72; Textual Criticism and Editorial Technique, 1973; Studies in Greek Elegy and Iambus, 1974; Hesiod, Works and Days (ed), 1978; Theognidis et Phocylidis fragmenta, 1978; Delectus ex Iambis et Elegis Graecis, 1980; Greek Metre, 1982; The Orphic Poems, 1983; Carmina Anacreontea, 1984; The Hesiodic Catalogue of Women, 1985; articles in classical periodicals. *Recreation:* strong music. *Address:* Royal Holloway and Bedford New College, Egham Hill, Egham TW20 0EX. *T:* Egham 34455; 42 Portland Road, Oxford OX2 7EY. *T:* 56060.

WEST, Michael Charles B.; *see* Beresford-West.

WEST, Morris (Langlo), AM 1985; novelist; *b* Melbourne, 26 April 1916; *s* of Charles Langlo West and Florence Guilfoyle Hanlon; *m* 1953, Joyce Lawford; three *s* one *d. Educ:* Melbourne Univ. (BA 1937). Taught modern langs and maths, NSW and Tas, 1933–39. Served, Lieutenant, AIF, South Pacific, 1939–43. Sec. to William Morris Hughes, former PM of Australia, 1943. FRSL; Fellow World Acad. of Art and Science. Hon. DLitt, Univ. of Santa Clara, 1969; Hon. DLitt Mercy Coll., NY, 1982. Internat. Dag Hammarskjold Prize (Grand Collar of Merit), 1978. *Publications:* Gallows on the Sand, 1955; Kundu, 1956; Children of the Sun, 1957; The Crooked Road, 1957 (Eng.: The Big Story); The Concubine, 1958; Backlash, 1958 (Eng.: The Second Victory); The Devil's Advocate, 1959 (National Brotherhood Award, National Council of Christians and Jews 1960; James Tait Black Memorial Prize, 1960; RSL Heinemann Award, 1960; filmed 1977); The Naked Country, 1960; Daughter of Silence (novel), 1961, (play), 1961; The Shoes of the Fisherman, 1963; The Ambassador, 1965; The Tower of Babel, 1968; The Heretic, a Play in Three Acts, 1970; (with R. Francis) Scandal in the Assembly, 1970; Summer of the Red Wolf, 1971; The Salamander, 1973; Harlequin, 1974; The Navigator, 1976; Proteus, 1979; The Clowns of God, 1981 (Universe Literary Prize, 1981); The World is Made of Glass, 1983 (play 1984); Cassidy, 1986. *Address:* c/o Maurice Greenbaum, Rosenman Colin Freund Lewis and Cohen, 575 Madison Avenue, New York, NY 10022, USA. *Clubs:* Royal Prince Alfred Yacht, Elanora Golf (Sydney).

WEST, Norman; Member (Lab) Yorkshire South, European Parliament, since 1984; *b* 26 Nov. 1935; *m;* two *s. Educ:* Barnsley; Sheffield Univ. Miner. Mem., South Yorks CC (Chm., Highways Cttee; Mem., anti-nuclear working party). Member: NUM; CND. Mem., Energy, Research and Technology Cttee, European Parlt, 1984–. *Address:* 43 Coronation Drive, Birdwell, Barnsley, South Yorks.

WEST, Peter; commentator/anchorman, for radio since 1947, for television since 1950; Chairman, West Nally Group (sports marketing), 1971–83; *b* 12 Aug. 1920; *s* of Harold William and Dorcas Anne West; *m* 1946, Pauline Mary Pike; two *s* one *d. Educ:* Cranbrook Sch.; RMC, Sandhurst. Served War of 1939–45: Duke of Wellington's Regt. TV/Radio commentaries every year: on Test matches, 1952–86; on Wimbledon, 1955–82; on Rugby Union, 1950–85; Olympics, 1948–60–64–68–72–76. Rugby Football Correspondent of The Times, 1971–82. TV shows: Chairman of: Why?, 1953; Guess my Story, 1953–54–55. Introduced: At Home, 1955; First Hand and It's Up to You, 1956–57; Box Office, 1957; Come Dancing, 1957–72 (incl.); Be Your Own Boss and Wish You Were Here, 1958; Get Ahead, 1958–62; Good Companions, 1958–62; First Years at Work (Schs TV), 1958–69 (incl.); Miss World, 1961–66 (incl.); Facing West, 1986. Children's TV: introd.: Question Marks, 1957; Ask Your Dad, 1958; What's New?, 1962–63–64. Radio: introd.: What Shall We Call It?, 1955; Sound Idea, 1958; Morning Call, 1960–61; Treble Chance, 1962; Sporting Chance, 1964; Games People Play, 1975. *Publications:* The Fight for the Ashes, 1953; The Fight for the Ashes, 1956; Flannelled Fool and Muddied Oaf (autobiog.), 1986. *Recreation:* gardening. *Address:* The Paddock, Duntisbourne Abbotts, Cirencester, Glos. *T:* Miserden 380.

WEST, Prunella Margaret Rumney, (Mrs T. L. West); *see* Scales, Prunella.

WEST, Prof. Richard Gilbert, FRS 1968; FSA; FGS; Fellow of Clare College, Cambridge, since 1954; Professor of Botany, University of Cambridge, since 1977, and Director, Subdepartment of Quaternary Research, since 1966; *b* 31 May 1926; *m* 1st, 1958; one *s;* 2nd, 1973, Hazel Gristwood; two *d. Educ:* King's School, Canterbury; Univ. of Cambridge. Univ. Demonstrator in Botany, 1957–60; Univ. Lecturer in Botany, 1960–67; Reader in Quaternary Research, 1967–75, Prof. of Palaeoecology, 1975–77, Univ. of Cambridge. Member: Council for Scientific Policy, 1971–73; NERC, 1973–76; Ancient Monuments Bd for England, 1980–84. Darwin Lecturer to the British Association, 1959; Lyell Fund, 1961, Bigsby Medal, 1969, Geological Society of London. Hon. MRIA. *Publications:* Pleistocene Geology and Biology, 1968, 2nd edn 1977; (jtly) The Ice Age in Britain, 1972, 2nd edn 1981; The Pre-glacial Pleistocene of the Norfolk and Suffolk coasts, 1980. *Address:* 3A Woollards Lane, Great Shelford, Cambs. *T:* Cambridge 842578; Clare College, Cambridge.

WEST, Dr Richard John, FRCP; Dean since 1982, and Senior Lecturer since 1975, St George's Hospital Medical School; Consultant Paediatrician, St George's Hospital, since 1975; *b* 8 May 1939; *s* of Cecil J. West and Alice B. West (*née* Court); *m* 1962, Jenny Winn Hawkins; one *s* two *d. Educ:* Tiffin Boys' Sch.; Middlesex Hospital Medical School (MB, BS, MD, DCH, DObstRCOG). FRCP 1979. Research Fellow, Inst. of Child Health, London, 1971–73; Sen. Registrar, Hosp. for Sick Children, London, 1973–74; Lectr, Inst. of Child Health, 1974–75. Member: Wandsworth HA, 1981–82; SW Thames RHA, 1982–. Mem., Governing Body, Tiffin Boys' Sch., 1983–86. *Publications:* Family Guide to Children's Ailments, 1983; research papers on metabolic diseases, incl. lipid disorders. *Recreations:* windmills, medical history, travel, reading. *Address:* 6 Dorset Road, Merton Park, SW19 3HA. *T:* 01–542 5119.

WEST, Dr Thomas Summers, FRSE, FRSC; Director, Macaulay Institute for Soil Research, Aberdeen, since 1975; Honorary Research Professor, University of Aberdeen, since 1983; *b* 18 Nov. 1927; *s* of late Thomas West and of Mary Ann Summers; *m* 1952, Margaret Officer Lawson, MA; one *s* two *d. Educ:* Tarbat Old Public Sch., Portmahomack; Royal Acad., Tain; Aberdeen Univ. (BSc 1st Cl. Hons Chemistry, 1949); Univ. of Birmingham (PhD 1952, DSc 1962). FRSC (FRIC 1962); FRSE 1979. Univ. of Birmingham: Sen. DSIR Fellow, 1952–55; Lectr in Chem., 1955–63; Imperial Coll., London: Reader in Analytical Chem., 1963–65; Prof. of Analytical Chem., 1965–75. Pres., Analytical Div., 1977–79, Sec. Gen., 1983–, IUPAC; Pres., Soc. for Analytical Chem., 1969–71; Mem. Royal Society's British National Cttee for Chem. (Chm., Analytical Sub-cttee), 1965–; Hon. Sec., Chemical Soc., 1972–75 (Redwood Lectr, 1974); Hon. Member: Bunseki Kagakukai (Japan), 1981; Fondation de la Maison de la Chimie (Paris), 1985. Meldola Medal, RIC, 1956; Instrumentation Medal, 1976, and Gold Medal, 1977, Chemical Soc.; Johannes Marcus Medal for Spectroscopy, Spectroscopic Soc. of Bohemia, 1977. *Publications:* Analytical Applications of Diamino ethane tetra acetic acid, 1958, 2nd edn 1961; New Methods of Analytical Chemistry, 1964; Complexometry with EDTA and Related Reagents, 1969. *Recreations:* gardening, motoring, reading, music, fishing. *Address:* 31 Baillieswells Drive, Bieldside, Aberdeen AB1 9AT. *T:* Aberdeen 868294.

WEST, Timothy Lancaster, CBE 1984; actor and director; *b* 20 Oct. 1934; *s* of Harry Lockwood West and late Olive Carleton-Crowe; *m* 1st, 1956, Jacqueline Boyer (marr. diss.); one *d;* 2nd, 1963, Prunella Scales, *qv;* two *s. Educ:* John Lyon Sch., Harrow; Regent Street Polytechnic. Entered profession as asst stage manager, Wimbledon, 1956; first London appearance, Caught Napping, Piccadilly, 1959; Mem., RSC, 1964–66; Prospect Theatre Co., 1966–72: Dr Samuel Johnson, Prospero, Bolingbroke, young Mortimer in Edward II, King Lear, Emerson in A Room with a View, Alderman Smuggler in The Constant Couple, and Holofernes in Love's Labour's Lost; Otto in The Italian Girl, 1968; Gilles in Abelard and Heloise, 1970; Robert Hand in Exiles, 1970; Gilbert in The Critic as Artist, 1971; Sir William Gower in Trelawny (musical), Bristol, 1972; Falstaff in Henry IV Pts I and II, Bristol, 1973; Shpigelsky in A Month in the Country, Chichester, 1974 (London, 1975); Brack in Hedda Gabler, RSC, 1975; Iago in Othello, Nottingham, 1976; with Prospect Co.: Harry in Staircase, 1976, Claudius in Hamlet, storyteller in War Music, and Enobarbus in Antony and Cleopatra, 1977; Ivan and Gottlieb in Laughter, and Max in The Homecoming, 1978; with Old Vic Co.: Narrator in Lancelot and Guinevere, Shylock in The Merchant of Venice, 1980; Beecham, Apollo, 1980, NZ, 1983; Uncle Vanya, Australia, 1982; Stalin in Master Class, Leicester, 1983, Old Vic, 1984; Charlie Mucklebrass in Big in Brazil, 1984; The War at Home, Hampstead, 1984; When We Are Married, Whitehall, 1986. *Directed:* plays for Prospect Co., Open Space, Gardner Centre, Brighton, and rep. at Salisbury, Bristol, Northampton and Cheltenham; own season, The Forum, Billingham, 1973; Artistic Dir, Old Vic Co., 1980–81. *Television includes:* Richard II, 1969; Edward II, and The Boswell and Johnson Show, 1970; Horatio Bottomley, 1972; Edward VII, 1973; Hard Times, 1977; Crime and Punishment, Churchill and the Generals, 1979 (RTS Award); Brass, 1982–84; The Last Bastion, 1984; The Nightingale Saga, Tender is the Night, 1985; The Monocled Mutineer, 1986. *Films:* The Looking-Glass War, 1968; Nicholas and Alexandra, 1970; The Day of the Jackal, 1972; Hedda, 1975; Joseph Andrews, and The Devil's Advocate, 1976; William Morris, 1977; Agatha, and The 39 Steps, 1978; The Antagonists, 1980; Murder is Easy, and Oliver Twist, 1981. Compiles and dir. recital progs; sound broadcaster. Director in Residence, Univ. of WA, 1982; Director: All Change Arts Ltd; Hiccombe Productions Ltd; World Student Drama Trust. Member: Arts Council Drama Panel, 1974–76, and Touring Cttee, 1978–80; Council, LAMDA, 1980–; Governor, Bristol Old Vic Trust, 1986–. *Recreations:* theatre history, travel, music, old railways. *Address:* c/o James Sharkey Associates Ltd, 15 Golden Square, W1.

WEST, Prof. William Dixon, CIE 1947; ScD, FGS, FNA (Geol.); Emeritus Professor of Applied Geology, Director of Ground Water Project, Madhya Pradesh, University of Saugar; *b* 1901; *s* of Arthur Joseph West. *Educ:* King's Sch., Canterbury; St John's Coll., Cambridge (BA; ScD). Former Director, Geological Survey of India; former Vice-Chancellor, Univ. of Saugar. Lyell Medal, Geological Soc. of London, 1950. *Address:* Department of Applied Geology, University of Saugar, Madhya Pradesh, India.

WEST CUMBERLAND, Archdeacon of; *see* Hodgson, Ven. T. R. B.

WEST HAM, Archdeacon of; *see* Dawes, Ven. P. S.

WEST-RUSSELL, Sir David (Sturrock), Kt 1986; **His Honour Judge West-Russell;** President of Industrial Tribunals for England and Wales, since 1984; *b* 17 July 1921; *o s* of late Sir Alexander West-Russell and late Agnes West-Russell; *m* Christine (*née* Tyler); one *s* two *d. Educ:* Rugby; Pembroke Coll., Cambridge. Commissioned Queen's Own Cameron Highlanders, 1941; Parachute Regt, 1942–46; served in N Africa, Italy, France,

Greece, Norway and Palestine (despatches, Major). Management Trainee, Guest Keen and Nettlefold, 1948–50; Harmsworth Law Scholar, 1952; called to Bar, Middle Temple, 1953, Bencher, 1986; SE Circuit; Dep. Chm., Inner London Quarter Sessions, 1966–72; Circuit Judge, 1972; Sen. Circuit Judge, Inner London Crown Court, 1979–82, Southwark Crown Court, 1983–84. Mem., Departmental Cttee on Legal Aid in Criminal Proceedings, 1964–65. Comr (NI Emergency Provisions Act), 1974–; Chairman: Lord Chancellor's Adv. Cttee on Appts of Magistrates for Inner London, 1976–; Home Sec's Adv. Bd on Restricted Patients, 1985–; Member: Inner London Probation Cttee, 1979–; Lord Chancellor's Adv. Cttee on the Trng of Magistrates, 1980–85; Judicial Studies Bd, 1980–84; Parole Bd, 1980–82. Pres., Inner London Magistrates' Assoc., 1979–85. *Recreations:* town gardening, country walking. *Address:* 24 Hamilton Terrace, NW8. *T:* 01–286 3718. *Club:* Garrick.

WESTALL, Rupert Vyvyan Hawksley, MA Cantab; Lieutenant Commander RN (retired); Head Master, Kelly College, Tavistock, Devon, 1939–59; *b* 27 July 1899; *s* of late Rev. William Hawksley Westall and Adela Clara Pope; *m* 1925, Sylvia G. D. Page (*d* 1979); two *s* three *d*. *Educ:* RN Colleges Osborne and Dartmouth; Queens' College, Cambridge. Royal Navy, 1912–22; served European War, 1914–18; served in HMS Goliath, HMS Canada, HMS Ure and four years in The Submarine Service; Service on East African Station and Gallipoli, 1914–15, Jutland, China Station; Queens' College, Cambridge, 1922–26 (Exhibitioner in History, MA 1926, 1st division 2nd class both parts History Tripos); Training College for Schoolmasters, Cambridge, 1925–26; VI form and Careers Master, Blundell's School, 1926–34; Head Master West Buckland School, 1934–38. *Address:* Penrose, 9 Kimberley Place, Falmouth, Cornwall TR11 3QL. *T:* Falmouth 313238.

WESTBROOK, Eric Ernest, CB 1981; Arts Consultant, since 1980; *b* 29 Sept. 1915; *s* of Ernest James and Helen Westbrook; *m* 1st, 1942, Ingrid Nyström; one *d*; 2nd, 1964, Dawn Sime. *Educ:* Alleyn's Sch., Dulwich; various schools of art. Lecturer for Arts Council of Gt Britain, 1943; Director, Wakefield City Art Gallery, Yorks, 1946; Chief Exhibitions Officer, Arts Council of Gt Britain, 1949; Director: Auckland City Art Gallery, NZ, 1952–55; National Gallery of Victoria, Melbourne, Aust., 1956–73; Director (Permanent Head), Ministry for the Arts, Victoria, 1973–80, retired. Hon. LLD Monash, 1974. Chevalier de l'Ordre des Arts et Lettres (France), 1972. *Publications:* Birth of a Gallery, 1968; various articles and reviews in arts and museum pubns. *Recreations:* music, gardening. *Address:* Lot 52, Alma Road, Panton Hill, Victoria 3759, Australia. *T:* 719–7585.

WESTBROOK, Neil Gowanloch, CBE 1981; Chairman, Trafford Park Estates plc; *b* 21 Jan. 1917; *s* of Frank and Dorothy Westbrook; *m* 1945, Hon. Mary Joan Fraser, *o d* of 1st Baron Strathalmond, CBE; one *s* one *d*. *Educ:* Oundle Sch.; Clare Coll., Cambridge (MA). FRICS. Served War of 1939–45: Sapper, 1939; Actg Lt-Col 1945 (despatches). Member: Council, CBI North West Region, 1982–; Inst. of Directors Greater Manchester Branch Cttee, 1972–86. Treas., Manchester Conservative Assoc., 1964–73, Dep. Chm., 1973–74, Chm., 1974–83; Chairman: Greater Manchester Co-ordinating Cttee, NW Area Cons. Assoc., 1977–86; Exchange Div. Cons. Assoc., 1973; Manchester Euro South Cons. Assoc., 1978–84; Member: NW Area F and GP Cttee, Cons. Party, 1974–; Cons. Bd of Finance, 1984–. Mem., Manchester City Council, 1949–71; Dep. Leader 1967–69; Lord Mayor 1969–70. Chm., North Western Art Galleries and Museums Service, 1965–68; Mem., Exec. Cttee, Museums Assoc., 1965–69. Pres., Central Manchester Br., Arthritis and Rheumatism Council, 1970. *Recreations:* football, fishing, horse racing. *Address:* White Gables, Prestbury, Cheshire. *T:* Prestbury 829337. *Clubs:* Carlton; Manchester Tennis and Racquets.

WESTBROOK, Roger; HM Diplomatic Service; High Commissioner in Negara Brunei Darussalam, since 1986; *b* 26 May 1941; *e s* of Edward George Westbrook and Beatrice Minnie Westbrook (*née* Marshall). *Educ:* Dulwich Coll.; Hertford Coll., Oxford (MA Modern History). Foreign Office, 1964; Asst Private Sec. to Chancellor of Duchy of Lancaster and Minister of State, FO, 1965; Yaoundé, 1967; Rio de Janeiro, 1971; Brasilia, 1972; Private Sec. to Minister of State, FCO, 1975; Head of Chancery, Lisbon, 1977; Dep. Head, News Dept, FCO, 1980; Dep. Head, Falkland Is Dept, FCO, 1982; Overseas Inspectorate, FCO, 1984. *Recreations:* doodling, sightseeing, theatre, reading, dining. *Address:* c/o Foreign and Commonwealth Office, SW1. *Club:* Travellers'.

WESTBURY, 5th Baron, *cr* 1861; **David Alan Bethell,** MC 1942; DL; *b* 16 July 1922; *s* of Captain The Hon. Richard Bethell (*d* 1929; *o c* of 3rd Baron); *S* brother, 1961; *m* 1947, Ursula Mary Rose James; two *s* one *d*. *Educ:* Harrow. 2nd Lieut 1940, Capt. 1944, Scots Guards. Equerry to the Duke of Gloucester, 1946–49. DL N Yorks, formerly NR Yorks, 1973. KStJ 1977. *Heir:* *s* Hon. Richard Nicholas Bethell, MBE 1979 [*b* 29 May 1950; *m* 1975, Caroline Mary, *d* of Richard Palmer; two *d*. *Educ:* Harrow; RMA Sandhurst. Major Scots Guards, 1978]. *Address:* Barton Cottage, Malton, North Yorkshire. *T:* Malton 2293.

WESTBURY, Prof. Gerald, FRCP, FRCS; Professor of Surgery since 1982, Dean since 1986, Institute of Cancer Research; Hon. Consultant Surgeon, Royal Marsden Hospital, since 1982; *b* 29 July 1927; *s* of Lew and Celia Westbury; *m* 1965, Hazel Frame; three *d*. *Educ:* St Marylebone Grammar Sch.; Westminster Med. Sch., Univ. of London (MB, BS (Hons) 1949); FRCS 1952; FRCP 1976. House Surg., Westminster and Royal Northern Hosps, 1949–50; RAF Med. Service, 1950–52; RSO, Brompton Hosp., 1952–53; Registrar and Sen. Registrar, Westminster Hosp., 1953–60; Fellow in Surgery, Harvard Med. Sch., 1957; Cons. Surg., Westminster Hosp., 1960–82; Hon. Cons. in Surgery to the Army, 1980–. Examiner, Univs of London, Edinburgh, Cambridge, Hong Kong; Hunterian Prof., RCS, 1963; Honyman Gillespie Lectr, Univ. of Edinburgh, 1965; Semon Lectr and Haddow Lectr, RSM, 1982. *Publications:* medical articles and contribs to text books. *Recreations:* music, bird watching. *Address:* 123 Hamilton Terrace, NW8 9QR. *T:* 01–624 2092. *Club:* Athenæum.

WESTBURY, (Rose) Marjorie; Singer and Actress; *b* 18 June 1905; *o d* of George and Adella Westbury, Langley, Near Birmingham. Won 4 year scholarship to RCM, London, 1927. Sang Gretel at Old Vic as operatic debut for Lilian Baylis, 1932. Began broadcasting (as singer), 1933; joined BBC Drama Repertory, 1942; Solveig in Peer Gynt; Ylena (Lorca); Miles and Flora in Turn of the Screw; Nora in The Doll's House; Elsa Strauss in the Henry Reed series (Emily Butter); Steve Temple in Paul Temple series; Susan Grantly in Barchester Chronicles. *Recreations:* gardening, cooking, sewing, croquet. *Address:* Copperdene, Budletts, Maresfield, E Sussex TN22 2EB. *T:* Uckfield 2806.

WESTCOTT, George Foss, MA, MIMechE; freelance, since 1957; *b* 6 Feb. 1893; *e s* of Rev. Arthur Westcott, 2nd *s* of Brooke Foss Westcott, Bishop of Durham; *m* 1938, Anne Esther Anderberg; two *d*. *Educ:* Sherborne; GNR Locomotive Works, Doncaster (Premium Apprentice); Queens' College, Cambridge (Exhibitioner). Served in European War, 1914–19, in ASC (MT) and RFC; Hons Mechanical Science Tripos, 1920; worked for Scientific and Industrial Research Department, 1920; Assistant at Science Museum, 1921; Keeper of Mechanical Engineering Collections, 1937; on loan to Admiralty Engineering Lab., 1939–41; Emergency Commn in RASC, 1941–42; Science Museum, 1942; Keeper of Dept of Land And Water Transport, 1950; retired 1953; re-engaged as Asst Keeper, 1953; finally retired from Civil Service, 1957; worked for Intercontinental Marketing Services Ltd, 1963; Reader, Acad. of Visual Arts, 1964; founded Basic Ideology Research Unit, 1967. Kt Internat., Mark Twain Soc., 1977. *Publications:* Science Museum Handbooks; Pumping Machinery, 1932; Mechanical and Electrical Engineering, 1955 (new edn, revised by H. P. Spratt, 1960); The British Railway Locomotive, 1803–1853, 1958; various Historical Synopses of Events Charts, 1922–56; The Conflict of Ideas, 1967; Christianity, Freethinking and Sex, 1968; Towards Intellectual Freedom: the development of a basic ideology, 1972, rev. edn 1974; The Science of Man, 1975, rev. edn 1984. *Recreations:* sociological research, reading, writing.

WESTCOTT, Prof. John Hugh, DSc(Eng), PhD, DIC; FRS 1983; FEng, FIEE, FBCS, FInstMC, FCGI, FinstD; Professor of Control Systems, Imperial College of Science and Technology, since 1970; Chairman: Feedback plc; Churchill Controls Ltd; *b* 3 Nov. 1920; *s* of John Stanley Westcott and Margaret Elisabeth Westcott (*née* Bass); *m* 1950, Helen Fay Morgan; two *s* one *d*. *Educ:* Wandsworth Sch.; City and Guilds Coll., London; Massachusetts Inst. of Technology. Royal Commission for the Exhibition of 1851 Senior Studentship; Apprenticeship BTH Co., Rugby. Radar Research and Develt Estabt, 1941–45; Lectr, Imperial Coll., 1951; Reader, 1956; Prof., 1961; Head of Computing and Control Dept, 1970–79. Control Commn for Germany, 1945–46. Consultant to: Bataafsche Petroleum Maatschappij (Shell), The Hague, Holland, 1953–58; AEI, 1955–69; ICI, 1965–69; George Wimpey & Son, 1975–80; Westland plc, 1983–85. Chm., Control and Automation Div., Instn of Electrical Engrs, 1968–69. Mem., Exec. Council of Internat. Fedn of Automatic Control, 1969–75; Chm., United Kingdom Automation Council, 1973–79; Pres., Inst. of Measurement and Control, 1979–80; Governor, Kingston Polytechnic, 1974–80. *Publications:* An Exposition of Adaptive Control, 1962; monographs and papers, mainly on Control Systems and related topics. *Recreations:* gardening, reading. *Address:* Department of Electrical Engineering, Imperial College, SW7 2BT. *T:* 01–589 5111; (home) Broadlawns, 8 Fernhill, Oxshott, Surrey.

WESTENRA, family name of **Baron Rossmore.**

WESTERMAN, Sir (Wilfred) Alan, Kt 1963; CBE 1962 (OBE 1957); EdD; MAEcon; Chairman, Australian Industry Development Corporation, 1971–83; *b* NZ, 25 March 1913; *s* of W. J. Westerman, Sydney, NSW; *m* 1969, Margaret, *d* of late B. H. White. *Educ:* Knox Grammar School; Universities of Tasmania, Melbourne and Columbia. Chairman, Commonwealth Tariff Board, 1958–60; Sec., Dept of Trade and Industry, Canberra, 1960–71. Director: Ampol Ltd; Philips Industries Holdings Ltd; Oak Systems of Australia Pty Limited; Chm., Stevedoring Industry Consultative Council, 1978–. *Recreation:* tennis. *Address:* PO Box 1483, Canberra, ACT 2601, Australia. *Clubs:* Commonwealth (Canberra); Athenæum (Melbourne); Union (Sydney).

WESTHEIMER, Prof. Gerald, FRS 1985; Professor of Physiology, University of California, Berkeley, since 1967; *b* Berlin, 13 May 1924; *s* of late Isaac Westheimer and Ilse Westheimer (*née* Cohn). *Educ:* Sydney Tech. Coll. (Optometry dip. 1943, Fellowship dip. 1949); Univ. of Sydney (BSc 1947); Ohio State Univ. (PhD 1953); postdoctoral training at Marine Biol. Lab., Woods Hole, 1957 and at Physiolog. Lab., Cambridge, 1958–59. Australian citizen, 1945; practising optometrist, Sydney, 1945–51; faculties of Optometry Schools: Univ. of Houston, 1953–54; Ohio State Univ., 1954–60; Univ. of California, Berkeley, 1960–67. Associate: Bosch Vision Res. Center, Salk Inst., 1984–; Neurosciences Res. Program, NY, 1985–; Chairman: Visual Scis Study Sect., NIH, 1977–79; Bd of Scientific Counsellors, Nat. Eye Inst., 1981–83; Bd of Editors, Vision Research, 1986–; service on numerous professional Cttees. Fellow or Member, scientific socs, UK and overseas. Tillyer Medal, Optical Soc. of America, 1978; Proctor Medal, Assoc. for Res. in Vision and Ophthalmology, 1979; von Sallmann Prize, 1986. *Publications:* research articles in sci. and professional optometric and ophth. jls; edtl work for sci. jls. *Recreations:* chamber music (violin), foundation and history of sensory physiology. *Address:* 582 Santa Barbara Road, Berkeley, Calif 94707, USA.

WESTLAKE, Prof. Henry Dickinson; Hulme Professor of Greek in the University of Manchester, 1949–72, now Professor Emeritus; *b* 4 Sept. 1906; *s* of C. A. Westlake and Charlotte M. Westlake (*née* Manlove); *m* 1940, Mary Helen Sayers; one *s* one *d*. *Educ:* Uppingham School; St John's College, Cambridge (Scholar). Strathcona Student, 1929; Assistant Lecturer, University College, Swansea, 1930–32; Fellow of St John's College, Cambridge, 1932–35; Assistant Lecturer, University of Bristol, 1936–37; Lecturer, King's College, Newcastle, 1937–46; Administrative Assistant, Ministry of Home Security, 1941–44; Reader in Greek, University of Durham, 1946–49; Dean of the Faculty of Arts, Univ. of Manchester, 1960–61; Pro-Vice-Chancellor, 1965–68. *Publications:* Thessaly in the Fourth Century BC, 1935; Timoleon and his relations with tyrants, 1952; Individuals in Thucydides, 1968; Essays on the Greek Historians and Greek History, 1969. Articles and reviews in learned periodicals. *Address:* West Lodge, Manor Farm Road, Waresley, Sandy, Bedfordshire SG19 3BX. *T:* Gamlingay 50877.

WESTLAKE, Peter Alan Grant, CMG 1972; MC 1943; *b* 2 Feb. 1919; *s* of A. R. C. Westlake, CSI, CIE, and late Dorothy Louise (*née* Turner) *m* 1943, Katherine Spackman; two *s*. *Educ:* Sherborne; Corpus Christi Coll., Oxford; Military College of Science. Served with 1st Regt RHA (Adjt 1942), and on the staff (despatches). HM Foreign Service (now Diplomatic Service), 1946–76: served in Japan and at Foreign Office; Joint Services Staff College, 1954; Israel, 1955; Japan, 1957; Administrative Staff Coll., 1961; Counsellor: Foreign Office, 1961; Washington, 1965; British High Commn, Canberra, 1967–71; Minister, Tokyo, 1971–76. Pres., Asiatic Soc. of Japan, 1972–74. UK Comr-General, Internat. Ocean Expo, Okinawa, 1975. BD Wales 1981, MSc Wales, 1981; Deacon, Church in Wales, 1981, Priest 1982. FRAS. Order of the Rising Sun, Japan. *Address:* 53 Church Street, Beaumaris, Anglesey.

WESTMEATH, 13th Earl of, *cr* 1621; **William Anthony Nugent;** Baron Delvin, by tenure temp. Henry II; by summons, 1486; Senior Master, St Andrew's School, Pangbourne; *b* 21 Nov. 1928; *s* of 12th Earl of Westmeath and Doris (*d* 1968), 2nd *d* of C. Imlach, Liverpool; *S* father, 1971; *m* 1963, Susanna Margaret, *o d* of J. C. B. W. Leonard, *qv*; two *s*. *Educ:* Marlborough Coll. Captain, RA, retired. *Heir:* *s* Hon. Sean Charles Weston Nugent, *b* 16 Feb. 1965. *Address:* Farthings, Rotten Row Hill, Bradfield, Berks. *T:* Bradfield 744426.

WESTMINSTER, 6th Duke of, *cr* 1874; **Gerald Cavendish Grosvenor;** DL; Bt 1622; Baron Grosvenor, 1761; Earl Grosvenor and Viscount Belgrave, 1784; Marquess of Westminster, 1831; commissioned Queens Own Yeomanry, 1973, Captain 1979, Major 1985; *b* 22 Dec. 1951; *s* of 5th Duke of Westminster, TD, and of Viola Dowager Duchess of Westminster, *qv*; *S* father, 1979; *m* 1978, Natalia, *d* of Lt-Col H. P. J. Phillips; two *d*. *Educ:* Harrow. Director: Hennell Ltd; Stuart Devlin Ltd; Claridges Hotel Ltd; Sun Alliance & London Group; Sutton Ridge Pty Ltd; Maritime Trust; Marcher Sound Ltd; Harland & Wolff Ltd. Governor: Royal Agricl Soc. of England; Internat. Students' Trust, 1977; Chester Teacher Training Coll., 1979; Court, Univ. of Manchester, 1980; Cawthorne's Endowed Sch., 1981; Pro-Chancellor, Univ. of Keele, 1986–. President: London Tourist Bd, 1980–; NW Industrialists' Council, 1979–; Chester City Conservative

Assoc., 1977–; London Fedn of Boys' Clubs, 1984–; St John's Ambulance, London Dist, 1983–. Patron: Worcs. CCC (Pres., 1984–86); British Holstein Soc.; British Kidney Patients Assoc. Trustee, Civic Trust, 1983–. Freeman: Chester, 1973; England, 1979; City of London, 1980. OStJ 1982. DL Cheshire, 1982. *Address:* Eaton Hall, Chester, Cheshire. *Clubs:* Brooks's, Cavalry, MCC; Royal Yacht Squadron.

WESTMINSTER, Viola Dowager Duchess of; Viola Maud Grosvenor; Lord Lieutenant of Co. Fermanagh, Northern Ireland, 1979–86; *b* 10 June 1912; *d* of 9th Viscount Cobham, KCB, TD, and Violet Yolande (*d* 1966), *y d* of Charles Leonard; *m* 1946, Lt-Col Robert George Grosvenor, later 5th Duke of Westminster (*d* 1979); one *s* (*see* Duke of Westminster) two *d*. *Educ:* privately. Served War in WAAF, 1939–46 (despatches). President for Co. Fermanagh: Girl Guides Assoc., NSPCC, Salvation Army, British Legion (Women's Sect.), SJAB. Pres., Show Cttee, Ulster Farming Soc. Member Governing Body, Royal Acad. of Music. Nat. Vice-Pres., Women's Section, British Legion, Ulster, 1954–68. Former President of societies in Chester: Music Soc., Male Voice Choir, Operatic Soc., Ladies' Choir, BRCS, CPRE, Marriage Guidance Council, LEPRA. Dame of Justice, Order of St John of Jerusalem, 1983 (Dame of Grace 1980). *Recreations:* music, trees, books. *Address:* Ely Island, Enniskillen, Co. Fermanagh, N Ireland. *T:* Springfield 224.

WESTMINSTER, Archbishop of, (RC), since 1976; **His Eminence Cardinal (George) Basil Hume;** *b* 2 March 1923; *s* of Sir William Hume, CMG, FRCP. *Educ:* Ampleforth Coll.; St Benet's Hall, Oxford; Fribourg Univ., Switzerland. Ordained priest 1950. Ampleforth College: Senior Modern Language Master, 1952–63; Housemaster, 1955–63; Prof. of Dogmatic Theology, 1955–63; Magister Scholarum of the English Benedictine Congregation, 1957–63; Abbot of Ampleforth, 1963–76. Cardinal, 1976. President: RC Bishops' Conf. of England and Wales, 1979–; Council of European Bishops' Confs, 1979–; Mem. Council for Secretariat of Internat. Synod of Bishops, 1978–. Hon. Bencher, Inner Temple, 1976. Hon. DD: Cantab, 1979; Newcastle upon Tyne, 1979; London, 1980; Oxon, 1981; York, 1982; Kent, 1983; Hon. DHL: Manhattan Coll., NY, 1980; Catholic Univ. of America, 1980. *Publications:* Searching for God, 1977; In Praise of Benedict, 1981; To Be a Pilgrim, 1984. *Address:* Archbishop's House, Westminster, SW1P 1QJ.

WESTMINSTER, Auxiliary Bishops of, (RC); *see* Butler, Rt Rev. B. C.; Guazzelli, Rt Rev. V.; Harvey, Rt Rev. P. J. B.; Mahon, Rt Rev. G. T.; and O'Brien, Rt Rev. J. J.

WESTMINSTER, Dean of; *see* Mayne, Very Rev. M. C. O.

WESTMORLAND, 15th Earl of *cr* 1624; **David Anthony Thomas Fane,** KCVO 1970; Baron Burghersh, 1624; late RHG; Master of the Horse, since 1978; Director, Sotheby Parke Bernet Group (Deputy Chairman, 1979, Chairman, 1980–82); *b* 31 March 1924; *e s* of 14th Earl of Westmorland and Hon. Diana Lister (*d* 1983), *widow* of Capt. Arthur Edward Capel, CBE, and *y d* of 4th Baron Ribblesdale; *S* father 1948; *m* 1950, Jane, *d* of Lt-Col Sir Roland Lewis Findlay, 3rd Bt, and Barbara Joan, *d* of late Maj. H. S. Garrard; two *s* one *d*. Served War of 1939–45 (wounded); resigned from RHG with hon. rank of Captain, 1950. A Lord in Waiting to the Queen, 1955–78. *Heir: s* Lord Burghersh, *qv*. *Address:* Kingsmead, Didmarton, Glos; 23 Chester Row, SW1. *Clubs:* Buck's, White's.

WESTMORLAND AND FURNESS, Archdeacon of; *see* Vaughan, Ven. P. St G.

WESTOBY, Jack Cecil, CMG 1975; retired, 1974; *b* 10 Dec. 1912; *s* of John William Westoby and Rose Ellen Miles; *m* 1941, Florence May Jackson; two *s*. *Educ:* Wheeler Street Council Sch., Hull; Hymers Coll., Hull; University Coll., Hull, BScEcon (London); FSS; FIS. Railway clerk, LNER, 1936–45; Statistician, BoT, 1945–52. Food and Agriculture Organisation of United Nations: Economist/Statistician, 1952–58; Chief, Forest Economics Br., 1958–62; Dep. Dir, Forestry Div., 1962–69; Dir of Program Co-ordination and Ops, Forestry Dept, 1970–74. Regents' Prof., Univ. of California, 1972. Foreign Member: Royal Agriculture and Forestry Acad. of Sweden, 1968; Italian Acad. of Forest Science, 1971; Finnish Forestry Soc., 1964; Soc. of Amer. Foresters, 1971; Hon. Life Mem., Commonwealth Forestry Soc. *Publications:* many studies and articles in official publications of FAO and in a wide variety of professional forestry jls. *Recreations:* music, theatre. *Address:* Calcioli, Via Collegalle 12, 50022 Greve-in-Chianti (FI), Italy. *T:* (055) 854.044.

WESTOLL, James, DL; *b* 26 July 1918; *s* of late James Westoll, Glingerbank, Longtown; *m* 1946, Sylvia Jane Luxmoore, MBE, *d* of late Lord Justice Luxmoore, Bilsington, Kent; two *s* two *d*. *Educ:* Eton; Trinity College, Cambridge (MA). Served War of 1939–45: Major, The Border Regiment (despatches). Called to Bar, Lincoln's Inn, 1952. Member, NW Electricity Board, 1959–66; Deputy Chm., Cumberland Quarter Sessions, 1960–71; Cumberland County Council: CC 1947; CA 1959–74; Chm., 1958–74; Chm., Cumbria Local Govt Reorganisation Jt Cttee, 1973; Chm., Cumbria CC, 1973–76. DL 1963, High Sheriff 1964, Cumberland. Warden, 1973–75, Master, 1983–84, Clothworkers' Company. Hon. LLD Leeds, 1984. KStJ 1983. *Recreations:* gardening, shooting. *Address:* Dykeside, Longtown, Carlisle, Cumbria CA6 5ND. *T:* Longtown 791235. *Clubs:* Boodle's, Farmers'; County and Border (Carlisle).

WESTOLL, Prof. Thomas Stanley, BSc, PhD Dunelm; DSc Aberdeen; FRS 1952; FRSE, FGS, FLS; J. B. Simpson Professor of Geology, University of Newcastle upon Tyne (formerly King's College, Newcastle upon Tyne, University of Durham), 1948–77, now Emeritus; Chairman of Convocation, Newcastle upon Tyne University, since 1979; *b* W Hartlepool, Durham, 3 July 1912; *e s* of Horace Stanley Raine Westoll; *m* 1st, 1939, Dorothy Cecil Isobel Wood (marr. diss. 1951); one *s*; 2nd, 1952, Barbara Swanson McAdie. *Educ:* West Hartlepool Grammar School; Armstrong (later King's) Coll., Univ. of Durham; University College, London. Senior Research Award, DSIR, 1934–37; Lecturer in Geology, Univ. of Aberdeen, 1937–48. Leverhulme Emeritus Res. Fellow, 1977–79. Alexander Agassiz Visiting Professor of Vertebrate Paleontology, Harvard University, 1952; Huxley Lectr, Univ. of Birmingham, 1967. J. B. Tyrell Fund, 1937, and Daniel Pidgeon Fund, 1939, Geological Soc. of London. President: Palæontological Assoc., 1966–68; Section C, British Assoc. for Advancement of Science, Durham, 1970; Geological Soc., 1972–74; Mem. Council, Royal Soc., 1966–68. Corr. Mem., Amer. Museum of Natural History; Hon. Life Mem., Soc. of Vertebrate Paleontology, USA, 1976. Hon. LLD Aberdeen, 1979. Murchison Medal, Geol. Soc. London, 1967; Clough Medal, Geol Soc. of Edinburgh, 1977; Linnean Gold Medal (Zool.), 1978. *Publications:* (ed) Studies on Fossil Vertebrates, 1958; (ed, with D. G. Murchison) Coal and Coal-bearing Strata, 1968; (ed, with N. Rast) Geology of the USSR, by D. V. Nalivkin, 1973; numerous papers and monographs on vertebrate anatomy and palæontology and geological topics, in several journals. *Recreations:* photography and numismatics. *Address:* Department of Geology, The University, Newcastle upon Tyne NE1 7RU; 21 Osborne Avenue, Newcastle upon Tyne NE2 1JQ. *T:* 81–1622.

WESTON, Bertram John, CMG 1960; OBE 1957; retired from the public service; Estate Factor to British Union Trust Ltd, 1964–81; *b* 30 March 1907; *o s* of late J. G. Weston, Kennington, Kent; *m* 1932, Irene Carey; two *d*. *Educ:* Ashford Grammar School; Sidney Sussex College, Cambridge (MA); Pretoria University, SA (MSc, Agric); Cornell University, USA (Post Grad.). Horticulturist, Cyprus, 1931; Asst Comr, Nicosia (on secondment), 1937; Administrative Officer, 1939. War Service, 1940–43 (Major). Commissioner for development and post-war construction, Cyprus, 1943; Commissioner, 1946; Administrative Officer Class I, 1951; Senior Administrative Officer, 1954; Senior Commissioner, 1958; Government Sec., St Helena, 1960–63; acted as Governor and C-in-C, St Helena, at various times during this period. *Recreations:* lawn tennis, gardening, watching cricket and other sports. *Address:* 10 Westfield Close, Uphill, Weston-super-Mare BS23 4XQ. *Club:* Royal Commonwealth Society.

WESTON, Bryan Henry; Chairman, Merseyside and North Wales Electricity Board, since 1985; *b* 9 April 1930; *s* of Henry James Weston and Rose Grace Weston; *m* 1956, Heather West; two *s* two *d*. *Educ:* St George Grammar School, Bristol; Bristol, Rutherford and Oxford Technical Colleges. CEng, MIEE; MBIM. South Western Electricity Board: Commercial Manager, 1973–75; Bd Mem., 1975; Exec. Mem., 1975–77; Dep. Chm., Yorkshire Electricity Bd, 1977–85. *Recreations:* caravanning, walking, gardening. *Address:* Fountainhead Cottage, Brassey Green, near Tarporley, Cheshire. *T:* Tarporley 3523.

WESTON, Rear-Adm. Charles Arthur Winfield, CB 1978; Admiral President, RN College, Greenwich, 1976–78; Appeals Secretary, King Edward VII's Hospital for Officers, since 1979; *b* 12 July 1922; *s* of late Charles Winfield Weston and of Edith Alice Weston; *m* 1946, Jeanie Findlay Miller; one *s* one *d*. *Educ:* Merchant Taylors' Sch. Entered RN as Special Entry Cadet, 1940; HM Ships: Glasgow, 1940; Durban, 1942; Staff of C-in-C Mediterranean, as Sec. to Captain of the Fleet, 1944–45 (despatches 1945); Sec. to Cdre in Charge Sheerness, 1946–47, to Flag Captain Home Fleet, HMS Duke of York, 1947–48; Loan Service, RAN, 1948–50; HM Ships: St Vincent, 1952–53; Ceres, 1954–55; Decoy, 1956; Sec. to DCNP (Trng and Manning), 1957–58, to DG Trng, 1959; CO HMS Jufair, 1960; Supply Officer, St Vincent, 1961–62; Sec. to Fleet Comdr Far East Fleet, 1963–64, to Second Sea Lord, 1965–67; sowc 1968; Chief Staff Officer (Q) to C-in-C Naval Home Comd, 1969–70; DNPTS, 1971; Director Defence Admin Planning Staff, 1972–74; Dir of Quartering (Navy), 1975. ADC to the Queen, 1976. Rear-Adm. 1976. Liveryman, Shipwrights' Co., 1979–. *Recreations:* cricket, golf, gardening, music. *Address:* Westacre, Liphook, Hants GU30 7NY. *T:* Liphook 723337. *Clubs:* MCC, Army and Navy.

WESTON, Christopher John; Chairman and Chief Executive: Phillips Son & Neale, since 1972; Glendining & Co., and subsidiaries, since 1972; *b* 3 March 1937; *s* of Eric Tudor Weston and Evelyn Nellie Weston; *m* 1969, Josephine Annabel Moir; one *d*. *Educ:* Lancing Coll. FIA (Scot.). Director: Phillips, 1964–; F & C Pacific Investment Trust, 1984–; Headline Book Publishing, 1986–. Chairman: Phillips Gp, 1972–; Soc. of Fine Art Auctioneers, 1973–; Bradford Peters (Holdings) Ltd, 1978–; Mornington Building Soc., 1984– (Dir, 1973–). Liveryman, Painters-Stainers' Co. FRSA (Mem. Council, 1985). *Recreations:* theatre, music. *Address:* 7 Blenheim Street, W1Y 0AS. *T:* 01–629 6602. *Club:* Oriental.

WESTON, Rev. David Wilfrid Valentine; Vicar, St John the Baptist, Pilling, since 1985; *b* 8 Dec. 1937; *s* of late Rev. William Valentine Weston and late Mrs Gertrude Hamilton Weston; *m* 1984, Helen Strachan Macdonald, *d* of James and Barbara Macdonald; one *s*. *Educ:* St Edmund's Sch., Canterbury. Entered Nashdom Abbey, 1960; deacon, 1967, priest, 1968; Novice Master, 1969–74; Prior, 1971–74; Abbot, 1974–84; Curate, St Peter's, Chorley, 1984–85. Freeman, City of London; Liveryman of Salters' Co. *Address:* The Vicarage, Pilling, Preston, Lancs PR3 6AA.
See also Ven. F. V. Weston.

WESTON, Ven. Frank Valentine; Archdeacon of Oxford and a Canon of Christ Church, Oxford, since 1982; *b* 16 Sept. 1935; *s* of William Valentine Weston and Gertrude Hamilton Weston; *m* 1963, Penelope Brighid, *d* of Marmaduke Carver Middleton Athorpe, formerly of Dinnington, Yorks; one *s* two *d*. *Educ:* Christ's Hospital; Queen's Coll., Oxford; Lichfield Theological Coll. BA 1960, MA 1964. Curate, St John the Baptist, Atherton, Lancs, 1961–65; Chaplain, 1965–69, Principal, 1969–76, College of the Ascension, Selly Oak, Birmingham; Vice-Pres., Selly Oak Colls, 1973–76; Principal and Pantonian Prof., Edinburgh Theological Coll., 1976–82. Court of Assistants, Salters' Co. *Publications:* (contrib.) Quel Missionnaire, 1971; (contrib.) Gestalten der Kirchengeschichte, 1984; contribs to Faith and Unity, Sobornost, Eglise Vivante. *Recreations:* wine, persons and song; exploring the countryside. *Address:* Archdeacon's Lodging, Christ Church, Oxford OX1 1DP. *T:* Oxford 243847.
See also Rev. D. W. V. Weston.

WESTON, Galen; *see* Weston, W. G.

WESTON, Garfield Howard; Chairman: Associated British Foods plc, since 1967; Fortnum and Mason, since 1978; *b* 28 April 1927; *s* of late Willard Garfield Weston and Reta Lila Howard; *m* 1959, Mary Ruth, *d* of late Major-Gen. Sir Howard Kippenberger; three *s* three *d*. *Educ:* Sir William Borlase School, Marlow; New College, Oxford; Harvard University (Economics). Man. Director: Ryvita Co. Ltd, 1951; Weston Biscuit Co., Aust., 1954; Vice-Chairman, Associated British Foods Ltd, 1960; Chm., George Weston Holdings Ltd, 1978. *Recreations:* gardening, tennis, walking. *Address:* Weston Centre, Bowater House, 68 Knightsbridge, SW1X 7LR. *T:* 01–589 6363. *Club:* Lansdowne.

WESTON, Geoffrey Harold, CBE 1975; FHSM; retired; Deputy Health Service Commissioner for England, Scotland and Wales, 1977–82; *b* 11 Sept. 1920; *s* of George and Florence Mary Weston; *m* 1953, Monica Mary Grace Comyns; three *d*. *Educ:* Wolverhampton Sch. War Service, 1940–46. Gp Sec., Reading and Dist Hosp. Management Cttee, 1955–65; Board Sec., NW Metropolitan Regional Hosp. Bd, 1965–73; Regional Administrator, NW Thames RHA, 1973–76. Member: Salmon Cttee, 1963–65; Whitley Councils: Mem. Management side of Optical Council, 1955–65, and of Nurses and Midwives Council, 1966–76; Mem., Working Party on Collab. between Local Govt and Nat. Health Service, 1973–74. Inst. of Health Service Administrators: Mem., Nat. and Reg. Councils, 1959–78 (Vice-Chm. of Council, 1968, Chm. 1969, Pres. of Inst., 1970). Bd Mem., London and Provincial Nursing Services Ltd, 1973–; Member: Mental Health Review Tribunal, 1982–; Oxford RHA, 1983–; Trustee, Goring Day Centre, 1978–. Parish Councillor, 1979–. *Recreations:* gardening, travel, dining with friends. *Address:* Little Mead, Goring on Thames, near Reading, Berks RG8 9ED. *T:* Goring on Thames 872881. *Club:* Royal Air Force.

WESTON, John; *see* Weston, P. J.

WESTON, Dr John Carruthers; General Manager, Northampton Development Corporation, 1969–77. *Educ:* Univ. of Nottingham. Admiralty Research, 1940–46; Plessey Co., 1946–47; Building Research Station, 1947–64; Chief Exec. Operational Div., Nat. Building Agency, 1964–65; Dir, Building Research Station, MPBW, 1966–69. *Recreations:* gardening, music, walking, reading and living.

WESTON, John Pix, BSc(Eng), BSc(Econ); CEng, FIEE, FBIM; investment consultant, since 1984; *b* 3 Jan. 1920; *s* of John Pix Weston and Margaret Elizabeth (*née Cox); m* 1948, Ivy (*née* Glover); three *s*. *Educ:* King Edward's Sch., Birmingham, 1931–36; Univ.

of Aston, 1946–50 (BSc(Eng), Hons); Univ. of London (LSE), 1954–57 (BSc(Econ), Hons). CEng 1953, FIEE 1966; FSS 1958; FREconS 1958; FBIM 1977. City of Birmingham: Police Dept, 1936–39; Electricity Supply Dept, 1939–48; Midlands Electricity Bd, 1948–50; English Electricity Co., 1950–51; NW Elec. Bd, 1951–58; Eastern Elec. Bd, 1958–60; Dep. Operating Man., Jamaica Public Services Co., 1960–61; Principal Asst Engr, Midlands Elec. Bd, 1961–64; Asst Ch. Commercial Officer, S of Scotland Elec. Bd, 1964–66; Sen. Econ. Adviser to Mrs Barbara Castle, MoT, 1966–69; Sen. Econ. and Chartered Engr, IBRD, 1968–70; Michelin Tyre Co., France, 1970–72; Dir of Post Experience Courses, Open Univ., 1972–75; Dir Gen., RoSPA, 1975–77; Gen. Sec., Birmingham Anglers' Assoc., 1977; Industrial Develt Officer, Argyll and Bute, 1977–79; Health, Safety and Welfare Officer, Newcastle Polytechnic, and Central Safety Advr, Northants CC, 1979; Chief Admin. Officer and Clerk to Governors, W Bromwich Coll. of Comm. and Tech., 1979–85. Hon. Sec. and Treasurer, Assoc. of Coll. Registrars and Administrators (W Midlands), 1982–85. Council Mem., Midlands Counties Photographic Fedn, 1984–86; Hon. Prog. Sec. and Council Mem., Birmingham Photographic Soc., 1981–86; MIES 1963; Mem., Assoc. of Public Lighting Engrs, 1962. Chm., Upper Marlbrook Residents' Assoc., 1982–. Page Prize, IEE, 1950; Rosebery Prize, Univ. of London, 1957. SBStJ 1962. *Publications:* papers, reports and other contribs on electricity, highways, educn (espec. function and progress of the Open University), safety, etc, to public bodies, congresses and conferences, UK and abroad. *Recreations:* cine photography (Programme Sec., Birmingham Photographic Soc., 1981–86), gardening, swimming, fell walking. *Address:* The Bungalow, Marlbrook Lane, Upper Marlbrook, Bromsgrove, Worcs. *T:* 021–445 2393. *Clubs:* Farmers', St John House; Birmingham Press.

WESTON, John William, CB 1979; Principal Assistant Solicitor, Board of Inland Revenue, 1967–80; *b* 3 Feb. 1915; *s* of Herbert Edward Weston, MA, and Emma Gertrude Weston; *m* 1943, Frances Winifred (*née* Johnson); two *s* one *d. Educ:* Berkhamsted Sch., Herts. Solicitor, 1937. Joined Inland Revenue, 1940; Sen. Legal Asst, 1948; Asst Solicitor, 1954. *Recreations:* tennis, golf. *Address:* 5 Dickerage Road, Kingston Hill, Surrey. *T:* 01–942 8130.

WESTON, Dame Margaret (Kate), DBE 1979; BScEng (London); CEng; FMA; Director of the Science Museum, 1973–86; *b* 7 March 1926; *o c* of late Charles Edward and Margaret Weston. *Educ:* Stroud High School; College of Technology, Birmingham (now Univ. of Aston). Engineering apprenticeship with General Electric Co. Ltd, followed in 1949 by development work, very largely on high voltage insulation problems. Joined Science Museum as an Assistant Keeper, Dept of Electrical Engineering and Communications, 1955; Deputy Keeper, 1962; Keeper, Dept of Museum Services, 1967–72. Mem., Ancient Monuments Bd for England, 1977–84. Mem., SE Elec. Bd, 1981–. Trustee, Hunterian Collection, 1981–. Governor, Imperial Coll. (FIC 1975). FMA 1976; Sen. Fellow, RCA, 1986; FRSA (Mem. Council, 1985–). Hon. Fellow, Newnham Coll., Cambridge, 1986. Hon. DEng Bradford, 1984; Hon. DSc: Aston, 1974; Salford, 1984. *Address:* 7 Shawley Way, Epsom, Surrey. *T:* Burgh Heath 55885.

WESTON, Michael Charles Swift, CVO 1979; HM Diplomatic Service; Counsellor, Cairo, 1984–86; *b* 4 Aug. 1937; *s* of late Edward Charles Swift Weston and of Kathleen Mary Weston (*née* Mockett); *m* 1959, Veronica Anne Tickner; two *s* one *d. Educ:* Dover Coll.; St Catharine's Coll., Cambridge (Exhibitioner). BA, MA. Joined HM Diplomatic Service, 1961; 3rd Sec., Kuwait, 1962; 2nd Sec., FCO, 1965; 1st Secretary: Tehran, 1968; UK Mission, New York, 1970; FCO, 1974; Counsellor, Jedda, 1977; RCDS, 1980; Counsellor (Information), Paris, 1981. *Recreations:* tennis, squash. *Address:* French Court, Pett, East Sussex TN35 4JA. *T:* Hastings 812306.

WESTON, (Philip) John, CMG 1985; HM Diplomatic Service; Minister, Paris, since 1985; *b* 13 April 1938; *s* of late Philip George Weston and Edith Alice Bray (*née* Ansell); *m* 1967, Margaret Sally Ehlers; two *s* one *d. Educ:* Sherborne; Worcester Coll., Oxford. 1st Cl. Hons, Honour Mods Classics and Lit. Hum. Served with Royal Marines, 1956–58. Entered Diplomatic Service, 1962; FO, 1962–63; Treasury Centre for Admin. Studies, 1964; Chinese Language student, Hong Kong, 1964–66; Peking, 1967–68; FO, 1969–71; Office of UK Permanent Representative to EEC, 1972–74; Asst Private Sec. to Sec. of State for Foreign and Commonwealth Affairs (Rt Hon. James Callaghan, Rt Hon. Anthony Crosland), 1974–76; Counsellor, Head of EEC Presidency Secretariat, FCO, 1976–77; Vis. Fellow, All Souls Coll., Oxford, 1977–78; Counsellor, Washington, 1978–81; Hd Defence Dept, FCO, 1981–84; Asst Under-Sec. of State, FCO, 1984–85. *Recreations:* fly-fishing, poetry, running, chess. *Address:* c/o Foreign and Commonwealth Office, SW1. *Club:* United Oxford & Cambridge University.

WESTON, Ronald; Commissioner of Customs and Excise, since 1983; *b* 17 Feb. 1929; *s* of late Arthur and Edna Weston; *m* 1953, Brenda Vera Townshend; two *s* one *d. Educ:* Swanwick Hall Grammar Sch., Derbyshire. Officer of Customs and Excise, 1952; Principal, 1972; Asst Secretary, Collector of Customs and Excise, Birmingham, 1977; Deputy Director, then Director, Outfield, 1982. *Recreations:* choral music, walking. *Address:* 4 Hill Rise, Rickmansworth, Herts WD3 2NZ. *T:* Rickmansworth 779121. *Club:* Moor Park Golf.

WESTON, W(illard) Galen; Chairman, since 1974, and President, since 1978, George Weston Ltd, Toronto; *b* England, 29 Oct. 1940; *s* of W. Garfield Weston and Reta Lila (*née* Howard); *m* Hilary Mary Frayne; one *s* one *d.* Chairman: Loblaw Companies Ltd; Brown Thomas Group Ltd (Eire); Vice-Chm., Fortnum & Mason plc (UK); Pres., Wittington Investments Ltd; Director: British Columbia Packers Ltd; National Tea Co. (US); Peter J. Schmidt Inc. (US); Canadian Imperial Bank of Commerce; Associated British Foods plc (UK). Pres. and Trustee, W. Garfield Weston Foundation. *Address:* Suite 2001, George Weston Ltd, 22 St Clair Avenue East, Toronto, Ont. M4T 2S3, Canada. *Clubs:* Toronto, York (Toronto); Guards' Polo.

WESTON, Rear-Adm. William Kenneth, CB 1956; OBE 1945; RN retired; *b* 8 November 1904; *s* of late William Weston; *m* 1934, Mary Ursula Shine; one *s* two *d. Educ:* RNC Osborne and Dartmouth. RNEC Keyham; RNC Greenwich. Served on staff of Flag Officer Destroyers, Pacific, 1945–46; Admiralty District Engineer Overseer, NW District, 1951–54; Staff of C-in-C Plymouth, 1954–58; retired, 1958. Court of Assistants of the Worshipful Company of Salters, 1959, Master, 1963. *Address:* Brackleyways, Hartley Wintney, Hants. *T:* Hartley Wintney 2546. *Club:* Naval and Military.

WESTWELL, Alan Reynolds, MSc; CEng, MIMechE, MIProdE; FCIT; Managing Director and Chief Executive, Strathclyde Buses Ltd, since 1986; *b* 11 April 1940; *s* of Stanley Westwell and Margaret (*née* Reynolds); *m* 1967, Elizabeth Aileen Birrell; two *s* one *d. Educ:* Old Swan Coll.; Liverpool Polytechnic (ACT Hons); Salford Univ. (MSc 1983). Liverpool City Transport Dept: progressively, student apprentice, Technical Asst, Asst Works Manager, 1956–67; Chief Engineer: Southport Corporation Transport Dept, 1967–69; Coventry Corp. Transport Dept, 1969–72; Glasgow Corp. Transport Dept, 1972–74; Director of Public Transport (responsible for bus/rail, airport, harbours), Tayside Regional Council, 1974–79; Dir Gen., Strathclyde PTE, 1979–86. President: Scottish Council of Confedn of British Road Passenger Transport, 1982–83 (Vice-Pres., 1981–82); Bus and Coach Council, Scotland, 1982–83; Vice Pres., Bus and Coach Council, UK, 1985–86. Chairman: IMechE, Automobile Div., Scottish Centre, 1982–84; CIT, Scottish Centre, 1983–84. *Publications:* various papers. *Recreations:* golf, swimming, tennis, music, modelling, reading. *Address:* 12 Glen Drive, Helensburgh, Dunbartonshire G84 9BJ. *T:* Helensburgh 71709. *Club:* Helensburgh Golf.

WESTWOOD, family name of **Baron Westwood.**

WESTWOOD, 2nd Baron, *cr* 1944, of Gosforth; **William Westwood;** Company Director; *b* 25 Dec. 1907; *s* of 1st Baron and Margaret Taylor Young (*d* 1916); *S* father 1953; *m* 1937, Marjorie, *o c* of Arthur Bonwick, Newcastle upon Tyne; two *s. Educ:* Glasgow, JP Newcastle upon Tyne, 1949. Dir of several private companies. Hon. Vice-Pres., Football Association, 1981 (Vice-Pres., 1974–81); Life Mem., Football League, 1981. FRSA; FCIS. *Heir: s* Hon. William Gavin Westwood [*b* 30 Jan. 1944; *m* 1969, Penelope, *er d* of Dr C. E. Shafto, Newcastle upon Tyne; two *s*]. *Address:* 12 Westfield Drive, Newcastle upon Tyne NE3 4XU.

WESTWOOD, Rt. Rev. William John; *see* Peterborough, Bishop of.

WETHERALL, Rev. Canon Theodore Sumner; *b* 31 May 1910; *s* of late Rev. A. S. Wetherall and Mrs G. V. M. Wetherall (*née* Bennett-Powell); *m* 1939, Caroline, 4th *d* of Dr Charles Milne; one *s* three *d. Educ:* St Edward's School, Oxford; Oriel College, Oxford. Exhibitioner at Oriel College, 1929; 1st Class Classical Mods, 1931; BA (2nd Class Lit. Hum.), 1933. Preparatory Schoolmaster, Wellesley House, Broadstairs, 1933–35; MA 1936; Liddon Student, 1936; Cuddesdon College, 1936–37; Asst Curate, St John's, Greengates, Bradford, 1937–39; Fellow and Chaplain, Corpus Christi College, Oxford, 1939–47, Dean, 1940–45, Vice-Pres., 1947; Principal of St Chad's College, Durham, 1948–65. Vicar of St Edward the Confessor, Barnsley, 1965–69; Vicar of Huddersfield, 1969–76. Select Preacher to the Univ. of Oxford, 1945–47; Chaplain in the Univ. of Oxford to Bishop of Derby, 1940–47, Examining Chaplain to Bishop of Oxford, 1946–47, to Bishop of Durham, 1948–65, to Bishop of Bradford, 1949–55; to Bishop of Wakefield, 1969–76; Surrogate for Marriages, 1969–76; Rural Dean of Huddersfield, 1969–76. Hon. Canon: Durham, 1958–65, Wakefield, 1970–76; Hon. Canon Emeritus, Wakefield, 1976–. *Address:* 2 Lomas Cottages, Litton, Buxton, Derbyshire SK17 8QR. *T:* Tideswell 871042.

WETHERELL, Alan Marmaduke, PhD; FRS 1971; Senior Physicist, CERN (European Organisation for Nuclear Research), Geneva, since 1963 (Division Leader, Experimental Physics Division, 1981–84); *b* 31 Dec. 1932; *s* of Marmaduke and Margaret Edna Wetherell; *m* 1957, Alison Morag Dunn (*d* 1974); one *s. Educ:* Univ. of Liverpool (BSc, PhD). Demonstrator in Physics, Univ. of Liverpool, 1956–57; Commonwealth Fund Fellow, California Inst. of Technology, Pasadena, Calif., 1957–59; Physicist, CERN, 1959–63. Vis. Prof., Dept of Physics, Univ. of Liverpool, 1981–. *Publications:* scientific papers in: Proc. Phys. Soc. (London), Proc. Roy. Soc. (London), Physical Review, Physical Review Letters, Physics Letters, Nuovo Cimento, Nuclear Physics, Nuclear Instruments and Methods, Yadernaya Fizika, Uspekhi Fizicheski Nauk. *Recreations:* skiing, water skiing. *Address:* 27 Chemin de la Vendee, 1213 Petit Lancy, Geneva, Switzerland. *T:* 022 928742.

WETTON, Philip Henry Davan; HM Diplomatic Service; Counsellor, Seoul, 1983–March 1987; *b* 21 Sept. 1937; *s* of late Eric Davan Wetton, CBE and Kathleen Valerie Davan Wetton; *m* 1983, Roswitha Kortner. *Educ:* Westminster; Christ Church, Oxford (MA). Unilever Ltd, 1958–65; FCO, 1965–68; served Tokyo, Osaka and FCO, 1968–73; Head of Division, later Director, Secretariat of Council of Ministers of European Communities, 1973–83. *Recreations:* rowing, music, astronomy. *Address:* c/o Foreign and Commonwealth Office, SW1.

WETZEL, Dave; Deputy Leader and Chair of Environmental Planning, London Borough of Hounslow, since 1986; *b* 9 Oct. 1942; *s* of Fred Wetzel and Ivy Donaldson; *m* 1973, Heather Allman; two *d. Educ:* Spring Grove Grammar Sch.; Southall Technical Coll., Ealing Coll., and the Henry George Sch. of Social Sciences (part-time courses). Student apprentice, 1959–62; Bus Conductor/Driver, 1962–65, Bus Official, 1965–69, London Transport; Br. Manager, Initial Services, 1969–70; Pilot Roster Officer, British Airways, 1970–74 (ASTMS Shop Steward); Political Organiser, Co-operative Soc., 1974–81; Member for Hammersmith N, GLC, 1981–86 (Transport Cttee Chair, 1981–86). Elected Mem. (Lab) Hounslow Borough Council, 1964. Editor, Civil Aviation News, 1978–81. *Recreations:* politics, Esperanto, camping. *Address:* 28 Penderel Road, Hounslow, Middlesex TW3 3QR. *Club:* Feltham Labour.

WEYER, Deryk Vander, CBE 1986; FIB, CBIM; Deputy Chairman, British Telecom, 1983–86; Director: Bank of England, since 1986 (Member, Board of Banking Supervision, since 1986); Barclays Bank PLC, since 1974; *b* 21 Jan. 1925; *s* of Clement Vander Weyer and Harriet Weyer; *m* 1950, Marguerite (*née* Warden); one *s* one *d. Educ:* Bridlington Sch. FIB 1972; CBIM (FBIM 1976). Joined Barclays Bank PLC, 1941: Asst Manager, Liverpool, 1956; Man., Chester Br., 1961; Local Dir, Liverpool, 1965; Asst Gen. Man., 1968; Gen. Man., 1969; Sen. Gen. Man., 1973; Vice-Chm., 1977–80; Chm., Barclays Merchant Bank Ltd, 1977–80; Dir, Barclays Bank Internat., 1977–83; Gp Dep. Chm., Barclays Bank, 1980–83; Chm., Barclays Bank UK, 1980–83. Pres., Institute of Bankers, 1979–81. Mem., Royal Commn on Distribn of Income and Wealth, 1977–79; part-time Dir, British Telecom. Corp., 1981–83. Chm., Bd of Companions, BIM, 1981–. Governor, Museum of London, 1978–83. *Recreations:* painting, music. *Address:* 1 Gatefield Cottages, High Road, Chipstead, Surrey CR3 3QR.

WEYMES, John Barnard, OBE 1975; HM Diplomatic Service, retired; Managing Director, Cayman Islands News Bureau, Grand Cayman, 1981–83; *b* 18 Oct. 1927; *s* of William Stanley Weymes and Irene Innes Weymes; *m* 1978, Beverley Pauline Gliddon; three *c* (by a previous marr.). *Educ:* Dame Allan's Sch., Newcastle upon Tyne; King's Coll., Durham Univ., Newcastle upon Tyne. Served HM Forces, 1945–48. Foreign Office, 1949–52; 3rd Sec., Panama City, 1952–56; 2nd Sec., Bogotá, 1957–60; Vice-Consul, Berlin, 1960–63; Dep-Consul, Tamsui, Taiwan, 1963–65; 1st Sec., FCO, 1965–68; Prime Minister's Office, 1968–70; Consul, Guatemala City, 1970–74; 1st Sec., FCO, 1974–77; Consul-Gen., Vancouver, 1977–78; Ambassador to Honduras, 1978–81. *Recreations:* outdoor sport, partic. cricket; chess, reading. *Address:* Nuthatches, Balcombe Green, Sedlescombe, Battle, E Sussex TN33 0QL. *T:* Sedlescombe 455. *Clubs:* MCC, Middlesex County Cricket; Rodmell Cricket, Sedlescombe Cricket, Sedlescombe Seniors.

WEYMOUTH, Viscount; Alexander George Thynn; *b* 6 May 1932; *s* of Marquess of Bath, *qv*; *m* 1969, Anna Gyarmathy; one *s* one *d. Educ:* Eton College; Christ Church, Oxford (BA, MA). Lieutenant in the Life Guards, 1951–52, and in Royal Wilts Yeomanry, 1953–57. Contested (Wessex Regionalist): Westbury, Feb. 1974; Wells, 1979; contested (Wessex Regionalist and European Federal Party) Wessex, European Election 1979. Pres., Verulam Inst., 1976–. Permanent exhibn of murals (painted 1964–69, opened to public 1973), in private apartments at Longleat House. Record, I Play the Host, singing own compositions, 1974. *Publications:* (as Alexander Thynn) (before 1976 Alexander Thynne) The Carry-cot, 1972; Lord Weymouth's Murals, 1974; A Regionalist Manifesto, 1975;

The King is Dead, 1976; Pillars of the Establishment, 1980. *Heir: s* Hon. Ceawlin Henry Laszlo Thynn, *b* 6 June 1974. *Address:* Longleat, Warminster, Wilts. *T:* Maiden Bradley 300.

WHADDON, Baron *cr* 1978 (Life Peer), of Whaddon in the County of Cambridgeshire; **(John) Derek Page;** Director: Cambridge Chemical Co. Ltd, since 1962; Microautomatics Ltd, since 1981; Rindalbourne, since 1985; Chairman: Daltrade, since 1983; Skorimpex-Rind, since 1985; *b* 14 Aug. 1927; *s* of John Page and Clare Page (*née* Maher); *m* 1st, 1948, Catherine Audrey Halls (*d* 1979); one *s* one *d*; 2nd, 1981, Angela Rixson. *Educ:* St Bede's College, Manchester; London University. External BSc (Soc.). MP (Lab) King's Lynn, 1964–70; contested (Lab) Norfolk NW, Feb. 1974. Mem., Council of Management, CoSIRA, 1975–82; Mem., E Anglia Economic Planning Council, 1975–80. *Recreation:* private pilot. *Address:* The Old Vicarage, Whaddon, Royston, Herts. *T:* Cambridge 207209. *Club:* Reform.

WHALE, John Hilary; Head of Religious Programmes, BBC Television, since 1984; *b* 19 Dec. 1931; *s* of Rev. Dr John Seldon Whale, *qv*; *m* 1957, Judith Laurie Hackett; one *s*. *Educ:* Winchester; Corpus Christi College, Oxford. BA Lit Hum 1955, MA 1958. Lieut, Intelligence Corps, 1950–51 (Nat. Service). Writing, acting and teaching, 1954–58; Section Anglaise, French radio, Paris, 1958–59; ITN, 1960–69: Political Corresp., 1963–67; US Corresp., Washington, 1967–69; Sunday Times, 1969–84: political staff, 1969–79; Religious Affairs Corresp., 1979–84; Asst Editor, 1981–84; leader-writer throughout; Dir, London programme, Univ. of Missouri Sch. of Journalism, 1980–83. Churchwarden, St. Mary's, Barnes, 1976–81. *Publications:* The Half-Shut Eye, 1969; Journalism and Government, 1972; The Politics of the Media, 1977; One Church, One Lord, 1979 (Winifred Mary Stanford Prize, 1980); (ed) The Pope from Poland, 1980; Put it in Writing, 1984; (contrib.) Why I am Still an Anglican, 1986; contribs to books, quarterlies, weeklies. *Address:* 28 St James's Walk, Clerkenwell, EC1R 0AP. *T:* 01–253 1008.

WHALE, Rev. John Seldon, MA (Oxon); DD (Glasgow); *b* 19 Dec. 1896; *s* of Rev. John Whale and Alice Emily Seldon; *m* Mary, *d* of Rev. H. C. Carter, MA; two *s* two *d* (and one *s* decd). *Educ:* Caterham School, Surrey; St Catherine's Society and Mansfield College, Oxford; 1st Class Hons Sch. of Mod. Hist. 1922; Magdalene College, Cambridge, 1933. Minister of Bowdon Downs Congregational Church, Manchester, 1925–29; Mackennal Professor of Ecclesiastical History, Mansfield College, Oxford, and Tutor in Modern History, St Catherine's, 1929–33; President of Cheshunt College, Cambridge, 1933–44; Headmaster of Mill Hill School, 1944–51; Visiting Professor of Christian Theology, Drew Univ., Madison, NJ, USA, 1951–53. Moderator of Free Church Federal Council, 1942–43; Select Preacher, Univ. of Cambridge, 1943, 1957; Warrack Lecturer, 1944; Russell Lecturer (Auburn and New York), 1936 and 1948; Alden Tuthill Lecturer, Chicago, 1952; Greene Lecturer, Andover, 1952; Currie Lecturer, Austin, Texas, 1953; Hill Lectr, St Olaf Coll., Minnesota, 1954; Visiting Lecturer, Univ. of Toronto, 1957; Danforth Scholar, USA, 1958; Sir D. Owen Evans Lectures, Aberystwyth, 1958. Visiting Professor, Univ. of Chicago, 1959; Senior Fellow of Council of Humanities, Princeton Univ., 1960. *Publications:* The Christian Answer to the Problem of Evil, 1936; What is a Living Church?, 1937; This Christian Faith, 1938; Facing the Facts, 1940; Christian Doctrine, 1941; The Protestant Tradition, 1955; Victor and Victim: the Christian doctrine of Redemption, 1960; Christian Reunion: historic divisions reconsidered, 1971; The Coming Dark Age, 1973 (Eng. trans. of Roberto Vacca's Il Medioevo Prossimo Venturo, 1972). *Address:* Wild Goose, Widecombe-in-the-Moor, Newton Abbot, S Devon TQ13 7TY. *T:* Widecombe-in-the-Moor 260.

See also J. H. Whale.

WHALEN, Geoffrey Henry; Managing Director, Peugeot Talbot Motor Co. Ltd, since 1984; *b* 8 Jan. 1936; *s* of Henry and Mabel Whalen; *m* 1961, Elizabeth Charlotte; two *s* three *d*. *Educ:* Magdalen College, Oxford. MA Hons Modern History; FIPM. National Coal Board, Scotland (industrial relations), 1959–66; Divl Personnel Manager, A. C. Delco Div., General Motors, Dunstable, 1966–70; British Leyland, 1970–78; Personnel Dir, Leyland Cars, 1975–78; Personnel Dir, Rank Hovis McDougall Bakeries Div., 1978–80; Personnel and Indust. Rel. Dir, Talbot Motor Co., 1980–81, Asst Man. Dir, 1981–84. *Address:* Victoria Lodge, 8 Park Crescent, Abingdon, Oxon OX14 1DF. *Club:* United Oxford & Cambridge University.

WHALLEY, Richard Carlton; Chairman: Ewden Associates Ltd, since 1981; Eaton and Booth Ltd, since 1984; John King and Co. Ltd, since 1985; Chairman and Chief Executive, Eaton and Booth Rolling Mills Ltd, since 1984; *b* Quetta, India, 4 July 1922; *s* of Frederick Seymour Whalley, MC, FCGI, MIMechE, and Gwendolen, *d* of Sir William Collingwood; *m* 1945, Mary Christian Bradley; two *s* twin *d*. *Educ:* Shrewsbury Sch.; 151 OCTU, Aldershot. Served War: Private, Royal Berkshire Regt, 1940; commissioned 2nd Lieut, Royal Corps of Signals, 1942; Captain and Adjt, 2nd Div. Signals, India, Assam, Burma, 1942–45 (despatches). War Office, AG II (O), 1945–48; GHQ Singapore, 1948–51. Vulcan Foundry Ltd: Asst Sec., 1952–58; Commercial Manager, 1958–60; Dep. Gen. Manager, 1960–65; Manager, English Electric Diesel Engine Div., 1965–67; Dir and Gen. Manager, Glacier Metal Co., 1968–70. 1970–78: Dep. Chm. and Managing Dir, Millspaugh Ltd; Chm. and Managing Dir, C. A. Harnden Ltd, Westbury Engrg Ltd, Hargreaves & Jennings Ltd, and T. Rowbottom Ltd; Director: Bertram-Scott Ltd; Sulzer Bros (UK) Ltd; Mem., Bd of British Shipbuilders (with special responsibility for personnel, indust. relations, and trng), 1978–80. Chairman: F. & M. Ducker Ltd, 1981–84; A. Spafford & Co. Ltd, 1981–82; Pennine Plastics Ltd, 1981–82; Director: Estridge & Ropner Ltd, 1981–84; Sheffield Photoco, 1983–84; Dep. Chm., Malacarp Group, 1982–84. *Recreations:* rowing, walking. *Address:* Sunnybank Farm, Bolsterstone, Sheffield S30 5ZL. *T:* Sheffield 883116. *Clubs:* National Liberal; Sheffield (Sheffield); London Rowing.

WHALLEY, Prof. William Basil; Professor of Chemistry and Head of Department of Pharmaceutical Chemistry, School of Pharmacy, 1961–82, now Emeritus Professor of Chemistry, University of London; *b* 17 Dec. 1916; *s* of William and Catherine Lucy Whalley; *m* 1945, Marie Agnes Alston; four *s* one *d*. *Educ:* St Edward's College, Liverpool; Liverpool University. BSc Hons 1938; PhD 1940; DSc 1952; FRIC 1950. MOS and ICI 1940–45. Lecturer, 1946–55, Sen. Lectr, 1955–57, Reader, 1957–61, in Organic Chemistry, at Liverpool University. *Publications:* contrib. on organic chemistry to several books: *eg* Heterocyclic Compounds, Vol. 7, Edited R. C. Elderfield, Wiley (New York); many pubns in Jl of Chem. Soc., Jl Amer. Chem. Soc., etc. *Recreations:* music and mountaineering. *Address:* 9 Peaks Hill, Purley, Surrey. *T:* 01–668 2244.

WHALLEY, Maj.-Gen. William Leonard, CB 1985; Colonel Commandant, Royal Army Ordnance Corps, since 1986; *b* 19 March 1930; *m* 1955, Honor Mary (*née* Golden); one *d*. *Educ:* Sir William Turner's Sch., Coatham. Joined Army (Nat. Service), 1948; sc 1962; Commander, RAOC, 1st Div., 1968–71; Dir of Ordnance Services, BAOR, 1980–83; Dir Gen. of Ordnance Services, MoD, 1983–85. Life Vice-Pres., Army Boxing Assoc. (Chm., 1983–85). *Recreations:* bridge, computers, cabinet making. *Address:* Midland Bank, 81 Church Street, Preston, Lancs PR1 3AA.

WHALLEY-TOOKER, Hyde Charnock, MA, LLM (Cantab), MA (Oxon); Emeritus Fellow of Downing College, Cambridge (Fellow, 1927–67, and Senior Tutor, 1931–47); University Lecturer in Law, 1931–67; *b* 1 Sept. 1900; *o s* of Edward Whalley-Tooker; *m* 1935, Frances, *er d* of late Thomas Halsted; one *d*. *Educ:* Eton; Trinity Hall, Cambridge; Balliol College, Oxford; Law Tripos Part I, Class I, 1921; Part II, Class I, 1922. *Address:* 5 Wilberforce Road, Cambridge. *T:* Cambridge 350073.

WHARNCLIFFE, 4th Earl of, *cr* 1876; **Alan James Montagu-Stuart-Wortley-Mackenzie;** Viscount Carlton, 1876; Baron Wharncliffe, 1826; *b* 23 March 1935; *o s* of 3rd Earl and late Lady Elfrida Wentworth Fitzwilliam, *d* of 7th Earl Fitzwilliam; *S* father 1953; *m* 1957, Aline Margaret, *d* of late R. F. D. Bruce, Wharncliffe Side, near Sheffield; one *d* (and one *d* decd). *Educ:* Eton. Joined RNVR, 1952; National Service, RN, 1953–55; RNSR, 1955–59. *Recreation:* shooting. *Heir: cousin* Alan Ralph Montagu-Scott-Wortley [*b* 27 July 1927; *m* 1952, Virginia Anne, *d* of W. Martin Claybaugh; two *s* one *d*]. *Address:* Wharncliffe House, Wortley, Sheffield S30 4DG. *T:* Sheffield 882331. *Clubs:* Lansdowne; Sheffield (Sheffield).

See also D. C. Mansel Lewis, Duke of Newcastle.

WHARTON, Barony *cr* 1544–5; in abeyance. *Co-heiresses:* Hon. Myrtle Olive Felix Robertson [*b* 20 Feb. 1934; *m* 1958, Henry MacLeod Robertson; three *s* one *d*]; Hon. Caroline Elizabeth Appleyard-List [*b* 28 Aug. 1935; *m* 1970, Commander Jonathon Cecil Appleyard-List, RN; one *d*].

WHARTON, Michael Bernard; author and journalist; 'Peter Simple' Columnist, Daily Telegraph, since 1960; *b* 19 April 1913; *s* of Paul Nathan and Bertha Wharton; *m* 1st, 1936, Joan Atkey (marr. diss. 1947); one *s*; 2nd 1952, Catherine Mary Derrington (marr. diss. 1972); one *d*; 3rd, 1974, Susan Moller. *Educ:* Bradford Grammar Sch.; Lincoln Coll., Oxford. Army service, Royal Artillery and General Staff, 1940–46. Scriptwriter and Producer, BBC, 1946–56; writer on Peter Simple column, Daily Telegraph, 1957–60. *Publications: as Michael Wharton:* (ed) A Nation's Security, 1955; Sheldrake (novel), 1958; The Missing Will (autobiog.), 1984; editor and mainly writer of ten anthologies of Peter Simple column, 1963–84; *under pseudonym Simon Crabtree:* Forgotten Memories, 1941; Hector Tumbler Investigates, 1943. *Recreations:* walking, gardening, Celtic studies. *Address:* Forge Cottage, Naphill Common, High Wycombe, Bucks. *T:* Naphill 3454.

WHATELEY, Dame Leslie Violet Lucy Evelyn Mary, DBE 1946 (CBE 1943); TD 1951; *b* 28 Jan. 1899; *d* of late Ada Lilian Hutton and late Col Evelyn F. M. Wood, CB, DSO, OBE; *m* 1st, 1922, W. J. Balfour; one *s*; 2nd, 1939, H. Raymond Whateley, Squadron-Leader, RAFVR. *Educ:* Convents of Society of HCJ, St Leonards-on-Sea and Cavendish Square. Private Secretary up to marriage, and then Social Welfare Work, including District Nursing Associations and Village Institutes. Director of Auxiliary Territorial Service, 1943–46; Hon. Col 668 (bn) HAA Regt RA (TA), 1948–53. Director World Bureau of Girl Guides/Girl Scouts, 1951–64; Administrator of Voluntary Services, Queen Mary's Hosp., Roehampton, 1965–74. Chevalier Légion d'Honneur, 1945; Order of Merit (USA), 1946. *Publications:* As Thoughts Survive, 1949; Yesterday, Today and Tomorrow, 1974. *Recreations:* gardening, writing. *Address:* c/o Lloyds Bank, 6 Pall Mall, SW1.

WHATLEY, Prof. Frederick Robert, FRS 1975; Sherardian Professor of Botany, Oxford University, since 1971; Fellow of Magdalen College, Oxford, since 1971; *b* 26 Jan. 1924; *s* of Frederick Norman Whatley and Maud Louise (*née* Hare); *m* 1951, Jean Margaret Smith Bowie; two *d*. *Educ:* Bishop Wordsworth's Sch., Salisbury; (Scholar) Selwyn Coll., Cambridge University (BA, PhD). Benn W. Levy Student, Cambridge, 1947. Sen. Lectr. in Biochemistry, Univ. of Sydney, 1950–53; Asst Biochemist, Univ. of California at Berkeley, 1954–58; Associate Biochemist, 1959–64; Guggenheim Fellowship (Oxford and Stockholm), 1960; Prof. of Botany, King's Coll., London, 1964–71. Vis. Fellow, ANU, 1979. *Publications:* articles and reviews in scientific jls. *Address:* Department of Plant Sciences, South Parks Road, Oxford OX1 3RA. *T:* Oxford 53391.

WHATLEY, William Henry Potts, OBE 1986; General Secretary, Union of Shop Distributive and Allied Workers, 1979–85; *b* 16 Dec. 1922; *s* of Arthur John and Ethel Whatley; *m* 1946, Margaret Ann Harrison. *Educ:* Gosforth Secondary School. Clerk, CWS, Newcastle upon Tyne, 1938; War Service, RAF, War of 1939–45; Area Organiser, USDAW, Bristol, 1948; National Officer, 1966; Chief Organising Officer, 1976; Member: TUC General Council, 1979–85; TUC Economic Cttee, 1979; Pres., EURO-FIET, 1982–. *Recreations:* gardening, reading. *Address:* 72 St Martin's Road, Ashton-on-Mersey, Sale, Cheshire. *T:* 061–973 3772.

WHEADON, Richard Anthony; Principal, Elizabeth College, Guernsey, since 1972; *b* 31 Aug. 1933; *s* of Ivor Cecil Newman Wheadon and Margarita Augusta (*née* Cash); *m* 1961, Ann Mary (*née* Richardson); three *s*. *Educ:* Cranleigh Sch. Balliol Coll., Oxford. MA (Physics). Commissioned RAF, 1955 (Sword of Honour); Air Radar Officer, 1955–57; Asst Master, Eton Coll., 1957–66; Dep. Head Master and Head of Science Dept, Dauntsey's Sch., 1966–71. Mem., Wilts Educn Cttee's Science Adv. Panel, 1967–71. Member: HMC; SHA; NAHT. Rowed bow for Oxford, 1954, for GB in European Championships and Olympic Games, 1956; Captain RAF VIII, 1956 and 1957; Olympic Selector and Nat. Coach, 1964–66. Contingent Comdr, Dauntsey's Sch. CCF, 1969–70. *Publication:* The Principles of Light and Optics, 1968. *Recreations:* French horn, photography, electronics, singing, sailing, words. *Address:* Elizabeth College, Guernsey, Channel Islands. *T:* Guernsey 26544. *Club:* East India, Devonshire, Sports and Public Schools.

WHEARE, Thomas David, MA; Headmaster of Bryanston School, since 1983; *b* 11 Oct. 1944; *s* of late Sir Kenneth Wheare, CMG, FBA, and of Lady (Joan) Wheare; *m* 1977, Rosalind Clare Spice; two *d*. *Educ:* Dragon Sch.; Magdalen College Sch., Oxford; King's Coll., Cambridge (BA, MA); Christ Church, Oxford (DipEd). Assistant Master, Eton College, 1967–76; Housemaster of School House, Shrewsbury School, 1976–83. *Recreation:* cooking. *Address:* Bryanston School, Blandford, Dorset DT11 0PX. *T:* Blandford 52728.

WHEATCROFT, George Shorrock Ashcombe; Professor of English Law, University of London, 1959–68, now Professor Emeritus; First Editor, British Tax Review, 1956–71, now Consulting Editor; first Editor of British Tax Encyclopedia, 1962–71, now Consulting Editor; Consulting Editor, Encyclopedia of Value Added Tax; Vice-Chairman, Hambro Life Assurance Ltd, 1971–79; Chairman, G. S. A. & M. Wheatcroft (Advisory Services) Ltd; Adviser to HM Customs and Excise on Value Added Tax, 1971–72; *b* 29 Oct. 1905; *s* of Hubert Ashcombe Wheatcroft and Jane (*née* Eccles); *m* 1930, Mildred Susan (*d* 1978), *d* of late Canon Walter Lock, DD, formerly Warden of Keble College, Oxford; two *s* one *d*. *Educ:* Rugby; New College, Oxford (MA). Qualified as Solicitor, 1929; partner in Corbin Greener and Cook, Solicitors, of 52 Bedford Row, London, 1930–51; Master of the Supreme Court (Chancery Division), 1951–59. Served as an officer in RASC, 1940–45; released in 1945 with hon. rank of Lt-Col (despatches twice). Mem., Payne Cttee on enforcement of civil debts. Past President British Chess Federation. Consulting Editor, Hambro Tax Guide, 1972–. Hon. Fellow: LSE, 1976; UC Buckingham,

1978. Hon. LLD Buckingham, 1979. *Publications:* The Taxation of Gifts and Settlements, 1953 (3rd edn 1958); The Law of Income Tax, Surtax and Profits Tax, 1962; Estate and Gift Taxation, 1965; Capital Gains Tax, 1965; Wheatcroft on Capital Gains Taxes (with A. E. W. Park), 1967; Corporation Tax (with J. E. Talbot), 1968; Sweet & Maxwell's Guide to the Estate Duty Statutes, 1969 (2nd edn 1972); Whiteman and Wheatcroft on Income Tax and Surtax, 1971; (with G. D. Hewson) Capital Transfer Tax, 1975; titles Discovery, Execution, Judgments and Orders and Practice and Procedure in Halsbury's Laws of England (3rd edn); articles on taxation and legal procedure in periodicals. *Recreations:* golf, bridge, chess (represented England at Stockholm in 1937). *Address:* Brackenhill, Gravel Path, The Common, Berkhamsted, Herts HP4 2PJ. *Club:* Reform.

WHEATCROFT, Stephen Frederick, OBE 1974; Director, Aviation and Tourism International Ltd, since 1983; *b* 11 Sept. 1921; *s* of late Percy and Fanny Wheatcroft; *m* 1st, 1943, Joy (*d* 1974), *d* of late Cecil Reed; two *s* one *d*; 2nd, 1974, Alison, *d* of late Arnold Dessau; two *s*. *Educ:* Latymer Sch., N9; London Sch. of Economics. BSc(Econ) 1942. Served War, Pilot in Fleet Air Arm, 1942–45. Commercial Planning Manager, BEA, 1946–53; Simon Research Fellow, Manchester Univ., 1953–55; private practice as Aviation Consultant, 1956–72; retained as Economic Adviser to BEA. Commns for Govts of: Canada, India, W Indies, E African Community, Afghanistan; Consultant to World Bank; Assessor to Edwards Cttee on British Air Transport in the Seventies; Mem. Bd, British Airways (Dir of Economic Develt), 1972–82. Governor, London Sch. of Economics. Vis. Prof., Univ. of Surrey. FRAeS, FCIT (Pres., 1978–79); FAIAA; CBIM. *Publications:* Economics of European Air Transport, 1956; Airline Competition in Canada, 1958; Air Transport Policy, 1966; articles in professional jls. *Recreation:* travel. *Address:* 20 Mallord Street, SW3. *T:* 01–351 1511. *Club:* Reform.

WHEATLEY, family name of **Baron Wheatley.**

WHEATLEY, Baron *cr* 1970 (Life Peer), of Shettleston, Glasgow; John Wheatley, PC 1947; one of the Senators of the College of Justice in Scotland, 1954–85; Lord Justice-Clerk, 1972–85; *b* 17 Jan. 1908; *s* of Patrick Wheatley and Janet Murphy; *m* 1935, Agnes Nichol; four *s* one *d*. *Educ:* St Aloysius Coll., Glasgow; Mount St Mary's Coll., Sheffield; Glasgow Univ. MA 1928; LLB 1930; called to Scottish Bar, 1932; Advocate-Depute, 1945–47 MP (Lab) East Edinburgh, 1947–54; Solicitor-General for Scotland, March-Oct. 1947; QC (Scotland) 1947; Lord Advocate, 1947–51. War of 1939–45, RA (Field) and later with Judge Advocate-General's Branch; Chm. Scottish Nurses' Salaries Cttee, 1945–47; Chm. Milk Enquiry in Scotland, 1946–47; Chm., Cttee on Teaching Profession (Scotland), 1961–63; Mem., Royal Commn on Penal Reform (England and Wales), 1964–66; Chairman: Exec. Cttee Royal Scottish Soc. for Prevention of Cruelty to Children, 1956–79; Royal Commn on Local Govt in Scotland, 1966–69; conducted enquiry into crowd safety at sports grounds, 1971–72. Hon. Pres., Age Concern (Scotland). Hon. LLD Glasgow, 1963; DUniv Stirling, 1976; Hon. FEIS. *Recreation:* golf. *Address:* 3 Greenhill Gardens, Edinburgh EH10 4BN. *T:* 031–229 4783.
See also T. Dalyell, Hon. John Wheatley.

WHEATLEY, Alan Edward, FCA; Senior Partner, Price Waterhouse (London Office), since 1985; *b* 23 May 1938; *s* of Edward and Margaret Wheatley (*née* Turner); *m* 1962, Marion Frances (*née* Wilson); two *s* one *d*. *Educ:* Ilford Grammar School. Chartered Accountant. Norton Slade, 1954–60, qualified 1960; joined Price Waterhouse, 1960; admitted to partnership, 1970; Mem., Policy Cttee, 1981–. Non-exec. Dir, EBS Investments (Bank of England sub.), 1977–; Govt Dir, Cable & Wireless, 1981–84, non-exec. Dep. Chm., 1984–85. Member: British Steel Corp., 1984–; Ind. Develt Adv. Bd, 1985–. Governor, Solefield School, 1985–. *Recreations:* golf, tennis, badminton. *Address:* Highcroft, Kippington Road, Sevenoaks, Kent. *T:* Sevenoaks 453088. *Club:* Wildernesse (Seal, Kent).

WHEATLEY, Sir Andrew; *see* Wheatley, Sir G. A.

WHEATLEY, Rear-Adm. Anthony; Flag Officer, Portsmouth, Naval Base Commander and Head of Establishment of Fleet Maintenance and Repair Organisation, since 1985; *b* 3 Oct. 1933; *yr s* of Edgar C. Wheatley and late Audrey G. Barton Hall; *m* 1962, Iona Sheila Haig; one *d*. *Educ:* Berkhamsted School; RN Coll., Dartmouth; RNEC, Manadon. HMS Ceylon, 1958-60; HMS Ganges, 1960–61; HMS Cambrian, 1962–64; Staff of RNEC, Manadon, 1964–67; Staff of Comdr British Navy Staff, Washington, 1967–69; HMS Diomede, 1970–72; Staff of C-in-C Fleet, 1972–74; Exec. Officer, RNEC Manadon, 1975–76; MoD Procurement Exec., 1977–79; British Naval Attaché, Brasilia, 1979–81; RCDS course 1982; HMS Collingwood (in Command), 1982–85. *Recreations:* cricket (Pres., RN Cricket Club), golf, music. *Address:* c/o Barclays Bank, 189 High Street, Berkhamsted, Herts HP4 1AY. *Clubs:* Army and Navy, Free Foresters.

WHEATLEY, Rev. Canon Arthur; Priest in Charge of St Columba's, Grantown-on-Spey and St John's, Rothiemurchus, since 1983; *b* 4 March 1931; *s* of George and Elizabeth Wheatley; *m* 1959, Sheena Morag Wilde; two *s* two *d*. *Educ:* Alloa Academy; Coates Hall Theol. Coll., Edinburgh. Deacon 1970, priest 1970, Dio. Brechin; 1st Curate's title, St Salvador's with St Martin's, Dundee, 1970–71; Curate in Charge, St Ninian's Mission, Dundee, 1971–76; Rector of Holy Trinity, Elgin with St Margaret's Church, Lossiemouth, Dio. Moray, Ross and Caithness, 1976–80; Canon of St Andrew's Cathedral, 1978–80; Provost, 1980–83; Canon of Inverness Cathedral, 1985–. Episcopalian Chaplain to HM Prison, Porterfield, 1980–. *Recreations:* shooting, fishing, bee keeping and motor cycling. *Address:* St Columba's Rectory, Grant Road, Grantown-on-Spey, Moray PH26 3ER.

WHEATLEY, Derek Peter Francis, QC 1981; Legal Adviser to Lloyds Bank, since 1976 (Deputy Legal Adviser, 1974–76); Chairman, Legal Committee, Committee of London and Scottish Bankers, since 1985; Member, Commercial Court Committee, since 1976; Barrister-at-Law; *b* 18 Dec. 1925; 3rd *s* of late Edward Pearse Wheatley, company director, and Gladys Wheatley; *m* 1955, Elizabeth Pamela, *d* of John and Gertrude Reynolds; two *s* one *d*. *Educ:* The Leys Sch., Cambridge; University Coll., Oxford (MA). Served War of 1939–45, Army, 1944–47: (short univ. course, Oxford, 1944); commissioned into 8th King's Royal Irish Hussars, 1945, Lieut. University Coll., Oxford, 1947–49; called to the Bar, Middle Temple, 1951; Member: Senate of Inns of Court and the Bar, 1975–78, 1982–85; Exec. Cttee, Bar Council, 1982–85. Deputy Coroner: to the Royal Household, 1959–64; for London, 1959–64; Recorder of the Crown Court, 1972–74. Vice-Pres., Bar Assoc. for Commerce, Finance and Industry, 1986– (Chm., 1982–83). *Publications:* articles in legal jls and The Times. *Recreation:* sailing. *Address:* Three The Wardrobe, Old Palace Yard, Richmond, Surrey. *T:* 01–940 6242. *Clubs:* Bar Yacht, Little Ship.

WHEATLEY, Sir (George) Andrew, Kt 1967; CBE 1960; MA; BCL; Clerk of the Peace and Clerk of Hampshire County Council, 1946–67; *b* 1908; *s* of late Robert Albert Wheatley; *m* 1937, Mary Vera Hunt; three *s* two *d*. *Educ:* Rugby and Exeter Coll., Oxford. Asst Solicitor: Pembrokeshire CC, 1932–34; East Suffolk CC, 1934–36; N Riding, Yorks, 1936–39; Dep. Clerk of the Peace and Dep. Clerk of Cumberland CC, 1939–42; Clerk of the Peace and Clerk of the Cumberland CC, 1942–46. Hon. Sec., Society of Clerks of the Peace of Counties and of Clerks of County Councils, 1961; former

Member: Local Government Advisory Panel, Dept of Technical Co-operation; Home Office Adv. Council on Child Care; Central Training Council in Child Care; Min. of Housing and Local Govt Departmental Cttee on Management in Local Govt; Royal Commn on Assizes and Quarter Sessions; Mem., English Local Govt Boundary Commn, 1971–78. DL Hants, 1967–70. *Address:* 7 Admiral's Close, Lymington SO41 9ET.

WHEATLEY, John Derek; Director General, The Sports Council, since 1983; *b* 24 July 1927; *s* of Leslie Sydney and Lydia Florence Wheatley; *m* 1956, Marie Gowers; one *s* one *d*. *Educ:* Sir Thomas Rich's Sch., Gloucester; Loughborough Coll., 1944–46 (Teacher's Cert.); Carnegie College of Physical Educn, 1952–53 (DipPE). Served RAF, 1946–52; Surrey Education Authority, 1953–54; Central Council of Physical Recreation: London and SE, 1954–58; Secretary, Northern Ireland, 1959–69; Principal Regional Officer, SW, 1970–72; Sports Council: Regional Director, SW, 1972–80; Director of Administrative Services, Headquarters, 1980–83. *Recreations:* gardening, bee keeping, running. *Address:* 1 Argyll Court, 82–84 Lexham Gardens, W8 5JB.

WHEATLEY, Hon. John Francis; Sheriff of Tayside Central and Fife at Perth, since 1980 (at Dunfermline, 1979–80); *b* 9 May 1941; *s* of Rt Hon. John Thomas Wheatley (Baron Wheatley), *qv; m* 1970, Bronwen Catherine Fraser; two *s*. *Educ:* Mount St Mary's Coll., Derbyshire; Edinburgh Univ. (BL). Called to the Scottish Bar, 1966; Standing Counsel to Scottish Develt Dept, 1971; Advocate Depute, 1975. *Recreations:* gardening, music. *Address:* Braefoot Farmhouse, Crook of Devon, Fossoway, Kinross-shire. *T:* Fossoway 212.

WHEATLEY, Maj.-Gen. Percival Ross, DSO 1943; late RAMC, retired; *b* Westbury, Wilts, 4 May 1909; *s* of late Rev. Percival Wheatley, Congregational Minister, and late Margaret Lettice Wheatley (*née* Wallis); *m* 1939, Dorothy Joan Fellows (*née* Brock); one *s*. *Educ:* St Dunstan's Coll., Catford; Guy's Hosp. Med. School. MB, BS (London), MRCS, LRCP, 1933; FRCS 1940. Commissioned Lieut RAMC, 1939; BEF as Surgical Specialist, Sept. 1939; 2nd in comd 16 Para. Field Ambulance, 1942, comdg, 1943; N Africa, 1942; Sicily and Italy, 1943; ADMS, 2nd Indian Airborne Div., 1944–46; Surgical Specialist, 1946–60: Catterick, Hamburg, Singapore, Japan, Millbank; seconded to Ghana Army, Surgical Specialist, 1960–61; Consultant Surgeon: FARELF, 1963–66; BAOR, 1966–67; Dir of Army Surgery and Consulting Surgeon to the Army, 1967–69. Surgeon, P&O Lines Ltd, 1969–77. FRSocMed; Senior Fellow: Brit. Orthopædic Assoc.; Assoc. of Surgeons of Great Britain and Ireland. QHS 1967–69. *Publication:* contrib. to Basic Surgery. *Recreation:* philately. *Address:* Sherwood, High Park Avenue, East Horsley, Surrey. *T:* East Horsley 2151. *Club:* Army and Navy.

WHEATON, Rev. Canon David Harry; Vicar of Christ Church, Ware, since 1986; *b* 2 June 1930; *s* of Harry Wheaton, MBE, and Kathleen Mary (*née* Frost); *m* 1956, Helen Joy Forrer; one *s* two *d*. *Educ:* Abingdon Sch.; St John's Coll., Oxford (Exhibnr; MA); London Univ. (BD (London Bible Coll.)); Oak Hill Theol Coll. NCO, Wiltshire Regt, 1948–49. Deacon, 1959; priest, 1960; Tutor, Oak Hill Coll., 1954–62; Rector of Ludgershall, Bucks, 1962–66; Vicar of St Paul, Onslow Square, S Kensington, 1966–71; Chaplain, Brompton Chest Hosp., 1969–71; Principal Oak Hill Theolog. Coll., 1971–86. Hon. Canon, Cathedral and Abbey Church of St Alban, 1976. *Publications:* contributed to: Baker's Dictionary of Theology, 1960; New Bible Dictionary, 1962; New Bible Commentary (rev.), 1970; Evangelical Dictionary of Theology, 1984; Here We Stand, 1986. *Recreations:* walking, carpentry and do-it-yourself. *Address:* Christ Church Vicarage, 15 Hanbury Close, Ware, Herts SG12 7BZ. *T:* Ware 3165.

WHEELDON, Rt. Rev. Philip William, OBE 1946; *b* 20 May 1913; *e s* of late Alfred Leonard Wheeldon and late Margaret Proctor Wheeldon (*née* Smith); *m* 1966, Margaret Redfearn. *Educ:* Clifton Coll., Bristol; Downing Coll., Cambridge; Westcott House Theological Coll. BA 1935, MA 1942. Deacon, 1937; Priest, 1938; Farnham Parish Church, Dio. Guildford, 1937–39; Chaplain to the Forces, 1939–46; Chaplain, 1st Bn Coldstream Guards, 1939–42; Senior Chaplain, 79th Armoured Div., 1942–43; Dep. Asst Chaplain-Gen. 12th Corps, 1943–45; 8th Corps, 1945–46; Hon. Chaplain to the Forces, 1946–; Domestic Chaplain to Archbishop of York, 1946–49, Hon. Chaplain, 1950–54; General Sec., CACTM, 1949–54; Prebendary of Wedmore II in Wells Cathedral, 1952–54; Suffragan Bishop of Whitby, 1954–61; Bishop of Kimberley and Kuruman, 1961–65; resigned, 1965; an Asst Bishop, Dio. Worcester, 1965–68; Bishop of Kimberley and Kuruman, 1968–76. Hon. Asst Bishop, Diocese of Worcester 1976–77, Diocese of Wakefield 1977–85. *Recreations:* music, gardening. *Address:* Westgate Close, Clifton, Brighouse, West Yorks HD6 4HJ.

WHEELER, Anthony; *see* Wheeler, H. A.

WHEELER, Arthur William Edge, CBE 1979 (OBE 1967); Chairman, Foreign Compensation Commission, since 1983; *b* 1 Aug. 1930; *e s* of Arthur William Wheeler and Rowena (*née* Edge); *m* 1956, Gay (*née* Brady); two *s* one *d*. *Educ:* Mountjoy Sch.; Trinity Coll., Dublin (Reid Prof.'s Prize, MA, LLB). Called to the Irish Bar, King's Inns, 1953; called to the Bar, Gray's Inn, 1960. Crown Counsel, Nigeria, 1955; Legal Sec. (Actg), Southern Cameroons, and Mem. Exec. Council and House of Assembly, 1958; Principal Crown Counsel, Fedn of Nigeria, 1961; Northern Nigeria: Dep. Solicitor Gen., 1964; Dir of Public Prosecutions, 1966; High Court Judge, 1967; Chief Judge (formerly Chief Justice), Kaduna State of Nigeria, 1975; Comr for Law Revision, northern states of Nigeria, 1980. Mem., Body of Benchers, Nigeria, 1975; Associate Mem., Commonwealth Parly Assoc. *Recreations:* sport, music. *Address:* c/o Foreign Compensation Commission, Alexandra House, Kingsway, WC2B 6TT. *Clubs:* Royal Commonwealth Society; Kildare Street & University (Dublin).

WHEELER, Charles (Cornelius-); journalist and broadcaster, since 1940; *b* 26 March 1923; *s* of late Wing-Comdr Charles Cornelius-Wheeler, RFC and RAFVR, and Winifred (*née* Rees); *m* 1961, Dip Singh; two *d*. *Educ:* Cranbrook School. Began journalism as tape-boy, Daily Sketch, 1940. Served War, Royal Marines, 1942–46; Captain 1944 (despatches NW Europe). Sub-editor, BBC Latin American Service, 1947–49; German Service Correspondent in Berlin, 1950–53; Talks writer, European Service, 1954–56; Producer, Panorama, 1956–58; S Asia Correspondent, 1958–62; Berlin Corresp., 1962–65; Washington Corresp., 1965–68; Chief Correspondent: USA, 1969–73; Europe, 1973–76; BBC Television News, 1977; Panorama, 1977–79; Newsnight, 1980–. Documentaries include: The Kennedy Legacy, Battle for Berlin. Poynter Fellow, Yale Univ., 1973. *Publication:* The East German Rising (with Stefan Brant), 1955. *Recreations:* gardening, travel. *Address:* c/o Lloyds Bank, Cox's and King's Branch, 6 Pall Mall, SW1.

WHEELER, Prof. David John, FRS 1981; Professor of Computer Science, Cambridge University, since Oct. 1978; Fellow of Darwin College, Cambridge, since 1967; *b* 9 Feb. 1927; *s* of Arthur William Wheeler and Agnes Marjorie (*née* Gudgeon); *m* 1957, Joyce Margaret Blackler. *Educ:* Camp Hill Grammar Sch., Birmingham; Hanley High Sch., Stoke on Trent; Trinity Coll., Cambridge. Research Fellow, Trinity Coll., Cambridge, 1951–57; Visiting Asst Prof., Univ. of Illinois, USA, 1951–53; Asst Director of Research, Cambridge Univ., 1956–66; Reader in Computer Science, Cambridge Univ., 1966–78.

Publication: The Preparation of Programs for an Electronic Digital Computer, 1951. *Address:* 131 Richmond Road, Cambridge CB4 3PS. *T:* Cambridge 351319.

WHEELER, Lt-Comdr Sir (Ernest) Richard, KCVO 1981 (CVO 1969; MVO 1965); MBE 1943; RN retd; Clerk of the Council and Keeper of Records, Duchy of Lancaster, 1970–81; *b* 21 July 1917; *s* of late Rev. Harold W. Wheeler, Burton Bradstock and Weston Turville, and Margaret Laura Wheeler; *m* 1st, 1939, Yvonne Burns (*d* 1973); one *d*; 2nd, 1974, Auriel Clifford. *Educ:* Marlborough Coll.; HMS Frobisher. Paymaster Cadet, RN, 1935; Lieut 1939; served: HM Ships Devonshire, Emerald, Office of C-in-C Med., 1940–42; Sec. to Chief of Staff, C-in-C Med., 1942–43; HMS Daedalus and Admty, 1944–47; Lt-Comdr 1947; retd (invalided), 1949. Asst Bursar, Epsom Coll., 1949–52; Chief Clerk, Duchy of Lancaster, 1952–70. *Address:* 40 The Street, Marden, Devizes, Wilts. *Club:* Army and Navy.

WHEELER, Frank Basil; HM Diplomatic Service; Counsellor, on loan to Department of Trade and Industry, since 1986; *b* 24 April 1937; *s* of late Harold Gifford Wheeler and Winifred Lucy Wheeler (*née* Childs); *m* 1st, 1959, Catherine Saunders Campbell (*d* 1979); one *s*; *m* 2nd, 1984, Alyson Ruth Lund (*née* Powell); two step *s* one step *d*. *Educ:* Mill Hill Sch. HM Forces, 1956–58. HM Foreign Service, 1958–: Foreign Office, 1958–61; Third Sec. (Commercial), Moscow, 1961–63; Asst Private Sec. to Minister of State, FO, 1963–65; Second Sec. (Commercial), Berne, 1965–67; First Sec., FO (later FCO), 1967–72; Wellington, 1972–75; FCO, 1975–77; Counsellor and Head of Chancery, Prague, 1977–79; Inspector, 1979–82; Head of Personnel Policy Dept, FCO, 1982–84; Counsellor and Head of Chancery, UK Delegn to NATO, Brussels, 1984–86. *Recreations:* music, tennis. *Address:* c/o Foreign and Commonwealth Office, SW1.

WHEELER, Sir Frederick (Henry), AC 1979; Kt 1967; CBE 1962 (OBE 1952); *b* 9 Jan. 1914; *s* of late A. H. Wheeler; *m* 1939, Peggy Hilda (*d* 1975), *d* of Basil P. Bell; one *s* two *d*. *Educ:* Scotch College; Melbourne University (BCom). State Savings Bank of Victoria, 1929–39; Treasury: Research Officer, 1939; Economist, 1944; Asst Sec., 1946; First Asst Sec., 1949–52; Treasurer Comptroller, ILO, Geneva, 1952–60; Chm., Commonwealth Public Service Bd, Canberra, 1961–71; Sec. to Treasury, Australia, 1971–79. Member: Aust. delegn to various British Commonwealth Finance Ministers' Conferences; Austr. Delegn Bretton Woods Monetary Conf.; UN Civil Service Adv. Bd, 1969–72; Commonwealth Govt Defence Review Cttee, 1981–82. Director: Amatil Ltd, 1979–84; Alliance Holdings Ltd, 1979–86. *Address:* 9 Charlotte Street, Red Hill, ACT 2603, Australia. *T:* 959 888. *Clubs:* (Pres. 1966–69) Commonwealth (Canberra); Royal Canberra Golf.

WHEELER, Geoffrey, CB 1952; *b* 22 Nov. 1909; *s* of late A. E. Wheeler; *m* 1937, Dorothy Mary Wallis; one *s* one *d*. *Educ:* Clay Cross School, Derbyshire; St John's Coll., Cambridge (Scholar). First Class Part I Historical Tripos, 1930; First Class Part II Historical Tripos, 1931. Entered Civil Service, 1932, and appointed to Board of Customs and Excise; Private Sec. to Sir Evelyn Murray, 1936; Principal, 1937; Assistant Secretary, 1943; Under-Secretary (Ministry of Defence), 1948; Under-Secretary: Min. of Aviation, 1964–67; Min. of Technology (Principal Estabt Officer), 1967–70; Min. of Aviation Supply, 1970–71; Asst Under Sec. of State (Personnel), Procurement Exec., MoD, 1971–72; Asst Dir, Civil Service Selection Bd, 1972–76. Pres., Groupe Statut EEC, 1977. Chm., London Derbyshire Soc., 1973–. *Recreations:* music; amateur theatre. *Address:* 57 Hillcrest Road, Purley, Surrey. *T:* 01–660 2858.

WHEELER, Lt-Col Geoffrey Edleston, CIE 1943; CBE 1948; Hon. MA University of Durham, 1955; Director of Central Asian Research Centre, 1953–68; *b* 22 June 1897; *s* of late Capt. Owen Wheeler, Leicestershire Regiment; *m* 1927, Irena Nicolaevna Boulatoff (*d* 1973); one *s*. *Educ:* Eastbourne Coll. Commissioned Queen's Regt 1915; served in France, 1915–17; transferred to Indian Army, 1918, 6th Gurkha Rifles; various Intelligence appointments in Turkey, Malta, and Palestine to 1925; Military Attaché, Meshed, 1926; Intelligence duties in Iraq, 1928–31; 7th Rajput Regt to 1936; General Staff, Army HQ, India, 1936–41; Director, Publications Division, Govt of India, 1941–46; Counsellor, British Embassy, Teheran, 1946–50. Sir Percy Sykes Memorial Medal, RCAS, 1967. *Publications:* Racial Problems in Soviet Muslim Asia; The Modern History of Soviet Central Asia; The Peoples of Soviet Central Asia. *Address:* c/o Lloyds Bank, 4 Station Approach, Tadworth, Surrey.

WHEELER, Rt. Rev. Monsignor Gordon; see Wheeler, W. G.

WHEELER, (Harry) Anthony, OBE 1973; RSA, FRIBA; President, Royal Scottish Academy, since 1983; Consultant, Wheeler & Sproson, Architects and Planning Consultants, Edinburgh and Kirkcaldy; *b* 7 Nov. 1919; *s* of Herbert George Wheeler and Laura Emma Groom; *m* 1944, Dorothy Jean Campbell; one *d*. *Educ:* Stranraer High Sch.; Royal Technical Coll., Glasgow; Glasgow School of Art; Univ. of Strathclyde (BArch). RIBA, DipTP, MRTPI. Glasgow Sch. of Architecture, 1937–48 (war service, Royal Artillery, 1939–46); John Keppie Scholar and Sir Rowand Anderson Studentship, 1948; RIBA Grissell Gold Medallist, 1948, and Neale Bursar, 1949. Assistant: to City Architect, Oxford, 1948; to Sir Herbert Baker & Scott, London, 1949; Sen. Architect, Glenrothes New Town, 1949–51; Sen. Lectr, Dundee Sch. of Arch., 1952–58; commenced private practice in Fife, 1952. Principal works include: Woodside Shopping Centre and St Columba's Parish Church, Glenrothes; Reconstruction of Giles Pittenweem; Redevelopment of Dysart and of Old Buckhaven; Town Centre Renewal, Grangemouth; Students' Union, Univ. of St Andrews; Hunter Building, Edinburgh Coll. of Art; St Peter's Episcopal Ch., Kirkcaldy. Member: Royal Fine Art Commn for Scotland, 1967–86; Scottish Housing Adv. Cttee, 1971–75; Trustee, Scottish Civic Trust, 1970–83; Pres., Royal Incorpn of Architects in Scotland, 1973–75; Vice-Pres., RIBA, 1973–75. RSA 1975 (ARSA 1963; Treasurer, 1978–80; Sec., 1980–83). 13 Saltire Soc. Awards for Housing and Reconstruction; 4 Civic Trust Awards. *Publications:* articles on civic design and housing in technical jls. *Recreations:* making gardens, sketching and water colours, fishing, music and drama. *Address:* Hawthornbank House, Dean Village, Edinburgh EH4 3BH. *T:* 031–225 2334. *Clubs:* Caledonian; New, Scottish Arts (Edinburgh).

WHEELER, Air Chief Marshal Sir (Henry) Neil (George), GCB 1975 (KCB 1969; CB 1967); CBE 1957 (OBE 1949); DSO 1943; DFC 1941 (Bar 1943); AFC 1954; *b* 8 July 1917; *s* of T. H. Wheeler, South African Police; *m* 1942, Elizabeth, *d* of late W. H. Weightman, CMG; two *s* one *d*. *Educ:* St Helen's College, Southsea, Hants. Entered Royal Air Force College, Cranwell, 1935; Bomber Comd, 1937–40; Fighter and Coastal Comds, 1940–45; RAF and US Army Staff Colls, 1943–44; Cabinet Office, 1944–45; Directing Staff, RAF Staff Coll., 1945–46; FEAF, 1947–49; Directing Staff, JSSC, 1949–51; Bomber Comd, 1951–53; Air Min., 1953–57. Asst Comdt, RAF Coll., 1957–59; OC, RAF Laarbruch, 1959–60; IDC, 1961; Min. of Defence, 1961–63; Senior Air Staff Officer, HQ, RAF Germany (2nd TAF), Sept. 1963–66; Asst Chief of Defence Staff (Operational Requirements), MoD, 1966–67, Deputy Chief of Defence Staff, 1967–68; Commander, FEAF, 1969–70; Air Mem. for Supply and Organisation, MoD, 1970–73; Controller, Aircraft, MoD Procurement Exec., 1973–75. ADC to the Queen, 1957–61. Director: Rolls-Royce Ltd, 1977–82; Flight Refuelling (Holdings) Ltd, 1977–85; Mem. Council, Air League; Liveryman, GAPAN, 1980, Master, 1986–87. FRAeS; CBIM. *Address:*

Boundary Hall, Cooksbridge, Lewes, East Sussex. *Clubs:* Royal Air Force, Flyfishers', City Livery.
See also Maj.-Gen. T. N. S. Wheeler.

WHEELER, John Daniel, JP; MP (C) Westminster North, since 1983 (City of Westminster, Paddington Division, 1979–83); Director-General, British Security Industry Association, since 1976; *b* 1 May 1940; *s* of late Frederick Harry Wheeler and of Constance Elsie (*née* Foreman); *m* 1967, Laura Margaret Langley; one *s* one *d*. *Educ:* county sch., Suffolk; Staff Coll., Wakefield. Home Office: Asst Prison Governor, 1967–74; Res. Officer (looking into causes of crime and delinquency and treatment of offenders), 1974–76. Prospective Parly Candidate, City of Westminster, Paddington, 1976–79. Dir, National Supervisory Council for Intruder Alarms, 1977–; Member: Home Office Standing Cttee on Crime Prevention, 1976–; Cons. Party National Adv. CPC Cttee, 1978–80; Home Affairs Select Cttee, 1979–; Chm., Home Affairs Sub-Cttee, Race Relations and Immigration, 1980–. Chm., Nat. Inspectorate of Security Guard Patrol and Transport Services, 1982–. Vice-Chairman: All Party Penal Affairs Gp, 1979–; Cons. Urban and New Towns Cttee, 1980–83; Jt Secretary: Cons. Home Affairs Cttee, 1980–; Cons. Greater London Area Members' Cttee, 1980–83 (Chm. 1983–). Director: IFSEC PLC, 1984–; One to One Inc. (a Pacific Telesis co.), 1984–. JP Inner London, 1978. *Publications:* Who Prevents Crime?, 1980; (jtly) The Standard Catalogue of the Coins of the British Commonwealth, 1642 to present day, 1980–. *Recreation:* enjoying life. *Address:* House of Commons, SW1A 0AA. *T:* 01–219 4615. *Club:* Carlton.

WHEELER, Sir John (Hieron), 3rd Bt *cr* 1920; formerly Chairman, Raithby, Lawrence & Co. Ltd, retired 1973; *b* 22 July 1905; 2nd *s* of Sir Arthur Wheeler, 1st Bt; *S* brother, Sir Arthur (Frederick Pullman) Wheeler, 1964; *m* 1929, Gwendolen Alice (*née* Oram); two *s*. *Educ:* Charterhouse. Engaged in Print. Served War of 1939–45, Trooper, RTR, 1941–45. After the war, returned to printing. *Recreations:* whittling, dry stone walling. *Heir: s* John Frederick Wheeler [*b* 3 May 1933; *m* 1963, Barbara Mary, *d* of Raymond Flint, Leicester; two *s* one *d*]. *Address:* 39 Morland Avenue, Leicester LE2 2PF. *Club:* Wig and Pen.

WHEELER, Hon. Sir Kenneth (Henry), Kt 1976; JP; Speaker of the Victorian Parliament, Australia, 1973–79; *b* 7 Sept. 1912; *s* of William Henry Wheeler and Alma Nellie Wheeler; *m* 1934, Hazel Jean Collins; one *s* one *d*. *Educ:* Mernda State Sch., Vic. Grazier and retail dairyman for 19 years. Municipal Councillor, 1950–59; Mayor, City of Coburg, Vic., 1955–56; elected to Parliament of Victoria for Essendon, 1958. Member: CPA; Victorian Parly Former Mems Assoc.; Life Mem., Coburg FC. Life Governor: Essendon Hosp.; Essendon Lions Club. *Recreations:* golf, football, exhibition of horses. *Address:* 2/1 High Road, Camberwell, Vic 3124, Australia. *Clubs:* Essendon; Coburg Rotary; Royal-Park Golf; Royal Automobile of Victoria.

WHEELER, Air Vice-Marshal Leslie William Frederick; Director-General of Personal Services (RAF), Ministry of Defence, 1983–84, retired; Panel Inspector for Public Inquiries, since 1984; *b* 4 July 1930; *s* of late George Douglas Wheeler and of Susan Wheeler; *m* 1960, Joan, *d* of late Harry Carpenter and of Evelyn Carpenter; two *d*. *Educ:* Creighton School, Carlisle. Commnd, 1952; Egypt and Cyprus, 1954–56; Specialist in Signals, 1958; Aden, 1958–60; V-force (Valiants), 1961–65; India (Staff Coll.), 1965–66; Headquarters Signals Command, 1966–69; OC 360 Sqdn, 1970–72; Dir, RAF Staff Coll., 1972–74; Electronic Warfare and Recce Operations, MoD, 1975–77; Stn Comdr, RAF Finningley, 1977–79; Air Cdre Policy & Plans, Headquarters RAF Support Comd, 1979–83. *Recreations:* walking, reading, DIY, philately. *Address:* c/o Midland Bank plc, Brampton, Cumbria. *Club:* Royal Air Force.

WHEELER, Michael Mortimer, QC 1961; *b* Westminster, 8 Jan. 1915; *o s* of late Sir Mortimer Wheeler, CH, CIE, MC, TD, and late Tessa Verney Wheeler, FSA; *m* 1939, Sheila, *e d* of late M. S. Mayou, FRCS; two *d*. *Educ:* Dragon School, Oxford; Rugby School; Christ Church, Oxford. Barrister: Gray's Inn, 1938; Lincoln's Inn, 1946 (Bencher 1967; Treasurer, 1986). Served throughout War of 1939–45, with RA (TA) in UK and Italy (Lt-Col 1945; despatches); TD 1961. *Address:* 114 Hallam Street, W1N 5LW. *T:* 01–580 7284. *Clubs:* Garrick, MCC.

WHEELER, Sir Neil; see Wheeler, Sir H. N. G.

WHEELER, Maj.-Gen. Norman; see Wheeler, Maj.-Gen. T. N. S.

WHEELER, Sir Richard; see Wheeler, Sir E. R.

WHEELER, Maj.-Gen. (retd) Richard Henry Littleton, CB 1960; CBE 1953; *b* 2 Nov. 1906; *s* of Maj. Henry Littleton Wheeler, CB, DSO, and Vera Gillum Webb; *m* 1941, Iris Letitia Hope; one *d*. *Educ:* Uppingham; RMA, Woolwich. 2nd Lt RA, 1926. Served War of 1939–45, 50th Division. Lt-Col 1942; Brigadier 1950; HQ Northern Army Group, 1958–61; Maj.-Gen. 1959. Col Comdt RA, 1963–71. *Recreations:* riding, music. *Address:* Manor Farm, Knighton, Sherborne, Dorset DT9 6QU. *Club:* Army and Navy.

WHEELER, (Selwyn) Charles (Cornelius-); see Wheeler, C. C.

WHEELER, Maj.-Gen. (Thomas) Norman (Samuel), CB 1967; CBE 1964 (OBE 1958); Chairman, John Elmes Beale Trust Co. Ltd, since 1983; *b* 16 June 1915; *e s* of late Thomas Henry Wheeler, S African Police; *m* 1939, Helen Clifford, *y d* of F. H. E. Webber, Emsworth, Hants; one *s* one *d*. *Educ:* South Africa; St Helen's College, Southsea; RMC Sandhurst. Commissioned Royal Ulster Rifles, 1935; Palestine Rebellion, 1937–39 (despatches). Served War of 1939–45 (despatches twice): Bde Major, 38 Irish Bde, 1941–42; MEF, 1942–43; British Military Mission to Albania, 1943–44; 2nd Bn Royal Ulster Rifles, 1944–45. AA & QMG 6th Airborne Div., 1945–46; Airborne Establishment, 1946–47; Mil. Asst to Adj.-Gen. to the Forces, 1949–50; UK Services Liaison Staff, Australia, 1951–52; GSO1 and Col GS, HQ Northern Army Group and HQ, BAOR, 1954–57; comd 1st Bn Royal Ulster Rifles Cyprus Rebellion, 1958–59 (despatches); comd 39 Inf. Bde Group, N Ireland, 1960–62; Chief of Staff 1st (British) Corps, BAOR, 1962–63; General Officer Commanding Second Division, 1964–66; Chief of Staff, Contingencies Planning, SHAPE, 1966–69; Chief of Staff, HQ, BAOR, 1969–71; retired, 1971. Dir and Sec., Independent Stores Assoc., 1971–76; Dep. Man. Dir, Associated Independent Stores Ltd, 1976–80; Chm., J. E. Beale Ltd, 1980–83. Independent Mem., Cinematograph Films Council, 1980–83. *Recreation:* travel. *Address:* Glebe House, Liston, Sudbury, Suffolk. *Clubs:* Army and Navy, Airborne, Special Forces.
See also Sir Neil Wheeler.

WHEELER, Rt. Rev. (William) Gordon, MA Oxon; Hon. DD Leeds; Bishop Emeritus of Leeds; *b* 5 May 1910; *o s* of late Frederick Wheeler and Marjorie (*née* Upjohn). *Educ:* Manchester Gram. Sch.; University Coll. and St Stephen's House, Oxford; Beda Coll., Rome. Curate: St Bartholomew's, Brighton, 1933; Curate, St Mary and All Saints, Chesterfield, 1934; Asst Chaplain, Lancing Coll., 1935. Received into Roman Catholic Church at Downside, 1936; Beda Coll., Rome, 1936–40; ordained priest, 1940; Asst St Edmund's, Lower Edmonton, 1940–44; Chaplain of Westminster Cathedral and Editor of Westminster Cathedral Chronicle, 1944–50; Chaplain to the Catholics in the University, London, 1950–54, and Ecclesiastical Adviser to the Union of Catholic Students, 1953–60; Privy Chamberlain to HH The Pope, 1952; Hon. Canon of Westminster, 1954, Administrator of Cathedral, 1954–65; Created Domestic Prelate to HH Pope Pius XII, 1955; Grand Cross Conventual Chaplain to the British Association of the Sovereign and Military Order of Malta; Coadjutor Bishop of Middlesbrough, 1964–66; Bishop of Leeds, 1966–85. *Publications:* Edited and contributed to Homage to Newman, 1945; Richard Challoner, 1947; The English Catholics, etc. Contribs to Dublin Review, The Tablet, Clergy Review, etc. *Address:* College of the Blessed Virgin, 62 Headingley Lane, Leeds, W Yorks LS6 2BX.

WHEELER, William Henry, CMG 1959; PhD (London); Chairman, Mark Laboratories Ltd, since 1960; *b* Petersfield, Hants, 5 March 1907; *s* of John William and Ellen Wheeler; *m* 1937, Mary Inkpen; no *c. Educ:* St Catharine's Coll., Cambridge (BA); Imperial Coll. of Science (DIC). Beit Memorial Research Fellow, Imperial Coll., 1931. Man. British Automatic Refrigerators, London, 1935; Government Scientific Service, 1937; Dir, Guided Weapons Research & Development, 1950; Head of UK Ministry of Supply Staff and Scientific Adviser to UK High Commission, Australia, 1955; Director of Explosives Research, Waltham Abbey, 1959. Man. Dir, 1961–82, and Dep. Chm., 1968–82, Urquhart Engineering Co. Ltd; Chairman: Urquhart Engineering Co. (Pty) Ltd, 1971–82; Urquhart Engineering GmbH, 1973–82; Dep. Chm., Steam and Combustion Engineering Ltd, 1973–82; Chm., Process Combustion Corp., USA, 1970–82. *Publications:* papers on Combustion and Detonation in Proc. and Trans. Royal Society, and on Rocket Propellants in Nature, Proc. of Inst. of Fuel and Instn of Chemical Engineers; papers on the Mechanism of Cavitation Erosion for DSIR and American Soc. of Mechanical Engineers. *Recreation:* private research laboratory. *Address:* Mark House, Ashmead Lane, Denham, Bucks.

WHEELER-BOOTH, Michael Addison John, MA; Reading Clerk, House of Lords, since 1983; *b* 25 Feb. 1934; *s* of Addison James Wheeler and Mary Angela Wheeler-Booth (*née* Blakeney-Booth); *m* 1982, Emily Frances Smith; one *d. Educ:* Leighton Park Sch.; Magdalen Coll., Oxford (Exhibnr; MA). Clerk, Parliament Office, House of Lords, 1960; seconded as Private Secretary to Leader of House and Government Chief Whip, 1965; seconded as Jt Sec., Inter-Party Conference on House of Lords Reform, 1967; Clerk of the Journals, 1970; Chief Clerk, Overseas and European Office, 1972, Principal Clerk, 1978. *Address:* Fir Tree Cottage, Sandford St Martin, Oxon OX5 4AG. *T:* Great Tew 632; 11 Dewhurst Road, W14 0ET. *T:* 01-602 0838.

WHEEN, Rear-Adm. Charles Kerr Thorneycroft, CB 1966; *b* 28 Sept. 1912; *s* of late F. T. Wheen, Holmbury, Chislehurst, Kent; *m* 1940, Veryan Rosamond, *d* of late William Acworth, Chobham; three *s* one *d. Educ:* RN College, Dartmouth. Entered RN as Cadet, 1926. Served War of 1939–45: China, The Nore, Admiralty, Normandy Landings, East Indies. Naval Attaché, Beirut, Amman and Addis Ababa, 1958–60; Director of Officers' Appointments (S), Admiralty, 1960–63; Flag Officer Admiralty Interview Board, 1964–66. Capt. 1956; Rear-Adm. 1964; retd 1966. Dir, Cement Makers Federation, 1967–79. Chm., Bd of Governors, Gordon Boys School, 1971–85. *Recreations:* golf, fishing. *Address:* Willow House, Philpot Lane, Chobham, Surrey. *T:* Chobham 8118.

WHELAN, Michael John, MA, PhD, DPhil; FRS 1976; Reader in the Physical Examination of Materials, Department of Metallurgy and Science of Materials, University of Oxford, since 1966; Fellow of Linacre College, Oxford, since 1967; *b* 2 Nov. 1931; *s* of William Whelan and Ellen Pound. *Educ:* Farnborough Grammar Sch.; Gonville and Caius Coll., Cambridge. FInstP. Fellow of Gonville and Caius Coll., 1958–66; Demonstrator in Physics, Univ. of Cambridge, 1961–65; Asst Dir of Research in Physics, Univ. of Cambridge, 1965–66. *Publications:* (co-author) Electron Microscopy of Thin Crystals, 1965; numerous papers in learned jls. *Recreation:* gardening. *Address:* 18 Salford Road, Old Marston, Oxford OX3 0RX. *T:* Oxford 244556.

WHELAN, Terence Leonard, NDD, MSTD; Editor, Ideal Home Magazine, since 1977; *b* 5 Dec. 1936; *s* of Thomas James and Gertrude Beatrice Whelan; *m* 1972, Margaret Elizabeth Bowen; two *s* one *d. Educ:* Oakfield Secondary School. NDD 1955; MSTD 1972. Studied Graphic Design at Beckenham College of Art, 1953–56. Art Editor, Publishers, Condé Nast, working on Vogue Pattern Book, Vogue South Africa and British Vogue, 1959–68; gained a number of Design and Art Direction awards during this period; Art Editor, 1968–74, Asst Editor/Art Director, 1974–77, Ideal Home magazine. *Publications:* writer and broadcaster on home improvements. *Recreation:* classical guitar. *Address:* Ideal Home magazine, King's Reach Tower, Stamford Street, SE1. *T:* 01-261 6474.

WHELER, Sir Edward (Woodford), 14th Bt *cr* 1660, of City of Westminster; Company Secretary, Robert Lewis (St James's) Ltd, since 1981; *b* 13 June 1920; *s* of Sir Trevor Wood Wheler, 13th Bt, and of Margaret Idris, *y d* of late Sir Ernest Birch, KCMG; *S* father, 1986; *m* 1945, Molly Ashworth, *e d* of Thomas Lever, Devon; one *s* one *d. Educ:* Radley College. Joined Army (RA), 1940; commnd Royal Sussex Regt, 1941; attached 15 Punjab Regt, IA, 1941–45; BAOR, 1945–47. Oversea Audit Service, Uganda and Ghana, 1948–58; Automobile Association of East Africa, Kenya, 1958–70; Benson & Hedges Ltd, 1971–81, Director 1979–81. Liveryman, Worshipful Co. of Pipe Makers and Tobacco Blenders, 1980; Freeman, City of London, 1980. *Heir: s* Trevor Woodford Wheler [*b* 11 April 1946; *m* 1974, Rosalie Margaret, *d* of late Ronald Thomas Stunt; two *s*]. *Address:* 25 Cavendish Road, Chesham, Bucks. *T:* Chesham 784766.

WHELON, Charles Patrick Clavell; a Recorder of the Crown Court, since 1978; *b* 18 Jan. 1930; *s* of Charles Eric Whelon and Margaret Whelon; *m* 1968, Prudence Mary (*née* Potter); one *s* one *d. Educ:* Wellington Coll.; Pembroke Coll., Cambridge (MA Hons). Called to Bar, Middle Temple, 1954. Liveryman of Vintners' Co., 1952–. *Recreations:* gardening, cartooning. *Address:* 2 Harcourt Buildings, Temple, EC4. *T:* 01-353 2112; Russets, Pyott's Hill, Old Basing, Hants RG24 0AP. *T:* Basingstoke 469964.

WHETSTONE, Rear-Adm. Anthony John, CB 1982; Director-General, National Television Rental Association, since 1983; *b* 12 June 1927; *s* of Albert Whetstone; *m* 1951, Elizabeth Stewart Georgeson; one *s* two *d. Educ:* King Henry VIII School, Coventry. Joined RN, 1945; specialised in submarines, 1949; Commanded: HMS Sea Scout, 1956–57; HMS Artful, 1959–61; HMS Repulse, 1968–70; HMS Juno, 1972–73; HMS Norfolk, 1977–78; Flag Officer Sea Training, 1978–80; Asst Chief of Naval Staff (Operations), 1981–83. Dir-Gen., Cable TV Assoc., 1983–86. FBIM 1979. *Recreations:* hill walking, fishing, amateur dramatics (Chm., Civil Service Drama Fedn). *Address:* 17 Anglesey Road, Alverstoke, Hants. *Club:* Army and Navy.

See also N. K. Whetstone.

WHETSTONE, (Norman) Keith, OBE 1983; VRD; Editor-in-Chief, The Birmingham Post and Birmingham Evening Mail series, since 1984; Director, Birmingham Post & Mail Ltd, since 1980; *b* 17 June 1930; *yr s* of Albert and Anne Whetstone; *m* 1952, Monica Joan Clayton, Leamington Spa; three *s. Educ:* King Henry VIII Sch., Coventry. Served Royal Navy, 1949–50, 1951–52; Lt Comdr (S) RNVR, retired, 1965. Coventry Evening Telegraph, 1950–51; Western Morning News, 1952–55; Birmingham Post, 1955–58; Coventry Evening Telegraph, 1958–63; Editor, Cambridge Evening News, 1964–70; Editor, Coventry Evening Telegraph, 1970–80; Ed.-in-Chief, Birmingham Evening Mail series, 1980–84. Nat. Pres., Guild of British Newspaper Editors, 1976–77. Mem. Press Council, 1980–86. *Recreations:* theatre, Rugby football, golf, squash. *Address:* Tudor House, Benton Green Lane, Berkswell, Coventry CV7 7AY. *T:* Berkswell 32323. *Club:* Quadrant (Coventry).

See also A. J. Whetstone.

WHEWAY, Albert James; Chairman, Hogg Robinson Group plc, since 1983; *b* 6 April 1922; *s* of Albert and Alice Wheway; *m* 1st, 1946, Joan Simpson; 2nd, 1984, Susannah Mary Gray (*née* Luesby). *Educ:* Kimberworth School, Rotherham. Cooper Bros (later Cooper Lybrand), 1946–53; S.G. Warburg, 1953–57; industry, 1957–63; Ionian Bank, 1963–70; internat. industry and commerce, 1970–. *Recreations:* art collecting, music. *Address:* Beaumont, Duddington, near Stamford, Lincs PE9 3QE. *T:* Duddington 237.

WHEWELL, Prof. Charles Smalley, PhD; Professor of Textile Industries, University of Leeds, 1963–77, Emeritus Professor 1977 (Professor of Textile Technology, 1954–63, Head of Department, 1963–75); *b* 26 April 1912; *m* 1937, Emma Stott, PhD; one *s. Educ:* Grammar School, Darwen, Lancs; University of Leeds (BSc, PhD). Research Chemist, Wool Industries Research Association, 1935–37. University of Leeds, 1937–77: Lecturer in Textile Chemistry; Lecturer in Textile Finishing; Senior Lecturer in Textile Chemistry; Reader in Textile Finishing; Pro-Vice-Chancellor, 1973–75. Pres., Textile Inst., 1977–79. Hon. Liveryman, Clothworkers' Company, 1970. Hon. Fellow: Huddersfield Polytechnic, 1977; Textile Inst., 1979. Textile Institute Medal, 1954; Warner Memorial Medal, 1960; Textile Institute Service Medal, 1971; Distinguished Service Award, Indian Inst. of Technol., Delhi, 1985. *Publications:* contrib. to: Chambers's Encyclopædia; Encyclopædia Britannica; British Wool Manual; Waterproofing and Water-repellency; Chemistry of Natural Fibres, ed Asquith, 1977; Oxford History of Technology, ed Williams; Jl Soc. of Dyers and Colourists; Jl Textile Inst. *Recreations:* music (organ), travel. *Address:* 8 Weetwood Avenue, Leeds LS16 5NF. *T:* Leeds 751654.

WHICHER, Peter George, CEng; FRAeS; MIEE; Consultant, Logica, since 1985; *b* 10 March 1929; *o s* of late Reginald George Whicher and Suzanne (*née* Dexter); *m* 1962, Susan Rosemary Strong; one *s* one *d. Educ:* Chichester High School. BSc(Eng) London 1948; CEng, MIEE 1957. STC, 1948–51; Flying Officer, RAF, 1951–53; Min. of Aviation, 1953; Principal Expert in Telecommunications, Eurocontrol Agency, Paris, 1962–64; Cabinet Office, 1964–66; Asst Dir, Telecommunications R & D, and Manager, Skynet Satellite Communications Project, Min. of Technology, 1967–71; Superintendent, Communications Div., RAE, 1971–73; Dir, Air Radio, MoD(PE), 1973–76; RCDS, 1977; Dir, Defence Sci. (Electronics), MoD, 1978–81; Dep. Dir, RAE, 1981–84. FRAeS 1985. *Publications:* papers for professional instns. *Recreations:* sailing, innovation, arts. *Address:* Logica, 64 Newman Street, W1. *Club:* Royal Ocean Racing.

WHICKER, Alan Donald; television broadcaster (Whicker's World); writer; *b* 2 Aug. 1925; *o s* of late Charles Henry Whicker and late Anne Jane Cross. *Educ:* Haberdashers' Aske's Sch. Capt., Devonshire Regt; Dir, Army Film and Photo Section, with 8th Army and US 5th Army. War Corresp. in Korea, For. Corresp., novelist, writer and radio Broadcaster. Joined BBC TV, 1957: Tonight programme (appeared nightly in filmed reports from around the world, studio interviews, outside broadcasts, Eurovision, and Telstar, incl. first Telstar two-way transmission at opening of UN Assembly, NY, 1962); TV Series: Whicker's World, 1959–60; Whicker Down Under, 1961; Whicker on Top of the World!, 1962; Whicker in Sweden, Whicker in the Heart of Texas, Whicker down Mexico Way, 1963; Alan Whicker Report series: The Solitary Billionaire (J. Paul Getty), etc; wrote and appeared in own series of monthly documentaries on BBC 2, subseq. repeated on BBC 1, under series title, Whicker's World, 1965–67 (31 programmes later shown around the world); BBC radio programmes and articles for The Listener, etc; left BBC, 1968. Various cinema films, incl. The Angry Silence. Mem., successful consortium for Yorkshire Television, 1967. Contrib. a documentary series to ITV, 1968. Completed 16 Documentaries for Yorkshire TV during its first year of operation, incl. Whicker's New World Series, and Specials on Gen. Stroessner of Paraguay, Count von Rosen, and Pres. Duvalier of Haiti; Whicker in Europe; Whicker's Walkabout; Broken Hill—Walled City; Gairy's Grenada; documentary series, World of Whicker; Whicker's Orient; Whicker within a Woman's World, 1972; Whicker's South Seas, Whicker way out West, 1973; Whicker's World, series on cities, 1974–77; Whicker's World—Down Under, 1976; Whicker's World: US, 1977 (4 progs); India, 1978 (7 progs); Indonesia, 1979; California, 1980 (6 progs); Peter Sellers Meml programme, 1980; Whicker's World Aboard the Orient Express, 1982; Around Whicker's World in 25 Years (3 YTV retrospect. progs), 1982; BBC TV, 1982–; Whicker's World—the First Million Miles (6 retrospect. progs), 1982; Whicker's World—a Fast Boat to China (4 QE2 progs), 1984; Whicker! (10 talk shows), 1984; Whicker's World—Living with Uncle Sam (10 progs), 1985; Whicker's World Down Under, 1986. BBC Radio: Chm., Start the Week; Whicker's Wireless World (3 series), 1983; Various awards, 1963–, incl. Screenwriters' Guild, best Documentary Script, 1963; Guild of Television Producers and Directors Personality of the Year, 1964; Silver Medal, Royal Television Soc., 1968; Dumont Award, Univ. of California, 1970; Best Interview Prog. Award, Hollywood Festival of TV, 1973; Dimbleby Award, BAFTA, 1978; TV Times Special Award, 1978. FRSA 1970. *Publications:* Some Rise by Sin, 1949; Away—with Alan Whicker, 1963; Best of Everything, 1980; Within Whicker's World: an autobiography, 1982; Whicker's Business Traveller's Guide (with BAA), 1983; Whicker's New World, 1985; Sunday newspaper columns; contrib. various internat. pubns. *Recreations:* people, photography, writing, travel, and reading (usually airline timetables). *Address:* Le Gallais Chambers, St Helier, Jersey.

WHIFFEN, David Hardy, MA, DPhil (Oxon), DSc (Birmingham); FRS 1966; FRSC; Professor of Physical Chemistry, 1968–85, Head of School of Chemistry, 1978–85, Pro-Vice-Chancellor, 1980–83, University of Newcastle upon Tyne (Dean of Science, 1974–77); *s* of late Noël H. and Mary Whiffen; *m* Jean P. Bell; four *s. Educ:* Oundle School; St John's College, Oxford (Scholar). Sometime Commonwealth Fund Fellow, Sen. Student of Commn for 1851 Exhibition. Formerly: Lectr in Chemistry, Univ. of Birmingham; Supt, Molecular Science Div., NPL. Vice-Chm., Newcastle HA, 1983–85 (Mem., Newcastle AHA, 1978–82, Newcastle HA, 1982–85). Pres., Faraday Div., RSC, 1981–83. *Publications:* papers in scientific jls.

WHINNEY, Rt. Rev. Michael Humphrey Dickens; *see* Southwell, Bishop of.

WHIPPLE, Prof. Fred Lawrence; Senior Scientist, Smithsonian Astrophysical Observatory, since 1973; Director, Smithsonian Institution Astrophysical Observatory, 1955–73; Phillips Professor of Astronomy, Harvard University, 1968–77; *b* 5 Nov. 1906; *s* of Harry Lawrence Whipple and Celestia Whipple (*née* MacFarland); *m* 1st, 1928, Dorothy Woods (divorced 1935); one *s*; 2nd, 1946, Babette Frances Samelson; two *d. Educ:* Long Beach High School, Calif; UCLA; Univ. of California, Berkeley. Lick Observatory Fellow, 1930–31; Staff Member, Harvard Univ., 1931–; Instructor, 1932–38; Lecturer, 1938–45; Assoc. Prof., 1945–50; Professor, 1950–; Chm. Dept of

Astronomy, 1949–56. US Nat. Cttee of Internat. Geophysical Year: Chm. Techn. Panel on Rocketry, 1955–59; Member: Techn. Panel on Earth Satellite Program, 1955–59; Working Group on Satellite Tracking and Computation, 1955–58; Scientific Advisory Bd to USAF, 1953–62; Cttee on Meteorology, Nat. Acad. of Sciences, Nat. Research Coun., 1958–; Special Cttees on Space Techn., Nat. Advisory Cttee for Aeronautics, 1958– (now NASA), US; Space Sciences Working Group on Orbiting Astronomical Observatories, Nat. Acad. of Sciences (Mem. Nat. Acad. of Sciences, 1959–); Advisory Panel to Cttee on Sci. and Astronautics of US House of Representatives, 1960–73; Amer. Philosophical Soc., Philadelphia; Amer. Acad. of Arts and Sciences, Boston; New York Acad. of Science, NY; several technical societies. Associate, Royal Astronomical Soc., 1970–. Benjamin Franklin Fellow, RSA, 1968–. Editor: Smithsonian Contributions to Astrophysics, 1956–73; Planetary and Space Science, 1958–. Hon. degrees: MA, Harvard Univ., 1945; DSc, Amer. Internat. Coll., 1958; DLitt, North-eastern Univ., 1961; DS, Temple Univ., 1961; LLD, CW Post Coll. of Long Island Univ., 1962. J. Lawrence Smith Medal of Nat. Acad. of Sciences, 1949; Donohue Medals, 1932, 1933, 1937, 1940, 1942 (received two medals that year); Presidential Certificate of Merit, 1948; Exceptional Service Award, US Air Force Scientific Adv. Bd, 1960; Space Flight Award, Amer. Astron. Soc., 1961; President's Award for Distinguished Federal Civilian Service, 1963; Space Pioneers Medallion, 1968; NASA Public Services Award, 1969; Kepler Medal, AAAS, 1971; Nat. Civil Service League's Civil Service Award, 1972; Henry Medal, Smithsonian Instn, 1973; Alumnus of the Year Award, UCLA, 1976; Gold Medal, Royal Astronomical Soc., 1983; and other foreign awards. *Publications:* Earth, Moon and Planets, 1942, 3rd edn 1968. Many technical papers in various astronomical and geophysical journals and books; popular articles in magazines and in Encyclopædia Britannica. *Recreation:* cultivation of roses. *Address:* Smithsonian Astrophysical Observatory, 60 Garden Street, Cambridge, Mass 02138, USA. *T:* Boston University 4–7383.

WHISHAW, Anthony Popham Law, ARA 1980; *b* 22 May 1930; *s* of Robert Whishaw and Joyce (*née* Wheeler); *m* 1957, Jean Gibson; two *d*. *Educ:* Tonbridg Sch.; Chelsea Sch. of Art (Higher Cert); Royal College of Art (ARCA). Travelling Schol., RCA; Abbey Minor Schol.; Spanish Govt Schol.; Abbey Premier Schol., 1982; Lorne Schol., 1982–83. John Moores Minor Painting Prize, 1982; (jtly) 1st Prize, Hunting Group Art Awards, 1986. *One-Man Exhibns:* Libreria Abril, Madrid, 1957; Rowland Browse and Delbranco, London, 1960, 1961, 1963, 1965, 1968; ICA, 1971; New Art Centre, 1972; Folkestone Arts Centre, 1973; Hoya Gall., London, 1974; Oxford Gall., Oxford, 1974; ACME, London, 1978; Newcastle upon Tyne Polytech. Gall., 1979; (with Martin Froy) New Ashgate Gall., Farnham, 1979; Nicola Jacobs Gall., London 1981; From Landscape, Kettle's Yard, Cambridge, Ferens Gall., Hull, Bede Gall., Jarrow, 1982–84; Works on Paper, Nicola Jacobs Gall., 1983; Paintings, Nicola Jacobs Gall., 1984; Mappin Art Gall., Sheffield, 1985; Large Paintings, RA 1986. *Group Exhibns:* Gimpel Fils, AIA Gall., Café Royal Centen., Towards Art (RCA), Camden Arts Centre, London, Ashmoleum Mus., Oxford, 1957–72; Brit. Drawing Biennale, Teesside, 1973; British Landscape, Graves Art Gall., Sheffield, Chichester Nat. Art, 1975; Summer Exhibn, RA, 1974–81; British Painting, 1952–77, RA, 1977; London Group, Whitechapel Open, 1978, A Free Hand, Arts Council (touring show), 1978; The British Art Show, Arts Council (touring), Recent Arts Council Purchases and Awards, Serpentine Gall., First Exhibition, Nicola Jacobs Gall., Tolly Cobbold (touring), 55 Wapping Artists, London, 1979; Four Artists, Nicola Jacobs Gall., Sculpture and Works on Paper, Nicola Jacobs, Wapping Open Studios, Hayward Annual, Hayward Gall., Whitechapel Open, Whitechapel Gall., John Moore's Liverpool Exhibn 12, 1980, Exhibn 13, 1982, Walker Art Gall., Liverpool; London Gp, S London Art Gall., Wapping Artists, 1981; Images for Today, Graves Art Gall., Sheffield, 1982; Nine Artists (touring), Helsinki, 1983; Tolly Cobbold/Eastern Arts Fourth (touring), 1983; Three Decades 1953–83, RA, 1983. *Works in Collections:* Arts Council of GB, Tate Gall., Coventry Art Gall., Leicester Art Gall., Nat. Gall. of Wales, Sheffield City Art Galls, Financial Times, Shell-BP, Museo de Bahia, Brazil, Nat. Gall. of Victoria, Melb., Seattle Mus. of Art, Bank of Boston, Chantrey Bequest, W Australia Art Gall., Bayer Pharmaceuticals, DoE, Nat. Westminster Bank, Power Art Gall., Aust. European Parlt, Ferens Art Gall. *Recreations:* chess, badminton. *Address:* 7a Albert Place, Victoria Road, W8 5PD. *T:* 01–937 5197.

WHISHAW, Sir Charles (Percival Law), Kt 1969; solicitor (retired); *b* 29 October 1909; 2nd *s* of late Montague Law Whishaw and Erna Louise (*née* Spies); *m* 1936, Margaret Joan, *e d* of late Col T. H. Hawkins, CMG, RMLI; one *s* two *d*. *Educ:* Charterhouse; Worcester College, Oxford. Called to Bar, Inner Temple, 1932; Solicitor, 1938; Partner in Freshfields, 1943–74. Trustee, Calouste Gulbenkian Foundn, 1956–81. Member: Iron and Steel Holding and Realisation Agency, 1953–67; Council, Law Soc., 1967–76. Comdr, Order of Prince Henry (Portugal), 1981. *Address:* Westcott Hill House, Westcott, Surrey RH4 3JY. *T:* Dorking 885315.

WHISTLER, Maj.-Gen. Alwyne Michael Webster, CB 1963; CBE 1959; retired, 1965; *b* 30 Dec. 1909; *s* of Rev. W. W. Whistler and Lilian Whistler (*née* Meade), Elsted, Sussex; *m* 1936, Margaret Louise Michelette, *d* of Brig.-Gen. Malcolm Welch, CB, CMG, JP, Stedham, Sussex; one *s* two *d*. *Educ:* Gresham's Sch., Holt; RMA Woolwich. 2nd Lt Royal Signals, 1929; served in India, 1932–44; War of 1939–45: Staff Coll., Camberley, 1944; Burma Campaign, 19 and 25 Indian Divs and XII Army, 1944–45 (despatches twice). ADPR, Berlin, 1946; GSO1 (Military Adviser), Military Governor of Germany, 1946–48; AQMG, War Office, 1949–50; JSSC 1950; Comdg Royal Signals, 3 Div., 1951–54; Col GS, War Office, 1955–57; Col Q Far ELF, 1957–58; Comdr Corps Royal Signals, 1 (British) Corps, BAOR, 1959–60; Signal Officer-in-Chief, War Office, 1960–62; Chairman, British Joint Communications Board, Ministry of Defence, 1962–64; Assistant Chief of the Defence Staff (Signals), 1964–65. Hon. Col Princess Louise's Kensington Regt (41st Signals) TA, 1963–66; Col Commandant, Royal Corps of Signals, 1964–68; Hon. Col 32nd (Scottish) Signal Regiment (V), 1967–72. Princess Mary Medal, Royal Signals Instn, 1978. Master of Fox Hounds, Nerbudda Vale Hunt, 1938–40. *T:* Wareham 2605.

WHISTLER, Laurence, CBE 1973 (OBE 1955); FRSL; engraver on glass; writer; *b* 21 Jan. 1912; *s* of Henry Whistler and Helen (*née* Ward); *yr b* of late Rex Whistler; *m* 1st, 1939, Jill (*d* 1944), *d* of Sir Ralph Furse, KCMG, DSO; one *s* one *d*; 2nd, 1950, Theresa, *yr sister* of Jill Furse; one *s* one *d*. *Educ:* Stowe; Balliol College, Oxford (Hon. Fellow 1974). BA Oxon (MA 1985). Chancellor's Essay Prize, 1934. Served War of 1939–45: private soldier, 1940; commissioned in The Rifle Brigade, 1941; Captain 1942. King's Gold Medal for Poetry, 1935 (first award); Atlantic Award for Literature, 1945. First Pres., Guild of Glass Engravers, 1975–80. *Work on glass includes:* goblets, etc, in point-engraving and drill, and engraved church windows and panels at: Sherborne Abbey; Moreton, Dorset; Checkendon, Oxon; Ilton, Som; Eastbury, Berks (window to Edward and Helen Thomas); Guards' Chapel, London; Stowe, Bucks; St Hugh's Coll., Oxford; Ashmansworth, Berks; Steep, Hants (windows to Edward Thomas); Hannington, Hants; Yalding, Kent (windows to Edmund Blunden); Thornham Parva, Suffolk; Salisbury Cathedral. *Exhibitions:* Agnews, Bond Street, 1969; Marble Hill, Twickenham, 1972; Corning Museum, USA, 1974; Ashmolean, 1976, 1985. *Publications include:* Sir John Vanbrugh (biography), 1938; The English Festivals, 1947; Rex Whistler, His Life and His Drawings, 1948; The World's Room (Collected Poems), 1949; The Engraved Glass of Laurence Whistler, 1952; Rex Whistler: The Königsmark Drawings, 1952; The Imagination of Vanbrugh and his Fellow Artists, 1954; The View From This Window (poems), 1956; Engraved Glass, 1952–58; The Work of Rex Whistler (with Ronald Fuller), 1960; Audible Silence (poems), 1961; The Initials in the Heart: the story of a marriage, 1964, rev. edn 1975; To Celebrate Her Living (poems), 1967; Pictures on Glass, 1972; The Image on the Glass, 1975; Scenes and Signs on Glass, 1985; The Laughter and the Urn: the life of Rex Whistler, 1985. *Address:* The Old Manor, Alton Barnes, Marlborough, Wilts. *T:* Woodborough 515.

WHISTON, Peter Rice, RSA 1977; ARIBA; FRIAS; Consultant Architect, since 1977; *b* 19 Oct. 1912; *s* of Thomas Whiston and Marie Barrett; *m* 1947, Kathleen Anne Parker (*d* 1983); one *s* four *d*. *Educ:* Holy Cross Acad.; Sch. of Architecture, Edinburgh Coll. of Art. RIBA Silver Medallist for Recognised Schs, 1937. Served War, Staff Captain RE, 1940–45. Articled, City Architect, Edinburgh, 1930–35; Partner, Dick Peddie McKay & Jamieson, 1937–38; Chief Architect, SSHA, 1946–49; Sen. Lectr, Sch. of Architecture, ECA, 1950–69; Dir, Arch. Conservation Studies, at Heriot Watt Univ., 1969–77. Visiting Lectr at Internat. Centre for Conservation, Rome, 1971; Ecclesiological Practice, 1950–77. *Works include:* Cistercian Abbey at Nunraw; St Margaret's, St Mark's and St Paul's, Edin.; St Columba, Cupar; St Mary Magdalene's, Perth; St Ninian's and St Leonard's, Dundee. Awarded Papal Knighthood of St Gregory for Services to Architecture, (KSG), 1969. *Recreations:* travel, sketching, painting. *Address:* 14 Grange Court, Edinburgh. *T:* 031–668 2720.

WHITAKER, Benjamin Charles George; author; Executive Director, Minority Rights Group, since 1971; *b* 15 Sept. 1934; 3rd *s* of late Maj.-Gen. Sir John Whitaker, 2nd Bt, CB, CBE, and late Lady Whitaker (*née* Snowden), Babworth, Retford, Notts; *m* 1964, Janet Alison Stewart; two *s* one *d*. *Educ:* Eton; New Coll., Oxford. BA (Modern History). Called to Bar, Inner Temple, 1959 (Yarborough-Anderson Scholar). Practised as Barrister, 1959–67. Extra-mural Lectr in Law, London Univ., 1963–64. MP (Lab) Hampstead, 1966–70; PPS to Minister of: Overseas Development, 1966; Housing and Local Govt, 1966–67; Parly Sec., ODM, 1969–70. Member: UN Human Rights Sub-Commn, 1975– (Vice-Chm., 1979); Goodman Cttee on Charity Law Reform, 1974–76; UK Nat. Commn for UNESCO, 1978–85; Chairman: UN Working Gp on Slavery, 1976–78; Defence of Literature and Arts Soc., 1976–82; City Poverty Cttee, 1971–83. *Publications:* The Police, 1964; (ed) A Radical Future, 1967; Crime and Society, 1967; Participation and Poverty, 1968; Parks for People, 1971; (ed) The Fourth World, 1972; The Foundations, 1974; The Police in Society, 1979; (contrib.) Human Rights and American Foreign Policy, 1979; UN Report on Slavery, 1982; (ed) Teaching about Prejudice, 1983; A Bridge of People, 1983; (ed) Minorities: a question of human rights?, 1984; UN Report on Genocide, 1985; The Global Connection, 1987; Gen. Editor, Sources for Contemporary Issues series (7 vols), 1973–75. *Address:* 13 Elsworthy Road, NW3.

See also Sir James Whitaker, Bt.

WHITAKER, David Haddon; Editorial Director, since 1980 and Chairman, since 1982, J. Whitaker & Sons, Ltd; Director: Standard Book Numbering Agency, since 1968; Teleordering Ltd, since 1983; Chairman, Gardners of Bexhill Ltd, since 1983; *b* 6 March 1931; *s* of late Edgar Haddon Whitaker, OBE and of Mollie Marian, *y d* of George and Louisa Seely; *m* 1st, 1959, Veronica Wallace (decd); two *s* two *d*; 2nd, 1976, Audrey Miller (marr. diss.). *Educ:* Marlborough; St John's Coll., Cambridge. Joined family firm of publishers, J. Whitaker & Sons, Ltd, 1955; Dir, 1966; Editor, The Bookseller, 1977–79. Member: Adv. Panel, Internat. Standard Book Numbering Agency (Berlin), 1979–; Adv. Panel, Registrar for Public Lending Right, 1983–; Library and Information Services Council, 1985–. Chm., Soc. of Bookmen, 1984–. *Recreations:* reading, walking. *Address:* 30 Jenner House, Hunter Street, WC1. *T:* 01–837 8109. *Clubs:* Garrick, Thames Rowing; Leander (Henley-on-Thames).

WHITAKER, Frank Howard, CMG 1969; OBE 1946; Secretary of the Metrication Board, 1969–74; *b* 9 Jan. 1909; *er s* of late Frank Harold Whitaker and late Edith Whitaker, Bradford; *m* 1937, Marjorie Firth (*d* 1984); no *c*. *Educ:* Thornton Grammar Sch.; Leeds University. LLB (1st cl. hons) 1929; Solicitor (1st cl. hons, D. Reardon and Wakefield and Bradford Prizeman), 1931. Legal Practice until 1939. Royal Air Force, 1940–46 (Sqdn Leader). Entered Civil Service as Principal, Board of Trade, 1946; Asst Sec., 1955; Export Credits Guarantee Dept, 1957, Under-Secretary, 1966. *Recreation:* mountaineering. *Address:* Tavistock, The Rowans, Gerrards Cross, Bucks.

WHITAKER, Sir James Herbert Ingham, 3rd Bt, *cr* 1936; Vice-Chairman, Halifax Building Society, since 1973, Chairman, London Advisory Board, since 1974; *b* 27 July 1925; *s* of late Maj.-Gen. Sir John Whitaker, 2nd Bt, CB, CBE, and Lady Whitaker (*née* Snowden); *S* father 1957; *m* 1948, Mary Elisabeth Lander Urling Clark (*née* Johnston), *widow* of Captain D. Urling Clark, MC; one *s* one *d*. *Educ:* Eton. Coldstream Guards, 1944. Served in North West Europe. Retired, 1947. Chm., Governing Body, Atlantic College. High Sheriff of Notts, 1969–70. *Recreation:* shooting. *Heir: s* John James Ingham Whitaker, BSc, FCA [*b* 23 October 1952; *m* 1981, Janey, *d* of L. J. R. Starke, New Zealand; one *s* one *d*]. *Address:* Babworth Hall, Retford, Notts. *T:* Retford 703454; Auchnafree, Dunkeld, Perthshire. *Club:* Boodle's.

See also B. C. G. Whitaker.

WHITAKER, Thomas Kenneth; President, Royal Irish Academy, since 1985; Chancellor, National University of Ireland, since 1976; Joint Chairman, Anglo-Irish Encounter, since 1983; *b* 8 Dec. 1916; *s* of Edward Whitaker and Jane O'Connor; *m* 1941, Nora Fogarty; five *s* one *d*. *Educ:* Christian Brothers' Sch., Drogheda; London Univ. (External Student; BScEcon, MScEcon). Irish CS, 1934–69 (Sec., Dept of Finance, 1956–69); Governor, Central Bank of Ireland, 1969–76; Dir, Bank of Ireland, 1976–85. Dir, Arthur Guinness Son & Co. Ltd, 1976–84. Chairman: Bord na Gaeilge, 1975–78; Agency for Personal Service Overseas, 1973–78; Mem., Seanad Éireann, 1977–82. Pres., Econ. and Social Res. Inst.; Chm. Council, Dublin Inst. for Advanced Studies. Hon. DEconSc National Univ. of Ireland, 1962; Hon. LLD: Univ. of Dublin, 1976; Queen's Univ. of Belfast, 1980; Hon. DSc NUU, 1984. Commandeur de la Légion d'Honneur, France, 1976. *Publications:* Financing by Credit Creation, 1947; Economic Development, 1958; Interests, 1983. *Recreations:* fishing, golf, music. *Address:* 148 Stillorgan Road, Donnybrook, Dublin 4, Ireland. *T:* Dublin 693474.

WHITBREAD, Samuel Charles, DL; Chairman, Whitbread & Co. plc, since 1984; *b* 22 Feb. 1937; *s* of late Major Simon Whitbread; *m* 1961, Jane Mary Hayter; three *s* one *d*. *Educ:* Eton College. Beds and Herts Regt, 1955–57. Joined Board, Whitbread & Co., 1972, Dep. Chm., Jan. 1984. Chm., Mid-Beds Conservative Assoc., 1969–72. Bedfordshire: JP, 1969–83; High Sheriff, 1973–74; DL, 1974; County Councillor, 1974–82. *Recreations:* shooting, travel, photography, music. *Address:* Southill Park, Biggleswade, Beds SG18 9LL. *T:* Hitchin 813272. *Club:* Brooks's.

WHITBREAD, William Henry, TD; MA Cantab; Past President, Whitbread and Company, Ltd, 1972–79 (Chairman, 1944–71, Managing Director, 1927–68); Chairman, Whitbread Investment Co. Ltd, 1956–77; Vice-President of the Brewers' Society (Chairman, 1952–53); Past-Master, Brewers' Company; Vice-Pres. Inst. of Brewing

(Chm. Res. Cttee, 1948–52); *b* 22 Dec. 1900; *s* of late Henry William Whitbread, Norton Bavant, Wiltshire; *m* 1st, 1927, Ann Joscelyne (*d* 1936), *d* of late Samuel Howard Whitbread, CB, Southill, Beds; two *s* one *d*; 2nd, 1941, Betty Parr, *d* of Samuel Russell, ICS; one *s* two *d*. *Educ:* Eton; Corpus Christi College, Cambridge. Lovat Scouts, 1920–41; served War of 1939–45: Lovat Scouts, 1939–41; Reconnaissance Corps, 1941–45; Parachutist. Chm. Parliamentary Cttee, Brewers' Society, 1948–52. Director: Barclays Bank Ltd, 1958–73; Eagle Star Insurance Co., 1958–74. Member Governing Body Aldenham School, 1929–61 (Chairman, 1948–58). President: BSJA, 1966–68; Shire Horse Soc., 1971–72; Member: National Hunt Committee, 1956–68; Jockey Club, 1968–; Hurlingham Club Polo Committee, 1932–45; Master, Trinity Foot Beagles, 1921–23. *Recreations:* shooting, fishing and sailing. *Address:* Hazelhurst, Bunch Lane, Haslemere, Surrey; The Heights, Kinlochewe, Ross-shire; Farleaze, near Malmesbury, Wilts. *Clubs:* Brooks's, Pratt's, Royal Thames Yacht; Royal Yacht Squadron.

See also J. F. Doble, Sir H. T. Tollemache, Bt.

WHITBY, Bishop Suffragan of, since 1983; **Rt. Rev. Gordon Bates;** *b* 16 March 1934; *s* of Ernest and Kathleen Bates; *m* 1960, Betty (*née* Vaux); two *d*. *Educ:* Kelham Theological Coll. (SSM). Curate of All Saints, New Eltham, 1958–62; Youth Chaplain in Gloucester Diocese, 1962–64; Diocesan Youth Officer and Chaplain of Liverpool Cathedral, 1965–69; Vicar of Huyton, 1969–73; Canon Residentiary and Precentor of Liverpool Cathedral and Diocesan Director of Ordinands, 1973–83. *Recreations:* golf, music, writing. *Address:* Handyside, 60 West Green, Stokesley, Cleveland TS9 5BD. *T:* Stokesley 710390.

WHITBY, Charles Harley, QC 1970; a Recorder of the Crown Court, Western Circuit, since 1972; *b* 2 April 1926; *s* of late Arthur William Whitby and Florence Whitby; *m* 1981, Eileen Scott. *Educ:* St John's, Leatherhead; Peterhouse, Cambridge. Open Schol., Peterhouse, 1943; served RAFVR, 1944–48; BA (History) 1st cl. 1949, MA 1951. Called to Bar, Middle Temple, 1952; Bencher, 1977; Mem. Bar Council, 1969–71, 1972–78. Mem., Criminal Injuries Compensation Bd, 1975–. Chm. Council, St John's Sch., Leatherhead, 1985 (Mem., 1977–). *Publications:* contrib. to Master and Servant in Halsbury's Laws of England, 3rd edn, Vol. 25, 1959 and Master and Servant in Atkin's Encyclopaedia of Court Forms, 2nd edn, Vol. 25, 1962. *Recreations:* golf, watching soccer, boating, fishing, swimming, theatre, cinema. *Address:* 12 King's Bench Walk, Temple, EC4. *T:* 01–583 0811. *Clubs:* United Oxford & Cambridge University, Royal Automobile (Steward, 1985–), Garrick; Woking Golf.

WHITBY, Mrs Joy; Director, Grasshopper Productions Ltd; *b* 27 July 1930; *d* of James and Esther Field; *m* 1954, Anthony Charles Whitby (*d* 1975); three *s*. *Educ:* St Anne's Coll., Oxford. Schools Producer, BBC Radio, 1956–62; Children's Producer, BBC Television, 1962–67; Executive Producer, Children's Programmes, London Weekend Television, 1967–70; freelance producer, writer, and book reviewer for The Times, 1970–76; Head of Children's Programmes, Yorkshire TV, 1976–85. Dir, Bd of Channel 4, 1980–84. Devised for television: Play School, 1964; Jackanory, 1965; The Book Tower, 1979; Under the Same Sky (EBU Drama Exchange), 1984; The Giddy Game Show, 1985. Independent film productions: Grasshopper Island, 1971; A Pattern of Roses, 1983; Emma and Grandpa, 1984. BAFTA Award and Prix Jeunesse (for Play School), 1965; Eleanor Farjeon Award for Services to Children's Books, 1979; Prix Jeunesse (for Book Tower), 1980. *Publications:* Grasshopper Island, 1971; Emma and Grandpa (4 vols), 1984; articles on different aspects of children's television in The Spectator, The Listener, School Bookshop, The New Era.

WHITBY, Professor Lionel Gordon, FRSE, FRCP, FRCPE, FRCPath; Professor of Clinical Chemistry, University of Edinburgh, since 1963; *b* 18 July 1926; *s* of late Sir Lionel Whitby, CVO, MC, MD, FRCP, Regius Prof. of Physic and Master of Downing Coll., Cambridge; *m* 1949, Joan Hunter Sanderson; one *s* two *d*. *Educ:* Eton; King's Coll., Cambridge; Middlesex Hosp. MA, PhD, MD, BChir. Fellow of King's College, Cambridge, 1951–55; W. A. Meek Schol., Univ. of Cambridge, 1951; Murchison Schol., RCP, 1958; Rockefeller Trav. Res. Fellow, Nat. Insts of Health Bethesda, Md, USA, 1959. Registrar and Asst Lectr in Chem. Path., Hammersmith Hosp. and Postgrad. Med. Sch. of London, 1958–60; Univ. Biochemist to Addenbrooke's Hosp., 1960–63, and Fellow of Peterhouse, 1961–62, Cambridge; Univ. of Edinburgh: Dean of Faculty of Medicine, 1969–72 and 1983–86; Curator of Patronage, 1978–; Vice-Principal, 1979–83. Member: Scientific Services Adv. Gp, SHHD, 1975–77; Laboratory Develt Adv. Group, DHSS, 1972–76; Screening Sub-Cttee of Standing Medical Adv. Cttee, 1975–81; Training Cttee, RCPath, 1977–79; GMC, 1986–; Adv. Council, British Library, 1986–. Guest Lectr, Amer. Chem. Soc., 1966; Vis. Prof. of Chemical Pathology, RPMS, 1974. Vice-Pres., RSE, 1983–86. Trustee, Nat. Library of Scotland, 1982–. *Publications:* (ed jointly) Principles and Practice of Medical Computing, 1971; (jointly) Lecture Notes on Clinical Chemistry, 1975, 3rd edn 1984; (jtly) Multiple Choice Questions on Clinical Chemistry, 1981; scientific papers on flavinglucosides, catecholamines and metabolites, several aspects of clin. chem., and early detection of disease by chemical tests. *Recreations:* gardening, photography. *Address:* 51 Dick Place, Edinburgh EH9 2JA. *T:* 031–667 4358; The Royal Infirmary, Edinburgh. *T:* 031–229 2477, ext. 2319.

WHITCOMBE, Maj.-Gen. Philip Sidney, CB 1944; OBE 1941; JP; *b* 3 Oct. 1893; *e s* of late Rt Rev. Robert Henry Whitcombe, DD, Bishop of Colchester; *m* 1919, Madeline Leila Brydges (*d* 1977), *d* of Canon Arthur Symonds, Over Tabley, Knutsford; one *s* (and one *s* decd). *Educ:* Winchester. Gazetted to ASC from Durham LI (Spec. Res.), June 1914; served with BEF in France and Flanders, Aug. 1914–18; DAD Transport, 1918–19; psc 1926; Bde Major, Madras, 1928–32; Bt Major, 1933; DAAG, N Comd, York, 1934–36; GSO 2 War Office, 1936–38; Bt Lt-Col 1939; served in France as ADS and T 1939–40 (despatches); AA and QMG 1940–41 (OBE); Gibraltar, Brig. i/c Admin., 1941–42; Col 1942; DA and QMG, BTNI, 1942–43; MGA Eastern Command, 1943–47; retired, 1947. Freeman of Shrewsbury, 1924. JP for Wilts, 1948. *Recreations:* cricket, fishing. Played cricket for Essex, 1922, the Army, 1925, and Berkshire, 1925–32. *Address:* The Grange, Lake, Amesbury, Wilts. *T:* Amesbury 23175. *Clubs:* Army and Navy, MCC.

WHITE, family name of **Baron Annaly** and **Baroness White.**

WHITE, Baroness *cr* 1970 (Life Peer), of Rhymney, Monmouth; **Eirene Lloyd White;** a Deputy Speaker, House of Lords, since 1979; *b* 7 Nov. 1909; *d* of late Dr Thomas Jones, CH; *m* 1948, John Cameron White (*d* 1968). *Educ:* St Paul's Girls' Sch.; Somerville Coll., Oxford. Ministry of Labour officer, 1933–37 and 1941–45; Political Correspondent, Manchester Evening News, 1945–49; contested (Lab) Flintshire, 1945; MP (Lab) East Flint, 1950–70. Nat. Exec. Cttee of the Labour Party, 1947–53, 1958–72, Chm. 1968–69; Parly Secretary, Colonial Office, 1964–66; Minister of State for Foreign Affairs, 1966–67; Minister of State, Welsh Office, 1967–70; Chm., Select Cttee on Eur. Communities, and Principal Dep. Chm. of Cttees, H of L, 1979–82. Mem., Royal Commn on Environmental Pollution, 1974–81. Governor: National Library of Wales, 1950–70; Brit. Film Inst. and National Film Theatre, 1959–64; Indep. Mem. Cinematograph Films Council, 1946–64. Chairman, Fabian Society, 1958–59; President: Nursery School Assoc., 1964–66; Nat. Council of Women (Wales); Council for Protection of Rural Wales; Lord President's nominee, Court of UCW, Aberystwyth; Member: UGC, 1977–80; Council, UWIST, Cardiff, 1981– (Chm., 1983–); Chairman: Internat. Cttee, Nat. Council of Social Service, 1973–77; Coleg Harlech, 1974–84; Adv. Cttee on Oil Pollution at sea, 1974–78; Land Authority for Wales, 1975–80; Dep. Chm., Metrication Bd, 1972–76; Vice-President: Commonwealth Countries League; Commonwealth Youth Exchange Council, 1976–79; Council for National Parks, 1985–; TCPA, 1983–. Hon. Fellow, Somerville College, Oxford, 1966. Hon. LLD: Wales, 1979; Queen's Univ., Belfast, 1981; Bath, 1983. *Publication:* The Ladies of Gregynog, 1985. *Address:* 64 Vandon Court, Petty France, SW1H 9HF. *T:* 01–222 5107; Treberfydd, Bwlch, Powys LD3 7PX. *Club:* Royal Commonwealth Society.

WHITE, Adrian N. S.; *see* Sherwin-White.

WHITE, Aidan Patrick; Journalist, The Guardian, since 1980; *b* 2 March 1951; *s* of Thomas White and Kathleen Ann McLaughlin. *Educ:* King's Sch., Peterborough. Dep. Gp Editor, Stratford Express, 1977–79. Mem., Press Council, 1978–80. National Union of Journalists: Mem. Exec. Council, 1974, 1976, 1977; Treasurer, 1984–86; Chm., National Newspapers Council, 1981; Internat. Fedn of Journalists Exec., 1986–. Vice-Chm., Campaign for Press and Broadcasting Freedom, 1983–84. *Address:* 92 Quilter Street, E2. *T:* 01–739 3598.

WHITE, Alan, CMG 1985; OBE 1973; HM Diplomatic Service; Ambassador to Bolivia, since 1985; *b* 13 Aug. 1930; *s* of William White and Ida (*née* Hall); *m* 1st, 1954, Cynthia Maidwell; two *s* one *d*; 2nd, 1980, Clare Corley Smith. SSC Army 1954 (Capt.); Hong Kong, 1959–63; MoD (Central), 1965; First Sec., FO (later FCO), 1966; Mexico City, 1969; First Sec., UK Disarmament Delegn, Geneva, 1974; Counsellor (Commercial), Madrid, 1976; Counsellor and Head of Chancery, Kuala Lumpur, 1980–83; Hd, Trade Relns and Exports Dept, FCO, 1983–85. *Recreations:* mountaineering, travel. *Address:* c/o Foreign and Commonwealth Office, SW1. *Club:* Royal Automobile.

WHITE, Prof. Alan Richard, BA, PhD; Ferens Professor of Philosophy in the University of Hull, since 1961; *b* Toronto, Canada, 9 Oct. 1922; *s* of late George Albert White and Jean Gabriel Kingston; *m* 1st, 1948, Eileen Anne Jarvis; one *s* two *d*; 2nd, 1979, Enid Elizabeth Alderson. *Educ:* Midleton College and Presentation College, Cork; Trinity College, Dublin. Dublin: Schol. and 1st class Moderator in Classics, 1st class Moderator in Mental and Moral Science; Boxing Pink; President of the 'Phil'; Univ. Student in Classics and Dep. Lecturer in Logic, 1945–46; Asst Lecturer, Lecturer, Sen. Lecturer in Philosophy, Univ. of Hull, 1946–61, Dean of Arts, 1969–71, Pro-Vice-Chancellor, 1976–79. Visiting Professor: Univ. of Maryland, 1967–68, 1980; Temple Univ., 1974; Simon Fraser Univ., 1983; Univ. of Delaware, 1986. Secretary, Mind Assoc., 1960–69, Pres., 1972. Pres., Aristotelian Soc., 1979–80. 42nd Dublin Rifles (LDF), 1941–45. *Publications:* G. E. Moore: A Critical Exposition, 1958; Attention, 1964; The Philosophy of Mind, 1967; (ed) The Philosophy of Action, 1968; Truth, 1970; Modal Thinking, 1975; The Nature of Knowledge, 1982; Rights, 1984; Grounds of Liability, 1985; articles in philosophical journals. *Recreations:* dilettantism and odd-jobbery. *Address:* The University, Hull HU6 7RX. *T:* Hull 46311.

WHITE, Hon. Sir Alfred (John), Kt 1971; Tasmanian Agent-General in London, 1959–71; *b* 2 Feb. 1902; British; *m* 1939, Veronica Louisa Punch; two *s* two *d*. Elected to Tasmanian Parliament, 1941; Minister for Health and Chief Secretary, 1946–48, then Chief Secretary and Minister for Labour and Industry, Shipping and Emergency Supplies until Jan. 1959. JP since 1934, and Territorial JP for the State of Tasmania in London, 1959. Appointed Agent-General for Tasmania in London for period of 3 years, Jan. 1959, re-appointed for a further period of 3 years, Jan. 1962; re-appointed 1967; re-appointed 1970; resigned 1971 and retired. Granted title of "Honourable" for life. *Recreations:* ski-ing, gardening, bowls and fishing. *Address:* 6 Clarke Avenue, Battery Point, Hobart, Tasmania 7000, Australia.

WHITE, Arthur John Stanley, CMG 1947; OBE 1932; *b* 28 Aug. 1896; *s* of A. R. White, DL, OBE, and of Minnie B. White, OBE (*née* Beauchamp); *m* 1932, Joan, *d* of R. O. Davies and *niece* of Lord Waring; four *s* one *d*. *Educ:* Marlborough College; Clare College, Cambridge (Scholar), MA 1930. Served European War, Wiltshire Regt, 1915–20, France and Ireland; Indian Civil Service, Burma, 1922; Under-Secretary, Home and Political Dept, 1924; Deputy Commissioner, 1928 (Burma Rebellion 1931–32, OBE); Secretary to Government of Burma, 1934; appointed to British Council as Dep. Sec.-Gen., 1937, Sec.-Gen. 1940–47, Controller, 1947–62. Retired 1962. Director, OPOS (Office for placing overseas boys and girls in British Schs), 1964–67. *Recreations:* hockey (International Trials, 1921 and 1922), cricket, tennis, shooting. *Address:* The Red House, Mere, Warminster, Wilts. *T:* Mere 860551. *Club:* East India, Devonshire, Sports and Public Schools.

WHITE, Rev. Barrington Raymond; Principal, Regent's Park College, Oxford, since 1972; *b* 28 Jan. 1934; *s* of Raymond Gerard and Lucy Mildred White; *m* 1957, Margaret Muriel Hooper; two *d*. *Educ:* Chislehurst and Sidcup Grammar Sch.; Queens' Coll., Cambridge (BA Theol, MA); Regent's Park Coll., Oxford (DPhil). Ordained, 1959; Minister, Andover Baptist Church, 1959–63; Lectr in Ecclesiastical History, Regent's Park Coll., Oxford, 1963–72. First Breman Prof. of Social Relations, Univ. of N Carolina at Asheville, 1976. FRHistS 1973. *Publications:* The English Separatist Tradition, 1971; Association Records of the Particular Baptists to 1660, Part I, 1971, Part II, 1973, Part III, 1974; Authority: a Baptist view, 1976; Hanserd Knollys and Radical Dissent, 1977; contrib. Reformation, Conformity and Dissent, ed R. Buick Knox, 1977; The English Puritan Tradition, 1980; contrib. Biographical Dictionary of British Radicals in the Seventeenth Century, ed Greaves and Zaller, 1982–84; The English Baptists of the Seventeenth Century, 1983; contribs to Baptist Qly, Jl of Theological Studies, Jl of Ecclesiastical History, Welsh Baptist Studies. *Recreation:* recorded music. *Address:* The Principal's Lodging, Regent's Park College, Oxford. *T:* Oxford 56093.

WHITE, Bryan Oliver; HM Diplomatic Service; Ambassador to Honduras and (non-resident) to El Salvador, since 1984; *b* 3 Oct. 1929; *s* of Thomas Frederick White and Olive May Turvey; *m* 1958, Helen McLeod Jenkins; one *s* two *d*. *Educ:* The Perse Sch.; Wadham Coll., Oxford (Lit.Hum.). HM Forces, 1948–49; FO, 1953; Kabul, Vienna, Conakry, Rio de Janeiro, the Cabinet Office, and Havana, 1953–79; Counsellor, Paris, 1980–82; Head of Mexico and Central America Dept, FCO, 1982–84. *Recreation:* the Romance languages. *Address:* c/o Foreign and Commonwealth Office, SW1.

WHITE, Byron R(aymond); Associate Justice of the Supreme Court of the United States since 1962; *b* Fort Collins, Colorado, 8 June 1917; *s* of Alpha White, Wellington, Colorado; *m* 1946, Marion Lloyd Stearns, *d* of Dr Robert L. Stearns; one *s* one *d*. *Educ:* Wellington High Sch.; Univ. of Colorado; Oxford Univ. (Rhodes Scholar); Yale Univ. Law Sch (before and after War). Served War of 1939–45: USNR, Naval Intell., Pacific (two Bronze Stars). Law Clerk to Chief Justice of the United States, 1946–47; law practice in Denver, Colorado, 1947–60, with firm of Lewis, Grant, Newton, Davis and Henry (later Lewis, Grant and Davis). Dep. Attorney-Gen., 1961–62. Phi Beta Kappa, Phi Gamma Delta. As a Democrat, he was a prominent supporter of John F. Kennedy in the

Presidential campaign of 1960. *Recreations:* ski-ing, paddle tennis, fishing. *Address:* US Supreme Court, 1 First Street NE, Washington, DC 20543, USA.

WHITE, Prof. Cedric Masey, DSc(Eng.), PhD; Professor Emeritus, University of London, 1966; Consultant for River and Coastal projects; *b* 19 Oct. 1898; *s* of Joseph Masey White, Nottingham; *m* 1st, 1921, Dorothy F. Lowe; 2nd, 1946, Josephine M. Ramage; one *d. Educ:* privately; University College, Nottingham. Served European War, in Tank Corps, 1917–19. Lecturer in Civil Engineering, Univ. of London, King's Coll., 1927–33; Reader in Civil Engineering, and Asst Prof. in Imperial Coll. of Science and Technology, 1933–45; Responsible for work of Hawksley Hydraulic Lab., 1933–66; Professor of Fluid Mechanics and Hydraulic Engineering, 1946–66. Completed various investigations for Admiralty, WO, MAP, etc, during War of 1939–45, and investigations of proposed river-structures for Hydro-Power here and abroad, 1946–56. Founder Member, Hydraulic Research Bd, 1946–51, 1959–67; sometime member of Research Committees of Instn of Civil Engineers; delegation on Hydrology to Internat. Union of Geodesy and Geophysics, 1939, 1948, 1951; Member: Council of British Hydromechanics Research Assoc., 1949–59; Internat. Assoc. for Hydraulic Research, 1947–59. Hon. ACGI, 1951. *Publications:* various engineering reports and scientific papers, chiefly on the motion of air and water. *Address:* 8 Orchard Close, East Budleigh, Devon. *T:* Budleigh Salterton 3559.

WHITE, Christopher John, PhD; Director, Ashmolean Museum, Oxford, since 1985; Fellow of Worcester College, Oxford, since 1985; *b* 19 Sept. 1930; *s* of Gabriel Ernest Edward Francis White, *qv*; *m* 1957, Rosemary Katharine Desages; one *s* two *d. Educ:* Downside Sch.; Courtauld Institute of Art, London Univ. BA (Hons) 1954, PhD 1970. Served Army, 1949–50; commnd, RA, 1949. Asst Keeper, Dept of Prints and Drawings, British Museum, 1954–65; Director, P. and D. Colnaghi, 1965–71; Curator of Graphic Arts, Nat. Gall. of Art, Washington, 1971–73; Dir of Studies, Paul Mellon Centre for Studies in British Art, 1973–85; Adjunct Prof. of History of Art, 1976–85; Associate Dir, Yale Center for British Art, 1976–85. Dutch Govt Schol., 1956; Hermione Lectr, Alexandra Coll., Dublin, 1959; Adjunct Prof., Inst. of Fine Arts, New York Univ., 1973 and 1976; Conference Dir, European-Amer. Assembly on Art Museums, Ditchley Park, 1975; Visiting Prof., Dept of History of Art, Yale Univ., 1976. Reviews Editor, Master Drawings, 1967–80. *Publications:* Rembrandt and his World, 1964; The Flower Drawings of Jan van Huysum, 1965; Rubens and his World, 1968; Rembrandt as an Etcher, 1969; (jtly) Rembrandt's Etchings: a catalogue raisonné, 1970; Dürer: the artist and his drawings, 1972; English Landscape 1630–1850, 1977; The Dutch Paintings in the Collection of HM The Queen, 1982; (ed) Rembrandt in Eighteenth Century England, 1983; Rembrandt, 1984; Peter Paul Rubens: man and artist, 1987; film (script and commentary), Rembrandt's Three Crosses, 1969; various exhibn catalogues; contribs to Burlington Mag., Master Drawings, etc. *Address:* 135 Walton Street, Oxford OX1 2HQ; *T:* Oxford 512289; 14 South Villas, NW1 9BS. *T:* 01–485 9148; Shingle House, St Cross, Harleston, Norfolk IP20 0NT. *T:* St Cross 264.

WHITE, Sir Christopher (Robert Meadows), 3rd Bt *cr* 1937, of Boulge Hall, Suffolk; *b* 26 Aug. 1940; *s* of Sir (Eric) Richard Meadows White, 2nd Bt, and Lady Elizabeth Mary Gladys (*d* 1950), *o d* of 6th Marquess Townshend; *S* father, 1972; *m* 1st, 1962, Anne Marie Ghislaine (marr. diss. 1968), *yr d* of Major Tom Brown, OBE; 2nd, 1968, Dinah Mary Sutton (marr. diss. 1972), Orange House, Heacham, Norfolk; 3rd, 1976, Ingrid Carolyn Jowett, *e d* of Eric Jowett, Great Baddow; two step *s. Educ:* Bradfield Coll., Berks. Imperial Russian Ballet School, Cannes, France, 1961; schoolmaster, 1961–72; Professore, Istituto Shenker, Rome, and Scuola Specialisti Aeronauta, Macerata, 1962–63; Housemaster, St Michael's Sch., Ingoldisthorpe, Norfolk, 1963–69. Hon. Pres., Warnborough House, Oxford, 1973–. Lieutenant, TA, Norfolk, 1969. *Recreations:* dogs, vintage cars, antiques.

WHITE, Christopher Stuart Stuart-; *see* Stuart-White.

WHITE, David Harry; Group Managing Director: British Road Services Ltd, since 1976; Pickfords, since 1982; NFC Property Group, since 1984; Director, since 1982, and a Deputy Chairman, since 1985, National Freight Consortium; non-executive Director, British Rail Property Board, since 1985; *b* 12 Oct. 1929; *s* of late Harry White, OBE, FCA, and Kathleen White; *m* 1971, Valerie Jeanne White; one *s* four *d. Educ:* Nottingham High Sch.; HMS Conway. Master Mariner's F. G. Certificate. Sea career, apprentice to Master Mariner, 1946–56; Terminal Manager, Texaco (UK) Ltd, 1956–64; Operations Manager, Gulf Oil (GB) Ltd, 1964–68; Asst Man. Dir, Samuel Williams Dagenham, 1968–70; Trainee to Gp Managing Director, British Road Services Ltd, 1970–76. Chm., Nottingham HA, 1986–. County Chm., Notts County Branch, King George's Fund for Sailors, 1985–. FCIT; CBIM. *Recreations:* football supporter (Forest), walking. *Address:* 8 Tennis Mews, The Park, Nottingham NG7 1EX. *Club:* Royal Automobile.

WHITE, Sir Dick (Goldsmith), KCMG 1960; KBE 1955 (CBE 1950; OBE 1942); formerly attached to Foreign and Commonwealth Office, retired 1972; *b* 20 Dec. 1906; *s* of Percy Hall White and Gertrude White (*née* Farthing); *m* 1945, Kathleen Bellamy; two *s. Educ:* Bishops Stortford Coll.; Christ Church, Oxford (Hon. Student, 1981); Universities of Michigan and California, USA. US Legion of Merit, Croix de Guerre (France). *Club:* Garrick.

See also J. A. White.

WHITE, Edward George, OBE 1976; HM Diplomatic Service, retired; *b* 30 June 1923; *s* of late George Johnson White, OBE, ISO, and Edith Birch; *m* 1st, 1945, Sylvia Shears; two *d*; 2nd, 1966, Veronica Pauline (*née* Crosling). *Educ:* Bec Secondary Sch., London SW; London Univ. Served RAF, 1941–47. Various consular and diplomatic appts in Guatemala, USA, Madagascar, Burma, Thailand and India; Dep. Head of Finance Dept, FCO, 1976–78; Counsellor (Admin), Bonn, 1978–79. *Recreation:* sailing. *Address:* 7 Crosslands, Thurlestone, Kingsbridge, Devon TQ7 3TF. *T:* Kingsbridge 560236.

WHITE, Edward Martin Everatt; Chief Executive, Buckinghamshire County Council, since 1980; *b* 22 Feb. 1938; *s* of Frank and Norah White; *m* 1969, Jean Catherine Armour; one *s* one *d. Educ:* Priory Boys' Grammar Sch., Shrewsbury; King's Coll., Cambridge (MA). Solicitor. Asst Solicitor, Lancs County Council, 1962–65; Sen. Asst Solicitor, then Asst Clerk, then Principal Asst Clerk, Kent County Council, 1965–72; Dep. Chief Exec., Somerset County Council, 1972–74; Chief Exec., Winchester City Council, 1974–80. *Recreations:* gardening, walking, other outdoor pursuits. *Address:* The Spinney, Sevenacres, Chilton Road, Long Crendon, Bucks HP18 9DU. *T:* Long Crendon 208914.

WHITE, Prof. Edwin George, PhD, DSc, BSc (Vet. Sci.), BSc (Physiol.), FRCVS; William Prescott Professor of Veterinary Preventive Medicine, University of Liverpool, 1950–76, now Emeritus; Pro-Vice-Chancellor, 1966–70; *b* 26 March 1911; *s* of Edwin White and Alice Maud White; *m* 1st, 1936, Grace Mary Adlington; two *d*; 2nd, 1974, Winefred Wright. *Educ:* Newport (Mon.) High School; Royal Veterinary College, London (Kitchener Scholarship); University College, London. Studentship for Research in Animal Health, 1933–35, for postgraduate study in Germany and England; Lecturer in Pathology, Royal Veterinary College, London, 1935; Reader in Pathology, 1939; Principal Scientific Officer, Rowett Research Inst., Bucksburn, Aberdeenshire, 1946; Director of East African Veterinary Research Organisation, 1947–49; Dean of Faculty of Vet. Sci., Univ. of Liverpool, 1961–65. Pres., RCVS, 1967–68. Chm., Granada Schs Adv. Cttee. Chm. Governors, Birkenhead High Sch. *Publications:* articles in various scientific journals since 1934. *Recreation:* gardening. *Address:* Afton, Neston Road, Burton, South Wirral, Cheshire L64 5SY. *T:* 051–336 4210. *Club:* Royal Commonwealth Society.

WHITE, Erica, FRBS (retired); Sculptor and Painter; *d* of Frederic Charles White, solicitor and Mildred S. Hutchings. *Educ:* St George's School, Harpenden; Slade School of Art (Sculpture Scholarship two years and Painting Prize); gained London University Diploma in Fine Arts; studied at Central School of Arts and Crafts; gained British Institution Scholarship in Sculpture; studied at Royal Acad. Schools (Silver and Bronze Medallist); awarded Feodora Gleichen Memorial Fund Grant; exhibited at Royal Academy and at Glasgow, Brighton, Bournemouth and other Art Galleries. *Recreations:* outdoor sports and music. *Address:* South Cliff Cottage, 3 South Cliff, Bexhill-on-Sea, Sussex TN39 3EJ. *T:* Bexhill 211013.

WHITE, Frank John; His Honour Judge White; a Circuit Judge, since 1974; *b* 12 March 1927; *s* of late Frank Byron White; *m* 1953, Anne Rowlandson, MBE, *d* of late Sir Harold Gibson Howitt, GBE, DSO, MC; two *s* two *d. Educ:* Reading Sch.; King's Coll., London. LLB, LLM (London). Sub-Lt, RNVR, 1945–47; called to the Bar, Gray's Inn, 1951; Mem., General Council of the Bar, 1969–73; Dep. Chm., Berkshire QS, 1970–72; a Recorder of the Crown Court, 1972–74. Member: Lord Chancellor's Adv. Cttee on Legal Aid, 1977–83; Judicial Studies Bd, 1985–. *Recreations:* walking, photography. *Address:* 8 Queen's Ride, SW13 0JB. *T:* 01–788 8903; Blauvac, Vaucluse, France. *Clubs:* Athenæum, Roehampton.

WHITE, Frank Richard, JP; executive director and industrial relations adviser; *b* Nov. 1939; *m*; three *c. Educ:* Bolton Tech. Coll. Member: Bolton CC, 1963–74; Greater Manchester CC, 1973–75; Bolton DC, 1986–. Member: NUGMW; IPM; Inst. of Management Services. Contested (Lab): Bury and Radcliffe, Feb. 1974; Bury North, 1983. MP (Lab) Bury and Radcliffe, Oct. 1974–1983; PPS to Minister of State, Dept of Industry, 1975–76; Asst Govt Whip, 1976–78; Opposition Whip, 1980–82; opposition spokesman on church affairs, 1980–83. Chairman: All Party Paper Industry Gp, 1979–83; NW Lab Gp, 1979–83; Mem., NW Regional Exec., Labour Party, 1986–. *Address:* 4 Ashdown Drive, Firwood Fold, Bolton, Lancs BL2 3AX.

WHITE, Sir Frederick William George, KBE 1962 (CBE 1954); PhD; FAA 1960; FRS 1966; Chairman, Commonwealth Scientific and Industrial Research Organization, 1959–70 (Deputy Chairman, 1957, Chief Executive Officer, 1949–57); *b* 26 May 1905; *s* of late William Henry White; *m* 1932, Elizabeth Cooper; one *s* one *d. Educ:* Wellington College, New Zealand; Victoria University College, Univ. of New Zealand (MSc 1928); Cambridge Univ. (PhD 1932). Postgrad. Schol. in Science, Univ. of NZ and Strathcona Schol., St John's Coll., Cambridge; Research in Physics, Cavendish Laboratory, 1929–31; Asst Lecturer in Physics, Univ. of London, King's Coll., 1931–36; Professor of Physics, Canterbury University Coll., NZ, 1937; Member, British Empire Cancer Campaign Soc., Canterbury Branch Cttee, 1938; Radio Research Cttee, DSIR NZ, 1937; Advisor to NZ Govt on radar research, 1939; seconded to Aust. CSIR, 1941; Chm., Radiophysics Adv. Bd, 1941; Chief, Div. of Radiophysics, 1942. Exec. Officer, 1945, Mem., Exec. Cttee, 1946, CSIR Aust. Radio Research Bd, 1942; Scientific Adv. Cttee, Aust. Atomic Energy Commn, 1953; FInstP; Fellow Aust. Instn of Radio Engrs. Hon. DSc: Monash Univ.; ANU; Univ. of Papua and New Guinea. *Publications:* scientific papers on nature of ionosphere over NZ and on propagation of radio waves; Electromagnetic Waves, 1934. *Recreation:* fishing. *Address:* 57 Investigator Street, Red Hill, Canberra, ACT 2603, Australia. *T:* 957424.

WHITE, Gabriel Ernest Edward Francis, CBE 1963; painter, etcher; Director of Art, Arts Council of Great Britain, 1958–70; *b* 29 Nov. 1902; *s* of late Ernest Arthur White and Alice White; *m* 1st, 1928, Elizabeth Grace (*d* 1958), *d* of late Auguste Ardizzone; two *s*; 2nd, 1963, Jane, *d* of late J. R. Kingdon and of Mrs Kingdon, Minehead; one *s* one *d. Educ:* Downside Sch.; Trinity Coll., Oxford. Staff Officer RE Camouflage, 1940–45; Asst Art Director, Arts Council of Great Britain, 1945–58. Order of the Aztec Eagle, 2nd class (Mexico). *Publications:* Sickert Drawings (in Art and Technics), 1952; Ardizzone, 1979; (illustrator) Rivers of Britain series, 1985–86. *Address:* 88 Holmdene Avenue, SE24. *T:* 01–274 9643.

See also C. J. White.

WHITE, Air Vice-Marshal George Alan, CB 1984; AFC 1973; Commandant, Royal Air Force Staff College, 1984–87; Director, Ground Air Training Systems (Cyprus) Ltd, since 1987; *b* 11 March 1932; *s* of James Magee White and Evangeline (*née* Henderson); *m* 1955, Mary Esmé (*née* Magowan); two *d. Educ:* University of London (LLB). Pilot, 1956; served in RAF Squadrons and OCUs, 1956–64; RAF Staff College, 1964; HQ Middle East Command, 1966–67; 11 Sqn, 1968–70; 5 Sqn, 1970–72; Nat. Defence Coll., 1972–73; in command, RAF Leuchars, 1973–75; Royal Coll. of Defence Studies, 1976; Dir of Ops (Air Defence and Overseas), 1977–78; SASO No 11 Group, 1979–80; Air Cdre Plans, HQ Strike Comd, 1981–82; Dep. Comdr, RAF Germany, 1982–84. FRAeS 1985. *Recreations:* sailing, hill walking, bridge. *Address:* PO Box 162, Paphos, Cyprus. *Club:* Royal Air Force.

WHITE, Sir George (Stanley James), 4th Bt *cr* 1904, of Cotham House, Bristol; *b* 4 Nov. 1948; *s* of Sir George Stanley Midelton White, 3rd Bt, and of Diane Eleanor, *d* of late Bernard Abdy Collins, CIE; *S* father, 1983; *m* 1st, 1974; one *d*; 2nd, 1979, Elizabeth Jane, *d* of Sir Reginald Verdon-Smith, *qv*; one *d. Educ:* Harrow School. *Heir:* none.

WHITE, Maj.-Gen. Gilbert Anthony, MBE 1944; *b* 10 June 1916; *s* of Cecil James Lawrence White and Muriel (*née* Collins); *m* 1939, Margaret Isabel Duncan Wallet; two *d. Educ:* Christ's Hosp., Horsham. Member of Lloyd's, 1938. Joined TA Artists Rifles, 1937; TA Commn, E Surrey Regt, 1939; served BEF, 1940, N Africa, 1943–44, Italy, 1944–45; Staff Coll., 1944; Instructor, Staff Coll., Haifa, 1946; with UK Delegn to UN, 1946–48; served on Lord Mountbatten's personal staff in MoD, 1960–61; idc 1965; BAOR, 1966–69; Chief, Jt Services Liaison Orgn, Bonn, 1969–71; retd 1971. Mem. Council, Guide Dogs for the Blind, 1971–. *Recreations:* golf, racing. *Address:* Speedwell, Tekels Avenue, Camberley, Surrey. *T:* Camberley 23812. *Club:* Army and Navy.

WHITE, Sir Gordon; *see* White, Sir V. G. L.

WHITE, Harold Clare, MBE 1967; HM Diplomatic Service, retired; Consul-General, Seattle, 1976–79; *b* 26 Oct. 1919; *s* of Alfred John White and Nora White; *m* 1951, Marie Elizabeth Richardson; two *d. Educ:* Grammar Sch., Warrington. Served War, Royal Signals, 1939–45. GPO, 1937–39 and 1946; FO, 1947; Third Sec., Djakarta, 1951; FO, 1955; Vice-Consul, Piraeus, Kirkuk, San Francisco, and Durban, 1957–64; 1st Secretary: Kinshasa, 1964; Kuala Lumpur, 1968; FCO, 1972; Dep. Consul-Gen., Chicago, 1974. *Recreations:* cricket, golf. *Address:* 31 Stuart Avenue, Eastbourne, East Sussex BN21 1SU. *T:* Eastbourne 31148. *Club:* Civil Service.

WHITE, Sir Harold (Leslie), Kt 1970; CBE 1962; MA; FLAA; FAHA; FASSA; National Librarian, National Library of Australia, Canberra, 1947–70; *b* Numurkah, Vic, 14 June 1905; *s* of late James White, Canterbury, Vic; *m* 1930, Elizabeth (MBE), *d* of Richard Wilson; two *s* two *d*. *Educ:* Wesley College, Melbourne; Queen's College, University of Melbourne. Commonwealth Parliamentary Library, 1923–67; National and Parliamentary Librarian, 1947–67. Visited US as Carnegie Scholar, 1939, and as first Australian under "Leaders and Specialists programme" of Smith Mundt Act, 1950. Represented Australia at various overseas Conferences, 1939–69. Chairman, Standing Cttee, Aust. Advisory Council on Bibliographical Services, 1960–70; Member: various Aust. cttees for UNESCO; Aust. Nat. Film Bd; UNESCO Internat. Cttee on Bibliography, Documentation and Terminology, 1961–64; Nat. Meml Cttee, 1975–; Chm., Adv. Cttee, Australian Encyclopaedia, 1970–; Governor, Australian Film Inst., 1958–77; Hon. Vice Pres., Library Assoc. of UK, 1970–. H. C. L. Anderson Award, Library Assoc. of Australia, 1983. *Publications:* (ed) Canberra: A Nation's Capital; contribs to various jls. *Address:* 27 Mugga Way, Canberra, ACT 2603, Australia.

WHITE, Sir Henry Arthur Dalrymple D.; *see* Dalrymple-White.

WHITE, Prof. James, CEng; Dyson Professor of Refractories Technology, University of Sheffield, 1956–73, now Emeritus; Dean of Faculty of Metallurgy, 1958–62; *b* 1 April 1908; *s* of late John White and Margaret E. White (*née* Laidlaw), Langholm, Dumfriesshire; *m* 1936, Elizabeth Kelly, Glasgow; one *s*. *Educ:* Langholm Acad. (Dux Medallist); Dumfries Acad. (Science Dux); Glasgow University. BSc 1st Cl. Hons Physical Chemistry, 1931; PhD 1935; DSc 1939. DSIR Research Scholarship, Roy. Technical Coll., Glasgow, 1931; Dr James McKenzie Prize for Research, 1933; Research Asst in Metallurgy, Roy. Technical Coll., 1933; Associateship of Roy. Technical Coll., 1934; Lectr in Metallurgy, Roy. Tech. Coll., 1935; Andrew Carnegie Research Scholarship of Iron and Steel Inst., 1936–38; Andrew Carnegie Gold Medallist of Iron and Steel Inst., 1939; Research Technologist in Refractories Industry, 1943; Lectr in Refractory Materials, Sheffield Univ., 1946; Reader in Ceramics, Sheffield Univ., 1952. FIM 1952; Founder FICeram 1955 (Hon. FICeram 1984); CEng 1977. FRSA 1972. Silver Jubilee Lectr, Glass and Ceramic Res. Inst., Calcutta. President: Sheffield Metallurgical Assoc., 1950; Refractories Assoc. of Great Britain, 1959–60; Chm. Clay Minerals Group, Mineralogical Society, 1959–61; British Ceramic Society: First Chm., Basic Science Section; Pres., 1961–62; Hon. Mem. 1983; Hon. Mem. Council, Iron and Steel Inst., 1961–62. Visiting Prof., Nat. Research Centre, Cairo, 1962; Student's Trust Fund Visiting Lectr, Univ. of the Witwatersrand, SA, 1964; Visiting Prof., Univ. of Illinois, 1966; Nat. Sci. Foundn Senior Foreign Scientist Fellowship, Univ. of Alfred, NY, 1968; R. B. Sosman Meml Lectr, Amer. Ceramic Soc., 1980. Fellow, Mineralogical Soc. of America, 1960; Hon. Mem., Iron and Steel Inst., 1973. Griffith Medal, Materials Science Club, 1971; (jtly) A. W. Allen Award, Amer. Ceramic Soc., 1982. *Publications:* scientific papers on ferrous metallurgy and refractory materials (some jointly). *Recreations:* sketching, motor-cars, walking. *Address:* 1 Chequers Close, Ranby, Retford DN22 8JX.

WHITE, James; MP (Lab) Glasgow (Pollok) since 1970; Managing Director, Glasgow Car Collection Ltd, since 1959; *m*; one *s* two *d*. *Educ:* Knightswood Secondary School. Served Eighth Army, War of 1939–45 (African and Italian Stars; Defence Medal). Mem. Commonwealth Parly Assoc. Delegns, Bangladesh, 1973, Nepal, 1981. *Address:* House of Commons, SW1; 23 Alder Road, Glasgow G43 2UU.

WHITE, James; Professor of the History of Painting, Royal Hibernian Academy, since 1968; External Lecturer in the History of Art, University College, Dublin, since 1955; *b* 16 Sept. 1913; *s* of Thomas John White and Florence Coffey; *m* 1941, Agnes Bowe; three *s* two *d*. *Educ:* Belvedere Coll., Dublin; privately in European museums and collections. Art Critic: Standard, 1940–50; Irish Press, 1950–59; Irish Times, 1959–62. Curator, Municipal Gallery of Modern Art, Dublin, 1960–64; Director, Nat. Gallery of Ireland, 1964–80. Chm., Irish Arts Council, 1978–84. Visiting Lectr in Univs and Socs in GB, Italy, USA, Canada. Pres., Friends of Nat. Collections of Ireland; Chairman: Internat. Council of Museums, Ireland; Irish Museums Assoc.; Irish Art Historians; Trustee, Chester Beatty Library of Oriental Art, Dublin. Radio and Television contribs: BBC, RTE, and in the USA. Irish Comr to Biennale at Venice and at Paris on various occasions; Organiser of Exhibns in Dublin, London, Paris, etc., incl. Paintings from Irish Collections, 1957. Corresp. Mem., Real Academia de Bellas Artes de San Fernando, 1975. Hon. LLD NUI, 1970. Arnold K. Henry Medal of RCS of Ireland. Chevalier, Légion d'Honneur, 1974; Order of Merit, Govt of Italy, 1977; Commander of the Order of Merit, Federal Republic of Germany, 1983. *Publications:* Irish Stained Glass (with Michael Wynne), 1963; The National Gallery of Ireland, 1968; Jack B. Yeats, 1971; John Butler Yeats and the Irish Renaissance, 1972; Masterpieces of the National Gallery of Ireland, 1978; Pauline Bewick: painting a life, 1985; monographs on Louis Le Brocquy, George Campbell, Brian Bourke; contributor to: Apollo, Art News, Studio, Connoisseur, Blackfriars, Manchester Guardian, The Furrow, Doctrine and Life, Art Notes, Merian, Werk, Das Munster, Hollandsche Art, La Biennale, La Revue Française, Il Milione, Encyclopaedia of Art, etc. *Recreations:* golf, swimming, gardening, bridge. *Address:* 15 Herbert Park, Ballsbridge, Dublin 4. *T:* 683723. *Club:* Kildare Street and University (Dublin).

WHITE, James Ashton V.; *see* Vallance White.

WHITE, John Alan; Deputy Chairman, Associated Book Publishers Ltd, 1963–68 (Managing Director, 1946–62); former Director: British Publishers Guild Ltd; Eyre & Spottiswoode Ltd; Chapman & Hall Ltd; Book Centre Ltd; *b* 20 June 1905; *e s* of Percy Hall White and Gertrude (*née* Farthing); *m* 1st, Marjorie Lovelace Vincent (*d* 1958); two *s*; 2nd, Vivienne Rosalie Musgrave. *Educ:* Bishops Stortford College. President, Publishers' Association, 1955–57; Chairman, National Book League, 1963–65. *Recreations:* reading, gardening. *Address:* Hayfield House, College Road, Cork, Ireland. *T:* Cork 21519. *Club:* Garrick.

See also Sir Dick Goldsmith White.

WHITE, Rev. Canon John Austin; Canon of Windsor, since 1982; *b* 27 June 1942; *s* of Charles White and Alice Emily (*née* Precious). *Educ:* The Grammar Sch., Batley, W Yorkshire; Univ. of Hull (BA Hons); College of the Resurrection, Mirfield. Assistant Curate, St Aidan's Church, Leeds, 1966–69; Asst Chaplain, Univ. of Leeds, 1969–73; Asst Director, post ordination training, Dio. of Ripon, 1970–73; Chaplain, Northern Ordination Course, 1973–82. Convenor, Nat. Standing Conf. on Care of the Dying, 1986–. *Publications:* various articles. *Recreations:* medieval iconography, drama, Italy, cooking. *Address:* 8 The Cloisters, Windsor Castle SL4 1NJ. *T:* Windsor 860409.

WHITE, Lt-Col John Baker, TD 1950; JP; *b* West Malling, Kent, 12 Aug. 1902; *s* of late J. W. B. White, Street End House, Canterbury; *m* 1925, Sybil Irene Erica (*d* 1980), *d* of late C. B. Graham, Onslow Gardens, SW1; one *s* one *d*. *Educ:* Stubbington House, Fareham; Malvern College. Worked on farms in Kent and Sussex to gain a basic knowledge of agriculture, 1920–22; worked in a circus to gain a wider knowledge of human nature, 1922; studied the structure of industry and social science in London and various industrial centres, 1922–24; worked as a voluntary helper in canteens for the unemployed and among distressed ex-service men; employed in the coal industry, 1924–26; Director Economic League, 1926–45, Publicity Adviser, 1945–76. Joined Territorial Army, London Rifle Brigade, 1934; served in Army as regimental soldier, on War Office staff with Political Intelligence Dept of FO, and Political Warfare Mission in the Middle East, 1939–45; Lieut-Colonel 1941. MP (C) Canterbury division of Kent, 1945–53. JP Kent, 1954. Pres., E Kent Fruit Show Soc.; Vice Pres., Canterbury Soc. *Publications:* Red Russia Arms, 1934; It's Gone for Good, 1941; The Soviet Spy System, 1948; The Red Network, 1953; The Big Lie, 1955; Pattern for Conquest, 1956; Sabotage is Suspected, 1957; True Blue, 1970. *Address:* Street End Place, near Canterbury, Kent CT4 5NP. *T:* Petham 265.

WHITE, Hon. Sir John (Charles), Kt 1982, MBE (mil.) 1942; Judge of High Court of New Zealand, retired 1981, sitting as retired Judge since 1982; *b* 1 Nov. 1911; *s* of Charles Gilbert White and Nora Addison Scott White; *m* 1943, Dora Eyre Wild; one *s* three *d*. *Educ:* Wellesley Coll., Wellington; John McGlashan Coll., Dunedin; Victoria University Coll., Wellington; Univ. of New Zealand (LLM Hons). Barrister and Solicitor of Supreme Court of New Zealand. Judge's Associate, 1937–38; served War, Middle East, Greece, Crete, Italy, 1940–45, final rank Major; formerly Dominion Vice-Pres., New Zealand Returned Services Assoc.; Private practice as barrister and solicitor, Wellington, 1945–66; Pres., Wellington Law Soc., Vice-Pres., NZ Law Soc., 1966; QC and Solicitor General of New Zealand, 1966; Judge of the Supreme Court (now High Court), 1970, retd 1981; Judge Advocate General of Defence Forces, 1966–. Actg Chief Justice, Solomon Islands, 1984. Pres., Solomon Is Court of Appeal, 1985–. Royal Comr, Inquiry into 1982 Fiji Gen. Election, 1983. Asst Editor, Sim's Practice & Procedure, 9th edn, 1955, and 10th edn 1966. *Recreations:* formerly Rugby, cricket, tennis, bowls. *Address:* 23 Selwyn Terrace, Wellington 1, New Zealand. *T:* 725–502. *Clubs:* Wellington; Dunedin; United Services Officers (Wellington).

WHITE, Prof. John Edward Clement Twarowski, CBE 1983; FSA; Durning-Lawrence Professor of the History of Art, since 1971, Vice-Provost, since 1984, University College, London; *b* 4 Oct. 1924; *s* of Brigadier A. E. White and Suzanne Twarowska; *m* 1950, Xenia Joannides. *Educ:* Ampleforth College; Trinity College, Oxford; Courtauld Institute of Art, University of London. Served in RAF, 1943–47. BA London 1950; Junior Research Fellow, Warburg Inst., 1950–52; PhD Lond. 1952; MA Manchester 1963. Lectr in History of Art, Courtauld Inst., 1952–58; Alexander White Vis. Prof., Univ. of Chicago, 1958; Reader in History of Art, Courtauld Inst., 1958–59; Pilkington Prof. of the History of Art and Dir of The Whitworth Art Gallery, Univ. of Manchester, 1959–66; Vis. Ferens Prof. of Fine Art, Univ. of Hull, 1961–62; Prof. of the History of Art and Chm., Dept of History of Art, Johns Hopkins Univ., USA, 1966–71. Member: Adv. Council of V&A, 1973–76; Exec. Cttee, Assoc. of Art Historians, 1974–81 (Chm., 1976–80); Art Panel, Arts Council, 1974–78; Vis. Cttee of RCA, 1977–; Armed Forces Pay Review Body, 1986–; Chm., Reviewing Cttee on Export of Works of Art, 1976–82 (Mem., 1975–82). Trustee, Whitechapel Art Gall., 1976– (Vice-Chm., 1985–). Membre Titulaire, 1983–, Membre du Bureau, 1986–, Comité International d'Histoire de l'Art. *Publications:* Perspective in Ancient Drawings and Painting, 1956; The Birth and Rebirth of Pictorial Space, 1957, 2nd edn 1967 (Italian trans. 1971); Art and Architecture in Italy, 1250–1400, 1966; Duccio: Tuscan Art and the Medieval Workshop, 1979; Studies in Renaissance Art, 1983; Studies in Late Medieval Italian Art, 1984; articles in Art History, Art Bulletin, Burlington Magazine, Jl of Warburg and Courtauld Institutes, Art Bulletin. *Address:* Department of The History of Art, University College, Gower Street, WC1; (home) 25 Cadogan Place, SW1. *Club:* Athenæum.

WHITE, John Sampson, AO 1982; CMG 1970; Secretary to the Governor, South Australia, 1976–82; *b* 9 June 1916; *s* of late W. J. White; *m* 1941, Dorothy G., *d* of late E. J. Griffin; one *s* one *d*. *Educ:* Black Forest Primary and Adelaide High Schs. AASA. Attorney-General's Dept, 1933–61. Served War, 2nd AIF, 1941–45, Captain. Asst Sec., Industries Develt Cttee, 1950, Sec., 1951–61; Sec., Land Agents' Bd, 1951–61; Sec. to Premier, SA, 1961–65; Mem., SA Superannuation Fund Bd, 1961–74; Sec., Premier's Dept, SA, 1965–74; Agent-Gen. for SA, 1974–76; Comr of Charitable Funds, 1964–74. Member: State Exec. Cttee, Meals on Wheels Inc., 1982–; Exec. Cttee, SA Br., Victoria League for Commonwealth Friendship, 1982–; Bd of Dirs, Service to Youth Council, 1982–84; Casino Supervisory Authy, 1983–86. Mem., Council of Governors, Presb. Girls' Coll., 1958–73. Freeman, City of London. *Recreations:* swimming, tennis. *Address:* 4 Evans Avenue, Mitcham, SA 5062, Australia. *Clubs:* Adelaide, Naval, Military and Air Force, Sturt (Adelaide).

WHITE, John William, CMG 1981; DPhil; FRSC; Professor of Physical and Theoretical Chemistry, Australian National University, Canberra, since 1985; *b* Newcastle, Australia, 25 April 1937; *s* of late George John White and of Jean Florence White; *m* 1966, Ailsa Barbara, *d* of A. A. and S. Vise, St Lucia, Brisbane; one *s* three *d*. *Educ:* Newcastle High Sch.; Sydney Univ. (MSc); Lincoln Coll., Oxford (1851 Schol., 1959; MA, DPhil). ICI Fellow, Oxford Univ.; Research Fellow, Lincoln Coll., 1962; University Lectr, Oxford, 1963–85, Assessor, 1981–82; Fellow, St John's Coll., Oxford, 1963–85 (Vice-Pres. 1973). Neutron Beam Coordinator, AERE, Harwell, 1974; Asst Director, 1975, Director 1977–80, Institut Laue-Langevin, Grenoble. Argonne Fellow, Argonne Nat. Lab. and Univ. of Chicago, 1985. Tilden Lectr, Chemical Soc., 1975; Liversidge Lectr, Sydney Univ., 1985. Member of Council: Epsom Coll., 1981–85; Wycliffe Hall, Oxford, 1983–85. FRSC 1982; FRACI 1985. Marlow Medal, Faraday Soc., 1969. *Publications:* various contribs to scientific jls. *Recreations:* family, squash, skiing. *Address:* 2 Spencer Street, Turner, ACT 2601, Australia. *T:* Canberra 486836.

WHITE, Sir John (Woolmer), 4th Bt *cr* 1922; *b* 4 Feb. 1947; *s* of Sir Headley Dymoke White, 3rd Bt and of Elizabeth Victoria Mary, *er d* of late Wilfrid Ingram Wrightson; *S* father, 1971. *Educ:* Hurst Court, Hastings; Cheltenham College. *Heir: uncle* Sir Lynton Stuart White, *qv*. *Address:* Salle Park, Norwich, Norfolk NR10 4SG.

WHITE, Lawrence John, CMG 1972; formerly Assistant Secretary, Board of Customs and Excise, 1961–75, retired; *b* 23 Feb. 1915; *s* of Arthur Yirrell White and Helen Christina White; *m* 1936, Ivy Margaret Coates; one *s*. *Educ:* Banbury Grammar Sch. Joined Customs and Excise, 1933; Commonwealth Relations Office, 1948–50; Customs and Excise, 1951–75. *Recreations:* reading, walking. *Address:* Peach Tree Cottage, Fifield, Oxon. *T:* Shipton under Wychwood 830806.

WHITE, Sir Lynton (Stuart), Kt 1985; MBE (mil.) 1943; TD 1950; DL; Chairman, Hampshire County Council, 1977–85; *b* 11 Aug. 1916; 2nd *s* of Sir Dymoke White, 2nd Bt, JP, DL, and late Lady White (*née* MacGowan); *heir-pres.* to nephew Sir John Woolmer White, Bt, *qv*; *m* 1945, Phyllis Marie Rochfort Worley, *er d* of Sir Newnham Arthur Worley, KBE; four *s* one *d*. *Educ:* Harrow; Trinity College, Cambridge (MA 1938). Associate RIBA, 1947–82. TA 1939, as 2nd Lieut RA; served War of 1939–45: UK, 1939–40; Far East, 1940–45 (despatches, 1943); Hon. Lieut-Col RA, TA, 1946; TARO, 1948–71. Member Hampshire CC, 1970; Vice-Chm., 1976. DL Hants 1977. *Recreations:* country pursuits, shooting. *Address:* Oxenbourne House, East Meon, Petersfield, Hants GU32 1QL. *Clubs:* United Oxford & Cambridge University, East India; Hampshire (Winchester).

WHITE, Michael Simon; theatre and film producer; *b* 16 Jan. 1936; *s* of Victor R. and Doris G. White; *m* 1965, Sarah Hillsdon (marr. diss. 1973); two *s* one *d*; 2nd, 1985, Louise M. Moores, *d* of late Nigel Moores; one *s*. *Educ:* Lyceum Alpinum, Zuoz, Switzerland; Pisa University; Sorbonne, Paris. Asst to Sir Peter Daubeny, 1956–61; *stage:* London productions include: Rocky Horror Show; Sleuth; America Hurrah; Oh, Calcutta!; The Connection; Joseph and the Amazing Technicolor Dreamcoat; Loot; The Blood Knot; A Chorus Line; Deathtrap; Annie; Pirates of Penzance; On Your Toes; *films:* include: Monty Python and the Holy Grail; Rocky Horror Picture Show; My Dinner with André; Ploughman's Lunch; Moonlighting; Strangers's Kiss; The Comic Strip Presents; The Supergrass; High Season. *Publication:* Empty Seats, 1984–. *Recreations:* art, ski-ing, racing. *Address:* 13 Duke Street, St James's, SW1. *T:* 01–839 3971. *Clubs:* Turf, Royal Automobile; Rocks (Los Angeles).

WHITE, Neville Helme; Stipendiary Magistrate for Humberside, since 1985; *b* 12 April 1931; *s* of Noel Walter White and Irene Helme White; *m* 1958, Margaret Jennifer Catlin; two *s* one *d*. *Educ:* Newcastle-under-Lyme High School. RAF, 1949–51. Partner, Grindey & Co., Solicitors, Stoke-on-Trent, 1960–85. Pres., N Staffs Law Soc., 1980–81. *Recreations:* music, walking, gardening, reading, all sports, paintings. *Address:* 20 Waltham Lane, Beverley, North Humberside HU17 8HB.

WHITE, Norman Arthur, PhD; CEng, FIMechE; Director and Principal Executive, Norman White Associates, since 1972; *b* Hetton-le-Hole, Durham, 11 April 1922; *s* of late Charles Brewster White and Lillian Sarah (*née* Finch); *m* 1st 1944, Joyce Marjorie Rogers (*d* 1982); one *s* one *d*; 2nd, 1983, Marjorie Iris Rushton. *Educ:* Luton Tech. Coll. (HNC 1943); Manchester Inst. of Sci. and Technol. (AMCT Hons 1948); London Univ. (BSc Eng (Hons) 1949); Univ. of Philippines (MSc 1955); Harvard Business Sch. (grad. AMP 1968); LSE (PhD 1973). CEng 1947; MRAeS; FInstPet; FInstE; FIMechE; FIMM. Industrial apprentice, George Kent, and D. Napier & Son, 1936–43; Flight Test Engr, Mil. Aircraft develt, 1943–45. Joined Royal Dutch/Shell Gp, 1945; Petroleum Res. Engr, Thornton Res. Centre, 1945–51; Tech. Manager, Shell Co. of Philippines, 1951–55; Shell International Petroleum: Div. Hd, later Dep. Manager, Product Develt Dept, 1955–61; special assignments in various countries, 1961–63; Gen. Manager, Lubricants, Bitumen and LPG Divs, 1963–66; Dir of Marketing Develt, 1966–68; Chief Exec., New Enterprises Div., London and The Hague, 1968–72; Chm. and Dir, Shell oil and mining cos, UK and overseas, 1963–72. Established Norman White Associates (specialists in technology based enterprises and international resources), 1972; Energy Advr, Hambros Bank, 1972–76; Chm./Dir, various petroleum exploration cos in UK, Netherlands, Canada and USA, 1974–; Chairman: KBC Process Technology, 1979–; Tesel plc, 1983–85 (Dir, 1980–); Ocean Thermal Energy Conversion Systems, 1982–; Petranol plc, 1986– (Dir, 1985–); Process Automation and Computer Systems, 1985–; Andaman Resources plc, 1986–; Dir, Environmental Resources, 1973–. Mem., Parly and Scientific Cttee, House of Commons, 1977–83; World Energy Conference: Member: British Nat. Cttee, 1977–; Conservation Commn, 1979–; World Pteroleum Congress: Dep. Chm., British Nat. Cttee, 1977–; Permanent Council, 1979–; Treasurer, 1983–; Member: Bd and World Council, Internat. Road Fedn, Geneva and Washington, 1964–72; UK CAA Cttee of Enquiry on Flight Time Limitations (Bader Cttee), 1972–73; Royal Soc./Inst. of Petroleum Delegn to People's Republic of China, 1985; Chm., China Technical Exchange Cttee, 1985–. Visiting Professor: Arthur D. Little Management Educn Inst., Boston, 1977–79; ASC, Henley, 1979– (Vis. Fellow 1976–79); Manchester Business Sch., 1981– (Vis. Industrial Dir 1971–81); Vis. Lectr, RCDS, 1981–85; Dep. Chm., Council of Management, Henley Centre for Forecasting, 1974–; London University: Member: Senate, 1974–; External Council, 1974–84; Governing Bd, Commerce Degree Bureau, 1975–84; Academic Adv. Bd in Engrg, 1976–85; Collegiate Council, 1984–; Cttee of Mangt, Inst. of US Studies, 1984–; Mem., Council of Mining and Metallurgical Instns, 1981–. Member Council: Inst. of Petroleum, 1975–81 (Vice-Pres., 1978–81); IMechE, 1980–85 (Chm., Engrg Management Div.). FRSA 1944; FBIM; MRI; Mem., RIIA; Founder Mem., British Inst. of Energy Econs. Associate, St George's House, Windsor Castle, 1972. Governor: King Edward VI Royal Grammar Sch., Guildford, 1976–; Reigate Grammar Sch., 1976–. Freeman, City of London, 1983; Liveryman: Worshipful Co. of Engineers, 1984; Co. of Spectacle Makers, 1986; Mem., Guild of Freemen, 1986. *Publications:* Financing the International Petroleum Industry, 1978; The International Outlook for Oil Substitution to 2020, 1983; contribs to professional jls in UK and Canada, on fluid mechanics, petroleum utilization, energy resources, R&D management, project financing and engrg management. *Recreations:* family and various others in moderation, country and coastal walking, wild life, browsing, international affairs, comparative religions, domestic odd-jobbing. *Address:* 9 Park House, 123–125 Harley Street, W1N 1HE. *T:* 01–935 7387; Green Ridges, Downside Road, Guildford, Surrey GU4 8PH. *T:* Guildford 67523. *Clubs:* Athenæum, City Livery, Inst. of Directors.

WHITE, Patrick Victor Martindale; Author; *b* 28 May 1912; *s* of Victor Martindale White and Ruth Withycombe. *Educ:* Cheltenham Coll.; King's Coll., Cambridge. Brought up partly in Australia, partly in England. First published while living in London before War of 1939–45. Served War with RAF, as Intelligence Officer, mainly in Middle East. Returned to Australia after War. Nobel Prize for Literature, 1973. *Publications: novels:* Happy Valley, 1939; The Living and the Dead, 1941 (new edn 1962); The Aunt's Story, 1946; The Tree of Man, 1954; Voss, 1957 (1st annual literary award of '1000 from W. H. Smith & Son, 1959); Riders in the Chariot, 1961; The Solid Mandala, 1966; The Vivisector, 1970; The Eye of the Storm, 1973; A Fringe of Leaves, 1976; The Twyborn Affair, 1979; Memoirs of Many in One, 1986; *plays:* The Ham Funeral, 1947; The Season at Sarsaparilla, 1961; A Cheery Soul, 1962; Night on Bald Mountain, 1962; Big Toys, 1977; Signal Driver, 1981; Netherwood, 1983; *short stories:* The Burnt Ones, 1964; The Cockatoos, 1974; *self-portrait:* Flaws in the Glass, 1981; *film:* The Night the Prowler, 1978. *Recreations:* friendship, cooking, gardening, listening to music, keeping dogs. *Address:* c/o Curtis Brown (Aust.) Pty Ltd, 27 Union Street, Paddington, NSW 2021, Australia.

WHITE, Adm. Sir Peter, GBE 1977 (KBE 1976; CBE 1960; MBE 1944); Associate Director, Education for Industrial Society, since 1980; *b* 25 Jan. 1919; *s* of William White, Amersham, Bucks; *m* 1947, Audrey Eileen, *d* of Ernest Wallin, Northampton; two *s*. *Educ:* Dover College. Secretary: to Chief of Staff, Home Fleet, 1942–43; to Flag Officer Comdg 4th Cruiser Sqdn, 1944–45; to Asst Chief of Naval Personnel, 1946–47; to Flag Officer, Destroyers, Mediterranean, 1948–49; to Controller of the Navy, 1949–53; to C-in-C Home Fleet and C-in-C Eastern Atlantic, 1954–55; Naval Asst to Chm. BJSM, Washington, and UK Rep. of Standing Group, NATO, 1956–59; Supply Officer, HMS Adamant, 1960–61; Dep. Dir of Service Conditions and Fleet Supply Duties, Admty, 1961–63; idc 1964; CO HMS Raleigh, 1965–66; Principal Staff Officer to Chief of Defence Staff, 1967–69; Dir-Gen. Fleet Services, 1969–71; Port Admiral, Rosyth, 1972–74; Chief of Fleet Support, 1974–77. Consultant, Wilkinson Match Ltd, 1978–79; Underwriting Member of Lloyd's, 1979–. Chm., Officers Pension Society. Mem. Foundn Cttee, Gordon Boys' Sch. *Address:* c/o Westminster Bank, 26 The Haymarket, SW1.

WHITE, Phyllis Dorothy; *see* James, Phyllis D.

WHITE, Raymond Walter Ralph, CMG 1982; Chairman, BP New Zealand, since 1984 (Director, since 1982); Deputy Chairman, Alcan New Zealand, since 1985 (Director, since 1982); Director: New Zealand Advisory Board, Westpac Banking Corporation, since 1982; New Zealand Guardian Trust Company, since 1983; Mair & Co. Ltd, since 1984; ICI New Zealand Ltd, since 1984; *b* 23 June 1923; *s* of Henry Underhill White and Ethel Annie White; *m* 1946, Nola Colleen Adin; one *s* two *d*. *Educ:* Palmerston North Technical High Sch.; Victoria Univ. FCA 1981; FCIS 1968; FBINZ 1982. Dep. Governor, 1967–77, Governor, 1977–82, Reserve Bank of NZ. Chm., NZ Inst. of Economic Research, 1984–. Chm., Meat Export Prices Cttee, 1984–. *Recreations:* golf, tennis, gardening. *Address:* 63 Chatsworth Road, Silverstream, New Zealand. *T:* Wellington 282084. *Club:* Wellington (NZ).

WHITE, Captain Richard Taylor, DSO 1940 (Bars 1941 and 1942); RN retired; *b* 29 Jan. 1908; *s* of Sir Archibald White, 4th Bt and *heir-pres.* to Sir Thomas White, *qv*; *m* 1936, Gabrielle Ursula Style; three *s* two *d*. *Educ:* RN College, Dartmouth. Served War of 1939–45 (DSO and two Bars). Retired 1955. *Address:* Tilts House, Boughton Monchelsea, Maidstone, Kent ME17 4JE.

WHITE, Robin Bernard G.; *see* Grove-White.

WHITE, Roger, FSA 1986; Secretary, Georgian Group, since 1984; *b* 1 Sept. 1950; *s* of Geoffrey and Zoe White. *Educ:* Ifield Grammar School; Christ's College, Cambridge (1st class Hons, Hist. of Art Tripos); Wadham College, Oxford. GLC Historic Buildings Div., 1979–83. *Publications:* John Vardy, 1985; contribs to Architectural Hist., Jl of Garden Hist., Country Life. *Recreations:* visiting and writing about historic buildings, walking, music. *Address:* The Georgian Group, 37 Spital Square, E1 6DY. *T:* 01–377 1722.

WHITE, Roger Lowrey, JP; Chairman, Calcumate UK Ltd, since 1985; Managing Director, Research Information Services (Westminster) Ltd; Director: Williamson Tea Holdings PLC, since 1972; WTH Finance Ltd, since 1981; Heavy Goods Vehicle Parking Ltd, since 1982; Associate Director, Cargill Attwood International, since 1971; *b* 1 June 1928; *o s* of late George Frederick White and Dorothy Jeanette White; *m* 1962, Angela Mary (*née* Orman), company director. *Educ:* St Joseph's Coll., Beulah Hill. National Vice-Chm., Young Conservatives, 1958–59; Founder Mem., Conservative Commonwealth Council; Mem. Council, London Borough of Bromley, 1964–68. MP (C) Gravesend, 1970–Feb. 1974. Mem., Asthma Research Council, 1973–. Freeman, City of London, 1953; Liveryman, Worshipful Co. of Makers of Playing Cards, 1975–; JP Inner London Area, 1965. *Recreations:* golf, fishing. *Address:* 74 Clifton Court, Aberdeen Place, NW8. *Club:* Carlton.

WHITE, Stephen Fraser; consulting engineer; *b* 13 May 1922; *s* of Robert and Iola White; *m* 1953, Judith Hamilton Cox; two *s* one *d*. *Educ:* Friars, Bangor; Nottingham Univ. BSc; FICE, MIWES, MIStructE. War Service in Indian Electrical and Mechanical Engineers, discharged 1947. G. H. Hill and Sons, Consulting Civil Engineers, 1947–59; Cardiff Corporation, 1959–62; Engineering Inspector, Min. of Housing and Local Govt, 1962–70; Dir of Water Engineering, Dept of the Environment, 1970–77; Sen. Technical Advr to Nat. Water Council, 1977–83. *Recreations:* golf, bridge. *Address:* 28 Biddenham Turn, Bedford. *T:* Bedford 53557.

WHITE, Terence de Vere, FRSL; *b* 29 April 1912; *s* of Frederick S. de Vere White, LLD, and Ethel (*née* Perry); *m* 1st, 1941, Mary O'Farrell (marr. diss. 1982); two *s* one *d*; 2nd, 1982, Hon. Victoria Glendinning, *qv*. *Educ:* St Stephen's Green Sch., Dublin; Trinity Coll., Dublin (BA, LLB). Admitted solicitor, 1933. Mem. Council, Incorporated Law Society, retd 1961. Literary Editor, The Irish Times, 1961–77. Vice-Chm., Board of Governors, National Gallery of Ireland; Trustee: National Library, 1946–79; Chester Beatty Library, 1959–80; Dir, Gate Theatre, 1969–81. Mem., Irish Academy of Letters, 1968; Hon. RHA 1968; Hon. Prof. of Literature, RHA, 1973; FRSL 1981. *Publications:* The Road of Excess, 1945; Kevin O'Higgins, 1948; The Story of the Royal Dublin Society, 1955; A Fretful Midge, 1957; A Leaf from the Yellow Book, 1958; An Affair with the Moon, 1959; Prenez Garde, 1962; The Remainder Man, 1963; Lucifer Falling, 1965; The Parents of Oscar Wilde, 1967; Tara, 1967; Leinster, 1968; Ireland, 1968; The Lambert Mile, 1969; The March Hare, 1970; Mr Stephen, 1971; The Anglo-Irish, 1972; The Distance and the Dark, 1973; The Radish Memoirs, 1974; Big Fleas and Little Fleas, 1976; Chimes at Midnight, 1977; Tom Moore, 1977; My Name is Norval, 1978; Birds of Prey, 1980; Johnnie Cross, 1983; contribs to 19th Century, Cambridge Review, Horizon, The Spectator, NY Times, Sunday Telegraph. *Recreation:* formerly riding. *Address:* c/o Allied Irish Banks, 100 Grafton Street, Dublin 2, Ireland. *Clubs:* Garrick; Kildare Street and University (Dublin).

WHITE, Thomas Anthony B.; *see* Blanco White.

WHITE, Sir Thomas Astley Woollaston, 5th Bt, *cr* 1802; JP; Hon. Sheriff for Wigtownshire, since 1963; *b* 13 May 1904; *s* of Sir Archibald Woollaston White, 4th Bt, and late Gladys Becher Love, *d* of Rev. E. A. B. Pitman; *S* father, 1945; *m* 1935, Daphne Margaret, *er d* of late Lt-Col F. R. I. Athill, CMG; one *d*. *Educ:* Wellington College. FRICS. JP Wigtownshire, 1952. *Heir:* *b* Capt. Richard T. White, *qv*. *Address:* Ha Hill, Torhousemuir, Wigtown, Newton Stewart DG8 9DJ. *T:* Wigtown 2238.

WHITE, Hon. Victoria de Vere, (Hon. Mrs Terence de Vere White); *see* Glendinning, Hon. V.

WHITE, Sir (Vincent) Gordon (Lindsay), KBE 1979; Chairman of the Board, Hanson Industries, since 1983; *b* 11 May 1923; *s* of late Charles White and Lily May (*née* Wilson); *m* 1974, Virginia Anne; one *s* (and two *d* by a former marriage). *Educ:* De Aston Sch., Lincs. Served War, 1940–46: SOE, Force 136, Captain. Chairman, family publishing business, Welbecson Ltd, 1947–65; Dep. Chm., Hanson Trust Ltd, 1965–73; Special Commn to open Hanson Trust's opportunities overseas, 1973–83. Mem. Bd and Chm., Internat. Cttee, Congressional Award, 1984–; Member: Council for Police Rehabilitation Appeal, 1985–; Bd of Dirs, Shakespeare Theatre, Folger Library, Washington, 1985–. Governor, BFI, 1982–84. Hon. Fellow, St Peter's Coll., Oxford, 1984. Nat. Voluntary Leadership Award, Congressional Award 1984; (with Lord Hanson) Aims of Industry Free Enterprise Award, 1985. *Recreations:* flying (holder of helicopter licence), riding, skiing, tennis. *Address:* 410 Park Avenue, New York, NY 10022, USA. *T:* (212) 759–8477. *Clubs:* Special Forces; Brook, Explorers' (New York); Mid-Ocean (Bermuda).

WHITE, Wilfrid H.; *see* Hyde White.

WHITE, William Kelvin Kennedy, CMG 1983; HM Diplomatic Service; High Commissioner to Zambia, since 1984; *b* 10 July 1930; *y s* of late Kennedy White, JP, Caldy, Cheshire, and Violet White; *m* 1957, Susan Margaret, *y d* of late R. T. Colthurst, JP, Malvern, Worcs; three *s*. *Educ:* Birkenhead Sch.; Merton Coll., Oxford. HM Forces, 1949–50 (2nd Lieut Manchester Regt); Lieut 13th (Lancs) Bn TA, 1950–54. Entered HM Foreign (later Diplomatic) Service, 1954; Foreign Office, 1954–56, attending UN Gen. Assemblies, 1954 and 1955; 3rd Sec., Helsinki, 1956–57; 2nd Sec., Commissioner-General's Office, Singapore, 1957–61; 2nd Sec., then 1st Sec., FO, 1961–66; 1st Sec.

(Commercial), Stockholm, 1966–69; 1st Sec., then Counsellor and Head of Republic of Ireland Dept, FCO, 1969–74; Counsellor, New Delhi, 1974–77; Head of South Asian Dept, FCO, 1978–80; Minister, Canberra, 1980–81; Dep. Chief Clerk and Chief Inspector, FCO, 1982–84. *Address:* c/o Foreign and Commonwealth Office, SW1. *Club:* Moreton CC.

WHITE-THOMSON, Very Rev. Ian Hugh; Dean of Canterbury, 1963–76; *b* 18 December 1904; *m* 1954, Wendy Ernesta Woolliams; two *s* two *d*. *Educ:* Harrow; Oxford. Deacon, 1929; Priest, 1930; Curacy, St Mary's, Ashford, Kent, 1929–34; Rector of S Martin's with St Paul's, Canterbury, 1934–39; Chaplain to Archbishop of Canterbury, 1939–47; Vicar of Folkestone, 1947–54; Archdeacon of Northumberland and Canon of Newcastle, 1955–63; Chaplain to King George VI, 1947–52, to the Queen, 1952–63; Examining Chaplain to Bishop of Newcastle, 1955–63. Hon. Canon of Canterbury Cathedral, 1950. Governor, Harrow School, 1947–62, 1965–70. Freeman, City of Canterbury, 1976. Hon. DCL Univ. of Kent at Canterbury, 1971. *Address:* Camphill, Harville Road, Wye, Ashford, Kent. *T:* Wye 812210.

WHITEHEAD, Edward Anthony, (Ted); playwright; theatre and film reviewer; *b* 3 April 1933; *s* of Edward Whitehead and Catherine Curran; *m* 1st, 1958, Kathleen Horton (marr. diss. 1976); two *d*; 2nd, 1976, Gwenda Bagshaw. *Educ:* Christ's Coll., Cambridge (MA). Military Service, King's Regt (Infantry), 1955–57. Evening Standard Award, and George Devine Award, 1971. *Publications:* The Foursome, 1972; Alpha Beta, 1972; The Sea Anchor, 1975; Old Flames, 1976; The Punishment, 1976; Mecca, 1977; World's End, 1981; The Man Who Fell in Love with his Wife, 1984. *Recreations:* soccer, pubs, music. *Address:* c/o Judy Daish Associates Ltd, 83 Eastbourne Mews, W2 6LQ. *T:* 01–262 1101.

WHITEHEAD, Frank Ernest; Deputy Director, Office of Population Censuses and Surveys, since 1982; *b* 21 Jan. 1930; *s* of Ernest Edward Whitehead and Isabel Leslie; *m* 1961, Anne Gillian Marston; three *s*. *Educ:* Leyton County High School; London School of Economics. BSc (Econ). National Service, RAF, 1948–49. Rio Tinto Co. Ltd, 1952–54; Professional Officer, Central Statistical Office, Fedn of Rhodesia and Nyasaland, 1955–64; Statistician, General Register Office, 1964–68; Chief Statistician, Min. of Social Security, later DHSS, 1968–77; Head of Social Survey Div., Office of Population Censuses and Surveys, 1977–82; Under Secretary, 1982. *Publications:* Social Security Statistics: Reviews of United Kingdom Statistical Sources, Vol. II (ed W. F. Maunder), 1974; contribs to Statistical News, Population Trends. *Recreations:* family history, unskilled garden labour. *Address:* Queensmead, Pilgrims Way, Kemsing, Kent TN15 6XA. *T:* Sevenoaks 61787.

WHITEHEAD, Frank Henry; Deputy Chairman, Macmillan Ltd, 1980–83; *b* 25 Sept. 1918; *s* of William George Whitehead and Annie S. Whitehead; *m* 1941, Gwendolyn Heather (*née* Ross); one *s* two *d*. *Educ:* Harrow County Sch.; LSE; London Sch. of Printing. Served War, RA, 1939–46. Joined Macmillan Ltd, 1937; Dir, 1963; Gp Man. Dir, 1965–80; non-exec. Dir, 1983–84. Liveryman, Stationers and Newspaper Makers Co. *Recreations:* reading, painting, music, gardening, photography. *Address:* 5 Briery Field, Chorleywood, Herts. *T:* Chorleywood 4721. *Clubs:* City Livery, Wig and Pen.
See also G. S. Whitehead.

WHITEHEAD, Garnet George Archie, DFC 1944; **His Honour Judge Whitehead;** a Circuit Judge, since 1977; *b* 22 July 1916; *s* of late Archibald Payne Whitehead and Margaret Elizabeth Whitehead; *m* 1946, Monica (*née* Watson); two *d*. *Educ:* Wisbech. Admitted Solicitor, 1949. Served War, 1939–45, RAF, Pilot, Bomber Comd and Transport Comd; demob. as Flt Lt, 1 Jan. 1947. Articled to Edmund W. Roythorne, MBE, Solicitor, Spalding. Formerly Senior Partner, Roythorne & Co., Solicitor, Boston, Lincs (Partner, 1950–77); a Recorder of the Crown Court, 1972–77. Formerly Alderman, Boston Borough Council; Mayor of Boston, 1969–70. *Recreations:* photography, walking. *Address:* 15 Burton Close, Boston, Lincs. *T:* Boston 64977.

WHITEHEAD, George Sydney, CMG 1966; LVO 1961; HM Diplomatic Service, retired; re-employed in Foreign and Commonwealth Office (Security Department), 1976–81; *b* 15 Nov. 1915; *s* of William George and Annie Sabina Whitehead; *m* 1948, Constance Mary Hart (*née* Vale); one *d* (and one step *d*). Educ: Harrow County Sch.; London Sch. of Economics. India Office, 1934. Armed Forces (Royal Artillery), 1940–45. Private Sec. to Parly Under-Sec. of State for India and Burma, 1945–46; British Embassy, Rangoon, 1947; CRO 1948–52; British High Commn, Canberra, 1952–55; Counsellor, British High Commn, Calcutta, 1958–61; Inspector, Commonwealth Service, 1961–64; Inspector, Diplomatic Service, 1965; Head of Asia Economic Dept, CO, 1966–67; Head of Commonwealth Trade Dept, CO, 1967–68; Head of Commodities Dept, FCO, 1968–69; Dep. High Comr and Minister (Commercial), Ottawa, 1970–72; Asst Under-Sec. of State, 1972–75, Dep. Chief Clerk, 1973–75, FCO. Vice-Pres., RIPA, 1985 (Mem. Council, 1977–84). *Recreations:* gardening, reading, walking. *Address:* 399 Pinner Road, Harrow, Mddx. *T:* 01–427 5872. *Clubs:* Civil Service, Royal Commonwealth Society; Middlesex County Cricket.
See also F. H. Whitehead.

WHITEHEAD, Graham Wright, CBE 1977; President, Jaguar Cars Inc., since 1983; Chairman, Jaguar Canada Inc., Ontario, since 1983; Director, Jaguar Cars Ltd, since 1982; Jaguar plc, since 1984; *m* Gabrielle Whitehead, OBE; one *s* one *d*. Joined Wolseley Motors, 1945; moved to US, 1959; Pres., BL Motors Inc., later Jaguar Rover Triumph Inc., NJ, 1968–83; Chm., Jaguar Rover Triumph Canada Inc., Ont, 1977–83. President: British-American Chamber of Commerce, NY, 1976–78; British Automobile Manufacturers Assoc., NY; St George's Soc. of NY. *Address:* 20 Meadow Place, Old Greenwich, Conn 06870, USA. *Club:* Riverside Yacht (Conn).

WHITEHEAD, Dr John Ernest Michael, FRCPath; Director of Public Health Laboratory Service, 1981–85; *b* 7 Aug. 1920; *s* of Dr Charles Ernest Whitehead and Bertha Whitehead; *m* 1946, Elizabeth Bacchus (*née* Cochran); one *s* one *d*. *Educ:* Merchant Taylors' Sch.; Gonville and Caius Coll., Cambridge (MA); St Thomas's Hosp. Med. Sch. (MB BChir, DipBact). Jun. Ho. appts, St Thomas' Hosp., 1944–47; Lectr in Bacteriology, St Thomas's Hosp. Med. Sch., 1948–51; Travelling Fellowship, State Serum Inst., Copenhagen, 1949–50; Asst Bacteriologist, Central Public Health Laboratory, 1952–53; Dep. Dir, Public Health Lab., Sheffield, 1953–58; Dir, Public Health Lab., Coventry, 1958–75; Cons. Microbiologist, Coventry Hosps, 1958–75; Dep. Dir, Public Health Laboratory Service, 1975–81. Hon. Lecturer: Univ. of Sheffield, 1954–58; Univ. of Birmingham, 1962–75. Vice-Pres., RCPath, 1983–86; Member: Adv. Cttee on Dangerous Pathogens, 1981–85; Adv. Cttee on Irradiated and Novel Foods, 1982–86; Expert Adv. Gp on AIDS, 1985; Consultant Advr in Microbiol., DHSS, 1982–85; Temporary Adviser and Chm., Working Gp on Safety Measures in Microbiology, WHO, 1976–82; Chm., Working Gp on Organisation and Administration of Public Health Laboratory Services, Council of Europe, 1977–79. *Publications:* chapters in The Pathological Basis of Medicine, ed R. C. Curran and D. G. Harnden, 1974; papers and reviews in med. microbiology in various med. and scientific jls. *Recreations:* house and garden maintenance, skiing, modern languages. *Address:* Martins, Lee Common, Great Missenden, Bucks HP16 9JP. *T:* The Lee 492. *Club:* Athenæum.

WHITEHEAD, Sir John (Stainton), KCMG 1986 (CMG 1976); CVO 1978; HM Diplomatic Service; Ambassador to Japan, since 1986; *b* 20 Sept. 1932; *s* of late John William and Kathleen Whitehead; *m* 1964, Mary Carolyn (*née* Hilton); two *s* two *d*. *Educ:* Christ's Hospital; Hertford Coll., Oxford (MA). HM Forces, 1950–52; Oxford, 1952–55; FO, 1955–56; 3rd Sec., later 2nd Sec., Tokyo, 1956–61; FO, 1961–64; 1st Sec., Washington, 1964–67; 1st Sec. (Economic), Tokyo, 1968–71; FCO, 1971–76, Head of Personnel Services Dept, 1973–76; Counsellor, Bonn, 1976–80; Minister, Tokyo, 1980–84; Dep. Under-Sec. of State (Chief Clerk), FCO, 1984–86. *Recreations:* music, travel, golf, tree-felling, walking, chess. *Address:* British Embassy, 1 Ichiban-cho, Chiyoda-ku, Tokyo 100, Japan; Bracken Edge, High Pitfold, Hindhead, Surrey. *T:* Hindhead 4162. *Club:* United Oxford & Cambridge University.

WHITEHEAD, Phillip; writer and television producer; Chairman: Statesman and Nation Publications Ltd, 1985; New Society Ltd, 1986; *b* 30 May 1937; adopted *s* of late Harold and Frances Whitehead; *m* 1967, Christine, *d* of T. G. Usborne; two *s* one *d*. *Educ:* Lady Manners' Grammar Sch., Bakewell; Exeter Coll., Oxford. President, Oxford Union, 1961. BBC Producer, 1961–67, and WEA Lecturer, 1961–65; Editor of This Week, Thames TV, 1967–70. Guild of TV Producers Award for Factual Programmes, 1969. Vice-Chm., Young Fabian Group, 1965; Chm., Fabian Soc., 1978–79 (Centenary Dir, 1983–84). Member: Annan Cttee on Future of Broadcasting, 1974–77; Council, Consumers' Assoc., 1982–. Director: Brook Productions, 1986; Goldcrest Film and Television Hldgs Ltd. MP (Lab) Derby N, 1970–83; Front bench spokesman on higher educn, 1980–83 and on the arts, 1982–83; Member: Procedure Cttee, 1977–79; Select Cttee on Home Affairs, 1979–81; PLP Liaison Cttee, 1975–79; Council of Europe Assembly, 1975–80. Contested (Lab): W Derbys, 1966, Derby N, 1983. Member: NUJ; NUR. Times columnist, 1983–85; Presenter, Credo series, LWT, 1983–84. FRSA 1983. *Publications:* (jtly) Electoral Reform: time for change, 1982; (contrib.) Fabian Essays in Socialist Thought, 1984; The Writing on the Wall, 1985. *Recreations:* walking, cinema, old model railways. *Address:* Mill House, Rowsley, Matlock, Derbys. *T:* Matlock 732659.

WHITEHEAD, Sir Rowland (John Rathbone), 5th Bt, *cr* 1889; *b* 24 June 1930; *s* of Major Sir Philip Henry Rathbone Whitehead, 4th Bt, and 1st wife Gertrude, *d* of J. C. Palmer, West Virginia, USA; *S* father, 1953; *m* 1954, Marie-Louise, *d* of Arnold Christian Gausel, Stavanger, Norway; one *s* one *d*. *Educ:* Radley; Trinity Hall, Cambridge (BA). Late 2nd Lieutenant RA. Chairman: Trustees, Rowland Hill Benevolent Fund, 1982–; Exec. Cttee, Standing Council of the Baronetage, 1984–; Founder Chm., Baronets' Trust, 1984–. Governor, Appleby Grammar Sch., 1964–. Liveryman, Worshipful Co. of Fruiterers'; Freeman, City of London. *Recreations:* poetry and rural indolence. *Heir:* *s* Lt Philip Henry Rathbone Whitehead [*b* 13 Oct. 1957. Late Welsh Guards]. *Address:* Sutton House, Chiswick Mall, W4 2PR. *T:* 01–994 2710; Walnut Tree Cottage, Fyfield, Lechlade, Glos GL7 3NT. *Clubs:* Reform, Arts.

WHITEHEAD, Ted; *see* Whitehead, E. A.

WHITEHEAD, Prof. Thomas Patterson, CBE 1985; MCB, FRCPath, FRSC; Professor of Clinical Chemistry, since 1968 and Dean, Faculty of Medicine and Dentistry, 1984–Oct. 1987, University of Birmingham; Consultant Biochemist, Queen Elizabeth Medical Centre, since 1960; *b* 7 May 1923; *m* 1947, Doreen Grace Whitton, JP; two *s* one *d*. *Educ:* Salford Royal Technical Coll.; Univ. of Birmingham (PhD). Biochemist to S Warwickshire Hospital Gp, 1950–60. Dir, Wolfson Research Laboratories, 1972–84. Council Mem., Med. Research Council, 1972–76; Mem., Health Service Research Bd, 1973–75; Chairman: Div. of Path. Studies, Birmingham, 1974–80; Board of Undergraduate Med. Educn, Birmingham, 1982–84; W Midlands RHA Res. Cttee, 1982–; DHSS Adv. Cttee on Assessment of Laboratory Standards, 1969–84; W Midlands RHA Scientific Services Cttee, 1984–. Consultant to: BUPA Medical Centre, London, 1969–; BUPA Hosps, London, 1983–; Centro Diagnostico Italiano, Milan, 1972–; WHO, Geneva, 1974–; JS Pathology Services, London, 1983–. Pres., Assoc. of Clinical Biochemists, 1981–83; Mem. Council, RCPath, 1982–84. Hon. MRCP 1985. Kone Award Lectr, 1983. Wellcome Prize, 1972; Dade Award, Geneva, 1975. *Publications:* Quality Control in Clinical Chemistry, 1976; papers in med. and scientific jls. *Recreation:* growing and exhibiting sweet peas. *Address:* 70 Northumberland Road, Leamington Spa CV32 6HB. *T:* Leamington Spa 21974. *Club:* Athenæum.

WHITEHORN, John Roland Malcolm, CMG 1974; Consultant Director, Lilly Industries Ltd, since 1978; *b* 19 May 1924; *s* of late Alan and Edith Whitehorn; *m* 1st, 1951, Josephine (*née* Plummer) (marr. diss. 1973); no *c*; 2nd, 1973, Marion FitzGibbon (*née* Gutmann). *Educ:* Rugby Sch. (Exhbnr); Trinity Coll., Cambridge (Exhbnr). Served War, 1943–46, RAFVR (Flying Officer). Joined FBI, 1947; Dep. Overseas Dir, 1960; Overseas Dir, 1963; Overseas Dir, CBI, 1965–68; a Dep. Dir-Gen., CBI, 1966–78; Dir, Mitchell Cotts plc, 1978–86. Member: BOTB, 1975–78; Bd, British Council, 1968–82; Gen. Adv. Council, BBC, 1976–82. *Address:* Casters Brook, Cocking, near Midhurst, W Sussex GU29 0KJ. *T:* Midhurst 3537. *Club:* Reform.
See also Katharine Whitehorn.

WHITEHORN, Katharine Elizabeth, (Mrs Gavin Lyall); Columnist, since 1960, Associate Editor, since 1980, The Observer; *b* London; *d* of late A. D. and E. M. Whitehorn; *m* 1958, Gavin Lyall, *qv*; two *s*. *Educ:* Blunt House; Roedean; Glasgow High School for Girls, and others; Newnham Coll., Cambridge. Publisher's Reader, 1950–53; Teacher-Secretary in Finland, 1953–54; Grad. Asst, Cornell Univ., USA, 1954–55; Picture Post, 1956–57; Woman's Own, 1958; Spectator, 1959–61. Member: Latey Cttee on Age of Majority, 1965–67; BBC Adv. Gp on Social Effects of Television, 1971–72; Board, British Airports Authority, 1972–77; Council, RSocMed, 1982–85. Dir, Nationwide Building Soc., 1983–. Rector, St Andrews Univ., 1982–85. Hon. LLD St Andrews, 1985. *Publications:* Cooking in a Bedsitter, 1960; Roundabout, 1961; Only on Sundays, 1966; Whitehorn's Social Survival, 1968; Observations, 1970; How to Survive in Hospital, 1972; How to Survive Children, 1975; Sunday Best, 1976; How to Survive in the Kitchen, 1979; View from a Column, 1981; How to Survive your Money Problems, 1983. *Recreation:* small river boat. *Address:* c/o The Observer, 8 St Andrew's Hill, EC4. *T:* 01–236 0202.
See also J. R. M. Whitehorn.

WHITEHOUSE, Dr David Bryn; Chief Curator, The Corning Museum of Glass, Corning, USA, since 1984; *b* 15 Oct. 1941, *s* of Brindley Charles Whitehouse and Alice Margaret Whitehouse; *m* 1st, 1963, Ruth Delamain Ainger; one *s* two *d*; 2nd, 1975, Elizabeth-Anne Ollemans; one *s* two *d*. *Educ:* King Edward's Sch., Birmingham; St John's Coll., Cambridge. MA, PhD; FSA; FRGS. Scholar, British Sch. at Rome, 1963–65; Wainwright Fellow in Near Eastern Archaeology, Univ. of Oxford, 1966–73; Dir, Sīrāf Expedn, 1966–73; Dir, British Inst. of Afghan Studies, 1973–74; Dir, British Sch. at Rome, 1974–84. Pres., Internat. Union of Institutes, 1980–81; Mem. Council, Internat. Assoc. for Classical Archaeology, 1974–84. Corresp. Mem., German Archaeological Inst.; Academician, Accademia Fiorentina dell'Arte del Disegno; Fellow: Pontificia Accademia Romana di Archeologia; Accademia di Archeologia, Lettere e Belle Arti, Naples. *Publications:* (jtly) Background to Archaeology, 1973; (jtly) The Origins of Europe, 1974;

(with Ruth Whitehouse) Archaeological Atlas of the World, 1975; (ed jtly) Papers in Italian Archaeology I, 1978; Siraf III: The Congregational Mosque, 1980; (with David Andrews and John Osborne) Papers in Italian Archaeology III, 1981; (with Richard Hodges) Mohammed, Charlemagne and the Origins of Europe, 1983; (jtly) Glass of the Caesars, 1987; The Medieval Pottery of Central and Southern Italy, 1987; The Collapse of Civilisation, 1987; many papers in Iran, Antiquity, Med. Archaeol., Papers of Brit. Sch. at Rome, etc. *Address:* The Corning Museum of Glass, One Museum Way, Corning, NY 14830–2253, USA. *T:* (607) 937 5371.

WHITEHOUSE, Mary, CBE 1980; Honorary General Secretary, National Viewers' and Listeners' Association, 1965–80, President since 1980; free lance journalist, broadcaster; *b* 13 June 1910; *d* of James and Beatrice Hutcheson; *m* 1940, Ernest R. Whitehouse; three *s*. *Educ:* Chester City Grammar Sch.; Cheshire County Training Coll. Art Specialist: Wednesfield Sch., Wolverhampton, 1932–40; Brewood Grammar Sch., Staffs, 1943; Sen. Mistress, and Sen. Art Mistress, Madeley Sch., Shropshire, 1960–64. Co-founder, "Clean up TV campaign", 1964. *Publications:* Cleaning Up TV, 1966; "Who Does She Think She Is?", 1971; Whatever Happened to Sex?, 1977; A Most Dangerous Woman?, 1982; Mightier than the Sword, 1985. *Recreations:* reading, gardening, walking. *Address:* Blachernae, Ardleigh, Colchester, Essex. *T:* Colchester 230123.

WHITEHOUSE, Walter Alexander; Professor of Theology, University of Kent, 1965–77; Master of Eliot College, University of Kent, 1965–69, and 1973–75; *b* 27 Feb. 1915; *e s* of Walter and Clara Whitehouse, Shelley, near Huddersfield; *m* 1st, 1946, Beatrice Mary Kent Smith (*d* 1971); 2nd, 1974, Audrey Ethel Lemmon. *Educ:* Penistone Gram. Sch.; St John's Coll., Cambridge; Mansfield Coll., Oxford. Minister of Elland Congregational Church, 1940–44; Chaplain at Mansfield College, Oxford, 1944–47; Reader in Divinity, Univ. of Durham, 1947–65. Principal of St Cuthbert's Soc., Univ. of Durham, 1955–60; Pro-Vice-Chancellor of Univ., and Sub-Warden, 1961–64. Minister at High Chapel, Ravenstonedale, 1977–82. Hon. DD Edinburgh, 1960. *Publications:* Christian Faith and the Scientific Attitude, 1952; Order, Goodness, Glory (Riddell Memorial Lectures), 1959; The Authority of Grace, 1981. *Address:* 37 Cotswold Green, Stonehouse, Glos.

WHITELAW, family name of **Viscount Whitelaw.**

WHITELAW, 1st Viscount *cr* 1983, of Penrith in the County of Cumbria; **William Stephen Ian Whitelaw,** CH 1974; MC; PC 1967; DL; Lord President of the Council and Leader of the House of Lords, since 1983; farmer and landowner; *b* 28 June 1918; *s* of late W. A. Whitelaw and Mrs W. A. Whitelaw, Monkland, Nairn; *m* 1943, Cecilia Doriel, 2nd *d* of late Major Mark Sprot, Riddell, Melrose, Roxburghshire; four *d*. *Educ:* Winchester Coll.; Trinity Coll., Camb. Reg. Officer, Scots Guards; Emergency Commn, 1939; resigned Commn, 1947. MP (C) Penrith and the Border Div. of Cumberland, 1955–83; PPS to Chancellor of the Exchequer, 1957–58 (to Pres. of BOT, 1956); Asst Govt Whip, 1959–61; a Lord Comr of the Treasury, 1961–62; Parly Sec., Min. of Labour, July 1962–Oct. 1964; Chief Opposition Whip, 1964–70; Lord Pres. of Council and Leader, House of Commons, 1970–72; Secretary of State for: N Ireland, 1972–73; Employment, 1973–74; Chm., Conservative Party, 1974–75; Dep. Leader of the Opposition and spokesman on home affairs, 1975–79; Home Secretary, 1979–83. Visiting Fellow, Nuffield Coll., Oxford, 1970–. DL Dunbartonshire, 1952–66; DL Cumbria, formerly Cumberland, 1967. *Recreations:* golf, shooting. *Heir:* none. *Address:* Ennim, Penrith, Cumbria. *Clubs:* White's, Carlton (Chm., 1986–); Royal and Ancient (Captain 1969–70).

See also Earl of Swinton.

WHITELAW, Billie; actress; *b* 6 June 1932; *d* of Perceval and Frances Whitelaw; *m* Robert Muller, writer; one *s*. *Educ:* Thornton Grammar Sch., Bradford. Appeared in: *plays:* Hotel Paradiso, Winter Garden, 1954 and Oxford Playhouse, 1956; Progress to the Park, Theatre Workshop and Saville, 1961; England our England, Prince's, 1962; Touch of the Poet, Venice and Dublin, 1962; National Theatre, 1963–65: Othello, London and Moscow; Hobson's Choice; Beckett's Play; Trelawny of the Wells; The Dutch Courtesan; After Haggerty, Criterion, 1971; Not I, Royal Court, 1973 and 1975; Alphabetical Order, Mayfair, 1975; Footfalls, Royal Court, 1976; Molly, Comedy, 1978; Happy Days, Royal Court, 1979; The Greeks, Aldwych, 1980; Passion Play, Aldwych, 1981; Rockaby and Enough, NY, 1981, with Footfalls, 1984, NT 1982, Riverside, 1986, Adelaide Fest., 1986, Purchase Fest., NY, 1986; Tales from Hollywood, NT, 1983; *films:* No Love for Johnny; Charlie Bubbles; Twisted Nerve; The Adding Machine; Start the Revolution Without Me; Leo the Last; Eagle in a Cage; Gumshoe; Frenzy; Night Watch; The Omen; Leopard in the Snow; The Water Babies; An Unsuitable Job for a Woman; Tangier; Slayground; Shadey; The Chain; *television:* No Trams to Lime Street; Lena Oh My Lena; Resurrection; The Skin Game; Beyond the Horizon; Anna Christie; Lady of the Camelias; The Pity of it all; Love on the Dole; A World of Time; You and Me; Poet Game; Sextet (8 plays); Napoleon and Love (9 plays: Josephine); The Fifty Pound Note (Ten from the Twenties); The Withered Arm (Wessex Tales); The Werewolf Reunion (2 plays); Two Plays by Samuel Beckett; Not I; Eustace and Hilda (2 plays); The Serpent Son; Happy Days (dir. by Beckett); Private Schulz; Last Summer's Child; A Tale of Two Cities; Jamaica Inn; Camille; Old Girlfriends; *radio plays:* The Master Builder; Hindle Wakes; Jane Eyre; The Female Messiah; Alpha Beta; The Cherry Orchard. Lectr on Beckett at US Univs of Santa Barbara, Stanford and Denver, 1985, at Balliol Coll., Oxford, 1986. Silver Heart Variety Club Award, 1961; TV Actress of Year, 1961, 1972; British Academy Award, 1968; US Film Critics Award, 1968; Variety Club of GB Best Film Actress Award, 1977; Evening News Film Award as Best Actress, 1977. Hon. DLitt Bradford 1981. *Recreation:* pottering about the house. *Address:* c/o Duncan Heath Associates Ltd, 162 Wardour Street, W1.

WHITELEY, family name of **Baron Marchamley.**

WHITELEY, Maj.-Gen. Gerald Abson, CB 1969; OBE 1952; *b* 4 March 1915; *s* of late Harry Whiteley, Walton Park, Bexhill; *m* 1943, Ellen Hanna (*d* 1973). *Educ:* Worksop Coll.; Emmanuel Coll., Cambridge (MA). Solicitor, 1938. Commissioned, RA, 1940; Maj., DJAG's Staff, ME, 1942–45. AAG, Mil. Dept, JAG's Office, WO, 1945–48; Asst Dir of Army Legal Services: FARELF, 1948–51; WO, 1952–53; Northern Army Gp, 1953–54; MELF, 1954–57; BAOR, 1957–60; Dep. Dir of Army Legal Services, BAOR, 1960–62; Col, Legal Staff, WO, 1962–64; Dir of Army Legal Services, MoD, 1964–69. *Recreations:* photography, walking. *Address:* 8 Kemnal Park, Haslemere, Surrey. *T:* Haslemere 2803. *Club:* Army and Navy.

WHITELEY, Sir Hugo Baldwin Huntington-; *see* Huntington-Whiteley, Sir H. B.

WHITELEY, Gen. Sir Peter (John Frederick), GCB 1979 (KCB 1976); OBE 1960; Lieutenant-Governor and Commander-in-Chief, Jersey, 1979–84; *b* 13 Dec. 1920; *s* of late John George Whiteley; *m* 1948, Nancy Vivian, *d* of late W. Carter Clayden; two *s* two *d*. *Educ:* Bishop's Stortford Coll.; Bembridge Sch.; Ecole des Roches. Joined Royal Marines, 1940; 101 Bde, 1941; HMS: Resolution, 1941; Renown, 1942; HMNZS Gambia, 1942; seconded to Fleet Air Arm, 1946–50; Adjt 40 Commando, 1951; Staff Coll., Camberley, 1954; Bde Major 3rd Commando Bde, 1957; Instructor, Staff Coll., Camberley, 1960–63; CO 42 Commando, 1965–66 (despatches, Malaysia, 1966); Col GS Dept of CGRM, 1966–68; Nato Defence Coll., 1968; Comdr 3rd Commando Bde, 1968–70; Maj.-Gen. Commando Forces, 1970–72; C of S, HQ Allied Forces Northern Europe, 1972–75; Commandant General, Royal Marines, 1975–77; C-in-C Allied Forces Northern Europe, 1977–79. Col Comdt, RM, 1985–; Hon. Col, 211 (Wessex) Field Hosp. RAMC (Volunteers), TA, 1985–. Mem., Union Jack Club Council, 1985–. Pres., W Devon Area, St Johns Ambulance Bde, 1985–. Trustee, Jersey Wildlife Preservation Trust. Governor: Bembridge Sch., 1981–; Kelly Coll., 1985–; St Michael's Sch., Tavistock, 1985–. Liveryman, Fletchers' Co., 1982; Guild of Freemen of City of London: Mem. Ct of Assistants, 1980–; Sen. Warden, 1986–. CBIM. KStJ 1980; Chevalier, Ordre de la Pléaiade, Assoc. of French Speaking Parliaments, 1984. *Publications:* contribs to Jane's Annual, NATO's Fifteen Nations, RUSI Jl, Nauticus. *Recreations:* music (Mem. Glyndebourne Festival Soc.), photography, painting, wood carving, sailing, dogs. *Address:* Stoneycross, Yealmpton, Devon. *Clubs:* Royal Yacht Squadron, Royal Western Yacht, Anchorites, Royal Marines Sailing, Royal Naval Sailing Assoc., Royal Norwegian Sailing.

WHITELEY, Samuel Lloyd; Deputy Chief Land Registrar, 1967–73; Legal Assistant to the Clerk to the Haberdashers' Company 1973–78, Freeman, 1978; *b* 30 April 1913; *s* of Rev. Charles Whiteley and Ann Letitia Whiteley; *m* 1939, Kathleen Jones; two *d*. *Educ:* George Dixon Sch.; Birmingham Univ. LLB (Hons) 1933. Admitted Solicitor, 1935; HM Land Registry, 1936; seconded Official Solicitor's Dept, 1939; RAF, 1940–46; HM Land Registry, 1946–73. *Recreation:* sport, as a reminiscent spectator. *Address:* 8 Stonehaven Court, Knole Road, Bexhill, Sussex. *T:* Bexhill 213191.

WHITEMAN, Elizabeth Anne Osborn, DPhil; FRHistS, FSA; JP; Tutor in Modern History 1946–85, Fellow 1948–85, and Vice-Principal 1971–81, Lady Margaret Hall, Oxford; *b* 10 Feb. 1918; *d* of Harry Whitmore Whiteman and Dorothy May (*née* Austin). *Educ:* St Albans High Sch.; Somerville Coll., Oxford (MA 1945, DPhil 1951). FRHistS 1954; FSA 1958. Served War, WAAF, 1940–45: served in N Africa and Italy (mentioned in despatches, 1943). Rep. of Women's Colls, Oxford Univ., 1960–61. Member: Hebdomadal Council, Oxford Univ., 1968–85; Academic Planning Bd, Univ. of Warwick, 1961–65; UGC, 1976–83. Trustee, Ruskin Sch. of Drawing, 1974–77. JP City of Oxford, 1962. *Publications:* (contrib.) Victoria County History, Wilts, Vol. III, 1956; (contrib.) New Cambridge Modern History, Vol. V, 1961; (contrib.) From Uniformity to Unity, ed Chadwick and Nuttall, 1962; (ed with J. S. Bromley and P. G. M. Dickson, and contrib.) Statesmen, Scholars and Merchants: Essays in eighteenth-century History presented to Dame Lucy Sutherland, 1973; (ed with Mary Clapinson) The Compton Census of 1676, 1986; contrib. hist. jls. *Address:* 5 Observatory Street, Oxford. *T:* Oxford 511009.

WHITEMAN, Peter George; QC 1977; barrister-at-law; Attorney and Counselor at Law, State of New York; Professor of Law, University of Virginia, since 1980; Member, Faculty of Laws, Florida University, since 1977; *b* 8 Aug. 1942; *s* of David Whiteman and Betsy Bessie Coster; *m* 1971, Katherine Ruth (*née* Ellenbogen); two *d*. *Educ:* Warwick Secondary Modern Sch.; Leyton County High Sch.; LSE (LLB, LLM with Distinction). Called to the Bar, Lincoln's Inn, 1967, Bencher, 1985. Lectr, London Univ., 1966–70. Visiting Professor: Virginia Univ., 1978; Univ. of California at Berkeley, 1980. Mem. Cttee, Unitary Tax Campaign (UK), 1982–. FRSA. Mem. Bd, Univ. of Virginia Jl of Internat. Law, 1981–. *Publications:* Whiteman and Wheatcroft on Capital Gains Tax, 1967, 3rd edn 1980; Whiteman and Wheatcroft on Income Tax, 1971, 2nd edn 1976; contrib. British Tax Encyc. *Recreations:* tennis, squash, mountain-walking, jogging, croquet. *Address:* 101 Dulwich Village, SE21 7BJ. *T:* 01–299 0858, (chambers) 01–353 0551; University of Virginia School of Law, Charlottesville, Va 22901, USA. *T:* (804) 924–3996.

WHITEMAN, William Meredith; MA; FRSA; writer on local history, caravanning and the countryside; Vice-President, Camping and Caravanning Club; *b* 29 May 1905; *m* 1931, Patricia Aileen Thornton (*d* 1954); three *d*; *m* 1965, Mary Moore (*née* Hall). *Educ:* St Albans School; St John's College, Cambridge. Founder, National Caravan Council; Hon. Secretary, 1939–49, Hon. Director, 1949–52. Director, Caravan Club, 1938–60. Vice-Pres., British Caravanners Club, 1948–77. Organiser, Moveable Dwelling Conference, 1947–49. Editor, The Caravan, 1938–61. Man. Editor, Link House Publications Ltd, 1942–70; UK Mem., Internat. Caravan Commn, 1947–70, Pres., 1957–70; Countryside Commn transit site study group, 1969–70; Mem., Exec. Cttee, Hampshire Council of Community Service, 1971–83; Vice-Pres., Petersfield Soc., 1986. Served on more than 50 cttees, working parties etc, on caravanning and camping. Hon. Life Mem., Caravan Club; Hon. Mem., Fédération Internationale de Camping et de Caravanning. *Publications:* books on camping and caravanning. *Recreation:* local history. *Address:* Northfield Cottage, Steep, Petersfield, Hants GU32 2DQ. *T:* Petersfield 63915.

WHITEMORE, Hugh John; dramatist; *b* 16 June 1936; *s* of Samuel George Whitemore and Kathleen Alma Whitemore (*née* Fletcher); *m* 1st, Jill Brooke (marr. diss.); 2nd, 1976, Sheila Lemon; one *s*. *Educ:* King Edward VI School, Southampton; RADA. *Stage:* Stevie, Vaudeville, 1977; Pack of Lies, Lyric, 1983; Breaking the Code, Haymarket, 1986; *television:* plays and dramatisations include: Elizabeth R (Emmy award, 1970); Cider with Rosie (Writer's Guild award, 1971); Country Matters (Writer's Guild award, 1972); Dummy (RAI Prize, Prix Italia, 1979); Concealed Enemies (Emmy award, Neil Simon Jury award, 1984); *films:* Stevie, 1980; The Return of the Soldier, 1982; 84 Charing Cross Road, 1986. *Publications:* (contrib) Elizabeth R, 1972; Stevie, 1977, new edn 1984; (contrib.) My Drama School, 1978; (contrib.) Ah, Mischief!, 1982; Pack of Lies, 1983; Breaking the Code, 1986. *Recreations:* music, movies, reading. *Address:* c/o Judy Daish Associates, 83 Eastbourne Mews, W2 6LQ. *T:* 01–262 1101. *Club:* Savile.

WHITEOAK, John Edward Harrison, MA, CIPFA; County Treasurer, Cheshire County Council, since 1981; *b* 5 July 1947; *s* of Frank Whiteoak, farmer, and Marion Whiteoak; *m* 1st, 1969, Margaret Elizabeth Blakey, teacher (decd); one *s* two *d*; 2nd, 1983, Karen Lynne Wallace Stevenson, MB ChB BSc. *Educ:* Sheffield Univ. (MA). CIPFA 1971. Joined Skipton RDC in 1966 and held various appts with Skipton UDC, Solihull MDC, Cleveland CC (Asst County Treasurer, 1976–79), Cheshire CC (Dep. County Treasurer, 1979–81). Financial Advr, ACC, 1984–. Member: Soc. of County Treasurers, 1981–; Accounting Standards Cttee, 1984–; CIPFA Accounting Panel, 1984–. *Publications:* articles for various local government journals. *Recreations:* tennis, squash. *Address:* Huntington Hall, Huntington, Chester CH3 6EA. *T:* (home) Chester 312901; (business) Chester 602000.

WHITESIDE, Dr Derek Thomas, FBA 1975; University Reader in History of Mathematics, Cambridge, since 1976; *b* 23 July 1932; *s* of Ernest Whiteside and Edith (*née* Watts); *m* 1962, Ruth Isabel Robinson; one *s* one *d*. *Educ:* Blackpool Grammar Sch.; Bristol Univ. (BA); Cambridge Univ. (PhD). Leverhulme Research Fellow, 1959–61; DSIR Research Fellow, 1961–63; Research Asst, 1963–72, Asst Dir of Research, 1972–76, Univ. of Cambridge. Médaille Koyré, Académie Internat. d'Histoire des Sciences, 1968; Sarton Medal, Amer. History of Sci. Soc., 1977. *Publications:* Patterns of Mathematical Thought in the later Seventeenth Century, 1961; (ed) The Mathematical Papers of Isaac

Newton, 1967–; articles in Brit. Jl Hist. Science, Jl for Hist. of Astronomy, etc. *Recreations:* a diversity of things unenergetic. *Address:* Whipple Science Museum, Free School Lane, Cambridge.

WHITFIELD, family name of **Baron Kenswood.**

WHITFIELD, Adrian; QC 1983; a Recorder of the Crown Court, since 1981; *b* 10 July 1937; *s* of Peter Henry Whitfield and Margaret Mary Burns; *m* 1st, 1962, Lucy Caroline Beckett (marr. diss.); two *d*; 2nd, 1971, Niamh O'Kelly; one *s* one *d*. *Educ:* Ampleforth Coll.; Magdalen Coll., Oxford (Demy; BA). 2nd Lieut, KOYLI (Nat. Service), 1956–58. Called to the Bar, Middle Temple, 1964; Member of Western Circuit; Asst Parliamentary Boundary Commissioner, 1976; Deputy Circuit Judge, 1978; Mem. of Senate, 1983–86. *Publications:* contribs on legal matters in medical and dental pubns. *Recreations:* reading, carpentry, country pursuits. *Address:* 47 Faroe Road, W14 0EL. *T:* 01–603 8982; Carpmael Building, Temple, EC4Y 7HT. *T:* 01–353 5537. *Club:* Hampshire.

WHITFIELD, Prof. Charles Richard, MD; FRCOG; FRCPGlas; Regius Professor of Midwifery in the University of Glasgow, since Oct. 1976; *b* 21 Oct. 1927; *s* of Charles Alexander and Aileen Muriel Whitfield; *m* 1953, Marion Douglas McKinney; one *s* two *d*. *Educ:* Campbell Coll., Belfast; Queen's Univ., Belfast (MD). House Surg. and Ho. Phys. appts in Belfast teaching hospitals, 1951–53; Specialist in Obstetrics and Gynaecology, RAMC (Lt-Col retd), 1953–64; Sen. Lectr/Hon. Reader in Dept of Midwifery and Gynaecology, Queen's Univ., Belfast, 1964–74; Consultant to Belfast teaching hosps, 1964–74; Prof. of Obstetrics and Gynaecology, Univ. of Manchester, 1974–76. *Publications:* (ed) Dewhurst's Obstetrics and Gynaecology for Postgraduates, 4th edn 1985; papers on perinatal medicine, pregnancy anaemia and other obstetric and gynaec. topics in med. and scientific jls. *Recreations:* food, travel, sun-worship. *Address:* Redlands, 23 Thorn Road, Bearsden, Glasgow G61 4BS.

WHITFIELD, Rev. George Joshua Newbold; General Secretary, Church of England Board of Education, 1969–74; *b* 2 June 1909; *s* of late Joshua Newbold and Eva Whitfield; *m* 1937, Dr Audrey Priscilla Dence, *d* of late Rev. A. T. Dence; two *s* two *d*. *Educ:* Bede Gram. Sch., Sunderland; King's Coll., Univ. of London; Bishops' Coll., Cheshunt. BA 1st cl. Hons, Engl. and AKC, 1930 (Barry Prizeman); MA 1935. Asst Master, Trin. Sch., Croydon, 1931–34; Sen. Engl. Master: Doncaster Gram. Sch., 1934–36; Hymers Coll., Hull, 1937–43; Headmaster: Tavistock Gram. Sch., 1943–46; Stockport Sch., 1946–50; Hampton Sch., 1950–68. Chief Examr in Engl., Univ. of Durham Sch. Exams Bd, 1940–43. Deacon, 1962; Priest, 1963. Member: Duke of Edinburgh's Award Adv. Cttee, 1960–66; Headmasters' Conf., 1964–68; Corporation of Church House, 1974–; Pres., Headmasters' Assoc., 1967; Chm., Exeter Diocesan Educn Cttee, 1981–. *Publications:* (ed) Teaching Poetry, 1937; An Introduction to Drama, 1938; God and Man in the Old Testament, 1949; (ed) Poetry in the Sixth Form, 1950; Philosophy and Religion, 1955; (jtly) Christliche Erziehung in Europa, Band I, England, 1975. *Recreations:* gardening, photography. *Address:* Bede Lodge, 31A Rolle Road, Exmouth, Devon EX8 2AW. *T:* Exmouth 274162. *Club:* Athenæum.

WHITFIELD, John; MP (C) Dewsbury, since 1983; *b* 31 Oct. 1941; *s* of Sydney Richard Whitfield and Mary Rishworth Whitfield; *m* 1967, Mary Ann Moy; three *s*. *Educ:* Sedbergh Sch.; Leeds Univ. (LLB). Solicitor, family firm of Whitfield Son and Hallam, of Batley, Dewsbury and Mirfield, 1965–83. Director: Caldaire Independent Hosp. Plc; Cullingworth Textiles Ltd. *Publications:* contribs to Law Society's Gazette. *Address:* The Old Rectory, Badsworth, Pontefract. *T:* Pontefract 45420. *Clubs:* House of Commons; Headingley Football; Hemsworth Conservative; Mirfield Constitutional; Tanfield Angling.

WHITFIELD, John Flett, JP, DL; Chairman, Surrey Police Authority, since 1985; Chairman of Police Committee, Association of County Councils, since 1985; *b* 1 June 1922; *s* of John and Bertha Whitfield; *m* 1946, Rosemary Elisabeth Joan Hartman; two *d*. *Educ:* Epsom Coll., Surrey. Served War, King's Royal Rifle Corps, 1939–46. HM Foreign Service, 1946–57; Director, Materials Handling Equipment (GB) Ltd, 1957–61; London Director, Hunslet Holdings Ltd, 1961–64. Director, Sunningdale Golf Club, 1973–77. Councillor: Berkshire CC, 1961–70; Surrey CC, 1970– (Chm., 1981–84). Contested (C) Pontefract, General Election, 1964. JP Berkshire 1971–, Chm. Windsor County Bench, 1978–80; DL Surrey 1982, High Sheriff, 1985–86. Chm., Surrey Univ. Council, 1986– (Vice-Chm., 1983–86). *Recreations:* golf, foreign languages, bookbinding. *Address:* 4 Holiday House, Sunningdale, Berks SL5 9RW. *T:* Ascot 20997. *Clubs:* Royal and Ancient Golf of St Andrews; Royal Cinque Ports Golf; Sunningdale Golf; Rye Golf.

WHITFIELD, Professor John Humphreys; Serena Professor of Italian Language and Literature in the University of Birmingham, 1946–74; *b* 2 Oct. 1906; *s* of J. A. Whitfield; *m* 1936, Joan Herrin, ARCA; two *s*. *Educ:* Handsworth Grammar School; Magdalen College, Oxford. William Doncaster Scholar, Magdalen Coll., 1925–29; Double First Class Hons in Mod. Langs, 1928, 1929; Paget Toynbee Prizeman, 1933. Asst Master, King Edward VII School, Sheffield, 1930–36; University Lecturer in Italian, Oxford University, 1936–46; Awarder to Oxford and Cambridge Schools Examination Bd, 1940–68. Part-time Temporary Assistant Civil Officer, Naval Intelligence Department, 1943. Chairman, Society for Italian Studies, 1962–74; Senior editor of Italian Studies, 1967–74. President: Dante Alighieri Society (Comitato di Birmingham), 1957–75; Assoc. of Teachers of Italian, 1976–77. Hon. Fellow, Inst. for Advanced Res. in the Humanities, Univ. of Birmingham, 1984. Barlow Lecturer on Dante, University College, London, 1958–59, Barlow Centenary Lecture, 1977; Donald Dudley Meml Lecture, Birmingham, 1980. Edmund G. Gardner Memorial Prize, 1959; Amedeo Maiuri Prize (Rome), 1965; Serena Medal for Italian Studies, British Acad., 1984. Commendatore, Ordine al Merito della Repubblica Italiana, 1972 (Cavaliere Ufficiale, 1960). *Publications:* Petrarch and the Renascence, 1943 (NY, 1966); Machiavelli, 1947 (NY, 1966); Petrarca e il Rinascimento (tr. V. Capocci, Laterza), 1949; Dante and Virgil, 1949; Giacomo Leopardi, 1954 (Italian tr. 1964); A Short History of Italian Literature, 1962 (Pelican, 1960, 5th edn 1980); The Barlow Lectures on Dante, 1960; Leopardi's Canti, trans. into English Verse, 1962; Leopardi's Canti, ed with Introduction and notes, 1967, rev. edn 1978; Discourses on Machiavelli, 1969; The Charlecote Manuscript of Machiavelli's Prince, facsimile edn with an Essay on the Prince, 1969; Castiglione: The Courtier, ed with introduction, 1974; Guarini: Il Pastor Fido, ed bilingual edn with introduction, 1976; Painting in Naples from Caravaggio to Giordano (trans. of Italian texts), 1982; articles and reviews contrib. to Modern Language Review, Italian Studies, History, Medium Aevum, Comparative Literature, Problemi della Pedagogia, Le parole e le Idee, Encyclopædia Britannica, Chambers's Encyclopædia, Hutchinson's Encyclopædia, Concise Encyclopædia of the Italian Renaissance, etc. *Festschrift:* Essays in Honour of John Humphreys Whitfield, 1975. *Address:* 2 Woodbourne Road, Edgbaston, Birmingham B15 3QH. *T:* 021–454 1035.

WHITFIELD, June Rosemary, OBE 1985; actress; *b* 11 Nov. 1925; *d* of John Herbert Whitfield and Bertha Georgina Whitfield; *m* 1955, Timothy John Aitchison; one *d*. *Educ:* Streatham Hill High School; RADA (Diploma 1944). Revue, musicals, pantomime, TV and radio; worked with Arthur Askey, Benny Hill, Frankie Howerd, Dick Emery, Bob Monkhouse, Leslie Crowther, Ronnie Barker; first worked with Terry Scott in 1969; *radio:* series include: Take It From Here (with Dick Bentley and Jimmy Edwards, 1953–60; *television:* series include: Fast and Loose (with Bob Monkhouse), 1954; Faces of Jim (with Jimmy Edwards), 1962, 1963; Beggar My Neighbour, 1966, 1967; Scott On . . . (with Terry Scott), 1969–73; Happy Ever After, 1974; Terry and June, 1979–. Freeman, City of London, 1982. *Address:* c/o April Young, 31 King's Road, SW3 4RP. *T:* 01–730 9922.

WHITFIELD LEWIS, Herbert John; *see* Lewis, H. J. W.

WHITFORD, Hon. Sir John (Norman Keates), Kt 1970; **Hon. Mr Justice Whitford;** a Judge of the High Court, Chancery Division, since 1970; *b* 24 June 1913; *s* of Harry Whitford and Ella Mary Keates; *m* 1946, Rosemary, *d* of John Barcham Green and Emily Paillard; four *d*. *Educ:* University College School; Munich University; Peterhouse, Cambridge. President, ADC. Called to the Bar: Inner Temple, 1935; Middle Temple, 1946 (Bencher 1970). Served with RAFVR, 1939–44: Wing Comdr, 1942; Chief Radar Officer and Dep. Chief Signals Officer, Air Headquarters Eastern Mediterranean; Advisor on patents and information exchanged for war purposes, HM Embassy, Washington, 1944–45. QC 1965. Member of Bar Council, 1968–70. Chm., Departmental Cttee on Law Relating to Copyright and Designs, 1974–76. *Address:* Royal Courts of Justice, WC2.

WHITHAM, Prof. Gerald Beresford, FRS 1965; Professor of Applied Mathematics, at the California Institute of Technology, Pasadena, Calif, since 1962; *b* 13 Dec. 1927; *s* of Harry and Elizabeth Ellen Whitham; *m* 1951, Nancy (*née* Lord); one *s* two *d*. *Educ:* Elland Gram. Sch., Elland, Yorks; Manchester University. PhD Maths, Manchester, 1953. Lectr in Applied Mathematics, Manchester Univ., 1953–56; Assoc. Prof., Applied Mathematics, New York Univ., 1956–59; Prof., Mathematics, MIT, 1959–62. FAAAS 1959. *Publications:* Linear and Nonlinear Waves, 1974; Lectures on Wave Propagation, 1979; research papers in Proc. Roy. Soc., Jl Fluid Mechanics, Communications on Pure and Applied Maths. *Address:* Applied Mathematics 217–50, California Institute of Technology, Pasadena, California 91125, USA.

WHITING, Alan; Under Secretary, Department of Trade and Industry, since 1985; *b* 14 Jan. 1946; *s* of Albert Edward and Marjorie Irene Whiting; *m* 1968, Annette Frances Pocknee; two *s* two *d*. *Educ:* Acklam Hall Grammar Sch., Middlesbrough; Univ. of East Anglia (BA Hons); University College London (MSc Econ). Research Associate and Asst Lectr, Univ. of East Anglia, 1967; Cadet Economist, HM Treasury, 1968; Economic Asst, DEA, and Min. of Technology, 1969; Economist, EFTA, Geneva, 1970; Economist, CBI, 1972; Economic Adviser, DTI, 1974; Sen. Econ. Adviser, 1979; Industrial Policy Div., Dept of Industry, 1983–85. *Publications:* (jtly) The Trade Effects of EFTA and the EEC 1959–1967, 1972; (ed) The Economics of Industrial Subsidies, 1975; articles in economic jls. *Recreations:* building, gardening, music, sailing. *Address:* The Willows, Larges Lane, Bracknell, Berks RG12 3AN. *T:* Bracknell 426948. *Club:* Littleton Sailing.

WHITING, Rev. Peter Graham, CBE 1984; Minister, Beechen Grove Baptist Church, since 1985; *b* 7 Nov. 1930; *s* of Rev. Arthur Whiting and late Mrs Olive Whiting; *m* 1960, Lorena Inns; two *s* three *d*. *Educ:* Yeovil Grammar Sch.; Irish Baptist Theol Coll., Dublin. Ordained into Baptist Ministry, 1956. Minister, King's Heath, Northampton, 1956–62; commnd RAChD, 1962; Regtl Chaplain, 1962–69 (Chaplain to 1st Bn The Parachutte Regt, 1964–66); Sen. Chaplain, 20 Armd Bde and Lippe Garrison, BAOR, 1969–72; Staff Chaplain, HQ BAOR, 1973–74; Sen. Chaplain, 24 Airportable Bde, 1974–75; Dep. Asst Chaplain Gen., W Midland Dist, Shrewsbury, 1975–78 (Sen. Chaplain, Young Entry Units, 1976–78); Asst Chaplain Gen., 1st British Corps, BAOR, 1978–81; Dep. Chaplain Gen. to the Forces (Army), 1981–85. QHC 1981–85. *Address:* 264 Hempstead Road, Watford, Herts WD1 3LY. *T:* (office) Watford 41858; (home) Watford 53197.

WHITLAM, Hon. (Edward) Gough, AC 1978; QC 1962; Australian Member, Executive Board of Unesco, since 1985 (Australian Ambassador to Unesco, 1983–86); Constitutional Commission, since 1985 (Joint Parliamentary Committee on Constitutional Review, 1956–59; Constitutional Conventions, 1973–76); Fellow, University of Sydney Senate, 1981–83 and since 1986; Prime Minister of Australia, 1972–75; *b* 11 July 1916; *s* of late H. F. E. Whitlam, Australian Crown Solicitor and Aust. rep. on UN Human Rights Commission; *m* 1942, Margaret Elaine, *d* of late Mr Justice Dovey, NSW Supreme Court; three *s* one *d*. *Educ:* University of Sydney. BA 1938; LLB 1946. RAAF Flight Lieut, 1941–45. Barrister, 1947; MP for Werriwa, NSW, 1952–78; Deputy Leader, Aust. Labor Party, 1960, Leader, 1967–77; Leader of the Opposition, 1967–72 and 1976–77; Minister for Foreign Affairs, 1972–73. Vis. Fellow, 1978–81, First Nat. Fellow, 1980–81, ANU; Vis. Prof., Harvard Univ., 1979. Chairman: Australia–China Council, 1986–; Australian Nat. Gall., 1987–. Pres., Australian Sect, Internat. Commn of Jurists, 1982–83. Hon. DLitt Sydney, 1981; Hon. LLD Philippines, 1974. Silver Plate of Honour, Socialist Internat., 1976. *Publications:* The Constitution *versus* Labor, 1957; Australian Foreign Policy, 1963; Socialism within the Constitution, 1965; Australia, Base or Bridge?, 1966; Beyond Vietnam: Australia's Regional Responsibility, 1968; An Urban Nation, 1969; A New Federalism, 1971; Urbanised Australia, 1972; Australian Public Administration and the Labor Government, 1973; Australia's Foreign Policy: New Directions, New Definitions, 1973; Road to Reform: Labor in Government, 1975; The New Federalism: Labor's Programs and Policies, 1975; Government of the People, for the People—by the People's House, 1975; On Australia's Constitution, 1977; Reform During Recession, 1978; The Truth of the Matter, 1979, 2nd edn 1983; The Italian Inspiration in English Literature, 1980; A Pacific Community, 1981; The Cost of Federalism, 1983; The Whitlam Government 1972–75, 1985. *Address:* 100 William Street, Sydney, NSW 2011, Australia.

WHITLEY, Elizabeth Young, (Mrs H. C. Whitley); social worker and journalist; *b* 28 Dec. 1915; *d* of Robert Thom and Mary Muir Wilson; *m* 1939, Henry Charles Whitley (Very Rev. Dr H. C. Whitley, CVO; *d* 1976); two *s* two *d* (and one *s* decd). *Educ:* Laurelbank School, Glasgow; Glasgow University. MA 1936; courses: in Italian at Perugia Univ., 1935, in Social Science at London School of Economics and Glasgow School of Social Science, 1938–39. Ran Girls' Clubs in Govan and Plantation, Glasgow, and Young Mothers' Clubs in Partick and Port Glasgow; Vice-Chm. Scottish Association of Girls' Clubs and Mixed Clubs, 1957–61, and Chm. of Advisory Cttee, 1958–59. Broadcast regular programme with BBC (Scottish Home Service), 1953. Member: Faversham Committee on AID, 1958–60; Pilkington Committee on Broadcasting, 1960–62. Columnist, Scottish Daily Express. Adopted as Parly candidate for SNP by West Perth and Kinross, 1968. *Publications:* Plain Mr Knox, 1960; The Two Kingdoms: the story of the Scottish covenanters, 1977; descriptive and centenary articles for Scottish papers, particularly Glasgow Herald and Scotland's Magazine. *Recreations:* reading, gardening. *Address:* The Glebe, Southwick, by Dumfries. *T:* Southwick 276.

WHITLEY, John Reginald; His Honour Judge Whitley; a Circuit Judge, since 1986; *b* 22 March 1926; *o s* of late Reginald Whitley and of Marjorie Whitley (*née* Orton); *m* 1966, Susan Helen Kennaway; one *d*. *Educ:* Sherborne Sch.; Corpus Christi Coll., Cambridge. Served War, Army, Egypt, Palestine, 1944–48; commissioned, KRRC, 1945. Called to the Bar, Gray's Inn, 1953; Western Circuit, 1953; a Recorder, 1978–86.

Recreation: golf. *Address:* Kingsrod, Friday's Hill, Kingsley Green, near Haslemere, Surrey GU27 3LL.

WHITLEY, Air Marshal Sir John (René), KBE 1956 (CBE 1945); CB 1946; DSO 1943; AFC 1937, Bar, 1956; *b* 7 September 1905; *s* of late A. Whitley, Condette, Pas de Calais, France; *m* 1st, 1932, Barbara Liscombe (*d* 1965); three *s* (and one *s* decd); 2nd, 1967, Alison (*d* 1986), *d* of Sir Nigel Campbell and *widow* of John Howard Russell; three step *s*. *Educ:* Haileybury. Entered Royal Air Force with a short-service commission, 1926; Permanent Commission, 1931; served in India, 1932–37; served in Bomber Command, 1937–45, as a Squadron Comdr, Station Comdr, Base Comdr and AOC 4 Group; HQ ACSEA Singapore, 1945; HQ India and Base Comdr, Karachi, 1946–47; Director of Organisation (Establishments), Air Ministry, 1948 and 1949; Imperial Defence College, 1950; AOA, 2nd Tactical Air Force, 1951 and 1952; AOC No 1 (Bomber) Group, 1953–56; Air Member for Personnel, 1957–59; Inspector-General, RAF, 1959–62; Controller, RAF Benevolent Fund, 1962–68, retd. *Address:* 2 Woodside Close, Woodside Avenue, Lymington SO41 8FH. *T:* Lymington 76920. *Clubs:* Royal Air Force; Royal Lymington Yacht, Island Sailing (IoW).

WHITLEY, Oliver John; Managing Director, External Broadcasting, British Broadcasting Corporation, 1969–72, retired; *b* 12 Feb. 1912; *s* of Rt Hon. J. H. Whitley, and Marguerite (*née* Marchetti); *m* 1939, Elspeth Catherine (*née* Forrester-Paton); four *s* one *d*. *Educ:* Clifton Coll.; New Coll., Oxford. Barrister-at-Law, 1935; BBC, 1935–41. Served in RNVR, 1942–46; Coastal Forces and Combined Ops. BBC 1946–: seconded to Colonial Office, 1946–49; Head of General Overseas Service, 1950–54; Assistant Controller, Overseas Services, 1955–57; Appointments Officer, 1957–60; Controller, Staff Training and Appointments, 1960–64; Chief Assistant to Dir-Gen., 1964–68. Valiant for Truth Award, Order of Christian Unity, 1974. *Recreations:* reading and gardening. *Address:* Greenacre, Ganavan Road, Oban, Argyll PA34 5TU. *T:* Oban 62555.

WHITLOCK, William Charles; *b* 20 June 1918; *s* of late George Whitlock and Sarah Whitlock, Sholing, Southampton; *m* 1943, Jessie Hilda, *d* of George Reardon of Armagh; five *s*. *Educ:* Itchen Gram. Sch.; Southampton Univ. Army Service, 1939–46. Apptd full-time Trade Union Officer, Area Organiser of Union of Shop, Distributive and Allied Workers, 1946. President, Leicester and District Trades Council, 1955–56; President, Leicester City Labour Party, 1956–57; President, North-East Leicester Labour Party, 1955–56, and 1958–59. Member East Midlands Regional Council of Labour Party, 1955–67, Vice-Chairman 1961–62, Chairman 1962–63. MP (Lab) Nottingham N, Oct. 1959–1983; Opposition Whip, House of Commons, 1962–64; Vice-Chamberlain of the Household, 1964–66; Lord Comr of Treasury, March 1966–July 1966; Comptroller of HM Household, July 1966–March 1967; Dep. Chief Whip and Lord Comr of the Treasury, March-July 1967; Under Sec. of State for Commonwealth Affairs, 1967–68; Parly Under-Sec. of State, FCO, 1968–69. Contested (Lab) Nottingham N, 1983. *Address:* 51 Stoughton Road, Stoneygate, Leicester.

WHITMORE, Sir Clive (Anthony), KCB 1983; CVO 1983; Permanent Under-Secretary of State, Ministry of Defence, since 1983; *b* 18 Jan. 1935; *s* of Charles Arthur Whitmore and Louisa Lilian Whitmore; *m* 1961, Jennifer Mary Thorpe; one *s* two *d*. *Educ:* Sutton Grammar Sch., Surrey; Christ's Coll., Cambridge (BA). Asst Principal, WO, 1959; Private Sec. to Permanent Under-Sec. of State, WO, 1961; Asst Private Sec. to Sec. of State for War, 1962; Principal, 1964; Private Sec. to Permanent Under-Sec. of State, MoD, 1969; Asst Sec., 1971; Asst Under-Sec. of State (Defence Staff), MoD, 1975; Under Sec., Cabinet Office, 1977; Principal Private Sec. to the Prime Minister, 1979–82; Dep. Sec., 1981. *Recreations:* gardening, listening to music. *Address:* Ministry of Defence, Whitehall, SW1. *Club:* Athenæum.

WHITMORE, Sir John (Henry Douglas), 2nd Bt *cr* 1954; *b* 16 Oct. 1937; *s* of Col Sir Francis Henry Douglas Charlton Whitmore, 1st Bt, KCB, CMG, DSO, TD, and of Lady Whitmore (*née* Ellis Johnsen); *S* father 1961; *m* 1st, 1962, Gunilla (marr. diss. 1969), *e d* of Sven A. Hansson, OV, KLH, Danderyd, and *o d* of Mrs Ella Hansson, Stockholm, Sweden; one *d*; 2nd, 1977, Diana Elaine, *e d* of Fred A. Becchetti, California, USA; one *s*. *Educ:* Stone House, Kent; Eton; Sandhurst; Cirencester. Occupation: active in personal development and social change. *Recreations:* ski-ing, squash, motor cycling. *Heir:* *s* Jason Whitmore, *b* 26 Jan. 1983. *Address:* 50 Guildford Road, SW8. *Club:* British Racing Drivers.

WHITNEY, John Norton Braithwaite; Director General, Independent Broadcasting Authority, since 1982; *b* 20 Dec. 1930; *s* of Dr Willis Bevan Whitney and Dorothy Anne Whitney; *m* 1956, Roma Elizabeth Hodgson; one *s* one *d*. *Educ:* Leighton Park Friends' Sch. Radio producer, 1951–64; formed Ross Radio Productions, 1951, and Autocue, 1955; founded Radio Antilles, 1963; Man. Dir, Capital Radio, 1973–82; Mem. Bd, National Theatre, 1982–; Founder Dir, Sagitta Prodns, 1968–82; Director: Duke of York's Theatre, 1979–82; Consolidated Productions (UK) Ltd, 1980–82; Friends' Provident Life Office, 1982– (Chm., Friends' Provident Stewardship Trust, 1985–). Chm. and Co-founder, Local Radio Assoc., 1964; Chm., Assoc. of Indep. Local Radio Contractors, 1973, 1974, 1975 and 1980. Wrote, edited and devised numerous television series, 1956–82. Founded Recidivists Anonymous Fellowship Trust, 1962; Member: RCM Centenary Develt Fund (formerly Appeal Cttee), 1982– (Chm., Media and Events Cttee, 1982–); Royal Jubilee Trusts Industry and Commerce Liaison Cttee, 1986– (Mem., Admin. Council of Trusts, 1981–85); Member Council: Royal London Aid Society, 1966–; Drake Fellowship, 1981–; Intermediate Technol. Gp, 1982–85. President: TV and Radio Industries Club, 1985–86 (Mem. Council, 1979–); London Marriage Guidance Council, 1983–; Vice President: Commonwealth Youth Exchange Council, 1982–85; British Maritime Charitable Foundn, 1983–; Chairman: Soundaround (National Sound Magazine for the Blind), 1981–; Artsline, 1983–; Trustee, Venture Trust, 1982–. Fellow and Vice Pres., RTS, 1986–; FRSA. Hon. Mem., RCM. *Recreations:* chess, photography, sculpture, looking at sunrises. *Address:* Independent Broadcasting Authority, 70 Brompton Road, SW3 1EY. *T:* 01–584 7011. *Clubs:* Garrick, Whitefriars, Pilgrims.

WHITNEY, Raymond William, OBE 1968; MP (C) Wycombe, Bucks, since April 1978; *b* 28 Nov. 1930; *o s* of late George Whitney, Northampton; *m* 1956, Sheila Margot Beswick Prince; two *s*. *Educ:* Wellingborough Sch.; RMA, Sandhurst; London Univ. (BA (Hons) Oriental Studies). Commnd Northamptonshire Regt, 1951; served in Trieste, Korea, Hong Kong, Germany; seconded to Australian Army HQ, 1960–63; resigned and entered HM Diplomatic Service, 1964; First Sec., Peking, 1966–68; Head of Chancery, Buenos Aires, 1969–72; FCO, 1972–73; Dep. High Comr, Dacca, 1973–76; FCO, 1976–78, Hd of Information Res. Dept and Hd of Overseas Inf. Dept, 1976–78. PPS to Treasury Ministers, 1979–80; Parly Under-Sec. of State, FCO, 1983–84, DHSS, 1984–86. Vice-Chm., Cons. Employment Cttee, 1980–83; Chm., Cons. For. Affairs Cttee, 1981–83; Mem., Public Accounts Cttee, 1981–83. *Publications:* articles on Chinese and Asian affairs in professional jls. *Recreations:* theatricals (performing, producing and writing), tennis, bridge, walking, wind-surfing. *Address:* The Dial House, Sunninghill, Berks SL5 0AG. *T:* Ascot 23164.

WHITSEY, Fred; Gardening Correspondent, Daily Telegraph, since 1971; *b* 18 July 1919; *m* 1947, Patricia Searle. *Educ:* outside school hours, and continuously since then. Assistant Editor, Popular Gardening, 1948–64, Associate Editor, 1964–67, Editor, 1967–82. Gardening correspondent, Sunday Telegraph, 1961–71. Gold Veitch Meml Medal, RHS, 1979; VMH 1986. *Publications:* Sunday Telegraph Gardening Book, 1966; Fred Whitsey's Garden Calendar, 1985; Garden for All Seasons, 1986; contribs to Country Life, New York Times and The Garden. *Recreations:* gardening, music. *Address:* Avens Mead, 20 Oast Road, Oxted, Surrey RH8 9DU.

WHITSEY, Rt. Rev. Hubert Victor; *b* 21 Nov. 1916; *s* of Samuel and Rachel Whitsey, Blackburn, Lancs; *m* 1950, Jean Margaret Bellinger; two *s* one *d*. *Educ:* Queen Elizabeth's Grammar Sch., Blackburn; Technical Coll., Blackburn; St Edmund Hall, Oxford (MA); Westcott House, Cambridge. Midland Bank, 1933–39. Royal Regt Artillery (TA), 1938–46 (Lt Col 1945). Asst Curate, Chorley, Lancs, 1949–51; Vicar: Farington, Lancs, 1952–55; St Thomas, Halliwell, Bolton, 1955–60; Asst Rural Dean, Bolton, 1957–60; Vicar: All Saints and Martyrs, Langley, Manchester, 1960–68; Downham, Lancs, 1968–71; Hon. Canon, Manchester Cathedral, 1963, Emeritus, 1968; Bishop Suffragan of Hertford, 1971–74; Bishop of Chester, 1974–81. *Recreations:* idleness, practicality. *Address:* Hill Top, Twiston, Clitheroe, Lancs BB7 4DB.

WHITTAKER, Air Vice-Marshal David, MBE 1967; Air Officer Administration and Air Officer Commanding Directly Administered Units, RAF Support Command, since 1986; *b* 25 June 1933; *s* of Lawson and Irene Whittaker; *m* 1956, Joyce Ann Noble; two *s*. *Educ:* Hutton Grammar School. Joined RAF, 1951; commissioned 1952; served No 222, No 3, No 26 and No 1 Squadrons, 1953–62; HQ 38 Group, 1962–63; HQ 24 Bde, 1963–65; Comd Metropolitan Comms Sqdn, 1966–68; RAF Staff Coll., 1968; Asst Air Adviser, New Delhi, 1969–70; RAF Leeming, 1971–73; Coll. of Air Warfare, 1973; Directing Staff, RNSC Greenwich, 1973–75; Staff of CDS, 1975–76; DACOS (Ops), AFCENT, 1977–80; RCDS 1980; Defence and Air Adviser, Ottawa, 1983–86. *Recreations:* fishing, gardening, travel. *Address:* Seronera, Copgrove, Harrogate, North Yorks. *T:* Copgrove 459. *Clubs:* Royal Air Force; Rideau (Ottawa).

WHITTALL, Harold Astley, CBE 1978; CEng; Chairman: B.S.G. International Ltd, since 1981; Ransome, Sims & Jefferies Ltd, since 1983 (Director since 1977; Deputy Chairman, 1981–83); Turriff Corporation, since 1986 (Deputy Chairman, 1985–86); Director, APV Holdings, since 1982; *b* 8 Sept. 1925; *s* of Harold and Margaret Whittall; *m* 1952, Diana Margharita Berner. *Educ:* Handsworth Grammar Sch., Birmingham; Aston and Birmingham Technical Colls. Gen. Manager, Belliss & Morcom, 1962; Managing Dir, Amalgamated Power Engineering, 1968, Chm., 1977–81; Dir, LRC Internat., 1982–85. Pres., Engineering Employers' Fedn, 1976–78; Chm., Engrg ITB, 1985–. *Address:* Brook Farmhouse, Whelford, near Fairford, Glos GL7 4DY. *T:* Cirencester 712393. *Clubs:* Royal Automobile, St James'.

WHITTALL, Michael Charlton, CMG 1980; OBE 1963; HM Diplomatic Service; Counsellor, Foreign and Commonwealth Office, since 1973; *b* 9 January 1926; *s* of Kenneth Edwin Whittall and Edna Ruth (*née* Lawson); *m* 1953, Susan Olivia La Fontain one *d*. *Educ:* Rottingdean; Rugby; Trinity Hall, Cambridge. Served RAF, 1944–48. Foreign Office, 1949; Salonika, 1949; British Middle East Office, 1952; Vice-Consul, Basra, 1953; FO, 1955; Second Secretary, Beirut, 1956; FO, 1958; First Secretary, Amman, 1959. *Recreations:* railways (GWR), birdwatching, walking, photography. *Address:* c/o Foreign and Commonwealth Office, SW1. *Club:* Royal Air Force.

WHITTAM, Prof. Ronald, FRS 1973; Emeritus Professor, Leicester University, since 1983 (Professor of Physiology, 1966–83); *b* 21 March 1925; *e s* of Edward Whittam and May Whittam (*née* Butterworth), Oldham, Lancs; *m* 1957, Christine Patricia Margaret, 2nd *d* of Canon J. W. Lamb; one *s* one *d*. *Educ:* Council and Technical Schools, Oldham; Univs of Manchester, Sheffield and Cambridge. BSc 1st Class Hons (Manchester); PhD (Sheffield and Cambridge). Served RAF, 1943–47. John Stokes Fellow, Dept of Biochem., Univ. of Sheffield, 1953–55; Beit Memorial Fellow, Physiological Lab., Cambridge, 1955–58; Mem. Scientific Staff, MRC Cell Metabolism Research Unit, Oxford, 1958–60; Univ. Lectr in Biochemistry, Oxford, 1960–66; Bruno Mendel Fellow of Royal Society, 1965–66; Dean of Fac. of Science, Leicester Univ., 1979–82. Mem. Editorial Bd of Biochem. Jl, 1963–67; Hon. Sec., 1969–74, Hon. Mem., 1986, Physiological Soc.; Mem. Biological Research Bd of MRC, 1971–74, Co-Chm., 1973–74; Member: Biological Sciences Cttee, UGC, 1974–82; Educn Cttee, Royal Soc., 1979–83; Chm., Biological Educn Cttee, Royal Soc. and Inst Biol., 1974–77. *Publications:* Transport and Diffusion in Red Blood Cells, 1964; scientific papers dealing with cell membranes. *Recreation:* walking. *Address:* 9 Guilford Road, Leicester LE2 2RD. *T:* Leicester 707132.

WHITTAM SMITH, Andreas; Editor, The Independent, since 1986; *b* 13 June 1937; *s* of Canon J. E. Smith and Mrs Smith (*née* Barlow); *m* 1964, Valerie Catherine, *d* of late Wing Comdr J. A. Sherry and of Mrs N. W. H. Wyllys; two *s*. *Educ:* Birkenhead Sch., Cheshire; Keble Coll., Oxford (BA). With N. M. Rothschild, 1960–62; Stock Exchange Gazette, 1962–63; Financial Times, 1963–64; The Times, 1964–66; Dep. City Editor, Daily Telegraph, 1966–69; City Editor, The Guardian, 1969–70; Editor, Investors Chronicle and Stock Exchange Gazette, and Dir, Throgmorton Publications, 1970–77; City Editor, Daily Telegraph, 1977–85; Dir, Newspaper Publishing PLC, 1986–. Hon. Treasurer, Nat. Council for One Parent Families, 1982–. Wincott award, 1975. *Recreations:* music, history. *Address:* 31 Brunswick Gardens, W8 4AW. *Club:* Garrick.

WHITTELL, James Michael Scott, OBE 1984; Secretary, British Council, and Head, Director General's Department since 1985; *b* 17 Feb. 1939; *s* of late Edward Arthur Whittell and Helen Elizabeth Whittell (*née* Scott); *m* 1962, Eleanor Jane Carling; three *s*. *Educ:* Gresham's School, Holt; Magdalen College, Oxford (MA, BSc); Manchester Univ. Teaching, Sherborne School, 1962–68, Nairobi School, 1968–72; British Council: Ibadan, Nigeria, 1973–76; Enugu, Nigeria, 1976–78; Director General's Dept, 1978–81; Rep., Algiers, 1981–85. *Recreations:* walking, mountaineering, books, music. *Address:* British Council, 10 Spring Gardens, SW1A 2BN. *Clubs:* Travellers', Alpine.

WHITTEMORE, Ernest William, MM 1944 and Bar 1945; Under-Secretary, Department of Health and Social Security, 1973–76; *b* 31 Aug. 1916; *s* of late Ernest William Whittemore and Hilda Whittemore; *m* 1942, Irene Mollie Hudson; two *d*. *Educ:* Raine's Sch., Stepney; King's Coll., London. BA Hons English. Receiver's Office, New Scotland Yard, 1934–35; Min. of Health, 1935–45; Royal Artillery, 1942–46; Min. of Nat. Insce (and successor depts), 1945–76. *Recreations:* bibliomania, travel, sweet peas. *Address:* 39 Montalt Road, Woodford Green, Essex IG8 9RS. *T:* 01–504 7028.

WHITTERIDGE, Prof. David, FRS 1953; FRSE 1951; Waynflete Professor of Physiology, University of Oxford, 1968–79, now Emeritus Professor; *b* 22 June 1912; 2nd *s* of Walter and late Jeanne Whitteridge; *m* 1938, Gweneth, Hon. FRCP, *d* of S. Hutchings; three *d*. *Educ:* Whitgift School, Croydon; Magdalen College, Oxford (1st cl. Physiology Finals, 1934); King's College Hospital. BSc 1936; BM, BCh 1937; DM 1945; FRCP 1966. Beit Memorial Fellowship, 1940; Schorstein Research Fellow, 1944; Fellow by Special Election, Magdalen College, Oxford, 1945–50; University Demonstrator in

Physiology, Univ. of Oxford, 1944–50; Prof. of Physiology, Univ. of Edinburgh, 1950–68. Fellow of Magdalen Coll., Oxford, 1968–79, Hon. Fellow, 1979. Leverhulme Vis. Prof., Univ. Delhi, 1967 and 1973; Lectures: Sherrington, RSM, 1972; Victor Horsley Meml, BMA, 1972; Bowman, OSUK, 1977; Bayliss Starling, Physiolog. Soc., 1979; G. Parr Meml, EEG Soc., 1980. Mem. Bd of Trustees, Nat. Lib. of Scotland, 1966–70. Physiological Society: Sec., 1947–51; Foreign Sec., 1980–86; Hon. Mem., 1982. Vice-Pres., RSE, 1956–59. Hon. Mem., Assoc. of British Neurologists, 1984; Foreign FNA, 1982. Feldberg Prize, Feldberg Foundn, 1962. *Publications:* papers on physiological topics in Jl Physiol., Brain, etc. *Address:* Winterslow, Lincombe Lane, Boar's Hill, Oxford OX1 5DZ. *T:* Oxford 735211.

See also R. A. Furtado, Sir G. C. Whitteridge.

WHITTERIDGE, Sir Gordon (Coligny), KCMG 1964 (CMG 1956); OBE 1946; *b* 6 Nov. 1908; *s* of late Walter Randall and Jeanne Whitteridge, Croydon; *m* 1st, 1938, Margaret Lungley (*d* 1942; one *s* one *d* decd 1942); 2nd, 1951, Jane (*d* 1979), twin *d* of Frederick J. Driscoll, Brookline, Mass, USA; one *s*; 3rd, 1983, Mrs Jill Stanley (*née* Belcham). *Educ:* Whitgift School, Croydon; Fitzwilliam Coll., Cambridge. Joined Consular Service, 1932; one of HM Vice-Consuls, Siam, 1933; Vice-Consul, Batavia, 1936; Acting Consul, Batavia, 1937, 1938, and 1939; Acting Consul, Medan, Sept. 1941–Feb. 1942. Employed at Foreign Office from June, 1942; promoted Consul (Grade II), Foreign Office, 1944, Consul, 1945. 1st Secretary, Moscow, 1948–49; Consul-General Stuttgart, 1949–51; Counsellor/Consul-Gen., 1950; Counsellor, Bangkok, 1951–56 (Chargé d'Affaires in 1952, 1953, 1954, 1955); Consul-Gen., Seattle, Wash, 1956–60; HM Consul-General, Istanbul, 1960–62; Ambassador: to Burma, 1962–65; to Afghanistan, 1965–68; retired, 1968. Chm., Anglo-Thai Soc., 1971–76; Hon. Treasurer: Soc. for Afghan Studies, 1972–83; Soc. for S Asian Studies, 1983–85. (Lay) Mem., Immigration Appeal Tribunal, 1970–81. *Publication:* Charles Masson of Afghanistan, 1986. *Recreations:* music, history. *Address:* Stonebank, Blighton Lane, The Sands, near Farnham, Surrey GU10 1PU. *Club:* Travellers'.

See also R. A. Furtado, Prof. D. Whitteridge.

WHITTET, Dr Thomas Douglas, CBE 1977; Chief Pharmacist, Department of Health and Social Security, 1967–78; *b* 4 Jan. 1915; *s* of late Thomas Douglas Whittet and Ellen Sloan Whittet (*née* Scott); *m* 1942, Doreen Mary Bowes; two *s*. *Educ:* Rosebank Sch., Hartlepool; Sunderland Polytechnic (Hon. Fellow 1980); University Coll., London (Fellow, 1979). PhC (now FPS) 1938; BSc (London) 1953; FRSC (FRIC 1955); CChem 1975; PhD (London) 1958. Mem., Coll. of Pharmacy Practice, 1982. Chief Chemist, Numol Ltd, 1939–41; hospital pharmacy, 1941–43; Chief Pharmacist and Lectr in Pharmacy: Charing Cross Hosp., 1943–47; University Coll. Hosp. and Med. Sch., 1947–65; Dep. Chief Pharmacist, Min. of Health, 1965–67. Member: Brit. Pharm. Codex Revis. Cttee, 1967–75; Joint Formulary Cttee, 1967–78; European Pharmacopoeia Commn, 1967–71; WHO Expert Adv. Cttee on Internat. Pharmacopoeia, 1948–; Council of Europe (Partial Agreement) Pharmaceutical Cttee, 1967–78; EEC Pharmaceutical Cttee and working parties, 1977–78. Consultant, UNIDO, 1978–. Mem. Cttee of Management, 1978–83, Mem. Adv. Cttee, 1984–, Chelsea Physick Garden (Freedom of Garden 1984). Master, Soc. of Apothecaries of London, 1982–83 (Sydenham Lectr, 1965; Delaune Lectr, 1977; Sir Hans Sloane Lectr, 1987; Chm., Faculty of Hist. and Philos. of Medicine and Pharmacy, 1975–78; Court Visitor, 1978–, Hon. LMSSA 1984). Lectures: Wright Meml, Sydney, 1972; Winch Meml, 1973; Harrison Meml (and Medallist), 1973; Todd Meml, 1980; Foundn, British Soc. for Hist. of Pharmacy, 1983; Thomas Vicary, RCS, 1986. Hon. Member: Royal Spanish Acad. of Pharmacy, 1958; Internat. Acad. of Pharmacy, 1965. Hon. DSc: Bath, 1968; Aston, 1974. Evans Gold Medal (Guild of Public Pharmacists), 1960; Charter Gold Medal, Pharm. Soc., 1978; Don Francke Medal, Amer. Soc. Hosp. Pharmacists, 1978. FRSocMed (Pres., Hist. of Medicine Section, 1981–83). *Publications:* Hormones, 1946; Diagnostic Agents, 1947; Sterilisation and Disinfection, 1965; The Apothecaries in the Great Plague of London of 1665, 1971; many papers on medical and pharmaceutical history; numerous papers in Jl of Pharmacy and Pharmacology and in Pharmaceutical Jl on pyrogens and fever and on drug stability. *Recreations:* overseas travel, especially Commonwealth; medical and pharmaceutical history. *Address:* Woburn Lodge, 8 Lyndhurst Drive, Harpenden, Herts. *T:* Harpenden 4376. *Clubs:* Royal Commonwealth Society; MCC.

WHITTICK, Richard James; Assistant Under-Secretary of State, Home Office, 1967–72; *b* 21 August 1912; *s* of Ernest G. Whittick and Grace M. Shaw; *m* 1938, Elizabeth Mason; two *s*. *Educ:* George Heriot's School; Edinburgh University. British Museum (Natural History), 1936; Home Office, 1940; Principal Private Secretary to Home Secretary, 1952–53; Assistant Secretary, 1953. *Recreations:* gardening, photography (ARPS 1983). *Address:* Coombe Cottage, Coombe, Sherborne, Dorset DT9 4BX. *T:* Sherborne 814488.

WHITTINGHAM, Charles Percival, BA, PhD Cantab; Head of Department of Botany, Rothamsted Experimental Station, since 1971; *b* 1922; *m* 1946, Alison Phillips; two *d*. *Educ:* St John's College, Cambridge. Professor of Botany, London University, at Queen Mary College, 1958–64; Head of Dept of Botany, 1967–71, and Prof. of Plant Physiology, 1964–71, Imperial Coll., Univ of London; Dean, Royal Coll. of Science, 1969–71; Hon. Dir, ARC Unit for Plant Physiology, 1964–71. Vis. Prof., Univ. of Nottingham, 1978–. *Publications:* Chemistry of Plant Processes, 1964; (with R. Hill) Photosynthesis, 1955; The Mechanism of Photosynthesis, 1974; contrib. to scientific journals. *Recreations:* music, travel. *Address:* Rothamsted Experimental Station, Harpenden, Herts.

WHITTINGTON, Charles Richard, MC 1944; Chamberlain of London, 1964–1973; *b* 8 March 1908; *er s* of late Charles Henry Whittington, Stock Exchange, and Vera Whittington; *m* 1938, Helen Irene Minnie, *d* of late Lieutenant-Colonel J. E. Hance, RHA; one *s* four *d*. *Educ:* Uppingham School. Served War of 1939–45. Member of The Stock Exchange, London, 1931–64. Liveryman Mercers' Company, 1931; Mem. of Court of Common Council for Ward of Broad Street, 1939–64; one of HM Lieutenants, City of London, 1964–73. *Recreation:* gardening. *Address:* Wood Cottage, Brampton Bryan, Bucknell, Salop SY7 0DH. *T:* Bucknell 291.

WHITTINGTON, Prof. Harry Blackmore, FRS 1971; Woodwardian Professor of Geology, Cambridge University, 1966–83; *b* 24 March 1916; *s* of Harry Whittington and Edith M. (*née* Blackmore); *m* 1940, Dorothy E. Arnold; no *c*. *Educ:* Handsworth Gram. Sch.; Birmingham University. Commonwealth Fund Fellow, Yale Univ., 1938–40; Lectr in Geology, Judson Coll., Rangoon, 1940–42; Prof. of Geography, Ginling Coll., Chengtu, W China, 1943–45; Lectr in Geology, Birmingham Univ., 1945–49; Harvard Univ.: Vis. Lectr, 1949–50; Assoc. Prof. of Geology, 1950–58; Prof. of Geology, 1958–66. Trustee: British Museum (Nat. History), 1980–; Uppingham Sch., 1983–. Hon. Fellow, Geol Soc. of America, 1983. Medal, Paleontol Soc., USA, 1983; Lyell Medal, Geological Soc., 1986. Hon. AM, Harvard Univ., 1950. *Publications:* The Burgess Shale, 1985; articles in Jl of Paleontology, Bulletin Geol. Soc. of Amer., Quarterly Jl Geol. Soc. London, Phil. Trans. Royal Soc., etc. *Address:* 20 Rutherford Road, Cambridge CB2 2HH. *Club:* Geological.

WHITTINGTON, Joseph Basil, OBE 1981; HM Diplomatic Service, retired; HM Consul-General, Rotterdam, 1977–80; *b* 24 Oct. 1921; *s* of Joseph and Margaret Whittington; *m* 1947, Hazel Joan Rushton; two *s* one *d*. *Educ:* Cotton Coll., North Staffs; St Philip's Grammar Sch., Birmingham. Post Office, 1938–48. Served Army, 1940–46; Captain, Royal Artillery. Regional Boards for Industry, 1948–52; Bd of Trade, 1952–64; Asst Trade Commissioner, Jamaica, 1953–55; Bahamas and Bermuda, 1955–57 and Jamaica, 1957–58; Trade Commissioner, Johannesburg, 1958–62 and Toronto, 1963–67; transf. to Diplomatic Service, 1964; Head of Chancery, First Sec. (Commercial) and Consul, Liberia, 1968–70; First Sec. (Economic/Commercial), Zambia, 1970–73 and Malta, 1974–77. *Recreations:* gardening, golf, walking. *Address:* Heathcote, Darlington Road, Bath BA2 6NL. *T:* Bath 61697.

WHITTINGTON, Thomas Alan, CB 1977; Circuit Administrator, North Eastern Circuit, 1974–81; *b* 15 May 1916; *o s* of late George Whittington, JP and Mary Elizabeth Whittington; *m* 1939, Audrey Elizabeth, *y d* of late Craven Gilpin, Leeds; four *s*. *Educ:* Uppingham Sch.; Leeds Univ. (LLB). Commnd W Yorks Regt (Leeds Rifles) TA, 1937, serving War of 1939–45 in UK and 14th Army in India (Major). Solicitor of Supreme Court, 1945; Clerk of the Peace, Leeds, 1952–70; Senior Partner, Marklands, Solicitors, Leeds, 1967–70, Consultant, 1981–; Under-Sec., Lord Chancellor's Office, 1970; Circuit Administrator, Northern Circuit, 1970–74. *Recreations:* fishing, gardening, holiday golf. *Address:* The Cottage, School Lane, Collingham, Wetherby LS22 5BQ. *T:* Collingham Bridge 73881.

WHITTINGTON-SMITH, Marianne Christine, (Mrs C. A. Whittington-Smith); *see* Lutz, M. C.

WHITTLE, Air Cdre Sir Frank, OM 1986; KBE 1948 (CBE 1944); CB 1947; Comdr, US Legion of Merit, 1946; RDI 1985; FRS 1947; FEng; MA Cantab; RAF, retired; *b* 1 June 1907; *s* of M. Whittle; *m* 1930, Dorothy Mary Lee (marr. diss. 1976); two *s*; *m* 1976, Hazel S. Hall. *Educ:* Leamington Coll.; No 4 Apprentices' Wing, RAF Cranwell; RAF Coll., Cranwell; Peterhouse, Cambridge (Mechanical Sciences Tripos, BA 1st Cl. Hons). No 4 Apprentices' Wing, RAF Cranwell, 1923–26; Flight Cadet, RAF Coll., Cranwell, 1926–28 (Abdy-Gerrard-Fellowes Memorial Prize); Pilot Officer, 111 (Fighter) Sqdn, 1928–29; Flying Instructors' Course, Central Flying Sch., 1929; Flying Instructor, No 2 Flying Training Sch., RAF Digby, 1930; Test Pilot, Marine Aircraft Experimental Estab., RAF Felixstowe, 1931–32; RAF Sch. of Aeronautical Engrg, Henlow, 1932–34; Officer i/c Engine Test, Engine Repair Section, Henlow, 1934 (6 mths); Cambridge Univ., 1934–37 (Post-Graduate year, 1936–37); Special Duty List, attached Power Jets Ltd for develt of aircraft gas turbine for jet propulsion, 1937–46; War Course, RAF Staff Coll., 1943; Technical Adviser to Controller of Supplies (Air), Min. of Supply, 1946–48; retd RAF, 1948. Hon. Technical Adviser: Jet Aircraft, BOAC, 1948–52; Shell Gp, 1953–57; Consultant, Bristol Siddeley Engines/Rolls Royce on turbo drill project, 1961–70. Mem. Faculty, US Naval Acad., Annapolis, Maryland, 1977–. Partnered late Flt-Lt G. E. Campbell in Crazy Flying RAF Display, Hendon, 1930; 1st flights of Gloster jet-propelled aeroplane with Whittle engine, May 1941. Freeman of Royal Leamington Spa, 1944. Hon. FRAeS; Hon. FAeSI; Hon. FIMechE; Founder Fellow, Fellowship of Engineering, 1976. Hon. Mem., Franklin Inst.; Hon. FAIAA; Hon. Mem., Société Royale Belge des Ingénieurs; Hon. Foreign Mem., Amer. Acad. Arts and Scis, 1976; For. Assoc., US Nat. Acad. of Engrg, 1978; Hon. Fellow, Soc. of Experimental Test Pilots, USA; Hon. MEIC. Hon. Fellow, Peterhouse. Hon. DSc: Oxon; Manchester; Leicester; Bath; Warwick; Exeter; Hon. LLD Edinburgh; Hon. ScD Cantab; Hon. DTech Trondheim. James Alfred Ewing Medal, ICE, 1944; Gold Medal, RAeS, 1944; James Clayton Prize, IMechE, 1946; Daniel Guggenheim Medal, USA, 1946; Kelvin Gold Medal, 1947; Melchett Medal, 1949; Rumford Medal, Royal Soc., 1950; Gold Medal, Fedn Aeronautique Internat., 1951; Churchill Gold Medal, Soc. of Engineers, 1952; Albert Gold Medal, Soc. of Arts, 1952; Franklin Medal, USA, 1956; John Scott Award, 1957; Goddard Award, USA, 1965; Coventry Award of Merit, 1966; International Communications (Christopher Columbus) Prize, City of Genoa, 1966; Tony Jannus Award, Greater Tampa Chamber of Commerce, 1969; James Watt Internat. Gold Medal, IMechE, 1977; Nat. Air and Space Mus. Trophy, 1986. *Publications:* Jet, 1953; Gas Turbine Aero-Thermodynamics, 1981. *Clubs:* Royal Air Force; Wings.

WHITTLE, Kenneth Francis, CEng, FIEE; CBIM; Chairman, South Western Electricity Board, since 1977; *b* 28 April 1922; *s* of Thomas Whittle and May Whittle; *m* 1945, Dorothy Inskip; one *s* one *d*. *Educ:* Kingswood Sch., Bath; Faculty of Technol., Manchester Univ. (BScTech). Served War, Electrical Lieut, RNVR, 1943–46. Metropolitan Vickers Elec. Co. Ltd, 1946–48; NW Div., CEGB, 1948–55; North West Electricity Board: various posts, 1955–64; Area Commercial Officer, Blackburn, 1964–69; Manager, Peak Area, 1969–71; Manager, Manchester Area, 1971–74; Chief Commercial Officer, 1974–75; Dep. Chm., Yorks Elec. Bd, 1975–77. *Recreation:* golf. *Address:* 8 Cambridge Road, Clevedon, Avon BS21 7HX. *T:* Clevedon 874017.

WHITTLE, Prof. Peter, FRS 1978; Churchill Professor of Mathematics of Operational Research, University of Cambridge, since 1967; *b* 27 Feb. 1927; *s* of Percy Whittle and Elsie Tregurtha; *m* 1951, Käthe Hildegard Blomquist; three *s* three *d*. *Educ:* Wellington Coll., New Zealand. Docent, Uppsala Univ., 1951–53; employed New Zealand DSIR, 1953–59, rising to Senior Principal Scientifc Officer; Lectr, Univ. of Cambridge, 1959–61; Prof. of Mathematical Statistics, Univ. of Manchester, 1961–67. Mem., Royal Soc. of NZ, 1981–. *Publications:* Hypothesis Testing in Time Series Analysis, 1951; Prediction and Regulation, 1963; Probability, 1970; Optimisation under Constraints, 1971; Optimisation over Time, 1982; Systems in Stochastic Equilibrium, 1986; contribs to Biometrika, Jl Roy. Statistical Soc., Proc. Camb. Phil. Soc., Proc. Roy. Soc. *Recreation:* guitar. *Address:* 268 Queen Edith's Way, Cambridge; Statistical Laboratory, University of Cambridge.

WHITTON, Cuthbert Henry; *b* 18 Feb. 1905; *s* of Henry and Eleanor Whitton; *m* 1938, Iris Elva Moody; one *d*. *Educ:* St Andrew's College, Dublin; Dublin University. Malayan Civil Service, 1929; Colonial Legal Service, 1939; Puisne Judge, Federation of Malaya, 1951; Puisne Judge, Supreme Court, Singapore, 1954; Foreign Compensation Commn, Legal Dept, 1959–71. *Recreations:* golf, gardening. *Address:* 5 Marsham Lodge, Marsham Lane, Gerrard's Cross, Bucks. *T:* 885608. *Clubs:* Royal Commonwealth Society; Kildare Street and University (Dublin).

WHITTON, Prof. Peter William; Deputy Vice-Chancellor, University of Melbourne, 1979–84, retired; *b* 2 Sept. 1925; *s* of William Whitton and Rosa Bungay; *m* 1950, Mary Katharine White; two *s* three *d*. *Educ:* Latymer Upper Sch., London; Southampton Univ. (BScEng); Imperial College of Science and Technology, London (DIC, PhD); ME Melbourne 1965. FIE(Aust). Engineering Cadet, English Electric Co., Preston, 1942–46; Wireless Officer, Royal Signals, Catterick and Singapore, 1946–48; Sen. Lectr in Mech. Engrg, Univ. of Melbourne, 1953–56; Head, Engrg Sect., ICI Metals Div. Research Dept, Birmingham, 1956–60; Foundation Prof. and Dean, Faculty of Engrg, Univ. of the West Indies, 1960–64; University of Melbourne: Prof. of Mech. Engrg, 1965–77, Emeritus Prof., 1977–; Dean, Faculty of Engrg, 1966; Principal, Royal Melbourne Inst. of Technology, 1977–78. *Publications:* various papers on metal forming, in Proc. IMechE, London, and Jl of Inst. of Metals, London. *Recreations:* reading, golf. *Address:* 425 Beach Road, Beaumaris, Victoria 3193, Australia.

WHITTUCK, Gerald Saumarez, CB 1959; *b* 13 Oct. 1912; *s* of late Francis Gerald Whittuck; *m* 1938, Catherine McCrea; two *s. Educ:* Cheltenham; Clare Coll., Cambridge. Air Ministry, 1935; Private Secretary to Secretary of State, 1944–46; Asst Under-Secretary of State: Air Ministry, 1955–63; War Office, 1963–64; MoD, 1964–71; Dir, Greenwich Hosp., 1971–74. Mem., Royal Patriotic Fund Corp., 1971–74. *Address:* 15A Greenaway Gardens, NW3. *T:* 01–435 3742.

WHITTY, John Lawrence; General Secretary, Labour Party, since 1985; *b* 15 June 1943; *s* of Frederick James and Kathleen May Whitty; *m* 1969, Tanya Margaret (separated); two *s. Educ:* Latymer Upper School; St John's College, Cambridge (BA Hons Economics). Hawker Siddeley Aviation, 1960–62; Min. of Aviation Technology, 1965–70; Trades Union Congress, 1970–73; General, Municipal, Boilermakers and Allied Trade Union (formerly GMWU), 1973–85. *Recreations:* theatre, cinema, swimming. *Address:* 106 Grove Park, SE5. *T:* 01–274 8348.

WHITWAM, Derek Firth, CEng, FRINA; RCNC; Director of Quality Assurance, Ministry of Defence, since 1985; *b* 7 Dec. 1932; *s* of Hilton and Marion Whitwam; *m* 1954, Pamela May (*née* Lander); one *s* one *d. Educ:* Royds Hall Sch., Huddersfield; Royal Naval Coll., Dartmouth; Royal Naval Engineering Coll., Manadon; Royal Naval Coll., Greenwich. Work on ship design, MoD (N) Bath, 1957–65; Rosyth Dockyard, 1965–68; Singapore Dockyard, 1968–70; DG Ships Bath, 1970–77; RCDS 1978; Production Manager, Rosyth Dockyard, 1979–80; Gen. Manager, Portsmouth Dockyard, 1981–84; Principal Dir of Planning and Policy, Chief Exec. Royal Dockyards, 1984–85. *Publications:* papers for Trans Royal Inst. of Naval Architects. *Recreations:* golf, music, walking. *Address:* Director of Quality Assurance (Industry), Building 22, Royal Arsenal West, Woolwich SE18 6ST.

WHITWELL, Stephen John, CMG 1969; MC; HM Diplomatic Service, retired; *b* 30 July 1920; *s* of Arthur Percy Whitwell and Marion Whitwell (*née* Greenwood). *Educ:* Stowe; Christ Church, Oxford. Coldstream Guards, 1941–47; joined HM Foreign Service (now Diplomatic Service), 1947; served: Tehran, 1947; FO, 1949; Belgrade, 1952; New Delhi, 1954; FO, 1958; Seoul, 1961. Polit. Adv. to C-in-C Middle East, Aden, 1964; Counsellor, Belgrade, 1965; Ambassador to Somalia, 1968–70; Head of East-West Contacts Dept, FCO, 1970–71. *Recreations:* reading, painting, looking at buildings. *Address:* Jervis Cottage, Aston Tirrold, Oxon. *Club:* Travellers'.

WHITWORTH, Francis John; Deputy Director-General, General Council of British Shipping, since 1980; Director, International Shipping Federation, since 1980; *b* 1 May 1925; *s* of late Captain Herbert Francis Whitworth, OBE, RNVR, and Helen Marguerite Whitworth (*née* Tait); *m* 1956, Auriol Myfanwy Medwyn Hughes; one *s* one *d. Educ:* Charterhouse (Jun. Schol.); Pembroke Coll., Oxford (Holford Schol.). MA Jurisprudence 1949). FBIM 1980 (MBIM 1967). Served War, Royal Marines, 1943–46. Called to Bar, Middle Temple, 1950. Joined Cunard Steam-Ship Co. as management trainee, 1950; service in USA and Canada, 1956–62; Personnel Director, 1965, Managing Dir Cunard Line, 1968, Group Admin Dir, 1969; joined British Shipping Fedn as Dep. Dir, Industrial Relations, 1972. Member, Nat. Maritime Board, 1962–; Chairman: Internat. Cttee of Passenger Lines, 1968–71; Atlantic Passenger Steamship Conf., 1970–71; Employers' Gp, Jt Maritime Commn of ILO, 1980–; Employers' Gp, Internat. Maritime (Labour) Conf. of ILO, 1986; Social Affairs Cttee, Comité des Assocs d'Armateurs des Communautés Européennes, 1983–; Mem., Econ. and Social Cttee, EEC, 1986–. Mem., Industrial Tribunals for England and Wales, 1978–. Mem. Council, King George's Fund for Sailors, 1980–. Governor, Nat. Sea Trng Schs, 1966–71 (Chm., 1980–). *Recreations:* racing, opera, music, cricket. *Address:* The Old School House, Farley Chamberlayne, Romsey, Hants SO5 0QR. *T:* Braishfield 68538. *Club:* United Oxford & Cambridge University.

WHITWORTH, Group Captain Frank, QC 1965; a Recorder of the Crown Court, 1972–82; *b* 13 May 1910; *o s* of late Daniel Arthur Whitworth, Didsbury, Manchester; *m* 1st, 1939, Mary Lucy (*d* 1979), *o d* of late Sir John Holdsworth Robinson, JP, Bingley, Yorks; no *c*; 2nd, 1980, Mrs Irene Lannon. *Educ:* Shrewsbury Sch.; Trinity Hall, Cambridge. Served with RAFVR (Special Duties), 1940–45, retired. Called to Bar, Gray's Inn, 1934. Member of Dorking and Horley RDC, 1939–68. Contested (C) St Helens, 1945. Judge of Courts of Appeal of Jersey and Guernsey, 1971–80. Master, Clockmakers' Co., 1962 and 1971. Trustee, Whiteley Village Homes, 1963. *Publications:* miscellaneous verse and articles. *Recreation:* farming. *Address:* Little Manor House, Westcott, near Dorking, Surrey. *T:* Dorking 889966; 13 King's Bench Walk, Temple, EC4. *T:* 01–353 7204. *Club:* United Oxford & Cambridge University.

WHITWORTH, Hugh Hope Aston, MBE 1945; Lay Assistant to the Archbishop of Canterbury, 1969–78; *b* 21 May 1914; *s* of Sidney Alexander Whitworth and Elsie Hope Aston; *m* 1st, 1944, Elizabeth Jean Boyes (*d* 1961); two *s* one *d*; 2nd, 1961, Catherine Helen Bell. *Educ:* Bromsgrove Sch.; Pembroke Coll., Cambridge (BA). Indian Civil Service, Bombay Province, 1937–47; Administrator, Ahmedabad Municipality, 1942–44; Collector and District Magistrate, Nasik, 1945–46; Board of Trade, 1947–55; Scottish Home Dept, 1955; Asst Sec., 1957; Under-Sec., Scottish Home and Health Dept, 1968–69. *Recreations:* travel, theatre, gardening. *Address:* 47 Orford Gardens, Strawberry Hill, Twickenham, Mddx TW1 4PL. *T:* 01–892 4672. *Club:* Royal Commonwealth Society.

WHITWORTH, Maj.-Gen. Reginald Henry, CB 1969; CBE 1963; MA; *b* 27 Aug. 1916; 2nd *s* of late Aymer William Whitworth and late Alice (*née* Hervey), Eton College; *m* 1946, June Rachel, *o d* of late Sir Bartle Edwards, CVO, MC, and of Daphne, MBE, *d* of late Sir Cyril Kendall Butler, KBE; two *s* one *d. Educ:* Eton; Balliol College, Oxford, 1st cl. Hons, Modern History, 1938; Laming Travelling Fellow, Queen's Coll., Oxford, 1938–39. 2nd Lt Grenadier Guards, 1940; GSO2, 78 Division, 1944; Bde Major, 24 Guards Brigade, 1945–46; GSO2, Staff College, Camberley, 1953–55; comdg 1st Bn Grenadier Guards, 1956–57; GSO1, SHAPE, 1958–59; Sen. Army Instructor, Jt Services Staff Coll., 1959–61; Comdr Berlin Infantry Bde Gp, 1961–63; DMS 1, Ministry of Defence, 1964–66; GOC: Yorkshire District, 1966–67; Northumbrian District, 1967–68; Chief of Staff, Southern Command, 1968–70. Bursar and Official Fellow, Exeter College, Oxford, 1970–81. Governor: Felsted Sch.; St Mary's, Wantage (Chm.). Chm., Army Museums Ogilby Trust. Bronze Star, USA, 1945. *Publications:* Field Marshal Earl Ligonier, 1958; Famous Regiments: the Grenadier Guards, 1974. *Recreations:* riding, fishing, military history. *Address:* Abbey Farm, Goosey, Faringdon, Oxon. *T:* Stanford in Vale 252. *Club:* Army and Navy.

WHYBREW, Edward Graham, (Ted); Under Secretary, Industrial Relations Division, Department of Employment, since 1985; *b* 25 Sept. 1938; *s* of Ernest Whybrew and Winifred (*née* Castle); *m* 1967, Julia Helen Baird; one *s* two *d. Educ:* Hertford Grammar Sch.; Balliol Coll., Oxford (BA 1961); Nuffield Coll., Oxford. Economist: NEDO, 1963; DEA, 1964–69; Dept of Employment, 1969–77; Asst Sec., Employment, Trng and Industrial Relations, Dept of Employment, 1977–85. *Publication:* Overtime Working in Great Britain, 1968. *Recreations:* cricket, horse riding, gardening. *Address:* 31 Hanover Gardens, SE11 5TN. *T:* 01–735 5336.

WHYTE, Sir Hamilton; *see* Whyte, Sir W. E. H.

WHYTE, Rev. James Aitken; Professor of Practical Theology and Christian Ethics, University of St Andrews, since 1958; *b* 28 Jan. 1920; 2nd *s* of late Andrew Whyte, Leith, and late Barbara Janet Pittillo Aitken; *m* 1942, Elisabeth, *er d* of Rev. G. S. Mill, MA, BSc, Kalimpong, India; two *s* one *d. Educ:* Daniel Stewart's Coll., Edinburgh; University of Edinburgh (Arts and Divinity), MA 1st Cl. Hons Phil., 1942. Ordained, 1945; Chaplain to the Forces, 1945–48; Minister of: Dunollie Road, Oban, 1948–54; Mayfield, Edinburgh, 1954–58. St Andrews University: Dean, Faculty of Divinity, 1968–72; Principal, St Mary's Coll., 1978–82. Guest Lectr, Inst. for the Study of Worship and Religious Architecture, Birmingham, 1965–66; Lectures: Kerr, Univ. of Glasgow, 1969–72; Croall, Univ. of Edinburgh, 1972–73. Pres., Soc. for Study of Theol., 1983–84. Hon. LLD Dundee, 1981. *Publications:* (ed jtly) Worship Now, 1972; contributor to various dictionaries, composite volumes, journals, etc. *Address:* 13 Hope Street, St Andrews, Fife. *Club:* New (Edinburgh).

WHYTE, John Stuart, CBE 1976; MSc(Eng); FEng 1980; FIEE; Chairman, Plessey Telecommunications (International) Ltd, since 1983; Deputy Chairman, Plessey Telecommunications and Office Systems Ltd, since 1985; *b* High Wycombe, 20 July 1923; *s* of late William W. Whyte and Ethel K. Whyte; *m* 1951, E. Joan M. (*née* Budd); one *s* one *d. Educ:* The John Lyon Sch., Harrow; Northampton Polytechnic, London Univ. BSc(Eng) (Hons), MSc(Eng). Post Office Radio Laboratory, Castleton, Cardiff, 1949–57; PO Research Station, Dollis Hill: Sen. Exec. Engr, 1957–61; Asst Staff Engr, 1961–65. Asst Sec., HM Treasury, 1965–68; Dep. Dir of Engrg, PO, 1968–71; Dir, Operational Programming, PO, 1971–75; Dir of Purchasing and Supply, 1975–76, Sen. Dir of Develt, 1977–79, Dep. Man. Dir, 1979–81, PO Telecommunications; Engr-in-Chief, Man. Dir (major systems), and Mem. Main Bd, British Telecom, 1981–83; Dir, British Telecommunications Systems Ltd, 1979–83; Chm., Astronet Corp., 1984–85; Pres., 1984–85, Chm., 1985–86, Stromberg Carlson Corp. Manager, Royal Instn, 1971–74 (Vice-Pres., 1972, 1973, 1974); Mem. Cttee of Visitors, 1975–78 (Chm., 1977–78), Chm., Membership Cttee, 1975–77. Mem., Nat. Electronics Council, 1977– (Mem. Exec. Cttee, 1977–; Dep. Chm., 1980–); Mem. Council, ERA, 1977–83. President: Instn of PO Electrical Engrs, 1977–82; Instn of British Telecommunications Engrs, 1982–83 (Hon. Mem., 1984); Mem. Council, IEE, 1980–84 (Vice-Pres., 1981–84); Chm. Professional Bd, 1981–84). Governor, Internat. Council for Computer Communication, 1985–. Liveryman, Scientific Instrument Makers' Co. Leader, British Hinku Expedn, 1979. *Publications:* various articles and papers in professional telecommunications jls. *Recreations:* mountaineering, photography, opera. *Address:* Wild Hatch, Coleshill Lane, Winchmore Hill, Amersham, Bucks HP7 0NT. *T:* Amersham 22663. *Clubs:* Alpine; Swiss Alpine (Berne).

WHYTE, (John) Stuart Scott, CB 1986; Under Secretary, Department of Health and Social Security, 1978–86; *b* 1 April 1926; *er s* of late Thomas and Mysie Scott Whyte, Sandycove, Co. Dublin; *m* 1950, Jocelyn Margaret, *o d* of late George Hawley, CBE, Edinburgh; two *s* one *d. Educ:* St Andrew's Coll., Dublin; Trinity Coll., Univ. of Dublin. BA 1947; LLB 1948. Asst Principal, Dept of Health for Scotland, 1948; Principal, 1955; Principal Private Sec. to Sec. of State for Scotland, 1959; Asst Sec., Scottish Develt Dept, 1962; Asst Sec., Cabinet Office, 1969; Asst Under-Sec. of State, Scottish Office, 1969–74; Under Sec., Cabinet Office, 1974–78. *Address:* 26 Langley Hill, Kings Langley, Herts. *T:* Kings Langley 64745; La Bâtisse, Bonin, 47120 Duras, France.

WHYTE, Lewis Gilmour, CBE 1973; FFA; Chairman: London and Manchester Assurance Co. Ltd, 1961–78; New York & Gartmore Investment Trust Ltd, 1972–79; Welfare Insurance Co. Ltd, 1974–78; Director: Associated Commercial Vehicles Ltd, 1953–78; Broadstone Investment Trust Ltd, 1953–78; *b* 9 Oct. 1906; *s* of Robert Whyte and Florence Smith; *m* 1st, 1935, Ursula Frances Ware (marr. diss. 1971); one *s* three *d*; 2nd, 1971, Diana Mary Campbell. *Educ:* Trinity Coll., Glenalmond. FFA 1929. Investment Manager, later Dir, Equity & Law Life Assurance Company Ltd, 1940–1953; Dir, Save & Prosper Group Ltd, 1950–63; Member: NCB, 1963–66; NFC, 1971–74; Dep. Chm., British Leyland Motor Corporation Ltd, 1968–72; Chm., Transport Holding Company, 1971–73. Receiver-General, Order of St John of Jerusalem, 1955–68. GCStJ 1969. *Publications:* Principles of Finance and Investment, vol. 1, 1949, vol. 2, 1950; One Increasing Purpose, 1984. *Recreations:* golf, gardening. *Address:* Queen's Cottage, Somerford Keynes, Cirencester, Glos GL7 6DN.

WHYTE, Stuart Scott; *see* Whyte, J. S. S.

WHYTE, Sir (William Erskine) Hamilton, KCMG 1985 (CMG 1979); HM Diplomatic Service; High Commissioner in Singapore, since 1985; *b* 28 May 1927; *s* of late William Hamilton Whyte; *m* 1953, Sheila Annie Duck; two *d* (and one *d* decd), *Educ:* King's Sch., Bruton; The Queen's Coll., Oxford. Served, Royal Navy, 1945–48. Civil Asst, War Office, 1952–55; HM Foreign (later Diplomatic) Service, 1955; Vienna, 1956; Bangkok, 1959; UK Mission to UN, New York, 1963; Foreign Office, 1966; Counsellor, HM Embassy, Kinshasa, Democratic Republic of the Congo, 1970–71; Dir-Gen., British Information Services, and Dep. Consul-General (Information), NY, 1972–76; Head of News Dept, FCO, 1976–79; Minister (Economic and Social Affairs), UK Mission to UN, New York, 1979–81; Ambassador and Dep. Perm. Rep. to UN, 1981–83; High Comr in Nigeria and Ambassador (non-resident) to Benin, 1983–84. *Recreations:* gardening, photography. *Address:* c/o Foreign and Commonwealth Office, SW1; The Lodge, Ford Lane, Ford, Sussex BN18 0DE. *T:* 551377. *Club:* Century Association (New York).

WIBBERLEY, Prof. Gerald Percy, CBE 1972; Ernest Cook Professor of Countryside Planning in the University of London, University College/Wye College, 1969–82; *b* 15 April 1915; *m* 1st, 1943, Helen Yeomans (*d* 1963); one *d*; 2nd, 1972, Peggy Samways. *Educ:* King Henry VIII Grammar Sch., Abergavenny; Univs of Wales, Oxford, and Illinois, USA. BSc, MS, PhD. Asst Lectr, Univ. of Manchester, 1940–41; E Sussex Agricultural Cttee: Dist Officer, 1941–43; Asst Exec. Officer, 1943–44; Min. of Agriculture: Asst Rural Land Utilisation Officer, 1944–49; Research Officer, Land Use, 1949–54; Univ. of London, Wye Coll.: Head of Dept of Economics, 1954–69, also Reader in Agricultural Economics, 1958–62; Prof. of Rural Economy, 1963–69; Fellow 1985. Dir, CoSIRA, 1968–86; Mem., Nature Conservancy Council, 1973–80; Pres., British Agricl Econs Soc., 1975–76. Chm., Rural Planning Services Ltd, 1972–82. Hon. Associate Mem. TPI, 1949–67; Hon. Mem., RTPI, 1967–. Hon. DSc Bradford, 1982. *Publications:* Agriculture and Urban Growth, 1959; (part author): The Agricultural Significance of the Hills, 1956; Land Use in an Urban Environment, 1960; Outdoor Recreation in the British Countryside, 1963; An Agricultural Land Budget for Britain 1965–2000, 1970; The Nature and Distribution of Second Homes in England and Wales, 1973; (jtly) Planning and the Rural Environment, 1976; Countryside Planning: a personal evaluation, 1982; contributor to Jls of: Agricl Economics, Land Economics, Town and Country Planning. *Recreations:* music, altering old houses, arguing about rural affairs. *Address:* Vicarage Cottage, 7 Upper Bridge Street, Wye, near Ashford, Kent. *T:* Wye 812377. *Club:* Farmers'.

WIBLIN, Derek John; Under Secretary, Principal Establishment and Finance Officer, Lord Chancellor's Department, since 1984; *b* 18 March 1933; *s* of Cyril G. H. Wiblin and

Winifred F. Wiblin (*née* Sandford); *m* 1960, Pamela Jeanne Hamshere; one *s* one *d*. *Educ:* Bishopshalt School, Hillingdon; Birmingham University (BSc Hons Chem 1954). RAF, 1954–57. Courtaulds Ltd, 1957–58; joined DSIR Building Research Station, 1958; Civil Service Commission, 1967–71; DoE, 1971–79; Ports Div., Dept of Transport, 1979–81; Estabs Div., DoE, 1981–83. *Recreations:* making violins, collecting books. *Address:* 19 Woodwaye, Watford, Herts WD1 4NN. *T:* Watford 28615. *Club:* Royal Air Force.

WICKBERG, Gen. Erik E.; Comdr of the Order of Vasa (Sweden), 1970; General of the Salvation Army, 1969–74; *b* 6 July 1904; *s* of David Wickberg, Commissioner, Salvation Army, and Betty (*née* Lundblad); *m* 1929, Ens. Frieda de Groot (*d* 1930); *m* 1932, Captain Margarete Dietrich (*d* 1976); two *s* two *d*; *m* 1977, Major Eivor Lindberg. *Educ:* Uppsala; Berlin; Stockholm. Salvation Army Internat. Training Coll., 1924–25, and Staff Coll., 1926; commissioned, 1925; appts in Scotland, Berlin, London; Divisional Commander, Uppsala, 1946–48; Chief Secretary, Switzerland, 1948–53; Chief Secretary, Sweden, 1953–57; Territorial Commander, Germany, 1957–61; Chief of the Staff, Internat. HQ, London, 1961–69; elected General of the Salvation Army, July 1969; assumed international leadership, Sept. 1969. Hon. LLD Choong Ang Univ., Seoul, 1970. Order of Moo-Koong-Wha, Korea, 1970; Grosses Verdienstkreuz, Germany, 1971; The King's golden medal (Sweden), 1980. *Publications:* In Darkest England Now, 1974; Inkallad (autobiography, in Swedish), 1978; articles in Salvation Army periodicals and Year Book. *Recreations:* reading, fishing, chess. *Address:* c/o The Salvation Army, Box 5090, 10240 Stockholm, Sweden.

WICKENS, Dr Alan Herbert, OBE 1980; FEng, FIMechE; Director of Engineering Development and Research, British Rail, since 1984; *b* 29 March 1929; *s* of Herbert Leslie Wickens and Sylvia Wickens; *m* 1953, Eleanor Joyce Waggott (*d* 1984); one *d*. *Educ:* Ashville Coll., Harrogate; Loughborough Univ. of Technol. (DLC Eng, BScEng London, 1951; DSc Loughborough, 1978). CEng, FIMechE 1971; MRAeS. Res. Engr, Sir W. G. Armstrong Whitworth Aircraft Ltd, Coventry, 1951–55; Gp Leader, Dynamics Analysis, Canadair Ltd, Montreal, 1955–59; Head of Aeroelastics Section, Weapons Res. Div., A. V. Roe & Co., Ltd, Woodford, 1959–62; British Rail: Supt, Res. Dept, 1962–67; Advanced Projs Engr, 1967–68; Dir of Advanced Projs, 1968–71; Dir of Labs, 1971–78; Dir of Research, 1978–84. Industrial Prof. of Transport Technol., Loughborough Univ. of Technol., 1972–76. Pres., Internat. Assoc. of Vehicle System Dynamics, 1981–86. Mem., Amer. Inst. Aeronautics and Astronautics. FBIS; FRSA. Hon. Fellow, Derbyshire Coll. of Higher Educn, 1984. Hon. DTech CNAA, 1978; Hon. Dr Open Univ, 1980. George Stephenson Res. Prize, IMechE, 1966; (jtly) MacRobert Award, 1975. *Publications:* papers on dynamics of railway vehicles, high speed trains and future railway technology, publ. by IMechE, Amer. Soc. of Mech. Engrs, Internat. Jl of Solids and Structures, and Jl of Vehicle System Dynamics. *Recreations:* gardening, travel, music. *Address:* Broomfields, 52 Broadway, Duffield, Derbyshire DE6 4BW. *T:* Derby 840341.

WICKERSON, John Michael; President, Law Society, 1986–87; *b* 22 Sept. 1937; *s* of Walter and Ruth Wickerson; *m* 1963, Shirley Maud Best; one *s*. *Educ:* Christ's Hospital; London University (LLB). Admitted solicitor, 1960; Mem. Council, Law Society, 1969 (Chm., Contentious Business Cttee; Vice-Pres., 1985–86); Pres., London Criminal Courts Solicitors Assoc., 1980–81; Mem., Matrimonial Causes Rules Cttee, 1982–. *Publication:* Motorist and the Law, 1975, 2nd edn 1982. *Recreation:* golf. *Address:* c/o Ormerod, Morris & Dumont, 10 High Street, Croydon, Surrey CR9 2BH. *T:* 01–686 3841.

WICKHAM, Rt. Rev. Edward Ralph; Assistant Bishop, Diocese of Manchester, since 1982; *b* 3 Nov. 1911; *s* of Edward Wickham, London; *m* 1944, Dorothy Helen Neville Moss, *d* of Prof. Kenneth Neville Moss, Birmingham; one *s* two *d*. *Educ:* University of London (BD); St Stephen's House, Oxford. Deacon, 1938; Priest, 1939; Curate, Christ Church, Shieldfield, Newcastle upon Tyne, 1938–41; Chaplain, Royal Ordnance Factory, Swynnerton, 1941–44; Curate-in-charge, Swynnerton, 1943–44; Diocesan Missioner to Industry, Sheffield, 1944–59; Hon. Chaplain to Bishop of Sheffield, 1950–59; Canon Residentiary, Sheffield, 1951–59; Bishop Suffragan of Middleton, 1959–82. Sir H. Stephenson Fellow, Sheffield University, 1955–57. Chm. Working Party, Gen. Synod Industrial Cttee, 1977 (report: Understanding Closed Shops); Chairman: Bd for Social Responsibility Working Party on The Future of Work, 1980; Royal Soc. of Arts Industry Year 1986 Churches' Cttee, 1985. Chm. Council, and Pro-Chancellor, Salford Univ., 1975–83. FRSA 1986. Hon. DLitt Salford, 1973. *Publications:* Church and People in an Industrial City, 1957; Encounter with Modern Society, 1964; Growth & Inflation, 1975; Growth, Justice and Work, 1985; contributions to: Theology, The Ecumenical Review, Industrial Welfare, etc. *Recreations:* mountaineering, rock-climbing. *Address:* 12 Westminster Road, Eccles, Manchester. *T:* 061–789 3144.

WICKHAM, Glynne William Gladstone; Professor of Drama, University of Bristol, 1960–82, now Emeritus; Dean of Faculty of Arts, 1970–72; *b* 15 May 1922; *s* of W. G. and Catherine Wickham; *m* 1954, Marjorie Heseltine (*née* Mudford); two *s* one *d*. *Educ:* Winchester College; New College, Oxford. Entered RAF, 1942; commissioned as Navigator, 1943; discharged as Flt Lt, 1946. BA, 1947; DPhil, 1951 (Oxon); President of OUDS, 1946–47. Asst Lecturer, Drama Dept, Bristol Univ., 1948; Senior Lecturer and Head of Dept, 1955. Worked sporadically as actor, script-writer and critic for BBC, from 1946; attended General Course in Broadcasting, BBC Staff Trg Sch., 1953. Travelled in America on Rockefeller Award, 1953. Visiting Prof., Drama Dept, State Univ. of Iowa, 1960; Ferens Vis. Prof. of Drama, Hull Univ., 1969; Vis. Prof. of Theatre History, Yale Univ., 1970; Killam Res. Prof., Dalhousie Univ., 1976–77; S. W. Brooks Vis. Prof., Univ. of Qld, 1983; Vis. Prof. in British Studies (Drama), Univ. of the South, Sewanee, 1984. Lectures: G. F. Reynolds Meml, Univ. of Colorado, 1960; Judith E. Wilson, in Poetry and Drama, Cambridge, 1960–61; Festvortrag, Deutsche Shakespeare Gesellschaft, 1973; Shakespeare, British Acad., 1984; British Council, in Europe, annually 1969–79. Directed: Amer. première, The Birthday Party, for Actors' Workshop, San Francisco, 1960; world première, Wole Soyinka's Brother Jero's Metamorphosis, 1974. Consultant to Finnish National Theatre and Theatre School on establishment of Drama Department in Univ. of Helsinki, 1963. Governor of Bristol Old Vic Trust, 1963–83; Vandyck Theatre, Bristol Univ., renamed Glynne Wickham Studio Theatre, 1983. Consultant to Univ. of E Africa on establishment of a Sch. of Drama in University Coll., Dar-es-Salaam, Tanzania, 1965; Dir, Theatre Seminar, for Summer Univ., Vaasa, Finland, 1965; External Examr to Sch. of Drama in Univ. of Ibadan, Nigeria, 1965–68. Chm., Nat. Drama Conf., Nat. Council of Social Service, 1970–76; Chm., and Chief Exec., Radio West plc (ILR Bristol), 1979–83; Pres., Soc. for Theatre Research, 1976–; Member: Adv. Cttee, British Theatre Museum, 1974–77; Culture Adv. Panel, UK Nat. Commn to UNESCO, 1984–86. Mem., Edit. Cttee, Shakespeare Survey, 1974–; Chairman: Adv. Bd, Theatre Research International, 1975–; Gen. Edit. Bd, Theatre in Europe: documents and sources, 1979–. Trustee, St Deiniol's Residential Library, Hawarden, 1985–. Hon. DLitt: Loughborough, 1984; Univ. of the South, Sewanee, 1984. *Publications:* Early English Stages 1300–1660, Vol. I (1300–1576), 1959, 2nd edn 1980; Vol. II (1576–1660, Pt 1), 1962; Vol. II (Pt 2), 1972; Vol. III, 1981; Editor: The Relationship between Universities and Radio, Film and Television, 1954; Drama in a World of Science, 1962; Gen. Introd. to the London Shakespeare, 6 vols (ed J. Munro), 1958; Shakespeare's Dramatic Heritage, 1969; The Medieval Theatre, 1974, 3rd edn 1986; English Moral Interludes, 1975, 2nd edn 1985; A History of the Theatre, 1985. *Recreations:* gardening and travel. *Address:* 6 College Road, Clifton, Bristol BS8 3JB. *T:* Bristol 34918. *Club:* Garrick.

WICKHAM, William Rayley; His Honour Judge Wickham; a Circuit Judge, since 1975; *b* 22 Sept. 1926; *s* of late Rayley Esmond Wickham and late Mary Joyce Wickham; *m* 1957, Elizabeth Mary (*née* Thompson); one *s* two *d*. *Educ:* Sedbergh Sch.; Brasenose Coll., Oxford (MA, BCL). Served War of 1939–45, Army, 1944–48. Called to Bar, Inner Temple, 1951. Magistrate, Aden, 1953; Chief Magistrate, Aden, 1958; Crown Counsel, Tanganyika, 1959; Asst to Law Officers, Tanganyika, 1961–63; practised on Northern Circuit, 1963–75; a Recorder of the Crown Court, 1972–75. *Recreations:* fell walking, music, amateur dramatics. *Address:* 115 Vyner Road South, Birkenhead. *T:* 051–652 2095.

WICKINS, David Allen; Chairman, The British Car Auction Group plc, since 1946; Director, Five Oaks Investments, since 1985; *b* 15 Feb. 1920; *s* of Samuel Wickins and Edith Hannah Robinson; *m* 1969, Karen Esther Young; one *s* five *d*. *Educ:* St George's College, Weybridge. Trained as chartered accountant with Deloitte & Co., attached to Johannesburg Consolidated Investment Co. and moved to S Africa, 1938, to work on audits for Rhodesian copper mines and sawmills. War of 1939–45: S African Naval Forces (18 months with Eastern Fleet); seconded to RN; served with UK Coastal Forces. Founded, Feb. 1946, Southern Counties Car Auctions, later The British Car Auction Group. Former Chairman: Attwoods plc; Group Lotus plc. *Recreations:* golf, sailing. *Address:* British Car Auction Group, Expedier House, Hindhead, Surrey. *T:* Hindhead 7440. *Clubs:* St James's, Royal Thames Yacht; Sunningdale Golf; Wentworth Golf.

WICKRAMASINGHE, Prof. Nalin Chandra, PhD, ScD; Professor and Head of Department of Applied Mathematics and Astronomy, University College, Cardiff, since 1973; *b* 20 Jan. 1939; *s* of Percival Herbert Wickramasinghe and Theresa Elizabeth Wickramasinghe; *m* 1966, Nelum Priyadarshini Pereira; one *s* two *d*. *Educ:* Royal Coll., Colombo, Sri Lanka; Univ. of Ceylon (BSc); Univ. of Cambridge (MA, PhD, ScD). Commonwealth Scholar, Trinity Coll., Cambridge, 1960; Powell Prize for English Verse, 1961; Jesus College, Cambridge: Research Fellow, 1963–66; Fellow, 1967–73; Tutor, 1970–73; Staff Mem., Inst. of Theoretical Astronomy, Univ. of Cambridge, 1968–73. Visiting Professor: Vidyodaya Univ. of Ceylon, Univ. of Maryland, USA, Univ. of Arizona, USA, Univ. of Kyoto, Japan, 1966–70; Univ. of W Ontario, 1974, 1976; UNDP Cons. and Scientific Advisor to President of Sri Lanka, 1970–81; Dir, Inst. of Fundamental Studies, Sri Lanka, 1982–83. Collaborator with Prof. Sir Fred Hoyle, and propounder with Hoyle of the theory of the space origin of life and of microorganisms. *Publications:* Interstellar Grains, 1967; (with F. D. Kahn and P. G. Mezger) Interstellar Matter, 1972; Light Scattering Functions for Small Particles with Applications in Astronomy, 1973; The Cosmic Laboratory, 1975; (with D. J. Morgan) Solid State Astrophysics, 1976; Fundamental Studies and the Future of Science, 1984; (with F. Hoyle): Lifecloud: the origin of life in the universe, 1978; Diseases From Space, 1979; The Origin of Life, 1980; Evolution From Space, 1981; Space Travellers, the Bringers of Life, 1981; From Grains to Bacteria, 1984; Living Comets, 1985; Archaeopteryx, the Primordial Bird: a case of fossil forgery, 1986; Viruses from Space; over 250 articles and papers in astronomical and scientific jls; contributor to anthologies of Commonwealth Poetry, incl. Young Commonwealth Poets '65, ed P. L. Brent, 1965. *Recreations:* photography, poetry—both writing and reading, history and philosophy of science. *Address:* University College, PO Box 78, Cardiff CF1 1XL. *T:* Cardiff 874201. *Club:* Icosahedron Dining (Cardiff).

WICKREME, A. S. K.; *see* Kohoban-Wickreme.

WICKREMESINGHE, Dr Walter Gerald, CMG 1954; OBE 1949; *b* 13 Feb. 1897; *s* of Peter Edwin Wickremesinghe and Charlotte Catherine Goonetilleka; *m* 1931, Irene Amelia Goontilleka; two *s* two *d*. *Educ:* Royal College, Colombo; Ceylon Medical College; London University (the London Hospital); Harvard University (School of Public Health). Licentiate in Medicine and Surgery (Ceylon), 1921; MRCS, LRCP, 1923; Master of Public Health (Harvard), 1926; Dr of Public Health (Harvard), 1927. Director of Medical and Sanitary Services, Ceylon, 1948–53. Chief Delegate from Ceylon at WHO. Assembly and Executive board, Geneva, 1952; Mem. UN Health Planning Mission to Korea, 1952; WHO Consultant, Manila, 1965; Chairman, Committee of Inquiry into Mental Health Services, Ceylon, 1966. (Hon.) FAPHA 1952. OStJ. *Publications:* contributions to Brit. Med. Jl; Ceylon Med. Jl; Trans. Soc. of Med. Officers of Health, Ceylon; Amer. Jl of Public Health. *Recreations:* golf, tennis, riding, swimming. *Address:* 48 Buller's Lane, Colombo 7, Sri Lanka. *T:* Colombo 81374. *Clubs:* Otter Aquatic, Royal Colombo Golf (Colombo); Nuwara Eliya Golf, Nuwara Eliya Hill; (Life Mem.) Health Dept Sports.

WICKS, Allan; Organist, Canterbury Cathedral, since 1961; *b* 1923; *s* of late Edward Kemble Wicks, Priest, and Nancie (*née* Murgatroyd); *m* 1955, Elizabeth Kay Butcher; two *d*. *Educ:* Leatherhead; Christ Church, Oxford. Sub-organist, York Minster, 1947; Organist, Manchester Cathedral, 1954. MusDoc Lambeth, 1974; Hon. DMus Kent, 1985. *Address:* The Old Farm House, Lower Hardres, Canterbury, Kent. *T:* Petham 253.

WICKS, David Vaughan, RE 1961 (ARE 1950); Technical Artist, Bank of England Printing Works, 1954–79, retired, Consultant, 1979–85; *b* 20 Dec. 1918; British; *m* 1948, Margaret Gwyneth Downs; one *s* one *d* (and one *s* decd). *Educ:* Wychwood, Bournemouth; Cranleigh School, Surrey. Polytechnic School of Art, 1936, silver medal for figure composition, 1938, 1939. Radio Officer, Merchant Navy, 1940–46. Royal College of Art, Engraving School, 1946–49, Diploma, ARCA Engraving. Taught Processes of Engraving at RCA, 1949–54. *Recreations:* gardening, bowls.

WICKS, Sir James, Kt 1972; Chief Justice of Kenya, 1971–82 and of Court of Appeal, 1977–82; *b* 20 June 1909; *s* of late James Wicks and late Mrs Wicks; *m* 1960, Doris Mary, *d* of late G. F. Sutton; no *c*. *Educ:* Royal Grammar Sch., Guildford; King's Coll., London (LLB); Christ Church, Oxford (MA, BLitt). Chartered Surveyor (PASI), 1931; called to the Bar, Gray's Inn, 1939; practised at Bar, 1939–40 and 1945–46. Served War: RAF (Sqdn Ldr), 1940–45 (despatches thrice). Crown Counsel Palestine, 1946–48; Magistrate, Hong Kong, 1948–53; Actg Additional Judge, Supreme Court, Hong Kong, 1948–49; Dist Judge, Hong Kong, 1953–58; Actg Puisne Judge, Hong Kong, 1953, 1955, 1957; High Court, Kenya: Puisne Judge, 1958–69, Sen. Puisne Judge, 1969–71. *Publication:* The Doctrine of Consideration, 1939. *Recreation:* golf. *Address:* Côte de Vauxlaurens, L'Hyvreuse, Cambridge Park, St Peter Port, Guernsey, Channel Islands. *Clubs:* Mombasa, Nairobi (Kenya).

WICKS, Sir James (Albert), Kt 1978; JP; Wanganui Computer Centre Privacy Commissioner, 1978–83; Acting District Court Judge, 1980–81; *b* 14 June 1910; *s* of Henry James Wilmont Wicks and Melanie de Rohan Wicks (*née* Staunton); *m* 1942 Lorna Margaret de la Cour; one *s* one *d*. *Educ:* Christchurch Boys' High Sch.; Canterbury Univ., NZ. LLM (Hons) Univ. of New Zealand. Admitted Barrister and Solicitor of Supreme Court of NZ, 1932; Notary Public, 1951; Lectr in Trustee Law, Canterbury

Univ., 1946–55; in practice as barrister and solicitor (in Christchurch), 1945–61; Mem. Council, Canterbury Dist Law Soc., 1954–61. Stipendiary Magistrate, 1961–78. JP 1963; Chairman: Magistrates' Courts' Rules Cttee, 1967–78; NZ Magistrates' Exec., 1973–78; Dept of Justice's Editorial Bd, 1968–78; Chairman: various Appeal Boards and Statutory Cttees, 1965–78; Teachers' Disciplinary Bd, 1978–82; Cttee of Inquiry into the Administration of the Electoral Act, 1979; Public Service Appeal Bd, 1982. Consultant to Govt of Niue on legal, judicial and law enforcement systems and policies, 1983. *Publications*: papers to Australian Inst. of Criminology, Feb. 1974, and Commonwealth Magistrates' Conf., Kuala Lumpur, Aug. 1975; contribs to NZ Law Jl, Commonwealth Judicial Jl. *Address*: 29 Glen Road, Kelburn, Wellington 5, New Zealand. *T*: 759–204. *Club*: Canterbury (Christchurch, NZ).

WICKS, Nigel Leonard, CBE 1979; Principal Private Secretary to the Prime Minister, since 1985; *b* 16 June 1940; *s* of Leonard Charles and Beatrice Irene Wicks; *m* 1969, Jennifer Mary (*née* Coveney) three *s*. *Educ*: Beckenham and Penge Grammar Sch.; Univ. of Cambridge (MA); Univ. of London (MA). The British Petroleum Co. Ltd, 1958–68; HM Treasury, 1968–75; Private Sec. to the Prime Minister, 1975–78; HM Treasury, 1978–83; Economic Minister, British Embassy, Washington, and UK Exec. Dir, IMF and IBRD, 1983–85. Mem. Bd, BNOC, 1980–82. *Address*: 10 Downing Street, SW1.

WICKS, Rt. Rev. Ralph Edwin, OBE 1982; ED 1964; Bishop of the Southern Region, Diocese of Brisbane, since 1985; *b* 16 Aug. 1921; *s* of Charles Thomas Wicks and Florence Maud Wicks (*née* White); *m* 1946, Gladys Hawgood (*d* 1981); one *s* one *d*. *Educ*: East State Sch. and State High Sch., Toowoomba, Qld; St Francis Theological Coll., Brisbane, Qld (LTh). Mem., Qld Public Service (Educn Dept), 1936–41; Theological Student, 1941–44; Asst Curate: Holy Trinity Ch., Fortitude Valley, Brisbane, 1944–47; St James' Ch., Toowoomba, Qld, 1947–48; Rector: Holy Trinity Ch., Goondiwindi, Qld, 1949–54; Holy Trinity Ch., Fortitude Valley, Brisbane, 1954–63; St James' Church, Toowoomba, Qld, 1963–72; Asst Bishop of Brisbane, 1973; Rector of St Andrew's Parish, Caloundra, and Commissary to Archbishop of Brisbane, 1983–85. Hon. Canon of St John's Cath., Brisbane, 1968; Archdeacon of Darling Downs, Qld, 1973. Chaplain to the Australian Army, 1949–70. *Recreations*: reading, gardening, music. *Address*: 7/90 Invermore Street, Mount Gravatt, Brisbane, Queensland, Australia.

WICKSTEAD, Cyril; Chairman, Eastern Electricity Board, 1978–82; Member, Electricity Council, 1978–82; *b* 27 Sept. 1922; *s* of John William and Mary Caroline Wickstead; *m* 1948, Freda May Hill; two *s*. *Educ*: Rowley Regis Central Sch.; City of Birmingham Commercial Coll. FCIS; CBIM. Served War, Royal Navy (Lieut RNVR), 1942–46. Midland Electric Corporation for Power Distribution Ltd: various positions, 1937–42; Asst Sec., 1946–48; Midlands Electricity Board: Sec., S Staffs and N Worcs Sub-Area, 1948–59; Dep. Sec. of Bd, 1959–63; Sec., 1964–72; Dep. Chm., 1972–77. Freeman, City of London, 1979. *Recreations*: walking, music, gardening, sport. *Address*: Little Acre, Colchester Road, Dedham, Colchester, Essex CO7 6DS.

WIDDAS, Prof. Wilfred Faraday, MB, BS; BSc; PhD; DSc; Professor of Physiology in the University of London, and Head of the Department of Physiology, Bedford College, 1960–81, now Professor Emeritus; *b* 2 May 1916; *s* of late Percy Widdas, BSc, mining engineer, and Annie Maude (*née* Snowdon); *m* 1940, Gladys Green (*d* 1983); one *s* two *d*. *Educ*: Durham School; University of Durham College of Medicine and Royal Victoria Infirmary, Newcastle upon Tyne. MB, BS 1938; BSc 1947; PhD 1953; DSc 1958. Assistant in General Practice, 1938–39. Served in RAMC, 1939–47; Deputy Assistant Director-General Army Medical Services, War Office (Major), 1942–47. Research Fellow, St Mary's Hospital Medical School, 1947–49; Lecturer and Sen. Lecturer in Physiology, St Mary's Hospital Medical School, 1949–55; Senior Lecturer in Physiology, King's College, 1955–56; University Reader in Physiology at King's College, 1956–60. FRSocMed. Member: Royal Institution of Gt Britain; Physiological Society. *Publications*: Membrane Transport of Sugars, chapter in Carbohydrate Metabolism and its Disorders; Permeability, chapter in Recent Advances in Physiology; also papers on similar topics in (chiefly) Jl of Physiology. *Recreations*: tennis, golf. *Address*: 67 Marksbury Avenue, Kew Gardens, Richmond, Surrey. *T*: 01–876 6374.

WIDDECOMBE, James Murray, CB 1968; OBE 1959; Director-General, Supplies and Transport (Naval), Ministry of Defence, 1968–70, retired; *b* 7 Jan. 1910; *s* of late Charles Frederick Widdecombe and late Alice Widdecombe; *m* 1936, Rita Noreen Plummer; one *s* one *d*. *Educ*: Devonport High Sch. Asst Naval Armament Supply Officer, Portsmouth, Holton Heath and Chatham, 1929–35; Dep. Naval Armt Supply Officer, Chatham, 1936; OC, RN Armt Depot, Gibraltar, 1936–40; Naval Armt Supply Officer: Admty, 1940–43; Levant, 1943–44. Capt. (SP) RNVR. Sen. Armt Supply Officer: Staff of C-in-C, Med., 1944–46; Admty, 1946–50; Asst Dir of Armt Supply, Admty, 1950–51, and 1956–59; Suptg Naval Armt Supply Officer, Portsmouth, 1951–53; Prin. Naval Armt Supply Officer, Staff of C-in-C, Far East, 1953–56; Dep. Dir of Armt Supply, Admiralty, 1959–61; Dir of Victualling, Admty, 1961–66; Head of RN Supply and Transport Service, MoD, 1966–68; special duties, Management Services, MoD, 1970–73. Gen. Sec., CS Retirement Fellowship, 1973–79. FBIM; FInstPS. *Recreations*: golf, gardening, amateur dramatics. *Address*: 1 Manor Close, Haslemere, Surrey GU27 1PP. *T*: Haslemere 2899. *Clubs*: Hindhead Golf, Navy Department Golfing Society.

WIDDICOMBE, David Graham; QC 1965; a Recorder, since 1985; *b* 7 Jan. 1924; *s* of Aubrey Guy Widdicombe and Margaret (*née* Puddy); *m* 1961, Anastasia Cecilia (*née* Leech) (marr. diss. 1983); two *s* one *d*. *Educ*: St Albans Sch.; Queen's Coll., Cambridge (BA 1st cl. Hons; LLB 1st cl. Hons; MA). Called to the Bar, Inner Temple, 1950, Bencher, 1973; Attorney at Law, State Bar of California, 1986. Mem., Cttee on Local Govt Rules of Conduct, 1973–74; Chairman: Oxfordshire Structure Plan Examination in Public, 1977; Cttee of Inquiry into Conduct of Local Authority Business, 1985–86. *Publication*: (ed) Ryde on Rating, 1968–83. *Address*: 2 Mitre Court Buildings, Temple, EC4Y 7BX. *T*: 01–583 1380; 5 Albert Terrace, NW1 7SU. *T*: 01–586 5209. *Clubs*: Athenæum, Garrick.

WIDDOWS, Air Commodore Charles; see Widdows, Air Commodore S. C.

WIDDOWS, Roland Hewlett; Special Commissioner of Income Tax, since 1977, Presiding Commissioner, since 1984; *b* 14 Aug. 1921; *s* of late A. E. Widdows, CB; *m* 1945, Diana Gweneth, *d* of late E. A. Dickson, Malayan Civil Service; two *s* one *d*. *Educ*: Stowe Sch.; Hertford Coll., Oxford (MA). Served in Royal Navy, Coastal Forces, 1941–45. Called to Bar, Middle Temple, 1948; entered Inland Revenue Solicitor's Office, 1951; Asst Solicitor, 1963; on staff of Law Commission, 1965–70; Lord Chancellor's Office, 1970–77; Under Secretary, 1972. *Recreation*: sailing. *Address*: 36 Gordon Road, Claygate, Surrey KT10 0PQ. *T*: Esher 62532. *Club*: United Oxford & Cambridge University.

WIDDOWS, Air Commodore (Stanley) Charles, CB 1959; DFC 1941 (despatches twice); RAF retired; People's Deputy, States of Guernsey, 1973–79; *b* 4 Oct. 1909; *s* of P. L. Widdows, Southend, Bradfield, Berkshire; *m* 1939, Irene Ethel, *d* of S. H. Rawlings, Ugley, Essex; two *s*. *Educ*: St Bartolomew's School, Newbury; No 1 School of Technical Training, RAF, Halton; Royal Air Force College, Cranwell. Commissioned, 1931; Fighting Area, RAF, 1931–32; RAF Middle East, Sudan and Palestine, 1933–37; Aeroplane and Armament Experimental Estab., 1937–40; OC 29 (Fighter) Sqdn, 1940–41; OC RAF West Malling, 1941–42; Gp Capt., Night Ops, HQ 11 and 12 Gp, 1942; SASO, No 85 (Base Defence) Gp, 1943–44, for Operation Overlord; Gp Capt. Organisation, Supreme HQ, Allied Expeditionary Air Force, 1944; OC, RAF Wahn, Germany, 1944–46; RAF Instructor, Sen. Officers War Course, RNC, Greenwich, 1946–48; Fighter Command, 1948–54; SASO HQ No 12 Gp; Chief Instructor, Air Defence Wing, School of Land/Air Warfare; Sector Commander, Eastern Sector. Imperial Defence College, 1955; Director of Operations (Air Defence), Air Ministry, 1956–58. *Address*: Les Granges de Beauvoir, Rohais, St Peter Port, Guernsey, CI. *T*: Guernsey 20219.

WIDDOWSON, Dr Elsie May, CBE 1979; FRS 1976; Department of Medicine, Addenbrooke's Hospital, Cambridge, since 1972; *b* 21 Oct. 1906; *d* of Thomas Henry Widdowson and Rose Widdowson. *Educ*: Imperial Coll., London (BSc, PhD); DSc London 1948. Courtauld Inst. of Biochemistry, Mddx Hosp., 1931–33; KCH, London, 1933–38; Cambridge University: Dept of Exper. Medicine, 1938–66; Infant Nutrition Res. Div., 1966–72. President: Nutrition Soc., 1977–80; Neonatal Soc., 1978–81. Hon. DSc Manchester, 1974. 2nd Bristol-Myers Award for Distinguished Achievement in Nutrition Res., 1982; 1st European Nutrition Award, Fedn of European Nutrition Socs, 1983; Rank Prize Funds Prize for Nutrition, 1984; McCollum Award, 1985; Atwater Award, 1986. *Publications*: (with R. A. McCance) The Composition of Foods, 1940 (2nd edn 1967); (with R. A. McCance) Breads White and Brown: Their Place in Thought and Social History, 1956; contrib. Proc. Royal Soc., Jl Physiol., Biochem. Jl, Brit. Jl Nut., Arch. Dis. Child., Lancet, BMJ, Nature, Biol. Neonate, Nut. Metabol., and Ped. Res. *Address*: Orchard House, 9 Boot Lane, Barrington, Cambridge. *T*: Cambridge 870219.

WIDDOWSON, Prof. Henry George; Professor of Education, University of London, at Institute of Education, since 1977; *b* 28 May 1935; *s* of George Percival Widdowson and Edna Widdowson; *m* 1966, Dominique Dixmier; two *s*. *Educ*: Alderman Newton's Sch., Leicester; King's Coll., Cambridge (MA); Univ. of Edinburgh (PhD). Lectr, Univ. of Indonesia, 1958–61; British Council Educn Officer, Sri Lanka, 1962–63; British Council English Language Officer, Bangladesh, 1963–64, 1965–68; Lectr, Dept of Linguistics, Univ. of Edinburgh, 1968–77. Editor, Jl of Applied Linguistics, 1980–85. *Publications*: Stylistics and the Teaching of Literature, 1975; Teaching Language as Communication, 1978, French edn 1981, Ital. edn 1982; Explorations in Applied Linguistics I, 1979; Learning Purpose and Language Use, 1983; Explorations in Applied Linguistics II, 1984; editor, English in Focus series, Communicative Grammar; papers in various jls. *Recreations*: reading poetry, rumination, walking. *Address*: 151 Sheen Road, Richmond upon Thames, Surrey. *T*: 01–948 0854.

WIDDUP, Malcolm, CB 1979; retired 1981; Under-Secretary, HM Treasury, 1971–80; *b* 9 May 1920; *s* of John and Frances Ellen Widdup; *m* 1947, Margaret Ruth Anderson; one *s* one *d*. *Educ*: Giggleswick Sch.; Trinity Coll., Oxford (MA). Served War, Army, RA and Staff, 1940–45. Ministry of Food, 1946–53; HM Treasury, 1953–55; Cabinet Office, 1955–57; HM Treasury, 1957–60; Min. of Health, 1960–62; HM Treasury, 1962–66; UK Delegn to OECD, 1966–68; HM Treasury, 1968–80; Sen. Clerk, House of Lords, 1980–81. *Recreations*: sailing, gardening, music. *Address*: 2 Manor Close, East Horsley, Leatherhead, Surrey.

WIESEL, Prof. Torsten Nils, MD; Head of Laboratory of Neurobiology, Rockefeller University, since 1983; *b* 3 June 1924; *s* of Fritz S. Wiesel and Anna-Lisa Wiesel (*née* Bentzer); *m* 1st, 1956, Teeri Stenhammar (marr. diss. 1970); 2nd, 1973, Ann Yee (marr. diss. 1981); one *d*. *Educ*: Karolinska Inst., Stockholm (MD 1954). Instructor, Dept of Physiol., Karolinska Inst., 1954–55; Asst, Dept of Child Psychiatry, Karolinska Hosp., Stockholm, 1954–55; Fellow in Ophthalmol., 1955–58, Asst Prof. of Ophthalmic Physiol., 1958–59, Johns Hopkins Univ. Med. Sch., Baltimore; Harvard Medical School: Associate in Neurophysiol. and Neuropharmacol., 1959–60; Asst Prof., 1960–67; Prof. of Physiol., 1967–68; Prof. of Neurobiol., 1968–74; Chm., Dept of Neurobiol., 1973–82; Robert Winthrop Prof. of Neurobiol., 1974–83. Lectures: Ferrier, Royal Soc., 1972; Grass, Soc. for Neurosci., 1976. Member: Amer. Physiol Soc.; AAAS; Amer. Acad. of Arts and Scis; Amer. Philosophical Soc.; Soc. for Neurosci. (Pres. 1978–79); Nat. Acad. of Scis; Swedish Physiol Soc.; Foreign Mem., Royal Soc., 1982; Hon. Mem., Physiolog. Soc., 1982. Hon. AM Harvard Univ., 1967; Hon. MD Linköping, 1982; Hon. Dr of Med. and Surg. Ancona Univ., 1982; Hon. DSc Pennsylvania, 1982. Awards and Prizes: Dr Jules C. Stein, Trustees for Research to Prevent Blindness, 1971; Lewis S. Rosenstiel, Brandeis Univ., 1972; Friedenwald, Assoc. for Res. in Vision and Ophthalmology, 1975; Karl Spencer Lashley, Amer. Phil. Soc., 1977; Louisa Gross Horwitz, Columbia Univ., 1978; Dickson, Pittsburgh Univ., 1979; Ledlie, Harvard Univ., 1980; Soc. for Scholars, Johns Hopkins Univ., 1980; Nobel Prize in Physiology or Medicine, 1981. *Publications*: (contrib.) Physiological and Biochemical Aspects of Nervous Integration, 1968; (contrib.) The Organization of the Cerebral Cortex, 1981; contribs to professional jls, symposia and trans of learned socs. *Address*: Rockefeller University, 1230 York Avenue, New York, NY 10021, USA. *T*: (212) 570–7661. *Club*: Harvard (Boston).

WIESNER, Dr Jerome Bert; Institute Professor, Massachusetts Institute of Technology, since 1980 (Provost, 1966–71; President, 1971–80); *b* 30 May 1915; *s* of Joseph and Ida Friedman Wiesner; *m* 1940, Laya Wainger; three *s* one *d*. *Educ*: University of Michigan, Ann Arbor, Michigan. PhD in electrical engineering, 1950. Staff, University of Michigan, 1937–40; Chief Engineer, Library of Congress, 1940–42; Staff, MIT Radiation Lab., 1942–45; Staff, Univ. of Calif Los Alamos Lab., 1945–46; Asst Prof. of Electrical Engrg, MIT, 1946; Associate Prof. of Electrical Engrg, 1947; Prof. of Electrical Engrg, 1950–64; Dir, Res. Lab. of Electronics, 1952–61. Special Assistant to the President of the USA, for Science and Technology, The White House, 1961–64; Director, Office of Science and Technology, Exec. Office of the President, 1962–64; Chm., Tech. Assessment Adv. Council, Office of Tech. Assessment, US Congress, 1976–78. Dean of Science, MIT, 1964–66. Member, Board of Directors: Faxon Co.; Automatix; Damon Biotech; New England TV Corp.; MacArthur Foundn. *Publications*: Where Science and Politics Meet, 1965; contrib.: Modern Physics for the Engineer, 1954; Arms Control, Disarmament and National Security, 1960; Arms Control, issues for the Public, 1961; Lectures on Modern Communications, 1961; technical papers in: Science, Physical Rev., Jl Applied Physics, Scientific American, Proc. Inst. Radio Engineers, etc. *Recreations*: photography, boating. *Address*: Massachusetts Institute of Technology, Building E15–207, Cambridge, Mass 02139, USA. *T*: 253–2800. *Clubs*: Cosmos (Washington, DC); Commercial, St Botolph's (Boston); Century, Harvard Club of New York City (NY).

WIESNER, Prof. Karel František, OC 1975; FRS 1969; FRSC 1957; University Professor, University of New Brunswick, since 1976 (Research Professor, 1964–76); *b* 25 Nov. 1919; *s* of Karel Wiesner, industrialist, Chrudim, Czechoslovakia, and Eugenie Storová, Prague; *m* 1942, Blanka Pevná; one *s* (and one *d* decd). *Educ*: Gymnasium Chrudim; Charles Univ., Prague. Asst, Dept of Physical Chem., Charles Univ., Prague, 1945–46; Post-doctoral Fellow, ETH Zürich, 1946–48; Prof. of Organic Chem., Univ. of New Brunswick, 1948–62; Associate Dir of Research, Ayerst Laboratories, Montreal,

1962–64. Mem., Pontifical Acad. of Scis, 1978. Hon. DSc: New Brunswick, 1970; Western Ontario, 1972; Montreal, 1975. Gunther Award, Amer. Chem. Soc., 1983; Izaak Walton Killam Meml Prize, 1986. Order of Kyril and Methodius, 1st cl. (Bulgaria), 1981. *Publications:* about 195 research papers in various scientific periodicals. *Recreations:* tennis, ski-ing, hunting. *Address:* 814 Burden Street, Fredericton, New Brunswick E3B 4C4, Canada. *T:* 4544007.

WIGAN, Sir Alan (Lewis), 5th Bt *cr* 1898; *b* 19 Nov. 1913; second *s* of Sir Roderick Grey Wigan, 3rd Bt, and Ina (*d* 1977), *o c* of Lewis D. Wigan, Brandon Park, Suffolk; *S* brother, 1979; *m* 1950, Robina, *d* of Sir Iain Colquhoun, 7th Bt, KT, DSO; one *s* one *d*. *Educ:* Eton; Magdalen College, Oxford. Commissioned Suppl. Reserve, KRRC, 1936; served with KRRC, 1939–46; wounded and taken prisoner, Calais, 1940. Director, Charrington & Co. (Brewers), 1939–70. Master, Brewers' Co., 1958–59. *Recreations:* shooting, fishing, golf. *Heir: s* Michael Iain Wigan [*b* 3 Oct. 1951; *m* 1984, Frances (marr. diss.), *d* of late Flt-Lt Angus Barr Faucett and of Mrs Antony Reid]. *Address:* Badingham House, Badingham, Woodbridge, Suffolk. *T:* Badingham 664; Moorburn, The Lake, Kirkcudbright. *Club:* Army and Navy.

WIGDOR, Lucien Simon, CEng, MRAeS; President, L. S. Wigdor Inc., New Hampshire, since 1984; Managing Director, L. S. Wigdor Ltd, since 1976; *b* Oct. 1919; *s* of William and Adèle Wigdor; *m* 1951, Marion Louise, *d* of Henry Risner; one *s* one *d*. *Educ:* Highgate Sch.; College of Aeronautical Engineering. Served War, RAF, early helicopter pilot, 1940–46 (Sqn Ldr); Operational Research, BEA: Research Engr, 1947–51; Manager, Industrial and Corporate Develt, Boeing Vertol Corp., USA, 1951–55; Managing Dir, Tunnel Refineries Ltd, 1955–69, Vice-Chm., 1969–72; Corporate Consultant, The Boeing Company, 1960–72; Dep. Dir-Gen., CBI, 1972–76; Chief Exec., Leslie & Godwin (Holdings) Ltd, 1977–78, Dir 1977–81; Chm., Weir Pumps Ltd, 1978–81; Director: The Weir Group, 1978–81; Rothschild Investment Trust, 1977–82; Zambian Engineering Services Ltd, 1979–84; Rothschild Internat. Investments SA, 1981–82. Special Adviser on Internat. Affairs, Bayerische Hypotheken-SPTund Wechsel-SPTBank AG, 1981–83; Consultant: Lazard Bros, 1982–84; Manufacturing and Financial Services Industries (L. S. Wigdor Inc.), 1984–. *Publications:* papers to Royal Aeronautical Soc., American Helicopter Soc. *Recreations:* ski-ing, experimental engineering. *Address:* Indian Point, Little Sunapee Road, PO Box 1035, New London, New Hampshire 03257, USA. *T:* (603) 526 4456. *Clubs:* Royal Air Force; Pilgrims (New York).

WIGGIN, Alfred William, (Jerry Wiggin); TD 1970; MP (C) Weston-super-Mare since 1969; *b* 24 Feb. 1937; *e s* of late Col Sir William H. Wiggin, KCB, DSO, TD, DL, JP, and late Lady Wiggin, Worcestershire; *m* 1964, Rosemary Janet (marr. diss. 1982), *d* of David L. D. Orr; two *s* one *d*. *Educ:* Eton; Trinity Coll., Cambridge. 2nd Lieut, Queen's Own Warwickshire and Worcestershire Yeomanry (TA), 1959; Major, Royal Yeomanry, 1975–78. Contested (C), Montgomeryshire, 1964 and 1966. PPS to Lord Balniel, at MoD, later FCO, 1970–74, and to Ian Gilmour, MoD, 1971–72; Parly Sec., MAFF, 1979–81; Parly Under-Sec. of State for Armed Forces, MoD, 1981–83. Promoted Hallmarking Act, 1973. Jt Hon. Sec., Conservative Defence Cttee, 1974–75; Vice-Chm., Conservative Agricultural Cttee, 1975–79; Chm., West Country Cons. Gp, 1978–79. General Rapporteur, Economic Cttee, North Atlantic Assembly, 1976–79. *Address:* House of Commons, SW1. *T:* 01–219 4522; The Court, Axbridge, Somerset. *T:* Axbridge 732527. *Clubs:* Beefsteak, Pratt's; Royal Yacht Squadron.

WIGGIN, Jerry; *see* Wiggin, A. W.

WIGGIN, Sir John (Henry), 4th Bt *cr* 1892; MC 1946; DL; Major, Grenadier Guards, retired; *b* 3 March 1921; *s* of Sir Charles Richard Henry Wiggin, 3rd Bt, TD, and Mabel Violet Mary (*d* 1961), *d* of Sir William Jaffray, 2nd Bt; *S* father, 1972; *m* 1st, 1947, Lady Cecilia Evelyn Anson (marr. diss. 1961; she *d* 1963), *yr d* of 4th Earl of Lichfield; two *s*; 2nd, 1963, Sarah, *d* of Brigadier Stewart Forster; two *s*. *Educ:* Eton; Trinity College, Cambridge. Served War of 1939–45 (prisoner-of-war). High Sheriff, 1976, DL 1985, Warwicks. *Heir: s* Charles Rupert John Wiggin, Major, Grenadier Guards [*b* 2 July 1949; *m* 1979, Mrs Mary Burnett-Hitchcock; one *s* one *d*. *Educ:* Eton]. *Address:* Honington Hall, Shipston-on-Stour, Warwicks. *T:* Shipston-on-Stour 61434.

WIGGINS, (Anthony) John; Under Secretary, Cabinet Office, since 1985; *b* 8 July 1938; *s* of Rev. Arthur Wiggins and Mavis Wiggins (*née* Brown); *m* 1962, Jennifer Anne Walkden; one *s* one *d*. *Educ:* Highgate Sch.; The Hotchkiss Sch., Lakeville, Conn, USA; Oriel Coll., Oxford (MA). Assistant Principal, HM Treasury, 1961; Private Sec. to Permanent Under Sec., Dept of Economic Affairs, 1964–66; Principal: Dept of Economic Affairs, 1966–67; HM Treasury, 1967–69; Harkness Fellow, Harvard Univ., 1969–71 (MPA 1970); Asst Sec., HM Treasury (various posts in Domestic Economy Sector), 1972–79; Principal Private Sec. to Chancellor of the Exchequer, 1980–81; Under Sec., Dept of Energy, 1981–84 (Head of Oil Policy (Home) Div., 1981–82, Head of Oil Div. and Mem. of BNOC, 1982–84). *Recreations:* mountaineering, skiing, opera. *Address:* St Anne's, Rowley Green Road, Arkley, Barnet, Herts EN5 3HH. *T:* 01–440 4072. *Club:* Alpine.

WIGGINS, David, FBA 1978; Fellow, and Praelector in Philosophy, University College, Oxford, since 1981; *b* 8 March 1933; *s* of Norman Wiggins and Diana Wiggins (*née* Priestley); *m* 1979, Jennifer Hornsby. *Educ:* St Paul's Sch.; Brasenose Coll., Oxford. BA 1955; MA 1958. Asst Principal, Colonial Office, London 1957–58. Jane Eliza Procter Vis. Fellow, Princeton Univ., 1958–59; Lectr, 1959, then Fellow and Lecturer, 1960–67, New College, Oxford; Prof. of Philosophy, Bedford Coll., Univ. of London, 1967–80. Visiting appointments: Stanford, 1964 and 1965; Harvard, 1968 and 1972; All Souls College, 1973; Princeton, 1980; Fellow, Center for Advanced Study in the Behavioral Sciences, Stanford, 1985–86. Mem., Indep. Commn on Transport, 1973–74; Chm., Transport Users' Consultative Cttee for the South East, 1977–79. *Publications:* Identity and Spatio-Temporal Continuity, 1967; Truth, Invention and the Meaning of Life, 1978; Sameness and Substance, 1980; Needs, Values, Truth: essays in the philosophy of value, 1986; philosophical articles in Philosophical Review, Analysis, Philosophy, Synthèse; articles on environmental and transport subjects in Spectator, Times, Tribune.

WIGGINS, John; *see* Wiggins, A. J.

WIGGINS, Rt. Rev. Maxwell Lester; Bishop of Victoria Nyanza, 1963–76; retired; *b* 5 Feb. 1915; *s* of Herbert Lester and Isobel Jane Wiggins; *m* 1941, Margaret Agnes (*née* Evans); one *s* two *d*. *Educ:* Christchurch Boys' High Sch., NZ; Canterbury University College, NZ (BA). Asst Curate, St Mary's, Merivale, NZ, 1938; Vicar of Oxford, NZ, 1941; CMS Missionary, Diocese Central Tanganyika, 1945; Head Master, Alliance Secondary Sch., Dodoma, 1948; Provost, Cathedral of Holy Spirit, Dodoma, 1949; Principal, St Philip's Theological Coll., and Canon of Cathedral of Holy Spirit, Dodoma, 1954; Archdeacon of Lake Province, 1956; Asst Bishop of Central Tanganyika, 1959; Asst Bishop of Wellington, 1976–81; Gen. Sec., NZ CMS, 1982–83. *Address:* 138A Hamilton Avenue, Christchurch 4, New Zealand.

WIGGLESWORTH, Gordon Hardy; Director: Quadrant Projects, since 1982; Alan Turner Associates, architects, planning and development consultants, since 1984; *b* 27 June 1920; *m* 1952, Cherry Diana Heath; three *d*. *Educ:* Highgate; University Coll., London; Architectural Association. ARIBA; AADipl. Served War of 1939–45: Royal Engineers, 1941–46. Architectural Assoc., 1946–48; private practice and Univ. of Hong Kong, 1948–52; private practice: London, 1952–54; Hong Kong, 1954–56; London, 1956–57. Asst Chief Architect, Dept of Education and Science, 1957–67; Dir of Building Develt, MPBW, later DoE, 1967–72; Principal Architect, Educn, GLC (ILEA), 1972–74; Housing Architect, GLC, 1974–80. FRSA. *Address:* 53 Canonbury Park South, N1 2JL. *T:* 01–226 7734.

WIGGLESWORTH, Sir Vincent (Brian), Kt 1964; CBE 1951; FRS 1939; MA, MD, BCh Cantab, FRES; Retired Director, Agricultural Research Council Unit of Insect Physiology (1943–67); Quick Professor of Biology, University of Cambridge, 1952–66; Fellow of Gonville and Caius College; *b* 17 April 1899; *s* of late Sidney Wigglesworth, MRCS; *m* 1928, Mabel Katherine (*d* 1986), *d* of late Col Sir David Semple, IMS; three *s* one *d*. *Educ:* Repton; Caius Coll., Cambridge (Scholar); St Thomas' Hosp. 2nd Lt RFA, 1917–18, served in France; Frank Smart Student of Caius College, 1922–24; Lecturer in Medical Entomology in London School of Hygiene and Tropical Medicine, 1926; Reader in Entomology in University of London, 1936–44; Reader in Entomology, in University of Cambridge, 1945–52. Fellow, Imperial College, London, 1977. Hon. Member: Royal Entomological Soc.; Physiological Soc.; Soc. Experimental Biology; Assoc. Applied Biology; International Confs of Entomology; Soc. of European Endocrinologists; Royal Danish Academy of Science; Amer. Philosophical Soc.; US Nat. Academy of Sciences; American Academy of Arts and Sciences; Kaiserliche Deutsche Akademie der Naturforscher, Leopoldina; Deutsche Entomologische Gesellschaft; Amer. Soc. of Zoologists; American Entomol. Soc.; USSR Acad. of Sciences; All-Union Entomol. Soc.; Entomol. Soc. of India; Société Zoologique de France; Société Entomologique de France, Société Entomologique d'Egypte; Entomological Society of the Netherlands; Schweizerische Entomologische Gesellschaft; Indian Academy of Zoology; Corresponding Member: Accademia delle Scienze dell' Istituto di Bologna; Société de Pathologie Exotique; Entomological Soc. of Finland; Dunham Lecturer, Harvard, 1945; Woodward Lecturer, Yale, 1945; Croonian Lecturer, Royal Society, 1948; Messenger Lecturer, Cornell, 1958; Tercentenary Lecturer, Royal Society, 1960. Royal Medal, Royal Society, 1955; Swammerdam Medal, Soc. Med. Chir., Amsterdam, 1966; Gregor Mendel Gold Medal, Czechoslovak Acad. of Science, 1967; Frink Medal, Zoological Soc., 1979; Wigglesworth Medal, Royal Entomological Soc., 1981. DPhil (*hc*) University, Berne; DSc (*hc*): Paris, Newcastle and Cambridge. *Publications:* Insect Physiology, 1934; The Principles of Insect Physiology, 1939; The Physiology of Insect Metamorphosis, 1954; The Life of Insects, 1964; Insect Hormones, 1970; Insects and the Life of Man, 1976; numerous papers on comparative physiology. *Address:* 14 Shilling Street, Lavenham, Suffolk. *T:* Lavenham 247293.

See also W. R. B. Wigglesworth.

WIGGLESWORTH, William Robert Brian; Deputy Director General of Telecommunications, since 1984; *b* 8 Aug. 1937; *s* of Sir Vincent Wigglesworth, *qv*; *m* 1969, Susan Mary, *d* of late Arthur Baker, JP, Lavenham; one *s* one *d*. *Educ:* Marlborough; Magdalen College, Oxford (BA). Nat. Service, 2nd Lieut, Royal Signals, 1956–58. Ranks, Hovis McDougall Ltd, 1961–70: trainee; Gen. Manager, Mother's Pride Bakery, Cheltenham; PA to Group Chief Exec.; Gen. Manager, Baughans of Colchester; Board of Trade, 1970; Fair Trading Div., Dept of Prices and Consumer Protection, 1975; Posts and Telecommunications Div., 1978, Inf. Tech. Div., 1982, Dept of Industry. *Recreations:* fishing, gardening, history. *Address:* Office of Telecommunications, Atlantic House, Holborn Viaduct, EC1 2HQ. *T:* 01–822 1604.

WIGHAM, Eric Leonard, CBE 1967; Labour Correspondent, The Times, 1946–69; *b* 8 Oct. 1904; *s* of Leonard and Caroline Nicholson Wigham; *m* 1929, Jane Dawson; one *d*. *Educ:* Ackworth and Bootham Schools; Birmingham University (MA). Reporter on Newcastle upon Tyne papers, 1925–32; Manchester Evening News, 1932–45; War Correspondent, The Observer and Manchester Evening News, 1944–45; Labour Correspondent, Manchester Guardian, 1945–46. Member, Royal Commission on Trade Unions and Employers' Associations, 1965–68. Order of King Leopold II (Belgium), 1945. *Publications:* Trade Unions, 1956; What's Wrong with the Unions?, 1961; The Power to Manage: a history of the Engineering Employers' Federation, 1973; Strikes and the Government 1893–1974, 1976, 2nd edn, 1893–1981, 1982; From Humble Petition to Militant Action: a history of the Civil and Public Services Association, 1903–1978, 1980. *Recreation:* gardening. *Address:* Link View, The Avenue, West Wickham, Kent BR4 0DX. *T:* 01–776 0397.

WIGHT, James Alfred, OBE 1979; FRCVS; practising veterinary surgeon, since 1939; author, since 1970; *b* 3 Oct. 1916; *s* of James Henry and Hannah Wight; *m* 1941, Joan Catherine Danbury; one *s* one *d*. *Educ:* Hillhead High Sch.; Glasgow Veterinary Coll. FRCVS 1982. Started in general veterinary practice in Thirsk, Yorks, 1940, and has been there ever since with the exception of war-time service with the RAF. Began to write at the ripe age of 50 and quite unexpectedly became a best-selling author of books on his veterinary experiences which have been translated into all European languages and many others, incl. Japanese. Hon. Mem., British Vet. Assoc., 1975. Hon. DLitt Heriot-Watt, 1979; Hon. DVSc Liverpool, 1983. *Publications:* (as James Herriot): If Only They Could Talk, 1970; It Shouldn't Happen to a Vet, 1972; All Creatures Great and Small, (USA) 1972; Let Sleeping Vets Lie, 1973; All Things Bright and Beautiful, (USA) 1973; Vet in Harness, 1974; Vets Might Fly, 1976; Vet in a Spin, 1977; James Herriot's Yorkshire, 1979; The Lord God Made Them All, 1981; The Best of James Herriot, 1982; Moses the Kitten (for children), 1984; Only One Woof (for children), 1985; James Herriot's Dog Stories, 1985. *Recreations:* music, dog-walking. *Address:* Mire Beck, Thirlby, Thirsk, Yorks YO7 2DJ.

WIGHTWICK, Charles Christopher Brooke, MA; HM Inspector of Schools, since 1980; *b* 16 Aug. 1931; *s* of Charles Frederick Wightwick and Marion Frances Wightwick (*née* Smith); *m* 1955, Pamela Layzell (marr. diss. 1986); one *s* two *d*; *m* 1986, Gillian Rosemary Anderson (*née* Dalziel). *Educ:* St Michael's, Otford Court; Lancing Coll.; St Edmund Hall, Oxford. BA 1954, MA 1958. Asst Master, Hurstpierpoint Coll., 1954–59; Head of German, Denstone Coll., 1959–65; Head of Languages, then Director of Studies, Westminster Sch., 1965–75; Head Master, King's College Sch., Wimbledon, 1975–80. FRSA 1980. *Publication:* (co-author) Longman Audio-Lingual German, 3 vols., 1974–78. *Recreations:* photography, running, judo, language. *Address:* 19 Nottingham Road, SW17 7EA. *T:* 01–767 6161.

WIGLEY, Dafydd; MP (Plaid Cymru) Caenarfon since Feb. 1974; President, Plaid Cymru, 1981–84; industrial economist; *b* April 1943; *s* of Elfyn Edward Wigley, former County Treasurer, Caernarfonshire CC; *m* Elinor Bennett (*née* Owen), *d* of Emrys Bennett Owen, Dolgellau; one *s* one *d* (and two *s* decd). *Educ:* Caernarfon Grammar Sch.; Rydal Sch., Colwyn Bay; Manchester Univ. Ford Motor Co., 1964–67; Chief Cost Accountant and Financial Planning Manager, Mars Ltd, 1967–71; Financial Controller, Hoover Ltd, Merthyr Tydfil, 1971–74. Mem., Merthyr Tydfil Borough Council, 1972–74. Vice-Chm., Parly Social Services Gp, 1985–; Mem., Select Cttee on Welsh Affairs, 1983–.

Sponsor, Disabled Persons Act, 1981. Vice-Pres., Nat. Fedn of Industrial Develt Authorities, 1981–. Member: Nat. Cttee for Electoral Reform; ASTMS. Pres., Spastic Soc. of Wales, 1985–. *Publication*: An Economic Plan for Wales, 1970. *Address*: House of Commons, SW1A 0AA.

WIGNER, Prof. Eugene P(aul); Thomas D. Jones Professor of Mathematical Physics of Princeton University, 1938–71, retired; *b* 17 Nov. 1902; *s* of Anthony and Elizabeth Wigner; *m* 1st, 1936, Amelia Z. Frank (*d* 1937); 2nd, 1941, Mary Annette Wheeler (*d* 1977); one *s* one *d*; 3rd, 1979, Eileen C. P. Hamilton. *Educ*: Technische Hochschule, Berlin, Dr Ing. 1925. Asst and concurrently Extraordinary Prof., Technische Hochschule, Berlin, 1926–35; Lectr, Princeton Univ., 1930, half-time Prof. of Mathematical Physics, 1931–36. Mem. Gen. Adv. Cttee to US Atomic Energy Commn, 1952–57, 1959–64; Director: Nat. Acad. of Sciences Harbor Project for Civil Defense, 1963; Civil Defense Project, Oak Ridge Nat. Lab., 1964–65. Pres., Amer. Physical Soc., 1956 (Vice-Pres., 1955); Member: Amer. Physical Soc.; Amer. Assoc. of Physics Teachers; Amer. Math. Soc.; Amer. Nuclear Soc.; Amer. Assoc. for Adv. of Scis; Sigma Xi; Franklin Inst.; German Physical Soc.; Royal Netherlands Acad. of Science and Letters, 1960; Foreign Mem., Royal Soc., 1970; Corresp. Mem. Acad. of Science, Göttingen, 1951; Austrian Acad. Sciences, 1968; Nat. Acad. Sci. (US); Amer. Philos. Soc.; Amer. Acad. Sci. Hon. Mem., Eötvös Lorand Soc., Hungary, 1976. Citation, NJ Sci. Teachers' Assoc., 1951. US Government Medal for Merit, 1946; Franklin Medal, 1950; Fermi Award, 1958; Atoms for Peace Award, 1960; Max Planck Medal of German Phys. Soc., 1961; Nobel Prize for Physics, 1963; George Washington Award, Amer. Hungarian Studies Assoc., 1964; Semmelweiss Medal, Amer. Hungarian Med. Assoc., 1965; US Nat. Medal for Science, 1969; Pfizer Award, 1971; Albert Einstein Award, 1972; Wigner Medal, 1978. Holds numerous hon. doctorates. *Publications*: Nuclear Structure (with L. Eisenbud), 1958; The Physical Theory of Neutron Chain Reactors (with A. M. Weinberg), 1958; Group Theory (orig. in German, 1931), English trans., NY, 1959 (trans. Hungarian, Russian, 1979); Symmetries and Reflections, 1967 (trans. Hungarian, Russian, 1971); Survival and the Bomb, 1969. *Address*: 8 Ober Road, Princeton, NJ 08540, USA. *T*: 609–924–1189. *Club*: Cosmos (Washington, DC).

WIGODER, family name of **Baron Wigoder**.

WIGODER, Baron *cr* 1974 (Life Peer), of Cheetham in the City of Manchester; **Basil Thomas Wigoder**, QC 1966; Chairman, British United Provident Association, since 1981; *b* 12 Feb. 1921; *s* of late Dr P. I. Wigoder and Mrs R. R. Wigoder, JP, Manchester; *m* 1948, Yoland Levinson; three *s* one *d*. *Educ*: Manchester Gram. Sch.; Oriel Coll., Oxford (Open Scholar, Mod. Hist.; MA 1946). Served RA, 1942–45. Pres. Oxford Union, 1946. Called to Bar, Gray's Inn, 1946, Master of the Bench, 1972. A Recorder of the Crown Court, 1972–84. BoT Inspector, Pinnock Finance (GB) Ltd, 1967. Member: Council of Justice, 1960–; Gen. Council of the Bar, 1970–74; Crown Court Rules Cttee, 1971–77; Council on Tribunals, 1980–; Home Office Adv. Cttee on Service Candidates, 1984–; Chm., Health Services Bd, 1977–80. Chm., Liberal Party Exec., 1963–65; Chm., Liberal Party Organising Cttee, 1965–66; Liberal Chief Whip, House of Lords, 1977–84 (Dep. Whip, 1976–77). Contested (L): Bournemouth, 1945 and by-election, Oct. 1945; Westbury, 1959 and 1964. Vice-President: Nuffield Hosps, 1981–; Statute Law Soc., 1984–; Mem. Court, Nene Coll., 1982–; Trustee, Oxford Union Soc., 1982–. *Recreations*: cricket, music. *Address*: House of Lords, SW1. *Clubs*: National Liberal, MCC.

WIGRAM, family name of **Baron Wigram**.

WIGRAM, 2nd Baron, *cr* 1935, of Clewer; **George Neville Clive Wigram**, MC 1945; JP; DL; *b* 2 Aug. 1915; *s* of Clive, 1st Baron Wigram, PC, GCB, GCVO, CSI, and Nora Mary (*d* 1956), *d* of Sir Neville Chamberlain, KCB, KCVO; *S* father 1960; *m* 1941, Margaret Helen (*d* 1986), *yr d* of late General Sir Andrew Thorne, KCB, CMG, DSO; one *s* two *d*. *Educ*: Winchester and Magdalen College, Oxford. Page of Honour to HM King George V, 1925–32; served in Grenadier Guards, 1937–57: Military Secretary and Comptroller to Governor-General of New Zealand, 1946–49; commanded 1st Bn Grenadier Guards, 1955–56. Governor of Westminster Hospital, 1967. JP Gloucestershire, 1959, DL 1969. Heir: *s* Major Hon. Andrew (Francis Clive) Wigram, MVO, Grenadier Guards [*b* 18 March 1949; *m* 1974, Gabrielle Diana, *y d* of late R. D. Moore; three *s*]. *Address*: Poulton Fields, Cirencester, Gloucestershire. *T*: Poulton 250. *Club*: Cavalry and Guards.

WIGRAM, Rev. Canon Sir Clifford Woolmore, 7th Bt, *cr* 1805; Vicar of Marston St Lawrence with Warkworth, near Banbury, 1945–83, also of Thenford, 1975–83; Non-Residentiary Canon of Peterborough Cathedral, 1973–83, Canon Emeritus since 1983; *b* 24 Jan. 1911; *er s* of late Robert Ainger Wigram and Evelyn Dorothy, *d* of C. W. E. Henslowe; *S* uncle, 1935; *m* 1948, Christobel Joan Marriott (*d* 1983), *d* of late William Winter Goode. *Educ*: Winchester; Trinity Coll., Cambridge. Asst Priest at St Ann's, Brondesbury, 1934–37; Chaplain Ely Theological College, 1937. *Heir*: *b* Maj. Edward Robert Woolmore Wigram, Indian Army [*b* 19 July 1913; *m* 1944, Viva Ann, *d* of late Douglas Bailey, Laughton Lodge, near Lewes, Sussex; one *d*. *Educ*: Winchester; Trinity Coll., Cambridge. Attached 2nd Batt. South Staffordshire Regt, Bangalore, 1935; Major, 19th KGO Lancers, Lahore, 1938]. *Address*: Little Lyon Mead, 40 High Street, Chard, Som TA20 1QL.

WIGRAM, Derek Roland, MA, BSc (Econ.); Headmaster of Monkton Combe School, near Bath, 1946–68; *b* 18 Mar. 1908; *er s* of late Roland Lewis Wigram and of Mildred (*née* Willock); *m* 1944, Catharine Mary, *d* of late Very Rev. W. R. Inge, KCVO, DD, former Dean of St Paul's; one *s* one *d*. *Educ*: Marlborough Coll.; Peterhouse, Cambridge (Scholar). 1st Class Hons Classical Tripos, 1929; 2nd Class Hons Economics and Political Science, London, 1943; Assistant Master and Careers Master, Whitgift School, Croydon, 1929–36; House Master and Careers Master, Bryanston School, 1936–46. Hon. Associate Mem., Headmasters' Conf. (Chm., 1963–64); Vice-Pres., CMS (Chm., Exec. Cttee, 1956–58, 1969–72); Patron, Oxford Conf. in Education; Mem., Council of Lee Abbey; Mem. Adv. Council and Associate Consultant, Christian Orgns Research and Adv. Trust. Bishops' Inspector of Theological Colls (Mem. Archbishops' Commn, 1970–71). *Publication*: (Jt Editor) Hymns for Church and School, 1964. *Address*: 23 The Pastures, Westwood, Bradford on Avon, Wilts. *T*: Bradford on Avon 2362.

WIIN-NIELSEN, Aksel Christopher, Fil.Dr; Director, Danish Meteorological Office, since 1984; *b* 17 Dec. 1924; *s* of Aage Nielsen and Marie Petre (*née* Kristoffersen); *m* 1953, Bente Havsteen (*née* Zimsen); three *d*. *Educ*: Univ of Copenhagen (MSc 1950); Univ. of Stockholm (Fil.Lic. 1957; Fil.Dr 1960). Danish Meteorol Inst., 1952–55; Staff Member: Internat. Meteorol Inst., Stockholm, 1955–58; Jt Numerical Weather Prediction Unit, Suitland, Md, USA, 1959–61; Asst Dir, Nat. Center for Atmospherical Research, Boulder, Colorado, 1961–63; Prof., Dept of Atmospheric and Oceanic Sci., Univ. of Michigan, 1963–73; Dir, European Centre for Medium-Range Weather Forecasts, Reading, 1974–79; Sec.-Gen., WMO, 1980–83. Member: Finnish Acad. of Arts and Scis; Royal Swedish Acad. of Sci.; Danish Acad. of Technical Scis, 1984–; Danish Royal Soc., 1986–; Hon. Mem., RMetS. Hon. DSc: Reading, 1982; Copenhagen, 1986. Buys Ballot Medal, Royal Netherlands Acad., 1982; Wihuri Internat. Prize, Finland, 1983. *Publications*:

Dynamic Meteorology, 1970; over 100 scientific publications. *Recreation*: tennis. *Address*: Solbakken 6, 3230 Graested, Denmark.

WILBERFORCE, family name of **Baron Wilberforce**.

WILBERFORCE, Baron, *cr* 1964 (Life Peer); **Richard Orme Wilberforce**, PC 1964; Kt 1961; CMG 1956; OBE 1944; a Lord of Appeal in Ordinary, 1964–82; Fellow, All Souls College, Oxford, since 1932; *b* 11 Mar. 1907; *s* of late S. Wilberforce; *m* 1947, Yvette, *d* of Roger Lenoan, Judge of Court of Cassation, France; one *s* one *d*. *Educ*: Winchester; New College, Oxford. Served War, 1939–46; returned to Bar, 1947; QC 1954; Judge of the High Court of Justice (Chancery Division), 1961–64; Bencher, Middle Temple, 1961. Chm. Exec. Council, Internat. Law Assoc.; Mem., Permanent Court of Arbitration; President: Fédération Internationale du Droit Européen, 1978; Appeal Tribunal, Lloyd's of London, 1983–. Jt Pres., Anti-Slavery Soc.; Vice-President: (jt) RCM; David Davies Meml Inst. Chancellor, Univ. of Hull, 1978–; Univ. of Oxford: High Steward, 1967–; Visitor, Wolfson Coll., 1974; Visitor, Linacre Coll., 1983; Hon. Fellow, New Coll., 1965. Hon. FRCM. Hon. Comp. Royal Aeronautical Society. Hon. Mem., Scottish Faculty of Advocates, 1978. Hon. DCL Oxon, 1968; Hon. LLD: London, 1972; Hull, 1973; Bristol, 1983. Diplôme d'Honneur, Corp. des Vignerons de Champagne. US Bronze Star, 1944. *Publications*: The Law of Restrictive Trade Practices, 1956; articles and pamphlets on Air Law and International Law. *Recreations*: the turf, travel, opera. *Address*: House of Lords, SW1. *Club*: Athenæum.

WILBERFORCE, Robert, CBE 1924; retired; *b* 8 Dec. 1887; 2nd *s* of H. E. Wilberforce; *m* 1914, Hope Elizabeth (*d* 1970), *d* of Schuyler N. Warren, New York. *Educ*: Beaumont and Stonyhurst; Balliol College, Oxford. BA 1912, Honour School of Modern History; War Trade Intelligence Department, 1915–16; Attaché HM Legation to Holy See, 1917–19; called to Bar, Inner Temple, 1921; Member of British Delegation to Washington Disarmament Conference, 1921–22; Carnegie Endowment International Mission to Vatican Library (arranged pubn, in assoc. with author, of Eppstein's Catholic Tradition of the Law of Nations), 1927; British Delegation to Geneva Disarmament Conference, 1932 and 1933; Director British Information Services, New York; retired 1952. As *g g s* of William Wilberforce, headed family deleg. at internat. thanksgiving service commemorating his life and work, Westminster Abbey, 1983. *Publications*: Meditations in Verse; Foreword to A Rug Primer, by Hope Elizabeth Wilberforce, 1979; articles and reviews in various periodicals. *Address*: St Teresa's, Corston, near Bath, Avon BA2 9AG. *T*: Saltford 2607.

WILBERFORCE, William John Antony, CMG 1981; HM Diplomatic Service; High Commissioner in Cyprus, since 1982; *b* 3 Jan. 1930; *s* of late Lt-Col W. B. Wilberforce and Cecilia (*née* Dormer); *m* 1953, Laura Lyon, *d* of late Howard Sykes, Englewood, NJ; one *s* two *d*. *Educ*: Ampleforth; Christ Church, Oxford. Army National Service, 2nd Lieut KOYLI, 1948–49. HM Foreign Service, 1953; served: Oslo, 1955–57; Berlin, 1957–59; Ankara, 1962–64; Abidjan, 1964–67; Asst Head of UN (Econ. and Social) Dept, 1967–70, and of Southern European Dept, 1970–72; Counsellor, 1972–74, and Head of Chancery, 1974–75, Washington; Hd of Defence Dept, FCO, 1975–78; Asst Under-Sec., RCDS, 1979; Leader of UK Delegn to Madrid Conf. on Security and Cooperation in Europe Review Meeting, with rank of Ambassador, 1980–82. Hon. DHum Wilberforce, 1973. *Recreations*: the turf, travel, gardening. *Address*: c/o Foreign and Commonwealth Office, SW1; Markington Hall, Harrogate, N Yorks. *T*: Ripon 87356. *Club*: Athenæum.

WILBRAHAM; *see* Bootle-Wilbraham, family name of Baron Skelmersdale.

WILBRAHAM, Sir Richard B.; *see* Baker Wilbraham.

WILBY, John Ronald William, CMG 1961; Professor of International Trade and Finance, Seattle University, 1967–81, now Emeritus; *b* 1 Sept. 1906; *s* of Thomas Wilby and Gertrude Snowdon; *m* 1944, Winifred Russell Walker; no *c*. *Educ*: Batley School; University of Leeds. Board of Inland Revenue, 1928–46; Board of Trade (Principal), 1946–49; First Secretary (Commercial), British Embassy, Washington, 1949–53; British Trade Commissioner, Ottawa, 1953–55; Principal British Trade Commissioner in Ontario, Canada, 1955–64; Consul-General in Seattle, 1964–67. *Recreations*: sailing, music. *Address*: 185 34th Avenue E, Seattle, Washington 98112, USA. *T*: EA5–6999.

WILCOCK, Prof. William Leslie; Professor of Physics, University College of North Wales, Bangor, since 1965; *b* 7 July 1922. *Educ*: Manchester Univ. (BSc, PhD). Imperial Coll. of Science and Technology, London, 1956–65, Reader in Applied Physics, 1961–65. Mem., SERC, 1981–85. *Publications*: Advances in Electronics and Electron Physics, vols 12–15 (ed jtly), 1960–61; numerous papers in scientific jls. *Address*: School of Physical and Molecular Sciences, University College of North Wales, Bangor LL57 2UW.

WILCOX, Albert Frederick, CBE 1967; QPM 1957; Chief Constable of Hertfordshire, 1947–69, retired; *b* 18 April 1909; *s* of late Albert Clement Wilcox, Ashley Hill, Bristol; *m* 1939, Ethel, *d* of late E. H. W. Wilmott, Manor House, Whitchurch, Bristol; one *s* two *d*. *Educ*: Fairfield Grammar School, Bristol. Joined Bristol City Police, 1929; Hendon Police Coll., 1934; Metropolitan Police, 1934–43. Served Allied Mil. Govt, Italy and Austria (Lt-Col), 1943–46. Asst Chief Constable of Buckinghamshire, 1946. Cropwood Fellowship, Inst. of Criminology, Cambridge, 1969. Pres. Assoc. of Chief Police Officers, Eng. and Wales, 1966–67; Chm. of Management Cttee, Police Dependents' Trust, 1967–69. Regional Police Commander (designate), 1962–69. Member, Parole Board, 1970–73. Criminological Res. Fellowship, Council of Europe, 1974–76. Barrister-at-Law, Gray's Inn, 1941. Mem. Edit. Bd, Criminal Law Review. *Publication*: The Decision to Prosecute, 1972. *Address*: 34 Roundwood Park, Harpenden, Herts.

WILCOX, David John Reed; **His Honour Judge David Wilcox**; a Circuit Judge, since 1985; *b* 8 March 1939; *s* of Leslie Leonard Kennedy Wilcox and Margaret Ada Reed Wilcox (*née* Rapson); *m* 1962, Wendy Feay Christine Whiteley; one *s* one *d*. *Educ*: Wednesbury Boys' High Sch.; King's Coll., London (LLB Hons). Called to the Bar, Gray's Inn, 1962. Directorate, Army Legal Services (Captain): Legal Staff, 1962–63; Legal Aid, Far East Land Forces, Singapore, 1963–65. Crown Counsel, Hong Kong, 1965–68; Member, Hong Kong Bar, 1968; in practice, Midland and Midland and Oxford Circuits, 1968–85; a Recorder of the Crown Court, 1979–85. *Recreations*: reading, gardening. *Address*: The Garden House, 14a Park Terrace, Nottingham NG1 5DN. *T*: Nottingham 473960.

WILCOX, Rev. Rt. David Peter; *see* Dorking, Bishop Suffragan of.

WILCOX, Desmond John; independent television producer/reporter; journalist and author; *b* 21 May 1931; *e s* of John Wallace Wilcox and Alice May Wilcox; *m* 1st, (marr. diss.); one *s* two *d*; 2nd, 1977, Esther Rantzen, *qv*; one *s* two *d*. *Educ*: Cheltenham Grammar Sch.; Christ's Coll., London; Outward Bound Sea Sch. Sail training apprentice, 1947; Deckhand, Merchant Marine, 1948; Reporter, weekly papers, 1949; commissioned Army, National Service, 1949–51; News Agency reporter, 1951–52; Reporter and Foreign Correspondent, Daily Mirror, incl. New York Bureau and UN, 1952–60; Reporter, This

Week, ITV, 1960–65; joined BBC 1965: Co-Editor/Presenter, Man Alive, 1965; formed Man Alive Unit, 1968; Head of General Features, BBC TV, 1972–80; Writer/Presenter, Americans, TV documentary, 1979; Presenter/Chm., Where it Matters, ITV discussion series, 1981; Producer/Presenter BBC TV series: The Visit, 1982, 1984–86; The Marriage, 1986; Presenter, 60 Minutes, BBC TV, 1983–84. SFTA Award for best factual programme series, 1967; Richard Dimbleby Award, SFTA, for most important personal contrib. in factual television, 1971. *Publications:* (jtly) Explorers, 1975; Americans, 1978; (with Esther Rantzen) Kill the Chocolate Biscuit: or Behind the Screen, 1981; (with Esther Rantzen) Baby Love, 1985. *Recreations:* offshore sail cruising, gardening, television. *Address:* 11 Lichfield Road, Kew Gardens, Surrey TW9 3JR. *T:* 01–940 6722. *Clubs:* Arts, BBC.

WILCOX, Esther Louise, (Mrs Desmond Wilcox); *see* Rantzen, E. L.

WILD, Dr David; Director of Professional Services, South West (Teaching) Regional Health Authority, since 1982; *b* 27 Jan. 1930; *s* of Frederick and Lena Wild; *m* 1954, Dr Sheila Wightman; one *s* one *d. Educ:* Manchester Grammar Sch.; Univ. of Manchester (MB, ChB); Univ. of Liverpool (DPH; FFCM, DMA). Deputy County Medical Officer, 1962, Area Medical Officer, 1974, West Sussex. Editor (with Dr Brian Williams), Community Medicine, 1978–84. *Publications:* contribs Jl Central Council of Health Educn, Medical Officer. *Recreation:* conversation. *Address:* 16 Brandy Hole Lane, Chichester, Sussex PO19 4RY. *T:* Chichester 527125; 13 Surrendale Place, W9. *T:* 01–289 7257. *Club:* Royal Society of Medicine.

WILD, David Humphrey; His Honour Judge Wild; a Circuit Judge, since 1972; *b* 24 May 1927; *s* of John S. Wild and Edith Lemarchand; *m* 1963, Estelle Grace Prowett, *d* of James Marshall, Aberdeen and Malaya; one *s. Educ:* Whitgift Middle Sch., Croydon. Served War of 1939–45, Royal Navy, 1944–48. Called to Bar, Middle Temple, 1951. Practised, London and SE Circuit, 1951–58, Midland Circuit, 1958–72; resident judge, Cambridge Crown Court, 1973–84. Councillor, Oundle and Thrapston RDC, 1968–72. Mem., St Catharine's Coll., Cambridge, 1973. *Publication:* The Law of Hire Purchase, 1960 (2nd edn, 1964). *Clubs:* Naval and Military, Savile; Luffenham Heath Golf.

WILD, Rt. Rev. Eric; Bishop Suffragan of Reading, 1972–82; an Assistant Bishop, Diocese of Oxford, since 1982; *b* 6 Nov. 1914; *s* of R. E. and E. S. Wild; *m* 1946, Frances Moyra, *d* of late Archibald and Alice Reynolds; one *s* one *d. Educ:* Manchester Grammar School; Keble College, Oxford. Ordained deacon 1937, priest 1938, Liverpool Cathedral; Curate, St Anne, Stanley, 1937–40; Curate, St James, Haydock, 1940–42; Chaplain, RNVR, 1942–46; Vicar, St George, Wigan, 1946–52; Vicar, All Saints, Hindley, 1952–59; Director of Religious Education, Dio. Peterborough, 1959–62; Rector, Cranford with Grafton Underwood, 1959–62; Canon of Peterborough, 1961, Emeritus, 1962; Gen. Sec. of National Society and Secretary of C of E Schools Council, 1962–67; Rector of Milton, 1967–72; Archdeacon of Berks, 1967–73. *Publications:* articles in periodicals; reviews, etc. *Recreations:* gardening and walking. *Address:* 2 Speen Place, Speen, Newbury, Berks. *Club:* Army and Navy.

WILD, Major Hon. Gerald Percy, AM 1980; MBE 1941; Company Director; Agent-General for Western Australia in London, 1965–71; *b* 2 Jan. 1908; *m* 1944, Virginia Mary Baxter; two *s* one *d. Educ:* Shoreham Gram. Sch., Sussex; Chivers Acad., Portsmouth, Hants. Served War of 1939–45 (despatches, MBE): Middle East, Greece, Crete, Syria, New Guinea and Moratai, Netherlands East Indies (Major). Elected MLA for Western Australia, 1947; Minister for Housing and Forests, 1950–53; Minister for Works and Water Supplies and Labour (WA), 1959–65. JP Perth (WA), 1953. *Recreations:* golf, tennis, cricket, football. *Address:* 80 Culeenup Road, North Yunderup, WA 6208, Australia. *T:* 450.1910. *Clubs:* East India, Devonshire, Sports and Public Schools, MCC; Naval and Military, Western Australia, West Australian Turf (WA).

WILD, Very Rev. John Herbert Severn, MA Oxon; Hon. DD Durham, 1958; Dean of Durham, 1951–73, Dean Emeritus, since 1973; *b* 22 Dec. 1904; *e s* of Right Rev. Herbert Louis Wild and Helen Christian, *d* of Walter Severn; *m* 1945, Margaret Elizabeth Everard, *d* of G. B. Wainwright, OBE, MB. *Educ:* Clifton Coll.; Brasenose College, Oxford (Scholar); represented Oxford against Cambridge at Three Miles, 1927; Westcott House, Cambridge. Curate of St Aidan, Newcastle upon Tyne, 1929–33; Chaplain-Fellow of University College, Oxford, 1933–45; Master, 1945–51; Hon. Fellow, 1951–; Select Preacher, Univ. of Oxford, 1948–49. Church Comr, 1958–73. ChStJ, 1966–. *Recreations:* fishing, walking. *Address:* Deacons Farmhouse, Rapps, Ilminster, Somerset TA19 9LG. *T:* Ilminster 3398. *Club:* United Oxford & Cambridge University.

WILD, Dr John Paul, AC 1986; CBE 1978; FRS 1970; FAA 1962; FTS 1978; Chairman and Chief Executive, Commonwealth Scientific and Industrial Research Organization, 1979–85 (Associate Member of Executive, 1977; Chief, Division of Radiophysics, 1971); *b* 1923; *s* of late Alwyn Howard Wild and late Bessie Delafield (*née* Arnold); *m* 1948, Elaine Poole Hull; two *s* one *d. Educ:* Whitgift Sch.; Peterhouse, Cambridge (Hon. Fellow 1982). ScD 1962. Radar Officer in Royal Navy, 1943–47; joined Research Staff of Div. of Radiophysics, 1947, working on problems in radio astronomy, esp. of the sun, later also radio navigation (Interscan aircraft landing system). Anglo-Australian Telescope Bd, 1973–82 (Chm., 1975–80); Bd, Interscan (Australia) Pty Ltd, 1978–84. For. Hon. Mem., Amer. Acad. of Arts and Scis, 1961; For. Mem., Amer. Philos. Soc., 1962; Corresp. Mem., Royal Soc. of Scis, Liège, 1969; For. Sec., Australian Acad. of Science, 1973–77. Edgeworth David Medal, 1958; Hendryk Arctowski Gold Medal, US Nat. Acad. of Scis, 1969; Balthasar van der Pol Gold Medal, Internat. Union of Radio Science, 1969; 1st Herschel Medal, RAS, 1974; Thomas Ranken Lyle Medal, Aust. Acad. of Science, 1975; Royal Medal, Royal Soc., 1980; Hale Medal, Amer. Astronomical Soc., 1980; ANZAAS Medal, 1984. Hon. DSc: ANU, 1979; Newcastle, 1982. *Publications:* numerous research papers and reviews on radio astronomy in scientific jls. *Address:* RMB, 338 Sutton Road, via Queanbeyan, NSW 2620, Australia.

WILD, John Vernon, CMG 1960; OBE 1955; Colonial Administrative Service, retired; *b* 26 April 1915; *m* 1st, 1942, Margaret Patricia Rendell (*d* 1975); one *d* (one *s* decd); 2nd, 1976, Marjorie Mary Lovatt Robertson. *Educ:* Taunton School; King's College, Cambridge. Senior Optime, Cambridge Univ., 1937. Colonial Administrative Service, Uganda: Assistant District Officer, 1938; Assistant Chief Secretary, 1950; Establishment Secretary, 1951; Administrative Secretary, 1955–60; Chairman, Constitutional Committee, 1959. Teacher and Lectr in Mathematics, 1960–76. *Publications:* The Story of the Uganda Agreement; The Uganda Mutiny; Early Travellers in Acholi. *Recreations:* cricket (Cambridge Blue, 1938), golf, music. *Address:* Maplestone Farm, Brede, near Rye, East Sussex TN31 6EP. *T:* Brede 882261. *Club:* Rye Golf.

WILD, Prof. Raymond, CEng, FIMechE, FIProdE; Head of Departments of Engineering and Management Systems, since 1977, and Production Technology, since 1984, Brunel University; *b* 24 Dec. 1940; *s* of Alice Wild and Frank Wild; *m* 1965, Carol Ann Mellor; one *s* one *d. Educ:* Stockport College; Bradford University. PhD (Management), MSc (Eng), MSc (Management); WhF. Engineering apprentice, Crossley Bros, 1957–62, design engineer, 1962–63, research engineer, 1963–65; postgrad. student, Bradford Univ., 1965–66; production engineer, English Electric, 1966–67; Res. Fellow then Senior Res. Fellow, Bradford Univ., 1967–73; Dir of Grad. Studies, Admin. Staff Coll., Henley, 1973–77, Mem., Senior Staff, Henley Management Coll., 1973–; Dir, Special Engineering Programme, Brunel Univ., 1977–84. FBIM, FRSA. *Publications:* The Techniques of Production Management, 1971; Management and Production, 1972, trans. Greek 1984; (with A. B. Hill and C. C. Ridgeway) Women in the Factory, 1972; Mass Production Management, 1972; (with B. Lowes) Principles of Modern Management, 1972; Work Organization, 1975; Concepts for Operations Management, 1977; Production and Operations Management, 1979, 3rd edn 1984; Operations Management: a policy framework, 1980, 2nd edn 1985; Essentials of Production and Operations Management, 1980, 2nd edn 1985; (ed) Management and Production Readings, 1981; Read and Explain (4 children's books on technology), 1982 and 1983, trans. French, Swedish, German, Danish; How to Manage, 1983; papers in learned jls. *Recreations:* writing, do it yourself, restoring houses, travel. *Address:* Broomfield, New Road, Shiplake, Henley on Thames, Oxon RG9 3LA. *T:* Wargrave 4102.

WILDE, Derek Edward, CBE 1978; Vice Chairman, 1972–77, and Director, 1969–83, Barclays Bank Ltd; Deputy Chairman, Charterhouse Group, 1980–83; *b* 6 May 1912; *s* of late William Henry Wilde and Ethel May Wilde; *m* 1940, Helen, *d* of William Harrison; (one *d* decd). *Educ:* King Edward VII School, Sheffield. Entered Barclays Bank Ltd, Sheffield, 1929; General Manager, 1961; Sen. General Manager, 1966–72. Dir, Yorkshire Bank Ltd, 1972–80; Chairman: Keyser Ullmann Holdings, 1975–81; Charterhouse Japhet, 1980–81. Governor, Midhurst Med. Res. Inst., 1970–85. Fellow, Inst. of Bankers (Hon. Fellow 1975). Hon. DLitt Loughborough, 1980. *Recreation:* gardening. *Address:* Ranmoor, Smarts Hill, Penshurst, Kent. *T:* Penshurst 870228,

WILDE, Peter Appleton; HM Diplomatic Service, retired; *b* 5 April 1925; *m* 1950, Frances Elisabeth Candida Bayliss; two *s. Educ:* Chesterfield Grammar Sch.; St Edmund Hall, Oxford. Army (National Service), 1943–47; Temp. Asst Lectr, Southampton, 1950; FO, 1950; 3rd Sec., Bangkok, 1951–53; Vice-Consul, Zürich, 1953–54; FO, 1954–57; 2nd Sec., Baghdad, 1957–58; 1st Sec., UK Delegn to OEEC (later OECD), Paris, 1958–61; 1st Sec., Katmandu, 1961–64; FO (later FCO), 1964–69; Consul-Gen., Lourenço Marques, 1969–71; Dep. High Comr, Colombo, 1971–73. Mem., Llanfihangel Rhosycorn Community Council, 1974–83. Member: Management Cttee, Carmarthenshire Pest Control Soc. Ltd, 1974–82; Council, Royal Forestry Soc., 1977–; Regional Adv. Cttee, Wales Conservancy, Forestry Commn, 1985– (Mem., Regional Adv. Cttee, S Wales Conservancy, 1983–85). *Recreation:* forestry. *Address:* Nantyperchyll, Gwernogle, Carmarthen, Dyfed SA32 7RR. *T:* Brechfa 241.

WILDENSTEIN, Daniel Leopold; art historian; President, Wildenstein Foundation Inc., since 1964; Chairman, Wildenstein & Co Inc., New York, since 1968 (Vice-President, 1943–59, President, 1959–68); *b* Verrières-le-Buisson, France, 11 Sept. 1917; *s* of Georges Wildenstein; *m* 1939, Martine Kapferer (marr. diss. 1968); two *s*; *m* 1978, Sylvia Roth. *Educ:* Cours Hattemer; Sorbonne (LèsL 1938). Gp Sec., French Pavilion, World's Fair, 1937; went to US, 1940; with Wildenstein & Co. Inc., New York, 1940–; Director: Wildenstein & Co. Inc., London, 1963–; Wildenstein Arte, Buenos Aires, 1963–. Dir, Gazette des Beaux Arts, 1963–; Dir of Activities, Musée Jacquemart-André, Paris, 1956–62; Musée Chaalis, Institut de France, Paris, 1956–62; organiser of art competitions (Hallmark art award). Mem., French Chamber of Commerce in US (Conseiller), 1942–; Founder (1947) and Mem, Amer. Inst. of France (Sec.). Mem., Institut de France (Académie des Beaux-Arts), 1971; Membre du Haut Comité du Musée de Monaco. *Publications:* Claude Monet, vol. 1, 1975, vols 2 and 3, 1979, vol. 4, 1985; Edouard Manet, vol. 1, 1976, vol. 2, 1977; Gustave Courbet, vol. 1, 1977, vol. 2, 1978. *Recreation:* horse racing (leading owner, 1977). *Address:* 48 avenue de Rumine, 1007 Lausanne, Switzerland; (office) 57 rue La Boétie, 75008 Paris, France. *T:* 563–01–00. *Clubs:* Brooks's; Turf and Field, Madison Square Garden (New York); Cercle de Deauville, Tir au Pigeon (Paris); Jockey (Buenos Aires).

WILDING, Richard William Longworth, CB 1979; Deputy Secretary, Head of Office of Arts and Libraries, Cabinet Office, since 1984; *b* 22 April 1929; *er s* of late L. A. Wilding; *m* 1954, Mary Rosamund de Villiers; one *s* two *d. Educ:* Dragon Sch., Oxford; Winchester Coll.; New Coll., Oxford (MA). HM Foreign Service, 1953–59; transf. to Home Civil Service, 1959; Principal, HM Treasury, 1959–67; Sec., Fulton Cttee on Civil Service, 1966–68; Asst Sec., Civil Service Dept, 1968–70; Asst Sec., Supplementary Benefits Commn, DHSS, 1970–72; Under-Sec., Management Services, 1972–76, Pay, 1976, CSD; Deputy Secretary: CSD, 1976–81; HM Treasury, 1981–83. *Publications:* (with L. A. Wilding) A Classical Anthology, 1954; Key to Latin Course for Schools, 1966; articles in Jl Public Administration, Social Work Today, Studies. *Recreations:* music, gardening. *Address:* 16 Middleway, NW11. *T:* 01–455 6245. *Club:* Royal Over-Seas League.

WILDISH, Vice-Adm. Denis Bryan Harvey, CB 1968; Director General of Personal Services and Training (Naval), 1970–72, retired; *b* 24 Dec. 1914; *s* of late Rear-Adm. Sir Henry William Wildish, KBE, CB; *m* 1941, Leslie Henrietta Jacob; two *d. Educ:* RNC Dartmouth; RNEC. Entered Royal Navy, 1928; Comdr 1948; Capt. 1957; Rear-Adm. 1966; Vice-Adm. 1970. Dir of Fleet Maintenance, 1962–64; Commodore Naval Drafting, 1964–66; Adm. Supt, HM Dockyard, Devonport, 1966–70. *Recreations:* cricket, painting. *Address:* Deans Farm, Weston, near Petersfield, Hants. *Clubs:* Army and Navy, MCC.

WILDSMITH, Brian Lawrence; artist and maker of picture books for young children; *b* 22 Jan. 1930; *s* of Paul Wildsmith and Annie Elizabeth Oxley; *m* 1955, Aurelie Janet Craigie Ithurbide; one *s* three *d. Educ:* de la Salle Coll.; Barnsley Sch. of Art; Slade Sch. of Fine Arts. Art Master, Selhurst Grammar School for Boys, 1954–57; freelance artist, 1957–. Production design, illustrations, titles and graphics for first USA-USSR Leningrad film co-production of the Blue Bird. Kate Greenaway Medal, 1962. *Publications:* ABC, 1962; The Lion and the Rat, 1963; The North Wind and the Sun, 1964; Mother Goose, 1964; 1; 2; 3;, 1965; The Rich Man and the Shoemaker, 1965; The Hare and the Tortoise, 1966; Birds, 1967; Animals, 1967; Fish, 1968; The Miller the Boy and the Donkey, 1969; The Circus, 1970; Puzzles, 1970; The Owl and the Woodpecker, 1971; The Twelve Days of Christmas, 1972; The Little Wood Duck, 1972; The Lazy Bear, 1973; Squirrels, 1974; Pythons Party, 1974; The Blue Bird, 1976; The True Cross, 1977; What the Moon Saw, 1978; Hunter and his Dog, 1979; Animal Shapes, 1980; Animal Homes, 1980; Animal Games, 1980; Animal Tricks, 1980; The Seasons, 1980; Professor Noah's Spaceship, 1980; Bears Adventure, 1981; The Trunk, 1982; Cat on the Mat, 1982; Pelican, 1982; The Apple Bird, 1983; The Island, 1983; All Fall Down, 1983; The Nest, 1983; Daisy, 1984; Who's Shoes, 1984; Toot Toot, 1984; Give a Dog a Bone, 1985; Goats Trail, 1986; My Dream, 1986; What a Tail, 1986. *Recreations:* squash, tennis, music (piano). *Address:* 11 Castellaras, 06370 Mouans-Sartoux, France. *T:* (93) 75.24.11. *Club:* Reform.

WILDY, Prof. (Norman) Peter (Leete); Professor of Pathology, and Fellow of Gonville and Caius College, University of Cambridge, since 1975; *b* 31 March 1920; *s* of late Eric Lawrence and Gwendolen Wildy; *m* 1945, Joan Audrey Kenion; one *s* two *d. Educ:* Eastbourne College; Caius Coll., Cambridge; St Thos Hosp., London. MRCS, LRCP

1944; MB, BChir 1948. RAMC, 1945–47. St Thomas's Hospital Medical School: Michael and Sydney Herbert and Leonard Dudgeon Res. Fellow, 1949–51; Lecturer in Bacteriology, 1952–57; Sen. Lectr in Bacteriology, 1957–58; Brit. Memorial Fellow in Virology, 1953–54; Asst Director, MRC Unit for Experimental Virus Research, Glasgow, 1959–63; Prof. of Virology, Univ. of Birmingham, 1963–75. FRSE 1962; FRCPath 1975; Hon. ARCVS 1985. *Publications:* articles on bacteria and viruses. *Address:* Cotton Hall, Cotton Hall Lane, Kedington, Haverhill, Suffolk.

WILEMAN, Margaret Annie, MA; Honorary Fellow since 1973 (President (formerly Principal), 1953–73), Hughes Hall, Cambridge; *b* 19 July 1908; *e d* of Clement Wileman and Alice (*née* Brinson). *Educ:* Lady Margaret Hall, Oxford, and the University of Paris. Scholar of Lady Margaret Hall, Oxford, 1927; First in Hons School of Mod. Langs, 1930; Zaharoff Travelling Scholar, 1931; Assistant, Abbey School, Reading, 1934; Senior Tutor, Queen's College, Harley Street, 1937; Lecturer, St Katherine's Coll., Liverpool, 1940; Resident Tutor, Bedford College, Univ. of London, 1944–53; Univ. Lectr, and Dir of Women Students, Dept of Educn, Cambridge Univ., 1953–73. *Address:* 5 Drosier Road, Cambridge CB1 2EY. *T:* Cambridge 351846. *Club:* University Women's.

WILES, Sir Donald (Alonzo), KA 1984, CMG 1965; OBE 1960; Executive Director, Barbados National Trust, since 1980; *b* 8 Jan. 1912; *s* of Donald Alonzo Wiles and Millicent Wiles; *m* 1938, Amelia Elsie Pemberton; two *d. Educ:* Harrison Coll., Barbados; Univs of London, Toronto, Oxford. Member of Staff of Harrison College, Barbados, 1931–45; Public Librarian, Barbados, 1945–50; Asst Colonial Secretary, Barbados, 1950–54; Permanent Secretary, Barbados, 1954–60; Administrator, Montserrat, 1960–64; Administrative Sec., Da Costa & Musson Ltd, 1965–79. *Recreations:* swimming, hiking, tennis. *Address:* Casa Loma, Sunrise Drive, Pine Gardens, St Michael, Barbados. *T:* 426–6875. *Club:* Bridgetown (Barbados).

WILES, Rev. Prof. Maurice Frank, FBA 1981; Canon of Christ Church, Oxford, and Regius Professor of Divinity, since 1970; *b* 17 Oct. 1923; *s* of late Sir Harold Wiles, KBE, CB, and of Lady Wiles; *m* 1950, Patricia Margaret (*née* Mowll); two *s* one *d. Educ:* Tonbridge School; Christ's College, Cambridge. Curate, St George's, Stockport, 1950–52; Chaplain, Ridley Hall, Cambridge, 1952–55; Lectr in New Testament Studies, Ibadan, Nigeria, 1955–59; Lectr in Divinity, Univ. of Cambridge, and Dean of Clare College, 1959–67; Prof. of Christian Doctrine, King's Coll., Univ. of London, 1967–70; Bampton Lectr, Univ. of Oxford, 1986. FKC 1972. *Publications:* The Spiritual Gospel, 1960; The Christian Fathers, 1966; The Divine Apostle, 1967; The Making of Christian Doctrine, 1967; The Remaking of Christian Doctrine, 1974; (with M. Santer) Documents in Early Christian Thought, 1975; Working Papers in Doctrine, 1976; What is Theology?, 1976; Explorations in Theology 4, 1979; Faith and the Mystery of God, 1982 (Collins Biennial Religious Book Award, 1983); God's Action in the World, 1986. *Address:* Christ Church, Oxford.

WILES, Prof. Peter John de la Fosse; Professor of Russian Social and Economic Studies, University of London, 1965–85, now Emeritus; *b* 25 Nov. 1919; *m* 1st, 1945, Elizabeth Coppin (marr. diss., 1960); one *s* two *d*; 2nd, 1960, Carolyn Stedman. *Educ:* Lambrook Sch.; Winchester Coll.; New Coll., Oxford. Royal Artillery, 1940–45 (despatches twice; mainly attached Intelligence Corps). Fellow, All Souls Coll., Oxford, 1947–48; Fellow, New Coll., Oxford, 1948–60; Prof., Brandeis Univ., USA, 1960–63; Research Associate, Institutet för Internationell Ekonomi, Stockholm, 1963–64. Visiting Professor: Columbia Univ., USA, 1958; City Coll. of New York, 1964 and 1967; Collège de France, 1972; Ecole des Sciences Politiques, 1979; Univ. of Windsor, Ont., 1986. *Publications:* The Political Economy of Communism, 1962; Price, Cost and Output (2nd edn), 1962; Communist International Economics, 1968; (ed) The Prediction of Communist Economic Performance, 1971; Economic Institutions Compared, 1977; Die Parallelwirtschaft, 1981; (ed) The New Communist Third World, 1981; (ed with Guy Routh) Economics in Disarray, 1985. *Recreations:* simple. *Address:* 23 Ridgmount Gardens, WC1.

WILFORD, Sir (Kenneth) Michael, GCMG 1980 (KCMG 1976; CMG 1967); HM Diplomatic Service, retired; Director, Lloyds Merchant Bank Ltd, since 1986 (Director, Lloyds Bank International, 1982–85); *b* Wellington, New Zealand, 31 Jan. 1922; *yr s* of late George McLean Wilford and late Dorothy Veronica (*née* Wilson); *m* 1944, Joan Mary, *d* of Captain E. F. B. Law, RN; three *d. Educ:* Wrekin College; Pembroke College, Cambridge. Served in Royal Engineers, 1940–46 (despatches). Entered HM Foreign (subseq. Diplomatic) Service, 1947; Third Sec., Berlin, 1947; Asst Private Secretary to Secretary of State, Foreign Office, 1949; Paris, 1952; Singapore, 1955; Asst Private Sec. to Sec. of State, Foreign Office, 1959; Private Sec. to the Lord Privy Seal, 1960; served Rabat, 1962; Counsellor (Office of British Chargé d'Affaires) also Consul-General, Peking, 1964–66; Visiting Fellow of All Souls, Oxford, 1966–67; Counsellor, Washington, 1967–69; Asst Under Sec. of State, FCO, 1969–73; Dep. Under Sec. of State, FCO, 1973–75; Ambassador to Japan, 1975–80. Chm., Royal Soc. for Asian Affairs, 1984–; Hon. Pres., Japan Assoc., 1981–. *Recreations:* golf, gardening. *Address:* Brook Cottage, Abbotts Ann, Andover, Hants. *T:* Andover 710509.

WILHELM, Most Rev. Joseph Lawrence, DD, JCD; former Archbishop of Kingston, Ontario, (RC); *b* Walkerton, Ontario, 16 Nov. 1909. *Educ:* St Augustine's Seminary, Toronto; Ottawa Univ., Ottawa, Ont. Ordained priest, Toronto, 1934. Mil. Chaplain to Canadian Forces, 1940–46 (MC, Sicily, 1943). Auxiliary Bishop, Calgary, Alberta, 1963–66; Archbishop of Kingston, Ont, 1967–82. Hon. DD Queen's Univ., Kingston, Ont, 1970. *Address:* The Anchorage, Belleville, Ont, Canada.

WILKES, Prof. Eric, OBE (civil) 1974 (MBE (mil.) 1943); DL; FRCP, FRCGP, FRCPsych; Professor of Community Care and General Practice, Sheffield University, 1973–83, now Emeritus; *b* 12 Jan. 1920; *s* of George and Doris Wilkes; *m* 1953, Jessica Mary Grant; two *s* one *d. Educ:* Royal Grammar Sch., Newcastle upon Tyne; King's Coll., Cambridge (MA); St Thomas' Hosp., SE1 (MB, BChir). Lt-Col, Royal Signals, 1944. General Medical Practitioner, Derbyshire, 1954–73. High Sheriff of S Yorkshire, 1977–78; Chm., Sheffield and Rotherham Assoc. for the Care and Resettlement of Offenders, 1976–83; Med. Director, St Luke's Nursing Home, Sheffield, 1971–86; Chairman: Sheffield Council on Alcoholism, 1976–83; Prevention Cttee, Nat. Council on Alcoholism, 1980–83; Trinity Day Care Trust, 1979–83; Sheffield Victim Support Scheme, 1983–84; Working Gp of National Cancer Sub-Cttee on Cancer Services in the Community, 1983–; Co-Chm., Help the Hospices, 1984– (Chm., Training and Educn Sub-Cttee); Pres., Inst. of Religion and Medicine, 1982–83. DL Derbys, 1984. Hon. Fellow, Sheffield City Polytechnic, 1985. Hon. MD Sheffield, 1986. *Publications:* The Dying Patient, 1982; Long-Term Prescribing, 1982; various chapters and papers, mainly on chronic and incurable illness. *Recreations:* gardening, fishing, natural history. *Address:* Grislow Field, Curbar, Sheffield S30 1XF. *T:* Baslow 2225.

See also Lyall Wilkes.

WILKES, Prof. John Joseph, FSA; FBA 1986; Professor of Archaeology of the Roman Provinces, University of London, since 1974; *b* 12 July 1936; *s* of Arthur Cyril Wilkes and Enid Cecilia Eustance; *m* 1980, Dr Susan Walker; one *s. Educ:* King Henry VIII Grammar Sch., Coventry; Harrow County Grammar Sch.; University Coll. London (BA); Univ. of Durham (St Cuthbert's Society) (PhD). FSA 1969. Research Fellow, Univ. of Birmingham, 1961–63; Asst Lectr in History and Archaeology, Univ. of Manchester, 1963–64; Lectr in Roman History, 1964–71, Sen. Lectr 1971–74, Univ. of Birmingham. Chm., Faculty of Archaeology, Hist. and Letters, British Sch. at Rome, 1979–83. Vis. Fellow, Inst. of Humanistic Studies, Pennsylvania State Univ., 1971. Mem., Ancient Monuments Bd for Scotland, 1981–. Vice-Pres., Soc. for Promotion of Roman Studies, 1978; Pres., London and Middx Archaeological Soc., 1982–85. Corresp. Mem., German Archaeol Inst., 1976. Governor, Mus. of London, 1981–. Editor, Britannia, 1980–84. *Publications:* Dalmatia (Provinces of Roman Empire series), 1969; (jtly) Diocletian's Palace: joint excavations in the southeast quarter, Pt 1, Split, 1972; (ed jtly) Victoria County History of Cambridgeshire, vol. VII, Roman Cambridgeshire, 1978; Rhind Lectures (Edinburgh), 1984; Diocletian's Palace, Split, 1986; papers, excavation reports and reviews in learned jls of Britain, Amer., and Europe. *Recreations:* listening to music, watching Association football. *Address:* Institute of Archaeology, 31–34 Gordon Square, WC1H 0PY. *T:* 01–387 6052.

WILKES, His Honour Lyall; a Circuit Judge (formerly Judge of the County Courts), 1964–82; *b* 19 May 1914; *e s* of George Wilkes, MBE and Doris Wilkes, Newcastle upon Tyne; *m* 1946, Margaret Tait, *e d* of Fred and Mabel Tait, Gateshead; four *d. Educ:* Newcastle Grammar School; Balliol Coll., Oxford (MA). Secretary Oxford Union Society, 1937. Joined Middlesex Regiment 1940; served one year in the ranks; active service North Africa, Italy and German-occupied Greece, attached Force 133; Major, 1944 (despatches). Called to Bar, Middle Temple, 1947; practised North-Eastern Circuit, 1947–64; Dep. Chm., County of Durham QS, 1961–64; Asst Recorder, Sheffield and Newcastle upon Tyne, 1960–62; MP (Lab) for Newcastle Central, 1945–51, when did not stand for re-election. Jt Pres., HM Council of Circuit Judges, 1981. Pres., Friends of Laing Art Gall., Newcastle upon Tyne, 1981–. *Publications:* (with Gordon Dodds) Tyneside Classical: the Newcastle of Grainger, Dobson and Clayton, 1964; Tyneside Portraits: studies in Art and Life, 1971; Old Jesmond and other poems (limited edn), 1975; (contrib.) New Poetry 3, 1977; John Dobson: Architect and Landscape Gardener, 1980; (contrib.) Shell Book of English Villages, 1980; (contrib.) The Oxford Book of Death, 1983; South and North and other poems, 1983; The Aesthetic Obsession: a portrait of Sir William Eden, Bt, 1985; (contrib.) Everyman Anthology of 2nd World War Poetry, 1985. *Recreation:* regretting the 20th century and avoiding its architecture. *Club:* Northern Counties (Newcastle-upon-Tyne).

See also Eric Wilkes.

WILKES, Maurice Vincent, MA, PhD; FRS 1956; FEng 1976; FIEE; FBCS; Member for Research Strategy, Olivetti Research Board, since 1986; Head of the Computer Laboratory, Cambridge (formerly Mathematical Laboratory), 1970–80; Professor of Computer Technology, 1965–80, now Emeritus Professor; Fellow of St John's College, since 1950; *b* 26 June 1913; *s* of late Vincent J. Wilkes, OBE; *m* 1947, Nina Twyman; one *s* two *d. Educ:* King Edward's School, Stourbridge; St John's College, Cambridge. Mathematical Tripos (Wrangler). Research in physics at Cavendish Lab.; Univ. Demonstrator, 1937. Served War of 1939–45, Radar and Operational Research. Univ. Lecturer and Acting Dir of Mathematical Laboratory, Cambridge, 1945; Dir of Mathematical Laboratory, 1946–70. Computer Engr, Digital Equipment Corp., USA, 1980–86; Adjunct Prof. of Computer Sci. and Elect. Engrg, MIT, 1981–85. Member: Measurement and Control Section Committee, IEE, 1956–59; Council, IEE, 1973–76; First President British Computer Soc., 1957–60, Distinguished Fellow 1973. Mem. Council, IFIP, 1960–63; Chm. IEE E Anglia Sub-Centre, 1969–70; Turing Lectr Assoc. for Computing Machinery, 1967. Foreign Hon. Mem., Amer. Acad. of Arts and Sciences, 1974; Foreign Corresponding Mem., Royal Spanish Acad. of Sciences, 1979; Foreign Associate: US Nat. Acad. of Engrg, 1977; US Nat. Acad. of Scis, 1980. Hon. DSc: Newcastle upon Tyne, 1972; Hull, 1974; Kent, 1975; City, 1975; Amsterdam, 1978; Munich, 1978; Hon. DTech Linköping, 1975. Harry Goode Award, Amer. Fedn of Inf. Processing Socs, 1968; Eckert-Mauchly Award, Assoc. for Computing Machinery and IEEE Computer Soc., 1980; McDowell Award, IEEE Computer Soc., 1981; Faraday Medal, IEE, 1981; Pender Award, Univ. of Pennsylvania, 1982. *Publications:* Oscillations of the Earth's Atmosphere, 1949; (joint) Preparations of Programs for an Electronic Digital Computer, Addison-Wesley (Cambridge, Mass), 1951, 2nd edn 1958; Automatic Digital Computers, 1956; A Short Introduction to Numerical Analysis, 1966; Time-sharing Computer System, 1968, 3rd edn 1975; (jtly) The Cambridge CAP Computer and its Operating System, 1979; Memoirs of a Computer Pioneer, 1985; papers in scientific jls. *Address:* Olivetti Research Ltd, 4a Market Hill, Cambridge CB2 3NJ. *T:* Cambridge 313542. *Club:* Athenæum.

WILKES, Richard Geoffrey, OBE 1969; TD 1959; DL; FCA; Partner, Price Waterhouse, Chartered Accountants, since 1969; *b* 12 June 1928; *s* of Geoffrey W. Wilkes and Kathleen (*née* Quinn); *m* 1953, Wendy Elaine, *d* of Rev. C. Ward; one *s* three *d. Educ:* Repton (Exhibnr). FCA 1952. Mem. Council, Inst. of Chartered Accountants in England and Wales, 1969– (Dep. Pres., 1979–80; Pres., 1980–81); Chm., UK Auditing Practices Cttee, 1976–78; International Federation of Accountants: UK Rep., 1983–; Mem. Council, 1983–; Dep. Pres., 1985–; Mem., Internat. Auditing Practices Cttee, 1978–79; Adviser on self-regulation, Lloyd's of London, 1983–85. Governor, CARE for the Mentally Handicapped, 1972–. Commnd RHA, 1947; CO 4/5th Bn Royal Leics Regt (TA), 1966–69; Col TAVR E Midlands Dist, 1969–73; ADC (TAVR) to the Queen, 1972–77. Dep. Hon. Col, Royal Anglian Regt (Leics), 1981–. Comdt, Leics Special Constab., 1972–79; Vice Chm., E Midlands TA&VRA (Chm., Leics Co. Cttee, 1980–). DL Leics, 1967. *Recreations:* shooting, sailing. *Address:* The Hermitage, Swingbridge Street, Foxton, Market Harborough, Leics LE16 7RH. *T:* East Langton 213. *Club:* Army and Navy.

WILKIE, Prof. Douglas Robert, FRS 1971; Jodrell Research Professor of Physiology, in the University of London, since 1979; *b* 2 Oct. 1922; *m* 1949, June Rosalind Hill (marr. diss. 1982); one *s. Educ:* Medical Student, University Coll. London, 1940–42 (Fellow, 1972); Yale Univ. (MD), 1942–43; University Coll. Hosp., MB, BS, 1944, MRCP 1945; FRCP 1972. Lectr, Dept of Physiology, UCL, 1948; Inst. of Aviation Medicine, Farnborough (Mil. Service), 1948–50; London University: Locke Research Fellowship (Royal Soc.), UCL, 1951–54; Readership in Experimental Physiology, UCL, 1954–65; Prof. of Experimental Physiology, 1965–69; Jodrell Prof., and Head of Physiology Dept, UCL, 1969–79. SRC Sen. Res. Fellowship, 1978. *Publications:* Muscle, 1968; contribs to learned jls, etc, mainly research on energetics of muscular contraction, and attempts to make thermodynamics simpler, recently, application of nuclear magnetic resonance in medicine. *Recreations:* sailing, friends, photography. *Address:* 2 Wychwood End, Stanhope Road, N6 5ND. *T:* 01–272 4024.

WILKIE, James, MA, FRSE; Secretary, Carnegie United Kingdom Trust, 1939–54; *b* Manchester, 1 June 1896; *er s* of late James Wilkie, Glasgow; *m* 1930, Ethel Susan (*d* 1984), *er d* of late W. H. Moore, JP, Killough, Co. Down; three *d. Educ:* Whitgift School; Brasenose College, Oxford (Dist. Litt. Hum. 1920). Served European War, 1914–19 (Captain, Machine Gun Corps, despatches twice, wounded, Order of Crown of Rumania) and War of 1939–45 (Major, Home Guard). Entered Board of Education, 1921 (Asst

Private Sec. to President, 1924–27), transferred to Empire Marketing Board, 1927–33; returned to Board of Education, 1933–39 (in charge of Metropolitan Div. and Sec. to Adult Education Cttee). Mem. Exec. Cttee: Newbattle Abbey Coll., 1939–54; Scottish Council of Social Service, 1944–54; Land Settlement Assoc., 1939–48; Nat. Central Library, 1939–50; Scottish Leadership Training Assoc., 1945–50; Member: NHS Executive Council for E Sussex, 1955–71; Advisory Council on Education in Scotland, 1948–51; Council of Nat. Federation of Young Farmers' Clubs, 1939–51; Vice-Pres.: Sussex Rural Community Council, Sussex Assoc. of Parish Councils; Irish Library Assoc., 1940–48; Pres., Library Assoc., 1951. *Address:* Charlwood Manor, Uckfield, Sussex.

WILKIN, (Frederick) John, CBE 1978 (OBE 1968); DFM 1943; Associate Member of Special Trustees, Charing Cross Hospital, since 1979; Member of Council, National Incorporated Beneficent Society, since 1968; *b* 15 Aug. 1916; *s* of late George Wilkin and Rosetta Christina Wilkin; *m* 1st, 1943, Marjorie Joan Wilson (*d* 1972); one *d*; 2nd, 1975, Laura Elizabeth Eason; one *s* one *d*. *Educ:* Southwark Central Sch.; Morley Coll., London. Served RAF, 1940–46: Navigator (12, 101 and 156 Sqdns); Permanent Award Pathfinder Badge. Asst Accountant, House of Commons, 1955, Chief Accountant, 1962–80; Secretary: House of Commons Members' Fund, 1962–81; Parliamentary Contributory Pensions Fund, 1965–80; Head of Admin Dept, House of Commons, 1980–81. Vice-Chm., Hammersmith and Fulham DHA, 1982–83. Mem., Guild of Freemen of City of London. *Recreations:* gardening, watching sport; formerly cricket, cycling, table tennis. *Address:* 14 Forest Ridge, Beckenham, Kent BR3 3NH. *T:* 01–650 5261. *Club:* Pathfinder.

WILKINS, Frederick Charles, CB 1963; *b* 10 July 1901; *s* of Richard Charles Wilkins; *m* 1926, Winifred Bertha Denham; one *d*. *Educ:* Portsmouth. Entered Admiralty Service, 1917; Naval Store Officer, 1939 (Asst 1923; Dep. 1936); Asst Dir of Stores, 1942; Capt. RNVR (attached to Brit. Pacific Fleet, 1944–46); Dep. Dir of Stores, 1955; Dir of Stores, Admiralty, 1960–64. *Recreation:* reading (Theology). *Address:* 9 Kenilworth Gardens, Kangaloon Road, Bowral, NSW 2576, Australia.

WILKINS, Sir Graham John, (Bob), Kt 1980; Chairman and Chief Executive, THORN EMI, since 1985; President, Beecham Group Ltd, since 1984 (Chairman and Chief Executive, 1975–84); *b* 22 Jan. 1924; *s* of George William and Anne May Wilkins; *m* 1945, Daphne Mildred Haynes. *Educ:* Yeovil Sch.; University Coll., South West of England, Exeter (BSc). Dir and Vice-Pres., Beecham (Canada) Ltd, 1954–59; C. L. Bencard Ltd, and Beecham Research Labs Ltd: Asst Man. Dir, 1959; Man. Dir, 1960; Dir, Beecham Pharmaceutical Div., 1962–64; Beecham Group Ltd: Dir and Chm., Pharmaceutical Div., 1964–72; Man. Dir (Pharmaceuticals), 1972; Exec. Vice-Chm., 1974; Chm., ICC UK, 1985– (Vice Chm., 1984–85); Director: Beecham Inc., 1967–86; Hill Samuel Gp Ltd, 1977–; THORN EMI (formerly Thorn Electrical Industries) Ltd, 1978–. Mem., Doctors' and Dentists' Remuneration Rev. Bd, 1980–. Vice-Chm., Proprietary Assoc. of GB, 1966–68; President: Assoc. of Brit. Pharmaceutical Industry, 1969–71 (Vice-Pres., 1968–69); European Fedn of Pharmaceutical Industries Assoc., 1978–82; Chm., Medico-Pharmaceutical Forum, 1971–73 (Vice-Chm., 1969–70). Mem., BOTB, 1977–80. Pres., Advertising Assoc., 1983–. Mem. Council, Sch. of Pharmacy, London Univ., 1984–. Hon. FRCP 1984. *Publications:* various papers on pharmaceutical industry. *Recreations:* golf, theatre-going. *Address:* THORN EMI plc, THORN EMI House, Upper St Martin's Lane, WC2H 9ED. *T:* 01–836 2444.

WILKINS, John Anthony Francis; Editor of The Tablet, since 1982; *b* 20 Dec. 1936; *s* of Edward Manwaring Wilkins and Ena Gwendolen Francis. *Educ:* Clifton Coll., Bristol (Scholar); Clare Coll., Cambridge (State Scholar, 1954; Major Scholar and Foundn Scholar; Classical Tripos 1959, Theol Tripos 1961; BA 1961). Served 1st Bn Glos Regt, 1955–57 (2nd Lieut). Planning Div., Marine Dept, Head Office of Esso Petroleum, London, 1962–63; Asst Editor: Frontier, 1964–67; The Tablet, 1967–72; features writer, BBC External Services, 1972–81; Producer, Radio 4, 1978. Ondas Radio Prize, 1973. *Recreation:* ornithology. *Address:* The Tablet, 48 Great Peter Street, SW1P 2HA. *T:* 01–222 7462.

WILKINS, Prof. Malcolm Barrett, FRSE 1972; Regius Professor of Botany, Glasgow University, since 1970; *b* 27 Feb. 1933; *s* of Barrett Charles Wilkins and Eleanor Mary Wilkins (*née* Jenkins); *m* 1959, Mary Patricia Maltby; one *s* (one *d* decd). *Educ:* Monkton House Sch., Cardiff; King's Coll., London. BSc 1955; PhD London 1958; AKC 1958; DSc 1972. Lectr in Botany, King's Coll., London, 1958–64; Rockefeller Foundn Fellow, Yale Univ., 1961–62; Research Fellow, Harvard Univ., 1962–63; Lectr in Biology, Univ. of East Anglia, 1964–65; Prof. of Biology, Univ. of East Anglia, 1965–67; Prof. of Plant Physiology, Univ. of Nottingham, 1967–70. Darwin Lectr, British Assoc. for Advancement of Science, 1967. Member: Biol. Sci. Cttee of SRC, 1971–74; Governing Body: Hill Farming Res. Orgn, 1971–80; Scottish Crops Research Inst, 1974–; Glasshouse Crops Res. Inst., 1979–; Exec. Cttee, Scottish Field Studies Assoc.; British Nat. Cttee for Biology, 1977–82; Life Science Working Gp, ESA, 1983–. Dir, West of Scotland Sch. Co.; Chm., Laurel Bank Sch. Co. Ltd. Cons. Editor in Plant Biology, McGraw-Hill Publishing Co., 1968–80; Managing Editor, Planta, 1977–. *Publications:* (ed) The Physiology of Plant Growth and Development, 1969; (ed) Advanced Plant Physiology, 1984; (ed) Plant Biology (series), 1981–; papers in Jl of Experimental Botany, Plant Physiology, Planta, Nature, Proc. Royal Soc. *Recreation:* sailing. *Address:* Department of Botany, The University, Glasgow G12 8QQ. *T:* 041–339 8855. *Club:* Caledonian.

WILKINS, Maurice Hugh Frederick, CBE 1963; MA, PhD; FRS 1959; Professor of Bio-physics, 1970–81, Emeritus Professor of Biophysics since 1981, and Fellow, since 1973, King's College, University of London; Director, Medical Research Council Cell Biophysics Unit, 1974–80 (Deputy Director, 1955–70, Director, 1970–72, Biophysics Unit; Director Neurobiology Unit, 1972–74); *b* 15 Dec. 1916; *s* of late Edgar Henry Wilkins and of Eveline Constance Jane (*née* Whittaker), both of Dublin; *m* 1959, Patricia Ann Chidgey; two *s* two *d*. *Educ:* King Edward's Sch., Birmingham: St John's College, Cambridge (Hon. Fellow, 1972). Research on luminescence of solids at Physics Department, Birmingham University, with Ministry of Home Security and Aircraft Production, 1938; PhD 1940; Manhattan Project (Ministry of Supply), Univ. of California (research on separation of uranium isotopes by mass spectrograph), 1944; Lectr in Physics, St Andrews Univ., 1945; MRC Biophysics Unit in Physics Department, King's College, London, 1946; Hon. Lecturer in the sub-department of Biophysics, 1958; Prof. of Molecular Biology, King's Coll., 1963–70. President: British Soc. for Social Responsibility in Science, 1969–; Food and Disarmament Internat., 1984–. Hon. Mem., Amer. Soc. of Biological Chemists, 1964; For. Hon. Mem., Amer. Acad. of Arts and Scis, 1970. Albert Lasker Award, Amer. Public Health Assoc., 1960. Hon. LLD Glasgow, 1972. (Jt) Nobel Prize for Medicine, 1962. *Publications:* papers in scientific journals on luminescence and topics in bio-physics, *eg* molecular structure of nucleic acids and structure of nerve membranes. *Address:* 30 St John's Park, SE3. *T:* 01–858 1817.

WILKINS, Lt-Gen. Sir Michael (Compton Lockwood), KCB 1985; OBE 1975; Commandant General, Royal Marines, since 1984; *b* 4 Jan. 1933; *s* of Eric Wilkins and Lucy (*née* Lockwood); *m* 1960, Anne Catherine (*née* Skivington); one *s* two *d*. *Educ:* Mill Hill School. Joined Royal Marines, 2nd Lieut, 1951; 40 Commando RM, 1954–56; Special Boat Sqdn, 1957–61; 41 Commando RM, 1961–62; RM Eastney, 1962–64; sc 1965; GSO2 (Ops) 17 Division, 1966–67; Plans Division, Naval Staff, 1968–69; Bde Major 3 Commando Bde, 1970–71; Directing Staff, Army Staff Coll., 1972–73; CO 40 Commando RM, 1974–75; NATO Defence Coll., 1976; Director of Drafting and Records, 1977–78; Comdr 3 Commando Bde, 1979–80; COS to Comdt Gen. RM, 1981–82; Maj.-Gen. Commando Forces RM, 1982–84. Pres., Royal Marines Saddle Club. *Recreations:* sailing, riding.

WILKINS, Nancy; barrister-at-law; *b* 16 June 1932; three *s* one *d*. *Educ:* School of St Helen and St Katharine, Abingdon, Berkshire. Called to the Bar, Gray's Inn, Nov. 1962; a Recorder, 1978–86. *Publication:* An Outline of the Law of Evidence (with late Prof. Sir Rupert Cross), 1964, 5th edn 1980. *Recreation:* grand-daughter. *Address:* 50 High Pavement, Nottingham.

WILKINS, William Albert, CBE 1965; *b* 17 Jan. 1899; *m* 1923, Violet Florrie Reed; three *s* one *d*. *Educ:* Whitehall Elementary School, Bristol. Linotype operator; commenced work at 13½ as an errand boy. Apprenticed to Thos Goulding, Printer, 6 Nelson St, Bristol. Later employed by Bristol Evening Times and Echo and Bristol Evening World. Actively engaged in politics since 1922; MP (Lab) Bristol South, 1945–70; Assistant Govt Whip (unpaid), 1947–62; a Lord Comr of the Treasury, 1950–51. Labour Party Rep., Council of Europe, Strasbourg, 1958–60. Member Typographical Association (now National Graphical Association), 1919–; Past member of Typographical Association Nat. Executive, Past President Bristol Branch, Past Pres. South-Western Group TA. Member of Bristol City Council, 1936–46. *Address:* 37 King Street, Two Mile Hill, Kingswood, Bristol. *T:* 673779.

WILKINSON, Rev. Canon Alan Bassindale, PhD; Priest-in-Charge of Darley with Thruscross and Thornthwaite, since 1984; *b* 26 Jan. 1931; *s* of late Rev. J. T. Wilkinson, DD; *m* 1975, Fenella Holland; two *s* one *d* of first marriage. *Educ:* William Hulme's Grammar Sch., Manchester; St Catharine's Coll., Cambridge; College of the Resurrection, Mirfield. MA 1958, PhD 1959 (Cambridge). Deacon, 1959; Priest, 1960; Asst Curate, St Augustine's, Kilburn, 1959–61; Chaplain, St Catharine's Coll., Cambridge, 1961–67; Vicar of Barrow Gurney and Lecturer in Theology, College of St Matthias, Bristol, 1967–70; Principal, Chichester Theol. Coll., 1970–74; Canon and Prebendary of Thorney, 1970–74, Canon Emeritus, 1975; Warden of Verulam House, Dir of Training for Auxiliary Ministry, dio. of St Albans, 1974–75; Lectr in Theology and Ethics, Crewe and Alsager Coll. of Higher Educn, 1975–78; Dir of Training, Diocese of Ripon, 1978–84; Hon. Canon, Ripon Cathedral, 1984. Hulsean Preacher, 1967–68; Select Preacher, Oxford Univ., 1982. Mem., Bd of Educn, Gen. Synod, 1981–85; Vice-Chm., Leeds Marriage and Personal Counselling Service, 1981–83. Governor: SPCK, 1982–; Coll. of Ripon and York St John, 1985–. *Publications:* The Church of England and the First World War, 1978; Would You Believe It?, 1980; More Ready to Hear, 1983; Christian Choices, 1983; Dissent or Conform?, 1986; contributor to: Cambridge Sermons on Christian Unity, 1966; Catholic Anglicans Today, 1968; A Work Book in Popular Religion, 1986; also to: Faith and Unity, Sobornost, Preacher's Quarterly, London Quarterly Holborn Review, Theology, Clergy Review, New Fire. *Recreations:* gardening, walking, cinema, Victorian architecture. *Address:* Darley Vicarage, Harrogate, North Yorks HG3 2QF. *T:* Harrogate 780771.

WILKINSON, Alexander Birrell; Sheriff of Tayside, Central and Fife at Falkirk, since 1986; *b* 2 Feb. 1932; *o s* of late Captain Alexander Wilkinson, MBE, The Black Watch and Isabella Bell Birrell; *m* 1965, Wendy Imogen, *d* of late Ernest Albert Barrett and of R. V. H. Barrett; one *s* one *d*. *Educ:* Perth Academy; Univs of St Andrews and Edinburgh. Walker Trust Scholar 1950, Grieve Prizeman in Moral Philosophy 1952, MA(Hons Classics) 1954, Univ. of St Andrews. National Service, RAEC, 1954–56. Balfour Keith Prizeman in Constitutional Law 1957, LLB (with distinction) 1959, Univ. of Edinburgh. Admitted to Faculty of Advocates, 1959; in practice at Scottish bar, 1959–69; Lecturer in Scots Law, Univ. of Edinburgh, 1965–69; Sheriff of Stirling, Dunbarton and Clackmannan at Stirling and Alloa, 1969–72; Prof. of Private Law, 1972–86, and Dean of Faculty of Law, 1974–76, Univ. of Dundee. A Chm. of Industrial Tribunals (Scotland). Chancellor: Dio. of Brechin, 1982–; Dio. of Argyll and the Isles, 1985–. Chairman: Central Scotland Marriage Guidance Council, 1970–72; Scottish Marriage Guidance Council, 1974–77; Legal Services Gp, Scottish Assoc. of CAB, 1979–83. *Publications:* (ed jtly) Gloag and Henderson's Introduction to the Law of Scotland, 8th edn 1980, 9th edn 1987; The Scottish Law of Evidence, 1986; articles in legal periodicals. *Recreations:* collecting books and pictures, reading, travel. *Address:* 267 Perth Road, Dundee DD2 1JP. *T:* Dundee 68939. *Clubs:* New (Edinburgh); University (Dundee).

WILKINSON, Prof. Andrew Wood, CBE 1979; ChM (Edinburgh); FRCSE; FRCS; Emeritus Professor of Pædiatric Surgery, University of London; Surgeon, Hospital for Sick Children, Great Ormond Street, since 1958; Hon. Consultant Pædiatric Surgeon, Post-graduate Medical School, Hammersmith, and Queen Elizabeth Hospital for Children; Civilian Consultant in Pediatric Surgery to RN; *b* 19 April 1914; *s* of Andrew W. and Caroline G. Wilkinson; *m* 1941, Joan Longair Sharp; two *s* two *d*. *Educ:* Univ. of Edinburgh. MB, ChB, Edin., 1937; ChM; (1st cl. hons and gold medal for thesis), 1949; FRCS Edin. 1940; FRCS Eng. 1959. Surg. specialist, Lt-Col RAMC, 1942–46. Syme Surgical Fellowship, Univ. of Edinburgh, 1946–49; Senior University Clinical Tutor in Surgery, 1946–51; Lecturer in Surgery, University of Edinburgh and Assistant Surgeon, Deaconess Hosp., Edinburgh, 1951–53; Sen. Lectr in Surgery, Univ. of Aberd. and Asst Surg., Roy. Inf. and Roy. Aberd. Hosp. for Sick Children, 1953–58; Nuffield Prof. of Paediatric Surgery, Inst. of Child Health, 1958–79. Dir, Internat. Sch. of Med. Scis, Ettore Majorana Foundn, 1970–. Royal College of Surgeons of Edinburgh: Mem. Council, 1964–73; Vice-Pres., 1973–76; Pres., 1976–79; Founder and Mem., Appeal Cttee, 1978–. Member: Armed Forces Med. Adv. Bd; Nat. Med. Consultative Cttee. Examr Primary and Final FRCS Ed.; Past Examiner: Univ. Glasgow, DCH London; Primary FRCSEng. Lectures: Tisdall, Canadian Med. Assoc., 1966; Mason Brown Meml, 1972; Forshall, 1979; Simpson Smith Meml, 1980; Tan Sri Datu Ismail Oration, Kuala Lumpur, 1980. Hunterian Prof., RCS, 1965. Visiting Prof. Univ. of Alexandria, 1965, Albert Einstein Coll. of Medicine, 1967. Member: Bd of Governors, Hosp. for Sick Children, 1972–80; Cttee of Management, Inst. of Child Health, 1959–79. Founder Mem., Scottish Surgical Pædiatric Soc.; Hon. Mem., and Past Pres., British Assoc. of Pediatric Surgeons, 1970–72 (Denis Browne Gold Medal, 1981). FRSocMed (Pres. Open Section, 1974–76). Hon. FRCSI; Hon. FRACS; Hon. FCPS (Pakistan); Hon. FCPS (S Africa); Hon. Fellow: Brasilian Soc. Pædiatric Surgery; Yugoslavian Pediatric Surgical Soc.; Greek Pædiatric Surgical Soc.; Amer. Acad. Pediatrics; Italian Pediatric Surgical Soc.; Pediatric Surgical Soc. of Ecuador; Hong Kong Surgical Soc.; Amer. Coll. Surgeons; Hon. Member: Neonatal Soc.; BPA; Peruvian Socs Pediatrics and Pædiatric Surgery; Hellenic Surgical Soc.; Assoc. of Surgeons of India; Corresp. Member: Scandinavian Pediatric Surgical Assoc.; Sicilian Calabrian Soc. of Pædiatric Surgery. *Publications:* Body Fluids in Surgery, 1955, 4th edn 1973 (Japanese edn, 1978); Recent Advances in Pædiatric Surgery, 1963, 3rd edn 1974 (Spanish edn, 1977); Parenteral Feeding, 1972; (jtly) Research in Burns, 1966; (ed jtly) Metabolism and the Response to Injury, 1976; Early Nutrition and Later

Development, 1976; (jt) Placental Transport, 1978; Inflammatory Bowel Disease, 1980; Investigation of Brain Function, 1981; Immunology of Breast Feeding, 1981; chapters, articles and reviews in various books, and surgical and other jls. *Recreations:* fishing, gardening, cooking, eating. *Address:* Auchenbrae, Rockcliffe, Dalbeattie, Kirkcudbrightshire DG5 4QF. *Club:* New (Edinburgh).

WILKINSON, Christopher Richard; Head of Division, Strategy for Information Technology and Telecommunications, Commission of the European Communities, since 1983; *b* 3 July 1941; *s* of Rev. Thomas Richard Wilkinson and Winifred Frances Wilkinson (*née* Steel); *m* 1965, Marie-Françoise Courthieu; one *s* one *d*. *Educ:* Hymers Coll., Kingston upon Hull; Heath Grammar Sch., Halifax; Selwyn Coll., Cambridge (MA). Commonwealth Economic Cttee, 1963–65; OECD, Paris and Madrid, 1965–66; World Bank, Washington DC and Lagos, 1966–73; EEC: Head of Div., Directorate Gen. for Regional Policy, 1973–78; Head of Div., Directorate Gen. for Internal Market and Industrial Affairs, 1978–82. Vis. Fellow, Center for Internat. Affairs, Harvard Univ., 1982–83. Vice-Pres., European School Parents Assoc., Brussels, 1974, 1976–77. *Recreations:* mountain walking, gardening, cooking. *Address:* Avenue des Frères Legrain 23, 1150 Brussels, Belgium; 81 Old Bank Road, Mirfield, West Yorkshire.

WILKINSON, Clive Victor; Financial and Commercial Director, Birmingham Repertory Theatre, since 1983; *b* 26 May 1938; *s* of Mrs Winifred Jobson; *m* 1961, Elizabeth Ann Pugh; two *d*. *Educ:* Four Dwellings Secondary Sch., Quinton; Birmingham Modern Sch. Birmingham City Council: Member, 1970–84; Leader, 1973–76 and 1980–82; Leader of Opposition, 1976–80, 1982–84. Dir, Nat. Exhibn Centre, 1973–84. Chm., CoSIRA, 1977–80; Dep. Chairman: AMA, 1974–76; Redditch Develt Corp., 1977–81. Chm., Sandwell DHA. Member: Develt Commn, 1977–86; Electricity Consumers Council, 1977–80; Council, Univ. of Birmingham, 1974–84. Hon. Alderman, City of Birmingham, 1984. *Recreations:* watching Birmingham City Football Club, playing squash. *Address:* 53 Middle Park Road, Birmingham B29 4BH. *T:* 021–475 1829.

WILKINSON, Sir (David) Graham (Brook), 3rd Bt *cr* 1941; *b* 18 May 1947; *s* of Sir (Leonard) David Wilkinson, 2nd Bt, DSC, and of Sylvia Ruby Eva Anne, *d* of Professor Bosley Alan Rex Gater; *S* father, 1972; *m* 1977, Sandra Caroline, *d* of Dr Richard Rossdale; two *d*. *Educ:* Millfield; Christ Church, Oxford.

WILKINSON, David Lloyd; Chief Executive Officer and General Secretary, Cooperative Union, since 1975; *b* 28 May 1937; *m* 1960; one *s* one *d*. *Educ:* Royds Hall Grammar Sch. ACIS; CSD. *Address:* 29 Mountfield Road, Waterloo, Huddersfield HD5 8RA. *T:* Huddersfield 27419.

WILKINSON, Sir Denys (Haigh), Kt 1974; FRS 1956; Vice-Chancellor, University of Sussex, 1976–Sept. 1987; *b* Leeds, Yorks, 5 September 1922; *o s* of late Charles Wilkinson and Hilda Wilkinson (*née* Haigh); *m* 1st, 1947, Christiane Andrée Clavier (marriage dissolved, 1967); three *d*; 2nd, 1967, Helen Sellschop; two step *d*. *Educ:* Loughborough Gram. Sch.; Jesus Coll. Cambridge (Fellow, 1944–59, Hon. Fellow 1961). BA 1943, MA, PhD 1947, ScD 1961. British and Canadian Atomic Energy Projects, 1943–46; Univ. Demonstrator, Cambridge, 1947–51; Univ. Lecturer, 1951–56; Reader in Nuclear Physics, Univ. of Cambridge, 1956–57; Professor of Nuclear Physics, Univ. of Oxford, 1957–59; Prof. of Experimental Physics, Univ. of Oxford, 1959–76, Head of Dept of Nuclear Physics, 1962–76; Student, Christ Church, Oxford, 1957–76, Emeritus Student, 1976, Hon. Student, 1979. Dir, Internat. Sch. of Nuclear Physics, Erice, Sicily, 1975–83. Mem. Governing Board of National Institute for Research in Nuclear Science, 1957–63 and 1964–65; Member: SRC, 1967–70; Wilton Park Acad. Council, 1979–83; Council, ACU, 1980–; Royal Commn for the Exhibn of 1851, 1983– (Chm., Science Scholarships Cttee, 1983–); Chairman: Nuclear Physics Board of SRC, 1968–70; Physics III Cttee, CERN, Geneva, 1971–75; Radioactive Waste Management Adv. Cttee, 1978–83; British Council Sci. Adv. Panel and Cttee, 1977–86; Pres., Inst. of Physics, 1980–82; Vice-Pres., IUPAP, 1985–. Lectures: Welch, Houston, 1957; Scott, Cambridge Univ., 1961; Rutherford Meml, Brit. Physical Soc., 1962; Graham Young, Glasgow Univ., 1964; Queen's, Berlin, 1966; Silliman, Yale Univ., 1966; Cherwell-Simon, Oxford Univ., 1970; Distinguished, Utah State Univ., 1971, 1983; Goodspeed-Richard, Pennsylvania Univ., 1973 and 1986; Welsh, Toronto Univ., 1975; Tizard Meml, Westminster Sch., 1975; Lauritsen Meml, Cal. Tech., 1976; Herbert Spencer, Oxford Univ., 1976; Schiff Meml, Stanford Univ., 1977; Racah Meml, Hebrew Univ. Jerusalem, 1977; Cecil Green, Univ. of BC, 1978; Distinguished Lectr, Univ. of Alberta, 1979; Wolfson, Oxford Univ., 1980; Waterloo-Guelph Distinguished Lectr, Guelph Univ., 1981; Herzberg, Ottawa, 1984; Solly Cohen Meml, Hebrew Univ., Jerusalem, 1985; Peter Axel Meml, Univ. of Ilinois, 1985. Walker Ames Prof., Univ. of Washington, 1968; Battelle Distinguished Prof., Univ. of Washington, 1970–71.; For. Mem., Royal Swedish Acad. of Scis, 1980. Holweck Medal, British and French Physical Socs, 1957; Hughes Medal, Royal Society, 1965; Bruce-Preller Prize, RSE, 1969; Bonner Prize, American Physical Soc., 1974; Royal Medal, Royal Soc., 1980; Guthrie Medal and Prize, Inst. of Physics, 1986. Hon. Mem., Mark Twain Soc, 1978. Hon. DSc: Saskatchewan, 1964; Utah State, 1975; Guelph, 1981; Hon. FilDr Uppsala, 1980. Comm. Bontemps Médoc et Graves, 1973. *Publications:* Ionization Chambers and Counters, 1951; (ed) Isospin in Nuclear Physics, 1969; (ed) Progress in Particle and Nuclear Physics, 1978–84; (ed jtly) Mesons in Nuclei, 1979; papers on nuclear physics and bird navigation. *Recreations:* mediæval church architecture and watching birds. *Address:* Gayles Orchard, Friston, Eastbourne, East Sussex BN20 0BA. *T:* East Dean 3333. *Clubs:* Athenæum, Achilles.

WILKINSON, Elizabeth Mary, PhD; FBA 1972; Professor of German, University College London, 1960–76, now Emeritus; *b* 17 Sept. 1909; *d* of Frank Wilkinson and Martha E. Gilleard, Keighley, Yorks. *Educ:* Whalley Range High Sch., Manchester; Bedford Coll., London (BA, PhD; Hon. Fellow 1985); DipEd Oxford. Vis. Prof., Univ. of Chicago, 1955; first Virginia C. Gildersleeve Prof., Barnard Coll., Columbia Univ., 1958; Prof.-at-Large of Cornell Univ., 1967–. President: English Goethe Soc., 1974–86; Modern Language Assoc., GB, 1964; Hon. Mem., Modern Language Assoc. of America, 1965. Governor, Bedford Coll., London. Korresp. Mitglied, Akademie der Wissenschaften zu Göttingen, 1973; Deutsche Akad. für Sprache und Dichtung, 1976. Hon. LLD Smith Coll., Mass, 1966; Hon. DLitt Kent, 1971. Medaille in Gold des Goethe-Instituts, 1965; Preis für Germanistik im Ausland der Deutschen Akad. für Sprache und Dichtung, 1974. German Editor, Notebooks of Samuel Taylor Coleridge, 1950–62 (vols 1 and 2); Editor, publications of the English Goethe Soc., 1951–70. *Publications:* Thomas Mann's Tonio Kröger, 1943; (with L. A. Willoughby) Schiller's Kabale und Liebe, 1944; J. E. Schlegel: A German Pioneer in Aesthetics, 1945, repr. 1973 (J. G. Robertson Prize); Edward Bullough's Aesthetics, 1957; (with L. A. Willoughby) Goethe: Poet and Thinker, 1962 (German edn 1974); (with L. A. Willoughby) Schiller: On the Aesthetic Education of Man, 1967 (German edn 1977); Goethe Revisited, 1983; contrib. to Encyclopædia Britannica, 1963. *Address:* 33 Queen Court, Queen Square, WC1.

WILKINSON, Prof. Sir Geoffrey, Kt 1976; FRS 1965; Sir Edward Frankland Professor of Inorganic Chemistry, University of London; *b* 14 July 1921; *s* of Henry and Ruth Wilkinson; *m* 1951, Lise Sølver, *o d* of Rektor Prof. Svend Aa. Schou, Copenhagen; two *d*. *Educ:* Todmorden Secondary Sch (Royal Scholar, 1939); Imperial Coll., London; USA. Junior Scientific Officer, Nat. Res. Council, Atomic Energy Div., Canada, 1943–46; Research Fellow: Radiation Lab., Univ. of Calif, Berkeley, Calif, USA, 1946–50; Chemistry Dept, Mass Inst. of Technology, Cambridge, Mass, USA, 1950–51; Asst Prof. of Chemistry, Harvard Univ., Cambridge, Mass, 1951–56; Prof. of Inorganic Chemistry at Imperial Coll., Univ. of London, 1956, Sir Edward Frankland Prof. 1978. Arthur D. Little Visiting Prof., MIT, 1967; Lectures: William Draper Harkins' Meml, Univ. of Chicago, 1968; Leermakers, Wesleyan Univ., 1975; First Mond, Chem. Soc., 1980; First Sir Edward Frankland, RSC, 1983. John Simon Guggenheim Fellow, 1954. Foreign Member: Roy. Danish Acad. of Science and Arts (math.-phys section), 1968; Amer. Acad. of Arts and Sciences, 1970; Foreign Assoc., Nat. Acad. of Scis, 1975; Centennial Foreign Fellow, Amer. Chem. Soc., 1976. Hon. Fellow, Lady Margaret Hall, Oxford, 1984. Hon. DSc: Edinburgh, 1975; Granada, 1976; Columbia, 1978; Bath, 1980. American Chem. Soc. Award in Inorganic Chemistry, 1965; Lavoisier Medal, Société Chimique de France, 1968; Chem. Soc. Award for Transition Metal Chemistry, 1972; (jtly) Nobel Prize for Chemistry, 1973; Consejero de Honor, Spanish Council for Scientific Res., 1974; Hiroshima Univ. Medal, 1978; Royal Medal, Royal Soc., 1981; Galileo Medal, Univ. of Pisa, 1983. *Publications:* (jtly) Advanced Inorganic Chemistry: a Comprehensive Text, 1962, 4th edn 1980; Basic Inorganic Chemistry, 1976; numerous in Physical Review, Journal of the American Chemical Society, etc. *Address:* Chemistry Department, Imperial College, SW7 2AY. *T:* 01–589 5111.

WILKINSON, Geoffrey Crichton, CBE 1986; AFC; Chief Inspector of Accidents (Aircraft), 1981–86; *b* 7 Nov. 1926; *s* of Col W. E. D. Wilkinson and Mrs E. K. Wilkinson; *m* 1958, Virginia Mary Broom; two *d*. *Educ:* Bedford Sch. Graduate, Empire Test Pilots Sch.; FRAES. Royal Indian Mil. Coll., 1943–44; served RN, 1944–47; aeronautical engrg course, 1948; served RAF, 1949–59 (Air Force Cross, 1956); Turner and Newall, 1959–61; Mercury Airlines, 1961–65; Accidents Investigation Br., 1965–86. Air Medal, USA, 1953. *Recreations:* sailing, skiing, music. *Address:* Buckingham House, 50 Hyde Street, Winchester, Hants SO23 7DY. *T:* Winchester 65823. *Clubs:* Royal Air Force; Royal Air Force Yacht (Hamble).

WILKINSON, Sir Graham Brook; *see* Wilkinson, Sir D. G. B.

WILKINSON, Jeffrey Vernon; Chairman, Plastics Processing Economic Development Committee, since 1985; *b* 21 Aug. 1930; *s* of late Arthur Wilkinson and Winifred May Allison; *m* 1955, Jean Vera Nurse; two *d*. *Educ:* Mathew Humberstone Foundation Sch.; King's Coll., Cambridge (MA); Sorbonne. FBCS, CBIM. Joined Joseph Lucas as graduate apprentice, 1954; Director, CAV, 1963; Director and General Manager, Diesel Equipment, CAV, 1967; Director: Simon Engineering, 1968; Joseph Lucas, 1974; Gen. Manager, Lucas Electrical, 1974; Divisional Man. Dir, Joseph Lucas Ltd, 1978; Jt Gp Man. Dir, Lucas Industries plc, 1980–84. Chm., Automotive Components Manufacturers, 1979–84; Mem. Council and Exec., SMMT, 1979–84. Liveryman, Wheelwrights Company, 1971–. *Recreations:* squash, water-skiing, swimming, reading, theatre, art. *Address:* Hillcroft, 15 Mearse Lane, Barnt Green, Birmingham B45 8HG. *T:* 021–445 1747.

WILKINSON, John Arbuthnot Ducane; MP (C) Ruislip Northwood, since 1979; *b* 23 Sept. 1940; 2nd *s* of late Denys Wilkinson and Gillian Wilkinson, Eton College; *m* 1969, Paula Adey, *o d* of Joseph Adey, East Herrington, Co. Durham; one *d*. *Educ:* Eton (King's Scholar); RAF Coll., Cranwell; Churchill Coll., Cambridge (2nd cl. Hons Mod. Hist.; MA). Flight Cadet, RAF Coll., Cranwell, 1959–61 (Philip Sassoon Meml Prize, qualified French Interpreter); commnd 1961; Flying Instructor, No 8 FTS, Swinderby, 1962. Churchill Coll., Cambridge, Oct. 1962–65. Trooper, 21st Special Air Service Regt (Artists'), TA, 1963–65; rejoined RAF 1965; Flying Instructor, RAF Coll., Cranwell, 1966–67; Tutor, Stanford Univ.'s British Campus, 1967; ADC to Comdr 2nd Allied Tactical Air Force, Germany, 1967; resigned RAF, 1967. Head of Universities' Dept, Conservative Central Office, 1967–68; Aviation Specialist, Cons. Research Dept, 1969; Senior Administration Officer (Anglo-French Jaguar Project), Preston Div., British Aircraft Corp., 1969–70; Tutor, Open Univ., 1970–71; Vis. Lectr, OCTU RAF Henlow, 1971–75; Chief Flying Instructor, Skywork Ltd, Stansted, 1974–75; Gen. Manager, General Aviation Div., Brooklands Aviation Ltd, 1975–76; PA to Chm., BAC, 1975–77; Senior Sales Executive, Eagle Aircraft Services Ltd, 1977–78; Sales Manager, Klingair Ltd, 1978–79. MP (C) Bradford W, 1970–Feb. 1974; Chm., Cons. Parly Aviation Cttee, 1983–85 (Jt Sec., 1972–74; Vice-Chm., 1979); Vice-Chm., Cons. Parly Defence Cttee, 1983–85 (Sec., 1972–74 and 1980–81); Member Select Committee on: Race Relations and Immigration, 1972–74; Sci. and Technol., 1972–74; contested (C) Bradford W, Feb. and Oct. 1974; PPS to Minister of State for Industry, 1979–80, to Sec. of State for Defence, 1981–82; Chairman: Anglo-Asian Cons. Soc., 1979–82; European Freedom Council, 1982–; Vice-Chm., Cons. Space Sub Cttee, 1983–85. Chm., Horn of Africa Council, 1984–. Delegate to Council of Europe (Chm., Space Sub-Cttee, 1984–) and WEU (Chm., Cttee on Scientific, Technological and Aerospace Questions, 1986–), 1979–. *Publications:* (jtly) The Uncertain Ally, 1982; pamphlets and articles on defence and politics. *Recreation:* flying. *Address:* c/o House of Commons, SW1. *Clubs:* Beefsteak, Royal Air Force.

WILKINSON, John Francis; Director, Public Affairs, BBC, 1980–85; *b* 2 Oct. 1926; *s* of late Col W. T. Wilkinson, DSO, and Evelyn S. Wilkinson (*née* Ward); *m* 1951, Alison, *d* of late Hugh and Marian Malcolm; two *s* one *d*. *Educ:* Wellington Coll.; Edinburgh Univ. Naval Short Course, 1944–45; Cambridge and London Univs Colonial Course, 1947–48. Served Royal Navy (Fleet Air Arm trainee pilot, 1945), 1945–47; HM Colonial Service, N Nigeria, 1949; Asst District Officer, Bida, 1949; Asst Sec., Lands and Mines, Kaduna, 1950; Private Sec. to Chief Comr, N Nigeria, 1951; transf. to Nigerian Broadcasting Corp., 1952; Controller: Northern Region, 1952–56; National Programme, Lagos, 1956–58; joined BBC African Service as African Programme Organiser, 1958; East and Central African Programme Organiser, 1961; BBC TV Production Trng Course and attachment to Panorama, 1963; Asst Head, 1964, Head, 1969, BBC African Service; attachment to Horizon, 1972; Head of Production and Planning, BBC World Service, 1976; Secretary of the BBC, 1977–80. Chm. of Governors, Centre for Internat. Briefing, Farnham Castle, 1977–. Vice-Pres., Royal African Soc., 1978–82. *Publications:* Broadcasting in Africa, in African Affairs (Jl of Royal African Soc.), 1972; contrib. to Broadcasting in Africa, a continental survey of radio and television, 1974. *Recreations:* sailing, occasional golf. *Address:* Orchard House, Kingsley Green, Haslemere, Surrey GU27 3LG. *T:* Haslemere 3897. *Club:* Royal Commonwealth Society.

WILKINSON, Dr John Frederick, FRCP, MD (Gold Medal), ChB, BSc (1st Cl. Hons Chem.), MSc, PhD Manchester, DSc (Hon.) Bradford; CChem, FRSC; author; Consulting Physician; Consulting Haematologist, United Manchester Hospitals; late Director of Department of Hæmatology, University and Royal Infirmary of Manchester; late Reader in Hæmatology, and Lecturer in Systematic Medicine, Univ. of Manchester; late Hon. Consulting Hæmatologist, The Christie Cancer Hospital, Holt Radium Institute and The Duchess of York Hospital for Babies, Manchester; Hon. Fellow and Editor, Manchester Medical Society; formerly President, European Hæmatological Soc.; Life Councillor, International Hæmatological Soc.; *b* Oldham, 10 June 1897; *s* of John Frederick Wilkinson, Oldham and Stockport, and Annie, *d* of late Reverend E. Wareham, DD,

Rector of Heaton Mersey; *m* 1964, Marion Crossfield, Major, WRAC. *Educ*: Arnold School, Blackpool; University of Manchester; Manchester Royal Infirmary. Served European War, 1916–19, RNAS, RN, and later attached Tank Corps, France; also served on Vindictive at Zeebrugge, 1918, and ballotted for Victoria Cross award; Chemical Research Manchester University, 1919–28; Medical Research since 1929; Regional Transfusion Officer, and Regional Adviser on Resuscitation, Ministry of Health, NW Region, 1940–46. Graduate Scholarship (Chemistry), 1920; Dalton Research Scholarship; Sir Clement Royds Research Fellowship; Medical (Graduate) Scholarship, 1923; Hon. Demonstrator in Crystallography; Research Asst in Physiology; Sidney Renshaw Physiology Prizeman; Gold Medal for Dissertation in Med., 1931, University of Manchester. RCP Lectures: Oliver Sharpey, 1948; Samuel Gee, 1977. Worshipful Society of Apothecaries, London: Liveryman, 1948; Osler Lectr, 1981; Hon. Fellow 1982 (Faculty of History and Philosophy of Medicine and Pharmacy). Freeman City of London, 1949. Hon. DSc Bradford, 1976. *Publications*: scientific and medical publications since 1920 in English and foreign journals, etc. Sections on Blood Diseases, Anæmias and Leukæmias in British Encyclopædia of Medical Practice, 1936, 1950 and yearly supplements since 1951, and in Encyclopædia of General Practice, 1964; Section on Emergencies in Blood Diseases, in Medical Emergencies, 1948 to date; ed Modern Trends in Diseases of the Blood, 1955, 1975; The Diagnosis and Treatment of Blood Diseases, 1973; ed, Section in Clinical Surgery, 1967; articles on antiques, Old English and continental apothecaries' drug jars, etc, in miscellaneous medical and art jls, 1970–. *Recreations*: motoring, antiques, travel, zoos, tropical fish keeping, lecturing, scouting. *Address*: Mobberley Old Hall, Knutsford, Cheshire WA16 7AB. *T*: Mobberley 2111.

WILKINSON, Kenneth Grahame, CBE 1979; Hon. DSc, BSc, FEng, FCGI, FRAeS, FCIT, FSLAET, CBIM; FRSA; aviation consultant; Director, British Rail Engineering, since 1982; Director, Airways Aero Associations Ltd; *b* 14 July 1917; *s* of Bertie and Dorothy Wilkinson; *m* 1941, Mary Holman Victory; one *s* one *d*. *Educ*: Shooter's Hill; Imperial Coll. (BSc, DIC). Sen. Scientific Officer, RAE, Farnborough, 1945; Performance and Analysis Supt, BEA, 1946–52; Manager, Fleet Planning Br., BEA, 1960; Chief Engr, BEA, 1964; Mem. Bd, BEA, 1968–72; Dep. Chief Exec. and Man. Dir (BEA Mainline), BEA, 1971–72, Chm. and Chief Exec., BEA, Sept.-Nov. 1972; Mem. Bd, BOAC, 1972; Rolls Royce (1971) Ltd: Man. Dir, 1972–74; Vice-Chm., 1974–76; Engineering Dir, British Airways, 1976–79. Chm., Air Transport and Travel Industry Trng Bd, 1981–82; Mem., BAB, 1971–72 and 1976–81 (Dep. Chm., 1979–80). Chm., BGA Techn. Cttee, 1946–48; Chm., BGA, 1970, Vice-Pres., 1972; Pres. RAeS, 1972. Vis. Prof., Cranfield Inst. of Technology, 1981–. Member: Cranwell Adv. Bd, 1970–73; Council, Cranfield Inst. of Technology, 1971– (Dep. Chm., 1983). *Publications*: Sailplanes of the World (with B. S. Shenstone): Vol. 1, 1960; Vol. 2, 1963; articles and papers to: Jl of Royal Aeronautical Soc.; Aircraft Engineering. *Recreations*: gliding, swimming, gardening, travel. *Address*: Pheasants, Mill End, Hambleden, Henley-on-Thames, Oxon RG9 3BL.

WILKINSON, Sir Martin; see Wilkinson, Sir R. F. M.

WILKINSON, Rt. Hon. Sir Nicolas Christopher Henry B.; see Browne-Wilkinson.

WILKINSON, Prof. Paul; Professor of International Relations, since 1979, and Head of the Department of Politics and International Relations, since 1985, University of Aberdeen; *b* 9 May 1937; *s* of late Walter Ross Wilkinson and of Joan Rosemary (*née* Paul); 1960, Susan; two *s* one *d*. *Educ*: Lower School of John Lyon; University Coll., Swansea, Univ. of Wales (BA (jt Hons Mod. Hist. and Politics), MA; Hon. Fellow, 1986). Royal Air Force regular officer, 1959–65. Asst Lecturer in Politics, 1966–68, Lectr in Politics, 1968–75, Sen. Lectr in Politics, 1975–77, University Coll., Cardiff; Reader, Univ. of Wales, 1978–79. Member: IBA Scottish Adv. Cttee, 1982–85; Academic Adv. Bd, Hughenden Foundn, 1986–; Trustee, Res. Foundn for Study of Terrorism, 1986–. Special Consultant, CBS Broadcasting Co., USA, 1986–. Editorial Adviser, Contemporary Review, 1980–; Mem., Editorial Board, Conflict Quarterly, 1980–. *Publications*: Social Movement, 1971; Political Terrorism, 1974; Terrorism versus Liberal Democracy, 1976; Terrorism and the Liberal State, 1977, rev. edn 1986; (jtly) Terrorism: theory and practice, 1978; Gen. Editor, Key Concepts in International Relations, 1980–; (ed) British Perspectives on Terrorism, 1981; The New Fascists, 1981, rev. edn 1983; Defence of the West, 1983; contribs to wide range of jls in Britain, USA and Canada. *Recreations*: modern art, poetry, walking. *Address*: Edward Wright Building, Dunbar Street, Old Aberdeen, Aberdeen AB9 2UB. *T*: Aberdeen 40241. *Club*: Savile.

WILKINSON, Sir Peter (Allix), KCMG 1970 (CMG 1960); DSO 1944; OBE 1944; HM Diplomatic Service, retired; *b* 15 April 1914; *s* of late Captain Osborn Cecil Wilkinson; *m* 1945, Mary Theresa (*d* 1984), *d* of late Algernon Villiers; two *d*. *Educ*: Rugby; Corpus Christi Coll., Cambridge. Commissioned in 2nd Bn Royal Fusiliers, 1935; active service in Poland (despatches), France, Italy and Balkans; retired with rank of Lieut-Colonel, 1947. Entered HM Foreign Service, appointed 1st Secretary at British Legation, Vienna, 1947; 1st Secretary at British Embassy, Washington, 1952; Secretary-General of Heads of Government Meeting at Geneva, 1955; Counsellor, HM Embassy, Bonn, 1955; Counsellor, Foreign Office, 1960–63; Under-Secretary, Cabinet Office, 1963–64; Senior Civilian Instructor at the Imperial Defence Coll., 1964–66; Ambassador to Vietnam, 1966–67; Under-Secretary, Foreign Office, 1967–68; Chief of Administration, HM Diplomatic Service, 1968–70; Ambassador to Vienna, 1970–71. Cross of Valour (Poland), 1940; Order of White Lion (IV Class) (Czechoslovakia), 1945. *Recreations*: gardening, sailing, fishing. *Address*: Mill House, Charing, Kent. *T*: Charing 2306. *Clubs*: White's, Army and Navy.

WILKINSON, Peter William, MC 1942; Director, Anglia Building Society, since 1978 (General Manager, 1978–83; Joint Chief General Manager, April-Dec. 1983); *b* 10 Dec. 1922; *s* of Frederic Walter Wilkinson, FCA, and Lillie Mary Wilkinson; *m* 1948, Cicely June (*née* Bettington); two *s* one *d*. *Educ*: Gresham's Sch., Holt. FCA; ACBSI. Served War of 1939–45 (MC). Joined Northampton Town and County Building Soc., 1963; Mem. Council, Building Socs Assoc., 1973–83; Chm., Midland Assoc. of Building Socs, 1978–79. *Recreations*: fishing, sailing, golf. *Address*: Tharfield, East Haddon, Northampton NN6 8DE. *Club*: Naval and Military.

WILKINSON, Philip William, FIB; Director, since 1979, and Group Chief Executive, since 1983, National Westminster Bank PLC; Director, International Westminster Bank Ltd, since 1982; *b* 8 May 1927; *m* 1951, Eileen Patricia (*née* Malkin); one *s* two *d*. *Educ*: Leyton County High School. Joined Westminster Bank, 1943; Chief Executive, Lombard North Central Ltd, 1975; General Manager, Related Banking Services Division, 1978; Dep. Group Chief Executive, 1980. *Recreations*: golf and watching sport. *Address*: 41 Lothbury, EC2P 2BP. *T*: 01–726 1266. *Club*: Royal Automobile.

WILKINSON, Rev. Canon Raymond Stewart; Rector of Solihull, since 1971; Chaplain to the Queen, since 1982; Hon. Canon of Birmingham, since 1976; *b* 5 June 1919; *s* of Sidney Ewart and Florence Miriam Wilkinson; *m* 1945, Dorothy Elinor Church; four *s*. *Educ*: Luton Grammar Sch.; King's Coll., London (AKC); Bishop's Coll., Cheshunt. Curate of Croxley Green, 1943–45; Vicar: S Oswald's, Croxley Green, 1945–50; Abbot's Langley, 1950–61; Rector of Woodchurch, 1961–71; Proctor in Convocation and Mem.,

Church Assembly, 1964–71. Member, various educnl governing bodies. *Publications*: To the More Edifying, 1952; The Church and Parish of Abbot's Langley, 1955; My Confirmation Search Book, 1962, 10th edn 1982; An Adult Confirmation Candidate's Handbook, 1964, 6th edn 1984; Gospel Sermons for Alternative Service Book, 1983; Learning about Vestments and Altar Serving, 1984; A Pocket Guide for Servers, 1985; The Essence of Anglicanism, 1986. *Recreations*: producing, acting in and conducting Gilbert and Sullivan operas; church architecture, organising youth holidays. *Address*: Solihull Rectory, West Midlands B91 3RQ. *T*: (home) 021–705 0069; (office) 021–705 5350. *Clubs*: Royal Commonwealth Society, Royal Society of Arts.

WILKINSON, Sir (Robert Francis) Martin, Kt 1969; Chairman: the Stock Exchange, London, 1965–March 1973; the Stock Exchange, March-June 1973 (Deputy Chairman, 1963–65); Chairman, Federation of Stock Exchanges in Great Britain and Ireland, 1965–73; *b* 4 June 1911; *e s* of late Sir Robert Pelham Wilkinson and Phyllis Marion Wilkinson; *m* 1936, Dora Esme, *d* of late William John Arendt and late Mrs Arendt; three *d*. *Educ*: Repton. Member, Stock Exchange, 1933; Partner in de Zoete & Gorton, 1936; Senior Partner, de Zoete & Bevan, 1970–76; Member of Council, Stock Exchange, 1959. Chm., Altifund, 1976–81; Dir, City of London Brewery Trust (Chm., 1977–78). One of HM Lieutenants, City of London, 1973–. Served with RAF 1940–45. *Recreations*: cricket, gardening. *Address*: Hurst-an-Clays, Ship Street, East Grinstead, W Sussex RH19 4EE. *Club*: City of London.

WILKINSON, Sydney Frank, CB 1951; Director of Administration, National Research Development Corporation, 1955–65; *b* 14 Dec. 1894; *s* of Charles James Carey Wilkinson; *m* 1924, Gladys Millicent Boorsma; one *s*. *Educ*: Strand Sch.; King's Coll., London. Entered Civil Service, National Health Insurance Commission, 1913; Commissioned RFA, 1918; Private Secretary to Minister of Food, 1920; Secretary to Parliamentary Conference on Reform of Licensing Law, 1921; Assistant Private Secretary to Sir Kingsley Wood, 1935; loaned to National Fitness Council, 1937; Private Secretary to Mr Walter Elliot and Mr Malcolm MacDonald, 1938–40; Security Executive, 1940–41; Director of Public Relations, Ministry of Health, 1941–43. Under-Secretary for Housing, Ministry of Housing and Local Government, 1951–54 (Ministry of Local Government and Planning, 1951; Ministry of Health, 1947–51). *Recreation*: golf. *Address*: 51 Cornwall Road, Cheam, Surrey SM2 6DU. *T*: 01–642 0374.

WILKINSON, William Henry Nairn; Chairman, Nature Conservancy Council, since 1983; *b* 22 July 1932; *e s* of late Denys and Gillian Wilkinson, of Eton College; *m* 1964, Katharine Louise Frederica, *er d* of late F. W. H. Loudon and of Lady Prudence Loudon; one *s* two *d*. *Educ*: Eton Coll. (King's Schol.); Trinity Coll., Cambridge (Major Scholar; MA). Council of Royal Society for the Protection of Birds, 1970–76 (Hon. Treasurer, 1971–76), and again, 1977–83 (Chm., Information Cttee, 1980–81, Hon. Treas., 1981–83); Council of the Game Conservancy, 1976, and Vice-Chm., 1981–83. Chm., TSL Thermal Syndicate plc, 1984– (Dir, 1976–); Director: Kleinwort Benson Ltd, 1973–85; John Mowlem and Co. plc, 1977–. Mem. Council, Winston Churchill Meml Trust, 1985–. FRSA. *Publications*: papers for ornithological conferences. *Recreations*: ornithology, opera and music, shooting, archaeology. *Address*: 119 Castelnau, Barnes, SW13 9EL; Pill House, Llanmadoc, Gower, West Glamorgan SA3 1DB. *Club*: Brooks's.

WILKINSON, Dr William Lionel, FEng 1980; Deputy Chief Executive, British Nuclear Fuels Ltd, since 1986 (Deputy Director, 1979–84; Technical Director, 1984–86); Member, Science and Engineering Research Council, since 1981; *b* 16 Feb. 1931; *s* of Lionel and Dorothy Wilkinson; *m* 1955, Josephine Anne Pilgrim; five *s*. *Educ*: Christ's Coll., Cambridge. MA, PhD, ScD; FIChemE. Salters' Res. Schol., Christ's Coll., Cambridge, 1953–56; Lectr in Chem. Engrg, UC Swansea, 1956–59; UKAEA Production Gp, 1959–67; Prof. of Chem. Engrg, Univ. of Bradford, 1967–79. *Publications*: Non-Newtonian Flow, 1960; contribs to sci. and engrg jls on heat transfer, fluid mechanics, polymer processing and process dynamics. *Recreations*: sailing, fell-walking. *Address*: Tree Tops, Legh Road, Knutsford, Cheshire WA16 8LP. *T*: Knutsford 53344.

WILKS, Jean Ruth Fraser, CBE 1977; Pro-Chancellor, Birmingham University, since 1985; *b* 14 April 1917; *d* of Mark Wilks. *Educ*: North London Collegiate Sch.; Somerville Coll., Oxford (MA; Hon. Fellow, 1985). Assistant Mistress: Truro High Sch., 1940–43; James Allen's Girls' Sch., Dulwich, 1943–51; Head Mistress, Hertfordshire and Essex High Sch., Bishop's Stortford, Hertfordshire, 1951–64; Head Mistress, King Edward VI High Sch. for Girls, Birmingham, 1965–77. Pres., Assoc. of Head Mistresses, 1972–74; Member: Public Schools Commn, 1968–70; Governing Council of Schools Council, 1972–75; Adv. Council on Supply and Trng of Teachers, 1973–78; Educn Cttee, Royal Coll. of Nursing, 1973–79; University Authorities Panel, 1982–. University of Birmingham: Mem. Council, 1971–; Chm., Academic Staffing Cttee, 1978–; Dep. Pro-Chancellor, 1979–85. Hon. Fellow, Somerville Coll., 1985 (Pres. ASM, 1982–85); Chm. Governors, Ellerslie, Malvern, 1982–. FCP 1978. Hon. LLD Birmingham, 1986. *Address*: 4 Hayward Road, Oxford OX2 8LW. *Club*: Naval and Military.

WILKS, Jim; see Wilks, Stanley David.

WILKS, Stanley David, (Jim Wilks), CB 1979; MIEx; Deputy Chairman (formerly Director General), Technology Transfer Group, since 1981; Director: Matthew Hall International Development, Ltd, since 1981; Hadson Petroleum International plc, since 1981; Hadson Corporation (USA), since 1985; Export Intelligence Ltd, since 1986; Consultant Director, Strategy International, since 1981; Regional Director, James Hallam Ltd, since 1984; *b* 1 Aug. 1920; *m* 1947, Dorothy Irene Adamthwaite; one *s* one *d*. *Educ*: Polytechnic Sch., London. Royal Armoured Corps, 1939–46; service with 48th Bn, Royal Tank Regt; 3rd Carabiniers, Imphal, 1944. Home Office, 1946–50; Board of Trade, later Dept of Trade, 1950–80: posts included 1st Sec., British Embassy, Washington, 1950–53; GATT, non-ferrous metals, ECGD, airports policy; Chief Exec., BOTB, 1975–80. Vice-Chm., Internat. Tin Council, 1968–69; Chm., Tech. Help for Exporters Management Cttee, BSI, 1982–. Chm., UK Wayfarer Assoc., 1982–. MIEx 1981. *Recreation*: dinghy racing. *Address*: 6 Foxgrove Avenue, Beckenham, Kent. *Clubs*: World Traders, Civil Service; Medway Yacht, Lloyd's Yacht.

WILL, Ronald Kerr; Deputy Keeper of Her Majesty's Signet, 1975–83; formerly Senior Partner, Dundas & Wilson, CS, Edinburgh; *b* 22 March 1918; 3rd *s* of late James Alexander Will, WS and late Bessie Kennedy Salmon, Dumfries; *m* 1953, Margaret Joyce, *d* of late D. Alan Stevenson, BSc, FRSE; two *s*. *Educ*: Merchiston Castle Sch.; Edinburgh Univ. Commnd King's Own Scottish Borderers, 1940; served with 1st Bn and in Staff appts (despatches); psc; GSO2. Writer to the Signet, 1950. Director: Scottish Equitable Life Assce Soc., 1965– (Chm., 1980–84); Scottish Investment Trust PLC, 1963–; Standard Property Investment PLC, 1972–. Mem. Council on Tribunals, 1971–76 and Chm. of Scottish Cttee, 1972–76. Governor, Merchiston Castle Sch., 1953–76. *Recreations*: shooting, fishing. *Address*: 3 Belgrave Place, Edinburgh EH4 3AN. *T*: 031–3328970. *Club*: New (Edinburgh).

WILLAN, Edward Gervase, CMG 1964; HM Diplomatic Service, retired; Ambassador to Czechoslovakia, 1974–77; *b* 17 May 1917; *er s* of late Captain F. G. L. Willan, RNR;

m 1944, Mary Bickley Joy, *d* of late Lieut-Colonel H. A. Joy, IAOC. *Educ:* Radley; Pembroke Coll., Cambridge (Exhibitioner, MA). Indian Civil Service, 1939–47; 2nd Secretary (from 1948, 1st Secretary) on staff of UK High Commissioner, New Delhi, 1947–49; appointed to HM Diplomatic Service, 1948; Foreign Office, 1949–52; 1st Secretary, HM Embassy, The Hague, 1953–55; 1st Secretary, HM Legation, Bucharest, 1956–58 (Chargé d'Affaires, 1956, 1957 and 1958); Head of Communications Dept, FO, 1958–62; Political Adviser to Hong Kong Government, 1962–65; Head of Scientific Relations Dept, FO, 1966–68; Minister, Lagos, 1968–70; Ambassador at Rangoon, 1970–74. *Recreations:* travel, walking, gardening. *Address:* Cherry Tree Cottage, Shappen Hill, Burley, Hants. *Club:* United Oxford & Cambridge University.

WILLAN, Prof. Thomas Stuart, MA, BLitt, DPhil; Professor of Economic History, University of Manchester, 1961–73, now Emeritus; *b* 3 Jan. 1910; 3rd *s* of Matthew Willan and Jane (*née* Stuart); unmarried. *Educ:* Queen Elizabeth's Sch., Kirkby Lonsdale; The Queen's Coll., Oxford. Asst Lecturer, School of Economics and Commerce, Dundee, 1934–35; University of Manchester: Asst Lecturer in History, 1935–45; Lecturer in History, 1945–47; Senior Lecturer in History, 1947–49; Reader in History, 1949–61. *Publications:* River Navigation in England, 1600–1750, 1936; The English Coasting Trade, 1600–1750, 1938; (ed with E. W. Crossley) Three Seventeenth-century Yorkshire Surveys, 1941; The Navigation of the Great Ouse between St Ives and Bedford in the Seventeenth Century, 1946; The Navigation of the River Weaver in the Eighteenth Century, 1951; The Muscovy Merchants of 1555, 1953; The Early History of the Russia Company, 1553–1603, 1956; Studies in Elizabethan Foreign Trade, 1959; (ed) A Tudor Book of Rates, 1962; The Early History of the Don Navigation, 1965; An Eighteenth-Century Shopkeeper, Abraham Dent of Kirkby Stephen, 1970; The Inland Trade, 1976; Elizabethan Manchester, 1980; articles in English Historical Review, Economic History Review, etc. *Address:* 3 Raynham Avenue, Didsbury, Manchester M20 0BW. *T:* 061–445 4771. *Club:* Penn.

WILLATT, Sir Hugh, Kt 1972; Secretary General of the Arts Council of Great Britain, 1968–75 (Member, 1958–68); *b* 25 April 1909; *m* 1945, Evelyn Gibbs, ARE, ARCA, (Rome Scholar); no *c. Educ:* Repton; Pembroke Coll., Oxford (MA). Admitted a Solicitor, 1934; Partner, Hunt, Dickins and Willatt, Nottingham, and later Partner in Lewis, Silkin & Partners, Westminster. Served War of 1939–45, in RAF. Member BBC Midland Regional Adv. Council, 1953–58; Member Arts Council Drama Panel, 1955–68 (Chairman, 1960–68); Chm. Bd, Nat. Opera Studio, 1977–; Member Board: National Theatre, 1964–68; Mercury Trust Ltd (Ballet Rambert) (Chm.), 1961–67; Nottingham Theatre Trust Ltd, 1949–60; Riverside Studios, Hammersmith (Chm., 1976–82); Visiting Arts Unit (Chm., 1977–83); English Stage Co. (Royal Court Theatre), 1976–. FRSA 1974. Hon. MA, University of Nottingham. *Address:* 4 St Peter's Wharf, Hammersmith Terrace, W6. *Club:* Garrick.

WILLCOCK, Kenneth Milner, QC 1972; **His Honour Judge Willcock;** a Circuit Judge, since 1972. MA; BCL. Called to Bar, Inner Temple, 1950. Dep. Chm., Somerset QS, 1969–71; a Recorder of the Crown Court, 1972. *Address:* Queen Elizabeth Building, Temple, EC4Y 9BS.

WILLCOCK, Prof. Malcolm Maurice; Professor of Latin, University College London, since 1980; *b* 1 Oct. 1925; *s* of late Dr Maurice Excel Willcock and Evelyn Clarice Willcock (*née* Brooks); *m* 1957, Sheena Gourlay; four *d. Educ:* Fettes Coll.; Pembroke Coll., Cambridge (MA). Served Royal Air Force, 1944–47. Research Fellow, Pembroke Coll., Cambridge, 1951–52; Sidney Sussex College: Fellow, 1952–65; Sen. Tutor, 1962–65; University of Lancaster: first Professor of Classics, 1965–79; Principal, Bowland Coll., 1966–79; Pro-Vice-Chancellor, 1975–79. *Publications:* ed, Plautus Casina, 1976; Companion to the Iliad, 1976; ed, Iliad of Homer, vol. 1 (Books I–XII) 1978, vol. 2 (Books XIII–XXIV) 1984; articles and reviews in classical jls. *Recreations:* squash, bridge. *Address:* 1 Lancaster Avenue, SE27. *T:* 01–761 5615.

WILLCOCKS, Sir David (Valentine), Kt 1977; CBE 1971; MC 1944; Musical Director of the Bach Choir since 1960; General Editor, OUP Church Music, since 1961; *b* 30 Dec. 1919; *s* of late T. H. Willcocks; *m* 1947, Rachel Gordon, *d* of late Rev. A. C. Blyth, Fellow of Selwyn Coll., Cambridge; two *s* two *d. Educ:* Clifton Coll.; King's Coll., Cambridge (MA; MusB). Chorister, Westminster Abbey, 1929–33; Scholar, Clifton Coll., 1934–38; FRCO, 1938; Scholar at College of St Nicolas (RSCM), 1938–39; Organ Scholar, King's Coll., Cambridge, 1939–40; Open Foundation Scholarship, King's Coll., Cambridge, 1940; Stewart of Rannoch Scholarship, 1940. Served War of 1939–45, 5th Bn DCLI, 1940–45. Organ Scholar, King's Coll., Cambridge, 1945–47; Fellow of King's Coll., Cambridge, 1947–51, Hon. Fellow, 1979; Organist of Salisbury Cathedral, 1947–50; Master of the Choristers and Organist, Worcester Cathedral, 1950–57; Fellow and Organist, King's Coll., Cambridge, 1957–73; Univ. Lectr in Music, Cambridge Univ., 1957–74; Univ. Organist, Cambridge Univ., 1958–74; Dir, RCM, 1974–84. Conductor: Cambridge Philharmonic Soc., 1947; City of Birmingham Choir, 1950–57; Bradford Festival Choral Soc., 1957–74; Cambridge Univ. Musical Soc., 1958–73. President: RCO, 1966–68; ISM, 1978–79; Old Cliftonian Soc., 1979–81; Nat. Fedn of Music Socs, 1980–. Freeman, City of London, 1981. FRSCM 1965; FRCM 1971; FRNCM 1977; FRSAMD 1982; Hon. RAM 1965; Hon. FTCL 1976; Hon. GSM 1980; Hon. Fellow, Royal Canadian College of Organists, 1967. Hon. MA Bradford, 1973; Hon. DMus: Exeter, 1976; Leicester, 1977; Westminster Choir Coll., Princeton, 1980; Bristol, 1981; Hon. DLitt Sussex, 1982; Hon. Dr of Sacred Letters, Trinity Coll., Toronto, 1985. *Publications:* miscellaneous choral and instrumental works. *Address:* 13 Grange Road, Cambridge. *T:* Cambridge 359559. *Clubs:* Athenæum, Arts.

WILLCOX, James Henry; Clerk of Public Bills, House of Commons, since 1982; *b* 31 March 1923; *s* of George Henry and Annie Elizabeth Willcox; *m* 1st, 1950, Winsome Rosemarie Adèle Dallas Ross (*d* 1984); one *s* one *d*; 2nd, 1985, Pamela, *widow* of Col John Lefroy Knyvett. *Educ:* St George's Coll., Weybridge; St John's Coll., Oxford (Schol.; MA). Served RNVR, 1942–45. Assistant Clerk, House of Commons, 1947; Sen. Clerk, 1951; Clerk of Standing Committees, 1975–76; Clerk of Overseas Office, 1976–77; Clerk of Private Bills, Examiner of Petitions for Private Bills and Taxing Officer, 1977–82. *Recreations:* walking, gardening. *Address:* Ibthorpe Farm House, Ibthorpe, near Andover, Hants SP11 0BN. *T:* Hurstbourne Tarrant 575. *Club:* Garrick.

WILLEBRANDS, His Eminence Cardinal Johannes Gerardus Maria; President, Vatican Secretariat for Promoting Christian Unity, since 1969; Archbishop of Utrecht and Primate of Holland, 1975–83; *b* Netherlands, 4 Sept. 1909. *Educ:* Warmond Seminary, Holland; Angelicum, Rome (Dr Phil.). Priest, 1934; Chaplain, Begijnhof Church, Amsterdam, 1937–40; Prof. of Philosophy, Warmond, 1940; Director, 1945; Pres., St Willibrord Assoc., 1946; organised Catholic Conf. on Ecumenical Questions, 1951; Sec., Vatican Secretariat for Promoting Christian Unity, 1960; Titular Bishop of Mauriana, 1964; Cardinal, 1969; Cardinal with the Title of St Sebastian, Martyr, 1975. Hon. Dr of Letters: Notre Dame Univ.; St Louis Univ.; St Olaf Coll., USA; St Thomas' Coll., St Paul's, Minn, 1979; Assumption Coll., Worcester, Mass, 1980; Hon. Dr of Theology: Catholic Univ. of Louvain, 1971; Leningrad Theological Acad, 1973; Catholic Univ.,

Lublin, Poland, 1985. *Publications:* Oecuménisme et Problèmes Actuels; reports on the ecumenical situation and articles on inter-church relationships. *Address:* Via dell'Erba 1, I-00193–Rome, Italy.

WILLESDEN, Area Bishop of, since 1985; **Rt. Rev. Thomas Frederick Butler;** *b* 1940; *s* of Thomas John Butler and Elsie Butler (*née* Bainbridge); *m* 1964, Barbara Joan Clark; one *s* one *d. Educ:* Univ. of Leeds (BSc 1st Cl. Hons, MSc, PhD). CEng; MIEE. College of the Resurrection, Mirfield, 1962–64; Curate: St Augustine's, Wisbech, 1964–66; St Saviour's, Folkestone, 1966–68; Lecturer and Chaplain, Univ. of Zambia, 1968–73; Acting Dean of Holy Cross Cathedral, Lusaka, Zambia, 1972; Chaplain to Univ. of Kent at Canterbury, 1973–80; Archdeacon of Northolt, 1980–85. Six Preacher, Canterbury Cathedral, 1979–84. *Recreations:* reading, mountain walking. *Address:* 173 Willesden Lane, Brondesbury, NW6 7YN. *T:* 01–451 0189.

WILLESEE, Hon. Donald Robert; Member of Senate for Western Australia, 1949–75; *b* 14 April 1916; *m*; four *s* two *d. Educ:* Carnarvon, Western Australia. Special Minister of State, Minister assisting Prime Minister, Minister assisting Minister for Foreign Affairs and Vice-Pres. of Exec. Council, 1972–73; Minister for Foreign Affairs, 1973–75; Leader of Opposition in the Senate, 1966–67; Deputy Leader of Opposition in Senate, 1969–72; Deputy Leader of Govt in Senate, 1972. *Recreation:* swimming. *Address:* 5 Walton Place, Quinns Rock, WA 6030, Australia.

WILLETT, Archibald Anthony; Investment Chairman, Cable & Wireless Pension Funds, since 1984; *b* 27 Jan. 1924; *s* of Reginald Beckett Willett and Mabel Alice (*née* Plaister); *m* 1948, Doris Marjorie Peat; one *s* one *d. Educ:* Oswestry High Sch.; Southall Grammar School. Lloyds Bank Ltd, 1940; Great Western Railway Co., 1941–42 and 1947–48; RAF (Signals Branch), 1942–47; Cable & Wireless Ltd, 1948–77; Dir, 1967–77; Dep. Man. Dir, 1971–72; Man. Dir, 1973–77. Bursar and Fellow, St Antony's Coll., Oxford, 1977–84; Fellow Emeritus 1984. MA Oxon 1977; FCIS 1963. *Recreations:* home and garden, walking, trout fishing. *Address:* St Antony's College, Oxford. *Clubs:* Royal Automobile; Exiles' (Twickenham).

WILLETT, Prof. Frank, CBE 1985; FRSE 1979; Director and Titular Professor, Hunterian Museum and Art Gallery, Glasgow, since 1976; *b* 18 Aug. 1925; *s* of Thomas Willett and Frances (*née* Latham); *m* 1950, Mary Constance Hewitt; one *s* three *d. Educ:* Bolton Municipal Secondary Sch.; University Coll., Oxford. MA (Oxon); Dip. Anthropology (Oxon). War damage clerk, Inland Revenue, 1940; RAF Linguist, Japanese, 1943–44. Keeper, Dept of Ethnology and Gen. Archaeology, Manchester Museum, 1950–58; Hon. Surveyor of Antiquities, Nigerian Federal Govt, 1956–57, 1958; Archaeologist and Curator, Mus. of Ife Antiquities, Nigerian Fed. Govt, 1958–63; Supply Teacher, Bolton Educn Cttee, 1963–64; Leverhulme Research Fellow, 1964; Research Fellow, Nuffield Coll., Oxford, 1964–66; Prof. of Art History, African and Interdisciplinary Studies, Northwestern Univ., Evanston, Ill, USA, 1966–76; Vis. Fellow, Clare Hall, Cambridge, 1970–71. Hon. Corresp. Member, Manchester Literary and Philosophical Soc., 1958–. *Publications:* Ife in the History of West African Sculpture, 1967, rev. edn, Ife: une Civilisation Africaine, 1971; African Art: An Introduction, 1971, rev. 1977; (with Ekpo Eyo) Treasures of Ancient Nigeria, 1980; articles in Encyc. Britannica, Man, Jl of Afr. Hist., Afr. Arts, Africa, Jl of Nigerian Historical Soc., Odu, SA Archaeol Bull., Archæometry; many conf. reports and chapters in several books. *Recreation:* relaxing. *Address:* Hunterian Museum, University of Glasgow, Glasgow G12 8QQ. *T:* 041–339 8855 (ext. 4285). *Club:* Royal Commonwealth Society.

WILLETT, Prof. Frederick John, AO 1984; DSC 1944; Vice-Chancellor, Griffith University, Queensland, 1972–84; *b* 26 Feb. 1922; *s* of E. Willett; *m* 1949, Jane Cunningham Westwater; one *s* two *d. Educ:* Fitzwilliam House, Cambridge. MA (Cambridge), MBA (Melb.). Observer, Fleet Air Arm, Atlantic, Mediterranean, Indian and Pacific theatres, 1939–46; served with British Naval Liaison Mission, Washington, 1942–43. Asst Director of Research in Industrial Management, Univ. of Cambridge, 1957–62; Sidney Myer Prof. of Commerce and Business Administration, Univ. of Melbourne, 1962–72, now Emeritus. Pro Vice-Chancellor, University of Melbourne, 1966–72. Mem., Aust.-China Council, 1979–82; Chm., Indonesian Social Sciences Project, 1983–86. Hon. LLD Melbourne, 1973; Hon. DEcon Qld, 1983; DUniv Griffith, 1983. FAIM. *Publications:* many articles and papers. *Address:* 576 Coronation Drive, Toowong, Qld 4066, Australia. *Club:* Queensland (Brisbane).

WILLETT, Guy William; a Recorder of the Crown Court, 1971–76; *b* 10 June 1913; *y s* of late William and late Florence Mary Anne Willett; *m* 1945, Elizabeth Evelyn Joan Radford; one *s* two *d. Educ:* Malvern; Gonville and Caius Coll., Cambridge (BA). Called to Bar, 1937; Western Circuit, 1938; Head of Chambers, Francis Taylor Building, Temple, 1961–77. Chm., Halstead Sch., 1958–74. *Recreations:* cricket, sailing, golf. *Address:* Sundial House, 24A High Street, Alderney, CI. *T:* Alderney 2911. *Clubs:* Westfield and District Cricket (Pres. 1946–74), Admiralty Ferry Crew Assoc., Alderney Golf, Alderney Society, Bar Yacht, Bar Golf.

WILLETTS, Bernard Frederick, PhD; CEng, FIMechE, FIProdE; CBIM; Deputy Chief Executive, Dubai Aluminium Company Ltd, since 1981; Non-Executive Director: Liverpool Daily Post and Echo, since 1976; Telephone Rentals Ltd, since 1981; *b* 24 March 1927; *s* of James Frederick Willetts and Effie Hurst; *m* 1952, Norah Elizabeth Law; two *s. Educ:* Birmingham Central Grammar Sch.; Birmingham Univ. (BSc); Durham Univ. (MSc, PhD). Section Leader, Vickers-Armstrong (Engineers) Ltd, 1954–58; Massey-Ferguson (UK) Ltd: Chief Engineer, 1959; Director, Engineering, 1962; Director, Manufacturing, 1965; Dep. Managing Director, 1967; Plessey Co. Ltd: Group Managing Director, Telecommunications, 1968; Main Board Director, 1969; Dep. Chief Exec., 1975–78; Vickers Ltd: Asst Managing Director, 1978; Man. Dir, 1980. Vice-Pres., Instn of Production Engineers, 1979–82. *Recreations:* gardening, squash, stamp collecting. *Address:* Suna Court, Pearson Road, Sonning-on-Thames, Berkshire. *T:* Reading 695050. *Clubs:* Lansdowne; Parkstone Yacht.

WILLEY, Rt. Hon. Frederick Thomas, PC 1964; Vice-President, Save the Children Fund; Barrister; *b* 1910; *s* of late Frederick and Mary Willey; *m* 1939, Eleanor, *d* of late William and Elizabeth Snowdon; two *s* one *d. Educ:* Johnston Sch.; St John's Coll., Cambridge Univ. (Full blue Soccer; 1st Class Hons Law; Blackstone Prizeman, Harmsworth Studentship, McMahon Studentship, etc.). Called to Bar, Middle Temple, 1936. MP (Lab) Sunderland, 1945–50, Sunderland N, 1950–83; PPS to Rt Hon. J. Chuter Ede, 1946–50; Chm., Select Cttee on Estimates and Mem. Select Cttees on Statutory Instruments and Public Accounts until 1950; Parly Sec. to Ministry of Food, 1950–51; Dir, North-Eastern Trading Estates Ltd, until 1950; River Wear Comr until 1950; Former Mem., Consultative Assembly of the Council of Europe and Assembly of WEU; Minister of Land and Natural Resources, 1964–67; Minister of State, Ministry of Housing and Local Government, 1967; Member, Select Committee on: Privileges; Members' Interests (former Chm.); former Chairman, Select Committee on: Race Relations and Immigration; Selection; Abortion (Amendment) Bill; Parly and Scientific Cttee. Chm., PLP, 1979–81. Vice-Pres., Youth Hostels Trust of England and Wales. Hon. Fellow, Sunderland Polytechnic. *Publications:* Plan for Shipbuilding, 1956; Education, Today and

Tomorrow, 1964; An Enquiry into Teacher Training, 1971; The Honourable Member, 1974; articles in various periodicals, legal and political. *Address:* 2 The Butts, Biddestone, Chippenham, Wilts SN14 7DY.

WILLIAMS; *see* Rees-Williams, family name of Baron Ogmore.

WILLIAMS, family name of **Baron Williams of Elvel.**

WILLIAMS OF ELVEL, Baron *cr* 1985 (Life Peer), of Llansantffraed in Elvel in the County of Powys; **Charles Cuthbert Powell Williams,** CBE 1980; Chairman, Berkeley Exploration and Production PLC, since 1982; *b* 9 Feb. 1933; *s* of late Dr Norman Powell Williams, DD, and Mrs Muriel de Lérisson Williams (*née* Cazenove); *m* 1975, Jane Gillian (*née* Portal), JP; one step *s*. *Educ.* Westminster Sch.; Christ Church, Oxford (MA); LSE. British Petroleum Co. Ltd, 1958–64; Bank of London and Montreal, 1964–66; Eurofinance SA, Paris, 1966–70; Baring Brothers and Co. Ltd, 1970–77 (Man. Dir, 1971–77); Chm., Price Commn, 1977–79; Man. Dir 1980–82, Chm. 1982–85, Henry Ansbacher & Co. Ltd; Chief Exec., Henry Ansbacher Holdings PLC, 1982–85. Parly Candidate (Lab), Colchester, 1964. Founder Mem, Labour Econ. Finance and Taxation Assoc. (Vice-Chm., 1975–77, 1979–83). Director: Pergamon Holdings Ltd; Hollis PLC; BPCC Printing Corp. PLC; Schütz Choir Ltd. FRSA. *Recreations:* cricket (Oxford Univ. CC, 1953–55, Captain 1955; Essex CCC, 1953–59); music, real tennis. *Address:* 48 Thurloe Square, SW7 2SX. *T:* 01–581 1783; Pant-y-Rhiw, Llansantffraed in Elvel, Powys LD1 5RH. *Clubs:* Reform, MCC.

WILLIAMS, Alan Frederick, PhD; Director, Medical Research Council Cellular Immunology Unit, since 1977; *b* 25 May 1945; *s* of Walter Alan and Mary Elizabeth Williams; *m* 1967, Rosalind Margaret Wright; one *s* one *d*. *Educ:* Box Hill High Sch., Melbourne; Melbourne Univ. (BAgrSc); Adelaide Univ. (PhD Biochem). Departmental Demonstrator, Biochemistry Dept, Oxford Univ., 1970–72; Jun. Research Fellow, Linacre Coll., Oxford, 1970–72; Staff Member, MRC Immunochemistry Unit, Oxford, 1972–77. *Publications:* contribs to biochemistry and immunology scientific jls. *Recreation:* gardening. *Address:* Sir William Dunn School of Pathology, University of Oxford, Oxford OX1 3RE. *T:* Oxford 57321.

WILLIAMS, Prof. Alan Harold; Professor in the Department of Economics, University of York, since 1968; *b* 9 June 1927; *s* of Harold George Williams and Gladys May Williams (*née* Clark); *m* 1953, June Frances Porter; two *s* one *d*. *Educ:* King Edward's, Birmingham; Univ. of Birmingham (BCom). Lecturer, Exeter Univ., 1954–63; Sen. Lectr and Reader, Univ. of York, 1964–68. Visiting Lecturer: MIT, 1957–58; Princeton, 1963–64; Director of Economic Studies, HM Treasury Centre for Administrative Studies, 1966–68. Member: Yorkshire Water Authority, 1973–76; DHSS Chief Scientists Research Cttee, 1973–78; Royal Commission on the NHS, 1976–78; various SSRC Cttees and Panels, 1973–; Nat. Water Council, 1980–83. Hon. DPhil Lund, 1977. *Publications:* Public Finance and Budgetary Policy, 1963; (with Robert Anderson) Efficiency in the Social Services, 1975; (with Robert Sugden) Principles of Practical Cost-Benefit Analysis, 1978; articles in Economica, Jl of Political Econ., Jl of Public Econs, Nat. Tax Jl, and elsewhere; numerous conf. papers on various aspects of public expenditure appraisal, esp. the NHS. *Recreations:* music, walking, teasing.

WILLIAMS, Rt. Hon. Alan John, PC 1977; MP (Lab) Swansea West since 1964; *b* 14 Oct. 1930; *m* 1957, Mary Patricia Rees, Blackwood, Mon; two *s* one *d*. *Educ:* Cardiff High Sch.; Cardiff College of Technology; University College, Oxford. BSc (London); BA (Oxon). Lecturer in economics, Welsh College of Advanced Technology; Free-lance Journalist. Joined Labour Party, 1950. Member: NATFHE (formerly of ATTI), 1958–; Fabian Society; Co-operative Party; National Union of Students delegation to Russia, 1954. Advr, Assoc. of First Div. Civil Servants, 1982–. Contested (Lab) Poole, 1959. PPS to Postmaster General, 1966–67; Parly Under-Sec., DEA, 1967–69; Parly Sec., Min. of Technology, 1969–70; Opposition Spokesman on Consumer Protection, Small Businesses, Minerals, 1970–74; Minister of State: Dept of Prices and Consumer Protection, 1974–76; DoI, 1976–79; Opposition spokesman on Wales, 1979–80; Shadow Minister for CS, 1980–83; opposition spokesman on trade and industry, 1983–; Dep. Shadow Leader of the House, 1983–. Chairman, Welsh PLP, 1966–67; Delegate, Council of Europe and WEU, 1966–67; Mem. Public Accts Cttee, 1966–67; Jt Chm., All-Party Minerals Cttee, 1979–. Sponsored by TSSA (Mem., 1984–). *Address:* House of Commons, SW1; Hill View, 96 Plunch Lane, Limeslade, Swansea. *Club:* Clyne Golf.

WILLIAMS, Alan Lee, OBE 1973; Warden, Toynbee Hall, since 1987; *b* 29 Nov. 1930; *m* 1963, Karen Scott Holloway (marr. diss. 1971); two *s*; *m* 1974, Jennifer Ford. *Educ:* Roan Sch., Greenwich; Ruskin Coll., Oxford. National Service, RAF, 1951–53; Oxford, 1954–56; National Youth Officer, Labour Party, 1956–62; MP (Lab) Hornchurch, 1966–70, Havering, Hornchurch, Feb. 1974–1979; PPS to Sec. of State for Defence, 1969–70, 1976; PPS to Sec. of State for NI, 1976–78; Dir-Gen., E-SU, 1979–86. Chm., Parly Lab. Party Defence Cttee, 1976–79; Member: FO Adv. Cttee on Disarmament and Arms Control, 1975–79; Adv. Council on Public Records, 1977–84; Chm., Delegn to 4th Cttee of UN, NY, 1969; Jt Editor, Labour Trades Union Press Service, 1975; Chairman: All Party Parly River Thames Group, 1974–79; Transport on Water Assoc.; Deputy Director, European Movement, 1970–71, Treasurer, 1972–79; Dir, British Atlantic Cttee, 1972–74, Chm., 1980–83; Vice Pres., European-Atlantic Gp, 1983–; Chm., Peace Through NATO, 1983–; Member: RUSI, 1968–; European Working Gp of Internat. Centre for Strategic and Internat. Studies, Georgetown Univ., Washington DC, 1974–; Trilateral Commn, 1976; Council, Council for Arms Control, 1982–. Joined SDP, 1981. Freeman: City of London, 1969; Co. of Watermen and Lightermen, 1952–. FRSA. *Publications:* Radical Essays, 1966; Europe or the Open Sea?, 1971; Crisis in European Defence, 1973; The European Defence Initiative: Europe's bid for equality, 1985; UN Assoc. pamphlet, UN and Warsaw and Nato Pacts; Fabian Soc. pamphlet on East/West Détente. *Recreations:* reading, history and novels, walking, camping. *Address:* 6 North Several, Blackheath, SE3 0QR. *T:* 01–852 3188. *Clubs:* Reform, Travellers', Pilgrims.

WILLIAMS, Albert; General Secretary, Union of Construction, Allied Trades and Technicians, since 1985; *b* 12 Feb 1927; *s* of William Arthur Williams and Phyllis Williams (*née* Barnes); *m* 1954, Edna Bradley; two *s*. *Educ:* Houldsworth School, Reddish; Manchester School of Building (1st and 2nd year ULCI Certs of Training). Apprentice bricklayer, Manchester City Corp., 1941; Armed Forces, 1944–48; bricklaying for various contractors; Member: Exec., Amalgamated Union of Building Trade Workers, 1958; Exec., Council of UCATT, 1971; Operatives' Side Sec., Nat. Jt Council for Building Industry, 1984–. *Recreations:* poetry and work. *Address:* UCATT House, 177 Abbeville Road, SW4 9RL. *T:* 01–622 2442.

WILLIAMS, (Albert) Clifford, BEM 1957; JP; Member: Welsh National Water Development Authority; Sports Council for Wales, 1972–75 (Vice-Chairman, Centre Committee; Chairman, Water Recreation Committee); *b* 28 June 1905; British; *s* of Daniel Williams, Blaina, Mon; *m* 1929, Beatrice Anne, *d* of Charles Garbett; one *d*. *Educ:* Primary Sch., Blaina, Mon. Trade Union Official, 1935–50. Mem. 21 years, Chm. 10 years, Usk Rivers Authority; Vice-Pres., former Assoc. of River Authorities. Administrator of Voluntary Hospitals, 40 years until 1969; Vice-Chm., N Monmouthshire HMC. County Councillor, Monmouthshire; Alderman, 1964–74; MP (Lab) Abertillery, April 1965–1970. *Recreations:* watching sports, Rugby football. *Address:* Brodawel, Abertillery Road, Blaina, Gwent NP3 3DZ. *T:* Blaina 379.

WILLIAMS, (Albert) Trevor; management scientist; *b* 7 April 1938; *s* of Ben and Minnie Williams; *m* 1st, 1970, Mary Lynn Lyster; three *s*; 2nd, 1978, Deborah Sarah Fraser Duncan (*née* Milne); one *s*. *Educ:* King George V Sch., Southport; Queens' Coll., Cambridge (MA); Cranfield Institute of Technology (MSc). Rotary Foundation Fellow, Univ. of Ghana, 1961–62; Business Operations Research Ltd: Director, 1965–68; various academic appointments, 1968–78, including: Sen. Lectr and Vis. Professor, Graduate School of Business, Cape Town Univ.; Sen. Research Fellow, Sussex Univ.; Vis. Associate Prof., Wisconsin Univ.; Vis. Prof., INSEAD. Dir, Novy Eddison and Partners, 1971–74; Dep.-Dir for Futures Research, Univ. of Stellenbosch, 1974–78; Dep. Chief Scientific Officer, Price Commission, 1978–79; Advisor on Technology Projects, Scottish Development Agency, 1979; Dir, Henley Centre for Forecasting, 1980–81; various consultancy assignments (incl. consultant and Sen. Industrial Advr, Monopolies and Mergers Commn), 1981–87. *Publication:* A Guide to Futures Studies, 1976. *Recreations:* tennis, reading. *Address:* Bodenham House, Dinedor, Hereford HR2 6LQ. *T:* Holme Lacy 243. *Club:* Institute of Directors.

WILLIAMS, Alexander, FInstP, FIQA; Under Secretary, Research and Technology Policy Division, Department of Trade and Industry, since 1981; *b* 30 March 1931; *s* of Henry and Dorothy Williams; *m* 1957, Beryl Wynne Williams (*née* Williams); one *s*. *Educ:* Grove Park Grammar Sch., Wrexham; University College of North Wales, Bangor (BSc). National Service, REME, 1953–55; Monsanto Chemicals, 1955–56; Southern Instruments, Camberley, 1956–59; National Physical Laboratory: Div. of Radiation Science, 1959–78; Head, Div. of Mechanical and Optical Metrology, 1978–81. *Publications:* A Code of Practice for the Detailed Statement of Accuracy (with P. J. Campion and J. E. Burns), 1973; numerous papers on measurements of radio-activity etc, to Internat. Jl of Applied Radiation and Isotopes, Nucl. Instruments and Methods, etc. *Recreations:* bell-ringing, music, opera, walking. *Address:* c/o Department of Trade and Industry, Ashdown House, SW1E 6RB.

WILLIAMS, Sir Alwyn, Kt 1983; PhD; FRS 1967; FRSE, MRIA, FGS; Principal and Vice-Chancellor of University of Glasgow, since 1976; *b* 8 June 1921; *s* of D. Daniel Williams and E. May (*née* Rogers); *m* 1949, E. Joan Bevan; one *s* one *d*. *Educ:* Aberdare Boys' Grammar Sch.; University College of Wales, Aberystwyth. PhD Wales. Fellow, Univ. of Wales, 1946–48. Harkness Fund Fellow at US National Museum, Washington, DC, 1948–50; Lecturer in Geology in University of Glasgow, 1950–54; Prof. of Geology, 1954–74, Pro-Vice-Chancellor, 1967–74, Queen's Univ. of Belfast; Lapworth Prof. of Geology, and Head of Dept, Univ. of Birmingham, 1974–76. Pres., Palaeontological Assoc., 1968–70. Trustee, British Museum (Nat. History), 1971–79, Chm. of Trustees, 1974–79. Member: Equip. and Phys. Sci. sub-cttees, UGC, 1974–76; NERC, 1974–76; Adv. Council, British Library, 1975–77; Scottish Tertiary Educn Adv. Council, 1983–; Adv. Bd for the Res. Councils, 1985–; Chm., Cttee on Nat. Museums and Galls in Scotland, 1979–81; Vice-Chm., Cttee of Vice-Chancellors and Principals, 1979–81. Pres., Royal Soc. of Edinburgh, 1985–86. Hon. Fellow, Geol Soc. of America, 1970–; For. Mem., Polish Academies of Science; Hon. Associate, BM (Nat. Hist.), 1981–; Hon. FRCPS; Hon. FDS RCPS; Hon. DSc: Wales, 1974; Belfast, 1975; Edinburgh, 1979; Hon. LLD Strathclyde, 1982. Bigsby Medal, 1961, Murchison Medal, 1973, Geol Soc.; Clough Medal, Edin. Geol. Soc., 1976; T. Neville George Medal, Glasgow Geol. Soc., 1984. *Publications:* contrib. to Trans Royal Socs of London and Edinburgh, Jl Geological Society; Geological Magazine; Washington Acad. of Sciences; Geological Societies of London and America; Palaeontology; Journal of Paleontology, etc. *Address:* The Principal's Lodging, 12 The University, Glasgow G12 8QG. *T:* 041–339 0383.

WILLIAMS, Sir Anthony (James), KCMG 1983 (CMG 1971); HM Diplomatic Service, retired; *b* 28 May 1923; *s* of late Bernard Warren Williams, FRCS, and Hon. Muriel B. Buckley; *m* 1955, Hedwig Gabrielle, Gräfin Neipperg; two *s* one *d* (and one *d* decd). *Educ:* Oundle; Trinity Coll., Oxford. Entered Foreign Service, 1945; served in: Prague; Montevideo; Cairo; UK Permanent Mission to UN, New York; Buenos Aires; UK Permanent Mission to 18 Nation Disarmament Conf., Western, United Nations and South East Asian Depts of Foreign Office. Counsellor, Head of Chancery, Moscow, 1965–67; IDC, 1968; Counsellor (Political), Washington, 1969–70; Ambassador at Phnom Penh, 1970–73; Minister, Rome, 1973–76; Ambassador to Libyan Arab Jamahariya, 1977–79, to Argentina, 1980–82; Leader, UK Delegn to Madrid Conf. on Security and Co-operation in Europe Rev. Meeting, with rank of Ambassador, 1982–83; UK Deleg., UN Human Rights Commn, Geneva, 1984–86. *Address:* Jolly's Farmhouse, Salehurst, Sussex TN32 5PS. *Clubs:* Beefsteak, United Oxford & Cambridge University, Canning.

WILLIAMS, Arthur Vivian, CBE 1969; General Manager and Solicitor, Peterlee (New Town) Development Corporation, 1948–74, and of Aycliffe (New Town) Development Corporation, 1954–74; *b* 2 Jan. 1909; *s* of N. T. and Gwendolen Williams; *m* 1937, Charlotte Moyra (*d* 1985), *d* of Dr E. H. M. Milligan; three *s* one *d*. *Educ:* William Hulme's Grammar Sch., Manchester; Jesus Coll., Oxford. BA (Oxon), Final Honour Sch. of Mod. Hist. Admitted as Solicitor, 1936; Dep. Town Clerk of Finchley, 1938–41; Town Clerk of Bilston, 1941–46; Town Clerk and Clerk of the Peace, Dudley, 1946–48. *Address:* 7 Majestic Court, Spring Grove, Harrogate.

WILLIAMS, Hon. Atanda F.; *see* Fatayi-Williams.

WILLIAMS, Rev. Austen; *see* Williams, Rev. S. A.

WILLIAMS, Basil Hugh G.; *see* Garnons Williams.

WILLIAMS, Bernard Arthur Owen, FBA 1971; Provost of King's College, Cambridge, since 1979; *b* 21 Sept. 1929; *s* of late O. P. D. Williams, OBE and of H. A. Williams; *m* 1955, Shirley Vivienne Teresa Brittain Catlin (*see* Mrs S. V. T. B. Williams) (marr. diss. 1974); one *d*; *m* 1974, Patricia Law Skinner; two *s*. *Educ:* Chigwell Sch., Essex; Balliol Coll., Oxford (Hon. Fellow 1984). BA (Oxon) 1951; MA 1954. Fellow of All Souls Coll., Oxford, 1951–54; RAF (Gen. Duties Br.), 1951–53; Fellow of New Coll., Oxford, 1954–59; Vis. Lectr, Univ. Coll. of Ghana, 1958–59; Lectr in Philosophy, Univ. Coll., London, 1959–64; Professor of Philosophy, Bedford College, London, 1964–67 (Hon. Fellow 1985); Knightbridge Prof. of Philosophy, Cambridge, and Fellow of King's Coll., Cambridge, 1967–79. Visiting Professor: Princeton Univ., USA, 1963; Harvard Univ., 1973; Univ. of California, Berkeley, 1986; Vis. Fellow, Inst. of Advanced Studies, ANU, 1969; Sen. Vis. Fellow, Princeton, 1978. Member: Public Schools Commn, 1965–70; Royal Commn on Gambling, 1976–78; Chm., Cttee on Obscenity and Film Censorship, 1977–79. Dir, English Nat. Opera (formerly Sadler's Wells Opera), 1968–. Foreign Hon. Mem., Amer. Acad. of Arts and Sciences, 1983. Hon. LittD Dublin, 1981. *Publications:* (ed with A. C. Montefiore) British Analytical Philosophy, 1966; Morality, 1972;

Problems of the Self, 1973; A Critique of Utilitarianism, 1973; Descartes: The Project of Pure Enquiry, 1978; Moral Luck, 1981; (ed with A. K. Sen) Utilitarianism and Beyond, 1982; Ethics and the Limits of Philosophy, 1985; articles in philosophical jls, etc. *Recreation:* music, particularly opera. *Address:* Provost's Lodge, King's College, Cambridge CB2 1ST; Kent House, Swaffham Prior, Cambs. *T:* Newmarket 741443.

WILLIAMS, Betty; *see* Williams, Elizabeth.

WILLIAMS, Sir Brandon M. R.; *see* Rhys Williams.

WILLIAMS, Prof. Sir Bruce (Rodda), KBE 1980; Vice-Chancellor and Principal of the University of Sydney, 1967–81; Director, Technical Change Centre, 1981–86; *b* 10 January 1919; *s* of late Reverend W. J. Williams; *m* 1942, Roma Olive Hotten; five *d. Educ:* Wesley College; Queen's College, University of Melbourne (BA 1939). MA Adelaide 1942; MA(Econ) Manchester, 1963. FASSA 1968. Lecturer in Economics, University of Adelaide, 1939–46 and at Queen's University of Belfast, 1946–50; Professor of Economics, University College of North Staffordshire, 1950–59; Robert Otley Prof., 1959–63, and Stanley Jevons Prof., 1963–67, Univ. of Manchester. Secretary and Joint Director of Research, Science and Industry Committee, 1952–59. Member, National Board for Prices and Incomes, 1966–67; Econ. Adviser to Minister of Technology, 1966–67; Member: Central Advisory Council on Science and Technology, 1967; Reserve Bank Board, 1969–81; Chairman: NSW State Cancer Council, 1967–81; Australian Vice Chancellors Cttee, 1972–74; Aust. Govt Cttee of Inquiry into Educn and Trng, 1976–79; Dep. Chm., Parramatta Hosps Bd, 1979–81. Editor, The Sociological Review, 1953–59, and The Manchester Sch., 1959–67. President Economics Section of British Assoc., 1964. Hon. DLitt: Keele, 1973; Sydney, 1982; Hon. DEcon Qld, 1980; Hon. LLD: Melbourne, 1981; Manchester, 1982; Hon. DSc Aston, 1982. *Publications:* The Socialist Order and Freedom, 1942; (with C. F. Carter): Industry and Technical Progress, 1957, Investment in Innovation, 1958, and Science in Industry, 1959; Investment Behaviour, 1962; Investment Proposals and Decisions, 1965; Investment, Technology and Growth, 1967; (ed) Science and Technology in Economic Growth, 1973; Systems of Higher Education: Australia, 1978; Education, Training and Employment, 1979; Living with Technology, 1982; (ed) Knowns and Unknowns in Technical Change, 1985; Attitudes to New Technologies and Economic Growth, 1986. *Address:* 106 Grange Road, W5 3PJ. *T:* 01–567 1526. *Club:* Athenæum.

WILLIAMS, Campbell (Sherston); *see under* Smith, Campbell (Sherston).

WILLIAMS, Catrin Mary, FRCS; Consultant Ear, Nose and Throat Surgeon, Clwyd Health Authority (North), since 1956; *b* 9 May 1922; *d* of late Alderman Richard Williams, JP, Pwllheli, and Mrs Margaret Williams; unmarried. *Educ:* Pwllheli Grammar Sch.; Welsh National Sch. of Medicine (BSc 1942, MB, BCh 1945). FRCS 1948. Co-Chm., Women's National Commn, 1981–83; Pres., Medical Women's Fedn, 1973–74; first Vice-Pres., Gymdeithas Feddygol Gymraeg (Welsh Med. Soc.), 1975–. *Recreations:* reading, embroidery. *Address:* Gwrych House, Abergele, Clwyd LL22 8EU. *T:* Abergele 822256.

WILLIAMS, Cecil Beaumont, CHB 1980; OBE 1963; Executive Director, Da Costa & Musson Ltd, Barbados, since 1980; *b* 8 March 1926; *s* of George Cuthbert and Violet Irene Williams; *m* 1952, Dorothy Marshall; two *s* one *d. Educ:* Harrison Coll., Barbados; Durham Univ.; Oxford Univ. BA, DipEd. Asst Master, Harrison Coll., 1948–54. Asst Sec., Govt Personnel Dept, and Min. of Trade, Industry and Labour (Barbados), 1954–56; Permanent Secretary: Min. of Educn, 1958; Min. of Trade, Industry and Labour, 1958–63; Dir, Economic Planning Unit, 1964–65; Manager, Industrial Develt Corp., 1966–67; High Comr to Canada, 1967–70; Permanent Sec., Min. of External Affairs, 1971–74; Ambassador to USA and Perm. Rep. to OAS, 1974–75; High Comr in UK, 1976–79. *Recreations:* music, tennis, reading, gardening. *Address:* Moonshine Hall, St George, Barbados.

WILLIAMS, Rear-Adm. Charles Bernard, CB 1980; OBE 1967; Flag Officer Medway and Port Admiral Chatham, 1978–80, retired; *b* 19 Feb. 1925; *s* of Charles Williams and Elizabeth (*née* Malherbe); *m* 1946, Patricia Mary, *d* of Henry Brownlow Thorp and Ellen Thorp; one *s* one *d. Educ:* Graeme Coll., Grahamstown SA; Royal Naval Engineering Coll., Plymouth. Served in HM Ships Nigeria, Hornet, Triumph, 1946–53; in charge: Flight deck trials unit, 1953; Naval Wing, Nat. Gas Turbine Estabt, 1956; Sen. Engr, HMS Cumberland, 1958; in charge Admiralty Fuel Experimental Station, 1960; Comdr 1960; Engineer Officer, HMS London, 1962; Staff Engr, Flag Officer ME, 1964; Duty Comdr, Naval Ops MoD (N), 1967; Captain 1969; Dep. Manager, Portsmouth Dockyard, 1969; Supt, Clyde Submarine Base, 1972; Captain, HMS Sultan, 1975; Rear-Adm. 1978. *Recreations:* sailing (Chm., Whitbread Round the World Race, 1981–), walking, music. *Address:* Green Shutters, Montserrat Road, Lee-on-Solent PO13 9LT. *T:* Lee-on-Solent 550816. *Clubs:* Royal Yacht Squadron; Royal Ocean Racing; Royal Southern Yacht; Royal Naval Sailing Association.

WILLIAMS, Dr Cicely Delphine, CMG 1968; retired (except on demand); *b* 2 Dec. 1893; *d* of James Rowland Williams, Kew Park, Jamaica (Dir of Educn, Jamaica) and Margaret E. C. Williams (*née* Farewell). *Educ:* Bath High Sch. for Girls; Somerville Coll., Oxford (Hon. Fellow, 1979); King's Coll. Hosp. DM, FRCP, DTM&H. Colonial Med. Service: appts, 1929–48. WHO Adv. in Maternal and Child Health, 1948–51; Research on Vomiting Sickness, 1951–53; Sen. Lectr in Nutrition, London, 1953–55; consulting visits to various countries, 1955–59; Visiting Professor: of Maternal and Child Health, Amer. Univ. of Beirut, 1959–64; Tulane Sch. of Public Health, New Orleans, 1971–; Adv. in Trng Progrs, Family Planning Assoc., 1964–67. Lectures: Milroy, RCP, 1958; Blackfan, Harvard Med. Sch., 1973; Balgopal Oration, Paediatric Soc., Katmandu, Nepal, 1981; Speaker, Pakistan Paediatric Assoc., 1982. Emeritus Professor of Maternal and Child Health, Nursing and Nutrition, Tulane Sch. of Public Health, 1974. Hon. FRSM 1976; Hon. Fellow: King's Coll. Hosp. Medical Sch, 1978; Green Coll., Oxford, 1985. Hon. DSc: Univ. of WI; Univ. of Maryland; Univ. of Tulane; Smith Coll., Northampton, Mass. James Spence Meml Medal, Br. Paed. Assoc., 1965; Goldberger Award in Clin. Nutrition, Amer. Med. Assoc., 1967; Dawson-Williams Award in Paediatrics, BMA (jt), 1973; Galen Medal, Worshipful Soc. of Apothecaries, London, 1984. Order of Merit, Jamaica, 1975. *Publications:* chapters in: Diseases of Children in the Tropics, 1954; Sick Children, 1956; The Matrix of Medicine, 1958; (with D. B. Jelliffe) Mother and Child Health: delivering the services, 1972; contrib. to: The Lancet, Archives of Diseases in Childhood (which reissued, 1982, as 'perhaps the most important ever published in the Archives', her paper A Nutritional Disease of Childhood, 1933), Tropical Pediatrics, etc. *Recreations:* people and solitude. *Address:* 24 Wyndham House, Plantation Road, Oxford OX2 6JJ. *T:* Oxford 50317. *Club:* Royal Commonwealth Society.

WILLIAMS, Clifford; *see* Williams, A. C.

WILLIAMS, Clifford; Associate Director, Royal Shakespeare Company, since 1963; *b* 30 Dec. 1926; *s* of George Frederick Williams and Florence Maud Williams (*née* Gapper); *m* 1st, 1952, Joanna Douglas (marr. diss. 1959); no *c*; 2nd, 1962, Josiane Eugenie Peset; two *d. Educ:* Highbury County Grammar Sch. Acted in London (These Mortals, Larissa, Wolves and Sheep, Great Catherine), and repertory theatres, 1945–48; founded and directed Mime Theatre Company, 1950–53; Dir of Productions: at Marlowe Theatre, Canterbury, 1955–56; at Queen's Theatre, Hornchurch, 1957. Directed at Arts Theatre, London: Yerma, 1957; Radio Rescue, 1958; Dark Halo, Quartet for Five, The Marriage of Mr Mississippi (all in 1959); Moon for the Misbegotten, The Shepherd's Chameleon, Victims of Duty (all in 1960); The Race of Adam, Llandaff Festival, 1961. Joined Royal Shakespeare Company, 1961; Directed: Afore Night Come, 1962; The Comedy of Errors, 1963. Productions for RSC in Stratford and London: The Tempest, The Representative, The Comedy of Errors (revival), 1963; Richard II, Henry IV Pts I and II (co-dir), Afore Night Come (revival), The Jew of Malta, 1964; The Merchant of Venice, The Jew of Malta (revival), The Comedy of Errors (revival), 1965; The Meteor, Twelfth Night, Henry IV Pts I and II (co-dir, revivals), 1966; Doctor Faustus, 1968; Major Barbara, 1970; The Duchess of Malfi, 1971; The Comedy of Errors (revival), 1972; The Taming of the Shrew, A Lesson in Blood and Roses, 1973; Cymbeline, 1974; The Mouth Organ, Too True to be Good, 1975; Wild Oats, 1976, 1979; Man and Superman, 1977; The Tempest, 1978; The Love-Girl and the Innocent, 1981; The Comedy of Errors, 1983; The Happiest Days of Your Life (revival), 1984; Il Candelaio, 1986. Other productions include: Our Man Crichton, 1964, and the Flying Dutchman, 1966, in London; The Gardener's Dog, 1965, and The Merry Wives of Windsor, 1967, for the Finnish National Theatre; Volpone at Yale Univ., 1967; Othello, for Bulgarian Nat. Theatre, 1968; Soldiers, New York and London, 1968; Dido and Aeneas, Windsor Festival, 1969; Famine, English Stage Soc., 1969; As You Like It, 1967, and Back to Methuselah, 1969, both for the Nat. Theatre of GB; The Winter's Tale, 1969, for Yugoslav Nat. Theatre; Sleuth, London, NY and Paris, 1970; Oh! Calcutta!, London and Paris, 1970; Emperor Henry IV, New York, 1973; As You Like It (revival), New York, 1974; What Every Woman Knows, London, 1974; Emperor Henry IV, London, 1974; Murderer, London, 1975; Mardi-Gras, London, 1976; Carte Blanche, London, 1976; Stevie, The Old Country, Rosmerholm, London, 1977; The Passion of Dracula, London, 1978; Richard III, Mexican Nat. Theatre, 1979; Threepenny Opera, 1979, and The Love-Girl and the Innocent, 1980, Aalborg; Born in the Gardens, London, 1980; Overhead, London, 1981; To Grandmother's House We Go, NY, 1981; The Carmelites, Aalborg, 1981; Othello, Bad Hersfeld, 1982; Chapter 17, London, 1982; Richard III, Madrid, 1983; Merry Wives of Windsor, USA, 1983; Scheherazade, Festival Ballet, 1983; Pack of Lies, London, 1983, NY, 1985; A Child's Christmas in Wales (revival), USA, 1983; Rise and Fall of the City of Mahagonny, Aalborg, 1984; Aren't We All?, London, 1984, NY, 1985; The Cherry Orchard, Tokyo, 1984; Measure for Measure, Norrköping, 1985; St Joan, British tour, 1985; Legends, USA, 1986; Breaking the Code, London, 1986; Aren't We All?, Australia, 1986. Also directed plays for the Arena Theatre, Triumph Theatre Co., Theatre Workshop, Guildford, Oxford, Coventry, Toronto, Los Angeles, Washington, Houston, Johannesburg, Edinburgh Festival; Malvern Festival; Dir, Man and Superman (film), 1986. Mem. Welsh Arts Council, 1963–72; Chairman: Welsh Nat. Theatre Co., 1968–72; British Theatre Assoc., 1977–; Chm., British Children's Theatre Assoc., 1968–71; Governor, Welsh Coll. of Music and Drama, 1981–. Associate Artist of Yugoslav Nat. Theatre, 1969; FTCL. *Publications:* (ed) John O'Keeffe, Wild Oats, 1977; *plays:* The Disguises of Arlecchino, 1951; The Sleeping Princess, 1953; The Goose Girl, 1954; The Secret Garden, 1955; (with Donald Jonson) Stephen Dedalus, 1956; *translations:* Ionesco, The Duel, Double Act, 1979; Pirandello, As You Desire Me, 1981; Chekhov, The Cherry Orchard, 1981. *Recreations:* motor boating, water-ski-ing. *Address:* 43 Onslow Square, SW7 3NJ; The Vineyard, Domaine du Chateauneuf, 06560 Valbonne, France.

WILLIAMS, Colin; *see* Welland, C.

WILLIAMS, Colin Hartley; Chief Press Relations Manager, National Westminster Bank, since 1983; *b* 7 Dec. 1938; *s* of late Gwilym Robert Williams and Margaret (*née* Hartley); *m* 1964, Carolyn (*née* Bulman); one *s* two *d. Educ:* Grangefield Grammar Sch., Stockton-on-Tees; University College of Wales, Aberystwyth (BA). Journalist: Evening Gazette, Middlesbrough, 1960–63; Today Magazine, Odhams Press, 1964; Daily Sketch, 1964–66; Senior Lecturer, International Press Inst., Nairobi, 1967–68; Corporate and Public Relations Executive, 1969–74; Press Officer, Corporation of City of London, 1975–76; Asst Dir, City Communications Centre, 1977, Exec. Dir, 1979–83; Exec. Dir, Cttee on Invisible Exports, 1982–83. *Publications:* articles on labour management, financial and communication topics. *Recreations:* writing, painting, golf. *Address:* 84 Clare Road, Prestwood, near Great Missenden, Bucks HP16 0NU. *T:* Great Missenden 4464. *Clubs:* Scribes Cellar; Chiltern Forest Golf.

WILLIAMS, Cyril Robert, CBE 1945; *b* 11 May 1895; *s* of Rev. F. J. Williams, MA; *m* 1928, Ethel Winifred Wise; two *d. Educ:* Wellington College, Berks; New College, Oxford. Dist Loco. Supt, Khartoum, Sudan Rlys, 1923; Asst Mech. Engineer (Outdoor), 1924; Loco. Running Supt, 1927; Works Manager, 1932; Asst Chief Mech. Engineer, 1936; Deputy General Manager, 1939; General Manager, 1941. JP Somerset, 1947–69. *Recreation:* philately. *Address:* Ballacree, Somerton, Somerset. *T:* Somerton 72408.

WILLIAMS, Dafydd Wyn J.; *see* Jones-Williams.

WILLIAMS, Prof. David, FRS 1984; Professor of Mathematical Statistics and Professorial Fellow, Clare College, Cambridge University, since 1985; *b* 9 April 1938; *s* of Gwyn Williams and Margaret Elizabeth Williams; *m* 1966, Sheila Margaret Harrison; two *d. Educ:* Jesus College, Oxford (DPhil); Grey College, Durham. Instructor, Stanford Univ., 1962; Lectr, Durham Univ., 1963; Shell Research Lectr, Statistical Lab., and Res. Fellow, Clare Coll., Cambridge, 1966; Lectr, 1969, Prof. of Maths, 1972, University Coll., Swansea. *Publications:* Diffusions, Markov processes, and martingales, vol. 1, Foundations, 1979; papers in Séminaire de probabilités and other jls. *Recreations:* music, cycling, walking. *Address:* 7 Moss Drive, Haslingfield, Cambridge CB3 7JB. *T:* Cambridge 872194.

WILLIAMS, Adm. Sir David, GCB 1977 (KCB 1975); DL; Governor and Commander-in-Chief, Gibraltar, 1982–85; a Gentleman Usher to The Queen, 1979–82, an Extra Gentleman Usher, since 1982; Vice Chairman, since 1985 and Member, since 1980, Commonwealth War Graves Commission; *b* 22 Oct. 1921; 3rd *s* of A. E. Williams, Ashford, Kent; *m* 1947, Philippa Beatrice Stevens; two *s. Educ:* Yardley Court Sch., Tonbridge; RN College, Dartmouth. Cadet, Dartmouth, 1935. Graduate, US Naval War Coll., Newport, RI. Served War of 1939–45 at sea in RN. Qual. in Gunnery, 1946; Comdr, 1952; Captain, 1960; Naval Asst to First Sea Lord, 1961–64; HMS Devonshire, 1964–66; Dir of Naval Plans, 1966–68; Captain, BRNC, Dartmouth, 1968–70; Rear-Adm. 1970; Flag Officer, Second in Command Far East Fleet, 1970–72; Vice-Adm. 1973; Dir-Gen. Naval Manpower and Training, 1972–74; Adm. 1974; Chief of Naval Personnel and Second Sea Lord, 1974–77; C-in-C Naval Home Comd, and ADC to the Queen, 1977–79, retired. Pres., Ex Services Mental Welfare Soc., 1979–. Hon. Liveryman, Fruiterers' Co.; KStJ 1982. FRSA. DL Devon, 1981. *Recreations:* sailing, tennis, gardening. *Address:* Brockholt, Strete, Dartmouth, Devon. *Clubs:* Army and Navy; Royal Dart Yacht; RN Sailing Association; Royal Yacht Squadron; Royal Western Yacht.

WILLIAMS, Rear-Adm. David Apthorp, CB 1965; DSC 1942; *b* 27 Jan. 1911; *s* of Thomas Pettit Williams and Vera Frederica Dudley Williams (*née* Apthorp); *m* 1951,

Susan Eastlake, 3rd *d* of late Dr W. H. Lamplough and *widow* of Surg. Cdr H. de B. Kempthorne, RN; one *s* two step *d*. *Educ:* Cheltenham College; Royal Naval Engineering College, Keyham. Joined RN, 1929. Served War, Engineer Officer, HMS Hasty, 1939–42 (DSC, despatches four times), 2nd Destroyer Flotilla, Med. Fleet, S Atlantic Stn, Home Fleet, E Med. Fleet; Sen. Engineer, HMS Implacable, 1942–45, Home Fleet, and 1st Aircraft Carrier Sqdn, British Pacific Fleet, Comdr (E) 1945; Capt. 1955; Rear-Adm. 1963; Dir Gen. Aircraft, Admiralty, 1962–64; Dir Gen., Aircraft (Naval), Ministry of Defence, 1964–65; retired list, 1965. CEng, MIMechE. *Recreations:* various. *Address:* 3 Ellachie Gardens, Alverstoke, Hants PO12 2DS. *T:* Gosport 583375. *Club:* Army and Navy.

WILLIAMS, David Barry, TD 1964; QC 1975; **His Honour Judge David Williams;** a Circuit Judge, since 1979; Deputy Senior Judge (non-resident), Sovereign Base Area, Cyprus, since 1983; *b* 20 Feb. 1931; *s* of Dr W. B. Williams and Mrs G. Williams, Garndiffaith, Mon; *m* 1961, Angela Joy Davies; three *s* one *d*. *Educ:* Cardiff High Sch. for Boys; Wellington Sch., Somerset; Exeter Coll., Oxford (MA). Served with South Wales Borderers, 1949–51, 2nd Bn Monmouthshire Regt (TA), 1951–67, retired (Major). Called to Bar, Gray's Inn, 1955; Wales and Chester Circuit, 1957. A Recorder of the Crown Court, 1972–79; Asst Comr, Local Govt Boundary Commn for Wales, 1976–79; Comr for trial of Local Govt election petitions, 1978–79. Chm., Legal Affairs Cttee, Welsh Centre for Internat. Affairs, 1980–; Mem., Court, University Coll., Cardiff, 1980–; Vice-Pres., UWIST, 1985– (Mem. Court and Council, 1981–; Vice-Chm. Council, 1983–). Liaison Judge for W Glamorgan; a Pres., Mental Health Review Tribunals, 1983–. *Recreations:* mountain walking, Rugby football. *Address:* 52 Cyncoed Road, Cardiff. *T:* Cardiff 498189. *Clubs:* Army and Navy; Cardiff and County (Cardiff).

WILLIAMS, David Carlton, PhD; retired; President and Vice-Chancellor, University of Western Ontario, 1967–77; *b* 7 July 1912; *s* of John Andrew Williams and Anna Williams (Carlton); *m* 1943, Margaret Ashwell Carson; one *s* one *d*. *Educ:* Gordon Bell and Kelvin High Schs; Univ. of Manitoba, Winnipeg (BA); Univ. of Toronto (MA, PhD, Psych.). Special Lectr in Psychology, Univ. of Toronto, 1946; Associate Prof. of Psychology, Univ. of Manitoba, 1947; Prof. and Head, Dept of Psychology, Univ. of Manitoba, 1948; Prof. of Psychology, Univ. of Toronto, 1949–58 (Cons. to Toronto Juvenile Ct Clinic, 1951–58); Dir of Univ. Extension, Univ. of Toronto, 1958; a Dir, John Howard Soc., Toronto, 1956–67; Mem., Royal Commn on Govt Organization, 1961; Chm., Ontario Commn on Freedom of Information and Individual Privacy, 1977. Vice-Pres., Univ. of Toronto, for Scarborough and Erindale Colls, 1963–67. Principal of Scarborough Coll., Univ. of Toronto, 1963; Principal of Erindale Coll., Univ. of Toronto, 1965. Chm., Council of Ontario Univs, 1970–73; Dir, Assoc. of Univs and Colls of Canada, 1970–; Chm. Bd, University Hosp., London, Ont, 1984–86. Hon. LLD: Univ. of Manitoba, 1969; Univ. Windsor, 1977; Univ. of Western Ontario, 1977; Toronto Univ., 1977. *Publications:* The Arts as Communication, 1963; University Television, 1965. *Recreations:* photography, music, swimming, fishing. *Address:* Apt 207, 1201 Richmond Street, London, Ontario N6A 3L6, Canada. *T:* 433–1436. *Clubs:* University, London, London Hunt and Country (all London, Ont); York (Toronto).

WILLIAMS, David Claverly, CVO 1970; CBE 1977; *b* 31 July 1917; *s* of late Rev. Canon Henry Williams, OBE, and late Ethel Florence Williams; *m* 1944, Elizabeth Anne Fraser; three *d*. *Educ:* Christ's Coll., Christchurch, NZ; Victoria Univ. of Wellington. Professional Exam. in Public Administration. Inland Revenue Dept, 1936–39. Served War, 2NZEF, Pacific and Middle East, 1939–46. NZ Forest Service, 1946–60; Official Sec. to the Governor-General of NZ, 1960–77; Sec./Manager, The Wellington Club (Inc.), 1978–82. *Address:* 4 Huia Road, Days Bay, Eastbourne, New Zealand. *Clubs:* Wellington (Wellington).

WILLIAMS, Prof. David Glyndwr Tudor; President, Wolfson College, University of Cambridge, since 1980; Rouse Ball Professor of English Law, Cambridge University, since 1983; *b* 22 Oct. 1930; *s* of late Tudor Williams, OBE (Headmaster of Queen Elizabeth Grammar Sch., Carmarthen, 1929–55), and late Anne Williams; *m* 1959, Sally Gillian Mary Cole; one *s* two *d*. *Educ:* Queen Elizabeth Grammar Sch., Carmarthen; Emmanuel Coll., Cambridge (MA, LLB, Hon. Fellow 1984). LLM Calif. Nat. Service, RAF, 1949–50. Called to the Bar, Lincoln's Inn, 1956, Hon. Bencher, 1985. Commonwealth Fund Fellow of Harkness Foundn, Berkeley and Harvard, 1956–58; Lecturer: Univ. of Nottingham, 1958–63; Univ. of Oxford, 1963–67 (Fellow of Keble Coll.); Emmanuel College, Cambridge: Fellow, 1967–80; Sen. Tutor and Tutor for Admissions, 1970–76; Reader in Public Law, Cambridge Univ., 1976–83. Vis. Fellow, ANU, Canberra, 1974; Allen, Allen and Hemsley Vis. Fellow, Law Dept, Univ. of Sydney, 1985. Pres., Nat. Soc. for Clean Air, 1983–85; Chm., Adv. Cttee on Animal Experiments, 1986–; Member: Clean Air Council, 1971–79; Royal Commn on Environmental Pollution, 1976–83; Commn on Energy and the Environment, 1978–81; Council on Tribunals, 1972–82; Berrill Cttee of Investigation, SSRC, 1982–83; Marre Cttee on Future of Legal Profession, 1986–. *Publications:* Not in the Public Interest, 1965; Keeping the Peace, 1967; (ed jtly) Administrative Law, in Halsbury's Laws of England, Vol. 1, 4th edn 1973; articles in legal jls. *Address:* Wolfson College, Cambridge CB3 9BB. *T:* Cambridge 64811.

WILLIAMS, Sir David Innes, Kt 1985; MD, MChir Cambridge, FRCS; Pro-Vice-Chancellor, University of London, since 1985; Chairman, Council for Postgraduate Medical Education in England and Wales, since 1985; Chairman Council, Imperial Cancer Research Fund, since 1982 (Member, since 1975); Consulting Urologist: Hospital for Sick Children, Great Ormond Street (Urologist, 1952–78); St Peter's Hospital, London (Surgeon, 1950–78); *b* 12 June 1919; *s* of late Gwynne E. O. Williams, MS, FRCS; *m* 1944, Margaret Eileen Harding; two *s*. *Educ:* Sherborne Sch.; Trinity Hall, Cambridge; Univ. College Hospital (Hon. Fellow, 1986). RAMC, 1945–48 (Major, Surg. Specialist). Urologist, Royal Masonic Hosp., 1963–72; Civilian Consultant Urologist to RN, 1974–84; Dir, BPMF, Univ. of London, 1978–86. Mem., Home Sec's Adv. Cttee on Cruelty to Animals, 1975–79. Mem., GMC, 1979– (Chm., Overseas Cttee, 1981–); Vice-Pres., RCS, 1983–85 (Mem. Council, 1974–86; Mem. Jt Consultants Cttee, 1983–85). FRSocMed (Past Pres., Urology Sect.); Hon. Member: British Assoc. Paediatric Surgeons (Denis Browne Medal, 1977); British Assoc. Urological Surgeons (Past Pres.; St Peter's Medal, 1967); Assoc. Française d'Urologie; Amer. Surgical Assoc.; Hon. FACS 1983; Hon. FRCSI 1984; Hon. FDSRCS. *Publications:* Urology of Childhood, 1958; Paediatric Urology, 1968, 2nd edn 1982; Scientific Foundations of Urology, 1976, 2nd edn 1982; various contributions to medical journals. *Address:* (office) Imperial Cancer Research Fund, Lincoln's Inn Fields, PO Box 123, WC2A 3PX; 66 Murray Road, SW19 4PE. *T:* 01–879 1042; The Old Rectory, East Knoyle, Salisbury, Wilts. *T:* 255.

WILLIAMS, Dr David Iorwerth, FRCP, FKC; Dean, King's College Hospital Medical School, 1966–77, now Dean Emeritus and Fellow; former Consultant in Dermatology, King's College Hospital; Consultant to Kuwait Health Office, London; *b* 7 May 1913; *s* of William Tom Williams and Mabel Williams (*née* Edwards); *m* 1939, Ethel Margaret Wiseman; one *s* (one *d* decd). *Educ:* Dulwich Coll. (Jun. and Sen. Scholar); King's College Hosp. Med. Sch. Warneford and Raymond Gooch Scholar; MB, BS 1938; FRCP 1953; AKC 1934; FKC 1977. RAMC, 1940–46, Lt-Col. Member: BMA; Brit. Assoc. of Dermatology (Past Pres. and Past Sec., Hon. Mem. 1979); Royal Soc. of Med. (Past Pres. Dermatology Section); West Kent Medico-Chirurgical Soc. (Past Pres.); Hon. (or Foreign) Member: American, Austrian, Danish, French and S African Dermatological Socs. Gold Medal of Brit. Assoc. of Dermatology, 1965. *Publications:* articles in various med. jls over last 40 yrs. *Recreations:* my stroke, music. *Address:* 28 South Row, SE3 0RY. *T:* 01–852 7060.

WILLIAMS, David John; *b* 10 July 1914; *s* of late James Herbert Williams and late Ethel (*née* Redman); unmarried. *Educ:* Lancing College; Christ Church, Oxford (MA). Called to Bar, Inner Temple, 1939. Postgrad. Dip. in Social Anthropology, LSE, 1965. Served War of 1939–45, Royal Artillery. Practised as Barrister, Norwich, 1946–51; Resident Magistrate, Tanganyika, 1951–56; Senior Resident Magistrate, 1956–60; Judge of High Court of Tanganyika, 1960–62; Lord Chancellor's Office, 1966–79. FRAI 1966. *Recreations:* the arts and travelling. *Address:* 10e Thorney Crescent, Morgan's Walk, SW11 3TR.

WILLIAMS, (David John) Delwyn; *b* 1 Nov. 1938; *s* of David Lewis Williams and Irena Violet Gwendoline Williams; *m* 1963, Olive Elizabeth Jerman; one *s* one *d*. *Educ:* Welshpool High School; University College of Wales, Aberystwyth. LLB. Solicitor with Lanyons, Shrewsbury. Company director. MP (C) Montgomery, 1979–83; former Member: Select Cttee on Wales; Statutory Instruments Cttee; Jt Sec., All-Party Leisure and Recreation Industry Cttee. Contested (C) Montgomery, 1983. Mem., British Field Sports Soc. *Recreations:* race horse owner; cricket, golf, small bore shooting. *Address:* Frondeg, Guilsfield, Welshpool, Powys SY21 9NQ. *T:* Welshpool 3400.

WILLIAMS, David Lincoln; Chairman and Managing Director, John Williams of Cardiff PLC, since 1983 (Director, since 1968); Chairman, Allied Profiles Ltd, since 1981; *b* 10 Feb. 1937; *s* of Lewis Bernard Williams and Eileen Elizabeth Cadogan; *m* 1959, Gillian Elisabeth, *d* of Dr William Phillips; one *s* one *d*. *Educ:* Cheltenham College. Chm., Cardiff Broadcasting PLC, 1979–84. President, Aluminium Window Assoc., 1971–72. Chm., Vale of Glamorgan Festival, 1978–; Nat. Chm., Friends of Welsh National Opera, 1980–. FInstD. Freeman, City of London, 1986; Liveryman, Founders' Co., 1986. *Recreations:* opera, skiing, fine weather sailing. *Address:* Rose Revived, Llantrithyd, Cowbridge, S Glam CF7 7UB. *T:* Bonvilston 357. *Club:* Cardiff and County (Cardiff).

WILLIAMS, David Oliver; General Secretary, Confederation of Health Service Employees, 1983–May 1987; *b* 12 March 1926; *m* 1949, Kathleen Eleanor Jones, Dinorwic; two *s* five *d* (and one *s* decd). *Educ:* Brynrefail Grammar Sch.; North Wales Hospital, Denbigh (RMN 1951). COHSE: full-time officer, Regional Secretary, Yorkshire Region, 1955; National Officer, Head Office, 1962; Sen. National Officer, 1969; Asst General Secretary, 1964. Chairman: Nurses and Midwives Whitley Council Staff Side, 1977–; General Whitley Council Staff Side, 1974–. Jubilee Medal, 1977. *Recreations:* walking, birdwatching, swimming, music. *Address:* 35 Onslow Gardens, Wallington, Surrey SM6 9QH. *T:* 01–669 3964.

WILLIAMS, David Wakelin, MSc, PhD; CBiol, FIBiol; retired as Director, Department of Agriculture and Fisheries for Scotland, Agricultural Scientific Services, 1963–73; *b* 2 Oct. 1913; *e s* of John Thomas Williams and Ethel (*née* Lock); *m* 1948, Margaret Mary Wills, BSc, *d* of late Rev. R. H. Wills; one *s*. *Educ:* Rhondda Grammar School, Porth; University College, Cardiff. Demonstrator, Zoology Dept, Univ. Coll., Cardiff, 1937–38; Lectr in Zoology and Botany, Tech. Coll., Crumlin, Mon., 1938–39; research work on nematode physiology, etc. (MSc, PhD), 1937–41; biochemical work on enzymes (Industrial Estate, Treforest), 1942–43. Food Infestation Control Inspector (Min. of Food), Glasgow; Sen. Inspector, W Scotland, 1945; Scotland and N Ireland, 1946. Prin. Scientific Officer, Dept Agriculture for Scotland, 1948; Sen. Prin. Scientific Officer, 1961; Dep. Chief Scientific Officer (Director), 1963. Chairman, Potato Trials Advisory Cttee, 1963–; FIBiol 1966 (Council Mem. Scottish Br., 1966–69). MBIM, 1970–76. *Publications:* various papers, especially for the intelligent layman, on the environment, and on pest control and its side effects. *Recreations:* writing, music, Hi-Fi, photography, computing. *Address:* 8 Hillview Road, Edinburgh EH12 8QN. *T:* 031–334 1108.

WILLIAMS, Delwyn; *see* Williams, D. J. D.

WILLIAMS, Dr Denis (John), CBE 1955; DSc; MD; FRCP; Hon. Consulting Neurologist: St George's Hospital; King Edward VII Hospital for Officers; Hon. Consulting Physician, National Hospital, Queen Square; Hon. Neurologist, Star and Garter Home, Richmond; Hon. Civil Consultant in Neurology, RAF, British Airways; Civil Consultant in Electro-encephalography, RAF and Army; *b* 4 Dec. 1908; *s* of Rev. Daniel Jenkin Williams, MA, BD, Aberayron and Elsie Leonora Edwards; *m* 1937, Joyce Beverley Jewson, MBE, JP, MB, BS, DPH; one *s* two *d* (and one *s* decd). *Educ:* Manchester Univ.; Harvard University. DSc (Physiol.), Manchester 1942 (MSc 1938, BSc 1929); MD (Gold Medal) Manchester 1935 (MB, ChB 1932); FRCP 1943 (MRCP 1937). After resident appts in Manchester and London, Prof. Tom Jones Meml Fellow in Surgery, Manchester Univ.; Halley Stewart Research Fellow, MRC, Nat. Hosp., Queen Square; Rockefeller Travelling Fellow in Neurology. Hon. Research Fellow, Harvard Univ. Wing Comdr RAF; Air Crew Research and Clinical Neurology in Royal Air Force, 1939–45, and seconded to RN; Physician, Departments of Applied Electrophysiology, St George's and National Hosps. Consultant Advr in neurology, DHSS, 1966–73. Lectr in Neurology, London Univ., 1946–75; Chairman: Academic Bd, Inst. of Neurology, 1965–74; Sec. of State's Hon. Med. Adv. Panel on Neurol Aspects of Safety in Driving, 1967–83. Editor, Brain, and Modern Trends in Neurology, 1954–75. Bradshaw Lectr, RCP, 1955; Scott-Heron Lectr, Belfast, 1960; Guest Lectr, Canadian Medical Assoc., 1963; Hugh Cairns Lectr, Adelaide, 1965; Bruce Hall Lectr, Sydney, 1965; Guest Lectr, RACP, 1965; Richardson Lectr, Toronto, 1974. Visiting Professor: Univ. of Cincinnati, 1963, 1969; St Vincent's Hosp. Sydney (Hon. Phys.), 1965. Mem. Council, 1960–63, Vice-Pres., 1976, 1977, Royal Coll. of Physicians (Chm., Cttee on Neurology, 1965–74); Pres., Sect. of Neurology, Roy Soc Med, 1967; Pres., Assoc. of British Neurologists 1972–74 (Sec., 1952–60); Hon. Member: American, Canadian and German Neurological Assocs; EEG Soc. Examr, RCP and various Univs. Governor, Nat. Hosp.; Trustee, Brain Res. Trust. Gowers Medal, UC and Nat. Hosps, London, 1974. *Publications:* articles on brain function, epilepsy, abnormal behaviour and electro-encephalography, in Brain, Modern Trends in Neurology, and other journals; Neurology, in Price's Medicine; Contrib. to Handbook of Neurology. *Recreations:* farming, gardening. *Address:* 11 Frognal Way, Hampstead, NW3 6XE. *T:* 01–435 4030; Woodlands House, Mathry, Dyfed. *T:* St Nicholas 677. *Clubs:* Wayfarers', Royal Air Force.

WILLIAMS, Derek Alfred H.; *see* Hutton-Williams.

WILLIAMS, Derrick; *see* Williams, R. D.

WILLIAMS, Doiran George; Principal Assistant Director of Public Prosecutions, since 1982; *b* 27 June 1926; *s* of Rev. Dr Robert Richard Williams and Dilys Rachel Williams; *m* 1st, 1949, Flora Samitz (decd); one *s* one *d*; 2nd, 1977, Maureen Dorothy Baker; one *d*. *Educ:* Hereford Cathedral Sch.; Colwyn Bay Grammar Sch.; Liverpool Coll.; John F.

Hughes Sch., Utica, NY. Served Army (Infantry), 1944–47. Called to the Bar, Gray's Inn, 1952; practised in Liverpool, 1952–58; Dept of Dir of Public Prosecutions, 1959, Asst Dir, 1977–82. Drama critic, Liverpool Evening Express, 1954–55; Lectr, Preston Polytechnic, 1956–57, Wallasey Tech. Coll., 1957–58. Sec., Liverpool Fabian Soc., 1956–58. Reader: Liverpool Dio., 1953–58; London Dio., 1959–63; Southwark Dio., 1964–; Member: Southwark Dio. Synod, 1971–73; Southwark Readers' Bd, 1977–. *Recreations:* arts, mountains, sport, wine. *Address:* c/o Director of Public Prosecutions, 4–12 Queen Anne's Gate, SW1. *T:* 01–213 3440.

WILLIAMS, Donald; *see* Williams, W. D.

WILLIAMS, Sir Donald Mark, 10th Bt *cr* 1866; *b* 7 Nov. 1954; *s* of Sir Robert Ernest Williams, 9th Bt, and of Ruth Margaret, *d* of Charles Edwin Butcher, Hudson Bay, Saskatchewan, Canada; *S* father, 1976; *m* 1982, Denise, *o d* of Royston H. Cory. *Educ:* West Buckland School, Devon. *Heir:* *b* Barton Matthew Williams, *b* 21 Nov. 1956. *Address:* Upcott House, Barnstaple, N Devon.

WILLIAMS, Douglas, CB 1977; CVO 1966; Deputy Secretary, Ministry of Overseas Development (later Overseas Development Administration), 1973–77, retired; *b* 14 May 1917; *s* of late James E. Williams and Elsie Williams; *m* 1948, Marie Jacquot; no *c*. *Educ:* Wolverhampton Sch.; Exeter Coll., Oxford. Served War, 1939–46 (despatches): Major, RA. Colonial Office, 1947; Principal, 1949; Colonial Attaché, Washington, 1956–60; Asst Sec., Colonial Office, 1961; transferred to ODM (later ODA), 1967, Under-Sec., 1968–73. Member: Bd, Crown Agents, 1978–84; EEC Econ. and Social Cttee, 1978–82; Governing Council, ODI, 1979–85. Chm., Exec. Cttee, Help the Aged and associated charities, 1985– (Trustee, 1984–). *Publications:* articles on human rights and economic development, British colonial history. *Address:* 14 Gomshall Road, Cheam, Sutton, Surrey. *T:* 01–393 7306. *Club:* United Oxford & Cambridge University.

WILLIAMS, Sir Dudley; *see* Dudley-Williams, Sir Rolf Dudley.

WILLIAMS, Dudley Howard, PhD, ScD; FRS 1983; Reader in Organic Chemistry, University of Cambridge, since 1974; Fellow of Churchill College, since 1964; *b* 25 May 1937; *s* of Lawrence Williams and Evelyn (*née* Hudson); *m* 1963, Lorna Patricia Phyllis, *d* of Anthony and Lorna Bedford; two *s*. *Educ:* Grammar Sch., Pudsey, Yorks; Univ. of Leeds (state schol.; BSc, PhD); MA, ScD Cantab. Post-doctoral Fellow and Research Associate, Stanford Univ., Calif, 1961–64; Sen. Asst in Research, 1964–66, Asst Dir of Research, 1966–74, Univ. of Cambridge. Nuffield Vis. Lectr, Sydney Univ., 1973; Visiting Professor: Univ. of California, Irvine, 1967; Univ. of Cape Town, 1972; Univ. of Wisconsin, 1975; Univ. of Copenhagen, 1976; ANU, 1980. Meldola Medal, RIC, 1966; Corday-Morgan Medal, 1968; Tilden Medal and Lectr, 1983. *Publications:* Applications of NMR in Organic Chemistry, 1964; Spectroscopic Methods in Organic Chemistry, 1966, 3rd edn 1980; Mass Spectrometry of Organic Compounds, 1967; Mass Spectrometry—Principles and Applications, 1981; papers in chemical and biochemical jls. *Recreations:* music, squash. *Address:* 7 Balsham Road, Fulbourn, Cambridge CB1 5BZ. *T:* Cambridge 880592.

WILLIAMS, Sir Edgar (Trevor), Kt 1973; CB 1946; CBE 1944; DSO 1943; DL; Emeritus Fellow, Balliol College, Oxford, since 1980; Chairman: Nuffield Provincial Hospitals Trust, since 1966; Nuffield Medical Benefaction, Oxford, since 1982; a Radcliffe Trustee, since 1960; Governor, St Edward's School, Oxford, since 1960; a Freeman of Chester; *b* 20 Nov. 1912; *e s* of late Rev. J. E. Williams; *m* 1938, Monica, *d* of late Professor P. W. Robertson; one *d*; *m* 1946, Gillian, *yr d* of late Major-General M. D. Gambier-Parry, MC; one *s* one *d*. *Educ:* Tettenhall College; KES, Sheffield; Merton College, Oxford (Chambers Postmaster, 1931–34; First Class, Modern History, 1934; Harmsworth Senior Scholar, 1934–35; Junior Research Fellow, 1937–39; MA 1938; Hon. Fellow, 1964–). FRHistS 1947. Asst Lectr, Univ. of Liverpool, 1936. Served War of 1939–45 (despatches thrice); 2nd Lieut (SRO), 1st King's Dragoon Guards, 1939; Western Desert, 1941; GSO1, Eighth Army (North Africa, 1942–43, Sicily and Italy, 1943); Brig., Gen. Staff I, 21st Army Gp, 1944–45; Rhine Army, 1945–46; Officer, US Legion of Merit, 1945; UN Security Council Secretariat, 1946–47. Fellow, Balliol Coll., Oxford, 1945–80; a Pro-Vice-Chancellor, Oxford Univ., 1968–80.; Sec., Rhodes Trust, 1951–80. Editor, DNB, 1949–80. Mem., Devlin Nyasaland Commn, 1959; UK Observer, Rhodesian elections, 1980. DL Oxfordshire, 1964–. President, OUCC, 1966–68 (Sen. Treasurer, 1949–61); Hon. Mem., American Hosp. Assoc., 1971. Hon. Fellow: Queen Elizabeth House, Oxford, 1975; Wolfson Coll., Oxford, 1981. Hon. LLD: Waynesburg Coll., Pa, 1947; Univ. of Windsor, Ontario, 1969; Hon. LHD, Williams Coll., Mass, 1965; Hon. PdD, Franklin and Marshall Coll., Pa, 1966; Hon. DLitt: Warwick, 1967; Hull, 1970; Mt Allison, NB, 1980; Liverpool, 1982; Hon. LittD: Swarthmore Coll., Pa, 1969; Sheffield, 1981. *Festschrift:* Oxford and the Idea of Commonwealth (ed A. F. Madden and D. K. Fieldhouse), 1982. *Address:* 94 Lonsdale Road, Oxford OX2 7ER. *T:* Oxford 515199. *Clubs:* Athenæum, Savile; MCC; Vincent's (Oxford).

WILLIAMS, Maj.-Gen. Edward Alexander Wilmot, CB 1962; CBE 1958; MC 1940; DL; *b* 8 June 1910; *s* of late Captain B. C. W. Williams, DL, JP, Herringston, Dorchester and late Hon. Mrs W. M. Williams (*er d* of 2nd Baron Addington); *m* 1943, Sybilla Margaret, *er d* of late Colonel O. A. Archdale, MBE, late The Rifle Brigade, West Knighton House, Dorchester; one *s* three *d*. *Educ:* Eton; Royal Military College. 2nd Lieut 60th Rifles, 1930; Adjutant, 2nd Battalion (Calais), 1938–39. Served War of 1939–45; commanded 1st Bn 60th Rifles, 1944; US Armed Forces Staff Coll. (course 1), 1947; Bt Lieut-Col, 1950; Directing Staff, Joint Services Staff College, 1950–52; commanded 2nd Bn 60th Rifles, 1954–55; Comdr 2nd Infantry Brigade, 1956–57; Imperial Defence College, 1958; Brigadier Author, War Office, 1959. GOC 2nd Div. BAOR, 1960–62: Chief of Staff, GHQ Far East Land Forces, May-Nov. 1962; General Officer Commanding Singapore Base District, 1962–63; Chairman, Vehicle Cttee, Min. of Defence, 1964; retired 1965; Colonel Commandant, 2nd Bn The Royal Green Jackets (The King's Royal Rifle Corps), 1965–70. DL Dorset, 1965; High Sheriff of Dorset, 1970–71. *Recreations:* fishing, shooting. *Address:* Herringston, Dorchester, Dorset. *T:* Dorchester 64122. *Clubs:* Army & Navy, Pratt's, Lansdowne; Royal Dorset Yacht.

WILLIAMS, Air Cdre Edward Stanley, CBE 1975 (OBE 1968); defence consultant; *b* 27 Sept. 1924; *s* of late William Stanley Williams and Ethel Williams; *m* 1947, Maureen Donovan; two *d*. *Educ:* Wallasey Central Sch.; London Univ. Sch. of Slavonic and E European Studies; St John's Coll., Cambridge (MPhil (Internat. Relations), 1982). Joined RAF, 1942; trained in Canada; service in flying boats, 1944; seconded BOAC, 1944–48; 18 Sqdn, Transport Comd, 1949; Instr, Central Navigation Sch., RAF Shawbury, 1950–52; Russian Language Study, 1952–54; Flying Appts MEAF, A&AEE, 216 Sqdn Transport Comd, 1954–61; OC RAF Element, Army Intell. Centre, 1961–64; Asst Air Attaché, Moscow, 1964–67; first RAF Defence Fellow, UCL, 1967–68; comd Jt Wing, Sch. of Service Intell., 1968–71; Chief, Target Plans, HQ Second ATAF, 1971–73; Chief Intell. Officer, HQ British Forces Near East, 1973–75; comd Jt Air Reconn. Intell. Centre, 1976–77; Defence and Air Attaché, Moscow, 1978–81, retired RAF, 1981. *Publications:* The Soviet Military, 1986; various articles in professional jls. *Recreations:* Russian studies, walking, photography. *Address:* c/o Midland Bank, 2 Liscard Way, Wallasey, Merseyside L44 5TR. *Club:* Royal Air Force.

WILLIAMS, Hon. Sir Edward (Stratten), KCMG 1983; KBE 1981; Commissioner-General of Expo 88, Brisbane, Australia, since 1984; *b* 29 Dec. 1921; *s* of Edward Stratten and Zilla Claudia Williams; *m* 1949, Dorothy May Murray; three *s* four *d* (and one *s* decd). *Educ:* Yungaburra State Sch., Qld; Mt Carmel Coll., Charters Towers, Qld; Univ. of London (LLB Hons). Served RAAF, UK and Aust., 1942–46. Barrister-at-Law, 1946; QC (Australia) 1965; Justice of Supreme Court of Qld, 1971–84. Chairman, Parole Board of Qld, 1976–83; Royal Commissioner, Aust. Royal Commn of Inquiry into Drugs, 1977–80; Member, Internat. Narcotics Control Board (UN), 1982–87. Director: Elders IXL Ltd, 1984–; Aust. Hydrocarbons NL, 1985–; Chm., Brisbane Crematorium Ltd, 1985–. Chairman, Commonwealth Games Foundn Brisbane (1982), 1976–83; Mem., Anti-Cancer Council, Queensland Cancer Fund, 1983–. Australian of the Year, 1982; Queenslander of the Year, 1983. *Publications:* Report of Australian Royal Commission of Inquiry into Drugs and associated reports. *Recreations:* horse racing, gardening, golf. *Address:* 150 Adelaide Street East, Clayfield, Queensland 4011, Australia. *T:* 2624802. *Clubs:* Brisbane, United Services, Queensland Turf (Chairman, 1980–), Rugby Union, BATC, Tattersall's, Albion Park Trotting, Far North Queensland Amateur Turf (all Queensland).

See also Sir H. S. Williams.

WILLIAMS, Edward Taylor, CMG 1962; MICE; retired as General Manager, Malayan Railway; civil engineering railway consultant with Henderson, Busby Partnership, consulting engineers and economists, since 1965; *b* Bolton, Lancashire, 15 October 1911; *s* of Edward and Harriet Williams; *m* 1940, Ethel Gertrude Bradley (*d* 1983); one step *s* one step *d*. *Educ:* Accrington Grammar School; Manchester College of Technology. LMS Rly, pupil engineer, 1929–36; Sudan Rly, Asst Civil Engr, 1936–38; Metropolitan Water Board, Civil Engr, 1939–41; Malayan Rly, 1941–62 (Gen. Man. 1959–62); Rly Advr, Saudi Govt Railroad, 1963–65. Interned in Singapore, in Changi and Sime Road, 1941–45. *Recreation:* travel. *Address:* The Courtyard, Gatchell House, Trull, Taunton, Somerset. *T:* Taunton 83641.

WILLIAMS, Elizabeth, (Betty), (Mrs J. T. Perkins); working for peace, since 1976; *b* 22 May 1943; *m* 1st, 1961, Ralph Williams (marr. diss.); one *s* one *d*; 2nd, 1982, James T. Perkins. *Educ:* St Dominic's Grammar School. Office Receptionist. Leader, NI Peace Movement, 1976–78. Hon. LLD, Yale Univ., 1977; Hon. HLD, Coll. of Sienna Heights, Michigan, 1977. Nobel Peace Prize (jtly), 1976; Carl-von-Ossietsky Medal for Courage, 1976. *Recreation:* gardening.

WILLIAMS, Emlyn, CBE 1962; MA; FRSL; *b* 1905; *m* Molly O'Shann (*d* 1970); two *s*. *Educ:* County School, Holywell; Geneva; Christ Church, Oxford (MA). Hon. LLD Bangor. *Plays:* A Murder has been Arranged; Glamour; Full Moon; Vigil; Vessels Departing; Spring, 1600; Night Must Fall; He Was Born Gay; The Corn is Green; The Light of Heart; The Morning Star; adaptation of A Month in the Country; The Druid's Rest; The Wind of Heaven; Trespass; Accolade; Someone Waiting; Beth; adaptation of The Master Builder; Cuckoo (also directed). In addition to acting in most of these, has acted at the Old Vic, also in The Winslow Boy, Lyric, 1946; The Wild Duck, Saville, 1955; Season at Stratford-on-Avon, 1956. Shadow of Heroes, Piccadilly, 1958. As Charles Dickens (solo performance), Lyric (Hammersmith), Criterion, Duchess, 1951, Golden Theatre (New York), Ambassadors, 1952. As Dylan Thomas (Growing Up: solo performance), Globe, 1955 and 1958, Long Acre Theatre (New York), Oct. 1957, Ambassadors, 1980; as Saki (solo performance), Apollo, 1977. Acted in: Three, Criterion, 1961; Daughter of Silence, New York, 1961; A Man For All Seasons, New York, 1962; The Deputy, New York, 1964; World Tour as Dickens, 1964–65; as Charles Dickens, Globe, 1965, and Haymarket, 1975; acted in A Month in the Country, Cambridge, 1965; Forty Years On, Apollo, 1969. *Films include:* The Last Days of Dolwyn (author, co-director, and star), 1948; Ivanhoe, 1950; Deep Blue Sea, 1955; I Accuse, 1957; The Wreck of the Mary Deare, 1959; The L-Shaped Room, 1962; Eye of the Devil, 1966; The Walking-Stick, 1969; David Copperfield, 1969. *Television includes:* The Deadly Game, 1982; Rumpole of the Bailey, 1983. *Publications:* (autobiog.) George, 1961; Beyond Belief, 1967; (autobiog.) Emlyn, 1973; (novel) Headlong, 1980. *Address:* 123 Dovehouse Street, SW3. *T:* 01–352 0208.

WILLIAMS, Brig. Eric Llewellyn Griffith G.; *see* Griffith-Williams.

WILLIAMS, Evelyn Faithfull M.; *see* Monier-Williams.

WILLIAMS, Sir Francis (John Watkin), 8th Bt *cr* 1798; QC 1952; *b* Anglesey, 24 Jan. 1905; *s* of Col Lawrence Williams, OBE, DL, JP (*d* 1958) (*gs* of 1st Bt); *S* brother, 1971; *m* 1932, Brenda, *d* of Sir John Jarvis, 1st Bt; four *d*. *Educ:* Malvern College; Trinity Hall, Cambridge. Barrister of Middle Temple, 1928. Served War of 1939–45; Wing Comdr, RAFVR. Recorder of Birkenhead, 1950–58; Recorder of Chester, 1958–71; Chm., Anglesey QS, 1960–71 (Dep. Chm., 1949–60); Chm., Flint QS, 1961–71 (Dep Chm., 1953–61); Dep. Chm., Cheshire QS, 1952–71; a Recorder of the Crown Court, 1972–74. JP Denbighshire, 1951–74; Chm. Medical Appeal Tribunal for N Wales Areas, 1954–57; High Sheriff: of Denbighshire, 1957, of Anglesey, 1963. Chancellor, Diocese of St Asaph, 1966–83. Freeman of City of Chester, 1960. *Heir:* *half-b* Lawrence Hugh Williams [*b* 25 Aug. 1929; *m* 1952, Sara Margaret Helen, 3rd *d* of Sir Harry Platt, Bt, *qv*; two *d*]. *Address:* Llys, Middle Lane, Denbigh, Clwyd. *T:* Denbigh 2984. *Clubs:* United Oxford & Cambridge University; Grosvenor (Chester).

See also Sir Charles Kimber, Bt.

WILLIAMS, Francis Julian, CBE 1986; JP; DL; Member of Prince of Wales' Council, Duchy of Cornwall, 1969–85; *b* 16 April 1927; 2nd *s* of late Alfred Martyn Williams, CBE, DSC; *m* Delia Fearne Marshall, *e d* of Captain and Mrs Campbell Marshall, St Mawes; two *s*. *Educ:* Eton; Trinity Coll., Cambridge (BA). RAF, 1945–48. Chm., Cambridge Univ. Conservative Assoc;, 1950; Pres., Cambridge Union, 1951. Contested (C) All Saints Div. of Birmingham, 1955. Mem., Devon and Cornwall Cttee, Lloyds Bank, 1971–. Succeeded to Caerhays, 1955. Pres., Cornwall Cricket Club. Mem., Cornwall CC, 1967– (Vice-Chm., 1974; Chm., 1980–). JP 1970, DL 1977, Cornwall. *Recreation:* gardening. *Address:* Caerhays Castle, Gorran, St Austell, Cornwall. *T:* Truro 501250. *Clubs:* Brooks's, White's.

WILLIAMS, Frank Denry Clement, CMG 1956; *b* 3 May 1913; *s* of Frank Norris Williams and Joanna Esther Williams; *m* 1941, Traute Kahn; no *c*. *Educ:* Leighton Park School, Reading; London School of Economics (BSc Econ.). Cadet, Colonial Administrative Service, 1946; Asst Financial Sec., Nigeria, 1952; Financial Secretary: Jamaica, 1954; Federation of Nigeria, 1956; Economic Adviser, Federation of Nigeria, 1957–58; Permanent Secretary, Prime Minister's Dept, Fedn of The W Indies, 1958–62; Financial Sec., The Gambia, 1962–65. *Recreations:* walking, languages. *Address:* 51 The Priory, London Road, Brighton, Sussex BN1 8QT.

WILLIAMS, Prof. Gareth Howel; Professor of Chemistry, University of London, 1967–84 (Head of Department of Chemistry, Bedford College, 1967–84), now Emeritus

Professor; b 17 June 1925; s of Morgan John and Miriam Williams, Treherbert, Glam; m 1955, Marie, BA, yr d of William and Jessie Mary Mitchell, Wanlockhead, Dumfriesshire; one s one d. Educ: Pentre Grammar Sch.; University Coll., London. BSc, PhD, DSc London; FRSC. Asst Lectr, then Lectr in Chemistry, King's Coll., Univ. of London, 1947–60; Research Fellow, Univ. of Chicago, 1953–54; Reader in Organic Chemistry, Birkbeck Coll., Univ. of London, 1960–67. Vis. Lectr, Univ. of Ife, Nigeria, 1965; Rose Morgan Vis. Prof., Univ. of Kansas, 1969–70; Vis. Prof., Univ. of Auckland, NZ, 1977. External Examr: Univ. of Rhodesia, 1967–70; Univ. of Khartoum, 1967–73, 1976–80; City Univ., 1968–74; Univ. of Surrey, 1974–76; Brunel Univ., 1980–85. Publications: Homolytic Aromatic Substitution, 1960; Organic Chemistry: a conceptual approach, 1977; (Editor) Advances in Free-Radical Chemistry, Vol. I, 1965, Vol. II, 1967, Vol. III, 1969, Vol. IV, 1972, Vol. V, 1975, Vol. VI, 1980; numerous papers in Jl Chem. Soc. and other scientific jls. Recreation: music. Address: Hillside, 22 Watford Road, Northwood, Mddx. T: Northwood 25297. Club: Athenæum.

WILLIAMS, Prof. Gareth Lloyd; Professor of Educational Administration, Institute of Education, University of London, since 1984; b 19 Oct. 1935; s of Lloyd and Katherine Enid Williams; m 1960, Elizabeth Ann Peck; two s one d. Educ: Creeting St Mary; Framlingham; Cambridge Univ. (MA). Res. Officer, Agricl Econs Res. Inst., Oxford Univ., 1959–62; Res. Fellow, OECD, Athens, 1962–64; Principal Administrator, OECD, Paris, 1964–68; Associate Dir, Higher Educn Res. Unit, LSE, 1968–73; Prof. of Educnl Planning, Univ. of Lancaster, 1973–84. Vis. Prof., Melbourne Univ., 1981–82. Specialist Adviser to Arts and Educn Sub-Cttee to House of Commons Cttee on Expenditure, 1972–76; Consultant to OECD, ILO, and UNESCO, 1968–. Member: Council, Policy Studies Inst., 1979–85; Governing Council for Soc. for Res. into Higher Educn, 1970– (Chm.,1978–80,1986–). Mem. Bd, Red Rose Radio PLC,1981–. FRSA 1982. Publications: (with Greenaway) Patterns of Change in Graduate Employment, 1973; (with Blackstone and Metcalf) The Academic Labour Market in Britain, 1974; Towards Lifelong Learning, 1978; (with Zabalza and Turnbull) The Economics of Teacher Supply, 1979; (with Woodhall) Independent Further Education, 1979; (with Blackstone) Response to Adversity, 1983; Higher Education in Ireland, 1985. Address: 11 Thornfield, Ashton Road, Lancaster. T: Lancaster 66002.

WILLIAMS, Gareth Wyn; QC 1978; a Recorder of the Crown Court, since 1978; b 5 Feb. 1941; s of Albert Thomas Williams and Selina Williams; m 1962, Pauline Clarke; one s two d. Educ: Rhyl Grammar Sch.; Queens' Coll., Cambridge (Open Schol. (History) 1958; Univ. Prize, Jurisprudence 1962; Foundn Schol. 1964; LLB (1st Cl.) 1964; MA 1965). Called to the Bar, Gray's Inn, 1965. Address: Southlake House, Shurlock Row, near Reading, Berks. T: Shurlock Row 617.

WILLIAMS, Geoffrey Guy; Deputy Chairman, J. Henry Schroder Wagg & Co. Ltd, since 1977; b 12 July 1930; s of late Captain Guy Williams, OBE, and Mrs Margaret Williams (née Thomas). Educ: Blundell's Sch., Christ's Coll., Cambridge (MA, LLB). Slaughter and May, Solicitors, 1952–66, Partner 1961; Dir, J. Henry Schroder Wagg & Co. Ltd, 1966, Vice-Chm. 1974. Chm., National Film Finance Corp., 1976–85 (Dir, 1970). Director: Bass plc, 1971–; Schroders plc, 1976–; John Brown plc, 1977–85. Chm., Issuing Houses Assoc., 1979–81. Recreations: reading, theatre, cinema. Address: 18G Eaton Square, SW1W 9DD. T: 01–235 5212. Club: Brooks's.

WILLIAMS, Geoffrey Milson John, FEng 1982; Senior Partner, Scott Wilson Kirkpatrick and Partners, consulting engineers, since 1966; b 28 Jan. 1923; s of John and Clementine Williams; m 1952, Margaret Brown; three d. Educ: Sidney Sussex College, Cambridge (MA). FICE, FIStructE, FASCE. Associated with Scott Wilson Kirkpatrick and Partners in various capacities, 1945–; mainly concerned with design, supervision of construction and project management of civil and structural engineering work; projects include: Hong Kong International Airport, 1952–70; Hong Kong Cross-Harbour Road Tunnel, 1960–; Shell Centre, 1957–62; Commercial Union Building, 1962–69; British Airways Base, 1950–75 and Fourth Passenger Terminal, 1979–, London Airport. Member of Council: ACE, 1972– (Chm., 1986–87); Fellowship of Engrg, 1984–; ICE, 1981–84, 1986–; Mem. for London Central, Engrg Assembly, 1984–; Chm., Engrg Council Regl Orgn for London, 1984–. FRSA. Publications: technical papers to ICE, IStructE, ASCE. Address: Clifton House, Euston Road, NW1 2RA. T: 01–388 6621. Clubs: Royal Automobile, Hurlingham.

WILLIAMS, (George Haigh) Graeme; QC 1983; barrister; a Recorder of the Crown Court, since 1981; b 5 July 1935; s of Leslie Graeme Williams and Joan Haigh Williams; m 1963, Anna Maureen Worrall; two d. Educ: Tonbridge Sch.; Brasenose Coll., Oxford (MA). Called to the Bar, Inner Temple, 1959. Address: 19 Murray Mews, NW1. T: 01–267 0817.

WILLIAMS, George Mervyn, CBE 1977; MC 1944; TD; Vice Lord-Lieutenant of Mid Glamorgan, since 1986; Chairman, South Wales Regional Board, Lloyds Bank, since 1977; b 30 Oct. 1918; yr s of late Owain Williams and late Mrs Williams; m 1st, Penelope (marr. diss. 1946), d of late Sir Frank Mitchell, KCVO; 2nd, Grizel Margaretta Cochrane, DStJ, d of late Major Walter Stewart, DSO; one s. Educ: Radley Coll. Served Royal Fusiliers, N Africa and Italy, 1939–46; Major, British Military Mission to Greece, 1945. Great Universal Stores, 1946–49; Christie-Tyler PLC, 1949–85, Chm. and Man. Dir, 1959–85; Director: Lloyds Bank plc, 1972–77; Lloyds Bank UK Management Ltd. Governor, United World Coll. of Atlantic, 1980–. JP 1965–70, High Sheriff 1966, DL 1967–86, Glamorgan. CStJ. Address: Llanharan House, Llanharan, Mid Glamorgan CF7 9NR. T: Llantrisant 226253; Craig y Bwla, Crickhowell, Powys NP8 1SU. T: Crickhowell 810413. Clubs: Brooks's; Cardiff and County (Cardiff).

WILLIAMS, George W.; see Wynn-Williams.

WILLIAMS, Gerald Wellington, JP; b 1903; s of Wellington Archbold Williams, JP, Shernfold Park, Frant, Sussex; m 1930, Mary Katharine Victoria (d 1981), d of Captain Joscelyn Heber-Percy, DL, JP, East Lymden, Ticehurst, Sussex; one s two d. Educ: Eton; Christ Church, Oxford (MA). RNVR, 1939 (Lt-Comdr 1942). MP (C) Tonbridge division of Kent, 1945–56, resigned. JP Tunbridge Wells, 1957; High Sheriff of Kent, 1968–69. Address: Maplehurst, Staplehurst, Tonbridge, Kent. T: Staplehurst 893237. Clubs: Carlton, MCC.

WILLIAMS, Prof. Glanmor, CBE 1981; FBA 1986; Professor of History, 1957–82, University College of Swansea; Chairman: Ancient Monuments Board (Wales), since 1983; Royal Commission on Ancient and Historical Monuments in Wales, since 1986 (Member, since 1962); b 5 May 1920; s of Daniel and Ceinwen Williams, Dowlais, Glam; m 1946, Margaret Fay Davies; one s one d. Educ: Cyfarthfa Grammar Sch., Merthyr Tydfil; Univ. Coll. of Wales, Aberystwyth. MA 1947; DLitt 1962. Univ. Coll. of Swansea: Asst Lectr in History, 1945; Sen. Lectr, 1952; a Vice-Principal, 1975–78. Nat. Governor, BBC, for Wales, 1965–71; Member: Historic Bldgs Council for Wales, 1962–; British Library Bd, 1973–80 (Chm., Adv. Council, 1981–85); Adv. Council on Public Records, 1974–82; Welsh Arts Council, 1978–81; Council, Nat. Museum of Wales, 1983–. Vice-Pres., UCW Aberystwyth, 1986–. Chm., Pantyfedwen Foundations,

1973–79; Pres., Cambrian Arch. Assoc., 1980. FRHistS 1954 (Vice-Pres., 1979–83); FSA 1978. Publications: Yr Esgob Richard Davies, 1953; The Welsh Church, 1962; Owen Glendower, 1966; Welsh Reformation Essays, 1967; (ed) Glamorgan County History, vol II 1984, vol. III 1971, vol. IV 1974, vol. V 1980; Religion, Language and Nationality in Wales, 1979; Grym Tafodau Tân, 1984; Henry Tudor and Wales, 1985; contrib. to: History, Welsh History Review, etc. Recreations: walking, gramophone, cine-photography. Address: 11 Grosvenor Road, Swansea. T: Swansea 204113. Club: National Liberal.

WILLIAMS, Glanville Llewelyn, QC 1968; FBA 1957; Fellow of Jesus College, Cambridge, 1955–78, Hon. Fellow, 1978, and Rouse Ball Professor of English Law in the University of Cambridge, 1968–78 (Reader, 1957–65; Professor, 1966); b 15 Feb. 1911; s of late B. E. Williams, Bridgend, Glam; m 1939, Lorna Margaret, d of late F. W. Lawfield, Cambridge; one s. Educ: Cowbridge; University College of Wales, Aberystwyth; St John's Coll., Cambridge. Called to the Bar, 1935; PhD (Cantab), 1936; Research Fellow of St John's Coll., 1936–42; LLD (Cantab), 1946; Reader in English Law and successively Professor of Public Law and Quain Professor of Jurisprudence, University of London, 1945–55; Carpentier Lecturer in Columbia Univ., 1956; Cohen Lecturer in Hebrew University of Jerusalem, 1957; first Walter E. Meyer Visiting Research Professor, New York Univ., 1959–60; Charles Inglis Thompson Guest Professor, University of Colorado, 1965. Special Consultant for the American Law Institute's Model Penal Code, 1956–58; Member: Standing Cttee on Criminal Law Revision, 1959–80; Law Commn's Working Party on Codification of Criminal Law, 1967; Cttee on Mentally Abnormal Offenders, 1972. Pres., Abortion Law Reform Assoc., 1962–. Hon. Bencher, Middle Temple, 1966. Fellow, Eugenics Soc.; For. Hon. Mem., Amer. Acad. of Arts and Scis, 1985. Ames Prize, Harvard, 1963; (joint) Swiney Prize, RSA, 1964. Hon. LLD: Nottingham, 1963; Wales, 1974; Glasgow, 1980; Hon. DCL Durham, 1984. Publications: Liability for Animals, 1939; chapters in McElroy's Impossibility of Performance, 1941; The Law Reform (Frustrated Contracts) Act (1943), 1944; Learning the Law, 1st edn 1945, 11th edn 1982; Crown Proceedings, 1948; Joint Obligations, 1949; Joint Torts and Contributory Negligence, 1950; Speedhand Shorthand, 1952, 8th edn 1980; Criminal Law; The General Part, 1st edn 1953, 2nd edn 1961; The Proof of Guilt, 1st edn 1955, 3rd edn 1963; The Sanctity of Life and the Criminal Law, American edn 1956, English edn 1958; The Mental Element in Crime, 1965; (with B. A. Hepple) Foundations of the Law of Tort, 1976, 2nd edn 1984; Textbook of Criminal Law, 1978, 2nd edn 1983; articles in legal periodicals. Address: Merrion Gate, Gazeley Road, Cambridge CB2 2HB. T: Cambridge 841175.

WILLIAMS, Rev. Dr Glen Garfield; General Secretary, Conference of European Churches, 1968–87; b 14 Sept. 1923; s of John Archibald Douglas Williams and Violet May (née Tucker); m 1945, Velia Cristina (née Baglio). Educ: Newport High Sch.; Universities of Wales (Cardiff), London, Tübingen. Military Service, 1943–47. Univ. studies, 1947–55. Minister, Dagnall Street Baptist Church, St Albans, 1955–59; European Area Secretary, World Council of Churches, Geneva, 1959–68. Hon. DTh Budapest, 1975; Hon. DD Bucharest, 1981. Order of St Vladimir, 1976, and St Sergius, 1979, Russian Orthodox Church; Order of St Mary Magdalene, 1980, Polish Orthodox Church. Publications: contrib. to Handbook on Western Europe, 1967, etc.; numerous articles, mainly in Continental journals. Recreations: travel, reading, archæology. Address: 139 Rue de Lausanne, 1202 Geneva, Switzerland. T: (022) 31.30.16. Club: Athenæum.

WILLIAMS, Graeme; see Williams, George H. G.

WILLIAMS, Air Vice-Marshal Graham Charles, AFC 1970 and Bar 1975; FRAeS; Assistant Chief of Defence Staff, Operational Requirements (Air), since 1986; b 4 June 1937; s of Charles Francis Williams and Molly (née Chapman); m 1962, Judith Teresa Ann Walker; one s one d. Educ: Marlborough College; RAF College, Cranwell. FRAeS 1984. 54 Sqn, 229 OCU, 8 Sqn, Empire Test Pilots' School, A Sqn, A&AEE, 1958–70; RAF Staff Coll., 1971; OC 3 Sqn, Wildenrath, 1972–74; Junior Directing Staff (Air), RCDS, 1975–77; OC RAF Brüggen, 1978–79; Group Captain Ops, HQ RAF Germany, 1980–82; CO Experimental Flying Dept, RAE, 1983; Comdt, Aeroplane and Armament Exptl Estabt, 1983–85; Dir, Operational Requirements, MoD, 1986. Harmon Internat. Trophy for Aviators, USA, 1970. Recreations: squash (Chm. RAFSRA), golf. Address: 3 The Ramparts, Sandwich, Kent. Club: Royal Air Force.

WILLIAMS, Rt. Rev. Gwilym Owen, DD Lambeth 1957; b 23 March 1913; s of Owen G. Williams; m 1941, Megan (d 1976), d of T. D. Jones; one s. Educ: Llanberis Gram. Sch.; Jesus Coll., Oxford, Hon Fellow, 1972. BA 1st Class Hons English, 1933; 1st Class Hons Theol. 1935; Gladstone Student at St Deiniol's Library, Hawarden, 1935; St Stephen's House, Oxford, 1936; MA 1937. Curate of Denbigh, 1937; Reader in Theology, St David's Coll., Lampeter, 1940; Warden of Church Hostel, Bangor; Lecturer in Theology, University Coll., Bangor; Canon of Bangor Cathedral, 1947; Warden and Headmaster, Llandovery Coll., 1948–49; Bishop of Bangor, 1957–82; Archbishop of Wales, 1971–82. Chaplain and Sub-Prelate of Order of St John of Jerusalem, 1965. Hon. DD Wales, 1985. Publication: The Church's Work, 1959. Recreations: fishing and walking. Address: Hafod-y-Bryn, Criccieth, Gwynedd LL52 0AH.

WILLIAMS, Sir Gwilym (Tecwyn), Kt 1970; CBE 1966; Director: Dalgety (UK) Ltd, 1975–83; Dalgety Spillers, 1980–83; b 1913; s of David and Margaret Williams; m 1936, Kathleen, d of John and Maria Edwards; two s one d. Educ: Llanfyllin CSS; Llysfasi Farm Inst.; Harper Adams Agric. Coll. Leader, Employers' side, Agricultural Wages Board, 1960–66; Director, FMC Ltd, 1962–75. Potato Marketing Board: Member, 1954–58; Chairman, 1955–58; Special Member, 1961–66. Member: Agric. NEDO, 1968–76; Econ. and Social Cttee, EEC, 1972–78; Adv. Council for Agriculture and Horticulture in England and Wales, 1973–82. National Farmers' Union: Mem. Council, 1948– (Life Mem., 1977); Vice-Pres., 1953, 1954, 1960–62; Dep. Pres., 1955, 1963–65; Pres., 1966–70. Chm. Governors, Harper Adams Agric. Coll., 1977–85. Recreations: trout fishing, shooting. Address: Red Gables, Longford, Newport, Salop. T: Newport (Salop) 810439. Club: Farmers'.

WILLIAMS, Very Rev. Harold Claude Noel; Provost of Coventry Cathedral, 1958–81; Provost Emeritus since 1981; b 6 Dec. 1914; s of Charles Williams and Elizabeth Malherbe, Grahamstown, S Africa; m 1940, Pamela Marguerite Taylor, Southampton; two s two d (and one d decd). Educ: Graeme Coll., S Africa; Durham Univ.; Southampton Univ. Ordained, 1938; Curate of Weeke, Winchester, 1938–40; Principal, St Matthew's Coll., S Africa, 1941–49; Vicar of Hyde, Winchester, 1950–54; Rector of St Mary's, Southampton, 1954–58. Hon. LLD Valparaiso Univ., USA. Grosse Verdienstkreuz des Verdienst Ordens, Federal Republic of Germany, 1967. Publications: African Folk Songs, 1948; (ed) Vision of Duty, 1963; Twentieth Century Cathedral, 1964; Coventry Cathedral and its Ministry, 1965; Nothing to Fear, 1967; Coventry Cathedral in Action, 1968; Basics and Variables, 1970; The Latter Glory, 1978; Order My Steps in Thy Way, 1982. Recreations: mountaineering and fishing. Address: 96 Stoney Road, Coventry CV3 6HY. T: Coventry 502561. Club: Alpine.

WILLIAMS, Air Vice-Marshal Harold Guy L.; see Leonard-Williams.

WILLIAMS, Harri Llwyd H.; *see* Hudson-Williams.

WILLIAMS, Rev. Harry Abbott; Community of the Resurrection, since 1969; *b* 10 May 1919; *s* of late Captain Harry Williams, RN, and Annie Williams. *Educ:* Cranleigh Sch.; Trinity Coll., Cambridge; Cuddesdon Coll., Oxford. BA 1941; MA 1945. Deacon, 1943; Priest, 1944. Curate of St Barnabas, Pimlico, 1943–45; Curate of All Saints, Margaret Street, 1945–48; Chaplain and Tutor of Westcott House, Cambridge, 1948–51; Fellow of Trinity Coll., Cambridge, 1951–69; Dean of Chapel, 1958–69, and Tutor, 1958–68; Exam. Chaplain to Bishop of London, 1948–69. Mem., Anglican delegation to Russian Orthodox Church, Moscow, 1956; Select Preacher, Univ. of Cambridge, 1950, 1958, 1975; Hulsean Preacher, 1962, 1975; Select Preacher, Univ. of Oxford, 1974. Licensed to officiate in Dio. of Ely, 1948–, Dio. of Wakefield, 1979–. *Publications:* Jesus and the Resurrection, 1951; God's Wisdom in Christ's Cross, 1960; The Four Last Things, 1960; The True Wilderness, 1965; True Resurrection, 1972; Poverty, Chastity and Obedience: the true virtues, 1975; Tensions, 1976; Becoming What I Am, 1977; The Joy of God, 1979; Some Day I'll Find You (autobiog.), 1982; contribs to: Soundings, 1962; Objections to Christian Belief, 1963; The God I Want, 1967. *Recreations:* idleness and religion. *Address:* House of the Resurrection, Mirfield, West Yorks WF14 0BN.

WILLIAMS, Rev. Dr (Henry) Howard; Minister, Bloomsbury Central Baptist Church, 1958–86; Moderator, Free Church Federal Council, 1984–85; *b* 30 April 1918; *s* of Rev. Henry James Williams and Edith Gwenllian Williams; *m* 1950, Athena Mary (*née* Maurice); three *s* one *d*. *Educ:* Mountain Ash Grammar Sch.; Rawdon Coll.; Leeds Univ. BA, BD, PhD. Minister: Blenheim Baptist Church, Leeds, 1943–53; Beechen Grove, Watford, 1953–58; Member: Baptist Union Council, 1954–; Central Religious Advisory Council, BBC, 1962–65; Religious Advisory Panel, ITA, 1965–70. Pres., Baptist Union of Great Britain and Ireland, 1965; Dir, Baptist Times Ltd. Hon. Life Mem., Central YMCA, London (former Dir). Mem. Editorial Bd, New Christian, 1965–70. *Publications:* Down to Earth, 1964; Noughts and Crosses, 1965; Old Memories and New Ways, 1965; The Song of the Devil, 1972; My Word, 1973; contributor to Expository Times. *Recreations:* now reduced to viewing the activity of others. *Address:* 162 Hendon Way, NW2 2NE. *T:* 01–455 6628.

WILLIAMS, Ven. Henry Leslie; Archdeacon of Chester, since 1975; *b* 26 Dec. 1919; *m* 1949, Elsie Marie; one *s*. *Educ:* Bethesda Gram. Sch.; St David's Coll., Lampeter (BA); St Michael's Coll., Llandaff. Deacon 1943, priest 1944, Bangor; Curate of Aberdovey, 1943–45; St Mary's, Bangor, 1945–48; Chaplain, HMS Conway, 1948–49; Curate, St Mary-without-the-Walls, Chester, 1949–53; Vicar of Barnston, Wirral, 1953–84. RD of Wirral North, 1967–75; Hon. Canon of Chester Cathedral, 1972–75. Mem., General Synod, 1978–80, 1985–. CF (TA), 1953–62. *Recreations:* fly-fishing, bee-keeping. *Address:* 25 Bartholomew Way, Westminster Park, Chester CH4 7NP. *T:* Chester 675417.

WILLIAMS, Sir Henry Morton Leech, Kt 1961; MBE 1945; farmer; Managing Director, Guest, Keen, Williams Ltd, 1952–62; President, Bengal Chamber of Commerce and Industry, and President, Associated Chambers of Commerce, India, 1960; *b* 1913; *s* of late O. R. Williams; *m* 1945, Bridget Mary, *d* of late C. G. Dowding; two *s* two *d*. *Educ:* Harrow; Corpus Christi Coll., Cambridge. Served War of 1939–45 (despatches, MBE), becoming Major, REME. CC Berkshire, 1967. *Address:* Grounds Farm, Uffington, Oxon SN7 7RD. *Club:* Oriental.

WILLIAMS, Sir (Henry) Sydney, Kt 1983; OBE 1978; company director; *b* 10 Jan. 1920; *s* of Edward Stratten Williams and Zilla Williams (*née* McHugh); *m* 1940, Joyce Veronica Meldon; four *s*. *Educ:* Mt Carmel Coll., Charters Towers, Qld, Aust. Served 7th Aust. Div. Cavalry Regt, ME and PNG, 1940–45; 51st Inf. Bn (Far North Qld Regt), 1947–57, Lt-Col Comd 1954–57. Chm. and Man. Dir, Air Queensland Ltd (formerly Bush Pilots Airways Ltd), 1960–86; Chairman: Willtrac Pty Ltd, 1964–; Radio 4 a.m., 1968–; Lizard Island Pty Ltd, 1970–; Director: Carlton & United Breweries (NQ) Ltd, 1964–; Placer Pacific Ltd. Member: Queensland Films Commn, 1974–; Queensland Art Gall., 1981–; Cairns Port Authority, 1982–; Life Mem., Cairns RSSAILA; Trustee, World Wildlife Fund, 1981–; Councillor, Enterprise Australia, 1980–; Pres., Far North Queensland Amateur Turf Club, 1959–; past Dep. Chm., Australian Tourist Commn; past Pres., Cairns Legacy Club. *Recreations:* fishing, bowls, golf. *Address:* 14 Bellevue Crescent, Edge Hill, Cairns, Queensland, Australia. *T:* 531489. *Clubs:* North Queensland (Townsville); United Services (Brisbane).
See also Hon. Sir Edward Williams.

WILLIAMS, Hilary a'Beckett E.; *see* Eccles-Williams.

WILLIAMS, Howard; *see* Williams, Henry H.

WILLIAMS, Hubert Glyn, AE 1944; a Recorder of the Crown Court, 1974–77; Senior Partner, Blake, Lapthorn, Rea & Williams, Solicitors, Portsmouth and District, 1973–83; *b* 18 Dec. 1912; *s* of John Christmas Williams and Florence Jane Williams (*née* Jones); *m* 1952, Audrey Elizabeth Righton; one *s* one *d*. *Educ:* Ruthin. Admitted solicitor, 1934 (2nd cl. Hons). Served War of 1939–45 (Sqdn Ldr; AE): AAF, 1939–41; RAFVR, 1941–45; UK, Egypt, E Africa, Palestine. Pres., Hampshire Inc. Law Soc., 1977–78. *Recreation:* cricket. *Address:* Twenty Nine, The Avenue, Alverstoke, Hants PO12 2JS. *T:* Gosport 583058. *Club:* MCC.

WILLIAMS, Hugo Mordaunt; writer; *b* 20 Feb. 1942; *s* of Hugh Williams, actor and playwright, and Margaret Vyner; *m* 1965, Hermine Demoriane; one *d*. *Educ:* Eton College. Asst Editor, London Magazine, 1961–70; television critic, 1983–, and poetry editor, 1984–, New Statesman. Henfield Writer's Fellowship, Univ. of East Anglia, 1981. Awards (for poetry): Eric Gregory, 1965; Cholmondeley, 1970; Geoffrey Faber Memorial Prize, 1979. *Publications: poems:* Symptoms of Loss, 1965; Sugar Daddy, 1970; Some Sweet Day, 1975; Love-Life, 1979; Writing Home, 1985; *travel:* All the Time in the World, 1966; No Particular Place to Go, 1981. *Address:* 3 Raleigh Street, N1. *T:* 01–226 1655.

WILLIAMS, Ian Malcolm Gordon, CBE 1960 (OBE 1954; MBE 1945); *b* 7 May 1914; *s* of late Thomas and Mabel Williams. *Educ:* Tatterford Sch., Norfolk; Leeds Univ.; Gonville and Caius Coll., Cambridge. President, Leeds University Students' Union, 1939. Volunteered Military Service, Sept. 1939; Officer Cadet, 123 OCTU; Commnd Royal Regt of Artillery, March 1940; NW Frontier of India and Burma, 1940–45, as Major, RA, and Mountain Artillery, Indian Army (despatches, MBE). Staff Officer, Hong Kong Planning Unit, 1946; Adjutant, Hong Kong Defence Force, 1946. Entered Colonial Administrative Service, 1946; was District Officer and Asst Colonial Secretary, Hong Kong, 1946–49; at Colonial Office, 1949–51; Senior Asst Secretary, Secretariat, Cyprus, 1951–53; Commissioner: of Paphos, 1953–55, of Larnaca, 1955–57, of Limassol, 1957–60; Chief Officer, Sovereign Base Areas of Akrotiri and Dhekelia, 1960–64; Member Administrator's Advisory Board; UK Chairman, Joint Consultative Board, 1960–64; Min. of Technology, 1965–67; DoE, 1967–71; Programme Dir, UN/Thai Programme for Drug Abuse Control in Thailand, 1972–79. Comdr, Most Noble Order of the Crown of Thailand, 1981. *Recreations:* art, Cypriot archæology, swimming. *Address:* White House, Adderbury, near Banbury, Oxfordshire. *Club:* East India, Devonshire, Sports and Public Schools.

WILLIAMS, (James) Vaughan, DSO 1942; OBE 1959; TD 1947; JP; Lord-Lieutenant for the County of West Glamorgan, since 1985; *b* 25 Oct. 1912; *s* of James Vaughan Williams, Merthyr Tydfil; *m* 1938, Mary Edith Jones (*d* 1972), *d* of G. Bryn Jones, OBE, JP, Merthyr Tydfil; two *d*. Local Govt Service, 1930–39. Commnd RE (TA), 1934; served War of 1939–45, BEF, France, Egypt, Italy, Berlin (despatches 1942 and 1943); psc 1946; Lt-Col TA, 1947–59; Hon. Col 53rd (W) Div. RE, 1959–67. Mem. Wales TA&VRA, 1968; Vice-Chm. Glam TA&VR Cttee, 1968; President, Swansea Branch: Royal British Legion; Royal Engrs Assoc.; Dunkirk Veteran Assoc.; Scout Council West Glamorgan; West Glam Council St John of Jerusalem; West Glam SSAFA. Past Chm., S Wales Assoc. ICE. DL Glam 1959; Lieut, W GLam, 1974; JP Glamorgan 1975. KStJ 1979. *Recreations:* travel, gardening. *Address:* 5 The Grove, Mumbles, Swansea, West Glamorgan. *T:* Swansea 68551. *Clubs:* Army and Navy; Bristol Channel Yacht.

WILLIAMS, John, OBE 1980; guitarist; *b* Melbourne, 24 April 1941. Studied with father, Segovia and at the Accademia Musicale Chigiana, Siena and RCM, London; since when has given many recitals, concerts, made TV and radio appearances worldwide, and recordings of both solo guitar, and chamber and orchestral music. Mem., Sky, 1979–84. Artistic Dir, South Bank Summer Music, 1984 and 1985. Hon. FRCM; Hon. FRNCM. *Recreations:* people, living, chess, table-tennis, music. *Address:* c/o Harold Holt Ltd, 31 Sinclair Road, W14.

WILLIAMS, John Brinley, FCIT; Managing Director, Associated British Ports (formerly British Transport Docks Board), since 1985 (Board Member since 1980; Joint Managing Director, 1982–85); *b* 18 Aug. 1927; *s* of late Leslie Williams and Alice Maud Williams; *m* 1951, Eileen (*née* Court) one *s* one *d*. *Educ:* Eveswell Sch., Newport. Asst Manager, Cardiff Docks, 1963–65; Commercial and Development Asst to Chief Docks Manager, South Wales Ports, 1965–67; Docks Manager: Cardiff and Penarth Docks, 1968–72; Hull Docks, 1972–75; Port Director: South Wales Ports, 1976–78; Southampton, 1978–82. *Recreations:* Rugby, open air pursuits. *Address:* Maes-y-Coed, Oakwood Road, Chandler's Ford, Hants. *T:* Chandler's Ford 69522. *Clubs:* Royal Southampton Yacht; Royal Southern Yacht (Hamble).

WILLIAMS, (John Bucknall) Kingsley; solicitor; *b* 28 July 1927; *s* of Charles Kingsley Williams and Margaret Elizabeth (*née* Bucknall); *m* 196 Brenda (*née* Baldwin); two *s*. *Educ:* Kingswood Sch., Bath; Trinity Hall, Cambridge (MA, LLB). Partner, Dutton Gregory & Williams, Solicitors, Winchester, 1956–. Chm., Wessex RHA, 1975–82. Member: Winchester City Council, 1966–73; Hampshire CC (ex-officio Mem., Planning and Health Cttees, 1971–73); Assoc. of County Councils, 1973–75; NHS Supply Council, 1980–82. Vice-Chm., Council, Southampton Univ., 1976–; Chm. of Governors, Winchester Sch. of Art, 1986–. *Address:* Danesacre, Worthy Road, Winchester, Hants SO23 7AD. *T:* (home) Winchester 52594; (office) Winchester 66363.

WILLIAMS, Ven. John Charles; Archdeacon of Worcester, 1975–80, now Archdeacon Emeritus; Residentiary Canon of Worcester Cathedral, 1975–80; *b* 17 July 1912; *s* of William and Edith Williams; *m* 1940, Agnes Mildred Hutchings, MA; one *s* one *d*. *Educ:* Cowbridge Sch.; St David's University Coll., Lampeter; University College, Oxford. Asst Curate, Christ Church, Summerfield, Birmingham, 1937–39; Asst Curate, Hales Owen, in charge of St Margaret's, Hasbury, 1939–43; Vicar: Cradley Heath, Staffs, 1943–48; Redditch, Worcs, 1948–59. Surrogate, 1951–71; Rural Dean of Bromsgrove, 1958–59; Rector, Hales Owen, 1959–70; Archdeacon of Dudley, 1968–75; Vicar of Dodderhill, 1970–75. Hon. Canon, Worcester Cathedral, 1965–75; Examng Chaplain to Bishop of Worcester, 1969–80; Dir, Worcester Diocesan Central Services, 1974–75; Director of Ordination Candidates, 1975–79. *Publication:* One Hundred Years, 1847–1947; A History of Cradley Heath Parish. *Recreations:* history of architecture, sailing. *Address:* The Old Vicarage, Norton with Lenchwick, Evesham, Worcs WR11 4TL. *Clubs:* Oxford University Occasionals, United Oxford & Cambridge University.

WILLIAMS, John Eirwyn F.; *see* Ffowcs Williams.

WILLIAMS, Prof. John Ellis Caerwyn, FBA 1978; FSA; Professor of Irish, University College of Wales, Aberystwyth, 1965–79, now Professor Emeritus; Director of Centre for Advanced Welsh and Celtic Studies, Aberystwyth, 1978–85; *b* 17 Jan. 1912; *s* of John R. Williams and Maria Williams; *m* 1946, Gwen Watkins. *Educ:* Ystalyfera Int. County Sch.; University Coll. of N Wales, Bangor (BA Hons: Latin 1933, Welsh 1934; MA); Nat. Univ. of Ireland, Dublin; TCD; United Theol Coll., Aberystwyth (BD 1944); Theol Coll., Bala. Research Lectr, UC of N Wales, Bangor, 1937–39; Fellow, Univ. of Wales, 1939–41; Lectr, 1945–51, Sen. Lectr, 1951–53, Prof. of Welsh, 1953–65, UC of N Wales. Leverhulme Fellow, 1963–64; Vis. Prof. Celtic, UCLA, 1968; Summer Sch., Harvard, 1968; Lectures: O'Donnell, in Celtic Studies, Oxford Univ., 1979–80; Dr Daniel Williams, Aberystwyth, 1983; Sir John Morris Jones, Oxford, 1983; R. T. Jenkins, Bangor, 1983. Chm., Welsh Acad., 1965–75; Cons. Editor, Univ. of Wales Welsh Dict. Fasc. xxiii–; Chm., Editorial Cttee, Welsh Acad. Dict., 1976–; Editor: Y Traethodydd, 1965–; Ysgrifau Beirniadol, i-xiii; Studia Celtica, i-xix; Llên y Llenor, 1983–. Mem. Council for Name Studies in Gt Britain and Ireland, 1965–. FSA 1975; Hon. DLitt: Celt., Univ. of Ireland, 1967; Univ. of Wales, 1983. Derek Allen Prize, British Acad., 1985. *Publications:* trans., Ystoriau ac Ysgrifau Pádraic Ó Conaire, 1947; trans., Yr Ebol Glas, 1954; Traddodiad Llenyddol Iwerddon, 1958; trans., Aderyn y Gwirionedd, 1961; Edward Jones, Maes-y-Plwm, 1963; ed, Llên a Llafar Môn, 1963; trans., I. Williams, Canu Taliesin (Poems of Taliesin), 1968; The Court Poet in Medieval Ireland, 1972; Y Storïwr Gwyddeleg a'i Chwedlau, 1972; Beirdd y Tywysogion—Arolwg 1970, in Llên Cymru, and separately 1972; ed, Literature in Celtic Countries, 1971; trans. Jakez Riou, An Ti Satanazet (Diawl yn y Tŷ), 1972; Canu Crefyddol y Gogynfeirdd (Darlith Goffa Henry Lewis), 1976; The Poets of the Welsh Princes, 1978; Cerddi'r Gogynfeirdd i Wragedd a Merched, 1979; (with Máirín Ní Mhuiríosa) Traidisiún Liteartha Na nGael, 1979; Geiriadurwyr y Gymraeg yng nghyfnod y Dadeni, 1983; contribs to Encyclopaedia Britannica, Bull. Bd of Celt. Studies, Celtica, Études Celt., Llên Cymru, etc. *Recreation:* walking. *Address:* University College of Wales, Aberystwyth SY23 2AX. *T:* Aberystwyth 3177; Iwerydd, 6 Pant-y-Rhos, Aberystwyth, Dyfed SY23 3QE. *T:* Aberystwyth 612959.

WILLIAMS, John Elwyn; His Honour Judge Williams; a Circuit Judge, since 1974; *b* 16 June 1921; *s* of Benjamin and Maria Williams; *m* 1st, Gwladys Margaret Vivian; two *s*; 2nd, Nancy Hilda. *Educ:* Cyfarthfa Castle Grammar Sch.; Aberystwyth University Coll.; University College London (LLB). Called to the Bar, Gray's Inn, 1950. *Recreations:* music, climbing. *Address:* Church Cottage, Belchamp Walter, Sudbury, Suffolk CO10 7AT.

WILLIAMS, John Griffith; QC 1985; a Recorder of the Crown Court, since 1984; *b* 20 Dec. 1944; *s* of Griffith John Williams, TD and Alison Williams; *m* 1971, Mair Tasker Watkins, *d* of Rt Hon. Sir Tasker Watkins, *qv*; two *d*. *Educ:* King's School, Bruton; The Queen's College, Oxford (MA). Served 4th Bn, RWF (TA), 1965–68; Welsh Volunteers (TAVR), 1968–71 (Lieut). Called to the Bar, Gray's Inn, 1968. *Recreation:* golf. *Address:*

144 Pencisely Road, Llandaff, Cardiff CF5 1DR. *T:* Cardiff 562981. *Clubs:* Cardiff and County, Cardiff Golf, Royal Porthcawl Golf.

WILLIAMS, Rev. John Herbert; Chaplain to the Royal Victorian Order and Chaplain of the Queen's Chapel of the Savoy, since 1983; *b* 15 Aug. 1919; *s* of Thomas and Mary Williams; *m* 1948, Joan Elizabeth (*née* Morgan); one *s Educ:* St David's Coll., Lampeter (BA Hons); Salisbury Theological Coll. Deacon 1943; priest 1944; Curate: Blaenavon (Gwent), 1943–46; Llanishen, Cardiff, 1946–48; Priest in Charge, Rogerstone (Gwent), 1948–51; Asst Chaplain, HM Prison, Manchester, 1951; Chaplain, HM Prison: Holloway, 1952; Birmingham, 1957; Wormwood Scrubs, 1964; South East Regional Chaplain, 1971; Deputy Chaplain General, Home Office Prison Dept, 1974–83; Priest-in-Ordinary to the Queen, 1980–83. *Recreations:* Rugby, classical music/opera, Francophile. *Address:* The Queen's Chapel of the Savoy, Strand, WC2; 18 Coombe Lane West, Kingston-upon-Thames. *T:* 01–942 1196. *Clubs:* Zion College, City Livery.

WILLIAMS, (John) Kyffin, OBE 1982; RA 1974 (ARA 1970); *b* 9 May 1918; *s* of Henry Inglis Wynne Williams and Essyllt Mary Williams (*née* Williams). *Educ:* Shrewsbury Sch.; Slade Sch. of Art. Sen. Art Master, Highgate Sch., 1944–73. One-man shows: Leicester Galleries, 1951, 1953, 1956, 1960, 1966, 1970; Colnaghi Galleries, 1948, 1949, 1965, 1970; Thackeray Gall., 1975, 1977, 1979, 1981, 1983, 1985. Pres., Royal Cambrian Acad., 1969–76. Winston Churchill Fellow, 1968. DL Gwynedd 1985. Hon. MA Wales, 1973. *Publication:* Across the Straits (autobiog.), 1973. *Recreations:* the countryside, sport. *Address:* Pwllfanogl, Llanfairpwll, Gwynedd LL61 6PD. *T:* Llanfairpwll 714693.

WILLIAMS, John Leighton; QC 1986; a Recorder of the Crown Court, since 1985; *b* 15 Aug. 1941; *s* of Reginald John Williams and Beatrice Beynon; *m* 1969, Sally Elizabeth Williams; two *s. Educ:* Neath Boys' Grammar School; King's College London (LLB); Trinity Hall, Cambridge (MA). Called to the Bar, Gray's Inn, 1964. *Address:* Farrar's Building, Temple, EC4. *T:* 01–583 9241.

WILLIAMS, Sir (John) Leslie, Kt 1974; CBE 1970; Chairman, Civil Service Appeal Board, 1977–78 (Deputy Chairman, 1973–77); Secretary General, Civil Service National Whitley Council (Staff Side), 1966–73; *b* 1 Aug. 1913; *s* of Thomas Oliver Williams and Mary Ellen Williams; *m* 1937, Florrie Read Jones; one *s. Educ:* Grove Park Grammar Sch., Wrexham, N. Wales. Civil Servant, 1931–46. Society of Civil Servants: Asst Secretary, 1947–49; Dep. General Secretary, 1949–56; General Secretary, 1956–66. Royal Institute of Public Administration: Executive Council Member, 1955–74; Chairman, 1968; Vice-Pres., 1974–84. Member Board of Governors: Nat. Hospitals for Nervous Diseases, 1962–82 (Chm., 1974–82); Hospital for Sick Children, 1976–81; Member: NW Metropolitan Regional Hospital Board, 1963–65; (part-time) UKAEA, 1970–80; Adv. Council, Civil Service Coll., 1970–76; (part-time) Pay Bd, 1974; Royal Commn on Standards of Conduct in Public Life, 1974–76; Armed Forces Pay Review Body, 1975–80; (part-time) Independent Chm., Conciliation Cttees NJC for Civil Air Transport, 1974–77; Standing Commn on Pay Comparability, 1979–80; London Adv. Gp on NHS, 1980–81. *Recreations:* cricket, gardening, music. *Address:* 26 Russell Green Close, Purley, Surrey. *T:* 01–660 9666.

WILLIAMS, John Melville; QC 1977; a Recorder, since 1986; *b* 20 June 1931; *o s* of late Baron Francis-Williams and late Lady (Jessie Melville) Francis-Williams; *m* 1955, Jean Margaret, *d* of Harold and Hilda Lucas, Huddersfield; three *s* one *d. Educ:* St Christopher Sch., Letchworth; St John's Coll., Cambridge (BA). Called to the Bar, Inner Temple, 1955, Bencher, 1985. Counsel to NUJ; a legal assessor to GMC; Mem., Indep. Review Body Under New Colliery Review Procedure, 1985–. *Recreations:* mountain scrambling and walking, indifferent golf. *Address:* Deers Hill, Sutton Abinger, near Dorking, Surrey. *T:* Dorking 730331; Cnoclochan, Scourie, by Lairg, Sutherland; 15 Old Square, Lincoln's Inn, WC2A 3UH. *T:* 01–831 0801.

WILLIAMS, John M(eredith); Chairman, Welsh Development Agency, since 1982; *b* 20 Oct. 1926; *s* of Gwynne Evan Owen Williams and Cicely Mary Innes; *m* 1953, Jean Constance (*née* Emerson); two *d. Educ:* Sherborne Sch., Dorset; Trinity Hall, Cambridge. Dir, BOC Gp, 1969–78; Chm., Newman Industries Ltd, 1980–82; Director: Stone-Platt Industries Ltd, 1981–82; Harland and Wolff Ltd, 1982–. Mem., Milk Marketing Bd, 1984–. *Address:* 95 Hurlingham Court, Ranelagh Gardens, SW6 3UR. *T:* 01–731 0686; Victuals Grove, St Briavels, Lydney, Glos. *T:* Dean 530494. *Clubs:* Hurlingham, Himalayan.

WILLIAMS, Rt. Rev. Monsignor John Noctor; Prelate of Honour, 1985; Principal Roman Catholic Chaplain (Army), since 1985; Vicar General, 1986; *b* 9 Aug. 1931; *s* of Thomas Williams and Anne Williams (*née* Noctor). *Educ:* St Anselm's Grammar School, Birkenhead; Ushaw College, Durham. Curate: St Laurence's, Birkenhead, 1956; St Joseph's, Sale, 1958; Our Lady's, Birkenhead, 1959–66. Army, Chaplains' Dept, 1966; 7 Armd Bde, 1966; Singapore, 1969; 6 Armd Bde, 1971; UN, Cyprus, 1972; Senior Chaplain: Hong Kong, 1976; 1 Div., 1978; N Ireland, 1980; HQ BAOR, 1982; SE District, 1984. *Recreations:* bridge, golf, motoring. *Address:* MoD Chaplains (Army), Bagshot Park, Bagshot, Surrey GU19 5PL. *T:* Bagshot 71717 (ext. 25). *Clubs:* Berkshire Golf, Worplesdon Golf.

WILLIAMS, John Peter Rhys, MBE 1977; FRCSEd; Consultant in Trauma and Orthopaedic Surgery, Princess of Wales Hospital, Bridgend, since 1986; *b* 2 March 1949; *s* of Peter Williams, MB, BCh and Margaret Williams, MB, BCh; *m* 1973, Priscilla Parkin, MB, BS, DObst, RCOG; three *d. Educ:* Bridgend Grammar School; Millfield; St Mary's Hosp. Med. School. MB, BS London 1973; LRCP, MRCS, 1973; Primary FRCS 1976; FRCSEd 1980. University Hosp., Cardiff, Battle Hosp., Reading, St Mary's Hosp., London, 1973–78; Surgical Registrar, 1978–80, Orthopaedic Registrar, 1980–82, Cardiff Gp of Hosps; Sen. Orthopaedic Registrar, St Mary's Hosp., London, 1982–86. Played Rugby for Bridgend, 1967–68, 1976–79 (Captain, 1978–79), 1980–81, for London Welsh, 1968–76; 1st cap for Wales, 1969 (Captain, 1978); British Lions tours, 1971, 1974; a record 55 caps for Wales, to 1981; won Wimbledon Lawn Tennis Junior Championship, 1966. *Publication:* JPR (autobiog.), 1979. *Recreations:* sport and music. *Address:* Llansannor Lodge, Llansannor, near Cowbridge, South Glamorgan. *Clubs:* Wig and Pen; Lord's Taverners'.

WILLIAMS, Captain Sir John (Protheroe), Kt 1967; CMG 1960; OBE 1950; *b* 1896; *m* 1st, 1921, Gladys Grieves (*d* 1962); one *s* three *d*; 2nd, 1964, Mrs Althea Florence Carr (widow). *Educ:* Queen Elizabeth's Grammar Sch., Carmarthen. Master Mariner; Chairman: Australian National Line, 1956–71; United Salvage Pty Ltd; City Ice & Cold Storage Pty Ltd; Penmore Pty Ltd; Snr Partner J. P. Williams & Associates, Penmore graziers. Officer in Charge on behalf of Bank of England, Salvage Operations of RMS Niagara, sunk in 438 ft of water, 1941, when £2,396,000 worth of gold bullion weighing 8½ tons was recovered. *Publication:* So Ends This Day (autobiog.), 1982. *Address:* 77 St Georges Road, Toorak, Victoria 3142, Australia. *T:* 2412440; Penmore, Bolinda, Victoria. *Clubs:* Australian (Melbourne and Sydney); Melbourne (Melbourne).

WILLIAMS, Sir John (Robert), KCMG 1982 (CMG 1973); HM Diplomatic Service, retired; Chairman, Board of Governors, Commonwealth Institute, since 1984; *b* 15 Sept. 1922; *s* of late Sydney James Williams, Salisbury; *m* 1958, Helga Elizabeth, *d* of Frederick Konow Lund, Bergen; two *s* two *d. Educ:* Sheen County School; Fitzwilliam House, Cambridge (Hon. Fellow 1984). Served War of 1939–45, with 1st Bn King's African Rifles in East Africa and Burma Campaign (Captain). Joined Colonial Office as Asst Principal, 1949; First Secretary, UK High Commission, New Delhi, 1956; Commonwealth Relations Office, 1958; Deputy High Commissioner in North Malaya, 1959–63; Counsellor, New Delhi, 1963–66; Commonwealth Office, 1966; Private Sec. to Commonwealth Secretary, 1967; Diplomatic Service Inspectorate, 1968; High Comr, Suva, 1970–74; Minister, Lagos, 1974–79 and concurrently Ambassador (non-resident) to Benin, 1976–79; Asst. Under-Sec. of State, FCO, 1979; High Comr in Kenya, 1979–82; Perm. British Rep. to UN Environment Prog. and to UN Centre for Human Settlements, 1979–82. *Recreations:* music, golf, gardening. *Address:* 3 York Avenue, SW14. *Clubs:* United Oxford & Cambridge University, Royal Over-Seas League (Mem., Gen. Council, 1983–).

WILLIAMS, John Towner; composer of film scores; *b* 8 Feb. 1932. *Educ:* Juilliard Sch., NY. Conductor, Boston Pops Orchestra, 1980–84. Hon. DMus: Berklee Coll. of Music, Boston, 1980; St Anselm Coll., Manchester, NH, 1981; Boston Conservatory of Music, 1982; Hon. DHL S Carolina, 1981; Hon. Dr of Fine Arts Northeastern Univ. (Boston), 1981; Hon. DMus, William Woods Coll., USA, 1982. Awards include Oscars for: Fiddler on the Roof (filmscore arrangement), 1971; Jaws, 1976; Star Wars, 1978; E.T., 1983; 14 Grammies, 2 Emmys and many other awards; 16 Academy Award nominations. *Composer of film scores:* The Secret Ways, 1961; Diamond Head, 1962; None but the Brave, 1965; How to Steal a Million, 1966; Valley of the Dolls, 1967; The Cowboys, 1972; The Poseidon Adventure, 1972; Tom Sawyer, 1973; Earthquake, 1974; The Towering Inferno, 1974; Jaws, 1975; Jaws 2, 1976; The Eiger Sanction, 1975; Family Plot, 1976; Midway, 1976; The Missouri Breaks, 1976; Raggedy Ann and Andy, 1977; Black Sunday, 1977; Star Wars, 1977; Close Encounters of the 3rd Kind, 1977; The Fury, 1978; Superman, 1978; Dracula, 1979; The Empire Strikes Back, 1980; Raiders of the Lost Ark, 1981; E. T. (The Extra Terrestial), 1982; Return of the Jedi, 1983; Indiana Jones and the Temple of Doom, 1984; many TV films. *Address:* 20th Century Fox, Music Department, PO Box 900, Beverly Hills, Calif 90213, USA.

WILLIAMS, John Trevor; HM Diplomatic Service, retired; *b* 12 Nov. 1921; *yr s* of Dr Griffith Williams and Monica Johnson; *m* 1953, Ena Ferguson Boyd (*d* 1974); two *d. Educ:* St Paul's Sch.; Jesus Coll., Oxford. Joined Royal Armoured Corps, 1941; served with 14th/20th King's Hussars in Middle East and Italy, 1943–45. Home Civil Service, 1947–67; joined HM Diplomatic Service, 1967; Counsellor, High Commn, Wellington, NZ, 1967–69; Nato Defence Coll., Rome, 1970; Counsellor, Dublin, 1970–72; Head of Commodities Dept, FCO, 1972; seconded to: N Ireland Office, 1972–73; DoE, 1973–76. *Recreations:* riding, theatre, looking for good restaurants. *Address:* 3 Ranelagh Gardens, SW6 3PA. *T:* 01–736 1733. *Club:* Hurlingham.

WILLIAMS, Maj.-Gen. John William C.; *see* Channing Williams.

WILLIAMS, Kenneth; actor; *b* 22 Feb. 1926; *s* of Charles George Williams and Louisa Alexandra (*née* Morgan). *Educ:* Lyulph Stanley Sch.; Bolt Court, London. Formerly lithograph draughtsman. Made first appearance on stage, Victoria Theatre, Singapore, playing the detective in Seven Keys to Baldpate, 1946, then Ninian in The First Mrs Fraser, Newquay Rep. Th., Cornwall, 1948; first London appearance as Slightly in Peter Pan, Scala, 1952; Dauphin in Saint Joan, Arts, 1954, transf. with this to St Martin's, 1955; Elijah in Orson Welles prodn of Moby Dick, Duke of York's, 1955; Montgomery in Sandy Wilson's The Buccaneer, Lyric, Hammersmith, 1955, subseq. Apollo, 1956; Maxime in Hotel Paradiso, Wintergarden, 1956; Kite in Wit to Woo, Arts, 1957; Green in Share My Lettuce, Lyric, Hammersmith, 1957, transf. to Comedy, 1957, and to Garrick, 1958; Portia in Cinderella, Coliseum, 1958. Starred in revue, Pieces of Eight, Apollo, 1959, and in One Over the Eight, Duke of York's, 1961. Played Julian in The Private Ear and the Public Eye, Globe, 1962; Jack in Gentle Jack, Queen's, 1963; Truscott in Loot, Arts, Cambridge, 1965; Bernard in Platinum Cat, Wyndham's, 1965; Drinkwater in Captain Brassbound's Conversion, Cambridge Th., 1971; Henry in My Fat Friend, Globe, 1972; Barillon in Signed and Sealed, Comedy, 1976; The Undertaking, Greenwich, later Fortune, 1979. Directed: Loot, Lyric Studio, 1980; Entertaining Mr Sloane, Lyric, Hammersmith, 1981. *Films:* Trent's Last Case; Beggar's Opera; The Seekers; Carry On series. *Television* series include: Hancock's Half Hour; International Cabaret; Kenneth Williams' Show; Whizz Kids Guide. Has broadcast regularly in Round the Horne, Stop Messing About, Just a Minute, etc. *Publications:* Acid Drops, 1980; Back Drops, 1983; Just Williams, 1985; I Only Have to Close My Eyes, 1986. *Recreations:* calligraphy, reading, music, walking. *Address:* ICM, 388/396 Oxford Street, W1N 9HE.

WILLIAMS, Kingsley; *see* Williams, J. B. K.

WILLIAMS, Kyffin; *see* Williams, John K.

WILLIAMS, Sir Leonard, KBE 1981; CB 1975; Director-General for Energy, Commission of the European Communities, 1976–81; *b* 19 Sept. 1919; *m* Anne Taylor Witherley; three *d. Educ:* St Olave's Grammar Sch.; King's Coll., London. Inland Revenue, 1938. War Service (RA), 1940–47. Ministry of Defence, 1948; NATO, 1951–54; Min. of Supply (later Aviation), 1954; Min. of Technology (later DTI), 1964; IDC 1966; Dep. Sec., 1973; Dept of Energy, 1974–76. *Address:* Blue Vines, Bramshott Vale, Liphook, Hants.

WILLIAMS, Leonard Edmund Henry, CBE 1981; DFC 1944; Chairman, Nationwide Building Society, since 1982 (Director, since 1975); *b* 6 Dec. 1919; *s* of William Edmund Williams; *m* 1946, Marie Harries-Jones; four *s* one *d. Educ:* Acton County Grammar School. FCA, FCBSI, IPFA; FRSA; CBIM. RAF, 1939–46. Acton Borough Council, 1935–39, Chief Internal Auditor 1946–49; Asst Accountant, Gas Council, 1949–53; Nationwide Building Society: Finance Officer, 1954–61; Dep. Gen. Man., 1961–67; Chief Exec., 1967–81. Director: Y. J. Lovell (Hldgs) plc, 1982–; Peachey Property Corp. plc, 1982–; Governor, BUPA Ltd, 1982–; Mem., Housing Corp., 1976–82. Chairman: Metrop. Assoc. of Building Socs, 1972–73; Building Socs Assoc., 1979–81 (Dep. Chm., 1977–79); Pres., Chartered Building Socs Inst., 1969–70; Vice-Pres., Internat. Union of Building Socs and Savings Assocs. *Publication:* Building Society Accounts, 1966. *Recreations:* golf, reading. *Address:* The Romanys, Albury Road, Burwood Park, Walton-on-Thames, Surrey KT12 5DY. *T:* Walton-on-Thames 242758. *Clubs:* Royal Air Force, Arts, City Livery.

WILLIAMS, Sir Leslie; *see* Williams, Sir J. L.

WILLIAMS, Ven. Leslie Arthur, MA; Archdeacon of Bristol, 1967–79; *b* 14 May 1909; *s* of Arthur and Susan Williams; *m* 1937, Margaret Mary, *d* of Richard Crocker; one *s* one *d. Educ:* Knutsford; Downing Coll., Cambridge. Curate of Holy Trinity, Bristol, 1934–37; Licensed to officiate, St Andrew the Great, Cambridge, 1937–40; Curate in Charge, St Peter, Lowden, Chippenham, 1940–42; Chaplain, RAFVR, 1942–46; Curate,

Stoke Bishop, 1946–47; Vicar: Corsham, Wilts, 1947–53; Bishopston, Bristol, 1953–60; Stoke Bishop, Bristol, 1960–67. Rural Dean of Clifton, 1966–67; Hon. Canon of Bristol, 1958. *Recreation:* gardening. *Address:* St Monica Home, Westbury on Trym, Bristol BS9 3UN. *Clubs:* Hawks (Cambridge); Savage (Bristol).

WILLIAMS, Leslie Henry; Deputy Chairman, Imperial Chemical Industries Ltd, 1960–67; Chairman, ICI Fibres Ltd, 1965–67; *b* 26 Jan. 1903; *s* of late Edward Henry Williams; *m* 1930, Alice, *d* of late Henry Oliver Harrison; one *s*. *Educ:* Highbury County Sch.; London Univ. (BSc). Joined ICI Ltd, Paints Division, 1929; appointed Director, 1943; Managing Director, 1946; Chairman, 1949; Director of ICI Main Board, 1957, Dep. Chm., 1960; Director, British Nylon Spinners Ltd, 1957–64; Director Ilford Ltd, 1958–67. FRIC 1945; President, Royal Institute of Chemistry, 1967–70. Member, Monopolies Commission, 1967–73. Hon. FRIC 1978. Hon. DSc Salford, 1972. *Recreations:* gardening, music. *Address:* Penny Green, West End Lane, Stoke Poges, Bucks. *T:* Farnham Common 3423.

WILLIAMS, Martin John, CVO 1983; OBE 1979; HM Diplomatic Service; Counsellor and Head of Chancery, Rome, since 1986; *b* 3 Nov. 1941; *s* of John Henry Stroud Williams and Barbara (*née* Benington); *m* 1964, Susan Dent; two *s*. *Educ:* Manchester Grammar Sch.; Corpus Christi Coll., Oxford (BA). Joined Commonwealth Relations Office, 1963; Private Sec. to Permanent Under Secretary, 1964; Manila, 1966; Milan, 1970; Civil Service College, 1972; FCO, 1973; Tehran, 1977; FCO, 1980; New Delhi, 1982. *Recreations:* music, theatre, Scottish dancing. *Address:* c/o Foreign and Commonwealth Office, SW1; British Embassy, via XX Settembre 80A, Rome, Italy. *T:* Rome 4755441; Clapham Lodge, Bawtree Close, Banstead Road South, Sutton, Surrey. *T:* 01–643 9958.

WILLIAMS, Mary Bridget; Counsellor and Deputy Head of UK Delegation on Mutual Reduction of Forces and Armaments and Associated Measures, Vienna, since 1984; *b* 14 Aug. 1933; *d* of Thomas and Mary O'Neil; *m* 1961, Robert Cameron Williams. *Educ:* University Coll. of S Wales and Monmouthshire, Univ. of Wales (BA Hons Phil; Pres. of Union and NUS Debating Tournament). Valuation Clerk, Inland Revenue, 1950–52; NCB, 1952–61 (incl. period as NCB Schol.); Lectr in Politics and Govt, Dir of Studies, and sometime Mem. Senate and Council, Univ. of Bath, 1961–73; entered Min. of Defence, 1974; Head, Gen. Finance Div. 1, 1980–84. *Recreations:* Tournament bridge, looking and listening. *Address:* c/o British Embassy, Reisnerstrasse 40, A1030 Wien, Austria. *T:* Vienna 73–15–75.

WILLIAMS, Sir Max; *see* Williams, Sir W. M. H.

WILLIAMS, Mrs Michael; *see* Dench, J. O.

WILLIAMS, Michael Leonard; actor; Associate Artist, Royal Shakespeare Company, since 1966; *b* 9 July 1935; *s* of Michael Leonard Williams and Elizabeth (*née* Mulligan); *m* 1971, Judith Olivia Dench, *qv*; one *d*. *Educ:* St Edward's Coll., Liverpool; RADA (Coronation Scholar). Début, Nottingham Playhouse, 1959; London début, Celebration, Duchess Theatre, 1961; joined RSC, 1963; rôles include: Puck in A Midsummer Night Dream, Filch in The Beggar's Opera, Eichmann in The Representative, 1963; Oswald in King Lear (also NY), Pinch in The Comedy of Errors, Kokol in Marat/Sade, Lodowick in The Jew of Malta, 1964; Dromio of Syracuse in The Comedy of Errors, Guildenstern in Hamlet, Herald in Marat/Sade (also NY), 1965; Arthur in Tango, 1966; Petruchio in The Taming of the Shrew, Orlando in As You Like It, 1967; Fool in King Lear, Troilus in Troilus and Cressida, 1968; Charles Courtly in London Assurance, 1970; Bassanio in The Merchant of Venice, Ferdinand in The Duchess of Malfi, title rôle in Henry V, 1971; Mole in Toad of Toad Hall, 1972; Stellio in Content to Whisper, 1973; Private Meek in Too True to be Good, 1975; title rôle in Schweyk in the Second World War, Dromio in The Comedy of Errors (musical version), Autolycus in The Winter's Tale, Fool in King Lear, 1976; title rôle in national tour, Quartermaine's Terms, 1982; Bob in Pack of Lies, 1983; George in Two Into One, 1984; *films* include: The Marat/Sade, 1966; Eagle in a Cage, 1969; Dead Cert, 1974; In Search of Alexander the Great, 1980; Enigma, 1981; Educating Rita, 1982; *television* includes: Elizabeth R, 1971; A Raging Calm, The Hanged Man, 1974; My Son, My Son, 1978; Love in a Cold Climate, 1980; Quest of Eagles, 1980; A Fine Romance, 1980–81, 1982. Chm., Catholic Stage Guild, 1977–. *Recreations:* family, tennis, pottering, gardening. *Address:* c/o Michael Whitehall, 125 Gloucester Road, SW7. *T:* 01–244 8466. *Club:* Garrick.

WILLIAMS, Prof. Michael Maurice Rudolph; Professor of Nuclear Engineering, University of Michigan, since 1987; Professor of Nuclear Engineering, Queen Mary College, University of London, 1970–86, Head of Department, 1980–86; *b* 1 Dec. 1935; *s* of late M. F. Williams and G. M. A. Denton; *m* 1958, Ann Doreen Betty; one *s* one *d*. *Educ:* Ewell Castle Sch.; Croydon Polytechnic; King's Coll., London; Queen Mary Coll., London. BSc, PhD, DSc; CEng; Fellow, Instn Nuclear Engrs (Vice-Pres., 1971); FInstP. Engr with Central Electricity Generating Board, 1962; Research Associate at Brookhaven Nat. Lab., USA, 1962–63; Lectr, Dept of Physics, Univ. of Birmingham, 1963–65; Reader in Nuclear Engrg, Queen Mary Coll., London Univ., 1965–70. Mem., Adv. Cttee on Safety of Nuclear Installations, 1983–86. Chm. of Governors, Ewell Castle Sch., 1976–79. Exec. Editor: Annals of Nuclear Energy; Progress in Nuclear Energy. Fellow American Nuclear Soc. *Publications:* The Slowing Down and Thermalization of Neutrons, 1966; Mathematical Methods in Particle Transport Theory, 1971; Random Processes in Nuclear Reactors, 1974; contribs to Proc. Camb. Phil. Soc., Nucl. Science and Engrg, Jl Nuclear Energy, Jl Physics. *Address:* Department of Nuclear Engineering, University of Michigan, Cooley Building, N Campus, Ann Arbor, Mich 48109, USA.

WILLIAMS, Sir Michael O.; *see* Williams, Sir Osmond.

WILLIAMS, Nicholas James Donald; Managing Director and Chief Executive, Don Engineering, 1977–84; President, Vinton Oil and Gas Co., 1980–85; *b* 21 Oct. 1925; *s* of late Nicholas Thomas Williams and Daisy Eustace (*née* Hollow); *m* 1st, 1947, Dawn Vyvyan (*née* Hill); one *s* one *d*; 2nd, 1955, Sheila Mary (*née* Dalgety); two *s* one *d*. *Educ:* St Erbyn's Sch., Penzance; Rugby Sch. (Scholar). Admitted Solicitor 1949. Served Royal Marines, 1943–47 (Captain). Partner, Nicholas Williams & Co., Solicitors, London, 1950; Senior Partner, Surridge & Beecheno, Solicitors, Karachi, 1955; Burmah Oil Co. Ltd: Legal Adviser, 1961; Co-ordinator for Eastern ops, 1963; Dir, 1965; Asst Man. Dir, 1967; Man. Dir and Chief Exec., 1969–75. Director: Flarebay Ltd, 1978–85; EBC Gp PLC, 1986–; Chm., Vintoil SA, 1984–85. *Recreation:* sailing. *Address:* Purlieus Farmhouse, Ewen, Cirencester, Glos. *Clubs:* Oriental, MCC, Royal Cornwall Yacht.

WILLIAMS, Nigel Christopher Ransome, CMG 1985; HM Diplomatic Service; Minister, Bonn, since 1985; *b* 29 April 1937; *s* of Cecil Gwynne Ransome Williams and Corinne Belden (*née* Rudd). *Educ:* Merchant Taylors' Sch.; St John's Coll., Oxford. Joined Foreign Service and posted to Tokyo, 1961; FO, 1966; Private Secretary: to Minister of State, 1968; to Chancellor of Duchy of Lancaster, 1969; UK Mission to UN, New York, 1970; FCO, 1973; Counsellor (Economic), Tokyo, 1976; Cabinet Office, 1980; Hd of UN Dept, FCO, 1980–84. *Address:* c/o Foreign and Commonwealth Office, SW1.

WILLIAMS, Noel Ignace B.; *see* Bond-Williams.

WILLIAMS, Norman; *see* Williams, R. N.

WILLIAMS, Sir Osmond, 2nd Bt, *cr* 1909; MC 1944; JP; *b* 22 April 1914; *s* of late Captain Osmond T. D. Williams, DSO, 2nd *s* of 1st Bt, and Lady Gladys Margaret Finch Hatton, *o d* of 13th Earl of Winchilsea; *S* grandfather, 1927; *m* 1947, Benita Mary, *yr d* of late G. Henry Booker, and Mrs Michael Burn; two *d*. *Educ:* Eton; Freiburg Univ. Royal Scots Greys, 1935–37, and 1939–45; served Palestine, Africa, Italy and NW Europe. Chm., Quarry Tours Ltd, 1973–77. Vice-Chm., Amnesty Internat. (British Sect.), 1971–74. Trustee: Internat. Prisoners of Conscience Fund; Festiniog Rly Trust; Mem., Merioneth Park Planning Cttee, 1971–74. Governor, Rainer Foundn Outdoor Pursuits Centre, 1964–76. JP 1960 (Chairman of the Bench, Ardudwy-uwch-Artro, Gwynedd, 1974–84). Chevalier, Order of Leopold II with Palm; Croix de Guerre with Palm (Belgium), 1940. *Recreations:* music, travelling. *Heir:* none. *Address:* Borthwen, Penrhyndeudraeth, Gwynedd. *Club:* Travellers'.

WILLIAMS, Owen Lenn; retired; Regional Financial and Development Adviser, St Vincent, West Indies, 1976–78; *b* 4 March 1914; *s* of Richard Owen Williams and Frances Daisy Williams (*née* Lenn); *m* 1959, Gisela Frucht. *Educ:* St Albans Sch.; London University. Asst Principal, Export Credit Guarantee Dept, 1938; Asst Principal, Treasury, 1939; UK High Commn, Ottawa, 1941; Principal, Treasury, 1945; Asst Treasury Representative, UK High Commn, New Delhi, 1953; Treasury Rep., UK High Commn, Karachi, 1955; Economic and Financial Adviser, Leeward Islands, 1957; Perm. Sec., Min. of Finance, Eastern Nigeria, 1959; Asst Sec., Treasury, 1962; Counsellor, UK Delegn to OECD, 1968–73; Gen. Fiscal Adviser to Minister of Finance, Sierra Leone, 1974–75. *Recreations:* music, travel. *Address:* c/o National Westminster Bank, Caxton House, SW1. *Club:* Reform.

WILLIAMS, Paul; Director, Backer Electric Co. Ltd; Consultant, P-E Consulting Services; *b* 14 Nov. 1922; *s* of late Samuel O. Williams and Esmée I. Williams (*née* Cail); *m* 1947, Barbara Joan Hardy (marr. diss. 1964); two *d*; *m* 1964, Gillian Foote, *e d* of A. G. Howland Jackson, Elstead, Surrey, and of Mrs E. J. Foote and step *d* of late E. J. Foote, Cascais, Portugal; one *d*. *Educ:* Marlborough; Trinity Hall, Cambridge (MA). MP (C) Sunderland South, (C 1953–57, Ind. C 1957–58, C 1958–64). Chairman, Monday Club, 1964–69. FInstD; FBIM. *Address:* 65 Perrymead Street, SW6. *T:* 01–731 0045. *Clubs:* Boodle's, Institute of Directors.

WILLIAMS, Paul H.; *see* Hodder-Williams.

WILLIAMS, Penry Herbert; Fellow and Tutor in Modern History, New College, Oxford, since 1964; *b* 25 Feb. 1925; *s* of late Douglas Williams and Dorothy Williams (*née* Murray); *m* 1952, June Carey Hobson, *d* of late George and Kathleene Hobson; one *s* one *d*. *Educ:* Marlborough Coll.; New Coll., Oxford, 1947–50; St Antony's Coll., Oxford, 1950–51. MA, DPhil Oxon. Served Royal Artillery, 1943–45, Royal Indian Artillery, 1945–47. Asst Lecturer in History, 1951–54, Lectr, 1954–63, Sen. Lectr, 1963–64, Univ. of Manchester. Fellow of Winchester Coll., 1978. Jt Editor, English Historical Review, 1982–. *Publications:* The Council in the Marches of Wales under Elizabeth I, 1958; Life in Tudor England, 1963; The Tudor Regime, 1979, paperback 1981; (ed, with John Buxton) New College, Oxford 1379–1979, 1979; contribs to learned jls. *Address:* New College, Oxford OX1 3BN; 53 Park Town, Oxford OX2 6SL. *T:* Oxford 57613.

WILLIAMS, Peter F.; *see* Firmston-Williams.

WILLIAMS, Peter H.; *see* Havard-Williams.

WILLIAMS, Peter Keegan; HM Diplomatic Service; Head of United Nations Department, Foreign and Commonwealth Office, since 1986; *b* 3 April 1938; *s* of William Edward Williams and Lilian (*née* Spright); *m* 1969, Rosamund Mary de Worms; two *d*. *Educ:* Calday Grange Grammar Sch.; Collège de Marcq-en-Baroeul (Nord); Univ. de Lille; Pembroke Coll., Oxford (MA). Joined Diplomatic Service, 1962; language student, MECAS, Lebanon, 1962; Second Sec., Beirut, 1963, Jedda, 1964; Commonwealth Office, 1967; First Sec., FCO, 1969; Director, Policy and Reference Div., British Information Services, New York, 1970; First Sec., FCO, 1973; First Sec., Head of Chancery and Consul, Rabat, 1976 (Chargé d'Affaires, 1978 and 1979); Counsellor, GATT, UK Mission, Geneva, 1979–83 (Chm. Panel, USA/Canada, 1980–81; Chm., Cttee on Finance, 1981–83); Ambassador, People's Democratic Republic of Yemen, 1983–85. *Recreations:* wine, walking. *Address:* c/o Foreign and Commonwealth Office, SW1. *Club:* United Oxford & Cambridge University.

WILLIAMS, Peter Lancelot, OBE 1971; editor, writer on dance, designer; chairman of committees on dance; *b* 12 June 1914; *s* of Col G. T. Williams and Awdrie Elkington. *Educ:* Harrow Sch.; Central Sch. of Art and Design, London. Dress designer with own business, 1934–39; Transport Officer, Civil Defence (Falmouth Div.), 1939–45; Head Designer, Jantzen Ltd, 1945–47; stage designer, 1947–. Arts Council of Great Britain, 1965–80: served on most panels with connections with ballet and music; resp. for ballet sect. on Opera and Ballet Enquiry, 1966–69 (led to develt of dance theatre throughout GB); Chm., Dance Advisory Cttee (formerly Dance Theatre Cttee), 1973–80. Chairman: Brit. Council's Drama Adv. Cttee, 1976–81; (also Founder), Dancers Pensions and Resettlement Fund, 1975–; Creative Dance Artists Ltd, 1979–; Royal Ballet Benevolent Fund 1984–; Gov., Royal Ballet, 1986–; Mem., most cttees concerned with dance: Royal Acad. of Dancing, Cecchetti Soc. Asst Editor, Ballet, 1949–50; Founder Editor/Art Dir, Dance and Dancers, 1950–80; Ballet Critic, Daily Mail, 1950–53; Dance Critic, The Observer, 1982–83 (Deputy, 1970–). *Publications:* Masterpieces of Ballet Design, 1981; contrib. articles, mainly on dance and theatre, to newspapers and magazines in GB and internationally. *Address:* Tredrea, Perranarworthal, Truro, Cornwall; 1 St Albans Studios, South End Row, W8.

WILLIAMS, Peter Michael, PhD; Chief Executive, Oxford Instruments Group plc, since 1985 (Managing Director, 1983–85); *b* 22 March 1945; *s* of Cyril Lewis and Gladys Williams; *m* 1970, Jennifer Margaret Cox; one *s*. *Educ:* Hymers College, Hull; Trinity College, Cambridge. MA, PhD. Mullard Research Fellow, Selwyn College, Cambridge, 1969–70; Lectr, Dept of Chemical Engineering and Chemical Technology, Imperial College, 1970–75; VG Instruments Group, 1975–82 (Dep. Man. Dir, 1979–82); Oxford Instruments Group plc, 1982–. Guardian Young Business Man of the Year, 1986. *Publications:* numerous contribs to jls relating to solid state physics. *Recreations:* ski-ing, gardening. *Address:* Yew Cottage, Old Boars Hill, Oxford OX1 5JJ. *T:* Oxford 739470.

WILLIAMS, Dr Peter Orchard, FRCP; Director: The Wellcome Trust, since 1965; Wellcome Institute for the History of Medicine, 1981–83; *b* 23 Sept. 1925; *s* of Robert Orchard Williams, CBE, and Agnes Annie Birkinshaw; *m* 1949, Billie Innes Brown; two *d*. *Educ:* Caterham Sch.; Queen's Royal College, Trinidad; St John's Coll., Cambridge (MA); St Mary's Hospital Medical School. MB, BChir 1950; MRCP 1952; FRCP 1970. House Physician, St Mary's Hospital, 1950–51; Registrar, Royal Free Hospital, 1951–52; Medical Specialist, RAMC, BMH Iserlohn, 1954; Medical Officer, Headquarters, MRC,

1955–60; Wellcome Trust: Asst and Dep. Scientific Secretary, 1960–64; Scientific Secretary, 1964–65. Vice-Pres., Royal Soc. of Tropical Med. and Hygiene, 1975–77; Member: Nat. Council of Soc. Services Cttee of Enquiry into Charity Law and Practice, 1974–76; BBC, IBA Central Appeals Adv. Cttee, 1978–83; DHSS Jt Planning Adv. Cttee, 1986–; Chairman: Foundations Forum, 1977–79; Assoc. of Med. Res. Charities, 1974–76, 1979–83; Hague Club (European Foundns), 1981–83. Hon. Fellow, LSHTM, 1986. Mary Kingsley Medal for Services to Tropical Medicine, Liverpool Sch. of Trop. Med., 1983. *Publications:* Careers in Medicine, 1952; papers in scientific journals. *Recreations:* gardening, travel, golf. *Address:* Symonds House, Symonds Street, Winchester SO23 9JS.

WILLIAMS, Sir Peter W.; *see* Watkin Williams.

WILLIAMS, Sir Philip; *see* Williams, Sir R. P. N.

WILLIAMS, Sir Ralph D. D.; *see under* Dudley-Williams, Sir Rolf (Dudley).

WILLIAMS, Prof. Raymond Henry; Fellow of Jesus College, Cambridge, since 1961; *b* 31 Aug. 1921; *s* of Henry Joseph Williams and Gwendolene Williams (*née* Bird); *m* 1942, Joyce Mary Dalling; two *s* one *d.* *Educ:* Abergavenny Grammar Sch.; Trinity Coll., Cambridge; MA, LittD. War service (ending as Captain), 21st Anti-Tank Regt, Guards Armoured Div., 1941–45; Staff Tutor in Literature, Oxford University Extra-Mural Delegacy, 1946–61; Univ. Reader in Drama, 1967–74, Professor of Drama, 1974–83, University of Cambridge. Mem., Arts Council, 1976–78. Vis. Prof. of Political Science, Stanford Univ., USA, 1973. DUniv Open, 1975; Hon. DLitt: Wales, 1980; Kent, 1984. General Editor, New Thinkers' Library, 1962–70. Editor: Politics and Letters, 1946–47; May Day Manifesto, 1968. *Publications:* Reading and Criticism, 1950; Drama from Ibsen to Eliot, 1952; Drama in Performance, 1954 (rev. edn 1968); Culture and Society, 1958; Border Country, 1960; The Long Revolution, 1961; Communications, 1962 (rev. edn 1976); Second Generation, 1964; Modern Tragedy, 1966; Public Inquiry, 1967; Drama from Ibsen to Brecht, 1968; The English Novel from Dickens to Lawrence, 1970; A Letter from the Country, 1971; Orwell, 1971; The Country and the City, 1973; Television: technology and cultural form, 1974; (ed) George Orwell, 1975; Keywords, 1976; Marxism and Literature, 1977; The Volunteers, 1978, 2nd edn 1985; (ed with Marie Axton) English Drama: forms and development, 1978; The Fight for Manod, 1979; Politics and Letters: interviews with New Left Review, 1979; Problems in Materialism and Culture, 1980; (ed) Contact: the history of human communications, 1981; Culture, 1981; Towards 2000, 1983; Writing in Society, 1983; Loyalties, 1985. *Recreation:* gardening. *Address:* Jesus College, Cambridge.

WILLIAMS, Raymond Lloyd, DPhil, DSc; CChem, FRSC; Director, Metropolitan Police Laboratory, since 1968; Visiting Professor in Chemistry, University of East Anglia, since 1968; *b* Bournemouth, 27 Feb. 1927; *s* of late Walter Raymond Williams and Vera Mary Williams; *m* 1956, Sylvia Mary Lawson Whitaker; one *s* one *d.* *Educ:* Bournemouth Sch.; St John's Coll., Oxford (schol.). Gibbs Univ. Schol. 1948, BA 1st Cl. Hons Nat Sci-Chem, MA, DPhil, DSc Oxon. Research Fellow, Pressed Steel Co., 1951–53; Commonwealth Fund Fellow, Univ. of California, Berkeley, 1953–54; progressively, Sen. Res. Fellow, Sen. Scientific Officer, Principal Sci. Officer, Explosives R&D Estab., 1955–60; PSO, Admiralty Materials Lab., 1960–62; Explosives R&D Establishment: SPSO, 1962; Supt, Analytical Services Gp, 1962–65; Supt, Non-metallic Materials Gp, 1965–68. External Examiner: Univ. of Strathclyde, 1983–85; KCL, 1986–. Theophilus Redwood Lectr, RSC, 1984. Jt Editor: Forensic Science International, 1978–; Forensic Science Progress, 1984–. Pres., Forensic Science Soc., 1983–85; Hon. Mem., Assoc. of Police Surgeons of GB, 1980. *Publications:* papers in scientific jls on spectroscopy, analytical chemistry, and forensic science. *Recreations:* lawn tennis (played for Civil Service and Oxfordshire: representative colours), squash rackets, carpentry. *Address:* 9 Meon Road, Bournemouth, Dorset BH7 6PN. *T:* Bournemouth 423446.

WILLIAMS, (Reginald) Norman, CB 1982; Assistant Registrar of Friendly Societies, since 1984; *b* 23 Oct. 1917; *s* of Reginald Gardnar Williams and Janet Mary Williams; *m* 1956, Hilary Frances West; two *s.* *Educ:* Neath Grammar Sch.; Swansea Univ. Served War: Captain RA and later Staff Captain HQ 30 Corps, 1940–46. Solicitor in private practice, 1947–48. Dept of Health and Social Security (formerly Min. of Nat. Insurance): Legal Asst, 1948; Sen. Legal Asst, 1959; Asst Solicitor, 1966; Principal Asst Solicitor, 1974; Under Sec., 1977–82. Member of Law Society. *Recreations:* golf, photography, reading. *Address:* Brecon, 23 Castle Hill Avenue, Berkhamsted, Herts HP4 1HJ. *T:* Berkhamsted 5291.

WILLIAMS, (Richard) Derrick, MA (Cantab); Principal, Gloucestershire College of Arts and Technology, since 1981; *b* 30 March 1926; *s* of Richard Leslie Williams and Lizzie Paddington; *m* 1949, Beryl Newbury Stonebanks; four *s.* *Educ:* St John's Coll., Cambridge. Asst Master, Lawrence Sherriff Sch., Rugby, 1950–51; Lectr, University Coll., Ibadan, Nigeria, 1951–52; Adult Tutor, Ashby-de-la-Zouch Community Coll., Leicestershire, 1952–54; Further Educn Organising Tutor, Oxfordshire, 1954–60; Asst Educn Officer: West Suffolk, 1960–65; Bristol, 1965–67; Dep. Chief Educn Officer, Bristol, 1967–73; Chief Educn Officer, County of Avon, 1973–76; Dir, Glos Inst. of Higher Educn, 1977–80. *Recreations:* cricket, music. *Address:* 5 Longs View, Charfield, Wotton-under-Edge, Glos. *T:* Dursley 844389.

WILLIAMS, Richard Hall; Under Secretary, Agriculture Department, Welsh Office, Cardiff, since 1981; *b* 21 Oct. 1926; *s* of Edward Hall Williams and Kitty Hall Williams; *m* 1949, Nia Wynn (*née* Jones); two *s* two *d.* *Educ:* Barry Grammar Sch., Glamorgan; University College of Wales, Aberystwyth (BScEcon Hons). Experience in university teaching, local government, industry, technical and management education before entering Civil Service, 1967; subsequent career within Welsh Office has included service in Health and Economic Planning Groups before entering Agriculture Dept, 1978. *Recreation:* enjoying all things Welsh. *Address:* Argoed, 17 West Orchard Crescent, Llandaff, Cardiff CF5 1AR. *T:* Cardiff 562472.

WILLIAMS, Robert Emmanuel; *b* 1 Jan. 1900; *o s* of David Williams and Gertrude Olive Williams (*née* Mansfield); *m* 1st, 1928, Rosamund May Taylor (*d* 1929); 2nd, 1938, Audrey Forbes Higginson; three *s* one *d.* *Educ:* Liverpool Institute; Liverpool Univ. (MSc); Brasenose Coll., Oxford (MA). Assistant Master: Ilkeston, Rugby, Lawrence Sheriff Sch., Repton, 1922–36; Lecturer, Oxford Univ. Department of Education, 1936–39; HM Inspector of Schools, 1939; Staff Inspector, 1945; Chief Inspector of Schools, Ministry of Education, 1952–61; Simon Senior Research Fellow, Manchester Univ., 1961–62; Lecturer in Education, London Univ. Institute of Education, 1962–67. *Publications:* contributions to School Science Review, Religion in Education. *Address:* Sea Crest, 10 Ryder's Avenue, Westgate-on-Sea, Kent CT8 8LN. *T:* Thanet 33521.

WILLIAMS, Sir Robert (Evan Owen), Kt 1976; MD, FRCP, FRCPath; FFCM; Director, Public Health Laboratory Service, 1973–81; Chairman, Advisory Committee on Genetic Manipulation, Health and Safety Executive, 1984–86 (Chairman, Genetic Manipulation Advisory Group, 1981–84); *b* 30 June 1916; *s* of Gwynne Evan Owen Williams and Cicely Mary (*née* Innes); *m* 1944, Margaret (*née* Lumsden); one *s* two *d.* *Educ:* Sherborne Sch., Dorset; University College, London and University College Hospital. Assistant Pathologist, EMS, 1941–42; Pathologist, Medical Research Council Unit, Birmingham Accident Hospital, 1942–46; on staff Public Health Laboratory Service, 1946–60 (Director, Streptococcus, Staphylococcus and Air Hygiene Laboratory, 1949–60); Prof. of Bacteriology, Univ. of London, at St Mary's Hosp. Med. Sch., 1960–73, Dean 1967–73. Mem. MRC, 1969–73. Pres., RCPath, 1975–78. Fellow, UCL, 1968. Hon. FRCPA, 1977; Hon. MD Uppsala, 1972; Hon. DSc Bath, 1977. *Publications:* (jt author) Hospital Infection, 1966; numerous publications in journals on bacteriological and epidemiological subjects. *Recreation:* horticulture. *Address:* Little Platt, Plush, Dorchester, Dorset DT2 7RQ. *T:* Piddletrenthide 320. *Club:* Athenæum.

WILLIAMS, Prof. Robert Joseph Paton, DPhil; FRS 1972; Royal Society Napier Research Professor at Oxford, since 1974; Fellow of Wadham College, Oxford, since 1955; *b* 25 Feb. 1926; *m* 1952, Jelly Klara (*née* Büchli); two *s.* *Educ:* Wallasey Grammar Sch.; Merton Coll., Oxford (MA, DPhil). FRSC. Rotary Foundn Fellow, Uppsala, 1950–51; Jun. Res. Fellow, Merton Coll., Oxford, 1951–55; Lectr, 1955–73, Reader in Inorganic Chemistry, 1973–74, Univ. of Oxford. Associate, Peter Bent Brigham Hosp., Boston, USA; Commonwealth Fellow, Mass, 1965–66. Liversidge Lectr, Chem. Soc., 1979; Bakerian Lectr, Royal Soc., 1981. Foreign Member: Acad. of Science, Portugal; Royal Swedish Acad. of Sciences, 1983; Royal Soc. of Science, Liège. Hon. DSc: Liège, 1980; Leicester, 1985. Tilden Medal, Chem. Soc., 1970; Keilin Medal, Biochem. Soc., 1972; Hughes Medal, Royal Soc., 1979; Chaire Bruylants Medal, Louvain, 1979; Krebs Medal, Europ. Biochem. Soc., 1985; Linderstrøm-Lang Medal, Copenhagen, 1986. *Publications:* (with C. S. G. Phillips) Inorganic Chemistry, 1965; (jtly) Nuclear Magnetic Resonance in Biology, 1977; (ed jtly) New Trends in Bio-Inorganic Chemistry, 1978; papers in Jl Chem. Soc., biochemical jls, etc. *Recreation:* walking in the country. *Address:* Wadham College, Oxford. *T:* Oxford 242564.

WILLIAMS, Robert Martin, CB 1981; CBE 1973; Chairman, State Services Commission, New Zealand, 1975–81; *b* 30 March 1919; *s* of late Canon Henry Williams; *m* Mary Constance, *d* of late Rev. Francis H. Thorpe; one *s* two *d.* *Educ:* Christ's Coll., NZ; Canterbury University College, NZ; St John's Coll., Cambridge. MA. 1st Class Hons Mathematics, Univ. Sen. Schol., Shirtcliffe Fellow, NZ, 1940; BA, 1st Class Hons Mathematics Tripos, Cantab, 1947; PhD Math. Statistics, Cantab, 1949. Mathematician at Radar Development Laboratory, DSIR, NZ, 1941–44; Member UK Atomic Group in US, 1944–45; Member, 1949–53, Director, 1953–62, Applied Mathematics Laboratory, DSIR, NZ; Harkness Commonwealth Fellow and Vis. Fellow, at Princeton Univ., 1957–58; State Services Commissioner, NZ Public Service, 1963–67; Vice-Chancellor: Univ. of Otago, Dunedin, 1967–73; ANU, 1973–75. Mem., NZ Metric Adv. Bd, 1969–73. Mem., Internat. Statistical Inst., 1961–. Chm., Cttee of Inquiry into Educnl TV, 1970–72. Carnegie Travel Award, 1969. Hon. LLD Otago, 1972. *Publications:* papers mainly on mathematical statistics and related topics. *Address:* 21 Wadestown Road, Wellington, New Zealand. *Club:* Wellington (Wellington, NZ).

WILLIAMS, Sir (Robert) Philip (Nathaniel), 4th Bt *cr* 1915; *b* 3 May 1950; *s* of Sir David Philip Williams, 3rd Bt and of Elizabeth Mary Garneys, *d* of late William Ralph Garneys Bond; *S* father, 1970; *m* 1979, Catherine Margaret Godwin, *d* of Canon Cosmo Pouncey, Tewkesbury; one *s* two *d.* *Educ:* Marlborough; St Andrews Univ. MA Hons. *Heir:* *s* David Robert Mark Williams, *b* 31 Oct. 1980. *Address:* Bridehead, Littlebredy, Dorchester, Dorset. *T:* Long Bredy 232. *Club:* MCC.

WILLIAMS, Maj.-Gen. Robin Guy, CB 1983; MBE 1969; retired; Chairman, Operation Raleigh, New Zealand, since 1986 (Vice-Chairman, 1985–86); *b* 14 Aug. 1930; *s* of John Upham and Margaret Joan Williams; *m* 1953, Jill Rollo Tyrie; one *s* two *d.* *Educ:* Nelson Coll., New Zealand. psc(UK) 1963, jssc(AS) 1972, rcds(UK) 1976. Commissioned RMC, Duntroon, 1952; 1 Fiji Inf. Regt Malaya, 1953–54; Adjt/Coy Comd 2 NZ Regt Malaya, 1959–61 Chief Instructor Sch. of Inf. (NZ), 1964–65; BM 28 Comwel Inf. Bde, Malaysia, 1965–68; CO 1 Bn Depot (NZ), 1969; CO 1 RNZIR (Singapore), 1969–71; GSO1 Field Force Comd (NZ), 1972–73; CofS Field Force Comd (NZ), 1973–74; Col SD, Army GS, 1974–75; Comd Field Force, 1977–79; ACDS (Ops/Plans), 1979–81; DCGS 1981; CGS, 1981–84. Chief Exec., Order of St John (NZ). *Recreations:* golf, swimming, walking. *Address:* 7A Ranikhet Way, Khandallah, Wellington 4, New Zealand. *T:* 793–968. *Club:* Wellington Golf (Heretaunga, NZ).

WILLIAMS, Sir Robin (Philip), 2nd Bt, *cr* 1953; Insurance Broker since 1952; Lloyd's Underwriter, 1961; 2nd Lieut, retired, RA; *b* 27 May 1928; *s* of Sir Herbert Geraint Williams, 1st Bt, MP, MSc, MEngAssoc, MInstCE; *S* father 1954; *m* 1955, Wendy Adèle Marguerite, *o d* of late Felix Joseph Alexander, London and Hong Kong; two *s.* *Educ:* Eton Coll.; St John's Coll., Cambridge (MA). 2nd Lieut, Royal Artillery, 1947. Vice-Chairman, Federation of Univ. Conservative and Unionist Assocs, 1951–52; Acting Chairman, 1952; Chairman of Bow Group (Conservative Research Society), 1954. Called to Bar, Middle Temple, 1954; Chm., Anti-Common Market League, 1969; Dir, Common Market Safeguards Campaign, 1973–76. Councillor, Haringey, 1968–74. *Publication:* Whose Public Schools?, 1957. *Heir:* *s* Anthony Geraint Williams, *b* 22 Dec. 1958. *Address:* 1 Broadlands Close, Highgate, N6.

WILLIAMS, Dr Roger Stanley, FRCP; Consultant Physician, King's College Hospital and Director, Liver Research Unit, King's College School of Medicine and Dentistry (formerly King's College Hospital and Medical School), since 1966; Consultant, Liver Research Unit Trust, since 1974; *b* 28 Aug. 1931; *s* of Stanley George Williams and Doris Dagmar Clatworthy; *m* 1st, 1954, Lindsay Mary Elliott (marr. diss. 1977); two *s* three *d*; 2nd, 1978, Stephanie Gay de Laszlo; one *s* two *d.* *Educ:* St Mary's Coll., Southampton; London Hosp. Med. Coll., Univ. of London. MB, BS (Hons), MD; MRCS, LRCP, MRCP, FRCP. House appointments and Pathology Asst, London Hospital, 1953–56; Jun. Med. Specialist, Queen Alexandra Hospital, Millbank, 1956–58; Medical Registrar and Tutor, Royal Postgrad. Med. Sch., 1958–59; Lectr in Medicine, Royal Free Hospital, 1959–65; Consultant Physician, Royal South Hants and Southampton General Hospital, 1965–66. Member: Adv. Gp on Hepatitis, DHSS, 1980–; Transplant Adv. Panel, DHSS, 1974–83; WHO Scientific Gp on Viral Hepatitis, Geneva, 1972. Rockefeller Travelling Fellowship in Medicine, 1962; Legg Award, Royal Free Hosp. Med. Sch., 1964; Melrose Meml Lecture, Glasgow, 1970; Goulstonian Lectr, RCP, 1970; Searle Lecture, Amer. Assoc. for the Study of Liver Diseases, 1972; Sir Ernest Finch Vis. Prof., Sheffield, 1974; Fleming Lecture, Glasgow Coll. of Physicians and Surgeons, 1975; Sir Arthur Hurst Meml Lecture, British Soc. of Gastroënterology, 1975; Skinner Lecture, Royal Coll. of Radiologists, 1978; Albert M. Snell Meml Lecture, Palo Alto Med. Foundn, 1981. Member: European Assoc. for the Study of the Liver, 1966– (Cttee Mem., 1966–70; Pres., 1983); Harveian Soc. of London (Sec., Councillor and Vice-Pres., 1963–70, Pres., 1974–75); British Assoc. for Study of Liver (formerly Liver Club) (Sec. and Treasurer, 1968–71; Pres., 1984–86); Royal Soc. of Medicine (Sec. of Section, 1969–71). *Publications:* Editor: Fifth Symposium on Advanced Medicine, 1969; Immunology of the Liver, 1971; Artificial Liver Support, 1975; Immune Reactions in Liver Disease, 1978; Drug Reactions and the Liver, 1981; Variceal Bleeding, 1982; author of over 800 scientific papers, review articles and book chapters. *Recreations:* tennis, sailing, opera. *Address:* Reed House, Satchell

Lane, Hamble, Hants. *T:* Southampton 453749; 8 Eldon Road, W8. *T:* 01–937 5301. *Clubs:* Saints and Sinners, Royal Ocean Racing; Royal Southern Yacht.

WILLIAMS, Sir Rolf D. D.; *see* Dudley-Williams.

WILLIAMS, Ronald Millward; DL; Member, Essex County Council, since 1970 (Chairman, 1983–86); *b* 9 Dec. 1922; *s* of George and Gladys Williams; *m* 1943, Joyce; one *s* two *d. Educ:* Leeds College of Technology. Electrical Engineer, then Industrial Eng Superintendent, Mobil Oil Co. Ltd, 1954–82. Member: Benfleet Urban Dist Council, 1960–74 (Chm. 1963–66, 1972–74); Castle Point Dist Council, 1974– (Chm. 1980–81); Leader Cons. Gp, Essex CC, 1977–83, 1986–. Chm., Southend Health Authority, 1982–. Chm., SE Essex Abbeyfield Soc., 1983–. DL Essex 1983. *Recreations:* supporter, football, cricket, bowls, tennis; video filming of countryside. *Address:* 41 Poors Lane, Hadleigh, Benfleet, Essex. *T:* Southend on Sea 559565.

WILLIAMS, Ronald William; Senior Adviser, Coopers & Lybrand Associates, since 1986; Director, Office of Manpower Economics, 1980–86 (on secondment); *b* 19 Dec. 1926; *yr s* of late Albert Williams and Katherine Teresa Williams (*née* Chilver). *Educ:* City of London Sch.; Downing Coll., Cambridge (BA, LLB). RN, 1945–48. Iraq Petroleum Co. Ltd, 1956–58; Philips Electrical Industries Ltd, 1958–64; Consultant, later Sen. Consultant, PA Management Consultants Ltd, 1964–69; Asst Sec., NBPI, 1969–71; Sen. Consultant, Office of Manpower Economics, 1971–73; Asst Sec., CSD, 1973–80; Under Sec. 1980; HM Treasury, 1982; Dept of Employment, 1986. *Recreations:* music, visual arts. *Address:* 126 Defoe House, Barbican, EC2Y 8DN. *T:* 01–638 5456.

WILLIAMS, Rev. Prof. Rowan Douglas; Lady Margaret Professor of Divinity, and Canon of Christ Church, Oxford, since 1986; *b* 14 June 1950; *s* of Aneurin Williams and Nancy Delphine Williams; *m* 1981, Hilary Jane Paul. *Educ:* Dynevor School, Swansea; Christ's College, Cambridge (BA 1971, MA 1975); Christ Church and Wadham College, Oxford (DPhil 1975). Lectr, College of the Resurrection, Mirfield, 1975–77; Chaplain, Tutor and Director of Studies, Westcott House, Cambridge, 1977–80; Univ. Lectr in Divinity, 1980–86, Fellow and Dean of Clare Coll., 1984–86, Cambridge Univ. Hon. Asst Priest, St George's, Cambridge, 1980–83; Canon Theologian, Leicester Cathedral, 1981–. *Publications:* The Wound of Knowledge, 1979; Resurrection, 1982; The Truce of God, 1983; (with Mark Collier) Beginning Now: peacemaking theology, 1984; contribs to Jl of Theological Studies, Downside Review, Eastern Churches Review, Sobornost, New Blackfriars. *Recreations:* music, fiction, languages. *Address:* Priory House, Christ Church, Oxford.

WILLIAMS, Roy; Deputy Secretary, Department of Trade and Industry, since 1984; *b* 31 Dec. 1934; *s* of Eric Williams and Ellen Williams; *m* 1959, Shirley, *d* of Captain and Mrs O. Warwick; one *s* one *d. Educ:* Liverpool Univ. (1st Cl. BA Econs). Asst Principal, Min. of Power, 1956; Principal, 1961; Harkness Commonwealth Fellow, Univs of Chicago and Berkeley, 1963–64; Principal Private Sec., Minister of Power and subseq. Paymaster Gen., 1969; Asst Sec., DTI, 1971; Principal Private Sec., Sec. of State for Industry, 1974; Under-Sec., DoI, later DTI, 1976–84. *Address:* Darl Oast, The Street, Ightham, Sevenoaks, Kent. *T:* Borough Green 883944.

WILLIAMS, Rev. Samuel Lewis; QHC 1986; RN; Principal Chaplain, Church of Scotland and Free Churches (Navy), since 1986; *b* 8 Jan. 1934; *s* of Thomas John Williams and Miriam Mary Williams (*née* West); *m* 1958, Mary Sansom (*née* Benjamin); one *s* one *d. Educ:* Pagefield College Public Day School, Newport, Gwent; Memorial Coll. (Congregational), Brecon. Local government officer, 1950–52; RAF, 1952–55; theol. training, 1955–58. Ordained Congregational (URC) Minister, 1958; Mill Street Congregational Church, Newport, Gwent, 1958–63; Bettws Congregational Church, 1963–68; Llanvaches Congregational Church, 1966–68; Free Churches Chaplain, St Woolas Hosp., Newport, 1964–68. Entered RN as Chaplain, 1968; served HMS: Seahawk, 1968–69; Hermes, 1969–70; Raleigh, 1970–71; Seahawk, 1971–73; Daedalus, 1973–74; served Malta, 1974–76; C-in-C Naval Home Comd staff, 1977–81; HMS Sultan, 1981–84; Flag Officer Scotland and NI staff, 1984–86; HMS Heron, 1986. *Recreations:* oil painting, golf, hill walking, music, gardening, Rugby. *Address:* Ministry of Defence (Navy), Lacon House, Theobalds Road, WC1X 8RY. *T:* 01–430 6842.

WILLIAMS, Rt. Hon. Shirley Vivien Teresa Brittain, PC 1974; Co-founder, Social Democratic Party, 1981, President since 1982; *b* 27 July 1930; *d* of late Prof. Sir George Catlin, and late Mrs Catlin, (Vera Brittain); *m* 1955, Prof. Bernard Arthur Owen Williams (marr. diss. 1974), *qv*; one *d. Educ:* eight schools in UK and USA; Somerville Coll., Oxford (MA), Hon. Fellow, 1970; Columbia Univ., New York. General Secretary, Fabian Soc., 1960–64 (Chm., 1980–81). MP: (Lab) Hitchin, 1964–74; (Lab) Hertford and Stevenage, 1974–79; (first-elected SDP MP) Crosby, Nov. 1981–1983; PPS, Minister of Health, 1964–66; Parly Sec., Min. of Labour, 1966–67; Minister of State: Education and Science, 1967–69; Home Office, 1969–70; Opposition spokesman on: Social Services, 1970–71, on Home Affairs, 1971–73; Prices and Consumer Protection, 1973–74; Sec. of State for Prices and Consumer Protection, 1974–76; Sec. of State for Educn and Science, 1976–79; Paymaster General, 1976–79. Chm., OECD study on youth employment, 1979. Mem., Labour Party Nat. Exec. Cttee, 1970–81. Visiting Fellow, Nuffield College, Oxford, 1967–75; Fellow, PSI, 1979–85; Visiting Faculty, Internat. Management Inst., Geneva; Fellow, Inst., of Politics, Harvard, 1979–80 (Mem., Sen. Adv., Council, 1986–); Director: Turing Inst., Glasgow; Learning by Experience Trust; Godkin Lectr, Harvard, 1980; Rede Lectr, Cambridge, 1980; Janeway Lectr, Princeton, 1981. Hon. DEd CNAA, 1969; Hon. Dr Pol. Econ.: Univ. of Leuven, 1976; Radcliffe Coll., Harvard, 1978; Leeds, 1980; Bath, 1980; Hon. LLD: Sheffield, 1980; Southampton, 1981; Hon. DLitt Heriot-Watt, 1980; Hon. DSc Aston, 1981. *Publications:* Politics is for People, 1981; Jobs for the 1980s; Youth Without Work, 1981; (jtly) Unemployment and Growth in the Western Economies, 1984; A Job to Live, 1985. *Recreations:* music, hill walking. *Address:* c/o SDP, 4 Cowley Street, SW1.

WILLIAMS, Rev. (Sidney) Austen, CVO 1980; Vicar of St Martin-in-the-Fields, 1956–84; Chaplain to the Queen's Household, 1961–82, Extra Chaplain since 1982; a Prebendary of St Paul's Cathedral, since 1973; *b* 23 Feb. 1912; *s* of Sidney Herbert and Dorothy Williams; *m* 1945, Daphne Joan McWilliam; one *s* one *d. Educ:* Bromsgrove School; St Catharine's College, Cambridge (MA); Westcott House, Cambridge. Curate of St Paul, Harringay, 1937–40. Chaplain, Toc H, France and Germany (POW), 1940–48. Curate of: All Hallows, Barking by the Tower, 1945–46; St Martin-in-the-Fields, 1946–51; Vicar of St Albans, Westbury Park, Clifton, Bristol, 1951–56. Freeman of the City of London, 1977. *Recreations:* photography, ornithology. *Address:* 37 Tulsemere Road, SE27. *T:* 01–670 7945.

WILLIAMS, Stanley; solicitor; Member, Mental Health Review Tribunal (Wales Region), since 1972; *b* 6 April 1911; *s* of Thomas and Sarah Elizabeth Williams; *m* 1948, Lily Ceridwen Evans; three *s* one *d. Educ:* Froncysyllte; Llangollen County Sch. (Schol.); Liverpool Univ. (LLB). Admitted Solicitor, 1934. Served War of 1939–45: ranks, 1940–43; commnd RAMC, 1943. Contested (Lab) Denbigh Division, 1959 and 1964. A Recorder of the Crown Court, 1972–75. Member: Bootle Corporation, 1934–38 and

1946–50; Denbighshire County Council, 1960–63; Wrexham Corporation, 1966–68; Noise Adv. Council, 1970. *Recreations:* music, walking, gardening. *Address:* Liddington, Wynnstay Lane, Marford, Wrexham, Clwyd. *T:* Gresford 2715.

WILLIAMS, Mrs Susan Eva, MBE 1959; Lord-Lieutenant of South Glamorgan, since 1985; *b* 17 Aug. 1915; *d* of Robert Henry Williams and Dorothy Marie Williams; *m* 1950, Charles Crofts Llewellyn Williams. *Educ:* St James's, West Malvern. WAAF, 1939–45. JP 1961, High Sheriff 1968, DL 1973, Glamorgan; Lieut, S Glam, 1981–85. *Recreation:* National Hunt racing. *Address:* Caercady, Welsh St Donats, Cowbridge, S Glamorgan CF7 7ST. *T:* Cowbridge 2346.

WILLIAMS, Sir Sydney; *see* Williams, Sir Henry S.

WILLIAMS, Prof. Thomas Eifion Hopkins, CBE 1980; CEng; Research Professor of Civil Engineering, University of Southampton, since 1983 (Professor of Civil Engineering, 1967–83); *b* 14 June 1923; *s* of David Garfield Williams and Annie Mary Williams (*née* Hopkins), Cwmtwrch, Brecon; *m* 1947, Elizabeth Lois Davies; one *s* two *d. Educ:* Ystradgynlais Grammar Sch.; Univ. of Wales (BSc, MSc); Univ. of Durham (PhD). FICE, MIStructE, FIHT, FCIT, FRSA. Research Stressman, Sir W. G. Armstrong-Whitworth Aircraft, 1945; Asst Engr, Trunk Roads, Glam CC, 1946; Asst Lectr Civil Engrg, UC Swansea, 1947; Lectr in Civil Engrg, King's Coll., Univ. of Durham, 1948; Resident Site Engr, R. T. James & Partners, 1952; Post-doctoral Visitor, Univ. of California at Berkeley, 1955; Vis. Prof., Civil Engrg, Northwestern Univ., 1957; Sen. Lectr, Reader and Prof. of Civil and Transport Engrg, King's Coll., Univ. of Durham (subseq. Univ. of Newcastle upon Tyne), 1958–67. Chairman: Civil Engrg EDC, 1976–78; Standing Adv. Cttee on Trunk Rd Assessment, Dept of Transport, 1980– (Mem., Adv. Cttee, 1977–80); Member: EDC Civil Engrg, 1967–76; Transport Cttee, SRC; Roads Engrg Bd, ICE; British Nat. Cttee, PIARC; Council and Transp. Engrg Bd, Inst. Highway Engrs (Pres. 1979–80); Public Policy Cttee, RAC, 1981–. Visitor, TRRL, 1982– (Mem., Adv. Cttee on Traffic and Safety, 1977–80). Mem. Council, Church Schools Co., 1982–. *Publications:* (Editor) Urban Survival and Traffic, 1961; Capacity, in Traffic Engineering Practice, 1963; Prediction of Traffic in Industrial Areas, 1966; Autostrade: Strategia, di sviluppo industriale e la vitalita delle nostre citta, 1965; Inter-City VTOL: Potential Traffic and Sites, 1969; Mobility and the Environment, 1971; (ed) Transportation and Environment: policies, plans and practice, 1973; Integrated Transport: developments and trends, 1976; Air, Rail and Road Inter-City Transport Systems, 1976; Land Use, Highways and Traffic, 1977; Motor Vehicles in a Changing World, 1978; Traffic Engineering 1960–81, 1981; Transport Policy: facts; frameworks; econometrics, 1983; Assessment of Urban Roads, 1986; contribs to Proc. ICE, Highway Engrs, IMunE, Road International, Traffic Engrg and Control, Segnalazioni Stradali, OTA/PIARC Confs. *Recreation:* music. *Address:* Willowdale, Woodlea Way, Ampfield, Romsey, Hants SO51 9DA. *T:* Chandler's Ford 3342. *Club:* Royal Automobile.

WILLIAMS, His Eminence Cardinal Thomas Stafford; *see* Wellington (NZ), Archbishop of, (RC).

WILLIAMS, Trevor; *see* Williams, A. T.

WILLIAMS, Trevor Illtyd, MA, BSc, DPhil, CChem, FRSC, FRHistS; scientific consultant and writer; *b* 16 July 1921; *s* of Illtyd Williams and Alma Mathilde Sohlberg; *m* 1st, 1945 (marriage dissolved, 1952); 2nd, 1952, Sylvia Irène Armstead; four *s* one *d. Educ:* Clifton College; Queen's College, Oxford. Nuffield Research Scholar, Sir William Dunn Sch. of Pathology, Oxford, 1942–45; Endeavour: Deputy Editor, 1945–54; Editor, 1954–74, 1977– (Consulting Scientific Editor, 1974–76); Editor, Outlook on Agriculture, 1982–. Academic Relations Advr, ICI Ltd, 1962–74. Chm., Soc. for the Study of Alchemy and Early Chemistry, 1967–86; Jt Editor, Annals of Science, 1966–74; Chairman: World List of Scientific Periodicals, 1966–; Adv. Cttee on the Selection of Low-priced Books for Overseas, 1982–84; Member: Steering Cttee, English Language Book Soc., 1984–; Adv. Council, Science Museum, 1972–84; Council, University Coll., Swansea, 1965–83. Vis. Fellow, ANU, 1981; Leverhulme Fellow, 1985. Dexter Award, Amer. Chem. Soc., for contribs to the history of chemistry, 1976. *Publications:* An Introduction to Chromatography, 1946; Drugs from Plants, 1947; (ed) The Soil and the Sea, 1949; The Chemical Industry Past and Present, 1953; The Elements of Chromatography, 1954; (ed, jtly) A History of Technology, 1954–58; (with T. K. Derry) A Short History of Technology, 1960; Science and Technology (Ch. III, Vol. XI, New Cambridge Mod. History); (rev. edn) Alexander Findlay's A Hundred Years of Chemistry, 1965; (ed) A Biographical Dictionary of Scientists, 1968; Alfred Bernhard Nobel, 1973; James Cook, 1974; Man the Chemist, 1976; (ed) A History of Technology, Vols VI and VII: The Twentieth Century, 1978; (ed) Industrial Research in the United Kingdom, 1980; A History of the British Gas Industry, 1981; A Short History of Twentieth Century Technology, 1982; (ed) European Research Centres, 1982; Florey: penicillin and after, 1984; numerous articles on scientific subjects, especially history of science and technology. *Recreations:* fishing, trade tokens. *Address:* 20 Blenheim Drive, Oxford OX2 8DG. *T:* Oxford 58591. *Club:* Athenæum.

WILLIAMS, Vaughan; *see* Williams, J. V.

WILLIAMS, Walter Gordon Mason, CB 1983; FRICS; Vice President, London Rent Assessment Panel, since 1984; *b* 10 June 1923; *s* of Rees John Williams, DSO and Gladys Maud Williams; *m* 1950, Gwyneth Joyce Lawrence; two *d. Educ:* Cardiff High Sch. FRICS. Joined Valuation Office, Inland Revenue, 1947; Superintending Valuer (N Midlands), 1969–73; Asst Chief Valuer, 1973–79; Dep. Chief Valuer, 1979–83. *Address:* 33A Sydenham Hill, SE26 6SH. *T:* 01–670 8580.

WILLIAMS, Prof. William David, MA, DPhil; Professor of German, Liverpool University, 1954–80; *b* 10 March 1917; *s* of William Williams and Winifred Ethel Williams (*née* Anstey); *m* 1946, Mary Hope Davis; one *s* one *d. Educ:* Merchant Taylors' School; St John's Coll., Oxford (MA, DPhil). Served War of 1939–45, with Sudan Defence Force, Middle East, and as Liaison Officer with Polish Army in Italy; Asst Lecturer in German, Leeds Univ., 1946; Lecturer in German, Oxford Univ., 1948–54; Pro-Vice-Chancellor, Liverpool Univ., 1965–68. *Publications:* Nietzsche and the French, 1952; The Stories of C. F. Meyer, 1962; reviews, etc, in Modern Language Review, and Erasmus. *Recreation:* gardening. *Address:* Strangers Corner, 5 Summerfield Rise, Goring-on-Thames, near Reading, Berks RG8 0DS. *T:* Goring-on-Thames 872603.

WILLIAMS, (William) Donald; *b* 17 Oct. 1919; 2nd *s* of Sidney Williams, Malvern; *m* 1945, Cecilia Mary (*née* Hirons); one *s. Educ:* Royal Grammar Sch., Worcester. Served War of 1939–45: Volunteer, 8th Bn Worcestershire Regt, May 1939; POW 1940 (Germany); escaped to Russia and was repatriated, 1945. Qualified as a Chartered Accountant, 1949. Partner in a Professional Practice, 1950–77, on own account as Financial Consultant, 1978–86, now retired. Director: Fiesta Foods Ltd; Kendalls of Malvern Ltd. Contested (C) Dudley, (Gen. Elec.), 1966; MP (C) Dudley, March 1968–1970; contested (C) Dudley East, 1979. CC Hereford/Worcester, 1973–81. Gov., Abberley Hall. *Recreations:* reading, travelling. *Address:* c/o Lächler, 71 Kilchgrund Strasse, 4125 Riehen, Basle, Switzerland. *Club:* Carlton.

WILLIAMS, Sir (William) Max (Harries), Kt 1983; solicitor; Senior Partner, Clifford-Turner, since 1984; *b* 18 Feb. 1926; *s* of Llwyd and Hilary Williams; *m* 1951, Jenifer, *d* of late Rt Hon. E. L. Burgin, LLD, and Mrs Burgin, JP; two *d. Educ:* Nautical Coll., Pangbourne. Served 178 Assault Field Regt RA, Far East (Captain), 1943–47. Admitted Solicitor, 1950. Mem. Council, 1962–85, Pres., 1982–83, Law Society. Mem., Crown Agents for Oversea Govts and Administration, 1982–86; Lay Mem., Stock Exchange Council, 1984–. Dir, Royal Insurance plc, 1985–. Chm., Review Bd for Govt Contracts, 1986–; Member: Royal Commission on Legal Services, 1976–79; Cttee of Management of Inst. of Advanced Legal Studies, 1980–86; Council, Wildfowl Trust (Hon. Treasurer, 1974–80). Mem., Amer. Law Inst., 1985–; Hon. Member: Amer. Bar Assoc.; Canadian Bar Assoc. Master, Solicitors' Co., 1986. Hon. LLD Birmingham, 1983. *Recreations:* fishing, ornithology. *Address:* 19 New Bridge Street, EC4V 6BY. *T:* 01–353 0211. *Clubs:* Garrick, Flyfishers'.

WILLIAMS, William Thomas, OBE 1980; ARCS; PhD, DSc (London); DIC; FIBiol; FLS; FAA 1978; with Australian Institute of Marine Science, Cape Ferguson, Townsville, 1980–85; pianoforte teacher (LMus Australia), since 1973; *b* 18 Apr. 1913; *o s* of William Thomas and Clara Williams. *Educ:* Stationers' Company's School, London; Imperial College of Science and Technology. Demonstrator in Botany, Imperial College, 1933–36; Lecturer in Biology, Sir John Cass' College, 1936–40. Served War, 1940–46; RA (Sjt), RAOC (2/Lt), REME (T/Major). Lecturer in Botany, Bedford College, London, 1946–51; Professor of Botany, University of Southampton, 1951–65; CSIRO Division of Computing Research, Canberra, Australia, 1966–68; Div. of Tropical Pastures, Brisbane, 1968–73; Chief Res. Scientist, CSIRO, 1970–73; with Townsville Lab., CSIRO, 1973–80. Sometime Secretary of Society for Experimental Biology, and of Sherlock Holmes Society of London. Past Editor, Journal of Experimental Botany. Hon. DSc Queensland, 1973. *Publications:* The Four Prisons of Man, 1971; (ed) Pattern Analysis in Agricultural Science, 1976; over 150 papers on plant physiology, numerical taxonomy and statistical ecology in scientific journals. *Recreations:* music, drinking beer. *Address:* 10 Surrey Street, Hyde Park, Townsville, Qld 4812, Australia.

WILLIAMS, Col William Trevor, FCIS; Director, Engineering Industries Association, since 1981; *b* 16 Oct. 1925; *s* of Francis Harold and Ellen Mabel Williams, Newton Manorbier; *m* 1951, Elizabeth, *d* of late Brig. Arthur Goldie; two *s* two *d. Educ:* Darwin Coll., Univ. of Kent (MA). FBIM, MCIT. Commissioned in Infantry, 1945; regimental service, India and Malaya, to 1949; seconded to Guyanese Govt, 1964, 1965; Commander, Maritime Air Regt, Far East, 1967–69; Project Office, National Defence Coll., 1970–71; Adviser, Ethiopian Govt, 1971–72; Col Q BAOR, 1973–76 (Chm., Berlin Budget Cttee); Head of Secretariat, MoD, 1976–77; Director, SATRA, 1979–80. *Publications:* military. *Recreations:* golf, photography. *Address:* Mill Lane, Harbledown, Canterbury. *T:* Canterbury 68170.

WILLIAMS, Yvonne Lovat; Secretary, Monopolies and Mergers Commission, 1974–79; *b* 23 Feb. 1920; *d* of late Wendros Williams, CBE and Vera Lovat Williams. *Educ:* Queenswood Sch., Hatfield; Newnham Coll., Cambridge. BA History 1941, MA 1946. Temp. Civil Servant, BoT, 1941–46; Asst Principal, BoT, 1946–48, Principal 1948–56; Treasury, 1956–58; BoT, 1958–63; Asst Sec., BoT, Min. Tech., DTI, 1963–73. *Recreations:* visiting friends, theatres and old places. *Address:* Flat 16, The Limes, Linden Gardens, W2 4ET. *T:* 01–727 9851.

WILLIAMS-BULKELEY, Sir Richard Harry David, 13th Bt, *cr* 1661; TD; JP; Lord Lieutenant of Gwynedd, 1974–83 (HM Lieutenant for the County of Anglesey, 1947–74); Member: Anglesey County Council, 1946–74 (Chairman, 1955–57); Mayor of Beaumaris, 1949–51; *b* 5 Oct. 1911; *s* of late Maj. R. G. W. Williams-Bulkeley, MC, and late Mrs V. Williams-Bulkeley; *S* grand-father, 1942; *m* 1938, Renée Arundell, *yr d* of Sir Thomas L. H. Neave, 5th Bt; two *s. Educ:* Eton. Served with 9th and 8th Bns Royal Welch Fusiliers, 1939–44, 2nd in Command of both Battalions and with Allied Land Forces South East Asia, specially employed, 1944–Sept. 1945, Lt-Col Comdt, Anglesey and Caernarvonshire Army Cadet Force, 1946–47 (resigned on appointment as HM Lieut). CStJ. *Recreations:* shooting, golf, hunting. *Heir:* *s* Richard Thomas Williams-Bulkeley [*b* 25 May 1939; *m* 1964, Sarah Susan, *er d* of Rt Hon. Sir Henry Josceline Phillimore, OBE; twin *s* one *d*]. *Address:* Plâs Meigan, Beaumaris, Gwynedd. *T:* Beaumaris 810345. *Club:* Boodle's.

WILLIAMS-THOMAS, Lt-Col Reginald Silvers, DSO 1940; TD; JP; DL; Commander of Crown (Belgium); Croix de Guerre; RA; Queen's Own Worcestershire Hussars; Glass Manufacturer; Director, Stevens and Williams Ltd; Lloyd's Underwriter; *b* 11 February 1914; *s* of late Hubert Silvers Williams-Thomas, Broome, Stourbridge, Worcestershire; *m* 1938, Esmée Florence Taylor; two *s* one *d*; *m* 1963, Sonia Margot Jewell, *d* of late Major M. F. S. Jewell, CBE, DL, Upton-on-Severn, Worcs. *Educ:* Shrewsbury School. JP Staffs, 1947; DL Worcestershire, 1954. Freeman of the City of London; Mem., Worshipful Co. of Glass-Sellers. *Publication:* The Crystal Years, 1984. *Recreations:* shooting, archery, fishing, gardening. *Address:* The Tythe House, Broome, near Stourbridge, West Midlands. *T:* Kidderminster 700632.

WILLIAMS-WYNN, Col Sir (Owen) Watkin, 10th Bt, *cr* 1688; CBE 1969; FRAgSs 1969; Lord Lieutenant of Clwyd, 1976–79; *b* 30 Nov. 1904; *s* of Sir Robert William Herbert Watkin Williams-Wynn, 9th Bt, KCB, DSO; *S* father 1951; *m* 1st, 1939, Margaret Jean (*d* 1961), *d* of late Col William Alleyne Macbean, RA, and Hon. Mrs Gerald Scarlett; one *s* (and one *s* decd); 2nd, 1968, Gabrielle Haden Matheson, *d* of late Herbert Alexander Caffin. *Educ:* Eton; RMA, Woolwich. Commnd RA, 1925; RHA, Instructor at Equitation Sch., Weedon; Adj. 61st (Carnarvon and Denbigh Yeo.) Medium Regt RA (TA), 1936–40; Major, 1940. Served with Regt as 2nd in command, France and Dunkirk; served with 18th Division, Singapore (despatches twice); Prisoner of War, Siam and Burmah Railway; Lt-Col comdg 361st Med. Regt RA (TA), 1946; Hon. Col 361 Med. Regt RA (TA), 1952–57. Liaison Officer to Min. of Agriculture for N Wales, 1961–70; Mem., Nature Conservancy for Wales, 1963–66. Master Flint and Denbigh Foxhounds, 1946–61; Joint Master, Sir W. W. Wynn's Hounds, 1957. JP 1937, DL 1947, Denbighshire; High Sheriff of Denbighshire, 1954; Vice-Lieutenant, Denbighshire, 1957–66, Lord Lieutenant 1966–74; Lieutenant of Clwyd, 1974–76. KStJ 1972. *Heir:* *s* David Watkin Williams-Wynn [*b* 18 Feb. 1940; *m* 1st, 1968, Harriet Veryan Elspeth, *d* of Gen. Sir Norman Tailyour, KCB, DSO; two *s* twin *d*; 2nd, 1983, Mrs Victoria Jane Dillon, *d* of late Lt-Col Ian Dudley De Ath, DSO, MBE]. *Address:* Llangedwyn, Oswestry, Salop. *T:* Llanrhaiadr 269. *Club:* Army and Navy.

WILLIAMS-WYNNE, Col John Francis, CBE 1972; DSO 1945; JP; FRAgS; Vice Lord-Lieutenant of Gwynedd, 1980–85 (Lieutenant, 1974–80; HM Lieutenant of Merioneth, 1957–74); Constable of Harlech Castle since 1964; *b* 9 June 1908; *s* of late Major F. R. Williams-Wynn, CB, and late Beatrice (*née* Cooper); *m* 1938, Margaret Gwendolen, *d* of late Rev. George Roper and late Mrs G. S. White; one *s* two *d. Educ:* Oundle; Magdalene College, Cambridge (MA Mech. Sciences). Commissioned in RA 1929; served NW Frontier, 1936; served War of 1939–45; psc Camberley; Brigade Major, RA 2 Div., 1940–41; 2 i/c 114 Fd Regt, 1942; GSO2 HQ Ceylon Comd, 1942; comd 160 Jungle Field Regt, RA, 1943–44; GSO1, GHQ India, 1945; GSO1, War Office, 1946–48; retd 1948; comd 636 (R Welch) LAA Regt, RA, TA, 1951–54; Subs. Col 1954. Hon. Col 7th (Cadet) Bn RWF, 1964–74. Contested (C) Merioneth, 1950. JP 1950, DL 1953, VL 1954, Merioneth. Chairman, Advisory Cttee, Min. of Agric. Experimental Husbandry Farm, Trawscoed, 1955–76. Part-time mem., Merseyside and N Wales Electricity Bd, 1953–65; National Parks Comr, 1961–66; Forestry Comr, 1963–65; Member: Regional Adv. Cttee N Wales Conservancy Forestry Commission, 1950–63; County Agric. Exec. Cttee, 1955–63 and 1967–71; Gwynedd River Board, 1957–63; Forestry Cttee of GB, 1966–76; Home Grown Timber Advisory Cttee, 1966–76; Prince of Wales's Cttee for Wales, 1970–79; President: Timber Growers Organisation, 1974–76; Royal Welsh Agric. Soc., 1968 (Chm. Council, 1971–77); Chairman: Agricl Adv. Cttee, BBC Wales, 1974–79; Flying Farmers' Assoc., 1974–. Pres., Merioneth Br., CLA, 1979–. Member: Airline Users Cttee, CAA, 1973–79; Sch. of Agric. Cttee, University Coll. N Wales, 1982–. Chm. and Man. Dir, Cross Foxes Ltd. *Recreations:* farming, forestry and flying. *Address:* Peniarth, Tywyn-Merioneth, Gwynedd. *T:* Tywyn 710328. *Clubs:* Army and Navy, Pratt's.

See also Hon. D. A. C. Douglas-Home.

WILLIAMSON, family name of **Baron Forres.**

WILLIAMSON, Brian; *see* Williamson, R. B.

WILLIAMSON, David Francis, CB 1984; Deputy Secretary, Cabinet Office, since 1983; *b* 8 May 1934; *s* of Samuel Charles Wathen Williamson and Marie Eileen Williamson (*née* Denney); *m* 1961, Patricia Margaret Smith; two *s. Educ:* Tonbridge Sch.; Exeter Coll., Oxford (MA). Entered Min. of Agriculture, Fisheries and Food, 1958; Private Sec. to Permanent Sec. and to successive Parly Secs, 1960–62; HM Diplomatic Service, as First Sec. (Agric. and Food), Geneva, for Kennedy Round Trade Negotiations, 1965–67; Principal Private Sec. to successive Ministers of Agric., Fisheries and Food, 1967–70; Head of Milk and Milk Products Div., Marketing Policy Div. and Food Policy Div., 1970–74; Under-Sec., Gen. Agricultural Policy Gp, 1974–76, EEC Gp, 1976–77; Dep. Dir Gen., Agriculture, European Commn, 1977–83; Dep. Sec., 1982. *Address:* St Anthony's, Manor Park, Chislehurst, Kent BR7 5QE. *T:* 01–467 9246.

WILLIAMSON, David Theodore Nelson, FRS 1968; Group Director of Engineering, Rank Xerox Ltd, 1974–76; Director, Xerox Research (UK) Ltd, 1975–76; retired; *b* 15 Feb. 1923; *s* of David Williamson and Ellie (*née* Nelson); *m* 1951, Alexandra Janet Smith Neilson; two *s* two *d. Educ:* George Heriot's Sch., Edinburgh; Univ. of Edinburgh. MO Valve Co. Ltd, 1943–46; Ferranti Ltd, Edinburgh, 1946–61; pioneered numerical control of machine tools, 1951; Manager, Machine Tool Control Div., 1959–61; Work on sound reproduction: Williamson amplifier, 1947, Ferranti pickup, 1949; collab. with P. J. Walker in developt of first wide-range electrostatic loud-speaker, 1951–56; Dir of Res. and Develt, Molins Ltd, 1961–74. Member: NEL Metrology and Noise Control Sub cttee, 1954–57; NEL Cttee on Automatic Design and Machine Tool Control, 1964–66; Min. of Technology Working Party on Computer-Aided Design, 1967; Penny Cttee on Computer-Aided Design, 1967–69; Steering Cttee, IAMTACT, 1967–69; SRC Mech. and Prod. Engrg Cttee, 1965–69; SRC Control Panel, 1966–69; Mech. Engrg EDC, 1968–74; SRC Engrg Bd, 1969–75; Adv. Cttee for Mech. Engrg, 1969–71; Court, Cranfield Inst. of Technology, 1970–79; Council and Exec. Cttee, British Hydrodynamics Research Assoc., 1970–73; Design Council (formerly CoID) Engrg Design Adv. Cttee, 1971–75; Council for Scientific Policy, 1972–73; Science Mus. Adv. Cttee, 1972–79; SRC Manufrg Technology Cttee, 1972–75 (Chm.); Mech. Engrg and Machine Tool Requirements Bd, DTI subseq. DoI, 1973–76; Council, Royal Soc., 1977–78. Hon. DSc: Heriot-Watt, 1971; Edinburgh, 1985. *Publications:* contrib. to: Electronic Engineers' Reference Book, 1959; Progress in Automation, 1960; Numerical Control Handbook, 1968; papers and articles on engrg subjects; NEDO Discussion Paper No 1, 1971. James Clayton Lecture, IMechE, 1968. *Recreations:* music, photography. *Address:* Villa Belvedere, La Cima 10, Tuoro-sul-Trasimeno, 06069 Pg, Umbria, Italy. *T:* (075) 826285.

WILLIAMSON, Dame (Elsie) Marjorie, DBE 1973; MSc, PhD (London); Principal, Royal Holloway College, University of London, 1962–73; *b* 30 July 1913; *d* of late Leonard Claude Williamson and Hannah Elizabeth Cary. *Educ:* Wakefield Girls' High School; Royal Holloway College. Demonstrator in Physics, Royal Holloway College, University of London, 1936–39; Lecturer in Physics, University College of Wales, Aberystwyth, 1939–45; Lecturer in Physics, Bedford Coll., Univ. of London, 1945–55; Principal, St Mary's Coll., Univ. of Durham, 1955–62; Deputy Vice-Chancellor, Univ. of London, 1970–71, 1971–72. Fellow, Bedford Coll., Univ. of London, 1975. A Manager, The Royal Instn, 1967–70, 1971–74. Mem., Commonwealth Scholarship Commn, 1975–83. *Publications:* Papers in various scientific periodicals. *Recreations:* music, gardening. *Address:* Priory Barn, Lower Raydon, Ipswich, Suffolk IP7 5QT. *T:* Hadleigh 824033.

WILLIAMSON, Frank Edger, QPM 1966; *b* 24 Feb. 1917; *s* of John and late Mary Williamson; *m* 1943, Margaret Beaumont; one *d. Educ:* Northampton Grammar Sch. Manchester City Police, 1936–61; Chief Constable: Carlisle, 1961–63; Cumbria Constabulary, 1963–67; HM Inspector of Constabulary, 1967–72. OStJ 1967. *Address:* Eagle Cottage, Alderley Park, Nether Alderley, Macclesfield, Cheshire SK10 4TD. *T:* Alderley Edge 583135.

WILLIAMSON, (George) Malcolm; Board Member, Post Office, and Managing Director, Girobank plc, since 1985; *b* 27 Feb. 1939; *s* of George and Margery Williamson; *m* 1963, Pamela; one *s* one *d. Educ:* Bolton School. FIB. Barclays Bank: Local Director, 1980; Asst Gen. Manager, 1981; Regional Gen. Manager, 1983–85. *Recreations:* mountaineering, golf, chess. *Address:* Martyr Worthy Place, Martyr Worthy, Winchester SO21 1AW. *T:* Winchester 78235. *Clubs:* Rucksack, Pedestrian (Manchester).

WILLIAMSON, Prof. James, CBE 1985; FRCPE; Visiting Professor, University of British Columbia, 1986; Professor of Geriatric Medicine, University of Edinburgh, 1976–86, now Emeritus; *b* 22 Nov. 1920; *s* of James Mathewson Williamson and Jessie Reid; *m* 1945, Sheila Mary Blair; three *s* two *d. Educ:* Wishaw High Sch., Lanarkshire; Univ. of Glasgow (MB ChB 1943); FRCPE 1959 (MRCPE 1949). Training in general medicine, incl. two years in general practice, later specialising in respiratory diseases, then in medicine of old age; Consultant Physician, 1954–73; Prof. of Geriatric Medicine in newly established Chair, Univ. of Liverpool, 1973–76. *Publications:* chapters in various textbooks; numerous articles in gen. med. jls and in jls devoted to subject of old age. *Recreations:* walking, reading. *Address:* 14 Ann Street, Edinburgh EH4 1PJ. *T:* 031–332 3568.

WILLIAMSON, Marshal of the Royal Air Force Sir Keith (Alec), GCB 1982 (KCB 1979); AFC 1968; Chief of the Air Staff, 1982–85; Air ADC to the Queen, 1982–85; *b* 25 Feb. 1928; *s* of Percy and Gertrude Williamson; *m* 1953, Patricia Anne, *d* of W/Cdr F. M. N. Watts; two *s* two *d. Educ:* Bancroft's Sch., Woodford Green; Market Harborough Grammar Sch.; RAF Coll., Cranwell. Commissioned, 1950; flew with Royal Australian Air Force in Korea, 1953; OC 23 Sqdn, 1966–68; Command, RAF Gütersloh, 1968–70;

RCDS 1971; Dir, Air Staff Plans, 1972–75; Comdt, RAF Staff Coll., 1975–77; ACOS (Plans and Policy), SHAPE, 1977–78; AOC-in-C, RAF Support Comd, 1978–80; AOC-in-C, RAF Strike Command and C-in-C, UK Air Forces, 1980–82. *Recreation:* golf. *Address:* c/o Midland Bank, 25 Notting Hill Gate, W11. *Club:* Royal Air Force.

WILLIAMSON, Malcolm; *see* Williamson, G. M.

WILLIAMSON, Malcolm Benjamin Graham Christopher, CBE 1976; composer, pianist, organist; Master of the Queen's Music, since 1975; *b* 21 Nov. 1931; *s* of Rev. George Williamson, Sydney, Australia; *m* 1960, Dolores Daniel; one *s* two *d. Educ:* Barker Coll., Hornsby, NSW; Sydney Conservatorium. Composer-in-Residence, Westminster Choir Coll., Princeton, NJ, 1970–71. Pres., Royal Philharmonic Orch., 1977–82. Ramaciotti Medical Research Fellow, Univ. of NSW, 1982–83; Vis. Prof. of Music, Strathclyde Univ., 1983–86. President: Beauchamp Sinfonietta, 1972–; Birmingham Chamber Music Soc., 1975–; Univ. of London Choir, 1976–; Sing for Pleasure, 1977–; British Soc. for Music Therapy, 1977–. Hon. DMus: Westminster Choir Coll., Princeton, NJ, 1970 (Hon. Fellow, 1971); Melbourne, 1982; Sydney, 1982; DUniv Open, 1983. *Compositions include: orchestral:* seven symphonies; Santiago de Espada Overture; Sinfonia Concertante; Sinfonietta; Concerto Grosso; Symphonic Variations; Fiesta; Ochre; Fanfarade; In Thanksgiving Sir Bernard Heinze; Himna Titu; *string orchestra:* Epitaphs for Edith Sitwell; Lament in memory of Lord Mountbatten of Burma; Ode for Queen Elizabeth; Symphony No 7; Lento for Strings; *concertos:* three Piano Concertos; Organ Concerto; Violin Concerto; Concerto for Two Pianos; Harp Concerto; *ballets:* The Display, 1964; Sun into Darkness, 1966; Astarte, 1974; Heritage, 1985; *operas:* Our Man in Havana, 1963; The Violins of Saint-Jacques, 1966; Lucky Peter's Journey, 1969; *chamber operas:* English Eccentrics, 1964; The Happy Prince, 1965; Julius Caesar Jones, 1965; Dunstan and the Devil, 1967; The Growing Castle, 1968; The Red Sea, 1972; *operatic sequence:* The Brilliant and the Dark, 1969; *cassations (mini-operas):* The Moonrakers; Knights in Shining Armour; The Snow Wolf; Genesis; The Stone Wall; The Winter Star; The Glitter Gang; The Terrain of the Kings; The Valley and the Hill; Le Pont du Diable; *vocal:* A Vision of Beasts and Gods; Celebration of Divine Love; Three Shakespeare Songs; Six English Lyrics; From a Child's Garden; Pietà; White Dawns; *symphonic song cycles:* Hammarskjöld Portrait, 1974; Les Olympiques, 1976; Tribute to a Hero, 1981; Next Year in Jerusalem—Poems of Jorge Luis Borges, 1985; *choral:* Symphony for Voices; In Place of Belief; The Death of Cuchulain; Love the Sentinel; The Musicians of Bremen; Canticle of Fire; The World at the Manger; *chorus with orchestra:* Symphony No 3 (The Icy Mirror), 1972; Ode to Music, 1973; Mass of Christ the King, 1977 (to celebrate the Queen's Silver Jubilee); A Pilgrim Liturgy—Cantata, 1984; Songs for a Royal Baby, 1985; *chamber music:* Variations for Cello and Piano; Concerto for Wind Quintet and Two Pianos; Serenade for Flute, Piano and String Trio; Pas de Quatre for Woodwind Quartet and Piano; Piano Quintet; Piano Trio; Champion Family Album; *piano:* two Sonatas; seven books of Travel Diaries; Five Preludes; Sonata for two Pianos; Ritual of Admiration; Himna Titu; *organ:* Fons Amoris; Resurgence du Feu; Symphony for Organ; Vision of Christ-Phoenix; Little Carols of the Saints; Peace Pieces; Mass of a Medieval Saint; The Lion of Suffolk; Mass of the People of God; *church music:* masses, cantatas, anthems, psalms, hymns. *Recreation:* reading. *Address:* Campion Press, Sandon, Buntingford, Herts SG9 0QW.

WILLIAMSON, Dame Marjorie; *see* Williamson, Dame E. M.

WILLIAMSON, Sir Nicholas Frederick Hedworth, 11th Bt, *cr* 1642; *b* 26 Oct. 1937; *s* of late Maj. William Hedworth Williamson (killed in action, 1942) and Diana Mary, *d* of late Brig.-Gen. Hon. Charles Lambton, DSO (she *m* 2nd, 1945, 1st Baron Hailes, PC, GBE, CH); *S* uncle, 1946. *Address:* Abbey Croft, Mortimer, Reading, Berks RG7 3PE. *T:* Mortimer 332324.

WILLIAMSON, Nicol; actor; *b* Hamilton, Scotland, 14 Sept. 1938. Dundee Rep. Theatre, 1960–61; Royal Court: That's Us, Arden of Faversham, 1961; A Midsummer Night's Dream, Twelfth Night, 1962; Royal Shakespeare Company, 1962; Nil Carborundum, The Lower Depths, Women Beware Women; Spring Awakening, Royal Court, 1962; Kelly's Eye, The Ginger Man, Royal Court, 1963; Inadmissible Evidence, 1964, 1978, Royal Court, Wyndham's 1965 (Evening Standard Best Actor Award); NY 1965 (NY Drama Critics Award); A Cuckoo in the Nest, Waiting for Godot, Miniatures, 1964; Sweeney Agonistes, Globe, 1965; Diary of a Madman, Duchess, 1967; Plaza Suite, NY, 1968; Hamlet, Round House, 1969 (Evening Standard Best Actor Award), NY and US tour, 1969; Midwinter Spring, Queen's, 1972; Circle in the Square, Uncle Vanya, NY, 1973; Royal Shakespeare Company, 1973–75: Corialanus, Midwinter Spring, Aldwych, 1973; Twelfth Night, Macbeth, Stratford 1974, Aldwych 1975; dir and title role, Uncle Vanya, Other Place, Stratford, 1974; Rex, NY, 1975; Inadmissible Evidence, NY, 1981; Macbeth, NY, BBC Shakespeare series, 1983; The Entertainer, NY, 1983. *Films:* Inadmissible Evidence, 1967; The Bofors Gun, 1968; Laughter in the Dark, 1968; The Reckoning, 1969; Hamlet, 1970; The Jerusalem File, 1971; The Wilby Conspiracy, 1974; The Seven Per Cent Solution, 1975; The Cheap Detective, The Goodbye Girl, Robin and Marion, 1977; The Human Factor, 1979; Excalibur, Venom, 1980; I'm Dancing as Fast as I Can, 1981. *Television:* The Word, 1977; Lord Mountbatten—the Last Viceroy, 1986. *Address:* c/o ICM, 388–396 Oxford Street, W1.

WILLIAMSON, Nigel; Editor, Tribune, since 1984; *b* 4 July 1954; *s* of Neville Albert and Anne Maureen Williamson; *m* 1976, Magali Patricia Wild; two *s. Educ:* Chislehurst and Sidcup Grammar School; University College London. Journalist, 1982–84, Literary Editor, 1984, Tribune. *Publications:* The SDP (ed), 1982; The New Right, 1984. *Recreations:* opera, cricket, gardening, boating. *Address:* Flat 2, 15 Shortlands Grove, Bromley, Kent. *T:* 01–466 5633. *Club:* Skyliners Cricket.

WILLIAMSON, Peter Roger; HM Diplomatic Service; Counsellor, Kuala Lumpur, since 1985; *b* 20 April 1942; *s* of Frederick W. and Dulcie R. Williamson; *m* 1977, Greta Helen Clare Richards; one *s* one *d. Educ:* Bristol Grammar Sch.; St John's Coll., Oxford (MA). Journalist and teacher, Far East, 1965–66; joined FCO, 1966; Kuala Lumpur, 1970; 1st Sec., FCO, 1973; Hong Kong, 1975; FCO, 1979. *Recreations:* squash, tennis, travel, theatre. *Address:* c/o Foreign and Commonwealth Office, SW1; British High Commission, Jalan Semantan, Wisma Damansara, Kuala Lumpur, Malaysia. *T:* Kuala Lumpur 941533. *Club:* Lake (Kuala Lumpur).

WILLIAMSON, Prof. Robert, FRCPath; Professor of Biochemistry, St. Mary's Hospital Medical School, University of London, since 1976; *b* 14 May 1938; *s* of John and Mae Williamson; *m* 1962, Patricia Anne Sutherland; one *s* one *d. Educ:* Bronx High School of Science, NY; Wandsworth Comprehensive School; University College London (BSc, MSc, PhD). Lectr, Univ. of Glasgow, 1963–67; Sen. Scientist (Molecular Biol.), Beatson Inst. for Cancer Research, Glasgow, 1967–76. Sen. Fellow, Carnegie Instn of Washington, Baltimore, 1972–73. External Examnr, Malaysia, Saudi Arabia. Member: UK Genetic Manipulation Adv. Cttee, 1976–; Grants Cttees, MRC, Cancer Research Campaign, Action Research for Crippled Child, Cystic Fybrosis Research Trust. Hon. MRCP 1986. Wellcome Award, Biochem. Soc., 1983. *Publications:* (ed) Genetic Engineering, vol. 1, 1981, vol. 2, 1982, vol. 3, 1982, vol. 4, 1983; articles in Nature, Cell, Procs of US Nat.

Acad. of Scis, Biochemistry, Nucleic Acids Research. *Recreations:* reading, sport. *Address:* The Old Baths and Washhouse, 71A Flask Walk, NW3. *T:* 01–723 0858.

WILLIAMSON, (Robert) Brian; Chairman, London International Financial Futures Exchange, since 1985; *b* 16 Feb. 1945; *m* 1986, Diane Marie Christine de Jacquier de Rosée. *Educ:* Trinity College, Dublin (MA). Personal Asst to Rt Hon. Maurice Macmillan (later Viscount Macmillan), 1967–71; Editor, International Currency Review, 1971; Man. Dir, Gerrard & National, 1978; Chm., GNI, 1985–. Mem., Securities and Investments Bd, 1986–. Mem. HAC, commissioned 1975. Contested (C) Sheffield Hillsborough, Feb. and Oct. 1974; prosp. parly cand., Truro, 1976–77. *Address:* 5 Whitehead's Grove, SW3. *T:* 01–589 1332. *Clubs:* Carlton; Kildare and University (Dublin).

WILLIAMSON, Rt. Rev. Robert Kerr; *see* Bradford, Bishop of.

WILLIAMSON, Prof. Robin Charles Noel, FRCS; Professor of Surgery, University of Bristol, since 1979; *b* 19 Dec. 1942; *s* of James Charles Frederick Lloyd Williamson and Helena Frances Williamson (*née* Madden); *m* 1967, Judith Marjorie (*née* Bull); three *s. Educ:* Rugby School; Emmanuel College, Cambridge; St Bartholomew's Hosp. Med. Coll. MA, MD, MChir (Cantab). Surgical Registrar, Reading, 1971–73; Sen. Surgical Registrar, Bristol, 1973–75; Res. Fellow, Harvard, 1975–76; Consultant Sen. Lectr, Bristol, 1977–79. Arris and Gale Lectr, RCS, 1977–78; Moynihan Fellow, Assoc. of Surgeons, 1979; Hunterian Prof., RCS, 1981–82; Pres., Pancreatic Soc. of GB and Ireland, 1984–85; Company Sec., British Jl of Surgery Soc., 1983–. Hallett Prize, RCS, 1970; Research Medal, British Soc. of Gastroenterology, 1982. *Publications:* (ed jtly) Colonic Carcinogenesis, 1982; (ed jtly) General Surgical Operations, 2nd edn 1987; numerous papers in surgical and med. jls. *Recreations:* travel, military uniforms and history. *Address:* 18 Woodstock Road, Redland, Bristol BS6 7EJ. *T:* Bristol 424334. *Club:* United Oxford & Cambridge University.

WILLINK, Sir Charles (William), 2nd Bt *cr* 1957; *b* 10 Sept. 1929; *s* of Rt Hon. Sir Henry Urmston Willink, 1st Bt, MC, QC (*d* 1973), and Cynthia Frances (*d* 1959), *d* of H. Morley Fletcher, MD, FRCP; *S* father, 1973; *m* 1954, Elizabeth, *d* of Humfrey Andrewes, Highgate, London; one *s* one *d. Educ:* Eton College (scholar); Trinity College, Cambridge (scholar). MA Cantab. Assistant Master: Marlborough College, 1952–54; Eton College, 1954–85 (Housemaster, 1964–77). *Publications:* (ed) Euripides' Orestes, 1986; articles in Classical Quarterly, 1966, 1968, 1971 and 1983. *Recreations:* bridge, field botany, music (bassoon). *Heir: s* Edward Daniel Willink, *b* 18 Feb. 1957. *Address:* 20 North Grove, Highgate, N6. *T:* 01–340 5129.

WILLIS, family name of **Baron Willis.**

WILLIS, Baron, *cr* 1963, of Chislehurst (Life Peer); **Edward Henry Willis;** FRTS; FRSA; playwright (as Ted Willis); Director: World Wide Pictures, since 1967; Capital Radio Ltd, since 1974; Leisure Technics Ltd, since 1983; Vitalcall Ltd, since 1983; *b* London, 13 Jan. 1918; *m* 1944, Audrey Hale; one *s* one *d. Educ:* Tottenham Central School. *Plays include:* Hot Summer Night, New, 1957; God Bless the Guv'nor, Unity, 1959; Woman in a Dressing Gown, 1962; A Slow Roll of Drums, 1964; Queenie, 1967; Mr Polly, 1977; Doctor on the Boil, 1978; Stardust, 1983; Cat and Mouse, 1985; Old Flames, 1986; *Television scripts:* Dixon of Dock Green Series, 1953–75; Sergeant Cork, 1963–67; Knock on any Door, 1964; Crime of Passion, 1970; Hunter's Walk, 1973; Black Beauty, 1979; Buckingham Palace Connection, 1981; Eine Heim für Tiere (Germany), 1984; *Films include:* Woman in a Dressing Gown, 1958 (Berlin Award); Flame in the Streets (play, Hot Summer Night), 1961; Bitter Harvest, 1963; A Long Way to Shiloh, 1969; Maneater, 1979; The Iron Man, 1983; Mrs Harris MP, 1984; Mrs Harris Goes to New York, 1985; The Left-Handed Sleeper, 1986. President, Writers Guild of GB, 1958–68, 1976–79. Mem., Sports Council, 1971–73. Awards include: Writers' Guild Zita, 1966, 1974; Internat. Writers' Guild Distinguished Writing, 1972; Variety Club of GB for Distinguished Service, 1974; Pye TV for Outstanding Service, 1983; RSA Silver Medal, 1966. *Publications:* Woman in a Dressing Gown and other TV plays, 1959; Whatever Happened to Tom Mix? (autobiography), 1970; *novels* Death May Surprise Us, 1974; The Left-Handed Sleeper, 1975; Man-eater, 1976; The Churchill Commando, 1977; The Buckingham Palace Connection, 1978 (Current Crime Cup); The Lions of Judah, 1979; The Naked Sun, 1980; The Most Beautiful Girl in the World, 1981; Spring at the Winged Horse, 1983; A Problem for Mother Christmas (children's novel), 1986. *Recreations:* tennis, Association football. *Address:* 5 Shepherds Green, Chislehurst, Kent BR7 6PB. *Club:* Garrick.

WILLIS, Charles Reginald; Director, Tiverton Gazette & Associated Papers Ltd, since 1971; Member, Press Council, 1967; *b* 11 June 1906; *s* of Charles and Marie Willis, Tiverton, Devon; *m* 1929, Violet Stubbs; one *d. Educ:* Tiverton Grammar Sch. Tiverton Gazette, 1922–27; North Western Daily Mail, 1927–29; Evening Chronicle, Newcastle upon Tyne, 1929–1935; Evening Chronicle, Manchester, 1935–42; Empire News, London, 1942–43; The Evening News, London, 1943 (Editor, 1954–66); Dir, Associated Newspapers Ltd, 1961–71; Editorial Dir, Harmsworth Publications, 1967–70. *Recreation:* cricket. *Address:* Howden Heyes, Ashley, Tiverton, Devon. *T:* Tiverton 254829. *Club:* Saints and Sinners.

WILLIS, Hon. Sir Eric (Archibald), KBE 1975; CMG 1974; Executive Director, Arthritis Foundation of Australia, since 1984; *b* 15 Jan. 1922; *s* of Archibald Clarence Willis and Vida Mabel Willis (*née* Buttenshaw); *m* 1951, Norma Dorothy Thompson (*née* Knight); two *s* one *d; m* 1982, Lynn Anitra Ward (*née* Roberts). *Educ:* Murwillumbah High Sch., NSW; Univ. of Sydney (BA Hons). MLA (Liberal) for Earlwood, NSW, 1950–78; Dep. Leader, NSW Parly Liberal Party, 1959–75, Leader, 1976–77; Minister for Labour and Industry, Chief Secretary and Minister for Tourism, 1965–71; Chief Sec. and Minister for Tourism and Sport, 1971–72; Minister for Education, 1972–76; Premier and Treasurer, 1976; Leader of the Opposition, NSW Parlt, 1976–77. Exec. Sec., Royal Australian Coll. of Ophthalmologists, 1978–83. *Recreation:* reading. *Address:* 5/94 Kurraba Road, Neutral Bay, NSW 2089, Australia. *T:* (02) 993432.

WILLIS, Rt. Hon. Eustace George, PC 1967; *b* 7 March 1903; *s* of Walter Willis and Rose Jane Eaton; *m* 1929, Mary Swan Ramsay Nisbet; one *d. Educ:* City of Norwich Sch. Engine Room Artificer, Royal Navy, 1919–30. Served Royal Artillery, 1942–45. Political Organiser, 1930–32; Bookseller and Lecturer for NCLC, 1932–64. MP (Lab), North Edinburgh, 1945–50, East Edinburgh, April 1954–70. Member: Select Cttee on Estimates, 1945–50, 1954–59; Central Adv. Cttee to Min. of Pensions, 1945–50; Mineral Development Cttee, 1946–48. Chairman: Edinburgh City Labour Party, 1952–54; Scottish Labour Party, 1954–55; Scottish Parliamentary Labour Party, 1961–63. Parliamentary Deleg. to Atlantic Congress, 1959, NATO, 1960–62. Minister of State, Scottish Office, 1964–67. Gen. Comr, Bd of Inland Revenue, 1972–78; Mem., Scottish Parole Bd, 1975–80. *Recreations:* book-collecting, music. *Address:* 31 Great King Street, Edinburgh EH3 6QR. *T:* 031–556 6941.

WILLIS, Vice-Adm. Sir (Guido) James, KBE 1981; AO 1976; Chief of Naval Staff, Department of Defence, Australia, 1979–82, retired; *b* 18 Oct. 1923; *s* of late Jack Rupert Law Willis and Théa Willis; *m* 1st, 1949; one *s* two *d*; 2nd, 1976, Marjorie J. Rogers.

Educ: Wesley Coll., Melbourne; Royal Australian Naval Coll. Imperial Defence Coll., 1967; Director General Operations and Plans, 1968–71; CO HMAS Melbourne, 1971–72; DDL Project Director, 1972–73; Chief of Naval Personnel, 1973–75; Chief of Naval Material, 1975–76; Asst Chief of Defence Force Staff, 1976–78; Flag Officer Commanding HMA Fleet, 1978–79. Commander 1956, Captain 1962, Rear-Adm. 1973, Vice-Adm. 1979. *Address:* PO Box 45, Tuross Head, NSW 2537, Australia. *T:* (044) 738 335.

WILLIS, Dr Hector Ford, CB 1960; Scientific Adviser, Ministry of Defence, 1962–70, retired; *b* 3 March 1909; *m* 1936, Marie Iddon (*née* Renwick). *Educ:* Howard Gardens High Sch.; University College, Cardiff; Trinity Coll., Cambridge. British Cotton Industry Research Association, 1935–38; Admiralty, 1938; Chief of the Royal Naval Scientific Service, 1954–62. US Medal of Freedom (Silver Palm), 1947. *Publications:* Papers in Proceedings of Royal Society, Philosophical Magazine, Proceedings of the Faraday Society. *Address:* Fulwood, Eaton Park, Cobham, Surrey.

WILLIS, Sir James; *see* Willis, Sir G. J.

WILLIS, His Honour John Brooke; a Circuit Judge (formerly County Court Judge), 1965–80; Barrister-at-Law; *b* 3 July 1906; *yr s* of William Brooke Willis and Maud Mary Willis, Rotherham; *m* 1929, Mary Margaret Coward (marr. diss., 1946); one *s* one *d*; *m* 1964, Terena Ann Steel (formerly Hood); two *d*. *Educ:* Bedford Modern Sch.; Sheffield Univ. Called to the Bar, Middle Temple, 1938, North Eastern Circuit. Served War of 1939–45. RAFVR, 1940–45, Sqdn Leader. Recorder, Rotherham, 1955–59, Huddersfield, 1959–65; Dep. Chm., W Riding of Yorks QS, 1958–71. Chairman, Medical Appeal Tribunal under the National Insurance (Industrial Injuries) Acts, 1953–65. *Address:* 14 Larchwood, Woodlands Drive, Rawdon, Leeds LS19 6JZ.

WILLIS, Maj.-Gen. John Brooker, CB 1981; independent defence and marketing consultant; *b* 28 July 1926; *s* of late William Noel Willis and of Elaine Willis; *m* 1959, Yda Belinda Jane Firbank; two *s* two *d*. *Educ:* privately, until 1941; Redhill Technical Coll. ptsc, jssc. Enlisted in Royal Navy (Fleet Air Arm) as Trainee Pilot; basic training in USA, 1944; returned to UK, transf. to Indian Army, attended Armoured OTS Ahmed Nagar, 1945; commnd 1947, joined 10th Royal Hussars; attended 13 Technical Staff Course, RMCS, 1958–60; Bt Lt-Col 1965, in comd 10th Hussars Aden; GSO1 (Armour) DS RMCS, 1968–69; Col GS MGO Secretariat, MoD, 1969–71; Dep. Comdt, RAC Centre, 1971–74; Sen. Officers' War Course, Greenwich, 1974; Dir, Projects (Fighting Vehicles), 1974–77; Dir Gen., Fighting Vehicles and Engr Equipment, 1977–81, retd. *Recreations:* golf, gardening, aviation, sailing. *Address:* c/o Lloyds Bank, 26 Hammersmith Broadway, W6 7AH. *Club:* Army and Navy.

WILLIS, John Henry, RBA, ARCA (London); artist; *b* Tavistock, 9 Oct. 1887; *s* of R. Willis, art dealer; *m*; one *s*. *Educ:* Armstrong Coll., Durham Univ.; Royal College of Art, South Kensington. Portrait and Landscape Painter. *Principal works:* Kiwi Hut, on the line RA, 1921; 'Twixt Devon and Cornwall, on the line RA, 1923; The Nant Francon Pass, on the line RA, 1924; *portraits:* M. C. Oliver, RA, 1922; Stanley, son of E. J. Miles, RA, 1923. *Address:* 20 Titchfield Gardens, Paignton, Devon. *T:* Paignton 556850.

WILLIS, Sir John (Ramsay), Kt 1966; Judge of the High Court of Justice, Queen's Bench Division, 1966–80; *b* 1908; *s* of Dr and Mrs J. K. Willis, Cranleigh, Surrey; *m*; two *s*. *Educ:* Lancing (Scholar); Trinity Coll., Dublin; BA, LLB (1st cl. Hons). Called to Bar, Gray's Inn, 1932; QC 1956. Royal Signals (TA), 1938–45; served War of 1939–45 (Lt-Col); GSO 1 14th Army. Bencher, Gray's Inn, 1953, Treasurer, 1969. Recorder of Southampton, 1965–66; Dep. Chairman, E Suffolk QS, 1965–71; Mem., Parole Bd, 1974–75. *Recreations:* mountaineering, gardening. *Clubs:* Garrick, Alpine.

WILLIS, John Trueman, DFM 1942; housing consultant; Director: Kingdomwide Housing Trust, since 1982; Unihab Ltd, since 1982; *b* 27 Oct. 1918; *s* of Gordon and Ethel Willis, Headington, Oxford; *m* 1947, Audrey Joan, *d* of Aubrey and Gertrude Gurden, Headington, Oxford; one *s* one *d*. *Educ:* Oxford High Sch., Oxford. Estates Management, Magdalen Coll., Oxford, 1935–36; Industrial Trng, Lockheed Hydraulic Brake Co., Leamington Spa, 1937–38. Served War of 1939–45: Pilot on 14 Sqdn RAF Middle East, 1940–42; PoW Stalag Luft III, Germany, 1943–45. Estates Management, 1946–64, Estates Sec., 1953–65, Magdalen Coll., Oxford; Rent Officer for Oxford, 1965–67; Sec. Housing Societies Charitable Trust, 1968–69; Director: Shelter, 1971–72 (Housing Dir, 1969–70); Liverpool Housing Trust, 1973–75; Castle Rock Housing Assoc., 1976–78. Mem., NEDO Housing Strategy Cttee, 1975–78. Vice-Chm., Housing Assocs Charitable Trust, 1980–. Promoted housing conf., Planning for Home Work, 1984. ICSA. *Publication:* Housing and Poverty Report, 1970. *Recreations:* diminishing. *Address:* 15 Manor Road, Hoylake, Wirral, Merseyside L47 3DE. *T:* 051-632 3873.

WILLIS, Joseph Robert McKenzie, CB 1952; CMG 1946; Deputy Chairman, Board of Inland Revenue, 1957–71; *b* 18 March 1909; 2nd *s* of Charles Frederick Willis and Lucy Alice McKenzie; *m* 1945, Elizabeth Browning, *er d* of James Ewing; one *s* one *d*. *Educ:* Eton; Christ Church, Oxford. Entered Inland Revenue Dept, 1932; Under Secretary, Central Economic Planning Staff, Treasury, 1948–49; Commissioner of Inland Revenue, 1949; Student of Imperial Defence Coll., 1948. Professorial Res. Fellow and Vis. Prof., Bath Univ., 1972–79. Specialist advr to Select Cttee on Wealth Tax, 1975. *Publications:* (with C. T. Sandford and D. J. Ironside): An Accessions Tax, 1973; An Annual Wealth Tax, 1975; (with P. J. W. Hardwick) Tax Expenditures in the United Kingdom, 1978. *Address:* Bunbury, Lower Shiplake, Henley-on-Thames, Oxon. *T:* Wargrave 2726.

WILLIS, Rear-Adm. Kenneth Henry George, CB 1981; Director General, Home Farm Trust Ltd, Bristol, since 1982; *m*; three *d*. *Educ:* Royal Naval Engineering Coll.; Royal Naval Coll.; Jesus Coll., Cambridge (BA 1949). Joined RN 1944; served at sea and in shore weapons depts; Resident Officer, Polaris Executive, Clyde Submarine Base, 1965–68; i/c training, HMS Collingwood, 1969–70; Asst Dir, Underwater Weapon Dept, 1970; sowc 1974; Dep. Dir, RN Staff Coll., Greenwich, 1975–76, Dir, 1976; CO HMS Collingwood, 1976–79; C of S to C-in-C, Naval Home Command, 1979–81, retired. FRSA. *Address:* c/o Barclays Bank, 1 Manvers Street, Bath, Avon.

WILLIS, Norman David; General Secretary, Trades Union Congress, since 1984; *b* 21 Jan. 1933; *s* of Victor J. M. and Kate E. Willis; *m* 1963, Maureen Kenning; one *s* one *d*. *Educ:* Ashford County Grammar Sch.; Ruskin and Oriel Colls, Oxford, 1955–59 (Hon. Fellow, Oriel Coll., 1984). Employed by TGWU, 1949; Nat. Service, 1951–53; PA to Gen. Sec., TGWU, 1959–70; Nat. Sec., Research and Educn, TGWU, 1970–74; TUC: Asst Gen. Sec., 1974–77, Dep. Gen. Sec., 1977–84. Councillor (Lab) Staines UDC, 1971–74. Member: NEDC, 1984–; Council, ODI, 1985–; Council, Motability, 1985–; Chm., Nat. Pensioners' Convention Steering Cttee, 1979–; Vice-President: IMS, 1985–; ETUC, 1984–; ICFTU, 1984–; WEA, 1985–; Trustee, Anglo-German Foundn for the Study of Industrial Soc., 1986–. *Recreations:* painting, poetry, natural history, architecture, canals. *Address:* TUC, Congress House, Great Russell Street, WC1B 3LS.

WILLIS, Lady; Olive Christine, CBE 1951; *b* 20 Nov. 1895; *d* of late Henry Edward Millar, Hampstead; *m* 1916, Lieut Algernon Usborne Willis (Admiral of the Fleet Sir Algernon U. Willis, GCB, KBE, DSO) (*d* 1976); two *d*. *Educ:* St Felix Sch., Southwold, Suffolk; Newnham Coll., Cambridge. Organised new Royal Naval Wives Voluntary Service, whereby older wives helped younger ones cope with separations of service life, 1946–50; started Under 5 Club, Valetta, Malta, 1946. Officer (Sister) Order of St John of Jerusalem, 1948. *Recreations:* appreciating gardens, reading, knitting. *Address:* c/o Lady Macdonald, Spinners Ash, Tilmore, Petersfield, Hants GU32 2JH.

WILLIS, Robert William Gaspard, MA; Founder and Headmaster of Copford Glebe School, 1958–69, Principal, 1969–72; *b* 22 Nov. 1905; *s* of Rev. W. N. Willis, founder and Headmaster for 38 years of Ascham St Vincent's, Eastbourne, and Sophia Caroline Baker; *m* 1930, Ernestine Ruth Kimber; two *s* two *d*. *Educ:* Ascham St Vincent's, Eastbourne; Eton Coll. (Foundation Scholar); Corpus Christi Coll., Cambridge (Scholar). Assistant Master at Malvern Coll., Worcs, 1927–39 (Mathematics and Classics); Senior Mathematical Master at The King's School, Macclesfield, Cheshire, 1939–41; Headmaster of Sir William Turner's School (Coatham School), Redcar, 1941–53; Headmaster of English High School for Boys, Istanbul, Turkey, 1953–57. Hon. Fellow, Huguenot Soc. of London. Hon. Life Mem., Gainsborough's House Soc., Sudbury. *Recreation:* golf. *Address:* 8 Links View, Newton Green, Sudbury, Suffolk. *T:* Sudbury 72522. *Clubs:* Royal Over-Seas League; Newton Green Golf.

WILLIS, His Honour Roger Blenkiron, TD; a Circuit Judge (formerly County Court Judge), 1959–81; *b* 22 June 1906; *s* of late William Outhwaite Willis, KC, and Margaret Alice (*née* Blenkiron); *m* 1933, Joan Eleanor Amy Good; two *d*. *Educ:* Charterhouse School; Emmanuel Coll., Cambridge. Barrister, Inner Temple, Nov. 1930. Joined Middlesex Yeomanry (TA), 1938. Served War of 1939–45. *Recreation:* golf. *Address:* 18 Turners Reach House, 9 Chelsea Embankment, SW3. *Clubs:* Garrick, MCC.

WILLIS, Stephen Murrell; His Honour Judge Willis; a Circuit Judge, since 1986; *b* 21 June 1929; *s* of late John Henry Willis and late Eileen Marian (*née* Heard), Hadleigh, Suffolk; *m* 1st, 1953, Jean Irene Eve; one *s* three *d*; 2nd, 1975, Doris Florence Davies (*née* Redding); two step *d*. *Educ:* (chorister) Christ Church Cathedral, Oxford; Bloxham Sch. (scholar). Admitted solicitor, 1955; Partner: Chamberlin Talbot & Bracey, Lowestoft and Beccles, Suffolk, 1955–63; Pearless, de Rougemont & Co., East Grinstead, Sussex, 1964–86; a Recorder, 1980–86. Founded The Suffolk Singers, 1960; Founder and Director, The Prodigal Singers and Gallery Band, 1964–. *Compositions:* mediaeval song settings for radio and theatre plays. *Recording:* (with The Prodigal Singers) Christmas Tree Carols. *Recreations:* performing early music, sailing, travel. *Address:* 8 Church Lane, East Grinstead, West Sussex RH19 3BA. *T:* East Grinstead 23687. *Clubs:* Noblemen and Gentlemen's Catch, Law Society, Law Society Yacht.

WILLIS, Ted; *see* Willis, Baron.

WILLISON, Lt-Gen. Sir David (John), KCB 1973; OBE 1958; MC 1945; Chief Royal Engineer, 1977–82; Consultant, County Bank, since 1985; President, Western Area, Hampshire, St John's Ambulance, 1987; *b* 25 Dec. 1919; *s* of Brig. A. C. Willison, DSO, MC; *m* 1941, Betty Vernon Bates; one *s* two *d*. *Educ:* Wellington; RMA Woolwich. 2/Lt RE, 1939; OC 17 and 246 Field Cos, 1944–45; Staff Coll., Camberley 1945; Brigade Major, Indian Inf. Brigade, Java, 1946; Malaya, 1947; WO, 1948–50; OC 16 Field Co., Egypt, 1950–52; GHQ MELF, 1952–53; OC, RE Troops, Berlin, 1953–55; Directing Staff, Staff Coll., Camberley, 1955–58; AQMG (Ops), HQ British Forces Aden, 1958–60; CO, 38 Engr Regt, 1960–63; Col GS MI/DI4, MoD, 1963–66; idc 1966; BGS (Intell.), MoD, 1967–70; BGS (Intell. and Security)/ACOS, G2, HQ NORTHAG, 1970–71; Dir of Service Intelligence, MoD, 1971–72; Dep. Chief Defence Staff (Int.), 1972–75; Dir Gen. of Intelligence, MoD, 1975–78. Col Comdt RE, 1973–82. Consultant on Internat. Affairs, Nat. Westminster Bank Gp, 1980–84. Freeman, City of London, 1981. *Recreations:* sailing, shooting. *Address:* Long Barton, Lower Pennington Lane, Lymington, Hampshire. *Clubs:* Naval and Military; Royal Lymington Yacht.

WILLISON, Sir John (Alexander), Kt 1970; OBE 1964; QPM 1968; DL; *b* 3 Jan. 1914; *s* of John Willison Gow Willison and Mabel Willison, Dalry, Ayrshire; *m* 1947, Jess Morris Bruce. *Educ:* Sedbergh School. Joined City of London Police, 1933; served with RNVR, 1943–46; Chief Constable: Berwick, Roxburgh and Selkirk, 1952–58; Worcestershire Constabulary, 1958–67; West Mercia Constabulary, 1967–74. DL Worcs 1968. KStJ 1973. *Address:* Ravenhills Green, Lulsley, near Worcester.

WILLMAN, John; General Secretary, Fabian Society, since 1985; *b* 27 May 1949; *s* of John Willman and Kate Willman (*née* Thornton); *m* 1978, Margaret Shanahan; one *s* one *d*. *Educ:* Bolton Sch.; Jesus Coll., Cambridge (BA); Westminster Coll., Oxford (CertEd). Teacher, Brentford Sch. for Girls, Brentford, Mddx, 1972–76; Financial Researcher, Money Which?, 1976–79; Editor, Taxes and Assessment (Inland Revenue Staff Fedn pubn), 1979–83; Pubns Manager, Peat, Marwick, Mitchell & Co., 1983–85. *Publications:* contributor to books on finance, economics and taxation; numerous articles. *Address:* (office) 11 Dartmouth Street, SW1H 9BN. *T:* 01–222 8877.

WILLMER, Prof. (Edward) Nevill, ScD; FRS 1960; Emeritus Professor of Histology, University of Cambridge, since 1969; Fellow of Clare College since 1936; *b* 15 Aug. 1902; 5th *s* of Arthur W. Willmer, Birkenhead; *m* 1939, Henrietta Noreen (Penny), 2nd *d* of H. Napier Rowlatt; two *s* two *d*. *Educ:* Birkenhead Sch.; Corpus Christi Coll., Oxford (Hon. Fellow, 1983). BA (Oxon) 1924; MA (Oxon) 1965; MSc (Manchester) 1927; ScD (Cambridge) 1944. Demonstrator and Assistant Lecturer in Physiology, Manchester, 1924–29; Lecturer in Histology, Cambridge, 1930–48; Reader, 1948–65, Prof., 1966–69. Editor, Biological Reviews, 1969–80. *Publications:* Tissue Culture, 1934; Retinal Structure and Colour Vision, 1946; Cytology and Evolution, 1960, 2nd edn 1970; (ed) Cells and Tissues in Culture, 1965; Old Grantchester, 1976; The River Cam, 1979; contrib. physiological and biological journals. *Recreations:* painting, gardening, walking. *Address:* Yew Garth, Grantchester, Cambridge. *T:* Cambridge 840360.

See also B. J. Davenport.

WILLMER, John Franklin, QC 1967; *b* 30 May 1930; *s* of Rt Hon. Sir (Henry) Gordon Willmer, OBE, TD and of Barbara, *d* of Sir Archibald Hurd; *m* 1st, 1958, Nicola Ann Dickinson (marr. diss. 1979); one *s* three *d*; 2nd, 1979, Margaret Lilian, *d* of Chester B. Berryman. *Educ:* Winchester; Corpus Christi Coll., Oxford. National Service, 2nd Lieut, Cheshire Regt, 1949–50; TA Cheshire Regt, 1950–51; Middlesex Regt, 1951–57 (Captain). Called to Bar, Inner Temple, 1955, Bencher, 1975. A Gen. Comr of Income Tax for Inner Temple, 1982. Member: panel of Lloyd's Arbitrators in Salvage Cases, 1967; panel from which Wreck Commissioners appointed, 1967–79. *Recreation:* walking. *Address:* Flat 4, 23 Lymington Road, NW6 1HZ. *T:* 01–435 9245. *Club:* United Oxford & Cambridge University.

WILLMER, Nevill; *see* Willmer, E. N.

WILLMOTT, Dennis James, QFSM 1981; Chief Fire Officer, Merseyside Fire Brigade, since 1983; *b* 10 July 1932; *s* of James Arthur Willmott and Esther Winifred Maude Willmott (*née* Styles); *m* 1958, Mary Patricia Currey; three *s*. *Educ:* St Albans County Grammar School. MIFireE. Regular Army Service, East Surrey Regt, 1950–51, Royal Norfolk Regt, 1951–57. London, Bucks, Hants and Isle of Wight Fire Brigades, 1957–74;

Dep. Chief Officer, Wilts Fire Brigade, 1974–76; Chief Staff Officer, 1976–81, Dep. Chief Officer, 1981–83, London Fire Brigade. *Recreation:* walking. *Address:* 7 Northwood Road, Prenton, Birkenhead, Merseyside L43 0SN. *T:* 051–608 2693; 27 Highlands, Potterne, Devizes, Wilts SN10 5NS. *T:* Devizes 5672. *Clubs:* Lyceum (Liverpool); Royal British Legion (Higher Bebington).

WILLMOTT, Maj.-Gen. Edward George, OBE 1979; President, Ordnance Board, since 1986; *b* 18 Feb. 1936; *s* of late T. E. Willmott and E. R. Willmott (*née* Murphy); *m* 1960, Sally Penelope (*née* Banyard); two *s* one *d*. *Educ:* Gonville and Caius Coll., Cambridge (MA). Commissioned RE 1956; psc 1968; active service, N Borneo 1963, N Ireland 1971, 1972, 1977; comd 8 Field Sqdn, 1971–73; 23 Engr Regt, 1976; 2 Armd Div. Engr Regt, 1977–78; 30 Engr Bde, 1981–82; RCDS 1983; Dep. Comdt RMCS, 1984–85; Vice-Pres. (Army), Ordnance Bd, 1985–86. *Recreations:* sailing, ski-ing, gardening. *Address:* c/o Lloyds Bank plc, 125 Colmore Row, Birmingham. *Club:* Institute of Directors.

WILLMOTT, Prof. John Charles, CBE 1983; PhD; Professor of Physics since 1964, and Director of the Physical Laboratories since 1967, Manchester University (a Pro-Vice-Chancellor, 1982–85); *b* 1 April 1922; *s* of Arthur George Willmott and Annie Elizabeth Willmott; *m* 1952, Sheila Madeleine Dumbell; two *s* one *d*. *Educ:* Bancroft's Sch., Woodford; Imperial Coll. of Science and Technol. (BSc, PhD). ARCS. Lectr in Physics, Liverpool Univ., 1948–58, Sen. Lectr, 1958–63. Mem., SERC (formerly SRC), 1978–83. *Publications:* Tables of Coefficients for the Analysis of Triple Angular Correlations of Gamma-rays from Aligned Nuclei, 1968; Atomic Physics, 1975; articles on nuclear structure in learned jls. *Address:* 37 Hall Moss Lane, Bramhall, Cheshire SK7 1RB. *T:* 061–439 4169.

WILLMOTT, Peter; Senior Fellow, Policy Studies Institute, since 1983; Visiting Professor of Social Policy and Administration, London School of Economics, since 1983; Hon. Research Fellow, Bartlett School of Architecture and Planning, University College London, since 1983; *b* 18 Sept. 1923; *s* of Benjamin Merriman Willmott and Dorothy Willmott (*née* Waymouth); *m* 1948, Phyllis Mary Noble; two *s*. *Educ:* Tollington Sch., London; Ruskin Coll., Oxford. BSc (Soc) (external) London. Research Asst, Labour Party, 1948–54; Institute of Community Studies: Res. Officer, 1954–60; Dep. Dir, 1960–64; Co-Dir, 1964–78; Chm., 1978–. Dir, Centre for Environmental Studies, 1978–80; Head of Central Policy Unit, GLC, 1981–83; Vis. Prof., Bartlett Sch. of Architecture and Planning, UCL, 1972–83. Vis. Prof., Ecole Pratique des Hautes Etudes, Univ. of Paris, 1972; Regents' Lectr, Univ. of California, 1982. *Publications:* (with Michael Young) Family and Kinship in East London, 1957; (with Michael Young) Family and Class in a London Suburb, 1960; The Evolution of a Community, 1963; Adolescent Boys of East London, 1966; (with Michael Young) The Symmetrical Family, 1973; (ed) Sharing Inflation? Poverty Report, 1976; (with Graeme Shankland and David Jordan) Inner London: policies for dispersal and balance, 1977; (with Charles Madge) Inner City Poverty in Paris and London, 1981; (with Roger Mitton and Phyllis Willmott) Unemployment, Poverty and Social Policy in Europe, 1983; Community in Social Policy, 1984; Social Networks, Informal Care and Public Policy, 1986. *Address:* 27 Kingsley Place, N6 5EA. *T:* 01–348 3958.

WILLOCHRA, Bishop of, since 1970; **Rt. Rev. Stanley Bruce Rosier;** *b* 18 Nov. 1928; *s* of S. C. and A. Rosier; *m* 1954, Faith Margaret Alice Norwood; one *s* three *d*. *Educ:* Univ. of WA; Christ Church, Oxford. Asst Curate, Ecclesall, Dio. of Sheffield, 1954; Rector of: Wyalkatchem, Dio. of Perth, 1957; Kellerberrin, Dio. of Perth, 1964; Auxiliary Bishop in Diocese of Perth, Western Australia, 1967–70. *Recreation:* natural history. *Address:* Bishop's House, PO Box 96, Gladstone, SA 5473, Australia. *T:* (office) 086–62249; (home) 086–622057.

WILLOTT, Brian; *see* Willott, W. B.

WILLOTT, Lt-Col Roland Lancaster, DSO 1940; OBE 1945; TD 1946; BSc; CEng, FIMechE; *b* 1 May 1912; *s* of Frederick John Willott and Gertrude May Leese; *m* 1960, Elisabeth Petersen. *Educ:* Wellington Sch. (Somerset); University of Wales. College Apprentice Metropolitan Vickers Electrical Co., Trafford Park, Manchester, 1931–33; Mechanical Engineer Metropolitan Vickers Co., 1933–36; Major RE 1939–41; Lt-Col CRE 1941–45; Colonel Commander Army Group RE, 1945 (despatches, DSO, OBE, Order of Leopold of Belgium, Croix de Guerre). Chief Engineer, John Summers & Sons Ltd, 1945–69, Dir, 1965–71; Group Chief Engineer, Shotton Works, BSC, 1969–72. *Address:* 5 Curzon Park South, Chester CH4 8AA. *T:* Chester 674049. *Club:* Army and Navy.

WILLOTT, (William) Brian, PhD; Head of Information Technology Division, Department of Trade and Industry, since 1984; *b* 14 May 1940; *s* of Dr William Harford Willott and Dr Beryl P. M. Willott; *m* 1970, Alison Leyland Pyke-Lees; two *s* two *d*. *Educ:* Trinity Coll., Cambridge (MA, PhD). Research Associate, Univ. of Maryland, USA, 1965–67; Asst Principal, Board of Trade, 1967–69; Principal: BoT, 1969–73; HM Treasury, 1973–75; Asst Sec., Dept of Industry, 1975–78; Secretary: Industrial Development Unit, DoI, 1978–80; NEB, 1980–81; Chief Exec., British Technology Gp (NEB and NRDC), 1981–84. *Recreations:* music, reading, ancient history, gardening. *Address:* Pembroke House, 11 Spencer Hill, Wimbledon, SW19 4PA. *T:* 01–946 1263. *Club:* Royal Automobile.

WILLOUGHBY, family name of **Baron Middleton.**

WILLOUGHBY DE BROKE, 21st Baron *cr* 1491; **Leopold David Verney;** *b* 14 Sept. 1938; *s* of 20th Baron Willoughby de Broke, MC, AFC, AE and of Rachel, *d* of Sir Bourchier Wrey, 11th Bt; *S* father, 1986; *m* 1965, Petra, 2nd *d* of Sir John Aird, 3rd Bt, MVO, MC; three *s*. *Educ:* Le Rosey; New College, Oxford. *Heir:* *s* Hon. Rupert Greville Verney, *b* 4 March 1966. *Address:* Ditchford Farm, Moreton-in-Marsh, Glos.

WILLOUGHBY DE ERESBY, Baroness (27th in line), *cr* 1313; **Nancy Jane Marie Heathcote-Drummond-Willoughby;** *b* 1 Dec. 1934; *d* of 3rd Earl of Ancaster, KCVO, TD, and Hon. Nancy Phyllis Louise Astor (*d* 1975), *d* of 2nd Viscount Astor; *S* to barony of father, 1983. *Heir:* *co-heiresses:* Lady Catherine Mary Clementina Hume [*b* 25 Sept. 1906; *m* 1st, 1935, John St Maur Ramsden (marr. diss. 1947), *s* of Sir John Frecheville Ramsden 6th Bt; one *d*; 2nd, 1948, Charles Wedderburn Hume (*d* 1974)]; Lady Priscilla Aird [*b* 29 Oct. 1909; *m* 1939, Col Sir John Renton Aird, 3rd Bt, MVO, MC; one *s* three *d*]. *Address:* Grimsthorpe, Bourne, Lincs. *T:* Edenham 222.

WILLOUGHBY, Ven. David Albert; Archdeacon of the Isle of Man, since 1982; Vicar of St George's with All Saints, Douglas, since 1980; *b* 8 Feb. 1931; *s* of John Robert and Jane May Willoughby; *m* 1959, Brenda Mary (*née* Watson); two *s*. *Educ:* Bradford Grammar School; St John's Coll., Univ. of Durham (BA, Dip. Theol.). Assistant Curate: St Peter's, Shipley, 1957–60; Barnoldswick with Bracewell, 1960–62; Rector of St Chad's, New Moston, Manchester, 1962–72; Vicar of Marown, Isle of Man, 1972–80; Rural Dean of Douglas, 1980–82. Chaplain, Noble's Hospital, Douglas, 1980–; Mem. Gen. Synod, 1982–; Church Commissioner for IOM, 1982–. *Recreations:* motor cycling, competition singing and involvement in light entertainment. *Address:* St George's with All Saints Vicarage, 16 Devonshire Road, Douglas, Isle of Man. *T:* Douglas 5430. *Club:* Victory Services.

WILLOUGHBY, Rear-Admiral Guy; CB 1955; *b* 7 Nov. 1902; *s* of Rev. Nesbit E. Willoughby, Vicar of Bickington, Devon, and of Marjorie Helen Willoughby (*née* Kaye); *m* 1923, Mary, *d* of J. G. W. Aldridge, AMICE, Wimbledon; one *s* one *d*. *Educ:* Osborne and Dartmouth. Joined Osborne, 1916; Sub-Lieut, 1923; qualified as a naval pilot 1925, and thereafter flew as a pilot in Naval and RAF Squadrons, embarked in various Carriers until 1936; Commander, 1937; Commander (Air) in Glorious, 1938–39; served on naval staff, Admiralty, 1940–41; comd HM Carrier Activity, 1942–43; Captain, 1943; Chief Staff Officer to Admiral Comdg Carriers in Eastern Fleet, 1944; Director of Air Warfare and Training (Naval Staff, Admiralty), 1945–46; Imperial Defence Coll., 1947; 4th Naval Member of Australian Commonwealth Navy Board and Cdre (Air), 1948–50; comd HM Carrier Eagle, 1951–52; Rear-Admiral 1953; Flag Officer, Flying Training, 1953–56, retired, 1956. *Address:* High Croft, South Woodchester, near Stroud, Glos. *T:* Amberley 2594. *Club:* Naval and Military.

WILLOUGHBY, Maj.-Gen. Sir John (Edward Francis), KBE 1967 (CBE 1963; OBE 1953); CB 1966; *b* 18 June 1913; *s* of Major N. E. G. Willoughby, The Middlesex Regt, and Mrs B. A. M. Willoughby, Heytesbury, Wiltshire; *m* 1938, Muriel Alexandra Rosamund Scott; three *d*. Commissioned, Middlesex Regt, 1933. Served War of 1939–45 with Middlesex Regt, BEF, 1940–41; OC 2 Middlesex Regt, 1943; GSO 1 220 Military Mission, USA, Pacific, Burma and UK, 1943–44; OC 1 Dorsets Regt, NW Europe, 1944; served with Middlesex Regt, FARELF, Korea, 1950–51; GSO1, 3 Inf. Div., UK and MELF, 1951–53; OC 1 Middlesex Regt, British Troops Austria, UK and MELF, 1954–56; Colonel, The Middlesex Regt, 1959–65; Chief of Staff, Land Forces, Hong Kong, 1961; GOC, 48 Inf. Div. (TA) and W Midland District, 1963–65; GOC Land Forces ME Comd, Inspector-Gen. of Federal Regular Army of S Arabia and Security Comdr Aden State, 1965–67; Adviser on Defence to Fedn of Arab Emirates, 1968–71.

WILLOUGHBY, Kenneth James; *b* 6 Nov. 1922; *y s* of late Frank Albert Willoughby and late Florence Rose (*née* Darbyshire); *m* 1943, Vera May Dickerson; one *s* one *d*. *Educ:* Hackney Downs (Grocers') Sch.; Selwyn Coll., Cambridge. Tax Officer, Inland Revenue, 1939; Royal Engineers, UK, Egypt, Italy, Austria, Greece, 1941–47 (despatches, Captain); Asst Auditor, Exchequer and Audit Dept, 1947; Asst Prin., Min. of Civil Aviation, 1949; Asst Private Sec. to Minister of Civil Aviation, 1950; Private Sec. to Perm. Sec., 1951; Principal, Min. of Transport (and later, Civil Aviation), 1951; Sec., Air Transport Adv. Council, 1957–61; Asst Sec., Min. of Aviation, 1962; Under-Secretary: Min. of Technology, 1968–70; DTI, 1970–74. *Recreations:* gardening, music, reading. *Address:* 84 Douglas Avenue, Exmouth, Devon EX8 2HG. *T:* Exmouth 271175.

WILLOUGHBY, Rt. Rev. Noel Vincent; *see* Cashel and Ossory, Bishop of.

WILLS, family name of **Baron Dulverton.**

WILLS, Arthur William, DMus (Dunelm), FRCO (CHM), ADCM; composer; Organist, Ely Cathedral, since 1958; *b* 19 Sept. 1926; *s* of Violet Elizabeth and Archibald Wills; *m* 1953, Mary Elizabeth Titterton; one *s* one *d*. *Educ:* St John's Sch., Coventry. Sub. Organist, Ely Cathedral, 1949; Director of Music, King's School, Ely, 1953–65; Prof., Royal Academy of Music, 1964. Mem. Council, RCO, 1966–; Examr to Royal Schs of Music, 1966–. Recital tours in Canada, Europe, USA, Australia and New Zealand; recording artist. Hon. RAM, Hon. FLCM, FRSCM. *Publications:* (contrib.) English Church Music, 1978; Organ, 1984; numerous musical compositions include: *organ:* Sonata, Trio Sonata, Christmas Meditations, Prelude and Fugue (Alkmaar), Tongues of Fire, Variations on Amazing Grace, Symphonia Eliensis, Concerto (organ, strings and timpani), The Fenlands (symphonic suite for brass band and organ), Etheldreda Rag (organ or piano); *brass band:* Overture: A Muse of Fire; *guitar:* Sonata, Pavane and Galliard, Hommage à Ravel, Four Elizabethan Love Songs (alto and guitar), Moods and Diversions, The Year of the Tiger, Suite Africana; *choral:* Missa Eliensis, The Child for Today (carol sequence), The Light Invisible (double choir, organ and percussion), Missa in Memoriam Benjamin Britten, An English Requiem, Jerusalem Luminosa (choir and organ), Ely (part-song for treble voices), Caedmon: a children's cantata; *vocal:* When the Spirit Comes (four poems of Emily Brontë), The Dark Lady (eight Shakespeare Sonnets). *Recreations:* travel, antique collecting, Eastern philosophy. *Address:* The Old Sacristy, The College, Ely, Cambs. *T:* Ely 2084. *Club:* Savage.

WILLS, Brian Alan, PhD; FPS, CChem, FRSC; Chief Pharmacist, Department of Health and Social Security, since 1978; *b* 17 Feb. 1927; *s* of late William Wills and Emily (*née* Hibbert); *m* 1955, Barbara Joan Oggelsby; one *d*. *Educ:* Univ. of Nottingham (BPharm); PhD (London). FPS 1972 (MPS 1949); FRSC (FRIC 1967, ARIC 1957); CChem 1975. Lecturer in Pharmaceutics, Sch. of Pharmacy, Univ. of London, 1951–57; Head of Research and Control Dept, Allen & Hanburys (Africa) Ltd, Durban, S Africa, 1957–62; Head of Control Div., Allen & Hanburys Ltd, London, E2, 1962–78. Member: British Pharmacopoeia Commn, 1973–; UK delegn to European Pharmacopoeia Commn, 1975–; UK delegn to Council of Europe Public Health Cttee (Partial Agreement) on Pharmaceutical Questions, 1979–; WHO Expert Adv. Panel on Internat. Pharmacopoeia and Pharmaceutical Preparations, 1979–. Vis. Professor: Univ. of Bath, 1979–83; Univ. of Bradford, 1984–. Member: Jt Formulary Cttee for British Nat. Formulary, 1979–; Pharmacy Working Party, Nat. Adv. Body for Local Authy Higher Educn, 1982–; Bd of Studies in Pharmacy, London Univ., 1979–; Council, Sch. of Pharmacy, London Univ., 1981–. *Publications:* papers on sterilisation and disinfection and on the preservation, stability and quality control of pharmaceutical preparations. *Address:* 8 Graces Maltings, Akeman Street, Tring, Herts HP23 6DL. *T:* Tring 4217.

WILLS, Sir David; *see* Wills, Sir H. D. H.

WILLS, Sir (David) Seton, 5th Bt *cr* 1904, of Hazelwood and Clapton-in-Gordano; FRICS; *b* 29 Dec. 1939; *s* of Major George Seton Wills (*d* 1979) (*yr s* of 3rd Bt) and Lilah Mary, *y d* of Captain Percy Richard Hare; *S* uncle, 1983; *m* 1968, Gillian, twin *d* of A. P. Eastoe; one *s* three *d*. *Educ:* Eton. *Heir:* *s* James Seton Wills, *b* 24 Nov. 1970. *Address:* Eastridge House, Ramsbury, Marlborough, Wilts SN8 2HJ.

WILLS, Helen; *see* Roark, H. W.

WILLS, Sir (Hugh) David (Hamilton), Kt 1980; CBE 1971 (MBE 1946); TD 1964; DL; *b* 19 June 1917; 2nd *s* of late Frederick Noel Hamilton Wills and of Margery Hamilton Sinclair; *m* 1949, Eva Helen, JP, *d* of late Major A. T. McMorrough Kavanagh, MC; one *s* one *d*. *Educ:* Eton; Magdalen Coll., Oxford. Served War of 1939–45 with Queen's Own Cameron Highlanders (TA): France 1940, Aruba 1941; GSO 3 (Ops) GHQ Home Forces, 1942–43; GSO 2 (Ops) Southern Command, 1943–44. Chairman of Trustees, Rendcomb Coll., 1955–83; Chm., Ditchley Foundation, 1972–83; Mem. Governing Body, Atlantic Coll., 1963–73, 1980–. High Sheriff Oxfordshire 1961, DL 1967. *Recreations:* fishing, sailing. *Address:* Sandford Park, Sandford St Martin, Oxford OX5 4AJ. *T:* Great Tew 238. *Clubs:* Boodle's, Ends of the Earth.

WILLS, Sir John Spencer; Kt 1969; FCIT; Chairman, British Electric Traction Co. Ltd, 1966–82 (Director, 1939–82, Managing Director, 1946–73, Deputy Chairman, 1951–66); Director and Chairman: National Electric Construction Co. Ltd, since 1945; Birmingham and District Investment Trust Ltd, since 1946; Electrical & Industrial Investment Co. Ltd, since 1946; *b* 10 Aug. 1904; *s* of Cedric Spencer Wills and Cécile Charlotte; *m* 1936, Elizabeth Drusilla Alice Clare Garcke; two *s*. *Educ:* Cleobury Mortimer Coll., Shropshire; Merchant Taylors' Sch., London. Asst to Secs, British Traction Co. Ltd and British Automobile Traction Ltd, 1922–23; Sec., Wrexham and Dist Transport Co. Ltd, 1924–26; Gen. Manager, E Yorks Motor Services Ltd, 1926–31, Dir and Chm., 1931–65; Chm., Birmingham & Midland Motor Omnibus Co. Ltd, 1946–68; Dir, 1947–73, Dep. Chm., 1953–71, Monotype Corp. Ltd; Man. Dir, 1947–67, Chm., 1947–78, Broadcast Relay Service Ltd, later Rediffusion Ltd; Chm., Associated-Rediffusion Ltd, later Rediffusion Television Ltd, 1954–78; Director and Chairman: E Midland Motor Services Ltd, 1931–44; Yorks Woollen Dist Transport Co. Ltd, 1931–43; Hebble Motor Services Ltd, 1932–45; Yorks Traction Co. Ltd, 1932–46; Mexborough & Swinton Traction Co. Ltd, 1933–47; Western Welsh Omnibus Co. Ltd, 1933–60; Crosville Motor Services Ltd, 1933–41; Ribble Motor Services Ltd, 1942–47; N Western Road Car Co. Ltd, 1943–45; S Wales Transport Co. Ltd, Swansea Improvements & Tramways Co. Ltd, 1943–46; Devon Gen. Omnibus and Touring Co. Ltd, 1946–47; Man. Dir, British and Foreign Aviation Ltd and Great Western and Southern Air Lines Ltd, 1938–42; Director: Olley Air Service Ltd, Channel Air Ferries Ltd, West Coast Air Services Ltd, Air Booking Co. Ltd, 1938–42; Air Commerce Ltd, 1939–42; Yorks Electric Power Co., 1942–48; Wembley Stadium Ltd, 1960–82 (Chm., 1965–82). Chm., Hull and Grimsby Sect., Incorp. Secs' Assoc. (now CIS), 1929–31; Member of Council: BET Fedn, 1933 (Pres., 1946–79); Public Road Transport Assoc. (formerly Public Transport Assoc.), 1943–68 (Chm., 1945–46; Hon. Mem., 1969), subseq. Confedn of British Road Passenger Transport Ltd (Hon. Mem., 1975); FCIT (Henry Spurrier Meml Lectr, 1946, Pres., 1950–51); Chairman: Omnibus Owners' Assoc., 1943–44; Nat. Council for Omnibus Industry, 1944–45 (Mem. 1940–66); Standing Cttee, Air Transport Sect., London Chamber of Commerce, 1953–65 (Mem. 1943; Dep. Chm. 1949). Governor, Royal Shakespeare Theatre, Stratford upon Avon, 1946–74; Mem. Council, Royal Opera House Soc., 1962–74; Trustee, LSO Trust, 1962–68; Vice-Patron, Theatre Royal Windsor Trust, 1965–. Member, UK Council, European Movement, 1966–. *Recreations:* complete idleness; formerly: flying, swimming, ski-ing, tennis, riding, shooting. *Address:* 1 Campden House Terrace, Kensington Church Street, W8 4BQ. *T:* 01–727 5981; Beech Farm, Battle, East Sussex. *T:* Battle 2950. *Clubs:* Naval and Military, East India, Devonshire, Sports, and Public Schools.

See also N. K. S. Wills.

WILLS, Sir John Vernon, 4th Bt, *cr* 1923; TD; FRICS; JP; Lord-Lieutenant and Custos Rotulorum of Avon, since 1974; Director: Bristol and West Building Society, since 1969 (Vice-Chairman, since 1982); Bristol Evening Post, since 1973 (Deputy Chairman, since 1978); Deputy Chairman, Bristol United Press, since 1980; Chairman, Bristol Waterworks Co., 1986 (Director, 1964–73; Deputy Chairman, 1983–86); Local Director, Barclays Bank, since 1981; *b* 3 July 1928; *s* of Sir George Vernon Proctor Wills, 2nd Bt, and Lady Nellie Jeannie, ARRC, JP, *y d* of late J. T. Rutherford, Abergavenny; *S* brother 1945; *m* 1953, Diana Veronica Cecil (Jane), *o d* of Douglas R. M. Baker, Winsford, Somerset; four *s*. *Educ:* Eton. Served Coldstream Guards, 1946–49; Lt-Col Comdg N Somerset and Bristol Yeomanry, 1965–67; Bt Col 1967; now TARO. Hon. Col, 37th (Wessex and Welsh) Signal Regt, T&AVR, 1975–. Chm., Wessex Water Auth., 1973–82; Mem., Nat. Water Council, 1973–82; Chm., Bristol Marketing Bd, 1984–. Pro-Chancellor, Univ. of Bath, 1979–. Pres., Royal Bath and West Southern Counties Soc., 1980. Member of Somerset CC. JP 1962, DL 1968, High Sheriff, 1968, Somerset. KStJ 1978. Hon. LLD Bristol, 1986. *Heir:* *s* David James Vernon Wills, *b* 2 Jan. 1955. *Address:* Langford Court, near Bristol, Avon. *T:* Wrington 862338. *Club:* Cavalry and Guards.

WILLS, Joseph Lyttleton; Hon. Mr Justice Wills, CBE 1965; FSA; Judge, Supreme Court, Windward Islands and Leeward Islands, WI, since 1955; *b* 24 June 1899; *m* 1940, Dorothy Cather; one *d*. *Educ:* Middle School, Georgetown, British Guiana; Queen's Coll., British Guiana; King's Coll., London. Barrister-at-law, Inner Temple, 1928; admitted to practice as Barrister-at-Law, British Guiana, 1930; Magistrate, 1947; Additional Puisne Judge of Supreme Court of British Guiana, 1953–55. Councillor of Georgetown, 1933; Deputy Mayor, 1942–43; Hon. Member of Legislative Council, British Guiana, 1933; President, British Guiana Labour Union and British Guiana Workers League; Chairman and Member of several public committees; Member Judicial Service Commn, British Guiana, 1963; Chairman, Income Tax (Appeal) Board of Review, Guyana, 1966. Chairman of British Guiana Congregational Union, 1949–53 and 1974–75. Jubilee Medal, 1935; Coronation Medal, 1953. *Recreations:* horse-riding, motoring and cricket. *Address:* Lyttleton House, 57 Chalmers Place, Stabroek, Georgetown, Guyana. *Clubs:* Royal Commonwealth Society (West Indian); Guyana Cricket, Maltenoes Sports (Guyana); Castries (WI).

WILLS, Nicholas Kenneth Spencer, FCA; Managing Director: British Electric Traction Co. plc, since 1982; Birmingham & District Investment Trust plc, since 1970; Electrical & Industrial Investment plc, since 1970; National Electric Construction plc, since 1971; Chairman: Initial plc, since 1979; BET Building Services Ltd, since 1984; Chief Executive, BET plc, since 1985; *b* 18 May 1941; *s* of Sir John Spencer Wills, *qv*; *m* 1st, 1973, Hilary Ann (marr. diss. 1983), *d* of N. C. Flood; two *s* two *d*; 2nd, 1984, Philippa Trench Casson. *Educ:* Rugby Sch.; Queens' Coll., Cambridge (MA). Binder Hamlyn & Co., 1963–67; Morgan Grenfell, 1967–70; Chairman: Argus Press Hldgs, 1974–83; Electrical Press, 1974–83; Boulton & Paul plc, 1979–84; Director: British Electric Traction Co. plc, 1975–; Bradbury, Agnew & Co. Ltd, 1974–83; Globe Investment Trust plc, 1977–; National Mutual Life Assce Soc., 1974–85; Drayton Consolidated, 1982–; St George Assce Co. Ltd, 1974–81; Colonial Securities Trust Co. Ltd, 1976–82; Cable Trust Ltd, 1976–77; Reg. Dir, City and West End, Nat. Westminster Bank, 1982–; American Chamber of Commerce (UK). Treasurer and Churchwarden, Church of St Bride, Fleet Street, 1978–; Asst, Worshipful Co. of Haberdashers', 1981–. CBIM; FCT. *Recreations:* shooting, sailing, trying to farm in the Highlands. *Address:* Stratton House, Stratton Street, Piccadilly, W1X 6AS. *T:* 01–629 8886. *Clubs:* White's, Royal Automobile; Clyde Cruising.

WILLS, Peter Gordon Bethune, TD 1967; Chairman, Sheppards Moneybrokers Ltd, 1985; *b* 25 Oct. 1931; *s* of P. L. B. Wills and E. W. Wills (*née* Stapleton) *Educ:* Malvern Coll.; Corpus Christi Coll., Cambridge, 1952–55 (MA). National Service with Royal Inniskilling Fusiliers, N Ireland and Korea, 1950–52; TA, London Irish Rifles, 1952–67. Joined Sheppards & Co. (later Sheppards and Chase), 1955, Partner, 1960–85. Member, Stock Exchange Council, 1973– (Dep. Chm., 1979–82). Director, Wills Group plc (formerly George Wills and Sons (Holdings) Ltd), 1969–, Vice-Chm., 1977–; Dir, BAII Holding, 1986. *Recreation:* collecting stamps. *Address:* Sheppards Moneybrokers Ltd, 20 Gresham Street, EC2V 7HT.

WILLS, Sir Seton; *see* Wills, Sir D. S.

WILLSON, Douglas James, CBE 1953; TD; *b* 30 Oct. 1906; *s* of late Ernest Victor Willson and late Mary Willson; *m* 1942, Morna Josephine, *d* of Stanley Hine; one *d*. *Educ:* Bishop's Stortford Coll., Herts. Admitted Solicitor, 1928; joined Customs and Excise, 1928. Served War, 1939–45, Lieut-Colonel, RA. Solicitor for Bd of Customs and Excise, 1963–71. *Publications:* Titles Purchase Tax and Excise in Halsbury's Encyclopædia of Laws of England, 3rd edn; Willson & Mainprice on Value Added Tax. *Recreations:* gardening and bird watching. *Address:* Dove Cottage, West Farleigh, Kent. *T:* Maidstone 812203.

WILLSON, Prof. (Francis Michael) Glenn; Vice-Chancellor, 1978–84, Emeritus Professor, since 1985, Murdoch University, Western Australia; Visiting Professor, University of California, Santa Cruz, since 1985; *b* 29 Sept. 1924; *s* of late Christopher Glenn Willson and late Elsie Katrine (*née* Mattick); *m* 1945, Jean (*née* Carlyle); two *d*. *Educ:* Carlisle Grammar Sch.; Manchester Univ. (BA Admin); Balliol and Nuffield Colls, Oxford (DPhil, MA). Merchant Navy, 1941–42; RAF, 1943–46; BOAC 1946–47. Research Officer, Royal Inst. of Public Admin, 1953–60; Res. Fellow, Nuffield Coll., Oxford, 1955–60; Lectr in Politics, St Edmund Hall, Oxford, 1958–60; Prof. of Govt, UC Rhodesia and Nyasaland, 1960–64; Dean, Faculty of Social Studies, UC Rhodesia and Nyasaland, 1962–64; Univ. of California, Santa Cruz: Prof. of Govt/Politics, 1965–74; Provost of Stevenson Coll., 1967–74; Vice-Chancellor, College and Student Affairs, 1973–74; Warden, Goldsmiths' Coll., London, 1974–75; Principal of Univ. of London, 1975–78. *Publications:* (with D.N. Chester) The Organization of British Central Government 1914–56, 2nd edn 1914–64, 1968; Administrators in Action, 1961; contrib. Public Admin, Polit. Studies, Parly Affairs, etc. *Address:* 32 Digby Mansions, Hammersmith Bridge Road, W6 9DF.

WILLSON, John Michael; HM Diplomatic Service; Ambassador to Ivory Coast, Burkina (formerly Upper Volta) and Niger, since 1983; *b* 15 July 1931; *e s* of late Richard and Kathleen Willson; *m* 1954, Phyllis Marian Dawn, *o c* of late William and Phyllis Holman Richards, OBE; two *s* two *d*. *Educ:* Wimbledon Coll.; University Coll., Oxford (MA); Trinity Hall, Cambridge. National Service, 1949–51. HM Colonial Service, N Rhodesia, 1955–64; Min. of Overseas Development, 1965–70 (seconded to British High Commn, Malta, 1967–70); joined HM Diplomatic Service, 1970; British Consulate-General, Johannesburg, 1972–75; FCO (W Indian and N American Depts), 1975–78; Special Counsellor for African Affairs, 1978; Secretary-General, Rhodesian Independence Conf., 1979; Salisbury (on staff of Governor of Rhodesia), 1979–80; Counsellor, Bucharest, 1980–82. *Recreations:* gardening, photography, music. *Address:* c/o Foreign and Commonwealth Office, SW1; c/o C. Hoare & Co., 37 Fleet Street, EC4P 4DQ. *Club:* Royal Commonwealth Society.

WILMINGTON, Joseph (Robert); JP; Chairman and Managing Director, Wilmington Employment Agencies Ltd, since 1966; *b* 21 April 1932; *s* of Joseph R. Wilmington and Magtilda Susanna Wilmington. *Educ:* Alsop High Sch., Liverpool; London Sch. of Economics. Mem., Liverpool City Council, 1962; Past Chm., Liverpool Liberal Party, 1965–67; Chairman: Personnel Cttee, Liverpool City Council; Markets Cttee, Liverpool City Council; Chief Whip; Lord Mayor of Liverpool, 1974–75. Chm., NW Fedn of Employment Consultants; Mem. Nat. Exec., Fedn of Employment Consultants; Mem. Inst. Employment Consultants. JP Liverpool, 1976. *Recreations:* koi keeping, music and the arts. *Address:* Jordaan, South Drive, Sandfield Park, Liverpool L12 1LH.

WILMOT, Air Vice-Marshal Aubrey S.; *see* Sidney-Wilmot.

WILMOT, Sir Henry Robert, 9th Bt *cr* 1759; *b* 10 April 1967; *s* of Sir Robert Arthur Wilmot, 8th Bt, and of Juliet Elvira, *e d* of Captain M. N. Tufnell, RN; *S* father, 1974. *Heir:* *b* Charles Sacheverel Wilmot, *b* 13 Feb. 1969. *Address:* Pitters Farmhouse, Sandy Lane, Chippenham, Wilts.

WILMOT, Sir John Assheton E.; *see* Eardley-Wilmot.

WILMOT, Robb; *see* Wilmot, R. W.

WILMOT, Robert William, (Robb Wilmot), CBE 1985; Chairman, Wilmot Enterprises Ltd, since 1984; Founder and Co-Chairman, European Silicon Structures, ES2, since 1985; Director, Octagon Investment Management, since 1986; Founder and Chairman, OASIS, since 1986; *b* 2 Jan. 1945; *s* of Thomas Arthur William Wilmot and Frances Mary Hull; *m* 1969, Mary Josephine Sharkey; two *s*. *Educ:* Royal Grammar Sch., Worcester; Nottingham Univ. BSc (1st cl. Hons) Electrical Engrg. Texas Instruments, 1966–81: European Technical Dir, France, 1973–74; Div. Dir, USA, 1974–78; Man. Dir, 1978–81; Asst Vice Pres., 1980; International Computers (ICL): Man. Dir, 1981–83; Chief Exec., 1983–84; Chm., 1985. Hon. DSc: Nottingham, 1983; City, 1984. *Recreations:* music, theatre, walking, vintage boats. *Address:* The White House, Bolney Road, Lower Shiplake, Henley-on-Thames, Oxon RG9 3PA. *T:* Wargrave 4252.

WILMOT-SITWELL, Peter Sacheverell; Joint Chairman, S. G. Warburg, Akroyd, Rowe & Pitman, Mullens Securities Ltd, since 1986; *b* 28 March 1935; *s* of Robert Bradshaw Wilmot-Sitwell and Barbara Elizabeth Fisher; *m* 1960, Clare Veronica Cobbold; two *s* one *d*. *Educ:* Eton Coll.; Oxford Univ., 1955–58 (BA, MA). Commnd Coldstream Guards, 1953–55. Trainee, Hambros Bank Ltd, 1958–59; Partner 1959–82, Sen. Partner 1982–86, Rowe & Pitman. *Recreations:* shooting, golf, tennis. *Address:* Portman House, Dummer, near Basingstoke, Hants RG25 2AD. *Clubs:* White's; Swinley Forest (Ascot).

WILMSHURST, Michael Joseph; HM Diplomatic Service; UK Permanent Representative to International Atomic Energy Agency, United Nations Industrial Development Organization, and to other UN Organizations, Vienna, since 1982, with personal rank of Ambassador; *b* 14 Sept. 1934; *s* of Mr and Mrs E. J. Wilmshurst; *m* 1958, Mary Elizabeth Kemp; one *s* one *d*. *Educ:* Latymer Upper Sch.; Christ's Coll., Cambridge. BA 1959. Entered Foreign Service, 1953. 2nd Lieut, Royal Signals, 1953–55. Asst Private Sec. to Foreign Secretary, 1960–62; 2nd Sec., The Hague, 1962–65; 1st Sec. (Commercial), Bogota, 1965–67; Western European Dept, FCO, 1968–70; 1st Sec. (Commercial), Cairo, 1970–73; Asst Head of Energy Dept, FCO, 1974–75; Asst Head of Energy and Arms Control and Disarmament Depts, 1975–77; Counsellor and Head of Joint Nuclear Unit, FCO, 1977–78; Consul, Guatemala City, 1978–81; Sabbatical, Stiftung Wissenschaft und Politik, Ebenhausen, 1982. *Publications:* Nuclear Non-Proliferation: can the policies of the Eighties prove more successful than those of the Seventies?, 1982; (contrib.) The International Nuclear Non-Proliferation System: challenges and choices, 1984. *Recreation:* reading. *Address:* c/o Foreign and Commonwealth Office, SW1.

WILSON; *see* McNair-Wilson.

WILSON, family name of **Barons Moran, Nunburnholme, Wilson, Wilson of Langside** and **Wilson of Rievaulx.**

WILSON, 2nd Baron, *cr* 1946, of Libya and of Stowlangtoft; **Patrick Maitland Wilson;** *b* 14 Sept. 1915; *s* of Field-Marshal 1st Baron Wilson, GCB, GBE, DSO, and Hester Mary (*d* 1979), *d* of Philip James Digby Wykeham, Tythrop House, Oxon; *S* father 1964; *m* 1945, Violet Storeen, *d* of late Major James Hamilton Douglas Campbell, OBE. *Educ:*

Eton; King's College, Cambridge. Served War of 1939–45 (despatches). *Heir:* none. *Address:* c/o Barclays Bank, Cambridge.

WILSON OF LANGSIDE, Baron *cr* 1969 (Life Peer); **Henry Stephen Wilson,** PC 1967; QC (Scot.) 1965; *b* 21 March 1916; *s* of James Wilson, Solicitor, Glasgow, and Margaret Wilson (*née* Young); *m* 1942, Jessie Forrester Waters; no *c*. *Educ:* High School, Glasgow; Univ. of Glasgow (MA, LLB). Joined Army, 1939; Commd 1940; Regl Officer, HLI and RAC, 1940–46. Called to Scottish Bar, 1946; Advocate-Depute, 1948–51. Sheriff-Substitute: Greenock, 1955–56; Glasgow, 1956–65; Solicitor-General for Scotland, 1965–67; Lord Advocate, 1967–70; Dir, Scottish Courts Administration, 1971–74; Sheriff Principal of Glasgow and Strathkelvin, 1975–77. Contested (Lab) Dumfriesshire, 1950, 1955, W Edinburgh, 1951; Mem. SDP, 1981–. *Recreations:* hill walking, gardening. *Address:* Dunallan, Kippen, Stirlingshire. *T:* Kippen 210. *Club:* Western (Glasgow).

WILSON OF RIEVAULX, Baron *cr* 1983 (Life Peer), of Kirklees in the County of West Yorkshire; **James Harold Wilson;** KG 1976; OBE 1945; PC 1947; FRS 1969; *b* 11 March 1916; *s* of late James Herbert and Ethel Wilson, Huddersfield, Yorks (formerly of Manchester); *m* 1940, Gladys Mary, *d* of Rev. D. Baldwin, The Manse, Duxford, Cambridge; two *s*. *Educ:* Milnsbridge Council Sch. and Royds Hall Sch., Huddersfield; Wirral Grammar Sch., Bebington, Cheshire; Jesus Coll., Oxford (Gladstone Memorial Prize, Webb Medley Economics Scholarship, First Class Hons Philosophy, Politics and Economics). Lecturer in Economics, New Coll., Oxford, 1937; Fellow of University Coll., 1938; Praelector in Economics and Domestic Bursar, 1945. Dir of Econs and Stats, Min. of Fuel and Power, 1943–44. MP (Lab) Ormskirk, 1945–50, Huyton, Lancs, 1950–83; Parly Sec. to Ministry of Works, 1945–March 1947; Sec. for Overseas Trade, March-Oct. 1947; Pres., BoT, Oct. 1947–April 1951; Chairman: Labour Party Exec. Cttee, 1961–62; Public Accounts Cttee, 1959–63; Leader, Labour Party, 1963–76; Prime Minister and First Lord of the Treasury, 1964–70, 1974–76; Leader of the Opposition, 1963–64, 1970–74. Chairman: Cttee to Review the Functioning of Financial Instns, 1976–80; British Screen Adv. Council, 1985–. Pres., Royal Statistical Soc., 1972–73. An Elder Brother of Trinity House, 1968. Hon. Fellow, Jesus and University Colleges, Oxford, 1963. Hon. Freeman, City of London, 1975. Hon. Pres., Great Britain-USSR Assoc., 1976–. Pres., Royal Shakespeare Theatre Co., 1976–. Chancellor, Bradford Univ., 1966–85. Hon. LLD: Lancaster, 1964; Liverpool, 1965; Nottingham, 1966; Sussex, 1966; Hon. DCL, Oxford, 1965; Hon. DTech., Bradford, 1966; DUniv: Essex, 1967; Open, 1974. *Publications:* New Deal for Coal, 1945; In Place of Dollars, 1952; The War on World Poverty, 1953; The Relevance of British Socialism, 1964; Purpose in Politics, 1964; The New Britain (Penguin), 1964; Purpose in Power, 1966; The Labour Government 1964–70, 1971; The Governance of Britain, 1976; A Prime Minister on Prime Ministers, 1977; Final Term: the Labour Government 1974–76, 1979; The Chariot of Israel, 1981; Harold Wilson Memoirs 1916–64, 1986. *Recreation:* golf. *Address:* House of Lords, SW1.

WILSON, Prof. Alan Geoffrey; Professor of Urban and Regional Geography, University of Leeds, since 1970; *b* 8 Jan. 1939; *s* of Harry Wilson and Gladys (*née* Naylor); *m* 1965, Christine Diane Snow (marr. diss. 1978). *Educ:* Corpus Christi Coll., Cambridge (MA). Scientific Officer, Rutherford High Energy Lab., 1961–64; Res. Officer, Inst. of Econs and Statistics, Univ. of Oxford, 1964–66; Math. Adviser, MoT, 1966–68; Asst Dir, Centre for Environmental Studies, London, 1968–70. Mem., Kirklees AHA, 1979–82; Vice-Chm., Dewsbury HA, 1982–85. Vice-Chm. Environment and Planning Cttee, ESRC, 1986–. Gill Meml Award, RGS, 1978. *Publications:* Entropy in Urban and Regional Modelling, 1970; Papers in Urban and Regional Analysis, 1972; Urban and Regional Models in Geography and Planning, 1974; (with M. J. Kirkby) Mathematics for Geographers and Planners, 1975, 2nd edn 1980; (with P. H. Rees) Spatial Population Analysis, 1977; (ed with P. H. Rees and C. M. Leigh) Models of Cities and Regions, 1977; Catastrophe Theory and Bifurcation: applications to urban and regional systems, 1981; (jtly) Optimization in Locational and Transport Analysis, 1981; Geography and the Environment: Systems Analytical Methods, 1981; (with R. J. Bennett) Mathematical Methods in Geography and Planning, 1985. *Recreations:* writing, dog walking, miscellaneous fads. *Address:* School of Geography, University of Leeds, Leeds LS2 9JT. *T:* Leeds 431751 ext 7176.

WILSON, Sir Alan (Herries), Kt 1961; FRS 1942; Chairman, Granville Venture Capital Ltd, since 1983; *b* 2 July 1906; *o s* of H. and A. Wilson; *m* 1934, Margaret Constance Monks (*d* 1961); two *s*. *Educ:* Wallasey Gram. Sch.; Emmanuel College, Cambridge. Smith's Prize, 1928; Adams Prize, 1931–32; Fellow of Emmanuel College, Cambridge, 1929–33; Fellow and Lecturer of Trinity College, Cambridge, 1933–45; University Lecturer in Mathematics in the University of Cambridge, 1933–45; joined Courtaulds Ltd, 1945; Man. Dir, 1954; Dep. Chm., 1957–62. Dir, Internat. Computers (Hldgs) Ltd, 1962–72; Chm., Glaxo Group Ltd, 1963–73. Chairman: Committee on Coal Derivatives, 1959–60; Committee on Noise, 1960–63; Nuclear Safety Adv. Committee, 1965–66; Central Adv. Water Cttee, 1969–74; Dep. Chm. and pt-time Mem., Electricity Council, 1966–76; Member: Iron and Steel Board, 1960–67; UGC, 1964–66; President: Inst. of Physics and Physical Soc., 1963–64; Nat. Society for Clean Air, 1965–66; Aslib, 1971–73. Chm. Governing Body, Nat. Inst. of Agricultural Engrg, 1971–76; Chm., Bd of Governors, Bethlem Royal and Maudsley Hosps., 1973–80. Prime Warden, Goldsmiths Co., 1969–70. Hon. Fellow: Emmanuel College, Cambridge; St Catherine's College, Oxford; UMIST. Hon. FIChemE; Hon. FInstP; Hon. FIMA. Hon. DSc: Oxford; Edinburgh. *Publications:* The Theory of Metals, 1936, 2nd edition 1953; Semi-conductors and Metals, 1939; Thermo-dynamics and Statistical Mechanics, 1957; many papers on atomic physics. *Address:* 65 Oakleigh Park South, Whetstone, N20 9JL. *T:* 01–445 3030. *Club:* Athenæum.

WILSON, Alan Martin; QC 1982; a Recorder of the Crown Court, since 1979; *b* 12 Feb. 1940; *s* of late Joseph Norris Wilson and Kate Wilson; *m* 1st, 1966, Pauline Frances Kibart (marr. diss. 1975); two *d*; 2nd, 1976, Julia Mary Carter; one *d*. *Educ:* Kilburn Grammar Sch.; Nottingham Univ. (LLB Hons). Called to the Bar, Gray's Inn, 1963; Dep. Circuit Judge, 1978. *Recreations:* rough shooting, sailing, poetry. *Address:* 6 King's Bench Walk, Temple, EC4Y 7DR; Langland House, Peopleton, near Pershore, Worcs WR10 2EE. *Clubs:* Sloane; Bar Yacht.

WILSON, Alexander, CBE 1986; FLA; Director General, British Library Reference Division, 1980–86; *b* 12 Feb. 1921; *s* of late William Wilson and Amelia Wilson; *m* 1949, Mary Catherin Traynor; two *s*. *Educ:* Bolton County Grammar Sch. FLA 1950; Hon. FLA 1984. Served War, RAF, 1941–46. Librarian at Bolton, Harrogate, Taunton, and Swindon, 1946–52; Dir of Library and Cultural Services, Dudley and later Coventry, 1952–72; Dir, Cheshire Libraries and Museums Service, 1972–79. Member: Library Adv. Council (England), 1971–74; British Library Bd, 1974–86. Pres., LA, 1986. *Publications:* contrib. books and periodicals on libraries and other cultural services. *Recreations:* walking, listening to music, lecturing and writing on professional subjects. *Address:* 1 Brockway West, Tattenhall, Chester CH3 9DN.

WILSON, Lt-Gen. Sir (Alexander) James, KBE 1974 (CBE 1966; MBE 1948); MC 1945; Chief Executive, Tobacco Advisory Council, 1983–85 (Chairman, 1977–83); Director, Standard Commercial Tobacco Co., since 1983; *b* 13 April 1921; *s* of Maj.-Gen. Bevil Thomson Wilson, CB, DSO, and of Florence Erica, *d* of Sir John Starkey, 1st Bt; *m* 1958, Hon. Jean Margaret Paul, 2nd *d* of 2nd Baron Rankeillour; two *s*. *Educ:* Winchester Coll.; New Coll., Oxford (BA, Law). Served War of 1939–45, North Africa and Italy, Rifle Bde (despatches); Adjt, IMA Dehra Dun, 1945–47; PS to C-in-C Pakistan, 1948–49; Co. Comdr, 1st Bn Rifle Bde, BAOR 1949 and 1951–52, Kenya 1954–55 (despatches); psc 1950; Bde Major 11th Armd Div., BAOR, 1952–54; Instr, Staff Coll. Camberley, 1955–58; 2nd in comd 3rd Green Jackets, BAOR, 1959–60; GSO1 Sandhurst, 1960–62; CO 1st Bn XX Lancs Fus, 1962–64; Chief of Staff, UN Force in Cyprus, 1964–66 (Actg Force Comdr, 1965–66); Comdr, 147 Inf. Bde TA, 1966–67; Dir of Army Recruiting, MoD, 1967–70; GOC NW District, 1970–72; Vice Adjutant General, MoD, 1972–74; GOC SE District, 1974–77. Dep. Col (Lancashire), RRF, 1973–77, Col, 1977–82; Hon. Col, Oxford Univ. OTC, 1978–82. Col Commandant: Queen's Division, 1974–77; RAEC, 1975–79; Royal Green Jackets, 1977–81. Chm., Council, RUSI, 1973–75. Member: Sports Council, 1973–82; Council, CBI, 1977–85; Pres., Army Cricket Assoc., 1973–76; Vice-Pres., Army Football Assoc., 1973–76, Chm., 1976–77, Pres., 1977–82; Hon. Vice-Pres., FA, 1976–82. Vice-Chm., NABC, 1977–; Chm., Crown and Manor Club, Hoxton, 1977–. Pres., Notts Assoc. of Boys and Keystone Clubs, 1986–. Association Football Correspondent, Sunday Times, 1957–; Review Editor, Army Quarterly, 1985–. *Publications:* articles and book reviews on mil. subjects and peacekeeping. *Recreations:* cricket, Association football. *Address:* 9 Hasker Street, SW3 2LE; Goldhill Farm House, Edingley, near Newark, Notts. *T:* Southwell 813308. *Clubs:* Travellers', MCC; Notts CC.

WILSON, Prof. Allan Charles, FRS 1986; Professor of Biochemistry, University of California, Berkeley, since 1964; *b* 18 Oct. 1934; *s* of Charles and Eunice Boyce Wilson; *m* 1958, Leona Greenbaum; one *s* one *d*. *Educ:* King's College, NZ; Otago Univ. (BSc 1955); Washington State Univ. (MS 1957); Univ. of California (PhD 1961). Postdoctoral Fellow, Brandeis Univ., 1961–64; Asst Prof., 1964–68, Associate Prof., 1968–72, Prof., 1972–, Univ. of California. Guggenheim Fellow: Weizmann Inst. and Nairobi Univ., 1972–73; Harvard Univ., 1979–80; MacArthur Fellow, John D. and Catherine T. MacArthur Foundn, 1986–. Mem., Amer. Acad. of Arts and Sciences, 1983. *Publications:* author and co-author of numerous papers in sci. jls. *Address:* 1004 Park Hills Road, Berkeley, Calif 94708, USA. *T:* (415) 848–1784.

WILSON, Andrew James; *see* Wilson, Snoo.

WILSON, Andrew N., FRSL; author; *b* 27 Oct. 1950; *s* of Jean Dorothy Wilson (*née* Crowder); *m* 1971, Katherine Duncan-Jones; two *d*. *Educ:* Rugby; New College, Oxford (MA). Chancellor's Essay Prize, 1971, and Ellerton Theological Prize, 1975. FRSL 1981. *Publications: novels:* The Sweets of Pimlico, 1977 (John Llewellyn Rhys Memorial Prize, 1978); Unguarded Hours, 1978; Kindly Light, 1979; The Healing Art, 1980 (Somerset Maugham Award, 1981; Arts Council National Book Award, 1981; Southern Arts Prize, 1981); Who was Oswald Fish?, 1981; Wise Virgin, 1982 (W. H. Smith Literary Award, 1983); Scandal, 1983; Gentlemen in England, 1985; Love Unknown, 1986; *non fiction:* The Laird of Abbotsford, 1980 (John Llewellyn Rhys Memorial Prize, 1981); A Life of John Milton, 1983; Hilaire Belloc, 1984; How Can We Know?, 1985; (jtly) The Church in Crisis, 1986. *Address:* c/o A. D. Peters, 10 Buckingham Street, WC2. *Club:* Travellers'.

WILSON, Andrew Thomas, CMG 1982; Chief Natural Resources Adviser, Overseas Development Administration, 1983–86, retired; *b* 21 June 1926; *s* of John Wilson, farmer, and Gertrude (*née* Lucas); *m* 1954, Hilda Mary (*née* Williams); two *d*. *Educ:* Cowley Sch.; Leeds Univ. (BSc); St John's Coll., Cambridge (DipAg); Imperial College of Tropical Agriculture (DTA). Colonial Service/HMOCS, Northern Rhodesia/Zambia, 1949–66: Agricultural Officer, 1949; Chief Agricl Officer, 1959; Chief Agricl Research Officer, 1961; Dep. Director of Agriculture, 1963; ODM/ODA: Agricl Adviser, British Development Div. in the Caribbean, 1967; FCO: Agricl Adviser, Nairobi and Kampala, 1969; ODM/ODA: Agricl Adviser, E Africa Development Div., 1974; Agricl Adviser, Middle East Development Div., 1976; Head of British Develt Div. in S Africa, 1979. *Recreations:* sport, gardening. *Clubs:* Farmers'; Nairobi (Kenya).

WILSON, Sir Angus (Frank Johnstone), Kt 1980; CBE 1968; CLit 1972; FRSL 1958; author; Professor of English Literature, University of East Anglia, 1966–78, now Emeritus; *b* 11 Aug. 1913; *s* of William Johnstone-Wilson, Dumfriesshire, and of Maude (*née* Caney), Durban, Natal, South Africa. *Educ:* Westminster School; Merton College, Oxford. Foreign Office, 1942–46. Deputy to Superintendent of Reading Room, British Museum, 1949–55. Began to write in 1946. Lectr, Internat. Assoc. of Professors of English, Lausanne, 1959; Ewing Lectr, Los Angeles, 1960; Bergen Lectr, Yale Univ., 1960; Wm Vaughan Moody Lectr, Chicago, 1960; Northcliffe Lectrs, Lond., 1961; Leslie Stephen Lectr, Cambridge, 1962–63; Lectr, Sch. of Eng. Studies, E Anglia Univ., 1963–66; Beckman Prof., Univ. of California, Berkeley, 1967; John Hinkley Vis. Prof., Johns Hopkins Univ., Baltimore, 1974; Visiting Professor: Univ. of Delaware, 1977, 1980, 1983; Univ. of Iowa, 1978; Georgia State Univ., 1979; Univ. of Michigan, 1979; Univ. of Minnesota, 1980; Univ. of Missouri, 1982; Andrew Mellon Vis. Prof., Univ. of Pittsburgh, 1981; Univ. of Arizona, 1984. Mem. Cttee, Royal Literary Fund, 1966. Mem. Arts Council, 1967–69; Chm., NBL, 1971–74. President: Powys Soc., 1970–80; Dickens Fellowship, 1974–75; Kipling Soc., 1981–; RSL, 1982–. Foreign Hon. Mem., Amer. Acad. and Inst. of Arts and Letters, 1980. Hon. DLitt: Leicester, 1977; East Anglia, 1979; Sussex, 1981; Hon. LittD Liverpool, 1979; Hon. Dr Sorbonne, 1983. Chevalier de l'Ordre des Arts et des Lettres, 1972. *Publications:* (short stories, novels, etc); The Wrong Set, 1949; Such Darling Dodos, 1950; Emile Zola, 1950; Hemlock and After (novel), 1952; For Whom The Cloche Tolls, 1953, 2nd edn, 1973; The Mulberry Bush (play) (prod Bristol, 1955, Royal Court Theatre, London, 1956); Anglo-Saxon Attitudes (novel), 1956; A Bit off the Map, 1957; The Middle Age of Mrs Eliot (novel), 1958 (James Tait Black Meml Prize; Prix du Meilleur Roman Etranger, Paris); The Old Men at the Zoo (novel), 1961; The Wild Garden, 1963; Late Call (novel), 1964 (adapted for TV, 1975); No Laughing Matter (novel), 1967; The World of Charles Dickens, 1970 (Yorkshire Post Book of the Year, 1970); (with Edwin Smith and Olive Cook) England, 1971; As If By Magic (novel), 1973; The Naughty Nineties, 1976; The Strange Ride of Rudyard Kipling, 1977; Setting the World on Fire (novel), 1980; (with Tony Garrett) East Anglia in Verse, 1982; Diversity and Depth in Fiction, 1983; (ed) The Viking Portable Dickens, 1983; Reflections in a Winter's Eye, 1986. TV plays: After the Show (perf. 1959); The Stranger (perf. 1960); The Invasion (perf. 1963). *Recreations:* gardening, travel. *Address:* Appartement 61, 7 Place de la République, 13210 St Remy de Provence, France. *T:* 90.92.34.36. *Club:* Athenæum.

WILSON, Anthony, FCA; Head of Government Accountancy Service and Accounting Adviser to HM Treasury, since 1984; *b* 17 Feb. 1928; *s* of late Charles Ernest Wilson and Martha Clarice Wilson (*née* Mee); *m* 1955, Margaret Josephine Hudson; two *s* one *d*. *Educ:* Giggleswick School. Associate Mem., Inst. of Internal Auditors. Royal Navy, 1946–49. John Gordon Walton & Co., 1945–46 and 1949–52; Price Waterhouse, 1952, Partner, 1961–84; HM Treasury, 1984–. Member: UK Govt Production Statistics Adv. Cttee, 1972–84; Accounting Standards Cttee, 1984–; Council, Inst. of Chartered

Accountants in England and Wales, 1985–. Mem. Management Cttee, SW Regl Arts Assoc., 1983–; Member: English Ceramic Circle, 1983–; Northern Ceramic Soc., 1976–. Liveryman: Needlemakers' Co.; Chartered Accountants' Co. FRSA 1983. *Recreations:* fishing, gardening, collecting pottery. *Address:* The Barn House, 89 Newland, Sherborne, Dorset DT9 3AG. *T:* Sherborne 815674. *Clubs:* Reform, Roehampton.

WILSON, Maj.-Gen. Arthur Gillespie, CBE 1955; DSO 1946; *b* 29 Sept. 1900; *s* of late Charles Wilson, originally of Glasgow, Scotland; *m* 1st, 1927, Edna D. L. Gibson (*d* 1940); no *c*; 2nd, 1953, Shirley H. Cruickshank, *d* of late Colin Campbell, Queenscliff, Victoria, Australia; no *c*. *Educ:* North Sydney Boys' High School, NSW, Australia; Royal Military College, Duntroon, Australia. Commissioned Aust. Staff Corps, 1921; served India with various Brit. and IA Artillery Units, 1924; commanded Roy. Aust. Artillery, Thursday Island, 1926–28; Staff College, Quetta, 1935–36; GSO3, AHQ 1938; continued to serve in various appts at AHQ until joined AIF 1940; GSO1 HQ AIF UK and then Assistant Mil. Liaison Officer, Australian High Commissioner's Office, UK, until 1943, when returned to Australia; served with AIF New Guinea Philippines and Borneo, 1943–45; DDSD(o) Land Headquarters, 1944–45; commanded British Commonwealth Base BCOF Japan, 1946–47; served various appts AHQ and HQ Eastern Command, 1947–52; Aust. Army Rep., UK, 1953–54; GOC, Central Command, Australia, 1954–57; retired 1957. *Address:* Leahurst Cottage, Crafers, South Australia 5152, Australia. *Club:* Naval, Military and Air Force (Adelaide).

WILSON, Prof. Arthur James Cochran, FRS 1963; Professor of Crystallography, Department of Physics, Birmingham University, 1965–82, now Emeritus; *b* 28 November 1914; *o s* of Arthur A. C. and Hildegarde Gretchen (*née* Geldert) Wilson, Springhill, Nova Scotia, Canada; *m* 1946, Harriett Charlotte, BSc, PhD, Sociologist (*née* Friedeberg); two *s* one *d. Educ:* King's Collegiate School, Windsor, Nova Scotia, Canada); Dalhousie University, Halifax, Canada (MSc); Massachusetts Institute of Technology (PhD); Cambridge University (PhD). 1851 Exhibition Scholar, 1937–40. Res. Asst, Cavendish Lab., Cambridge, 1940–45; Lecturer, 1945, and Senior Lecturer, 1946, in Physics, University College, Cardiff; Professor of Physics, University College, Cardiff, 1954–65. Visiting Professor: Georgia Inst. of Technology, 1965, 1968, 1971; Univ. of Tokyo, 1972. Editor of Structure Reports, 1948–59; Editor of Acta Crystallographica, 1960–77; Assoc. Editor, Proc. Royal Society, 1978–83; Editor of International Tables for Crystallography, 1982–. Member: Exec. Cttee, Internat. Union of Crystallography, 1954–60 and 1978–81 (Vice-Pres., 1978–81); ICSU Abstracting Bd (now Internat. Council for Scientific and Technical Information), 1971–77, 1980–86 (Vice-Pres.). *Publications:* X-ray Optics, 1949 (Russian edn 1951, 2nd edn 1962); Mathematical Theory of X-ray Powder Diffractometry, 1963 (French edn 1964, German edn 1965); Elements of X-ray Crystallography, 1970; (with L. V. Azároff and others) X-ray Diffraction, 1974; (ed jtly) Crystallographic Statistics: Progress and Problems, 1982; (ed) Structure and Statistics in Crystallography, 1985; numerous papers in Proc. Phys. Soc., Proc. Roy. Soc., Acta Cryst., etc. *Address:* Crystallographic Data Centre, University Chemical Laboratory, Cambridge CB2 1EW. *Clubs:* Sierra (San Francisco); Swiss Alpine.

WILSON, Sir Austin (George), Kt 1981; OBE 1958; retired; *b* 6 Nov. 1906; *s* of George Wilson and Lydia Mary Wilson; *m* 1936, Ailsa Blanche (*née* Percy); one *s. Educ:* Auckland Grammar Sch. FCIS; FNZSocA; FInstD. Director: NZ Forest Products Ltd, 1959–79 (Chm., 1968–73 and 1977–79); Auckland Gas Co. Ltd, 1959–85 (Chm., 1963–85); NZ Insurance Co. Ltd, 1961–82 (Chm., 1967–71); E. Lichtenstein & Co. Ltd, 1961–84; Nestles (NZ) Ltd, 1962–80; Plessey (NZ) Ltd, 1968–83 (Chm., 1970–83); Progressive Enterprises Ltd, 1971–79; NZI Finance Corporation Ltd, 1972–84 (Chm., 1972–84); Nissan Datsun Holdings Ltd, 1971–83 (Chm., 1973–82). Mem., Auckland Harbour Board, 1947–56 (Chm., 1953–55); Auckland Harbour Bd Sinking Fund Comr, 1963–. Life Member: Auckland Chamber of Commerce, 1963; NZ Bureau of Importers, 1978; Gas Assoc. of New Zealand, 1978. *Recreation:* lawn bowls. *Address:* 3/19 Victoria Avenue, Remuera, Auckland 5, New Zealand. *T:* 549743. *Clubs:* Northern, Rotary of Auckland (Pres., 1958) (Auckland).

WILSON, Austin Peter; Assistant Under Secretary of State, since 1981; Head of Home Office Equal Opportunities Department, since 1982; *b* 31 March 1938; *s* of Joseph and Irene Wilson; *m* 1962, Norma Louise, *y d* of D. R. Mill; one *s* two *d. Educ:* Leeds Grammar Sch.; St Edmund Hall, Oxford (BA). Entered Home Office, 1961; Private Secretary to Minister of State, 1964–66; Principal, 1966; Secretary, Deptl Cttee on Death Certification and Coroners (Brodrick Cttee), 1968–71; Asst Sec., 1974, Prison Dept; seconded to N Ireland Office, 1977–80; Asst Under Secretary of State, Criminal Justice Dept, 1981. *Recreations:* theatre, walking, exploring France. *Address:* Home Office, Queen Anne's Gate, SW1. *T:* 01–213 3000.

WILSON, Rear-Adm. Barry Nigel; Flag Officer Sea Training, since 1986; *b* 5 June 1936; *s* of Rear-Adm. G. A. M. Wilson, CB, and of Dorothy Wilson; *m* 1961, Elizabeth Ann (*née* Hardy); one *s* one *d. Educ:* St Edward's Sch., Oxford; Britannia Royal Naval Coll. Commanded: HMS Mohawk, 1973–74; HMS Cardiff, 1978–80; RCDS 1982; Dir Navy Plans, 1983–85. *Recreations:* campanology, gardening. *Address:* c/o Naval Secretary, Old Admiralty Building, Whitehall, SW1. *T:* 01–218 9000.

WILSON, Lt-Col Blair Aubyn S.; *see* Stewart-Wilson.

WILSON, Prof. Brian Graham; Vice-Chancellor, University of Queensland, since 1979; *b* 9 April 1930; *s* of Charles Wesley Wilson and Isobel Christie (*née* Ferguson); *m* 1st, 1959, Barbara Elizabeth Wilkie; two *s* one *d;* 2nd, 1978, Margaret Jeanne Henry. *Educ:* Queen's Univ., Belfast (BSc Hons); National Univ. of Ireland (PhD Cosmic Radiation). Post-doctoral Fellow, National Research Council, Canada, 1955–57; Officer in Charge, Sulphur Mt Lab., Banff, 1957–60; Associate Res. Officer, 1959–60; Associate Prof. of Physics, Univ. of Calgary, 1960–65, Prof., 1965–70, Dean of Arts and Science, 1967–70; Prof. of Astronomy and Academic Vice-Pres., Simon Fraser Univ., 1970–78. Hon. LLD Calgary. *Publications:* numerous, on astrophysics, in learned jls. *Recreations:* fishing, swimming. *Address:* 55 Walcott Street, St Lucia, Queensland 4067, Australia. *T:* (07)870 8757.

WILSON, Brian Harvey, CBE 1972 (MBE 1944); solicitor, retired; *b* 4 Sept. 1915; *o s* of Sydney John Wilson, MC, and Bessie Mildred (*née* Scott); *m* 1941, Constance Jane (*née* Gee); one *s. Educ:* Manchester Grammar Sch.; (Exhibitioner) Corpus Christi Coll., Cambridge (MA, LLB). Chief Asst Solicitor, Warrington, 1946–48; Dep. Town Clerk: Grimsby, 1948–53; Ilford, 1953–56; Town Clerk, Hampstead, 1956–65 (now Camden); Town Clerk and Chief Exec., London Borough of Camden, 1965–77; Hon. Clerk to Housing and Works Cttee, London Boroughs Assoc., 1965–79; Chm., Metropolitan Housing Trust, 1978–85. Chm., Royal Inst. of Public Administration, 1973–75. Member: Uganda Resettlement Board, 1972–73; DoE Study Gp on Agrément, 1978. Chairman: Public Examn, Glos Structure Plan, 1980; Indep. Inquiry into death of Maria Mehmedagi, 1981; GLC Independent Inquiry into financial terms of GLC housing transferred to London Boroughs and Districts, 1984–85. *Address:* Old Housing, Fifield, Oxon. *T:* Shipton-under-Wychwood 830695.

WILSON, Brian William John Gregg, MA; MBIM; Headmaster, Campbell College, Belfast, since 1977; *b* 16 June 1937; *s* of Cecil S. and Margaret D. Wilson; *m* 1969, Sara Remington (*née* Hollins); two *d. Educ:* Sedbergh Sch., Yorks; Christ's Coll., Cambridge (MA). NI short service commn, RIrF, 1955–57. Asst Master, Radley Coll., 1960–65; Housemaster, King's Sch., Canterbury, 1965–73; Dir of Studies, Eastbourne Coll., 1973–76. Member: Central Religious Adv. Cttee, BBC/ITV, 1982–; Management Cttee, NISTRO, 1980–. Hon. Sec., Ancient History Cttee, JACT, 1967–77. *Publications:* (with W. K. Lacey) Res Publica, 1970; (with D. J. Miller) Stories from Herodotus, 1973. *Recreations:* fives, squash, golf, cricket, hockey, etc; translating, theology, stock market, drama. *Address:* Headmaster's House, Campbell College, Belfast BT4 2ND. *T:* Belfast 63076.

WILSON, Brig. Charles Edward T.; *see* Tryon-Wilson.

WILSON, Sir Charles Haynes, Kt 1965; MA Glasgow and Oxon; Principal and Vice-Chancellor of University of Glasgow, 1961–76; *b* 16 May 1909; 2nd *s* of late George Wilson and Florence Margaret Hannay; *m* 1935, Jessie Gilmour Wilson; one *s* two *d. Educ:* Hillhead High School; Glasgow Univ.; Oxford Univ. Glasgow University Faulds Fellow in Political Philosophy, 1932–34. Lecturer in Political Science, London School of Economics, 1934–39; Fellow and Tutor in Modern History, Corpus Christi College, Oxford, 1939–52. Junior Proctor, 1945; Faculty Fellow, Nuffield College. Visiting Professor in Comparative Government at Ohio State Univ., 1950; Principal, The University College of Leicester, 1952–57; Vice-Chancellor, Univ. of Leicester, 1957–61. Chairman: Commn on Fourah Bay Coll., Sierra Leone, 1957; Miners' Welfare Nat. Schol. Scheme Selec. Cttee, 1959–64; Acad. Planning Bd for Univ. of E Anglia, 1960; Member: Academic Planning Cttee and Council of UC of Sussex, 1958; Acad. Adv. Cttee, Royal Coll. of Science and Technology, Glasgow (now Univ. of Strathclyde), 1962; British Cttee of Selection for Harkness Fellowships of Commonwealth Fund, 1962–67; Heyworth Cttee on Social Studies, 1962; Acad. Planning Bd, Univ. of Stirling, 1964; Chairman, Cttee of Vice-Chancellors and Principals, 1964–67; Chm., Assoc. of Commonwealth Univs, 1966–67 and 1972–74. Mem., Museums and Galleries Commn (formerly Standing Commn on Museums and Galleries), 1976–83. Hon. Fellow: Corpus Christi Coll., Oxford, 1963; LSE, 1965. Hon. LLD: Glasgow, 1957; Leicester, 1961; Rhodes Univ., 1964; Queen's Univ., Kingston, Ont, 1967; Ohio State Univ., 1969; Pennsylvania, 1975; Hon. DLitt: Strathclyde, 1966; NUU, 1976; Heriot-Watt, 1977; Hon. DCL East Anglia, 1966. Comdr, St Olav (Norway), 1966; Chevalier, Legion of Honour, 1976. *Address:* Whinnymuir, Dalry, Castle Douglas DG7 3TT. *T:* Dalry 218. *Club:* Royal Scottish Automobile.

WILSON, Prof. Charles Henry, CBE 1981; LittD; FBA 1966; Fellow of Jesus College, Cambridge, since 1938; Professor of Modern History, Cambridge University, 1965–79; *b* 16 Apr. 1914; *s* of Joseph Edwin Wilson and Louisa Wilson. *Educ:* De Aston Grammar Sch., Lincs; Jesus Coll., Cambridge. DLitt Cambridge, 1976. Studied in Holland and Germany, 1937–38. Served in RNVR and Admiralty, 1940–45. Univ. Lecturer in History, 1945–64, Reader in Modern Economic History, 1964–65, Cambridge Univ.; Bursar of Jesus Coll., 1945–55. Ford Lecturer in English History, Oxford Univ., for 1968–69. Vis. Prof., Univ. of Tokyo, 1974. Prof. of History and Civilization, European Univ. Inst., Florence (seconded from Cambridge), 1976–79, Vis. Prof. 1980–81. Member: Lord Chancellor's Adv. Council on Public Records, 1972–77; Adv. Council, Business History Unit (LSE), 1981. Jt Ed., Econ. Hist. Review, 1960–67; Mem. Editorial Cttee, Jl of European Econ. Hist. (Rome), 1975–. Governor, British Inst. of Florence, 1979–; British Acad. deleg. to European Science Foundn, 1980. British Govt Representative, Anglo-Netherlands Cultural Commn, 1956–72. Corres. Fellow: Royal Danish Acad. of Arts and Science, 1970; Royal Belgian Acad., 1973. Manager, Istituto Datini, Prato, 1971. Hon. Vice-Pres., RHistS, 1981. LittD (*hc*) Univ. of Groningen, 1964; Univ. of Louvain, 1977. Comdr, Order of Oranje-Nassau, 1973. *Publications:* Anglo-Dutch Commerce and Finance in 18th Century, 1940; Holland and Britain, 1945; History of Unilever, 1954; Profit and Power, 1957; Mercantilism, 1958, 5th edn, 1971; (with William Reader) Men and Machines, 1958; A Memoir of Sir Ellis Hunter, 1962; A Man and His Times, 1962; England's Apprenticeship 1603–1763, 1965, 2nd edn 1985; Unilever, 1945–65, 1968; The Dutch Republic and the Civilization of the Seventeenth Century, 1968; Economic History and the Historian, 1969; Queen Elizabeth and the Revolt of the Netherlands, 1970; Parliaments, Peoples and Mass Media, 1970; The Relevance of History (Brussels), 1975; (chapter) Colonialism in Africa, Vol. 4 1975; The Transformation of Europe, 1976; (ed with N. G. Parker) The Sources of European Economic History, 1977; Il Cammino verso l'industrializzone (Bologna), 1979; Cambridge Economic History of Europe: (ed jtly with Prof. E. E. Rich, and contrib.) Vol. IV 1967, Vol. V 1977; New Cambridge Modern History: (chapters on economic history) Vol. VII 1957, Vol. XI 1962; (ed. and contrib.) Geoffrey Heyworth, A Memoir, 1985; First With the News: a history of W. H. Smith 1792–1972, 1985; numerous articles. *Recreation:* music. *Address:* Jesus College, Cambridge. *Club:* University Pitt (Cambridge).

WILSON, Charles Martin; Editor, The Times, since 1985; *b* 18 Aug. 1935; *s* of Adam and Ruth Wilson; *m* 1st, 1968, Anne Robinson (marr. diss. 1973); one *d;* 2nd, 1980, Sally Angela O'Sullivan; one *s* one *d. Educ:* Eastbank Academy, Glasgow. News Chronicle, 1959–60; Daily Mail, 1960–71; Dep. Northern Editor, Daily Mail, 1971–74; Asst Editor, London Evening News, 1974–76; Editor, Glasgow Evening Times, Glasgow Herald, Scottish Sunday Standard, 1976–82; Exec. Editor, The Times, 1982, Dep. Editor, 1983. *Recreations:* reading, horse racing. *Address:* The Times, PO Box 481, Virginia Street, E1. *T:* 01–481 4100. *Club:* Reform.

WILSON, (Christopher) David, CBE 1968; MC 1945; Chairman: Southern Television Ltd, 1976–81 (Managing Director, 1959–76); Southstar Television International, 1976–81; Beaumont (UK) Ltd, 1979–81; *b* 17 Dec. 1916; *s* of late Anthony James Wilson, Highclere, Worplesdon, Surrey; *m* 1947, Jean Barbara Morton Smith; no *c. Educ:* St George's Sch., Windsor; Aldenham. Served War of 1939–45: Captain RA, in India, Middle East and Italy. Business Manager, Associated Newspapers Ltd, 1955–57; Dir, Associated Rediffusion Ltd, 1956–57; Gen. Manager, Southern Television Ltd, 1957–59; Chm., ITN Ltd, 1969–71. Mem. Council, Southampton Univ.; Vice-Pres., Southern Arts Assoc.; Mem. Exec. Cttee, South East Arts Assoc.; Trustee, Chichester Festival Theatre Trust Ltd; Dir, Canterbury New Theatre Ltd. FCA 1947. *Recreations:* sailing, music. *Address:* Little Croft, Upham, Hants. *T:* Durley 204. *Clubs:* MCC; Royal Southern Yacht.

WILSON, Christopher Maynard, DIC, PhD; Chairman, Microsystems Group PLC, since 1984; *b* 19 Dec. 1928; *s* of late George Henry Cyril Wilson and of Adelaide Flora Marie Wilson; *m* 1953, Elizabeth Ursula Canning; one *s* two *d. Educ:* King Edward VII Sch., Sheffield; Worksop Coll., Notts; Imperial Coll., London Univ. (BSc, ARCS, DIC, PhD). National Service, RAF, 1947–49. Ferranti Computers, 1953–63; Ferranti merged with ICT, 1963, ICT merged with English Electric Computers to become ICL, 1968; Manager, UK Sales, 1968–70; Director: Marketing and Product Strategy, 1970–72; Internat. Div., 1972–77; Man. Dir, International Computers Ltd, 1977–81. *Recreations:*

squash, tennis, gardening, golf. *Address:* Tiles Cottage, Forest Road, Winkfield Row, near Bracknell, Berks.

WILSON, Clifford; Professor of Medicine, University of London, at the London Hospital and Director, Medical Unit, The London Hospital, 1946–71, now Emeritus Professor; *b* 27 Jan. 1906; *m* 1936, Kathleen Hebden; one *s* one *d. Educ:* Balliol College, Oxford. Brackenbury Scholar, Balliol Coll., Oxford, 1924; 1st Class Oxford Final Hons School of Nat. Sciences, 1928; House Physician, etc., London Hospital, 1931–34; Rockefeller Travelling Fellow, 1934–35; Research Fellow, Harvard Univ.; Asst Director, Medical Unit, London Hosp., 1938; Univ. Reader in Medicine, London Hosp., 1940; Major RAMC, Medical Research Section, 1942–45. President Renal Association, 1963–64. Examiner MRCP, 1960–; Censor, RCP, 1964–66; Senior Censor and Senior Vice-Pres., 1967–68. Dean, Faculty of Medicine, Univ. of London, 1968–71. *Publications:* sections on renal diseases and diseases of the arteries in Price's Text Book of Medicine; papers on renal disease, hypertension, arterial disease and other medical subjects, 1930–70. *Address:* The White Cottage, Woodgreen, Fordingbridge, Hants.

WILSON, Clive Hebden; Under Secretary, Children, Maternity, Prevention Division, Department of Health and Social Security, since 1986; *b* 1 Feb. 1940; *s* of Joseph and Irene Wilson; *m* 1976, Jill Garland Evans; one *d. Educ:* Leeds Grammar Sch.; Corpus Christi Coll., Oxford. Joined Civil Service, 1962; Ministry of Health: Asst Principal, 1962–67; Asst Private Sec. to Minister of Health, 1965–66; Principal, 1967–73; Assistant Secretary: DHSS, 1973–77; Cabinet Office, 1977–79; DHSS, 1979–82; Under Sec., 1982; Dir of Estabs (HQ), DHSS, 1982–84; Child Care Div., DHSS, 1984–86. *Recreations:* squash, walking, gardening.

WILSON, Prof. Colin Alexander St John, FRIBA; Professor of Architecture, Cambridge University, since 1975; Fellow, Pembroke College, Cambridge, since 1977; Architect (own private practice); *b* 14 March 1922; *yr s* of late Rt Rev. Henry A. Wilson, CBE, DD; *m* 1st, 1955, Muriel Lavender (marr. diss. 1971); 2nd, 1972, Mary Jane Long; one *s* one *d. Educ:* Felsted Sch.; Corpus Christi Coll., Cambridge, 1940–42 (MA); Sch. of Architecture, London Univ., 1946–49 (Dip. Lond.). Served War, RNVR, 1942–46. Asst in Housing Div., Architects Dept, LCC, 1950–55; Lectr at Sch. of Architecture, Univ. of Cambridge, 1955–69; Fellow, Churchill Coll., Cambridge, 1962–71. Practised in assoc. with Sir Leslie Martin, 1955–64: on bldgs in Cambridge (Harvey Court, Gonville and Caius Coll.; Stone Building, Peterhouse); Univ. of Oxford, Law Library; Univ. of Leicester, Science Campus; Univ. of London, Royal Holloway Coll. In own practice Buildings include: Extension to Sch. of Architecture, Cambridge; Research Laboratory, Babraham; Extension to British Museum; The British Library, St Pancras (commenced construction, 1982); various residences; Projects for Liverpool Civic and Social Centre, and Group Headquarters and Research Campus for Lucas Industries Ltd. Vis. Critic to Yale Sch. of Architecture, USA, 1960, 1964 and 1983; Bemis Prof. of Architecture, MIT, USA, 1970–72. Trustee: Tate Gall., 1973–80; Nat. Gall., 1977–80. *Publications:* articles in: The Observer; professional jls in UK, USA, France, Spain, Japan, Germany, Norway, Italy, Switzerland, etc. *Address:* 31A Grove End Road, NW8. *T:* 01–286 8306; 2 Grantchester Road, Cambridge. *T:* Cambridge 357776; (office) Colin St John Wilson & Partners, Highbury Crescent Rooms, 70 Ronalds Road, N5 1XW. *T:* 01–354 2030.

WILSON, Colin Henry; author; *b* Leicester, 26 June 1931; *s* of Arthur Wilson and Annetta Jones; *m* Dorothy Betty Troop; one *s*; *m* Joy Stewart; two *s* one *d. Educ:* The Gateway Secondary Technical School, Leicester. Left school at 16. Laboratory Asst (Gateway School), 1948–49; Civil Servant (collector of taxes), Leicester and Rugby, 1949–50; national service with RAF, AC2, 1949–50. Various jobs, and a period spent in Paris and Strasbourg, 1950; came to London, 1951; various labouring jobs, long period in plastic factory; returned to Paris, 1953; labouring jobs in London until Dec. 1954, when began writing The Outsider: has since made a living at writing. Visiting Professor: Hollins Coll., Va, 1966–67; Univ. of Washington, Seattle, 1967; Dowling Coll., Majorca, 1969; Rutgers Univ., NJ, 1974. Plays produced: Viennese Interlude; The Metal Flower Blossom; Strindberg. *Publications:* The Outsider, 1956; Religion and the Rebel, 1957; The Age of Defeat, 1959; Ritual in the Dark, 1960; Adrift in Soho, 1961; An Encyclopædia of Murder, 1961; The Strength to Dream, 1962; Origins of the Sexual Impulse, 1963; The Man without a Shadow, 1963; The World of Violence, 1963; Rasputin and the Fall of the Romanovs, 1964; The Brandy of the Damned (musical essays), 1964; Necessary Doubt, 1964; Beyond the Outsider, 1965; Eagle and Earwig, 1965; The Mind Parasites, 1966; Introduction to The New Existentialism, 1966; The Glass Cage, 1966; Sex and the Intelligent Teenager, 1966; The Philosopher's Stone, 1968; Strindberg (play), 1968; Bernard Shaw: A Reassessment, 1969; Voyage to a Beginning, 1969; Poetry and Mysticism, 1970; The Black Room, 1970; A Casebook of Murder, 1970; The God of the Labyrinth, 1970; Lingard, 1970; (jtly) The Strange Genius of David Lindsay, 1970; The Occult, 1971; New Pathways in Psychology, 1972; Order of Assassins, 1971; Tree by Tolkien, 1973; Hermann Hesse, 1973; Strange Powers, 1973; The Schoolgirl Murder Case, 1974; Return of the Lloigor, 1974; A Book of Booze, 1974; The Craft of the Novel, 1975; The Space Vampires, 1976 (filmed as Lifeforce, 1985); Men of Strange Powers, 1976; Enigmas and Mysteries, 1977; The Geller Phenomenon, 1977; Mysteries, 1978; Mysteries (play), 1979; The Quest for Wilhelm Reich, 1979; The War Against Sleep: the philosophy of Gurdjieff, 1980; Starseekers, 1980; Frankenstein's Castle, 1981; (ed with John Grant) The Directory of Possibilities, 1981; Poltergeist!, 1981; Access to Inner Worlds, 1982; The Criminal History of Mankind, 1983; (with Donald Seaman) Encyclopaedia of Modern Murder, 1983; Psychic Detectives, 1983; The Janus Murder Case, 1984; The Essential Colin Wilson, 1984; The Personality Surgeon, 1985; contribs to: The Spectator, Audio, Books and Bookmen, Hi-Fi News, Sunday Times, Sunday Telegraph, etc. *Recreations:* collecting gramophone records, mainly opera; mathematics. *Address:* Tetherdown, Trewallock Lane, Gorran Haven, Cornwall. *Club:* Savage.

WILSON, Maj.-Gen. Dare; *see* Wilson, Maj.-Gen. R. D.

WILSON, David; *see* Wilson, C. D.

WILSON, Sir David, 3rd Bt *cr* 1920; solicitor; *b* 30 Oct. 1928; *s* of Sir John Mitchell Harvey Wilson, 2nd Bt, KCVO, and Mary Elizabeth (*d* 1979), *d* of late William Richards, CBE; *S* father, 1975; *m* 1955, Eva Margareta, *e d* of Tore Lindell, Malmö, Sweden; two *s* one *d. Educ:* Deerfield Acad., Mass., USA; Harrow School; Oriel Coll., Oxford (Brisco Owen Schol.). Barrister, Lincoln's Inn, 1954–61; admitted Solicitor, 1962; Partner in Simmons & Simmons, EC2, 1963–. *Heir: s* Thomas David Wilson [*b* 6 Jan. 1959; *m* 1984, Valerie, *er d* of Vivian Stogdale, Shotover, Oxford]. *Address:* Tandem House, Queen's Drive, Oxshott, Leatherhead, Surrey KT22 0PH. *Clubs:* Arts; Royal Southern Yacht.

WILSON, David Clive, CMG 1985; PhD; HM Diplomatic Service; Assistant Under-Secretary of State, Foreign and Commonwealth Office, since 1984; *b* 14 Feb. 1935; *s* of Rev. William Skinner Wilson and Enid Wilson; *m* 1967, Natasha Helen Mary Alexander; two *s. Educ:* Trinity Coll., Glenalmond; Keble Coll., Oxford (schol., MA); PhD London 1973. National Service, The Black Watch, 1953–55; entered Foreign Service, 1958; Third Secretary, Vientiane, 1959–60; Language Student, Hong Kong, 1960–62; Second, later First Secretary, Peking, 1963–65; FCO, 1965–68; resigned, 1968; Editor, China

Quarterly, 1968–74; Vis. Scholar, Columbia Univ., New York, 1972; rejoined Diplomatic Service, 1974; Cabinet Office, 1974–77; Political Adviser, Hong Kong, 1977–81; Hd, S European Dept, FCO, 1981–84. Oxford Univ. Somaliland Expedn, 1957; British Mt Kongur Expedn (NW China), 1981. *Recreations:* mountaineering, ski-ing, reading. *Address:* c/o Foreign and Commonwealth Office, SW1. *Clubs:* Athenæum, Alpine.

WILSON, Sir David (Mackenzie), Kt 1984; FBA 1981; Director of the British Museum, since 1977; *b* 30 Oct. 1931; *e s* of Rev. Joseph Wilson; *m* 1955, Eva, *o d* of Dr Gunnar Sjögren, Stockholm; one *s* one *d. Educ:* Kingswood Sch.; St John's Coll., Cambridge (LittD; Hon. Fellow, 1985); Lund Univ., Sweden. Research Asst, Cambridge Univ., 1954; Asst Keeper, British Museum, 1954–64; Reader in Archaeology of Anglo-Saxon Period, London Univ., 1964–71; Prof. of Medieval Archaeology, Univ. of London, 1971–76; Jt Head of Dept of Scandinavian Studies, UCL, 1973–76. Slade Prof., Cambridge, 1985–86. Mem., Ancient Monuments Bd for England, 1976–84. Governor, Museum of London, 1976–81; Trustee: Nat. Museums of Scotland, 1985–; Nat. Museums of Merseyside, 1986–. Crabtree Orator 1966. Member: Royal Swedish Acad. of Sci.; Royal Acad. of Letters, History and Antiquities, Sweden; German Archaeological Inst.; Royal Gustav Adolf's Acad. of Sweden; Royal Soc. of Letters of Lund; Vetenskapssocieteten, Lund; Royal Soc. of Sci. and Letters, Gothenburg; Royal Soc. of Sci., Uppsala; Royal Norwegian Soc. of Sci. and Letters; FSA; Hon. MRIA; Hon. Mem., Polish Archaeological and Numismatic Soc.; Sec., Soc. for Medieval Archaeology, 1957–77; Pres., Viking Soc., 1968–70; Pres., Brit. Archaeological Assoc., 1962–68. Hon. Fil.Dr Stockholm; Hon. Dr Phil Aarhus; Hon. DLitt Nottingham. Félix Neuburgh Prize, Gothenburg Univ., 1978. Order of Polar Star, 1st cl. (Sweden), 1977. *Publications:* The Anglo-Saxons, 1960, 3rd edn 1981; Anglo-Saxon Metalwork 700–1100 in British Museum, 1964; (with O. Klindt-Jensen) Viking Art, 1966; (with G. Bersu) Three Viking Graves in the Isle of Man, 1969; The Vikings and their Origins, 1970, 2nd edn 1980; (with P. G. Foote) The Viking Achievement, 1970 (Dag Strömbäck Prize, Royal Gustav Adolf's Acad., 1975); (with A. Small and C. Thomas) St Ninian's Isle and its Treasure, 1973; The Viking Age in the Isle of Man, 1974; (ed) Anglo-Saxon Archaeology, 1976; (ed) The Northern World, 1980; The Forgotten Collector, 1984; Anglo-Saxon Art, 1984; The Bayeux Tapestry, 1985, etc. *Address:* British Museum, WC1; The Lifeboat House, Castletown, Isle of Man. *Club:* Athenæum.

WILSON, Des; Campaign Director, Friends of the Earth International, since 1985; Chairman, Campaign for Freedom of Information, since 1984; President of the Liberal Party, Sept. 1986–87; *b* 5 March 1941; *s* of Albert H. Wilson, Oamaru, New Zealand; *m* 1985, Jane Dunmore; one *s* one *d* by a previous marriage. *Educ:* Waitaki Boys' High Sch., New Zealand. Journalist-Broadcaster, 1957–67; Director, Shelter, Nat. Campaign for the Homeless, 1967–71; Head of Public Affairs, RSC, 1974–76; Editor, Social Work Today, 1976–79; Dep. Editor, Illustrated London News, 1979–81; Chm., 1981–85, Project Advr, 1985–, CLEAR (Campaign for Lead-Free Air). Member: Nat. Exec., Nat. Council for Civil Liberties, 1971–73; Cttee for City Poverty, 1972–73; Bd, Shelter, 1982– (Trustee, 1982–); Trustee, Internat. Year of Shelter for the Homeless (UK), 1985–87. Columnist, The Guardian, 1968–70; Columnist, The Observer, 1971–75; regular contributor, Illustrated London News, 1972–85. Contested (L) Hove, 1973, 1974; Liberal Party: Mem. Council, 1973–74 and 1984–85; Mem., Nat. Exec., 1984–85; Pres., NLYL, 1984–85. *Publications:* I Know It Was the Place's Fault, 1970; Des Wilson's Minority Report (a diary of protest), 1973; So you want to be Prime Minister: a personal view of British politics, 1979; The Lead Scandal, 1982; Pressure, the A to Z of Campaigning in Britain, 1984; (ed) The Environmental Crisis, 1984; (ed) The Secrets File, 1984; The Citizen Action Handbook, 1986. *Address:* 46 Arundel Street, Brighton, Sussex.

WILSON, Dr Douglas George, CB 1984; Chief Government Medical Officer, Queensland, 1968–84; retired 1984; Senior Lecturer in Forensic Medicine, University of Queensland, since 1968; *b* 21 Jan. 1924; *s* of William John Wilson and Mary Catherine Mitchell; *m* 1951, Heloise, *d* of J. J. McCormack; one *s. Educ:* St Joseph's College, Nudgee, Qld. MB BS Qld 1952; DPH Sydney 1965; Dip. Med. Jurisp., Soc. of Apothecaries of London, 1975. War service, 2nd AIF, 1942–44; RAAMC, 1953. Resident MO, Brisbane Gen. Hosp., 1952–53; private practice, Caloundra, 1954–65; Dep. MOH, NSW Dept of Public Health, 1965–67. Founder Dep. Chm., Qld Road Safety Council Res. Cttee, 1975–; Mem., Traffic Adv. Cttee, 1968–84; Dep. Chm. Med. Div. and Mem. Internat. Med. Commn, XII Commonwealth Games, Brisbane, 1982. Nat. Health and MRC Travelling Fellowship in Forensic Medicine, 1975; Fulbright Sen. Schol. in Traffic Medicine, Central Missouri State Univ., 1978. Member: British Acad. of Forensic Scis; Forensic Sci. Soc.; Internat. Assoc. for Accident and Traffic Medicine; Aust. and Pacific Area Police Med. Officers' Assoc. Foundation Chairman: Sunshine Coast Br., Arthritis Foundn of Aust., 1985; Qld Estuarine Res. Gp, 1985. Gold Medal, Internat. Assoc. for Accident and Traffic Medicine, 1985. SBStJ 1978. *Publications:* Rationale of the Determination of Blood Alcohol Concentration by Breath Analysis (Training Manual), 1968; numerous papers on alcohol, drugs and traffic safety, forensic subjects in learned jls. *Recreations:* swimming, boating, golf, tropical fruit farming. *Address:* 3 Alfred Street, Caloundra, Qld 4551, Australia. *T:* (071) 91 1610. *Clubs:* University of Queensland (Brisbane); Caloundra Golf, Caloundra Power Boat, Caloundra Returned Services.

WILSON, Ellis; *see* Wilson, H. E. C.

WILSON, Lt-Col Eric Charles Twelves, VC 1940; retired; *b* 2 October 1912; *s* of late Rev. C. C. C. Wilson; *m* 1943, Ann (from whom he obtained a divorce, 1953), *d* of Major Humphrey Pleydell-Bouverie, MBE; two *s*; *m* 1953, Angela Joy, *d* of Lt-Col J. McK. Gordon, MC; one *s. Educ:* Marlborough; RMC, Sandhurst. Commissioned in East Surrey Regt, 1933; seconded to King's African Rifles, 1937; seconded to Somaliland Camel Corps, 1939; Long Range Desert Gp, 1941–42; Burma, 1944; seconded to N Rhodesia Regt, 1946; retd from Regular Army, 1949; Admin Officer, HM Overseas Civil Service, Tanganyika, 1949–61; Dep. Warden, London House, 1962, Warden, 1966–77. Hon. Sec., Anglo-Somali Soc., 1972–77. *Publication:* Stowell in the Blackmore Vale, 1986. *Recreation:* country life. *Address:* Woodside Cottage, Stowell, Sherborne, Dorset. *T:* Templecombe 70264.

WILSON, Frank Richard, CMG 1963; OBE 1946; Controller of Administration, Commonwealth Development Corporation, 1976–80; retired HMOCS Oct. 1963; *b* 26 Oct. 1920; *er s* of late Sir Leonard Wilson, KCIE and the late Muriel Wilson; *m* 1947, Alexandra Dorothy Mary (*née* Haigh); two *s. Educ:* Oundle Sch.; Trinity Hall, Cambridge (1939–40 only). Commnd Indian Army, 1941; retired as Lieut-Col, 1946. Joined Colonial Administrative Service (later HMOCS) in Kenya, 1947; District Comr, 1950–56; Private Sec. to the Governor, 1956–59; Provincial Comr, Central Province, 1959–63; Civil Sec., Central Region, 1963. With Commonwealth Develt Corp., 1964–80. *Address:* Chelsea House, Mickleton, Chipping Campden, Glos.

WILSON, Geoffrey; Chairman, Wells, O'Brien & Co., since 1972; *b* 11 July 1929; *m* 1962, Philomena Mary Kavanagh; one *s* one *d. Educ:* Bolton County Grammar Sch.; Univ. of Birmingham; Linacre Coll., Oxford. PE Consulting Group, 1958–63; British Railways, 1963–71; Mem., BR Bd, 1968–71, Chief Exec. (Railways), 1971. Member:

Council, Royal Inst. of Public Admin, 1970–71; Council, Inst. of Transport, 1970–71. *Recreations:* golf, gardening, painting. *Address:* 5 Lancaster Court, Well Place, Cheltenham, Glos.

WILSON, Hon. Geoffrey Hazlitt, FCA, FCMA; Chief Executive since 1981, and Chairman since 1982, Delta Group plc; *b* 28 Dec. 1929; *yr s* of 1st Baron Moran, MC, MD, FRCP, and Lady Moran, MBE; *m* 1955, Barbara Jane Hebblethwaite; two *s* two *d.* *Educ:* Eton; King's Coll., Cambridge (BA Hons). JDipMA. Articled to Barton Mayhew (now Ernst & Whinney), 1952; Chartered Accountant 1955; joined English Electric, 1956; Dep. Comptroller, 1965; Financial Controller (Overseas), GEC, 1968; joined Delta Group as Financial Dir, Cables Div., 1969; elected to Main Board as Gp Financial Dir, 1972; Jt Man. Dir, 1977; Dep. Chief Executive, 1980. Director: Blue Circle Industries plc, 1980–; English & International Trust Ltd, 1978–; W Midlands and Wales Regl Bd, Nat. Westminster Bank PLC, 1985–. Member: Council, Inst. of Cost and Management Accountants, 1972–78; Accounting Standards Cttee, 1978–79; Inflation Accounting Steering Gp, 1976–80; London Metal Exchange, 1982–; Engrg Industries Council, 1985–; Chm., 100 Gp of Chartered Accountants, 1979–80 (Hon. Mem., 1985). Mem. Management Bd, Engineering Employers Fedn, 1979–83 (Vice-Pres., 1983–86; Dep. Pres., 1986–); Chm., EEF Cttee on Future of Wage Bargaining, 1980. Member: Administrative Council, Royal Jubilee Trusts, 1979–, Hon. Treas., 1980–; Council, Winchester Cathedral Trust, 1985–; Council, St Mary's Hosp. Med. Sch., 1985–. Mem. Ct of Assistants, Chartered Accountants' Co., 1982–, Jun. Warden, 1986–87. *Recreations:* family, reading, vintage cars. *Address:* Delta Group, 1 Kingsway, WC2B 6XF. *T:* 01–836 3535. *Clubs:* Boodle's, Royal Automobile.

WILSON, Sir Geoffrey Masterman, KCB 1969 (CB 1968); CMG 1962; Chairman, Oxfam, 1977–83; *b* 7 April 1910; 3rd *s* of late Alexander Cowan Wilson and Edith Jane Brayshaw; *m* 1946, Julie Stafford Trowbridge (marr. diss. 1979); two *s* two *d.* *Educ:* Manchester Grammar School; Oriel College, Oxford. Chairman, Oxford Univ. Labour Club, 1930; Pres., Oxford Union, 1931. Harmsworth Law Scholar, Middle Temple, 1931; called to Bar, Middle Temple, 1934. Served in HM Embassy, Moscow, and Russian Dept of Foreign Office, 1940–45. Cabinet Office, 1947; Treasury, 1948; Director, Colombo Plan Technical Co-operation Bureau, 1951–53; Under-Secretary, Treasury, 1956–58; Deputy Head of UK Treasury Delegn and Alternate Exec. Dir for UK, Internat. Bank, Washington, 1958; Vice-President, International Bank, Washington, 1961; Deputy Secretary, ODM, 1966–68, Permanent Secretary, 1968–70; Dep. Sec.-Gen. (Economic), Commonwealth Secretariat, 1971. Chm., Race Relations Bd, 1971–77. Hon. Fellow, Wolfson Coll., Cambridge, 1971. *Address:* 4 Polstead Road, Oxford.

See also Prof. J. E. Meade, Prof. R. C. Wilson, S. S. Wilson.

WILSON, Geoffrey Studholme, CMG 1961; Commissioner of Police, Tanganyika Police Force, 1958–62; *b* 5 June 1913; *s* of late J. E. S. Wilson; *m* 1936, Joy Noel, *d* of Capt. C. St G. Harris-Walker; two *s.* *Educ:* Radley College. Joined Hong Kong Police, 1933; Commissioner of Police, Sarawak Constabulary, 1953–58. King's Police Medal, 1950. OStJ 1961. *Recreations:* golf, fishing, sailing. *Address:* c/o The Hong Kong & Shanghai Banking Corporation, 9 Waterloo Place, SW1Y 4BE. *Club:* Hong Kong (Hong Kong).

WILSON, George; *see* Wilson, W. G.

WILSON, George Pritchard Harvey, CMG 1966; JP; Chairman, Victorian Inland Meat Authority, 1973–77 (Deputy Chairman, 1970–73); *b* 10 March 1918; *s* of late G. L. Wilson; *m* 1945, Fay Hobart Duff; two *s* one *d.* *Educ:* Geelong Grammar School. Nuffield Scholar (Farming), 1952. Council Member, Monash University, 1961–69; Royal Agricultural Society of Victoria: Councillor, 1950; President, 1964–73; Trustee, 1968–. Member: Victoria Promotion Cttee, 1968–81; Victoria Economic Develt Corp., 1981–82. JP 1957. *Recreation:* fishing. *Address:* Wilson House, Berwick, Victoria 3806, Australia. *T:* Berwick 7071271. *Clubs:* Melbourne, Royal Automobile Club of Victoria (Melbourne).

WILSON, Gerald Robertson; Under Secretary, Industry Department for Scotland, since 1984; *b* 7 Sept. 1939; *s* of Charles Robertson Wilson and Margaret Wilson (*née* Early); *m* 1963, Margaret Anne, *d* of late John S. and Agnes Wight; one *s* one *d.* *Educ:* Holy Cross Academy, Edinburgh; University of Edinburgh. MA. Asst Principal, Scottish Home and Health Dept, 1961–65; Private Sec. to Minister of State for Scotland, 1965–66; Principal, Scottish Home and Health Dept, 1966–72; Private Sec. to Lord Privy Seal, 1972–74, to Minister of State, Civil Service Dept, 1974; Asst Sec., Scottish Economic Planning Dept, 1974–77; Counsellor, Office of the UK Perm. Rep. to the European Communities, Brussels, 1977–82; Asst Sec., Scottish Office, 1982–84. *Recreation:* music. *Address:* c/o Industry Department for Scotland, Alhambra House, 45 Waterloo Street, Glasgow G2 6AT. *Club:* Royal Commonwealth Society.

WILSON, (Gerald) Roy; Deputy Director of Savings (Under Secretary), Department for National Savings, since 1986; *b* 11 Jan. 1930; *s* of late Fred Wilson and Elsie Wilson (*née* Morrison); *m* 1965, Doreen Chadderton; one *s* one *d.* *Educ:* High School, Oldham. Min. of Works, 1947; HM Stationery Office, 1949; Post Office Savings Dept, 1957; PO HQ, 1963; National Girobank, 1966; Dept for National Savings, 1969–; Controller, Savings Certificate and SAYE Office, Durham, 1978. FBIM. *Recreations:* Rotarian; swimming, and its organisation and teaching, reading, drawing, photography, watching other sports. *Address:* c/o Department for National Savings, Charles House, 375 Kensington High Street, W14 8SD. *Clubs:* Civil Service; Dunelm (Durham); Durham City Swimming, Durham City Cricket.

WILSON, Gilbert; *b* 2 March 1908; *s* of J. E. Wilson; *m* 1934, Janet Joy Turner; two *d.* *Educ:* Auckland Grammar School. Served with 2nd NZEF, Middle East, 1940–43. Joined National Bank of New Zealand, 1924; joined Reserve Bank of New Zealand, 1935; Dep. Chief Cashier, 1948–53; Chief Cashier, 1953–56; Dep. Governor, 1956–62; Governor, 1962–67; also Alternate Governor for New Zealand of International Monetary Fund, 1962–67. *Address:* 41 Mere Road, Taupo, New Zealand.

WILSON, Gordon; *see* Wilson, Robert G.

WILSON, Gordon Wallace, CB 1986; Under Secretary, Ministry of Agriculture, Fisheries and Food, 1975–86; *b* 14 July 1926; *s* of late John Wallace Wilson and of Mrs Joyce Elizabeth Grace Sherwood-Smith; *m* 1951, Gillian Maxwell (*née* Wood); three *s.* *Educ:* King's Sch., Bruton; Queen's Coll., Oxford (BA PPE). Entered Civil Service (War Office), 1950; Principal Private Sec. to Sec. of State for War, 1962; Asst Sec., MoD, 1964; Dir, Centre of Admin Studies, HM Treasury, 1965; Asst Sec., DEA, 1968; HM Treasury, 1969. *Recreations:* tennis, carpentry, gardening, camping. *Address:* 61 Ottways Lane, Ashtead, Surrey. *T:* Ashtead 72898.

WILSON, Graeme McDonald, CMG 1975; British Civil Aviation Representative (Far East), 1964–81, retired; *b* 9 May 1919; *s* of Robert Linton McDonald Wilson and Sophie Hamilton Wilson (*née* Milner); *m* 1968, Yabu Masae; three *s.* *Educ:* Rendcomb Coll., Glos; Schloss Schule Salem, Germany; Lincoln Coll., Oxford; Gray's Inn, London. Served in Fleet Air Arm, 1939–46. Joined Home Civil Service, 1946. Private Sec. to Parly Sec., Min. of Civil Aviation, 1946–49; Planning 1, 1949–53; Dep. UK Rep. on Council of ICAO, 1953–56; Lt-Comdr (A) (O) (Ph) (q) RCNR, 1954; Internat. Relations 1, Min. of Transport and Civil Aviation, 1956–61; Asst Sec. Interdependence, Exports and Electronics, Min. of Aviation, 1961–64; seconded to Foreign Service as Counsellor and Civil Air Attaché, at twelve Far Eastern posts, 1964. Ford Foundn Fellow, Nat. Translation Center, Austin, Texas, 1968–69. UN Expert on Air Services Agreements, 1984. *Publications:* Face At The Bottom Of The World: translations of the modern Japanese poetry of Hagiwara Sakutaro, 1969; (trans., with Ito Aiko) I Am a Cat, 1971; (trans., with Atsumi Ikuko) Three Contemporary Japanese Poets, 1972; (trans., with Ito Aiko) Ten Nights of Dream, 1973; Nihon no Kindaishi to Gendaishi no Dai Yon-sho: Hagiwara Sakutaro, 1974; (trans., with Ito Aiko) I Am a Cat II, 1979; (trans., with Ito Aiko) I Am a Cat III, 1985; articles on East Asian literature and poems (mostly Japanese, Chinese, Vietnamese and Korean trans). *Address:* 42 Cranford Avenue, Exmouth, Devon. *T:* Exmouth 264786. *Clubs:* Naval; PEN Club of Japan (Tokyo).

WILSON, Sir Graham (Selby), Kt 1962; MD, FRCP, DPH (London); FRS 1978; late Captain Royal Army Medical Corps (Special Reserve); Hon. Lecturer, Department of Bacteriology and Immunology, London School of Hygiene and Tropical Medicine, 1964–70; Director of the Public Health Laboratory Service, 1941–63; KHP, 1944–46; *b* 10 Sept. 1895; *m* Mary Joyce (*d* 1976), *d* of Alfred Ayrton, Chester; two *s.* *Educ:* Epsom College; King's Coll., London; Charing Cross Hospital, London; Governors' Clinical Gold Medal, Charing Cross Hospital, and Gold Medal, University of London, MB, BS; Specialist in Bacteriology, Royal Army Med. Corps, 1916–20; Demonstrator in Bacteriology, Charing Cross Hospital Medical School, 1919–22; Lecturer in Bacteriology, University of Manchester, 1923–27; Reader in Bacteriology, University of London, 1927–30; Prof. of Bacteriology as applied to Hygiene, London School of Hygiene and Tropical Medicine, 1930–47; William Julius Mickle Fellowship, University of London, 1939. Member: Council, RCP, 1938–40; of several cttees on tuberculosis, poliomyelitis and other infectious diseases; Weber-Parkes prize, RCP 1942; Milroy Lecturer, RCP, 1948; Hon. Fellow, Amer. Public Health Assoc., 1953; Hon. Fellow: Royal Soc. of Health, 1960; London Sch. of Hygiene and Tropical Medicine, 1976; Hon. FRSocMed, 1971; Hon. FRCPath, 1972. Czechoslovak Medical Society, Jan Evangelista Purkyně, 1963; Bisset Hawkins Medal, RCP, 1956; Marjory Stephenson Memorial Prize, 1959; Stewart Prize, 1960; Buchanan Medal, Royal Society, 1967; Harben Gold Medal, 1970; Jenner Meml Medal, 1975. Hon. LLD (Glasgow) 1962. *Publications:* The Principles of Bacteriology and Immunity (with late Professor W. W. C. Topley and Sir Ashley Miles), 6th edn 1975, (also with Dr M. T. Parker) 7th edn 1984; The Hazards of Immunization, 1967; The Bacteriological Grading of Milk (with collaborators), 1935; The Pasteurization of Milk, 1942; The Brown Animal Sanatory Institution, 1979; numerous papers on bacteriological subjects. *Address:* 11 Morpeth Mansions, Morpeth Terrace, SW1P IER. *Club:* Athenæum.

WILSON, Harold; His Honour Judge Harold Wilson; a Circuit Judge, since 1981 (Midland and Oxford Circuit); *b* 19 Sept. 1931; *s* of late Edward Simpson Wilson; *m* 1973, Jill Ginever, *d* of late Charles Edward Walter Barlow; one step *s* one step *d*; three *s* one *d* by previous marriage. *Educ:* St Albans Sch.; Sidney Sussex Coll., Cambridge (State Scholar; MA). Commnd service, RAF, RAFVR, RAuxAF, 1950–disbandment. Administrative Trainee, KCH, 1954–56; Schoolmaster, 1957–59. Called to the Bar, Gray's Inn, 1958 (Holker Exhbr; runner-up, Lee Essay Prize, 1959); Oxford Circuit, 1960–70 (Circuit Junior, 1964–65); Midland and Oxford Circuit, 1971–75; Dep. Chm., Monmouthshire Quarter Sessions, 1970; a Recorder, Midland and Oxford Circuit, 1971–75; Chm. of Industrial Tribunals, Birmingham, 1976–81; designated Judge, Coventry Crown Ct, 1983–; Liaison Judge, 1986–; Hon. Recorder of Coventry, 1986–. Member: Matrimonial Causes Rules Cttee, 1985–; W Midlands Probation Cttee, 1985–. *Recreations:* watching rugby football, reading and listening to music. *Address:* 2 Harcourt Buildings, Temple, EC4Y 9DB. *T:* 01–353 6961. *Club:* Royal Air Force.

WILSON, Harold Arthur Cooper B.; *see* Bird-Wilson.

WILSON, Harry; *see* Wilson of Langside, Baron.

WILSON, (Harry) Ellis (Charter), MB, ChB; DSc; FRCPGlas; retired as Lecturer in Pathological Biochemistry at Royal Hospital for Sick Children, Glasgow; *b* 26 July 1899; *s* of Harry James and Margaret Williamina Wilson. *Educ:* Glasgow Academy and University. Carnegie Scholar, 1923; studied in Würzburg, 1926; Assistant in Institute of Physiology, Glasgow University, 1924; a Rockefeller Fellowship tenable in USA, 1926; carried out research in New York and the Mayo Clinic, Rochester; Carnegie Teaching Fellow in Institute of Physiology, Glasgow University, 1930; studied (research) in Germany, 1931; Professor of Biochemistry and Nutrition, The All-India Institute of Hygiene and Public Health, Calcutta, 1934–37, and Professor of Chemistry, The Medical College, Calcutta, 1935–37. *Publications:* papers on biochemical subjects in various journals. *Recreations:* golf, travel. *Address:* Redholm, 5 West Chapelton Avenue, Bearsden, Glasgow; The Royal Hospital for Sick Children, Yorkhill, Glasgow.

WILSON, Harry Lawrence L.; *see* Lawrence-Wilson.

WILSON, Henry Braithwaite; Assistant Under-Secretary of State, Home Office, 1963–71; *b* 6 Aug. 1911; *s* of Charles Braithwaite Wilson and Ellen Blanche Hargrove; *m* 1936, Margaret Bodden; two *s* two *d.* *Educ:* Leighton Park School; Lincoln College, Oxford. Editorial work for Joseph Rowntree Social Service Trust, 1933–40; Sub-Warden, Toynbee Hall, 1940–41; Home Office: Temp. Administrative Asst, 1941–44; Sec., Departmental Cttee on War Damaged Licensed Premises and Reconstruction, 1942–44; Principal, 1944 (estab. 1946); Asst Sec., 1956. *Address:* Arran, Yew Tree Road, Grange over Sands, Cumbria LA11 7AA. *T:* Grange 3488.

WILSON, (Henry) James; Chief Chancery Registrar, 1979–82, retired; *b* 3 Sept. 1916; *s* of Alfred Edgar and Margaret Ethel Wilson; *m* 1st, 1940, Felicity Sidney (*née* Daniels) (*d* 1971); one *s* two *d*; 2nd, 1972, Peggy Frances (*née* Browne). *Educ:* Wrekin College. Territorial Army, Westminster Dragoons, 1936; embodied for war service, 1939; commissioned, later Captain Royal Tank Regt. Admitted Solicitor, 1938; joined Chancery Registrar's Office, 1946; Chancery Registrar, 1961. *Recreations:* gardening, opera. *Address:* Ingleside Ferbies, Speldhurst, Kent TN3 0NS. *T:* Langton 3172. *Club:* Wig and Pen.

WILSON, Henry Moir, CB 1969; CMG 1965; MBE 1946; PhD, BSc, FRAeS; *b* 3 Sept. 1910; 3rd *s* of late Charles Wilson, Belfast; *m* 1937, Susan Eveline Wilson; one *s* three *d.* *Educ:* Royal Belfast Academical Institution, Queen's Univ., Belfast. Apprentice in Mech. Eng, Combe Barbour, Belfast, 1927–31; QUB, 1927–31 (part-time) and 1931–34 (full-time); BSc with 1st Class Hons in Elect. Eng, 1932; PhD 1934 (Thesis on High Voltage Transients on Power Transmission Lines). College Apprentice, Metropolitan-Vickers, Manchester, 1934–35. Joined RAF Educational Service, 1935; commissioned RAFVR, 1939; Senior Tutor, RAF Advanced Armament Course, Ft. Halstead, 1943–46; Senior Educ. Officer, Empire Air Armament School, Manby (Acting Wing Comdr), 1946–47. Joined Ministry of Supply, 1947, as Senior Principal Sci. Officer, Supt Servo Div., Guided Projectile Estab., Westcott, 1947; Supt Guidance and Control Div. Guided Weapons Dept,

RAE, 1947–49; Head of Armament Dept, RAE, 1949–56. Dep. Chief Sci. Officer, 1952; Chief Scientific Officer, 1956; Director-General, Aircraft Equipment Research and Devel., Ministry of Aviation, 1956–62; Head, Defence Research and Development Staff, British Embassy, Washington, DC, 1962–65; Dep. Chief Scientist (Army), 1965–66, Chief Scientist (Army), 1967–70; Dir, SHAPE Tech. Centre, 1970–75. Hon. DSc QUB, 1971. *Recreations*: golf, gardening. *Address*: 7 Carlinwark Drive, Camberley, Surrey.

WILSON, Prof. Henry Wallace, PhD; CPhys, FInstP; FRSE; physicist; Director, Scottish Universities' Research and Reactor Centre, 1962–85; Personal Professor of Physics, Strathclyde University, 1966–85, now Emeritus; *b* 30 Aug. 1923; *s* of Frank Binnington Wilson and Janet (*née* Wilson); *m* 1955, Fiona McPherson Martin, *d* of Alfred Charles Steinmetz Martin and Agnes Mary (*née* McPherson); three *s*. *Educ*: Allan Glen's Sch., Glasgow; Glasgow Univ. (BSc, PhD Physics). AInstP 1949, FInstP 1962; FRSE 1963. Wartime work as Physicist, Explosives Res. Div., ICI, Ardeer. Asst Lectr, Natural Philosophy Dept, Glasgow Univ., 1947–51; post-doctoral Res. Fellow, Univ. of Calif, Berkeley, 1951–52; Lectr, Nat. Phil. Dept, Glasgow Univ., 1952–55; Leader of Physical Measurements Gp, UKAEA, Aldermaston, 1955–62 (Sen. Principal Scientific Officer, 1958). Hon. Scientific Advr, Nat. Mus. of Antiquities of Scotland, 1969. Mem., Nuclear Safety Cttee, 1964–, and Consultant, SSEB; Mem., Radioactive Substances Adv. Cttee, 1966–70. Inst. of Physics: Mem. Council, 1970–71; Chm., Scottish Br., 1969–71; mem. several cttees; Royal Soc. of Edinburgh: Mem. Council, 1966–69, 1976–79; Vice Pres., 1979–81. Member: Brit. Nuclear Energy Soc.; British Mass Spectrometry Soc. (Chm., 1977–79). *Publications*: contributions to: Alpha, Beta and Gamma-ray Spectroscopy, ed K. Siegbahn, 1965; Activation Analysis, ed Lenihan and Thomson, 1965; Modern Aspects of Mass Spectrometry, ed R. I. Reed, 1968; Encyclopaedic Dictionary of Physics, ed J. Thewlis, 1973; papers on radioactivity, low energy nuclear physics, meson physics, mass spectrometry, isotope separation, effects of radiation, and reactor physics, in Phil. Mag., Nature, Phys. Rev., Proc. Phys. Soc., etc. *Recreations*: sailing, hill-walking, industrial archaeology (esp. canal history), photography. *Address*: Ashgrove, The Crescent, Busby, Glasgow G76 8HT. *T*: 041–644 3107.

WILSON, Ian D.; *see* Douglas-Wilson.

WILSON, Very Rev. Ian George MacQueen; Dean of Argyll and the Isles, since 1979; Rector of St John's, Ballachulish and St Mary's, Glencoe, 1978–85; *b* 6 March 1920; *s* of Joseph and Mary Wilson; *m* 1952, Janet Todd Kyle. *Educ*: Edinburgh Theological College. Deacon 1950, priest 1951; Curate, St Margaret's, Glasgow, 1950–52; Priest-in-charge, St Gabriel's, Glasgow, 1952–57; Rector: Christ Church, Dalbeattie, 1957–61; St John's, Baillieston, 1961–64; St Paul's, Rothesay, 1964–75; Canon, St John's Cathedral, Oban, 1973; Priest-in-charge, St Peter's, Stornoway, 1975–78; Officiating Chaplain, RAF, Stornoway, 1975–78; Synod Clerk, Diocese of Argyll and the Isles, 1977–79. Hon. LTh, St Mark's Inst. of Theology, 1974. *Address*: The Parsonage, Ardchattan, Bonawe, Oban, Argyll PA37 1RL. *T*: Bonawe 228.

WILSON, Ian Matthew, CB 1985; Secretary of Commissions for Scotland, since 1987; *b* 12 Dec. 1926; *s* of Matthew Thomson Wilson and Mary Lily Barnett; *m* 1953, Anne Chalmers; three *s*. *Educ*: George Watson's Coll.; Edinburgh Univ. (MA). Asst Principal, Scottish Home Dept, 1950; Private Sec. to Perm. Under-Sec. of State, Scottish Office, 1953–55; Principal, Scottish Home Dept, 1955; Asst Secretary: Scottish Educn Dept, 1963; SHHD, 1971; Asst Under-Sec. of State, Scottish Office, 1974–77; Under Sec., Scottish Educn Dept, 1977–86. *Address*: 1 Bonaly Drive, Edinburgh EH13 0EJ. *T*: 031–441 2541. *Club*: Royal Commonwealth Society.

WILSON, Sir James; *see* Wilson, Sir A. J.

WILSON, James; *see* Wilson H. J.

WILSON, Brig. James, CBE 1986; Chief Executive, Livingston Development Corporation, 1977–April 1987; *b* 12 March 1922; *s* of late Alexander Robertson Wilson and Elizabeth Wylie Wilson (*née* Murray); *m* 1949, Audrie Veronica, *er d* of late A. W. and O. V. Haines; three *d*. *Educ*: Irvine Royal Academy; Edinburgh Academy; Aberdeen Univ. Commissioned RA, 1941; served War with 71 (West Riding) Field Regt, N Africa and Italy, 1941–45; Instructor, Sch. of Artillery, India, 1945–47; Adjt, Sussex Yeo.; 1948–49; active service in Malaya and ME, 1950–53; psc 1954; DAQMG, War Office, 1955–57; Instructor, Staff Coll., 1959–61; CO, 439 (Tyne) Light Air Defence Regt, 1964–67; AQMG, Northern Comd, 1967–68; Col GS SD, HQ BAOR, 1969–71; AMA and DCBAS, Washington, 1972–73; DQMG, HQ UKLF, 1974–77. Member: Executive Council, TCPA (Scotland), 1977–87; Edin. Univ. Careers Adv. Cttee, 1982–86; Scottish Cttee, Inst. of Dirs, 1983–86; Dir, Edinburgh Chamber of Commerce, 1979–82. Mem., Royal Artillery Council for Scotland, 1979–; Chm., W Lothian SSAFA, 1983–87. FBIM 1980. *Recreations*: golf, sailing, bridge. *Address*: 10 Merchiston Avenue, Edinburgh EH10 4NY. *T*: 031–229 7017. *Clubs*: Army and Navy; New (Edinburgh); Hon. Co. of Edinburgh Golfers.

WILSON, Dr James Maxwell Glover, FRCP, FRCPE, FFCM; Senior Principal Medical Officer, Department of Health and Social Security, 1972–76; *b* 31 Aug. 1913; *s* of late James Thomas Wilson and Mabel Salomons; *m* Lallie Methley; three *s*. *Educ*: King's College Choir Sch., Cambridge; Oundle Sch.; St John's Coll., Cambridge; University College Hosp., London. MA, MB, BChir (Cantab). Clinical appts, London and Cambridge, 1937–39. Served War, RAMC (Major, 6th Airborne Div.), 1939–45. Hospital appts, London and Edinburgh, 1945–54; medical work on tea estates in India, 1954–57; Medical Staff, Min. of Health (later DHSS), concerned with the centrally financed research programme, 1957–76; Sen. Res. Fellow, Inf. Services Div., Common Services Agency, Scottish Health Service, 1976–81. Lectr (part-time), Public Health Dept, London Sch. of Hygiene and Tropical Med., 1968–72. *Publications*: (with G. Jungner) Principles and Practice of Screening for Disease (WHO), 1968; contribs to med. jls, mainly on screening for disease. *Recreations*: reading, walking, fishing. *Address*: Millhill House, 77 Millhill, Musselburgh, Midlothian EH21 7RP. *T*: 031–665 5829.

WILSON, James Noel, ChM, FRCS; retired; Consultant Orthopædic Surgeon: Royal National Orthopædic Hospital, London, National Hospitals for Nervous Diseases, Queen Square and Maida Vale, 1962–84, and Surgeon i/c of Accident Unit, RNOH, Stanmore, 1955–84; Teacher of Orthopædics, Institute of Orthopædics, University of London; retired; *b* Coventry, 25 Dec. 1919; *s* of Alexander Wilson and Isobel Barbara Wilson (*née* Fairweather); *m* 1945, Patricia Norah McCullough; two *s* two *d*. *Educ*: King Henry VIII Sch., Coventry; University of Birmingham. Peter Thompson Prize in Anatomy, 1940; Sen. Surgical Prize, 1942; Arthur Foxwell Prize in Clinical Medicine, 1943; MB, ChB 1943; MRCS, LRCP, 1943; FRCS 1948; ChM (Birmingham) 1949; House Surgeon, Birmingham General Hospital, 1943; Heaton Award as Best Resident for 1943. Service in RAMC, Nov. 1943–Oct. 1946, discharged as Captain; qualified as Parachutist and served with 1st Airborne Division. Resident surgical posts, Birmingham General Hospital and Coventry and Warwickshire Hospital, 1947–49; Resident Surgical Officer, Robert Jones and Agnes Hunt Orthopædic Hospital, Oswestry, 1949–52; Consultant Orthopædic Surgeon to Cardiff Royal Infirmary and Welsh Regional Hospital Board, 1952–55.

President: World Orthopaedic Concern, 1979–84; Orthopaedic Section, RSocMed, 1982–83; former Mem. Brit. Editorial Bd, Jl of Bone and Joint Surgery; Fellow, and formerly Editorial Sec., British Orthopædic Assoc. (BOA Travelling Fellowship to USA, 1954); FRSocMed. Life Mem., Bangladesh Orthopaedic Soc.; Hon. Mem., Egyptian Orthopaedic Assoc. *Publications*: Sections in Butterworth's Operative Surgery; (ed) Watson Jones Fractures and Joint Injuries, 6th edn 1982; chapters and articles on orthopædic subjects to various books and journals. *Recreations*: golf, gardening and photography. *Address*: The Chequers, Waterdale, near Watford, Herts. *T*: Garston 672364. *Club*: Airborne.

WILSON, Air Vice-Marshal James Stewart, CBE 1959; Civil Consultant in Preventive Medicine to the Royal Air Force, since 1983; *b* 4 Sept. 1909; *s* of late J. Wilson, Broughty Ferry, Angus, and late Helen Fyffe Wilson; *m* 1937, Elizabeth Elias; one *s* (and one *s* decd). *Educ*: Dundee High Sch.; St Andrews Univ. (MB, ChB). DPH (London) 1948; FFCM(RCP) 1974. House Surgeon, Dundee Royal Infirmary, 1933; House Surgeon, Arbroath Infirmary, 1934; Commissioned Royal Air Force, 1935. Served North Africa, 1942–45. Director Hygiene and Research, Air Ministry, London, 1956–59; Principal Medical Officer, Flying Training Command, 1959–61; Director-General of Medical Services, Royal Australian Air Force, 1961–63. QHP 1961–65; Principal Medical Officer, Bomber Command, 1963–65, retired. Special Adviser in Epidemiology and Applied Entomology, Inst. of Community Medicine, RAF Halton, 1965–83. *Publications*: articles (jointly) on respiratory virus infections, in medical journals. *Recreations*: golf, fishing, shooting. *Address*: Eucumbene, Buckland, Aylesbury, Bucks. *T*: Aylesbury 630062. *Club*: Royal Air Force.

WILSON, Sir James (William Douglas), 5th Bt *cr* 1906; farmer; *b* 8 Oct. 1960; *s* of Captain Sir Thomas Douglas Wilson, 4th Bt, MC, and of Pamela Aileen, *d* of Sir Edward Hanmer, 7th Bt; *S* father, 1984; *m* 1985, Julia Margaret Louise, fourth *d* of J. C. F. Mutty, Mulberry Hall, Melbourn, Cambs. *Educ*: London Univ. (BA Hons French). *Heir*: none. *Address*: Lillingstone Lovell Manor, Buckingham MK18 5BQ. *T*: Lillingstone Dayrell 237.

WILSON, Sir John (Foster), Kt 1975; CBE 1965 (OBE 1955); Director, Royal Commonwealth Society for the Blind, 1950–83, Vice-President 1983; Senior Consultant, United Nations Development Programme, International Initiative Against Avoidable Disablement (IMPACT), since 1983; President, International Agency for the Prevention of Blindness, 1974–83; *b* 20 Jan. 1919; *s* of late Rev. George Henry Wilson, Buxton, Derbys; *m* 1944, Chloe Jean McDermid, OBE 1981; two *d*. *Educ*: Worcester College for the Blind; St Catherine's, Oxford (MA Jurisprudence, Dipl. Public and Social Administration; Hon. Fellow, 1984). Asst Secretary, Royal National Inst. for the Blind, 1941–49; Member, Colonial Office Delegation investigating blindness in Africa, 1946–47. Proposed formation of Royal Commonwealth Society for Blind; became its first Director, 1950; extensive tours in Africa, Asia, Near and Far East, Caribbean and N. America, 1952–67; world tours, 1958, 1963, 1978; formulated Asian plan for the Blind 1963, and African Plan for the Blind, 1966. Internat. Member of World Council for Welfare of Blind and Hon. Life Mem., World Blind Union; Founder Member, National Fedn of Blind (President, 1955–60); Pres., Internat. Agency for the Prevention of Blindness, 1974–83. Helen Keller International Award, 1970; Lions Internat. Humanitarian Award, 1978; World Humanity Award, 1979; Albert Lasker Award, 1979. *Publications*: Blindness in African and Middle East Territories, 1948; Ghana's Handicapped Citizens, 1961; Travelling Blind, 1963; (ed) World Blindness and its Prevention, 1980; various on Commonwealth affairs, rehabilitation and blindness. *Recreations*: current affairs, travel, writing, tape-recording, wine-making. *Address*: 22 The Cliff, Roedean, Brighton, East Sussex BN2 5RE. *T*: Brighton 607667. *Club*: Royal Commonwealth Society.

WILSON, Sir John Gardiner, Kt 1982; CBE 1972; Chairman, Australian Paper Manufacturers Ltd, 1978–84; *b* 13 July 1913; *s* of J. S. Wilson; *m* 1944, Margaret Louise De Ravin; three *d*. *Educ*: Melbourne Grammar Sch.; Clare Coll., Cambridge (MA 1935). Served RAE, AIF, 1939–46, Col. With J. S. Wilson & Co., actuaries and sharebrokers, 1934–39; Mem., Melbourne Stock Exchange, 1935–47; joined Australian Paper Manufacturers, 1947: Dep. Man. Dir, 1953–59; Man. Dir, 1959–78. Former Director: Vickers Australia; Vickers Cockatoo Dockyard Pty. *Address*: 6 Woorigoleen Road, Toorak, Vic 3142, Australia. *Clubs*: Melbourne, Australian, Royal Melbourne Golf (Melbourne).

WILSON, Prof. John Graham; Cavendish Professor of Physics, 1963–76 (Professor, 1952–63), Pro-Vice-Chancellor, 1969–71, University of Leeds; now Emeritus Professor; *b* 28 April 1911; *er s* of J. E. Wilson, Hartlepool, Co. Durham; *m* 1938, Georgiana Brooke, *o d* of Charles W. Bird, Bisley, Surrey; one *s* one *d*. *Educ*: West Hartlepool Secondary Sch.; Sidney Sussex Coll., Cambridge. Member of teaching staff, University of Manchester, 1938–52; Reader in Physics, 1951. University of York: Member, Academic Planning Board, 1960–63; Member of Council, 1964–84; Chairman, Joint Matriculation Board, 1964–67. DUniv York, 1975; Hon. DSc Durham, 1977. *Publications*: The Principles of Cloud Chamber Technique, 1951. Editor of Progress in Cosmic Ray Physics, 1952–71; (with G. D. Rochester), Cloud Chamber Photographs of the Cosmic Radiation, 1952. Papers on cosmic ray physics, articles in jls. *Recreation*: gardening. *Address*: 23 Newall Hall Park, Otley, West Yorks LS21 2RD. *T*: Otley 465184.

WILSON, J(ohn) Greenwood, MD, FRCP, DPH; Fellow of King's College, University of London; formerly: Group Medical Consultant, Health and Hygiene, FMC Ltd; Medical Officer of Health, Port and City of London (first holder of dual appointment; MOH Port of London, 1954, MOH, City of London, in addition, 1956); *b* 27 July 1897; 2nd *s* of late Rev. John Wilson, Woolwich; *m* 1st, 1929, Wenda Margaret Hithersay Smith (marr. diss. 1941); one *s* two *d*; 2nd, 1943, Gwendoline Mary Watkins (*d* 1975); one *d*. *Educ*: Colfe Grammar Sch.; Westminster Hospital, University of London. Served European War, S. Lancashire Regt, RFC and RAF, 1916–19 (wounded). Various hospital appointments, London and provinces and some general practice, 1923–28; subseq. MOH and Sch. Medical Officer posts; then MOH City and Port of Cardiff, Sch. MO, Cardiff Education Authority, and Lecturer in Preventive Medicine, Welsh Nat. School of Medicine, 1933–54. President, Welsh Br. Society of Med. Officers of Health, 1940–45. Member Nat. Adv. Council for recruitment of Nurses and Midwives, 1943–56. Governor, St Bart's Hospital Medical College. Formerly Examiner in Public Health, RCPS (London); Vice-President (Past Chairman of Council) and Hon. Fellow, Royal Society of Health. Hon. Sec., Assoc. of Sea and Air Port Health Authorities of British Isles, 1936–43; Member, Central Housing Advisory Cttee, 1936–56; Member Royal Commission on Mental Health, 1954–57; Chairman, City Division, BMA, 1962–63; Vice-President (Past Chairman), National House-Building Council. Hon. Fellow American Public Health Association. OStJ 1953. *Publications*: Diptheria Immunisation Propaganda and Counter Propaganda, 1933; Public Health Law in Question and Answer, 1951; numerous contributions to med., scientific and tech. publications. *Recreations*: theatre, music, swimming. *Address*: Flat 5, Holmoaks House, 47 Bromley Road, Beckenham BR3 2PA. *T*: 01–658 8250. *Club*: Wig and Pen.

WILSON, Ven. John Hewitt, CB 1977; Canon Emeritus of Lincoln Cathedral, since 1980; Rector of The Heyfords with Rousham and Somerton, diocese of Oxford, since 1981; *b* 14 Feb. 1924; 2nd *s* of John Joseph and Marion Wilson; *m* 1951, Gertrude Elsie Joan Weir; three *s* two *d*. *Educ:* Kilkenny Coll., Kilkenny; Mountjoy Sch., Dublin; Trinity Coll., Dublin. BA 1946, MA 1956. Curate, St George's Church, Dublin, 1947–50. Entered RAF, 1950: RAF Coll., Cranwell, 1950–52; Aden, 1952–55; RAF Wittering, 1955–57; RAF Cottesmore, 1957–58; RAF Germany, 1958–61; Staff Chaplain, Air Ministry, 1961–63; RAF Coll., Cranwell, 1963–66; Asst Chaplain-in-Chief: Far East Air Force, 1966–69; Strike command, 1969–73; Chaplain-in-Chief, RAF, 1973–80. QHC 1973–80. *Recreations:* Rugby football, tennis, gardening, theatre. *Address:* Glencree, Philcote Street, Deddington, Oxford OX5 4TB. *T:* Deddington 38903. *Club:* Royal Air Force.

WILSON, John James, CEng, FIEE; CBIM; Chairman, London Electricity Board, since 1986; *b* 16 Feb. 1932; *s* of Norval John Wilson and Edna May (*née* Smith); *m* 1961, Connie Catherina Boldt Salomonsson; one *s*. *Educ:* Royal Grammar Sch., Worcester; College of Technology, Birmingham (BSc). Successive engineering appts, Midlands Electricity Bd, Southern Electricity Bd, 1955–68; Southern Electricity Board: Dist Manager, Swindon, 1968–69; Dist Manager, Reading, 1969–72; Area Manager, Portsmouth, 1972–77; Midlands Electricity Board: Chief Engineer, 1977–79; Dep. Chairman, 1979–82; Chairman, 1982–86. *Recreations:* golf, gardening.

WILSON, Sir John (Martindale), KCB 1974 (CB 1960); a Vice-President, Civil Service Retirement Fellowship, since 1982; *b* 3 Sept. 1915; *e s* of late John and Kate Wilson; *m* 1941, Penelope Beatrice, *e d* of late Francis A. Bolton, JP, Oakamoor, Staffs; one *s* one *d*. *Educ:* Bradfield Coll.; Gonville and Caius Coll., Cambridge. BA (Cantab), 1st Class Law Trip., 1937; MA 1946. Asst Principal, Dept of Agriculture for Scotland, 1938; Ministry of Supply, 1939; served War, 1939–46 (despatches) with Royal Artillery in India and Burma; Private Sec. to Minister of Supply, 1946–50; Asst Sec., 1950; Under-Sec., 1954; Cabinet Office, 1955–58; MoD, 1958–60; Dep. Sec., Min. of Aviation, 1961–65; Dep. Under-Sec. of State, MoD, 1965–72; Second Permanent Under-Sec. of State (Admin), MoD, 1972–75. Chairman: Crown Housing Assoc., 1975–78; CS Appeal Bd, 1978–81 (Dep. Chm., 1975–78); Civil Service Retirement Fellowship, 1978–82. *Recreation:* gardening. *Address:* Bourne Close, Bourne Lane, Twyford, near Winchester, Hants. *T:* Twyford 713488. *Club:* Army and Navy.

WILSON, Dr John Murray, MBE 1964; Controller, Home Division, British Council, 1985–86; *b* 25 July 1926; *s* of Maurice John and Mary Ellen Wilson (*née* Murray); *m* 1957, Audrey Miriam Simmons; one *s* one *d*. *Educ:* Selwyn Avenue Junior, Highams Park; Bancroft's School, Essex; St John's College, Oxford (MA Botany 1952; DPhil 1957; *prox. acc.* Christopher Welch Scholarship 1951). Served RAF, 1945–48. British Council, 1955–: Science Dept, 1955–58; Chile, 1958–62; Brazil, 1962–66; India, 1966–71; Dep. Rep./Sci. Officer, Italy, 1971–74; Sci. Officer, Germany, 1974–79; Dep. Rep., Germany, 1979–81; Dep. Controller, Home Div., 1981–85. *Publications:* (with J. L. Harley) papers in New Phytologist. *Recreations:* gardening, photography, messing about. *Address:* c/o Personnel Records, The British Council, 10 Spring Gardens, SW1A 2BN.

WILSON, John Spark, CBE 1979 (OBE 1969); Assistant Commissioner, Traffic and Technical Support Department, Metropolitan Police, 1977–82, retired; *b* 9 May 1922; *s* of John Wilson and Elizabeth Kidd Wilson; *m* 1948, Marguerite Chisholm Wilson; two *s* one *d*. *Educ:* Logie Central Sch., Dundee. Joined Metropolitan Police, 1946; Special Branch, 1948–67; Detective Chief Supt, 1968; Comdr, 1969; went to Wales re Investiture of Prince of Wales, 1969; Dep. Asst Comr (CID), 1972; Asst Comr (Crime), 1975. *Recreations:* football, Rugby, boxing.

WILSON, Prof. John Stuart Gladstone, MA, DipCom; Professor of Economics and Commerce in the University of Hull, 1959–82, now Emeritus Professor; Head of Department, 1959–71, and 1974–77; *b* 18 Aug. 1916; *s* of Herbert Gladstone Wilson and Mary Buchanan Wilson (*née* Wylie); *m* 1943, Beryl Margaret Gibson, *d* of Alexander Millar Gibson and Bertha Noble Gibson; no *c*. *Educ:* University of Western Australia. Lecturer in Economics: University of Tasmania, 1941–43; Sydney, 1944–45; Canberra, 1946–47; LSE, 1948–49. Reader in Economics, with special reference to Money and Banking, Univ. of London, 1950–59; Dean, Faculty of Social Sciences and Law, Univ. of Hull, 1962–65; Chairman, Centre for S-E Asian Studies, Univ. of Hull, 1963–66. Hackett Research Student, 1947; Leverhulme Research Award, 1955. Economic Survey of New Hebrides on behalf of Colonial Office, 1958–59; Consultant, Trade and Payments Dept, OECD, 1965–66; Consultant with Harvard Advisory Development Service in Liberia, 1967; headed Enquiry into Sources of Capital and Credit to UK Agriculture, 1970–73; Consultant, Directorate Gen. for Agric., EEC, 1974–75; Specialist Adviser, H of C Select Cttee on Nationalised Industries, 1976; Consultant, Cttee on Financial Markets, OECD, 1979–81; Dir, Centre for Jt Study of Economics, Politics and Sociology, 1980–82; SSRC Grant for comparative study of banking policy and structure, 1977–81; Leverhulme Emeritus Fellow, 1983–84. Mem. Cttee of Management, Inst. of Commonwealth Studies, London, 1960–77, Hon. Life Mem., 1980; Governor, SOAS, London, 1963–. Member: Yorkshire Council for Further Education, 1963–67; Nat. Advisory Council on Education for Industry and Commerce, 1964–66; Languages Bd, CNAA, 1978–83; Sec.-General, Société Universitaire Européenne de Recherches Financières, 1968–72, Pres., 1973–75, Vice-Pres., 1977–83. Editor, Yorkshire Bulletin of Economic and Social Research, 1964–67; Mem., Editorial Adv. Bd, Modern Asian Studies, 1966–. *Publications:* French Banking Structure and Credit Policy, 1957; Economic Environment and Development Programmes, 1960; Monetary Policy and the Development of Money Markets, 1966; Economic Survey of the New Hebrides, 1966; (ed with C. R. Whittlesey) Essays in Money and Banking in Honour of R. S. Sayers, 1968, repr. 1970; Availability of Capital and Credit to United Kingdom Agriculture, 1973; (ed with C. F. Scheffer) Multinational Enterprises—Financial and Monetary Aspects, 1974; Credit to Agriculture—United Kingdom, 1975; The London Money Markets, 1976; (ed with J. E. Wadsworth and H. Fournier) The Development of Financial Institutions in Europe, 1956–1976, 1977; Industrial Banking: a comparative survey, 1978; Banking Policy and Structure: a comparative analysis, 1986; contribs. to Banking in the British Commonwealth (ed R. S. Sayers), 1952 and to Banking in Western Europe (ed R. S. Sayers), 1962; A Decade of the Commonwealth, 1955–64, ed W. B. Hamilton and others, 1966; to International Encyclopaedia of the Social Sciences; Encyclopaedia Britannica, 15th edn; Economica, Economic Journal, Journal of Political Econ., Economic Record. *Recreations:* gardening, theatre, art galleries, photography. *Address:* Department of Economics and Commerce, The University, Hull, North Humberside. *Club:* Reform.

WILSON, John Tuzo, CC (Canada) 1974; OBE 1946; FRS 1968; FRSC 1949; Chancellor, York University, Toronto, 1983–86; Professor of Geophysics, University of Toronto, 1946–74, Emeritus Professor, 1977; Director-General, Ontario Science Centre, 1974–85; *b* Ottawa, 24 Oct. 1908; *s* of John Armitstead Wilson, CBE, and Henrietta L. Tuzo; *m* 1938, Isabel Jean Dickson; two *d*. *Educ:* Ottawa; Universities of Toronto (Governor-General's medal, Trinity Coll., 1930; Massey Fellow, 1930), Cambridge (ScD), and Princeton (PhD). Asst Geologist, Geological Survey of Canada, 1936–46; Principal, Erindale Coll., Univ. of Toronto, 1967–74. Regimental service and staff appointments, Royal Canadian Engrs, UK and Sicily, 1939–43; Director, Opl. Research, Nat. Defence HQ, Ottawa (Colonel), 1944–46. President, International Union of Geodesy and Geophysics, 1957–60; Visiting Prof.: Australian Nat. Univ., 1950 and 1965; Ohio State Univ., 1968; California Inst. of Technology, 1976. Member Nat. Research Council of Canada, 1957–63; Member Defence Res. Board, 1958–64. Canadian Delegation to Gen. Ass., UNESCO, 1962, 1964, 1966. President: Royal Society of Canada, 1972–73; Amer. Geophysical Union, 1980–82. Overseas Fellow, Churchill Coll., Cambridge, 1965; Trustee, Nat. Museums of Canada, 1967–74. Hon. Fellow: Trinity Coll., University of Toronto, 1962; St John's Coll., Cambridge, 1981; Hon. FRSE 1986. Foreign Associate, Nat. Acad. of Sciences, USA, 1968; Foreign Hon. Mem., Amer. Acad. of Arts and Sciences; For. Mem., Royal Swedish Acad. of Sciences, 1981; Associé, Académie Royale de Belgique, 1981. Holds hon. doctorates and hon. or foreign memberships and medals, etc, in Canada and abroad. Vetlesen Prize, Columbia Univ., 1978; Britannica Award, 1986. OC (Canada) 1970. *Publications:* One Chinese Moon, 1959; Physics and Geology (with J. A. Jacobs and R. D. Russell), 1959; IGY Year of the New Moons, 1961; (ed) Continents Adrift, 1972; Unglazed China, 1973; (ed) Continents Adrift and Continents Aground, 1976; scientific papers. *Recreations:* travel, sailing, Hong Kong junk. *Address:* 27 Pricefield Road, Toronto M4W 1Z8, Canada. *T:* 923–4244. *Clubs:* Arts and Letters, York (Toronto).

WILSON, John Veitch D.; *see* Drysdale Wilson.

WILSON, John Warley; His Honour Judge John Wilson; a Circuit Judge, since 1982; *b* 13 April 1936; *s* of John Pearson Wilson and Nancy Wade Wilson (*née* Harston); *m* 1962, Rosalind Mary Pulford. *Educ:* Warwick Sch.; St Catharine's Coll., Cambridge (MA). Called to the Bar, Lincoln's Inn, 1960, in practice, 1960–82; a Recorder of the Crown Court, 1979–82. Dep. Chairman, West Midlands Agricultural Land Tribunal, 1978–82. *Recreation:* gardening. *Address:* Victoria House, Farm Street, Harbury, Leamington Spa CV33 9LR. *T:* Harbury 612572.

WILSON, Joseph Albert; Secretary to the Cabinet, Sierra Leone Government, 1968; Barrister-at-Law; *b* 22 Jan. 1922; *e s* of late George Wilson; *m* 1947, Esther Massaquoi; two *s* four *d* (and one *s* decd). *Educ:* St Edward's Secondary Sch., Freetown, Sierra Leone; University of Exeter, (DPA); Middle Temple. Graded Clerical Service, Sierra Leone Government, 1941–47; family business, 1948–51; Secretary, Bonthe District Council, 1951–59; Administrative Officer, Sierra Leone Government, rising to rank of Cabinet Secretary, 1959–; High Comr from Sierra Leone to UK, 1967–68. Manager (Special Duties), SLST Ltd, 1959; Dir, National Diamond Mining Co. (Sierra Leone) Ltd. Mem., Court of Univ. of Sierra Leone. *Recreations:* tennis, golf. *Address:* 14 Syke Street, Brookfields, Freetown, Sierra Leone. *T:* 2590.

WILSON, Mrs (Katherine) Muriel (Irwin), OBE 1985; Chairman and Chief Executive, Equal Opportunities Commission for Northern Ireland, 1981–84; *b* 3 Dec. 1920; *d* of Francis Hosford and Martha Evelyn (*née* Irwin); *m* 1949, William George Wilson; one *s*. *Educ:* Methodist Coll., Belfast; The Queen's University of Belfast (DPA); MBIM. Northern Ireland Civil Service, 1939–49; N Ireland Health Service, 1949–73: Eastern Special Care Management Cttee (Services for the Mentally Handicapped): Asst Sec., 1963–71; Gp Sec. and Chief Admin. Officer, 1971–73; Asst Chief Admin. Officer (Personnel and Management Services), Northern Health and Social Services Board, 1973–81. Chm. NI Div., 1977–79, National Vice-Pres. 1979–81, United Kingdom Fedn of Business and Professional Women; Mem. Bd, Labour Relations Agency (NI), 1976–81; Member: NI Adv. Cttee, Independent Broadcasting Authority, 1978–83; NI Council, RIPA, 1985–. *Recreations:* swimming, reading.

WILSON, Sir Keith (Cameron), Kt 1966; Member of House of Representatives for Sturt, South Australia, 1949–54, 1955–66; *b* 3 Sept. 1900; *s* of Algernon Theodore King Wilson; *m* 1930, Elizabeth H., *d* of late Sir Lavington Bonython; two *s* one *d*. *Educ:* Collegiate School of St Peter, Adelaide; University of Adelaide. LLB 1922. Admitted to Bar, 1922. Served War of 1939–45: Gunner, 2nd AIF, 1940; Middle East, 1940–43; Major. Senator for South Australia, 1938–44. Chm., Aged Cottage Homes Inc., 1952–71; Past President: Blinded Welfare Fund; Good Neighbour Council of SA, 1968–72; Queen Elizabeth Hosp. Research Foundn; Legacy. *Publication:* Wilson-Uppill Wheat Equalization Scheme, 1938. *Address:* 79 Tusmore Avenue, Tusmore, SA 5065, Australia. *T:* 315578. *Club:* Adelaide (Adelaide).

WILSON, Prof. Kenneth Geddes, PhD; Professor of Physics, since 1983 and Director, Center for Theory and Simulation in Science and Engineering, since 1985, Cornell University; *b* 8 June 1936; *s* of Edgar Bright Wilson and Emily Fisher Buckingham; *m* 1982, Alison Brown. *Educ:* Harvard Univ. (AB); Calif Inst. of Technol. (PhD). Asst Prof. of Physics, Cornell Univ., 1963. Hon. PhD: Harvard, 1981; Chicago, 1976. Nobel Prize for Physics, 1982. *Publications:* (ed jtly) Broken Scale Invariance and the Light Cone, 1971; Quarks and Strings on a Lattice, 1975; (contrib.) New Pathways in High Energy Physics, Vol. II 1976; (contrib.) New Developments in Quantum Field Theory and Statistical Mechanics, 1977; (contrib.) Recent Developments in Gauge Theories, 1980; contrib. Jl of Math. Phys, Nuovo Cimento, Acta Phys. Austriaca, Phys Rev., Jl of Chem. Phys, Comm. Math. Phys, Phys Reports, Advances in Maths, Rev. of Mod. Phys, Scientific American; symposia and conf. papers. *Address:* 316 Newman Laboratory, Cornell University, Ithaca, NY 14853, USA. *T:* (607) 255–5169; Center for Theory and Simulation in Science and Engineering, 265 Olin Hall, Cornell University. *T:* (607) 255 8686.

WILSON, Rev. Canon Leslie Rule; Hon. Canon of Holy Cross Cathedral, Geraldton, since 1966; *b* 19 July 1909; *y s* of late Rev. John and Mary Adelaide Wilson; *m* 1984, Mrs Margaret Nunns, *widow* of R. C. Nunns, Stocksfield. *Educ:* Royal Grammar Sch., Newcastle upon Tyne; University College, Durham; Edinburgh Theological College. Asst Priest, Old St Paul's, Edinburgh, 1934–36; Rector of Fort William, 1936–42, with Nether Lochaber and Portree, 1938–42; Canon of Argyll and The Isles, 1940–42; Education Officer, 1942–45; Welfare Officer, SEAC (Toc H), 1945–46; Vicar of Malacca, Malaya, 1946–50; Principal Probation Officer, Federation of Malaya, 1950–52; Vicar of Kuching, Sarawak, 1952–55; Provost and Canon of St Thomas' Cathedral, Kuching, 1955–59; Rector of Geraldton, W Australia, 1960–64; Dean of Geraldton, 1964–66 (Administrator, Diocese of NW Australia, 1966); Archdeacon of Carpentaria, 1966–67; Rector of Winterbourne Stickland with Turnworth and Winterbourne Houghton, 1967–69; Vicar of Holmside, 1969–74; retired 1974; permission to officiate, Diocese of Durham, 1975–. Commissary for Bp of NW Australia, 1966–83. Founder and Chairman, Parson Woodforde Society, 1968–75 (Hon. Life Pres., 1975). *Recreations:* reading, genealogy. *Address:* 11 Norwich Close, Great Lumley, Chester-le-Street, Co. Durham DH3 4QL. *T:* Chester-le-Street 892366.

WILSON, Leslie William, JP; Director-General, Association of Special Libraries and Information Bureaux (Aslib), 1950–78, retired; *b* 26 Sept. 1918; *s* of Harry Wilson and Ada Jane Wilson; *m* 1942, Valerie Jones; one *s* two *d*. *Educ:* Cambridgeshire High Sch.; Trinity Hall, Cambridge (Open Scholar, MA Mod. Langs). Army Service, India, 1940–46. Foreign Editor, Times Educnl Supplement, 1946–50. Hon. Fellow, Internat. Fedn for

Documentation, 1978; Hon. Member: Inst. of Information Scientists, 1977; US Special Libraries Assoc., 1978; Aslib, 1978. JP Mddx, 1971. *Publications:* publ. extensively in scientific and library jls. *Address:* 29 St Peter's Road, St Margaret's-on-Thames, Mddx TW1 1QY. *T:* 01-892 6742.

WILSON, Sir (Mathew) Martin, 5th Bt, *cr* 1874; *b* 2 July 1906; *s* of Lieut-Colonel Sir Mathew Richard Henry Wilson, 4th Bt, and Hon. Barbara Lister (*d* 1943), *d* of 4th Baron Ribblesdale; *S* father, 1958. *Educ:* Eton. *Heir: nephew* Brig. Mathew John Anthony Wilson, OBE, MC [*b* 2 Oct. 1935; *m* 1962, Janet Mary, *e d* of late E. W. Mowll, JP; one *s* one *d*]. *Address:* 1 Sandgate Esplanade, Folkestone, Kent.

WILSON, Mrs Muriel; *see* Wilson, K. M. I.

WILSON, Nigel Guy, FBA 1980; Fellow and Tutor in Classics, Lincoln College, Oxford; *b* 23 July 1935; *s* of Noel Wilson and Joan Lovibond. *Educ:* University Coll. Sch.; Corpus Christi Coll., Oxford (1st Cl. Classics (Mods) 1955; 1st Cl. Lit. Hum. 1957; Hertford Scholar 1955; Ireland and Craven Scholar 1955; Derby Scholar 1957). Lectr, Merton Coll., Oxford, 1957–62; Lincoln College, Oxford: Fellow, 1962–; Tutor in Classics, 1962–. Jt Editor, Classical Rev., 1975–87. Ospite Linceo, Scuola normale superiore, Pisa, 1977; Vis. Prof., Univ. of Padua, 1985. Gaisford Lectr, 1983. Gordon Duff Prize, 1968. *Publications:* (with L. D. Reynolds) Scribes and Scholars, 1968, 2nd edn 1974; An Anthology of Byzantine Prose, 1971; Medieval Greek Bookhands, 1973; St Basil on the Value of Greek Literature, 1975; Scholia in Aristophanis Acharnenses, 1975; (with D. A. Russell) Menander Rhetor, 1981; Scholars of Byzantium, 1983; articles and reviews in various learned jls. *Recreations:* bridge, squash. *Address:* Lincoln College, Oxford. *T:* Oxford 279794.

WILSON, Norman George, CMG 1966; Commercial Director, ICI of Australia Ltd, 1972–73; Deputy Chairman, Fibremakers Ltd, 1972–73; *b* 20 Oct. 1911; *s* of P. Wilson; *m* 1939, Dorothy Gwen, *d* of late Sir W. Lennon Raws; one *s* two *d*. *Educ:* Melbourne University (BCE). Joined ICI Australia Ltd, 1935: Exec. positions, 1936–48; General Manager, Dyes and Plastics Group, 1949–54; Director, 1959–73; Managing Director: Dulux Pty Ltd, 1954–62; Fibremakers Ltd, 1962–72. Business Adviser to Dept of Air, and Dep. Chm. Defence Business Board, Commonwealth Government, 1957–76; Chairman Production Board, Dept of Manufacturing Industries, Commonwealth Government, 1960–76. Mem., Export Develt Council, Dept of Trade and Industry, Commonwealth Govt, 1966–72. Mem. Bd, Victorian Railways, 1973–83; Dep. Chm., Victorian Conservation Trust, 1973–83. FInstD, FAIM. *Recreations:* golf, farming. *Address:* Apartment 14, 18 Lansell Road, Toorak, Victoria 3142, Australia. *T:* Melbourne 241 4438; The Highlands, Kerrie, Romsey, Vic 3434, Australia. *T:* 054 270232. *Clubs:* Australian (Melbourne); Royal Melbourne Golf, Melbourne Cricket, Victoria Racing.

WILSON, Peter Humphrey St John, CB 1956; CBE 1952; Deputy Under Secretary of State, Department of Employment and Productivity, 1968–69, retired (Deputy Secretary, Ministry of Labour, 1958–68); *b* 1 May 1908; *e s* of late Rt Rev. Henry A. Wilson, CBE, DD; *m* 1939, Catherine Laird (*d* 1963), *d* of late H. J. Bonser, London; three *d*. *Educ:* Cheltenham Coll. (Schol.); Corpus Christi Coll., Cambridge (Foundation Schol.). Assistant Principal, Ministry of Labour, 1930; Principal, 1936; Regional Controller, Northern Region, 1941; Controller, Scotland, 1944; Under Secretary, 1952. *Recreations:* reading, music, grand-children. *Address:* Thorntree Cottage, Blackheath, near Guildford, Surrey. *T:* Guildford 893758.

WILSON, Prof. Peter Northcote; Professor of Agriculture and Rural Economy and Head of School of Agriculture, University of Edinburgh, since 1984; Principal, East of Scotland College of Agriculture, since 1984; *b* 4 April 1928; *s* of Llewellyn W. C. M. Wilson and F. Louise Wilson; *m* 1950, Maud Ethel (*née* Bunn); two *s* one *d*. *Educ:* Whitgift School; Wye College, Univ. of London (BSc (Agric), MSc, PhD); Univ. of Edinburgh (Dip. Animal Genetics). FIBiol. Lectr in Agriculture, Makerere Coll., UC of E Africa, 1951–57; Sen. Lectr in Animal Production, Imperial Coll. of Tropical Agriculture, 1957–61; Prof. of Agriculture, Univ. of W Indies, 1961–64; Senior Scientist, Unilever Res. Lab., 1964–68; Agricl Dir, SLF Ltd (Unilever), 1968–71; Chief Agricl Advr, BOCM Silcock Ltd (Unilever), 1971–83. Vis. Prof. Univ. of Reading, 1975–83. Pres., Brit. Soc. of Animal Production, 1977. Sec.-Gen., Council of Scottish Agricl Colls, 1985. *Publications:* Agriculture in the Tropics, 1965, 2nd edn 1980; Improved Feeding of Cattle and Sheep, 1981; numerous papers in learned jls. *Recreations:* hill walking, photography, foreign travel, philately. *Address:* 8 St Thomas' Road, Edinburgh EH9 2LQ. *T:* 031-667 3182. *Club:* Farmers'.

WILSON, Quintin Campbell, OBE 1975; HM Inspector of Constabulary for Scotland, 1975–79; *b* 19 Nov. 1913; *s* of William Wilson and Mary (*née* Cowan); *m* 1939, Adelia Campbell Scott; two *s*. *Educ:* Barr Primary Sch.; Girvan High Sch. Halifax Borough Police, April 1936; Ayrshire Constabulary, Nov. 1936; Chief Supt, Police Research and Planning Branch, Home Office, London, 1965; Dep. Chief Constable, Ayrshire, 1966; Chief Constable, Ayrshire, 1968–75. *Recreation:* golf. *Address:* 15 Portmark Avenue, Alloway, Ayr KA7 4DN. *T:* Alloway 43034.

WILSON, Prof. Raymond; Professor of Education, since 1968, Chairman of School of Education, 1969–76 and since 1980, University of Reading; *b* 20 Dec. 1925; *s* of John William Wilson and Edith (*née* Walker); *m* 1950, Gertrude Mary Russell; two *s* one *d*. *Educ:* London Univ. (BA English, 1st Cl.). Teacher, secondary schs, 1950–57; English Master, subseq. Chief English Master, Dulwich Coll., 1957–65; Lectr, Southampton Univ., 1965–68. *Publications:* numerous textbooks and anthologies; papers on English and related studies; occasional poet. *Address:* Roselawn, Shiplake, Henley-on-Thames, Oxon. *T:* Wargrave 2528. *Club:* Royal Commonwealth Society.

WILSON, Sir Reginald (Holmes), Kt 1951; BCom; FCIT; CBIM; Scottish Chartered Accountant; Director of business and finance companies; *b* 1905; *o s* of Alexander Wilson and Emily Holmes Wilson; *m* 1st, 1930, Rose Marie von Arnim; one *s* one *d*; 2nd, 1938, Sonia Havell. *Educ:* St Peter's Sch., Panchgani; St Lawrence, Ramsgate; London Univ. BCom. Partner in Whinney Murray & Co., 1937–72; HM Treasury, 1940; Principal Assistant Secretary, Ministry of Shipping, 1941; Director of Finance, Ministry of War Transport, 1941; Under-Secretary, Ministry of Transport, 1945; returned to City, 1946; Joint Financial Adviser, Ministry of Transport, 1946; Member of Royal Commission on Press, 1946; Vice-Chairman, Hemel Hempstead Development Corporation, 1946–56; Adviser on Special Matters, CCG, 1947. Comptroller BTC, 1947, Member BTC, 1953, Chm. E Area Board, 1955–60, Chm. London Midland Area Board, 1960–62; Dep. Chm. and Man. Dir, Transport Holding Co., 1962–67; Chairman: Transport Holding Co., 1967–70; Nat. Freight Corp., 1969–70; Transport Develt Gp, 1971–74 (Dep. Chm., 1970–71); Thos Cook & Son Ltd, 1967–76. Mem., Cttee of Enquiry into Civil Air Transport, 1967–69. Chm., Bd for Simplification of Internat. Trade Procedures, 1976–79. Award of Merit, Inst. Transport, 1953; President, Inst. Transport, 1957–58. Governor, LSE, 1954–58; Chairman, Board of Governors: Hospitals for Diseases of the Chest, 1960–71; National Heart Hospital, 1968–71; National Heart and Chest Hospitals, 1971–80; Chm., Cardiothoracic Inst., 1960–80; UK Rep., Council of Management, Internat. Hosp. Fedn, 1973–79. *Publications:* various papers on transport matters. *Recreations:* music, walking. *Address:* 49 Gloucester Square, W2 2TQ. *Clubs:* Athenæum, Oriental.

WILSON, Prof. Richard Middlewood; Professor of English Language, University of Sheffield, 1955–73; *b* 20 Sept. 1908; *e s* of late R. L. Wilson, The Grange, Kilham, Driffield, E Yorks; *m* 1938, Dorothy Muriel, *y d* of late C. E. Leeson, Eastgate House, Kilham, Driffield; one *d*. *Educ:* Woodhouse Grove School; Leeds University. Asst Lecturer, Leeds Univ., 1931, Lecturer, 1936; Senior Lecturer and Head of Dept of English Language, Sheffield Univ., 1946. *Publications:* Sawles Warde, 1939; Early Middle English Literature, 1939; (with B. Dickins) Early Middle English Texts, 1951; The Lost Literature of Medieval England, 1952; (with D. J. Price) The Equatorie of the Planetis, 1955; articles and reviews. *Recreation:* cricket. *Address:* 9 Endcliffe Vale Avenue, Sheffield S11 8RX. *T:* Sheffield 663431.

WILSON, Richard Thomas James; Head of Personnel Management Group, on loan to Cabinet Office (Management and Personnel Office), since 1986; *b* 11 Oct. 1942; *s* of late Richard Ridley Wilson and Frieda Bell (*née* Finlay); *m* 1972, Caroline Margaret, *y d* of Rt Hon. Sir Frank Lee, GCMG, KCB and of Lady Lee; one *s* one *d*. *Educ:* Radley Coll.; Clare Coll., Cambridge (Exhibnr; BA 1964, LLB 1965). Called to the Bar, Middle Temple, 1965. Joined BoT as Asst Principal, 1966; Private Sec. to Minister of State, BoT, 1969–71; Principal: Cabinet Office, 1971–73; Dept of Energy, 1974; Asst Sec., 1977–82; Under Sec., 1982; Prin. Estabt and Finance Officer, Dept of Energy, 1982–86. *Address:* Old Bakery, Dinton, Aylesbury, Bucks HP17 8UW. *T:* Aylesbury 748321.

WILSON, Prof. Robert, CBE 1978; FRS 1975; Perren Professor of Astronomy and Director of the Observatories, University College London, since 1972; *s* of Robert Graham Wilson and Anne Wilson. *Educ:* King's Coll., Newcastle upon Tyne; Univ. of Edinburgh. BSc (Physics), Newcastle, 1948; PhD (Astrophysics), Edin., 1952. SSO, Royal Observatory, Edinburgh, 1952–57; Research Fellow, Dominion Astrophysical Observatory, Canada, 1957–58; Leader of Plasma Spectroscopy Gp, CTR Div., Harwell, 1959–61; Head of Spectroscopy Div., Culham Laboratory, 1962–68; Dir, Science Research Council's Astrophysics Research Unit, Culham, 1968–72; Dean, Faculty Sci., UCL, 1982–85. Member: SERC, 1985–; NERC, 1985–; Chm., British National Cttee for Space Res., 1983–. Foreign Mem., Société Royale des Sciences, Liège; Vice-Pres., Internat. Astronomical Union, 1979–85; Member: Internat. Acad. of Astronautics, 1985; COSPAR Bureau, 1986–. (Jtly) Herschel Medal, RAS, 1986. *Publications:* papers in many jls on: optical astronomy, plasma spectroscopy, solar physics, ultraviolet astronomy.

WILSON, Robert Donald; farmer; Chairman: Mersey Regional Health Authority, since 1982; Electricity Consultative Council (North West), since 1981; *b* 6 June 1922; *s* of John and Kate Wilson; *m* 1946, E. Elizabeth Ellis. *Educ:* Grove Park Sch., Wrexham, Clwyd. Served RAF, 1940–46. Tyre industry, 1946–60; farming, 1954–; Director of various farming and property companies; Member of Lloyd's, 1970–; Board Mem. (part-time), North West Electricity Bd (NORWEB), 1981–. Chairman: Ayrshire Cattle Soc., 1966–67; Cheshire Br., CLA, 1980–82; Nat. Staff Cttee, Admin, Catering and Other Services, 1983–85. Vice-Chm. Governors, Cheshire Coll. of Agric., 1980–84. High Sherriff, Cheshire, 1985–86. FRSA 1986. *Recreations:* fishing, shooting. *Address:* The Oldfields, Pulford, Chester, Cheshire CH4 9EJ. *T:* Rossett 570207. *Clubs:* Farmers'; City (Chester).

WILSON, (Robert) Gordon; MP (SNP) Dundee East since Feb. 1974; Chairman, Scottish National Party, since 1979; formerly solicitor in private practice; *b* 16 April 1938; *s* of R. G. Wilson; *m* 1965, Edith M. Hassall; two *d*. *Educ:* Douglas High Sch.; Edinburgh Univ. (BL); Dundee Univ. (LLD). Nat. Sec., SNP, 1963–71; Exec. Vice-Chm., 1972–73; Sen. Vice-Chm., 1973–74; Chm., 1979–. SNP Parly Spokesman: on Energy, 1974–79; on Home Affairs, 1975–76; on Devolution (jt responsibility), 1976–79. Dep. Leader, SNP, 1974–79. Rector, Dundee Univ., 1983–86. *Recreations:* reading, walking, photography. *Address:* 48 Monifieth Road, Broughty Ferry, Dundee DD5 2RX. *T:* Dundee 79009; 01-219 3494/4474.

WILSON, Prof. Robert McLachlan, PhD; FBA 1977; Professor of Biblical Criticism, University of St Andrews, 1978–83; *b* 13 Feb. 1916; *er s* of Hugh McL. Wilson and Janet N. (*née* Struthers); *m* 1945, Enid Mary, *d* of Rev. and Mrs F. J. Bomford, Bournemouth, Hants; two *s*. *Educ:* Greenock Acad.; Royal High Sch., Edinburgh; Univ. of Edinburgh (MA 1939, BD 1942); Univ. of Cambridge (PhD 1945). Minister of Rankin Church, Strathaven, Lanarkshire, 1946–54; Lectr in New Testament Language and Literature, St Mary's Coll., Univ. of St Andrews, 1954, Sen. Lectr, 1964, Prof., 1969–78. Vis. Prof., Vanderbilt Divinity Sch., Nashville, Tenn, 1964–65. Pres., Studiorum Novi Testamenti Societas, 1981–82. Hon. Mem., Soc. of Biblical Literature, 1972–. Associate Editor, New Testament Studies, 1967–77, Editor 1977–83; Mem., Internat. Cttee for publication of Nag Hammadi Codices, and of Editorial Bd of Nag Hammadi Studies monograph series. Hon. DD Aberdeen, 1982. *Publications:* The Gnostic Problem, 1958; Studies in the Gospel of Thomas, 1960; The Gospel of Philip, 1962; Gnosis and the New Testament, 1968; (ed) English trans., Hennecke-Schneemelcher, NT Apocrypha: vol. 1, 1963 (2nd edn 1973); vol. 2, 1965 (2nd edn 1974); (ed) English trans., Haenchen, The Acts of the Apostles, 1971; (ed) English trans., Foerster, Gnosis: vol. 1, 1972; vol. 2, 1974; (ed and trans., jtly) Jung Codex treatises: De Resurrectione, 1963; Epistula Jacobi Apocrypha, 1968; Tractatus Tripartitus, pars I, 1973, partes II et III, 1975; (ed) Nag Hammadi and Gnosis, 1978; (ed) The Future of Coptology, 1978; (ed jtly) Text and Interpretation, 1979; (ed) English trans., Rudolph, Gnosis, 1983; articles in British, Amer. and continental jls. *Recreation:* golf. *Address:* 10 Murrayfield Road, St Andrews, Fife. *T:* St Andrews 74331.

WILSON, Dr Robert Woodrow; Head, Radio Physics Research Department, AT&T Bell Laboratories, since 1976; *b* 10 Jan. 1936; *s* of Ralph Woodrow Wilson and Fannie May Willis; *m* 1958, Elizabeth Rhoads Sawin; two *s* one *d*. *Educ:* Rice Univ. (BA Physics, 1957); Calif Inst. of Technol. (PhD 1962). Post-doctoral Fellowship, Calif Inst. of Technol., 1962–63; Mem. Technical Staff, Bell Labs, Holmdel, NJ, 1963–76. Member: Phi Beta Kappa; Amer. Acad. of Arts and Sciences, 1978; US Nat. Acad. of Science, 1979. Hon. degrees: Monmouth Coll., 1979; Jersey City State Coll., 1979; Thiel Coll., 1980. Henry Draper Award, 1977; Herschel Award, RAS, 1977; (jtly) Nobel Prize for Physics, 1978. *Publications:* contrib. to Astrophys. Jl. *Recreations:* running, skiing. *Address:* 9 Valley Point Drive, Holmdel, NJ 07733, USA. *T:* (201) 671–7807.

WILSON, Prof. Roger Cowan; Professor of Education, University of Bristol, 1951–71, Emeritus 1971; Visiting Professor: University of Malawi, 1966; Harvard University, 1968; *b* 3 August 1906; 2nd *s* of Alexander Cowan Wilson and Edith Jane Brayshaw; *m* 1931, Margery Lilian, *y d* of late Rev. C. W. Emmet, Fellow of University College, Oxford, and Gertrude Weir; one *s* one *d*. *Educ:* Manchester Grammar School; The Queen's College, Oxford (Exhibitioner); Manchester College of Technology. Chairman, OU Labour Club, 1927; President, Oxford Union, 1929; First Cl. in Philosophy, Politics and Economics, 1929. Apprentice in Cotton Industry, 1929–35; Talks Staff of BBC, 1935–40; dismissed from BBC as conscientious objector; General Secretary, Friends Relief Service, 1940–46; head of Dept of Social Studies, University College, Hull, 1946–51.

Mem., Colonial Office and Min. of Overseas Develt adv. cttees and consultative missions, 1957–71. Senior Adviser on Social Affairs, United Nations Operation in the Congo, 1961–62. Chairman: Bd of Visitors, Shepton Mallet Prison, 1966–70; Council for Voluntary Action, South Lakeland, 1974–79; Cumbria Council on Alcoholism, 1979–81; Clerk, London Yearly Meeting of Society of Friends, 1975–78. JP Bristol, 1954–67. Médaille de la Reconnaisance Française, 1948. *Publications:* Frank Lenwood, a biography, 1936; Authority, Leadership and Concern, a study of motive and administration in Quaker relief work, 1948; Quaker Relief, 1940–48, 1952; The Teacher: instructor or educator, 1952; (with Kuenstler and others) Social Group Work in Great Britain, 1955; Difficult Housing Estates, 1963; (jtly) Social Aspects of Urban Development, 1966; Jesus the Liberator, 1981. *Recreations:* gardener's boy, walking, Quaker interests. *Address:* Peter Hill House, Yealand Conyers, near Carnforth, Lancs. *T:* Carnforth 733519.

See also D. M. Emmet, J. E. Meade, Sir Geoffrey Wilson and S. S. Wilson.

WILSON, Rt. Rev. Roger Plumpton, KCVO 1974; DD (Lambeth), 1949; Clerk of the Closet to the Queen, 1963–75; *b* 3 Aug. 1905; *s* of Canon Clifford Plumpton Wilson, Bristol, and Hester Marion Wansey; *m* 1935, Mabel Joyce Avery, Leigh Woods, Bristol; two *s* one *d. Educ:* Winchester Coll. (Exhibitioner); Keble Coll., Oxford (Classical Scholar). Hon. Mods in Classics 1st Class, Lit. Hum. 2nd Class, BA 1928; MA 1932. Classical Master, Shrewsbury Sch., 1928–30, 1932–34; Classical Master, St Andrew's Coll., Grahamstown, S Africa, 1930–32. Deacon, 1935; Priest, 1936; Curacies: St Paul's, Prince's Park, Liverpool, 1935–38; St John's, Smith Square, SW1, 1938–39; Vicar of South Shore, Blackpool, 1939–45; Archdeacon of Nottingham and Vicar of Radcliffe on Trent, 1945–49; also Vicar of Shelford (in plurality), 1946–49; Bishop of Wakefield, 1949–58; Bishop of Chichester, 1958–74. Chm., Church of England Schools Council, 1957–71; Mem., Presidium, Conf. of European Churches, 1967–74. *Recreations:* Oxford University Authentics Cricket Club, Oxford University Centaurs Football Club, golf. *Address:* Kingsett, Wrington, Bristol. *Club:* Royal Commonwealth Society.

WILSON, Sir Roland, KBE 1965 (CBE 1941); Kt 1955; Chairman: Commonwealth Banking Corporation, 1966–75; Qantas Airways Ltd, 1966–73; Wentworth Hotel, 1966–73; Director: The MLC Ltd, 1969–79; ICI Australia, 1967–74; economic and financial consultant; *b* Ulverstone, Tasmania, 7 April 1904; *s* of Thomas Wilson; *m* 1930, Valeska (*d* 1971), *d* of William Thompson; *m* 1975, Joyce, *d* of Clarence Henry Chivers. *Educ:* Devonport High School; Univ. of Tasmania; Oriel College, Oxford; Chicago University. Rhodes Scholar for Tasmania, 1925; BCom 1926, Univ. of Tasmania; Dipl. in Economics and Political Science 1926, and DPhil 1929, Oxon; Commonwealth Fund Fellow, 1928, and PhD 1930, Chicago. Pitt Cobbett Lecturer in Economics, Univ. of Tasmania, 1930–32; Director of Tutorial Classes, Univ. of Tasmania, 1931–32; Asst Commonwealth Statistician and Economist, 1932; Economist, Statistician's Branch, Commonwealth Treasury, 1933; Commonwealth Statistician and Economic Adviser to the Treasury, Commonwealth of Australia, 1936–40 and 1946–51; Sec. to Dept Labour and Nat. Service, 1941–46; Chairman Economic and Employment Commission, United Nations, 1948–49. Secretary to Treasury, Commonwealth of Australia, 1951–66; Member Bd: Commonwealth Bank of Australia, 1951–59; Reserve Bank of Australia, 1960–66; Qantas Empire Airways, 1954–73; Commonwealth Banking Corp., 1960–75. Hon. LLD Tasmania, 1969. *Publications:* Capital Imports and the Terms of Trade, 1931; Public and Private Investment in Australia, 1939; Facts and Fancies of Productivity, 1946. *Address:* 64 Empire Circuit, Forrest, Canberra, ACT 2603, Australia. *T:* 95–2560. *Club:* Commonwealth (Canberra).

WILSON, Maj.-Gen. (Ronald) Dare, CBE 1968 (MBE 1949); MC 1945; MA Cantab; DL; retired; current interests farming, forestry and worldwide national park research; *b* 3 Aug. 1919; *s* of Sydney E. D. Wilson and Dorothea, *d* of George Burgess; *m* 1973, Sarah, *d* of Sir Peter Stallard, *qv*; two *s. Educ:* Shrewsbury Sch.; St John's Coll. Cambridge (Pt I 1939, BA 1972). Commissioned into Royal Northumberland Fusiliers, 1939; served War, 1939–45: BEF 1940, ME and NW Europe (MC, despatches 1946); 6th Airborne Div., 1945–48; 1st Bn Parachute Regt, 1949; MoD, 1950; Royal Northumberland Fusiliers: Korea, 1951; Kenya, 1953; GSO2, Staff Coll., Camberley, 1954–56; AA&QMG, 3rd Div., 1958–59; comd 22 Special Air Service Regt, 1960–62; Canadian Nat. Defence Coll., 1962–63; Col GS 1(BR) Corps BAOR, 1963–65; comd 149 Infantry Bde (TA), 1966–67; Brig. 1966; Brig., AQ ME Comd, 1967; Maj.-Gen. 1968; Dir, Land/Air Warfare, MoD, 1968–69; Dir, Army Aviation, MoD, 1970–71. Exmoor Nat. Park Officer, 1974–78. Observer, UK Cttee for Internat. Nature Conservation; Consultant to Fedn of Nature and Nat. Parks of Europe. Speaker for E-SU in USA. Church Warden, Church of St George, Morebath, Devon. Helicopter and light aircraft pilot; Mem., Army Cresta Run Team and Army Rifle VIII; captained British Free-Fall Parachute Team, 1962–65; Chm., British Parachute Assoc., 1962–65. FRGS. DL Somerset, 1979. Royal Aero Club Silver Medal, 1967. *Publications:* Cordon and Search, 1948; contribs to military jls. *Recreations:* country pursuits, travelling, winter sports. *Address:* Combeland, Dulverton, Somerset. *Club:* Flyfishers'.

WILSON, Hon. Sir Ronald (Darling), KBE 1979; CMG 1978; Justice of the High Court of Australia, since 1979; Chancellor, Murdoch University, since 1980; *b* 23 Aug. 1922; *s* of Harold Wilson and Jean Ferguson Wilson (*née* Darling); *m* 1950, Leila Amy Gibson Smith; three *s* two *d. Educ:* Geraldton State School; Univ. of Western Australia (LLB Hons; Hon. LLD 1980); Univ. of Pennsylvania (LLM). Assistant Crown Prosecutor, Western Australia, 1954–59; Chief Crown Prosecutor, WA, 1959–61; Crown Counsel, WA, 1961–69; QC 1963; Solicitor General, WA, 1969–79. Moderator, Presbyterian Church in Western Australia, 1965; Moderator, WA Synod, Uniting Church in Australia, 1977–79. *Address:* 88 Webster Street, Nedlands, WA 6009, Australia. *T:* 386 4500. *Club:* Weld (Perth).

WILSON, Ronald Marshall, CBE 1982; sole proprietor, Ronnie Wilson, Chartered Surveyors, since 1983; Director: Central Farmers Ltd, since 1971; Sherfield (Investments), since 1983; Chairman, Nightingale Secretariat PLC, since 1985; Consultant, Wright Oliphant, since 1983; *b* 6 March 1923; *s* of Marshall Lang Wilson and Margaret Wilson Wilson; *m* 1948, Marion Robertson Scobie (marr. diss. 1985); two *s. Educ:* Sedbergh; London Univ. (BSc Estate Management 1950). Served War of 1939–45: North Irish Horse; Court Orderly Officer, Wüppertal War Crimes Trial, 1946. Partner, Bell-Ingram, Chartered Surveyors, 1957–83. Royal Institution of Chartered Surveyors: Mem. General Council, 1973–; President, 1979–80; Mem. Land Agency and Agricl Divisional Council, 1970–77 (Chm., 1974–75); Chm., Internat. Cttee, 1976–78. *Publications:* articles on technical and professional subjects, incl. Planning in the Countryside. *Recreations:* golf, fishing, shooting. *Address:* 66 Alexandra Road, Kew, Richmond, Surrey TW9 2BS. *T:* 01–948 4976. *Club:* Farmers'.

WILSON, Roy; *see* Wilson, G. R.

WILSON, Sheriff Roy Alexander, WS; Sheriff of Grampian, Highlands and Islands at Elgin, since 1975; *b* 22 Oct. 1927; *s* of Eric Moir Wilson and Jean Dey Gibb; *m* 1954, Alison Mary Craig; one *s* one *d. Educ:* Drumwhindle Sch.; Aberdeen Grammar Sch.; Merchiston Castle Sch.; Lincoln Coll., Oxford Univ. (BA); Edinburgh Univ. (LLB); Thow Scholarship in Scots Law, 1952. WS; NP. Solicitor, 1953. Partner, subseq. Sen. Partner, Messrs Allan McNeil & Son, WS, Edinburgh, 1957–75. Chm., indust. relations tribunals, 1971–75. Rotarian; Past President: Moray Caring Assoc.; Moray Rugby Club; Treasurer, Fochabers Curling Club. *Recreations:* golf, curling, spectator sports, reading. *Address:* Deansford, Bishopmill, Elgin, Moray. *T:* Elgin 7339. *Club:* Elgin.

WILSON, Roy Vernon, CEng, MICE; Director, Eastern Region, Property Services Agency, Department of the Environment, 1980–82; *b* 23 July 1922; *s* of Alfred Vincent Wilson and late Theresa Elsie Wilson; *m* 1951, Elsie Hannah Barrett; three *s. Educ:* Cheadle Hulme Sch.; Manchester Univ. (BScTech Hons). Served Royal Engineers, 1942–44. Civil Engineer, local govt, 1945–51; Harlow Develt Corp., 1951–54; Air Ministry Works Directorate. Warrington, 1954–59; Newmarket, 1959–62; Germany, 1962–65; District Works Officer: Wethersfield, 1965–67; Mildenhall, 1967–72; Area Officer, Letchworth (PSA), 1972–76; Regional Director, Cyprus (PSA), 1976–79; Chief Works Officer, Ruislip, 1979. *Recreations:* lacrosse (earlier years), golf, tennis. *Address:* 12 Diomed Drive, Great Barton, Bury St Edmunds, Suffolk IP31 2TD. *Club:* Civil Service.

WILSON, Samuel; Lord Mayor of Belfast, June 1986–87; *b* 4 April 1953; *s* of Alexander and Mary Wilson. *Educ:* Methodist Coll., Belfast; The Queen's Univ., Belfast (BScEcon; PGCE). Teacher of Economics, 1975–83; Researcher in N Ireland Assembly, 1983–86. Councillor, Belfast CC, 1981–; Press Officer for Democratic Unionist Party, 1982–. *Publications:* The Carson Trail, 1982; The Unionist Case—The Forum Report Answered, 1984. *Recreations:* reading, motor cycling, windsurfing. *Address:* 19 Jocelyn Gardens, Belfast. *T:* Belfast 59934.

WILSON, Sandy; composer, lyric writer, playwright; *b* 19 May 1924; *s* of George Walter Wilson and Caroline Elsie (*née* Humphrey). *Educ:* Elstree Preparatory School; Harrow School; Oriel College, Oxford (BA Eng. Lit.). Contributed material to Oranges and Lemons, Slings and Arrows, 1948; wrote lyrics for touring musical play Caprice, 1950; words and music for two revues at Watergate Theatre, 1951 and 1952; (musical comedy) The Boy Friend for Players' Theatre, 1953, later produced in West End and on Broadway, 1954, revival, Comedy, 1967 (also directed), revival, Old Vic, 1984; (musical play) The Buccaneer, 1955; Valmouth (musical play, based on Firbank's novel), Lyric, Hammersmith and Savile Theatre, 1959, New York, 1960, revival, Chichester, 1982; songs for Call It Love, Wyndham's Theatre, 1960; Divorce Me, Darling! (musical comedy), Players' Theatre, 1964, Globe, 1965; music for TV series, The World of Wooster, 1965–66; music for As Dorothy Parker Once Said, Fortune, 1969; songs for Danny la Rue's Charley's Aunt (TV), 1969; wrote and performed in Sandy Wilson Thanks the Ladies, Hampstead Theatre Club, 1971; His Monkey Wife, Hampstead, 1971; The Clapham Wonder, Canterbury, 1978; Aladdin, Lyric, Hammersmith, 1979. *Publications:* This is Sylvia (with own illustrs), 1954; The Boy Friend (with own illustrs), 1955; Who's Who for Beginners (with photographs by Jon Rose), 1957; Prince What Shall I Do (illustrations, with Rhoda Levine), 1961; The Poodle from Rome, 1962; I Could Be Happy (autobiog.), 1975; Ivor, 1975; Caught in the Act, 1976; The Roaring Twenties, 1977. *Recreations:* visiting the National Film Theatre and writing musicals. *Address:* 2 Southwell Gardens, SW7. *T:* 01–373 6172. *Club:* Players' Theatre.

WILSON, Snoo; writer, since 1969; *b* 2 Aug. 1948; *s* of Leslie Wilson and Pamela Mary Wilson; *m* 1976, Ann McFerran; two *s* one *d. Educ:* Bradfield Coll.; Univ. of East Anglia (BA English and American Studies). Associate Director, Portable Theatre, 1970–75; Dramaturge, Royal Shakespeare Co., 1975–76; Script Editor, Play for Today, 1976. Henfield Fellow, Univ. of E Anglia, 1978; US Bicentennial Fellow in Playwriting, 1981–82. Adapted Gounod's La Colombe, Buxton Fest., 1983. *Filmscript:* Shadey, 1986. *Publications: plays:* Layby (jtly), 1972; Pignight, 1972; The Pleasure Principle, 1973; Blowjob, 1974; Soul of the White Ant, 1976; England England, 1978; Vampire, 1978; The Glad Hand, 1978; A Greenish Man, 1978; The Number of the Beast, 1982; Flaming Bodies, 1982; Grass Widow, 1983; Loving Reno, 1983; Hamlyn, 1984, etc; *novels:* Spaceache, 1984; Inside Babel, 1985; *opera:* Orpheus in the Underworld (new version), 1984. *Recreations:* beekeeping, space travel. *Address:* 41 The Chase, SW4 0NP.

WILSON, Stanley John, CBE 1981; FCIS; Chairman, Burmah Oil (South Africa) (Pty) Ltd, since 1982; Managing Director, 1975–82 and Chief Executive, 1980–82, The Burmah Oil Co. Ltd; *b* 23 Oct. 1921; *s* of Joseph Wilson and Jessie Cormack; *m* 1952, Molly Ann (*née* Clarkson); two *s. Educ:* King Edward VII Sch., Johannesburg Witwatersrand Univ. CA (SA); ASAA, ACMA; FCIS 1945; CBIM; FInst Pet. 1945–73: Chartered Accountant, Savory & Dickinson; Sec. and Sales Man., Rhodesian Timber Hldgs; Chm. and Chief Exec. for S Africa, Vacuum Oil Co.; Reg. Vice Pres. for S and E Asia, Mobil Petroleum; Pres., Mobil Sekiyu; Pres., subseq. Reg. Vice Pres. for Europe, Mobil Europe Inc.; Pres., Mobil East Inc., and Reg. Vice Pres. for Far East, S and SE Asia, Australia, Indian Sub-Continent, etc, 1973–75. Underwriting Mem. of Lloyd's. Freeman, City of London; Liveryman, Basketmakers' Co. FRSA. *Recreations:* golf, shooting, fishing. *Address:* The Jetty, PO Box 751, Plettenberg Bay, Cape Province, 6600, South Africa. *T:* Plettenberg Bay 9624. *Clubs:* City of London, Royal Automobile; Royal & Ancient Golf; Tidworth Garrison Golf; City (Cape Town); Rand (Johannesburg); Heresewentien (SA).

WILSON, Stanley Livingstone, CMG 1966; DSO 1943; Visiting Surgeon, Dunedin Hospital, 1937–66, Hon. Consulting Surgeon, Dunedin Hospital, since 1966; *b* 17 April 1905; *s* of Robert and Elizabeth Wilson; *m* 1930, Isabel, *d* of William Kirkland; two *s* one *d. Educ:* Dannevirke High School; University of Otago. Univ. Entrance Schol., 1923; MB, ChB 1928; FRCS 1932; FRACS 1937. Resident Surgeon, Dunedin Hosp., Royal Northern and St Mary's Hosps, London, 1929–37. NZ Medical Corps, Middle East; Solomons, 1940–44; OC 2 NZ Casualty Clearing Station, Pacific, 1943–44. President, Otago BMA, 1948; Council, RACS 1951–63 (President, 1961–62). Examiner in Surgery, Univ. of Otago, 1952–65; Court of Examiners, RACS, 1948–60; Mem., Otago Hosp. Bd, 1965–74. Hon. Fellow, American Coll. of Surgeons, 1963. Hon. DSc Otago, 1975. *Recreation:* golf. *Address:* 27 Burwood Avenue, Dunedin, NW1, New Zealand. *T:* 741.061. *Club:* Dunedin (Dunedin).

WILSON, Stephen Shipley, CB 1950; Keeper of Public Records, 1960–66; *b* 4 Aug. 1904; *s* of Alexander Cowan Wilson and Edith Jane Brayshaw; *m* 1933, Martha Mott, *d* of A. B. Kelley and Mariana Parrish, Philadelphia, Pa; two *s* one *d. Educ:* Leighton Park; Queen's Coll., Oxford. Fellow, Brookings Inst., Washington, DC, 1926–27; Instructor, Columbia University, New York City, 1927–28; Public Record Office, 1928–29; Ministry of Transport, 1929–47; Ministry of Supply, 1947–50; Iron and Steel Corporation of Great Britain, 1950–53, and Iron and Steel Holding and Realisation Agency, 1953–60. Historical Section, Cabinet Office, 1966–77. *Address:* 3 Willow Road, NW3 1TH. *T:* 01–435 0148. *Club:* Reform.

See also J. E. Meade, Sir Geoffrey Wilson, R. C. Wilson.

WILSON, Prof. Thomas, CBE 1959; Professor of Tropical Hygiene, Liverpool School of Tropical Medicine, University of Liverpool, 1962–71; *b* 5 Nov. 1905; *s* of R. H. Wilson, OBE, Belfast; *m* 1930, Annie Cooley; two *s* one *d. Educ:* Belfast Royal Academy; Queen's Univ., Belfast. MB, BCh, BAO (Belfast) 1927; DPH (Belfast) 1929; DTM, DTH (Liverpool) 1930; MD (Belfast) 1952. MO, Central Health Bd, FMS 1930; Health Officer,

Malayan Med. Service, 1931; Lieut and Capt., RAMC (POW in Malaya and Thailand), 1942–45; Sen. Malaria Research Officer, Inst. for Med. Res., Fedn of Malaya, 1949; Dir, Inst. for Med. Res., Fedn of Malaya, 1956; Sen. Lectr in Tropical Hygiene, Liverpool Sch. of Trop. Med., Univ. of Liverpool, 1959. *Publications*: (with T. H. Davey) Davey and Lightbody's Control of Disease in the Tropics, 1965, 4th edn 1971; contrib. to Hobson's Theory and Practice of Public Health, 3rd edn 1969, 5th edn 1979; articles in medical journals on malaria and filariasis. *Recreation*: golf. *Address*: 77 Strand Road, Portstewart, N Ireland.

WILSON, Prof. Thomas, OBE 1945; FBA 1976; FRSE 1980; Adam Smith Professor of Political Economy, University of Glasgow, 1958–82; Hon. Fellow, London School of Economics, 1979; *b* 23 June 1916; *s* of late John Bright and Margaret G. Wilson, Belfast; *m* 1943, Dorothy Joan Parry, LVO; one *s* two *d*. *Educ*: Queen's University, Belfast; London School of Economics. Mins of Economic Warfare and Aircraft Production, 1940–42; Prime Minister's Statistical Branch, 1942–45. Fellow of University College, Oxford, 1946–58; Faculty Fellow of Nuffield College, Oxford, 1950–54; Vis. Fellow, All Souls Coll., Oxford, 1974–75; Editor, Oxford Economic Papers, 1948–58. Vice-Chm., Scottish Council's Cttee of Inquiry into the Scottish Economy, 1960–61; Nuffield Foundation Visiting Prof., Univ. of Ibadan, 1962. Economic Consultant to Govt of N Ireland, 1964–65, 1968–70; to Sec. of State for Scotland, 1963–64 and 1970–83; Shipbuilding Industry Cttee, 1965; Assessor, DoE, 1984–. Dir, Scottish Mutual Assce Soc. (Chm., 1978–81). DUniv Stirling, 1982. *Publications*: Fluctuations in Income and Employment, 1941; (ed) Ulster under Home Rule, 1955; Inflation, 1960; Planning and Growth, 1964; (ed) Pensions, Inflation and Growth, 1974; (ed with A. S. Skinner) Essays on Adam Smith, 1975; (ed with A. S. Skinner) The Market and the State, 1976; The Political Economy of Inflation (British Acad. Keynes Lecture), 1976; (with D. J. Wilson) The Political Economy of the Welfare State, 1982; Inflation, Unemployment and the Market, 1985. *Recreations*: sailing, hill walking. *Address*: 1 Chatford House, The Promenade, Clifton, Bristol BS8 3NG. *T*: Bristol 730741. *Club*: Athenæum.

WILSON, Thomas Marcus; Assistant Under-Secretary, Ministry of Defence (Procurement Executive), 1971–73; retired; *b* 15 April 1913; *s* of Reverend C. Wilson; *m* 1939, Norah Boyes (*née* Sinclair) (*d* 1984); no *c*. *Educ*: Manchester Grammar School; Jesus College, Cambridge. Asst Principal, Customs and Excise, 1936; Private Secretary: to Board of Customs and Excise, 1939; to Chm. Bd, 1940; Principal, 1941; lent to Treasury, 1942; lent to Office of Lord President of Council, 1946; Asst Sec., 1947; seconded: Min. of Food, 1949; Min. of Supply, 1953, Under-Sec., 1962, and Prin. Scientific and Civil Aviation Adv. to Brit. High Comr in Australia, also Head of Defence Research and Supply Staff, 1962–64; Under-Secretary: Min. of Aviation, 1964–67; Min. of Technology, 1967–70; Min. of Aviation Supply, 1970–71; MoD, 1971–73. *Recreations*: reading, music, painting and travel, especially in France. *Address*: Flat 6, 21 Queen Square, Bath.

WILSON, William; DL; *b* 28 June 1913; *s* of Charles and Charlotte Wilson; *m* 1939, Bernice Wilson; one *s*. *Educ*: Wheatley St Sch.; Cheylesmore Sch.; Coventry Jun. Technical School. Qual. as Solicitor, 1939. Entered Army, 1941; served in N Africa, Italy and Greece; demobilised, 1946 (Sergeant). Contested (Lab) Warwick and Leamington, 1951, 1955, March 1957, 1959. MP (Lab) Coventry S, 1964–74, Coventry SE, 1974–83; Mem., Commons Select Cttee on Race Relations and Immigration, 1970–79. Mem., Warwicks CC, 1958–70 (Leader Labour Group), re-elected 1972. DL County of Warwick, 1967. *Recreations*: gardening, theatre, watching Association football. *Address*: Avonside House, High Street, Barford, Warwickshire. *T*: Barford 624278.

WILSON, Prof. William Adam; Lord President Reid Professor of Law, University of Edinburgh, since 1972; *b* 28 July 1928; *s* of Hugh Wilson and Anne Adam. *Educ*: Hillhead High Sch., Glasgow; Glasgow Univ. MA 1948, LLB 1951. Solicitor, 1951. Lectr in Scots Law, Edinburgh Univ., 1960, Sen. Lectr 1965. Dep. Chm., Consumer Protection Adv. Cttee, 1974–82. *Publications*: (with A. G. M. Duncan) Law of Trusts, Trustees and Executors, 1975; Introductory Essays on Scots Law, 1978, 2nd edn 1984; Law of Debt, 1981; articles in legal jls. *Address*: 2 Great Stuart Street, Edinburgh EH3 6AW. *T*: 031–225 4958.

WILSON, William Desmond, OBE 1964 (MBE 1954); MC 1945; DSC (USA) 1945; HM Diplomatic Service, retired; Deputy High Commissioner, Kaduna, Nigeria, 1975–81; *b* 2 Jan. 1922; *s* of late Crozier Irvine Wilson and Mabel Evelyn (*née* Richardson); *m* 1949, Lucy Bride; two *s*. *Educ*: Royal Belfast Acad. Instn; QUB; Trinity Coll., Cambridge. Joined Indian Army, 1941; served with 10 Gurkha Rifles, India and Italy, 1942–46 (Major). Colonial Admin. Service: Northern Nigeria, 1948–63 (MBE for Gallantry, 1954); retd as Permanent Sec.; joined Foreign (subseq. Diplomatic) Service, 1963; First Sec., Ankara, 1963–67; UN (Polit.) Dept, FO, 1967; First Sec. and Head of Chancery, Kathmandu, 1969–74; Counsellor, 1975; Sen. Officers' War Course, RNC Greenwich, 1975. *Recreations*: shooting, riding. *Address*: The Spinney, Forge Hill, Pluckley, Kent TN27 0SJ. *T*: Pluckley 300. *Clubs*: East India, St Stephen's Constitutional.

WILSON, (William) George, OBE 1960; Director, Paul James & George Wilson Ltd, Health Services Development Advisers, since 1983; *b* 19 Feb. 1921; *s* of late William James Wilson and late Susannah Wilson; *m* 1948, Freda Huddleston; three *s*. Min. of Health, 1939. Served War, Army, in India and Ceylon, 1940–46. Min. of Nat. Insurance, 1947; Asst Principal, Colonial Office, 1947; Principal, CO, 1950–57 (Adviser, UK Delegn to UN Gen. Assembly, 1951); Financial Sec., Mauritius, 1957–60; Asst Sec., MoH, 1962; Consultant, Hosp. Design and Construction, Middle East and Africa, 1968–70; Asst Sec., DHSS, 1971; Under-Sec., DHSS, 1972–81. *Recreation*: book collecting. *Address*: Clarghyll Hall, Alston, Cumbria. *Clubs*: Wig and Pen, Royal Commonwealth Society, Sloane.

WILSON, Rt. Rev. William Gilbert; *see* Kilmore, Elphin and Ardagh, Bishop of.

WILSON, William Lawrence, CB 1967; OBE 1954; retired as Deputy Secretary, Department of the Environment, now Consultant; *b* 11 Sept. 1912; *s* of Joseph Osmond and Ann Wilson; *m* C. V. Richards; two *s*. *Educ*: Stockton on Tees Secondary School; Constantine College, Middlesbrough. BSc (London), FIMechE, Whitworth Prizeman. Apprentice, ICI Billingham 1928–33; Technical Asst, ICI, 1933–36; Assistant Engineer, HMOW, 1937; subsequently Engineer, 1939; Superintending Engineer, (MOW) 1945; Assistant Chief Engineer, 1954; Chief Engineer, 1962; Deputy Secretary, MPBW later DoE, 1969–73. Pres., Assoc. of Supervising Electrical Engineers. FRSA; Hon. FCIBSE. Coronation Medal. *Publications*: papers on Radioactive Wastes; contrib. to World Power Conference, USSR and USA. *Recreations*: cricket, fishing, watching all forms of sport. *Address*: Oakwood, Chestnut Avenue, Rickmansworth, Herts. *T*: Rickmansworth 774419.

WILSON, William Napier M.; *see* Menzies-Wilson.

WILSON-JOHNSON, David Robert; baritone; *b* 16 Nov. 1950; *s* of Sylvia Constance Wilson and Harry Kenneth Johnson. *Educ*: Wellingborough School; British Institute, Florence; St Catharine's College, Cambridge (BA Hons 1973); Royal Acad. of Music. NFMS Award, 1977; Gulbenkian Fellowship, 1978–81. Royal Opera House, Covent Garden: We Come to the River (debut), 1976; Billy Budd, 1982; L'Enfant et les

Sortillèges, 1983; Le Rossignal, 1983; Les Noces, Boris Godunov, 1984; Die Zauberflöte, 1985; Turandot, 1987; Wigmore Hall recital début, 1977; BBC Proms début, 1981; appearances at Glyndebourne, Edinburgh, and other UK and overseas venues; numerous recordings. Hon. ARAM 1982. *Recreations*: swimming, slimming, gardening and growing walnuts at Dordogne house. *Address*: 28 Englefield Road, N1 4ET. *T*: 01–254 0941.

WILSON JONES, Prof. Edward, FRCP, FRCPath; Professor of Dermatopathology since 1974, and Dean since 1980, Institute of Dermatology, University of London; *b* 26 July 1926; *s* of Percy George Jones and Margaret Louisa Wilson; *m* 1952, Hilda Mary Rees; one *s* one *d*. *Educ*: Oundle Sch.; Trinity Hall, Cambridge (MB, BChir 1951); St Thomas' Hosp., London. FRCP 1970; FRCPath 1975. National Service, Army, 1953–54. House Surgeon (Ophthalmic), St Thomas' Hosp., 1951; House Physician (Gen. Medicine), St Helier Hosp., Carshalton, 1951–52; House Physician (Neurology and Chest Diseases), St Thomas' Hosp., 1955; Registrar (Gen. Medicine), Watford Peace Meml Hosp., 1955–57; Registrar (Derm.), St Thomas' Hosp., 1957–60; Inst. of Dermatology, St John's Hosp. for Diseases of the Skin: Sen. Registrar (Derm.), 1960–62; Sen. Registrar (Dermatopath.), 1962–63; Sen. Lectr (Dermatopath.), 1963–74; Hon. Consultant, St John's Hosp. for Diseases of Skin, 1974–. *Publications*: (contrib.) Textbook of Dermatology, ed Rook, Wilkinson and Ebling, 3rd edn 1979; articles on dermatopath. subjects in British Jl of Derm., Arch. of Derm., Acta Dermatovenereologica, Dermatologica, Clin. and Exptl Derm., Histopath., and in Human Path. *Recreation*: art history. *Address*: Institute of Dermatology, St John's Hospital for Diseases of the Skin, 5 Lisle Street, WC2H 7BJ.

WILTON, 7th Earl of, *cr* 1801; **Seymour William Arthur John Egerton;** Viscount Grey de Wilton, 1801; *b* 29 May 1921; *s* of 6th Earl and Brenda (*d* 1930), *d* of late Sir William Petersen, KBE; *S* father, 1927; *m* 1962, Mrs Diana Naylor Leyland. *Heir*: (by special remainder) *kinsman* Baron Ebury, *qv*. *Address*: c/o Messrs Warrens, 20 Hartford Road, Huntingdon, Cambs PE18 6QE. *Club*: White's.

WILTON, Sir (Arthur) John, KCMG 1979 (CMG 1967); KCVO 1979; MC 1945; MA; HM Diplomatic Service, retired; Chairman, Arab-British Centre, since 1981; *b* 21 Oct. 1921; *s* of Walter Wilton and Annetta Irene Wilton (*née* Perman); *m* 1950, Maureen Elizabeth Alison Meaker; four *s* one *d*. *Educ*: Wanstead High School; Open Schol., St John's Coll., Oxford, 1940. Commissioned, Royal Ulster Rifles, 1942; served with Irish Brigade, N Africa, Italy and Austria, 1943–46. Entered HM Diplomatic Service, 1947; served Lebanon, Egypt, Gulf Shaikhdoms, Roumania, Aden, and Yugoslavia; Dir, Middle East Centre for Arabic Studies, Shemlan, 1960–65; Ambassador to Kuwait, 1970–74; Asst Under-Sec. of State, FCO, 1974–76; Ambassador to Saudi Arabia, 1976–79; Dir, London House for Overseas Graduates, 1979–86. FRSA 1982. Hon. LLD. *Recreations*: reading, gardening. *Address*: Wilmere Lodge, Middleton Stoney, Oxon OX6 8SQ.

WILTS, Archdeacon of; *see* Smith, Ven. B. J.

WILTSHIRE, Earl of; **Christopher John Hilton Paulet;** *b* 30 July 1969; *s* and *heir* of Marquess of Winchester, *qv*.

WILTSHIRE, Edward Parr, CBE 1965; HM Diplomatic Service, retired; *b* 18 Feb. 1910; 2nd *s* of late Major Percy Wiltshire and Kathleen Olivier Lefroy Parr Wiltshire, Great Yarmouth; *m* 1942, Gladys Mabel Stevens; one *d*. *Educ*: Cheltenham College; Jesus College, Cambridge. Entered Foreign Service, 1932. Served in: Beirut, Mosul, Baghdad, Tehran, Basra, New York (one of HM Vice-Consuls, 1944); promoted Consul, 1945; transf. Cairo, 1946 (Actg Consul-Gen., 1947, 1948); transf. Shiraz (having qual. in Arabic, and subseq. in Persian); Consul, Port Said, 1952; 1st Sec. and Consul: Baghdad, 1952, Rio de Janeiro, 1957; promoted Counsellor, 1959; Political Agent, Bahrain, 1959–63; Consul-General, Geneva, 1963–67; Dir, Diplomatic Service Language Centre, London, 1967–68; worked for Council for Nature (Editor, Habitat), 1968–69; Consul, Le Havre, 1969–75. Hon. Associate, BM (Nat. Hist.), 1980. *Publications*: The Lepidoptera of Iraq, 1957; A Revision of the Armadini, 1979. *Recreations*: music, entomology. *Address*: Wychwood, High Road, Cookham, Berks SL6 9JS.

WILTSHIRE, Sir Frederick Munro, Kt 1976; CBE 1970 (OBE 1966); FTS 1976; Managing Director: Wiltshire File Co. Pty Ltd, Australia, 1938–77; Wiltshire Cutlery Co. Pty Ltd, 1959–77; Director: Repco Ltd, 1966–81; Australian Paper Manufacturers Ltd, 1966–83; *b* 1911; *m* 1938, Jennie L., *d* of F. M. Frencham; one *d*. Chm., Dept of Trade and Industry Adv. Cttee on Small Businesses, 1968; Chm., Cttees of Inquiry, etc. Mem., Executive, CSIRO, 1974–78. Past Pres., Aust. Industries Develt Assoc.; Member, Manufacturing Industries Adv. Council, 1957–77 (Vice-Pres. 1972); Industrial Member, Science and Industry Forum of Aust. Acad. of Science, 1967–80; FAIM (Councillor, 1955–59). *Address*: 38 Rockley Road, South Yarra, Vic 3141, Australia. *Clubs*: Athenæum (Melbourne); Kingston Heath Golf (Aust.).

WIMALASENA, Nanediri; High Commissioner in London for Sri Lanka, 1977–80; Deputy Director General, Greater Colombo Economic Commission of Sri Lanka; *b* 22 March 1914; *m* 1938, Prema Fernando; one *s* two *d*. *Educ*: Ananda Coll., Colombo; Ceylon University Coll.; Ceylon Law Coll. Attorney-at-Law. Elected member, Kandy Municipal Council, 1946, remaining a member for an unbroken period of 21 years; Dep. Mayor of Kandy, 1946; Mayor of City of Kandy, 1963. Elected Member of Parliament for Senkadagala: March-July 1960; again, 1965, then re-elected 1970–May 1977; Dep. Minister of Finance, 1965–70. *Recreations*: tennis, hiking. *Address*: 55 Ward Place, Colombo 7, Sri Lanka.

WIMBORNE, 3rd Viscount, *cr* 1918; **Ivor Fox-Strangways Guest;** Baron Wimborne, 1880; Baron Ashby St Ledgers, 1910; Bt 1838; Chairman, Harris and Dixon Holdings Ltd, since 1976; *b* 2 Dec. 1939; *s* of 2nd Viscount and of Dowager Viscountess Wimborne; *S* father, 1967; *m* 1st, 1966, Victoria Ann (marr. diss. 1981), *o d* of late Col Mervyn Vigors, DSO, MC; one *s*; 2nd, 1983, Mrs Venetia Margaret Barker, *er d* of Richard Quarry; one *d*. *Educ*: Eton. Chairman, Harris & Dixon Group of Cos, 1972–76 (Man. Dir, 1967–71). Jt Master, Pytchley Hounds, 1968–76. *Heir*: *s* Hon. Ivor Mervyn Vigors Guest, *b* 19 Sept. 1968. *Clubs*: Travellers', Cercle Interalliée, Polo (Paris).

WIMBUSH, Rt. Rev. Richard Knyvet; an Assistant Bishop, Diocese of York, since 1977; *b* 18 March 1909; *s* of late Rev. Canon J. S. Wimbush, Terrington, Yorks, and late Judith Isabel Wimbush, *d* of Sir Douglas Fox; *m* 1937, Mary Margaret, *d* of Rev. E. H. Smith; three *s* one *d*. *Educ*: Haileybury Coll.; Oriel Coll., Oxford; Cuddesdon Coll. 2nd cl. Classical Mods 1930; BA 1st cl. Theol. 1932; MA 1935. Deacon, 1934; Priest, 1935; Chaplain, Cuddesdon Coll., Oxon, 1934–37; Curate: Pocklington, Yorks, 1937–39; St Wilfrid, Harrogate, 1939–42. Rector, Melsonby, Yorks, 1942–48; Principal, Edinburgh Theological Coll., 1948–63; Bishop of Argyll and the Isles, 1963–77; Primus of the Episcopal Church in Scotland, 1974–77; Priest-in-charge of Etton with Dalton Holme, dio. York, 1977–83. Canon of St Mary's Cathedral, Edinburgh, 1948–63; Exam. Chap. to Bp of Edinburgh, 1949–62; Select Preacher, Oxford Univ., 1971. *Recreations*: gardening, walking. *Address*: 5 Tower Place, York YO1 1RZ. *Club*: New (Edinburgh).

WINCH, Prof. Donald Norman, FBA 1986; Professor, History of Economics, University of Sussex, since 1969; Pro-Vice-Chancellor (Arts and Social Studies), since 1986; *b* 15

April 1935; *s* of Sidney and Iris Winch; *m* 1983, Doreen Lidster. *Educ:* Sutton Grammar Sch.; LSE (BSc Econ 1956); Princeton Univ. (PhD 1960). Vis. Lectr, Univ. of California, 1959–60; Lectr in Economics, Univ. of Edinburgh, 1960–63; University of Sussex: Lectr, 1963–66; Reader, 1966–69; Dean, Sch. of Social Scis, 1968–74. Visiting Fellow: Sch. of Social Sci., Inst. for Advanced Study, Princeton, 1974–75; King's Coll., Cambridge, 1983; History of Ideas Unit, ANU, 1983; Vis. Prof., Tulane Univ., 1984. Publications Sec., Royal Economic Soc., 1971–; Review Editor, Economic Jl, 1976–83. *Publications:* Classical Political Economy and Colonies, 1965; James Mill: selected economic writings, 1966; Economics and Policy, 1969; (with S. K. Howson) The Economic Advisory Council 1930–1939, 1976; Adam Smith's Politics, 1978; (with S. Collini and J. W. Burrow) That Noble Science of Politics, 1983; Malthus, 1987. *Address:* University of Sussex, Brighton BN1 9QN. *T:* Brighton 678028.

WINCHESTER, 18th Marquess of, *cr* 1551; **Nigel George Paulet;** Baron St John of Basing, 1539; Earl of Wiltshire, 1550; Premier Marquess of England; *b* 23 Dec. 1941; *s* of George Cecil Paulet (*g g g s* of 13th Marquess) (*d* 1961), and Hazel Margaret (*d* 1976), *o d* of late Major Danvers Wheeler, RA, Salisbury, Rhodesia; *S* kinsman, 1968; *m* 1967, Rosemary Anne, *d* of Major Aubrey John Hilton; two *s* one *d*. *Heir: s* Earl of Wiltshire, *qv*. *Address:* Lydford Cottage, 35 Whyteladies Lane, Borrowdale, Harare, Zimbabwe.

WINCHESTER, Bishop of, since 1985; **Rt. Rev. Colin Clement Walter James;** *b* 20 Sept. 1926; *yr s* of late Canon Charles Clement Hancock James and Gwenyth Mary James; *m* 1962, Margaret Joan Henshaw; one *s* two *d*. *Educ:* Aldenham School; King's College, Cambridge (MA, Hons History); Cuddesdon Theological College. Assistant Curate, Stepney Parish Church, 1952–55; Chaplain, Stowe School, 1955–59; BBC Religious Broadcasting Dept, 1959–67; Religious Broadcasting Organizer, BBC South and West, 1960–67; Vicar of St Peter with St Swithin, Bournemouth, 1967–73; Bishop Suffragan of Basingstoke, 1973–77; Canon Residentiary of Winchester Cathedral, 1973–77; Bishop of Wakefield, 1977–85. Member of General Synod, 1970–; Chairman: Church Information Cttee, 1976–79; C of E's Liturgical Commn, 1986–. Chm., BBC and IBA Central Religious Adv. Cttee, 1979–84. President: Woodard Corp., 1978–; RADIUS, 1980–. Chm., USPG, 1985–. *Recreations:* theatre, travelling. *Address:* Wolvesey, Winchester, Hants SO23 9ND.

WINCHESTER, Dean of; *see* Beeson, Very Rev. T. R.

WINCHESTER, Archdeacon of; *see* Clarkson, Ven. A. G.

WINCHESTER, Ian Sinclair, CMG 1982; HM Diplomatic Service; Assistant Under-Secretary of State (Director of Communications and Technical Services), Foreign and Commonwealth Office, since 1985; *b* 14 March 1931; *s* of Dr Alexander Hugh Winchester, FRCS(Ed), and late Mary Stewart (*née* Duguid); *m* 1957, Shirley Louise Milner; three *s*. *Educ:* Lewes County Grammar Sch., Sussex; Magdalen Coll., Oxford. Foreign Office, 1953; Third Sec. (Oriental), Cairo, 1955–56; FO, 1956–60; Asst Political Agent, Dubai, 1960–62; Actg Political Agent, Doha, 1962; First Sec. (Inf.), Vienna, 1962–65; First Sec. (Commercial), Damascus, 1965–67; FO (later FCO), 1967–70; Counsellor, Jedda, 1970–72; Counsellor (Commercial), Brussels, 1973–76; FCO, 1976–81; Minister, Jedda, 1982–83. *Address:* c/o Foreign and Commonwealth Office, SW1A 2AH.

WINCHILSEA, 16th Earl of, *cr* 1628, **AND NOTTINGHAM,** 11th Earl of, *cr* 1675; **Christopher Denys Stormont Finch Hatton,** Bart 1611; Viscount Maidstone, 1623; Bart English, 1660; Baron Finch, 1674; Custodian of Royal Manor of Wye; *b* 17 Nov. 1936; *er s* of 15th Earl and Countess Gladys Széchényi (*d* 1978) (who obtained a divorce, 1946; she *m* 1954, Arthur Talbot Peterson), 3rd *d* of Count László Széchényi; *S* father, 1950; *m* 1962, Shirley, *e d* of late Bernard Hatfield, Wylde Green, Sutton Coldfield; one *s* one *d*. *Heir: s* Viscount Maidstone, *qv*. *Address:* South Cadbury House, Yeovil, Somerset.

WINCKLES, Kenneth, MBE 1945; business consultant; *b* 17 June 1918; *s* of Frank and Emily Winckles; *m* 1941, Peggy Joan Hodges; one *s* one *d*. *Educ:* Lower School of John Lyon, Harrow. FCA. Served War, Army, 1939–46, demobilised Lt-Col. Company Secretary, Scribbans-Kemp Ltd, 1947–48; Rank Organisation, 1948–67: Director and Gp Asst Managing Dir; Managing Dir, Theatre Div.; Dir, Southern Television Ltd; Dir, Rank-Xerox Ltd; Chm., Odeon Theatres (Canada) Ltd; Chm., Visnews Ltd. Chm. and Man. Dir, United Artists Corp, 1967–69; Man. Dir, Cunard Line Ltd, 1969–70; Dir, Hill Samuel Gp Ltd, 1971–80. Director: Horserace Totalisator Bd, 1974–76; CAA, 1978–80. An Underwriting Member of Lloyd's, 1977–. *Publication:* The Prctice of Successful Business Management, 1986. *Recreations:* golf, swimming, gardening, music. *Address:* Moor House, Fishers Wood, Sunningdale, Ascot, Berks SL5 0JF. *T:* Ascot 24800.

WINDER, Col John Lyon C.; *see* Corbett-Winder.

WINDEYER, Sir Brian (Wellingham), Kt 1961; FRCP, FRCS, FRCSE, FRSM, FRCR, DMRE; Vice-Chancellor, University of London, 1969–72; Professor of Radiology (Therapeutic), Middlesex Hospital Medical School, University of London, 1942–69; Dean, Middlesex Hospital Medical School, 1954–67; formerly Director: Meyerstein Institute of Radiotherapy, Middlesex Hospital; Radiotherapy Department, Mount Vernon Hospital; Cons. Adviser in Radiotherapy to Ministry of Health; *b* 7 Feb. 1904; *s* of Richard Windeyer, KC, Sydney, Australia; *m* 1st, 1928, Joyce Ziele, *d* of Harry Russell, Sydney; one *s* one *d*; 2nd, 1948, Elspeth Anne, *d* of H. Bowry, Singapore; one *s* two *d*. *Educ:* Sydney C of E Grammar Sch.; St Andrew's Coll., Univ. of Sydney. Sydney Univ. Rugby Team, 1922–27; combined Australian and NZ Univs Rugby Team, 1923; coll. crew, 1922–26. MB, BS Sydney, 1927; FRCSE 1930; DMRE Cambridge, 1933; FFR (now FRCR) 1940; FRCS (ad eundem) 1948; MRCP 1957. Formerly House Physician, House Surgeon and Radium Registrar, Royal Prince Alfred Hosp., Sydney; Asst, Fondation Curie, Paris, 1929–30; Middlesex Hospital: Radium Officer, 1931; MO i/c Radiotherapy Dept, 1936; Medical Comdt, 1940–45; Dir, EMS Radiotherapy Dept, Mt Vernon Hosp., 1940–46; Dean, Faculty of Medicine, Univ. of London, 1964–68. Skinner Lectr, Faculty of Radiologists, 1943 (Pres. of Faculty, 1949–52); Hunterian Prof., RCS, 1951. Pres., Radiology Section, RSM, 1958–59. Chairman: Radio-active Substances Adv. Cttee, 1961–70; Nat. Radiological Protection Bd, 1970–78; Academic Council, Univ. of London, 1967–69; Matilda and Terence Kennedy Inst. of Rheumatology, 1970–77; Inst. of Educn, Univ. of London, 1974–83; Council, RSA, 1973–78. Member: Royal Commn on Med. Educn; Grand Council and Exec. Cttee, British Empire Cancer Campaign; British Inst. of Radiology (late Mem. Council); Med. Soc. of London; MRC, 1958–62 and 1968–71; Clinical Research Bd, 1954–62 (Chm., 1968); main Cttee, until 1977, Cttee 4, 1965–69, Internat. Commn on Radiological Protection; Royal Hosp. and Home for Incurables, Putney (Chm., Res. Adv. Cttee); a Vice Pres., Royal Surgical Aid Soc. (formerly Chm.). Co-opted Mem. Council, RCS, to rep. radiology, 1948–53. Former Chm., Throgmorton Club. Mem. Court, 1963–78, Master, 1972–73, Apothecaries' Soc. Hon. Mem., Amer. Radium Soc., 1948. Hon. FRACS, 1951; Hon. FCRA (now FRACR) 1955; Hon. FACR 1966. Hon. DSc: British Columbia, 1952; Wales, 1965; Cantab, 1971; Hon. LLD Glasgow, 1968; Hon. MD Sydney, 1979. *Publications:* various articles on cancer and radiotherapy. *Recreations:* golf, gardening. *Address:* 9 Dale Close, St Ebbe's, Oxford OX1 1TU. *T:* Oxford 242816. *Club:* Athenæum.

WINDEYER, Rt. Hon. Sir (William John) Victor, PC 1963; KBE 1958 (CBE (mil.) 1944); CB 1953; DSO (and bar), 1942; ED; Justice of the High Court of Australia, 1958–72, retired; *b* 28 July 1900; *s* of W. A. Windeyer, Sydney, NSW; *m* 1934, Margaret Moor Vicars; three *s* one *d*. *Educ:* Sydney Grammar Sch.; University of Sydney (MA, LLB). Admitted to Bar of NSW, 1925; KC (NSW) 1949; sometime lecturer in Faculty of Law, University of Sydney. Lieut AMF (Militia), 1922; War of 1939–45; Lieut-Colonel comdg 2/48 Bn, AIF, 1940–42 (including siege of Tobruk); Brig. comdg 20th Australian Inf. Bde, AIF, 1942–46 (El Alamein, New Guinea, Borneo); Major-General and CMF Member, Australian Military Board, 1950–53; Retired List, 1957. Trustee, Sydney Grammar Sch., 1943–70; Member of Senate, University of Sydney, 1949–59, Dep. Chancellor, 1953–58; Hon. Col, Sydney University Regiment, 1956–66; Member Council Australian National University, 1951–55. Director: Colonial Sugar Refining Co., 1953–58; Mutual Life and Citizens Assurance Co., 1954–58. Chairman Trustees, Gowrie Scholarship Fund, 1964–86. Vice-President, Selden Society, 1965–; Pres., NSW Branch, Australian Scouts Assoc., 1970–78. Hon. Member, Society Public Teachers of Law; Hon. Bencher, Middle Temple, 1972–. Hon. Fellow, Royal Aust. Hist. Soc., 1976–. Hon. LLD Sydney, 1975. *Publications:* The Law of Wagers, Gaming and Lotteries, 1929; Lectures on Legal History, 1938, 2nd edn 1949, rev. 1957; numerous articles and lectures on legal and historical subjects. *Address:* Peroomba, Harrington Avenue, Turramurra, NSW 2074, Australia. *Clubs:* Australian, Pioneers (Sydney); Elanora Country (Narrabeen).

WINDHAM, William Ashe Dymoke; Chairman, Skelmersdale Development Corporation, 1979–85; (Deputy Chairman, 1977); *b* 2 April 1926; *s* of late Lt-Col Henry Steuart Windham and Marjory Russell Dymock; *m* 1956, Alison Audrey, *d* of late Maj. P. P. Curtis and Ellinor Kidston; two *s* one *d*. *Educ:* Bedford; Christ's Coll., Cambridge (schol.; MA). CEng, MIChemE. Gen. Manager, Runcorn Div., Arthur Guinness Son & Co. (GB), 1972–84. Mem., Runcorn Develt Corp., 1975–77. Chm., Halton Dist Sports Council, 1973–76; first Chm., Halton Sports and Recreational Trust, 1975–81; Mem., Cttee of Management Henley Royal Regatta, 1973–; rowed for: Cambridge, 1947 and 1951; England, Empire Games, 1950; GB, European Championships, 1950 and 1951 (Gold Medal); Olympic Games, 1952. Chm., Gt Budworth Church Restoration Trust, 1982–84. *Recreations:* shooting, fishing. *Address:* Upper Felin-newydd, Llandefalle, Brecon, Powys LD3 0NE. *T:* Llyswen 338. *Clubs:* Hawks (Cambridge); Leander (Henley).

WINDHAM, Brig. William Russell S.; *see* Smijth-Windham.

WINDLE, Terence Leslie William; Director, Directorate General for Agriculture, European Commission, since 1980; *b* 15 Jan. 1926; *s* of Joseph William Windle and Dorothy Windle (*née* Haigh); *m* 1957, Joy Winifred Shield; one *s* two *d*. *Educ:* Gonville and Caius College, Cambridge (MA); London University (Colonial Course). Colonial/HMOCS: Nigeria, 1951–59; Zambia, 1959–69 (Under Sec., Min. of Natural Resources and Tourism); Home Civil Service, MAFF, 1969–73; Commn of EC, 1973–. *Address:* 200 rue de la Loi, 1049 Brussels, Belgium. *T:* Brussels 235 5426.

WINDLESHAM, 3rd Baron, *cr* 1937; **David James George Hennessy,** CVO 1981; PC 1973; Bt 1927; Chairman: The Parole Board, since 1982; Trustees of the British Museum, since 1986 (Trustee, since 1981); *b* 28 Jan. 1932; *s* of 2nd Baron Windlesham; *S* father, 1962; *m* 1965, Prudence Glynn, (*d* 1986); one *s* one *d*. *Educ:* Ampleforth; Trinity Coll., Oxford (MA; Hon. Fellow 1982). Chairman, Bow Group, 1959–60, 1962–63; Member, Westminster City Council, 1958–62. Minister of State, Home Office, 1970–72; Minister of State for Northern Ireland, 1972–73; Lord Privy Seal and Leader of the House of Lords, 1973–74. Mem., Cttee of Privy Counsellors on Ministerial Memoirs, 1975. Man. Dir, Grampian Television, 1967–70. Jt Man. Dir, 1974–75, Man. Dir, 1975–81, Chm., 1981, ATV Network; Director: The Observer, 1981–; W. H. Smith & Son (Holdings), 1986–. Vice-Pres., Royal Television Soc., 1977–82. Jt Dep. Chm., Queen's Silver Jubilee Appeal, 1977; Dep. Chm., The Royal Jubilee Trusts, 1977–80; Chairman: Oxford Preservation Trust, 1979–; Oxford Society, 1985–; Mem, Museums and Galleries Commn, 1984–86; Trustee: Charities Aid Foundn, 1977–81; Community Service Volunteers, 1981–. Vis. Fellow, All Souls Coll., Oxford, 1986. *Publications:* Communication and Political Power, 1966; Politics in Practice, 1975; Broadcasting in a Free Society, 1980. *Heir: s* Hon. James Hennessy, *b* 9 Nov. 1968. *Address:* House of Lords, SW1A 0PW.

WINDSOR, Viscount; Ivor Edward Other Windsor-Clive; *b* 19 Nov. 1951; *s* and *heir* of 3rd Earl of Plymouth, *qv*; *m* 1979, Caroline, *d* of Frederick Nettlefold and Hon. Mrs Juliana Roberts; two *s*. *Educ:* Harrow; Royal Agricl Coll., Cirencester. Co-founder, and Dir, Centre for the Study of Modern Art, 1973. *Recreation:* cricket. *Heir: s* Hon. Robert Other Ivor Windsor-Clive, *b* 25 March 1981. *Address:* The Stables, Oakly Park, Ludlow, Shropshire.

WINDSOR, Dean of; *see* Mann, Rt Rev. M. A.

WINDSOR-CLIVE, family name of **Earl of Plymouth.**

WINFIELD, Dr Graham; Chief Executive, Overseas Division, BOC Group, since 1979; *b* 28 May 1931; *s* of Josiah and Gladys Winfield; *m* 1959, Olive Johnson; three *s* one *d*. *Educ:* Univ. of Liverpool (BSc, PhD Chemistry). Chemist, Min. of Supply, 1956–57; Lectr, Univ. of Liverpool, 1957–58; Chief Chemist, later Develt Manager, Ciba ARL, 1958–62; Develt Manager, MaxMeyer Co., Milan, 1962–63; BOC Group, 1963–: R&D, marketing, gen. management; Chief Exec., Metals Div. UK, 1969–74; Chief Exec., Gases Div. UK, 1974–79. Non-exec. Dir., Baker Perkins Group, 1984–. Mem., ESRC, 1985–. *Publications:* numerous papers in pure and applied chemistry. *Recreations:* golf, bridge, music, reading. *Address:* Milford, Chinnor Road, Bledlow Ridge, near High Wycombe, Bucks. *T:* (office) Camberley 77222.

WINFIELD, Peter Stevens, FRICS; Senior Partner, Healey & Baker, London, Amsterdam, Brussels, New York, Paris, St Helier, Jersey, since 1975; Property Consultant, Manders (Holdings) plc, since 1985; *b* 24 March 1927; *s* of late Harold Stevens Winfield and Susan Cooper; *m* 1955, Mary Gabrielle Kenrick; four *s* two *d*. *Educ:* Sloane Sch., Chelsea; West London College of Commerce. Served Royal Artillery, 1944–48. Joined Healey & Baker, 1951. Governor, Guy's Hospital, 1973–74, Special Trustee, 1974–; Director, London Auction Mart Ltd, 1970–, Chairman, 1980–; Member: Lloyd's of London, 1978–; Property Investment Cttee of Save & Prosper Gp Ltd, 1980–; Horserace Totalisator Bd, 1981–. Liveryman: Worshipful Company of Farriers, 1967–; Worshipful Company of Feltmakers, 1972 , Asst to the Court, 1979–. *Recreations:* horseracing, cricket. *Address:* 29 St George Street, W1A 3BG. *T:* 01-629 9292. *Clubs:* Buck's, City Livery, United & Cecil, MCC, Turf.

WING, Prof. John Kenneth, MD, PhD; DPM; FRCPsych; Director, Medical Research Council Social Psychiatry Unit, since 1965; Professor of Social Psychiatry, Institute of Psychiatry and London School of Hygiene and Tropical Medicine, since 1970; *b* 22 Oct. 1923. *Educ:* Strand Sch.; University College London (MB, BS, MD, PhD). Served RNVR, 1942–46, Lieut (A). Mem., MRC, 1985– (Chm., Neurosciences Bd, 1985–). Hon. Consultant Psychiatrist, Maudsley and Bethlem Royal Hosp., 1960–. Advr to H of C Social Services Cttee, 1984–85. Hon. MD Heidelberg, 1977. *Publications:* (ed) Early

Childhood Autism, 1966, 2nd edn 1975 (trans. Italian 1970, German 1973); (with G. W. Brown) Institutionalism and Schizophrenia, 1970; (with J. E. Cooper and N. Sartorius) Description and Classification of Psychiatric Symptoms, 1974 (trans. German 1978, French 1980, Japanese 1981); Reasoning about Madness, 1978 (trans. Portuguese 1978, German 1982, Italian 1983); ed, Schizophrenia: towards a new synthesis, 1978; ed (with R. Olsen), Community Care for the Mentally Disabled, 1979; (with J. Leach) Helping Destitute Men, 1979; (ed jtly) What is a Case?, 1981; (ed jtly) Handbook of Psychiatric Rehabilitation, 1981; (with L. G. Wing) Psychoses of Uncertain Aetiology, vol. III of Cambridge Handbook of Psychiatry, 1982. *Address*: Institute of Psychiatry, de Crespigny Park, SE5 8AF. *T*: 01–703 5411.

WINGATE, Captain Sir Miles (Buckley), KCVO 1982; FNI; Deputy Master and Chairman of the Board of Trinity House, London, since 1976; *b* 17 May 1923; *s* of Terrence Wingate and Edith Wingate; *m* 1947, Alicia Forbes Philip; three *d. Educ*: Taunton Grammar Sch.; Southampton and Prior Park Coll., Somerset. Master Mariner. Apprenticed to Royal Mail Lines Ltd, 1939; first Comd, 1957; elected to Bd of Trinity House, 1968. Commonwealth War Graves Comr, 1986–. Vice-President: Seamen's Hosp. Soc., 1980–; Royal Alfred Seafarers Soc., 1980–; British Maritime Charitable Foundn, 1983–; Pres., Internat. Assoc. of Lighthouse Authorities, 1985– (Vice-Pres., 1980–85); Dep. Chm., Gen. Council, King George's Fund for Sailors, 1983; Mem., Cttee of Management, RNLI, 1976–; Council, Missions to Seamen, 1982–. Liveryman: Hon. Co. of Master Mariners, 1970–; Worshipful Co. of Shipwrights, 1980–; Freeman, Watermen and Lightermen's Co., 1984. Governor, Pangbourne Coll., 1982–. *Recreation*: golf. *Address*: Trinity House, Tower Hill, EC3N 4DH. *T*: 01–480 6601. *Clubs*: Royal Thames Yacht; Hove Deep Sea Anglers.

WINGATE, His Honour William Granville; QC 1963; a Circuit Judge (formerly a County Court Judge), 1967–86; *b* 28 May 1911; *s* of Colonel George and Mary Ethel Wingate; *m* 1960, Judith Rosemary Evatt; one *s* one *d. Educ*: Brighton Coll.; Lincoln Coll., Oxford (BA). Called to Bar, Inner Temple, 1933; Western Circuit. Served Army, 1940–46. Dep. Chm., Essex QS, 1965–71. Member: Bar Council, 1961–67; County Court Rule Cttee, 1971–80; Lord Chancellor's Legal Aid Adv. Cttee, 1971–77; Lord Chancellor's Law Reform Cttee, 1974–. Chm., Brighton Coll. Council, 1978–86. *Recreation*: sailing. *Address*: 2 Garden Court, Temple, EC4. *T*: 01–353 4741; Cox's Mill, Dallington, Heathfield, Sussex. *Clubs*: Royal Corinthian Yacht (Commodore, 1965–68), Bar Yacht (Commodore, 1972–76).

WINGFIELD, family name of **Viscount Powerscourt**.

WINGFIELD DIGBY; *see* Digby.

WINGFIELD DIGBY, Ven. Stephen Basil, MBE 1944; Archdeacon of Sarum, 1968–79; Canon Residentiary, 1968–79, and Treasurer, 1971–79, Salisbury Cathedral; *b* 10 Nov. 1910; *m* 1940, Barbara Hatton Budge; three *s* one *d. Educ*: Marlborough Coll.; Christ Church, Oxford; Wycliffe Hall, Oxford. Asst Master, Kenton Coll., Kenya, 1933–36; Curate, St Paul's, Salisbury, 1936–38; Priest-in-Charge, St George's, Oakdale, Poole, 1938–47. CF (temp.), 1939–45; SCF, 7th Armoured Div., 1943–45. Vicar of Sherborne with Castleton and Lillington, 1947–68. RD of Sherborne and Canon of Salisbury Cathedral, 1954–68. *Recreations*: fishing, gardening. *Address*: 77 Banks Road, Sandbanks, Poole, Dorset.

WINKS, Prof. Robin W(illiam Evert), MA, PhD; Randolph W. Townsend Professor of History, and Master of Berkeley College, Yale University, since 1957; *b* 5 Dec. 1930; *s* of Evert McKinley Winks and Jewell Sampson; *m* 1952, Avril Flockton, Wellington, NZ; one *s* one *d. Educ*: Univ. of Colorado (BA Hons 1952, MA 1953); Victoria Univ., NZ (Cert. 1952); Johns Hopkins Univ. (PhD 1957). Dir, Office of Special Projects and Foundns, Yale Univ., 1974–76. Chm., Council of Masters, Yale Univ., 1978–84, 1986–. Smith-Mundt Prof., Univ. of Malaya, 1962; Vis. Prof., Univ. of Sydney, 1963; Vis. Fellow, Inst. of Commonwealth Studies, 1966–67; Guggenheim Fellow, 1976–77; Vis. Prof. of Economics, Univ. of Stellenbosch, 1983; Fellow, Amer. Sch. for Research, 1985. Cultural Attaché, Amer. Embassy, London, 1969–71; Advisor to Dept of State, 1971–. Chm., Nat. Park Service Adv. Bd, 1981–83; Trustee, Nat. Parks and Conservation Assoc. Mem. Council on For. Relations. FRHistS; Fellow, Explorers' Club. Hon. MA Yale 1967; Hon. DLitt Univ. of Nebraska, 1976. *Publications*: Canada and the United States, 1960 (2nd edn 1973); The Cold War, 1964 (2nd edn 1977); Historiography of the British Empire-Commonwealth, 1966; Malaysia, 1966, 2nd edn 1979; Age of Imperialism, 1969; Pastmasters, 1969; The Historian as Detective, 1969; The Blacks in Canada, 1971; Slavery, 1972; An American's Guide to Britain, 1977, 3rd edn 1987; Other Voices, Other Views, 1978; The Relevance of Canadian History, 1979; Western Civilization, 1979; Detective Fiction, 1980; The British Empire, 1981; Modus Operandi, 1982; History of Civilization, 1984; Cloak and Gown, 1987; articles in Amer. Hist. Rev. *Recreations*: travel, old maps, detective fiction. *Address*: 403A Yale Station, New Haven, Conn 06520, USA. *Clubs*: Athenæum, Royal Commonwealth Society; Yale (NY).

WINLAW, Ashley William Edgell, OBE 1968; TD 1953; retired; *b* 8 Feb. 1914; *s* of Rev. G. P. K. Winlaw, Morden, Surrey, and Minnie Ashley, Kidlington, Yorks. *Educ*: Winchester Coll.; St John's Coll., Cambridge (MA). Master, Aldenham Sch., 1936–39; Master, Shrewsbury Sch., 1939–40; served War, 1940–46; Intelligence Corps, Special Forces, Airborne (Lt-Col; retired as Hon. Major). Master, Rugby Sch., 1946–54; Master, Kent Sch., Connecticut, USA, 1950–51; Headmaster, Achimota Sch., Accra, Ghana, 1954–59; Principal, Government Cadet Coll., Hasan Abdal, W Pakistan, 1959–65; Director of Studies, British Inst., Santiago, Chile, 1965–66; Principal, Federal Govt Coll., Warri, Nigeria, 1966–69; English Master: Bishops Senior Sch., Mukono, Uganda, 1969–72; Blantyre Secondary Sch., Blantyre, Malaŵi, 1972–75; Mangochi Secondary Sch., Mangochi, Malaŵi, 1975–78; Lectr in English, The Polytechnic, Univ. of Malaŵi, 1978–80. Tamgha-i-Pakistan (TPk), Pakistan, 1964. *Recreations*: sports, sailing, drama, painting. *Address*: Ann Page Cottage, 28 High Street, Aldeburgh, Suffolk IP15 5AB. *T*: Aldeburgh 3206. *Clubs*: Special Forces, MCC, Free Foresters, I Zingari.

WINN, family name of **Barons Headley** and **St Oswald**.

WINN, Air Vice-Marshal Charles Vivian, CBE 1963; DSO 1945; OBE 1950; DFC 1941; AOC Scotland and Northern Ireland 1972–73; *b* 20 April 1918; *s* of C. A. Winn, Cardiff, Past Pres. of Shipping Fedn, and D. B. Winn (née Thomas); *m* 1946, Suzanne Patricia (née Baily); one *s* one *d. Educ*: St Peter's Sch., Weston-super-Mare; Wycliffe Coll. Station Comdr, Felixstowe, 1951 (Queen's Commendation for Bravery, 1953); DP2, Air Ministry, 1953; Station Comdr: Weston Zoyland, 1955; Laarbruch, 1957; SASO, 38 Gp, 1960; Chief of Plans and Ops, Far East, Nov. 1962; Dir of Ops, MoD (Air), 1965; Air Comdr, Malta, 1968; Chief of Plans, SHAPE, 1971. Chief Recreation Officer, Anglian Water Authority, 1974–84. Chm., Ex-Services Mental Welfare Soc., 1982–; Mem., Air League. MBIM. *Address*: The Cottage, Green End, Great Stukeley, Huntingdon, Cambs. *Clubs*: Royal Air Force; Union (Malta).

WINNER, Dame Albertine (Louise), DBE 1967 (OBE 1945); President, St Christopher's Hospice; *b* 4 March 1907; *d* of Isidore and Annie Winner, 4k Portman Mansions, W1.

Educ: Francis Holland Sch., Clarence Gate; University College, London, and University College Hospital. BSc (Hons Physiology) 1929; MRCS, LRCP, 1932; MBBS London, 1933 (University Gold Medal); MD (London), 1934; MRCP (London) 1935; FRCP (London) 1959; FFCM 1973. Hon. Assistant Physician, Elizabeth Garrett Anderson Hospital, 1937; Hon. Physician, Mothers' Hospital, Clapton, 1937. Service with RAMC, 1940–46 (Lieut-Colonel). Service with Ministry of Health, 1947–67 (Dep. CMO). Hon. Consultant for Women's Services to the Army, 1946–70. Visiting Lecturer, London School of Economics, 1951–63. Fellow, University College, London, 1965; Linacre Fellow, RCP, 1967–78. QHP 1965–68. *Publications*: articles in Lancet, Public Health, etc. *Recreations*: gardening, Japanese prints, music, people, opera. *Address*: 35 Gordon Mansions, Torrington Place, WC1E 7HG. *T*: 01–636 1921. *Club*: University Women's.

WINNER, Prof. Harold Ivor, MA, MD, FRCP, FRCPath; Professor of Medical Microbiology, University of London, at Charing Cross Hospital Medical School, 1965–83, now Emeritus; Consulting Microbiologist, Charing Cross Hospital, (Consultant Microbiologist, 1954–83); *b* 1 June 1918; *y s* of late Jacob Davis and Janet Winner; *m* 1945, Nina (*d* 1986), *e d* of Jacques and Lily Katz; two *s. Educ*: St Paul's Sch.; Downing Coll., Cambridge (Maj. Schol.); University College Hospital Medical School. 1st class hons, Nat. Scis Tripos Cambridge, 1939. House Surgeon, Addenbrooke's Hospital, Cambridge, 1942; served RAMC, 1942–44; Asst Pathologist, EMS, 1945–48 and NW Group Laboratory, Hampstead, 1948–50; Lecturer, Sen. Lecturer, and Reader in Bacteriology, Charing Cross Hospital Medical Sch., 1950–64; Mem. School Council, 1967–69 and 1977–83. Member: Univs' Cttee on Safety, 1981–; Adv. Cttee on Dangerous Pathogens, 1981–84. Examiner: Examining Board in England, 1962–77; Royal Coll. of Surgeons, 1971–76; Royal Coll. of Pathologists, 1975–; universities at home and overseas. Founder Fellow and Archivist, RCPath; formerly Pres. and Hon. Editor, Section of Pathology, and Vice-Pres., Sect. of Comparative Medicine, RSM; Chm., Med. Scis Historical Soc., 1982–83; Vis. Prof., Guest Lectr and corresp. Mem., various univs and medical insts at home and overseas. *Publications*: Candida albicans (jointly), 1964; Symposium on Candida Infections (jointly), 1966; Microbiology in Modern Nursing, 1969; Microbiology in Patient Care, 1973, 2nd edn 1978; Louis Pasteur and Microbiology, 1974; chapters in medical books; papers in medical, scientific and nursing journals. *Recreations*: listening to music, looking at pictures and buildings, gardening, travel. *Address*: 48 Lyndale Avenue, NW2 2QA. *T*: 01–435 5959.

WINNER, Michael Robert; Chairman: Scimitar Films Ltd, Michael Winner Ltd, Motion Picture and Theatrical Investments Ltd, since 1957; *b* 30 Oct. 1935; *s* of George Joseph and Helen Winner. *Educ*: St Christopher's Sch., Letchworth; Downing Coll., Cambridge Univ. (MA). Film critic and Fleet Street journalist and contributor to: The Spectator, Daily Express, London Evening Standard, etc. Panellist, Any Questions, BBC radio. Entered Motion Pictures, 1956, as Screen Writer, Asst Director, Editor. Mem. Council, Directors' Guild of Great Britain, 1983–; Chief Censorship Officer 1983–. Films include: Play It Cool (Dir), 1962; The Cool Mikado (Dir and Writer), 1962; West Eleven (Dir), 1963; The System (Prod. and Dir), 1963; You Must Be Joking (Prod., Dir, Writer), 1965; The Jokers (Prod., Dir, Writer), 1966; I'll Never Forget What's 'isname (Prod. and Dir), 1967; Hannibal Brooks (Prod., Dir, Writer), 1968; The Games (Prod. and Dir), 1969; Lawman (Prod. and Dir), 1970; The Nightcomers (Prod. and Dir), 1971; Chato's Land (Prod. and Dir), 1971; The Mechanic (Dir), 1972; Scorpio (Prod. and Dir), 1972; The Stone Killer (Prod. and Dir), 1973; Death Wish (Prod. and Dir), 1974; Won Ton Ton The Dog That Saved Hollywood (Prod. and Dir), 1975; The Sentinel (Prod., Dir, Writer), 1976; The Big Sleep (Prod., Dir, Writer), 1977; Firepower (Prod., Dir), 1978; Death Wish Two (Prod., Dir, Writer), 1981; The Wicked Lady (Prod., Dir, Writer), 1982; Scream for Help (Prod., Dir), 1984; Death Wish Three (Prod. and Dir), 1985. Theatre productions: The Tempest, Wyndhams, 1974; A Day in Hollywood A Night in the Ukraine, 1978. Founder and Chm., Police Meml Trust, 1984–. *Recreations*: walking around art galleries, museums, antique shops. *Address*: 6/8 Sackville Street, W1X 1DD. *T*: 01–734 8385.

WINNICK, David Julian; MP (Lab) Walsall North, since 1979; *b* Brighton, 26 June 1933; *s* of late Eugene and Rose Winnick; *m* 1968, Bengi Rona (marr. diss.), *d* of Tarik and Zeynep Rona. *Educ*: secondary school; London Sch. of Economics (Dip. in Social Admin). Army National Service, 1951–53. Branch Secretary, Clerical and Administrative Workers' Union, 1956–62 (now APEX); Mem. Exec. Council, 1978–, Vice-Pres., 1983–, APEX. Advertisement Manager, Tribune, 1963–66. Employed by a voluntary organisation, 1970–79. Chm., UK Immigrants Adv. Service, 1984–. Contested (Lab) Harwich, 1964; MP (Lab) Croydon South, 1966–70; contested (Lab): Croydon Central, Oct. 1974; Walsall N, Nov. 1976. Member: Select Cttee on the Environment, 1979–83; Home Affairs Cttee, 1983–. Member: Willesden Borough Council, 1959–64; London Borough of Brent Council, 1964–66 (Chairman, Children Cttee, 1965–66). Contributor to socialist and trade union journals. *Recreations*: walking, cinema, theatre, reading. *Address*: House of Commons, SW1A 0AA.

WINNIFRITH, Sir (Alfred) John (Digby), KCB 1959 (CB 1950); *b* 16 Oct. 1908; *s* of Rev. B. T. Winnifrith; *m* 1935, Lesbia Margaret (*d* 1981), *d* of late Sir Arthur Cochrane, KCVO; two *s* one *d. Educ*: Westminster School; Christ Church, Oxford. Entered Board of Trade, 1932; transferred to HM Treasury, 1934; Asst Sec., War Cabinet Office and Civil Sec., Combined Operations HQ, 1942–44, till return to HM Treasury; Third Secretary, HM Treasury, 1951–59; Permanent Secretary, Ministry of Agriculture, Fisheries and Food, 1959–67; Dir-Gen., National Trust, 1968–70. Trustee, British Museum (Natural History), 1967–72; Member: Royal Commn on Environmental Pollution, 1970–73; Commonwealth War Graves Commn, 1970–83; Hops Marketing Board, 1970–78. Hon. ARCVS 1974. *Address*: Hallhouse Farm, Appledore, Kent. *T*: Appledore 264.

WINNING, Most Rev. Thomas J.; *see* Glasgow, Archbishop of, (RC).

WINNINGTON, Sir Francis Salwey William, 6th Bt, *cr* 1755; Lieut, late Welsh Guards; *b* 24 June 1907; *er s* of late Francis Salwey Winnington, *e s* of 5th Bt and Blanch, *d* of Commander William John Casberd-Boteler, RN; *S* grandfather, 1931; *m* 1944, Anne, *o d* of late Captain Lawrence Drury-Lowe; one *d. Educ*: Eton. Served War of 1939–45 (wounded, prisoner). Owns 4700 acres. *Heir*: *b* Colonel Thomas Foley Churchill Winnington, MBE, Grenadier Guards [*b* 16 Aug. 1910; *m* 1944, Lady Betty Marjorie Anson, *er d* of 4th Earl of Lichfield; two *s* two *d*]. *Address*: Brockhill Court, Shelsley Beauchamp, Worcs. *Club*: Cavalry and Guards.
See also Viscount Campden.

WINNINGTON-INGRAM, Edward John; Managing Director, Associated Newspapers Group, since 1986; *b* 20 April 1926; *s* of Rev. Preb. Edward Francis and Gladys Winnington-Ingram; *m* 1st, 1953, Shirley Lamotte (marr. diss. 1968); two *s*; 2nd, 1973, Elizabeth Linda Few Brown. *Educ*: Shrewsbury; Keble Coll., Oxford (BA). Served RN (Sub-Lieut), 1944–47. Joined Associated Newspapers, 1949; Circulation Manager, Daily Mail, 1960–65; Gen. Manager, Daily Mail Manchester, 1965–70; helped create Northprint Manchester Ltd, a jt printing consortium with Manchester Guardian and Evening News and Associated, 1969; Dir, Associated Newspapers, 1971; Managing Director: Harmsworth Publishing, 1973; Mail on Sunday, 1982; Dir, Associated Newspapers Holdings, 1983. *Recreations:* tennis, shooting (badly), beagling, gardening, music, defending the 1662 Prayer Book. *Address:* Old Manor Farm, Cottisford, Brackley, Northants NN13 5SW. *T:* Finmere 367. *Clubs:* Buck's, Roehampton.

WINNINGTON-INGRAM, Prof. Reginald Pepys, FBA 1958; Professor of Greek Language and Literature in the University of London (King's College), 1953–71, now Professor Emeritus; Fellow of King's College, since 1969; *b* 22 Jan. 1904; *s* of late Rear-Admiral and late Mrs C. W. Winnington-Ingram; *m* 1938, Mary, *d* of late Thomas Cousins. *Educ:* Clifton Coll., Trinity Coll., Cambridge. BA 1925; MA 1929; Scholar of Trinity Coll., 1922, Fellow, 1928–32; 1st Class Classical Tripos, Part I, 1923; Waddington Schol., 1924; 1st Class Classical Tripos, Part II, 1925; Charles Oldham Classical Schol., 1926. Asst Lecturer and Lecturer, University of Manchester, 1928, 1930 and 1933; Reader in Classics, University of London (Birkbeck College), 1934–48. Temp. Civil Servant, Ministry of Labour and National Service, 1940–45 (Asst Secretary, 1944); Professor of Classics in the University of London (Westfield Coll.), 1948–53; J. H. Gray Lectures, Cambridge Univ., 1956. Vis. Prof., Univ. of Texas at Austin, 1971, 1973; Vis. Aurelio Prof., Boston Univ., 1975. President, Society for the Promotion of Hellenic Studies, 1959–62 (Hon. Secretary, 1963–82, Hon. Mem., 1983). Director, University of London Inst. of Classical Studies, 1964–67. Hon. DLitt: Glasgow, 1969; London, 1985. *Publications:* Mode in Ancient Greek Music, 1936; Euripides and Dionysus, 1948; (ed) Aristides Quintilianus, *De Musica*, 1963; Sophocles: an interpretation, 1980; Studies in Aeschylus, 1983; contribs to classical and musical journals, dictionaries, etc. *Recreation:* music. *Address:* 12 Greenhill, NW3 5UB. *T:* 01–435 6843. *Club:* Athenæum.

WINSKILL, Air Commodore Sir Archibald (Little), KCVO 1980 (CVO 1973); CBE 1960; DFC 1941 and Bar 1943; AE 1944; Extra Equerry to The Queen; *b* 24 Jan. 1917; *s* of late James Winskill; *m* 1947, Christiane Amilie Pauline, *d* of M. Bailleux, Calais, France; one *s* one *d.* War of 1939–45: Fighter Pilot: Battle of Britain; European and North African Theatres. Post-war: Air Adviser to Belgian Govt; Station Cmdr, RAF Turnhouse and Duxford; Gp Capt. Ops Germany; Air Attaché, Paris; Dir of Public Relations, MoD (RAF); Captain of the Queen's Flight, 1968–82. Liveryman, GAPAN, 1978–; Freedom of City of London, 1978. MRAeS. *Recreation:* golf. *Address:* Anchors, Coastal Road, West Kingston Estate, East Preston, West Sussex. *T:* Rustington 775439. *Club:* Royal Air Force.

WINSTANLEY, family name of **Baron Winstanley.**

WINSTANLEY, Baron *cr* 1975 (Life Peer), of Urmston in Greater Manchester; **Michael Platt Winstanley;** TV and radio broadcaster, author, journalist, columnist, medical practitioner; Chairman, Countryside Commission, 1978–80; *b* Nantwich, Cheshire, 27 Aug. 1918; *e s* of late Dr Sydney A. Winstanley; *m* 1st, 1945, Nancy Penney (marr. diss. 1952); one *s*; 2nd, 1955, Joyce M. Woodhouse; one *s* one *d. Educ:* Manchester Grammar Sch.; Manchester Univ. President, Manchester Univ. Union, 1940–41; Captain, Manchester Univ. Cricket Club, 1940–42; Captain Combined English Univs Cricket Team, 1941; Ed. University magazine, 1941–42. MRCS LRCP, 1944. Resident Surgical Officer, Wigan Infirmary, 1945; Surgical Specialist, RAMC, 1946; GP, Urmston, Manchester, 1948–66; MO, Royal Ordnance Factory, Patricroft, 1950–66; Treasury MO and Admiralty Surgeon and Agent, 1953–66; Member Lancs Local Med. Cttee, 1954–66; Member Lancs Exec. Council, 1956–65. Spokesman for Manchester Div. of BMA, 1957–65. Member Liberal Party Council, 1962–66. Contested (L) Stretford, 1964; MP (L) Cheadle, 1966–70; MP (L) Hazel Grove, Feb.-Sept. 1974. Chairman Liberal Party Health Cttee, 1965–66; Liberal Party Spokesman on health, Post Office and broadcasting. TV and radio broadcaster, 1957–; own series on Indep. TV and BBC. Member: BBC Gen. Adv. Council, 1967–70; Post Office Bd, 1978–80; Water Space Amenity Commn, 1980–82. President: Fluoridation Soc., 1984–; Gingerbread, 1984–; Birth Control Campaign, 1984–; Chm., Groundwork Trust, 1980–. A Dep. Pro-Chancellor, Univ. of Lancaster, 1986–. *Publications:* Home Truths for Home Doctors, 1963; The Anatomy of First-Aid, 1966; The British Ombudsman, 1970; Tell Me, Doctor, 1972; Know Your Rights, 1975; cricket columnist, Manchester Evening News, 1964–65; weekly personal column, Manchester Evening News, 1970–76; articles on current affairs, health, etc. *Recreations:* cricket; golf; playing the bagpipes. *Address:* Hare Hall, Dunnerdale, Broughton-in-Furness, Cumbria. *Clubs:* National Liberal, Authors'.

WINSTANLEY, John, MC 1944; TD 1951; FRCS 1957; Hon. Consultant Ophthalmic Surgeon, St Thomas' Hospital, since 1983 (Ophthalmic Surgeon, 1960–83); Hon. Ophthalmic Surgeon, Royal Hospital, Chelsea, since 1963; *b* 11 May 1919; 3rd *s* of late Captain Bernard Joseph Winstanley and Grace Taunton; *m* 1959, Jane Frost; one *s* two *d. Educ:* Wellington Coll., Berks; St Thomas's Hosp. Med. Sch. (MB, BS 1951). Served 4th Bn Queen's Own Royal West Kent Regt, 1937–46 (despatches BEF, 1940). Resident med. appts, St Thomas' and Moorfields Eye Hosps, 1951–56; Chief Clin. Asst, Moorfields Eye Hosp., 1956–60; Sen. Registrar, St Thomas' Hosp., 1956–60; recog. teacher of ophthalmol., St Thomas' Hosp., 1960–83; Ophth. Surg., Lewisham and Greenwich Health Dists, 1959–70; Hon. Ophthalmic Surgeon: Queen Alexandra's Mil. Hosp., Millbank, 1966–72; Queen Elizabeth Mil. Hosp., Woolwich, 1972–83. Hon. Civilian Consultant in Ophthalmol. to MOD (Army), 1971–83. Examiner in Ophthalmology (DipOphth of Examining Bd of RCP and RCS, 1968–72; Mem. Court of Examiners, RCS, 1972–78). FRSM 1963 (Vice-Pres., Sect. of Ophth., 1979); Member: Ophthal. Soc. UK, 1958– (Hon. Sec. 1966–68, Vice-Pres. 1980–83); Faculty of Ophthalmologists, 1958–, Mem. Council, 1973–, Vice-Pres., 1979–; Mem. Council, Medical Protection Soc., 1979–. Liveryman, Soc. of Apothecaries, 1965 (Mem. Livery Cttee, 1982). *Publications:* chapter, Rose's Medical Ophthalmology, 1983; papers on ophthalmic topics and med. hist. in med. jls. *Recreations:* shooting, fishing, medical history. *Address:* The Churchill Clinic, 80 Lambeth Road, SE1 7PW. *T:* 01–928 5633; 10 Pembroke Villas, The Green, Richmond, Surrey TW9 1QF. *T:* 01–940 6247. *Clubs:* Army and Navy, Flyfishers'.

WINSTON, Charles Edward, CMG 1974; FRACS; Consulting Surgeon: Sydney Hospital, Australia, since 1958; Royal South Sydney Hospital, since 1963; *b* 3 June 1898; *s* of James Percival and Annie Elizabeth Winston; *m* 1933; one *d. Educ:* Sydney Boys' High Sch.; Univ. of Sydney. MB, ChM. Bd Dir, 1958, Vice Pres., 1968–82, and Patron, 1982–, Sydney Hosp. *Publications:* papers on surgical problems to MJA. *Recreations:* golf, bowls, fishing. *Address:* 683 New South Head Road, Rose Bay, NSW 2029, Australia. *T:* 371–7728.

WINSTON, Clive Noel; Assistant Director, Federation Against Copyright Theft Ltd; *b* 20 April 1925; *s* of George and Alida Winston; *m* 1952, Beatrice Jeanette; two *d. Educ:* Highgate Sch.; Trinity Hall, Cambridge (BA). Admitted solicitor, 1951. Joined Metropolitan Police, 1951; Dep. Solicitor, Metropolitan Police, 1982–85. Chairman, Union of Liberal and Progressive Synagogues, 1981–85 (Vice-Pres., 1985–). *Recreations:* golf, gardening. *Address:* (office) 19 Wells Street, W1. *T:* 01–637 8972.

WINSTON-FOX, Mrs Ruth, JP; Co-Chairman, Women's National Commission, 1979–81 (Member, since 1971); *b* 12 Sept. 1912; *d* of Major the Rev. Solomon Lipson, Hon. SCF, and Tilly Lipson (*née* Shandel); *m* 1st, 1938, Laurence Winston (*d* 1949); two *s* one *d*; 2nd, 1960, Goodwin Fox (*d* 1974). *Educ:* St Paul's Girls' Sch.; London Univ. BSc Household and Social Sci.; Home Office Child Care Cert. Mental Hosps Dept and Child Care Dept, LCC, 1936–39; Dep. Centre Organiser, WVS, Southgate, 1941–45; Southgate Borough Council: Member, 1945–65; Alderman, 1955–65; Mayor of Southgate, 1958–59, Dep. Mayor, 1959–61; Sen. Officer, Adoptions Consultant, Social Services Dept, Herts CC, 1949–77. Member: London Rent Assessment Panel and Tribunals, 1975–; Review Cttee for Secure Accommodation, London Borough of Enfield, 1982–; Bd of Deputies of British Jews, 1960– (Chm. Educn Cttee, 1974–80; voluntary nat. organiser, exhibn Jewish Way of Life, 1978–); Vice-Pres., Internat. Council of Jewish Women, 1974– (Chairman: Status of Women Cttee, 1966–75; Inter-Affiliate Travel Cttee, 1975–81); Mem. Governing Body, World Jewish Congress, 1981–; Co-Chm., Jewish Community Exhibn Centre, 1984–. Founder, one of first Day Centres for the Elderly in GB, Ruth Winston House, Southgate Old People's Centre, opened by Princess Alexandra, 1961, and again, 1972; Vice-President: Southgate Old People's Welfare Cttee, 1974–; Southgate Horticultural Soc.; President: League of Jewish Women, 1969–72; First Women's Lodge, England, 1972–74; Enfield Marriage Guidance Council, 1984–. JP Mddx Area GLC, 1954–. *Publications:* articles only. *Recreations:* five grandchildren, travel, voluntary service. *Address:* 4 Morton Crescent, Southgate, N14 7AH. *T:* 01–886 5056. *Clubs:* University Women's, Bnai Brith.

WINSTONE, (Frank) Reece, FRPS; self employed, since 1925; illustrative photographer, since 1937; book designer, publisher and distributor, since 1957; *b* 3 Sept. 1909; *s* of John Ephraim Winstone and Lillian Kate (*née* Reece); *m* 1937, Dorothy Agnes Attrill; one *s. Educ:* Bristol Cathedral Sch. FRPS 1976. Partner, father's menswear business, 1925–36. *Publications:* Bristol As It Was, 1939–1914, 1957 (5th edn 1978); Bristol As It Was, 1914–1900, 1957 (3rd edn 1972); Bristol Today, 1958 (4th edn 1971); Bristol in the 1890's, 1960 (3rd edn 1973); Bristol in the 1940's, 1961 (2nd edn 1970); Bristol in the 1880's, 1962 (2nd edn 1978); Bristol As It Was, 1950–1953, 1964 (2nd edn 1970); Bristol As It Was, 1879–1874, 1965 (3rd edn 1984); Bristol As It Was, 1874–1866, 1966 (2nd edn 1971); Bristol As It Was, 1866–1860, 1967 (2nd edn 1972); Bristol Fashion, 1968; Bristol in the 1850's, 1968 (2nd edn 1978); Bristol As It Was, 1953–1956, 1969, (2nd edn 1979); Bristol's Earliest Photographs, 1970 (2nd edn 1975); Bristol Tradition, 1970; Bristol in the 1920's, 1971 (2nd edn 1977); Bristol As It Was, 1956–1959, 1972 (2nd edn 1986); Bristol Blitzed, 1973 (2nd edn 1976); Bristol's Trams, 1974; Bristol As It Was, 1913–1921, 1976; Bristol's Suburbs in the 1920's and 1930's, 1977; Bristol As It Was, 1928–1933, 1979; Bath As It Was, 1980; Bristol As It Was, 1960–1962, 1981; Bristol As It Was, 1845–1900, 1983; Bristol's Suburbs Long Ago, 1985; Bristol As It Was, 1934–1936, 1986; (ed) Bristol's History: Vol. 1, 1966 (3rd edn 1980); Vol. 2, 1975; (ed) Miss Ann Green of Clifton, 1974; (ed) History of Bristol's Suburbs, 1977. *Recreations:* local preservation societies, motoring, the gramophone, serious broadcast programmes, reading. *Address:* 23 Hyland Grove, Henbury Hill, Bristol BS9 3NR. *T:* Bristol 503646.

WINT, Dr Arthur Stanley, CD 1973; MBE 1954; FRCS; private medical practitioner; formerly Doctor and Surgeon in charge, Linstead General Hospital, Jamaica; *b* 25 May 1920; *s* of John Samuel Wint and Hilda Wint; *m* 1949, Norma Wint (*née* Marsh); three *d. Educ:* Calabar High School; Excelsior College, Jamaica; St Bartholomew's Medical School. MB BS; FRCS. Served RAF, 1942–47; Medical School, 1947–53. Participated in international athletics, 1936–53; Olympics 1948: Gold medal, 400 m; Silver medal, 800 m; Olympics 1952: Gold medal, 4x400 m Relay; Silver medal, 800 m. Medical Practitioner, 1953–73. Jamaican High Comr in the UK, 1974–78. FICS 1972; DMJ (Clin), 1975. Hon. DLitt Loughborough, 1982. *Recreations:* badminton, swimming, walking. *Address:* 21 King Street, Linstead, St Catherine, Jamaica, WI. *Club:* Polytechnic Harriers.

WINTER, Rt. Rev. Allen Ernest; *b* 8 Dec. 1903; *o s* of Ernest Thomas and Margaret Winter, Malvern, Vic; *m* 1939, Eunice Eleanor, 3rd *d* of Albert and Eleanor Sambell; three *s* two *d. Educ:* Melbourne C of E Grammar School; Trinity Coll., Univ. of Melbourne (BA 1926, MA 1928); University Coll., Oxford (BA 1932, MA 1951); Australian College of Theology (ThL 1927, ThD 1951 iur. dig.). Deacon, 1927, priest, 1928, Melbourne; Curate, Christ Church, S Yarra, 1927–29; on leave, Oxford, 1929–32; Curate, St James', Ivanhoe, 1932–35; Minister of Sunshine, 1935–39; Incumbent of St Luke's, Brighton, Melb., 1939–48; Chaplain, AIF, 1942–46; Incumbent of Christ Church, Essendon, 1948–49; Canon-Residentiary and Rector of All Saints' Cathedral, Bathurst, 1949–51; Bishop of St Arnaud, 1951–73; Chaplain, St John's Coll., Morpeth, NSW, 1974. *Address:* Lis Escop, 11 Bella Vista Road, North Caulfield, Vic 3161, Australia. *T:* 03–509–2554.

WINTER, Charles Milne, FIBScot; Group Chief Executive, Royal Bank of Scotland Group plc, since 1985 (Director, since 1981); *b* 21 July 1933; *s* of David and Annie Winter; *m* 1957, Audrey Hynd; one *s* one *d. Educ:* Harris Acad., Dundee. FIBScot 1979. Served RAF, 1951–53. Joined The Royal Bank of Scotland, 1949; Exec. Dir, 1981–86; Man. Dir, 1982–85; Dep. Gp Chief Exec., 1985. Dir, Williams & Glyn's Bank, 1982–85 (Man. Dir, March-Oct. 1985). Pres., Inst. of Bankers in Scotland, 1981–83; Chm., Cttee of Scottish Clearing Bankers, 1983–85. *Recreations:* golf, choral music. *Address:* 4 Charteris Park, Longniddry, East Lothian EH32 0NY. *T:* Longniddry 52340. *Clubs:* Caledonian, New (Edinburgh).

WINTER, Frederick Thomas, CBE 1963; racehorse trainer since 1964; *b* 20 Sept. 1926; *s* of Frederick Neville Winter and Ann (*née* Flanagan); *m* 1956, Diana Pearson; three *d* (incl. twins). *Educ:* Ewell Castle. Served as Lieut, 6th Bn Para. Regt, 1944–47. Jockey, Flat, 1939–42; National Hunt jockey, 1947–64. *Recreations:* golf, gardening. *Address:* Uplands, Lambourn, Berks. *T:* Lambourn 71438.

WINTER, Prof. Gerald Bernard, FDS RCS; Professor and Head of Department of Children's Dentistry, since 1966, Dean and Director of Studies since 1983, Institute of Dental Surgery, University of London; *b* 24 Nov. 1928; *s* of Morris Winter and Edith (*née* Malter); *m* 1960, Brigitte Eva Fleischhacker; one *s* one *d. Educ:* Coopers' Company's Sch.; London Hospital Med. Coll. (BDS, MB BS); DCH London. Ho. Surg./Ho. Phys., London Hosp. Med. Coll., 1955–59; Lectr in Children's Dentistry, Royal Dental Hosp., London, 1959–62; Cons. Dent. Surg., Eastman Dental Hosp., 1962–. Hon. Sec. 1962–65, Pres. 1970–71, Brit. Paedodontic Soc.; Hon. Gen. Sec., Internat. Assoc. of Dentistry for Children, 1971–79; Founder Chm., Brit. Soc. of Dentistry for the Handicapped, 1976–77. *Publications:* A Colour Atlas of Clinical Conditions in Paedodontics (with R. Rapp), 1979; 75 chapters and sci. papers. *Recreations:* theatre, music, gardening. *Address:* Institute of Dental Surgery, Eastman Dental Hospital, Gray's Inn Road, WC1X 8LD. *T:* 01–837 3646; (private) 1 Hartfield Close, Elstree, Herts. *T:* 01–953 3403.

WINTERBOTHAM, Group Captain Frederick William, CBE 1943; author; *b* 16 April 1897; *s* of late F. Winterbotham, Painswick, Gloucestershire; *m* 1st, 1921; one *s* two *d*; *m* 1947; one *d. Educ:* Charterhouse; Christ Church, Oxon. Royal Gloucestershire Hussars, 1915; RFC and RAF, 1916–19; Pedigree Stock Breeder, 1920–29; Air Staff and Foreign Office, 1929–45; BOAC 1945–48. *Publications:* Secret and Personal, 1969; The

Ultra Secret, 1974; The Nazi Connection, 1978. *Address:* Bridleways, Tarrant Monkton, Blandford, Dorset. *Club:* Royal Air Force.

WINTERBOTTOM, family name of **Baron Winterbottom.**

WINTERBOTTOM, Baron, *cr* 1965 (Life Peer), of Clopton in the county of Northampton; **Ian Winterbottom;** Chairman: Dynavest Ltd, since 1982; Anglo Global Limited, since 1984; *b* 6 April 1913; *s* of G. H. Winterbottom, Horton House, Northants, and Georgina MacLeod; *m* 1st, 1939, Rosemary Mills (marr. diss. 1944); one *s*; 2nd, 1944, Irene Eva, (Ira), Munk; two *s* one *d*. *Educ:* Charterhouse; Clare Coll., Cambridge. Worked in textile and engineering trades in Manchester, Derby, and Bamberg and Cologne, Germany. Captain Royal Horse Guards; served War of 1939–45, NW European Campaign; ADC and subsequently Personal Assistant to Regional Commissioner, Hamburg, 1946–49. MP (Lab) Nottingham Central, 1950–55; Parly Under Sec. of State, Royal Navy, MoD, 1966–67; Parly Sec., MPBW, 1967–68; Parly Under-Sec. of State, RAF, MoD, 1968–70; opposition spokesman on defence, 1970–74; a Lord in Waiting (Govt Whip), 1974–78; spokesman on: defence, 1974–78; trade and industry, 1976–78; resigned from Govt, 1978; Founder Mem., SDP. Deleg., UN Trusteeship Council, 1974; Founder Mem., House of Lords All-Party Defence Study Gp; Member: Parly and Scientific Cttee; CPA; Anglo-Nigerian Soc. Director: Winterbottom Bookcloth Co., 1955–57; Venesta Internat., 1957–66, 1970–74 (Chm., 1972–74); Chairman: Centurion Housing Association, 1980–; Collins Aircraft Co., 1980–; Consultant, C. Z. Scientific Instruments Ltd, 1980–. *Recreations:* birdwatching, music. *Address:* Woodland Place, St Briavels, Lydney, Glos GL15 6RT. *T:* Dean 530396. *Club:* Athenæum.

WINTERBOTTOM, Michael, MA, DPhil; FBA 1978; Fellow and Tutor in Classics, Worcester College, Oxford, since 1967; *b* 22 Sept. 1934; *s* of Allan Winterbottom and Kathleen Mary (*née* Wallis); *m* 1st, 1963, Helen Spencer (marr. diss. 1983); two *s*; 2nd, 1986, Nicolette Janet Streatfeild Bergel. *Educ:* Dulwich Coll.; Pembroke Coll., Oxford. 1st Cl. Hon. Mods and Craven Schol., 1954; 1st Cl. Lit. Hum. and Derby Schol., 1956; Domus Sen. Schol., Merton Coll., 1958–59; Research Lectr, Christ Church, 1959–62. MA 1959, DPhil 1964 (Oxon). Lectr in Latin and Greek, University Coll. London, 1962–67. *Dhc* Besançon, 1985. *Publications:* (ed) Quintilian, 1970; (with D. A. Russell) Ancient Literary Criticism, 1972; Three Lives of English Saints, 1972; (ed and trans.) The Elder Seneca, 1974; (ed with R. M. Ogilvie) Tacitus, *Opera Minora*, 1975; (ed and trans.) Gildas, 1978; Roman Declamation, 1980; (ed with commentary) The Minor Declamations ascribed to Quintilian, 1984; articles and reviews in jls. *Recreations:* travel and plans for travel, hill walking. *Address:* 172 Watton Street, Oxford. *T:* Oxford 515727.

WINTERBOTTOM, Sir Walter, Kt 1978; CBE 1972 (OBE 1963); retired; *b* 31 March 1913; *s* of James Winterbottom and Frances Holt; *m* 1942, Ann Richards; one *s* two *d*. *Educ:* Chester Coll. of Educn; Carnegie Coll. of Physical Educn. Schoolmaster, Oldham; Lectr, Carnegie Coll. of Phys. Educn; Wing Comdr, RAF, 1939–45; Dir of Coaching and Manager of England Team, Football Assoc., 1946–62; Gen. Sec., Central Council of Physical Recreation, 1963–72; Dir, The Sports Council, 1965–78. *Publications:* technical, on association football. *Recreations:* golf, bowls. *Address:* 15 Orchard Gardens, Cranleigh, Surrey. *T:* Cranleigh 271593.

WINTERSGILL, Dr William, FFCM; Specialist in Community Medicine, York Health Authority, since 1984; Member, Research and Advisory Committee, Cambridge Applied Nutrition, Toxicology and Biosciences Ltd, since 1984; *b* 20 Dec. 1922; *s* of Fred Wintersgill and May Wintersgill; *m* 1952, Iris May Holland; three *d*. *Educ:* Barnsley Holgate Grammar Sch.; Leeds Medical Sch., Univ. of Leeds (MB, ChB). MRCGP, MFCM; FFCM 1983. House Surgeon, 1948, and Registrar, 1948–49, Pontefract Infirmary; Principal, Gen. Practice, Snaith, Yorks, 1950–66; Dept of Health and Social Security (formerly Min. of Health): Reg. MO, 1967–70; SMO, 1970–72; PMO, 1972–76; SPMO 1976–84. Chm., British Assoc. of Community Physicians, 1985–. *Recreations:* gardening, antique collecting (silver especially), playing the piano, painting, old buildings. *Address:* Chandler's Cottage, Flawith, York. *T:* Tollerton 310; Pinfold Cottage, Alne, York.

WINTERTON, 7th Earl, *cr* 1766 (Ireland); **Robert Chad Turnour;** Baron Winterton, *cr* 1761 (Ireland); Viscount Turnour, 1766 (Ireland); Royal Canadian Air Force; *b* 13 Sept. 1915; *s* of Cecil Turnour (*d* 1953), Saskatoon, Sask.; *S* kinsman, 1962; *m* 1st, 1941, Kathleen Ella (*d* 1969), *d* of D. B. Whyte; 2nd, 1971, Marion Eleanor, *d* of late Arthur Phillips. *Educ:* Nutana Coll., Canada. Joined RCAF, 1940; with Canadian NATO Force Sqdn, Sardinia, 1957–58. *Heir:* *b* Noel Cecil Turnour, DFM, CD [*b* 11 Dec. 1919; *m* 1941, Evelyn Isobel, *d* of J. C. A. Oulton; three *s*. Formerly Flt Lieut, RCAF].

WINTERTON, (Jane) Ann; MP (C) Congleton, since 1983; *b* 6 March 1941; *d* of Joseph Robert Hodgson and Ellen Jane Hodgson; *m* 1960, Nicholas R. Winterton, *qv*; two *s* one *d*. *Educ:* Erdington Grammar Sch. for Girls. *Recreations:* music, theatre, tennis. *Address:* Whitehall Farm, Newbold Astbury, Congleton, Cheshire CW12 3NH.

WINTERTON, Maj.-Gen. Sir John; *see* Winterton, Maj.-Gen. Sir (Thomas) John.

WINTERTON, Nicholas Raymond; MP (C) Macclesfield since Sept. 1971; *b* 31 March 1938; *o s* of late N. H. Winterton, Lysways House, Longdon Green, near Rugeley, Staffs; *m* 1960, Jane Ann Hodgson (*see* J. A. Winterton); two *s* one *d*. *Educ:* Bilton Grange Prep. Sch.; Rugby Sch. Commnd 14th/20th King's Hussars, 1957–59. Sales Exec. Trainee, Shell-Mex and BP Ltd, 1959–60; Sales and Gen. Manager, Stevens and Hodgson Ltd, Birmingham (Co. engaged in sale and hire of construction equipment), 1960–71. Chairman: CPC Cttee, Meriden Cons. Assoc., 1966–68; Midland Branch, Contractors Mech. Plant Engrs Assoc., 1968–69. Member: W Midlands Cons. Council, 1966–69, 1971–72; Central Council, Nat. Union of Cons. and Unionist Assocs, 1971–72. Contested (C) Newcastle-under-Lyme, Oct. 1969, 1970; Jt Vice Chm., Anglo Danish Parly Gp; Vice-Chm., All Party Parly British Swedish Gp; Treas., All Party Parly British Indonesian Gp; Chairman: All Party Parly Textile Gp; All Party Parly British Namibia Gp; All Party Parly Gp for Paper and Board Industry; Vice Chairman: British South Africa Parly Gp; UK Falkland Is Gp; Cons. Parly Sports and Recreation Cttee, 1979–84. County Councillor, Atherstone Div. Warwickshire CC, 1967–72. President: Macclesfield Fermain Club; Poynton Community Centre; N Staffs Polytechnic Conservative Assoc.; Wigan Young Conservatives; Vice-President: NW Area Young Conservative Assoc.; Macclesfield and Congleton District Scout Council; Cheshire Scout Assoc.; Upton Priory Youth Centre, Macclesfield; E Cheshire Hospice. Hon. Mem., Macclesfield Lions Club; Hon. Life Mem., Macclesfield Rugby Union Football Club; Patron: Macclesfield and District Sheep Dog Trials Assoc; Internat. Centre for Child Studies. President, Macclesfield Branch: Riding for the Disabled; Multiple Sclerosis Soc. Pres., Bollington Light Opera Gp; Life Mem., Poynton Gilbert and Sullivan Soc. Liveryman, Weavers' Co.; Freeman of the City of London. *Recreations:* Rugby football, squash, hockey, tennis, swimming, horse riding. *Address:* Whitehall Farm, Mow Lane, Newbold Astbury, Congleton, Cheshire. *Club:* Lighthouse.

WINTERTON, Maj.-Gen. Sir (Thomas) John (Willoughby), KCB 1955 (CB 1946); KCMG 1950; CBE 1942 (OBE 1940); DL; retired; *b* 13 April 1898; *e s* of H. J. C. Winterton, Lichfield, Staffs; *m* 1921, Helen (*d* 1976), *d* of late H. Shepherd Cross, Hamels Park, Herts; three *s*. *Educ:* Oundle; RMA, Woolwich. Served European War, 1917–18; Burma, 1930–32; War of 1939–45; Dep. Comr Allied Commission for Austria, 1945–49; British High Commissioner and C-in-C in Austria, 1950; Military Governor and Commander, British/US Zone Free Territory of Trieste, 1951–54, retired Jan. 1955. ADC to the King, 1948–49. Colonel Comdt 1st Green Jackets 43rd and 52nd (formerly the Oxfordshire and Buckinghamshire Light Infantry), 1955–60. Formerly President, S Berks Conservative and Unionist Assoc. (Chairman, 1958–65). Formerly Member St John Council for Berkshire (Chairman, 1962–64); a Vice-Pres., Royal Humane Society, 1973– (Cttee Mem., 1962–73). DL, Berkshire, 1966. CStJ 1969. *Address:* Craven Lodge, Speen, Newbury, Berks. *T:* Newbury 40525. *Club:* Army and Navy.

WINTERTON, William Ralph, FRCS, FRCOG; Consultant Gynaecological Surgeon Emeritus, Middlesex Hospital; Surgeon, Hospital for Women, Soho Square; Obstetric Surgeon, Queen Charlotte's Maternity Hospital; Archivist to the Middlesex Hospital; *b* 24 June 1905; *o s* of late Rev. William Charles Winterton; *m* 1934, Kathleen Margaret, 2nd *d* of late Rev. D. Marsden; two *s* two *d*. *Educ:* Marlborough Coll.; Gonville and Caius Coll., Cambridge; Middlesex Hospital. MA; MB, BChir. House appointments, Middlesex Hospital, 1929–31; Gynæcological Registrar, Middlesex Hospital, 1934–36. Examr in Obstetrics to Universities of Cambridge, London, Glasgow, Ibadan, Dar-es-Salaam, and to Royal College of Obstetricians and Gynæcologists. Fellow of the Royal Society of Medicine, President Obstetric Section, 1960–61. Governor: Bancroft's Sch., Woodford Green, 1960–75; Howell's Sch., Denbigh (Vice-Chairman). Court of Assistants of the Drapers' Company (Master, 1964–65). Past President, Guild of Med. Bellringers. *Publications:* Aids to Gynæcology; (jointly) Queen Charlotte's Textbook of Obstetrics. Contributions to Medical Journals. *Recreations:* fishing, gardening, change ringing, and Do-it-yourself. *Address:* 26 De Walden Street, W1M 7PH. *T:* 01-935 8751; Youngloves, Rushden, Herts SG9 0SP. *T:* Broadfield 217.

WINTON, Walter; Keeper, Department of Electrical Engineering, Telecommunications and Loan Circulation, Science Museum, 1976–80; *b* 15 May 1917; *m* 1942, Dorothy Rickard; two *s* one *d*. *Educ:* Glossop Grammar Sch.; Manchester Univ. (BSc and Teacher's Diploma). Royal Ordnance Factories, Chemist, 1940–45. Taught Science, Harrow County and Greenford, 1945–50; Assistant and Deputy Keeper, Science Museum, 1950–67; Keeper: Dept of Loan Circulation, Mining and Marine Technol., 1968–73; Dept of Museum Services, 1973; Dept of Mechanical and Civil Engrg and Loan Circulation, 1973–76. *Publications:* contrib. to journals. *Recreations:* Scottish dancing, sailing, fell-walking. *Address:* The Old Workhouse, Harefield, Middlesex. *T:* 01–420 2103.

WINTOUR, Audrey Cecelia; *see* Slaughter, A. C.

WINTOUR, Charles Vere, CBE 1978 (MBE (mil.) 1945); journalist; Editorial Consultant to the London Daily News; *b* 18 May 1917; *s* of late Maj.-Gen. F. Wintour, CB, CBE; *m* 1st, 1940, Eleanor Trego Baker (marr. diss. 1979), *er d* of Prof. R. J. Baker, Harvard Univ.; two *s* two *d* (and one *s* decd); 2nd 1979, Mrs Audrey Slaughter, *qv*. *Educ:* Oundle Sch.; Peterhouse, Cambridge. BA 1939; MA 1946. Royal Norfolk Regt, 1940; GSO2 Headquarters of Chief of Staff to the Supreme Allied Commander (Designate) and SHAEF, 1943–45 (despatches). Joined Evening Standard, 1946: Dep. Editor, 1954–57; Editor, 1959–76 and 1978–80; Managing Dir, 1978–79; Chm., 1968–80; Asst Editor, Sunday Express, 1952–54; Managing Editor, Daily Express, 1957–59, Managing Dir, 1977–78; Editor: Sunday Express Magazine, 1981–82; UK Press Gazette, 1985–86; Director: Evening Standard Co. Ltd, 1959–82; Express (formerly Beaverbrook) Newspapers Ltd, 1964–82; TV-am (News) Ltd, 1982–84; AGB Communications, 1984–85; Wintour Publications, 1984–85. Mem., Press Council, 1979–81. Croix de Guerre (France) 1945; Bronze Star (US) 1945. *Publication:* Pressures on the Press, 1972. *Recreations:* theatre-going, reading newspapers. *Address:* 5 Alwyne Road, N1 2HH. *T:* 01–359 4590. *Club:* Garrick.

WISBECH, Archdeacon of; *see* Fleming, Ven. D.

WISDOM, Prof. Arthur John Terence Dibben, MA; Professor of Philosophy, University of Oregon, 1968–72; Fellow of Trinity College, Cambridge; *b* 1904; *s* of Rev. H. C. Wisdom and Edith S. Wisdom. *Educ:* Aldeburgh Lodge School; Fitzwilliam House (now College), Cambridge (Hon. Fellow, Fitzwilliam Coll., 1978). BA 1924; MA 1934. Lecturer in Moral Sciences, Trinity Coll., Cambridge; Prof. of Philosophy, Cambridge Univ., 1952–68. DU Essex, 1978. *Publications:* Other Minds, 1952; Philosophy and Psycho-Analysis, 1952; Paradox and Discovery, 1966. Contributions to Mind and to Proceedings of the Aristotelian Society. *Address:* 154 Stanley Road, Cambridge.

WISDOM, Norman; Actor/Comedian; has starred regularly on stage and television since 1952. First film Trouble in Store, in 1953 (winning an Academy Award) since which has starred in 19 major films in both England and America; two Broadway awards for stage musical, Walking Happy; numerous Royal Performances, both film and stage. *Recreations:* all sports. *Address:* c/o Eric Glass Ltd, 28 Berkeley Square, W1X 6HD.

WISE, family name of **Baron Wise.**

WISE, 2nd Baron, *cr* 1951, of King's Lynn; **John Clayton Wise;** farmer; *b* 11 June 1923; *s* of 1st Baron Wise and of Kate Elizabeth, *e d* of late John Michael Sturgeon; *S* father, 1968; *m* 1946, Margaret Annie, *d* of Frederick Victor Snead, Banbury; two *s*. *Heir:* *s* Hon. Christopher John Clayton Wise, PhD, BSc Hons [*b* 19 March 1949. *Educ:* Norwich School; Univ. of Southampton. Plant Scientist]. *Address:* Martlets, Blakeney, Norfolk NR25 7NP.

WISE, Mrs Audrey; Member, National Executive Committee of the Labour Party, since 1982; *d* of George and Elsie Crawford Brown; *m* John Wise; one *s* one *d*. Shorthand typist. MP (Lab) Coventry South West, Feb. 1974–1979. Contested (Lab) Woolwich, 1983; prospective parly candidate (Lab) Preston, 1985–. *Publications:* Women and the Struggle for Workers' Control, 1973; Eyewitness in Revolutionary Portugal, 1975. *Recreations:* family life, camping, walking, reading. *Address:* 99 Wolverhampton Road, Stafford. *T:* Stafford 59490.

WISE, Derek; *see* Wise, R. D.

WISE, Prof. Douglass, OBE 1980; FRIBA; Director, Institute of Advanced Architectural Studies, University of York, since 1975; *b* 6 Nov. 1927; *s* of Horace Watson Wise and Doris Wise; *m* 1958, Yvonne Jeannine Czeiler; one *s* one *d*. *Educ:* King's Coll., Newcastle, Durham Univ. (BArch; DipTP). Lecturer in Architecture, 1959–65, Prof. of Architecture, 1965–69, Head of Dept of Architecture, 1969–75, Newcastle Univ. Principal, Douglass Wise & Partners, Architects, 1959–. RIBA: Chm., Moderators, 1969–75; Chm., Examinations Cttee, 1969–75; Mem. Council, 1976–79; Chm., Heads of Schools Cttee, 1971–73; Mem. Bd of Management, North Eastern Housing Assoc., 1967–76 (Vice-Chm., 1974–76); Mem. Council, Newcastle Polytechnic, 1974–77; past Mem. Council, Senate and Court, Newcastle Univ.; Governor, Building Centre Trust, London, 1976–. *Publications:* contribs to various technical jls on housing, continuing educn and architectural theory. *Recreations:* painting, natural history. *Address:* The Institute of Advanced Architectural Studies, The King's Manor, York YO1 2EP. *T:* York 24919.

WISE, Ernie; *see* Wiseman, Ernest.

WISE, Prof. Michael John, CBE 1979; MC 1945; PhD; FRGS; Emeritus Professor of Geography, University of London; *b* Stafford, 17 August 1918; *s* of Harry Cuthbert and Sarah Evelyn Wise; *m* 1942, Barbara Mary, *d* of C. L. Hodgetts, Wolverhampton; one *s* one *d*. *Educ:* Saltley Grammar School, Birmingham; University of Birmingham. BA (Hons Geography) Birmingham, and Mercator Prize in Geography, 1939; PhD Birmingham, 1951. Served War, Royal Artillery, 80th LAA Regt, 1941–44, 5th Bn The Northamptonshire Regt, 1944–46, in Middle East and Italy; commissioned, 1941, Major, 1944. Assistant Lecturer, Univ. of Birmingham, 1946–48, Lecturer in Geography, 1948–51; London School of Economics: Lecturer in Geography, 1951–54; Sir Ernest Cassel Reader in Economic Geography, 1954–58; Prof. of Geography, 1958–83; Pro-Director, 1983–85. Chm., Departmental Cttee of Inquiry into Statutory Smallholdings, 1963–67; Mem., Dept of Transport Adv. Cttee on Landscape Treatment of Trunk Roads, 1971– (Chm., 1981–). Mem., UGC for Hong Kong, 1966–73. Recorder, Sect. E, Brit. Assoc. for Advancement of Science, 1955–60 (Pres., 1965); President: Inst. of British Geographers, 1974; IGU, 1976–80 (Vice-Pres., 1968–76); Geographical Assoc., 1976–77 (Hon. Treasurer, 1967–76, Hon. Mem., 1983); Mem., SSRC, 1976–82; Chm., Council for Extra-Mural Studies, Univ. of London, 1976–83; Chm., Exec. Cttee, Assoc. of Agriculture, 1972–83 (Vice-Pres., 1983–); Mem. Adv. Cttees, UN Univ., 1976–82; Hon. Sec., RGS, 1963–73, Vice-Pres., 1975–78, Hon. Vice-Pres., 1978–80, 1983–, Pres., 1980–82. Chm., Birkbeck Coll., 1983– (Governor, 1968–). Erskine Fellow, Univ. of Canterbury, NZ, 1970. Hon. Life Mem., Univ. of London Union, 1977. Hon. Member: Assoc. of Japanese Geographers, 1980; Geog. Soc. of Mexico, 1984; Geog. Soc. of Poland, 1986; Membre d'Honneur, Société de Géographie, 1983. FRSA. DUniv Open, 1978; Hon. DSc Birmingham, 1982. Received Gill Memorial award of RGS, 1958; RGS Founder's Medal, 1977; Alexander Kőrösi Csoma Medal, Hungarian Geographical Soc., 1980; Tokyo Geographical Soc. Medal, 1981; Lauréat d'Honneur, IGU, 1984. *Publications:* Hon. Editor, Birmingham and its Regional Setting, 1951; A Pictorial Geography of the West Midlands, 1958; General Consultant, An Atlas of Earth Resources, 1979; General Consultant, The Great Geographical Atlas, 1982; (consultant and contrib.) The Ordnance Survey Atlas of Great Britain, 1982; numerous articles on economic and urban geography. *Recreation:* music. *Address:* 45 Oakleigh Avenue, N20. *T:* 01–445 6057. *Club:* Athenæum.

WISE, Peter Anthony Surtees; Assistant Commissioner (Commercial), Hong Kong Government Office, London, since 1978; also (non-resident) Counsellor (Hong Kong Trade Affairs), Helsinki, Oslo, Stockholm, Vienna, since 1980; *b* 26 June 1934; *s* of late J. A. S. (Tony) Wise and Lenore Dugdale; *m* 1956, Elizabeth Muirhead Odhams; two *s*. *Educ:* Royal Naval College, Dartmouth. Served Royal Navy, 1948–56 (invalided). Marconi Instruments Ltd, 1956–60; Vickers Ltd, 1961–74; First Secretary, later Counsellor (Hong Kong Affairs), UK Mission, Geneva, 1974–78. *Address:* Field House, Boxford, Berks RG16 8DN. *T:* Boxford 302. *Club:* Hong Kong (Hong Kong).

WISE, Very Rev. Randolph George, VRD 1964; Dean of Peterborough, since 1981; *b* 20 Jan. 1925; *s* of George and Agnes Lucy Wise; *m* 1951, Hazel Hebe Simpson; four *d*. *Educ:* St Olave's and St Saviour's Grammar School; Queen's Coll., Oxford (MA); Lincoln Theological Coll.; Ealing Technical Coll. (DMS). Served RNVR, 1943–47. Assistant Curate: Lady Margaret, Walworth, 1951–53; Stocksbridge, Sheffield, 1953–55; Vicar of Lady Margaret, Walworth, 1955–60; Vicar of Stocksbridge, 1960–66; Bishop of London's Industrial Chaplaincy, 1966–76; Guild Vicar, St Botolph, Aldersgate, 1972–76; Rector of Notting Hill, 1976–81. Member of Plaisterers' Company. *Recreations:* music, sculling. *Address:* The Deanery, Peterborough PE1 1XS. *T:* Peterborough 62780. *Club:* Naval.

WISE, (Reginald) Derek, CBE 1977; Partner, Wise & Mercer, Paris, since 1983; *b* 29 July 1917; *s* of Reginald and Rita Wise; *m* 1957, Nancy Brenta Scialoya; two *s* one *d*. *Educ:* St Paul's Sch. Admitted solicitor, 1947. Served War of 1939–45, RA and Intell. Partner, Theodore Goddard, Paris, 1957–82. Legal Adviser, British Embassy, Paris, 1962–. *Address:* 203 bis Boulevard St Germain, 75007 Paris, France. *T:* 4222.07.94. *Club:* Travellers' (Paris).

WISEMAN, C. L., MA; Headmaster, Queen's College, Taunton, 1926–53; retired, 1953; *b* 20 April 1893; *s* of late Rev. F. L. Wiseman and Elsie Daniel; *m* 1946, Christine Irene, *d* of Sir William Savage, MD; *m* 1972, Patricia Joan Wragge, *d* of Prebendary R. Wragge-Morley. *Educ:* King Edward's School, Birmingham; Peterhouse, Cambridge (Scholar). Instructor Lt RN, 1915–19; Senior Mathematical Master, Kingswood School, Bath, 1921–26. *Recreation:* music. *Address:* 11 Park Lane, Milford-on-Sea, Lymington, Hants SO41 0PT.

WISEMAN, Prof. Donald John, OBE 1943; DLit; FBA 1966; FSA; Professor of Assyriology in the University of London, 1961–82, Emeritus 1982; *b* 25 Oct. 1918; *s* of Air Cdre Percy John Wiseman, CBE, RAF; *m* 1948, Mary Catherine, *d* of P. O. Ruoff; three *d*. *Educ:* Dulwich College; King's College, London. BA (London); AKC, McCaul Hebrew Prize, 1939; FKC 1982. Served War of 1939–45, in RAFVR. Ops, 11 Fighter Group, 1939–41; Chief Intelligence Officer, Mediterranean Allied Tactical Air Forces with Rank of Group Capt., 1942–45. Heap Exhibitioner in Oriental Languages, Wadham Coll., Oxford, 1945–47; MA 1949. Asst Keeper, Dept of Egyptian and Assyrian, later Western Asiatic, Antiquities, British Museum, 1948–61. Epigraphist on archæological excavations at Nimrud, Harran, Rimah; Jt Dir of British School of Archæology in Iraq, 1961–65, Chm. 1970–. Pres., Soc. for Old Testament Studies, 1980; Chm., Tyndale House for Biblical Research, Cambridge, 1957–86. Corresp. Mem., German Archæological Inst., 1961. Editor, Journal IRAQ, 1953–78; Joint Editor, Reallexion der Assyriologie, 1959–83. Bronze Star (USA), 1944. *Publications:* The Alalakh Tablets, 1953; Chronicles of Chaldaean Kings, 1956; Cuneiform Texts from Cappadocian Tablets in the British Museum, V, 1956; Cylinder-Seals of Western Asia, 1958; Vassal-Treaties of Esarhaddon, 1958; Illustrations from Biblical Archæology, 1958; Catalogue of Western Asiatic Seals in the British Museum, 1963; Peoples of Old Testament Times, 1973; Archaeology and the Bible, 1979; Essays on the Patriarchal Narratives, 1980; Nebuchadrezzar and Babylon, 1985; contrib. to journals. *Address:* Low Barn, 26 Downs Way, Tadworth, Surrey KT20 5DZ. *T:* Tadworth 3536.

WISEMAN, Ernest, OBE 1976; **(Ernie Wise);** *b* 27 Nov. 1925; *s* of Harry and Connie Wiseman; *m* 1953, Doreen Blyth. *Educ:* Council School. Career in show business: radio, variety, TV, films. First double act (with E. Morecambe), at Empire Theatre, Liverpool, 1941; first broadcast, 1943; BBC and ITV television series, 1955–84 (Soc. of Film and Television Arts Best Light Entertainment Award, 1973); series sold to Time Life, USA, 1980; Morecambe and Wise Tribute Show, Bring Me Sunshine, 1984; The Best of Morecambe and Wise, BBC, 1984; What's My Line, 1985; Too Close for Comfort, 1985; Los Angilla's. *Awards:* BAFTA (formerly SFTA), 1963, 1971, 1972, 1973, 1977; Silver Heart, 1964; Water Rats, 1970; Radio Industries, 1971, 1972; Sun Newspaper, 1973; Sun, 1974; Water Rats Distinguished Services, 1974; TV Times Hall of Fame Award, 1980–81; Commendation, 1981, Special Mention, 1982, HM Queen Mother's Award, Keep Britain Tidy; Best Dressed Man Award, 1983; Variety Club of GB award for work for deprived children, 1983; TV Times Award, 1985. Telethon for Children's Charity, NZ, 1985. Freeman, City of London, 1976. *Films:* The Intelligence Men, 1964; That Riviera Touch, 1965; The Magnificent Two, 1966; (for TV) Night Train to Murder, 1983. *Publications:* (with E. Morecambe): Eric and Ernie: an autobiography of Morecambe and Wise, 1973; Scripts of Morecambe and Wise, 1974; Morecambe and Wise Special, 1977; There's No Answer to That, 1981. *Recreations:* boating, tennis, swimming, jogging. *Address:* Thames Television, Teddington Lock, TW11 9NT.

WISEMAN, Sir John William, 11th Bt, *cr* 1628; *b* 16 March 1957; *o s* of Sir William George Eden Wiseman, 10th Bt, and Joan Mary, *d* of late Arthur Phelps, Harrow; *S* father, 1962; *m* 1980, Nancy, *d* of Casimer Zyla, New Britain, Conn; two *d*. *Educ:* Millfield Sch.; Univ. of Hartford, Conn, USA. *Heir: kinsman* Thomas Alan Wiseman [*b* 8 July 1921; *m* 1946, Hildemarie Domnik; (one *s* one *d* decd)]. *Address:* 395 North Road, Sudbury, Mass 01776, USA.

WISEMAN, Prof. Timothy Peter, DPhil; FSA; FBA 1986; Professor of Classics, University of Exeter, since 1977; *b* 3 Feb. 1940; *s* of Stephen Wiseman and Winifred Agnes Wiseman (*née* Rigby); *m* 1962, Doreen Anne Williams. *Educ:* Manchester Grammar Sch.; Balliol Coll., Oxford (MA 1964; DPhil 1967). FSA 1977. Rome Schol. in Classical Studies, British Sch. at Rome, 1962–63; University of Leicester: Asst Lectr in Classics, 1963–65; Lectr, 1965–73; Reader in Roman History, 1973–76. Vis. Associate Prof., Univ. of Toronto, 1970–71. *Publications:* Catullan Questions, 1969; New Men in the Roman Senate, 1971; Cinna the Poet, 1974; Clio's Cosmetics, 1979; (with Anne Wiseman) Julius Caesar: The Battle for Gaul, 1980; (ed) Roman Political Life, 1985; Catullus and his World, 1985; Roman Studies Literary and Historical, 1987. *Address:* Classics Department, The University, Exeter EX4 4QH. *T:* Exeter 263263.

WISHART, Maureen; *see* Lehane, M.

WISTRICH, Enid Barbara, PhD; Principal Lecturer in Public Administration, Middlesex Polytechnic, since 1979; *b* 4 Sept. 1928; *d* of Zadik Heiber and Bertha Brown; *m* 1950, Ernest Wistrich, *qv*; two *c* (and one *c* decd). *Educ:* Froebel Institute Sch.; Brackley High Sch.; St Paul's Girls' Sch.; London School of Economics (BScEcon, PhD). Research Asst, LSE, 1950–52; Instructor, Mt Holyoke Coll., Mass, USA, 1952–53; Research Officer, Royal Inst. of Public Administration, 1954–56; Sen. Res. Officer, LSE, 1969–72; NEDO, 1977–79. Councillor (Lab): Hampstead Metropolitan Bor. Council, 1962–65; London Bor. of Camden, 1964–68 and 1971–74; GLC, ILEA, 1973–77. Chm., Hampstead Community Health Council, 1986–. Governor: British Film Inst., 1974–81 (also Actg Chm., 1977–78); National Film Sch., 1978–82; Founder Trustee and Vice-Chm., Areopagitica Educnl Trust, 1980–; Chm. of Governors, Heathlands Sch. for Autistic Children, 1976–86. *Publications:* Local Government Reorganisation: the first years of Camden, 1972; I Don't Mind the Sex, It's the Violence: film censorship explored, 1978; The Politics of Transport, 1983; articles in Political Qly, Local Government Studies, Jl of Media Law and Practice, Teaching Public Administration, etc. *Recreations:* experiencing the arts, admiring nature, fussing round the family. *Address:* 37B Gayton Road, NW3. *T:* 01–435 8796.

WISTRICH, Ernest, CBE 1973; Director, European Movement (British Council), 1969–86; Editor, The European Enterprise, since 1986; *b* 22 May 1923; *s* of Dr Arthur and Mrs Eva Wistrich; *m* 1950, Enid Barbara (*née* Heiber), *qv*; two *c* (and one *c* decd). *Educ:* Poland; University Tutorial Coll., London. Served in RAF, 1942–46; Timber Merchant, 1946–67; Dir, Britain in Europe, 1967–69; Councillor, Hampstead Borough Council, 1959–65; Camden Borough Council, Alderman 1964–71, Councillor 1971–74; Chm., Camden Cttee for Community Relations, 1964–68; Mem., Skeffington Cttee on Public Participation in Planning, 1968–69. Contested (Lab): Isle of Thanet, 1964; Hendon North, 1966; Cleveland, 1979; contested (SDP) London Central, 1984, European Parly elections. Editor of various jls. *Publications:* contrib. Into Europe, Facts, New Europe and other jls. *Recreations:* music, walking. *Address:* 37B Gayton Road, NW3. *T:* 01–435 8796; (office) 01–839 3120. *Club:* National Liberal.

WITHALL, Maj.-Gen. William Nigel James, CB 1982; Marketing Director, and Member, Board of Directors, Singer Link-Miles Ltd, since 1985 (Consultant, 1984); *b* 14 Oct. 1928; *s* of late Bernard Withall and Enid (*née* Hill); *m* 1952, Pamela Hickman; one *s* one *d*. *Educ:* St Benedict's; Birmingham Univ. (Civil Engrg degree). Commnd RE, 1950; served in Hong Kong, Gulf States, Aden, Germany and India; Staff Coll., 1961; Sqdn Comd, 73 Fd Sqdn, 1964–66; Jt Services Staff Coll., Latimer, 1967; Mil. Asst to MGO, 1968–70; CO 26 Engr Regt, BAOR, 1970–72; Bde Comd, 11 Engr Bde, 1974–76; NDC, India, 1977; No 259 Army Pilots Course, 1978; Dir, Army Air Corps, 1979–83. Col Comdt RE, 1984–. Chm., Army Football Assoc., 1980–81; Pres., Army Cricket Assoc., 1981–83. Freeman, City of London, 1981; Liveryman, GAPAN, 1981. *Recreations:* cricket, squash, all games, reading, walking. *Address:* c/o Barclays Bank, High Street, Andover, Hants. *Clubs:* City Livery, MCC.

WITHERINGTON, Giles Somerville Gwynne; Chairman, 1982–87, Member of Council, since 1980, Save the Children Fund; *b* 7 June 1919; *s* of Iltid Gwynne Witherington and Alice Isabel Gage Spicer; *m* 1951, Rowena Ann Spencer Lynch; one *s* three *d*. *Educ:* Charterhouse; University Coll., Oxford (MA). War Service, Royal Artillery, UK, N Africa, Italy, 1939–46 (despatches). Joined Spicers Ltd, 1946, Jt Managing Director, 1960; joined Reed International Ltd: Director, 1963; Dep. Chm., 1976; retired, 1982. Mem. Council, Textile Conservation Centre, 1984. Hon. LLD Birmingham, 1983. *Recreations:* shooting, gardening, modern art, travel. *Address:* Bishops, Widdington, Saffron Walden, Essex CB11 3SQ; Flat 2, 11 Netherton Grove, Netherton, SW10 9TQ. *Club:* Arts.

WITHERS, Googie, (Mrs John McCallum), AO 1980; Actress since 1932; *b* Karachi, India, 12 March 1917; *d* of late Captain E. C. Withers, CBE, CIE, RIM, and late Lizette Catherine Wilhelmina van Wageningen; *m* 1948, John Neil McCallum, *qv*; one *s* two *d*. *Educ:* Fredville Park, Nonnington, Kent; Convent of the Holy Family, Kensington. Started as dancer in Musical Comedy. First film contract at age of 17; has acted in over 50 pictures, starring in 30. *Films include:* One of our Aircraft is Missing; The Silver Fleet; On Approval; Loves of Joanna Godden; It Always Rains on Sunday; White Corridors; Nickel Queen. *Plays include:* They Came to a City; Private Lives; Winter Journey; The Deep Blue Sea; Waiting for Gillian; Janus. Stratford on Avon Season, 1958: Beatrice in Much Ado About Nothing; Gertrude in Hamlet. The Complaisant Lover, New York, 1962; Exit the King, London, 1963; Getting Married, Strand, 1967; Madame Renevsky in The Cherry Orchard, Mrs Cheveley in An Ideal Husband, 1972; Lady Kitty in The Circle, Chichester Festival Theatre, 1976, Haymarket, 1977 (nominated for SWET best actress award), Toronto, 1978; Lady Bracknell in The Importance of Being Earnest, Chichester, 1979; Time and the Conways, Chichester, 1983; Lady Sneerwell in The School for Scandal, Duke of York's, 1984 (also European tour); The Chalk Garden, Chichester, 1986. Tours: 1959, Australia and NZ with: Roar Like a Dove, The Constant Wife and Woman in a Dressing Gown; 1964, excerpts Shakespeare (Kate, Margaret of Anjou, Beatrice, Portia, Rosalind, Cleopatra); 1965, Australia and NZ, with Beekman Place; 1968,

Australia, with Relatively Speaking; 1969–70, Australia and NZ, with Plaza Suite; 1978–80, Australia, NZ and Far East, with The Kingfisher; 1981, UK tour, The Cherry Orchard, The Skin Game, Dandy Dick; 1984–85, UK and Australia, Stardust. TV appearances in drama including The Public Prosecutor; Amphitryon 38; The Deep Blue Sea (Best Actress, 1954); Last Year's Confetti, Court Circular, 1971; Knightsbridge, 1972; The Cherry Orchard, 1973; series Within These Walls, 1974–76 (Best Actress of the Year, 1974); Time after Time (TV film), 1985; Hotel du Lac (TV film), 1985; Northanger Abbey (TV film), 1986. *Recreations:* music, travel, reading, interior decorating. *Address:* 1740 Pittwater Road, Bay View, NSW 2104, Australia; c/o Coutts & Co., 440 Strand, WC2.

WITHERS, John Keppel Ingold D.; *see* Douglas-Withers.

WITHERS, Senator Rt. Hon. Reginald (Greive), PC 1977; Senator (L) for Western Australia, since 1966; *b* 26 Oct. 1924; *s* of late F. J. Withers and I. L. Greive; *m* 1953, Shirley Lloyd-Jones; two *s* one *d. Educ:* Bunbury; Univ. of WA (LLB). Barrister-at-law 1953. Served War, RAN, 1942–46. Councillor, Bunbury Municipal Council, 1954–56; Mem., Bunbury Diocesan Council, 1958–59, Treasurer, 1961–68. State Vice-Pres., Liberal and Country League of WA, 1958–61, State Pres., 1961–65; Mem., Federal Exec. of Liberal Party, 1961–65; Fed. Vice-Pres., Liberal Party, 1962–65. Govt Whip in Senate, 1969–71; Leader of Opposition in Senate, 1972–75; Special Minister of State, Minister for Capital Territory, Minister for Media, and Minister for Tourism and Recreation, Nov.-Dec. 1975; Vice-Pres. of Exec. Council, Leader of Govt in Senate, and Minister for Admin. Services, 1975–78. Sec., SW Law Soc., 1955–68. *Recreations:* swimming, reading, painting. *Address:* 23 Malcolm Street, West Perth, WA 6005, Australia. *T:* (09)3214608.

WITHERS, Roy Joseph, CBE 1983; FEng 1983; Vice Chairman, Davy Corporation plc, since 1983; Chairman, Vosper Thornycroft (Holdings) Ltd, since 1985; Deputy Chairman, Transmark, since 1985 (Director, since 1978); *b* 18 June 1924; *s* of Joseph Withers and Irene Ada Withers (*née* Jones); *m* 1947, Pauline M. G. Johnston; four *s. Educ:* T School, Kingston upon Thames; Trinity College, Cambridge (1st. cl. Hons Mech. Scis Tripos). ICI, 1948–55; Humphreys & Glasgow, 1955–63; Engineering Dir, then Man. Dir, Power-Gas Corp. (subsid. of Davy Corp.), 1963–71; Chief Exec., Davy Powergas International, 1972–73; Man. Dir, Davy Corp., 1973–83. Dir, A. Monk & Co., 1983–. Mem., BOTB, 1983–86; Chm., Overseas Projects Board, 1983–86. Hon. FIChemE. *Recreations:* painting, golf, walking. *Address:* Spaniards Court, 41 Ingram Avenue, Hampstead, NW11 6TG. *T:* 01–455 0267. *Clubs:* Carlton; Hampstead Golf.

WITHERS, Rupert Alfred; Director, Dalgety Ltd, 1969–83 (Deputy Chairman and Managing Director, 1969–71; Chairman, 1972–77); *b* 29 Oct. 1913; *o s* of late Herbert Withers, FRAM and Marguerite (*née* Elzy); *m*; three *d. Educ:* University College School. Fellow Institute of Chartered Accountants, 1938. Secretary and Chief Accountant, Gloster Aircraft Co. Ltd, 1940–44; a Senior Partner of Urwick Orr & Partners Ltd until 1959; Man. Dir, Ilford Ltd, 1959–64; Chm. and Chief Executive, 1964–68. *Recreations:* music, books, theatre. *Address:* Epwell Mill, Banbury, Oxon OX15 6HG. *T:* Swalcliffe 327; 11K Stuart Tower, Maida Vale, W9. *T:* 01–286 8706. *Clubs:* Savile, Buck's.

WITHY, George; Assistant Editor (night), Liverpool Echo, since 1972; *b* Birkenhead, 15 May 1924; *er s* of George Withy and Alma Elizabeth Withy (*née* Stankley); *m* 1950, Dorothy Betty, *e c* of Bertram Allen and Dorothy Gray, Northfield, Birmingham; two *d. Educ:* Birkenhead Park High Sch. Served War, Royal Artillery, Britain and NW Europe, 1942–47. Trainee and Reporter, Birkenhead News, 1940; Chief Reporter, Redditch Indicator, 1948; District Reporter, Birmingham Post and Mail, 1950; Editor, Redditch Indicator, 1952. Joined Liverpool Daily Post 1960: successively Sub-Editor, Dep. Chief Sub-Editor, Asst News Editor, Chief Sub-Editor. Chief Sub-Editor, Liverpool Echo, 1970. Inst. of Journalists, 1962: successively Sec. and Chm., Liverpool District; Convenor, NW Region; Chm., Salaries and Conditions Bd, 1973–; Vice-Pres. and then Pres., 1975; Fellow 1975. Chm., Nat. Council for the Trng of Journalists, 1974, 1982 (Mem., 1970; Vice-Chm., 1973, 1981; Chm., North-West Adv. Trng Cttee, 1974–76, 1983–85); Mem., Newspaper Trng Cttee, Printing and Publishing Industry Trng Bd; Mem., Press Council, 1973–79. *Recreations:* writing on Rugby Union football, gardening, reading, philately. *Address:* 3 Woodside Road, Irby, Wirral, Merseyside L61 4UL. *T:* 051–648 2809.

WITNEY, Kenneth Percy, CVO; *b* 19 March 1916; *s* of late Rev. Thomas and of Dr Myfanwy Witney, S India; *m* 1947, Joan Tait; one *s* one *d. Educ:* Eltham Coll.; Wadham Coll., Oxford (Schol.). BA Hons Mod. History, 1938; MA 1975. Min. of Home Security, 1940; Private Sec. to Parly Under-Sec., 1942–44; Home Office, 1945; Asst Private Sec. to Home Sec., 1945–47; Colonial Office (Police Div.), 1955–57; Asst Sec., Home Office, 1957; Asst Under-Sec. of State, Home Office, 1969–76. Special Consultant to Royal Commn on Gambling, 1976–78. Chm., Kent Fedn of Amenity Socs, 1982–85. *Publications:* The Jutish Forest, 1976; The Kingdom of Kent, 1982; contribs to Econ. Hist. Rev., Archaeologia Cantiana. *Recreations:* local history, gardening. *Address:* 1 Loampits Close, Tonbridge, Kent. *T:* Tonbridge 352971; 37 Paradise Row, Sandwich, Kent. *Club:* United Oxford & Cambridge University.

WITT, Rt. Rev. Howell Arthur John; *see* Bathurst, Bishop of.

WITT, Maj.-Gen. John Evered, CB 1952; CBE 1948; MC 1918; retired from Army, 1953; *b* 15 Jan. 1897; *s* of late Rev. A. R. Witt, Royal Army Chaplains' Department; *m* 1st, 1924, Kathleen Phyllis Outram (*d* 1968); one *s*; 2nd, 1969, Mrs Cynthia Myrtle Margaret Reynolds (*d* 1982), *yr d* of late Dr Geoffrey Eden, FRCP. *Educ:* King's Sch., Canterbury. RMC Sandhurst, 1914; 2nd Lt ASC, Dec. 1914; BEF, 1915–19; BAOR, 1919–21; UK, 1921–23; BAOR, 1923–26; UK, 1926; India, 1927; Egypt, 1927–32; UK, 1932–46; Director of Supplies and Transport, BAOR, 1946–48; FarELF, 1948–49 (despatches); Director of Supplies and Transport, Middle East Land Forces, 1950–53. *Address:* c/o Barclay's Bank, 101 Victoria Road, Aldershot, Hants.

WITTE, Prof. William, FRSE; Professor of German in the University of Aberdeen, 1951–77; *b* 18 Feb. 1907; *o s* of W. G. J. and E. O. Witte; *m* 1937, Edith Mary Stenhouse Melvin; one *s* one *d. Educ:* Universities of Breslau, Munich, Berlin. MA, DLit (London); PhD (Aberdeen); FRSE 1978. Assistant, Department of German: Aberdeen, 1931–36; Edinburgh, 1936–37; Lecturer, Department of German, Aberdeen, 1937; Head of Dept, 1945; Reader in German, 1947. Gold Medal, Goethe Inst., 1971. Cross of the Order of Merit (Federal Republic of Germany), 1974. *Publications:* Modern German Prose Usage, 1937; Schiller, 1949; ed Schiller's Wallenstein, 1952; ed Two Stories by Thomas Mann, 1957; Schiller and Burns, and Other Essays, 1959; ed Schiller's Wallensteins Tod, 1962; ed Schiller's Maria Stuart, 1965; ed Goethe's Clavigo, 1973; contributions to collective works; articles in Modern Language Review, German Life and Letters, Oxford German Studies, Publications of the English Goethe Society, Publications of the Carlyle Soc., Aberdeen Univ. Rev., Wisconsin Monatshefte, Schiller-Jahrbuch, Forum for Modern Language Studies, Encyclopædia Britannica, etc. *Recreations:* gardening, motoring. *Address:* 41 Beechgrove Terrace, Aberdeen AB2 4DS. *T:* 643799.

WITTEVEEN, Dr (Hendrikus) Johannes, Commander, Order of Netherlands Lion; Commander, Order of Orange Nassau; Board Member: Royal Dutch Petroleum Co., 1971–73 and since 1978; Robeco, 1971–73 and since 1979 (Adviser, 1971–73); Nationale-Nederlanden, since 1979; Adviser for International Affairs, Amro Bank, Amsterdam, since 1979; Member, European Advisory Council, General Motors, since 1978; *b* Zeist, Netherlands, 12 June 1921; *m* 1949, Liesbeth de Vries Feyens; two *s* one *d. Educ:* Univ. Rotterdam (DrEcons). Central Planning Bureau, 1947–48; Prof., Univ. Rotterdam, 1948–63; Mem. Netherlands Parlt, First Chamber, 1959–63 and 1971–73, and Second Chamber, 1965–67; Minister of Finance, Netherlands, 1963–65 and 1967–71; First Deputy Prime Minister, 1967–71; Managing Director, IMF, 1973–78. Chm., Group of Thirty, 1979–85, Hon. Chm., 1985–; Mem., Internat. Council, Morgan Guaranty Trust Co. of NY, 1978–85; Bd Mem., Thyssen-Bornemisza NV, 1978–86. Grand Cross, Order of Crown (Belgium); Order of Oak Wreath (Luxemburg); Order of Merit (Fed. Republic Germany). *Publications:* Loonshoogte en Werkgelegenheid, 1947; Growth and Business Cycles, 1954; articles in Economische Statistische Berichten, Euromoney. *Recreation:* hiking. *Address:* Wassenaar, Waldeck Pyrmontlaan 15, The Netherlands.

WITTIG, Prof. Georg, Dr Phil; *b* Berlin, 16 June 1897; *s* of Prof. Gustav Wittig and Martha (*née* Dombrowski); *m* 1930, Waltraut Ernst (*d* 1978 two *d. Educ:* Wilhelms-Gymnasium, Kassel; Marburg Univ. Lecturer, Marburg Univ., 1926–32; Division Director, Technische Hochschule, Braunschweig, 1932–37; Prof., Univs of Braunschweig, Freiburg and Tübingen, 1937–56; Prof., Heidelberg Univ., 1956–67, emeritus, 1967–. Member: Acad. of Sciences, Munich and Heidelberg; l'Acad. Française; Soc. Quimica del Perú; Leopoldina Halle; Hon. Member: Swiss Chem. Assoc.; New York Acad. of Scis; Chem. Soc., London; Soc. Chim. de France. Hon. doctorates, Sorbonne and Hamburg. Nobel Prize (jointly) 1979; many earlier awards, incl. Otto Hahn Prize, 1967; Karl Ziegler Prize, 1975. Ordens Grosses Verdienstkreuz, 1980. *Publications:* Textbook on Stereochemistry, 1930; numerous articles in jls on Metallorganic, Ylid and Carbanion Chemistry. *Recreations:* painting, music, hiking, mountain climbing. *Address:* Bergstrasse 35, 69 Heidelberg, Federal Republic of Germany. *T:* 40945.

WITTON-DAVIES, Ven. Carlyle; Archdeacon Emeritus of Oxford, since 1985; *b* 10 June 1913; *s* of late Prof. T. Witton Davies, DD, and Hilda Mabel Witton Davies (*née* Everett); *m* 1941, Mary Rees, BA, *o d* of late Canon W. J. Rees, St Asaph, Clwyd; three *s* four *d. Educ:* Friars School, Bangor; University College of N Wales, Bangor; Exeter College, Oxford; Cuddesdon College, Oxford; Hebrew University, Jerusalem. Exhib., University Coll. of N Wales, Bangor, 1930–34; BA (Wales), 1st Cl. Hons Hebrew, 1934; BA (Oxon), 2nd Cl. Hons Theology, 1937; Junior Hall Houghton Septuagint Prize, Oxford, 1938, Senior, 1939; MA (Oxon), 1940; Deacon, 1937, Priest, 1938, St Asaph; Assistant Curate, Buckley, 1937–40; Subwarden, St Michael's College, Llandaff, 1940–44; Examining Chaplain to Bishop of Monmouth, 1940–44; Adviser on Judaica to Anglican Bishop in Jerusalem, 1944–49; Examining Chaplain to Bishop in Jerusalem, 1945–49; Canon Residentiary of Nazareth in St George's Collegiate Church, Jerusalem, 1947–49; Dean and Precentor of St David's Cathedral, 1949–57; Examining Chaplain to Bishop of St David's, 1950–57; Chaplain, Order of St John of Jerusalem, 1954–; Archdeacon of Oxford and Canon of Christ Church, Oxford, 1957–82, Sub Dean, 1972–82 (Student Emeritus of Christ Church, 1982–); Examining Chaplain to Bishop of Oxford, 1965–82. Chairman, Council of Christians and Jews, 1957–78 (Vice-Pres., 1978–); Mem., Archbishops' Commn on Crown Appointments, 1962–64; Censor Theologiae, Christ Church, 1972–75, 1978–80; Member, Convocation of Canterbury, and Church Assembly/General Synod of C of E, 1957–75, 1978–80. First recipient, Sir Sigmund Sternberg Award, 1979. *Publications:* Journey of a Lifetime, 1962; (part translated) Martin Buber's Hasidism, 1948; (translated) Martin Buber's The Prophetic Faith, 1949; contrib. to Oxford Dictionary of the Christian Church, 1957; contrib. to The Mission of Israel, 1963. *Recreations:* music, lawn tennis, swimming, travel. *Address:* 199 Divinity Road, Oxford OX4 1LS. *T:* Oxford 247301.

WITTY, (John) David, CBE 1985; Chairman, London Enterprise Property Co., 1984–85; *b* 1 Oct. 1924; *s* of late Harold Witty and Olive Witty, Beverley; *m* 1955, Doreen Hanlan; one *s. Educ:* Beverley Grammar Sch.; Balliol Coll., Oxford (MA). Served War, RN, 1943–46. Asst Town Clerk, Beverley, 1951–53; Asst Solicitor: Essex CC, 1953–54; Hornsey, 1954–60; Dep. Town Clerk: Kingston upon Thames, 1960–65; Merton, 1965–67; Asst Chief Exec., Westminster, 1967–77, Chief Exec., 1977–84. Lawyer Mem., London Rent Assessment Panel, 1984–. Hon. Sec., London Boroughs Assoc., 1978–84. Order of Infante D. Henrique (Portugal), 1978; Order of Right Hand (Nepal), 1980; Order of King Abdul Aziz (Saudi Arabia), 1981; Order of Oman, 1982; Order of Orange-Nassau, 1982. *Recreation:* golf. *Address:* 14 River House, The Terrace, Barnes, SW13 0NR.

WIX, Ethel Rose; Special Commissioner of Income Tax, 1977–86; *b* 1 Nov. 1921; *d* of Michael Wix and Anna Wix (*née* Snyder). *Educ:* Henrietta Barnett Sch.; Cheltenham Ladies' Coll.; University Coll. London (BA Hons 1942); Hull University Coll. (Cert Ed 1943). Special Operations Executive, 1944–45; lived in S Africa, 1948–54; work for S African Inst. of Race Relations, 1950–54; Africa Bureau, London, 1955–56; Solicitor of Supreme Court, 1960; Partner, Herbert Oppenheimer, Nathan & Vandyk, 1960–75; General Commissioner of Income Tax, 1976–78. Mem. Council: Richmond Fellowship, 1975–85; Trinity Hospice, Clapham, 1981–; Cheltenham Ladies' Coll., 1983–; St Christopher's Hospice, 1985–. *Publications:* papers on Cost of Living, 1951, and Industrial Feeding Facilities, 1953, for S African Inst. of Race Relations; summary of Royal Commn Report on E Africa, 1956, for Africa Bureau. *Recreations:* reading, cooking, theatre. *Address:* 5 Phillimore Gardens, W8 7QG. *T:* 01–937 8899. *Clubs:* Reform, University Women's, Special Forces.

WODEHOUSE, family name of **Earl of Kimberley.**

WODEHOUSE, Lord; John Armine Wodehouse; Systems Programmer, Glaxo, since 1979; *b* 15 Jan. 1951; *s* and *heir* of 4th Earl of Kimberley, *qv*; *m* 1973, Hon. Carol Palmer, MA (Oxon), *er d* of Baron Palmer, *qv*; one *s* one *d. Educ:* Eton; Univ. of East Anglia. BSc (Chemistry) 1973; MSc (Physical Organic Chemistry) 1974. FRSA. Research Chemist, Glaxo, 1974–79. Chm., UK Info Users Gp, 1981–83. Fellow, British Interplanetary Soc., 1984 (Associate Fellow, 1981–83). *Recreations:* interest in spaceflight, photography, computing, fantasy role playing games. *Heir: s* David Simon John Wodehouse, *b* 10 Oct. 1978. *Address:* Derry House, North End, Henley-on-Thames, Oxon RG9 6LQ.

WOGAN, Michael Terence, (Terry); jobbing broadcaster; *b* 3 Aug. 1938; *s* of Michael Thomas and Rose Wogan; *m* 1965, Helen Joyce; two *s* one *d. Educ:* Crescent Coll., Limerick, Ireland; Belvedere Coll., Dublin. Joined RTE as Announcer, 1963, Sen. Announcer, 1964–66; various programmes for BBC Radio, 1965–67; Late Night Extra, BBC Radio, 1967–69; The Terry Wogan Show, BBC Radio One, 1969–72, BBC Radio Two, 1972–84; television shows include: Lunchtime with Wogan, ATV; BBC: Come Dancing; Song for Europe; The Eurovision Song Contest; Children in Need; Wogan's Guide to the BBC; Blankety-Blank; Wogan. Awards include: Pye Radio Award, 1980; Radio Industries Award (Radio Personality 3 times; TV Personality, 1982, 1984, 1985); TV Times TV Personality of the Year (8 times); Daily Express Award (twice); Carl Alan Award (3 times); Variety Club of GB: Special Award, 1982; Showbusiness Personality, 1984. *Publications:* Banjaxed, 1979; The Day Job, 1981; To Horse, To Horse, 1982.

Recreations: tennis, golf, swimming, reading, writing. *Address:* c/o Jo Gurnett, 2 New Kings Road, SW6 4SA. *Clubs:* Lord's Taverners; London Irish Rugby Football; Stoke Poges Golf; Temple Golf (Henley-on-Thames).

WOLEDGE, Brian; Emeritus Professor of French Language and Literature, University of London; Fielden Professor of French, University College, London, 1939–71; Hon. Research Fellow, University College London; *b* 16 Aug. 1904; *m* 1933, Christine Mary Craven; one *s* one *d*. *Educ:* Leeds Boys' Modern School; University of Leeds. BA (Leeds) 1926; MA (Leeds) 1928; Docteur de l'Université de Paris, 1930; Asst Lecturer in French, University College, Hull, 1930–32; Lecturer in French, University of Aberdeen, 1932–39. Visiting Andrew Mellon Professor of French, University of Pittsburg, 1967. Docteur *hc* de l'Université d'Aix-Marseille, 1970. *Publications:* L'Atre périlleux; études sur les manuscrits, la langue et l'importance littéraire du poème, 1930; L'Atre périlleux, roman de la Table ronde (Les Classiques français du moyen âge 76), 1935; Bibliographie des romans et nouvelles en prose française antérieurs à 1500, 1954, repr. 1975, Supplement 1975; The Penguin Book of French Verse, Vol. 1, To the Fifteenth Century, 1961; Répertoire des premiers textes en prose française, 842–1210 (with H. P. Clive), 1964; La Syntaxe des substantifs chez Chrétien de Troyes, 1979; Commentaire sur Yvain (Le Chevalier au Lion) de Chrétien de Troyes, Vol. 1, 1986. *Address:* 28a Dobbins Lane, Wendover, Aylesbury, Bucks. *T:* Wendover 622188.

WOLF, Prof. Peter Otto, FEng; FICE; FIWES; FRMetS; FASCE; Consultant; Professor and Head of Department of Civil Engineering, 1966–82, The City University, London, now Professor Emeritus; *b* 9 May 1918; *s* of Richard Wolf and Dora (*née* Bondy); *m* 1s 1944, Jennie Robinson; two *s* one *d*; 2nd, 1977, Janet Elizabeth Robertson. *Educ:* University of London (BScEng). Assistant under agreement to C. E. Farren, Cons. Engr, 1941–44; Civilian Asst, a Dept of the War Office, 1944–45; Engineer (Chief Designer, Loch Sloy Project), under James Williamson, Cons. Engr, 1945–47; Engineer for Mullardoch Dam (Affric Project), John Cochrane & Sons Ltd, 1947–49; Imperial College of Science and Technology: Lectr in Fluid Mechanics and Hydraulic Engrg, 1949–55; Reader in Hydrology in Univ. of London, 1955–66. Private consultancy, London, 1950–. Chm., Cttee on Flood Protection Res., MAFF, 1984–85. Visiting Professor: Stanford Univ., Calif, 1959–60, 1961–64; Cornell Univ., 1963. Hon. Mem., BHRA, 1984–. Hon. DrIng Technological Univ. of Dresden, 1986. *Publications:* trans. and ed, Engineering Fluid Mechanics, by Charles Jaeger, 1956; papers in Proc. ICE, Jl IWE, UNESCO Reports, UNESCO Nature and Resources, Proc. Internat. Water Resources Assoc., etc. *Recreations:* classical music, reading, ski-ing, sailing, walking. *Address:* 69 Shepherds Hill, N6 5RE. *T:* 01–340 6638. *Club:* Athenæum.

WOLFE, Prof. James Nathan; Professor of Economics, University of Edinburgh, 1964–84, now Emeritus; *b* 16 Sept. 1927; *s* of late Jack Wolfe and of Rose (*née* Segal); *m* 1954, Monica Anne Hart; one *d*. *Educ:* Westhill High Sch., Montreal; McGill Univ. (BA 1948, MA 1949); Glasgow Univ.; Queen's and Nuffield Colls, Oxford. BLitt (Oxon) 1952. Lecturer in Political Economy, Univ. of Toronto, 1952–60; Prof. of Economics, Univ. of California, Berkeley and Santa Barbara, 1960–64; Brookings Research Prof., 1963–64. Economic Consultant: to Nat. Economic Develt Office, 1963–64; to Sec. of State for Scotland, 1965–72; to Dept of Economic Affairs, 1965–69; Member, Inter-deptl Cttee on Long Term Population Distribution, 1966–69. Visiting Scholar, Stanford Univ., 1982. *Publications:* ed, Government and Nationalism in Scotland, 1969; The Economics of Technical Information Systems, 1974; ed (with C. I. Phillips) Clinical Practice and Economics, 1977; (with M. Pickford) The Church of Scotland: an economic survey, 1980; articles in learned jls. *Recreations:* travel, reading, Canadiana. *Address:* 3 St Margaret's Road, Edinburgh EH9 1AZ. *T:* 031–447 6645. *Clubs:* New, Scottish Arts (Edinburgh).

WOLFE, William Cuthbertson; President, Scottish National Party, 1980–82; *b* 22 Feb. 1924; *s* of late Major Tom Wolfe, TD, and Katie Cuthbertson; *m* 1953, Arna Mary, *d* of late Dr Melville Dinwiddie, CBE, DSO, MC; two *s* two *d*. *Educ:* Bathgate Academy; George Watson's Coll., Edinburgh. CA. Army service, 1942–47, NW Europe and Far East; Air OP Pilot. Hon. Publications Treas., Saltire Society, 1953–60; Scout County Comr, West Lothian, 1960–64; Hon. Pres. (Rector), Students' Assoc., Heriot-Watt Univ., 1966–69. Contested (SNP) West Lothian, 1962, 1964, 1966, 1970, Feb. and Oct. 1974, 1979; Chm., SNP, 1969–79. *Publication:* Scotland Lives, 1973. *Address:* Burnside Forge, Burnside Road, Bathgate, W Lothian. *T:* Bathgate 54785.

WOLFENDALE, Prof. Arnold Whittaker, PhD, DSc; FRS 1977; FInstP, FRAS; Professor of Physics, University of Durham, since 1965; *b* 25 June 1927; *s* of Arnold Wolfendale and Doris Wolfendale; *m* 1951, Audrey Darby; twin *s*. *Educ:* Univ. of Manchester (BSc Physics 1st Cl. Hons 1948, PhD 1953, DSc 1970). FInstP 1958; FRAS 1973. Asst Lectr, Univ. of Manchester, 1951, Lectr, 1954; Univ. of Durham: Lectr, 1956; Sen. Lectr, 1959; Reader in Physics, 1963; Head of Dept, 1973–77, 1980–83, 1986–. Chm., Northern Reg. Action Cttee, Manpower Services Commn's Job Creation Prog., 1975–78. Pres., RAS, 1981–83. *Publications:* Cosmic Rays, 1963; (ed) Cosmic Rays at Ground Level, 1973; (ed) Origin of Cosmic Rays, 1974; (ed jtly and contrib.) Origin of Cosmic Rays, 1981; (ed) Gamma Ray Astronomy, 1981; (ed) Progress in Cosmology, 1982; (with P. V. Ramana Murthy) Gamma Ray Astronomy, 1986; original papers on studies of cosmic radiation and aspects of astrophysics. *Recreations:* walking, gardening, foreign travel. *Address:* Ansford, Potters Bank, Durham. *T:* Durham 45642.

WOLFF, Frederick Ferdinand, CBE 1975; TD 1945; Chairman: Rudolf Wolff & Co. Ltd, 1965–81; Wolff Steel Ltd, Swansea, since 1982; *b* 13 Oct. 1910; *s* of Philip Robert Wolff and Irma Wolff; *m* 1937, Natalie Winifred Virginia Byrne; two *s* three *d* (incl. twin *s* and *d*). *Educ:* Shirley House Prep. Sch., Watford, Herts; Beaumont Coll., Old Windsor, Berks. Oxfordshire and Bucks LI, 1939–45 (Captain). Joined Rudolf Wolff & Co., 1929; Partner, 1951. Chairman: London Metal Exchange Committee, 1970–77 (Mem. Cttee, 1961–77; Mem. Bd, 1963–83); Fedn of Commodity Assocs, 1971–77; Mem., Cttee on Invisible Exports, 1971–. AAA Champion 440 yards, 1933; British Gold Medallist, 4 × 400 metres relay team, Olympic Games, Berlin, 1936. *Recreations:* golf, racing. *Address:* 11 Shardeloes, Amersham, Bucks HP7 0RL. *T:* Amersham 5081. *Clubs:* London Athletic, Gresham, Directors; Beaconsfield Golf.

WOLFF, Prof. Heinz Siegfried, FIBiol; Director, Brunel Institute for Bioengineering, Brunel University, since 1983; *b* 29 April 1928; *s* of Oswald Wolff and Margot (*née* Saalfeld); *m* 1953, Joan Eleanor Stephenson; two *s*. *Educ:* City of Oxford Sch.; University Coll. London (BSc(Hons)Physiology). National Institute for Medical Research: Div. of Human Physiology, 1954–62; Hd, Div. of Biomedical Engrg, 1962–70; Hd, Bioengrg Div., Clinical Res. Centre of MRC, 1970–83. European Space Agency: Chm., Life Science Working Gp, 1976–82; Mem., Sci. Adv. Cttee, 1978–82; Chm., Microgravity Adv. Cttee, 1982–. Chm., Microgravity Panel, Brit. Nat. Space Centre, 1986–. *Television series:* BBC TV Young Scientist of the Year (contributor), 1968–81; BBC2: Royal Instn Christmas Lectures, 1975; Great Egg Race, 1978–; Great Experiments, 1985–86. *Publications:* Biomedical Engineering, 1969 (German, French, Japanese and Spanish trans, 1970–72); about 120 papers in sci. jls and contribs to books. *Recreations:* working, lecturing to children, dignified practical joking. *Address:* Brunel Institute for Bioengineering, Brunel University, Uxbridge, Mddx UB8 3PH.

WOLFF, John Arnold Harrop, CMG 1963; *b* 14 July 1912; *er s* of late Arnold H. Wolff, Halebarns, Cheshire; *m* 1939, Helen Muriel McCracken, Howth, Co. Dublin; one *s* one *d*. *Educ:* Haileybury College; Peterhouse, Cambridge. Colonial Administrative Service, Kenya: District Officer, 1935–59; Provincial Commissioner, 1959–63; Civil Secretary, Rift Valley Region, 1963; retired, Nov. 1963. *Recreations:* gardening, golf. *Address:* Wallflowers, Bloxham, Oxon.

WOLFF, Michael, PSIAD; FRSA; Director: the Consortium, since 1985; the Hunger Project, since 1979; *b* 12 Nov. 1933; *s* of Serge Wolff and Mary (*née* Gordon); *m* 1976, Susan Kent; one *d*. *Educ:* Gresham Sch., Holt, Norfolk; Architectural Association Sch. of Architecture. Designer: Sir William Crawford & Partners, 1957–61; BBC Television, 1961–62; Main Wolff & Partners, 1964–65; with Wolff Olins Ltd as a founder and Creative Director, 1965–83. President: D and AD, 1971; SIAD, 1985–87. *Recreations:* enjoying a family, seeing. *Address:* 9 Cumberland Gardens, WC1. *T:* 01–833 0007; (office) 49 Wellington Street, WC2E 7BN. *T:* 01–379 6492.

WOLFF, Prof. Otto Herbert, CBE 1985; MD, FRCP; Nuffield Professor of Child Health, University of London, 1965–85, now Emeritus Professor; Dean of the Institute of Child Health, 1982–85; *b* 10 Jan. 1920; *s* of Dr H. A. J. Wolff; *m* 1952, Dr Jill Freeborough; one *s* one *d*. *Educ:* Peterhouse, Cambridge; University College Hospital, London. Lieut and Capt. RAMC, 1944–47. Resident Medical Officer, Registrar and Sen. Med. Registrar, Birmingham Children's Hospital, 1948–51; Lecturer, Sen. Lectr, Reader, Dept of Pædiatrics and Child Health, Univ. of Birmingham, 1951–64. Senator, London Univ.; Representative of London Univ. on GMC. Past Pres., British Pædiatric Assoc.; Member: Royal Society of Medicine; American Pædiatric Society; New York Academy of Sciences; Amer. Academy of Pediatrics; European Soc. for Paediatric Research; European Soc. for Paediatric Gastroenterology; Deutsche Akad. der Naturforscher Leopoldina. Corresp. Member: Société Française de Pédiatrie; Société Suisse de Pédiatrie; Österreichische Gesellschaft für Kinderheilkunde; Società Italiana di Pediatria; Deutsche Gesellschaft für Kinderheilkunde; Fellow, Indian Acad. of Pediatrics. Dawson Williams Meml Prize, BMA, 1984. *Publications:* chapter on Disturbances of Serum Lipoproteins in Endocrine and Genetic Diseases of Childhood (ed L. I. Gardner); chapter on Obesity in Recent Advances in Paediatrics (ed David Hull); articles in Lancet, British Medical Journal, Archives of Disease in Childhood, Quarterly Jl of Medicine, etc. *Recreation:* music. *Address:* 53 Danbury Street, N1 8LE. *T:* 01–226 0748.

WOLFF, Rosemary Langley; Member, Police Complaints Authority, since 1985 (Member, Police Complaints Board, 1977–85); *b* 10 July 1926; *er d* of late A. C. V. Clarkson; *m* 1956, Michael Wolff, JP (*d* 1976); two *d*. *Educ:* Haberdashers' Aske's Sch. Mem., Community Relations Commn, 1973–77. Manager of various primary schs in North Kensington and Tower Hamlets, 1963–; Governor, City College; Chm., Conservative Contact Group, 1973–77; Mem., Managing Cttee, Working Ladies' Guild. *Address:* 13 Holland Park, W11 3TH. *T:* 01–727 9051.

WOLFSON, family name of **Baron Wolfson.**

WOLFSON, Baron *cr* 1985 (Life Peer), of Marylebone in the City of Westminster; **Leonard Gordon Wolfson,** Kt 1977; Chairman and a Founder Trustee, Wolfson Foundation; Joint Chairman and Managing Director, Great Universal Stores (Director, 1952); Chairman, Burberrys Ltd; *b* 11 Nov. 1927; *s* of Sir Isaac Wolfson, 1st Bt, *qv*; *m* 1949, Ruth, *d* of E. A. Sterling; four *d*. *Educ:* King's School, Worcester. Hon. Fellow: St Catherine's Coll., Oxford; Wolfson Coll., Cambridge; Wolfson Coll., Oxford; Worcester Coll., Oxford; UCL; LSHTM 1985; QMC 1985. Patron, Royal College of Surgeons, 1976. Hon. FRCP 1977. Hon. FBA 1986. Hon. PhD: Tel Aviv, 1971; Hebrew Univ., 1978; Hon. DCL: Oxon, 1972; East Anglia, 1986; Hon. LLD: Strathclyde, 1972; Dundee, 1979; Cantab, 1982; London, 1982; Hon. DSc: Hull, 1977; Wales, 1984; Hon. DHL Bar Ilan Univ., 1983. *Recreations:* history, economics, golf. *Address:* Universal House, 251 Tottenham Court Road, W1A 1BZ.

WOLFSON, Sir David, Kt 1984; Non-executive Director, Stewart Wrightson Holdings PLC, since 1985; *b* 9 Nov. 1935; *s* of Charles Wolfson and Hylda Wolfson; *m* 1st, 1962, Patricia E. Rawlings (marr. diss. 1967); 2nd, 1967, Susan E. Davis; two *s* one *d*. *Educ:* Clifton Coll.; Trinity Coll., Cambridge (MA); Stanford Univ., California (MBA). Great Universal Stores, 1960–78, Director 1973–78; Secretary to Shadow Cabinet, 1978–79; Chief of Staff, Political Office, 10 Downing Street, 1979–85. Chm., Alexon Group PLC (formerly Steinberg Group PLC), 1982–86. Hon. FRCR, 1978. *Recreations:* golf, bridge. *Clubs:* Portland; Sunningdale; Woburn.

WOLFSON, (Geoffrey) Mark; MP (C) Sevenoaks, since 1979; Director, Hambros Bank, since 1973 (Head of Personnel, 1970–85); *b* 7 April 1934; *s* of late Captain V. Wolfson, OBE, VRD, RNR, and Dorothy Mary Wolfson; *m* 1965, Edna Webb (*née* Hardman); two *s*. *Educ:* Eton Coll.; Pembroke Coll., Cambridge (MA). Served Royal Navy, 1952–54; Cambridge, 1954–57; Teacher in Canada, 1958–59; Warden, Brathay Hall Centre, Westmorland, 1962–66; Head of Youth Services, Industrial Soc., 1966–69. PPS to Minister of State for NI, 1983–84, to Minister of State for Defence Procurement, 1984–85. Officer, Cons. Backbench Employment Cttee, 1981–83. *Recreations:* fell walking, rowing coaching, travel.

WOLFSON, Sir Isaac, 1st Bt *cr* 1962; FRS 1963; Hon. Fellow: Weizmann Institute of Science, Israel; St Edmund Hall, Oxford; Jews' College; Lady Margaret Hall, Oxford; Founder Fellow, Wolfson College, Oxford; Joint Chairman, The Great Universal Stores Ltd; *b* 17 Sept. 1897; *m* 1926, Edith Specterman (*d* 1981); one *s*. *Educ:* Queen's Park School, Glasgow. Joined The Great Universal Stores Ltd, 1932. Member, Worshipful Company of Pattenmakers; Member, Grand Council, Cancer Research Campaign; Hon. Pres., Weizmann Institute of Science Foundation; Trustee, Religious Centre, Jerusalem; Patron, Royal College of Surgeons; Founder, and Pres., 1975– (formerly Chm.), and Trustee, Wolfson Foundation which was created in 1955 mainly for the advancement of health, education and youth activities in the UK and Commonwealth. Fellow, Royal Postgrad. Med. Sch., 1972; Hon. FRCP 1959; Hon. FRCS 1969; Hon. FRCP&S Glasgow. Hon. DCL Oxford, 1963; Hon. LLD: London, 1958; Glasgow, 1963; Cambridge, 1966; Manchester, 1967; Strathclyde, 1969; Brandeis Univ., US 1969; Nottingham, 1971; Hon. PhD Jerusalem, 1970. Einstein Award, US, 1967; Herbert Lehmann Award, US, 1968. Freeman, City of Glasgow, 1971. *Heir:* *s* Lord Wolfson, *qv*.

WOLFSON, Mark; *see* Wolfson, G. M.

WOLKIND, Jack, CBE 1978; Director, St Katharine-by-the-Tower Ltd, since 1985; *b* 16 Feb. 1920; *s* of Samuel and Golda Wolkind; *m* 1945, Bena Sternfeld; two *s* one *d*. *Educ:* Mile End Central Sch.; King's Coll., London. LLB Hons, LLM (London). Admitted Solicitor, 1953. Army service to 1945. Dep. Town Clerk and Solicitor, Stepney Borough Council, 1952–65; Chief Exec. (formerly Town Clerk), Tower Hamlets, 1964–85. Mem., London Residuary Body. Indep. Mem., Kessler Foundn, 1986. Governor: Toynbee Hall,

1981–; QMC, Univ. of London, 1981– (Hon. Fellow, 1985). FRSA 1980; Fellow, City of London Poly., 1985. *Recreations:* reading, music. *Address:* 45 Gordon Avenue, Stanmore, Mddx HA7 3QQ. *Club:* City Livery.

WOLLASTON, Henry Woods; Standing Counsel to General Synod of the Church of England, 1981–83; *b* 14 Nov. 1916; *s* of Sir Gerald Woods Wollaston, KCB, KCVO; *m* 1944, Daphne Margaret Clark; one *s* two *d. Educ:* Harrow School; Cambridge Univ. (MA). Barrister-at-law. Served War, Captain, Grenadier Guards, 1940–46. Legal Adviser's Branch, Home Office, 1946; Principal Asst Legal Adviser, 1977–80. Master of the Haberdashers' Company, 1974–75. *Publications:* Jervis on Coroners, 9th edn, 1957; Court of Appeal, 1968; Parker's Conduct of Parliamentary Elections, 1970; Halsbury's Laws of England: 3rd edn, titles, Coroners, Elections, Police; 4th edn, title Elections; British Official Medals for Coronations and Jubilees, 1978. *Recreations:* real tennis, lawn tennis. *Address:* 2 Ashtead House, Ashtead, Surrey KT21 1LU.

WOLLHEIM, Prof. Richard Arthur, FBA 1972; Visiting Mills Professor, University of California, Berkeley, since 1985; Emeritus Grote Professor in the University of London; *b* 5 May 1923; *s* of Eric Wollheim; *m* 1st, 1950, Anne, *yr d* of Lieutenant-Colonel E. G. H. Powell (marr. diss. 1967); two *s*; 2nd, 1969, Mary Day, *er d* of Robert S. Lanier, NYC; one *d. Educ:* Westminster School; Balliol College, Oxford (MA). Served in the Army, N Europe, 1942–45 (POW during Aug. 1944). Assistant Lecturer in Philosophy, University College, London, 1949; Lecturer, 1951; Reader, 1960; Grote Prof. of Philosophy of Mind and Logic in Univ. of London, 1963–82; Prof. of Philosophy, Columbia Univ., 1982–85. Visiting Professor: Columbia Univ., 1959–60, 1970; Visva-Bharati Univ., Santiniketan, India, 1968; Univ. of Minnesota, 1972; Graduate Centre, City Univ. of NY, 1975; Univ. of California, Berkeley, 1981; Harvard Univ., 1982. Power Lectr, Univ. of Sydney, 1972; Leslie Stephen Lectr, Univ. of Cambridge, 1979; William James Lectr, Harvard Univ., 1982; Andrew W. Mellon Lectr, Nat. Gall., Washington, 1984. Pres., Aristotelian Soc., 1967–68; Vice-Pres., British Soc. of Aesthetics, 1969–. Mem., American Acad. of Arts and Scis, 1986. Hon. Affiliate, British Psychoanalytical Soc. *Publications:* F. H. Bradley, 1959, rev. edn 1969; Socialism and Culture, 1961; On Drawing an Object (Inaugural Lecture), 1965; Art and its Objects, 1968, 2nd edn with suppl. essays, 1980; A Family Romance (fiction), 1969; Freud, 1971; On Art and the Mind (essays and lectures), 1973; The Good Self and the Bad Self (Dawes Hicks lecture), 1976; The Sheep and the Ceremony (Leslie Stephen lecture), 1979; The Thread of Life, 1984; Painting as an Art, 1987; edited: F. H. Bradley, Ethical Studies, 1961; Hume on Religion, 1963; F. H. Bradley, Appearance and Reality, 1968; Adrian Stokes, selected writings, 1972; Freud, a collection of critical essays, 1974; J. S. Mill, Three Essays, 1975; (with Jim Hopkins) Philosophical Essays on Freud, 1982; articles in anthologies, philosophical and literary jls. *Address:* 20 Ashchurch Park Villas, W12.

WOLMER, Viscount; William Lewis Palmer; *b* 1 Sept. 1971; *s* and *heir* of 4th Earl of Selborne, *qv*.

WOLPE, Berthold Ludwig, OBE 1983; RDI 1959; graphic designer and teacher; *b* 29 Oct. 1905; *s* of Simon Wolpe and Agathe (*née* Goldschmidt); *m* 1941, Margaret Leslie Smith; two *s* two *d. Educ:* studied lettering and graphic design under Rudolf Koch, Offenbach Art Sch., 1924–27; goldsmith work under Theodor Wende, Pforzheim Art Sch., 1928. Assistant to Rudolf Koch, 1929–34; Teacher at Frankfurt Art Sch., 1930–33; worked with Ernest Ingham, Fanfare Press, London, 1935–40; joined Faber & Faber, designing and decorating books, book jackets and bindings, 1941; taught at Camberwell School of Art, 1949–53; Tutor, 1956–65, Vis. Lectr, 1965–75, Royal College of Art; teaching at City & Guilds of London Sch. of Art, 1975–. Lyell Reader in Bibliography, Oxford Univ., 1981–82. Designed printing types: Hyperion, Albertus, Tempest, Sachsenwald, Pegasus, Decorata. Retrospective exhibitions: V&A Mus., 1980; Nat. Library of Scotland, Edinburgh, 1982; Klingspor Mus., Offenbach, 1983. Hon. Member: Double Crown Club; Soc. of Scribes and Illuminators, 1977; Bund Deutscher Buchkuenstler, 1982; Vice-Pres., Printing Historical Soc., 1977; Hon. Fellow, Soc. of Designer-Craftsmen, 1984. Dr *hc* RCA 1968. Frederic W. Goudy Award, Rochester Inst. of Tech., New York, 1982; Silver Medal, Town of Offenbach, 1983; Ehrenurkunde, Maximilian Gesellschaft, Hamburg, 1985. *Publications:* Schriftvorlagen, 1934; (jtly) ABC Buechlein, 1934, 2nd edn 1977; Handwerkerzeichen, 1936; Marken und Schmuckstuecke, 1937; Fanfare Ornaments, 1938; A Newe Booke of Copies 1574, 1959, 2nd edn 1961; (jtly) Renaissance Handwriting, 1960; Vincent Figgins Type Specimens 1801 and 1815, 1967; Freedom of the Press: Broadsides, 1969; Steingruber Architectural Alphabet, 1972. *Recreations:* collecting material for studies of history of craftsmanship, of printing and calligraphy. *Address:* 140 Kennington Park Road, Lambeth, SE11 4DJ. *T:* 01–735 7450.

WOLPERT, Prof. Lewis, DIC, PhD; FRS 1980; Professor of Biology and Head of Department of Anatomy and Biology as Applied to Medicine (formerly Department of Biology as Applied to Medicine), Middlesex Hospital Medical School, since 1966; *b* 19 Oct. 1929; *s* of William and Sarah Wolpert; *m* 1961; two *s* two *d. Educ:* King Edward's Sch., Johannesburg; Univ. of Witwatersrand (BScEng); Imperial Coll., London (DIC); King's Coll., London (PhD). Personal Asst to Director of Building Research Inst., S African Council for Scientific and Industrial Research, 1951–52; Engineer, Israel Water Planning Dept, 1953–54; King's College, London: Asst Lectr in Zoology, 1958–60; Lectr in Zoology, 1960–64; Reader in Zoology, 1964–66. Chairman: Cell Board, MRC, 1984–; Scientific Inf. Cttee, Royal Soc., 1983–; President: British Soc. for Cell Biology, 1985–; Inst. of Information Scientists, 1986–87. Lectures: Steinhaus, Univ. of California at Irvine, 1980; van der Horst, Univ. of Witwatersrand, Johannesburg, 1981; Bidder, Soc. for Experimental Biology, Leicester, 1982; Swirling, Dana-Faber, Boston, 1985; Lloyd-Roberts, RCP, 1986. Hon. MRCP. Scientific Medal, Zoological Soc., 1968. *Publications:* articles on cell and developmental biology in scientific jls. *Recreation:* tennis. *Address:* Department of Anatomy and Biology as Applied to Medicine, Middlesex Hospital Medical School, Cleveland Street, W1P 6DB.

WOLRIGE-GORDON, Patrick; *b* 10 Aug. 1935; *s* of late Captain Robert Wolrige-Gordon, MC and Joan Wolrige-Gordon; *m* 1962, Anne, *o d* of late Peter D. Howard and Mrs Howard; one *s* two *d. Educ:* Eton; New College, Oxford. MP (C) Aberdeenshire East, Nov. 1958–Feb. 1974. Liveryman Worshipful Company of Wheelwrights, 1966. *Recreations:* reading, walking, music. *Address:* Ythan Lodge, Newburgh, Aberdeenshire. *Club:* Royal Over-Seas League.

See also John MacLeod of MacLeod.

WOLSELEY, Sir Charles Garnet Richard Mark, 11th Bt, *cr* 1628; Partner, Smiths Gore, Chartered Surveyors, since 1979 (Associate Partner, 1974); *b* 16 June 1944; *s* of Capt. Stephen Garnet Hubert Francis Wolseley, Royal Artillery (*d* 1944, of wounds received in action), and of Pamela, *yr d* of late Capt. F. Barry and Mrs Lavinia Power, Wolseley Park, Rugeley, Staffs; *S* grandfather, Sir Edric Charles Joseph Wolseley, 10th Bt, 1954; *m* 1st, 1968, Anita Maria (marr. diss. 1984), *er d* of late H. J. Fried, Epsom, Surrey; one *s* three *d*; 2nd, 1984, Mrs Imogene Brown. *Educ:* St Bede's School, near Stafford; Ampleforth College, York. FRICS. *Recreations:* shooting, fishing, gardening. *Heir: s* Stephen Garnet Hugo Charles Wolseley, *b* 2 May 1980. *Address:* Wolseley Park, Rugeley, Staffs. *T:* Rugeley 2346; North End, Easton, Winchester, Hants. *T:* Itchen Abbas 212. *Clubs:* Farmers'; English XX Rifle (Bisley Camp, Brookwood).

WOLSELEY, Sir Garnet, 12th Bt, *cr* 1744–45 (Ireland); emigrated to Ontario, Canada, 1951; *b* 27 May 1915; *s* of late Richard Bingham and Mary Alexandra Wolseley; *S* cousin (Rev. Sir William Augustus Wolseley), 1950; *m* 1950, Lillian Mary, *d* of late William Bertram Ellison, Wallasey. *Educ:* New Brighton Secondary Sch. Served War of 1939–45, Northants Regt, Madagascar, Sicily, Italy and Germany. Boot Repairer Manager, 1946. *Address:* 73 Dorothy Street, Brantford, Ontario, Canada. *T:* 753–7957.

WOLSTENCROFT, Alan, CB 1961; Director, National Counties Building Society (Chairman, 1979–84); *b* 18 Oct. 1914; *yr s* of late Walter and Bertha Wolstencroft; *m* 1951, Ellen, *d* of late W. Tomlinson. *Educ:* Lancaster Royal Grammar Sch.; Caius Coll., Cambridge (MA 1st Cl. Classical Tripos). Assistant Principal, GPO, 1936. Served War of 1939–45: Royal Engineers (Postal Section), France and Middle East. Principal GPO, 1945; Assistant Secretary, GPO, 1949; Secretary, Independent Television Authority, 1954; General Post Office: Director of Personnel, 1955; Director of Postal Services, 1957; Director of Radio Services, 1960–64; Deputy Director General, 1964–67; Man. Dir Posts, 1967, Posts and GIRO, 1968; Adviser on Special Projects to Chm. of Post Office Corporation, 1969–70; Sec. to Post Office, 1970–73; retired. *Address:* Green Court, 161 Long Lane, Tilehurst, Reading RG3 6YW.

WOLSTENHOLME, Sir Gordon (Ethelbert Ward), Kt 1976; OBE (mil.) 1944; MA, MB, BChir; MRCS, FRCP, FIBiol; Harveian Librarian, Royal College of Physicians, since 1979; *b* Sheffield, 28 May 1913; *m* 1st; one *s* two *d*; 2nd; two *d. Educ:* Repton; Corpus Christi Coll., Cambridge; Middlesex Hosp. Med. Sch. Served with RAMC, 1940–47 (OBE); France, UK, ME and Central Mediterranean; specialist and advr in transfusion and resuscitation; OC Gen. Hosp. in Udine and Trieste; Dir, Ciba Foundn, 1949–78. Mem., GMC, 1973–83; Chm., Genetic Manipulation Adv. Gp, 1976–78. Founder Mem. 1954, Treasurer 1955–61, Mem. Exec. Bd 1961–70, UK Cttee for WHO; Organizer and Advr, Haile Selassie I Prize Trust, 1963–74; Advr, La Trinidad Med. Centre, Caracas, 1969–78. Royal Society of Medicine: Hon. Sec. 1964–70; Pres. Library (Sci. Res) Sect., 1968–70; Chm. Working Party on Soc's Future, 1972–73; Pres., 1975–77, 1978; Zoological Society: Scientific Fellow and Vice-Pres.; Member: Finance Cttee, 1962–69; Council, 1962–66, 1967–70, 1976–80; Chm., Nuffield Inst. for Comparative Medicine, 1969–70; Chm. Governors, Inst. for Res. into Mental and Multiple Handicap, 1973–77. Founder Mem. 1950, Hon. Treasurer 1956–69, Renal Assoc. of GB; Chm. Congress Prog. Cttee, 1962–64, Mem. Finance Cttee 1968–72, Internat. Soc. for Endocrinology; Trustee and Mem. Res. Bd, Spastics' Soc., 1963–67; Founder Chm., European Soc. for Clinical Investigation, 1966–67 (Boerhaave Lectr, 1976); Mem. Council 1969–75, Sponsor 1976–, Inst. for Study of Drug Dependence; Dir, Nuffield Foundn Inquiry into Dental Educn, 1978–80; Chm., Dental Res. Strategy Gp, 1986–. Member: Council, Westfield Coll., London Univ., 1965–73; Planning Bd, University College at Buckingham, 1969. Chm., Anglo-Ethiopian Soc., 1967–70. Mem. Ct of Assistants, Soc. of Apothecaries, 1969– (Master, 1979–80; Chm., Faculty of Hist. and Philosophy of Med. and Pharmacy, 1973–75; Visitor, 1975–78); Chm., Skin Diseases Res. Fund, 1980–85. Vis. Prof., UCSD, 1982, 1983, 1984. Dir, IRL Press Ltd, 1980–. Trustee: Foulkes Foundn; Tibble Trust; Lorch Foundn; Trustee, 1978–, Chm. Acad. Bd, St George's Univ. Sch. of Med., Grenada. Mem. Bd, Dahlem Konferenzen. Vice-Pres., ASLIB, 1979–82. Pres., Brit. Soc. Hist. Medicine, 1983–85. Patron, FRAME. Hon. Life Governor, Middlesex Hosp., 1938. Hon. FACP, 1975; Hon. Fellow: Hunterian Soc., 1975 (Orator 1976); Royal Acad. of Med. in Ireland, 1976; European Soc. for Clinical Investigation, 1979; RSocMed, 1982; Faculty of Hist. Med. Pharm., 1982. Hon. Member: Swedish Soc. of Endocrinology, 1955; Soc. of Endocrinology, 1959; Swiss Acad. of Med. Sciences, 1975; Assoc. Med. Argentina, 1977; Internat. Assoc. for Dental Res., 1984; Foreign Mem., Swedish Med. Soc., 1959; Hon. For. Mem., Amer. Acad. of Arts and Scis, 1981. Hon. LLD Cambridge, 1968; Hon. DTech Brunel, 1981; Hon. MD Grenada, 1982. Linnaeus Medal, Royal Swedish Acad. Sci., 1977; Pasteur Medal, Paris, 1982; Gold Medal: Perugia Univ., 1961; (class 1A) Italian Min. of Educn, 1961. Tito Lik, 1945; Chevalier, Légion d'Honneur, 1959; Star of Ethiopia, 1966. *Publications:* (ed) Ciba Foundation vols, 1950–78; Royal College of Physicians: Portraits, vol. I (ed with David Piper), 1964, vol. II (ed with John Kerslake), 1977; (ed with Valerie Luniewska) Munk's Roll, vol. VI, 1982; vol. VII, 1984; (jtly) Portrait of Irish Medicine, 1984. *Recreations:* walking, photography. *Address:* 10 Wimpole Mews, W1M 7TF. *T:* 01–486 3884.

WOLTERS, Very Rev. Conrad Clifton; Chaplain to the Society of St Margaret, 1976–85; Provost Emeritus of Newcastle, since 1976; *b* 3 April 1909; *e s* of Frederick Charles and Gertrude Elizabeth Wolters; *m* 1937, Joyce Cunnold; one *s. Educ:* privately; London College of Divinity; St John's College, Durham. ALCD 1932; LTh 1932; BA 1933; MA 1936. Curate: Christ Church, Gipsy Hill, SE19, 1933–37; Christ Church, Beckenham, 1937–41; Vicar, St Luke's, Wimbledon Park, 1941–49; Rector, Sanderstead, Surrey, 1949–59; Canon of Newcastle, 1959–62; Vicar of Newcastle and Provost of the Cathedral, 1962–76. *Publications:* (ed) Cloud of Unknowing, 1960; (ed) Revelations of Divine Love, 1966; (ed) The Fire of Love, 1971; (ed) The Cloud of Unknowing and Other Works, 1978; (ed) A Study of Wisdom, 1980. *Address:* Flat 1, 7 Chatsworth Gardens, Eastbourne, Sussex BN20 7JP. *T:* Eastbourne 648871.

WOLTERS, Gwyneth Eleanor Mary; a Commissioner of Inland Revenue, 1971–78; *d* of late Prof. and Mrs A. W. Wolters. *Educ:* Abbey Sch., Reading; Reading Univ.; Newnham Coll., Cambridge. Entered Inland Revenue Dept, 1947. *Address:* 45 Albert Road, Caversham, Reading. *T:* Reading 472605.

WOLTON, Harry; QC 1982; a Recorder, since 1985; *b* 1 Jan. 1938; *s* of late Harry William Wolton and Dorothy Beatrice Wolton; *m* 1971, Julie Rosina Josephine Lovell (*née* Mason); three *s. Educ:* King Edward's Sch., Birmingham; Univ. of Birmingham. Called to the Bar, Gray's Inn, 1969. *Recreations:* gardening, family. *Address:* Armscote Farm, Armscote, Stratford upon Avon, Warwickshire CV37 8DQ. *T:* Ilmington 234; 10 St Luke's Street, Chelsea, SW3. *T:* 01–352 5056.

WOLVERHAMPTON, Bishop Suffragan of, since 1985; **Rt. Rev. Christopher John Mayfield;** *b* 18 Dec. 1935; *s* of Dr Roger Bolton Mayfield and Muriel Eileen Mayfield; *m* 1962, Caroline Ann Roberts; two *s* one *d. Educ:* Sedbergh School; Gonville and Caius Coll., Cambridge (MA 1961); Linacre House, Oxford (Dip. Theology). Deacon 1963, priest 1964, Birmingham; Curate of St Martin-in-the-Bull Ring, Birmingham, 1963–67; Lecturer at St Martin's, Birmingham, 1967–71; Chaplain at Children's Hospital, Birmingham, 1967–71; Vicar of Luton, 1971–80 (with East Hyde, 1971–76); RD of Luton, 1974–79; Archdeacon of Bedford, 1979–85. MSc Cranfield, 1984. *Recreations:* marriage, evangelism, walking. *Address:* 61 Richmond Road, Merridale, Wolverhampton WV3 9JH. *T:* Wolverhampton 23008.

WOLVERSON COPE, F(rederick); *see* Cope.

WOLVERTON, 6th Baron *cr* 1869; **John Patrick Riversdale Glyn,** CBE 1974; *b* 17 April 1913; *s* of Maurice G. C. Glyn (*d* 1920) (*g s* of 1st Baron) and Hon. Maud Grosvenor (*d* 1948), *d* of 2nd Baron Ebury; *S* cousin, 1986; *m* 1937, Audrey Margaret Stubbs; two *s* two *d*. *Educ:* Eton; New Coll., Oxford. Major, Grenadier Guards. A Man. Dir, Glyn, Mills & Co., 1950–70; Chairman: John Govett & Co. Ltd, 1970–75; Govett European Trust Ltd, 1972–75; Alexanders Discount Co. Ltd, 1961–81; Yorkshire Bank Ltd, 1970–81; Agricultural Mortgage Corp. Ltd, 1964–82; First National Finance Corp. Ltd, 1975–85 (Dep. Chm. 1974–75). Mem., Develt Commn, 1965–81. FIB 1978. *Recreations:* fishing, shooting. *Heir:* *s* Hon. Christopher Richard Glyn [*b* 5 Oct. 1938; *m* 1st, 1961, Carolyn Jane (marr. diss. 1967), *yr d* of late Antony N. Hunter; two *d*; 2nd, 1975, Mrs Frances S. E. Stuart Black]. *Address:* The Dower House, Chute Standen, near Andover, Hants SP11 9EE. *T:* Chute Standen 228. *Clubs:* Boodle's, Pratt's.

See also H. B. Glyn.

WOMBWELL, Sir George (Philip Frederick), 7th Bt *cr* 1778; *b* 21 May 1949; *s* of Sir (Frederick) Philip (Alfred William) Wombwell, 6th Bt, MBE, and late Ida Elizabeth, *er d* of Frederick J. Leitch; *S* father, 1977; *m* 1974, (Hermione) Jane, *e d* of T. S. Wrightson; one *s* one *d*. *Educ:* Repton. *Heir:* *s* Stephen Philip Henry Wombwell, *b* 12 May 1977. *Address:* Newburgh Priory, Coxwold, York YO6 4AS.

WOMERSLEY, Denis Keith, CBE 1974; HM Diplomatic Service, retired; *b* 21 March 1920; *s* of late Alfred Womersley, Bradford, Yorks, and late Agnes (*née* Keighley); *m* 1955, Eileen Georgina, *d* of late George and Margaret Howe. *Educ:* Christ's Hospital; Caius Coll., Cambridge (Hons, MA). Served War, HM Forces, 1940–46. Entered Foreign (later Diplomatic) Service, 1946; Foreign Office, 1948, Control Commn Germany, 1952; Vienna, 1955; Hong Kong, 1957, FO, 1960; Baghdad, 1962; FO, 1963; Aden, 1966; Beirut, 1967; FCO, 1969–71; Bonn, 1971–74; Counsellor, FCO, 1974–77. FRSA 1976. *Recreations:* violin-playing, photography, Abbeyfield Soc. work. *Club:* Christ's Hospital (Horsham).

WOMERSLEY, J(ohn) Lewis, CBE 1962; RIBA; FRTPI; FRSA; Retired Partner, Hugh Wilson and Lewis Womersley, Chartered Architects and Town Planners (Partner, 1964–77); *b* 12 Dec. 1910; *s* of Norman Womersley and Elizabeth Margaret Lewis; *m* 1936, Jean Roberts; two *s*. *Educ:* Huddersfield College. Asst Architect, private practices in London and Liverpool, 1933–46; Borough Architect and Town Planning Officer, Northampton, 1946–53; City Architect, Sheffield, 1953–64. Past Member Council, RIBA (Vice-President, 1961–62). Member: Central Housing Adv. Cttee, 1956–61, Parker Morris Cttee on Housing Standards, 1958–60, Min. of Housing and Local Govt; North West Econ. Planning Council, 1965–72; Manchester Conservation Areas and Historic Buildings Panel, 1970–77 (Chm., 1974–77); Chm., Manchester's Albert Meml Restoration Appeal Cttee, 1976–78. Works include housing, Manchester Education Precinct Plan, Huddersfield Polytechnic, Develt Plan and Central Services Building, central area redevelopment. RIBA DistTP, 1956. Hon. LLD Sheffield, 1966; Hon. MA Manchester, 1978. *Publication:* Traffic Management in the Lake District National Park, 1972. *Recreations:* reading, gardening. *Address:* 44 St Germains, Bearsden, Glasgow G61 4AB.

WOMERSLEY, Sir Peter (John Walter), 2nd Bt *cr* 1945; Personnel Manager, Beecham Group; *b* 10 November 1941; *s* of Capt. John Womersley (*o s* of 1st Bt; killed in action in Italy, 1944), and of Betty, *d* of Cyril Williams, Elstead, Surrey; *S* grandfather, 1961; *m* 1968, Janet Margaret Grant; two *s* two *d*. *Educ:* Aldro; Charterhouse; RMA, Sandhurst. Entered Royal Military Academy (Regular Army), 1960; Lt, King's Own Royal Border Regt, 1964, retd 1968. *Publication:* (with Neil Grant) Collecting Stamps, 1980. *Heir:* *s* John Gavin Grant Womersley, *b* 7 Dec. 1971. *Address:* Sunnycroft, The Street, Bramber, near Steyning, Sussex.

WONFOR, Andrea Jean; Director of Programmes, Tyne Tees Television Ltd, since 1983; *b* 31 July 1944; *d* of George Duncan and Audrey Joan Player; *m* 1st, 1967, Patrick Masefield (marr. diss. 1973); one *d*; 2nd, 1974, Geoffrey Wonfor; one *d*. *Educ:* Simon Langton Girls School, Canterbury; New Hall, Cambridge (BA). Graduate trainee, Granada Television, 1966–67; Tyne Tees Television: Researcher, 1969; Director, 1973; Head of Children's and Young People's Programmes, 1976. *Recreations:* reading, music. *Address:* Fell Pasture, Ingoe, Matfen, Northumberland. *T:* Stamfordham 487.

WONTNER, Sir Hugh (Walter Kingwell), GBE 1974; Kt 1972; CVO 1969 (MVO 1950); Chairman: Claridge's and the Berkeley Hotels, London, since 1948; Lancaster Hotel, Paris, since 1973; a Director, The Savoy, since 1940 (Chairman, 1948–84; Managing Director, 1941–79); Chairman and Managing Director, The Savoy Theatre, since 1948; Clerk of the Royal Kitchens, since 1953, and a Catering Adviser in the Royal Household, since 1938; Underwriting Member of Lloyd's, since 1937; *b* 22 Oct. 1908; *er s* of Arthur Wontner, actor-manager; *m* 1936, Catherine, *o d* of Lieut T. W. Irvin, Gordon Highlanders (*d* of wounds, France, 1916); two *s* one *d*. *Educ:* Oundle and in France. On staff of London Chamber of Commerce, 1927–33; Asst Sec., Home Cttee, Associated Chambers of Commerce of India and Ceylon, 1930–31; Sec., London Cttee, Burma Chamber of Commerce, 1931; Gen. Sec., Hotels and Restaurants Assoc. of Great Britain, 1933–38; Asst to Sir George Reeves-Smith at The Savoy, 1938–41; Director, The Savoy Hotel Ltd, 1940; Sec., Coronation Accommodation Cttee, 1936–37, Chm., 1953; a British delegate, Internat. Hotel Alliance, 1933–38; Pres., Internat. Hotel Assoc., 1961–64, Mem. of Honour, 1965–. Chairman: Exec. Cttee, British Hotels and Rests Assoc., 1957–60 (Vice-Chm., 1952–57; Vice-Chm. of Council, 1961–68; Chm., London Div., 1949–51); Chm. of Council, British Hotels, Restaurants and Caterers Assoc., 1969–73; London Hotels Information Service, 1952–56; Working Party, Owners of Historic Houses open to the public, 1965–66; Historic Houses Cttee, BTA, 1966–77. Member: Historic Buildings Council, 1968–73; British Heritage Cttee, 1977–; Heritage of London Trust, 1980–; Barbican Centre Cttee, 1979–84; Board of BTA, 1950–69; LCC Consultative Cttee, Hotel and Restaurant Technical School, 1933–38; Court of Assistants, Irish Soc., 1967–68, 1971–73; Vis. Cttee, Holloway Prison, 1963–68. Governor: University Coll. Hosp., 1945–53 (Chm., Nutrition Cttee, 1945–52); Christ's Hosp., 1963–. Trustee: College of Arms Trust; Southwark Cathedral Develt Trust; D'Oyly Carte Opera Trust; Morden Coll., Blackheath; Chm., Temple Bar Trustees; Vice Pres., The Pilgrims. Chm., Eurocard International, 1964–78. Liveryman: Worshipful Co. of Feltmakers, 1934– (Master, 1962–63 and 1973–74); Clockmakers, 1967– (Warden, 1971–; Master, 1975–76); Hon. Liveryman: Worshipful Co. of Launderers', 1970; Plaisterers, 1975; Chancellor, The City Univ., 1973–74; one of HM Lieuts and a JP for the City of London, 1963–80, Chief Magistrate, 1973–74; Freeman of the City, 1934, Alderman for Broad Street Ward, 1963–79, Sheriff, 1970–71; Lord Mayor of London, 1973–74. Hon. Citizen, St Emilion, 1974; Freeman of the Seychelles, 1974. Order of Cisneros, Spain, 1964; Officer, L'Etoile Equatoriale, 1970; Médaille de Vermeil, City of Paris, 1972; Ordre de l'Etoile Civique, 1972; Officier du Mérite Agricole, 1973; Comdr, Nat. Order of the Leopard, Zaire, 1974; Knight Comdr, Order of the Dannebrog, 1974; Order of the Crown of Malaysia, 1974; Knight Comdr, Royal Swedish Order of the Polar Star, 1980. KStJ 1973 (OStJ 1971). Hon. DLitt 1973. *Recreations:* genealogy, acting. *Address:* 1 Savoy Hill, WC2. *T:* 01–836 1533. *Clubs:* Garrick, City Livery.

WOOD, family name of **Earl of Halifax** and **Baron Holderness.**

WOOD, Alan John, CBE 1971; Tan Sri (Malaysia) 1972; Assistant Director, Trade Development, Delaware River Port Authority, World Trade Division, Camden, NJ, USA, since 1983; *b* 16 Feb. 1925; *s* of late Lt-Col Maurice Taylor Wood, MBE; *m* 1950 (marr. diss.); one *s* one *d*; *m* 1978, Marjorie Anne (*née* Bennett). *Educ:* King Edward VI Royal Grammar Sch., Guildford, Surrey, UK. Served Army, 1943–47; demobilised rank Captain. Various exec. and managerial positions with Borneo Motors Ltd, Singapore and Malaya, 1947–64 (Dir, 1964); Dir, Inchcape Bhd, 1968–73, Exec. Dep. Chm. 1973–74; Exec. Vice Pres., Sowers, Lewis, Wood Inc., Old Greenwich, Conn, 1975–78; Gen. Man., India, Singer Sewing Machine Co., 1979–82. Pres., Malaysian Internat. Chamber of Commerce, 1968–72; Chm., Nat. Chambers of Commerce of Malaysia, 1968 and 1972. Panglima Setia Mahkota (Hon.), 1972. *Recreation:* tennis. *Address:* 34 Treaty Drive, Wayne, Pa 19087, USA. *Clubs:* Oriental; Lake, Royal Selangor Golf (Kuala Lumpur); Penang (Penang).

WOOD, Sir Alan Marshall M.; *see* Muir Wood.

WOOD, Alfred Arden, TD 1960; FRIBA, FRTPI; Director of Area Conservation, English Heritage, since 1986 (Chief Architect Planner, 1984–86); *b* 8 Sept. 1926; *s* of late Henry Arden Wood, AMIMechE, and Victoria Wood (*née* Holt); *m* 1957, Dorinda Rae (*née* Hartley); one *s* one *d*. *Educ:* Ashville Coll., Harrogate; Harrogate Grammar Sch.; Hertford Coll., Oxford; Leeds Schs of Architecture and Town Planning. Dip. and Dip. with Dist. Served 8th Royal Tank Regt, Leeds Rifles TA and Westminster Dragoons TA, 1944–62. Architect, Stockholm CC, Harlow New Town, W Riding CC, Leeds CC, Glasgow Corp., partner in private practice, 1951–65; City Planning Officer, Norwich, 1965–72; County Planner, Hereford and Worcester CC, 1972–73; County Architect and Planner, W Midlands CC, 1973–84. Buildings and other works include: housing in Harlow, Leeds and Glasgow, 1953–65; conservation, 1965–72, and first pedestrianisation in UK, Norwich, 1967; conservation, Jewellry Quarter, Birmingham, 1980–84; Birmingham Internat. Airport, 1984. Member: Historic Buildings Council for England, 1969–84; RTPI Council, 1969–75; UK Exec. European Architectural Heritage Year, 1975 (Chm., Heritage Grants Cttee); Preservation Policy Gp, 1967–70; Environmental Bd, 1975–78; Comr, Indep. Transport Commn, 1972–74. Prof., Centre for the Conservation of Historic Towns and Bldgs, Katholieke Univ., Leuven, Belgium, ex Coll. of Europe, Bruges, 1976–; External Examiner at several univs; adviser, at various times, Council of Europe, Strasbourg, and OECD, Paris; lecture tours to N America, 1967, 1976, 1980, 1983, 1985, 1986; conf. addresses in Paris, Rome, Berlin, Amsterdam, Brussels, Zürich, London and elsewhere, 1965–; occasional broadcaster. Civic Trust awards, 1969, 1971. *Publications:* contributions to jls of learned societies. *Recreations:* cities, buildings, travel, railways, music. *Address:* The Hall Barn, Dunley, Worcestershire DY13 0TX; 71 Gloucester Street, Pimlico, SW1V 4EA.

WOOD, Andrew Marley, CMG 1986; HM Diplomatic Service; Ambassador to Yugoslavia, since 1985; *b* 2 Jan. 1940; *s* of Robert George Wood; *m* 1st, 1972, Melanie LeRoy Masset (*d* 1977); one *s*; 2nd, 1978, Stephanie Lee Masset; one *s* one *d*. *Educ:* Ardingly Coll.; King's Coll., Cambridge (MA 1965). Foreign Office, 1961; Moscow, 1964; Washington, 1967; FCO, 1970; seconded to Cabinet Office, 1971; First Sec., FCO, 1973; First Sec. and Hd of Chancery, Belgrade, 1976; Counsellor, 1978; Hd of Chancery, Moscow, 1979; Hd of W European Dept, 1982, Hd of Personnel Operations Dept, 1983, FCO. *Address:* c/o Foreign and Commonwealth Office, SW1A 2AH.

WOOD, Sir Anthony John P.; *see* Page Wood.

WOOD, Anthony Richard; HM Diplomatic Service; Counsellor, Foreign and Commonwealth Office, since 1984; *b* 13 Feb. 1932; *s* of late Rev. T. J. Wood and of Phyllis Margaret (*née* Bold); *m* 1966, Sarah Drew (marr. diss. 1973); one *s* one *d*. *Educ:* St Edward's Sch.; Worcester Coll., Oxford (BA). HM Forces, 1950–52. British Sch. of Archaeology in Iraq, Nimrud, 1956; joined HM Foreign Service, 1957; served: Beirut, 1957; Bahrain, 1958; Paris, 1959; Benghazi, 1962; Aden, 1963; Basra, 1966; Tehran, 1970; Muscat, 1980. *Recreations:* walking, singing. *Address:* c/o Foreign and Commonwealth Office, SW1. *Clubs:* Army and Navy, Royal Green Jackets.

WOOD, Ven. Arnold; Archdeacon of Cornwall and Canon Residentiary (Librarian), Truro Cathedral, since 1981; *b* 24 Oct. 1918; *s* of Harry and Annie Wood; *m* 1945, Dorothy Charlotte Tapper; two *d*. *Educ:* Holy Trinity School, Halifax; London Univ. (Dip. Economics). Commissioned, RASC, 1939–49. Legal Adviser and Man. Director, CMI Engineering Co. Ltd, 1949–63; student, Clifton Theological Coll., 1963–65; Curate, Kirkheaton, W Yorks, 1965–67; Vicar, Mount Pellon, W Yorks, 1967–73; Rector of Lanreath and Vicar of Pelynt, 1973–81; Rural Dean, West Wivelshire, dio. Truro, 1976–81. Warden, Community of the Epiphany, 1985–. Mem., General Synod, 1985–. Gen. Comr of Income Tax, 1977–. *Recreations:* walking, bowls, music. *Address:* Archdeacon's House, 39 Tregolls Road, Truro, Cornwall TR1 1LE. *T:* Truro 72866.

WOOD, Sir (Arthur) Michael, Kt 1985; CBE 1977; Director General, African Medical and Research Foundation, retired; *b* 28 Jan. 1919; *s* of Arthur Henry Wood and Katherine Mary Altham Wood (*née* Cumberlege); *m* 1943, Susan Studd Buxton; two *s* two *d*. *Educ:* Winchester College; London Univ. (MB BS 1944); Middlesex Hosp. Med. School; MRCS, LRCP 1943; FRCS 1946. House Surgeon, Casualty Surgical Officer and Registrar, Middlesex Hosp., 1943–47; training in gen. and plastic surgery; Marks Fellow in Plastic Surgery, 1955; consultant surgeon to Nairobi Hosp., Aga Khan Hosp., Gertrude's Garden Children's Hosp., Kenyatta Nat. Hosp. and Kilimanjaro Christian Med. Centre, at various times, 1950–83. Co-founder, African Med. and Res. Foundn, 1957 (and E African flying doctor services); President: Capricorn Africa Soc., 1959; Assoc. of Surgeons of E Africa, 1971; Chm., Food and Agric. Res. Mission, 1985. Hon. DHL Manhattan Coll., NY, 1985. Bronze Medal, Royal African Soc.; Raoul Wallenberg Humanitarian Award, 1986. *Publications:* The Principles of the Treatment of Trauma, 1962; Go an Extra Mile, 1978; numerous med. papers and articles. *Recreations:* farming, flying, skiing. *Address:* Mbagathi Ridge, Karen, PO Box 24277, Nairobi, Kenya. *T:* 882362. *Clubs:* Royal Commonwealth Society; Muthaiga Country; Aero Club of East Africa.

WOOD, Charles Gerald; FRSL 1984; writer for films, television and the theatre, since 1962; *b* 6 Aug. 1932; *s* of John Edward Wood, actor and Catherine Mae (*née* Harris), actress; *m* 1954, Valerie Elizabeth Newman, actress; one *s* one *d*. *Educ:* King Charles I Sch., Kidderminster; Birmingham Coll. of Art. Corp., 17/21st Lancers, 1950–55; Factory worker, 1955–57; Stage Manager, advertising artist, cartoonist, scenic artist, 1957–59; Bristol Evening Post, 1959–62. Mem. Drama Adv. Panel, South Western Arts, 1972–73. Consultant to Nat. Film Develt Fund, 1980–82. *Wrote plays:* Prisoner and Escort, John Thomas, Spare, (Cockade), Arts Theatre, 1963; Meals on Wheels, Royal Court, 1965; Don't Make Me Laugh, Aldwych, 1966; Fill the Stage with Happy Hours, Nottingham Playhouse, Vaudeville Theatre, 1967; Dingo, Bristol Arts Centre, Royal Court, 1967; H, National Theatre, 1969; Welfare, Liverpool Everyman, 1971; Veterans, Lyceum, Edinburgh, Royal Court, 1972; Jingo, RSC, 1975; Has 'Washington' Legs?, Nat. Theatre, 1978; Red Star, RSC, 1984; Across from the Garden of Allah, Comedy, 1986. *Screenplays include:* The Knack, 1965 (Grand Prix, Cannes; Writers Guild Award for Best Comedy); Help!, 1965; How I Won the War, 1967; The Charge of the Light Brigade, 1968; The

Long Day's Dying, 1969; Cuba, 1980; Wagner, 1983; Red Monarch, 1983; Puccini, 1984; The Battle of the Yarmouk, 1984; Tumbledown, 1985; *adapted*: Bed Sitting Room, 1973. Numerous television plays incl. Prisoner and Escort, Drums Along the Avon, Drill Pig, A Bit of a Holiday, A Bit of an Adventure, Do As I Say, Love Lies Bleeding, Dust to Dust; creator of Gordon Maple in series, Don't Forget to Write; Company of Adventurers (series for CBC), 1986; My Family and Other Animals (series for BBC), 1987. Evening Standard Awards, 1963, 1973. *Publications*: plays: Cockade, 1965; Fill the Stage with Happy Hours, 1967; Dingo, 1967; H, 1970; Veterans, 1972; Has 'Washington' Legs?, 1978. *Recreations*: military and theatrical studies; gardening. *Address*: c/o Fraser and Dunlop Scripts Ltd, 91 Regent Street, W1R 8RU. *Clubs*: Dramatists', British Playwrights' Mafia.

WOOD, Rear-Adm. Christopher Lainson; Director General, Fleet Support Policy and Services, since 1986; *b* 9 Feb. 1936; *s* of Gordon and Eileen Wood; *m* 1962, Margot; two *s* one *d. Educ*: Pangbourne College. MInstAM, MNI; FBIM. Seaman Officer, RN, 1954; joined submarine service, 1958; CO's qualifying course, 1966; in comd, HMS Ambush, 1966–68; JSSC, 1970; nuclear submarine training, 1971; in comd, HMS Warspite, 1971–73; Staff of FO Submarines, 1973–75; Staff of Dir, Naval Op. Requirements, 1975–77; Underwater Weapons Acceptance, 1978–81; Dep. Dir, Naval Op. Requirements, 1981–83; Dir Gen., Underwater Weapons, 1983–85. *Recreations*: music, choral society, fishing, cycling, camping. *Address*: c/o Midland Bank, 55 Victoria Street, Grimsby, South Humberside DN31 1UX. *Club*: Royal Commonwealth Society.

WOOD, Rt. Rev. Clyde Maurice; *see* Northern Territory (Australia), Bishop of the.

WOOD, David; actor, playwright, composer, theatrical producer and director; *b* 21 Feb. 1944; *s* of Richard Edwin Wood and Audrey Adele Wood (*née* Fincham) *m* 1975, Jacqueline Stanbury; two *d. Educ*: Chichester High Sch. for Boys; Worcester Coll., Oxford. BA (Hons). Acted with OUDS and ETC at Oxford; first London appearance in ETC prodn, Hang Down Your Head and Die (also co-writer), Comedy, 1964; later performances include: A Spring Song, Mermaid, 1964; Dr Faustus (OUDS), 1966; Four Degrees Over, Edinburgh Festival and Fortune, 1966 (also contrib. lyrics and sketches); repertory, 1966–69; RSC's After Haggerty, Aldwych 1970, and Criterion 1971; A Voyage Round My Father, Greenwich, 1970, Toronto, 1972; Me Times Me, tour, 1971; Mrs Warren's Profession, 1972, and revue Just the Ticket, 1973; Thorndike, Leatherhead; The Provok'd Wife, Greenwich, 1973; Jeeves, Her Majesty's, 1975; Terra Nova, Chichester, 1980. *Films include*: If . . ., 1968; Aces High, 1975; Sweet William, 1978; North Sea Hijack, 1979. *TV series include*: Mad Jack, Fathers and Sons, Cheri, Disraeli, The Avengers, Van der Valk, Danger UXB, Huntingtower, Enemy at the Door, Jackanory, Jim'll Fix It, When the Boat Comes In, The Brack Report. Various revues in collaboration with John Gould; music and lyrics, The Stiffkey Scandals of 1932, Queen's, 1967; with John Gould formed Whirligig Theatre, touring children's theatre company, 1979; has directed one of own plays on tour and at Sadler's Wells Theatre, annually 1979–; has performed David Wood Magic and Music Show in theatres all over UK, incl. Polka Theatre, Arts Theatre and Purcell Room, 1983–. *TV series scripts*: Chips Comic; Chish 'n' Fips; Seeing and Doing; *screenplay*: Swallows and Amazons, 1974. *Publications*: *musical plays for children*: (with Sheila Ruskin) The Owl and the Pussycat went to see . . ., 1968; (with Sheila Ruskin) Larry the Lamb in Toytown, 1969; The Plotters of Cabbage Patch Corner, 1970; Flibberty and the Penguin, 1971; The Papertown Paperchase, 1972; Hijack over Hygenia, 1973; Old Mother Hubbard, 1975; The Gingerbread Man, 1976; Old Father Time, 1976; (with Tony Hatch and Jackie Trent) Rock Nativity, 1976; Nutcracker Sweet, 1977; Mother Goose's Golden Christmas, 1977; Tickle, 1978; Babes in the Magic Wood, 1978; There Was an Old Woman . . . , 1979; Cinderella, 1979; Aladdin, 1981; (with Dave and Toni Arthur) Robin Hood, 1981; Dick Whittington and Wondercat, 1981; Meg and Mog Show, 1981; The Ideal Gnome Expedition, 1982; Jack and the Giant, 1982; The Selfish Shellfish, 1983; (with ABBA and Don Black) Abbacadabra, 1984; (with Dave and Toni Arthur) Jack the Lad, 1984; (with Peter Pontzen) Dinosaurs and all that Rubbish, 1985; The Seesaw Tree, 1986; The Old Man of Lochnagar (based on book by HRH the Prince of Wales), 1986; various revues; *books for children*: The Gingerbread Man, 1985; (with Geoffrey Beitz): The Operats of Rodent Garden, 1984; The Discorats, 1985; articles in Drama, London Drama. *Recreations*: writing, conjuring, collecting old books. *Address*: c/o Margaret Ramsay Ltd, 14A Goodwin's Court, St Martin's Lane, WC2. *T*: 01–240 0691. *Club*: Green Room.

WOOD, Sir David (Basil) H.; *see* Hill-Wood.

WOOD, Maj.-Gen. Denys Broomfield, CB 1978; Independent Inquiry Inspector, since 1984; General Commissioner for Taxes, since 1986; *b* 2 Nov. 1923; *s* of late Percy Neville Wood and Meryl Broomfield; *m* 1948, Jennifer Nora Page, *d* of late Air Cdre William Morton Page, CBE; one *s* two *d. Educ*: Radley; Pembroke Coll., Cambridge. MA: CEng, FIMechE. Commissioned into REME, 1944; war service in UK and Far East, 1944–47; Staff Captain, WO, 1948–49; Instructor, RMA, Sandhurst, 1949–52; Staff Coll., 1953; DAA&QMG, 11 Infantry Bde, 1955–57; OC, 10 Infantry Workshop, Malaya, 1958–60; jssc 1960; Directing Staff, Staff Coll., 1961–63; Comdr, REME, 3rd Div., 1963–65; Operational Observer, Viet Nam, 1966–67; Col GS, Staff Coll., 1967–69; idc 1970; Dir, Administrative Planning, 1971–73; Dep. Military Sec. (2), 1973–75; Dir of Army Quartering, 1975–78. Exec. Sec., 1978–82, Sec., 1982–84, CEI. Col Comdt, REME, 1978–84. FRSA. *Recreations*: walking, gardening, reading. *Address*: Elmtree House, Hurtmore, Godalming, Surrey. *T*: Godalming 6936. *Club*: Army and Navy.

WOOD, Derek Alexander; QC 1978; a Recorder, since 1985; *b* 14 Oct. 1937; *s* of Alexander Cecil Wood and Rosetta (*née* Lelyveld); *m* 1961, Sally Teresa Clarke, *d* of Lady Elliott and step *d* of Sir Norman Elliott, *qv*; two *d. Educ*: Tiffin Boys' Sch., Kingston-upon-Thames; University Coll., Oxford (MA, BCL). Called to the Bar, Middle Temple, 1964. Dept of the Environment: Mem., Adv. Gp on Commercial Property Develt, 1975–78; Mem., Property Adv. Gp, 1978–; Mem., Working Party on New Forms of Social Ownership and Tenure in Housing, 1976. Dep. Chm., Soc. of Labour Lawyers, 1978–. Mem. Council, London Bor. of Bromley, 1975–78. *Recreation*: music. *Address*: Chatham House, Gosshill Road, Chislehurst, Kent BR7 5NS. *T*: 01–467 8475.

WOOD, Prof. Derek Rawlins, FIBiol; Dean of Faculty of Medicine and Professor of Applied Pharmacology, University of Leeds, 1969–86; *b* 16 May 1921; *s* of Frederick Charles Wood and Ruth Dorothy (*née* Rawlins); *m* 1945, Mary Elizabet Caldwell; two *s* two *d* (and one *s* decd). *Educ*: Wm Hulme's Grammar Sch., Manchester; Brasenose Coll. and Radcliffe Infirmary, Oxford. BM BCh, BSc, MA Oxford. House Physician, Radcliffe Inf., 1945; Demonstrator, Pharmacology, Oxford, 1945–46; Lectr 1946, Sen. Lectr 1952–57, Pharmacology, Univ. of Sheffield; J. H. Hunt Travelling Schol., 1949; J. H. Brown Fellow, Pharmacol., Yale, 1955–56; Associate Prof., Pharmacol., McGill Univ., 1957–60; Prof. and Head of Dept of Pharmacol., Univ. of Leeds, 1960–69. Hon. Sec., 1952–57, Hon. Treas., 1964–70, Brit. Pharmacol. Soc.; Member: Brit. Pharmacopoeia Commn, 1969–79; GMC, 1969–86; Gen. Dental Council, 1971–86; Leeds Reg. Hosp. Bd, 1969–74; Bd of Governors, United Leeds Hosps, 1969–74; Leeds AHA (T), 1974–82; Leeds DHA, West and East, 1982–84. Chairman, University Hosps Assoc., 1978–81.

Mem. Court: Univs of Bradford, 1970–, and Sheffield, 1966–79. Hon. MPS. *Publications*: Dental Pharmacology and Therapeutics (with L. E. Francis), 1961; contribs to Brit. Jl Pharmacol., Jl Physiol., and others. *Recreations*: gardening, music. *Address*: 27 Shire Oak Road, Leeds LS6 2DD. *T*: Leeds 752579.

WOOD, Dudley Ernest; Secretary, Rugby Football Union, since 1986; *b* 18 May 1930; *s* of Ernest Edward and Ethel Louise Wood; *m* 1955, Mary Christina; two *s. Educ*: Luton Grammar School; St Edmund Hall, Oxford (BA Modern Languages). ICI 1954; Petrochemicals and Plastics Division, ICI: Overseas Manager, 1977–82; Sales and Marketing Manager, 1982–86. Rugby Football: Oxford Blue, 1952, 1953; played for Bedford, Rosslyn Park, Waterloo, Streatham-Croydon, East Midlands; Hon. Life Mem., Squash Rackets Assoc., 1984. *Recreations*: Rugby Football, squash, dog breeding (golden retriever), travel, Middle East affairs. *Address*: Rugby Football Union, Twickenham, Middx. *T*: 01–892 8161. *Clubs*: East India, Royal Over-Seas League.

WOOD, Prof. Edward James; Professor of Latin, University of Leeds, 1938–67, Professor Emeritus, 1967; Pro-Vice-Chancellor, University of Leeds, 1957–59; *b* 3 Sept. 1902; *s* of James M. A. Wood, Advocate in Aberdeen; *m* 1933, Marion Grace Chorley; one *s* one *d. Educ*: Aberdeen Grammar School; Aberdeen University; Trinity College, Cambridge. Lectr in Classics, Manchester University, 1928; Professor of Latin, Aberystwyth, 1932. *Publications*: contributions to: Classical Review, Gnomon. *Address*: 35 Barleyfields Road, Wetherby, West Yorks. *T*: Wetherby 62488.

WOOD, Eric; Finance Officer, University of Bristol, since 1979; *b* 22 Sept. 1931; *s* of Herbert Francis and Eva Wood; *m* 1955, Erica Twist; three *d. Educ*: West Hartlepool Grammar Sch.; Blandford Grammar Sch.; St Peter's Coll., Oxford (MA). IPFA. National Service, Army, 1950–51. Finance Depts, Cheshire, Durham and Notts County Councils, 1954–65; Finance Dept, London Transport, 1965–67; Asst Treasurer, GLC, 1967–73; Dir, CIPFA, 1973–79. *Publications*: articles in prof. accountancy press. *Recreations*: skiing, squash. *Address*: 14 Alexandra Road, Clifton, Bristol BS8 2DD. *T*: Bristol 730881.

WOOD, Francis Gordon, FIA; Deputy Chief General Manager, Prudential Assurance Co. Ltd, 1982–85; non-Executive Director, Prudential Corporation, since 1985 (Director, 1984); *b* 30 Oct. 1924; *s* of Francis R. and Florence A. Wood; *m* 1950, Margaret Parr; two *d. Educ*: Alleyne's Grammar School, Stone, Staffs. ACII. Prudential Assurance Co. Ltd, 1941–85; Dir, 1981. *Recreation*: golf. *Address*: 6 Matching Lane, Bishop's Stortford, Herts CM23 2PP. *T*: Bishop's Stortford 52197.

WOOD, Sir Frederick (Ambrose Stuart), Kt 1977; Hon. Life President, Croda International Ltd, since 1987 (Managing Director, 1953–85, Executive Chairman, 1960–85, non-executive Chairman, 1985–86); *b* 30 May 1926; *s* of Alfred Phillip Wood, Goole, Yorkshire, and Patras, Greece, and Charlotte Wood (*née* Barnes), Goole, Yorkshire, and Athens, Greece; *m* 1947, J. R. (Su) King; two *s* one *d. Educ*: Felsted Sch., Essex; Clare Coll., Cambridge. Served War, Sub-Lt (A) Observer, Fleet Air Arm, 1944–47. Trainee Manager, Croda Ltd, 1947–50; Pres., Croda Inc., New York, 1950–53. Chm., Nat. Bus Co., 1972–78. Mem., 1973–78, Chm., 1979–83, NRDC; Chm. NEB, 1981–83; Chm., British Technology Gp, 1981–83. Mem., Nationalised Industries Chms' Gp, 1975–78. Chm. British Sect., Centre Européen d'Entreprise Publique, 1976–78. Hon. LLD Hull, 1983. *Address*: Plaster Hill Farm, Churt, Surrey. *T*: Headley Down 712134. *Club*: Carlton.

WOOD, Prof. Emer. Frederick Lloyd Whitfeld, CMG 1974; Professor Emeritus, Victoria University, 1969; *b* 29 Sept. 1903; *s* of Prof. G. A. Wood and Eleanor Madeline Wood (*née* Whitfeld), Sydney; *m* 1932, Joan Myrtle, *d* of E. L. Walter, Sydney; one *s* one *d* (and one *s* one *d* decd). *Educ*: Sydney Grammar Sch.; Univ. of Sydney (BA); Balliol Coll., Oxford (MA). Univ. Medals History and Philos., Sydney. Frazer Scholar, Univ. of Sydney, 1925; Goldsmith Sen. Student, Oxford, 1929; Lectr in History, Univ. of Sydney, 1930–34; Actg Lectr in History, Balliol Coll., 1929 and 1937; Prof. of History, Victoria Univ., Wellington, NZ, 1935–69. Carnegie Vis. Fellow, Royal Inst. of Internat. Affairs, London, 1952–53. Res. Dir, NZ Inst. of Internat. Affairs, 1974. *Publications*: The Constitutional Development of Australia, 1933; Concise History of Australia, 1935; New Zealand in the World, 1940; Understanding New Zealand, 1944; revised edns as This New Zealand, 1946, 1952 and 1958; The New Zealand People at War, Political and External Affairs, 1958; contrib. NZ Jl of History, DNB. *Recreation*: walking. *Address*: 4 Gladstone Terrace, Wellington, New Zealand. *T*: Wellington 726–818.

WOOD, Maj.-Gen. Harry Stewart, CB 1967; TD 1950; *b* 16 Sept. 1913; *e s* of late Roland and Eva M. Wood; *m* 1939, Joan Gordon, *d* of Gordon S. King; two *s* (and one *s* decd). *Educ*: Nautical Coll., Pangbourne. Civil Engineer (inc. articled trg), 1931–39. Commnd RA (TA), 1937. Served War of 1939–45: Regimental Service, Sept. 1939–June 1944; subseq. Technical Staff. Dep. Dir of Artillery, Min. of Supply (Col), 1958–60; Dep. Dir of Inspection (Brig.), 1960–62; Sen. Mil. Officer, Royal Armament Research and Development Estab. (Brig.), 1962–64; Vice-President, Ordnance Board, 1964–66, President, 1966–67. Maj.-Gen. 1964; retd, 1967. Legion of Merit, degree of Legionnaire (USA), 1947. *Recreations*: home and garden, motor sport. *Address*: Brook House, Faygate, near Horsham, Sussex. *T*: Faygate 342.

WOOD, Sir Henry (Peart), Kt 1967; CBE 1960; Principal, Jordanhill College of Education, Glasgow, 1949–71, retired; *b* 30 Nov. 1908; *s* of T. M. Wood, Bedlington, Northumberland; *m* 1937, Isobel Mary, *d* of W. F. Stamp, Carbis Bay, Cornwall; one *s* two *d. Educ*: Morpeth Grammar Sch.; Durham University. BSc 1930, MSc 1934, Durham; MA 1938, MEd 1941, Manchester. Lecturer, Manchester University, 1937–44; Jordanhill College of Education: Principal Lecturer, 1944–46; Vice-Principal, 1947–49. Part-time Lectr, Glasgow Univ., 1972–78; Assessor in Educn, Strathclyde Univ., 1972–82; Vis. Prof. in Educn, Strathclyde Univ., 1978–84. Hon. LLD: Glasgow, 1972; Strathclyde, 1982. *Address*: 15a Hughenden Court, Hughenden Road, Glasgow G12 9XP. *T*: 041–334 3647.

See also R. F. M. Wood.

WOOD, Humphrey; *see* Wood, J. H. A.

WOOD, Ian Clark, CBE 1982; Chairman since 1981, and Managing Director since 1967, John Wood Group plc; Chairman, J. W. Holdings Ltd, since 1981; *b* 21 July 1942; *s* of John Wood and Margaret (*née* Clark); *m* 1970, Helen Macrae; three *s. Educ*: Aberdeen Univ. (BSc Psychology, First Cl. Hons). Joined John Wood Group, 1964. Board Member: Scottish Develt Agency, 1984–; Sea Fish Industry Authy, 1981–; Member: Aberdeen Harbour Bd; Offshore Energy Technology Bd. CBIM 1983. Hon. LLD Aberdeen, 1984. Queen's Silver Jubilee Medal, 1977. *Recreations*: family, squash, reading. *Address*: Marchmont, 42 Rubislaw Den South, Aberdeen AB2 6BB. *T*: Aberdeen 313625.

WOOD, John; actor. *Educ*: Bedford Sch.; Jesus Coll., Oxford (Pres. OUDS). Old Vic Co., 1954–56; Camino Real, Phoenix, 1957; The Making of Moo, Royal Court, 1957; Brouhaha, Aldwych, 1958; The Fantasticks, Apollo, 1961; Rosencrantz and Guildenstern are Dead, NY, 1967; Exiles, Mermaid, 1970; joined Royal Shakespeare Company, 1971; Enemies, The Man of Mode, Exiles, The Balcony, Aldwych, 1971; The Comedy of

Errors, Stratford, 1972; Julius Caesar, Titus Andronicus, Stratford, 1972, Aldwych, 1973; Collaborators, Duchess, 1973; A Lesson in Blood and Roses, The Place, 1973; Sherlock Holmes, Travesties (Evening Standard Best Actor Award, 1974; Tony Award, 1976), Aldwych, 1974, NY, 1974; The Devil's Disciple, Ivanov, Aldwych, 1976; Death Trap, NY, 1978; Undiscovered Country, Richard III, Nat. Theatre, 1979; Piaf, Wyndham's, 1980; The Provok'd Wife, Nat. Theatre, 1980. Television: A Tale of Two Cities, Barnaby Rudge, 1964–65; The Victorians, 1965; The Duel, 1966. Films: Nicholas and Alexandra, 1971; Slaughterhouse Five, 1972; War Games, 1983. *Address:* c/o Royal Shakespeare Company, Barbican Centre, Silk Street, EC2Y 8DS.

WOOD, John; Deputy Director of Public Prosecutions, since 1985, and Head of Legal Services, Crown Prosecution Service, since 1986; *b* 11 Jan. 1931; *s* of Thomas John Wood and Rebecca Grand; *m* 1958, Jean Iris Wood; two *s*. *Educ:* King's College Sch., Wimbledon. Admitted Solicitor, 1955. Director of Public Prosecutions: Legal Assistant, 1958; Sen. Legal Asst, 1963; Asst Solicitor, 1971; Asst Director, 1977; Principal Asst Dir, 1981. *Recreations:* cricket, badminton, music, theatre. *Address:* 4–12 Queen Anne's Gate, SW1. *T:* 01–213 3661.

WOOD, John Edwin, PhD; Director, British Aerospace, Naval and Electronic Systems Division, Bristol, since 1984; *b* 24 July 1928; *s* of late John Stanley Wood and Alice (*née* Hardy); *m* 1953, Patricia Edith Wilson Sheppard (marr. diss. 1978); two *s* two *d*. *Educ:* Darlington Grammar Sch.; Univ. of Leeds (BSc, PhD). Joined Royal Naval Scientific Service at HM Underwater Countermeasures and Weapons Estabt, 1951; Admiralty Underwater Weapons Estabt, 1959; Head of Acoustic Research Div., 1968; Head of Sonar Dept, 1972; Admiralty Surface Weapons Establishment: Head of Weapons Dept, 1976; Head of Communications, Command and Control Dept, 1979; Chief Scientist (Royal Navy), and Director General Research (A), 1980; joined Sperry Gyroscope (now British Aerospace), Bracknell, 1981. Pres., Gp 12, Council of British Archaeology, 1984–. *Publications:* Sun, Moon and Standing Stones, 1978, 2nd edn 1980; papers and book reviews in technical and archaeological jls. *Recreations:* archaeology, fell-walking. *Address:* 7 Pennant Hills, Bedhampton, Havant, Hants PO9 3JZ. *T:* Havant 471411. *Club:* Civil Service.

WOOD, (John) Humphrey (Askey); Managing Director, Consolidated Gold Fields plc, since 1979; *b* 26 Nov. 1932; *s* of late Lt-Col Edward Askey Wood and Irene Jeanne Askey Wood; *m* 1st, 1965, Jane Holland; one *s*; 2nd, 1981, Katherine Ruth Stewart Reardon (*née* Peverley); one step *s* one step *d*. *Educ:* Abberley Hall; Winchester College; Corpus Christi College, Cambridge. MA (Mech. Scis). De Havilland Aircraft Co. Ltd, 1956; Hawker Siddeley Aviation Ltd, 1964, Dir and Gen. Manager, Manchester, 1969–76; Man. Dir, Industrial and Marine Div., Rolls-Royce Ltd, 1976–79; Chm., Amey Roadstone Corp., 1979–86. Director: Gold Fields of South Africa Ltd, 1986–; Blue Tee Corp., 1986–. Vice-Pres., Nat. Council of Building Material Producers, 1985–. Mem. Council, CBI, 1983–. *Recreations:* fly fishing, sailing, painting. *Address:* 31 Charles II Street, St James's Square, SW1Y 4AG. *T:* 01–930 9677.

WOOD, Hon. Sir John (Kember), Kt 1977; MC 1944; **Hon. Mr Justice Wood;** a Judge of the High Court of Justice, Family Division, since 1977; Judge of Employment Appeals Tribunal, since 1985; *b* 8 Aug. 1922; *s* of John Roskruge Wood and Gladys Frances (*née* Kember); *m* 1952, Kathleen Ann Lowe; one *s* one *d*. *Educ:* Shrewsbury Sch.; Magdalene Coll., Cambridge. Served War of 1939–45: Rifle Brigade, 1941–46; ME and Italy; PoW, 1944. Magdalene Coll., 1946–48. Barrister (Lincoln's Inn), 1949, Bencher, 1977; QC 1969; a Recorder of the Crown Court, 1975–77. Mem., Parole Bd, 1986–. *Recreations:* sport, travel. *Address:* Royal Courts of Justice, WC2. *Clubs:* Garrick, MCC; Hawks (Cambridge).

WOOD, John Laurence; Keeper, Department of Printed Books, British Library, 1966–76; retired; *b* 27 Nov. 1911; *s* of J. A. Wood and Clara Josephine (*née* Ryan); *m* 1947, Rowena Beatrice Ross; one *s* one *d*. *Educ:* Bishop Auckland; Merton Coll., Oxford (BA); Besançon; Paris. Lecteur, Univ. of Besançon, 1934; Asst Cataloguer, British Museum, 1936; seconded to Foreign Office, 1941; Asst Keeper, British Museum, 1946; Deputy Keeper, 1959. Editor, Factotum, 1978–. *Publications:* (trans.) The French Prisoner, Garneray, 1957; (trans.) Contours of the Middle Ages, Genicot, 1967. *Recreation:* bookbinding. *Address:* 88 Hampstead Way, NW11. *T:* 01–455 4395.

WOOD, John Peter; Editor, 1971–86, Consultant Editor, since 1986, Amateur Gardening; *b* 27 March 1925; *s* of Walter Ralph Wood and Henrietta Martin; *m* 1956, Susan Maye White; one *s* one *d*. *Educ:* Grove Park Grammar Sch.; Seale Hayne Agricultural Coll. (NDH and Dip. in Hort., of College). FIHort 1986. Served War, 1943–46. Horticultural studies, 1946–52; Amateur Gardening: Asst Editor, 1952–66; Dep. Editor, 1966–71. *Publications:* Amateur Gardening Handbook—Bulbs, 1957; Amateur Gardening Picture Book—Greenhouse Management, 1959. *Recreations:* gardening, choral singing, sailing. *Address:* 1 Charlton House Court, Charlton Marshall, Blandford, Dorset. *T:* Blandford 54653.

WOOD, Joseph Neville, (Johnnie), CBE 1978; Director General, The General Council of British Shipping, 1975–78; *b* 25 October 1916; *o s* of late Robert Hind Wood and Emily Wood, Durham; *m* 1st, 1944, Elizabeth May (*d* 1959); three *d*; 2nd, 1965, Josephine Samuel (*née* Dane) (*d* 1985); 3rd, 1986, Frances Howarth. *Educ:* Johnston School, Durham; London School of Economics. Entered Civil Service (Board of Trade), 1935; Ministry of War Transport, 1940; jssc 1950; Ministry of Transport: Asst Sec., 1951; Far East Representative, 1952–55; Under-Sec., 1961; Chief of Highway Administration, 1967–68. Joined Chamber of Shipping of the UK, 1968, Dep. Dir, 1970, Dir, 1972–78. Mem., Baltic Exchange, 1968–; Director: Finance for Shipping Ltd, 1978–82; Ship Mortgage Finance Co. Ltd, 1978–83. Mem. Chichester DC, 1979–. Dep. Chm., Shipwrecked Fishermen and Mariners Royal Benevolent Soc., 1983–. FCIT 1976. Freeman, City of London, 1978. Officier, Ordre de Mérite Maritime, 1950. *Recreation:* gardening. *Address:* Barbers Cottage, Heyshott, Midhurst, Sussex. *T:* Midhurst 4282.

WOOD, Kenneth Maynard; consultant; *b* 4 Oct. 1916; *s* of late Frederick Cavendish Wood and Agnes Maynard; *m* Patricia Rose; two *s* two *d* (by previous marriage), and three step *s*. *Educ:* Bromley County School. Cadet, Merchant Navy, 1930–34; electrical and mechanical engineering, 1934–37; started own company radio, television and radar development, 1937–39; sold business and joined RAF, transferred for development of electronic equipment, 1939–46; started Kenwood Manufacturing Co. Ltd, 1946; Managing Director, 1946 until take-over by Thorn Electrical Industries Ltd, 1968; Chm. and Man. Dir, Dawson-Keith Group of Companies, 1972–80; Chm, Hydrotech Systems Ltd. Fellow, Inst. of Ophthalmology. *Recreation:* golf. *Address:* Dellwood Cottage, Wheatsheaf Enclosure, Liphook, Hants. *T:* Liphook 723108.

WOOD, Leonard George, CBE 1978; Director of Parent Board, 1965–80, and Group Director of Music, 1966–78, EMI Ltd; *s* of Leonard George Wood and Miriam (*née* Barnes); *m* 1936, Christine Florence Reason (*d* 1978). *Educ:* Bishopshalt Sch., Hillingdon, Mddx; London Univ. (BCom). Served War, RAF: Sgt, Airfield Controller, 1943; commnd Flying Control Officer, 1944–46. Asst Record Sales Manager, UK, EMI Ltd, 1939, Record Sales Man., 1947; EMI Records Ltd: Gen. Man., 1957; Man. Dir, 1959–66; Chm., 1966–78; EMI Ltd: Gp Divl Dir, 1961; Gp Asst Man. Dir, 1973–77. Internat. Fedn of Producers of Phonograms and Videograms: Chm. Council, 1968–73; Pres., 1973–76; Vice Pres. and Mem. Bd, 1967–81, Emeritus Vice-Pres., 1981–82; Mem. Bd, IFPI (Secretariat) Ltd, 1979–81. Hon. Pres., Brit. Phonographic Industry, 1980– (Chm., 1973–80); Governor, Brit. Inst. of Recorded Sound, 1974–78; Dep. Chm., Phonographic Performance Ltd, 1967–80; Chm., Record Merchandisers Ltd, 1975–81; FRSA 1971–85. *Publication:* paper to RSA on growth and develt of recording industry. *Address:* Lark Rise, 39 Howards Thicket, Gerrards Cross, Bucks SL9 7NT. *T:* Gerrards Cross 884233.

WOOD, Leslie Walter; General Secretary, Union of Construction, Allied Trades and Technicians, 1978–85, retired; Member, TUC General Council, 1979–85; *b* 27 Nov. 1920; *s* of Walter William Wood and Alice Bertha Wood (*née* Clark); *m* 1945 Irene Gladys Emery; two *d*. *Educ:* Birmingham Central Technical Coll.; Ruskin Coll., Oxford. Apprenticed carpenter and joiner, 1935; RAF, 1939–45; Asst Workers' Sec., Cadbury's Works Council, 1948–49; full time employment in Union, 1953–85; Asst Gen. Sec., Amalgamated Soc. of Woodworkers, 1962. Mem. Council, ACAS, 1980–85. *Publication:* A Union to Build (history of Building Trades Unionism), 1979. *Recreations:* golf, swimming, bridge. *Address:* 67 Chestnut Grove, South Croydon, Surrey. *T:* 01–657 7852.

WOOD, Rt. Rev. Mark; *see* Wood, Rt Rev. S. M.

WOOD, Rt. Rev. Maurice Arthur Ponsonby, DSC 1944; MA; RNR; an Hon. Assistant Bishop, Diocese of London, since 1985; *b* 26 Aug. 1916; *o s* of late Arthur Sheppard Wood and of Jane Elspeth Dalzell Wood (*née* Piper); *m* 1st, 1947, Marjorie (*née* Pennell) (*d* 1954); two *s* one *d*; 2nd, 1955, M. Margaret (*née* Sandford); two *s* one *d*. *Educ:* Monkton Combe Sch.; Queens' Coll., Cambridge (MA); Ridley Hall, Cambridge. Curate, St Paul's, Portman Square, 1940–43. Royal Naval Chaplain, 1943–47 (still a Chap. to Commando Assoc.); attached RM Commandos, 1944–46; Chaplain, RNR, 1971. Rector, St Ebbe's, Oxford, 1947–52; Vicar and RD of Islington, and Pres. Islington Clerical Conf., 1952–61; Principal, Oak Hill Theological Coll., Southgate, N14, 1961–71; Prebendary of St Paul's Cathedral, 1969–71; Bishop of Norwich, 1971–85; Abbot of St Benet's, 1971–85. Proctor in Convocation of Canterbury and Mem. House of Clergy and Gen. Synod of Church of England (formerly Church Assembly), 1954–85; Member: Archbishops' Council on Evangelism, 1966–71; Church Comrs' Houses Cttee, 1980–85. Chairman: Theological Colls Principals' Conf., 1970–71; Anglican Council of Boys' Brigade; Norfolk Water Safety Assoc, 1966–71; Norwich RSPCA, 1971–85; The Mansion Trust (India), 1984– (and Trustee); Order of Christian Unity, 1986–; Pres., Hildenborough Hall Christian Conf. Centre, 1970–85; Vice-Pres. Bible Churchmen's Missionary Soc.; Trustee, Mary Whitehouse Trust, 1986–; Council Member: British Atlantic Council, 1985–; Commonwealth Human Ecology Council, 1986–. Governor: Monkton Combe Sch., Bath; Gresham's Sch., Holt, 1971–85; Visitor, Langley Sch., Norfolk. Mission work with Dr Billy Graham in Tokyo, Toronto, Virginia, Osaka, Boston, Amsterdam. Mem., House of Lords, 1975–85. *Publications:* Like a Mighty Army, 1956; Comfort in Sorrow, 1957; Your Suffering, 1959; Christian Stability, 1968; To Everyman's Door, 1968; Into the Way of Peace, 1982; This is our Faith, 1985. *Recreations:* swimming, painting, (still) supporting Norwich City FC. *Address:* 36 Biddulph Mansions, Biddulph Road, W9 1HX. *Club:* Royal Commonwealth Society.

WOOD, Sir Michael; *see* Wood, Sir A. M.

WOOD, Norman, CBE 1965; Director: Co-operative Wholesale Society Ltd, 1942–64; Manchester Ship Canal Co., 1954–64; Associated British Foods Ltd, 1964–75, retired; *b* 2 Oct. 1905; *m* 1st, 1933, Ada Entwisle (*d* 1974); two *s* one *d*; 2nd, 1976, Nita Miller. *Educ:* Bolton Co. Grammar Sch.; Co-operative Coll. Nat. Exec. Co-operative Party, and Central Board of Co-operative Union, 1934; Ministry of Information, 1939; Chocolate and Sugar Confectionery War-time Assoc., 1942; British Tourist and Holidays Board (later BTA), 1947–70 (Dep. Chm., 1964–67); Plunkett Foundation, 1948– (Vice-Pres. 1972–); Cake and Biscuit Alliance, 1948; Wheat Commission, 1950; Domestic Coal Consumers Council, 1950; Coronation Accommodation Cttee, 1952. Member: British and Irish Millers, 1950–64; White Fish Authority, 1959–63; Food Res. Adv. Cttee, 1961–65; DTI Japan Trade Adv. Cttee, 1971–; Exec. Mem., British Food Export Council, 1970–75. Chairman: Food and Drink Cttee, British Week, Toronto, 1967, Tokyo, 1969; Chm., ten Food and Drink Missions to Hong Kong and Japan, 1968–76; Dir, Fedn of Agricl Co-ops (UK) Ltd, 1975–; Mem., Lab Party Study Gp on Export Services and Organisation, 1974; Founder Mem., SDP; Pres., Epsom & Ewell Area Party, SDP. *Recreations:* walking, music. *Address:* 17 Wallace Fields, Epsom, Surrey KT17 3AX. *T:* 01–393 9052. *Club:* Oriental.

WOOD, Peter (Lawrence); theatrical and television director; Associate Director, National Theatre, since 1978; *b* 8 Oct. 1928; *s* of Frank Wood and Lucy Eleanor (*née* Meeson). *Educ:* Taunton School; Downing College, Cambridge. Resident Director, Arts Theatre, 1956–57; The Iceman Cometh, Arts, 1958; The Birthday Party, Lyric, Hammersmith, 1958; Maria Stuart, Old Vic, 1958; As You Like It, Stratford, Canada, 1959; The Private Ear and The Public Eye, Globe, 1962, Morosco, New York, 1963; Carving a Statue, Haymarket, 1964; Poor Richard, Helen Hayes Theatre, New York, 1964; Incident at Vichy, Phœnix, 1966; The Prime of Miss Jean Brodie, Wyndham's, 1966; White Liars, and Black Comedy, 1968; In Search of Gregory (film), 1968–69; Design for Living, Los Angeles, 1971; Jumpers, Burgtheater, Vienna, 1973, Billy Rose Theatre, NY, 1974; Dear Love, Comedy, 1973; Macbeth, LA, 1975; The Mother of Us All (opera), Santa Fé, 1976; Long Day's Journey into Night, LA, 1977; Cosi Fan Tutte, Santa Fé, 1977; She Stoops to Conquer, Burgtheater, Vienna, 1978; Night and Day, Phoenix, 1978, NY, 1979; Il Seraglio, Glyndebourne, 1980; Don Giovanni, Covent Garden, 1981; Macbeth, Staatsoper, Vienna, 1982; The Real Thing, Strand, 1982; Orione (opera), Santa Fé, 1983; Orion, King's Theatre, Edinburgh, 1984; Jumpers, Aldwych, 1985. *Royal Shakespeare Company:* Winter's Tale, 1960; The Devils, 1961; Hamlet, 1961; The Beggar's Opera, 1963; Co-Dir, History Cycle, 1964; Travesties, 1974 (NY, 1975); *National Theatre:* The Master Builder, 1964; Love for Love, 1965 (also Moscow); Jumpers, 1972; The Guardsman, The Double Dealer, 1978; Undiscovered Country, 1979; The Provok'd Wife, 1980; On the Razzle, 1981; The Rivals, 1983; Rough Crossing, 1984; Love for Love, 1985; Dalliance, 1986; The Threepenny Opera, 1986. *Television:* Hamlet, USA, 1970; Long Day's Journey Into Night, USA, 1973; Shakespeare, episode I, ATV, 1976; Double Dealer, Granada, 1980. *Recreations:* swimming, sailing, travelling. *Address:* 11 Warwick Avenue, W9.

WOOD, Ralph; His Honour Judge Wood; a Circuit Judge since 1972; *b* 26 April 1921; *o s* of late Harold and Dorothy Wood, Wilmslow, Cheshire. *Educ:* Wilmslow Prep. Sch.; King's Sch., Macclesfield; Exeter Coll., Oxford. Served War of 1939–45: commissioned Somerset LI, and served in England, India and Manipur, 1941–46. Called to Bar, Gray's Inn, 1948; practised on Northern Circuit; JP Co. Lancs, 1970–; Dep. Chm., Lancashire QS, 1970–71. *Address:* 38 Hawthorn Lane, Wilmslow, Cheshire SK9 5DG. *T:* Wilmslow 522673.

WOOD, (René) Victor; Director: Coalite Group PLC; Sun Life Assurance Society plc; Wemyss Development Co. Ltd; Chandos Insurance Co. Ltd; Colbourne Insurance Co.

Ltd; Alpwood Holdings PLC; PM Associates Ltd; Criterion Holdings Ltd; Chairman, Leonard Grouse Associates Ltd; *b* 1925. *Educ:* Jesus Coll., Oxford (BA). FFA. Chief Exec., 1969–79, Chm. 1974–79, Hill Samuel Insurance and Shipping Holdings Ltd; Chm., Lifeguard Assurance, 1976–84. Vice-Pres., British Insurance Brokers Assoc., 1981–84. *Publications:* (with Michael Pilch): Pension Schemes, 1960; New Trends in Pensions, 1964; Pension Scheme Practice, 1967; Company Pension Schemes, 1971; Managing Pension Schemes, 1974; Pension Schemes, 1979. *Address:* Little Woodbury, Newchapel, near Lingfield, Surrey RH7 6HR. *T:* Lingfield 832054.

WOOD, Prof. Richard Frederick Marshall, RD 1976; FRCSG, FRCS; Professor of Surgery, St Bartholomew's Hospital Medical College, University of London, and Hon. Consultant Surgeon, City and Hackney Health District, since 1984; *b* 6 Jan. 1943; *s* of Sir Henry Peart Wood, *qv*; *m* 1968, Christine Crawford Smith Jamieson; two *s*. *Educ:* Glasgow Acad.; Univ. of Glasgow (MB ChB 1967, MD 1976); MA Oxon 1981. FRCS 1972; FRCSG 1972. Surgeon Lt-Comdr, RNR, 1973–. Jun. surgical appts at Western Infirmary, Glasgow, 1967–74; Lectr and Sen. Lectr in Surgery, Univ. of Leicester, 1974–81; Hon. Consultant Surgeon, Leics AHA, 1977; Clinical Reader in Surgery and Fellow of Green Coll., Oxford Univ., and Hon. Consultant Surgeon, Oxford AHA, 1981–84. Vis. Fellow, Peter Bent Brigham Hosp., Boston, 1980; Hunterian Prof., RCS, 1985. Mem., Management Cttee, UK Transplant Service, 1980–. Sec., Surgical Res. Soc., 1987–. Fellow, Assoc. of Surgeons of GB; Member Editorial Board: British Jl of Surgery; Transplantation. *Publications:* Renal Transplantation: a clinical handbook, 1983; Surgical Aspects of Haemodialysis, 1983; papers and chapters in textbooks on transplantation, and surgical topics. *Recreations:* music, sailing. *Address:* 25 Turney Road, Dulwich, SE21. *T:* 01–670 2658.

WOOD, Rt. Rev. Richard James; *b* 25 Aug. 1920; *s* of Alexander and Irene Wood; *m* 1st, 1946, Elsa Magdalena de Beer (*d* 1969); one *s* one *d* (twins); 2nd, 1972, Cathleen Anne Roark; two *d*. *Educ:* Oldham Hulme Grammar School; Regent St Polytechnic; Wells Theological Coll. Electrical Officer, RAF, then with Ceylon Fire Insurance Assoc. Curate, St Mary's, Calne, 1952–55; Curate, St Mark's Cathedral, George, S Africa, 1955–58; Rector, Christ Church, Beaufort West, 1958–62; Vicar of St Andrew's, Riversdale, 1962–65; Chaplain, S African Defence Force, 1965–68; Asst, St Alban's, E London, 1968; Rector of St John's, Fort Beaufort, 1969–71; Rector of Keetmanshoop, dio. Damaraland, 1971; Priest-in-Charge of Grace Church and St Michael's, Windhoek and Canon of St George's Cathedral, 1972; Vicar Gen. and Suffragan Bishop of Damaraland, 1973–75; expelled by S Africa, 1975; Hon. Asst Bishop of Damaraland, 1976–; Sec. to The Africa Bureau, 1977; Priest-in-Charge of St Mary, Lowgate, Hull, Chaplain to Hull Coll. of Higher Education and Hon. Asst Bishop of York, 1978–79; at St Mark's Theolog. Coll., Dar es Salaam, 1979–83; Interim Rector: St Matthew's, Wheeling, W Virginia, 1983–84; Trinity, Martinsburg, W Virginia, 1984–. Hon. Life Mem., Hull Univ. Student Union. *Recreations:* general home interests.

WOOD, Robert Eric, CBE 1972; Director, City of Leicester Polytechnic, 1969–73; *b* 6 May 1909; *e s* of Robert and Emma Wood; *m* 1935, Beatrice May Skinner (*d* 1983); one *s* one *d*. *Educ:* Birkenhead Inst.; Liverpool Univ. BSc 1st cl. hons, MSc; FInstP. Lectr and Demonstrator, Liverpool Univ., 1930; Lecturer: Borough Road Trng Coll., 1931; Kingston Techn. Coll., 1934; Woolwich Polytechnic, 1939; Head of Physics Dept, Wigan Techn. Coll., 1942; Principal: Grimsby Techn. Coll., 1947; Leicester Regional Coll. of Technology, 1953. Assoc. of Principals of Technical Instns: Hon. Sec., 1960–65; Pres., 1965–66; Chm., Interim Cttee of Polytechnic Directors, 1969–70; Mem. Council, CNAA, 1964–70; Mem., Council for Techn. Educn and Trng in Overseas Countries, 1962–66; Vice-Chm., Nat. Adv. Council on Educn for Industry and Commerce, 1967–72. Hon. FCFI. *Address:* Capler, Peppers Lane, Burton Lazars, Melton Mowbray, Leics. *T:* Melton Mowbray 64576.

WOOD, Robert Noel; Jungian analysis, since 1982, psychotherapy training, since 1984, Westminster Pastoral Foundation; *b* 24 Dec. 1934; *s* of Ernest Clement Wood, CIE and Lucy Eileen Wood; *m* 1962, Sarah Child (marr. diss. 1981); one *s* one *d*. *Educ:* Sherborne Sch.; New Coll., Oxford (BA Hons PPE); LSE (Rockefeller Student; Certif. in Internat. Studies); Certif. in Pastoral Counselling, Westminster Pastoral Foundn, 1985. Nat. Service Commn, RHA, 1953–55. Dep. Res. Dir, Internat. Div., Economist Intelligence Unit Ltd, 1959–65; Inst. of Econs and Statistics, Oxford, 1965–70; Sen. Economist, Min. of Econ. Affairs and Develt Planning, Tanzania, 1966–69; Dir of Studies, Overseas Develt Inst., 1970–74; Adviser to House of Commons Select Cttee on Overseas Develt, 1973–74; Dir, Overseas Develt Inst., 1974–82. Chm., Friends of the Union Chapel, 1983–; Mem., Religious Soc. of Friends (Quakers), 1982–. Gov., Quintin Kynaston Sch., 1974–86. *Publications:* contrib. Bull. Oxford Inst. of Econs and Statistics, ODI Rev. *Recreations:* Victorian artists, listening to music, singing, swimming, Arsenal football club, poetry, Jung. *Address:* 19 Baalbec Road, N5 1QN. *T:* 01–226 4775.

WOOD, Roger L.; *see* Leigh-Wood.

WOOD, Rt. Rev. Roland Arthur; *see* Saskatoon, Bishop of.

WOOD, Prof. Ronald Karslake Starr, FRS; Professor of Plant Pathology, Imperial College, University of London, since 1964; *s* of Percival Thomas Evans Wood and Florence Dix Starr; *m* 1947, Marjorie Schofield; one *s* one *d*. *Educ:* Ferndale Grammar Sch.; Imperial College. Royal Scholar, 1937; Forbes Medal, 1941; Huxley Medal, 1950. Research Asst to Prof. W. Brown, 1941; Directorate of Aircraft Equipment, Min. of Aircraft Production, 1942; London University: Lectr, Imperial Coll., 1947; Reader in Plant Pathology, 1955; Prof. of Plant Pathology, 1964; Head of Dept of Pure and Applied Biol., Imperial Coll., 1981–84. Commonwealth Fund Fellow, 1950; Research Fellow, Connecticut Agric. Experiment Stn, 1957. Mem. Council, British Mycological Soc., 1948; Sec., Assoc. of Applied Biologists; Mem., Parly and Sci. Cttee; Mem., Biological Council, 1949; Consultant, Nat. Fedn of Fruit and Potato Trades, 1955; Mem. council, Inst. of Biology, 1956; Chm., Plant Pathology Cttee, British Mycological Soc.; Mem. Governing Body, Nat. Fruit and Cider Inst., Barnes Memorial Lectr, 1962; Sec., First Internat. Congress of Plant Pathology, 1965; Mem. Governing Body, East Malling Research Stn, 1966 (Vice-Chm.); Pres., Internat. Soc. for Plant Pathology, 1968; Mem., Nat. Cttee for Biology, 1978; Chm., British Nat. Sub-Cttee for Botany, 1978; Dean, RCS, 1975–78. Scientific Dir, NATO Advanced Study Institute, Pugnochiuso, 1970, Sardinia, 1975, Cape Sounion, 1980; Consultant, FAO/UNDP, India, 1976. Fellow, Amer. Phytopathological Soc., 1972; Corres. Mem., Deutsche Phytomedizinische Gesellschaft, 1973. Otto-Appel-Denkmünster, 1978. Thurburn Fellow, Univ. of Sydney, 1979; Sir C. V. Raman Prof., Univ. of Madras, 1980; Regents' Lectr, Univ. of California, 1981. *Publications:* Physiological Plant Pathology, 1967; (ed) Phytotoxins in Plant Diseases, 1972; (ed) Specifity in Plant Diseases, 1976; (ed) Active Defence Mechanisms in Plants, 1981; numerous papers in Annals of Applied Biology, Annals of Botany, Phytopathology, Trans British Mycological Soc. *Recreation:* gardening. *Address:* Pyrford Woods, Pyrford, near Woking, Surrey. *T:* Byfleet 43827.

WOOD, Sir Russell (Dillon), KCVO 1985 (CVO 1979; MVO 1975); VRD 1964; Lt-Comdr, RNR; Deputy Treasurer to the Queen, 1969–85; *b* 16 May 1922; *s* of William G. S. Wood, Whitstable, Kent, and Alice Wood; *m* 1948, Jean Violet Yelwa Davidson, *d* of Alan S. Davidson, Sutton Valence, Kent; one *s* three *d*. *Educ:* King's Sch., Canterbury. Fleet Air Arm Pilot, 1940–46 (despatches twice). Qual. as Chartered Accountant, 1951; financial management career with major public companies, 1951–68. *Recreations:* private flying, sailing, shooting. *Address:* The Old Forge, Dunwich, Suffolk IP17 3DU. *T:* Westleton 595. *Clubs:* Army and Navy; East Anglian Flying, Aldeburgh Yacht.

WOOD, Sam, MSc; Director of Statistics and Business Research, Post Office, 1965–72, retired; *b* 10 Oct. 1911; *m* 1940, Lucy Greenhalgh Whittaker; two *d*. *Educ:* Glossop Grammar School, Derbyshire; University of Manchester. Gaskell Open Scholarship, Derbyshire Major Scholarship, 1929; BSc (1st cl. Hons) Maths; Bishop Harvey Goodwin Research Scholarship, 1932; MSc 1933. Civil Service: GPO, 1933–34; National Assistance Board, 1934–43; Min. of Aircraft Production, 1943–46; Treasury, 1946–50; GPO: Statistician, 1950; Chief Statistician, 1954. *Publications:* articles in Jl of Inst. of Statisticians, British Jl of Industrial Relations. *Address:* Boxhedge House, Astwood Road, Cranfield, Bedford. *T:* Bedford 750392.

WOOD, Rt. Rev. (Stanley) Mark; *see* Ludlow, Bishop Suffragan of.

WOOD, Terence Courtney; HM Diplomatic Service; Visiting Fellow, Center for International Affairs, Harvard University, since 1986; *b* 6 Sept. 1936; *s* of Courtney and Alice Wood; *m* 1st, 1962, Kathleen Mary Jones (marr. diss. 1981); one *s* one *d*; 2nd, 1982, Diana Humphreys-Roberts. *Educ:* King Edward VI Sch., Chelmsford; Trinity Coll., Cambridge. BA Hons 1960. RA, 1955–57 (2nd Lieut). Information Officer, FBI (later CBI), 1963–67; entered HM Diplomatic Service, 1968; Foreign Office, 1968–69; 1st Sec., Rome, 1969–73; FCO, 1973–77; Counsellor (Economic and Commercial), New Delhi, 1977–81; Political Advr and Hd of Chancery, Brit. Mil. Govt, Berlin, 1981–84; Hd of S Asian Dept, FCO, 1984–86. sowc, Royal Naval Coll., Greenwich, 1977. *Recreations:* music, painting. *Address:* c/o Foreign and Commonwealth Office, SW1. *Club:* Travellers'.

WOOD, Rev. Prof. Thomas; D. J. James Professor of Pastoral Theology, St David's University College, Lampeter, 1957–84; Emeritus Professor, University of Wales, 1984; Deputy Principal, St David's University College, 1971–77; Head of Department of Pastoral Theology, 1957–77, of Theology, 1977–83, of Theology and Religious Studies, 1983–84; *b* 30 April 1919; *o s* of Willie Wood and Mabel (*née* Gaffey), Batley, Yorks; *m* 1945, Joan Ashley Pollard (*d* 1984); three *s*. *Educ:* Batley Grammar Sch.; Univ. of Leeds (BA 1st Cl. Hons English 1941; BD 1945; MA with Dist. 1947); Coll. of the Resurrection, Mirfield. Deacon 1943, priest 1944. Asst Curate, St Anne's, Worksop, 1943–47; Sen. Asst Curate, Mansfield Parish Church, 1947–52; Vicar of Seascale, 1952–57. Chm., Ch. in Wales Working Party on Marriage and Divorce, 1972–75. Member: Southwell Dioc. Cttee for Post-ordination Trng, 1948–52; Social and Indust. Commn of Ch. Assembly, 1949–50; Churches' Council on Gambling, 1965–78; Doctrinal Commn of Ch. in Wales, 1969–85; Ch. in Wales Adv. Commn on Ch. and Society, 1973–85. An Ecclesiastical Judge, Provincial Ct of Ch. in Wales, 1976–. Bishop's Selector, CACTM, 1955–66; Select Preacher, Univ. of Cambridge, 1961. *Publications:* English Casuistical Divinity during the Seventeenth Century, 1952; The Pastoral Responsibility of the Church Today, 1958; Five Pastorals, 1961; Some Moral Problems, 1961; Chastity Not Outmoded, 1965; (contrib.) A Dictionary of Christian Ethics, 1967; A New Dictionary of Christian Ethics, 1986; articles and revs in Theol., Ch. Qtly Rev., Jl Theol Studies, Ch. in Wales Qtly, Trivium. *Address:* 26 Manor Park Close, York YO3 6UZ.

WOOD, Timothy John Rogerson; MP (C) Stevenage, since 1983; *b* 13 Aug. 1940; *s* of Thomas Geoffrey Wood and Norah Margaret Annie (*née* Rogerson); *m* 1969, Elizabeth Mary Spencer; one *s* one *d*. *Educ:* King James's Grammar Sch., Knaresborough, Yorks; Manchester Univ. (BSc Maths). Joined Ferranti Ltd as Lectr in Computer Programming, 1962; joined ICT Ltd (later ICL), 1963; subseq. involved in develt of ICL systems software; Sen. Proj. Management Consultant advising on introdn of large computer systems, 1977; Sen. Proj. Manager on application systems, 1981; resigned from ICL, 1983. PPS to Minister for Armed Forces, 1986–. Chm., Wokingham Cons. Assoc., 1980–83; Vice Chairman: National Assoc. of Cons. Graduates, 1975–76; Thames Valley Euro Constituency Council, 1979–83; Member: Bow Gp, 1962– (Mem. Council, 1968–71); Bracknell DC, 1975–83 (Leader, 1976–78); Bd, Bracknell Develt Corp., 1977–82. *Publications:* Bow Group pamphlets on educn, computers in Britain, and the Post Office. *Recreations:* gardening, chess, reading. *Address:* Sylvan Lodge, Millfield Lane, St Ippolyts, Hitchin, Herts SG4 7NH. *T:* Hitchin 36480.

WOOD, Victor; *see* Wood, R. V.

WOOD, Victoria; writer and comedienne; *b* 19 May 1953; *d* of Stanley and Helen Wood; *m* 1980, Geoffrey Durham. *Educ:* Bury Grammar School for Girls; Univ. of Birmingham (BA Drama, Theatre Arts). Performed regularly on television and radio as singer/songwriter, 1974–78. First stage play, Talent, performed at Crucible Th., Sheffield, 1978; TV production of this, broadcast, 1979 (3 National Drama awards, 1980); wrote Good Fun, stage musical, 1980; wrote and performed, TV comedy series: Wood and Walters, 1981–82; Victoria Wood As Seen On TV, 1st series 1985 (Broadcasting Press Guilds Award; BAFTA Awards, best Light Entertainment Programme, best Light Entertainment Performance); 2nd series 1986. Appeared in stage revues, Funny Turns, Duchess Th., 1982, Lucky Bag, Ambassadors, 1984. *Publications:* Victoria Wood Song Book, 1984; Up to you, Porky, 1985. *Recreation:* playing piano. *Address:* c/o Richard Stone, 18–20 York Buildings, WC2N 6JU. *T:* 01–839 6421.

WOOD, Walter; Town Clerk, City of Birmingham, 1972–74; *b* Bolton, 11 Jan. 1914; *s* of Walter Scott Wood; *m* 1939, Hilda Maude, *d* of Albert Forrester; two *s*. *Educ:* Canon Slade Sch., Bolton; Victoria Univ., Manchester (LLB). Served with RAF, 1940–45. Admitted solicitor, 1937 (Daniel Reardon and Clabon prizeman); legal associate member, RTPI, 1948; Asst Solicitor, Bradford, 1937. Swansea, 1939; Dep. Town Clerk, Grimsby, 1947; Principal Asst Solicitor, Sheffield, 1948; Asst Town Clerk, Birmingham, 1952; Dep. Town Clerk, Birmingham, 1960. Panel Inspector, DoE, 1974–85. Governor, Solihull Sch., 1974–84. Pres., Birmingham Law Soc., 1976. Pres., West Midland Rent Assessment Panel, 1980–84. *Recreations:* swimming, philately. *Address:* 43 Sandgate Road, Hall Green, Birmingham B28 0UN. *T:* 021–744 1195.

WOOD, Rt. Rev. Wilfred Denniston; *see* Croydon, Bishop Suffragan of.

WOOD, Sir William (Alan), KCVO 1978; CB 1970; Second Crown Estate Commissioner, 1968–78; Ombudsman, Mirror Group Newspapers, since 1985; Chairman, London and Quadrant Housing Trust, since 1980; *b* 8 Dec. 1916; *m* 1st, 1943, Zoë (*d* 1985), *d* of Rev. Dr D. Frazer-Hurst; two *s* two *d*; 2nd, 1985, Mrs Mary Hall (*née* Cowper). *Educ:* Dulwich Coll.; Corpus Christi Coll., Cambridge (Scholar). Ministry of Home Affairs, N. Ireland, 1939. Lieut, RNVR, 1942–46. Ministry of Town and Country Planning, 1946; Minister's Private Secretary, 1951; Principal Regional Officer (West Midlands), Ministry of Housing and Local Government, 1954; Asst Secretary, 1956; Under-Secretary, 1964–68. Chm. Council, King Alfred Sch., 1966–78, Pres. 1978–. *Address:* 93 Crawford Street, W1H 1AT. *T:* 01–724 0685; Maplewood, 40 Picklers Hill, Abingdon, Oxon OX14 2BB. *T:* Abingdon 20515. *Club:* Athenæum.

WOODALL, Alec; MP (Lab) Hemsworth since Feb. 1974; *b* 20 Sept. 1918; *m* 1950; one *s* one *d. Educ:* South Road Elementary School. Colliery official. PPS to Sec. of State for Trade, 1976–78. *Address:* 2 Grove Terrace, Hemsworth, West Yorkshire WF9 4BQ. *T:* Hemsworth 613897.

WOODALL, Mary, CBE 1959; PhD; DLitt; FSA; FMA; London Adviser to Felton Trust, Melbourne, 1965–75; *b* 6 March 1901. *Educ:* Cheltenham Ladies' Coll.; Somerville Coll., Oxford. Voluntary, British Museum Dept of Prints and Drawings. WRVS Regional Administrator, 1938–42; Temp. Principal, Ministry of Health and Ministry of Supply, 1942–45; Keeper, Dept of Art, 1945–56, Director, 1956–64, City Museum and Art Gallery, Birmingham. Trustee, Nat. Gallery, 1968–76. Fellow of University College, London, 1958. *Publications:* Gainsborough's Landscape Drawings, 1939; Thomas Gainsborough, 1949; The Letters of Thomas Gainsborough, 1962. *Recreations:* travelling, painting. *Club:* University Women's.

WOODBINE PARISH, Sir David (Elmer), Kt 1980; CBE 1964; Chairman, City and Guilds of London Institute, 1967–79, Life Vice-President, 1979; *b* 29 June 1911; *o s* of late Walter Woodbine Parish and Audrey Makins; *m* 1939, Mona Blair McGarel, BA (Arch), ARIBA, *o d* of late Charles McGarel Johnston, Glynn, Co. Antrim; two *d. Educ:* Sandroyd; Eton; Lausanne, Switzerland. Chm. and Man. Dir, Holliday and Greenwood Ltd, 1953–59; Chm., Bovis Ltd, 1959–66; Dep. Chm., Marine and General Mutual Life Assurance Soc., 1976–86 (Dir, 1971–86). Chm., Jt Mission Hosp. Equip. Bd (ECHO), 1973–78. President: London Master Builders Assoc., 1952; Nat. Fedn of Building Trades Employers, 1960; Vice-Pres., Internat. Fedn of European Contractors of Building and Public Works, 1967–71; Member: Regional Adv. Council for Technological Educn, London and Home Counties, 1952–69; Architects Registration Council, 1952–72; Nat. Adv. Council for Educn in Industry and Commerce, 1953–78; BIM Council, 1953–62, Bd of Fellows, 1966–72; Nat. Council for Technological Awards, 1955–61; Bd of Building Educn, 1955–66; Building Res. Bd, 1957–60; Industrial Training Council, 1958–64; Council, British Employers' Confedn, 1959–65; Council Foundn for Management Educn, 1959–65; British Productivity Council, 1961–70 (Chm., Educn and Trng Cttee, 1963–70); Human Sciences Cttee (SRC), 1963–66; Construction Industry Training Bd, 1964–70. Chairman: UK Nat. Cttee, Internat. Apprentice Competition, 1962–70; MPBW Working Party on Res. and Information, 1963; Nat. Examinations Bd for Supervisory Studies, 1964–73; Mem., Nat. Jt Consult. Cttee of Architects, Quantity Surveyors and Builders, 1958–70 (Chm. 1966–68); Chm., Dept of Health and Social Security Cttee of Inquiry on Hosp. Building Maintenance and Minor Capital Works, 1968–70; Member: Court, Russia Co., 1937–84; Court, City Univ., 1967–72; Bd of Governors, The Polytechnic, Regent Street, 1967–70; Court, Polytechnic of Central London, 1970–76; Governing Body, Imperial Coll. of Science and Technology, 1971–81. Vice-Chm., Bd of Governors, St Thomas' Hosp., 1967–74 (Chm., Rebuilding Cttee, 1968–76); Chairman: Council, St Thomas's Hosp. Med. Sch., 1970–82; St Thomas' Dist Educn Adv. Council, 1974–81; Florence Nightingale Museum Trust, 1982–86; Member: Nightingale Fund Council, 1974–84; Bd of Governors, Bethlem Royal Hosp. and Maudsley Hosp., 1975–78; Council of Governors, Utd Medical and Dental Schs of Guy's and St Thomas's Hosps, 1982–85. Chm., Sussex Area, Royal Sch. of Church Music, 1981–85. Master, Clothworkers' Co., 1974–75 (Warden, 1962–64; Chm., Angel Court Develt, 1969–80). Mem. Bd of Governors, Clothworkers' Foundation, 1977–. FCIOB (FIOB 1940); FRSA 1953; CBIM (FBIM 1957). Fellow, Imperial Coll., 1976; Hon. FCGI 1979. Hon. LLD Leeds, 1975. *Publications:* contribs to technical jls concerned with construction. *Recreations:* travel and music. *Address:* The Glebe Barn, Pulborough, West Sussex RH20 2AF. *T:* Pulborough 2613; 5 Lurgan Mansions, Sloane Square, SW1W 8BH. *T:* 01–730 6512. *Club:* Boodle's.

WOODCOCK, Dr George, FRGS; Editor, Canadian Literature, 1959–77; author; *b* 8 May 1912; *s* of Samuel Arthur Woodcock and Margaret Gertrude Woodcock (*née* Lewis); *m* 1949, Ingeborg Hedwig Elisabeth Linzer. *Educ:* Sir William Borlase's Sch., Marlow. Editor, Now, London, 1940–47; freelance writer, 1947–54; Lectr in English, Univ. of Washington, 1954–56; Lectr, Asst Prof. and finally Associate Prof. of English, Univ. of British Columbia, 1956–63; Lectr in Asian Studies, Univ. of British Columbia, 1966–67. At the same time continued writing books and talks; also plays and documentaries for Canadian Broadcasting Corporation. Prepared a series of nine documentary films for CBC, on South Pacific, 1972–73. Hon. LLD: Victoria, 1967; Winnipeg, 1975; Hon. DLitt: Sir George Williams Univ., 1970; Univ. of Ottawa, 1974; Univ. of British Columbia, 1977. John Simon Guggenheim Fellow, 1950; Canadian Govt Overseas Fellow, 1957; Canada Council: Killam Fellow, 1970; Senior Arts Fellow, 1975. Governor-General's Award for Non-Fiction, 1967; Molson Prize, 1973; UBC Medal for Popular Biography, 1973 and 1976. FRSC 1968, FRGS 1971. *Publications:* William Godwin, 1946; The Anarchist Prince, 1950; Proudhon, 1956; To the City of the Dead, 1956; Selected Poems, 1967; Anarchism, 1962; Faces of India, 1964; The Greeks in India, 1966; The Crystal Spirit: a study of George Orwell, 1966; Canada and the Canadians, 1970; Dawn and the Darkest Hour, 1971; Gandhi, 1971; Rejection of Politics, 1972; Herbert Read, 1972; Who Killed the British Empire?, 1974; Gabriel Dumont, 1975; Notes on Visitations, 1975; South Sea Journey, 1976; Peoples of the Coast, 1977; Thomas Merton, Monk and Poet, 1978; Two Plays, 1978; The Canadians, 1980; The World of Canadian Writing, 1980; The George Woodcock Reader, 1980; The Mountain Road, 1981; Confederation Betrayed, 1981; Taking It to the Letter, 1981; Letter to the Past, 1982; Collected Poems, 1983; British Columbia: a celebration, 1983; Orwell's Message, 1984; Strange Bedfellows, 1985; The Walls of India, 1985; The University of British Columbia, 1986; Northern Spring, 1987; Beyond the Blue Mountains, 1987; also many articles. *Recreation:* travel. *Address:* 6429 McCleery Street, Vancouver, BC V6N 1G5, Canada. *T:* 604–266–9393. *Club:* Faculty (Vancouver).

WOODCOCK, Gordon, FCA, CIPFA; County Treasurer of Staffordshire, 1973–83. Served War, Royal Navy, 1942–46. City Treasurer's Dept: Birmingham, 1937–42 and 1946–54; Stoke-on-Trent, 1954–73; City Treasurer of Stoke-on-Trent, 1971–73.

WOODCOCK, John, CBE 1983; QPM 1976; CBIM; HM Inspector of Constabulary, since 1983; *b* 14 Jan. 1932; *s* of late Joseph Woodcock and of Elizabeth May Woodcock (*née* Whiteside); *m* 1953, Kathleen Margaret Abbott; two *s* one *d. Educ:* Preston, Lancs, elementary schs; Preston Technical Coll. Police cadet, Lancashire Constabulary, 1947–50; Army Special Investigation Branch, 1950–52; Constable to Chief Inspector, Lancashire Constabulary, 1952–65; Supt and Chief Supt, Bedfordshire and Luton Constabulary, 1965–68; Asst Chief Constable, 1968–70, Dep. Chief Constable, 1970–74, Gwent Constabulary; Dep. Chief Constable, Devon and Cornwall Constabulary, 1974–78; Chief Constable: N Yorkshire Police, 1978–79; S Wales Constabulary, 1979–83. Intermed. Comd Course, Police Coll., 1965, Sen. Comd Course, 1968; Study, Bavarian Police, 1977; European Discussion Centre, 1977; Internat. Police Course (Lectr), Sicily, Rome, 1978. FBI, Nat. Exec., Washington, 1981. Vice-Pres., Welsh Assoc. of Youth Clubs, 1981–; Chm., South Wales Cttee, Royal Jubilee and Prince's Trusts, 1983–85; Member: Admin. Council, Royal Jubilee Trusts, 1981–85; Prince's Trust Cttee for Wales, 1981–85; Mem., Governing Body, World College of the Atlantic, 1980–85. OStJ 1981; KSG 1984.

Recreations: squash, badminton, walking. *Address:* Home Office, Block A, Government Buildings, Whittington Road, Worcester WR5 2PA. *Clubs:* Special Forces; Hon. Member, Swansea Lions.

WOODCOCK, John Charles; cricket writer; *b* 7 Aug. 1926; *s* of late Rev. Parry John Woodcock and Norah Mabel Woodcock (*née* Hutchinson). *Educ:* Dragon Sch.; St Edward's Sch., Oxford; Trinity Coll., Oxford (MA; OUHC *v* Cambridge, 1946, 1947). Manchester Guardian, 1952–54; Cricket Correspondent to The Times, 1954–, and to Country Life, 1962–; Editor, Wisden Cricketers' Almanack, 1980–86; has covered 29 Test tours, 1950–, to Australia, 13 times, S Africa, W Indies, New Zealand, India and Pakistan. *Publications:* The Ashes, 1956; (with E. W. Swanton) Barclays World of Cricket, 1980, 2nd edn 1986. *Recreations:* the countryside, golf. *Address:* The Curacy, Longparish, near Andover, Hants SP11 6PB. *T:* Longparish 259. *Clubs:* MCC, Flyfishers'; Vincent's (Oxford); St Enodoc Golf.

WOODCOCK, Michael, (Mike), JP; MP (C) Ellesmere Port and Neston, since 1983; *b* 10 April 1943; *s* of Herbert Eric Woodcock and Violet Irene Woodcock; *m* 1969, Carole Ann (*née* Berry); one *s* one *d. Educ:* Queen Elizabeth's Grammar Sch., Mansfield, Notts. Successively: Accountant, Personnel Officer, Management Development Adviser, Head of Small Business Development Unit, Consultant, Vice-Pres. of US Corp., Founder of four UK companies. Underwriting Mem. of Lloyds. Parly Advr, Chamber of Coal Traders. JP Mansfield, Notts, 1971. *Publications:* People at Work, 1975; Unblocking Your Organisation, 1978; Team Development Manual, 1979 (UK and USA); Organisation Development Through Teambuilding, 1981 (UK and USA); The Unblocked Manager, 1982 (UK and USA); 50 Activities for Self Development, 1982 (UK and USA); Manual of Management Development, 1985. *Recreation:* walking. *Address:* House of Commons, SW1. *Clubs:* Farmers', Royal Commonwealth Society.

WOODCOCK, Thomas; Somerset Herald, since 1982; *b* 20 May 1951; *s* of Thomas Woodcock, Hurst Green, Lancs, and Mary, *d* of William Woodcock, Holcombe, Lancs. *Educ:* Eton; University Coll., Durham (BA); Darwin Coll., Cambridge (LLB). Called to Bar, Inner Temple, 1975. Research Assistant to Sir Anthony Wagner, Garter King of Arms, 1975–78; Rouge Croix Pursuivant, 1978–82. *Recreation:* genealogy. *Address:* 47 Regents Park Road, NW1. *T:* 01–722 5166; College of Arms, Queen Victoria Street, EC4. *T:* 01–236 3634. *Club:* Travellers'.

WOODD WALKER, Geoffrey Basil, FRCS; retired as a Consultant Surgeon (West London Hospital, 1930–65); *b* 9 June 1900; *s* of Basil Woodd Walker, MD, and Margaret Jane Routledge; *m* 1932, Ulla Troili; two *s. Educ:* Rugby Sch.; King's Coll., Cambridge; St Mary's Hospital. MA Cambridge; MB, BCh; MRCS, LRCP London; FRCS 1928. *Recreation:* zoology (FZS). *Address:* 33 Lexden Road, Colchester, Essex CO3 3PX. *Club:* Athenæum.

WOODFIELD, Sir Philip (John), KCB 1983 (CB 1974); CBE 1963; Chairman, London and Metropolitan Government Staff Commission, since 1984; Chairman, Irish Soldiers and Sailors Land Trust, 1986; *b* 30 Aug. 1923; *s* of late Ralph Woodfield; *m* 1958, Diana Margaret, *d* of Sydney Herington; three *d. Educ:* Alleyn's Sch., Dulwich; King's Coll., London. Served War of 1939–45: Royal Artillery, 1942–47 (Captain). Entered Home Office, 1950; Asst Private Secretary to Home Secretary, 1952; Federal Government of Nigeria, 1955–57; Home Office, 1957–60; Private Secretary to the Prime Minister, 1961–65; Asst Sec. 1965–67, Asst Under-Sec. of State, 1967–72, Home Office; Deputy Sec., NI Office, 1972–74, Home Office, 1974–81; Perm. Under-Sec. of State, NI Office, 1981–83. Secretary to Commonwealth Immigration Mission, 1965; Secretary to Lord Mountbatten's inquiry into prison security, Nov.-Dec. 1966. *Recreation:* music. *Address:* c/o Lloyds Bank, 6 Pall Mall, SW1. *Clubs:* Garrick, Beefsteak.

WOODFORD, Maj.-Gen. David Milner, CBE 1975; Commandant, Joint Service Defence College, 1984–86, retired; *b* 26 May 1930; *s* of late Major R. M. Woodford, MC, and Marion Rosa Woodford (*née* Gregory); *m* 1959, Mary E. Jones. *Educ:* Prince of Wales Sch., Nairobi; Wadham Coll., Oxford (BA). RCDS, psc and jsdc. National Service, then Regular, 1st Royal Fusiliers, Korea, 1953, then Regtl service, Egypt, Sudan, UK, 1953–55; ADC/GOC Berlin, 1956–58; Adjt 1RF, Gulf, Kenya, 1958–59; Coy Comd 1RF, Malta, Cyprus, Libya, 1959–61; GSO3 Div./Dist, UK, 1962; sc Camberley, 1963; GSO2 MO 1, then MA/VCGS, 1964–66; Coy Comd 1RF, BAOR, UK, Gulf and Oman, 1966–68; GSO1 (DS) Staff Coll., 1968–70; CO 3 RRF, Gibraltar, UK, N Ireland, 1970–72; Col GS NEARELF (Cyprus), 1973–75; Comd 3 Inf. Bde (N Ireland), 1976–77; Dep. Col, RRF, 1976–81; RCDS 1978; D Comd and COS SE Dist, UK, 1979–80; ACGS (Training and Combat Develt), 1981–82; Sen. Army Mem., RCDS, 1982–84. Col RRF, 1982–86. *Recreations:* literary, historical; passionate golfer. *Address:* c/o Regimental Headquarters, The Royal Regiment of Fusiliers, HM Tower of London, EC3N 4AB. *Clubs:* Army and Navy, New Zealand Golf.

WOODFORD, Brigadier Edward Cecil James, CBE 1946; DSO 1943; *b* 1901; *s* of late Major Edward Francis Woodford, York and Lancaster Regt; *m* 1949, Joanne Eileen, *d* of Peter Charles Mayer, Washington, DC, USA; one *s* two *d. Educ:* Bedford Sch.; RMC Sandhurst; Staff Coll., Camberley, 1936–37; Nat. War Coll., USA, 1949. 2nd Lieut, York and Lancaster Regt, 1920. Served War of 1939–45, N Africa, Iraq, Persia, Sicily, Italy, Burma, French Indo-China; Lieut-Colonel, 1942, Brigadier, 1945. Commander, Lubbecke District, BAOR, 1952–55, retired 1955. *Address:* 6457 Cameron Forest Lane, Apt 1-E, Charlotte, NC 28210, USA.

WOODGATE, Joan Mary, CBE 1964; RRC 1959; Matron-in-Chief, Queen Alexandra's RN Nursing Service, 1962–66, retired; *b* 30 Aug. 1912; *d* of Sir Alfred Woodgate, CBE, and Louisa Alice (*née* Digby). *Educ:* Surbiton High Sch., Surrey. Trained at St George's Hospital, 1932–36, Sister, 1937–38; Queen Charlotte's Hospital, 1936. Joined QARNNS, 1938; served Middle East and Far East; HM Hospital Ship, Empire Clyde, 1945–47; HM Hospital Ship, Maine, 1953–54; Principal Matron: RNH Haslar, 1959–61; RNH Malta, 1961–62. OStJ 1959; QHNS, 1962–64. Member, Commonwealth War Graves Commn, 1966–83. *Recreations:* gardening, country pursuits. *Address:* Tiptoe, near Lymington, Hants. *Club:* English-Speaking Union.

WOODHALL, David Massey; Chief Executive, Commission for New Towns, since 1982; *b* 25 Aug. 1934; *s* of Douglas J. D. and Esme Dorothy Woodhall; *m* 1954, Margaret A. Howarth; two *s. Educ:* Bishop Holgate's Sch., Barnsley; Royds Hall, Huddersfield; Henley Administrative Staff Coll. Dip. Leeds Sch. of Architecture and Town Planning, West Riding CC, 1951–60; Cumberland CC, 1960–63; Northamptonshire CC, 1963–82: County Planning Officer, 1971–80; Asst Chief Executive, 1980–82. *Recreations:* motor-racing, fell walking, food and wine. *Address:* 5 Kylestrome House, Cundy Street, SW1W 9JT. *T:* 01–730 0989; 62 Stradbroke Road, Southwold, Suffolk. *T:* Southwold 724494.

WOODHAM, Professor Ronald Ernest; Professor of Music, Reading University, 1951–77; *b* 8 Feb. 1912; *s* of Ernest Victor Woodham, Beckenham, Kent; *m* 1949, Kathleen Isabel, *e d* of P. J. Malone; three *s. Educ:* Sherborne Sch.; Royal College of Music, London; Christ Church, Oxford. BA, DMus; FRCO, ARCM. Assistant Director of Music, Bradfield Coll., 1936. Served in RASC, in Middle East and Italy, 1939–45 (despatches). Acting Director of Music, Bradfield Coll., 1946; Director of Music, Sherborne Sch., 1946; Cramb Lecturer in Music, Glasgow Univ., 1947–51. *Address*: 8 Sutton Gardens, St Peter Street, Winchester, Hants SO23 8HP.

WOODHAMS, Ven. Brian Watson; Archdeacon of Newark, 1965–79, Archdeacon Emeritus since 1980; Hon. Canon of Southwell Minister, 1960–79; Rector of Staunton with Flawborough and Kilvington, 1971–79; *b* 16 Jan. 1911; *s* of Herbert and Florence Osmond Woodhams; *m* 1941, Vera Charlotte White; one *s*. *Educ*: Dover Coll.; Oak Hill Theological Coll.; St John's Coll., University of Durham. LTh 1934, BA 1936, Durham. Deacon, 1936; Priest, 1937. Curate: St Mary Magdalene, Holloway, 1936–39; St James-the-Less, Bethnal Green, 1939–41; Christ Church, New Malden, i/c of St John, New Malden, 1941–43; Vicar: St Mark, Poplar, 1943–45; St James-the-Less, Bethnal Green, 1945–50; St Jude's, Mapperley, Nottingham, 1950–65; Farndon with Thorpe-by-Newark, 1965–71. Proctor in York Convocation, 1955–65. Chairman, Southwell Diocesan Board of Women's Work, 1966–79. *Recreations*: children's and refugee work; joys and problems of retirement; interested in sport (local FA football referee). *Address*:: 2 Lunn Lane, Collingham, Newark, Notts. *T*: Newark 892207.

WOODHOUSE, family name of **Baron Terrington.**

WOODHOUSE, Ven. Andrew Henry, DSC 1945; MA; Archdeacon of Hereford and Canon Residentiary, Hereford Cathedral, since 1982; *b* 30 Jan. 1923; *s* of H. A. Woodhouse, Dental Surgeon, Hanover Square, W1, and Woking, Surrey, and Mrs P. Woodhouse; unmarried. *Educ*: Lancing Coll.; The Queen's Coll., Oxford. MA 1949. Served War, RNVR, 1942–46 (Lieut). Oxford, 1941–42 and 1946–47; Lincoln Theological Coll., 1948–50. Deacon, 1950; Priest, 1951; Curate of All Saints, Poplar, 1950–56; Vicar of St Martin, West Drayton, 1956–70; Rural Dean of Hillingdon, 1967–70; Archdeacon of Ludlow and Rector of Wistanstow, 1970–82. *Recreations*: photography, walking. *Address*: The Archdeacon's House, The Close, Hereford HR1 2NG. *T*: Hereford 272873. *Club*: Naval.

WOODHOUSE, Rt. Hon. Sir (Arthur) Owen, KBE 1981; Kt 1974; DSC 1944; PC 1974; Founding President, Law Commission, New Zealand, since 1986; a Judge of the Supreme Court, New Zealand, 1961–86; a Judge of the Court of Appeal, 1974–86, President of the Court of Appeal, 1981–86; *b* Napier, 18 July 1916; *s* of A. J. Woodhouse: *m* 1940, Margaret Leah Thorp; four *s* two *d*. *Educ*: Napier Boys' High Sch.; Auckland Univ. (LLB). Served War of 1939–45, Lt-Comdr in RNZNVR on secondment to RN; service in MTBs; liaison officer with Yugoslav Partisans, 1943; Asst to Naval Attaché, HM Embassy Belgrade, 1945. Joined Lusk, Willis & Sproule, barristers and solicitors, 1946; Crown Solicitor, Napier, 1953; appointed Judge of Supreme Court, 1961. Chm., Royal Commn on Compensation and Rehabilitation in respect of Personal Injury in NZ, 1966–67, and of inquiry into similar questions in Australia, 1973–74. Hon. LLD: Victoria Univ. of Wellington, 1978; Univ. of York, Toronto, 1981. *Recreations*: music, golf. *Address*: Law Commission, Box 2590, Wellington, New Zealand. *Clubs*: Northern (Auckland); Hawkes Bay (Napier); Wellesley, Wellington (Wellington).

WOODHOUSE, Ven. (Charles) David (Stewart); Archdeacon of Warrington, since 1981; Vicar of St Peter's, Hindley, since 1981; *b* 23 Dec. 1934; *s* of Rev. Hector and Elsie Woodhouse. *Educ*: Silcoates School, Wakefield; Kelham Theological College. Curate of St Wilfrid's, Halton, Leeds, 1959–63; Youth Chaplain, Kirkby Team Ministry, Diocese of Liverpool, 1963–66; Curate of St John's, Pembroke, Bermuda, 1966–69; Asst Gen. Secretary, CEMS, 1969–70; Gen. Sec., 1970–76; Rector of Ideford, Ashcombe and Luton and Domestic Chaplain to Bishop of Exeter, 1976–81. Hon. Canon, Liverpool Cathedral, 1983. *Address*: The Vicarage, Wigan Road, Hindley WN2 3DF. *T*: Wigan 55505.

WOODHOUSE, Hon. (Christopher) Montague, DSO 1943; OBE 1944; MA (Oxon); *b* 11 May 1917; 2nd *s* of 3rd Baron Terrington, KBE; *b* and *heir-pres.* to 4th Baron Terrington, *qv*; *m* 1945, Lady Davina, *d* of 2nd Earl of Lytton, KG, PC, GCSI, GCIE, and *widow* of 5th Earl of Erne; two *s* one *d*. *Educ*: Winchester; New Coll., Oxford (Craven and Hertford Schols, Gaisford Prizeman; Hon. Fellow, 1982). First Cl. Hon. Mods, 1937; First Class Lit. Hum., 1939; MA 1947; Lord Justice Holker Schol. Gray's Inn, 1939; enlisted RA, 1939, commissioned 1940; Colonel, Aug. 1943, in command of Allied Military Mission to Greek Guerillas in German-occupied Greece (despatches twice, DSO, OBE, Officer of Legion of Merit (USA), Commander of Order of the Phoenix, with Swords (Greece)). Served in HM Embassy, Athens, 1945, Tehran, 1951; Secretary-General, Allied Mission for Observing Greek Elections, 1946; worked in industry 1946–48; Asst Secretary, Nuffield Foundation, 1948–50; Foreign Office, 1952; Director-General, RIIA, and Dir. of Studies, 1955–59; MP (C) Oxford, 1959–66 and 1970–Sept. 1974; Parliamentary Secretary, Ministry of Aviation, 1961–62; Joint Under-Secretary of State, Home Office, July 1962–Oct. 1964. Dir, Educn and Training, CBI, 1966–70. President, Classical Assoc., 1968; Chm. Council, RSL, 1977–86. Fellow of Trinity Hall, Cambridge, 1950; Visiting Fellow, Nuffield Coll., Oxford, 1956; Vis. Prof., King's Coll., London, 1978. FRSL 1951. Special Mem., Acad. of Athens, 1980. *Publications*: Apple of Discord, 1948; One Omen, 1950; Dostoievsky, 1951; The Greek War of Independence, 1952; Britain and the Middle East, 1959; British Foreign Policy since the Second World War, 1961; Rhodes (with late J. G. Lockhart), 1963; The New Concert of Nations, 1964; The Battle of Navarino, 1965; Post-War Britain, 1966; The Story of Modern Greece, 1968; The Philhellenes, 1969; Capodistria: the founder of Greek independence, 1973; The Struggle for Greece (1941–1949), 1976; Something Ventured, 1982; Karamanlis: the restorer of Greek democracy, 1982; The Rise and Fall of the Greek Colonels, 1985; Gemistos Plethon: the last of the Hellenes, 1986; numerous articles, translations, broadcasts. *Address*: Willow Cottage, Latimer, Bucks. *T*: Little Chalfont 2627.

WOODHOUSE, Ven. David; *see* Woodhouse, Ven. C. D. S.

WOODHOUSE, Henry, CB 1975; Principal Assistant Solicitor and Head of Transport Branch of Legal Directorate, Departments of the Environment and Transport, until 1978, now retired; *b* 12 July 1913; *s* of Frank and Florence A. Woodhouse, Cradley Heath, Warley, W Midlands; *m* 1941, Eileen Mary, *d* of Harry and Florence C. Roach, Cradley Heath; two *d*. *Educ*: King Edward's Sch., Birmingham; St John's Coll., Oxford (MA). Solicitor, 1938; served in HM Forces, 1940–46: Lt-Col in Legal Div., Control Commn for Germany, 1945–46; entered Treasury Solicitor's Dept, 1946; Asst Treasury Solicitor, 1955–69; Principal Asst Treasury Solicitor, 1969–71; Principal Asst Solicitor, DoE, later Depts of the Environment and Transport, 1972–78. *Publications*: articles in The Conveyancer. *Recreations*: Methodist local preacher, photography, gardening. *Address*: Three Ways, Birchall, Leek, Staffs ST13 5RA. *T*: Leek 372814.

WOODHOUSE, James Stephen; Headmaster, Lancing College, since 1981; *b* 21 May 1933; *s* of late Rt Rev. J. W. Woodhouse, sometime Bishop of Thetford, and late Mrs K. M. Woodhouse; *m* 1957, Sarah, *d* of late Col Hubert Blount, Cley, Norfolk; three *s* one *d*. *Educ*: St Edward's Sch.; St Catharine's Coll., Cambridge. BA (English) Cantab, 1957; MA 1961. Nat. Service, 14th Field Regt RA, 1953. Asst Master, Westminster Sch., 1957; Under Master and Master of the Queen's Scholars, 1963; Headmaster, Rugby Sch., 1967–81. Chairman: NABC Religious Adv. Cttee, 1971–; Bloxham Project, 1972–77;

Head Masters' Conf., 1979; Joint Standing Cttee of HMC, IAPS and GSA, 1981–86; Vice-Chm., E-SU Schoolboy Scholarship Cttee, 1973–77. *Recreations*: sailing, music, hill walking. *Address*: The Old Farmhouse, Lancing College, Lancing, West Sussex BN15 0RW.

WOODHOUSE, Hon. Montague; *see* Woodhouse, Hon. C. M.

WOODHOUSE, Rt. Hon. Sir Owen; *see* Woodhouse, Rt Hon. Sir A. O.

WOODHOUSE, Ven. Samuel Mostyn Forbes; Archdeacon of London and Canon Residentiary of St Paul's, 1967–78, Archdeacon Emeritus and Canon Emeritus, 1978; Archdeacon to Retired Clergy, Bath and Wells, since 1978; Chairman, Retired Clergy Association, since 1980; *b* 28 April 1912; *s* of Rev. Major James D. F. Woodhouse, DSO, and Elsie Noel Woodhouse, Water, Manaton, Devon; *m* 1939, Patricia Daniel; two *s* one *d*. *Educ*: Shrewsbury; Christ Church, Oxford; Wells Theological Coll. BA 1934; MA 1942. Deacon, 1936, Priest, 1937, Diocese of Blackburn; Curate, Lancaster Priory, 1936–39. Chaplain to the Forces (Army), 1939–45 (despatches thrice). Vicar, Holy Trinity, South Shore, Blackpool, 1945–49; Vicar of Leominster, 1949–57; Rural Dean of Leominster, 1956–57; Rector of Bristol City Parish Church (St Stephen's), 1957–67. *Recreations*: painting, architecture. *Address*: Under Copse Cottage, Redhill, Wrington, Bristol BS18 7SH. *T*: Wrington 862711. *Clubs*: Leander; Vincent's (Oxford).

WOODLAND, Austin William, CBE 1975; PhD; FGS; Hon. Professorial Fellow, University College of Swansea and Cardiff, since 1980; *b* Mountain Ash, Mid Glamorgan, 4 April 1914; *er s* of William Austin Woodland and Sarah Jane (*née* Butler); *m* 1939, Nesta Ann Phillips (*d* 1981); one *s* one *d*. *Educ*: Mountain Ash Co. Sch.; University Coll. of Wales, Aberystwyth (BSc Hons Geol., PhD). Lyell Fund, Geol Soc., 1947; FGS 1937. Temp. Asst Lectr in Geol., Manchester Univ., 1937; Demonstrator in Geol., QUB, 1937–39; Geologist, Geol Survey of GB (now incorp. in Inst. of Geol Sciences), 1939; Dist Geologist, 1957–62; Asst Dir (Northern England), 1962–71; Dep. Dir, 1971–75; Director: Inst. of Geol Sciences, 1976–79; Geol Survey of Northern Ireland, 1976–79; Geol Adv. to Minister of Overseas Develt, 1976–79. President: Yorks Geol Soc., 1966–68; Sect. C (Geol.), BAAS, Swansea, 1971 (Mem. Council, 1970–73; Mem. Gen. Cttee, 1973–); Vice-Pres., Geol Soc., 1968–70 (Mem. Council, 1967–70). Sec.-Gen., 6th Internat. Congress of Carboniferous Stratigraphy and Geol., Sheffield, 1967; Geol Adviser, Aberfan Disaster Tribunal, 1966–67. Major, Special Geol Sect., RE (AER), 1948–57. *Publications*: Geology of district around Pontypridd and Maesteg, 1964; (ed) Petroleum and the Continental Shelf of North West Europe, 1975; papers on geol aspects of manganese, coal, water supply, engrg applications. *Recreations*: golf, stamp collecting, gardening. *Address*: 60 Dan-y-Bryn Avenue, Radyr, Cardiff. *T*: Cardiff 843330.

WOODLEY, Ven. Ronald John; Archdeacon of Cleveland, since 1985; *b* 28 Dec. 1925; *s* of John Owen Woodley and Maggie Woodley; *m* 1959, Patricia Kneeshaw; one *s* two *d*. *Educ*: Montagu Road School, Edmonton; St Augustine's Coll., Canterbury; Bishops' Coll., Cheshunt. Deacon 1953, priest 1954; Curate: St Martin, Middlesbrough, 1953–58; Whitby, 1958–61; Curate in Charge 1961–66, and Vicar 1966–71, The Ascension, Middlesbrough; Rector of Stokesley, 1971–85; RD of Stokesley, 1977–84. Canon of York, 1982–. *Recreations*: gardening, walking. *Address*: Park House, Rosehill, Great Ayton, Middlesbrough, Cleveland TS9 6BH. *T*: Great Ayton 723221.

WOODLOCK, Jack Terence; Under-Secretary, Department of Health and Social Security, 1969–79, retired; *b* 10 July 1919; *s* of late James Patrick and Florence Woodlock; *m* 1941, Joan Mary Taylor; three *s* one *d*. *Educ*: Bromley Grammar School. Entered Civil Service, 1936; served in Royal Artillery, 1939–45; Ministry of Health, 1945; Asst Principal 1946; Principal 1950; Principal Private Sec. to Minister, 1958–59; Asst Sec. 1959. *Recreations*: gardening, camping. *Address*: 9 Berens Way, Chislehurst, Kent. *T*: Orpington 22895.

WOODROFFE, Most Rev. George Cuthbert Manning, KBE 1980 (CBE 1973); MA, LTh; *b* 17 May 1918; *s* of James Manning Woodroffe and Evelyn Agatha (*née* Norton); *m* 1947, Aileen Alice Connell; one *s* one *d* (and one *s* decd). *Educ*: Grenada Boys' Secondary School; Codrington Coll., Barbados. Clerk in Civil Service, 1936–41; Codrington Coll. (Univ. of Durham), 1941–44; Deacon 1944; Priest 1945; Asst Priest, St George's Cath., St Vincent, 1944–47; Vicar of St Simon's, Barbados, 1947–50; Rector: St Andrew, 1950–57; St Joseph, 1957–62; St John, 1962–67; Rural Dean of St John, Barbados, 1965–67; Sub-Dean and Rector of St George's Cathedral, St Vincent, Windward Islands, 1967–69; Bishop of Windward Islands, 1969–86; Archbishop of West Indies, 1980–86. Vice-Chm., Anglican Consultative Council, 1974. Chm., Vis. Justices St Vincent Prisons, 1968–76. Mem., Prerogative of Mercy Cttee, St Vincent, 1969–. Member: Bd of Educn, Barbados, 1964–67; National Trust of St Vincent, 1967– (Chm., 1972–82); Council, Univ. of the West Indies, 1980–83; Chm., Bd of Governors, Alleyne Sch., Barbados, 1951–57. Hon. DD Nashotah House, USA, 1980; Hon. LLD Univ. of the West Indies, 1981. *Recreations*: music, driving, detective tales and novels, military band music. *Address*: PO Box 919, Murray Road, St Vincent, West Indies. *T*: St Vincent 809 45 61277. *Club*: Royal Commonwealth Society.

WOODROFFE, Jean Frances, (Mrs J. W. R. Woodroffe), CVO 1953; *b* 22 Feb. 1923; *d* of late Capt. A. V. Hambro; *m* 1st, 1942, Capt. Hon. Vicary Paul Gibbs, Grenadier Guards (killed in action, 1944), *er s* of 4th Baron Aldenham; one *d* (and one *d* decd); 2nd, 1946, Rev. Hon. Andrew Charles Victor Elphinstone (*d* 1975), 2nd *s* of 16th Lord Elphinstone, KT; one *s* (*see* 18th Lord Elphinstone) one *d*; 3rd, 1980, Lt-Col John William Richard Woodroffe. Lady-in-Waiting to the Queen as Princess Elizabeth, 1945; Extra Woman of the Bedchamber to the Queen, 1952–. *Address*: Maryland, Worplesdon, Guildford, Surrey GU3 3RB. *T*: Worplesdon 232629.

WOODROOFE, Sir Ernest (George), Kt 1973; PhD, FInstP, FIChemE; *b* 6 Jan. 1912; *s* of late Ernest George Woodroofe and Ada (*née* Dickinson); *m* 1st, 1938, Margaret Downes (*d* 1961); one *d*; 2nd, 1962, Enid Grace Hutchinson Arnold. *Educ*: Cockburn High Sch.; Leeds Univ. Staff of Loders & Nucoline Ltd, 1935–44; Staff of British Oil & Cake Mills Ltd, 1944–50; Mem., Oil Mills Executive of Unilever Ltd, 1951–55; Director of British Oil & Cake Mills Ltd, 1951–55; Head of Research Division of Unilever Ltd, 1955–61; Director: United Africa Co. Ltd, 1961–63; Unilever NV, 1956–74; Chm., Unilever Ltd, 1970–74 (Dir, 1956–74; Vice-Chm., 1961–70); Trustee, Leverhulme Trust, 1962–82 (Chm., 1974–82). President, International Society for Fat Research, 1962. Member Cttee of Enquiry into the Organisation of Civil Science, 1962–63; a Vice-Pres., Soc. of Chemical Industry, 1963–66; Member: Tropical Products Inst. Cttee, 1964–69; Council for Nat. Academic Awards, 1964–67; Cttee of Award of the Commonwealth Fund, 1965–70; Royal Commn for the Exhbn of 1851, 1968–; British Gas Corp., 1973–81. Director: Schroders Ltd, 1974–; Burton Group Ltd, 1974–83; Guthrie Corp. Ltd, 1974–82. Chairman: Review Body on Doctors' and Dentists' Remuneration, 1975–79; CBI Research Cttee, 1966–69. Governor, London Business Sch., 1970–75 (Dep. Chm., 1973–75). Hon. ACT Liverpool, 1963; Hon. Fellow, University of Manchester Inst. of Science and Technology, 1968; Hon. LLD Leeds, 1968; DUniv Surrey, 1970; Hon. DSc: Cranfield, 1974; Liverpool, 1980. Vis. Fellow, Nuffield Coll., Oxford, 1972–80. Comdr.

Order of Orange Nassau (Netherlands), 1972. *Recreations:* fishing, golf. *Address:* 44 The Street, Puttenham, Surrey. *T:* Guildford 810977. *Club:* Athenæum.

WOODROW, Maj.-Gen. (Albert) John, MBE 1949; *b* 3 June 1919; *s* of late Frederick Henry Woodrow, Portsmouth; *m* 1944, Elizabeth, *d* of late Major Sir John Theodore Prestige, Bourne Park, Bishopsbourne, Kent; two *s* one *d*. *Educ:* Nunthorpe. Commnd Royal Signals, 1940; served War of 1939–45 in NW Europe and Burma (despatches); British Mission to Burma, 1948–49; exchange duty Canada, 1954–56; CO 1 Div. Sigs, 1961–63; British Army Staff, Washington, 1963–65; Comdr Trng Bde Royal Signals, 1965–68; Dir of Public Relations Army, 1968–70; GOC Wales, 1970–73. Col Comdt, Royal Corps of Signals, 1970–77. Dir of Army Security, 1973–78, retired. *Address:* Hookers Green, Bishopsbourne, Canterbury, Kent. *Club:* Army and Navy.

WOODROW, David, CBE 1979; retired solicitor; *b* 16 March 1920; *s* of late Sydney Melson Woodrow and late Edith Constance (*née* Farmer); *m* 1st, 1950, Marie-Armande (marr. diss.), *d* of late Benjamin Barrios, KBE, and late Lady Ovey; two *d*; 2nd, 1983, Mary Miley, *d* of late Rupert Alexander Whitamore and Sally Whitamore. *Educ:* Shrewsbury; Trinity Coll., Oxford (MA). Commnd Royal Artillery, 1940; served SE Asia; POW Java and Japan, 1942–45. Admitted Solicitor, 1949. Chairman: Reading and District HMC, 1966–72; Oxford Regional Hosp. Bd, 1972–74; RHA, 1973–78; NHS Nat. Staff Cttee, Administrative and Clerical Staff, 1975–79. *Recreations:* painting and making and mending things. *Address:* Dobsons, Brightwell-cum-Sotwell, Wallingford, Oxon. *T:* Wallingford 36170. *Club:* Leander (Henley-on-Thames).

WOODROW, Gayford William; HM Diplomatic Service, retired; Consul, Algeciras, 1982–85; *b* 21 Feb. 1922; *s* of William Alexander Woodrow and Charlotte Louise (*née* Ellis); *m* 1946, Janine Suzanne Marcelle Jannot; one *s*. *Educ:* Brockley County School. Served War, RAF, 1941–46. Foreign Office, 1946; Caracas, 1949; Vice Consul: Barcelona, 1952; Panama, 1954; Consul: Cairo, 1960; Alexandria, 1961; First Sec. and Consul, Warsaw, 1962; Consul: Valencia, 1965; Jerusalem, 1969; First Sec., Ottawa, 1976; Consul General, Tangier, 1978–80; Asst, Consular Dept, FCO, 1980–81. *Recreations:* walking, swimming, archaeology, gardening. *Address:* Apartment 3, Pitt House, Chudleigh, Devon TQ13 0EL.

WOODROW, Maj.-Gen. John; *see* Woodrow, A. J.

WOODRUFF, Prof. Alan Waller, CMG 1978; Professor of Medicine, University of Juba, Sudan, since 1981; Wellcome Professor of Clinical Tropical Medicine, London School of Hygiene and Tropical Medicine, 1952–81; Hon. Consultant in Tropical Diseases to: the Army, 1956–81; British Airways, since 1962; *b* 27 June 1916; *s* of late William Henry Woodruff, Sunderland, and Mary Margaret Woodruff; *m* 1946, Mercia Helen, *d* of late Leonard Frederick Arnold, Dorking, and Amy Elizabeth Arnold; two *s* one *d*. *Educ:* Bede Collegiate Sch., Sunderland; Durham Univ. MB, BS 1939, MD 1941, Durham; DTM&H England, 1946; PhD London, 1952; FRCP 1953; FRCPE 1960. House Physician and House Surgeon, Royal Victoria Infirmary, Newcastle upon Tyne, 1939–40; MO and Med. Specialist, RAFVR, 1940–46; Med. Registrar, Royal Victoria Infirmary, Newcastle upon Tyne, 1946–48; Sen. Lectr in Clinical Tropical Medicine, London Sch. of Hygiene and Trop. Medicine, 1948–52; First Asst, 1948–52, Physician, 1952–81, Hosp. for Tropical Diseases, University Coll. Hosp., London; Lectr in Tropical Medicine, Royal Free Hosp. Sch. of Medicine, 1952–81; William Julius Mickle Fellow, Univ. of London, 1959. Lectures: Goulstonian, RCP, 1954; Lettsomian, Med. Soc. of London, 1969; Watson-Smith, RCP, 1970; Halliburton Hume, Newcastle-upon-Tyne, 1981. Orator, Reading Pathological Soc., 1976. Member: WHO Expert Adv. Panel on Parasitic Diseases, 1963–; Med. Cttee of Overseas Develt Administration; Visiting Professor at Universities: Alexandria, 1963; Ain Shams, Cairo, 1964; Baghdad, 1966, 1968, 1971, 1974; Mosul, 1977–79; Basrah, 1973–74; Makerere, 1973; Khartoum, 1974, 1978; Benghazi, 1976–80. Mem., Assoc. of Physicians of GB and Ireland; President: Durham Univ. Soc., 1963–73; Royal Soc. of Tropical Medicine and Hygiene, 1973–75; Medical Soc. of London, 1975–76; Section of History of Medicine, Royal Soc. Med., 1977–. Hon. Mem., Burma Med. Assoc., 1966; Hon. Mem., Société de Pathologie Exotique, Paris; Hon. Associate Mem., Soc. Belge de Médecine Tropicale, 1965; Hon. Mem., Brazilian Soc. of Tropical Medicine. Katherine Bishop Harman Prize, BMA, 1951; Cullen Prize, RCPE, 1982. Hon. RE 1979. Gold Medal of Univ. of Pernambuco, Brazil, 1980. *Publications:* (with S. Bell) A Synopsis of Infectious and Tropical Diseases, 1968; (ed) Alimentary and Haematological Aspects of Tropical Disease, 1970; (ed) Medicine in the Tropics, 1974, 2nd edn 1984; sections in: Paediatrics for the Practitioner (ed Gaisford and Lightwood); Medicine (ed Richardson); contribs to BMJ, Lancet, Trans Royal Soc. Trop. Medicine and Hygiene, W African Med. Jl, E African Med. Jl, Newcastle Med. Jl, Practitioner, Clinical Science, Proc. Nutrition Soc., etc. *Recreation:* engraving. *Address:* 122 Ferndene Road, SE24 0BA. *T:* 01–274 3578; University of Juba, PO Box 82, Juba, Sudan. *Clubs:* Athenæum; Sunderland (Sunderland).

WOODRUFF, Harry Wells, CMG 1966; retired, 1972; *b* 31 Oct. 1912; *s* of Leonard Wells Woodruff and Rosina Woodruff; *m* 1938, Margaret Bradley; one *d*. *Educ:* Reigate Grammar Sch.; London Univ. Trade Comr, Johannesburg, 1946–51; Trade Comr and Economic Adviser to High Commissioner: Salisbury, 1951–55; Kuala Lumpur, 1957–61; Commercial Counsellor, Canberra, 1962–66; Economic Adviser to Foreign Office, 1966–68; Asst Sec., Dept of Trade and Industry (formerly Bd of Trade), 1968–72. *Publication:* (jointly) Economic Development in Rhodesia and Nyasaland, 1955. *Recreation:* painting. *Address:* 387 Sandbanks Road, Poole, Dorset.

WOODRUFF, Prof. Sir Michael (Francis Addison), Kt 1969; FRS 1968; FRCS; DSc, MS (Melbourne); Emeritus Professor of Surgery, University of Edinburgh, and Surgeon, Edinburgh Royal Infirmary, 1957–76; Director, Nuffield Transplantation Surgery Unit, Edinburgh, 1968–76; *b* 3 April 1911; *s* of late Prof. Harold Addison Woodruff and Margaret Ada (*née* Cooper); *m* 1946, Hazel Gwenyth Ashby; two *s* one *d*. *Educ:* Wesley Coll., Melbourne; Queen's Coll., University of Melbourne. MB, BS (Melbourne) 1937, MD 1940, MS 1941; FRCS 1946. Captain, Australian Army Medical Corps, 1940–46. Tutor in Surgery, Univ. of Sheffield, 1946–48; Lecturer in Surgery, Univ. of Aberdeen, 1948–52; Hunterian Prof., RCS, 1952; Travelling Fellow, WHO, 1949; Prof. of Surgery, Univ. of Otago, Dunedin, NZ, 1953–56; Prof. of Surgery, Univ. of Edinburgh, 1957–76. Pres., Transplantation Soc., 1972–74. A Vice-Pres., Royal Soc., 1979. Associé Etranger, Académie de Chirurgie, 1964; Hon. Fellow American Surgical Assoc., 1965; Korrespondierendem Mitglied, Deutsche Gesellschaft für Chirurgie; Hon. FACS 1975; Hon. FRCPE 1982. Lister Medal, 1969; Gold Medal, Soc. of Apothecaries, 1974. *Publications:* (Joint) Deficiency Diseases in Japanese Prison Camps, 1951; Surgery for Dental Students, 1954; Transplantation of Tissues and Organs, 1960; (essays) On Science and Surgery, 1977; The Interaction of Cancer and Host, 1980; articles on surgical topics and on experimental tissue transplantation. *Recreations:* music, sailing. *Address:* The Bield, 506 Lanark Road, Juniper Green, Edinburgh EH14 5DH. *Clubs:* Athenæum; New (Edinburgh); Royal Forth Yacht.

WOODRUFF, Philip; *see* Mason, Philip.

WOODRUFF, William Charles, CBE 1985; FRAeS; *b* 14 Aug. 1921; *s* of late Thomas and Caroline Woodruff; *m* 1946, Ethel May Miles (*d* 1981); one *s* one *d*. *Educ:* St George's, Ramsgate. RAF, 1941–46: Navigator/Observer, 1409 Flight; POW Germany, 1943–45. Seconded Air Min., 1945, and later Min. of Civil Aviation for Air Traffic Control planning; various air traffic control appts at Hurn, Northolt, Southern Centre, Heston and MTCA Hdqrs, 1946–56; Air Traffic Control Officer i/c Heathrow, 1956–62; Sec. of Patch Long-term Air Traffic Control Planning Group, 1960–61; Dep. Dir, 1962–67, Dir, 1967–69, Civil Air Traffic Ops; National Air Traffic Services: Jt Field Comdr, 1969–74; Dep. Controller, 1974–77; Controller, 1977–81. Assessor, Stanstead/Heathrow Airports Public Inquiries, 1981–84. Guild of Air Traffic Control Officers: Clerk, 1952–56; Master, 1956. *Publications:* articles on aviation subjects. *Address:* 25 Chichester Avenue, Ruislip, Mddx.

WOODS, Brian; His Honour Judge Woods; a Circuit Judge, since 1975; *b* 5 Nov. 1928; *yr s* of late E. P. Woods, Woodmancote, Cheltenham; *m* 1957, Margaret, *d* of late F. J. Griffiths, Parkgate, Wirral; three *d*. *Educ:* City of Leicester Boys' Sch.; Nottingham Univ. (LLB 1952). National Service, RAF, 1947–49. Called to the Bar, Gray's Inn, 1955; Midland Circuit; Dep. Chm., Lincs (Lindsey) QS, 1968. Chancellor, Diocese of Leicester, 1977–79; Reader, dio. of Leicester, 1970–79, dio. of Lichfield, 1978–. Member Council: S Mary and S Anne's Sch., Abbots Bromley, 1977–; Ellesmere Coll., 1983–84. Mem., Law Adv. Cttee, Nottingham Univ., 1979–; a Legal Mem., Trent Region Mental Health Review Tribunal, 1983–. Fellow, Midland Div., Woodard Corp., 1979–. *Recreations:* daughters, musical music, taking photographs. *Address:* c/o Circuit Administrator, 2 Newton Street, Birmingham B4 7LU.

WOODS, Maj.-Gen. Charles William, CB 1970; MBE 1952; MC 1944; Chairman, Douglas Haig Memorial Homes, since 1975; *b* 21 March 1917; *s* of late Captain F. W. U. Woods and of Mrs M. E. Woods, Gosbrook House, Binfield Heath, Henley-on-Thames; *m* 1940, Angela Helen Clay; one *d* (one *s* decd). *Educ:* Uppingham Sch.; Trinity Coll., Cambridge (MA). Commnd into Corps of Royal Engineers, 1938; served War of 1939–45, N Africa, Sicily, Italy, NW Europe (D Landings with 50th Div.); Staff Coll., Camberley, 1946; served in Korea, 1951–52; comd 35 Corps Engineer Regt, BAOR, 1959–60; Dep. Military Secretary, 1964–67; Dir of Manning (Army), 1967–70. Col Comdt, RE, 1973–78. Chm., RE Assoc., 1971–77. *Recreations:* sailing, ski-ing. *Address:* Riversdale Cottage, Boldre, Lymington, Hants SO4 8PE. *T:* Lymington 73445. *Clubs:* Naval and Military, Royal Ocean Racing, Royal Cruising, Ski Club of Great Britain; Royal Lymington Yacht, Royal Engineer Yacht, Island Sailing (Cowes).

WOODS, Christopher Matthew, CMG 1979; MC 1945; HM Diplomatic Service; Special Operations Executive Adviser, Foreign and Commonwealth Office, since 1982; *b* 26 May 1923; *s* of Matthew Grosvenor Woods; *m* 1954, Gillian Sara Rudd (*d* 1985); four *s* one *d*. *Educ:* Bradfield Coll.; Trinity Coll., Cambridge. HM Forces, KRRC and SOE, 1942–47; Foreign Office, 1948; served Cairo, Tehran, Milan, Warsaw, Rome; FO, later FCO, 1967. *Address:* 10 St John's Street, Woodbridge, Suffolk IP12 1Eb. *T:* Woodbridge 7881.

WOODS, Sir Colin (Philip Joseph), KCVO 1977; CBE 1973; QPM 1980; Director and Consultant, Securicor and Securicor International, since 1982; *b* London, 20 April 1920; *s* of late Michael Woods, Sub-divisional Inspector, Metropolitan Police; *m* 1941, Gladys Ella May (*née* Howell); one *d*. *Educ:* LCC Primary and Secondary Schs; Finchley Grammar Sch. Served War, in 60th Rifles and RUR, 1939–46. Metropolitan Police: Constable, through ranks, to Dep. Comdr; Commander, Traffic Dept, 1966–67; Head of Management Services, 1968; Comdt, National Police Coll., 1969–70; Asst Comr (Traffic Dept), 1970; Asst Comr (Crime), 1972; Dep. Comr, 1975–77; HM Chief Inspector of Constabulary, 1977–79; Comr, Australian Federal Police, 1979–82. *Recreations:* walking, gardening, caravanning. *Address:* Doversmead, Littleworth Road, The Sands, Farnham, Surrey GU10 1JW. *T:* Runfold 2514.

WOODS, Most Rev. Frank, KBE 1972; Archbishop of Melbourne, 1957–77; Primate of Australia, 1971–77; *b* 6 April 1907; *s* of late Rt Rev. E. S. Woods, DD, Bishop of Lichfield; *m* 1936, Jean Margaret Sprules; two *s* two *d*. *Educ:* Marlborough; Trinity Coll., Cambridge. Deacon, 1931; priest, 1932; Curate of Portsea Parish Church, 1932–33; Chaplain, Trinity Coll., Cambridge, 1933–36; Vice-principal, Wells Theological Coll., 1936–39; Chaplain to the Forces, 1939–45; Vicar of Huddersfield, 1945–52; Suffragan Bishop of Middleton, 1952–57. Proctor in Convocation, 1946–51; Chaplain to the King, 1951–52; Chaplain, Victoria Order of St John, 1962. Hon. Fellow, Trinity Coll., Melbourne, 1981. Hon. DD Lambeth, 1957; Hon. LLD Monash, 1979. *Recreation:* walking. *Address:* 2 Hughes Street, N Balwyn, Victoria 3104, Australia. *Clubs:* Melbourne, Australian (Melbourne).

See also Rt Rev. R. W. Woods.

WOODS, Maj.-Gen. Henry Gabriel, CB 1979; MBE 1965; MC 1945; General Officer Commanding North East District, 1976–80, retired; Head, Centre for Industrial and Educational Liaison (West and North Yorkshire), since 1980; Vice Lord-Lieutenant, North Yorkshire, since 1985; *b* 7 May 1924; *s* of late G. S. Woods and F. C. F. Woods (*née* McNevin); *m* 1953, Imogen Elizabeth Birchenough Dodd; two *d*. *Educ:* Highgate Sch.; Trinity Coll., Oxford (MA 1st Cl. Hons Mod. History). FBIM. psc, jssc, rcds. Commnd 5th Royal Inniskilling Dragoon Guards, 1944; served NW Europe, 1944–45; Korea, 1951–52; Adjt, 1952–53; Sqdn Leader, 1954–55 and 1960–62; Army Staff Coll., 1956; Jt Services Staff Coll., 1960; Mil. Asst to Vice CDS, MoD, 1962–64; comd 5th Royal Inniskilling Dragoon Gds, 1965–67; Asst Mil. Sec. to C-in-C BAOR, 1968–69; Comdt, RAC Centre, 1969–71; RCDS, 1972; Mil. Attaché, Brit. Embassy, Washington, 1973–75. Chairman: SATRO Panel, 1982–83; W and N Yorks Regl Microelectronics Educn Programme, 1982–86; Yorks and Humberside Industry/Educn Council, 1982–; Bradford and W Yorks Br., BIM, 1982–84; N Yorks Scouts, 1982–; Yorks Region, Royal Soc. of Arts, 1982–; Member: Yorks Br. Exec. Cttee, Inst. of Dirs, 1982–; Yorks Br. Exec. Cttee, British Assoc. for Advancement of Sci., 1982–. Mem., York Area Mental Health Appeals Cttee. Mem. Council, Univ. of Leeds, 1980–. Chm., 5th Royal Inniskilling Dragoon Guards Regtl Assoc. Pres. York and Humberside Br., Royal Soc. of St George, 1986–. DL N Yorks, 1984. FRSA. Officier, Ordre de Léopold, Belgium, 1965. *Publication:* Change and Challenge: the story of 5th Royal Inniskilling Dragon Guards, 1978. *Recreations:* hunting, fencing, sailing, military history. *Address:* Grafton House, Tockwith, York YO5 8PY. *T:* Tockwith 735. *Clubs:* Cavalry and Guards; Ends of the Earth (UK section), Trinity Society.

WOODS, Ivan; *see* Woods, W. I.

WOODS, Rev. Canon John Mawhinney; *b* 16 Dec. 1919; *s* of Robert and Sarah Hannah Woods. *Educ:* Edinburgh Theological College. Deacon 1958, for St Peter's, Kirkcaldy, Fife; priest, 1959; Rector of Walpole St Peter, Norfolk, 1960–75; Provost, St Andrew's Cathedral, Inverness, 1975–80; Rector of The Suttons with Tydd, 1980–85; Canon of Inverness, 1980–. *Address:* Sudbury House, 1 Purfleet Place, King's Lynn, Norfolk PE30 1JH.

WOODS, Prof. Leslie Colin, BE, MA, DPhil, DSc; Professor of Mathematics (Theory of Plasma), University of Oxford, and Fellow of Balliol College, Oxford, since 1970; *b* Reporoa, NZ, 6 Dec. 1922; *s* of A. B. Woodhead, Sandringham, NZ; *m* 1st, 1943; five *d*; 2nd, 1977, Dr Helen Troughton. *Educ:* Auckland Univ. Coll.; Merton Coll., Oxford. Fighter pilot, RNZAF, Pacific Area, 1942–45. Rhodes Schol., Merton Coll., Oxford, 1948–51; Scientist (NZ Scientific Defense Corps) with Aerodynamics Div., NPL Mddx, 1951–54; Senior Lectr in Applied Maths, Sydney Univ., 1954–56; Nuffield Research Prof. of Engineering, Univ. of New South Wales, 1956–60; Fellow and Tutor in Engrg Science, Balliol Coll., Oxford, 1960–70; Reader in Applied Maths, Oxford, 1964–70. Hon. DSc Auckland, 1983. *Publications:* The Theory of Subsonic Plane Flow, 1961; Introduction to Neutron Distribution Theory, 1964; The Thermodynamics of Fluid Systems, 1975; many research papers in aerodynamics and plasma physics in Proc. Royal Soc., Physics of Fluids, etc. *Recreations:* music, sailing. *Address:* Balliol College, Oxford.

WOODS, Rt. Rev. Robert Wilmer, KCVO 1971; MA; Assistant Bishop, Diocese of Gloucester, since 1982; Prelate of the Most Distinguished Order of St Michael and St George, since 1971; *b* 15 Feb. 1914; *s* of late Edward Woods, Bishop of Lichfield, and Clemence (*née* Barclay); *m* 1942, Henrietta Marion (JP 1966), *d* of late K. H. Wilson; two *s* three *d*. *Educ:* Gresham's Sch., Holt; Trinity Coll., Cambridge. Asst Sec., Student Christian Movement, 1937–42; Chaplain to the Forces, 1942–46 (despatches, 1944); Vicar of South Wigston, Leicester, 1946–51; Archdeacon of Singapore and Vicar of St Andrew's Cathedral, 1951–58; Archdeacon of Sheffield and Rector of Tankersley, 1958–62; Dean of Windsor, 1962–70; Domestic Chaplain to the Queen, 1962–70; Register of the Most Noble Order of the Garter, 1962–70; Bishop of Worcester, 1970–81. Secretary, Anglican/Methodist Commn for Unity, 1965–74; Member: Council, Duke of Edinburgh's Award Scheme, 1968; Public Schools Commn, 1968–70; Governor, Haileybury Coll.; Pres, Queen's Coll., Birmingham, and Chm. Council, 1970–; Chairman: Windsor Festival Co., 1969–71; Churches Television Centre, 1969–79; Dir, Christian Aid, 1969. Chm., Birmingham and Hereford and Worcester Bd, MSC, 1976–83. Visitor, Malvern Coll., 1970–81. *Publication:* Robin Woods: an autobiography, 1986. *Recreations:* sailing, shooting, painting. *Address:* Torsend House, Tirley, Gloucester GL19 4EU. *T:* Tirley 327.

See also Most Rev. F. Woods.

WOODS, Timothy Phillips, MA, DPhil; Head of History, Trent College, since 1985; *b* 24 Dec. 1943; *s* of late Arthur Phillips Woods and of Katherine Isabella Woods; *m* 1969, Erica Lobb. *Educ:* Cordwalles Prep. Sch., Natal; Michaelhouse Sch., Natal; Rhodes Univ. (BA Hons, MA; UED); Oxford Univ. (DPhil). Cape Province Rhodes Scholar, 1968; Felsted School: Asst Master, 1971; Head of History, 1975; Headmaster, Gresham's Sch. 1982–85. *Recreations:* cricket, hockey, squash, gardening, music, history and architecture of cathedrals. *Address:* 63 Curzon Street, Long Eaton, Nottingham NG10 4FG. *T:* Nottingham 720927. *Club:* Vincent's (Oxford).

WOODS, (William) Ivan; 3rd *s* of late William and Anna Woods, Annaghmore, Co. Armagh; *m* (1st wife *d* 1965); one *s* one *d*; 2nd, 1966, Florence Margaret, *o d* of late William and Florence Sloan, Ach-na-mara, Donaghadee, Co. Down; one *s* two *d*. *Educ:* Ranelagh Sch., Athlone; Mountjoy Sch., Dublin. Accountant, Min. of Finance for N Ire., 1962; N Ire. Govt Liaison Officer in London, 1963; Dir of Office of Parliamentary Commissioner for Administration, NI, 1969; Dir of Office of Commissioner for Complaints, NI, 1969; Dep. Sec., Dept of Finance for NI, 1973–76. Sec., Milibern Trust, 1976–79. *Recreations:* golf, sailing. *Address:* 112 Warren Road, Donaghadee, Co. Down BT21 0PQ. *T:* Donaghadee 883568. *Clubs:* Portaferry Sailing, Mitchels GA (Co. Down).

WOODWARD, Hon. Sir (Albert) Edward, Kt 1982; OBE 1969; Judge of Federal Court of Australia, since 1977; *b* 6 Aug. 1928; *s* of Lt-Gen. Sir Eric Winslow Woodward, KCMG, KCVO, CB, CBE, DSO, and Amy Freame Woodward (*née* Weller); *m* 1950, Lois Thorpe; one *s* six *d*. *Educ:* Melbourne C of E Grammar Sch.; Melbourne Univ. (LLM). Practising barrister, 1953–72; QC 1965; Judge, Commonwealth Industrial Court and Supreme Court of Australian Capital Territory, 1972–. Chairman, Armed Services Pay Inquiry, 1972; Royal Commissioner: Aboriginal Land Rights, 1973–75; into Australian Meat Industry, 1981–82; President, Trade Practices Tribunal, 1974–76; Director-General of Security, 1976–81. Chairman: Victorian Dried Fruits Bd, 1963–72; Nat. Stevedoring Industry Conf. and Stevedoring Industry Council, 1965–72; Australian Defence Force Academy Council, 1985–; Schizophrenia Australia, 1985–. Chm. Council, Camberwell Grammar Sch., 1983–. *Address:* 63 Tivoli Road, South Yarra, Victoria 3141, Australia. *T:* (03) 240 8404.

WOODWARD, Prof. C(omer) Vann; Sterling Professor of History, Yale University, 1961–77, now Emeritus Professor; *b* 13 Nov. 1908; *s* of Hugh Allison Woodward and Bess (*née* Vann); *m* 1937, Glenn Boyd MacLeod; one *s*. *Educ:* Emory Univ. (PhB); Universities of Columbia (MA), North Carolina (PhD). Asst Professor of History, University of Florida, 1937–39; Visiting Asst Professor of History, University of Virginia, 1939–40; Assoc. Professor of History, Scripps Coll., 1940–43; Assoc. Professor of History, Johns Hopkins University, 1946; Professor of American History, Johns Hopkins Univ., 1947–61. Served with US Naval Reserve, 1943–46. Commonwealth Lecturer, UCL, 1954; Harold Vyvyan Harmsworth Professor of American History, University of Oxford, 1954–55; Literary Award, Nat. Inst. of Arts and Letters, 1954, etc. Corresp. Fellow: British Academy, 1972, RHistS, 1978. Member: American Academy of Arts and Sciences; American Philosophical Society; Nat. Inst. of Arts and Letters; American Historical Assoc. (President, 1969); Orgn of American Historians (President, 1968–69). Hon. degrees: MA Oxon, 1954; LLD: N Carolina, 1959; Arkansas, 1961; Michigan, 1971; LittD: Emory, 1963; William and Mary, 1964; Princeton, 1971; Columbia, 1972; DLitt Cambridge, 1975. *Publications:* Tom Watson: Agrarian Rebel, 1938; The Battle for Leyte Gulf, 1947; Origins of the New South (1877–1913), 1951 (Bancroft Prize, 1952); Reunion and Reaction, 1951; The Strange Career of Jim Crow, 1955; The Burden of Southern History, 1960; American Counterpoint, 1971; Thinking Back, 1986; (ed) The Comparative Approach to American History, 1968; (ed) Mary Chesnut's Civil War, 1981 (Pulitzer Prize, 1982). *Address:* 83 Rogers Road, Hamden, Conn 06517, USA.

WOODWARD, Hon. Sir Edward; *see* Woodward, Hon. Sir A. E.

WOODWARD, Edward, OBE 1978; actor and singer, since 1946; *b* 1 June 1930; *s* of Edward Oliver Woodward and Violet Edith Woodward; *m* 1952, Venetia Mary Collett; two *s* one *d*; one *d*. *Educ:* Kingston Coll.; RADA. *Stage:* Castle Theatre, Farnham, 1946; appeared for some years in rep. cos throughout England and Scotland; first appearance on London stage, Where There's a Will, Garrick, 1955; Mercutio in Romeo and Juliet, and Laertes in Hamlet, Stratford, 1958; Rattle of a Simple Man, Garrick, 1962; Two Cities (musical), 1968; Cyrano in Cyrano de Bergerac, and Flamineo in The White Devil, Nat. Theatre Co., 1971; The Wolf, Apollo, 1973; Male of the Species, Piccadilly, 1975; On Approval, Theatre Royal Haymarket, 1976; The Dark Horse, Comedy, 1978; starred in and directed Beggar's Opera, 1980; Private Lives, Australia, 1980; The Assassin, Greenwich, 1982; Richard III, Ludlow Fest., 1982; has appeared in 3 prodns in NY; *films:* Becket, 1966; File on the Golden Goose, 1968; Hunted, 1973; Sitting Target, Young Winston, The Wicker Man, 1974; Stand Up Virgin Soldiers, 1977; Breaker Morant, 1980; The Appointment, 1981; Who Dares Wins, Forever Love, Merlin and the Sword, 1982; Champions, 1983; Christmas Carol, 1984; King David, Uncle Tom's Cabin, 1986. Over 200 TV prodns, inc. Callan (TV series and film, and in Wet Job, 1981); The Trial of Lady Chatterley, Blunt Instrument, 1980; Churchill: The Wilderness Years, 1981; Killer Contract, 1984; The Equalizer (series), 1985; 12 long-playing records (singing) and 3 records (poetry). Many national and internat. acting awards. *Recreations:* boating, geology. *Address:* c/o Eric Glass Ltd, 28 Berkeley Square, W1X 6HD. *T:* 01–629 7162. *Clubs:* Garrick, Green Room, Wellington.

WOODWARD, Geoffrey Frederick, RIBA; jssc; Assistant Director General of Design Services, Property Services Agency, Department of the Environment, 1983–84; *b* 29 June 1924; *s* of Joseph Frederick and Edith Mary Woodward; *m* 1953, Elizabeth Marjory McCubbin; four *s*. *Educ:* Wirral Grammar School for Boys; Trinity College, Cambridge Univ.; School of Architecture, Liverpool Univ. (BArch). Architects' Dept: Hertfordshire CC, 1952–56; British Transport Commn, 1956–60; Directorate of Army Works, 1960–63; Directorate of Research & Development, Min. of Public Building and Works, 1963–67; Directorate of Works (Married Quarters), MPBW, 1967–70; Directorate of Works (Navy Home), PSA, 1970–71; Director of Works (Navy Home), PSA, 1971–75; Director, Directorate General of Design Services, Design Office, 1975–78; Under Sec., PSA, DoE, 1978; Dir of Architectural Services, 1978–81; Dir, Diplomatic and Post Office Services, 1981–83. jssc 1963. *Recreations:* motoring, walking. *Address:* Little Orchard, Cuddington Way, Cheam, Sutton, Surrey SM2 7JA. *T:* 01–643 1964.

WOODWARD, Geoffrey Royston; Under-Secretary, Ministry of Agriculture, Fisheries and Food, 1970–81; *b* 26 June 1921; *o s* of James Edward Woodward and Gwendolen May (*née* Dodridge); *m* 1st, 1947, Marjorie Beatrice Bishop (marr. diss. 1974); three *s*; 2nd, 1974, Doreen Parker, MBE. *Educ:* Bradford Grammar Sch. Entered Civil Service, 1938; served RAFVR, 1941–46 (Flt-Lt, despatches). Joined Min. of Agriculture and Fisheries, 1948. *Recreation:* armchair archaeology. *Address:* 3 Gilbert Court, Green Vale, W5 3AX. *Club:* Reform.

WOODWARD, Vice-Adm. Sir John (Forster), KCB 1982; Deputy Chief of Defence Staff (Commitments), 1985–April 1987; *b* Penzance, Cornwall, 1 May 1932; *s* of late T. Woodward and of M. B. M. Woodward; *m* 1960, Charlotte Mary McMurtrie; one *s* one *d*. *Educ:* Royal Naval College, Dartmouth. Under training, Home Fleet, until 1953; Submarine Specialist, serving in HMS Sanguine, Porpoise, Valiant, and commanding HMS Tireless, Grampus and Warspite, from 1953; Min. of Defence and senior training posts, from 1971, plus comd HMS Sheffield, 1976–77; Director of Naval Plans, 1978–81; Flag Officer, First Flotilla, 1981–83, Sen. Task Gp Comdr, S Atlantic, during Falklands Campaign, Apr.-July 1982; Flag Officer, Submarines, and Comdr, Submarines Eastern Atlantic, 1983–84. Hon. Liveryman, Glass Sellers' Co., 1982. *Recreations:* sailing, philately, skiing. *Address:* c/o The Naval Secretary, Ministry of Defence, Old Admiralty Building, Whitehall, SW1. *Clubs:* Tamesis (Teddington); Royal Yacht Squadron (Cowes); Royal Naval Sailing Association (Portsmouth); Hayling Island Sailing.

WOODWARD, Rev. Max Wakerley; Methodist Minister, retired 1973; *b* 29 Jan. 1908; *s* of Alfred Woodward, Methodist Minister, and Mabel (*née* Wakerley); *m* 1934, Kathleen May Beaty; three *s* one *d*. *Educ:* Orme Sch., Newcastle; Kingswood Sch., Bath; Handsworth Coll., Birmingham. Missionary to Ceylon, 1929–42; Chaplain, Royal Navy, 1942–46; Minister: Leamington Spa, 1946–50; Finsbury Park, 1950–54; Harrow, 1954–58; Wesley's Chapel, London, 1958–64; Secretary, World Methodist Council, 1964–69; Minister, Bromley, Kent, 1969–73. Exchange Preacher, Univ. Methodist Church, Baton Rouge, La, 1957. Dir, Methodist Newspaper Co. Ltd, 1962–84. *Publication:* One At London, 1966. *Recreations:* gardening, stamp collecting. *Address:* 6a Field End Road, Pinner, Mddx HA5 2QL. *T:* 01–429 0608.

WOODWARD, William Charles; QC 1985; Midland and Oxford Circuit, since 1964; *b* 27 May 1940; *s* of Wilfred Charles Woodward and Annie Stewart Woodward (*née* Young); *m* 1965, Carolyn Edna Johns; two *s* one *d*. *Educ:* South County Junior Sch.; Nottingham High Sch.; St John's Coll., Oxford (BA Jurisp). Marshall to Sir Donald Finnemore, Michaelmas 1962. Called to the Bar, Inner Temple, 1964; pupillage with Brian J. Appleby, QC; Nottingham practice. Member: Nottingham Univ. Law Adv. Cttee; E Midlands Area Cttee, Law Soc. *Recreations:* family, friends, holidays. *Address:* (chambers) 24 The Ropewalk, Nottingham NG1 5EF. *T:* Nottingham 472581. *Clubs:* Pre War Austin Seven; Nottingham and Notts United Services.

WOOF, Robert Edward; Member and former official, National Union of Mineworkers; *b* 24 Oct. 1911; *m* Mary Bell (*d* 1971); one *d*. *Educ:* Elementary School. Began work in the mines at an early age, subsequently coal face worker. Member of the Labour Party, 1937–; MP (Lab) Blaydon, Co. Durham, Feb. 1956–1979. Member Durham County Council, 1947–56. *Address:* 10 Ramsay Road, Chopwell, Newcastle upon Tyne NE17 7AG.

WOOF, Robert Samuel, PhD; Reader in English Literature, University of Newcastle upon Tyne, since 1971; *b* 20 April 1931; *s* of William Woof and Annie (*née* Mason); *m* 1958, Pamela Shirley Moore; two *s* two *d*. *Educ:* Lancaster Royal Grammar School; Pembroke College, Oxford (MA); University of Toronto (PhD). Goldsmith Travelling Fellow, 1953–55; Lectr, Univ. of Toronto, 1958–61; University of Newcastle: Lord Adams of Ennerdale Fellow, 1961–62; Lectr, 1962; Leverhulme Fellow, 1983–84. Vice-Chm., Northern Arts Assoc., 1974–81; Hon. Keeper of Collections, Trustees of Dove Cottage, Grasmere, 1974–, Hon. Sec. and Treasurer, 1978–. Mem., Arts Council, 1982–: Vice-Chm., 1982–, acting Chm, 1985–, Drama Panel; Chm., Literature Panel, 1984– (Vice-Chm., 1983–84). *Publications:* (ed) T. W. Thompson, Wordsworth's Hawkshead, 1970; The Wordsworth Circle, 1979; (with Peter Bicknell) The Discovery of the Lake District 1750–1810, 1982; (with Peter Bicknell) The Lake District Discovered 1810–50, 1983; Thomas De Quincey: an English opium-eater 1785–1859, 1985; (with David Thomason) Derwentwater, the Vale of Elysium, 1986. *Recreations:* the arts, the Lake District. *Address:* 4 Burdon Terrace, Jesmond, Newcastle upon Tyne. *T:* Newcastle 2812680.

WOOLDRIDGE, Ian Edmund; Sports Columnist, Daily Mail, since 1972; BBC Television documentary reporter and writer; *b* 14 Jan. 1932; *s* of late Edmund and Bertha Wooldridge; *m* 1st, Veronica Ann Churcher; three *s*; 2nd, Sarah Margaret Chappell Lourenço. *Educ:* Brockenhurst Grammar School. New Milton Advertiser, 1948; Bournemouth Times, 1953; News Chronicle, 1956; Sunday Dispatch, 1960; Daily Mail, 1961. Columnist of Year, 1975 and 1976; Sportswriter of Year, 1972, 1974, 1981, in British Press Awards. *Publications:* Cricket, Lovely Cricket, 1963; (with Mary Peters) Mary P, 1974; (with Colin Cowdrey) MCC: The Autobiography of a Cricketer, 1976; The Best of Wooldridge, 1978; Travelling Reserve, 1982. *Recreations:* travel, golf, Beethoven and dry Martinis. *Address:* 11 Collingham Gardens, SW5 0HS. *Club:* Scribes.

WOOLF, Harry, PhD; Director, Institute for Advanced Study, Princeton, USA, since 1976; *b* 12 Aug. 1923; *s* of Abraham Woolf and Anna (*née* Frankman) *m* 1961, Patricia

A. Kelsh; two s two d. *Educ*: Univ. of Chicago (BS Physics and Maths 1948; MA Physics and History 1949); Cornell Univ. (PhD Hist. of Science 1955). Served US Army, 1943–46. Instructor: Boston Univ., Mass, 1953–55; Brandeis Univ., Waltham, Mass, 1954–55; Univ. of Washington, Seattle: Asst Prof., Associate Prof., and Prof., 1955–61; Johns Hopkins University: Prof., Hist. of Science Dept, 1961–76 (Chm. of Dept, 1961–72); Provost, 1972–76; Princeton University: Mem. Adv. Council, Depts of Philosophy, 1980–84, and of Comparative Lit., 1982–86. Pres., Chm. of Bd, Johns Hopkins Program for Internat. Educn in Gynecology and Obstetrics, Inc., 1973–76, Trustee 1976–; Mem. Adv. Bd, Smithsonian Research Awards, 1975–79; Member: Vis. Cttee Student Affairs, MIT, 1973–77; Corporation Vis. Cttee, Dept of Linguistics and Philosophy, MIT, 1977 83; Nat. Adv. Child Health and Human Develt Council, NIH, 1977–80; Mem. Vis. Cttee, Research Center for Language Sciences, Indiana Univ., 1977–80; Trustee: Associated Universities Inc., Brookhaven Nat. Laboratories, Nat. Radio Astronomy Observatory, 1972–82; Hampshire Coll., Amherst, Mass, 1977–81; Merrill Lynch Cluster C Funds, 1982–; Trustee-at-Large, Univs Research Assoc. Inc., Washington, DC (Fermi Nat. Accelerator Lab.), 1978–, Chm. Bd 1979–. Member: Corp. Visiting Cttee for Dept of Physics, MIT, 1979–; Council on Foreign Relations Inc., 1979–; Adv. Panel, WGBH, NOVA, 1979–; Internat. Research and Exchanges Bd, NY, 1980–; Scientific Adv. Bd, Wissenschaftskolleg zu Berlin, 1981–; Adv. Bd, New Perspective Fund, Inc., Los Angeles, 1980–83; Adv. Council, SCI/TECH Inc.; Bd of Dirs, Alex. Brown Cash Reserve Fund, Inc., Baltimore, 1981–; Bd of Dirs, BioTechnica Internat., 1981–; Bd of Dirs, W. Alton Jones Cell Science Center, 1982–86; Adv. Council, Dept of Comparative Literature, 1982–86; Adv. Council, Nat. Science Foundn, 1984–; Bd of Trustees, Rockefeller Foundn, 1984–; Dir-at-large, Amer. Cancer Soc., 1982–. Member: Académie Internat. d'Histoire des Sciences; Amer. Philosoph. Soc.; Phi Beta Kappa; Sigma Xi (also Bicentennial Lectr, 1976). Editor, ISIS Internat. Review, 1958–64; Associate Editor, Dictionary of Scientific Biog., 1970–80; Mem. Editl Bd, Interdisciplinary Science Revs, 1975–; Mem. Editl Adv. Bd, The Writings of Albert Einstein, 1977–. Fellow, Amer. Acad. of Arts and Scis. Hon. DSc: Whitman Coll., 1979; Amer. Univ., Washington DC, 1982; Hon. LHD: Johns Hopkins Univ., 1983; St Lawrence Univ. 1986. *Publications*: The Transits of Venus: a study in eighteenth-century science, 1959, repr. 1981; (ed) Quantification: essays in the history of measurement in the natural and social sciences, 1961; (ed) Science as a Cultural Force, 1964; (ed and contrib.) Some Strangeness in the Proportion: a centennial symposium to celebrate the achievements of Albert Einstein, 1980; (ed) The Analytic Spirit: essays in the history of science, 1981. *Address*: Institute for Advanced Study, Princeton, NJ 08540, USA. *T*: (609) 734–8200. *Clubs*: Century Association (New York); Cosmos (Washington, DC).

WOOLF, Rt. Hon. Sir Harry (Kenneth), Kt 1979; PC 1986; **Rt. Hon. Lord Justice Woolf;** a Lord Justice of Appeal, since 1986; *b* 2 May 1933; *s* of Alexander Woolf and Leah Woolf (*née* Cussins); *m* 1961, Marguerite Sassoon, *d* of George Sassoon; three *s*. *Educ*: Fettes Coll.; University Coll., London (LLB; Fellow, 1981). Called to Bar, Inner Temple, 1954; Bencher, 1976. Commnd (Nat. Service), 15/19th Royal Hussars, 1954; seconded Army Legal Services, 1955; Captain 1955. Started practice at Bar, 1956. A Recorder of the Crown Court, 1972–79; Jun. Counsel, Inland Revenue, 1973–74; First Treasury Junior Counsel (Common Law), 1974–79; a Judge of the High Court of Justice, Queen's Bench Div., 1979–86; Presiding Judge, SE Circuit, 1981–84. Member: Senate, Inns of Court and Bar, 1981–85 (Chm., Accommodation Cttee, 1982–85); Management Cttee, Inst. of Advanced Legal Studies, 1985– (Chm., 1986–); President: Assoc. of Law Teachers, 1985–; Anglo-Jewish Archives, 1985–. *Address*: Royal Courts of Justice, Strand, WC2. *Club*: Garrick.

WOOLF, Sir John, Kt 1975; film and television producer; Chairman, Romulus Films Ltd, since 1948; Managing Director, since 1967 and Chairman, since 1982, British & American Film Holdings Plc; Director, First Leisure Corporation Plc, since 1982; Executive Director, Drama, Anglia Television, since 1983; *s* of Charles M. and Vera Woolf; *m* 1955, Ann Saville; two *s*. *Educ*: Institut Montana, Switzerland. War of 1939–45 (Bronze Star (USA), 1945): Asst Dir, Army Kinematography, War Office, 1944–45. Executive Director, Anglia TV Group PLC, 1958–83. Member: Cinematograph Films Council, 1969–79; Bd of Governors, Services Sound & Vision Corp. (formerly Services Kinema Corp.), 1974–83; Trustee and Mem. Exec. Council, Cinema and Television Benevolent Fund. Freeman, City of London. FRSA. Films produced by Romulus Group include: The African Queen, Pandora and the Flying Dutchman, Moulin Rouge, I am a Camera, Carrington VC, Beat the Devil, Story of Esther Costello, Room at the Top, Wrong Arm of the Law, The L-Shaped Room, Term of Trial, Life at the Top, Oliver!, Day of the Jackal, The Odessa File. Productions for Anglia TV include: 80 Tales of the Unexpected; Miss Morrison's Ghosts; The Kingfisher; Edwin; Love Song. Personal awards include: British Film Academy Award for Best Film of 1958: Room at the Top; Oscar and Golden Globe for Best Film of 1969: Oliver!; special awards for contribution to British film industry from Cinematograph Exhibitors Assoc., 1969, Variety Club of GB, 1974. *Address*: 36 Park Lane, W1Y 3LE. *T*: 01–493 7741.

WOOLF, John Moss, CB 1975; Deputy Chairman of the Board of Customs and Excise, and Director-General (Customs and Establishments), 1973–78; *b* 5 June 1918; *o s* of Alfred and Maud Woolf; *m* 1940, Phyllis Ada Mary Johnson; one *d*. *Educ*: Drayton Manor Sch.; Honourable Society of Lincoln's Inn. Barrister-at-law, 1948. War Service, 1939–46 (Captain, RA). Inland Revenue, 1937. Asst Principal, Min. of Fuel and Power, 1948; HM Customs and Excise, 1950: Principal, 1951; Asst Sec., 1960; Chm., Valuation Cttee, Customs Cooperation Council, Brussels, 1964–65; National Bd for Prices and Incomes, 1965; Under-Secretary, 1967; Asst Under-Sec. of State, Dept of Employment and Productivity, 1968–70; HM Customs and Excise: Comr, 1970; Dir of Establishments and Organisation, 1971–73. Advr on Price Problems, Govt of Trinidad & Tobago, 1968. Assoc. of First Div. Civil Servants: Mem. of Exec. Cttee, 1950–58 and 1961–65; Hon. Sec., 1952–55; Chm., 1955–58 and 1964–65; Mem., Civil Service National Whitley Council (Staff Side), 1953–55. Leader of Review Team to examine responsibilities of the Directors of the Nat. Museums and Galleries, 1978–79; Review of Organisation and Procedures of Chancery Div. of High Court, 1979–81; Overseas Adviser to CEGB, 1979–82. Commandeur d'Honneur, Ordre du Bontemps de Médoc et des Graves, 1973; Hon. Borgenerális (Hungary), 1974. *Publications*: Report on Control of Prices in Trinidad and Tobago (with M. M. Eccleshall), 1968; Report of the Review Body on the Chancery Division of the High Court (with Lord Justice Oliver and R. H. H. White), 1981. *Recreations*: reading, gardening. *Address*: West Lodge, 113 Marsh Lane, Stanmore, Mddx HA7 4TH. *T*: 01–952 1373. *Club*: Civil Service.

WOOLFORD, Harry Russell Halkerston, OBE 1970; Consultant, formerly Chief Restorer, National Gallery of Scotland; *b* 23 May 1905; *s* of H. Woolford, engineer; *m* 1932, Nancy Philip; one *d*. *Educ*: Edinburgh. Studied art at Edinburgh Coll. of Art (Painting and Drawing) and RSA Life School (Carnegie Travelling Scholarship, 1928), London, Paris and Italy; afterwards specialized in picture restoration. FMA; FIIC. Hon. Mem., Assoc. of British Picture Restorers, 1970. Hon. MA Dundee, 1976. *Address*: Dean Park, Golf Course Road, Bonnyrigg, Midlothian EH19 2EU. *T*: 031–663 7949. *Club*: Scottish Arts.

WOOLFSON, Mark; Consultant and Director of Consortium, Pollution Control Consultants, since 1972; a Partner, Posford Parry & Partners, since 1976; *b* 10 Nov. 1911; *s* of Victor Woolfson and Sarah (*née* Kixman); *m* 1940, Queenie Carlis; two *d*. *Educ*: City of London. Student Engr, Lancashire Dynamo & Crypto, until 1936; Engr, ASEA Electric Ltd, 1936–40; War Service, RNVR, 1940–46 (Lt-Comdr); MPBW, later DoE, 1946–71, Chief Mech. and Electr. Engineer, 1969–71. FIMechE, FIEE. *Publications*: papers in Jls of Instns of Civil, Mechanical and Elect. Engrs. *Recreations*: tennis, gardening, golf. *Address*: 3 Runnelfield, Harrow, Mddx. *T*: 01–422 1599.

WOOLFSON, Prof. Michael Mark, FRS 1984; FRAS; FInstP; Professor of Theoretical Physics, since 1965, and Head of Department of Physics, since 1982, University of York; *b* 9 Jan. 1927; *s* of Maurice and Rose Woolfson; *m* 1951, Margaret (*née* Frohlich); two *s* one *d*. *Educ*: Jesus College, Oxford (MA); UMIST (PhD, DSc). Royal Engineers, 1947–49. Research Assistant: UMIST, 1950–52; Cavendish Lab., Cambridge, 1952–54; ICI Fellow, Univ. of Cambridge, 1954–55; Lectr, 1955–61, Reader, 1961–65, UMIST. *Publications*: Direct Methods in Crystallography, 1961; An Introduction to X-Ray Crystallography, 1970; papers in learned jls. *Recreations*: gardening, wine making. *Address*: 124 Wigton Lane, Leeds LS17 8RZ. *T*: Leeds 687890.

WOOLHOUSE, Prof. Harold William; Director, John Innes Institute, and Professor of Biological Sciences, University of East Anglia, since 1980; *b* 12 July 1932; *s* of William Everson Woolhouse and Frances Ella Woolhouse; *m* 1959, Leonie Marie Sherwood; two *s* one *d*. *Educ*: Univ. of Reading (BSc); Univ. of Adelaide (PhD). Lecturer and Sen. Lectr, Sheffield Univ., 1960–69; Professor of Botany, Leeds Univ., 1969–80. Vis. Professor, USC, Los Angeles, 1968; Andrew D. White Professor at Large, Cornell Univ., 1983–. *Publications*: research papers on plant senescence, photosynthesis, metal toxicity and tolerance, and physiology of adaptation. *Recreations*: poetry, music, poultry breeding, gardening. *Address*: Old Sun House, 65 Damgate, Wymondham, Norfolk.

WOOLLAM, John Victor; Barrister-at-Law; *b* 14 Aug. 1927; *s* of Thomas Alfred and Edie Moss Woollam; *m* 1964, Lavinia Rosamond Ela, *d* of S. R. E. Snow; two *s*. *Educ*: Liverpool Univ. Called to the Bar, Inner Temple. Contested (C) Scotland Div. of Liverpool, 1950; MP (C) W Derby Div. of Liverpool, Nov. 1954–Sept. 1964; Parliamentary Private Sec. to Minister of Labour, 1960–62. *Recreation*: philately. *Address*: 27 Sandford Walk, Newtown, Exeter EX1 2ES.

WOOLLASTON, Sir (Mountford) Tosswill, Kt 1979; painter (abandoned other occupations, 1966); *b* 11 April 1910; *s* of John Reginald Woollaston and Charlotte Kathleen Frances (*née* Tosswill); *m* 1936, Edith Winifred Alexander; three *s* one *d*. *Educ*: Huinga Primary; Stratford (NZ) Secondary; brief brushes with art schools, Christchurch, 1931; King Edward Technical Coll., Dunedin, 1932. Member, The Group, Christchurch, 1935–; a few private but enthusiastic supporters; work featured in Art in New Zealand, 1937. Doldrums, 1950s: Auckland City Art Gallery began purchasing work, 1958, other galleries followed; overseas travel grant, NZ Arts Council, 1961; reputation increased. Govt purchases for embassies overseas, early sixties; Peter McLeavey, Dealer, Wellington, took over selling, 1967. *Publications*: The Faraway Hills (Auckland City Art Gall. Associates), 1962; ERUA (48 drawings of a boy, with text—Paul), 1966; Sage Tea (autobiog.), 1981. *Recreation*: gardening. *Address*: RD3, Motueka, New Zealand. *T*: Motueka 88425.

WOOLLCOMBE, Rt. Rev. Kenneth John; a Canon Residentiary of St Paul's, since 1981; Precentor, since 1982; *b* 2 Jan. 1924; *s* of late Rev. E. P. Woollcombe, OBE, and Elsie Ockenden Woollcombe; *m* 1st, 1950, Gwendoline Rhona Vyvien Hodges (*d* 1976); three *d*; 2nd, 1980, Deaconess Juliet Dearmer; one *d*. *Educ*: Haileybury Coll., Hertford; St John's Coll., Oxford; Westcott House, Cambridge. Sub-Lieut (E) RNVR, 1945. Curate, St James, Grimsby, 1951; Fellow, Chaplain and Tutor, St John's Coll., Oxford, 1953, Hon. Fellow, 1971; Professor of Dogmatic Theology, General Theological Seminary, New York, 1960; Principal of Episcopal Theological Coll., Edinburgh, 1963; Bishop of Oxford, 1971–78; Asst Bishop, Diocese of London, 1978–81. Chm., SPCK, 1973–79; Mem., Central Cttee, World Council of Churches, 1975–83; Chm., Churches' Council for Covenanting, 1978–82; Co-Chm., English Anglican-RC Cttee, 1985–; Judge in Court of Ecclesiastical Causes Reserved, 1984–. Hon. Chaplain, Glass Sellers' Co., 1978–. STD Univ. of the South, Sewanee, USA, 1963; Hon. DD Hartford, Conn, 1975. *Publications*: (contrib.) The Historic Episcopate, 1954; (jointly) Essays on Typology, 1957. *Address*: 5 Amen Court, EC4M 7BU.

WOOLLER, Arthur, CBE 1967; HM Diplomatic Service, retired; *b* 23 May 1912; *s* of Joseph Edward Wooller and Sarah Elizabeth (*née* Kershaw); *m* 1944, Frances, *e d* of Justice A. L. Blank, ICS; three *s*. *Educ*: Bradford Grammar School; Corpus Christi College, Oxford. ICS, Bengal, 1935; Indian Foreign and Political Service, 1939; UK Trade Comr, New Zealand, 1947; First Sec. (Commercial), Ottawa, 1953; UK Trade Comr, Toronto, 1959; British Trade Comr, Hong Kong, 1960; Principal British Trade Comr, Bombay, 1963; British Deputy High Commissioner in Western India, Bombay, 1965–68; High Comr in Mauritius, 1968–70; Economic Advr, FCO, 1970–72. *Recreation*: gardening. *Address*: c/o Midland Bank, High Street, Harpenden, Herts. *Club*: United Oxford & Cambridge University.

WOOLLETT, Maj.-Gen. John Castle, CBE 1957 (OBE 1955); MC 1945; MA Cantab; FICE; Principal Planning Inspector, Department of the Environment, 1971–81; *b* 5 Nov. 1915; *o s* of John Castle Woollett and Lily Bradley Woollett, Bredgar, Kent; *m* 1st, 1941, Joan Eileen Stranks (marr. diss. 1957); two *s* (and one *s* decd); 2nd, 1959, Helen Wendy Willis; two step *s*. *Educ*: St Benedict's Sch.; RMA Woolwich; St John's Coll., Cambridge. Joined RE, 1935; 23 Field Co., 1938–40 (BEF, 1939–40); 6 Commando 1940–42; Major Comdg 16 Field Sqdn and 16 Assault Sqdn RE, 1942–45 (BLA, 1944–45); Student, Staff Coll., Camberley, 1946; DAAG and GSO2, Brit. Service Mission to Burma, 1947–50; Major Comdg 51 Port Sqdn RE, 1950; Instructor, Staff Coll., Camberley, 1950–53; Lt-Col Comdg 28 Field Engr Regt, 1954–55 (Korea); Bt Lt-Col 1955; Comdr Christmas Is, 1956–57; GSO1, Northern Army Gp, 1957–59; Col GS, US Army Staff Coll., Fort Leavenworth, 1959–61; DQMG (Movements), BAOR, 1962–64; Brig. Comdg Hants Sub District and Transportation Centre, RE, 1964–65; Sch. of Transport, 1965–66; Dep. Engr-in-Chief, 1966–67; Maj.-Gen., Chief Engineer, BAOR, 1967–70, retired. Col Comdt, RE, 1973–78. Pres., Instn of RE, 1974–79. *Recreations*: cruising, shooting. *Address*: 42 Rhinefield Close, Brockenhurst, Hants. *Clubs*: Army and Navy, Royal Ocean Racing, Royal Cruising; Island Sailing (Cowes), Royal Lymington Yacht.

WOOLLEY, David Rorie, QC 1980; barrister-at-law; a Recorder of the Crown Court, since 1982; *b* 9 June 1939; *s* of Albert and Ethel Woolley. *Educ*: Winchester Coll.; Trinity Hall, Cambridge (BA Hons Law). Called to the Bar, Middle Temple, 1962. Vis. Scholar, Wolfson Coll., Cambridge, 1982–. Inspector, DoE inquiry into Nat. Gall. extension, 1984. *Publications*: Town Hall and the Property Owner, 1965; contribs to various legal jls. *Recreations*: opera, mountaineering, real tennis. *Address*: 2 Mitre Court Buildings, Temple, EC4. *T*: 01–583 1355. *Clubs*: MCC; Swiss Alpine.

WOOLLEY, John Maxwell, MBE 1945; TD 1946; Clerk, Merchant Taylors' Company, and Clerk to The Governors, Merchant Taylors' School, 1962–80; *b* 22 March 1917; *s* of Lt-Col Jasper Maxwell Woolley, IMS (Retd) and Kathleen Mary Woolley (*née* Waller); *m* 1952, Esme Adela Hamilton-Cole; two *s. Educ:* Cheltenham College; Trinity College, Oxford. BA (Oxon) 1938, MA (Oxon) 1962. Practising Solicitor, 1950–55; Asst Clerk, Merchant Taylors' Company, 1955–62. *Address:* 26 Vallance Gardens, Hove, East Sussex BN3 2DD. *T:* Brighton 733200. *Club:* Hove.

WOOLLEY, Sir Richard (van der Riet), Kt 1963; OBE 1953; FRS 1953; Director, South African Astronomical Observatory, 1972–76; Hon. Fellow, University House, Australian National University, since 1955; Hon. Fellow, Gonville and Caius College, Cambridge, since 1956; *b* Weymouth, Dorset, 24 April 1906; *s* of Paymaster Rear-Admiral Charles E. A. Woolley, CMG, RN; *m* 1st, 1932, Gwyneth Jane Margaret (*née* Meyler) (*d* 1979); 2nd, 1979, Emily May Patricia Marples (*d* 1985); 3rd, 1985, Sheila Gillham. *Educ:* Allhallows School, Honiton; University of Cape Town; Gonville and Caius College, Cambridge; MSc Cape Town; MA, ScD Cantab; Hon. LLD Melbourne. Commonwealth Fund Fellow, at Mt Wilson Observatory, California, 1929–31; Isaac Newton Student, Cambridge Univ., 1931–33; Chief Assistant, R Observatory, Greenwich, 1933–37; John Couch Adams Astronomer, Cambridge, 1937–39; Commonwealth Astronomer, 1939–55; Astronomer Royal, 1956–71. Hon. Professor of Astronomy in Australian National University, 1950–. Visiting Prof. of Astronomy, Univ. of Sussex, 1966–. Pres., Royal Astronomical Soc., 1963–65. Vice-Pres., International Astronomical Union, 1952–58; Pres., Australian and New Zealand Assoc. for the Advancement of Science, Melbourne meeting, 1955. Hon. DrPhil Uppsala, 1956; Hon. DSc: Cape Town, 1969; Sussex, 1970. Corresp. Mem. de la Société Royale des Sciences de Liège, 1956. Master, Worshipful Co. of Clockmakers, 1969. Gold Medal, RAS, 1971. *Publications:* (with Sir Frank Dyson) Eclipses of the Sun and Moon, 1937; (with D. W. N. Stibbs) The Outer Layers of a Star, 1953. *Address:* 4 Myrtle Street, Somerset West, Cape, South Africa. *Club:* Athenæum.

WOOLLEY, Roy Gilbert; His Honour Judge Woolley; a Circuit Judge, since 1976; *b* 28 Nov. 1922; *s* of John Woolley and Edith Mary Woolley; *m* 1953, Doreen, *d* of Humphrey and Kathleen Morris; two *s* two *d. Educ:* Overton and Marchwiel Primary Schs; Deeside Secondary Sch.; UCL (LLB Hons 1949). Served War, 1939–45, Air Gunner, RAF. Christopher Tancred Student, Lincoln's Inn, 1948; called to the Bar, 1951; Wales and Chester Circuit; Recorder, 1975. Reader: Diocese of Chester, 1955–; Diocese of Lichfield, 1977–. *Recreations:* outdoor pursuits, incl. horse riding, gardening, shooting; interested in music, poetry, art and antique furniture. *Address:* Henlle Hall, St Martins, Oswestry, Salop SY10 7AX. *T:* Oswestry 661257.

WOOLLEY, Russell; *see* Woolley, A. R.

WOOLLEY, William Edward, CBE 1974; DL; Chairman, Cupal Ltd, since 1947; Director, Secto Co. Ltd, since 1947; *b* 17 March 1901; *s* of William Woolley, JP, and Eleanor Woolley; *m* 1929, Marion Elizabeth Aspinall (*d* 1982); one *s* one *d. Educ:* Woodhouse Grove School, Yorkshire; Edinburgh University. MP (Nat L) for Spen Valley Division of Yorkshire, 1940–45; Parliamentary Private Secretary to Minister of Health, 1943, to Minister of Aircraft Production, 1945. JP; Chairman: Blackburn Borough Magistrates, 1956–72; Gen. Comrs Income Tax, Lancs Adv. Cttee, 1974–76; Gen Comrs Income Tax, Blackburn District, 1960–76; Blackburn and District Hosp. Management Cttee, 1952–74; Manchester Regional Hosp. Staff Cttee, 1966–74; Pres., Blackburn and District Council of Social Service. Contested (Nat L) Brighouse and Spenborough, General elections, 1950, 1951. DL Lancs, 1975. *Address:* Billinge Crest, Billinge End Road, Blackburn, Lancs BB2 6PY. *TA* and *T:* Blackburn 53449.

WOOLMAN, (Joseph) Roger; Under Secretary (Legal), Department of Trade and Industry, since 1985; *b* 13 Feb. 1937; *s* of late Maurice Wollman and Hilda Wollman; *m* 1973, Elizabeth, *d* of late Eric Ingham; one *s* one *d. Educ:* Perse School, Cambridge; Trinity Hall, Cambridge (Exhibnr); BA (Law Tripos), MA). Solicitor, 1974; Legal Asst, Office of Fair Trading, 1976; Senior Legal Asst, Dept of Trade, 1978; Asst Solicitor, DTI, 1981. *Recreations:* golf, travel. *Address:* 5 Ferncroft Avenue, NW3. *T:* 01-435 3944.

WOOLMER, Kenneth John; Lecturer, School of Economic Studies, Leeds University, since 1983; *b* 25 April 1940; *s* of Joseph William and Gertrude May Woolmer; *m* 1961, Janice Chambers; three *s. Educ:* Gladstone Street County Primary, Rothwell, Northants; Kettering Grammar Sch.; Leeds Univ. (BA Econs). Research Fellow, Univ. of West Indies, 1961–62; Teacher, Friern Rd Sec. Mod. Sch., London, 1963; Lecturer: Univ. of Leeds (Economics), 1963–66; Univ. of Ahmadu Bello, Nigeria, 1966–68; Univ. of Leeds, 1968–79. Councillor: Leeds CC, 1970–78; West Yorkshire MCC, 1973–80 (Leader, 1975–77; Leader of Opposition, 1977–79). Chairman, Planning and Transportation Cttee, Assoc. of Metropolitan Authorities, 1974–77. MP (Lab) Batley and Morley, 1979–83; Opposition spokesman on trade, shipping and aviation, 1981–83; Mem., Select Cttee on Treasury and Civil Service, 1980–81; Chm., 1981, Vice-Chm., 1982, PLP Economics and Finance Gp. Contested (Lab) Batley and Spen, 1983. *Recreations:* all forms of sport, espec. soccer, Rugby Union and League, cricket and swimming. *Address:* 54 Moor Grange View, Leeds LS16 5BJ.

WOOLSEY, Rt. Rev. Gary Frederick; *see* Athabasca, Bishop of.

WOOLTON, 3rd Earl of, *cr* 1956; **Simon Frederick Marquis;** Baron Woolton, 1939; Viscount Woolton, 1953; Viscount Walberton, 1956; *b* 24 May 1958; *s* of 2nd Earl of Woolton and of Cecily Josephine (later Lady Forres, now Countess Lloyd George of Dwyfor), *e d* of Sir Alexander Gordon Cumming, 5th Bt; *S* father, 1969. *Educ:* Eton College; St Andrews Univ. (MA Hons). *Address:* 5 Lincoln Street, SW3; Glenogil, by Forfar, Angus. *Clubs:* White's, Brooks's; New (Edinburgh); Royal and Ancient.

WOOLVERTON, Kenneth Arthur; Head of Latin America, Caribbean and Pacific Department, Overseas Development Administration of the Foreign and Commonwealth Office, 1985–86; *b* 4 Aug. 1926; *s* of Arthur Eliott Woolverton and Lilian Woolverton; *m* 1957, Kathleen West; one *s. Educ:* Orange Hill Grammar Sch. Colonial Office, 1950–61; CRO, 1961–66 (2nd Sec., Jamaica); Min. of Overseas Development, 1966–79; Hd of Middle East Develt Div., ODA, 1979–81; Hd of British Develt Div. in the Caribbean, ODA, 1981–84. *Recreations:* photography, archaeology, sailing. *Address:* 47 Durleston Park Drive, Great Bookham, Surrey. *T:* Bookham 54055. *Club:* Farmers'.

WOOLWICH, Bishop Suffragan of, since 1984; **Rt. Rev. Albert Peter Hall;** *b* 2 Sept. 1930; *s* of William Conrad Hall and Bertha Gladys Hall; *m* 1957, Valerie Jill Page; two *s. Educ:* Queen Elizabeth Grammar School, Blackburn; St John's Coll., Cambridge (MA Mod. Langs); Ridley College, Cambridge. Deacon 1955, priest 1956; Curate: St Martin, Birmingham, 1955–60; St Mary Magdalene, Avondale, Zimbabwe, 1960; Rector of Avondale, Zimbabwe, 1963–70; Rector of Birmingham, 1970–84. *Recreations:* squash, mountain walking. *Address:* 8B Hillyfields Crescent, Brockley, SE4 1QA.

WOON, Peter William; Head of BBC Operations, North America, since 1985; *b* 12 Dec. 1931; *s* of Henry William Woon and Gwendoline Constance Woon; *m* 1969, Diana Jean Ward; two *s. Educ:* Christ's Hospital. 2nd Lieut Royal Signals, 1954–56; Reporter, Bristol Evening Post, 1949–54 and 1956–58; air corresp., Daily Express, 1958–61; BBC: reporter, 1961–66; Asst Editor, TV News, 1966–69; Editor, Radio News, 1969–75; Head of Information, 1975–77; Editor, News and Current Affairs, radio, 1977–80; Editor, TV News, 1980–85. *Recreations:* theatre, reading, TV, sailing (one day). *Address:* c/o BBC, 630 Fifth Avenue, New York, USA. *T:* New York (212) 603–6501.

WOOSTER, Clive Edward Doré; consultant; *b* 3 Nov. 1913; *s* of Edward Doré Wooster; *m*; two *s*; *m* 1970, Patricia Iris (formerly Dewey). *Educ:* Private School, Southend-on-Sea. Private offices, 1930–40; War Service, Captain RA, 1940–46. Local Authority Offices and LCC, 1946–51; Ministry of Education, 1951–58; University Grants Cttee, 1958–59; Works Directorate, War Office, 1959–63; Dir of Building Management, MPBW, 1963–69; Dep. Chief Architect, Min. of Housing and Local Govt, 1969; Dir, Housing Develt, DoE, 1972–74, retired. RIBA Technical Standards Cttee, 1960–64; RIBA Building Controls Panel Chairman, 1960–63; RIBA Management Handbook Cttee, 1963–67; RIBA Council, 1970–72. *Publications:* Lectures on architectural and building management subjects; contrib. to professional journals. *Address:* 141 Harefield Road, Rickmansworth, Herts WD3 1PB. *T:* Rickmansworth 775401.

WOOTTON OF ABINGER, Baroness *cr* 1958 (Life Peer), of Abinger Common, **(Barbara Frances),** CH 1977; MA; holds Hon. Doctorates from Columbia (NY), Nottingham, Essex, Liverpool, Aberdeen, York, Hull, Aston in Birmingham, Bath, Southampton, Warwick, Cambridge; and London; *b* Cambridge, 1897; *d* of late Dr James Adam, Senior Tutor of Emmanuel Coll., Cambridge and Mrs Adam, sometime Fellow of Girton Coll., Cambridge; *m* 1st, 1917, John Wesley Wootton (*d* of wounds, 1917), Earl of Derby Research Student, Trinity College, Cambridge; 2nd, 1935, George Percival Wright (*d* 1964). *Educ:* Perse High School for Girls, Cambridge; Girton Coll., Cambridge (MA Cantab). Director of Studies and Lecturer in Economics, Girton Coll., 1920–22; Research Officer Trades Union Congress and Labour Party Joint Research Department, 1922–26; Principal, Morley College for Working Men and Women, 1926–27; Director of Studies for Tutorial Classes, University of London, 1927–44; Professor of Social Studies, University of London, 1948–52; Nuffield Research Fellow, Bedford College, University of London, 1952–57. A Governor of the BBC, 1950–56; a Deputy-Speaker in House of Lords, 1967–. Member: Departmental Cttee, Nat. Debt and Taxation, 1924–27; Royal Commission on Workmen's Compensation, 1938; Interdepartmental Cttee on Shop Hours, 1946–49; Royal Commn on the Press, 1947; UGC, 1948–50; Royal Commn on the Civil Service, 1954; Interdepartmental Cttee on the Business of the Criminal Courts, 1958–61; Council on Tribunals, 1961–64; Interdepartmental Cttee on the Criminal Statistics, 1963–67; Royal Commn on Penal System, 1964–66; Penal Adv. Council, 1966–79; Adv. Council on Misuse of Drugs, 1971–74; Chm., Countryside Commn, 1968–70 (Nat. Parks Commn, 1966–68). JP in the Metropolitan Courts, 1926–70 (on the Panel of Chairmen in the Metropolitan Juvenile Courts, 1946–62). Hon. Fellow: Girton Coll., Cambridge, 1965–; Bedford Coll., London, 1964–; Royal Coll. of Psychiatrists, 1979. *Publications:* (as Barbara Wootton): Twos and Threes, 1933; Plan or No Plan, 1934; London's Burning, 1936; Lament for Economics, 1938; End Social Inequality, 1941; Freedom Under Planning, 1945; Testament for Social Science, 1950; The Social Foundations of Wage Policy, 1955; Social Science and Social Pathology, 1959; Crime and the Criminal Law, 1964; In a World I Never Made, 1967; Contemporary Britain, 1971; Incomes Policy: an inquest and a proposal, 1974; Crime and Penal Policy, 1978; frequent contributor to New Society and other sociological journals. *Recreation:* country life. *Address:* Holmesdale Park, Nutfield, Surrey RH1 4HT. *T:* Nutfield Ridge 2738.

WOOTTON, Godfrey; *see* Wootton, N. G.

WOOTTON, Gordon Henry; His Honour Judge Wootton; a Circuit Judge, since 1980; *b* 23 April 1927; *s* of William Henry Wootton and Winifred Beatrice Wootton; *m* 1st, 1953, Camilla Bowes (marr. diss. 1979); two *s*; 2nd, 1979, Eileen Mary North. LLB Hons. Captain, RE, 1947. Called to the Bar, Middle Temple, 1952; Resident Magistrate, Uganda, 1954–62; a Recorder of the Crown Court, 1975–80. *Address:* Beech-Hurst, Abbotswood, Greenhill, Evesham, Worcs WR11 4NS.

WOOTTON, Harold Samuel, CMG 1942; FCIS; JP; Town Clerk of Melbourne, 1935–54, retired; *b* Ballan, Vic, 13 Dec. 1891; *s* of late John Richard Wootton, Tatura, Goulburn Valley, Victoria; *m* 1914, Anne, *d* of late Joseph Biggs; one *s* one *d. Educ:* State School, Waranga, Victoria; Central Business College, Melbourne. Junior Clerk, Melbourne Town Hall, 1909; Deputy Town Clerk, 1923. *Recreation:* bowls. *Address:* Unit 2, 11 Robert Street, Noosaville, Qld 4566, Australia. *Clubs:* St Kilda Bowling, Tewantin Bowling (Queensland).

WOOTTON, Ian David Phimester, MA, MB, BChir, PhD, FRSC, FRCPath, FRCP; Professor of Chemical Pathology, Royal Postgraduate Medical School, University of London, 1963–82; *b* 5 March 1921; *s* of D. Wootton and Charlotte (*née* Phimester); *m* 1946, Veryan Mary Walshe; two *s* two *d. Educ:* Weymouth Grammar School; St John's College, Cambridge; St Mary's Hospital, London. Research Assistant, Postgraduate Med. School, 1945; Lecturer, 1949; Sen. Lecturer, 1959; Reader, 1961. Consultant Pathologist to Hammersmith Hospital, 1952. Member of Medical Research Council Unit, Cairo, 1947–48; Major, RAMC, 1949; Smith-Mundt Fellow, Memorial Hosp., New York, 1951. Chief Scientist (Hosp. Scientific and Technical Services), DHSS, 1972–73. *Publications:* Microanalysis in Medical Biochemistry, 1964, ed 6th edn, 1982; Biochemical Disorders in Human Disease, 1970; papers in medical and scientific journals on biochemistry and pathology. *Recreations:* carpentry, boating, beekeeping. *Address:* Cariad Cottage, Cleeve Road, Goring, Oxon RG8 9DB. *T:* Goring 873050.

WOOTTON, (Norman) Godfrey; Stipendiary Magistrate for Merseyside, since 1976; *b* 10 April 1926; *s* of H. N. and E. Wootton, Crewe, Cheshire. *Educ:* The Grammar Sch., Crewe; Liverpool Univ. (LLB). Called to Bar, Gray's Inn, 1951. Joined Northern Circuit, 1951. A Recorder of the Crown Court, 1972. *Recreations:* travel, photography. *Address:* Magistrates' Court, Dale Street, Liverpool L2 2JQ. *Club:* Athenæum (Liverpool).

WOOTTON, Ronald William; Assistant Secretary, Overseas Development Administration, since 1976; *b* 7 April 1931; *s* of William George and Lilian Wootton; *m* 1954, Elvira Mary Gillian Lakeman; one *s* one *d. Educ:* Christ's College, Finchley. Served Royal Signals, 1950–52. Colonial Office, 1952–63; Commonwealth Relations Office, 1963–65; ODM/ODA, 1965–; Head of British Develt Div. in the Pacific, 1982–85. *Address:* 16 The Heath, Chaldon, Surrey. *T:* Caterham 44903.

WOOZLEY, Prof. Anthony Douglas, MA; University Professor Emeritus of Philosophy and Law, University of Virginia, since 1983; *b* 14 Aug. 1912; *o s* of David Adams Woozley and Kathleen Lucy Moore; *m* 1937, Thelma Suffield (marr. diss. 1978), *e d* of late Frank Townshend, Worcester; one *d. Educ:* Haileybury College; Queen's College, Oxford. Open Scholar, Queen's College, 1931–35; 1st Cl. Class. Hon. Mods, 1933; 1st Cl. Lit. Hum., 1935; John Locke Schol., 1935. Served War, 1940–46 (despatches); commissioned King's Dragoon Guards, 1941; served N Africa, Italy, Greece, Egypt, Syria, Palestine; Major. Fellow of All Souls College, 1935–37; Fellow and Praelector in

Philosophy, Queen's Coll., 1937–54; Librarian, 1938–54; Tutor, Queen's College, 1946–54; University Lecturer in Philosophy, 1947–54; Senior Proctor, 1953–54; Prof. of Moral Philosophy, Univ. of St Andrews, 1954–67; University of Virginia: Prof. of Philosophy, 1966; Commonwealth Prof. of Philosophy, 1974–77; Commonwealth Prof. and Univ. Prof. of Philosophy and Law, 1977–83. Editor of The Philosophical Quarterly, 1957–62; Editor, Home University Library, 1962–68. Visiting Professor of Philosophy: Univ. of Rochester, USA, 1965; Univ. of Arizona, 1972. *Publications:* (ed) Thomas Reid's Essays on the Intellectual Powers of Man, 1941; Theory of Knowledge, 1949; (with R. C. Cross) Plato's Republic: a Philosophical Commentary, 1964; (ed) John Locke's Essay Concerning Human Understanding, 1964; Law and Obedience, 1979; articles and reviews in Mind, etc. *Address:* 655 Kearsarge Circle, Charlottesville, Va 22901, USA.

WORCESTER, Marquess of; Henry John Fitzroy Somerset; ARICS; *b* 22 May 1952; *s* and *heir* of 11th Duke of Beaufort, *qv*. *Educ:* Eton; Cirencester Agricultural College. With Morgan Grenfell Laurie Ltd (formerly Michael Laurie & Partners), London, 1977–. *Recreations:* hunting, shooting, golf, tennis, skiing, rock music. *Address:* 28 Halsey Street, SW3 2PT. *T:* 01–584 6592. *Club:* Turf.

WORCESTER, Bishop of, since 1982; **Rt. Rev. Philip Harold Ernest Goodrich;** *b* 2 Nov. 1929; *s* of Rev. Canon Harold Spencer Goodrich and Gertrude Alice Goodrich; *m* 1960, Margaret Metcalfe Bennett; four *d*. *Educ:* Stamford Sch.; St John's Coll., Cambridge (MA); Cuddesdon Theological Coll. Curate, Rugby Parish Church, 1954–57; Chaplain, St John's Coll., Cambridge, 1957–61; Rector of the South Ormsby Group of Parishes, 1961–68; Vicar of Bromley, 1968–73; Diocesan Director of Ordinands, Rochester, 1974–82; Bishop Suffragan of Tonbridge, 1974–82. *Recreations:* gardening, music, walking, looking at buildings. *Address:* Bishop's House, Hartlebury Castle, Kidderminster, Worcs DY11 7XX.

WORCESTER, Archdeacon of; *see* Bentley, Ven. F. W. H.

WORCESTER, Robert Milton; Chairman, since 1973 and Managing Director, since 1969, Market & Opinion Research International (MORI) Ltd; *b* 21 Dec. 1933; *s* of late C.M. and Violet Ruth Worcester, of Kansas City, Mo, USA; *m* 1st, 1958, Joann (*née* Ransdell); two *s*; 2nd, 1982, Margaret Noel (*née* Smallbone). *Educ:* Univ. of Kansas (BSc). Consultant, McKinsey & Co., 1962–65; Controller and Asst to Chm., Opinion Research Corp., 1965–68. Past Pres., World Assoc. for Public Opinion Research. Member: Council, WWF (UK); Exec. Cttee, Democrats Abroad (UK); Pilgrims' Soc.; Scientific Activities Cttee, Internat. Social Science Council, Unesco; Programme Cttee, Ditchley Foundn. Consultant: The Times; Sunday Times; Economist. Frequent broadcaster and speaker on British and Amer. politics. MBIM. *Publications:* edited: Consumer Market Research Handbook, 1971, 3rd edn 1986; (with M Harrop) Political Communications, 1982; Political Opinion Polling: an international review, 1983; (with Lesley Watkins) Private Opinions, Public Polls, 1986; columnist, The Times; papers in tech. and prof. jls. *Recreations:* choral music (St Bartholomew's Hospital Choir), gardening, scuba diving, ski-ing. *Address:* 32 Old Queen Street, SW1H 9HP. *T:* 01–222 0232. *Clubs:* Reform, Hurlingham.

WORDEN, Prof. Alastair Norman; Professor of Toxicology, University of Bath, 1973–85; Chairman, Huntingdon Research Centre, 1951–78, Founder, since 1978; Hon. Professor of Toxicology, since 1978, Adviser to Department of Biochemistry, since 1985, University of Surrey; Chairman, Cambridge Applied Nutrition, Toxicology of Biosciences Group, since 1981; *b* 23 April 1916; *s* of Dr. C. Norman and Elizabeth Worden; *m* 1st, 1942, Agnes Marshall Murray; one *s*; 2nd, 1950, Dorothy Mary Jensen (*née* Peel), MA (Fellow and Steward, Lucy Cavendish Coll., Cambridge); two *s* one *d*. *Educ:* Queen Elizabeth's Sch., Barnet; St John's Coll. and Sch. of Clinical Medicine, Cambridge (MA, MB, BChir, PhD); Royal Veterinary, Birkbeck and University Colls, London (DVetMed, DSc). DrVetMed Zurich; FRCPath; FRCVS; FAAVCT; FRSC; FIBiol; CBiol; FLS, LSA, CChem; FIBM; FBIRA. Research Student, Lister Inst. of Preventive Medicine and Univ. Cambridge, 1938–41; Res. Officer, Univ. Cambridge, 1941–45; Milford Res. Prof., and Jt Hd, Dept of Biochemistry, Univ. Wales, 1945–50; Fellow and Co-ordinator of Environmental Studies, Wolfson (formerly University) Coll., Cambridge, 1971–83, Emeritus Fellow 1983, Mem. Council, 1974–78; Expert Pharmacologue-Toxicologue Specialisé du Ministère de la Santé Publique, France, 1974–. Member: ARC Tech. Cttees on Calf and Pig Diseases, 1944; Jt ARC Agricl Improvement Council Cttee on Grassland Improvement Station, 1946; ARC Res. (Frazer) Cttee on Toxic Chemicals, 1961; MAFF British Agrochemicals Jt Medical Panel, 1961; Zool Soc. Lond., Animal Husbandry and Welfare Cttee, 1954–, Hon. Res. Associate 1979–; Japan Pharmacol. Soc. 1970; Asociación Medica Argentina, 1974; Royal Society Study Gp on Long Term Toxic Effects, 1975–78; MAFF Res. Consultative Cttee on Food Safety, 1985–; Sec., FRAME Toxicity Cttee, 1979–; Chm., Inst. of Food Techologists, 1973–74. Governor, Taverham Hall Educnl Trust, 1968–; Mem. Papworth-Huntingdon HMC, 1970–74; Trustee: Lucy Cavendish Coll., Cambridge, 1975–; Cambridge Univ. Vet. Sch., 1981–. President: Hunts Br., Historical Assoc., 1967–; Hunts Fauna and Flora Soc., 1965–; Beds and Hunts Naturalist Trust; Chm., Mammal Soc. British Isles, 1953–54; Pres., Hunts Football League; Vice Pres., Hunts CCC, FA, and Referees' Assoc.; Life Member: CUCC; CURUFC. Mem. Worshipful Soc. Apothecaries, 1971. Freeman, City of London, 1974. Editor: Animal Behaviour, 1950–65; Toxicology Letters, 1977–. *Publications:* Laboratory Animals, 1947; (with Harry V. Thompson) The Rabbit, 1956; Animal Health, Production and Pasture, 1964; Animals and Alternatives in Research, 1983; (with John Marks and D. V. Parke) The Future of Predictive Safety Evaluation, 1968; numerous papers on nutrition, biochemistry and toxicology. *Recreations:* history, natural history, sport, travel. *Address:* Cross Keys Orchard, Hemingford Abbots, Cambs PE18 9AE. *T:* Huntingdon 62434. *Clubs:* Athenæum, United Oxford & Cambridge University, Farmers', No 10; Sette of Odd Volumes; MCC, Lancashire CCC, Middlesex CCC, Surrey CCC, Blackpool FC.

WORDIE, Sir John (Stewart), Kt 1981; CBE 1975; VRD 1963; barrister-at-law; *b* 15 Jan. 1924; *s* of late Sir James Mann Wordie, CBE, Hon. LLD, and of Lady Wordie (*née* Henderson); *m* 1955, Patricia Gladys Kynoch, Keith, Banffshire, *d* of Lt-Col G. B. Kynoch, CBE, TD, DL; four *s*. *Educ:* Winchester Coll.; St John's Coll., Cambridge (MA; LLM). Served RNVR, 1942–46. Comdr RNR, 1967; Comdr London Div. RNR, 1969–71. Cambridge, 1946–49; Called to the Bar, Inner Temple, 1950; in practice at the Bar, 1951–. Chairman: Burnham, Pelham and Soulbury Cttees, 1966–; Wages Councils; Mem., Agricultural Wages Bd for England and Wales, 1974–; Dep. Chm. and Mem., Central Arbitration Cttee, 1976–. Mem. Court of Assistants, Salters' Co., 1971–, Master, 1975. *Recreations:* shooting, sailing and boating, athletics, tennis. *Address:* Shallows Cottage, Breamore, Fordingbridge, Hants. *T:* Breamore 432. *Clubs:* Travellers', Army and Navy, Royal Ocean Racing; Hawks (Cambridge); Royal Tennis Court (Hampton Court); Clyde Corinthian Yacht.

WORDLEY, Ronald William; Managing Director, HTV Ltd, since 1978 (Chairman, 1985–86); *b* 16 June 1928; *s* of William Wordley and Elizabeth Anne Hackett; *m* 1953, Pamela Mary Offord; two *s* one *d* (and one *s* decd). *Educ:* Barnet Grammar Sch.; City of London Coll.; RMA, Sandhurst. Regular Army Officer: 2/Lieut RA, 1948; regtl duty, UK, Far East and Europe; Liaison Officer, RM Commando Bde, 1951, Captain; Air OP Pilot, 1953; Army Light Aircraft Sch., 1955; seconded Army Air Corps Cadre, 1957; resigned commn, 1958. Unilever (United Africa Co.), 1958–59; Anglia Television Ltd: Sales Exec., 1959; Gen. Sales Manager, 1962; Dep. Sales Controller, 1964; joined Harlech Consortium as Sales Controller, 1967; Sales Dir on bd of HTV Ltd, 1971. Director: Instock Ltd; Independent Television Publications Ltd; (also Mem. Council), Independent Television Cos Assoc. Ltd; HTV Gp plc; HTV Equipment Ltd; HTV Property Ltd. Mem., Inst. of Marketing; FRSA 1983. *Recreations:* music, travel, golf, swimming. *Address:* 6 Spring Leigh, Leigh Woods, Bristol, Avon. *T:* (office) Bristol 778366. *Clubs:* Clifton (Bristol); Crews Hill Golf (Mddx), Bristol and Clifton Golf, Burnham and Berrow Golf.

WORDSWORTH, Barry; conductor; *b* 20 Feb. 1948; *s* of Ronald and Kathleen Wordsworth; *m* 1970, Ann Barber; one *s*. *Educ:* Royal College of Music. Conductor, Royal Ballet, 1974–84; Music Dir, Sadler's Wells Opera, 1982–84, New Sadler's Wells Opera. Joint winner, Sargent Conductor's Prize, 1970; Tagore Gold Medal, RCM, 1970. *Recreations:* swimming, photography, cooking. *Address:* 20 Charlton Place, N1 8AJ. *T:* 01–354 2181.

WORKMAN, Charles Joseph, TD 1966; Part-time Chairman, Industrial Tribunals for Scotland, since 1986; *b* 25 Aug. 1920; *s* of Hugh William O'Brien Workman and Annie Shields; *m* 1949, Margaret Jean Mason; one *s* two *d*. *Educ:* St Mungo's Acad., Glasgow; Univ. of Glasgow (MA 1950, LLB 1952). Admitted solicitor, 1952. Served War, 1939–45: France, Belgium, Holland, Germany; commnd Second Fife and Forfar Yeomanry, RAC, 1942; Captain, 1945; served Intell. Corps TA and TAVR, 1954–69; Bt Lt-Col 1969; Hon. Col, Intell. and Security Gp (V), 1977–86. Entered Office of Solicitor to Sec. of State for Scotland as Legal Asst, 1955; Sen. Legal Asst, 1961; Asst Solicitor, 1966; Dep. Solicitor to Sec. of State, 1976; Dir, Scottish Courts Administration, 1978–82; Senior Dep. Sec. (Legal Aid), Law Soc. of Scotland, 1982–86. Chm., Public Service and Commerce Gp, Law Soc. of Scotland, 1977–78. Founder Mem., Edinburgh Chamber Music Trust, 1977–. *Publication:* (contrib.) Stair Memorial Encyclopaedia of Laws of Scotland. *Recreations:* hill walking, swimming, music. *Address:* Green Lane Cottage, Lasswade, Midlothian EH18 1HE. *Clubs:* Army and Navy; New (Edinburgh).

WORKMAN, Robert Little, CB 1974; Under-Secretary, HM Treasury, 1967–74; *b* 30 Oct. 1914; *s* of late Robert Workman and Jesse Little; *m* 1940, Gladys Munroe Foord; two *d*. *Educ:* Sedbergh Sch.; Clare Coll., Cambridge. Economist, Export Credits Guarantee Dept, 1938–49; HM Treasury: Principal, 1949–59; Asst Secretary, 1959–66. Member, St Pancras Borough Council, 1945–49. *Recreations:* building and the visual arts. *Address:* Flatts Farm, Hawstead, Suffolk. *T:* Sicklesmere 497.

WORKMAN, Timothy; a Metropolitan Stipendiary Magistrate, since 1986; *b* 18 Oct. 1943; *s* of Gordon and late Eileen Workman; *m* 1971, Felicity Ann Caroline Western; one *s* one *d*. *Educ:* Ruskin Grammar Sch., Croydon. Probation Officer, Inner London, 1967–69; admitted Solicitor, 1969; Solicitor, subseq. Partner, C. R. Thomas & Son, later Lloyd Howorth & Partners, Maidenhead, 1969–85. *Recreations:* ski-ing, pottery. *Address:* Orchard House, Fleet Hill, Finchampstead, Berks RG11 4LA. *T:* Eversley 733315. *Club:* Medico-Legal.

WORLOCK, Most Rev. Derek John Harford; *see* Liverpool, Archbishop of, (RC).

WORMALD, Brian Harvey Goodwin, MA; University Lecturer in History, Cambridge, 1948–79; Fellow of Peterhouse, 1938–79, Emeritus Fellow 1979; *b* 24 July 1912; *s* of late Rev. C. O. R. Wormald and Mrs A. W. C. Wormald (*née* Brooks); *m* 1946, Rosemary, *d* of E. J. B. Lloyd; four *s*. *Educ:* Harrow; Peterhouse, Cambridge (Scholar). BA 1934 (1st Class Hons Hist. Tripos, Parts I and II); Members Prize (English Essay), 1935; Strathcona Research Student, St John's College, 1936–38; Prince Consort Prize, 1938; MA 1938. Chaplain and Catechist, Peterhouse, 1940–48; Dean, 1941–44; Tutor, 1952–62. Select Preacher, Cambridge, 1945 and 1954. Junior Proctor, 1951–52. Received into Catholic Church, 1955. *Publication:* Clarendon: Politics, History and Religion, 1951. *Address:* c/o Peterhouse, Cambridge. *Club:* Travellers'.

WORMALD, Maj.-Gen. Derrick Bruce, DSO 1944; MC 1940, Bar 1945; Director-General of Fighting Vehicles and Engineer Equipment, Ministry of Defence, 1966–70, retired; *b* 28 April 1916; 2nd *s* of late Arthur and Veronica Wormald; *m* 1953, Betty Craddock; two *d*. *Educ:* Bryanston Sch.; RMA Sandhurst. Commnd into 13/18 Royal Hussars (QMO), 1936; served in India, 1936–38, BEF, 1939–40 and BLA, 1944–45; Comd, 25th Dragoons, India, 1945–47; Staff Coll., Quetta, 1947; War Office, 1948–50; Comdr, 1st Armoured Car Regt of Arab Legion, 1951–52; Comdr Arab Legion Armoured Corps, 1953–54; jssc 1955; GSO1, 11th Armoured Div., 1956; Comd, 3rd The King's Own Hussars, 1956, and The Queen's Own Hussars, 1958; Comdr, Aden Protectorate Levies, 1959–61; Comdr, Salisbury Plain Sub District, 1962–65. Col, 13th/18th Royal Hussars (QMO), 1974–79. Order of El Istiqlal (Jordan), 1953. *Recreations:* shooting, fishing, sailing. *Address:* Ballards, Wickham Bishops, Essex CM8 3JJ. *T:* Maldon 891218. *Club:* Cavalry and Guards.

WORMALD, Dame Ethel (May), DBE 1968; JP; DL; *b* 19 Nov. 1901; *d* of late John Robert Robinson, Journalist, Newcastle upon Tyne; *m* 1923, Stanley Wormald, MA, MEd, BSc (decd); two *s*. *Educ:* Whitley Bay High Sch.; Leeds Univ. (BA, DipEd). Liverpool City Councillor, 1953–67; Lord Mayor of Liverpool, 1967–68. President, Assoc. of Education Cttees, 1961–62; Chairman, Liverpool Education Cttee, 1955–61, and 1963–67. Mem. Court, Liverpool Univ. JP Liverpool, 1948–; DL Lancaster, 1970, Merseyside, 1974. *Address:* 26 Princes Park Mansions, Liverpool L8 3SA. *T:* 051–728 8670.

WORMALD, Peter John; Under Secretary, Department of Health and Social Security, since 1978; *b* 10 March 1936; *s* of late H. R. and G. A. Wormald; *m* 1962, Elizabeth North; three *s*. *Educ:* Doncaster Grammar Sch.; The Queen's Coll., Oxford (MA). Assistant Principal, Min. of Health, 1958, Principal, 1963; HM Treasury, 1965–67, Asst Sec., 1970. *Recreations:* music, golf, contract bridge. *Address:* 31 Wilton Crescent, SW19 3QY. *T:* 01–540 5760. *Club:* United Oxford & Cambridge University.

WORMELL, Prof. Donald Ernest Wilson; Fellow Emeritus, Trinity College, Dublin; *b* 5 Jan. 1908; *yr s* of Thomas Wilson and Florence Wormell; *m* 1941, Daphne Dillon Wallace; three *s* one *d*. *Educ:* Perse School. Schol., St John's Coll., Cambridge, 1926; Sandys Student, 1930; Henry Fund Fellow, 1931; Sterling Research Fellow, Yale, 1932; PhD Yale, 1933. Fellow, St John's Coll., Cambridge, 1933–36; Asst Lecturer in Classics, University College, Swansea, 1936–39; employed by Air Ministry and Foreign Office, 1942–44; Fellow, TCD, 1939–78; Prof. of Latin, Univ. of Dublin, 1942–78, Public Orator, 1952–69; Vice-Provost, TCD, 1973–74. Leverhulme Res. Fellow, 1954. MRIA; Mem., Inst. for Advanced Study, Princeton, USA, 1967–68. *Publications:* (with H. W. Parke) The Delphic Oracle, 1956; (jtly) Ovid's Fasti, 1978; articles on classical literature and ancient history in learned periodicals. *Recreation:* music. *Address:* 44 Seaview Park, Shankill, Co. Dublin. *T:* Dublin 823404.

WORRALL, Alfred Stanley, CBE 1983 (OBE 1975); *b* 28 Jan. 1912; *s* of Rev. Sidney A. Worrall and Margaret Worrall (*née* White); *m* 1936, Mary Frances Marshall; one *s* two *d* (and one *s* decd). *Educ:* King Edward's Sch., Bath; St Catharine's Coll., Cambridge (Schol.; MA); BD London. Teaching posts at St George's Sch., Bristol, 1935–38, Leeds Grammar Sch., 1938–49; war service in Non-combatant Corps (bomb disposal) and coal mining, 1941–46; Headmaster: Rock Ferry High Sch., 1949–57; Sir Thomas Rich's Sch., 1957–61; Methodist Coll., Belfast, 1961–74, retired. Member, Methodist Conference, 1955, 1959, 1961–64, also of the Conf. in Ireland, 1966–83. Pres., Ulster Headmasters' Assoc., 1966–68; Chairman: BBC Religious Adv. Council, N Ireland, 1968–73; Arts Council of N Ire., 1974–82; New Ulster Movement, 1974–79; Chm. of Governors, Stranmillis Coll. of Educn, 1974–83; Mem., Radio Telefis Eireann Authority, Dublin, 1979–83; Chm., Libr. and Inf. Services Council, NI, 1982–83. Hon. Life Mem., SHA, 1980. Hon. LLD QUB, 1974. *Publications:* (with Cahal B. Daly) Ballymascanlon: a venture in Irish inter-church dialogue, 1978; (with Eric Gallagher) Christians in Ulster 1969–80, 1982. *Recreations:* travel, enjoyment of the arts. *Address:* 27 Selly Park Road, Birmingham B29 7PH. *T:* 021-471 5140.

WORRALL, Denis John, PhD; South African Ambassador to the Court of St. James's, since 1984; *b* 29 May 1935; *s* of Cecil John Worrall and Hazel Worrall; *m* 1965, Anita Ianco; three *s*. *Educ:* Univ. of Cape Town (BA Hons, MA); Univ. of South Africa (LLB); Cornell Univ. (PhD). Teaching and research positions, Univs of Natal, S Africa, Ibadan, Witwatersrand, California, Cornell; Rearch Prof. and Dir, Inst. of Social and Economic Research, Rhodes Univ., 1973. Senator, 1974; elected to Parlt, 1977; Chm., Constitutional Cttee, President's Council, 1981; Ambassador to Australia, 1983–84. Advocate of Supreme Court of S Africa. *Publication:* South Africa: government and politics, 1970. *Recreations:* tennis, reading, music. *Address:* South African Embassy, South Africa House, Trafalgar Square, WC2N 5DP.

WORRALL, Air Vice-Marshal John, CB 1963; DFC 1940; retired; Managing Director, The Advertising Agency Poster Bureau Ltd, 1964–65; *b* 9 April 1911; *o s* of late J. R. S. Worrall, Thackers, Bombay, India; *m* 1967, Barbara Jocelyne, *er d* of late Vincent Ronald Robb. *Educ:* Cranleigh; Royal Air Force Coll., Cranwell. Commission Royal Air Force, 1931; flying duties No 1 Sqdn, 1932, No 208 Sqdn, 1933–36; language study, Peking, 1936–39; commanded No 32 (F) Sqdn Biggin Hill, 1940; Fighter Control, Biggin Hill, 1940; Fighter and Transport Staff and Unit, 1941–45 (despatches 1944); RAF Staff Coll., 1945; Senior Personnel Staff Officer, HQ Transport Command, 1945–48; OC, RAF West Malling and Metropolitan Sector, 1948–49; OC, RAF Kai Tak, Hong Kong, 1949–51; HQ Home Command, 1952–53; Air Ministry, Organisation Branch, 1953–54; OC Eastern Sector, 1954–56; AOA, HQ Flying Training Command, 1956–58; Assistant Chief of Air Staff (Training), 1958–60; SASO, NEAF, 1960–63; retired from RAF, 1963. Chairman RAF Ski and Winter Sports Assoc., 1953–60, Vice-President, 1960–68; Chairman, Battle of Britain Fighter Assoc., 1958–60. *Recreations:* ski-ing, sailing. *Address:* Es Forti 109, Cala d'Or, Mallorca, Spain; c/o National Westminster Bank, 155 North Street, Brighton, East Sussex.

WORSFOLD, Reginald Lewis, CBE 1979; Member for Personnel, British Gas Corporation (formerly Gas Council), 1973–80, retired; *b* 18 Dec. 1925; *s* of Charles S. and Doris Worsfold; *m* 1st, 1952, Margot Kempell (marr. diss. 1974); one *s* one *d*; 2nd, 1982, Christine McKeown. *Educ:* School of Technology, Art and Commerce, Oxford; London Sch. of Economics. MIPM. Served War of 1939–45: Lieut 44 Royal Marine Commandos, 1943–46. Organising Commissioner, Scout Council of Nigeria, 1947–49; Personnel Manager: British European Airways, 1953–65; W Midlands Gas Bd, 1965–69; Gas Council: Dep. Personnel Dir, 1969–70; Personnel Dir, 1970–72. *Recreations:* sailing, camping, music. *Address:* Beck House, 43 Wychwood Grove, Chandler's Ford, Hants SO5 1FQ. *T:* Chandler's Ford 69873.

WORSKETT, Prof. Roy, RIBA; MRTPI; Consultant Architect, Architectural Planning Partnership, Horsham, since 1985 (partner, 1982–85); *b* 3 Sept. 1932; *s* of Archibald Ellwood Worskett and Dorothy Alice Roffey; two *s* one *d*. *Educ:* Collyer's Sch., Horsham; Portsmouth Sch. of Architecture. MRTPI 1975; RIBA 1955. Architect's Dept, LCC, 1957–60; Architect, Civic Trust, London, 1960–63; Historic Areas Div., DoE (formerly MPBW), 1963–74; City Architect and Planning Officer, Bath City Council, and Prof. of Urban Conservation, Sch. of Architecture, Bath Univ., 1974–79; Consultant Head, Conservation Section, Crafts Council, 1979–82. Consultant Architect: Bath CC, 1979–83; Salisbury DC, 1980–; Consultant: Ford Foundn in India, 1982–; Council of Europe, 1984–. Chm., Conservation Cttees, Crafts Adv. Cttee, 1974–79; Member: Heritage Educn Group, 1976–; Council for Urban Study Centres, TCPA, 1977–80; Council of Management, Architectural Heritage Fund, 1977–. Pres., Urban Design Gp, 1983–84. Vis. Prof., Internat. Centre for Conservation, Rome, 1972–. *Publications:* The Character of Towns, 1968; articles in architect. and planning magazines. *Recreation:* looking and listening in disbelief. *Address:* 32 Smithbarn, Horsham, Sussex. *T:* Horsham 61781.

WORSLEY, Lord; Charles John Pelham; *b* 5 Nov. 1963; *s* and *heir* of 7th Earl of Yarborough, *qv*.

WORSLEY, Air Cdre Geoffrey Nicolas Ernest T. C.; *see* Tindal-Carill-Worsley.

WORSLEY, Very Rev. Godfrey Stuart Harling; Dean Emeritus of Gibraltar, since 1969; *b* 4 Dec. 1906; *o s* of late Rev. A. E. Worsley, Rector of Georgeham; *m* 1933, Stella Mary, *o c* of late H. S. Church, Croyde Manor, N Devon; two *s* one *d*. *Educ:* Dean Close, Cheltenham; London College of Divinity. Deacon, 1929; Priest, 1931; Asst Curate, Croydon Parish Church, 1930–33; CF, Ireland, Malta, Catterick, 1933–43; SCF, W Africa, Greece, Cyprus, 1943–49; DACG, N Midland District and Malta, 1949–54; Rector of Kingsland, 1954–60; Rural Dean of Leominster, 1956–60; Prebendary de Cublington in Hereford Cathedral, and Proctor in Convocation, Diocese of Hereford, 1959–60; Dean of Gibraltar and Rural Dean of Southern Spain, and officiating chaplain RN, 1960–69; Rector of Pen Selwood, 1969–79. *Address:* Arrow Cottage, Eardisland, Leominster, Herefordshire.

WORSLEY, Lt-Gen. Sir John (Francis), KBE 1966 (OBE 1951); CB 1963; MC 1945; retired, 1968; *b* 8 July 1912; *s* of Geoffrey Worsley, OBE, ICS, and Elsie Margaret (*née* Macpherson); *m* 1942, Barbara Elizabeth Jarvis (*née* Greenwood); one *s* three *d* (and two step *d*). *Educ:* Radley; Royal Military Coll., Sandhurst. Unattached List, Indian Army (attached Queen's Own Cameron Highlanders), 1933; 3rd Bn 2nd Punjab Regt, 1934; served NW Frontier, India, 1935 and 1936–37; War of 1939–45, Middle East and SE Asia; Staff Coll., Quetta, 1941; Comd 2nd Bn 1st Punjab Regt, 1945; York and Lancaster Regt, 1947; Joint Services Staff Coll., 1951; Comd 1st Bn The South Lancashire Regt (Prince of Wales's Volunteers), 1953; Secretary, Joint Planning Staff, Ministry of Defence, 1956; Comd 6th Infantry Brigade Group, 1957; Imperial Defence Coll., 1960; General Officer Commanding 48 Division (Territorial Army) and West Midland District, 1961–63; Commandant, Staff Coll., Camberley, 1963–66; Commander, British Forces, Hong Kong, 1966–68. *Address:* Castleton House, Sherborne, Dorset. *Club:* Army and Navy.

WORSLEY, Sir Marcus; *see* Worsley, Sir W. M. J.

WORSLEY, Michael Dominic Laurence; QC 1985; *b* 9 Feb. 1926; *s* of Paul Worsley and Magdalen Teresa Worsley; *m* 1962, Pamela (*née* Philpot) (*d* 1980); one *s* (and one *s* decd); *m* 1986, Jane, *d* of Percival and Mary Sharpe. *Educ:* Bedford School; Inns of Court School of Law. RN 1944–45. Lived in Africa, 1946–52; called to the Bar, Inner Temple, 1955, Bencher, 1980; Standing Prosecuting Counsel to Inland Revenue, 1968–69; Treasury Counsel at Inner London Sessions, 1969–71; Junior Treasury Counsel, 1971–74, Senior Treasury Counsel, 1974–84, CCC. *Recreations:* music, travelling, walking. *Address:* 6 King's Bench Walk, Temple, EC4Y 7DR. *T:* 01–583 0410. *Clubs:* Garrick; Thomas More Society.

WORSLEY, Gen. Sir Richard (Edward), GCB 1982 (KCB 1976); OBE 1964; joined Pilkington Bros, 1982; Chairman, Electro-Optical Division, Pilkington Group, since 1984 (Chief Executive, 1982–86); Chairman: Barr and Stroud, since 1982; Pilkington PE, since 1982; *b* 29 May 1923; *s* of H. H. K. Worsley, Grey Abbey, Co. Down; *m* 1st, 1959, Sarah Anne Mitchell; one *s* one *d*; 2nd, 1980, Caroline, Duchess of Fife, *er d* of Baron Forteviot, *qv*. *Educ:* Radley Coll. Served War: commissioned into Rifle Bde, 1942, Middle East and Italian Campaigns, 1942–45. Instr, RMA Sandhurst, 1948–51; Malayan Emergency, 1956–57; Instr, Staff Coll., Camberley, 1958–61; CO, The Royal Dragoons, 1962–65; Comdr, 7th Armoured Bde, 1965–67; Imperial Defence Coll., 1968; Chief of Staff, Far East Land Forces, 1969–71; GOC 3rd Div., 1972–74; Vice-QMG, MoD, 1974–76; GOC 1 (Br) Corps, 1976–78; QMG, 1979–82. Freeman: City of London, 1983; Glass Sellers' Co., 1984. *Recreations:* shooting, ornithology. *Address:* c/o Barclays Bank, 27 Regent Street, SW1. *Club:* Cavalry and Guards.

WORSLEY, Sir (William) Marcus (John), 5th Bt *cr* 1838; JP; DL; Deputy Chairman, The National Trust, since 1986 (Chairman, Properties Committee, since 1980); *b* 6 April 1925; *s* of Colonel Sir William Arthington Worsley, 4th Bt, and Joyce Morgan (*d* 1979), *d* of Sir John Fowler Brunner, 2nd Bt; *S* father, 1973; *m* 1955, Hon. Bridget Assheton, *d* of 1st Baron Clitheroe, PC, KCVO; three *s* one *d*. *Educ:* Eton; New Coll., Oxford. Green Howards, 1943–47 (Lieut seconded to Royal West African Frontier Force). BA Hons (Oxford) Modern History, 1949. Programme Assistant, BBC European Service, 1950–53. Contested (C) Keighley, 1955; MP (C) Keighley, 1959–64, Chelsea, 1966–Sept. 1974; Parliamentary Private Secretary: to Minister of Health, 1960–61; to Minister without Portfolio, 1962–64; to Lord President of the Council, 1970–72. Second Church Estates Commissioner, 1970–74; a Church Commissioner, 1976–84. Pres., Royal Forestry Soc. of England, Wales and N Ireland, 1980–82 (Vice-Pres., 1976–80); Chm., Yorks Reg. Cttee, Nat. Trust, 1969–80. JP 1957, DL 1978, North Yorks; High Sheriff of North Yorks, 1982. *Recreations:* walking, reading. *Heir:* *s* William Ralph Worsley, ARICS, *b* 12 Sept. 1956. *Address:* Hovingham Hall, York YO6 4LU. *T:* Hovingham 206. *Clubs:* Boodle's; Yorkshire (York).

WORSTHORNE, Peregrine Gerard; Editor, Sunday Telegraph, since 1986; *b* 22 Dec. 1923; *s* of Col Koch de Gooreynd, OBE (who assumed surname of Worsthorne by deed poll, 1921), and of Baroness Norman, *qv*; *m* 1950, Claude Bertrand de Colasse; one *d*. *Educ:* Stowe; Peterhouse, Cambridge (BA); Magdalen Coll., Oxford. Commnd Oxf. and Bucks LI, 1942; attached Phantom, GHQ Liaison Regt, 1944–45. Sub-editor, Glasgow Herald, 1946; Editorial staff: Times, 1948–53; Daily Telegraph, 1953–61; Deputy Editor, Sunday Telegraph, 1961–76, Associate Editor, 1976–86. . *Publications:* The Socialist Myth, 1972; Peregrinations: selected pieces, 1980. *Recreations:* tennis, reading. *Address:* 6 Kempson Road, SW6 4PU; Westerlies, Wivenhoe, Essex. *T:* Wivenhoe 2886. *Clubs:* Beefsteak, Garrick.

See also S. P. E. C. W. Towneley.

WORSWICK, (George) David (Norman), CBE 1981; FBA 1979; Director, National Institute of Economic and Social Research, 1965–82; *b* 18 Aug. 1916; *s* of Thomas Worswick, OBE, and Eveline (*née* Green); *m* 1940, Sylvia, *d* of A. E. Walsh, MBE; one *s* two *d* (and one *s* decd). *Educ:* St Paul's Sch.; New Coll., Oxford (Scholar). Final Hons (Maths), 1937; Dipl. in Economics and Political Science, 1938. Research staff, Oxford Univ. Institute of Statistics, 1940–60; Fellow and Tutor in Economics, Magdalen Coll., Oxford, 1945–65 (Sen. Tutor, 1955–57; Vice-President, 1963–65; Emeritus Fellow, 1969). Vis. Prof. of Economics, MIT, 1962–63. Mem., SSRC, 1966–70. President: Sect. F, British Assoc., 1971; Royal Econ. Soc., 1982–84. Hon. DSc City, 1975. *Publications:* Joint Editor: The British Economy 1945–50, 1952; The British Economy in the 1950's, 1962; (ed) The Free Trade Proposals, 1960; (jt) Profits in the British Economy 1909–1938, 1967; (ed) Uses of Economics, 1972; (ed) The Concept and Measurement of Involuntary Unemployment, 1976; (ed) Education and Economic Performance, 1985; articles in academic jls. *Recreation:* squash. *Address:* 25 Beech Croft Road, Oxford OX2 7AY. *T:* Oxford 52486. *Club:* United Oxford & Cambridge University.

WORTH, Abbot of; *see* Farwell, Rt Rev. G. V.

WORTH, George Arthur, MBE; JP; Farmer and Landowner; *b* 3 May 1907; *s* of late Arthur Hovendon Worth; *m* 1935, Janet Maitland, *d* of late Air Chief Marshal Sir A. M. Longmore, GCB, DSO; two *s* two *d*. *Educ:* Marlborough Coll.; Sidney Sussex Coll., Cambridge. Served War of 1939–45, RAF. JP Parts of Holland, Lincs, 1939; High Sheriff of Lincolnshire, 1948–49; DL Lincs, 1950–73. *Address:* 5 Church Lane, Manton, Oakham, Leics.

See also H. B. H. Carlisle.

WORTH, Irene, Hon. CBE 1975; actress; *b* 23 June 1916. *Educ:* University of California, Los Angeles (BE). Antoinette Perry Award for distinguished achievement in the Theatre, 1965. First appeared as Fenella in Escape Me Never, New York, 1942; debut on Broadway as Cecily Harden in The Two Mrs Carrolls, Booth Theatre, 1943. Studied for six months with Elsie Fogerty, 1944–45. Subsequently appeared frequently at Mercury, Bolton's, Q, Embassy, etc. Parts include: Anabelle Jones in Love Goes to Press, Duchess Theatre, 1946 (after Embassy); Ilona Szabo in The Play's the Thing, St James's, 1947 (after tour and Lyric, Hammersmith); Eileen Perry in Edward my Son, Lyric, 1948; Lady Fortrose in Home is Tomorrow, Cambridge Theatre, 1948; Olivia Raines in Champagne for Delilah, New, 1949; Celia Coplestone in The Cocktail Party, New, 1950 (after Edinburgh Festival, 1949; Henry Miller Theatre, New York, 1950); Desdemona in Othello, Old Vic, 1951; Helena in Midsummer Night's Dream, Old Vic, 1952; Catherine de Vausselles in The Other Heart, Old Vic, 1952; Lady Macbeth in Macbeth, Desdemona in Othello, Helena in Midsummer Night's Dream, Catherine de Vausselles in The Other Heart, Old Vic tour of S Africa, 1952; Portia in The Merchant of Venice, Old Vic, 1953; Helena in All's Well That Ends Well and Queen Margaret in Richard III, First Season Shakespeare Festival Theatre, Stratford, Ont, Canada, 1953; Frances Farrar in A Day By The Sea, Haymarket, 1953–54; Alcestis in A Life in the Sun, Edinburgh Festival, 1955; leading rôles in: The Queen and the Rebels, Haymarket, 1955; Hotel Paradiso, Winter Garden, 1956; Mary Stuart, Phœnix Theatre, NY, 1957, Old Vic, 1958; The Potting Shed, Globe Theatre, London, 1958; Rosalind in As You Like It, Shakespeare Festival Theatre, Stratford, Ont, 1959; Albertine Prine in Toys in the Attic, Hudson Theatre, New York, 1960 (NY Newspaper Guild Page One Award); Season at Royal Shakespeare Theatre, Stratford,

1962; Goneril in King Lear, Aldwych, 1962; Doctor Mathilde von Zahnd in The Physicists, Aldwych, 1963; Clodia Pulcher in The Ides of March, Haymarket, 1963; World tour of King Lear for Royal Shakespeare Company, 1964; Alice in Tiny Alice, Billy Rose Theatre, New York, 1965 (Tony award 1965), Aldwych, 1970; Hilde in A Song at Twilight, Anne in Shadows of the Evening, Anna-Mary in Come into the Garden Maud (Noël Coward Trilogy), Queen's, 1966 (Evening Standard Award); Hesione Hushabye in Heartbreak House, Chichester and Lyric, 1967 (Variety Club of GB Award, 1967); Jocasta in Seneca's Oedipus, National Theatre, 1968; Hedda in Hedda Gabler, Stratford, Ont, 1970; worked with internat. Co. for Theatre Res., Paris and Iran, 1971; Notes on a Love Affair, Globe, 1972; Madame Arkadina, The Seagull, Chichester, 1973; Hamlet, Ghosts, The Seagull, Greenwich, 1974; Sweet Bird of Youth, Lake Forest, Washington, New York, 1975 (Tony Award, 1975; Jefferson Award, 1975); The Cherry Orchard, NY, 1977; Happy Days, NY, 1979; The Lady from Dubuque, NY, 1980; L'Olimpiade, Edinburgh Fest., 1982; The Chalk Garden, NY, 1982; The Physicists, Washington, 1983; The Golden Age, NY, 1984; Coriolanus, Nat. Theatre, 1984; The Bay at Nice, Nat. Theatre, 1986; Lake Forest, Ill, productions: Misalliance, 1976; Old Times, 1977; After the Season, 1978. *Films:* Order to Kill, 1957 (British Film Academy Award for Best Woman's Performance, 1958); The Scapegoat, 1958; King Lear (Goneril), 1970; Nicholas and Alexandra, 1971; Eye Witness, 1980. Daily Mail National Television Award, 1953–54, and has subseq. appeared on television and acted with CBC Television in NY and Canada; Coriolanus (BBC Shakespeare series), 1984. Hon. Dr Arts Tufts Univ. Whitbread Anglo-American Award for Outstanding Actress, 1967; Drama Desk Award, 1977; NY Theatre Hall of Fame, 1979. *Recreation:* music. *Address:* c/o ICM Sixth Floor, Milton Goldman, 40 West 57th Street, New York, NY 10019, USA.

WORTHINGTON, Edgar Barton, CBE 1967; MA, PhD; environmental consultant; *b* 13 Jan. 1905; *s* of Edgar Worthington and Amy E. Beale; *m* 1st, 1930, Stella Desmond Johnson (*d* 1978); three *d*; 2nd, 1980, Harriett Stockton, Cape Cod. *Educ:* Rugby; Gonville and Caius Coll., Cambridge. Expeditions to African Lakes, 1927–31; Balfour Student, 1930–33, and Demonstrator in Zoology, Cambridge Univ., 1933–37; Scientist for the African Research Survey, 1934–37; Mungo Park Medal, RSGS, 1939; Director of Laboratories and Secretary of Freshwater Biological Assoc., Windermere, 1937–46; Scientific Adviser to Middle East Supply Centre, 1943–45; Development Adviser, Uganda, 1946; Scientific Secretary to Colonial Research Council, 1946–49, to E Africa High Commission, 1950–51; Secretary-General to Scientific Council for Africa South of the Sahara, 1951–55; Deputy Director-General (Scientific) Nature Conservancy, 1957–65; Scientific Dir, Internat. Biological Programme, 1964–74; Pres., Cttee on Water Res. of Internat. Council of Scientific Unions, 1973–77. Order of Golden Ark (Netherlands), 1976; Member of Honour, IUCN, 1978. *Publications:* (with Stella Worthington) Inland Waters of Africa, 1933; Science in Africa, 1938; Middle East Science, 1946; Development Plan for Uganda, 1947; (with T. T. Macan) Life in Lakes and Rivers, 1951, rev. edn 1973; Science in the Development of Africa, 1958; (ed) Man-made Lakes: problems and environmental effects, 1973; Evolution of the IBP, 1975; (ed) Arid Land Irrigation: problems and environmental effects, 1976; The Nile, 1978; The Ecological Century, 1983; official reports and papers in scientific journals. *Recreations:* field sports and farming. *Address:* Colin Godmans, Furner's Green, Uckfield, East Sussex. *T:* Chelwood Gate 322. *Clubs:* Athenæum, Farmers'.

WORTHINGTON, Air Vice-Marshal (Retired) Sir Geoffrey (Luis), KBE 1960 (CBE 1945); CB 1957; idc; psa; Director-General of Equipment, Air Ministry, 1958–61, retired; *b* 26 April 1903; *s* of late Commander H. E. F. Worthington, RN; *m* 1931, Margaret Joan, *d* of late Maj.-Gen. A. G. Stevenson, CB, CMG, DSO; two *s* one *d*. *Educ:* HMS Conway; Eastbourne Coll. RAF Coll., Cranwell, 1921. Joined RAF, 1922; resigned 1924; re-joined, 1926, in Stores Branch; RAF Staff Coll., 1934. Served War of 1939–45 (despatches, CBE): HQ Maintenance Comd, 1939–43; Air Cdre, 1943; HQ AEAF, 1944; SHAEF, 1944–45; Air Comd, Far East, 1945–47; Director of Equipment B, Air Ministry, 1948–49; idc 1950; Director of Equipment D, Air Ministry, 1951–53; AOC No 42 Group, Maintenance Comd, 1954–55; Air Vice-Marshal, 1956; AOC No 40 Group, 1955–58. Comdr US Legion of Merit, 1955. *Address:* 30 Brickwall Close, Burnham-on-Crouch, Essex. *T:* Maldon 782388. *Clubs:* Royal Air Force; Royal Burnham Yacht.

WORTHINGTON, George Noel; His Honour Judge Worthington; a Circuit Judge, since 1979; *b* 22 June 1923; *s* of late George Errol Worthington and Edith Margaret Boys Worthington; *m* 1954, Jacqueline Kemble Lightfoot, 2nd *d* of late G. L. S. Lightfoot and Mrs Lightfoot, Carlisle; one *s* one *d* (and one *s* decd). *Educ:* Rossall Sch., Lancashire. Served War of 1939–45 in Royal Armoured Corps, 1941–46. Admitted a solicitor, 1949; a Recorder of the Crown Court, 1972–79. Liveryman, Wax Chandlers' Co. *Recreation:* gardening. *Address:* 33 Cromwell Grove, W6 7RQ. *T:* 01–602 5965. *Club:* Border and County (Carlisle).

WORTLEY, Prof. Ben Atkinson, CMG 1978; OBE 1946; QC 1969; LLD (Manchester), LLM (Leeds); Hon. Docteur de l'Univ. de Rennes (1955); Strasbourg (1965); membre de l'Institut de droit international, 1967 (associé 1956); Professor of Jurisprudence and International Law, University of Manchester, 1946–75, now Emeritus; Barrister of Gray's Inn, 1947; *b* 16 Nov. 1907; *o s* of late John Edward Wortley and late Mary Cicely (*née* King), Huddersfield; *m* 1935, Kathleen Mary Prynne (*d* 1982); two *s* one *d*. *Educ:* King James's Grammar Sch., Almondbury; Leeds Univ.; France. Law Society Open Schol., 1925; 1st Class Hons LLB, 1928, and at Law Society's Final, 1929, also D. Reardon Prizeman. Practised full-time till 1931. Taught Law, London School Econ., 1931–33; Manchester Univ., 1933–34; Birmingham Univ., 1934–36; Manchester Univ., 1936–; visiting Prof. Tulane Univ., New Orleans, 1959. Ministry of Home Security, 1939–43; Instructor Commander RN (temp.), 1943–46. Member: Inst. Advanced Legal Studies, 1947–77; Council, UNIDROIT, 1950–75; Society of Public Teachers of Law (President, 1964–65); an editor, Rev. Diritto Europeo and British Yearbook of International Law. Member Royal Netherlands Academy, 1960; Commendatore (Italy), 1961; Correspondent Hellenic Inst. for International and Foreign Law, and of Belgian Society for Comparative Law. Representative of HM Government at International Confs at The Hague, 1951, 1956, 1960, 1964, and at New York, 1955 and 1958. Sometime Mem., Lord Chancellor's Cttee on Conflict of Laws. Hon. DCL Durham, 1975. Hon. Brother, de la Salle Order, 1973; KSS, 1975. *Publications:* Expropriation in Public International Law, 1959; Jurisprudence, 1967; part editor, Dicey's Conflict of Laws, 1949; (ed) UN, The First Ten Years, 1957; (ed) Law of the Common Market, 1974; lectures, 1939, 1947, 1954 and 1958 (published by Hague Acad. of Internat. Law); (ed) 13 vols Schill lectures; numerous articles. *Recreations:* garden, law of war, literature. *Address:* 24 Gravel Lane, Wilmslow, Cheshire SK9 6LA. *T:* Wilmslow 522810. *Club:* Athenæum.

WOUK, Herman; author, US; *b* New York, 27 May 1915; *s* of Abraham Isaac Wouk and Esther Wouk (*née* Levine); *m* 1945, Betty Sarah Brown; two *s* (and one *s* decd). *Educ:* Townsend Harris High Sch.; Columbia Univ. (AB). Radio script writer, 1935–41; Vis. Professor of English, Yeshiva Univ., 1952–57; Presidential consultative expert to the United States Treasury, 1941. Served United States Naval Reserve, 1942–46, Deck Officer (four campaign stars). Member Officers' Reserve Naval Services. Trustee, College of the Virgin Islands, 1961–69. Columbia University Medal for excellence, 1952; Alexander Hamilton Medal, Columbia Univ., 1980. Hon. LHD, Yeshiva Univ., New York City, 1954; Hon. DLit: Clark Univ., 1960; American Internat. Coll., 1979. *Publications: novels:* Aurora Dawn (American Book of the Month), 1947; The City Boy, 1948; The Caine Mutiny (Pulitzer Prize), 1951; Marjorie Morningstar, 1955; Youngblood Hawke, 1962; Don't Stop The Carnival, 1965; The Winds of War, 1971 (televised 1983); War and Remembrance, 1978; Inside, Outside, 1985; *plays:* The Traitor, 1949; The Caine Mutiny Court-Martial, 1953; Nature's Way, 1957; *non-fiction:* This Is My God, 1959, rev. edn 1973. *Address:* c/o BSW Literary Agency, 3255 N Street, NW, Washington, DC 20007, USA. *Clubs:* Cosmos, Metropolitan (Washington); Bohemian (San Francisco); Century (New York).

WRAGG, Prof. Edward Conrad; Director, Exeter University School of Education, since 1978; *b* 26 June 1938; *s* of George William and Maria Wragg; *m* 1960, Judith (*née* King); one *s* two *d*. *Educ:* King Edward VII Grammar Sch., Sheffield; Durham Univ. (BA Hons German Cl. 1; Postgrad. CertEd, Cl. 1); Leicester Univ. (MEd); Exeter Univ. (PhD). Asst Master, Queen Elizabeth Grammar Sch., Wakefield, 1960–64; Head of German, Wyggeston Boys' Sch., Leicester, 1964–66; Lectr in Education, Exeter Univ., 1966–73; Prof. of Educn, Nottingham Univ., 1973–78; Prof. of Educn and Dir of Sch. of Educn, Exeter Univ., 1978–. Pres., British Educnl Research Assoc., 1981–82; Specialist Adviser, Parliamentary Select Cttee, 1976–77; Chm., School Broadcasting Council for UK, 1981–; Member: Educnl Res. Bd, SSRC, 1974–78; Educn Sub-Cttee, UGC, 1981–. Presenter of radio and TV series and items on education, including Chalkface (Granada), Crisis in Education (BBC), The Education Roadshow (BBC), Pebble Mill at One (BBC). Editor, Research Papers in Education. *Publications:* Teaching Teaching, 1974; Teaching Mixed Ability Groups, 1976; Classroom Interaction, 1976; A Handbook for School Governors, 1980; Class Management and Control, 1981; A Review of Teacher Education, 1982; Swineshead Revisited, 1982; Classroom Teaching Skills, 1984; Pearls from Swineshire, 1984; The Domesday Project, 1985; Education: an action guide for parents, 1986; frequent contributor to Guardian, Times Educnl Supp. (regular columnist), Times Higher Educn Supp. *Recreations:* football playing, watching and coaching; cooking, running, writing, music. *Address:* 14 Doriam Close, Exeter EX4 4RS. *T:* Exeter 77052.

WRAGG, John, ARA 1983; sculptor; *b* 20 Oct. 1937; *s* of Arthur and Ethel Wragg. *Educ:* York Sch. of Art; Royal Coll. of Art. *Work in Public Collections:* Israel Mus., Jerusalem; Tate Gall.; Arts Council of GB; Arts Council of NI; Contemp. Art Soc.; Wellington Art Gall., NZ; work in private collections in GB, America, Canada, France and Holland. *One-man Exhibitions:* Hanover Gall., 1963, 1966 and 1970; Galerie Alexandre Iolas, Paris, 1968; York Fest., 1969; Bridge Street Gall., Bath, 1982; Quinton Green Fine Art, London, 1985; *Exhibitions:* Lords Gall., 1959; L'Art Vivant, 1965–68; Arts Council Gall., Belfast, 1966; Pittsburgh Internat., 1967; Britische Kunst heute, Hamburg, Fondn Maeght, and Contemp. Art Fair, Florence, 1968; Bath Fest. Gall., 1977; Artists Market, 1978; Biennale di Scultura di Arese, Milan, and King Street Gall., Bristol, 1980; Galerie Bollhagen Worpswede, N Germany, 1981 and 1983. Sainsbury Award, 1960; Winner of Sainsbury Sculpture Comp., King's Road, Chelsea, 1966; Arts Council Major Award, 1977. *Relevant Publications:* chapters and articles about his work in: Neue Dimensionen der Plastic, 1964; Contemporary British Artists, 1979; British Sculpture in the Twentieth Century, 1981; Studio Internat., Art & Artiste, Sculpture Internat., Arts Rev., and The Artist. *Recreation:* walking. *Address:* 4 Lansdowne Terrace, Morris Lane, Devizes, Wilts SN10 1NX. *T:* Devizes 5819.

WRAIGHT, Sir John (Richard), KBE 1976; CMG 1962; HM Diplomatic Service, retired; company consultant and company director, since 1976; *b* 4 June 1916; *s* of late Richard George Wraight; *m* 1947, Marquita Elliott. Served War of 1939–45 with Honourable Artillery Company and RHA, Western Desert and Libya; Ministry of Economic Warfare Mission in the Middle East, Cairo, 1944. Economic Warfare Adviser, HQ Mediterranean Allied Air Forces, Italy, June-Dec. 1944. Foreign Office, 1945; Special Assistant to Chief of UNRRA Operations in Europe, 1946. Entered Foreign (subseq. Diplomatic) Service, 1947; British Embassy: Athens, 1948; Tel Aviv, 1950; Washington, 1953; Asst Head of Economic Relations Dept, Foreign Office, 1957; Counsellor (Commercial): Cairo, 1959; Brussels and Luxembourg, 1962 (UK Comr on Tripartite Commn for Restitution of Monetary Gold, Brussels, 1962–68); Minister and Consul-General, Milan, 1968–73; Ambassador to Switzerland, 1973–76. Pres., Greater London SW Scout County, 1977–. Commander of the Order of the Crown (Belgium), 1966. *Recreations:* music, travel, gardening, birdwatching. *Address:* AIDCOM International PLC, 25 Wellington Street, WC2E 7DW.

WRAN, Hon. Neville Kenneth, QC (NSW) 1968; Consultant to New South Wales Government for NSW Bicentennial Council, since 1986; Member, Australian Bicentennial Authority, since 1986; Premier of New South Wales, 1976–86. *Educ:* Fort Street Boys' High Sch., Sydney; Sydney Univ. (LLB). Solicitor before admission to Bar of NSW, 1957. Joined Australian Labor Party, 1954: Branch and Electorate Council positions; Mem., Central Exec., NSW Br; Nat. Pres., 1980–86. Elected to Legislative Council, 1970; Dep. Leader of Opposition, 1971; Leader of Opposition, Legislative Council, 1972; MLA for Bass Hill, Nov. 1973–1986; Leader of Opposition, Dec. 1973–76. Is especially interested in law reform, civil liberties, industrial relations, conservation and cultural matters. Member: NSW Legal and Constitutional Cttee; Federal Legal and Constitutional Cttee; NSW Bar Assoc. *Recreations:* reading, walking, swimming, tennis, cycling. *Address:* GPO Box 4545, Sydney, NSW 2001, Australia. *Club:* Sydney Labor (Hon. Life Mem.).

WRATTEN, Donald Peter; Director, National Counties Building Society, since 1985; *b* 8 July 1925; *er s* of late Frederick George and Marjorie Wratten; *m* 1947, Margaret Kathleen (*née* Marsh); one *s* one *d*. *Educ:* Morehall Elem. Sch. and Harvey Grammar Sch., Folkestone; London Sch. of Economics. Storehand, temp. clerk, meteorological asst (Air Min.), 1940–43; service with RAF Meteorological Wing, 1943–47. LSE, 1947–50. Joined Post Office, 1950; Private Sec. to Asst Postmaster Gen., 1955–56; seconded to Unilever Ltd, 1959; Private Sec. to Postmaster Gen., 1965–66; Head of Telecommunications Marketing Div., 1966–67; Director: Eastern Telecommunications Region, 1967–69; Exec. Dir, Giro and Remittance Services, 1969–74 (Sen. Dir, 1970–74); Sen. Dir, Data Processing Service, 1974–75; Sen. Dir, Telecom Personnel, 1975–81. Member: Industrial Adv. Panel, City Univ. Business Sch., 1974–81 (Chm., 1977–81); Court, Cranfield Inst. of Technology, 1976–81; Business Educn Council, 1977–83; Council, Intermediate Technology Develt Gp, 1982–85. *Recreations:* travel, topography, photography, consumer affairs, do-it-yourself. *Address:* 10 Homefield Road, Radlett, Herts WD7 8PY. *T:* Radlett 4500.

WRAXALL, 2nd Baron, *cr* 1928, of Clyst St George, Co. Devon; **George Richard Lawley Gibbs;** DL; *b* 16 May 1928 (for whom Queen Mary was sponsor); *er s* of 1st Baron and Hon. Ursula Mary Lawley, OBE 1945, RRC (*d* 1979), *e d* of 6th Baron Wenlock; *S* father 1931. *Educ:* Eton; RMA Sandhurst. Coldstream Guards, 1948–53; Lieut North Somerset Yeomanry/44 Royal Tank Regt (TA), Dec. 1958; Captain, 1962; Major, 1965; retired 1967. Chairman: N Somerset Conservative Assoc., 1970–74; Avon County Scout Council, 1976–; Mem., Exec. Cttee, Woodard Corporation, 1983–; Chm.

Governors, St Katherine's Sch., Avon, 1976–81; Fellow, Woodard Schs (Western Div.), 1979–. DL Avon, 1974. *Heir*: *b* Hon. Sir Eustace Hubert Beilby Gibbs, *qv*. *Address*: Tyntesfield, Wraxall, Bristol, Avon BS19 1NU. *T*: Flax Bourton 2923. *Clubs*: Royal Automobile, Cavalry and Guards; Clifton (Bristol).

WRAXALL, Sir Charles (Frederick Lascelles), 9th Bt *cr* 1813; Assistant Accountant, British Steel Corporation, since 1981; *b* 17 Sept. 1961; *s* of Sir Morville William Lascelles Wraxall, 8th Bt, and of Lady (Irmgard Wilhelmina) Wraxall; *S* father, 1978; *m* 1983, Lesley Linda, *d* of William Albert and Molly Jean Allan. *Educ*: Archbishop Tenison's Grammar School, Croydon. *Recreations*: stamp and postcard collection, watching football. *Heir*: *b* Peter Edward Lascelles Wraxall, *b* 30 March 1967.

WRAY, Prof. Gordon Richard, FRS 1986; FEng 1980; Professor and Head of Department of Mechanical Engineering, Loughborough University of Technology, since 1970; *b* 30 Jan. 1928; *s* of Joseph and Letitia Wray (*née* Jones); *m* 1954, Kathleen Senior; one *s* one *d*. *Educ*: Bolton Tech. Coll., Univ. of Manchester (BScTech, MScTech, PhD); DSc Loughborough; FIMechE, FTI; FRSA. Engineering apprentice, Bennis Combustion, Bolton, 1943; Design draughtsman, Dobson & Barlow, Bolton, 1946; Sir Walter Preston Scholar, Univ. of Manchester, 1949; Develt Engineer, Platts (Barton), 1952; Lectr in Mech. Engrg, Bolton Tech. Coll., 1953; Lectr in Textile Engrg, UMIST, 1955; Reader in Mech. Engrg, Loughborough Univ., 1966–70. Springer Vis. Prof., Univ. of California, Berkeley, 1977. Member: DoI Chief Scientist's Requirements Bd, 1974–75; CEI/CSTI Interdisciplinary Bd, 1978–83; SEFI Cttee on Innovation, Brussels, 1980–82; Royal Soc. Working Gp on Agricl Engrg, 1981–82; SERC Applied Mechanics Cttee, 1982–85; Fellowship of Engrg Working Party on DoI Requirements Bds, 1982; SERC Working Party on Engrg Design, 1983; Royal Soc. Sectional Cttee 4 (i), 1985; Cttee, Engrg Profs Conf., 1985. Mem. Council, IMechE, 1964–67 (Chm., Manip. and Mech. Handling Machinery Gp, 1969–71); IMechE Prizes: Viscount Weir, 1959; Water Arbitration, 1972; James Clayton, 1975; Warner Medal, Textile Inst., 1976; S. G. Brown Award and Medal, Royal Soc., 1978; Engrg Merit Award, ASME, 1977. *Publications*: (contrib.) Textile Engineering Processes, ed Nissan, 1959; Modern Yarn Production from Man-made Fibres, 1960; Modern Developments in Weaving Machinery, 1961; An Introduction to the Study of Spinning, 3rd edn 1962; (contrib.) Contemporary Textile Engineering, ed Happey, 1982; numerous papers to learned jls. *Recreations*: fell-walking, photography, theatre, music, gardening, DIY. *Address*: Stonestack, Rempstone, Loughborough, Leics LE12 6RH. *T*: Wymeswold 880043.

WRAY, Martin Osterfield, CMG 1956; OBE 1954; *b* 14 June 1912; *s* of late C. N. O. Wray; *m* 1938, Lilian Joyce, *d* of late R. W. Playfair, Nairobi, Kenya; one *s* two *d*. *Educ*: St George's Sch., Harpenden; Wadham Coll., Oxford. Colonial Administrative Service in Uganda, 1935; Administrative Secretary, Zanzibar, 1949; Administrative Secretary to High Commissioner for Basutoland, the Bechuanaland Protectorate and Swaziland, 1952; Resident Commissioner, Bechuanaland Protectorate, 1955–59; Chief Secretary, Northern Rhodesia, 1959–62. *Address*: Prospect House, East Knoyle, Wilts. *Club*: Royal Commonwealth Society.

WRENBURY, 3rd Baron, *cr* 1915; **John Burton Buckley;** Partner, Thomson Snell and Passmore, since 1974; *b* 18 June 1927; *s* of 2nd Baron and Helen Malise (*d* 1981), 2nd *d* of late His Honour John Cameron Graham of Ballewan, Stirlingshire; *S* father, 1940; *m* 1st, 1956, Carolyn Joan Maule (marr. diss., 1961), *o d* of Lt-Col Ian Burn-Murdoch, OBE, of Gartincaber, Doune, Perthshire; 2nd, 1961, Penelope Sara Frances, *o d* of Edward D. Fort, The White House, Sixpenny Handley, Dorset; one *s* two *d*. *Educ*: Eton Coll.; King's Coll., Cambridge. Deputy Legal Adviser to the National Trust, 1955–56; Partner, Freshfield's, Solicitors, 1956–74. *Heir*: *s* Hon. William Edward Buckley, *b* 19 June 1966. *Address*: Oldcastle, Dallington, near Heathfield, East Sussex. *T*: Rushlake Green 830400. *Club*: Oriental.

WREY, Sir (Castel Richard) Bourchier, 14th Bt, *cr* 1628; *b* 27 March 1903; *s* of late Edward Castel Wrey and Katharine Joan, *d* of Rev. John Dene; *S* uncle, 1948; *m* 1946, Alice Sybil, *d* of Dr Lubke, Durban, S Africa; two *s*. *Educ*: Oundle. Served War of 1939–45; 2nd Lieut, RASC (Supp. Res.), France, 1939–40 (invalided); joined RN as ordinary seaman, 1940; Lieut, RNVR, 1942. *Heir*: *s* George Richard Bourchier Wrey [*b* 2 Oct. 1948; *m* 1981, Hon. Caroline Lindesay-Bethune, *d* of Earl of Lindsay, *qv*; one *s*]. *Address*: Hollamoor Farm, Tawstock, Barnstaple, N Devon; 511 Currie Road, Durban, South Africa.

WRIGGLESWORTH, Ian William; MP (SDP) Stockton South, since 1983 (Teesside, Thornaby, Feb. 1974–1983 (Lab and Co-op, 1974–81, SDP, 1981–83)); *b* Dec. 1939; *s* of Edward and Elsie Wrigglesworth; *m* Patricia Truscott; two *s* one *d*. *Educ*: Stockton Grammar Sch.; Stockton-Billingham Technical Coll; Coll. of St Mark and St John, Chelsea. Formerly: Personal Assistant to Gen. Sec., NUT; Head of Research and Information Dept of Co-operative Party; Press and Public Affairs Manager of National Giro. PPS to Mr Alec Lyon, Minister of State, Home Office, 1974; PPS to Rt Hon. Roy Jenkins, Home Secretary, 1974–76; Opposition spokesman on Civil Service, 1979–80; SDP spokesman on industry, 1981, on home affairs, 1982, on industry and economic affairs, 1983–. *Address*: House of Commons, SW1.

WRIGHT, Alan John; a Master of the Supreme Court, Supreme Court Taxing Office, since 1972; *b* 21 April 1925; *s* of late Rev. Henry George Wright, MA and Winifred Annie Wright; *m* 1952, Alma Beatrice Ridding; two *s* one *d*. *Educ*: St Olave's and St Saviour's Grammar Sch., Southwark; Keble Coll., Oxford. BA 1949, MA 1964. Served with RAF, India, Burma and China, 1943–46. Solicitor 1952; in private practice with Shaen Roscoe & Co., 1952–71; Legal Adviser to Trades Union Congress, 1955–71. *Recreations*: Germanic studies, walking, physical fitness training, travel, youth work, industrial law. *Address*: 21 Brockley Park, Forest Hill, SE23 1PT.

WRIGHT, Alec Michael John, CMG 1967; *b* Hong Kong, 19 Sept. 1912; *s* of Arthur Edgar Wright and Margery Hepworth Chapman; *m* 1948, Ethel Surtees; one *d*. *Educ*: Brentwood Sch. ARICS 1934; ARIBA 1937. Articled pupil followed by private practice in London. Joined Colonial Service, 1938; appointed Architect in Hong Kong, 1938. Commissioned Hong Kong Volunteer Defence Force, 1941; POW in Hong Kong, 1941–45. Chief Architect, Public Works Dept, Hong Kong, 1950; Asst Director of Public Works, 1956; Dep. Director, 1959; Director, 1963–69; Commissioner for Hong Kong in London, 1969–73. *Address*: 13 Montrose Court, Exhibition Road, SW7 2QG. *T*: 01–584 4293. *Club*: Hong Kong (Hong Kong).

See also Sir Denis Wright.

WRIGHT, Hon. Alison Elizabeth, JP; writer and consultant on the economy of Spain, since 1970; Member, Commonwealth Development Corporation, since 1984; *b* 5 Jan. 1945; *d* of Baron Franks, *qv*; *m* 1973, Stanley Harris Wright, *qv*. *Educ*: Headington School, Oxford; Downe House, Newbury; St Anne's College Oxford (BA PPE). Research Officer, Overseas Development Institute, 1965–69; research in Spain, 1970–72. Member: Heilbron Cttee on Law of Rape, 1975; Top Salaries Review Body, Nov. 1984, resigned April 1985. JP Inner London 1978; Mem., Inner London Exec. Cttee, Magistrates' Assoc., 1980–82. *Publications*: The Less Developed Countries in World Trade (with M. Zammit Cutajar), 1969; The Spanish Economy 1959–1976, 1977; contribs to Economist Intelligence Unit and other publications. *Recreations*: reading, theatre. *Address*: 6 Holly Place, Holly Walk, NW3 6QU. *T*: 01–435 0237.

WRIGHT, Sir Allan Frederick, KBE 1982; farmer; Chairman of Directors, NZ Rural Banking and Finance Corporation; Director: Farmers' Mutual Insurance Group; Mair & Co.; NZ Railways Corporation; NZ Skin Pool Co-operative; *b* Darfield, 25 March 1929; *s* of Quentin A. Wright; *m* 1953, Dorothy June Netting; three *s* two *d*. *Educ*: Christ's Coll., Christchurch. Nat. Pres., Young Farmers' Clubs, 1957–58; President: N Canterbury Federated Farmers, 1971–74; Federated Farmers of NZ, 1977–81 (formerly Sen. Nat. Vice-Pres.). Mem., NZ Cricket Bd of Control, 1967–; Manager, NZ Cricket Team to England, 1983. Mem. Council, Lincoln Coll., 1974–. *Recreations*: cricket (played for N Canterbury), rugby, golf. *Address*: Annat, RD Sheffield, Canterbury, New Zealand.

WRIGHT, Arthur Francis Stevenson, MBE 1945; FRIBA, FRIAS; architect principal in private practice, since 1949, consultant, since 1983; *b* 15 Feb. 1918; *s* of Arthur and Alice Wright; *m* 1946, Catherine Grey Linton; one *d*. *Educ*: Morgan Academy; College of Art, Dundee (DipArch 1948). Served War, Royal Engineers (Major), 1940–46. FRIBA 1956; FRIAS 1954 (Pres., 1975–77); FCIOB (FIOB 1974); FCIArb (FIArb 1976). Chm., Jt Standing Cttee of Architects, Surveyors and Builders in Scotland, 1973–75. *Recreations*: fishing, golf. *Address*: Hillside of Prieston, Tealing, Dundee DD4 0RG. *T*: Tealing 279.

WRIGHT, (Arthur Robert) Donald, OBE 1984; *b* 20 June 1923; *s* of late Charles North Wright and Beatrice May Wright; *m* 1948, Helen Muryell Buxton; two *s* three *d*. *Educ*: Bryanston Sch.; Queens' Coll., Cambridge. War Service (commnd 1943), NW Europe (despatches) and India, 1942–46. Taught at: University Coll. Sch., 1948–50; The Hill School, Pennsylvania, 1950; Leighton Park School, 1950–52; Marlborough College (Housemaster), 1953–63; Headmaster, Shrewsbury Sch., 1963–75. Chm., HMC, 1971. Appointments' Sec. to Archbishops of Canterbury and York, 1975–84 and Sec., Crown Appointments Commn, 1977–84. Governor, King's Coll. Sch., Wimbledon; Chm., Council, Benenden School, 1976–86; Mem., Council, William Temple Foundn. *Recreations*: music, writing. *Address*: Mill Barn, Coulston, near Westbury, Wilts BA13 4NY.

WRIGHT, Basil Charles; Film Producer; *b* 12 June 1907; *s* of Major Lawrence Wright, TD, and Gladys Marsden. *Educ*: Sherborne; Corpus Christi Coll., Cambridge. Mawson Schol., CCC, 1926; BA (Hons), Classics and Economics. Concerned with John Grierson and others in development of Documentary Film, 1929–; directed, among many films: Song of Ceylon (Gold Medal and Prix du Gouvernement, Brussels), 1935; (with Harry Watt) Night Mail, 1936; Waters of Time, 1951; (with Paul Rotha) World Without End, 1953; (with Gladys Wright) took film expedition to Greece and made The Immortal Land, 1957 (Council of Europe Award, 1959) and Greek Sculpture (with Michael Ayrton), 1959; A Place for Gold, 1960; Visiting Lectr on Film Art, Univ. of Calif, Los Angeles, 1962 and 1968; Senior Lectr in Film History, Nat. Film Sch., 1971–73; Vis. Prof. of Radio, TV and Film, Temple Univ., Philadelphia, 1977–78. Producer, Crown Film Unit, 1945. Governor: Bryanston School, 1949–; British Film Institute, 1953; Fellow, British Film Academy, 1955; Council Mem., Roy. Coll. of Art, 1954–57. Gold Cross, Royal Order of King George I, Greece, 1963. *Publications*: The Use of the Film, 1949; The Long View, 1974. *Recreations*: opera, ballet, gardening. *Address*: Little Adam Farm, Frieth, Henley-on-Thames, Oxon. *Club*: Savile.

WRIGHT, Beatrice Frederika, (Lady Wright); Vice-President, Royal National Institute for the Deaf, since 1978; President, Hearing Dogs for the Deaf, since 1983; *b* New Haven, Connecticut; *d* of Mr and Mrs F. Roland Clough; *m* 1st, 1932, John Rankin Rathbone (Flight Lieut, RAFVR, MP, killed in action, 1940); one *s* one *d*; 2nd, 1942, Paul Hervé Giraud Wright (*see* Sir Paul Wright); one *d*. *Educ*: Ethel Walker School, Simsbury, Conn; Radcliffe College, Oxford. MP (U) Bodmin Div. of Cornwall, 1941–45. *Address*: 3 Ormonde Gate, SW3 4EU.

See also J. R. Rathbone.

WRIGHT, Billy; *see* Wright, W. A.

WRIGHT, Claud William, CB 1969; Deputy Secretary, Department of Education and Science, 1971–76; *b* 9 Jan. 1917; *s* of Horace Vipan Wright and Catherine Margaret Sales; *m* 1947, Alison Violet Readman; one *s* four *d*. *Educ*: Charterhouse; Christ Church, Oxford (MA). Assistant Principal, War Office, 1939; Private, Essex Regiment, 1940; 2nd Lieut, KRRC, 1940; War Office, rising to GSO2, 1942–45; Principal, War Office, 1944; Min. of Defence: Principal, 1947; Asst Sec., 1951; Asst Under-Sec. of State, 1961–68; Dep. Under-Sec. of State, 1968–71. Chm., Cttee on Provincial Museums and Galleries, 1971–73. Research Fellow, Wolfson Coll., Oxford, 1977–83. Lyell Fund, 1947, R. H. Worth Prize, 1958, Geological Society of London; Foulerton Award, Geologists Association, 1955; Stamford Raffles Award, Zoological Society of London, 1965. Phillips Medal, Yorks Geol. Soc., 1976. President, Geologists Assoc., 1956–58. Hon. Associate, British Museum (Nat. Hist.), 1973; fil.Dr *hc* Uppsala, 1979. *Publications*: (with W. J. Arkell *et al*) vol. on Ammonites, 1957, (with W. K. Spencer) on Starfish, 1966, in Treatise on Invertebrate Palaeontology; (with J. S. H. Collins) British Cretaceous Crabs, 1972; (with W. J. Kennedy) Ammonites of the Middle Chalk, 1981; (with W. J. Kennedy) Ammonites of the Lower Chalk, pt I, 1984; (with A. B. Smith) British Cretaceous Echinoidea, pt I, 1987; papers in geological, palaeontological and archaeological journals. *Recreations*: palaeontology, natural history, gardening, archæology. *Address*: Old Rectory, Seaborough, Beaminster, Dorset DT8 3QY. *T*: Broadwindsor 68426. *Club*: Athenæum.

WRIGHT, David John; HM Diplomatic Service; Head of Personnel Services Department, Foreign and Commonwealth Office, since 1985; *b* 16 June 1944; *s* of J. F. Wright; *m* 1968, Sally Ann Dodkin; one *s* one *d*. *Educ*: Wolverhampton Grammar Sch.; Peterhouse, Cambridge (MA). Third Secretary, FO, 1966; Third Sec., later Second Sec., Tokyo, 1966–72; FCO, 1972–75; Ecole Nationale d'Administration, Paris, 1975–76; First Sec., Paris, 1976–80; Private Sec. to Secretary of the Cabinet, 1980–82; Counsellor (Economic), Tokyo, 1982–85. *Recreations*: running, cooking, military history, rock music. *Address*: c/o Foreign and Commonwealth Office, SW1A 2AH.

WRIGHT, Sir Denis (Arthur Hepworth), GCMG 1971 (KCMG 1961; CMG 1954); HM Diplomatic Service, retired; *b* 23 March 1911; *s* of late A. E. Wright, Hong Kong, and Margery Hepworth Chapman, York; *m* 1939, Iona Craig, Bolney, Sussex; no *c*. *Educ*: Brentwood School; St Edmund Hall, Oxford, Hon. Fellow 1972. Asst Advertising Manager to Gallaher & Co. (Tobacco Manufacturers), 1935–39. Employed from outbreak of war as Vice-Consul on economic warfare work at HM Consulate at Constantza (Roumania), 1939–41. Vice-Consul-in-charge of HM Consulate at Trebizond (Turkey), 1941–43; Acting-Consul-in-charge of HM Consulate, Mersin (Turkey), 1943–45; First Secretary (Commercial) to HM Embassy, Belgrade, 1946–48; Superintending Trade Consul at Chicago for Middle-Western Region of USA, 1949–51; Head of Economic Relations Department in the Foreign Office, 1951–53; appointed Chargé d'Affaires, Tehran, on resumption of diplomatic relations with Persia, Dec. 1953; Counsellor, HM

Embassy, Tehran, 1954–55; Asst Under-Sec., FO, 1955–59; Ambassador to Ethiopia, 1959–62; Asst Under-Sec., FO, 1962; Ambassador to Iran, 1963–71. Dir, Shell Transport & Trading Co., Standard Chartered Bank, and Mitchell Cotts Gp, 1971–81. Governor, Oversea Service, Farnham Castle, 1972–86; Mem. Council, British Inst. of Persian Studies, 1973– (Pres., 1978–); Chm., Iran Soc., 1976–79. Hon. Fellow St Antony's Coll., Oxford, 1976. *Publications:* Persia (with James Morris and Roger Wood), 1969; The English Amongst the Persians, 1977; The Persians Amongst the English, 1985. *Address:* Duck Bottom, Haddenham, Aylesbury, Bucks. *Club:* Travellers'.

See also A. M. J. Wright.

WRIGHT, Desmond Garforth, QC 1974; *b* 13 July 1923; *s* of late Arthur Victor Wright and Doris Greensill; *m* 1952, Elizabeth Anna Bacon; one *s* one *d. Educ:* Giggleswick; Royal Naval Coll., Greenwich; Worcester Coll., Oxford (MA). Cholmondley Scholar of Lincoln's Inn. Served War of 1939–45: RNVR, 1942–46. Staff of Flag Officer Malaya Forward Area, 1946. Called to Bar, Lincoln's Inn, 1950, Bencher, 1981. *Publication:* Wright on Walls, 1954. *Recreations:* cartology, conversation, skiing on snow. *Address:* 22 Old Buildings, Lincoln's Inn, WC2A 3UJ. *T:* 01–405 2072. *Club:* RNVR.

WRIGHT, Donald; *see* Wright, A. R. D.

WRIGHT, Prof. Donald Arthur, MSc, DSc; FInstP; FRAS; Honorary Research Fellow in Archaeology, University of Durham, since 1976; *b* Stoke-on-Trent, 29 March 1911; *m* 1937, Mary Kathleen Rimmer; one *s* one *d. Educ:* Orme School, Newcastle-under-Lyme; University of Birmingham. 1st Class Hons BSc 1932; MSc 1934; DSc Birmingham 1955. Research Physicist, GEC, Wembley, 1934–59; Head of Solid Physics Laboratory, Research Labs, GEC, Wembley, 1955–59; Prof. of Applied Physics, Univ. of Durham, 1960–76. Fellow Institute of Physics, 1946. Member of Board, Institute of Physics, 1957–64. Mem. of Council, Physical Society, 1955–58, Hon. Treasurer, 1958–60. *Publications:* Semiconductors, 1950 (revd edn 1965); Thermoelectric Cooling in Progress in Cryogenics, Vol. I, 1959; Thermoelectric Generation in Direct Generation of Electricity, 1965; many papers on electron emission and solid-state physics in learned journals. *Recreations:* music, formerly tennis. *Address:* Museum of Archaeology, Fulling Mill, Durham; 16 St Mary's Close, Shincliffe, Durham DH1 2ND. *T:* Durham 48408.

WRIGHT, Sir Douglas; *see* Wright, Sir R. D.

WRIGHT, Mrs Edmund Gordon; *see* Cross, H. M.

WRIGHT, (Edmund) Kenneth, MA, FCA; Chartered Accountant; Partner in Dearden, Farrow, 1940–76; *b* 10 Dec. 1909; *s* of late William Ameers Wright and Martha Wright; *m* 1942, Daisy, *d* of late Rev. T. W. Thornton and Mrs Thornton; one *s* one *d. Educ:* preparatory schs in Southern Africa; Leighton Park Sch.; St Catharine's Coll., Cambridge (Engl. and Economics Triposes). ACA 1937, FCA 1945. London Ambulance Service, 1940–45. Chm., London and Dist Soc. of Chartered Accountants, 1957–58; Mem. Council, Inst. of Chartered Accountants, 1959–76 (Dep. Pres., 1972, Pres., 1973). Governor, Leighton Park Sch., 1949–84. *Publications:* numerous books and papers on fiscal and accountancy subjects in national and professional press, including: The Development of an Accounting Practice, 1965; Professional Goodwill and Partnership Annuities, 1967; (with Andrew Tappin) Financial Planning for Individuals, 1970, 3rd edn 1979; (with Malcolm Penney and Derek Robinson) Capital Transfer Tax Planning, 1975, 4th edn 1984. *Recreations:* gardening, philately, writing, walking. *Address:* Old Orchard, Sevenoaks Road, Ightham, Kent. *T:* Borough Green 882374. *Club:* Reform.

WRIGHT, Sir Edward (Maitland), Kt 1977; MA, DPhil, LLD, DSc; FRSE; Research Fellow, University of Aberdeen, since 1976; *b* 1906; *s* of M. T. Wright, Farnley, Leeds; *m* 1934, Elizabeth Phyllis, *d* of H. P. Harris, Bryn Mally Hall, N Wales; one *s. Educ:* Jesus Coll. and Christ Church, Oxford; Univ. of Göttingen. Master, Chard School, Somerset, 1923–26; Scholar, Jesus College, Oxford, 1926–30; Senior Scholar, Christ Church, 1930–33; Lecturer, King's College, London, 1932–33; Lecturer, Christ Church, 1933–35; Flt Lieut, RAFVR, 1941–43; Principal Scientific Officer, Air Ministry, 1943–45; Prof. of Mathematics, 1935–62, Vice-Principal, 1961–62, Principal and Vice-Chancellor, 1962–76, Univ. of Aberdeen. Member: Anderson Cttee on Grants to Students, 1958–60; Hale Cttee on Univ. Teaching Methods, 1961–64; Scottish Universities Entrance Bd, 1948–62 (Chm. 1955–62); Royal Commission on Medical Education, 1965–67. Vice-Pres., RUSI, 1969–72. Hon. LLD: St Andrews, 1963; Pennsylvania, 1975; Aberdeen, 1978; Hon. DSc Strathclyde, 1974. Hon. Fellow, Jesus College, Oxford, 1963. Macdougall-Brisbane Prize, RSE, 1952; Sen. Berwick Prize, London Math. Soc., 1978. Gold Medal of the Order of Polonia Restituta of the Polish People's Republic, 1978. *Publications:* Introduction to the Theory of Numbers (with Professor G. H. Hardy), 1938, 5th edn 1979; mathematical papers in scientific journals. *Address:* 16 Primrosehill Avenue, Cults, Aberdeen. *T:* Aberdeen 861185. *Club:* Caledonian.

WRIGHT, Eric; Regional Director, Yorkshire and Humberside Region, Department of Trade and Industry, since 1985; *b* 17 Nov. 1933; *s* of Alec Wright and Elsie (*née* Worthington); *m* 1955, Pauline Sutton; three *s* (and one *s* decd). *Educ:* Wolstanton Grammar Sch.; Keble Coll., Oxford (BA 1st Cl. Hons Mod. Hist.). 2nd Lieut RASC, 1955–57. Ministry of Fuel and Power, 1957–65; Civil Service Commission, 1965–67; Min. of Technology, 1968–70; Sloan Fellow, London Business Sch., 1970–71; Principal Private Sec. to Secretary of State, DTI, 1971–72; Dept of Trade, 1972–77; Dept of Industry, 1977–83, Under Sec., 1979. *Recreations:* music, tennis, chess. *Address:* 5 West Hill, South Croydon, Surrey CR2 0SB. *T:* 01–657 4569.

WRIGHT, Eric David, CB 1975; Member, Parole Board for England and Wales, 1978–83; Deputy Under-Secretary of State, Home Office, and Director-General, Prison Service, 1973–77; *b* 12 June 1917; *s* of Charles Henry and Cecelia Wright; *m* 1944, Doris (*née* Nicholls); one *s. Educ:* Ealing County Grammar School. Joined War Office, 1935; Principal, 1945; seconded to Dept of the Army, Australia, 1951; Asst Secretary, 1955; Command Secretary, BAOR, 1955–58; Imperial Defence College, 1964; Asst Under-Sec. of State, MoD, 1965; on loan to Home Office, Police Dept, 1970–73. *Address:* 32 Valley Road, Rickmansworth, Herts WD3 4DS.

WRIGHT, Prof. Esmond; Emeritus Professor of American History, University of London, since 1983; Vice-President, Automobile Association, since 1985 (Vice-Chairman and Hon. Treasurer, 1971–85); *b* 5 Nov. 1915; *m* 1945, Olive Adamson. *Educ:* University of Durham (Open Entrance Schol.); Univ. of Virginia (Commonwealth Fund Fellow). War Service, 1940–46, demobilised as Lt-Col, 1946. Glasgow Univ., 1946–67; Prof. of Modern History, 1957–67. MP (C) Glasgow, Pollok, March 1967–1970; Dir, Inst. of US Studies and Prof. of American History, Univ. of London, 1971–83; Principal, Swinton Cons. Coll., 1972–76. Chm., Border TV, 1981–85 (Vice-Chm., 1976–81). Founder-Mem., British Association for American Studies (Chm., 1965–68). Mem., Marshall Aid Commemoration Commn, 1966–83; Vice-Chm., British Road Fedn, 1981–85. FRHistS, FRSA. Hon. LHD Pennsylvania, 1983; Hon. DLitt New Brunswick, 1984. *Publications:* A Short History of our own Times, 1951; George Washington and the American Revolution, 1957; The World Today, 1961, 4th edn 1978; Fabric of Freedom, 1961, 2nd edn 1978; (ed) Illustrated World History, 1964; Benjamin Franklin and American Independence, 1966; (ed) Causes and Consequences of the American Revolution, 1966; (ed) American Themes, 1967; American Profiles, 1967; (ed) Benjamin Franklin, a profile, 1970; A Time for Courage, 1971; A Tug of Loyalties, 1974; Red, White and True Blue, 1976; (with A. G. Nicolson) Europe Today, 1979; The Great Little Madison (British Academy Lecture), 1981; The Fire of Liberty, 1983; (ed) History of the World: Pre-History to Renaissance, 1985; Franklin of Philadelphia, 1986; The last five hundred years, 1986; articles in periodicals. *Address:* 31 Tavistock Square, WC1H 9EZ. *T:* 01–387 5534. *Club:* Athenæum.

WRIGHT, Frederick Matthew, OBE 1976 (MBE 1945); General Manager, British Railways, Western Region and Member of British Railways (Western) Board, 1972–76; *b* 26 June 1916; *s* of Thomas Bell Wright and Ethel Johnson; *m* 1940, Claire Agnes (*née* Cook); one *s* one *d. Educ:* Rutherford Coll., Newcastle upon Tyne. FCIT; FInstM. Joined LNER, 1933. Served with Royal Engrs in France, Madagascar, Africa and India, 1939–45. British Railways: posts in traffic depts, 1945–61; Eastern Region: Commercial Supt, Great Northern Line, 1961; Divisional Man., Doncaster, 1964; Asst Gen. Man., York, 1968; Mem., BR (Eastern) Bd, 1969; Dep. Gen. Man., York, 1970. Chm., Bournemouth Helping Services Council, 1978; Vice Chm., E Dorset Community Proj. Agency, 1981–83. Dorset County Dir, St John Ambulance Assoc., 1976–81. OStJ 1975, CStJ 1980. *Recreations:* gardening, soccer, Rugby, cricket (critic). *Club:* Parkstone Yacht (Parkstone).

WRIGHT, Georg Henrik von, GCVO (Hon.); MA; Research Professor in the Academy of Finland, 1961–86; *b* Helsingfors, 14 June 1916; *s* of Tor von Wright and Ragni Elisabeth Alfthan; *m* 1941, Maria Elisabeth von Troil, CVO (Hon.); one *s* one *d. Educ:* Svenska Normallyceum, Helsingfors; Helsingfors Univ. Helsingfors University: Lectr and Acting Prof. of Philosophy, 1943–46; Prof. of Philosophy, 1946–61 (also in Univ. of Cambridge, 1948–51); Prof. at Large, Cornell Univ., 1965–77; Chancellor of Abo Academy, 1968–77; Visiting Professor: Cornell Univ., 1954 and 1958; Univ. Calif., Los Angeles, 1963; Univ. Pittsburg, 1966; Univ. Karlsruhe, 1975; Lectures: Shearman Meml, University Coll., London, 1956; Gifford, Univ. of St Andrews, 1959–60; Tarner, Trinity Coll., Cambridge, 1969; Woodbridge, Columbia Univ., 1972; Nellie Wallace, Univ. of Oxford, 1978; Tanner, Helsingfors Univ., 1984. President: Internat. Union of History and Philosophy of Science, 1963–65; Acad. of Finland, 1968–69; Philosophical Soc. of Finland, 1962–73; Institut International de Philosophie, 1975–78. Fellow: Finnish Soc. of Sciences (Pres., 1966–67, Hon. Fellow 1978); New Soc. of Letters, Lund; Royal Swedish Academy of Sciences; Royal Soc. of Letters, Lund; British Academy; Royal Swedish Academy of Letters, History and Antiquities; Finnish Acad. of Sciences; Royal Danish Acad. of Sciences and Letters; Royal Acad. of Arts and Sciences, Uppsala; Norwegian Acad. of Science and Letters; Royal Acad. of Science, Trondheim; European Acad. of Arts, Sciences and Humanities; Hon. Foreign Mem., Amer. Acad. of Arts and Sciences. Sometime Fellow, Trinity College, Cambridge, Hon. Fellow 1983. Hon. degrees: Helsingfors Univ. (doctor of pol. sci.); Univ. of Liverpool (DLitt); Univ. of Lund (doctor of philosophy); Turku Univ. (doctor of philosophy); Saint Olaf Coll., Northfield, Minn. (doctor of humane letters); Tampere Univ. (doctor of soc. sci.); Univ. of Buenos Aires. Wilhuri Foundn Internat. Prize, 1976. *Publications:* The Logical Problem of Induction, 1941, rev. edn 1957; Den logiska Empirismen, 1943; Über Wahrscheinlichkeit, 1945; A Treatise on Induction and Probability, 1951; An Essay in Modal Logic, 1951; Logical Studies, 1957; The Varieties of Goodness, 1963; The Logic of Preference, 1963; Norm and Action, 1963; An Essay in Deontic Logic, 1968; Time, Change, and Contradiction, 1969; Explanation and Understanding, 1971; Causality and Determinism, 1974; Freedom and Determination, 1980; Wittgenstein, 1982; Philosophical Papers I-III, 1983–84. *Address:* 4 Skepparegatan, Helsingfors, Finland.

WRIGHT, George Henry, MBE 1977; Regional Secretary, Wales, Transport and General Workers Union, since 1972; Chairman, Wales Co-operative Development Centre, since 1983; *b* 11 July 1935; *s* of William Henry and Annie Louisa Wright; *m* 1956, Margaret Wright; two *d. Educ:* Tinkers Farm Sch., Birmingham. Car worker, 1954–65. T&GWU: District Officer, West Bromwich, 1966–68; District Secretary, Birmingham, 1968–72. Gen. Sec., Wales TUC, 1974–84. Member: MSC Wales, 1976–; Employment Appeal Tribunal, 1985–. *Recreations:* fishing, gardening. *Address:* 5 Kidwelly Court, Caerphilly, Mid Glamorgan, Wales. *T:* Caerphilly 885434.

WRIGHT, George Paul; Chief Superintendent, Royal Signals and Radar Establishment, Ministry of Defence, Baldock, 1976–80; *b* 27 April 1919; *s* of late George Maurice Wright, CBE, and of late Lois Dorothy Wright (*née* Norburn); *m* 1957, Jean Margaret Reid, *d* of Lt-Col Charles Alexander Reid Scott, DSO and Marjorie Reid Scott (*née* Mackintosh); one *s* one *d. Educ:* Bishops Stortford Coll.; Magdalen Coll., Oxford. BA 1948, MA 1951; FInstP. Admty Signal Estabt, 1939–45; Services Electronics Research Lab., 1945–57; Dept of Physical Research, Admty, 1957–63; Services Electronics Research Lab., 1963–76 (Dir, 1972–76). *Recreations:* music, sailing, gardening. *Address:* Tilekiln Farmhouse, Earls Colne, Colchester, Essex. *T:* Earls Colne 2432. *Clubs:* United Oxford & Cambridge University, Civil Service; Blackwater Sailing.

WRIGHT, Gerard, QC 1973; *b* 23 July 1929; *s* of Leo Henry and Catherine M. F. Wright; *m* 1950, Betty Mary Fenn; one *s* two *d. Educ:* Stonyhurst Coll.; Lincoln Coll., Oxford (BA, BCL). Served in Army, 1947–49, rank T/Captain. Called to Bar, Gray's Inn, 1954 (Arden Scholar, Barstow Scholar); Northern Circuit. KHS 1974; KCHS 1979; Auxiliaire de l'Hospitalité de Notre Dame de Lourdes, 1982, Titulaire 1985. *Publication:* Test Tube Babies—a Christian view (with others), 1984. *Recreations:* skiing, sailing, squash. *Address:* Pine Lodge, Coral Ridge, Noctorum, Birkenhead, Merseyside L43 7XE. *T:* 051–652 4138; Melbourne House, 21 North John Street, Liverpool L2 5QU. *T:* 051–236 0718.

WRIGHT, Prof. H(enry) Myles; FRIBA; FRTPI; Lever Professor of Civic Design, University of Liverpool, 1954–75, now Emeritus Professor; University Planning Consultant, 1957–77; *b* 9 June 1908; *s* of H. T. Wright, Gosforth, Newcastle upon Tyne; *m* 1939, Catharine Noble (*d* 1981), *y d* of Very Rev. H. N. Craig, Dean of Kildare; two *d. Educ:* Fettes College, Edinburgh (Foundationer); King's College, Newcastle upon Tyne; St John's College, Cambridge. Assistant in various private offices, 1930–35; Asst Editor, The Architects' Journal, and in private practice, 1935–40; Partner in firm of Sir William Holford, 1948–54; principally engaged on planning proposals for Cambridge and Corby New Town. Member British Caribbean Federal Capital Commn, 1956. *Publications:* The Planner's Notebook, 1948; Cambridge Planning Proposals, 1950, and Corby New Town (with Lord Holford), 1952; Land Use in an Urban Environment (Editor and contributor), 1961; The Dublin Region: Preliminary and Final Reports, 1965 and 1967; Lord Leverhulme's Unknown Venture, 1982; other technical publications. *Recreations:* walking, reading. *Address:* 9 Pine Hey, Neston, S Wirral, Cheshire L64 3TJ.

WRIGHT, Hugh Raymond, MA; Headmaster, Gresham's School, Holt, since 1985; *b* 24 Aug. 1938; *s* of Rev. Raymond Blayney Wright and Alice Mary Wright (*née* Hawksworth); *m* 1962, Jillian Mary McIlDowie Meiklejohn; three *s. Educ:* Kingswood Sch., Bath; The Queen's Coll., Oxford (Bible Clerk; MA Lit. Hum.). Asst Master, Brentwood Sch., 1961–64; Cheltenham Coll., 1964–79; Hd of Classics, 1967–72; Housemaster, Boyne House, 1971–79; Headmaster, Stockport Grammar Sch., 1979–85.

Chm., NW Dist, HMC, 1983; Chm., HMC Community Service Sub-Cttee, 1985–(Mem., 1980–); Mem., Admty Interview Bd Panel, 1982–. FRSA 1984. *Publication*: film strips and notes on The Origins of Christianity and the Medieval Church, 1980. *Recreations*: music, theatre, hill walking, wildfowl, gardening, Rugby football, tennis. *Address*: Lockhart House, Gresham's School, Holt, Norfolk NR25 6DZ. *T*: Holt 713739. *Club*: East India.

WRIGHT, Prof. Jack Clifford, MA, BA; Professor of Sanskrit in the University of London, at the School of Oriental and African Studies, since 1964; *b* 5 Dec. 1933; *s* of Jack and Dorothy Wright, Aberdeen; *m* 1958, Hazel Chisholm (*née* Strachan), Crathes, Banchory; one *s*. *Educ*: Robert Gordon's Coll., Aberdeen; Univ. of Aberdeen (MA Hons in French and German, 1955); University of Zürich; Univ. of London (BA Hons in Sanskrit, 1959). Lectr in Sanskrit, 1959–64, Head, Dept of Indology and Mod. Langs and Lits of S Asia, 1970–83, SOAS, Univ. of London. *Address*: School of Oriental and African Studies, University of London, WC1E 7HP.

WRIGHT, Adm. Jerauld, DSM (US) (twice); Silver and Bronze Star Medals; Legion of Merit (US); USN retired; US Ambassador to Nationalist China, 1963–65; *b* Amherst, Mass., 4 June 1898; *s* of Gen. William Mason Wright and Marjorie R. (Jerauld) Wright; *m* 1938, Phyllis B. Thompson; one *s* one *d*. *Educ*: US Naval Academy. Ensign, USN, 1917; promoted through grades to Admiral, 1954; Executive Staff of US Naval Academy; operational staff appointments for N African, Sicilian and Italian landings; Mem., Gen. Mark Clark's Expedition to North Africa, 1942; Comd British Sub. HMS Seraph in evacuation of Gen. Henri Giraud from S France to Gibraltar, 1942; Staff Adv. to Sir Andrew B. Cunningham, RN, in N African invasion, 1942; Staff Comdr, 8th Fleet in Sicily and Salerno landings, 1943. Comdr, USS Santa Fe, Pacific, 1943–44; Comdr Amphibious Group Five, 1944–45; Comdr Cruiser Div. Six, 1945; Asst Chief of Naval Operations for Fleet Readiness, 1945–48; Comdr. Amphibious Force, US Atlantic Fleet, 1949–51; US Rep. NATO Standing Group, Washington, 1951–52; C-in-C US Naval Forces, E Atlantic and Medit., 1952–54; Supreme Allied Commander, Atlantic, and C-in-C Western Atlantic Area, NATO, 1954–60; C-in-C Atlantic (US Unified Command), and C-in-C Atlantic Fleet, 1954–60. Pres. US Naval Inst., 1959. Holds Hon. doctorates in Laws and Science. Awarded foreign decorations. *Address*: (home) 4101 Cathedral Avenue, Washington, DC 20016, USA. *Clubs*: Metropolitan, Alibi, Chevy Chase (Washington); Knickerbocker, Brook (New York).

WRIGHT, Joe Booth, CMG 1979; HM Diplomatic Service, retired; Ambassador to Ivory Coast, Upper Volta and Niger, 1975–78; *b* 24 Aug. 1920; *s* of Joe Booth Wright and Annie Elizabeth Wright; *m* 1st, 1945, Pat (*née* Beaumont); one *s* two *d*; 2nd, 1967, Patricia Maxine (*née* Nicholls). *Educ*: King Edward VI Grammar Sch., Retford; Univ. of London. BA Hons, French. GPO, 1939–47. Served War, HM Forces: RAOC, Intelligence Corps, 1941–46. Entered Foreign Office, 1947; FO, 1947–51; Vice-Consul, Jerusalem, 1951; Consul, Munich, 1952, and Basra, 1954; Dep. Consul, Tamsui, 1956; FO, 1959–64; Consul, Surabaya, 1964; Consul, Medan, 1965–67; First Sec. (Information), Nicosia, 1968; Head of Chancery and Consul, Tunis, 1968–71; Consul-General: Hanoi, 1971–72; Geneva, 1973–75. Mem., Inst. of Linguists and Translators' Guild, 1982–. *Publications*: Francophone Black Africa Since Independence, 1981; Zaire Since Independence, 1983; Paris As It Was, 1985. *Recreations*: cricket, film-going, music, writing. *Address*: 29 Brittany Road, St Leonards-on-Sea, East Sussex TN38 0RB. *Club*: Royal Over-Seas League.

WRIGHT, Captain John, DSC 1944; RN (retd); Assistant Managing Director and General Manager, Marconi Underwater Systems Ltd, Portsmouth, 1982–84, retired; *b* 30 April 1921; *s* of Percy Robert and Lucy Ada Wright; *m* 1946, Ethel Lumley Sunderland; one *s* two *d*. *Educ*: Liverpool Univ. (Part I for BSc). MIEE; Silver Medal, City and Guilds. Served War: RNVR, 1942; 16th Destroyer Flotilla, 1942; HMS Birmingham, 1943; HMS Diadem, 1943. Devonport Gunnery Sch., 1946; HMS Collingwood, 1948; BJSM, USA, 1951; Admiralty Surface Weapons Estabt, 1952; HMS Cumberland, 1956; Naval Ordnance Div., 1958; British Naval Staff, USA, 1960; Polaris Technical Dept, 1964; HM Dockyard, Chatham, 1968; RN retd 1972; Gen. Manager, HM Dockyard, Devonport, 1972–77; Gen. Man., Marconi Space and Defence Systems Ltd, Portsmouth, 1981–82. *Recreations*: fishing, gardening. *Address*: Oakdene, 21 Blackbrook Park Avenue, Fareham, Hants PO15 5JN. *T*: Fareham 280512.

WRIGHT, John Hurrell C.; *see* Collier-Wright.

WRIGHT, John Keith; JP; economic and financial consultant; Under Secretary, Overseas Development Administration, Foreign and Commonwealth Office (formerly Ministry of Overseas Development), 1971–84; *b* 30 May 1928; *s* of late James Wright and Elsie Wright, Walton-on-Thames, Surrey; *m* 1958, Thérèse Marie-Claire, *er d* of René Aubenas, Paris. *Educ*: Tiffins' Sch.; King's Coll., Cambridge (MA Hist., 1950; Dipl. in Economics, 1954; Gladstone Memorial Prize, 1954); Yale Univ. OEEC, Paris: Economics and Statistics Directorate, 1951–52; Agriculture and Food Directorate, 1954–56; UK Atomic Energy Authority, 1956–61; Chief Scientific Adviser's staff, MoD, 1961–66 (UK Delegn to 18 Nation Disarmament Conf., 1962–64); Sen. Econ. Adviser, CRO, 1966–68; Head of Economists Dept and subseq. Dir (Economic), FCO, 1968–71. Chm., Economists' Panel, First Division Assoc., 1973–75. Dir, Sadlers Wells (Trading) Ltd, 1983–. Member: Court of Governors, London Sch. of Hygiene and Tropical Medicine, 1979–81; Councils, Queen Elizabeth Coll., 1982–85, King's Coll., 1984–, Univ. of London; Trustee, Thomson Foundn, 1985–. JP Dover and East Kent, 1983–. Has exhibited at Royal Academy. *Publications*: articles on economic subjects and on nuclear strategy. *Recreations*: economic and military history, music, amateur radio (G4IOL). *Address*: 47 Brunswick Gardens, W8; Bowling Corner, Sandwich, Kent. *Clubs*: Athenæum, Beefsteak.

WRIGHT, (John) Michael, QC 1974; a Recorder of the Crown Court, since 1974; *b* 26 Oct. 1932; *s* of Prof. John George Wright, DSc, MVSc, FRCVS, and Elsie Lloyd Razey; *m* 1959, Kathleen, *er d* of F. A. Meanwell; one *s* two *d*. *Educ*: King's Sch., Chester; Oriel Coll., Oxford. BA Jurisprudence 1956, MA 1978. Served Royal Artillery, 1951–53. Called to Bar, Lincoln's Inn (Tancred Student), 1957, Bencher 1983; Leader, SE Circuit, 1981–83; Chm. of the Bar, 1983–84 (Vice-Chm., 1982–83). Member: Bar Council, 1972–; Senate of the Four Inns of Court, 1973–74; Senate of the Inns of Court and the Bar, 1975–84. Mem. Supreme Court Rules Cttee, 1973–74. Legal Assessor to the Disciplinary Cttee, RCVS, 1983–. Hon. Member: American Bar Assoc.; Canadian Bar Assoc. *Recreations*: books, music. *Address*: 2 Crown Office Row, Temple, EC4Y 7HJ. *T*: 01–353 9337; Old Coombe House, Sharpthorne, W Sussex.

WRIGHT, Sir (John) Oliver, GCMG 1981 (KCMG 1974; CMG 1964); GCVO 1978; DSC 1944; HM Diplomatic Service, retired; re-appointed, Ambassador to Washington, 1982–86; *b* 6 March 1921; *m* 1942, Lillian Marjory Osborne; three *s*. *Educ*: Solihull School; Christ's College, Cambridge (MA; Hon. Fellow 1981; pre-elected Master, May 1982, resigned July 1982). Served in RNVR, 1941–45. Joined HM Diplomatic Service, Nov. 1945; served: New York, 1946–47; Bucharest, 1948–50; Singapore, 1950–51; Foreign Office, 1952–54; Berlin, 1954–56; Pretoria, 1957–58. Imperial Defence College, 1959. Asst Private Sec. to Sec. of State for Foreign Affairs, 1960; Counsellor and Private Sec., 1963; Private Sec. to the Prime Minister, 1964–66 (to Rt Hon. Sir Alec Douglas-

Home, and subseq. to Rt Hon. Harold Wilson); Ambassador to Denmark, 1966–69; seconded to Home Office as UK Rep. to NI Govt, Aug. 1969–March 1970; Chief Clerk, HM Diplomatic Service, 1970–72; Dep. Under-Sec. of State, FCO, 1972–75; Ambassador to Federal Republic of Germany, 1975–81. Director: Siemens Ltd, 1981–82; Amalgamated Metal Corp., April–July 1982. Distinguished Vis. Prof., Univ. of S. Carolina. Bd Mem., British Council, 1981–82, 1986–. Trustee, British Museum, 1986–; Chm., British Königswinter Steering Cttee. Hon. DHL Univ. of Nebraska, 1983; Hon. DL Rockford Coll., Ill, 1985. Grand Cross, German Order of Merit, 1978. *Recreations*: theatre, gardening. *Address*: Burstow Hall, near Horley, Surrey. *T*: Horley 783494. *Club*: Travellers'.

WRIGHT, Joseph, OBE 1978; FPS; FCIS; Secretary (Chief Executive), National Pharmaceutical Association (formerly National Pharmaceutical Union), 1961–81; *b* 7 Jan. 1917; *s* of late Thomas Wright and Margaret (*née* Cardwell); *m* 1942, Margaretta May Hart Talbot, BA, MPS; two *s* two *d*. *Educ*: Blackpool Boys' Grammar Sch.; Chelsea Polytechnic. Dip., Chem. and Druggist and PhC examinations. Called to the Bar, Middle Temple, 1952. In retail pharmacy, 1933–47, incl. 4 years apprenticeship in Blackpool, with subseq. experience in London. Served war, RAF, commnd wireless navigator, Coastal Comd. On staff, Pharm. Section, Min. of Health, 1947–48; joined NPU, 1948: Asst Sec., 1949, Dep. Sec., 1955, Sec. and Manager, 1961; Dir, NPA Gp, 1971 (Gp comprises Nat. Pharm. Assoc. Ltd, Chemists' Def. Assoc. Ltd, Pharmacy Mutual Insce Co. Ltd, Pharm. and Gen. Prov. Soc., NPU Ltd (t/a NPA Sces), NPU Holdings Ltd). Director: NPU Holdings Ltd, 1965–81; NPU Ltd, 1971–81; Indep. Chemists Marketing Ltd, 1972–81; NPU Marketing Ltd, 1966–81; Member: Standing Pharm. Adv. Cttee, 1964–82; Poisons Bd, 1963–84; Panel of Fellows of Pharm. Soc., 1965–82; Gen. Practice Sub-Cttee, PSGB, 1963–81; Bd, Nat. Chamber of Trade, 1973–82; Trade & Professional Alliance, 1975–81; Legislation & Taxation Cttee, Nat. Ch. of Trade, 1964–81; Adviser to Pharm. Services Negotiating Cttee, 1977–81. Hon. Life Mem., S African Retail Chem. and Druggists Assoc., 1974; Distinguished Service Award, Pharmacy Guild of Aust., 1978. Charter Gold Medal of Pharmaceutical Soc. of GB, 1980. Liveryman, Worshipful Soc. of Apoth. of London, 1978–. Freedom of City of London. *Recreations*: reading, travel, amateur radio (G0AJO) and—intermittently—grandchildren. *Address*: 116 Wynchgate, Winchmore Hill, N21 1QU. *T*: 01–886 1645.

WRIGHT, Judith, (Mrs J. P. McKinney); writer; *b* 31 May 1915; *d* of late Phillip Arundell Wright, CMG, and Ethel Mabel (*née* Bigg); *m* J. P. McKinney; one *d*. *Educ*: NSW Correspondence Sch.; New England Girls' Sch.; Sydney Univ. Secretarial work, 1938–42; Univ. Statistician (Univ. of Queensland), 1945–48. Creative Arts Fellow, ANU, 1974; Australia Council Senior Writers' Fellowship, 1977. Dr of Letters (Hon.): Univ. of New England, 1963; Univ. of Sydney, 1976; Monash Univ., 1977; ANU, 1981; Univ. of NSW, 1985. Encyclopædia Britannica Writer's Award, 1965; Robert Frost Medallion, Fellowship of Australian Writers, 1975; Asan World Prize, Asan Meml Assoc., 1984. FAHA 1970. *Publications*: verse: The Moving Image, 1946; Woman to Man, 1950; The Gateway, 1953; The Oxford Book of Australian Verse, 1954; The Two Fires, 1955; Birds, 1960; Five Senses, 1963; The Other Half, 1966; Collected Poems, 1971; Alive, 1972; Fourth Quarter, 1976; The Double Tree, 1978; Phantom Dwelling, 1985; prose: The Generations of Men, 1955; New Land New Language, 1956; Preoccupations in Australian Poetry, 1964; The Nature of Love, 1966; Because I Was Invited, 1975; Charles Harpur, 1977; The Coral Battleground, 1977; The Cry for the Dead, 1981; We Call for a Treaty, 1985; four books for children; also critical essays and monographs. *Recreation*: gardening. *Address*: c/o Post Office, Braidwood, NSW 2622, Australia.

WRIGHT, Kenneth; *see* Wright, E. K.

WRIGHT, Kenneth Campbell, OBE 1973; PhD; HM Diplomatic Service; Foreign and Commonwealth Office, since 1985; *b* 31 May 1932; *s* of James Edwin Wright and Eva Rebecca Wright (*née* Sayers) *m* 1958, Diana Yolande Binnie; one *s* two *d*. *Educ*: George Heriot's Sch., Edinburgh; Univs of Edinburgh (MA 1st Cl. Hons Mod Langs, PhD) and Paris (LèsL). Short-service commission, Royal Air Force, 1957–60. Lecturer, Inst. Politique Congolais and Lovanium Univ., Congo (Zaire), 1960–63; Lectr, later Sen. Lectr, Dept of Modern Languages, Univ. of Ghana, 1963–65; entered HM Diplomatic Service, 1965; FO, 1965–68; First Sec., Bonn, 1968–72; FCO, 1972–75; First Sec., later Counsellor, UK Permanent Representation to the European Communities, Brussels, 1975–79; FCO, 1979–82; Counsellor, Paris, 1982–85. *Recreations*: people, places, books. *Address*: c/o Foreign and Commonwealth Office, SW1. *Club*: Athenæum.

WRIGHT, Lance Armitage, RIBA; Associate Director, International Committee of Architectural Critics, since 1978; *b* 25 Dec. 1915; *s* of Edmund Lancelot Wright and Elizabeth Helen (*née* Bonser); *m* 1942, Susan Melville Foster; two *s* two *d*. *Educ*: Haileybury; University Coll. London; Architectural Assoc. Sch. Architect in private practice, 1946–73; Registrar, Royal West of England Academy Sch. of Architecture, 1950–53; Technical Editor, The Architects Journal, 1954; Editor, The Architectural Review, 1973–80. Chevalier, Order of St Gregory the Great, 1971. *Publication*: (with D. A. C. A. Boyne) Architects Working Details, vols 4–15, 1953–69. *Address*: 18 Holly Hill, Hampstead, NW3 6SE.

WRIGHT, Prof. Margaret S.; *see* Scott Wright.

WRIGHT, Martin; Information Officer, National Association of Victims Support Schemes, since 1985; *b* 24 April 1930; *s* of late Clifford Kent Wright and Rosalie Wright, Stoke Newington; *m* 1957, Louisa Mary Nicholls; three *s* two *d*. *Educ*: Repton; Jesus Coll., Oxford. Librarian, Inst. of Criminology, Cambridge, 1964–71; Dir, Howard League for Penal Reform, 1971–81. Mem. Council, The Cyrenians, 1969–80 (Chm., Cambridge Cyrene Community (formerly Cambridge Simon Community), 1965–71). ALA 1960. *Publications*: (ed) The Use of Criminological Literature, 1974; Making Good: Prisons, Punishment and Beyond, 1982. *Recreation*: suggesting improvements. *Address*: 19 Hillside Road, SW2 3HL. *T*: 01–671 8037.

WRIGHT, Michael; *see* Wright, J. M.

WRIGHT, Michael Thomas; JP; Publisher: Country Life, since 1984 (Editor, 1973–84, Editor in Chief, 1980–84); Practical Woodworking, since 1985; Television, since 1985; Editorial Consultant, Country Life Books, since 1978; Editor in Chief and Publisher, Antique Dealer and Collectors' Guide, since 1982; *b* 10 Dec. 1936; *o c* of Thomas Manning Wright and Hilda Evelyn Wright (*née* Whiting); *m* 1964, Jennifer Olga Angus, 2nd *d* of C. B. Angus, Singapore; two *s*. *Educ*: Bristol Grammar Sch.; Gonville and Caius Coll., Cambridge (MA); Trinity Coll., Dublin. Member, Honourable Society of Gray's Inn. Churchwarden, St Michael's Parish Church, Highgate, 1974–79; Chm., Highgate Soc., 1985–. Judge, RICS/The Times Conservation Awards, 1976–86. Mem., DoE Working Party on Rural Settlements. Formerly: Financial Analyst, Ford Motor Co. Asst Sec., Town Planning Inst.; Editor, Town Planning Inst. Jl; Asst Editor, Country Life; Managing Editor, Journal of Royal Inst. of British Architects; Dep. Editor, Country Life. FRSA 1980. *Publications*: contrib. articles to: TPI Jl, RIBA Jl; Water Space; Country Life.

Recreations: music, tennis, walking; participation in local amenity society work. *Address:* 7 Fitzwarren Gardens, Highgate, N19 3TR. *T:* 01–272 2971. *Club:* Travellers'.

WRIGHT, Sir Oliver; *see* Wright, Sir J. O.

WRIGHT, Sir Patrick (Richard Henry), KCMG 1984 (CMG 1978); HM Diplomatic Service; Permanent Under-Secretary of State and Head of the Diplomatic Service, since 1986; *b* 28 June 1931; *s* of late Herbert H. S. Wright and of Rachel Wright (*née* Green), Haslemere, Surrey; *m* 1958, Virginia Anne Gaffney; two *s* one *d.* *Educ:* Marlborough; Merton Coll. (Postmaster), Oxford (MA). Served Royal Artillery, 1950–51; joined Diplomatic Service, 1955; Middle East Centre for Arabic Studies, 1956–57; Third Secretary, British Embassy, Beirut, 1958–60; Private Sec. to Ambassador and later First Sec., British Embassy, Washington, 1960–65; Private Sec. to Permanent Under-Sec., FO, 1965–67; First Sec. and Head of Chancery, Cairo, 1967–70; Dep. Political Resident, Bahrain, 1971–72; Head of Middle East Dept, FCO, 1972–74; Private Sec. (Overseas Affairs) to Prime Minister, 1974–77; Ambassador to: Luxembourg, 1977–79; Syria, 1979–81; Dep. Under-Sec. of State, FCO, 1982–84; Ambassador to Saudi Arabia, 1984–86. *Recreations:* music, philately, walking. *Address:* c/o Foreign and Commonwealth Office, King Charles Street, SW1. *Club:* United Oxford & Cambridge University.

WRIGHT, Sir Paul (Hervé Giraud), KCMG 1975 (CMG 1960); OBE 1952; FRSA; HM Diplomatic Service, retired; Chairman: Irvin Great Britain Ltd, since 1979; British American Arts Association, since 1983; Governor, Westminster Cathedral Choir School, since 1981; *b* 12 May 1915; *o s* of late Richard Hervé Giraud Wright; *m* 1942, Beatrice Frederika Rathbone (*see* Beatrice Wright), *widow* of Flt-Lt J. R. Rathbone, MP; one *d.* *Educ:* Westminster. Employed by John Lewis Partnership Ltd, 1933–39. Served HM Forces, War of 1939–45; Major, KRRC; HQ 21 Army Group, 1944–45 (despatches). Contested (L) NE Bethnal Green, 1945. Asst Dir, Public Relations, National Coal Bd, 1946–48; Dir, Public Relations, Festival of Britain, 1948–51. HM Foreign Service: Paris and New York, 1951–54; Foreign Office, 1954–56; The Hague, 1956–57; Head of Information, Policy Dept in FO, 1957–60; Cairo, 1960–61; UK Delegn to N Atlantic Council, 1961–64; Minister (Information), Washington, 1965–68, and Dir-Gen., British Inf. Services, NY, 1964–68; Ambassador to Congo (Kinshasa) and to Republic of Burundi, 1969–71; Ambassador to the Lebanon, 1971–75. Special Rep. of Sec. of State for Foreign and Commonwealth Affairs, 1975–78. Hon. Sec. Gen., London Celebrations Cttee for Queen's Silver Jubilee, 1977; Vice-Chm., The American Fest., 1985. *Publication:* A Brittle Glory (autobiog.), 1986. *Address:* 3 Ormonde Gate, SW3 4EU. *Club:* Garrick.

WRIGHT, Peter, OBE 1982; Chief Constable, South Yorkshire Police, since 1983; *b* Stockport, 21 July 1929; *s* of Henry Wright and late Elizabeth (*née* Burton); *m* 1950, Mary Dorothea (*née* Stanway); one *s.* *Educ:* Edgeley Roman Catholic Sch.; Stockport Technical School. RN, 1947–49. Manchester City Police, 1954, to Chief Superintendent, Greater Manchester, 1975; Asst Chief Constable, 1975–79, Dep. Chief Constable, 1979–82, Merseyside. *Recreations:* walking, gardening. *Address:* Chief Constable's Office, South Yorkshire Police, Snig Hill, Sheffield S3 8LY. *T:* Sheffield 78522. *Club:* Royal Commonwealth Society.

WRIGHT, Peter Harold, VC 1944; late Company Sergeant-Major, Coldstream Guards; farmer; *b* 10 Aug. 1916, British; *m* 1946, Mollie Mary Hurren, Wenhaston; one *s* two *d.* *Educ:* Brooke, Norfolk (elementary school). Left school at 14 and worked on father's farm up to the age of 20. Joined Coldstream Guards, 1936; sailed for Egypt, 1937. Served in Egypt, Palestine, Syria and throughout the Libyan campaign and North Africa, took part in the landing at Salerno, Italy, Sept. 1943; demobilised, 1945. *Address:* Poplar Farm, Helmingham, Stowmarket, Suffolk.

WRIGHT, Peter Robert, CBE 1985; Director, Sadler's Wells Royal Ballet, since 1977; *b* 25 Nov. 1926; *s* of Bernard and Hilda Mary Wright; *m* 1954, Sonya Hana; one *s* one *d.* *Educ:* Bedales School. Dancer: Ballet Jooss, 1945–47, 1951–52; Metropolitan Ballet, 1947–49; Sadler's Wells Theatre Ballet, 1949–51, 1952–56; Ballet Master, Sadler's Wells Opera, and Teacher, Royal Ballet Sch., 1956–58; freelance choreographer and teacher, 1958–61; Ballet Master and Asst Dir, Stuttgart Ballet, 1961–63; BBC Television Producer, 1963–65; freelance choreographer, 1965–69; Associate Dir, Royal Ballet, 1969–77. *Creative Works:* Ballets: A Blue Rose, 1957; The Great Peacock, 1958; Musical Chairs, 1959; The Mirror Walkers, 1962; Quintet, 1962; Namouna, 1963; Designs for Dancers, 1963; Summer's Night, 1964; Danse Macabre, 1964; Variations, 1964; Concerto, 1965; Arpege, 1974; El Amor Brujo, 1975; Summertide, 1976; own productions of classics: Giselle: Stuttgart, 1966; Cologne, 1967; Royal Ballet, 1968 and 1985; Canadian National Ballet, 1970; Munich, 1976; Dutch National Ballet, 1977; Houston, Texas, 1979; Frankfurt, 1980; Rio de Janeiro, Brazil, 1982; Winnipeg, 1982; The Sleeping Beauty: Cologne, 1968; Royal Ballet, 1968; Munich, 1974; Dutch National Ballet, 1981; Sadler's Wells Royal Ballet, 1984; Coppelia: Royal Ballet, 1976; Sadler's Wells Royal Ballet, 1979; Swan Lake: Sadler's Wells Royal Ballet, 1981, 1986; Munich, 1984; Nutcracker: Royal Ballet, 1984. Evening Standard Award for Ballet, 1982. *Recreations:* potter, gardener. *Address:* c/o Royal Opera House, Covent Garden, WC2E 7QA. *T:* 01–240 1200.

WRIGHT, Hon. Sir Reginald Charles, Kt 1978; *b* Tasmania, 10 July 1905; *s* of John and Emma Wright; *m* 1930, Evelyn Arnett; two *s* four *d.* *Educ:* Devonport St High Sch., Tasmania; Univ. of Tasmania. BA, LLB. Admitted Tasmanian Bar, 1928; Lectr in Law, Univ. of Tasmania, 1931–46; Captain, Aust. Field Artillery, AIF, 1941–44; Pres., Liberal Party, Tasmania, 1945–46; MHA for Franklin, Tasmania, and Deputy Leader of Opposition, Tasmanian House of Assembly, 1946–49; Senator (Lib) for Tasmania, 1949–78; Minister for Works and Minister assisting Minister for Trade and Industry and in charge of Tourist Activities, 1968–72. *Address:* Wallys Farm, Central Castra, Tasmania, Australia. *Clubs:* Naval and Military, Ulverstone.

See also Sir R. D. Wright.

WRIGHT, Maj.-Gen. Richard Eustace John G.; *see* Gerrard-Wright.

WRIGHT, Sir Richard (Michael) C.; *see* Cory-Wright.

WRIGHT, Robert Anthony Kent, QC 1973; *b* 7 Jan. 1922; *s* of Robert and Eva Wright; *m* 1956, Gillian Elizabeth Drummond Hancock. *Educ:* Hilton Coll., Natal, S Africa; St Paul's Sch., London; The Queen's Coll., Oxford (MA). Indian Army, 1942–46, Major. Oxford, 1946–48. Called to Bar, Lincoln's Inn, 1949, Bencher 1979. *Recreations:* music, sailing, golf, walking. *Address:* 24 Old Buildings, Lincoln's Inn, WC2A 3UJ. *T:* 01–242 5532. *Clubs:* National Liberal; Bosham Sailing (Bosham); Royal Wimbledon Golf (Wimbledon).

WRIGHT, Very Rev. Ronald (William Vernon) Selby, CVO 1968; TD; DD; FRSE; FSA Scotland; JP; Minister Emeritus of the Canongate (The Kirk of Holyroodhouse), Edinburgh, and of Edinburgh Castle (Minister, 1936–77); Extra Chaplain to the Queen in Scotland, 1961–63 and since 1978 (Chaplain, 1963–78); Chaplain to The Queen's Bodyguard for Scotland, Royal Company of Archers, since 1973; *b* 12 June 1908; *s* of late Vernon O. Wright, ARCM, and late Anna Gilberta, *d* of Major R. E. Selby; unmarried. *Educ:* Edinburgh Academy; Melville Coll.; Edinburgh Univ. (MA; Hon. DD 1956); New Coll. Edinburgh. Warden, St Giles' Cathedral Boys' Club, 1927–36, and Canongate Boys' Club (formerly St Giles'), 1937–78. Cadet Officer, The Royal Scots, 1927–31; Student-Asst at St Giles' Cathedral, 1929–36; Asst Minister of Glasgow Cathedral, 1936; Warden of first Scottish Public Schools' and Clubs' Camp, 1938; Chaplain to 7th/9th (Highlanders) Bn The Royal Scots, 1938–42 (France, 1940), 1947–49; Senior Chaplain to the Forces: 52nd (Lowland) Div., 1942–43; Edinburgh Garrison, 1943; Middle East Forces, 1943–44; NE London, 1944; 10th Indian Div., CMF, 1944–45 (despatches); Hon. SCF, 1945–. Special Preacher, Oxford Univ., 1944; Select Preacher, Cambridge Univ., 1947; Visiting Preacher: Aberdeen Univ., 1946, 1953, 1965, 1973; St Andrews Univ., 1951, 1956, 1967, 1973; Glasgow Univ., 1955, 1973; Edinburgh Univ., 1959; Birmingham Univ., 1959; Hull Univ., 1967; Dundee Univ., 1973. Chaplain to, the Lord High Comr, 1959, and 1960. Conducted numerous series of religious broadcasts for BBC as Radio Padre, toured for War Office and BBC all Home Comds in 1942 and 1943 and MEF, 1943–44; toured transit camps etc in Italy, Austria, S Germany, etc, 1945; toured, for Church of Scotland: India, 1972; for HM Forces: Hong Kong 1973; Singapore, 1973. Moderator, Presbytery of Edinburgh, 1963; Moderator, Gen. Assembly of the Church of Scotland, 1972–73. Chm., Edinburgh and Leith Old People's Welfare Council, 1956–69; Extraordinary Dir, The Edinburgh Academy, 1973–; Hon. Church of Scotland Chaplain to: Fettes Coll., 1957–60, 1979–82, 1984–86 (Hon. Mem., 1983); Loretto Sch., 1960–84 (Hon. Old Lorettonian, 1976); Edinburgh Acad., 1966–73; Hon. Mem. Cargilfield Sch., 1985; Chaplain to: Governor of Edinburgh Castle, 1959–; Merchant Co. of Edinburgh, 1973–82; ChStJ 1976; President: Scottish Church Soc., 1971–74; Scottish Assoc. of Boys Clubs; Vice-Pres., Old Edinburgh Club; Hon. Pres. Scottish Churches FA; Patron, Lothian Amateur FA. Mem. Edinburgh Educn Cttee, 1960–70. JP Edinburgh, 1963. Cross of St Mark, 1970. *Publications:* Asking Why (with A. W. Loos), 1939; The Average Man, 1942; Let's Ask the Padre, 1943; The Greater Victory, 1943; The Padre Presents, 1944; Small Talks, 1945; Whatever the Years, 1947; What Worries Me, 1950; Great Men, 1951; They Looked to Him, 1954; Our Club, 1954; The Kirk in the Canongate, 1956; The Selfsame Miracles, 1957; Our Club and Panmure House, 1958; Roses in December, 1960; The Seven Words, 1964; An Illustrated Guide to the Canongate, 1965; Take up God's Armour, 1967; The Seven Dwarfs, 1968; Haply I May Remember, 1970; In Christ We Are All One, 1972; Seven Sevens, 1977; Another Home, 1980; edited and contributed to Asking Them Questions, 1936; A Scottish Camper's Prayer Book, 1936; I Attack, 1937; Asking Them Questions-Second Series, 1938; Front Line Religion, 1941; Soldiers Also Asked, 1943; Asking Them Questions-Third Series, 1950; Asking Them Questions (a Selection), 1953; The Beloved Captain: Essays by Donald Hankey, 1956; (with L. Menzies and R. A. Knox) St Margaret, Queen of Scotland, 1957; A Manual of Church Doctrine (with T. F. Torrance), 1960; Fathers of the Kirk, 1960; Asking Them Questions, a new series, 1972, 1973; contrib. to Chambers's Encyclopædia, DNB, etc. Editor, Scottish Forces' Magazine (quarterly), 1941–76. *Recreation:* after trying to run Boys' Clubs and Camps, 1927–78, now enjoying a busy retirement. *Address:* The Queen's House, 36 Moray Place, Edinburgh EH3 6BX. *T:* 031–226 5566. *Clubs:* Athenæum; New (Hon. Mem.) (Edinburgh).

WRIGHT, Sir Rowland (Sydney), Kt 1976; CBE 1970; Director, Blue Circle Industries PLC, 1978–86 (Chairman 1978–83); Chairman, Blue Circle Trust, since 1983; Chancellor, Queen's University, Belfast, since 1984; *b* 4 Oct. 1915; *s* of late Sydney Henry Wright and Elsie May; *m* 1940, Kathleen Mary Hodgkinson, BA; two *s* one *d.* *Educ:* High Pavement Sch., Nottingham; UC Nottingham. BSc London; FRSC. Joined ICI Ltd, Dyestuffs Div., 1937; Production Dir, Imperial Chemical (Pharmaceuticals) Ltd, 1955–57; Production Dir, Dyestuffs Div., 1957–58; Research Dir, 1958–61; Jt Man. Dir, ICI Ltd Agricultural Div., 1961–63, Chm. 1964–65; Personnel Dir, ICI Ltd, 1966–70; Dep. Chm., ICI Ltd, 1971–75, Chm., 1975–78; Director: AE&CI Ltd, 1970–75 (Dep. Chm., 1971–75); Royal Insurance Co., 1973–79; Barclays Bank Ltd, 1977–84; Hawker Siddeley Group, 1979–; Shell Transport & Trading Co. Ltd, 1981–86. Chm., Reorganisation Commn for Eggs, 1967–68; Past Mem. Council, Foundn for Management Educn; Mem. Council, Chemical Industries Assoc., 1968–73; Pres. Inst. of Manpower Studies, 1971–77, Hon. Pres., 1977–; Vice-Pres., Soc. of Chemical Industry, 1971–74; Mem., British Shippers' Council, 1975–78; Trustee: Civic Trust, 1975–78; Westminster Abbey Trust, 1984–. Mem. Court, Univ. of Sussex, 1983–. Governor, London Graduate School of Business Studies, 1975–78. FRSA 1970–; CBIM 1975; FIChemE; Mem., Royal Instn, 1971–. Hon. LLD: St Andrews, 1977; Belfast, 1978; Nottingham, 1978; Hon. DSc QUB, 1985. *Recreations:* gardening, photography. *Club:* Athenæum.

WRIGHT, Sir (Roy) Douglas, AK 1983; FRACP; Professor Emeritus; Chancellor, University of Melbourne, since 1980; Consultant, Howard Florey Institute, since 1975; *b* 7 Aug. 1907; *s* of John Forsyth Wright and Emma Maria Wright; *m* 1st, 1932, Julia Violet Bell; one *s* one *d;* 2nd, 1964, Meriel Antoinette Winchester Wilmot. *Educ:* Devonport State High Sch., Tasmania; Univ. of Tasmania; Univ. of Melbourne (MB, BS 1929; MS 1931; DSc 1941). DSc ANU, 1967. Sen. Lectr, Pathology, Univ. of Melbourne, 1932–38; Surgeon, Royal Melbourne Hosp. and Associate Surgeon, Austin Hosp., 1934–38; University of Melbourne: Prof. of Physiology, 1939–71; Consulting Physiologist, Clinical Hosps, 1940–71; Dean, Faculty of Medicine, 1947, 1951; Mem. Council, 1963–. Mem. Council, ANU, 1946–76; Chm. Exec., 1948–71, Medical Dir, 1971–75, Cancer Inst. of Victoria; Originating Dir, Howard Florey Inst. for Experimental Physiology and Medicine, 1971–. Hon. LLD: ANU, 1977; Melbourne, 1980. *Publications:* reports and articles in jls of pathology, anatomy, physiology, endocrinology. *Recreations:* gardening, reading, public affairs. *Address:* Howard Florey Institute, University of Melbourne, Vic 3052, Australia. *Club:* Graduate Union (Melbourne).

See also Hon. Sir R. C. Wright.

WRIGHT, Roy Kilner; Deputy Editor, The London Standard (formerly Evening Standard), since 1979; *b* 12 March 1926; *s* of Ernest Wright and Louise Wright; *m* 1st (marr. diss.); two *d;* 2nd, 1969, Jane Barnicoat (*née* Selby). *Educ:* elementary sch., St Helens, Lancs. Jun. Reporter, St Helens Reporter, 1941; Army Service; Sub-Editor: Middlesbrough Gazette, 1947; Daily Express, Manchester, 1951; Daily Mirror, London, 1952; Features Editor, Daily Express, London; Dep. Editor, Daily Express, 1976, Editor, 1976–77; Dir, Beaverbrook Newspapers, 1976–77; Senior Asst Editor, Daily Mail, 1977. *Address:* 25 Foskett Road, SW6. *T:* 01–736 0403; Girards, Broadchalke, Wilts. *T:* Salisbury 780385.

WRIGHT, Roy William, CBE 1970; MIEE; Director, 1957–85, Deputy Chairman and Deputy Chief Executive, 1965–75, The Rio Tinto-Zinc Corporation; Director: Davy Corporation Ltd, 1976–85; A. P. V. Holdings Ltd, 1976–85; Transportation Systems and Market Research, 1978–85; *b* 10 Sept. 1914; *s* of late Arthur William Wright; *m* 1939, Mary Letitia, *d* of late Llewelyn Davies; two *d.* *Educ:* King Edward VI Sch., Chelmsford; Faraday House Coll., London. Served War of 1939–45, S African Navy and RN in S Atlantic, N Atlantic and Arctic; Lt-Comdr 1944. Joined Rio Tinto Co. Ltd, 1952; Man. Dir, Rio Tinto Canada, 1956; Director: Rio Tinto Co. Ltd, 1957; Lornex Mining Co., Vancouver, 1970–79; Rio Algom Ltd, Toronto, 1960–80; Palabora Mining Co., Johannesburg, 1963–80; Rio Tinto South Africa Ltd, Johannesburg, 1960–79. Chairman:

Process Plant Expert Cttee, Min. of Technology, 1968; Econ. Develt Cttee for Electronics Industry, NEDO, 1971–76. *Address*: Cobbers, Forest Row, East Sussex RH18 5JZ. *T*: Forest Row 2009. *Clubs*: Athenæum, Royal Automobile; Toronto (Toronto).

WRIGHT, Rt. Rev. Royston Clifford; *see* Monmouth, Bishop of.

WRIGHT, Sewall; Professor Emeritus of Genetics, University of Wisconsin, since 1960; *b* 21 Dec. 1889; *s* of Philip Green Wright and Elizabeth Quincy Sewall; *m* 1921, Louise Lane Williams; two *s* one *d*. *Educ*: Lombard Coll.; University of Illinois; Harvard Univ. BS Lombard Coll., 1911; MS Illinois, 1912; ScD Harvard, 1915. Senior Animal Husbandman, US Dept of Agriculture, 1915–25; University of Chicago: Assoc. Professor of Zoology, 1926–29; Professor of Zoology, 1930–37; Ernest D. Burton Distinguished Service Professor, 1937–54; Leon J. Cole Professor of Genetics, University of Wisconsin, 1955–60; Hitchcock Professor, University of California, 1943; Fulbright Professor, University of Edinburgh, 1949–50. Hon. Member, Royal Society of Edinburgh; Foreign Member: Royal Society, London (Darwin Medal 1980); Royal Danish Acad. of Sciences and Letters. Hon. ScD: Rochester, 1942; Yale, 1949; Harvard, 1951; Knox Coll., 1957; Western Reserve, 1958; Chicago, 1959; Illinois, 1961; Wisconsin, 1965; State Univ. of NY at Stony Brook, 1984; Hon. LLD, Michigan State, 1955. Nat. Medal of Science, 1966; Balzan Prize, 1984. *Publications*: Evolution and the Genetics of Populations, vol. 1, 1968, vol. 2, 1969, vol. 3, 1977, vol. 4, 1978; numerous papers on genetics of characters of guinea pig, population genetics, theory of evolution and path analysis. *Recreation*: travel. *Address*: 6209 Mineral Point Road, Madison, Wisconsin 53705, USA. *Club*: University (Madison).

WRIGHT, Sheila Rosemary Rivers; *b* 22 March 1925; *d* of Daniel Rivers Wright and Frances Grace Wright; *m* 1949, Ronald A. Gregory; two *c*. Social Science Cert. 1951; BScSoc London External 1956. Personnel Officer, 1951–57; Social Worker, 1957–74. Councillor: Birmingham CC, 1956–78; West Midlands CC, 1973–81. MP (Lab) Birmingham, Handsworth, 1979–83. Member, Birmingham Reg. Hosp. Bd and W Midlands RHA, 1966–80. *Address*: 41 Beaudesert Road, Birmingham B20 3TQ. *T*: 021–554 9840.

WRIGHT, Shirley Edwin McEwan; industrial consultant; *b* 4 May 1915; *s* of Alfred Coningsby Wright and Elsie Derbyshire; *m* 1939, Dora Fentem; one *s* three *d*. *Educ*: Herbert Strutt Sch., Belper; Coll. of Technology, Manchester; Univ. of Sheffield. BEng, CEng, FIMechE. Metropolitan Vickers, 1932, ICI Explosives Div., 1938; Asst Chief Engr, ICI Nobel Div., 1955; Dir, Irvine Harbour Bd, 1962; Engrg and Techn Dir, ICI Nobel Div., 1965; Pres., Philippine Explosives Corp., 1970; Chief Exec., Livingston Develt Corp., 1972–77; Dir, Premix-Fibreglass, 1978–80. *Recreations*: cricket, golf. *Address*: Hazeldene, West Kilbride, Ayrshire. *T*: West Kilbride 822659.

WRIGHT, Stanley Harris; Partner, Price Waterhouse and Partners, since 1985; Chairman, Wolstenholme Rink PLC, since 1982 (Director, since 1980); Director, Royal Trust Company of Canada, since 1984; *b* 9 April 1930; *er s* of John Charles Wright and Doris Wright; *m* 1st, 1957, Angela Vivien Smith (marr. diss. 1973); one *s*; 2nd, 1973, Alison Elizabeth Franks (*see* Hon. A. E. Wright). *Educ*: Bolton Sch.; Merton Coll., Oxford (Postmaster); 1st cl. hons PPE. Asst Principal, BoT, 1952–55; 2nd Sec., UK Delegn to OEEC, Paris, 1955–57; Principal, HM Treasury, 1958–64; 1st Sec. (Financial), British Embassy, Washington, 1964–66; Asst Sec., HM Treasury, 1966–68; Lazard Bros & Co. Ltd, 1969 and 1970 (Dir 1969); Under-Sec., HM Treasury, 1970–72. Exec. Dir, Lazard Bros & Co. Ltd, 1972–81; Director: Wilkinson Match Ltd, 1974–81; Scripto Inc., 1977–81; Law Land Co., 1979–81; Exec. Chm., International Commercial Bank PLC, 1981–83. Member: Layfield Cttee on Local Government Finance, 1974–76; Armstrong Cttee on Budgetary Reform, 1979–80; Mem. and Dir of Studies, CBI Wkg Pty on Tax Reform, 1984–85; Chm., British Bankers Assoc. Fiscal Cttee, 1974–80. Mem. Council, Westfield Coll., 1977–. *Recreations*: various. *Address*: 6 Holly Place, NW3. *Clubs*: Reform, MCC.

WRIGHT, Prof. Verna, FRCP; Professor of Rheumatology, University of Leeds, since 1970; Consultant Physician in Rheumatology, Leeds Area Health Authority (A) Teaching, and Yorkshire Regional Health Authority, since 1964; Co-Director, Bioengineering Group for Study of Human Joints, University of Leeds, since 1964; *b* 31 Dec. 1928; *s* of Thomas William and Nancy Eleanor Wright; *m* 1953, Esther Margaret Brown; five *s* four *d*. *Educ*: Bedford Sch.; Univ. of Liverpool (MB ChB 1953, MD 1956). FRCP 1970 (MRCP 1958). House Officer, Broadgreen Hosp., Liverpool, 1953–54; Sen. Ho. Officer, Stoke Mandeville Hosp., 1954–56; Research Asst, Dept of Clin. Medicine, Univ. of Leeds, 1956–58; Research Fellow, Div. of Applied Physiology, Johns Hopkins Hosp., Baltimore, 1958–59; Lectr, Dept of Clin. Med., Univ. of Leeds, 1960–64; Sen. Lectr, Dept of Medicine, Univ. of Leeds, 1964–70. Adv. Fellow to World Fedn of Occupational Therapists, 1980–. President: Heberden Soc., 1976–77; British Assoc. for Rheumatology and Rehabilitation, 1978–80; Soc. for Research in Rehabilitation, 1978; Soc. for Back Pain Research, 1977–79. Member, Johns Hopkins Soc. for Scholars, USA, 1978–. *Publications*: Lubrication and Wear in Joints, 1969; (with J. M. H. Moll) Seronegative Polyarthritis, 1976; Clinics in Rheumatic Diseases: Osteoarthrosis, 1976; (with I. Haslock) Rheumatism for Nurses and Remedial Therapists, 1977; (with D. Dowson) Evaluation of Artificial Joints, 1977; (with D. Dowson) Introduction to the Biomechanics of Joints and Joint Replacement, 1981; The Relevance of Christianity in a Scientific Age, 1981; (with H. A. Bird) Applied Drug Therapy of the Rheumatic Diseases, 1982; Topical Reviews in Rheumatic Disorders, vol. 2, 1982; Clinics in Rheumatic Diseases: osteoarthritis, 1982; Clinics in Rheumatic Diseases: measurement of joint movement, 1982; Bone and Joint Disease in the Elderly, 1983; (with R. A. Dickson) Integrated Clinical Science: musculo-skeletal disease, 1984; Personal Peace in a Nuclear Age, 1985. *Recreations*: interdenominational Christian youth work, voracious reader. *Address*: Inglehurst, Park Drive, Harrogate HG2 9AY. *T*: Harrogate 502326.

WRIGHT, William Alan, CIE 1945; AFC; *b* 27 Nov. 1895; *s* of Rev. Thomas Wright and Annie Pedley; *m* 1948, Elizabeth Ada, *d* of A. E. Garrott, Launceston, Tasmania; one *s* one *d*. *Educ*: Oundle. 2nd Lieut, Leicestershire Regt, Jan, 1915; joined the Royal Flying Corps, Sept. 1916; Captain about July 1917 (Chevalier of Crown of Belgium and Belgian Croix de Guerre); transferred to RAF on its formation (AFC); joined Indian Civil Service, 1921, and served in Burma, acting Judge Rangoon High Court in 1939; with Government of India, War Dept, 1942–45, as Deputy Secretary, and then as officiating Joint Secretary; Deputy Director of Civil Affairs, Burma, Brig. 1945; Judge Rangoon High Court, 1945–48. *Address*: Salween, 10 Smithers Street, Lorne, Victoria 3232, Australia.

WRIGHT, William Ambrose, (Billy Wright), CBE 1959; Controller of Sport, Central Independent Television Ltd, since 1982 (Head of Sport and Outside Broadcasts, ATV Network Ltd, 1966–81); *b* 6 Feb. 1924; *m* 1958, Joy Beverley; two *d*, and one step *s*. *Educ*: Madeley Secondary Modern Sch. Professional Footballer; became Captain, Wolverhampton Wanderers Football Club; played for England 105 times; Captain of England 90 times; Manager of Arsenal Football Club, 1962–66. FA Cup Winners medal; 3 Football League Winners Medals. *Publications*: Captain of England; The World's my

Football Pitch. *Recreations*: golf, cricket. *Address*: 87 Lyonsdown Road, New Barnet, Herts.

WRIGHT, Prof. William David, ARCS, DIC, DSc; Professor of Applied Optics, Imperial College of Science and Technology, 1951–73; *b* 6 July 1906; *s* of late William John Wright and Grace Elizabeth Ansell; *m* 1932, Dorothy Mary Hudson; two *s*. *Educ*: Southgate County Sch.; Imperial Coll. Research engineer at Westinghouse Electric and Manufacturing Co., Pittsburgh, USA, 1929–30; research and consultant physicist to Electric and Musical Industries, 1930–39. Lecturer and Reader in Technical Optics Section, Imperial Coll., 1931–51. Kern Prof. of Communications, Rochester Inst. of Technol., USA, 1984–85. Chm. Physical Soc. Colour Group, 1941–43; Vice-Pres., Physical Soc., 1948–50; Sec., International Commn for Optics, 1953–66; Chairman: Physical Soc. Optical Group, 1956–59; Colour Group (GB), 1973–75; Pres., International Colour Assoc., 1967–69. Hon. DSc City Univ., 1971. *Publications*: The Perception of Light, 1938; The Measurement of Colour, 4th edn, 1969; Researches on Normal and Defective Colour Vision, 1946; Photometry and the Eye, 1950; The Rays are not Coloured, 1967. About 80 original scientific papers, mainly dealing with colour and vision. *Address*: 68 Newberries Avenue, Radlett, Herts WD7 7EP. *T*: Radlett 5306.

WRIGHT, Most Rev. William Lockridge, DD, DCL, LLD; *b* 8 Sept. 1904; *s* of Rev. Canon J. de Pencier Wright and Lucy Lockridge; *m* 1936, Margaret Clare, BA; two *s* two *d*. *Educ*: Queen's University, Kingston, Ontario; Trinity College, Toronto (Hon. Fellow 1983). LTh 1927. Curate St George's, Toronto, 1926–28; Incumbent St James', Tweed, 1928–32; Curate Christ's Church Cathedral, Hamilton, 1932–36; Rector St George's Church, Toronto, 1936–40; Rector St Luke's Cathedral, Sault Ste Marie, 1940–44; Dean St Luke's Cathedral, 1941–44; Bishop of Algoma, 1944; Archbishop of Algoma and Metropolitan of Ontario, 1955–74; Acting Primate of the Anglican Church of Canada, Aug. 1970–Jan. 1971. DD (juris dig.) 1941; DCL (Bishop's Univ. Lennoxville), 1953; DD (*hc*) Wycliffe Coll., Toronto, 1956; Huron Coll., 1957; Montreal Diocesan Coll., 1958; LLD (*hc*) Laurentian University of Sudbury, Ont, 1964. *Recreations*: ice hockey, rugby football. *Address*: Box 637, Sault Ste Marie, Ontario P6A 5N2, Canada.

WRIGHTSON, Sir (Charles) Mark (Garmondsway), 4th Bt *cr* 1900; Director, Hill Samuel & Co. Ltd, since 1984; *b* 18 Feb. 1951; *s* of Sir John Garmondsway Wrightson, 3rd Bt, TD, and of Hon. Rosemary, *y d* of 1st Viscount Dawson of Penn, GCVO, KCB, KCMG, PC; *S* father, 1983; *m* 1975, Stella Virginia, *d* of late George Dean; three *s*. *Educ*: Eton; Queens' Coll., Cambridge (BA 1972). Called to the Bar, Middle Temple, 1974. Joined Hill Samuel & Co. Ltd, 1977. *Heir*: *s* Barnaby Thomas Garmondsway Wrightson, *b* 5 Aug. 1979. *Address*: 39 Westbourne Park Road, W2.
See also Oliver Wrightson.

WRIGHTSON, Oliver; His Honour Judge Wrightson; a Circuit Judge, since 1978; *b* 28 May 1920; *y s* of Col Sir Thomas Garmondsway Wrightson, 2nd Bt, TD. *Educ*: Eton; Balliol Coll., Oxford. Served with Coldstream Guards, 1942–46, Captain. Called to Bar, Lincoln's Inn, 1950. A Recorder of the Crown Court, 1972–78. *Recreations*: lawn tennis, music, theatre. *Address*: The Bridge House, Eryholme, Darlington, Yorks. *Club*: Northern Counties (Newcastle upon Tyne).

WRIGLEY, Prof. Edward Anthony, (Tony), PhD; FBA 1980; Professor of Population Studies, London School of Economics and Political Science, since 1979; Fellow of Peterhouse, Cambridge, since 1958; *b* 17 Aug. 1931; *s* of Edward Ernest Wrigley and Jessie Elizabeth Wrigley; *m* 1960, Maria Laura Spelberg; one *s* three *d*. *Educ*: King's Sch., Macclesfield; Peterhouse, Cambridge (MA, PhD). William Volker Res. Fellow, Univ. of Chicago, 1953–54; Lectr in Geography, Cambridge, 1958–74; Tutor, Peterhouse, 1962–64, Sen. Bursar, 1964–74; Co-Dir, SSRC Cambridge Gp for History of Population and Social Structure, 1974–. Mem., Inst. for Advanced Study, Princeton, 1970–71; Hinkley Vis. Prof., Johns Hopkins Univ., 1975; Tinbergen Vis. Prof., Erasmus Univ., Rotterdam, 1979. Pres., British Soc. for Population Studies, 1977–79; Chm., Population Investigation Cttee, 1984–. Editor, Economic History Review, 1986–. *Publications*: Industrial Growth and Population Change, 1961; (ed) English Historical Demography, 1966; Population and History, 1969; (ed) Nineteenth Century Society, 1972; (ed) Identifying People in the Past, 1973; (ed with P. Abrams) Towns in Societies, 1978; (with R. S. Schofield) Population History of England, 1981; (ed jtly) The Works of Thomas Robert Malthus, 1986. *Recreations*: gardening, violin making. *Address*: 13 Sedley Taylor Road, Cambridge CB2 2PW. *T*: Cambridge 247614.

WRIGLEY, Air Vice-Marshal Henry Bertram, CB 1962; CBE 1956; DL; Senior Technical Staff Officer, Royal Air Force Fighter Command, 1960–64, retired; Sales Manager Air Weapons, Hawker Siddeley Dynamics, 1964–76; *b* 24 Nov. 1909; *s* of Frederick William Wrigley and Anne Jeffreys, Seascale, Cumberland; *m* 1935, Audrey, *d* of C. S. Boryer, Portsmouth; one *d*. *Educ*: Whitehaven Grammar Sch.; RAF Coll., Cranwell. 33 Squadron, 1930; HMS Glorious 1931; HMS Eagle, 1933; long Signals Course, 1934; various signals appointments until 1937; RAF Signals Officer, HMS Glorious, 1938; served War of 1939–45, X Force, Norway, 1940; Fighter Command, 1940–43; HQ South East Asia, 1943–46; RAF Staff Coll., 1946; comd Northern Signals Area, 1947–50; jssc 1950; Inspector, Radio Services, 1950–52; Chief Signals Officer, 2nd TAF, 1952–54; Director of Signals (I), Air Ministry, 1954–57; Guided Weapons (Air), Min. of Aviation, 1957–60. DL, Hertfordshire, 1966. *Recreation*: gardening. *Address*: Boonwood, Turpin's Chase, Oaklands Rise, Welwyn, Herts. *T*: Welwyn 5231. *Club*: Royal Air Force.

WRIGLEY, Prof. Jack, CBE 1977; Professor of Education, since 1967 and Deputy Vice-Chancellor, since 1982, University of Reading; *b* 8 March 1923; *s* of Harry and Ethel Wrigley; *m* 1946, Edith Baron; two *s*. *Educ*: Oldham High Sch.; Manchester Univ. BSc, MEd (Manch.); PhD (Queen's, Belfast). Asst Mathematics Teacher: Stretford Grammar Sch., 1946–47; Chadderton Grammar Sch., 1948–50; Research Asst, Manchester Univ., 1950–51; Lectr in Educn: Queen's Univ., Belfast, 1951–57; Univ. of London Inst. of Educn, 1957–62; Research Adviser, Curriculum Study Gp in Min. of Educn, 1962–63; Prof. of Educn, Univ. of Southampton, 1963–67; Dir of Studies, Schools Council, 1967–75. Member: Bullock Cttee on Teaching of Reading and other uses of English, 1972–74; SSRC, Mem. Council and Chm. Educnl Res. Bd, 1976–81. *Publications*: (ed) The Dissemination of Curriculum Development, 1976; Values and Evaluation in Education, 1980; contrib. learned jls. *Recreations*: chess (Ulster Chess Champion, 1957), theatre, foreign travel. *Address*: 68 Grosvenor Road, Caversham, Reading, Berks RG4 0ES. *T*: Reading 471812.

WRIGLEY, Michael Harold, OBE 1971; HM Diplomatic Service; retired; *b* 30 July 1924; *e s* of Edward Whittaker Wrigley and Audrey Margaret Wrigley; *m* 1950, Anne Phillida Brewis; two *s* two *d*. *Educ*: Harrow; Worcester Coll., Oxford. Served War of 1939–45: Rifle Brigade, 1943–47. HM Diplomatic Service, 1950; served HM Embassies: Brussels, 1952–54; Bangkok, 1956–59; Office of Commissioner-Gen. for South-East Asia, Singapore, 1959–60; HM Embassy, Bangkok (again), 1961–64 and 1966–71; Counsellor, Kuala Lumpur, 1971–74; Counsellor, FCO, 1974–76. Mem., North Yorkshire CC,

1977–85. *Recreations:* shooting, racing. *Address:* Ganton Hall, Scarborough, N Yorks. *T:* Sherburn 70223. *Clubs:* Turf, Jockey; Royal Bangkok Sports (Bangkok).

WRIGLEY, Tony; *see* Wrigley, E. A.

WRINTMORE, Eric George; His Honour Judge Wrintmore; a Circuit Judge, since 1984; *b* 11 June 1928; *s* of Rev. F. H. and Muriel Wrintmore; *m* 1951, Jean Blackburn; two *s* one *d. Educ:* Stationers' Company's Sch.; King's Coll. London (LLB Hons). Called to Bar, Gray's Inn, 1955; full-time Chm., Industrial Tribunals, 1971; Regional Chm., Industrial Tribunals, 1976–84; a Dep. Circuit Judge, 1980–83; a Recorder, 1983–84. *Recreations:* sailing, squash, golf. *Address:* Central Office of the Industrial Tribunals, 93 Ebury Bridge Road, SW1W 8RE. *Clubs:* Chichester Yacht; Ifield Golf and Country.

WRIXON-BECHER, Major Sir William F.; *see* Becher.

WROATH, John Herbert; His Honour Judge Wroath; a Circuit Judge, since 1984; *b* 24 July 1932; *s* of Stanley Wroath and Ruth Ellen Wroath; *m* 1959, Mary Bridget Byrne; two *s* one *d. Educ:* Ryde Sch., Ryde, IoW. Admitted Solicitor, 1956; private practice, 1958–66; Registrar, Isle of Wight County Court, 1965; County Prosecuting Solicitor, 1966; full-time County Court Registrar, 1972; a Recorder of the Crown Court, 1978–84. *Recreations:* sailing, bowling, reading, painting. *Address:* Little Barn Cottage, Portloe, Cornwall. *T:* Truro 501548. *Clubs:* Royal London Yacht; Cowes Island Sailing (Cowes).

WROE, David Charles Lynn; Under Secretary, Regional Policy Directorate, and Director of Statistics, Department of the Environment, since 1982; *b* 20 Feb. 1942; *m* 1966, Susan Higgitt; three *d. Educ:* Reigate Grammar Sch.; Trinity Coll., Cambridge (MA); Trinity Coll., Oxford (Cert. Statistics); Birkbeck Coll., London (MSc). Min. of Pensions and National Insurance, 1965–68; Central Statistical Office, 1968–70, 1973–75, 1976–82; secondment to Zambian Govt, 1971–72; Secretariat of Royal Commission on Distribution of Income and Wealth, 1975–76. *Address:* Department of the Environment, 2 Marsham Street, SW1.

WRONG, Henry Lewellys Barker, CBE 1986; Director (formerly General Administrator), Barbican Centre, since 1970; *b* Toronto, Canada, 20 April 1930; *s* of Henry Arkel Wrong and Jean Barker Wrong; *m* 1966, Penelope Hamilton Norman; two *s* one *d. Educ:* Trinity Coll., Univ. of Toronto (BA). Stage and business administration, Metropolitan Opera Assoc., New York, 1952–64; Director Programming, National Arts Center, Ottawa, 1964–68; Director, Festival Canada Centennial Programme, 1967. Hon. DLitt City, 1985. Centennial Medal, Govt of Canada, 1967. *Address:* Yew Tree House, Much Hadham, Herts SG10 6AJ. *T:* Much Hadham 2106; Barbican Centre, EC2Y 8DS. *Clubs:* Mark's; Badminton and Rackets (Toronto).

WROTH, Prof. Charles Peter, MA, PhD, DSc; FEng, MICE; FGS; Professor of Engineering Science, University of Oxford, since 1979; Fellow of Brasenose College, Oxford, since 1979; *b* 2 June 1929; *s* of late Charles Wroth and Violet Beynon Wroth (*née* Jenour); *m* 1954, Mary Parlane Wroth (*née* Weller); two *s* two *d. Educ:* Marlborough Coll.; Emmanuel Coll., Cambridge (MA, PhD). Schoolmaster, Felsted Sch., 1953–54; Research Student, Univ. of Cambridge, 1954–58; Engineer, G. Maunsell & Partners, London, 1958–61; University of Cambridge: Lectr in Engineering, 1961–75; Reader in Soil Mechanics, 1975–79; Fellow of Churchill Coll., 1963–79. Chairman, British Geotechnical Soc., 1979, 1980, 1981. *Publications:* (with A. N. Schofield) Critical State Soil Mechanics, 1968; contribs to learned jls on soil mechanics and foundation engineering. *Recreations:* golf, Real tennis. *Address:* Department of Engineering Science, Parks Road, Oxford OX1 3PJ. *Clubs:* MCC; Hawks, Jesters.

WROTTESLEY, family name of **Baron Wrottesley.**

WROTTESLEY, 6th Baron *cr* 1838; **Clifton Hugh Lancelot de Verdon Wrottesley;** Bt 1642; *b* 10 Aug. 1968; *s* of Hon. Richard Francis Gerard Wrottesley (*d* 1970) (2nd *s* of 5th Baron) and of Georgina Anne (who *m* 1982, Lt-Col Jonathan L. Seddon-Brown), *er d* of Lt-Col Peter Thomas Clifton, *qv*; *S* grandfather, 1977. *Heir: uncle* Hon. Mark Wrottesley, *b* 21 June 1951. *Address:* c/o Barclays Bank, 8 High Street, Eton, Windsor, Berks.

WU Shu-Chih, Hon. Alex, CBE 1983 (OBE 1973); JP; company director; Chairman, Fidelity Management Ltd, since 1965; Vice-Chairman, Dai Nippon Printing Co. (HK) Ltd, since 1973; *b* 14 Sept. 1920; *s* of Wu Chao-Ming and Yeh Huei-Cheng; *m* 1946; three *s* three *d. Educ:* National South West Associated Univ., Kunming, China. Director: Hong Kong & Yaumati Ferry Co. Ltd, 1976–; Green Island Cement Co. Ltd, 1978–; Hong Kong Aircraft Engineering Co. Ltd, 1983–; Asia Dairy Industries (HK) Ltd, 1983–; BSR Internat. PLC, 1984–; Longman Group (Far East) Ltd, 1984–; Chevalier (HK) Ltd, 1984–; Nat. Electronics (Consolidated) Ltd, 1984–; Proprietor, Sino-Scottish Trading Co., 1960–; Publisher, Sino-American Publishing Co., 1960. MLC, Hong Kong, 1975–85. FBIM 1979. Hon. Pres., Hong Kong Printers Assoc., 1983. JP Hong Kong, 1973. Fellow, Hong Kong Management Assoc., 1983; FIOP 1984. *Recreations:* classical music, Western and Peking opera, tennis, soccer, swimming, contract bridge. *Address:* 14/F, Hart House, 12–14 Hart Avenue, Tsimshatsui, Kowloon, Hong Kong. *T:* 3–668789. *Clubs:* Rotary of Hong Kong, Hong Kong; Royal Hong Kong Jockey; Royal Hong Kong Golf.

WULSTAN, Prof. David; Gregynog Professor of Music, University College of Wales, Aberystwyth, since 1983; *b* 18 Jan. 1937; *s* of Rev. Norman and (Sarah) Margaret Jones; *m* 1965, Susan Nelson Graham; one *s. Educ:* Royal Masonic Sch., Bushey; Coll. of Technology, Birmingham; Magdalen Coll., Oxford (Academical Clerk, 1960; Burrowes Exhibr, 1961; Mackinnon Sen. Schol., 1963; Fellow by examination, 1964). MA, BSc, BLitt; ARCM. Lectr in History of Music, Magdalen Coll., Oxford, 1968–78; also at St Hilda's and St Catherine's Colls; Vis. Prof., Depts of Near Eastern Studies and Music, Univ. of California, Berkeley, 1977; Statutory (Sen. Lectr), University Coll., Cork, 1979, Prof. of Music, 1980–83. Dir, Clerkes of Oxenford (founded 1961); appearances at Cheltenham, Aldeburgh, York, Bath, Flanders, Holland, Krakow, Zagreb, Belgrade Fests, BBC Proms; many broadcasts and TV appearances, gramophone recordings; also broadcast talks, BBC and abroad. *Publications:* Septem Discrimina Vocum, 1983; Tudor Music, 1985; editor: Gibbons, Church Music, Early English Church Music, vol. 3, 1964, vol. 27, 1979; Anthology of Carols, 1968; Anthology of English Church Music, 1971; Play of Daniel, 1976; Victoria, Requiem, 1977; Tallis, Puer Natus Mass, 1977; Coverdale Chant Book, 1978; Sheppard, Complete Works, 1979–; Weelkes, Ninth Service, 1980; many edns of anthems, services etc; entries in Encyclopédie de Musique Sacrée, 1970; chapter in A History of Western Music, ed Sternfeld, 1970; articles and reviews in learned jls. *Recreations:* badminton, tennis, cooking, eating. *Address:* Tŷ Isaf, Llanilar, near Aberystwyth, Dyfed SY23 4NP. *T:* Llanilar 229.

WUTTKE, Hans A., Dr jr; German banker; Executive Vice President, International Finance Corporation (World Bank Group), 1981–84; *b* Hamburg, 23 Oct. 1923; *m* 1st, 1957, Marina M. Schorsch (marr. diss. 1976); two *s* two *d*; 2nd, 1982, Jagoda M. Buič. *Educ:* Univs of Cologne and Salamanca. Dresdner Bank AG, 1949–54; Daimler-Benz AG, 1954–61; Partner, M. M. Warburg-Brinckmann, Wirtz and Co., Hamburg, 1961–75; Executive Director, S. G. Warburg and Co. Ltd, London, 1962–75; Man. Dir, Dresdner Bank AG, Frankfurt, 1975–80; Chm., Deutsch-Süd-Amerikanische Bank AG, 1975–80. Mem. Board several European companies; Mem. Bd, German Development Co., Cologne, 1962–80; Chairman: East Asia Assoc., 1963–73; Comité Européen pour le Progrès Economique et Social (CEPES), 1976–. *Address:* Apt 321, Watergate South, 700 New Hampshire Avenue NW, Washington, DC 20037, USA; (office) 9 Motcomb Street, SW1X 8LA. *T:* 01-235 3691; *Telex* 896711.

WYATT, Arthur Hope, CMG 1980; HM Diplomatic Service; High Commissioner to Ghana and Ambassador (non-resident) to Togo, since 1986; *b* 12 Oct. 1929; *s* of Frank and Maggie Wyatt, Anderton, Lancs; *m* 1957, Barbara Yvonne, *d* of Major J. P. Flynn, late Indian Army; two *d. Educ:* Bolton School. Army, 1947–50; FO, 1950–52; 3rd Sec., Ankara, 1952–56; 2nd Sec., Phnom Penh, 1956–58; 2nd Sec., Ankara, 1958–61; FO, 1962–66; 1st Sec., Bonn, 1966–70; FCO, 1970–72; Counsellor and Head of Chancery, Lagos, 1972–75; Dep. High Comr, Valletta, 1975–76; Diplomatic Service Inspector, 1977–79; Counsellor (Econ. and Comm.) and Consul-Gen., Tehran, 1979–80; Counsellor, Ankara, 1981–84; Minister, Lagos, 1984–86. *Recreations:* golf, football, bridge, stamp collecting. *Address:* c/o Foreign and Commonwealth Office, SW1A 2AH. *T:* 01–839 7010.

WYATT, (Christopher) Terrel, FEng, FICE, FIStructE; Chairman, Costain Group PLC, since 1980; *b* 17 July 1927; *s* of Lionel Harry Wyatt and Audrey Vere Wyatt; *m* 1970, Geertruida; four *s. Educ:* Kingston Grammar Sch.; Battersea Polytechnic (BScEng); Imperial Coll. (DIC). FICE 1963; FIStructE 1963; FEng 1980. Served RE, 1946–48. Charles Brand & Son Ltd, 1948–54; Richard Costain Ltd, 1955–: Dir, 1970–; Gp Chief Exec., 1975–80; Dep. Chm., 1979–80. *Recreation:* sailing. *Address:* Lower Hawksfold, Fernhurst, near Haslemere, Surrey GU27 3NR. *T:* Haslemere 54538.

WYATT, David Joseph, CBE 1977; Director, International Division, British Red Cross Society, since 1985; HM Diplomatic Service, 1949–85; *b* 12 Aug. 1931; *s* of late Frederick Wyatt and of Lena (*née* Parr); *m* 1957, Annemarie Angst (*d* 1978); two *s* one *d. Educ:* Leigh Grammar Sch. National Service, RAF, 1950–52. Entered Foreign Service, 1949; Berne, 1954; FO, 1957–61; Second Sec., Vienna, 1961; First Sec., Canberra, 1965; FCO, 1969–71; First Sec., Ottawa, 1971; Counsellor, 1974; seconded Northern Ireland Office, Belfast, 1974–76; Counsellor and Head of Chancery, Stockholm, 1976–79; Under Sec. on loan to Home Civil Service, 1979–82; UK Mission to UN during 1982 General Assembly (personal rank of Ambassador); Minister and Dep. Comdt, British Mil. Govt, Berlin, 1983–85. *Address:* c/o British Red Cross Society, 9 Grosvenor Crescent, SW1.

WYATT, Gavin Edward, CMG 1965; Consultant; *b* 12 Jan. 1914; *s* of Edward A. Wyatt and Blanche M. Muller; *m* 1950, Mary Mackinnon, *d* of John Macdonald, Oban; one *s* one *d. Educ:* Newton Abbot Grammar Sch. CEng, FIEE 1951; FIMechE 1962. Engineer and Manager, East African Power & Lighting Co. Ltd, Tanganyika and Kenya, 1939–57; Chief Exec. Officer and General Manager, Electricity Corp. of Nigeria, 1957–62; Man. Director, East Africa Power & Lighting Co. Ltd, 1962–64; World Bank, 1965–76, retired as Dir, Projects Dept, Europe, Middle East and North Africa Region. *Recreation:* gardening. *Address:* Holne Bridge Lodge, Ashburton, South Devon.

WYATT, Terrel; *see* Wyatt, C. T.

WYATT, Sir Woodrow (Lyle), Kt 1983; Chairman, Horserace Totalisator Board, since 1976; *b* 4 July 1918; *y s* of late Robert Harvey Lyle Wyatt and Ethel Morgan; *m* 1957, Lady Moorea Hastings (marr. diss., 1966), *e d* of 15th Earl of Huntingdon, *qv*; one *s*; *m* 1966, Veronica, *widow* of Baron Dr Laszlo Banszky Von Ambroz; one *d. Educ:* Eastbourne Coll.; Worcester Coll., Oxford, MA. Served throughout War of 1939–45 (despatches for Normandy); Major, 1944. Founder and Editor, English Story, 1940–50; Editorial Staff, New Statesman and Nation, 1947–48; Weekly Columnist: Reynolds News, 1949–61; Daily Mirror, 1965–73; Sunday Mirror, 1973–83; News of the World, 1983–. Began Panorama with Richard Dimbleby, 1955; under contract BBC TV, 1955–59; introduced non-heat-set web offset colour printing to England, 1962. MP (Lab), Aston Div. of Birmingham, 1945–55, Bosworth Div. of Leicester, 1959–70; Member of Parly Delegn to India, 1946; Personal Asst to Sir Stafford Cripps on Cabinet Mission to India, 1946; Parly Under-Sec. of State, and Financial Sec., War Office, May-Oct. 1951. Contested (Lab) Grantham Div. of Lincolnshire, 1955. Mem. Council, Zoological Soc. of London, 1968–71, 1973–77. *Publications:* The Jews at Home, 1950; Southwards from China, 1952; Into the Dangerous World, 1952; The Peril in Our Midst, 1956; Distinguished for Talent, 1958; Turn Again, Westminster, 1973; The Exploits of Mr Saucy Squirrel, 1976; The Further Exploits of Mr Saucy Squirrel, 1977; What's Left of the Labour Party?, 1977; To the Point, 1981; Confessions of an Optimist (autobiog.), 1985. *Address:* 19 Cavendish Avenue, NW8. *T:* 01–286 9020.

WYETH, Andrew Newell; artist; landscape painter; *b* 12 July 1917; *s* of Newell and Caroline Wyeth; *m* 1940, Betsy Merle James; two *s. Educ:* privately. First one man exhibn, William Macbeth Gall., NY, 1937; subsequent exhibitions include: Doll & Richards, Boston, 1938, 1940, 1942, 1944; Cornell Univ., 1938; Macbeth Gall., 1938, 1941, 1943, 1945; Art Inst. of Chicago, 1941; Museum of Modern Art, NYC, 1943; Dunn Internat. Exhibn, London, 1963; one man exhibns: M. Knoedler and Co., NYC, 1953, 1958; MIT, Cambridge, 1966; The White House, Washington DC, 1970; Tokyo, 1974; retrospectives: Metropolitan Museum, NY, 1976; RA, 1980 (1st by living American artist); Tokyo, 1974, 1979. Member: Nat. Inst. of Arts and Letters (Gold Medal, 1965); Amer. Acad. of Arts and Sciences; Amer. Acad. of Arts and Letters (Medal of Merit, 1947); Académie des Beaux-Arts, 1977; Hon. Mem., Soviet Acad. of the Arts, 1978. Presidential Medal of Freedom, 1963; Einstein Award, 1967. Hon. AFD: Colby Coll., Maine, 1954; Harvard, 1955; Dickinson, 1958; Swarthmore, 1958; Nasson Coll., Maine, 1963; Temple Univ., 1963; Maryland, 1964; Delaware, 1964; Northwestern Univ., 1964; Hon. LHD Tufts, 1963. *Address:* Chadds Ford, Pa 19317, USA.

WYFOLD, 3rd Baron, *cr* 1919, of Accrington; **Hermon Robert Fleming Hermon-Hodge;** 3rd Bt, *cr* 1902; retired 1985 as Director, Robert Fleming Holdings, and other companies; *b* 26 June 1915; *s* of 2nd Baron and Dorothy (*d* 1976), *e d* of late Robert Fleming, Joyce Grove, Oxford; *S* father, 1942. *Educ:* Eton; Le Rosey, Switzerland. Captain, Grenadier Guards (RARO), 1939–65. *Heir:* none. *Address:* Sarsden House, Churchill, Oxfordshire. *T:* Kingham 226. *Clubs:* Carlton, Pratt's; Metropolitan (New York).

WYKEHAM, Air Marshal Sir Peter, KCB 1965 (CB 1961); DSO 1943 and Bar 1944; OBE 1949; DFC 1940 and Bar 1941; AFC 1951; technical consultant, since 1969; *b* 13 Sept. 1915; *s* of Guy Vane and Audrey Irene Wykeham-Barnes; family changed name by Deed Poll, 1955, from Wykeham-Barnes to Wykeham; *m* 1949, Barbara Priestley, RIBA, AAdip., *d* of late J. B. Priestley, OM; two *s* one *d. Educ:* RAF Halton. Commissioned, 1937; served with fighter sqns, 1937–43 (commanded Nos 73, 257 and 23 sqns); commanded fighter sectors and wings, 1943–45; Air Ministry, 1946–48; Test Pilot, 1948–51; seconded to US Air Force, Korea, 1950; commanded fighter stations, 1951–53; NATO, 1953–56; staff appointments, 1956–59; AOC No 38 Gp, RAF, 1960–62; Dir, Jt

Warfare Staff, Min. of Defence, Aug. 1962–64. Comdr, FEAF, 1964–66; Dep. Chief of Air Staff, 1967–69. Chairman: Slingsby Aviation PLC; Wykehams Ltd; Anglo-European Liaison Ltd. FRAeS 1968; FBIM. Chevalier, Order of Dannebrog, 1945; US Air Medal, 1950. *Publications:* Fighter Command, 1960; Santos-Dumont, 1962. *Recreations:* sailing, writing. *Address:* Green Place, Stockbridge, Hampshire. *Club:* Royal Automobile.

WYKES, James Cochrane, MA (Cantab); *b* 19 Oct. 1913; *m* 1938, Cecile Winifred Graham, *e d* of J. Graham Rankin; one *s* one *d. Educ:* Oundle Sch.; Clare Coll., Cambridge (Open Exhibn in Classics). Asst Master, Loretto Sch., 1935–51; Headmaster, St Bees Sch., 1951–63; Head of Educational Broadcasting, ATV Network, 1963–66; Inner London Education Authority: Dir of Television, 1966–75; Television Adviser, 1975–78. Chm., Nat. Educnl Closed Circuit Television Assoc., 1970–72. Served War of 1939–45: Black Watch (RHR), 1940–44. *Publication:* Caesar at Alexandria, 1951. *Recreations:* walking, fishing, ornithology, music. *Address:* 14 Norman Court, Hemingford Grey, Huntingdon, Cambs. *T:* Huntingdon 67803. *Club:* New (Edinburgh).

WYLD, Martin Hugh; Chief Restorer, National Gallery, since 1979; *b* 14 Sept. 1944; *s* of John Wyld and Helen Leslie Melville; one *s* one *d. Educ:* Harrow School. Assistant Restorer, National Gallery, 1966. *Recreation:* travel. *Address:* 21 Grafton Square, SW4 0DA. *T:* 01–720 2627. *Clubs:* Colony Room, MCC.

WYLDBORE-SMITH, Maj.-Gen. Sir (Francis) Brian, Kt 1980; CB 1965; DSO 1943; OBE 1944; General Officer Commanding, 44th Division (TA) and Home Counties District, 1965–68; Director, Conservative Board of Finance, since 1970; *b* 10 July 1913; *s* of Rev. W. R. Wyldbore-Smith and Mrs D. Wyldbore-Smith; *m* 1944, Hon. Molly Angela Cayzer, *d* of 1st Baron Rotherwick; one *s* four *d. Educ:* Wellington Coll.; RMA, Woolwich. Served Middle East, Italy, France and Germany, 1941–45; Military Adviser to CIGS, 1947–49; GSO1, 7 Armoured Div., 1951–53; Comd 15/19 King's Royal Hussars, 1954–56; IDC 1959; BGS Combat Development, 1959–62; Chief of Staff to Commander-in-Chief, Far East Command, 1962–64. Col, 15/19 Hussars, 1970–77. *Recreations:* hunting, shooting. *Address:* Grantham House, Grantham, Lincs. *T:* Grantham 64705. *Clubs:* Buck's, Naval and Military.

WYLIE, Rt. Hon. Lord; Norman Russell Wylie, PC 1970; VRD 1961; a Senator of the College of Justice in Scotland, since 1974; *b* 26 Oct. 1923; *o s* of late William Galloway Wylie and late Mrs Nellie Smart Wylie (*née* Russell), Elderslie, Renfrewshire; *m* 1963, Gillian Mary, *yr d* of late Dr R. E. Verney, Edinburgh; three *s. Educ:* Paisley Grammar Sch.; St Edmund Hall, Oxford (Hon. Fellow, 1975); Univs of Glasgow and Edinburgh. BA (Oxon) 1948; LLB (Glasgow) 1951. Admitted to Faculty of Advocates, 1952; QC (Scotland) 1964. Appointed Counsel to Air Ministry in Scotland, 1956; Advocate-Depute, 1959; Solicitor-General for Scotland, April-Oct. 1964. MP (C) Pentlands Div., Edinburgh, Oct. 1964–Feb. 1974; Lord Advocate, 1970–74. Trustee, Carnegie Trust for Univs of Scotland, 1976–; Chm., Scottish Nat. Cttee, English-Speaking Union of the Commonwealth, 1978–84. Served in Fleet Air Arm, 1942–46; subseq. RNR; Lt-Comdr, 1954. *Recreations:* shooting, sailing. *Address:* 30 Lauder Road, Edinburgh EH9 2JF. *T:* 031–667 8377. *Clubs:* New (Edinburgh); Royal Highland Yacht.

WYLIE, Sir Campbell, Kt 1963; ED; QC; *b* NZ, 14 May 1905; *m* 1933, Leita Caroline Clark (*d* 1984); no *c. Educ:* Dannevirke High Sch.; Auckland Grammar Sch.; Univ. of New Zealand. LLM 1st Class hons (Univ. of New Zealand), 1928; Barrister and Solicitor (New Zealand), 1928; Barrister-at-law, Inner Temple, 1950. Was in private practice, New Zealand, until 1940. War service, 1940–46 (despatches). Crown Counsel, Malaya, 1946; Senior Federal Counsel, 1950; Attorney-General: Barbados, 1951; British Guiana, 1955; The West Indies, 1956; Federal Justice, Supreme Court of The West Indies, 1959–62; Chief Justice, Unified Judiciary of Sarawak, N Borneo and Brunei, 1962–63; Chief Justice, High Court in Borneo, 1963–66; Law Revision Commissioner, Tonga, 1966–67; Chief Justice, Seychelles, 1967–69; Comr for Law Revision and Reform, Seychelles, 1970–71. QC 1952 (Barbados), 1955 (British Guiana). *Address:* River Lodge, 53 Stanhill Drive, Chevron Island, Surfers Paradise, Queensland 4217, Australia. *T:* 385532.

WYLIE, Derek; *see* Wylie, W. D.

WYLIE, Rt. Hon. Norman Russell; *see* Wylie, Rt Hon. Lord.

WYLIE, (William) Derek, FRCP, FRCS, FFARCS; Consulting Anaesthetist, St Thomas' Hospital, SE1; Consultant Anaesthetist, The Royal Masonic Hospital, 1959–82; Dean, St Thomas's Hospital Medical School, 1974–79; Adviser in Anaesthetics to the Health Service Commissioner, since 1974; *b* 24 Oct. 1918; *s* of Edward and Mabel Wylie, Huddersfield; *m* 1945, Margaret Helen, 2nd *d* of F. W. Toms, Jersey, CI (formerly Dep. Inspector-Gen., Western Range, Indian Police); one *s* two *d.* (and one *s* decd). *Educ:* Uppingham Sch.; Gonville and Caius Coll., Cambridge (MA; MB, BChir); St Thomas's Hosp. Med. Sch. MRCP 1945, FFARCS 1953, FRCP 1967, FRCS 1972. Resident posts at St Thomas' Hosp., 1943–45. Served RAFVR, 1945–47, Wing Comdr. Apptd Hon. Staff, St Thomas' Hosp., 1946; Consultant, 1948; Sen. Cons. Anaesthetist, 1966–79; Cons. Anaesthetist, The National Hosp. for Nervous Diseases, 1950–67. Examiner: FFARCS, 1959–72; FFARCSI, 1966–78. Mem., Bd of Faculty of Anaesthetists, RCS, 1960–70 (Dean, 1967–69; Vice-Dean, 1965–66; Bernard Johnson Adviser in Postgraduate Studies, 1959–67; Faculty Medal, 1984); Mem. Council, RCS, 1967–69; FRSM (Mem. Council, 1962–72; Hon. Treas., 1964–70; Pres., Section of Anaesthetics, 1963); Mem., Bd of Governors, St Thomas' Hosp., 1969–74; elected Mem. Council, Med. Defence Union (Vice-Pres., 1962–82, Pres., 1982–). Jenny Hartmann Lectr, Basle Univ., 1961; Clover Lectr and Medallist, RCS(Eng), 1974. Pres., Assoc. of Anaesthetists of GB and Ireland, 1980–82, Hon. Mem., 1984. Hon. Citizen of Dallas, USA, 1963; Hon. FFARCSI, 1971; Hon. FFARACS, 1984. Henry Hill Hickman Medal, RSM, 1983. *Publications:* The Practical Management of Pain in Labour, 1953; A Practice of Anaesthesia, 3rd edn, 1972 (jtly with Dr H. C. Churchill-Davidson); papers in specialist and gen. med. jls. *Recreations:* reading, travel, philately. *Address:* St John's Cottage, Nursery Lane, Fairwarp, Uckfield, East Sussex TN22 3BD. *T:* Nutley 2822. *Club:* Royal Automobile.

WYLLIE, Prof. Peter John, PhD; FRS 1984; Professor of Geology and Chairman of Division of Geological and Planetary Sciences, California Institute of Technology, since 1983; *b* 8 Feb. 1930; *s* of George William and Beatrice Gladys Wyllie (*née* Weaver); *m* 1956, Frances Rosemary Blair; two *s* one *d* (and one *d* decd). *Educ:* Univ. of St Andrews. BSc 1952 (Geology and Physics); BSc 1955 (1st cl. hons Geology); PhD 1958 (Geology). Glaciologist, 1950, Geologist, 1952–54, British N Greenland Expdn; Asst Lectr in Geology, Univ. of St Andrews, 1955–56; Research Asst, 1956–58, Asst Prof. of Geochemistry, 1958–59, Pennsylvania State Univ.; Research Fellow in Chemistry, 1959–60, Lectr in Exptl Petrology, 1960–61, Leeds Univ.; Associate Prof. of Petrology, Pennsylvania State Univ., 1961–65 (Acting Head, Dept Geochem. and Mineralogy, 1962–63); University of Chicago; Prof. of Petrology and Geochem., 1965–77; Master Phys. Scis, Collegiate Div., Associate Dean of Coll. and of Phys. Scis Div., 1972–73; Homer J. Livingston Prof., 1978–83; Chm., Dept of Geophysical Scis, 1979–82. Pres., Internat. Mineralogical Assoc., 1986–. Foreign Associate, US Nat. Acad. of Scis, 1981; Fellow, Amer. Acad. of Arts and Scis, 1982; Corresponding Fellow, Edin. Geol Soc., 1985–. Hon. DSc St Andrews, 1974. Polar Medal, 1954; Wollaston Medal, Geol Soc. of London, 1982. *Publications:* Ultramafic and Related Rocks, 1967; The Dynamic Earth, 1971; The Way the Earth Works, 1976; numerous papers in sci. jls. *Address:* 2150 Kinclair Drive, Pasadena, Calif 91107, USA. *T:* 818–791–9164. *Club:* Arctic (Cambridge).

WYLLIE, Robert Lyon, CBE 1960; DL; JP; FCA; *b* 4 March 1897; *s* of Rev. Robert Howie Wyllie, MA, Dundee; *m* 1924, Anne, *d* of Thomas Rutherford, Harrington, Cumberland; two *d. Educ:* Hermitage Sch., Helensburgh; Queen's Park Sch., Glasgow. Served European War, 1914–18, with Lothians and Border Horse (France). Chartered Accountant, 1920; FCA 1949. Dir, Ashley Accessories Ltd; Life Vice-President, Cumberland Development Council Ltd. Formerly Chairman: W Cumberland Industrial Develt Co. Ltd; W Cumberland Silk Mills Ltd; Cumberland Develt Council Ltd; Whitehaven & Dist Disablement Advisory Cttee, and Youth Employment Cttee; Vice-Chm. W Cumberland Hosp. Management Cttee; Hon. Treas., NW Div., YMCA. JP 1951; DL Cumbria (formerly Cumberland), 1957–84. OStJ 1976. *Recreation:* fishing. *Address:* The Cottage, Papcastle, Cockermouth, Cumbria. *T:* Cockermouth 823292.

WYLLIE, William Robert Alexander; Chairman and Chief Executive, Asia Securities Ltd, Hong Kong, since 1971; Chairman, BSR, since 1982; *b* 9 Oct. 1932; *s* of Robert Wyllie and Marion Margaret Rae (*née* McDonald); *m* 1959, Ann Helena Mary (*née* Lewis) (*d* 1986); two *s* one *d. Educ:* Scarborough State Sch., Perth, W Australia; Perth Technical Coll. (qual. Automobile and Aeronautical Engrg). MIRTE. Sen. Exec./Br. Manager, Wearne Bros Ltd, Malaysia/Singapore, 1953–64; Man. Dir, Harpers Internat. Ltd, Hong Kong, 1964–73; Chm. and Chief Exec., China Engineers Holdings Ltd, Hong Kong, 1973–75; Deputy Chairman and Chief Executive: Hutchison Internat. Ltd, Hong Kong, 1975–Dec. 1977; Hutchison Whampoa Ltd, Hong Kong, Jan. 1978–June 1979 (Chm. and Chief Exec., 1979–80). FInstD 1980. *Recreations:* power boating, water skiing, Scuba diving, restoration of vintage cars. *Address:* Asia Securities Ltd, 16/F Sutherland House, 3 Chater Road, Hong Kong. *T:* (office) 5–8105500; (home) 5–8094946. *Clubs:* British Racing Drivers, Bentley Owners; Hong Kong, American, Shek O Country, Royal Hong Kong Jockey, Royal Hong Kong Yacht (Hong Kong).

WYMAN, John Bernard, MBE 1945; FRCS; FFARCS; Consultant Anaesthetist, Westminster Hospital, 1948–81; Dean, Westminster Medical School, 1964–81 (Sub-Dean, 1959–64); *b* 24 May 1916; *s* of Louis Wyman and Bertha Wyman; *m* 1948, Joan Dorothea Beighton; three *s* one *d. Educ:* Davenant Foundn Sch., London; King's Coll., London (Fellow 1980); Westminster Med. Sch. MRCS, LRCP 1941; DA 1945; FFARCS 1953; FRCS 1981. Military Service, 1942–46: Major RAMC; N Africa, Italy and India. Cons. Anaesthetist, Woolwich War Memorial Hospital Hosp., 1946–64; formerly Hon. Anaesthetist, Italian Hosp. Hunterian Prof., RCS, 1953. Member: Bd of Governors, Westminster Hosp., 1959–74; Sch. Council, Westminster Med. Sch., 1959–81; Croydon AHA, 1974–75; Kensington and Chelsea and Westminster AHA, 1975–81. *Publications:* chapters in med. text books and papers in gen. and specialist jls on anaesthesia and med. educn. *Recreation:* gardening. *Address:* Chilling Street Cottage, Sharpthorne, Sussex. *T:* Sharpthorne 810281. *Club:* Savage.

WYNDHAM, family name of **Baron Egremont and Leconfield.**

WYNDHAM, Sir Harold (Stanley), Kt 1969; CBE 1961; retired from Department of Education, New South Wales; *b* Forbes, NSW, Australia, 27 June 1903; *s* of late Stanley Charles Wyndham; *m* 1936, Beatrice Margaret, *d* of Rt. Rev. A. C. Grieve; three *s. Educ:* Fort Street Boys' High Sch.; Univ. of Sydney (MA Hons, Cl. I); Stanford Univ. (EdD). Lectr, Sydney Teachers' Coll., 1925–27 and 1934; Teacher, NSW Dept of Educn, 1928–32; Carnegie Fellow, Stanford, 1932–33; Head of Research and Guidance, NSW Dept of Educn, 1935–40; Inspector of Schools, 1940–41. Flt Lt (A&SD Br.), RAAF, 1942–43; Commonwealth Dept of Post-War Reconstruction, 1944–46 (Leader, Aust. Delegn, Constituent Meeting for UNESCO, London, 1945); Sec., NSW Dept of Educn, 1948–51; Dep. Dir-Gen. of Educn, 1951–52; Dir-Gen. and Permanent Head, Dept of Education, 1952–68, Macquarie Univ., Professorial Fellow, 1969–75, Hon. Professorial Fellow, 1976–. Mem. Aust. Delegn to: UNESCO, 1958 and 1966; Commonwealth Educn Conf., Oxford, 1959. Vis. Fellow to Canada, 1966; Fellow and Past-Pres., Aust. Coll. of Educn; Mem., Nat. Library Council of Australia, 1962–73; Chm., Soldiers' Children Educn Bd, Dept of Veterans' Affairs, 1964–84. *Publications:* Class Grouping in the Primary School, 1932; Ability Grouping, 1934; articles in a number of professional jls. *Recreations:* music, gardening. *Address:* 3 Amarna Parade, Roseville, NSW 2069, Australia. *T:* 406–4129. *Club:* University (Sydney).

WYNDHAM-QUIN, family name of **Earl of Dunraven.**

WYNFORD, 8th Baron, *cr* 1829; **Robert Samuel Best;** MBE 1953; DL; Lt-Col Royal Welch Fusiliers; *b* 5 Jan. 1917; *e s* of 7th Baron and Evelyn (*d* 1929), *d* of late Maj.-Gen. Sir Edward S. May, KCB, CMG; *S* father, 1943; *m* 1941, Anne Daphne Mametz, *d* of late Maj.-Gen. J. R. Minshull Ford, CB, DSO, MC; one *s* two *d. Educ:* Eton; RMC, Sandhurst. 2nd Lieut, RWF, 1937; served BEF; GHQ Home Forces; North Africa (Croix de Guerre); Egypt; Italy; wounded, 1944; Instructor, Staff College, 1945–46; War Office, 1947–49; OC Depot, RWF, 1955–57; Instructor Joint Service Staff Coll., 1957–60; RARO 1960. DL Dorset, 1970. *Heir: s* Hon. John Philip Best [*b* 23 Nov. 1950; *m* 1981, Fenella Christian Mary, *o d* of Arthur Reginald Danks]. *Address:* Wynford House, Wynford Eagle, Dorchester, Dorset DT2 0ET. *TA* and *T:* Maiden Newton 20241. *Club:* Army and Navy.

WYNGAARDEN, James Barnes, MD; FRCP; Director, National Institutes of Health, since 1982; *b* 19 Oct. 1924; *s* of Martin Jacob Wyngaarden and Johanna Kempers Wyngaarden; *m* 1946, Ethel Dean Vredevoogd (marr. diss. 1976); one *s* four *d. Educ:* Calvin College; Western Michigan University; University of Michigan. MD 1948; FRCP 1984. Investigator, NIH, 1953–56; Associate Prof. of Medicine, Duke Univ. Med. Center, 1956–61; Prof. of Medicine, Duke Univ. Med. Sch., 1961–65; Chairman, Dept of Medicine: Univ. of Pennsylvania Med. Sch., 1965–67; Duke Univ. Med. Sch., 1967–82. Hon. DSc: Michigan, 1980; Ohio, 1984; Illinois, 1985. *Publications:*(ed jtly) The Metabolic Basis of Inherited Disease, 1960, 5th edn 1983; (with O. Spurling and A. DeVries) Purine Metabolism in Man, 1974; (with W.N. Kelley) Gout and Hyperuricemia, 1976; (with L. H. Smith) Review of Internal Medicine; a self-assessment guide, 1979, 3rd edn 1985; (ed jtly) Cecil Textbook of Medicine, 15th edn 1979, 17th edn 1985. *Recreations:* tennis, ski-ing, painting. *Address:* National Institutes of Health, Building 1, Room 124, Bethesda, Maryland 20205, USA. *T:* 301/496–2433.

WYNN, family name of **Baron Newborough.**

WYNN, Arthur Henry Ashford; Adviser on Standards, Department of Trade and Industry (formerly Ministry of Technology), 1965–71; *b* 22 Jan. 1910; *s* of late Prof. William Henry Wynn, MD, MSc; *m* 1938, Margaret Patricia Moxon; three *s* one *d. Educ:* Oundle Sch.; Trinity Coll., Cambridge (Entrance Scholar, Nat. Science and Mathematics; MA). Barrister-at-Law, Lincoln's Inn, 1939; Director of Safety in Mines Research Establishment, Ministry of Fuel and Power, 1948–55; Scientific Member of National

Coal Board, 1955–65; Member: Advisory Council on Research and Development, Ministry of Power, 1955–65; Safety in Mines Research Advisory Board, 1950–65; Exec. Cttee, British Standards Institution, 1966–71; Advisory Council on Calibration and Measurement, 1967–71; Chairman: Standing Joint Cttee on Metrication, 1966–69; Adv. Cttee on Legal Units of Measurement, 1969–71. *Publications:* (with Margaret Wynn): The Protection of Maternity and Infancy in Finland, 1974; The Right of Every Child to Health Care in France, 1974; Nutrition Counselling in Canada, 1975; Prevention of Handicap of Perinatal Origin in France, 1976; Prevention of Preterm Birth, 1977; Prevention of Handicap and Health of Women, 1979; Prevention of Handicap of Early Pregnancy Origin, 1981; Lead and Human Reproduction, 1982. *Address:* 9 View Road, N6. *T:* 01–348 1470.

WYNN, Sir (Owen) Watkin W.; *see* Williams-Wynn.

WYNN, Terence Bryan; Editor, Your Court (house journal of Lord Chancellor's Department), since 1985; *b* 20 Nov. 1928; *o s* of late Bernard Wynn and Elsie Wynn (*née* Manges); unmarried. *Educ:* St Cuthbert's Grammar Sch., Newcastle upon Tyne. Started as jun. reporter with Hexham Courant, Northumberland, 1945; Blyth News, 1947–48; Shields Evening News, 1948–50; Sunderland Echo, 1950–53; Reporter with Daily Sketch, 1953–58; News Editor, Tyne Tees Television, 1958, then Head of News and Current Affairs, 1960–66; Editorial Planning, BBC Television News, 1966–67; Sen. Press and Information Officer with Land Commn, 1967–71; Sen. Inf. Officer, HM Customs and Excise, 1971–72; Editor, The Universe, 1972–77; Editor, Liberal News, and Head of Liberal Party Orgn's Press Office, 1977–83; Regl Press Officer, MSC, COI, London and SE Region, 1983–85. Helped to found and first Editor of Roman Catholic monthly newspaper, Northern Cross. Chm., Catholic Writers' Guild, 1967–70 (Hon. Vice-Pres., 1970); Judge for British Television News Film of the Year Awards, 1961–64; Mem. Mass Media Commn, RC Bishops' Conf. of England and Wales, 1972–83. *Publication:* Walsingham, a modern mystery play, 1975. *Recreations:* reading, writing, talking. *Address:* (office) Trevelyan House, Great Percy Street, SW1P 4LS; Bosco Villa, 30 Queen's Road, South Benfleet, Essex SS7 1JW. *T:* South Benfleet 792033.

WYNN-WILLIAMS, George, MB, BS London; FRCS; FRCOG; Surgeon, Chelsea Hospital for Women; Consulting Obstetrician to City of Westminster; Consulting Gynæcologist, Chelsea Hospital for Women; Consulting Obstetric Surgeon, Queen Charlotte's Hospital; Consulting Gynæcologist to the Civil Service; Teacher in Gynæcology and Obstetrics, London University; *b* 10 Aug. 1912; *er s* of William Wynn-Williams, MRCS, LRCP, and Jane Anderson Brymer, Caernarvon, N Wales; *m* 1943, Penelope, *o d* of 1st and last Earl Jowitt of Stevenage, PC, and Lesley McIntyre; two *s* one *d*. *Educ:* Rossall; King's Coll.; Westminster Hospital. MRCS, LRCP 1937; MB, BS (London) 1938; MRCOG 1941; FRCS 1943; FRCOG 1967. Alfred Hughes Anatomy Prize, King's Coll.; Chadwick Prize in Clinical Surgery, Forensic Medicine and Public Health Prizes, Westminster Hospital. Various appointments 1937–41; Chief Asst and Surgical Registrar and Grade I Surgeon, EMS, 1941–45; Acting Obst. and Gynæcol. Registrar, Westminster Hosp., 1941–46; Surgeon-in-Charge, Mobile Surg. Team to Portsmouth and Southampton, June-Oct. 1944; Chief Asst, Chelsea Hosp. for Women, 1946–47; Obst. Registrar, Queen Charlotte's Hosp., 1946–50; Cons. Obstetrician, Borough of Tottenham; Cons. Gynæcologist, Weir Hosp. Surgical Tutor, Westminster Hosp., 1941–46; Obst. and Gynæcol. Tutor, Westminster Hosp., 1941–48; Lectr and Demonstrator to Postgrad. Students, Queen Charlotte's Hosp., 1946–50; Lectr to Postgrad. Students, Chelsea Women's Hosp., 1946–; Examiner, Central Midwives' Board; Recognized Lectr of London Univ.; Assoc. Examiner in Obst. and Gynæcol., Worshipful Co. of Apothecaries. Woodhull Lectr, Royal Instn, 1978. Member: BMA; Soc. for Study of Fertility; The Pilgrims. FRSM. *Publications:* (jtly) Queen Charlotte's Text Book of Obstetrics; contributions to medical journals, including Human Artificial Insemination, in Hospital Medicine, 1973; Infertile Patients with Positive Immune Fluorescent Serum, 1976; Spermatazoal Antibodies treated with Condom Coitus, 1976; The Woodhull Lecture on Infertility and its Control, 1978. *Recreations:* tennis, shooting, fishing. *Address:* 48 Wimpole Street, W1M 7DG. *T:* 01–487 4866; 39 Hurlingham Court, SW6; The Hall, Wittersham, Isle of Oxney, Kent. *Clubs:* Hurlingham, Chelsea Arts, English-Speaking Union, Oriental; Rye Golf.

WYNNE, Prof. Charles Gorrie, FRS 1970; BA, PhD; Senior Research Fellow, Imperial College, London, since 1978 (Director, Optical Design Group, 1960–78); Chairman, IC Optical Systems Ltd, since 1978; Professor of Optical Design, University of London, 1969–78, now Emeritus; Consultant to the Royal Greenwich Observatory, Herstmonceux Castle, Sussex; *b* 18 May 1911; *s* of C. H. and A. E. Wynne; *m* 1937, Jean Richardson; one *s* one *d*. *Educ:* Wyggeston Grammar Sch., Leicester; Exeter Coll., Oxford (Scholar). Optical Designer, Taylor Taylor & Hobson Ltd, 1935–43; Wray (Optical Works) Ltd, 1943–60, latterly Director. Hon. Sec. (business), Physical Soc., 1947–60; Hon. Sec., Inst. of Physics and Physical Soc., 1960–66. Editor, Optica Acta, 1954–65. Thomas Young Medal, Inst. of Physics, 1971; Gold Medal, Royal Astronomical Soc., 1979; Rumford Medal, Royal Soc., 1982. *Publications:* scientific papers on aberration theory and optical instruments in Proc. Phys. Soc., Mon. Not. RAS, Astrophys. Jl, Optica Acta, etc. *Address:* Morar, Boreham Street, near Hailsham, Sussex. *T:* Herstmonceux 832234.

WYNNE, David; sculptor, since 1949; *b* Lyndhurst, Hants, 25 May 1926; *s* of Comdr Charles Edward Wynne and Millicent (*née* Beyts); *m* 1959, Gillian Mary Leslie Bennett (*née* Grant); two *s*, and one step *s* one step *d*. *Educ:* Stowe Sch.; Trinity Coll., Cambridge. FZS; FRSA. Served RN, 1944–47: minesweepers and aircraft carriers (Sub-Lieut RNVR). No formal art training. First exhibited at Leicester Galls, 1950, and at Royal Acad., 1952. One-man Exhibitions: Leicester Galls, 1955, 1959; Tooth's Gall., 1964, 1966; Temple Gall., 1964; Findlay Galls, New York, 1967, 1970, 1973; Covent Garden Gall., 1970, 1971; Fitzwilliam Museum, Cambridge, 1972; Pepsico World HQ, New York, 1976; Agnew's Gall., 1983; retrospective, Cannizaro House, 1980; also various mixed exhibns. Large works in public places: Magdalen Coll., Oxford; Malvern Girls' Coll.; Civic Centre, Newcastle upon Tyne; Lewis's, Hanley; Ely Cathedral; Birmingham Cath.; Church of St Paul, Ashford Hill, Berks; Ch. of St Thomas More, Bradford-on-Avon; Mission Ch., Portsmouth; Fountain Precinct, Sheffield; Bowood House, Wilts; Risen Christ and 2 seraphim, west front of Wells Cathedral, 1985; London: Albert Bridge; British Oxygen Co., Hammersmith; Cadogan Place Gardens and Cadogan Sq.; Crystal Palace Park; Guildhall; Longbow House; St Katharine-by-the-Tower; Taylor Woodrow; Wates Ltd, Norbury; also London Road, Kingston-upon-Thames; Elmsleigh Centre, Staines; IPC HQ, Sutton; USA: Ambassador Coll., Texas, and Ambassador Coll., Calif; Atlantic Richfield Oil Co., New Mexico; Lakeland Meml Hosp., Wis; First Fed. Savings, Mass; Pepsico World HQ, Purchase, NY; Playboy Hotel and Casino, Atlantic City, NJ; Sarasota, Fla; Mayo Foundation, Minn; Sherman, Texas; also Perth, WA. Bronze portrait heads include: Sir Thomas Beecham, 1956; Sir John Gielgud, 1962; Yehudi Menuhin, 1963; The Beatles, 1964; Kokoschka, 1965; Sir Alec Douglas-Home, 1966; Robert, Marquess of Salisbury, 1967; The Prince of Wales, 1969; Lord Baden-Powell, 1971; Virginia Wade, 1972; The Queen, 1973; King Hassan of Morocco, 1973; Air Chief Marshal Lord Dowding, 1974; The Begum Aga Khan, 1975; Pele, 1976; Lord Hailsham, 1977; Prince Michael of Kent, 1977; Earl Mountbatten of Burma, 1981; Paul Daniels, 1982; Jackie Stewart, 1982; Portrait Figures: Arnold Palmer, 1983; Björn Borg, 1984; other sculptures: Fred Perry, AELTC, 1984; Shergar and jockey, 1981; Shareef Dancer and groom, 1984; Cresta Rider, St Moritz, 1985. Designed: Common Market 50 pence piece of clasped hands, 1973; the Queen's Silver Jubilee Medal, 1977 (with new effigy of the Queen wearing St Edward's Crown); King Hassan, for Moroccan coinage. *Publication:* The Messenger, a sculpture by David Wynne, 1982. *Relevant publications:* T. S. R. Boase, The Sculpture of David Wynne 1949–1967, 1968; Graham Hughes, The Sculpture of David Wynne 1968–1974, 1974. *Recreations:* active sports, poetry, music. *Address:* 12 South Side, SW19. *T:* 01–946 1514. *Clubs:* Garrick, Hurlingham, Queen's; Leander (Henley-on-Thames); 1st and 3rd Trinity Boat; St Moritz Tobogganing; The Royal Tennis Court (Hampton Court Palace).

WYNNE, Col J. F. W.; *see* Williams-Wynne.

WYNNE-EDWARDS, Vero Copner, CBE 1973; MA, DSc; FRS 1970; FRSE, FRSC; Regius Professor of Natural History, University of Aberdeen, 1946–74, Vice Principal, 1972–74; *b* 4 July 1906; 3rd *s* of late Rev. Canon John Rosindale Wynne-Edwards and Lilian Agnes Streatfeild; *m* 1929, Jeannie Campbell, *e d* of late Percy Morris, Devon County Architect; one *s* one *d*. *Educ:* Leeds Grammar Sch.; Rugby Sch.; New Coll., Oxford. 1st Class Hons in Natural Science (Zoology), Oxford, 1927; Senior Scholar of New Coll., 1927–29; Student Probationer, Marine Biological Laboratory, Plymouth, 1927–29; Assistant Lecturer in Zoology, Univ. of Bristol, 1929–30; Asst Prof. of Zoology, McGill Univ., Montreal, 1930–44; Associate Prof., 1944–46. Canadian representative, MacMillan Baffin Island expedition, 1937; Canadian Fisheries Research Board expeditions to Mackenzie River, 1944, and Yukon Territory, 1945; Baird Expedition to Central Baffin Island, 1950. Visiting Prof. of Conservation, University of Louisville, Kentucky, 1959, Commonwealth Universities Interchange Fellow New Zealand, 1962; Leverhulme Emeritus Fellowship, 1978–80. Jt Editor, Journal of Applied Ecology, 1963–68. Member: Nature Conservancy, 1954–57; Red Deer Commn (Vice-Chm.), 1959–68; Royal Commn on Environmental Pollution, 1970–74; President: British Ornithologists' Union, 1965–70; Scottish Marine Biological Assoc., 1967–73; Section D, British Assoc., 1974; Chairman: NERC, 1968–71; DoE and Scottish Office Adv. Cttees on Protection of Birds, 1970–78; Scientific Authority for Animals, DoE, 1976–77. For. Mem., Societas Scientiarum Fennica, 1965; Hon. Mem., British Ecological Soc., 1977. Hon. FIBiol 1980. Hon. DUniv Stirling, 1974; Hon. LLD Aberdeen, 1976. Godman-Salvin Medal, British Ornithologists' Union, 1977; Neill Prize, RSE, 1977; Frink Medal, Zoological Soc., 1980. *Publications:* Animal Dispersion in relation to social behaviour, 1962; Evolution through Group Selection, 1986; (contrib.) Leaders in the Study of Animal Behaviour, ed D. A. Dewsbury, 1985; scientific papers on ornithology (esp. oceanic birds), animal populations. *Recreation:* skiing. *Address:* Ravelston, William Street, Torphins, Via Banchory, Aberdeenshire AB3 4JR. *Club:* Naval and Military.

WYNNE MASON, Walter, CMG 1967; MC 1941; *b* 21 March 1910; *y s* of late George and Eva Mason, Wellington, NZ; *m* 1945, Freda Miller, *d* of late Frederick and Lilian Miller, Woodford, Essex; two *s* one *d*. *Educ:* Scots Coll., NZ; Victoria University College, NZ (MA). NZ Govt Education Service 1934–39; served NZ Army, 1939–46; NZ War Histories, 1947–48; NZ Diplomatic Service, 1949–54; Chief, Middle East, Commonwealth War Graves Commission, 1954–56, Dir of External Relations and Deputy to Dir-Gen., 1956–70; Mem., Sec. of State for Environment's panel of independent Inspectors, 1972–77. *Publication:* Prisoners of War, 1954. *Recreations:* lawn tennis, theatre, music. *Address:* Keene House, Hillier Road, Guildford, Surrey. *T:* Guildford 572601.

WYNTER, Sir Luther (Reginald), Kt 1977; CBE 1966 (OBE 1962, MBE 1950); MD; FICS; private medical practitioner, Antigua, since 1927; *b* 15 Sept. 1899; *s* of Thomas Nathaniel Wynter and Pauline Jane Wynter; *m* 1927, Arah Adner Busby. *Educ:* Wolmers High Sch., Jamaica; Coll. of City of Detroit, USA; Dalhousie Univ. (MD, CM); Moorfields Hosp. (DOMS). FICS (Ophthalmology) 1969. Gen. med. practitioner, Hamilton, Ont, Canada, 1925–27; actg govt radiologist, Antigua, 1937–51; ophthalmologist, Antigua, 1953–64, hon. consulting ophthalmologist, 1966–. Nominated Mem., Antigua Govt, 1956–66; Senator and Pres. of Senate, 1967–68 (often acting as Governor or Dep. to Governor). Hon. LLD: Univ. of the West Indies, 1972; Dalhousie, 1975. *Recreation:* learning to play bridge. *Address:* PO Box 154, St John's, Antigua, West Indies. *T:* (office) St John's 22027, (home) Hodges Bay 22102. *Clubs:* (Hon. Life Mem.) Mill Reef, (Hon. Mem.) Lions (Antigua).

Y

YALE, David Eryl Corbet, FBA 1980; Reader in English Legal History, Cambridge University, since 1969; Fellow, Christ's College, since 1950; *b* 31 March 1928; *s* of Lt-Col J. C. L. Yale and Mrs Beatrice Yale (*née* Breese); *m* 1959, Elizabeth Ann, *d* of C. A. B. Brett, Belfast; two *s*. *Educ*: Malvern Coll., Worcs; Queens' Coll., Cambridge (BA 1949, LLB 1950, MA 1953). Called to the Bar, Inner Temple, 1951; Asst Lectr and Lectr in Law, Cambridge Univ., 1952–69. Literary Dir, Selden Soc. *Publications*: various, mainly in field of legal history. *Recreation*: fishing. *Address*: Christ's College, Cambridge. *T*: Cambridge 334900.

YALOW, Rosalyn Sussman, PhD; Senior Medical Investigator, Veterans Administration, since 1972; *b* 19 July 1921; *d* of Simon Sussman and Clara (*née* Zipper); *m* 1943, Aaron Yalow; one *s* one *d*. *Educ*: Hunter Coll., NYC (AB Physics and Chemistry, 1941); Univ. of Ill, Urbana (MS Phys. 1942, PhD Phys. 1945). Diplomate, Amer. Bd of Radiol., 1951. Asst in Phys., Univ. of Ill, 1941–43, Instr, 1944–45; Lectr and Temp. Asst Prof. in Phys., Hunter Coll., 1946–50. Veterans Admin Hospital, Bronx, NY: Consultant, Radioisotope Unit, 1947–50; Physicist and Asst Chief, Radioisotope Service, 1950–70 (Actg Chief, 1968–70); Chief, Nuclear Medicine Service, 1970–80; Dir, Solomon A. Berson Res. Lab., 1973–; Chief, VA Radioimmunoassay Ref. Lab., 1969–. Consultant, Lenox Hill Hosp., NYC, 1952–62. Res. Prof., Dept of Med., Mt Sinai Sch. of Med., 1968–74, Distinguished Service Prof., 1974–79; Distinguished Prof.-at-Large, Albert Einstein Coll. of Med., Yeshiva Univ., NY, 1979–. Chm., Dept of Clin. Sciences, Montefiore Hosp. and Med. Center, Bronx, NY, 1980–. IAEA Expert, Instituto Energia Atomica, Brazil, 1970; WHO Consultant, Radiation Med. Centre, India, 1978; Sec., US Nat. Cttee on Med. Physics, 1963–67. Member: President's Study Gp on Careers for Women, 1966–67; Med. Adv. Bd, Nat. Pituitary Agency, 1968–71; Endocrinol. Study Sect., Nat. Insts of Health, 1969–72; Cttee for Evaluation of NPA, Nat. Res. Council, 1973–74; Council, Endocrine Soc., 1974– (Koch Award, 1972; Pres., 1978); Bd of Dirs, NY Diabetes Assoc., 1974–. Member: Editorial Adv. Council, Acta Diabetologica Latina, 1975–77; Ed. Adv. Bd, Encyclopaedia Universalis, 1978–; Ed. Bd, Mt Sinai Jl of Medicine, 1976–79; Ed. Bd, Diabetes, 1976–79. Fellow: NY Acad. of Sciences (Chm., Biophys. Div., 1964–65; A. Cressy Morrison Award in Nat. Sci., 1975); Radiation Res. Soc.; Amer. Assoc. of Physicists in Med.; Biophys. Soc.; Amer. Diabetes Assoc. (Eli Lilly Award, 1961; Commemorative Medallion, 1972; Banting Medal, 1978; Rosalyn S. Yalow Res. and Develt Award estabd 1978); Amer. Physiol Soc.; Soc. of Nuclear Med. Associate Fellow in Phys., Amer. Coll. of Radiol. Member: Nat. Acad. of Sciences; Amer. Acad. Arts and Sciences; Foreign Associate, French Acad. of Medicine. Hon. DSc and Hon. DHumLett from univs and med. colls in the US, France, Argentina, Canada. Nobel Prize in Physiology or Medicine, 1977; VA Exceptional Service Award, 1975 and 1978. Has given many distinguished lectures and received many awards and prizes from univs and med. socs and assocs. *Publications*: over 400 papers and contribns to books, research reports, proceedings of conferences and symposia on radioimmunoassay of peptide hormones and related subjects, since 1944. *Address*: 3242 Tibbett Avenue, Bronx, NY 10463, USA. *T*: (212) KI 3–7792.

YAMAZAKI, Toshio; Japanese Ambassador to the Court of St James's, since 1985; *b* 13 Aug. 1922; *s* of Takamaro Yamazaki and Konoe Yamazaki; *m* 1955, Yasuko Arakawa; one *s* one *d*. *Educ*: Tokyo University (Faculty of Law). 2nd Sec., Japanese Embassy, London, 1955–59; Dir, British Commonwealth Div., European and Oceanic Affairs Bureau, Min. of Foreign Affairs, 1962–64; Counsellor, Permt Mission to UN, New York; 1964–67; Dir, Financial Affairs Div., Minister's Secretariat, Min. of Foreign Affairs, 1967–70; Dep. Dir-Gen., Treaties Bureau, 1970; Minister, Washington, 1971–74; Dir-Gen., Amer. Affairs Bureau, Min. of Foreign Affairs, 1974–77; Dep. Vice-Minister for Admin, 1978–80; Ambassador to Egypt, 1980–82, to Indonesia, 1982–84. Order of Republic, 1st cl. (Egypt), 1982; Banda 2nd cl., Orden del Aguila Azteca (Mexico), 1978; Grosses Verdienstkreuz mit Stern (FRG), 1979. *Recreation*: golf. *Address*: Embassy of Japan, 46 Grosvenor Street, W1X 0BA. *T*: 01–493 6030. *Clubs*: Royal Wimbledon Golf, Sunningdale Golf.

YAMEY, Prof. Basil Selig, CBE 1972; FBA 1977; Professor of Economics, University of London, 1960–84, now Emeritus; Member (part-time), Monopolies and Mergers Commission, 1966–78; *b* 4 May 1919; *s* of Solomon and Leah Yamey; *m* 1948, Helen Bloch (*d* 1980); one *s* one *d*. *Educ*: Tulbagh High Sch.; Univ. of Cape Town; LSE. Lectr in Commerce, Rhodes Univ., 1945; Senior Lectr in Commerce, Univ. of Cape Town, 1946; Lectr in Commerce, LSE, 1948; Associate Prof. of Commerce, McGill Univ., 1949; Reader in Economics, Univ. of London, 1950. Trustee: National Gall., 1974–81; Tate Gall., 1979–81; Member: Council, National Trust, 1979–81; Museums and Galls Commn, 1983–84; Cinematograph Films Council, 1969–73; Mem. Committee of Management: Courtauld Inst., 1981–84; Warburg Inst., 1981–84. *Publications*: Economics of Resale Price Maintenance, 1954; (jt editor) Studies in History of Accounting, 1956; (with P. T. Bauer) Economics of Under-developed Countries, 1957; (jt editor) Capital, Saving and Credit in Peasant Societies, 1963; (with H. C. Edey and H. Thomson) Accounting in England and Scotland, 1543–1800, 1963; (with R. B. Stevens) The Restrictive Practices Court, 1965; (ed) Resale Price Maintenance, 1966; (with P. T. Bauer) Markets, Market Control and Marketing Reform: Selected Papers, 1968; (ed) Economics of Industrial Structure, 1973; (jt editor) Economics of Retailing, 1973; (jt editor) Debits, Credits, Finance and Profits, 1974; (with B. A. Goss) Economics of Futures Trading, 1976; Essays on the History of Accounting, 1978; (jt editor) Stato e Industria in Europa: Il Regno Unito, 1979; Further Essays on the History of Accounting, 1983; Arte e Contabilità, 1986; articles on economics, economic history and law in learned journals. *Address*: 36 Hampstead Way, NW11. *T*: 01–455 5810.

YANG, Chen Ning; physicist, educator; Einstein Professor and Director, Institute for Theoretical Physics, State University of New York at Stony Brook, New York, since 1966; *b* Hofei, China, 22 Sept. 1922; *s* of Ke Chuen Yang and Meng Hwa Lo; *m* 1950, Chih Li Tu; two *s* one *d*. Naturalized 1964. *Educ*: National Southwest Associated Univ., Kunming, China (BSc), 1942; University of Chicago (PhD), 1948. Institute for Advanced Study, Princeton, NJ: Member, 1949–55; Prof. of Physics, 1955–65; several DSc's from universities. Member of Board: Rockefeller Univ., 1970–76; AAAS, 1976–80; Salk Inst., 1978–; Ben Gurion Univ.; Member: Amer. Phys. Soc.; Nat. Acad. Sci.; Amer. Philos. Soc., Sigma Xi; Brazilian, Venezuelan and Royal Spanish Acads of Sci. Nobel Prize in Physics, 1957; Einstein Commemorative Award in Sciences, 1957; Rumford Prize, 1980. *Publications*: contrib. to Physical Review, Reviews of Modern Physics. *Address*: (home) 14 Woodhull Cove, Setauket, New York 11733, USA; (office) State University of New York at Stony Brook, New York 11790, USA.

YANG, Ti-Liang; Hon. Mr Justice Yang; Justice of Appeal, Hong Kong, since 1980; Judge of the High Court, Hong Kong, since 1975; *b* 30 June 1929; *s* of late Shao-nan Yang and Elsie (*née* Chun); *m* 1954, Eileen Barbara (*née* Tam); two *s*. *Educ*: The Comparative Law Sch. of China; Soochow Univ., Shanghai; UCL (LLB Hons 1953). Called to the Bar (with honours), Gray's Inn, 1954. Magistrate, Hong Kong, 1956; Sen. Magistrate, 1963; Rockefeller Fellow, London Univ., 1963–64; District Judge, Dist Court, 1968; Puisne Judge, Supreme Court, 1975. Chairman: Kowloon Disturbances Claims Assessment Bd, 1966, Compensation Bd, 1967; Commn of Inquiry into the Rainstorm Disasters, 1972; Commn of Inquiry into the Leung Wing-sang Case, 1976; Commn of Inquiry into the MacLennan Case, 1980; Law Reform Commn (Chm., Sub-cttee on law relating to homosexuality), 1980. Mem., Chinese Lang. Cttee (Chm. Legal Sub-cttee), 1970. Former Vice Chm., Bd of Trustees, Chung Chi Coll. Vice Chm., Hong Kong Sea Cadet Corps; Hon. President: Hong Kong Scouts Assoc.; Hong Kong Discharged Prisoners' Aid Soc.; Soc. Against Child Abuse. Adviser, Hong Kong Juvenile Care Centre. Former Council Member: Univ. of Hong Kong; Chinese Univ. of Hong Kong; Hong Kong Baptist Coll.; Chairman: Chief Justice's Working Party on Voir Dire Proceedings and Judges' Rules, 1979; University and Polytechnic Grants Cttee, 1981–84; Hong Kong Univ. Council, 1985–. Pres., Rotary Club of Hong Kong, 1983. Hon. LLD Chinese Univ. of Hong Kong, 1984. *Publications*: contrib. Internat. and Comparative Law Qly. *Recreations*: philately, reading, walking, oriental ceramics, travelling, music. *Address*: 30 Lowlands, 2 Eton Avenue, NW3; Supreme Court, Hong Kong. *T*: Hong Kong 5–239728. *Clubs*: Athenæum; Hong Kong, Hong Kong Country, Royal Hong Kong Jockey, Hong Kong Gun (Hong Kong).

YANKOV, Alexander; Professor of International Law, Sofia State University, 1968; Deputy Minister for Foreign Affairs, Bulgaria, 1976; *b* 22 June 1924; *m* 1949, Eliza; one *s* one *d*. *Educ*: Sofia State Univ. Law Sch. (PhD Internat. Law); Hague Acad. of Internat. Law. Asst Prof. of Internat. Law, 1951–54, Associate Prof. 1957–64, Sofia State Univ. Sec., Internat. Union of Students, Prague, 1954–57; Counsellor, Perm. Mission of Bulgaria to UN, mem. delegns to sessions of UN Gen. Assembly, 1965–68; Vice-Chm., UN Cttee on Peaceful Uses of Sea-bed, 1968–73; Ambassador of Bulgaria to Court of St James's, 1972–76; Ambassador and Perm. Rep. to UN, 1977–80. Mem., Perm. Court of Arbitration at The Hague, 1971; Mem. Court of Arbitration to Bulgarian Chamber of Commerce, 1970–. Pres., 8th Assembly, IMCO, 1973–75; Head of Bulgarian Delegn, 3rd UN Conf. on Law of the Sea; Chm., 3rd Cttee, UN Conf. on Law of the Sea, NY 1973, Caracas 1974, Geneva 1975, NY 1976, 1977, 1982; Chm., 4th Cttee, London Conf. on Marine Pollution by Ships, 1973; Member: Exec. Council, Internat. Law Assoc., 1973–; Internat. Law Commn, 1977–. Order 9 Sept. 1944, 1959; Order of Freedom of the People, 1960; Order of Cyril and Methodius, 1962; Order of People's Republic of Bulgaria, 1974 (all Bulgaria). *Publications*: The European Collective Security System, 1958; Reservations to the Declaration of Acceptance of Compulsory Jurisdiction of the International Court of Justice, 1961; The Peace Treaty with the Two German States and its Legal Effects, 1962; Principles of International Law as Applied to the Treaty Practice of Bulgaria, 1964; The United Nations: Legal Status and International Personality, 1965; Exploration and Uses of the Sea-bed: a new legal framework, 1970; United Nations Declaration on Principles of Friendly Relations and Progressive Development of International Law, 1971; United Nations and Development of International Trade Law, 1971, etc. *Recreations*: theatre, swimming. *Address*: Sofia State University, Ruski 15, Sofia, Bulgaria; Complex Lenin, Block 73, 1111–Sofia, Bulgaria.

YAPP, Sir Stanley Graham, Kt 1975; Chairman, West Midlands County Council, 1983–84 (Leader, 1973–77; Vice-Chairman, 1982–83); Member, Birmingham City Council, later Birmingham District Council, 1961–77 (Leader, 1972–74); *s* of late William and of Elsie Yapp; *m* 1961, Elisbeth Wise (marr. diss.); one *d*; *m* 1974, Carol Matheson (marr. diss.); one *s*; *m* 1983, Christine Horton. Member, West Midlands Economic Planning Council (Chm., Transport Cttee); Member many bodies both local and national, inc.: Vice-Chm. LAMSAC; Member: Local Govt Trng Board; Nat. Jt Councils on pay and conditions; AMA; BR Adv. Bd, Midlands and N Western Reg., 1977–79; Chm., West Midlands Planning Authorities Conf., 1973–75, Vice-Chm. 1975–77. Governor, BFI, 1977–79. FBIM. *Publications*: contribs to Local Government Chronicle, Municipal Journal, Rating and Valuation. *Recreations*: astronomy, reading walking. *Address*: 172 York Road, Hall Green, Birmingham B28 8LE.

YARBOROUGH, 7th Earl of, *cr* 1837; **John Edward Pelham;** Baron Yarborough, Baron Worsley, 1794; Major Grenadier Guards, retired 1952; Vice Lord-Lieutenant (formerly Vice-Lieutenant), Lincolnshire, since 1964; JP; *b* 2 June 1920; *s* of 6th Earl of Yarborough; *S* father, 1966; *m* 1957, Mrs Ann Duffin, *d* of late John Herbert Upton, Ingmire Hall, Yorkshire; one *s* three *d*. *Educ*: Eton; Trinity College, Cambridge. Contested

(C) Grimsby, 1955. President: Midland Area, British Legion, 1959–60, East Midland Area, 1960–62; Nat. Exec. Council, British Legion, 1962–73; Patron, E Midlands Area, 1974–. High Sheriff of Lincolnshire, 1964; Hon. Col, 440 Light AD Regt, RA (TA), 1965–69, Humber Regt, RA T&AVR, 1969–71; Dep. Hon. Col, 2nd Bn, Yorkshire Volunteers, 1971–72. JP, Parts of Lindsey, 1965. *Recreations:* shooting, sailing. *Heir: s* Lord Worsley, *qv*. *Address:* Brocklesby Park, Habrough, South Humberside DN37 8PL. *T:* Roxton 60242. *Clubs:* Cavalry and Guards, Boodle's; Royal Yacht Squadron.

YARBURGH-BATESON; *see* de Yarburgh-Bateson, family name of Baron Deramore.

YARDE, Air Vice-Marshal Brian Courtenay, CVO 1953; CBE 1949; psa; *b* 5 September 1905; *s* of late John Edward Yarde, Crediton, Devon, and Bedford; *m* 1927, Marjorie, *d* of late W. Sydney Smith, Bedford; two *d*. *Educ:* Bedford School; RAF College, Cranwell (Sword of Honour), 1926. Served War of 1939–45 in France, Malaya, Middle East, UK (despatches thrice); Deputy Director of Bomber Operations, Air Ministry, 1945; Senior Director, RAF Staff College, 1946–47; Station Commander, Gatow, 1947–49 (Berlin Airlift); Provost Marshal and Chief of the Royal Air Force Police, 1951–53; Air Officer Commanding No. 62 Group, 1953–54. Air Commodore, 1951; Acting Air Vice-Marshal, 1954; Commandant-General of the Royal Air Force Regiment and Inspector of Ground Combat Training, 1954–57, retired. Chairman, Courtenay Caterers Ltd, Andover. Officer American Legion of Merit. *Address:* Wiremead, East Cholderton, Andover, Hants SP11 8LR. *T:* Weyhill 2265.

YARDE-BULLER, family name of **Baron Churston.**

YARDLEY, Prof. David Charles Miller; Chairman, Commission for Local Administration in England, since 1982; *b* 4 June 1929; *s* of Geoffrey Miller Yardley and Doris Woodward Yardley (*née* Jones); *m* 1954, Patricia Anne Tempest Olver; two *s* two *d*. *Educ:* The Old Hall Sch., Wellington; Ellesmere Coll., Shropshire; Univ. of Birmingham (LLB, LLD); Univ. of Oxford (MA, DPhil). Called to Bar, Gray's Inn, 1952. RAF Flying Officer (nat. service), 1949–51. Bigelow Teaching Fellow, Univ. of Chicago, 1953–54; Fellow and Tutor in Jurisprudence, St Edmund Hall, Oxford, 1953–74; CUF Lectr, Univ. of Oxford, 1954–74; Sen. Proctor, Univ. of Oxford, 1965–66; Barber Prof. of Law, Univ. of Birmingham, 1974–78; Head of Dept of Law, Politics and Economics, Oxford Poly., 1978–80; Rank Foundn Prof. of Law, University Coll. at Buckingham, 1980–82. Visiting Prof. of Law, Univ. of Sydney, 1971. Constitutional Consultant, Govt of W Nigeria, 1956; Chm., Thames Valley Rent Tribunal, 1963–82; Vice-Pres., Cambs Chilterns and Thames Rent Assessment Panel, 1966–82; Oxford City Councillor, 1966–74; Chm. of Governors, St Helen's Sch., Abingdon, 1967–81; Chm., Oxford Area Nat. Ins. Local Appeal Tribunal, 1969–82. *Publications:* Introduction to British Constitutional Law, 1960, 6th edn, 1984; A Source Book of English Administrative Law, 1963, 2nd edn, 1970; The Future of the Law, 1964; Geldart's Elements of English Law, 7th edn, 1966–9th edn, 1984; Hanbury's English Courts of Law, 4th edn, 1967; Hanbury and Yardley, English Courts of Law, 5th edn, 1979; Principles of Administrative Law, 1981, 2nd edn, 1986; (with I. N. Stevens) The Protection of Liberty, 1982. *Recreations:* lawn tennis, squash racquets, theatre, cats. *Address:* 9 Belbroughton Road, Oxford OX2 6UZ. *T:* Oxford 54831. *Clubs:* United Oxford & Cambridge University, Royal Air Force.

YARMOUTH, Earl of; Henry Jocelyn Seymour; *b* 6 July 1958; *s* and *heir* of 8th Marquess of Hertford, *qv*.

YARNOLD, Rev. Edward John, SJ; DD; Tutor in Theology, Campion Hall, Oxford, since 1964 (Master, 1965–72; Senior Tutor, 1972–74); *b* 14 Jan. 1926; *s* of Edward Cabré Yarnold and Agnes (*née* Deakin). *Educ:* St Michael's Coll., Leeds; Campion Hall, Oxford (MA); Heythrop College (STL). Taught classics at St Francis Xavier's Coll., Liverpool, 1954–57; ordained, 1960; taught classics at St Michael's Coll., Leeds, 1962–64. Sarum Lectr, Univ. of Oxford, 1972–73. Assoc. Gen. Sec., Ecumenical Soc. of Blessed Virgin Mary, 1975–; Mem., Anglican-Roman Catholic Internat. Commn, 1970–81 and 1983–. Lectr (part-time), Heythrop Coll., London, 1978–80; Vis. Prof., Univ. of Notre Dame, 1982–. Order of St Augustine, 1981. *Publications:* The Theology of Original Sin, 1971; The Awe-Inspiring Rites of Initiation, 1972; The Second Gift, 1974; (with H. Chadwick) Truth and Authority, 1977; (ed jtly and contrib.) The Study of Liturgy, 1978; They are in Earnest, 1982; Eight Days with the Lord, 1984; (ed jtly and contrib.) The Study of Spirituality, 1986; articles in learned jls. *Recreations:* opera, cricket. *Address:* Campion Hall, Oxford OX1 1QS. *T:* Oxford 726811 or 240861.

YARNOLD, Patrick; HM Diplomatic Service; Counsellor and Head of Chancery, Belgrade, since 1985; *b* 21 March 1937; *s* of late Leonard Francis Yarnold and Gladys Blanche Yarnold (*née* Merry); *m* 1961, Caroline, *er d* of Andrew J. Martin; two *d*. *Educ:* Bancroft's School. HM Forces, 1955–57. Joined HM Foreign (now Diplomatic) Service, 1957; served: FO, 1957–60; Addis Ababa, 1961–64; Belgrade, 1964–66; FO (later FCO), 1966–70; 1st Sec., Head of Chancery, Bucharest, 1970–73; 1st Sec. (Commercial), Bonn, 1973–76; FCO, 1976–79; Counsellor (Economic and Commercial), Brussels, 1980–83; Consul-Gen., Zagreb, 1983–85. *Recreations:* travel, photography, walking, genealogy, local history, reading, etc. *Address:* c/o Foreign and Commonwealth Office, SW1A 2AH.

YARROW, Dr Alfred, FFCM; Senior Principal Medical Officer, Department of Health and Social Security, 1977–84; *b* 25 May 1924; *s* of Leah and step *s* of Philip Yarrow; *m* 1953, Sheila Kaufman; two *d*. *Educ:* Hackney Downs Grammar Sch.; Edinburgh Univ. (MB, ChB); London Sch. of Hygiene and Trop. Medicine (Hons DPH). Foundn FFCM 1972. Dep. Area MO, Tottenham and Hornsey, 1955–60; Area MO, SE Essex, 1960–65; MOH, Gateshead, 1965–68; Dir, Scottish Health Educn Unit, 1968–73; SMO, DHSS, 1973–77. Temp. Consultant, WHO, 1975–76. Brit. Council Lectr, 1975; Council of Europe Fellow, 1978. *Publications:* So Now You Know About Smoking, 1975; Politics, Society and Preventive Medicine, 1986; scientific papers on demography, epidemiology, preventive medicine and health educn. *Recreations:* walking, travelling, reading. *Address:* 9/4 Nof Harim, Jerusalem, Israel. *T:* 535792.

YARROW, Sir Eric Grant, 3rd Bt, *cr* 1916; MBE (mil.) 1946; DL; President, Yarrow PLC, 1985–86 (Chairman, 1962–85); Chairman, Clydesdale Bank PLC, since 1985 (Director since 1962, Deputy Chairman, 1975–85); Director, Standard Life Assurance Co., since 1958; *b* 23 April 1920; *o s* of Sir Harold Yarrow, 2nd Bt and 1st wife, Eleanor Etheldreda (*d* 1934); *S* father, 1962; *m* 1st, 1951, Rosemary Ann (*d* 1957), *yr d* of late H. T. Young, Roehampton, SW15; one *s*; 2nd, 1959, Annette Elizabeth Françoise (marr. diss. 1975), *d* of late A. J. E. Steven, Ardgay; three *s* (including twin *s*); 3rd, 1982, Mrs Joan Botting, *d* of late R. F. Masters, Piddinghoe, Sussex. *Educ:* Marlborough Coll.; Glasgow Univ. Served apprenticeship, G. & J. Weir Ltd. Served Burma, 1942–45; Major RE, 1945. Asst Manager Yarrow & Co., 1946; Dir, 1948; Man. Dir, 1958–67. Mem. Council, RINA, 1957–; Vice-Pres., 1965; Hon. Vice-Pres., 1972. Mem., General Cttee, Lloyd's Register of Shipping, 1960; Prime Warden, Worshipful Co. of Shipwrights, 1970; Deacon, Incorporation of Hammermen of Glasgow, 1961–62; Retired Mem. Council, Institution of Engineers & Shipbuilders in Scotland; Mem. Council, Inst. of Directors, 1983–. Pres., Scottish Convalescent Home for Children, 1957–70; Hon. Pres., Princess Louise Scottish Hospital at Erskine, 1986– (Chm., 1980–86). President: Smeatonian Soc. of Civil Engineers, 1983; Marlburian Club, 1984; OStJ. DL Renfrewshire, 1970. *Recreations:* golf, shooting. *Heir: e s* Richard Grant Yarrow [*b* 21 March 1953; *m* 1982, Sheila, *er d* of Ronald Allison, *qv*]. *Address:* Cloak, Kilmacolm, Renfrewshire PA13 4SD. *T:* Kilmacolm 2067. *Clubs:* Army and Navy; Royal Scottish Automobile.

YARWOOD, Dame Elizabeth (Ann), DBE 1969; JP; DL; *b* 25 Nov. 1900; *d* of Henry and Margaret Gaskell; *m* 1918, Vernon Yarwood; two *s*. *Educ:* Whitworth Street High Sch., Manchester. Councillor, Manchester City Council, 1938–74, Alderman, 1955–74; Lord Mayor of Manchester, 1967–68. Director: Manchester & Salford Co-operative Society Ltd, 1955; Manchester Ship Canal, 1964. Vice-Pres., Manchester County Girl Guides Assoc. Freeman of the City of Manchester, 1974. Hon. MA Manchester, 1978. JP Manchester, 1945; DL Lancs, 1974. *Recreation:* reading.

YARWOOD, Michael Edward, OBE 1976; entertainer, since 1962; *b* 14 June 1941; *s* of Wilfred and Bridget Yarwood; *m* 1969, Sandra Burville; two *d*. *Educ:* Bredbury Secondary Modern Sch., Cheshire. First television appearance, 1963; *BBC TV:* Three of a Kind, 1967; Look—Mike Yarwood, and Mike Yarwood in Persons (series), 1971–82; *ATV:* Will the Real Mike Yarwood Stand Up? (series), 1968; *Thames:* Mike Yarwood in Persons, 1983–84, 1985–86. Royal Variety performances, 1968, 1972, 1976, 1981. Variety Club of Gt Britain award for BBC TV Personality of 1973; Royal Television Society award for outstanding creative achievement in front of camera, 1978. Mem., Grand Order of Water Rats, 1968. *Publications:* And This Is Me, 1974; Impressions of my life (autobiog.), 1986. *Recreations:* golf, tennis. *Address:* Weybridge, Surrey. *Club:* Lord's Taverners.

YASS, Irving; Under Secretary, Department of Transport, since 1982; *b* 20 Dec. 1935; *s* of late Abraham and Fanny Yass; *m* 1962, Marion Leighton; two *s* one *d*. *Educ:* Harrow County Grammar School for Boys; Balliol Coll., Oxford (Brackenbury Schol.; BA). Assistant Principal, Min. of Transport and Civil Aviation, 1958; Private Sec. to Joint Parliamentary Secretary, 1960; HM Treasury, 1967–70; Asst Secretary, Dept of the Environment, 1971; Secretary, Cttee of Inquiry into Local Govt Finance, 1974–76; Dept of Transport, 1976–. *Address:* Department of Transport, 2 Marsham Street, SW1. *T:* 01–212 4054.

YASSUKOVICH, Stanislas Michael; Chairman, Merrill Lynch Europe Ltd, since 1985; *b* 5 Feb. 1935; *s* of Dimitri and Denise Yassukovich; *m* 1961, Diana (*née* Townsend); two *s* one *d*. *Educ:* Deerfield Academy; Harvard University. US Marine Corps, 1957–61. Joined White, Weld & Co., 1961: posted to London, 1962; Branch Manager, 1967; General Partner, 1969; Managing Director, 1969; European Banking Co. Ltd: Managing Director, 1973; Group Dep. Chm., 1983. *Publications:* articles in financial press. *Recreations:* hunting, shooting, polo. *Address:* Merrill Lynch, 27 Finsbury Square, EC2A 1AQ. *T:* 01–382 8473. *Clubs:* Buck's, Turf; Travellers' (Paris); Brook (New York); Union (US).

YATES, Alfred, CBE 1983; FBPsS; Director, National Foundation for Educational Research in England and Wales, 1972–83; *b* 17 Nov. 1917; *s* of William Oliver Yates and Frances Yates; *m* 1943, Joan Mary Lawrence-Fellows; one *s* one *d*. *Educ:* Farnworth Grammar Sch.; Sheffield Univ. (BA); Oxford Univ. (MA); QUB (MEd). FBPsS 1957. Served War, Army, 1940–46: Captain, REME. Schoolmaster, Launceston Coll., Cornwall, 1939–40; Lectr, QUB, 1946–51; Sen. Res. Officer, NFER, 1951–59; Sen. Tutor, Dept of Educnl Studies, Oxford Univ., 1959–72. FCP 1981. *Publications:* Admission to Grammar Schools, 1957; Grouping in Education, 1966; An Introduction to Educational Measurement, 1968; The Role of Research in Educational Change, 1971; The Organisation of Schooling, 1971. *Recreations:* reading, theatre, watching Association football and cricket. *Address:* 46 London Road, Wheatley, Oxford. *T:* Wheatley 3315.

YATES, Anne; *see* Yates, E. A.

YATES, (Edith) Anne, (Mrs S. J. Yates), CBE 1972; *b* 21 Dec. 1912; *d* of William Blakeman and Frances Dorothea (*née* Thacker); *m* 1935, Stanley James Yates; two *s* one *d*. *Educ:* Barrs' Hill Girls' Sch., Coventry. County Councillor, 1955, County Alderman, 1966, Notts; Chm., Notts CC, Feb. 1968–March 1974. Chairman: Midlands Tourist Bd, 1971–76; E Midlands Sports Council, 1972–77; Indep. Chm., Nat. Cttee on Recreation Management Trng, 1976–82 (Yates Report, 1984); Member: Sports Council, 1971–74; E Midlands Council of Sport and Recreation, 1977–82; MSC, 1974–76; East Midlands Regional MSC, 1977–82; English Tourist Bd, 1975–78; Nat. Water Council, 1973–79 (Chm., Water Training Cttee, 1973–79); Bd for Distributing Hotel and Catering and Leisure Services, BTEC, 1984–. *Recreations:* reading, music, theatre. *Address:* Manor Close, Rolleston, Newark, Notts. *T:* Southwell 813362.

YATES, Frank, CBE 1963; ScD; FRS 1948; Honorary Scientist, Rothamsted Experimental Station, since 1968 (formerly Head of Statistics Department and Agricultural Research Statistical Service, and Deputy Director); *b* 1902; *s* of Percy and Edith Yates, Didsbury, Manchester; *m* 1939, Pauline (*d* 1976), *d* of Vladimir Shoubersky; *m* 1981, Ruth, *d* of William James Hunt, Manchester. *Educ:* Clifton; St John's Coll., Cambridge. Research Officer and Mathematical Adviser, Gold Coast Geodetic Survey, 1927–31; Rothamsted Experimental Station, 1931, Dept of Statistics, 1933, Agric. Res. Statistical Service, 1947, Dep. Dir, 1958; Scientific Adviser to various Mins, UNO, FAO, 1939–; Wing Comdr (Hon.) RAF, 1943–45; Mem. UN Sub-Commn on Statistical Sampling, 1947–52. Sen. Res. Fellow, Imperial Coll., 1969–74; Sen. Vis. Fellow, Imperial Coll., 1974–77. Pres., British Computer Society, 1960–61; Pres., Royal Statistical Society, 1967–68. Royal Medal of the Royal Society, 1966. Hon. DSc London, 1982. *Publications:* Design and Analysis of Factorial Experiments, 1937; (with R. A. Fisher) Statistical Tables for Biological, Medical and Agricultural Research, 1938 (6th edn 1963); Sampling Methods for Censuses and Surveys, 1949 (4th edn 1981); Experimental Design: Selected Papers, 1970. Numerous scientific papers. *Recreation:* mountaineering. *Address:* Stackyard, Rothamsted, Harpenden, Herts AL5 2BQ. *T:* Harpenden 2732. *Club:* Athenæum.

YATES, Ian Humphrey Nelson; General Manager and Chief Executive, The Press Association Ltd, since 1975; *b* 24 Jan. 1931; *s* of James Nelson Yates and Martha (*née* Nutter); *m* 1956, Daphne J. Hudson, MCSP; three *s*. *Educ:* Lancaster Royal Grammar Sch.; Canford Sch., Wimborne. Royal Scots Greys, Germany and ME (National Service Commn), 1951–53. Management Trainee, Westminster Press Ltd, 1953–58 (Westmorland Gazette, and Telegraph & Argus, Bradford); Asst to Man. Dir, King & Hutchings Ltd, Uxbridge, 1958–60; Bradford and District Newspapers: Asst Gen. Man., 1960; Gen. Man., 1964; Man. Dir, 1969–75; Dir, Westminster Press Planning Div., 1969–75. Director: Universal News Services Ltd; Tellex Monitors Ltd, 1986–. President: Young Newspapermen's Assoc., 1966; Yorks Newspaper Soc., 1968. Member: Council, Newspaper Soc., 1970–75; Council, Commonwealth Press Union, 1977–; Vice-Pres., Alliance of European News Agencies, 1984–; Chm., New Media Cttee. *Recreations:* walking, reading, theatre. *Address:* Woodbury, 11 Holmwood Close, East Horsley, Surrey. *T:* East Horsley 3873.

YATES, Ivan R., CBE 1982; FEng 1983; Deputy Chief Executive (Engineering), since 1986, Deputy Managing Director (Aircraft), since 1985, Director, since 1982, British

Aerospace PLC; *b* 22 April 1929; *m* 1967, Jennifer Mary Holcombe; one *s* one *d*. *Educ:* Liverpool Collegiate Sch.; Liverpool Univ. (BEng 1st Class Hons). FIMechE; FRAeS; FAIAA; CBIM. Graduate Apprentice, English Electric, Preston, 1950, Chief Project Engr, 1959; Project Manager, Jaguar, 1966; British Aircraft Corporation: Special Dir, Preston Div., 1970; Dir, Preston, Warton Div., 1973; Dir, Aircraft Projects, 1974; Director: SEPECAT SA, 1976; Panavia GmbH, 1977; British Aerospace: Man. Dir, Warton, 1978; Dir of Engrg and Project Assessment, Aircraft Gp, 1981; Chief Exec., Aircraft Gp, 1983. Mem., Technology Requirements Bd, 1985–. British Silver Medal, 1979, Gold Medal, 1985, RAeS. FRSA 1985. *Publications:* various papers and lectures. *Recreations:* walking, ski-ing, painting, music. *Address:* British Aerospace PLC, 100 Pall Mall, SW1Y 5HR. *T:* 01–930 1020.

YATES, Rt. Rev. John; *see* Gloucester, Bishop of.

YATES, Peter (James); film director/producer and theatre director; *b* 24 July 1929; *s* of Col Robert L. Yates and Constance Yates; *m* 1960, Virginia Pope; two *s* one *d* (and one *d* decd). *Educ:* Charterhouse; Royal Academy of Dramatic Art. Entered film industry, 1956. *Films directed:* Summer Holiday, 1962; One Way Pendulum, 1964; Robbery, 1966; Bullitt, 1968; John and Mary, 1969; Murphy's War, 1970; The Hot Rock, 1971; The Friends of Eddie Coyle, 1972; For Pete's Sake, 1973; Mother, Jugs and Speed, 1975; The Deep, 1976; Breaking Away (dir and prod.), 1979 (nominated 1980 Academy Awards, Director and Producer); The Janitor (dir and prod.), 1980; Krull, 1982; The Dresser (dir and prod.), 1983 (nominated 1984 Academy Awards, Dir and Producer); Eleni, 1984; The House on Sullivan Street (dir and prod.), 1986. *Theatre directed:* The American Dream, Royal Court, 1961; The Death of Bessie Smith, (London) 1961; Passing Game, (New York) 1977; Interpreters, (London) 1985. *Recreations:* tennis, sailing, skiing. *Address:* 1 West 72nd Street, New York, NY 10023, USA.

YATES-BELL, John Geoffrey, FRCS; retired; Consultant Urologist to King's College Hospital; *b* 6 Dec. 1902; *s* of John Bell, FRCVS, and Matilda Bell, London; *m* 1932, Winifred Frances Hordern (*née* Perryman) (*d* 1979); one *s* one *d*. *Educ:* St Dunstan's College; King's College, London. MB, BS London 1926; FRCS 1930. King's College Hospital: House Surgeon, 1926–28; Surgical Registrar, 1928–29; Junior Urological Surgeon, 1930; Hon. Urological Surgeon, 1937. Emeritus Urological Surgeon, Epsom and Leatherhead Hosps. President, Urological Section, RSM, 1952 (Vice-Pres. 1939); Fellow Internat. Soc. of Urology, 1934; Founder Member, British Assoc. of Urological Surgeons (Hon. Treas., 1954–56). *Publications:* Kidney and Ureter, Stone (British Surgical Practice), 1950; Mythology of Greece and Rome, 1980; articles in British Jl of Urology, Jl of Urology, Medical Press, Lancet, etc. *Recreation:* lawn tennis. *Address:* 7 Andorra Court, Widmore Road, Bromley, Kent BR1 3AE. *T:* Bromley 2451.

YEATES, W(illiam) Keith, MD, MS; FRCS; FRCSEd (without examination); Honorary Consultant Urologist, Newcastle University Hospitals, since 1985 (Consultant Urologist, 1951–85); Hon. Senior Lecturer, Institute of Urology, University of London, since 1981; Chairman, Intercollegiate Board in Urology, since 1984; *b* 10 March 1920; *s* of William Ravensbourne Yeates and Winifred (*née* Scott); *m* 1946, Jozy McIntyre Fairweather; one *s* one *d*. *Educ:* Glasgow Academy; Whitley Bay Grammar Sch.; King's Coll., Newcastle, Univ. of Durham. Consultant Advr in Urology, DHSS, 1978–84. Chm., Specialist Adv. Cttee in Urology, Jt Cttee on Higher Surgical Trng, RCS, 1984–86. Visiting Professor: Universities of: Baghdad, 1974, 1978; California, LA, 1976; Texas, Dallas, 1976; Delhi, 1977; Cairo, 1978; Kuwait, 1980; Guest Prof., New York section, Amer. Urolog. Assoc., 1977, 1985; Principal Guest Lectr, Urolog. Soc. of Australasia, 1977; Guest Lecturer: Italian Urolog. Assoc., 1978; Yugoslavian Urolog. Assoc., 1980; Vis. Lectr, Rio de Janeiro, 1975; Mem., Internat. Soc. of Urology, 1958–; Sen. Mem., European Assoc. of Urology, 1986– (Foundn Mem., 1974–86); Hon. Member: Urolog. Soc. of Australasia, 1977; Canadian Urological Assoc., 1981. President: N of England Surgical Soc., 1971–72; British Assoc. of Urological Surgeons, 1980–82 (Vice-Pres., 1978–80, St Peter's Medal, 1983). British Journal of Urology: Editor, 1973–78; Chm., Editorial Cttee, 1978–84; Consulting Editor, 1985–. *Publications:* various papers, chapters in text books on Urology, particularly on bladder dysfunction and male infertility. *Address:* 22 Castleton Grove, Jesmond, Newcastle upon Tyne NE2 2HD. *T:* Tyneside 2814030; 71 King Henry's Road, NW3 3QU. *T:* 01–586 7633.

YEEND, Sir Geoffrey (John), AC 1986; Kt 1979; CBE 1976; FAIM; consultant; Director, AMATIL Ltd, since 1986; *b* 1 May 1927; *s* of Herbert J. Yeend and Ellen Yeend; *m* 1952, Laurel, *d* of L. G. Mahoney; one *s* one *d*. *Educ:* Canberra High Sch.; Canberra University Coll., Melbourne Univ. (BCom). Served RAE, AIF, 1945–46. Dept of Post War Reconstruction, 1947–49; Prime Minister's Dept, 1950–86; Private Sec. to Prime Minister, 1952–55; Asst Sec., Aust. High Commn, London, 1958–61; Dep. Sec., 1972–77; Head of Dept and Sec. to Cabinet, 1978–86. Mem. and leader of Aust. delegns to internat. confs. Mem., Adv. Council on Aust. Archives, 1985–. Aust. Eisenhower Fellow, 1971. FAIM 1982. Internat. Hockey Fedn: Councillor, 1959–66; Vice-Pres., 1967–76; Member of Honour, 1979. *Recreations:* golf, fishing. *Address:* 1 Loftus Street, Yarralumla, ACT 2600, Australia. *T:* 062 813266. *Clubs:* Commonwealth (Canberra); Royal Canberra Golf.

YELLOWLEES, Sir Henry, KCB 1975 (CB 1971); Consultant, European Region, World Health Organization, since 1985; Chief Medical Officer, Department of Health and Social Security, Department of Education and Science and Home Office, 1973–83; *b* 1919; *s* of late Henry Yellowlees, OBE, Psychiatrist of Bath. *Educ:* Stowe Sch.; University Coll., Oxford. MA, BM, BCh Oxon 1950. FRCP 1971 (MRCP 1966, LRCP 1950); FFCM 1972; FRCS 1983 (MRCS 1950). Pilot, RAF, 1941–45. Resident Med. Officer, Mddx Hosp., London, 1951–54; Asst Senior Med. Officer, South West Regional Hosp. Bd, 1954–59; Dep. Sen. Admin. Med. Officer, North West Metropolitan Regional Hosp. Bd, 1959–63; Principal Med. Officer, Min. of Health, 1963–65 (seconded); Senior Principal Med. Officer, 1965–67 (established); Dep. Chief Med. Officer, 1967–72, 2nd Chief Med. Officer, 1972–73, Dept of Health and Social Security. Member: Medical Research Council, 1974–83; Gen. Medical Council, 1979–; Health Services Supervisory Bd, 1983–. Hon. FRCP Glasgow, 1974; Hon. FRCPsych, 1977; Fellow Brit. Inst. of Management, 1974–83; Vice-Pres., Mental After-Care Assoc.; Hon. Mem., Nat. Assoc. of Clinical Tutors. *Address:* 43 Sandwich House, Sandwich Street, WC1H 9PR.

YEMM, Prof. Edmund William, BA, DPhil Oxon; Melville Wills Professor of Botany, University of Bristol, 1955–74, Emeritus Professor 1974; *b* 16 July 1909; *s* of William H. Yemm and Annie L. Brett; *m* 1935, Marie Solari; one *s* three *d*. *Educ:* Wyggeston School, Leicester; Queen's College, Oxford. Foundation, Schol., Queen's Coll., 1928; Christopher Welch Schol., 1931. Major, REME, 1942–45. Research Fellow, Queen's Coll., 1935–38; Lecturer, Univ. of Bristol, 1939–49; Reader in Botany, Univ. of Bristol, 1950–55; Pro-Vice-Chancellor, Bristol Univ., 1970–73. Fellowship, Rockefeller Foundation, 1954; Vis. Prof., Western Reserve Univ., 1966–67. *Publications:* scientific papers in Proc. Royal Soc., New Phytologist, Biochemical Jl, Jl of Ecology, Jl of Experimental Botany. *Recreations:* cricket, gardening; formerly football (Oxford Univ. Assoc. Football Blue, 1929–31). *Address:* The Wycke, 61 Long Ashton Road, Bristol BS18 9HW. *T:* Long Ashton 392258.

YENDELL, Rear-Adm. William John, CB 1957; RN, retired; *b* 29 Dec. 1903; *e s* of late Charles Yendell; *m* 1937, Monica Duncan; one *d*. *Educ:* RN Colleges Osborne and Dartmouth. Qualified Gunnery Officer, 1929; commanded HM Ships: Bittern, 1938; Shah, 1943–45; Glasgow, 1950; Superb, 1950. Director of Naval Ordnance, 1951–54; Assistant Chief of Naval Staff (Warfare), 1954–57. Naval ADC 1954–. Comdr, 1937; Captain, 1945. *Recreations:* painting and most games. *Address:* The Bell Cottage, Newtonmore, Inverness-shire. *T:* Newtonmore 344. *Club:* Royal Naval and Royal Albert Yacht (Portsmouth).

YENTOB, Alan; Head of Music and Arts, BBC Television, since 1985; *b* 11 March 1947; *s* of Isaac Yentob and Flora Yentob (*née* Khazam). *Educ:* King's School, Ely; Univ. of Grenoble; Univ. of Leeds (LLB). BBC general trainee, 1968; producer/director, 1970–; arts features, incl. Omnibus; Editor, Arena, 1978–85; Co-Editor, Omnibus, 1985. Member: Bd of Directors, Riverside Studios, 1984–; BFI Production Board, 1985–. *Recreations:* swimming, books. *Address:* 99 Blenheim Crescent, W11.

YEO, Douglas; Director, Shell Research Ltd, Thornton Research Centre, 1980–85; *b* 13 June 1925; *s* of Sydney and Hylda Yeo; *m* 1947, Joan Elisabeth Chell; two *d*. *Educ:* Secondary Sch., St Austell; University Coll., Exeter (BSc London). Expedn on locust control, Kenya, 1945. HMOCS, 1948–63; Tropical Pesticides Research Inst., Uganda and Tanzania, 1948–61 (Scientific Officer, 1948–51, Sen. Scientific Officer, 1951–57, Prin. Scientific Officer, 1957–61). Internat. African Migratory Locust Control Organisation, Mali: on secondment, 1958, 1960; Dir and Sec. Gen., 1961–63. Shell Research Ltd: Research Dir, Woodstock Agricultural Research Centre, 1963–69, Dir, 1969–76; Dir, Biosciences Lab., Sittingbourne, 1976–80. Mem. Council, RHBNC, London Univ., 1985–. FIBiol. *Publications:* papers in Bulletin Ent. Res., Bull. WHO, Anti-Locust Bull., Qly Jl Royal Met. Soc., Jl Sci. Fd. Agric., Plant Protection Confs, etc. *Recreations:* sailing, hill walking, fishing. *Address:* Tremarne, Tremarne Close, Feock, Truro TR3 6SB. *Club:* Royal Corinthian Yacht (Burnham on Crouch).

YEO, Kok Cheang, CMG 1956; MD; MB; BS; DPH; DTM&H; *b* 1 April 1903; *s* of Yeo Kim Hong; *m* Florence, *d* of late Sir Robert Ho-tung, KBE; one *s* two *d*. *Educ:* Hong Kong University; Cambridge University; London School of Hygiene and Tropical Medicine. MB, BS, Hong Kong, 1925, MD, 1930; DTM&H (England) 1927; DPH, Cambridge, 1928. Assistant Medical Officer of Health, Hong Kong, 1928; Lecturer and Examiner in public health, Hong Kong University, 1936–37; Official JP 1938; Chinese Health Officer, senior grade, 1939–47; Deputy Director of Health Services, and Vice-Chairman of Urban Council, 1947–50; Deputy Director of Medical and Health Services, 1950–52; member of Legislative Council, Hong Kong, 1951–57; Director of Medical and Health Services, Hong Kong, 1952–58; Professor of Social Medicine, Hong Kong University, 1953–58; retd 1958. *Address:* Uplands, Netherfield Hill, Battle, East Sussex TN33 0LH.

YEO, Timothy Stephen Kenneth; MP (C) Suffolk South, since 1983; *b* 20 March 1945; *s* of late Dr Kenneth John Yeo and Norah Margaret Yeo; *m* 1970, Diane Helen Pickard; one *s* one *d*. *Educ:* Charterhouse; Emmanuel Coll., Cambridge. Asst Treas., Bankers Trust Co., 1970–73; Director, Worcester Engineering Co. Ltd, 1975–86. Dir, Spastics Soc., 1980–83, Mem., Exec. Council, 1984–86. Mem., Social Services Select Cttee, 1985–. Jt Sec., Cons. Pty Finance Cttee, 1984–. Hon. Treasurer, International Voluntary Service, 1975–78. Trustee: African Palms, 1970–85; Tanzania Development Trust, 1980–; Chm., Tadworth Court Trust, 1983–. *Publication:* Public Accountability and Regulation of Charities, 1983. *Recreation:* skiing. *Address:* House of Commons, SW1A 0AA. *T:* 01–219 3000. *Clubs:* Carlton; Sudbury Conservative (Sudbury); Royal St George's (Sandwich).

YEOMAN, Maj.-Gen. Alan; Commander Communications, British Army of the Rhine, since 1984; *b* 17 Nov. 1933; *s* of George Smith Patterson Yeoman and Wilhelmina Tromans Elwell; *m* 1960, Barbara Joan Davies; two *s* one *d*. *Educ:* Dame Allan's School, Newcastle upon Tyne. Officer Cadet, RMA Sandhurst, 1952; commnd Royal Signals, 1954; served Korea, Malaysia, Singapore, Cyprus, UK, BAOR and Canada, 1954–70 (Staff Coll., 1963); CO 2 Div. Sig. Regt, BAOR, 1970–73; HQ 1 (BR) Corps, BAOR, 1973–74; MoD, 1974–77; Col AQ, HQLF Cyprus, 1978–79; Comd Trng Gp, Royal Signals and Catterick Garrison, 1979–82; Brig. AQ, HQ 1 (BR) Corps, BAOR, 1982–84. *Recreations:* golf, cricket, ski-ing. *Address:* c/o Lloyds Bank, Catterick Garrison, North Yorks. *Clubs:* Army and Navy, MCC.

YEOMAN, Prof. Michael Magson, PhD; FRSE; Regius Professor of Botany, University of Edinburgh, since 1978; *b* 16 May 1931; *s* of Gordon Yeoman and Mabel Ellen (*née* Magson), Newcastle upon Tyne; *m* 1962, Erica Mary Lines; two *d*. *Educ:* Gosforth Grammar Sch.; King's Coll., Univ. of Durham (BSc 1952, MSc 1954, PhD 1960); FRSE 1980. National Service, Royal Corps of Signals, 1954–56. Demonstrator in Botany, King's Coll., Newcastle upon Tyne, 1957–59; Edinburgh University: Lectr in Botany, 1960; Sen. Lectr, 1968; Reader, 1973; Dean, Fac. of Science, 1981–84. Vis. Prof., Nenu, Changchung, China, 1986–. Member: Governing Bodies, Nat. Vegetable Res. Stn and Scottish Plant Breeding Stn, 1978–82; SERC Biological Scis Cttee, 1982–85; SERC Biotechnology Management Cttee, 1983–85; British Nat. Cttee for Biology, 1981–. Mem. Council, RSE, 1985– (Fellowship Sec., 1986–). Governor: East of Scotland Coll. of Agriculture, 1984–; Scottish Crops Res. Inst., 1986–. Trustee, Edinburgh Botanic Gdn (Sibbald) Trust, 1986–. Mem., Editorial Bds of Jl of Experimental Botany, 1981–85, Plant Science Letters, 1974–83, and New Phytologist (Trustee). *Publications:* (ed) Cell Division in Higher Plants, 1976; (jtly) Laboratory Manual of Plant Cell and Tissue Culture, 1982; (ed) Plant Cell Technology, 1986; contrib. scientific jls; chapters, articles and revs in books. *Recreations:* military history, photography, gardening, walking. *Address:* 9 Glenlockhart Valley, Edinburgh EH14 1DE. *T:* 031–443 8540.

YEOMAN, Philip Metcalfe, MD; FRCS; Consultant Orthopaedic Surgeon, Bath, since 1964; *b* 29 April 1923; *s* of William Yeoman, MD and Dorothy Young; *m* 1947, Idonea Evelyn Mary Scarrott; two *s* one *d*. *Educ:* Sedbergh; Cambridge (MA, MB BChir, MD); University Coll. Hosp. London. Flight Lieut, RAF Hosp., Ely, 1950–52. Lectr, Inst. of Orthopaedics, 1959–64. Mem. Council, RCS, 1984– (Mem., Court of Exmrs, 1980–; Hunterian Prof., 1983); Vice-Pres., British Orthopaedic Assoc., 1984–85 (Robert Jones Gold Medal, 1963; North American Travelling Fellow, 1964; Mem. Council, 1981–84); President: Section of Orthopaedics, RSocMed, 1983; North American Travelling Fellows, 1981–83. *Publications:* chapters on peripheral nerve injuries, brachial plexus injuries, bone tumours, surgical management of Rheumatoid arthritis of the cervical spine. *Recreations:* golf, gardening. *Address:* Broadmead, Monkton Combe, near Bath. *T:* Limpley Stoke 3294. *Club:* Army and Navy.

YERBURGH, family name of **Baron Alvingham.**

YERBY, Frank Garvin; Novelist; *b* 5 September 1916; *s* of Rufus Garvin Yerby and Wilhelmina Smythe; *m* 1956, Blanca Calle Pérez; two *s* two *d* of former marriage. *Educ:* Haines Institute; Paine College; Fisk Univ.; Univ. of Chicago. Teacher, Florida Agricultural and Mechanical Coll., 1939; Southern Univ. (Baton Rouge, Louisiana), 1940–41; War work: laboratory technician, Ford Motor Company, Detroit, 1941–44;

Ranger Aircraft, New York, 1944–45; writer since 1944; O. Henry Award for short story, 1944. *Publications:* The Foxes of Harrow, 1946; The Vixens, 1947; The Golden Hawk, 1948; Pride's Castle, 1949; Floodtide, 1950; A Woman Called Fancy, 1951; The Saracen Blade, 1952; The Devil's Laughter, 1953; Benton's Row, 1954; The Treasure of Pleasant Valley, 1955; Captain Rebel, 1956; Fairoaks, 1957; The Serpent and the Staff, 1958; Jarrett's Jade, 1959; Gillian, 1960; The Garfield Honor, 1961; Griffin's Way, 1962; The Old Gods Laugh, 1964; An Odor of Sanctity, 1965; Goat Song, 1967; Judas, My Brother, 1968; Speak Now, 1969; The Man from Dahomey, 1970; The Girl from Storyville, 1972; The Voyage Unplanned, 1974; Tobias and the Angel, 1975; A Rose for Ana María, 1976; Hail the Conquering Hero, 1977; A Darkness at Ingraham's Crest, 1978; Western, 1983; Devilseed, 1984; McKenzie's Hundred, 1985. *Recreations:* photography, painting. *Address:* c/o Wm Morris Agency, 1350 Avenue of the Americas, New York, NY 10019, USA. *Clubs:* Authors Guild (New York); Real Sociedad Hipica Española (Madrid).

YOCKLUNN, Sir John (Soong Chung), KCVO 1977; Kt 1975; Chief Librarian, Gippsland Institute of Advanced Education, since 1983; *b* Canton, China, 5 May 1933; *s* of late Charles Soong Yocklunn and Wui Sin Yocklunn, formerly of W Australia; *m* 1981, Patricia Ann Mehegan. *Educ:* Northam High Sch., W Australia; Univ. of W Australia (BA); Aust. Nat. Univ. (BA); Univ. of Sheffield (MA). ALA; ALAA. Dept of the Treasury, Canberra, 1959–63; Nat. Library of Australia, Canberra, 1964–67; Librarian-in-Charge, Admin Coll. of Papua New Guinea, Port Moresby, 1967–69; Exec. Officer, Public Service Board of Papua New Guinea, 1969–70; Librarian, Admin Coll. 1970–72; Principal Private Sec. to Chief Minister, 1972–73; study in UK, under James Cook Bicentenary Schol., 1973–74; on return, given task of organising a national library; Sen. Investigation Officer, Public Services Commn, 1974–77; Asst Sec. (Library Services), Dept of Educn (National Librarian of PNG), 1978–83. Chm., PNG Honours and Awards Cttee, 1975–83; Advr on Honours to PNG Govt, 1984–85; Consultant on estabt of new honours system, 1985–87. Vice-Pres., Pangu Pati, 1968–72; Nat. Campaign Manager for Pangu Pati for 1972 general elections in Papua New Guinea; Treasurer, Pangu Pati, 1973–80. Asst Dir, Visit of Prince of Wales to PNG, 1975; Dir, Visits of the Queen and Prince Philip to PNG, 1977 and 1982. Trustee, 1986–, Chm. of Friends, 1985–, Mus. of Chinese Australian Hist. *Publications:* The Charles Barrett Collection of Books relating to Papua New Guinea, 1967, 2nd edn 1969; articles on librarianship and politics in various jls. *Recreations:* book collecting, languages, cooking. *Address:* Gippsland Institute of Advanced Education, Churchill, Victoria 3842, Australia. *T:* (office) (051) 22 0420; (home) (051) 34 8303.

YOFFEY, Joseph Mendel, DSc, MD, FRCS; Visiting Professor, Hebrew University of Jerusalem, since 1969; Professor of Anatomy, University of Bristol, 1942–67, now Professor Emeritus; *b* 10 July 1902; *s* of Rabbi Israel Jacob Yoffey and Pere Jaffe; *m* 1940, Betty Gillis, LLB; three *d. Educ:* Manchester Grammar School; Univ. of Manchester. Leech Research Fellow, University of Manchester, 1926–27; Research Scholar, BMA, 1928–29; House Surgeon, Manchester Royal Infirmary, 1929–30; Asst Lectr in Anatomy, Univ. of Manchester, 1930; Senior Lectr in Anatomy, University College of South Wales and Monmouthshire, Cardiff; Hunterian Prof., RCS England, 1933 and 1940; Fellow of Rockefeller Foundn, 1937–39. Visiting Professor: Univ. of Washington, 1958; Univ. of Calif., San Francisco, 1967–68; John Curtin Sch. of Medical Research, ANU, 1968–69. Hon. Life Mem., Reticulendotheliol Soc., 1978; Hon. Mem., Amer. Assoc. of Anatomists, 1980. John Hunter Triennial Medal, RCS, 1968. Hon. LLD Manchester, 1973. Knight First Class of the Order of the Dannebrog (Denmark), 1959. *Publications:* Quantitative Cellular Hæmatology, 1960; Bone Marrow Reactions, 1966; (with Dr F. C. Courtice) Lymphatics, Lymph and the Lymphomyeloid Complex, 1970; Bone Marrow in Hypoxia and Rebound, 1973; (with M. Tavassoli) Bone Marrow: structure and function, 1983; numerous scientific papers. *Recreations:* music, walking, modern Hebrew. *Address:* 1 Rehov Degania, Beth Hakerem, Jerusalem, Israel. *T:* Jerusalem 525738.

YONG NYUK LIN; Member, Presidential Council for Minority Rights, Singapore; *b* Seremban, Malaya, 24 June 1918; *s* of late Yong Thean Yong and Chen Shak Moi; *m* 1939, Kwa Geok Lan; two *d. Educ:* Raffles Coll., Singapore. Science Master, King George V Sch., Seremban, Malaya, 1938–41; with Overseas Assurance Corp., Singapore, 1941 (resigned, as Gen. Manager, 1958). Legislative Assemblyman, Singapore, 1959–65, MP 1965–79; Minister for Educn, 1959–63; Chm., Singapore Harbour Bd, 1961–62; Minister for: Health, 1963–68; Communications, 1968–75; Minister without Portfolio, 1975–76; High Comr in London, 1975–76. Chm., Singapore Land/Marina Centre Development Private Ltd. *Address:* 50 Oei Tiong Ham Park, Singapore 1026.

YONGE, Dame (Ida) Felicity (Ann), DBE 1982 (MBE 1958); Special Adviser in Government Chief Whip's Office, 1979–83; *b* 28 Feb. 1921; *d* of Comdr W. H. N. Yonge, RN, and Kathleen Yonge. *Educ:* Convent of the Holy Child, St Leonard's-on-Sea. Served WRNS (2nd Officer), 1940–46. Purser's Office, P&OSN Co., 1947–50; Private Secretary: to Chairman of the Conservative Party, 1951–64; to Leader of the Opposition, 1964–65; to Opposition Chief Whip, 1965–70 and 1974–79; to Leader of House of Commons, 1970–74. *Recreations:* gardening, bridge. *Address:* 58 Leopold Road, Wimbledon, SW19 7JF.

YORK, Archbishop of, since 1983; **Most Rev. and Rt. Hon. John Stapylton Habgood,** PC 1983; MA, PhD; *b* 23 June 1927; *s* of Arthur Henry Habgood, DSO, MB, BCh, and Vera (*née* Chetwynd-Stapylton); *m* 1961, Rosalie Mary Anne Boston; two *s* two *d. Educ:* Eton; King's Coll., Cambridge (Hon. Fellow, 1986); Cuddesdon Coll., Oxford. Univ. Demonstrator in Pharmacology, Cambridge, 1950–53; Fellow of King's Coll., Cambridge, 1952–55; Curate of St Mary Abbots, Kensington, 1954–56; Vice-Principal of Westcott House, Cambridge, 1956–62; Rector of St John's Church, Jedburgh, 1962–67; Principal of Queen's College, Birmingham, 1967–73; Bishop of Durham, 1973–83. Moderator, Church and Society Sub-Unit, WCC. Hon. DD: Durham, 1975; Cambridge, 1984. *Publications:* Religion and Science, 1964; A Working Faith, 1980; Church and Nation in a Secular Age, 1983. *Recreation:* carpentry. *Address:* Bishopthorpe, York YO2 1QE. *Club:* Athenæum.

YORK, Dean of; *see* Southgate, Very Rev. J. E.

YORK, Archdeacon of; *see* Stanbridge, Ven. L. C.

YORK, Christopher, DL; *b* 27 July 1909; *s* of late Col Edward York; *m* 1934, Pauline Rosemary, *d* of late Sir Lionel Fletcher, CBE; one *s* three *d. Educ:* Eton; RMC Sandhurst. Joined The Royal Dragoons, India, 1930; retired, 1934, on to Supplementary Reserve; rejoined Regt, 1939, rank Major; joined Land Agents Soc., 1934, and passed examinations, acting as Land Agent until elected MP; MP (U) Harrogate Division, 1950–54 (Ripon Division of the West Riding, 1939–50); DL West Riding of Yorkshire, Later N Yorkshire, 1954; High Sheriff of Yorkshire, 1966. Pres., RASE, 1979. Hon. Fellow, Royal Veterinary Coll., 1971. *Recreation:* writing. *Address:* South Park, Long Marston, York. *TA* and *T:* Rufforth 357. *Clubs:* Boodle's, Carlton; Yorkshire (York).

YORK, Michael, (Michael York-Johnson); actor; *b* 27 March 1942; *s* of Joseph Johnson and Florence Chown; *m* 1968, Patricia Frances McCallum. *Educ:* Hurstpierpoint College; Bromley Grammar School; University College, Oxford (BA). *Stage:* Dundee Repertory Theatre, 1964; National Theatre Co., 1965; Outcry, NY, 1973; Bent, NY, 1980; Cyrano de Bergerac, Santa Fe, 1981; *films:* The Taming of the Shrew, 1966; Accident, 1966; Romeo and Juliet, 1967; Cabaret, 1971; England Made Me, 1971; The Three Musketeers, 1973; Murder on the Orient Express, 1974; Logan's Run, 1975; The Riddle of the Sands, 1978; Success is the Best Revenge, 1984; Dawn, 1985; Vengeance, 1986; *television:* Jesus of Nazareth, 1976; A Man Called Intrepid, 1978; For Those I Loved, 1981; The Weather in the Streets, 1983; The Master of Ballantrae, 1983; Space, 1984; The Far Country, 1985; Are you my Mother?, 1986. *Publication:* (contrib.) The Courage of Conviction, 1986. *Recreations:* travel, music, collecting theatrical memorabilia.

YORK, Susannah; actress and writer; *b* 9 Jan. 1942; *d* of William Fletcher and Joan Bowring; *m* 1960, Michael Wells (marr. diss. 1976); one *s* one *d. Educ:* Marr Coll., Troon, Scotland; RADA, London. *Films* include: The Greengage Summer, 1961; Freud, 1962; Tom Jones, 1963; A Man for All Seasons, 1966; The Killing of Sister George, 1968; They Shoot Horses, Don't They, 1969; Zee and Co., 1971; Images, 1972. *Theatre* includes: Wings of a Dove, 1964; A Singular Man, 1965; The Maids, 1974; Peter Pan, 1977; The Singular Life of Albert Nobbs, 1978; Hedda Gabler, New York 1981, London 1982; Agnes of God, 1983; The Human Voice (own trans. of Cocteau), 1984; Fatal Attraction, Haymarket, 1985; The Apple Cart, Haymarket, 1986. TV series We'll Meet Again, 1982. *Publications:* In Search of Unicorns, 1973, rev. edn 1984; Larks Castle, 1975, rev. edn, 1985; (ed) The Big One, 1984. *Recreations:* family, writing, gardening, reading, houses, riding, languages, travelling, theatre, cinema, walking. *Address:* c/o Jeremy Conway, 109 Eagleton House, Jermyn Street, W1.

YORK-JOHNSON, Michael; *see* York, M.

YORKE, family name of **Earl of Hardwicke.**

YORKE, Richard Michael, QC 1971; a Recorder of the Crown Court, 1972–83; *b* 13 July 1930; *e s* of Gilbert Victor Yorke, Civil Engineer. *Educ:* Solihull Sch., Warwickshire; Balliol Coll., Oxford (MA). Commissioned 2nd Lt, RA, July 1949 (Prize of Honour, Best Officer Cadet); Lieut, Honourable Artillery Company, 1951; Captain, 1953. Asst to Sec., British Road Services, 1953–56. Called to Bar, Gray's Inn, 1956 (Lee Prizeman), Bencher 1981; Inner Temple, *ad eund.*, 1968; Barrister, Supreme Court of NSW and High Court of Australia, 1972; QC NSW 1974. Consultant, Bodington & Yturbe, Paris, 1973–82. Contested (C): Durham, 1966; Loughborough, Feb. and Oct. 1974. Pres., Civil Aviation Review Bd, 1972–75. Vice-Chm., Senate/Law Soc. Jt Working Party on Banking Law, 1975–83; Member: Special Panel, Transport Tribunal, 1976–85; Panel of Arbitrators, Amer. Arbitrators Assoc., 1983–; Supporting Mem., London Maritime Arbitrators Assoc., 1984–; Mem., CIArb, 1985–. Voluntary Governor, Bart's Hospital, 1974; Governor, Sadler's Wells Trust, 1985–. *Recreations:* skiing, sailing, tennis, flying. *Address:* 4 and 5 Gray's Inn Square, Gray's Inn, WC1R 5AY. *T:* 01–404 5252. *Telex:* 895 3743 Gralaw; *Cables:* Graylegal; (home) 5 Cliveden Place, SW1W 8LA. *T:* 01–730 6054; Eden Roc, Rue de Ransou, 1936 Verbier, Switzerland. *T:* (26) 76504; La Mandragore, Tourrette-sur-Loup, AM, France. *T:* (93) 24 18 08. *Clubs:* Cavalry and Guards, Royal Ocean Racing, St Stephen's Constitutional; Hurlingham; Island Sailing (Cowes).

YORKSHIRE, EAST RIDING, Archdeacon of; *see* Vickers, Ven. M. E.

YOUDE, Sir Edward, GCMG 1983 (KCMG 1977; CMG 1968); MBE 1949; Governor and Commander-in-Chief, Hong Kong, since 1982; *b* 19 June 1924; *m* 1951, Pamela Fitt; two *d. Educ:* Sch. of Oriental and African Studies, Univ. of London. RNVR, 1943–46. Joined Foreign Office, 1947; Third Sec., Nanking and Peking, 1948; Foreign Office, 1951; Second Sec., Peking, 1953; First Secretary: Washington, 1956–59; Peking, 1960–62; Foreign Office, 1962–65; Counsellor and Head of Chancery, UK Mission to UN, 1965–69; Private Secretary to the Prime Minister, 1969–70; IDC, 1970–71; Head of Personnel Services Dept, FCO, 1971–73; Asst Under-Sec. of State, FCO, 1973–74; Ambassador to China, 1974–78; Dep. Under-Sec. of State (Chief Clerk), FCO, 1978; Dep. to Permanent Under-Sec. of State, and Chief Clerk, FCO, 1980–82. *Recreations:* walking, theatre, music. *Address:* Government House, Hong Kong.

YOUDS, His Honour Edward Ernest; a Circuit Judge, Bedford, 1972–85; *b* 21 Nov. 1910; *s* of late Edward Youds. *Educ:* Birkenhead Sch.; Magdalene Coll., Cambridge. BA, LLB (Hons) Cantab. Called to Bar, Gray's Inn, 1936. Practised on Northern Circuit as Barrister-at-law. Served 1940–45, France and Germany (despatches, 1945). Dep. Chm., Lancs County Sessions, 1961–66; County Court Judge, 1966–69; Puisne Judge, High Court, Uganda, 1969–72.

YOUELL, Rev. Canon George; *b* 23 Dec. 1910; *s* of late Herbert Youell, Beccles; *m* 1st, 1936, Gertrude Barron (*d* 1982), *d* of late J. Irvine, West Hartlepool; two *s* three *d;* 2nd, 1983, Mary Nina, *d* of late Revd H. G. Phillipson. *Educ:* Beccles; St Michaels; Hartley Coll., Manchester; St Stephen's House, Oxford; Univ. of Keele (MA 1969). Ordained, 1933; Curate, St John's, Chester, 1933; Clerical Dir of Industrial Christian Fellowship, 1937; chaplain attached to 2nd Bn Grenadier Guards (BEF and Guards Armoured Div.), 1939; Sen. Chaplain to Forces: Nigeria, 1942; Woolwich and SE London, 1944; Nigeria and Gold Coast, 1945; Rector of Ightfield with Calverhall, Salop, 1947; Rural Dean of Leek, 1952–56; Vicar of Leek, 1952–61; Archdeacon of Stoke-upon-Trent, 1956–70; Vicar of Horton, Leek, 1968–70; Chaplain, Univ. of Keele, 1961–68; Hon. Canon, Lichfield Cathedral, 1967–70; Canon Residentiary of Ely Cathedral, 1970–81; Vice-Dean and Treas., 1973–81. *Publications:* Africa Marches, 1949; contributor on colonial and sociological affairs to the Guardian, 1947–51. *Recreations:* fell walking, gardening. *Address:* Stranton Cottage, Wattisfield Road, Walsham le Willows, near Bury St Edmunds, Suffolk. *T:* Walsham le Willows 8888.

YOUENS, Ven. Archdeacon John Ross, CB 1970; OBE 1959; MC 1946; Chaplain to the Queen 1969–84; Senior Treasurer, Corporation of the Sons of the Clergy, 1982–84; *b* 29 Sept. 1914; *e s* of late Canon F. A. C. Youens; *m* 1940, Pamela Gordon Lincoln (*née* Chandler); one *s* (two *d* decd). *Educ:* Buxton Coll.; Kelham Theological Coll. Curate of Warsop, Notts, 1939–40. Commissioned RA Chaplains' Dept, 1940; Aldershot and SE Comd, 1940–42; Sen. Chaplain: 59 Inf. Div., 1942; Chatham, 1943; 2nd Army Troops, June 1944; Guards Armd Div., Nov. 1944–45; 3rd Inf. Div. in Egypt and Palestine, 1945–48; 7th Armd Div. in Germany, 1948–50; Aldershot, 1950–51; DACG, Egypt, 1951–53; Tripoli, 1953–54; Sen. Chaplain, RMA Sandhurst, 1955–58; DACG, Gibraltar, 1958–60; ACG War Office, 1960–61, Rhine Army, 1961–66; Chaplain General to the Forces, 1966–74; Archdeacon Emeritus, 1974. Dep. Chairman, Keston Coll., Centre for the Study of Religion and Communism (Mem. Council, 1975–84). *Address:* Fir Tree Cottage, Stedham, near Midhurst, W Sussex GU29 0QN. *T:* Midhurst 3588. *Clubs:* Cavalry and Guards (Hon. Mem.), MCC.

YOUENS, Sir Peter (William), Kt 1965; CMG 1962; OBE 1960; *b* 29 April 1916; 2nd *s* of late Canon F. A. C. Youens; *m* 1943, Diana Stephanie, *d* of Edward Hawkins, Southacre, Norfolk; two *d. Educ:* King Edward VII's School, Sheffield; Wadham College,

Oxford. MA (Oxon), 1938. Joined Colonial Administrative Service; naval service, 1939–40. Sub-Lt, Cadet S. L., 1939; Asst Dist Comr, 1942; Dist Comr, 1948; Colony Comr and Member, Sierra Leone Legislative Council, 1950; Asst Sec., Nyasaland, 1951; Dep. Chief Sec., 1953–63; Secretary to the Prime Minister and to the Cabinet, Malawi, 1964–66 (Nyasaland, 1963–64); Mem., Nyasaland Legislative Council, 1954–61. Retired, 1966. Exec. Dir, Lonrho Ltd, 1966–69, Non-Exec. Dir, 1980–81, Exec. Dir, 1981–; Partner, John Tyzack & Partners Ltd, 1969–81; Dir, Oxford Playhouse Company (Anvil Productions Ltd), 1978–. *Address:* The Old Parsonage, Hurstborne Priors, Whitchurch, Hants. *Clubs:* East India, Devonshire, Sports and Public Schools; Vincent's (Oxford).

YOUNG, family name of **Baron Kennet, Baroness Young** and **Barons Young of Dartington** and **Young of Graffham.**

YOUNG; *see* Hughes-Young, family name of Baron St Helens.

YOUNG, Baroness *cr* 1971 (Life Peer), of Farnworth in the County Palatine of Lancaster; **Janet Mary Young;** PC 1981; Minister of State, Foreign and Commonwealth Office, since 1983; *b* 23 Oct. 1926; *d* of John Norman Leonard Baker and Phyllis Marguerite Baker (*née* Hancock); *m* 1950, Geoffrey Tyndale Young; three *d. Educ:* Dragon School Oxford, Headington School, and in America; St Anne's Coll., Oxford; MA (Politics, Philosophy and Economics); Hon. Fellow, 1978. Baroness in Waiting (Govt Whip), 1972–73; Parly Under-Sec. of State, DoE, 1973–74; Minister of State, DES, 1979–81; Chancellor, Duchy of Lancaster, 1981–82; Leader of House of Lords, 1981–83; Lord Privy Seal, 1982–83. A Vice-Chm., Cons. Party Organisation, 1975–83, Dep. Chm., 1977–79. Co-Chm., Women's Nat. Commn, 1979–83. Councillor Oxford City Council, 1957; Alderman, 1967–72; Leader of Conservative Group, 1967–72. Dir, UK Provident Instn, 1975–79. Mem., BR Adv. Bd, Western Reg., 1977–79. Hon. FICE. Hon. DCL Mt Holyoke Coll., 1982. *Recreation:* music. *Address:* House of Lords, SW1A 0PW.

YOUNG OF DARTINGTON, Baron *cr* 1978 (Life Peer), of Dartington in the County of Devon; **Michael Young,** BSc (Econ), MA, PhD; Director, Institute of Community Studies since 1953; Deputy Chairman, Dartington Hall, since 1980 (Trustee, since 1942); *b* 9 Aug. 1915; father a musician, mother a writer; *m* 1st, 1945, Joan Lawson; two *s* one *d*; 2nd, 1960, Sasha Moorsom; one *s* one *d. Educ:* Dartington Hall Sch.; London Univ. Barrister, Gray's Inn. Dir of Political and Economic Planning, 1941–45; Sec., Research Dept, Lab. Party, 1945–51. Chairman: Social Science Research Council, 1965–68; Dartington Amenity Research Trust, 1967–; Internat. Extension Coll., 1970–; Nat. Consumer Council, 1975–77; Mutual Aid Centre, 1977–; Coll. of Health, 1983–; Argo Venture, 1984–; Dir, Mauritius Coll. of the Air, 1972; Member: Central Adv. Council for Education, 1963–66; NEDC, 1975–78; Policy Cttee, SDP, 1981–83; President: Consumer's Assoc., 1965– (Chm., 1956–65); National Extension Coll., 1971– (Chm., 1962–71); Adv. Centre for Educn, 1976– (Chm., 1959–76). Chm., Tawney Soc., 1982–84. Fellow, Churchill Coll., Cambridge, 1961–66; Vis. Prof. of Extension Educn, Ahmadu Bello Univ., Nigeria, 1974; Regents' Lectr, UCLA, 1985. Hon. LittD Sheffield, 1965; DUniv Open, 1973; Hon. DLitt Adelaide, 1974; Hon. LLD Exeter, 1982. Hon. Fellow: LSE, 1978; Plymouth Polytechnic, 1980; QMC, 1983. *Publications:* Family and Kinship in East London (with Peter Willmott), 1957; The Rise of the Meritocracy, 1958; Family and Class in a London Suburb (with Peter Willmott), 1960; Innovation and Research in Education, 1965; Learning Begins at Home (with Patrick McGeeney), 1968; (ed) Forecasting and the Social Sciences, 1968; The Symmetrical Family (with Peter Willmott), 1973; (ed) The Poverty Report, 1974 and 1975; (with Marianne Rigge) Mutual Aid in a Selfish Society, 1979; (with others) Distance Teaching for the Third World, 1980; The Elmhirsts of Dartington—the creation of an Utopian Community, 1982; (with Marianne Rigge) Revolution From Within: co-operatives and co-operation in British industry, 1983; Social Scientist as Innovator, 1984. *Recreation:* painting. *Address:* 18 Victoria Park Square, E2 9PF.

YOUNG OF GRAFFHAM, Baron *cr* 1984 (Life Peer), of Graffham in the County of W Sussex; **David Ivor Young;** PC 1984; Secretary of State for Employment, since 1985; *b* 27 Feb. 1932; *s* of late Joseph and of Rebecca Young; *m* 1956, Lita Marianne Shaw; two *d. Educ:* Christ's Coll., Finchley; University Coll., London (LLB Hons). Admitted solicitor, 1956. Exec., Great Universal Stores Ltd, 1956–61; Chairman: Eldonwall Ltd, 1961–75; Manufacturers Hanover Property Services Ltd, 1974–84; Dir, Town & City Properties Ltd, 1972–75. Chairman: British ORT, 1975–80, Pres., 1980–82; Admin. Cttee, World ORT Union, 1980–84. Dir, Centre for Policy Studies, 1979–82 (Mem., Management Bd, 1977); Mem., English Industrial Estates Corp., 1980–82; Chm., Manpower Services Commn, 1982–84. Industrial Adviser, 1979–80, Special Adviser, 1980–82, DoI; Minister without Portfolio, 1984–85. Mem., NEDC, 1982–. Chm., Internat. Council of Jewish Social and Welfare Services, 1981–84. Hon. FRPS, 1981. *Recreations:* golf, fishing, computing. *Address:* c/o 88 Brook Street, W1. *Clubs:* Savile; West Sussex Golf.
See also B. A. Rix.

YOUNG, Prof. Alec David, OBE 1964; MA; FRS 1973; FEng; AFAIAA; Professor and Head of the Department of Aeronautical Engineering, Queen Mary College, London University, 1954–78, now Emeritus; Vice-Principal, Queen Mary College, 1966–78; *b* 15 Aug. 1913; *s* of Isaac Young and Katherine (*née* Freeman); *m* 1st, 1937, Dora Caplan (*d* 1970); two *s* one *d*; 2nd, 1971, Rena Waldmann (*née* Szafer). *Educ:* Caius Coll., Cambridge. Wrangler, Mathematical Tripos, 1935. Research Student in Aeronautics, Cambridge, 1935–36; Mem. of staff, Aerodynamics Dept, Royal Aircraft Estab., 1936–46; College of Aeronautics: Senior Lectr and Dep. Head of Dept of Aerodynamics, 1946–50; Prof. and Head of Dept of Aerodynamics, 1950–54. Dean, Faculty of Engineering, Univ. of London, 1962–66; Mem. Senate, Univ. of London, 1970–78. Mem. various Cttees of Aeronautical Research Council, Chm. of Council, 1968–71. Chm., Bd of Direction, Von Karman Institute for Fluid Dynamics, 1964; Mem., Advisory Bd, RAF Coll., Cranwell, 1966. Gold Medal, 1972, Royal Aeronautical Soc. (Past Chm., Aerodynamics Data Sheets Cttee); FRAeS, 1951, Hon. FRAeS 1984; FEng 1976. Ludwig Prandtl Ring, Deutsche Gesellschaft für Luft-und Raumfahrt, 1976; Von Karman Medal, AGARD, 1979. Commandeur de l'Ordre de Leopold, 1976. Fellow QMC, 1980. Editor, Progress in Aerospace Sciences, 1983. *Publications:* various, of Aeronautical Research Council, Coll. of Aeronautics Reports series; articles in Aeronautical Quarterly and Jl of Royal Aeronautical Soc., Quarterly Jl of Mechanics and Applied Mathematics, and Aircraft Engineering. Co-author of An Elementary Treatise on the Mechanics of Fluids, 1960, 2nd edn 1970; Aircraft Excrescence Drag, 1981. *Recreations:* drama, sketching. *Address:* 70 Gilbert Road, Cambridge CB4 3PD. *T:* Cambridge 354625.

YOUNG, Alexander, FRNCM; retired as free-lance concert and opera singer; Head of Department of Vocal Studies, Royal Northern College of Music, Manchester, 1973–86; *b* London; *m* 1948, Jean Anne Prewett; one *s* one *d. Educ:* secondary; (scholar) Royal Coll. of Music, London; studied in London with late Prof. Pollmann, of Vienna State Academy. FRNCM 1977. Served War, HM Forces, 1941–46. Has regular engagements with the BBC and has sung in the USA, Canada, and most European countries, as well as frequently in Britain. First operatic rôle (tenor), as Scaramuccio in Strauss' Ariadne, Edin. Fest., with Glyndebourne Opera, 1950; parts at Glyndebourne, and began broadcasting for BBC, 1951 (subseq. incl. opera, oratorio, recitals, light music, etc). First appearances: with English Opera Group, world Première of Lennox Berkeley's opera, A Dinner Engagement, 1954; also appeared at Royal Festival Hall, several times with Sir Thomas Beecham, in Mozart Requiem; at Sadler's Wells Opera, as Eisenstein in Die Fledermaus, 1959, and subsequently in many roles such as: Ramiro in La Cenerentola; title role in Count Ory; Almaviva in The Barber of Seville; notable roles include: Tom in Stravinsky's Rake's Progress (which he created for British audiences); David in Die Meistersinger; title role in Mozart's Idomeneo. At Covent Garden sang in: Strauss's Arabella; Britten's A Midsummer Night's Dream. Oratorio roles include: Evangelist in Bach Passions; Elgar's Dream of Gerontius; Britten's War Requiem. Was regularly engaged by Welsh National Opera and Scottish Opera. Many commercial recordings, especially of Handel oratorios and operas, as well as The Rake's Progress conducted by the composer. Lieder recitals a speciality. *Recreation:* railway modelling.

YOUNG, Andrew; Mayor of Atlanta, Georgia, since 1982; *b* New Orleans, La, 12 March 1932; *s* of Andrew J. Young and Daisy Fuller; *m* 1954, Jean Childs; one *s* three *d. Educ:* Howard Univ., USA; Hartford Theological Seminary. Ordained, United Church of Christ, 1955; Pastor, Thomasville, Ga, 1955–57; Associate Dir for Youth Work, Nat. Council of Churches, 1957–61; Admin. Christian Educn Programme, United Church of Christ, 1961–64; Mem. Staff, Southern Christian Leadership Conf., 1961–70; Exec. Dir, 1964–70; Exec. Vice-Pres., 1967–70; elected to US House of Representatives from 5th District of Georgia, 1972 (first Black Congressman from Georgia in 101 years); re-elected 1974 and 1976; US Ambassador to UN, 1977–79. Chairman: Atlanta Community Relations Commn, 1970–72; National Democratic voter registration drive, 1976; during 1960s organized voter registration and community develt programmes. Holds numerous hon. degrees and awards. *Address:* The Office of the Mayor, 68 Mitchell Street SW, Atlanta, Georgia 30303, USA.

YOUNG, Bertram Alfred, OBE 1980; dramatic critic, since 1964, and arts editor, 1971–77, The Financial Times; *b* 20 Jan. 1912; *y* (twin) *s* of Bertram William Young and Dora Elizabeth Young (*née* Knight); unmarried. *Educ:* Highgate. Served with Artists Rifles, 1930–35, and Lancs Fusiliers, KAR and Staff, 1939–48; Asst Editor, Punch, 1949–62; Dramatic Critic, Punch, 1962–64. Mem., British Council Drama Adv. Cttee, 1973–83; Pres., Critics' Circle, 1978–80. Hon. Kentucky Col, 1980. *Publications:* Tooth and Claw, 1958; How to Avoid People, 1963; Bechuanaland, 1966; Cabinet Pudding, 1967; Colonists from Space, 1979; The Mirror up to Nature, 1982; The Rattigan Version, 1986; author of about 20 radio plays broadcast 1938–49. *Recreation:* music (consumer only). *Address:* Clyde House, Station Street, Cheltenham GL50 3LX. *T:* Cheltenham 581485. *Club:* Garrick.

YOUNG, Air Vice-Marshal Brian Pashley, CB 1972; CBE 1960 (OBE 1944); Commandant General, RAF Regiment, 1968–73; *b* 5 May 1918; *s* of Kenneth Noel Young and Flora Elizabeth Young, Natal, S Africa; *m* 1942, Patricia Josephine, *d* of Thomas Edward Cole, Bedford; three *s* two *d. Educ:* Michaelhouse, Natal, SA; RAF Coll., Cranwell. Fighter Comd, UK and France, 1938–40 (wounded); Hosp., 1941–42; Coastal Comd, N Ire and Western Isles, 1942–43; Aden and Persian Gulf, 1944; Staff Coll., Haifa, 1945; Middle East, 1946–47; Air Min., 1948–50; Bomber Comd HQ No 1 Gp, Hemswell/Gaydon, 1951–57; HQ Bomber Comd, 1958–60; NATO, Fontainebleau, Asst Chief of Staff, Intelligence, 1960–62; IDC 1963; AOC, Central Reconnaisance Estabt, 1964–67. Planning Inspector, DoE, 1973–83. Rep. RAF: athletics, 1939, Rugby, 1947–48. *Address:* Chapel Walk House, The Street, Didmarton, Glos. *Club:* Royal Air Force.

YOUNG, Sir Brian (Walter Mark), Kt 1976; MA; Chairman, Christian Aid, since 1983; *b* 23 Aug. 1922; *er s* of late Sir Mark Young, GCMG and Josephine (*née* Price); *m* 1947, Fiona Marjorie, *o d* of late Allan, 16th Stewart of Appin, and Marjorie (*née* Ballance); one *s* two *d. Educ:* Eton (King's Schol.); King's College, Cambridge (Schol.). Served in RNVR, mainly in destroyers, 1941–45. First class hons in Part I, 1946, and Part II, 1947, of Classical Tripos; Porson Prize, 1946; Winchester Reading Prize, 1947; BA 1947; MA 1952. Assistant Master at Eton, 1947–52; Headmaster of Charterhouse, 1952–64; Dir, Nuffield Foundn, 1964–70; Dir-Gen., IBA (formerly ITA), 1970–82. Member: Central Advisory Council for Education, 1956–59 (Crowther Report); Central Religious Adv. Cttee of BBC and ITA, 1960–64; Bd of Centre for Educn Develt Overseas, 1969–72; Arts Council of GB, 1983–; Exec. Cttee, British Council of Churches, 1983–; Chm., Associated Bd of the Royal Schs of Music, 1984–. A Managing Trustee, Nuffield Foundn, 1978–; Trustee: Lambeth Palace Liby, 1984–; Imperial War Mus., 1985–. Hon. DLitt Heriot-Watt, 1980. *Publications:* Via Vertendi, 1952; Intelligent Reading (with P. D. R. Gardiner), 1964. *Recreations:* music, travel, history, problems. *Address:* Hill End, Woodhill Avenue, Gerrards Cross, Bucks. *T:* Gerrards Cross 887793.

YOUNG, Rev. Canon (Cecil) Edwyn, CVO 1983; Chaplain, The Queen's Chapel of the Savoy, and Chaplain of the Royal Victorian Order, 1974–83; Chaplain to the Queen, 1972–83; *b* 29 April 1913; *er s* of Cecil Morgan Young and Doris Edith Virginia Young, Colombo, Ceylon; *m* 1944, Beatrice Mary, *e d* of Percy Montague Rees and Beatrice Rees; two *s* one *d. Educ:* Radley Coll.; Dorchester Missionary College. Curate, St Peter's, London Docks, 1936–41; Priest in Charge, St Francis, N Kensington, 1941–44; Rector of Broughton with Ripton Regis, 1944–47; Vicar of St Silas, Pentonville, 1947–53; Rector of Stepney, 1953–64, and Rural Dean of Stepney, 1959–64; Prebendary of St Paul's, 1959–64; Rector and Rural Dean of Liverpool, 1964–73; Canon Diocesan, 1965–73. Commissary, Diocese of North Queensland, 1959–, Canon to the Ordinary, 1974–. Chaplain: Worshipful Co. of Distillers, 1974–; Weavers' Co., 1977–; to Chm., Freight Forwarders Inst., 1974–. Pres., Sion College, 1963–64. Hon. Chaplain, HCIMA. *Publications:* Young and Graceful, 1962; No Fun Like Work, 1970; (contrib.) Father Groser, East End Priest, 1971. *Recreations:* meeting people; wild flowers; the theatre, especially music hall; watching cricket. *Address:* Flat 1, 45 Brunswick Square, Hove, Sussex. *Clubs:* Greenroom, City Livery.

YOUNG, Christopher Godfrey; His Honour Judge Young; a Circuit Judge, since 1980; *b* 9 Sept. 1932; *s* of the late Harold Godfrey Young, MB, ChB, and Gladys Mary Young; *m* 1969, Jeanetta Margaret (*d* 1984), *d* of Halford and Dorothy Vaughan; one *s. Educ:* Bedford Sch.; King's Coll., Univ. of London (LLB Hons 1954). Called to the Bar, Gray's Inn, 1957; Midland and Oxford Circuit, 1959; a Recorder of the Crown Court, 1975–79. Chm., Maidwell with Draughton Parish Council, 1973–76. *Recreations:* music, natural history, gardening. *Address:* Stockshill House, Duddington, near Stamford, Lincs. *Club:* Northampton and County (Northampton).

YOUNG, Colin, OBE 1976; Director, National Film and Television School of Great Britain, since 1970; *b* 5 April 1927; *s* of Colin Young and Agnes Holmes Kerr Young; *m* 1960, Kristin Ohman; two *s. Educ:* Bellahouston Academy, Glasgow; Univs of Glasgow, St Andrews and California (Los Angeles). Theatre and film critic, Bon Accord, Aberdeen, 1951; cameraman, editor, writer, director, 1953–; producer, 1967–; UCLA (Motion Pictures): Instructor, 1956–59; Asst Prof., 1959–64; Assoc. Prof., 1964–68; Prof., 1968–70, Head, Motion Picture Div., Theater Arts Dept, UCLA, 1964–65; Chm., Dept of Theater Arts, 1965–70. Res. Associate, Centre Nat. de Recherche Scientifique, Paris,

1984; Andrew W. Mellon Vis. Prof. in Humanities, Rice Univ., Houston, Texas, 1985–86. Vice-Chm., 1972–76, Chm., 1976–, Edinburgh Film Festival; Governor, BFI, 1974–80. Member: Arts Council Film Cttee, 1972–76; Public Media Panel, Nat. Endowment for Arts, Washington, 1972–77; Gen. Adv. Council, BBC, 1973–78; Council of Management, BAFTA, 1974–81; Exec. Cttee, Centre International de Liaison des Ecoles de Cinéma et de Télévision, 1974– (Pres., 1980–); Nat. Film Finance Corp., 1979–85. FBKS 1975. Chm., Cttee on Educational Policy, UCLA, 1968–69. London Editor, Film Quarterly, 1970– (Los Angeles Editor, 1958–68). Michael Balcon Award, BAFTA, 1983. *Publications:* various articles in collections of film essays including Principles of Visual Anthropology, 1975; experimental film essay for Unesco, 1963; ethnographic film essay for Unesco, 1966; contribs to Film Quarterly, Sight and Sound, Jl of Aesthetic Education, Jl of the Producers Guild of America, Kosmorama (Copenhagen), etc. *Address:* National Film and Television School, Beaconsfield, Bucks.

YOUNG, David Edward Michael, QC 1980; *b* 30 Sept. 1940; *s* of George Henry Edward Young and Audrey Young; *m* 1968, Ann de Bromhead; two *d*. *Educ:* Monkton Combe Sch.; Hertford Coll., Oxford (MA). Called to the Bar, Lincoln's Inn, 1966; practising at Chancery Bar, specialising in indust. property work (patents, trade marks, copyright and restrictive trade practices). *Publication:* (co-ed) Terrell on the Law of Patents, 12th edn 1971, 13th edn 1982; Passing Off, 1985. *Recreations:* field sports, tennis, ski-ing. *Address:* Gussage House, Gussage All Saints, Wimborne, Dorset BH21 5ET.

YOUNG, (David) Junor; HM Diplomatic Service; Counsellor (Commercial), Bonn, since 1986; *b* 23 April 1934; *m* 1954, Kathleen Brooks; two *s* two *d*. *Educ:* Robert Gordon's College. Joined Foreign Office, 1951; served Berlin, Ankara, South Africa, DSAO, Port Louis, Belgrade, 1951–75; Consul (Comm.), Stuttgart, 1978–81; First Sec., Kampala, 1981–84; Consul Gen., Hamburg, 1984–86. *Recreations:* fishing, shooting. *Address:* c/o Foreign and Commonwealth Office, SW1A 2AH; Pine Cottage, Hintlesham, Suffolk. *Club:* Naval and Military.

YOUNG, Rt. Rev. David Nigel de Lorentz; *see* Ripon, Bishop of.

YOUNG, Lt-Gen. Sir David (Tod), KBE 1980; CB 1977; DFC 1952; Chairman, Cairntech Ltd, Edinburgh, since 1983; GOC Scotland and Governor of Edinburgh Castle, 1980–82; *b* 17 May 1926; *s* of late William Young and Davina Tod Young; *m* 1950, Joyce Marian Melville; two *s*. *Educ:* George Watson's Coll., Edinburgh. Commissioned, The Royal Scots (The Royal Regt), 1945 (Col, 1975–80). Attached Glider Pilot Regt, 1949–52; Bt Lt-Col, 1964; Mil. Asst to Dep. Chief of Gen. Staff, MoD, 1964–67; commanded 1st Bn The Royal Scots (The Royal Regt), 1967–69; Col Gen. Staff, Staff Coll., 1969–70; Comdr, 12th Mechanized Bde, 1970–72; Dep. Mil. Sec., MoD, 1972–74; Comdr Land Forces, NI, 1975–77; Dir of Infantry, 1977–80. Col Comdt: Scottish Div., 1980–82; UDR, 1986–. Pres., ACFA, Scotland, 1984–. HM Comr, Queen Victoria Sch., Dunblane, 1984–. Chm., St Mary's Cathedral Workshop Ltd, 1986–. Chm. Scottish Cttee, Marie Curie Meml Foundn, 1986– (Mem., 1983–); Governor, St Columba's Hospice, Edinburgh, 1986–. *Recreations:* golf, shooting, spectator of sports. *Address:* c/o Royal Bank of Scotland plc, 83 Princes Street, Edinburgh EH2 2ER. *Clubs:* Royal Scots, New (Edinburgh).

YOUNG, David Wright; MP (Lab) Bolton South East, since 1983 (Bolton East, Feb. 1974–1983); teacher; *b* Greenock, Scotland, 12 Oct. 1930. *Educ:* Greenock Academy; Glasgow Univ.; St Paul's Coll., Cheltenham. Head of History Dept; subseq. insurance executive. Joined Labour Party, 1955; contested: South Worcestershire, 1959; Banbury, 1965; Bath, 1970. PPS to Sec. of State for Defence, 1977–79. Formerly Alderman, Nuneaton Borough Council; Councillor, Nuneaton District Council. Chm., Coventry East Labour Party, 1964–68. Member: NUPE; Co-operative Party. Is especially interested in comprehensive educn, defence, pensions, economics. *Recreations:* reading, motoring. *Address:* House of Commons, SW1A 0AA.

YOUNG, Donald Anthony, FIGasE; Regional Chairman, British Gas plc Southern (formerly Southern Region, British Gas Corporation), since 1983; *b* 23 June 1933; *s* of Cyril Charles Young and Sarah Young; *m* 1960, June (*née* Morrey); two *d*. *Educ:* Stockport Secondary Sch. FIGasE 1969. National Service, 2nd Lieut REME, 1953–55. North Western Gas Bd, 1949–60; E Midlands Gas Bd, 1960–68; Gas Council Terminal Manager, Bacton Natural Gas Reception Terminal, 1968–70; Gas Council Plant Ops Engr, 1970–77; Regional Dep. Chm., N Thames Gas, 1977–79; Dir (Operations), Prodn & Supply Div., British Gas HQ, 1979–83. CBIM 1986. *Recreations:* gardening, walking. *Address:* c/o British Gas plc Southern, 80 St Mary's Road, Southampton SO9 5AT.

YOUNG, Dr Edith Isabella, CBE 1964; *b* 7 March 1904; *d* of William Ross Young and Margaret Ramsay Young (*née* Hill). *Educ:* High School of Stirling; Univ. of Glasgow. BSc 1924, MA (1st cl. Hons Mathematics and Natural Philosophy) 1925. HM Inspector of Schools, Scottish Educn Dept, 1935–64; HM Inspector, in charge of Dundee and Angus, 1946–52; HM Chief Inspector, Highland Div., 1952–64. UNESCO expert on the teaching of science in Yugoslavia, Oct. 1956–Feb. 1957; UK Deleg., UNESCO Conf., Belgrade, 1960; Mem. Council for Technical Educn and Trg for Overseas Countries, 1964–68 (Chm., Women's Gp); UK Deleg. to Commonwealth Conf. on Trg of Technicians in Huddersfield, 1966; Co-Chm., Women's Nat. Commn, 1971–73; Pres., 1967–70, Hon. Vice-Pres. (for life), 1983, British Fedn of Univ. Women. Chairman: Northern Area Nurse Trng Cttee, 1967–81; Inverness Hosp. Bd, 1968–74. Hon. LLD Southampton, 1967. *Recreations:* sundry. *Address:* 36 Broadstone Park, Inverness IV2 3LA. *T:* Inverness 233216. *Clubs:* Royal Over-Seas League, University Women's.

YOUNG, Edward Preston, DSO 1944; DSC 1943; writer and retired book designer; *b* 17 Nov. 1913; *m* 1st, 1945, Diana Lilian Graves (marr. diss.); two *d*; 2nd, 1956, Mary Reoch Cressall. *Educ:* Highgate Sch. Served War, 1940–45: RNVR; entered submarine service 1940 (despatches, DSC); first RNVR officer to command operational submarine, 1943 (DSO, Bar to DSC); temp. Commander RNVR, 1945. Man. Dir, Rainbird Publishing Gp Ltd, 1970–73. *Publications:* One of Our Submarines, 1952; Look at Lighthouses, 1961; The Fifth Passenger, 1962; Look at Submarines, 1964. *Address:* 15 Maple Walk, Rustington, W Sussex.

YOUNG, Rev. Canon Edwyn; *see* Young, Rev. Canon C. E.

YOUNG, Eric, OBE 1976; HM Diplomatic Service, retired; Editor, Control Risks Information Services, since 1984; *b* 16 Nov. 1924; *s* of late Robert Young, MBE, and Emily Florence Young, Doncaster; *m* 1949, Sheila Hutchinson; three *s* one *d*. *Educ:* Maltby Grammar Sch.; Sheffield Univ. (BA 1948). Served War, RN, 1943–46. Editorial staff: Sheffield Telegraph, 1948; Western Morning News, 1951; Daily Dispatch, 1952; Manchester Guardian, 1953; PRO, NCB, Manchester, 1958; Dep. Dir, UK Inf. Office, Tanganyika and Zanzibar, 1960; First Secretary: (Inf.), Dar es Salaam, 1961; (Aid), Kaduna, 1963; Commonwealth Office (later FCO), 1967; Madras, 1969; Head of Chancery, Reykjavik, 1973 (Hd of Brit. Interests Section, French Embassy, during breach of diplomatic relations, 1976); Dep. High Comr, Bombay, 1977; High Comr, Seychelles, 1980–83. *Recreations:* music, books, living in England. *Address:* c/o Midland Bank, 11 Stamford New Road, Altrincham, Cheshire WA14 1BW. *Club:* Royal Over-Seas League.
See also Air Vice-Marshal G. Young.

YOUNG, Eric William, BEng (Hons); MIMechE, MIEE; *b* 26 March 1896; 2nd *s* of Colonel C. A. Young, CB, CMG; *m* 1936, Mrs Olive Bruce. *Educ:* Epsom Coll.; Shrewsbury Sch.; Liverpool Univ. (BEng Hons, 1922). Served RE (T) (Lieut) 1913–19. Metropolitan Vickers Ltd, 1922–26; Technical Manager, Electrolux Ltd, 1926–39; Rootes Ltd: General Manager, Aero Engine Factories, 1939–45; Director and General Manager, Sunbeam Talbot Ltd, 1945–46; Director, Rootes Export Co. Ltd, 1946–47; Sales Director, Harry Ferguson Ltd, 1947–53; Managing Director, Eastern Hemisphere Division, Massey-Ferguson Ltd, 1953 56; Vice-Chm., Massey-Ferguson Holdings Ltd, 1956–65, Chm., 1965–70. *Recreations:* golf, gardening. *Address:* Childerstone, Liphook, Hampshire GU30 7AP. *T:* Liphook 722125. *Club:* Liphook Golf.

YOUNG, Sir Frank (George), Kt 1973; DSc, PhD (London), MA (Cantab); FRS 1949; CChem, FRSC; Sir William Dunn Professor of Biochemistry, University of Cambridge, 1949–75; now Professor Emeritus; Master of Darwin College, Cambridge, 1964–76, Hon. Fellow 1977; Hon. Fellow of Trinity Hall, Cambridge, since 1965 (Fellow, 1949–64); Fellow of University College, London; *b* 25 March 1908; *er s* of late Frank E. Young, Dulwich; *m* 1933, Ruth (MB, BS, MRCPsych), *o c* of Thomas Turner, Beckenham, Kent; three *s* (one *d* decd). *Educ:* Alleyn's Sch., Dulwich; University Coll., London. Beit Memorial Fellow at University Coll., London, University of Aberdeen and University of Toronto, 1932–36; Member of Scientific Staff, Medical Research Council, at Nat. Inst. for Med. Research, 1936–42; Professor of Biochemistry, University of London, 1942–49 (at St Thomas's Hosp. Med. Sch., 1942–45, UCL, 1945–49). Syndic, CUP, 1951–64; Mem. Council of Senate, Cambridge, 1965–68; Chm., Clinical Sch. Planning Cttee, Univ. of Cambridge, 1969–76. Vice Pres. and Hon. Mem., British Diabetic Assoc., 1948–; Member: Medical Res. Council, 1950–54; Commission on Higher Educ. for Africans in Central Africa, 1952; Inter-University Council for Higher Education Overseas, 1961–73; Commission on new Chinese University in Hong Kong, 1962–63; Medical Sub-Cttee, UGC, 1964–73; Board of Governors of United Cambridge Hospitals, 1964–68; Royal Commn on Medical Educn, 1965–68; Council, British Nutrition Foundn, 1967–80; Council of Nestlé Foundn, Lausanne, 1972–80. Trustee, Kennedy Memorial Trust, 1964–76. President: European Assoc. for the Study of Diabetes, 1965–68, Hon. Mem., 1973; British Nutrition Foundn, 1970–76; Internat. Diabetes Fedn, 1970–73 (Hon. Pres., 1973–); Vice-Pres. and Mem. of Exec. Bd, Internat. Council of Scientific Unions, 1970–73. Chairman: Smith Kline and French Trustees (UK), 1963–77; Clinical Endocrinology Cttee (MRC), 1965–72; Adv. Cttee on Irradiation of Food (UK), 1967–80; Mem. Executive Council, Ciba Foundation, 1954–67, Chm. 1967–77, Trustee, 1967–83. Croonian Lecturer, Royal Society, 1962. Named lectureships held abroad: Renziehausen, Pittsburg, 1939; Sterling, Yale, 1939; Jacobæus, Oslo, 1948; Dohme, Johns Hopkins, 1950; Banting, Toronto, 1950; Banting, San Francisco, 1950; Richardson, Harvard, 1952; Hanna, Western Reserve, 1952; Woodward, Yale, 1958; Brailsford Robertson, Adelaide, 1960; Upjohn, Atlantic City, 1963. Hon. Member: Consejo Superior de Investigaciones Cientificas, Madrid; Biochemical Soc. and Soc. for Endocrinology, and Hon. or corresp. member of many foreign medical and scientific bodies. Hon. FRCP. Hon. LLD Aberdeen; Hon. DSc Zimbabwe; Doctor *hc:* Catholic University of Chile; Univ. Montpellier. Coronation Medal, 1953. *Publications:* scientific papers in Biochemical Journal and other scientific and medical journals on hormonal control of metabolism, diabetes mellitus, and related topics. *Address:* 11 Bentley Road, Cambridge CB2 2AW. *T:* Cambridge 352650.

YOUNG, Frieda Margaret, OBE 1969; HM Diplomatic Service, retired; *b* 9 April 1913; *d* of Arthur Edward Young. *Educ:* Wyggeston Grammar Sch., Leicester; Wycombe Abbey Sch., Bucks; and in France and Germany. Home Office, 1937–39; Min. of Home Security, 1939–41; MOI 1941–44; Paris 1944–48; Tehran 1948–51; Vienna 1951–54; FO 1954–57; First Secretary and Consul, Reykjavik, 1957–59; Consul, Cleveland, 1959–62; FO 1962–65; Consul, Bergen, 1965–68; Consul-General, Rotterdam, 1968–73. *Recreations:* travel, photography, bird-watching. *Address:* 6 Lady Street, Lavenham, Suffolk. *Club:* Royal Commonwealth Society.

YOUNG, Gavin Neil B.; *see* Barr Young.

YOUNG, George Bell, CBE 1976; Managing Director, East Kilbride Development Corporation, since 1973 (and Stonehouse, 1973–77); *b* 17 June 1924; *s* of late George Bell Young and late Jemima Mackinlay; *m* 1946, Margaret Wylie Boyd (decd); one *s*; *m* 1979, Joyce Marguerite McAteer. *Educ:* Queens Park, Glasgow. MIEx 1958; MInstM 1969; FBIM 1982. RNVR, 1942–45, Lieut (destroyers and mine-sweepers). Journalist and Feature Writer, Glasgow Herald, 1945–48; North of Scotland Hydro-Electric Board, 1948–52; Chief Exec. (London), Scottish Council (Development and Industry), 1952–68; Gen. Man., E Kilbride Develt Corp., 1968–73. Mem. Council, Nat. Trust for Scotland, 1974–79; Dir, Royal Caledonian Schools, 1957–85; Chm., East Kilbride and District National Savings Cttee, 1968–78; Trustee, Strathclyde Scanner Campaign; Scottish Chm., British Heart Foundn, 1975–79 (Mem., East Kilbride Cttee, 1970–; Pres., Scottish Appeal, 1980–). Hon. Vice-Pres., East Kilbride Dist Sports Council, 1984. Chm., E Kilbride Cttee, Order of St John (CStJ 1979). FRSA 1968; FInstM 1984; Mem., Amer. Inst. of Corporate Asset Managers, 1985. Member: Saints and Sinners Club of Scotland (Hon. Sec., 1982–); Royal Glasgow Inst. of the Fine Arts; The Merchants House of Glasgow; Cttee of 20 Nat. Children's Homes for Scotland. *Recreations:* golf, fishing. *Address:* 4 Newlands Place, East Kilbride, Lanarkshire. *T:* East Kilbride 30094. *Clubs:* Caledonian; Royal Scottish Automobile (Glasgow).

YOUNG, George Kennedy, CB 1960; CMG 1955; MBE 1945; *b* 8 April 1911; *s* of late George Stuart Young and Margaret Kennedy, Moffat, Dumfriesshire; *m* 1939, Géryke, *d* of late Dr M. A. G. Harthoorn, Batavia, Dutch EI. *Educ:* Dumfries Acad.; Univs of St Andrews, Giessen, Dijon, Yale, MA (First Class Hons Mod. Langs) 1934; Commonwealth Fund Fellowship, 1934–36; MA (Political Science), Yale, 1936; Editorial staff The Glasgow Herald, 1936–38; British United Press, 1938–39. Served War of 1939–45; commissioned KOSB 1940 (despatches, E Africa, 1941); specially employed list, Italy and W Europe, 1943–45. Berlin correspondent, British United Press, 1946. Joined HM Foreign Service, 1946; Vienna, 1946; Economic Relations Dept, FO, 1949; British Middle East Office, 1951; Ministry of Defence, 1953–61; Under-Secretary, 1960. Kleinwort, Benson Ltd, 1961–76; Pres., Nuclear Fuel Finance SA, 1969–76. Medal of Freedom (Bronze Palm), 1945. *Publications:* Masters of Indecision, 1962; Merchant Banking, 1966; Finance and World Power, 1968; Who Goes Home?, 1969; Who is my Liege?, 1972; Subversion, 1984. *Recreations:* music, reading, swimming, walking. *Address:* 37 Abbotsbury House, W14. *T:* 01-603 8432.

YOUNG, Sir George (Samuel Knatchbull), 6th Bt, *cr* 1813; MP (C) Ealing, Acton, since Feb. 1974; *b* 16 July 1941; *s* of Sir George Young, 5th Bt, CMG, and Elisabeth (*née* Knatchbull-Hugessen); *S* father 1960; *m* 1964, Aurelia Nemon-Stuart, *er d* of late Oscar Nemon, and of Mrs Nemon-Stuart, Boar's Hill, Oxford; two *s* two *d*. *Educ:* Eton; Christ Church, Oxford (Open Exhibitioner); MA Oxon, MPhil Surrey. Economist, NEDO, 1966–67; Kobler Research Fellow, University of Surrey, 1967–69; Economic Adviser,

PO Corp., 1969–74. Councillor, London Borough of Lambeth, 1968–71; Mem., GLC, for London Borough of Ealing, 1970–73. An Opposition Whip, 1976–79; Parly Under Sec. of State, DHSS, 1979–81, DoE, 1981–86. Chm., Acton Housing Assoc., 1972–79. *Publications:* Accommodation Services in the UK 1970–1980, 1970; Tourism, Blessing or Blight?, 1973. *Recreations:* squash, bicycling. *Heir:* s George Horatio Young, b 11 Oct. 1966. *Address:* House of Commons, SW1A 0AA.

YOUNG, Gerard Francis, CBE 1967; DL; CEng, FIMechE; HM Lord-Lieutenant and Custos Rotolurum, for South Yorkshire, 1974–85; President, Tempered Group Ltd; *b* 5 May 1910; *s* of Smelter J. Young, MICE, and Edith, *d* of Sir John Aspinall, Pres. ICE and Pres. IMechE; *m* 1937, Diana Graham Murray, MA, BSc, JP, *d* of Charles Graham Murray, MD; two *s* three *d*. *Educ:* Ampleforth College. Engrg Apprentice, LNER, Doncaster. Entered family firm, The Tempered Spring Co. Ltd (later Tempered Group Ltd), 1930; Dir, 1936; Man. Dir, 1942; Chm., 1954–78. Dir, 1958, Chm., 1967–80, Sheffield Area Board, Sun Alliance & London Insurance Group; Dir, National Vulcan Engineering Insce Group, 1962–79. Member: Nat. Bd for Prices and Incomes, 1968–71; Top Salaries Review Body, 1971–74; Armed Forces Pay Review Body, 1971–74; Gen. Comr of Income Tax, 1947–74 (Chm., Don Div., 1968–74). Dir, Crucible Theatre Trust Ltd, 1967–75; Sec., Assoc. of Christian Communities in Sheffield, 1940–46; Chm., Radio Hallam Ltd, 1973–79; Trustee, Sheffield Town Trust (Town Collector, 1978–81); Chm., J. G. Graves Charitable Fund, 1974–85; Chm., Freshgate Foundn, 1979–86; President: Council of St John, South and West Yorks, 1979–85; Yorks Volunteers Council, 1980–81; TAVRA Yorks & Humberside, 1983–85 (Vice-Pres., 1974–82). Univ. of Sheffield: Mem. Council, 1943; Treas., 1947–51; Pro-Chancellor, 1951–67; Chm., 1956–67; Life Mem. of Court, 1983. Mem. Bd of Govs, United Sheffield Hosps, 1948–53 (Chm. of Finance Cttee, 1948–50); Chm., Royal Hosp., 1951–53. Master, Company of Cutlers in Hallamshire, 1961–62. JP Sheffield, 1950–85. High Sheriff of Hallamshire, 1973–74; DL West Riding of Yorks, 1974. Hon. LLD Sheffield, 1962. KStJ 1976; GCSG 1974. *Recreations:* gardening, 13 grandchildren. *Address:* 69 Carsick Hill Crescent, Sheffield S10 3LS. *T:* Sheffield 302834. *Club:* Sheffield (Sheffield).
See also H. J. S. Young.

YOUNG, Air Vice-Marshal Gordon, CBE 1963; retired; *b* 29 May 1919; *s* of late Robert Young, MBE, and late Emily Florence Young, Doncaster; *m* 1943, Pamela Doris Weatherstone-Smith; two *d*. *Educ:* Maltby Grammar School; Sheffield Univ. Served War of 1939–45, Flying Boat Ops S Atlantic and Western Approaches (despatches); Air Min., 1945–47; Asst Air Attaché, Moscow, 1949–52; OC No 204 Sqdn, 1954–55; RAF Staff Coll., 1956; OC Flying Wing, RAF St Mawgan, 1958–60; Asst Chief, Comdrs-in-Chief Mission to Soviet Forces in Germany, 1960–63; OC RAF Wyton, 1963–65; Air Attaché, Bonn, 1966–68; SASO Coastal Command, 1968–69; COS No 18 (M) Gp, 1969–71. *Recreation:* bird-watching (MBOU 1969). *Address:* PO Box 24, Bath, Ont K0H 1G0, Canada. *T:* 613–352–3498. *Club:* Royal Air Force.
See also Eric Young.

YOUNG, Most Rev. Sir Guilford; *see* Hobart, Archbishop of, (RC).

YOUNG, Hon. Sir Harold (William), KCMG 1983; Senator for South Australia, 1967–83, President of the Senate, 1981–83, retired; *b* 30 June 1923; *s* of Frederick James Garfield Young and Edith Mabel Scott; *m* 1952, Eileen Margaret Downing; two *s* two *d*. *Educ:* Prince Alfred Coll., Adelaide. Wheat farmer and grazier prior to entering Parliament. Government Whip in the Senate, 1971–72; Opposition Whip, 1972–75; Shadow Spokesman on the Media, 1975; Chm., Govt Members' Cttee on National Resources, Energy and Trade, 1976–81. *Recreations:* tennis, skiing, fishing. *Address:* 32 Greenwood Grove, Urrbrae, SA 5064, Australia. *T:* (08) 79–1805. *Clubs:* South Australian Police (Adelaide); National Press (Canberra).

YOUNG, Maj.-Gen. Hugh A., CB 1946; CBE 1945; DSO 1944; CD 1954; Vice-President, Central Mortgage and Housing Corporation since 1947; *b* 3 April 1898; *s* of Andrew and Emily Young, Winnipeg; *m* 1927; one *s* one *d*. *Educ:* Winnipeg Collegiate; University of Manitoba (BSc Elec. Engineering, 1924). RC Signals, 1924; Staff Coll., Camberley, England, 1933–34; various General Staff appointments during the war; commanded Inf. Bde, operations Normandy, 1944; QMG Canadian Army, 1944–47; retired, 1947. Dep. Minister of Department of Resources and Development, and Comr of NW Territories, Canada, 1950–53; Dep. Minister, Dept of Public Works, 1953–63.

YOUNG, Hugo John Smelter; journalist; *b* 13 Oct. 1938; *s* of Gerard Francis Young, *qv*; *m* 1966, Helen Mason; one *s* three *d*. *Educ:* Ampleforth Coll.; Balliol Coll., Oxford (BA Jurisprudence). Yorkshire Post, 1961; Harkness Fellow, 1963; Congressional Fellow, US Congress, 1964; The Sunday Times, 1965–84: Chief Leader Writer, 1966–77; Political Editor, 1973–84; Jt Dep. Editor, 1981–84; Political Columnist, The Guardian, 1984–; Dir, The Tablet, 1985–. Columnist of the Year: British Press Awards, 1980, 1983, 1985; Granada TV What the Papers Say Awards, 1985. *Publications:* (jtly) The Zinoviev Letter, 1966; (jtly) Journey to Tranquillity, 1969; The Crossman Affair, 1974; (jtly) No, Minister, 1982; (jtly) But, Chancellor, 1984; (jtly) The Thatcher Phenomenon, 1986. *Address:* c/o The Guardian, 119 Farringdon Road, EC1.

YOUNG, Jimmy; *see* Young, L. R.

YOUNG, John Allen, CBE 1975; Chairman and Managing Director, Young & Co.'s Brewery, since 1962; *b* 7 Aug. 1921; *e s* of late William Allen Young and of Joan Barrow Simonds; *m* 1951, Yvonne Lieutenant, Liège; one *s*. *Educ:* Nautical Coll., Pangbourne; Corpus Christi Coll., Cambridge (BA Hons Econs). Served War, 1939–45: Lt-Comdr (A) RNVR; comd 888 Naval Air Sqdn (despatches). Runciman Ltd, 1947; Moor Line, 1949; Young & Co.'s Brewery, 1954–. Chairman: Foster-Probyn Ltd; Cockburn & Campbell; RI Shipping Ltd. Gen. Comr of Taxes, 1965–. President: London Carthorse Parade Soc., 1957–68; Shire Horse Soc., 1963–64 (Treas., 1962–73); Greater London Horse Show, 1972–74; Battersea Scouts, 1974–86. Chairman: Bd of Governors, Nat. Hosps for Nervous Diseases, 1982–86 (Mem. Bd, 1972–86; Chm. Finance, 1974–82); Nat. Hosps Develt Foundn, 1984–; Dep. Chm., Inst. of Neurology, 1982–86 (Chm., Jt Res. Adv. Cttee, 1973–82); Governor, Chalfont Centre for Epilepsy, 1983–; Trustee: Brain Research Trust, 1983–86; Licensed Trade Charities Trust, 1984–. *Recreations:* music, sailing. *Address:* Moonsbrook Cottage, Wisborough Green, West Sussex. *T:* Wisborough Green 700355. *Club:* Royal Yacht Squadron (Cowes).

YOUNG, Major John Darling, JP; Lord-Lieutenant of Buckinghamshire, 1969–84; *b* 4 Jan. 1910; *o s* of late Sir Frederick Young; *m* 1934, Nina (*d* 1974), *d* of late Lt-Col H. W. Harris; three *d*. *Educ:* Eton and Oxford (BA). Commissioned The Life Guards, 1932–46; Middle East and Italy, 1940–44. Member Bucks Agricultural Executive Cttee, 1947–58. Pres., Eastern Wessex TA&VRA, 1976–78. DL 1958, High Sheriff, 1960, JP 1964, CC 1964–77, CA 1969–74, Buckinghamshire. KStJ 1969. *Address:* Thornton Hall, Thornton, Milton Keynes MK17 0HB. *T:* Buckingham 813234. *Clubs:* Turf, Cavalry and Guards.

YOUNG, Sir John (Kenyon Roe), 6th Bt *cr* 1821; Senior Buyer; *b* 23 April 1947; *s* of Sir John William Roe Young, 5th Bt, and Joan Minnie Agnes (*d* 1958), *d* of M. M. Aldous; *S* father, 1981; *m* 1977, Frances Elise, *o d* of W. R. Thompson; one *s*. *Educ:* Hurn Court; Napier College. Joined RN, 1963; transferred to Hydrographic Branch, 1970; qualified Hydrographic Surveyor, 1977; retired from RN, 1979; attended Napier Coll., 1979–80. Mem. Hydrographic Soc. *Recreations:* Rugby, golf. *Heir:* *s* Richard Christopher Roe Young, *b* 14 June 1983. *Address:* Bolingey, 159 Chatham Road, Maidstone, Kent ME14 2ND.

YOUNG, Hon. Sir John (McIntosh), KCMG 1975; **Hon. Mr Justice Young;** Lieutenant-Governor of Victoria and Chief Justice of the Supreme Court of Victoria, Australia, since 1974; *b* Melbourne, 17 Dec. 1919; *s* of George David Young, Glasgow, and Kathleen Mildred Young, Melbourne; *m* 1951, Elisabeth Mary, *yr d* of late Dr Edward Wing Twining, Manchester; one *s* two *d*. *Educ:* Geelong Grammar Sch.; Brasenose Coll., Oxford (MA); Inner Temple; Univ. of Melbourne (LLB). Served War: Scots Guards, 1940–46 (Captain 1943); NW Europe (despatches), 1945. Admitted Victorian Bar, 1948; Associate to Mr Justice Dixon, High Court of Australia, 1948; practice as barrister, 1949–74; Hon. Sec., Victorian Bar Council, 1950–60; Lectr in Company Law, Univ. of Melbourne, 1957–61; Hon. Treas., Medico Legal Soc. of Vic., 1955–65 (Vice-Pres., 1966–68; Pres., 1968–69). QC (Vic.) 1961; admitted Tasmanian Bar, 1964, QC 1964; NSW Bar, 1968, QC 1968; Consultant, Faculty of Law, Monash Univ., 1968–74. Mem., Bd of Examiners for Barristers and Solicitors, 1969–72; Mem. Council, Geelong Grammar Sch., 1974; Pres., Victorian Council of Legal Educn and Victoria Law Foundn, 1974–. Vice-Pres., Scout Assoc. of Australia, 1985– (Pres., Victorian Br., 1974–); Pres., St John Council for Victoria, 1975–82; KStJ 1977; Chancellor, Order of St John in Australia, 1982–. Hon. Col, 4th/19th Prince of Wales's Light Horse, 1978–; Rep. Hon. Col, RAAC, 1986–; Hon. Air Cdre, No 21 (City of Melbourne) Sqn, RAAF, 1986–. Hon. LLD Monash, 1986. *Publications:* (co-author) Australian Company Law and Practice, 1965; articles in legal jls. *Recreations:* riding, golf. *Address:* 17 Sorrett Avenue, Malvern, Victoria 3144, Australia. *Clubs:* Cavalry and Guards; Melbourne, Australian (Melbourne).

YOUNG, John Richard Dendy; Attorney of Supreme Court, South Africa, since 1984; *b* 4 Sept. 1907; 5th *s* of James Young and Evelyn Maud Hammond; *m* 1946, Patricia Maureen Mount; four *s* two *d*. *Educ:* Hankey, Cape Province, SA; Humansdorp, CP, SA; University, South Africa (External). Joined Public Service, S Rhodesia, 1926; resigned to practise at Bar, 1934; joined Military Forces, 1940; active service, North Africa, Sicily and Italy; commissioned in the field; demobilised, 1945. QC 1948; MP Southern Rhodesia, 1948–53; Member Federal Assembly, 1953–56; Judge of the High Court of Rhodesia, 1956–68; Chief Justice, Botswana, 1968–71; Advocate of Supreme Court of SA, 1971–84; Sen. Counsel, 1979–84; Judge of Appeal, Lesotho, Swaziland, Botswana, 1979–84. *Recreations:* swimming, walking. *Address:* 8 Tulani Gardens, Greenfield Road, Kenilworth, Cape, 7700, South Africa.

YOUNG, John Robertson; HM Diplomatic Service; Counsellor, Damascus, since 1984; *b* 21 Feb. 1945; *s* of late Francis John Young and of Marjorie Elizabeth Young; *m* 1967, Catherine Suzanne Françoise Houssait; one *s* two *d*. *Educ:* King Edward VI Sch., Norwich; Leicester Univ. (BA 1st C1. Hons, French). Entered FCO, 1967; MECAS, Lebanon, 1968; Third Sec., Cairo, 1970; Second Sec., FCO, 1972; Private Sec. to Minister of State, 1975; First Sec., Paris, 1977; Asst Head, Western European Dept, FCO, 1982. *Recreations:* music, acting. *Address:* c/o Foreign and Commonwealth Office, SW1; 23 Keildon Road, SW11; Les Choiseaux, Artannes-sur-Indre, Tours, France. *Club:* Cruising Association.

YOUNG, John Zachary, MA; FRS 1945; Professor of Anatomy, University College, London, 1945–74, now Emeritus, Hon. Fellow, 1975; engaged in research at Oxford University, Marine Biology Station, Plymouth, and Duke Marine Laboratory, Beaufort, N Carolina; *b* 18 March 1907; *s* of Philip Young and Constance Maria Lloyd; *m* Phyllis Heaney; one *s* one *d*; *m* Raymonde Parsons; one *d*. *Educ:* Wells House, Malvern Wells; Marlborough Coll.; Magdalen Coll., Oxford (Demy). Senior Demy, Magdalen Coll., 1929, Christopher Welch Scholar, 1928, Naples Biological Scholar, 1928, 1929; Fellow of Magdalen Coll., Oxford, 1931–45 (Hon. Fellow, 1975); University Demonstrator in Zoology and Comparative Anatomy, Oxford, 1933–45; Rockefeller Fellow, 1936. Fullerton Professor of Physiology, Royal Institution, 1958–61. Pres., Marine Biol Assoc., 1976–. Foreign Member: Amer. Acad. of Arts and Scis; Amer. Philosophical Soc.; Accademia dei Lincei. Hon. FBA 1986. Hon. DSc: Bristol, 1965; McGill, 1967; Durham, 1969; Bath, 1973; Duke, 1978; Oxford, 1979; Hon. LLD: Glasgow, 1975; Aberdeen, 1980. Royal Medal, Royal Society, 1967; Linnean Gold Medal, 1973; Jan Swammerdam Medal, Amsterdam Soc. for Natural Scis and Medicine, 1980. *Publications:* The Life of Vertebrates, 1950, 3rd edn 1981; Doubt and Certainty in Science, 1951; The Life of Mammals, 1957; A Model of the Brain, 1964 (lectures); The Memory System of the Brain, 1966; An Introduction to the Study of Man, 1971; The Anatomy of the Nervous System of *Octopus vulgaris*, 1971; Programs of the Brain, 1978; scientific papers, mostly on the nervous system. *Recreation:* walking. *Address:* 1 The Crossroads, Brill, Bucks. *T:* Brill 237412; Department of Psychology, South Parks Road, Oxford.

YOUNG, Joyce Jean, SRN, RMN; Regional Nursing Officer, Oxford, since 1984; *b* 16 Nov. 1936; *d* of Leslie Cyril and Frances May Lyons. *Educ:* Cowes High School, Isle of Wight. General Nurse training, Essex County Hosp., Colchester, 1955–58; Mental Nurse training, Severalls Hosp., Colchester, 1959–60; Ward Sister posts, gen. and psych. hosps, 1960–70; Clinical Nurse Advr, Hosp. Adv. Service, 1970–72; Regl Nurse Advr, SE Metrop. Hosp. Bd for Mental Illness, Mental Handicap and Elderly Services, 1972–74; Dist Nursing Officer, Tunbridge Wells Health Dist., 1974–80; Chief Nursing Officer, Brighton HA, 1980–84. *Publications:* (contrib.) Impending Crisis of Old Age (Nuffield Provincial Trust), 1981; articles in Nursing Times and Nursing Mirror. *Recreations:* gardening, wild life. *Address:* The Thatched Cottage, Idbury, West Oxfordshire. *T:* Shipton-under-Wychwood 830882.

YOUNG, Junor; *see* Young, D. J.

YOUNG, Kenneth Middleton, CBE 1977; Vice Chairman, since 1986, and Board Member, since 1972 (currently for Personnel and Corporate Resources), Post Office Corporation; *b* 1 Aug. 1931; *s* of Cyril W. D. Young and Gwladys Middleton Young; *m* 1958, Brenda May Thomas; one *s* one *d*. *Educ:* Neath Grammar Sch.; University Coll. of Wales, Aberystwyth; Coll. of Science and Technology, Univ. of Manchester. BA (Hons) 1952. Pilot Officer/Navigator, General Duties (Aircrew), RAF, 1952–54. Asst Personnel Manager, Elliott-Automation Ltd, 1955–59; Collective Agreements Manager, later Salary Administration Manager, Massey-Ferguson (UK) Ltd, 1959–64; Personnel Adviser, Aviation Div., Smiths Industries Ltd, 1964–66; Group Personnel Manager, General Electric Company Ltd, and Dir, GEC (Management) Ltd, 1966–71. Member: Management Bd, Engineering Employers Fedn, 1971; CBI Employment Policy Cttee, 1978–84; Employment Appeal Tribunal, 1985–; Council, Inst. of Manpower Studies; London Business Sch. Liaison Cttee. FIPM. *Recreations:* photography; Chelsea Football Club. *Address:* Ingleton, Main Drive, Gerrards Cross, Bucks. *T:* Gerrards Cross 885422.

YOUNG, Leslie, DSc (London), PhD, FRSC; Professor of Biochemistry in the University of London, and Head of the Department of Biochemistry, St Thomas's Hospital Medical School, London, SE1, 1948–76, now Professor Emeritus; Hon. Consultant, St Thomas'

Hospital; *b* 27 Feb. 1911; *o c* of John and Ethel Young; *m* 1939, Ruth Elliott; one *s*. *Educ:* Sir Joseph Williamson's Mathematical Sch., Rochester; Royal College of Science, London; University College, London. Sir Edward Frankland Prize and Medal of Royal Institute of Chemistry, 1932; Bayliss-Starling Memorial Scholar in Physiology, University Coll., London, 1933–34; Asst Lectr in Biochemistry, University College, London, 1934–35; Commonwealth Fund Fellow in Biochemistry at Washington Univ. Medical School and Yale Univ., USA, 1935–37; Lectr in Biochemistry, University Coll., London, 1937–39; Assoc. Prof. of Biochemistry, Univ. of Toronto, 1939–44; chemical warfare research for the Dept of Nat. Defence, Canada, 1940–46; Prof. of Biochemistry, Univ. of Toronto, 1944–47; Reader in Biochemistry, University Coll., London, 1947–48. Hon. Sec., The Biochemical Soc., 1950–53; Vice-Pres., The Royal Institute of Chemistry, 1964–66, Mem., Bd of Governors, St Thomas' Hosp., 1970–74; Chm. of Council, Queen Elizabeth Coll., London Univ., 1975–80, Hon. Fellow, 1980. *Publications:* (with G. A. Maw) The Metabolism of Sulphur Compounds, 1958; papers on chem. and biochem. subjects in various scientific journals. *Address:* 23 Oaklands Avenue, Esher, Surrey KT10 8HX. *T:* 01–398 1262. *Club:* Athenæum.

YOUNG, Sir Leslie (Clarence), Kt 1984; CBE 1980; DL; Chairman, British Waterways Board, since 1984; Director: Bank of England, since 1986; National Westminster Bank, since 1986; *b* 5 Feb. 1925; *s* of late Clarence James Young and of Ivy Isabel Young; *m* 1949, Muriel Howard Pearson; one *s* one *d*. *Educ:* London School of Economics (BScEcon). Courtaulds Ltd: held range of senior executive appts, incl. chairmanship of number of gp companies, 1948–68; J. Bibby & Sons Ltd, 1968–86: Managing Director, J. Bibby Agriculture Ltd, 1968; Chm. and Man. Dir, J. Bibby Food Products Ltd, 1970; Gp Man. Dir, 1970, Dep. Chm. and Man. Dir, 1977, Chm., 1979–86, J. Bibby & Sons Ltd. Chairman: NW Regional Council, CBI, 1976–78; NW Industrial Development Board, 1978–81; Merseyside Develt Corp., 1981–84. Trustee, Civic Trust for the North West, 1978–83. Regional Dir, N Regional Bd, National Westminster Bank PLC, 1979–, Chm., 1986–; Non-Exec. Dir, Granada Television Ltd, 1979–84; Dir, Pioneer Mutual Insce Co., 1986–. Chm. Trustees, Nat. Museums and Galls on Merseyside, 1986–. Member Council: N of England Zoological Soc., 1979–; Royal Liverpool Philharmonic Soc., 1980–. DL Merseyside, 1983. *Recreations:* fly-fishing, walking, shooting. *Address:* Overwood, Vicarage Lane, Burton, South Wirral L64 5TJ. *T:* 051–336 5224. *Club:* Carlton.

YOUNG, Leslie Ronald, (Jimmy Young), OBE 1979; Presenter, Jimmy Young Programme, BBC Radio Two, since 1973 (Radio One, 1967–73); *b* 21 Sept.; *s* of Frederick George Young and Gertrude Woolford; *m* 1st, 1946, Wendy Wilkinson (marr. diss.); one *d*; 2nd, 1950, Sally Douglas (marr. diss.). *Educ:* East Dean Grammar Sch., Cinderford, Glos. RAF, 1939–46. First BBC radio broadcast, songs at piano, 1949; pianist, singer, bandleader, West End, London, 1950–51; first theatre appearance, Empire Theatre, Croydon, 1952; regular theatre appearances, 1952–; first radio broadcast introd. records, Flat Spin, 1953; BBC TV Bristol, Pocket Edition series, 1955; first introd. radio Housewives' Choice, 1955; BBC radio series, incl.: The Night is Young, 12 o'clock Spin, Younger Than Springtime, Saturday Special, Keep Young, Through Till Two, 1959–65; presented progs, Radio Luxembourg, 1960–68. BBC TV: series, Jimmy Young Asks, 1972; The World of Jimmy Young, 1973. First live direct BBC broadcasts to Europe from Soviet Union, Jimmy Young Programme, 16 and 17 May 1977; Jimmy Young Programmes broadcast live from Egypt and Israel, 9 and 12 June 1978, from Zimbabwe-Rhodesia, 9 and 10 Aug. 1979; Host for Thames TV of first British Telethon, 2nd and 3rd Oct. 1980; Jimmy Young Programmes live from Tokyo, 26th, 27th and 28th May 1981, from Sydney, 4–8 Oct. 1982, from Washington DC, 3–7 Oct. 1983. ITV series: Whose Baby?, 1973; Jim's World, 1974; The Jimmy Young Television Programme, 1984, 1985, 1986. Hit Records: 1st, Too Young, 1951; Unchained Melody, The Man From Laramie, 1955 (1st Brit. singer to have 2 consec. no 1 hit records); Chain Gang, More, 1956; Miss You, 1963. Weekly Column, Daily Sketch, 1968–71. Hon. Mem. Council, NSPCC, 1981–. Freeman, City of London, 1969. Variety Club of GB Award, Radio Personality of the Year, 1968; Sony Award, Radio Personality of the Year, 1985. Silver Jubilee Medal, 1977. *Publications:* Jimmy Young Cookbook: No 1, 1968; No 2, 1969; No 3, 1970; No 4, 1972; (autobiogs) JY, 1973, Jimmy Young, 1982; contrib. magazines, incl. Punch, Woman's Own. *Address:* c/o Broadcasting House, Portland Place, W1A 1AA. *Clubs:* Wig and Pen; Wigan Rugby League Social.

YOUNG, Mark; General Secretary, British Air Line Pilots' Association, since 1974; *b* 7 June 1929; *s* of Arnold Young and Florence May (*née* Lambert) *m* 1st, 1952, Charlotte Maria (*née* Rigol) (*d* 1978); two *s* two *d*; 2nd, 1979, Marie-Thérèse, (Mollie) (*née* Craig); one *s*. *Educ:* Pendower Technical Sch., Newcastle upon Tyne. Electrician, 1944–61; Head of Res., ETU, 1961; National Officer, ETU, 1963–73. *Recreations:* flying, ballooning, golf, tennis. *Address:* (office) 81 New Road, Harlington, Hayes, Mddx UB3 5BG.

YOUNG, Sir Norman (Smith), Kt 1968; formerly Chairman: Pipelines Authority of South Australia; South Australian Brewing Co. Ltd; South Australian Oil and Gas Corporation Pty Ltd; News Ltd; Elder Smith Goldsbrough Mort Ltd; Bradmill Ltd; *b* 24 July 1911; *s* of Thomas and Margaret Young; *m* 1936, Jean Fairbairn Sincock; two *s* one *d*. *Educ:* Norwood High Sch.; University of Adelaide. Member: Adelaide City Council, 1949–60; Municipal Tramways Trust, 1951–67 (Dep. Chairman); Royal Commn on Television, 1953–54; Bankruptcy Law Review Cttee, 1956–62. Fellow, Inst. of Chartered Accountants, 1933; FASA, 1932; Associate in Commerce, University of Adelaide, 1930. *Publication:* Bankruptcy Practice in Australia, 1942. *Address:* 256 Stanley Street, North Adelaide, South Australia 5006, Australia. *T:* 2673688.

YOUNG, Brig. Peter, DSO 1942; MC 1942 and two Bars 1943; military historian; Captain-Generall, The Sealed Knot Society of Cavaliers and Roundheads, since 1968; *b* 28 July 1915; *s* of Dallas H. W. Young, MBE, and Irene Barbara Lushington Mellor; *m* 1950, Joan Duckworth; no *c*. *Educ:* Monmouth Sch.; Trinity Coll., Oxford. 2nd Lieut, Bedfordshire and Hertfordshire Regt, 1937. Served War of 1939–45: BEF Dunkirk (wounded), 1940; No 3 Commando, 1940; raids on Guernsey, 1940; Lofoten and Vaagso, 1941, Dieppe, 1942, Sicily and Italy, 1943; comd No 3 Commando, 1943–44; Normandy, 1944; Arakan, 1944–45; comd 1st Commando Bde, 1945–46. Commanded 9th Regt Arab Legion, 1953–56. Reader in Military History, Royal Military Acad., Sandhurst, 1959–69. Gen. Editor, Military Memoirs series, 1967–; Editor, Purnell's History of First World War, 1970–72; Editor in Chief, Orbis' World War II, 1972–74; TV Consultant: Churchill and the Generals, 1980; 1798, The Year of the French, 1981; By The Sword Divided, 1st series 1983 (Mil. Consultant), 2nd series 1984 (Historical Adviser). Vice-President: Commando Assoc.; Naseby Preservation Soc.; Military Historical Soc.; Chm., Cheriton 1644 Assoc. FSA 1960; FRGS 1968. Order of El Istiqlal (Jordan) 3rd Class, 1954. *Publications:* Bedouin Command, 1956; Storm from the Sea, 1958; The Great Civil War (with late Lt-Col Alfred H. Burne, DSO), 1959; Cromwell, 1962; Hastings to Culloden (with John Adair), 1964; World War 1939–45, 1966; Edgehill, 1642: The Campaign and the Battle, 1967; The British Army, 1642–1970, 1967; The Israeli Campaign, 1967, 1967; (ed) Decisive Battles of the Second World War, 1967; Charge (with Lt-Col J. P. Lawford), 1967; (jt editor) The Civil War: Richard Atkyns and John Gwyn, 1967; Oliver Cromwell, 1968; Commando, 1969; Cropredy Bridge, 1644 (with Margaret Toynbee), 1970; Marston Moor, 1644, 1970; (ed with Lt-Col J. P. Lawford) History of the British Army, 1970; Chasseurs of the Guard, 1971; The Arab Legion, 1971; George Washington's Army, 1972; (ed) John Cruso, Militarie Instructions for the Cavall'rie, 1972; Blücher's Army, 1973; Armies of the English Civil War, 1973; (with Lt-Col J. P. Lawford) Wellington's Masterpiece, 1973; (ed and contrib.) The War Game, 1973; (ed and contrib.) The Machinery of War, 1973; (with R. Holmes) The English Civil War, 1974; Atlas of the Second World War, 1974; (with M. Toynbee) Strangers in Oxford, 1974; (with W. Emberton) The Cavalier Army, 1974; (ed with Brig. M. Calvert) A Dictionary of Battles: 1816–1976, 1977; 1815–1915, 1977; 1715–1815, 1978; (with W. Emberton) Sieges of the Great Civil War, 1642–1646, 1978; Civil War England, 1981; D-Day, 1981; The Fighting Man, 1981; Naseby 1645: the campaign and the battle, 1985; numerous articles in Army Historical Research Journal and Chambers's Encyclopædia. *Recreations:* equitation, wargaming. *Address:* Flat 3, Twyning Manor, Tewkesbury, Glos GL20 6DB. *Clubs:* Savage, The Sette of Odd Volumes.

YOUNG, Ven. Peter Claude; Archdeacon Emeritus of Cornwall and Canon Emeritus of Truro Cathedral; *b* 21 July 1916; *s* of Rev. Thomas Young and of Mrs Ethel Ashton Young; *m* 1944, Marjorie Désirée Rose; two *s*. *Educ:* Exeter Sch.; Exeter Coll., Oxford; Wycliffe Hall, Oxford. BA 1938, BLitt 1940, MA 1942, MLitt 1980, Oxon. Asst Curate of Ottery St Mary, 1940–44; Asst Curate of Stoke Damerel, i/c of St Bartholomew's, Milehouse, Plymouth, 1944–47; Rector of Highweek, Newton Abbot, 1947–59; Vicar of Emmanuel, Plymouth, 1959–65; Archdeacon of Cornwall and Canon Residentiary of Truro Cathedral, 1965–81; Examining Chaplain to Bishop of Truro, 1965–81. *Recreations:* motoring, fishing, reading. *Address:* 31 Princes Road, Cheltenham, Glos. *T:* Cheltenham 39955.

YOUNG, Priscilla Helen Ferguson, CBE 1982; Director, Central Council for Education and Training in Social Work, 1971–86; *b* 25 Nov. 1925; *d* of Fergus Ferguson Young and Helen Frances Graham (*née* Murphy). *Educ:* Kingsley Sch., Leamington Spa; Univ. of Edinburgh (MA). Social Worker: London Family Welfare Assoc., 1947–51; Somerset CC Children's Dept, 1951–53; Oxford City Children's Dept, 1953–58 (Dep. Children's Officer); Child and Family Services, Portland, Me, USA, 1958–61; Lectr/Sen. Lectr, Sch. of Social Work, Univ. of Leicester, 1961–71. Hon. Fellow, Sheffield City Polytechnic, 1977. *Publication:* The Student and Supervision in Social Work Education, 1967. *Recreations:* growing plants, clay modelling.

YOUNG, Sir Richard (Dilworth), Kt 1970; BSc, FIMechE; CBIM; Chairman, Boosey & Hawkes Ltd, 1979–84 (Deputy Chairman, 1978–79); Director: Rugby Portland Cement Co., since 1968; Commonwealth Finance Development Corp. Ltd, 1968–86; Warwick University Science Park Ltd, since 1983; Retirement Securities Ltd, since 1983; *b* 9 April 1914; *s* of Philip Young and Constance Maria Lloyd; *m* 1951, Jean Barbara Paterson Lockwood, *d* of F. G. Lockwood; four *s*. *Educ:* Bromsgrove; Bristol Univ. Joined Weldless Steel Tube Co. Ltd, 1934; served with Tube Investments companies in production and engineering capacities until 1944; Representative of TI in S America and Man. Dir of Tubos Britanicos (Argentina) Ltda, 1945–50; Man. Dir of TI (Export) Ltd, 1950–53; Sales Dir of TI Aluminium Ltd, 1953–56; Asst to Chm. of Tube Investments Ltd, 1957–60; Dir, 1958; Asst Man. Dir, 1959; Man. Dir, 1961–64; Chairman: Park Gate Iron & Steel Co., 1959–64; Raleigh Industries Ltd, 1960–64; Alfred Herbert Ltd: Dep. Chm., 1965–66; Chm., 1966–74; Man. Dir, 1969–70; Director: Ingersoll Milling Machine Co., USA, 1967–71; Ingersoll Engineers Inc., 1976–86. Member: Council BIM, 1960–65; Council, CBI, 1967–74; Council, IMechE, 1969–76; Adv. Cttee on Scientific Manpower, 1962–65; SSRC, 1973–75; Council, Warwick Univ., 1966–; Central Adv. Council on Science and Technol., 1967–70; SRC Engineering Bd, 1974–76. *Address:* Bearley Manor, Bearley, near Stratford-on-Avon, Warwickshire. *T:* Stratford-on-Avon 731220. *Club:* Athenæum.

YOUNG, Sir Robert Christopher M.; *see* Mackworth-Young.

YOUNG, Robert Henry; Consultant Orthopædic Surgeon, St George's Hospital, SW1, since 1946; Hon. Consultant, St Peter's Hospital, Chertsey, since 1939; *b* 6 Oct. 1903; *s* of James Allen Young and Constance Barrow Young; *m* 1st, 1929, Nancy Willcox; 2nd, 1961, Norma, *d* of Leslie Williams; two *s*. *Educ:* Sherborne Sch.; Emmanuel Coll., Cambridge; St Thomas' Hospital, SE1. *Publications:* numerous articles in leading medical journals. *Address:* 111 Harley Street, W1. *Clubs:* United Oxford & Cambridge University, Buck's.

YOUNG, Sir Roger (William), Kt 1983; MA; STh, LHD, FRSE; Principal of George Watson's College, Edinburgh, 1958–85; *b* 15 Nov. 1923; *yr s* of late Charles Bowden Young and Dr Ruth Young, CBE; *m* 1950, Caroline Mary Christie; two *s* two *d*. *Educ:* Dragon Sch., Oxford; Westminster Sch. (King's Scholar); Christ Church, Oxford (Scholar). Served War of 1939–45, RNVR, 1942–45. Classical Mods, 1946, Lit Hum 1948. Resident Tutor, St Catharine's, Cumberland Lodge, Windsor, 1949–51; Asst Master, The Manchester Grammar Sch., 1951–58. 1st Class in Archbishop's examination in Theology (Lambeth Diploma), 1957. Participant, US State Dept Foreign Leader Program, 1964. Scottish Governor, BBC, 1979–84. Member: Edinburgh Marriage Guidance Council, 1960–75; Scottish Council of Christian Educn Movement, 1960–81 (Chm., 1961–67; Hon. Vice-Pres., 1981–85); Gen. Council of Christian Educn Movement, 1985–; Management Assoc., SE Scotland, 1965–85; Educational Research Bd of SSRC, 1966–70; Court, Edinburgh Univ., 1967–76; Public Schools Commn, 1968–70; Consultative Cttee on the Curriculum, 1972–75; Adv. Cttee, Scottish Centre for Studies in Sch. Administration, 1972–75; Royal Soc. of Edinburgh Dining Club, 1972–; Scottish Adv. Cttee, Community Service Volunteers, 1973–78; Edinburgh Festival Council, 1970–76; Independent Schs Panel of Wolfson Foundn, 1978–82; Gen. Adv. Council of BBC, 1978–79; Scottish Council of Independent Schs, 1978–85; Royal Observatory Trust, Edin., 1981–; Council, RSE, 1982–85. Hon. Sec., Headmasters' Assoc. of Scotland, 1968–72, Pres., 1972–74; Chairman: HMC, 1976; BBC Consult. Gp on Social Effects of TV, 1978–79; Bursary Bd, Dawson International Ltd, 1977–85. Trustee, Campion Sch., Athens, 1984–; Chm. Council, Cheltenham Ladies' Coll., 1986–; Mem., Governing Body, Westminster Sch., 1986–. Conducted Enquiry on Stirling Univ., 1973. Hon. LHD, Hamilton Coll., Clinton, NY, 1978. *Publications:* Lines of Thought, 1958; Everybody's Business, 1968; Everybody's World, 1970; Report on the Policies and Running of Stirling University 1966–1973, 1973. *Recreations:* gardening, photography, climbing, golf, knitting. *Address:* 11 Belgrave Terrace, Bath, Avon BA1 5JR. *T:* Bath 336940. *Club:* East India.

YOUNG, Sheriff Sir Stephen Stewart Templeton, 3rd Bt, *cr* 1945; Sheriff of North Strathclyde, since 1984; advocate; *b* 24 May 1947; *s* of Sir Alastair Young, 2nd Bt, and Dorothy Constance Marcelle (*d* 1964), *d* of late Lt-Col Charles Ernest Chambers, and *widow* of Lt J. H. Grayburn, VC, 43rd LI; *S* father, 1963; *m* 1974, Viola Margaret Nowell-Smith, *d* of Prof. P. H. Nowell-Smith, *qv* and Perilla Thyme (she *m* 2nd, Lord Roberthall, *qv*); two *s*. *Educ:* Rugby; Trinity Coll., Oxford; Edinburgh Univ. Voluntary Service Overseas, Sudan, 1968–69. Sheriff of Glasgow and Strathkelvin, March-June 1984.

Heir: s Charles Alastair Stephen Young, *b* 21 July 1979. *Address:* Glen Rowan, Shore Road, Cove, Dunbartonshire G84 0NU.

YOUNG, Wayland; *see* Kennet, Baron.

YOUNG, William Hilary, CMG 1957; HM Diplomatic Service, retired; Ambassador to Colombia 1966–70; *b* 14 Jan. 1913; *s* of late Rev. Arthur John Christopher Young and Ethel Margaret (*née* Goodwin); *m* 1946, Barbara Gordon Richmond, *d* of late Gordon Park Richmond; one *s* one *d*. *Educ:* Marlborough Coll.; Emmanuel Coll., Cambridge. Entered Consular Service, 1935; served HM Legation, Tehran, 1938–41; Foreign Office, 1941–45; 1st Secretary, 1945; Berlin (Political Division, Control Commission), 1945–48; HM Legation, Budapest, 1948–50; attached to IDC, 1951; Counsellor: UK High Commn, New Delhi, 1952–54; Foreign Office, 1954–57; Minister, Moscow, 1957–60; Senior Civilian Instructor, IDC, 1960–62; Minister, British Embassy, Pretoria and Cape Town, 1962–65; Fellow, Harvard University Center for Internat. Affairs, 1965–66. *Address:* Blackmoor, Four Elms, Edenbridge, Kent.

YOUNG, Hon. William Lambert, JP; High Commissioner for New Zealand in UK, 1982–85; concurrently Ambassador to Ireland and High Commissioner in Nigeria, 1982–85; *b* 13 Nov. 1913; *s* of James Young and Alice Gertrude Annie Young; *m* 1946, Isobel Joan Luke; one *s* four *d*. *Educ:* Wellington Coll. Commenced work, 1930; spent first 16 yrs with farm servicing co., interrupted by War Service, N Africa with Eighth Army, 1940–43; took over management of wholesale distributing co. handling imported and NZ manufactured goods; Gen. Man. of co. manufg and distributing radios, records, electronic equipment and owning 32 retail stores, 1956; purchased substantial interest in importing and distributing business, 1962. MP (National) Miramar, 1966–81; Minister of Works and Develt, 1975–81. Formerly Chairman: National Roads Bd; National Water and Soil Authority; NZ Fishing Licensing Authority. Formerly: Director: Johnsons Wax of NZ Ltd (subsid. of USA Co.); Howard Rotovator Co. Ltd; AA Mutual Insurance Co.; J. J. Niven Ltd; NZ Motor Bodies Ltd; Trustee, Wellington Savings Bank. Pres., Star Boating Club; Mem. Council, NZ Amateur Rowing Assoc. Life Mem., AA of Wellington (Mem. Council, 1976–). JP 1962. *Address:* 31 Moana Road, Kelburn, Wellington 5, New Zealand. *Club:* Wellington (Wellington, NZ).

YOUNG, Sir William Neil, 10th Bt, *cr* 1769; Director, Kleinwort Benson International Investment Ltd, since 1982; *b* 22 Jan. 1941; *s* of Captain William Elliot Young, RAMC (killed in action 27 May 1942), and Mary, *d* of late Rev. John Macdonald; *S* grandfather, 1944; *m* 1965, Christine Veronica Morley, *o d* of R. B. Morley, Buenos Aires; one *s* one *d*. *Educ:* Wellington Coll.; Sandhurst. Captain, 16th/5th The Queen's Royal Lancers, retired 1970. *Recreations:* ski-ing, sailing, tennis, shooting. *Heir: s* William Lawrence Elliot Young, *b* 26 May 1970. *Address:* 22 Elm Park Road, SW3. *Clubs:* Cavalry and Guards; Hong Kong (Hong Kong).

YOUNG-HERRIES, Sir Michael Alexander Robert; *see* Herries.

YOUNGER, family name of **Viscount Younger of Leckie.**

YOUNGER OF LECKIE, 3rd Viscount, *cr* 1923; **Edward George Younger;** OBE 1940; 3rd Bt of Leckie, *cr* 1911; Lord-Lieutenant, Stirling and Falkirk (formerly of County of Stirling), 1964–79; Colonel, Argyll and Sutherland Highlanders (TA); *b* 21 Nov. 1906; *er s* of 2nd Viscount and Maud (*d* 1957), *e d* of Sir John Gilmour, 1st Bt; *S* father 1946; *m* 1930, Evelyn Margaret, MBE (*d* 1983), *e d* of late Alexander Logan McClure, KC; three *s* one *d*. *Educ:* Winchester; New Coll., Oxford. Served War of 1939–45 (OBE). *Heir: s* Hon. George (Kenneth Hotson) Younger, *qv. Address:* Leckie, Gargunnock, Stirling. *T:* Gargunnock 281. *Club:* New (Edinburgh).
See also Hon. R. E. G. Younger.

YOUNGER, Maj.-Gen. Allan Elton, DSO 1944; OBE 1962; MA; Director-General, Royal United Services Institute for Defence Studies, 1976–78; *b* 4 May 1919; *s* of late Brig. Arthur Allan Shakespear Younger, DSO, and late Marjorie Rhoda Younger (*née* Halliley); *m* 1942, Diana Lanyon; three *d*. *Educ:* Gresham's; RMA Woolwich; Christ's Coll., Cambridge. Commnd RE, 1939; France and Belgium, 1940; France, Holland and Germany, 1944–45; Burma, 1946–47; Malaya, 1948; Korea, 1950–51; RMA Sandhurst, 1954–57; Bt Lt-Col 1959; comd 36 Corps Engineer Regt in UK and Kenya, 1960–62; Instructor US Army Comd and Gen. Staff Coll., Fort Leavenworth, 1963–66; Programme Evaluation Gp, 1966–68; Chief Engr, Army Strategic Comd, 1968–69; COS, HQ Allied Forces Northern Europe, Oslo, 1970–72; Sen. Army Mem., Directing Staff, RCDS, 1972–75. Col Comdt, RE, 1974–79. Member Council: British Atlantic Cttee; Lord Kitchener Nat. Meml Fund. Silver Star (US), 1951. *Publications:* contribs to RUSI Jl, Military Review (USA). *Recreations:* ski-ing, writing. *Address:* The Manor House, Twyford, near Winchester, Hants. *T:* Twyford 712514. *Club:* Army and Navy.

YOUNGER, Charles Frank Johnston, DSO 1944; TD 1952; *b* 11 Dec. 1908; *s* of late Major Charles Arthur Johnston Younger, King's Dragoon Guards; *m* 1935, Joanna, *e d* of late Rev. John Kyrle Chatfield, BD, MA, LLB; one *d*. *Educ:* Royal Naval Coll., Dartmouth. Served Royal Navy, 1926–37; resigned commn to enter William Younger & Co. Ltd, Brewers, Edinburgh, 1937. Served War of 1939–45 (despatches, DSO); RA (Field), 15th Scottish Division, 1939–41; 17th Indian Light Div., Burma, 1942–45; commanded 129th Lowland Field Regt, RA, 1942–45 and 278th Lowland Field Regt RA (TA), 1946–52 (Lt-Col). Director: William Younger & Co. Ltd, 1945–73; Scottish & Newcastle Breweries Ltd, 1946–73; Dir, Bank of Scotland, 1960–79. Vice Pres., Brewers' Soc., 1964– (Chm., 1963–64); Chairman: Parly Cttee, 1961–63; Survey Cttee, 1967–75). Chm., Scottish Union & National Insurance Co., 1954–57, 1966–68, Dep. Chm., 1968–79; Dir, Norwich Union and Associated Cos, 1966–79, Vice-Chm., 1976–79. Chm., Scottish Adv. Bd, 1976–80. UK deleg. to EFTA Brewing Ind. Council, 1964–73; Mem. Council, CBI, 1965–73. Mem., Worshipful Company of Brewers. Mem., Royal Company of Archers (Queen's Body Guard for Scotland). Freeman of the City of London. *Recreations:* country pursuits. *Address:* Painsthorpe Hall, Kirby Underdale, York Y04 1RQ. *T:* Bishop Wilton 342. *Clubs:* Boodle's, Pratt's.
See also Earl of Halifax.

YOUNGER, Rt. Hon. George (Kenneth Hotson), TD 1964; PC 1979; DL; MP (C) Ayr, since 1964; Secretary of State for Defence, since 1986; *b* 22 Sept. 1931; *e s* and *heir* of 3rd Viscount Younger of Leckie, *qv; m* 1954, Diana Rhona, *er d* of Captain G. S. Tuck, RN, Little London, Chichester, Sussex; three *s* one *d*. *Educ:* Cargilfield Sch., Edinburgh; Winchester Coll.; New Coll., Oxford. Commnd in Argyll and Sutherland Highlanders, 1950; served BAOR and Korea, 1951; 7th Bn Argyll and Sutherland Highlanders (TA), 1951–65; Hon. Col, 154 (Lowland) Transport Regt, RCT, T&AVR, 1977–85. Director: George Younger & Son Ltd, 1958–68; J. G. Thomson & Co. Ltd, Leith, 1962–66; Maclachlans Ltd, 1968–70; Tennant Caledonian Breweries Ltd, 1977–. Contested (U) North Lanarkshire, 1959; Unionist Candidate for Kinross and West Perthshire, 1963, but stood down in favour of Sir A. Douglas-Home. Scottish Conservative Whip, 1965–67; Parly Under-Sec. of State for Develt, Scottish Office, 1970–74; Minister of State for Defence, 1974; Sec. of State for Scotland, 1979–86. Chm., Conservative Party in Scotland, 1974–75 (Dep. Chm., 1967–70). Brig., Queen's Body Guard for Scotland (Royal Company

of Archers). DL Stirlingshire, 1968. *Recreations:* music, tennis, sailing, golf. *Address:* Easter Leckie, Gargunnock, Stirlingshire. *T:* Gargunnock 274. *Clubs:* Caledonian; Highland Brigade.
See also Hon. R. E. G. Younger.

YOUNGER, Maj.-Gen. Sir John William, 3rd Bt *cr* 1911; CBE 1969 (MBE 1945); Commissioner-in-Chief, St John Ambulance Brigade, 1980–86; *b* 18 Nov. 1920; *s* of Sir William Robert Younger, 2nd Bt, and of Joan Gwendoline Johnstone (later Mrs Dennis Wheatley; she *d* 1982); *S* father, 1973; *m* 1st, 1948, Mrs Stella Jane Dodd (marr. diss. 1952), *d* of Rev. John George Lister; one *s* one *d*; 2nd, 1953, Marcella Granito, Princess Pignatelli Di Belmonte, *d* of Prof. Avv. R. Scheggi. *Educ:* Canford Sch.; RMC Sandhurst. Served War 1939–45, Middle East (PoW) (MBE); 2nd Lt, Coldstream Gds, 1939; Lt Col 1959; AQMG, HQ London Dist, 1961–63; Col 1963; AAG, War Office, 1963–65; Brig. 1967; Dep. Dir, Army Staff Duties, MoD, 1967–70; Dir of Quartering (A), MoD, 1970–73; Maj.-Gen. 1971; Dir, Management and Support of Intelligence, 1973–76. Mem., various Civil Service Commn and Home Office Interview Bds. Dep. Comr, St John Ambulance Bde, London (Prince of Wales's) Dist, 1978. KStJ 1980. *Recreations:* golf, photography, travel. *Heir: s* Julian William Richard Younger, *b* 10 Feb. 1950. *Address:* 23 Cadogan Square, SW1X 0HU. *Club:* Boodle's.

YOUNGER, Hon. Robert Edward Gilmour; Sheriff of Tayside, Central and Fife, since 1982; *b* 25 Sept. 1940; third *s* of 3rd Viscount Younger of Leckie, *qv; m* 1972, Helen Jane Hayes; one *s* one *d*. *Educ:* Cargilfield Sch., Edinburgh; Winchester Coll.; New Coll., Oxford (MA); Edinburgh Univ. (LLB); Glasgow Univ. Advocate, 1968; Sheriff of Glasgow and Strathkelvin, 1979–82. *Recreation:* out of doors. *Address:* Old Leckie, Gargunnock, Stirling, Scotland FK8 3BN. *T:* Gargunnock 213.
See also Rt. Hon. G. K. H. Younger.

YOUNGER, Sir William McEwan, 1st Bt, *cr* 1964, of Fountainbridge; DSO 1942; DL; Chairman: Scottish & Newcastle Breweries Ltd, 1960–69 (Managing Director, 1960–67); The Second Scottish Investment Trust Company Ltd, 1965–75; *b* 6 Sept. 1905; *y s* of late William Younger, Ravenswood, Melrose; *m* 1st, 1936, Nora Elizabeth Balfour (marr. diss., 1967); one *d*; 2nd, 1983, June Peck. *Educ:* Winchester; Balliol Coll., Oxford (Hon. Fellow 1984). Served War of 1939–45 (despatches, DSO); Western Desert, 1941–43; Italy, 1943–45; Lt-Col, RA. Hon. Sec., Scottish Unionist Assoc., 1955–64; Chm., Conservative Party in Scotland, 1971–74. Mem. Queen's Body Guard for Scotland. Director: British Linen Bank, 1955–71; Scottish Television, 1964–71; Chm., Highland Tourist (Cairngorm Development) Ltd, 1966–78. DL Midlothian, later City of Edinburgh, 1956–84. *Recreations:* mountaineering and fishing. *Heir: none. Address:* Little Hill Cottage, Harpsden, Henley-on-Thames, Oxon RG9 4HR. *T:* Henley-on-Thames 574339; 27 Moray Place, Edinburgh EH3 6DA. *T:* 031–225 8173. *Clubs:* Carlton, Alpine; New (Edinburgh).

YOUNGSON, Prof. Alexander John; Chairman, Royal Fine Art Commission for Scotland, since 1983 (Member, 1972–74); Emeritus Professor, Australian National University, since 1980; *b* 28 Sept. 1918; *s* of Alexander Brown, MA, MB, ChB and Helen Youngson; *m* 1948, Elizabeth Gisborne Naylor; one *s* one *d*. *Educ:* Aberdeen Grammar Sch.; Aberdeen Univ. Pilot, Fleet Air Arm, 1940–45. MA Aberdeen Univ., 1947; Commonwealth Fellow, 1947–48. Lecturer, University of St Andrews, 1948–50; Lecturer, University of Cambridge, 1950–58; Prof. of Political Economy 1963–74, and Vice-Principal, 1971–74, Univ. of Edinburgh; Dir, Res. Sch. of Social Scis, ANU, 1974–80; Prof. of Econs, Univ. of Hong Kong, 1980–82. Hon. FRIAS 1984. DLitt Aberdeen Univ., 1952. *Publications:* The American Economy, 1860–1940, 1951; Possibilities of Economic Progress, 1959; The British Economy, 1920–1957, 1960; The Making of Classical Edinburgh, 1966; Overhead Capital, 1967; After the Forty-Five, 1973; Beyond the Highland Line, 1974; Scientific Revolution in Victorian Medicine, 1979; (ed) China and Hong Kong: the economic nexus, 1983; The Prince and the Pretender, 1985; contrib. to various journals devoted to economics and economic history. *Recreation:* gardening. *Address:* 48 Blacket Place, Edinburgh EH9 1RJ.

YOUNIE, Edward Milne, OBE 1978; HM Diplomatic Service, retired; Consultant, Trefoil Associates, since 1983; *b* 9 Feb. 1926; *s* of John Milne and Mary Dickie Younie; *m* 1st, 1952, Mary Groves (*d* 1976); 2nd, 1979, Mimi Barkley. *Educ:* Fettes Coll. (Scholar); Gonville and Caius Coll., Cambridge (Scholar) (BA Hons). RN, 1944–46. HM Colonial Service, Tanganyika, 1950–62; FCO, 1963; Johannesburg, 1964–67; Blantyre, 1967–69; First Secretary: Lagos, 1972–76; Nairobi, 1977–79; Salisbury, 1979–81 (Counsellor, 1980); FCO, 1981–82. *Recreations:* golf, tennis, music. *Address:* Glebe House, Kippen, Stirling. *Club:* Brooks's.

YOUNSON, Maj.-Gen. Eric John, OBE 1952; BSc; CEng, FRAeS, FBIM, FIIM, FRSA; Industrial Consultant; Clerk to the Worshipful Company of Scientific Instrument Makers, since 1976; *b* 1 March 1919; *o s* of late Ernest M. Younson, MLitt, BCom, Jarrow; *m* 1946, Jean Beaumont Carter, BA; three *d*. *Educ:* Jarrow Grammar Sch.; Univ. of Durham; Royal Military Coll. of Science. Served War of 1939–45: commissioned, RA, 1940; UK and NW Europe (despatches). Directing Staff, RMCS, 1953–55; Atomic Weapons Research Estab., 1957–58; Attaché (Washington) as rep. of Chief Scientific Adviser, 1958–61; Head of Defence Science 3, MoD, 1961–63; Dep. Dir of Artillery, 1964–66; Dir of Guided Weapons Trials and Ranges, Min. of Technology, 1967–69; Vice-Pres., Ordnance Board, 1970–72, Pres., 1972–73; retired 1973; Sen. Asst Dir, Central Bureau for Educnl Visits and Exchanges, 1973–74; Dep. Dir, SIMA, 1974–78; Sec.-Gen., EUROM, 1975–77. Freeman, City of London, 1981. *Publications:* articles on gunnery and scientific subjects in Service jls; occasional poetry. *Recreations:* photography, electronics. *Address:* 9 Montague Close, SE1. *T:* 01–403 3300; 7 Pondwick Road, Harpenden, Herts. *T:* Harpenden 5892. *Club:* Army and Navy.

YPRES, 3rd Earl of, *cr* 1922; Viscount, *cr* 1916; of Ypres and of High Lake; **John Richard Charles Lambart French;** *b* 30 Dec. 1921; *o s* of 2nd Earl and Olivia Mary (*d* 1934), *d* of Maj.-Gen. Thomas John; *S* father, 1958; *m* 1st, 1943, Maureen Helena (marr. diss. 1972), *d* of Major H. John Kelly, US Foreign Service (retd), and of Mrs Kelly, Stow Bedon Hall, Attleborough, Norfolk; three *d*; 2nd, 1972, Deborah, *d* of R. Roberts, Liverpool; one *d*. *Educ:* Winchester; Trinity Coll., Dublin. Served War of 1939–45 as Captain, King's Royal Rifle Corps. *Heir: none.*

YUDKIN, John, MA, PhD, MD, BCh (Cambridge); BSc (London); FRCP, FRSC, FIBiol; Professor of Nutrition, University of London, at Queen Elizabeth College, 1954–71, Emeritus Professor, since 1971; *b* 8 August 1910; 3rd *s* of Louis and Sarah Yudkin, London; *m* 1933, Emily Himmelweit; three *s*. *Educ:* Hackney Downs (formerly Grocers' Company) School, London; Chelsea Polytechnic; Christ's Coll., Cambridge; London Hospital. Research in Biochemical Laboratory, Cambridge, 1931–36; Research in Nutritional Laboratory, Cambridge, 1938–43; Benn Levy Research Student, 1933–35; Grocers' Company Research Scholar, 1938–39; Sir Halley Stewart Research Fellow, 1940–43; Dir of Medical Studies, Christ's Coll., Cambridge, 1940–43; Prof. of Physiology, Queen Elizabeth Coll., 1945–54; Fellow, Queen Elizabeth Coll., London, 1976. William Julius Mickle Fellow, 1961–62. *Publications:* This Slimming Business, 1958; The Complete Slimmer, 1964; Changing Food Habits, 1964; Our Changing Fare, 1966; Pure, White and Deadly, 1972; This Nutrition Business, 1976; A-Z of Slimming, 1977; Penguin Encyclopaedia of Nutrition, 1985; numerous articles on biochemistry and nutrition in scientific and medical journals. *Address:* 20 Wellington Court, Wellington Road, St John's Wood, NW8. *T:* 01–586 5586.

YUKAWA, Morio, Hon. GCVO; Japanese diplomatist; *b* 23 Feb. 1908; *m* 1940, Teiko Kohiyama; two *s. Educ:* Tokyo Imperial Univ. (Law Dept). Joined Diplomatic Service, and apptd Attaché, London, 1933; Dir, Trade Bureau of Economic Stabilization Bd (Cabinet), 1950; Dir, Econ. Affairs Bureau (For. Min.), 1951; Counsellor, Paris, 1952; Dir, Internat. Co-op. Bureau (For. Min.), 1954; again Dir, Econ. Affairs Bureau, 1955; Ambassador to The Philippines, 1957–61; Dep. Vice-Minister (For. Min.), 1961–63; Ambassador to Belgium, 1963–68; concurrently Ambassador to Luxembourg and Chief of Japanese Mission to European Economic Community, 1964–68; Ambassador to Court of St James's, 1968–72. Grand Master of Ceremonies, Imperial Household, Tokyo, 1973–79. First Order of Sacred Treasure and many other decorations, inc. Hon. GCVO 1971. *Publications:* articles and brochures, principally on historical subjects. *Recreations:* golf, theatre, history and biography. *Address:* Sanbancho Hilltop, 5–10 Sanbancho, Chiyoda-ku, Tokyo, Japan. *Clubs:* Tokyo, Nihon, Gakushikai (Tokyo); Hodogaya Country (Yokohama).

YUKON, Bishop of, since 1981; **Rt. Rev. Ronald Curry Ferris;** *b* 2 July 1945; *s* of Herald Bland Ferris and Marjorie May Ferris; *m* 1965, Janet Agnes (*née* Waller); two *s* four *d. Educ:* Toronto Teachers' Coll. (diploma); Univ. of W Ontario (BA); Huron Coll., London, Ont. (MDiv). Teacher, Pape Avenue Elem. School, Toronto, 1965; Principal Teacher, Carcross Elem. School, Yukon, 1966–68. Incumbent, St Luke's Church, Old Crow, Yukon, 1970–72; Rector, St Stephen's Memorial Church, London, Ont., 1973–81. Hon. DD, Huron Coll., London, Ont., 1982. *Address:* 41 Firth Road, Whitehorse, Yukon Y1A 4R5, Canada.

Z

ZACHARIAH, Joyce Margaret; Secretary of the Post Office, 1975–77; *b* 11 Aug. 1932; *d* of Robert Paton Emery and Nellie Nicol (*née* Wilson); *m* 1978, George Zachariah. *Educ:* Earl Grey Sch., Calgary; Hillhead High Sch., Glasgow; Glasgow Univ. (MA 1st cl. Hons French and German, 1956). Post Office: Asst Principal, 1956; Private Sec. to Dir Gen., 1960; Principal, 1961; Asst Sec., 1967; Dir, Chairman's Office, 1970. *Address:* Vårflodsgatan 17, 41712 Gothenburg, Sweden.
See also E. J. Emery.

ZACHAROV, Prof. Vasilii, (Basil), PhD, DSc; Invited Professor, University of Geneva, since 1984; *b* 2 Jan. 1931; *s* of Viktor Nikiforovich Zakharov and Varvara Semyenovna (*née* Krzak); *m* 1959, Jeanne (*née* Hopper) one *s* one *d*. *Educ:* Latymer Upper Sch.; Univ. of London (BSc: Maths 1951, Phys 1952; MSc 1958; PhD 1960; DIC 1960; DSc 1977). MInstP. Research in Computer systems and applications, Birkbeck Coll., 1953–56; digital systems development, Rank Precision Instruments, 1956–57; Research Fellow, Imperial Coll., 1957–60; Physicist, European Organisation for Nuclear Res. (CERN), Geneva, 1960–65; Reader in Experimental Physics, Queen Mary Coll., London, 1965–66; Head of Computer Systems and Electronics Div., as Sen. Principal Sci. Officer, SRC Daresbury Laboratory, 1966–69, Dep. Chief Sci. Officer, 1970–78; Dir, London Univ. Computing Centre, 1978–80, and Prof. of Computing Systems, 1979–80; Sen. Associate, CERN, Geneva, 1981–83. Vis Scientist: JINR Dubna, USSR, 1965; CERN, 1971–72; Consultant to AERE Harwell, 1965; Vis. Prof. of Physics, QMC London, 1968; Vis. Prof., Westfield Coll., 1974–78. Member, SRC Comp. Sci. Cttee, 1974–77. *Publications:* Digital Systems Logic, 1968; scientific papers in professional jls on photoelectronics, computer systems, elementary particle physics and computer applications. *Recreations:* collecting Russian miscellanea, skiing, shooting; grape growing, wine making, wine drinking. *Address:* The Firs, Oldcastle, Cheshire SY14 7NE.

ZAHEDI, Ardeshir; Ambassador of Iran to the United States, 1959–61 and 1973–79; Ambassador of Iran to Mexico, 1973–76; *b* Tehran, 16 Oct. 1928; *s* of General Fazlollah and Khadijeh Zahedi; *m* 1957, HIH Princess Shahnaz Pahlavi (marr. diss., 1964); one *d*. *Educ:* American Coll. of Beirut; Utah State Univ. (BS). Treasurer, Jt Iran-American Commn, and Asst to Dir of Point 4 Program, 1950; took part in revolution led by Gen. Zahedi which overthrew Mossadegh, 1953; Special Adviser to Prime Minister, 1953; Chamberlain to HIM the Shahanshah of Iran, 1954–59; Head of Iranian Students Program, 1959–60; Head of Mission representing Iran at 150th Anniv. Celebrations in Argentina, 1960; Ambassador of Iran to the Court of St James's, 1962–66; Foreign Minister of Iran, 1967–71. Represented Iranian Govt: at signing of Treaty banning Nuclear Tests, London, 1963; at Independence Celebrations, Bahamas, 1973. Hon. Doctorates: Utah State Univ., 1951; Chungang Univ. of Seoul, 1969; East Texas State, 1973; Kent State Univ., 1974; St Louis Univ., 1975. Holds decorations from Iran and 23 other countries incl. Iranian Taj with Grand Cordon First Class, 1975. *Recreations:* hunting, shooting.

ZAHIRUDDIN bin Syed Hassan, Tun Syed, SMN, PSM, DUNM, SPMP, JMN, PJK; Governor of Malacca, since 1975; *b* 11 Oct. 1918; *m* 1949, Toh Puan Halimah, *d* of Hj. Mohd. Noh; five *s* five *d*. *Educ:* Malay Coll., Kuala Kangsar; Raffles Coll., Singapore (Dip.Arts). Passed Cambridge Sch. Cert. Malay Officer, Tanjong Malim, etc, 1945–47; Dep. Asst Dist Officer, 1948; Asst Dist Officer, 1951–54; 2nd Asst State Sec., Perak, 1955; Registrar of Titles and Asst State Sec. (Lands), Perak, 1956; Dist Officer, Batang Padang, Tapah, 1957; Dep. Sec., Public Services Commn, 1958; Principal Asst Sec. (Service), Fedn Estabt Office, Kuala Lumpur, 1960; State Sec., Perak, 1961; Permanent Sec.: Min. of Agric. and Co-operatives, Kuala Lumpur, 1963; Min. of Educn, Kuala Lumpur, 1966; Dir-Gen., Public Services Dept, Kuala Lumpur, 1969; retd, 1972. High Comr for Malaysia in London, 1974–75. Chm., Railway Services Commn, Kuala Lumpur, 1972–. Chairman: Special Cttee on Superannuation in the Public Services, 1972, and Statutory Bodies; Bd of Governors, Malay Coll., Kuala Kangsar; Interim Council of Nat. Inst. of Technology; Central Bd. Vice-Pres., Subang Nat. Golf Club, 1972–74. Hon. GCVO 1974. *Recreation:* golf. *Address:* Seri Melaka, Malacca, Malaysia.

ZAIDI, Bashir Husain, Syed, CIE 1941; Padma Vibhushan 1976; Director of several industrial concerns; *b* 1898; *s* of Syed Shaukat Husain Zaidi; *m* 1937, Qudsia Abdullah (*d* 1960); two *s* one *d*. *Educ:* St Stephen's College, Delhi; Cambridge University. Called to Bar, Lincoln's Inn, 1923; served Aligarh Univ., 1923–30; entered Rampur State service, 1930; Chief Minister Rampur State, UP, 1936–49; Member: Indian Constituent Assembly, 1947–49, Indian Parliament, 1950–52; Indian Delegation to Gen. Assembly of UN, 1951; Indian Parliament (Lok Sabha), 1952–57; (Rajya Sabha) 1964–70; Govt of India's Commn of Inquiry on Communal Disturbances, 1967–69. Chm., Associated Journals Ltd, 1952–77. Vice-Chancellor, Aligarh Muslim University, 1956–62. Leader, Good Will Mission to 9 Afro-Asian countries, 1964; Leader, Cultural Delegn to participate in Afghan Independence Week celebrations, 1965. Trustee: HEH the Nizam's Trusts, 1962–; Youth Hostels Assoc. of India, 1970–. Member: Governing Body, Dr Zakir Husain Coll., New Delhi, 1974–; Ct, Aligarh Muslim Univ., 1983–. DLitt *hc*: Aligarh 1964; Kanpur, 1974. *Address:* Zaidi Villa, Jamianagar, New Delhi, India.

ZAMBONI, Richard Frederick Charles, FCA; Managing Director, since 1979 and a Vice-Chairman, since 1986, Sun Life Assurance Society plc; Chairman: Sun Life Investment Management Services, since 1985; Sun Life Trust Management, since 1985; Sun Life Direct Marketing, since 1986; *b* 28 July 1930; *s* of Alfred Charles Zamboni and Frances Hosler; *m* 1960, Pamela Joan Marshall; two *s* one *d*. *Educ:* Monkton House Sch., Cardiff. Gordon Thomas & Pickard, Chartered Accountants, 1948–54; served Royal Air Force, 1954–56; Peat Marwick Mitchell & Co., 1956–58; British Egg Marketing Board, 1959–70, Chief Accountant, from 1965; Sun Life Assurance Society plc, 1971–, Director, 1975–. Deputy Chairman: Life Offices' Assoc., 1985 (Mem., Management Cttee, 1981–85); Assoc. of British Insurers, 1986– (Dep. Chm., 1985–86, Chm., 1986–, Life Insurance Council); Member: Council, Chartered Insurance Inst., 1983–85; Life Assurance and Unit Trust Regulatory Orgn's steering gp, 1985–86; Hon. Treasurer, Insurance Institute of London, 1982–85. Member, Management Cttee, Effingham Housing Assoc. Ltd, 1980–86; Director: Worldtech Ventures Ltd, 1981–; Avon Enterprise Fund PLC, 1984–. Pres., Insurance Offices RFU, 1985–. *Recreations:* ornithology, gardening, tennis. *Address:* Long Meadow, Beech Avenue, Effingham, Leatherhead, Surrey KT24 5PH. *T:* Bookham 58211.

ZAMYATIN, Leonid Mitrofanovich; Soviet Ambassador to the Court of St James's, since 1986; *b*. Nizhni Devitsk, 9 March 1922; *m* 1946; one *d*. *Educ:* Moscow Aviation Inst.; Higher Diplomatic School. Mem., CPSU, 1944–, Mem. Central Cttee, 1976–; Min. of Foreign Affairs, 1946; First Sec., Counsellor on Political Questions, USSR Mission to UN, 1953–57; Soviet Dep. Rep., Preparatory Cttee, later Bd of Governors, IAEA, 1957–59; Soviet Rep., IAEA, 1959–60; Dep. Head, American Countries Dept, Min. of Foreign Affairs, 1960–62; Head of Press Dept, 1962–70; Mem., Collegium of Ministry, 1962–70; Dir-Gen., TASS News Agency, 1970–78, Govt Minister, 1972–; Dep. to USSR Supreme Soviet, 1970–; Chief, Dept of Internat. Inf., Central Cttee, CPSU, 1978–86. Mem., Commn for Foreign Relations, Soviet of Nationalities, 1974–. Lenin Prize 1978; USSR Orders and medals incl. Order of Lenin (twice). *Address:* Soviet Embassy, 13 Kensington Palace Gardens, W8 4QX. *T:* 01–229 3628.

ZANDER, Prof. Michael; Professor of Law, London School of Economics, since 1977 (Convener, Law Department, since 1984); Legal Correspondent of The Guardian, since 1963; *b* 16 Nov. 1932; *s* of Dr Walter Zander and Margaret Magnus; *m* 1965, Betsy Treeger; two *c*. *Educ:* Royal Grammar Sch., High Wycombe; Jesus Coll., Cambridge (BA Law, double 1st Cl. Hons; LLB 1st Cl. Hons; Whewell Scholar in Internat. Law); Harvard Law Sch. (LLM). Solicitor of the Supreme Court. National Service, RA, 1950–52, 2nd Lieut. Cassel Scholar, Lincoln's Inn, 1957, resigned 1959; New York law firm, 1958–59; articled with City solicitors, 1959–62; Asst Solicitor with City firm, 1962–63; London Sch. of Economics: Asst Lectr, 1963; Lectr, 1965; Sen. Lectr, 1970; Reader, 1970. *Publications:* Lawyers and the Public Interest, 1968; (ed) What's Wrong with the Law?, 1970; (ed) Family Guide to the Law, 1971 (2nd edn 1972); Cases and Materials on the English Legal System, 1973 (4th edn 1984); (with B. Abel-Smith and R. Brooke) Legal Problems and the Citizen, 1973; Social Workers, their Clients and the Law, 1974 (3rd edn 1981); A Bill of Rights?, 1975 (3rd edn 1985); Legal Services for the Community, 1978; (ed) Pears Guide to the Law, 1979; The Law-Making Process, 1980 (2nd edn 1985); The State of Knowledge about the English Legal Profession, 1980; The Police and Criminal Evidence Act 1984, 1985; articles in Criminal Law Rev., Mod. Law Rev., Law Soc.'s Gazette, New Law Jl, Solicitors' Jl, Amer. Bar Assoc. Jl, New Society, etc. *Recreations:* reform, the cello. *Address:* 12 Woodside Avenue, N6 4SS. *T:* 01–883 6257.

ZANGWILL, Prof. Oliver Louis, FRS 1977; Professor of Experimental Psychology, University of Cambridge, 1952–81, now Emeritus; *b* 29 Oct. 1913; *yr s* of Israel Zangwill, author and dramatist, and Edith Ayrton Zangwill; *m* 1st, 1947, Joy Sylvia (marr. diss. 1976), *d* of late Thomas Moult; one *s* decd; 2nd, 1976, Shirley Florence Tribe, BDS (Edin.); one *s* (adopted). *Educ:* University College School, London; King's College, Cambridge (BA 1935, MA 1939). Natural Science Tripos, Part I, Class 2, 1934; Moral Science Tripos, Part II, Class 1, with special distinction, 1935. Research Student, Cambridge Psychological Laboratory, 1935–40; Psychologist, Brain Injuries Unit, Edinburgh 1940–45; Asst Director, Institute of Experimental Psychology, Oxford, 1945–52; Senior Lecturer in General Psychology, Univ. of Oxford, 1948–52. Visiting Psychologist, Nat. Hosp. for Nervous Diseases, Queen Square, London, 1947–79, Hon. Res. Fellow, 1979; Hon. Consulting Psychologist to United Cambridge Hospitals, 1969–. Editor, Quart. Jl Exper. Psychology, 1958–66. President: Sect. J. Brit. Assoc. Adv. Sci., 1963; Experimental Psychology Soc., 1962–63; British Psychological Soc., 1974–75. Mem., Biological Research Board, Medical Research Council, 1962–66. Professorial Fellow, 1955–, Supernumerary Fellow, 1981–, King's Coll., Cambridge. Mem., Assoc. of British Neurologists, 1973. Hon. For. Mem., Soc. Française de Neurologie, 1971. Sir Frederic Bartlett Lectr, 1971; Stolz Lectr, Guy's Hosp., 1979. Kenneth Craik Award, St John's Coll., Cambridge, 1977–78. DUniv Stirling, 1979; ScD St Andrew's, 1980. Hon. FRCPsych 1980. *Publications:* An Introduction to Modern Psychology, 1950; Cerebral Dominance and its relation to psychological function, 1960; Jt Author and Jt Editor: Current Problems in Animal Behaviour, 1961; Amnesia, 1966, 2nd edn 1977; Lateralisation or Language in the Child, 1981; Handbook of Psychology, vol. 1, General Psychopathology, 1982; papers in psychological and medical journals. *Recreations:* reading, natural history. *Address:* 247 Chesterton Road, Cambridge. *T:* Cambridge 65750.

ZANZIBAR AND TANGA, Bishop of; *see* Tanzania, Archbishop of.

ZARNECKI, Prof. George, CBE 1970; MA, PhD; FSA; FBA 1968; Professor of History of Art, University of London, 1963–82, now Emeritus Professor (Reader, 1959–63); Deputy Director, Courtauld Institute of Art, 1961–74; *b* 12 Sept. 1915; *m* 1945, Anne Leslie Frith; one *s* one *d*. *Educ:* Cracow Univ. MA Cracow Univ., 1938; PhD Univ. of London, 1950. Junior Asst, Inst. of History of Art, Cracow Univ., 1936–39. Served war of 1939–45 as lance-corporal in Polish Army; in France, 1939–40 (Polish Cross of Valour and Croix de Guerre, 1940); prisoner of war, 1940–42; interned in Spain, 1942–43; in Polish Army in UK, 1943–45. On staff of Courtauld Institute of Art, Univ. of London, 1945–82. Slade Professor of Fine Art, Univ. of Oxford, 1960–61. Vice-President: Soc. of Antiquaries of London, 1968–72; British Soc. of Master Glass Painters, 1976–; British

Archaeol Assoc., 1979–; Member: Corpus Vitrearum Medii Aevi Cttee, British Acad., 1956–85; Conservation Cttee, Council for Places of Worship, 1969–75; Royal Commn on Historical Monuments, 1971–84; Arts Sub-Cttee of UGC, 1972–77; Publications Cttee, British Acad., 1978–84; Sub-Cttee for Higher Doctorates, CNAA, 1978–82; Chm., Corpus of Anglo-Saxon Sculpture Cttee, British Acad., 1979–84; Chm., Working Cttee organizing Arts Council exhibition, English Romanesque Art 1066–1200, 1984. Inst. for Advanced Study, Princeton, 1966. Hon. DLitt: Warwick, 1978; East Anglia, 1981; Hon. LittD Dublin, 1984. Gold Medal, Soc. of Antiquaries, 1986. Gold Medal of Merit (Poland), 1978. *Publications:* English Romanesque Sculpture 1066–1140, 1951; Later English Romanesque Sculpture 1140–1210, 1953; English Romanesque Lead Sculpture, 1957; Early Sculpture of Ely Cathedral, 1958; Gislebertus, sculpteur d'Autun, 1960 (English edn, 1961), Romanesque Sculpture at Lincoln Cathedral, 1964; La sculpture à Payerne, Lausanne, 1966; 1066 and Architectural Sculpture (Proceedings of Brit. Acad.), 1966; Romanik (Belser Stilgeschichte, VI), 1970 (English edn, Romanesque Art, 1971); The Monastic Achievement, 1972; (contrib.) Westminster Abbey, 1972; Art of the Medieval World, 1975; Studies in Romanesque Sculpture, 1979; articles in archaeological journals. *Address:* 22 Essex Park, N3 1NE. *T:* 01–346 6497.

ZEALLEY, Christopher Bennett; Director since 1970 and Trustee since 1976, Dartington Hall Trust; Chairman, White Hart Holdings PLC; *b* 5 May 1931; *s* of Sir Alec Zealley and Lady Zealley (*née* King); *m* 1966, Ann Elizabeth Sandwith one *s* one *d*. *Educ:* Sherborne Sch.; King's Coll., Cambridge (MA Law). Commnd RNVR, 1953; ICI Ltd, 1955–66; IRC, 1967–70. Chairman: Public Interest Research Centre, 1972–; Social Audit Ltd, 1972–; Consumers' Assoc., 1976–81; Trustee, Charities Aid Foundn, 1982–. Director: JT Group Ltd; Grant Instruments Ltd; Good Food Club Ltd. *Recreation:* music. *Address:* Culverwood, Rattery, South Brent, Devon. *Club:* Naval.

ZEEMAN, Prof. Erik Christopher, FRS 1975; Professor, Director of Mathematics Research Centre, University of Warwick, since 1964; Senior Fellow, Science Research Council, since 1976; *b* 4 Feb. 1925; *s* of Christian Zeeman and Christine Zeeman (*née* Bushell); *m* 1960, Rosemary Gledhill; three *s* two *d*. *Educ:* Christ's Hospital; Christ's Coll., Cambridge (MA, PhD). Commonwealth Fellow, 1954; Fellow of Gonville and Caius Coll., Cambridge, 1953–64; Lectr, Cambridge Univ., 1955–64. Visiting Prof. at various institutes, incl.: IAS; Princeton; IHES, Paris; IMPA, Rio; Royal Instn, 1983–; also at various univs, incl.: California, Florida, Pisa. Hon. Dr, Strasbourg. *Publications:* numerous research papers on topology, dynamical systems, and applications to biology and the social sciences, in various mathematical and other jls. *Recreation:* family. *Address:* 40 Warwick New Road, Leamington Spa. *T:* Leamington 26997.

ZEFFIRELLI, G. Franco (Corsi); opera, film and theatrical producer and designer since 1949; *b* 12 February 1923. *Educ:* Florence. Designer: (in Italy): A Streetcar Named Desire; Troilus and Cressida; Three Sisters. Has produced and designed numerous operas at La Scala, Milan, 1952 , and in all the great cities of Italy, at world-famous festivals, and in UK and USA; *operas include:* Lucia di Lammermoor, Cavalleria Rusticana, and Pagliacci (Covent Garden, 1959, 1973); Falstaff (Covent Garden, 1961); L'Elisir D'Amore (Glyndebourne, 1961); Don Giovanni, and Alcina (Covent Garden, 1962); Tosca, Rigoletto (Covent Garden, 1964, 1966, 1973, Metropolitan, NY, 1985); Don Giovanni (Staatsoper-Wien, 1972); Otello (Metropolitan, NY, 1972); Antony and Cleopatra (Metropolitan, NY, 1973); Otello (La Scala, 1976); La Bohème (Metropolitan, NY, 1981); Turandot (La Scala, 1983, 1985); *stage:* Romeo and Juliet (Old Vic, 1960); Othello (Stratford-on-Avon), 1961; Amleto (National Theatre), 1964; After the Fall (Rome), 1964; Who's Afraid of Virginia Woolf (Paris), 1964, (Milan), 1965; La Lupa (Rome), 1965; Much Ado About Nothing (National Theatre), 1966; Black Comedy (Rome), 1967; A Delicate Balance (Rome), 1967; Saturday, Sunday, Monday (Nat. Theatre), 1973; Filumena, Lyric, 1977; *films:* The Taming of the Shrew, 1965–66; Florence, Days of Destruction, 1966; Romeo and Juliet, 1967; Brother Sun, Sister Moon, 1973; Jesus of Nazareth, 1977; The Champ, 1979; Endless Love, 1981; La Traviata, 1983; Cavalleria Rusticana, 1983; Otello, 1986. Produced Beethoven's Missa Solemnis, San Pietro, Rome, 1971. *Publication:* Zeffirelli (autobiog.), 1986. *Address:* Via due Macelli 31, Rome.

ZEHETMAYR, John Walter Lloyd, VRD 1963; FICFor; Senior Officer for Wales and Conservator South Wales, Forestry Commission, 1966–81, retired; Member, Brecon Beacons National Park Committee, since 1982; Chairman, Forestry Safety Council, since 1986; *b* 24 Dec. 1921; *s* of late Walter Zehetmayr and late Gladys Zehetmayr; *m* 1945, Isabell (Betty) Neill-Kennedy; two *s* one *d*. *Educ:* St Paul's, Kensington; Keble Coll., Oxford (BA). Served RNVR, 1942–46 (despatches); now Lt Cdr RNR retired. Forestry Commission: Silviculturist, 1948–56; Chief Work Study Officer, 1956–64; Conservator West Scotland, 1964–66. Mem. Prince of Wales' Cttee, 1970–81 and 1983–85. *Publications:* Experiments in Tree Planting on Peat, 1954; Afforestation of Upland Heaths, 1960; The Gwent Small Woods Project 1979–84, 1985; Forestry in Wales, 1985. *Recreations:* garden, conservation, skiing. *Address:* The Haven, Augusta Road, Penarth, S Glam CF6 2RH.

ZEIDLER, Sir David (Ronald), Kt 1980; CBE 1971; FAA 1985; FRACI; FIChemE; Chairman and Managing Director, ICI Australia, 1973–80, retired; *s* of Otto William and Hilda Maude Zeidler; *m* 1943, June Susie Broadhurst; four *d*. *Educ:* Scotch Coll., Melbourne; Melbourne Univ. (MSc). CSIRO, 1941–52; joined ICI Australia, 1952: Research Manager, 1953; Development Manager, 1959; Controller, Dyes and Fabrics Gp, 1962; Dir, 1963; Man. Dir, 1971; Dep. Chm., 1972. Chm., Metal Manufacturers Ltd, 1981–; Director: Amatil Ltd, 1979–; Broken Hill Prop. Co. Ltd, 1978–; Commercial Bank of Australia Ltd, 1974–; Australian Foundation Investment Co. Ltd, 1982–; past Director: ICI New Zealand Ltd; IMI Australia Ltd. Vice-Pres., Walter and Eliza Hall Inst. of Med. Res., 1972–; Dep. Chm., Queen's Silver Jubilee Trust, 1977–. Chairman: Govt Inquiry into Elec. Generation and Power Sharing in SE Aust., 1980–81; Defence Industry Cttee, 1981–84; Member, or past Mem., cttees concerned with prof. qualifications, defence industry, educn and trng, internat. business co-operation. Member: Aust.-Japan Businessmen's Co-operation Cttee, 1978–80; Aust.-NZ Businessmen's Council Ltd, 1978–80; Sir Robert Menzies Meml Trust, 1978–80; Council, Aust. Acad. of Technol Scis, 1979– (Vice-Pres., 1970–71; Pres., 1983–); Council, Science Museum of Victoria, 1964–82; Commerce and Industry Cttee, 1978–85, and Defence Industry Cttee, 1977–84 (Chm., 1981–84), Victorian Div. of Aust. Red Cross Soc.; Inst. of Dirs; Royal Society, Victoria; Royal Soc. for Encouragement of Arts Manuf. and Commerce in London; Cook Society. *Recreations:* tennis, ski-ing, golf. *Address:* 45/238 The Avenue, Parkville, Victoria 3052, Australia. *T:* 387 5720. *Clubs:* Melbourne, Australian (Melb. and Sydney), Commonwealth (Canberra), Sciences.

ZELLICK, Prof. Graham John, PhD; Professor of Public Law, since 1982, and Dean of the Faculty of Laws, since 1986, in the University of London; Dean of the Faculty of Laws and Head of the Department of Laws at Queen Mary College, since 1984; *b* 12 August 1948; *s* of R. H. and B. Zellick; *m* 1975, Jennifer Temkin, LLM, Barrister, Lectr in Law, LSE; one *s* one *d*. *Educ:* Christ's Coll., Finchley; Gonville and Caius Coll., Cambridge (MA, PhD); Stanford Univ. Ford Foundn Fellow, Stanford Law Sch., 1970–71; Lectr, 1971–78, Reader in Law, 1978–82, QMC, London Univ. Vis. Fellow, Centre of Criminology, 1978–79, and Vis. Prof. of Law, 1975, 1978–79, Toronto Univ. Lectures: Noel Buxton, 1983; Webber, 1986; Sir Gwilym Morris, 1986. Member: Council and Exec. Cttee, Howard League for Penal Reform, 1973–82; Jellicoe Cttee on Bds of Visitors of Prisons, 1973–75; Sub Cttee on Crime and Criminal Justice, 1984–, and Sub Cttee on Police Powers and the Prosecution Process, 1985–, ESRC; Lord Chancellor's Legal Aid Adv. Cttee, 1985–; Newham Dist Ethics Cttee, 1985–86; Data Protection Tribunal, 1985–; Chm., Prisoners' Advice and Law Service, 1984–; Dep. Chm., Justice Cttee on Prisoners' Rights, 1981–83. Governor: Pimlico Sch., 1973–77; QMC, 1983–; Member: Senate, London Univ, 1985–; Council, Univ. Coll. Sch., 1983–; Academic Adv. Cttee, Jews' Coll., 1984–; Court of Governors: Polytechnic of Central London, 1973–77; Polytechnic of N London, 1986–; Chm , Lawyers' Gp, 1984 , and Mem. Council of Management and Trustee, 1985–, Tel Aviv Univ. Trust. JP Inner London (N Westminster), 1981–85. Editor: European Human Rights Reports, 1978–82; Public Law, 1981–86; Member of Editorial Board: British Jl of Criminology, 1980–; Public Law, 1981–; Howard Jl of Criminal Justice, 1984–. *Publications:* (contrib.) Halsbury's Laws of England, 4th edn 1982; contribs to collections of essays, pamphlets, the national press, and professional and learned periodicals incl. British Jl of Criminology, Criminal Law Rev., Modern Law Rev., Public Law, Univ. of Toronto Law Jl. *Address:* Faculty of Laws, Queen Mary College, E1 4NS. *T:* 01–980 4811; 14 Brookfield Park, NW5 1ER. *T:* 01–485 8219. *Club:* Reform.

ZEMAN, Prof. Zbyněk Anthony Bohuslav; Research Professor in European History, since 1982, and Professorial Fellow of St Edmund Hall, since 1983, Oxford University; *b* Prague, 18 Oct. 1928; *s* of late Jaroslav and Růžena Zeman; *m* 1956, Sarah Anthea Collins (separated); two *s* one *d*. *Educ:* London and Oxford Universities. BA (Hons) London, DPhil Oxon. Research Fellow, St Antony's Coll., Oxford, 1958–61, and Mem. editorial staff, The Economist, 1959–62; Lectr in Modern History, Univ. of St Andrews, 1963–70; Head of Research, Amnesty International, 1970–73; Director, East-West SPRL (Brussels) and European Cooperation Research Gp, 1974–76; Prof. of Central and SE European Studies and Dir, Comenius Centre, Lancaster Univ., 1976–82. *Publications* include: The Break-up of the Habsburg Empire 1914–1918, 1961; Nazi Propaganda, 1964; (with W. B. Scharlau) The Merchant of Revolution, A Life of Alexander Helphand (Parvus), 1965; Prague Spring, 1969; A Diplomatic History of the First World War, 1971; (ed jtly) International Yearbook of East-West Trade, 1975; The Masaryks, 1976; (with Jan Zoubek) Comecon Oil and Gas, 1977; Selling the War: art and propaganda in the First World War, 1978; Heckling Hitler: caricatures of the Third Reich, 1984. *Recreations:* skiing, squash, cooking. *Address:* St Edmund Hall, Oxford.

ZETLAND, 3rd Marquess of; **Lawrence Aldred Mervyn Dundas;** Bt 1762; Baron Dundas, 1794; Earl of Zetland, 1838; Earl of Ronaldshay (UK), 1892; DL; Temporary Major Yorkshire Hussars (TA); *b* 12 Nov. 1908; *er s* of 2nd Marquess of Zetland, KG, PC, GCSI, GCIE, FBA, and Cicely, *d* of Colonel Mervyn Archdale; *S* father, 1961; *m* 1936, Penelope, *d* of late Col Ebenezer Pike, CBE, MC; three *s* one *d*. *Educ:* Harrow; Trinity Coll., Cambridge. ADC on Staff of Viceroy of India, 1930–31. DL, North Yorks, 1965. *Heir: s* Earl of Ronaldshay, *qv*. *Address:* Aske, Richmond, North Yorks DL10 5HJ. *T:* Richmond (Yorks) 3222; 59 Cadogan Place, SW1. *T:* 01–235 6542. *Clubs:* All England Lawn Tennis, Jockey.

ZETTER, Paul Isaac, CBE 1981; Chairman, Zetters Group Ltd, since 1972; *b* 9 July 1923; *s* of late Simon and Esther Zetter; *m* 1954, Helen Lore Morgenstern; one *s* one *d*. *Educ:* City of London Sch. Army, 1941–46. Family business, 1946–; became public co., 1965. Chm., Southern Council for Sport and Recreation, 1985–; Mem., Sports Council, 1985–; Governor, 1975–, and Hon. Vice-Pres., 1985–, Sports Aid Foundation (Chm., 1976–85). Mem., Glovers' Co., 1981–; Freeman, City of London, 1981. *Publication:* It Could Be Verse, 1976. *Recreations:* varied water sports, walking, trout breeding, member of the Test and Itchen Fishing Association Ltd. *Address:* 86 Clerkenwell Road, EC1P 1ZS. *Club:* Royal Automobile.

ZETTERLING, Mai Elizabeth; Actress, films and stage, film director, writer; *b* 24 May 1925; *d* of Joel and Lina Zetterling; *m* 1st, 1944, Tutte Lemkow; one *s* one *d*; 2nd, 1958, David John Hughes (marr. diss. 1977). *Educ:* Stockholm, Sweden. Graduate of Royal Theatre School of Drama, Stockholm. First appeared as Cecilia in Midsummer Dream in the Workhouse, Blanche Theatre, Stockholm, Oct. 1941. Stage successes (all at Royal Theatre, Stockholm) include: Janet in St Mark's Eve; Agnes in The Beautiful People; Brigid in Shadow and Substance; Maria in Twelfth Night; Nerissa in Merchant of Venice; Electra in Les Mouches; Adela in House of Bernarda. First appearance in London, as Hedwig in The Wild Duck, St Martin's, Nov. 1948; subsequently Nina in The Seagull, Lyric, Hammersmith, and St James's, 1949; Eurydice in Point of Departure, Lyric, Hammersmith and Duke of York's, 1950; Karen in The Trap, Duke of York's, 1952; Nora Helmer in A Doll's House, Lyric, Hammersmith, 1953; Poppy in The Count of Clérambard, Garrick, 1955; Thérèse Tard in Restless Heart, St James's, 1957; Tekla in Creditors, Lyric, Hammersmith, 1959, etc. *Swedish films* include: Frenzy, Iris, Rain Follows Dew, Music in the Dark, A Doll's House, Swinging on a Rainbow. *English films* include: Frieda, The Bad Lord Byron, Quartet, Portrait from Life, Lost People, Blackmailed, Hell is Sold Out, Tall Headlines, Desperate Moment, Faces in the Dark, Offbeat, The Main Attraction, and Only Two Can Play, Scrubbers. *United States films* include: Knock on Wood, Prize of Gold, and Seven Waves Away. Director of documentary films for BBC; Dir and Prod and co-writer with David Hughes of short film The War Game; 1st Award at Venice for Narrative Shorts, 1963; Director: Swedish full-length films, Alskande Par, (Eng.) Loving Couples, 1965; Night Games, 1966 (and *see infra*); Dr Glas, 1968; Flickorna, (Eng.) The Girls, 1968; Writer and Director: Visions of Eight (Olympics film), USA, 1972; Vincent the Dutchman, (award 1973); We Have Many Names (and actress), Sweden, 1975; The Moon is a Green Cheese, Sweden, 1976; The Native Squatter (for Canadian TV), Sweden, 1977; Lady Policeman (Granada TV documentary), 1979; Of Seals and Men (with Greenland trade dept), 1979; Love, Canada, 1980; Love and Marriage (Canadian TV documentary) (co-writer and director) Scrubbers (feature film, England); Amorosa (feature film, Sweden), 1986; Dir and Deviser, Playthings, Vienna English Theatre, New Half Moon Theatre, 1980. *Publications:* The Cat's Tale (with David Hughes), 1965; Night Games (novel), 1966; Shadow of the Sun (short stories), 1975; Bird of Passage (novel), 1976; Rains Hat (children's book), 1979; Ice Island (novel), 1979; All Those Tomorrows (autobiog.), 1985. *Recreations:* gardening, cooking, philosophical ESP, alchemy. *Address:* c/o Douglas Rae Management Ltd, 28 Charing Cross Road, W1.

ZHUKOV, Georgi Alexandrovich; Hero of Socialist Labour (1978); Orders of: Lenin (2); October Revolution; Red Banner of Labour (2); Red Star; Joliot-Curie Medal; Columnist of Pravda, since 1962; Alternate Member, Central Committee, CPSU, since 1976 (elected by XXV and XXVI Congresses of CPSU); MP since 1962; Member, Foreign Relations Committee, USSR Supreme Soviet, since 1966; Chairman, Soviet-French parliamentary group, since 1966; President, Soviet Committee of Peace, since 1983; Member Presidium, World Peace Council, since 1974; Vice-President, Soviet-American Institute, since 1961; President, Society USSR-France, since 1958; Secretary,

Moscow writing organization, since 1970; *b* 1908. *Educ:* Lomonosov Inst., Moscow. Corresp.: local papers in Lugansk, Kharkov, 1927–32; Komsomolskaya Pravda, 1932–46 (Mem. Editorial Bd); Pravda, 1946–47; Pravda in Paris, 1947–52; Foreign Editor of Pravda, 1952–57; Chairman, USSR Council of Ministers' State Committee for Cultural Relations with Foreign Countries, 1957–62. Mem., Central Auditing Cttee of CPSU, 1956–76, elected by XX, XXII, XXIII and XXIV Congresses of CPSU. Prizes: Lenin (for Journalism); Vorovsky; Union of Soviet Journalists; internat. organization of journalists. *Publications:* Border, 1938; Russians and Japan, 1945; Soldier's Life, 1946; American Notes (essays), 1947; The West After War, 1948; Three Months in Geneva, 1954; Taming Tigers, 1961; Japan, 1962; Meetings in Transcarpathia, 1962; One MIG from a Thousand, 1963, 2nd edn 1979; These Seventeen Years, 1963; Silent Art, 1964; The People of the Thirties, 1964; Vietnam, 1965; America, 1967; The People of the Forties, 1968, 2nd edn 1975; From Battle to Battle: letters from the ideological struggle front, 1970; Chilean Diary, 1970; The USA on the Threshold of the Seventies, 1970; The People in the War (about Vietnam), 1972; 33 Visas, 1972; Times of Great Changes, 1973; Alex and others, 1974; Poisoners, 1975; The War: the beginning and the end, 1975; Letters from Rambouillet, 1975; European Horizons, 1975; Thirty Conversations with TV Viewers, 1977; Town's Beginning, 1977; Thoughts of Unthinkable, 1978; Society without Future, 1978; The Tale of Dirty Tricks, 1978; Roots, 1980; Pioneer Builders, 1982; Rocketing Steps, 1983; Journey through Indo-China, 1984; Journalists, 1984; Where is peace—there life, 1985. *Address:* 24 Pravda Street, Moscow, USSR.

ZIEGLER, Henri Alexandre Léonard, Ingénieur Général Air; Grand Officier, Légion d'Honneur; Croix de Guerre (1939–45); Rosette de la Résistance; Hon. CBE; Hon. CVO; Legion of Merit (US); French Aviation Executive; *b* Limoges, 18 Nov. 1906; *s* of Charles Ziegler and Alix Mousnier-Buisson; *m* 1932, Gillette Rizzi; three *s* one *d*. *Educ:* Collège Stanislas, Paris; Ecole Polytechnique (Grad.); Ecole Nationale Supérieure de l'Aéronautique. Officer-Pilot in French Air Force, 1928 (5000 hours); Tech. Officer, Min. of Aviation, 1929; Dep. Dir of Flight Test Centre, 1938; Foreign Missions: Gt Britain, USA, Germany, Poland, USSR. War of 1939–45: Dep. Buying Mission, USA, Dec. 1939; French Resistance, 1941–44; Col and Chief of Staff, Forces Françaises de l'Intérieur (London), 1944. Dir-Gen., Air France, 1946–54. Dir of Cabinet: of J. Chaban-Delmas (Min. of Public Works, Transport and Tourism), 1954; of Gen. Cormiglion-Molignier (Min. of Public Works), 1955–56; Admin. Dir-Gen., Ateliers d'aviation Louis Breguet, 1957–67. Pres. Dir-Gen., Sud Aviation, 1968; Pres. Dir-Gen., Soc. Nationale Industrielle Aérospatiale, 1970–73; Pres., Airbus Industrie, 1970–74. Pres., Air Alpes, 1961–76; Pres., Forum Atomique Européen, 1956–60; Admin. Inst. du Transport Aérien, 1969–77; Pres., Union Syndicale des Industries Aérospatiales, 1971–74. Mem., Amicale des anciens des essais en vol. Hon. Fellow, Soc. of Experimental Test Pilots; Hon. FRAeS. *Publication:* La Grande Aventure de Concorde, 1976. *Recreation:* alpinism. *Address:* 55 boulevard Lannes, 75116 Paris, France. *T:* 45.04.61.53. *Club:* Aéro-Club de France (Paris).

ZIEGLER, Philip Sandeman; author; *b* 24 Dec. 1929; *s* of Major Colin Louis Ziegler, DSO, DL, and Mrs Dora Ziegler (*née* Barnwell); *m* 1st, 1960, Sarah Collins; one *s* one *d*; 2nd, 1971, Mary Clare Charrington; one *s*. *Educ:* Eton; New Coll., Oxford (1st Cl. Hons Jurisprudence; Chancellor's Essay Prize). Entered Foreign Service, 1952; served in Vientiane, Paris, Pretoria and Bogotà; resigned 1967; joined William Collins and Sons Ltd, 1967, Editorial Dir 1972, Editor-in-Chief, 1979–80, resigned when apptd to write official biog. of Earl Mountbatten of Burma. Chm., The London Library, 1979–85. FRSL 1975; FRHS 1979. *Publications:* Duchess of Dino, 1962; Addington, 1965; The Black Death, 1968; William IV, 1971; Omdurman, 1973; Melbourne, 1976 (W. H. Heinemann Award); Crown and People, 1978; Diana Cooper, 1981; Mountbatten, 1985; Elizabeth's Britain 1926 to 1986, 1986. *Address:* 22 Cottesmore Gardens, W8 5PR. *T:* 01–937 1903; Picket Orchard, Ringwood, Hants. *T:* Ringwood 3258. *Club:* Brooks's.

ZIENKIEWICZ, Prof. Olgierd Cecil, FRS 1979; FEng 1979; Professor and Head of Civil Engineering Department, since 1961, and Director, Institute for Numerical Methods in Engineering, since 1976, University of Wales at Swansea; *b* Caterham, 18 May 1921; *s* of Casimir Zienkiewicz and Edith Violet (*née* Penny); *m* 1952, Helen Jean (*née* Fleming), Toronto; two *s* one *d*. *Educ:* Katowice, Poland; Imperial Coll., London. BSc (Eng); ACGI; PhD; DIC; DSc (Eng); DipEng; FICE; FASCE. Consulting engrg, 1945–49; Lectr, Univ. of Edinburgh, 1949–57; Prof. of Structural Mechanics, Northwestern Univ., 1957–61. Naval Sea Systems Comd Res. Prof., Monterey, Calif, 1979–80. Hon. Founder Mem., GAMNI, France. Chairman: Cttee on Analysis and Design, Internat. Congress of Large Dams; Jt Computer Cttee, Instn of Civil Engineers. Mem. Council, ICE, 1972–75 (Chm., S Wales and Mon. Br.); Telford Premium, ICE, 1963–67. General Editor, Internat. Jl Numerical Methods in Engineering; Member Editorial Board: Internat. Jl Solids and Structures; Internat. Jl Earthquakes and Structural Mechanics; Internat. Jl Rock Mechanics, Numerical and Analytical Methods in Geomechanics. James Clayton Fund Prizes, IMechE, 1967, 1973. For. Associate, US Nat. Acad. of Engrg, 1981; For. Mem., Polish Acad. of Sci., 1985. Hon. Dr, Lisbon, 1972; Hon. DSc: NUI, 1975; Northwestern Univ., Illinois, 1984; Norwegian Inst. of Technol., Trondheim, 1985; Hon. DSci Free Univ., Brussels, 1982. FCGI 1979. James Alfred Ewing Medal, ICE, 1980; Newmark Medal, ASCE, 1980; Worcester Reed Warner Medal, ASME, 1980. *Publications:* Stress Analysis, 1965; Rock Mechanics, 1968; Finite Element Method, 1967, 3rd edn 1977; Optimum Design of Structures, 1973; Finite Elements in Fluids, 1975; Numerical Methods in Offshore Engineering, 1977; Finite Elements and Approximation, 1983; numerous papers in Jl ICE, Jl Mech. Sci., Proc. Royal Soc., Internat. Jl of Num. Methods in Engrg, etc. *Recreations:* sailing, skin-diving. *Address:* 29 Somerset Road, Langland, Swansea SA3 4PG. *T:* Swansea 68776. *Clubs:* Athenæum; Rotary (Mumbles); Mumbles Yacht.

ZIJLSTRA, Jelle; Central Banker; President, Netherlands Bank, 1967–81; *b* 27 Aug. 1918; *s* of Ane Zijlstra and Pietje Postuma; *m* 1946, Hetty Bloksma; two *s* three *d*. *Educ:* Netherlands Sch. of Economics. Asst, Netherlands Sch. of Economics, 1945; Prof., Theoretical Economics, 1948–52; Prof., Public Finance, 1963–66, Free Univ. of Amsterdam; Minister of Economic Affairs, 1952–58; of Finance, 1959–63; Prime Minister, 1966–67. Mem., Chm. Board, and Pres., BIS, 1967–82; Governor, IMF, 1967–. *Publications:* Planned Economy, 1947; The Velocity of Money and its Significance for the Value of Money and for Monetary Equilibrium, 1948; Economic Order and Economic Policy, 1952. *Recreations:* sailing, ski-ing. *Address:* Park Oud-Wassenaar 1, 44 2243 BX, Wassenaar, The Netherlands.

ZILKHA, Selim Khedoury; Chairman and Chief Executive Officer, SKZ Inc., Houston, Texas, since 1986; *b* 7 April 1927; *s* of Khedoury Aboodi Zilkha and Louise (*née* Bashi); *m* (marr. diss.); one *s* one *d*. *Educ:* English Sch., Heliopolis, Egypt; Horace Mann Sch. for Boys, USA; Williams Coll., USA (BA Major Philos.). Dir, Zilkha & Sons Inc., USA, 1947–; Chm. and Man. Dir, Mothercare Ltd and associated cos, 1961–82; Dir, Habitat Mothercare Gp, 1982; Chairman: Amerfin Co. Ltd, GB, 1955–68; Spirella Co. of Great Britain Ltd, 1957–62; Chm./Jt Man. Dir, Lewis & Burrows Ltd, 1961–64; Chm. and Chief Exec. Officer, Towner Petroleum Co., Houston, 1983–85. *Recreations:* bridge, backgammon, golf, tennis, horse racing. *Address:* 750 Lausanne Road, Los Angeles, Calif 90077, USA. *Clubs:* Portland; Sunningdale Golf; Travellers' (Paris).

ZIMAN, Prof. John Michael, FRS 1967; Visiting Professor in Departments of Social and Economic Studies and Humanities, Imperial College of Science and Technology, since 1982; *b* 16 May 1925; *s* of late Solomon Netheim Ziman, ICS, retired, and Nellie Frances Ziman (*née* Gaster); *m* 1951, Rosemary Milnes Dixon; two adopted *s* two adopted *d*. *Educ:* Hamilton High Sch., NZ; Victoria University Coll., Wellington, NZ; Balliol Coll., Oxford. Junior Lectr in Mathematics, Oxford Univ., 1951–53; Pressed Steel Co. Ltd Research Fellow, Oxford Univ., 1953–54; Lectr in Physics, Cambridge Univ., 1954–64; Fellow of King's Coll., Cambridge, 1957–64; Editor of Cambridge Review, 1958–59; Tutor for Advanced Students, King's Coll., Cambridge, 1959–63; Prof. of Theoretical Physics, 1964–69, Melville Wills Prof. of Physics, 1969–76, Dir, H. H. Wills Physics Lab., 1976–81, Henry Overton Wills Prof. of Physics, 1976–82, Univ. of Bristol. Rutherford Memorial Lectr in India and Pakistan, 1968. Chairman: Council for Science and Society; European Assoc. for Study of Science and Technology; Member: Scientific Council, Internat. Centre for Theoretical Physics, Trieste, 1970–79; CNAA, 1982–. Hon. DSc Victoria Univ. of Wellington, NZ, 1985. Jt Editor, Science Progress, 1965–. *Publications:* Electrons and Phonons, 1960; Electrons in Metals, 1963; (with Jasper Rose) Camford Observed, 1964; Principles of the Theory of Solids, 1965; Public Knowledge, 1968; Elements of Advanced Quantum Theory, 1969; The Force of Knowledge, 1976; Reliable Knowledge, 1978; Models of Disorder, 1979; Teaching and Learning about Science and Society, 1980; Puzzles, Problems and Enigmas, 1981; An Introduction to Science Studies, 1984; (with Paul Sieghart and John Humphrey) The World of Science and the Rule of Law, 1986; numerous articles in scientific jls. *Address:* Science Policy Support Group, 114 Cromwell Road, SW7 4ES. *T:* 01–373 7171.

ZINN, Major William Victor, CEng, FICE, FIStructE; MEIC (Canada), MSCE (France); retired; Principal of W. V. Zinn & Associates, International Consulting Civil and Structural Engineers, 1934–80; *b* 7 July 1903; *s* of late Roman Reuben Zinn and Bertha Zinn (*née* Simon); *m* 1st, 1934, Laure (*d* 1960), *d* of Chaim and Fleur Modiano, London; one *s* one *d*; 2nd, 1963, Monica (*d* 1985), *d* of late Alan Ribton-Turner and Josephine Ribton-Turner (*née* Carey). *Educ:* University College Sch. and University Coll., London. BSc(Eng), MConsE London. War Service, 14th Army Burma, Major RE (retd), 1939–45. Sen. Partner: Haigh Zinn & Associates, Haigh Zinn & Humphreys, and Airport Development Consultants; New Steelworks, Guest Keen & Nettlefolds, Cardiff, 1932–35; Consultant assisting UKAEA and Min. of Works on Atomic Power Stations at Harwell, Windscale, Capenhurst, Calder Hall, Chapel Cross and Dounreay, 1952–56. *Works:* London Hilton Hotel and Royal Garden Hotel; London Govt Offices: Min. of Transport, Min. of Housing, Min. of Works, Dept of Postmaster-Gen., Central Electricity Authority and Min. of Civil Aviation; County Halls: Devon, Gloucester, Norfolk, Lanarkshire, 1954–66; Housing Projects for UK Local Authorities, totalling over 53,000 dwellings, 1934–69; overseas: Princes Bldg and Mandarin Hotel, also Brit. Mil. Hosp., Hong Kong, 1965; Feasibility Reports for World Bank: Teesta Barrage, and Chandpur Irrigation Project (East Pakistan), 1960–62; Ceylon Water Supplies and Drainage for World Health Organisation of the UNO, 1968; development of new techniques for deep underground city excavations, 1960–66; Engineering Consultant for Livingston New Town, Scotland, 1968; Tsing Yi Bridge (2,000 ft), Hong Kong, 1973; underground car park, Houses of Parliament, Westminster, 1974. *Publications:* Economical Construction of Deep Basements, 1968; Detailing by Computer, 1969; Phenomena and Noumena, 1980; Global Philosophy, 1981. *Recreation:* Theravada Buddhism. *Address:* High Trees, Mont Sohier, St Brelades Bay, Jersey, Channel Islands.

See also Rt Hon. J. D. Mabon.

ZINNEMANN, Fred; Film Director since 1934; *b* Austria, 29 April 1907; *s* of Dr Oskar Zinnemann, Physician and Anna F. Zinnemann; *m* 1936, Renée Bartlett; one *s*. *Educ:* Vienna Univ. (Law School). First film, The Wave (documentary) directed for Mexican Govt, 1934; initiated, with others, school of neo-realism in American cinema, directing among other films: The Seventh Cross, 1943; The Search, 1948; The Men, 1949; Teresa, 1950; High Noon, 1951; Member of the Wedding, 1952; From Here to Eternity, 1953. Later films include: Oklahoma!, 1956; The Nun's Story, 1959; The Sundowners, 1960; Behold a Pale Horse, 1964; A Man for All Seasons, 1966; The Day of the Jackal, 1973; Julia, 1977; Five Days One Summer, 1982. Member: Amer. Film Inst. (co-founder and ex-trustee); Acad. of Motion Picture Arts; Directors' Guild of America (2nd Vice-Pres., 1960–64); Hon. Pres., Directors' Guild of Great Britain, 1983. Fellow, BAFTA, 1978. Awards include: Academy Award, Los Angeles, 1951, 1954, 1967; Film Critics' Award, NY, 1952, 1954, 1960, 1967; Golden Thistle Award, Edinburgh, 1965; Moscow Film Festival Award, 1965; D. W. Griffith Award, 1970; Donatello Award, Florence, 1978. Gold Medal of City of Vienna, 1967. Order of Arts and Letters, France, 1982. *Publication:* article on directing films, Encyclopædia Britannica. *Recreations:* mountain climbing, chamber music. *Address:* 128 Mount Street, W1. *T:* 01–499 8810. *Club:* Sierra (San Francisco).

ZOBEL de AYALA, Jaime; Chairman and President, Ayala Corporation, since 1983; Chairman, Bank of the Philippine Islands, since 1985; *b* 18 July 1934; *s* of Alfonso Zobel de Ayala and Carmen Pfitz y Herrero; *m* 1958, Beatriz Miranda; two *s* five *d*. *Educ:* La Salle, Madrid; Harvard Univ. (BA, Arch. Scis). Major, Philippine Air Force (Res.). Philippine Ambassador to the Court of St James's and concurrently to Scandinavian countries, 1970–74. Mem., Camera Club of the Philippines, 1978–; Associate, RPS, 1984. Hon. Dr of Business Management De La Salle Univ., 1985. Comendador de la Orden del Merito Civil, Spain, 1968; Chevalier des Arts et des Lettres, 1980. *Recreation:* photography. *Address:* Ayala Corporation, Makati, Metro Manila, D-708, Philippines. *Clubs:* White's; Fox (Harvard).

ZOLEVEKE, Sir Gideon (Asatori Pitabose), KBE 1983 (MBE 1968); retired as public servant, 1973 and as politician, 1980; farmer since 1980; *b* 3 Aug. 1922; *s* of Pita Pitabose and Mata Taburana; *m* 1954, Melody Sukuluta'a Watanamae; three *s* three *d* (and one *s* decd). *Educ:* primary schs, Solomon Is; secondary sch. and tertiary educn, Fiji. Dip. in Surgery and Medicine, Fiji Sch. of Medicine, Suva; DCMHE London. Served British Solomon Is Protectorate Defence Force, 1942–45 (Pacific Stars). Govt MO, 1951–62; Sen. Health Educn Officer, 1962–73; Mem., Governing Council, 1973–74 (Chm., Works and Public Utilities); MLA, 1974–78 (Backbencher, 1975–76); Minister of: Works and Public Utilities, 1974–75; Home Affairs, April-July 1975; Educn, July-Nov. 1975; Agriculture and Lands, 1976–78; Health and Med. Services, 1978–80. Mem. and leader, various govt delegns, 1953–. Mem., Solomon Is Public Service Commn, 1981–; Chm., Solomon Is Electricity Authy Bd of Management, 1983–. Founder and first Pres., Solomon Is Med. Officers Assoc., 1952–69; President: W Pacific Br.,BMA, 1961–70; Choiseul People's Assoc., 1955–71; Civil Servants Assoc., British Solomon Is Protectorate, 1966–67; Solomon Is Br., BRCS, 1974–78 (BRCS award, 1978; Life Mem., 1982); Solomon Is Red Cross, 1978–82; St John's Primary Sch., Rove, Honiara, 1968–76; Honiara Club, 1963–68. *Publications:* A Man from Choiseul (autobiog.), 1980; (contrib.) Lands in the Solomon Islands, 1982; (contrib.) Solomon Island Politics, 1983. *Recreations:* writing, reading. *Address:* Kaiti Hill, PO Box 243, Honiara, Solomon Islands. *T:* Honiara 22730.

ZOUCHE, 18th Baron, *cr* 1308, of Haryngworth; **James Assheton Frankland;** Bt 1660; company director; President, Multiple Sclerosis Society of Victoria, since 1981; *b* 23 Feb.

1943; *s* of Major Hon. Sir Thomas William Assheton Frankland, 11th Bt, and Mrs Robert Pardoe (*d* 1972), *d* of late Captain Hon. Edward Kay-Shuttleworth; *S* to father's Btcy 1944; *S* grandmother, 17th Baroness Zouche, 1965; *m* 1978, Sally Olivia, *y d* of R. M. Barton, Diss, Norfolk; one *s* one *d*. *Educ*: Lycée Jaccard, Lausanne. Served 15/19th the King's Royal Hussars, 1963–68. *Heir*: *s* Hon. William Thomas Assheton Frankland [*b* 23 July 1984]. *Address*: Barbon Manor, Kirkby Lonsdale, Cumbria. *Clubs*: Cavalry and Guards; Melbourne (Melbourne).

ZSÖGÖD, Géza B. G.; *see* Grosschmid-Zsögöd, G. B.

ZUCKER, Kenneth Harry, QC 1981; a Recorder of the Crown Court, since 1982; *b* 4 March 1935; *s* of Nathaniel and Norma Zucker; *m* 1961, Ruth Erica, *y d* of Dr H. Brudno; one *s* one *d*. *Educ*: Westcliff High Sch.; Exeter Coll., Oxford, 1955–58 (MA). Served in Royal Air Force, 1953–55. Bacon Scholar, Gray's Inn, 1958; Called to Bar, Gray's Inn, 1959; Atkin Scholar, Gray's Inn, 1959. *Recreations*: reading, walking, photography. *Address*: 60 Gurney Drive, N2 0DE. *T*: 01–458 1556.

ZUCKERMAN, family name of **Baron Zuckerman**.

ZUCKERMAN, Baron *cr* 1971 (Life Peer), of Burnham Thorpe, Norfolk; **Solly Zuckerman,** OM 1968; KCB 1964 (CB 1946); Kt 1956; MA, MD, DSc; MRCS, FRCP; FRS 1943, FIBiol, Hon. FRCS, Hon. FPS; President, British Industrial Biological Research Association, since 1974; Visitor, Bedford College, 1968–85; *b* Cape Town, 1904; *m* 1939, Lady Joan Rufus Isaacs, *er d* of 2nd Marquess of Reading; one *s* one *d*. *Educ*: S African College Sch.; Univ. of Cape Town (Libermann Scholar); University Coll. Hosp., London (Goldsmid Exhibnr). Demonstrator of Anatomy, Univ. of Cape Town, 1923–25; Union Res. Scholar, 1925; Res. Anatomist to Zoological Soc. of London and Demonstrator of Anatomy, UCL, 1928–32; Res. Associate and Rockefeller Res. Fellow, Yale Univ., 1933–34; Beit Meml Res. Fellow, 1934–37, Univ. Demonstrator and Lectr in Human Anatomy, 1934–45, Oxford Univ.; William Julius Mickle Fellow, Univ. of London, 1935; Hunterian Prof., Royal Coll. of Surgeons, 1937; Sands Cox Prof. of Anatomy, Univ. of Birmingham, 1943–68; Professor-at-Large, Univ. of E Anglia, 1969–74. Scientific Adviser, Combined Operations HQ; Scientific Advr on planning, AEAF, MAAF, SHAEF, 1939–46 (Gp Capt. (Hon.) RAF, 1943–46); Member: Min. of Works Sci. Cttee, 1945–47; Cttee on Future Sci. Policy (Barlow Cttee), 1946–48; Min. of Fuel and Power Sci. Adv. Cttee, 1948–55; Associate Mem., Ordnance Bd, 1947–69, Emeritus 1969–; Dep. Chm., Adv. Council on Sci. Policy, 1948–64; Mem., Agricl Res. Council, 1949–59; Chairman: Cttee on Sci. Manpower, 1950–64; Natural Resources (Technical) Cttee, 1951–64; UK Delegate, Nato Science Cttee, 1957–66; Mem., BBC Gen. Adv. Council, 1957–62; Chairman: Cttee on Management and Control of Research and Devslt, 1958–61; Defence Research Policy Cttee, 1960–64; Chief Scientific Adviser: to Sec. of State for Defence, 1960–66; to HM Govt, 1964–71; Chm., Central Adv. Cttee for Science and Technology, 1965–70; UK Delegate on UN disarmament working gps, 1966–71; Trustee, British Museum (Natural History), 1967–77; Chm., Hosp. Sci. and Tech. Services Cttee, 1967–68; Mem., Royal Commn on Environmental Pollution, 1970–74; Chm., Commn on Mining and the Environment, 1971–72; Mem., WHO Adv. Cttee on Med. Research, 1973–77. President: Parly and Sci. Cttee, 1973–76; Assoc., of Learned and Professional Soc. Publishers, 1973–77; Fauna Preservation Soc., 1974–81; Zoological Soc. of London, 1977–84 (Hon. Sec., 1955–77; Hon. Fellow, 1984); Bath Inst. of Med. Engrg, 1980–. Lectures: Gregynog, UC Wales, 1956; Mason, Univ. of Birmingham, 1957; Caltech Commencement, 1959; Lees Knowles, Cambridge, 1965; Maurice Lubbock, Oxford, 1967; Maurice Bloch, Glasgow, 1969; Trueman Wood, RSA, 1969; Compton, MIT, 1972; Edwin Stevens, RoySocMed, 1974; Romanes, Oxford, 1975; Rhodes, S Africa, 1975; Jubilee, Imperial Coll., 1982; E. A. Lane, Clare Coll., Cambridge, 1983; Keith Morden Meml, Portland State Univ., 1985. Medal of Freedom with Silver Palm (USA); Chevalier de la Légion d'Honneur. Fellow, University College, London; Fellow Commoner, Christ's College, Cambridge; Gold Medal, Zoological Soc. of London, 1971; Hon. Member: Academia das Ciencias, Lisboa; Anatomical Soc.; Physiological Soc.; Soc. for Endocrinology; Foreign Member: Amer. Philosophical Soc., Amer. Acad. of Arts and Sciences; Assoc. Mem. (Emeritus), Ordnance Bd; Professor Emeritus: Univ. of Birmingham, Univ. of E Anglia. Dr *hc* Bordeaux, 1961; Hon. DSc: Sussex, 1963; Jacksonville, USA, 1964; Bradford, 1966; Hull, 1977; Columbia, USA, 1977; East Anglia, 1980; Reading, 1984; Hon. LLD: Birmingham, 1970; St Andrews, 1980. *Publications*: The Social Life of Monkeys and Apes, 1932, 2nd edn 1981; Functional Affinities of Man, Monkeys and Apes, 1933; (ed, anonymous) Science in War, 1940; A New System of Anatomy, 1961, 2nd edn, 1981; (ed) The Ovary, 2 vols, 1962, 2nd edn 1977; Scientists and War, 1966; Beyond the Ivory Tower, 1970; From Apes to Warlords (autobiography), 1978; (ed) Great Zoos of the World, 1980; Science Advisers, Scientific Advisers and Nuclear Weapons, 1980; Nuclear Illusion and Reality, 1982; Star Wars in a Nuclear World, 1986; contribs to scientific jls since 1925. *Address*: University of East Anglia, Norwich NR4 7TJ. *Clubs*: Beefsteak, Brooks's.

ZUKERMAN, Pinchas; concert violinist; *b* Tel Aviv, Israel, 16 July 1948; *s* of Jehuda and Miriam Zukerman; *m* 1968, Eugenia Rich, flautist; two *d*. *Educ*: Juilliard School of Music. Début, USA, 1969; Europe, 1970. Violin soloist with every major orchestra in USA and Europe; tours of USA, Europe, Israel, Scandinavia, Australia; extensive recordings. Music Director: South Bank Festival, 1978–80; St Paul Chamber Orch., 1980–81, 1981–82. First prize, Leventritt Internat. Violin Competition, 1967. *Recreations*: tennis, horseback riding. *Address*: c/o Shirley Kirshbaum & Associates, 711 West End Avenue, New York, NY 10025, USA. *T*: (212) 222–4843.

ZULU, Rt. Rev. Alphaeus Hamilton; Chairman, KwaZulu Development Corporation, since 1978; Speaker, KwaZulu Legislative Assembly, since 1978; *b* 29 June 1905; *m* 1929, Miriam Adelaide Magwaza (*d* 1983); one *s* five *d* (and one *d* decd). *Educ*: St Chad's Coll., Ladysmith (qual. teacher); Univ. of S Africa. BA (dist. Soc. Anthrop.) 1938; LTh 1940. Deacon, 1940; Priest, 1942. Curate of St Faith's Mission, Durban, 1940–52, Priest-in-charge, 1952–60; Suffragan Bishop of St John's (formerly St John's, Kaffraria), 1960–66; Bishop of Zululand, 1966–75. Jt Pres., World Council of Churches, 1968–75. DD Rhodes Univ., 1977; Hon. PhD: Natal, 1974; Univ. of Zululand, 1979. *Recreation*: tennis. *Address*: PO Box 177, Edendale, Natal 4505, S Africa.

ZULUETA, Sir Philip Francis de, Kt 1963; Chairman, Tanks Consolidated Investments Ltd, since 1983 (Director, since 1969); Member: Advisory Board, Société Générale de Belgique, since 1982; London Committee, Hongkong and Shanghai Banking Corporation, since 1974; Director: Union Minière, since 1969; Banque Belge Ltd, 1981; Imperial Continental Gas Association, 1982; Sofina, 1983; Abbott Laboratories, 1983; *b* 2 Jan. 1925; *o s* of late Professor Francis de Zulueta; *m* 1955, Hon. Marie-Louise, *e d* of 2nd Baron Windlesham; one *s* one *d*. *Educ*: Beaumont; New College, Oxford (Scholar). MA. Welsh Guards, NW Europe, 1943–47 (Capt., 1945). Foreign Service, 1949: Moscow, 1950–52; Private Sec. to successive Prime Ministers (Lord Avon, Mr Macmillan, Sir A. Douglas-Home), 1955–64. Asst Sec., HM Treasury, 1962. Resigned from Foreign Service and joined Philip Hill-Higginson, Erlangers, 1964; Dir, Hill Samuel & Co., 1965–72; Chief Exec., 1973–76, Chm., 1976–81, Antony Gibbs Holdings Ltd; Special Adviser to Bd, Hongkong and Shanghai Banking Corp., 1981–85. Member: Adv. Council, BBC, 1967–71; Franco-British Council, 1972– (Chm., British Section, 1981–); Exec. Cttee, Trilateral Commn, 1973–; Council, CBI, 1982–85; Zoological Soc., 1982–. Chm., Corporate Affairs Cttee, Inst. of Dirs, 1981–. Hon. Treasurer, Africa Centre, 1965–. Kt of Honour and Devotion, SMO Malta, 1965; Officer de la Légion d'Honneur, 1984. *Address*: 3 Westminster Gardens, Marsham Street, SW1P 4JA. *T*: 01–828 2448. Eastgate House, Eastgate, West Sussex PO20 6UT. *T*: Eastergate 2108. *Clubs*: Beefsteak, Pratt's, White's; Jockey (Paris).

ZUNTZ, Prof. Günther, FBA 1956; DrPhil (Marburg); Emeritus Professor, Manchester University; Professor of Hellenistic Greek, 1963–69; *b* 28 Jan. 1902; *s* of Dr Leo Zuntz and Edith (*née* Bähring); *m* 1947, Mary Alyson Garratt; two *s* one *d*. *Educ*: Bismarck-Gymnasium, Berlin-Wilmersdorf; Berlin, Marburg, Göttingen and Graz Universities. Teacher, Odenwaldschule, 1924–26; Teacher, Marburg Gymnasium and Kassel Gymnasium, 1926–32; worked for Monumenta Musicae Byzantinae, in Copenhagen, 1935–39, in Oxford, 1939–47; Librarian, Mansfield College, Oxford, 1944–47; Senior Lecturer, Manchester University, 1947–55 (Reader, 1955–63). Corresponding Member: Oesterreich. Akad. der Wissenschaften, 1974; Heidelberger Akademie der Wissenschaften, 1985. Dr.phil *hc* Tübingen, 1983. *Publications*: Hölderlins Pindar-Übersetzung, 1928; (with C. Höeg) Prophetologium, i–vi, 1939–71; The Ancestry of the Harklean New Testament, 1945; The Text of the Epistles, 1953; The Political Plays of Euripides, 1955, corrected repr., 1963; The Transmission of the Plays of Euripides, 1965; Persephone, 1971; Opuscula Selecta, 1972; Ein griechischer Lehrgang, 3 vols, 1983; Drei Kapitel zur Griechischen Metrik, 1984; articles in many learned journals. *Recreation*: music. *Address*: 1 Humberstone Road, Cambridge CB4 1JD. *T*: 357789.

ZURENUO, Rt. Rev. Sir Zurewe (Kamong), Kt 1981; OBE 1971; Head Bishop of Evangelical Lutheran Church of Papua New Guinea, 1973–82; *b* 5 July 1920; *s* of Zurenuo and Kbasung (previously the people took only one name and were known by none other); *m* 1941, Eleju; two *s* three *d* (and one *s* decd). *Educ*: Lutheran Mission schools (8 years in formal schools and 2 years teacher trng). Began teaching in Lutheran Schools, 1939, interrupted by illness, 1946; also did pastoral work; became Church Secretary of Sattelberg Circuit of Lutheran Church, 1953, and was elected General Secretary of Evangelical Lutheran Church of New Guinea, 1962; ordained, 1966. Instrumental in leading the church from mission status to indigenous church status; played a leading role in writing the constitution of the church; active in community affairs and inter-church relations; Chairman, Melanesian Council of Churches, 1970–73; established Lae City Christian Council, 1972 (Chm., 1972–82). *Address*: Evangelical Lutheran Church of Papua New Guinea, PO Box 80, Lae, Papua New Guinea.